Collins COBUILD

ADVANCED

DICTIONARY

of American English

English/Japanese

Collins COBUILD Advanced Dictionary of American English, English/Japanese

Heinle
President: *Dennis Hogan*
Editorial Director: *Joe Dougherty*
Publisher: *Sherrise Roehr*
VP, Director of Content Development: *Anita Raducanu*
Development Editor: *Katherine Carroll*
Director of Product Marketing: *Amy T. Mabley*
Director of Global Marketing: *Ian Martin*
Executive Marketing Manager: *Jim McDonough*
Sr. Field Marketing Manager: *Donna Lee Kennedy*
Product Marketing Manager: *Katie Kelley*
Content Project Manager: *Dawn Marie Elwell*
Asset Development Coordinator: *Noah Vincelette*
Sr. Frontlist Buyer: *Mary Beth Hennebury*
Editors: *Grant Barrett, Catherine Weller*
Front and End Matter Typeset: *Parkwood Composition Service, Inc.*
Illustrators: *See pgs. 1407–1408 for illustration and photo credits.*
Cover Layout: *Dawn Marie Elwell*
Printer: *China Translation and Printing Services Ltd*

Heinle
25 Thomson Place
Boston, Massachusetts 02210
USA

elt.heinle.com

In-text features including: Picture Dictionary, Thesaurus, Word Links, Word Partnerships, Word Webs, and supplements including: Guide to Key Features, Activity Guide, Brief Grammar Reference, Brief Writer's Handbook, Brief Speaker's Handbook, Words That Frequently Appear on TOEFL® and TOEIC,® Text Messaging and Emoticons, Academic Word List, USA States and Capitals, Geographical Place and Nationalities

Collins COBUILD
Founding Editor-in-Chief: *John Sinclair*
Publisher: *Elaine Higgleton*
Publishing Management: *Morven Dooner, Alison Macaulay*
For the English text
    Contributors: *Maree Airlee, Carol Braham, Carol-June Cassidy, Rosalind Combley, Pat Cook, Helen Forrest, Robert Grossmith, Orin Hargraves, Dana Darby Johnson, Cindy Mitchell, Marianne Noble, Susan Norton, Sue Ogden, Enid Pearsons, Elizabeth Potter, Maggie Seaton, Laura Wedgeworth*
For the Japanese text
    Consultants: *Toshio Saito, PhD, Professor Emeritus, Osaka University, Japan; Akasegawa Shiro, Lago Institute of Language; Kenji Nagoshi*
    Translators: *Reiko Abe Boughen, Sanae Burgess, Akiko Stenson, Keiko Gardner, Hiromi Green, Reiko Inoue Bendtsen, Hiroyuki Ishizuka, Sachiko Shibanuma, Miyoko Yamashita*
Computing support: Thomas Callan
Typeset: Wordcraft

Printed in China.
1 2 3 4 5 6 7 8 9 10   11 10 09 08 07

Harper Collins Publishers
Westerhill Road
Bishopbriggs
Glasgow
G64 2QT
Great Britain

www.collins.co.uk

First Edition 2008

For permission to use material from this text or product, submit a request online at
http://www.thomsonrights.com
http://www.collins.co.uk/rights

Library of Congress Cataloging-in-Publication Data has been applied for.

Book: 978-1-4240-1938-0
Book + CD-ROM: 978-1-4240-0079-1
CD-ROM: 978-1-4240-1939-7

Photo and illustration credits can be found on pages 1407–1408, which constitutes a continuation of this copyright page.

CONTENTS

ACKNOWLEDGEMENTS

The publishers would like to acknowledge the following for their invaluable contribution to the original COBUILD concept:

John Sinclair
Patrick Hanks
Gwyneth Fox
Richard Thomas

Stephen Bullion, Jeremy Clear, Rosalind Combley, Susan Hunston, Ramesh Krishnamurthy, Rosamund Moon, Elizabeth Potter

Jane Bradbury, Joanna Channell, Alice Deignan, Andrew Delahunty, Sheila Dignen, Gill Francis, Helen Liebeck, Elizabeth Manning, Carole Murphy, Michael Murphy, Jonathan Payne, Elaine Pollard, Christina Rammell, Penny Stock, John Todd, Jenny Watson, Laura Wedgeworth, John Williams

We would like to acknowledge the assistance of the many hundreds of individuals and companies who have kindly given permission for copyright material to be used in the Bank of English™. The written sources include many national and regional newspapers in Britain and overseas; magazines and periodical publishers; and book publishers in Britain, the United States and Australia. Extensive spoken data has been provided by radio and television broadcasting companies; research workers at many universities and other institutions; and numerous individual contributors. We are grateful to them all.

Consultant

Paul Nation

Reviewers — Japan

Ichiro Akano
Kyoto Gaikokugo University
Kyoto, Japan

Caroline Lloyd
Hiroshima YMCA Language School
Hiroshima, Japan

James Ronald
Hiroshima Shudo University
Hiroshima, Japan

Yukio Tono
Tokyo Gaikokugo University
Tokyo, Japan

Tomohiro Yanagi
Chubu University
Kasugai City, Aichi, Japan

Guide to Key Features

Through a collaborative initiative, Collins COBUILD and Heinle is co-publishing a dynamic new line of learner's dictionaries offering unparalleled pedagogy and learner resources.

With innovations such as Definitions*PLUS* and Vocabulary Builders, the *Collins COBUILD Advanced Dictionary of American English, English/Japanese* transforms the learner's dictionary from an occasional reference into the ultimate resource and must-have dictionary for language learners.

Definitions*PLUS*

- **Definitions*PLUS* Collocations**—Each definition is written in simple, natural English and shows which words are most typically used with the target word.
- **Definitions*PLUS* Grammar**—Each definition includes the most representative grammatical patterns to help the learner use English correctly.
- **Definitions*PLUS* Natural English**—Each definition is a model of how to use the language appropriately and idiomatically.

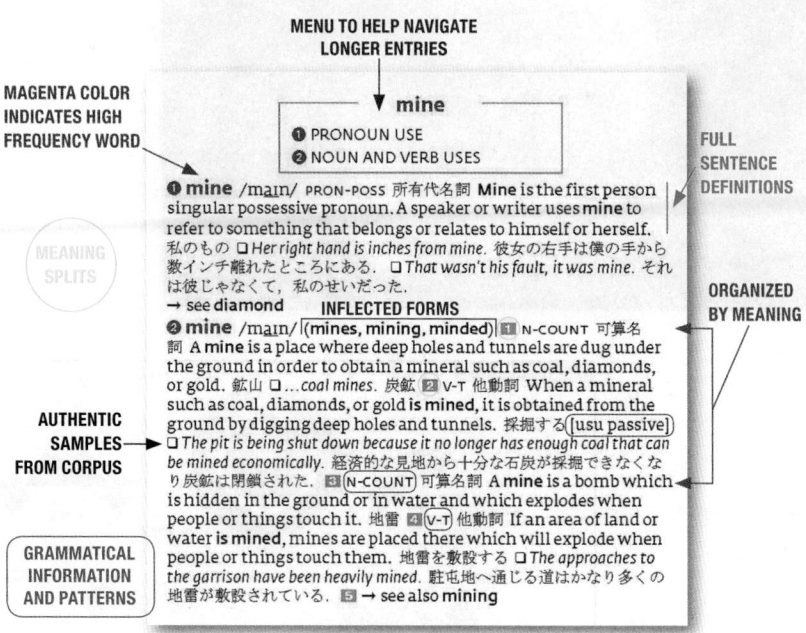

BANK *of* ENGLISH

The Bank of English™ is the original and the most current computerized corpus of authentic American English. This robust research tool was used to create each definition. All sample sentences are drawn from the rich selection that the corpus offers.

Vocabulary Builders

Over 3,000 pedagogical features encourage curiosity and exploration, which in turn builds the learner's bank of active and passive vocabulary knowledge. The "Vocabulary Builders" outlined here enhance vocabulary acquisition, increase language fluency, and improve accurate communication. They provide the learner with a greater depth and breadth of knowledge of the English language. The *Collins COBUILD Advanced Dictionary of American English, English/Japanese* offers a level of content and an overall learning experience unmatched in other dictionaries.

"**Picture Dictionary**" boxes illustrate vocabulary and concepts. The words are chosen for their usefulness in an academic setting, frequently showing a concept or process that benefits from a visual presentation.

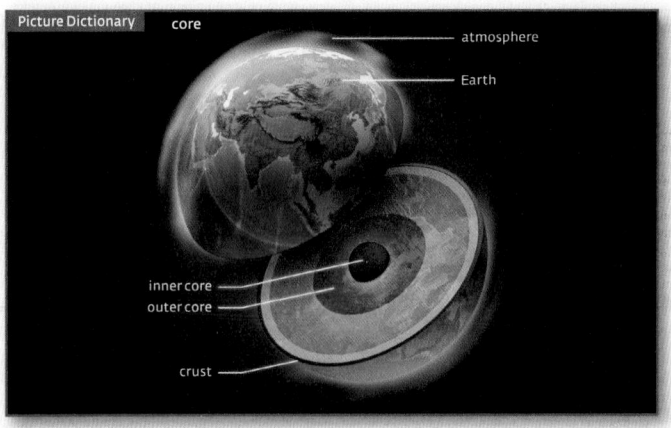

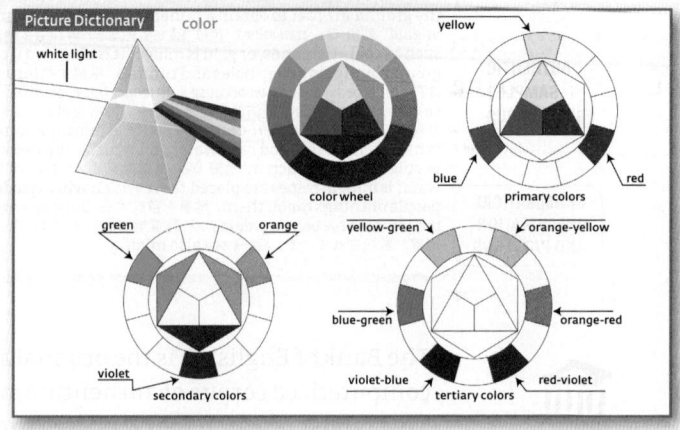

"**Word Webs**" present topic-related vocabulary through encyclopedia-like readings combined with stunning art, creating opportunities for deeper understanding of the language and concepts. All key words in bold are defined in the dictionary. Upon looking up one word, learners discover other related words that draw them further into the dictionary and the language. The more sustained time learners spend exploring words, the greater and richer their language acquisition is. The "Word Webs" encourage language exploration.

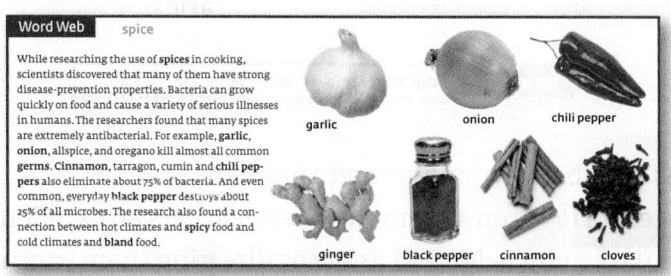

Word Web   spice

While researching the use of **spices** in cooking, scientists discovered that many of them have strong disease-prevention properties. Bacteria can grow quickly on food and cause a variety of serious illnesses in humans. The researchers found that many spices are extremely antibacterial. For example, **garlic, onion**, allspice, and oregano kill almost all common germs. **Cinnamon**, tarragon, cumin and **chili peppers** also eliminate about 75% of bacteria. And even common, everyday **black pepper** destroys about 25% of all microbes. The research also found a connection between hot climates and spicy food and cold climates and **bland** food.

garlic   onion   chili pepper
ginger   black pepper   cinnamon   cloves

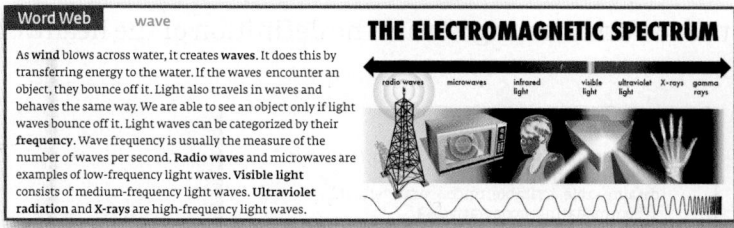

Word Web   wave

As **wind** blows across water, it creates **waves**. It does this by transferring energy to the water. If the waves encounter an object, they bounce off it. Light also travels in waves and behaves the same way. We are able to see an object only if light waves bounce off it. Light waves can be categorized by their **frequency**. Wave frequency is usually the measure of the number of waves per second. **Radio waves** and microwaves are examples of low-frequency light waves. **Visible light** consists of medium-frequency light waves. **Ultraviolet radiation** and **X-rays** are high-frequency light waves.

THE ELECTROMAGNETIC SPECTRUM

radio waves   microwaves   infrared light   visible light   ultraviolet light   X-rays   gamma rays

Chosen based on frequency in the Bank of English™, "**Word Partnerships**" show high-frequency word patterns, giving the complete collocation with the headword in place to clearly demonstrate use. The numbers refer the student to the correct meaning within the definition of the word that collocates with the headword.

Word Partnership   trust は次の語句と使われる:

V.   **build** trust, **create** trust, **place** trust **in** *someone* 2
    learn to trust 1
ADJ.   **mutual** trust 2
    charitable trust 10
N.   trust *your* **instincts**, trust *someone's* **judgment** 6
    investment trust 9

Word Partnership   moment は次の語句と使われる:

ADV.   **a** moment **ago, just a** moment 1
N.   moment **of silence**, moment **of thought** 1
V.   **stop for a** moment, **take a** moment, **think for a** moment, **wait a** moment 1
ADJ.   **an awkward** moment, **a critical** moment, **the right** moment 2

"**Word Links**" exponentially increase language awareness by showing how words are built in English, something that will be useful for learners in all areas of academic work as well as in daily communication. Focusing on prefixes, suffixes, and word roots, each "Word Link" provides a simple definition of the building block and then gives three examples of it used in a word. Providing three examples encourages learners to look up these words to further solidify understanding.

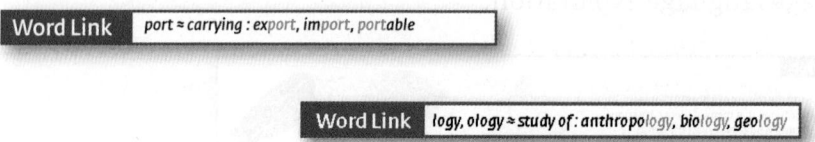

"**Thesaurus**" entries offer both synonyms and antonyms for high frequency words. An extra focus on synonyms offers learners an excellent way to expand vocabulary knowledge and usage by directing them to other words they can research in the dictionary. The numbers refer the student to the correct meaning within the definition of the headword.

CD-ROM

A valuable enhancement to the learning experience, the *Collins COBUILD Advanced Dictionary of American English, English/Japanese, CD-ROM* offers learners a fast and simple way to explore words and their meanings while working on a computer.

- **Search** definitions, sample sentences, Word Webs, and Picture Dictionary boxes.
- **"PopUp" Dictionary:** Find the definition of a word while working in any computer application.
- **Audio pronunciation with record and playback** provides pronunciation practice.
- **"My Dictionary"** allows learners to create a personalized tool by adding their own words, definitions, and sample sentences.
- **Bookmarks** allow learners to save and organize vocabulary. There are 75 bookmark folders already created with topic-related vocabulary to act as a springboard for vocabulary learning.

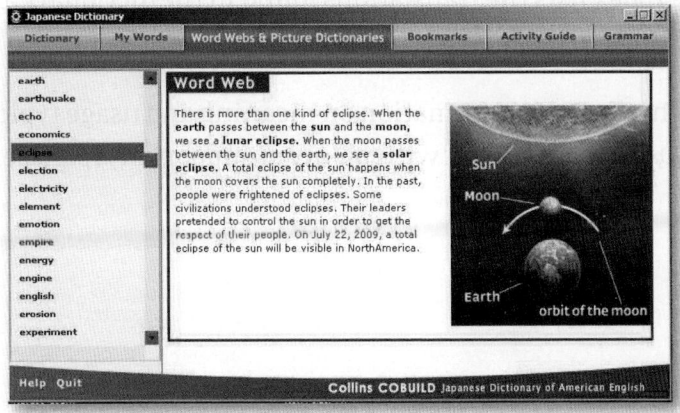

By using the resources found in this volume, learners will discover that the *Collins COBUILD Advanced Dictionary of American English, English/Japanese* is something that they want to delve into and spend time exploring, not just something to flip through for a quick answer. As they investigate options for words that will best serve their individual communicative needs at any given point, learners will find more opportunities for learning than they have ever seen in a traditional reference tool. This will become their ultimate resource and partner in their language learning journey.

Benefits of Semibilingual Dictionary

Collins COBUILD and Heinle are pleased to offer a new type of dictionary for Japanese learners of English. The *Collins COBUILD Advanced Dictionary of American English, English/Japanese* is a semibilingual dictionary designed for high intermediate or advanced level learners of English.

- This semibilingual dictionary includes all the features of a COBUILD monolingual dictionary, such as full sentence definitions and corpus-based examples.
- Additionally, for learners who feel they would benefit from access to Japanese translations, they are included for all definitions, senses, examples, and explanatory terms.
- The Japanese translations are presented on the same page as the English text but in separate, parallel column for easy reference.
- Japanese translations are included to complement the English material and provide additional support to the learner when they encounter a difficult word or expression.
- The index lists the translations found in the dictionary and directs the learner, in Japanese, to the relevant English entry.

Thus users have all the information on meaning and usage typically found in COBUILD dictionaries, but with plenty of support in Japanese.

JOHN SINCLAIR
Founding Editor-in-Chief, Collins COBUILD Dictionaries
1933-2007

John Sinclair was Professor of Modern English Language at the University of Birmingham for most of his career; he was an outstanding scholar, one of the very first modern corpus linguists, and one of the most open-minded and original thinkers in the field. The COBUILD project in lexical computing, funded by Collins, revolutionized lexicography in the 1980s, and resulted in the creation of the largest corpus of English language texts in the world.

Professor Sinclair personally oversaw the creation of this very first electronic corpus, and was instrumental in developing the tools needed to analyze the data. Having corpus data allowed Professor Sinclair and his team to find out how people really use the English language, and to develop new ways of structuring dictionary entries. Frequency information, for example, allowed him to rank senses by importance and usefulness to the learner (thus the most common meaning should be put first); and the corpus highlights collocates (the words which go together), information which had only been sketchily covered in previous dictionaries. Under his guidance, his team also developed a full-sentence defining style, which not only gave the user the sense of a word, but showed that word in grammatical context.

When the first *Collins COBUILD Dictionary of English* was published in 1987, it revolutionized dictionaries for learners, completely changed approaches to dictionary-writing, and led to a new generation of corpus-driven dictionaries and reference materials for English language learners.

Professor Sinclair worked on the Collins COBUILD range of titles until his retirement, when he moved to Florence, Italy and became president of the Tuscan Word Centre, an association devoted to promoting the scientific study of language. He remained interested in dictionaries until his death, and the Collins COBUILD range of dictionaries remains a testament to his revolutionary approach to lexicography and English language learning. Professor Sinclair will be sorely missed by everyone who had the great pleasure of working with him.

Introduction

A dictionary is probably the single most important reference book that a learner of English can buy. At Collins we do our best to ensure that our dictionaries live up to all expectations. This **Collins Cobuild Advanced Dictionary of American English, English/Japanese** is a new type of dictionary. It is especially designed for Japanese learners who already have a good working knowledge of English, but who may not be entirely comfortable using a monolingual English dictionary. All the features of a monolingual dictionary are included, with Japanese translations provided for all senses, examples and explanatory terms. The dictionary also includes an index which lists alphabetically the translations found in the dictionary and which directs you to the relevant English entry through the medium of Japanese.

The corpus

The **Collins Cobuild Advanced Dictionary of American English, English/Japanese** like all Collins dictionaries, is based on a corpus, the Bank of English ™, part of the Collins Word Web, which now contains over 650 million words of contemporary English. The corpus is central to the compilation of COBUILD dictionaries. It enables the dictionary editors to look at how the language works and make evidence-based statements about the meanings, patterns, and uses of words with confidence and accuracy.

Content

A dictionary must present the most important facts about language, and dictionary compilers need good evidence to be able to make their selections. It is much easier to decide which words to include, and which to omit, when we have accurate statistical information from such a vast database of language as the Bank of English ™. This enables the compilers to look at the relative frequency of words and to identify and highlight the 2,500 most frequently used words in English. These words account for over 75% of all English usage, so it is easy to see why they are important.

Definitions

One of the most distinctive feature of all COBUILD dictionaries is the use of full English sentences in the definitions, explaining the meaning in the way that one person might explain it to another. They give the user much more than the meaning of the word they are looking up, and also contain information on usage, register, typical context, and syntax. The fullness of the definitions will give learners of English confidence as they learn what words and phrases mean and how they are used.

Examples

All of the examples in this dictionary have been selected from the Bank of English ™, and have been chosen carefully to show the collocates of a word—other words that are frequently used with the word we are defining—and the patterns in which it is used. Since the examples are genuine pieces of text, you can be sure that they show the word in use in a natural context.

Set structures

For each definition, the word or phrase being defined is printed in **bold**. In addition, we have identified and highlighted in **bold** words which combine with the headword to make a very important or set grammatical structure or collocational pattern, for example, *A* **band of** *people is . . . If you* **say** *something* **to yourself,** *you think it . . . If you are* **unable to** *do something, it is . . .*

Coverage

Today's learners of English need to be aware of the variation of language in different parts of the English-speaking world. The **Collins Cobuild Advanced Dictionary of American**

English, English/Japanese includes useful notes to identify vocabulary and expressions from those parts of the world, particularly American and British English.

Usage notes
Throughout the text we have included a number of notes which give additional information about how words are used. There is a variety of useful information contained in these notes, which help to clarify important distinctions in usage and in grammar.

Culture notes
Extra information on culturally significant events, institutions, traditions and customs is given in the form of a note following the relevant entry. These notes are intended to help you gain a greater understanding of life and culture in English-speaking countries.

Complex entries
Entries which are long or complex are given a special treatment to make them easier to navigate. A menu shows what sections the entry is divided into, and how they are ordered, so that you can immediately go to the correct section to find the meaning you want. For example, **mean** is divided into three sections, corresponding to its verb, adjective, and noun uses. The same principle is used for **hold**, where there is an important sense distinction running through its uses.

Grammatical information
Where relevant, useful information about the grammatical patterns is provided. This information appears immediately before the examples which further clarify the patterns.

Guide to the Dictionary Entries

Definitions
One of the features of the **Collins Cobuild Advanced Dictionary of American English, English/Japanese** is that the definitions are written in full sentences, using vocabulary and grammatical structures that occur naturally with the word being explained. This enables us to give a lot of information about the way a word or meaning is used by speakers of the language. Whenever possible, words are explained using simpler and more common words. This gives us a natural defining vocabulary with most words in our definitions being among the 2,500 commonest words of English. A Japanese translation is given for each sense of each word. For example, the verb **bask** has two senses, each of which has a Japanese translation:

If you **bask in** the sunshine, you lie somewhere sunny and enjoy the heat.
If you **bask in** someone's approval, favor, or admiration, you greatly enjoy their positive reaction toward you.

An individual sense of an English word may have more than one Japanese translation. For example, the noun **jealousy** has two different Japanese translations.

Information about collocates and structure

In our definitions, we show the typical collocates of a word: that is, the other words that are used with the word we are defining. For example, the definition of meaning 1 of the adjective **savory** says:

> **Savory** food has a salty or spicy flavor rather than a sweet one.

This shows that you use the adjective **savory** to describe food, rather than other things.

Meaning 1 of the verb **wag** says:

> When a dog **wags** its tail, it repeatedly waves its tail from side to side.

This shows that the subject of meaning 1 of **wag** refers to a dog, and the object of the verb is "tail".

Information about Japanese collocations, if any, is given after the translation.

> **Abstention** is a formal act of not voting either for or against a proposal: 棄（投票の）

Information about grammar

The definitions also give information about the grammatical structures in which a word is used. For example, meaning 1 of the adjective **candid** says:

> When you are **candid** about something or with someone, you speak honestly.

This shows that you use **candid** with the preposition "about" with something and "with" with someone.

Other definitions show other kinds of structure. Meaning 1 of the verb **soften** says:

> If you **soften** something or if it **softens**, it becomes less hard, stiff, or firm.

This shows that the verb is used both transitively and intransitively. In the transitive use, you have a human subject and a non-human object. In the intransitive use, you have a non-human subject.

Finally, meaning 1 of **compel** says:

> If a situation, a rule, or a person **compels** you to do something, they force you to do it.

This shows you what kinds of subject and object to use with **compel**, and it also shows that you typically use the verb in a structure with a to-infinitive.

Information about context and usage

In addition to information about collocation and grammar, definitions also can be used to convey your evaluation of something, for example to express your approval or disapproval. For example, here is the definition of **unhelpful**:

> If you say that someone or something is **unhelpful**, you mean that they do not help you or improve a situation, and may even make things worse.

In this definition, the expressions "if you say that", and "you mean that" indicate that these words are used subjectively, rather than objectively.

Other kinds of definition

We sometimes explain grammatical words and other function words by paraphrasing the word in context. For example, meaning 3 of **through** says:

> To go **through** a town, area, or country means to travel across it or in it.

In many cases, it is impossible to paraphrase the word, and so we explain its function instead. For example, the definition of **unfortunately** says:

> You can use **unfortunately** to introduce or refer to a statement when you consider that it is sad or disappointing, or when you want to express regret.

Lastly, some definitions are expressed as if they are cross-references. For example:

> **rd.** is a written abbreviation for **road**.
> **e-commerce** is the same as **e-business**.

If you need to know more about the words **road** or **e-business**, you look at those entries.

Style and Usage

Some words or meanings are used mainly by particular groups of people, or in particular social contexts. In this dictionary, where relevant, the definitions also give information about the kind of people who are likely to use a word or expression, and the type of social situation in which it is used.

In terms of geographical diversity, this dictionary focuses on American and British English using evidence from the Bank of English ™. Where relevant, the American or British form is shown at its equivalent word or meaning.

This information is usually placed at the end of the definition, in small capitals and within square brackets. If more than one type of information is provided, they are given in a list. The Japanese translation of this information is provided after the Japanese translation of the sense.

Geographical labels

AM: used mainly by speakers and writers in the US, and in other places where American English is used or taught. Where relevant the British equivalent is provided.

BRIT: used mainly by speakers and writers in Britain, and in other places where British English is used or taught. Where relevant the American equivalent is provided.

Other geographical labels are used in the text to refer to English as it is spoken in other parts of the world, e.g. AUSTRALIAN, NORTHERN ENGLISH, SCOTTISH.

Style labels

BUSINESS: used mainly when talking about the field of business, e.g. **annuity**

COMPUTING: used mainly when talking about the field of computing, e.g. **chat room**

DIALECT: used in some dialects of English, e.g. **ain't**

FORMAL: used mainly in official situations, or by political and business organizations, or when speaking or writing to people in authority, e.g. **gracious**

HUMOROUS: used mainly to indicate that a word or expression is used in a humorous way, e.g. **gents**

INFORMAL: used mainly in informal situations, conversations, and personal letters, e.g. **pep talk**

JOURNALISM: used mainly in journalism, e.g. **glass ceiling**

LEGAL: used mainly in legal documents, in law courts, and by the police in official situations, e.g. **manslaughter**

LITERARY: used mainly in novels, poetry, and other forms of literature, e.g. **plaintive**

MEDICAL: used mainly in medical texts, and by doctors in official situations, e.g. **psychosis**

MILITARY: used mainly when talking or writing about military terms, e.g. **armor**

OFFENSIVE: likely to offend people, or to insult them; words labeled OFFENSIVE should therefore usually be avoided, e.g. **cripple**

OLD-FASHIONED: generally considered to be old-fashioned, and no longer in common use, e.g. **dashing**

SPOKEN: used mainly in speech rather than in writing, e.g. **pardon**

TECHNICAL: used mainly when talking or writing about objects, events, or processes in a specialist subject, such as business, science, or music, e.g. **biotechnology**

TRADEMARK: used to show a designated trademark, e.g. **hoover**

VULGAR: used mainly to describe words which could be considered taboo by some people; words labeled VULGAR should therefore usually be avoided, e.g. **bloody**

WRITTEN: used mainly in writing rather than in speech, e.g. **avail**

PRAGMATICS LABELS

Many uses of words need more than a statement of meaning to be properly explained. People use words to do many things: give invitations, express their feelings, emphasize what they are saying, and so on. The study and description of the way in which people use language to do these things is called **pragmatics**.

In the dictionary, we draw attention to certain pragmatic aspects of words and phrases of English, paying special attention to those that, for cultural and linguistic reasons, we feel may be confusing to learners. The following labels are used:

APPROVAL: used to show that you approve of the person or thing you are talking about, e.g. **angelic**

DISAPPROVAL: used to show that you disapprove of the person or thing you are talking about, e.g. **brat**

EMPHASIS: used to emphasize the point you are making, e.g. **never-ending**

FEELINGS: used to express your feelings about something, or towards someone, e.g. **unfortunately**

FORMULAE: used in particular situations such as greeting and thanking people, or acknowledging something, e.g. **hi, congratulations**

POLITENESS: used to express politeness, sometimes even to the point of being euphemistic. e.g. **elderly**

VAGUENESS: used to show how certain you are about the truth or validity of your statements; this is sometimes called "hedging" or "modality", e.g. **presumably**

PRONUNCIATION

The basic principle underlying the suggested pronunciations is "If you pronounce it like this, most people will understand you." The pronunciations are therefore broadly based on the two most widely taught accents of English, GenAm or General American for American English, and RP or Received Pronunciation for British English.

For the majority of words, a single pronunciation is given, as most differences between American and British pronunciation are systematic. Where the usual British pronunciation differs from the usual American pronunciation more significantly, a separate transcription is given after the code BRIT. Where more than one pronunciation is common in either American or British English, alternative pronunciations are given.

The pronunciations are the result of a program of monitoring spoken English and consulting leading reference works. The transcription system has developed from original work by Dr David Brazil for the Collins COBUILD English Language Dictionary. The symbols used in the dictionary are adapted from those of the International Phonetic Alphabet (IPA), as standardized in the English Pronouncing Dictionary by Daniel Jones (14th Edition, revised by AC Gimson and SM Ramsaran 1988).

IPA Symbols

Vowel Sounds

ɑ	calm, ah
æ	act, mass
ɑɪ	dive, cry
ɑʊ	out, down
ɛ	met, lend, pen
eɪ	say, weight
ɪ	fit, win
i	feed, me
ɒ	lot, spot
oʊ	note, coat
ɔ	claw, maul
ɔɪ	boy, joint
ʊ	could, stood
u	you, use
ʌ	fund, must
ə	first vowel in about
i	second vowel in very
u	second vowel in actual

Consonant Sounds

b	bed, rub
d	done, red
f	fit, if
g	good, dog
h	hat, horse
j	yellow, you
k	king, pick
l	lip, bill
ᵊl	handle, panel
m	mat, ram
n	not, tin
ᵊn	hidden, written
p	pay, lip
r	run, read
s	soon, bus
t	talk, bet
v	van, love
w	win, wool
x	loch
z	zoo, buzz
ʃ	ship, wish
ʒ	measure, leisure
ŋ	sing, working
tʃ	cheap, witch
θ	thin, myth
ð	then, bathe
dʒ	joy, bridge

Notes

/æ/ or /ɑ/

There are a number of words which use the /æ/ sound in GenAm and in most accents of English, but /ɑ/ in RP, such as 'bath' which is pronounced /bæθ/ in GenAm and /bɑθ/ in RP. This affects some words in which this vowel is followed by the sounds /f/, /nd/, /ns/, /nt/, /ntʃ/, /s/, /θ/. For example, 'graph', 'command', 'answer', 'can't', 'ranch', 'class' and 'bath' are pronounced /græf/, /kəmænd/, /ænsər/, /kænt/, /ræntʃ/, /klæs/ and /bæθ/ in GenAm, but /grɑf/, /kəmɑnd/, /ɑnsəʳ/, /kɑnt/, /rɑntʃ/, /klɑs/ and /bɑθ/ in RP. However, there are exceptions to this such as "land" /lænd/. In these cases, we show only the GenAm version as it is a common and acceptable pronunciation for British English, even though it is not RP.

/r/

In most accents of English, including GenAm, 'r' is always pronounced. One of the main ways in which RP differs is that 'r' is only pronounced as /r/ when the next sound is a vowel. Thus, in RP, 'far gone' is pronounced /fɑ gɒn/ but 'far out' is pronounced /fɑr aʊt/. Similarly, 'fire', 'flour', 'fair', 'near' and 'pure' are pronounced /faɪər/, /flaʊər/, /fɛər/, /nɪər/ and /pyʊər/ in GenAm, but /faɪə/, /flaʊə/, /fɛə/, /nɪə/ and /pyʊə/ in RP.

/oʊ/

This symbol is used to represent the sound /oʊ/ in GenAm, and also the sound /əʊ/ in RP, as these sounds are almost entirely equivalent.

/ᵊl/ and /ᵊn/

These show that /l/ and /n/ are pronounced as separate syllables:

handle /hændᵊl/
hidden /hɪdᵊn/

Stress

Stress is shown by underlining the vowel in the stressed syllable:

two /t<u>u</u>/
result /rɪz<u>ʌ</u>lt/
disappointing /d<u>ɪ</u>səp<u>ɔ</u>ɪntɪŋ/

When a word is spoken in isolation, stress falls on the syllables which have vowels which are underlined. If there is one syllable underlined, it will have primary stress.

'TWO'
'reSULT'

If two syllables are underlined, the first will have secondary stress, and the second will have primary stress:

'DISapPOINTing'

A few words are shown with three underlined syllables, for example 'disqualification' /d<u>ɪ</u>skwɒlɪfɪk<u>eɪ</u>ʃᵊn/. In this case, the third underlined syllable will have primary stress, while the secondary stress may be on the first or second syllable:

'DISqualifiCAtion' or 'disQUALifiCAtion'

GenAm usually prefers 'dis-', while RP tends to prefer 'DIS-'.

In the case of compound words, where the pronunciation of each part is given separately, the stress pattern is shown by underlining the headword: '<u>off</u>-peak', '<u>first</u>-class', but 'cake pan'.

Stressed syllables

When words are used in context, the way in which they are pronounced depends upon the information units that are constructed by the speaker. For example, a speaker could say:

1   'the reSULT was disapPOINTing'
2   'it was a DISappointing reSULT'
3   'it was VERy disappointing inDEED'

In (3), neither of the two underlined syllables in disappointing /dɪsəpɔɪntɪŋ/ receives either primary or secondary stress. This shows that it is not possible for a dictionary to predict whether a particular syllable will be stressed in context.

It should be noted, however, that in the case of adjectives with two stressed syllables, the second syllable often loses its stress when it is used before a noun:

'an OFF-peak FARE'
'a FIRST-class SEAT'

Two things should be noted about the marked syllables:

1   They can take primary or secondary stress in a way that is not shared by the other syllables.
2   Whether they are stressed or not, the vowel must be pronounced distinctly; it cannot be weakened to /ə/, /ɪ/ or /ʊ/.

These features are shared by most of the one-syllable words in English, which are therefore transcribed in this dictionary as stressed syllables:

two /tu/
inn /ɪn/
tree /tri/

Unstressed syllables

It is an important characteristic of English that vowels in unstressed syllables tend not to be pronounced clearly. Many unstressed syllables contain the vowel /ə/, a neutral vowel which is not found in stressed syllables. The vowels /ɪ/ , or /ʊ/, which are relatively neutral in quality, are also common in unstressed syllables.

Single-syllable grammatical words such as 'shall' and 'at' are often pronounced with a weak vowel such as /ə/. However, some of them are pronounced with a more distinct vowel under certain circumstances, for example when they occur at the end of a sentence. This distinct pronunciation is generally referred to as the strong form, and is given in this dictionary after the word STRONG.

shall /ʃəl, STRONG ʃæl/
at /ət, STRONG æt/

LIST OF GRAMMATICAL NOTATIONS

Word classes

adjective	ADJ
adverb	ADV
auxiliary verb	AUX
color word	COLOR
combining form	COMB
conjunction	CONJ
convention	CONVENTION
determiner	DET
exclamation	EXCLAM
fraction	FRACTION
modal verb	MODAL
count noun	N-COUNT
collective count noun	N-COUNT-COLL
family noun	N-FAMILY
noun in names	N-IN-NAMES
mass noun	N-MASS
plural noun	N-PLURAL
proper noun	N-PROPER
collective proper noun	N-PROPER-COLL
singular noun	N-SING
collective singular noun	N-SING-COLL
title noun	N-TITLE
uncount noun	N-UNCOUNT
collective uncount noun	N-UNCOUNT-COLL
variable noun	N-VAR
collective variable noun	N-VAR-COLL
vocative noun	N-VOC
negative	NEG
number	NUM
ordinal	ORD
phrasal verb	PHRASAL VERB
phrasal verb-link	PHRASAL VERB-LINK
phrasal passive verb	PHRASAL VERB-PASSIVE
phrasal reciprocal verb	PHRASAL VERB-RECIP
phrase	PHRASE
predeterminer	PREDET
preposition	PREP
pronoun	PRON
emphatic pronoun	PRON-EMPH
indefinite pronoun	PRON-INDEF
negative indefinite pronoun	PRON-INDEF-NEG
negative pronoun	PRON-NEG
plural pronoun	PRON-PLURAL
possessive pronoun	PRON-POSS
reciprocal pronoun	PRON-RECIP
reflexive pronoun	PRON-REFL
emphatic reflexive pronoun	PRON-REFL-EMPH
relative pronoun	PRON-REL
singular pronoun	PRON-SING
quantifier	QUANT
negative quantifier	QUANT-NEG
plural quantifier	QUANT-PLURAL
question word	QUEST
sound word	SOUND
intransitive verb	V-I
link verb	V-LINK
passive verb	V-PASSIVE
reciprocal verb	V-RECIP
passive reciprocal verb	V-RECIP-PASSIVE
transitive verb	V-T
passive transitive verb	V-T PASSIVE
intransitive or transitive verb	V-T/V-I

Words and abbreviations used in patterns

adjective group	adj
superlative form	adj-superl
adverb group	adv
word or phrase indicating an amount of something	amount
broad negative	brd-neg
clause	cl
color word	color
comparative form	compar
continuous	cont
definite noun group	def-n
definite noun group with an uncount noun	def-n-uncount
definite noun group with a noun in the plural	def-pl-n
determiner	det
past participle of a verb	-ed
noun group, adjective, adverb, or prepositional phrase	group
imperative	imper
infinitive form of a verb	inf
present participle of a verb	-ing
interrogative	interrog
clause beginning with *like*	like
noun or noun group	n
names of places or institutions	names
negative word	neg
proper noun	n-proper
number	num
uncount noun or noun group with an uncount noun	n-uncount
ordinal	ord
particle, part of a phrasal verb	P
passive voice	passive
plural	pl
noun in the plural, plural noun group, co-ordinated noun group	pl-n
plural number	pl-num
possessive	poss
prepositional phrase or preposition	prep
pronoun	pron
indefinite pronoun	pron-indef
reflexive pronoun	pron-refl
relative pronoun	pron-rel
question word	quest
singular	sing
noun in the singular	sing-n
supplementary information accompanying a noun	supp
'that'-clause	that
the to-infinitive form of a verb	to-inf
usually	usu
verb or verb group	v
continuous verb	v-cont
link verb	v-link
wh-word, clause beginning with a wh-word	wh

Explanation of Grammatical Terms

Introduction

For each use of each word in this dictionary, grammar information is provided. For a very few words, such as abbreviations, contractions and some words of foreign origin, no grammar is given, because the words do not belong to any word class, or are used so freely that every example could be given a different word class, e.g. *AD, ditto, must've*.

The grammar information that is given is of three types:

1. the word class of the word: e.g. **PHRASAL VERB, N-COUNT, ADJ, QUANT**
2. restrictions or extensions to its behavior, compared to other words of that word class: e.g. **usu passive, usu sing, also no det**
3. the patterns that the word most frequently occurs in: e.g. **N** *of* **n, ADJ that, ADV with v**

For all word classes, the patterns are given immediately before the examples they accompany.

The word class of the word being explained is in CAPITAL LETTERS. The order of items in a pattern is the order in which they normally occur in a sentence. Words in *italics* are words (not word classes) that occur in the pattern. Alternatives are separated by a slash (/).

Word classes

ADJ

An **adjective** can be graded or ungraded, or be in the comparative or the superlative form, e.g. *He has been absent from his desk for two weeks . . . the most accurate description of the killer to date . . . The eldest child was a daughter called Fatiha.*

Adjective patterns

ADJ n The adjective is always used before a noun, e.g. *. . . a governmental agency.*

usu ADJ n The adjective is usually used before a noun. It is sometimes used after a link verb.

v-link ADJ The adjective is used after a link verb such as *be* or *feel*, e.g. *He felt unwell.* Adjectives with this label are sometimes used in other positions such as after the object of a verb such as *make* or *keep*, but never before a noun.

usu v-link ADJ The adjective is usually used after a link verb. It is sometimes used before a noun.

ADJ after v The adjective is used after a verb that is not a link verb, e.g. *I wore a white dress and was barefoot.*

n ADJ The adjective comes immediately after a noun, e.g. *between archaeology proper and science-based archaeology.*

det ADJ The adjective comes immediately after a determiner and before any other adjectives, and sometimes comes before numbers, e.g. *You owe a certain person a sum of money.* If the dictionary does not show that an adjective is used only or mainly in the pattern **ADJ n** and **v-link ADJ**, this means that the adjective is used freely in both patterns.

These main adjective patterns are sometimes combined with other patterns.

ADV

An **adverb** can be graded or ungraded, or be in the comparative or the superlative form. e.g. *Much of our behavior is biologically determined . . . I'll work hard . . . Inflation is below 5% and set to fall further . . . those areas furthest from the coast.*

AUX

An **auxiliary verb** is used with another verb to add particular meanings to that verb, for example, to form the continuous aspect or the passive voice, or to form negatives and interrogatives. The verbs *be, do, get* and *have* have some senses in which they are auxiliary verbs.

COLOR

A **color word** refers to a color. It is like an adjective, e.g. *the blue sky . . . The sky was blue*, and also like a noun, e.g. *She was dressed in red . . . several shades of yellow*.

COMB

A **combining form** is a word which is joined with another word, usually with a hyphen, to form compounds, e.g. *strawberry-flavored, business-speak*. The word class of the compound is also given, e.g. **COMB in ADJ, COMB in N-UNCOUNT**.

CONJ

A **conjunction** usually links elements of the same grammatical type, such as two words or two clauses, e.g. *She and Simon had already gone . . . I sat on the chair to unwrap the package while he stood by*.

CONVENTION

A **convention** is a word or a fixed phrase which is used in conversation, for example when greeting someone, apologizing, or replying, e.g. *hello, sorry, no comment*.

DET

A **determiner** is a word that is used at the beginning of a noun group, e.g. *a tray, more time, some books, this amount*. It can also be used to say who or what something belongs or relates to e.g. *his face, my house*, or to begin a question e.g. *Whose car were they in?*

EXCLAM

An **exclamation** is a word or phrase which is spoken suddenly, loudly, or emphatically in order to express a strong emotion such as shock or anger. Exclamations are often followed by exclamation marks, e.g. *good heavens! Ouch!*

FRACTION

A **fraction** is used in numbers, e.g. *five and a half, two and two thirds*; before *of* and a noun group, e.g. *half of the money, a third of the children, an eighth of Russia's grain*; after *in* or *into*, e.g. *in half, into thirds*. A fraction is also used like a count noun, e.g. *two halves, the first quarter of the year*.

MODAL

A **modal** is used before the infinitive form of a verb, e.g. *You may go*. In questions, it comes before the subject, e.g. *Must you speak?* In negatives, it comes before the negative word, e.g. *They would not like this*. It does not inflect, for example, it does not take an -s in the third person singular, e.g. *She can swim*.

N-COUNT

A **count noun** has a plural form, usually made by adding -s. When it is singular, it must have a determiner in front of it, such as *the, her,* or *such*, e.g. *My cat is getting fatter . . . She's a good friend*.

N-COUNT-COLL

A **collective count noun** is a count noun which refers to a group of people or things. It behaves like a count noun, but when it is in the singular form it can be used with either a singular or plural verb, e.g. *Their audience are much younger than the average . . . The British audience has a huge appetite for serials . . . Audiences are becoming more selective*.

N-FAMILY

A **family noun** refers to a member of a family, e.g. *father, mommy,* and *granny*. Family nouns are count nouns which are typically used in the singular, and usually follow a possessive determiner. They are also vocative nouns. They are also proper nouns, used with no determiner, e.g. *My mommy likes marzipan . . . Tell them I didn't do it, Mommy . . . Mommy's always telling me I'm too old for dolls.*

N-IN-NAMES

The **noun** occurs **in names** of people, things, or institutions.

N-MASS

A **mass noun** typically combines the behavior of both count and uncount nouns in the same sense. It is used like an uncount noun to refer to a substance. It is used like a count noun to refer to a brand or type, e.g. *Rinse in cold water to remove any remaining detergent . . . Wash it in hot water with a good detergent . . . We used several different detergents in our stain-removal tests.*

N-PLURAL

A **plural noun** is always plural, and is used with plural verbs. If a pronoun is used to stand for the noun, it is a plural pronoun such as *they* or *them*, e.g. *These clothes are ready to wear . . . He expressed his condolences to the families of people who died in the incident.* Plural nouns which end in *-s* usually lose the *-s* when they come in front of another noun, e.g. *pants, pants leg.* If they refer to a single object which has two main parts, such as *jeans* and *glasses*, the expression *a pair of* is sometimes used, e.g. *a pair of jeans.* This is shown as **N-PLURAL: also** *a pair of* **N**.

N-PROPER

A **proper noun** refers to one person, place, thing, or institution, and begins with a capital letter. Many proper nouns are used without a determiner, e.g. . . . *Earth;* some must be used with *the*, and this is indicated: **N-PROPER,** *the* **N**, e.g. *the* UK.

N-PROPER-COLL

A **collective proper noun** is a proper noun which refers to a group of people or things. It can be used with either a singular or a plural verb, e.g. *The Senate is expected to pass the bill shortly . . . The Houses of Parliament are the British parliament.*

N-SING

A **singular noun** is always singular, and needs a determiner, e.g. . . . *to respect the environment . . . Maureen was the epitome of sophistication.* When only *a* or *the* is used, this is indicated: **N-SING: a N** or **N-SING:** *the* **N**, e.g. *The traffic slowed to a crawl . . . We dropped to the ground.*

N-SING-COLL

A **collective singular noun** is a singular noun which refers to a group of people or things. It behaves like a singular noun, but can be used with either a singular or plural verb, e.g. *The enemy were pursued for two miles . . . Their defense has now conceded 12 goals in six games.*

N-TITLE

A **title noun** is used to refer to someone who has a particular role or position. Titles come before the name of the person and begin with a capital letter, e.g. *The Chancellor of the Exchequer.*

N-UNCOUNT

An **uncount noun** refers to things that are not normally counted or considered to

be individual items. Uncount nouns do not have a plural form, and are used with a singular verb. They do not need determiners, e.g. . . . *an area of outstanding natural beauty*.

N-UNCOUNT-COLL

A **collective uncount noun** is an uncount noun which refers to a group of people or things. It behaves like an uncount noun, but can be used with either a singular or plural verb, e.g. . . . *Hearts is one of the four suits in a pack of playing cards . . . Hearts are trumps*.

N-VAR

A **variable noun** typically combines the behavior of both count and uncount nouns in the same sense (see **N-COUNT, N-UNCOUNT**). The singular form occurs freely both with and without determiners. Variable nouns also have a plural form, usually made by adding *-s*. Some variable nouns when used like uncount nouns refer to abstract things like *hardship* and *technology*, and when used like count nouns refer to individual examples or instances of that thing, e.g. *Technology is changing fast . . . They should be allowed to wait for cheaper technologies to be developed*. Others refer to objects which can be mentioned either individually or generally, like *potato* and *salad*: you can talk about *a potato, potatoes,* or *potato*.

N-VAR-COLL

A **collective variable noun** is a variable noun which refers to a group of people or things. It behaves like a variable noun, but when it is singular it can be used with either a singular or a plural verb, e.g. *The management is doing its best to improve the situation*.

N-VOC

A **vocative noun** is used when speaking directly to someone or writing to them. Vocative nouns do not need a determiner, but some may be used with a possessive determiner, e.g. *Thank you, darling . . . How are you, my darling?*

NEG see **PRON-INDEF-NEG, PRON-NEG, QUANT-NEG**

NUM

A **number** is a word such as *three* and *hundred*. Numbers such as *one, two, three* are used like determiners, e.g. *three bears*; like adjectives, e.g. *the four horsemen*; like pronouns, e.g. *She has three cases and I have two*; and like quantifiers, e.g. *Six of the boys stayed behind*. Numbers such as *hundred, thousand, million* always follow a determiner or another number, e.g. *two hundred people, the thousand horsemen, She has a thousand dollars and I have a million, A hundred of the boys stayed behind*.

ORD

An **ordinal** is a type of number. Ordinals are used like adjectives, e.g. *He was the third victim*; like pronouns, e.g. *the second of the two teams*; like adverbs, e.g. *The other team came first*; and like determiners, e.g. *Fourth place goes to Timmy*.

PHRASAL VERB

A **phrasal verb** consists of a verb and one or more particles e.g. *look after, look back, look down on*. Some phrasal verbs are reciprocal, link or passive verbs.

PHRASE

Phrases are groups of words which are used together with little variation and which have a meaning of their own, e.g. *The emergency services were working against the clock*.

PREDET

A **predeterminer** is used in a noun group before *a, the,* or another determiner, e.g. *What a terrific idea! . . . both the children . . . all his life*.

PREFIX

A **prefix** is a letter or group of letters, such as *un-* or *multi-*, which is added to the beginning of a word in order to form another word. For example, the prefix *un-* is added to *happy* to form *unhappy*

PREP

A **preposition** begins a prepositional phrase and is followed by a noun group or a present participle. Patterns for prepositions are shown in the dictionary only if they are restricted in some way. For example, if a preposition occurs only before a present participle, it is shown as **PREP -ing.**

PREP-PHRASE

A **phrasal preposition** is a phrase which behaves like a preposition, e.g. *Prices vary according to the quantity ordered.*

PRON

Pronouns are used like noun groups, to refer to someone or something that has already been mentioned or whose identity is known, e.g. *They produced their own shampoos and hair-care products, all based on herbal recipes . . . two bedrooms, each with three beds.* Some pronouns are further classified, for example as **PRON-EMPH, PRON-INDEF,** and so on.

PRON-EMPH

Emphatic pronouns are words like *all, both,* and *each,* when they are used to emphasize another noun or pronoun, e.g. *We each have different needs and interests . . . I wish you both a good trip.*

PRON-INDEF

Indefinite pronouns are words like *anyone, anything, everyone,* and *something,* e.g. *Why would anyone want that job? . . . after everything else in his life had changed.*

PRON-INDEF-NEG

Negative indefinite pronouns are words like *none, no-one,* and *nothing,* e.g. *He searched for a sign of recognition on her face, but there was none . . . Do our years together mean nothing?*

PRON-NEG

Negative pronouns are words like *neither,* e.g. *Neither seemed likely to be aware of my absence for long.*

PRON-PLURAL

Plural pronouns are the plural personal pronouns, which include *we, us, they,* and *them,* e.g. *Neither of us forgot about it.*

PRON-POSS

A **possessive pronoun** is used to say who or what something belongs to or relates to. The possessive pronouns are *mine, yours, his, hers, ours* and *theirs,* e.g. *That wasn't his fault, it was mine . . . The author can report other people's results which more or less agree with hers.*

PRON-RECIP

The **reciprocal pronouns** are *each other* and *one another,* e.g. *We looked at each other in silence.*

PRON-REFL

Reflexive pronouns are pronouns which are used as the object of a verb or preposition when they refer to the same person or thing as the subject of the verb. They are used in the same positions as other pronouns. The reflexive pronouns are *myself, yourself, himself, herself, itself, oneself, ourselves, yourselves,* and *themselves,* e.g. *I asked myself what I would have done in such a situation . . . One must apply oneself to the present.*

PRON-REFL-EMPH

Emphatic reflexive pronouns are reflexive pronouns which are used for emphasis, often after another pronoun or at the end of a clause, e.g. *A wealthy man like yourself is bound to make an enemy or two along the way . . . The president himself is on a visit to Beijing . . . I made it myself.*

PRON-REL

Relative pronouns are words like *which* and *who*, that introduce relative clauses. They are the subject or object of the verb in the relative clause, or the object of a preposition, e.g. *. . . those who eat out for a special occasion . . . The largest asteroid is Ceres, which is about a quarter the size of the moon.*

PRON-SING

Singular pronouns are the singular personal pronouns, which include *I, me, he, him, she, her, it,* and *one,* e.g. *He didn't mean to be cruel but I cried my eyes out.*

QUANT

A **quantifier** comes before *of* and a noun group, e.g. *most of the house.* If there are any restrictions on the type of noun group, this is indicated: **QUANT** *of* **def-n** means that the quantifier occurs before *of* and a definite noun group, e.g. *Most of the kids have never seen the sea.*

QUANT-NEG

Negative quantifiers are words like *neither*, e.g. *Neither of us felt like going out.*

QUANT-PLURAL

Plural quantifiers are words like *billions* and *millions* which are followed by *of* and a noun group, e.g. *. . . for billions of years.*

QUEST

A **question word** is a wh-word that is used to begin a question, e.g. *Why didn't he stop me?*

SOUND

Sound words are used before or after verbs such as *go* and *say*, e.g. *Suddenly there was a loud crack.*

SUFFIX

A **suffix** is a letter or group of letters such as *–ly* or *–ness*, which is added to the end of a word in order to form a new word, usually of a different word class, e.g. *quick, quickly.*

V-I

An **intransitive verb** is one which takes an indirect object or no object, e.g. *The problems generally fall into two categories . . . As darkness fell outside, they sat down to eat.*

V-LINK

A **link verb** connects a subject and a complement. Most link verbs do not occur in the passive voice, e.g. *be, become, taste, feel.*

V-RECIP

Reciprocal verbs describe processes in which two or more people, groups, or things interact mutually: they do the same thing to each other, or participate jointly in the same action or event. Reciprocal verbs are used where the subject is both participants, e.g. *Fred and Sally met . . .* The participants can also be referred to separately, e.g. *Fred met Sally . . . Fred argued with Sally.* These patterns are reciprocal because they also mean that *Sally met Fred* and *Sally argued with Fred.* Note that many reciprocal verbs can also be used in

a way that is not reciprocal. For example, *Fred and Sally kissed* is reciprocal, but *Fred kissed Sally* is not reciprocal (because it does not mean that Sally also kissed Fred).

V-RECIP-PASSIVE
A **passive reciprocal verb** behaves like both a passive verb and a reciprocal verb, e.g. *He never believed he and Susan would be reconciled*.

V-T
A **transitive verb** is one which takes a direct object, e.g. *He mailed me the contract*.

V-T PASSIVE
A **passive verb** occurs in the passive voice only, e.g. *The company is rumored to be a takeover target*.

V-T/V-I
Some verbs may be **transitive** or **intransitive** depending on how they are used, e.g. *He opened the window and looked out... The flower opens to reveal a bee*.

Words and abbreviations used in patterns
In a pattern, the element in capital letters represents the word in the entry. All the other elements are in small letters. Items in *italics* show the actual word that is used, such as *of*. Items in roman print show the word class or type of clause that is used. For example:

> **N** *of* **n** means that the word being explained is a noun (**N**), and it is followed in the sentence by the word *of* and another noun or noun group (**n**).
> **ADV adj/adv** means that the word being explained is an adverb (**ADV**), and it is followed in the sentence by an adjective (**adj**) or (/) another adverb (**adv**).

When the word in the entry occurs in a pattern, the element in capital letters is **N** for any kind of noun, **ADJ** for any kind of adjective, and so on. **PHR** is used for a phrase, and **N** is used to represent a noun in a phrase.

Words used to structure information in patterns
after: **after v** means after a verb. The word is used either immediately after the verb, or after the verb and another word or phrase, or in a marked position at the beginning of the clause. For example, the adverb **mildly** is used:

> immediately after a verb: *Have a nice time, dear, and drive carefully*.
> after a verb and its object: *Use a flash and position the camera carefully*.
> at the beginning of a clause: *Carefully make a cut with a small knife*.

The phrase **on hold** is used:

> immediately after a verb: *Everything is on hold until we know more*.
> after a verb and its object: *He put his retirement on hold*.

also: used with some nouns to show that the word is used in a way that is not typical of that type of noun. For example, **also N in pl** means that unlike most uncount nouns, this noun also has a plural form and use. **Also** is used with some adverbs and adjectives to show a pattern that is less common than the other patterns mentioned. For example, **usu ADV with v**, **also ADV adj** means that the adverb is usually used with a verb but is also used before an adjective.

before: **before v** means before a verb. The word is used before the main element in a verb group. For example, the adverb **already** is used:

> before the whole verb group: *those who already know of the delights of skiing*.
> immediately before the main element in the group: *They had already voted for him at the first ballot*.

no: used to indicate that a verb is not used in a particular way, for example **no passive**, or that a singular noun is also used without a determiner: **also no det**.

oft: used to indicate that a word or phrase often occurs in a particular pattern or behaves in a particular way.

only: used to indicate that a verb is always used in a particular way, for example **only cont**.

usu: used to indicate that a word or phrase usually occurs in a particular pattern or behaves in a particular way.

with: with is used when the position of a word or phrase is not fixed. This means that the word or phrase sometimes comes before the named word class and sometimes comes after it. For example, **quickly** at **quick 1** has the pattern **ADV** *with* **v**. It occurs:

after the verb: *Cussane worked quickly and methodically;*
before the verb: *She quickly looked away and stared down at her hands.*

In addition, **with cl** is used when the word sometimes occurs at the beginning of the clause, sometimes at the end, and sometimes in the middle. For example, **seriously** has the pattern **ADV with cl**. It occurs:

at the beginning of the clause: *Seriously, I only watch TV in the evenings.*
at the end of the clause: *All of us react favorably to those who take our views seriously.*
in the middle of the clause: *This approach is now seriously out of step with the times.*

Elements used in patterns

adj: stands for **adjective group.** This may be one word, such as "happy", or a group of words, such as "very happy" or "as happy as I have ever been".
e.g. **adj N: read** 8 . . . *Ben Okri's latest novel is a good read.*

adj-compar: stands for **comparative adjective.** This is used to indicate an adjective group with the comparative form of the adjective.
e.g. ADJ-compar *than*: **old** 2 . . . *Bill was six years older than David.*

adj-superl: stands for **superlative adjective.** It is used to indicate an adjective group with the superlative form of the adjective.
e.g. **ADV adj-superl: positively** 1 . . . *This is positively the last chance for the industry to establish such a system.*
e.g. **ORD adj-superl: second** 2 . . . *the party is still the second strongest in Italy.*

adv: stands for **adverb group.** This may be one word, such as "slowly", or a group of words, such as "extremely slowly" or "more slowly than ever".
e.g. **adv ADV: else** 1 . . . *I never wanted to live anywhere else.*

amount: means **word or phrase indicating an amount of something,** such as "a lot", "nothing", "three percent", "four hundred pounds", "more", or "much".
e.g. **amount** *and* **ADV: above** 2 . . . *Banks have been charging 25 percent and above for unsecured loans.*

brd-neg: stands for **broad negative,** that is, a clause which is negative in meaning. It may contain a negative element such as "no-one", "never", or "hardly", or may show that it is negative in some other way.
e.g. **oft** *with* **brd-neg: approve** 1 . . . *Not everyone approves of the festival.*

cl: stands for **clause.**
e.g. **cl ADV: anyway** 4 . . . *What do you want from me, anyway?*

color: means **color word,** such as "red", "green", or "blue".
e.g. **ADJ color: pastel** . . . *pastel pink, blue, peach, and green.*

compar: stands for **comparative form of an adjective or adverb.**

    e.g. **ADV compar: even** 2 . . . *On television he made an even stronger impact as an interviewer.*

cont: stands for **continuous.** It is used when indicating that a verb is always, usually, or never used in the continuous.

    e.g. **only cont: die** 4 . . . *I'm dying for a breath of fresh air.*

    no cont: adore 1 . . . *She adored her parents and would do anything to please them.*

def-n: stands for **definite noun group.** A definite noun group is a noun group that refers to a specific person or thing, or a specific group of people or things, that is known and identified.

    e.g. **QUANT** *of* **def-n: whole** 1 . . . *I was cold throughout the whole of my body.*

def-pl-n: stands for **definite noun group with a noun in the plural.**

    e.g. **QUANT** *of* **def-pl-n: many** 1 . . . *It seems there are not very many of them left in the sea.*

det: stands for **determiner.** A determiner is a word that comes at the beginning of a noun group, such as "the", "her", or "those".

    e.g. **det ADJ: following** 2 . . . *We went to dinner the following Monday evening.*

-ed: stands for **past participle of a verb,** such as "decided", "gone", or "taken".

    e.g. **ADV -ed: freshly** . . . *freshly baked bread.*

group: stands for **noun group, adjective, adverb, or prepositional phrase.**

    e.g. **ADV group: strictly** . . . *He seemed fond of her in a strictly professional way.*

imper: stands for **imperative.** It is used when indicating that a verb is always or usually used in the imperative.

    e.g. **only imper** and **inf: beware** . . . *Beware of being too impatient with others.*

inf: stands for **infinitive form of a verb,** such as "decide", "go", or "sit".

    e.g. **ADJ to-inf: duty-bound** . . . *I felt duty-bound to help.*

    ADV to-inf: yet 7: . . . *She has yet to spend a Christmas with her husband.*

-ing: stands for **present participle of a verb,** such as "deciding", "going", or "taking".

    e.g. **PREP -ing: before** 2 . . . *He spent his early life in Sri Lanka before moving to Canada.*

it: means an "introductory" or "dummy" *it.* It does not refer to anything in a previous sentence or in the world; it may refer to what is coming later in the clause or it may refer to things in general.

    e.g. **oft** *it* **v-link ADJ to-inf: nice** 7 . . . *It's nice to meet you.*

n: stands for **noun** or **noun group.** If the **n** element occurs in a pattern with something that is part of a noun group, such as an adjective or another noun, it represents a noun. If the **n** element occurs in a pattern with something that is not part of a noun group, such as a verb or preposition, it represents a noun group. The noun group can be of any kind, including a pronoun.

    e.g. **ADJ n: abiding:** . . . *He has a genuine and abiding love of the craft.*

names: means **names of places or institutions.**

    e.g. **oft in names: requiem** 2 . . . *a performance of Verdi's Requiem.*

neg: stands for **negative words,** such as "not", or "never".

    e.g. **with neg: dream** 6 . . . *I wouldn't dream of making fun of you.*

n-proper: stands for **proper noun.** A proper noun is the name of a particular person or thing.

    e.g. usu **n-proper N: lookalike** . . . a Marilyn Monroe lookalike.

num: stands for **number.**

    e.g. **num ADV: odd** 3 . . . *How many pages was it, 500 odd?*

n-uncount: stands for **uncount noun** or **noun group with an uncount noun.** An uncount noun is a noun which has no plural form and which is sometimes used with no determiner.

    e.g. **QUANT**of **n-uncount: touch** 13 . . . *She thought she just had a touch of flu.*

ord: stands for **ordinal,** such as "first", or "second".

    e.g. **ord ADJ n: generation** 4 . . . *second generation Jamaicans in New York.*

passive: stands for **passive voice.** It is used when indicating that a verb usually or never occurs in the passive voice.

    e.g. **usu passive: expel** 1 . . . *More than five-thousand high school students have been expelled for cheating.*

pl: stands for **plural.**

pl-n: stands for **noun in the plural, plural noun group,** or **co-ordinate noun group** (two or more noun groups joined by a co-ordinating conjunction).

    e.g. **PREP pl-n: between** 2 . . . *I spent a lot of time in the early Eighties travelling between Waco and El Paso.*

pl-num: stands for **plural number.** A plural number is a number which is used only in the plural.

    e.g. **PREP poss pl-num: in** 5 . . . *young people in their twenties.*

poss: stands for **possessive.** Possessives which come before the noun may be a possessive determiner, such as "my", "her", or "their", or a possessive formed from a noun group, such as "the horse's". Possessives which come after the noun are of the form "of n", such as "of the horse".

    e.g.**usu pl, with poss: ancestor** 1 . . . *our daily lives, so different from those of our ancestors.*

prep: stands for **prepositional phrase** or **preposition.**

    prep PRON: him 1 . . . *Is Sam there? Let me talk to him.*

pron: stands for **pronoun.** A pronoun is a word such as "I", "it", or "them" which is used like a noun group. It refers to someone or something that has already been mentioned or whose identity is known.

    e.g. **PREP pron: before** 12 . . . *Everyone in the room knew it was the single hardest task before them.*

pron-indef: stands for **indefinite pronoun.** An indefinite pronoun is a word like *anyone, anything, everyone* and *something.*

    e.g. **pron-indef ADJ: else** 2 . . . *I expect everyone else to be truthful.*

pron-refl: stands for **reflexive pronoun,** such as "yourself", "herself", or "ourselves".

    e.g. **PREP pron-refl: among** 9 . . . *The girls stood aside, talking among themselves.*

quest: stands for **question word.** A question word is a wh-word such as "what", "how", or "why" which is used to begin a question.

    e.g. **quest ADV: ever** 6 . . . *Why ever didn't you tell me?*

sing: stands for **singular.**

sing-n: stands for **noun in the singular.**

    e.g. **PREDET det sing-n: all** 2 . . . *She's worked all her life.*

supp: stands for **supplementary information accompanying a noun.** Supplementary information that comes before a noun may be given by a determiner, possessive, adjective, or noun modi·er. Supplementary information that comes after the noun may be given by a prepositional phrase or a clause.

    e.g. **supp N: park** 2 . . . *a science and technology park.*

that: stands for **"that"-clause**. The clause may begin with the word "that", but does not necessarily do so.

    e.g. **usu N that: conviction** 1 . . . *It is our conviction that a step forward has been taken.*

to-inf: stands for **to-infinitive form of a verb**.

    e.g. **v-link ADJ to-inf: inclined** 2 . . . *I am inclined to agree with Alan.*

v: stands for **verb or verb group**. It is not used to represent a link verb. See also the explanations of **after, before** and **with**.

    e.g. **v PRON: her** 1 . . . *I told her I had something to say.*

    v PREP n: at 10 . . . *She opened the door and stood there, frowning at me.*

v-link: stands for **link verb**. A link verb is a verb such as "be" which connects a subject and a complement.

    e.g. **v-link ADJ: down** 3 . . . *The computer's down again.*

wh: stands for **wh-word**, or **clause beginning with a wh-word,** such as "what", "why", "when", "how", "if", or "whether".

    e.g. **ADJ about n/wh: tight-lipped** 1 . . . *Military officials are still tight-lipped about when their forces will launch a ground offensive.*

Activity Guide Contents

ACTIVITY GUIDE

---

1. USING YOUR BRAIN

Word Web Activities	Word Link Activities
Choosing the Right Definition	Practice with Pragmatics

1. **Word Web Activities**

   Use the Word Web feature entitled *brain* to answer the following questions about the brain.

   a. Which part tells you it's time to eat? _____

   b. Which part helps you learn to speak? _____

   c. Which part makes sure you stand up straight? _____

   d. Which part controls your heartbeat? _____

   e. Which part is wrapped around the outside of the brain? _____

2. **Choosing the Right Definition**

   Study the four numbered definitions for "brain." Then write the number of the definition that relates to each sentence below.

   a. _____ Angela mastered the new computer program in one day. She has some <u>brain</u>!

   b. _____ Some studies show that people with larger <u>brains</u> are more intelligent than people with smaller <u>brains</u>.

   c. _____ They say that Martin is the <u>brains</u> behind the success of the company.

   d. _____ If you'll just use your <u>brain</u> you'll make the right decision.

   e. _____ In proportion to the size of its body, the elephant's <u>brain</u> is very small.

3. **Word Link Activities**

   a. The definition of brain says that it "enables you to think." The prefix in the word *enable* is _____.

   b. Find the Word Link for this prefix. What does the prefix mean? _____

   c. What two other words with this prefix do you find?

   _____ _____

   Guess what each word means. Then check your answers by looking up the words.

4. **Practice with Pragmatics**

    Study the information about the fourth meaning in the definition of *brain*.

    Read the four sentences below. Write *Yes* if the sentence uses the term appropriately, and *No* if the usage is inappropriate.

    a. _____ I think Anna was the brains behind the kids' plan to skip school on Friday.

    b. _____ History states that Einstein was the brains behind the discovery of the theory of relativity.

    c. _____ The president said that the governor was the brains behind the economic recovery in her state.

    d. _____ I supplied the money, but Mike was the brains behind the surprise party.

ANSWER KEY:

1. **a.** medulla oblongata; **b.** cerebrum; **c.** cerebellum; **d.** medulla oblongata; **e.** cerebrum

2. **a.** 2; **b.** 1; **c.** 4; **d.** 2; **e.** 1

3. **a.** -en; **b.** to make or put; **c.** enact, encode

4. **a.** Yes; **b.** No; **c.** No; **d.** Yes

2. GOING IN CIRCLES

Grammar Activities Picture Dictionary Activities	Word Link Activities

1. **Grammar Activities**

   Many different words are based on the word *circle*. Write the part of speech of each underlined word—noun, verb, or adjective. Use your dictionary to check your answers.

   a. The moon was perfectly <u>circular</u> last night. _____

   b. The students arranged the chairs in a <u>circle</u>. _____

   c. Vitamin E improves the <u>circulation</u> of the blood. _____

   d. Airplanes sometimes <u>circle</u> several times before landing. _____

   e. Please open the window so the air can <u>circulate</u>. _____

   f. What is the <u>circulation</u> of the *New York Times*? _____

   g. Did the teacher <u>circle</u> your mistakes? _____

   h. I like <u>circular</u> eyeglasses, not square ones. _____

2. **Picture Dictionary Activities—A**

   a. How many other shapes can you think of besides the circle? Write your list below.

   _____

   Look at the Picture Dictionary feature for *shapes* and check your answers.

   b. Which two shapes most closely resemble the circle?

   _____   _____

3. **Picture Dictionary Activities—B**

   Study the Picture Dictionary feature titled *area*. Pay special attention to how to find the area of a circle.

   a. What do you call the distance from the center of the circle to the outside edge? _____

   b. What do you call the line that runs around the outside of the circle? _____

   c. What do you call the line that runs across the circle from one side to the other? _____

   d. What is the formula for finding the area of a circle? _____

   e. If a circle has a radius of 3 inches, what is its area. Use $\pi = 3.14$. _____

4. **Word Link Activities**

   a. The first four letters of the word *circle* form a Word Link. Look at the information in the Word Link for *circ-*.
   What words besides *circle* appear there?
   _____ _____

   b. Rewrite each word below. Then look it up in the dictionary and identify it as *verb*, *noun*, or *adjective*.

   _____, _____ _____, _____
   (word)   (part of speech)   (word)   (part of speech)

   c. Complete each sentence below with the correct word from b.

   1. Blood _____ around the body.

   2. A tree fell on the power lines and broke the electrical _____.

ANSWER KEY:

1. **a.** adjective; **b.** noun; **c.** noun; **d.** verb; **e.** verb; **f.** noun; **g.** verb; **h.** adjective
2. **a.** Answers will vary; **b.** ellipse, oval
3. **a.** radius; **b.** circumference; **c.** diameter; **d.** πr^2; **e.** 28.26 inches
4. **a.** circuit, circulate; **b.** circuit, noun; circulate, verb; **c1.** circulates; **c2.** circuit

3. TRANSPORTATION

Choosing the Right Definition Word Web Activities	Dictionary Research Word Link Activities

1. **Choosing the Right Definition**

   Study the numbered definitions for *transportation*. Then write the number of the definition that relates to each sentence below.

   a. _____ The <u>transportation</u> of nuclear waste through large cities can be dangerous.

   b. _____ Using mass <u>transportation</u> helps the environment.

   c. _____ Many schools provide <u>transportation</u> for children in the form of school buses.

   d. _____ Subways provide rapid <u>transportation</u>.

   e. _____ Bad weather slows down most forms of <u>transportation</u>.

2. **Word Web Activities**

   Use the Word Web feature titled *ship* to answer the following questions. Look up these words in the dictionary to check your answers.

   a. What do you call things other than people that are carried on ships?   _____

   b. What do you call the place where a ship stops?   _____

   c. What do you call the person who steers a large ship?   _____

   d. What do you call the place where a plane can land on a large ship?   _____

3. **Dictionary Research**

   a. Reread the definition of *transportation*. Write your own definition of the word *goods* as it is used in the definition.

   _____

   b. Look up the word *goods* in the dictionary and complete these sentences.

   Goods are things that people make and then later _____ .

   Goods are things that people _____ and can move from one place to another.

4. **Word Link Activities**

   The first four letters of the word *transportation* form a Word Link. Look at the information in the Word Link for *trans-*.

   a. What does the Word Link *trans-* mean? _____

   b. What are the three Word Links for *trans*?

   _____   _____   _____

   c. Complete each sentence below with the correct word from b. Check your answers by looking up each word in the dictionary.

   1. I don't know how to read Chinese. Can you _____ this letter for me?
   2. After the president of the college left, there was a period of _____ before a new one was appointed.
   3. You'll have to take two buses to get there. You can _____ from the 101 to the 145 at Main Street.

ANSWER KEY:

1. a. 3; b. 2; c. 1; d. 2; e. 3

2. a. cargo; b. port; c. captain; d. flight deck

3. a. Answers will vary.; b. sell, own

4. a. across; b. transfer, transition, translate; c1. translate; c2. transition; c3. transfer

4. TRIAL BY JURY

Dictionary Research	Word Link Activities
Word Web Activities	Choosing the Right Definition
Word Partnership Activities	

1. **Dictionary Research**
    Study the first numbered definition for the word *trial*. Think about the meaning of the four words listed below. Then match each word with the correct definition. Look up these words in the dictionary if you are not sure.

    _____ **a.** judge
    _____ **b.** guilty
    _____ **c.** jury
    _____ **d.** evidence

    1. something you see that causes you to believe something is true
    2. a person who decides how a law in applied
    3. responsible for a crime
    4. group of people who decide if a person is guilty or not

    If a person is accused of a crime and a grand jury calls for a trial, the defendant must appear in court. Study the information in the definitions for *appear*. Then write the number of the definition that relates to each sentence below.

    _____ **e.** The sun finally <u>appeared</u> at about 11:00 in the morning.
    _____ **f.** Clive <u>appeared</u> in court on Monday morning at 9:00.
    _____ **g.** My favorite band <u>appeared</u> at the Roxy last weekend.
    _____ **h.** Linda <u>appears</u> to be very healthy.

2. **Word Web Activities**
    Study the Word Web feature titled *trial*. Then use bold words from this Word Web feature to complete the following sentences. Look up any words you aren't sure of.
    a. The defendant will get a trial by _____.
    b. The defendant may or may not _____ guilty.
    c. The person who accused the defendant is the _____.
    d. The _____ will tell what they know about the crime.
    e. The words the witnesses say is called their _____.
    f. In the end, the judge will deliver a _____ .

3. **Word Partnership Activities**

Study the Word Partnerships feature for the word *jury*. Pay special attention to the phrases below. Then match each phrase with the correct definition. Look up the words in the dictionary if you are not sure.

_____ **a.** jury convicts
_____ **b.** hung jury
_____ **c.** jury duty

1. a jury that can't agree on a verdict
2. a jury finds someone guilty
3. a citizen's obligation to serve on a jury

4. **Word Link Activities**

Study the Word Link feature for the root *il*.

a. What definition do you find for the root *il*?   _____

Which of the words means the following?
Look up the words in the dictionary if you are not sure.
b. a person who is unable to read   _____
c. something that is against the law   _____

5. **Choosing the Right Definition**

Study the first four numbered definitions for *trial*. Then write the number of the definition that relates to each sentence below.
a. _____ Sitting through that movie was a real <u>trial</u> for me.
b. _____ You should give aspirin a <u>trial</u> before you ask for anything stronger.
c. _____ The murderer's <u>trial</u> lasted for six weeks.
d. _____ The boss gave me a three-week <u>trial</u> to see if I could handle the responsibilities.

ANSWER KEY:

1. **a.** 2; **b.** 3; **c.** 4; **d.** 1; **e.** 3; **f.** 7; **g.** 6; **h.** 2
2. **a.** jury; **b.** plead; **c.** plaintiff; **d.** witnesses; **e.** testimony; **f.** verdict
3. **a.** 2; **b.** 1; **c.** 3
4. **a.** not; **b.** illiterate; **c.** illegal
5. **a.** 3; **b.** 2; **c.** 1; **d.** 2

5. NEWSPAPER

Word Web Activities	Word Link Activities
Thesaurus Activities	Choosing the Right Definition
Dictionary Research	Grammar Activities

1. **Word Web Activities**

   Study the information in the Word Web feature entitled *newspaper*.
   Then answer the questions below. Write T for *true* or F for *false*.

   _____ **a.** The *Weekly Journal* was a British newspaper.

   _____ **b.** This newspaper contained some anti-British stories.

   _____ **c.** The British governor went to prison.

   _____ **d.** Zenger was found guilty.

   _____ **e.** The first amendment to the Constitution guarantees the
   freedom of the press.

2. **Thesaurus Activities**

   The two words below are sometimes used to describe an article in a newspaper:

   - story
   - report

   Read the dictionary definition for the word *story*. Then study the thesaurus feature for
   this word.

   a. Which numbered meanings of the word *story* apply to
   a newspaper story? _____

   b. What two words does the thesaurus give relating to the
   second definition? _____

   Look up any of these words that you don't understand.

   Read the dictionary definition for the word *report*. Then study the thesaurus feature
   for this word.

   c. Which numbered meanings of the word *report* apply to
   a newspaper story? _____

3. **Dictionary Research**

   Review the Word Web feature entitled *newspaper*. Then look up the word *article*.
   Study the five meanings. Write the number of the meaning that relates to the
   underlined word in each sentence.

   _____ **a.** Some people disagreed with several <u>articles</u> in the U.S. Constitution.

   _____ **b.** The use of the definite <u>article</u> can be confusing at times.

   _____ **c.** There were two <u>articles</u> about the football game in today's newspaper.

   _____ **d.** Words starting with a consonant sound take the <u>article</u> *a*.

   _____ **e.** We left several <u>articles</u> in the trunk of our rental car.

4. Word Link Activities

Read the definitions of the following item as it appears in the dictionary after the word *news*:

- news conference

Then answer the questions about these words.

   a. Look up the Word Link for *con-* as in *convene*. What does *con-* mean? _____

   b. Which of the sample words after *con-* means "to call
      a meeting together?" _____

   c. Which of the sample words means "general agreement?" _____

5. Choosing the Right Definition

Look up the word *news* and study the four definitions. Write the number of the definition that relates to how the word *news* is used in each sentence below.

   _____ a. The fire in the public library was big <u>news</u>.

   _____ b. I saw a full report on the <u>news</u> last night.

   _____ c. <u>News</u> about the economy is always on page 2.

   _____ d. I have some good <u>news</u> to tell you.

6. Grammar Activities

Read the dictionary entry for *report* and also read the surrounding entries that contain the word *report*. Then write the word forms described below using the root word *report*.

   a. A noun that means the same as "newspaper article." _____

   b. An adjective form of the word *report* as in the phrase
      "a _____ coup." _____

   c. A noun that describes a person who writes newspaper stories. _____

   d. A verb that tells what a reporter does. A reporter _____. _____

ANSWER KEY:

1. **a.** F; **b.** T; **c.** F; **d.** F; **e.** T

2. **a.** 2, 5; **b.** account, report; **c.** 2, 3

3. **a.** 3; **b.** 4; **c.** 1; **d.** 4; **e.** 2

4. **a.** together; **b.** convene; **c.** consensus

5. **a.** 4; **b.** 3; **c.** 2; **d.** 1

6. **a.** report; **b.** reported; **c.** reporter; **d.** reports

6. THE HUMAN BODY

Choosing the Right Definition Picture Dictionary Activities	Word Partnership Activities Word Link Activities

1. **Choosing the Right Definition**
   Study the definitions for the word *body*. Then write the number of the definition that relates to each sentence below.
   - _____ **a.** Congress is the largest law-making <u>body</u> in the country.
   - _____ **b.** My arms and legs got sunburned, but my <u>body</u> didn't.
   - _____ **c.** The introduction was interesting, but the <u>body</u> of the essay was boring.
   - _____ **d.** This beer has real <u>body</u>!
   - _____ **e.** When you dive into a pool, your whole <u>body</u> goes under the water.
   - _____ **f.** The Library of Congress contains a large <u>body</u> of information about American history.
   - _____ **g.** The <u>body</u> of the plane was painted blue, but the wings were bright red.
   - _____ **h.** The police found a <u>body</u> buried in the back yard.
   - _____ **i.** The Pacific Ocean is the largest <u>body</u> of water in the world.
   - _____ **j.** There is a small <u>body</u> of sports fans who like to watch violent wrestling matches.

2. **Picture Dictionary Activities**
   a. How many parts of the human body can you name? Start with the head and finish with the foot. Write your list below.

   _____

   Look at the Picture Dictionary feature for *body*. Which parts of the body did you miss?

   _____

   b. What are the four parts of the leg shown in the picture?

   _____

   c. What are the three parts of the arm shown in the picture?

   _____

3. **Word Partnership Activities**
   Look up the word *knee* in the dictionary.
   a. What is the plural form of the word *knee*? _____
   b. What is the past tense form of the verb *knee*? _____

   Study the Word Partnership feature for *knee*. Then complete the four sentences below using the word *knee* before or after one of these words: *bent, injury, left, weak*. Use each of these words one time.
   c. Luke sprained his _____ _____ skiing.
   d. I'm getting sick. I feel dizzy and _____ _____.
   e. He suffered a minor _____ _____ at Friday's game.
   f. My trainer says it's important to keep my _____ _____ when lifting weights.

4. **Word Link Activities**

   The definition of *body* says that it is all of your "physical" parts. Read the definition of *physical* and then study the Word Link that accompanies it.

   a. What does the Word Link *physi* mean? _____

   b. What synonym for *doctor* appears in the Word Link? _____

ANSWER KEY:

1. **a.** 4; **b.** 2; **c.** 6; **d.** 10; **e.** 1; **f.** 9; **g.** 7; **h.** 3; **i.** 8; **j.** 5

2. **a.** Answers will vary.; **b.** foot, ankle, knee, thigh; **c.** hand, wrist, elbow

3. **a.** knees; **b.** kneed; **c.** left knee; **d.** weak-kneed; **e.** knee injury; **f.** knees bent

4. **a.** of nature; **b.** physician

7. ORCHESTRA

Word Web Activities Picture Dictionary Activities Word Partnership Activities	Word Link Activities Choosing the Right Definition Dictionary Research

1. **Word Web Activities**

   Study the information in the Word Web feature entitled *orchestra*. Then answer the questions below. Write T for *true* or F for *false*.

   _____ **a.** A symphony orchestra usually has more than 100 players.

   _____ **b.** The largest section of the orchestra is the string section.

   _____ **c.** The double bass plays in the string section.

   _____ **d.** The brass section needs to play very loud.

   _____ **e.** The timpani is part of the brass section.

2. **Picture Dictionary Activities**

   a. Look at the Picture Dictionary feature for the word *brass*. The largest brass instrument shown is the _____.

   b. Look at the Picture Dictionary feature for the word *percussion*. The three percussion instruments that can play melodies are the x_____, the m_____, and the c_____.

3. **Word Partnership Activities**

   The job of a symphony orchestra is to *perform* for the public. Look up the word *perform* in the dictionary.

   a. Write the number of the definition that applies to music.   _____

   Study the Word Partnership feature for *perform*. Then complete the four sentences below using the word perform before or after one of these words or phrases: *tasks, ability to, miracles, well*. Use each of these words or phrases one time.

   b. Some people believe holy people can _____ _____.

   c. The violinist's cold affected his _____ _____.

   d. The new truck _____ _____ on the icy roads.

   e. Doctors believe the brains of adults and children _____ _____ in different ways.

4. **Word Link Activities**

   a. Look up the Word Link for *sym*. What does *sym* mean?   _____

   b. Look up the Word Link for *phon*. What does *phon* mean?   _____

   c. A <u>symphony</u> is a piece of music for an orchestra to _____ _____.

5. **Choosing the Right Definition**

Reread the Word Web feature for the word *orchestra*. Several of the words in this feature have multiple meanings.

Study the definitions for the word *composition*. Then write the number of the definition that relates to each sentence below.

_____ **a.** The <u>composition</u> of furniture in the store window was very attractive.

_____ **b.** Have you written any new <u>compositions</u> for the piano lately?

Study the definitions for the word *section*. Then write the number of the definition that relates to each sentence below.

_____ **c.** Did you read the <u>section</u> that tells how much interest you have to pay?

_____ **d.** Which <u>section</u> of the city do you live in?

Study the definitions for the word *instrument*. Then write the number of the definition that relates to each sentence below.

_____ **e.** The piano is my favorite <u>instrument</u>.

_____ **f.** The dentist placed the <u>instruments</u> on the shelf.

6. **Dictionary Research**

a. Study the definitions for the word *string*. Then find the one that applies to musical instruments. Complete the sentence with the correct phrase.

The brass section needs to play softer. I can't hear _____ _____.

b. Find the dictionary entries that contain the word *symphony*.

Symphony orchestras usually play _____ music.

ANSWER KEY:

1. **a.** F; **b.** T; **c.** T; **d.** F; **e.** F
2. **a.** tuba; **b.** (x)ylophone, (m)arimba, (c)himes
3. **a.** 3; **b.** perform miracles; **c.** ability to perform; **d.** performed well; **e.** perform tasks
4. **a.** together; **b.** sound; **c.** sound together
5. **a.** 1; **b.** 2; **c.** 1; **d.** 2; **e.** 2; **f.** 1
6. **a.** the strings; **b.** classical

8. COOKING

Word Web Activities	Thesaurus Activities
Picture Dictionary Activities	Grammar Activities
	Dictionary Research

1. **Word Web Activities**
    As you complete this activity, look up any words you aren't sure of.

    Read the definitions for the words *cook* and *cooking*. Then study the Word Web feature entitled *cooking* to answer the following questions.
    a. Which bold word means the opposite of *tough*? _____
    b. Which bold word means *absorb food* into your body? _____

    Now study the Word Web feature entitled *spice* to answer the following questions.
    c. Which spice is the least effective in killing germs? _____
    d. What kind of food do people in cold climates usually like? _____

    Now study the Word Web feature entitled *pan* to answer the following questions.
    e. Cooking pans made of what material are very heavy? _____
    f. Copper pans are usually covered with a thin layer of what metal? _____

2. **Picture Dictionary Activities—A**
    Look at the Picture Dictionary feature for *cook*. Then complete the sentences.
    a. If you want to make coffee, you have to _____ the water.
    b. You need an oven if you want to _____, _____, or _____ food.
    c. When you put food in a wire container with boiling water under it, you _____ the food.
    d. When you turn a slice of bread brown by cooking it you _____ it.
    e. When you cook food in an oven very close to the flame, you _____ it.

3. **Picture Dictionary Activities—B**
    Look at the Picture Dictionary feature for *egg*. Then answer the questions below. Look up any words you aren't sure of. Write T for *true* or F for *false*.
    _____ **a.** The scrambled eggs have peppers in them.
    _____ **b.** The omelet has meat in it.
    _____ **c.** The hard-boiled egg has a round yolk.
    _____ **d.** The quiche is in a frying pan.

4. **Thesaurus Activities**
    Find the Thesaurus feature with the word *cook*. Then complete the sentences using words from the feature. Look up any words you aren't sure of.

    a. The noun meaning "given" is _____.
    b. Yeast is the ingredient that _____ bread rise.
    c. If the meal is cooked but it has gotten cold, you might just _____ the food.
    d. Busy people tend to eat meals that are simple to _____.

5. **Grammar Activities**

Read the definitions for *cook* and *cooking*. Identify the part of speech of each underlined word below—noun, verb, or adjective.

a. My sister's <u>cooking</u> is fantastic. _____

b. When you make pies, you should use <u>cooking</u> apples. _____

c. On Sunday I <u>cooked</u> dinner for my family. _____

d. My husband is a very good <u>cook</u>. _____

6. **Dictionary Research**

Look at other words and phrases that follow the word *cook* in the dictionary.

a. Which one describes a collection of recipes? _____

b. Which one describes the food of a certain nation? _____

ANSWER KEY:

1. **a.** tender; **b.** digest; **c.** black pepper; **d.** bland; **e.** cast iron; **f.** tin

2. **a.** boil; **b.** roast, bake, broil; **c.** steam; **d.** toast; **e.** broil

3. **a.** F; **b.** T; **c.** T; **d.** F

4. **a.** chef; **b.** makes; **c.** heat up; **d.** prepare

5. **a.** noun; **b.** adjective; **c.** verb; **d.** noun

6. **a.** cookbook; **b.** cooking

9. ENERGY

Choosing the Right Definition Word Web Activities	Word Link Activities Grammar Activities

1. **Choosing the Right Definition**
   Study the four numbered definitions for *energy*. Then write the number of the definition that relates to each sentence below.
   a. ____ She's putting all her <u>energies</u> into her children instead of going back to work.
   b. ____ My children have more <u>energy</u> than I do.
   c. ____ One problem with nuclear <u>energy</u> is that it produces radioactive waste.
   d. ____ You should put more <u>energy</u> into your homework.
   e. ____ Which <u>energy</u> source do you think is the cleanest?
   f. ____ Conserve your <u>energy</u>. Go to bed early.

2. **Word Web Activities**
   Use the Word Web feature titled *energy* to answer the following questions. Answer each question with one of the bold words in the Word Web feature.
   a. What kind of power plants were built in the 1970s? _____
   b. What kind of gas is still used for home heating? _____
   c. What was the primary energy source for American settlers? _____
   d. What was the source of electrical power in the early 1900s? _____

3. **Word Link Activities**
   Look up the Word Link in the list below. Then match each Word Link with the correct definition.

Word Link	Definition
____ a. hydr	1. without
____ b. free	2. cause to be
____ c. electr	3. one who acts as
____ d. ate	4. water
____ e. ar	5. electric

4. **Grammar Activities**
   Review the dictionary entry for *energy* as well as the entry that appears just before it. Then complete each sentence with the correct form of a word starting with the letters *energ-*. Identify the part of speech of each word you use—noun, verb, adjective, or adverb.

Sentences	Part of Speech
a. Celia is very _____ today.	_____
b. I don't know what happened to all my _____. I'm really tired.	_____
c. David washed the car _____.	_____

ANSWER KEY:
1. **a.** 3; **b.** 1; **c.** 4; **d.** 2; **e.** 4; **f.** 1
2. **a.** nuclear; **b.** natural; **c.** wood; **d.** coal
3. **a.** 4; **b.** 1; **c.** 5; **d.** 2; **e.** 3
4. **a.** energetic, adjective; **b.** energy, noun; **c.** energetically, adverb

10. UNION

Word Web Activities Word Link Activities	Choosing the Right Definition Style and Pragmatics

1. **Word Web Activities**
   Use the Word Web feature titled *union* to answer the following questions. Each answer is one of the bold words in the feature. Look up each word in the dictionary to check your answer.

   a. What do you call people who work in offices? _____ employees

   b. What do you call an increase in someone's pay? a _____

   c. What do you call the money workers take home each week? _____

   d. What do you call the action workers take when they refuse to work? a _____

   e. What do you call the hours an employee works each day? a _____

2. **Word Link Activities**
   The first three letters of the word *union* form a Word Link. Look at the information in the Word Link for *uni*.

   a. What does the word link *uni* mean? _____

   b. What are the three word links for *uni*?

   _____   _____   _____

   c. Complete each sentence below with the correct word from b. Check your answers by looking up each word in the dictionary.

   1. The police officers were all wearing the same dark blue _____.

   2. The boss made a _____ decision that the workday would begin at 8:00 AM.

   3. Leaders of the _____ asked to meet with the company's managers.

3. **Choosing the Right Definition**
   Review the Word Web feature entitled *union* and notice how the word *strike* is used. Then look up the word *strike* in the dictionary. The first definition is the one that relates to labor union activity. Study the other numbered definitions. Then write the number of the definition that relates to each sentence below.

   a. _____ The tsunami struck without warning.

   b. _____ When the hammer struck the rock, it broke into several pieces.

   c. _____ The injured man had been struck on the head.

4. **Style and Pragmatics**

   Look at the dictionary definition of *strike* again. Three of the meanings contain a boxed note like this: | BUSINESS | Read all the definitions and find as many of these pragmatics notes as you can. Write the numbers below.

   a. Which two definitions relate to business situations? _____ and _____
   b. Which definition relates to literary situations? _____
   c. Which uses of *strike* are considered formal? _____

ANSWER KEY:

1. **a.** white-collar; **b.** raise; **c.** wages; **d.** strike; **e.** workday

2. **a.** one; **b.** uniform, unilateral, union; **c. 1.** uniform; **2.** unilateral; **3.** union

3. **a.** 5; **b.** 4; **c.** 2

4. **a.** 1, 2; **b.** 13; **c.** 2, 3, 4, 15

11. BANK

Word Web Activities Choosing the Right Definition Dictionary Research	Word Partnership Activities Thesaurus Activities

1. **Word Web Activities**

   Study the Word Web feature entitled *bank*. Answer each question with one of the bold words in the feature.

   a. What is the verb that means "to take money out?" _____

   b. What two things does a borrower pay back? _____

   and _____

   c. What do you use to get money out of an ATM? a _____

   d. Which word means the same as *loan*? _____

2. **Choosing the Right Definition**

   Look up the word *bank* in the dictionary. The circled numbers indicate three very different uses of the word *bank*. Write the number of the usage that relates to each sentence below.

   _____ a. The airplane <u>banked</u> before it landed.

   _____ b. The park was located on the <u>banks</u> of the Genesee River.

   _____ c. Most <u>banks</u> are closed on Sunday.

   Study the three noun meanings under the first use of *bank*—the section with the ① next to it. Write the number of the usage that relates to each sentence below.

   _____ d. A new <u>bank</u> just opened on the corner.

   _____ e. There is a large <u>bank</u> of vocabulary words in a dictionary.

   _____ f. The World <u>Bank</u> helps poor countries develop new businesses.

3. **Dictionary Research**

   Look at other words and phrases that follow the word *bank* in the dictionary. Several of them include the word *bank* followed by another word. Use the correct word to fill in the blanks after the word *bank* in the sentences below.

   a. My bank _____ is $352.25.

   b. I've lost my bank _____ so I can't use the ATM.

   c. I opened a new bank _____ and received a checkbook and check register.

4. **Word Partnership Activities**
   Study the Word Partnerships feature for the word *borrow*. Use one of the phrases in this feature to complete each sentence below. If necessary, look up new words in these phrases in the dictionary.
   a. When his business burned down, Michael had to _____ _____ to put up a new building.
   b. To get money to pay for college, parents sometimes _____ _____ the value of their house.
   c. Your _____ _____ _____ money can be limited if you have a bad credit rating.
   d. I decided to _____ _____ my brother instead of going to a bank.

5. **Thesaurus Activities**
   a. Look up the word *money*. Find the Thesaurus feature with this word. What five words and phrases do you find?
   _____   _____   _____   _____   _____
   b. Guess which of these words and phrases go with each definition below. Then look up the definition the words in the dictionary and check your answers.
      1. Which two items mean "coins and bills that you can use to pay for things"?
      _____   _____
      2. Which item means "a large amount of money and property"?   _____
      3. Which item means "money used to start a business"?   _____
      4. Which item means "amounts of money available to be spent"?   _____

ANSWER KEY:
1. **a.** withdraw; **b.** principal, interest; **c.** bank card; **d.** lend
2. **a.** 3; **b.** 2; **c.** 1; **d.** 2; **e.** 4; **f.** 1
3. **a.** balance; **b.** card; **c.** account
4. **a.** borrow heavily; **b.** borrow against; **c.** ability to borrow; **d.** borrow from
5. **a.** capital, cash, currency, funds, wealth;
   b. 1. cash, currency; **2.** wealth; **3.** capital; **4.** funds

12. WATER

Word Web Activities	Word Link Activities
Picture Dictionary Activities	
Choosing the Right Definition	

1. **Word Web Activities**
   Use the Word Web feature entitled *water* to answer the following questions.
   a. What happens when the sun warms lakes and rivers?
      Some of the water in them _____.
   b. What is the gas that is created during evaporation called?
      It's called _____ _____.
   c. What happens to water when it forms clouds?
      It _____.
   d. What are the three types of precipitation?
      They are rain, _____, and snow.

2. **Picture Dictionary Activities**
   Look at the Picture Dictionary feature for *clouds*. Then complete the sentences correctly.
   a. Long, thin wispy clouds are _____ clouds.
   b. Flat, gray rain clouds are called _____ clouds.
   c. Fluffy, white clouds that look like cotton are _____ clouds.
   d. Very tall, thin, fluffy white clouds are _____ clouds.

3. **Choosing the Right Definition**
   Study the numbered definitions for *cloud*. Then write the number of the definition that relates to each sentence below.
   _____ a. The ongoing argument between the couple <u>clouded</u> their vacation fun.
   _____ b. There wasn't a <u>cloud</u> in the sky.
   _____ c. The glass quickly <u>clouded</u> after I added ice cubes to my drink.
   _____ d. His anxiety <u>clouded</u> his understanding of the situation.
   _____ e. A <u>cloud</u> of smoke rose from the volcano.

4. **Work Link Activities**
   The first four letters of the word *cycle* form a Word Link. Look at the information in the Word Link for *cycl*.
   a. What does the Word Link *cycl* mean?   _____
   b. Which sample word describes a series of things?   _____
   c. Which sample word describes a pattern that repeats over and over? _____
   d. Which sample word describes a vehicle with two wheels?   _____

ANSWER KEY:
1. **a.** evaporates; **b.** water vapor; **c.** condenses; **d.** sleet
2. **a.** cirrus; **b.** nimbus; **c.** cumulus; **d.** cumulonimbus
3. **a.** 4; **b.** 1; **c.** 5; **d.** 3; **e.** 2
4. **a.** circle; **b.** cycle; **c.** cyclical; **d.** bicycle

13. PARK

Word Web Activities	Choosing the Right Definition
Grammar Activities	Word Partnership Activities
Picture Dictionary Activities	Thesaurus Activities

1. **Word Web Activities**
   Study the Word Web feature entitled *park*. Answer each question with one of the bold words in the feature. Look up any words you aren't sure of.

   a. Which part of the park features animals?   the _____

   b. Which part of the park do older people seem to prefer?   the _____

   c. What do you call food eaten while sitting on a blanket
   in the park?   a _____

   d. Where do people play tennis?   on a tennis _____

2. **Grammar Activities**
   Read the definitions for *park* and *parking*. Write the part of speech of each underlined word below—noun, verb, or adjective.

   a. We couldn't find <u>parking</u> on the street, so we had to
   use a parking garage.   _____

   b. Where did you <u>park</u> the car?   _____

   c. We left the car on a street near the <u>park</u>.   _____

   d. Sarah <u>parked</u> the car at a parking meter.   _____

3. **Picture Dictionary Activities**
   Study the Picture Dictionary feature entitled *baseball* and answer these questions.

   a. What does the catcher use to catch the ball?   a _____

   b. What does the pitcher stand on?   the pitcher's _____

   Study the Picture Dictionary feature entitled *tennis* and answer these questions.

   c. What do you call the person who supervises the game?   the _____

   d. What long feature is in the middle of the tennis court?   a _____

   e. What is the line at the side of the tennis court called?   a _____

4. **Choosing the Right Definition**
   Study the numbered dictionary definitions for *diamond*. Then write the number of the definition that relates to each sentence below.

   _____ a. Tony put a <u>diamond</u> on my three of hearts.

   _____ b. Baseball is played on a <u>diamond</u>.

   _____ c. I love my <u>diamond</u> earrings.

   Study the numbered dictionary definitions for *court*. Then write the number of the definition that relates to each sentence below.

   _____ d. I'll meet you at the tennis <u>court</u>.

   _____ e. The King of France had his <u>court</u> at Versailles.

   _____ f. After his accident, Roy had to appear in <u>court</u>.

5. **Word Partnership Activities**

Study the Word Partnership feature for *catch*. Then complete the four sentences below using the word *catch* before or after one of these words or phrases: *ball, play, the train, a fish, my eye*. Use each item one time.

a. In baseball you will hurt your hand if you try to catch a _____ without a glove.

b. I have to catch _____ to Fairfield right after class.

c. Many baseball players _____ catch between innings in a game.

d. I wanted to catch _____ for our dinner.

e. The waiter was trying to catch _____ because he finally had a free table.

6. **Thesaurus Activities**

In an athletic competition, one player or team tries to *beat* the other. Study the information in the thesaurus entry which works with three other meanings for the word *beat*. Then write the number of the meaning in the thesaurus that relates to each sentence below.

_____ a. <u>Beat</u> the eggs until they are stiff.

_____ b. I could hear the baby's heart <u>beat</u>.

_____ c. He was so angry he <u>beat</u> on the door with his fists.

ANSWER KEY:

1. a. zoo; b. gardens; c. picnic; d. court

2. a. noun; b. verb; c. noun; d. verb

3. a. glove; b. mound; c. referee; d. net; e. sideline

4. a. 3; b. 4; c. 1; d. 3; e. 4; f. 5

5. a. ball; b. the train; c. play; d. a fish; e. my eye, my attention

6. a. 5; b. 3; c. 1

14. STARS AND ASTRONOMERS

Word Web Activities	Thesaurus Activities
Choosing the Right Definition	Word Link Activities
Word Partnership Activities	

1. **Word Web Activities**

   Use the Word Web feature entitled *star* to answer the following questions.
   Look up these words in the dictionary to check your answers.

   a. What is a group of stars called?   a _____
   b. What do people call the idea that the stars control our lives?   _____
   c. What is the scientific study of the stars called?   _____
   d. Which star is used to guide ships on the sea?   the _____

   Use the Word Web feature entitled *astronomer* to answer this question:

   e. Galileo was an astronomer who thought that the center of the
      universe was the _____.

2. **Choosing the Right Definition**

   Study the first five numbered definitions for *star*. Then write the number of the
   definition that relates to each sentence below.

   a. _____ I only eat in restaurants that get at least four <u>stars</u>.
   b. _____ Eric is <u>starring</u> in a new TV comedy called " Just for You."
   c. _____ It was cloudy last night and we couldn't see any <u>stars</u>.
   d. _____ Madonna is my favorite singing <u>star</u>.
   e. _____ The flag of the United States has 50 <u>stars</u> on it.

3. **Word Partnership Activities**

   Reread the Word Web feature for *star*. Find the word *object* in the second sentence.
   Look up the word *object* in the dictionary and read the definitions.

   a. The first meaning of *object* is *something that has a fixed* _____ or _____.
   b. The second meaning of *object* is _____ or _____.

   Study the Word Partnership feature for the noun form of *object*. Then complete the
   four sentences below using the word *object* and one of these words: *foreign,
   inanimate, moving, solid*. Use each of these words one time. Look up any words you
   aren't sure of.

   c. Dogs are not usually interested in an _____ _____.
   d. We watched as the magician passed a _____ _____ through a mirror.
   e. A fast-_____ _____ has a high speed.
   f. If a child swallows a _____ _____ call a doctor for advice.

4. **Thesaurus Activities**

Reread the Word Web feature entitled *astronomer*. Notice the word *observe* near the end of the feature. Look up *observe* in the dictionary and study the Thesaurus entry that accompanies it. Which of the words in the box goes with each sentence below?

| notice   celebrate   study |

a. Americans <u>observe</u> Independence Day on July 4th. _____

b. I checked the level of the water every hour, but I didn't <u>observe</u> any change. _____

c. Jane Goodall would <u>observe</u> the chimps carefully for hours without moving. _____

5. **Word Link Activities**

The first four letters of the word *astronomer* form a Word Link. Look at the information in the Word Links for *astro*.

a. What does the Word Link *astro* mean? _____

b. What are the three Word Links for *astro*? _____   _____   _____

c. Complete each sentence below with the correct word from b. Check your answers by looking up each word in the dictionary.

1. This symbol (*) is called the _____.

2. You need a telescope to study _____.

3. You have to know how to fly a plane before you can study to become an _____.

d. Reread the Word Web feature for *star*. Find the word *astrology*. It contains two Word Links. You have studied the Word Link *astro*. Now find the Word Link *logy*.

1. What does *logy* mean? _____

2. So the literal meaning of *astrology* is the _____ of _____.

ANSWER KEY:

1. **a.** constellation; **b.** astrology; **c.** astronomy; **d.** North Star; **e.** sun
2. **a.** 3; **b.** 5; **c.** 1; **d.** 4; **e.** 2
3. **a.** shape, form; **b.** aim, purpose; **c.** inanimate object; **d.** solid object; **e.** moving object; **f.** foreign object
4. **a.** celebrate; **b.** notice; **c.** study
5. **a.** star; **b.** asterisk, astronaut, astronomy; **c1.** asterisk; **c2.** astronomy; **c3.** astronaut; **d. 1.** study of; **2.** study, stars

15. FOOD

| Word Web Activities | Picture Dictionary Activities |
| Thesaurus Activities | Choosing the Right Definition |

1. **Word Web Activities**
   Study the information in the Word Web feature entitled *food*. Then answer the
   questions below. Write T for *true* or F for *false*.
   _____ **a.** Snakes are herbivores.
   _____ **b.** Mice are predators.
   _____ **c.** Green plants store energy from the sun.

2. **Thesaurus Activities**
   The Word Web feature for *food* says that a hawk is a <u>top predator</u>. Find the Thesaurus
   feature with the word *top*. Then complete the sentences using words from the feature.
   Look up any words you aren't sure of.
   a. The adjective meanings for *top* are _____, _____, and _____.
   b. Which adjective best describes the hawk's position as a <u>top predator</u>? _____
   c. Which two noun meanings describe the <u>top</u> of a mountain? _____
   and _____

3. **Picture Dictionary Activities**
   Study the Picture Dictionary feature for *dessert*. Then answer the questions below.
   Look up any words you aren't familiar with.
   a. Which three desserts don't have to be cooked? _____, _____, and _____
   b. Which two desserts are usually very cold? _____ and _____
   c. Which dessert is always brown? _____
   d. Which dessert is made mostly of eggs? _____
   e. Which dessert is made mostly of a white grain? _____

4. **Choosing the Right Definition**
   The word *feed* is related to the word *food*. Look up the word *feed* in the dictionary.
   Then write the number of the definition that relates to each sentence below.
   a. _____ My mother always <u>feeds</u> the children dinner early on Friday nights.
   b. _____ The squirrels in our yard like to <u>feed</u> on the seed we leave for the birds.
   c. _____ Newborn babies usually <u>feed</u> every three hours.
   d. _____ We collected money to <u>feed</u> the hurricane victims in Louisiana.

ANSWER KEY:

1. **a.** F; **b.** F; **c.** T
2. **a.** best, first-rate, finest; **b.** best; **c.** peak, summit
3. **a.** ice cream, sundae, fruit salad; **b.** ice cream, sundae; **c.** brownie; **d.** custard; **e.** rice pudding
4. **a.** 1; **b.** 3; **c.** 4; **d.** 2

16. ECONOMICS AND BUSINESS

Word Web Activities	Word Link Activities
Word Partnership Activities	Choosing the Right Definition
Picture Dictionary Activities	

1. **Word Web Activities**

   Study the Word Web feature entitled *economics*. Then use bold words from this Word Web feature to complete the following sentences. Look up any words you aren't sure of.

   a. Tasks that a worker performs are called _____.

   b. The word that describes how much of something is available on the market is _____.

   c. Products manufactured in a factory are called _____.

   d. The amount of money a country possesses is called its _____.

2. **Word Partnership Activities**

   Study the Word Partnerships feature for the word *business*. Pay special attention to the phrases below. Then match each word with the correct definition. Look up these words in the dictionary if you are not sure.

   _____ **a.** business casual
   _____ **b.** business owner
   _____ **c.** online business
   _____ **d.** unfinished business
   _____ **e.** go out of business

   1. Internet orders
   2. person who owns a company
   3. an appropriate but informal way to dress
   4. close a business permanently
   5. a situation that is still a problem

3. **Picture Dictionary Activities**

   Most businesses require an office. Study the Picture Dictionary feature for *office*. Use the words in this feature to answer these questions.

   a. What do you need if you make a mistake in typing a name on an envelope? _____

   b. Where do people keep old letters and other documents? in a _____

   c. What do you use to make an important word or name stand out in your notes? a _____

   d. What do you use to permanently attach two pieces of paper together? a _____

   e. What is the name of a worker's space that has only three walls? a _____

4. **Word Link Activities**

Review the Word Web feature for *economics*. This feature contains two words with important Word Links. Look up the Word Links below and answer the following questions. Look up any words you don't know in the dictionary.

a. What does *micro* mean? _____

b. Which word in this link names an instrument used to look at tiny objects? _____

c. What does *tribute* as in the word *distribute* mean? _____

d. Which word in this link means the same as "give"? _____

e. Which word means "a quality or characteristic that someone possesses"? _____

5. **Choosing the Right Definition**

Reread the Word Web feature for *economics*. Several words in this feature have multiple meanings.

Study the definitions for the word *capital*. Then write the number of the definition that relates to each sentence below.

_____ a. The capital of New York State is Albany.

_____ b. They need a lot of capital to start their business.

_____ c. Always begin a proper name with a capital letter.

Study the definitions for the word *service*. Then write the number of the definition that relates to each sentence below.

_____ d. The service in this restaurant is usually very good.

_____ e. We attended a service in memory of the flood victims.

Study the definitions for the word *demand*. Then write the number of the definition that relates to each sentence below.

_____ f. The demand for fresh water is high in desert areas.

_____ g. I demand an explanation for you actions last night.

ANSWER KEY:

1. a. services; b. supply; c. goods; d. wealth
2. a. 3; b. 2; c. 1; d. 5; e. 4
3. a. correction fluid; b. file cabinet; c. highlighter; d. stapler; e. cubicle
4. a. small; b. microscope; c. giving; d. contribute; e. attribute
5. a.4; b. 1; c. 6; d. 11; e. 12; f. 4; g. 1

17. ART

Word Web Activities	Word Link Activities
Thesaurus Activities	Style and Pragmatics
	Choosing the Right Definition

1. **Word Web Activities**
   Use the Word Web feature titled *art* to answer the following questions.
   a. What inspired the term "Impressionism"?   a painting by _____
   b. In what part of the world did Impressionism start?   in _____
   c. What did the Impressionists usually paint?   _____
   d. What elements did they emphasize in their paintings?   _____ and color
   e. The art of what country influenced the Impressionists?   _____

2. **Thesaurus Activities**
   The Word Web feature for *art* says that the Impressionists were interested in light and color. Find the Thesaurus feature with the word *light*. Then complete the sentences using words from the feature. Look up any words you aren't sure of.
   a. The noun meanings for *light* are _____, _____, _____, _____, and _____.
   b. Which noun meaning best describes the soft light of a fire when there are no flames? _____
   c. Which noun meaning describes the happiness on a person's face? _____
   d. Which adjective describes a room with a lot of windows facing south? _____

3. **Word Link Activities**
   Review the Word Web feature for *art* noting the words *realistic* and *depict*.
   Look up the Word Link below and answer the questions. Look up any words you don't know in the dictionary.
   a. What does the Word Link *real* mean?   _____
   b. Which word in this link means "to make something happen"? _____
   c. Which word in this link means "actually"?   _____
   d. What does *ist* mean?   _____
   e. Which word describes someone who works in a drugstore? _____
   f. What does the Word Link *pict* mean?   _____
   g. Which word in this link means "charming and pretty"? _____
   h. Which word in this link means "show or illustrate"? _____

4. **Style and Pragmatics**

Here are several words that use the root *real: real, realize, really*. Look up each word in the dictionary. Look for notes about pragmatics in a box following sample sentences that include these words. Locate the following notes and copy the sample sentence below.

a. Describe how much something sold for. ⌐FORMAL⌐

_____

b. Emphasize a description by using *real* + adjective. ⌐AM, INFORMAL⌐

_____

5. **Choosing the Right Definition**

The Word Web feature for *art* says that the Impressionists stopped painting in their *studios*. Study the four numbered definitions for *studio*. Then write the number of the definition that relates to each sentence below.

a. ____ The TV show originated in a <u>studio</u> in New York City.

b. ____ Because he couldn't afford a one-bedroom apartment, he lived in a <u>studio</u>.

c. ____ The photographer has a large <u>studio</u> with large windows.

d. ____ Most of the large movie <u>studios</u> are located in Hollywood.

ANSWER KEY:

1. **a.** Monet; **b.** Europe; **c.** landscapes; **d.** light; **e.** Japan
2. **a.** brightness, gleam, glow, radiance, shine; **b.** glow; **c.** radiance/glow; **d.** sunny
3. **a.** actual; **b.** realize; **c.** really; **d.** one who practices; **e.** pharmacist; **f.** painting;
   g. picturesque; **h.** depict
4. **a.** A selection of correspondence from P.G. Wodehouse realized 2,000 dollars.;
   b. He is finding prison life real tough.
5. **a.** 2; **b.** 4; **c.** 1; **d.** 3

18. TELEVISION

Word Web Activities Thesaurus Activities Word Link Activities	Choosing the Right Definition Grammar Activities Dictionary Research

1. **Word Web Activities**
   Use the Word Web feature entitled *television* to answer the following questions. Look up any words you don't know in the dictionary.
   a. What kind of tube was used in old-fashioned televisions? a _____ tube
   b. What are the tiny dots of light on a TV screen called? _____
   c. What are the three sources of TV signals? _____,

   _____,

   and _____.
   d. How many pixels per square inch does a high-definition
      TV have? _____

2. **Thesaurus Activities**
   The Word Web feature for *television* says that high-definition televisions have a very *clear picture*.
   a. Read the dictionary definition for the word *clear*. *Clear* is used to describe a TV picture that is easy to _____.
   Study the thesaurus feature for *clear*.
   b. Which numbered definition of *clear* relates to the weather? _____
   c. Which word in the thesaurus entry means the opposite of *dark*? _____
   Read the dictionary definition for the word *picture*. Then study the thesaurus feature for this word.
   d. Which meaning of the word *picture* applies to a television picture? _____
   e. Look at the verb meanings of *picture* in the thesaurus entry. They describe a picture that exists only in a person's _____.

3. **Word Link Activities**
   Television
   a. Look up the Word Link for *tele*. What does *tele* mean? _____
   b. What does the word *vision* mean? _____
   c. So television is something that lets you _____ things at a _____.

4. **Choosing the Right Definition**
    Reread the Word Web feature for *television*. Pay special attention to the words *screen* and *station*.
    Study the numbered definitions for *screen*. Then write the number of the definition that relates to each sentence below.
    _____ **a.** We put a screen in front of the window to keep out the light.
    _____ **b.** Did they screen your luggage at the airport?
    Study the numbered definitions for *station*. Then write the number of the definition that relates to each sentence below.
    _____ **c.** We live only three blocks from the subway station.
    _____ **d.** Which station is showing the soccer game tonight?

5. **Grammar Activities**
    The Word Web feature says that cathode-ray tubes are used to *produce* a television picture. Many different words are based on the word *produce*. Write the part of speech of each underlined word—noun, verb, adjective, or adverb. Use your dictionary to check your answers.

a. I always buy my produce in the fruit market on the corner.	_____
b. There are so many new products on the market, I don't know which to buy.	_____
c. A lot of movie production takes place on the streets of New York.	_____
d. I am the most productive early in the morning.	_____
e. The thief produced a gun from his pocket.	

6. **Dictionary Research**
    Look at the words and phrases that follow the word *screen* in the dictionary.
    a. Which one describes something you find on a computer?   _____
    b. Which one describes something that will later become a movie?   _____

ANSWER KEY:

1. **a.** cathode-ray; **b.** pixels; **c.** ground stations, satellites, cables; **d.** two million

2. **a.** see; **b.** 3; **c.** bright; **d.** image; **e.** mind

3. **a.** distance; **b.** see; **c.** see, distance

4. **a.** 4; **b.** 8; **c.** 1; **d.** 3

5. **a.** noun; **b.** noun; **c.** noun; **d.** adjective; **e.** verb

6. **a.** screensaver; **b.** screenplay

19. MONEY

Word Web Activities	Choosing the Right Definition
Word Partnership Activities	Dictionary Research
Thesaurus Activities	

1. **Word Web Activities**
   Study the Word Web feature entitled *money* and answer the following questions.
   a. Which word in the feature means the same as *trade*? _____
   b. What form of ocean life was used as money at one time? _____
   c. Were the first coins round? _____
   d. What country had the first circular coins? _____
   e. Which two metals were used by the Lydians to make coins? _____ and
      _____

2. **Word Partnership Activities**
   Look up the word *buy* in the dictionary.
   a. What is the past tense of the verb *buy*?
   b. Which meaning of *buy* is found in this sentence?
      I bought myself a few minutes by raising my hand and asking questions.
      meaning number _____
   Study the Word Partnership feature for *buy*. Then complete the four sentences below
   using the word *buy* before or after one of these words or phrases: *online, and sell, presents,
   afford to*. Use each of these items one time.
   c. I can't _____ _____ a flat screen TV. I don't have enough money.
   d. If you _____ _____ stocks at the right time, you can get rich.
   e. Is it safe to _____ _____ ?

3. **Thesaurus Activities**
   Study the Thesaurus feature for *money*. Look up each synonym given in order to
   understand the differences in meaning. Then complete each sentence below with the
   correct word.
   a. A single _____ is now in use in all European countries.
   b. I never use _____ . I prefer to pay by credit card or check.
   c. I don't have the amount of _____ I need to start my own business.
   d. The group decided to raise _____ to help people with AIDS.
   e. The discovery of oil brought great _____ to the Middle East.

4. **Choosing the Right Definition**

   Study the numbered definitions for *bill*. Then write the number of the definition that relates to each sentence below.

   _____ a. Please ask the waiter to bring the <u>bill</u>.

   _____ b. The duck put its <u>bill</u> into the water.

   _____ c. My electric <u>bill</u> this month was over $100.

   _____ d. My favorite band is <u>billed</u> to perform at Madison Square Garden next summer.

   _____ e. He handed me three crisp, new dollar <u>bills</u>.

   _____ f. The singer was <u>billed</u> as the next Madonna.

   _____ g. The mechanic <u>billed</u> us for some work he didn't do.

   _____ h. Congress passed a <u>bill</u> that prohibited smoking in hospitals.

5. **Dictionary Research**

   The Word Web feature for *money* says that the Lydians *minted* three types of coins. Look up the word *mint* in the dictionary. Then write the number of the definition that relates to each sentence below.

   a. Which numbered meaning of *mint* is used in the Word Web feature?   _____

   b. Which meaning names a spice people cook with?   _____

   c. Which meaning names a type of candy?   _____

   d. Which meaning tells where money is manufactured?   _____

ANSWER KEY:

1. **a.** barter; **b.** cowrie shells; **c.** no; **d.** China; **e.** gold, silver

2. **a.** bought; **b.** 3; **c.** afford to buy; **d.** buy and sell; **e.** buy online

3. **a.** currency; **b.** cash; **c.** capital; **d.** funds; **e.** wealth

4. **a.** 6; **b.** 9; **c.** 1; **d.** 7; **e.** 3; **f.** 8; **g.** 2; **h.** 4

5. **a.** 4; **b.** 1; **c.** 2; **d.** 3

20. POLLUTION AND THE GREENHOUSE EFFECT

Word Web Activities	Word Link Activities
Word Partnership Activities	Choosing the Right Definition
	Dictionary Research

1. **Word Web Activities**

   Use the Word Web feature entitled *pollution* to answer the following questions.
   Look up any words you aren't familiar with.

   a. *Smog* is a combination of smoke and _____.

   b. Factories in the Midwest cause _____ that falls in the East.

   c. A substance used to kill insects is called a _____.

   Use the Word Web feature entitled *the greenhouse effect* to answer these questions.

   d. Energy that comes from the sun is called _____ radiation.

   e. Gasoline is an example of a _____ fuel.

   f. The average temperature of the earth is going _____.

2. **Word Partnership Activities**

   Notice how the word *cause* is used in the Word Web features for *pollution* and *the greenhouse effect*. Next study the Word Partnerships feature for the word *cause*. Use the correct Word Partnership phrase to complete each sentence below. If necessary, look up new words in the dictionary.

   a. Scientists are looking for answers. They want to _____ global warming.

   b. My cold isn't serious at all. There's no _____.

   c. Doctors say cigarette smoking may _____.

   d. They want to know why their dog died. The vet is looking for the _____.

3. **Word Link Activities**

   The Word Web feature for *pollution* talks about *exhaust*.

   a. The prefix in the word *exhaust* is _____.

   b. Find the Word Link for this prefix. What does the prefix mean? _____

   Which of the words means the same as the following? Look up the words in the dictionary if you are not sure.

   c. to leave _____

   d. to break into many pieces _____

   e. to go beyond _____

4. **Choosing the Right Definition**

The Word Web feature for *the greenhouse effect* mentions carbon dioxide and other *gases*. Study the five numbered definitions for *gas*. Then write the number of the definition that best relates to each sentence below.

_____ **a.** I need to put some gas in the car before we leave this afternoon.

_____ **b.** The soldiers were gassed by a small group of enemy troops.

_____ **c.** Our new stove uses gas instead of electricity.

_____ **d.** Cigarette smoke contains poisonous gases.

_____ **e.** Oxygen is a gas that plants give off.

5. **Dictionary Research**

The Word Web feature for *the greenhouse effect* says that global average *temperature* has risen over the past hundred years. Search the Word Webs to find the answers to the following questions about temperature .

	Word Web feature	Question	Answer
a.	sun	The temperature of the sun is _____.	_____
b.	climate	In the last 100 years, the earth's temperature has increased by _____.	_____
c.	wind	Air flows from one place to another because of the _____ in temperature from one area to another.	_____
	element	Oxygen is a gas at _____ temperature.	_____
	cooking	Heating food to a high temperature kills _____.	_____

ANSWER KEY:

1. **a.** fog; **b.** acid rain; **c.** pesticide; **d.** solar; **e.** fossil; **f.** up

2. **a.** determine the cause of; **b.** cause for concern; **c.** cause cancer; **d.** cause of death

3. **a.** ex; **b.** away, from, out; **c.** exit; **d.** explode; **e.** exceed

4. **a.** 4; **b.** 5; **c.** 1; **d.** 3; **e.** 2

5. **a.** 15 million degrees Celsius; **b.** about 1° Fahrenheit; **c.** difference; **d.** room; **e.** bacteria

21. BRIDGES AND DAMS

Word Web Activities	Word Partnership Activities
Thesaurus Activities	Word Link Activities
Grammar Activities	Practice with Pragmatics

1. **Word Web Activities**

   Study the Word Web feature for *bridge*. Then match each number below with the correct description.

Word Link	Definition
____ **a.** 1⁺ mile	1. The height in feet of the Akashi Kaikyo Bridge
____ **b.** 1883	2. When the Brooklyn Bridge was built
____ **c.** 120,000	3. The length of the Evergreen Point Floating Bridge
____ **d.** 1,000	4. How many cars cross the Brooklyn Bridge every day
____ **e.** 8.5	5. The strength of an earthquake that the Akashi Kaikyo Bridge can withstand
____ **f.** 12,828	6. The length of the Akashi Kaikyo Bridge

   Read the Word Web feature for *dam*. Then answer the questions below. Write T for *true* or F for *false*.

   ____ **g.** The world's first dam was built near Memphis.

   ____ **h.** The world's first dam prevented flooding.

   ____ **i.** Hydroelectric dams provide 20% of the world's electricity.

   ____ **j.** The Itapu Dam took 10 years to build.

2. **Thesaurus Activities**

   The Word Web feature for *dam* states that dams help protect valuable forest *lands*. Find the Thesaurus feature with the word *land*. Then complete the sentences below using words from this thesaurus feature. Look up any words you aren't sure of.

   a. Someday I will return to the _____ of my birth.

   b. Harry doesn't own a house, but he does own some _____ outside of town.

   c. We weren't sure when the train would _____.

   d. Do you live in a safe _____ ?

3. **Grammar Activities**

   The Word Web feature for *dam* describes the world's longest *suspension* bridge. Study the list of words that are formed from the word *suspend*. Identify the part of speech of each underlined word below—noun, verb, or adjective. Use the dictionary to check any you aren't sure of.

   a. I drove over a large rock and damaged the car's suspension. _____

   b. The airline suspends flights during storms. _____

   c. I use suspenders instead of a belt. _____

   d. I couldn't stand the suspense so I asked the teacher what my grade was. _____

4. **Word Partnership Activities**

   Study the Word Partnerships feature for the word *build*. Use one of the phrases in this feature to complete each sentence below. If necessary, look up new words in these phrases in the dictionary.

   a. Students need to speak English as much as possible to _____.

   b. Leo works out at the gym and has a very _____ .

   c. Many female ballet dancers have a _____ .

   d. The government will _____ to connect all the major cities in the country.

   e. Tax revenue often helps to _____ and _____ .

5. **Word Link Activities**

   Reread the Word Web feature entitled *dam*. Notice the words *constructed* and *endanger*. Look these words up in the dictionary.

   a. Which one relates to building something? _____

   b. Which one relates to destroying something? _____

   There are two Word Links in the word *constructed—con* and *struct*. Look up these Word Links.

   c. What does the Word Link *con* mean? _____

   d. What does the Word Link *struct* mean? _____

   e. So the word *construct* means to _____ something _____.

   The first two letters of *endanger* are a Word Link. Look at the Word Link for *en*.

   f. What does the word link *en* mean? _____

   g. So the word *endanger* means to _____ someone or something in danger.

6. **Practice with Pragmatics**

   Study the information about the fourth meaning in the definition of *bridge*. Read the four sentences below. Write *Yes* if the sentence uses the term appropriately, and *No* if the usage is inappropriate.

   a. ____ Some scientists believe that it is possible to bridge the gap between human and machine.

   b. ____ Museums are a bridge between past and present.

   c. ____ The summit failed to bridge differences on free trade between the two nations.

   d. ____ The president tried to build bridges with Europe.

ANSWER KEY:

1. **a.** 3; **b.** 2; **c.** 4; **d.** 1; **e.** 5; **f.** 6; **g.** T; **h.** F; **i.** T; **j.** F

2. **a.** country; **b.** acreage/real estate; **c.** arrive; **d.** area

3. **a.** noun; **b.** verb; **c.** noun; **d.** noun

4. **a.** build confidence; **b.** athletic/strong build; **c.** slender build; **d.** build roads; **e.** build bridges, build schools

5. **a.** constructed; **b.** endanger; **c.** together, with; **d.** building; **e.** building, together; **f.** making, putting; **g.** put

6. **a.** yes; **b.** no; **c.** yes; **d.** no

22. CLONE

Word Web Activities	Word Link Activities
Thesaurus Activities	Choosing the Right Definition
	Grammar Activities

1. **Word Web Activities**
   Study the Word Web feature entitled *clone*. Then use bold words from this feature to complete the following sentences. Look up any words you aren't sure of.
   a. Maria's computer is _____ to mine.
   b. I need to give them a _____ of my driver's license.
   c. The girls look like _____, but they were born a year apart.
   d. Each _____ in your body contains DNA.
   e. Scientists use _____ to create new types of plants.

2. **Thesaurus Activities**
   Find the Thesaurus feature for the word *natural*. Then complete the sentences using words from the feature. Look up any words you aren't sure of.
   a. It is _____ for new students to be a little nervous at first.
   b. This doesn't look like _____ leather to me. I think it's plastic.
   c. Please accept my _____ apology for what I said.
   d. Farm-grown strawberries are good, but _____ strawberries are better.

3. **Word Link Activities**
   Find the word *identical* in the Word Web feature for *clone*. Study the Word Link feature for the root *ident*.
   a. What does the Word Link *ident* mean? _____
   Write the word in this Word Link that matches each definition below. Look up the words in the dictionary if you are not sure.
   b. your passport or driver's license _____
   c. exactly the same _____
   d. unknown or nameless _____
   Find the word *donate* in the Word Web feature for *clone*. Study the Word Link feature for the root *don*.
   e. What does the Word Link *don* mean? _____
   Write the word in this Word Link that matches each definition below. Look up the words in the dictionary if you are not sure.
   f. to forgive someone _____
   g. someone who gives something away _____
   h. to give money or goods to an organization _____

4. **Choosing the Right Definition**
    Clones are produced by *genetic engineering.* Study the numbered definitions for *engineer.*
    Then write the number of the definition that relates to each sentence below.
    ___ **a.** A famous civil <u>engineer</u> designed that bridge.
    ___ **b.** The building <u>engineer</u> repaired the water heater.
    ___ **c.** The <u>engineer</u> told the captain that the ship would never make it back to port.
    ___ **d.** They <u>engineered</u> the car in such a way that it would get good gas mileage.
    ___ **e.** My "accidental" meeting with Rosa was actually <u>engineered</u> by her sister.

5. **Grammar Activities**
    Review the dictionary entry for *genetic* as well as the five entries that follow it.
    Then complete each sentence with the correct word or phrase.
    a. The study of how characteristics are passed from parents to children is
    called _____ .
    b. The science of changing the genetic structure of a plant or animal is called _____.
    c. Plants and animals whose genes have been changed have _____ genes.

ANSWER KEY:
1. **a.** identical; **b.** copy; **c.** twins; **d.** cell; **e.** genetic engineering
2. **a.** normal; **b.** genuine; **c.** sincere; **d.** wild
3. **a.** same; **b.** identification; **c.** identical; **d.** unidentified; **e.** giving; **f.** pardon; **g.** donor;
    h. donate
4. **a.** 1; **b.** 2; **c.** 3; **d.** 4; **e.** 5
5. **a.** genetics; **b.** genetic engineering; **c.** genetically modified

Aa

A also **a** /eɪ/ (**A's, a's**) N-VAR 可変性名詞 **A** is the first letter of the English alphabet. 英語アルファベットの第1文字

a /ə, STRONG eɪ/ also **an** /ən, STRONG æn/

> **A** or **an** is the indefinite article. It is used at the beginning of noun groups that refer to only one person or thing. The form **an** is used in front of words that begin with vowel sounds.

> **A** または **an** は不定冠詞であり、1人か1つの物しか指さない名詞群の始めに用いられる。**an** 形は母音で始まる語の前で用いられる。

1 DET 限定詞 You use **a** or **an** when you are referring to someone or something for the first time or when people may not know which particular person or thing you are talking about. (漠然と) 1つの、1人の □*A waiter entered with a tray bearing a glass and a bottle of whiskey.* ウェイターがウィスキー1びんとグラス1個をのせた盆を持って入ってきた。□*He started eating an apple.* 彼はりんごを食べ始めた。**2** DET 限定詞 You use **a** or **an** when you are referring to any person or thing of a particular type and do not want to be specific. 誰か、何か □*I suggest you leave it to an expert.* それは専門家に任せた方がいいと思うよ。□*Bring a sleeping bag.* 寝袋を持って来て下さい。**3** DET 限定詞 You use **a** or **an** in front of an uncount noun when that noun follows an adjective, or when the noun is followed by words that describe it more fully. 不可算名詞が形容詞を伴う場合、また不可算名詞が説明の言葉を伴う場合に使う。□*The islanders exhibit a constant happiness with life.* その島の住人はいつも幸せそうだ。**4** DET 限定詞 You use **a** or **an** in front of a mass noun when you want to refer to a single type or make of something. (質量名詞の前に置き) 1種の □*Bollinger "RD" is a rare, highly prized wine.* ボランジェ RDは希少で非常に貴重なワインだ。**5** DET 限定詞 You use **a** in quantifiers such as **a lot, a little,** and **a bit.** 数量詞の前に付ける。□*I spend a lot on expensive jewelry and clothing.* 私は高価な宝石と衣服にたくさんお金をかける。**6** DET 限定詞 You use **a** or **an** to refer to someone or something as a typical member of a group, class, or type. 一というもの □*Some parents believe a boy must learn to stand up and fight like a man.* 男の子というものは男らしく立ち上がって戦えるようにならなくては、と考える親もいる。**7** DET 限定詞 You use **a** or **an** in front of the names of days, months, or festivals when you are referring to one particular instance of that day, month, or festival. (曜日、月、祝日などの前に置き) ある □*The interview took place on a Friday afternoon.* 面接はある金曜の午後に行われた。**8** DET 限定詞 You use **a** or **an** when you are saying what someone is or what job they have. 職業について説明する時に使う。□*I explained that I was an artist.* 私は芸術家だと説明した。**9** DET 限定詞 You use **a** or **an** instead of the number "one," especially with words of measurement such as "hundred," "hour," and "meter," and with fractions such as "half," "quarter," and "third." (数量を表す言葉に付けて) 1 □*...more than a thousand acres of land.* 1,000エーカー以上の土地 **10** DET 限定詞 You use **a** or **an** in expressions such as **eight hours a day** to express a rate or ratio. (数量を表す言葉に付けて) 一につき、一当たり □*Prices start at $13.95 a yard for printed cotton.* 綿プリントの値段は1ヤード当たり13.95ドルからです。

A & E /eɪ ən i/ N-UNCOUNT 不可算名詞 **A & E** is the same as the **ER.** 救急外来 [BRIT 英国英語]

aback /əbæk/ PHRASE 句 If you are **taken aback by** something, you are surprised or shocked by it and you cannot respond at once. 不意を打たれて □*Roland was taken aback by our strength of feeling.* ローランドは我々の強い気持ちにめんくらった。

aban|don /əbændən/ (**abandons, abandoning, abandoned**)
1 V-T 他動詞 If you **abandon** a place, thing, or person, you leave the place, thing, or person permanently or for a long time, especially when you should not do so. 捨てる □*He claimed that his parents had abandoned him.* 彼は両親に捨てられたと主張した。**2** V-T 他動詞 If you **abandon** an activity or piece of work, you stop doing it before it is finished. あきらめる □*The authorities have abandoned any attempt to distribute food in an orderly fashion.* 当局は整然と食料を配布しようとする試みをすっかりあきらめた。**3** V-T 他動詞 If you **abandon** an idea or way of thinking, you stop having that idea or thinking in that way. 断念する □*Logic had prevailed and he had abandoned the idea.* 論理が勝って、彼はその考えを断念していた。**4** N-UNCOUNT 不可算名詞 If you say that someone does something **with abandon,** you mean that they behave in a wild, uncontrolled way and do not think or care about how they should behave. 勝手気まま [DISAPPROVAL 不賛成] [usu 'with' N] □*He approached life with reckless abandon – I don't think he himself knew what he was going to do next.* 彼は向こう見ずな奔放さで人生を生きてきた。彼自身、次に自分が何をしようとしているのか分かっていなかったと思う。**5** → see also **abandoned 6** PHRASE 句 If people **abandon ship,** they get off a ship because it is sinking. 船を捨てる □*At the captain's order, they abandoned ship.* 船長の命令で彼らは船を離れた。

> **Thesaurus** *abandon* また次を参照:
>
> v.　desert, leave, quit; (*ant.*) stay **1**
>　　break off, give up, quit, stop;
>　　(*ant.*) continue **2**

aban|doned /əbændənd/ ADJ 形容詞 An **abandoned** place or building is no longer used or occupied. 放棄された □*The digging had left a network of abandoned mines and tunnels.* 採掘の後、廃鉱になった鉱床と坑道が網目状に残った。

aban|don|ment /əbændənmənt/ **1** N-UNCOUNT 不可算名詞 The **abandonment of** a place, thing, or person is the act of leaving it permanently or for a long time, especially when you should not do so. 放棄 □*...memories of her father's complete abandonment of her.* 彼女が父親に完全に捨てられた思い出 **2** N-UNCOUNT 不可算名詞 The **abandonment of** a piece of work or activity is the act of stopping doing it before it is finished. 断念、中止 □*Constant rain forced the abandonment of the next day's competitions.* 絶え間ない雨に、翌日の競技は中止せざるをえなかった。

abate /əbeɪt/ (**abates, abating, abated**) V-I 自動詞 If something bad or undesirable **abates,** it becomes much less strong or severe. 和らぐ [FORMAL 形式ばった] □*The storms had abated by the time they rounded Cape Horn.* 彼らがホーン岬を回る頃には嵐はないでいた。

ab|bey /æbi/ (**abbeys**) N-COUNT 可算名詞 An **abbey** is a church with buildings attached to it in which monks or nuns live or used to live. 大修道院

ab|bre|vi|ate /əbrivieɪt/ (**abbreviates, abbreviating, abbreviated**) V-T 他動詞 If you **abbreviate** something, especially a word or a piece of writing, you make it shorter. 短縮する、略する □*The creators of the original X-Men abbreviated the title of its sequel to simply X2.* 原作『X-メン』の制作者たちは続編の題名を単に『X2』に短縮した。

ab|bre|via|tion /əbrivieɪʃ°n/ (**abbreviations**) N-COUNT 可算名詞 An **abbreviation** is a short form of a word or phrase, made by leaving out some of the letters or by using only the first letter of each word. 短縮、略語 □*The abbreviation for Kansas is KS.* カンザス州の短縮形はKSである。

ab|di|cate /æbdɪkeɪt/ (**abdicates, abdicating, abdicated**) **1** V-I 自動詞 If a king or queen **abdicates,** he or she gives up being king or queen. 退位する □*The last French king was Louis Philippe, who abdicated in 1848.* 最後のフランス王はルイ・フィリップで、1848年に退位した。●**ab|di|ca|tion** /æbdɪkeɪʃ°n/ N-UNCOUNT 不可算名詞 退位 □*the most serious royal crisis since the abdication of Edward VIII.* エドワード8世の退位以来の最も深刻な王室の危機 **2** V-T 他動詞 If you say that someone has **abdicated** responsibility for something, you disapprove of them because they have refused to accept responsibility for it any longer. 放棄する [FORMAL 形式ばった, DISAPPROVAL 不賛成] □*Many parents simply abdicate all responsibility for their children.* 実際子供に対する責任をすべて放棄している親が多い。●**ab|di|ca|tion** N-UNCOUNT 不可算名詞 放棄 □*There had been a complete abdication of responsibility.* 責任が完全に放棄されていた。

ab|do|men /æbdoumən/ (**abdomens**) N-COUNT 可算名詞 Your **abdomen** is the part of your body below your chest where your stomach and intestines are. 腹部 [FORMAL 形式ばった] □*He went into the hospital to undergo tests for a pain in his abdomen.* 彼は腹部の痛みの検査を受けるため入院した。

ab|domi|nal /æbdɒmɪn°l/ ADJ 形容詞 **Abdominal** is used to describe something that is situated in the abdomen or forms part of it. 腹部の [FORMAL 形式ばった] [ADJ n] □*...vomiting, diarrhea, and abdominal pain.* 嘔吐、下痢、および腹痛。

ab|duct /æbdʌkt/ (**abducts, abducting, abducted**) V-T 他動詞 If someone **is abducted** by another person, he or she is taken away

illegally, usually using force. 誘拐する，拉致する □*He was on his way to the airport when his car was held up and he was abducted by four gunmen.* 彼は空港に向かっている途中で4人の銃を持った男に車を止められて誘拐された. ● **ab|duc|tion** /æbdʌkʃ°n/ N-VAR 可変的名詞 誘拐，拉致 □*The U. N. World Food Program confirmed the abduction of eight of its workers in northern Darfur.* 国連世界食糧計画はダルフール北部で職員8名が拉致されたことを確認した.

ab|er|ra|tion /æbəreɪʃ°n/ (aberrations) N-VAR 可変的名詞 An **aberration** is an incident or way of behaving that is not typical. 常軌を逸脱すること [FORMAL 形式ばった] □*It became very clear that the incident was not just an aberration; it was not just a single incident.* その事件がただの常軌を逸した事件ではないことが極めて明白になった．それはただの単発的な事件ではなかったのだ.

abide /əbaɪd/ (abides, abiding, abided) **1** PHRASE 句 If you **can't abide** someone or something, you dislike them very much. 我慢できない □*I can't abide people who take up their minds.* 私は優柔不断な人には我慢ならない. **2** → see also **abiding, law-abiding**
▶ **abide by** PHRASAL VERB 句動詞 If you **abide by** a law, agreement, or decision, you do what it says you should do. 守る，従う □*They have got to abide by the rules.* 彼らは規則に従わねばならない.

abid|ing /əbaɪdɪŋ/ ADJ 形容詞 An **abiding** feeling, memory, or interest is one that you have for a very long time. 永続的な，変わらない [ADJ with n] □*He has a genuine and abiding love of the craft.* 彼はその工芸の仕事に心からの変わらぬ愛情を抱いている.

abil|ity /əbɪlɪti/ (abilities) **1** N-SING 単数名詞 Your **ability to** do something is the fact that you can do it. 能力 □*The public never had faith in his ability to handle the job.* 国民は彼がその職務をうまくやれるとは決して信じていなかった. **2** N-VAR 可変的名詞 Your **ability** is the quality or skill that you have which makes it possible for you to do something. 才能 □*Her drama teacher spotted her ability.* 演劇の先生が彼女の才能を見抜いた. □*Does the school cater to all abilities?* その学校はあらゆる才能に対応していますか. **3** PHRASE 句 If you do something **to the best of** your **abilities** or **to the best of** your **ability**, you do it as well as you can. できる限り □*I take care of them to the best of my abilities.* 私はできる限り彼らの面倒を見ている.

Do not confuse **ability** with **capability** and **capacity**. You often use **ability** to say that someone can do something well. □*He had remarkable ability as a musician. …the ability to bear hardship.* A person's **capability** is the amount of work they can do and how well they can do it. □*…a job that was beyond the capability of one man. …the director's ideas of the capability of the actor.* If someone has a particular **capacity**, a **capacity** for something, or a **capacity** to do something, they have the qualities required to do it. **Capacity** is a more formal word than **ability**. □*…their capacity for hard work. …his capacity to see the other person's point of view.*

Thesaurus ability また次を参照:

| N. | capability, competence **1** |
| | craft, knack, skill, technique **2** |

Word Partnership ability は次の語句と使われる:

N.	lack of ability **1**
V.	ability to handle, have the ability, lack the ability **1 2**
ADJ.	natural ability **2**

ab|ject /æbdʒɛkt/ ADJ 形容詞 You use **abject** to emphasize that a situation or quality is extremely bad. 悲惨な [EMPHASIS 強調] □*Both of them died in abject poverty.* 彼らは2人とも極貧の中で死んだ.

ablaze /əbleɪz/ **1** ADJ 形容詞 Something that is **ablaze** is burning very fiercely. 燃え立って [v-link ADJ, v-link ADJ] □*Stores, houses, and vehicles were set ablaze.* 店や家や車が放火され炎上した. **2** ADJ 形容詞 If a place is **ablaze with** lights or colors, it is very bright because of them. 光り輝いている [v-link ADJ] □*The chamber was ablaze with light.* その部屋は明かりで光り輝いていた.

able /eɪb°l/ (abler /eɪblər/, ablest /eɪblɪst/) **1** PHRASE 句 If you **are able to** do something, you have skills or qualities which make it possible for you to do it. できる，能力がある □*The older child should be able to prepare a simple meal.* その年長の子供なら簡単な食事は作れるはずだ. □*The company says they're able to keep pricing competitive.* その会社は競争価格を維持できると言っている.

Can, could, and **be able to** are all used to talk about a person's ability to do something. They are followed by the infinitive form of a verb. You use **can** or a present form of **be able to** to refer to the present, although **can** is more common. □*They can all read and write… The snake is able to catch small mammals.* You use **could** or a past form of **be able to** to refer to the past, and "will" or "shall" with **be able to** to refer to the future. **Be able to** is used if you want to refer to doing something at a particular time. □*After treatment he was able to return to work.* **Can** and **could** are used to talk about possibility. **Could** refers to a particular occasion and **can** to more general situations. □*Many jobs could be lost… Too much salt can be harmful.* When talking about the past, you use **could have** and a past participle. □*It could have been much worse.* You also use **can** for the present and **could** for the past to talk about rules or what people are allowed to do. □*They can leave at any time.* Note that when making requests either **can** or **could** may be used. □*Can I have a drink?… Could we put the fire on?* However, **could** is always used for suggestions. □*You could phone her and ask.*

2 PHRASE 句 If you **are able to** do something, you have enough freedom, power, time, or money to do it. できる，可能である □*You'll be able to read in peace.* あなたは静かに読書できるでしょう. □*Have you been able to have any kind of contact?* 何らかの連絡が取れましたか?

Note that **able** and **capable** are both used to say that someone can do something. When you say that someone is **able** to do something, you mean that they can do it either because of their knowledge or skill, or because it is possible. □*He wondered if he would be able to climb over the rail… They were able to use their profits for new investments.* Note that if you use a past tense, you are saying that someone has actually done something. □*We were able to reduce costs.* When you say that someone is **capable** of doing something, you mean either that they have the knowledge and skill to do it, or that they are likely to do it. □*The workers are perfectly capable of running the organization themselves… She was quite capable of falling asleep.* You can say that someone is **capable** of a particular feeling or action. □*He's capable of loyalty… Bowman could not believe him capable of murder.* You can also use "**capable of**" when talking about what something such as a car or machine can do. □*The car was capable of 110 miles per hour.* If you describe someone as **able** or **capable**, you mean that they do things well. □*He's certainly a capable gardener.*

3 ADJ 形容詞 Someone who is **able** is very intelligent or very good at doing something. 優れた □*…one of the brightest and ablest members of the government.* 政府の最も聡明で最も有能なメンバーの1人

able-bodied /eɪb°l bɒdid/ ADJ 形容詞 An **able-bodied** person is physically strong and healthy, rather than weak or disabled. 健常の □*The gym can be used by both able-bodied and disabled people.* その体育館は健常者も障害者も利用できる. ● N-PLURAL 複数名詞 The **able-bodied** are people who are able-bodied. 健常者 □*No doubt such robots would be very useful in the homes of the able-bodied, too.* たぶんそのようなロボットは健常者の家でも大いに役立つだろう.

ably /eɪbli/ ADV 副詞 **Ably** means skillfully and successfully. うまく，立派に [ADV with v] □*He was ably assisted by a number of members from other branches.* 彼は他の支店からの多くの同僚にしっかりと支援された.

ab|nor|mal /æbnɔrm°l/ ADJ 形容詞 Someone or something that is **abnormal** is unusual, especially in a way that is troublesome. 異常な [FORMAL 形式ばった] □*…abnormal heart rhythms and high anxiety levels.* 異常な心拍と高い不安レベル ● **ab|nor|mal|ly** ADV 副詞 異常に □*…abnormally high levels of glucose.* 異常に高いブドウ糖値.

ab|nor|mal|ity /æbnɔrmælɪti/ (abnormalities) N-VAR 可変性名詞 An **abnormality** in something, especially in a person's body or behavior, is an unusual part or feature of it that may be worrying or dangerous. 異常 [FORMAL 形式ばった] □*Further scans are required to confirm the diagnosis of an abnormality.* 異常の診断を確認するにはさらに精密検査が必要だ.

aboard /əbɔrd/ PREP 前置詞 If you are **aboard** a ship or plane, you are on it or in it. （船や飛行機の）中へ，（船や飛行機に）乗って □*She invited 750 people aboard the luxury yacht, the Savarona.* 彼女は750人を豪華ヨット「サヴァロナ号」に招待した. ● ADV 副詞 **Aboard** is also an adverb. （船や飛行機に）乗って [ADV after v] □*It had taken two hours to load all the people aboard.* 乗客全員を乗せるのに2時間かかっていた.

abol|ish /əbɒlɪʃ/ (abolishes, abolishing, abolished) V-T 他動詞 If someone in authority **abolishes** a system or practice, they formally put an end to it. 廃止する □*An Illinois House committee voted Thursday to abolish the death penalty.* イリノイ州下院の委員会が木曜日に死刑の廃止を採決した.

Thesaurus	*abolish* また次を参照 :
v.	eliminate, end; (ant.) continue

abo|li|tion /ˌæbəlɪʃⁿn/ N-UNCOUNT 不可算名詞 The **abolition of** something such as a system or practice is its formal ending. 廃止 ❑ *The abolition of slavery in Brazil and the Caribbean closely followed the pattern of the United States.* ブラジルとカリブ諸島の奴隷制度廃止は米国の例にすっかりならったものである.

abomi|nable /əbɒmɪnəbⁿl/ ADJ 形容詞 Something that is **abominable** is very unpleasant or bad. ひどく嫌な, 言語道断な ❑ *The president described the killings as an abominable crime.* その殺人事件は憎むべき犯罪であると大統領は述べた.

Abo|rigi|nal /ˌæbərɪdʒɪnⁿl/ (Aboriginals) also aboriginal ▪ N-COUNT 可算名詞 An **Aboriginal** is an Australian Aborigine. アボリジニー（オーストラリア先住民） ❑ *He remained fascinated by the Aboriginals' tales.* 彼はアボリジニーの物語にずっと魅了されていた. ▪ 2 ADJ 形容詞 **Aboriginal** means belonging or relating to the Australian Aborigines. アボリジニーの [ADJ n] ❑ ...aboriginal art. アボリジニーの芸術

Abo|rigi|ne /ˌæbərɪdʒɪni/ (Aborigines) N-COUNT 可算名詞 **Aborigines** are members of the tribes that were living in Australia when Europeans arrived there. アボリジニー ❑ ...Bigge Island, an area sacred to Aborigines for more than 20,000 years. 2万年以上アボリジニーの聖地であったビッグ島

abort /əbɔːrt/ (aborts, aborted, aborting) ▪ V-T 他動詞 If an unborn baby **is aborted**, the pregnancy is ended deliberately and the baby is not born alive. 中絶する ❑ *Her lover walked out on her after she had aborted their child.* 彼女が子供を中絶した後, 恋人は彼女を見捨てた. ▪ 2 V-T 他動詞 If someone **aborts** a process, plan, or activity, they stop it before it has been completed. 中止する ❑ *When the decision was made to abort the mission, there was great confusion.* その任務を中止する決定がなされると, 大混乱が起こった.

abor|tion /əbɔːrʃⁿn/ (abortions) N-VAR 可変性名詞 If a woman has an **abortion**, she ends her pregnancy deliberately so that the baby is not born alive. 中絶 ❑ *He and his girlfriend had been going out together for a year when she had an abortion.* 彼の女友達が妊娠中絶したとき, 彼と彼女はすでに1年間つきあっていた.

abor|tive /əbɔːrtɪv/ ADJ 形容詞 An **abortive** attempt or action is unsuccessful. 不成功の [FORMAL 形式ばった] ❑ ...an abortive attempt to prevent the current president from taking office. 今の社長の就任を阻止しようとして不発に終わった企て

abound /əbaʊnd/ (abounds, abounding, abounded) V-I 自動詞 If things **abound**, or if a place **abounds with** things, there are very large numbers of them. たくさんある, 富む [FORMAL 形式ばった] ❑ *Stories abound about when he was in charge.* 彼が責任者だった頃の逸話は多い.

about /əbaʊt/

In addition to the uses shown below, **about** is used after some verbs, nouns, and adjectives to introduce extra information. **About** is also often used after verbs of movement, such as "walk" and "drive," especially in British English, and in phrasal verbs such as "set about."

下記の用法に加えて, **about** は情報を追加するために動詞, 名詞, 形容詞の後に使われる. **About** はまたしばしば, 特に英国英語で **walk** や **drive** のような移動の動詞と共に使われるし, また **set about** のような句動詞にも使われる.

▪ PREP 前置詞 You use **about** to introduce who or what something relates to or concerns. 〜について ❑ *She knew a lot about food.* 彼女は食物についてたくさん知っていた. ❑ *He never complains about his wife.* 彼は決して妻の愚痴を言わない. ▪ 2 PREP 前置詞 When you mention the things that an activity or institution is **about**, you are saying what it involves or what its aims are. 〜を目的として, 〜を必要として ❑ *Leadership is about the ability to implement change.* リーダーシップとは改革を実行する能力のことだ. ▪ 3 PREP 前置詞 You use **about** after some adjectives to indicate the person or thing that a feeling or state of mind relates to. 〜のことについて ❑ *"I'm sorry about Patrick," she said.* 「パトリックのことは気の毒だったわね」と彼女は言った. ▪ 4 PREP 前置詞 If you do something **about** a problem, you take action in order to solve it. 〜に対して ❑ *Rachel was going to do something about Jacob.* レイチェルはジェイコブのことを何とかしようとしていた. ▪ 5 PREP 前置詞 When you say that there is a particular quality **about** someone or something, you mean that they have this quality. 〜には ❑ *There was a warmth and passion about him I never knew existed.* 彼にはそれまで私が全然知らなかった温かさと情熱があった. ▪ 6 PREP 前置詞 If you put something **about** a person or thing, you put it around them. 〜の回りに [mainly BRIT 主に英国英語; AM usually **around** 米国英語

では通常 **around**] ▪ 7 ADV 副詞 **About** is used in front of a number to show that the number is not exact. およそ, 約 [ADV num] ❑ *The rate of inflation is running at about 2.7 percent.* インフレーション率は約2.7パーセントに達している. ▪ 8 ADV 副詞 If someone or something moves **about**, they keep moving in different directions. あちこちに [mainly BRIT 主に英国英語] [ADV after v] [AM usually **around** 米国英語では通常 **around**] PREP 前置詞 ● **About** is also a preposition. 〜のあちこちへ [mainly BRIT 主に英国英語] [AM usually **around** 米国英語では通常 **around**] ▪ 9 ADJ 形容詞 If someone or something is **about**, they are present or available. 手近にいて, 利用できて [mainly BRIT 主に英国英語] [v-link ADJ] [AM usually **around** 米国英語では通常 **around**] ▪ 10 ADJ 形容詞 If you are **about to** do something, you are going to do it very soon. If something is **about to** happen, it will happen very soon. 今まさに〜しようとしていて [v-link ADJ to-inf] ❑ *I think he's about to leave.* 彼は今出かけるところだと思うわ. ❑ *Argentina had lifted all restrictions on trade and visas are about to be abolished.* アルゼンチンは全ての貿易規制を撤廃したし, 間もなくビザも廃止されようとしている. ▪ 11 **how about** → see **how** ▪ 12 **what about** → see **what** ▪ 13 **just about** → see **just** ▪ 14 PHRASE 句 If someone is **out and about**, they are going out and doing things, especially after they have been unable to for a while. (病人が) 外に出られるようになって ❑ *Despite considerable pain she has been getting out and about almost as normal.* かなりひどい痛みにもかかわらず, 彼女はほとんど普通に出歩いている.

above /əbʌv/ ▪ PREP 前置詞 If one thing is **above** another one, it is directly over it or higher than it. 〜の上に, 〜より上に ❑ *He lifted his hands above his head.* 彼は両手を頭上に上げた. ❑ *Apartment 46 was a quiet apartment, unlike the one above it.* アパートの46号室は, その上の部屋と違って静かだった. ● ADV 副詞 **Above** is also an adverb. 上に ❑ *A long scream sounded from somewhere above.* 長い悲鳴がどこか上の方から聞こえてきた. ❑ ...a picture of the new plane as seen from above. 新しい飛行機を上から見た写真. ▪ 2 PREP 前置詞 If an amount or measurement is **above** a particular level, it is greater than that level. 〜を超えて ❑ *The temperature crept up to just above 40 degrees.* 気温がいつの間にか40度を少し超えた. ❑ *Victoria Falls has had above average levels of rainfall this year.* ビクトリア滝では今年の降雨量が平均を上回った. ● ADV 副詞 **Above** is also an adverb. より上で [amount "and" ADV] ❑ *Banks have been charging 25 percent and above for unsecured loans.* 銀行は無担保貸付に25パーセント以上の利子を取っている. ▪ 3 PREP 前置詞 If you hear one sound **above** another, it is louder or clearer than the second one. 〜より目立った ❑ *Then there was a woman's voice, rising shrilly above the barking.* その時, 女の金切り声がほえ声を超えて聞こえてきた. ▪ 4 PREP 前置詞 If someone is **above** you, they are in a higher social position than you or in a position of authority over you. (身分や地位など) 〜より上に ❑ *I married above myself.* 私は身分不相応な結婚をした. ● ADV 副詞 **Above** is also an adverb. 上で ['from' ADV] ❑ *The policemen admitted beating the student, but said they were acting on orders from above.* 警官たちは学生に暴行を加えたことを認めたが, 上からの命令でやっているのだと述べた. ▪ 5 PREP 前置詞 If you say that someone thinks they are **above** something, you mean that they act as if they are too good or important for it. 〜を超越した, 〜をしない [DISAPPROVAL 不賛成] ❑ *This was clearly a failure by someone who thought he was above failure.* これは明らかに自分は失敗しないと過信している者による失敗だった. ▪ 6 PREP 前置詞 If someone is **above** criticism or suspicion, they cannot be criticized or suspected because of their good qualities or their position. 〜を受けない [v-link PREP n] ❑ *He was a respected academic and above suspicion.* 彼は立派な学者で, 疑われるような人物ではなかった. ▪ 7 PREP 前置詞 If you value one person or thing **above** any other, you value them more or consider that they are more important. 〜より優先して, 〜より重んじて ❑ ...his tendency to put the team above everything. チームを何よりも優先する彼の性向 ▪ 8 **over and above** → see **over** ▪ 9 **above the law** → see **law** ▪ 10 **above board** → see **board** ▪ 11 ADV 副詞 In writing, you use **above** to refer to something that has already been mentioned or discussed. 上で, 前に ❑ *Several conclusions could be drawn from the results described above.* 上述の結果からいくつかの結論を引き出すことができるであろう. ● N-SING-COLL 集合的単数名詞 **Above** is also a noun. 上記, 前述 ❑ *For additional information, contact any of the above.* これ以上のことにつきましては, 上記のいずれかにご連絡下さい. ● ADJ 形容詞 **Above** is also an adjective. 上記の, 前述の [ADJ n] ❑ *For a copy of their brochure, write to the above address.* それらのパンフレットがご入り用の方は, 上記あて先までお便り下さい.

Above and **over** are both used to talk about position and height. If something is higher than something else and the two things are imagined as being positioned along a vertical line, you can use either **above** or **over**. ❑ *He opened a cupboard above the sink... She leaned forward until her face was over the basin.* However, if something is higher than something else but the two things are regarded as being wide or horizontal rather than tall or vertical, you have to use **above**. ❑ *The trees rose above the row of houses.* **Above** and **over** are both used to talk about measurements, for example, when you are talking about a point that is higher than another point on a scale. ❑ *Any money earned over that level is taxed. ...everybody above five feet eight inches in height.* You use **over** to say that a distance or period of time is longer than the one mentioned. ❑ *...a height of over twelve thousand feet... Our relationship lasted for over a year.*

abra|sive /əbreɪsɪv/ **1** ADJ 形容詞 Someone who has an **abrasive** manner is unkind and rude. 不快な ❑ *His abrasive manner has won him an unenviable notoriety.* 彼の不快なマナーにありがたくない評判が立った. **2** ADJ 形容詞 An **abrasive** substance is rough and can be used to clean hard surfaces. 研磨する ❑ *...a new all-purpose, non-abrasive cleaner that cleans and polishes all metals.* どんな金属でも表面を傷付けずピカピカに磨き上げる新しい万能洗剤.

abreast /əbrest/ **1** ADV 副詞 If people or things walk or move **abreast**, they are next to each other, side by side, and facing in the same direction. 横に並んで ❑ *The steep sidewalk was too narrow for them to walk abreast.* その急な歩道は彼らが横に並んで歩くには狭すぎた. **2** PHRASE 句 If you **keep abreast** of a subject, you know all the most recent facts about it. 〜に遅れを取らない ❑ *He will be keeping abreast of the news.* 彼ならいつもそのニュースの最新情報をつかんでいるだろう.

abroad /əbrɔd/ ADV 副詞 If you go **abroad**, you go to a foreign country, usually one that is separated from the country where you live by an ocean or a sea. 海外へ ❑ *I would love to go abroad this year, perhaps to the South of France.* 今年は海外へ行きたい. たぶん南フランスかな. ❑ *He will stand in for Mr. Goh when he is abroad.* 郷氏が海外に行っているときは彼が代理を務める予定である.

ab|rupt /əbrʌpt/ **1** ADJ 形容詞 An **abrupt** change or action is very sudden, often in a way that is unpleasant. 突然の, 急な ❑ *Rosie's idyllic world came to an abrupt end when her parents' marriage broke up.* 両親の結婚が破たんしたとき, ロージーの牧歌的な世界は突然終わった. ●**ab|rupt|ly** ADV 副詞 [ADV with v] 突然に ❑ *He stopped abruptly and looked my way.* 彼は突然立ち止まって私の方を見た. **2** ADJ 形容詞 Someone who is **abrupt** speaks in a rude, unfriendly way. ぶっきらぼうな ❑ *He was abrupt to the point of rudeness.* 彼は無作法なくらいぶっきらぼうだった. ●**ab|rupt|ly** ADV 副詞 ❑ *"Good night, then," she said abruptly.* 「じゃあ, おやすみ」 と彼女はぶっきらぼうに言った.

ab|sence /æbs³ns/ (absences) **1** N-VAR 可変性名詞 Someone's **absence** from a place is the fact that they are not there. 不在, 欠席 ❑ *...a bundle of letters which had arrived for me in my absence.* 留守中に私宛に届いていた手紙の束 **2** N-SING 単数名詞 The **absence** of something from a place is the fact that it is not there or does not exist. ないこと, 無 ❑ *The presence or absence of clouds can have an important impact on temperature.* 雲の有無で温度に大きな影響が出ることがある.

ab|sent /æbs³nt/ **1** ADJ 形容詞 If someone or something is **absent from** a place or situation where they should be or where they usually are, they are not there. 不在の, 欠席の ❑ *He has been absent from his desk for two weeks.* 彼は2週間欠勤している. **2** ❑ *The pictures, too, were absent from the walls.* それらの絵も壁にかかっていなかった. **2** ADJ 形容詞 If someone appears **absent**, they are not paying attention because they are thinking about something else. ぼんやりの, 放心した ❑ *"Nothing," Rosie said in an absent way.* 「何でもないわ」 とロージーが上の空で言った. ●**ab|sent|ly** /æbs³ntli/ ADV 副詞 ぼんやりして, 上の空で ❑ *He nodded absently.* 彼は上の空で頷いた. **3** ADJ 形容詞 [ADJ n] An **absent** parent does not live with his or her children. 別居している ❑ *...absent fathers who fail to pay toward the costs of looking after their children.* 子供の養育費を支払うのを怠る別居の父親たち **4** PREP 前置詞 If you say that **absent** one thing, another thing will happen, you mean that if the first thing does not happen, the second thing will happen. 〜がなければ [AM 米国英語, FORMAL 形式ばった] ❑ *Absent a solution, people like Sue Godfrey will just keep on fighting.* もし問題解決に至らなければ, スー・ゴッドフリーのような人たちはひたすら闘い続けるだろう.

ab|sen|tee /æbs³nti/ (absentees) **1** N-COUNT 可算名詞 An **absentee** is a person who is expected to be in a particular place but who is not there. 欠席者 ❑ *At least two of the three other absentees also had justifiable reasons for being away.* 他の3人の欠席者のうち少なくとも2人にも欠席のもっともな理由があった. **2** ADJ 形容詞 **Absentee** is used to describe someone who is not there to do a particular job in person. 不在者の [ADJ n] ❑ *Absentee fathers will be*

forced to pay child support. 不在の父親は強制的に子供の養育費を払わされるようになる. **3** ADJ 形容詞 In elections in the United States, if you vote by **absentee** ballot or if you are an **absentee** voter, you vote in advance because you will be unable to go to the polling place. 不在投票者の [AM 米国英語] [ADJ n] ❑ *He has already voted by absentee ballot.* 彼は既に不在者投票で投票を済ませた. → see **election**

absent-minded ADJ 形容詞 Someone who is **absent-minded** forgets things or does not pay attention to what they are doing, often because they are thinking about something else. ぼんやりしている, 上の空の ❑ *In his later life he became even more absent-minded.* 晩年には彼はのうっかりがなお一層ひどくなった. ●**absent-mindedly** ADV 副詞 [ADV with v] 上の空で, うっかりと ❑ *Elizabeth absent-mindedly picked a thread from his lapel.* エリザベスは上の空で彼の折り襟から糸をつまみ取った.

ab|so|lute /æbsəlut/ (absolutes) **1** ADJ 形容詞 **Absolute** means total and complete. 完全な ❑ *It's not really suited to absolute beginners.* それは全くの初心者にはあまり向いていない. **2** ADJ 形容詞 You use **absolute** to emphasize something that you are saying. (後に続く言葉を強調して) 絶対の [EMPHASIS 強調] [ADJ n] ❑ *About 12 inches wide is the absolute minimum you should consider.* 最低でも幅, 約12インチは見ておかないといけない. **3** ADJ 形容詞 An **absolute** ruler has complete power and authority over his or her country. 絶対的な, 専制的な [ADJ n] ❑ *He ruled with absolute power.* 彼は絶対的な権力で支配した. **4** ADJ 形容詞 **Absolute** is used to say that something is definite and will not change even if circumstances change. 確固たる ❑ *John brought the absolute proof that we needed.* ジョンは私たちが必要としていた確たる証拠を持って来た. **5** ADJ 形容詞 An amount that is expressed in **absolute** terms is expressed as a fixed amount rather than referring to variable factors such as what you earn or the effects of inflation. 絶対的な [ADJ n] ❑ *In absolute terms their wages remain low by national standards.* それだけで見ると, 彼らの賃金は全国の標準からするとまだ低い. **6** ADJ 形容詞 **Absolute** rules and principles are believed to be true, right, or relevant in all situations. 完全無欠の ❑ *There are no absolute rules.* 完全な規則などはない. **7** N-COUNT 可算名詞 An **absolute** is a rule or principle that is believed to be true, right, or relevant in all situations. 絶対不変なもの ❑ *This is one of the few absolutes in U.S. constitutional law.* 合衆国憲法の中でもこれは数少ない絶対不変の法規の1つだ.

ab|so|lute|ly /æbsəlutli/ **1** ADV 副詞 **Absolutely** means totally and completely. 全く, 絶対に [EMPHASIS 強調] ❑ *Joan is absolutely right.* ジョウンが全く正しい. ❑ *I absolutely refuse to get married.* 結婚するのは絶対にお断りする. **2** ADV 副詞 Some people say **absolutely** as an emphatic way of saying yes or of agreeing with someone. They say **absolutely not** as an emphatic way of saying no or of disagreeing with someone. 全くだ, そのとおり [EMPHASIS 強調] [ADV as reply] ❑ *"It's worrying that they're doing things without training though, isn't it?" — "Absolutely."* 「でも彼らが訓練も受けずにやっているのは心配だね?」 「全くだ. 」

ab|sorb /əbsɔrb, -zɔrb/ (absorbs, absorbing, absorbed) **1** V-T 他動詞 If something **absorbs** a liquid, gas, or other substance, it soaks it up or takes it in. 吸収する ❑ *Plants absorb carbon dioxide from the air and moisture from the soil.* 植物は空気中から二酸化炭素を, また土壌から水分を吸収する. **2** V-T 他動詞 If something **absorbs** light, heat, or another form of energy, it takes it in. 取り込む ❑ *A household radiator absorbs energy in the form of electric current and releases it in the form of heat.* 家庭用暖房器は電流の形でエネルギーを取り込み, それを熱の形で放出する. **3** V-T 他動詞 If a group is **absorbed into** a larger group, it becomes part of the larger group. 吸収合併する ❑ *City schools were absorbed into the countywide school district.* 市立校は郡単位の学区に合併吸収された. **4** V-T 他動詞 If something **absorbs** a force or shock, it reduces its effect. 緩和する ❑ *...footwear which does not absorb the impact of the foot striking the ground.* 足が地面を蹴る衝撃を緩和しない靴 **5** V-T 他動詞 If a system or society **absorbs** changes, effects, or costs, it is able to deal with them. 負担できる, 対応できる ❑ *The banks would be forced to absorb large losses.* 銀行が多額の損失を負担せざるを得なくなるであろう. **6** V-T 他動詞 If something **absorbs** something valuable such as money, space, or time, it uses up a great deal of it. 使い尽くす ❑ *It absorbed vast amounts of capital that could have been used for investment.* それは投資に回すこともできたであろう巨額の資金を使い果たした. **7** V-T 他動詞 If you **absorb** information, you learn and understand it. 理解する, (知識・学問を) 身に付ける ❑ *Too often he only absorbs half the information in the manual.* 彼がマニュアルの内容を半分しか把握していないのはしょっちゅうだ. **8** V-T 他動詞 If something **absorbs** you, it interests you a great deal and takes up all your attention and energy. 夢中にさせる ❑ *...a second career which absorbed her more completely than her acting ever had.* それまでの女優業よりも完全に彼女を虜 (とりこ) にした別の仕事 **9** → see also **absorbed, absorbing**

ab|sorbed /əbsɔrbd, -zɔrbd/ ADJ 形容詞 If you are **absorbed in** something or someone, you are very interested in them and they take up all your attention and energy. 夢中になって [v-link ADJ]

They were completely absorbed in each other. 彼らはお互いにすっかり心を奪われていた.

ab|sor|bent /əbsɔrbənt, -zɔrbənt/ ADJ 形容詞 **Absorbent** material soaks up liquid easily. 吸収性のある □ *The towels are highly absorbent.* それらのタオルは吸収性が高い.

ab|sorb|ing /əbsɔrbɪŋ, -zɔrbɪŋ/ ADJ 形容詞 An **absorbing** task or activity interests you a great deal and takes up all your attention and energy. 夢中にさせる, とても興味深い *"Two Sisters" is an absorbing read.* 『姉妹』はとても面白い読み物だ.

ab|sorp|tion /əbsɔrpʃ°n, -zɔrpʃ°n/ **1** N-UNCOUNT 不可算名詞 The **absorption of** a liquid, gas, or other substance is the process of it being soaked up or taken in. 吸収 □ *This controls the absorption of liquids.* これで液体の吸収を調節する. **2** N-UNCOUNT 不可算名詞 The **absorption of** a group **into** a larger group is the process of it becoming part of the larger group. 吸収, 併合 □ *...Serbia's absorption into the Ottoman Empire.* オスマン帝国へのセルビアの併合

ab|stain /æbsteɪn/ (abstains, abstaining, abstained) **1** V-I 自動詞 If you **abstain from** something, usually something you want to do, you deliberately do not do it. 控える, やめる [FORMAL 形式ばった] □ *Abstain from sex or use condoms.* セックスをしないか, そうでなければコンドームを使うように. **2** V-I 自動詞 If you **abstain** during a vote, you do not use your vote. 棄権する □ *Three countries abstained in the vote.* 票決で3か国が棄権した.

ab|sten|tion /æbstenʃ°n/ (abstentions) N-VAR 可変性名詞 **Abstention** is a formal act of not voting either for or against a proposal. 棄権 (投票の) □ *...a vote of sixteen in favor, three against, and one abstention.* 賛成16, 反対3, 棄権1の投票結果.

ab|sti|nence /æbstɪnəns/ N-UNCOUNT 不可算名詞 **Abstinence** is the practice of abstaining from something such as alcoholic drink or sex, often for health or religious reasons. 断つこと, 節制 □ *...six months of abstinence.* 6か月間の節制

ab|stract /æbstrækt/ (abstracts) **1** ADJ 形容詞 An **abstract** idea or way of thinking is based on general ideas rather than on real things and events. 抽象的な □ *...starting with a few abstract principles.* いくつかの抽象的な原則から始めて □ *It's not a question of some abstract concept of justice.* それは正義とかいう抽象的な概念の問題ではない. **2** ADJ 形容詞 In grammar, an **abstract** noun refers to a quality or idea rather than to a physical object. 観念的な [ADJ n] □ *...abstract words such as glory, honor, and courage.* 栄光, 名誉, 勇気といった観念的な言葉. **3** ADJ 形容詞 **Abstract** art makes use of shapes and patterns rather than showing people or things. 抽象芸術の □ *A modern abstract painting takes over one complete wall.* 現代抽象画は壁1面分のスペースを取る. **4** PHRASE 句 When you talk or think about something **in the abstract**, you talk or think about it in a general way, rather than considering particular things or events. 抽象的に □ *Money was a commodity she never thought about except in the abstract.* お金というものは彼女が抽象的に考える以外に決して考えたことがないものった. **5** N-COUNT 可算名詞 An **abstract** is an abstract work of art. 抽象芸術作品 □ *His abstracts are held in numerous collections.* 彼の抽象作品は多くのコレクションに加えられている. **6** N-COUNT 可算名詞 An **abstract of** an article, document, or speech is a short piece of writing that gives the main points of it. 概要 □ *It might also be necessary to supply an abstract of the review of the literature as well.* その文献の論評の概要も用意する必要があるかもしない.

ab|strac|tion /æbstrækʃ°n/ (abstractions) N-VAR 可変性名詞 An **abstraction** is a general idea rather than one relating to a particular object, person, or situation. 抽象概念 [FORMAL 形式ばった] □ *Is it worth fighting a big war, in the name of an abstraction like sovereignty?* 主権というような抽象概念の名の下に大戦争をする価値があるだろうか?

ab|surd /æbsɜrd, -zɜrd/ ADJ 形容詞 If you say that something is **absurd**, you are criticizing it because you think that it is ridiculous or that it does not make sense. ばかげた [DISAPPROVAL 不賛成] □ *That's absurd.* それはばかげている. □ *It's absurd to suggest that they knew what was going on but did nothing.* 何が起こっているか知りながら彼らが何もしなかったと言うなんておかしい. N-SING 単数名詞 • **The absurd** is something that is absurd. ばかげたこと [FORMAL 形式ばった] ['the' N] □ *Connie had a sharp eye for the absurd.* コニーにはばかげたことを敏感に見分ける力があった. • **ab|surd|ly** ADV 副詞 ばからしいほど □ *Prices were still absurdly low, in his opinion.* 彼の考えでは, 価格がまだばからしいほど低い. • **ab|surd|ity** /æbsɜrdɪti, -zɜrd-/ (absurdities) N-VAR 可変性名詞 不合理さ, ばかばかしさ □ *I find myself growing increasingly angry at the absurdity of the situation.* そんな不合理な状況に, 私は自分の中でだんだん怒りが込み上げてくる.

abun|dance /əbʌndəns/ N-SING-COLL 集合的単数名詞 An **abundance of** something is a large quantity of it. 豊富 [usu N 'of' n, also 'in' N] □ *This area of Mexico has an abundance of safe beaches*

and a pleasing climate. メキシコのこの地域は多くの安全な浜辺と心地よい気候に恵まれている.

abun|dant /əbʌndənt/ ADJ 形容詞 Something that is **abundant** is present in large quantities. 豊富な □ *There is an abundant supply of cheap labor.* 安い労働力がふんだんにある.

abuse (abuses, abusing, abused)

The noun is pronounced /əbyus/. The verb is pronounced /əbyuz/.

名詞は /əbyus/ と発音される. 動詞は /əbyuz/ と発音される.

1 N-UNCOUNT 不可算名詞 **Abuse** of someone is cruel and violent treatment of them. 虐待 [also N in pl] □ *...investigation of alleged child abuse.* 児童虐待疑惑の捜査 □ *...victims of sexual and physical abuse.* 性的虐待と暴行の犠牲者たち. **2** N-UNCOUNT 不可算名詞 **Abuse** is extremely rude and insulting things that people say when they are angry. 悪態 □ *I was left shouting abuse as the car sped off.* 悪態をわめき散らす車を残し, 車はすごい勢いで走り去った. **3** N-VAR 可変性名詞 **Abuse** of something is the use of it in a wrong way or for a bad purpose. 悪用, 乱用 [with supp] □ *What went on here was an abuse of power.* ここで続いていたことは権力の乱用であった. **4** V-T 他動詞 If someone **is abused**, they are treated cruelly and violently. 虐待する □ *Janet had been abused by her father since she was eleven.* ジャネットは11歳の時から父親に虐待されていた. □ *...parents who feel they cannot cope or might abuse their children.* 自分の子供に対処できない, あるいは子供を虐待してしまうかもしれないと感じている親たち. **5** V-T 他動詞 You can say that someone **is abused** if extremely rude and insulting things are said to them. 口汚くののしる □ *He alleged that he was verbally abused by other soldiers.* 彼は他の兵士達から言葉による嫌がらせを受けたと主張した. **6** V-T 他動詞 If you **abuse** something, you use it in a wrong way or for a bad purpose. 悪用する □ *He showed how the rich and powerful can abuse their position.* 彼は裕福で権力を持った者たちがいかにその地位を悪用できるかを明らかにした.

abu|sive /əbyusɪv/ **1** ADJ 形容詞 Someone who is **abusive** behaves in a cruel and violent way toward other people. 乱暴な □ *He became violent and abusive toward Ben's mother.* 彼はベンの母親に乱暴するようになった. **2** ADJ 形容詞 **Abusive** language is extremely rude and insulting. 侮辱的な □ *I did not use any foul or abusive language.* 私は絶対暴言を吐いていなかった.

abys|mal /əbɪzm°l/ ADJ 形容詞 If you describe a situation or the condition of something as **abysmal**, you think that it is very bad or poor in quality. ひどく悪い □ *The general standard of racing was abysmal.* レースの全体的な水準がひどく低い. • **abys|mal|ly** ADV 副詞 底知れないほどに □ *The group for the most part found the standard of education abysmally low.* そのグループの人たちはたいてい教育水準が極端に低いのに気づいた.

abyss /æbɪs/ (abysses) **1** N-COUNT 可算名詞 An **abyss** is a very deep hole in the ground. 底なしの深い穴 [LITERARY 文語的] □ *The torrent, swollen by the melting snow, plunges into a tremendous abyss.* 雪解け水で膨れ上がった激流が巨大な深淵になだれ込む. **2** N-COUNT 可算名詞 If someone is on the edge or brink of an **abyss**, they are about to enter into a very frightening or threatening situation. 奈落の底 [LITERARY 文語的] □ *...a warning that the Middle East was on the brink of an abyss.* 中東が奈落の淵に立っているという警告

aca|dem|ic /ækədemɪk/ (academics) **1** ADJ 形容詞 **Academic** is used to describe things that relate to the work done in schools, colleges, and universities, especially work that involves studying and reasoning rather than practical or technical skills. 学問的な [ADJ n] □ *Their academic standards are high.* 彼らの学問的水準は高い. • **aca|dem|ical|ly** /ækədemɪkli/ ADV 副詞 学問的に □ *He is academically gifted.* 彼は学問的才能がある. **2** ADJ 形容詞 [ADJ n] **Academic** is used to describe things that relate to schools, colleges, and universities. 学校の, 大学の □ *...the start of the last academic year.* 昨年の学年度の始め **3** ADJ 形容詞 **Academic** is used to describe work, or a school, college, or university, that places emphasis on studying and reasoning rather than on practical or technical skills. 学究的な □ *The author has settled for a more academic approach.* 筆者はより学究的な手法を取ることにした. **4** ADJ 形容詞 Someone who is **academic** is good at studying. 学力のある □ *The system is failing most disastrously among less academic children.* その制度は学力の低い子供たちの間ではまことに惨たんたる失敗となっている. **5** ADJ 形容詞 You can say that a discussion or situation is **academic** if you think it is not important because it has no real effect or cannot happen. 理論上の, 非現実的な □ *Who wants to*

hear about contracts and deadlines that are purely academic? 全く非現実的な契約や期限に誰が耳を貸すだろうか？ **6** N-COUNT 可算名詞 An **academic** is a member of a university or college who teaches or does research. 大学人，学者 □A group of academics say they can predict house prices through a computer program. ある研究者グループによると，コンピュータプログラムで住宅価格が予想できそうだ。

acad|emy /əkǽdəmi/ (**academies**) **1** N-COUNT 可算名詞 **Academy** is sometimes used in the names of schools and colleges, especially those specializing in particular subjects or skills, or private high schools in the United States. 専門学校，（私立の）ハイスクール □He is an English teacher at the Seattle Academy for Arts and Sciences. 彼はシアトル文理学院の英語教師です。 **2** N-IN-NAMES 名称中の名詞 **Academy** appears in the names of societies formed to improve or maintain standards in a particular field. 学会 □...the American Academy of Psychotherapists. アメリカ心理療法士学会

ac|cel|er|ate /ækséləreɪt/ (**accelerates, accelerating, accelerated**) **1** V-T/V-I 他動詞/自動詞 If the process or rate of something **accelerates** or if something **accelerates** it, it gets faster and faster. 加速する □Growth will accelerate to 2.9 percent next year. 来年成長率は加速して2.9パーセントになるであろう。 **2** V-I 自動詞 When a moving vehicle **accelerates**, it goes faster and faster. （車などが）速度を上げる □Suddenly the car accelerated. 急に車がスピードを上げた。

ac|cel|era|tion /ækséləréɪʃən/ **1** N-UNCOUNT 不可算名詞 The **acceleration** of a process or change is the fact that it is getting faster and faster. 加速，促進 □He has also called for an acceleration of political reforms. 彼は政治改革の促進も呼びかけている。 **2** N-UNCOUNT 不可算名詞 **Acceleration** is the rate at which a car or other vehicle can increase its speed, often seen in terms of the time that it takes to reach a particular speed. 加速 □Acceleration to 60 mph takes a mere 5.7 seconds. 時速60マイルまで加速するのにたった5.7秒しかからない。 **3** N-UNCOUNT 不可算名詞 **Acceleration** is the rate at which the speed of an object increases. 加速度 [TECHNICAL 技術的]
→ see **motion**

ac|cel|era|tor /ækséləreɪtər/ (**accelerators**) N-COUNT 可算名詞 The **accelerator** in a car or other vehicle is the pedal that you press with your foot in order to make the vehicle go faster. アクセル □He eased his foot off the accelerator. 彼はアクセルを緩めた。

ac|cent /ǽksɛnt/ (**accents**) **1** N-COUNT 可算名詞 Someone who speaks with a particular **accent** pronounces the words of a language in a distinctive way that shows which country, region, or background they come from. なまり □He had developed a slight southern accent. 彼はかすかな南部なまりを身に付けていた。 **2** N-COUNT 可算名詞 An **accent** is a short line or other mark which is written above certain letters in some languages and which indicates the way those letters are pronounced. アクセント □...an acute accent. 鋭アクセント（発音記号の強調記号）

Word Partnership	accent は次の語句と使われる：
ADJ.	**American/French** accent, **regional** accent, **thick** accent **1**
ADV.	**heavily** accented **1**
V.	**have an** accent **1** **put the** accent **on 2**

ac|cen|tu|ate /æksɛ́ntʃueɪt/ (**accentuates, accentuating, accentuated**) V-T 他動詞 To **accentuate** something means to emphasize it or make it more noticeable. 強調する □His shaven head accentuates his large round face. 彼の坊主頭は大きな丸顔を目立たせている。

ac|cept /æksɛ́pt/ (**accepts, accepting, accepted**) **1** V-T/V-I 他動詞/自動詞 If you **accept** something that you have been offered, you say yes to it or agree to take it. 受け入れる，受け取る □Eventually Esteban persuaded her to accept an offer of marriage. ついにエステバンは彼女を説得して結婚の申し込みを承諾させた。 □All those invited to next week's peace conference have accepted. 来週の平和会議へ招待された全員が受諾した。 **2** V-T 他動詞 If you **accept** an idea, statement, or fact, you believe that it is true or valid. 認める □I do not accept that there is any kind of crisis in American science. 私はアメリカの科学になんらかの危機があるなどとは認めない。 □I don't think they would accept that view. 私は彼らがその考え方を認めないだろうと思う。 **3** V-T 他動詞 If you **accept** a plan or an intended action, you agree to it and allow it to happen. 受け入れる，了承する □The Council will have to decide if it should accept his resignation. 評議会が開かれて彼の辞任を受け入れるべきかどうかを決定する予定である。 **4** V-T 他動詞 If you **accept** an unpleasant fact or situation, you get used to it or recognize that it is necessary or cannot be changed. 甘受する □People will accept suffering that can be shown to lead to a greater good. 国民は痛みでもより大きな利益になることが示せるものであれば甘受するだろう。 □Urban dwellers often accept noise as part of city life. 都市の住人は騒音を都市生活の一部として受け入れてい

ることが多い。 **5** V-T 他動詞 If a person, company, or organization **accepts** something such as a document, they recognize that it is genuine, correct, or satisfactory and agree to consider it or handle it. 受理する □We took the unusual step of contacting newspapers to advise them not to accept the advertising. 我々は新聞社と連絡を取って各社がその広告を受け付けないように忠告するという異例の手段をとった。 **6** V-T 他動詞 If an organization or person **accepts** you, you are allowed to join the organization or use the services that are offered. 入会する，入社する □All-male groups will not be accepted. 男性だけのグループは入れません。 **7** V-T 他動詞 If a person or a group of people **accepts** you, they begin to be friendly toward you and are happy with who you are or what you do. （人柄や行動を）受け入れる □As far as my grandparents were concerned, they've never had a problem accepting me. 私の祖父母に関する限り，彼らが私を受け入れるのに何の問題もなかった。 □Many men still have difficulty accepting a woman as a business partner. 多くの男性はいまだに女性を仕事のパートナーとして受け入れるのに抵抗を感じている。 **8** V-T 他動詞 If you **accept** the responsibility or blame for something, you recognize that you are responsible for it. （責任などを）負う，受け入れる □The company cannot accept responsibility for loss or damage. 会社は紛失や損傷の責任を負えません。 **9** V-T 他動詞 If you **accept** someone's advice or suggestion, you agree to do what they say. 受け入れる，従う □The army refused to accept orders from the political leadership. 軍は政府の命令に従うことを拒否した。 **10** V-T 他動詞 If a machine **accepts** a particular kind of thing, it is designed to take it and deal with it or process it. 対応する □The new parking meters don't accept dollar bills. 新しい駐車メーターはドル紙幣に対応していない。 **11** → see also **accepted**

Thesaurus	accept また次を参照：
V.	receive, take; (ant.) refuse, reject **1** acknowledge, agree to, recognize; (ant.) object, oppose, refuse **2 3** endure, live with, tolerate; (ant.) disallow, reject **4**

ac|cept|able /ækséptəbəl/ **1** ADJ 形容詞 **Acceptable** activities and situations are those that most people approve of or consider to be normal. 容認できる □It is becoming more acceptable for women to drink. 女性の飲酒はますます受け入れられてきている。 ● **ac|cept|abil|ity** /ækséptəbíliti/ N-UNCOUNT 不可算名詞 容認性 □This assumption played a considerable part in increasing the social acceptability of divorce. この考え方が離婚の社会的容認性を増すのに少なからぬ役割を果たした。 ● **ac|cept|ably** /ækséptəbli/ ADV 副詞 容認されるように □The aim of discipline is to teach children to behave acceptably. しつけの目的は子供たちにちゃんとしたふるまいを身に付けさせることにある。 **2** ADJ 形容詞 If something is **acceptable to** someone, they agree to consider it, use it, or allow it to happen. 受け入れられる □They have thrashed out a compromise formula acceptable to Moscow. 彼らはモスクワに受け入れられるような妥協案を入念に練り上げた。 **3** ADJ 形容詞 If you describe something as **acceptable**, you mean that it is good enough or fairly good. まあまあの □On the far side of the street was a restaurant that looked acceptable. 通りの向こう側に一見よさそうなレストランがあった。 ● **ac|cept|ably** ADV 副詞 （完全ではないが）満足できる程度に □...a method that provides an acceptably accurate solution to a problem. 問題に対してまずまずの正確な解決を与える方法

Thesaurus	acceptable また次を参照：
ADJ.	adequate, decent, passable, satisfactory **3**

ac|cept|ance /ækséptəns/ (**acceptances**) **1** N-VAR 可変性名詞 **Acceptance of** an offer or a proposal is the act of saying yes to it or agreeing to it. 受理 □The Party is being degraded by its acceptance of secret donations. その政党は秘密の献金を受け取って堕落しつつある。 **2** N-UNCOUNT 不可算名詞 If there is **acceptance** of an idea, most people believe or agree that it is true. 容認 □...a theory that is steadily gaining acceptance. 着実に認められつつある学説。 **3** N-UNCOUNT 不可算名詞 Your **acceptance of** a situation, especially an unpleasant or difficult one, is an attitude or feeling that you cannot change it and that you must get used to it. 甘受 □The most impressive thing about him is his calm acceptance of whatever comes his way. 彼の最も印象的なところは何が起ころうとも冷静に甘受するところだ。 **4** N-UNCOUNT 不可算名詞 **Acceptance** of someone into a group means beginning to think of them as part of the group and to act in a friendly way toward them. 受け入れ □A very determined effort by society will ensure that the disabled achieve real acceptance and integration. 社会の非常に果敢な努力があれば，障害者が真に社会に受け入れられ融合できるようになるであろう。

ac|cept|ed /ækséptɪd/ **1** ADJ 形容詞 **Accepted** ideas are agreed by most people to be correct or reasonable. 容認された □There is no generally accepted definition of life. 生命というものに対し世間一般に認められた定義はない。 **2** → see also **accept**

ac|cess /ǽksɛs/ (**accesses, accessing, accessed**) **1** N-UNCOUNT 不可算名詞 If you have **access to** a building or other place, you

are able or allowed to go into it. 立ち入り ❑ *The facilities have been adapted to give access to wheelchair users.* その施設は車椅子で出入りできるよう改造されている. ❑ *For logistical and political reasons, scientists have only recently been able to gain access to the area.* 兵站(へいたん)学的および政治的な理由から，科学者がその地域に立ち入れるようになったのはごく最近である. **2** N-UNCOUNT 不可算名詞 If you have **access to** something such as information or equipment, you have the opportunity or right to see it or use it. 利用権 ❑ *...a Code of Practice that would give patients access to their medical records.* 患者に自身の医療記録を閲覧する権利を与えるような開業規則 **3** N-UNCOUNT 不可算名詞 If you have **access to** a person, you have the opportunity or right to see them or meet them. 面会 ❑ *He was not allowed access to a lawyer.* 彼は弁護士への接見が許されなかった. **4** V-T 他動詞 If you **access** something, especially information held on a computer, you succeed in finding or obtaining it. (コンピュータや情報に)アクセスする，入手する ❑ *You've illegally accessed and misused confidential security files.* あなたは機密のセキュリティーファイルに違法にアクセスして，悪用した.

ac|ces|sible /æksɛsɪbəl/ **1** ADJ 形容詞 If a place or building is **accessible** to people, it is easy for them to reach it or get into it. If an object is **accessible**, it is easy to reach. 行きやすい，近づきやすい ❑ *The center is easily accessible to the general public.* そのセンターは一般市民が行きやすい. ●**ac|ces|sibil|ity** /æksɛsɪbɪlɪti/ N-UNCOUNT 不可算名詞 近づきやすさ ❑ *...the easy accessibility of the area.* その地域への行きやすさ **2** ADJ 形容詞 If something is **accessible** to people, they can easily use it or obtain it. 利用できる，入手しやすい ❑ *The aim of any reform of legal aid should be to make the system accessible to more people.* 法的支援のどんな改正の目的もその制度をより多くの人が利用できるようにすることであるべきだ. ●**ac|ces|sibil|ity** N-UNCOUNT 不可算名詞 利用しやすさ，入手しやすさ ❑ *...growing public concern about the cost, quality and accessibility of health care.* 医療の費用，質や受けやすさについて増大する国民の不安 **3** ADJ 形容詞 If you describe a book, painting, or other work of art as **accessible**, you think it is good because it is simple enough for people to understand and appreciate easily. 理解しやすい [APPROVAL 賛成] ❑ *Both say they want to write literary books that are accessible to a general audience.* 両人とも一般の読者に分かりやすい文芸書を書きたいとのことだ. ●**ac|ces|sibil|ity** N-UNCOUNT 不可算名詞 分かりやすさ ❑ *Seminar topics are chosen for their accessibility to a general audience.* セミナーには一般聴講者に分かりやすいトピックが選ばれている.
→ see **disability**

ac|ces|so|ry /æksɛsəri/ (**accessories**) **1** N-COUNT 可算名詞 **Accessories** are items of equipment that are not usually essential, but can be used with or added to something else in order to make it more efficient, useful, or decorative. 付属品 ❑ *...an exclusive range of hand-made bedroom and bathroom accessories.* 寝室と浴室用の選び抜かれた手作り小物ひとそろい. **2** N-COUNT 可算名詞 **Accessories** are articles such as belts and scarves which you wear or carry but which are not part of your main clothing. 服飾品，アクセサリー ❑ *It also has a good range of accessories, including sunglasses, handbags and belts.* サングラス，ハンドバッグ，ベルトなど，いろんな種類のアクセサリーもある. **3** N-COUNT 可算名詞 If someone is guilty of being an **accessory to** a crime, they helped the person who committed it, or knew it was being committed but did not tell the police. 従犯者 [LEGAL 法律的] ❑ *She had been charged with being an accessory to the embezzlement of funds from a cooperative farm.* 彼女は共同農場の資金使い込みの従犯者として起訴されていた.

ac|cess time (**access times**) N-COUNT 可算名詞 **Access time** is the time that is needed to get information that is stored in a computer. アクセス時間 [COMPUTING コンピューティング] ❑ *This system helps speed up access times.* このシステムはアクセス時間の短縮に役立つ.

ac|ci|dent /æksɪdənt/ (**accidents**) **1** N-COUNT 可算名詞 An **accident** happens when a vehicle hits a person, an object, or another vehicle, causing injury or damage. 交通事故 ❑ *She was involved in a serious car accident last week.* 彼女は先週ひどい車の交通事故に遭った. **2** N-COUNT 可算名詞 If someone has an **accident**, something unpleasant happens to them that was not intended, sometimes causing injury or death. 事故，災難 ❑ *5,000 people die every year because of accidents in the home.* 毎年5千人が家の中の事故で死亡している. **3** N-VAR 可変性名詞 If something happens **by accident**, it happens completely by chance. 偶然に ❑ *She discovered the problem by accident during a visit to a nearby school.* 彼女は近くの学校を訪れている時に偶然その問題を発見した.

Thesaurus *accident* また次を参照:
N.	casualty, mishap **2**
	chance **3**

Word Partnership *accident* は次の語句と使われる:
N.	**car** accident **1**
	the cause of an accident **1** **2**
ADJ.	**bad** accident, **a tragic** accident **1** **2**
V.	**cause an** accident, **insure against** accident, **killed in** the accident, **report an** accident **1** **2**
PREP.	**without** accident **3**
	by accident **3**

ac|ci|den|tal /æksɪdɛntəl/ ADJ 形容詞 An **accidental** event happens by chance or as the result of an accident, and is not intended. 偶然の，不慮の ❑ *...the tragic accidental shooting of his younger brother.* 弟を誤って撃ってしまった悲劇的な事件 ●**ac|ci|den|tal|ly** /æksɪdɛntli/ ADV 副詞 [ADV with v] 偶然に，誤って ❑ *A policeman accidentally killed his two best friends with a single bullet.* 警官が1発の銃弾で2人の親友を誤って殺してしまった.

ac|ci|dent and emer|gen|cy (**accident and emergencies**) N-COUNT 可算名詞 **Accident and emergency** is the same as **emergency room**. 救急外来 [BRIT 英国英語]

Word Link *claim ≈ shouting : acclaim, clamor, exclaim*

ac|claim /əkleɪm/ (**acclaims, acclaiming, acclaimed**) **1** V-T 他動詞 If someone or something **is acclaimed**, they are praised enthusiastically. 絶賛する [FORMAL 形式ばった] [usu passive] ❑ *The restaurant has been widely acclaimed for its excellent French cuisine* そのレストランは素晴らしいフランス料理で広く賞賛を受けている. ❑ *He was acclaimed as America's greatest filmmaker.* 彼はアメリカの最も偉大な映画制作者として賞賛された. ●**ac|claimed** ADJ 形容詞 賞賛を受けている，評価の高い ❑ *She has published six highly acclaimed novels.* 彼女は高く評価された小説を6冊出版している. **2** N-UNCOUNT 不可算名詞 **Acclaim** is public praise for someone or something. 絶賛，賞賛 [FORMAL 形式ばった] ❑ *Angela Bassett has won critical acclaim for her excellent performance.* アンジェラ・バセットはその素晴らしい演技で評論家の絶賛を浴びた.

ac|cli|ma|tize /əklaɪmətaɪz/ (**acclimatizes, acclimatizing, acclimatized**) V-T/V-I 他動詞/自動詞 **Acclimatize** means the same as **acclimate**. 順応させる，慣らす[他動詞]，順応する，慣れる[自動詞] ❑ *The athletes are acclimatizing to the heat by staying in Monte Carlo.* 競技選手たちはモンテカルロに滞在して暑さに慣れてきている. [FORMAL 形式ばった] ❑ *This year he has left for St. Louis early to acclimatize himself.* 今年は彼は順応するために早めにセントルイスへ発った.

ac|co|lade /ækəleɪd/ (**accolades**) N-COUNT 可算名詞 If someone is given an **accolade**, something is done or said about them which shows how much people admire them. 賞賛，栄誉 [FORMAL 形式ばった] ❑ *The Nobel Prize has become the ultimate accolade in the sciences.* ノーベル賞は科学分野で最高の栄誉となった. ❑ *He won accolades as one of America's top test pilots.* 彼はアメリカの最高の試験飛行士の1人として賞賛を浴びた.

ac|com|mo|date /əkɒmədeɪt/ (**accommodates, accommodating, accommodated**) **1** V-T 他動詞 If a building or space can **accommodate** someone or something, it has enough room for them. 収容する [no cont] ❑ *The school was not big enough to accommodate all the children.* その学校は子供たち全員を収容できるほど大きくなかった. **2** V-T 他動詞 To **accommodate** someone means to provide them with a place to live or stay. 泊める ❑ *...a hotel built to accommodate guests for the wedding of King Alfonso.* アルフォンソ王の結婚式の招待客を泊めるために建てられたホテル **3** V-T 他動詞 If something is planned or changed to **accommodate** a particular situation, it is planned or changed so that it takes this situation into account. (状況・条件に)適応させる [FORMAL 形式ばった] ❑ *The roads are built to accommodate gradual temperature changes.* 道路は漸進的な温度変化に適応するように造られている.

ac|com|mo|dat|ing /əkɒmədeɪtɪŋ/ ADJ 形容詞 If you describe someone as **accommodating**, you like the fact that they are willing to do things in order to please you or help you. 世話好きな，親切な [APPROVAL 賛成] ❑ *Eddie was among the most approachable athletes on the team, always very accommodating to me.* エディーはチームの中で一番親しみやすい選手の1人で，いつも私に大変親切にしてくれた.

ac|com|mo|da|tion /əkɒmədeɪʃən/ (**accommodations**) **1** N-UNCOUNT 不可算名詞 **Accommodations** are buildings or rooms where people live or stay. 宿泊施設 [AM 米国英語] [also N in pl] ❑ *The government will provide temporary accommodations for up to three thousand homeless people.* 政府はホームレスが3千人まで泊まれる仮の宿泊施設を用意する. **2** N-UNCOUNT 不可算名詞 **Accommodation** is space in buildings or vehicles that is available for certain things, people, or activities. (特定の物・人・活動のための)スペース [FORMAL 形式ばった] ❑ *Their offices are housed in rented accommodation in a modernized wing of the Mathematics Institute.* 彼らのオフィスは数学研究所の現代的に改修された一翼の賃貸部分に入っている.

A

ac|com|pa|ni|ment /əkʌmpənimənt/ (accompaniments)
1 N-COUNT 可算名詞 The **accompaniment** to a song or tune is the music that is played at the same time as it and forms a background to it. 伴奏 ❑ He sang "My Funny Valentine" and "Wanted" to musical director Jim Steffan's piano accompaniment. 彼はジム・ステファン音楽ディレクターのピアノ伴奏に合わせて『マイ・ファニー・バレンタイン』と『ウォンテッド』を歌った. **2** N-COUNT 可算名詞 An **accompaniment** is something that goes with another thing. 添え物 ❑ This recipe makes a good accompaniment to ice cream. このレシピはアイスクリームによく合う. ● PHRASE 句 If one thing happens **to the accompaniment of** another, they happen at the same time. 一について

ac|com|pa|ny /əkʌmpəni/ (accompanies, accompanying, accompanied) **1** V-T 他動詞 If you **accompany** someone, you go somewhere with them. ついて行く [FORMAL 形式ばった] ❑ Ken agreed to accompany me on a trip to Africa. ケンはアフリカ旅行に私と同行することを承知した. ❑ She was accompanied by her younger brother. 彼女は弟を連れていた. **2** V-T 他動詞 If one thing **accompanies** another, it happens or exists at the same time, or as a result of it. 伴って起こる，結果として起こる [FORMAL 形式ばった] ❑ This volume of essays was designed to accompany an exhibition in Seattle. このエッセー集はシアトルでの展覧会に合わせてまとめられたものである. **3** V-T 他動詞 If you **accompany** a singer or a musician, you play one part of a piece of music while they sing or play the main tune. 伴奏をする ❑ On Meredith's new recording, Eddie Higgins accompanies her on all but one song. メレディスの新しいアルバムでは，エディ・ヒギンズが1曲を除いて全曲を伴奏している.

ac|com|plice /əkʌmplɪs/ (accomplices) N-COUNT 可算名詞 Someone's **accomplice** is a person who helps them to commit a crime. 共犯者 ❑ Witnesses said the gunman immediately ran to a motorcycle being ridden by an accomplice. 目撃者たちは拳銃強盗がただちに共犯者の運転しているバイクに向かって走っていったと述べた.

ac|com|plish /əkʌmplɪʃ/ (accomplishes, accomplishing, accomplished) V-T 他動詞 If you **accomplish** something, you succeed in doing it. 成し遂げる ❑ If we'd all work together, I think we could accomplish our goal. もし私たちがみんな一協力し合えば，目標を達成できると思います.

Thesaurus　　accomplish また次を参照 :

v.　　achieve, complete, gain, realize, succeed

ac|com|plished /əkʌmplɪʃt/ ADJ 形容詞 If someone is **accomplished** at something, they are very good at it. 熟練した，堪能な [FORMAL 形式ばった] ❑ She is an accomplished painter and a prolific author of stories for children. 彼女は熟練した画家であり，また多作の童話作家である.

ac|com|plish|ment /əkʌmplɪʃmənt/ (accomplishments) N-COUNT 可算名詞 An **accomplishment** is something remarkable that has been done or achieved. 業績，成果 ❑ For a novelist, that's quite an accomplishment. 小説家にとってこれはたいした成果だ.

ac|cord /əkɔːd/ (accords, according, accorded) **1** N-COUNT 可算名詞 An **accord** between countries or groups of people is a formal agreement; for example, to end a war. 合意 ❑ UNITA was legalized as a political party under the 1991 peace accords. 1991年の和平合意によりUNITAは合法的な政党となった. **2** V-T 他動詞 If you **are accorded** a particular kind of treatment, people act toward you or treat you in that way. 認容する [他動詞]，彼の前任者は，同様の大歓声で迎えられた. [FORMAL 形式ばった] ❑ On his return home, the government accorded him the rank of Colonel. 彼が帰国すると政府は大佐の地位を与えた. **3** → see also **according to** **4** PHRASE 句 If something happens **of its own accord**, it seems to happen by itself, without anyone making it happen. ひとりでに ❑ In many cases the disease will clear up of its own accord. 多くの場合，その病気は自然に快癒する. **5** PHRASE 句 If you do something **of your own accord**, you do it because you want to, without being asked or forced. 自発的に ❑ He did not quit as France's prime minister of his own accord. 彼は自発的に仏首相の座を辞したのではなかった.

ac|cord|ance /əkɔːdns/ PHRASE 句 If something is done **in accordance with** a particular rule or system, it is done in the way that the rule or system says that it should be done. に従って ❑ Entries which are illegible or otherwise not in accordance with the rules will be disqualified. 判別できない記入または規定に従わない記入は無効となります.

ac|cord|ing|ly /əkɔːdɪŋli/ **1** ADV 副詞 You use **accordingly** to introduce a fact or situation that is a result or consequence of something that you have just referred to. それゆえに ❑ We have a different background, a different history. Accordingly, we have the right to different futures. 私たちは背景も歴史も違っている. それゆえに，異なる未来を持つ権利がある. **2** ADV 副詞 If you consider a situation and then act **accordingly**, the way you act depends on the nature of the situation. しかるべく [ADV after v] ❑ It is a difficult job and they should be paid accordingly. 難しい仕事なので，相応の支払いを受けるべきだ.

ac|cord|ing to **1** PHRASE 句 If someone says that something is true **according to** a particular person, book, or other source of information, they are indicating where they got their information. ～によると ❑ The van raced away, according to police reports, and police gave chase. 警察の報告によると，そのバンは慌てて走り去り，警察が追跡した. **2** PHRASE 句 If something is done **according to** a particular set of principles, these principles are used as a basis for the way it is done. ～に則って ❑ They both played the game according to the rules. 双方がルールに則って試合を戦った. **3** PHRASE 句 If something varies **according to** a changing factor, it varies in a way that is determined by this factor. ～に応じて ❑ Prices vary according to the quantity ordered. 価格は注文数量に応じて変わる. **4** PHRASE 句 If something happens **according to plan**, it happens in exactly the way that it was intended to happen. 予定通り ❑ If all goes according to plan, the first concert will be Tuesday evening. すべて予定通り進めば，最初の演奏会は火曜の夕方だ.

ac|count /əkaʊnt/ (accounts, accounting, accounted) **1** N-COUNT 可算名詞 If you have an **account** with a bank or a similar organization, you have an arrangement to leave your money there and take some out when you need it. 口座 ❑ Some banks make it difficult to open an account. 口座の開設が難しい銀行もある. **2** N-COUNT 可算名詞 In business, a regular customer of a company can be referred to as an **account**, especially when the customer is another company. 顧客 [BUSINESS 実業] ❑ All three Internet agencies boast they've won major accounts. インターネット代理業3社が大手顧客を獲得したと得意げに言っている. **3** N-COUNT 可算名詞 **Accounts** are detailed records of all the money that a person or business receives and spends. 会計簿 [BUSINESS 実業] ❑ He kept detailed accounts. 彼は会計簿を詳細に記録した. **4** N-COUNT 可算名詞 An **account** is a written or spoken report of something that has happened. 説明 ❑ He gave a detailed account of what happened on the fateful night. 彼は運命の夜に起こった出来事を事細かに説明した. **5** → see also **accounting, bank account, checking account, deposit account**

> Do not confuse **account** and **bill**. When you have an **account** with a bank, you leave your money in the bank and take it out when you need it. When you have to pay for things such as electricity or a work done by a repairman, you get a **bill**.

6 PHRASE 句 If you say that something is true **by all accounts** or **from all accounts**, you believe it is true because other people say so. だれに聞いても ❑ He is, by all accounts, a superb teacher. だれに聞いても彼は優秀な教師だ. **7** PHRASE 句 If you say that something is **of no account** or **of little account**, you mean that it is very unimportant and is not worth considering. 取るに足りない [FORMAL 形式ばった] ❑ These obscure groups were of little account in either national or international politics. これらの無名の集団は，内外政策の両方でほとんど重要性がない. **8** PHRASE 句 If you buy or pay for something **on account**, you pay nothing or only part of the cost at first, and pay the rest later. 掛けで，分割払いで，内金として ❑ He was ordered to pay the company $500,000 on account pending a final assessment of his liability. 負債の最終評価が定まるまで，彼は一部として会社に対して50万ドルの支払いを命じられた. **9** PHRASE 句 You use **on account of** to introduce the reason or explanation for something. ～のため ❑ The president declined to deliver the speech himself, on account of a sore throat. 大統領は，喉の痛みのため自ら演説することを辞退した. **10** PHRASE 句 Your feelings **on** someone's **account** are the feelings you have about what they have experienced or might experience, especially when you imagine yourself to be in their situation. (だれか)の 身になって ❑ Mollie told me what she'd done and I was really scared on her account. モリーは自分のしたことを私に語り，私は彼女の身になって本当に恐ろしく感じた. **11** PHRASE 句 If you tell someone not to do something **on your account**, you mean that they should do it only if they want to, and not because they think it will please you. ～のために [SPOKEN 口語] ❑ Don't leave on my account. 私のためにだったら行かないで. **12** PHRASE 句 If you say that something should **on no account** be done, you are emphasizing that it should not be done under any circumstances. 決して一ない [EMPHASIS 強調] ❑ On no account should the mixture come near boiling. 混合液は決して沸騰させないこと. **13** PHRASE 句 If you do something **on your own account**, you do it because you want to and without being asked, and you take responsibility for your own action. 自分のため，自分の責任で ❑ I told him if he withdrew it was on his own account. それを撤回するかどうかは彼自身の責任だと私は彼に言った. **14** PHRASE 句 If you **take** something **into account**, or **take account of** something, you consider it when you are thinking about a situation or deciding what to do. 考慮に入れる ❑ The defendant asked for 21 similar offenses to be taken into account. 被告人は21件の類似の違反を考慮に入れるよう求めた. **15** PHRASE 句 If someone is **called, held,** or **brought to account** for something they have done wrong, they are made to explain why they did it, and are often criticized or punished for it. 釈明を求められる ❑ Individuals who repeatedly provide false

information should be called to account for their actions. 繰り返し虚偽の情報を流した個人は、その行為について釈明を求められることになります. ⓰ PHRASE 句動詞 If you say that someone **gave a good account of** themselves in a particular situation, you mean that they performed well, although they may not have been completely successful. 立派に振る舞う ❑*We have been hindered by our lack of preparation, but I'm sure we will give a good account of ourselves.* 準備不足が響いてはいるが、我々は立派に振る舞えると私は確信している.

Word Partnership	*account* は次の語句と使われる:
N.	account **balance**, **bank** account, account **number**, **savings** account ①
V.	**access your** account, **open an** account ① **give a detailed** account ④ **take** *something* **into** account ⑭
ADJ.	**blow-by-blow** account ④

▶ **account for** ① PHRASAL VERB 句動詞 If a particular thing **accounts for** a part or proportion of something, that part or proportion consists of that thing, or is used or produced by it. 占める ❑*Computers account for 5% of the country's commercial electricity consumption.* コンピューターは、その国の商用電力消費の5%を占める. ② PHRASAL VERB 句動詞 If something **accounts for** a particular fact or situation, it causes or explains it. 説明する, 原因となる ❑*The gene they discovered today doesn't account for all those cases.* 彼らが今日発見した遺伝子が、そうしたすべての場合を説明するわけではない. ③ PHRASAL VERB 句動詞 If you can **account for** something, you can explain it or give the necessary information about it. 説明する ❑*How do you account for the company's alarmingly high staff turnover?* その会社の不安になるほどの離職率の高さをどう説明しますか. ④ PHRASAL VERB 句動詞 If someone has to **account for** an action or policy, they are responsible for it, and may be required to justify it to other people or be punished if it fails. 責任を取る ❑*The president and the president alone must account for his government's reforms.* 大統領が、そして大統領のみが政府の改革に責任を持たねばならない. ⑤ PHRASAL VERB 句動詞 If a sum of money **is accounted for** in a budget, it has been included in that budget for a particular purpose. 計上する ❑*The really heavy costs have been accounted for.* 多額の費用は計上されている.
→ see **bank**, **history**

ac|count|able /əkaʊntəbəl/ ADJ 形容詞 If you are **accountable to** someone **for** something that you do, you are responsible for it and must be prepared to justify your actions to that person. 責任がある ❑*Public officials can finally be held accountable for their actions.* 公務員は最終的に自分の行いの説明責任があります. ● **ac|count|abil|ity** /əkaʊntəbɪliti/ N-UNCOUNT 不可算名詞 責任 ❑*...a drive toward democracy and greater accountability.* 民主主義とより大きな責任に向けての推進力

ac|count|an|cy /əkaʊntənsi/ N-UNCOUNT 不可算名詞 **Accountancy** is the theory or practice of keeping financial accounts. 会計事務, 会計学 [BRIT 英国英語; AM **accounting** 米国英語 **accounting**]

ac|count|ant /əkaʊntənt/ (accountants) N-COUNT 可算名詞 An **accountant** is a person whose job is to keep financial accounts. 会計士

ac|count|ing /əkaʊntɪŋ/ ① N-UNCOUNT 不可算名詞 **Accounting** is the activity of keeping detailed records of the amounts of money a business or person receives and spends. 会計 ❑*...the accounting firm of Leventhal & Horwath.* リーベンサル・アンド・ホーワス会計事務所 ② → see also **account**

ac|cru|al /əkruəl/ (accruals) N-COUNT 可算名詞 In finance, the **accrual** of something such as interest or investments is the adding together of interest or different investments over a period of time. 定期的に累増する金額 [BUSINESS 実業] ❑*After an employee has 25 years of service, there is no further accrual of benefits.* 勤続25年を越える従業員については、手当てはそれ以上累増しない.

ac|crue /əkru/ (accrues, accruing, accrued) V-T/V-I 他動詞/自動詞 If money or interest **accrues**, it gradually increases in amount over a period of time. 生じる ❑*I owed $5,000 - part of this was accrued interest.* 5000ドルを借りた - この一部は経過利息だ. [BUSINESS 実業] ❑*While they may use a credit card for convenience, affluent people never let interest charges accrue.* 裕福な人は、便宜上クレジットカードを使うかもしれないが、利子を累積させることはない.

ac|cu|mu|late /əkyumyəleɪt/ (accumulates, accumulating, accumulated) V-T/V-I 他動詞/自動詞 When you **accumulate** things or when they **accumulate**, they collect or are gathered over a period of time. 蓄積する ❑*Lead can accumulate in the body until toxic levels are reached.* 鉛は毒性量に達するまで体内に蓄積しうる.

ac|cu|mu|la|tion /əkyumyəleɪʃən/ (accumulations) ① N-COUNT 可算名詞 An **accumulation of** something is a large number of things that have been collected together or acquired over a period of time. 蓄積 ❑*...an accumulation of experience*

and knowledge. 経験と知識の蓄積 ② N-UNCOUNT 不可算名詞 **Accumulation** is the collecting together of things over a period of time. 蓄積 ❑*...the accumulation of capital and the distribution of income.* 資本の蓄積と所得の分配

ac|cu|ra|cy /ækyərəsi/ ① N-UNCOUNT 不可算名詞 The **accuracy** of information or measurements is their quality of being true or correct, even in small details. 正確さ ❑*Every care has been taken to ensure the accuracy of all information given in this leaflet.* この冊子に盛り込まれたすべての情報の正確さを確保するため、あらゆる注意が払われてきた. ② N-UNCOUNT 不可算名詞 If someone or something performs a task, for example, hitting a target, **with accuracy**, they do it in an exact way without making a mistake. 正確 ❑*...weapons that could fire with accuracy at targets 3,000 yards away.* 3000ヤード離れた標的を正確に爆破できる兵器

ac|cu|rate /ækyərɪt/ ① ADJ 形容詞 **Accurate** information, measurements, and statistics are correct to a very detailed level. An **accurate** instrument is able to give you information of this kind. 正確な, 精密な ❑*Police have stressed that this is the most accurate description of the killer to date.* 警察は、これが今のところ最も正確な殺人犯の人物像であることを強調した. ● **ac|cu|rate|ly** ADV 副詞 正確に ❑*The test can accurately predict what a bigger explosion would do.* この試験によって、より大きな爆発が起こった結果を正確に予測しうる. ② ADJ 形容詞 An **accurate** statement or account gives a true or fair judgment of something. 的確な ❑*Stalin gave an accurate assessment of the utility of nuclear weapons.* スターリンは核兵器の有効性を的確に評価した. ● **ac|cu|rate|ly** ADV 副詞 [ADV with v] 的確に ❑*What many people mean by the word "power" could be more accurately described as "control."* 「権力」という言葉が意味するものは、「支配」というほうが的確かもしれない. ③ ADJ 形容詞 You can use **accurate** to describe the results of someone's actions when they do or copy something correctly or exactly. 厳密な ❑*We require grammar and spelling to be accurate.* 文法および綴りの厳密さが求められる. ④ ADJ 形容詞 An **accurate** weapon or throw reaches the exact point or target that it was intended to reach. You can also describe a person as **accurate** if they fire a weapon or throw something in this way. 精密な ❑*His throws were long, hard and accurate, as always.* 彼の投擲(とうてき)は、いつもどおり飛距離があり強力で的を外しませんでした. ● **ac|cu|rate|ly** ADV 副詞 [ADV with v] 精密に ❑*He hit the golf ball powerfully and accurately.* 彼は強力かつ正確にゴルフボールを打った.

Thesaurus	*accurate* また次を参照:
ADJ.	right, true; (*ant*.) inaccurate ② correct, precise, rigorous ③

ac|cu|sa|tion /ækyuzeɪʃən/ (accusations) ① N-VAR 可変性名詞 If you make an **accusation** against someone, you criticize them or express the belief that they have done something wrong. 非難 ❑*Kim rejects accusations that country music is over-sentimental.* キムはカントリー音楽が感傷的に過ぎるという非難を退けた. ② N-COUNT 可算名詞 An **accusation** is a statement or claim by a witness or someone in authority that a particular person has committed a crime, although this has not yet been proved. 告発, 告訴 ❑*...people who have made public accusations of rape.* 強姦に関して公に告発を行った人々

ac|cuse /əkyuz/ (accuses, accusing, accused) ① V-T 他動詞 If you **accuse** someone **of** doing something wrong or dishonest, you say or tell them that you believe that they did it. 非難する ❑*My mom was really upset because he was accusing her of having an affair with another man.* 私の母がひどく動揺していたのは彼に別の男と関係を持ったと非難されたからだ. ② V-T 他動詞 If you **are accused of** a crime, a witness or someone in authority states or claims that you did it, and you may be formally charged with it and put on trial. 起訴する ❑*Her assistant was accused of theft and fraud by the police.* 彼女の助手は、窃盗と詐欺に問われ警察に起訴された. ❑*He faced a total of seven charges, all accusing him of lying in his testimony.* 彼は全7件の罪に問われ、そのすべてにおいて偽証のかどで告訴されている. ③ → see also **accused** ④ PHRASE 句 If someone **stands accused** of something, they have been accused of it. 告発を受ける ❑*The candidate stands accused of breaking promises even before he's in office.* その候補者は、職務に就く前にすでに公約違反で告発を受けています.

Thesaurus	*accuse* また次を参照:
V.	blame, charge, implicate; (*ant*.) absolve, exonerate, vindicate ① ②

ac|cused /əkyuzd/ (accused)

Accused is both the singular and the plural form.

Accused は単数形でも複数形でもある.

N-COUNT 可算名詞 You can use **the accused** to refer to a person or a group of people charged with a crime or on trial for it. 被告

[LEGAL] 法律的 ❑ *The accused is alleged to be a member of a right-wing gang.* 被告は右翼の一員と言われている.

ac|cus|tom /əkʌstəm/ (**accustoms, accustoming, accustomed**) ❶ V-T 他動詞 If you **accustom yourself** or another person **to** something, you make yourself or them become used to it. 慣れさせる [他動詞] ❑ *She tried to accustom herself to the tight bandages.* 彼女はきつい包帯に慣れようとした. [FORMAL 形式ばった] ❷ → see also **accustomed**

ac|cus|tomed /əkʌstəmd/ ❶ ADJ 形容詞 If you are **accustomed to** something, you know it so well or have experienced it so often that it seems natural, unsurprising, or easy to deal with. 慣れている [v-link ADJ 'to' n/-ing] ❑ *I was accustomed to being the only child at a table full of adults.* 私は子供の頃, 大人ばかりの食卓に着くことに慣れていた. ❷ ADJ 形容詞 When your eyes become **accustomed to** darkness or bright light, they adjust so that you start to be able to see things, after not being able to see properly at first. 順応している [v-link ADJ 'to' n] ❑ *My eyes were becoming accustomed to the gloom and I was able to make out a door at one side of the room.* 私の目は暗がりに順応し始め, 部屋の片側に扉を見分けられた.

Word Partnership *accustomed は次の語句と使われる:*

N.	accustomed **to the heat** ❶
	accustomed **to the dark(ness)** ❷
V.	become accustomed, get accustomed, grow accustomed ❶❷
ADV.	gradually accustomed, long accustomed ❶❷

ace /eɪs/ (**aces**) ❶ N-COUNT 可算名詞 An **ace** is a playing card with a single symbol on it. In most card games, the ace of a particular suit has either the highest or the lowest value of the cards in that suit. エース, 1の札 ❑ *...the ace of hearts.* ハートのエース ❷ N-COUNT 可算名詞 If you describe someone such as a sports player as an **ace**, you mean that they are very good at what they do. エース, 主力選手 [JOURNALISM ジャーナリズム] ❑ *Despite the loss of their ace early in the game, Seattle beat the Brewers 6-5.* 試合の早い段階でエースを失ったにもかかわらず, シアトルはブルワーズを6対5で下した. ● ADJ 形容詞 **Ace** is also an adjective. 一流の [ADJ n] ❑ *...ace horror-film producer Lawrence Woolsey.* 一流の恐怖映画製作者ローレンス・ウールジー ❸ N-COUNT 可算名詞 In tennis, an **ace** is a serve which is so fast that the other player cannot reach the ball. 相手が返球できない打球 ❑ *Agassi believed he had served an ace at 5-3 (40-30) in the deciding set.* 決勝戦の5対3 (40対30) で, アガシはサービス・エースを放ったと信じた. ❹ PHRASE 句 Something that is an **ace in the hole** is an advantage which you have over an opponent or rival, and which you can use if necessary. 切り札 [v-link PHR, PHR after v] ❑ *Our superior technology is our ace in the hole.* 卓越した技術が我々の切り札だ.

ache /eɪk/ (**aches, aching, ached**) ❶ V-I 自動詞 If you **ache** or a part of your body **aches**, you feel a steady, fairly strong pain. 痛む [自動詞] ❑ *The glands in her neck were swollen, her head was throbbing and she ached all over.* 彼女は, 首のリンパ腺が腫れ, 頭がうずき, 全身が痛んだ. ❑ *My leg is giving me much less pain but still aches when I sit down.* 足の痛みははるかにやわらいだが, 座るときにはまだ痛む. ❷ N-COUNT 可算名詞 An **ache** is a steady, fairly strong pain in a part of your body. 痛み ❑ *You feel nausea and aches in your muscles.* 吐き気と筋肉痛を感じる. ❸ PHRASE 句 You can use **aches and pains** to refer in a general way to any minor pains that you feel in your body. うずきと痛み ❑ *It seems to ease all the aches and pains of a hectic and tiring day.* 忙しくて疲れる一日の全身の痛みが和らぐようだ. ❹ → see also **headache, heartache, stomach ache**

Thesaurus *ache また次を参照:*

| V. | hurt, throb ❶ |
| N. | pain, pang, sore ❷ |

achieve /ətʃiːv/ (**achieves, achieving, achieved**) V-T 他動詞 If you **achieve** a particular aim or effect, you succeed in doing it or causing it to happen, usually after a lot of effort. 達成する ❑ *There are many who will work hard to achieve these goals.* こうした目標を達成するために力を尽くす人は多い.

Thesaurus *achieve また次を参照:*

| V. | accomplish, bring about; (ant.) fail, lose, miss |

achieve|ment /ətʃiːvmənt/ (**achievements**) ❶ N-COUNT 可算名詞 An **achievement** is something that someone has succeeded in doing, especially after a lot of effort. 業績 ❑ *It was a great achievement that a month later a global agreement was reached.* ひと月後に包括的合意に至ったことは大きな業績だった. ❷ N-UNCOUNT 不可算名詞 **Achievement** is the process of achieving something. 達成 ❑ *It is only the achievement of these goals that will finally bring lasting peace.* 最終的に永続的平和をもたらすのはこれらの目標が成就すること

とによってである.

achiev|er /ətʃiːvər/ (**achievers**) N-COUNT 可算名詞 A high **achiever** is someone who is successful in their studies or their work, usually as a result of their efforts. A low **achiever** is someone who achieves less than those around them. 達成者 ❑ *High achievers at the company are in line for cash bonuses.* その会社で優れた業績を上げた者は現金賞与の支給対象となる.

acid /æsɪd/ (**acids**) ❶ N-MASS 質量名詞 An **acid** is a chemical substance, usually a liquid, which contains hydrogen and can react with other substances to form salts. Some acids burn or dissolve other substances that they come into contact with. 酸 ❑ *...citric acid.* クエン酸 ❷ ADJ 形容詞 An **acid** substance contains acid. 酸性の ❑ *These shrubs must have an acid, lime-free soil.* これらの低木は, 酸性で石灰を含まない土壌を必要とする. ● **acid|ity** /əsɪdɪti/ N-UNCOUNT 不可算名詞 [oft N 'of' n] 酸性度 ❑ *...the acidity of rainwater.* 雨水の酸性度

acid|ic /əsɪdɪk/ ADJ 形容詞 **Acidic** substances contain acid. 酸性の ❑ *Dissolved carbon dioxide makes the water more acidic.* 溶解した二酸化炭素が水の酸性度を高める.

acid rain N-UNCOUNT 不可算名詞 **Acid rain** is rain polluted by acid that has been released into the atmosphere from factories and other industrial processes. Acid rain is harmful to the environment. 酸性雨 → see **pollution**

ac|knowl|edge /æknɒlɪdʒ/ (**acknowledges, acknowledging, acknowledged**) ❶ V-T 他動詞 If you **acknowledge** a fact or a situation, you accept or admit that it is true or that it exists. 受け入れる ❑ *Naylor acknowledged, in a letter to the judge, that he was a drug addict.* 裁判官への手紙で, ネイラーは自分が薬物中毒者であることを認めた. [FORMAL 形式ばった] ❑ *Belatedly, the government has acknowledged the problem.* 遅ればせながら政府は問題を認めた. ❷ V-T 他動詞 If someone's achievements, status, or qualities **are acknowledged**, they are known about and recognized by a lot of people, or by a particular group of people. 認める ❑ *He is also acknowledged as an excellent goalkeeper.* 彼は優秀なゴールキーパーとしても定評がある. ❸ V-T 他動詞 If you **acknowledge** a message or letter, you write to the person who sent it in order to say that you have received it. 受け取ったことを伝える ❑ *The army sent me a postcard acknowledging my request.* 軍は私の要求の受け取り確認の葉書を送ってきた. ❹ V-T 他動詞 If you **acknowledge** someone, for example, by moving your head and or smiling, you show that you have seen and recognized them. 認識する ❑ *He saw her but refused to even acknowledge her.* 彼は彼女を見たはずだが, そのことを意識することすら拒んだ.

Thesaurus *acknowledge また次を参照:*

| V. | accept, admit, grant ❶ |
| | recognize; (ant.) ignore ❷ – ❹ |

ac|knowl|edg|ment /æknɒlɪdʒmənt/ (**acknowledgments**) also **acknowledgement** ❶ N-SING 単数名詞 An **acknowledgment** is a statement or action which recognizes that something exists or is true. 認容 [also no det] ❑ *The president's resignation appears to be an acknowledgment that he has lost all hope of keeping the country together.* 大統領は辞職することで国をまとめる希望を完全に失ったことを認めたように思える. ❷ N-PLURAL 複数名詞 The **acknowledgments** in a book are the section in which the author thanks all the people who have helped him or her. 献辞 ❑ *...two whole pages of acknowledgments.* 全2ページに及ぶ献辞 ❸ N-UNCOUNT 不可算名詞 A gesture of **acknowledgment**, such as a smile, shows someone that you have seen and recognized them. 認知 [also 'a' N] ❑ *Farling smiled in acknowledgment and gave a bow.* ファーリングは, 相手に気づいたことを示すため微笑んでお辞儀した.

acne /ækni/ N-UNCOUNT 不可算名詞 If someone has **acne**, they have a skin condition which causes a lot of pimples on their face and neck. にきび ❑ *She wore no makeup, and her face was dotted with acne.* 彼女は化粧しておらず, 顔にはにきびがあった.

acorn /eɪkɔːrn/ (**acorns**) N-COUNT 可算名詞 An **acorn** is a pale oval nut that is the fruit of an oak tree. どんぐり

acous|tic /əkuːstɪk/ (**acoustics**) ❶ ADJ 形容詞 An **acoustic** guitar or other instrument is one whose sound is produced without any electrical equipment. 電気装置を用いない ❷ N-COUNT 可算名詞 If you refer to the **acoustics** of a space, you are referring to the structural features which determine how well you can hear music or speech in it. 音響効果 [ADJ n] ❑ *In this performance, Rattle had the acoustics of the Symphony Hall on his side.* この演奏では, シンフォニー・ホールの音響効果がラトルにとって有利に働いた. ❸ N-UNCOUNT 不可算名詞 **Acoustics** is the scientific study of sound. 音響学 ❑ *...his work in acoustics.* 音響学における彼の業績

ac|quaint /əkweɪnt/ (**acquaints, acquainting, acquainted**) ❶ V-T 他動詞 If you **acquaint** someone **with** something, you tell

them about it so that they know it. If you **acquaint yourself with** something, you learn about it. 知らせる [他動詞] □ *Have steps been taken to acquaint breeders with their right to apply for licenses?* 種畜家に免許を申し込む権利があることを知らせるための手順はとったのか. [FORMAL 形式ばった] **2** → see also **acquainted**

ac|quaint|ance /əkweɪntəns/ (**acquaintances**) **1** N-COUNT 可算名詞 An **acquaintance** is someone who you have met and know slightly, but not well. 知人 □ *He exchanged a few words with the proprietor, an old acquaintance of his.* 彼は旧知の経営者とわずかに言葉を交わした. **2** N-VAR 可変性名詞 If you have an **acquaintance** **with** someone, you have met them and you know them. 知り合い □ *...a writer who becomes involved in a real murder mystery through his acquaintance with a police officer.* 警察官と知り合いになり現実の殺人事件と関わるようになった作家 **3** PHRASE 句 When you **make** someone's **acquaintance**, you meet them for the first time and get to know them a little. 知り合いになる [FORMAL 形式ばった] □ *I first made his acquaintance in the early 1960s.* 1960年代初頭に彼と知り合いになった.

ac|quaint|ed /əkweɪntɪd/ **1** ADJ 形容詞 If you are **acquainted** **with** something, you know about it because you have learned it or experienced it. 知っている [FORMAL 形式ばった] [v-link ADJ 'with' n] □ *He was well acquainted with the literature of Latin America.* 彼はラテンアメリカ文学に精通している. **2** ADJ 形容詞 If you get or become **acquainted with** someone that you do not know, you talk to each other or do something together so that you get to know each other. You can also say that two people get or become **acquainted**. 知り合いである [v-link ADJ] □ *At first the meetings were a way to get acquainted with each other.* 最初, その会議はお互いを知り合うための手段だった. **3** → see also **acquaint**

ac|quire /əkwaɪər/ (**acquires, acquiring, acquired**) **1** V-T 他動詞 If you **acquire** something, you buy or obtain it for yourself, or someone gives it to you. 取得する □ *General Motors acquired a 50% stake in Saab for about $400m.* ゼネラルモーターズはサーブ社株式の50%を約4億ドルで取得した. [FORMAL 形式ばった] **2** V-T 他動詞 If you **acquire** something such as a skill or a habit, you learn it, or develop it through your daily life or experience. 身につける □ *I've never acquired a taste for wine.* ワインの味はいまだにわからない. **3** V-T 他動詞 If someone or something **acquires** a certain reputation, they start to have that reputation. 獲得する □ *During her film career, she acquired a reputation as a strong-willed, outspoken woman.* 彼女は映画人生で強靭な意志を持つ率直に発言する女性という評判を得た.

ac|quir|er /əkwaɪərər/ (**acquirers**) N-COUNT 可算名詞 In business, an **acquirer** is a company or person who buys another company. 買収者 [BUSINESS 実業] □ *...the ability of corporate acquirers to finance large takeovers.* 大規模な買収資金を調達する企業の能力

ac|qui|si|tion /ækwɪzɪʃən/ (**acquisitions**) **1** N-VAR 可変性名詞 If a company or business person makes an **acquisition**, they buy another company or part of a company. 買収 [BUSINESS 実業] □ *...the acquisition of a profitable paper recycling company.* 利益を生む古紙再生会社の買収 **2** N-COUNT 可算名詞 If you make an **acquisition**, you buy or obtain something, often to add to things that you already have. 買い入れ □ *How did you go about making this marvelous acquisition then?* それでこの素晴らしい買い付けにどんなふうに取り組んだのかな. **3** N-UNCOUNT 不可算名詞 The **acquisition** of a skill or a particular type of knowledge is the process of learning it or developing it. 習得 □ *...language acquisition.* 言語習得

ac|quit /əkwɪt/ (**acquits, acquitting, acquitted**) V-T 他動詞 If someone **is acquitted** of a crime in a court of law, they are formally declared not to have committed the crime. 放免する [usu passive] □ *Mr. Castorina was acquitted of attempted murder.* カストリーナ氏は殺人未遂容疑で無罪になった.

ac|quit|tal /əkwɪtəl/ (**acquittals**) N-VAR 可変性名詞 **Acquittal** is a formal declaration in a court of law that someone who has been accused of a crime is innocent. 無罪判決 □ *...the acquittal of six police officers charged with beating up a suspect.* 容疑者殴打の容疑がかかっていた警官6名の無罪判決 □ *The jury voted 8-to-4 in favor of acquittal.* 陪審員の投票は8対4で無罪を支持しました.

acre /eɪkər/ (**acres**) N-COUNT 可算名詞 An **acre** is an area of land measuring 4,840 square yards or 4,047 square meters. 土地の広さの単位 □ *The property consists of two acres of land.* その不動産は2エーカーの土地からなる.

ac|ri|mo|ni|ous /ækrɪmoʊniəs/ ADJ 形容詞 **Acrimonious** words or quarrels are bitter and angry. 痛烈な [FORMAL 形式ばった] □ *The acrimonious debate on the agenda ended indecisively.* その議題についての痛烈な討論は漠然とした結論に終わった.

| Word Link | onym ≈ name : acronym, anonymous, synonym |

ac|ro|nym /ækrənɪm/ (**acronyms**) N-COUNT 可算名詞 An **acronym** is a word composed of the first letters of the words in a phrase, especially when this is used as a name. An example of an acronym is NATO which is made up of the first letters of the "North Atlantic Treaty Organization." 頭字語

across /əkrɔs/

| In addition to the uses shown below, **across** is used in phrasal verbs such as "come across," "get across," and "put across." |
| 下記の用法に加えて, **across** は come across, get across, put across のような句動詞に使われる. |

1 PREP 前置詞 If someone or something goes **across** a place or a boundary, they go from one side of it to the other. 横切って □ *She walked across the floor and lay down on the bed.* 彼女は部屋を横切りベッドに横たわった. □ *He watched Karl run across the street to Tommy.* 彼はカールが通りを横切りトミーに向かって走るのを見た. ● ADV 副詞 **Across** is also an adverb. 横切って [ADV after v] □ *Richard stood up and walked across to the window.* リチャードは立ち上がり, 窓のほうに歩いた. **2** PREP 前置詞 If something is situated or stretched **across** something else, it is situated or stretched from one side of it to the other. 横断して □ *...the floating bridge across Lake Washington in Seattle.* シアトルのワシントン湖を横断してかかる浮橋 □ *He scrawled his name across the bill.* 彼は勘定書の端から端に自分の名前を無造作に書いた. ● ADV 副詞 **Across** is also an adverb. 反対側まで [ADV after v] □ *Trim toenails straight across using nail clippers.* 爪切りを使って足の爪をまっすぐに切る. **3** PREP 前置詞 If something is lying **across** an object or place, it is resting on it and partly covering it. かかって □ *She found her clothes lying across the chair.* 彼女は自分の服が椅子 (いす) にかかっているのを見た. **4** PREP 前置詞 Something that is **across** something such as a street, river, or area is on the other side of it. 向こう側の □ *Anyone from the houses across the road could see him.* 道の向こう側の家からは誰でも彼を見ることができた. ● ADV 副詞 **Across** is also an adverb. 向こう側に □ *They parked across from the Castro Theater.* 彼らはカストロ劇場の向こう側に駐車した. **5** PREP 前置詞 You use **across** to say that a particular expression is shown on someone's face. 全体に □ *An enormous grin spread across his face.* 彼の顔に満面の笑みが広がった. **6** PREP 前置詞 If someone hits you **across** the face or head, they hit you on that part. 対して □ *Graham hit him across the face with the gun, then pushed him against the wall.* グレアムは銃で彼の顔を殴りつけ, 彼を壁に押し付けた. **7** PREP 前置詞 When something happens **across** a place or organization, it happens equally everywhere within it. 全体で □ *The movie opens across the country on December 11.* その映画は12月11日に全国で公開される. **8** PREP 前置詞 When something happens **across** a political, religious, or social barrier, it involves people in different groups. またがって □ *...parties competing across the political spectrum.* 政界勢力を横断し競合する諸政党 **9** **across** **the board** → see **board** **10** ADV 副詞 If you look **across** at a place, person, or thing, you look toward them. 方向に □ *He glanced across at his sleeping wife.* 彼は眠っている妻のほうに視線を向けた. □ *She rose from the chair and gazed across at him.* 彼女は椅子 (いす) から身を起こし, 彼のほうをじっと見た. **11** ADV 副詞 **Across** is used in measurements to show the width of something. 幅で [amount ADV] □ *This hand-decorated plate measures 14 inches across.* この手工芸の皿は直径14インチ.

acryl|ic /ækrɪlɪk/ N-UNCOUNT 不可算名詞 **Acrylic** material is artificial and is manufactured by a chemical process. アクリル □ *...her pink acrylic sweater.* 彼女の桃色をしたアクリルのセーター

act /ækt/ (**acts, acting, acted**) **1** V-I 自動詞 When you **act**, you do something for a particular purpose. 行動する □ *The deaths occurred when police acted to stop widespread looting and vandalism.* 警察が略奪と破壊の横行を食い止めるべく行動したときに, 死者が発生した. **2** V-I 自動詞 If you **act on** advice or information, you do what has been advised or suggested. 従って行動する □ *A patient will usually listen to the doctor's advice and act on it.* 患者は, 医者の忠告を聞き, それに従うものだ. **3** V-I 自動詞 If someone **acts** in a particular way, they behave in that way. 振舞う □ *...a gang of youths who were acting suspiciously.* 挙動不審の若者の一団 □ *He acted as if he hadn't heard any of it.* 彼はそのことをまったく聞いていないかのごとく振舞った. **4** V-I 自動詞 If someone or something **acts** **as** a particular thing, they have that role or function. 役を務める □ *Among his other duties, he acted both as the ship's surgeon and as chaplain for the men.* 他の職務に加え, 彼は船医および乗組員のための司祭の役を務めた. **5** V-I 自動詞 If someone **acts** in a particular way, they pretend to be something that they are not. 装う □ *Chris acted astonished as he examined the note.* クリスはその覚書を調べ, 驚いたふりをした. **6** V-I 自動詞 When professionals such as lawyers **act for** you, or **act on** your **behalf**, they are employed by you to deal with a particular matter. 代理を務める □ *Daniel Webster acted for Boston traders while still practicing in New Hampshire.* ダニエル・ウェブスターは, ニュー・ハンプシャーで開業しながら, ボストンの商人の代理を務めた. **7** V-I 自動詞 If a force or substance **acts** on something or someone, it has a certain effect on them. 作用する □ *He's taking a dangerous drug: it acts very fast on the central nervous system.* 彼は危険な薬を服用した. それは極めて短時間で中枢神経に作用する. **8** V-I 自動詞 If you **act** in a play or film, you have a part in it. 演じる □ *She confessed to her parents her desire to act.* 彼女は両親に女優になりたい気持ちを打ち明けた. **9** N-COUNT 可算名詞 An **act** is a single thing that someone does. 行為 [FORMAL 形式ばった]

[oft N 'of' n] ❏ *Language interpretation is the whole point of the act of reading.* 言葉の解釈は読むという行為の核心だ. **10** N-COUNT 可算名詞 An **Act** is a law passed by the government. 制定法 ❏ *...an Act of Congress.* 下院制定法 **11** N-COUNT 可算名詞 An **act** in a play, opera, or ballet is one of the main parts into which it is divided. 幕 [oft N num] ❏ *Act II contained one of the funniest scenes I have ever witnessed.* 第二幕に今まで見た中でも特に面白い場面があった. **12** N-COUNT 可算名詞 An **act** in a show is a short performance which is one of several in the show. 出し物 ❏ *This year numerous bands are playing, as well as comedy acts.* 今年は喜劇に加え, 多くの楽団が演奏している. **13** N-SING 単数名詞 If you say that someone's behavior is an **act**, you mean that it does not express their real feelings. 演技 ❏ *His anger was real. It wasn't an act.* 彼の怒りは本物だった. 演技ではなかった. **14** PHRASE 句 If you **catch** someone **in the act**, you discover them doing something wrong or committing a crime. 現場を押さえる ❏ *The men were caught in the act of digging up buried explosives.* 男たちは地中の爆発物を掘り起こしている現場を押さえられた. **15** PHRASE 句 If someone who has been behaving badly **cleans up** their **act**, they start to behave in a more acceptable or responsible way. 行いを改める [INFORMAL くだけた] ❏ *The nation's advertisers need to clean up their act.* その国の広告主は行いを改める必要がある. **16** PHRASE 句 If you **get in on the act**, you take part in or take advantage of something that was started by someone else. 割り込む [INFORMAL くだけた] ❏ *In the 1970s Kodak, anxious to get in on the act, launched its own instant camera.* 1970年代にコダックは流れに乗ろうとして, 自社のインスタント・カメラを発売した. **17** PHRASE 句 You say that someone was **in the act of** doing something to indicate what they were doing when they were seen or interrupted. 最中 ❏ *Ken was in the act of paying his bill when Neil came up behind him.* ニールが背後にやってきたとき, ケンは支払いの最中だった. **18** PHRASE 句 If you **get** your **act together**, you organize your life or your affairs so that you are able to achieve what you want or to deal with something effectively. 行動に一貫性を持たせる [INFORMAL くだけた] ❏ *The government should get its act together.* 政府がしっかりするべきだ. **19** to **act the fool** → see **fool**

Word Partnership   act は次の語句と使われる:

PREP.	act **like** 5
N.	an acting **career** 8
	acts of vandalism, act of **violence** 9
	act **one/two/three** 11
V.	**caught** in the act 14
	get in on the act 16

act|ing /ǽktɪŋ/ **1** N-UNCOUNT 不可算名詞 **Acting** is the activity or profession of performing in plays or films. 演技 [oft N n] ❏ *She returned to London to pursue her acting career.* 彼女は演技の経歴を積むためロンドンに戻った. **2** ADJ 形容詞 You use **acting** before the title of a job to indicate that someone is doing that job temporarily. 代行の [ADJ n] ❏ *The new acting president has a reputation of being someone who is independent.* 新しい大統領代行は独立心に富む人物との評判である.

ac|tion /ǽkʃⁿn/ (**actions, actioning, actioned**) **1** N-UNCOUNT 不可算名詞 **Action** is doing something for a particular purpose. 行動 ❏ *The government is taking emergency action to deal with a housing crisis.* 政府は住宅危機に対処するための緊急行動をとっている. **2** N-UNCOUNT 不可算名詞 The fighting which takes place in a war can be referred to as **action**. 戦闘 ❏ *Our leaders have generally supported military action if it proves necessary.* 我々の指導者たちは, 必要であるとわかれば, 概して軍事行動を支持してきた. **3** N-COUNT 可算名詞 An **action** is something that you do on a particular occasion. 行為 ❏ *As always, Peter had a reason for his action.* いつものようにピーターのしたことには理由があった. **4** N-VAR 可変性名詞 To take legal **action** or to bring a legal **action** against someone means to bring a case against them in a court of law. 訴訟 [LEGAL 法律的] ❏ *Two leading law firms are to prepare legal actions against tobacco companies.* 二つの大手法律事務所が煙草会社に対する訴訟を起こそうとしている. **5** ADJ 形容詞 An **action** movie is a film in which a lot of dangerous and exciting things happen. An **action** hero is the main character in one of these films. 活劇の [ADJ n] **6** V-T 他動詞 If you **action** something that needs to be done, you deal with it. 対応する [BUSINESS 実業] [usu passive] ❏ *Documents can be actioned, or filed immediately.* 文書は, ただちに対応するかファイルするかのいずれかだ. **7** PHRASE 句 If someone or something is **out of action**, they are injured or damaged and cannot work or be used. 故障中 ❏ *He's been out of action for 16 months with a serious knee injury.* 16か月前から膝の深刻な故障で, 16か月間活動していない. **8** PHRASE 句 If someone wants to have **a piece of the action** or **a slice of the action**, they want to take part in an exciting activity or situation, especially in order to make money or become more important. 割り当て ❏ *In the late 1990s, investors big and small wanted a piece of the dot.com action.* 1990年代の終盤, 大小の投資家がインターネット・ブームに乗り遅れまいとした. **9** PHRASE 句 If you **put** an idea or policy **into action**, you begin to use it or cause

it to operate. 実践する ❏ *They have excelled in learning the lessons of business management theory, and putting them into action.* 彼らは企業経営理論の習得およびその実践に卓越している. → see **genre, motion**

Word Partnership   action は次の語句と使われる:

N.	**course** of action, **plan of** action 1
V.	**take** action 1
ADJ.	**disciplinary** action 1
	military action 2
	legal action 4

ac|ti|vate /ǽktɪveɪt/ (**activates, activating, activated**) V-T 他動詞 If a device or process **is activated**, something causes it to start working. 作動させる [他動詞] ❏ *Video cameras with night vision can be activated by movement.* 暗視機能を備えたビデオカメラは動きに反応して作動させることが可能だ. [usu passive]

ac|tive /ǽktɪv/ **1** ADJ 形容詞 Someone who is **active** moves around a lot or does a lot of things. 活動的な ❏ *With three active little kids running around, there was plenty to keep me busy.* 3人の元気な子供たちが走り回り, あれやこれやで忙しい. **2** ADJ 形容詞 If you have an **active** mind or imagination, you are always thinking of new things. 活発な ❏ *...the tragedy of an active mind trapped by failing physical health.* 衰える肉体的健康に捕われた活発な精神の悲劇 **3** ADJ 形容詞 If someone is **active** in an organization, cause, or campaign, they do things for it rather than just giving it their support. 積極的な ❏ *We should play an active role in politics, both at the national and local level.* 我々は, 国と地域両方のレベルで積極的な政治的役割を果たすべきだ. ●**ac|tive|ly** ADV 副詞 積極的に ❏ *They actively campaigned for the vote.* 彼らは積極的に有権者への政治運動を行った. **4** ADJ 形容詞 [ADJ n] **Active** is used to emphasize that someone is taking action in order to achieve something, rather than just hoping for it or achieving it in an indirect way. 積極的な [EMPHASIS 強調] ❏ *Companies need to take active steps to increase exports.* 企業は輸出拡大のため積極的な手段をとる必要がある. ●**ac|tive|ly** ADV 副詞 積極的に ❏ *They have never been actively encouraged to take such risks.* 彼らはかつてそうした危険を引き受けることを積極的に奨励されたことはなかった. **5** ADJ 形容詞 If you say that a person or animal is **active** in a particular place or at a particular time, you mean that they are performing their usual activities or performing a particular activity. 活動している ❏ *Guerrilla groups are active in the province.* その地方ではゲリラ集団が活動している. **6** ADJ 形容詞 An **active** volcano has erupted recently or is expected to erupt soon. 活動中の ❏ *...molten lava from an active volcano.* 活火山から流れた溶岩 **7** ADJ 形容詞 An **active** substance has a chemical or biological effect on things. 効力のある ❏ *The active ingredient in some of the mouthwashes was simply detergent.* 実効成分が単に洗浄剤だという口腔洗浄液もある. **8** N-SING 単数名詞 In grammar, the **active** or the **active voice** means the forms of a verb which are used when the subject refers to a person or thing that does something. For example, in "I saw her yesterday," the verb is in the active. Compare **passive**. 能動態

Word Partnership   active は次の語句と使われる:

N.	active **imagination** 2
	active **role** 4
	active **ingredient** 7
ADV.	**politically** active 3

ac|tiv|ist /ǽktɪvɪst/ (**activists**) N-COUNT 可算名詞 An **activist** is a person who works to bring about political or social changes by campaigning in public or working for an organization. 政治活動家 ❏ *The police say they suspect the attack was carried out by animal rights activists.* 警察は, その攻撃は動物の権利擁護運動の活動家によってなされた疑いがあるといっている. ❏ *Dobson blames activist judges for undermining families with favorable gay-marriage rulings.* ドブソンは, 同性愛者同士の結婚に有利な裁定をなした政治活動家の判事を, 家族制度を損なうとして非難した.

ac|tiv|ity /æktɪvɪti/ (**activities**) **1** N-UNCOUNT 不可算名詞 **Activity** is a situation in which a lot of things are happening or being done. 活動 ❏ *Changes in the money supply affect the level of economic activity and the interest rate.* 通貨供給量の変化は経済活動の水準と金利に影響を及ぼす. ❏ *Children are supposed to get 60 minutes of physical activity every day.* 子供は一日に60分の運動をするべきです. **2** N-COUNT 可算名詞 An **activity** is something that you spend time doing. 活動 ❏ *For lovers of the great outdoors, activities range from canoeing to bird watching.* 野外活動愛好家には, カヌーから野鳥観察までさまざまな活動があります. **3** N-PLURAL 複数名詞 The **activities** of a group are the things that they do in order to achieve their aims. 行動 ❏ *...a jail term for terrorist activities.* テロ活動に実刑

a

activity は次の語句と使われる：

N.	**level of** activity ⬛1
ADJ.	**criminal** activity, **extra-curricular** activity, **physical** activity ⬛2

ac|tor /ˈæktər/ (actors) N-COUNT 可算名詞 An **actor** is someone whose job is acting in plays or films. "Actor" in the singular usually refers to a man, but some women who act prefer to be called "actors" rather than "actresses". 俳優、役者 ❏ *His father was an actor in the Cantonese Opera Company.* 彼の父親は広東オペラの役者だった.
→ see **theater**

ess ≈ female : actress, heiress, princess

ac|tress /ˈæktrɪs/ (actresses) N-COUNT 可算名詞 An **actress** is a woman whose job is acting in plays or films. 女優 ❏ *She's not only a great dramatic actress but she's also very funny.* 彼女は優れた女優であるのみならず、とても面白い人物だ.

ac|tual /ˈæktʃuəl/ ⬛1 ADJ 形容詞 You use **actual** to emphasize that you are referring to something real or genuine. 本当の [EMPHASIS 強調] [ADJ n] ❏ *The segments are filmed using either local actors or the actual people involved.* その場面は、実際の役者または実際の関係者を使い撮影されている. ⬛2 ADJ 形容詞 You use **actual** to contrast the important aspect of something with a less important aspect. 実際の [EMPHASIS 強調] [ADJ n] ❏ *She had compiled pages of notes, but she had not yet gotten down to doing the actual writing.* 彼女は複雑なメモをまとめたが、まだ実際の書く行為にはいたっていない.

Do not confuse **actual** and **real**. You use **actual** to emphasize that what you are referring to is real or genuine, or to contrast different aspects of something. You use **real** to describe things that exist rather than being imagined or theoretical. ❏ *Robert squealed in mock terror, then in real pain.* Note that you only use **actual** in front of a noun. You do not say that something "is actual." Note also that **actual** is not used to refer to something which is happening now, at the present time. For this meaning, you need to use adjectives such as **current** or **present**.

ac|tu|al|ly /ˈæktʃuəli/ ⬛1 ADV 副詞 You use **actually** to indicate that a situation exists or happened, or to emphasize that it is true. 本当に [EMPHASIS 強調] ❏ *One afternoon, I got bored and actually fell asleep for a few minutes.* ある午後、私は退屈にて数分間本当に眠りこけた. ⬛2 ADV 副詞 You use **actually** when you are correcting or contradicting someone. 実は [EMPHASIS 強調] [ADV with cl] ❏ *No, I'm not a student. I'm a doctor, actually.* 私は学生じゃありません。実は医者なんですよ. ⬛3 ADV 副詞 You can use **actually** when you are politely expressing an opinion that other people might not have expected from you. 実は [POLITENESS 丁寧] [ADV with cl] ❏ *"Do you think it's a good idea to socialize with one's patients?" — "Actually, I do, I think it's a great idea."* 「患者とつきあうのがいいと思うか？」 － 「実は、素晴らしいことだと思っている」 ⬛4 ADV 副詞 You use **actually** to introduce a new topic into a conversation. 実のところ [ADV with cl] ❏ *Well actually, John, I called you for some advice.* ジョン、実のところちょっと意見を聞きたいんだが.

Note that **actually** and **really** are both used to emphasize statements. **Actually** is used to emphasize what is true or genuine in a situation, often when this is surprising, or a contrast with what has just been said. ❏ *All the characters in the novel actually existed… He actually began to cry.* It can also be used to be precise or to correct someone. ❏ *No one was actually drunk… We couldn't actually see the garden.* You use **really** in conversation to emphasize something that you are saying. ❏ *I really think he's sick.* When you use **really** in front of an adjective or adverb, it has a similar meaning to "very." ❏ *This is really serious.*

acu|men /ˈækyʊmən/ N-UNCOUNT 不可算名詞 **Acumen** is the ability to make good judgments and quick decisions. 眼識

acu|punc|ture /ˈækyʊpʌŋktʃər/ N-UNCOUNT 不可算名詞 **Acupuncture** is the treatment of a person's illness or pain by sticking small needles into their body at certain places. 鍼 ❏ *I had acupuncture in my lower back.* 腰にはりを打ってもらった.

acute /əˈkyut/ ⬛1 ADJ 形容詞 You can use **acute** to indicate that an undesirable situation or feeling is very severe or intense. 激しい ❏ *The war has aggravated an acute economic crisis.* 戦争のため深刻な経済危機が一層悪化した. ❏ *The report has caused acute embarrassment to the government.* その報告は政府にひどい当惑をもたらした. ⬛2 ADJ 形容詞 An **acute** illness is one that becomes severe very quickly but does not last very long. Compare **chronic**. 急性の [MEDICAL 医学の] [ADJ n] ❏ *…a patient with acute rheumatoid arthritis.* 急性リウマチ性関節炎の患者 ⬛3 ADJ 形容詞 If a person's or animal's sight, hearing, or sense of smell is **acute**, it is sensitive and powerful. 鋭敏な ❏ *When she lost her sight, her other senses grew more acute.* 彼

女は視力を失い、それ以外の感覚がさらに鋭くなった. ⬛4 ADJ 形容詞 An **acute** angle is less than 90°. Compare **obtuse** angle. 鋭い ⬛5 ADJ 形容詞 An **acute** accent is a symbol that is placed over vowels in some languages in order to indicate how that vowel is pronounced or over one letter in a word to indicate where it is stressed. You refer to a letter with this accent as, for example, e **acute**. For example, there is an acute accent over the letter "e" in the French word "café." [ADJ n, n ADJ]

acute|ly /əˈkyutli/ ADV 副詞 If you feel or notice something **acutely**, you feel or notice it very strongly. 鋭く ❏ *He was acutely aware of the odor of cooking oil.* 彼は調理油の臭いを敏感に意識した.

ad /æd/ (ads) N-COUNT 可算名詞 An **ad** is an advertisement. 広告 [INFORMAL くだけた] ❏ *She replied to a lonely hearts ad she spotted in the New York Times.* 彼女はニューヨーク・タイムズで見つけた交際相手募集広告に返事を出した.

AD /ˌeɪ ˈdi/ You use **AD** in dates to indicate the number of years or centuries that have passed since the year in which Jesus Christ is believed to have been born. Compare **BC**. 西暦紀元 ❏ *The original castle was probably built about AD 860.* もともとの城は紀元860年頃に建造されたようだ. ❏ *The cathedral was destroyed by the Great Fire of 1136 AD.* 大聖堂は紀元1136年のロンドン大火で破壊された.

ada|mant /ˈædəmənt/ ADJ 形容詞 If someone is **adamant** about something, they are determined not to change their mind about it. 不屈の ❏ *The president is adamant that he will not resign.* 大統領は強硬に辞職を拒んでいる. ● **ada|mant|ly** ADV 副詞 頑固に ❏ *She was adamantly opposed to her husband taking this trip.* 彼女は、夫の旅行に頑なに反対していた.

a|dapt /əˈdæpt/ (adapts, adapting, adapted) ⬛1 V-T/V-I 他動詞/自動詞 If you **adapt** to a new situation or **adapt yourself** to it, you change your ideas or behavior in order to deal with it successfully. 順応させる [他動詞]、順応する [自動詞] ❏ *The world will be different, and we will have to be prepared to adapt to the change.* 世界は変わるだろうし、我々はその変化に順応する覚悟が必要だろう. ⬛2 V-T 他動詞 If you **adapt** something, you change it to make it suitable for a new purpose or situation. ❏ *Shelves were built to adapt the library for use as an office.* 書斎を事務所として使うために棚を作った. ⬛3 → see also **adapted**

adapt また次を参照：

V.	acclimate, adjust, conform ⬛1
	modify, revise ⬛2

adapt|able /əˈdæptəbəl/ ADJ 形容詞 If you describe a person or animal as **adaptable**, you mean that they are able to change their ideas or behavior in order to deal with new situations. 順応性がある ❏ *By making the workforce more adaptable and skilled, he hopes to attract foreign investment.* 彼は労働者の順応性と技能を高めることで、海外投資を引き寄せたいと考えている. ● **adapt|abil|ity** /əˌdæptəˈbɪlɪti/ N-UNCOUNT 不可算名詞 順応性 ❏ *The adaptability of wool is one of its great attractions.* 順応性は羊毛の大きな魅力のひとつだ.

ad|ap|ta|tion /ˌædæpˈteɪʃən/ (adaptations) ⬛1 N-COUNT 可算名詞 An **adaptation** of a book or play is a film or a television program that is based on it. 改作 ❏ *Branagh won two awards for his screen adaptation of Shakespeare's Henry the Fifth.* ブラナーはシェークスピアのヘンリー5世を映画に翻案し二つの賞を授賞した. ⬛2 N-UNCOUNT 不可算名詞 **Adaptation** is the act of changing something or changing your behavior to make it suitable for a new purpose or situation. 適応 ❏ *Most living creatures are capable of adaptation when compelled to do so.* 大部分の生物は、そのように強いられれば適応することができる.

adaptation また次を参照：

N.	adjustment, alteration, modification ⬛2

a|dapt|ed /əˈdæptɪd/ ADJ 形容詞 If something is **adapted to** a particular situation or purpose, it is especially suitable for it. 適合した [v-link ADJ 'to/for' n] ❏ *The camel's feet, well adapted for dry sand, are useless on mud.* ラクダの足は、乾燥した砂地には適しているが、ぬかるみには向かない.

add /æd/ (adds, adding, added) ⬛1 V-T 他動詞 If you **add** one thing **to** another, you put it in or on the other thing, to increase, complete, or improve it. 加える [他動詞] ❏ *Add the grated cheese to the sauce.* おろしたチーズをソースに加える ❏ *Since 1908, chlorine has been added to drinking water.* 1908年以来、飲用水に塩素が加えられました. ⬛2 V-T 他動詞 If you **add** numbers or amounts **together**, you calculate their total. 足す [他動詞] ❏ *Banks add all the interest and other charges together.* 銀行は利息と他の料金をすべて合計する. ⬛3 V-I 自動詞 If one thing **adds to** another, it makes the other thing greater in degree or amount. 増す [自動詞] ❏ *This latest incident will add to the pressure on the White House.* この最新の事件がホワイトハウスへの圧力を高めることになる. ⬛4 V-T 他動詞 To **add** a particular quality **to** something means to cause it to have that quality. 添え

ら [他動詞] ❑ *The generous amount of garlic adds flavor.* にんにくをたっぷりと使い，香りをつける。 **5** V-T 他動詞 If you **add** something when you are speaking, you say something more. 言い足す[他動詞] ❑*"You can tell that he is extremely embarrassed," Mr. Montoya added.* 「彼が極めてきまりの悪い思いをしていることがわかります」モントヤ氏はそう付け加えた。 **6** V-I 自動詞 If you can **add**, you are able to calculate the total of numbers or amounts. 足し算をする ❑*More than a quarter of seven-year-olds cannot add properly.* 7歳児の4分の1以上はまともに足し算ができない。 [AM 米国英語]

▶ **add in** PHRASAL VERB 句動詞 If you **add in** something, you include it as a part of something else. 算入する ❑*Once the vegetables start to cook add in a couple of tablespoons of water.* 野菜に火が通ると大さじ2杯の水を加える。

▶ **add on** **1** PHRASAL VERB 句動詞 If one thing **is added on** to another, it is attached to the other thing, or is made a part of it. 付け足す ❑*Vacationers can also add on a week in Florida before or after the cruise.* 観光客はクルーズ旅行の前か後にさらにフロリダで1週間過ごすこともできる。 **2** PHRASAL VERB 句動詞 If you **add on** an extra amount or item to a list or total, you include it. 追加する ❑*Many loan application forms automatically add on insurance.* 融資申込書の多くは自動的に保険を追加するようになっている。 **3** PHRASAL VERB 句動詞 If you **add on**, you increase the size of a house or other building by constructing one or more extra rooms. 増築する ❑*Investors who cannot afford a larger property now can add on when they have more money.* 今，大き目の物件を買えない投資家が，資金ができたときに増築することができる。 [AM 米国英語]

▶ **add up** **1** PHRASAL VERB 句動詞 If you **add up** numbers or amounts, or if you **add** them **up**, you calculate their total. 合算する ❑*Add up the total of those six games.* その6試合の合計を計算する。 ❑*We just added all the numbers up and divided one by the other.* すべての数字を足し合わせ，それぞれの数字で割っただけだ。 **2** PHRASAL VERB 句動詞 If facts or events do not **add up**, they make you confused about a situation because they do not seem to be consistent. If something that someone has said or done **adds up**, it is reasonable and sensible. つじつまが合う ❑*Police said they arrested Olivia because her statements did not add up.* 警察は，供述のつじつまが合わないためオリビアを逮捕したと言った。 **3** PHRASAL VERB 句動詞 If small amounts of something **add up**, they gradually increase. 積もる ❑*Even small savings, 5 cents here or 10 cents there, can add up.* ここで5セント，あそこで10セントというわずかな節約でも積もり貯まる。

▶ **add up to** PHRASAL VERB 句動詞 If amounts **add up to** a particular total, they result in that total when they are put together. 合計～になる ❑*For a hit show, profits can add up to millions of dollars.* 番組が当たれば，利益は総計数百万ドルにもなりえる。

Thesaurus *add また次を参照:*

V.	put on, throw in **1**
	calculate, tally, total; (ant.) reduce, subtract **2**
	augment, increase; (ant.) lessen, reduce **3**

---

add|ed /ǽdɪd/ **1** ADJ 形容詞 You use **added** to say that something has more of a particular thing or quality. 追加の [ADJ n] ❑*For added protection choose moisturizing lipsticks with a sunscreen.* 追加の防護対策として，日焼け防止効果のある保湿用リップスティックを選んでください。

add|ed value N-UNCOUNT 不可算名詞 In marketing, **added value** is something that makes a product more appealing to customers. 付加価値 [BUSINESS 実業] ❑*We can create significant added value by pushing the brand into other areas.* そのブランドを他の領域に広げることで，かなりの付加価値を創出することができる。

ad|dict /ǽdɪkt/ (**addicts**) **1** N-COUNT 可算名詞 An **addict** is someone who takes harmful drugs and cannot stop taking them. 中毒患者 ❑*He's only 24 years old and a drug addict.* 彼はまだ24歳なのに麻薬中毒だ。 **2** N-COUNT 可算名詞 If you say that someone is an **addict**, you mean that they like a particular activity very much and spend as much time doing it as they can. 愛好者 ❑*She is a TV addict and watches as much as she can.* 彼女は大のテレビ好きで，見られるだけ見ている。

ad|dict|ed /ədɪ́ktɪd/ **1** ADJ 形容詞 Someone who is **addicted to** a harmful drug cannot stop taking it. 中毒の ❑*Many of the women are addicted to heroin and cocaine.* 多くの女性がヘロインとコカインの中毒に陥っている。 **2** ADJ 形容詞 If you say that someone is **addicted to** something, you mean that they like it very much and want to spend as much time doing it as possible. 夢中である ❑*She had become addicted to golf.* 彼女はゴルフに夢中になった。

ad|dic|tion /ədɪ́kʃən/ (**addictions**) **1** N-VAR 可変性名詞 **Addiction** is the condition of taking harmful drugs and being unable to stop taking them. 中毒 ❑*She helped him fight his drug addiction.* 彼女は彼が薬物中毒と戦うのを助けた。 **2** N-VAR 可変性名詞 An **addiction to** something is a very strong desire or need for it. 熱中 ❑*He needed money to feed his addiction to gambling.* 彼の賭け事への耽溺（たんでき）を続けるため金が必要だった。

Word Partnership *addiction は次の語句と使われる:*

N.	**drug** addiction **1**
V.	**feed an** addiction, **fight against** addiction **2**
ADJ.	**long-term** addiction **2**
PREP.	addiction **to something** **2**

---

ad|dic|tive /ədɪ́ktɪv/ **1** ADJ 形容詞 If a drug is **addictive**, people who take it cannot stop taking it. 中毒性の ❑*Cigarettes are highly addictive.* たばこは中毒性が高い。 **2** ADJ 形容詞 Something that is **addictive** is so enjoyable that it makes you want to do it or have it a lot. 癖になる ❑*Video movie-making can quickly become addictive.* ビデオでの映画作成は，癖になりやすい。

ad|di|tion /ədɪ́ʃən/ (**additions**) **1** PHRASE 句 You use **in addition** when you want to mention another item connected with the subject you are discussing. 加えて ❑*The web site provides regional weather reports, a shipping forecast and gale warnings. In addition, visitors can download satellite images of the U.S.* そのウェブサイトでは，地域の天気予報，海上気象予報，強風警報を提供している。さらにアメリカの衛星画像のダウンロードもできる。 **2** N-COUNT 可算名詞 An **addition to** something is a thing which is added to it. 追加 ❑*This is a fine book; a worthy addition to the series.* これはいい本だ。叢書（そうしょ）に追加する価値がある。 **3** N-COUNT 可算名詞 An **addition** is a new room or building which is added to an existing building or group of buildings. 増築部分 [AM 米国英語] [oft N 'to' n] ❑*The couple said they spent $20,000 on building an addition to their kitchen.* その夫婦は台所の増築のため2万ドルを費やしたと言った。 **4** N-UNCOUNT 不可算名詞 The **addition of** something is the fact that it is added to something else. 追加 ❑*It was completely refurbished in 1987, with the addition of a picnic site.* それは1987年にピクニック場を加え，完全に新装した。 **5** N-UNCOUNT 不可算名詞 **Addition** is the process of calculating the total of two or more numbers. 足し算 ❑*...simple addition and subtraction problems using whole numbers.* 整数を使った単純な足し算と引き算の問題
→ see **mathematics**

ad|di|tion|al /ədɪ́ʃənəl/ ADJ 形容詞 **Additional** things are extra things apart from the ones already present. 追加の ❑*The U.S. is sending additional troops to the region.* アメリカはその地域に追加部隊を投入している。

ad|di|tion|al|ly /ədɪ́ʃənəli/ ADV 副詞 You use **additionally** to introduce something extra such as an extra fact or reason. さらに [ADV with cl] ❑*All teachers are qualified to teach their native language. Additionally, we select our teachers for their engaging personalities.* 教師全員がそれぞれの母語を教える資格を持っています。さらに人間的魅力も教師の選定基準です。

ad|di|tive /ǽdɪtɪv/ (**additives**) N-COUNT 可算名詞 An **additive** is a substance which is added in small amounts to foods or other things in order to improve them or to make them last longer. 添加物 ❑*Strict safety tests are carried out on food additives.* 食品添加物には厳格な安全試験が行われる。

add-on (**add-ons**) N-COUNT 可算名詞 An **add-on** is an extra piece of equipment, especially computer equipment, that can be added to a larger one which you already own in order to improve its performance or its usefulness. 拡張機器，増設機器 ❑*To use this software, you don't need a CD-ROM drive or any expensive add-ons for your computer.* このソフトの使用に際し，CD-ROMドライブなどの高額な増設機器は不要です。

ad|dress (**addresses, addressing, addressed**)

The noun is pronounced /ədrɛ́s/ or /ǽdrɛs/. The verb is pronounced /ədrɛ́s/.
名詞は /ədrɛ́s/ または /ǽdrɛs/ と発音される。動詞は /ədrɛ́s/ と発音される。

1 N-COUNT 可算名詞 Your **address** is the number of the house or apartment and the name of the street and the town where you live or work. 住所 ❑*The address is 2025 M Street, NW, Washington, DC, 20036.* 住所は，2025 M Street, NW, Washington, DC, 20036です。 **2** N-COUNT 可算名詞 The **address** of a website is its location on the Internet, for example, www.thomson.com. アドレス [COMPUTING コンピューティング] ❑*Full details, including the website address to log on to, are at the bottom of this page.* ログオンするウェブサイトのアドレスなど，詳細はこのページの最後を御覧ください。 **3** V-T 他動詞 If a letter, envelope, or parcel **is addressed to** you, your name and address have been written on it. あて先を書く ❑*Applications should be addressed to: The business affairs editor.* 応募書類は経済担当編集長宛に送付してください。 [usu passive] **4** V-T 他動詞 If you **address** a group of people, you give a speech to them. 演説する ❑*He is due to address a conference on human rights next week.* 来週，彼は人権に関する会議で演説することになっている。 ● N-COUNT 可算名詞 **Address** is also a noun. 演説 ❑*He had scheduled an address to the American people for the evening of May 27.* 5月27日の夕方，彼はアメリカ国民に向け演説する予定だ。

Thesaurus   *address* また次を参照：

N.   lecture, speech, talk ④

Word Partnership   *address* は次の語句と使われる：

N.   **name and** address, **street** address ①
      address **remarks to** ④
ADJ. **permanent** address ①
      public address, **inaugural** address ④

ad|dress book (**address books**) ① N-COUNT 可算名詞 An **address book** is a book in which you write people's names and addresses. 住所録 ② N-COUNT 可算名詞 An **address book** is a computer file which contains a list of e-mail addresses. アドレス帳 [COMPUTING コンピューティング]

adept /ædépt/ ADJ 形容詞 Someone who is **adept at** something can do it skillfully. 熟達した □ He's usually very adept at keeping his private life out of the media. 通常，彼はメディアから私生活を守るすべに長（た）けている.

ad|equa|cy /ǽdɪkwəsi/ N-UNCOUNT 不可算名詞 **Adequacy** is the quality of being good enough or great enough in amount to be acceptable. 妥当性 □ There are questions to be raised about the adequacy of the inmates' legal representation. 服役者の法的代理人使用の妥当性に関して提言すべき問題がある.

ad|equate /ǽdɪkwɪt/ ADJ 形容詞 If something is **adequate**, there is enough of it or it is good enough to be used or accepted. 十分な □ One in four people worldwide are without adequate homes. 全世界の4人にひとりが必要最低限の家を持っていない. □ She is prepared to offer me an amount adequate to purchase another house. 彼女は私がもう一軒の家を購入するのに十分な額を提供するつもりだ. ● **ad|equate|ly** ADV 副詞 Many students are not adequately prepared for higher education. 多くの学生が高等教育をうけるための十分な準備ができていない.

ad|here /ædhíər/ (**adheres, adhering, adhered**) ① V-I 自動詞 If you **adhere to** a rule or agreement, you act in the way that it says you should. 厳守する □ All members of the association adhere to a strict code of practice. 協会の会員全員が厳しい行動規範を厳守している. ② V-I 自動詞 If something **adheres** to something else, it sticks firmly to it. 付着する □ Small particles adhere to the seed. 小さな粒子が種に付着する.

ad|he|sive /ædhíːsɪv/ (**adhesives**) ① N-MASS 質量名詞 An **adhesive** is a substance such as glue, which is used to make things stick firmly together. 接着剤 □ Glue the mirror in with a strong adhesive. 強力な接着剤で鏡を中に貼り付ける. ② ADJ 形容詞 An **adhesive** substance is able to stick firmly to something else. 接着性の □ ...adhesive tape. 粘着テープ

ad hoc /æd hɒk/ ADJ 形容詞 An **ad hoc** activity or organization is not planned in advance, but is done or formed only because a particular situation has made it necessary. 特にこの問題についてのみ □ "I would accept opportunities in TV on an ad hoc basis," he said. 「特別の場合に限りテレビに出てもかまわない」と彼は言った.

ad|ja|cent /ædʒéɪsᵊnt/ ADJ 形容詞 If one thing is **adjacent to** another, the two things are next to each other. 隣接した □ He sat in an adjacent room and waited. 彼は隣室で座って待った. □ The schools were adjacent but there were separate doors. それらの学校は隣接しているが，入り口は別々だ.

ad|jec|tive /ǽdʒɪktɪv/ (**adjectives**) N-COUNT 可算名詞 An **adjective** is a word such as "big," "dead," or "financial" that describes a person or thing, or gives extra information about them. Adjectives usually come before nouns or after linking verbs. 形容詞

ad|join /ədʒɔ́ɪn/ (**adjoins, adjoining, adjoined**) V-T 他動詞 If one room, place, or object **adjoins** another, they are next to each other. 隣接する □ The doctor's bedroom adjoined his wife's and the door between the rooms was always open. 医者の寝室は妻の隣で，ふたつの部屋を仕切る扉はいつも開いていた. [FORMAL 形式ばった]

ad|journ /ədʒɜ́ːrn/ (**adjourns, adjourning, adjourned**) V-T/V-I 他動詞/自動詞 If a meeting or trial **is adjourned** or if it **adjourns**, it is stopped for a short time. 延期する □ The proceedings have now been adjourned until next week. 現在，訴訟は来週まで延期することになった.

ad|journ|ment /ədʒɜ́ːrnmənt/ (**adjournments**) N-COUNT 可算名詞 An **adjournment** is a temporary stopping of a trial, inquiry, or other meeting. 延期 □ The court ordered a four-month adjournment. 裁判所は4ヶ月の休廷を命じた.

ad|just /ədʒʌ́st/ (**adjusts, adjusting, adjusted**) ① V-T/V-I 他動詞/自動詞 When you **adjust to** a new situation, you get used to it by changing your behavior or your ideas. 適応させる [自動詞] □ We have been preparing our fighters to adjust themselves to civil society. 我々は戦士たちが市民社会に適応するよう準備させてきた. □ I felt I had adjusted to the idea of being a mother very well. 自分が母親であるという考えにかなり慣れてきたように感じ

た. ② V-T 他動詞 If you **adjust** something, you change it so that it is more effective or appropriate. 調節する [他動詞] □ To attract investors, Panama has adjusted its tax and labor laws. 投資家を誘致するため，パナマは税法と労働法を整備した. ③ V-T 他動詞 If you **adjust** something such as your clothing or a machine, you correct or alter its position or setting. 調節する [他動詞] □ Liz adjusted her mirror and then edged the car out of its parking space. リズは鏡を調節し，車をゆっくりと駐車スペースから出した. ④ V-T/V-I 他動詞/自動詞 If you **adjust** your vision or if your vision **adjusts**, the muscles of your eye or the pupils alter to cope with changes in light or distance. 調整する [自動詞]，調整する [他動詞] □ He stopped to try to adjust his vision to the faint starlight. かすかな星の光に自分の目を合わせようと彼は立ち止まった.

ad|just|able /ədʒʌ́stəbᵊl/ ADJ 形容詞 If something is **adjustable**, it can be changed to different positions or sizes. 調整できる □ The bags have adjustable shoulder straps. バッグには長さを調整できる肩ひもが付いている.

Thesaurus   *adjustable* また次を参照：

ADJ.   adaptable, adaptive, changeable; (ant.) fixed

ad|just|ment /ədʒʌ́stmənt/ (**adjustments**) ① N-COUNT 可算名詞 An **adjustment** is a small change that is made to something such as a machine or a way of doing something. 調整 □ Compensation could be made by adjustments to taxation. 税調整による補償が可能だろう. □ Investment is up by 5.7% after adjustment for inflation. 投資額はインフレ調整後で5.7%増加しています. ② N-COUNT 可算名詞 An **adjustment** is a change in a person's behavior or thinking. 改めること □ He will have to make major adjustments to his thinking if he is to survive in office. 根本的に考え方を改めない限り，彼はこのまま会社でやっていくのは難しいでしょう.

ad|man /ǽdmæn/ (**admen**) N-COUNT 可算名詞 An **adman** is someone who works in advertising. 広告マン [INFORMAL くだけた] □ He was the most brilliant adman that any of us knew. 彼はだれもが認める優秀な広告マンだった.

ad|min /ǽdmɪn/ ① ADJ 形容詞 **Admin** is an abbreviation of **administrative**. 管理上の；行政上の ② N-UNCOUNT 不可算名詞 **Admin** is the activity or process of organizing an institution or organization. **Admin** is an abbreviation of **administration**. 運営，管理 [BRIT 英国英語, INFORMAL くだけた]

ad|min|is|ter /ædmɪ́nɪstər/ (**administers, administering, administered**) ① V-T 他動詞 If someone **administers** something such as a country, the law, or a test, they take responsibility for organizing and supervising it. 治める；執行する □ The plan calls for the U.N. to administer the country until elections can be held. 計画では選挙が実施できるようになるまでは国連がその国を統治することになる. ② V-T 他動詞 If a doctor or a nurse **administers** a drug, they give it to a patient. 投与する [FORMAL 形式ばった] □ The physician may prescribe but not administer the drug. 医師は薬を処方するだけで投与はしない.

ad|min|is|tra|tion /ædmɪnɪstréɪʃᵊn/ (**administrations**) ① N-UNCOUNT 不可算名詞 **Administration** is the range of activities connected with organizing and supervising the way that an organization or institution functions. 運営，管理 □ Too much time is spent on administration. 運営に費やされる時間があまりに多い. ② N-UNCOUNT 不可算名詞 The **administration** of something is the process of organizing and supervising it. 指揮，執行 □ Standards in the administration of justice have degenerated. 裁判制度の水準が下がってきています. ③ N-SING 単数名詞 The **administration** of a company or institution is the group of people who organize and supervise it. 経営陣 □ They would like the college administration to exert more control over the fraternity. 彼らは理事会に対しもっと男子学生クラブをしっかり監督することを要望している. ④ N-COUNT 可算名詞 You can refer to a country's government as the **administration**; used especially in the United States. 政権 □ O'Leary served in federal energy posts in both the Ford and Carter administrations. オリアリー氏はフォードおよびカーター政権下でエネルギー省長官を務めた.

ad|min|is|tra|tive /ædmɪ́nɪstreɪtɪv/ ADJ 形容詞 **Administrative** work involves organizing and supervising an organization or institution. 管理上の □ Other industries have had to sack managers to reduce administrative costs. 他の業界ではすでに経営者を解雇して経費の削減を余儀なくされている.

ad|min|is|tra|tor /ædmɪ́nɪstreɪtər/ (**administrators**) N-COUNT 可算名詞 An **administrator** is a person whose job involves helping to organize and supervise the way that an organization or institution functions. 経営者 □ On Friday the company's administrators sought permission from a Melbourne court to keep operating. 会社の経営者は金曜日メルボルン裁判所に営業継続の許可申請を出した.

ad|mi|rable /ǽdmɪrəbᵊl/ ADJ 形容詞 An **admirable** quality or action is one that deserves to be praised and admired. りっぱな □ She did an admirable job of holding the audience's attention. 聴

衆の注意をそらさない彼女の技術は見事だった． ●**ad|mi|rably** /ˈædmɪrəbli/ ADV 副詞 りっぱに ❑*Peter had dealt admirably with the sudden questions about Keith.* 突然キースのことを聞かれたが，ピーターはうまく切り抜けた．

ad|mi|ral /ˈædmərəl/ (admirals) N-COUNT; N-TITLE 可算名詞，称号名詞 An **admiral** is a very senior officer who commands a navy. 海軍大将 ❑*...Admiral Hodges.* ホッジズ大将．

ad|mi|ra|tion /ˌædmɪˈreɪʃ°n/ N-UNCOUNT 不可算名詞 **Admiration** is a feeling of great liking and respect for a person or thing. 敬服；賞賛 ❑*I have always had the greatest admiration for him.* 彼のことはいつも実に素晴らしいと思っている．

ad|mire /ədˈmaɪər/ (admires, admiring, admired) **1** V-T 他動詞 If you **admire** someone or something, you like and respect them very much. 褒める ❑*I admired her when I first met her and I still think she's marvelous.* 彼女に初めて会ったとき素晴らしい人だと思ったが，今でもその気持ちに変わりはない． ❑*He admired the way she had coped with life.* 彼女は人生のピンチをうまく切り抜けてきたと彼は感心した． **2** V-T 他動詞 If you **admire** someone or something, you look at them with pleasure. 見とれる ❑*We took time to stop and admire the view.* 私たちは立ち止まってゆっくりと景色を楽しんだ．

Thesaurus admire また次を参照：

v. esteem, honor, look up to, respect **1**

ad|mir|er /ədˈmaɪərər/ (admirers) N-COUNT 可算名詞 If you are an **admirer** of someone, you like and respect them or their work very much. 愛好家，ファン ❑*He was an admirer of her grandfather's paintings.* 彼は彼女の祖父の描いた絵が大好きだった．

ad|mis|sion /ədˈmɪʃ°n/ (admissions) **1** N-VAR 可変性名詞 **Admission** is permission given to a person to enter a place, or permission given to a country to enter an organization. **Admission** is also the act of entering a place. 入場許可；入場 ❑*Students apply for admission to a particular college.* 学生らはそれぞれの大学に願書を提出する． **2** N-VAR 可変性名詞 An **admission** is a statement that something bad, unpleasant, or embarrassing is true. 白状 ❑*By his own admission, he is not playing well.* 彼自身も認めているように，最近の彼は不調である． **3** N-PLURAL 複数名詞 **Admissions** to a place such as a school or university are the people who are allowed to enter or join it. 入学者 ❑*Each school sets its own admissions policy.* 各校は独自の入学選考基準を設けている． **4** N-UNCOUNT 不可算名詞 **Admission** at a park, museum, or other place is the amount of money that you pay to enter it. 入場料 ❑*Gates open at 10:30 a.m. and admission is free.* 入場ゲートの開門は午前10時半，入場は無料． ●N-UNCOUNT 不可算名詞 **Admission** is also used before a noun. 入場 ❑*The admission price is $8 for adults.* 入場料は大人で8ドルである．

→ see hospital

ad|mit /ədˈmɪt/ (admits, admitting, admitted) **1** V-T/V-I 他動詞/自動詞 If you **admit** that something bad, unpleasant, or embarrassing is true, you agree, often unwillingly, that it is true. (事実であると) 認める ❑*I am willing to admit that I do make mistakes.* 私が間違いを犯さないなんてとても言えませんよ． ❑*Up to two thirds of 14 to 16 year olds admit to buying alcohol illegally.* 14～16歳の子どもたちの3人に2人がお酒を買ったことがあると認めています． ❑*None of these people will admit responsibility for their actions.* この人たちのなかで自分のしたことに責任を認めるような人はいないだろう． **2** V-T 他動詞 If someone **is admitted to** a hospital, they are taken into the hospital for treatment and kept there until they are well enough to go home. 入院させる ❑*She was admitted to the hospital with a soaring temperature.* 彼女は急な高熱に襲われ病院に収容された． **3** V-T 他動詞 If someone **is admitted to** an organization or group, they are allowed to join it. (入会などを) 許可する ❑*He was admitted to the Académie Culinaire de France.* 彼はフランス料理アカデミーへの入学を認められた． **4** V-T 他動詞 To **admit** someone **to** a place means to allow them to enter it. (入場を) 許可する ❑*Embassy security personnel refused to admit him or his wife.* 夫妻は大使館に入ろうとしたがうち1人が警備員に拒否された．

Word Partnership admit は次の語句と使われる：

v. ashamed to admit, be the first to admit, must admit, willing to admit **1**
N. admit defeat **1**
CONJ. admit that **1**

ad|mit|ted|ly /ədˈmɪtɪdli/ ADV 副詞 You use **admittedly** when you are saying something that weakens the importance or force of your statement. 認めざるを得ないが [ADV with cl/group] ❑*It's only a theory, admittedly, but the pieces fit together.* たしかに憶測と言われればそのとおりだが，話のつじつまは合う．

ado|les|cence /ˌædəˈlɛs°ns/ N-UNCOUNT 不可算名詞 **Adolescence** is the period of your life in which you develop from being a child into being an adult. 思春期 ❑*Some young people suddenly become self-conscious and tongue-tied in early adolescence.* 思春期に入ると急に自意識が芽生え恥ずかしくて口を利かなくなる子どもがいる．

→ see child

ado|les|cent /ˌædəˈlɛs°nt/ (adolescents) **1** ADJ 形容詞 **Adolescent** is used to describe young people who are no longer children but who have not yet become adults. It also refers to their behavior. 思春期の ❑*It is important that an adolescent boy should have an adult in whom he can confide.* 思春期の男の子にとって大切なのは何でも打ち明けられる大人がいることだ． **2** N-COUNT 可算名詞 An **adolescent** is an adolescent boy or girl. 思春期の子ども ❑*Young adolescents are happiest with small groups of close friends.* 思春期になると仲のよい数人の友だちといるときがいちばん楽しい．

→ see age

Word Link opt ≈ choosing : adopt, opt, optional

adopt /əˈdɒpt/ (adopts, adopting, adopted) **1** V-T 他動詞 If you **adopt** a new attitude, plan, or way of behaving, you begin to have it. 採用する ❑*The United Nations General Assembly has adopted a resolution calling on all parties in the conflict to seek a political settlement.* 国連総会において採択された決議では，紛争のすべての当事者に政治的解決を図るように求めている． ●**adop|tion** /əˈdɒpʃ°n/ N-UNCOUNT 不可算名詞 採用 ❑*The group is working to promote the adoption of broadband wireless access over long distances.* グループでは遠距離間でのブロードバンド無線アクセスの採用を進めている． **2** V-T/V-I 他動詞/自動詞 If you **adopt** someone else's child, you take it into your own family and make it legally your son or daughter. 養子にする [他動詞]，養子をもらう [自動詞] ❑*There are hundreds of people desperate to adopt a child.* 養子を切望する人たちは何百人もいる． ●**adop|tion** (adoptions) N-VAR 可変性名詞 養子縁組み ❑*They gave their babies up for adoption.* 彼らは赤ちゃんを養子に出した．

Thesaurus adopt また次を参照：

v. approve, endorse, support; (ant.) refuse, reject **1**
care for, raise, take in **2**

adop|tive /əˈdɒptɪv/ ADJ 形容詞 Someone's **adoptive** family is the family that adopted them. 里親の [ADJ n] ❑*He was brought up by adoptive parents in Kentucky.* 彼はケンタッキーの里親のもとで育てられた．

ador|able /əˈdɔrəb°l/ ADJ 形容詞 If you say that someone or something is **adorable**, you are emphasizing that they are very attractive and you feel great affection for them. かわいらしい [EMPHASIS 強調] ❑*By the time I was 30, we had three adorable children.* 30才になるまでに3人の子宝に恵まれた．

ado|ra|tion /ˌædəˈreɪʃ°n/ N-UNCOUNT 不可算名詞 **Adoration** is a feeling of great admiration and love for someone or something. 敬愛 ❑*She needs and wants to be loved with overwhelming passion and adoration.* 彼女が必要とし求めているのは激しいまでの情熱と愛情を注いでくれる相手だ．

→ see emotion

adore /əˈdɔr/ (adores, adoring, adored) **1** V-T 他動詞 If you **adore** someone, you feel great love and admiration for them. 敬愛する [no cont] ❑*She adored her parents and would do anything to please them.* 彼女は両親のことを深く愛していたので，二人が喜びそうなことは何でもしてあげた． **2** V-T 他動詞 If you **adore** something, you like it very much. 大好きだ [INFORMAL くだけた] [no cont] ❑*My mother adores bananas and eats two a day.* バナナは母の大好物で日に2本食べる．

adorn /əˈdɔrn/ (adorns, adorning, adorned) V-T 他動詞 If something **adorns** a place or an object, it makes it look more beautiful. 飾る ❑*His watercolor designs adorn a wide range of books.* 彼の水彩画はさまざまな本の装丁に使われている．

adrena|lin /əˈdrɛn°lɪn/ also **adrenaline** N-UNCOUNT 不可算名詞 **Adrenalin** is a substance which your body produces when you are angry, scared, or excited. It makes your heart beat faster and gives you more energy. アドレナリン ❑*That was my first big game in months and the adrenalin was going.* 何か月ぶりかの大切な試合だったのでどきどきした．

adrift /əˈdrɪft/ **1** ADJ 形容詞 If a boat is **adrift**, it is floating on the water and is not tied to anything or controlled by anyone. 漂流して [v-link ADJ, v n ADJ] ❑*They were spotted after three hours adrift in a dinghy.* 彼らはゴムボートで3時間漂流したのち発見された． **2** ADJ 形容詞 If someone is **adrift**, they feel alone with no clear idea of what they should do. 途方に暮れて [v-link ADJ, v n ADJ] ❑*Amy had the growing sense that she was adrift and isolated.* エイミーは自分があてもなく一人ぼっちなのだとひしひしと感じた．

adult /əˈdʌlt/ (adults) **1** N-COUNT 可算名詞 An **adult** is a mature, fully developed person. An **adult** has reached the age when they are legally responsible for their actions. 大人，成人 ❑*Becoming a father signified that he was now an adult.* 父親になって彼は大人の仲間入りをした． **2** N-COUNT 可算名詞 An **adult** is a fully

developed animal. 成体 ❑ …*a pair of adult birds*. 一つがいの成鳥 **3** ADJ 形容詞 **Adult** means relating to the time when you are an adult, or typical of adult people. 大人の [ADJ n] ❑ *I've lived most of my adult life in Arizona*. 成人してからはほとんどアリゾナで暮らしてきた. **4** ADJ 形容詞 You can describe things such as films or books as **adult** when they deal with sex in a very clear and open way. 成人向けの ❑ …*an adult movie*. 成人映画.
→ see **age**

Thesaurus　　*adult* また次を参照：

N.	grown-up, man, woman **1**
ADJ.	full-grown **3**

adul|ter|ate /ədʌ́ltəreɪt/ (**adulterates, adulterating, adulterated**) V-T 他動詞 If something such as food or drink **is adulterated**, someone has made its quality worse by adding water or cheaper products to it. 混ぜ物をして質を落とす [usu passive] ❑ *The food had been adulterated to increase its weight*. その食品は混ぜ物をして重量を増やしていた.

adul|tery /ədʌ́ltəri/ N-UNCOUNT 不可算名詞 If a married person commits **adultery**, they have sex with someone that they are not married to. 不倫 ❑ *She is going to divorce him on the grounds of adultery*. 彼女は不倫が原因で離婚する.

Word Link　　*hood ≈ state, condition : adulthood, childhood, manhood*

adult|hood /ədʌ́lthʊd/ N-UNCOUNT 不可算名詞 **Adulthood** is the state of being an adult. 成人であること ❑ *Few people nowadays are able to maintain friendships into adulthood*. 最近では、大人になってからも学生時代の友だちと付き合い続けることは難しくなった.

ad|vance /ædvǽns/ (**advances, advancing, advanced**) **1** V-I 自動詞 To **advance** means to move forward, often in order to attack someone. 進軍する ❑ *Reports from Chad suggest that rebel forces are advancing on the capital*. チャドからの情報によると反政府軍は首都に向かって進撃している模様です. ❑ *According to one report, the water is advancing at a rate of between 8 and 10 inches a day*. ある情報筋では洪水は一日に8−10インチの割合で広がっている. **2** V-I 自動詞 To **advance** means to make progress, especially in your knowledge of something. 向上する ❑ *Medical technology has advanced considerably*. 医療技術は大幅に向上した. **3** → see also **advanced** **4** V-T 他動詞 If you **advance** someone a sum of money, you lend it to them, or pay it to them earlier than arranged. 前貸しする、前払いする ❑ *I advanced him some money, which he would repay on our way home*. 彼にお金を立て替えてやったが、帰り道で返してもらうことになっていた. **5** V-T 他動詞 To **advance** an event, or the time or date of an event, means to bring it forward to an earlier time or date. 早める ❑ *Too much protein in the diet may advance the aging process*. たんぱく質を過剰に摂取すると老化を早める恐れがある. **6** V-T 他動詞 If you **advance** a cause, interest, or claim, you support it and help to make it successful. 促進する ❑ *When not producing art of his own, Oliver was busy advancing the work of others*. オリバーは自分の制作活動以外の時間は他の芸術家の制作の手伝いに忙しかった. **7** N-COUNT 可算名詞 An **advance** is money lent or paid to someone before they would normally receive it. 前払い ❑ *She was paid a $100,000 advance for her next two novels*. 彼女は次に書く小説2本の前金として10万ドルを受け取った. **8** N-VAR 可変性名詞 An **advance** is a forward movement of people or vehicles, usually as part of a military operation. 前進 ❑ *In an exercise designed to be as real as possible, they simulated an advance on enemy positions*. 実戦を想定した演習では部隊は敵地へ進撃する訓練を行いました. **9** N-VAR 可変性名詞 An **advance** in a particular subject or activity is progress in understanding it or in doing it well. 改善 ❑ *Air safety has not improved since the dramatic advances of the 1970s*. 空の安全は1970年代に飛躍的に高まったが、その後は改善が見られない. **10** N-SING 単数名詞 If something is an **advance on** what was previously available or done, it is better in some way. 改善されたもの [usu 'a' N 'on' n] ❑ *This could be an advance on the present situation*. これで現状が改善されるかもしれない. **11** ADJ 形容詞 **Advance** booking, notice, or warning is done or given before an event happens. 事前の [ADJ n] ❑ *They don't normally give any advance notice about which building they're going to inspect*. どの建物が検査対象になるかは、事前に通知されることはありません. **12** PHRASE 句 If you do something **in advance**, you do it before a particular date or event. 前もって ❑ *The subject of the talk is announced a week in advance*. 会談の議題は1週間前に発表される.

Thesaurus　　*advance* また次を参照：

V.	improve **2**
N.	allowance, credit, loan, pre-payment, retainer **6**
ADJ.	early, prior **10**
ADV.	beforehand, previously **11**

Word Partnership　　*advance* は次の語句と使われる：

V.	advance **and retreat** **1**
ADJ.	**technological** advance **2**
N.	**cash** advance **3**
	advance **a cause** **5**
	advance **knowledge**, advance **notice**, advance **purchase**, advance **reservations** **10**

ad|vanced /ædvǽnst/ **1** ADJ 形容詞 An **advanced** system, method, or design is modern and has been developed from an earlier version of the same thing. 最新の ❑ …*a superpower equipped with the most advanced military technology in the world*. 最先端の軍事技術をもった超大国. **2** ADJ 形容詞 A country that is **advanced** has reached a high level of industrial or technological development. 先進の ❑ *Agricultural productivity remained low by comparison with advanced countries like the United States*. アメリカなどの先進国に比べ、農業の生産性は低いままだった. **3** ADJ 形容詞 An **advanced** student has already learned the basic facts of a subject and is doing more difficult work. An **advanced** course of study is designed for such students. 上級の ❑ *The course is suitable for beginners and advanced students*. そのコースが対象とする学生は初心者、上級者を問わない. **4** ADJ 形容詞 Something that is at an **advanced** stage or level is at a late stage of development. 進行した ❑ *Medicare is available to victims of advanced kidney disease*. 重度の腎臓病患者もメディケアが使える.

Thesaurus　　*advanced* また次を参照：

ADJ.	cutting-edge, foremost, latest, sophisticated **1**

ad|vance|ment /ædvǽnsmənt/ (**advancements**) **1** N-UNCOUNT 不可算名詞 **Advancement** is progress in your job or in your social position. 昇進、出世 ❑ *He cared little for social advancement*. 彼にとっては出世などどうでもよかった. **2** N-VAR 可変性名詞 The **advancement of** something is the process of helping it to progress or the result of its progress. 促進 ❑ *Her work for the advancement of the status of women in India was recognized by the whole nation*. インドの女性の地位向上に果たした彼女の功績は広く国民から認められた.

ad|van|tage /ædvǽntɪdʒ, -vǽn-/ (**advantages**) **1** N-COUNT 可算名詞 An **advantage** is something that puts you in a better position than other people. 有利な点 ❑ *They are breaking the law in order to obtain an advantage over their competitors*. 彼らが違法行為に走るのは競争相手よりも先を行こうとしているからです. **2** N-COUNT 可算名詞 An **advantage** is a way in which one thing is better than another. 有利 ❑ *The great advantage of home-grown oranges is their magnificent flavor*. 自家栽培オレンジの大きな特長はその素晴らしい風味である. **3** N-UNCOUNT 不可算名詞 **Advantage** is the state of being in a better position than others who are competing against you. 優位 ❑ *Men have created a social and economic position of advantage for themselves over women*. これまで男性は女性に対して社会的にも経済的にも優位な立場を築いてきた. **4** PHRASE 句 If you **take advantage of** something, you make good use of it while you can. 活用する ❑ *I intend to take full advantage of this trip to buy the things we need*. 今回の旅行を十分活用して必要なものは買うつもりだ. **5** PHRASE 句 If someone **takes advantage of** you, they treat you unfairly for their own benefit, especially when you are trying to be kind or to help them. 付け込む ❑ *She took advantage of him even after they were divorced*. 彼女は離婚してからも彼が優しいのをいいことに付け上がっていた. **6** PHRASE 句 If you use or turn something **to your advantage**, you use it in order to benefit from it, especially when it might be expected to harm or damage you. 逆手に取る ❑ *The government has not been able to turn today's demonstration to its advantage*. 現在のところ政府は今日行われたデモを逆手に利用するような方策をとっていない.

Word Partnership　　*advantage* は次の語句と使われる：

ADJ.	**competitive** advantage, **unfair** advantage **1**
V.	**have an** advantage **1**
	take advantage **of** *someone/something* **4**
	use to *someone's* advantage **6**

ad|van|ta|geous /ædvənteɪdʒəs/ ADJ 形容詞 If something is **advantageous** to you, it is likely to benefit you. 好都合な ❑ *Free exchange of goods was advantageous to all*. 商品が自由に交換できることはだれにとっても好都合だった.

ad|vent /ædvɛnt/ N-UNCOUNT 不可算名詞 The **advent of** an important event, invention, or situation is the fact of it starting or coming into existence. 出現、到来 [FORMAL 形式ばった] ❑ *The advent of the computer has brought this sort of task within the bounds of possibility*. コンピュータの出現によりこうした作業が可能になってきた.

ad|ven|ture /ædvɛntʃər/ (adventures) **1** N-COUNT 可算名詞 If someone has an **adventure**, they become involved in an unusual, exciting, and somewhat dangerous trip or series of events. 冒険 ❑ I set off for a new adventure in Alaska on the first day of the new year. 元日にアラスカへの冒険旅行に出発した. **2** N-UNCOUNT 不可算名詞 **Adventure** is excitement and willingness to do new, unusual, or somewhat dangerous things. 冒険心 ❑ Their cultural backgrounds gave them a spirit of adventure. 文化的な背景が彼らの旺盛な冒険心を育てた.

ad|ven|tur|ous /ædvɛntʃərəs/ **1** ADJ 形容詞 Someone who is **adventurous** is willing to take risks and to try new methods. Something that is **adventurous** involves new things or ideas. 冒険心のある; 冒険的な ❑ Warren was an adventurous businessman. ウォレンは進取の気性に富んだ実業家だった. **2** ADJ 形容詞 Someone who is **adventurous** is eager to visit new places and have new experiences. 冒険好きな ❑ He had always wanted an adventurous life in the tropics. 彼は熱帯地方で冒険に満ちた生活をしたいとかねてから思っていた.

ad|verb /ædvɜrb/ (adverbs) N-COUNT 可算名詞 An **adverb** is a word such as "slowly," "now," "very," "politically," or "fortunately" which adds information about the action, event, or situation mentioned in a clause. 副詞

ad|verb phrase (adverb phrases) N-COUNT 可算名詞 An **adverb phrase** or **adverbial phrase** is a group of words based on an adverb, such as "very slowly" or "fortunately for us." An adverb phrase can also consist simply of an adverb. 副詞句

ad|ver|sar|ial /ædvərsɛəriəl/ ADJ 形容詞 If you describe something as **adversarial**, you mean that it involves two or more people or organizations who are opposing each other. 敵対する [FORMAL 形式ばった] ❑ In our country there is an adversarial relationship between government and business. わが国では政府と企業は敵対している.

ad|ver|sary /ædvərsɛri/ (adversaries) N-COUNT 可算名詞 Your **adversary** is someone you are competing with, or arguing or fighting against. 敵 ❑ His political adversaries would like to discredit him. 政敵は彼の信用に傷をつけようと狙っている.

ad|verse /ædvɜrs/ ADJ 形容詞 **Adverse** decisions, conditions, or effects are unfavorable to you. 不利な ❑ The police said Mr. Hadfield's decision would have no adverse effect on the progress of the investigation. 警察は, ハドフィールド氏の決断によって捜査の進展が妨げられることはないとした. ● **ad|verse|ly** ADV 副詞 [ADV with v] 不利に ❑ Price changes must not adversely affect the living standards of the people. 物価の変動によって, 国民の生活水準に悪影響が出るようなことがあってはならない.

ad|ver|sity /ædvɜrsɪti/ (adversities) N-VAR 可変性名詞 **Adversity** is a very difficult or unfavorable situation. 苦境 ❑ He showed courage in adversity. 彼は打たれ強かった.

ad|vert /ædvɜrt/ (adverts) N-COUNT 可算名詞 An **advert** is an announcement in a newspaper, on television, or on a poster about something such as a product, event, or job. 広告, コマーシャル [BRIT 英国英語] AM 米国英語 **ad**]

ad|ver|tise /ædvərtaɪz/ (advertises, advertising, advertised) **1** V-T/V-I 他動詞/自動詞 If you **advertise** something such as a product, an event, or a job, you tell people about it in newspapers, on television, or on posters in order to encourage them to buy the product, go to the event, or apply for the job. 宣伝する, 広告を出す ❑ The company is spending heavily to advertise its strongest brands. 会社は稼ぎ頭となっているブランドの宣伝に大金を費やしている. ❑ In 1991, the house was advertised for sale at $49,000. 1991年にその家は4万9千ドルで売りに出た. **2** V-I 自動詞 If you **advertise for** someone to do something for you, for example, to work for you or share your accommodation, you announce it in a newspaper, on television, or on a bulletin board. 募集する ❑ We advertised for staff in a local newspaper. 当社は地方紙で社員を募集した. **3** V-T 他動詞 If you do not **advertise** the fact that something is the case, you try not to let other people know about it. おおっぴらにする [usu with brd-neg] ❑ There is no need to advertise the fact that you are a single

woman. きみが独身であることをいいふらすことはないよ. **4** → see also **advertising**

ad|ver|tise|ment /ædvərtaɪzmənt/ (advertisements) **1** N-COUNT 可算名詞 An **advertisement** is an announcement in a newspaper, on television, or on a poster about something such as a product, event, or job. 広告, 宣伝 [WRITTEN 書き言葉] ❑ Miss Parrish recently placed an advertisement in the local newspaper. パリッシュさんは最近地方紙に広告を出しました. **2** N-COUNT 可算名詞 If you say that an example of something is **an advertisement for** that thing in general, you mean that it shows how good that thing is. 好例 ❑ The Treviso team was an effective advertisement for the improving state of Italian club rugby. トレビゾチームは, イタリアのクラブラグビーの復調ぶりを端的に示した.

ad|ver|tis|er /ædvərtaɪzər/ (advertisers) N-COUNT 可算名詞 An **advertiser** is a person or company that pays for a product, event, or job to be advertised in a newspaper, on television, or on a poster. 広告主 ❑ When will advertisers stop bombarding women with images of unattainable beauty? 到達しがたい美のイメージを女性に植えつけようとする広告はいったいいつまで続くのだろうか.

ad|ver|tis|ing /ædvərtaɪzɪŋ/ N-UNCOUNT 不可算名詞 **Advertising** is the activity of creating advertisements and making sure people see them. 広告業 ❑ I work in advertising. 私は広告業界で働いている.
→ see Word Web: **advertising**

ad|ver|tis|ing agen|cy → see **ad agency**

ad|ver|tis|ing cam|paign → see **ad campaign**

ad|vice /ædvaɪs/ N-UNCOUNT 不可算名詞 If you give someone **advice**, you tell them what you think they should do in a particular situation. 助言 ❑ Don't be afraid to ask for advice about ordering the meal. 食事を注文するときは遠慮なくウェーターに聞けばよい.

Thesaurus	advice また次を参照:
N.	counsel, guidance, help, information, input; (ant.) opinion, recommendation, suggestion

Word Partnership	advice は次の語句と使われる:
PREP.	**against** advice
V.	**ask for** advice, **give** advice, **need some** advice, **take** advice
ADJ.	**bad/good** advice **expert** advice

Note that **advice** is an uncount noun. You can say **a piece of advice** or **some advice**, but you cannot say "an advice" or "advices." Do not confuse **advice** and **advise**. **Advise** is the verb that is connected with **advice**.

ad|vice col|umn|ist (advice columnists) N-COUNT 可算名詞 An **advice columnist** is a person who writes a column in a newspaper or magazine in which they reply to readers who have written to them for advice on their personal problems. 人生相談回答者 [AM 米国英語] ❑ ...the advice columnist at the local paper. 地方紙の人生相談回答者.

ad|vis|able /ædvaɪzəbəl/ ADJ 形容詞 If you tell someone that it **is advisable to** do something, you are suggesting that they should do it, because it is sensible or is likely to achieve the result they want. 望ましい, 賢明な [FORMAL 形式ばった] [v-link ADJ] ❑ Because of the popularity of the region, it is advisable to book hotels or campsites in advance. その地域は人気が高いので, ホテルやキャンプ場は前もって予約しておいたほうがよい.

ad|vise /ædvaɪz/ (advises, advising, advised) **1** V-T 他動詞 If you **advise** someone to do something, you tell them what you think they should do. 忠告する ❑ The minister advised him to leave as soon as possible. 大臣は彼にできるだけ早くに立ち去るよう勧めた. ❑ I would strongly advise against it. それは絶対やめておいたほう

Word Web　advertising

It's impossible to avoid **advertisements**. In our homes, **newspaper, magazine,** and **television** ads compete for our attention. **Posters, billboards,** and **flyers** greet us the moment we walk out the door. **Advertising agencies** stay busy thinking up new ways to get our attention. We have company **logos** on our clothes. Our e-mail is full of **spam,** and pop-ups slow us down as we surf the Web. Product **placements** sneak into movies and TV shows. "Ad wrapping" turns cars into moving signboards. Advertisers have even tried **subliminal** advertising in TV **commercials**. It's no wonder that this is called the **consumer** age.

がよいと思いますよ. ② V-T 他動詞 If an expert **advises** people on a particular subject, he or she gives them help and information on that subject. 助言する ❑ ...*an officer who advises undergraduates from the University on money matters.* 学生の経済的問題の相談に乗るカウンセラー.

Word Partnership   *advise* は次の語句と使われる:

PREP.	advise **against** ①
N.	advise *someone* **to** ①
ADV.	**strongly** advise ①

Do not confuse **advise** and **advice**. **Advice** is the noun that is connected with the verb **advise**. If you **advise** someone to do something, you tell them what you think they should do. If you **suggest** something, however, you mention it as an idea or plan for someone to think about, perhaps together with other ideas or plans. You can also **suggest** doing something, or **suggest** that someone does something. ❑ *Your bank manager will probably suggest a loan... I suggested inviting Jim... I suggest that you leave this to me.*

ad|vis|er /ædvaɪzər/ (advisers) also **advisor** N-COUNT 可算名詞 An **adviser** is an expert whose job is to give advice to another person or to a group of people. 顧問 ❑ *In Washington, the president and his advisers spent the day in meetings.* ワシントンでは大統領と顧問が丸一日会議に費やしました.

Word Link   *ory* ≈ relating to : advisory, contradictory, predatory

ad|vi|so|ry /ædvaɪzəri/ (advisories) ① N-COUNT 可算名詞 An **advisory** is an official announcement or report that warns people about bad weather, diseases, or other dangers or problems. 注意報, 警報 [AM 米国英語] ❑ *26 states have issued health advisories.* 26州が健康に関する勧告を出しました. ② ADJ 形容詞 An **advisory** group regularly gives suggestions and help to people or organizations, especially about a particular subject or area of activity. 諮問の [FORMAL 形式ばった] ❑ *...members of the advisory committee on the safety of nuclear installations.* 核施設の安全性に関する諮問委員会のメンバー.

ad|vo|ca|cy /ædvəkəsi/ ① N-SING 単数名詞 Someone's **advocacy of** a particular action or plan is their act of recommending it publicly. 支持 [FORMAL 形式ばった] ❑ *I support your advocacy of free trade.* 貴紙の自由貿易を擁護する立場を支持します. ② N-UNCOUNT 不可算名詞 An **advocacy** group or organization is one that tries to influence the decisions of a government or other authority. 圧力団体 [AM 米国英語] ❑ *Consumer advocacy groups are not so enthusiastic about removing restrictions on the telephone companies.* 消費者団体は電話会社の規制を撤廃することにあまり乗り気でない.

Word Link   *voc* ≈ speaking : advocate, vocabulary, vocal

ad|vo|cate (advocates, advocating, advocated)

The verb is pronounced /ædvəkeɪt/. The noun is pronounced /ædvəkɪt/.

動詞は /ædvəkeɪt/ と発音される. 名詞は /ædvəkɪt/ と発音される.

① V-T 他動詞 If you **advocate** a particular action or plan, you recommend it publicly. 支持する [FORMAL 形式ばった] ❑ *Mr. Williams is a conservative who advocates fewer government controls on business.* ウィリアム氏は保守主義者で, 企業活動に対する政府の規制緩和を支持している. ② N-COUNT 可算名詞 An **advocate of** a particular action or plan is someone who recommends it publicly. 支持者 [FORMAL 形式ばった] ❑ *He was a strong advocate of free market policies and a multi-party system.* 彼は自由市場政策と複数政党制の強く擁護した. ③ N-COUNT 可算名詞 An **advocate for** a particular group is a person who works for the interests of that group. 支援者 [AM 米国英語] ❑ *...advocates for the homeless.* ホームレスの支援者. ④ N-COUNT 可算名詞 An **advocate** is a lawyer who speaks in favor of someone or defends them in a court of law. 弁護人 [LEGAL 法律的]

Word Partnership   *advocate* は次の語句と使われる:

ADJ.	**leading** advocate, **strong** advocate ②
PREP.	advocate **of** *something* ②
	advocate **for** *something/someone* ③

Word Link   *aer* ≈ air : aerial, aerobics, aerosol

aer|ial /ɛəriəl/ (aerials) ① ADJ 形容詞 You talk about **aerial** attacks and **aerial** photographs to indicate that people or things on the ground are attacked or photographed by people in airplanes. 航空機による [ADJ n] ❑ *Weeks of aerial bombardment had destroyed factories and highways.* 何週間にもわたる空襲で工場や幹線道路が破壊された. ❑ *Patterns that are invisible on the ground can be the most striking part of an aerial photograph.* 地上では分からないパターンが見えることが航空写真の最大の特長といえる. ② N-COUNT 可算名詞 An **aerial** is a device that receives television or radio signals. アンテナ [mainly BRIT 主に英国英語; AM usually antenna 米国英語では通常 antenna]

aero|bics /ɛəroʊbɪks/ N-UNCOUNT 不可算名詞 **Aerobics** is a form of exercise which increases the amount of oxygen in your blood, and strengthens your heart and lungs. The verb that follows **aerobics** may be either singular or plural. エアロビクス [oft N n] ❑ *I'd like to join an aerobics class to improve my fitness.* エアロビクス教室に入って健康を増進したいです.

aero|dy|nam|ic /ɛəroʊdaɪnæmɪk/ ADJ 形容詞 If something such as a car has an **aerodynamic** shape or design, it goes faster and uses less fuel than other cars because the air passes over it more easily. 流線形の ❑ *The secret of the machine lies in the aerodynamic shape of the one-piece, carbon-fiber frame.* このマシンの秘密は流線形に一体成型した炭素繊維フレームにある.

aero|plane /ɛərəpleɪn/ (aeroplanes) An **aeroplane** is a vehicle with wings and one or more engines that enable it to fly through the air. 飛行機 [BRIT 英国英語; AM airplane 米国英語 airplane]

aero|sol /ɛərəsɒl/ (aerosols) N-COUNT 可算名詞 An **aerosol** can or spray is a small container in which a liquid such as paint or deodorant is kept under pressure. When you press a button, the liquid is forced out as a fine spray or foam. エアゾール [usu N n] ❑ *...an aerosol can of insecticide.* スプレー式の殺虫剤.

aes|thet|ic /ɛsθɛtɪk/ also **esthetic** ① ADJ 形容詞 **Aesthetic** is used to talk about beauty or art, and people's appreciation of beautiful things. 美の, 美的な ❑ *...products chosen for their aesthetic appeal as well as their durability and quality.* 耐久性や品質だけでなく美しいデザインで選ばれた製品. ② N-SING 単数名詞 The **aesthetic** of a work of art is its aesthetic quality. 美しさ ❑ *He responded very strongly to the aesthetic of this particular work.* 彼はこの作品の美しさに強く引かれた. ● **aes|theti|cal|ly** /ɛsθɛtɪkli/ ADV 副詞 美的に ❑ *A statue which is aesthetically pleasing to one person, however, may be repulsive to another.* 同じ彫像を見て美しいと思う人もいれば不快に思う人もいる.

af|fable /æfəbl/ ADJ 形容詞 Someone who is **affable** is pleasant and friendly. 愛想がよい ❑ *Mr. Brooke is an extremely affable and approachable man.* ブルック氏はとても気さくで近寄りやすい人だ.

af|fair /əfɛər/ (affairs) ① N-SING 単数名詞 If an event or a series of events has been mentioned and you want to talk about it again, you can refer to it as **the affair**. ❑ *The administration has mishandled the whole affair.* 現政権はすべての点でこの問題の扱いを誤ってきた. ② N-SING 単数名詞 You can refer to an important or interesting event or situation as "**the ... affair**." 事件 [MAINLY JOURNALISM 主にジャーナリズム] ❑ *...the damage caused to the CIA and FBI in the aftermath of the Watergate affair.* ウォーターゲート事件の余波としてCIAとFBIが受けた被害. ③ N-SING 単数名詞 You can describe the main quality of an event by saying that it is a particular kind of **affair**. 用事 ❑ *Michael said that his planned 10-day visit would be a purely private affair.* マイケルによれば, 計画中の10日間の訪問はあくまで私的なものということです. ④ N-COUNT 可算名詞 If two people who are not married to each other have an **affair**, they have a sexual relationship. 不倫 ❑ *Married male supervisors were carrying on affairs with female subordinates in the office.* 既婚の上司が部下の女性社員と不倫していました. ⑤ → see also **love affair** ⑥ N-PLURAL 複数名詞 You can use **affairs** to refer to all the important facts or activities that are connected with a particular subject. 事情, 事態 ❑ *He does not want to interfere in the internal affairs of another country.* 彼は他国の内政に干渉するつもりはない. ⑦ → see also **current affairs, state of affairs** ⑧ N-PLURAL 複数名詞 Your **affairs** are all the matters connected with your life that you consider to be private and normally deal with yourself. 身の回りのこと ❑ *The unexpectedness of my father's death meant that his affairs were not entirely in order.* 父は突然亡くなったので, すっかり身の回りの整理ができていたわけではなかった.

af|fect /əfɛkt/ (affects, affecting, affected) ① V-T 他動詞 If something **affects** a person or thing, it influences them or causes them to change in some way. 影響する ❑ *Nicotine adversely affects the functioning of the heart and arteries.* ニコチンは心臓と動脈の働きに悪影響を及ぼす. ❑ *More than seven million people have been affected by drought.* 干ばつの被害を受けた人たちは7百万人を超えます. ② V-T 他動詞 If a disease **affects** someone, it causes them to become ill. 冒す ❑ *Arthritis is a crippling disease which affects people all over the world.* 関節炎は身体が不自由になる病気でその患者は世界中にいる. ③ V-T 他動詞 If something or someone **affects** you, they make you feel a strong emotion, especially sadness or pity. 動揺させる ❑ *If Jim had been more independent, the divorce would not have affected him as deeply.* もっと自立していたらジムも離婚でこんなに落ち込むことはなかったろう.

Note that the noun that comes from **affect** is **effect**. You can say that something **affects** you, or that it has an **effect** on you. ❏ *...the effect that noise has on people in factories.* You can also talk about the **effect** of something. ❏ *...the effect of the anesthetic.* **Effect** can also be a verb. If you **effect** something such as a change or a repair, you make it happen or do it. This is a fairly formal word. ❏ *She had effected a few hasty repairs.*

af|fec|tion /əfɛkʃⁿn/ (affections) **1** N-UNCOUNT 不可算名詞 If you regard someone or something with **affection**, you like them and are fond of them. 好意 ❏ *She thought of him with affection.* 彼女は彼に好意を抱いていた. **2** N-PLURAL 複数名詞 Your **affections** are your feelings of love or fondness for someone. 愛情 ❏ *Caroline is the object of his affections.* キャロラインこそ彼の意中の人だ. → see **love**

Word Link ate ≈ filled: affectionate, compassionate, considerate

af|fec|tion|ate /əfɛkʃənɪt/ ADJ 形容詞 If you are **affectionate**, you show your love or fondness for another person in the way that you behave toward them. 愛情にあふれた ❏ *They seemed devoted to each other and were openly affectionate.* 二人は熱愛の仲らしく, そのしぐさは愛情にあふれていた. ● **af|fec|tion|ate|ly** ADV 副詞 [ADV with v] 愛情を込めて ❏ *He looked affectionately at his niece.* おいを見つめる彼の目には愛情がこもっていた.

af|fi|da|vit /æfɪdeɪvɪt/ (affidavits) N-COUNT 可算名詞 An **affidavit** is a written statement that you swear is true and that may be used as evidence in a court of law. 宣誓供述書 [LEGAL 法律的] ❏ *In his sworn affidavit, Roche outlined a history of actions against him by the church.* ロッシュは宣誓供述書おいて教会がこれまで彼にしてきたことのあらましを述べた.

af|fili|ate (affiliates, affiliating, affiliated)

The noun is pronounced /əfɪliɪt/. The verb is pronounced /əfɪlieɪt/.

名詞は /əfɪliɪt/ と発音される. 動詞は /əfɪlieɪt/ と発音される.

1 N-COUNT 可算名詞 An **affiliate** is an organization which is officially connected with another, larger organization or is a member of it. 系列会社; 加盟団体 [FORMAL 形式ばった] ❏ *The World Chess Federation has affiliates in around 120 countries.* 国際チェス連盟は世界約120ヶ国に支部がある. **2** V-I 自動詞 If an organization **affiliates with** another larger organization, it forms a close connection with the larger organization or becomes a member of it. 提携する; 加盟する [FORMAL 形式ばった] ❏ *He wanted to affiliate with a U.S. firm because he needed expert advice in legal affairs.* 彼はあるアメリカ企業との提携を望んでいたが, それは法律問題で専門家の助言を必要としていたからであった.

af|filia|tion /əfɪlieɪʃⁿn/ (affiliations) N-VAR 可変性名詞 If one group has an **affiliation** with another group, it has a close or official connection with it. 提携 [FORMAL 形式ばった] ❏ *The kidnappers had no affiliation with any militant group.* 誘拐犯はどの武装グループとも関係がなかった.

af|fin|ity /əfɪnɪti/ N-SING 単数名詞 If you have an **affinity** with someone or something, you feel that you are similar to them or that you know and understand them very well. 親近感 ❏ *He has a close affinity with the landscape and people he knew when he was growing up.* 彼は子どもの頃に見た風景や出会った人々に深い愛着がある.

Word Link firm ≈ making strong: affirm, confirm, infirm

af|firm /əfɜrm/ (affirms, affirming, affirmed) **1** V-T 他動詞 If you **affirm** that something is true or that something exists, you state firmly and publicly that it is true or exists. 断言する; 表明する [FORMAL 形式ばった] ❏ *The court affirmed that the information can be made public under the Freedom of Information Act.* 裁判では, 情報自由法に従ってその情報を公開できるという下級審の判決を支持した. ❏ *...a speech in which he affirmed a commitment to lower taxes.* 減税の公約を再表明した演説. ● **af|firma|tion** /æfərmeɪʃⁿn/ N-VAR 可変性名詞 (affirmations) 断言; 表明 ❏ *The North Atlantic Treaty begins with the affirmation that its parties "reaffirm their faith in the purposes and principles of the Charter of the United Nations."* 北大西洋条約はその冒頭で, 加盟国が「国連憲章の目的と原則に従う」ことを表明している. **2** V-T 他動詞 If an event **affirms** something, it shows that it is true or exists. 確認する [FORMAL 形式ばった] ❏ *Everything I had accomplished seemed to affirm that opinion.* 私がこれまでやってきたことからすれば, その意見に間違いはないと感じた. ● **af|firma|tion** N-UNCOUNT 不可算名詞 [also 'a' n] 確認 ❏ *The ruling was a welcome affirmation of the constitutional right to free speech.* 判決は, 憲法の保障する言論の自由を擁護した歓迎すべき判決だった.

af|firma|tive /əfɜrmətɪv/ **1** ADJ 形容詞 An **affirmative** word or gesture indicates that you agree with what someone has said or that the answer to a question is "yes." 賛成の, 肯定的な [FORMAL 形式ばった] ❏ *Haig was desperately eager for an affirmative answer.* ヘイグは色よい返事がくるのをひらすら待った. **2** ADJ 形容詞 In grammar, an **affirmative** clause is positive and does not contain a negative word. 肯定の **3** PHRASE 句 If you reply to a question **in the affirmative**, you say "yes" or make a gesture that means "yes." 肯定の返事で [FORMAL 形式ばった] ❏ *He asked me if I was ready. I answered in the affirmative.* 彼は準備はできたかと聞いたので, 私はできていると答えた.

af|firma|tive ac|tion N-UNCOUNT 不可算名詞 **Affirmative action** is the policy of giving jobs and other opportunities to members of groups such as racial minorities or women who might not otherwise have them. 少数派優遇策 [AM 米国英語] ❏ *Despite nearly a decade of affirmative action since apartheid was dismantled, few black sportsmen have reached the top level.* アパルトヘイトが撤廃され少数派優遇策が実施されて10年近くになるが, 黒人でトップレベルに到達した選手はほとんどいない.

Word Link fix ≈ fastening : affix, prefix, suffix

af|fix /æfɪks/ (affixes) N-COUNT 可算名詞 An **affix** is a letter or group of letters, for example, "un-" or "-y," which is added to either the beginning or the end of a word to form a different word with a different meaning. For example, "un-" is added to "kind" to form "unkind." Compare **prefix** and **suffix**. 接辞

af|flict /əflɪkt/ (afflicts, afflicting, afflicted) V-T 他動詞 If you **are afflicted by** pain, illness, or disaster, it affects you badly and makes you suffer. 苦しめる, 悩ます [FORMAL 形式ばった] ❏ *Italy has been afflicted by political corruption for decades.* イタリアは何十年にもわたって政治腐敗に悩まされてきた. ❏ *There are two main problems which afflict people with hearing impairments.* 聴覚障害のある人たちを苦しめている大きな問題が2つあります.

Word Link flict ≈ striking : affliction, conflict, inflict

af|flic|tion /əflɪkʃⁿn/ (afflictions) N-VAR 可変性名詞 An **affliction** is something that causes physical or mental suffering. 病気; 苦悩 [FORMAL 形式ばった] ❏ *Hay fever is an affliction that arrives at an early age.* 花粉症は若い頃に発症する病気である.

af|flu|ence /æfluəns/ N-UNCOUNT 不可算名詞 **Affluence** is the state of having a lot of money or a high standard of living. 裕福 [FORMAL 形式ばった] ❏ *The postwar era was one of new affluence for the working class.* 戦後に労働階級が裕福になった時期がありました.

af|flu|ent /æfluənt/ ADJ 形容詞 If you are **affluent**, you have a lot of money. 裕福な ❏ *Cigarette smoking used to be more common among affluent people.* かつては裕福な人たちの間でも喫煙は一般的であった. ● N-PLURAL 複数名詞 **The affluent** are people who are affluent. 裕福な人たち ❏ *The diet of the affluent has not changed much over the decades.* 裕福な人の食事は過去数十年ほとんど変化がない.

af|ford /əfɔrd/ (affords, affording, afforded) **1** V-T 他動詞 If you **cannot afford** something, you do not have enough money to pay for it. (経済的に) 余裕がある ❏ *My parents can't even afford a new refrigerator.* 両親は新しい冷蔵庫を買う余裕さえない. ❏ *The arts should be available to more people at prices they can afford.* 芸術は多くの人たちが低料金で楽しめるようにすべきである. **2** V-T 他動詞 If you say that you cannot **afford** to do something or allow it to happen, you mean that you must not do it or must prevent it from happening because it would be harmful or embarrassing to you. (〜する) わけにいかない ❏ *We can't afford to wait.* ただ待っているわけにはいかない.

Word Partnership afford は次の語句と使われる:

v.	afford to buy/pay **1**
	can/could afford, can't/couldn't afford **1 2**
	afford to lose **2**
ADJ.	able/unable to afford **1 2**

af|ford|able /əfɔrdəbⁿl/ ADJ 形容詞 If something is **affordable**, most people have enough money to buy it. 手ごろな ❏ *...the availability of affordable housing.* 手ごろな価格の住宅が購入できる可能性.

af|front /əfrʌnt/ (affronts, affronting, affronted) **1** V-T 他動詞 If something **affronts** you, you feel insulted and hurt because of it. 侮辱する [FORMAL 形式ばった] ❏ *One recent example, which particularly affronted Kasparov, was at the European team championship in Hungary.* 最近の例としてはハンガリーでの欧州チーム選手権があるが, これはカスパロフにとってとりわけ屈辱的な試合だった. **2** N-COUNT 可算名詞 If something is an **affront to** you, it is an obvious insult to you. 侮辱 ❏ *It's an affront to human dignity to keep someone alive like this.* こんなふうに人を生かしておくことは人間の尊厳を侮辱するようなものだ.

afield /əfild/ PHRASE 句 **Further afield** or **farther afield** means in places or areas other than the nearest or most obvious one. 遠く離れて ❏ *They enjoy participating in a wide variety of activities, both locally and further afield.* 参加者たちは地元や遠方で開かれるさまざまな活動を楽しんだ.

afloat /əfloʊt/ ① ADV 副詞 If someone or something is **afloat**, they remain partly above the surface of water and do not sink. 浮かんで ❑ *They talked modestly of their valiant efforts to keep the tanker afloat.* 彼らはタンカーが沈没しないように果敢な行動に出たが、そのときのようすを淡々と語った. ② ADV 副詞 If a person, business, or country stays **afloat** or is kept **afloat**, they have just enough money to pay their debts and continue operating. 破産せずに [BUSINESS 実業] ❑ *A number of efforts were being made to keep the company afloat.* 会社が破産しないようにあらゆる努力が払われた.

afoot /əfʊt/ ADJ 形容詞 If you say that a plan or scheme is **afoot**, it is already happening or being planned, but you do not know much about it. 進行中で、計画中で [v-link ADJ] ❑ *Everybody knew that something awful was afoot.* 大変な事態が迫っていることにだれもが気づいていた.

afore|men|tioned /əfɔrmɛnʃ°nd/ ADJ 形容詞 If you refer to **the aforementioned** person or subject, you mean the person or subject that has already been mentioned. 前述の [FORMAL 形式ばった] [det ADJ, usu 'the' ADJ n] ❑ *This is the draft of a declaration that will be issued at the end of the aforementioned U.N. conference.* これは前述の国連会議の最後に発表される宣言の草案である.

afore|said /əfɔrsɛd/ ADJ 形容詞 **Aforesaid** means the same as **aforementioned**. 前述の [FORMAL 形式ばった] [det ADJ, usu 'the' ADJ n] ❑ *…the aforesaid organizations and institutions.* 前述した組織や機関.

afraid /əfreɪd/ ① ADJ 形容詞 If you are **afraid of** someone or **afraid to** do something, you are frightened because you think that something very unpleasant is going to happen to you. 恐れて [v-link ADJ] ❑ *She did not seem at all afraid.* 彼女が恐れているようすは全く見られなかった. ❑ *I was afraid of the other boys.* 他の男の子たちが怖かったんです. ② ADJ 形容詞 If you are **afraid for** someone else, you are worried that something horrible is going to happen to them. 心配して [v-link ADJ] ❑ *She's afraid for her family in Somalia.* 彼女はソマリアにいる家族のことを心配しています. ③ ADJ 形容詞 If you are **afraid** that something unpleasant will happen, you are worried that it may happen and you want to avoid it. 心配して（でないかと）[v-link ADJ] ❑ *I was afraid that nobody would believe me.* だれも私のことを信じてくれないのではないかと心配でした. ④ PHRASE 句 If you want to apologize to someone or to disagree with them in a polite way, you can say **I'm afraid**. 残念ながら [SPOKEN 口語, POLITENESS 丁寧さ] ❑ *We don't have anything like that, I'm afraid.* 申し訳ございませんが、こちらではそのような商品は扱っておりません.

Thesaurus	*afraid* また次を参照:
ADJ.	alarmed, fearful, frightened, petrified, scared, terrified ① worried ③

Word Partnership	*afraid* は次の語句と使われる:
PREP.	afraid of *someone/something* ①
V.	be afraid ① – ③

---

afresh /əfrɛʃ/ ADV 副詞 If you do something **afresh**, you do it again in a different way. 新たに [ADV after v] ❑ *They believe that the only hope for the French left is to start afresh.* フランスに残された唯一の望みといえば、再出発することしかないと彼らは思っている.

African-American (**African-Americans**) N-COUNT 可算名詞 **African-Americans** are black people living in the United States who are descended from families that originally came from Africa. アフリカ系アメリカ人 ❑ *Today African-Americans are 12 percent of the population.* アフリカ系アメリカ人は現在人口の12%を占めています. ● ADJ 形容詞 **African-American** is also an adjective. アフリカ系アメリカ人の ❑ *…a group of African-American community leaders.* 黒人社会の指導者たちの組織.

The term **African-American** is used in the USA to describe people whose ancestors came from Africa. Some people prefer to use the term **black**.

---

aft /æft/ ADV 副詞 If you go **aft** in a boat or plane, you go to the back of it. If you are **aft**, you are in the back. 船尾に; 尾翼に ❑ *I went aft to take my turn at the helm.* 船尾に行ってかじ取りを交代した.

af|ter /æftər/

In addition to the uses shown below, **after** is used in phrasal verbs such as "ask after," "look after," and "take after."

下記の用法に加えて、**after** は ask after, look after, take after のような句動詞に使われる.

---

① PREP 前置詞 If something happens **after** a particular date or event, it happens during the period of time that follows that date or event. あとに ❑ *After May 19, strikes were occurring on a daily basis.* 5月19日以降ストライキは連日起こっていた. ❑ *After breakfast Amy took a taxi to the station.* 朝食を済ますとエイミーはタクシーで駅に向かった. ● CONJ 接続詞 **After** is also a conjunction. （して）あとで ❑ *After Don told me this, he spoke of his mother.* ドンはこう言ってから母親のことを話した. ② PREP 前置詞 If you do one thing **after** doing another, you do it during the period of time that follows the other thing. （して）から [PREP -ing] ❑ *After completing and signing it, please return the form to us in the envelope provided.* 用紙に記入し署名した上で同封の封筒でご返送ください. ③ PREP 前置詞 You use **after** when you are talking about time. For example, if something is going to happen during **the day after** or **the weekend after** a particular time, it is going to happen during the following day or during the following weekend. （の）次の [n PREP n] ❑ *She's leaving the day after tomorrow.* 彼女はあさって出発する. ● ADV 副詞 **After** is also an adverb. あとに [ADV after v] ❑ *Tomorrow. Or the day after.* 明日かあさって. ④ PREP 前置詞 If you go **after** someone, you follow or chase them. あとを追って ❑ *Alice said to Gina, "Why don't you go after him, he's yours?"*「どうして追っかけていかないの、あなたの息子でしょ」とアリスはジーナに言った. ⑤ PREP 前置詞 If you are **after** something, you are trying to get it. ねらって ❑ *They were after the money.* 彼らの目当ては金なのだ. ⑥ PREP 前置詞 If you call, shout, or stare **after** someone, you call, shout, or stare at them as they move away from you. 後ろから ❑ *"Come back!" he called after me.*「帰って来てくれ」と彼は私を呼びとめた. ⑦ PREP 前置詞 If you tell someone that one place is a particular distance **after** another, you mean that it is situated beyond the other place and further away from you. 離れて ❑ *…a station 134 miles after the train starts its journey.* 列車の始発地点から134マイル離れた駅. ⑧ PREP 前置詞 If one thing is written **after** another thing on a page, it is written following it or underneath it. あとに ❑ *I wrote my name after Penny's at the bottom of the page.* ページの下にあったペニー名前のあとに自分の名前を書いた. ⑨ PREP 前置詞 You use **after** in order to give the most important aspect of something when comparing it with another aspect. 次いで ❑ *After Germany, America is Britain's second-biggest customer.* イギリスにとって、アメリカはドイツに次ぐ第2位の輸出国である. ⑩ PREP 前置詞 To be named **after** someone means to be given the same name as them. ちなんで ❑ *He persuaded Virginia to name the baby after him.* 何とかバージニアを説得して彼は赤ちゃんに自分の名前をつけることができた. ⑪ PREP 前置詞 **After** is used when telling the time. If it is, for example, **ten after six**, the time is ten minutes past six. 過ぎ [AM 米国英語] ⑫ CONVENTION 慣習表現 If you say "**after you**" to someone, you are being polite and allowing them to go in front of you or through a doorway before you do. どうぞお先に [POLITENESS 丁寧さ] ⑬ after all → see all

---

You use **after**, **afterward**, and **later** to talk about things that happen following the time when you are speaking, or following a particular event. Expressions such as "not long" and "shortly" can also be used with **after**. ❑ *After dinner she spoke to him… I returned to England after visiting India… Shortly after, she called me.* **Afterward** can be used when you do not need to mention the particular time or event. ❑ *Afterward we went to a nightclub.* You can also use words such as "soon" and "shortly" with **afterward**. ❑ *Soon afterward, he came to the clinic.* You can use **later** to refer to a time or situation that follows the time when you are speaking. ❑ *I'll go and see her later.* "A little," "much," and "not much" can also be used with **later**. ❑ *A little later, the lights went out… I learned all this much later.* You can use **after**, **afterward**, or **later** following a phrase that mentions a period of time, in order to say when something happens. ❑ *…five years after his death… She wrote about it six years afterward… Ten minutes later he left the house.*

---

⑭ PHRASE 句 If you do something to several things **one after the other** or **one after another**, you do it to one, then the next, and so on, with no break between your actions. 次から次と ❑ *…a lawyer who wins three cases, one after another.* 相次いで3件の訴訟に勝利した弁護士. ⑮ PHRASE 句 If something happens **day after day** or **year after year**, it happens every day or every year, for a long time. 来る日も来る日も; 毎年毎年 ❑ *…people who'd been coming here year after year.* 毎年のようにやってきた人たち.

after- /æftər-/ COMB IN ADJ 形容詞の複合 **After-** is added to nouns to form adjectives which indicate that something takes place or exists after an event or process. （の）あとの [ADJ n] ❑ *…an after-dinner speech.* テーブルスピーチ.

after|market /æftərmɑrkɪt/ ① N-SING 単数名詞 The **aftermarket** is all the related products that are sold after an item, especially a car, has been bought. アフターマーケット [BUSINESS 実業] ❑ *The company serves the national automotive aftermarket with a broad range of accessory and recreational-vehicle products.* 会社は国内の自動車アフターマーケット向けにアクセサリーやRV車向け製品を幅広く供給している. ② N-SING 単数名詞 The **aftermarket** in stocks and bonds is the buying and selling of them after they have been issued. 流通市場 [BUSINESS 実業] ❑ *It's illegal to get into a formal*

A

agreement with investors that they'll buy in the aftermarket. 流通市場で株式を購入するように投資家と正式な契約を結ぶのは違法行為である.

after|math /ˈæftərmæθ/ N-SING 単数名詞 **The aftermath of** an important event, especially a harmful one, is the situation that results from it. 余波 □ In the aftermath of the coup, the troops opened fire on the demonstrators. クーデターの余波が残るなか, 軍隊はデモ参加者に向けて発砲した.

after|noon /ˌæftərˈnuːn/ (afternoons) N-VAR 可変性名詞 The **afternoon** is the part of each day that begins at lunchtime and ends at about six o'clock. 午後 □ He's arriving in the afternoon. 彼は午後に到着する. □ He had stayed in his room all afternoon. 彼は午後はずっと部屋にこもっていた.

after|shave /ˈæftərʃeɪv/ (aftershaves) also after-shave N-MASS 質量名詞 **Aftershave** is a liquid with a pleasant smell that men sometimes put on their faces after shaving. アフターシェーブローション □ ...a bottle of aftershave. アフタシェイブローションのびん.

after|ward /ˈæftərwərd/ also afterwards ADV 副詞 If you do something or if something happens **afterward**, you do it or it happens after a particular event or time that has already been mentioned. その後 [ADV with cl] □ Shortly afterward, police arrested four suspects. その後まもなく警察は4人の容疑者を逮捕した.

> You use **after**, **afterward**, and **later** to talk about things that happen following the time when you are speaking, or following a particular event. Expressions such as "not long" and "shortly" can also be used with **after**. □ After dinner she spoke to him... I returned to England after visiting India... Shortly after, she called me. **Afterward** can be used when you do not need to mention the particular time or event. □ Afterward we went to a night club. You can also use words such as "soon" and "shortly" with **afterward**. □ Soon afterward, he came to the clinic. You can use **later** to refer to a time or situation that follows the time when you are speaking. □ I'll go and see her later. "A little," "much," and "not much" can also be used with **later**. □ A little later, the lights went out... I learned all this much later. You can use **after**, **afterward**, or **later** following a phrase that mentions a period of time, in order to say when something happens. □ ...five years after his death... She wrote about it six years afterward... Ten minutes later he left the house.

again /əˈgɛn, əˈgeɪn/ **1** ADV 副詞 You use **again** to indicate that something happens a second time, or after it has already happened before. 余波 □ He kissed her again. 彼はもう一度彼女にキスした. □ Again there was a short silence. 再びしばしの沈黙があった. **2** ADV 副詞 You use **again** to indicate that something is now in a particular state or place that it used to be in. もとの状態に戻って [ADV after v] □ He opened his attaché case, removed a folder, then closed it again. 書類かばんを開けてフォルダを取り出すと元どおりかばんを閉じた. **3** ADV 副詞 You can use **again** when you want to point out that there is a similarity between the subject that you are talking about now and a previous subject. また [ADV cl] □ Again the pregnancy was very similar to my previous two. 今回の妊娠もこれまで2回の妊娠と非常に似ていた. **4** ADV 副詞 You can use **again** in expressions such as **but again**, **then again**, and **there again** when you want to introduce a remark that contrasts with or weakens something that you have just said. その一方で [ADV with cl] □ You may be happy to buy imitation leather, and then again, you may wonder what you're getting for your money. 合成皮革の製品を気に入って買おうとしたとたん, 今度は値段に見合う値打ちがあるのか気になってくることがある. **5** ADV 副詞 You can add **again** to the end of your question when you are asking someone to tell you something that you have forgotten or that they have already told you. でしたっけ [SPOKEN 口語] [cl ADV] □ Sorry, what's your name again? すみません, お名前は何とおっしゃいましたっけ. **6** ADV 副詞 You use **again** in expressions such as **half as much again** when you are indicating how much greater one amount is than another amount that you have just mentioned or are about to mention. さらに…だけ [BRIT 英国英語] [amount ADV] □ A similar wine from France would cost you half as much again. 同じようなフランスワインだったら値段は1倍半する. **7** PHRASE 句 You can use **again and again** or **time and again** to emphasize that something happens many times. 何度も何度も [EMPHASIS 強調] □ He would go over his work again and again until he felt he had it right. 彼は納得がいくまで何度も繰り返して課題を見直すことがよくありました. **8** now and again → see now **9** once again → see once

against /əˈgɛnst, əˈgeɪnst/

> In addition to the uses shown below, **against** is used in phrasal verbs such as "come up against," "guard against," and "hold against."

> 下記の用法に加えて, **against** は come up against, guard against, hold against のような句動詞に使われる.

1 PREP 前置詞 If one thing is leaning or pressing **against** another, it is touching it. もたれて □ She leaned against him. 彼女は彼に寄りかかった. □ On a table pushed against a wall there were bottles of beer and wine. 壁際にぴったり寄せたテーブルにはビールとワインのびんが置かれていた. **2** PREP 前置詞 If you are **against** something such as a plan, policy, or system, you think it is wrong, bad, or stupid. 反対して □ Taxes are unpopular – it is understandable that voters are against them. 税金は人気がないものだが, 有権者が税金を嫌がる気持ちもよく分かる. □ Joan was very much against commencing drug treatment. ジョーンは薬物療法を始めることに大反対した. ● ADV 副詞 **Against** is also an adverb. 反対して [ADV after v] □ The vote for the suspension of the party was 283 in favor with 29 against. その政党の活動を停止するかどうかは投票の結果賛成283票に対し反対29票でした. **3** PREP 前置詞 If you compete **against** someone in a game, you try to beat them. 対戦して □ This is the first of two games against Denver in the next five days. ここ5日間に対デンバー戦が2試合行われるが, これはその最初の試合である. **4** PREP 前置詞 If you take action **against** someone or something, you try to harm them. 対抗して □ Security forces are still using violence against opponents of the government. 治安部隊は今なお反政府勢力に対し暴力を行使しています. **5** PREP 前置詞 If you take action **against** a possible future event, you try to prevent it. 予防して □ Experts have been discussing how to improve the fight against crime. 専門家たちはどうしたら犯罪を減らせるかについて議論してきた. **6** PREP 前置詞 If you do something **against** someone's wishes, advice, or orders, you do not do what they want you to do or tell you to do. 逆らって □ He discharged himself from the hospital against the advice of doctors. 彼は医者の忠告も聞かずに退院した. **7** PREP 前置詞 If you do something in order to protect yourself **against** something unpleasant or harmful, you do something that will make its effects on you less serious if it happens. 備えて □ Any business needs insurance against ordinary risks such as fire, flood, and breakage. どのような業務でも, 火災, 洪水, 傷害など通常起こりうる危険に備えた保険が必要がある. **8** PREP 前置詞 If something is **against** the law or **against** the rules, there is a law or a rule which says that you must not do it. 違反して □ It is against the law to detain you against your will for any length of time. どれだけの時間であっても相手の意思に反して拘束するのは違法行為である. **9** PREP 前置詞 If you are moving **against** a current, tide, or wind, you are moving in the opposite direction to it. 逆らって □ ...swimming upstream against the current. 流れに逆らって上流へ泳いでいる. **10** PREP 前置詞 If something happens or is considered **against** a particular background of events, it is considered in relation to those events, because those events are relevant to it. 背景として □ The profits rise was achieved against a backdrop of falling metal prices. 収益拡大の背景には金属価格の下落がある. **11** PREP 前置詞 If something is measured or valued **against** something else, it is measured or valued by comparing it with the other thing. 対照して □ Our policies have to be judged against a clear test: will it improve the standard of education? 政策の評価にあたっては, 教育水準の向上に寄与するかどうかという明確な基準にしたがって判断すべきである. **12** PREP 前置詞 The odds **against** something happening are the chances or odds that it will not happen. 反対の [n PREP] □ The odds against him surviving are incredible. 彼が助かる見込みはほとんどない. ● ADV 副詞 **Against** is also an adverb. 反対の [ADV after v] □ What were the odds against? そうならなかった可能性はどれくらいあったのか. **13** PHRASE 句 If you **have** something **against** someone or something, you dislike them. 嫌いになる理由がある □ Have you got something against women, Les? レス, 女嫌いになる何かわけでもあるの? **14** up against → see up **15** against the clock → see clock

age /eɪdʒ/ (ages, aging or ageing, aged) **1** N-VAR 可変性名詞 Your **age** is the number of years that you have lived. 年齢 □ She has a nephew who is just ten years of age. 彼女にはまだ10歳のおいがいる. □ At the age of sixteen he qualified for a place at the University of North Carolina. 彼は16歳でノースカロライナ大学への入学を果たした. **2** N-VAR 可変性名詞 The **age** of a thing is the number of years since it was made. 年数 □ In the room looks in keeping with the age of the building. 部屋にあるものすべてが古い建物とうまく調和している. **3** N-UNCOUNT 不可算名詞 **Age** is the state of being old or the process of becoming older. 老齢; 老化 □ Perhaps he has grown wiser with age. もしかしたら彼は年を重ねるより賢くなったのかもしれない. □ This cologne, like wine, improves with age. このオーデコロンはワインのように年を経るごとに香りがよくなる. **4** V-T/V-I 他動詞/自動詞 When someone **ages**, or when something **ages** them, they seem much older and less strong or less alert. 老けさせる [他動詞], 年をとる [自動詞] □ He had always looked so young, but he seemed to have aged in the last few months. これまでずっと若々しかった彼だが, ここ数か月で老けたような気がした. **5** N-COUNT 可算名詞 An **age** is a period in history. 時代 □ ...the age of steam and steel. 蒸気機関と鉄鋼業の時代. **6** N-COUNT 可算名詞 You can say **an age** or **ages** to mean a very long time. 長い間 [INFORMAL くだけた] □ He waited what seemed an age. 彼はずいぶん長い間待った気がした. **7** → see also **aged**, **aging**, **middle age** → see Picture Dictionary: **age**

Picture Dictionary — age

infant   toddler   teenager / adolescent   woman   man   senior citizen

CHILD	ADULT	
YOUNG	MIDDLE AGED	ELDERLY

aged

> Pronounced /eɪdʒd/ for meaning ▪, and /eɪdʒɪd/ for meanings ▪ and ▪.
>
> ▪ の意味では /eɪdʒd/ と, ▪ ▪ と の意味では /eɪdʒɪd/と発音される.

▪ ADJ 形容詞 You use **aged** followed by a number to say how old someone is. 一歳 □ *Alan has two children, aged eleven and nine.* アランには11歳と9歳になる2人の子供がいる. ▪ ADJ 形容詞 **Aged** means very old. 年とった [ADJ n] □ *She has an aged parent who's capable of being very difficult.* 彼女にはときどき気難しくなる年老いた親がいる. ▪ N-PLURAL 複数名詞 You can refer to all people who are very old as **the aged**. 老人, 高齢者 □ *The American Society on Aging provides resource services to those dealing with the aged.* アメリカ老年問題協会では, 日頃から高齢者に接する人たちに情報を提供している. ▪ → see also **middle-aged**

age|ing → see **age, aging**

agen|cy /eɪdʒənsi/ (agencies) ▪ N-COUNT 可算名詞 An **agency** is a business that provides a service on behalf of other businesses. 代理店 [BUSINESS 実業] □ *We had to hire maids through an agency.* ルームキーパーを雇うのに仲介業者を通す必要があった. ▪ → see also **ad agency, employment agency** ▪ N-COUNT 可算名詞 An **agency** is a government organization responsible for a certain area of administration. 行政機関 □ *She is calling for a collaboration of local, state and federal agencies to deal with the problem.* 彼女は地元, 州, 連邦の各機関が協調しながらこの問題に対処するように求めている.

→ see **advertising**

agen|da /ədʒɛndə/ (agendas) ▪ N-COUNT 可算名詞 You can refer to the political issues that are important at a particular time as an **agenda**. 政治問題 □ *Does television set the agenda on foreign policy?* 何が重要な外交問題なのかを決めているのはテレビなのでしょうか. ▪ → see also **hidden agenda** ▪ N-COUNT 可算名詞 An **agenda** is a list of the items that have to be discussed at a meeting. 議題 □ *This is sure to be an item on the agenda next week.* この問題は間違いなく来週の会議の議題として取り上げられる.

<table>
<tr><td colspan="2">Word Partnership   agenda は次の語句と使われる:</td></tr>
<tr><td>ADJ.</td><td>domestic/legislative/political agenda, hidden agenda ▪</td></tr>
<tr><td>V.</td><td>set the agenda ▪ ▪</td></tr>
<tr><td>PREP.</td><td>on the agenda ▪</td></tr>
</table>

agent /eɪdʒənt/ (agents) ▪ N-COUNT 可算名詞 An **agent** is a person who looks after someone else's business affairs or does business on their behalf. 代理人, 仲介者 [BUSINESS 実業] □ *You are*

buying direct, rather than through an agent. 仲介業者を通さずに直接購入している. ▪ → see also **travel agent** ▪ N-COUNT 可算名詞 An **agent** in the arts world is a person who gets work for an actor or musician, or who sells the work of a writer to publishers. マネジャー; 作家エージェント □ *My literary agent thinks it is not unreasonable to expect $500,000 in total.* 作家エージェントによれば, 総額50万ドルという数字は高すぎることはないという. ▪ N-COUNT 可算名詞 An **agent** is a person who works for a country's secret service. スパイ, 諜報員 □ *All these years he's been an agent for the East.* 彼はこれまで長年にわたって共産圏のスパイをしてきた. ▪ N-COUNT 可算名詞 A chemical that has a particular effect or is used for a particular purpose can be referred to as a particular kind of **agent**. 薬品, 薬剤 □ *...the bleaching agent in white flour.* 精白小麦粉に含まれる漂白剤.

→ see **concert**

age of con|sent N-SING 単数名詞 The **age of consent** is the age at which a person can legally agree to having a sexual relationship. 性行為同意年齢 ['the' N] □ *He was under the age of consent.* 彼は同意年齢に達していなかった.

age-old ADJ 形容詞 An **age-old** story, tradition, or problem has existed for many generations or centuries. 代々にわたる [WRITTEN 書き言葉] □ *This age-old struggle for control had led to untold bloody wars.* この長年にわたる支配権争いによって, 血なまぐさい戦争が幾度となく繰り返されてきた.

ag|gra|vate /ægrəveɪt/ (aggravates, aggravating, aggravated) ▪ V-T 他動詞 If someone or something **aggravates** a situation, they make it worse. 悪化させる □ *Stress and lack of sleep can aggravate the situation.* ストレスと睡眠不足が加わるとさらに状況は悪くなります. ▪ V-T 他動詞 If someone or something **aggravates** you, they make you annoyed. いらいらさせる [INFORMAL くだけた] □ *What aggravates you most about this country?* この国の問題でいちばん頭にくることは何ですか. ● **ag|gra|vat|ing** ADJ 形容詞 いらいらさせる □ *You don't realize how aggravating you can be.* どれほど周りをいらいらさせることがあるか分かっちゃいないだろう. ● **ag|gra|va|tion** /ægrəveɪʃ°n/ (aggravations) N-VAR 可変性名詞 腹立たしさ □ *I just couldn't take the aggravation.* 腹立たしくてどうにも我慢ならなかった.

ag|gre|gate /ægrɪgɪt/ ADJ 形容詞 An **aggregate** amount or score is made up of several smaller amounts or scores added together. 総計の [ADJ n] □ *The rate of growth of GNP will depend upon the rate of growth of aggregate demand.* 経済成長率は総需要の成長率に左右される.

ag|gres|sion /əgrɛʃ°n/ (aggressions) ▪ N-UNCOUNT 不可算名詞 **Aggression** is a quality of anger and determination that makes you ready to attack other people. 攻撃性 □ *Aggression is by no means a male-only trait.* 攻撃性は何も男性にだけ見られる特徴ではない. ▪ N-VAR 可変性名詞 **Aggression** is violent and attacking

A

behavior. 攻撃 ❏ ...the threat of massive military aggression. 大規模な軍事攻撃の恐れ.
→ see **anger**

Word Partnership	aggression は次の語句と使われる:

N.	**act** of aggression 1
PREP.	aggression **against** 2
ADJ.	**military** aggression, **physical** aggression 2

ag|gres|sive /əgrɛsɪv/ 1 ADJ 形容詞 An **aggressive** person or animal has a quality of anger and determination that makes them ready to attack other people. 攻撃的な ❏ Some children are much more aggressive than others. 子供のなかにはけんかっ早い子がいる. ❏ These fish are very aggressive. この魚はどう猛である. ● **ag|gres|sive|ly** ADV 副詞 攻撃的に ❏ They'll react aggressively. 彼らは攻撃的な行動に出るでしょう. 2 ADJ 形容詞 People who are **aggressive** in their work or other activities behave in a forceful way because they are very eager to succeed. 積極的な ❏ He is respected as a very aggressive and competitive executive. 彼は精力的で競争心の旺盛な経営者として尊敬を集めている. ● **ag|gres|sive|ly** ADV 副詞 積極的に ❏ ...countries noted for aggressively pursuing energy efficiency. 省エネルギーを積極的に推進しているとして知られる国々.

ag|gres|sor /əgrɛsər/ (**aggressors**) N-COUNT 可算名詞 The **aggressor** in a fight or battle is the person, group, or country that starts it. 攻撃者 ❏ They have been the aggressors in this conflict. 彼らはこの争いでは常に攻撃側でした.

Word Link	griev ≈ heavy, serious : ag**griev**ed, **griev**ance, **griev**e

ag|grieved /əgriːvd/ ADJ 形容詞 If you feel **aggrieved**, you feel upset and angry because of the way in which you have been treated. 不当な扱いを受けた, 立腹した ❏ I really feel aggrieved at this sort of thing. 私にそんなことをするなんて本当に腹立たしいわ.

aghast /əgɑːst, əgæst/ ADJ 形容詞 If you are **aghast**, you are filled with horror and surprise. (恐怖や驚嘆のあまり) 仰天して [FORMAL 形式ばった] [ADJ after v] ❏ While she watched, aghast, his eyes glazed over as his life flowed away. 彼女がおびえて見守る中, 彼の命が退潮するにつれ目の生気も失われた.

ag|ile /ædʒəl/ 1 ADJ 形容詞 Someone who is **agile** can move quickly and easily. 機敏な ❏ At 20 years old he was not as strong, as fast, as agile as he is now. 二十の時, 彼は今ほど頑健で速く敏捷ではなかった. ● **agil|ity** /ədʒɪlɪti/ N-UNCOUNT 不可算名詞 敏捷さ ❏ She blinked in surprise at his agility. 彼女は彼の敏捷さにびっくりして目をしばたたいた. 2 ADJ 形容詞 If you have an **agile** mind, you think quickly and intelligently. 頭の切れる ❏ She was quick-witted and had an extraordinarily agile mind. 彼女は機転が利くし, とりわけ頭の切れる人だった. ● **agil|ity** N-UNCOUNT 不可算名詞 (頭の回転の) 鋭さ ❏ His intellect and mental agility have never been in doubt. これまで彼の知性や思考の鋭さが疑問視されることはなかった.

ag|ing /eɪdʒɪŋ/ also ageing 1 ADJ 形容詞 Someone or something that is **aging** is becoming older and less healthy or efficient. 老化している ❏ John lives with his aging mother. ジョンは年を取りつつある母親と暮らしている. 2 N-UNCOUNT 不可算名詞 **Aging** is the process of becoming old or becoming worn out. 老化 ❏ The only signs of aging are the flecks of grey that speckle his dark hair. 彼に現れた唯一の老化現象は, 黒髪にぽつぽつと混じる白髪だけだ.

agi|tate /ædʒɪteɪt/ (**agitates, agitating, agitated**) 1 V-I 自動詞 If people **agitate for** something, they protest or take part in political activity in order to get it. (世論を) 扇動する ❏ The women who worked in these mills had begun to agitate for better conditions. これらの工場で働いていた女性工員たちが, 労働条件改善に立ち上がったのです. 2 V-T 他動詞 If you **agitate** something, you shake it so that it moves about. かきまぜる ❏ All you need to do is gently agitate the water with a finger or paintbrush. 指か筆でその水をそっとかきまぜればいいのです. [FORMAL 形式ばった] 3 V-T 他動詞 If something **agitates** you, it worries and makes you unable to think clearly or calmly. (心を) かき乱す ❏ Carl and Martin may inherit their grandmother's possessions when she dies. The thought agitates her. 祖母の死後, カールとマーティンが遺産を相続するだろう. そう考えると彼女の心は乱れた.

agi|tat|ed /ædʒɪteɪtɪd/ ADJ 形容詞 If someone is **agitated**, they are very worried or upset, and show this in their behavior, movements, or voice. 動揺している ❏ Susan seemed agitated about something. スーザンは何かに動揺しているようだった.

agi|ta|tion /ædʒɪteɪʃən/ N-UNCOUNT 不可算名詞 If someone is in a state of **agitation**, they are very worried or upset, and show this in their behavior, movements, or voice. 興奮 ❏ Danny returned to Father's house in a state of intense agitation. ダニーはとても興奮して父親の家に戻ってきた.

ag|nos|tic /ægnɒstɪk/ (**agnostics**) N-COUNT 可算名詞 An **agnostic** believes that it is not possible to know whether God exists or not. Compare **atheist**. 不可知論者 ❏ For the last twenty-three or twenty-four years I have been an agnostic. 23, 4年前から私は不

可知論者である.
→ see **religion**

ag|nos|ti|cism /ægnɒstɪsɪzəm/ N-UNCOUNT 不可算名詞 **Agnosticism** is the belief that it is not possible to say definitely whether or not there is a God. Compare **atheism**. 不可知論

ago /əgoʊ/ ADV 副詞 You use **ago** when you are referring to past time. For example, if something happened one year **ago**, it is one year since it happened. If it happened a long time **ago**, it is a long time since it happened. (今から) 一前に ❏ He was killed a few days ago in a skiing accident. 彼は数日前, スキーの事故で亡くなった. ❏ The meeting is the first ever between the two sides since the war there began 14 years ago. その会議は, そこで14年前に戦争が始まって以来, 両陣営が初めて開くものです.

You only use **ago** when you are talking about a period of time measured back from the present. If you are talking about a period measured back from some earlier time, you use **before** or **previously**. ❏ He had died a month before... She had rented the apartment some fourteen months previously. You use **for** to say how long a period lasts in the past, present, or future, or how much time passes without something happening. ❏ She slept for eight hours... He will be away for three weeks... I hadn't seen him for four years. You use **since** to say when a period of time started. ❏ She has been with the group since it began. ...the first civilian president since the coup 17 years ago. You also use **since** to refer to the last time that something happened, or to how much time passes without something happening. ❏ She hadn't eaten since breakfast... It was a long time since she had been to church.

Word Link	agon ≈ struggling : **agon**ize, ant**agon**ist, prot**agon**ist

ago|nize /ægənaɪz/ (**agonizes, agonizing, agonized**) V-I 自動詞 If you **agonize over** something, you feel very anxious about it and spend a long time thinking about it. 悩む ❏ Perhaps he was agonizing over the moral issues involved. おそらく彼はそれにかかわる道徳的な問題で悩んでいたのだろう.

ago|niz|ing /ægənaɪzɪŋ/ 1 ADJ 形容詞 Something that is **agonizing** causes you to feel great physical or mental pain. 苦痛な ❏ He did not wish to die the agonizing death of his mother and brother. 彼は母や兄のように苦しみながら死にたくはなかった. 2 ADJ 形容詞 **Agonizing** decisions and choices are very difficult to make. 苦渋の ❏ He now faced an agonizing decision about his immediate future. 今, 彼は自分の将来について苦渋の決断を迫られていた.

ago|ny /ægəni/ N-UNCOUNT 不可算名詞 **Agony** is great physical or mental pain. 苦痛 ❏ A new machine may save thousands of animals from the agony of drug tests. 新しい機械が多くの動物を薬剤試験の苦痛から解放する可能性がある.

agree /əgriː/ (**agrees, agreeing, agreed**) 1 V-RECIP 相互動詞 If people **agree with** each other about something, they have the same opinion about it or say that they have the same opinion. 合意する, 賛成する ❏ Both have agreed on the need for the money. 双方とも資金の必要性で一致した. ❏ So we both agree there's a problem? じゃあ, 何か問題だってことでいいよね. ❏ I agree with you that the open system is by far the best. オープンな制度が断然に優れているというご意見に賛成です. ❏ "It's appalling." —"It is. I agree." 「ひどいもんだな」「まったくだよ」❏ I agree with every word you've just said. すべてあなたのおっしゃるとおりですね. 2 V-RECIP 相互動詞 If people **agree on** something, they all decide to accept or do something. 合意に達する ❏ The warring sides have agreed on an unconditional ceasefire. 交戦当事者双方は無条件停戦の合意に達しました. 3 V-RECIP 相互動詞 In grammar, if a word **agrees with** a noun or pronoun, it has a form that is appropriate to the number or gender of the noun or pronoun. For example, in "He hates it," the singular verb agrees with the singular pronoun "he." (文法上の性や数が) 一致する [V 'with' n, pl-n V] 4 V-T/V-I 他動詞/自動詞 If you **agree to** do something, you say that you will do it. If you **agree to** a proposal, you accept it. 承諾する ❏ He agreed to pay me for the drawings. 彼は私に図面代を払うことを承諾しました. 5 V-I 自動詞 If you **agree with** an action or suggestion, you approve of it. 認める ❏ You didn't want to ask anybody whether they agreed with what you were doing. 君は自分がやっていることが認められるかどうかを人に聞きたくなかったんだ. 6 V-RECIP 相互動詞 If one account of an event or one set of figures **agrees with** another, the two accounts or sets of figures are the same or are consistent with each other. 一致する ❏ His second statement agrees with facts as stated by the other witnesses. 彼の二度目の陳述は, 他の証人が陳述した事実と一致した. 7 PHRASE 句 If two people who are arguing about something **agree to disagree** or **agree to differ**, they decide to stop arguing because neither of them is going to change their opinion. 見解の不一致を認める ❏ You and I are going to have to agree to disagree then. それじゃあ君と僕では意見が合うはずなんてないな. 8 → see also **agreed**

Thesaurus

agree また次を参照：

v.   concur; (ant.) disagree **1**
    consent, OK/okay **4**

agree|able /əgríəbᵊl/ **1** ADJ 形容詞 If something is **agreeable**, it is pleasant and you enjoy it. 快い □ *...workers in more agreeable and better paid occupations.* より良い環境や給与条件で働く人たち. **2** ADJ 形容詞 If someone is **agreeable**, they are pleasant and try to please people. 感じのよい □ *...sharing a bottle of wine with an agreeable companion.* 感じのよい仲間とワインを飲む

agreed /əgríd/ **1** ADJ 形容詞 If people are **agreed on** something, they have reached a joint decision on it or have the same opinion about it. 意見が一致して [v-link ADJ] □ *Okay, so are we agreed on going north?* よし，じゃあ，みんな北に向かっていいね. **2** → see also **agree**

Word Link

ment ≈ state, condition : agreement, management, movement

agree|ment /əgrímənt/ **(agreements)** **1** N-COUNT 可算名詞 An **agreement** is a formal decision about future action that is made by two or more countries, groups, or people. 協定 □ *It looks as though a compromise agreement has now been reached.* どうやら妥協による協定が結ばれたようです. **2** N-UNCOUNT 不可算名詞 **Agreement on** something is a joint decision that a particular course of action should be taken. 合意 □ *A spokesman said, however, that the two men had not reached agreement on the issues discussed.* しかし，報道官は，2人が議論された件で合意に至らなかったと述べた. **3** N-UNCOUNT 不可算名詞 **Agreement** with someone means having the same opinion as they have. 同意 □ *The judge kept nodding in agreement.* 裁判官は同意してうなずいていた. **4** PHRASE 句 If you are **in agreement with** someone, you have the same opinion as they have. 同意して **5** N-UNCOUNT 不可算名詞 **Agreement** to a course of action means allowing it to happen or giving it your approval. 同意 □ *The clinic doctor will then write to your doctor to get his agreement.* 担当医に同意を求める手紙を出すでしょう. **6** PHRASE 句 If you are **in agreement with** a plan or proposal, you approve of it. 賛同して

Word Partnership

agreement は次の語句と使われる：

N.   **terms of an** agreement, **trade** agreement, **peace** agreement **1**
V.   **enter into an** agreement, **sign an** agreement **1**
  reach an agreement **1** **2** **4**

ag|ri|busi|ness /ǽgribɪznɪs/ N-UNCOUNT 不可算名詞 **Agribusiness** is the various businesses that produce, sell, and distribute farm products, especially on a large scale. 農業関連産業 [BUSINESS 実業] □ *Many of the old agricultural collectives are now being turned into agribusiness corporations.* 古くからの農業共同体の多くが，今では農業関連産業に転じ始めています.

ag|ri|cul|tur|al /ǽgrɪkʌltʃərəl/ ADJ 形容詞 **Agricultural** means involving or relating to agriculture. 農業の □ *Farmers struggling for survival strip the forests for agricultural land.* 生き残りをかけた農家が，農地獲得のために森を裸にしています.
→ see **farm**

ag|ri|cul|ture /ǽgrɪkʌltʃər/ N-UNCOUNT 不可算名詞 **Agriculture** is farming and the methods that are used to raise and take care of crops and animals. 農業 □ *Strong both in industry and agriculture, Ukraine produces much of the grain for the nation.* 確固とした農工業を持つウクライナは，穀物のほとんどを国内自給しています.
→ see **industry**

aground /əgráʊnd/ ADV 副詞 If a ship runs **aground**, it touches the ground in a shallow part of a river, lake, or the sea, and gets stuck. 座礁して [ADV after v] □ *The ship ran aground where there should have been a depth of 35 ft.* その船は，深さが35フィートあったはずの場所で座礁した.

ah /ɑ/ EXCLAM 感嘆詞 **Ah** is used in writing to represent a noise that people make in conversation, for example, to acknowledge or draw attention to something, or to express surprise, relief or disappointment. ああ [FEELINGS 感情] □ *Ah, so many questions, so little time.* ああ，問題が山積みなのに時間がないよ.

ahead

❶ ADVERB USES
❷ PREPOSITION USES

❶ ahead /əhɛ́d/

In addition to the uses shown below, **ahead** is used in phrasal verbs such as "get ahead," "go ahead," and "press ahead."

下記の用法に加えて，**ahead** は **get ahead, go ahead, press ahead** のような句動詞に使われる.

1 ADV 副詞 Something that is **ahead** is in front of you. If you look **ahead**, you look directly in front of you. 前を □ *Brett looked straight ahead.* ブレットはまっすぐ前を見た. □ *The road ahead was now blocked solid.* 前方は流れの止まった大渋滞だった. **2** ADV 副詞 You use **ahead** with verbs such as "push," "move," and "forge" to indicate that a plan, program, or organization is making fast progress. 進めて [ADV after v] □ *Western countries were moving ahead with plans to send financial aid to all of the former Soviet republics.* 西側諸国は旧ソ連の共和国全てに財政支援を行う計画を推し進めていた. **3** ADV 副詞 If you are **ahead** in your work or achievements, you have made more progress than you expected to and are performing well. (予定，計画など) 上回って □ *First half profits have charged ahead from $127.6m to $134.2m.* 上半期の利益は1億2760万ドルから1億3420万ドルに伸長した. **4** ADV 副詞 If a person or a team is **ahead** in a competition, they are winning. 優勢で □ *Australia was ahead throughout the game.* オーストラリアは試合中終始優勢でした. □ *The Communists are comfortably ahead in the opinion polls.* 世論調査では共産党がかなりの優勢です. **5** ADV 副詞 **Ahead** also means in the future. この先 □ *A much bigger battle is ahead for the president.* 議長にはさらに大きな戦いが控えている. **6** ADV 副詞 If you prepare or plan something **ahead**, you do it some time before a future event so that everything is ready for that event to take place. 前もって [ADV after v] □ *The government wants figures that help it to administer its policies and plan ahead.* 政府は，政策や計画の実施に先だって有用な数字を望んでいる. **7** ADV 副詞 If you go **ahead**, or if you go on **ahead**, you go in front of someone who is going to the same place so that you arrive there some time before they do. 先に [ADV after v] □ *I went ahead and waited with Sean.* 私は先に行って，ショーンと待っていた.

❷ ahead
⇨ **Please look at category 6 to see if the expression you are looking for is shown under another headword.** **1** PHRASE 句 If someone is **ahead of** you, they are directly in front of you. If someone is moving **ahead of** you and you and moving in the same direction. 前方に □ *I saw a man in a blue jacket thirty yards ahead of me.* 青いジャケットを着た男が30ヤード前方に見えた. **2** PHRASE 句 If an event or period of time lies **ahead of** you, it is going to happen or take place soon or in the future. 前途に (時間的に) □ *I tried to think about all the problems that were ahead of me tomorrow.* 私は明日起こりうる全ての問題について考えようとしていた. □ *Heather had been awake all night thinking about the future that lay ahead of her.* ヘザーは自分の将来をあれこれ考えて一晩中起きていた. **3** PHRASE 句 In a competition, if a person or team does something **ahead of** someone else, they do it before the second person or team. 〜より先に □ *Robert Millar finished 1 minute and 35 seconds ahead of the Frenchman.* ロバート・ミラーはフランス人選手より1分35秒早くゴールしました. **4** PHRASE 句 If something happens **ahead of** schedule or **ahead of** time, it happens earlier than was planned. 〜より早く □ *The election was held six months ahead of schedule.* 選挙は予定より6か月早く実施されました. **5** PHRASE 句 If someone is **ahead of** someone else, they have made more progress and are more advanced in what they are doing. 勝って □ *Henry generally stayed ahead of the others in the academic subjects.* ヘンリーは勉強では概して他の者より先に進んでいた. **6 one step ahead of** someone or something → see **step** **7 ahead of** your **time** → see **time**

Word Partnership

ahead は次の語句と使われる：

ADV.   **straight** ahead **❶ 1**
V.   **lie** ahead, **look** ahead **❶ 1 5**
  move ahead **❶ 2**
  get ahead **❶ 4**
  plan ahead **❶ 6**
  go ahead **❶ 7**
PREP.   ahead **of schedule/time ❷ 2 3**
  in the days/months/years ahead **❷ 2 5**

aid /éɪd/ **(aids, aiding, aided)** **1** N-UNCOUNT 不可算名詞 **Aid** is money, equipment, or services that are provided for people, countries, or organizations who need them but cannot provide them for themselves. 支援 □ *...regular flights carrying humanitarian aid to Cambodia.* カンボジアへ人道支援を運ぶ定期航空便. □ *They have already pledged billions of dollars in aid.* 彼らはすでに数10億ドルの支援を誓約している. **2** N-UNCOUNT 不可算名詞 If you perform a task **with the aid of** something, you need or use that thing to perform that task. 助け □ *He succeeded with the aid of a completely new method he discovered.* 彼は自分が発見した斬新な方式を用いて成功を収めた. **3** V-T 他動詞 To **aid** a country, organization, or person means to provide them with money, equipment, or services that they need. 支援する □ *...U.S. efforts to aid Kurdish refugees.* 米国のクルド難民支援への取り組み. ●**-aided** COMB IN ADJ 形容詞の複合

ーの援助による ❏...*government-aided research*. 政府助成研究. **4** V-T 他動詞 To **aid** someone means to help or assist them. 助ける ❏...*a software system to aid managers in advanced decision-making*. 高度な意思決定を補助するソフトウェア・システム. [WRITTEN 書き言葉] ●N-UNCOUNT 不可算名詞 **Aid** is also a noun. 助け ❏ *He was forced to turn for aid to his former enemy*. 彼はかつての敵に助けを求めざるを得なかった. **5** V-T/V-I 他動詞/自動詞 If something **aids** a process, it makes it easier or more likely to happen. 促進する [他動詞], 助けとなる [自動詞] ❏ *The survey suggests that the export sector will continue to aid the economic recovery*. 調査によると, 輸出部門が引き続き経済回復を促進すると予測されています. ❏ *Calcium may aid in the prevention of colon cancer*. カルシウムには大腸がんの予防効果があると期待されています. **6** N-COUNT 可算名詞 An **aid** is an object, device, or technique that makes something easier to do. 助けとなるもの ❏ *The book is an invaluable aid to teachers of literature*. その本は文学教師には非常に貴重な参考書だ. **7** → see also **first aid** **8** PHRASE 句 If you **come** or **go to** someone's **aid**, you try to help them when they are in danger or difficulty. 助けに来る, 助けに行く ❏ *Dr. Fox went to the aid of the dying man despite having been injured in the crash*. フォックス先生は自分自身の衝突事故で負傷していたが, 瀕死の男性を助けに行った.

aide /eɪd/ (**aides**) **1** N-COUNT 可算名詞 An **aide** is an assistant to someone who has an important job, especially in government or in the armed forces. 補佐官 ❏ *A close aide to the prime minister repeated that Israel would never accept it*. イスラエルがそれをのむことはないと, 首相側近は繰り返した. **2** → see also **teacher's aide**

AIDS /eɪdz/ N-UNCOUNT 可算名詞 **AIDS** is a disease that destroys the natural system of protection that the body has against other diseases. **AIDS** is an abbreviation for **acquired immune deficiency syndrome**. エイズ ❏...*people suffering from AIDS*. エイズを患う人たち

Word Partnership   *AIDS* は次の語句と使われる:

N.	AIDS **activists**, AIDS **epidemic**, AIDS **patient**, AIDS **research**, **spread** of AIDS, AIDS **victims**
V.	**infected** with AIDS

ail|ing /eɪlɪŋ/ ADJ 形容詞 An **ailing** organization or society is in difficulty and is becoming weaker. 不振の ❏ *The rise in overseas sales is good news for the ailing American economy*. 外国での販売増は, 不振にあえぐアメリカ経済には良いニュースです.

ail|ment /eɪlmənt/ (**ailments**) N-COUNT 可算名詞 An **ailment** is an illness, especially one that is not very serious. (慢性的な軽い) 病気 ❏ *The pharmacist can assist you with the treatment of common ailments*. 一般的な病気の治療なら薬剤師があなたのお役に立ちます.

aim /eɪm/ (**aims, aiming, aimed**) **1** V-I 自動詞 If you **aim for** something or **aim to** do something, you plan or hope to achieve it. ねらう ❏ *He said he would aim for the 100-meter world record at the world championships in August*. 彼は8月の世界選手権で100メートルの世界記録をねらいたいとコメントした. ❏ *Businesses will have to aim at long-term growth*. 各企業は長期的成長を目標にしなければならなくなるだろう. ❏ *The program aims to educate and prepare students for a challenging career*. そのプログラムは, 生徒たちが訓練の結果やりがいのある仕事に就けるようにするものです. **2** V-I 自動詞 If you **aim to** do something, you decide or want to do it. 意図する, ーしたいと思う [自動詞] ❏ *I didn't aim to get caught*. つかまるつもりはなかった. [AM 米国英語, INFORMAL くだけた] **3** V-T 他動詞 If your actions or remarks **are aimed at** a particular person or group, you intend that the person or group should notice them and be influenced by them. (言葉や注意に) 向ける [usu passive] ❏ *His message was aimed at the undecided middle ground of Israeli politics*. 彼のメッセージはイスラエルの無党派に向けられたものだった. **4** V-T/V-I 他動詞/自動詞 If you **aim** a weapon or object at something or someone, you point it toward them before firing or throwing it. ねらう ❏ *When he appeared again, he was aiming the rifle at Wade*. 次に現れたとき, 彼はライフルでウエイドをねらっていた. ❏...*a missile aimed at the arms factory*. 兵器工場に照準を定めたミサイル. **5** V-T 他動詞 If you **aim** a kick or punch at someone, you try to kick or punch them. ねらう ❏ *They set on him, punching him in the face and aiming kicks at his shins*. 彼らは, 彼の顔を殴ったり, すねをけったりして攻撃した. **6** N-COUNT 可算名詞 The **aim** of something that you do is the purpose for which you do it or the result that it is intended to achieve. 目的 ❏ *The aim of the festival is to increase awareness of Hindu culture and traditions*. 祭は, ヒンドゥーの文化伝統への認識を高めることを目的としている. **7** V-T 他動詞 If an action or plan **is aimed at** achieving something, it is intended or planned to achieve it. 目標にする ❏ *The new measures are aimed at tightening existing sanctions*. 新しい措置は, 現行の制裁の強化が目標です. **8** N-SING 単数名詞 Your **aim** is your skill or action in pointing a weapon or other object at its target. 照準を定める ❏ *He stood with the gun gripped in his right hand and his left hand steadying his aim*. 彼は右手で銃を握り, 左手でしっかりと照準を定めて立っていた. **9** PHRASE 句 When you **take aim**, you point a weapon or object at someone or something, before firing or throwing it. ねらいを定める ❏ *She had spotted a man*

with a shotgun taking aim. 彼女は男がショットガンでねらっていると気づいていた.

Word Partnership   *aim* は次の語句と使われる:

PREP.	aim **for**, aim **to** **1**
	aim **at** **3**
	aim **of** **6**
ADJ.	**primary/sole/ultimate** aim **6**
V.	**take** aim **9**

Word Link   *less = without : aimless, harmless, worthless*

aim|less /eɪmləs/ ADJ 形容詞 A person or activity that is **aimless** has no clear purpose or plan. 目的のない ❏ *After several hours of aimless searching they were getting low on fuel*. 彼らはあてどなく数時間捜索した結果, 燃料切れになりつつあった. ●**aim|less|ly** ADV 副詞 [ADV after v] あてどなく ❏ *I wandered around aimlessly*. 私はあてどなく歩き回った.

ain't /eɪnt/ People sometimes use **ain't** instead of "am not," "aren't," "isn't," "haven't," and "hasn't." Many people consider this use to be incorrect. ain't は am not, aren't, isn't, haven't, hasn't などの代わりに使われるが, この用法を誤りとみなす人も多い. ❏ *Well, it's obvious, ain't it?* 見え透いてるじゃねえか. [DIALECT 方言, SPOKEN 口語]

air /ɛər/ (**airs, airing, aired**) **1** N-UNCOUNT 不可算名詞 **Air** is the mixture of gases that forms the Earth's atmosphere and that we breathe. 空気 ❏ *Drafts help to circulate air*. 通風装置は空気の循環を促す. ❏ *Keith opened the window and leaned out into the cold air*. キースは窓を開け, 冷たい外気に身を乗り出した. **2** N-UNCOUNT 不可算名詞 **Air** is used to refer to travel in aircraft. 航空交通 ❏ *Air travel will continue to grow at about 6% per year*. 航空機利用の旅行は, 約6%の年率で増加し続ける見込みだ. **3** N-SING 単数名詞 **The air** is the space around things or above the ground. 空 ❏ *Government troops broke up the protest by firing their guns in the air*. 政府軍は空砲を撃ってデモ隊を解散させた. **4** V-T 他動詞 If a broadcasting company **airs** a television or radio program, they show it on television or broadcast it on the radio. 放送する ❏ *Tonight PBS will air a documentary called "Democracy In Action."* PBSは今夜, ドキュメンタリー番組『戦う民主主義』を放送する. [mainly AM 主に米国英語] ●**air|ing** N-SING 単数名詞 放送 ❏...*the airing of a new television commercial that attacked the president's war record*. 大統領の戦歴を非難する新しいテレビコマーシャルの放送 **5** V-T 他動詞 If you **air** a room or building, you let fresh air into it. 換気する ❏ *One day a week her mother cleaned and aired each room*. 週に1度, 彼女のおかあさんは全ての部屋の掃除と換気を行った. **6** PHRASE 句 If you do something to **clear the air**, you do it in order to resolve any problems or disagreements that there might be. (疑惑や心配を) 解く ❏...*an inquiry just to clear the air and settle the facts of the case*. 疑惑を解き, 事件の真相を究明する公式調査. **7** PHRASE 句 If something is **in the air** it is felt to be present, but it is not talked about. 漂って (雰囲気などが) ❏ *There was great excitement in the air*. 大いなる興奮に包まれていた. **8** PHRASE 句 If someone is **on the air**, they are broadcasting on radio or television. If a program is **on the air**, it is being broadcast on radio or television. If it is **off the air**, it is not being broadcast. 放送中の ❏ *We go on the air, live, at 11:30 a.m.* 午前11時30分から生放送だ. **9** PHRASE 句 If someone or something disappears **into thin air**, they disappear completely. If someone or something appears **out of thin air**, they appear suddenly and mysteriously. 見えなくなって, どこからともなく ❏ *He had materialized out of thin air; I had not seen or heard him coming*. 彼はどこからともなく現れたんだよ. 姿も気配もまったくなかったのに.

→ see Word Web: **air**

→ see **erosion, flight, fly, respiratory, wind**

air|bag /ɛərbæg/ (**airbags**) also **air bag** N-COUNT 可算名詞 An **airbag** is a safety device in a car that automatically fills with air if the car crashes, and is designed to protect the people in the car when they are thrown forward in the crash. エアバッグ

→ see **car**

air base (**air bases**) also **airbase** N-COUNT 可算名詞 An **air base** is a center where military aircraft take off or land and are serviced, and where many of the center's staff live. 空軍基地 ❏...*the largest U.S. air base in Saudi Arabia*. サウジアラビア最大の米空軍基地.

air|borne /ɛərbɔrn/ **1** ADJ 形容詞 If an aircraft is **airborne**, it is in the air and flying. 飛行中の [v-link ADJ] ❏ *The pilot did manage to get airborne*. パイロットはなんとか浮上した. **2** ADJ 形容詞 **Airborne** troops use parachutes to get into enemy territory. 空挺 [ADJ n] ❏ *The allies landed thousands of airborne troops*. 連合軍は空挺部隊数千人を上陸させた. **3** ADJ 形容詞 **Airborne** means in the air or carried in the air. 空中を漂う ❏ *Many people are allergic to airborne pollutants such as pollen*. 多くの人が花粉などの空気中の浮遊物にアレルギー反応を示す.

→ see **pollution**

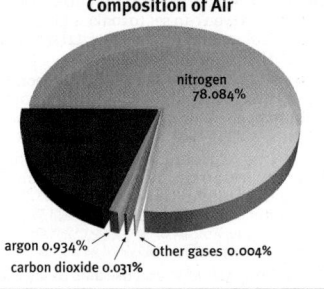

Word Web   air

The **air** we breathe contains seventeen different **gases**. Surprisingly, it is composed mostly of **nitrogen**, not **oxygen**. Recently, human activities have created imbalances in the earth's **atmosphere**. The widespread burning of coal and oil increased levels of **carbon dioxide** gas. Scientists believe this air **pollution** may be responsible for **global warming**. Certain chemical compounds used in air conditioners, agricultural processes, and manufacturing are the problem. With less protection from the sun, the air temperature rises. This leads to harmful effects on people, agriculture, animals, and the natural environment.

Composition of Air
nitrogen 78.084%
argon 0.934%   other gases 0.004%
carbon dioxide 0.031%

air-conditioned ADJ 形容詞 If a room or vehicle is **air-conditioned**, the air in it is kept cool and dry by means of a special machine. 冷暖房の効いた、エアコン付きの ❑ *...our new air-conditioned trains.* エアコン付きの新車

air-condition|ing N-UNCOUNT 不可算名詞 **Air-conditioning** is a method of providing buildings and vehicles with cool dry air. 空調

air|craft /ˈɛərkræft/ (aircraft)

Aircraft is both the singular and the plural form.

Aircraft は単数形でも複数形でもある。

N-COUNT 可算名詞 An **aircraft** is a vehicle that can fly, for example, an airplane or a helicopter. 航空機 ❑ *The return flight of the aircraft was delayed.* 航空機は帰路で遅れました。
→ see **fly**

air|field /ˈɛərfild/ (airfields) N-COUNT 可算名詞 An **airfield** is an area of ground where aircraft take off and land. It is smaller than an airport. 飛行場

air force (air forces) N-COUNT 可算名詞 An **air force** is the part of a country's armed forces that is concerned with fighting in the air. 空軍 ❑ *...the United States Air Force.* 米空軍

air|lift /ˈɛərlɪft/ (airlifts, airlifting, airlifted) 🄵 N-COUNT 可算名詞 An **airlift** is an operation to move people, troops, or goods by air, especially in a war or when land routes are closed. 空輸 ❑ *President Garcia has ordered an airlift of food, medicines and blankets.* ガルシア大統領は食糧、薬品、毛布の空輸を指示した。 🄶 V-T 他動詞 If people, troops, or goods **are airlifted** somewhere, they are carried by air, especially in a war or when land routes are closed. 空輸する ❑ *The injured were airlifted to a hospital in Dayton.* 負傷者はデイトンの病院に空輸された。

air|line /ˈɛərlaɪn/ (airlines) N-COUNT 可算名詞 An **airline** is a company that provides regular services carrying people or goods in airplanes. 航空会社 ❑ *...the world's largest discount airline.* 世界最大手のディスカウント航空会社。

air|lin|er /ˈɛərlaɪnər/ (airliners) N-COUNT 可算名詞 An **airliner** is a large airplane that is used for carrying passengers. 旅客機

air|mail /ˈɛərmeɪl/ N-UNCOUNT 不可算名詞 **Airmail** is the system of sending letters, parcels, and goods by air. 航空郵便 ❑ *...an airmail letter.* 航空郵便書状

air|man /ˈɛərmən/ (airmen) N-COUNT 可算名詞 An **airman** is a man who flies aircraft, especially one who serves in his country's air force. パイロット、空軍兵 ❑ *...an American airman.* 米空軍兵

air|plane /ˈɛərpleɪn/ (airplanes) N-COUNT 可算名詞 An **airplane** is a vehicle with wings and one or more engines that enable it to fly through the air. 飛行機 [AM 米国英語]
→ see **fly**

air|port /ˈɛərpɔrt/ (airports) N-COUNT 可算名詞 An **airport** is a place where aircraft land and take off, and that has buildings and facilities for passengers. 空港 ❑ *...Heathrow Airport, the busiest international airport in the world.* 世界で最も飛行機の発着が多いヒースロー空港。

air|port tax (airport taxes) N-VAR 可変性名詞 **Airport tax** is a tax that airline passengers have to pay in order to use an airport. 空港税 ❑ *Overnight return flights cost from $349 including airport taxes.* 帰路の夜間便は空港税込みで349ドルからだ。

air rage N-UNCOUNT 不可算名詞 **Air rage** is aggressive or violent behavior by airline passengers. 旅客機内での暴力行為 ❑ *Most air rage incidents involve heavy drinking.* 機内での暴力行為の大半は飲み過ぎが関係。

air raid (air raids) N-COUNT 可算名詞 An **air raid** is an attack by military aircraft in which bombs are dropped. 空爆 ❑ *The war began with overnight air raids on Baghdad and Kuwait.* 戦争はバグダッドとクエートへの夜間空爆で始まりました。

air|space /ˈɛərspeɪs/ also air space N-UNCOUNT 不可算名詞 A country's **airspace** is the part of the sky that is over that country and is considered to belong to it. 領空 ❑ *Forty minutes later, they left Colombian airspace.* 40分後、彼らはコロンビアの領空を離れた。

air|tight /ˈɛərtaɪt/ also air-tight 🄵 ADJ 形容詞 If a container is **airtight**, its lid fits so tightly that no air can get in or out. 気密性の ❑ *Store the cookies in an airtight container.* クッキーは密閉容器に入れてください。 🄶 ADJ 形容詞 An **airtight** alibi, case, argument, or agreement is one that has been so carefully put together that nobody will be able to find a fault in it. すきのない、完璧な [AM 米国英語] ❑ *If she could just establish the time the picture had been taken, Mick would have an airtight alibi.* 彼女がその写真の撮影時間を立証できたら、ミックには完璧なアリバイになる。
→ see **can**

air traf|fic con|trol|ler (air traffic controllers) N-COUNT 可算名詞 An **air traffic controller** is someone whose job is to organize the routes that aircraft should follow, and to tell pilots by radio which routes they should take. 航空管制官

air|waves /ˈɛərweɪvz/ also air waves N-PLURAL 複数名詞 The **airwaves** is used to refer to the activity of broadcasting on radio and television. For example, if someone says something over the **airwaves**, they say it on the radio or television. 放送電波 [JOURNALISM ジャーナリズム] ❑ *The election campaign has been fought not in street rallies but on the airwaves.* 選挙戦は街頭演説ではなく放送で繰り広げられた。

airy /ˈɛəri/ (airier, airiest) ADJ 形容詞 If a building or room is **airy**, it has a lot of fresh air inside, usually because it is large. 風通しのよい ❑ *The bathroom has a light and airy feel.* そのバスルームは明るく風通しがよい。

aisle /aɪl/ (aisles) N-COUNT 可算名詞 An **aisle** is a long narrow gap that people can walk along between rows of seats in a public building such as a church or between rows of shelves in a supermarket. 通路 ❑ *...the frozen food aisle.* 冷凍食品売り場

a.k.a. /ˌeɪ keɪ ˈeɪ/ also aka **a.k.a.** is an abbreviation for "also known as." **a.k.a.** is used especially when referring to someone's nickname or stage name. 別名— ❑ *From the very beginning, Stuart Leslie Goddard, a.k.a. Adam Ant, knew he was to be a star.* スチュアート・レスリー・ゴダード、別名アダム・アントは、最初の最初から自分はスターになると意識していた。

alarm /əˈlɑrm/ (alarms, alarming, alarmed) 🄵 N-UNCOUNT 可算名詞 **Alarm** is a feeling of fear or anxiety that something unpleasant or dangerous might happen. 警戒感 ❑ *The news was greeted with alarm by senators.* そのニュースは上院議員に警戒感を抱かせた。 🄶 V-T 他動詞 If something **alarms** you, it makes you afraid or anxious that something unpleasant or dangerous might happen. 怖がらせる [他動詞] ❑ *We could not see what had alarmed him.* 我々は彼が何を怖れていたのかわからなかった。 🄷 N-COUNT 可算名詞 An **alarm** is an automatic device that warns you of danger, for example, by ringing a bell. 警報 ❑ *He heard the alarm go off.* 彼は警報音が鳴り出すのを聞いた。 🄸 N-COUNT 可算名詞 An **alarm** is the same as an **alarm clock**. 目覚まし時計 ❑ *Dad set the alarm for eight the next day.* お父さんは翌朝8時に目覚まし時計をセットした。 🄹 → see also **alarmed, alarming, car alarm, false alarm, fire alarm** 🄺 PHRASE 句 If you say that something sets **alarm bells ringing**, you mean that it makes people feel worried or concerned about something. 警戒させる ❑ *This has set the alarm bells ringing in Moscow.* このことでモスクワは警戒した。 🄻 PHRASE 句 If you **raise the alarm** or **sound the alarm**, you warn people of danger. 警告した ❑ *His family raised the alarm when he had not come home by 9 pm.* 彼が9時までに帰宅しなかったとき家族は注意した。

Word Partnership   alarm は次の語句と使われる：

V.	**cause** alarm 🄵
	set the alarm 🄷
	raise/sound the alarm 🄻
N.	alarm **system** 🄷

alarm clock (**alarm clocks**) N-COUNT 可算名詞 An **alarm clock** is a clock that you can set to make a noise so that it wakes you up at a particular time. 目覚まし時計 ❏ *I set my alarm clock for 4:30.* 目覚まし時計を4時30分にセットした.

alarmed /əlɑrmd/ ADJ 形容詞 If someone is **alarmed**, they feel afraid or anxious that something unpleasant or dangerous might happen. 警戒して ❏ *They should not be too alarmed by the press reports.* あんまり新聞報道に神経質になってはいけない.

alarm|ing /əlɑrmɪŋ/ ADJ 形容詞 Something that is **alarming** makes you feel afraid or anxious that something unpleasant or dangerous might happen. 警戒心をいだかせる ❏ *The disease has spread at an alarming rate.* その病気は恐るべく速さで広がった. ● **alarm|ing|ly** ADV 副詞 警戒心をいだかせるほど ❏ *...the alarmingly high rate of heart disease.* 恐るべく高い心臓病発生率

alas /əlæs/ ADV 副詞 You use **alas** to say that you think that the facts you are talking about are sad or unfortunate. (挿入的に用いて) 残念なことに [FORMAL 形式ばった, FEELINGS 感情] [ADV with cl] ❏ *Such scandals have not, alas, been absent.* その類のスキャンダルは, 残念だが, これまでもなくはなかった.

al|be|it /ɔlbiːɪt/ ADV 副詞 You use **albeit** to introduce a fact or comment that reduces the force or significance of what you have just said. 一にもかかわらず [FORMAL 形式ばった] [ADV with cl/ group] ❏ *Charles's letter was indeed published, albeit in a somewhat abbreviated form.* 確かにチャールズの手紙は公表されたが, いくぶん省略された形ではあったが.

al|bum /ælbəm/ (**albums**) ■ N-COUNT 可算名詞 An **album** is a collection of songs that is available on a CD, record, or cassette. アルバム ❏ *Chris likes music and has a large collection of albums and cassettes.* クリスは音楽好きで, アルバムやカセットをたくさん持っている. ❏ *Oasis release their new album on July 1.* オアシスは7月1日にニューアルバムをリリースする. ② N-COUNT 可算名詞 An **album** is a book in which you keep things such as photographs or stamps that you have collected. アルバム ❏ *Theresa showed me her photo album.* テリーザは自分のアルバムを見せてくれた.

Word Partnership album は次の語句と使われる:

ADJ.	**debut/first/latest/new** album, **live** album **solo** album ■
V.	**produce/release an** album ■
	photo album ②

---

al|co|hol /ælkəhɔl/ (**alcohols**) ■ N-UNCOUNT 不可算名詞 Drinks that can make people drunk, such as beer, wine, and whiskey, can be referred to as **alcohol**. アルコール(飲料) ❏ *Do either of you smoke cigarettes or drink alcohol?* どちら様か, おたばこを吸われますか, それともアルコールを飲まれますか. ② N-MASS 質量名詞 **Alcohol** is a colorless liquid that is found in drinks such as beer, wine, and whiskey. It is also used in products such as perfumes and cleaning fluids. アルコール ❏ *...low-alcohol beer.* 低アルコールビール

al|co|hol|ic /ælkəhɔlɪk/ (**alcoholics**) ■ N-COUNT 可算名詞 An **alcoholic** is someone who cannot stop drinking large amounts of alcohol, even when this is making them ill. アルコール依存症 ❏ *He showed great courage by admitting on television that he is an alcoholic.* 彼は勇気を振るい, 自分がアルコール依存者であることをテレビで公表した. ② ADJ 形容詞 **Alcoholic** drinks are drinks that contain alcohol. アルコールの ❏ *The serving of alcoholic drinks was forbidden after six o'clock.* 6時以降にアルコール飲料を出すことが禁じられた.

al|co|hol|ism /ælkəhɔlɪzəm/ N-UNCOUNT 不可算名詞 People who suffer from **alcoholism** cannot stop drinking large quantities of alcohol. アルコール依存症 ❏ *...a physician who specialized in the problems of alcoholism.* アルコール依存症の専門医

ale /eɪl/ (**ales**) N-MASS 質量名詞 **Ale** is a kind of strong beer. エール(ビールの一種) ❏ *...our selection of ales and spirits.* 当店が選んだエールとスピリッツ

alert /əlɜrt/ (**alerts, alerting, alerted**) ■ ADJ 形容詞 If you are **alert**, you are paying full attention to things around you and are able to deal with anything that might happen. 警戒した ❏ *We all have to stay alert.* 常に警戒が必要です. ● **alert|ness** N-UNCOUNT 不可算名詞 即応力 ❏ *The drug improved mental alertness.* その薬で頭の回転が良くなった. ② ADJ 形容詞 If you are **alert to** something, you are fully aware of it. 油断なく警戒して ❏ *The bank is alert to the danger.* 銀行はその危険性に注意していた. ③ N-COUNT 可算名詞 An **alert** is a situation in which people prepare themselves for something dangerous that might happen soon. 警戒態勢 ❏ *There has been criticism of how his administration handled last week's terrorism alert.* 先週のテロ警戒への政府の対応には批判があった. ④ V-T 他動詞 If you **alert** someone **to** a situation, especially a dangerous or unpleasant situation, you tell them about it. 注意を喚起する [他動詞] ❏ *He wanted to alert people to the activities of the group.* 彼は, 一派の行動に対して人々の注意を喚起したいと思った.

た. ⑤ PHRASE 句 If you are **on the alert for** something, you are ready to deal with it if it happens. 一を警戒して, 一に目を光らせて ❏ *They want to be on the alert for similar buying opportunities.* 彼らは同じような買いの好機に常に注意を払いたいと思っている.
→ see **hypnosis**

al|gae /ældʒi, ælgaɪ/ N-PLURAL 複数名詞 **Algae** are plants with no stems or leaves that grow in water or on damp surfaces. 藻, 藻類 ❏ *...an effort to control toxic algae in Green Lake.* グリーンレークの有毒藻類の増殖を抑える試み
→ see **plant**

al|ge|bra /ældʒɪbrə/ N-UNCOUNT 不可算名詞 **Algebra** is a type of mathematics in which letters are used to represent possible quantities. 代数
→ see **mathematics**

Word Link ali ≈ other : alias, alibi, alien

---

ali|as /eɪliəs/ (**aliases**) ■ N-COUNT 可算名詞 An **alias** is a false name, especially one used by a criminal. 偽名 ❏ *Using an alias, he had rented a house in Des Moines.* 彼は偽名を使ってデモインに家を借りた. ② PREP 前置詞 You use **alias** when you are mentioning another name that someone, especially a criminal or an actor, is known by. 別名は ❏ *Richard Thorp, alias Alan Turner, said yesterday: "It is a sad time for both of us."* リチャード・ソープ, 別名アラン・ターナーは昨日「我々双方にとって悲しいときだ」とコメントした.

ali|bi /æləbaɪ/ (**alibis**) N-COUNT 可算名詞 If you have an **alibi**, you can prove that you were somewhere else when a crime was committed. アリバイ ❏ *He manages to persuade both his wife and girlfriend to provide him with an alibi.* 彼はアリバイ作りのため妻と愛人の両方をまんまと説き伏せる.

al|ien /eɪliən/ (**aliens**) ■ ADJ 形容詞 よそ者の **Alien** means belonging to a different country, race, or group, usually one you do not like or are frightened of. よそ者の [FORMAL 形式ばった, DISAPPROVAL 不賛成] ❏ *He said they were opposed to what he described as the presence of alien forces in the region.* 彼は, 彼らが反対しているのはその地域内の外国軍の存在だと表現した. ② ADJ 形容詞 If something is **alien to** you or to your normal feelings or behavior, it is not the way you would normally feel or behave. 異質な [FORMAL 形式ばった] [v-link ADJ 'to' n] ❏ *Such an attitude is alien to most businessmen.* そのような態度はビジネスマンの大半にはなじみのないものだ. ③ N-COUNT 可算名詞 An **alien** is someone who is not a legal citizen of the country in which they live. 在留外人 [LEGAL 法律的] ❏ *Both women had hired illegal aliens for child care.* その女性はどちらも, 子供の世話をさせるため不法滞在者を雇っていた. ④ N-COUNT 可算名詞 In science fiction, an **alien** is a creature from outer space. 異星人 ❏ *...aliens from another planet.* 地球外惑星からの異星人

al|ien|ate /eɪliəneɪt/ (**alienates, alienating, alienated**) ■ V-T 他動詞 If you **alienate** someone, you make them become unfriendly or unsympathetic toward you. 疎遠にする ❏ *The government cannot afford to alienate either group.* 政府は二派のうち一派でも支持を失うわけにはいかない. ② V-T 他動詞 To **alienate** a person **from** someone or something that they are normally linked with causes them to be emotionally or intellectually separated from them. 遠ざける ❏ *His second wife, Alice, was determined to alienate him from his two boys.* 二人目の妻, アリスは, 決然として彼を二人の息子から引き離そうとした.

alight /əlaɪt/ (**alights, alighting, alighted**) ■ ADJ 形容詞 If something is **alight**, it is burning. 燃えて [v n ADJ, v-link ADJ] ❏ *Several buildings were set alight.* 建物数軒が燃やされた. ② ADJ 形容詞 If someone's eyes are **alight** or if their face is **alight**, the expression in their eyes or on their face shows that they are feeling a strong emotion such as excitement or happiness. (目や顔が喜びや興奮に)輝いて [LITERARY 文語的] [v-link ADJ] ❏ *She paused and turned, her face alight with happiness.* 彼女は立ち止まって振り返った. その顔は幸せに輝いていた. ③ V-I 自動詞 If a bird or insect **alights** somewhere, it lands there. 降り立つ ❏ *A thrush alighted on a branch of the pine tree.* ツグミが松の枝に降り立った. [LITERARY 文語的] ④ V-I 自動詞 When you **alight** from a train, bus, or other vehicle, you get out of it after a trip. (乗り物から)降りる [FORMAL 形式ばった] [自動詞]

align /əlaɪn/ (**aligns, aligning, aligned**) ■ V-T 他動詞 If you **align yourself with** a particular group, you support them because you have the same political aim. 提携させる ❏ *When war broke out, they aligned themselves with the rebel forces.* 戦争が起こると, 彼らは反乱軍と手を結んだ. ② V-T 他動詞 If you **align** something, you place it in a certain position in relation to something else, usually parallel to it. (位置や向きを)調整する ❏ *A tripod will be useful to align and steady the camera.* カメラの位置調整や固定には三脚を使うといいでしょう.

align|ment /əlaɪnmənt/ (**alignments**) ■ N-VAR 可変性名詞 An **alignment** is support for a particular group, especially in politics, or for a side in a quarrel or struggle. 提携 ❏ *The church should have no political alignment.* 教会は, 政治的な協力関係を持つべきではない. ② N-UNCOUNT 不可算名詞 The **alignment** of something is its

position in relation to something else or to its correct position. 配置 □ *They shunned the belief that there is a link between the alignment of the planets and events on the Earth.* 彼らは，惑星の配置と地球上の現象に関係があるという確信を遠ざけました.

Word Link
like ≈ similar : alike, childlike, likeness

alike /əláɪk/ **1** ADJ 形容詞 If two or more things are **alike**, they are similar in some way. 似ている [v-link ADJ] □ *We looked very alike.* 私たちはみかけがよく似ていた. **2** ADV 副詞 **Alike** means in a similar way. よく似て [ADV after v] □ *They even dressed alike.* 彼らは服装までそっくりだった.

Thesaurus
alike また次を参照:

ADJ.　comparable, equal, equivalent, matching, parallel, similar; (*ant.*) different **1**

alive /əláɪv/ **1** ADJ 形容詞 If people or animals are **alive**, they are not dead. 生きている [v-link ADJ] □ *She does not know if he is alive or dead.* 彼女は彼の生死を知らない. **2** ADJ 形容詞 If you say that someone seems **alive**, you mean that they seem to be very lively and to enjoy everything that they do. 生き生きとした □ *She seemed more alive and looked forward to getting up in the morning.* 彼女はますます活気にあふれているようで，朝起きるのを楽しみにしていた. **3** ADJ 形容詞 If an activity, organization, or situation is **alive**, it continues to exist or function. 存続して [v-link ADJ, 'keep' n ADJ] □ *The big factories are trying to stay alive by cutting costs.* 大工場はコスト削減により生き残りを図っています. **4** ADJ 形容詞 If a place is **alive with** something, there are a lot of people or things there and it seems busy or exciting. 〜でにぎわって，〜でいっぱいの [v-link ADJ] □ *The river was alive with birds.* 川は多くの鳥でにぎわっていた. **5** PHRASE 句 If people, places, or events **come alive**, they start to be lively again after a quiet period. If someone or something **brings** them **alive**, they cause them to come alive. 活気を取り戻す，生き返らせる □ *The doctor's voice had come alive and his small eyes shone.* 医者の声が再び聞こえてくると，彼の小さな瞳は輝いた. **6** PHRASE 句 If a story or description **comes alive**, it becomes interesting, lively, or realistic. If someone or something **brings** it **alive**, they make it seem more interesting, lively, or realistic. 生き生きとする，生き生きとさせる □ *She made history come alive with tales from her own memories.* 彼女は自分の思い出話を交えて歴史を生き生きと語った.

Word Partnership
alive は次の語句と使われる:

ADJ.　**dead** or **alive 1**
ADV.　alive **and well 1**
　　　still alive **1 3**
V.　**found** alive, **keep** *someone/something* alive **1**
　　　stay alive **1 3**
　　　feel alive **1 5**
　　　come alive **5 6**

all
❶ EVERYTHING, THE WHOLE OF SOMETHING
❷ EMPHASIS
❸ OTHER PHRASES

❶ all /ɔ́l/ **1** PREDET 前限定詞 You use **all** to indicate that you are referring to the whole of a particular group or thing or to everyone or everything of a particular kind. すべて □ *...the restaurant that Hugh and all his friends go to.* ヒューと友達全員が通うレストラン ● DET 限定詞 **All** is also a determiner. すべての □ *There is built-in storage space in all bedrooms.* 全ベッドルームに作りつけの収納スペースがある. □ *He was passionate about all literature.* 彼は文学のすべてに夢中だった. ● QUANT 数量詞 **All** is also a quantifier. すべての □ *He was told to pack up all of his letters and personal belongings.* 彼は手紙と私物の全部を荷物にまとめるように言われた. ● PRON 代名詞 **All** is also a pronoun. すべての物・人 □ *The only salon produces its own shampoos and hair-care products, all based on herbal recipes.* 唯一のサロンが，オリジナルのシャンプーとヘアケア製品をすべてハーブ処方で製造している. ● PRON-EMPH 強調的代名詞 **All** is also an emphasizing pronoun. (強調の代名詞) すべて [n PRON v] □ *Milk, oily fish and eggs all contain vitamin D.* 牛乳，脂肪の多い魚，卵は，すべてがビタミンDを含んでいる.

All is often used to mean the same as **whole** but when used in front of plurals, **all** and **whole** have different meanings. For example, if you say "**All the buildings have been destroyed,**" you mean that every building has been destroyed. If you say "**Whole buildings have been destroyed,**" you mean that some buildings have been destroyed completely. Note that when **all** is used to consider a group, this means that the group has more than two members. To refer to two people or things, you use **both**. □ *Tony and Bob both laughed.* You use **every** to refer to all the members of a group that has more than two members. □ *He listened to every news bulletin. ...an equal chance for every child.* You use **each** to refer to every person or thing in a group when you are thinking about them as individuals. Note that **each** can be used to refer to both members of a pair. □ *Each apartment has two bedrooms... We each carried a suitcase.* Note that **each** and **every** are only used with singular nouns.

2 DET 限定詞 You use **all** to refer to the whole of a particular period of time. 〜の間ずっと □ *George had to cut grass all afternoon.* ジョージは午後はずっと芝を刈らなければならなかった. ● PREDET 前限定詞 **All** is also a predeterminer. すべての [PREDET det sing-n] □ *She's worked all her life.* 彼女はこれまでずっと働きづめだ. ● QUANT 数量詞 **All** is also a quantifier. 全体，全部 [QUANT 'of' def-n] □ *He spent all of that afternoon polishing the silver.* 彼は午後ずっと銀食器を磨いていた. **3** PRON 代名詞 You use **all** to refer to a situation or to life in general. 一切 □ *All is silent on the island now.* 今，島は静寂につつまれている. **4** PHRASE 句 **All but** a particular person or thing means everyone or everything except that person or thing. 〜のほかは □ *The general was an unattractive man to all but his most ardent admirers.* 司令官に強く心酔している人たちを除いて，誰も彼に魅力を感じていなかった. **5** PHRASE 句 You use **all but** to say that something is almost the case. ほとんど □ *The concrete wall that used to divide this city has now all but gone.* この町を分断していたコンクリートの壁は，今ではほとんどなくなった. **6** PHRASE 句 **In all** means in total. 合計で □ *There was evidence that thirteen people in all had taken part in planning the murder.* 全部で13人がその殺人事件の計画にかかわっていたとの証拠が挙がった. **7** PHRASE 句 You use **all in all** to introduce a summary or general statement. 概して □ *We both thought that all in all it might not be a bad idea.* 私たちは二人とも，それは大体において悪い考えではないかもしれないと思った.

Word Partnership
all は次の語句と使われる:

V.　have it all, have seen it all **❶ 1**
N.　all **ages**, all **kinds/sorts**, all the **way ❶ 1**
　　　all **day/night**, all the **time ❶ 2**
ADJ.　all **alone**, all **clear**, all **right ❶ 3**
PREP.　in all **❶ 1**
　　　above all **❷ 6**
　　　at all **❷ 8**
　　　of all **❷ 10 – 12**
　　　all of **❷ 13**
　　　after all **❸ 3**

❷ all /ɔ́l/ **1** DET 限定詞 You use **all** in expressions such as **in all sincerity** and **in all probability** to emphasize that you are being sincere or that something is very likely. 後に続く名詞の程度を強調する決定詞 □ *In all fairness he had to admit that she was neither dishonest nor lazy.* 彼は，できる限り公平に見て彼女は不正直でも怠惰でもないと認めざるを得なかった. [EMPHASIS 強調] **2** PRON 代名詞 You use **all** at the beginning of a clause when you are emphasizing that something is the only thing that is important. 万事 [EMPHASIS 強調] □ *He said all that remained was to agree to a time and venue.* 彼は，あとは開催時間と場所を承諾するだけだと述べた. □ *Do you ever want to do is go shopping!* 君はいつも買い物にいくことしか考えてないんだ. **3** ADV 副詞 You use **all** to emphasize that something is completely true, or happens everywhere or always, or on every occasion. すべてを [EMPHASIS 強調] [ADV prep/adv] □ *He loves animals and he knows all about them.* 彼は動物を愛しており，そのすべてを知っている. □ *He was doing it all by himself.* 彼はそれを全部自分でやった. **4** ADV 副詞 **All** is used in structures such as **all the more** or **all the better** to mean even more or even better than before. 一層 □ *The living room is decorated in pale colors that make it all the more airy.* 居間の内装は淡い色が基調で，さらに風通しがよさそうに感じる. **5** PRON-EMPH 強調的代名詞 You use **all** in expressions such as **seen it all** and **done it all** to emphasize that someone has had a lot of experience of something. あらゆること [EMPHASIS 強調] □ *They've seen it all, so it takes a lot to rattle them.* 彼らは経験豊富なので，多少のことでは動揺しない. **6** PHRASE 句 You say **above all** to indicate that the thing you are mentioning is the most important point. とりわけ，何よりも [EMPHASIS 強調] □ *Above all, chairs should be comfortable.* 何より，いすの座り心地が大切だ. **7** PHRASE 句 You use **and all** when you want to emphasize that what you are talking about includes the thing mentioned, especially when this is surprising or unusual. 〜など [EMPHASIS]

強調] ❑ *He dropped his hot dog on the pavement and someone's dog ate it, mustard and all.* 彼が道にホットドッグを落とすと，誰かの犬がマスタードまですっかり食べてしまった。 **8** PHRASE 句 You use **at all** at the end of a clause to give emphasis in negative statements, conditional clauses, and questions. 全く〜ない [EMPHASIS 強調] ❑ *Robin never really liked him at all.* ロビンは実際，彼を全く好きではなかった。 **9** PHRASE 句 You use **for all** in phrases such as **for all I know**, and **for all he cares**, to emphasize that you do not know something or that someone does not care about something. 恐らくは〜，〜にはどうでもよいことだが [EMPHASIS 強調] ❑ *For all we know, he may not even be in this country.* 恐らく，彼はこの国に存在しないかもしれない。 **10** PHRASE 句 You use **of all** to emphasize the words "first" or "last," or a superlative adjective or adverb. 〜の中でとりわけ [EMPHASIS 強調] ❑ *First of all, answer these questions.* まず最初に，これらの問に答えなさい。 **11** PHRASE 句 You use **of all** in expressions such as **of all people** or **of all things** when you want to emphasize someone or something surprising. よりによって [EMPHASIS 強調] ❑ *One group of women, sitting on the ground, was singing, of all things, "Greensleeves."* 地べたに座った女性のグループは，よりによって，『グリーンスリーブス』を歌っていた。 **12** PHRASE 句 You use **of all** in expressions like **of all the nerve** or **of all the luck** to emphasize how angry or surprised you are at what someone else has done or said. (他人の言動に驚いて) なんていうのだ [FEELINGS 感情] ❑ *Of all the lazy, indifferent, unbusinesslike attitudes to have!* なんて怠惰で，無頓着で，ビジネスの場にふさわしくない態度をしているのか。 **13** PHRASE 句 You use **all of** before a number to emphasize how small or large an amount is. (数の大小を強調して) わずか〜，たっぷり〜 [EMPHASIS 強調] ❑ *It took him all of 41 minutes to score his first goal.* 彼が初ゴールを決めるまで，ゆうに41分かかった。

❸ all /ɔl/ **1** ADV 副詞 You use **all** when you are talking about an equal score in a game. For example, if the score is three **all**, both players or teams have three points. 同点で [amount ADV] **2** PHRASE 句 You use **after all** when introducing a statement that supports or helps explain something you have just said. そもそも〜だから ❑ *I thought you might know somebody. After all, you're the man with connections.* あなたなら誰か知ってる人がいると思ってたわ。そもそも，あなたは顔が広いから。 **3** PHRASE 句 You use **after all** when you are saying that something that you thought might not be the case is in fact the case. 結局 ❑ *I came out here on the chance of finding you at home after all.* あなたが家にいるかと思って結局ここに来たのよ。

Note that you do not use **after all** if you want to talk about what happens at the end of a long period, instead you use **at last, finally, in the end, lastly**, or **last of all**. You use **at last** or **finally** when you have been waiting for or expecting something for a long time. **At last** usually comes at the end of a sentence. ❑ *The storm that had threatened came at last.* **Finally** usually comes at the beginning of a sentence or before a verb. ❑ *After another search they finally located the house.* You also use **finally** to talk about something that is the last in a series of things. ❑ *He lived in Turkey, France, Norway, and finally Mexico.* You use **in the end** when talking about something that happens after a long time or a long process. ❑ *Perhaps the police got him in the end... In the end, Peter seemed quite happy.* You use **lastly** to talk about the last of a series of people or things. ❑ *I went through the bathroom, the bedroom, and lastly the living room.* You use **last of all** to emphasize that there is nobody or nothing else after the person or thing you mention. ❑ *Last of all came the cat.*

4 PHRASE 句 You use **for all** to indicate that the thing mentioned does not affect or contradict the truth of what you are saying. 〜にもかかわらず ❑ *For all its beauty, Prague could soon lose some of the individuality that the communist years helped to preserve.* プラハは美しい都市だが，共産主義時代に保たれていた個性はもうすぐ失われるかもしれない。 **5** PHRASE 句 You use **all that** in statements with negative meaning when you want to weaken the force of what you are saying. 思うほどに〜ない [SPOKEN 口語, VAGUENESS あいまいさ] ❑ *He wasn't all that much older than we were.* 彼は私たちよりそれほど年上ではありませんでした。 **6** PHRASE 句 You can say **that's all** at the end of a sentence when you are explaining something and want to emphasize that nothing more happens or is the case. 〜だけだ。 ❑ *"Why do you want to know that?" he demanded. —"Just curious, that's all."* 彼は「なぜそれが知りたいの」と詰め寄った。「ちょっと興味があったの。それだけよ。」 **7** PHRASE 句 You use **all very well** to suggest that you do not really approve of something or you think that it is unreasonable. まことに結構だが [DISAPPROVAL 不賛成] ❑ *It is all very well to urge people to give more to charity when they have less, but is it really fair?* もっと寄付してくれるように頼むのはまことに結構だが，それは正しいことだろうか。

all- /ɔl-/ **1** COMB IN ADJ 形容詞の複合 **All-** is added to nouns or adjectives in order to form adjectives that describe something as consisting only of the thing mentioned or as having only the quality indicated. それだけで構成された [usu ADJ n] ❑ *The all-star*

cast includes Jeremy Irons. そのオールスター番組にはジェレミー・アイアンズも出演する。 **2** COMB IN ADJ 形容詞の複合 **All-** is added to present participles or adjectives in order to form adjectives that describe something as including or affecting everything or everyone. 非常に〜な [usu ADJ n] ❑ *Nursing a demented person is an all-consuming task.* 痴呆症の介護は非常に体力を要する仕事だ。 **3** COMB IN ADJ 形容詞の複合 **All-** is added to nouns in order to form adjectives that describe something as being suitable for or including all types of a particular thing. 名詞に付加して，『何にでも対応できる〜』，といった形容詞を作る。 ❑ *He wanted to form an all-party government of national unity.* 彼は全政党参加の挙国一致政府を組織したいと思っていた。 [usu ADJ n]

Allah /ælə, ˈælɑ/ N-PROPER 固有名詞 **Allah** is the name of God in Islam. アラー (の神) ❑ *Allah be praised!* アラーの神をたたえよ。

all-around **1** ADJ 形容詞 An **all-around** person is good at a lot of different skills, academic subjects, or sports. 万能の，オールラウンドの [ADJ n] ❑ *He is a great all-around player.* 彼は優秀なオールラウンドプレーヤーである。 **2** ADJ 形容詞 **All-around** means doing or relating to all aspects of a job or activity. 全般にわたる [ADJ n] ❑ *He demonstrated the all-around skills of a quarterback.* 彼はクォーターバックの技術全般を見せた。

al|lay /əˈleɪ/ (allays, allaying, allayed) V-T 他動詞 If you **allay** someone's fears or doubts, you stop them feeling afraid or doubtful. 和らげる [他動詞] ❑ *He did what he could to allay his wife's myriad fears.* 彼は妻のとめどない恐怖感を和らげようと最善を尽くした。 [FORMAL 形式ばった]

al|le|ga|tion /æləˈgeɪʃ°n/ (allegations) N-COUNT 可算名詞 An **allegation** is a statement saying that someone has done something wrong. 申し立て，主張 ❑ *The company has denied the allegations.* その会社はそうした主張は真実でないと否定した。

Word Partnership allegation は次の語句と使われる：

V.	**deny an** allegation, **make an** allegation
PREP.	allegation **of**
CONJ.	allegation **that**

al|lege /əˈlɛdʒ/ (alleges, alleging, alleged) V-T 他動詞 If you **allege that** something bad is true, you say it but do not prove it. (証明はできないが) 断言する [FORMAL 形式ばった] ❑ *She alleged that there was rampant drug use among the male members of the group.* 彼女はグループの男性メンバーの薬物使用が甚だしいと断言した。 ❑ *The accused is alleged to have killed a man.* その被告は殺人の嫌疑をかけられている。

al|leged /əˈlɛdʒd/ ADJ 形容詞 An **alleged** fact has been stated but has not been proved to be true. 〜であるとされている [FORMAL 形式ばった] [ADJ n] ❑ *They have begun a hunger strike in protest at the alleged beating.* 彼らは暴行疑惑に異議を唱えてハンガーストライキを始めた。 ● **al|leg|ed|ly** /əˈlɛdʒɪdli/ ADV 副詞 伝えられるところでは ❑ *His van allegedly struck the two as they were crossing a street.* 男が運転するトラックが横断中の2人をはねた模様である。

Thesaurus alleged また次を参照：

ADJ.	questionable, supposed, suspicious; (ant.) certain, definite, sure

al|le|giance /əˈlidʒ°ns/ (allegiances) N-VAR 可変性名詞 Your **allegiance** is your support for and loyalty to a particular group, person, or belief. 忠誠 ❑ *My allegiance to Kendall and his company ran deep.* 私のケンダルと彼の会社への忠誠心は深かった。

al|ler|gic /əˈlɜrdʒɪk/ **1** ADJ 形容詞 If you are **allergic to** something, you become ill or get a rash when you eat it, smell it, or touch it. 〜アレルギーの [v-link ADJ 'to' n] ❑ *I'm allergic to cats.* 私は猫アレルギーなんです。 **2** ADJ 形容詞 If you have an **allergic** reaction to something, you become ill or get a rash when you eat it, smell it, or touch it. アレルギー性の [ADJ n] ❑ *Soy milk can cause allergic reactions in some children.* 豆乳にアレルギー反応を起こす子供もいる。
→ see **peanut**

al|ler|gy /ˈælərdʒi/ (allergies) N-VAR 可変性名詞 If you have a particular **allergy**, you become ill or get a rash when you eat, smell, or touch something that does not normally make people ill. アレルギー ❑ *Food allergies can result in an enormous variety of different symptoms.* 食物アレルギーは実にさまざまな症状を引き起こす。

al|le|vi|ate /əˈliviˌeɪt/ (alleviates, alleviating, alleviated) V-T 他動詞 If you **alleviate** pain, suffering, or an unpleasant condition, you make it less intense or severe. 緩和する ❑ *Nowadays, a great deal can be done to alleviate back pain.* 今では，多岐にわたる腰痛緩和法がある。 [FORMAL 形式ばった] ● **al|le|via|tion** /əˌliviˈeɪʃ°n/ N-UNCOUNT 不可算名詞 [usu N 'of' n] 軽減 ❑ *Their energies were focused on the alleviation of the refugees' misery.* 彼らは難民の窮状を少しでも良くしようと力を注いだ。

al|ley /ǽli/ (**alleys**) N-COUNT 可算名詞 An **alley** is a narrow passage or street with buildings or walls on both sides. 路地, 通路

al|li|ance /əláɪəns/ (**alliances**) **1** N-COUNT 可算名詞 An **alliance** is a group of countries or political parties that are formally united and working together because they have similar aims. 同盟, 連合 □ The two parties were still too much apart to form an alliance. 両党の立場にはいまだ距離があり, 連合体制はとれなかった. **2** N-COUNT 可算名詞 An **alliance** is a relationship in which two countries, political parties, or organizations work together for some purpose. 提携, 協力 [oft N 'with/between' n] □ The Socialists' electoral strategy has been based on a tactical alliance with the Communists. 社会党の選挙戦略は共産党と戦術協力することを基本とした.

Word Partnership	alliance は次の語句と使われる:
PREP.	alliance **between**, alliance **with** **1** **2**
V.	**form an** alliance **1** **2**
N.	**members of an** alliance **1** **2**
ADJ.	**military/political** alliance **1** **2**

al|lied /əláɪd/ **1** ADJ 形容詞 **Allied** forces or troops are armies from different countries who are fighting on the same side in a war. 連合した [ADJ n] □ ...the approaching Allied forces. 接近する連合軍. **2** ADJ 形容詞 **Allied** countries, troops, or political parties are united by a political or military agreement. 同盟の [ADJ n, v-link ADJ 'to' n] □ ...forces from three allied nations. 三国同盟の部隊. **3** ADJ 形容詞 If one thing or group is **allied** to another, it is related to it because the two things have particular qualities or characteristics in common. 関連した [v-link ADJ 'to/with' n, ADJ n] □ ...lectures on subjects allied to health, beauty and fitness. 健康, 美容, フィットネスに関する科目の講義.

al|li|ga|tor /ǽlɪgeɪtər/ (**alligators**) N-COUNT 可算名詞 An **alligator** is a large reptile with short legs, a long tail, and very powerful jaws. ワニ □ There are numerous signs warning people not to feed the alligators in the area. この地区ではワニにえさを与えないよう警告する看板が数多く立てられている.

al|lo|cate /ǽləkeɪt/ (**allocates, allocating, allocated**) V-T 他動詞 If one item or share of something **is allocated to** a particular person or **for** a particular purpose, it is given to that person or used for that purpose. 割り当てる □ Tickets are limited and will be allocated to those who apply first. 枚数に限りがあるため, チケットは先着順で割り当てられる. □ The 1985 federal budget allocated $7.3 billion for development programs. 1985年の連邦予算では, 開発計画に73億ドルが当てられた.

al|lo|ca|tion /ǽləkéɪʃn/ (**allocations**) **1** N-COUNT 可算名詞 An **allocation** is an amount of something, especially money, that is given to a particular person or used for a particular purpose. 割当て □ A State Department spokeswoman said that the aid allocation for Pakistan was still under review. 国務省報道官によると, パキスタンへの支援割当額はいまだ再考中とのことだ. **2** N-UNCOUNT 不可算名詞 The **allocation** of something is the decision that it should be given to a particular person or used for a particular purpose. 配分 □ Town planning and land allocation had to be coordinated. 都市計画と土地配分は調整が必要だった.

al|lot /əlɒt/ (**allots, allotting, allotted**) V-T 他動詞 If something **is allotted to** someone, it is given to them as their share. 割り当てる □ The seats are allotted to the candidates who have won the most votes. 議席は最も得票の多かった候補者達に割り当てられた. [usu passive]

all-out also **all out** ADJ 形容詞 You use **all-out** to describe actions that are carried out in a very energetic and determined way, using all the resources available. 全力をあげての [ADJ n] □ He launched an all-out attack on his critics. 彼は批判者に対し徹底して反撃し始めた.

al|low /əláʊ/ (**allows, allowing, allowed**) **1** V-T 他動詞 If someone **is allowed to** do something, it is all right for them to do it and they will not get into trouble. 許可する □ The children are allowed to watch TV after school. 子供たちは学校が終わってからテレビを見ることを許される. □ Smoking will not be allowed. 喫煙は許されないだろう. **2** V-T 他動詞 If you **are allowed** something, you are given permission to have it or are given it. 許可する □ Gifts like chocolates or flowers are allowed. チョコレートや花などの贈り物は許されます. **3** V-T 他動詞 If you **allow** something **to** happen, you do not prevent it. させておく [他動詞] □ He won't allow himself to fail. 彼は自分の失敗を許さないだろう. **4** V-T 他動詞 If one thing **allows** another thing **to** happen, the first thing creates the opportunity for the second thing to happen. させる [他動詞] □ The compromise will allow him to continue his free market reforms. 譲歩によって, 彼の自由市場改革の継続が可能になった. □ ...an attempt to allow the Muslim majority a greater share of power. イスラム系の多数派に一層の勢力を持たせようとする試み. **5** V-T 他動詞 If you **allow** a particular length of time or a particular amount of something **for** a particular

purpose, you include it in your planning. 割り当てる □ Please allow 28 days for delivery. 配達まで28日を見込んでください.

▶ **allow for** PHRASAL VERB 句動詞 If you **allow for** certain problems or expenses, you include some extra time or money in your planning so that you can deal with them if they occur. 考慮に入れておく □ You have to allow for a certain amount of error. ある程度の誤差は見越さねばならない.

Thesaurus	allow また次を参照:
V.	approve, consent, support, tolerate; (ant.) disallow, forbid, prohibit, prevent **2** let **3**

Word Partnership	allow は次の語句と使われる:
V.	allow *someone* to do *something* **1** **2** continue to allow, refuse to allow **1** – **3**
N.	allow **time** **5**

al|low|ance /əláʊəns/ (**allowances**) **1** N-COUNT 可算名詞 An **allowance** is money that is given to someone, usually on a regular basis, in order to help them pay for the things that they need. 手当 □ She gets an allowance for taking care of Amy. 彼女はエイミーの養育手当をもらっている. **2** N-COUNT 可算名詞 A child's **allowance** is money that is given to him or her every week or every month by his or her parents. 小遣い [mainly AM 主に米国英語] □ When you give kids an allowance make sure they save some of it. お小遣いを渡す場合, その一部を貯金させなさい. **3** N-COUNT 可算名詞 A particular type of **allowance** is an amount of something that you are allowed in particular circumstances. 許容量 □ Most of our flights have a baggage allowance of 44 lbs per passenger. 当社の無料手荷物許容重量は, ほとんどの便で1人当たり44ポンドです. **4** N-COUNT 可算名詞 Your tax **allowance** is the amount of money that you are allowed to earn before you have to start paying income tax. 控除額 [BRIT 英国英語; AM personal exemption 米国英語 personal exemption] **5** PHRASE 句 If you **make allowances for** something, you take it into account in your decisions, plans, or actions. 〜を考慮にいれる □ They'll make allowances for the fact it's affecting our performance. 彼らはそれが業績に影響することを考慮するだろう. □ She tried to make allowances for his age. 彼女は彼の年齢を考慮しようとした. **6** PHRASE 句 If you **make allowances for** someone, you accept behavior from them that you would not normally accept, because of a problem that they have. 〜を大目に見る □ He's tired so I'll make allowances for him. 彼は疲れているから大目に見よう.

all right **1** ADJ 形容詞 If you say that someone or something is **all right**, you mean that you find them satisfactory or acceptable. 満足のいく, 許容できる [v-link ADJ] □ I consider you a good friend, and if it's all right with you, I'd like to keep it that way. 私はあなたを良いお友達だと思っているんだが, もしあなたがよければ, このままの関係でいたい. □ He's an all right kind of guy really. [INFORMAL くだけた] [ADJ n] □ He's an all right kind of guy really. 彼はいいひとだよ. **2** ADJ 形容詞 If someone or something is **all right**, they are well or safe. 大丈夫な [v-link ADJ] □ All she's worried about is whether he is all right. 彼女が心配で仕方なかったのは彼の安否だ. **3** ADV 副詞 If you say that something happens or goes **all right**, you mean that it happens in a satisfactory or acceptable manner. 満足な [ADV after v] □ Things have thankfully worked out all right. ありがたいことに, 事はうまく進んできた. **4** CONVENTION 慣習表現 You say "**all right**" when you are agreeing to something. (同意して) その通りだ [FORMULAE 決まり文句] □ "I think you should go now." — "All right." 「もう出発しないといけないんじゃない」「ほんとだ」 **5** CONVENTION 慣習表現 You say "**all right?**" after you have given an instruction or explanation to someone when you are checking that they have understood what you have just said, or checking that they agree with or accept what you have just said. わかったかい □ Peter, you get half the fees. All right? ピーター, おまえの取り分は半分だ. いいかい. **6** CONVENTION 慣習表現 If someone in a position of authority says "**all right**", and suggests talking about or doing something else, they are indicating that they want you to end one activity and start another. そこまででいい. □ All right, Bob. You can go now. そこまででいいよ, ボブ. もう帰っていいよ. **7** CONVENTION 慣習表現 You say "**all right**" during a discussion to show that you understand something that someone has just said, and to introduce a statement that relates to it. (相手の言葉に同意し, 自分の意見を付加して) 分かったよ. それならー □ I said there was no room in my mother's house, and he said, "All right, come to my studio and paint." 母さんの家では描く場所がないって言ったわ. そしたら, 彼は「分かったよ. じゃあ, ぼくのアトリエで描いたら」って言ったの. **8** CONVENTION 慣習表現 You say **all right** before a statement or question to indicate that you are challenging or threatening someone. よし (文頭で用いる間投詞. その後には相手をおどしたり, 相手にくってかかったりする言葉が続く) □ All right, who are you and what are you doing in my office? よし, 君は何者で, 私のオフィスで何をしてるか言ってみろ.

A

all-round → see **all-around**

all-time ADJ 形容詞 You use **all-time** when you are comparing all the things of a particular type that there have ever been. For example, if you say that something is the **all-time** best, you mean that it is the best thing of its type that there has ever been. 空前の [ADJ n] ❏ The president's popularity nationally is at an all-time low. 国内での大統領の人気は過去最低です.

al|lude /əlud/ (alludes, alluding, alluded) V-I 自動詞 If you **allude to** something, you mention it in an indirect way. ほのめかす [FORMAL 形式ばった] ❏ With friends, she sometimes alluded to a feeling that she herself was to blame for her son's predicament. 彼女が時々友達に漏らしたところでは, 息子がこんな目にあったのは自分のせいだと感じているようだった.

al|lure /əlʊər/ N-UNCOUNT 不可算名詞 The **allure** of something or someone is the pleasing or exciting quality that they have. 魅力 ❏ It's a game that has really lost its allure. 全く退屈なゲームになってしまいました.

al|lu|sion /əluʒⁿn/ (allusions) N-VAR 可変性名詞 An **allusion** is an indirect reference to someone or something. ほのめかすこと ❏ This last point was understood to be an allusion to the long-standing hostility between the two leaders. 最後の点については, 2人の指導者の間の長年にわたるライバル意識を暗に触れたものとされました.

ally (allies, allying, allied)

> The noun is pronounced /ælaɪ/. The verb is pronounced /əlaɪ/.
>
> 名詞は /ælaɪ/ と発音される. 動詞は /əlaɪ/ と発音される.

■ N-COUNT 可算名詞 A country's **ally** is another country that has an agreement to support it, especially in war. 同盟国 ❏ Washington would not take such a step without its allies' approval. アメリカ政府は同盟国からの支持が得られない限り, そうした措置を取ることはないだろう. ■ N-COUNT 可算名詞 If you describe someone as your **ally**, you mean that they help and support you, especially when other people are opposing you. 味方 ❏ He is a close ally of the president. 彼は大統領の側近です. ■ N-PLURAL 複数名詞 The **Allies** were the armed forces that fought against Germany and Japan in World War II. 連合軍 ❏ ...Germany's surrender to the Allies. ドイツの連合軍に対する降伏. ■ V-T 他動詞 If you **ally yourself** with someone or something, you give your support to them. 同盟する; 支持する ❏ He will have no choice but to ally himself with the new movement. 彼はその新たな動向に追随していくほかないでしょう. ■ → see also **allied**

al|mighty /ɔlmaɪti/ ■ N-PROPER 固有名詞 The **Almighty** is another name for God. You can also refer to **Almighty God**. 全能なる神 ❏ Adam sought guidance from the Almighty. アダムは全能なる神の導きを請うた. ■ EXCLAM 感嘆詞 People sometimes say **God Almighty** or **Christ Almighty** to express their surprise, anger, or horror. These expressions could cause offense. なんだって; ちくしょう; うわー [FEELINGS 感情]

al|mond /ɑmənd, æm-, ælm-/ (almonds) ■ N-VAR 可変性名詞 **Almonds** are pale oval nuts. They are often used in cooking. アーモンド ❏ ...sponge cake flavored with almonds. アーモンド風味のスポンジケーキ. ■ N-VAR 可変性名詞 An **almond** or an **almond tree** is a tree on which almonds grow. アーモンドの木 ❏ On the left was a plantation of almond trees. 左にはアーモンドの大農場が広がっていた.

al|most /ɔlmoʊst/ ADV 副詞 You use **almost** to indicate that something is not completely the case but is nearly the case. ほぼ— ❏ The couple had been dating for almost three years. 2人は付き合って3年近くになっていた. ❏ The effect is almost impossible to describe. その影響たるやほとんど言葉では表せない. ❏ He contracted Spanish flu, which almost killed him. 彼はスペイン風邪にかかり危うく命を失うところだった.

Thesaurus

　　　　　　　almost また次を参照:

ADV.　about, most, practically, virtually

alone /əloʊn/ ■ ADJ 形容詞 When you are **alone**, you are not with any other people. 一人きりで [v-link ADJ] ❏ There is nothing so fearful as to be alone in a combat situation. 戦闘のさなか味方が一人もいないときほど恐ろしいものはない. ●ADV 副詞 **Alone** is also an adverb. ひとりで [ADV after v] ❏ She has lived alone in this house for almost five years now. 彼女がこの家にひとりで暮らし始めてもう5年近くになる. ■ ADJ 形容詞 If one person is **alone with** another person, or if two or more people are **alone**, they are together, without anyone else present. —きりで [v-link ADJ] ❏ I couldn't imagine why he would want to be alone with me. 彼がどうして私と二人きりになろうとしたのか全く見当がつかなかった. ■ ADJ 形容詞 If you say that you are **alone** or feel **alone**, you mean that nobody who is with you, or nobody at all, cares about you. 孤独で [v-link ADJ] ❏ Never in her life had she felt so alone, so abandoned. 彼女は人生でこれほど孤独を感じ見捨てられた気分になったことはなかった. ■ ADJ 形容詞 If someone is **alone in** doing something, they are the only person doing it, and so are different from other people. —の点で

並ぶ者はいない [v-link ADJ] ❏ Am I alone in recognizing that these two statistics have quite different implications? 2つの数字の意味するところが全く違っていると気づいたのはこの私だけだろうか. ●ADV 副詞 **Alone** is also an adverb. ただ—だけ ❏ I alone was sane, I thought, in a world of crazy people. まともなのはこの私一人で, 周りはみな頭がいかれているかのように思えた. ■ ADV 副詞 You say that one person or thing **alone** does something when you are emphasizing that only one person or thing is involved. 単独で [EMPHASIS 強調] [n ADV] ❏ You alone should determine what is right for you. 自分に何がふさわしいかは本人が決めることだ. ■ ADV 副詞 If you say that one person or thing **alone** is responsible for part of an amount, you are emphasizing the size of that part and the size of the total amount. 単に—だけで [EMPHASIS 強調] [n ADV] ❏ CNN alone is sending 300 technicians, directors and commentators. CNNだけでも総勢300名に及ぶ技術者やディレクターや解説者を送り込んでいる. ■ ADV 副詞 When someone does something **alone**, they do it without help from other people. 自分ひとりで [ADV after v] ❏ Bringing up a child alone should give you a sense of achievement. 片親で子供を育て上げれば達成感が得られるはずだ. ■ PHRASE 句 If you **go it alone**, you do something without any help from other people. ひとりでやる [INFORMAL くだけた] ❏ I missed the stimulation of working with others when I tried to go it alone. ひとりでやろうとしたとたん, 人と一緒に働いているときの刺激がないことに気づいた. ■ to **leave** someone or something **alone** → see **leave** ■ **let alone** → see **let**

Thesaurus

　　　　　　　alone また次を参照:

ADJ.　solitary, unaccompanied; (ant.) crowded, together ■ friendless ■

along /əlɔŋ/

> In addition to the uses shown below, **along** is used in phrasal verbs such as "go along with," "play along," and "string along."
>
> 下記の用法に加えて, **along** は **go along with, play along, string along** のような句動詞に使われる.

■ PREP 前置詞 If you move or look **along** something such as a road, you move or look toward one end of it. —に沿って ❏ Pedro walked along the street alone. ペドロは通りを一人歩いた. ❏ The young man led Mark Ryle along a corridor. 若い男は廊下を歩いてマーク・ライルを案内した. ■ PREP 前置詞 If something is situated **along** a road, river, or corridor, it is situated in it or beside it. —の端から端までずっと ❏ ...enormous traffic jams all along the roads. 延々と続くひどい交通渋滞. ■ ADV 副詞 When someone or something moves **along**, they keep moving in a particular direction. どんどん進んで [ADV after v] ❏ She skipped and danced along. 彼女はスキップやダンスをしながらどんどん進んだ. ❏ He raised his voice a little, talking into the wind as they walked along. 彼は一緒に歩きながら, 少し声を張り上げて風に向かって話すみたいに話した. ■ ADV 副詞 If you say that something is going **along** in a particular way, you mean that it is progressing in that way. 進んで [ADV after v] ❏ ...the negotiations which have been dragging along interminably. だらだらと長引くだけの交渉. ■ ADV 副詞 If you take someone or something **along** when you go somewhere, you take them with you. 一緒に, 連れ立って [ADV after v] ❏ This is open to women of all ages, so bring along your friends and colleagues. 女性でしたらご年齢は問いませんので, ご友人やご同僚と一緒においでください. ■ ADV 副詞 If someone or something is coming **along** or is sent **along**, they are coming or being sent to a particular place. ある場所へ行く, 来る [ADV after v] ❏ She invited everyone she knew to come along. 彼女は知人にはみな声をかけて参加するように頼んだ. ■ PHRASE 句 You use **along with** to mention someone or something else that is also involved in an action or situation. —と一緒に ❏ The baby's mother escaped from the fire along with two other children. 赤ん坊の母親は他の2人の子供とともに火事から逃れました. ■ PHRASE 句 If something has been true or been present **all along**, it has been true or been present throughout a period of time. ずっと ❏ I've been fooling myself all along. 最初からずっと勘違いしてたんだ. ■ **along the way** → see **way**

along|side /əlɔŋsaɪd/ ■ PREP 前置詞 If one thing is **alongside** another thing, the first thing is next to the second. —の横を ❏ He crossed the street and walked alongside Central Park. 彼は道路を渡るとセントラルパーク沿いを歩いた. ●ADV 副詞 **Alongside** is also an adverb. 並んで [ADV after v] ❏ He waited several minutes for a car to pull up alongside. 彼は数分待つと1台の車が道路わきに止まった. ■ PREP 前置詞 If you work **alongside** other people, you all work together in the same place. —と一緒に ❏ He had worked alongside Frank and Mark and they had become friends. 彼はフランクやマークと一緒に働いているうちに友達になった.

aloof /əluf/ ADJ 形容詞 Someone who is **aloof** is not very friendly and does not like to spend time with other people. よそよそしい [DISAPPROVAL 不賛成] ❏ He seemed aloof and detached. 彼はよそよそしく打ち解けないようすだった.

aloud /əlaʊd/ ■ ADV 副詞 When you say something, read, or

laugh **aloud**, you speak or laugh so that other people can hear you. 声に出して [ADV after v] ❑ *When we were children, our father read aloud to us.* 子供の頃、父は私どもに本を読んでくれた. ❷ PHRASE 句 If you **think aloud**, you express your thoughts as they occur to you, rather than thinking first and then speaking. 何も考えずに話す ❑ *He really must be careful about thinking aloud. Who knew what he might say?* 彼は思ったことをそのまま口に出してしまうから、十分気をつけてもらわないとだめだ. 何を言い出すか誰ひとり分からなかったのだ.

al|pha|bet /ǽlfəbɛt, -bɪt/ (**alphabets**) N-COUNT 可算名詞 An **alphabet** is a set of letters usually presented in a fixed order which is used for writing the words of a particular language or group of languages. アルファベット ❑ *The modern Russian alphabet has 31 letters.* 現代ロシア語のアルファベットは31文字ある.

al|pha|beti|cal /ǽlfəbɛtɪkəl/ ADJ 形容詞 **Alphabetical** means arranged according to the normal order of the letters in the alphabet. アルファベット順の [ADJ n] ❑ *Their herbs and spices are arranged in alphabetical order on narrow open shelves.* ハーブや香辛料はアルファベット順にして戸のついていない幅の狭い棚に並べられている.

al|pine /ǽlpaɪn/ ADJ 形容詞 **Alpine** means existing in or relating to mountains, especially the ones in Switzerland. アルプスの ❑ *...grassy, alpine meadows.* アルプスの高山帯の草地.

al|ready /ɔːlrédi/ ❶ ADV 副詞 You use **already** to show that something has happened, or that something had happened before the moment you are referring to. Some speakers use **already** with the simple past tense of the verb instead of a perfect tense. すでに ❑ *They had already voted for him at the first ballot.* 彼らはすでに1回目の投票で彼に投票していた. ❑ *She says she already told the neighbors not to come over for a couple of days.* 彼女の話では、すでに近所の人にはここ2日は訪ねてこないように言ってあるそうです. ❷ ADV 副詞 You use **already** to show that a situation exists at this present moment or that it exists at an earlier time than expected. You use **already** after the verb "be" or an auxiliary verb, or before a verb if there is no auxiliary. When you want to add emphasis, you can put **already** at the beginning of a sentence. もうすでに ❑ *The authorities believe those security measures are already paying off.* 当局によれば、安全対策の効果はもうすでに出始めているとしています. ❑ *He was already rich.* 彼はもうそのときは金持ちだった. ❑ *Already, she is thinking ahead.* もうすでに彼女は次のことを考えている.

> **Already** is often used to add emphasis or to suggest that it is surprising that something has happened so soon. ❑ *They were already eating their lunch.* If you say that something is **still** happening or is **still** the case, you are usually emphasizing your surprise that it has been happening or has been the case for so long. ❑ *She was still looking at me... There are still plenty of horses around here.* You use **yet** in negative sentences and in questions. It is often used to add emphasis, to suggest surprise that something has not happened, or to say that it will happen later. ❑ *Have you seen it yet?... The troops could not yet see the shore... It isn't dark yet.* In British English, **already** and **yet** are usually used with the present perfect tense. ❑ *I have already started knitting baby clothes... Have they said sorry yet?* In American English, a past tense is commonly used. ❑ *She already told the neighbors not to come... I didn't get any sleep yet.* This usage is becoming more common in British English.

al|right /ɔːlráɪt/ → see **all right**

also /ɔːlsoʊ/ ❶ ADV 副詞 You can use **also** to give more information about a person or thing, or to add another relevant fact. さらに ❑ *The book also includes an appendix with a listing of all U.S. presidents.* その本の付録には歴代大統領の一覧表が付いている. ❑ *He is an asthmatic who is also anemic.* 彼はぜんそく持ちで貧血気味だ. ❷ ADV 副詞 You can use **also** to indicate that something you have just said about one person or thing is true of another person or thing. 同様に ❑ *General Geichenko was a survivor. His father, also a top-ranking officer, had perished during the war.* ゲイチェンコ将軍は生き延びた. 彼の父もまた最高将校だったが、戦時中に非業の死を遂げた. ❑ *This rule has also been applied in the case of a purchase of used tires and tubes.* 中古のタイヤやチューブを購入する際もこの規則が適用されてきた.

> **Also** and **too** are similar in meaning. **Also** never comes at the end of a clause, whereas **too** usually comes at the end. ❑ *He was also an artist and lived in Cleveland... He's a singer and an actor too.*

Thesaurus	*also* また次を参照:
ADV.	additionally, furthermore, plus, still ❶ and, likewise, too ❷

| **Word Link** | *alt* ≈ high : *altar, altitude, exalted* |

al|tar /ɔ́ːltər/ (**altars**) N-COUNT 可算名詞 An **altar** is a holy table in a church or temple. 祭壇 ❑ *...the high altar of the cathedral.* 大聖堂の高い祭壇.

al|ter /ɔ́ːltər/ (**alters, altering, altered**) V-T/V-I 他動詞/自動詞 If something **alters** or if you **alter** it, it changes. 変える [他動詞], 変わる [自動詞] ❑ *Nothing has altered and the deadline still stands.* 今のところ何一つ変更がないので期限にも変わりはない.

al|tera|tion /ɔ̀ːltəréɪʃən/ (**alterations**) ❶ N-COUNT 可算名詞 An **alteration** is a change in or to something. 変更 ❑ *Making some simple alterations to your diet will make you feel fitter.* 食事を少し変えるだけで体調がよくなる. ❷ N-UNCOUNT 不可算名詞 The **alteration** of something is the process of changing it. 手直し ❑ *Her jacket was at the boutique waiting for alteration.* 寸法を直してもらうのにジャケットをブティックに預けていた.

al|ter|nate (**alternates, alternating, alternated**)

> The verb is pronounced /ɔ́ːltərneɪt/. The adjective and noun are pronounced /ɔ́ːltɜːrnɪt/.
>
> 動詞は /ɔ́ːltərneɪt/ と発音される. 形容詞と名詞は /ɔ́ːltɜːrnɪt/ と発音される.

❶ V-RECIP 相互動詞 When you **alternate** two things, you keep using one then the other. When one thing **alternates with** another, the first regularly occurs after the other. 互い違いにする; 互い違いになる ❑ *Her aggressive moods alternated with gentle or more cooperative states.* 彼女には反抗的になったりおとなしく協調的になったりした. ❑ *Now you just alternate layers of that mixture and eggplant.* それからナスと混ぜ合わせたものと交互に重ねていきます. ❷ ADJ 形容詞 **Alternate** actions, events, or processes regularly occur after each other. 交互の [ADJ n] ❑ *They were streaked with alternate bands of color.* 2色のしま模様になっていた. ● **al|ter|nate|ly** ADV 副詞 代わる代わるに ❑ *He could alternately bully and charm people.* 彼はみんなをいじめることもあれば喜ばせることもあった. ❸ ADJ 形容詞 [ADJ n] If something happens on **alternate** days, it happens on one day, then happens on every second day after that. In the same way, something can happen in **alternate** weeks, years, or other periods of time. 一つおきの ❑ *Lesley had agreed to Jim going skiing in alternate years.* レスリーはジムと話し合って1年おきにスキーに行くことにした. ❹ ADJ 形容詞 You use **alternate** to describe a plan, idea, or system which is different from the one already in operation and can be used instead of it. 代わりの [ADJ n] ❑ *His group was forced to turn back and take an alternate route.* 一行は来た道を行ったり来たり戻って、別のルートを選ぶよりほかはなかったのです. ❺ N-COUNT 可算名詞 An **alternate** is a person or thing that replaces another, and can act or be used instead of them. 代わり [AM 米国英語] ❑ *In most jurisdictions, twelve jurors and two alternates are chosen.* 多くの裁判管轄区では陪審員12名と補欠2名を選ぶ.

al|ter|na|tive /ɔːltɜ́ːrnətɪv/ (**alternatives**) ❶ N-COUNT 可算名詞 If one thing is an **alternative** to another, the first can be found, used, or done instead of the second. 代わりとなるもの ❑ *New ways to treat arthritis may provide an alternative to painkillers.* 新しい関節炎の治療法がこれまでの鎮痛剤による治療に取って代わるかもしれない. ❷ ADJ 形容詞 An **alternative** plan or offer is different from the one that you already have, and can be done or used instead. 代わりとなる [ADJ n] ❑ *There were alternative methods of travel available.* 他の交通手段で旅行することもできた. ❸ ADJ 形容詞 **Alternative** is used to describe something that is different from the usual things of its kind, or the usual ways of doing something, in modern Western society. For example, an **alternative** lifestyle does not follow conventional ways of living and working. 従来の価値観に縛られない [ADJ n] ❑ *...unconventional parents who embraced the alternative lifestyle of the Sixties.* 従来の価値観に捉われない60年代の新しい生き方を選んだ親たち. ❹ ADJ 形容詞 **Alternative** medicine uses traditional ways of curing people, such as medicines made from plants, massage, and acupuncture. 代替の [ADJ n] ❑ *...alternative health care.* 代替医療. ❺ ADJ 形容詞 **Alternative** energy uses natural sources of energy such as the sun, wind, or water for power and fuel, rather than oil, coal, or nuclear power. 代替の [ADJ n]

al|ter|na|tive|ly /ɔːltɜ́ːrnətɪvli/ ADV 副詞 You use **alternatively** to introduce a suggestion or to mention something different from what has just been stated. あるいは [ADV with cl] ❑ *Hotels are generally of a good standard and not too expensive. Alternatively you could stay in an apartment.* 全般的にホテルは質もよく宿泊料も高くない. ホテルの代わりにアパートを借りる手もある.

al|though /ɔːlðóʊ/ ❶ CONJ 接続詞 You use **although** to introduce a subordinate clause which contains a statement that contrasts with the statement in the main clause. 一だけれども ❑ *Although he is known to only a few, his reputation among them is very great.* 彼を知る者は少ないが、その人たちの間での評判はとてもよい. ❷ CONJ 接続詞 You use **although** to introduce a subordinate clause which contains a statement that makes the main clause of the sentence seem surprising or unexpected. 一にもかかわらず ❑ *Although I was only six, I can remember seeing it on TV.* まだ

ほんの6歳だったのにテレビで見たのを覚えている. **3** CONJ 接続詞 You use **although** to introduce a subordinate clause which gives some information that is relevant to the main clause but modifies the strength of that statement. たとえ－でも □*He was in love with her, although a man seldom puts that name to what he feels.* 彼は彼女を愛していた. とはいえ男がその思いを愛と呼ぶようなことはまずない. **4** CONJ 接続詞 You use **although** when admitting a fact about something that you regard as less important than a contrasting fact. －だけれども □*Although they're expensive, they last forever and never go out of style* 高価なものだが長持ちするし飽きもこない.

Thesaurus
although また次を参照：

CONJ. despite, though, while **1** – **4**

Word Link
alt ≈ high : *alt*ar, *alt*itude, ex*alt*ed

al|ti|tude /ǽltɪtud/ (**altitudes**) N-VAR 可変性名詞 If something is at a particular **altitude**, it is at that height above sea level. 海抜 □*The aircraft had reached its cruising altitude of about 39,000 feet.* 航空機は巡航高度の約3万9千フィートに達していた.

al|to|geth|er /ɔ̀ltəgɛ́ðər/ **1** ADV 副詞 You use **altogether** to emphasize that something has stopped, been done, or finished completely. 完全に [EMPHASIS 強調] [ADV after v] □*When Artie stopped calling altogether, Julie found a new man.* アーティがすっかり姿を見せなくなってから，ジュリーは新しい男を見つけた. **2** ADV 副詞 You use **altogether** in front of an adjective or adverb to emphasize a quality that someone or something has. 全く [EMPHASIS 強調] [ADV adj/adv] □*The choice of language is altogether different.* 言葉の選び方がまるで違っています. **3** ADV 副詞 You use **altogether** to modify a negative statement and make it less forceful. 全く－というわけではない □*We were not altogether sure that the comet would miss the Earth.* すい星は地球に衝突しないと言い切れるわけではありません. **4** ADV 副詞 You can use **altogether** to introduce a summary of what you have been saying. 要するに [ADV with cl] □*Altogether, it was a delightful town garden, peaceful and secluded.* 総じていえば心地のよい都会の庭園で. 穏やかでひっそりとしたたたずまいを見せていた. **5** ADV 副詞 If several amounts add up to a particular amount **altogether**, that amount is their total. 合計で [ADV with amount] □*Brando received eight Oscar nominations altogether.* ブランドは計8部門でアカデミー賞の候補となった.

al|tru|ism /ǽltruɪzəm/ N-UNCOUNT 不可算名詞 **Altruism** is unselfish concern for other people's happiness and welfare. 利他主義 □*Fortunately, volunteers are not motivated by self-interest, but by altruism.* 幸いなことにボランティアの人たちは，自分のためでなく人の役に立ちたいと思って活動している.

alu|min|ium /ǽlyumɪ́niəm/ → see aluminum

alu|mi|num /əlúmɪnəm/ N-UNCOUNT 不可算名詞 **Aluminum** is a lightweight metal used, for example, for making cooking equipment and aircraft parts. アルミニウム [AM 米国英語] □*...aluminum cans.* アルミ缶.

al|ways /ɔ́lweɪz/ **1** ADV 副詞 If you **always** do something, you do it whenever a particular situation occurs. If you **always** did something, you did it whenever a particular situation occurred. いつも [ADV before v] □*She's always late for everything.* 彼女ったら，時間どおりに来たためしがないんだから. □*Always lock your garage.* ガレージには必ず鍵をかけること. **2** ADV 副詞 If something is **always** the case, was **always** the case, or will **always** be the case, it is, was, or will be the case all the time, continuously. いつでも □*We will always remember his generous hospitality.* 彼が温かくもてなしてくれたことはずっと忘れない. □*He has always been the family solicitor.* 彼は昔からこの家の弁護士だ. **3** ADV 副詞 If you say that something is **always** happening, especially something that annoys you, you mean that it happens repeatedly. しじゅう－ばかりしている [ADV before v-cont] □*She was always moving things around.* 彼女はしょっちゅう模様替えばかりしていた. **4** ADV 副詞 You use **always** in expressions such as **can always** or **could always** when you are making suggestions or suggesting an alternative approach or method. いつでも ['can/could' ADV inf] □*If you can't find any decent apples, you can always try growing them yourself.* よいりんごが見つからなかったら，いつでも自分で作ってみてください. **5** ADV 副詞 You can say that someone **always** was, for example, awkward or lucky to indicate that you are not surprised about what they are doing or have just done. もともと [ADV before v] □*She's going to be fine. She always was pretty strong.* 彼女はよくなるよ. もともと体は丈夫なほうなんだから.

Do not confuse **always** and **ever**. If something **always** happens, it happens regularly or on every occasion. □*I would always ask for the radio to be turned down... He's always been an active person.* If something is **always** the case, it is true at all times. □*No matter what she did, she would always be forgiven.* You use **ever**, for example in negative sentences, questions, and with superlatives, to talk about any time at all when referring to the past, present, or future. □*No one ever came...Will I ever see France? ...the nicest thing anyone's ever said to me.*

Thesaurus
always また次を参照：

ADV. consistently, constantly, regularly, repeatedly **1** **3** continuously, endlessly; (ant.) never, rarely **2**

am /əm, STRONG æm/ **Am** is the first person singular of the present tense of **be**. **Am** is often shortened to 'm in spoken English. The negative forms are "I am not" and "I'm not." In questions and tags in spoken English, these are usually changed to "aren't I." －である；－にいる

AM /éɪ ɛm/ **AM** is a method of transmitting radio waves that can be used to broadcast sound. **AM** is an abbreviation for 'amplitude modulation.' 振幅変調

a.m. /éɪ ɛm/ also **am** **a.m.** is used after a number to show that you are referring to a particular time between midnight and noon. Compare **p.m.** 午前 □*The program starts at 9 a.m.* 番組は午前9時に始まる.

amal|gam|ate /əmǽlgəmeɪt/ (**amalgamates, amalgamating, amalgamated**) V-RECIP 相互動詞 When two or more things, especially organizations, **amalgamate** or **are amalgamated**, they become one large thing. 合併する □*The firm has amalgamated with another company.* その会社は他の会社と合併しました. □*The chemical companies had amalgamated into a vast conglomerate.* 化学会社の合併によって巨大なコングロマリットが誕生した. ● **amal|gama|tion** /əmælgəméɪʃⁿn/ (**amalgamations**) N-VAR 可変性名詞 合併 □*Athletics South Africa was formed by an amalgamation of two organizations.* 南アフリカ陸上競技連盟は2つの組織の合併によって生まれた.

amass /əmǽs/ (**amasses, amassing, amassed**) V-T 他動詞 If you **amass** something such as money or information, you gradually get a lot of it. 蓄積する □*How had he amassed his fortune?* 彼はどのようにして財産を蓄えただろうか.

Word Link
eur ≈ one who does : *am*at*eur*, chauff*eur*, entrepr*eneur*

ama|teur /ǽmətʃɚr, -tʃʊər/ (**amateurs**) **1** N-COUNT 可算名詞 An **amateur** is someone who does something as a hobby and not as a job. まで □*Jerry is an amateur who dances because he feels like it.* ジェリーは素人ダンサーでとにかく好きで踊っている. **2** ADJ 形容詞 **Amateur** sports or activities are done by people as a hobby and not as a job. アマチュアの [ADJ n] □*...professional athletes and amateur runners.* プロの選手とアマチュアの走者.

amaze /əméɪz/ (**amazes, amazing, amazed**) V-T/V-I 他動詞／自動詞 If something **amazes** you, it surprises you very much. びっくりさせる □*He amazed us by his knowledge of Colorado history.* 彼はコロラドの歴史をよく知っていたのでみんなびっくりした. □*The "Riverside" restaurant promises a variety of food that never ceases to amaze!* 当店リバーサイドレストランでは，お客様に必ず満足いただける数々のメニューをご用意しております. ● **amazed** ADJ 形容詞 びっくりした □*Most of the cast was amazed by the play's success.* 芝居の成功にほとんどの出演者が驚きました.

Word Partnership
amaze は次の語句と使われる：

V. continue to amaze, never cease to amaze
N. amaze **your friends**

amaze|ment /əméɪzmənt/ N-UNCOUNT 不可算名詞 **Amazement** is the feeling you have when something surprises you very much. 驚き [oft 'in' n] □*I stared at her in amazement.* 驚きの目で彼女を見つめた.

amaz|ing /əméɪzɪŋ/ ADJ 形容詞 You say that something is **amazing** when it is very surprising and makes you feel pleasure, approval, or wonder. びっくりするような □*It's amazing that we can remember with a little prompting.* 少しのヒントがあれば思い出せるのだからびっくりする. ● **amaz|ing|ly** ADV 副詞 びっくりするほど □*She was an amazingly good cook.* 彼女の料理の腕前はそれは見事なものだった.

Thesaurus
amazing また次を参照：

ADJ. astonishing, astounding, extraordinary, incredible; (ant.) stunning, wonderful

am|bas|sa|dor /æmbǽsədər/ (**ambassadors**) N-COUNT 可算名詞 An **ambassador** is an important official who lives in a foreign country and represents his or her own country's interests there. 大使 □ …the German ambassador to Poland. ドイツの駐ポーランド大使.

am|ber /æmbər/ ■ N-UNCOUNT 不可算名詞 **Amber** is a hard yellowish-brown substance used for making jewelry. こはく [usu N n] □ …an amber choker with matching earrings. こはくのチョーカーとそれにぴったりのイヤリング. ■ COLOR 色彩語 **Amber** is used to describe things that are yellowish-brown in color. こはく色; こはく色の □ A burst of sunshine sent a beam of amber light through the window. 太陽の光がぱっと輝くと、こはく色の光の束が窓から差し込んだ. ■ COLOR 色彩語 An **amber** traffic light is yellow. 黄色 □ Cars did not stop when the lights were on amber. 信号は黄色だったが車は止まらず進んだ.

am|bi|ence /æmbiəns/ also **ambiance** N-SING 単数名詞 The **ambience** of a place is the character and atmosphere that it seems to have. 雰囲気 [LITERARY 文語的] □ The overall ambience of the room is cozy. 部屋全体の雰囲気が心地よい.

am|bi|gu|ity /æmbɪgyúɪti/ (**ambiguities**) N-VAR 可変性名詞 If you say that there is **ambiguity** in something, you mean that it is unclear or confusing, or it can be understood in more than one way. あいまいさ □ There is considerable ambiguity about what this part of the agreement actually means. 契約書のこの部分が実際どういう意味なのか、かなりあいまいである.

am|bigu|ous /æmbɪgyuəs/ ADJ 形容詞 If you describe something as **ambiguous**, you mean that it is unclear or confusing because it can be understood in more than one way. あいまいな □ This agreement is very ambiguous and open to various interpretations. この協定は非常にあいまいなのでどのようにも解釈できます. ● **am|bigu|ous|ly** ADV 副詞 あいまいに □ The national conference on democracy ended ambiguously. 民主主義をテーマにした全国会議は決着を見ないまま閉幕した.

am|bi|tion /æmbɪ́ʃⁿn/ (**ambitions**) ■ N-COUNT 可算名詞 If you have an **ambition** to do or achieve something, you want very much to do it or achieve it. 念願 □ His ambition is to sail around the world. 彼の夢はヨットで世界一周することだ. ■ N-UNCOUNT 不可算名詞 **Ambition** is the desire to be successful, rich, or powerful. 野心 □ Even when I was young I never had any ambition. 若い頃ですら野心とは全く無縁だった.

am|bi|tious /æmbɪʃəs/ ■ ADJ 形容詞 Someone who is **ambitious** has a strong desire to be successful, rich, or powerful. 野心のある □ Chris is so ambitious, so determined to do it all. クリスは全部やってしまおうとやる気満々だ. ■ ADJ 形容詞 An **ambitious** idea or plan is on a large scale and needs a lot of work to be carried out successfully. 大がかりな □ The ambitious project was completed in only nine months. 大がかりなプロジェクトだったがわずか9か月で完了した.

Thesaurus	ambitious また次を参照:
ADJ.	aspiring ■
	challenging, difficult ■

am|biva|lent /æmbɪvələnt/ ADJ 形容詞 If you say that someone is **ambivalent about** something, they seem to be uncertain whether they really want it, or whether they really approve of it. 相反する感情をもつ □ She remained ambivalent about her marriage. 彼女は結婚するかどうかずっと迷っていた.

am|bu|lance /æmbyələns/ (**ambulances**) N-COUNT 可算名詞 An **ambulance** is a vehicle for taking people to and from a hospital. 救急車 [also 'by' N]

am|bush /æmbʊʃ/ (**ambushes, ambushing, ambushed**) ■ V-T 他動詞 If a group of people **ambush** their enemies, they attack them after hiding and waiting for them. 待ち伏せする □ The Guatemalan army says rebels ambushed and killed 10 patrolmen. グアテマラ軍の発表では、反乱軍兵士から待ち伏せ攻撃を受けパトロール中の兵士10人が死亡しました. ■ N-VAR 可変性名詞 An **ambush** is an attack on someone by people who have been hiding and waiting for them. 待ち伏せ攻撃 □ Three civilians were killed in guerrilla ambushes. ゲリラ兵の待ち伏せ攻撃で村民3人が死亡した.

amen /ɑ́mɛn, eɪ́-/ CONVENTION 慣習表現 **Amen** is said by Christians at the end of a prayer. アーメン □ In the name of the Father and of the Son and of the Holy Ghost, amen. 父と子と聖霊との御名において、アーメン.

ame|nable /əmíːnəbⁿl, əmɛ́nə-/ ADJ 形容詞 If you are **amenable to** something, you are willing to do it or accept it. 素直に応じる □ The Jordanian leader seemed amenable to attending a conference. ヨルダンの首相は会議への出席を受け入れた模様です.

amend /əmɛ́nd/ (**amends, amending, amended**) ■ V-T 他動詞 If you **amend** something that has been written such as a law, or something that is said, you change it in order to improve it or

make it more accurate. 修正する □ The president agreed to amend the constitution and allow multi-party elections. 大統領は、複数政党による選挙制を導入することの憲法改正に同意しました. ■ PHRASE 句 If you **make amends** when you have harmed someone, you show that you are sorry by doing something to please them. 償いをする □ He wanted to make amends for causing their marriage to fail. 結婚を破綻させてしまったことに対して彼は償いたいと思った.

amend|ment /əmɛ́ndmənt/ (**amendments**) ■ N-VAR 可変性名詞 An **amendment** is a section that is added to a law or rule in order to change it. 修正案; 修正条項 □ …an amendment to the defense bill 国防法案に対する修正案. ■ N-COUNT 可算名詞 An **amendment** is a change that is made to a piece of writing. 修正

amen|ity /əmɛ́niti/ (**amenities**) N-COUNT 可算名詞 **Amenities** are things such as shopping centers or sports facilities that are provided for people's convenience, enjoyment, or comfort. 娯楽施設 [usu pl] □ The hotel amenities include health clubs, conference facilities, and banqueting rooms. ホテルにはヘルスクラブ、会議場、宴会場などが備わっている.

→ see hotel

Ameri|can foot|ball (**American footballs**) ■ N-UNCOUNT 不可算名詞 **American football** is a game that is played by two teams of eleven players using an oval-shaped ball. Players try to score points by passing or carrying the ball to their opponents' end of the field, or by kicking it over a bar fixed between two posts. アメリカンフットボール [BRIT 英国英語; AM **football** 米国英語**football**] ■ N-COUNT 可算名詞 An **American football** is an oval-shaped ball used for playing American football. アメリカンフットボールのボール [BRIT 英国英語; AM **football** 米国英語**football**]

ami|able /eɪmiəbⁿl/ ADJ 形容詞 Someone who is **amiable** is friendly and pleasant to be with. 気だてのよい [WRITTEN 書き言葉] □ She had been surprised at how amiable and polite he had been. 彼女が驚いていたのは、彼がいつも優しくて礼儀正しいことだった.

ami|cable /æmɪkəbⁿl/ ADJ 形容詞 When people have an **amicable** relationship, they are pleasant to each other and solve their problems without quarreling. 友好的な □ The meeting ended on reasonably amicable terms. お互いがほぼ満足できる条件で話し合いがついた. ● **ami|cably** /æmɪkəbli/ ADV 副詞 [ADV with v] 友好的に □ He hoped the dispute could be settled amicably. 紛争が平和裏に解決することを彼は期待した.

amid /əmɪd/

The form **amidst** is also used, but is old-fashioned.

amidst 形も使われるが、古風である.

PREP 前置詞 If something happens **amid** noises or events of some kind, it happens while the other things are happening. 〜の最中に □ Workers are sifting through the wreckage of the airliners amid growing evidence that the disasters were the work of terrorists. 機体の残骸調査が進むなか、この大惨事がテロによるものだという疑いが強まっている.

amiss /əmɪ́s/ ADJ 形容詞 If you say that something is **amiss**, you mean there is something wrong. 具合の悪い [v-link ADJ] □ Their instincts warned them something was amiss. 彼らは本能的に何かおかしいと感じた.

am|mo|nia /əmóʊniə/ N-UNCOUNT 不可算名詞 **Ammonia** is a colorless liquid or gas with a strong, sharp smell. It is used in making household cleaning substances. アンモニア

am|mu|ni|tion /æmyʊnɪ́ʃⁿn/ ■ N-UNCOUNT 不可算名詞 **Ammunition** is bullets and rockets that are made to be fired from weapons. 弾薬 □ He had only seven rounds of ammunition for the revolver. 拳銃には弾が7発しか入ってなかった. ■ N-UNCOUNT 不可算名詞 You can describe information that you can use against someone in an argument or discussion as **ammunition**. (自分の側に) 有利な情報 □ The improved trade figures have given the government fresh ammunition. 貿易収支が改善したことで、政府は批判をかわすための新たな論拠を手に入れました.

am|ne|sia /æmníːʒə/ N-UNCOUNT 不可算名詞 If someone is suffering from **amnesia**, they have lost their memory. 記憶喪失 □ People suffering from amnesia don't forget their general knowledge of objects. 記憶喪失になっても、身の回りのものについての一般的な知識は失われることはない.

am|nes|ty /æmnɪsti/ (**amnesties**) ■ N-VAR 可変性名詞 An **amnesty** is an official pardon granted to a group of prisoners by the state. 恩赦 □ Activists who were involved in crimes of violence will not automatically be granted amnesty. 暴力犯罪に関わった活動家に対しては、すぐさま恩赦が認められることはないでしょう. ■ N-COUNT 可算名詞 An **amnesty** is a period of time during which people can admit to a crime or give up weapons without being punished. (法の執行の) 赦免期間 □ The government has announced an immediate amnesty for rebel fighters. 政府は反乱軍兵士に対して武器を捨て投降すれば直ちに赦免すると発表しました.

A

among /əmʌn/

The form **amongst** is also used, but is more old-fashioned.

amongst 形も使われるが、やや古風である。

1 PREP 前置詞 Someone or something that is situated or moving **among** a group of things or people is surrounded by them. 一に混じって □...youths in their late teens sitting among adults. 大人で座っている10代後半の若者たち。 **2** PREP 前置詞 If you are **among** people of a particular kind, you are with them and having contact with them. 一の中で □Things weren't so bad, after all. I was among friends again. いろいろあったけど、たいしたことにはならなかった。友だちともまた付き合うようになった。 **3** PREP 前置詞 If someone or something is **among** a group, they are a member of that group and share its characteristics. 一の中に □A fifteen-year-old girl was among the injured. 負傷者の中には15歳の少女もいました。 **4** PREP 前置詞 If you want to focus on something that is happening within a particular group of people, you can say that it is happening **among** that group. 一の間で □Homicide is the leading cause of death among black men. 黒人男性の第1の死因は他殺です。 **5** PREP 前置詞 If something happens **among** a group of people, it happens within the whole of that group or between the members of that group. 一の間で □The calls for reform come as intense debate continues among the leadership over the next five-year economic plan. 改革が叫ばれるなか、次期経済5か年計画をめぐり指導部内の議論が激しさを増しています。 **6** PREP 前置詞 If something such as a feeling, opinion, or situation exists **among** a group of people, most of them have it or experience it. 一の間で □There was some concern among book and magazine retailers after last Wednesday's news. 先週水曜の報道以後、本や雑誌を扱う小売業者の間に不安が広がった。 **7** PREP 前置詞 If something applies to a particular person or thing **among others**, it also applies to other people or things. 他と共に □...a news conference attended among others by our foreign affairs correspondent. 本社海外特派員などの報道関係者が出席した記者会見。 **8** PREP 前置詞 If something is shared **among** a number of people, some of it is given to all of them. 一の間で □Most of the furniture was left to the neighbors or distributed among friends. 家具はほとんど近所の人や友人に譲ったり配ったりした。 **9** PREP 前置詞 If people talk, fight, or agree **among themselves**, they do it together, without involving anyone else. 一の間で [PREP pron-refl] □The girls stood aside, talking among themselves, looking over their shoulders at the boys. 女の子たちは脇によってひそひそ話をしながら、男の子たちを肩越しにのぞき込んだ。

If there are more than two people or things, you should use **among**. If there are only two people or things you should use **between** □...an area between Mars and Jupiter. You can also talk about relationships **between** or **among** people or things, and discussions **between** or **among** people. □...an argument between his mother and another woman. Note that if you are **between** things or people, the things or people are on either side of you. If you are **among** things or people, they are all around you □...the bag standing on the floor between us. ...the sound of a pigeon among the trees.

amongst /əmʌnst/ PREP 前置詞 **Amongst** means the same as **among**. 一の間で [OLD-FASHIONED 古風な]

amor|tize /æmərtaɪz/ (amortizes, amortizing, amortized) V-T 他動詞 In finance, if you **amortize** a debt, you pay it back in regular payments. 返済する [BUSINESS 実業] □There's little advantage to amortizing the loan, especially on a 30 or 40-year basis. ローンによる返済はほとんどメリットはなく、30年や40年のローンの場合は特にメリットがない。

amount /əmaʊnt/ (amounts, amounting, amounted) **1** N-VAR 可算変化名詞 The **amount of** something is how much there is, or how much you have, need, or get. 総額; 総量 □He needs that amount of money to survive. 生きていくためにはその程度のお金が必要です。 □I still do a certain amount of work for them. 今でもそこの仕事はある程度やってます。 **2** V-I 自動詞 If something **amounts to** a particular total, all the parts of it add up to that total. 合計で一になる □Consumer spending on sports-related items amounted to $9.75 billion. 消費者がスポーツのために使うお金は97億5千万ドルに達する。

You should avoid using a plural noun after **amount of**; instead you should use **number of** with a plural noun. □...the number of people out of work.

▶ **amount to** PHRASAL VERB 句動詞 If you say that one thing **amounts to** something else, you consider the first thing to be the same as the second thing. 一に等しい □The banks have what amounts to a monopoly. 銀行はいわば独占状態にある。

amp /æmp/ (amps) **1** N-COUNT 可算名詞 An **amp** is the same as an **ampere**. アンペア □Use a 3 amp fuse for equipment up to 720 watts. 3アンペアのヒューズは最高720ワットの装置まで使用できます。 **2** N-COUNT 可算名詞 An **amp** is the same as an **amplifier**. アンプ [INFORMAL くだけた]

am|pere /æmpɪər, æmpɪər/ (amperes) N-COUNT 詞 An **ampere** is a unit used for measuring electric current. The abbreviation **amp** is also used. アンペア

am|pheta|mine /æmfɛtəmin/ (amphetamines) N-MASS 質量名詞 **Amphetamine** is a drug that increases people's energy, makes them excited, and reduces their desire for food. アンフェタミン

Word Link　ampl ≈ large : ample, amplifier, amplify

am|ple /æmp°l/ (ampler, amplest) ADJ 形容詞 If there is an **ample** amount of something, there is enough of it and usually some extra. たっぷりの □There'll be ample opportunity to relax, swim and soak up some sun. のんびりしたり泳いだり日光浴したりする機会は十分あるでしょう。 ● **am|ply** ADV 副詞 十分に □This collection of his essays and journalism amply demonstrates his commitment to democracy. 評論と寄稿記事からなるこの本には、民主主義に対する彼の熱い思いが十分に表れています。

am|pli|fi|er /æmplɪfaɪər/ (amplifiers) N-COUNT 可算名詞 An **amplifier** is an electronic device in a radio or stereo system that causes sounds or signals to get louder. アンプ

am|pli|fy /æmplɪfaɪ/ (amplifies, amplifying, amplified) **1** V-T 他動詞 If you **amplify** a sound, you make it louder, usually by using electronic equipment. 増幅する □This landscape seemed to trap and amplify sounds. この地形のせいで音が閉じ込められて大きくなったと考えられた。 ● **am|pli|fi|ca|tion** /æmplɪfɪkeɪʃ°n/ N-UNCOUNT 不可算名詞 増幅 □...a voice that needed no amplification. マイクのいらない大きな声。 **2** V-T 他動詞 To **amplify** something means to increase its strength or intensity. 拡大する □The mist had been replaced by a kind of haze that seemed to amplify the heat. 霧が濃くなるにつれて気温も上昇したようです。

am|pu|tate /æmpyʊteɪt/ (amputates, amputating, amputated) V-T 他動詞 To **amputate** someone's arm or leg means to cut all or part of it off in an operation because it is diseased or badly damaged. (手術で)切断する □To save his life, doctors amputated his legs. 医師は彼の両足を切断して命を救いました。 ● **am|pu|ta|tion** /æmpyʊteɪʃ°n/ (amputations) N-VAR 可変性名詞 切断手術 □He lived only hours after the amputation. 切断手術を受けたが数時間の命だった。

amuse /əmyuz/ (amuses, amusing, amused) **1** V-T 他動詞 If something **amuses** you, it makes you want to laugh or smile. 笑わせる □The thought seemed to amuse him. その思いつきが彼には面白かったようだ。 **2** V-T 他動詞 If you **amuse yourself**, you do something in order to pass the time and not become bored. 楽しく過ごす □I need distractions. I need to amuse myself so I won't keep thinking about things. 僕には気分転換が必要だ。楽しく過ごしてあれこれ考え込まないことだ。 **3** → see also **amused**, **amusing**

amused /əmyuzd/ ADJ 形容詞 If you are **amused by** something, it makes you want to laugh or smile. 面白がる □Sara was not amused by Franklin's teasing. フランクリンがからかったが、セイラにはちっとも面白くなかった。

amuse|ment /əmyuzmənt/ (amusements) **1** N-UNCOUNT 不可算名詞 **Amusement** is the feeling that you have when you think that something is funny or amusing. おかしさ; 面白味 □He stopped and watched with amusement to see the child so absorbed. 彼は足を止めて、熱中している子供のようすを面白そうに眺めた。 **2** N-UNCOUNT 不可算名詞 **Amusement** is the pleasure that you get from being entertained or from doing something interesting. 楽しみ □I stumbled sideways before landing flat on my back, much to the amusement of the rest of the guys. 横によろけて大の字に倒れたので、みんなに大笑いされた。 **3** N-COUNT 可算名詞 **Amusements** are ways of passing the time pleasantly. 娯楽 □People had very few amusements to choose from. There was no radio, or television. 当時は娯楽と呼べるものはほとんどなかった。ラジオもテレビもなかった。 **4** N-PLURAL 複数名詞 **Amusements** are games, rides, and other things that you can enjoy, for example, at an amusement park or resort. レジャー施設 □...a place full of swings and amusements. ぶらんこや乗り物などがたくさんある場所。

amus|ing /əmyuzɪn/ ADJ 形容詞 Someone or something that is **amusing** makes you laugh or smile. おかしい □He had a terrific sense of humor and could be very amusing. 彼のユーモアのセンスは抜群でね、そりゃ面白いことがあったよ。 ● **amus|ing|ly** ADV 副詞 面白く □The article must be amusingly written. 記事は面白く書かなければならない。

an /ən, STRONG æn/ DET 限定詞 **An** is used instead of "a," the indefinite article, in front of words that begin with vowel sounds.

anaemia /əniːmiə/ → see **anemia**

anaemic /əniːmɪk/ → see **anemic**

an|aes|thet|ic /ænɪsθɛtɪk/ → see **anesthetic**

anaes|the|tist /ənɪsθətɪst/ (anaesthetists) N-COUNT 可算名詞 An **anaesthetist** is a doctor who specializes in giving anesthetics to patients. 麻酔医 [BRIT 英国英語; AM **anesthesiologist** 米国英語 **anesthesiologist**]

anal /eɪnˀl/ ADJ 形容詞 **Anal** means relating to the anus of a person or animal. 肛門の ❑ ...anal injuries. 肛門部の外傷.

analog /ǽnɔlɔg/ (analogs)

> The spelling **analogue** is sometimes used for the adjective, and usually used for the noun.
>
> つづりの **analogue** は形容詞に使われることもあるが通常は名詞に使われる.

■ ADJ 形容詞 **Analog** technology involves measuring, storing, or recording an infinitely variable amount of information by using physical quantities such as voltage. アナログの ❑ The analog signals from the videotape are converted into digital code. ビデオテープのアナログ信号はデジタル信号に変換される. ■ ADJ 形容詞 An **analog** watch or clock shows what it is measuring with a pointer on a dial rather than with a number display. Compare **digital**. アナログ式の ■ N-COUNT 可算名詞 If one thing is an **analog** of another, it is similar in some way. 類似したもの [FORMAL 形式ばった] ❑ No model can ever be a perfect analog of nature itself. 模型である限り実物を完全に再現することなどありえない.

analogous /ənǽləgəs/ ADJ 形容詞 If one thing is **analogous** to another, the two things are similar in some way. ～と類似した [FORMAL 形式ばった] ❑ Marine construction technology like this is very complex, somewhat analogous to trying to build a bridge under water. こうした海洋建築技術は非常に複雑なもので, 例えて言うなら水中に橋を作るようなものです.

analogy /ənǽlədʒi/ (analogies) N-COUNT 可算名詞 If you make or draw an **analogy** between two things, you show that they are similar in some way. 類似性 ❑ The analogy between music and fragrance has stuck. こうした音楽と香りの共通性が心から離れない.

Word Partnership analogy は次の語句と使われる:

PREP.	analogy **between**
V.	**draw** an analogy, **make** an analogy
ADJ.	**false** analogy

analyse /ǽnəlaɪz/ → see **analyze**

analysis /ənǽlɪsɪs/ (analyses /ənǽlɪsiːz/) ■ N-VAR 可変性名詞 **Analysis** is the process of considering something carefully or using statistical methods in order to understand it or explain it. 分析 ❑ Sporting greatness defies analysis – but we know it when we see it. 一流のプレーがどんなものかは分析のしようもないが, そうしたプレーのすばらしさは見るだけで分かる. ■ N-VAR 可変性名詞 **Analysis** is the scientific process of examining something in order to find out what it consists of. 分析 ❑ They collect blood samples for analysis at a national laboratory. 血液サンプルを採取し国立の研究所へ分析に出す. ■ N-COUNT 可算名詞 An **analysis** is an explanation or description that results from considering something carefully. 分析結果 ❑ Coming up after the newscast, an analysis of the president's domestic policy. ニュースの後は大統領の国内政策について掘り下げてお伝えします.

analyst /ǽnəlɪst/ (analysts) ■ N-COUNT 可算名詞 An **analyst** is a person whose job is to analyze a subject and give opinions about it. 評論家 ❑ ...a political analyst. 政治評論家. ■ N-COUNT 可算名詞 An **analyst** is someone, usually a doctor, who examines and treats people who have emotional problems. 精神分析医 ❑ My analyst warned me that I liked married men too much. 精神分析医は, 私には既婚男性に強く引かれる傾向があると注意した.

analytic /ænəlɪtɪk/ ADJ 形容詞 **Analytic** means the same as **analytical**. 分析的な [mainly AM 主に米国英語]

analytical /ænəlɪtɪkˀl/ ADJ 形容詞 An **analytical** way of doing something involves the use of logical reasoning. 分析的な ❑ I have an analytical approach to every survey. 私はどのような調査でも分析的な手法を使う.

analyze /ǽnəlaɪz/ (analyzes, analyzing, analyzed) ■ V-T 他動詞 If you **analyze** something, you consider it carefully or use statistical methods in order to fully understand it. 分析する ❑ McCarthy was asked to analyze the data from the first phase of trials of the vaccine. マッカーシーはワクチンの第1段階の試験データを分析するように依頼された. ■ V-T 他動詞 If you **analyze** something, you examine it using scientific methods in order to find out what it consists of. 分析する ❑ We haven't had time to analyze those samples yet. 今のところこれらの試料を分析する時間はありません.

Thesaurus analyze また次を参照:

V.	consider, examine, inspect ■
	break down, dissect ■

anarchic /ænɑrkɪk/ ADJ 形容詞 If you describe someone or something as **anarchic**, you disapprove of them because they do not recognize or obey any rules or laws. 無政府状態の [DISAPPROVAL 不賛成] ❑ ...anarchic attitudes and complete disrespect

for authority. 無政府主義的な思想と権力の完全否定.

anarchism /ǽnɑrkɪzəm/ N-UNCOUNT 不可算名詞 **Anarchism** is the belief that the laws and power of governments should be replaced by people working together freely. 無政府主義 ❑ He advocated anarchism as the answer to social problems. 彼は社会問題の解決策として無政府主義を主張した.

anarchist /ǽnɑrkɪst/ (anarchists) ■ N-COUNT 可算名詞 An **anarchist** is a person who believes in anarchism. 無政府主義者 [oft N n] ❑ West Berlin always had a large anarchist community. 西ベルリンには以前から無政府主義者たちが作るコミュニティーがありました. ■ ADJ 形容詞 If someone has **anarchist** beliefs or views, they believe in anarchism. 無政府主義の [ADJ n] ❑ He was apparently quite converted from his anarchist views. どうやら彼は無政府主義的な思想からすっかり足を洗ったようだった.

Word Link arch ≈ rule : an**arch**y, hier**arch**y, mon**arch**

anarchy /ǽnɑrki/ N-UNCOUNT 不可算名詞 If you describe a situation as **anarchy**, you mean that nobody seems to be paying any attention to rules or laws. 無政府状態 [DISAPPROVAL 不賛成] ❑ The school's liberal, individualistic traditions were in danger of slipping into anarchy. その学校には自由と個性を尊ぶ伝統があったが, そのために混乱状態に陥る危険があった.

anatomical /ænətɒmɪkˀl/ ADJ 形容詞 **Anatomical** means relating to the structure of the bodies of people and animals. 解剖学上の ❑ ...minute anatomical differences between insects. 昆虫の微細な解剖学的な相違.

anatomy /ənǽtəmi/ ■ N-UNCOUNT 不可算名詞 **Anatomy** is the study of the structure of the bodies of people or animals. 解剖学 ❑ ...a course in anatomy. 解剖学講座. ■ N-COUNT 可算名詞 You can refer to your body as your **anatomy**. からだ [HUMOROUS ユーモアのある] ❑ The ball hit him in the most sensitive part of his anatomy. ボールが彼の急所に当たった.

→ see **medicine**

ancestor /ǽnsestər/ (ancestors) ■ N-COUNT 可算名詞 Your **ancestors** are the people from whom you are descended. 先祖, 祖先 [usu pl, with poss] ❑ ...our daily lives, so different from those of our ancestors. 祖先の頃とは全く違う現代の日常生活. ■ N-COUNT 可算名詞 An **ancestor of** something modern is an earlier thing from which it developed. 原種 ❑ The direct ancestor of the modern cat was the Kaffir cat of ancient Egypt. 現在のイエネコの直接の祖先とされているる. 古代エジプトのリビアネコである.

ancestral /ænsestrəl/ ADJ 形容詞 You use **ancestral** to refer to a person's family in former times, especially when the family is important and has property or land that they have had for a long time. 先祖の ❑ ...the family's ancestral home in southern Germany. 南ドイツにある一族の先祖代々の屋敷.

ancestry /ǽnsestri/ (ancestries) N-COUNT 可算名詞 Your **ancestry** is the fact that you are descended from certain people. 家系 ❑ ...a family who could trace their ancestry back to the sixteenth century. 16世紀まで家系をたどれる名家.

anchor /ǽŋkər/ (anchors, anchoring, anchored) ■ N-COUNT 可算名詞 An **anchor** is a heavy hooked object that is dropped from a boat into the water at the end of a chain in order to make the boat stay in one place. いかり ■ N-COUNT 可算名詞 The **anchor** on a television or radio program, especially a news program, is the person who presents it. ニュースキャスター [mainly AM 主に米国英語] ❑ He worked in the news division of ABC – he was the anchor of its 15-minute evening newscast. 彼はABCのニュース部門で働きました. 夕方の15分のニュース番組でニュースキャスターを務めました. ■ V-T/V-I 他動詞/自動詞 When a boat **anchors** or when you **anchor** it, its anchor is dropped into the water in order to make it stay in one place. いかりを降ろす ❑ We could anchor off the pier. 埠頭(ふとう)の沖に停泊することも可能だ. ■ V-T 他動詞 If an object **is anchored** somewhere, it is fixed to something to prevent it moving from that place. 固定される ❑ The roots anchor the plant in the earth. 根は植物をしっかり地面に固定する. ■ V-T 他動詞 The person who **anchors** a television or radio program, especially a news program, is the person who presents it and acts as a link between interviews and reports that come from other places or studios. ニュースキャスターを務める [mainly AM 主に米国英語] ❑ Viewers saw him anchoring a five-minute summary of regional news. テレビに映っていたのは, 彼がニュースキャスターとしてローカルニュースを5分間で要約しているところだった. ■ N-COUNT 可算名詞 An **anchor** is the main store in a mall or shopping center. 核店舗 [AM 米国英語] ❑ A clothing store is to be a key anchor in a new development planned on the vacant lot. 更地に建設が予定されている開発計画では衣料品店が核店舗となる. ■ PHRASE 句 If a boat is **at anchor**, it is floating in a particular place and is prevented from moving by its anchor. 停泊して ❑ Sailboats lay at anchor in the narrow waterway. 帆船は狭い運河に停泊していた.

ancient /eɪnʃənt/ ■ ADJ 形容詞 **Ancient** means belonging to the distant past, especially to the period in history before the end of the Roman Empire. 古代の [ADJ n] ❑ They believed ancient Greece

and Rome were vital sources of learning. 彼らは古代ギリシャやローマが学問の重要なよりどころだと考えていました。 **2** ADJ 形容詞 **Ancient** means very old, or having existed for a long time. 大昔の；古来の ❏ *...ancient Jewish tradition.* 古来から続くユダヤの伝統。
→ see **history**

an|cil|lary /ǽnsəleri/ ADJ 形容詞 The **ancillary** workers in an institution are the people such as cleaners and cooks whose work supports the main work of the institution. 補助的な [ADJ n] ❏ *...ancillary staff.* 補助職員。

and /ənd, STRONG ǽnd/ **1** CONJ 接続詞 You use **and** to link two or more words, groups, or clauses. 〜と〜 ❏ *When he returned, she and Simon had already gone.* 彼が戻ってきたときは，彼女とサイモンはすでに行ってしまった後だった。 ❏ *I'm going to write good jokes and become a good comedian.* 面白いネタを書き集めて，芸達者なお笑いタレントになろうと思っています。 **2** CONJ 接続詞 You use **and** to link two words or phrases that are the same in order to emphasize the degree of something, or to suggest that something continues or increases over a period of time. ますます，〜も〜も [EMPHASIS 強調] ❏ *Learning becomes more and more difficult as we get older.* 年を取るにつれて学習はますます難しくなる。 ❏ *We talked for hours and hours.* 何時間も何時間も話しました。 **3** CONJ 接続詞 You use **and** to link two statements about events when one of the events follows the other. それから ❏ *I waved goodbye and went down the stone harbor steps.* 手を振って別れると港の石段を降りた。 **4** CONJ 接続詞 You use **and** to link two statements when the second statement continues to point that has been made in the first statement. さらに ❏ *You could only really tell the effects of the disease in the long term, and five years wasn't long enough.* 病気の後遺症はいつまでも残り，5年程度では治まらない。 **5** CONJ 接続詞 You use **and** to link two clauses when the second clause is a result of the first clause. 〜だから ❏ *All through yesterday crowds have been arriving and by midnight thousands of people packed the square.* 昨日は終日人が押し寄せたで，深夜になると広場は数千人の群衆で埋めつくされました。 **6** CONJ 接続詞 You use **and** to interrupt yourself in order to make a comment on what you are saying. それも ❏ *Danielle was among the last to find out, and as often happens, too, she learned of it only by chance.* ダニエルが気づいたのはみんなが気づいてからだった。それもよくあるようにたまたま気がついただけだった。 **7** CONJ 接続詞 You use **and** at the beginning of a sentence to introduce something else that you want to add to what you have just said. Some people think that starting a sentence with **and** is ungrammatical, but it is now quite common in both spoken and written English. さらに ❏ *Commuter airlines fly to out-of-the-way places.* コミュータ航空は地方都市に飛んでいます。利用者はビジネスマンです。 **8** CONJ 接続詞 You use **and** to introduce a question that follows logically from what someone has just said. それで ❏ *"He used to be so handsome."—"And now?"* 「昔はすごくハンサムだったのよ」「で今はどうなの」 **9** CONJ 接続詞 **And** is used by broadcasters and people making announcements to change a topic or to start talking about a topic they have just mentioned. それでは ❏ *And now the drought in Sudan.* さて次はスーダンの干ばつのニュースです。 **10** CONJ 接続詞 You use **and** to indicate that two numbers are to be added together. 〜足す〜 ❏ *What does two and two make?* 2たす2はいくら？ **11** CONJ 接続詞 **And** is used before a fraction that comes after a whole number. 〜と〜 ❏ *McCain spent five and a half years in a prisoner-of-war camp in Vietnam.* マケインはベトナムの捕虜収容所で5年半過ごしました。 **12** CONJ 接続詞 You use **and** in numbers larger than one hundred, after the words "hundred" or "thousand" and before other numbers. (数詞を結んで) 〜と〜 ❏ *We printed two hundred and fifty invitations.* 招待状を250枚印刷した。

an|ec|do|tal /ǽnɪkdoʊt°l/ ADJ 形容詞 **Anecdotal** evidence is based on individual accounts, rather than on reliable research or statistics, and so may not be valid. 聞いた話に基づく ❏ *Anecdotal evidence suggests that sales in the Southwest have slipped.* 聞くところによれば，南西部の売上は落ちているという。

an|ec|dote /ǽnɪkdoʊt/ (anecdotes) N-VAR 可変性名詞 An **anecdote** is a short, amusing account of something that has happened. エピソード ❏ *Pete was telling them an anecdote about their*

mother. ピートは彼らに母さんの面白い話を聞かせてやっていた。

anemia /ənímiə/ N-UNCOUNT 不可算名詞 **Anemia** is a medical condition in which there are too few red cells in your blood, causing you to feel tired and look pale. 貧血 ❏ *She suffered from anemia and even required blood transfusions.* 彼女は貧血に苦しんでいたが，輸血しなければならないほど重症だった。

anemic /ənímɪk/ ADJ 形容詞 Someone who is **anemic** suffers from anemia. 貧血症の ❏ *Tests showed that she was very anemic.* 検査の結果，重症の貧血だと分かった。

an|es|thesi|olo|gist /ǽnɪsθiziɒlədʒɪst/ (anesthesiologists) N-COUNT 可算名詞 An **anesthesiologist** is a doctor who specializes in giving anesthetics to patients. 麻酔医 [AM 米国英語]

Word Link *a, an ≈ not, without : anesthetic, anorexia, atheism*
---

an|es|thet|ic /ǽnɪsθɛtɪk/ (anesthetics) N-MASS 質量名詞 **Anesthetic** is a substance that doctors use to stop you feeling pain during an operation, either in the whole of your body when you are unconscious, or in a part of your body when you are awake. 麻酔薬 ❏ *The operation is carried out under a general anesthetic.* 手術は全身麻酔で行われる。

anes|the|tist /ənɛsθətɪst/ (anesthetists) N-COUNT 可算名詞 An **anesthetist** is a nurse or other person who gives an anesthetic to a patient. 麻酔士 [AM 米国英語]

anew /ənú/ ADV 副詞 If you do something **anew**, you do it again, often in a different way from before. 新たに [WRITTEN 書き言葉] [ADV after v] ❏ *She's ready to start anew.* 彼女は一から出直す覚悟でいる。

an|gel /éɪndʒ°l/ (angels) **1** N-COUNT 可算名詞 **Angels** are spiritual beings that some people believe are God's servants in heaven. 天使 ❏ *The artist usually painted his angels with multi-colored wings.* その画家は天使の翼を描くのにたいてい多くの色を使った。 **2** N-COUNT 可算名詞 You can call someone you like very much an **angel** in order to show affection, especially when they have been kind to you or done you a favor. 親切な人 [FEELINGS 感情] ❏ *Thank you a thousand times, you're an angel.* 本当にありがとう，親切な人。 **3** N-COUNT 可算名詞 If you describe someone as an **angel**, you mean that they seem to be very kind and good. 天使のような人 [APPROVAL 賛成] ❏ *Papa thought her an angel.* 父さんには彼女が天使のように思えた。

an|gel|ic /ændʒɛlɪk/ **1** ADJ 形容詞 You can describe someone as **angelic** if they are, or seem to be, very good, kind, and gentle. 天使のような [APPROVAL 賛成] ❏ *...an angelic face.* 天使のような顔。 **2** ADJ 形容詞 **Angelic** means like angels or relating to angels. 天使の [ADJ n] ❏ *...angelic choirs.* 天使の聖歌隊。

an|ger /ǽŋgər/ (angers, angering, angered) **1** N-UNCOUNT 不可算名詞 **Anger** is the strong emotion that you feel when you think that someone has behaved in an unfair, cruel, or unacceptable way. 怒り ❏ *He cried with anger and frustration.* 彼は怒りと失望のあまり叫んだ。 **2** V-T 他動詞 If something **angers** you, it makes you feel angry. 怒らせる ❏ *The decision to allow more offshore oil drilling angered some Californians.* 新たな海洋掘削が認められたことに対し，カリフォルニア住民の間から怒りの声が上がった。
→ see Word Web: **anger**
→ see **emotion**

an|gle /ǽŋg°l/ (angles) **1** N-COUNT 可算名詞 An **angle** is the difference in direction between two lines or surfaces. Angles are measured in degrees. 角度 ❏ *The boat is now leaning at a 30 degree angle.* ボートは現在30度傾いています。 **2** → see also **right angle** **3** N-COUNT 可算名詞 An **angle** is the shape that is created where two lines or surfaces join together. とがったところ ❏ *...the angle of the blade.* 刃。 **4** N-COUNT 可算名詞 An **angle** is the direction from which you look at something. (ものを見る) 角度 ❏ *Thanks to the angle at which he stood, he could just see the sunset.* ちょうど立っていた場所から夕日をかろうじて見ることができた。 **5** N-COUNT 可算名詞 You can refer to a way of presenting something or thinking about it as a particular **angle**. 視点 ❏ *He was considering the idea from all angles.* 彼はあらゆる角度からそのことを検討していた。 **6** PHRASE 句 If something is **at an angle**, it is leaning in

---

Word Web anger

Anger can be a positive thing. Until it surfaces, we may not realize how **upset** we are about a situation. Anger can give us a sense of our own power. Showing someone how **annoyed** we are with them may lead them to change their behavior. Anger also helps release **tension** in **frustrating** situations. This allows us to move on with our lives. But anger has its downside. It's hard to think clearly when we're **furious**. We may use bad judgment. **Rage** can also prevent us from seeing the truth about ourselves. And when anger turns into **aggression**, people get hurt.

Word Web animation

TV **cartoons** are one of the most popular forms of **animation**. Each **episode** begins with a storyline. Once the **script** is final, cartoonists make up storyboards. The director uses them to plan how the **artists** will **illustrate** the episode. First the illustrators **draw** some **sketches**. Next they draw a few key **frames** for each **scene**. Animators turn these into moving storyboards. This version of the cartoon looks unfinished. The producers review it and suggest changes. After they make these changes, the artists fill in the missing frames. This makes the movements of the characters look smooth and natural.

a particular direction so that it is not straight, horizontal, or vertical. 斜めに ❑ *An iron bar stuck out at an angle.* 鉄の棒が斜めに突き出ていた.
→ see **mathematics**

an|gler /ǽŋglər/ (**anglers**) N-COUNT 可算名詞 An **angler** is someone who fishes with a fishing rod as a hobby. 釣り人

an|gling /ǽŋglɪŋ/ N-UNCOUNT 不可算名詞 **Angling** is the activity or sport of fishing with a fishing rod. 魚釣り

an|gry /ǽŋgri/ (**angrier, angriest**) ADJ 形容詞 When you are **angry**, you feel strong dislike or impatience about something. 怒った ❑ *Are you angry with me for some reason?* 何か私に腹を立ててることでもあるの. ❑ *I was angry about the rumors.* そのうわさには腹が立った. ❑ *An angry mob gathered outside the courthouse.* 怒った暴徒は裁判所の外に押し寄せた. ● **an|gri|ly** /ǽŋgrɪli/ ADV 副詞 [ADV with v] 怒って ❑ *Officials reacted angrily to those charges.* 役人はそうした非難に憤慨しました.

Angry is normally used to talk about someone's mood or feelings on a particular occasion. If someone is often angry, you can describe them as **bad-tempered**. ❑ *She's a bad-tempered young lady.* If someone is very angry, you can describe them as **furious**. ❑ *Senior police officers are furious at the blunder.* If they are less angry, you can describe them as **annoyed** or **irritated**. ❑ *The premier looked annoyed but calm.* ...*a man irritated by the barking of his neighbor's dog.* Typically, someone is **irritated** by something because it happens constantly or continually. If someone is often irritated, you can describe them as **irritable**.

Thesaurus angry また次を参照：

ADJ. bitter, enraged, mad; (*ant.*) content, happy, pleased

Word Partnership angry は次の語句と使われる：

PREP. angry **about** *something*, angry **at** *someone/something*, angry **with** *someone*
V. **get** angry, **make** *someone* angry
N. angry **mob**

angst /ǽŋst/ N-UNCOUNT 不可算名詞 **Angst** is a feeling of anxiety and worry. 不安感 [JOURNALISM ジャーナリズム] ❑ *Many kids suffer from acne and angst.* 多くの子供たちがにきびに悩み，思春期の不安を抱えている.

an|guish /ǽŋgwɪʃ/ N-UNCOUNT 不可算名詞 **Anguish** is great mental suffering or physical pain. 激痛；苦悩 ❑ *Mark looked at him in anguish.* マークは苦痛に満ちた顔で彼を見た.

an|guished /ǽŋgwɪʃt/ ADJ 形容詞 **Anguished** means showing or feeling great mental suffering or physical pain. 苦悩に満ちた；苦悩に満ちた [WRITTEN 書き言葉] ❑ *She let out an anguished cry.* 彼女は苦痛のあまり叫び声をあげた.

an|gu|lar /ǽŋgyʊlər/ ADJ 形容詞 **Angular** things have shapes that seem to contain a lot of straight lines and sharp points. 角ばった ❑ *He had an angular face with prominent cheekbones.* 彼は角ばった顔でほお骨が突き出ていた.

Word Link anim ≈ alive, mind : animal, animated, unanimous

ani|mal /ǽnɪməl/ (**animals**) ❶ N-COUNT 可算名詞 An **animal** is a living creature such as a dog, lion, or rabbit, rather than a bird, fish, insect, or human being. 哺乳動物 ❑ *He was attacked by wild animals.* 彼は野生動物に襲われました. ❷ N-COUNT 可算名詞 Any living creature other than a human being can be referred to as an **animal**. （人間以外の）動物 ❑ *Language is something that fundamentally distinguishes humans from animals.* 言葉こそ，人間を動物から根本的に区別するものである. ❸ N-COUNT 可算名詞 Any living creature, including a human being, can be referred to as an **animal**. （植物に対して）動物 ❑ *Watch any young human being, or any other young animal.* 人の子供でも動物の子供でも見るとよい. ❹ ADJ 形容詞 **Animal** products come from animals rather than from

plants. 動物性の ❑ ...*food high in animal fats such as red meat and dairy products.* 赤身の肉や乳製品のような動物性脂肪の多い食べ物.
→ see **earth, pet**

Word Partnership animal は次の語句と使われる：

N. **plant** and animal ❶
  cruelty to animals, animal **hide**, animal **kingdom**, animal **noises**, animal **shelter** ❷
ADJ. **domestic** animal, **stuffed** animal, **wild** animal ❷

ani|mate (**animates, animating, animated**)

The adjective is pronounced /ǽnɪmət/. The verb is pronounced /ǽnɪmeɪt/.

形容詞は /ǽnɪmət/ と発音される. 動詞は /ǽnɪmeɪt/ と発音される.

❶ ADJ 形容詞 Something that is **animate** has life, in contrast to things like stones and machines which do not. 生命のある ❑ *Natural philosophy involved the study of all aspects of the material world, animate and inanimate.* 自然哲学では，生命の有無に関係なく物質世界をあらゆる側面から研究した. ❷ V-T 他動詞 To **animate** something means to make it lively or more cheerful. 活気づける ❑ *There was precious little about the cricket to animate the crowd.* そのクリケットの試合は観客を熱狂させるような試合ではなかった.

ani|mat|ed /ǽnɪmeɪtɪd/ ❶ ADJ 形容詞 Someone who is **animated** or who is having an **animated** conversation is lively and is showing their feelings. 活発な ❑ *She was seen in animated conversation with the singer Yuri Marusin.* 彼女は歌手のユリ・マルシンと楽しくおしゃべりしているところを目撃された. ❷ ADJ 形容詞 An **animated** film is one in which puppets or drawings appear to move. アニメの [ADJ n] ❑ *Disney has returned to what it does best: making full-length animated feature films.* 再びディズニーは最も得意とする長編アニメ映画の制作の分野に戻った.

ani|ma|tion /ænɪméɪʃⁿn/ (**animations**) ❶ N-UNCOUNT 不可算名詞 **Animation** is the process of making films in which drawings or puppets appear to move. アニメ製作 ❑ *The films are a mix of animation and full-length features.* アニメもあれば長編映画もあります. ❷ N-COUNT 可算名詞 An **animation** is a film in which drawings or puppets appear to move. アニメ映画 ❑ *This film is the first British animation sold to an American network.* この映画は，アメリカのテレビネットワークが初めて購入したイギリスのアニメ作品である.
→ see Word Web: **animation**

ani|mos|ity /ænɪmɒsɪti/ (**animosities**) N-UNCOUNT 不可算名詞 **Animosity** is a strong feeling of dislike and anger. **Animosities** are feelings of this kind. 敵意 [also N in pl] ❑ *There's a long history of animosity between the two nations.* 2国間には長い憎悪の歴史があります.

an|kle /ǽŋkⁿl/ (**ankles**) N-COUNT 可算名詞 Your **ankle** is the joint where your foot joins your leg. 足首 ❑ *John twisted his ankle badly.* ジョンは足首をひどくねんざした.
→ see **body, foot**

an|nex (**annexes, annexing, annexed**)

The verb is pronounced /ænéks/. The noun is pronounced /ǽneks/.

動詞は /ænéks/ と発音される. 名詞は /ǽneks/ と発音される.

❶ V-T 他動詞 If a country **annexes** another country or an area of land, it seizes it and takes control of it. 併合する ❑ *Rome annexed the Nabatean kingdom in AD 106.* ローマは西暦106年にナバテア王国を併合した. ● **an|nexa|tion** /ænekséɪʃⁿn/ (**annexations**) N-COUNT 可算名詞 併合 ❑ *Indonesia's annexation of East Timor never won the acceptance of the United Nations.* インドネシアによる東ティモールの併合が国連の承認を受けることはなかった. ❷ N-COUNT 可算名詞 An **annex** is a building joined to or next to a larger main building. 別館 [AM 米国英語] ❑ ...*setting up a museum in an annex to the theater.*

A

劇場に隣接して博物館を建設中.

an|ni|hi|late /ənaɪleɪt/ (**annihilates, annihilating, annihilated**) ◱ V-T 他動詞 To **annihilate** something means to destroy it completely. 全滅させる，絶滅させる ❑ There are lots of ways of annihilating the planet. 地球を破滅させる方法はいくらでもある. ●**an|ni|hi|la|tion** /ənaɪleɪʃən/ N-UNCOUNT 不可算名詞 全滅，絶滅 ❑ ...the threat of nuclear war and annihilation of the human race. 核戦争と人類滅亡の脅威. ◲ V-T 他動詞 If you **annihilate** someone in a contest or argument, you totally defeat them. 完全に負かす ❑ The Dutch annihilated the Olympic champions 5-0. オランダはオリンピックの優勝チームに5対0で圧勝した.

Word Link   ann ≈ year : anniversary, annual, annum

an|ni|ver|sa|ry /ænɪvɜrsəri/ (**anniversaries**) N-COUNT 可算名詞 An **anniversary** is a date that is remembered or celebrated because a special event happened on that date in a previous year. 記念日 ❑ Vietnam is celebrating the one hundredth anniversary of the birth of Ho Chi Minh. ベトナムではホーチミンの生誕100周年を祝っています.

an|no|tate /ænouteɪt/ (**annotates, annotating, annotated**) V-T 他動詞 If you **annotate** written work or a diagram, you add notes to it, especially in order to explain it. 注釈をつける ❑ Historians annotate, check and interpret the diary selections. 歴史家は日記の抄録を注釈し調査し解釈する.

Word Link   nounce ≈ reporting : announce, denounce, pronounce

an|nounce /ənaʊns/ (**announces, announcing, announced**) ◱ V-T 他動詞 If you **announce** something, you tell people about it publicly or officially. 発表する，公表する ❑ He will announce tonight that he is resigning from office. 彼は今夜辞職を表明します. ❑ She was planning to announce her engagement to Peter. ピーターとの婚約発表を予定していた. ◲ V-T 他動詞 If you **announce** a piece of news or an intention, especially something that people may not like, you say it loudly and clearly, so that everyone you are with can hear it. 知らせる. ❑ Peter announced that he had no intention of wasting his time at any university. ピーターは大学なんかで時間を無駄にする気はないと言ってのけた. ◳ V-T 他動詞 If an airport or rail employee **announces** something, they tell the public about it by means of a loudspeaker system. 放送する ❑ The loudspeaker announced the arrival of the train. スピーカーから電車の到着を知らせるアナウンスが流れた.

Thesaurus   announce また次を参照：

v.   advertise, declare, make public, reveal;
     (ant.) withhold ◱

an|nounce|ment /ənaʊnsmənt/ (**announcements**) ◱ N-COUNT 可算名詞 An **announcement** is a statement made to the public or to the media that gives information about something that has happened or that will happen. 公表 ❑ She made her announcement after talks with the president. 大統領との会談後に彼女は会見に臨んだ. ◲ N-COUNT 可算名詞 An **announcement** in a public place, such as a newspaper or the window of a store, is a short piece of writing telling people about something or asking for something. お知らせ ❑ The Seattle Times publishes brief announcements of religious events every Saturday. シアトルタイムズ紙には毎週土曜日に宗教行事の案内欄が掲載される. ◳ N-SING 単数名詞 The **announcement of** something that has happened is the act of telling people about it. 発表 ❑ ...the announcement of their engagement. 二人の婚約発表.

Word Partnership   announcement は次の語句と使われる：

ADJ.   **formal** announcement, **public** announcement, **surprise** announcement, **official** announcement ◱
V.   **make an** announcement ◱

an|nounc|er /ənaʊnsər/ (**announcers**) ◱ N-COUNT 可算名詞 An **announcer** is someone who introduces programs on radio or television or who reads the text of a radio or television advertisement. アナウンサー ❑ The radio announcer said it was nine o'clock. ラジオのアナウンサーが9時を告げた. ◲ N-COUNT 可算名詞 The **announcer** at a train station or airport is the person who makes the announcements. アナウンス係 ❑ The announcer apologized for the delay. 遅れをわびるアナウンスがあった.

an|noy /ənɔɪ/ (**annoys, annoying, annoyed**) ◱ V-T 他動詞 If someone or something **annoys** you, it makes you fairly angry and impatient. いらいらさせる，むっとさせる ❑ Try making a note of the things that annoy you. いらいらすることがあったら書き留めていけば. ❑ It annoyed me that I didn't have time to do more ironing. アイロンがけの時間が足りなくていらいらした. ◲ → see also **annoyed, annoying**

an|noy|ance /ənɔɪəns/ (**annoyances**) ◱ N-UNCOUNT 不可算名詞 **Annoyance** is the feeling that you get when someone makes you feel fairly angry or impatient. いらだち ❑ To her annoyance the

stranger did not go away. 困ったことにそのよそ者は立ち去らなかった. ◲ N-COUNT 可算名詞 An **annoyance** is something that makes you feel angry or impatient. 迷惑なもの ❑ Snoring can be more than an annoyance. いびきは周りの迷惑程度では済まないことがある.

an|noyed /ənɔɪd/ ◱ ADJ 形容詞 If you are **annoyed**, you are fairly angry about something. いらいらした，むっとした ❑ She is hurt and annoyed that the authorities have banned her from working with children. 彼女の気分が晴れないのは当局からの命令で子供に接する仕事ができないからだ. ◲ → see also **annoy**
→ see **anger**

an|noy|ing /ənɔɪɪŋ/ ADJ 形容詞 Someone or something that is **annoying** makes you feel fairly angry and impatient. うっとうしい ❑ You must have found my attitude annoying. きっと私の態度をうっとうしく思ったんでしょ.

an|nual /ænyuəl/ (**annuals**) ◱ ADJ 形容詞 **Annual** events happen once every year. 年に一度の [ADJ n] ❑ The issues will be voted on at the company's annual meeting on April 21 in Wilmington. 議題は4月21日にウィルミントンで開催される会社の年次総会で票決にかけられる. ●**an|nual|ly** ADV 副詞 [ADV with v] 年に一度 ❑ Companies report to their shareholders annually. 会社は株主に対し年次報告を行う. ◲ ADJ 形容詞 **Annual** quantities or rates relate to a period of one year. 1年間の [ADJ n] ❑ The electronic and printing unit has annual sales of about $80 million. 電子・印刷部門の年間売上は8千万ドルに及ぶ. ●**an|nual|ly** ADV 副詞 1年間で ❑ El Salvador produces 100,000 tons of refined copper annually. エルサルバドルは年間10万トンの精錬銅を生産する. ◳ N-COUNT 可算名詞 An **annual** is a book or magazine that is published once a year. 年間誌，年鑑 ❑ I looked for Wyman's picture in my high-school annual. 高校のアルバムでワイマンの写真を捜した. ◴ N-COUNT 可算名詞 An **annual** is a plant that grows and dies within one year. 1年生植物 ❑ Maybe this year I'll sow brilliant annuals everywhere. 今年は色鮮やかな一年草をあちこちに植えようかなあ.
→ see **plant**

an|nu|ity /ənuiti/ (**annuities**) N-COUNT 可算名詞 An **annuity** is an investment or insurance policy that pays someone a fixed sum of money each year. 年金 [BUSINESS 実業] ❑ He received a paltry annuity of $100. 彼が1年に受け取る年金はたったの100ドルだった.

an|nul /ənʌl/ (**annuls, annulling, annulled**) V-T 他動詞 If an election or a contract **is annulled**, it is declared invalid, so that legally it is considered never to have existed. 無効になる [usu passive] ❑ Opposition party leaders are now pressing for the entire election to be annulled. 野党の党首は選挙そのものの無効を要求しています.

an|num /ænəm/ → see **per annum**

anoma|ly /ənɒməli/ (**anomalies**) N-COUNT 可算名詞 If something is an **anomaly**, it is different from what is usual or expected. 例外，異常 [FORMAL 形式ばった] ❑ The space shuttle had stopped transmitting data, a very serious anomaly for the mission. スペースシャトルからの送信が途絶え，任務に支障をきたす深刻な事態が発生した.

Word Link   onym ≈ name : acronym, anonymous, synonym

anony|mous /ənɒnɪməs/ ◱ ADJ 形容詞 If you remain **anonymous** when you do something, you do not let people know that you were the person who did it. 匿名の ❑ You can remain anonymous if you wish. 匿名でも構いません. ❑ An anonymous benefactor stepped in to provide the prize money. 匿名の寄贈者が賞金の提供を申し出た. ●**ano|nym|ity** /ænɒnɪmiti/ N-UNCOUNT 不可算名詞 匿名 ❑ Both mother and daughter, who have requested anonymity, are doing fine. 匿名を望んでいる母子はともに元気にしています. ●**anony|mous|ly** ADV 副詞 匿名で ❑ The latest photographs were sent anonymously to the magazine's headquarters. 最近の写真が匿名で雑誌の発行元に送られてきた. ◲ ADJ 形容詞 Something that is **anonymous** does not reveal who you are. 名前を明かさない ❑ Of course, that would have to be by anonymous vote. もちろん，無記名投票ということになるでしょう. ●**ano|nym|ity** N-UNCOUNT 不可算名詞 名前を明かさないこと ❑ He claims many more people would support him in the anonymity of a voting booth. 記入ボックスによる無記名投票にすれば自分の支持者はずっと増えるだろうとしている.

ano|rak /ænəræk/ (**anoraks**) N-COUNT 可算名詞 An **anorak** is a warm waterproof jacket, usually with a hood. アノラック [mainly BRIT 主に英国英語]

Word Link   a, an ≈ not, without : anesthetic, anorexia, atheism

ano|rexia /ænərɛksiə/ N-UNCOUNT 不可算名詞 **Anorexia** or **anorexia nervosa** is an illness in which a person has an overwhelming fear of becoming fat, and so refuses to eat enough and becomes thinner and thinner. 拒食症

ano|rex|ic /ænərɛksɪk/ (**anorexics**) ADJ 形容詞 If someone is **anorexic**, they are suffering from anorexia and so are very thin. 拒食症の ❑ Claire had been anorexic for three years. クレアの拒食症は3年間続いた. ●N-COUNT 可算名詞 An **anorexic** is someone who is

anorexic. 拒食症の患者 ❏ *Not eating makes an anorexic feel in control.* 拒食症になると何も食べないことで気持ちが落ち着く.

an|oth|er /ənʌ́ðər/ ■ DET 限定詞 **Another** thing or person means an additional thing or person of the same type as one that already exists. もう1つの; もう1人の ❏ *Divers this morning found the body of another American sailor drowned during yesterday's ferry disaster.* 今朝ダイバーが捜索していたところ, 昨日のフェリー事故で溺れたもう1人のアメリカ人乗組員が遺体で発見されました. ● PRON-SING 単数代名詞 **Another** is also a pronoun. もう1つ, もう1人 ❏ *The demand generated by one factory required the construction of another.* 1カ所の工場では需要を賄いきれず, 新たな工場の建設が必要になった. ■ DET 限定詞 You use **another** when you want to emphasize that an additional thing or person is different from one that already exists. 別の, ほかの ❏ *I think he's just going to deal with this problem another day.* 彼はこの問題についていずれ対処すると思います. ● PRON-SING 単数代名詞 **Another** is also a pronoun. 別のもの, 別の人 ❏ *He didn't really believe that any human being could read another's mind.* 誰でも人の心が読めるということを彼はあまり信じていなかった. ■ DET 限定詞 You use **another** at the beginning of a statement to link it to a previous statement. もう1つの ❏ *Another time of great excitement for us boys was when war broke out.* 僕たち少年の心を沸き立たせたもう1つの事件は戦争の勃発 (ぼっぱつ) だった. ■ DET 限定詞 You use **another** before a word referring to a distance, length of time, or other amount, to indicate an additional amount. さらに ❏ *Continue down the same road for another 2 miles until you reach the church of Santa Maria.* この道をさらに2マイル進むとサンタマリア教会に着く. ■ PRON-RECIP 相互代名詞 You use **one another** to indicate that each member of a group does something to or for the other members. お互いに [v PRON, prep PRON] ❏ *...women learning to help themselves and one another.* 人に頼らず自分で努力することや互いに助け合うことを学んでいる女性たち.

Do not confuse **another** and **other**. When you are talking about **another** thing or person, you often mean one more of the same type. ❏ *Rick's got another camera... I waited another few minutes.* You use **other** to refer to more than one type of person or thing, usually followed by a plural count noun but sometimes by an uncount noun. ❏ *Other boys were arriving now... There was certainly other evidence.* When you are talking about two people or things and have already referred to one of them, you refer to the second one as **the other** or **the other one**. ❏ *One daughter was a baby, the other a girl of twelve.* When you are talking about several people or things and have already referred to one or more of them, you usually refer to the remaining ones as **the others**. ❏ *Jack and the others paid no attention.* More people or things of the same type are referred to simply as **others**. ❏ *Some writers are better than others.* **Other** can also be used after words such as "the," "few," or "any," and after numbers. ❏ *...the other side of the room... I love my son, like any other mother. ...the Hogans and three other couples.*

■ PHRASE 句 If you talk about **one** thing **after another**, you are referring to a series of repeated or continuous events. 次々と起こる— ❏ *They had faced one difficulty after another with bravery and dedication.* 彼らは次々と起こる困難にひたむきに立ち向かった. ■ PHRASE 句 You use **or another** in expressions such as **one kind or another** when you do not want to be precise about which of several alternatives or possibilities you are referring to. 何かのもの ❏ *...family members and visiting artists of one kind or another crowding the huge kitchen.* 広いキッチンにあふれ返る家族や客として呼ばれたいろんな分野の芸術家たち.

Word Partnership		*another* は次の語句と使われる:
ADV.	yet another ■	
N.	another chance, another day, another one ■ another man/woman, another thing ■	
V.	tell one from another ■	
PRON.	one another ■	

an|swer /ǽnsər/ (answers, answering, answered) ■ V-T/V-I 他動詞/自動詞 When you **answer** someone who has asked you something, you say something back to them. 答える ❏ *Just answer the question.* ただ質問に答えなさい. ❏ *He paused before answering.* 彼は少し間をおいてから答えた. ❏ *Williams answered that he had no specific proposals yet.* ウィリアムズは今のところ具体的な提案はないと答えました. ■ V-T/V-I 他動詞/自動詞 If you **answer** a letter or advertisement, you write to the person who wrote it. 返事を出す ❏ *Did he answer your letter?* 彼から手紙の返事があった? ■ V-T/V-I 他動詞/自動詞 When you **answer** the telephone, you pick it up when it rings. When you **answer** the door, you open it when you hear a knock on the bell. 応答する ❏ *She answered her phone on the first ring.* 1回鳴ったところで電話に出た. ● N-COUNT 可算名詞 **Answer** is also a noun. 応答 ❏ *I knocked at the front door and there was no answer.* 玄関をノックしたが返事はなかった. ■ V-T 他

動詞 When you **answer** a question in a test or quiz, you write or say something in an attempt to give the facts that are asked for. 答える ❏ *Always read an exam all the way through at least once before you start to answer any questions.* 必ず一度は試験問題全体に目を通してから問題に答えるようにしなさい. ■ V-T/V-I 他動詞/自動詞 If someone or something **answers** a particular description or **answers to** it, they have the characteristics described. 一致する ❏ *Two men answering the description of the suspects tried to enter Switzerland.* 犯人の特徴と一致する二人組の男がスイスへ入国しようとしました. ■ N-COUNT 可算名詞 An **answer** is something that you say when you **answer** someone. 返答 [also 'in' N 'to' N] ❏ *Without waiting for an answer, he turned and went in through the door.* 彼は返事を聞かないまま, くるりと向きを変えるとドアから中へ入っていった. ■ N-COUNT 可算名詞 An **answer** is a letter that you write to someone who has written to you. 返事 [also 'in' N 'to' N] ❏ *I wrote to him but I never had an answer back.* 彼に手紙を書いたが返事をもらったためしがなかった. ■ N-COUNT 可算名詞 An **answer to** a problem is a solution to it. 解決策 ❏ *There are no easy answers to the problems facing the economy.* 経済が直面している問題を簡単に解決する手立てはない. ■ N-COUNT 可算名詞 Someone's **answer to** a question in a test or quiz is what they write or say in an attempt to give the facts that are asked for. 答え ❏ *Simply marking an answer wrong will not help the student to get future examples correct.* ただ不正解にするだけでは, 生徒が正しい答えを導き出せるように してやることはできない. ■ N-COUNT 可算名詞 Your **answer to** something that someone has said or done is what you say or do in response to it or in defense of yourself. 応答 [also 'in' N 'to' N] ❏ *In answer to speculation that she wouldn't finish the race, she boldly declared her intention of winning it.* レースを完走できないのではないかという予想に対し, 大胆にも彼女は優勝すると言ってのけた. ■ PHRASE 句 If you say that someone will not **take no for an answer**, you mean that they go on trying to make you agree to something even after you have refused. 有無を言わせない ❏ *She is tough, unwilling to take no for an answer.* 彼女は頑固で相手に有無を言わせない.

▶ **answer back** PHRASAL VERB 句動詞 If someone, especially a child, **answers back**, they speak rudely to you when you speak to them. 口答えをする [BRIT 英国英語] ❏ *My youngest child is eight and she has started answering back too.* 一番下の娘が8歳で口答えもするようになった.

▶ **answer for** ■ PHRASAL VERB 句動詞 If you have to **answer for** something bad or wrong you have done, you are punished for it. 責任をとる ❏ *He must be made to answer for his terrible crimes.* 彼には自分が犯した恐ろしい罪を償わせる必要があります. ■ PHRASE 句 If you say that someone **has a lot to answer for**, you are saying that their actions have led to problems which you think they are responsible for. 〜に対し大きな責任がある ['have' inflects]

Thesaurus		*answer* また次を参照:
V.	reply, respond ■ ■	

Word Partnership		*answer* は次の語句と使われる:
V.	refuse to answer ■ – ■	
	have an answer ■ – ■	
	wait for an answer ■ ■ ■	
	find the answer ■ ■	
N.	answer a question ■ ■	
	answer the door/telephone ■	
DET.	no answer ■	
ADJ.	correct/right answer, wrong answer ■ ■	
	straight answer ■	

an|swer|ing ma|chine (answering machines) N-COUNT 可算名詞 An **answering machine** is a device that you connect to your telephone to record telephone calls while you are out. 留守番電話

ant /ǽnt/ (ants) N-COUNT 可算名詞 **Ants** are small crawling insects that live in large groups. アリ ❏ *Ants swarmed up out of the ground and covered her shoes and legs.* アリの群れが土の中から出てきて彼女の靴や足にたかった.

an|tago|nism /æntǽgənɪzəm/ (antagonisms) N-UNCOUNT 不可算名詞 **Antagonism** between people is hatred or dislike between them. **Antagonisms** are instances of this. 敵意 [also N in pl] ❏ *There is still much antagonism between environmental groups and the oil companies.* 環境団体と石油会社の対立は依然として根深いものがあります.

Word Link	agon ≈ struggling : *agonize, antagonist, protagonist*

an|tago|nist /æntǽgənɪst/ (antagonists) N-COUNT 可算名詞 Your **antagonist** is your opponent or enemy. 敵対者 ❏ *Spassky had never previously lost to his antagonist.* スパスキーはそれまで対戦相手に一度も負けたことがなかった.

A

Word Link *ant ≈ not, opposite : antagonize, Antarctic, antonym*

an|tago|nize /æntǽgənaɪz/ (**antagonizes, antagonizing, antagonized**) V-T 他動詞 If you **antagonize** someone, you make them feel angry or hostile toward you. 反感をもたせる □ *He didn't want to antagonize her.* 彼女の反感を買いたくはなかった.

Ant|arc|tic /æntɑ́ːrktɪk/ N-PROPER 固有名詞 **The Antarctic** is the area around the South Pole. 南極
→ see **globe**

ante /ǽnti/ ◼ N-SING 単数名詞 In card games such as poker, the **ante** is the sum of money staked by the players before the cards are dealt. 賭け金 ◻ PHRASE 句 If you up the **ante** or raise the **ante**, you increase your demands when you are in dispute or fighting for something. 要求を引き上げる [JOURNALISM ジャーナリズム] □ *Whenever they reached their goal, they upped the ante, setting increasingly complex challenges for themselves.* 彼らは目標を1つ達成するごとに次の目標を掲げてさらなる難問に挑戦した.

an|ten|na /æntɛ́nə/ (**antennae** /æntɛ́ni/ or **antennas**)

Antennas is the usual plural form for meaning ◻.

Antennas は ◻ を意味するための通常の複数形である.

◼ N-COUNT 可算名詞 The **antennae** of something such as an insect or crustacean are the two long, thin parts attached to its head that is used to feel things with. 触角 ◻ N-COUNT 可算名詞 An **antenna** is a device or a piece of wire that sends and receives television or radio signals and is usually attached to a radio, television, car, or building. アンテナ

an|them /ǽnθəm/ (**anthems**) N-COUNT 可算名詞 An **anthem** is a song that is used to represent a particular nation, society, or group and that is sung on special occasions. 国歌；賛歌 ◻ *The band played the Czech anthem.* 楽隊がチェコ国歌を演奏した.

an|thol|ogy /ænθɒ́lədʒi/ (**anthologies**) N-COUNT 可算名詞 An **anthology** is a collection of writings by different writers published together in one book. 作品集，選集 ◻ *...an anthology of poetry.* 詩選集.

Word Link *logy, ology ≈ study of : anthropology, biology, geology*

an|thro|pol|ogy /ænθrəpɒ́lədʒi/ N-UNCOUNT 不可算名詞 **Anthropology** is the scientific study of people, society, and culture. 人類学 ● **an|thro|polo|gist** /ænθrəpɒ́lədʒɪst/ (**anthropologists**) N-COUNT 可算名詞 人類学者 ◻ *...an anthropologist who had been in China for three years.* 中国に3年間滞在した人類学者.

Word Link *anti ≈ against : antibiotic, antibody, antidote*

anti|bi|ot|ic /æntibaɪɒ́tɪk, -taɪ-/ (**antibiotics**) N-COUNT 可算名詞 **Antibiotics** are medical drugs used to kill bacteria and treat infections. 抗生物質 ◻ *Your doctor may prescribe antibiotics.* 医者は抗生物質を処方するかもしれない.
→ see **medicine**

anti|body /ǽntibɒdi, ǽntaɪ-/ (**antibodies**) N-COUNT 可算名詞 **Antibodies** are substances that a person's or an animal's body produces in their blood in order to destroy substances that carry disease. 抗体 ◻ *Such women carry antibodies which make their blood more likely to clot during pregnancy.* そのような女性は妊娠中に血栓ができやすくなる抗体を持っている.

an|tici|pate /æntɪ́sɪpeɪt/ (**anticipates, anticipating, anticipated**) ◼ V-T 他動詞 If you **anticipate** an event, you realize in advance that it may happen and you are prepared for it. 予想する ◻ *At the time we couldn't have anticipated the result of our campaigning.* 当時は我々の運動がどうような結果をもたらすか全く予想できなかった. ◻ *It is anticipated that the equivalent of 192 full-time jobs will be lost.* 予想では正社員192人分の仕事が失われることになる. ◻ V-T 他動詞 If you **anticipate** a question, request, or need, you do what is necessary or required before the question, request, or need occurs. 前もって対処する ◻ *What Jeff did was to anticipate my next question.* ジェフは私が次に何を質問するか見越していました.

an|tici|pa|tion /æntɪsɪpéɪʃᵊn/ ◼ N-UNCOUNT 不可算名詞 **Anticipation** is a feeling of excitement about something pleasant or exciting that you know is going to happen. 期待 ◻ *There's been an atmosphere of anticipation around here for a few days now.* この周辺ではここ数日来期待感が高まっている. ◻ PHRASE 句 If something is done **in anticipation of** an event, it is done because people believe that event is going to happen. 〜を予想して ◻ *Troops in the Philippines have been put on full alert in anticipation of trouble during a planned general strike.* フィリピン軍は厳戒態勢を敷き，予定されているゼネストによる不測の事態に備えています.

anti|clock|wise /æntiklɒ́kwaɪz, æntaɪ-/ also **anti-clockwise** ADV 副詞 If something is moving **anticlockwise**, it is moving in the opposite direction to the direction in which the hands of a clock move. 反時計回りに [BRIT 英国英語；AM **counterclockwise** 米国英語 **counterclockwise**] ● ADJ 形容詞 **Anticlockwise** is also an adjective. 反時計回りの [ADJ n] ◻ *...an*

anticlockwise route around the coast. 沿岸部を反時計回りに進むルート.

an|tics /ǽntɪks/ N-PLURAL 複数名詞 **Antics** are funny, silly, or unusual ways of behaving. 悪ふざけ，ばかなまね ◻ *Elizabeth tolerated Sarah's antics.* エリザベスはサラの悪ふざけを大目に見てやった.

anti|dote /ǽntidoʊt/ (**antidotes**) ◼ N-COUNT 可算名詞 An **antidote** is a chemical substance that stops or controls the effect of a poison. 解毒剤 ◻ *When he returned, he noticed their sickness and prepared an antidote.* 外から戻ってきた彼は彼らの病状に気づくと解毒剤を準備した. ◻ N-COUNT 可算名詞 Something that is an **antidote to** a difficult or unpleasant situation helps you to overcome the situation. 解決法 ◻ *Massage is a wonderful antidote to stress.* マッサージはストレス解消に大きな効果がある.

an|tipa|thy /æntɪ́pəθi/ N-UNCOUNT 不可算名詞 **Antipathy** is a strong feeling of dislike or hostility toward someone or something. 嫌悪，反感 [FORMAL 形式ばった] ◻ *...the voting public's antipathy toward the president.* 有権者の大統領に対する反感.

Word Link *antiq ≈ old : antiquated, antique, antiquity*

anti|quat|ed /ǽntikweɪtɪd/ ADJ 形容詞 If you describe something as **antiquated**, you are criticizing it because it is very old or old-fashioned. 時代遅れの [DISAPPROVAL 不賛成] ◻ *Many factories are so antiquated they are not worth saving.* 工場の多くは老朽化が進んでいるため残しておく価値はありません.

an|tique /æntíːk/ (**antiques**) N-COUNT 可算名詞 An **antique** is an old object such as a piece of china or furniture that is valuable because of its beauty or rarity. 骨董（こっとう）品 アンティーク ◻ *...a genuine antique.* 本物の骨董品.

an|tiq|uity /æntíkwɪti/ (**antiquities**) ◼ N-UNCOUNT 不可算名詞 **Antiquity** is the distant past, especially the time of the ancient Egyptians, Greeks, and Romans. 古代 ◻ *...famous monuments of classical antiquity.* 古代の有名な遺跡. ◻ N-COUNT 可算名詞 **Antiquities** are things such as buildings, statues, or coins that were made in ancient times and have survived to the present day. 古代の遺物 ◻ *...collectors of Roman antiquities.* 古代ローマの美術品を収集するコレクター.

anti|sep|tic /æntəsɛ́ptɪk/ (**antiseptics**) N-MASS 質量名詞 **Antiseptic** is a substance that kills germs and harmful bacteria. 消毒剤，消毒薬 ◻ *She bathed the cut with antiseptic.* 彼女は傷口を消毒した.
→ see **medicine**

anti|so|cial /æntisóʊʃᵊl, æntaɪ-/ ADJ 形容詞 Someone who is **antisocial** is unwilling to meet and be friendly with other people. 社交嫌いの ◻ *...a generation of teenagers who will become aggressive and antisocial.* すぐにけんかをしたり人付き合いを嫌ったりする10代の子供たち.

an|tith|esis /æntíθəsɪs/ (**antitheses** /æntíθəsiːz/) N-COUNT 可算名詞 The **antithesis** of something is its exact opposite. 正反対 [FORMAL 形式ばった] ◻ *The antithesis of the Middle Eastern buyer is the Japanese.* 中東の購入者と好対照なのが日本人だ.

anti|trust /æntitrʌ́st, æntaɪ-/ ADJ 形容詞 In the United States, **antitrust** laws are intended to stop big companies taking over their competitors, fixing prices with their competitors, or interfering with free competition in any way. 独占禁止の [ADJ n] ◻ *The jury found that the NFL had violated antitrust laws.* 全米フットボールリーグは独占禁止法に違反したという陪審の評決が出た.

anti-virus also **antivirus** ADJ 形容詞 **Anti-virus** software is software that protects a computer against viruses. ウィルス対策の [ADJ n]

anus /éɪnəs/ (**anuses**) N-COUNT 可算名詞 A person's **anus** is the hole from which feces leaves their body. こう門 [MEDICAL 医学の]

anxi|ety /æŋzáɪɪti/ (**anxieties**) N-UNCOUNT 不可算名詞 **Anxiety** is a feeling of nervousness or worry. 不安 [also N in pl] ◻ *Her voice was full of anxiety.* 彼女の声は不安に満ちていた.

anx|ious /ǽŋkʃəs/ ◼ ADJ 形容詞 If you are **anxious to** do something or **anxious that** something should happen, you very much want to do it or very much want it to happen. 切望して [v-link ADJ] ◻ *Both the Americans and the Russians are anxious to avoid conflict in South Asia.* アメリカもロシアも南アジアでの紛争が回避されることを強く望んでいます. ◻ *He is anxious that there should be no delay.* 遅れが出ないことを強く願っています. ◻ ADJ 形容詞 If you are **anxious**, you are nervous or worried about something. 心配して ◻ *The foreign minister admitted he was still anxious about the situation in the country.* 外相はその国の情勢に依然として懸念を持っていることを認めました. ● **anx|ious|ly** ADV 副詞 [ADV with v] 切望して；心配して ◻ *They are waiting anxiously to see who will succeed him.* 彼の後任は誰になるか固唾（かたず）をのんで見守っている.

a

Word Partnership *anxious* は次の語句と使われる:

PREP. anxious **for** *something* ◼1
anxious **about** *something* ◼2
v. **become/feel/get/seem** anxious, anxious **to do** *something*, **make** *someone* anxious ◼2

any /ɛni/ ◼1 DET 限定詞 You use **any** in statements with negative meaning to indicate that no thing or person of a particular type exists, is present, or is involved in a situation. 何も (〜ない) 誰も (〜ない) □*I'm not making any promises.* 約束なんかしません. □*We are doing this all without any support from the hospital.* こうしたことをすべて病院からの支援を受けずにやっています. □*It is too early to say what effect, if any, there will be on the workforce.* 雇用者に影響が出るとしても、それがどんな影響なのかを話すのは今は早すぎる. ● QUANT 数量詞 **Any** is also a quantifier. □*You don't know any of my friends.* 私の友達は1人も知らないでしょ. ● PRON 代名詞 **Any** is also a pronoun. □*The children needed new school clothes and Kim couldn't afford any.* 子供たちに新しい制服を買ってやらなければならなかったが、キムにはそのお金がなかった. [PRON after v] ◼2 DET 限定詞 You use **any** in questions and conditional clauses to ask whether there is some of a particular thing or some of a particular group of people, or to suggest that there might be. いくらかの、何人かの □*Do you speak any foreign languages?* 何か外国語は話しますか. ● QUANT 数量詞 **Any** is also a quantifier. 一のうち何か、一のうち何か □*Introduce foods one at a time and notice if you feel uncomfortable with any of them.* 食品は1品ずつ試し、気分が悪くなるものがないか気をつける. ● PRON 代名詞 **Any** is also a pronoun. 誰か、何か [PRON after v] □*If any bright thoughts occur to you pass them straight to me. Have you got any?* 何か名案が浮かんだらすぐに教えてください. もう何かありますか. ◼3 DET 限定詞 You use **any** in positive statements when you are referring to someone or something of a particular kind that might exist, occur, or be involved in a situation, when their exact identity or nature is not important. どの一でも □*Any actor will tell you that it is easier to perform than to be themselves.* 役者なら誰でも地でいくよりも演技するほうが楽だと言うだろう. ● QUANT 数量詞 **Any** is also a quantifier. どの一でも □*Nealy disappeared two days ago, several miles away from any of the fighting.* ニーリーは2日前に姿を消したが、戦闘のあったどの場所からも数マイル離れたところでした. ● PRON 代名詞 **Any** is also a pronoun. 誰でも、どれでも □*Clean the mussels and discard any that do not close.* ムール貝を洗いますが、殻が開いたままのものは捨てます. ◼4 ADV 副詞 You can also use **any** to emphasize a comparative adjective or adverb in a negative statement. いくらかでも [EMPHASIS 強調] [ADV compar] □*I can't see things getting any easier for graduates.* 卒業生にとって状況が好転したとは言いがたい. ◼5 PHRASE 句 If you say that someone or something is **not just any** person or thing, you mean that they are special in some way. ただの一ではない □*Finzer is not just any East Coast businessman.* フィンザーはアメリカ東海岸の実業家だが、ただ者ではない.

Any is mainly used in questions and negative sentences. You use **not any** instead of **some** in negative sentences. □*There isn't any money.*

◼6 PHRASE 句 If something does not happen or is not true **any longer**, it has stopped happening or is no longer true. もはや □*I couldn't keep the tears hidden any longer.* もはや涙を隠すこともできなかった. ◼7 **in any case** → see **case** ◼8 **by any chance** → see **chance** ◼9 **in any event** → see **event** ◼10 **any old** → see **old** ◼11 **at any rate** → see **rate**

Word Partnership *any* は次の語句と使われる:

ADV. **almost** any, any **better**, any **further**, **hardly** any, any **longer**, any **more** ◼1
N. any **difference**, any **good**, any **idea**, any **kind**, any **luck**, any **minute/moment** (now), any **number of** *something*, any **questions** ◼3
PREP. any **(one) of** *something*, at any **point/time**, at any **rate**, **by** any **chance**, **by** any **means**, **in** any **case**, **in** any **way**, **without** any ◼3

any|body /ɛnibɒdi, -bʌdi/ PRON-INDEF 不定代名詞 **Anybody** means the same as **anyone**. 誰でも

any|how /ɛnihaʊ/ ◼1 ADV 副詞 **Anyhow** means the same as **anyway**. とにかく ◼2 ADV 副詞 If you do something **anyhow**, you do it in a careless or untidy way. いいかげんに [ADV after v] □*Her discarded books were piled up just anyhow.* 彼女の捨てた本が乱雑に積み上がっていた.

any|more /ɛnimɔr/ also **any more** ADV 副詞 If something does not happen or is not true **anymore**, it has stopped happening or is no longer true. もはや [ADV after v] □*I don't ride my motorbike much anymore.* バイクにはあまり乗らなくなった. □*I couldn't trust him anymore.* 彼のことがもう信用できなくなった.

any|one /ɛniwʌn/

The form **anybody** is also used.

anybody 形も使われる.

◼1 PRON-INDEF 不定代名詞 You use **anyone** or **anybody** in statements with negative meaning to indicate in a general way that nobody is present or involved in an action. 誰にも □*I won't tell anyone I saw you here.* ここで会ったなんて誰にも言わないから. □*You needn't talk to anyone if you don't want to.* 嫌なら誰にも話さなくていい. ◼2 PRON-INDEF 不定代名詞 You use **anyone** or **anybody** in questions and conditional clauses to ask or talk about whether someone is present or doing something. 誰か □*Why would anyone want that job?* そんな仕事など誰がしたいだろう. □*How can anyone look sad at an occasion like this?* こんような場で悲しそうな人なんているだろうか. ◼3 PRON-INDEF 不定代名詞 You use **anyone** or **anybody** before words that indicate the kind of person you are talking about. 一のような人 [PRON cl/group] □*I always had been the person who achieved things before anyone else at my age.* これまでずっと同い年の誰よりも先にやってしまうタイプの人間でした. □*It's not a job for anyone who is slow with numbers.* 数字に弱い人には向かない仕事です. ◼4 PRON-INDEF 不定代名詞 You use **anyone** or **anybody** to refer to a person when you are emphasizing that it could be any person out of a very large number of people. 誰でも [EMPHASIS 強調] □*Anyone could be doing what I'm doing.* 誰だって私と同じことをやっているかもしれない. ◼5 PHRASE 句 You use **anyone who is anyone** and **anybody who is anybody** to refer to people who are important or influential. 有力者 □*It seems anyone who's anyone in business is going to the conference.* 会議には業界の大物たちが顔を揃えるようだ.

Do not confuse **anyone** with **any one**. **Anyone** always refers to people. In the phrase **any one**, "one" is a pronoun or a determiner that can refer to either a person or a thing, depending on the context. It is often followed by the word **of**. □*Parting from any one of you for even a short time is hard… None of us stay in any one place for a very long time.* In these examples, **any one** is a more emphatic way of saying **any**. **Anyone** or **anybody** is mainly used in questions and negative sentences. You use **not anyone** instead of **someone** in negative sentences. □*There isn't anyone here… There isn't anybody here.*

any|place /ɛnipleɪs/ ADV 副詞 **Anyplace** means the same as **anywhere**. どこにも [AM 米国英語, INFORMAL くだけた] [ADV after v] □*She didn't have anyplace to go.* 彼女にはどこにも行くあてがなかった.

any|thing /ɛniθɪŋ/ ◼1 PRON-INDEF 不定代名詞 You use **anything** in statements with negative meaning to indicate in a general way that nothing is present or that an action or event does not or cannot happen. 何も □*We can't do anything.* 何もできない. □*She couldn't see or hear anything at all.* 彼女は全く見ることも聞くこともできなかった. ◼2 PRON-INDEF 不定代名詞 You use **anything** in questions and conditional clauses to ask or talk about whether something is present or happening. 何か □*What happened? Is anything wrong?* 何かあったの、どうしたの. □*Did you find anything?* 何か見つけたの？ ◼3 PRON-INDEF 不定代名詞 You can use **anything** before words that indicate the kind of thing you are talking about. 一の種類のもの [PRON cl/group] □*More than anything else, he wanted to become a teacher.* 何よりも彼は先生になりたかった. □*Anything that's cheap this year will be even cheaper next year.* 今年安いものは来年さらに安くなるだろう. ◼4 PRON-INDEF 不定代名詞 You use **anything** to emphasize a possible thing, event, or situation, when you are saying that it could be any one of a very large number of things. 何でも [EMPHASIS 強調] □*He is young, fresh, and ready for anything.* 彼は若いし元気いっぱいで何でも来いといった感じです. ◼5 PRON-INDEF 不定代名詞 You use **anything** in expressions such as **anything near**, **anything close to** and **anything like** to emphasize a statement that you are making. 一のようなもの [EMPHASIS 強調] [PRON prep] □*Doctors have decided the only way he can live anything near a normal life is to give him an operation.* 医者が下した診断では、普通に近い生活を送りたければ彼は手術するよりほかはない. ◼6 PRON-INDEF 不定代名詞 When you do not want to be exact, you use **anything** to talk about a particular range of things or quantities. 何でも [PRON 'from' n 'to' n, PRON 'between' n 'and' n] □*Chinese herbs that have cured anything from colds to broken bones.* 風邪から骨折まで何にでも効く漢方薬.

Anything is mainly used in questions and negative sentences. You use **not anything** instead of **something** in negative sentences. □*There isn't anything here.*

◼7 PHRASE 句 You use **anything but** in expressions such as **anything but quiet** and **anything but attractive** to emphasize that something is not the case. 全く一ない [EMPHASIS 強調] □*There's no evidence that Christopher told anyone to say anything but the truth.* クリストファーが誰かに嘘の発言をさせたという証拠は何一つありません. ◼8 PHRASE 句 You can say that you **would not** do something **for anything** to emphasize that you definitely

A

would not want to do or be a particular thing. 何が何でも一ない [INFORMAL, SPOKEN 口語、くだけた, EMPHASIS 強調] ❑ I wouldn't want to move for anything in the world. 何が何でもここを離れるつもりはない. ◙ PHRASE 句 You use if anything, especially after a negative statement, to introduce a statement that adds to what you have just said. どちらかといえば ❑ I never had to clean up after the lodgers. If anything, they did most of the cleaning. 下宿人が散らかして後片付けしたことは一度もなかったです. それどころか掃除はたいがいしてもらっていました. ◉ PHRASE 句 You can add or anything to the end of a clause or sentence in order to refer vaguely to other things that are or may be similar to what you just mentioned. 一か何か [INFORMAL, SPOKEN くだけた, 口語, VAGUENESS あいまいさ] ❑ Listen, if you talk to Elizabeth or anything make sure you let everyone know, will you. いい, エリザベスに話すようなことがあったらちゃんとみんなに知らせてよ, わかったわね.

> **Word Partnership** anything は次の語句と使われる:
>
> ADJ. anything **left**, anything **more** ◙
> **ready for** anything ◘
> PREP. anything **like** ◍
> anything **but** ◎

any|time /ɛnitaɪm/ ADV 副詞 You use anytime to mean a point in time that is not fixed or set. いつでも ❑ The college admits students anytime during the year. 大学では学生を一年中受け入れている. ❑ He can leave anytime he wants. 彼はいつでも好きなときに出て行くがよい.

any|way /ɛniweɪ/

> The form anyhow is also used.
>
> anyhow 形も使われる.

◙ ADV 副詞 You use anyway or anyhow to indicate that a statement explains or supports a previous point. いずれにしても [ADV with cl] ❑ I'm certain David's told you his business troubles. Anyway, it's no secret that he owes money. デービッドから仕事で困っている話は聞いているはずだ. いずれにしても, やつが借金していることは秘密でも何でもないんだ. ◙ ADV 副詞 You use anyway or anyhow to suggest that a statement is true or relevant in spite of other things that have been said. とにかく [ADV with cl] ❑ I don't know why I settled on Miami, but anyway I did. どうしてマイアミに落ち着くことになったのか自分でも分からないけど, とにかくそう決めたんだ. ◙ ADV 副詞 You use anyway or anyhow to correct or modify a statement, for example, to limit it to what you definitely know to be true. 正確に言えば [cl/group ADV] ❑ Mary Ann doesn't want to have children. Not right now, anyway. メアリー・アンは子供が欲しくないんだって. 少なくとも今はね. ◙ ADV 副詞 You use anyway or anyhow to indicate that you are asking what the real situation is or what the real reason for something is. それはそうと [cl ADV] ❑ What do you want from me, anyway? それはそうと, 私に何をしてほしいの. ◙ ADV 副詞 You use anyway or anyhow to indicate that you are leaving out some details in a story and are passing on to the next main point or event. ともかく [ADV with cl] ❑ I was told to go to Denver for this interview. It was a very amusing affair. Anyhow, I got the job. デンバーに行って面接を受けろと言われてね. そりゃ面白かった. とにかくそういうことで採用が決まったんだ. ◙ ADV 副詞 You use anyway or anyhow to change the topic or return to a previous topic. それはそうと [ADV cl] ❑ "I've got a terrible cold." — "Have you? Oh dear. Anyway, so you're not going to go away this weekend?" 「ひどい風邪をひいちゃったよ」「あらまあ, そうなの. それじゃ週末出かけるというってのは取り止めね」 ◙ ADV 副詞 You use anyway or anyhow to indicate that you want to end the conversation. それじゃ [ADV cl] ❑ "Anyway, I'd better let you have your dinner. Bye." それじゃ, もう夕食の時間だし, じゃーね.

any|ways /ɛniweɪz/ ADV 副詞 Anyways is a nonstandard or dialectal form of anyway. とにかく [AM 米国英語, SPOKEN 口語] ❑ Well, anyways, she said it wasn't safe. まあとにかく, 危なかったという話だよ.

any|where /ɛniwɛər/ ◙ ADV 副詞 You use anywhere in statements with negative meaning to indicate that a place does not exist. どこにも ❑ I haven't got anywhere to live. どこも住むところがないんです. ◙ ADV 副詞 You use anywhere in questions and conditional clauses to ask or talk about a place without saying exactly where you mean. どこかへ ❑ Did you try to get help from anywhere? どこかへ助けを求めてみたの? ◙ ADV 副詞 You use anywhere before words that indicate the kind of place you are talking about. 一のどこかで [ADV cl/group] ❑ He'll meet you anywhere you want. どこでもあなたが望む場所で会ってくれるよ. ◙ ADV 副詞 You use anywhere to refer to a place when you are emphasizing that it could be any of a large number of places. どこでも [EMPHASIS 強調] ❑ ...jokes that are so funny they always work anywhere. いつでもどこでもうける面白いジョーク. ◙ ADV 副詞 When you do not want to be exact, you use anywhere to refer to a particular range of things. ざっと見て ❑ His shoes cost anywhere

from $200 up. 彼の靴はざっと見て200ドルは下らない. ◙ ADV 副詞 You use anywhere in expressions such as anywhere near and anywhere close to to emphasize a statement that you are making. 一の近くのどこかに [EMPHASIS 強調] ❑ There weren't anywhere near enough empty boxes. 空箱の数が全然足りなかった.

> **Anywhere** is mainly used in questions and negative sentences. You use not anywhere instead of somewhere in negative sentences. ❑ He isn't going anywhere.

> **Word Partnership** anywhere は次の語句と使われる:
>
> V. **can/could happen** anywhere, **get** anywhere, **go** anywhere ◙ – ◙
> PREP. anywhere **in the world** ◙ – ◙
> anywhere **near** ◙

apart
❶ POSITIONS AND STATES
❷ INDICATING EXCEPTIONS AND FOCUSING

❶ apart /əpɑrt/

> In addition to the uses shown below, apart is used in phrasal verbs such as "grow apart" and "take apart."
>
> 下記の用法に加えて, apart は grow apart や take apart のような句動詞に使われる.

◙ ADV 副詞 When people or things are apart, they are some distance from each other. 離れて ❑ He was standing a bit apart from the rest of us, watching us. 彼はみんなからは少し離れたところに立ってこっちを見ていた. ◙ ADV 副詞 Ray and sister Renee lived just 25 miles apart from each other. レイと妹のレネの家はたった25マイルしか離れていなかった. ◙ ADV 副詞 If two people or things move apart or are pulled apart, they move away from each other. 離れて [ADV after v] ❑ John and Isabelle moved apart, back into the sun. ジョンとイザベルは別れてまた日なたに出ていった. ◙ ADV 副詞 If two people are apart, they are no longer living together or spending time together, either permanently or just for a short time. 別れて, 離れて ❑ It was the first time Jane and I had been apart for more than a few days. ジェーンと僕が数日以上も離れ離れになるのは初めてだった. ◙ ADV 副詞 If you take something apart, you separate it into the pieces that it is made of. If it comes or falls apart, its parts separate from each other. ばらばらに [ADV after v] ❑ When the clock stopped he took it apart, found what was wrong, and put the whole thing together again. 時計が動かなくなると彼は分解して原因を見つけまた元通りにした. ◙ ADV 副詞 If something such as an organization or relationship falls apart, or if something tears it apart, it can no longer continue because it has serious difficulties. 崩壊して, 破綻して [ADV after v] ❑ Any manager knows that his company will start falling apart if his attention wanders. 経営者なら誰でも本人の注意力が散漫になったとたんに会社が傾き始めることを知っている. ◙ ADV 副詞 If something sets someone or something apart, it makes them different from other people or things. ほかとは違って ❑ What really sets Mr. Thaksin apart is that he comes not from Southern China, but from northern Thailand. タクシン氏を特に際立たせているのは中国南部ではなくタイ北部の出身であるという点だ. ◙ ADJ 形容詞 If people or groups are a long way apart on a particular topic or issue, they have completely different views and disagree about it. 意見が相違して [v-link amount ADJ, oft ADJ 'on' n] ❑ Their concept of a performance and our concept were miles apart. 演技に対する考え方が彼らと我々ではおよそ離れています. ◙ PHRASE 句 If you can't tell two people or things apart, they look exactly the same to you. 区別がつかない ❑ I can still only tell Mark and Dave apart by the color of their shoes! いまでもマークとデーブを見分けるときはいつも靴の色で見分けるんです.

> **Word Partnership** apart は次の語句と使われる:
>
> ADV. **far** apart ◙
> N. **miles** apart ◙
> V. **take** apart ◙
> **drive** apart, **fall** apart, **tear** apart ◙
> **set** someone/something apart ◙
> **tell** apart ◙

❷ apart /əpɑrt/ ◙ PHRASE 句 Apart from means the same as aside from. 一以外は, 一を除くと ◙ ADV 副詞 You use apart when you are making an exception to a general statement. 一以外に [n ADV] ❑ This was, New York apart, the first American city I had ever been in where people actually lived downtown. ニューヨーク市を除いたら, 都心に人が暮らしているアメリカの都市を訪れるのはこれが初めてだった.

apart|heid /əpɑ́rthaɪt/ N-UNCOUNT 不可算名詞 **Apartheid** was a political system in South Africa in which people were divided into racial groups and kept apart by law. アパルトヘイト ❑ *He praised her role in the struggle against apartheid.* 彼はアパルトヘイトとの戦いで彼女が果たした役割を褒めたたえた.

apart|ment /əpɑ́rtmənt/ (apartments) N-COUNT 可算名詞 An **apartment** is a separate set of rooms for living in, in a house or a building with other apartments. アパート (の一室)；マンション (の一室) [mainly AM 主に米国英語] ❑ *Christina has her own apartment, with her own car.* 彼女は自分のマンションと車を持っている.
→ see **city**

apart|ment build|ing (apartment buildings) also apartment house N-COUNT 可算名詞 An **apartment building** or **apartment house** is a tall building that contains different apartments. アパート，マンション [AM 米国英語] ❑ *...the Manhattan apartment house where they live.* 彼らが暮らすマンハッタンのマンション.

apa|thet|ic /æ̀pəθɛ́tɪk/ ADJ 形容詞 If you describe someone as **apathetic**, you are criticizing them because they do not seem to be interested in or enthusiastic about doing anything. 無関心の，やる気がない[DISAPPROVAL 不賛成] ❑ *Even the most apathetic students are beginning to sit up and listen.* 全くやる気のなかった生徒にも上体を起こして話に耳を傾け始めている.

Word Link path ≈ feeling : apathy, empathy, sympathy

apa|thy /ǽpəθi/ N-UNCOUNT 不可算名詞 You can use **apathy** to talk about someone's state of mind if you are criticizing them because they do not seem to be interested in or enthusiastic about anything. 無関心，無気力[DISAPPROVAL 不賛成] ❑ *They told me about isolation and public apathy.* 彼らは孤独感と社会の無関心について話してくれた.

ape /eɪp/ (apes, aping, aped) ■ N-COUNT 可算名詞 **Apes** are chimpanzees, gorillas, and other animals in the same family. 類人猿 ❑ *...chimpanzees and other apes.* チンパンジーなどの類人猿. ■ V-T 他動詞 If you **ape** someone's speech or behavior, you imitate it. 物まねをする ❑ *Modeling yourself on someone you admire is not the same as aping all they say or do.* 尊敬する人を手本にするといっても，その人のあらゆる言動を真似ればよいわけではありません.
→ see **primate**

ap|er|ture /ǽpərtʃər/ (apertures) ■ N-COUNT 可算名詞 An **aperture** is a narrow hole or gap. すき間 [FORMAL 形式ばった] ❑ *Through the aperture he could see daylight.* すき間から太陽の光が見えました. ■ N-COUNT 可算名詞 In photography, the **aperture** of a camera is the size of the hole through which light passes to reach the film. 絞り ❑ *Use a small aperture and position the camera carefully.* 絞りを絞ってカメラの位置に気をつけます.

apex /eɪpɛks/ (apexes) ■ N-SING 単数名詞 The **apex of** an organization or system is the highest and most important position in it. 最高の地位 ❑ *At the apex of the party was its central committee.* 党の最高意思決定機関は中央委員会でした. ■ N-COUNT 可算名詞 The **apex of** something is its pointed top or end. 先端 ❑ *The hangar is 103 feet high at the apex of its roof.* 格納庫の屋根の先端までの高さは103フィートある.

apiece /əpí̱s/ ■ ADV 副詞 If people have a particular number of things **apiece**, they have that number each. 1人につき [amount ADV] ❑ *He and I had two fish apiece.* 彼も僕も2匹ずつ釣った. ■ ADV 副詞 If a number of similar things are for sale at a certain price **apiece**, that is the price for each one of them. 1個につき [amount ADV] ❑ *Entire roast chickens were sixty cents apiece.* ローストチキンは1羽60セントだった.

apolo|get|ic /əpɒ̀lədʒɛ́tɪk/ ADJ 形容詞 If you are **apologetic**, you show or say that you are sorry for causing trouble for someone, for hurting them, or for disappointing them. 謝罪して ❑ *The hospital staff were very apologetic but that couldn't really compensate.* 病院職員は深く謝罪したが，これで償いが済んだわけではなかった. ● apolo|get|ically /əpɒ̀lədʒɛ́tɪkli/ ADV 副詞 [ADV with v] ❑ *"It's of no great literary merit," he said, almost apologetically.* 「文芸的な価値は何もないですね」と彼はすまなさそうに言った.

apolo|gize /əpɒ́lədʒaɪz/ (apologizes, apologizing, apologized) V-I 自動詞 When you **apologize to** someone, you say that you are sorry that you have hurt them or caused trouble for them. You can say "**I apologize**" as a formal way of saying sorry. 謝罪する ❑ *I apologize for being late, but I have just had a message from the hospital.* 遅刻して申し訳ございません，ちょうど病院から連絡があったものですから. ❑ *He apologized to the people who had been affected.* 彼は被害を受けてきた人たちに対し謝罪を表しました.

Word Link log ≈ reason, speech : apology, dialogue, logic

apol|ogy /əpɒ́lədʒi/ (apologies) ■ N-VAR 可変性名詞 An **apology** is something that you say or write in order to tell

someone that you are sorry that you have hurt them or caused trouble for them. 謝罪 ❑ *I didn't get an apology.* 謝罪はなかった. ❑ *We received a letter of apology.* 詫び状が来た. ■ N-PLURAL 複数名詞 If you offer or make your **apologies**, you apologize. 謝罪する [FORMAL 形式ばった] ❑ *When Mary finally appeared, she made her apologies to Mrs. Velasquez.* ようやく姿を現したメアリーはベラスケスさんに謝罪した.

Word Partnership apology は次の語句と使われる:

ADJ.	formal/public apology ■
N.	letter of apology ■
V.	demand an apology, owe someone an apology ■ make an apology ■

apos|tro|phe /əpɒ́strəfi/ (apostrophes) N-COUNT 可算名詞 An **apostrophe** is the mark ' when it is written to indicate that one or more letters have been left out of a word, as in "isn't" and "we'll." It is also added to nouns to form possessives, as in "Mike's car." アポストロフィ

ap|pall /əpɔ́l/ (appalls, appalling, appalled) V-T 他動詞 If something **appalls** you, it disgusts you because it seems so bad or unpleasant. がくぜんとさせる，ぞっとさせる ❑ *The new-found strength of local militancy appalls many observers.* 現地での新たな戦闘の激化は監視団に大きな衝撃を与えている.

ap|palled /əpɔ́ld/ ADJ 形容詞 If you are **appalled** by something, you are shocked or disgusted because it is so bad or unpleasant. がく然として，ぞっとして ❑ *She said that the Americans are appalled at the statements made at the conference.* 彼女の話では，アメリカ国民は会議の声明を聞いてあ然としているということです.

ap|pall|ing /əpɔ́lɪŋ/ ■ ADJ 形容詞 Something that is **appalling** is so bad or unpleasant that it shocks you. ひどい，ぞっとする ❑ *They have been living under the most appalling conditions for two months.* 彼らの全くひどい生活状態は2ヶ月間も続いている. ● ap|pall|ing|ly ADV 副詞 ぞっとするほど ❑ *He says that he understands why they behaved so appallingly.* 彼らがなぜあんなひどい振る舞いをしたのか，彼にはそれが分かるという. ■ ADJ 形容詞 You can use **appalling** to emphasize that something is very extreme or severe. ひどい [EMPHASIS 強調] ❑ *I developed an appalling headache.* ひどい頭痛がするようになった. ● ap|pall|ing|ly ADV 副詞 ひどく ❑ *It's been an appallingly busy morning.* 今朝は忙しいったらありゃしない. → see also **appall**

ap|pa|rat|us /æ̀pərǽtəs, -réɪ-/ (apparatuses) ■ N-VAR 可変性名詞 The **apparatus** of an organization or system is its structure and method of operation. 構成，機構 ❑ *For many years, the country had been buried under the apparatus of the regime.* 長年にわたってその国は強権的な支配のもとにあった. ■ N-VAR 可変性名詞 **Apparatus** is the equipment, such as tools and machines, which is used to do a particular job or activity. 器具，装置 ❑ *One of the boys had to be rescued by firemen wearing breathing apparatus.* 少年のうち1人は呼吸器をつけた消防士に救出された.

ap|par|ent /əpǽrənt/ ■ ADJ 形容詞 An **apparent** situation, quality, or feeling seems to exist, although you cannot be certain that it does exist. 見たところ [ADJ n] ❑ *I was a bit depressed by our apparent lack of progress.* うまくいかなくていないようで少しがっかりした. ■ ADJ 形容詞 If something is **apparent** to you, it is clear and obvious to you. 明らかな [v-link ADJ] ❑ *It has been apparent that in other areas standards have held up well.* 明らかに言えることは，他の地域では高い水準が維持されていることである. ■ PHRASE 句 If you say that something happens **for no apparent reason**, you cannot understand why it happens. 原因不明の ❑ *The person may become dizzy for no apparent reason.* 原因不明のめまいが起こることもある.

ap|par|ent|ly /əpǽrəntli/ ■ ADV 副詞 You use **apparently** to indicate that the information you are giving is something that you have heard, but you are not certain that it is true. どうもらしい [VAGUENESS あいまいさ] ❑ *Apparently the girls are not at all amused by the whole business.* 女の子たちは今度のことを全く快く思っていないようだ. ■ ADV 副詞 You use **apparently** to refer to something that seems to be true, although you are not sure whether it is or not. 見たところでは ❑ *The recent deterioration has been caused by an apparently endless recession.* 近年の経済悪化の原因は出口のない不況にある.

ap|peal /əpí̱l/ (appeals, appealing, appealed) ■ V-I 自動詞 If you **appeal to** someone **to** do something, you make a serious and urgent request to them. 訴える ❑ *He appealed to voters to go to the polls tomorrow.* 明日は投票に出かけるよう彼は有権者に訴えた. ❑ *He will appeal to the state for an extension of unemployment benefits.* 彼は政府に対し失業手当の受給期間の延長を求めるつもりだ. ■ V-I 自動詞 If you **appeal** a decision to someone in authority, you formally ask them to change it. 上訴する；（判定などに）抗議する ❑ *We intend to appeal the verdict.* この評決を不服として上訴するつもりです. ■ V-I 自動詞 If something **appeals to** you, you find it attractive or interesting. 魅力がある ❑ *On the other*

hand, the idea appealed to him. 一方でその考えに興味をひかれる部分もあった. **4** N-COUNT 可算名詞 An **appeal** is a serious and urgent request. 訴え ❏He has a message from King Fahd, believed to be an appeal for Arab unity. 彼はファハド国王からの親書を携えており, アラブ諸国の結束を求めた内容だと考えられます. **5** N-COUNT 可算名詞 An **appeal** is an attempt to raise money for a charity or for a good cause. 募金協力の呼びかけ ❏...an appeal to save a library containing priceless manuscripts. 貴重な写本を所蔵する図書館の存続のための募金活動. **6** N-VAR 可変性名詞 An **appeal** is a formal request for a decision to be changed. 上訴; (判定などの) 抗議 ❏They took their appeal to the Supreme Court. 彼らは最高裁に上訴した. **7** N-UNCOUNT 不可算名詞 The **appeal** of something is a quality that people find attractive or interesting. 魅力 ❏Its new title was meant to give the party greater public appeal. 名称の変更には国民にアピールするねらいがありました. **8** → see also **appealing**
→ see trial

Word Partnership　appeal は次の語句と使われる:

PREP.	appeal **to** *someone* **1** **2** **6**
	appeal **to a court** **2**
	appeal **for** *something* **5**
V.	appeal a **case/decision** **2** **6**
	make an appeal **4** – **6**

ap|peal|ing /əpiːlɪŋ/ **1** ADJ 形容詞 Someone or something that is **appealing** is pleasing and attractive. 魅力的な ❏There was a sense of humor to what he did that I found very appealing. 彼のやり方にはユーモアのセンスがあってとても興味をひかれた. **2** ADJ 形容詞 An **appealing** expression or tone of voice indicates to someone that you want help, advice, or approval. 訴えかけるような ❏She gave him a soft appealing look that would have melted solid ice. 彼女の優しく訴えるようなまなざしは硬い氷をも溶かすほどだった. **3** → see also **appeal**

ap|pear /əpɪər/ (appears, appearing, appeared) **1** V-LINK 連結動詞 If you say that something **appears** to be the way you describe it, you are reporting what you believe or what you have been told, though you cannot be sure it is true. 一のようだ [VAGUENESS あいまいさ] [no cont] ❏There appears to be increasing support for the leadership to take a more aggressive stance. 政府に対しさらに強硬な姿勢を望む声が高まっているようだ. **2** V-LINK 連結動詞 If someone or something **appears to** have a particular quality or characteristic, they give the impression of having that quality or characteristic. 一のように見える [no cont] ❏She did her best to appear more self-assured than she felt. 彼女は実際より自信があるように見せようと必死でした. ❏He is anxious to appear a gentleman. 彼は自分のことを紳士と思われたくてしかたがない. **3** V-I 自動詞 When someone or something **appears**, they move into a position where you can see them. 現れる ❏A woman appeared at the far end of the street. 1人の女が通りのずっと向こうに現れた. **4** V-I 自動詞 When something new **appears**, it begins to exist or reaches a stage of development where its existence can be noticed. 現れる ❏...small white flowers which appear in early summer. 初夏に咲く小さな白い花. **5** V-I 自動詞 When something such as a book **appears**, it is published or becomes available for people to buy. 出版される ❏I could hardly wait for "Boys' Life" to appear each month. 毎月『ボーイズ・ライフ』が出るのがほんと待ちきれないよ. **6** V-I 自動詞 When someone **appears in** something such as a play, a show, or a television program, they take part in it. 出演する ❏Jill Bennett became John Osborne's fourth wife, and appeared in several of his plays. ジョン・オズボーンの4番目の妻となったジル・ベネットは彼の書いた数本の芝居に出演した. **7** V-I 自動詞 When someone **appears before** a court of law or **before** an official committee, they go there in order to answer charges or to give information as a witness. 出廷する; 出席する ❏The defendants are expected to appear in federal court today. 本日被告が連邦裁判所に出廷する予定だ.

Thesaurus　appear また次を参照:

V.	seem **1**
	look like, resemble, seem **2**
	arrive, show up, turn up; (ant.) disappear, vanish **3**

ap|pear|ance /əpɪərəns/ (appearances) **1** N-COUNT 可算名詞 When someone makes an **appearance** at a public event or in a broadcast, they take part in it. 出演 ❏It was the president's second public appearance to date. 大統領が国民の前に姿を現したのはこれで2度目です. **2** N-SING 単数名詞 Someone's or something's **appearance** is the way that they look. 外見 ❏She used to be so fussy about her appearance. 以前の彼女は外見にとてもうるさかった. **3** N-SING 単数名詞 The **appearance of** someone or something in a place is their arrival there, especially when it is unexpected. 出現 ❏The sudden appearance of a few bags of rice could start a riot. 思いがけなく数袋の米が運ばれてきただけでも暴動に発展することがあります. **4** N-SING 単数名詞 The **appearance of** something new is its coming into existence or use. 登場 ❏Flowering plants were

making their first appearance, but were still a rarity. 顕花植物が登場し始めるがまだ珍しかった. **5** N-SING 単数名詞 If something has the **appearance** of a quality, it seems to have that quality. 一感 ❏We tried to meet both children's needs without the appearance of favoritism or unfairness. 子供たちの要求に応えるときはえこひいきしているとか公平でないと思われないように気をつけた. **6** PHRASE 句 If something is true **by all appearances, from all appearances,** or **to all appearances,** it seems from what you observe or know about it that it is true. どう見ても ❏He was a small and by all appearances an unassuming man. 小柄でどこから見ても控えめそうな男だった.

Word Partnership　appearance は次の語句と使われる:

N.	**court** appearance **1**
ADJ.	**public** appearance **1**
	physical appearance **2**
	sudden appearance **3**
V.	**make an** appearance **1** **3**
	change *your* appearance **2**
	give/have an appearance **of** **5**

ap|pease /əpiːz/ (appeases, appeasing, appeased) V-T 他動詞 If you try to **appease** someone, you try to stop them from being angry by giving them what they want. なだめる; 譲歩する [DISAPPROVAL 不賛成] ❏Gandhi was accused by some of trying to appease both factions of the electorate. ガンジーが一部から受けた批判は, 対立する有権者の双方に譲歩しているというものでした.

ap|pease|ment /əpiːzmənt/ N-UNCOUNT 不可算名詞 **Appeasement** means giving people what they want to prevent them from harming you or being angry with you. 懐柔, 宥和(ゆうわ) [FORMAL 形式ばった, DISAPPROVAL 不賛成] ❏He denied there is a policy of appeasement. 彼は懐柔策の存在を否定した.

Word Link　pend ≈ hanging : appendix, depend, pendant

ap|pen|dix /əpɛndɪks/ (appendixes)

The plural form **appendices** /əpɛndɪsiːz/ is usually used for meaning **2**.

複数形 **appendices** /əpɛndɪsiːz/ は通常 **2** の意味に使われる.

1 N-COUNT 可算名詞 Your **appendix** is a small closed tube inside your body that is attached to your digestive system. 虫垂 ❏...a burst appendix. 虫垂の破裂. **2** N-COUNT 可算名詞 An **appendix to** a book is extra information that is placed after the end of the main text. 付録 ❏The survey results are published in full as an appendix to Mr. Barton's discussion paper. 調査結果の全容はバートン氏の審議文書の終りで報告されている.

ap|pe|tite /æpɪtaɪt/ (appetites) **1** N-VAR 可変性名詞 Your **appetite** is your desire to eat. 食欲 ❏He has a healthy appetite. 食欲が旺盛です. **2** N-COUNT 可算名詞 Someone's **appetite for** something is their strong desire for it. 願望 ❏...his appetite for success. 成功に対する強い願望.

ap|pe|tiz|ing /æpɪtaɪzɪŋ/ ADJ 形容詞 **Appetizing** food looks and smells good, so that you want to eat it. 食欲をそそる ❏...the appetizing smell of freshly baked bread. 焼きたてのパンのおいしそうなにおい.

ap|plaud /əplɔːd/ (applauds, applauding, applauded) **1** V-T/V-I 他動詞/自動詞 When a group of people **applaud**, they clap their hands in order to show approval, for example, when they have enjoyed a play or concert. 拍手する ❏The audience laughed and applauded. 観客は笑い声を上げて拍手した. **2** V-T 他動詞 When an attitude or action **is applauded,** people praise it. 称賛される ❏He should be applauded for his courage. 彼の勇気は称賛されて当然だ. ❏This last move can only be applauded. 最後の行動は称賛に値する.

ap|plause /əplɔːz/ N-UNCOUNT 不可算名詞 **Applause** is the noise made by a group of people clapping their hands to show approval. 拍手かっさい ❏They greeted him with thunderous applause. 彼は割れんばかりの大かっさいで迎えられました.

ap|ple /æpªl/ (apples) N-VAR 可変性名詞 An **apple** is a round fruit with smooth red, yellow, or green skin and firm white flesh. りんご ❏I want an apple. りんごが欲しい. ❏...his ongoing search for the finest varieties of apple. 最高級種のりんごを今なお求め続けていること.

This fruit has been used as a nickname for New York City: The Big Apple. Other nicknames include: The Windy City (Chicago), Mile High City (Denver), The Motor City (Detroit), Beantown (Boston), and Tinseltown (Hollywood).

ap|plet /æplɪt/ (applets) N-COUNT 詞 An **applet** is a computer program contained within a page on the World Wide Web that transfers itself to your computer and runs automatically while you are looking at that Web page. アプレット

ap|pli|ance /əplaɪəns/ (appliances) N-COUNT 可算名詞 An **appliance** is a device or machine in your home that you use to do

a job such as cleaning or cooking. Appliances are often electrical. 家庭用器具 [FORMAL 形式ばった] ❑ *He could also learn to use the vacuum cleaner, the washing machine and other household appliances.* 掃除機や洗濯機などの家電製品の使い方も覚えるだろう。

ap|pli|ca|ble /ǽplɪkəb³l, əplɪkə-/ ADJ 形容詞 Something that is **applicable to** a particular situation is relevant to it or can be applied to it. 当てはまる ❑ *What is a reasonable standard for one family is not applicable for another.* ある家族にはもっともなことでも別の家族には当てはまらない。

ap|pli|cant /ǽplɪkənt/ (applicants) N-COUNT 可算名詞 An **applicant for** something such as a job or a college is someone who makes a formal written request to be considered for it. 応募者，志願者 ❑ *We have had lots of applicants for these positions.* この職には多くの応募が集まっています。

ap|pli|ca|tion /ǽplɪkeɪʃ³n/ (applications) ◼ N-COUNT 可算名詞 An **application for** something such as a job or membership of an organization is a formal written request for it. 応募，申し込み ❑ *His application for membership of the organization was rejected.* 彼は団体への加入を申し込んだが断られた。 ◻ N-COUNT 可算名詞 In computing, an **application** is a piece of software designed to carry out a particular task. アプリケーション ❑ *The service works as a software application that is accessed via the internet.* 本サービスを提供するアプリケーションにはインターネットからアクセスできます。 ◻ N-VAR 可変性名詞 The **application of** a rule or piece of knowledge is the use of it in a particular situation. 適用，利用 ❑ *Students learned the practical application of the theory they had learned in the classroom.* 学生は授業で習った理論を実際に応用することを学んだ。 ◻ N-UNCOUNT 不可算名詞 **Application** is hard work and concentration on what you are doing over a period of time. 専念 ❑ *...his immense talent, boundless energy and unremitting application.* 彼の素晴らしい才能，みなぎる力，そしてたゆまぬ努力。

> **Word Partnership** *application* は次の語句と使われる:
>
> V.   accept/reject an application, file/submit an application, fill out an application ◼
> N.   college application, application form, grant/loan application, job application, membership application ◼
>   application software ◻
> ADJ. practical application ◻

ap|plied /əplάɪd/ ADJ 形容詞 An **applied** subject of study has a practical use, rather than being concerned only with theory. 応用〜 [ADJ n] ❑ *...Applied Physics.* 応用物理。
→ see make-up, science

ap|ply /əplάɪ/ (applies, applying, applied) ◼ V-T/V-I 他動詞/自動詞 If you **apply for** something such as a job or membership of an organization, you write a letter or fill out a form in order to ask formally for it. 申し込む ❑ *I am continuing to apply for jobs.* 今も職に応募し続けています。 ❑ *They may apply to join the organization.* 彼らは団体への加入を申し込むかもしれない。 ◻ V-T 他動詞 If you **apply yourself to** something or **apply** your mind to something, you concentrate hard on doing it or on thinking about it. 専念する ❑ *Scymanski has applied himself to this task with considerable energy.* シマンスキーは大いに精力を傾けてその仕事に集中した。 ◻ V-I 自動詞 If something such as a rule or a remark **applies to** a person or in a situation, it is relevant to the person or the situation. 当てはまる [no cont] ❑ *The convention does not apply to us.* 協定は我々には適用されない。 ❑ *The rule applies where a person owns stock in a corporation.* この規則は会社の株を所有している者に適用される。 ◻ V-T 他動詞 If you **apply** something such as a rule, system, or skill, you use it in a situation or activity. 適用する ❑ *The government appears to be applying the same principle.* 政府も同じ方針を適用しているようだ。 ◻ V-T 他動詞 A name that is **applied to** someone or something is used to refer to them. 用いられる ❑ *...a biological term that cannot be applied to a whole culture.* 一般には使われない生物学の専門用語。 ◻ V-T 他動詞 If you **apply** something **to** a surface, you put it on or rub it into the surface. 加える；塗る ❑ *The right thing would be to apply direct pressure to the wound.* 傷口を直接押さえるのがよいだろう。 ◼ → see also applied

> **Word Partnership** *apply* は次の語句と使われる:
>
> PREP. apply for admission, apply for a job ◼
> N.   laws/restrictions/rules apply ◻
>   apply make-up, apply pressure ◻

ap|point /əpɔ́ɪnt/ (appoints, appointing, appointed) ◼ V-T 他動詞 If you **appoint** someone to a job or official position, you formally choose them for it. 任命する，指名する ❑ *It made sense to appoint a banker to this job.* 銀行出身者をこの役職にあてたのは順当。 ❑ *The president has appointed a civilian as defense secretary.* 大統領は国防長官に民間人を登用しました。 ◻ → see also appointed

> **Word Partnership** *appoint* は次の語句と使われる:
>
> N.   appoint judges, appoint a leader, appoint members

ap|point|ed /əpɔ́ɪntɪd/ ADJ 形容詞 If something happens at the **appointed** time, it happens at the time that was decided in advance. 指定された [FORMAL 形式ばった] [ADJ n] ❑ *The appointed hour of the ceremony was drawing nearer.* 式典の予定時刻が迫っていた。

ap|point|ment /əpɔ́ɪntmənt/ (appointments) ◼ N-VAR 可変性名詞 The **appointment** of a person to a particular job is the choice of that person to do it. 任命，指名 ❑ *His appointment to the cabinet would please the right wing.* 彼の入閣は右派には朗報だろう。 ◻ N-COUNT 可算名詞 An **appointment** is a job or position of responsibility. 役職 ❑ *Mr. Fay is to take up an appointment as a researcher.* フェイ氏は研究員の職を引き受けるつもりです。 ◻ N-COUNT 可算名詞 If you have an **appointment with** someone, you have arranged to see them at a particular time, usually in connection with their work or for a serious purpose. 約束，予約 ❑ *She has an appointment with her accountant.* 彼女は会計士と会う約束がある。 ◻ PHRASE 句 If something can be done **by appointment**, people can arrange in advance to do it at a particular time. 予約で ❑ *Viewing is by appointment only.* 見学には予約が必要だ。

> **Thesaurus** *appointment* また次を参照:
>
> N.   date, engagement, meeting ◻

> **Word Partnership** *appointment* は次の語句と使われる:
>
> PREP. appointment to something ◼
>   appointment with someone ◻
>   by appointment ◻
> N.   appointment book ◻
> V.   have/make/schedule an appointment ◻

ap|prais|al /əpréɪz³l/ (appraisals) ◼ N-VAR 可変性名詞 If you make an **appraisal** of something, you consider it carefully and form an opinion about it. 認識 ❑ *What is needed in such cases is a calm appraisal of the situation.* そうした場合に必要なのは落ち着いて状況を把握することだ。 ◻ N-VAR 可変性名詞 **Appraisal** is the official or formal assessment of the strengths and weaknesses of someone or something. Appraisal often involves observation or some kind of testing. 評価 ❑ *One of the most important tools for organizational improvement is the performance appraisal.* 組織を改善させる最も重要な手段の1つは業績評価です。 ◻ N-COUNT 可算名詞 An **appraisal** is a judgement that someone makes about how much money something such as a house or a company is worth. 査定 [AM 米国英語] ❑ *It may also be necessary to get a new appraisal of the property.* 資産の新たな査定をうけることも必要かもしれません。

ap|praise /əpréɪz/ (appraises, appraising, appraised) ◼ V-T 他動詞 If you **appraise** something or someone, you consider them carefully and form an opinion about them. 評価する [FORMAL 形式ばった] ❑ *This prompted many employers to appraise their selection and recruitment policies.* これがきっかけで多くの雇用主が新社員の選考と採用の方法を評価するようになった。 ◻ V-T 他動詞 When experts **appraise** something, they decide how much money it is worth. 査定する [AM 米国英語] ❑ *His estate is now appraised at a figure near $1,000,000.* 彼の地所は現在100万ドル近い価格に査定されている。

ap|pre|ci|ate /əpríːʃieɪt/ (appreciates, appreciating, appreciated) ◼ V-T 他動詞 If you **appreciate** something, for example, a piece of music or good food, you like it because you recognize its good qualities. よさがわかる ❑ *Anyone can appreciate our music.* だれでも私たちの音楽のよさがわかる。 ◻ V-T 他動詞 If you **appreciate** a situation or problem, you understand it and know what it involves. 認識する ❑ *She never really appreciated the depth and bitterness of the family's conflict.* 彼女は家族の争いがどんなに深くて激しいものかを決して本当には認識していなかった。 ◻ V-T 他動詞 If you **appreciate** something that someone has done for you or is going to do for you, you are grateful for it. 感謝する ❑ *Peter stood by me when I most needed it. I'll always appreciate that.* ピーターは最も必要な時に私の味方になってくれた。私はそのことをいつまでも感謝する。 ◻ V-I 自動詞 If something that you own **appreciates** over a period of time, its value increases. 値上がりする ❑ *They don't have any confidence that houses will appreciate in value.* 彼らは住宅価格が上昇するとは全然確信を持っていない。

> **Word Partnership** *appreciate* は次の語句と使われる:
>
> V.   fail to appreciate ◼ – ◻
> ADV. fully appreciate ◼ – ◻
> N.   appreciate someone's concern/support ◻
>   appreciate in value ◻

A

ap|pre|cia|tion /əpriːʃieɪʃⁿn/ ■ N-SING 単数名詞 **Appreciation** of something is the recognition and enjoyment of its good qualities. 鑑賞力 [also no det, oft N 'of' n] □ ...an investigation into children's understanding and appreciation of art. 児童の芸術に対する理解と鑑賞力の調査 ■ N-SING 単数名詞 Your **appreciation for** something that someone does for you is your gratitude for it. 感謝 [also no det] □ He expressed his appreciation for what he called Saudi Arabia's moderate and realistic oil policies. 彼は穏健で現実的と彼が呼ぶサウジアラビアの石油政策に対する感謝の気持ちを表明した. ■ N-SING 単数名詞 An **appreciation of** a situation or problem is an understanding of what it involves. 理解 [also no det] □ They have a stronger appreciation of the importance of economic incentives. 彼らは経済的な動機の重要性をいっそう強く理解している. ■ N-UNCOUNT 不可算名詞 **Appreciation** in the value of something is an increase in its value over a period of time. 上昇 □ You have to take capital appreciation of the property into account. あなたはあの土地の資産価値の上昇を考慮に入れなければなりません.

ap|pre|cia|tive /əpriːʃiətɪv, -ʃeɪtɪv/ ■ ADJ 形容詞 An **appreciative** reaction or comment shows the enjoyment that you are getting from something. 満足そうな □ There is a murmur of appreciative laughter. 満足そうな低い笑い声が聞える. ■ ADJ 形容詞 If you are **appreciative of** something, you are grateful for it. 感謝して □ We have been very appreciative of their support. 我々は彼らの支援を大変感謝している.

ap|pre|hen|sion /æprɪhɛnʃⁿn/ (**apprehensions**) N-VAR 可変性名詞 **Apprehension** is a feeling of fear that something bad may happen. 不安 [FORMAL 形式ばった] □ It reflects real anger and apprehension about the future. それは将来についての真の怒りと不安を反映している.

ap|pre|hen|sive /æprɪhɛnsɪv/ ADJ 形容詞 Someone who is **apprehensive** is afraid that something bad may happen. 不安な □ People are still terribly apprehensive about the future. 人々はまだ将来についてひどく不安である.

ap|pren|tice /əprɛntɪs/ (**apprentices, apprenticing, apprenticed**) ■ N-COUNT 可算名詞 An **apprentice** is a young person who works for someone in order to learn their skill. 徒弟, 見習い □ I started off as an apprentice and worked my way up. 私は見習いから始めて苦労してはい上がった. ■ V-T 他動詞 If a young person **is apprenticed to** someone, they go to work for them in order to learn their skill. 徒弟に出す [usu passive] □ I was apprenticed to a plumber when I was fourteen. 私は14歳の時, 配管工の見習いになった.

ap|pren|tice|ship /əprɛntɪsʃɪp/ (**apprenticeships**) N-VAR 可変性名詞 Someone who has an **apprenticeship** works for a fixed period of time for a person who has a particular skill in order to learn the skill. **Apprenticeship** is the system of learning a skill like this. 見習い期間 □ After serving his apprenticeship as a toolmaker, he became a manager. 工作機械製作工の見習い期間を終了した後, 彼は主任になった.

ap|proach /əproʊtʃ/ (**approaches, approaching, approached**) ■ V-T/V-I 他動詞/自動詞 When you **approach** something, you get closer to it. 近づく □ He didn't approach the front door at once. 彼はすぐには正面玄関に近づかなかった. □ When I approached, they grew silent. 私が近づくと彼らは黙り込んだ. ● N-COUNT 可算名詞 **Approach** is also a noun. 近づくこと □ At their approach the little boy ran away and hid. 彼らが近づくとその小さい男の子は逃げて隠れた. ■ V-T 他動詞 If you **approach** someone **about** something, you speak to them about it for the first time, often making an offer or request. 話をもちかける [no cont] □ When Brown approached me about the job, my first reaction was of disbelief. ブラウンが私にその仕事の話を持ちかけたとき, 私はまず彼の言うことを疑った. □ He approached me to create and design the restaurant. 彼はそのレストランを立案設計するように私に話を持ちかけた. ● N-COUNT 可算名詞 **Approach** is also a noun. 働きかけ □ There had already been approaches from buyers interested in the whole of the group. グループ全体の買収に関心のある者たちからすでに働きかけがあった. ■ V-T 他動詞 When you **approach** a task, problem, or situation in a particular way, you deal with it or think about it in that way. 取り組む □ The Bank has approached the issue in a practical way. その銀行は現実的な方法でその問題に取り組んできた. ■ V-I 自動詞 As a future time or event **approaches**, it gradually gets nearer as time passes. 近づく □ As autumn approached, the plants and colors in the garden changed. 秋が近づくにつれて庭の植物や色彩に変化が見られた. ● N-SING 単数名詞 **Approach** is also a noun. 近づくこと □ ...the festive spirit that permeated the house with the approach of Christmas. クリスマスが近づくにつれて家じゅうにあふれたお祭り気分 ■ V-T 他動詞 As you **approach** a future time or event, time passes so that you gradually get nearer to it. 近づく □ There is a need for understanding and cooperation as we approach the summit. サミットが近づくにつれて理解と協調が必要である. ■ V-T 他動詞 If something **approaches** a particular level or state, it almost reaches that level or state. (状態に) 近づく □ Oil prices have approached their highest level for almost ten years. 石油価格はほぼ10年間最高のレベルに近づ

いていた. ■ N-COUNT 可算名詞 An **approach to** a place is a road, path, or other route that leads to it. 通じる道 □ The path serves as an approach to the boathouse. その小道はボート小屋へ行く道となっている. ■ N-COUNT 可算名詞 Your **approach to** a task, problem, or situation is the way you deal with it or think about it. 取り組み方 □ We will be exploring different approaches to gathering information. 我々は情報収集の異なる手法を探究する予定です.

Thesaurus approach また次を参照:

V. close in, near; (ant.) go away, leave ■
N. attitude, method, technique ■

Word Partnership approach は次の語句と使われる:

N. approach a problem ■
PREP. approach to something ■ ■
V. adopt/take an approach ■
ADJ. different/new/novel approach, hands-on approach ■

ap|pro|pri|ate /əproʊpriɪt/ ADJ 形容詞 Something that is **appropriate** is suitable or acceptable for a particular situation. 適切な □ It is appropriate that Hispanic names dominate the list. ラテンアメリカ系の名前がリストの大半を占めるのは適切だ. □ Dress neatly and attractively in an outfit appropriate to the job. 仕事にふさわしい服装できちんと魅力的に身支度しなさい. ● **ap|pro|pri|ate|ly** ADV 副詞 適切に □ Behave appropriately and ask intelligent questions. 適切にふるまい, 気のきいた質問をしなさい.

Thesaurus appropriate また次を参照:

ADJ. correct, fitting, relevant, right; (ant.) improper, inappropriate, incorrect

ap|prov|al /əpruːvⁿl/ (**approvals**) ■ N-UNCOUNT 不可算名詞 If you win someone's **approval for** something that you ask for or suggest, they agree to it. 承認 □ ...efforts to win congressional approval for an aid package for Moscow. モスクワ向けの一括援助に対する議会の承認を得る努力 □ The chairman has also given his approval for an investigation into the case. 会長はまたその事件の調査に許可を与えた. ■ N-UNCOUNT 不可算名詞 If someone or something has your **approval**, you like and admire them. 称賛, 好意 □ His son had an obsessive drive to gain his father's approval. 彼の息子は父親の称賛を得ることに異常なほど執着していた. ■ N-VAR 可変性名詞 **Approval** is a formal or official statement that something is acceptable. 認可 □ The testing and approval of new drugs will be speeded up. 新薬の治験と認可はより迅速に処理される予定です.

Word Partnership approval は次の語句と使われる:

V. gain approval, meet with approval, seek approval, win approval ■ – ■
N. approval rating ■
approval process ■
ADJ. final approval, subject to approval ■

ap|prove /əpruːv/ (**approves, approving, approved**) ■ V-I 自動詞 If you **approve of** an action, event, or suggestion, you like it or are pleased about it. 賛成する [oft with brd-neg] □ Not everyone approves of the festival. お祭りに賛成しない人もいる. ■ V-I 自動詞 If you **approve of** someone or something, you like and admire them. 好意を持つ [oft with brd-neg] □ You've never approved of Henry, have you? 君は1度もヘンリーに好意を持ったことはないでしょうね. ■ V-T 他動詞 If someone in a position of authority **approves** a plan or idea, they formally agree to it and say that it can happen. 承認する □ The Russian Parliament has approved a program of radical economic reforms. ロシアの議会は抜本的な経済改革計画を承認した. ■ → see also **approved**

Thesaurus approve また次を参照:

V. agree to, authorize, permit; (ant.) disapprove, reject ■

Word Partnership approve は次の語句と使われる:

ADJ. likely to approve ■ ■
PREP. approve of something/someone ■
N. approve a plan ■

ap|proved /əpruːvd/ ADJ 形容詞 An **approved** method or course of action is officially accepted as appropriate in a particular situation. 公認の □ The approved method of cleaning is industrial sandblasting. 公認の清浄方法は工業用砂吹きです. □ Approved methods might include destruction of nests and eggs, and the trapping and destruction of geese. 公認の方法にはことによると巣と卵の駆除や, わなによるガチョウの捕獲・駆除が含まれるかもしれない.

Word Link proxim ≈ near : *approximate, approximation, proximity*

ap|prox|i|mate (approximates, approximating, approximated)

The adjective is pronounced /əprɒksɪmət/. The verb is pronounced /əprɒksɪmeɪt/.

形容詞は /əprɒksɪmət/ と発音される。動詞は /əprɒksɪmeɪt/ と発音される。

1 ADJ 形容詞 An **approximate** number, time, or position is close to the correct number, time, or position, but is not exact. およその □ *The approximate cost varies from around $150 to $250.* およその費用は約150ドルから250ドルになる。● **ap|prox|i|mate|ly** ADV 副詞 [ADV num] おおよそ □ *Approximately $150 million is to be spent on improvements.* おおよそ1億5000万ドルが改修工事に使われる予定である。**2** ADJ 形容詞 An idea or description that is **approximate** is not intended to be precise or accurate, but to give some indication of what something is like. 大体の □ *They did not have even an approximate idea what the Germans really wanted.* 彼らはドイツ人が真に何を望んでいるかについておおよその理解すらしていなかった。**3** V-T 他動詞 If something **approximates** something else, it is similar to it but is not exactly the same. 近づく □ *The mixture described below will approximate it, but is not exactly the same.* 以下に説明する混合物はそれに近いものになろうが、すっかり同じではない。

ap|prox|i|ma|tion /əprɒksɪmeɪʃ°n/ (approximations)

1 N-COUNT 可算名詞 An **approximation** is a fact, object, or description which is similar to something else, but which is not exactly the same. 近似 □ *That is a fair approximation of the way in which the next boss is being chosen.* それが次期社長を選んでいるやり方の大体の構図だ。**2** N-COUNT 可算名詞 An **approximation** is a number, calculation, or position that is close to a correct number, time, or position, but is not exact. 近似値 □ *Clearly that's an approximation, but my guess is there'll be a reasonable balance.* 明らかにこれが近い数値だが、まずまずの残高があるだろうと私は思う。□ *As we know, 365.25 is only an approximation.* 周知の通り、365.25は近似値に過ぎない。

Apr. Apr. is a written abbreviation for **April**. 4月

apri|cot /eɪprɪkɒt/ (apricots) **1** N-VAR 可変性名詞 An **apricot** is a small, soft, round fruit with yellowish-orange flesh and a large seed inside. アンズ □ *...12 oz apricots, halved and pitted.* 半分に切り、種を取った12オンスのアンズ **2** COLOR 色彩語 **Apricot** is used to describe things that are yellowish-orange in color. アンズ色 □ *The bridesmaids wore apricot and white organza.* 花嫁の付き添い役の女性たちはアンズ色と白のオーガンザを着ていた。

April /eɪprɪl/ (Aprils) N-VAR 可変性名詞 **April** is the fourth month of the year in the Western calendar. 4月 □ *The changes will be introduced in April.* 変更は4月に導入される予定だ。

On April 1 people in Britain and America play all sorts of tricks and practical jokes on each other. People who fall for these tricks are called **April Fools**. Sometimes even the media join in the fun, inventing news stories and publishing spoof reports, for example, about spaghetti growing on trees in Italy.

apron /eɪprən/ (aprons) N-COUNT 可算名詞 An **apron** is a piece of clothing that you put on over the front of your normal clothes and tie around your waist, especially when you are cooking, in order to prevent your clothes from getting dirty. エプロン

apt /æpt/ **1** ADJ 形容詞 An **apt** remark, description, or choice is especially suitable. 適切な □ *The words of this report are as apt today as in 1929.* この報告書の文言は1929年当時と同様に現在でも当てはまる。● **apt|ly** ADV 副詞 適切に □ *...the beach in the aptly named town of Oceanside.* オーシャンサイドというぴったりの名称の町の海辺 **2** ADJ 形容詞 [v-link ADJ to-inf] If someone is **apt to do** something, they often do it and so it is likely that they will do it again. （〜し）やすくて □ *She was apt to raise her voice and wave her hands about.* 彼女はよく声を荒げ、手を振り回した。**3** ADJ 形容詞 An **apt** student is intelligent and able to understand things easily. 利発な [ADJ n] □ *She had taught him French and he had been an apt student.* 彼女は彼にフランス語を教えたことがあるが、彼は覚えの早い学生だった。

ap|ti|tude /æptɪtud/ (aptitudes) N-VAR 可変性名詞 Someone's **aptitude for** a particular kind of work or activity is their ability to learn it quickly and to do it well. 素質 □ *He drifted into publishing and discovered an aptitude for working with accounts.* 彼はいつの間にか出版業についていたが、経理の素質があることに気づいた。

aquat|ic /əkwætɪk/ **1** ADJ 形容詞 An **aquatic** animal or plant lives or grows on or in water. 水生の □ *The pond is small but can support many aquatic plants and fish.* 池は小さいが、多くの水生植物や魚が生息する。**2** ADJ 形容詞 **Aquatic** means relating to water. 水産の □ *...our aquatic resources.* 我々の水産資源

Arab /ærəb/ (Arabs) **1** N-COUNT 可算名詞 **Arabs** are people who speak Arabic and who come from the Middle East and parts of North Africa. アラブ人 **2** ADJ 形容詞 **Arab** means belonging or relating to Arabs or to their countries or customs. アラブ人の □ *On the surface, it appears little has changed in the Arab world.* 表面的にはアラブ世界はほとんど変わっていないように見える。

ar|able /ærəb°l/ ADJ 形容詞 **Arable** farming involves growing crops such as wheat and barley rather than keeping animals or growing fruit and vegetables. **Arable** land is land that is used for arable farming. 耕作の、耕作に適する □ *...arable farmers.* 農耕者

ar|bi|trage /ɑrbɪtrɑʒ/ N-UNCOUNT 不可算名詞 In finance, **arbitrage** is the activity of buying securities or currency in one financial market and selling it at a profit in another. 裁定取引、さや取り [BUSINESS 実業] □ *Astute Singaporeans quickly spotted an arbitrage opportunity.* 抜け目のないシンガポール人たちは裁定取引の機会を目ざとく見つけた。

ar|bi|trary /ɑrbɪtreri/ ADJ 形容詞 If you describe an action, rule, or decision as **arbitrary**, you think that it is not based on any principle, plan, or system. It often seems unfair because of this. 恣意(しい)的な、勝手な [DISAPPROVAL 不賛成] □ *Arbitrary arrests and detention without trial were common.* 恣意的逮捕と裁判なしの拘留が普通だった。● **ar|bi|trari|ly** /ɑrbɪtreərɪli/ ADV 副詞 [ADV with v] 恣意的に □ *The victims were not chosen arbitrarily.* 被害者は恣意的に選ばれたわけではなかった。

ar|bi|trate /ɑrbɪtreɪt/ (arbitrates, arbitrating, arbitrated) V-I 自動詞 When someone in authority **arbitrates between** two people or groups who are in dispute, they consider all the facts and make an official decision about who is right. 調停する、仲裁する □ *He arbitrates between investors and members of the association.* 彼は投資家と協会員の間を調停する。

ar|bi|tra|tion /ɑrbɪtreɪʃ°n/ N-UNCOUNT 不可算名詞 **Arbitration** is the judging of a dispute between people or groups by someone who is not involved. 調停、仲裁 □ *The matter is likely to go to arbitration.* その件は仲裁に付される見込みである。

arc /ɑrk/ (arcs) **1** N-COUNT 可算名詞 An **arc** is a smoothly curving line or movement. 弧 □ *The helicopter made a slow arc, passing over the mound but not stopping.* ヘリコプターはゆっくりと弧を描きながら止まらずに小山を越えて行った。**2** N-COUNT 可算名詞 In geometry, an **arc** is a part of the line that forms the outside of a circle. 円弧 [TECHNICAL 技術的]

ar|cade /ɑrkeɪd/ (arcades) **1** N-COUNT 可算名詞 An **arcade** is a place where you can play games on machines which work when you put money in them. ゲームセンター **2** → see also **video arcade 3** N-COUNT 可算名詞 An **arcade** is a covered passage where there are stores or market stalls. アーケード [mainly BRIT 主に英国英語] □ *...a shopping arcade.* アーケード商店街

arch /ɑrtʃ/ (arches, arching, arched) **1** N-COUNT 可算名詞 An **arch** is a structure that is curved at the top and is supported on either side by a pillar, post, or wall. アーチ門 **1** When she passed under the arch leading out of the park, Mira whooped with delight. マイラは公園の外に通じるアーチ門をくぐると歓声を上げた。**2** N-COUNT 可算名詞 An **arch** is a curved line or movement. アーチ形 □ *...the arch of the fishing rods.* 釣竿のカーブ **3** N-COUNT 可算名詞 The **arch** of your foot is the curved section at the bottom in the middle. 土踏まず □ *"Good girl," said Frank, winding the bandages around the arch of her foot.* 「いい子だ」とフランクは彼女の土踏まずに包帯を巻きながら言った。**4** → see also **arched 5** V-T/V-I 他動詞/自動詞 If you **arch** a part of your body such as your back or if it **arches**, you bend it so that it forms a curve. アーチ形にする □ *Don't arch your back, keep your spine straight.* 背中を丸めず、背骨をまっすぐに伸ばしていなさい。

→ see **architecture, foot**

arch- /ɑrtʃ/ COMB IN N-COUNT 可算名詞の複合 **Arch-** combines with nouns referring to people to form new nouns that refer to people who are extreme examples of something. For example, your **archrival** is the rival you most want to beat. 第1の □ *Neither he nor his archrival, Giuseppe De Rita, won.* 彼も好敵手のジュゼッペ・デ・リータも勝たなかった。

ar|chae|ol|ogy /ɑrkiɒlədʒi/ also **archeology** N-UNCOUNT 不可算名詞 **Archaeology** is the study of the societies and peoples of the past by examining the remains of their buildings, tools, and other objects. 考古学 ● **ar|chaeo|logi|cal** /ɑrkiəlɒdʒɪk°l/ ADJ 形容詞 [ADJ n] 考古学の □ *...one of the region's most important archaeological sites.* その地域で考古学的に最も重要な遺跡の1つ ● **ar|chae|olo|gist** /ɑrkiɒlədʒɪst/ (archaeologists) N-COUNT 可算名詞 考古学者 □ *The archaeologists found a house built around 300 BC, with a basement and attic.* 考古学者たちは紀元前300年頃に建てられた地下室と屋根裏部屋付きの家屋を発見した。

ar|cha|ic /ɑrkeɪɪk/ ADJ 形容詞 **Archaic** means extremely old or extremely old-fashioned. ごく古い □ *...archaic laws that are very seldom used.* ほとんど適用されることのないごく古い法律

arch|bishop /ɑrtʃbɪʃəp/ (archbishops) N-COUNT; N-TITLE 可算名詞、称号名詞 In the Roman Catholic, Orthodox, and Anglican Churches, an **archbishop** is a bishop of the highest rank, who is in charge of all the bishops and priests in a particular country or

Word Web architecture

The Colosseum (sometimes spelled Coliseum) in Rome is a great **architectural** triumph of the ancient world. This amphitheater, built in the first century BC, could hold 50,000 spectators. It was used for animal fights, human executions, and staged combat. The elliptical shape allowed spectators to be closer to the action. It also prevented participants from hiding in the corners. The **arches** are an important part of the **building**. They are an example of a Roman improvement to the simple arch. Each arch is supported by a **keystone** in the top center. The **design** of the Colosseum has influenced the design of thousands of other public venues. Many modern day sports stadiums are the same shape.

region. 大司教, 大主教 ❏ ...*the Roman Catholic archbishop of Colorado Springs.* コロラド・スプリングスのローマカトリック教会の大司教

arched /ɑrtʃt/ **1** ADJ 形容詞 An **arched** roof, window, or doorway is curved at the top. アーチ形の ❏ *From the television room an arched doorway leads in to the hall.* テレビ室からアーチ形のドアを通るとホールに出る. **2** ADJ 形容詞 An **arched** bridge has arches as part of its structure. アーチのある ❏ *She led them up some stairs and across a little arched stone bridge.* 彼女は彼らを導き何段かの階段を上り, 小さな石のそり橋を渡った.

arch|eol|ogy /ɑrkiɒlədʒi/ → see **archaeology**

arche|typ|al /ɑrkɪtaɪpᵊl/ ADJ 形容詞 Someone or something that is **archetypal** has all the most important characteristics of a particular kind of person or thing and is a perfect example of it. 典型的な [FORMAL 形式ばった] ❏ ...*the archetypal American middle-class family living in the suburbs.* 郊外に住む典型的なアメリカの中産階級家族

→ see **myth**

arche|type /ɑrkɪtaɪp/ (**archetypes**) N-COUNT 可算名詞 An **archetype** is something that is considered to be a perfect or typical example of a particular kind of person or thing, because it has all their most important characteristics. 典型 [FORMAL 形式ばった] ❏ *He came to this country 20 years ago and is the archetype of the successful Asian businessman.* 彼はこの国に20年前に移住したが, 成功したアジア人実業家の典型だ.

archi|tect /ɑrkɪtɛkt/ (**architects**) **1** N-COUNT 可算名詞 An **architect** is a person who designs buildings. 建築家 **2** N-COUNT 可算名詞 The **architect of** an idea, event, or institution is the person who invented it or made it happen. 立案者 [oft N 'of' n] ❏ *James Madison was the principal architect of the constitution.* ジェームス・マディソンは憲法の主な立案者だった.

archi|tec|tur|al /ɑrkɪtɛktʃərəl/ ADJ 形容詞 **Architectural** means relating to the design and construction of buildings. 建築上の ❏ ...*Tibet's architectural heritage.* チベットの建築遺産 ●**archi|tec|tur|al|ly** ADV 副詞 建築的に ❏ *The old city center is architecturally rich.* 市の古い中心部はいい建築が豊富にある.

archi|tec|ture /ɑrkɪtɛktʃər/ N-UNCOUNT 不可算名詞 **Architecture** is the art of planning, designing, and constructing buildings. 建築術 ❏ *He studied classical architecture and design in Rome.* 彼はローマで古典派の建築術と設計を学んだ. **2** N-UNCOUNT 不可算名詞 The **architecture** of a building is the style in which it is designed and constructed. 建築様式 ❏ ...*modern architecture.* 近代的な建築様式

→ see Word Web: **architecture**

ar|chive /ɑrkaɪv/ (**archives, archiving, archived**) **1** N-COUNT 可算名詞 **Archives** are a collection of documents and records that contain historical information. You can also use **archives** to refer to the place where archives are stored. 古文書, 公文書, 古文書保管所 ❏ ...*the State Library's archives.* 州立図書館の古文書 **2** ADJ 形容詞 **Archive** material is information that comes from archives. 古文書の [ADJ n] ❏ ...*archive material.* 古文書の資料 **3** V-T 他動詞 If you **archive** material such as documents or data, you store it in an archive. 古文書保管所に保管する ❏ *The system will archive the information so agencies can review it in detail.* そのシステムはその情報を保管して政府機関が詳細に再検討できるようにするであろう.

arc|tic /ɑrktɪk/ **1** N-PROPER 固有名詞 **The Arctic** is the area of the world around the North Pole. It is extremely cold and there is very little light in winter and very little darkness in summer. 北極地方 ❏ ...*winter in the Arctic.* 北極地方の冬 **2** ADJ 形容詞 If you describe a place or the weather as **arctic**, you are emphasizing that it is extremely cold. 極寒の [INFORMAL くだけた, EMPHASIS 強調] ❏ *The bathroom, with its spartan pre-war facilities, is positively arctic.* 戦前の質素な設備しかない風呂場は全く寒い.

→ see Picture Dictionary: **Arctic**

→ see **globe**

ar|dent /ɑrdᵊnt/ ADJ 形容詞 **Ardent** is used to describe someone who has extremely strong feelings about something or someone. 熱烈な ❏ *He's been one of the most ardent supporters of the administration's policy.* 彼は政府の政策の最も熱烈な支持者の１人だった.

ar|du|ous /ɑrdʒuəs/ ADJ 形容詞 Something that is **arduous** is difficult and tiring, and involves a lot of effort. つらい ❏ ...*a long, hot and arduous trip.* 長くて暑いつらい旅

are /ər, STRONG ɑr/ **Are** is the plural and the second person singular of the present tense of the verb **be**. **Are** is often shortened to **'re** after pronouns in spoken English. beの二人称単数および各人称複数の現在形. 口語では-'reと短縮されることが多い.

area /ɛəriə/ (**areas**) **1** N-COUNT 可算名詞 An **area** is a particular part of a town, a country, a region, or the world. 地域 ❏ ...*the large number of community groups in the area.* その地域の多数の地域社会 ❏ *The survey was carried out in both urban and rural areas.* 調査は都市と農村の両地域で実施された. **2** N-COUNT 可算名詞 Your **area** is the part of a town, country, or region where you live. An organization's **area** is the part of a town, country, or region that it is responsible for. 地区 ❏ *Local authorities have been responsible for the running of schools in their areas.* 地方自治体はその地区にある学校の運営に責任を負ってきた. **3** N-COUNT 可算名詞 A particular **area** is a piece of land or part of a building that is used for a particular activity. 場所 ❏ ...*a picnic area.* ピクニック場 **4** N-COUNT 可算名詞 An **area** is a particular place on a surface or object, for example, on your body. 部分 ❏ *You will notice that your baby has two soft areas on the top of his head.* 赤ちゃんの頭のてっぺんには柔らかい部分が2か所あるのに気づくでしょう. **5** N-COUNT 可算名詞 You can use **area** to refer to a particular subject or topic, or to a particular part of a larger, more general situation or activity. 分野 ❏ ...*the politically sensitive area of social security.* 社会保障という政治的に微妙な分野 **6** N-VAR 可変性名詞 The **area** of a surface such as a piece of land is the amount of flat space or ground that it covers, measured in square units. 面積 ❏ *The islands cover a total area of 400 square miles.* 島々は合計400平方マイルの面積に及んでいます. **7** → see also **gray area**

→ see Picture Dictionary: **area**

Thesaurus	*area* また次を参照:
N.	district, place, region, vicinity **1** **2**

Picture Dictionary — Arctic

snow · polar bear · arctic fox · ice · seal · iceberg · lichen · whale

---

<table>
<tr><td colspan="2">Word Partnership   area は次の語句と使われる·</td></tr>
<tr><td>ADJ.</td><td>metropolitan area, rural/suburban/urban area, surrounding area ■
local area, remote area ■
residential area, restricted area ■</td></tr>
<tr><td>N.</td><td>downtown area ■ ■
tourist area ■</td></tr>
<tr><td>PREP.</td><td>throughout the area ■ ■
area of expertise ■</td></tr>
</table>

area code (**area codes**) N-COUNT 可算名詞 The **area code** for a particular place is the series of numbers that you have to dial before someone's personal number if you are making a telephone call to that place from a different area. 市外局番 [mainly AM 主に米国英語] □ *The area code for western Pennsylvania is 412.* ペンシルバニア州西部の市外局番は412です.

arena /ərínə/ (**arenas**) ■ N-COUNT 可算名詞 An **arena** is a place where sports, entertainments, and other public events take place. It has seats around it where people sit and watch. 競技場 □ *...the largest indoor sports arena in the world.* 世界最大の屋内運動競技場 ■ N-COUNT 可算名詞 You can refer to a field of activity, especially one where there is a lot of conflict or action, as an **arena** of a particular kind. 活躍の舞台 □ *He made it clear he had no intention of withdrawing from the political arena.* 彼は政界から退く意図が全くないことを明らかにした.

aren't /ɑrnt, ɑrənt/ ■ **Aren't** is the usual spoken form of "are not." 口語で用いられる are not の短縮形 ■ **Aren't** is the form of "am not" that is used in questions or tags in spoken English.

arguably /ɑrgyuəbli/ ADV 副詞 You can use **arguably** when you are stating your opinion or belief, as a way of giving more authority to it. おそらく □ *They are arguably the most important band*

since The Rolling Stones. 彼らはまず間違いなくローリングストーンズ以来最も重要なバンドだ.

ar|gue /ɑrgyu/ (**argues, arguing, argued**) ■ V-RECIP 相互動詞 If one person **argues with** another, they speak angrily to each other about something that they disagree about. You can also say that two people **argue**. 言い争う □ *The committee is concerned about players' behavior, especially arguing with referees.* 委員会は選手の態度, 特に審判員と言い争うことについて憂慮している. ■ V-RECIP 相互動詞 If you **argue with** someone **about** something, you discuss it with them, with each of you giving your different opinions. 議論する □ *He was arguing with the king about the need to maintain the cavalry at full strength.* 彼は騎兵隊を全員維持する必要性について国王と議論していた. □ *They are arguing over foreign policy.* 彼らは外交政策について議論している. ■ V-I 自動詞 If you tell someone not to **argue with** you, you want them to do or believe what you say without protest or disagreement. 反対の意見を言う [usu imper with neg] □ *Don't argue with me.* 私につべこべ言うな. ■ V-T 他動詞 If you **argue that** something is true, you state it and give the reasons why you think it is true. 主張する □ *His lawyers are arguing that he is unfit to stand trial.* 彼の弁護士団は彼が体調を崩して裁判を受ける状態にはないと主張している. ■ V-I 自動詞 If you **argue for** something, you say why you agree with it, in order to persuade people that it is right. If you **argue against** something, you say why you disagree with it, in order to persuade people that it is wrong. 賛否の議論をする □ *The report argues against tax increases.* 報告書は増税に反対の立場を取っている.

<table>
<tr><td colspan="2">Thesaurus   argue また次を参照:</td></tr>
<tr><td>V.</td><td>bicker, disagree, fight, quarrel; (ant.) agree ■
debate, discuss, dispute ■
claim ■</td></tr>
</table>

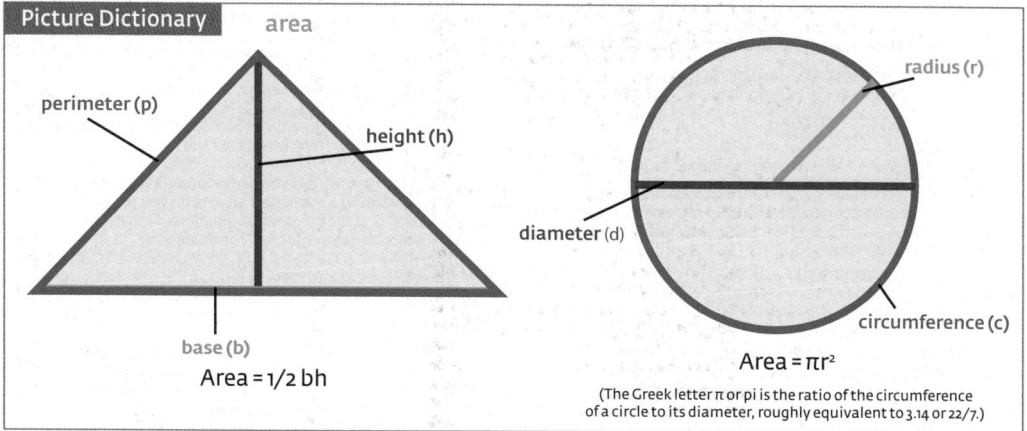

Picture Dictionary — area

perimeter (p) · height (h) · base (b)

Area = 1/2 bh

radius (r) · diameter (d) · circumference (c)

$$\text{Area} = \pi r^2$$

(The Greek letter π or pi is the ratio of the circumference of a circle to its diameter, roughly equivalent to 3.14 or 22/7.)

Word Partnership *argue* は次の語句と使われる:

PREP.	argue **with** *someone/something* **1** – **3**
	argue **about/over** *something* **1** **2**
	argue **against/for** *something* **5**
N.	argue **a case**, **critics** argue, **officials** argue,
	opponents/supporters argue **5**

ar|gu|ment /ɑrgyəmənt/ (**arguments**) **1** N-VAR 可変性名詞 An **argument** is a statement or set of statements that you use in order to try to convince people that your opinion about something is correct. 論拠 ❑ *There's a strong argument for lowering the price.* 価格を引き下げる有力な論拠がある. ❑ *The doctors have set out their arguments against the proposals.* 医師たちはそれらの提案に反対する理由を述べた. **2** N-VAR 可変性名詞 An **argument** is a discussion or debate in which a number of people put forward different or opposing opinions. 議論，論争 ❑ *The incident has triggered fresh arguments about the role of the extreme right in U.S. politics.* その事件は米国政治における極右派の役割についての新たな論争のきっかけとなった. **3** N-COUNT 可算名詞 An **argument** is a conversation in which people disagree with each other angrily or noisily. 口論 ❑ *Anny described how she got into an argument with one of the marchers.* アニーはデモ行進者の1人と口論になった状況を説明した. **4** N-UNCOUNT 不可算名詞 If you accept something without **argument**, you do not question it or disagree with it. 議論すること ❑ *He complied without argument.* 彼は異議を唱えずに応じた.

Do not confuse **argument** and **dispute**. An **argument** is a disagreement between people who may or may not know each other. ❑ *She had an argument with her father about practicing the piano… Travis got in an argument with another motorist.* A **Dispute** is a serious argument that can last for a long time. **Disputes** generally occur between organizations, political parties, or countries. ❑ *…a 10-year-old dispute over crude oil.* Note that **dispute** can also be a verb. ❑ *Opponents dispute the value of Japan's research.*

Word Partnership *argument* は次の語句と使われる:

ADJ.	**persuasive** argument **1**
	heated argument **3**
V.	**support an** argument **1**
	get into an argument, **have an** argument **3**
PREP.	argument **against/for** **2**
	without argument **4**

arid /ærɪd/ ADJ 形容詞 **Arid** land is so dry that very few plants can grow on it. 乾燥した ❑ *…new strains of crops that can withstand arid conditions.* 乾燥した状態に耐えられる新しい系統の穀物

arise /əraɪz/ (**arises, arising, arose, arisen** /ərɪzən/) **1** V-I 自動詞 If a situation or problem **arises**, it begins to exist or people start to become aware of it. 発生する ❑ *…if a problem arises later in the pregnancy.* 妊娠後期に問題が発生すれば **2** V-I 自動詞 If something **arises from** a particular situation, or **arises out of** it, it is created or caused by the situation. 生じる ❑ *This serenity arose in part from Rachel's religious beliefs.* この心の平静はある程度レイチェルの信仰によるものだった.

Word Partnership *arise* は次の語句と使われる:

N.	**complications/differences/issues/problems/**
	opportunities/questions arise **1**
PREP.	arise **from/out of** **1** **2**

Word Link *cracy ≈ rule by : aristocracy, bureaucracy, democracy*

aris|toc|ra|cy /ærɪstɒkrəsi/ (**aristocracies**) N-COUNT-COLL 集合可算名詞 The **aristocracy** is a class of people in some countries who have a high social rank and special titles. 貴族階級 ❑ *…a member of the aristocracy.* 貴族階級の1員

Word Link *crat ≈ power : aristocrat, bureaucrat, democrat*

aris|to|crat /ærɪstəkræt, ərɪst-/ (**aristocrats**) N-COUNT 可算名詞 An **aristocrat** is someone whose family has a high social rank, especially someone who has a title. 貴族 ❑ *…a wealthy southern aristocrat.* 裕福な南部の貴族

aris|to|crat|ic /ərɪstəkrætɪk/ ADJ 形容詞 **Aristocratic** means belonging to or typical of the aristocracy. 貴族の，貴族的な ❑ *…a wealthy, aristocratic family.* 裕福な貴族一家

arith|me|tic /ərɪθmɪtɪk/ **1** N-UNCOUNT 不可算名詞 **Arithmetic** is the part of mathematics that is concerned with the addition, subtraction, multiplication, and division of numbers. 算数 ❑ *…teaching the basics of reading, writing and arithmetic.* 読み書きと算数の基礎を教えること **2** N-UNCOUNT 不可算名詞 You can use **arithmetic** to refer to the process of doing a particular sum

or calculation. 計算 ❑ *4,000 women put in ten rupees each, which if my arithmetic is right adds up to 40,000 rupees.* 4千人の女性が10ルピーずつ出したので，私の計算が正しければ合計4万ルピーとなる. **3** N-UNCOUNT 不可算名詞 If you refer to **the arithmetic** of a situation, you are concerned with those aspects of it that can be expressed in numbers, and how they affect the situation. 数字 ❑ *The arithmetic was discouraging. In less than two months, they had used up six months' worth of food.* 数字は思わしくなかった. 彼らは2か月も経たないうちに6か月分の食料を使い果たしていたのだ.
→ see **mathematics**

arm

❶ PART OF YOUR BODY OR OF SOMETHING ELSE
❷ WEAPONS

❶ arm /ɑrm/ (**arms**) **1** N-COUNT 可算名詞 Your **arms** are the two long parts of your body that are attached to your shoulders and that have your hands at the end. 腕 ❑ *She stretched her arms out.* 彼女は両腕を伸ばした. **2** N-COUNT 可算名詞 The **arm** of a chair is the part on which you rest your arm when you are sitting down. ひじかけ ❑ *Mack gripped the arms of the chair.* マックは椅子のひじかけをぐっとつかんだ. **3** N-COUNT 可算名詞 An **arm** of an object is a long thin part of it that sticks out from the main part. 腕に似たもの ❑ *…the lever arm of the machine.* その機械のレバー **4** N-COUNT 可算名詞 An **arm** of land or water is a long thin area of it that is joined to a broader area. 岬，分流 ❑ *…a small area of woodland between two arms of a small stream.* 小川の2つの分流に挟まれた狭い林地 **5** N-COUNT 可算名詞 An **arm** of an organization is a section of it that operates in a particular country or that deals with a particular activity. 部門 ❑ *The agency is the central research and development arm of the Department of Defense.* その機関は国防総省の中央研究開発部門です. **6** N-COUNT 可算名詞 The **arm** of a piece of clothing is the part of it that covers your arm. 袖 ❑ *…coats that were short in the arms.* 袖の短かったコート **7** PHRASE 句 If two people are walking **arm in arm**, they are walking together with their arms linked. 腕を組んで ❑ *He walked from the court arm in arm with his wife.* 彼は裁判所から妻と腕を組み合って歩いた. **8** PHRASE 句 If you hold something **at arm's length**, you hold it away from your body with your arm straight. 腕を伸ばした距離で ❑ *He struck a match, and held it at arm's length.* 彼はマッチをすり，腕を伸ばしてそれを持った. **9** PHRASE 句 If you **keep** someone **at arm's length**, you avoid becoming too friendly or involved with them. よそよそしく ❑ *She had always kept the family at arm's length.* 彼女はいつも家族によそよそしかった. **10** PHRASE 句 If you welcome some action or change **with open arms**, you are very pleased about it. If you welcome a person **with open arms**, you are very pleased about their arrival. 心から [APPROVAL 賛成] ❑ *They would no doubt welcome the action with open arms.* 彼らはおそらくその行動を心から歓迎するだろう. **11** PHRASE 句 If you **twist** someone's **arm**, you persuade them to do something. 無理に強いる [INFORMAL くだけた] ❑ *She had twisted his arm to get him to invite her.* 彼女は彼に無理やりに自分を招待させていた.
→ see **body, war**

Word Partnership *arms* は次の語句と使われる:

PREP.	arms **around** ❶ **1**
V.	arms **crossed/folded**; **hold/take in** *your* arms, **join/**
	link arms ❶ **1**
ADJ.	**open/outstretched** arms ❶ **1**
V.	**bear** arms ❷ **1**
N.	arms **control**, arms **embargo**, arms **sales** ❷ **1**

❷ arm /ɑrm/ (**arms, arming, armed**) **1** N-PLURAL 複数名詞 **Arms** are weapons, especially bombs and guns. 兵器 [FORMAL 形式ばった] ❑ *Soldiers searched their house for illegal arms.* 兵士たちは違法の武器を見つけようと彼らの家を捜索した. **2** V-T 他動詞 If you **arm** someone **with** a weapon, you provide them with a weapon. 武装する ❑ *She'd been so terrified that she had armed herself with a loaded rifle.* 彼女はひどくおびえていたので装填したライフルで身を固めていた. **3** V-T 他動詞 If you **arm** someone **with** something that will be useful in a particular situation, you provide them with it. 供給する ❑ *She thought that if she armed herself with all the knowledge she could gather she could handle anything.* 彼女は手に入れられる知識をすべて身につければ，どんなことにも対応できると思った. **4** → see also **armed 5** PHRASE 句 A person's right to **bear arms** is their right to own and use guns, as a means of defense. 武器を所有する ❑ *…a country where the right to bear arms is enshrined in the constitution.* 武器を所有する権利が憲法で認められている国 **6** PHRASE 句 If one group or country **takes up arms against** another, they prepare to attack and fight them. 戦端を開く ❑ *They threatened to take up arms against the government if their demands were not met.* 彼らは要求が入れられなければ政府に対して武器を取って戦うと脅かした. **7** PHRASE 句 If people are **up in arms**

about something, they are very angry about it and are protesting strongly against it. 憤慨して □ *Patient advocates are up in arms over the possible closure of the psychiatric hospital.* 患者の代弁者たちはその精神病院の閉鎖の可能性に憤慨している.

ar|ma|ments /ɑrməmənts/ N-PLURAL 複数名詞 **Armaments** are weapons and military equipment belonging to an army or country. 軍備 □ *...global efforts to reduce nuclear and other armaments.* 核兵器やその他の軍備を縮小する世界的努力

arm|chair /ɑrmtʃɛər/ (**armchairs**) **1** N-COUNT 可算名詞 An **armchair** is a big comfortable chair that has a support on each side for your arms. 肘掛け椅子 □ *She was sitting in an armchair with blankets wrapped around her.* 彼女は毛布で身をくるん, 肘掛け椅子に座っていた. **2** ADJ 形容詞 An **armchair** critic, fan, or traveler knows about a particular subject from reading or hearing about it rather than from practical experience. 実践の伴わない [ADJ n] □ *This great book is ideal for both the traveling supporter and the armchair fan.* この立派な本は追っかけサポーターとテレビ観戦するファンの両方に向いている.

armed /ɑrmd/ **1** ADJ 形容詞 Someone who is **armed** is carrying a weapon, usually a gun. 武装した □ *City police said the man was armed with a revolver.* 市の警察はその男が拳銃で武装していると述べた. □ *...a barbed-wire fence patrolled by armed guards.* 武器を持った警備員がパトロールする有刺鉄線を張った柵 **2** ADJ 形容詞 An **armed** attack or conflict involves people fighting with guns or carrying weapons. 武器を使った [ADJ n] □ *They had been found guilty of armed robbery.* 彼らは武器強盗で有罪の判決を受けていた. **3** → see also **arm**

armed forces N-PLURAL 複数名詞 The **armed forces** or the **armed services** of a country are its military forces, usually the army, navy, marines, and air force. 軍隊 □ *Every member of the armed forces is a hero.* その軍隊は全員が勇士だ.

ar|mor /ɑrmər/ **1** N-UNCOUNT 不可算名詞 In former times, **armor** was special metal clothing that soldiers wore for protection in battle. よろいかぶと □ *...knights in armor.* 甲冑 (かっちゅう) 姿の騎士 **2** N-UNCOUNT 不可算名詞 **Armor** consists of tanks and other military vehicles used in battle. 機甲部隊 [MILITARY 軍事的] □ *U.S. Army troops and armor blocked access to the main palace grounds.* 米国陸軍部隊と機甲部隊が本宮殿敷地への通路をふさいだ. **3** N-UNCOUNT 不可算名詞 **Armor** is a hard, usually metal, covering that protects a vehicle against attack. 装甲 □ *...a formidable warhead that can penetrate the armor of most tanks.* たいていの戦車の装甲を貫通できる恐るべき弾頭 **4** **knight in shining armor** → see **knight**
→ see **army**

ar|mored /ɑrmərd/ **1** ADJ 形容詞 **Armored** vehicles are equipped with a hard metal covering in order to protect them from gunfire and other missiles. 装甲した □ *More than forty armored vehicles carrying troops have been sent into the area.* 部隊を輸送している装甲車が40台以上その地域に派遣された. **2** ADJ 形容詞 **Armored** troops are troops in armored vehicles. 装甲した □ *These front-line defenses are backed up by armored units in reserve.* こうした前線の防衛力は予備の機甲部隊の後援を受けている.

ar|mory /ɑrməri/ (**armories**) **1** N-COUNT 可算名詞 A country's **armory** is all the weapons and military equipment that it has. 兵器類 □ *Nuclear weapons will play a less prominent part in NATO's armory in the future.* 核兵器は将来NATO北大西洋条約機構の兵器類の中で今ほど重要な役割を持たなくなるであろう. **2** N-COUNT 可算名詞 An **armory** is a place where weapons, bombs, and other military equipment are stored. 兵器庫 □ *...a failed attempt to steal weapons from an armory.* 兵器庫から兵器を盗もうとして失敗した企て **3** N-COUNT 可算名詞 In the United States, an **armory** is a building used by the National Guard or Army Reserve for meetings and training. 州軍・予備軍施設 □ *The National Guard says an armory in Fairmont has opened to shelter stranded motorists.* 州軍によると, フェアモントの州軍施設が立ち往生したドライバーの避難所に開放されている.

arm|pit /ɑrmpɪt/ (**armpits**) N-COUNT 可算名詞 Your **armpits** are the areas of your body under your arms where your arms join your shoulders. わきの下 □ *I shave my armpits every couple of days.* 私は1日おきにわきの下をそる.

army /ɑrmi/ (**armies**) **1** N-COUNT-COLL 集合可算名詞 An **army** is a large organized group of people who are armed and trained to fight on land in a war. Most armies are organized and controlled by governments. 陸軍 □ *Perkins joined the Army in 1990.* パーキンスは1990年に陸軍に入隊した. **2** N-COUNT-COLL 集合可算名詞 An **army of** people, animals, or things is a large number of them, especially when they are regarded as a force of some kind. 大勢 □ *...data collected by an army of volunteers.* 大勢のボランティアによって収集されたデータ
→ see Word Web: **army**

aro|ma /əroʊmə/ (**aromas**) N-COUNT 可算名詞 An **aroma** is a strong, pleasant smell. 香り □ *...the wonderful aroma of freshly baked bread.* 焼きたてのパンの素晴らしい香り

aroma|thera|py /əroʊməθɛrəpi/ N-UNCOUNT 不可算名詞 **Aromatherapy** is a type of treatment which involves massaging the body with special fragrant oils. 芳香療法

aro|mat|ic /ærəmætɪk/ ADJ 形容詞 An **aromatic** plant or food has a strong, pleasant smell of herbs or spices. 芳香の □ *...an evergreen shrub with deep green, aromatic leaves.* 深緑で芳香を放つ葉をつけた常緑低木

arose /əroʊz/ **Arose** is the past tense of **arise**. ariseの過去形

around /əraʊnd/

> **Around** is an adverb and a preposition. In British English, the word "round" is often used instead. **Around** is often used with verbs of movement, such as "walk" and "drive," and also in phrasal verbs such as "get around" and "turn around."

> **Around** は副詞と前置詞である. 英国英語では単語 **round** がしばしばその代わりに用いられる. **Around** はしばしば **walk** や **drive** のような移動の動詞と共に用いられ, また **get around** や **turn around** のような句動詞にも用いられる.

1 PREP 前置詞 To be positioned **around** a place or object means to surround it or to be on all sides of it. To move **around** a place means to go along its edge, back to your starting point. ーのまわりに □ *She looked at the papers around her.* 彼女は身のまわりにある書類を見た. □ *Today she wore her hair down around her shoulders.* 今日彼女は肩のまわりに髪を垂らしていた. ● ADV 副詞 **Around** is also an adverb. まわりに [n ADV] □ *...a village with a rocky river, a ruined castle and hills all around.* 岩石の多い川と廃城とあたり一面に丘のある村 **2** PREP 前置詞 If you move **around** a corner or obstacle, you move to the other side of it. If you look **around** a corner or obstacle, you look to see what is on the other side. ーを曲がったところに □ *The photographer stopped clicking and hurried around the corner.* 写真家はシャッターを押すのを止め, 急いで角を曲がった. **3** PREP 前置詞 If you move **around** a place, you travel through it, going to most of its parts. If you look **around** a place, you look at every part of it. ーのあちこちに □ *I've been walking around Moscow and the town is terribly quiet.* 私はモスクワを歩き回っていましたが, 町はすごく静かです. ● ADV 副詞 **Around** is also an adverb. ぐるっと [ADV after v] □ *He backed away from the edge, looking all around at the flat horizon.* 彼はへりから後退して, 平らな地平線をぐるっと見回した. **4** PREP 前置詞 If someone moves **around** a place, they move through various

---

Word Web   army

The first Roman **army** was a poorly organized **militia band**. Its members had no **weapons** such as **swords** or **spears**. After the Etruscans, an advanced society from west-central Italy, **conquered** Rome, things changed. Then the Roman army became a powerful force. They learned how to **deploy** their **troops** to **fight** more effective **battles**. By the first century BC, the Roman army realized the importance of protective equipment. They started using bronze **helmets**, chain mail **armor**, and wooden **shields**. They fought many **military campaigns** and won many **wars**.

A

parts of that place without having any particular destination. —のあちこちに ❑ *These days much of my time is spent weaving my way around cocktail parties.* 最近はカクテルパーティーであちこち人混みを縫うようにして進むのに私の時間の大半を費やしている. ● ADV 副詞 **Around** is also an adverb. 動き回って [ADV after v] ❑ *My mornings are spent rushing around after him.* 午前中はもっぱら彼の後を追って走り回っている. ⁵ PREP 前置詞 You use **around** to say that something happens in different parts of a place or area. —のあちこちで ❑ *Police in South Africa say ten people have died in scattered violence around the country.* 南アフリカの警察によると，国内のあちこちで起きた散発的な暴動で10人の死者が出ている. ❑ *Elephants were often to be found in swamps in eastern Kenya around the Tana River.* ケニア東部のターナ川沿いでは沼地に象が頻繁に見られた. ● ADV 副詞 **Around** is also an adverb. あちこちと ❑ *What the hell do you think you're doing following me around?* 君は私に付きまとって一体何をしていると思っているんだ. ⁶ PREP 前置詞 The people **around** you are the people whom you come into contact with, especially your friends and relatives, and the people you work with. —の周囲の ❑ *We change our behavior by observing the behavior of those around us.* 私たちは周囲の人々の行動を観察することによって自らの行動を変える. ⁷ PREP 前置詞 If something such as a film, a discussion, or a plan is based **around** something, that thing is its main theme. —に基づいて ❑ *The novel is a political thriller loosely based around current political issues.* その小説は現在の政治問題に大体基づいた政治的スリラーものです. ⁸ PREP 前置詞 When you are giving measurements, you can use **around** to talk about the distance along the edge of something round. —の周囲が ❑ *She was 5 foot 4 inches, 38 around the chest, 28 around the waist and 40 around the hips.* 彼女は身長5フィート4インチ，胸囲38インチ，ウエスト28インチ，ヒップ40インチだった. ⁹ ADV 副詞 If you turn **around**, you turn so that you are facing in the opposite direction. ぐるりと向きを変えて [ADV after v] ❑ *I turned around and wrote the title on the blackboard.* 私はぐるりと向きを変えて黒板に題名を書いた. ¹⁰ ADV 副詞 If you go **around** to someone's house, you visit them. 立ち寄って [ADV after v] ❑ *She helped me unpack my things and then we went around to see the other girls.* 彼女は私が荷物の中味を取り出すのを手伝ってくれて，それから私たちは他の女の子たちに会いに行った. ¹¹ ADV 副詞 You use **around** in expressions such as **sit around** and **hang around** when you are saying that someone is spending time in a place and not doing anything very important. ぶらぶらして [ADV after v] ❑ *I'm just going to be hanging around twiddling my thumbs.* 私は何もせずにぶらぶら時を過ごすつもりだ. ● PREP 前置詞 **Around** is also a preposition. —のあたりにぶらぶらして ❑ *He used to skip lessons and hang around the harbor with some other boys.* 彼は授業をサボって何人かの他の少年たちと港のあたりをぶらついていたものだった. ¹² ADV 副詞 If you move things **around**, you move them so that they are in different places. あちこちに [ADV after v] ❑ *Furniture in the classroom should not be changed around without warning the blind child.* あの目の不自由な子供に注意せずに教室の家具をあちこち動かしてはいけません. ¹³ ADV 副詞 If a wheel or object turns **around**, it turns. ぐるぐると [ADV after v] ❑ *The boat started to spin around in the water.* その船は水の中でぐるぐる回転し始めた. ¹⁴ ADV 副詞 If someone or something is **around**, they exist or are present in a place. そこらに ❑ *You haven't seen my publisher anywhere around, have you?* 私の出版業者をどこかそこらで見かけませんでしたか. ¹⁵ ADV 副詞 You use **around** in expressions such as **this time around** or **to come around** when you are describing something that has happened before or things that happen regularly. また巡ってきて ❑ *Senator Bentsen has declined to get involved this time around.* ベンツェン上院議員は今回は関与することを断った. ¹⁶ ADV 副詞 **Around** means approximately. およそ ❑ *My salary was around $45,000 plus a car and expenses.* 私の給料は約4万5千ドルで，車と諸経費も払っている. ● PREP 前置詞 **Around** is also a preposition. あたり ❑ *He expects the elections to be held around November.* 彼は選挙が11月あたりに実施されると見ている.

When you are talking about movement in no particular direction, you can use **around** or **about**. **Around** is more common in American English. ❑ *It's so romantic up here, flying around in a small plane… Police officers walk about with guns on their hips.* When you are talking about something being generally present or available, you can use **around** or **about**: again, **around** is more common in American English. ❑ *There is a lot of talent around at the moment… There are not that many jobs about.*

¹⁷ PHRASE 句 **Around about** means approximately. およそ [SPOKEN 口語] ❑ *There is an outright separatist party but it only scored around about 10 percent in the vote.* 徹底的な分離主義の政党が1つあるが，投票ではおよそ10%しか獲得しなかった. **the other way around** → see **way**

arous|al /ərˈaʊzᵊl/ ¹ N-UNCOUNT 不可算名詞 **Arousal** is the state of being sexually excited. (性的な) 興奮 ❑ *…sexual arousal.* 性的興奮 ² N-UNCOUNT 不可算名詞 **Arousal** is a state in which you feel excited or very alert, for example, as a result of fear, stress, or anger. 刺激されること ❑ *Thinking angry thoughts can provoke strong*

physiological arousal. 腹立たしいことを考えると強力な生理的刺激を受けることがある.

arouse /ərˈaʊz/ (**arouses, arousing, aroused**) ¹ V-T 他動詞 If something **arouses** a particular reaction or attitude in people, it causes them to have that reaction or attitude. 引き起こす ❑ *His revolutionary work in linguistics has aroused intense scholarly interest.* 言語学に関する彼の革命的な著作は強い学問的関心を喚起した. ² V-T 他動詞 If something **arouses** a particular feeling or instinct that exists in someone, it causes them to experience that feeling or instinct strongly. 刺激する ❑ *The smell of frying bacon aroused his hunger.* ベーコンを焼く匂いは彼の空腹感を刺激した. ³ V-T 他動詞 If you **are aroused** by something, it makes you feel sexually excited. 性的に刺激する [usu passive] ❑ *Some men are aroused when their partner says erotic words to them.* 相手の女がエロチックな言葉を口にすると性的に興奮する男もいる.

ar|range /ərˈeɪndʒ/ (**arranges, arranging, arranged**) ¹ V-T 動詞 If you **arrange** an event or meeting, you make plans for it to happen. 手配する ❑ *She arranged an appointment for Friday afternoon at four-fifteen.* 彼女は金曜日の午後4時15分の約束をまとめた. ² V-T/V-I 他動詞/自動詞 If you **arrange** with someone **to** do something, you make plans with them to do it. 手はずを整える ❑ *I've arranged to see him on Friday morning.* 私は金曜の朝に彼と会うことにした. ❑ *It was arranged that the party would gather for lunch in Grant Park.* 一行は昼食のためにグラント公園に集合する手はずになっていた. ³ V-T/V-I 他動詞/自動詞 If you **arrange** something **for** someone, you make it possible for them to have it or to do it. 手配する ❑ *I will arrange for someone to take you around.* 私はだれかがあなたを案内してまわるように手配をします. ❑ *The hotel manager will arrange for a babysitter.* ホテルの支配人がベビーシッターを手配します. ❑ *Mr. Dambar had arranged a dinner for the three of them.* ダンバー氏は彼ら3人のためにディナーを手配していた. ⁴ V-T 他動詞 If you **arrange** things somewhere, you place them in a particular position, usually in order to make them look attractive or neat. 配置する ❑ *When she has a little spare time she enjoys arranging dried flowers.* 彼女は少し暇な時にはドライフラワーをいけるのを楽しんでいます. ⁵ V-T 他動詞 If a piece of music **is arranged by** someone, it is changed or adapted so that it is suitable for particular instruments or voices, or for a particular performance. 編曲する [usu passive] ❑ *The songs were arranged by another well-known bass player, Ron Carter.* それらの歌は別の有名なバス演奏家のロン・カーターにより編曲された.

ar|range|ment /ərˈeɪndʒmənt/ (**arrangements**) ¹ N-COUNT 可算名詞 **Arrangements** are plans and preparations that you make so that something will happen or be possible. 準備，手配 ❑ *The staff is working frantically on final arrangements for the summit.* 職員は首脳会談のための最後の準備に必死に働いている. ❑ *She telephoned Ellen, but made no arrangements to see her.* 彼女はエレンに電話したが，彼女に会う手はずは整えなかった. ² N-COUNT 可算名詞 An **arrangement** is an agreement that you make with someone to do something. 取り決め [also 'by' N] ❑ *The caves can be visited only by prior arrangement.* 洞窟 (どうくつ) は予約でしか見物できません. ³ N-COUNT 可算名詞 An **arrangement** of things, for example, flowers or furniture, is a group of them displayed in a particular way. 配列 ❑ *The house was always decorated with imaginative flower arrangements.* その家はいつも想像性に富んだ生け花で飾られていた. ⁴ N-COUNT 可算名詞 If someone makes an **arrangement** of a piece of music, they change it so that it is suitable for particular voices or instruments, or for a particular performance. 編曲 ❑ *…an arrangement of a well-known piece by Mozart.* モーツアルトの有名な曲の編曲

Word Partnership	*arrangement* は次の語句と使われる:
ADJ.	**informal/formal**, **special** arrangement, **temporary/ permanent** arrangement ¹ ‑ ³
N.	**flower** arrangement, **seating** arrangement ³

ar|ray /ərˈeɪ/ (**arrays**) ¹ N-COUNT-COLL 集合可算名詞 An **array** of different things or people is a large number or wide range of them. 様々なもの ❑ *As the deadline approached she experienced a bewildering array of emotions.* 締め切りが近づくにつれ，彼女はまごつくほどの様々な種類の感情を体験した. ² N-COUNT 可算名詞 An **array of** objects is a collection of them that is displayed or arranged in a particular way. ずらりと並んだもの ❑ *We visited the local markets and saw wonderful arrays of fruit and vegetables.* 私たちは地元の市場を訪れ，すばらしくずらりと並んだ果物や野菜を見た.

Word Partnership	*array* は次の語句と使われる:
ADJ.	**broad/vast/wide** array, **impressive/dizzying** array ¹ ²
PREP.	array **of** *something* ¹ ²

ar|rears /ərˈɪərz/ ¹ N-PLURAL 複数名詞 **Arrears** are amounts of money that you owe, especially regular payments that you should have made earlier. 滞納金 ❑ *They have promised to pay the*

arrears over the next five years. 彼らは今後5年間にわたって滞納金を支払うと約束しました. **2** PHRASE 句 If someone is **in arrears** with their payments, or falls **into arrears**, they have not paid the regular amounts of money that they should have paid. 滞納して ❑ …the 300,000 households who are more than six months in arrears with their mortgages. ローンの支払いが6か月を超えて滞納している30万の世帯 **3** PHRASE 句 If sums of money such as wages or taxes are paid **in arrears**, they are paid at the end of the period of time to which they relate, for example, after a job has been done and the wages have been earned. 後払いで ❑ Interest is paid in arrears after you use the money. 利子はお金を使ってからの後払いになっています.

ar|rest /ərɛst/ (arrests, arresting, arrested) **1** V-T 他動詞 If the police **arrest** you, they take charge of you and take you to a police station, because they believe you may have committed a crime. 逮捕する ❑ Police arrested five young men in connection with one of the attacks. 警察はその襲撃の1つに関連して5人の若者を逮捕した. ●N-VAR 可変性名詞 **Arrest** is also a noun. 逮捕 ❑ …a substantial reward for information leading to the arrest of the bombers. 爆破犯人たちの逮捕につながる情報に対する多額の賞金. ❑ Police chased the fleeing terrorists and later made two arrests. 警察は逃げるテロリストの後を追いかけ, 後で2名を逮捕した. **2** V-T 他動詞 If something or someone **arrests** a process, they stop it from continuing. 食い止める [FORMAL 形式ばった] ❑ The sufferer may have to make major changes in his or her life to arrest the disease. 患者は病気の進行を食い止めるために生活上の大きな変化を強いられるかもしれない. **3** → see also **house arrest**

ar|ri|val /əraɪvᵊl/ (arrivals) **1** N-VAR 可変性名詞 When a person or vehicle arrives at a place, you can refer to their **arrival**. 到着 ❑ …the day after his arrival in Wichita. ウィチタに彼が到着した翌日 ❑ He was dead on arrival at the nearby hospital. 彼は近くの病院に到着した時には死んでいた. **2** N-VAR 可変性名詞 When someone starts a new job, you can refer to their **arrival** in that job. 着任 ❑ …the power vacuum created by the arrival of a new president. 新大統領の就任で生まれた権力の空白 **3** N-SING 単数名詞 When something is brought to you or becomes available, you can refer to its **arrival**. 出現 ❑ I was flicking idly through a newspaper while awaiting the arrival of orange juice and coffee. 私はオレンジジュースとコーヒーが出てくるのを待っている間, 新聞を漫然とめくって読んでいました. **4** N-SING 単数名詞 When a particular time comes or a particular event happens, you can refer to its **arrival**. 到来 ❑ He celebrated the arrival of the New Year with a bout of drinking that nearly killed him. 彼は新年の到来を祝って死にそうになるほど酒盛りをした. **5** N-COUNT 可算名詞 You can refer to someone who has just arrived at a place as a new **arrival**. 到着した人 ❑ A high proportion of the new arrivals are skilled professionals. 新来者の多くは熟練した専門家です.

Word Partnership	*arrival* は次の語句と使われる:
N.	**time** of arrival **1**
PREP.	arrival **at** *someplace*, **on** arrival **1** arrival **of** *something* **1 3 4**
ADJ.	**early/late** arrival **1** **new** arrival, **recent** arrival **5**
V.	**awaiting** the arrival **1 3 4**

ar|rive /əraɪv/ (arrives, arriving, arrived) **1** V-I 自動詞 When a person or vehicle **arrives** at a place, they come to it from somewhere else. 到着する ❑ Fresh groups of guests arrived. 新しい客がいく組も到着した. ❑ …a small group of commuters waiting for their train, which arrived on time. 時間通りに到着した電車を待っていた少人数の通勤客 **2** V-I 自動詞 When you **arrive** at a place, you come to it for the first time in order to stay, live, or work there. 渡来する, 来る ❑ …in the old days before the European settlers arrived in the country. ヨーロッパの移民がその国に渡来する前の古い時代に **3** V-I 自動詞 When something such as a letter or meal **arrives**, it is brought or delivered to you. 届く ❑ Breakfast arrived while he was in the bathroom. 彼がバスルームを使っている間に朝食が届いた. **4** V-I 自動詞 When something such as a new product or invention **arrives**, it becomes available. 出てくる ❑ Several long-awaited movies will finally arrive in the stores this month. 長い間待たされたいくつかの映画が今月やっと店頭に出る予定だ. **5** V-I 自動詞 When a particular moment or event **arrives**, it happens, especially after you have been waiting for it or expecting it. 到来する ❑ The time has arrived when I need to give up smoking. 私が禁煙しなければならない時がやって来た. **6** V-I 自動詞 When you **arrive at** something such as a decision, you decide something after thinking about it or discussing it. 達する ❑ …if the jury cannot arrive at a unanimous decision. 陪審員が全員一致の決定に達することができない場合には

You use both **arrive** and **reach** to talk about coming to a particular place. You can use **arrive** to emphasize being in a place rather than traveling to it. ❑ When I arrived in England I was exhausted. **Reach** is always followed by a noun or pronoun referring to a place and you can use it to emphasize the effort required to get there. ❑ To reach the capital might not be easy. **Arrive at** and **reach** can also be used to say that someone eventually makes a decision or finds the answer to something. ❑ It took hours to arrive at a decision…They were unable to reach a decision.

Thesaurus	*arrive* また次を参照:
v.	enter, land, pull in, reach; (ant.) depart **1**

ar|ro|gant /ærəgənt/ ADJ 形容詞 Someone who is **arrogant** behaves in a proud, unpleasant way toward other people because they believe that they are more important than others. 横柄な [DISAPPROVAL 不賛成] ❑ He was so arrogant. 彼はとても横柄だった. ❑ That sounds arrogant, doesn't it? それは人に聞えますね. ●**ar|ro|gance** N-UNCOUNT 不可算名詞 横柄さ ❑ At times the arrogance of those in power is quite blatant. 時として権力者の横柄さは全く露骨である.

ar|row /ærou/ (arrows) **1** N-COUNT 可算名詞 An **arrow** is a long thin weapon that is sharp and pointed at one end and that often has feathers at the other end. An arrow is shot from a bow. 矢 ❑ Warriors armed with bows and arrows and spears have invaded their villages. 弓と矢と槍で武装した戦士が彼らの村を襲って来た. **2** N-COUNT 可算名詞 An **arrow** is a written or printed sign that consists of a straight line with another line bent at a sharp angle at one end. This is a printed arrow: ➔ 矢印 ❑ A series of arrows points the way to the modest grave of Andrei Sakharov. 一連の矢印がアンドレー・サハロフの質素な墓への道を指している.

arse /ɑrs/ (arses) N-COUNT 可算名詞 Your **arse** is your buttocks. 尻 [BRIT 英国英語, INFORMAL, VULGAR くだけた, 下品な]

ar|se|nal /ɑrsənᵊl/ (arsenals) **1** N-COUNT 可算名詞 An **arsenal** is a large collection of weapons and military equipment held by a country, group, or person. 兵器 ❑ Russia is committed to destroying most of its nuclear arsenals. ロシアはその核兵器の大半を破棄することを約束している. **2** N-COUNT 可算名詞 An **arsenal** is a building where weapons and military equipment are stored. 兵器庫

ar|son /ɑrsᵊn/ N-UNCOUNT 不可算名詞 **Arson** is the crime of deliberately setting fire to a building or vehicle. 放火 ❑ …a terrible wave of rioting, theft and arson. 暴動, 窃盗, 放火のひどい急増

art /ɑrt/ (arts) **1** N-UNCOUNT 不可算名詞 **Art** consists of paintings, sculpture, and other pictures or objects that are created for people to look at and admire or think deeply about. 芸術作品, 美術品 ❑ …the first exhibition of such art in the West. このような芸術作品の西欧諸国での最初の展覧会 ❑ …contemporary and modern American art. アメリカの現代美術品 **2** N-UNCOUNT 不可算名詞 **Art** is the activity or educational subject that consists of creating paintings, sculptures, and other pictures or objects for people to look at and admire or think deeply about. 美術 ❑ …a painter, content to be left alone with her all-absorbing art. 美術に没頭する存分没頭する画家 ❑ …Savannah College of Art and Design. サバンナ美術デザイン大学 **3** N-VAR 可変性名詞 **The arts** are activities such as music, painting, literature, film, and dance, which people can take part in for enjoyment, or to create works that express certain meanings or ideas of beauty. 芸術, 芸術全般 ❑ Catherine the Great was a patron of the arts and sciences. エカテリーナ大帝は芸術と科学の後援者であった. **4** N-PLURAL 複数名詞 At a university or college, **arts** are subjects such as history, literature, or languages in contrast to scientific subjects. 人文科学 ❑ …arts and social science graduates. 人文科学と社会科学の卒業生 **5** ADJ 形容詞 **Arts** or **art** is used to describe theaters that show plays or films that are intended to make the audience think deeply about the content, and not simply to entertain them. 芸術の [ADJ n] ❑ …a lower Manhattan art theater. マンハッタン南部の芸術劇場 **6** N-COUNT 可算名詞 If you describe an activity as an **art**, you mean that it requires skill and that people learn to do it by instinct or experience, rather than by learning facts or rules. 技術 ❑ …pioneers who transformed clinical medicine from an art to a science. 臨床医学を技術から科学に変えた先駆者たち **7** → see also **fine art, martial art, state-of-the-art, work of art**
→ see Word Web: **art**
→ see culture, drawing, gallery

ar|te|fact /ɑrtɪfækt/ → see **artifact**

ar|tery /ɑrtəri/ (arteries) **1** N-COUNT 可算名詞 **Arteries** are the tubes in your body that carry blood from your heart to the rest of your body. Compare **vein**. 動脈 ❑ …patients suffering from blocked arteries. 動脈閉塞(へいそく)の患者 **2** N-COUNT 可算名詞 You can refer to an important main route within a complex road, railroad, or river system as an **artery**. 幹線道路 ❑ …Connecticut

Word Web art

The **Impressionist** movement in **painting** began in Europe during the second half of the 19th century. The Impressionists abandoned traditional **realistic** depictions of people and objects painted in **studios**. They often painted **landscapes**,

emphasizing light and color in their **interpretations** of everyday life. Among these painters were French artists Paul Cézanne, Pierre Renoir, and Claude Monet. The word "Impressionist" has its origin in the name of a Monet painting, "Impression, Sunrise." Japanese prints had an effect on the Impressionist movement. The Impressionists appreciated the use of contrasting dark and bright colors found in these prints.

Ave., one of the main arteries of Washington. ワシントンの主要幹線の1つであるコネチカット通り

ar|thrit|ic /ɑrθrɪtɪk/ **1** ADJ 形容詞 **Arthritic** is used to describe the condition, the pain, or the symptoms of arthritis. 関節炎の [ADJ n] ❑ *I developed serious arthritic symptoms and chronic sinusitis.* 私は重い関節炎の症状と慢性副鼻腔炎になった **2** ADJ 形容詞 An **arthritic** person is suffering from arthritis, and cannot move very easily. **Arthritic** joints or hands are affected by arthritis. 関節炎の者 ❑ *...an elderly lady who suffered with arthritic hands.* 手が関節炎で苦しんでいた年配の女性

Word Link itis ≈ inflammation : arthritis, hepatitis, meningitis

ar|thri|tis /ɑrθraɪtɪs/ N-UNCOUNT 不可算名詞 **Arthritis** is a medical condition in which the joints in someone's body are swollen and painful. 関節炎 ❑ *I have a touch of arthritis in the wrist.* 私は手首に軽い関節炎がある.

ar|ti|choke /ɑrtɪtʃoʊk/ (artichokes) N-VAR 可変性名詞 **Artichokes** or **globe artichokes** are round green vegetables that have fleshy leaves arranged like the petals of a flower. アーティチョーク

Word Link cle ≈ small : article, cubicle, particle

ar|ti|cle /ɑrtɪkᵊl/ (articles) **1** N-COUNT 可算名詞 An **article** is a piece of writing that is published in a newspaper or magazine. 記事 ❑ *...a newspaper article.* 新聞記事 ❑ *According to an article in Newsweek the drug could have side effects.* ニューズウィークの記事によれば, その薬には副作用がありえるだろう. **2** N-COUNT 可算名詞 You can refer to objects as **articles** of some kind. 物品 ❑ *...articles of clothing.* 衣料品 ❑ *He had stripped the house of all articles of value.* 彼は価値のある物を全て家から持ち出していた. **3** N-COUNT 可算名詞 An **article of** a formal agreement or document is a section of it that deals with a particular point. 条項 ❑ *The country appears to be violating several articles of the convention.* その国は協定のいくつかの条項に違反していると思われる. **4** N-COUNT 可算名詞 In grammar, an **article** is a kind of determiner. In English, "a" and "an" are called the **indefinite article**, and "the" is called **the definite article**. 冠詞 **5** PHRASE 句 If you describe something as **the genuine article**, you are emphasizing that it is genuine, and often that it is very good. 本物 [EMPHASIS 強調] ❑ *The vodka was the genuine article.* ウォッカは本物だった.
→ see **newspaper**

ar|ticu|late (articulates, articulating, articulated)

The adjective is pronounced /ɑrtɪkyəlɪt/. The verb is pronounced /ɑrtɪkyəleɪt/.

形容詞は /ɑrtɪkyəlɪt/ と発音される. 動詞は /ɑrtɪkyəleɪt/ と発音される.

1 ADJ 形容詞 If you describe someone as **articulate**, you mean that they are able to express their thoughts and ideas easily and well. はっきり表現できる [APPROVAL 賛成] ❑ *She is an articulate young woman.* 彼女は自分の考えをはっきり言える若い女性だ. **2** V-T 他動詞 When you **articulate** your ideas or feelings, you express them clearly in words. はっきり表現する [FORMAL 形式ばった] ❑ *The president has been accused of failing to articulate an overall vision in foreign affairs.* 大統領は外交問題に関する全般的な展望をはっきり示さなかったことを非難されている. **3** V-T 他動詞 If you **articulate** something, you say it very clearly, so that each word or syllable can be heard. はっきり発音する ❑ *He articulated each syllable.* 彼は各音節をはっきり発音した.

ar|ticu|lat|ed /ɑrtɪkyəleɪtɪd/ ADJ 形容詞 An **articulated** vehicle, especially a bus, is made in two or more sections that are joined together by metal bars, so that the vehicle can turn more easily. 連結式の

Word Link fact, fic ≈ making : artifact, artificial, factor

ar|ti|fact /ɑrtɪfækt/ (artifacts) N-COUNT 可算名詞 An **artifact** is an ornament, tool, or other object that is made by a human being, especially one that is historically or culturally interesting. 工芸品 ❑ *They also repair broken religious artifacts.* 彼らは壊れた宗教用工芸品も修理する.
→ see **history**

ar|ti|fi|cial /ɑrtɪfɪʃᵊl/ **1** ADJ 形容詞 **Artificial** objects, materials, or processes do not occur naturally and are created by human beings, often using science or technology. 人工の ❑ *The city is dotted with small lakes, natural and artificial.* その都市には小さな天然湖や人造湖が点在する. ❑ *...a wholefood diet free from artificial additives, colors and flavors.* 人工添加物, 着色料, 調味料の入っていない自然食品 ● **ar|ti|fi|cial|ly** ADV 副詞 人工的に ❑ *...artificially sweetened lemonade.* 人工甘味料入りレモネード **2** ADJ 形容詞 An **artificial** state or situation exists only because someone has created it, and therefore often seems unnatural or unnecessary. 不自然な, 人為的な ❑ *Even in the artificial environment of an office, our body rhythms continue to affect us.* 事務所という人為的な環境の中でさえ, 私たちは人体のリズムの影響を常に受けている. ● **ar|ti|fi|cial|ly** ADV 副詞 人為的に ❑ *...state subsidies that have kept retail prices artificially low.* 小売価格を人為的に低く保ってきている国庫補助金

Thesaurus artificial また次を参照:

ADJ. manmade, manufactured, synthetic, unnatural; (ant.) natural **1 2**

ar|ti|fi|cial in|tel|li|gence N-UNCOUNT 不可算名詞 **Artificial intelligence** is a type of computer technology concerned with making machines work in an intelligent way, similar to the way that the human mind works. 人工知能

ar|til|lery /ɑrtɪləri/ **1** N-UNCOUNT 不可算名詞 **Artillery** consists of large, powerful guns that are transported on wheels and used by an army. 砲, 大砲 ❑ *Using tanks and heavy artillery, they seized the town.* 戦車や重砲を用いて彼らは町を占拠した. **2** N-SING-COLL 集合的単数名詞 **The artillery** is the section of an army that is trained to use large, powerful guns. 砲兵隊 ❑ *From 1935 to 1937 he was in the artillery.* 1935年から1937年まで彼は砲兵隊に所属していた.

Word Link ist ≈ one who practices : artist, chemist, pharmacist

art|ist /ɑrtɪst/ (artists) **1** N-COUNT 可算名詞 An **artist** is someone who draws or paints pictures or creates sculptures as a job or a hobby. 芸術家 ❑ *...the studio of a great artist.* 偉大な芸術家の仕事場 ❑ *Each poster is signed by the artist.* ポスターには1枚1枚にそのアーティストのサインがある. **2** N-COUNT 可算名詞 An **artist** is a person who creates novels, poems, films, or other things which can be considered as works of art. 作家 ❑ *His books are enormously easy to read, yet he is a serious artist.* 彼の本はずば抜けて読みやすいが, それにもかかわらず本格的な作家である. **3** N-COUNT 可算名詞 An **artist** is a performer such as a musician, actor, or dancer. 芸能人 ❑ *...a popular artist who has sold millions of records.* 何百万枚ものレコードを売り上げている人気アーティスト
→ see **animation**

ar|tis|tic /ɑrtɪstɪk/ **1** ADJ 形容詞 Someone who is **artistic** is good at drawing or painting, or arranging things in a beautiful way. 芸術の ❑ *They encourage boys to be sensitive and artistic.* 彼らは少年たちを励まして感受性と芸術性を伸ばす. **2** ADJ 形容詞 **Artistic** means relating to art or artists. 芸術の ❑ *...the campaign for artistic freedom.* 芸術の自由を求める運動 ● **ar|tis|ti|cal|ly** /ɑrtɪstɪkli/ ADV 副詞 芸術的に ❑ *...artistically gifted children.* 芸術的才能のある子供たち **3** ADJ 形容詞 An **artistic** design or arrangement is beautiful. 美しい, 趣のある ❑ *...an artistic arrangement of stone paving.* 石畳の趣のある敷き方 ● **ar|tis|ti|cal|ly** ADV 副詞 美しく ❑ *...artistically carved*

vessels. 美しく彫られた器

art|is|try /ˈɑrtɪstri/ N-UNCOUNT 不可算名詞 **Artistry** is the creative skill of an artist, writer, actor, or musician. 芸術的技量, 芸術性 ❑ ...his artistry as a cellist. 彼のチェロ奏者としての芸術的技量

---

as

❶ CONJUNCTION AND PREPOSITION USES

❷ USED WITH OTHER PREPOSITIONS AND CONJUNCTIONS

---

❶ as /əz, STRONG æz/

⟳ Please look at category ⓬ to see if the expression you are looking for is shown under another headword. **❶** CONJ 接続詞 If something happens **as** something else happens, it happens at the same time. ～している時に ❑ Another policeman has been injured as fighting continued this morning. 今朝も闘争が続く中、警官がもう 1名負傷した。❑ All the jury's eyes were on him as he continued. 彼が続けると陪審員全員が彼に注目した。**❷** CONJ 接続詞 You use **as** to say how something happens or is done, or to indicate that something happens or is done in the same way as something else. ～と同様に、～のように ❑ I'll behave toward them as I would like to be treated. 私が受けたいと思うような取り扱い方で彼らに対するつもりだ。❑ Today, as usual, he was wearing a three-piece suit. 今日もいつものように彼は3つぞろいの背広を着ていた。**❸** CONJ 接続詞 You use **as** to introduce short clauses that comment on the truth of what you are saying. ～のとおり ❑ As you can see, we're still working. ご覧のとおり、私たちはまだ働いています。**❹** CONJ 接続詞 You can use **as** to mean "because" when you are explaining the reason for something. ～だから、～なので ❑ Enjoy the first hour of the day. This is important as it sets the mood for the rest of the day. その日の最初の1時間を楽しむこと。これでその日の気分が決まるので、重要です。**❺** PHRASE 句 You use the structure **as...as** when you are comparing things. 同じぐらい ❑ I never went through a final exam that was as difficult as that one. 私はあれほどに難しい学年末試験を受けたことは全くなかった。• PHRASE 句 **As** is also a conjunction. ～ほど ❑ Being a mother isn't as bad as I thought at first! 母親になることは最初に思ったほど悪くないわ。**❻** PHRASE 句 You use **as...as** to emphasize amounts of something. (量の多寡を強調して) ～もの、～しか [EMPHASIS 強調] ❑ She gets as many as eight thousand letters a month. 彼女のところに は、月に8千通ものたくさんの手紙が届く。

You can use **as**, **because**, **since**, or **for** to give an explanation for something. **Because** is the most common of these, and is used when answering a question beginning with 'why'. You can use **as** or **since** instead of **because** to introduce a clause containing a reason for something, especially in writing. ❑ The size of the room is important as it will dictate the type of desk you choose... Since the juice is quite strong, you should always dilute it. In stories, **for** is sometimes used to explain or justify something. ❑ He seemed to be in need of company, for he suddenly went back into the house. Note that **because** is a conjunction, and is used to link two ideas within one sentence. ❑ I just forgot because I was nervous.

---

❼ PHRASE 句 You say **as it were** in order to make what you are saying sound less definite. いわば [VAGUENESS あいまいさ] ❑ I'd understood the words, but I didn't, as it were, understand the question. 単語は理解できたけど、まあいわば質問の意味が分からなかったんだ。**❽** PHRASE 句 You use expressions such as **as it is, as it turns out**, and **as things stand** when you are making a contrast between a possible situation and what actually happened or is the case. 実際は ❑ I want to work at home on a Tuesday but as it turns out sometimes it's a Wednesday or a Thursday. 火曜日には家で仕事をしたいと思っているのだが、実際には水曜日か木曜日になってしまうことも時々ある。**❾** PREP 前置詞 You use **as** when you are indicating what someone or something is or is thought to be, or what function they have. ～として ❑ He has worked as a diplomat in the U.S., Sudan and Saudi Arabia. 彼は米国とスーダンとサウジアラビアで外交官として働いてきた。❑ The news apparently came as a complete surprise. そのニュースはまったくの不意打ちだったようだ。**❿** PREP 前置詞 If you do something **as** a child or **as** a teenager, for example, you do it when you are a child or a teenager. ～のころ ❑ She loved singing as a child and started vocal training at 12. 子供のころ彼女は歌うことが好きで12歳で声楽の訓練を始めた。**⓫** PREP 前置詞 You use **as** in expressions like **as a result** and **as a consequence** to indicate how two situations or events are related to each other. ～だから、～ので ❑ As a result of the growing fears about home security, more people are arranging for someone to stay in their home when they're away. 家の防犯に関する不安が増大している結果として、留守をするときは留守番を頼む人が増えている。**⓬** as ever → see ever **⓭** as a matter of fact → see fact **⓮** as follows → see follow **⓯** as long as → see long **⓰** as opposed to → see opposed **⓱** as regards → see regard **⓲** as soon as → see soon **⓳** as such → see such **⓴** as well → see well **㉑** as well as → see well **㉒** as yet → see yet

---

Word Partnership *as* は次の語句と使われる:

V.	**act** as, (also) **known** as, **describe** as, **perceived/seen** as, **serve/use** as, **treat** as ❶ ❷
ADJ.	as **good** ❶ ❷
N.	**reputation** as ❶ ❾
	as **a result** ⓫
PREP.	as **for/to something** ❷ ❶ ❷
	as **of** ❷ ❸
CONJ.	as **if/though** ❷ ❹

❷ as /əz, STRONG æz/ **❶** PHRASE 句 You use **as for** and **as to** at the beginning of a sentence in order to introduce a slightly different subject that is still connected to the previous one. ～は どうかと言えば ❑ I don't know why the guy yelled at me. And as for going back there, certainly I would never go back, for fear of receiving further abuse. あの男がなぜ私をどなりつけたのかわからない。あそこに戻るかどうかと言えば、また悪態をつかれる恐れがあるので私は戻るつもりは全然ない。**❷** PHRASE 句 You use **as to** to indicate what something refers to. ～については ❑ They should make decisions as to whether the student needs more help. その学生にもっと支援が必要かどうかについては彼らが判断を下すべきである。**❸** PHRASE 句 If you say that something will happen **as of** a particular date or time, you mean that it will happen from that time on. ～の時点において ❑ The border, effectively closed since 1981, will be opened as of January the 1st. 1981年以来事実上閉鎖されていた国境が1月1日付で開かれるであろう。**❹** PHRASE 句 You use **as if** and **as though** when you are giving a possible explanation for something or saying that something appears to be the case when it is not. あたかも～のように ❑ Anne shrugged, as if she didn't know. アンはあたかも知らないかのように肩をすくめた。

asap /eɪ eɪ eɪ piː/ ADV 副詞 **asap** is an abbreviation for "as soon as possible." 至急に [ADV after v] ❑ The colonel ordered, "I want two good engines down here asap." 大佐は「大至急まともなエンジンを2台こちらに送ってくれ」と命じた。

as|bes|tos /æsˈbɛstəs, æz-/ N-UNCOUNT 不可算名詞 **Asbestos** is a gray material that does not burn and that was used in the past as a protection against fire or heat. Clothing and mats are sometimes made from it. 石綿、アスベスト ❑ ...asbestos gloves. 石綿手袋

Word Link *scend ≈ climbing : ascend, condescend, descend*

as|cend /əˈsɛnd/ (ascends, ascending, ascended) **❶** V-T 他動詞 [WRITTEN 書き言葉] If you **ascend** a hill or staircase, you go up it. 登る [WRITTEN 書き言葉] ❑ Mrs. Clayton had to hold Lizzie's hand as they ascended the steps. 階段を登るときクレイトン夫人はリジーの手を握らなければならなかった。**❷** V-I 自動詞 If a staircase or path **ascends**, it leads up to a higher position. 上がる [WRITTEN 書き言葉] ❑ A number of staircases ascend from the cobbled streets onto the ramparts. 丸石を敷いた街路から城壁に上がる階段がいくつかある。**❸** V-I 自動詞 If something **ascends**, it moves up, usually vertically or into the air. 上方に動く [WRITTEN 書き言葉] ❑ Keep the drill centered in the borehole while it ascends and descends. ドリルが上下する間は試錐孔(しすいこう)の中心に保つこと。**❹** → see also **ascending**

as|cend|ing /əˈsɛndɪŋ/ **❶** ADJ 形容詞 If a group of things is arranged in **ascending** order, each thing is bigger, greater, or more important than the thing before it. 上昇的な [ADJ n] ❑ Now draw or trace ten dinosaurs in ascending order of size. では恐竜の絵を10個小さいものから順に描くか写すかして下さい。**❷** → see also **ascend**

as|cent /əˈsɛnt/ (ascents) **❶** N-COUNT 可算名詞 An **ascent** is an upward journey, especially when you are walking or climbing. 登り ❑ In 1955 he led the first ascent of Kangchenjunga, the world's third highest mountain. 1955年に彼は世界第3位の高峰、カンチェンジュンガ初登頂の先頭に立った。**❷** N-COUNT 可算名詞 An **ascent** is an upward slope or path, especially when you are walking or climbing. 上り坂 ❑ It was a tough course over a gradual ascent before the big climb of Bluebell Hill. ブルーベル丘の本格的な登りの前にゆるやかな上り坂を登っていくきついコースだった。**❸** N-COUNT 可算名詞 An **ascent** is an upward, vertical movement. 上昇 ❑ Burke pushed the button and the elevator began its slow ascent. バークがボタンを押すと、エレベータはゆっくり上昇し始めた。

Word Link *cert ≈ determined, true : ascertain, certificate, certify*

as|cer|tain /æsərˈteɪn/ (ascertains, ascertaining, ascertained) V-T 他動詞 If you **ascertain** the truth about something, you find out what it is, especially by making a deliberate effort to do so. 確かめる [FORMAL 形式ばった] ❑ Through doing this, the teacher will be able to ascertain the extent to which the child understands what he is reading. こうすると、その児童が読んでいるものをどこまで理解しているかを教師が確かめることができるであろう。❑ Once they had ascertained that he was not a spy, they agreed to release him. 彼がスパイでないことを確認するとすぐに、彼らは彼を釈放することに同意した。

as|cribe /əˈskraɪb/ (ascribes, ascribing, ascribed) **❶** V-T 他動

詞 If you **ascribe** an event or condition **to** a particular cause, you say or consider that it was caused by that thing. 〜のせいと見なす [FORMAL 形式ばった] ❑ *An autopsy eventually ascribed the baby's death to sudden infant death syndrome.* 検死により幼児の死因は最終的に小児突然死症候群とされた. ❷ V-T 他動詞 If you **ascribe** a quality **to** someone, you consider that they possess it. 持っていると見なす [FORMAL 形式ばった] ❑ *We do not ascribe a superior wisdom to government or the state.* 政府または国家に優れた知恵があるとは思われない.

ash /æʃ/ (**ashes**) ❶ N-UNCOUNT 不可算名詞 **Ash** is the gray or black powdery substance that is left after something is burned. You can also refer to this substance as **ashes**. 灰 [also N in pl] ❑ *A cloud of volcanic ash is spreading across wide areas of the Philippines.* もうもうたる火山灰がフィリピンの広範な地域に広がってきている. ❑ *He brushed the cigarette ash from his sleeve.* 彼はそでからタバコの灰を払い落とした. ❷ N-PLURAL 複数名詞 A dead person's **ashes** are their remains after their body has been cremated. 遺灰 ❑ *And she asks him to go back there after her death and scatter her ashes on the lake.* しかも彼女は彼に自分の死後あそこに戻って湖に遺灰をまいてと頼むのだ. ❸ N-VAR 可変性名詞 An **ash** is a tree that has smooth gray bark and loses its leaves in winter. トネリコ ● N-UNCOUNT 不可算名詞 **Ash** is the wood from this tree. トネリコ材 ❑ *The rafters are made from ash.* そのたる木はトネリコ材でできている.
→ see **fire, glass, volcano**

ashamed /əʃeɪmd/ ❶ ADJ 形容詞 If someone is **ashamed**, they feel embarrassed or guilty because of something they do or they have done, or because of their appearance. 恥じ入って [v-link ADJ] ❑ *I felt incredibly ashamed of myself for getting so angry.* あんなに腹を立てたのを自分でもとても恥ずかしく思った. ❷ ADJ 形容詞 If you are **ashamed of** someone, you feel embarrassed to be connected with them, often because of their appearance or because you disapprove of something they have done. 恥じて [v-link ADJ 'of' n] ❑ *I've never told this to anyone, but it's true, I was terribly ashamed of my mom.* 今までだれにもこのことを話したことはないが, 実際に私はおふくろをものすごく恥じていた.

ashore /əʃɔr/ ADV 副詞 Someone or something that comes **ashore** comes from the sea onto the shore. 岸に, 浜に ❑ *Oil has come ashore on a ten-mile stretch to the east of Anchorage.* アンカレッジの東部10マイルにわたり油が海岸に漂着した.

ash|tray /æʃtreɪ/ (**ashtrays**) N-COUNT 可算名詞 An **ashtray** is a small dish in which smokers can put the ash from their cigarettes and cigars. 灰皿

Asian /eɪʒ³n/ (**Asians**) ADJ 形容詞 Someone or something that is **Asian** comes from or is associated with Asia. Americans use this term especially to refer to China, Korea, Thailand, Japan, or Vietnam. British people use this term especially to refer to India, Pakistan, and Bangladesh. アジアの ❑ *...Asian music.* アジア音楽 ● N-COUNT 可算名詞 An **Asian** is a person who comes from or is associated with a country or region in Asia. アジア人 ❑ *Many of the shops were run by Asians.* 店の多くがアジア人の経営であった.

> The word **Asian** is used to describe people from Asia, but the word **Oriental** is considered a derogatory term, and should be used only to refer to inanimate objects such as art, music, or history.

aside /əsaɪd/

> In addition to the uses shown below, **aside** is used in phrasal verbs such as "cast aside," "stand aside," and "step aside."
>
> 下記の用法に加えて, **aside** は **cast aside, stand aside, step aside** のような句動詞に使われる.

❶ ADV 副詞 If you move something **aside**, you move it to one side of you. わきに [ADV after v] ❑ *Sarah closed the book and laid it aside.* サラは本を閉じて傍らに置いた. ❷ ADV 副詞 If you take or draw someone **aside**, you take them a little way away from a group of people in order to talk to them in private. わきへ [ADV after v] ❑ *Latoya grabbed him by the elbow and took him aside.* ラトーヤは彼のひじをつかんでわきへ連れて行った. ❸ ADV 副詞 If you move **aside**, you get out of someone's way. わきに [ADV after v] ❑ *She had been standing in the doorway, but now she stepped aside to let them pass.* 彼女はそれまで戸口に立っていたが, わきに退いて彼らを通した. ❹ ADV 副詞 If you set something such as time, money, or space **aside** for a particular purpose, you save it and do not use it for anything else. 別にして, とっておいて [ADV after v] ❑ *While many parents are putting money aside for college tuition, some are taking on another big expense: buying cars for their teenagers.* 大学の授業料のために金をためている親は多いが, 10代の子供のために車を買うなどそれ以外にも多額の出費をしている親もいる. ❺ ADV 副詞 If you brush or sweep **aside** a feeling or suggestion, you reject it. 退ける [ADV after v] ❑ *Talk to a friend who will really listen and not brush aside your feelings.* ちゃんと聞いてくれて, あなたの気持ちを軽くあしらわない友だちと話しなさい. ❻ ADV 副詞 You use **aside** to indicate that you have finished talking about something, or that you are leaving it out of your

discussion, and that you are about to talk about something else. 抜きにして ❑ *Leaving aside the tiny minority who are clinically depressed, most people who have bad moods also have very good moods.* 機嫌の悪い人の大部分は機嫌にかかっているごく少数の人は別にして, 機嫌の悪い人の大部分は機嫌が大変良いこともある. ❼ PHRASE 句 You use **aside from** when you are making an exception to a general statement. 除いて ❑ *The room was empty aside from one man seated beside the fire.* 暖炉のそばに坐っている1人の男を除いて部屋は空っぽだった. ❽ PHRASE 句 You use **aside from** to indicate that you are aware of one aspect of a situation, but that you are going to focus on another aspect. 〜のほかに ❑ *Quite aside from her tiredness, Amanda seemed unnaturally abstracted.* 疲れていたのを全く別にしても, アマンダは異様にぼんやりしているようだった.

ask /ɑsk, æsk/ (**asks, asking, asked**) ❶ V-T/V-I 他動詞/自動詞 If you **ask** someone something, you say something to them in the form of a question because you want to know the answer. 尋ねる ❑ *"How is Frank?" he asked.* 「フランクはどうしている？」と彼は尋ねた. ❑ *I asked him his name.* 私は彼に名前を聞いた. ❑ *She asked me if I'd enjoyed my dinner.* 彼女は私に食事が楽しかったかどうか聞いた. ❑ *Maybe we should adopt the policy of "don't ask, don't tell."* 我々はたぶん「聞かざる・言わざる」の方策を取るべきなのかもしれない. ❷ V-T 他動詞 If you **ask** someone **to** do something, you tell them that you want them to do it. (〜するように) 頼む ❑ *We had to ask him to leave.* 私たちは彼に立ち去るよう求めなければならなかった. ❸ V-T 他動詞 If you **ask to** do something, you tell someone that you want to do it. (〜させてほしいと) 頼む ❑ *I asked to see the Director.* 私は所長に会わせてもらいたいと言った. ❹ V-I 自動詞 If you **ask for** something, you say that you would like it. 求める ❑ *I decided to go to the next house and ask for food.* 私は隣の家に行って食べ物を頼もうと決めた. ❺ V-I 自動詞 If you **ask for** someone, you say that you would like to see or speak to them. 面会を求める ❑ *There's a man at the gate asking for you.* 君に会いたい男が門のところにいるよ. ❻ V-T 他動詞 If you **ask** someone's permission, opinion, or forgiveness, you try to obtain it by making a request. 求める ❑ *Please ask permission from whoever pays the phone bill before making your call.* 電話をする前に電話代を払う人の許可を取ってください. ❼ V-T 他動詞 If you **ask** someone **to** an event or place, you invite them to go there. 招待する ❑ *Couldn't you ask Juan to the party?* ホアンをパーティーに招待していただけないでしょうか? ❽ V-T 他動詞 If someone is **asking** a particular price for something, they are selling it for that price. 請求する ❑ *Mr. Pantelaras was asking $6,000 for his collection.* パンテララス氏は自分のコレクションに対して6千ドル請求していた. ❾ CONVENTION 慣習表現 You reply "**don't ask me**" when you do not know the answer to a question, usually when you are annoyed or surprised that you have been asked. 知らないよ [FEELINGS 感情] ❑ *"She's got other things on her mind, wouldn't you think?" "Don't ask me," murmured Chris. "I've never met her."* 「彼女は何かほかのことで悩んでいるのじゃないかって思わない？」「そんなの知らないよ, 彼女に全く会ったことないのだから」とクリスはつぶやいた. ❿ PHRASE 句 You can say "**if you ask me**" to emphasize that you are stating your personal opinion. 私に言わせれば [EMPHASIS 強調] ❑ *He was nuts, if you ask me.* 私に言わせれば, 彼はばかだったんだ. ⓫ PHRASE 句 If you say that someone is **asking for trouble** or is **asking for it**, you mean that they are behaving in a way that makes it very likely that they will get into trouble. 自ら災いを招くようなことをする ❑ *To go ahead with the match after such clear advice had been asking for trouble.* そんな明確な忠告をよそに試合を進めるのは自ら災難を招くようなものだった.

Thesaurus	ask また次を参照:
v.	demand, interrogate, question, quiz; (*ant.*) answer, reply, respond ❶
	beg, plead, request; (*ant.*) command, insist ❻

Word Partnership	ask は次の語句と使われる:
ADJ.	**afraid to ask** ❶
DET.	**ask how/what/when/where/who/why** ❶
CONJ.	**ask if/whether** ❶
N.	**ask a question** ❶
	ask for help ❹
	ask forgiveness, ask *someone's* opinion, ask **permission** ❻
PREP.	**ask about** ❶
	ask for ❹ ❺
	ask to ❷ ❸ ❼
v.	**come to ask, have to ask** ❶
	don't ask me ❾

ask|ing price (**asking prices**) N-COUNT 可算名詞 The **asking price** of something is the price that the person selling it says that they want for it, although they may accept less. 言い値 ❑ *Offers 15% below the asking price are unlikely to be accepted.* 言い値より15％下回る付け値は受け入れられないだろう.

asleep /əslip/ ❶ ADJ 形容詞 Someone who is **asleep** is sleeping. 眠って [v-link ADJ] ❑ *My four-year-old daughter was asleep on the sofa.* 私の4歳の娘はソファーで眠っていた. ❷ ADJ 形容詞 If you say that your arm or leg is **asleep**, you mean that it is numb, for example because you have been sitting in an awkward position. しびれて [mainly AM 主に米国英語] ❑ *Her left leg was asleep from sitting on the floor.* 床に座っていたので彼女の左足がしびれていた. ❸ PHRASE 句 When you **fall asleep**, you start sleeping. 寝入る ❑ *Sam snuggled down in his pillow and fell asleep.* サムは枕に頭を沈めて横たわり眠りについた. ❹ PHRASE 句 Someone who is **fast asleep** or **sound asleep** is sleeping deeply. ぐっすり寝込んで ❑ *They were both fast asleep in their beds.* 彼らは2人とも自分のベッドでぐっすり寝込んでいた.
→ see **sleep**

as|para|gus /əspærəgəs/ N-UNCOUNT 不可算名詞 **Asparagus** is a vegetable that is long and green and has small shoots at one end. It is cooked and usually served whole. アスパラガス

as|pect /æspɛkt/ (aspects) ❶ N-COUNT 可算名詞 An **aspect** of something is one of the parts of its character or nature. 面, 局面 ❑ *Climate and weather affect every aspect of our lives.* 気候と天候は私たちの生活のすべての面に影響する. ❑ *He was interested in all aspects of the work here.* 彼はここの仕事のあらゆる面に興味を持っていた. ❷ N-COUNT 可算名詞 The **aspect** of a building or window is the direction in which it faces. 向き [FORMAL 形式ばった] ❑ *The house had a southwest aspect.* その家は南西向きだった.

Word Partnership   aspect は次の語句と使われる:

DET.	another/any/every aspect ❶
ADJ.	most important aspect, particular aspect ❶
PREP.	aspect of something ❶ ❷

as|pira|tion /æspəreɪʃ°n/ (aspirations) N-VAR 可変性名詞 Someone's **aspirations** are their desire to achieve things. 向上心, 志望 ❑ *...the needs and aspirations of our pupils.* 当校の生徒のニーズと志望 ❑ *He is unlikely to send in the army to quell nationalist aspirations.* 彼が民族主義的な野望を鎮圧するために軍隊を送り込むことはないであろう.

Word Link   spir ≈ breath : aspire, inspire, respiratory

as|pire /əspaɪər/ (aspires, aspiring, aspired) ❶ V-I 自動詞 If you **aspire** to something such as an important job, you have a strong desire to achieve it. 志望する ❑ *...people who aspire to public office.* 官公庁を志望する人たち ❑ *Rice aspired to go to college.* ライスは大学進学を切望した. ❷ → see also **aspiring**

as|pi|rin /æspərɪn, -prɪn/ (aspirins)

The form **aspirin** can also be used for the plural.
aspirin 形は複数にも使える.

N-VAR 可変性名詞 **Aspirin** is a mild drug that reduces pain and fever. アスピリン

as|pir|ing /əspaɪərɪŋ/ ❶ ADJ 形容詞 If you use **aspiring** to describe someone who is starting a particular career, you mean that they are trying to become successful in it. 向上心に燃えた [ADJ n] ❑ *Many aspiring young artists are advised to learn by copying the masters.* 若い芸術家の卵の多くは大家の作品を模写して学ぶように助言される. ❷ → see also **aspiring**

ass /æs/ (asses) ❶ N-COUNT 可算名詞 Your **ass** is your buttocks. しり [AM 米国英語, INFORMAL くだけた, VULGAR 下品な] ❑ *I jumped back and fell on my ass.* 私は後ろに飛び退いてしりもちをついた. ❷ N-COUNT 可算名詞 If you describe someone as an **ass**, you think that they are silly or do silly things. ばか [INFORMAL くだけた, DISAPPROVAL 不賛成] ❑ *He was generally disliked and regarded as a pompous ass.* 彼は一般に嫌われていて気取ったばか者と見なされていた. ❸ N-COUNT 可算名詞 An **ass** is an animal related to a horse but that is smaller and has long ears. ロバ ❑ **cover** your **ass** → see **cover** ❹ a pain in the **ass** → see **pain**

as|sail|ant /əseɪlənt/ (assailants) N-COUNT 可算名詞 Someone's **assailant** is a person who has physically attacked them. 攻撃者 [FORMAL 形式ばった] ❑ *Other partygoers rescued the injured man from his assailant.* 他のパーティー出席者たちが負傷した男性を暴行者の手から救い出した.

as|sas|sin /əsæsɪn/ (assassins) N-COUNT 可算名詞 An **assassin** is a person who assassinates someone. 暗殺者 ❑ *He saw the shooting and memorized the license plate of the assassin's car.* 彼はその狙撃を目撃して暗殺者の自動車のナンバーを記憶した.

as|sas|si|nate /əsæsɪneɪt/ (assassinates, assassinating, assassinated) V-T 他動詞 When someone important is **assassinated**, they are murdered as a political act. 暗殺する ❑ *Would the U.S. be radically different today if Kennedy had not been assassinated?* もしケネディーが暗殺されなかったら, 今日のアメリカは完全に違ったものになっているだろうか. ●**as|sas|si|na|tion** /əsæsɪneɪʃ°n/ (assassinations) N-VAR 可変性名詞 暗殺 ❑ *She would*

like an investigation into the assassination of her husband. 彼女は夫の暗殺について捜査してもらいたいと思っている. ❑ *He lives in constant fear of assassination.* 彼は絶えず暗殺を恐れて生活している.

as|sault /əsɔlt/ (assaults, assaulting, assaulted) ❶ N-COUNT 可算名詞 An **assault** by an army is a strong attack made on an area held by the enemy. 襲撃 ❑ *The rebels are poised for a new assault on the government garrisons.* 反乱者たちは政府軍の駐屯地を新たに襲撃する態勢にある. ❷ ADJ 形容詞 **Assault** weapons such as rifles are intended for soldiers to use in battle rather than for purposes such as hunting. 攻撃用の [ADJ n] ❸ N-VAR 可変性名詞 An **assault** on a person is a physical attack on them. 暴行 [oft N 'on/upon' n] ❑ *The attack is one of a series of savage sexual assaults on women in the university area.* その暴行事件は大学地区で起こった女性に対する一連の残忍な性的暴力事件の1つである. ❹ V-T 他動詞 To **assault** someone means to physically attack them. 襲う ❑ *The gang assaulted him with iron bars.* ギャング一味は彼を鉄の棒で襲った.

as|sem|ble /əsɛmb°l/ (assembles, assembling, assembled) ❶ V-T/V-I 他動詞/自動詞 When people **assemble** or when someone **assembles** them, they come together in a group, usually for a particular purpose such as a meeting. 集める [他動詞], 集まる [自動詞] ❑ *There wasn't even a convenient place for students to assemble between classes.* 授業の合間に学生が集まるのに便利な場所すらなかった. ❷ V-T 他動詞 To **assemble** something means to collect it together or to fit the different parts of it together. 組み立てる ❑ *Greenpeace managed to assemble a small flotilla of inflatable boats to waylay the ship at sea.* グリーンピースは海上でその船を待ち伏せするためにゴムボートの小型船隊を編成することができた.
→ see **industry**

as|sem|bly /əsɛmbli/ (assemblies) ❶ N-COUNT 可算名詞 An **assembly** is a large group of people who meet regularly to make decisions or laws for a particular region or country. 会議 ❑ *...the campaign for the first free election to the National Assembly.* 国民議会の初の自由選挙を求める運動 ❷ N-COUNT 可算名詞 An **assembly** is a group of people gathered together for a particular purpose. 集会, 集会参加者 ❑ *He waited until complete quiet settled on the assembly.* 彼は集会の場が完全に静かになるまで待った. ❸ N-UNCOUNT 不可算名詞 When you refer to rights of **assembly** or restrictions on **assembly**, you are referring to the legal right that people have to gather together. 集会 [FORMAL 形式ばった] ❑ *The U.S. Constitution guarantees free speech, freedom of assembly and equal protection.* 合衆国憲法は自由な言論と会合の自由と平等な保護を保障する. ❹ N-UNCOUNT 不可算名詞 The **assembly** of a machine, device, or object is the process of fitting its different parts together. 組み立て ❑ *For the rest of the day, he worked on the assembly of an explosive device.* その日の残りの時間の間, 彼は爆破装置の組み立てに取り組んだ. ❺ N-VAR 可変性名詞 In a school, an **assembly** is a gathering of all the teachers and students for a particular purpose. 全校集会 ❑ *Recently named the nation's top girls' basketball player, she will be honored this morning at a school assembly.* 最近全国トップの女子バスケット選手に指名された彼女は, 今朝全校集会で表彰されるでしょう.
→ see **mass production**

as|sent /əsɛnt/ (assents, assenting, assented) ❶ N-UNCOUNT 不可算名詞 If someone gives their **assent** to something that has been suggested, they formally agree to it. 同意 ❑ *He gave his assent to the proposed legislation.* 彼は提案された立法に同意した. ❷ V-I 自動詞 If you **assent** to something, you agree to it or agree with it. 同意する ❑ *I assented to the request of the American publishers to write this book.* 私はアメリカの出版社からの本書の執筆依頼を受け入れた.

as|sert /əsɜrt/ (asserts, asserting, asserted) ❶ V-T 他動詞 If someone **asserts** a fact or belief, they state it firmly. 断言する, 主張する [FORMAL 形式ばった] ❑ *Mr. Helm plans to assert that the bill violates the First Amendment.* ヘルム氏はその法案は米国憲法修正第1条に反すると主張する計画だ. ❑ *The defendants, who continue to assert their innocence, are expected to appeal.* 無罪を主張し続けている被告たちは控訴するよう予想される. ●**as|ser|tion** /əsɜrʃ°n/ (assertions) N-VAR 可変性名詞 断言, 主張 ❑ *There is no concrete evidence to support assertions that the recession is truly over.* 不況が本当に終わったという主張を裏付ける具体的な証拠は一切ない. ❷ V-T 他動詞 If you **assert** your authority, you make it clear by your behavior that you have authority. 行使する ❑ *After the war, the army made an attempt to assert its authority in the south of the country.* 戦後, 軍は国の南部でその権力を行使しようとした. ●**as|ser|tion** N-UNCOUNT 不可算名詞 (権力・権威の) 主張, 行使 ❑ *The decision is seen as an assertion of his authority within the company.* その決定は彼が会社内での権力を主張するために下したものと見られている. ❸ V-T 他動詞 If you **assert** your right or claim to something, you insist that you have the right to it. (権利などを) 主張する ❑ *The republics began asserting their right to govern themselves.* それらの共和国は自治権を主張し始めた. ●**as|ser|tion** N-UNCOUNT 不可算名詞 主張 ❑ *These institutions have made the assertion of ethnic identity possible.* これらの制度によって少数民族が独自性を主張することが可能になった. ❹ V-T 他動詞 If you **assert yourself**, you speak and act in a forceful way, so that people take notice of you. 強く主張する ❑ *He's speaking up and asserting himself and doing things he enjoys.* 彼は自由に物を言い自分の考えを強

く主張し自分の好きなことをしている.

as|ser|tive /əsɜ́rtɪv/ ADJ 形容詞 Someone who is **assertive** states their needs and opinions clearly, so that people take notice. 自己主張の強い □*Women have become more assertive in the past decade.* 過去10年間に女性たちがいっそう自分の意見をはっきり言うようになった. ● **as|ser|tive|ness** N-UNCOUNT 不可算名詞 主張性 □*Chantelle's assertiveness stirred up his deep-seated sense of inadequacy.* シャンテルのはっきりした物の言い方が彼の心の奥深くに潜む無能感を呼び起こした.

as|sess /əsɛ́s/ (assesses, assessing, assessed) **1** V-T 他動詞 When you **assess** a person, thing, or situation, you consider them in order to make a judgment about them. 判断する, 評価する □*The test was to assess aptitude rather than academic achievement.* そのテストは学力よりもむしろ適性を評価するためだった. □*It would be a matter of assessing whether she was well enough to travel.* それは彼女が旅行できるほど元気かどうかの判断次第だろう. **2** V-T 他動詞 When you **assess** the amount of money that something is worth or should be paid, you calculate or estimate it. 査定する □*Ask them to send you information on how to assess the value of your belongings.* あなたの財産価値を査定する方法についての情報を送ってもらうように彼らに頼みなさい.

as|sess|ment /əsɛ́smənt/ (assessments) **1** N-VAR 可変性名詞 An **assessment** is a consideration of someone or something and a judgment about them. 評価 □*There is little assessment of the damage to the natural environment.* 自然環境の被害はほとんど評価されていない. **2** N-VAR 可変性名詞 An **assessment** of the amount of money that something is worth or that should be paid is a calculation or estimate of the amount. 査定 □*Tax assessment is all about comparing values of similar properties.* 税金の査定はもっぱら類似の不動産の価値を比較することである.

as|ses|sor /əsɛ́sər/ (assessors) N-COUNT 可算名詞 An **assessor** is a person who is employed to calculate the value of something, or the amount of money that should be paid, for example, in tax. 査定者, 査定官 [BUSINESS 実業]

as|set /ǽsɛt/ (assets) **1** N-COUNT 可算名詞 Something or someone that is an **asset** is considered useful or helps a person or organization to be successful. 強み, 利点 □*Our creativity in the field of technology is our greatest asset.* 技術分野での私どもの独創力が私どもの最大の強みです. **2** N-PLURAL 複数名詞 The **assets** of a company or a person are all the things that they own. 資産 [BUSINESS 実業] □*By the end of 1989 the group had assets of $3.5 billion.* 1989年末にはこの企業グループの資産は35億ドルであった.

asset-stripping N-UNCOUNT 不可算名詞 If a person or company is involved in **asset-stripping**, they buy companies cheaply, sell off their assets to make a profit, and then close the companies down. 資産の収奪 [BUSINESS 実業, DISAPPROVAL 不賛成]

as|sign /əsáɪn/ (assigns, assigning, assigned) **1** V-T 他動詞 If you **assign** a piece of work **to** someone, you give them the work to do. 割り当てる □*When I taught, I would assign a topic to children that they would write about.* 私が教えていた時には子供たちに作文を書く課題を与えたものだった. □*Later in the year, she'll assign them research papers.* 年度の後半に彼女は彼らに研究論文を課すだろう. **2** V-T 他動詞 If you **assign** something **to** someone, you say that it is for their use. 与える □*The selling broker is then required to assign a portion of the commission to the buyer broker.* 売り手の仲買人はその時点で買い手の仲買人に手数料の一部を与えなければならない. **3** V-T 他動詞 If someone **is assigned to** a particular place, group, or person, they are sent there, usually in order to work at that place or for that person. 配属する, 任命する [usu passive] □*I was assigned to Troop A of the 10th Cavalry.* 第10機甲部隊のA中隊に配属された. □*Did you choose Russia or were you simply assigned there?* 君はロシアを自分から選んだのか, それとも単にそこに配属されたのか? **4** V-T 他動詞 If you **assign** a particular function or value **to** someone or something, you say they have it. 付ける, 帰する □*Under the system, each business must assign a value to each job.* この制度では各企業は仕事1つ1つに評価をつけなければならない.

as|sign|ment /əsáɪnmənt/ (assignments) N-COUNT 可算名詞 An **assignment** is a task or piece of work that you are given to do, especially as part of your job or studies. 課題, 宿題 □*The assessment for the course involves written assignments and practical tests.* このコースの成績評価はレポートと実地試験でされる.

Thesaurus *assignment* また次を参照:

N. chore, duty, job, task

Word Link simil ≈ similar : a**simil**ate, dis**simil**ar, **simil**arity

as|simi|late /əsɪ́mɪleɪt/ (assimilates, assimilating, assimilated) **1** V-T/V-I 他動詞/自動詞 When people such as immigrants **assimilate into** a community or when that community **assimilates** them, they become an accepted part of it. 同化する [他動詞/自動詞] □*There is every sign that new Asian-*

Americans are just as willing to assimilate. 新参のアジア系アメリカ人も全く同様に進んで同化しようとしている兆候が十分見られる. □*His family tried to assimilate into the white and Hispanic communities.* 彼の家族は白人社会とラテンアメリカ系社会に同化しようとした. ● **as|simi|la|tion** /əsɪmɪleɪ́ʃən/ N-UNCOUNT 不可算名詞 同化 □*They promote social integration and assimilation of minority ethnic groups into the culture.* 少数民族のグループを社会的に受け入れ文化的に同化させることを彼らは推し進めている. **2** V-T 他動詞 If you **assimilate** new ideas, customs, or techniques, you learn them or adopt them. 吸収する, 理解する □*My mind could only assimilate one impossibility at a time.* 私の頭はありえないようなことは1度に1つしか理解できない. ● **as|simi|la|tion** N-UNCOUNT 不可算名詞 吸収 □*This technique brings life to instruction and eases assimilation of knowledge.* この方法により授業が活性化され, 知識を吸収するのが簡単になる.

→ see **culture**

as|sist /əsɪ́st/ (assists, assisting, assisted) **1** V-T 他動詞 If you **assist** someone, you help them to do a job or task by doing part of the work for them. 手伝う □*The family decided to assist me with my chores.* 家族が私の雑用を手伝うことを決めた. **2** V-T/V-I 他動詞/自動詞 If you **assist** someone, you give them information, advice, or money. 助ける □*The public is urgently requested to assist police in tracing this man.* 警察はこの男の捜索に協力するように国民にしきりと呼びかけている. □*International organizations intensified their activities to locate victims and assist with relief efforts.* 国際的な諸団体が罹災者を見つけて救援努力で援助する活動を強化した. **3** V-T/V-I 他動詞/自動詞 If something **assists** in doing a task, it makes the task easier to do. 手を貸す □*...a chemical that assists in the manufacture of proteins.* たんぱく質の生産を補助する化学物質 □*Our sales representatives can assist you in selecting suitable investments.* 当社の販売員はあなたに合った投資をお選びお手伝いができます.

as|sis|tance /əsɪ́stəns/ **1** N-UNCOUNT 不可算名詞 If you give someone **assistance**, you help them do a job or task by doing part of the work for them. 援助 [oft with poss] □*Since 1976 he has been operating the shop with the assistance of volunteers.* 彼は1976年以来ボランティアの助けを得て店を経営している. **2** N-UNCOUNT 不可算名詞 If you give someone **assistance**, you give them information or advice. 手助け □*Any assistance you could give the police will be greatly appreciated.* 皆様が警察に提供できるどんな手がかりでも大いに感謝いたします. **3** N-UNCOUNT 不可算名詞 If someone gives a person or country **assistance**, they help them by giving them money. 援助 [oft supp N] □*...a viable program of economic assistance.* 経済援助の実行可能な計画 **4** N-UNCOUNT 不可算名詞 If something is done **with the assistance of** a particular thing, that thing is helpful or necessary for doing it. 助け □*The translations were carried out with the assistance of a medical dictionary.* それらの翻訳は医学辞書を参照して成し遂げられた. **5** PHRASE 句 Someone or something that is **of assistance** to you is helpful or useful to you. 役立つ □*Can I be of any assistance?* 何かお役に立てますでしょうか? **6** PHRASE 句 If you **come to** someone's **assistance**, you take action to help them. 人を援助する □*They are appealing to the world community to come to Jordan's assistance.* 彼らは国際社会にヨルダンの支援をするよう呼びかけている.

Word Partnership *assistance*は次の語句と使われる:

V. need/require assistance **1**
provide assistance **1** **2** **6**
ADJ. emergency assistance, medical assistance, technical assistance **2**
financial assistance **3**

as|sis|tant /əsɪ́stənt/ (assistants) **1** ADJ 形容詞 **Assistant** is used in front of titles or jobs to indicate a slightly lower rank. For example, an assistant director is one rank lower than a director in an organization. 補佐の [ADJ N] □*...the assistant secretary of defense.* 国防次官補 **2** N-COUNT 可算名詞 Someone's **assistant** is a person who helps them in their work. 助手 □*Kalan called his assistant, Hashim, to take over while he went out.* カランは助手のハシムに自分が出かけている間代行するように命じた. **3** N-COUNT 可算名詞 An **assistant** is a person who works in a store selling things to customers. 店員 □*The assistant took and checked the price on the back cover.* 店員は本を手に取り裏表紙の値段を確認した.

Word Link soci ≈ companion : as**soci**ate, **soci**al, **soci**ology

as|so|ci|ate (associates, associating, associated)

The verb is pronounced /əsóʊʃieɪt, -sieɪt/. The noun and adjective are pronounced /əsóʊʃiɪt, -siɪt/.

動詞は /əsóʊʃieɪt, -sieɪt/ と発音される. 名詞と形容詞は /əsóʊʃiɪt, -siɪt/ と発音される.

1 V-T 他動詞 If you **associate** someone or something **with** another thing, the two are connected in your mind. 結びつけて考える □*Through science we've got the idea of associating progress*

a

with the future. 科学のおかげで我々は進歩を未来と結びつけて考えている. **2** V-T 他動詞 If you **are associated with** a particular organization, cause, or point of view, or if you **associate yourself with** it, you support it publicly. 関係させる ❑*I haven't been associated with the project over the last year.* 私はそのプロジェクトに過去1年間携わっていない. **3** V-I 自動詞 If you say that someone **is associating with** another person or group of people, you mean they are spending a lot of time in the company of people you do not approve of. 交際する ❑*What would they think if they knew that they were associating with a murderer?* 彼らが人殺しとつきあっていると分かったらどう思うだろうか. **4** N-COUNT 可算名詞 Your **associates** are the people you are closely connected with, especially at work. 提携者, 仲間 ❑...*the restaurant owner's business associates*. そのレストラン所有者の仕事提携者 **5** N-COUNT 可算名詞 An **associate** is a retail worker who does not have previous experience or qualifications. 見習い店員 ❑*Be sure to get help from the sales associates before buying.* 買う前に必ずあの販売員見習いたちに聞いてください. **6** ADJ 形容詞 **Associate** is used before a rank or title to indicate a slightly different or lower rank or title. 副 (地位, 肩書き等) [ADJ n] ❑*Mr. Lin is associate director of the Institute.* リン氏は研究所の副所長である.

as|so|ci|at|ed /əsóʊʃièiṭɪd, -siei-/ **1** ADJ 形容詞 If one thing is **associated with** another, the two things are connected with each other. 関連した ❑*These symptoms are particularly associated with migraine headaches.* これらの症状は特に片頭痛と関連性がある. **2** ADJ 形容詞 **Associated** is used in the name of a company that is made up of a number of smaller companies that have joined together. 連合した [ADJ n] ❑...*the Associated Press.* A P通信

as|so|cia|tion /əsóʊʃièiʃ⁰n, -siei-/ (**associations**) **1** N-COUNT 可算名詞 An **association** is an official group of people who have the same job, aim, or interest. 協会 ❑...*the National Basketball Association.* 全国バスケットボール協会 **2** N-COUNT 可算名詞 Your **association with** a person or a thing such as an organization is the connection that you have with them. つながり ❑...*the company's six-year association with retailer J.C. Penney Co.* その会社の小売業者J.C. ペニー会社との6年間の提携 **3** N-COUNT 可算名詞 If something has particular **associations** for you, it is connected in your mind with a particular memory, idea, or feeling. 思い出, 連想 ❑*He has a shelf full of things, each of which has associations for him.* 彼には物でいっぱいの棚があるが, それらはそれぞれ彼にとって思い出の品である. **4** PHRASE 句 If you do something **in association with** someone else, you do it together. 共同して ❑*The changes I instigated in association with the board 18 months ago were because I love this company.* 私が18か月前に理事会と共同してそれらの改革を進めさせたのは, この会社を愛しているからこそだった.

→ see **memory**

as|sort|ed /əsɔ́rtɪd/ ADJ 形容詞 A group of **assorted** things is a group of similar things that are of different sizes or colors or have different qualities. 各種取りそろえた ❑*It should be a great week, with overnight stops in assorted hotels in the Adirondacks.* アディロンダック山地の各種のホテルに1泊ずつし, きっと素晴らしい1週間になるでしょう.

as|sort|ment /əsɔ́rtmənt/ (**assortments**) N-COUNT 可算名詞 An **assortment** is a group of similar things that are of different sizes or colors or have different qualities. 各種取りそろえた物 ❑...*an assortment of cheese.* チーズ各種

Word Link *sume ≈ taking : assume, consume, presume*

as|sume /əsúm/ (**assumes, assuming, assumed**) **1** V-T 他動詞 If you **assume that** something is true, you imagine that it is true, sometimes wrongly. 思い込む, 想定する ❑*It is a misconception to assume that the two continents are similar.* その2つの大陸が似ていると思うのは誤解である. ❑*If mistakes occurred, they were assumed to be the fault of the commander on the spot.* 間違いが起これば, それは当然現地の司令官の過失だと見なされた. **2** V-T 他動詞 If someone **assumes** power or responsibility, they take power or responsibility. 担う, 引き受ける ❑*Mr. Cross will assume the role of CEO with a team of four directors.* クロス氏が4名の重役陣を率いて最高経営責任者に就任するであろう. **3** V-T 他動詞 If you **assume** a particular expression or way of behaving, you start to look or behave in this way. 装う, ふりをする ❑*He managed to assume an air of calm.* 彼はどうにか平静を装うことができた.

Word Partnership *assume は次の語句と使われる:*

V.	let's assume *that*, tend to assume **1**
ADV.	assume so **1**
	automatically assume **1 2**
N.	assume the worst **1**
	assume control/power, assume responsibility, assume a role **2**

as|sum|ing /əsúmɪŋ/ CONJ 接続詞 You use **assuming** or **assuming that** when you are considering a possible situation or

event, so that you can think about the consequences. 仮定して ❑*"Assuming you're right,"* he said, *"there's not much I can do about it, is there?"* 「君が正しいと仮定すると, それについて僕にできることは大してないじゃないか」と彼は言った.

Word Link *sumpt ≈ taking : assumption, consumption, presumption*

as|sump|tion /əsʌ́mpʃ⁰n/ (**assumptions**) N-COUNT 可算名詞 If you make an **assumption that** something is true or will happen, you accept that it is true or will happen, often without any real proof. 仮定, 憶測 ❑*You would be making an assumption that's not based on any fact that you could report.* 君は報告できるような事実に基づかない憶測をしているだけではないか.

Word Partnership *assumption は次の語句と使われる:*

ADJ.	assumption **based on**, **common** assumption, **underlying** assumption
V.	**challenge an** assumption, **make an** assumption

as|sur|ance /əʃʊ́ərəns/ (**assurances**) **1** N-VAR 可変性名詞 If you give someone an **assurance that** something is true or will happen, you say that it is definitely true or will definitely happen, in order to make them feel less worried. 保証 ❑*He would like an assurance that other forces will not move into the territory that his forces vacate.* 彼の部隊が立ち退く地域には他の部隊が進入しないことを彼は保証しているのだ. **2** N-UNCOUNT 不可算名詞 If you do something **with assurance**, you do it with a feeling of confidence and certainty. 自信 ❑*Masur led the orchestra with assurance.* マズアは自信を持ってオーケストラを指揮した.

as|sure /əʃʊ́ər/ (**assures, assuring, assured**) **1** V-T 他動詞 If you **assure** someone that something is true or will happen, you tell them that it is definitely true or will definitely happen, often in order to make them less worried. 安心させる ❑*He hastened to assure me that there was nothing traumatic to report.* 彼は何も衝撃的な知らせはないと私をまずは安心させた. ❑*"Are you sure the raft is safe?"* she asked anxiously. *"Couldn't be safer,"* Max assured her confidently. 「本当にそのいかだは安全なの？」と彼女は心配そうに尋ねた. 「最高に安全だよ」とマックスは自信ありげに彼女をなだめた. **2** → see also **assured 3** V-T 他動詞 To **assure** someone of something means to make certain that they will get it. 保証する ❑*His performance yesterday morning assured him of a record eighth medal.* 昨日の朝の彼の出来栄えのおかげで, 彼は過去最多の8つ目のメダル獲得が確実になった. **4** PHRASE 句 You use phrases such as **I can assure you** or **let me assure you** to emphasize the truth of what you are saying. 大丈夫だ, 本当ですよ [EMPHASIS 強調] ❑*I can assure you that the animals are well cared for.* 動物たちの世話が十分行き届いていることは保証できますよ.

as|sured /əʃʊ́ərd/ **1** ADJ 形容詞 Someone who is **assured** is very confident and relaxed. 自信を持った ❑*He was infinitely more assured than in his more recent concert appearances.* 彼は最近のコンサート出演の時よりもはるかに自信を持っていた. **2** ADJ 形容詞 If something is **assured**, it is certain to happen. 確かな [v-link ADJ] ❑*Our victory is assured; nothing can stop us.* 我々の勝利は確実だ. 何ものもじゃまだてはできない. **3** ADJ 形容詞 If you are **assured of** something, you are certain to get it or achieve it. 保証された [v-link ADJ 'of' n] ❑*Laura Davies is assured of a place in the Olympic team.* ローラ・デーヴィスはオリンピックチーム入りを保証されている. **4** PHRASE 句 If you say that someone **can rest assured that** something is the case, you mean that it is definitely the case, so they do not need to worry about it. 安心している [EMPHASIS 強調] ❑*Their parents can rest assured that their children's safety will be of paramount importance.* 子供たちの安全が最も大切にされるでしょうから親たちは安心していられる.

Word Link *aster, astro ≈ star : asterisk, astronaut, astronomy*

as|ter|isk /æstərɪsk/ (**asterisks**) N-COUNT 可算名詞 An **asterisk** is the sign *. It is used especially to indicate that there is further information about something in another part of the text. 星印

asth|ma /ǽzmə/ N-UNCOUNT 不可算名詞 **Asthma** is a lung condition that causes difficulty in breathing. ぜんそく

asth|mat|ic /æzmǽtɪk/ (**asthmatics**) **1** N-COUNT 可算名詞 People who suffer from asthma are sometimes referred to as **asthmatics**. ぜんそく患者 ❑*I have been an asthmatic from childhood and was never able to play any sports.* 子供のころから私はぜんそく持ちで, どんな運動も全くできなかった. ● ADJ 形容詞 **Asthmatic** is also an adjective. ぜんそくにかかった ❑*One child in ten is asthmatic.* 子供のうち10人に1人はぜんそく持ちである. **2** ADJ 形容詞 **Asthmatic** means relating to asthma. ぜんそく性の [ADJ n] ❑...*asthmatic breathing.* ぜんそく性呼吸

aston|ish /əstɒ́nɪʃ/ (**astonishes, astonishing, astonished**) V-T 他動詞 If something or someone **astonishes** you, they surprise you very much. ひどく驚かす ❑*My news will astonish you.* 私の知ら

A

せにあなたはびっくりするよ.

aston|ished /əstɒnɪʃt/ ADJ 形容詞 If you are **astonished** by something, you are very surprised about it. ひどく驚いた □ *They were astonished to find the driver was a six-year-old boy.* 彼らは車を運転しているのが6歳の男の子だと分かってひどくびっくりした.

aston|ish|ing /əstɒnɪʃɪŋ/ ADJ 形容詞 Something that is **astonishing** is very surprising. 全く驚くばかりの □ *...an astonishing display of physical strength.* 全く驚くべき体力の発揮 ● **aston|ish|ing|ly** ADV 副詞 全く驚くほどに □ *Andrea was an astonishingly beautiful young woman.* アンドレアは全く驚くほど美しい若い女性だった.

aston|ish|ment /əstɒnɪʃmənt/ N-UNCOUNT 不可算名詞 **Astonishment** is a feeling of great surprise. 大きな驚き □ *I spotted a shooting star which, to my astonishment, was bright green in color.* 私は流れ星を見つけたのだが, ひどく驚いたことにそれは鮮やかな緑色だった.

astound /əstaʊnd/ (**astounds, astounding, astounded**) V-T 他動詞 If something **astounds** you, you are very surprised by it. びっくり仰天させる □ *He used to astound his friends with feats of physical endurance.* 彼は身体の耐久力を発揮しては友だちを仰天させたものだった.

astound|ing /əstaʊndɪŋ/ ADJ 形容詞 If something is **astounding**, you are shocked or amazed that it could exist or happen. 仰天させるような, どえらい □ *The results are quite astounding.* その結果は全く驚くべきものだ.

astray /əstreɪ/ ■ PHRASE 句 If you **are led astray** by someone or something, you behave badly or foolishly because of them. 道を踏み外させる, 堕落させる □ *The judge thought he'd been led astray by older children.* 年上の子供たちのせいで彼が道を踏み外したのだと判事は考えた. ② PHRASE 句 If someone or something **leads** you **astray**, they make you believe something that is not true, causing you to make a wrong decision. 迷わす □ *The testimony would inflame the jurors, and lead them astray from the facts of the case.* その証言は陪審員を刺激してこの事件に関する諸事実から目をそらさせることになるだろう. ③ PHRASE 句 If something **goes astray**, it gets lost while it is being taken or sent somewhere. 紛失する □ *Many items of mail being sent to her have gone astray.* 彼女あての郵便物の多くが紛失してしまった.

astride /əstraɪd/ PREP 前置詞 If you sit or stand **astride** something, you sit or stand with one leg on each side of it. またがって □ *...three youths who stood astride their bicycles and stared.* 自転車にまたがりじっと見つめていた若者3人

as|trolo|ger /əstrɒlədʒər/ (**astrologers**) N-COUNT 可算名詞 An **astrologer** is a person who uses astrology to try to tell you things about your character and your future. 星占い師

as|trol|ogy /əstrɒlədʒi/ N-UNCOUNT 不可算名詞 **Astrology** is the study of the movements of the planets, sun, moon, and stars in the belief that these movements can have an influence on people's lives. 占星術
→ see **star**

Word Link	
aster, astro ≈ star : *aster*isk, *astro*naut, *astro*nomy	

as|tro|naut /æstrənɔt/ (**astronauts**) N-COUNT 可算名詞 An **astronaut** is a person who is trained for traveling in a spacecraft. 宇宙飛行士

Word Link	
er, or ≈ one who does, that which does : *astronomer*, *author*, *writer*	

as|trono|mer /əstrɒnəmər/ (**astronomers**) N-COUNT 可算名詞 An **astronomer** is a scientist who studies the stars, planets, and other natural objects in space. 天文学者
→ see Word Web: **astronomer**
→ see **galaxy, telescope**

as|tro|nomi|cal /æstrənɒmɪkəl/ ■ ADJ 形容詞 If you describe

an amount, especially the cost of something as **astronomical**, you are emphasizing that it is very large. けた外れに大きな [EMPHASIS 強調] □ *Houses in the subdivision are going for astronomical prices.* この分譲地の住宅はけた外れな高値で売りに出ている. ② ADJ 形容詞 **Astronomical** means relating to astronomy. 天文学の □ *...the American Astronomical Society.* アメリカ天文学会

as|trono|my /əstrɒnəmi/ N-UNCOUNT 不可算名詞 **Astronomy** is the scientific study of the stars, planets, and other natural objects in space. 天文学
→ see **star**

as|tute /əstut/ ADJ 形容詞 If you describe someone as **astute**, you think they show an understanding of behavior and situations, and are skillful at using this knowledge to their own advantage. 機敏な, 抜け目がない □ *She was politically astute.* 彼女は政治的に目先がきく.

asy|lum /əsaɪləm/ (**asylums**) ■ N-UNCOUNT 不可算名詞 If a government gives a person from another country **asylum**, they allow them to stay, usually because they are unable to return home safely for political reasons. (亡命者の) 保護, 亡命 □ *He applied for asylum in 1987 after fleeing the police back home.* 彼は自国で警察の手から逃れて, 1987年に亡命を申請した. ② N-COUNT 可算名詞 An **asylum** is a psychiatric hospital. 精神病院 [OLD-FASHIONED 古風な]

asy|lum seek|er (**asylum seekers**) N-COUNT 可算名詞 An **asylum seeker** is a person who is trying to get asylum in a foreign country. 亡命希望者 □ *Fewer than 7% of asylum seekers are accepted as political refugees.* 亡命希望者のうち政治的亡命者として受け入れられるのは7パーセントに満たない.

at /ət, STRONG æt/

> In addition to the uses shown below, **at** is used after some verbs, nouns, and adjectives to introduce extra information. **At** is also used in phrasal verbs such as "have at" and "play at".

> 下記の用法に加えて, **at** は情報を追加するために1部の動詞, 名詞, 形容詞の後に使われる. **At** はまた **have at** や **play at** のような句動詞にも使われる.

■ PREP 前置詞 You use **at** to indicate the place or event where something happens or is situated. (場所) で, (場合) において □ *He will be at the airport to meet her.* 彼が空港に行って彼女を出迎えるでしょう. □ *I didn't like being alone at home.* 私は家に1人でいるのは嫌いだった. □ *They agreed to meet at a restaurant in Soho.* 彼らはソーホーのレストランで会うことを申し合わせた. ② PREP 前置詞 If you are **at** something such as a table, a door, or someone's side, you are next to it or them. (隣接したところ) で □ *An assistant sat typing away at a table beside him.* 助手が彼のそばでテーブルについて絶え間なくタイプを打っていた. □ *At his side was a beautiful young woman.* 彼のそばには美しい若い女性がいた. ③ PREP 前置詞 When you are describing where someone or something is, you can say that they are **at** a certain distance. You can also say that one thing is **at** an angle in relation to another thing. (距離, 角度) で □ *The two journalists followed at a discreet distance.* その2人の記者が目立たない距離をとって後をつけた. ④ PREP 前置詞 If something happens **at** a particular time, that is the time when it happens or begins to happen. (時点) で □ *The funeral will be carried out this afternoon at 3:00.* 葬儀は本日午後3時に執り行われます. ⑤ PREP 前置詞 If you do something **at** a particular age, you do it when you are that age. (年齢の) 時に □ *Zachary started playing violin at age 4.* ザカリーは4歳の時にバイオリンを弾き始めた. ⑥ PREP 前置詞 If someone is **at** a particular school or college, they go there regularly to study. 〜に (在籍している) □ *Their daughter is a sophomore at Yale.* 彼らの娘はエール大学の2年生だ. ⑦ PREP 前置詞 You use **at** to express a rate, frequency, level, or price. (割合, 頻度など) で □ *I drove back down the highway at normal speed.* 私は高速道路を普通の速度で運転して戻った. □ *Check the oil at regular intervals, and have the car serviced regularly.* オイルを定期的にチェックし, 車の

Word Web astronomer

The Italian **astronomer** Galileo Galilei did not invent the telescope. However, he was the first person to use it to study **celestial** bodies. He recorded his findings. What Galileo saw through the telescope supported the theory that the **planet** Earth is not the center of the universe. This theory was written by the Polish astronomer Nicolaus Copernicus in 1530. Copernicus said that all the planets in the universe revolve around the **sun**. In 1609, Galileo used a telescope to observe the **craters** on Earth's **moon**. He also discovered the four largest **satellites** of the planet Jupiter. These four bodies are called the Galilean moons.

保守点検も定期的に受けること. **8** PREP 前置詞 You use **at** before a number or amount to indicate a measurement. (数量) で [PREP amount] ❑ *...as unemployment stays pegged at three million.* 失業者数は3百万人でとどまっているので **9** PREP 前置詞 If you look **at** someone or something, you look toward them. If you direct an object or a comment **at** someone, you direct it toward them. (方角, 方向) を ❑ *He looked at Michael and laughed.* 彼はマイケルを見て笑った. **10** PREP 前置詞 You can use **at** after verbs such as "smile" or "wave" and before nouns referring to people to indicate that you have put on an expression or made a gesture that someone is meant to see or understand. 向かって (〜する) [V PREP n] ❑ *She opened the door and stood there, frowning at me.* 彼女はドアを開けてそこに立ち, 眉をひそめて私を見た. **11** PREP 前置詞 If you point or gesture **at** something, you move your arm or head in its direction so that it will be noticed by someone you are with. (対象) を [V PREP n] ❑ *He pointed at the empty bottle and the waitress quickly replaced it.* 彼が空になったびんを指さすと, ウェートレスはすばやく取り替えた. **12** PREP 前置詞 If you are working **at** something, you are dealing with it. If you are aiming **at** something, you are trying to achieve it. (対象・目標に) 向かって ❑ *She has worked hard at her marriage.* 彼女は結婚生活がうまくいくように大変努力してきた. **13** PREP 前置詞 If something is done **at** someone's invitation or request, it is done as a result of it. (招待や依頼に) 応じて [PREP n with poss] ❑ *She left the light on in the bathroom at his request.* 彼女は彼の頼みで浴室の電気を付けっぱなしにした. **14** PREP 前置詞 You use **at** to say that someone or something is in a particular state or condition. (状況・状態) に [v-link PREP n] ❑ *I am afraid we are not at liberty to disclose that information.* 残念ながら, 私たちの一存ではその情報を公開できません. **15** PREP 前置詞 You use **at** before a possessive pronoun and a superlative adjective to say that someone or something has more of a particular quality than at any other time. (最高の〜) で ❑ *When I'm on the soccer field, I'm at my happiest.* 私はサッカー場にいるときが一番幸せです. **16** PREP 前置詞 You use **at** to say how something is being done. (方法) で ❑ *Three people were killed by shots fired at random from a minibus.* ミニバスからの乱射で3人が死亡した. **17** PREP 前置詞 You use **at** to show that someone is doing something repeatedly. (繰り返す行為の対象) に [V PREP n] ❑ *She lowered the handkerchief which she had kept dabbing at her eyes.* 彼女はしきりに涙をぬぐっていたハンカチを下ろした. **18** PREP 前置詞 You use **at** to indicate an activity or task when saying how well someone does it. (活動, 仕事など) が ❑ *I'm good at my work.* 私は仕事がうまい. **19** PREP 前置詞 You use **at** to indicate what someone is reacting to. 〜に対して ❑ *Elena was annoyed at having had to wait so long for him.* エレナは彼に長々と待たされたことに腹を立てた. **20 at all** → see **all**

ate /eɪt/ **Ate** is the past tense of **eat**. 食べた

Word Link *a, an ≈ not, without : anesthetic, anorexia, atheism*

athe|ism /eɪθiɪzəm/ N-UNCOUNT 不可算名詞 **Atheism** is the belief that there is no God. Compare **agnosticism**. 無神論 ❑ *Many young people were rejecting the atheism of their Communist rulers.* 若者の多くが共産主義支配者たちの無神論を受け入れなくなってきていた.

athe|ist /eɪθiɪst/ (**atheists**) N-COUNT 可算名詞 An **atheist** is a person who believes that there is no God. Compare **agnostic**. 無神論者

ath|lete /æθliːt/ (**athletes**) **1** N-COUNT 可算名詞 An **athlete** is a person who does any kind of physical sports, exercise, or games, especially in competitions. 運動選手 ❑ *Mark Spitz was a great athlete.* マーク・スピッツは偉大な運動選手だった. **2** N-COUNT 可算名詞 You can refer to someone who is fit and athletic as an **athlete**. スポーツマン, 運動能力のある人 ❑ *I was no athlete.* 私はスポーツが全然だめだった.

ath|let|ic /æθletɪk/ **1** ADJ 形容詞 **Athletic** means relating to athletes and athletics. 運動競技の [ADJ n] ❑ *They have been given college scholarships purely on athletic ability.* 彼らは単に運動能力があるだけで大学の奨学金をもらっている. **2** ADJ 形容詞 An **athletic** person is fit, and able to perform energetic movements easily. 強健な ❑ *Xandra is an athletic 36-year-old with a 21-year-old's body.* ザンドラは身体的には21歳といえる強健な36歳の男である.

ath|let|ics /æθletɪks/ **1** N-UNCOUNT 不可算名詞 **Athletics** refers to any kind of physical sports, exercise, or games. 運動競技 [AM 米国英語] ❑ *...students who play intercollegiate athletics.* 大学対抗の運動競技に出場する学生たち **2** N-UNCOUNT 不可算名詞 **Athletics** refers to track and field sports such as running, the high jump, and the javelin. 陸上競技 [mainly BRIT 主に英国英語; AM **track and field** 米国英語 **track and field**]

at|las /ætləs/ (**atlases**) N-COUNT 可算名詞 An **atlas** is a book of maps. 地図帳

ATM /eɪ tiː ɛm/ (**ATMs**) N-COUNT 可算名詞 An **ATM** is a machine that allows people to take out money from their bank account by using a special card. **ATM** is an abbreviation for "automated teller machine." 現金自動預け払い機 [mainly AM 主に米国英語] ❑ *Keep your ATM card in a safe place.* ATMのカードは安全な場所に保管してください. → see **bank**

Word Link *sphere ≈ ball : atmosphere, hemisphere, sphere*

at|mos|phere /ætməsfɪər/ (**atmospheres**) **1** N-COUNT 可算名詞 A planet's **atmosphere** is the layer of air or other gases around it. 大気圏 ❑ *The shuttle Columbia will re-enter Earth's atmosphere tomorrow morning.* スペースシャトル・コロンビア号は明朝に地球の大気圏に再突入する予定である. **2** N-COUNT 可算名詞 The **atmosphere** of a place is the air that you breathe there. 空気 ❑ *These gases pollute the atmosphere of towns and cities.* これらのガスが都市の空気を汚染する. **3** N-SING 単数名詞 The **atmosphere** of a place is the general impression that you get of it. (周囲の) 状況, 雰囲気 ❑ *There's still an atmosphere of great hostility and tension in the city.* 市内ではまだひどい敵対行為と緊張の状況が続いている. **4** N-UNCOUNT 不可算名詞 If a place or an event has **atmosphere**, it is interesting. 趣き ❑ *The old harbor is still full of atmosphere and well worth visiting.* その古い港はまだ風情に満ちていて, 訪問する価値が十分あります.
→ see **air, core, earth, greenhouse, meteor, moon, water**

at|mos|pher|ic /ætməsfɛrɪk/ **1** ADJ 形容詞 **Atmospheric** is used to describe something that relates to the Earth's atmosphere. 大気の ❑ *...atmospheric gases.* 大気中のガス **2** ADJ 形容詞 If you describe a place or a piece of music as **atmospheric**, you like it because it has a particular quality that is interesting or exciting and makes you feel a particular emotion. 趣のある, ムードのある [APPROVAL 賛成] ❑ *One of the most atmospheric corners of Prague is the old Jewish ghetto.* プラハで最も趣きのある地区の1つは旧ユダヤ人街です.

atom /ætəm/ (**atoms**) N-COUNT 可算名詞 An **atom** is the smallest amount of a substance that can take part in a chemical reaction. 原子 ❑ *...the news that Einstein's former colleagues Otto Hahn and Fritz Strassmann had split the atom.* アインシュタインの元同僚オットー・ハーンとフリッツ・シュトラスマンが原子を分裂させたという報道
→ see **element**

atom|ic /ətɒmɪk/ **1** ADJ 形容詞 **Atomic** means relating to power that is produced from the energy released by splitting atoms. 原子の ❑ *...atomic energy.* 原子力 **2** ADJ 形容詞 **Atomic** means relating to the atoms of substances. 原子の [ADJ n] ❑ *...the atomic number of an element.* 元素の原子番号

atro|cious /ətroʊʃəs/ **1** ADJ 形容詞 If you describe something as **atrocious**, you are emphasizing that its quality is very bad. ひどく悪い [EMPHASIS 強調] ❑ *I remain to this day fluent in Hebrew, while my Arabic is atrocious.* 私はヘブライ語が今でも流暢 (りゅうちょう) だが, 私のアラビア語はひどいものだ. **2** ADJ 形容詞 If you describe someone's behavior or their actions as **atrocious**, you mean that it is unacceptable because it is extremely violent or cruel. 凶悪な ❑ *The judge said he had committed atrocious crimes against women.* 彼は女性に対して凶悪な犯罪を犯したと判事が述べた.

atroc|ity /ətrɒsɪti/ (**atrocities**) N-VAR 可変性名詞 An **atrocity** is a very cruel, shocking action. 残虐行為 ❑ *The killing was cold-blooded, and those who committed this atrocity should be tried and punished.* この殺害事件は冷酷なものであり, この残虐な行為を犯した者は裁判にかけ処罰すべきである.

at|tach /ətætʃ/ (**attaches, attaching, attached**) **1** V-T 他動詞 If you **attach** something **to** an object, you join it or fasten it to the object. 取り付ける ❑ *We attach labels to things before we file them away.* 我々はとじ込んで整理する前にラベルを付ける. [For further information, please contact us on the attached form. 詳しい情報をご希望の方は別紙の様式でご連絡下さい. **2** V-T 他動詞 In computing, if you **attach** a file to a message that you send to someone, you send it with the message but separate from it. 添付する ❑ *It is possible to attach executable program files to e-mail.* 実行プログラムファイルを電子メールに添付することができる. **3** → see also **attached 4 no strings attached** → see **string**

at|tached /ətætʃt/ **1** ADJ 形容詞 If you are **attached to** someone or something, you like them very much. 愛情を抱いて [v-link ADJ 'to' n] ❑ *She is very attached to her family and friends.* 彼女は家族と友だちが大好きだ. **2** ADJ 形容詞 If someone is **attached to** an organization or group of people, they are working with them, often only for a short time. 所属して [v-link ADJ 'to' n] ❑ *Ford was attached to the 101st Airborne Division.* フォードは第101空挺師団に所属していた.

at|tach|ment /ətætʃmənt/ (**attachments**) **1** N-VAR 可変性名詞 If you have an **attachment to** someone or something, you are fond of them or loyal to them. 愛着 ❑ *As a teenager she formed a strong attachment to one of her teachers.* 10代の頃, 彼女は教師の1人に強い思附の情を抱いた. **2** N-COUNT 可算名詞 An **attachment** is a device that can be fixed onto a machine in order to enable it to do different jobs. 付属部品 ❑ *Some models come with attachments for dusting.* ほこり除去のための付属品のついた型もいくつかあ

る。 **3** N-COUNT 可算名詞 In computing, an **attachment** is a file which is attached separately to a message that you send to someone. 添付ファイル □When you send an e-mail you can also send a file as an attachment and that file can be a graphic, a program, a sound or whatever. 電子メール送信の際，ファイルも添付して送信でき，そのファイルは画像，プログラム，音声などどんなものでもかまわない。

at|tack /ətǽk/ (attacks, attacking, attacked) **1** V-T/V-I 他動詞/自動詞 To **attack** a person or place means to try to hurt or damage them using physical violence. 攻撃する [他動詞/自動詞] □Fifty civilians in Masawa were killed when government planes attacked the town. 政府軍の飛行機がマサワを攻撃したとき，一般人に50人の死者が出た。 □He bundled the old lady into her hallway and brutally attacked her. 彼は彼女を廊下に追い出して，残忍に襲った。 □They found the least defended area and attacked. 彼らは最も防御の薄い地域を見つけ攻撃した。 ● N-VAR 可変性名詞 **Attack** is also a noun. 攻撃 □...a campaign of air attacks on strategic targets. 戦略目標への空爆作戦 **2** V-T 他動詞 If you **attack** a person, belief, idea, or act, you criticize them strongly. 非難する □He publicly attacked the people who've been calling for secret ballot nominations. 彼は無記名投票による指名を要求してきた人々を公然と非難した。 ● N-VAR 可変性名詞 **Attack** is also a noun. 非難 [usu with supp] □The role of the state as a prime mover in planning social change has been under attack. 社会的変化の計画の主導者としての国家の役割が激しく非難されている。 **3** V-T 他動詞 If something such as a disease, a chemical, or an insect **attacks** something, it harms or spoils it. 襲う，おかす □The virus seems to have attacked his throat. 彼ののどはウィルスにおかされたうだ。 ● N-UNCOUNT 不可算名詞 **Attack** is also a noun. 発病 [also N in pl] □The virus can actually destroy those white blood cells, leaving the body wide open to attack from other infections. ウィルスは実際にこれらの白血球を破壊することがあり，体を他の感染に対して無防備な状態にさらす。 **4** V-T 他動詞 If you **attack** a job or a problem, you start to deal with it in an energetic way. 猛然と取りかかる □Any attempt to attack the budget problem is going to have to in some way deal with those issues. 予算問題に着手するための試みは，全てなんらかの形でこうした問題を取り扱わねばならない。 **5** V-T/V-I 他動詞/自動詞 In games such as soccer, when one team **attacks** the opponent's goal, they try to score a goal. 攻撃する [他動詞/自動詞] □Now the U.S. is controlling the ball and attacking the opponent's goal. 今，アメリカ側がボールを持ち，相手のゴールを攻撃しています。 □The goal was just reward for their decision to attack constantly in the second half. 後半は絶え間なく攻撃しようとする決意への報いとしてゴールを決めることができた。 ● N-COUNT 可算名詞 **Attack** is also a noun. 攻撃 □Lee was at the hub of some incisive attacks in the second half. リーは後半の何度かの機敏な攻撃の要であった。 **6** N-COUNT 可算名詞 An **attack** of an illness is a short period in which you suffer badly from it. 発作 □It had brought on an attack of asthma. それがぜんそくの発作を引き起こした。 **7** → see also **counterattack, heart attack** → see **war**

Thesaurus *attack* また次を参照：

V.	assault, hit, invade; (ant.) defend **1**
	abuse, blame, criticize; (ant.) defend, praise **2**
	deal with, tackle; (ant.) avoid, ignore, put off **4**
N.	invasion **1**
	abuse, criticism, libel, slander; (ant.) defense **2**
	bout, fit **6**

Word Partnership *attack* は次の語句と使われる：

N.	**terrorist** attack **1**
ADJ.	**sudden/surprise** attack **1**
	personal attack **2**
V.	**launch/lead/plan** an attack **1 2**
PREP.	attack **on/against**, **under** attack **1 2**
	attack **of** something **6**

at|tack|er /ətǽkər/ (attackers) N-COUNT 可算名詞 You can refer to a person who attacks someone as their **attacker**. 攻撃者 □There were signs that she struggled with her attacker before she was stabbed. 彼女が刺される前に犯人ともみ合った形跡があった。

at|tain /ətéɪn/ (attains, attaining, attained) V-T 他動詞 If you **attain** something, you gain it or achieve it, often after a lot of effort. 達成する [FORMAL 形式ばった] □Jim is halfway to attaining his pilot's license. ジムは飛行士免許取得の道の半ばにいる。

at|tain|ment /ətéɪnmənt/ (attainments) **1** N-UNCOUNT 不可算名詞 The **attainment** of an aim is the achieving of it. 達成 [FORMAL 形式ばった] □...the attainment of independence. 独立の達成 **2** N-COUNT 可算名詞 An **attainment** is a skill you have learned or something you have achieved. 技能 [FORMAL 形式ばった] □...their educational attainments. 彼らの学業成績

Word Link *tempt ≈ trying : at*tempt, *tempt*ation, *tempt*ed

at|tempt /ətémpt/ (attempts, attempting, attempted)

1 V-T 他動詞 If you **attempt to** do something, especially something difficult, you try to do it. 試みる □The only time that we attempted to do something like that was in the city of Philadelphia. そのようなことを試みた唯一の機会は，フィラデルフィア市でのことだった。 **2** N-COUNT 可算名詞 If you make an **attempt to** do something, you try to do it, often without success. 企て □...a deliberate attempt to destabilize the defense. 守りを崩すための手の込んだ企て **3** N-COUNT 可算名詞 An **attempt on** someone's life is an attempt to kill them. 襲撃 □...an attempt on the life of the former Iranian prime minister. 前イタリア首相の暗殺の企て

Thesaurus *attempt* また次を参照：

V.	strive, tackle, take on, try **1**
N.	effort, try, venture **2**

Word Partnership *attempt* は次の語句と使われる：

V.	attempt **to control/find/prevent/solve** **1**
	make an attempt **2**
	attempt **suicide** **3**
ADJ.	**any** attempt, **desperate** attempt, **failed/successful** attempt **2**
N.	**assassination** attempt **3**

at|tempt|ed /ətémptɪd/ ADJ 形容詞 An **attempted** crime or unlawful action is an unsuccessful effort to commit the crime or action. 未遂の [ADJ n] □...a case of attempted murder. 殺人未遂事件

at|tend /əténd/ (attends, attending, attended) **1** V-T/V-I 他動詞/自動詞 If you **attend** a meeting or other event, you are present at it. 出席する [他動詞/自動詞] □Thousands of people attended the funeral. 数千人が葬儀に参列した。 □The meeting will be attended by finance ministers from many countries. 会合には多くの国の財務大臣が出席するだろう。 □The senator was invited but was unable to attend. 上院議員は招待されたが出席できなかった。 **2** V-T 他動詞 If you **attend** an institution such as a school, college, or church, you go there regularly. 通う □They attended college together at the University of Pennsylvania. 彼らは共にペンシルバニア大学に通った。 **3** V-I 自動詞 If you **attend to** something, you deal with it. If you **attend to** someone who is hurt or injured, you care for them. 世話をする，専心する □He took a short leave of absence to attend to personal business. 彼は自分の仕事に専念するため短期の休暇をとった。

at|tend|ance /əténdəns/ (attendances) **1** N-UNCOUNT 不可算名詞 Someone's **attendance** at an event or an institution is the fact that they are present at the event or go regularly to the institution. 出席 □Her attendance in school was sporadic. 彼女はときどき登校した。 **2** N-VAR 可変性名詞 The **attendance** at an event is the number of people who are present at it. 出席者数 □Rain played a big part in the air show's drop in attendance. 航空ショーの観客数の下落は雨の影響が大きかった。

at|tend|ant /əténdənt/ (attendants) **1** N-COUNT 可算名詞 An **attendant** is someone whose job is to serve or help people in a place such as a gas station or a parking lot. 係員 □Tony Williams was working as a parking lot attendant in Los Angeles. トニー・ウィリアムズはロサンゼルスで駐車場係員として働いていた。 **2** → see also **flight attendant** **3** N-COUNT 可算名詞 The **attendants** at a wedding are people such as the bridesmaids and the ushers, who accompany or help the bride and groom. 付添い人 □If the bride pays, she has the right to decide on the style of dress worn by her attendants. 花嫁が支払うなら，彼女には自分の付添い人の着る服装の様式を決める権利がある。

at|ten|tion /əténʃ°n/ **1** N-UNCOUNT 不可算名詞 If you give someone or something your **attention**, you look at it, listen to it, or think about it carefully. 注意 □You have my undivided attention. あなたには私が全面的な注意を払っている。 □Later he turned his attention to the desperate state of housing in the city. 後に彼はその市の悲惨な住宅事情に注意を向けた。 **2** N-UNCOUNT 不可算名詞 **Attention** is great interest that is shown in someone or something, particularly by the general public. 注目 □Volume Two, subtitled "The Lawyers," will also attract considerable attention. 『法律家』という副題を持つ第2巻もかなりの注目を集めるだろう。 **3** N-UNCOUNT 不可算名詞 If someone or something is getting **attention**, they are being dealt with or cared for. 配慮 □Each year more than two million household injuries need medical attention. 毎年家庭で起こる怪我の2百万件以上は医療措置が必要である。 **4** N-UNCOUNT 不可算名詞 If you **bring** something **to** someone's **attention** or **draw** their **attention** to it, you tell them about it or make them notice it. 注意 □If we don't keep bringing this to the attention of the people, nothing will be done. 我々がこのことに人々の注意を向けなければ，何もできないだろう。 **5** PHRASE 句 If someone or something **attracts** your **attention** or **catches** your **attention**, you suddenly notice them. 注意を引く □A faint aroma of coffee attracted his attention. コーヒーのかすかな香りが彼の注意を引いた。 **6** PHRASE 句 If you **pay attention to** someone, you

watch them, listen to them, or take notice of them. If you **pay no attention to** someone, you behave as if you are not aware of them or as if they are not important. 注意を払う ❑ *More than ever before, the food industry is paying attention to young consumers.* これまでにないほどに食料産業は若年消費者に注意を払っている. **7** PHRASE 句 When people **stand at attention**, they stand straight with their feet together and their arms at their sides. 気を付けの姿勢をとる ❑ *Soldiers in full combat gear stood at attention.* 完全防備の戦士たちが直立不動の姿勢をとった.

Word Partnership
attention は次の語句と使われる:

PREP.	attention **to** detail **1**
ADJ.	careful/close/undivided attention **1**
	special attention **1 – 3**
	unwanted attention **2**
	medical attention **3**
V.	catch *someone's* attention, focus attention, turn attention **to** *someone/something* **1 5**
	call/direct *someone's* attention **4**
	draw attention **4**
	attract attention **5**
	pay attention **6**
N.	center of attention **1**

at|ten|tive /ətɛntɪv/ **1** ADJ 形容詞 If you are **attentive**, you are paying close attention to what is being said or done. 注意深い ❑ *He wishes the government would be more attentive to detail in their response.* 彼は政府が彼らの反応の細目までよりいっそう心配りをすることを望んでいる. ● **at|ten|tive|ly** ADV 副詞 注意深く ❑ *He questioned Chrissie, and listened attentively to what she told him.* 彼はクリシーに質問し, 彼女が彼に語ることに注意深く耳を傾けた. **2** ADJ 形容詞 Someone who is **attentive** is helpful and polite. 思いやりのある ❑ *At society parties he is attentive to his wife.* 社交パーティーの場では, 彼は妻に対して思いやりを示す.

at|test /ətɛst/ (**attests, attesting, attested**) V-T/V-I 他動詞/自動詞 To **attest** something or **attest to** something means to say, show, or prove that it is true. 証明する [他動詞/自動詞] ❑ *Police records attest to his long history of violence.* 警察の記録が彼の長きに渡る暴行の履歴を立証する. [FORMAL 形式ばった]

at|tic /ætɪk/ (**attics**) N-COUNT 可算名詞 An **attic** is a room at the top of a house just below the roof. 屋根裏部屋 → see house

at|ti|tude /ætɪtud/ (**attitudes**) N-VAR 可変性名詞 Your **attitude to** something is the way that you think and feel about it, especially when this shows in the way you behave. 態度 ❑ *...the general change in attitude toward handicapped people.* 障害を持つ人々に対する態度の一般的な変化 ❑ *Being unemployed produces negative attitudes to work.* 失業状態は働くことへの消極的な態度を生み出す.

Word Partnership
attitude は次の語句と使われる:

PREP.	attitude **about/toward**
ADJ.	bad attitude, **negative/positive** attitude, **new** attitude, **progressive** attitude
V.	**change your** attitude

at|tor|ney /ətɜrni/ (**attorneys**) **1** N-COUNT 可算名詞 In the United States, an **attorney** or **attorney-at-law** is a lawyer. 弁護士 ❑ *...a prosecuting attorney.* 検察官 ❑ *At the hearing, her attorney did not enter a plea.* 審問で彼女の弁護士は無罪の申し立てをしなかった. **2** → see also state's attorney → see trial

Attorney General (**Attorneys General**) N-COUNT 可算名詞 A country's **Attorney General** is its chief law officer, who advises its government or ruler. 司法長官

at|tract /ətrækt/ (**attracts, attracting, attracted**) **1** V-T 他動詞 If something **attracts** people or animals, it has features that cause them to come to it. 引き寄せる ❑ *The Cardiff Bay project is attracting many visitors.* カーディフ湾の計画が多くの観光客を呼び込んでいる. **2** V-T 他動詞 If someone or something **attracts** you, they have particular qualities which cause you to like or admire them. If a particular quality **attracts** you **to** a person or thing, it is the reason why you like them. 引き付ける ❑ *He wasn't sure he'd got it right, although the theory attracted him by its logic.* 論理性ゆえにその理論は彼を引き付けたが, それが正しいかどうかの確信はなかった. **3** V-T 他動詞 If you **are attracted to** someone, you are interested in them sexually. 魅惑する ❑ *In spite of her hostility, she was attracted to him.* 敵意を感じながらも, 彼女は彼に魅せられた. ● **at|tract|ed** ADJ 形容詞 [v-link ADJ] 魅惑された ❑ *He was nice looking, but I wasn't deeply attracted to him.* 彼はハンサムだったが, 私は彼にそれほどの魅力を感じなかった. **4** V-T 他動詞 If something **attracts** support, publicity, or money, it receives support, publicity, or money. 誘致する ❑ *President Mwinyi said his country would also like to attract investment from private companies.* ムウィニ大

統領は自国で民間企業からの投資も誘致したいと述べた. **5** to **attract** someone's **attention** → see **attention** → see **magnet**

at|trac|tion /ətrækʃ°n/ (**attractions**) **1** N-UNCOUNT 不可算名詞 **Attraction** is a feeling of liking someone, and often of being sexually interested in them. 魅力 ❑ *Our level of attraction to the opposite sex has more to do with our inner confidence than how we look.* 異性を引き付ける魅力の強さは見かけよりも内なる自信と関係している. **2** N-COUNT 可算名詞 An **attraction** is a feature that makes something interesting or desirable. 魅力 ❑ *...the attractions of living on the waterfront.* 水辺の生活の魅力 **3** N-COUNT 可算名詞 An **attraction** is something that people can go to for interest or enjoyment, for example, a famous building. 呼び物 ❑ *The walled city is an important tourist attraction.* その城壁に囲まれた都市は重要な観光名所だ.

at|trac|tive /ətræktɪv/ **1** ADJ 形容詞 A person who is **attractive** is pleasant to look at. 魅力的な ❑ *She's a very attractive woman.* 彼女はとても魅力のある女性だ. ❑ *I thought he was very attractive and obviously very intelligent.* 彼のことはとても魅力的で, 明らかにとても聡明な方だと思った. ● **at|trac|tive|ness** N-UNCOUNT 不可算名詞 魅力 ❑ *Most of us would maintain that physical attractiveness does not play a major part in how we react to the people we meet.* たいていの人が, 肉体的魅力は人と出合った際の反応に大きな影響を及ぼさないと主張するだろう.

> When you are describing someone's appearance, you generally use **pretty** and **beautiful** to describe women, girls, and babies. **Beautiful** is a much stronger word than **pretty**. The equivalent word for a man is **handsome**. **Good-looking** and **attractive** can be used to describe people of either sex. **Pretty** can also be used to modify adjectives and adverbs but is less strong than **very**. In this sense, **pretty** is informal.

2 ADJ 形容詞 Something that is **attractive** has a pleasant appearance or sound. 魅力的な ❑ *The apartment was small but attractive, if rather shabby.* そのアパートは, 多少傷んではいるものの, 小さいが魅力的だった. **3** ADJ 形容詞 You can describe something as **attractive** when it seems worth having or doing. 興味をそそる ❑ *Smoking is still attractive to many young people who see it as glamorous.* 喫煙はいまだにそれを魅惑的だとみなす多くの若者を引きつけている.

Thesaurus
attractive また次を参照:

ADJ.	appealing, charming, good-looking, pleasant; (*ant.*) repulsive, ugly, unappealing, unattractive **1 2**

Word Link
tribute ≈ giving : **attribute, contribute, distribute**

at|trib|ute (**attributes, attributing, attributed**)

> The verb is pronounced /ətrɪbyut/. The noun is pronounced /ætrɪbyut/.
>
> 動詞は /ətrɪbyut/ と発音される. 名詞は /ætrɪbyut/ と発音される.

1 V-T 他動詞 If you **attribute** something **to** an event or situation, you think that it was caused by that event or situation. 帰する ❑ *Women tend to attribute their success to external causes such as luck.* 女性は自分の成功を運などの外的な要因のせいにする傾向がある. **2** V-T 他動詞 If you **attribute** a particular quality or feature **to** someone or something, you think that they have it. (物や人に性質などが) あるとする ❑ *People were beginning to attribute superhuman qualities to him.* 人々は彼に超人的な要素を認め始めていた. **3** V-T 他動詞 If a piece of writing, a work of art, or a remark **is attributed to** someone, people say that they wrote it, created it, or said it. (特定の作家の) 手になるものとする [usu passive] ❑ *This, and the remaining frescoes, are not attributed to Giotto.* この作品およびその残っているフレスコ画はジョットの手になるものではない. **4** N-COUNT 可算名詞 An **attribute** is a quality or feature that someone or something has. 属性 ❑ *Cruelty is a normal attribute of human behavior.* 残酷さは人間行動の正常な性質である.

auber|gine /oʊbɜrʒin/ N-VAR 可変性名詞 → see **eggplant**

auburn /ɔbərn/ COLOR 色彩語 **Auburn** hair is reddish brown. 赤褐色の ❑ *...a tall woman with long auburn hair.* 長い赤褐色の髪の背の高い女性

auc|tion /ɔkʃ°n/ (**auctions, auctioning, auctioned**) **1** N-VAR 可変性名詞 An **auction** is a public sale where items are sold to the person who offers the highest price. 競売 ❑ *The painting is expected to fetch up to $400,000 at auction.* その絵画は競売で40万ドルの値をつけると期待されている. **2** V-T 他動詞 If something **is auctioned**, it is sold in an auction. 競売にかける ❑ *Eight drawings by French artist Jean Cocteau will be auctioned next week.* 来週フランス人芸術家ジャン・コクトーの8点の素描が競売にかけられる. ▸ **auction off** PHRASAL VERB 句動詞 If you **auction off** something, you sell it to the person who offers most for it, often at an auction.

A

競売で売る ❑Any fool could auction off a factory full of engineering machinery. どんな愚か者でも機械設備を満載した工場を競売で処分することはできるだろう.

auc|tion|eer /ɔːkʃənɪər/ (**auctioneers**) N-COUNT 可算名詞 An **auctioneer** is a person in charge of an auction. 競売人

auda|cious /ɔːdeɪʃəs/ ADJ 形容詞 Someone who is **audacious** takes risks in order to achieve something. 大胆な ❑...an audacious plan to win the presidency. 大統領の地位を勝ち取るための大胆な計画 ❑He was known for risky tactics that ranged from audacious to outrageous. 彼は大胆なものから無法とも言えるものまで危険な戦略をとることで知られていた.

audac|ity /ɔːdæsɪti/ N-UNCOUNT 不可算名詞 **Audacity** is audacious behavior. 大胆さ ❑I was shocked at the audacity of the gangsters. 私は暴力団員たちの大胆さに衝撃を受けた.

audible /ɔːdɪbəl/ ADJ 形容詞 A sound that is **audible** is loud enough to be heard. 聞こえる ❑The Colonel's voice was barely audible. 大佐の声はかろうじて聞き取れた. ● **audibly** /ɔːdɪbli/ ADV 副詞 聞こえるように ❑Frank sighed audibly. フランクは聞き取れるほどのため息をついた.

audi|ence /ɔːdiəns/ (**audiences**) **1** N-COUNT-COLL 集合可算名詞 The **audience** at a play, concert, film, or public meeting is the group of people watching or listening to it. 聴衆 ❑The entire audience broke into loud applause. 聴衆全員が盛大な拍手を送った. **2** N-COUNT-COLL 集合可算名詞 The **audience** for a television or radio program consists of all the people who watch or listen to it. 視聴者 ❑The concert will be broadcast to a worldwide television audience estimated at one billion. その演奏会は世界中の推定10億人のテレビ視聴者に放送されるでしょう. **3** N-COUNT-COLL 集合可算名詞 The **audience** of a writer or artist is the people who read their books or look at their work. 読者, 支持者 ❑Say's writings reached a wide audience during his lifetime. セイの著作は, 彼の生涯を通じて広範な読者を得た.

→ see **concert**, **theater**

audio /ɔːdioʊ/ ADJ 形容詞 **Audio** equipment is used for recording and reproducing sound. 音の [ADJ n] ❑The software was the first to offer access to audio and video files. そのソフトは音声ファイルおよび動画ファイルを扱うことのできる初めてのものであった.

audio|tape /ɔːdioʊteɪp/ also **audio tape** N-UNCOUNT 不可算名詞 **Audiotape** is magnetic tape used to record sound. 音声テープ ❑Unfortunately, fewer than 5 percent of books are now available in Braille or audiotape. 残念ながら, 点字あるいは音声テープで入手できる書籍は5パーセント未満である.

audio|visual /ɔːdioʊvɪʒuəl/ also **audio-visual** ADJ 形容詞 **Audio-visual** equipment and materials involve both recorded sound and pictures. 視聴覚の [ADJ n]

audit /ɔːdɪt/ (**audits, auditing, audited**) V-T 他動詞 When an accountant **audits** an organization's accounts, he or she examines the accounts officially in order to make sure that they have been done correctly. (会計の) 監査をする ❑Each year they audit our accounts and certify them as being true and fair. 毎年彼らは我々の会計を監査し, 真正かつ公正であることを認証する. ● N-COUNT 可算名詞 **Audit** is also a noun. 監査 ❑The bank first learned of the problem when it carried out an internal audit. その銀行は内部監査を行い, 初めてその問題を把握した.

audi|tion /ɔːdɪʃən/ (**auditions, auditioning, auditioned**) **1** N-COUNT 可算名詞 An **audition** is a short performance given by an actor, dancer, or musician so that a director or conductor can decide if they are good enough to be in a play, film, or orchestra. 審査, オーディション ❑...an audition for a Broadway musical. ブロードウェイのミュージカルのためのオーディション **2** V-T/V-I 他動詞/自動詞 If you **audition** or if someone **auditions** you, you do an audition. 審査する [他動詞], 審査を受ける [自動詞] ❑I was auditioning for the part of a jealous girlfriend. 私は嫉妬深い恋人役のオ

ーディションを受けていた. ❑They're auditioning new members for the cast of "Miss Saigon" today. 今日『ミス・サイゴン』の配役のための新人のオーディションを行っている.

audi|tor /ɔːdɪtər/ (**auditors**) N-COUNT 可算名詞 An **auditor** is an accountant who officially examines the accounts of organizations. 監査官

audi|to|rium /ɔːdɪtɔːriəm/ (**auditoriums** or **auditoria** /ɔːdɪtɔːriə/) **1** N-COUNT 可算名詞 An **auditorium** is the part of a theater or concert hall where the audience sits. 観客席 ❑Anderson was to sing at the Constitution Hall auditorium. アンダーソンは憲法記念館で歌う予定だった. **2** N-COUNT 可算名詞 An **auditorium** is a large room, hall, or building that is used for events such as meetings and concerts. 講堂 [AM 米国英語] ❑...a high school auditorium. 高校の講堂

Aug. Aug. is a written abbreviation for **August**. 8月

aug|ment /ɔːgmɛnt/ (**augments, augmenting, augmented**) V-T 他動詞 To **augment** something means to make it larger, stronger, or more effective by adding something to it. 増大させる [FORMAL 形式ばった] ❑While searching for a way to augment the family income, she began making dolls. 家計収入を増やす方途を探っている間に, 彼女は人形作りを始めた.

August /ɔːgəst/ (**Augusts**) N-VAR 可変性名詞 **August** is the eighth month of the year in the Western calendar. 8月 ❑The world premiere took place in August 1956. 世界初演は1956年8月に行われた. ❑The trial will resume on August the twenty-second. 公判は8月22日に再開する.

aunt /ænt, ɑːnt/ (**aunts**) N-FAMILY; N-TITLE 家族名詞, 称号名詞 Someone's **aunt** is the sister of their mother or father, or the wife of their uncle. 叔母, 伯母 ❑She wrote to her aunt in Alabama. 彼女はアラバマのおばに手紙を書いた.

→ see **family**

auntie /ænti, ɑːnti/ (**aunties**) also **aunty** N-FAMILY; N-TITLE 家族名詞, 称号名詞 Someone's **auntie** is their aunt. おばちゃん [INFORMAL くだけた] ❑His uncle is dead, but his auntie still lives here. 彼のおじは亡くなったが, おばさんはまだここで暮らしている.

au pair /oʊ pɛər/ (**au pairs**) N-COUNT 可算名詞 An **au pair** is a young person from a foreign country who lives with a family in order to learn the language and who helps to take care of the children. オペア

aura /ɔːrə/ (**auras**) N-COUNT 可算名詞 An **aura** is a quality or feeling that seems to surround a person or place or to come from them. 雰囲気 ❑She had an aura of authority. 彼女には威光がただよっていた.

aus|pices /ɔːspɪsɪz/ PHRASE 句 If something is done **under the auspices of** a particular person or organization, or **under** someone's **auspices**, it is done with their support and approval. 後援で [FORMAL 形式ばった] ❑...to meet and discuss peace under the auspices of the United Nations. 国連の後援で会合を持ち, 平和に関して討議するため

aus|tere /ɔːstɪər/ **1** ADJ 形容詞 If you describe something as **austere**, you approve of its plain and simple appearance. 質素な [APPROVAL 賛成] ❑...a cream linen suit and austere black blouse. 乳白色の亜麻布のスーツと質素な黒のブラウス **2** ADJ 形容詞 If you describe someone as **austere**, you disapprove of them because they are strict and serious. 厳格な [DISAPPROVAL 不賛成] ❑I found her a rather austere, distant, somewhat cold person. 彼女はかなり厳格で, よそよそしく, どことなく冷たい人物であると思われた. **3** ADJ 形容詞 An **austere** way of life is one that is simple and without luxuries. 簡素な ❑The life of the troops was still comparatively austere. 部隊の生活はやはり比較的簡素だ. **4** ADJ 形容詞 An **austere** economic policy is one that reduces people's living standards sharply. 耐乏の ❑...a set of very austere economic measures to control inflation. インフレ抑制のため極めて切り詰めた一連の経済政策

aus|ter|ity /ɔːstɛrɪti/ N-UNCOUNT 不可算名詞 **Austerity** is a situation in which people's living standards are reduced because of economic difficulties. 耐乏 ❑...the years of austerity which followed the war. 戦後の耐乏生活の数年間

authen|tic /ɔːθɛntɪk/ **1** ADJ 形容詞 An **authentic** person, object, or emotion is genuine. 真正の ❑...authentic Italian food. 本物のイタリアの食べ物 ❑She has authentic charm whereas most people simply have nice manners. たいていの人が単に礼儀正しいだけであるのに, 彼女は真の魅力を備えている. ● **au|then|tic|ity** /ɔːθɛntɪsɪti/ N-UNCOUNT 不可算名詞 本物であること ❑There are factors, however, that have cast doubt on the statue's authenticity. しかしながら, その立像が本物であることを疑わせる要素がある. **2** ADJ 形容詞 If you describe something as **authentic**, you mean that it is such a good imitation that it is almost the same as or as good as the original. 忠実な [APPROVAL 賛成] ❑...patterns for making authentic frontier-style clothing. 開拓時代の様式に忠実な服をつくるための型紙 **3** ADJ 形容詞 An **authentic** piece of information or account of something is reliable and accurate. 信頼できる ❑I had obtained the authentic details about the birth of the organization. その組織の成立に

a

関して信頼できる詳細を入手していた.

> **Word Link** er, or ≈ one who does, that which does : astronomer, author, writer

author /ɔθər/ (authors) **1** N-COUNT 可算名詞 The **author** of a piece of writing is the person who wrote it. 著者 [oft N 'of' n] ❑ ...Jill Phillips, author of the book "Give Your Child Music." 『子供に音楽を』という本の著者, ジル・フィリップ **2** N-COUNT 可算名詞 An **author** is a person whose job is writing books. 作家 ❑ Haruki Murakami is Japan's best-selling author. 村上春樹は日本のベストセラー作家だ.

author|ise /ɔθəraɪz/ → see **authorize**

> **Word Link** arian ≈ believing in, having : authoritarian, humanitarian, vegetarian

authori|tar|ian /əθɔrɪtɛəriən/ ADJ 形容詞 If you describe a person or an organization as **authoritarian**, you are critical of them controlling everything rather than letting people decide things for themselves. 権威主義の, 独裁主義的な [DISAPPROVAL 不賛成] ❑ Senior officers could be considering a coup to restore authoritarian rule. 上級将校たちは独裁主義的支配を回復するためのクーデターを考えているかもしれないだろう.

authori|ta|tive /əθɔrɪteɪtɪv/ **1** ADJ 形容詞 Someone or something that is **authoritative** gives an impression of power and importance and is likely to be obeyed. 権威のある ❑ He has a commanding presence and deep, authoritative voice. 彼は堂々とした外見と太くて低い権威のある声を持っている **2** ADJ 形容詞 Someone or something that is **authoritative** has a lot of knowledge of a particular subject. 権威ある, 信頼できる ❑ The first authoritative study of polio was published in 1840. ポリオに関する最初の信頼にたる研究は1840年に出版された.

author|ity /əθɔrɪti/ (authorities) **1** N-PLURAL 複数名詞 The **authorities** are the people who have the power to make decisions and to make sure that laws are obeyed. 官憲 ❑ This provided a pretext for the authorities to cancel the elections. このことは官憲が選挙を中止する口実を与えた. **2** N-COUNT 可算名詞 An **authority** is an official organization or government department that has the power to make decisions. 公共機関 ❑ ...the Philadelphia Parking Authority. フィラデルフィア市駐車担当局 **3** → see also **local authority** **4** N-COUNT 可算名詞 Someone who is an **authority** on a particular subject knows a lot about it. 権威, 大家 ❑ He's universally recognized as an authority on Russian affairs. 彼は世界中でロシア問題に関する権威と見なされている. **5** N-UNCOUNT 不可算名詞 **Authority** is the right to command and control other people. 権力 ❑ A family member in a family business has a position of authority and power. 家族経営の会社では家族の1員が権力の地位にいる. **6** N-UNCOUNT 不可算名詞 If someone has **authority**, they have a quality which makes other people take notice of what they say. 権威 ❑ He had no natural authority and no capacity for imposing his will on others. 彼には自然な権威が欠けており, 自分の意思を他人に押し付ける能力もない. **7** N-UNCOUNT 不可算名詞 **Authority** is official permission to do something. 認可 ❑ The prison governor has refused to let him go, saying he must first be given authority from his own superiors. まず自分自身の上司の認可が必要だと言い, 刑務所長は彼の釈放を拒んだ.

author|ize /ɔθəraɪz/ (authorizes, authorizing, authorized) V-T 他動詞 If someone in a position of authority **authorizes** something, they give their official permission for it to happen. 認可する ❑ It would certainly be within his power to authorize a police raid like that. そのような警察の踏み込み捜査を認可することは, 間違いなく彼の権限に含まれるだろう. ●**authori|za|tion** /ɔθərɪzeɪʃ³n/ N-VAR 可変性名詞 (authorizations) 認可 ❑ The United Nations will approve his request for authorization to use military force to deliver aid. 国際連合は援助実施のための軍事力行使の認可を求める彼の要求を受け入れるだろう.

autism /ɔtɪzəm/ N-UNCOUNT 不可算名詞 **Autism** is a severe mental disorder that makes someone unable to respond to other people. 自閉症

auto /ɔtoʊ/ (autos) N-COUNT 可算名詞 An **auto** is a car. 自動車 [AM 米国英語] ❑ ...the auto industry. 自動車産業

auto|bio|graphi|cal /ɔtoʊbaɪəgræfɪkªl/ ADJ 形容詞 An **autobiographical** piece of writing relates to events in the life of the person who has written it. 自伝的な ❑ ...a highly autobiographical novel of a woman's search for identity. 女性の自己探求に関する極めて自伝的な小説

auto|bi|og|ra|phy /ɔtəbaɪɒgrəfi/ (autobiographies) N-COUNT 可算名詞 Your **autobiography** is an account of your life, which you write yourself. 自伝 ❑ He published his autobiography last fall. 彼は昨秋自伝を出版した.

> **Word Link** graph ≈ writing : autograph, biography, graph

auto|graph /ɔtəgræf/ (autographs, autographing, autographed) N-COUNT 可算名詞 An **autograph** is the signature of someone famous that is specially written for a fan to keep. 自署 ❑ He went backstage and asked for her autograph. 彼は彼女のサインをもらうため舞台裏に行った. **2** V-T 他動詞 If someone famous **autographs** something, they put their signature on it. 自署する ❑ I autographed a copy of one of my books. 私は自分の著作の1つの1冊にサインした.

auto|mate /ɔtəmeɪt/ (automates, automating, automated) V-T 他動詞 To **automate** a factory, office, or industrial process means to put in machines that can do the work instead of people. 自動化する ❑ He wanted to use computers to automate the process. 彼はその過程を自動化するためにコンピュータを使いたかった. ●**auto|ma|tion** /ɔtəmeɪʃ³n/ N-UNCOUNT 不可算名詞 自動化 ❑ In the last ten years automation has reduced the work force here by half. この10年間の自動化により, ここの労働力は半減した. → see **factory**

auto|mat|ed /ɔtəmeɪtɪd/ ADJ 形容詞 An **automated** factory, office, or industrial process uses machines to do the work instead of people. 自動化した ❑ The equipment was made on highly automated production lines. その備品は高度に自動化した生産ラインで作られた.

> **Word Link** auto ≈ self : automatic, automobile, autonomy

auto|mat|ic /ɔtəmætɪk/ (automatics) **1** ADJ 形容詞 An **automatic** machine or device is one that has controls that enable it to perform a task without needing to be constantly operated by a person. **Automatic** methods and processes involve the use of such machines. 自動の ❑ Modern trains have automatic doors. 現代の列車には自動ドアがある. **2** ADJ 形容詞 An **automatic** weapon is one that keeps firing shots until you stop pulling the trigger. 自動の [ADJ n] ❑ Three gunmen with automatic rifles opened fire. 自動式ライフルを持った3人の殺し屋が発砲した. ●N-COUNT 可算名詞 **Automatic** is also a noun. 自動式機械 ❑ He drew his automatic and began running in the direction of the sounds. 彼は自動小銃を抜き取り, 音の方向に走り始めた. **3** ADJ 形容詞 An **automatic** action is one that you do without thinking about it. 不随意の ❑ All of the automatic body functions, even breathing, are affected. 呼吸までをも含む全ての不随意的身体機能が影響を受ける. ●**auto|mati|cal|ly** /ɔtəmætɪkli/ ADV 副詞 不随意で ❑ You will automatically wake up after this length of time. この時間が経過するとひとりでに目が覚めるでしょう. **4** N-COUNT 可算名詞 An **automatic** is a car in which the gears change automatically as the car's speed increases or decreases. オートマチック車

> **Word Link** mobil ≈ moving : automobile, mobile, mobilize

auto|mo|bile /ɔtəməbil/ (automobiles) N-COUNT 可算名詞 An **automobile** is a car. 自動車 [mainly AM 主に米国英語] ❑ ...the automobile industry. 自動車産業 → see **car**

autono|mous /ɔtɒnəməs/ **1** ADJ 形容詞 An **autonomous** country, organization, or group governs or controls itself rather than being controlled by anyone else. 自治権のある ❑ They proudly declared themselves part of a new autonomous province. 彼らは新しい自治区の1員となることを誇らかに宣言した. **2** ADJ 形容詞 An **autonomous** person makes their own decisions rather than being influenced by someone else. 自立した, 自律できる ❑ He treated us as autonomous individuals who had to learn to make up our own minds about issues. 彼は物事を自分で決めることを知らねばならない自立した個人として我々を扱った.

autono|my /ɔtɒnəmi/ **1** N-UNCOUNT 不可算名詞 **Autonomy** is the control or government of a country, organization, or group by itself rather than by others. 自律, 自立 ❑ Activists stepped up their demands for local autonomy last month. 先月活動家たちは地方自治を求める彼らの要求を強めた. **2** N-UNCOUNT 不可算名詞 **Autonomy** is the ability to make your own decisions about what to do rather than being influenced by someone else or told what to do. 自主性 [FORMAL 形式ばった] ❑ Each of the area managers enjoys considerable autonomy in the running of his own area. 各地域責任者は, その担当地域の運営に関してかなりの自主決定権をもっている.

autop|sy /ɔtɒpsi/ (autopsies) N-COUNT 可算名詞 An **autopsy** is an examination of a dead body by a doctor who cuts it open in order to try to discover the cause of death. 検視 ❑ Macklin had the grim task of carrying out an autopsy on his friend. マックリンには自分の友人の検視をするというつらい仕事があった.

autumn /ɔtəm/ (autumns) N-VAR 可変性名詞 **Autumn** is the season between summer and winter when the weather becomes cooler and the leaves fall off the trees. 秋 [mainly BRIT 主に英国英語; AM usually **fall** 米国英語では通常 **fall**]

aux|il|ia|ry /ɔgzɪlyəri, -zɪləri/ (auxiliaries) **1** ADJ 形容詞 **Auxiliary** equipment is extra equipment that is available for use when necessary. 予備の [ADJ n] ❑ ...an auxiliary motor. 予備発動機 **2** ADJ 形容詞 **Auxiliary** staff and troops assist other staff and troops. 補助の [ADJ n] ❑ The government's first concern was to augment the army and auxiliary forces. 政府の第1の関心事は陸軍と予備戦力を拡

A

大することであった. 3 N-COUNT 可算名詞 An **auxiliary** is a person who is employed to assist other people in their work. Auxiliaries are often medical workers or members of the armed forces. 助手 ❑ *Nursing auxiliaries provide basic care, but are not qualified nurses.* 看護助手は基礎的な世話をするが，有資格看護士ではない. 4 N-COUNT 可算名詞 In grammar, an **auxiliary** or **auxiliary verb** is a verb that is used with a main verb, for example, to form different tenses or to make the verb passive. In English, the basic auxiliary verbs are "be," "have," and "do." Modal verbs such as "can" and "will" are also sometimes called auxiliaries. 助動詞

avail /əveɪl/ (avails, availing, availed) 1 PHRASE 句 If you do something **to no avail** or **to little avail**, what you do fails to achieve what you want. 全く役に立たない，ほとんど役に立たない [WRITTEN 書き言葉] ❑ *His efforts were to no avail.* 彼の努力はむだに終わった. 2 V-T 他動詞 If you **avail yourself of** an offer or an opportunity, you accept the offer or make use of the opportunity. (機会を) 利用する [FORMAL 形式ばった] ❑ *Guests should feel at liberty to avail themselves of your facilities.* 訪問者が自由に施設を利用できると思えるようにすべきだ.

avail|able /əveɪləbᵊl/ 1 ADJ 形容詞 If something you want or need is **available**, you can find it or obtain it. 手に入る ❑ *Since 1978, the amount of money available to buy books has fallen by 17%.* 1978年以来，本の購入に使える金額は17パーセント落ち込んでいる. ❑ *The store has about 500 autographed copies of the book available for purchase.* その店はその本の署名本を約500部抱えていて，購入可能である. ● avail|abil|ity /əveɪləbɪliti/ N-UNCOUNT 不可算名詞 入手可能性 ❑ *...the easy availability of guns.* 銃が容易に入手できること 2 ADJ 形容詞 [v-link ADJ] Someone who is **available** is not busy and is therefore free to talk to you or to do a particular task. 求めに応じられる ❑ *Mr. Leach is on holiday and was not available for comment.* リーチ氏は休暇を取っており，コメントをもらえなかった.

Thesaurus		*available* また次を参照:
ADJ.	accessible, handy, obtainable, usable 1	
	free, unoccupied 2	

Word Partnership		*available* は次の語句と使われる:
N.	available **information**, available **opportunities/options**, available **resources** 1	
ADV.	**readily** available, **widely** available **currently/now** available 1 2	
PREP.	available **on request** 1	
	available **for something** 2	
V.	**make yourself** available 2	

ava|lanche /ævəlæntʃ/ (avalanches) N-COUNT 可算名詞 An **avalanche** is a large mass of snow that falls down the side of a mountain. 雪崩

avant-garde /ævɒŋɡɑrd/ ADJ 形容詞 **Avant-garde** art, music, theater, and literature is very modern and experimental. 前衛的な ❑ *...avant-garde concert music.* 前衛的な演奏会用音楽

avenge /əvɛndʒ/ (avenges, avenging, avenged) V-T 他動詞 If you **avenge** a wrong or harmful act, you hurt or punish the person who is responsible for it. 復しゅうする ❑ *He has devoted the past five years to avenging his daughter's death.* 彼は娘の死の敵を討つためにこの5年間費やしてきた.

av|enue /ævɪnyu, -nu/ (avenues) 1 N-IN-NAMES 名称中の名詞 **Avenue** is sometimes used in the names of streets. The written abbreviation **Ave.** is also used. 通り ❑ *...the most expensive apartments on Park Avenue.* 公園通りに面した最も高価なアパート 2 N-COUNT 可算名詞 An **avenue** is a wide, straight road, especially one with trees on either side. 大通り

av|er|age /ævərɪdʒ, ævrɪdʒ/ (averages, averaging, averaged) 1 N-COUNT 可算名詞 An **average** is the result that you get when you add two or more numbers together and divide the total by the number of numbers you added together. 平均 ❑ *Take the average of those ratios and multiply by a hundred.* この比率の平均を取って100倍する. ● ADJ 形容詞 **Average** is also an adjective. 平均の [ADJ n] ❑ *The average price of goods rose by just 2.2%.* 商品の平均価格はちょうど2.2パーセントだけ上がった. 2 N-SING 単数名詞 You use **average** to refer to a number or size that varies but is always approximately the same. 標準 ❑ *It takes an average of ten weeks for a house sale to be completed.* 住宅販売の完了には通常10週間を要する. 3 N-SING 単数名詞 An amount or quality that is **the average** is the normal amount or quality for a particular group of things or people. 並み ❑ *35% of staff time was being spent on repeating work, about the average for a service industry.* サービス産業の通例として，従業員の労働時間の35パーセントが繰り返し作業に費やされていた. ● ADJ 形容詞 **Average** is also an adjective. 並みの ❑ *$2.20 for a beer is average.* ビール1本2.2ドルは普通である. 4 ADJ 形容詞 An **average** person or thing is typical or normal. 標準的な [ADJ n] ❑ *The average adult man burns 1,500 to 2,000 calories per day.* 標準的な成人男性は1日1,500

から2,000カロリーを消費する. 5 ADJ 形容詞 Something that is **average** is neither very good nor very bad, usually when you had hoped it would be better. 並みの ❑ *I was only average academically.* 私は学問的には平凡な人間に過ぎなかった. 6 V-T 他動詞 To **average** a particular amount means to do, get, or produce that amount as an average over a period of time. 平均する ❑ *We averaged 42 miles per hour.* 我々は平均時速42マイル出した. 7 PHRASE 句 You say **on average** or **on the average** to indicate that a number is the average of several numbers. 平均で ❑ *Shares rose, on average, by 38%.* 株価は平均で38パーセント上昇した.

aver|sion /əvɜrʒᵊn/ (aversions) N-VAR 可変性名詞 If you have an **aversion to** someone or something, you dislike them very much. 嫌悪 ❑ *Many people have a natural and emotional aversion to insects.* 昆虫に自然でかつ感情的な嫌悪感を抱いている人が多い.

avert /əvɜrt/ (averts, averting, averted) 1 V-T 他動詞 If you **avert** something unpleasant, you prevent it from happening. 避ける ❑ *Talks with the teachers' union over the weekend have averted a strike.* 週末の教職員組合との話し合いでストライキが回避された. 2 V-T 他動詞 If you **avert** your eyes or gaze **from** someone or something, you look away from them. 反らす ❑ *He avoids any eye contact, quickly averting his gaze when anyone approaches.* 彼は誰とも眼を合わせようとせず，誰かが近づくとすばやく目を反らす.

aviary /eɪvieri/ (aviaries) N-COUNT 可算名詞 An **aviary** is a large cage or covered area in which birds are kept. 鳥類飼育場

avia|tion /eɪvieɪʃᵊn/ N-UNCOUNT 不可算名詞 **Aviation** is the operation and production of aircraft. 航空術 ❑ *...the aviation industry.* 航空産業

avid /ævɪd/ ADJ 形容詞 You use **avid** to describe someone who is very enthusiastic about something that they do. 熱心な ❑ *He misses not having enough books because he's an avid reader.* 彼は大変な読書家であるので，手元に十分な本を欠かすことはない. ● av|id|ly ADV 副詞 [ADV with v] 熱心に ❑ *Thank you for a most entertaining magazine, which I read avidly each month.* 大変に面白い雑誌をありがとう. それを毎月夢中で読んでいます.

avo|ca|do /ævəkɑdoʊ/ (avocados) N-VAR 可変性名詞 **Avocados** are pear-shaped vegetables, with hard skins and large seeds, which are usually eaten raw. アボカド

avoid /əvɔɪd/ (avoids, avoiding, avoided) 1 V-T 他動詞 If you **avoid** something unpleasant that might happen, you take action in order to prevent it from happening. 避ける ❑ *The pilots had to take emergency action to avoid a disaster.* 飛行士たちは惨事を避けるため緊急行動をとらねばならなかった. 2 V-T 他動詞 If you **avoid** doing something, you choose not to do it, or you put yourself in a situation where you do not have to do it. 避ける ❑ *By borrowing from dozens of banks, he managed to avoid giving any of them an overall picture of what he was up to.* 何十もの銀行から融資を受けることで，どこの銀行にも彼がやろうとしていることの全体像を知られることをなんとか避けた. 3 V-T 他動詞 If you **avoid** a person or thing, you keep away from them. When talking to someone, if you **avoid** the subject, you keep the conversation away from a particular topic. 避ける ❑ *She eventually had to lock herself in the women's restroom to avoid him.* ついに彼女は彼を避けるため女性用トイレに入り鍵をかけねばならなかった. 4 V-T 他動詞 If a person or vehicle **avoids** someone or something, they change the direction they are moving in, so that they do not hit them. よける ❑ *The driver had ample time to brake or swerve and avoid the woman.* 運転手には，ブレーキをかけるか，ハンドルを切ってその女性をよける十分な時間があった.

Thesaurus		*avoid* また次を参照:
V.	abstain, bypass, evade, shun; *(ant.)* confront, embrace, face, seek 1 – 4	

await /əweɪt/ (awaits, awaiting, awaited) 1 V-T 他動詞 If you **await** someone or something, you wait for them. 待つ [FORMAL 形式ばった] ❑ *Very little was said as we awaited the arrival of the chairman.* 議長の到着を待つ間，ほとんどなにも発言はなかった. 2 V-T 他動詞 Something that **awaits** you is going to happen or come to you in the future. 待ち受ける [FORMAL 形式ばった] ❑ *A surprise awaited them in Wal-Mart.* ウォルマートで驚くべきことが彼らを待ち受けていた.

Thesaurus		*await* また次を参照:
V.	anticipate, count on, expect, hope 1	

Word Link		*wak* ≈ being awake : *a*wake, *a*wakening, wake

awake /əweɪk/ 1 ADJ 形容詞 Someone who is **awake** is not sleeping. 目が覚めて [v-link ADJ, ADJ after v] ❑ *I don't stay awake at night worrying about that.* 夜あのことを気にかけて眠れないなどということはない. 2 PHRASE 句 Someone who is **wide awake** is fully awake and unable to sleep. 完全に目を覚まして ❑ *I could not relax and still felt wide awake.* 私はくつろぐことが出来ず，まだすっかり目

を覚ましていた.
→ see **dream, sleep**

Word Partnership *awake* は次の語句と使われる:

V.	keep *someone* awake, lie awake, stay awake 1
ADV.	fully awake, half awake 1
	wide awake 2

---

awak|en|ing /əweɪkənɪŋ/ (**awakenings**) 1 N-COUNT 名詞 The **awakening** of a feeling or realization is the start of it. 目覚め ❏ ...the awakening of national consciousness in people. 人民の国家意識の目覚め 2 PHRASE 句 If you have a **rude awakening**, you are suddenly made aware of an unpleasant fact. つらい目覚め ❏ It was a rude awakening to learn after I left home that I wasn't so special anymore. 家を離れてから、もはや自分がそれほど特別に大切な人でないことを思い知るのは、つらい現実との直面だった.

award /əwɔrd/ (**awards, awarding, awarded**) 1 N-COUNT 可算名詞 An **award** is a prize or certificate that a person is given for doing something well. 賞 ❏ The Institute's annual award is presented to organizations that are dedicated to democracy and human rights. その協会の年度賞は民主主義と人権に献身的な組織に与えられる. 2 N-COUNT 可算名詞 In law, an **award** is a sum of money that a court decides should be given to someone. 裁定額 ❏ ...worker's compensation awards. 労働者の補償額 3 V-T 他動詞 If someone **is awarded** something such as a prize or an examination mark, it is given to them. 授賞する ❏ She was awarded the prize for both films. 彼女は両方の映画でその賞を与えられた. 4 V-T 他動詞 To **award** something **to** someone means to decide that it will be given to that person. 授与する ❏ We have awarded the contract to a New York-based company. ニューヨークに拠点を置く会社に請け負わせることにした.

Word Link *war* ≈ *watchful* : a**war**e, be**war**e, **war**y

---

aware /əwɛər/ 1 ADJ 形容詞 If you are **aware** of something, you know about it. 気づいて [v-link ADJ] ❏ Smokers are well aware of the dangers to their own health. 喫煙者は自分自身の健康への危険をよく知っている. ❏ He should have been aware of what his junior officers were doing. 彼は自分の下級将校たちのしていることに気づくべきだった. ● **aware|ness** N-UNCOUNT 不可算名詞 気づき ❏ The 1980s brought an awareness of green issues. 1980年代に環境問題への意識形成がなされた. 2 ADJ 形容詞 [v-link ADJ] If you are **aware** of something, you realize that it is present or is happening because you hear it, see it, smell it, or feel it. 気づいて ❏ She was acutely aware of the noise of the city. 彼女はその市の騒音に鋭く気づいた.

Word Partnership *aware* は次の語句と使われる:

ADV.	acutely/vaguely aware, fully aware, painfully aware, well aware 1 2
V.	become aware 1 2
PREP.	aware of *something/someone*, aware that 1 2

---

awash /əwɒʃ/ 1 ADJ 形容詞 If a place is **awash with** something, it contains a large amount of it. 満たされて [v-link ADJ] ❏ This is a company that is awash with cash. ここは現金をたっぷりと持った会社だ. 2 ADJ 形容詞 If the ground or a floor is **awash**, it is covered in water, often because of heavy rain or as the result of an accident. 冠水して [v-link ADJ] ❏ The bathroom floor was awash. 浴室の床に水があふれていた.

away /əweɪ/

Away is often used with verbs of movement, such as "go" and "drive," and also in phrasal verbs such as "do away with" and "fade away."

Away はしばしば **go** や **drive** のような移動の動詞と共に用いられ、また **do away with** や **fade away** のような句動詞にも用いられる.

1 ADV 副詞 If someone or something moves or is moved **away** from a place, they move or are moved so that they are no longer there. If you are **away** from a place, you are not in the place where people expect you to be. 離れて ❏ An injured policeman was led away by colleagues. けがをした警官が同僚に連れて行かれた. ❏ He walked away from his car. 彼は自分の車から歩いて離れた. ❏ Jason was away on a business trip. ジェイソンは出張で留守だった. 2 ADV 副詞 If you look or turn **away from** something, you move your head so that you are no longer looking at it. 離れて ❏ She quickly looked away and stared down at her hands. 彼女はすばやく視線をそらし、自分の両手をじっと見下ろした. 3 ADV 副詞 If you put something **away**, you put it where it should be. If you hide someone or something **away**, you put them in a place where nobody can see them or find them. あちらへ [ADV after v] ❏ I put my journal away and prepared for bed. 私は日記を脇にやり、寝る準備をした. ❏ All her letters were carefully filed away in folders. 彼女の手紙は全て書類入れに注意深く整

理保存されていた. 4 ADV 副詞 You use **away** to talk about future events. For example, if an event is a week **away**, it will happen after a week. 先に ['be' amount ADV] ❏ ...the Washington summit, now only just over two weeks away. 今やわずか2週間と少し後に迫っているワシントン首脳会談. 5 ADV 副詞 When a sports team plays **away**, it plays on its opponents' playing court or field. 遠征地で [ADV after v] ❏ ...a sensational 4-3 victory for the team playing away. 遠征地での対戦でチームの4対3の驚くべき勝利 ● ADJ 形容詞 **Away** is also an adjective. 遠征地の [ADJ n] ❏ Pittsburgh is about to play an important away game. ピッツバーグは重要な遠征試合をするところだ. 6 ADV 副詞 You can use **away** to say that something slowly disappears, becomes less significant, or changes so that it is no longer the same. 消えて [ADV after v] ❏ So much snow has already melted away. あんなにたくさんの雪がもう融け去った. ❏ His voice died away in a whisper. 彼の声はささやきになって絶えてしまった. 7 ADV 副詞 You use **away** to show that there has been a change or development from one state or situation to another. 去って ❏ British courts are increasingly moving away from sending young offenders to prison. 英国の法廷はますます若年犯罪者を刑務所に送らなくなっている. 8 ADV 副詞 You can use **away** to emphasize a continuous or repeated action. 絶えず [EMPHASIS 強調] [ADV after v] ❏ He would often be working away on his word processor late into the night. 彼はしばしば夜遅くまでワープロで作業を続けていたものだ. 9 ADV 副詞 You use **away** to show that something is removed. 除いて [ADV after v] ❏ If you take my work away I can't be happy anymore. あなたに仕事を奪われれば、もう私は幸せではおられません. 10 PHRASE 句 If something is **away from** a person or place, it is at a distance from that person or place. 離れて ❏ The two women were sitting as far away from each other as possible. その2人の女性はお互いにできるだけ離れて座っていた. 11 **right away** → see **right**

Word Partnership *away* は次の語句と使われる:

V.	back away, blow away, break away, chase *someone* away, drive away, hide away, move away, walk away
	get away, go away 1 6
	stay away 1 9 10
	look/turn away 2
	put away, throw away 3
	pull/take/wash *something* away 6
ADJ.	far away 1 4 10
N.	away from home 1 10

---

awe /ɔ/ (**awes, awed**) 1 N-UNCOUNT 不可算名詞 **Awe** is the feeling of respect and amazement that you have when you are faced with something wonderful and often rather frightening. 畏（おそ）れ ❏ She gazed in awe at the great stones. 彼女は畏怖（いふ）の念でその巨石群を見つめた. 2 V-T 他動詞 If you **are awed by** someone or something, they make you feel respectful and amazed, though often rather frightened. 畏れさせる [usu passive, no cont] ❏ I am still awed by David's courage. 私はまだデヴィッドの勇気に畏敬（いけい）を感じている.

Word Link *some* ≈ *causing* : awe**some**, fear**some**, trouble**some**

---

awe|some /ɔsəm/ 1 ADJ 形容詞 An **awesome** person or thing is very impressive and often frightening. おそるべき ❏ ...the awesome responsibility of sending men into combat. 兵士を戦場に送り込むという重大な責任 2 ADJ 形容詞 If you describe someone or something as **awesome**, you are emphasizing that you think that they are very impressive or extraordinary. 並外れた [INFORMAL くだけた, EMPHASIS 強調] ❏ Melvill called the flight "mind-blowing" and "awesome." メルヴィルはその飛行を「肝をつぶすよう」で「すさまじい」と表現した.

aw|ful /ɔfəl/ 1 ADJ 形容詞 If you say that someone or something is **awful**, you dislike that person or thing or you think that they are not very good. ひどい ❏ We met and I thought he was awful. 我々は出会い、私は彼を嫌なやつだと思った. ❏ ...an awful smell of paint. 塗料のひどい臭い 2 ADJ 形容詞 If you say that something is **awful**, you mean that it is extremely unpleasant, shocking, or bad. ひどい ❏ Her injuries were massive. It was awful. 彼女のけがは大きかった. ひどい有様だった. 3 ADJ 形容詞 If you look or feel **awful**, you look or feel ill. 気分が悪い [v-link ADJ] ❏ I hardly slept at all and felt pretty awful. 私はほとんどまったく眠れず、かなり気分が悪かった. 4 ADJ 形容詞 You can use **awful** with noun groups that refer to an amount in order to emphasize how large that amount is. すごい [EMPHASIS 強調] [ADJ n] ❏ I've got an awful lot of work to do. 私はする仕事がすごくたくさんある. ● **aw|ful|ly** ADV 副詞 すごく ❏ The caramel looks awfully good. キャラメルはすごくおいしそうだ.

Thesaurus *awful* また次を参照:

ADJ.	bad, dreadful, horrible, terrible; (*ant.*) good, nice, pleasing 1 2

awhile /əwaɪl/ ADV 副詞 **Awhile** means for a short time. しばら く □ *He worked awhile as a pharmacist in Cincinnati.* 彼はしばらくシン シナティで薬剤師として働いた.

awk|ward /ɔkwərd/ ◼ ADJ 形容詞 An **awkward** situation is embarrassing and difficult to deal with. 気まずい □ *I was the first to ask him awkward questions but there'll be harder ones to come.* 彼に 気まずい質問をしたのは私が初めてだったが，これからはもっと厄 介な質問があるだろう. ● **awk|ward|ly** ADV 副詞 [ADV adj/-ed] 気 まずく □ *There was an awkwardly long silence.* 気詰まりな長い沈黙 があった. ◼ ADJ 形容詞 Something that is **awkward to** use or carry is difficult to use or carry because of its design. A job that is **awkward** is difficult to do. 扱いにくい □ *It was small but heavy enough to make it awkward to carry.* それは小さかったが，重たくて運 びづらかった. ● **awk|ward|ly** ADV 副詞 [ADV -ed] 不格好に □ *The front window switches are awkwardly placed on the dashboard.* フロント ガラスのスイッチが計器盤の上に不細工に並んでいる. ◼ ADJ 形容詞 An **awkward** movement or position is uncomfortable or clumsy. ぎこちない □ *Amy made an awkward gesture with her hands.* エイミー は両手でぎこちない仕草をした. ● **awk|ward|ly** ADV 副詞 [ADV with v] ぎこちなく □ *He fell awkwardly and went down in agony clutching his right knee.* 彼は無様に転び，痛みのあまり右ひざを抱え倒れこん だ. ◼ ADJ 形容詞 Someone who feels **awkward** behaves in a shy or embarrassed way. きまりが悪い □ *Women frequently say that they feel awkward taking the initiative in sex.* 女性は性交の主導権をとること にきまり悪さを感じると女性がしばしば言っている. ● **awk|ward|ly** ADV 副詞 [ADV with v] 気まずげに □ *"This is Malcolm," the girl said awkwardly, to fill the silence.* 「こちらがマルコムです」と少女は沈黙か ら逃れるために気まずげに言った.

Thesaurus	*awkward* また次を参照:
ADJ.	delicate, embarrassing, sticky, uncomfortable ◼
	bulky, cumbersome, difficult ◼
	blundering, bumbling, uncoordinated, ungraceful ◼

awoke /əwouk/ **Awoke** is the past tense of **awake**. awakeの過 去形

awok|en /əwoukən/ **Awoken** is the past participle of **awake**. awakeの過去分詞

ax /æks/ (**axes, axing, axed**) ◼ N-COUNT 可算名詞 An **ax** is a tool used for cutting wood. It consists of a heavy metal blade that is sharp at one edge and attached by its other edge to the end of a long handle. おの ◼ V-T 他動詞 If someone's job or something such as a public service or a television program is **axed**, it is ended suddenly and without discussion. 打ち切る [usu passive] □ *Community projects are being axed by hard-pressed social services departments.* 地域の諸計画が社会福祉事業部門の財政難のため中止に 追い込まれている.

axes

Pronounced /æksɪz/ for meaning ◼, and /æksiz/ for meaning ◼.

◼ の意味では /æksɪz/ と，◼ /の意味では /æksiz/ と発音さ れる.

◼ **Axes** is the plural of **ax**. axの複数形 ◼ **Axes** is the plural of **axis**. axisの複数形

axis /æksɪs/ (**axes**) ◼ N-COUNT 可算名詞 An **axis** is an imaginary line through the middle of something. 軸 □ ...*the tilt of the Earth's axis.* 地軸の傾き ◼ N-COUNT 可算名詞 An **axis** of a graph is one of the two lines on which the scales of measurement are marked. 軸 □ *The level of spiritual achievement is plotted along the Y axis, and the degree of physical health is plotted along the X axis.* 精神的 成熟度はY軸に表し，身体的健康度はX軸に表す.

→ see **graph, moon**

Bb

B also b /biː/ (**B's, b's**) N-VAR 可変性名詞 **B** is the second letter of the English alphabet. 英語アルファベットの第2字

B2B /ˌbiː tuː ˈbiː/ N-UNCOUNT 不可算名詞 **B2B** is the selling of goods and services by one company to another using the Internet. **B2B** is an abbreviation for "business to business." 企業間取引, B2B [BUSINESS 実業] ❑ *American analysts have been somewhat cautious in estimating the size of the B2B market.* 米国のアナリストは、B2B市場規模の推定にいささか慎重であった.

B2C /ˌbiː tuː ˈsiː/ N-UNCOUNT 不可算名詞 **B2C** is the selling of goods and services by businesses to consumers using the Internet. **B2C** is an abbreviation for "business to consumer." 企業と一般消費者の取引, B2C [BUSINESS 実業] ❑ *B2C companies look particularly vulnerable with 19 per cent of them now worth little more than the cash on their balance sheets.* B2C企業は、現在貸借対照表上の現金以上の価値を持たないものが19%にもたらし、とりわけ脆弱に見える.

bab|ble /ˈbæbəl/ (**babbles, babbling, babbled**) ❶ V-I 自動詞 If someone **babbles**, they talk in a confused or excited way. ペチャクチャしゃべる ❑ *Momma babbled on and on about how he was ruining me.* ママは、彼がいかに私を甘やかしてだめにしているかについてくどくどとしゃべった. ❑ *They all babbled simultaneously.* 彼ら全員が一斉にがやがやと話した. ❷ N-SING 単数形名詞 You can refer to people's voices as a **babble of** sound when they are excited and confused, preventing you from understanding what they are saying. がやがやいう話し声 ❑ *Kemp knocked loudly so as to be heard above the high babble of voices.* ケンプはうるさいざわめきの中でも聞こえるように大きな音を立ててノックした.

baby /ˈbeɪbi/ (**babies**) ❶ N-COUNT 可算名詞 A **baby** is a very young child, especially one that cannot yet walk or talk. 赤ん坊 ❑ *She used to take care of me when I was a baby.* 彼女は私を赤ん坊のころ面倒をみてくれた. ❑ *My wife has just had a baby.* 妻は子供を生んだばかりだ. ❷ N-COUNT 可算名詞 A **baby** animal is a very young animal. 生まれたての動物 [usu N n] ❑ *...a baby elephant.* 象の赤ちゃん ❸ N-COUNT 可算名詞 If you refer to someone as a **baby**, you mean that they are behaving in a cowardly way or they are being too sensitive about something. 子供っぽい人 [DISAPPROVAL 不賛成] ❑ *I know he's an ex-champion boxer, but he can be a big baby sometimes! He hates spiders.* 彼ったら元ボクシング選手権保持者なのに、時々まるで子供みたいにクモを恐がるんだ. ❹ ADJ 形容詞 **Baby** vegetables are vegetables picked when they are very small. ベビー [ADJ n] ❑ *Cook the baby potatoes in their skins.* ベビーポテトを皮の付いたまま料理する. ❺ N-VOC; N-COUNT 呼格名詞, 可算名詞 Some people use **baby** as an affectionate way of addressing someone, especially a young woman, or referring to them. かわいい人 [INFORMAL くだけた] ❑ *You have to wake up now, baby.* さあ、そろそろ起きる時間よ、あなた.

→ see **child**

Word Partnership *baby* は次の語句と使われる:

N.	baby boy/girl/sister, baby clothes, baby food, baby names, baby talk ❶
V.	deliver a baby, have a baby ❶
ADJ.	new/newborn baby, unborn baby ❶

baby car|riage (**baby carriages**) N-COUNT 可算名詞 A **baby carriage** is a small vehicle in which a baby can lie as it is pushed along. 乳母車 [AM 米国英語]

baby|sit /ˈbeɪbisɪt/ (**babysits, babysitting, babysat**) V-T/V-I 他動詞/自動詞 If you **babysit for** someone or **babysit** their children, you look after their children while they are out. 子守をする ❑ *I promised to babysit for Mrs. Plunkett.* 私はプランケット夫人にベビーシッターの約束をした. ❑ *She had been babysitting him and his four-year-old sister.* 彼女は彼と4歳の妹の子守をしていた. ● **baby|sitter** N-COUNT 可算名詞 (**babysitters**) ベビーシッター ❑ *It can be difficult to find a good babysitter.* よいベビーシッターを見付けるのは難しいことがある.

bach|elor /ˈbætʃələr/ (**bachelors**) N-COUNT 可算名詞 A **bachelor** is a man who has never married. 独身の男 ❑ *...America's most eligible bachelor.* アメリカで結婚相手として最も望ましい男性

→ see **wedding**

---

back

❶ ADVERB USES
❷ OPPOSITE OF FRONT; NOUN AND ADJECTIVE USES
❸ VERB USES

❶ back /bæk/

In addition to the uses shown below, **back** is also used in phrasal verbs such as "date back" and "fall back on."

下に示された用法に加えて、**back** は date back や fall back on のような句動詞にも使われる.

↻ **Please look at category** 🔟 **to see if the expression you are looking for is shown under another headword.** ❶ ADV 副詞 If you move **back**, you move in the opposite direction to the one in which you are facing or in which you were moving before. 後ろへ ❑ *She stepped back from the door expectantly.* 彼女は予期したようにドアから後ずさりした. ❑ *He pushed her away and she fell back on the wooden bench.* 彼は彼女を押しやったので、彼女は木製ベンチにしりもちをついた. ❷ ADV 副詞 If you go **back** somewhere, you return to where you were before. 元の場所へ ❑ *I went back to bed.* 私は寝に戻った. ❑ *I'll be back as soon as I can.* できるだけすぐに戻ります. ❸ ADV 副詞 If someone or something is **back** in a particular state, they were in that state before and are now in it again. 元の状態へ ❑ *The rail company said it expected services to get slowly back to normal.* 鉄道会社は、業務は徐々に正常に復旧すると予測していると発表した. ❹ ADV 副詞 If you give or put something **back**, you return it to the person who had it or to the place where it was before you took it. If you get or take something **back**, you then have it again after not having it for a while. 元の場所に ❑ *She handed the knife back.* 彼女はナイフを返した. ❑ *Put it back in the freezer.* 冷凍庫に戻しなさい. ❺ ADV 副詞 If you put a clock or watch **back**, you change the time shown on it so that it shows an earlier time, for example, when the time changes to standard time. 元の状態に [ADV after v] ❑ *The clocks go back at 2 o'clock tomorrow morning.* 明朝2時に夏時間が終わる. ❻ ADV 副詞 If you write or call **back**, you write to or telephone someone after they have written to or telephoned you. If you look **back** at someone, you look at them after they have started looking at you. 返す ❑ *They wrote back to me and told me I didn't have to do it.* 彼らは返信で、その必要はなかったと伝えてきた. ❑ *If the phone rings, say you'll call back after dinner.* 電話が鳴ったら、夕食の後折り返し電話すると言いなさい. ❼ ADV 副詞 You can say that you go or come **back to** a particular point in a conversation to show that you are mentioning or discussing it again. もとの〜へ ❑ *Can I come back to the question of policing once again?* もう一度警察活動の質問に戻ってもよいですか. ❽ ADV 副詞 If something is or comes **back**, it is fashionable again after it has been unfashionable for some time. 返る ❑ *Short skirts are back.* 短いスカートがまた流行りになった. ❾ ADV 副詞 If someone or something is kept or situated **back from** a place, they are at a distance away from it. 離れて ❑ *Keep back from the edge of the platform.* プラットフォームの端に近づかないでください. ❑ *I'm a few miles back from the border.* 私は国境から数マイル離れたところにいる. 🔟 ADV 副詞 If something is held or tied **back**, it is held or tied so that it does not hang loosely over something. 抑えて [ADV after v] ❑ *The curtains were held back by tassels.* カーテンは広がらないように飾り房で留められている. ⓫ ADV 副詞 If you lie or sit **back**, you move your body backward into a relaxed sloping or flat position, with your head and body resting on something. 後方へ [ADV after v] ❑ *She lay back and stared at the ceiling.* 彼女は寝転んで天井を見詰めた. ⓬ ADV 副詞 If you look or shout **back** at someone or something, you turn to look or shout at them when they are behind you. 後方に ❑ *Nick looked back over his shoulder and then stopped, frowning.* ニックは振り向き、まゆをひそめて立ち止まった. ⓭ ADV 副詞 You use **back** in expressions like **back in Chicago** or **back at the house** when you are giving an account, to show that you are going to start talking about what happened or was happening in the place you mention. 戻って ❑ *Meanwhile, back in Everett, Marc Fulmer is busy raising money to help get the project off the ground.* 一方のエバレットでは、マーク・フルマーがプロジェクトの発足を助けるために金策に奔走している. ⓮ ADV 副詞 If you talk

about something that happened **back** in the past or several years **back**, you are emphasizing that it happened quite a long time ago. さかのぼって [EMPHASIS 強調] □ *The story starts back in 1950, when I was five.* 話は私が5歳だった1950年の昔から始まる. **15** ADV 副詞 If you think **back to** something that happened in the past, you remember it or try to remember it. 振り返って □ *I thought back to the time in 1975 when my son was desperately ill.* 息子の病気が重篤だった1975年のころを回想した. **16** PHRASE 句 If someone moves **back and forth**, they repeatedly move in one direction and then in the opposite direction. 前後に □ *He paced back and forth.* 彼は行ったり来たり歩いた. **17** to **cast** your **mind back** → see **mind**

❷ back /bæk/ (backs)

⇨ Please look at category **11** to see if the expression you are looking for is shown under another headword. **1** N-COUNT 可算名詞 A person's or animal's **back** is the part of their body between their head and their legs that is on the opposite side to their chest and stomach. 背 □ *Her son was lying peacefully on his back.* 彼女の息子は安らかにあおむけに休んでいた. □ *She turned her back to the audience.* 彼女は観客に背を向けた. **2** N-COUNT 可算名詞 The **back** of something is the side or part of it that is toward the rear or farthest from the front. The back of something is normally not used or seen as much as the front. 後部 □ *...a room at the back of the shop.* 店舗の奥にある部屋 □ *She raised her hands to the back of her neck.* 彼女は首の後ろに両手を伸ばした. **3** ADJ 形容詞 **Back** is used to refer to the side or part of something that is toward the rear or farthest from the front. 後方の [ADJ n] □ *He opened the back door.* 彼は勝手口を開けた. □ *Ann could remember sitting in the back seat of their car.* アンは, 彼らの車の後部座席に座っていたことを思い出せた. **4** N-COUNT 可算名詞 The **back** of a chair or sofa is the part that you lean against when you sit on it. 背もたれ □ *There was a pink sweater on the back of the chair.* 背もたれにピンクのセーターがかけられていた. **5** N-COUNT 可算名詞 The **back** of something such as a piece of paper or an envelope is the side that is less important. 裏面 □ *Send your answers on the back of a postcard or sealed, empty envelope.* はがきまたは封をした空の封筒の裏面に答えを書いてお送りください. **6** N-COUNT 可算名詞 The **back** of a book is the part nearest the end, where you can find the index or the notes, for example. 巻末 □ *The index at the back of the book lists both brand and generic names.* 本の巻末にある索引にはブランド名と一般名が一覧表示されている. **7** N-UNCOUNT 不可算名詞 You use **out back** to refer to the area behind a house or other building. You also use **in back** to refer to the rear part of something, especially a car or building. 裏手, 後ろ [AM 米国英語] □ *Dan informed her that he would be out back on the patio cleaning his shoes.* ダンは裏手にある中庭で靴を洗っていると彼女に伝えた. □ *...the trees in back of the building.* 建物の後ろにある木 **8** PHRASE 句 If you say that something was done **behind** someone's **back**, you disapprove of it because it was done without them knowing about it, in an unfair or dishonest way. 陰で [DISAPPROVAL 不賛成] □ *You eat her food, enjoy her hospitality and then criticize her behind her back.* きみは彼女の料理を食べ, 温かいもてなしを受けておきながら彼女の陰口をたたくのか. **9** PHRASE 句 If two or more things are done **back to back**, one follows immediately after the other without any interruption. 連続して □ *...two half-hour shows, which will be screened back to back.* 30分の番組が2つ連続して放映される. **10** → see also **back-to-back** **11** PHRASE 句 If you are wearing something **back to front**, you are wearing it with the back of it at the front of your body. If you do something **back to front**, you do it the wrong way around, starting with the part that should come last. 後ろ前に, 後先逆に [mainly BRIT 主に英国英語; AM usually **backward** 米国英語では通常 **backward**] **12** to **take** a **back seat** → see **seat**

→ see **body**

❸ back /bæk/ (backs, backing, backed) **1** V-I 自動詞 If a building **backs onto** something, the back of it faces in the direction of that thing or touches the edge of that thing. 背後が～に接する □ *He lives in a loft that backs onto Friedman's Bar.* 彼は裏側がフリードマンのバーに接する屋根裏部屋に住んでいる. **2** V-T/V-I 他動詞/自動詞 When you **back** a car or other vehicle somewhere or when it **backs** somewhere, it moves backward. 後退させる [他動詞] 後退する [自動詞] □ *He backed his car out of the drive.* 彼は車道から車を後退させた. **3** V-T 他動詞 If you **back** a person or a course of action, you support them, for example, by voting for them or giving them money. 後援する □ *His defense says it has found a new witness to back his claim that he is a victim of mistaken identity.* 弁護団は, 彼が人違いされているという主張を支持する新しい証人を見つけたと言う. **4** V-T 他動詞 If you **back** a particular person, team, or horse in a competition, you predict that they will win, and usually you bet money that they will win. 賭ける □ *She backed the Detroit Lions to beat the Chicago Bears by at least 20-10.* 彼女は, デトロイト・ライオンズがシカゴ・ベアーズより少なくとも20対10で破ることに賭けた. **5** V-T 他動詞 If a singer **is backed by** a band or by other singers, they provide the musical background for the singer. 伴奏をする [usu passive] □ *She chose to be backed by a classy trio of acoustic guitar, bass and congas.* 彼女は, アコースティックギター, ベースとコ

ンガのしゃれたトリオに伴奏してもらうことにした.

▶ **back away** **1** PHRASAL VERB 句動詞 If you **back away from** a commitment that you made or something that you were involved with in the past, you try to show that you are no longer committed to it or involved with it. 後退する □ *The company backed away from plans to cut their pay by 15%.* 会社は賃金を15%削減する計画を撤回した. **2** PHRASAL VERB 句動詞 If you **back away**, you walk backward away from someone or something, often because you are frightened of them. 後ずさりする □ *James got to his feet and started to come over, but the girls hastily backed away.* ジェームスは立ち上がって近づこうとしたが, 彼女たちはそそくさと後ずさりした.

▶ **back down** PHRASAL VERB 句動詞 If you **back down**, you withdraw a claim, demand, or commitment that you made earlier, because other people are strongly opposed to it. 撤回する □ *It's too late to back down now.* 今更引き下がることはできない.

▶ **back off** **1** PHRASAL VERB 句動詞 If you **back off**, you move away in order to avoid problems or a fight. 退却する □ *They backed off in horror.* 恐ろしさのあまり彼らは退却した. **2** PHRASAL VERB 句動詞 If you **back off from** a claim, demand, or commitment that you made earlier, or if you **back off**, you withdraw it. 撤回する □ *A spokesman says the president has backed off from his threat to boycott the conference.* 報道官は, 大統領は会議をボイコットするという威嚇を撤回したと伝えた.

▶ **back out** PHRASAL VERB 句動詞 If you **back out**, or if you **back out** of something, you decide not to do something that you previously agreed to do. 取り消す □ *The Hungarians backed out of the project in 1989 on environmental grounds.* ハンガリーは, 環境問題を根拠に1989年にプロジェクトから手を引いた.

▶ **back up** **1** PHRASAL VERB 句動詞 If someone or something **backs up** a statement, they supply evidence to suggest that it is true. 支持する □ *Radio signals received from the galaxy's center back up the black hole theory.* 銀河系の中心から受信された無線信号はブラックホール理論を裏づけた. **2** PHRASAL VERB 句動詞 If you **back up** a computer file, you make a copy of it that you can use if the original file is damaged or lost. バックアップする [COMPUTING コンピューティング] □ *Make a point of backing up your files at regular intervals.* 必ずファイルを定期的にバックアップしなさい. **3** PHRASAL VERB 句動詞 If an idea or intention is **backed up** by action, action is taken to support or confirm it. 裏づける □ *The secretary general says the declaration must now be backed up by concrete and effective actions.* 事務総長は, 今後申告は具体的かつ有効な行為によって証明されなければならないと述べている. **4** PHRASAL VERB 句動詞 If you **back** someone **up**, you show your support for them. 支援する □ *His employers backed him up.* 彼の従業員は彼の後ろ盾になった. **5** PHRASAL VERB 句動詞 If you **back** someone **up**, you help them by confirming that what they are saying is true. 確認する □ *The girl denied being there, and the man backed her up.* その少女はそこにいたことを否定し, 男性がそれを裏づけた. **6** PHRASAL VERB 句動詞 If you **back up**, the car or other vehicle that you are driving moves back a short distance. 後退させる □ *Back up, Hans.* バックスせろ, ハンス. **7** PHRASAL VERB 句動詞 If you **back up**, you move backward a short distance. 後ずさりする □ *I backed up carefully until I felt the wall against my back.* 私は背中が壁に接触するまで注意深く後ずさりした. **8** PHRASAL VERB 句動詞 When a car **backs up** or when you **back** it **up**, the car is driven backward. 後退する [AM 米国英語] **9** → see also **backup**

back|bone /bækboʊn/ (backbones) **1** N-COUNT 可算名詞 Your **backbone** is the column of small linked bones down the middle of your back. 背骨 **2** N-UNCOUNT 不可算名詞 If you say that someone has no **backbone**, you think that they do not have the courage to do things which need to be done. 勇気 [oft with brd-neg] □ *You might be taking drastic measures and you've got to have the backbone to do that.* 思い切った対策を取るのならそれを行う気概がないとだめだ.

back|date /bækdeɪt/ (backdates, backdating, backdated) also **back-date** V-T 他動詞 If a document or an arrangement is **backdated**, it is valid from a date before the date when it is completed or signed. さかのぼって発効する □ *The contract that was signed on Thursday morning was backdated to March 11.* 木曜日朝に署名された契約は3月11日に日付をさかのぼって発効された.

back|er /bækər/ (backers) N-COUNT 可算名詞 A **backer** is someone who helps or supports a project, organization, or person, often by giving or lending money. 後援者 □ *I was looking for a backer to assist me in the attempted buyout.* 私は計画された買収で私を援助してくれる後援者を探していた.

back|fire /bækfaɪər/ (backfires, backfiring, backfired) **1** V-I 自動詞 If a plan or project **backfires**, it has the opposite result to the one that was intended. 予期に反した結果をもたらす □ *The president's tactics could backfire.* 大統領の策略は裏目に出るかもしれない. **2** V-I 自動詞 When a motor vehicle or its engine **backfires**, it produces an explosion in the exhaust pipe. 不整爆発をする □ *The car backfired.* 車がバックファイアを起こした.

b

back|ground /bǽkgraʊnd/ (**backgrounds**) ■ N-COUNT 可算名詞 Your **background** is the kind of family you come from and the kind of education you have had. It can also refer to such things as your social and racial origins, your financial status, or the type of work experience that you have. 経歴, 素性 □ The Warners were from a Jewish working-class background. ワーナー兄弟はユダヤ人労働階級の出自だった. ② N-COUNT 可算名詞 The **background** to an event or situation consists of the facts that explain what caused it. 背景 □ The background to the current troubles is provided by the dire state of the country's economy. 現在の問題の遠因はその国の悲惨な経済事情にある. □ The meeting takes place against a background of continuing political violence. その会議は政治的暴力を背景に開催される. ⑤ N-SING 単数名詞 The **background** is sounds, such as music, that you can hear but that you are not listening to with your full attention. 背景で □ I kept hearing the sound of applause in the background. 背景で, 拍手かっさいがずっと聞こえていた. ❹ N-COUNT 可算名詞 You can use **background** to refer to the things in a picture or scene that are less noticeable or important than the main things or people in it. 背景 □ ...roses patterned on a blue background. 青地につけられたばらの模様

Word Partnership background は次の語句と使われる:

ADJ.	cultural/ethnic/family background, educational background ■
N.	background check ■ background information/knowledge ■ ② background story ② background music/noise ⑤
PREP.	in the background ⑤ ❹ against a background ❹
V.	blend into the background ❹

back|ing /bǽkɪŋ/ (**backings**) ■ N-UNCOUNT 不可算名詞 If someone has the **backing of** an organization or an important person, they receive support or money from that organization or person in order to do something. 後援 □ He said the president had the full backing of his government to negotiate a deal. 彼は, 大統領は協約交渉において政府の全面的支持を得たと言った. ② N-VAR 可変性名詞 A **backing** is a layer of something such as cloth that is put onto the back of something in order to strengthen or protect it. 裏打ち □ The table mats and coasters have a non-slip, soft green backing. テーブルマットとコースターには滑り止めの柔らかい緑の裏打ちがついている.

back|lash /bǽklæʃ/ N-SING 単数名詞 A **backlash against** a tendency or recent development in society or politics is a sudden, strong reaction against it. 反発 □ ...the male backlash against feminism. フェミニズムに対する男性の反発.

back|log /bǽklɒg/ (**backlogs**) N-COUNT 可算名詞 A **backlog** is a number of things which have not yet been done but which need to be done. 仕残し □ There is a backlog of repairs and maintenance in schools. 学校には修理と保守の残務がある.

back pay N-UNCOUNT 不可算名詞 **Back pay** is money which an employer owes an employee for work that he or she did in the past. 未払賃金 [BUSINESS 実業] □ He will receive $6,000 in back pay. 彼は未払給料として6千ドルを受け取る.

back|side /bǽksaɪd/ (**backsides**) N-COUNT 可算名詞 Your **backside** is the part of your body that you sit on. 臀部 [INFORMAL くだけた] □ The lad fell backwards, landing on his backside. 少年は後ろ向きに倒れてしりもちをついた.

back|stage /bǽkstéɪdʒ/ ADV 副詞 In a theater, **backstage** refers to the areas behind the stage. 舞台裏 [ADV after v] □ He went backstage and asked for her autograph. 彼は楽屋に彼女を訪ねてサインを賴った. ● ADJ 形容詞 **Backstage** is also an adjective. 舞台裏の [ADJ n] □ ...a backstage pass. 舞台裏への通行証
→ see **theater**

back|stroke /bǽkstroʊk/ N-UNCOUNT 不可算名詞 **Backstroke** is a swimming stroke that you do lying on your back. 背泳 [also 'the' N] □ "I see you know how to swim very well," she said, watching him do the backstroke. 彼が背泳ぎをするのを見ながら, 「水泳がとてもうまいのね」と彼女は言った.

back|up /bǽkʌp/ (**backups**) also **back-up** ■ N-VAR 可変性名詞 **Backup** consists of extra equipment, resources, or people that you can get help or support from if necessary. 予備, 予備の □ There is no emergency back-up immediately available. すぐに使える緊急予備はなかった. ② N-VAR 可変性名詞 If you have something such as a second piece of equipment or set of plans as **backup**, you have arranged for them to be available for use in case the first one does not work. 予備品 □ Every part of the system has a backup. システムの部品それぞれに予備がある. ⑤ N-COUNT 可算名詞 The **backup** of a song is the music that is sung or played to accompany the main tune. 伴奏

バックコーラスの歌手 □ Sharon also sang backup for Barry Manilow. シャロンはバリー・マニロウのバックコーラスもした. ❹ N-COUNT 可算名詞 A **backup** is a long line of traffic stretching back along a road, which moves very slowly or not at all, for example, because of roadwork or an accident. 渋滞 [AM 米国英語] □ There was a seven-mile backup on the freeway. 高速道路には7マイルの渋滞があった.
→ see **concert**

back|ward /bǽkwərd/

In British English, **backwards** is much more common than **backward** when used as an adverb.

英国英語では **backwards** は, 副詞として用いられたときには **backward** よりもずっと普通である.

■ ADJ 形容詞 A **backward** movement or look is in the direction that your back is facing. 後ろ向きの [ADJ n] □ He unlocked the door of apartment two and disappeared inside after a backward glance at Larry. 彼はアパート2のドアの鍵を開け, 振り返ってラリーをちらりと見てから中に消えた. ② ADJ 形容詞 If someone takes a **backward** step or a step **backward**, they do something that does not change or improve their situation, but causes them to go back a stage. 退歩的な □ The current U.S. farm bill, however, is a big step backward. しかし, 現在の米国農業法案は大きな退歩である. ⑤ ADJ 形容詞 A **backward** country or society does not have modern industries and machines. 発たちの遅い □ We need to accelerate the pace of change in our backward country. 後進的な私たちの国では, 変化を加速しなければならない. ❹ ADJ 形容詞 A **backward** child has difficulty in learning. 知恵の遅れた [OFFENSIVE 無礼な] □ ...research into teaching techniques to help backward children. 知恵の遅れた子供を助けるための教授法の研究 ⑤ ADV 副詞 If you move or look **backward**, you move or look in the direction that your back is facing. 後ろ向きに [ADV after v] □ The diver flipped over backward into the water. ダイバーは背中からひっくりかえって水に入った. □ He took two steps backward. 彼は2歩後ろに下がった. ⑥ ADV 副詞 If you do something **backward**, you do it in the opposite way to the usual way. 逆に [ADV after v] □ He works backward, building a house from the top downward. 彼は家を上から下へと, 逆のやり方で建てる. ⑦ ADV 副詞 You use **backward** to indicate that something changes or develops in a way that is not an improvement, but is a return to old ideas or methods. 逆行的に □ This country is going backward. この国は悪い方向に向かっている. ⑧ PHRASE 句 If someone or something moves **backward and forward**, they move repeatedly first in one direction and then in the opposite direction. 前後に □ Using a gentle, sawing motion, draw the floss backward and forward between the teeth. そっとのこぎりを引くような感じで, フロスを歯の間に入れて前後に引きます.

back|water /bǽkwɔtər/ (**backwaters**) ■ N-COUNT 可算名詞 A **backwater** is a place that is isolated. 孤立した場所 □ ...a quiet rural backwater. 静かな片田舎 ② N-COUNT 可算名詞 If you refer to a place or institution as a **backwater**, you think it is not developing properly because it is isolated from ideas and events in other places and institutions. 時代に取り残された場所 [DISAPPROVAL 不賛成] □ The state's high schools remain an educational backwater where dropout rates are rising. この州の高校は, 教育面で取り残されており, 中退率が高まっている. □ This agency will be relegated to the backwaters of Washington. この機関はワシントンのへき地に追いやられる.

back|yard /bǽkjɑrd/ (**backyards**) also **back yard** ■ N-COUNT 可算名詞 A **backyard** is an area of land at the back of a house. 裏庭 ② N-COUNT 可算名詞 If you refer to a country's own **backyard**, you are referring to its own territory or to somewhere that is very close and where that country wants to influence events. 領分 □ They seem to think that if it isn't happening in their own backyard, it isn't worth worrying about. 彼らは自分の身近で起こっていないのなら心配はいらないと思っているようだった.

ba|con /béɪkən/ N-UNCOUNT 不可算名詞 **Bacon** is salted or smoked meat which comes from the back or sides of a pig. ベーコン □ ...bacon and eggs. ベーコンと卵

bac|te|ria /bæktɪ́əriə/ N-PLURAL 複数名詞 **Bacteria** are very small organisms. Some bacteria can cause disease. 細菌 □ Chlorine is added to kill bacteria. 殺菌のために塩素が添加されている.
→ see **can**

bac|te|rial /bæktɪ́əriəl/ ADJ 形容詞 **Bacterial** is used to describe things that relate to or are caused by bacteria. 細菌の [ADJ n] □ Cholera is a bacterial infection. コレラは細菌感染である.

bad /bǽd/ (**worse, worst**)

In meaning ⑨, the comparative form is **badder** and the superlative form is **baddest**.

⑨を意味する場合は, 比較級形が **badder** で, 最上級形が **baddest** である.

■ ADJ 形容詞 Something that is **bad** is unpleasant, harmful, or

B

undesirable. 悪い ❑ *The bad weather conditions prevented the plane from landing.* 悪天候のために飛行機は着陸できなかった. ❑ *Divorce is bad for children.* 離婚は子供にとって悪いことだ. **2** ADJ 形容詞 You use **bad** to indicate that something unpleasant or undesirable is severe or great in degree. ひどい ❑ *Glick had a bad accident two years ago and had to give up farming.* グリックは2年前にひどい事故にあって農業をやめなければならなかった. ❑ *The floods are described as the worst in nearly fifty years.* この洪水はここ50年間で最悪といわれている. **3** ADJ 形容詞 A **bad** idea, decision, or method is not sensible or not correct. 間違った ❑ *Giving your address to a man you don't know is a bad idea.* 知らない男の人に住所を教えるのはまずい. ❑ *The worst thing you can do is underestimate an opponent.* 最悪なのは敵を過小評価することだ. **4** ADJ 形容詞 If you describe a piece of news, an action, or a sign as **bad**, you mean that it is unlikely to result in benefit or success. 好ましくない ❑ *The closure of the project is bad news for her staff.* プロジェクトの終止は彼女の職員にとってはまずい事態である. ❑ *It was a bad start in my relationship with Warr.* 私とウォーの関係のまずい始まりかただった. **5** ADJ 形容詞 Something that is **bad** is of an unacceptably low standard, quality, or amount. 不良な ❑ *Many old people in the United States are living in bad housing.* 米国では多くの高齢者が粗悪な住居に住んでいる. ❑ *The schools' main problem is that teachers' pay is so bad.* 学校の主要な問題は、教師の賃金が非常に低いことである. **6** ADJ 形容詞 Someone who is **bad at** doing something is not skillful or successful at it. 下手な ❑ *Howard was so bad at basketball.* ハワードはバスケットボールが非常に苦手だった. ❑ *He was a bad driver.* 彼は運転が下手だ. **7** ADJ 形容詞 If you say that it is **bad** that something happens, you mean it is unacceptable, unfortunate, or wrong. 不都合な, 不運な, 不当な ❑ *Not being able to hear doesn't seem as bad to the rest of us as not being able to see.* ほかの我々には、聴こえないことは、見えないことほど悪くないように思える. **8** ADJ 形容詞 You can say that something is **not bad** to mean that it is quite good or acceptable, especially when you are rather surprised about this. まんざらな [with neg] ❑ *"How much is he paying you?" — "Oh, five thousand." — "Not bad."* 「彼からいくらもらっているの.」「ああ, 5千.」「悪くないね.」❑ *That's not a bad idea.* それはなかなかの考えだ. **9** ADJ 形容詞 If you describe someone or something as **bad**, you mean that they are very good. 素晴らしい [INFORMAL くだけた] [usu ADJ n] ❑ *...the baddest bass music from Miami, featuring Dr. Boom & The Dominator.* ドクター・ブームとザ・ドミネーターをフィーチャーするマイアミ発最高のベース音楽 **10** ADJ 形容詞 A **bad** person has morally unacceptable attitudes and behavior. 邪悪な ❑ *I was selling drugs, but I didn't think I was a bad person.* 私は麻薬を売っていたけれど, 自分が悪人だとは思っていなかった. **11** ADJ 形容詞 A **bad** child disobeys rules and instructions or does not behave in a polite and correct way. いうことを聞かない, 行儀の悪い ❑ *You are a bad boy for repeating what I told you.* 私が言ったことを繰り返すなんて, お前は行儀の悪い子だ. **12** ADJ 形容詞 If you are in a **bad** mood, you are angry and behave unpleasantly to people. 不快な ❑ *She is in a bit of a bad mood because she's just given up smoking.* 彼女はたばこをやめたばかりなのでちょっと機嫌が悪い. **13** ADJ 形容詞 If you **feel bad about** something, you feel sorry or guilty about it. 気の毒に思って, 遺憾 ❑ *You don't have to feel bad about relaxing.* 気兼ねなくくつろいでいいのだよ. ❑ *I feel bad that he's doing most of the work.* 仕事のほとんどを彼がやっているのを気の毒に思う. **14** ADJ 形容詞 If you have a **bad** back, heart, leg, or eye, it is injured, diseased, or weak. 病んだ ❑ *Joe has a bad back so we have a hard bed.* ジョーの腰痛のため, 私たちは固いベッドで寝ている. **15** ADJ 形容詞 Food that has **gone bad** is not suitable to eat because it has started to decay. 腐った ❑ *They bought so much beef that some went bad.* 彼らは牛肉を買い過ぎて, 一部は腐ってしまった. **16** ADJ 形容詞 **Bad** language is language that contains offensive words such as swear words. 下品な ❑ *I don't like to hear bad language in the street.* 街頭で下品な言葉を聞きたくない. **17** → see also **worse**, **worst** **18** **bad blood** → see **blood** **19** **bad luck** → see **luck** **20** to **get a bad press** → see **press**

Thesaurus	*bad* また次を参照:
ADJ.	damaging, dangerous, harmful; (*ant.*) good **1**
	inferior, poor, unsatisfactory; (*ant.*) acceptable, good, satisfactory **5** **6**
	disobedient, naughty; (*ant.*) nice, obedient, well-behaved **11**
	rancid, rotten, spoiled; (*ant.*) fresh, good **15**

bad debt (**bad debts**) N-COUNT 可算名詞 A **bad debt** is a sum of money that has been lent but is not likely to be repaid. 回収不能金 ❑ *The bank set aside 1.1 billion dollars to cover bad debts from business failures.* 銀行は, 企業倒産による焦げつきに対応するために110億ドルの引当金を積んでおいた.

badge /bˈædʒ/ (**badges**) **1** N-COUNT 可算名詞 A **badge** is a piece of metal, cloth or plastic which you wear or carry to show that you work for a particular organization, or that you have achieved something. 記章, メダル ❑ *...a police officer's badge.* 警官のバッジ **2** N-COUNT 可算名詞 A **badge** is a small piece of metal or plastic

which you wear in order to show that you support a particular movement, organization, or person. You fasten a badge to your clothes with a pin. バッジ [BRIT 英国英語; AM **button** 米国英語 **button**]

badg|er /bˈædʒər/ (**badgers**, **badgering**, **badgered**) **1** N-COUNT 可算名詞 A **badger** is a wild animal which has a white head with two wide black stripes on it. Badgers live underground and usually come up to feed at night. アナグマ **2** V-T 他動詞 If you **badger** someone, you repeatedly tell them to do something or repeatedly ask them questions. しつこく悩ます ❑ *She badgered her doctor time and again, pleading with him to do something.* 彼女は何か手を施すようしつこく泣きついて医師を困らせた. ❑ *They kept phoning and writing, badgering me to go back.* 彼らは電話や手紙で戻るようにしつこくせがんだ.

bad|ly /bˈædli/ (**worse**, **worst**) **1** ADV 副詞 If something is done **badly** or goes **badly**, it is not very successful or effective. 悪く [ADV with v] ❑ *I was angry because I played so badly.* 自分があまりにまずいプレーをしたので腹が立った. ❑ *The whole project was badly managed.* プロジェクト全体の管理がまずかった. **2** ADV 副詞 If someone or something is **badly** hurt or **badly** affected, they are severely hurt or affected. 甚だしく ❑ *The bomb destroyed a police station and badly damaged a church.* 爆弾は警察署を破壊し, 教会を大破した. ❑ *One man was killed and another badly injured.* 1人は死亡し, もう1人は重症を負った. **3** ADV 副詞 If you want or need something **badly**, you want or need it very much. 大いに [ADV with v] ❑ *Why do you want to go so badly?* なぜそんなにまで行きたいのか. **4** ADV 副詞 If someone behaves **badly** or treats other people **badly**, they act in an unkind, unpleasant, or unacceptable way. まずく [ADV with v] ❑ *They have both behaved very badly and I am very hurt.* 彼らは2人とも非常に見苦しい振る舞いをしたので, 私はとても傷ついている. **5** ADV 副詞 If something reflects **badly** on someone or makes others think **badly** of them, it harms their reputation. 悪く [ADV after v] ❑ *Teachers know that low exam results will reflect badly on them.* 教師たちは試験結果が悪いと自分に悪評がたつことを知っている. **6** ADV 副詞 If a person or their job is **badly** paid, they are not paid very much for what they do. (賃金が) 悪く ❑ *You may have to work part-time, in a badly paid job.* きみはパートタイムで賃金の悪い仕事をしなければならないかもしれない. **7** → see also **worse**, **worst**

Thesaurus	*badly* また次を参照:
ADV.	carelessly, poorly, unsuccessfully; (*ant.*) well **1**
	deeply, desperately, seriously; (*ant.*) mildly **2**
	greatly **3**

bad|ly off → see **bad off**

bad off (**worse off**, **worst off**) **1** ADJ 形容詞 If you are **bad off**, you are in a bad situation. 恵まれていない [mainly AM 主に米国英語] [usu v-link ADJ] ❑ *But there were other people worse off than me at the hospital, linked up to respirators and unable to walk.* でも, 病院では人工呼吸器につながれて歩けない, 私よりもっと困っている人たちがほかにいる. **2** ADJ 形容詞 If you are **bad off**, you do not have much money. 暮らし向きが悪い [usu v-link ADJ] ❑ *An independent study found that the owners are not as bad off as they say, and most are making money.* 独自の調査によると, オーナーは彼らがいうほど暮らし向きが悪いわけではなく, 大部分がお金をもうけていることがわかった.

bad-tempered ADJ 形容詞 Someone who is **bad-tempered** is not very cheerful and gets angry easily. 気難しい ❑ *When his headaches developed, Nick became bad-tempered and even violent.* 頭痛がすると, ニックは不機嫌になり, 暴力的にさえなった.

Angry is normally used to talk about someone's mood or feelings on a particular occasion. If someone is often angry, you can describe them as **bad-tempered**. ❑ *She's a bad-tempered young lady.* If someone is very angry, you can describe them as **furious**. ❑ *Senior police officers are furious at the blunder.* If they are less angry, you can describe them as **annoyed** or **irritated**. ❑ *The premier looked annoyed but calm. ... a man irritated by the barking of his neighbor's dog.* Typically, someone is **irritated** by something because it happens constantly or continually. If someone is often irritated, you can describe them as **irritable**.

baf|fle /bˈæfl/ (**baffles**, **baffling**, **baffled**) V-T 他動詞 If something **baffles** you, you cannot understand it or explain it. 当惑させる ❑ *An apple tree producing square fruit is baffling experts.* 角ばった実を結ぶりんごの木に専門家は面食らっている. ● **baf|fling** ADJ 形容詞 調べてもわからない ❑ *I was constantly ill, with a baffling array of symptoms.* 不可解な症状が次々と現れ, 私は常に病気だった.

bag /bˈæg/ (**bags**) **1** N-COUNT 可算名詞 A **bag** is a container made of thin paper or plastic, for example, one that is used in stores to put things in that a customer has bought. 袋 **2** N-COUNT 可算名詞 You can use **bag** to refer to a bag and its contents, or to the contents only. 1袋, 1袋の中身 ❑ *...a bag of candy.* キャンディー1袋 **3** N-COUNT 可算名詞 A **bag** is a strong container with one or two handles, used to carry things in. かばん

b

She left the hotel carrying a shopping bag. 彼女は買い物袋を下げてホテルを出た. **4** N-COUNT 可算名詞 You can use **bag** to refer to a bag and its contents, or to the contents only. 1袋, 1袋の中身 □Mama came in the back door carrying two bags of groceries. お母さんは食料品の入った袋を2つ抱えて勝手口から入ってきた. **5** N-COUNT 可算名詞 A **bag** is the same as a **handbag**. ハンドバッグ **6** N-PLURAL 複数名詞 If you have **bags** under your eyes, you have folds of skin there, usually because you have not had enough sleep. たるみ □The bags under his eyes have grown darker. 彼の目の下にできたくまは色が濃くなった. **7** → see also **sleeping bag** → see **tea**

bag|gage /bǽgɪdʒ/ N-UNCOUNT 不可算名詞 Your **baggage** consists of the bags that you take with you when you travel. 手荷物 □The passengers went through immigration control and collected their baggage. 乗客は入国管理を通り, 手荷物を受け取った. **2** N-UNCOUNT 不可算名詞 You can use **baggage** to refer to someone's emotional problems, fixed ideas, or prejudices. 情緒的な問題, 固定観念 □How much emotional baggage is he bringing with him into the relationship? 彼は心の悩みをどのくらいつきあいに持ち込んでいるのか.

Baggage is an uncount noun. You can have **a piece of baggage** or **some baggage** but you cannot have "a baggage" or "some baggages." Both British and American speakers can refer to everything that travelers carry as their **bags**. American speakers can also call an individual suitcase a **bag**. In British English, people normally use **luggage** when they are talking about everything that travelers carry. **Baggage** is a more technical word and is used for example when discussing airports or travel insurance. In American English, **luggage** refers to empty bags and suitcases and **baggage** refers to bags and suitcases with their contents.

---

bag|gage car (baggage cars) N-COUNT 可算名詞 A **baggage car** is a railroad car, often without windows, which is used to carry luggage, goods, or mail. 荷物車 [AM 米国英語] □The coffin was loaded into the baggage car of the train. ひつぎは列車の荷物車に積まれた.

bag|gy /bǽgi/ (baggier, baggiest) ADJ 形容詞 If a piece of clothing is **baggy**, it hangs loosely on your body. ぶかぶかの □...a baggy sweater. だぶだぶのセーター

bail /béɪl/ (bails, bailing, bailed)

The spelling **bale** is also used for meaning **4**, and for meanings **1** and **3** of the phrasal verb.

つづりの **bale** は**4**を意味するのにも使われ, また句動詞の**1**と**3**の意味にも使える.

---

1 N-UNCOUNT 不可算名詞 **Bail** is a sum of money that an arrested person or someone else puts forward as a guarantee that the arrested person will attend their trial in a law court. 保釈金 □He was freed on bail pending an appeal. 上訴までの間, 彼は保釈された. **2** N-UNCOUNT 不可算名詞 **Bail** is permission for an arrested person to be released after bail has been paid. 保釈 □Bilal was held without bail after a court appearance in Detroit. ビラルはデトロイトでの出廷後, 保釈を認められずに拘留された. **3** V-T 他動詞 If someone **is bailed**, they are released while they are waiting for their trial, after paying an amount of money to the court. 保釈する [usu passive] □He was bailed to appear on 26 August. 彼は8月26日に出廷する条件で保釈された. **4** V-I 自動詞 If you **bail**, you use a container to remove water from a boat or from a place which is flooded. (ボートなどから水を) くみだす □We kept her afloat for a couple of hours by bailing frantically. 僕らは必死に水をくみだして船を2, 3時間浮かしておいた. ● PHRASAL VERB 句動詞 **Bail out** means the same as **bail**. くみだす □A crew was sent down the shaft to close it off and bail out all the water. シャフトを閉め, すべての水をかきだすために, 乗組員1名がシャフトを伝って船底に送られた. **5** PHRASE 句 If someone who has been arrested **makes bail**, or if another person **makes bail** for them, the arrested person is released on bail. 保釈金を納める □Guerrero was ultimately arrested, but he made bail and fled to Colombia. グエロは最終的に逮捕されたが, 保釈金を納めてコロンビアに逃げた. **6** PHRASE 句 If a prisoner **jumps bail**, he or she does not come back for his or her trial after being released on bail. 保釈中に行方をくらます □He had jumped bail last year while being tried on drug charges. 昨年, 彼は麻薬関連容疑で裁判にかけられている間, 保釈中に行方をくらました.

▶ **bail out** **1** PHRASAL VERB 句動詞 If you **bail** someone **out**, you help them out of a difficult situation, often by giving them money. 救済する □They will discuss how to bail the economy out of its slump. 彼らは経済不振の救済法を協議する. **2** PHRASAL VERB 句動詞 If you **bail** someone **out**, you pay bail on their behalf. 代わりに保釈金を支払う □He has been jailed eight times. Each time, friends bailed him out. 彼は8回投獄された. 毎回友人が保証金を支払って彼を刑務所から出した. **3** PHRASAL VERB 句動詞 If a pilot **bails out of** an aircraft

that is crashing, he or she jumps from it, using a parachute to land safely. 落下傘で脱出する □Reid was forced to bail out of the crippled aircraft. リードは操縦不能になった飛行機から落下傘で脱出せざるをえなくなった. **4** → see **bail 4**

bail|iff /béɪlɪf/ (bailiffs) N-COUNT 可算名詞 A **bailiff** is an official in a court of law who deals with tasks such as keeping control in court. 執行吏 [AM 米国英語] □The court bailiff said jurors did not wish to speak to news media until the sentencing. 廷吏は, 陪審員は判決まで報道機関と話すことを望まないと言った.

bait /béɪt/ (baits, baiting, baited) **1** N-VAR 可変性名詞 **Bait** is food which you put on a hook or in a trap in order to catch fish or animals. えさ □Vivien refuses to put down bait to tempt wildlife to the waterhole. ビビアンは野生動物を水飲み場におびき寄せるためにえさを置くことを拒否している. **2** V-T 他動詞 If you **bait** a hook or trap, you put bait on it or in it. (釣りばり・わなに) えさをつける □He baited his hook with pie. 彼は釣りばりにえさとしてパイをつけた. □The boys dug pits and baited them so that they could spear their prey. 少年たちはえじきを突き刺すことができるように, 穴を掘ってえさを入れた. **3** N-UNCOUNT 不可算名詞 To use something as **bait** means to use it to trick or persuade someone to do something. 誘い [also 'a' N] □Television programs are essentially bait to attract an audience for commercials. テレビ番組は基本的に視聴者が宣伝を見るよう導くものだ. **4** V-T 他動詞 If you **bait** someone, you deliberately try to make them angry by teasing them. なぶる □He delighted in baiting his mother. 彼は母親をいじめて楽しんだ. **5** **Bait and switch** is used to refer to a sales technique in which goods are advertised at low prices in order to attract customers, although only a small number of the low-priced goods are available. おとり商法 □The classy piano bar next to Maddalena's really sells 11 dishes for the advertised price at lunch. There's no bait and switch here. マダリーナの家の隣にあるしゃれたピアノバーは, 昼食時に, 11種の料理を宣伝通りの値段で出している. 実際には高くついたりはしない.

bake /béɪk/ (bakes, baking, baked) **1** V-T/V-I 他動詞/自動詞 If you **bake**, you spend some time preparing and mixing together ingredients to make bread, cakes, pies, or other food which is cooked in the oven. (パンや菓子などを天火で) 焼く [no passive] □How did you learn to bake cakes? ケーキの焼き方をどうやって習ったの. 私はケーキなどを焼くのが大好きだ. ● **baking** N-UNCOUNT 不可算名詞 [also 'the' N] パン焼き □On a Thursday she used to do all the baking. 彼女は木曜日にパン焼き仕事を全部していたものだった. **2** V-T/V-I 他動詞/自動詞 When a cake or bread **bakes** or when you **bake** it, it cooks in the oven without any extra liquid or fat. 焼ける, 焼く □Bake the cake for 35 to 50 minutes. ケーキを35分から50分焼きます. □The batter rises as it bakes. 焼けると生地が膨らみます. **3** → see also **baking** → see **cook**

bak|er /béɪkər/ (bakers) N-COUNT 可算名詞 A **baker** is a person whose job is to bake and sell bread, pastries, and cakes. パン製造販売人 **2** N-COUNT 可算名詞 A **baker** or a **baker's** is a store where bread and cakes are sold. パン屋 [mainly BRIT 主に英国英語; AM usually **bakery** 米国英語では通常 **bakery**]

Word Link ery ≈ place where something happens : bakery, fishery, refinery

---

bak|ery /béɪkəri, béɪkri/ (bakeries) N-COUNT 可算名詞 A **bakery** is a building where bread, pastries, and cakes are baked, or the store where they are sold. パン菓子類製造販売店 □A smell of bread drifted from some distant bakery. 遠くの製パン所からパンの香りが漂ってきた.

bak|ing /béɪkɪŋ/ **1** ADJ 形容詞 You can use **baking** to describe weather on a day that is very hot indeed. 焼けつくような □...a baking July day. 焼けつくように暑い7月のある日 □The coffins stood in the baking heat surrounded by mourners. ひつぎは哀悼者に囲まれ, 灼熱下におかれていた. **2** → see also **baking**

bal|ance /bǽləns/ (balances, balancing, balanced) **1** V-T/V-I 他動詞/自動詞 If you **balance** something somewhere, or if it **balances** there, it remains steady and does not fall. 均衡をとる □I balanced on the ledge. 私はへりの上でバランスをとった. **2** N-UNCOUNT 不可算名詞 **Balance** is the ability to remain steady when you are standing up. 平衡 □The medicines you are currently taking could be affecting your balance. 現在あなたが服用している薬は平衡感覚に支障を与えるかもしれません. **3** V-RECIP 相互動詞 If you **balance** one thing **with** something different, each of the things has the same strength or importance. 釣り合わせる □Balance spicy dishes with mild ones. 薬味を利かせた料理と一緒に辛味の穏やかな料理を出して釣り合いをもたせる. □The government has to find some way to balance these two needs. 政府はこれらの2つのニーズの均衡を保つための何らかの方法を探さなくてはならない. □Supply and demand on the currency market will generally balance. 通貨市場の供給と需要は全般的に釣り合うだろう. ● **bal|anced** ADJ 形容詞 釣り合いのとれた □This book is a well balanced biography. この本はうまく均整のとれた伝記だ. **4** N-SING 単数名詞 A **balance** is a situation in which all the different parts are equal in strength or importance. 均衡

B

...*the ecological balance of the forest.* 森林の生態系的均衡 **5** N-SING 単数名詞 If you say that **the balance** tips in your favor, you start winning or succeeding, especially in a conflict or contest. 優勢 □...*a powerful new gun which could tip the balance of the war in their favor.* 戦況を彼らの優勢に変える可能性のある強力な新しい銃 **6** V-T 他動詞 If you **balance** one thing **against** another, you consider its importance in relation to the other one. はかりにかける □*She carefully tried to balance religious sensitivities against democratic freedom.* 彼女は、宗教的感受性と民主的自由を慎重にはかりにかけようとした。 **7** V-T 他動詞 If someone **balances** their budget or if a government **balances** the economy of a country, they make sure that the amount of money that is spent is not greater than the amount that is received. 帳尻を合わせる □*He balanced his budgets by rigid control over public expenditure.* 彼は公共支出を厳重に管理して予算の帳尻を合わせた。 **8** V-T/V-I 他動詞/自動詞 If you **balance** your books or make them **balance**, you prove by calculation that the amount of money you have received is equal to the amount that you have spent. 帳簿の清算をする □...*teaching them to balance the books.* 帳簿の清算を彼らに教えること **9** N-COUNT 可算名詞 The **balance** in your bank account is the amount of money you have in it. 残高 □*I'd like to check the balance in my account please.* 私の口座の残高を確認したいのですが。 **10** N-SING 単数名詞 The **balance** of an amount of money is what remains to be paid for something or what remains when part of the amount has been spent. 残額 □*They were due to pay the balance on delivery.* 彼らは納品時に残額を支払うことになっていた。 **11** → see also **bank balance 12** PHRASE 句 If you **keep** your **balance**, for example, when standing in a moving vehicle, you remain steady and do not fall over. If you **lose** your **balance**, you become unsteady and fall over. 平衡を保つ □*She was holding onto the rail to keep her balance.* 彼女は平衡を保つためにレールにつかまっていた。 **13** PHRASE 句 If you are **off balance**, you are in an unsteady position and about to fall. 平衡を失って □*A gust of wind knocked him off balance and he fell face down in the mud.* 突風に打たれて彼は平衡を失い、ぬかるみにうつむけに倒れた。 **14** PHRASE 句 You can say **on balance** to indicate that you are stating an opinion after considering all the relevant facts or arguments. すべてを考慮すると □*On balance he agreed with Christine.* 結局のところ、彼はクリスティーンに同意した。
→ see **bank, brain**

Word Partnership balance は次の語句と使われる:

V.	**keep/lose** your balance, **restore** balance **11**
	check a balance, **maintain** a balance **9 10**
	pay a balance **10**
ADJ.	**delicate** balance **1 4**
	balance **due, outstanding** balance **10**
N.	balance **a budget 7**
	account balance, balance **transfer 9**

bal|anced /bǽlənst/ **1** ADJ 形容詞 A **balanced** report, book, or other document takes into account all the different opinions on something and presents information in a fair and reasonable way. 均整のとれた [APPROVAL 賛成] □*a fair, balanced, comprehensive report.* 公正で均整のとれた包括的な報告書 **2** ADJ 形容詞 Something that is **balanced** is pleasing or useful because its different parts or elements are in the correct proportions. 平均のとれた [APPROVAL 賛成] □...*a balanced diet.* 完全栄養食 **3** ADJ 形容詞 Someone who is **balanced** remains calm and thinks clearly, even in a difficult situation. (性格的、精神的に) 安定した [APPROVAL 賛成] □*I have to prove myself as a respectable, balanced person.* 自分が社会的な地位のある、落ち着いた人物であることを証明する必要がある。 **4** → see also **balance**

bal|ance of pay|ments (**balances of payments**) N-COUNT 可算名詞 A country's **balance of payments** is the difference, over a period of time, between the payments it makes to other countries for imports and the payments it receives from other countries for exports. 国際収支 [BUSINESS 実業] □...*the chronic American balance-of-payments deficit of the 1960s.* 1960年代における米国国際収支の慢性的な赤字

bal|ance of trade (**balances of trade**) N-COUNT 可算名詞 A country's **balance of trade** is the difference in value, over a period of time, between the goods it imports and the goods it exports. 貿易収支 [BUSINESS 実業] [usu sing] □*As other nations grow and spend more money on American products, the balance of trade should even out.* ほかの国々が発展し、もっと米国製品を買うようになれば、貿易収支の均衡はとれるはずだ。

bal|ance sheet (**balance sheets**) N-COUNT 可算名詞 A **balance sheet** is a written statement of the amount of money and property that a company or person has, including amounts of money that are owed or are owing. **Balance sheet** is also used to refer to the general financial state of a company. 貸借対照表 [BUSINESS 実業] □*Rolls-Royce needed a strong balance sheet.* ロールスロイスは堅調なバランスシートを必要としていた。

bal|co|ny /bǽlkəni/ (**balconies**) **1** N-COUNT 可算名詞 A **balcony** is a platform on the outside of a building, above ground level, with a wall or railing around it. バルコニー **2** N-SING 単数名詞 The **balcony** in a theater or cinema is an area of seats above the main seating area. 桟敷

bald /bɔ́ld/ (**balder, baldest**) **1** ADJ 形容詞 Someone who is **bald** has little or no hair on the top of their head. はげ頭の □*The man's bald head was beaded with sweat.* その男性ははげ頭にビーズのような汗をかいていた。 ●**bald|ness** N-UNCOUNT 不可算名詞 はげ □*He wears a cap to cover a spot of baldness.* 彼ははげを隠すために帽子をかぶっている。 **2** ADJ 形容詞 If a tire is **bald**, its surface has worn down and it is no longer safe to use. 擦り減った **3** ADJ 形容詞 [ADJ n] A **bald** statement is in plain language and contains no extra explanation or information. あからさまの □*The bald truth is he's just not happy.* むきだしの真実は、彼がとにかく幸せでないことだ。 ●**bald|ly** ADV 副詞 [ADV with v] 大胆に □*"The leaders are outdated," he stated baldly. "They don't relate to young people."* 彼は大胆にも「指導者は時代遅れだ」、「若者の気持ちがわかっていない」と発言した。

bald|ing /bɔ́ldɪŋ/ ADJ 形容詞 Someone who is **balding** is beginning to lose the hair on the top of their head. 頭のはげかかった □*He wore a straw hat to keep his balding head from getting sunburned.* 彼ははげかかった頭が日焼けしないよう麦わら帽子をかぶった。

bale /béɪl/ (**bales, baling, baled**) **1** N-COUNT 可算名詞 A **bale** is a large quantity of something such as hay, cloth, or paper, tied together tightly. 俵 □...*bales of hay.* 干し草の俵 **2** V-T 他動詞 If something such as hay, cloth, or paper **is baled**, it is tied together tightly. 梱包する □*Once hay has been cut and baled, it has to go through some chemical processes.* 干し草は切断して梱(こり)にしたあと、化学処理を行う必要がある。 **3** → see also **bail**

ball /bɔ́l/ (**balls, balling, balled**) **1** N-COUNT 可算名詞 A **ball** is a round or oval object that is used in games such as tennis, baseball, football, and soccer. ボール □...*a golf ball.* ゴルフボール **2** N-COUNT 可算名詞 A **ball** is something or an amount of something that has a round shape. 球形の物 □*Thomas screwed the letter up into a ball.* トーマスは手紙をくしゃにして丸めた。 **3** V-T/V-I 他動詞/自動詞 When you **ball** something or when it **balls**, it becomes round. 球になる [自動詞] 球にする [他動詞] □*He picked up the sheets of paper, and balled them tightly in his fists.* 彼は紙切れを取り上げ、握りこぶしでかたく丸めた。 **4** N-COUNT 可算名詞 The **ball of** your foot or **the ball of** your thumb is the rounded part where your toes join your foot or where your thumb joins your hand. (手足の親指などの) 付け根の丸く膨らんだ部分 **5** N-COUNT 可算名詞 A **ball** is a large formal social event at which people dance. 舞踏会 □*My Mama and Daddy used to have a grand Christmas ball every year.* 私のお母さんとお父さんは毎年クリスマスには華やかなダンスパーティーを開いていたものだった。 **6** PHRASE 句 If you are **having a ball**, you are having a very enjoyable time. 楽しいひとときを過ごす [INFORMAL くだけた] □*Outside the boys were sitting on the ground and, judging by the gales of laughter, they were having a ball.* ドッという笑い声から察するに、外では、少年たちが地べたに座って、楽しいときを過ごしているようだった。

▶ **ball up** PHRASAL VERB 句動詞 If you **ball up** a task or activity, you do it very badly, making a lot of mistakes. 台なしにする [AM 米英語, INFORMAL, VULGAR くだけた、下品な] □*The government has totally balled up the whole assessment process by going to the system they did.* 政府は新しいシステムに移行することにより評価プロセス全体を混乱させた。
→ see **foot, golf, soccer**

Word Partnership ball は次の語句と使われる:

V.	**bounce/catch/hit/kick/throw** a ball **11**
	roll into a ball **2**
N.	**bowling/golf/soccer/tennis** ball, **crystal** ball, ball **field,** ball **game 11**
	snow ball **2**
PREP.	ball **of** something **2**

bal|lad /bǽləd/ (**ballads**) **1** N-COUNT 可算名詞 A **ballad** is a long song or poem which tells a story in simple language. 詩歌曲 □...*an eighteenth-century ballad about some lost children called the Babes in the Wood.* 『森のふたりの幼い子ども』という迷子のことを歌った18世紀のバラード **2** N-COUNT 可算名詞 A **ballad** is a slow, romantic, popular song. バラード □*"You Don't Know Paris" is one of the most beautiful ballads that he ever wrote.* 『You Don't Know Paris』は彼がこれまでに書いたものの中でも特に美しいバラードだ。

bal|let /bǽleɪ/ (**ballets**) **1** N-UNCOUNT 不可算名詞 **Ballet** is a type of very skilled and artistic dancing with carefully planned movements. バレエ [also 'the' n, oft N n] □*I trained as a ballet dancer.* 私はバレエダンサーとして修行した。 **2** N-COUNT 可算名詞 A **ballet** is an artistic work that is performed by ballet dancers. バレエ曲 □*The performance will include the premiere of three new ballets.* 公演には初演のバレエ曲3作品が含まれる。

b

bal|loon /bəlun/ (**balloons, ballooning, ballooned**) ■ N-COUNT 可算名詞 A **balloon** is a small, thin, rubber bag that you blow air into so that it becomes larger and rounder or longer. Balloons are used as toys or decorations. 風船 □ She popped a balloon with her fork. 彼女はフォークで風船を突き刺した. ❷ N-COUNT 可算名詞 A **balloon** is a large, strong bag filled with gas or hot air, which can carry passengers in a container that hangs underneath it. 気球 □ They are to attempt to be the first to circle the Earth non-stop by balloon. 彼らは気球による初の無着陸世界一周を試みようとしている. ❸ V-I 自動詞 When something **balloons**, it increases rapidly in amount. 急増する □ The jail's female and minority populations have both ballooned in recent years. 近年, 刑務所の女性と少数派の数がともに急増した. → see **fly**

bal|loon mort|gage (**balloon mortgages**) N-COUNT 可算名詞 A **balloon mortgage** is a mortgage on which the repayments are relatively small until the large final payment. バルーンモーゲージ [AM 米国英語]

bal|lot /bælət/ (**ballots, balloting, balloted**) ■ N-COUNT 可算名詞 A **ballot** is a secret vote in which people select a candidate in an election, or express their opinion about something. 無記名投票 □ The result of the ballot will not be known for two weeks. 無記名投票の結果がわかるまでには2週間かかる. ❷ N-COUNT 可算名詞 A **ballot** is a piece of paper on which you indicate your choice or opinion in a secret vote. 無記名投票用紙 □ Election boards will count the ballots by hand. 選挙管理委員会は無記名投票用紙を手で数える. ❸ V-T 他動詞 If you **ballot** a group of people, you find out what they think about a subject by organizing a secret vote. 無記名投票を行う □ The union said they would ballot members on whether to strike. 労働組合はストライキを実行するか否かについて組合員投票を行うと言った. → see **election, vote**

ball|park /bɔlpɑrk/ (**ballparks**) also **ball park** ■ N-COUNT 可算名詞 A **ballpark** is a park or stadium where baseball is played. 野球場 □ ...one of the oldest and most beautiful ballparks in baseball. 野球史上, 最古で最も美しい野球場の1つ ❷ ADJ 形容詞 A **ballpark** figure or **ballpark** estimate is an approximate figure or estimate. おおよその [ADJ n] □ I can't give you anything more than just sort of a ballpark figure. あなたにはおおざっぱな数字しか言えない.

balm /bɑm/ (**balms**) ■ N-MASS 質量名詞 **Balm** is a sweet-smelling oil that is obtained from some tropical trees and used to make creams that heal wounds or reduce pain. 芳香性の塗り薬 □ ...a jar of lip balm. リップクリームの瓶 ❷ N-UNCOUNT 不可算名詞 If you refer to something as **balm**, you mean that it makes you feel better. いやすもの [APPROVAL 賛成] [also 'a' n] □ The place is balm to the soul. ここは魂の慰安所だ.

bam|boo /bæmbu/ (**bamboos**) N-VAR 可変性名詞 **Bamboo** is a tall tropical plant with hard, hollow stems. The young shoots of the plant can be eaten and the stems are used to make furniture. 竹 □ ...huts with walls of bamboo. 壁が竹でできた小屋

ban /bæn/ (**bans, banning, banned**) ■ V-T 他動詞 To **ban** something means to state officially that it must not be done, shown, or used. 禁止する □ Canada will ban smoking in all offices later this year. カナダは今年中に事務所での喫煙を全面禁止する. □ Last year arms sales were banned. 武器の販売は昨年禁止された. ❷ N-COUNT 可算名詞 A **ban** is an official ruling that something must not be done, shown, or used. 禁止令 □ The general lifted the ban on political parties. 将軍は政党禁止令を解除した. ❸ V-T 他動詞 If you **are banned from** doing something, you are officially prevented from doing it. 禁止する □ He was banned from driving for three years. 彼は3年間の運転免許停止処分を受けた.

Thesaurus	ban また次を参照:
V.	bar, forbid, prohibit; (ant.) allow, legalize, permit ■
N.	prohibition; (ant.) approval, sanction ❷

ba|nal /bənɑl, -næl, beɪnɑl/ ADJ 形容詞 If you describe something as **banal**, you do not like it because you think it is so ordinary that it is not at all effective or interesting. 凡庸な [DISAPPROVAL 不賛成] □ The text is banal. この文章は陳腐だ.

ba|na|na /bənænə/ (**bananas**) N-VAR 可変性名詞 **Bananas** are long curved fruit with yellow skins. バナナ □ ...a bunch of bananas. 1房のバナナ

band /bænd/ (**bands, banding, banded**) ■ N-COUNT-COLL 集合可算名詞 A **band** is a small group of musicians who play popular music such as jazz, rock, or pop. バンド □ He was a drummer in a rock band. 彼はロックバンドのドラマーだった. ❷ N-COUNT-COLL 集合可算名詞 A **band** is a group of musicians who play brass and percussion instruments. 楽団 □ Bands played German marches. 楽団はドイツの行進曲を演奏した. ❸ N-COUNT-COLL 集合可算名詞 A **band** of people is a group of people who have joined together because they share an interest or belief. 団 □ Bands of government soldiers, rebels and just plain criminals have been roaming some neighborhoods. 政府軍兵士, 反政府勢力および単なる犯罪者の集団が近隣を徘 (はい) 回していた. ❹ N-COUNT 可算名詞 A **band** is a flat,

narrow strip of cloth which you wear around your head or wrists, or which forms part of a piece of clothing. 帯状のひも □ Almost all hospitals use a wrist-band of some kind with your name and details on it. ほとんどすべての病院で, リストバンドに名前や詳細を記したものが使用されている. ❺ N-COUNT 可算名詞 A **band** is a strip of something such as color, light, land, or cloth that contrasts with the areas on either side of it. 筋 □ ...bands of natural vegetation between strips of crops. 農作物の畝の間に筋になって生えた自生植物 ❻ N-COUNT 可算名詞 A **band** is a strip or loop of metal or other strong material which strengthens something, or which holds several things together. 帯輪 □ Surgeon Geoffrey Horne placed a metal band around the knee cap to help it knit back together. 外科医ジェフリー・ホーンは接合を助けるため, ひざの皿に金属帯を巻いた. ❼ → see also **elastic band, rubber band** ❽ N-COUNT 可算名詞 A **band** is a range of numbers or values within a system of measurement. 帯域 □ For an initial service, a 10 megahertz-wide band of frequencies will be needed. 初期サービスでは, 周波数10メガヘルツ帯域が必要であろう.

▶ **band together** PHRASAL VERB 句動詞 If people **band together**, they meet and act as a group in order to try and achieve something. 結束する □ Women banded together to protect each other. 女性はお互いを守るために結束した. → see **army, concert, radio**

band|age /bændɪdʒ/ (**bandages, bandaging, bandaged**) ■ N-COUNT 可算名詞 A **bandage** is a long strip of cloth that is wrapped around a wounded part of someone's body to protect or support it. 包帯 □ We put some ointment and a bandage on his knee. 私たちは彼のひざに軟こうを塗って包帯で巻いた. ❷ V-T 他動詞 If you **bandage** a wound or part of someone's body, you tie a bandage around it. 包帯をする □ Apply a dressing to the wound and bandage it. 傷に包帯を当てて巻きなさい. ● PHRASAL VERB 句動詞 **Bandage up** means the same as **bandage**. 包帯をする □ I bandaged the leg up and gave her aspirin for the pain. 私は彼女の脚に包帯を当て, 痛み止めにアスピリンを与えた.

Band-Aid (**Band-Aids**) ■ N-VAR 可変性名詞 商標 A **Band-Aid** is a small piece of sticky tape that you use to cover small cuts or wounds on your body. バンドエード [mainly AM 主に米国英語, TRADEMARK 商標] ❷ ADJ 形容詞 If you refer to a **Band-Aid** solution to a problem, you mean that you disapprove of it because you think that it will only be effective for a short period. 間に合わせの [DISAPPROVAL 不賛成] [ADJ n] □ We need long-term solutions, not short-term Band-Aid ones. 我々には短期の応急処置ではなく, 長期的な解決法が必要である.

B & B /bi ən bi/ (**B&Bs**) → see **bed and breakfast**

ban|dit /bændɪt/ (**bandits**) N-COUNT 可算名詞 Robbers are sometimes called **bandits**, especially if they are found in areas where the law has broken down. 山賊 □ This is real bandit country. ここは本当の無法国だ.

band|wagon /bændwægən/ (**bandwagons**) ■ N-COUNT 可算名詞 You can refer to an activity or movement that has suddenly become fashionable or popular as a **bandwagon**. 時流 □ ...the environmental bandwagon. 環境問題という時流 ❷ N-COUNT 可算名詞 If someone, especially a politician, jumps or climbs **on the bandwagon**, they become involved in an activity or movement because it is fashionable or likely to succeed and not because they are really interested in it. 時流にのった動き [DISAPPROVAL 不賛成] □ In recent months many conservative politicians have jumped on the anti-immigrant bandwagon. ここ数ヵ月, 多くの保守的な政治家が移民排斥の時流に乗っている.

band|width /bændwɪdθ/ (**bandwidths**) N-VAR 可変性名詞 A **bandwidth** is the range of frequencies used for a particular telecommunications signal, radio transmission, or computer network. 帯域幅 □ To cope with this amount of data, the system will need a bandwidth of around 100mhz. この量のデータを取り扱うためには, システムは約100MHzの帯域幅を必要とする.

bang /bæŋ/ (**bangs, banging, banged**) ■ N-COUNT; SOUND 可算名詞, 音声語 A **bang** is a sudden loud noise such as the noise of an explosion. 大きな破裂音 □ I heard four or five loud bangs. 私は大きな破裂音を4, 5回聞いた. □ She slammed the door with a bang. 彼女は大きな音を立ててドアをバタンと閉めた. ❷ V-I 自動詞 If something **bangs**, it makes a sudden loud noise, once or several times. 大きな音を何回か立てる □ The engine spat and banged. エンジンはうなって爆発音を立てた. ❸ V-T/V-I 他動詞/自動詞 If you **bang** a door or if it **bangs**, it closes suddenly with a loud noise. バタンと閉める [自動詞] □ ...the sound of doors banging. ドアがバタンと閉まる音 □ All up and down the street the windows bang shut. 通りの窓はすべてバタンと閉まっていた. ❹ V-T/V-I 他動詞/自動詞 If you **bang on** something or if you **bang** it, you hit it hard, making a loud noise. バンと強打する □ We could bang on the desks and shout till they let us out. 我々は彼らが外に出してくれるまで机を強打し, 叫び続けることができた. ❺ V-T 他動詞 If you **bang** something on something or if you **bang** it down, you quickly and violently put it on a surface, because you are angry. たたきつける □ She banged his dinner on the table. 彼女は彼の夕食をテーブルにたたきつけた. ❻ V-T

他動詞 If you **bang** a part of your body, you accidentally knock it against something and hurt yourself. ぶつける ❑ *She'd fainted and banged her head.* 彼女は気を失って, 頭がぶつけ. ● N-COUNT 可算名詞 **Bang** is also a noun. 強打 ❑ *...a nasty bang on the head.* 頭のひどい強打 ▪ V-I 自動詞 If you **bang into** something or someone, you bump or knock them hard, usually because you are not looking where you are going. ぶつかる ❑ *I didn't mean to bang into you.* きみにぶつかるつもりはなかったんだ. ▪ ADV 副詞 You can use **bang** to emphasize expressions that indicate an exact position or an exact time. まさしく [EMPHASIS 強調] [ADV prep] ❑ *...bang in the middle of the track.* ちょうどトラックの真ん中に ▪ PHRASE 句 If something begins or ends **with a bang**, it begins or ends with a lot of energy, enthusiasm, or success. 勢いよく [PHR after v] ❑ *Her career began with a bang in 1986.* 彼女の職歴は1986年に華々しく始まった.

Word Partnership *bang は次の語句と使われる:*

V.	**hear a** bang ▪
ADJ.	**loud** bang ▪
PREP.	**with a** bang ▪
	bang **on** *something* ▪
	bang **into** ▪
ADV.	bang **down** ▪
N.	bang *your* **head** ▪

bangs /bǽŋz/ N-PLURAL 複数名詞 **Bangs** are hair that is cut so that it hangs over your forehead. 切り下げ前髪 [AM 米国英語] ❑ *My bangs were cut short, but the rest of my hair was long.* 私の前髪は短く切られていたが, 他の部分は長かった.

ban|ish /bǽnɪʃ/ (banishes, banishing, banished) ▪ V-T 他動詞 If someone or something **is banished from** a place or area of activity, they are sent away from it and prevented from entering it. 追放する ❑ *John was banished from England.* ジョンはイギリスから追放された. ❑ *I was banished to the small bedroom upstairs.* 私は2階の小さな寝室に追いやられた. ▪ V-T 他動詞 If you **banish** something unpleasant, you get rid of it. 払いのける ❑ *...a public investment program intended to banish the recession.* 景気回復のための公共投資計画.

Thesaurus *banish また次を参照:*

V.	ban, deport, evict, exile; (*ant.*) embrace, invite, welcome ▪

bank

❶ FINANCE AND STORAGE
❷ AREAS AND MASSES
❸ OTHER VERB USES

❶ **bank** /bǽŋk/ (banks, banking, banked) ▪ N-COUNT 可算名詞 A **bank** is an institution where people or businesses can keep their money. 銀行 ❑ *Students should look to see which bank offers them the service that best suits their financial needs.* 学生はどの銀行が金銭的なニーズに最適のサービスを提供しているかよく調べるべきだ. ▪ N-COUNT 可算名詞 A **bank** is a building where a bank offers its services. 銀行の建物 ▪ V-I 自動詞 If you **bank with** a particular bank, you have an account with that bank. （銀行に）口座を持つ取引をする ❑ *I have banked with Coutts & Co. for years.* 私は長年, クーツ銀行と取引をしている. ▪ N-COUNT 可算名詞 You use **bank** to refer to a store of something. For example, a blood **bank** is a store of blood that is kept ready for use. 貯蔵所 ❑ *...a national data bank of information on hospital employees.* 病院職員に関する情報の全国データバンク.
→ see Word Web: **bank**

❷ **bank** /bǽŋk/ (banks) ▪ N-COUNT 可算名詞 The **banks of** a river, canal, or lake are the raised areas of ground along its edge.

（川や運河, 湖などの）土手 注防 ❑ *We pedaled north along the east bank of the river.* 我々は東の川岸に沿って北へ自転車をこいだ. ▪ N-COUNT 可算名詞 A **bank** of ground is a raised area of it with a flat top and one or two sloping sides. 斜面 ❑ *...lounging on the grassy bank.* 草に覆われた斜面をぶらぶらしながら. ▪ N-COUNT 可算名詞 A **bank of** something is a long high mass of it. （雪や雲などの）積み重なったもの 塊 ❑ *A bank of clouds had built up along the western horizon.* 東の地平線に沿って雲の塊がわき上がっていた. ▪ N-COUNT 可算名詞 A **bank of** things, especially machines, switches, or dials, is a row of them, or a series of rows. （機械やスイッチ, ダイヤルなどの）列 並び ❑ *The typical laborer now sits in front of a bank of dials.* 典型的な作業員が今ダイヤルの列の前に座る.

❸ **bank** /bǽŋk/ (banks, banking, banked) V-I 自動詞 When an aircraft **banks**, one of its wings rises higher than the other, usually when it is changing direction. （飛行機が旋回する時に）機体を傾ける ❑ *A single-engine plane took off and banked above the highway in front of him.* 単発小型機が離陸し, 彼の眼前の高速道路の上で機体を傾け旋回した.
▶ **bank on** PHRASAL VERB 句動詞 If you **bank on** something happening, you expect it to happen and rely on it happening. 当てにする, 頼りにする ❑ *Everyone is banking on an economic rebound to help ease the state's fiscal problems.* 景気回復により国の財政問題が緩和するよう誰もが期待している.

bank ac|count (bank accounts) N-COUNT 可算名詞 A **bank account** is an arrangement with a bank which allows you to keep your money in the bank and to take some out when you need it. 銀行口座 ❑ *Paul had at least 17 different bank accounts.* ポールは銀行口座を少なくとも17は持っていた.

bank bal|ance (bank balances) N-COUNT 可算名詞 Your **bank balance** is the amount of money that you have in your bank account at a particular time. 銀行残高 ❑ *Do you wish to use the Internet simply to check your bank balance?* 銀行残高を確認するためだけにインターネットを使いたいのですか?

bank card (bank cards) also **bankcard** ▪ N-COUNT 可算名詞 A **bank card** is a plastic card that your bank gives you so you can get money from your bank account using a cash machine. It is also called an **ATM** card. キャッシュカード ▪ N-COUNT 可算名詞 A **bank card** is a credit card that is supplied by a bank. クレジットカード [AM 米国英語]
→ see **bank**

bank check (bank checks) N-COUNT 可算名詞 A **bank check** is a check that you can buy from a bank in order to pay someone who is not willing to accept a personal check. 銀行小切手 ❑ *Payments should be made by credit card or bank check in U.S. dollars.* 支払いは米ドル建てでクレジットカードまたは銀行小切手にて行う.

bank|er /bǽŋkər/ (bankers) N-COUNT 可算名詞 A **banker** is someone who works in banking at a senior level. 銀行家 ❑ *...an investment banker.* 投資銀行家.

bank holi|day (bank holidays) N-COUNT 可算名詞 A **bank holiday** is a public holiday. 公休日 [mainly BRIT 主に英国英語; AM usually **national holiday** 米国英語では通常 **national holiday**]

bank|ing /bǽŋkɪŋ/ N-UNCOUNT 不可算名詞 **Banking** is the business activity of banks and similar institutions. 銀行業務 ❑ *...the online banking revolution.* オンライン・バンキング革命.
→ see **industry**

bank|note /bǽŋknoʊt/ (banknotes) also **bank note** N-COUNT 可算名詞 **Banknotes** are pieces of paper money. 紙幣 ❑ *...a shopping bag full of banknotes.* 紙幣がいっぱい詰まった買い物袋.

bank rate (bank rates) N-COUNT 可算名詞 The **bank rate** is the rate of interest at which a bank lends money, especially the minimum rate of interest that banks are allowed to charge, which is decided from time to time by the country's central bank. 銀行割引歩合 ❑ *The United States reduced its main bank rate ten days ago.* 米国は10日前に主要金利を引き下げた.

Word Web bank

Most people deposit **money** into **checking accounts** and **savings accounts**. Money can be **withdrawn** from a checking account by writing a **check** or using a **bank card** at an automated teller machine (**ATM**). People record these **transactions** in a **check register**. People **balance** their accounts using their monthly **bank statements**. Customers can also **bank online** at their bank's website. When people **deposit** money into a savings account they earn **interest** from the bank for the use of the money. A bank uses its customers' money to make **loans**. Banks **lend** money for mortgages, car loans, student loans, and business loans. The **borrower** pays back the **principal** amount **borrowed**, plus interest.

b

bank|roll /bǽŋkroʊl/ (bankrolls, bankrolling, bankrolled) V-T 他動詞 To **bankroll** a person, organization, or project means to provide the financial resources that they need. 融資する, 財政援助をする [mainly AM 主に米国英語, INFORMAL くだけた] ❑ *The company has bankrolled a couple of local movies.* その会社は2本の地元映画に資金を提供した。

bank|rupt /bǽŋkrʌpt/ (bankrupts, bankrupting, bankrupted) **1** ADJ 形容詞 People or organizations that go **bankrupt** do not have enough money to pay their debts. 破産した [BUSINESS 実業] ❑ *If the firm cannot sell its products, it will go bankrupt.* もし製品が売れなかったら, その会社は倒産するだろう。 **2** V-T 他動詞 To **bankrupt** a person or organization means to make them go bankrupt. 破産させる [BUSINESS 実業] ❑ *The move to the market nearly bankrupted the firm and its director.* 市場への動きで, その会社と取締役は危うく破産するところだった。 **3** N-COUNT 可算名詞 A **bankrupt** is a person who has been declared bankrupt by a court of law. 支払い不能者 ❑ *In total, 80% of bankrupts are men.* 合計すると, 破産者の80パーセントが男性である。 **4** ADJ 形容詞 If you say that something is **bankrupt**, you are emphasizing that it lacks any value or worth. (価値などを) 欠く [EMPHASIS 強調] ❑ *He really thinks that European civilization is morally bankrupt.* 彼はヨーロッパ文明が道徳観念が完全に欠如していると本当に考えている。

bank|rupt|cy /bǽŋkrʌptsi/ (bankruptcies) **1** N-UNCOUNT 不可算名詞 **Bankruptcy** is the state of being bankrupt. 破産状態 [BUSINESS 実業] ❑ *Pan Am is the second airline in two months to file for bankruptcy.* パンナムはこの2か月で破産申請を行った2番目の航空会社だ。 **2** N-COUNT 可算名詞 A **bankruptcy** is an instance of an organization or person going bankrupt. 破産 [BUSINESS 実業] ❑ *The number of corporate bankruptcies climbed in August.* 企業倒産件数は8月に上昇した。

Word Partnership	*bankruptcy* は次の語句と使われる:
V.	**force into** bankruptcy **1**
	avoid bankruptcy **1 2**
	declare bankruptcy, **file for** bankruptcy **1**
N.	bankruptcy **law**, bankruptcy **protection 1 2**

bank state|ment (bank statements) N-COUNT 可算名詞 A **bank statement** is a printed document showing all the money paid into and taken out of a bank account. Bank statements are usually sent by a bank to a customer at regular intervals. 銀行取引明細書

ban|ner /bǽnər/ (banners) **1** N-COUNT 可算名詞 A **banner** is a long strip of cloth with something written on it. Banners are usually attached to two poles and carried during a protest or rally. 横断幕 ❑ *A large crowd of students followed the coffin, carrying banners and shouting slogans denouncing the government.* 大勢の学生が横断幕を掲げ, 政府を非難するスローガンを叫びながらひつぎの後に続いた。 **2** PHRASE 句 If someone does something **under the banner of** a particular cause, idea, or belief, they do it saying that they support that cause, idea, or belief. ～の旗の下に ❑ *Russia was the first country to forge a new economic system under the banner of Marxism.* ロシアはマルクス主義の旗の下に新しい経済制度を作り上げた最初の国だ。

ban|ner ad (banner ads) N-COUNT 可算名詞 A **banner ad** is a rectangular advertisement on a web page that contains a link to the advertiser's website. バナー広告 ❑ *See our banner ad at this site!* このサイトにある我社のバナー広告をご覧下さい!

ban|quet /bǽŋkwɪt/ (banquets) N-COUNT 可算名詞 A **banquet** is a grand formal dinner. 豪華な宴会 ❑ *...this week's Greater Cleveland Sports Commission awards banquet.* 今週のグレータークリーブランド・スポーツ委員会の受賞パーティー。 ❑ *...a wedding banquet.* 結婚披露宴。

ban|ter /bǽntər/ N-UNCOUNT 不可算名詞 **Banter** is teasing or joking talk that is amusing and friendly. 冗談, (機知に富み親しみを込めた) からかい ❑ *As she closed the door, she heard Tom exchanging good-natured banter with Jane.* 彼女がドアを閉める時に, トムがジェーンと気のいい冗談を交わしているのが聞こえた。

bap|tism /bǽptɪzəm/ (baptisms) N-VAR 可変性名詞 A **baptism** is a Christian ceremony in which a person is baptized. Compare **christening**. 洗礼 ❑ *Infants prepared for baptism should be dressed in pure white.* 洗礼を受ける子供は純白の衣装につつまれるべきだ。

bap|tize /bǽptaɪz/ (baptizes, baptizing, baptized) V-T 他動詞 When someone is **baptized**, water is put on their heads or they are covered with water as a sign that their sins have been forgiven and that they have become a member of the Christian church. Compare **christen**. 洗礼を施す [usu passive] ❑ *At this time she decided to become a Christian and was baptized.* この時, 彼女はキリスト教徒になることを決意し洗礼を受けた。

bar /bɑr/ (bars, barring, barred) **1** N-COUNT 可算名詞 A **bar** is a place where you can buy and drink alcoholic drinks. バー, 酒場 [mainly AM 主に米国英語] ❑ *...Devil's Herd, the city's most*

popular country and western bar. その街で最も人気のカントリー・アンド・ウェスタン・バー「デビルズ・ハード」。 **2** → see also **snack bar, wine bar 3** N-COUNT 可算名詞 A **bar** is a room in a hotel or other establishment where alcoholic drinks are served. (ホテルの) バー ❑ *Last night in the hotel there was some talk in the bar about drugs.* 昨夜, そのホテルのバーで麻薬について話している人がいた。 **4** N-COUNT 可算名詞 A **bar** is a counter on which alcoholic drinks are served. (バーの) カウンター ❑ *Michael was standing alone by the bar when Brian rejoined him.* ブライアンが再会した時, マイケルはバーのカウンターに一人で立っていた。

There are a number of names that can be applied to businesses serving alcohol. The most common is **bar**. In the UK, there are **pubs**, which sometimes also serve light meals. **Nightclubs** also serve drinks along with music or entertainment. However, a **snack bar** does not serve alcohol, just drinks and soft drinks.

5 N-COUNT 可算名詞 A **bar** is a long, straight, stiff piece of metal. (金属の) 細長い棒 ❑ *...a brick building with bars across the ground floor windows.* 1階の窓に格子を張り巡らせたれんがの建物。 **6** PHRASE 句 If you say that someone is **behind bars**, you mean that they are in prison. 獄中にいる ❑ *Fisher was behind bars last night, charged with attempted murder.* フィッシャーは昨夜, 殺人未遂の容疑で刑務所にいた。 **7** N-COUNT 可算名詞 A **bar of** something is a piece of it which is roughly rectangular. (棒状・長方形の) かたまり ❑ *What is your favorite chocolate bar?* あなたはどのチョコバーが好き? **8** V-T 他動詞 If you **bar** a door, you place something in front of it or a piece of wood or metal across it in order to prevent it from being opened. かんぬきをかける ❑ *For added safety, bar the door to the kitchen.* 念のため, 台所のドアにかんぬきをかけよう。 **9** V-T 他動詞 If you **bar** someone's way, you prevent them from going somewhere or entering a place, by blocking their path. (道や入り口を) ふさぐ ❑ *Harry moved to bar his way.* ハリーは彼の行く手をさえぎった。 **10** V-T 他動詞 If someone is **barred from** a place or **from** doing something, they are officially forbidden to go there or to do it. 禁止する [usu passive] ❑ *Amnesty workers have been barred from the country since 1982.* 1982年以来, アムネスティの職員は同国への立ち入りを禁止されている。 **11** N-COUNT 可算名詞 If something is a **bar to** doing a particular thing, it prevents someone from doing it. 障害, 制約 ❑ *One of the fundamental bars to communication is the lack of a universally spoken, common language.* 対話の根本的な妨げの一つは世界共通語がないことだ。 **12** PREP 前置詞 You can use **bar** when you mean "except." For example, all the work **bar** the laundry means all the work except the laundry. ～を除いて [mainly BRIT 主に英国英語] ❑ *Bar a plateau in 1989, there has been a rise in inflation ever since the mid-1980s.* 1989年の停滞期を除けば, 1980年代半ばからずっと物価が上昇している。 **13** → see also **barring 14** N-SING 単数名詞 The **bar** is used to refer to the profession of any kind of lawyer in the United States, or of a barrister in England. 法曹界 [oft N n] ❑ *Less than a quarter of graduates from the law school pass the bar exam on the first try.* 初めて司法試験を受けて合格する法学大学院卒業生の数は全体の四分の一以下だ。 **15** N-COUNT 可算名詞 In music, a **bar** is one of the several short parts of the same length into which a piece of music is divided. 小節 ❑ *She sat down at the piano and played a few bars of a Chopin Polonaise.* 彼女はピアノに向かい, ショパンのポロネーズを何小節か弾いた。

→ see **gymnastics, soap**

Word Partnership	*bar* は次の語句と使われる:
ADJ.	**full** bar, **gay** bar, **local** bar **1**
	candy/chocolate bar **6**
N.	bar **and grill**, bar **and lounge**, bar **owner, restaurant and** bar, **sports** bar, bar **stool 1**
	bar **of soap 6**
	bar **a door 7**
	bar **exam 12**
PREP.	**behind a** bar **3**
	bar *someone* **from 9**

bar|bar|ic /bɑrbǽrɪk/ ADJ 形容詞 If you describe someone's behavior as **barbaric**, you strongly disapprove of it because you think that it is extremely cruel or uncivilized. 野蛮な, 荒っぽい [DISAPPROVAL 不賛成] ❑ *This barbaric treatment of animals has no place in any decent society.* 動物に対するこの残虐な扱いは, まともな社会では決して許されない。

bar|ba|rism /bɑrbərɪzəm/ N-UNCOUNT 不可算名詞 If you refer to someone's behavior as **barbarism**, you strongly disapprove of it because you think that it is extremely cruel or uncivilized. 野蛮, 残虐な行為 [DISAPPROVAL 不賛成] ❑ *We do not ask for the death penalty; barbarism must not be met with barbarism.* 我々は死刑を要求しない。残虐な行為に残虐な行為で返してはならない。

bar|becue /bɑrbɪkyu/ (barbecues, barbecuing, barbecued) also **barbeque** or **Bar-B-Q 1** N-COUNT 可算名詞 A **barbecue** is a piece of equipment which you use for cooking on in the open air. バーベキューの器具 (焼き網や串など) **2** N-COUNT 可算名詞

If someone has a **barbecue**, they cook food on a barbecue in the open air. バーベキュー □ *On New Year's Eve we had a barbecue on the beach.* 大晦日に海辺でバーベキューをした. **2** V-T 他動詞 If you **barbecue** food, especially meat, you cook it on a barbecue. (火や炭の上で) あぶり焼く □ *Tuna can be grilled, fried or barbecued.* まぐろはグリルで焼いても、揚げ物にしても、バーベキューにしてもいい. □ *Here's a way of barbecuing corn-on-the-cob that I learned from my uncle.* これは私の叔父が教えてくれたトウモロコシの焼き方だよ. → see **cook**

> A **barbecue** is a popular style of cooking during the summer. Meat with a spicy sauce is cooked on a metal grill over an open fire. Some food may not be spiced, such as hamburgers, hot dogs, or corn on the cob, and this is cooked over the fire as well. North Americans may also call this event a **cookout**. In South Africa a barbecue is called a **braai** (pronounced like the word "cry"), and is a very common social or family gathering.

barbed wire /bɑrbd waɪər/ N-UNCOUNT 不可算名詞 **Barbed wire** is strong wire with sharp points sticking out of it, and is used to make fences. 有刺鉄線 □ *The factory was surrounded by barbed wire.* その工場には鉄条網が張り巡らされていた.

bar|bell /bɑrbɛl/ (**barbells**) N-COUNT 可算名詞 A **barbell** is a long bar with adjustable weights on either side that people lift to strengthen their arm and shoulder muscles. バーベル □ *She lifted the barbell in her left hand.* 彼女は左手でバーベルを持ち上げた.

bar|ber /bɑrbər/ (**barbers**) **1** N-COUNT 可算名詞 A **barber** is a man whose job is cutting men's hair. 理髪師 (通常、男性の髪を理髪する男性のことをいう) □ *My father marched me over to Otto, the local barber, to have my hair cut short.* 父は私を地元の散髪屋オットーのところへ引っ張って行き、髪を短く切らせた. **2** N-SING 単数名詞 A **barber's** is a store where a barber works. 理髪店 [mainly BRIT 主に英国英語; AM usually **barber shop** 米国英語では通常 **barber shop**]

bar chart (**bar charts**) N-COUNT 可算名詞 A **bar chart** is the same as a **bar graph**. 棒グラフ

bar code (**bar codes**) also **barcode** N-COUNT 可算名詞 A **bar code** is an arrangement of numbers and parallel lines that is printed on products to be sold in stores. The bar code can be read by computers. バーコード → see **laser**

bare /bɛər/ (**barer, barest, bares, baring, bared**) **1** ADJ 形容詞 If a part of your body is **bare**, it is not covered by any clothing. (衣服や靴などを) 身につけていない □ *She was wearing only a thin robe over a flimsy nightgown, and her feet were bare.* 彼女は薄いネグリジェの上に薄いバスローブをまとっただけで、足は裸足だった. **2** ADJ 形容詞 A **bare** surface is not covered or decorated with anything. むき出しの □ *They would have liked bare wooden floors throughout the house.* 彼らなら家中むき出しのフローリングが好みだったろうな. **3** ADJ 形容詞 If a tree or a branch is **bare**, it has no leaves on it. (木が) 裸の □ *...an old, twisted tree, many of its limbs brittle and bare.* もろい裸の枝を付け、曲がりくねった古い木. **4** ADJ 形容詞 If a room, cupboard, or shelf is **bare**, it is empty. 空っぽの □ *His fridge was bare apart from three very withered tomatoes.* 彼の冷蔵庫にはしなび切ったトマト3つ以外、何も入っていなかった. **5** ADJ 形容詞 An area of ground that is **bare** has no plants growing on it. 不毛の □ *That's probably the most bare, bleak, barren and inhospitable island I've ever seen.* それは私が見てきた中で恐らく最も寒々しく荒涼とした島だ. **6** ADJ 形容詞 If someone gives you the **bare** facts or the **barest** details of something, they tell you only the most basic and important things. 最低限の [det ADJ n] □ *Newspaper reporters were given nothing but the bare facts by the superintendent in charge of the investigation.* 新聞記者たちは捜査の担当警視監から最低限の情報しか与えてもらえなかった. **7** ADJ 形容詞 If you talk about the **bare** minimum or the **bare** essentials, you mean the very least that is necessary. 必要最小限の [det ADJ n] □ *The army would try to hold the western desert with a bare minimum of forces.* 軍は砂漠の西部を必要最小限の部隊で守ろうとするだろう. **8** ADJ 形容詞 **Bare** is used in front of an amount to emphasize how small it is. たった [EMPHASIS 強調] ['a' ADJ amount] □ *Sales are growing for premium wines, but at a bare 2 percent a year.* 上質ワインの売り上げが伸びているが、年間わずか2パーセントに過ぎない. **9** V-T 他動詞 If you bare something, you uncover it and show it. あらわにする [WRITTEN 書き言葉] □ *Walsh bared his teeth in a grin.* ウォルシュはにやりと笑って歯をむき出した. **10** PHRASE 句 If someone does something with their **bare hands**, they do it without using any weapons or tools. 素手で □ *Police believe the killer punched her to death with his bare hands.* 警察は殺人犯が素手で彼女を殴り殺したと信じている. **11** bare bones → see **bone**

Thesaurus
bare また次を参照:

ADJ.	naked, nude, undressed; (ant.) clothed, dressed **1**
	arid, barren, bleak **5**
V.	disclose, expose, reveal, show; (ant.) cover, hide **9**

bare-bones **1** ADJ 形容詞 If you describe something as **bare-bones**, you mean that it is reduced to the smallest size, amount, or number that you need. 必要最小限の [usu ADJ n] □ *The mayor will have to slash the city's already bare-bones budget.* 市長は既にぎりぎりの市の予算をさらに大幅削減しないといけなくなる. **2** → see also **bone 4**

bare|foot /bɛərfʊt/ ADJ 形容詞 Someone who is **barefoot** is not wearing anything on their feet. 裸足の □ *I wore a white dress and was barefoot.* 私は白いドレスを身にまとい、足は素足だった.

bare|ly /bɛərli/ **1** ADV 副詞 You use **barely** to say that something is only just true or only just the case. かろうじて、ほとんど~ない □ *Anastasia could barely remember the ride to the hospital.* アナスタシアは病院に運ばれたことをかすかに覚えていた. □ *It was 90 degrees and the air conditioning barely cooled the room.* 気温は華氏90度で、部屋のエアコンはほとんど効いていなかった. **2** ADV 副詞 If you say that one thing had **barely** happened when something else happened, you mean that the first event was followed immediately by the second. ~してすぐに [ADV before v] □ *The water had barely come to a simmer when she cracked four eggs into it.* お湯が沸くやいなや、彼女はそこへ卵を4つ割って入れた.

bar|gain /bɑrgɪn/ (**bargains, bargaining, bargained**) **1** N-COUNT 可算名詞 Something that is a **bargain** is good value, usually because it has been sold at a lower price than normal. 特価品 □ *At this price the wine is a bargain.* この値段でそのワインはお買い得だ. **2** N-COUNT 可算名詞 A **bargain** is an agreement, especially a formal business agreement, in which two people or groups agree what each of them will do, pay, or receive. 契約 □ *I'll make a bargain with you. I'll play hostess if you'll include Matthew in your guest list.* 取引しましょう。もしマシューをあなたのゲストリストに加えてくれるなら、私が女主人役をするわ. **3** V-I 自動詞 When people **bargain with** each other, they discuss what each of them will do, pay, or receive. 取引の交渉をする、駆け引きをする ( ) □ *They prefer to bargain with individual clients, for cash.* 彼らは個々の顧客と現金で取引の交渉をすることを好む. ● **bar|gain|ing** N-UNCOUNT 不可算名詞 交渉、取引 □ *The government has called for sensible pay bargaining.* 政府は常識的な賃金交渉を求めた. **4** PHRASE 句 You use **into the bargain** or **in the bargain** when mentioning an additional quantity, feature, fact, or action, to emphasize the fact that it is also involved. さらに [EMPHASIS 強調] □ *This machine is designed to save you effort, and keep your work surfaces tidy into the bargain.* この機械であなたの作業が楽になる上に、作業台がすっきりします. ▶ **bargain for** or **bargain on** PHRASAL VERB 句動詞 If you have not **bargained for** or **bargained on** something that happens, you did not expect it to happen and so feel surprised or worried by it. 期待する □ *The effects of this policy were more than the government had bargained for.* この政策の効果は政府が期待していた以上のものだった.

Thesaurus
bargain また次を参照:

N.	deal, discount, markdown **1**
	agreement, deal, understanding **2**
V.	barter, haggle, negotiate **3**

Word Partnership
bargain は次の語句と使われる:

V.	find/get a bargain **1**
	make/strike a bargain **2**
N.	bargain **hunter**, bargain **price**, bargain **rates 1**
	part of the bargain **2**
PREP.	bargain **with** *someone* **3**

barge /bɑrdʒ/ (**barges, barging, barged**) **1** N-COUNT 可算名詞 A **barge** is a long, narrow boat with a flat bottom. Barges are used for carrying heavy loads, especially on rivers and canals. 平底の荷船 [also 'by' N] □ *Carrying goods by train costs nearly three times more than carrying them by barge.* 鉄道輸送は、荷船運送に比べ3倍近くの費用がかかる. **2** V-I 自動詞 If you **barge into** a place or **barge through** it, you rush or push into it in a rough and rude way. 押しかける [INFORMAL くだけた] □ *Students tried to barge into the secretariat buildings.* 学生たちは事務局の建物に押し入ろうとした. **3** V-I 自動詞 If you **barge into** someone or **barge past** them, you bump against them roughly and rudely. ぶつかる [INFORMAL くだけた] □ *He would barge into them and kick them in the shins.* 彼なら彼らにぶつかって向こうずねを蹴っているだろう. → see **ship** ▶ **barge in** or **barge in on** PHRASAL VERB 句動詞 If you **barge in** or **barge in on** someone, you rudely interrupt what they are doing or saying. 割り込む [INFORMAL くだけた] □ *I'm sorry to barge in like this, but I have a problem I hope you can solve.* でも困っていて、あなたなら解決できないかと願っているの.

bar graph (**bar graphs**) N-COUNT 可算名詞 A **bar graph** is a graph that uses parallel rectangular shapes to represent changes in the size, value, or rate of something or to compare the amount of something relating to a number of different countries or

groups. 棒グラフ ❑ *They made a bar graph to display the results.* 彼らは結果を棒グラフで示した.
→ see **graph**

bar-hop (**bar-hops, bar-hopping, bar-hopped**) V-I 自動詞 If a person **bar-hops**, they go from one bar to another having drinks in each one. （飲み屋を）はしごする [AM 米国英語, INFORMAL くだけた] ❑ *…a yearly rite-of-passage in which graduating seniors bar-hop from morning until late afternoon.* 卒業する学生が朝から夕方まではしご酒をする毎年恒例の通過儀式.

bari|tone /bærɪtoʊn/ (**baritones**) N-COUNT 可算名詞 In music, a **baritone** is a man with a fairly deep singing voice that is lower than that of a tenor but higher than that of a bass. バリトン（男声のテノールとバスの中間）❑ *…the young American baritone Monte Pederson.* アメリカの若手バリトン歌手モンテ・ピダーソン

bark /bɑrk/ (**barks, barking, barked**) ❶ V-I 自動詞 When a dog **barks**, it makes a short, loud noise, once or several times. （犬やきつねが）ほえる ❑ *Don't let the dogs bark.* 犬をほえさせないようにして下さい. ● N-COUNT 可算名詞 **Bark** is also a noun. ほえる声 ❑ *The Doberman let out a string of roaring barks.* ドーベルマンがひどくほえ立てた. ❷ V-I 自動詞 If you **bark at** someone, you shout at them aggressively in a loud, rough voice. どなる ❑ *I didn't mean to bark at you.* きみにどなるつもりはなかったんだ. ❸ N-UNCOUNT 不可算名詞 **Bark** is the tough material that covers the outside of a tree. 樹皮 ❹ to be **barking up the wrong tree** → see **tree**

bar|ley /bɑrli/ N-UNCOUNT 不可算名詞 **Barley** is a grain that is used to make food, beer, and whiskey. 大麦 ❑ *…fields of ripening wheat and barley.* 小麦と大麦が実りつつある畑.

bar|maid /bɑrmeɪd/ (**barmaids**) N-COUNT 可算名詞 A **barmaid** is a woman who serves drinks behind a bar. 女性のバーテン [mainly BRIT 主に英国英語; AM **bartender** 米国英語]

bar|man /bɑrmən/ (**barmen**) N-COUNT 可算名詞 A **barman** is a man who serves drinks behind a bar. 男性のバーテン [mainly BRIT 主に英国英語; AM **bartender** 米国英語]

barn /bɑrn/ (**barns**) N-COUNT 可算名詞 A **barn** is a building on a farm in which animals, animal food, or crops can be kept. （家畜の）小屋，（餌や作物の）納屋
→ see Picture Dictionary: **barn**

ba|rom|eter /bərɒmɪtər/ (**barometers**) ❶ N-COUNT 可算名詞 A **barometer** is an instrument that measures air pressure and shows when the weather is changing. 気圧計 ❑ *A man in camp took a barometer reading at half-hour intervals.* キャンプの男は30分毎に気圧計の数字をはかった. ❷ N-COUNT 可算名詞 If something is a **barometer** of a particular situation, it indicates how things are changing or how things are likely to develop. （世論などの）指標，バロメーター ❑ *In past presidential elections, Missouri has been a barometer of the rest of the country.* 過去の大統領選挙で，ミズーリ州は全国の指標となっている.

baro|met|ric /bærəmɛtrɪk/ **Barometric** pressure is the atmospheric pressure that is shown by a barometer. 気圧計の ADJ 形容詞
→ see **forecast, weather**

bar|on /bærən/ (**barons**) ❶ N-COUNT; N-TITLE 可算名詞，称号名詞 A **baron** is a man who is a member of the lowest rank of the nobility. 男爵 [BRIT 英国英語] ❑ *…their stepfather, Baron Michael Distemple.* 彼らの義理の父であるマイケル・ディステンプル男爵. ❷ N-COUNT 可算名詞 You can use **baron** to refer to someone who controls a large part of a particular industry or activity and who is therefore extremely powerful. （その業界の）実力者 ❑ *…the battle against the drug barons.* 麻薬王たちとの戦い.

bar|rage /bərɑʒ/ (**barrages, barraging, barraged**)

Pronounced /bərɪdʒ/ for meaning ❹.

❹ の意味では /bərɪdʒ/ と発音される.

❶ N-COUNT 可算名詞 A **barrage** is continuous firing on an area with large guns and tanks. 爆撃 ❑ *The artillery barrage on the city was the heaviest since the ceasefire.* その街への爆撃は停戦以来，最も激しいものだった. ❷ N-COUNT 可算名詞 A **barrage of** something such as criticism or complaints is a large number of them directed at someone, often in an aggressive way. （批判や苦情，質問などの）集中攻撃 ❑ *He was faced with a barrage of angry questions from the floor.* 彼は議員席から怒りの質問をやつぎばやに浴びた. ❸ V-T 他動詞 If you **are barraged** by people or things, you have to deal with a great number of people or things you would rather avoid. やつぎばやに浴びせる [usu passive] ❑ *Doctors are complaining about being barraged by drug-company salesmen.* 医師たちは製薬会社の販売員が次々訪れてくることに苦情を訴えている. ❹ N-COUNT 可算名詞 A **barrage** is a structure that is built across a river to control the level of the water. （川の）せき ❑ *…a hydro-electric tidal barrage.* 潮の干満による水力発電ダム.

bar|rel /bærəl/ (**barrels, barreling** or **barrelling, barreled** or **barrelled**) ❶ N-COUNT 可算名詞 A **barrel** is a large, round container for liquids or food. （液体や食料を入れる）たる ❑ *The wine is aged for almost a year in oak barrels.* そのワインはオーク材のたるでほぼ1年寝かせた. ❷ N-COUNT 可算名詞 In the oil industry, a **barrel** is a unit of measurement equal to 42 gallons (159 liters). バレル（石油の容量を表す単位．1バレルは42ガロンまたは159リットル．）❑ *In 1989, Kuwait was exporting 1.5 million barrels of oil a day.* 1989年にクウェートは一日150万バレルの石油を輸出していた. ❸ N-COUNT 可算名詞 The **barrel** of a gun is the tube through which the bullet moves when the gun is fired. 銃身 ❑ *He pushed the barrel of the gun into the other man's open mouth.* 彼は銃身をもう一人の男の口の中に押し込んだ. ❹ V-I 自動詞 If a vehicle or person is **barreling** in a particular direction, they are moving very quickly in that direction. 疾走する [mainly AM 主に米国英語] ❑ *The car was barreling down the street at a crazy speed.* その車は通りを恐ろしいスピードで疾走していた. ❺ PHRASE 句 If you say, for example, that someone moves or buys something **lock, stock, and barrel**, you

Picture Dictionary — **barn**

hay · barn · pasture · orchard · greenhouse · plow · tractor · yard · cow · sheep · pig

B

are emphasizing that they move or buy every part or item of it. すべて、一切合財（いっさいがっさい）[EMPHASIS 強調] ❑ *They received a verbal offer to buy the company lock, stock and barrel.* 彼らはその会社の一切を買収する申し出を口頭で受けた.

N.	bottom of the **barrel**, wine **barrel** 🔢
	barrel of oil 🔢
	barrel of a gun 🔢
PREP.	**barrel down** toward *somewhere* 🔢

barrel-chested ADJ 形容詞 A **barrel-chested** man has a large, rounded chest. 胸のがっしりした ❑ *A barrel-chested young man entered the bedroom.* 胸のがっしりした若者が寝室に入った.

bar|ren /bǽrən/ 🔢 ADJ 形容詞 A **barren** landscape is dry and bare, and has very few plants and no trees. 不毛の ❑ *...the Tibetan landscape of high barren mountains.* 高い不毛の山々がそびえるチベットの風景. 🔢 ADJ 形容詞 **Barren** land consists of soil that is so poor that plants cannot grow in it.（土が）やせた ❑ *He wants to use the water to irrigate barren desert land.* 彼はやせた砂漠をかんがいするためにその水を使いたい. 🔢 ADJ 形容詞 If you describe something such as an activity or a period of your life as **barren**, you mean that you achieve no success during it or that it has no useful results. 実を結ばない [WRITTEN 書き言葉] [oft ADJ 'of' n] ❑ *...an empty exercise barren of utility.* 無益な虚しい実行. 🔢 ADJ 形容詞 If you describe a room or a place as **barren**, you do not like it because it has almost no furniture or other objects in it. 味気ない [WRITTEN 書き言葉, DISAPPROVAL 不賛成] [oft ADJ 'of' n] ❑ *The room was austere, nearly barren of furniture or decoration.* その部屋はほとんど家具も装飾もなく味気なかった.

| ADJ. | desolate, empty, infertile, sparse, sterile; (ant.) fertile, lush, rich 🔢 🔢 |

bar|ri|cade /bǽrɪkeɪd/ (**barricades, barricading, barricaded**) 🔢 N-COUNT 可算名詞 A **barricade** is a line of vehicles or other objects placed across a road or open space to stop people from getting past, for example, during street fighting or as a protest. バリケード ❑ *Large areas of the city have been closed off by barricades set up by the demonstrators.* デモ参加者によって張り巡らされたバリケードで都市の大部分が閉鎖されている. 🔢 V-T 他動詞 If you **barricade** something such as a road or an entrance, you place a barricade or barrier across it, usually to stop someone from getting in. バリケードでふさぐ ❑ *The rioters barricaded streets with piles of blazing tires.* 暴徒は燃え盛るタイヤを積み上げて通りをふさいだ. 🔢 V-T 他動詞 If you **barricade** yourself inside a room or building, you place barriers across the door or entrance so that other people cannot get in.（バリケードを築いて）立てこもる ❑ *The students have barricaded themselves into their dormitory building.* 学生たちは寮の中に立てこもっている.

bar|ri|er /bǽriər/ (**barriers**) 🔢 N-COUNT 可算名詞 A **barrier** is something such as a rule, law, or policy that makes it difficult or impossible for something to happen or be achieved. 障害 ❑ *Duties and taxes are the most obvious barrier to free trade.* 関税や税金は自由貿易の最も明らかな障害となっている. 🔢 N-COUNT 可算名詞 A **barrier** is a problem that prevents two people or groups from agreeing, communicating, or working with each other. 障壁 ❑ *There is no reason why love shouldn't cross the age barrier.* 愛は年齢の壁を超えられるはずだ. ❑ *She had been waiting for Simon to break down the barrier between them.* 彼女はサイモンが心を開いてくれるのを待っていた. 🔢 N-COUNT 可算名詞 A **barrier** is something such as a fence or wall that is put in place to prevent people from moving easily from one area to another. 柵, 防壁 ❑ *The demonstrators broke through heavy police barriers.* デモ参加者は警察の頑丈な柵を破ってきた. 🔢 N-COUNT 可算名詞 A **barrier** is an object or layer that physically prevents something from moving from one place to another.（移動や進行を妨げる）障害物 ❑ *A severe storm destroyed a natural barrier between the house and the lake.* 激しい嵐が家と湖の間にあった自然の障害物を破壊した. 🔢 N-SING 単数名詞 You can refer to a particular number or amount as a **barrier** when you think it is significant, because it is difficult or unusual to go above it.（数の）大台 ❑ *They are fearful that unemployment will soon break the barrier of three million.* 彼らは失業者数が間もなく300万人の大台に乗ることを恐れている.

ADJ.	**psychological** barrier, **racial** barrier 🔢
N.	**language** barrier 🔢
	police barrier 🔢
	barrier **islands/reef** 🔢
PREP.	barrier **between** 🔢 – 🔢
V.	**break down a** barrier, **cross a** barrier 🔢 – 🔢

bar|ring /bɑ́rɪŋ/ PREP 前置詞 You use **barring** to indicate that the person, thing, or event that you are mentioning is an exception to your statement. がなければ ❑ *Barring accidents, I believe they will succeed.* 事故がなければ、彼らは成功するはずだ.

bar|ris|ter /bǽrɪstər/ (**barristers**) N-COUNT 可算名詞 In England and Wales, a **barrister** is a lawyer who represents clients in the higher courts of law. Compare **solicitor**. 法廷弁護士（英国の法廷で答弁する権限を持つ.）

bar|room /bɑ́rum/ (**barrooms**) also **bar-room** N-COUNT 可算名詞 A **barroom** is a room or building in which alcoholic drinks are served over a counter.（ホテルなどの）バー, カクテルラウンジ [mainly AM 主に米国英語] ❑ *...a barroom brawl.* バーでのけんか.

bar|tender /bɑ́rtɛndər/ (**bartenders**) N-COUNT 可算名詞 A **bartender** is a person who serves drinks behind a bar. バーテンダー [AM 米国英語]

bar|ter /bɑ́rtər/ (**barters, bartering, bartered**) V-T/V-I 他動詞/自動詞 If you **barter** goods, you exchange them for other goods, rather than selling them for money. 物々交換する ❑ *They have been bartering wheat for cotton and timber.* 彼らは小麦を綿や材木と物々交換している. ❑ *The market-place and street were crowded with those who'd come to barter.* 市場や通りは物々交換に来た人々でごった返している. ● N-UNCOUNT 不可算名詞 **Barter** is also a noun. 物々交換 ❑ *Overall, barter is a very inefficient means of organizing transactions.* 全体的に見ると、物々交換は取引を体系化するには非常に効率が悪い方法だ. → see **money**

base /beɪs/ (**bases, basing, based, baser, basest**) 🔢 N-COUNT 可算名詞 The **base** of something is its lowest edge or part. 基部 ❑ *There was a bike path running along this side of the wall, right at its base.* 壁のこちら側の基部に沿って自転車道が走っていた. 🔢 N-COUNT 可算名詞 The **base** of something is the lowest part of it, where it is attached to something else. 付け根 ❑ *The surgeon placed catheters through the veins and arteries near the base of the head.* 外科医は頭の付け根近くの静脈と動脈にカテーテルを入れた. 🔢 N-COUNT 可算名詞 The **base** of an object such as a box or vase is the lower surface of it that touches the surface it rests on. 底 ❑ *Remove from the heat and plunge the base of the pan into a bowl of very cold water.* 火からなをおろし、すぐに冷水の入ったボウルに底を浸す. 🔢 N-COUNT 可算名詞 The **base** of an object that has several sections and that rests on a surface is the lower section of it. 底面 ❑ *The mattress is best on a solid bed base.* そのマットレスの下に敷くのは硬いベッドベースが最適だ. 🔢 N-COUNT 可算名詞 A **base** is a layer of something which will have another layer added to it. 下地 ❑ *Mix together the cream cheese, yogurt and honey, and spread over the meringue base.* クリームチーズとヨーグルト、はちみつを混ぜ、メレンゲの下地の上に広げる. 🔢 N-COUNT 可算名詞 A position or thing that is a **base** for something is one from which that thing can be developed or achieved. 基点 ❑ *The post will give him a powerful political base from which to challenge the Kremlin.* その地位は彼が次にクレムリンを狙うための強力な政治的足がかりとなるだろう. 🔢 V-T 他動詞 If you **base** one thing **on** another thing, the first thing develops from the second thing. 基づかせる ❑ *He based his conclusions on the evidence given by the captured prisoners.* 彼の結論は捕えられた捕虜の証言に基づくものだ. ● **based** ADJ 形容詞 [v-link ADJ 'on/upon' n] ーを基にした ❑ *Three of the new products are based on traditional herbal medicines.* 新製品のうち3つは伝統的な薬草剤からできている. 🔢 N-COUNT 可算名詞 A company's client **base** or customer **base** is the group of regular clients or customers that the company gets most of its income from. 基盤 [BUSINESS 実業] ❑ *The company has been expanding its customer base using trade magazine advertising.* その会社は業界紙に広告を載せて顧客基盤を拡大しつつある. 🔢 N-COUNT 可算名詞 A military **base** is a place that part of the armed forces works from. 基地 ❑ *Gunfire was heard at an army base close to the airport.* 空港の近くの陸軍基地で銃声が聞こえた. 🔢 N-COUNT 可算名詞 Your **base** is the main place where you work, stay, or live. 拠点,（活動, 居住, 滞在の主な）場所 ❑ *For most of the spring and early summer her base was her home in Connecticut.* 春から初夏にかけて彼女はだいたいコネチカット州にある自宅にいた. 🔢 N-COUNT 可算名詞 If a place is a **base** for a certain activity, the activity can be carried out at that place or from that place. 拠点, 出発点 ❑ *The two hotels are attractive bases from which to explore southeast Tuscany.* その2つのホテルはトスカナの南東部を探訪するのに格好の拠点となる. 🔢 N-COUNT 可算名詞 The **base** of a substance such as paint or food is the main ingredient of it, to which other substances can be added. 主成分, ベース ❑ *Just before cooking, drain off any excess marinade and use it as a base for a sauce.* 料理する前に, 余分な漬け汁をこしてソースのベースとして使う. 🔢 N-COUNT 可算名詞 A **base** is a system of counting and expressing numbers. The decimal system uses base 10, and the binary system uses base 2. 基数 [also N num] 🔢 N-COUNT 可算名詞 A **base** in baseball or softball is one of the places at each corner of the diamond on the field. A player who is at **first base, second base,** or **third**

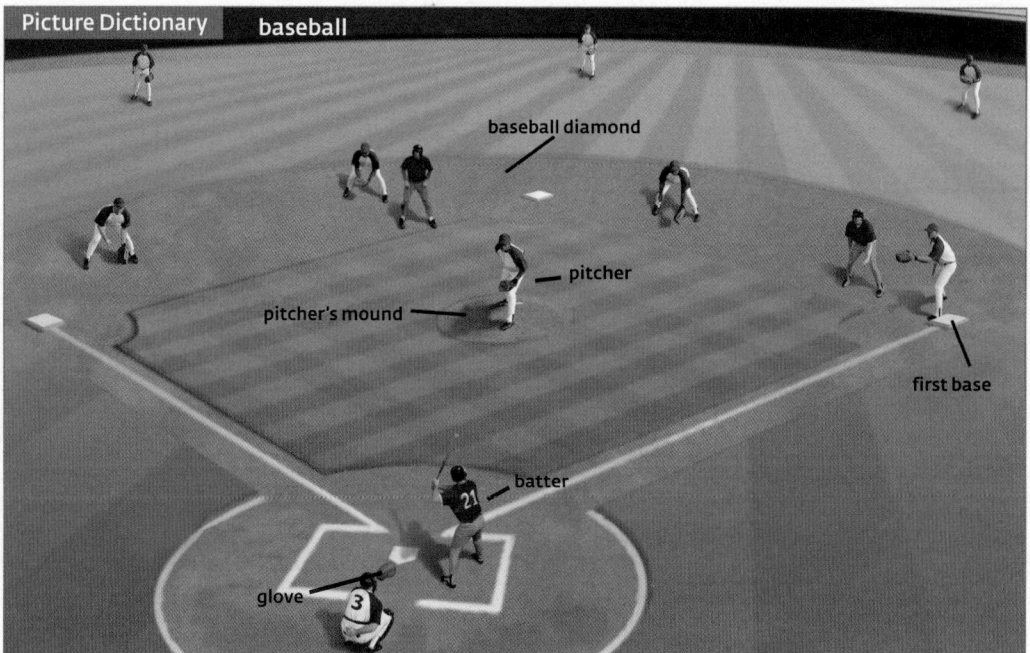

Picture Dictionary **baseball**

baseball diamond

pitcher

pitcher's mound

first base

batter

glove

b

base, is standing at the first, second, or third base in a clockwise direction from home plate. (野球やソフトボールの) ベース, 塁 ❑ *The first runner to reach second base in the game was John Flaherty.* その試合で二塁へ出た最初のランナーはジョン・フラハティだった. **15** ADJ 形容詞 **Base** is used to describe a price or someone's income when this does not include any additional amounts. 基本的の [ADJ n] ❑ *...an increase of more than twenty percent on the base pay of a typical worker.* 標準的な労働者の基本給が20パーセント以上の上昇.
→ see **area**, **baseball**

Word Partnership	base は次の語句と使われる:
N.	**knowledge** base, **tax** base **6**
	client/customer base, **fan** base **8**
	base **camp**, **home** base, base **of operation** **10 11**
	base **hit/run** **14**
ADJ.	**military/naval** base **9**
	stolen base **14**

base|ball /beɪsbɔl/ (baseballs) **1** N-UNCOUNT 不可算名詞 **Baseball** is a game played by two teams of nine players. Each player from one team hits a ball with a bat and then tries to run around three bases and get to home plate before the other team can get the ball back. Compare **softball**. 野球 **2** N-COUNT 可算名詞 A **baseball** is a small hard ball which is used in the game of baseball. 野球ボール
→ see Picture Dictionary: **baseball**
→ see **park**

Although it isn't the most watched sport anymore, **baseball** is still called "America's Pastime." A player who wants to reach his goal usually dreams of playing in the Major League and winning the World Series.

base|ball cap (baseball caps) N-COUNT 可算名詞 A **baseball cap** is a close-fitting cap with a curved part at the front that sticks out above your eyes. 野球帽 ❑ *He often wore a baseball cap.* 彼はよく野球帽をかぶっていた.
→ see **clothing**

based /beɪst/ ADJ 形容詞 If you are **based** in a particular place, that is the place where you live or do most of your work. See also **base**. 〜を拠点とした [v-link ADJ] ❑ *Both firms are based in Kent.* どちらの会社もケントを拠点にしている.

base|ment /beɪsmənt/ (basements) N-COUNT 可算名詞 The **basement** of a building is a floor built partly or completely below ground level. 地階, 地下室 ❑ *They bought an old schoolhouse to live in and built a workshop in the basement.* 彼らは古い校舎を居住用に購入し, 地下に作業場を作った.
→ see **house**

bases

Pronounced /beɪsɪz/ for meaning **1**. Pronounced /beɪsiz/ and hyphenated ba|ses for meaning **2**.
/beɪsɪz/の意味では **1** と発音される. /beɪsiz/の意味では **2** と発音されて, ba|sesとハイフンで結ばれる.

1 Bases is the plural of **base**. baseの複数形 **2 Bases** is the plural of **basis**. basisの複数形

bash /bæʃ/ (bashes, bashing, bashed) **1** N-COUNT 可算名詞 A **bash** is a party or celebration, especially a large one held by an official organization or attended by famous people. 盛大なパーティー [INFORMAL くだけた] ❑ *He threw one of the biggest showbiz bashes of the year as a 36th birthday party for Jerry Hall.* 彼はジェリー・ホールの36歳の誕生日を祝うため, 芸能人を招いたその年最大級のパーティーを開いた. **2** V-T 他動詞 If someone **bashes** you, they attack you by hitting or punching you hard. 殴りつける [INFORMAL くだけた] ❑ *If someone tried to bash my best friend they would have to bash me as well.* 誰かが私の親友を殴るなら, 私をも殴らなくてはならないだろう. ❑ *I bashed him on the head and dumped him in the water.* 私は彼の頭を殴り, 水の中へ放り込んだ. **3** V-T 他動詞 If you **bash** something, you hit it hard in a rough or careless way. 強打する [INFORMAL くだけた] ❑ *Too many golfers try to bash the ball out of sand. That spells disaster.* 非常に多くの人がバンカーから脱出しようとボールを強打するが, それは最悪の事態を招く.

ba|sic /beɪsɪk/ **1** ADJ 形容詞 You use **basic** to describe things, activities, and principles that are very important or necessary, and on which others depend. 基本的な ❑ *...the basic skills of reading, writing and communicating.* 読み, 書き, 意思をやりとりする基本的な権利だ. **2** ADJ 形容詞 **Basic** goods and services are very simple ones which every human being needs. You can also refer to people's **basic** needs for such goods and services. 必要最小限の ❑ *...shortages of even the most basic foodstuffs.* 最も必要最小限の食料品でさえ不足. ❑ *Hospitals lack even basic drugs for surgical operations.* 病院には外科手術に最低必要な薬さえない. **3** ADJ 形容詞 If one thing is **basic to** another, it is absolutely necessary to it, and the second thing cannot exist, succeed, or be imagined without it. ❑ *...an oily liquid, basic to the manufacture of a host of other chemical substances.* 他の多くの化学物質の製造に必要不可欠な油性液体. **4** ADJ 形容詞 You can use **basic** to emphasize that you are referring to what you consider to be the most important aspect of a situation, and that you are not concerned with less important details. 基礎的な [EMPHASIS 強調] [ADJ n] ❑ *There are three basic types of tea.* 紅茶には主に3つの種類がある. ❑ *The basic design changed little from that patented by Edison more than 100 years ago.* 基本的なデザインは100年以上も前にエジソンが特許を取った頃からほとんど変わらなかった. **5** ADJ 形容詞 You can use **basic** to describe something that is very simple in style

and has only the most necessary features, without any luxuries. 簡易の ❏We provide 2-person tents and basic cooking and camping equipment. こちらからは二人用テントと簡単な調理器具およびキャンプ道具を用意します。 ❷ ADJ 形容詞 The **basic** rate of income tax is the lowest or most common rate, which applies to people who earn average incomes. 基本になる [ADJ n] ❏All this is to be done without any big increases in the basic level of taxation. これは、すべて基本税率内での大幅増税なくして実施される。

Thesaurus
basic また次を参照:

| ADJ. | essential, fundamental, key, main, necessary, principal, vital; (*ant.*) nonessential, secondary ❶ – ❹ |

Word Partnership
basic は次の語句と使われる:

| N. | basic **right** ❶
basic **idea**, basic **principles/values**, basic **problem**, basic **questions**, basic **skills**, basic **understanding** ❶ ❹
basic (**health**) **care**, basic **needs** ❷ |
| ADJ. | **most** basic, basic **types of** *something* ❶ – ❺ |

BA|SIC /beɪsɪk/ also **Basic** N-UNCOUNT 不可算名詞 **BASIC** is a computer language that uses common English words. **BASIC** is an abbreviation for "Beginner's All-Purpose Symbolic Instruction Code." ベーシック, BASIC言語（コンピュータのプログラミング言語の一つ）[COMPUTING コンピューティング]

ba|si|cal|ly /beɪsɪkli/ ❶ ADV 副詞 You use **basically** for emphasis when you are stating an opinion, or when you are making an important statement about something. つまり [EMPHASIS 強調] [ADV with cl/group] ❏This gun is designed for one purpose – it's basically to kill people. この銃が作られた目的は一つ。つまり人を殺すことだ。 ❷ ADV 副詞 You use **basically** to show that you are describing a situation in a simple, general way, and that you are not concerned with less important details. 要するに ❏Basically you've got two choices. 要するに、きみには2つ選択肢があるわけだ。

ba|sics /beɪsɪks/ ❶ N-PLURAL 複数名詞 The **basics** of something are its simplest, most important elements, ideas, or principles, in contrast to more complicated or detailed ones. 基礎 ❏They will concentrate on teaching the basics of reading, writing and arithmetic. 彼らは読み、書き、計算の基礎を教えることに専念する。 ❏A strong community cannot be built until the basics are in place. 強い共同体は基礎がなければ築けない。 ❷ N-PLURAL 複数名詞 **Basics** are things such as simple food, clothes, or equipment that people need in order to live or to deal with a particular situation. 必需品 ❏...supplies of basics such as bread and milk. パンや牛乳のような必需品の供給。

ba|sin /beɪsⁿn/ (**basins**) ❶ N-COUNT 可算名詞 A **basin** is a large or deep bowl that you use for holding liquids. たらい ❏Water dripped into a basin at the back of the room. 部屋の奥のたらいに水のしずくがしたたっていた。 ❷ N-COUNT 可算名詞 A **basin of** something such as water is an amount of it that is contained in a basin. （水など）たらい一杯分 ❏We were given a basin of water to wash our hands in. 手を洗うための水をたらいに一杯もらった。 ❸ N-COUNT 可算名詞 A **basin** is a sink. 洗面台 ❏...a cast-iron bathtub with a matching basin. 鋳鉄（ちゅうてつ）製の浴槽とそろいの洗面台。 ❹ N-COUNT 可算名詞 The **basin** of a large river is the area of land around it from which streams run down into it. 流域 ❏...the Amazon basin. アマゾン川流域。 ❺ N-COUNT 可算名詞 In geography, a **basin** is a particular region of the world where the Earth's surface is lower than in other places. 盆地, 海盆 [TECHNICAL 技術的] ❏...countries around the Pacific Basin. 太平洋海盆周辺の国々。
→ see lake, plumbing

ba|sis /beɪsɪs/ (**bases** /beɪsiːz/) ❶ N-SING 単数名詞 If something is done **on** a particular **basis**, it is done according to that method, system, or principle. 根本原理 ❏We're going to be meeting there on a regular basis. 私たちは定期的にそこで会う予定だ。 ❏They want all groups to be treated on an equal basis. 彼らは全てのグループを公平に扱うよう求めている。 ❷ N-SING 単数名詞 If you say that you are acting **on** the **basis of** something, you are giving that as the reason for your action. 根拠 ❏McGregor must remain confined, on the basis of the medical reports we have received. 我々が受け取った医療報告によると、マクレガーは依然外出禁止だ。 ❸ N-COUNT 可算名詞 The **basis** of something is its starting point or an important part of it from which it can be further developed. 基盤 ❏Both factions have broadly agreed that the U.N. plan is a possible basis for negotiation. どちらの党派も国連が交渉の基盤になり得ることにおおむね同意している。 ❹ N-COUNT 可算名詞 The **basis** for something is a fact or argument that you can use to prove or justify it. 論証 ❏...Japan's attempt to secure the legal basis to send troops overseas. 海外派兵の法的根拠を固めようという日本の試み。

Word Partnership
basis は次の語句と使われる:

ADJ.	**equal** basis, **on a** daily/regular/weekly basis, **on a** voluntary basis ❶
PREP.	**on the** basis **of** *something* ❷ – ❹ basis **for** *something* ❸ ❹
V.	**serve as a** basis, **provide a** basis ❸ ❹

ba|sis point (**basis points**) N-COUNT 可算名詞 In finance, a **basis point** is one hundredth of a percent (.01%). ベーシス・ポイント（債券や株式などの単位で，1%の100分の1。1ベーシス・ポイント(bp)は0.01%。）[BUSINESS 実業] ❏The dollar climbed about 30 basis points during the morning session. 午前中の取引でドルは約30ベーシス・ポイント上昇した。

bask /bɑːsk, bæsk/ (**basks, basking, basked**) ❶ V-I 自動詞 If you **bask in** the sunshine, you lie somewhere sunny and enjoy the heat. 日光浴をする ❏All through the hot, still days of their vacation Amy basked in the sun. 暑くて穏やかな休暇中、エイミーはずっと日光浴をしていた。 ❷ V-I 自動詞 If you **bask in** someone's approval, favor, or admiration, you greatly enjoy their positive reaction toward you. （賞賛や尊敬，恩恵を）受ける ❏He has spent a month basking in the adulation of the fans back in Jamaica. 彼は出身のジャマイカでファンの追従を浴びてひと月を過ごした。

bas|ket /bɑːskɪt, bæs-/ (**baskets**) ❶ N-COUNT 可算名詞 A **basket** is a stiff container that is used for carrying or storing objects. Baskets are made from thin strips of materials such as straw, plastic, or wire woven together. かご, バスケット ❏...big wicker picnic baskets filled with sandwiches. サンドイッチがいっぱい詰まったやなぎ編みのピクニックバスケット。 ❷ N-COUNT 可算名詞 You can use **basket** to refer to a basket and its contents, or to the contents only. かごの中身 ❏...a small basket of fruit and snacks. 果物やお菓子が入った小さなかご。 ❸ N-COUNT 可算名詞 In economics, a **basket of** currencies or goods is the average or total value of a number of different currencies or goods. 同類の集まり [BUSINESS 実業] ❏The dollar has fallen 6.5 percent this year against a basket of currencies from its largest trading partners. ドルは最大貿易相手国の通貨バスケットに対し、今年は6.5パーセント下落した。

basket|ball /bɑːskɪtbɔːl, bæs-/ (**basketballs**) ❶ N-UNCOUNT 不可算名詞 **Basketball** is a game in which two teams of five players each try to score goals by throwing a large ball through a circular net fixed to a metal ring at each end of the court. バスケットボール ❷ N-COUNT 可算名詞 A **basketball** is a large ball which is used in the game of basketball. バスケットボールに使われるボール

bas|ket|ry /bæskɪtri/ ❶ N-UNCOUNT 不可算名詞 **Basketry** is baskets made by weaving together thin strips of materials such as wood. 編みかご ❷ N-UNCOUNT 不可算名詞 **Basketry** is the activity of making baskets. かご細工 ❏Eva specializes in one of the most difficult techniques of basketry. エーバはかご細工の最も難しい技術の一つを専門に扱っている。

bass (**basses**)

Pronounced /beɪs/ for meanings ❶ to ❹, and /bæs/ for meaning ❺. The plural of the noun in meaning ❺ is **bass**.

/beɪs/ から❶の意味では❹と発音され，/bæs/ の意味では❺と発音される。❺を意味する名詞の複数形は **bass** である。

❶ N-COUNT 可算名詞 A **bass** is a man with a very deep singing voice. バス歌手 ❏...the great Russian bass Chaliapin. 偉大なロシア人バス歌手シャリアピン。 ❷ ADJ 形容詞 A **bass** drum, guitar, or other musical instrument is one that produces a very deep sound. 低音楽器 [ADJ n] ❏...bass guitarist Dee Murray. ベーシスト，ディー・マレー。 ❸ N-VAR 可変性名詞 In popular music, a **bass** is a bass guitar or a **double bass**. ベースギター，ダブルベース ❏...Dave Ranson on bass and Kenneth Blevins on drums. デイブ・ランソンがベースとドラムを ❹ N-UNCOUNT 不可算名詞 On a stereo system or radio, the **bass** is the ability to reproduce the lower musical notes. The **bass** is also the knob that controls this. 低音, 低音の調整つまみ ❏Larger models give more bass. 型が大きくなるほど低音がよく利く。 ❺ N-VAR 可変性名詞 **Bass** are edible fish that are found in rivers and the sea. There are several types of bass. （魚の）バス, すずき ❏They unloaded their catch of cod and bass. 彼らは漁獲したタラとスズキを降ろした。 ● N-UNCOUNT 不可算名詞 **Bass** is a piece of this fish eaten as food. バスの切り身 ❏...a large fresh fillet of sea bass. 新鮮なシーバスの大きな切り身。

bas|si|net /bæsɪnɛt/ (**bassinets**) N-COUNT 可算名詞 A **bassinet** is a small bed for a baby that is like a basket. 赤ちゃん用のかご型ベッド ❏My baby slept safe from harm in her white wicker bassinet. 私の赤ちゃんは白い編みかごのベッドで安らかに眠った。

bas|ti|on /bæstʃən/ (**bastions**) N-COUNT 可算名詞 If a system or organization is described as a **bastion of** a particular way of life, it is seen as being important and effective in defending that way of life. **Bastion** can be used both when you think that this way of life should be ended and when you think it should be defended. 要塞, とりで [FORMAL 形式ばった] ❏...a town which had been a bastion of

---

Word Web　　bat

Bats fly like birds, but they are **mammals**. Female bats give birth to live young and produce milk. Bats are **nocturnal**, searching for food at night and sleeping during the day. They **roost** upside down in dark, quiet places such as caves and attics. People think that bats drink blood, but only **vampire bats** do this. Most bats eat fruit or insects. As bats fly they make high-pitched sounds that bounce off objects. This echolocation is a kind of **radar** that guides them.

---

white prejudice. 白人による偏見の要塞となっていた町. ❑...a bastion of spiritual freedom. 精神的自由のとりで.

bat /bæt/ (bats, batting, batted) **1** N-COUNT 可算名詞 A bat is a specially shaped piece of wood that is used for hitting the ball in baseball, softball, or cricket. （野球やソフトボール，クリケットの）バット ❑...a baseball bat. 野球バット. **2** V-I 自動詞 When you bat, you have a turn at hitting the ball with a bat in baseball, softball, or cricket. 打席に立つ ❑Pettitte hurt an elbow tendon while batting. ペティットは打撃中にひじのけんを痛めた. **3** N-COUNT 可算名詞 A bat is a small flying animal that looks like a mouse with wings made of skin. Bats are active at night. こうもり **4** PHRASE 句 If something happens **right off the bat**, it happens immediately. すぐに [AM 米国英語] ❑He learned right off the bat that you can't count on anything in this business. 彼はきみがこの仕事で孤立奮闘していることを即座に見抜いた.
→ see Word Web: bat
→ see flower

bat|boy /bætbɔɪ/ (batboys) N-COUNT 可算名詞 A batboy is a boy whose job is to take care of equipment that belongs to a baseball team. バットボーイ（野球チームの道具を管理する人）[AM 米国英語] ❑If you are a batboy, then you are holding the bat for the baseball players. きみがバットボーイなら野球選手のためにバットを持っておくものだ.

batch /bætʃ/ (batches) N-COUNT 可算名詞 A batch of things or people is a group of things or people of the same kind, especially a group that is dealt with at the same time or is sent to a particular place at the same time. 群れ ❑...the current batch of trainee priests. 見習い中の司祭の一群. ❑She brought a large batch of newspaper clippings. 彼女は新聞の切り抜きの束を持って来た. ❑I baked a batch of cookies. 私はクッキーをひと焼きした.

bath /bæθ/ (baths, bathing, bathed)

When the form **baths** is the plural of the noun it is pronounced /bæðz/. When it is the present tense of the verb, it is pronounced /bɑθs/ or /bæθs/.

baths形は名詞の複数形のときは，/bæðz/と発音される．動詞の現時形に使われるときは，/bɑθs/か/bæθs/と発音される．

1 N-COUNT 可算名詞 A bath is the process of washing your body in a bathtub. 入浴 ❑The midwife gave him a warm bath. 助産婦が彼に産湯を使わせた. **2** N-COUNT 可算名詞 When you take a bath, you sit or lie in a bathtub filled with water in order to wash your body. 風呂につかること ❑Take a shower instead of a bath. 風呂につかる代わりにシャワーを浴びて下さい. **3** V-T 他動詞 If you bath someone, especially a child, you wash them in a bathtub. 入浴させる [BRIT 英国英語; AM 米国英語 bathe] **4** N-COUNT 可算名詞 A bath is a container, usually a long rectangular one, which you fill with water and sit in while you wash your body. 浴槽 [BRIT 英国英語; AM bathtub 米国英語] When you bath, you take a bath. 入浴する [BRIT 英国英語; AM bathe 米国英語 bathe] **5** N-COUNT 可算名詞 A bath or a baths is a public building containing a swimming pool, and sometimes other facilities that people can use to wash or take a bath. 公共のプール（風呂が付いていることもある）❑...a thriving town with houses, government buildings and public baths. 住宅や官公庁，プールがあり栄えている街. **6** N-COUNT 可算名詞 A bath is a container filled with a particular liquid, such as a dye or an acid, in which particular objects are placed, usually as part of a manufacturing or chemical process. （化学処理に使う液体の）溶液器 ❑...a developing photograph placed in a bath of fixer. 定着液に浸した現像中の写真.

bathe /beɪð/ (bathes, bathing, bathed) **1** V-I 自動詞 When you bathe, you take a bath. 入浴する [AM 米国英語] ❑At least 60% of us now bathe or shower once a day. 今や我々の少なくとも60パーセントが一日一回，入浴するかシャワーを浴びている. **2** V-T 他動詞 If you bathe someone, especially a child, you wash them in a bathtub. （子供などの体を）風呂桶で洗う [AM 米国英語] ❑Back home, Shirley plays with, feeds and bathes the baby. 家ではシャーリーが赤ちゃんの相手をし，ミルクを飲ませ風呂に入れている. **3** V-I 自動詞 If you bathe in a sea, river, or lake, you swim, play, or wash yourself in it. Birds and animals can also bathe. 水浴びをする [mainly BRIT 主に英国英語, FORMAL 形式ばった] ❑The police have warned the city's inhabitants not to bathe in the polluted river. 警察は街の住民に汚染さ

れた川で水浴びをしないよう警告している. ●N-SING 単数名詞 Bathe is also a noun. 水浴び ❑They took an early morning bathe in the lake. 彼らは早朝に湖で水浴びをした. ●bath|ing /beɪðɪŋ/ N-UNCOUNT 不可算名詞 沐浴 ❑Bathing is not allowed. 沐浴禁止. **4** V-T 他動詞 If you bathe a part of your body or a wound, you wash it gently or soak it in a liquid. 浸して洗う ❑Bathe the infected area in a salt solution. 化膿している部分を食塩水で洗いなさい. **5** V-T 他動詞 If a place is bathed in light, it is covered with light, especially a gentle, pleasant light. （光を）浴びせる ❑The arena was bathed in warm sunshine. その競技場は暖かい太陽の光を浴びていた. ❑I was led to a small room bathed in soft red light. 私は柔らかい赤い明かりがともる小部屋に通された. **6** → see also sunbathe

bath|room /bæθrum/ (bathrooms) **1** N-COUNT 可算名詞 A bathroom is a room in a house that contains a bathtub or shower, a sink, and sometimes a toilet. 浴室 **2** N-SING 単数名詞 A bathroom is a room in a house or public building that contains a sink and toilet. 化粧室 [mainly AM 主に米国英語] ❑She had gone in to use the bathroom. 彼女は化粧室に入っていた. **3** PHRASE 句 People say that they **are going to the bathroom** when they want to say that they are going to use the toilet. お手洗いに行く [POLITENESS 丁寧さ] ❑Although he had been treated with antibiotics, he went to the bathroom repeatedly. 彼は抗生物質の治療を受けていたが，何度もトイレに行っていた. **4** PHRASE 句 You can say that someone **goes to the bathroom** to mean that they get rid of waste substances from their body, especially when you want to avoid using words that you think may offend people. 排尿する，排便する（婉曲用法）[mainly AM 主に米国英語, POLITENESS 丁寧さ] ❑I had to go to the bathroom, but I didn't want to use that awful outhouse. So I went off in the woods. お手洗いに行きたかったけど，あの汚い野外便所を使いたくなかったので，森の中に入って行った.
→ see house, plumbing

Thesaurus　　　　bathroom また次を参照:

N.	lavatory, boys'/girls'/ladies'/men's/women's room; (ant.) powder room, restroom, toilet, washroom **1** **2**

---

bath salts N-PLURAL 複数名詞 You dissolve bath salts in bath water to make the water smell pleasant and as a water softener. バスソルト（入浴剤）❑She poured all of the bath salts into the swirling water of the tub. 彼女は浴槽の渦巻くお湯にバスソルトを全部あけた.

bath|tub /bæθtʌb/ (bathtubs) N-COUNT 可算名詞 A bathtub is a long, usually rectangular container that you fill with water and sit in to wash your body. 浴槽 [AM 米国英語] ❑...a gigantic pink marble bathtub. 巨大なピンクの大理石の浴槽.

ba|ton /bætɒn/ (batons) **1** N-COUNT 可算名詞 A baton is a light, thin stick used by a conductor to conduct an orchestra or a choir. 指揮棒 ❑The maestro raises his baton. 巨匠が指揮棒を振り上げた. **2** N-COUNT 可算名詞 In track and field or track events, a baton is a short stick that is passed from one runner to another in a relay race. リレーのバトン ❑...their biggest relay outing since dropping the baton in Edmonton last August. 彼らが昨年8月にエドモントンでバトンを落として以来，最大の大きなリレー試合. **3** N-COUNT 可算名詞 A baton is a short heavy stick which is sometimes used as a weapon by the police. こん棒 [BRIT 英国英語; AM billy, billy club, nightstick 米国英語 billy, billy club, nightstick]

bat|tal|ion /bətælyən/ (battalions) **1** N-COUNT 可算名詞 A battalion is a large group of soldiers that consists of three or more companies. 大隊，大部隊 ❑Ten hours later Anthony was ordered to return to his battalion. 10時間後，アントニーは大隊に戻るよう指令された. **2** N-COUNT 可算名詞 A battalion of people is a large group of them, especially a well-organized, efficient group that has a particular task to do. （統制の取れた）大群 ❑There were battalions of highly paid publicists to see that such news didn't make the press. ニュースが報道されないようにと高給取りの広報係が大勢いた.

bat|ter /bætər/ (batters, battering, battered) **1** V-T 他動詞 To batter someone means to hit them many times, using fists or a heavy object. めった打ちにする ❑The passengers were battered by flying luggage and cargo as the cabin lost pressure. 航空機の客室の気圧が下がり，乗客は飛び交う荷物や積み荷にあちこちぶつかった. ❑A karate expert battered a man to death. 空手のたち人が男を殴り殺した. ●bat|tered ADJ 形容詞 打ちのめされた ❑Her battered body was

discovered in a field. 打ちのめされた彼女の体が畑で発見された. **2** V-T 他動詞 If someone **is battered**, they are regularly hit and badly hurt by a member of their family or by their partner. 虐待する ❑ …evidence that the child was being battered. その子供が虐待されていた証拠. ❑ …boys who witness fathers battering their mothers. 父親が母親に暴力を振るうのを目の当たりにする少年たち. ●**bat|ter|ing** N-UNCOUNT 不可算名詞 暴行 ❑ Leaving the relationship does not mean that the battering will stop. 関係を絶つと暴力が止むというわけではない. **3** V-T 他動詞 [usu passive] If a place **is battered** by wind, rain, or storms, it is seriously damaged or affected by very bad weather. (雨や風が) 激しく打ちつける ❑ The country has been battered by winds of between fifty and seventy miles an hour. その国は時速50から70マイルの強風にあおられている. **4** V-T 他動詞 If you **batter** something, you hit it many times, using your fists or a heavy object. 乱打する ❑ They were battering the door, they were trying to break in. 彼らはドアを叩き壊して中に乱入しようとしていた. **5** N-VAR 可変性名詞 **Batter** is a mixture of flour, eggs, and milk that is used in cooking. (小麦粉や卵を使った) 生地 ❑ …pancake batter. パンケーキの生地 **6** N-COUNT 可算名詞 In sports such as baseball and softball, a **batter** is a person who hits the ball with a wooden bat. (野球やソフトボールの) バッター ❑ …batters and pitchers. バッターとピッチャー. **7** → see also **battered, battering**
→ see **baseball**

bat|tered /bǽtərd/ ADJ 形容詞 Something that is **battered** is old and in poor condition because it has been used a lot. 使い古した ❑ He drove up in a battered old car. 彼はボロボロの古い車でやって来た.

bat|ter|ing /bǽtərɪŋ/ (batterings) N-COUNT 可算名詞 If something takes a **battering**, it suffers very badly as a result of a particular event or action. 痛手 ❑ The industry's reputation has taken a battering and its image needs to be restored. その業界の評判は痛手をこうむり, イメージの挽回が必要となっている.

bat|tery /bǽtəri/ (batteries) **1** N-COUNT 可算名詞 **Batteries** are small devices that provide the power for electrical items such as radios and children's toys. 電池 ❑ The shavers come complete with batteries. その電気かみそりは電池付きです. ❑ …a battery-operated cassette player. 電池式のカセット・プレーヤー. **2** N-COUNT 可算名詞 A car **battery** is a rectangular box containing acid that is found in a car engine. It provides the electricity needed to start the car. (車の) バッテリー ❑ …a car with a dead battery. バッテリーのあがった車. **3** N-UNCOUNT 不可算名詞 **Battery** is the crime of hitting or beating someone. [mainly AM 主に米国英語 LEGAL 法律用] ❑ Lawrence punched a man in a Los Angeles nightclub and was charged with battery. ローレンスはロサンゼルスのナイトクラブで男を殴り, 暴行罪で告訴された. **4** → see also **assault and battery** **5** N-COUNT 可算名詞 A **battery of** equipment such as guns, lights, or computers is a large set of it kept together in one place. 一群 ❑ They stopped beside a battery of abandoned guns. 捨てられた銃がずらりと並んでいるそばで彼らは立ち止まった. **6** N-COUNT 可算名詞 A **battery of** people or things is a very large number of them. 勢ぞろい ❑ …a battery of journalists and television cameras. 並み居る新聞記者やテレビカメラ.
→ see **cellphone**

bat|tle /bǽtl/ (battles, battling, battled) **1** N-VAR 可変性名詞 A **battle** is a violent fight between groups of people, especially one between military forces during a war. 戦闘 ❑ …the victory of King William III at the Battle of the Boyne. ボイン川の戦いでのウィリアム3世の勝利. ❑ …a gun battle between police and drug traffickers. 警察と麻薬密売人の銃撃戦. **2** N-COUNT 可算名詞 A **battle** is a conflict in which different people or groups compete in order to achieve success or control. 闘争 ❑ …an unfolding political battle over jobs and the economy. 雇用と経済をめぐる政治闘争の展開. ❑ …the eternal battle between good and evil in the world. 世の中の善と悪との果てしない戦い. **3** N-COUNT 可算名詞 You can use **battle** to refer to someone's efforts to achieve something in spite of very difficult circumstances. 奮闘 ❑ …the battle against crime. 犯罪対策の闘い. ❑ She has fought a constant battle with her weight. 彼女はいつも減量に努めている. **4** V-RECIP 相互動詞 To **battle with** an opposing group means to take part in a fight or contest against them. You can also say that one group or person **is battling** another. 戦う ❑ In one town thousands of people battled with police and several were reportedly wounded. ある街で何千もの人が警察と衝突し, 何人かが負傷したと伝えられた. ❑ The sides must battle again for a quarter-final place on December 16. 12月16日に両チームは準々決勝進出をかけて再び戦わなければならない. **5** V-T/V-I 他動詞/自動詞 To **battle** means to try

hard to do something in spite of very difficult circumstances. You can also **battle** something, or **battle against** something or **with** something. 奮闘する ❑ Doctors battled throughout the night to save her life. 医師団は彼女の命を救うため夜を徹して治療に当たった. ❑ Firefighters are still battling the two blazes. 消防士たちは今も2つの火事の消火のため奮闘している. **6** PHRASE 句 If one group or person **battles it out with** another, they take part in a fight or contest against each other until one of them wins or a definite result is reached. You can also say that two groups or two people **battle it out**. 最後まで戦い抜く ❑ She will now battle it out with 50 other hopefuls for a place in the last 10. これから彼女は最後の10人に残るため他の50人の候補者と競うことになる.
→ see **army**

bat|tle fa|tigue N-UNCOUNT 不可算名詞 **Battle fatigue** is a mental condition of anxiety and depression caused by the stress of fighting in a war. 戦争疲労 ❑ …a man suffering from battle fatigue. 戦争疲労を患う男性.

battle|field /bǽtᵊlfiːld/ (battlefields) **1** N-COUNT 可算名詞 A **battlefield** is a place where a battle is fought. 戦場 ❑ …the struggle to save America's Civil War battlefields. アメリカの南北戦争の戦場を保存するための努力. **2** N-COUNT 可算名詞 You can refer to an issue or field of activity over which people disagree or compete as a **battlefield**. 論争の場 ❑ …the domestic battlefield of family life. 家庭にある家族生活葛藤の場.

battle|ground /bǽtᵊlɡraʊnd/ → see **battlefield**

battle|ship /bǽtᵊlʃɪp/ (battleships) N-COUNT 可算名詞 A **battleship** is a very large, heavily armed warship. 戦艦

bawl /bɔːl/ (bawls, bawling, bawled) **1** V-I 自動詞 If you say that a child **is bawling**, you are annoyed because it is crying loudly. 大声で泣く ❑ One of the toddlers was bawling, and the other had a runny nose. 幼児の一人は泣きわめいていたし, もう一人は鼻水を垂らしていた. **2** V-T/V-I 他動詞/自動詞 If you **bawl**, you shout in a very loud voice, for example, because you are angry or you want people to hear you. 大声で叫ぶ ❑ When I came back to the hotel Laura and Peter were shouting and bawling at each other. 私がホテルに戻ると, ローラとピーターが大声でどなり合っていた. ❑ Then a voice bawled: "Lay off! I'll kill you, you little rascal!" その時, 「やめろ!いたずら小僧め, 殺してやる!」と叫ぶ声が聞こえた. ●PHRASAL VERB 句動詞 **Bawl out** means the same as **bawl**. 大声で叫ぶ ❑ Someone in the audience bawled out "Not him again!" 「またこいつか!」と観客の一人が大声で叫んだ.
▶ **bawl out** PHRASAL VERB 句動詞 If someone **bawls** you **out**, they tell you angrily. しかりつける [INFORMAL くだけた] ❑ I was bawled out at school for not doing my homework. 宿題をしなかったので学校でしかりつけられた.

bay /beɪ/ (bays, baying, bayed) **1** N-COUNT 可算名詞 A **bay** is a part of a coast where the land curves inward. 湾 ❑ …a short ferry ride across the bay. 湾の向う側はフェリー船ですぐの距離 ❑ …the Bay of Bengal. ベンガル湾 **2** N-COUNT 可算名詞 A **bay** is a partly enclosed area, inside or outside a building, that is used for a particular purpose. 仕切り部分 ❑ The animals are herded into a bay, then butchered. 動物は仕切り部分に集められた後で, 屠殺 (とさつ) される **3** N-COUNT 可算名詞 A **bay** is an area of a room that extends beyond the main walls of a house, especially an area with a large window at the front of a house. (建物の) 張り出した部分 **4** ADJ 形容詞 A **bay** horse is reddish-brown in color. 鹿毛の ❑ …a 10-year-old bay mare. 10歳の鹿毛の雌馬 **5** V-I 自動詞 If a number of people **are baying for** something, they are demanding something angrily, usually that someone should be punished. 叫んで求める [usu cont] ❑ The referee ignored players baying for a penalty. 審判員はペナルティを求める叫び声を無視した. ❑ Opposition politicians have been baying for his blood. 野党の政治家たちは彼の血を要求した. **6** V-I 自動詞 If a dog or wolf **bays**, it makes loud, long cries. (太い声で) ほえる ❑ A dog suddenly howled, baying at the moon. 犬は月を見て突然遠ぼえした. **7** PHRASE 句 If you **keep** something or someone **at bay**, or **hold** them **at bay**, you prevent them from reaching, attacking, or affecting you. 寄せつけない ❑ Eating oranges keeps colds at bay. オレンジを食べると風邪を引かない.

bayo|net /beɪənɪt, beɪənɛt/ (bayonets) N-COUNT 可算名詞 A **bayonet** is a long, sharp blade that can be attached to the end of a rifle and used as a weapon. 銃剣

ba|zaar /bəzɑːr/ (bazaars) **1** N-COUNT 可算名詞 In areas such as the Middle East and India, a **bazaar** is a place where there are

many small stores and stalls. (中東, インドなどの)商店街 □*Kamal was a vendor in Cairo's open-air bazaar.* カマールはカイロの露天商店街の商人だった. **2** N-COUNT 可算名詞 A **bazaar** is a sale to raise money for charity. バザー □*...a church bazaar.* 教会のバザー

BBC /ˌbiː biː ˈsiː/ N-PROPER 固有名詞 The **BBC** is a British organization which broadcasts programs on radio and television. **BBC** is an abbreviation for "British Broadcasting Corporation." BBC(英国放送協会) ['ðə' N] □*The concert will be broadcast live by the BBC.* コンサートはBBCによって生放送される.

BB gun /ˈbiː biː gʌn/ (**BB guns**) N-COUNT 可算名詞 A **BB gun** is a type of airgun that fires small round bullets that are called **BBs**. BBガン [AM 米国英語] □*Sims was carrying a BB gun at the time he was shot.* シムズは撃たれた時, BBガンを持っていた.

BC /ˌbiː ˈsiː/ also **B.C.** You use **BC** in dates to indicate a number of years or centuries before the year in which Jesus Christ is believed to have been born. Compare **AD**. 紀元前 □*The brooch dates back to the fourth century BC.* そのブローチは紀元前4世紀のものだ.

BCE /ˌbiː siː ˈiː/ also **B.C.E.** Non-Christians often use **BCE** instead of **BC** in dates. **BCE** indicates a number of years or centuries before the year in which Jesus Christ is believed to have been born. **BCE** is an abbreviation for "before the Common Era." Compare **AD**, **BC**, and **CE**. 共通紀元前 □*...Lao-tzu, a sixth-century BCE Chinese teacher.* 共通紀元前6世紀の中国の教師, 老子 □*The Babylonian Empire was conquered by the Persian Empire in 539 BCE.* バビロン帝国は共通紀元前539年にペルシャ帝国に征服された.

be

❶ AUXILIARY VERB USES
❷ OTHER VERB USES

❶ be /bi, STRONG biː/ (**am, are, is, being, was, were, been**)

In spoken English, forms of **be** are often shortened, for example "I am" can be shortened to "I'm" and "was not" can be shortened to "wasn't."

口語英語では **be** の諸形はしばしば短縮される. 例えば, **I am** は **I'm** に短縮できるし, **was not** は **wasn't** に短縮できる.

1 AUX 助動詞 You use **be** with a present participle to form the continuous tenses of verbs. ～しているところである □*This is happening in every school throughout the country.* これは国中のあらゆる学校で起こっている. □*She didn't always think carefully about what she was doing.* 彼女は自分がしていることについていつも注意深く考えていた訳ではない. **2 be going to →** see **going** **3** AUX 助動詞 You use **be** with a past participle to form the passive voice. ～される □*Her husband was killed in a car crash.* 彼女のご主人は自動車の衝突事故で亡くなった. □*Similar action is being taken by the U.S. government.* 同様の処置がアメリカ政府によって取られている. **4** AUX 助動詞 You use **be** with an infinitive to indicate that something is planned to happen, that it will definitely happen, or that it must happen. ～することになっている □*The talks are to begin tomorrow.* 議論は明日開始することになっている. □*It was to be Johnson's first meeting with the board in nearly a month.* それはジョンソンにとってほぼ1か月ぶりの役員会との打ち合わせになるはずだった. **5 be about to →** see **about** **6** AUX 助動詞 You use **be** with an infinitive to say or ask what should happen or be done in a particular situation, how it should happen, or who should do it. ～すべきだ □*What am I to do without her?* 私は彼女なしでどうしたらいいのか. □*Who is to say which of them had more power?* 彼らのうちの誰がより大きな権力を持っていたと誰が言えよう. **7** AUX 助動詞 You use **was** and **were** with an infinitive to talk about something that happened later than the time you are discussing, and was not planned or certain at that time. ～する運命である □*He started something that was to change the face of China.* 彼が始めたことによって中国が変貌することになるのだった. **8** AUX 助動詞 You can say that something is **to be seen**, heard, or found in a particular place to mean that people can see it, hear it, or find it in that place. ～することができる □*Little traffic was to be seen on the streets.* 通りの交通量は少なかった.

❷ be /bi, STRONG biː/ (**am, are, is, being, was, were, been**)

In spoken English, forms of **be** are often shortened, for example "I am" can be shortened to "I'm" and "was not" can be shortened to "wasn't."

口語英語では **be** の諸形はしばしば短縮される. 例えば, **I am** は **I'm** に短縮できるし, **was not** は **wasn't** に短縮できる.

1 V-LINK 連結動詞 You use **be** to introduce more information about the subject, such as its identity, nature, qualities, or position. ～である □*She's my mother.* 彼女は私の母だ. □*He is a very attractive man.* 彼は大変魅力的な男だ. □*He is fifty and has been through two marriages.* 彼は50歳で2度結婚したことがある. □*The sky was black.* 空は黒ずんでいた. □*He's still alive, isn't he?* 彼はまだ生きているんだね. **2** V-LINK 連結動詞 You use **be**, with "it" as the subject, in clauses where you are describing something or giving your judgment of a situation. (～ということ)である □*It was too chilly for swimming.* 泳ぐのには寒すぎた. □*Sometimes it is necessary to say no.* 断らなければならないときもある. □*It is likely that investors will face losses.* 投資家は損失を被りそうだ. □*It's nice having friends to chat to.* おしゃべりできる友がいることはいいことだ. **3** V-LINK 連結動詞 You use **be** with the impersonal pronoun "there" in expressions like **there is** and **there are** to say that something exists or happens. (～が)ある □*Clearly there is a problem here.* 明らかにこの点には問題がある. □*There are very few cars on this street.* この通りには車がほとんど走っていない. **4** V-LINK 連結動詞 You use **be** as a link between a subject and a clause and in certain other clause structures, as shown below. (～ということで)ある □*Our greatest problem is convincing them.* 我々の最大の問題は彼らを納得させることだ. □*All she knew was that I'd had a broken marriage.* 彼女が知っていたのは私が結婚に失敗したということだけだった. □*Local residents said it was as if there had been a nuclear explosion.* 地元の住民はまるで核爆発が起こったかのようだったと語った. **5** V-LINK 連結動詞 You use **be** in expressions like **the thing is** and **the point is** to introduce a clause in which you make a statement or give your opinion. (～ということで)ある [SPOKEN 口語] □*The fact is, the players gave everything they had.* 重要なことは, 選手がベストを尽くしたということである. **6** V-LINK 連結動詞 The form "**be**" is used occasionally instead of the normal forms of the present tense, especially after "whether." ～であろうと [FORMAL 形式ばった] □*They should then be able to refer you to the appropriate type of practitioner, whether it be your GP, dentist, or optician.* 家庭医, 歯科医または眼科医であろうと, その後で適切な医者に紹介してもらうことができるはずだ. **7** PHRASE 句 If you talk about what would happen **if it wasn't for** someone or something, you mean that they are the only thing that is preventing it from happening. ～さえなければ □*I could happily move back into an apartment if it wasn't for the fact that I'd miss my garden.* 庭がなくなることさえなければ, 喜んでマンションに戻るのだが.

beach /biːtʃ/ (**beaches, beaching, beached**) **1** N-COUNT 可算名詞 A **beach** is an area of sand or stones beside the ocean. 浜 □*...a beautiful sandy beach.* 美しい砂浜 **2** V-T/V-I 他動詞/自動詞 If something such as a boat **beaches**, or if it is **beached**, it is pulled or forced out of the water and onto land. (～に) 乗り上げる □*We beached the canoe, running it right up the bank.* 私たちはカヌーを浅瀬に近づけ, 岸に乗り上げた. □*The boat beached on a mud flat.* そのボートは平瀬に乗り上げた.

→ see Word Web: **beach**

You can use **beach**, **coast**, and **shore** to talk about the piece of land beside a stretch of water. A **beach** is a flat area of sand or pebbles next to the ocean. The **coast** is the area of land that lies alongside the ocean. You may be referring just to the land close to the ocean, or to a wider area that extends further inland. The **shore** is the area of land along the edge of the ocean, a lake, or a wide river.

Word Web   beach

Beaches have a natural cycle of build-up and **erosion**. Ocean currents, wind, and **waves** move **sand** along the **coast**. In certain spots, some of the sand gets left behind. The **surf** deposits it on the beach. Then the wind blows it into **dunes**. As currents change, they **erode** sand from the beach. High waves carry beach sand seaward. This process raises the seafloor. As the water gets shallower, the waves become smaller. Then they begin depositing sand on the beach. At the same time, small **pebbles** smash into each other. They break up and form new sand.

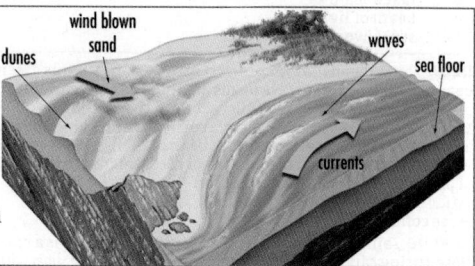

B

Word Partnership *beach* は次の語句と使われる:

PREP.	**along the** beach, **at/on the** beach ◼
N.	beach **chair**, beach **club/resort**, beach **vacation** ◼
V.	**lie on the** beach, **walk on the** beach ◼
ADJ.	**nude** beach, **private** beach, **rocky** beach, **sandy** beach ◼

beach chair (**beach chairs**) N-COUNT 可算名詞 A **beach chair** is a simple chair with a folding frame, and a piece of canvas as the seat and back. **Beach chairs** are usually used on the beach, on a ship, or in the yard. ビーチチェア [AM 米国英語] □ *People sprawl in beach chairs or sit under umbrellas.* 人々はビーチチェアに寝そべるかパラソルの下に座る.

beach|wear /biʧwɛər/ N-UNCOUNT 算名詞 **Beachwear** is the things people wear for swimming. ビーチウェア [mainly AM 主に米国英語] □ *There is a boutique where beachwear and sportswear are on sale.* ビーチウェアとスポーツウェアの特売をやっている店がある.

bea|con /biːkən/ (**beacons**) ◼ N-COUNT 可算名詞 A **beacon** is a light or a fire, usually on a hill or tower, that acts as a signal or a warning. ビーコン □ *...a huge office tower with aircraft warning beacons on the roof.* 屋根に航空機警戒ビーコンのある巨大なオフィスビル ◻ N-COUNT 可算名詞 If someone acts as a **beacon to** other people, they inspire or encourage them. 心の光明 □ *She is a beacon of hope for women navigating the darkest passage of their lives.* 彼女は人生の辛酸をなめて暮らす女性に希望の光を与えます.

bead /biːd/ (**beads**) ◼ N-COUNT 可算名詞 **Beads** are small pieces of colored glass, wood, or plastic with a hole through the middle. Beads are often put together on a piece of string or wire to make jewelry. ビーズ □ *...a string of beads.* 数珠つなぎ ◻ N-COUNT 可算名詞 A **bead of** liquid or moisture is a small drop of it. しずく □ *...beads of blood.* 血のしずく
→ see **glass**

beak /biːk/ (**beaks**) N-COUNT 可算名詞 A bird's **beak** is the hard curved or pointed part of its mouth. くちばし □ *...a black bird with a yellow beak.* 黄色いくちばしのクロウタドリ
→ see **bird**

beak|er /biːkər/ (**beakers**) ◼ N-COUNT 可算名詞 A **beaker** is a large cup or glass. 広口コップ [AM 米国英語] ◻ N-COUNT 可算名詞 A **beaker** is a glass or plastic jar which is used in chemistry. ビーカー

beam /biːm/ (**beams, beaming, beamed**) ◼ V-T/V-I 他動詞/自動詞 If you say that someone **is beaming**, you mean that they have a big smile on their face because they are happy, pleased, or proud about something. にっこりとする [WRITTEN 書き言葉] □ *Frances beamed at her friend with undisguised admiration.* フランシスは称賛の気持ちを込めて友たちににっこりとした. □ *"Welcome back," she beamed.* 「ようこそお帰りなさい」と彼女はにっこりとしながら言った. ◻ N-COUNT 可算名詞 A **beam** is a line of energy, radiation, or particles sent in a particular direction. 光線 □ *...high-energy laser beams.* 高エネルギーのレーザー光線 ◼ V-T/V-I 他動詞/自動詞 If radio signals or television pictures **are beamed** somewhere, they are sent there by means of electronic equipment. 放送する □ *The interview was beamed live across America.* そのインタビューはアメリカ中で生放送された. □ *The Sci-Fi Channel began beaming into 10 million American homes this week.* SFチャンネルは今週、のアメリカの1000万所帯に放送され始めた. ◼ N-COUNT 可算名詞 A **beam of** light is a line of light that shines from an object such as a lamp. 光線 □ *A beam of light slices through the darkness.* 一条の光線が暗闇を切るように進む. ◼ N-COUNT 可算名詞 A **beam** is a long thick bar of wood, metal, or concrete, especially one used to support the roof of a building. 梁(はり) □ *The ceilings are supported by oak beams.* 天井はオーク材の梁によって支えられている.
→ see **gymnastics, laser**

Word Partnership *beam* は次の語句と使われる:

PREP.	beam **at** *someone* ◼
	beam **down (on something)** ◼
N.	**laser** beam ◻
	beam **of light** ◼
ADJ.	**steel/wooden** beam ◼

bean /biːn/ (**beans**) ◼ N-COUNT 可算名詞 **Beans** such as green beans, French beans, or fava beans are the seeds of a climbing plant or the long thin cases which contain those seeds. エンドウ ◻ N-COUNT 可算名詞 **Beans** such as soybeans and kidney beans are the dried seeds of other types of bean plants. 豆 ◼ N-COUNT 可算名詞 **Beans** such as coffee beans or cocoa beans are the seeds of plants that are used to produce coffee, cocoa, and chocolate. (豆に似た)実
→ see **coffee**

bean|ie /biːni/ (**beanies**) N-COUNT 可算名詞 A **beanie** is a small, close-fitting cap. ビーニー帽 □ *He bursts into a breakfast diner with*

his hair under a woolen beanie. 彼は毛織りのビーニー帽をかぶり、ダイナーにいきなり入る.

bear
❶ VERB USES
❷ NOUN USES

❶ **bear** /bɛər/ (**bears, bearing, bore, borne**)
➭ Please look at category ◼ to see if the expression you are looking for is shown under another headword. ◼ V-T 他動詞 If you **bear** something somewhere, you carry it or take it there. 持って行く [LITERARY 文語的] □ *They bore the oblong hardwood box into the kitchen and put it on the table.* 彼らは硬材でできただ円形の箱を台所に持って行き、テーブルの上に置いた. ◻ V-T 他動詞 If you **bear** something such as a weapon, you hold it or carry it with you. 持つ [FORMAL 形式ばった] □ *...the constitutional right to bear arms.* 武器を持つ憲法上の権利 ◼ V-T 他動詞 If one thing **bears** the weight of something else, it supports the weight of that thing. 支える □ *The ice was not thick enough to bear the weight of marching men.* その氷は行進する男たちの重みを支えられるだけの厚みがなかった. ◼ V-T 他動詞 If something **bears** a particular mark or characteristic, it has that mark or characteristic. の跡(特質)がある □ *The houses bear the marks of bullet holes and the streets are practically deserted.* 家々は銃弾であいた穴の痕跡(こんせき)があり、街路にはほとんど人通りがない. □ *...notepaper bearing the presidential seal.* 大統領の印章のある便箋(びんせん) ◼ V-T 他動詞 If you **bear** an unpleasant experience, you accept it because you are unable to do anything about it. 耐える □ *They will have to bear the misery of living in constant fear of war.* 彼らは常に戦争を恐れながら生活する惨めさに耐えねばならないだろう. ◼ V-T 他動詞 If you can't **bear** someone or something, you dislike them very much. 我慢する [with neg] □ *I can't bear people who make judgements and label me.* 私のことを決めつけてレッテルを貼る人たちが我慢できない. ◼ V-T 他動詞 When a woman **bears** a child, she gives birth to him or her. 生む [OLD-FASHIONED 古風な] □ *Emma bore a son called Karl.* エマはカールと言う名の息子を産んだ. □ *She bore him a daughter, Susanna.* 彼女は彼との間に娘のスザンナを産んだ. ◼ V-T 他動詞 If someone **bears** the cost of something, they pay for it. (費用を)もつ □ *Patients should not have to bear the costs of their own treatment.* 患者は治療費を負担すべきではない. ◼ V-T 他動詞 If you **bear** the responsibility for something, you accept responsibility for it. 負う □ *If a woman makes a decision to have a child alone, she should bear that responsibility alone.* 一人で子供を持つと決めた女性はその責任を一人で負うべきである. ◼ V-T 他動詞 If one thing **bears** no resemblance or no relationship to another thing, they are not at all similar. (関係などを)もつ [usu with brd-neg] □ *Their daily menus bore no resemblance whatsoever to what they were actually fed.* 日替わりメニューは実際に供されるものとは全く似ていなかった. ◼ V-T 他動詞 When a plant or tree **bears** flowers, fruit, or leaves, it produces them. 結ぶ □ *As the plants grow and start to bear fruit they will need a lot of water.* 植物は成長し実を結び始めるに従い、大量の水を必要とする. ◼ V-T 他動詞 If something such as a bank account or an investment **bears** interest, interest is paid on it. (利子を)生む [BUSINESS 実業] □ *The eight-year bond will bear annual interest of 10.5%.* 8年物の債券の利子は年率10.5%です. ◼ V-I 自動詞 If you **bear** left or **bear** right when you are driving or walking along, you turn and continue in that direction. (ある方向に)向かう □ *Traveling north on 309 to Center Valley, bear right at the fork onto Route 378 North.* 309号線を北のセンターヴァリー方面に進み、分岐点で右に折れ、378号線北方に進む. ◼ → see also **bore, borne** ◼ to **bear the brunt** of → see **brunt** ◼ to **bear fruit** → see **fruit** ◼ to **grin and bear it** → see **grin** ◼ to **bear in mind** → see **mind**

▶ **bear out** PHRASAL VERB 句動詞 If someone or something **bears** a person **out** or **bears out** what that person is saying, they support what that person is saying. 裏づける □ *Recent studies have borne out claims that certain perfumes can bring about profound psychological changes.* 最近の調査は、一部の香水が大きな心理的変化をもたらすという主張の裏づけとなった.

▶ **bear with** PHRASAL VERB 句動詞 If you ask someone to **bear with** you, you are asking them to be patient. 辛抱する □ *If you'll bear with me, Frank, just let me try to explain.* フランク、ちょっと待って. 私に説明させて.

Thesaurus *bear* また次を参照:

V.	**carry, lug, move, transport** ❶ ◼
	endure, put up with, stand, tolerate ❶ ◼
	produce, yield ❶ ◼ ◼

Word Partnership	bearは次の語句と使われる:
N.	bear **a burden/weight** ❶ ① ③ ⑤
	bear **responsibility** ❶ ⑨
	bear **fruit** ❶ ⑪
	bear **interest** ❶ ⑫
ADV.	bear **left/right** ❶ ⑬

❷ bear /bɛ͟ər/ (bears) **1** N-COUNT 可算名詞 A **bear** is a large, strong wild animal with thick fur and sharp claws. クマ **2** N-COUNT 可算名詞 In the stock market, **bears** are people who sell shares in expectation of a drop in price, in order to make a profit by buying them back again after a short time. Compare **bull**. 弱気の売り手 [BUSINESS 実業]
→ see **Arctic**

bear|able /bɛ͟ərəb³l/ ADJ 形容詞 If something is **bearable**, you feel that you can accept it or deal with it. 我慢できる □A cool breeze made the heat bearable. 涼しい風のおかげで暑さをしのぐことができた.

beard /bɪ͟ərd/ (beards) N-COUNT 可算名詞 A man's **beard** is the hair that grows on his chin and cheeks. あごひげ □He's decided to grow a beard. 彼はあごひげを伸ばすことに決めた.

beard|ed /bɪ͟ərdɪd/ ADJ 形容詞 A **bearded** man has a beard. あごひげのある □...a bearded 40-year-old sociology professor. あごひげを生やした40歳の社会学の教授

bear|er /bɛ͟ərər/ (bearers) **1** N-COUNT 可算名詞 The **bearer of** something such as a message is the person who brings it to you. 運ぶ人 □I hate to be the bearer of bad news. 悪い知らせを伝える者にはなりたくない. **2** N-COUNT 可算名詞 A **bearer** of a particular thing is a person who carries it, especially in a ceremony. 運ぶ人 [FORMAL 形式ばった] □He was the U.S. flag bearer at the 1976 Montreal Games. 彼は1976年のモントリオール五輪でアメリカの旗手だった. **3** N-COUNT 可算名詞 The **bearer of** something such as a document, a right, or an official position is the person who possesses it or holds it. 保持者 [FORMAL 形式ばった] □...the traditional bourgeois notion of the citizen as a bearer of rights. 権利の保持者としての伝統的なブルジョワ的観念

bear|ing /bɛ͟ərɪŋ/ (bearings) **1** PHRASE 句 If something **has a bearing on** a situation or event, it is relevant to it. 関係 □Experts generally agree that diet has an important bearing on your general health. 専門家は概して日常の飲食物は人の健康状態に大きく関係していると考えている. **2** N-SING 単数名詞 Someone's **bearing** is the way in which they move or stand. ふるまい [LITERARY 文語的] □She later wrote warmly of his bearing and behavior. 彼女は後で彼のふるまいと態度について好意的に書いた. **3** PHRASE 句 If you **get your bearings** or **find** your bearings, you find out where you are or what you should do next. If you **lose** your bearings, you do not know where you are or what you should do next. 立場がわかる；位置を確認する；立場がわからなくなる □A sightseeing tour of the city is included to help you get your bearings. 市内観光が含まれていますので土地に慣れることができます.

bear|ish /bɛ͟ərɪʃ/ ADJ 形容詞 In the stock market, if there is a **bearish** mood, prices are expected to fall. Compare **bullish**. 弱気の [BUSINESS 実業] □Dealers said investors remain bearish. ディーラーは投資家は弱気のままだと言った.

bear mar|ket (bear markets) N-COUNT 可算名詞 A **bear market** is a situation in the stock market when people are selling a lot of shares because they expect the shares will decrease in value and they will be able to make a profit by buying them again after a short time. Compare **bull market**. 弱気市場 [BUSINESS 実業] □Is the bear market in equities over? 株式の弱気市場は終わったか.

beast /bi͟st/ (beasts) N-COUNT 可算名詞 You can refer to an animal as a **beast**, especially if it is large, dangerous, or unusual one. けだもの [LITERARY 文語的] □...the threats our ancestors faced from wild beasts. 私たちの祖先が直面した野生動物による脅威

beat /bi͟t/ (beats, beating, beaten)

The form **beat** is used in the present tense and is the past tense.
beat 形は現在形に使われ、過去形でもある.

1 V-T 他動詞 If you **beat** someone or something, you hit them very hard. 殴打する □My wife tried to stop them and they beat her. 私の妻は止めようとしたが彼らは彼女を殴打した. **2** V-I 自動詞 To **beat on, at**, or **against** something means to hit it hard, usually several times or continuously for a period of time. バタバタ動く □There was dead silence but for a fly beating against the glass. ハエが窓ガラスでブンブン羽音をさせている以外に物音一つしなかった. □Nina managed to free herself and began beating at the flames with a pillow. ニーナは何とか身動きがとれるようになり、炎を枕でたたき始めた. ●N-SING 単数名詞 **Beat** is also a noun. 打つ音 □...the rhythmic beat of the surf. 打ち寄せる波のリズムある音 ●**beat|ing** N-SING 単数名詞 打つこと □The silence was broken only by the beating of the rain. 沈黙は雨音で壊された. **3** V-I 自動詞 When

your heart or pulse **beats**, it continually makes regular rhythmic movements. 鼓動する □I felt my heart beating faster. 私は心臓の鼓動が早まるのを感じた. ●N-COUNT 可算名詞 **Beat** is also a noun. 鼓動 □He could hear the beat of his heart. 彼は自分の心臓の鼓動を聞くことができた. ●**beat|ing** N-SING 単数名詞 鼓動 □I could hear the beating of my heart. 私は心臓の鼓動を聞くことができた. **4** V-T/V-I 他動詞/自動詞 If you **beat** a drum or similar instrument, you hit it in order to make a sound. You can also say that a drum **beats**. たたく □When you beat the drum, you feel good. 太鼓をたたくと爽快に感じる. □...drums beating and pipes playing. 太鼓が鳴り、バグパイプが奏される ●N-SING 単数名詞 **Beat** is also a noun. (太鼓を)打つ音 □...drums beating until they start to thicken. 太鼓のリズミカルな音 **5** N-COUNT 可算名詞 The **beat** of a piece of music is the main rhythm that it has. (ロックなどの)強烈なリズム □...the thumping beat of rock music. ロックの強烈なリズム **6** N-COUNT 可算名詞 In music, a **beat** is a unit of measurement. The number of beats in a measure of a piece of music is indicated by two numbers at the beginning of the piece. 拍子 □It's got four beats to a measure. それは1小節4拍子ある. **7** V-T 他動詞 If you **beat** eggs, cream, or butter, you mix them thoroughly using a fork or beater. (卵などを)強くかきまぜる □Beat the eggs and sugar until they start to thicken. 卵と砂糖をどろどろするまで強くかきまぜます. **8** V-T/V-I 他動詞/自動詞 When a bird or insect **beats** its wings or when its wings **beat**, its wings move up and down. (鳥が翼を)羽ばたく □Beating their wings they flew off. 翼を羽ばたいて飛び去った. **9** V-T 他動詞 If you **beat** someone in a competition or election, you defeat them. 負かす □In yesterday's game, Switzerland beat the United States two to one. 昨日の試合でスイスは2対1でアメリカを負かした. **10** V-T 他動詞 If someone **beats** a record or achievement, they do better than it. (一を) 破る □He was as eager as his Captain to beat the record. 彼は主将と同じくらい記録を破ることに熱心だった. **11** V-T 他動詞 If you **beat** something that you are fighting against, for example, an organization, a problem, or a disease, you defeat it. 打ち勝つ □It became clear that the Union was not going to beat the government. 組合は政府に打ち勝つことはないことが明瞭になった. **12** V-T 他動詞 [usu passive] If an attack or an attempt is **beaten off** or is **beaten back**, it is stopped, often temporarily. 停止する □The rescuers were beaten back by strong winds and currents. 救助隊は強い風と潮流のため、救助を停止した. **13** V-T 他動詞 If you say that one thing **beats** another, you mean that it is better than it. (一に) まさる [INFORMAL くだけた] [no cont] □Being boss of a software firm beats selling insurance. ソフトウェア会社の経営者であることは保険を売ることにまさっている. **14** V-T 他動詞 To **beat** a time limit or an event means to achieve something before that time or event. 決まった時間より早く終える □They were trying to beat the midnight deadline. 彼らは真夜中の締め切り前に作業を終えようとしていた. **15** N-COUNT 可算名詞 A police officer's or journalist's **beat** is the area for which he or she is responsible. 受け持ち区域 □A policeman was patrolling his regular beat, when he saw a group of boys milling about the street. 警察官は担当区域を巡回していたとき少年たちが群がって通りをうろうろしているのを見かけた. **16** → see also **beating** **17** PHRASE 句 If you intend to do something but someone **beats** you **to it**, they do it before you do. (人を)出し抜く □Don't be too long about it or you'll find someone has beaten you to it. 余りぐずぐずしていると誰かがあなたを出し抜くかもしれない. **18** To **beat** someone **at their own game** → see **game**
▶ **beat up** PHRASAL VERB 句動詞 If someone **beats** a person **up**, they hit or kick the person many times. (人を)ひどい目にあわせる □Then they actually beat her up as well. それから彼らは彼女をひどい目にあわせた.
→ see **drum**

Thesaurus	beat また次を参照:
V.	hit, pound, punch; (ant.) caress, pat, pet ①
	flutter, quiver, vibrate ③ ⑧
	mix, stir, whip ⑦

Word Partnership	beatは次の語句と使われる:
N.	beat **a rug** ①
	heart beat ③
	beat **a drum** ④
	beat **eggs**
	beat **a deadline** ⑭
PREP.	beat **against, beat on** ②
	on/to a beat ⑤ ⑥
PRON.	beat **its/their wings** ⑧

beat|en /bi͟t³n/ **1** **Beaten** is the past participle of **beat**. beatの過去分詞 **2** PHRASE 句 A place that is **off the beaten track** is in an area where not many people live or go. よく知られていない場所 □Tiny secluded beaches can be found off the beaten track. こじんまりとした静かな海岸は人のあまりこない場所にある.

beat|ing /bi͟tɪŋ/ (beatings) **1** N-COUNT 可算名詞 If someone is given a **beating**, they are hit hard many times, especially with

B

something such as a stick. ひどくたたくこと ❑ ...*the investigation into the beating of an alleged car thief.* 自動車泥棒容疑者の殴打事件に関する調査 **2** N-SING 単数名詞 If something such as a business, a political party, or a team takes a **beating**, it is defeated by a large amount in a competition or an election. 敗北 ❑ *Our firm has taken a terrible beating in recent years.* 我々の会社は近年競争で大敗した.

Beau|jo|lais /ˈbouʒəleɪ/ (**Beaujolais**) also **beaujolais** N-VAR 可変性名詞 **Beaujolais** is a type of red wine that comes from the region of eastern France called Beaujolais. ボージョレー ❑ ...*a fruity Beaujolais.* 果実味のあるボージョレー

Word Link ful ≈ filled with : beautiful, careful, dreadful

---

beau|ti|ful /ˈbyutɪfəl/ **1** ADJ 形容詞 A **beautiful** person is very attractive to look at. 美しい ❑ *She was a very beautiful woman.* 彼女は大変な美人だった. **2** ADJ 形容詞 If you describe something as **beautiful**, you mean that it is very attractive or pleasing. すばらしい ❑ *New England is beautiful.* ニューイングランドは素晴らしい. ❑ *It was a beautiful morning.* それは素晴らしい朝だった. ● **beau|ti|ful|ly** /ˈbyutɪfli/ ADV 副詞 立派に ❑ *The children behaved beautifully.* 子供たちは立派にふるまった. **3** ADJ 形容詞 You can describe something that someone does as **beautiful** when they do it very skillfully. 見事な ❑ *That's a beautiful shot!* あれは見事なショットだ. ● **beau|ti|ful|ly** ADV 副詞 見事に ❑ *The Sixers played beautifully.* シックサーズは見事にプレーした.

When you are describing someone's appearance, you usually use **beautiful** and **pretty** to describe women, girls, and babies. **Beautiful** is a much stronger word than **pretty**. The equivalent word for a man is **handsome. Good-looking** and **attractive** can be used to describe people of either sex.

Thesaurus beautiful また次を参照:

ADJ. gorgeous, lovely, pretty, ravishing, stunning; (*ant.*) grotesque, hideous, homely, ugly **1**

---

beau|ty /ˈbyuti/ (**beauties**) **1** N-UNCOUNT 不可算名詞 **Beauty** is the state or quality of being beautiful. 美 ❑ ...*an area of outstanding natural beauty.* 特別自然美観地域 **2** N-COUNT 可算名詞 A **beauty** is a beautiful woman. 美人 [JOURNALISM ジャーナリズム] ❑ *She is known as a great beauty.* 彼女は大変な美人として知られている. **3** N-COUNT 可算名詞 You can say that something is a **beauty** when you think it is very good. 見事なもの [INFORMAL くだけた] ❑ *It was the one opportunity in the game – the pass was a real beauty, but the shot was poor.* それは試合の一つのチャンスだった、パスは実に見事だがショットはよくなかった. **4** N-COUNT 可算名詞 The **beauties** of something are its attractive qualities or features. 良さ [LITERARY 文語的] ❑ *He was beginning to enjoy the beauties of nature.* 彼は自然の良さを満喫し始めていた. **5** ADJ 形容詞 **Beauty** is used to describe people, products, and activities that are concerned with making women look beautiful. 美容 [ADJ n] ❑ *Additional beauty treatments can be booked in advance.* 追加のビューティトリートメントを予約できます. **6** N-COUNT 可算名詞 If you say that a particular feature is the **beauty of** something, you mean that this feature is what makes the thing so good. 美点 ❑ *There would be no effect on animals – that's the beauty of such water-based materials.* 動物には全く影響しない. それが水性素材のよさだ.

beau|ty mark (**beauty marks**) N-COUNT 可算名詞 A **beauty mark** is a small, dark spot on the skin that is supposed to add to a woman's beauty. 美人ぼくろ [AM, AUSTRALIAN 米国英語, オーストラリア英語] ❑ ...*that cute little beauty mark on Teri Hatcher's lower lip.* テリー・ハッチャーの下唇にある可愛くて小さな美人ぼくろ

bea|ver /ˈbivər/ (**beavers**) **1** N-COUNT 可算名詞 A **beaver** is a furry animal with a big flat tail and large teeth. Beavers use their teeth to cut wood and build dams in rivers. ビーバー **2** N-UNCOUNT 不可算名詞 **Beaver** is the fur of a beaver. ビーバーの毛皮 [oft N n] ❑ ...*a coat with a huge beaver collar.* ビーバーの毛皮でできた大きな襟付きのコート

be|came /bɪˈkeɪm/ **Became** is the past tense of **become.** become の過去形

be|cause /bɪˈkɔz, bɪˈkʌz/ **1** CONJ 接続詞 You use **because** when stating the reason for something. ～なので ❑ *He is called Mitch, because his name is Mitchell.* 彼の名前はミッチェルなのでミッチと呼ばれている. ❑ *Because it is an area of outstanding natural beauty, the number of boats available for hire on the river is limited.* それは特別自然美観地域なので川で借りられるボートの数は限られている. **2** CONJ 接続詞 You use **because** when stating the explanation for a statement you have just made. というのは ❑ *Maybe they just didn't want to ask too many questions, because they rented us a room without even asking to see our papers.* 多分彼らは余り多くの質問をしたくなかったのだろう. というのは彼らは身分証明書も要求せずに私たちに部屋を貸したからだ. ❑ *The president has played a shrewd diplomatic game because from the outset he called for direct talks.* 大統領は抜け目のない外交の駆け引きをした. 最初から彼は直接協議を呼びかけてい

たからだ. **3** PHRASE 句 If an event or situation occurs **because of** something, that thing is the reason or cause. ～のために ❑ *Many families break up because of a lack of money.* 多くの家族がお金が足りないために崩壊する.

beck|on /ˈbɛkən/ (**beckons, beckoning, beckoned**) **1** V-T/V-I 他動詞/自動詞 If you **beckon to** someone, you signal to them to come to you. 手まねで招く ❑ *He beckoned to the waiter.* 彼はウェーターに合図した. ❑ *I beckoned her over.* 私は彼女にこちらに来るよう合図した. **2** V-I 自動詞 If something **beckons**, it is so attractive to someone that they feel they must become involved in it. 招く ❑ *All the attractions of the peninsula beckon.* 半島の観光名所全てが招く **3** V-I 自動詞 If something **beckons for** someone, it is very likely to happen to them. 招く ❑ *The big time beckons for Billy Dodds.* ビリー・ドッズに成功が訪れる.

be|come /bɪˈkʌm/ (**becomes, becoming, became**)

The form **become** is used in the present tense and is the past participle.

---

become 形は現在形に使われ, 過去分詞でもある.

---

1 V-LINK 連結動詞 If someone or something **becomes** a particular thing, they start to change and develop into that thing, or start to develop the characteristics mentioned. (～に) なる ❑ *I first became interested in Islam during my nursing training.* 私は, 看護の養成訓練の最中にイスラム教に関心を持つようになった. **2** V-T 他動詞 If something **becomes** someone, it makes them look attractive or it seems right for them. 似合う [no passive, no cont] ❑ *Does khaki become you?* カーキ色はあなたに似合うか. **3** PHRASE 句 If you wonder **what** has **become of** someone or something, you wonder where they are and what has happened to them. ～が (どう) なる ❑ *She thought constantly about her family; she might never know what had become of them.* 彼女はいつも家族のことを考えた. 彼女は家族の行く末を知ることがないかもしれない.

bed /bɛd/ (**beds**) **1** N-COUNT 可算名詞 A **bed** is a piece of furniture that you lie on when you sleep. ベッド [also prep N] ❑ *We finally went to bed at about 4am.* 私たちは午前4時ごろやっと寝た. ❑ *By the time we got back from dinner, Nona was already in bed.* 私たちがディナーから戻った頃にはもうノーナは寝ていた. **2** N-COUNT 可算名詞 If a place such as a hospital or a hotel has a particular number of **beds**, it is able to hold that number of patients or guests. ベッド数 **3** N-COUNT 可算名詞 A **bed** in a garden or park is an area of ground that has been specially prepared so that plants can be grown in it. 苗床 ❑ ...*beds of strawberries and rhubarb.* ストロベリーとルーバーブの苗床 **4** N-COUNT 可算名詞 A **bed** of shellfish or plants is an area in the sea or in a lake where a particular type of shellfish or plant is found in large quantities. 床 ❑ *The whole lake was rimmed with thick beds of reeds.* 湖は水際全体にアシが厚い層をなしていた. **5** N-COUNT 可算名詞 The sea **bed** or a river **bed** is the ground at the bottom of the sea or of a river. 水底, 川床 ❑ *For three weeks a big operation went on to recover the wreckage from the sea bed.* 水底から難破貨物を回収する大作業が3週間続いた. **6** N-COUNT 可算名詞 A **bed** of rock is a layer of rock that is found within a larger area of rock. 単層 ❑ *Between the white limestone and the grayish pink limestone is a thin bed of clay.* 白い石灰石と灰色がかったピンクの石灰石の間には薄い粘土層がある. **7** N-COUNT 可算名詞 If a recipe or a menu says that something is served on a **bed of** a food such as rice or vegetables, it means it is served on a layer of that food. 土台 ❑ *Heat the curry thoroughly and serve it on a bed of rice.* カレーをよく温め, ご飯の上にかけます. **8** N-COUNT 可算名詞 On a vehicle such a truck or a pickup, the **bed** is the long, flat part at the back where goods are carried. 荷台 ❑ *They loaded about a ton of canned goods into the covered bed of a pickup truck.* 彼らは小型トラックの荷台に約1トンの缶詰を積んだ. **9** → see also **bedding 10** PHRASE 句 To **go to bed with** someone means to have sex with them. (異性と) 寝る ❑ *I went to bed with him once, just once.* 彼とは一度寝たことがあるわ, 一度だけね. **11** PHRASE 句 When you **make** the **bed**, you neatly arrange the sheets and covers of a bed so that it is ready to sleep in. ベッドを整える ❑ *He had made the bed after breakfast.* 彼は朝食後にベッドを整えた. **12** bed of roses → see rose → see Picture Dictionary: **bed** → see lake, sleep

---

Word Partnership bed は次の語句と使われる:

ADJ. asleep in bed, double/single/twin bed, ready for bed **1**
V. be sick in bed, get into bed, go to bed, lie (down) in bed, put *someone* to bed **1**
PREP. in/out of bed, under the bed **1** bed *of something* **7**

---

bed and break|fast (**bed and breakfasts**) also **bed-and-breakfast 1** N-UNCOUNT 不可算名詞 **Bed and breakfast** is a system of accommodations in a hotel or guest house, in which you pay for a room for the night and for breakfast the following

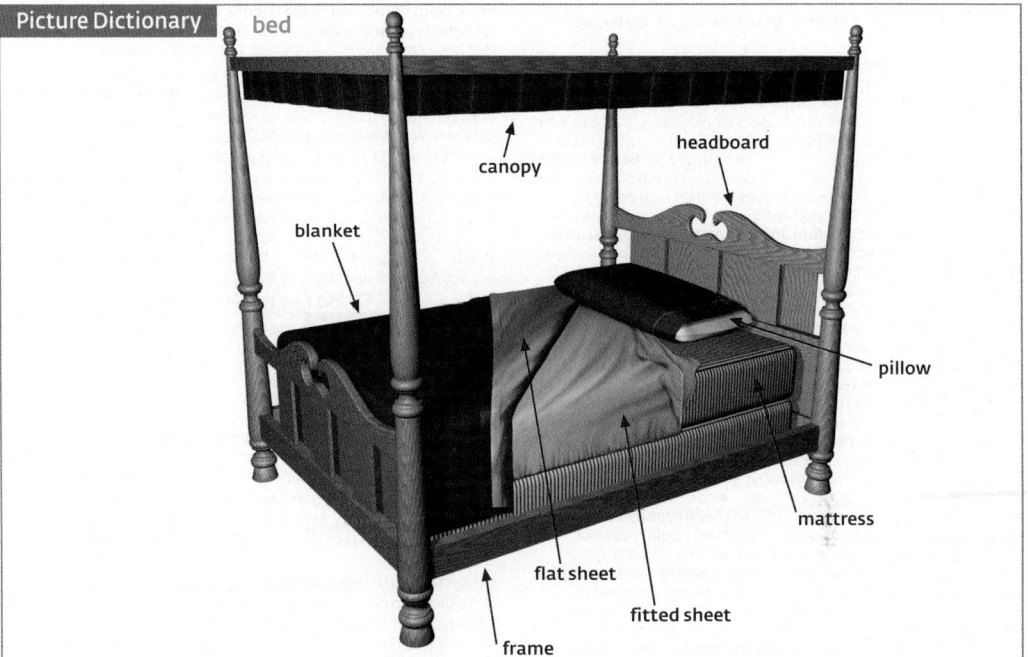

Picture Dictionary bed

canopy

headboard

blanket

pillow

mattress

flat sheet

fitted sheet

frame

morning. The abbreviation **B&B** is also used. 朝食付き宿泊 ❑ *Bed and breakfast costs from $50 per person per night.* 朝食付き宿泊料金はお一人様1泊50米ドルからです. **2** N-COUNT 可算名詞 A **bed and breakfast** is a guest house that provides bed and breakfast accommodations. The abbreviation **B&B** is also used. 朝食付き民宿（B&B）❑ *The restored home is now a bed-and-breakfast.* その修復された家は現在は朝食付き民宿になっています.

bed|clothes /bɛdklouz, -klouðz/ N-PLURAL 複数名詞 **Bedclothes** are the sheets and covers that you put over yourself when you get into bed. 寝具 [OLD-FASHIONED 古風な] ❑ *Momma was cleaning inside, changing the bedclothes.* ママは，寝具を換えて室内を掃除していた.

bed|ding /bɛdɪŋ/ N-UNCOUNT 不可算名詞 **Bedding** is sheets, blankets, and covers that are used on beds. 寝具類 ❑ *...a crib with two full sets of bedding.* 2セットの寝具付きのベビーベッド

bed|room /bɛdrum/ (**bedrooms**) **1** N-COUNT 可算名詞 A **bedroom** is a room used for sleeping in. 寝室 ❑ *...the spare bedroom.* 客用寝室 **2** ADJ 形容詞 If you refer to a place as a **bedroom community** or **suburb**, you mean that most of the people who live there travel to work in a city or another, larger town a short distance away. ベッドタウンの [AM 米国英語] [ADJ n] ❑ *This town is becoming a bedroom community of Columbus, 20 miles to the north.* この町は北20マイルのところにあるコロンバスのベッドタウンになりつつある.
→ see **house**

bed|side /bɛdsaɪd/ **1** N-SING 単数名詞 Your **bedside** is the area beside your bed. ベッドわき [usu N n] ❑ *She put a cup of tea down on the bedside table.* 彼女はベッドわきのテーブルに紅茶のカップを置いた. **2** N-SING 単数名詞 If you talk about being at someone's **bedside**, you are talking about being near them when they are ill in bed. （病人の）枕元 ❑ *She kept vigil at the bedside of her critically ill son.* 彼女は危篤の息子の枕元で徹夜の付き添いをした.

bee /biː/ (**bees**) N-COUNT 可算名詞 A **bee** is an insect with a yellow-and-black striped body that makes a buzzing noise as it flies. Bees make honey, and can sting. ミツバチ ❑ *A bee buzzed in the flowers.* ミツバチが草花の中をブンブン飛んだ.
→ see **flower**

beef /biːf/ (**beefs, beefing, beefed**) N-UNCOUNT 不可算名詞 **Beef** is the meat of a cow, bull, or ox. ビーフ ❑ *...roast beef.* ローストビーフ ❑ *...beef stew.* ビーフシチュー
▸ **beef up** PHRASAL VERB 句動詞 If you **beef up** something, you increase, strengthen, or improve it. 強化する ❑ *...a campaign to beef up security.* 保安を強化するキャンペーン ❑ *Both sides are still beefing up their military strength.* 両方ともまだ軍事力を強化中だ.
→ see **meat**

Beem|er /biːmər/ (**Beemers**) also **Beamer** N-COUNT 可算名

詞 Some people refer to a BMW automobile as a **Beemer**. ビーマー [INFORMAL くだけた] ❑ *The Beemer's door swung open and Markus Salkow stepped out.* ビーマーのドアがスーッと開き，マーカス・サルカウが出てきた.

been /bɪn/ **1** **Been** is the past participle of **be**. beの過去分詞 **2** V-I 自動詞 If you have **been** to a place, you have gone to it or visited it. 今までに行ったことがある ❑ *He's already been to Tunisia, and is to go on to Morocco and Mauritania.* 彼は既にチュニジアに行ったことがあり，モロッコとモーリタニアに行く予定だ.

beep|er /biːpər/ (**beepers**) N-COUNT 可算名詞 A **beeper** is a portable device that makes a beeping noise, usually to tell you to phone someone or to remind you to do something. ポケットベル ❑ *His beeper sounded and he picked up the telephone.* 彼のポケットベルが鳴り，彼は電話を取った.

beer /bɪər/ N-MASS 質量名詞 **Beer** is an alcoholic drink made from grain. ビール ❑ *He sat in the kitchen drinking beer.* 彼は台所に座りビールを飲んでいた. ● N-COUNT 可算名詞 A glass, can, or bottle of beer can be referred to as a **beer**. ビール一杯 ❑ *Would you like a beer?* ビール一杯いかがですか？

<table>
<tr><td colspan="2">**Word Partnership** beer は次の語句と使われる：</td></tr>
<tr><td>N.</td><td>**bottle of** beer, beer **bottle/can**, **case/six-pack of** beer, **glass/pint of** beer, beer **garden**, beer **keg**</td></tr>
<tr><td>ADJ.</td><td>**cold** beer, **imported** beer, **light** beer</td></tr>
<tr><td>V.</td><td>**drink/sip (a)** beer</td></tr>
</table>

beet /biːt/ (**beets**) **1** N-UNCOUNT 不可算名詞 **Beet** is a crop with a thick round root. ビート ❑ *...fields of sweetcorn and beet.* トウモロコシとビートの畑 **2** N-VAR 可変性名詞 **Beets** are dark red roots that are eaten as a vegetable. They are often preserved in vinegar. ビートの根 [AM 米国英語] ❑ *It comes with a garnish of red beets, white cottage cheese and blueberries.* つけ合せは赤いビートの根，白いコテージチーズとブルーベリーです.
→ see **sugar**

bee|tle /biːtəl/ (**beetles**) N-COUNT 可算名詞 A **beetle** is an insect with a hard covering to its body. 甲虫

beet|root /biːtrut/ → see **beet 2**

be|fit /bɪfɪt/ (**befits, befitting, befitted**) V-T 他動詞 If something **befits** a person or thing, it is suitable or appropriate for them. （一に）ふさわしい [FORMAL 形式ばった] ❑ *They offered him a post befitting his seniority and experience.* 彼らは彼の年功と経験にふさわしいポストを提供した.

be|fore /bɪfɔːr/

In addition to the uses shown below, **before** is used in the phrasal verbs "go before" and "lay before."

下記の用法に加えて，**before** は **go before** および **lay before** の句動詞に使われる．

1 PREP 前置詞 If something happens **before** a particular date, time, or event, it happens earlier than that date, time, or event. —よりも前に □ *Annie was born a few weeks before Christmas.* アニーはクリスマスの数週間前に生まれた． □ *Before World War II, women were not recruited as intelligence officers.* 第二次世界大戦前，女性は諜報（ちょうほう）部員に採用されなかった． □ PREP 接続詞 **Before** is also a conjunction. （—するに）先立って □ *Stock prices had climbed close to the peak they'd registered before the stock market crashed in 1987.* 株価は1987年の株式市場最落前の最高値近くまで下落した． **2** PREP 前置詞 If you do one thing **before** doing something else, you do it earlier than the other thing. （—する）前に [PREP -ing] □ *He spent his early life in Sri Lanka before moving to Canada.* 彼はカナダに移住する前，若い頃スリランカに住んでいた． □ CONJ 接続詞 **Before** is also a conjunction. （—するに）先立って □ *He took a cold shower and then toweled off before he put on fresh clothes.* 彼は冷たいシャワーをあび，タオルで身体を拭いてから洗いたての服を着た． **3** ADV 副詞 You use **before** when you are talking about time. For example, if something happened the day **before** a particular date or event, it happened during the previous day. 以前に [N ADV] □ *The war had ended only a month or so before.* 戦争は約1か月前に終わっていた． □ PREP 前置詞 **Before** is also a preposition. —よりも前に [N PREP N] □ *It's interesting that he sent me the book twenty days before the deadline for my book.* 彼が私の本の締め切りよりも20日前にその本を私に送ってきたのは興味深いことだ． □ CONJ 接続詞 **Before** is also a conjunction. —より前に □ *Kelman had a book published in the U.S. more than a decade before a British publisher would touch him.* ケルマンは英国の出版社が接触する10年以上前に米国で本を出版していた． **4** CONJ 接続詞 If you do something **before** someone else can do something, you do it when they have not yet done it. —する前に □ *Before Gallacher could catch up with the ball, Nadlovu had beaten him to it.* ギャラチャーがボールに追いつく前にナドロブは彼を出し抜いた． **5** ADV 副詞 If someone has done something **before**, they have done it on a previous occasion. If someone has not done something **before**, they have never done it. 以前に [ADV after v] □ *I've been here before.* 私はここに以前来たことがある． □ *I had met Professor Lown before.* 私はローン教授に以前会ったことがある． **6** CONJ 接続詞 If there is a period of time or if several things are done **before** something happens, it takes that amount of time or effort for this thing to happen. （—する）までに □ *It was some time before the door opened in response to his ring.* 彼のベルを聞いてドアが開くまでにしばらくかかった． **7** CONJ 接続詞 If a particular situation has to happen **before** something else happens, this situation must happen or exist in order for the other thing to happen. （—するに）先立って □ *There was additional work to be done before all the troops would be ready.* 軍隊全体の準備が万全になるには追加作業をしなければならなかった． **8** PREP 前置詞 If someone is **before** something, they are in front of it. —の面前に [FORMAL 形式ばった] □ *They drove through a tall iron gate and stopped before a large white villa.* 彼らは高い鉄の門を車で走りぬけ，白い大邸宅の前で止まった． **9** PREP 前置詞 If you tell someone that one place is a certain distance **before** another, you mean that they will come to the first place first. —より手前に □ *The station is on the right, one mile before downtown Romney.* 駅は右側，ロムニーの都心部より1マイル手前にある． **10** PREP 前置詞 If you appear or come **before** an official person or group, you go there and answer questions. （質問に答える人の）面前に □ *The governor will appear before the committee next Tuesday.* 理事は来週の火曜日，委員会に出る． **11** PREP 前置詞 If something happens **before** a particular person or group, it is seen by or happens while this person or this group is present. —の見守る中で □ *The game followed a colorful opening ceremony before a crowd of seventy-four thousand.* 観衆7万4千人が見守る華やかな開会式の後で試合が始まった． **12** PREP 前置詞 If you have something such as a trip, a task, or a stage of your life **before** you, you must do it or live through it in the future. —に直面して [PREP pron] □ *Everyone in the room knew it was the single hardest task before them.* 部屋の中の全員がそれが自分たちにとって最大の課題だと知っていた． **13** PREP 前置詞 When you want to say that one person or thing is more important than another, you can say that they come **before** the other person or thing. —に先んじて [V PREP N] □ *Her husband and her children came before her needs.* 彼女は夫と子供を自分の要求することより優先した． **14** **before long** → see **long**

Thesaurus *before* また次を参照:

ADV already, earlier, previously; (ant.) after **3** **5**

before|hand /bɪfɔrhænd/ ADV 副詞 If you do something **beforehand**, you do it earlier than a particular event. 事前に □ *How could she tell beforehand that I was going to go out?* 私が外出することを彼女はどうやって事前に知ったのでしょうか．

be|friend /bɪfrɛnd/ (**befriends, befriending, befriended**) V-T 他動詞 If you **befriend** someone, especially someone who is lonely

or far from home, you make friends with them. （—の）友となる □ *The film's about an elderly woman and a young nurse who befriends her.* その映画は年配の女性とその友となる若い看護婦の話です．

beg /beg/ (**begs, begging, begged**) **1** V-T/V-I 他動詞/自動詞 If you **beg** someone **to** do something, you ask them very anxiously or eagerly to do it. （—してほしいと）懇願する □ *I begged him to come back to New York with me.* 私は彼に一緒にニューヨークに戻ってくるよう懇願した． □ *We are not going to beg for help anymore.* 私たちは助けを請うつもりはない． **2** V-T/V-I 自動詞 If someone who is poor **is begging**, they are asking people to give them food or money. 施しを請う [oft cont] □ *I was surrounded by people begging for food.* 私は食べ物を請い求める人々に囲まれた． □ *...homeless people begging on the streets.* 通りでこじきをするホームレスの人々 □ *She was living alone, begging food from neighbors.* 彼女は隣人に食べ物を請い求めながら独居生活をしていた． **3** **I beg your pardon** → see **pardon**

Word Partnership *beg* は次の語句と使われる:

V.	beg and plead **1**
PREP.	beg for *something* **1** **2**
N.	beg for help/mercy **1** **2**
	beg for food/money **2**
	beg *(someone's)* pardon/forgiveness **3**

be|gan /bɪɡæn/ **Began** is the past tense of **begin**. beginの過去形

beg|gar /begər/ (**beggars**) N-COUNT 可算名詞 A **beggar** is someone who lives by asking people for money or food. こじき □ *There are no beggars on the street in Vienna.* ウィーンの通りにはこじきはいない．

be|gin /bɪɡɪn/ (**begins, beginning, began, begun**) **1** V-T 他動詞 To **begin** to do something means to start doing it. （—し）始める □ *He stood up and began to move around the room.* 彼は立ち上がり，部屋を動き回り始めた． □ *The weight loss began to look more serious.* 体重の減少はより深刻に見え始めた． **2** V-T/V-I 他動詞/自動詞 When something **begins** or when you **begin** it, it takes place from a particular time onward. 始まる □ *The problems began last November.* その問題は去る11月に始まった． □ *He has just begun his fourth year in hiding.* 彼は隠れてからちょうど4年目が始まった． **3** V-T/V-I 他動詞/自動詞 If you **begin with** something, or **begin by** doing something, this is the first thing you do. （—から）開始する □ *Could I begin with a few formalities?* まず形式的手続きから始めてよいですか． □ *...a businessman who began by selling golf shirts from the trunk of his car.* 車のトランクに積んだゴルフ用のシャツを販売することから始めた事業家 □ *He began his career flipping hamburgers.* 彼の職業生活はハンバーガーを焼くことから始まった． **4** V-T/V-I 他動詞/自動詞 You use **begin** to mention the first thing that someone says. 口を切る [no cont] □ *"Professor Theron," he began, "I'm very pleased to see you."* 「セロン教授」と彼は口を切った．「お会いできて嬉しいです」 □ *He didn't know how to begin.* 彼はどうやって会話を始めてよいのか分からなかった． **5** V-I 自動詞 If one thing **began as** another thing, it first existed as the other thing before it changed into its present form. 始まる [no cont] □ *What began as a local festival has blossomed into an international event.* 地元のお祭りとして始まったものが国際的行事に発展した． **6** V-I 自動詞 If you say that a thing or place **begins** somewhere, you are talking about one of its limits or edges. —から出る [no cont] □ *The fate line begins close to the wrist.* 運命線は手首の近くから出る． **7** V-I 自動詞 If a word **begins with** a particular letter, that is the first letter of that word. —で始まる [no cont] □ *The first word begins with an F.* 最初の単語はFで始まる． **8** PHRASE 句 You use **to begin with** when you are talking about the first stage of a situation, event, or process. 最初は □ *It was great to begin with but now it's difficult.* 最初は素晴らしかったが今は大変だ． **9** PHRASE 句 You use **to begin with** to introduce the first of several things that you want to say. まず第一に □ *"What do scientists you've spoken with think about that?" — "Well, to begin with, they doubt it's going to work."* 「あなたが話を聞いた科学者たちはそれについてどう考えますか．」「まず第一に，彼らはそれに効果があるとは思っていません．」

Begin, start, and commence all have a similar meaning, although commence is more formal and is not normally used in conversation. *The meeting is ready to begin... He tore the list up and started a fresh one ... an alternative to commencing the process of European integration.* Note that begin, start, and commence can all be followed by an -ing form or a noun, but only begin and start can be followed by a "to" infinitive.

Thesaurus *begin* また次を参照:

V. commence, kick off, start; (ant.) end, stop **2**

Word Partnership	*begin* は次の語句と使われる:
ADV.	begin **again/anew**, begin **immediately/soon**, **suddenly** begin 1
V.	**expected/scheduled** to begin, begin **to show**, begin **to understand** 1 2
ADJ.	**ready** to begin 1 2
N.	begin **a process** 1
PREP.	begin **by doing** *something* 8 to begin **with** 8 9

be|gin|ner /bɪgɪnər/ (**beginners**) N-COUNT 可算名詞 A **beginner** is someone who has just started learning to do something and cannot do it very well yet. 初心者 ❏ *The course is suitable for both beginners and advanced students.* そのコースは初心者と上級者の両方の学生に適している.

be|gin|ning /bɪgɪnɪŋ/ (**beginnings**) ■ N-COUNT 可算名詞 The **beginning of** an event or process is the first part of it. 始まり ❏ *This was also the beginning of her recording career.* これは彼女の最初のレコーディングでもあった. ◛ N-PLURAL 複数名詞 The **beginnings of** something are the signs or events which form the first part of it. 初期 ❏ *The discussions were the beginnings of a dialogue with Moscow.* その協議はモスクワとの対話の初期だった. ◜ N-SING 単数名詞 The **beginning of** a period of time is the time at which it starts. 初め ❏ *The wedding will be at the beginning of March.* 結婚式は3月の初めに行なわれる. ◝ N-COUNT 可算名詞 The **beginning of** a piece of written material is the first words or sentences of it. 初め ❏ *...the question that was raised at the beginning of this chapter.* この章の最初に出た質問 ◞ N-PLURAL 複数名詞 If you talk about the **beginnings** of a person, company, or group, you are referring to their backgrounds or origins. 起源 ❏ *His views come from his own humble beginnings.* 彼の考えはそのつつましい生い立ちからきたものだ.

Thesaurus	*beginning* また次を参照:
N.	birth, conception, genesis; (*ant*.) conclusion, end 1 inception, introduction, start; (*ant*.) conclusion, end 3

Word Partnership	*beginning* は次の語句と使われる:
PREP.	beginning **of** *something*, **from/since** the beginning 1 – 3 **in** the beginning 2
ADV.	**just** the beginning 1 – 3
ADJ.	**a new** beginning 1 – 4

be|gun /bɪgʌn/ **Begun** is the past participle of **begin**. *begin*の過去分詞

be|half /bɪhæf/ ■ PHRASE 句 If you do something on someone's **behalf**, you do it for that person as their representative. ～に代わって ❏ *She made an emotional public appeal on her son's behalf.* 彼女は息子に代わって感情のこもった言葉で公に訴えた. ◛ PHRASE 句 If you feel, for example, embarrassed or angry on someone's **behalf**, you feel embarrassed or angry for them. ～のために ❏ *"What do you mean?" I asked, offended on Liddie's behalf.* 「どういう意味なの」と私はリディのために腹を立てて聞いた.

be|have /bɪheɪv/ (**behaves, behaving, behaved**) ■ V-I 自動詞 The way that you **behave** is the way that you do and say things, and the things that you do and say. ふるまう ❏ *I couldn't believe these people were behaving in this way.* 私はこうした人々がこのようにふるまっているのを信じられなかった. ◛ V-T/V-I 他動詞/自動詞 If you **behave** or **behave yourself**, you act in the way that people think is correct and proper. 行儀よくする ❏ *You have to behave.* 行儀よくしなければなりません. ◜ V-I 自動詞 In science, the way that something **behaves** is the things that it does. 反応する ❏ *Under certain conditions, electrons can behave like waves rather than particles.* 一定の条件下で, 電子は素粒子ではなく波動のように作用することがある.

Word Partnership	*behave* は次の語句と使われる:
ADV.	behave **badly/well** 1
PREP.	behave **toward** *someone* 1
PRON.	behave **themselves/yourself** 1 2

be|hav|ior /bɪheɪvyər/ (**behaviors**) ■ N-VAR 可変性名詞 People's or animals' **behavior** is the way that they behave. You can refer to a typical and repeated way of behaving as a **behavior**. ふるまい ❏ *Make sure that good behavior is rewarded.* よいふるまいは報いられるようにしなさい. ❏ *...human sexual behavior.* 人間の性的行動 ◛ N-UNCOUNT 不可算名詞 In science, the **behavior** of something is the way that it behaves. 性質 ❏ *It will be many years before anyone can predict a hurricane's behavior with much accuracy.* ハリケーンの性質を正確に予測できるようになるまでには何年もかかるだろう. ◜ PHRASE 句 If someone is on their **best behavior**, they are trying very hard to behave well. 行儀をよくする ❏ *The 1,400 fans were on their best behavior and filed out peacefully at the end.* 1400人のファンは行儀よく, 最後は静かに列を作って退場した.

Thesaurus	*behavior* また次を参照:
N.	action, conduct 1

Word Partnership	*behavior* は次の語句と使われる:
V.	**change** *someone's* behavior 1
N.	**human** behavior, behavior **pattern**, behavior **problems** 1
ADJ.	**aggressive/criminal** behavior, **bad/good** behavior **learned** behavior 1 2

be|hav|ior|al /bɪheɪvyərəl/ ADJ 形容詞 **Behavioral** means relating to the behavior of a person or animal, or to the study of their behavior. 行動の [ADJ n] ❏ *...emotional and behavioral problems.* 感情および行動面での問題

be|hind /bɪhaɪnd/ (**behinds**)

In addition to the uses shown below, **behind** is also used in a few phrasal verbs, such as "fall behind" and "lie behind."

下に示された用法に加えて, **behind** は fall behind や lie behind のような少数の句動詞にも使われる.

■ PREP 前置詞 If something is **behind** a thing or person, it is on the other side of them from you, or nearer their back rather than their front. 後ろに ❏ *I put one of the cushions behind his head.* 私は彼の頭の後ろにクッションを置いた. ❏ *They were parked behind the truck.* 彼らはトラックの後ろに駐車した. ● ADV 副詞 **Behind** is also an adverb. 後ろに ❏ *Rising into the hills behind are 800 acres of parkland.* 800エーカーの緑地が裏の方に丘まで広がっている. ◛ PREP 前置詞 If you are walking or traveling **behind** someone or something, you are following them. ～のあとに ❏ *Keith wandered along behind him.* キースは彼のあとをぶらぶら歩いた. ● ADV 副詞 **Behind** is also an adverb. 後ろに [ADV after v] ❏ *The troopers followed behind, every muscle tensed for the sudden gunfire.* 突然の砲撃で騎兵らは全身の筋肉を緊張させ後ろについていった. ◜ PREP 前置詞 If someone is **behind** a desk, counter, or bar, they are on the other side of it from where you are. ～の後ろに ❏ *The colonel was sitting behind a cheap wooden desk.* 大佐は安物の木製の机の後ろ側に座っていた. ◝ PREP 前置詞 When you shut a door or gate **behind** you, you shut it after you have gone through it. (人の) 去った後の [PREP pron] ❏ *I walked out and closed the door behind me.* 私は退室し, ドアを閉めた. ◞ N-COUNT 可算名詞 Your **behind** is the part of your body that you sit on. 尻 ◟ PREP 前置詞 The people, reason, or events **behind** a situation are the causes of it or are responsible for it. ～の陰に ❏ *It is still not clear who was behind the killing.* 誰が陰で殺害に加担したのかはまだ明らかでない. ◠ PREP 前置詞 If something or someone is **behind** you, they support you and help you. ～を支持して [PREP pron] ❏ *He had the state's judicial power behind him.* 彼は州の司法権力の後ろ盾を受けていた. ◡ PREP 前置詞 If you refer to what is **behind** someone's outside appearance, you are referring to a characteristic which you cannot immediately see or is not obvious, but which you think is there. ～の裏に (隠れて) ❏ *What lay behind his anger was really the hurt he felt at Grace's refusal.* 彼の怒りの裏に本当にあったのはグレースの拒否で感じた痛みだった. ◢ PREP 前置詞 If you are **behind** someone, you are less successful than them, or have done less or advanced less. ～に敗れて ❏ *She finished second behind the American, Ann Cody, in the 800 meters.* 彼女は800メートルでアメリカ人のアン・コーディに敗れ, 2位だった. ● ADV 副詞 **Behind** is also an adverb. ～より劣って ❏ *The rapid development of technology means that she is now far behind, and will need retraining.* 技術が急速に進歩したため, 彼女は現在かなり遅れを取り, 再訓練を受ける必要がある. ◣ PREP 前置詞 If an experience is **behind** you, it happened in your past and will not happen again, or no longer affects you. (人) にとって過ぎ去って [PREP pron] ❏ *Maureen put the nightmare behind her.* モーリーンは悪夢を過去のことにした. ◤ PREP 前置詞 If you have a particular achievement **behind** you, you have managed to reach this achievement, and other people consider it to be important or valuable. 過去に ['have/with' n PREP pron] ❏ *He has 20 years of loyal service to Barclays Bank behind him.* 彼には20年間バークレイズ銀行に忠実に勤め上げた経験がある. ◥ PREP 前置詞 If something is **behind** schedule, it is not as far advanced as people had planned. If someone is **behind** schedule, they are not progressing as quickly at something as they had planned. ～に遅れて ❏ *The work is 22 weeks behind schedule.* 作業は予定より22週間遅れている. ◧ ADV 副詞 If you stay **behind**, you remain in a place after other people have gone. 残って [ADV after v] ❏ *About 1,200 personnel will remain behind to take care of the air base.* 約1200名の人員が残って空軍基地の世話をすることになっている. ◨ ADV 副詞 If you leave something or someone **behind**, you do not take them with you when you go. 残して [ADV after v] ❏ *The rebels fled*

into the mountains, leaving behind their weapons and supplies. 反乱軍は武器や物資を残して山に逃走した. **15 to do** something **behind** someone's **back** → see **back 16 behind bars** → see **bar 17 behind the scenes** → see **scene 18 behind the times** → see **time**

beige /beɪʒ/ COLOR 色彩語 Something that is **beige** is pale brown in color. ベージュ色 ❏ *The walls are beige.* 壁の色はベージュだ.

be|ing /biːɪŋ/ (**beings**) **1** Being is the present participle of **be.** be の現在分詞 **2** V-LINK 連結動詞 **Being** is used in nonfinite clauses when you are giving the reason for something. 〜であるので ❏ *It being a Sunday, the old men had the day off.* 日曜なので亭主たちは仕事が休みだった. ❏ *Little boys, being what they are, might decide to play on it.* 少年たちはやはり少年なのでその上で遊ぶかもしれない. **3** N-COUNT 可算名詞 You can refer to any real or imaginary creature as a **being.** もの ❏ *People expect a horse to perform like a car, with no thought for its feelings as a living being.* 人々は, 馬が感情のある生き物であることを理解せずに自動車のように走るのを期待する. **4** → see also **human being 5** N-UNCOUNT 不可算名詞 **Being** is existence. Something that is **in being** or comes **into being** exists. 実存 ❏ *Abraham Maslow described psychology as "the science of being."* エイブラハム・マスローは心理学を「実存の科学」と呼んだ. **6** → see also **well-being 7 other things being equal** → see **equal 8 for the time being** → see **time**

be|lat|ed /bɪleɪtɪd/ ADJ 形容詞 A **belated** action happens later than it should have. 遅れた [FORMAL 形式ばった] ❏ *...the government's belated attempts to alleviate the plight of the poor.* 貧困層の苦境を和らげようとする遅ればせながらの政府の試み.

belch /beltʃ/ (**belches, belching, belched**) **1** V-I 自動詞 If someone **belches,** they make a sudden noise in their throat because air has risen up from their stomach. げっぷする ❏ *Garland covered his mouth with his hand and belched discreetly.* ガーランドは手で口をおおい, 目立たないようにげっぷをした. ● N-COUNT 可算名詞 **Belch** is also a noun. げっぷ ❏ *He drank and stifled a belch.* 彼は飲んでげっぷを抑えた. **2** V-T/V-I 他動詞/自動詞 If a machine or chimney **belches** smoke or fire, or if smoke or fire **belches** from it, large amounts of smoke or fire come from it. 噴出する ❏ *Tired old trucks were struggling up the road below us, belching black smoke.* くたびれた古いトラックは黒い煙を噴出しながら私たちの下の道を苦労しながら登っていた. ● PHRASAL VERB 句動詞 **Belch out** means the same as **belch.** 噴き出す ❏ *The power-generation plant belched out five tons of ash an hour.* 発電所は1時間に5トンの灰を噴き出した.

be|lea|guered /bɪliːgərd/ ADJ 形容詞 A **beleaguered** person, organization, or project is experiencing a lot of difficulties, opposition, or criticism. 窮地に陥った [FORMAL 形式ばった] ❏ *There have been seven coup attempts against the beleaguered government.* 窮地に陥った政府に対しては7回クーデターの試みがあった.

be|lie /bɪlaɪ/ (**belies, belying, belied**) **1** V-T 他動詞 If one thing **belies** another, it hides the true situation and so creates a false idea or image of someone or something. (実際の姿を)間違って示す ❏ *Her looks belie her 50 years.* 彼女はとても50歳には見えない. **2** V-T 他動詞 If one thing **belies** another, it proves that the other thing is not true or genuine. (〜と)矛盾する ❏ *The facts of the situation belie his testimony.* 状況の真相は彼の証言と一致しない.

be|lief /bɪliːf/ (**beliefs**) **1** N-UNCOUNT 不可算名詞 **Belief** is a feeling of certainty that something exists, is true, or is good. 信じること ❏ *One billion people throughout the world are Muslims, united by belief in one god.* 世界中の10億人はイスラム教徒で, 唯一神の存在を信じることで団結している. **2** N-PLURAL 複数名詞 Your religious or political **beliefs** are your views on religious or political matters. 信仰 ❏ *He refuses to compete on Sundays because of his religious beliefs.* 彼は信仰のため日曜日に競技に参加することを拒否する. **3** N-SING 単数名詞 If it is your **belief** that something is the case, it is your strong opinion that it is the case. 確信 ❏ *It is our belief that improvements in health care will lead to a stronger, more prosperous economy.* 我々は医療の改善は経済の強化と繁栄につながることを確信している. **4** PHRASE 句 You use **beyond belief** to emphasize that something is true to a very great degree or that it happened to a very great degree. 信じられないほどの [EMPHASIS 強調] ❏ *We are devastated, shocked beyond belief.* 我々は信じられないほどにショックを受け, 途方に暮れている. **5** PHRASE 句 If you do one thing **in the belief that** another thing is true or will happen, you do it because you think, usually wrongly, that it is true or will happen. (〜ということ)確信 ❏ *Civilians had broken into the building, apparently in the belief that it contained food.* 一般人は食料が保管されていると信じ込み, ビルに乱入したようだ.

→ see **religion**

Thesaurus belief また次を参照:

| N. | dogma, faith, ideology, principle **2** |
| | assumption, opinion **3** |

Word Partnership belief は次の語句と使われる:

PREP.	belief **in** something **1**
	beyond belief **4**
N.	belief **in God 1 2**
ADJ.	**religious/spiritual** belief **1 2**
	firm belief, **strong** belief, **widespread** belief **1 3**
	(contrary to) popular belief **1 3 5**
V.	**hold** a belief **1 3**

be|liev|able /bɪliːvəbəl/ ADJ 形容詞 Something that is **believable** makes you think that it could be true or real. 信じられる ❏ *...believable evidence.* 信用できる証拠

be|lieve /bɪliːv/ (**believes, believing, believed**) **1** V-T 他動詞 If you **believe** that something is true, you think it is true, but you are not sure. 考える [FORMAL 形式ばった] ❏ *Experts believe that the coming drought will be extensive.* 専門家は来るべき干ばつは大規模になると考えている. ❏ *We believe them to be hidden here in this apartment.* それらはここのアパートに隠されていると考えている. **2** V-T 他動詞 If you **believe** someone or if you **believe** what they say or write, you accept that they are telling the truth. 信じる ❏ *He did not sound as if he believed her.* 彼が彼女を信じたようには聞こえなかった. ❏ *Never believe anything a married man says about his wife.* 既婚の男性が妻の話をしても何も信じるな. **3** V-I 自動詞 If you **believe** in fairies, ghosts, or miracles, you are sure that they exist or happen. If you **believe in** a god, you are sure of the existence of that god. 存在を信じる ❏ *I don't believe in ghosts.* 幽霊がいるとは思わない. **4** V-I 自動詞 If you **believe in** a way of life or an idea, you are in favor of it because you think it is good or right. 価値を認める ❏ *He believed in marital fidelity.* 彼は夫婦の貞節を信じた. **5** V-I 自動詞 If you **believe in** someone or what they are doing, you have confidence in them and think that they will be successful. 信頼する ❏ *If you believe in yourself you can succeed.* 自分を信じれば成功することができる.

Note that when you are using the verb **believe** with a **that**-clause in order to state a negative opinion or belief, you normally make **believe** negative, rather than the verb in the **that**-clause. For instance, it is more usual to say "❏ *I didn't believe that she could do it...*" than "❏ *He believed that she couldn't do it.*" The same applies to other verbs with a similar meaning, such as **consider, suppose,** and **think.** ❏ *I don't consider that you kept your promise ... I don't suppose he ever saw it ... I don't think he saw me.*

Thesaurus believe また次を参照:

| V. | consider, guess, speculate, think **1** |
| | accept, buy, trust **2** |

be|liev|er /bɪliːvər/ (**believers**) **1** N-COUNT 可算名詞 If you are a great **believer** in something, you think that it is good, right, or useful. 信じる人 ❏ *Mom was a great believer in herbal medicines.* かあちゃんは熱心な薬草治療の信者だった. **2** N-COUNT 可算名詞 A **believer** is someone who is sure that God exists or that their religion is true. 信者 ❏ *I made no secret of the fact that I was not a believer.* 信者ではないという事実を少しも隠さなかった.

bell /bel/ (**bells**) **1** N-COUNT 可算名詞 A **bell** is a device that makes a ringing sound and is used to give a signal or to attract people's attention. ベル ❏ *I had just enough time to finish eating before the bell rang and I was off to my first class.* ベルが鳴る前にぎりぎりで食べ終わって, 最初の授業に出かけていった. **2** N-COUNT 可算名詞 A **bell** is a hollow metal object shaped like a cup which has a piece hanging inside it that hits the sides and makes a sound. 鐘 ❏ *My brother, Nick, was born on a Sunday, when all the church bells were ringing.* 弟のニックは日曜日に生まれたが, ちょうど教会の鐘がすべて鳴っていたときだった. **3** PHRASE 句 If you say that something **rings a bell,** you mean that it reminds you of something, but you cannot remember exactly what it is. どこかで聞いた覚えがある [INFORMAL くだけた] ❏ *The name doesn't ring a bell.* その名前は聞いた記憶がない.

bel|lig|er|ent /bɪlɪdʒərənt/ ADJ 形容詞 A **belligerent** person is hostile and aggressive. 好戦的な ❏ *...the belligerent statements from both sides which have led to fears of war.* 戦争の危惧を招いた両者の敵対的な声明 ● **bel|lig|er|ence** N-UNCOUNT 不可算名詞 闘争的な態度 ❏ *He could be accused of passion, but never belligerence.* 彼が非難されるのは激情であっても闘争的ではありえない.

bel|low /beloʊ/ (**bellows, bellowing, bellowed**) **1** V-T/V-I 他動詞/自動詞 If someone **bellows,** they shout angrily in a loud, deep voice. どなる ❏ *"I didn't ask to be born!" she bellowed.* 「生んでくれないって頼まなかったわよ!」と彼女はどなった. ❏ *She prayed she wouldn't come in and find them there, bellowing at each other.* 彼女は入ったとき彼らがどなりあっているのを見ませんようにと願った. ● N-COUNT 可算名詞 **Bellow** is also a noun. ほえ声 ❏ *I was distraught and let out a bellow of tearful rage.* わたしは取り乱して涙ながらに激怒

のうなり声を放った． **2** V-I 自動詞 When a large animal such as a bull or an elephant **bellows**, it makes a loud and deep noise. 大きな鳴き声 □ *A heifer bellowed in her stall.* 雌の子牛は牛舎で大きな鳴き声を上げた． **3** N-COUNT 可算名詞 A **bellows** is or **bellows** are a device used for blowing air into a fire in order to make it burn more fiercely. ふいご [also 'a pair of' N]

bell pep|per (bell peppers) N-COUNT 可算名詞 A **bell pepper** is a hollow green, red, or yellow vegetable with seeds. アマトウガラシ, ピーマン [mainly AM 主に米国英語]

bel|ly /bέli/ (bellies) N-COUNT 可算名詞 The **belly** of a person or animal is their stomach or abdomen. 腹 □ *She laid her hands on her swollen belly.* 彼女は大きくなったお腹に両手を置いた． □ ...*a horse with its belly ripped open.* 腹を引き裂かれた馬

be|long /bilɔ́ŋ/ (belongs, belonging, belonged) **1** V-I 自動詞 If something **belongs to** you, you own it. 所有物である [no cont] □ *The house had belonged to her family for three or four generations.* その家は彼女の家系が三代か四代続けて所有していた． **2** V-I 自動詞 You say that something **belongs to** a particular person when you are guessing, discovering, or explaining that it was produced by or is part of that person. 属する [no cont] □ *The handwriting belongs to a male.* その筆跡は男のものである． **3** V-I 自動詞 If someone **belongs to** a particular group, they are a member of that group. 所属する [no cont] □ *I used to belong to a youth club.* 以前はユースクラブに入っていた． **4** V-I 自動詞 If something or someone **belongs in** or **to** a particular category, type, or group, they are of that category, type, or group. 部類に入る [no cont] □ *The judges could not decide which category it belonged in.* 裁判官たちはそれがどの分類に入るか決めかねた． **5** V-I 自動詞 If something **belongs to** a particular time, it comes from that time. 属する [no cont] □ *The pictures belong to an era when there was a preoccupation with high society.* それらの絵は上流社会に執着のあった時代に属する． **6** V-I 自動詞 If you say that something **belongs to** someone, you mean that person has the right to it. 資格がある [no cont] □ ...*but the last word belonged to Rosanne.* しかし最終決定権はロザンナにあった． **7** V-I 自動詞 If you say that a time **belongs to** a particular system or way of doing something, you mean that that time is or will be characterized by it. 一の性質がある [no cont] □ *The future belongs to democracy.* 将来は民主主義の時代である． **8** V-I 自動詞 If a baby or child **belongs to** a particular adult, that adult is his or her parent or the person who is looking after him or her. 一のものである [no cont] □ *He deduced that the two children belonged to the couple.* 彼は二人はその夫婦の子供だと推定した． **9** V-I 自動詞 If a person or thing **belongs in** a particular place or situation, that is where they should be. ふさわしい [no cont] □ *You don't belong here.* ここはきみの来る所じゃない． □ *They need to feel they belong.* 彼らには帰属感が必要である．

Word Partnership belong は次の語句と使われる：

PREP.	belong **to** someone **1** **2** **8**
	belong **to a club/group/organization** **3**
ADV.	belong **together** **4** **5**
	back **where** you belong **9**
V.	someone/something **doesn't** belong **9**

be|long|ings /bilɔ́ŋiŋz/ N-PLURAL 複数名詞 Your **belongings** are the things that you own, especially things that are small enough to be carried. 見の回り品 □ *I collected my belongings and left.* 見の回り品を集めて出ていった．

be|lov|ed /bilʌ́vid/ ADJ 形容詞 A **beloved** person, thing, or place is one that you feel great affection for. 最愛の [ADJ n] □ *He lost his beloved wife last year.* 彼は去年最愛の妻を亡くした．

be|low /bilóu/ **1** PREP 前置詞 If something is **below** something else, it is in a lower position. 一より下に □ *He appeared from the apartment directly below Leonard's.* レナードのアパートの部屋の真下の部屋から彼が現れた． □ *The sun had already sunk below the horizon.* 太陽は既に地平線の下に沈んでいた． ● ADV 副詞 **Below** is also an adverb. 下に □ *We climbed rather perilously down a rope-ladder to the boat below.* 少々危険をおかして下にあるボートまで縄ばしごを降りていった． □ ...*a view to the street below.* 下のほうにある道の眺め **2** PHRASE 句 If something is **below ground** or **below the ground**, it is in the ground. 地下の □ *They have designed a system which pumps up water from nearly 1,000 feet below ground.* 地下1,000フィート近くのところから水をポンプでくみ上げる装置を設計した． **3** ADV 副詞 You use **below** in a piece of writing to refer to something that is mentioned later. 下記の □ *Please write to me at the address below.* 下記の住所でわたしに手紙を書いてください． **4** PREP 前置詞 If something is **below** a particular amount, rate, or level, it is less than that amount, rate, or level. 一より下の □ *Night temperatures can drop below 15 degrees Celsius.* 夜の温度は摂氏15度より下がることもある． ● ADV 副詞 **Below** is also an adverb. 下で □ ...*temperatures at zero or below.* 零度以下の温度 **5** PREP 前置詞 If someone is **below** you in an organization, they are lower in rank. 一より低く □ *Such people often experience less stress than those in the ranks immediately below them.* このような人たちは、すぐ下の階級の人たちに比べて経験するストレスが軽い場合が大い． **6** below par → see par

Word Partnership below は次の語句と使われる：

ADV.	**directly** below, **far/significantly/substantially/well** below, **just/slightly** below **1**
N.	below **the surface** **1**
	below **ground** **2**
	below **the belt/waist**, below **cost**, below **freezing**, below **the poverty level/line**, below **zero** **4**
V.	**dip/drop/fall** below **1** **4**
	described below, **listed** below, **see** below **3**
ADJ.	below **average**, below **normal** **4**

below the belt → see **belt**

belt /bέlt/ (belts, belting, belted) **1** N-COUNT 可算名詞 A **belt** is a strip of leather or cloth that you fasten around your waist. ベルト □ *He wore a belt with a large brass buckle.* 彼は大きな真ちゅう製バックルの付いたベルトを締めていた． **2** → see also **safety belt**, **seat belt** **3** N-COUNT 可算名詞 A **belt** in a machine is a circular strip of rubber that is used to drive moving parts or to move objects along. ベルト □ *The turning disk is connected by a drive belt to an electric motor.* 回転ディスクは駆動ベルトで電気モーターに接続されている． **4** → see also **conveyor belt** **5** N-COUNT 可算名詞 A **belt** of land or sea is a long, narrow area of it that has some special feature. 地帯 □ *Miners in Zambia's northern copper belt have gone on strike.* ザンビアの北部産銅地帯の鉱夫たちはストに入った． **6** → see also **commuter belt**, **green belt** **7** V-T 他動詞 If someone **belts** you, they hit you very hard. If someone **belts** something, they hit it very hard. 強く殴る [INFORMAL くだけた] □ *"Is it right she belted old George in the gut?" she asked.* 「彼女がジョージじいさんの腹に一発くらわしたって本当なの？」と彼女が聞いた． □ *Torrealba belted the ball into the left-field bleachers.* トレアルバは左翼の外野席に打球をたたきこんだ． ● N-COUNT 可算名詞 **Belt** is also a noun. 強く打つこと □ *Father would give you a belt over the head with the scrubbing brush.* 父さんならあんたの頭にタワシでガツンとやるよ． **8** V-I 自動詞 If you **belt** somewhere, you move or travel there very fast. 突っ走る [INFORMAL くだけた] □ *Darren and I belted down the stairs and ran out of the house.* ダレンと僕は階段を駆け下りて家の外に走り出た． **9** PHRASE 句 Something that is **below the belt** is cruel and unfair. 卑劣なこと □ *Do you think it's a bit below the belt what they're doing?* やつらが今していることはちょっと卑劣だと思うかい？ **10** PHRASE 句 If you have to **tighten** your **belt**, you have to spend less money and manage without things because you have less money than you used to have. 耐乏生活をする □ *Clearly, if you are spending more than your income, you'll need to tighten your belt.* もしきみが収入以上に金を使っているなら、明らかに切り詰める必要があるだろう． **11** PHRASE 句 If you have something **under** your **belt**, you have already achieved it or done it. たち成済みで □ *Clare is now a full-time author with six books, including four novels, under her belt.* クレアは今では小説4冊を含む6冊を出版済みの本業作家である．

▶ **belt out** PHRASAL VERB 句動詞 If you **belt out** a song, you sing or play it very loudly. 大きな声で歌う [INFORMAL くだけた] □ *He belted out Sinatra and Beatles hits.* 彼はシナトラやビートルズのヒット曲を大声で歌った．

belt|way /bέltwei/ (beltways) N-COUNT 可算名詞 A **beltway** is a road that goes around a city or town, to keep traffic away from the center. 環状道路 [AM 米国英語] □ *Interstate 295 is a 20-mile beltway that bypasses Jacksonville's busy downtown area.* 州間道路295号線は、ジャクソンビルの混雑した下町エリアをバイパスする20マイルの環状道路である．

be|mused /bimyúzd/ ADJ 形容詞 If you are **bemused**, you are puzzled or confused. 困惑している □ *He was rather bemused by children.* 子供たちに多少困惑していた．

bench /bέntʃ/ (benches) **1** N-COUNT 可算名詞 A **bench** is a long seat of wood or metal that two or more people can sit on. ベンチ □ *He sat down on a park bench.* 彼は公園のベンチに座った． **2** N-COUNT 可算名詞 A **bench** is a long, narrow table in a factory or laboratory. 作業台 □ ...*the laboratory bench.* ラボの作業台 **3** N-SING-COLL 集合的単数名詞 In a court of law, **the bench** is the judge or magistrates. 判事官，判事 □ *The chairman of the bench adjourned the case until October 27.* 裁判長は10月27日まで休廷にした．

Word Link mark ≈ boundary, sign : bench**mark**, book**mark**, trade**mark**

bench|mark /bέntʃmɑrk/ (benchmarks) also bench mark N-COUNT 可算名詞 A **benchmark** is something whose quality or quantity is known and which can therefore be used as a standard with which other things can be compared. 基準 □ *The truck industry is a benchmark for the economy.* トラック産業は経済の比較基準である．

bend /bέnd/ (bends, bending, bent) **1** V-I 自動詞 When you **bend**, you move the top part of your body downward and forward. Plants and trees also **bend**. 身を曲げる □ *I bent over and kissed her cheek.* 身をかがめて彼女のほほにキスした． □ *She bent and picked*

up a plastic bucket. 彼女はかがんでプラスチックのバケツを取り上げた. **2** V-T 他動詞 When you **bend** your head, you move your head forward and downward. 曲げる ❑ Rick appeared, bending his head a little to clear the top of the door. リックはドアの上端にぶつけないように頭を少しかがめながら現れた. **3** V-T/V-I 他動詞/自動詞 When you **bend** a part of your body such as your arm or leg, or when it **bends**, you change its position so that it is no longer straight. 曲げる [他動詞] 曲がる [自動詞] ❑ These cruel devices are designed to stop prisoners from bending their legs. これらの残酷な装置は, 囚人が足を曲げられないよう設計されている. ●**bent** ADJ 形容詞 曲がった ❑ Keep your knees slightly bent. ひざを少し曲げたままにしてください. **4** V-T 他動詞 If you **bend** something that is flat or straight, you use force to make it curved or to put an angle in it. 曲げる ❑ Bend the bar into a horseshoe. 棒を曲げて蹄 (てい) 鉄にする. ●**bent** ADJ 形容詞 曲がった ❑ ...a length of bent wire. ある長さの曲がったワイヤ **5** V-T/V-I 他動詞/自動詞 When a road, beam of light, or other long thin thing **bends**, or when something **bends** it, it changes direction to form a curve or angle. 屈曲させる [他動詞] 屈曲する [自動詞] ❑ The road bent slightly to the right. 道は少し右へ折れた. **6** N-COUNT 可算名詞 A **bend** in a road, pipe, or other long thin object is a curve or angle in it. カーブ; 角 ❑ The crash occurred on a sharp bend. 衝突は急なカーブのところで発生した. **7** V-T 他動詞 If you **bend** rules or laws, you interpret them in a way that allows you to do something they would not normally allow you to do. 曲げて解釈する ❑ A minority of officers were prepared to bend the rules. 官僚中の少数は規則を曲げる覚悟であった. **8** N-PLURAL 複数名詞 If deep-sea divers suffer from **the bends**, they experience severe pain and difficulty in breathing as a result of coming to the surface of the ocean too quickly. 潜函 (かん) 病 ❑ New evidence suggests that exercise could protect divers from the bends. 新しい証拠によれば, 運動することでダイバーは潜函病を予防できる可能性があるということだ. **9** → see also **bent**

be|neath /bɪniθ/ **1** PREP 前置詞 Something that is **beneath** another thing is under the other thing. 一の下に ❑ She could see the muscles of his shoulders beneath his T-shirt. 彼女にはTシャツの下の彼の肩の筋肉が見えた. ❑ Four levels of parking beneath the theater was not enough. その劇場の下にある4階の駐車場は充分ではなかった. ●ADV 副詞 **Beneath** is also an adverb. 下で ❑ On a shelf beneath he spotted a photo album. その下の棚に彼はアルバムを見つけた. **2** PREP 前置詞 If you talk about what is **beneath** the surface of something, you are talking about the aspects of it which are hidden or not obvious. 一に隠れて ❑ ...emotional strains beneath the surface. 表面の下に隠れた精神的過労 ❑ Somewhere deep beneath the surface lay a caring character. 表面のどこか奥深くに優しい性格が潜んでいた. **3** PREP 前置詞 If you say that someone or something is **beneath** you, you feel that they are not good enough for you or not suitable for you. 一にふさわしくない ❑ They decided she was marrying beneath her. 彼らは, 彼女が自分より身分の低い人と結婚しようとしていると判断した.

ben|efac|tor /bɛnɪfæktər/ (benefactors) N-COUNT 可算名詞 A **benefactor** is someone who helps a person or organization by giving them money. 恩恵を施す人 ❑ In his old age he became a benefactor of the arts. 老境に入って彼は美術の後援者となった.

ben|efi|cial /bɛnɪfɪʃ^əl/ ADJ 形容詞 Something that is **beneficial** helps people or improves their lives. ためになる ❑ ...vitamins that are beneficial to our health. 健康に有益なビタミン類

ben|efi|ci|ary /bɛnɪfɪʃieri/ (beneficiaries) **1** N-COUNT 可算名詞 Someone who is a **beneficiary of** something is helped by it. 受益者 ❑ One of the main beneficiaries of the early election is thought to be the former president. 早期選挙が有利となった主な人々の中には元大統領も入っていると考えられている. **2** N-COUNT 可算名詞 The **beneficiaries** of a will are legally entitled to receive money or property from someone when that person dies. 遺産受取人 ❑ ...one of the beneficiaries of the will made by the late Mr. Steil. 故スタイル氏が書いた遺書の遺産受取人のひとり

ben|efit /bɛnɪfɪt/ (benefits, benefiting or benefitting, benefited or benefitted) **1** N-VAR 可変性名詞 The **benefit of** something is the help that you get from it or the advantage that results from it. 利益 ❑ Each family farms individually and reaps the benefit of its labor. 各家族がそれぞれ農業を営み, 各自の労働

の成果を得る. ❑ I'm a great believer in the benefits of this form of therapy. このような形の療法がもたらす利益は確実にあると信じている. **2** N-UNCOUNT 不可算名詞 If something is **to** your **benefit** or is **of benefit to** you, it helps you or improves your life. 得 ❑ This could now work to Albania's benefit. これは今アルバニアのためになるかもしれない. **3** V-T/V-I 他動詞/自動詞 If you **benefit from** something or if it **benefits** you, it helps you or improves your life. 役に立つ, 利益を得る ❑ Both sides have benefited from the talks. 両者とも協議を通して利益を享受した. **4** N-UNCOUNT 不可算名詞 If you have the **benefit** of some information, knowledge, or equipment, you are able to use it so that you can achieve something. 利点 ❑ Steve didn't have the benefit of a formal college education. スティーブには正式な大学教育という強みがなかった. **5** N-VAR 可変性名詞 **Benefits** are money or other advantages which come from your job, the government, or an insurance company. 給付金 ❑ McCary will receive about $921,000 in retirement benefits. マッカリィは退職金として約921,000ドルを受け取るだろう. ❑ ...the skyrocketing cost of health care and medical benefits. 急上昇している健康医療保険給付金コスト **6** N-COUNT 可算名詞 A **benefit**, or a benefit concert or dinner, is an event that is held in order to raise money for a particular charity or person. 慈善的な催し [oft N n] ❑ ...a memorial benefit concert for the Bonhoeffer endowment. ボンヘッファー寄付金の記念慈善コンサート **7** → see also **fringe benefit** **8** PHRASE 句 If you give someone the **benefit of the doubt**, you treat them as if they are telling the truth or as if they have behaved properly, even though you are not sure that this is the case. 疑わしきは罰せず ❑ At first I gave him the benefit of the doubt. 最初は疑わしい点を彼の有利に解釈した. **9** PHRASE 句 If you say that someone is doing something **for the benefit of** a particular person, you mean that they are doing it for that person. 一のために ❑ You need people working for the benefit of the community. 地域社会のために働く人たちが必要だ.

be|nevo|lent /bɪnɛvələnt/ ADJ 形容詞 If you describe a person in authority as **benevolent**, you mean that they are kind and fair. 情け深い ❑ The company has proved to be a most benevolent employer. その会社は最も情け深い雇用主であることが立証された. ●**be|nevo|lence** N-UNCOUNT 不可算名詞 慈悲の心 ❑ A bit of benevolence from people in power is not what we need. 権力者のちょっとした慈悲の心を我々は必要としているのではない.

be|nign /bɪnaɪn/ **1** ADJ 形容詞 You use **benign** to describe someone who is kind, gentle, and harmless. 穏やかな ❑ They are normally a more benign audience. 普通はもっと穏やかな観客である. ●**be|nign|ly** ADV 副詞 穏やかに ❑ I just smiled benignly and stood back. ただ穏やかに笑って, 後ろに下がっていた. **2** ADJ 形容詞 A **benign** substance or process does not have any harmful effects. 穏やかな ❑ We're taking relatively benign medicines and we're turning them into poisons. 私たちは比較的穏やかな薬を用いて, それらの薬を毒に変えている. **3** ADJ 形容詞 A **benign** tumor will not cause death or serious harm. 良性の [MEDICAL 医学の] ❑ It wasn't cancer, only a benign tumor. がんではなくて単なる良性しゅようであった. **4** ADJ 形容詞 **Benign** conditions are pleasant or make it easy for something to happen. 穏やかな ❑ They enjoyed an especially benign climate. 彼らは特に穏やかな気候を楽しんだ.

bent /bɛnt/ **1** **Bent** is the past tense and past participle of **bend**. bend の過去形および過去分詞形 **2** ADJ 形容詞 If an object is **bent**, it is damaged and no longer has its correct shape. 曲がった ❑ The trees were all bent and twisted from the wind. 木々は風のため曲がりゆがんでいた. **3** ADJ 形容詞 If a person is **bent**, their body has become curved because of old age or disease. 体の曲がった [WRITTEN 書き言葉] ❑ ...a bent, frail, old man. 腰の曲がった弱々しい老人 **4** ADJ 形容詞 If someone is **bent on** doing something, especially something harmful, they are determined to do it. 固く決心している [DISAPPROVAL 不賛成] [v-link ADJ 'on/upon' n/-ing] ❑ He's bent on suicide. 彼は自殺を決心している. **5** N-SING 単数名詞 If you have a **bent for** something, you have a natural ability to do it or a natural interest in it. 好み ❑ His bent for natural history directed him towards his first job. 博物学好きが彼を最初の仕事に導いた. **6** N-SING 単数名詞 If someone is **of** a particular **bent**, they hold a particular set of beliefs. 傾向 ❑ ...economists of a socialist bent. 社会主義的傾向のある経済学者

be|queath /bɪkwið/ (bequeaths, bequeathing, bequeathed) V-T 他動詞 If you **bequeath** your money or property **to** someone, you legally state that they should have it when you die. 遺言で譲る [FORMAL 形式ばった] ❑ He bequeathed all his silver to his children.

be|reaved /bɪrivd/ ADJ 形容詞 A **bereaved** person is one who has a relative or close friend who has recently died. 後に残された ❑ *Mr. Dinkins visited the bereaved family to offer comfort.* ディンキンズ氏は遺族を弔問した.

be|reave|ment /bɪrivmənt/ (**bereavements**) N-VAR 可変性名詞 **Bereavement** is the sorrow you feel or the state you are in when a relative or close friend dies. 死別 ❑ *When Mary died Anne did not share her brother's sense of bereavement.* メアリーが死んだとき, アンは弟 (弟) が感じた死別の悲しみをわかちあえなかった.

be|reft /bɪrɛft/ ADJ 形容詞 If a person or thing is **bereft of** something, they no longer have it. 失って [FORMAL 形式ばった] ❑ *The place seemed to be utterly bereft of human life.* その場所は人間らしい生活など全くないように思えた.

ber|ry /bɛri/ (**berries**) N-COUNT 可算名詞 **Berries** are small, round fruit that grow on a bush or a tree. Some berries are edible, for example, blackberries and raspberries. ベリー

berth /bɜrθ/ (**berths, berthing, berthed**) ◼ PHRASE 句 If you give someone or something **a wide berth**, you avoid them because you think they are unpleasant or dangerous, or simply because you do not like them. 避ける ❑ *She gives showbiz parties a wide berth.* 彼女は芸能界のパーティを敬遠している. ◻ N-COUNT 可算名詞 A **berth** is a bed on a ship or train. 寝台 ❑ *Goldring booked a berth on the first boat he could.* ゴルドリングはできる限り早い船に寝台を予約した. ◼ N-COUNT 可算名詞 A **berth** is a space in a harbor where a ship stays for a period of time. 停泊所 ❑ *...the slow passage through the docks to the ship's berth.* ドックを通って船の停泊所までのろのろと通行 ◼ V-I 自動詞 When a ship **berths**, it sails into harbor and stops at the quay. 停泊する ❑ *As the ship berthed in New York, McClintock was with the first immigration officers aboard.* その船がニューヨークに停泊したとき, マクリントックは最初に乗船した入国管理官たちと一緒だった.

be|set /bɪsɛt/ (**besets, besetting**)

The form **beset** is used in the present tense and is the past tense and past participle.

beset 形は現在形に使われ, 過去形と過去分詞でもある.

V-T 他動詞 If someone or something **is beset by** problems or fears, they have many problems or fears which affect them severely. つきまとわれる ❑ *The country is beset by severe economic problems.* その国は深刻な経済問題に取り囲まれている. ❑ *The discussions were beset with difficulties.* 討議には障害がつきまとった.

be|side /bɪsaɪd/ ◼ PREP 前置詞 Something that is **beside** something else is at the side of it or next to it. 〜の横に ❑ *On the table beside an empty plate was a pile of books.* テーブルの上にある空の皿の横には本が積み重ねられていた. ◻ → see also **besides** ◼ PHRASE 句 If you are **beside yourself** with anger or excitement, you are extremely angry or excited. 我を忘れて ❑ *He had shouted down the phone at her, beside himself with anxiety.* 彼は不安のため我を忘れて, 電話口で彼女にどなりつけて黙らせた. ◼ **beside the point** → see **point**

be|sides /bɪsaɪdz/ ◼ PREP 前置詞 **Besides** something or **beside** something means in addition to it. 〜に加えて ❑ *I think she has many good qualities besides being very beautiful.* 彼女はたいそう美しい上に, 優れた点もたくさんあるとわたしは思う. ● ADV 副詞 **Besides** is also an adverb. 〜のうえ [cl ADV] ❑ *You get to sample lots of baked things and take home masses of cookies besides.* オーブンで焼いたものをたくさん試食できるし, そのうえクッキーも山ほど家に持って帰ることができるよ. ◻ ADV 副詞 **Besides** is used to emphasize an additional point that you are making, especially one that you consider to be important. さらにまた ❑ *The house was out of our price range and too big anyway. Besides, I'd grown fond of our little rented house.* その家はわたしたちの予算枠を超えていて, とにかく大きすぎた. おまけにわたしは今の小さな借家が好きになっていた.

Do not confuse **besides, except, except for,** and **unless.** You use **besides** to introduce extra things in addition to the ones you are mentioning already. ❑ *Fruit will give you, besides enjoyment, a source of vitamins.* However, note that if you talk about "the only thing" or "the only person" **besides** a particular person or thing, **besides** means the same as "apart from." ❑ *He was the only person besides Gertrude who talked to Guy.* You use **except** to introduce the only things, situations, people, or ideas that a statement does not apply to. ❑ *All of his body relaxed except his right hand... Travelling was impossible, except in the cool of the morning.* You use **except for** before something that prevents a statement from being completely true. ❑ *The classrooms were silent, except for the scratching of pens on paper... I had absolutely no friends except for Tom.* **Unless** is used to introduce the only situation in which something will take place or be true. ❑ *In the 1940s, unless she wore gloves a woman was not properly dressed... You must not give compliments unless you mean them.*

be|siege /bɪsidʒ/ (**besieges, besieging, besieged**) ◼ V-T 他動詞 If you **are besieged by** people, many people want something from you and continually bother you. 押し寄せる [usu passive] ❑ *She was besieged by the press and the public.* 彼女は報道陣や公衆に取り囲まれた. ◻ V-T 他動詞 If soldiers **besiege** a place, they surround it and wait for the people in it to stop fighting or resisting. 包囲する ❑ *The main part of the army moved to Sevastopol to besiege the town.* 陸軍の本隊は町を包囲するために, セバストポルに移動した.

best /bɛst/ ◼ **Best** is the superlative of **good**. (**good**の最上級) 最もよい ❑ *If you want further information the best thing to do is have a word with the driver as you get on the bus.* もっと知りたかったら, いちばんいいのはバスに乗るときに運転手に相談することだ. ◻ **Best** is the superlative of **well**. (**well**の最上級) 最も ❑ *James Fox is best known as the author of "White Mischief," and he is currently working on a new book.* ジェームズ・フォックスは『白い炎の女』の作者として最もよく知られており, 現在は新しい本を執筆中だ. ◼ N-SING 単数名詞 The **best** is used to refer to things of the highest quality or standard. 最良のもの ❑ *We offer only the best to our clients.* お客様には最良のものしか提供いたしません. ◼ N-SING 単数名詞 Someone's **best** is the greatest effort or highest achievement or standard that they are capable of. 最上 ❑ *Miss Blockey was at her best when she played the piano.* ブロッキー嬢はピアノを弾いたときが最高であった. ◼ N-SING 単数名詞 If you say that something is the **best** that can be done or hoped for, you think it is the most pleasant, successful, or useful thing that can be done or hoped for. 最善のもの ❑ *A draw seems the best they can hope for.* 期待できるのは引き分けが精一杯のように思える. ◼ ADV 副詞 If you like something **best** or like it the **best**, you prefer it. 最も ❑ *The thing I liked best about the show was the music.* 僕でいちばんよかったのは音楽だった. ❑ *Mother liked it best when Daniel got money.* ダニエルが金を得たときが母はいちばん好きだった. ◼ **Best** is used to form the superlative of compound adjectives beginning with "good" and "well." For example, the superlative of "well-known" is "best-known." (複合語で最上級) 最もよく ◼ → see also **second best** ◼ PHRASE 句 You use **best of all** to indicate that what you are about to mention is the thing that you prefer or that has most advantages out of all the things you have mentioned. いちばんよいことには ❑ *It was comfortable and cheap: best of all, most of the rent was being paid by two American friends.* そこは快適で安かった: いちばんよいことには, 家賃のほとんどはアメリカ人の友たち2人が払っていたことだった. ◼ PHRASE 句 If someone does something **as best** they **can**, they do it as well as they can, although it is very difficult. 精一杯よく ❑ *Let's leave people to get on with their jobs and do them as best they can.* 人々が自分たちの仕事に取り組んでできるだけうまく仕事をするように, 自由にやらせよう. ◼ PHRASE 句 You use **at best** to indicate that even if you describe something as favorably as possible or if it performs as well as it possibly can, it is still not very good. いくらよくても ❑ *This policy, they say, is at best confused and at worst non-existent.* この方針は, よく言って支離滅裂, 悪くいえばないに等しいそうだ. ◼ PHRASE 句 If you **do** your **best** or **try** your **best** to do something, you try as hard as you can to do it, or do it as well as you can. 全力を尽くす ❑ *I'll do my best to find out.* 全力を尽くして調べてみよう. ◼ PHRASE 句 If you say that something is **for the best**, you mean it is the most desirable or helpful thing that could have happened or could be done, considering all the circumstances. 最善の結果となるように ❑ *Whatever the circumstances, parents are supposed to know what to do for the best.* どのような状況であっても, 親は最善の結果となるにはどうすればいいのか知っているものだ. ◼ PHRASE 句 If you say that a particular person **knows best**, you mean that they have a lot of experience and should therefore be trusted to make decisions for other people. 〜の権威である ❑ *He was convinced that doctors and dentists knew best.* 医者や歯医者がいちばん頼りになると彼は確信していた. ◼ **to the best of** your **ability** → see **ability** ◼ **to hope for the best** → see **hope** ◼ **to the best of** your **knowledge** → see **knowledge** ◼ **best of luck** → see **luck** ◼ **the best of both worlds** → see **world**

be|stow /bɪstoʊ/ (**bestows, bestowing, bestowed**) V-T 他動詞 To **bestow** something on someone means to give or present it to them. 授ける [FORMAL 形式ばった] ❑ *The United States bestowed honorary citizenship upon England's World War II prime minister, Sir Winston Churchill.* 合衆国は, 第二次世界大戦時の英国首相ウィンストン・チャーチル卿に名誉市民権を授けた.

best|sell|er /bɛstsɛlər/ (**bestsellers**) N-COUNT 可算名詞 A **bestseller** is a book of which a great number of copies has been sold. ベストセラー ❑ *By mid-August the book was a bestseller.* 8月中旬までにはその本はベストセラーとなった.

best-selling also **bestselling** ◼ ADJ 形容詞 A **best-selling** product such as a book is very popular and a large quantity of it has been sold. ベストセラーの [ADJ n] ◻ ADJ 形容詞 A **best-selling** author is an author who has sold a very large number of copies of his or her book. ベストセラーの [ADJ n]

bet /bɛt/ (bets, betting)

The form **bet** is used in the present tense and is the past tense and past participle.

bet 形は現在形に使われ，過去形と過去分詞でもある。

B

1 V-T/V-I 他動詞/自動詞 If you **bet on** the result of a horse race, football game, or other event, you give someone a sum of money which they give you back with extra money if the result is what you predicted, or which they keep if it is not. 賭(か)ける □*Jockeys are forbidden to bet on the outcome of races.* 騎手が競馬の結果に賭けることは禁止されている。 ● N-COUNT 可算名詞 Bet is also a noun. 賭(か)け □*Do you always have a bet on the Kentucky Derby?* ケンタッキーダービー競馬にいつも賭けをするかい？ ● **bet|ting** N-UNCOUNT 不可算名詞 賭(か)け事 □*…his thousand-dollar fine for illegal betting.* 彼の違法な賭け事に対する千ドルの罰金 **2** N-COUNT 可算名詞 A **bet** is a sum of money which you give to someone when you bet. 賭(か)け金 □*You can put a bet on almost anything these days.* 今日ではほとんど何にでも賭け金を出すことができる。 **3** V-T/V-I 他動詞/自動詞 If someone **is betting** that something will happen, they are hoping or expecting that it will happen. きっと—だと思う [JOURNALISM ジャーナリズム] □*The party is betting that the presidential race will turn into a battle for younger voters.* 党は大統領選は若い投票者獲得の戦いになると予測している。 □*People were betting on a further easing of credit conditions.* 融資条件はさらに緩くなると人々は予測していた。 **4** You use expressions such as "**I bet**," "**I'll bet**," and "**you can bet**" to indicate that you are sure something is true. うけあう [INFORMAL くだけた] □*I bet you were good at games when you were at school.* きみは学校に行っていたときは絶対競技が得意だったとうけあうね。 □*I'll bet they'll taste out of this world.* 絶対この世のものとは思えない味がするとうけあうよ。 **5** PHRASE 句 If you tell someone that something is a **good bet**, you are suggesting that it is the thing or course of action that they should choose. いい策 [INFORMAL くだけた] □*Your best bet is to choose a guest house.* 最善の策は旅館を選ぶことだ。 **6** PHRASE 句 If you say that it is a **good bet** or a **safe bet** that something is true or will happen, you are saying that it is extremely likely to be true or to happen. ほぼ確実なこと [INFORMAL くだけた] □*It is a safe bet that the current owners will not sell.* 現在の所有者たちが売ろうとしないことはほぼ確実だ。 **7** PHRASE 句 You use **I bet** or **I'll bet** in reply to a statement to show that you agree with it or that you expected it to be true, usually when you are annoyed or amused by it. もちろん [INFORMAL, SPOKEN くだけた，口語, FEELINGS 感情] □*"I'd like to ask you something," I said. "I bet you would," she grinned.* 「ちょっと聞きたいことがあるんだけど」とわたしは言った。「もちろんそうでしょうね。」と彼女はにっこり笑った。 **8** PHRASE 句 You say **I bet** or **I'll bet** in reply to a statement to show that you do not believe it or you doubt that it is true. まさか □*"I only kiss girls," said John. Then he blushed. "I'll bet," said Lisa.* 「女の子としかキスしないさ」とジョンが言った。そして赤くなった。「さあどうだか。」とリサが言った。 **9** PHRASE 句 You can use **my bet is** or **it's my bet** to give your personal opinion about something, when you are fairly sure that you are right. わたしの意見は—だ [INFORMAL くだけた] □*My bet is that next year will be different.* 来年は違うと絶対思うね。
→ see lottery

Word Partnership	bet は次の語句と使われる:
N.	bet **money 1**
PREP.	bet **against** *someone/something*, bet **on** *something* **1 2**
V.	**lose/win** a bet, **make** a bet, **place** a bet **1 2**
ADJ.	**willing** to bet **4** **best** bet, **good** bet, **safe** bet **5 6**

be|tray /bɪtreɪ/ (betrays, betraying, betrayed) **1** V-T 動詞 If you **betray** someone who loves or trusts you, your actions hurt and disappoint them. 裏切る □*When I tell someone I will not betray his confidence I keep my word.* 私が誰かに信頼を裏切らないと言うときは，約束を守る。 **2** V-T 他動詞 If someone **betrays** their country or their friends, they give information to an enemy, putting their country's security or their friends' safety at risk. 敵に売り渡す □*They offered me money if I would betray my associates.* 仲間を売るつもりはないとわたしに金で誘いをかけてきた。 **3** V-T 他動詞 If you **betray** an ideal or your principles, you say or do something which goes against those beliefs. 背く □*We betray the ideals of our country when we support capital punishment.* 死刑を支持すれば，我々の国の理想に背くことになる。 **4** V-T 他動詞 If you **betray** a feeling or quality, you show it without intending to. うっかり表わす □*She studied his face, but it betrayed nothing.* 彼女は彼の顔を注意して見たが，何事も読み取れなかった。

be|tray|al /bɪtreɪəl/ (betrayals) N-VAR 可変性名詞 A **betrayal** is an action which betrays someone or something, or the fact of being betrayed. 裏切り □*She felt that what she had done was a betrayal of Patrick.* 彼女は自分がしたことはパトリックへの裏切りだと感じた。

---

better
❶ COMPARING STATES AND QUALITIES
❷ GIVING ADVICE
❸ VERB USES

❶ **bet|ter** /bɛtər/ **1** **Better** is the comparative of **good**. (well の比較級) よりよい **2** **Better** is the comparative of **well**. (well の比較級) 気分がよりよい **3** ADV 副詞 If you like one thing **better than** another, you like it more. もっとよく [ADV after v] □*I like your interpretation better than the one I was taught.* あなたの解釈の方が教わった解釈よりも好きだ。 □*They liked it better when it rained.* 雨が降ったときの方が好きだった。 **4** ADJ 形容詞 If you are **better** after an illness or injury, you have recovered from it. If you feel **better**, you no longer feel so ill. 気分がよりよい [v-link ADJ] □*He is much better now, he's fine.* 彼は今はずっとよくなって，元気だ。 **5** PRON 代名詞 If you say that you expect or deserve **better**, you mean that you expect or deserve a higher standard of achievement, behavior, or treatment from people than they have shown you. より優れているもの □*We expect better of you in the future.* 将来はもっと向上して欲しい。 **6** **Better** is used to form the comparative of compound adjectives beginning with "good" and "well." For example, the comparative of "well-off" is "better-off." (goodやwellの複合語で比較級) よりよい **7** PHRASE 句 If something changes **for the better**, it improves. 良い方向へ □*He dreams of changing the world for the better.* 世界を好転させようと夢見る。 **8** PHRASE 句 If a feeling such as jealousy, curiosity, or anger **gets the better of** you, it becomes too strong for you to hide or control. 優勢になる □*She didn't allow her emotions to get the better of her.* 感情に負けて冷静さを失わないように自分を戒めた。 **9** PHRASE 句 If you **get the better of** someone, you defeat them in a contest, fight, or argument. 負かす □*He is used to tough defenders, and he usually gets the better of them.* 彼はタフな防御に慣れていて，普通は競り勝つ。 **10** PHRASE 句 If someone **knows better than to** do something, they are old enough or experienced enough to know it is the wrong thing to do. —くらいの分別がある □*She knew better than to argue with Adeline.* アデラインと言い争うほどばかではなかった。 **11** PHRASE 句 If you **know better than** someone, you have more information, knowledge, or experience than them. 一層の知識や情報を持つ □*He thought he knew better than I did, though he was much less experienced.* 彼は私に比べて経験はずっと少なかったが，自分の方が物事をよく知っていると考えた。 **12** CONVENTION 慣習表現 You say "**That's better**" in order to express your approval of what someone has said or done, or to praise or encourage them. その方がいい □*"I came to ask your advice – no, to ask for your help." — "That's better. And how can I help you?"* 「教えて欲しいと思って - いや，助けて欲しいと思って来た。」 - 「そうこなくっちゃいけねえ。で，どのように助けて欲しいんだい？」 **13** PHRASE 句 You can say "**so much the better**" or "**all the better**" to indicate that it is desirable that a particular thing is used, done, or available. それだけいっそう □*The fog had come in; so much the better for us to make our sneaking away.* 霧が満ちていた。ひそかに立ち去るにはいっそう都合がよかった。 **14** PHRASE 句 If you intend to do something and then **think better of it**, you decide not to do it because you realize it would not be sensible. 考え直す □*Alberg opened his mouth, as if to protest. But he thought better of it.* アルバーグは抗議するかのように口を開いたが，考え直した。 **15** to be **better than nothing** → see **nothing**

Word Partnership	better は次の語句と使われる:
N.	better **idea**, **nothing** better ❶ **1**
V.	**make** *something* better ❶ **1** **look** better ❶ **1 4** **feel** better, **get** better ❶ **2 4** **deserve** better ❶ **5**
ADV.	**any** better, **even** better, better **than** ❶ **1 2** **much** better ❶ **1 3 4**

❷ **bet|ter** /bɛtər/ **1** PHRASE 句 You use **had better** or **'d better** when you are advising, warning, or threatening someone, or expressing an opinion about what should happen. —するのがよい □*It's half past two. I think we had better go home.* 2時半だ。家に帰るほうがいいと思うよ。 □*You'd better run if you're going to get your ticket.* 券を手に入れるつもりなら，走ったほうがいい。 ● ADV 副詞 In spoken English, people sometimes use **better** without 'had' or 'be' before it. It has the same meaning. betterだけで使われることもある。 □*Better not say too much aloud.* あまり大声で言わないほうがいい。 **2** PHRASE 句 You can say that someone **is better** doing one thing than another, or **it is better** doing one thing than another, to advise someone about what they should do. —するほうが賢明だ □*Wouldn't it be better putting a time-limit on the task?* その作業に時間制限をするほうがよくないかい？ **3** PHRASE 句 If you say that someone would **be better off** doing something, you are advising them to do it or expressing the opinion that it would benefit

them to do it. 〜したほうが利益がある ❑ *If you've got bags you're better off taking a taxi.* バッグがあるならタクシーを使うほうがいい.

❸ **bet|ter** /bɛtər/ (betters, bettering, bettered) ■ V-T 他動詞 If someone **betters** a high achievement or standard, they achieve something higher. しのぐ ❑ *His throw bettered the American junior record set in 2003.* 彼の投げた距離は、2003年の全米ジュニア記録をしのいだ. ■ V-T 他動詞 If you **better** your situation, you improve your social status or the quality of your life. If you **better yourself**, you improve your social status. 改善する ❑ *He had dedicated his life to bettering the lot of the oppressed people of South Africa.* 彼は南アフリカで虐げられた多くの人の境遇を改善するために人生を捧げる決意をしていた.

be|tween /bɪtwiːn/

In addition to the uses shown below, **between** is used in a few phrasal verbs, such as "come between."

下記の用法に加えて，**between** は **come between** のような少数の句動詞に使われる.

■ PREP 前置詞 If something is **between** two things or is **in between** them, it has one of the things on one side of it and the other thing on the other side. (空間) 〜の間に ❑ *She left the table to stand between the two men.* 彼女はテーブルを離れて二人の男の間に立った. ■ PREP 前置詞 If people or things travel **between** two places, they travel regularly from one place to the other and back again. (場所) 〜の間を [PREP pl-n] ❑ *I spent a lot of time in the early Eighties traveling between Waco and El Paso.* 80年代の初めはワコとエルパソの間を行き来して過ごした. ■ PREP 前置詞 A relationship, discussion, or difference **between** two people, groups, or things is one that involves them both or relates to them both. (関係) 〜の間の [PREP pl-n] ❑ *I think the relationship between patients and doctors has got a lot less personal.* 患者と医者との間の関係は人格的な部分が非常に少なくなったと思う. ❑ *There have been intensive discussions between the two governments in recent days.* ここ数日間二か国の政府の間で集中検討が続いている. ■ PREP 前置詞 If something stands **between** you and what you want, it prevents you from having it. 間に立ちはだかる [PREP n 'and' n] ❑ *His sense of duty often stood between him and the enjoyment of life.* 義務感が彼と人生の楽しみとの間にたびたび立ちはだかった. ■ PREP 前置詞 If something is **between** two amounts or ages, it is greater or older than the first one and smaller or younger than the second one. (数量) 〜から〜までの間で [PREP num 'and' num] ❑ *Increase the amount of time you spend exercising by walking between 15 and 20 minutes.* 15分から20分歩いて運動にかける時間を増やしなさい. ■ PREP 前置詞 If something happens **between** or **in between** two times or events, it happens after the first time or event and before the second one. (時間) 〜から〜までの間に ❑ *The canal was built between 1793 and 1797.* その運河は1793年から1797年の間に建設された. ● ADV 副詞 **Between** or **in between** is also an adverb. 合間に [ADV with cl/group] ❑ *My life had been a journey from crisis to crisis with only a brief time in between.* わたしの人生は危機から危機へ旅路でその合間にわずかな時間があるだけだった. ■ PREP 前置詞 If you must choose **between** two or more things, you must choose just one of them. 〜のうちからひとつを [PREP pl-n] ❑ *Students will be able to choose between English, French and Russian as their first foreign language.* 学生は第一外国語として英語，フランス語，ロシア語のなかから一つ選ぶことができる. ■ PREP 前置詞 If people or places have a particular amount of something **between** them, this is the total amount that they have. みんな合わせて [PREP pron] ❑ *The three sites employ 12,500 people between them.* 三か所の拠点間で合計12,500人を雇用している. ■ PREP 前置詞 When something is divided or shared **between** people, they each have a share of it. (分配，共有) 〜の間で [PREP pl-n] ❑ *There is only one bathroom shared between eight bedrooms.* 寝室8部屋で共用のバスルームがひとつしかなかった.

If there are only two people or things you should use **between**. If there are more than two people or things, you should use **among**. You can also talk about relationships **between** or **among** people or things, and discussions **between** or **among** people. ❑ *...an argument between his mother and another woman.* .... *an opportunity to discuss these issues among themselves.* Note that if you are **between** things or people, the things or people are on either side of you. If you are **among** things or people, they are all around you. ❑ *...the bag standing on the floor between us.* .... *the sound of a pigeon among the trees.*

Word Partnership *between は次の語句と使われる:*

N.	**line** between, **link** between ■
	between **countries/nations**, **difference** between, **relationship** between ■
	choice between ■
V.	**caught** between ■
	choose/decide/distinguish between ■
ADV.	*somewhere* in between ■ ■

bev|er|age /bɛvərɪdʒ/ (beverages) N-COUNT 可算名詞 **Beverages** are drinks. 飲み物 [WRITTEN 書き言葉] ❑ *Alcoholic beverages are served in the hotel lounge.* アルコール類はホテルのラウンジに用意されています. ❑ *...artificially sweetened beverages.* 人工甘味料入り飲み物 → see **sugar**

Word Link *war ≈ watchful : aware, beware, wary*

be|ware /bɪwɛər/ V-I 自動詞 If you tell someone to **beware of** a person or thing, you are warning them that the person or thing may harm them or be dangerous. 用心する [only imper and inf] ❑ *Beware of being too impatient with others.* 他人に向かってせっかちになり過ぎないように注意しなさい. ❑ *Motorists were warned to beware of slippery conditions.* スリップしやすい道路状況に用心するようドライバーたちは警告を受けた.

be|wil|dered /bɪwɪldərd/ ADJ 形容詞 If you are **bewildered**, you are very confused and cannot understand something or decide what you should do. うろたえる ❑ *Some shoppers looked bewildered by the sheer variety of goods for sale.* セール商品の全くの種類の多さに一部の買い物客はまごついているように見えた.

be|wil|der|ing /bɪwɪldərɪŋ/ ADJ 形容詞 A **bewildering** thing or situation is very confusing and difficult to understand or to make a decision about. うろたえさせる ❑ *A glance along his bookshelves reveals a bewildering array of interests.* 彼の本棚をざっと見ただけでも，あっけにとられるような幅の広い趣味がわかる.

be|wil|der|ment /bɪwɪldərmənt/ N-UNCOUNT 不可算名詞 **Bewilderment** is the feeling of being bewildered. うろたえ ❑ *He shook his head in bewilderment.* 彼は当惑して頭を振った.

be|witch /bɪwɪtʃ/ (bewitches, bewitching, bewitched) V-T 他動詞 If someone or something **bewitches** you, you are so attracted to them that you cannot think about anything else. 魅惑する ❑ *She was not moving, as if someone had bewitched her.* 彼女はまるで魅惑されたように，動かなかった. ● **be|witch|ing** ADJ 形容詞 魅惑するような ❑ *Frank was a quiet young man with bewitching brown eyes.* フランクはうっとりするような茶色の目をした物静かな若者であった.

be|yond /bɪyɒnd/ ■ PREP 前置詞 If something is **beyond** a place or barrier, it is on the other side of it. 〜の向こうに ❑ *On his right was a thriving vegetable garden and beyond it a small orchard of apple trees.* 彼の右手にはよく育った菜園があり，その向こうはりんごの木の小さな果樹園であった. ● ADV 副詞 **Beyond** is also an adverb. 向こうに ❑ *The house had a fabulous view out to the Strait of Georgia and the Rockies beyond.* 家からの眺めはすばらしく，目の前にジョージア海峡，その向こうにはロッキー山脈が見えた. ■ PREP 前置詞 If something happens **beyond** a particular time or date, it continues after that time or date has passed. 〜を過ぎて ❑ *Few jockeys continue race-riding beyond the age of 40.* 40歳を過ぎて競馬を続ける騎手はほとんどいない. ● ADV 副詞 **Beyond** is also an adverb. 過ぎて [cl 'and' ADV] ❑ *The financing of home ownership will continue through the 1990s and beyond.* 持ち家への資金提供は1990年代とその後も続くでしょう. ■ PREP 前置詞 If something extends **beyond** a particular thing, it affects or includes other things. 〜を越えて ❑ *His interests extended beyond the fine arts to international politics and philosophy.* 彼の興味は美術のほかに国際政治や哲学まで及んだ. ■ PREP 前置詞 You use **beyond** to introduce an exception to what you are saying. 〜以外に ❑ *He appears to have almost no personal staff, beyond a secretary who can't make coffee.* コーヒーも入れられない秘書のほかには個人のスタッフはほとんど誰もいないようだ. ■ PREP 前置詞 If something goes **beyond** a particular point or stage, it progresses or increases so that it passes that point or stage. 〜を越えて ❑ *Their five-year relationship was strained beyond breaking point.* 彼らの5年間の関係は忍耐の限度を越えて緊迫していた. ■ PREP 前置詞 If something is, for example, **beyond** understanding or **beyond** belief, it is so extreme in some way that it cannot be understood or believed. 〜できないほどの ❑ *What Jock had done was beyond my comprehension.* ジョックがしたことはわたしには理解できなかった. ■ PREP 前置詞 If you say that something is **beyond** someone, or **beyond** their control, you mean that they cannot deal with it. 〜の及ばないところに ❑ *The situation was beyond her control.* 状況は彼女の手に負えなかった. ■ **beyond** your wildest dreams → see **dream**

Word Link *bi ≈ two : biannual, bicycle, bilingual*

bi|an|nual /baɪænyuəl/ ADJ 形容詞 A **biannual** event happens twice a year. 年2回の ❑ *You will need to have a routine biannual examination.* 年2回規定の検査を受ける必要があるでしょう. ● **bi|an|nu|al|ly** ADV 副詞 [ADV after v] 年2回に ❑ *Only since 1962 has the show been held biannually.* 1962年になって始めてショーは半年毎に開かれるようになった.

bias /baɪəs/ (biases, biasing, biased) ■ N-VAR 可変性名詞 **Bias** is a tendency to prefer one person or thing to another, and to favor that person or thing. ひいき ❑ *...his desire to avoid the appearance of bias in favor of one candidate or another.* 特定候補者をひいきしていると思われたくないという彼の強い願望 ■ V-T 他動詞 To **bias** someone means to influence them in favor of a particular choice. 偏らせる

B

❑*We mustn't allow it to bias our teaching.* わたしたちの教えがそのために偏らないようにしなければならない.

bi|ased /ˈbaɪəst/ **1** ADJ 形容詞 If someone is **biased**, they prefer one group of people to another, and behave unfairly as a result. You can also say that a process or system is **biased**. 偏った ❑*He seemed a bit biased against women in my opinion.* わたしの意見では, 彼は女性に対して少し偏見を持っているように見えた. **2** ADJ 形容詞 If something is **biased toward** one thing, it is more concerned with it than with other things. 偏した [v-link ADJ 'toward' n] ❑*University funding was tremendously biased toward scientists.* 大学予算はものすごく科学者に有利に偏っていた.

Bi|ble /ˈbaɪbəl/ (Bibles) **1** N-PROPER 固有名詞 **The Bible** is the holy book on which the Jewish and Christian religions are based. 聖書 **2** N-COUNT 可算名詞 A **bible** is a copy of the Bible. 聖書 ❑*...a publisher of bibles and hymn books.* 聖書や賛美歌集の出版者
→ see **religion**

bib|li|cal /ˈbɪblɪkəl/ ADJ 形容詞 **Biblical** means contained in or relating to the Bible. 聖書の ❑*The community, whose links with Syria date back to biblical times, is mainly elderly.* 聖書の時代からシリアとゆかりのあるその共同体は年配者が大部分だ.

bib|li|og|ra|phy /ˌbɪbliˈɒɡrəfi/ (bibliographies) **1** N-COUNT 可算名詞 A **bibliography** is a list of books on a particular subject. 関係書目 ❑*At the end of this chapter there is a select bibliography of useful books.* この章の最後に有益な書籍を選んだ目録がある. **2** N-COUNT 可算名詞 A **bibliography** is a list of the books and articles that are referred to in a particular book. 参照書目録 ❑*...the full bibliography printed at the end of the second volume.* 第2巻の最後に印刷されている全ての引用文献

bick|er /ˈbɪkər/ (bickers, bickering, bickered) V-RECIP 相互動詞 When people **bicker**, they argue or quarrel about unimportant things. つまらないことで口論する ❑*I went into medicine to care for patients, not to waste time bickering over budgets.* 患者の世話をするために医療の世界に入ったのであって, 予算の件でつまらない口論をして時間をむだ遣いするためではない. ❑*...as states bicker over territory.* 国が領土について口論する間 ● **bick|er|ing** N-UNCOUNT 不可算名詞 口論 ❑*The election will end months of political bickering.* その選挙で何か月も続いた政治論争が終結するだろう.

Word Link **bi ≈ two : biannual, bicycle, bilingual**

Word Link **cycl ≈ circle : bicycle, cycle, cyclical**

bi|cy|cle /ˈbaɪsɪkəl/ (bicycles) N-COUNT 可算名詞 A **bicycle** is a vehicle with two wheels which you ride by sitting on it and pushing two pedals with your feet. You steer it by turning a bar that is connected to the front wheel. 自転車
→ see Word Web: **bicycle**

bid /bɪd/ (bids, bidding)

The form **bid** is used in the present tense and is the past tense and past participle.

bid 形は現在形に使われ, 過去形と過去分詞でもある.

1 N-COUNT 可算名詞 A **bid for** something or a **bid to** do something is an attempt to obtain it or do it. 手に入れようとする努力 [JOURNALISM ジャーナリズム] ❑*...Sydney's successful bid for the 2000 Olympic Games.* 成功したシドニーの2000年オリンピック招致努力 **2** N-COUNT 可算名詞 A **bid** is an offer to pay a particular amount of money for something that is being sold. つけ値 ❑*Hanson made an agreed takeover bid of $351 million.* ハンソン社は3.51億ドルで合意済みの株式公開買付をした. **3** V-T/V-I 他動詞/自動詞 If you **bid** **for** something or **bid to** do something, you try to obtain it or do it. 名乗りをあげる ❑*Singapore Airlines is rumored to be bidding for a management contract to run both airports.* シンガポール航空は両空港運営の管理契約に名乗りをあげるとうわさされている. **4** V-I 自動詞 If you **bid for** something that is being sold, you offer to pay a particular amount of money for it. 値をつける ❑*She wanted to bid for it.* 彼女はそれに値をつけて競り落としたかった. ❑*The bank announced its intention to bid.* その銀行は入札する意図を発表した.

bid|der /ˈbɪdər/ (bidders) **1** N-COUNT 可算名詞 A **bidder** is someone who offers to pay a certain amount of money for something that is being sold. If you sell something to the highest **bidder**, you sell it to the person who offers the most money for it. せり手 ❑*The sale will be made to the highest bidder subject to a reserve price being attained.* 最低価格がたち成立することを条件とした最高価格を提示したせり手に売られる. **2** N-COUNT 可算名詞 A **bidder for** something is someone who is trying to obtain it or do it. 入札者 ❑*Vodafone is among successful bidders for two licenses to develop cellphone systems in Greece.* ボーダフォンは, ギリシャで携帯電話システム開発のための事業免許入札で選定された業者の1社だ.

bid price (bid prices) N-COUNT 可算名詞 The **bid price** of a particular stock or share is the price that investors are willing to pay for it. 買い呼び値 [BUSINESS 実業] ❑*Investors feel that the bid price undervalues the company.* 投資家たちはその買い呼び値は当該会社を過小評価していると感じている.

big /bɪɡ/ (bigger, biggest) **1** ADJ 形容詞 A **big** person or thing is large in physical size. 大きい ❑*Australia's a big country.* オーストラリアは大きな国だ. ❑*Her husband was a big man.* 彼女の夫は大男だった. **2** ADJ 形容詞 Something that is **big** consists of many people or things. 大規模の ❑*The crowd included a big contingent from Cleveland.* 群衆の中にはクリーブランドからの大規模な派遣団もいた. **3** ADJ 形容詞 If you describe something such as a problem, increase, or change as a **big** one, you mean it is great in degree, extent, or importance. 重要な ❑*Her problem was just too big for her to tackle on her own.* 問題は彼女がひとりで取り組むには大きすぎた. **4** ADJ 形容詞 A **big** organization employs many people and has many customers. 大規模な ❑*...one of the biggest companies in Italy.* イタリア最大級の企業 **5** ADJ 形容詞 If you say that someone is **big in** a particular organization, activity, or place, you mean that they have a lot of influence or authority in it. 偉い [INFORMAL くだけた] [ADJ n, v-link ADJ 'in' n] ❑*Their father was very big in the army.* 彼らの父親は陸軍で非常に偉かった. **6** ADJ 形容詞 If you call someone a **big** bully or a **big** coward, you are emphasizing your disapproval of them. 大変ひどい [INFORMAL くだけた, EMPHASIS 強調] [ADJ n] ❑*His personality changed. He turned into a big bully.* 彼の人柄が変わった. 大変ひどい弱いものいじめになった. **7** ADJ 形容詞 Children often refer to their older brother or sister as their **big** brother or sister. 年上の [ADJ n] ❑*She always introduces me as her big sister.* 彼女は, いつもわたしのことを姉さんと人に紹介する. **8** ADJ 形容詞 **Big** words are long or rare words which have meanings that are difficult to understand. おおげさな [INFORMAL くだけた] ❑*They use a lot of big words.* おおげさな言葉をたくさん使う. **9** PHRASE 句 If you **make it big**, you become successful or famous. 偉くなる [INFORMAL くだけた] ❑*Capone was an underdog hero, a poor boy who made it big.* カポネは偉くなった貧しい少年であり, 負け犬の英雄であった. **10** PHRASE 句 If you **think big**, you make plans on a large scale, often using a lot of time, effort, or money. 野心的に考える ❑*Maybe we're not thinking big enough.* まだ野心が充分でないのかもしれないぜ.

Big, **large**, and **great** are all used to talk about size. In general, **large** is more formal than **big**, and **great** is more formal than **large**. **Big** and **large** are normally used to describe objects, but you can also use **big** to suggest that something is important or impressive. ❑*...his influence over the big advertisers.* You normally use **great** to emphasize the importance of someone or something. ❑*...the great English architect, Inigo Jones.* However, you can also use **great** to suggest that something is impressive because of its size. ❑*The great bird of prey was a dark smudge against the sun.* You can use **large** or **great**, but not **big**, to describe amounts. ❑*...a large amount of blood on the floor.* ...*the coming of tourists in great numbers.* Both **big** and **great** can be used to emphasize the intensity of something, although **great** is more formal. ❑*It gives me great pleasure to welcome you... Most of them act like big fools.* Remember that **great** has several other meanings, when it does not refer to size, but to something that is remarkable, very good, or enjoyable.

Word Web **bicycle**

A Scotsman named Kirkpatrick MacMillan invented the first **bicycle** with **pedals** around 1840. Early bicycles had wooden or metal **wheels**. However, by the mid-1800s **tyres** with tubes appeared. Modern **racing bikes** are very lightweight and aerodynamic. The wheels have fewer **spokes** and the tyres are very thin and smooth. **Mountain bikes** allow riders to ride up and down steep hills on dirt trails. These bikes have fat, knobby tyres for extra traction. The **tandem** is a bicycle for two people. It has about the same **wind resistance** as a one-person bike. But with twice the power, it goes faster.

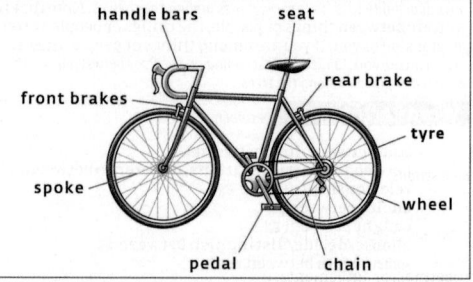

handle bars · seat · rear brake · front brakes · tyre · spoke · wheel · pedal · chain

Thesaurus	*big* また次を参照:
ADJ.	enormous, huge, large, massive; (ant.) little, small, tiny **1**
	considerable, significant, substantial; (ant.) insignificant, unimportant **3**
	important, influential, prominent **5**

big busi|ness 1 N-UNCOUNT 不可算名詞 **Big business** is business which involves very large companies and very large sums of money. 大規模ビジネス ❑ *Big business will never let petty nationalism get in the way of a good deal.* ビッグビジネスがつまらない一国主義に利益の邪魔をさせることは断じてないだろう. **2** N-UNCOUNT 不可算名詞 Something that is **big business** is something which people spend a lot of money on, and which has become an important commercial activity. 大型事業 ❑ *Online dating is big business in the United States.* 合衆国では出会い系サイトは大きな事業だ.

big deal 1 N-SING 単数名詞 If you say that something is a **big deal**, you mean that it is important or significant in some way. 一大事 [INFORMAL くだけた] ❑ *I felt the pressure on me, winning was such a big deal for the whole family.* 大げさにしかかってくるプレッシャーを感じた. 家族全員にとって優勝することは一大事だった. **2** PHRASE 句 If someone **makes a big deal out of** something, they make a fuss about it or treat it as if it were very important. 大げさに騒ぎ立てる [INFORMAL くだけた] ❑ *The Joneses make a big deal out of being "different."* ジョーンズ一家は「自分たちは並みとは違う」と大げさに騒ぎ立てる. **3** CONVENTION 慣習表現 You can say "**big deal**" to someone to show that you are not impressed by something that they consider important or impressive. 大げさな話だ [INFORMAL くだけた, FEELINGS 感情] ❑ *"You'll miss The Brady Bunch." — "Big deal."* 「ブレイディ一味がいなくなるとお前は寂しくなるなあ.」 - 「なんだつまらん.」

big|ot /bɪgət/ (**bigots**) N-COUNT 可算名詞 If you describe someone as a **bigot**, you mean that they are bigoted. 偏狭者 [DISAPPROVAL 不賛成] ❑ *Anyone who opposes them is branded a racist, a bigot, or a homophobe.* 彼らに反対する人たちは誰でも、人種差別主義者、偏狭者、ホモ嫌いと烙 (らく) 印を押される.

big|ot|ed /bɪgətɪd/ ADJ 形容詞 Someone who is **bigoted** has strong, unreasonable prejudices or opinions and will not change them, even when they are proved to be wrong. 偏屈な [DISAPPROVAL 不賛成] ❑ *He was bigoted and racist.* 偏屈で人種差別主義者であった.

big|ot|ry /bɪgətri/ N-UNCOUNT 不可算名詞 **Bigotry** is the possession or expression of strong, unreasonable prejudices or opinions. 偏狭 ❑ *He deplored religious bigotry.* 彼は宗教的頑迷を遺憾に思った.

big time also **big-time 1** ADJ 形容詞 You can use **big time** to refer to the highest level of an activity or sport where you can achieve the greatest amount of success or importance. If you describe a person as **big time**, you mean they are successful and important. 一流の [INFORMAL くだけた] ❑ *He took a long time to settle in to big-time football.* 一流フットボールに慣れるまで長い時間がかかった. **2** N-SING 単数名詞 If someone hits **the big time**, they become famous or successful in a particular area of activity. 一流 [INFORMAL くだけた] ❑ *He hit the big time with films such as Ghost and Dirty Dancing.* 彼は『ニューヨークの幻』や『ダーティダンシング』などの映画で一流スターにのし上がった. **3** ADV 副詞 You can use **big time** if you want to emphasize the importance or extent of something that has happened. 非常に [INFORMAL くだけた, EMPHASIS 強調] [ADV after v] ❑ *Mike Edwards has tasted success big time.* マイク・エドワーズはすごい成功を経験したことがある.

bike /baɪk/ (**bikes, biking, biked**) **1** N-COUNT 可算名詞 A **bike** is a bicycle. 自転車 [INFORMAL くだけた] ❑ *When you ride a bike, you exercise all of the leg muscles.* 自転車に乗れば足の筋肉を全部運動することになる. **2** N-COUNT 可算名詞 A **bike** is a motorcycle. オートバイ [INFORMAL くだけた] ❑ *She parked her bike in the alley.* 彼女はオートバイを路地に駐車した. **3** V-I 自動詞 To **bike** somewhere means to go there on a bicycle. 自転車で行く [INFORMAL くだけた] ❑ *I biked home from the beach.* 海岸から自転車で家に帰った.
→ see **bicycle**

bik|er /baɪkər/ (**bikers**) **1** N-COUNT 可算名詞 **Bikers** are people who ride around on motorcycles, usually in groups. オートバイを乗りまわす人 ❑ *There are always fights going on between rival bikers.* 対立暴走族同士でけんかが絶えない. **2** N-COUNT 可算名詞 People who ride bicycles are called **bikers**. 自転車に乗る人 [AM 米国英語] ❑ *And as the morning begins moving toward noon, look out for more bikers and pedestrians.* それから、午前、昼近くなると自転車に乗る人や歩行者が増えていくので注意しなさい.

bi|ki|ni /bɪkini/ (**bikinis**) N-COUNT 可算名詞 A **bikini** is a two-piece swimsuit worn by women. ビキニ

bi|lat|er|al /baɪlætərəl/ ADJ 形容詞 **Bilateral** negotiations, meetings, or agreements, involve only the two groups or

countries that are directly concerned. 2者がかかわる [FORMAL 形式ばった] [ADJ n] ❑ *...bilateral talks between Britain and America.* 英米2国間の協議 ● **bi|lat|er|al|ly** ADV 副詞 双方で ❑ *The agreement provided for disputes and differences between the two neighbors to be solved bilaterally.* その合意は近隣2か国の論争や紛争を当事者同士で解決するための備えだった.

Word Link	*bi* = two : b**i**annual, b**i**cycle, b**i**lingual
Word Link	*lingu* = language : bi**lingu**al, **lingu**ist, **lingu**istic

bi|lin|gual /baɪlɪŋgwəl/ **1** ADJ 形容詞 **Bilingual** means involving or using two languages. 2言語併用の [ADJ n] ❑ *...bilingual education.* 2言語併用教育 **2** ADJ 形容詞 Someone who is **bilingual** can speak two languages equally well, usually because they learned both languages as a child. 2言語を話す ❑ *He is bilingual in an Asian language and English.* 彼はアジアの言語と英語の2か国語を話す.

bill /bɪl/ (**bills, billing, billed**) **1** N-COUNT 可算名詞 A **bill** is a written statement of money that you owe for goods or services. 請求書 ❑ *They couldn't afford to pay the bills.* 請求書の支払いをする余裕がなかった. ❑ *He paid his bill for the newspapers promptly.* 新聞代をすぐに払った.

> Do not confuse **account** and **bill**. When you have an **account** with a bank, you leave your money in the bank and take it out when you need it. When you have to pay for things such as electricity or a work done by a repairman, you get a **bill**.

2 V-T 他動詞 If you **bill** someone **for** goods or services you have provided them with, you give or send them a bill stating how much money they owe you for these goods or services. 請求書を送る [no cont] ❑ *Are you going to bill me for this?* わたしにこれを請求するつもりですか? **3** N-COUNT 可算名詞 A **bill** is a piece of paper money. 紙幣 [AM 米国英語] ❑ *The case contained a large quantity of U.S. dollar bills.* そのケースには多量のアメリカ紙幣が入っていた. **4** N-COUNT 可算名詞 In government, a **bill** is a formal statement of a proposed new law that is discussed and then voted on. 議案 ❑ *This is the toughest crime bill that Congress has passed in a decade.* これは下院が過去10年間で承認した中で最も厳しい犯罪対策法案だ. **5** N-SING 単数名詞 The **bill** of a show or concert is a list of the entertainers who will take part in it. プログラム ❑ *Bob Dylan topped the bill.* ボブ・ディランはコンサートの主役だった. **6** N-SING 単数名詞 The **bill** in a restaurant is a piece of paper on which the price of the meal you have just eaten is written and which you are given before you pay. 勘定書 [mainly BRIT 主に英国英語; AM usually **check** 米国英語では通常 **check**] **7** V-T 他動詞 If someone **is billed to** appear in a particular show, it has been advertised that they are going to be in it. 番組に発表する [usu passive] ❑ *She was billed to play the Wicked Queen in "Snow White."* 彼女は『白雪姫』の継母を演じると発表された. ● **bill|ing** N-UNCOUNT 不可算名詞 番付け位置 ❑ *...their quarrels over star billing.* スターの番付でのけんか **8** V-T 他動詞 If you **bill** a person or event **as** a particular thing, you advertise them in a way that makes people think they have particular qualities or abilities. ビラで広告する ❑ *They bill it as California's most exciting museum.* カリフォルニアで最高のエキサイティングな博物館と宣伝している. **9** N-COUNT 可算名詞 A bird's **bill** is its beak. くちばし **10** PHRASE 句 If you say that someone or something **fits the bill** or **fills the bill**, you mean that they are suitable for a particular job or purpose. 必要条件を満たす ❑ *If you fit the bill, send a CV to Rebecca Rees.* もし必要条件を満たしているのであれば、履歴書をレベッカ・リーズに送ってください.

Word Partnership	*bill* は次の語句と使われる:
N.	electricity/gas/phone bill, hospital/hotel bill **1**
	dollar bill **3**
V.	pay a bill **1**
	pass a bill, sign a bill, vote on a bill **4**

bill|board /bɪlbɔrd/ (**billboards**) N-COUNT 可算名詞 A **billboard** is a very large board on which advertising is displayed. ビルボード
→ see **advertising**

bill|fold /bɪlfoʊld/ (**billfolds**) N-COUNT 可算名詞 A **billfold** is a small wallet, usually made of leather or plastic, where you can keep paper money and credit cards. 札入れ [AM 米国英語] ❑ *...a billfold containing fifteen dollars.* 15ドルが入った札入れ

bil|liards /bɪljərdz/

> The form **billiard** is used as a modifier.

> **billiard** 形は修飾語として使われる.

1 N-UNCOUNT 不可算名詞 **Billiards** is a game played on a large table, in which you use a long stick called a cue to hit balls against each other or against the walls around the sides of the table. ビリヤード [AM 米国英語] **2** N-UNCOUNT 不可算名詞 **Billiards** is a game played on a large table, in which you use a long

stick called a cue to hit balls against each other or into pockets around the sides of the table. ビリヤード [BRIT 英国英語; AM **pool** 米国英語 **pool**]

bil|lion /bɪlyən/ (billions)

> The plural form is **billion** after a number, or after a word or expression referring to a number, such as "several" or "a few."
>
> 複数形は数の後、あるいは **several** や **a few** のような数を指す単語や表現の後では **billion** である.

1 NUM 数詞 A **billion** is a thousand million. 10億 □ *The Ethiopian foreign debt stands at 3 billion dollars.* エチオピアの対外債務は30億ドルにちたする. **2** QUANT-PLURAL 複数数量詞 If you talk about **billions** of people or things, you mean that there is a very large number of them but you do not know or do not want to say exactly how many. 無数 [QUANT 'of' pl-n] □ *Biological systems have been doing this for billions of years.* 生物系はこれを悠久の昔から行ってきた. ● PRON 代名詞 You can also use **billions** as a pronoun. 何十億 □ *He thought that it must be worth billions.* それには何十億という価値があるに違いないと彼は思った.

bil|lion|aire /bɪlyənɛər/ (billionaires) N-COUNT 可算名詞 A **billionaire** is an extremely rich person who has money or property worth at least a thousand million dollars. 億万長者

Bill of Rights N-SING 単数名詞 A **Bill of Rights** is a written list of citizens' rights which is usually part of the constitution of a country. 権利章典 □ *And what are your rights according to the Bill of Rights?* 権利章典の4つの人権とは何だね.

bil|low /bɪloʊ/ (billows, billowing, billowed) **1** V-I 自動詞 When something made of cloth **billows**, it swells out and moves slowly in the wind. 膨らむ □ *The curtains billowed in the breeze.* そよ風でカーテンがふわっと膨らんだ. □ *Her pink dress billowed out around her.* 彼女のピンクのドレスは風をはらんで膨れあがった. **2** V-I 自動詞 When smoke or cloud **billows**, it moves slowly upward or across the sky. 渦巻く □ *...thick plumes of smoke billowing from factory chimneys.* 工場の煙突からもうもうと吐き出され大きくうねる煙 □ *Steam billowed out from under the hood.* ボンネットの下から蒸気が吹き出した. **3** N-COUNT 可算名詞 A **billow** of smoke or dust is a large mass of it rising slowly into the air. 渦 □ *...smoke stacks belching billows of almost solid black smoke.* ほとんど黒一色の煙をもうもうと噴出させる煙突

bil|ly /bɪli/ (billies) N-COUNT 可算名詞 A **billy** or **billy club** is a short heavy stick which is sometimes used as a weapon by the police. 警棒 [AM 米国英語]

bi|month|ly /baɪmʌnθli/ **1** ADJ 形容詞 A **bimonthly** event or publication happens or appears every two months. 隔月の [usu ADJ n] □ *...bimonthly assemblies.* 2か月に1度の総会 ● ADV 副詞 **Bimonthly** is also an adverb. 隔月に □ *Under the new plan, customers would pay $45 bimonthly, instead of $18 a month – a substantial increase.* 新規計画では、顧客は1か月に18ドルではなく隔月に45ドルを支払い、大幅な値上げとなる. **2** ADJ 形容詞 A **bimonthly** event or publication happens or appears twice every month. 半月ごとの [AM 米国英語] □ *In November, it will start bimonthly publication, and in January it goes weekly.* 11月には月2回の刊行を始め、1月に週刊化する. ● ADV 副詞 **Bimonthly** is also an adverb. 半月ごとに □ *...people who get paid weekly, bimonthly and monthly.* 週に1回、月に2回および月に1回給料を受け取る人たち

bin /bɪn/ (bins) **1** N-COUNT 可算名詞 A **bin** is a container that you keep or store things in. 貯蔵所 □ *...big steel storage bins.* スチールの収納箱 **2** N-COUNT 可算名詞 A **bin** is a container that you put garbage or trash in. ごみ箱 [mainly BRIT 主に英国英語; AM usually **garbage can, trash can** 米国英語では通常 **garbage can, trash can**]

bi|na|ry /baɪnəri/ **1** ADJ 形容詞 The **binary** system expresses numbers using only the two digits 0 and 1. It is used especially in computing. 二進法の [usu ADJ n] □ *The message contains Unicode characters and has been sent as a binary attachment.* メッセージはユニコード文字を含み、バイナリの添付ファイルとして送信された. **2** N-UNCOUNT 不可算名詞 **Binary** is the binary system of expressing numbers. 二進法 □ *The machine does the calculations in binary.* マシンは二進で演算を行う.

bi|na|ry code (binary codes) N-VAR 可変性名詞 **Binary code** is a computer code that uses the binary number system. バイナリコード [COMPUTING コンピューティング] □ *The instructions are translated into binary code, a form that computers can easily handle.* 命令はコンピューターが容易に扱うことのできるバイナリコードに翻訳される.

bind /baɪnd/ (binds, binding, bound) **1** V-T 他動詞 If something **binds** people **together**, it makes them feel as if they are all part of the same group or have something in common. 団結させる □ *It is the memory and threat of persecution that binds them together.* 彼らを結束させているのは迫害の記憶と脅威である. □ *...the social and political ties that bind the U.S. to Britain.* 米国と英国を結束させる社会的および政治的結びつき **2** V-T 他動詞 If you **are bound** by something such as a rule, agreement, or restriction, you are forced or required to act in a certain way. 義務を負わせる □ *All*

pharmacists are bound by the society's rules of confidentiality. すべての薬剤師は、社会の機密保持規定を守らねばならない. □ *The authorities will be bound by convention than the world of banking.* 当局は、法律によりあらゆる容疑者を逮捕するよう義務づけられる. ● **bound** ADJ 形容詞 [v-link ADJ 'by' n] 束縛された □ *The world of advertising is obviously less bound by convention than the world of banking.* 広告業界は、銀行業界よりも慣習による束縛が明らかに少ない. **3** V-T 他動詞 If you **bind** something or someone, you tie rope, string, tape, or other material around them so that they are held firmly. 巻く □ *Bind the ends of the cord together with thread.* ひもの末端に糸を巻いて束ねなさい. □ *...the red tape which was used to bind the files.* ファイルを束ねるために使われた赤いテープ **4** V-T 他動詞 When a book is **bound**, the pages are joined together and the cover is put on. 製本する □ *Each volume is bound in bright-colored cloth.* 各本は鮮やかな色で布装される. □ *Their business came from a few big publishers, all of whose books they bound.* 彼らは大規模出版社数社の製本を一手に請け負っていた.

bind|ing /baɪndɪŋ/ (bindings) **1** ADJ 形容詞 A **binding** promise, agreement, or decision must be obeyed or carried out. 拘束力のある □ *...proposals for a legally binding commitment on nations to stabilize emissions of carbon dioxide.* 各国に二酸化炭素排出量の安定化を法的に義務づける提案 **2** N-VAR 可変性名詞 The **binding** of a book is its cover. 装丁 □ *Its books are noted for the quality of their paper and bindings.* その会社の本は紙と装丁の質が高いことで有名だ. **3** N-VAR 可変性名詞 **Binding** is a strip of material that you put around the edge of a piece of cloth or other object in order to protect or decorate it. 玉縁 □ *...the Regency mahogany dining table with satinwood binding.* サテンウッドの縁取りのついたマホガニーのダイニングテーブル **4** → see also **bind**

binge /bɪndʒ/ (binges, bingeing, binged) **1** N-COUNT 可算名詞 If you go on a **binge**, you do too much of something, such as drinking alcohol, eating, or spending money. どんちゃん騒ぎ [INFORMAL くだけた] □ *She went on occasional drinking binges.* 彼女は時折深酒をした. **2** V-I 自動詞 If you **binge**, you do too much of something, such as drinking alcohol, eating, or spending money. どんちゃん騒ぎをする [INFORMAL くだけた] □ *I haven't binged since 1986.* 1986年以来無茶はしていない.

bin|go /bɪŋgoʊ/ **1** N-UNCOUNT 不可算名詞 **Bingo** is a game in which each player has a card with numbers on it. Someone calls out numbers and if you are the first person to have all your numbers called out, you win the game. ビンゴ □ *...a bingo hall.* ビンゴ場 **2** EXCLAM 感嘆詞 You can say '**bingo!**' when something pleasant happens, especially in a surprising, unexpected, or sudden way, or to show that you have just achieved or discovered something. やった □ *She grinned. "Wow, bingo! Got it in one."* 「やったね！一発で正解」と彼女はにっこり笑った.

bin|ocu|lars /bɪnɒkyələrz/ N-PLURAL 複数名詞 **Binoculars** consist of two small telescopes joined together side by side, which you look through in order to look at things that are a long distance away. 双眼鏡 [also 'a pair of' N]

bio|chemi|cal /baɪoʊkɛmɪkəl/ ADJ 形容詞 **Biochemical** changes, reactions, and mechanisms relate to the chemical processes that happen in living things. 生化学的の [ADJ n] □ *Starvation brings biochemical changes in the body.* 飢餓は体に生化学的変化をもたらす.

Word Link	chem ≈ chemical : biochemist, chemical, chemistry

bio|chem|ist /baɪoʊkɛmɪst/ (biochemists) N-COUNT 可算名詞 A **biochemist** is a scientist or student who studies biochemistry. 生化学者

bio|chem|is|try /baɪoʊkɛmɪstri/ **1** N-UNCOUNT 不可算名詞 **Biochemistry** is the study of the chemical processes that occur in living things. 生化学 **2** N-UNCOUNT 不可算名詞 The **biochemistry** of a living thing is the chemical processes that occur in it or are involved in it. 生化学的組成 □ *...the effects of air pollutants on the biochemistry of plants or animals.* 大気汚染物質が植物や動物の生化学的組成に及ぼす影響

Word Link	bio ≈ life : biodegradable, biography, biology

bio|degrad|able /baɪoʊdɪgreɪdəbəl/ ADJ 形容詞 Something that is **biodegradable** breaks down or decays naturally without any special scientific treatment, and can therefore be thrown away without causing pollution. 微生物で分解される □ *...a natural and totally biodegradable plastic.* 完全生分解性の天然プラスチック

bi|og|raph|er /baɪɒgrəfər/ (biographers) N-COUNT 可算名詞 Someone's **biographer** is a person who writes an account of their life. 伝記作家 □ *...Picasso's biographer.* ピカソの伝記作家

bio|graphi|cal /baɪəgræfɪkəl/ ADJ 形容詞 **Biographical** facts, notes, or details are concerned with the events in someone's life. 伝記の □ *The book contains few biographical details.* この本には伝記的情報はほとんどない.

Word Link	bio ≈ life : biodegradable, biography, biology

b

Word Link | graph ≈ writing : auto*graph*, bio*graphy*, *graph*

bi|og|ra|phy /baɪɒɡrəfi/ (biographies) **1** N-COUNT 可算名詞 A **biography** of someone is an account of their life, written by someone else. 伝記 □ ...recent biographies of Stalin. 最近書かれたスターリンの伝記 **2** N-UNCOUNT 不可算名詞 **Biography** is the branch of literature which deals with accounts of people's lives. 伝記文学 □ ...a volume of biography and criticism. 伝記と評論の本
→ see **library**

bio|logi|cal /baɪəlɒdʒɪkᵊl/ **1** ADJ 形容詞 **Biological** is used to describe processes and states that occur in the bodies and cells of living things. 生物学上の □ The living organisms somehow concentrated the minerals by biological processes. どうしたものか，生物は生体内作用により無機物を濃縮した． ● **bio|logi|cal|ly** /baɪəlɒdʒɪkli/ ADV 副詞 生物学的に □ Much of our behavior is biologically determined. 我々の行動の多くは生物学的に決定される． **2** ADJ 形容詞 [ADJ n] **Biological** is used to describe activities concerned with the study of living things. 生物学の □ ...all aspects of biological research associated with leprosy. ハンセン病に関連した生物学的研究の全局面 **3** ADJ 形容詞 **Biological** weapons and **biological** warfare involve the use of bacteria or other living organisms in order to attack human beings, animals, or plants. 細菌などを使った □ Such a war could result in the use of chemical and biological weapons. こういった戦争は化学兵器および生物兵器の使用を引き起こすかもしれない． **4** ADJ 形容詞 **Biological** pest control is the use of bacteria or other living organisms in order to destroy other organisms which are harmful to plants or crops. 生物の [ADJ n] □ ...a consultant on biological control of agricultural pests. 農業害虫生体駆除のコンサルタント **5** ADJ 形容詞 A child's **biological** parents are the man and woman who caused him or her to be born, rather than other adults who raise him or her. 生物学上の [ADJ n] □ ...foster parents for young teenagers whose biological parents have rejected them. 実父母によって拒まれた十代の若者の里親
→ see **war, zoo**

Word Link | logy, ology ≈ study of : anthropo*logy*, bio*logy*, geo*logy*

bi|ol|ogy /baɪɒlədʒi/ **1** N-UNCOUNT 不可算名詞 **Biology** is the science which is concerned with the study of living things. 生物学 ● **bi|olo|gist** /baɪɒlədʒɪst/ N-COUNT 可算名詞 (biologists) 生物学者 □ ...biologists studying the fruit fly. ショウジョウバエを研究する生物学者 **2** N-UNCOUNT 不可算名詞 The **biology** of a living thing is the way in which its body or cells behave. 生態 □ The biology of these diseases is terribly complicated. これら疾病の生態は大変複雑である．

bi|op|sy /baɪɒpsi/ (biopsies) N-VAR 可変性名詞 A **biopsy** is the removal and examination of fluids or tissue from a patient's body in order to discover why they are ill. 生体組織検査 □ James had a biopsy of the tumor over his right ear. ジェームズは右耳上にできたしゅようの生検を受けた．

Word Link | techn ≈ art, skill : bio*techn*ology, *techn*ical, *techn*ician

bio|tech|nol|ogy /baɪoʊteknɒlədʒi/ N-UNCOUNT 不可算名詞 **Biotechnology** is the use of living parts such as cells or bacteria in industry and technology. 生物工学 [TECHNICAL 技術的] □ ...the Scottish biotechnology company that developed Dolly the cloned sheep. クローン羊のドリーを開発したスコットランドのバイオテクノロジー企業
→ see **technology**

birch /bɜrtʃ/ (birches) N-VAR 可変性名詞 A **birch** is a type of tall tree with thin branches. カバの木

bird /bɜrd/ (birds) **1** N-COUNT 可算名詞 A **bird** is a creature with feathers and wings. Female birds lay eggs. Most birds can fly. 鳥 **2** → see also **early bird** **3** PHRASE 句 If you refer to two people as **birds of a feather**, you mean that they have the same interests or are very similar. 同類 □ We're birds of a feather, you and me, Mr. Plimpton. プリンプトンさん，あなたと私は同じ穴のむじなですよ． **4** PHRASE 句 A **bird in the hand** is something that you already have and do not want to risk losing by trying to get something else. 手中の鳥，しっかり握った利得 □ Another temporary discount may not be what you want, but at least it is a bird in the hand. 一時的にさらに

割り引きされるのを望まないかもしれませんが，それは少なくともあなたの手中にあるのですよ． **5** PHRASE 句 If you say that a **little bird** told you about something, you mean that someone has told you about it, but you do not want to say who it was. ある人から聞いた □ Incidentally, a little bird tells me that your birthday's coming up. ところで，ある人からあなたの誕生日がもうすぐと聞きました． **6** PHRASE 句 If you say that doing something will **kill two birds with one stone**, you mean that it will enable you to achieve two things that you want to achieve, rather than just one. 一石で二鳥を仕留める □ We can talk about Union Hill while I get this business over with. Kill two birds with one stone, so to speak. 私がこの仕事を片付ける間にユニオンヒルについても検討できます．いわば一挙両得です．
→ see Word Web: **bird**
→ see **pet**

bird flu N-UNCOUNT **Bird flu** is a virus that can be transmitted from chickens, ducks, and other birds to people. 鳥インフルエンザ

Biro /baɪroʊ/ (Biros) 商標 N-COUNT A **Biro** is the same as a **ballpoint**. ボールペン

birth /bɜrθ/ (births) **1** N-VAR 可変性名詞 When a baby is born, you refer to this event as his or her **birth**. 誕生 □ It was the birth of his grandchildren that gave him greatest pleasure. 彼は初孫の誕生を無上に喜んだ． □ She weighed 5lb 7oz at birth. 彼女の出生時体重は51ポンド7オンスだった． **2** N-UNCOUNT 不可算名詞 You can refer to the beginning or origin of something as its **birth**. 始まり □ ...the birth of popular democracy. 大衆民主主義の出現 **3** N-UNCOUNT 不可算名詞 Some people talk about a person's **birth** when they are referring to the social position of the person's family. 素性 □ ...men of low birth. 家柄の悪い人 **4** → see also **date of birth** **5** PHRASE 句 If, for example, you are French **by birth**, you are French because your parents are French, or because you were born in France. 生まれは □ Sadrudin was an Iranian by birth. サドルディンの生まれはイランだった． **6** PHRASE 句 When a woman **gives birth**, she produces a baby from her body. 生む □ She's just given birth to a baby girl. 彼女はたった今女の子を出産した． **7** PHRASE 句 To **give birth to** something such as an idea means to cause it to start to exist. 原因となる □ In 1980, strikes at the Lenin shipyards gave birth to the Solidarity trade union. 1980年レーニンに造船所で起こったストライキに端を発して労働組合「連帯」が生まれた． **8** PHRASE 句 The country, town, or village **of** your **birth** is the place where you were born. 出生地 □ He left the town of his birth five years later for Australia. 彼は，5年前に生まれた町を後にしてオーストラリアに渡った．

Word Partnership | birth は次の語句と使われる：

ADJ.	**premature** birth **1**
N.	birth **of a baby/child**, birth **certificate**, birth **control**, birth **and death**, birth **defect**, birth **rate 1**
	date of birth **1 4**
	birth **of a nation 2**
PREP.	**at** birth, **before** birth **1**
	by birth **3 5**
V.	**give** birth **6 7**

birth cer|tifi|cate (birth certificates) N-COUNT 可算名詞 Your **birth certificate** is an official document that gives details of your birth, such as the date and place of your birth, and the names of your parents. 出生証明書

birth con|trol N-UNCOUNT 不可算名詞 **Birth control** means planning whether to have children, and using contraception to prevent having them when they are not wanted. 産児制限 □ Today's methods of birth control make it possible for a couple to choose whether or not to have a child. 今日の避妊法により，夫婦は子供を生むか生まないかを選択できる．

birth|day /bɜrθdeɪ, -di/ (birthdays) N-COUNT 可算名詞 Your **birthday** is the anniversary of the date on which you were born. 誕生日 □ On his birthday she sent him presents. 彼女は彼の誕生日にプレゼントを送った．

birth|place /bɜrθpleɪs/ (birthplaces) **1** N-COUNT 可算名詞 Your **birthplace** is the place where you were born. 出生地 [WRITTEN 書き言葉] □ ...Bob Marley's birthplace in the village of Nine

Word Web | bird

Many scientists today believe that birds evolved from avian dinosaurs. Recently many links have been found. Like birds, these dinosaurs laid their **eggs** in **nests**. Some had **wings**, **beaks**, and **claws** similar to modern birds. But perhaps the most dramatic link was found in 2001. Scientists in China discovered a well-preserved *Sinornithosaurus*, a bird-like dinosaur with **feathers**. This dinosaur is believed to be related to a prehistoric bird, the *Archaeopteryx*.

Sinornithosaurus

B

Mile. ボブ・マーリーの生まれ故郷はナインマイルの村だ. **2** N-COUNT 可算名詞 The **birthplace of** something is the place where it began. 発生地 ロ…*Athens, the birthplace of the ancient Olympics*. アテネ, 古代オリンピック発生の地.

birth rate (birth rates) also **birth-rate** N-COUNT 可算名詞 The **birth rate** in a place is the number of babies born there for every 1000 people during a particular period of time. 出生率 ロ*America's birth rate fell to a record low last year*. 米国の出生率は昨年史上最低に落ち込んだ.
→ see **population**

bis|cuit /bɪskɪt/ (biscuits) **1** N-COUNT 可算名詞 A **biscuit** is a small round dry cake that is made with baking powder, baking soda, or yeast. 柔らかい菓子パン [AM 米国英語] **2** N-COUNT 可算名詞 A **biscuit** is a small flat cake that is crisp and usually sweet. ビスケット [BRIT 英国英語; AM **cookie** 米国英語 **cookie**] **3** PHRASE 句 **Take the biscuit** means the same as **take the cake**. 際立っている, 最低だ [BRIT 英国英語]

bi|sex|ual /baɪsɛkʃuəl/ (bisexuals) ADJ 形容詞 Someone who is **bisexual** is sexually attracted to both men and women. 両性愛の ● N-COUNT 可算名詞 **Bisexual** is also a noun. 両性愛者 ロ*He was an active bisexual*. 彼は性的に活発な両性愛者だった.

bish|op /bɪʃəp/ (bishops) **1** N-COUNT; N-TITLE; N-VOC 可算名詞, 称号名詞, 呼格名詞 A **bishop** is a clergyman of high rank in the Roman Catholic, Anglican, and Orthodox churches. 司教, 主教 **2** N-COUNT 可算名詞 In chess a **bishop** is a piece that can be moved diagonally across the board on squares that are the same color. ビショップ
→ see **chess**

bis|tro /bɪstroʊ/ (bistros) N-COUNT 可算名詞 A **bistro** is a small, informal restaurant or a bar where food is served. 小料理屋

bit /bɪt/ (bits) **1** QUANT 数量詞 **A bit of** something is a small amount of it. 少量 [QUANT 'of' n-uncount] ロ*All it required was a bit of work*. ちょっと働くだけでよかった. **2** PHRASE 句 **A bit** means to a small extent or degree. It is sometimes used to make a statement less extreme. 少しだけ, 幾らか [VAGUENESS あいまいさ] ロ*This girl was a bit strange*. この少女は少し変わっていた. ロ*I think people feel a bit more confident*. 人々は幾分自信を高めていると思う. **3** PHRASE 句 You can use **a bit of** to make a statement less forceful. For example, the statement "It's a bit of a nuisance" is less forceful than "It's a nuisance." 幾分 [VAGUENESS あいまいさ] ロ*It's all a bit of a mess*. 全体がちょっと散らかってるんだ. ロ*Students have always been portrayed as a bit of a joke*. いつも学生はちょっとした物笑いの種として描かれてきた. **4** PHRASE 句 **Quite a bit** means quite a lot. 大いに ロ*They're worth quite a bit of money*. それらは非常に高価だ. ロ*Things have changed quite a bit*. 状況はかなり変化した. **5** PHRASE 句 You use **a bit** before "more" or "less" to mean a small amount more or a small amount less. 幾らか ロ*I still think I have a bit more to offer*. まだ幾らかお手伝いできると思う. ロ*Maybe we'll hear a little bit less noise*. いくらか騒音が小さくなるかもしれない. **6** PHRASE 句 If you do something **a bit** or do something **for a bit**, you do it for a short time. ちょっとの間 ロ*Let's wait a bit*. ちょっと待とう. ロ*I hope there will be time to talk a bit — or at least ask you about one or two things this evening*. 今夜ちょっと話できればいいが. 少なくともひとつふたつ質問できればね. **7** N-COUNT 可算名詞 A **bit** of something is a small part or section of it. 小部分 ロ*Only a bit of the barley remained*. ほんの少しだけ大麦が残った ロ*Now comes the really important bit*. ここからが本当に重要な部分なんだ. **8** N-COUNT 可算名詞 A **bit** of something is a small piece of it. 小片 ロ*Only a bit of string looped round a nail in the doorpost held it shut*. 側柱の釘の回りに巻かれた短いひもだけで, それを閉じていた. **9** N-COUNT 可算名詞 You can use **bit** to refer to a particular item or to one of a group or set of things. For example, a **bit** of information is an item of information. 一片 ロ*There was one bit of vital evidence which helped win the case*. 訴訟を勝利に導いたひとつの貴重な証言があった. **10** N-COUNT 可算名詞 In computing, a **bit** is the smallest unit of information that is held in a computer's memory. It is either 1 or 0. Several bits form a byte. ビット **11** N-COUNT 可算名詞 A **bit** is 12½ cents; mainly used in expressions such as two **bits**, which means 25 cents, or **four bits**, which means 50 cents. 12セント半 [AM 米国英語, INFORMAL OR OLD-FASHIONED くだけた, または古風な] ロ*They weren't worth four bits*. それらは無価値だった. **12** **Bit** is the past tense of **bite**. biteの過去形 **13** PHRASE 句 If something happens **bit by bit**, it happens in stages. 徐々に ロ*Bit by bit I began to understand what they were trying to do*. 彼らが何をしようとしていたのか少しずつわかり始めた. **14** PHRASE 句 If you **do your bit**, you do something that, to a small or limited extent, helps to achieve something. おのれの分を尽くす [BRIT 英国英語; AM **do your part** 米国英語 **do your part**] **15** PHRASE 句 You say that one thing is **every bit as** good, interesting, or important **as** another to emphasize that the first thing is just as good, interesting, or important as the second. どの点も [EMPHASIS 強調] ロ*My dinner jacket is every bit as good as his*. 僕のタキシードはどの点からみても彼のに負けない. **16** PHRASE 句 If you say that something is **a bit much**, you

are annoyed because you think someone has behaved in an unreasonable way. 度がすぎる [INFORMAL くだけた, FEELINGS 感情] ロ*Her stage outfit of hot pants, over-the-knee boots and a tube top was a bit much*. ホットパンツ, ひざ上ブーツとチューブトップという彼女の舞台衣装はちょっとやりすぎだった. **17** PHRASE 句 You use **not a bit** to emphasize a strong negative statement. 少しも〜でない [EMPHASIS 強調] ロ*I'm really not a bit surprised*. 驚いたなんてとんでもない. **18** PHRASE 句 You can use **bits and pieces** to refer to a collection of different things. 寄せ集め [INFORMAL くだけた] ロ*The drawers are full of bits and pieces of armor*. 引き出しはごちゃごちゃの防護具でいっぱいだ.

bitch /bɪtʃ/ (bitches, bitching, bitched) **1** N-COUNT 可算名詞 If someone calls a woman a **bitch**, they are saying in a very rude way that they think she behaves in a very mean or unkind way. 意地の悪い女 [INFORMAL, OFFENSIVE, VULGAR くだけた, 無礼な, 下品な, DISAPPROVAL 不賛成] → see also **son of a bitch** **2** V-I 自動詞 If you say that someone **is bitching about** something, you mean that you disapprove of the fact that they are complaining about it in an unpleasant way. 不平を言う [INFORMAL くだけた, DISAPPROVAL 不賛成] [oft cont] ロ*They're forever bitching about everybody else*. 彼らは絶えず他人の愚痴をこぼしている. **4** N-COUNT 可算名詞 A **bitch** is a female dog. 雌イヌ

bite /baɪt/ (bites, biting, bit, bitten) **1** V-T/V-I 他動詞/自動詞 If you **bite** something, you use your teeth to cut into it, for example, in order to eat it or break it. If an animal or person **bites** you, they use their teeth to hurt or injure you. かむ ロ*Both sisters bit their nails as children*. 姉妹は2人とも子供のころ爪をかむ癖があった. ロ*He bit into his sandwich*. 彼はサンドイッチにかぶりついた. ロ*Every year in this country more than 50,000 children are bitten by dogs*. この国では毎年5万人以上の子供が犬にかまれている. **2** N-COUNT 可算名詞 A **bite** of something, especially food, is the action of biting it. かむこと ロ*He took another bite of apple*. 彼はりんごをもう一口かじった. **3** N-COUNT 可算名詞 A **bite** of food is the amount of food you take into your mouth when you bite it. 一口 ロ*Look forward to eating the food and enjoy every bite*. わくわくするような料理を心行くまでお楽しみください. **4** N-SING 単数名詞 If you have **a bite** to eat, you have a small meal or a snack. 軽食 [INFORMAL くだけた] ロ*It was time to go home for a little rest and a bite to eat*. そろそろ家に帰って, すこし休んで何か軽く食べよう. **5** V-T/V-I 他動詞/自動詞 If a snake or a small insect **bites** you, or if it **bites**, it makes a mark or hole in your skin, and often causes the surrounding area of your skin to become painful or itchy. 刺す [他動詞] 刺す [自動詞] ロ*When an infected mosquito bites a human, spores are injected into the blood*. 人間が感染した蚊に刺されると, 血液中に胞子が注入される. **6** N-COUNT 可算名詞 A **bite** is an injury or a mark on your body where an animal, snake, or small insect has bitten you. 刺傷 ロ*Any dog bite, no matter how small, needs immediate medical attention*. 犬にかまれたらどんなに小さい傷であってもすぐに医者に診てもらわなければならない. **7** V-I 自動詞 When an action or policy begins to **bite**, it begins to have a serious or harmful effect. 効果を発する ロ*As the sanctions begin to bite there will be more political difficulties ahead*. 制裁措置が効果を発揮し始めると, 政治的問題は増えるだろう. **8** V-I 自動詞 If an object **bites** into a surface, it presses hard against it or cuts into it. 食い込む ロ*There may even be some wire or nylon biting into the flesh*. 針金かナイロンが肌に食い込むことさえあるかもしれない. **9** N-UNCOUNT 不可算名詞 If you say that a food or drink has **bite**, you like it because it has a strong or sharp taste. 強くてシャープな味わい ロ*The olive salad has to have bite and tang*. オリーブサラダはパンチの効いた風味にしてください. **10** V-I 自動詞 If a fish **bites** when you are fishing, it takes the hook or bait at the end of your fishing line in its mouth. えさに食いつく ロ*After half an hour, the fish stopped biting and we moved on*. 30分後, 魚が食わなくなったので僕らは別の場所に移った. ● N-COUNT 可算名詞 **Bite** is also a noun. えさにつくこと ロ*I don't get a bite in a few minutes I lift the rod and twitch the bait*. 数分の内に魚が食いつかなければ, さおを上げてえさを引っ張ろう. **11** PHRASE 句 If someone **bites the hand that feeds** them, they behave badly or in an ungrateful way toward someone who they depend on. 恩をあだで返す ロ*She may be cynical about the film industry, but ultimately she has no intention of biting the hand that feeds her*. 彼女は映画業界について冷笑的かもしれないが, 結局のところ, 恩をあだで返すつもりはない. **12** PHRASE 句 If you **bite** your **lip** or your **tongue**, you stop yourself from saying something that you want to say, because it would be the wrong thing to say in the circumstances. 唇をかんで（言いたいこと）をこらえる ロ*I must learn to bite my lip*. 言いたいことを言わないってことを学ばなければ. **13** **to bite the bullet** → see **bullet** **14** **to bite the dust** → see **dust**

bit|ing /baɪtɪŋ/ **1** ADJ 形容詞 **Biting** wind or cold is extremely cold. 刺すような ロ*…a raw, biting northerly wind*. 冷え冷えと身を切るような北風. **2** ADJ 形容詞 **Biting** criticism or wit is very harsh or unkind, and is often caused by such feelings as anger or dislike. 鋭い ロ*…the author's biting satire on the church*. その作家の鋭い教会風刺

bit|map /bɪtmæp/ (bitmaps, bitmapping, bitmapped)

N-COUNT 可算名詞 A **bitmap** is a type of graphics file on a computer. ビットマップ [COMPUTING コンピューティング] □ ...bitmap graphics for representing complex images such as photographs. 写真など複雑な画像を表示するためのビットマップ画像 ● V-T 他動詞 **Bitmap** is also a verb. ビットマップ化された □ Bitmapped maps require huge storage space. ビットマップ形式の地図は大量のディスクスペースを必要とする.

bit|ten /bɪtⁿn/ **Bitten** is the past participle of **bite**. biteの過去分詞

bit|ter /bɪtər/ (**bitterest, bitters**) **1** ADJ 形容詞 In a **bitter** argument or conflict, people argue very angrily or fight very fiercely. 痛烈な □ ...the scene of bitter fighting during the Second World War. 第2次世界大戦中の激烈な戦闘の場面 □ ...a bitter attack on the government's failure to support manufacturing. 政府が製造業を援助できなかったことに対する痛烈な攻撃 ● **bit|ter|ly** ADV 副詞 痛烈に □ Any such thing would be bitterly opposed by most of the world's democracies. そういうものはすべて、世界中の大多数の民主主義国家により、猛烈に反対されるだろう. ● **bit|ter|ness** N-UNCOUNT 不可算名詞 痛烈さ □ The rift within the organization reflects the growing bitterness of the dispute. 組織内の亀裂は論争の激しさを反映している **2** ADJ 形容詞 If someone is **bitter** after a disappointing experience or after being treated unfairly, they continue to feel angry about it. つらい □ She is said to be very bitter about the way she was fired. 彼女は解雇のされかたに非常に憤慨しているらしい. ● **bit|ter|ly** ADV 副詞 ひどく □ "And he sure didn't help us," Grant said bitterly. 「もちろん彼は助けてはくれなかった」とグラントは憎々しげに言った. ● **bit|ter|ness** N-UNCOUNT 不可算名詞 つらみ □ I still feel bitterness and anger towards the person who knocked me down. 僕を打ち負かしたやつへの、僕はいまだに恨み、憎悪している. **3** ADJ 形容詞 A **bitter** taste is sharp, not sweet, and often slightly unpleasant. 苦い □ The leaves taste rather bitter. 葉っぱはかなり苦い. **4** ADJ 形容詞 A **bitter** experience makes you feel very disappointed. You can also use **bitter** to emphasize feelings of disappointment. つらい □ The decision was a bitter blow from which he never quite recovered. 決定は苦痛の一撃となり、彼が完全に立ち直ることはなかった. □ A great deal of bitter experience had taught him how to lose gracefully. 彼は多くの苦い経験から潔く負ける方法を学んだ. ● **bit|ter|ly** ADV 副詞 ひどく □ I was bitterly disappointed to have lost yet another race so near the finish. ゴール寸前でまたもや競争に負けてひどく落胆した. **5** ADJ 形容詞 **Bitter** weather, or a bitter wind, is extremely cold. 寒さの厳しい □ Outside, a bitter east wind was accompanied by flurries of snow. 外ではにわか雪の混じった肌を刺すような東風が吹いている. ● **bit|ter|ly** ADV 副詞 [ADV adj] 刺すように □ It's been bitterly cold here in Moscow. ここモスクワでは身を切るような寒さが続いている. **6 a bitter pill → see pill**
→ see taste

bit|ter|ly /bɪtərli/ ADV 副詞 You use **bitterly** when you are describing an attitude which involves strong, unpleasant emotions such as anger or dislike. ひどく [ADV adj] □ We are bitterly upset at what has happened. 僕らは起こった事件にひどくろうばいしている.

bi|week|ly /baɪwiːkli/ ADJ 形容詞 A **biweekly** event or publication happens or appears every two weeks. 隔週の [AM 米国英語] [ADJ n] □ He used to see them at the biweekly meetings. 彼は隔週開かれる会議で彼らに会っていたのだった. □ ...Beverage Digest, the industry's biweekly newsletter. 『ビバレッジ・ダイジェスト』、2週間に1回発行される業界のニュースレター ● ADV 副詞 **Biweekly** is also an adverb. 隔週に [ADV with v] □ The group meets on a regular basis, usually weekly or biweekly. グループは定期的に、たいてい毎週または隔週に集まっている.

bi|zarre /bɪzɑːr/ ADJ 形容詞 Something that is **bizarre** is very odd and strange. 奇妙な □ The game was also notable for the bizarre behavior of the team's manager. 試合は監督の突飛な行動でも注目に値した. ● **bi|zarre|ly** ADV 副詞 奇妙に □ She dressed bizarrely. 彼女の服装は一風変わっていた.

black /blæk/ (**blacker, blackest, blacks, blacking, blacked**) **1** COLOR 色彩語 Something that is **black** is of the darkest color that there is, the color of the sky at night when there is no light at all. 黒 □ She was wearing a black coat with a white collar. 彼女は襟の白い黒のコートを着ていた. □ He had thick black hair. 彼の髪は濃く黒い. **2** ADJ 形容詞 A **black** person belongs to a race of people with dark skins, especially a race originally from Africa. 黒人の □ He worked for the rights of black people. 彼は黒人の権利を守るために尽くした. □ Sherry is black, tall, slender and soft-spoken. シェリーは黒人で背が高くほっそりしていてやさしい話し方をする. **3** N-COUNT 可算名詞 Black people are sometimes referred to as **blacks**. This use could cause offense. 黒人 □ There are about thirty-one million blacks in the U.S. 米国には約3千百万の黒人がいる. **4** ADJ 形容詞 **Black** coffee or tea has no milk or cream added to it. ミルクやクリームの入っていない [ADJ n, v n ADJ] □ A cup of black tea or black coffee contains no calories. ミルクやクリームを入れないお茶やコーヒーのカロリーはゼロである. **5** ADJ 形容詞 If you describe a situation as **black**, you are emphasizing that it is very bad indeed. 希望のない [EMPHASIS 強調] □ It was, he said later, one of the blackest days of his

political career. 後になって彼は政治人生のなかで最も陰うつな日々だったと述べた. **6** ADJ 形容詞 If someone is in a **black** mood, they feel very miserable and depressed. 暗い □ In late 1975, she fell into a black depression. 1975年後半、彼女は暗たんとした憂うつに襲われた. **7** PHRASE 句 If a person or an organization is **in the black**, they do not owe anyone any money. 黒字で □ Remington's operations in Japan are now in the black. レミントンの日本事業は黒字に転じた.
▶ **black out 1** PHRASAL VERB 句動詞 If you **black out**, you lose consciousness for a short time. 一時意識を失う □ I could feel blood draining from my face. I wondered whether I was about to black out. 顔から血の気が引いていくのを自覚し、失神するかと思った. **2** PHRASAL VERB 句動詞 If a place **is blacked out**, it is in darkness, usually because it has no electricity supply. 真っ暗にする □ Large parts of Lima were blacked out after electricity pylons were blown up. 送電塔が爆破され、リマの広い範囲が停電で真っ暗になった. **3** PHRASAL VERB 句動詞 If a film or a piece of writing **is blacked out**, it is prevented from being broadcast or published, usually because it contains information which is secret or offensive. 放送を禁じる □ TV pictures of the demonstration were blacked out. デモのテレビ放映は禁止された. **4** PHRASAL VERB 句動詞 If you **black out** a piece of writing, you color over it in black so that it cannot be seen. 黒で塗りつぶす □ U.S. government specialists went through each page, blacking out any information a foreign intelligence expert could use. 米国政府の専門家は各ページをチェックして他国の情報活動専門家が利用できそうな情報すべてを黒く塗りつぶした. **5** PHRASAL VERB 句動詞 If you **black out** the memory of something, you try not to remember it because it upsets you. 抹消する □ I tried not to think about it. I blacked it out. It was the easiest way of coping. 私はそれについて考えないようにした. 私は記憶から抹消した. これが最も簡単な対処法だった.
6 → see also blackout
→ see coffee

black and white also **black-and-white 1** COLOR 色彩語 In a **black and white** photograph or film, everything is shown in black, white, and gray. 白黒の □ ...old black and white film footage. 古い白黒の映像 □ ...a black-and-white photo of the two of us together. 私たちが一緒に写った白黒写真 **2** ADJ 形容詞 A **black and white** television set shows only black and white pictures. 白黒の **3** ADJ 形容詞 A **black and white** issue or situation is one that involves issues that seem simple and therefore easy to make decisions about. 明白な □ But this isn't a simple black and white affair, Marianne. マリアンヌ、これはそんな単純明快な問題じゃないんだ. **4** PHRASE 句 You say that something is **in black and white** when it has been written or printed, and not just said. 書き物になった □ He'd seen the proof in black and white. 彼は証拠を書面で確認した.

black|berry /blækbɛri/ (**blackberries**) **1** N-COUNT 可算名詞 A **blackberry** is a small, soft black or dark purple fruit. ブラックベリー **2** N-COUNT 可算名詞 商標 A **Blackberry** is a portable, wireless computing device that allows you to send and receive email. BlackBerry [COMPUTING コンピューティング, TRADEMARK]

black|board /blækbɔːrd/ (**blackboards**) N-COUNT 可算名詞 A **blackboard** is a dark-colored board that you can write on with chalk. Blackboards are often used by teachers in the classroom. 黒板 [AM also **chalkboard** 米国英語、また **chalkboard**]

black|en /blækən/ (**blackens, blackening, blackened**) **1** V-T/V-I 他動詞/自動詞 To **blacken** something means to make it black or very dark in color. Something that **blackens** becomes black or very dark in color. 黒くする [他動詞] 黒くなる [自動詞] □ The married women of Shitamachi maintained the custom of blackening their teeth. 下町の既婚女性はおはぐろの慣習を守った. **2** V-T 他動詞 If someone **blackens** your character, they make other people believe that you are a bad person. 悪く言う □ They're trying to blacken our name. 彼らは我々に汚名をきせようとしている.

black eye (**black eyes**) N-COUNT 可算名詞 If someone has a **black eye**, they have a dark-colored bruise around their eye. 目のまわりの黒いあざ □ He punched her in the face, giving her a black eye. 彼は彼女の顔を殴って目のまわりに黒あざを作った.

black|list /blæklɪst/ (**blacklists, blacklisting, blacklisted**) **1** N-COUNT 可算名詞 If someone is on a **blacklist**, they are seen by a government or other organization as being one of a number of people who cannot be trusted or who have done something wrong. ブラックリスト □ A government official disclosed that they were on a secret blacklist. 政府高官が、彼らが機密のブラックリストに載っていることを発表した. **2** V-T 他動詞 If someone **is blacklisted** by a government or organization, they are put on a blacklist. ブラックリストに載せる [usu passive] □ He has been blacklisted since being convicted of possessing marijuana in 1969. 彼は、1969年に大麻所持で有罪判決を受けて以来ブラックリストに載っている.

black|mail /blækmeɪl/ (**blackmails, blackmailing, blackmailed**) **1** N-UNCOUNT 不可算名詞 **Blackmail** is the action of threatening to reveal a secret about someone, unless they do something you tell them to do, such as giving you money. 恐喝 □ It looks like the pictures were being used for blackmail. 写真は恐喝に使われていたようだ. **2** N-UNCOUNT 不可算名詞 If you describe

an action as emotional or moral **blackmail**, you disapprove of it because someone is using a person's emotions or moral values to persuade them to do something against their will. 脅迫 [DISAPPROVAL 不賛成] ❑ *The tactics employed can range from overt bullying to subtle emotional blackmail.* 使われる手口は，あからさまないじめから巧妙な感情的脅迫までいろいろとある. ■ V-T 他動詞 If one person **blackmails** another person, they use blackmail against them. 脅迫する ❑ *He told her their affair would have to stop, because Jack Smith was blackmailing him.* 彼はジャック・スミスに恐喝されているから，関係を清算しなければならないだろうと彼女に告げた. ❑ *The government insisted that it would not be blackmailed by violence.* 政府は暴力による脅しには屈しないと強調した. ● **black|mail|er** N-COUNT 可算名詞 (**blackmailers**) 恐喝者 ❑ *The nasty thing about a blackmailer is that his starting point is usually the truth.* 恐喝者の厄介な点は，通常事実を押さえていることだ.

black mar|ket (**black markets**) N-COUNT 可算名詞 If something is bought or sold **on the black market**, it is bought or sold illegally. やみ市 ❑ *There is a plentiful supply of arms on the black market.* やみ市では有り余るほどの武器が出回っている.

black|out /blǽkaʊt/ (**blackouts**) also **black-out** ■ N-COUNT 可算名詞 A **blackout** is a period of time during a war in which towns and buildings are made dark so that they cannot be seen by enemy planes. 灯火管制 ❑ *...blackout curtains.* 暗幕カーテン ❷ N-COUNT 可算名詞 If a **blackout** is imposed on a particular piece of news, journalists are prevented from broadcasting or publishing it. 報道管制 ❑ *...a media blackout imposed by the Imperial Palace.* 皇室によって課された報道管制 ❸ N-COUNT 可算名詞 If there is a power **blackout**, the electricity supply to a place is temporarily cut off. 停電 ❑ *There was an electricity black-out in a large area in the north of the country.* 国の北部の広範囲にわたって停電があった. ■ N-COUNT 可算名詞 If you have a **blackout**, you temporarily lose consciousness. 一時的意識喪失 ❑ *I suffered a black-out which lasted for several minutes.* 私は数分間意識を失くした.

black|smith /blǽksmɪθ/ (**blacksmiths**) N-COUNT 可算名詞 A **blacksmith** is a person whose job is making things by hand out of metal that has been heated to a high temperature. かじ屋

black|top /blǽktɒp/ N-UNCOUNT 不可算名詞 **Blacktop** is a hard black substance which is used as a surface for roads. アスファルト [AM 米国英語] ❑ *...waves of heat rising from the blacktop.* アスファルトから立ち上る熱波

blad|der /blǽdər/ (**bladders**) N-COUNT 可算名詞 Your **bladder** is the part of your body where urine is stored until it leaves your body. See also **gall bladder**. ぼうこう ❑ *...an opportunity to empty a full bladder.* 一杯になった膀胱を空にする機会

blade /bleɪd/ (**blades**) ■ N-COUNT 可算名詞 The **blade** of a knife, ax, or saw is the edge, which is used for cutting. 刃 ❑ *Many of them will have sharp blades.* その多くには鋭い刃がつけられる. ❷ N-COUNT 可算名詞 The **blades** of a propeller are the long, flat parts that turn around. 羽根 ❸ N-COUNT 可算名詞 The **blade** of an oar is the thin flat part that you put into the water. 水かき ■ N-COUNT 可算名詞 A **blade** of grass is a single piece of grass. 葉 ❑ *Brian began to tear blades of grass from between the bricks.* ブライアンはれんがの間から生えた草をちぎり始めた.
→ see **silverware**

blame /bleɪm/ (**blames, blaming, blamed**) ■ V-T 他動詞 If you **blame** a person or thing **for** something bad, or if you **blame** something bad **on** somebody, you believe or say that they are responsible for it or that they caused it. とがめる ❑ *The commission is expected to blame the army for many of the atrocities.* 委員会は，残虐行為の多くを陸軍の責任にすると予想される. ❑ *Ms. Carey appeared to blame her breakdown on EMI's punishing work schedule.* キャリーさんは心身衰弱をEMIの課する苛酷な仕事のスケジュールのせいにしているようだった. ● N-UNCOUNT 不可算名詞 **Blame** is also a noun. 非難 ❑ *Nothing could relieve my terrible sense of blame.* 私の強烈な罪の意識を和らげることのできるものはない. ❷ N-UNCOUNT 不可算名詞 The **blame for** something bad that has happened is the responsibility for causing it or letting it happen. 責任 ❑ *I'm not going to sit around and take the blame for a mistake he made.* 私は手をこまねいて，彼が犯した間違いの責任をとるつもりはない. ❸ V-T 他動詞 If you say that you do not **blame** someone **for** doing something, you mean that you consider it was a reasonable thing to do in the circumstances. 無理もない [usu with brd-neg] ❑ *I do not blame them for trying to make some money.* 彼らがお金を稼ごうとしているのを責めはしない. ■ PHRASE 句 If someone is **to blame** for something bad that has happened, they are responsible for causing it. 責がある ❑ *If their forces were not involved, then who is to blame?* 彼らの部隊がかかわっていないというのなら，一体誰が悪いのだ. ❺ PHRASE 句 If you say that someone **has only** themselves **to blame** or **has no one but** themselves **to blame**, you mean that they are responsible for something bad that has happened to them and that you have no sympathy for them. 自分以外に文句の持っていきどころがない ❑ *My life is ruined and I suppose I only have myself to blame.* 私の人生は丸つぶれで自分の責任でしかないと思う.

	Word Partnership	*blame* は次の語句と使われる:
N.	blame **the victim** ■	
V.	**tend to** blame ■	
	lay blame, **share the** blame ■ ❷	
	can hardly blame *someone* ❸	

blanch /blɑːntʃ/ (**blanches, blanching, blanched**) ■ V-I 自動詞 If you **blanch**, you suddenly become very pale. 顔色を蒼白にする ❑ *Simon's face blanched as he looked at Sharpe's blood-drenched uniform.* 血まみれになったシャープのユニフォームを見てサイモンは蒼白になった. ❷ V-I 自動詞 If you say that someone **blanches at** something, you mean that they find it unpleasant and do not want to be involved with it. 顔色を変える ❑ *Everything he had said had been a mistake. He blanched at his miscalculations.* 彼の言ったことはすべて間違いだった. 自分の誤算に彼は青ざめた.

bland /blænd/ (**blander, blandest**) ■ ADJ 形容詞 If you describe someone or something as **bland**, you mean that they are rather dull and unexciting. つまらない ❑ *Serle has a blander personality than Howard.* サールはハワードよりも穏やかな性格をしている. ❑ *It sounds like a commercial: easy on the ear but bland and forgettable.* 宣伝文句のように聞こえる. 響きはよいが退屈ですぐ忘れてしまう. ❷ ADJ 形容詞 Food that is **bland** has very little flavor. 刺激の少ない ❑ *It tasted bland and insipid, like warmed cardboard.* まるで温めた厚紙のように，味もすっぱもなかった.
→ see **spice**

blank /blæŋk/ (**blanks**) ■ ADJ 形容詞 Something that is **blank** has nothing on it. 空白の ❑ *We could put some of the pictures over on that blank wall over there.* そこの何もない壁に写真をいくつか飾ったらどうだろう. ❑ *He tore a blank page from his notebook.* 彼はノートから白紙のページを1枚破り取った. ❷ N-COUNT 可算名詞 A **blank** is a space which is left in a piece of writing or on a printed form for you to fill in particular information. 空白 ❑ *Put a word in each blank to complete the sentence.* 抜けている単語を埋めて文章を完成させなさい. ❸ ADJ 形容詞 If you look **blank**, your face shows no feeling, understanding, or interest. うつろな ❑ *Abbot looked blank. "I don't quite follow, sir."* アボットはとぼけた顔で「何のことかわかりません」と言った. ● **blank|ly** ADV 副詞 [ADV with v] ぼんやりと ❑ *She stared at him blankly.* 彼女はぽかんと彼を見つめた. ■ N-SING 単数名詞 If your mind or memory is a **blank**, you cannot think of anything or remember anything. 空白 ❑ *I'm sorry, but my mind is a blank.* すみません，でも何も覚えていないのです. ❺ N-COUNT 可算名詞 **Blanks** are gun cartridges which contain explosive but do not contain a bullet, so that they cause no harm when the gun is fired. 空砲 ❑ *...a starter pistol which only fires blanks.* 空砲だけのスタータービストル ❻ → see also **point-blank** ❼ PHRASE 句 If your mind **goes blank**, you are suddenly unable to think of anything appropriate to say, for example in reply to a question. からっぽになる

blank check (**blank checks**) ■ N-COUNT 可算名詞 If someone is given a **blank check**, they are given the authority to spend as much money as they need or want. 白紙式小切手 ❑ *We are not prepared to write a blank check for companies that have run into trouble.* トラブルに陥った企業に自由に金を使わせる用意はない. ❷ N-COUNT 可算名詞 If someone is given a **blank check**, they are given the authority to do what they think is best in a particular situation. 自由 ❑ *He has, in a sense, been given a blank check to negotiate the new South Africa.* 彼は，いうなれば，新しい南アフリカについて自由に交渉する権限を与えられたのだ.

blan|ket /blǽŋkɪt/ (**blankets, blanketing, blanketed**) ■ N-COUNT 可算名詞 A **blanket** is a large square or rectangular piece of thick cloth, especially one that you put on a bed to keep you warm. 毛布 ❷ N-COUNT 可算名詞 A **blanket of** something such as snow is a continuous layer of it which hides what is below or beyond it. 一面に覆うもの ❑ *The mud disappeared under a blanket of snow.* ぬかるみは一面の雪に隠れた. ❸ V-T 他動詞 If something such as snow **blankets** an area, it covers it. 一面に覆う ❑ *More than a foot of snow blanketed parts of Michigan.* ミシガンの一部は1フィート以上の深さの雪に覆われた. ■ ADJ 形容詞 You use **blanket** to describe something when you want to emphasize that it affects or refers to every person or thing in a group, without any exceptions. 全体に通ずる [EMPHASIS 強調] [ADJ n] ❑ *There's already a blanket ban on foreign unskilled labor in Japan.* 日本では，非熟練外国人労働はすでに全面的に禁止されている.
→ see **bed**

blare /bleər/ (**blares, blaring, blared**) V-I 自動詞 If something such as a siren or radio **blares**, it makes a loud, unpleasant noise. わめきたてる ❑ *The fire engines were just pulling up, sirens blaring.* 消防車はサイレンを鳴らしながらちょうど止まろうとしていた. ❑ *Music blared from the apartment behind me.* 私の家の裏にあるアパートから音楽が鳴り響いた. ● N-SING 単数名詞 **Blare** is also a noun. 音響 ❑ *...the blare of a radio through a thin wall.* 薄い壁を通して鳴り響くラジオの音 ● PHRASAL VERB 句動詞 **Blare out** means the same as **blare**. 鳴り響く ❑ *Music blares out from every café.* 音楽がどのカフェからも響く.

blas|phe|my /blǽsfəmi/ (**blasphemies**) N-VAR 変性名詞
You can describe something that shows disrespect for God or a religion as **blasphemy**. ぼうとく □ *He has acted out every kind of blasphemy, including dressing up as the pope in Rome.* ローマで法王のように着飾るなど、彼はありとあらゆる不敬を働いた。

blast /blǽst/ (**blasts, blasting, blasted**) **1** N-COUNT 可算名詞 A **blast** is a big explosion, especially one caused by a bomb. 突風 □ *250 people were killed in the blast.* 暴風により250人が死亡した。 **2** V-T 他動詞 If something **is blasted** into a particular place or state, an explosion causes it to be in that place or state. If a hole **is blasted** in something, it is created by an explosion. 爆発する、爆破する □ *There is a risk that toxic chemicals might be blasted into the atmosphere.* 有毒化学品が大気に吐き出される危険がある。 □ *The explosion which followed blasted out the wall of her apartment.* それに続く爆発が彼女のアパートの壁を爆破した。 **3** V-T 他動詞 If workers **are blasting** rock, they are using explosives to make holes in it or destroy it, for example, so that a road or tunnel can be built. 爆破する □ *Local workmen were blasting the rock face beside the track in order to make it wider.* 路線を拡張するために現地労働者が岩肌を爆破していた。 **4** V-T 他動詞 To **blast** someone means to shoot them with a gun. 撃つ [JOURNALISM ジャーナリズム] □ *A son blasted his father to death after a lifetime of bullying, a court was told yesterday.* 昨日、裁判所では生涯いじめに悩んだ息子は父を撃ち殺したとの証言があった。 ● N-COUNT 可算名詞 **Blast** is also a noun. 爆発 □ *Anthony died from a shotgun blast to the face.* アンソニーはショットガンで撃たれて死亡した。 **5** V-T 他動詞 If someone **blasts** their way somewhere, they get there by shooting at people or causing an explosion. 爆発させる □ *The police were reported to have blasted their way into the house using explosives.* 警察は爆発物を使用して家に突入したと伝えられた。 **6** V-T 他動詞 If something **blasts** water or air somewhere, it sends out a sudden, powerful stream of it. 噴射する □ *Blasting cold air over it makes the water evaporate.* それに冷たい空気を噴射すると、水を蒸発させる。 ● N-COUNT 可算名詞 **Blast** is also a noun. 強いひと吹き □ *Blasts of cold air swept down from the mountains.* 山から一陣の寒風が吹き下りた。 **7** V-T/V-I 他動詞/自動詞 If you **blast** something such as a car horn, or if it **blasts**, it makes a sudden, loud sound. If something **blasts** music, or music **blasts**, the music is very loud. 突然大きな音を出す [自動詞] 鳴り響く [他動詞] □ *...drivers who do not blast their horns.* 警笛を鳴らさないドライバー ● N-COUNT 可算名詞 **Blast** is also a noun. 大きな音 □ *The buzzer suddenly responded in a long blast of sound.* ブザーは突然大きく長い音をたてた。 **8** N-SING 単数名詞 If you say that something was a **blast**, you mean that you enjoyed it very much. 楽しいひと時 [INFORMAL くだけた] □ *He went sledding with his daughter. "It was a blast," he said later.* 彼は娘とそり滑りに行った。その後で「最高だった」と言った。 **9** PHRASE 句 If something such as a radio or a heater is on **full blast**, or on **at full blast**, it is producing as much sound or power as it is able to. 全力で □ *In many of those homes the television is on full blast 24 hours a day.* それらの家庭の多くでは、1日24時間テレビが音量いっぱいでつけっぱなしにされている。

▶ **blast off** PHRASAL VERB 句動詞 When a space rocket **blasts off**, it leaves the ground at the start of its journey. 打ち上げる □ *Columbia is set to blast off at 1:20 a.m. Eastern Time tomorrow.* コロンビア号は東部標準時間で明朝1時20分に打ち上げられることになっている。

bla|tant /bléɪtᵊnt/ ADJ 形容詞 You use **blatant** to describe something bad that is done in an open or very obvious way. 露骨な [EMPHASIS 強調] □ *Outsiders will continue to suffer the most blatant discrimination.* 外国人は極めて露骨な差別を受け続けるだろう。 □ *...a blatant attempt to spread the blame for the fiasco.* 大失敗の責任を他者多数に転嫁しようとするあからさまな企て ● **bla|tant|ly** ADV 副詞 露骨に □ *...a blatantly sexist question.* 性差別まるだしの質問

bla|tant|ly /bléɪtᵊntli/ ADV 副詞 **Blatantly** is used to add emphasis when you are describing states or situations that you think are bad. はなはだしく [EMPHASIS 強調] □ *It became blatantly obvious to me that the band wasn't going to last.* 私にとって、バンドが長く続かないことはもはや疑う余地がなくなった。 □ *For years, blatantly false assertions have gone unchallenged.* 何年もの間、まぎれもなく誤った主張が通ってきた。

blaze /bléɪz/ (**blazes, blazing, blazed**) **1** V-I 自動詞 When a fire **blazes**, it burns strongly and brightly. 燃え立つ □ *Three people died as wreckage blazed, and rescuers fought to release trapped drivers.* 残骸が炎上して3人が死亡、救助隊は閉じ込められた運転者の救出のため奮闘した。 □ *The log fire was blazing merrily.* 暖炉はパチパチと盛んに燃えていた。 **2** N-COUNT 可算名詞 A **blaze** is a large fire which is difficult to control and which destroys a lot of things. 火炎 [JOURNALISM ジャーナリズム] □ *Some 4,000 firefighters are battling the blaze.* およそ4千人の消防士が燃え広がる火炎と戦っている。 **3** V-I 自動詞 If something **blazes with** light or color, it is extremely bright. 輝く [LITERARY 文語的] □ *The gardens blazed with color.* 庭は色彩に輝いた。 ● N-COUNT 可算名詞 **Blaze** is also a noun. 強い輝き □ *I wanted the front garden to be a blaze of color.* 前庭を燃え立つような色彩で飾りたかった。 **4** N-SING 単数名詞 A **blaze of** publicity or attention is a great amount of it. 激発 □ *He was arrested in a blaze of publicity.* 彼は誰もが多大な好奇心をそそぐ中で逮捕された。 **5** V-I 自動詞 If guns **blaze**, or **blaze away**, they fire continuously, making a lot of noise. 連射する □ *Guns were blazing, flares going up and the sky was lit up all around.* 銃がどんどん発射されると、閃（せん）光が燃え上がり、空全体が明るくなった。 **6** with all guns blazing → see **gun**

blaz|er /bléɪzər/ (**blazers**) N-COUNT 可算名詞 A **blazer** is a kind of light jacket for men or women that is also often worn by members of a particular group. ブレザー

blaz|ing /bléɪzɪŋ/ ADJ 形容詞 The **blazing** sun or **blazing hot** weather is very hot. 燃えるような [ADJ n] □ *Quite a few people were eating outside in the blazing sun.* 炎天下の戸外で食事する人はわずかだった。

bleach /blíːtʃ/ (**bleaches, bleaching, bleached**) **1** V-T 他動詞 If you **bleach** something, you use a chemical to make it white or pale in color. 漂白する □ *These products don't bleach the hair.* これらの製品は髪を漂白しない。 □ *...bleached pine tables.* 脱色された松のテーブル **2** V-T/V-I 他動詞/自動詞 If the sun **bleaches** something, or something **bleaches**, its color gets paler until it is almost white. 白くする [他動詞] 白くなる [自動詞] □ *The tree's roots are stripped and hung to season and bleach.* 木の根っこは皮をむいたあと、乾燥し白くなるようつるす。 □ *He has hair which is naturally black but which has been bleached by the sun.* 彼の髪はもともと黒だが、日にさらされて色が薄くなっている。 **3** N-MASS 質量名詞 **Bleach** is a chemical that is used to make cloth white, or to clean things thoroughly and kill germs. 漂白剤

bleak /blíːk/ (**bleaker, bleakest**) **1** ADJ 形容詞 If a situation is **bleak**, it is bad, and seems unlikely to improve. （将来の見通しなどが）厳しい □ *The immediate outlook remains bleak.* 短期見通しは暗い。 ● **bleak|ness** N-UNCOUNT 不可算名詞 荒涼としていること □ *The continued bleakness of the American job market was blamed.* 米国で厳しい雇用状況が続いていることが原因とされた。 **2** ADJ 形容詞 If you describe a place as **bleak**, you mean that it looks cold, empty, and unattractive. 荒涼たる □ *The island's pretty bleak.* その島はかなり寒々としている。 **3** ADJ 形容詞 When the weather is **bleak**, it is cold, dull, and unpleasant. 寒冷な □ *The weather can be quite bleak on the coast.* 沿岸の天候は非常に寒冷になる。 **4** ADJ 形容詞 If someone looks or sounds **bleak**, they look or sound depressed, as if they have no hope or energy. 打ち沈んだ □ *His face was bleak.* 彼は陰気な顔をしていた。 ● **bleak|ly** ADV 副詞 陰気に □ *"There is nothing left," she says bleakly.* 「もう何も残っていない」と彼女は悲しそうに言った。

bleed /blíːd/ (**bleeds, bleeding, bled**) **1** V-I 自動詞 When you **bleed**, you lose blood from your body as a result of injury or illness. 出血する □ *His head had struck the sink and was bleeding.* 彼は流しに頭をぶつけて血を流していた。 □ *He was bleeding profusely.* 彼は大量に出血していた。 ● **bleed|ing** N-UNCOUNT 不可算名詞 出血 □ *This results in internal bleeding.* これは内出血を起こす。 **2** V-I 自動詞 If the color of one substance **bleeds into** the color of another substance that it is touching, it goes into the other thing so that its color changes in an undesirable way. 浸出する □ *The coloring pigments from the skins are not allowed to bleed into the grape juice.* 皮の色素がグレープジュースに混じってはならない。 **3** V-T 他動詞 If someone **is being bled**, money or other resources are gradually being taken away from them. （金品などを）搾り取る [DISAPPROVAL 不賛成] □ *We have been gradually bled for twelve years.* 私たちは12年間少しずつ搾り取られた。

blem|ish /blémɪʃ/ (**blemishes, blemishing, blemished**) **1** N-COUNT 可算名詞 A **blemish** is a small mark on something that spoils its appearance. きず □ *Every piece is closely scrutinized, and if there is the slightest blemish on it, it is rejected.* 各部品は厳重に検査され、少しでもきずがあれば不合格となる。 **2** N-COUNT 可算名詞 A **blemish on** something is a small fault in it. 欠点 □ *This is the one blemish on an otherwise resounding success.* 欠点が1つあることを除けば大成功だ。 **3** V-T 他動詞 If something **blemishes** someone's character or reputation, it spoils it or makes it seem less good than it was in the past. 傷つける □ *He wasn't about to blemish that pristine record.* 彼は、完全無欠な記録に傷をつけるつもりはまったくなかった。

blend /blénd/ (**blends, blending, blended**) **1** V-RECIP 相互動詞 If you **blend** substances together or if they **blend**, you mix them together so that they become one substance. 混ぜる □ *Blend the butter with the sugar and beat until light and creamy.* バターと砂糖を混ぜ合わせ、ふわっとクリーム状になるまで泡立てる。 □ *Blend the ingredients until you have a smooth cream.* 滑らかなクリームになるまで材料を混ぜ合わせる。 **2** N-COUNT 可算名詞 A **blend of** things is a mixture or combination of them that is useful or pleasant. 融合 □ *The public areas offer a subtle blend of traditional charm with modern amenities.* 公共エリアは伝統的な魅力と現代的な快適を融合している。 □ *...a blend of wine and sparkling water.* ワインとソーダ水のミックス **3** V-RECIP 相互動詞 When colors, sounds, or styles **blend**, they come together or are combined in a pleasing way. 融合する □ *You could paint the walls and ceilings the same color so they blend together.* 壁と天井が調和するように、同じ色で塗ったらどうだね。 **4** V-T 他動

詞 If you **blend** ideas, policies, or styles, you use them together in order to achieve something. 融合する □ *His vision is to blend Christianity with "the wisdom of all world religions."* 彼の構想はキリスト教と『世界の全宗教の知恵』を融合させることである.

bless /blɛs/ (**blesses, blessing, blessed**) **1** V-T 他動詞 When someone such as a priest **blesses** people or things, he or she asks for God's favor and protection for them. 神の恩恵を祈る □ *...asking for all present to bless this couple and their loving commitment to one another.* ご同席の方々全員が, この夫婦のお互いに対する愛と貞節を祝福してくださるようお願いします. **2** CONVENTION 慣習表現 **Bless** is used in expressions such as "God bless" or "bless you" to express affection, thanks, or good wishes. ありがたい [INFORMAL, SPOKEN くだけた, 口語, FEELINGS 感情] □ *"Bless you, Eva," he whispered.* 「くしゃみに福あり」と彼はささやいた. **3** CONVENTION 慣習表現 You can say "**bless you**" to someone who has just sneezed. くしゃみに福あり [SPOKEN 口語, FORMULAE 決まり文句] **4** → see also **blessed, blessing**

bless|ed

> Pronounced /blɛst/ for meaning **1**, and /blɛsɪd/ for meaning **2**.
>
> **1** の意味では /blɛst/ と, **2** の意味では /blɛsɪd/ と発音される.

1 ADJ 形容詞 If someone is **blessed with** a particular good quality or skill, they have that good quality or skill. に恵まれる [v-link ADJ 'with' n] □ *Both are blessed with an uncommon ability to fix things.* 二人とも並外れた調整能力に恵まれている. **2** ADJ 形容詞 You use **blessed** to describe something that you think is wonderful, and that you are grateful for or relieved about. 喜ばしい [APPROVAL 賛成] [ADJ n] □ *The birth of a live healthy baby is a truly blessed event.* 赤ちゃんが元気で無事に生まれるのは本当に喜ばしいことだ. ●**bless|ed|ly** ADV 副詞 幸いにも □ *...a wall still blessedly warm from the day's sun.* 日中晴れていたため幸いにも壁はまだ温かい. **3** → see also **bless**

bless|ing /blɛsɪŋ/ (**blessings**) **1** N-COUNT 可算名詞 A **blessing** is something good that you are grateful for. ありがたいもの □ *Rivers are a blessing for an agricultural country.* 農業国にとって川は天からの恵みである. **2** N-COUNT 可算名詞 If something is done with someone's **blessing**, it is done with their approval and support. 承認 [with poss] □ *With the blessing of the White House, a group of Democrats in Congress is meeting to find additional budget cuts.* 政府の支持を得て, 民主党下院議員団は追加の予算削減のため会合を開いている. **3** N-COUNT 可算名詞 A **blessing** is a prayer asking God to look kindly upon the people who are present or the event that is taking place. 神への祈り □ *The Reverend Chris Long led the prayers and pronounced the blessing.* クリス・ロング牧師は祈とうを行い祈りの言葉を唱えた. **4** → see also **bless**

blew /blu/ **Blew** is the past tense of **blow**. blow の過去形

blight /blaɪt/ (**blights, blighting, blighted**) **1** N-VAR 可変名詞 You can refer to something as a **blight** when it causes great difficulties, and damages or spoils other things. 傷つけるもの □ *This discriminatory policy has made been a blight on America.* この差別的な政策がアメリカに暗い影を落としてきた. **2** V-T 他動詞 If something **blights** your life or your hopes, it damages and spoils them. If something **blights** an area, it spoils it and makes it unattractive. 損なう [他動詞] □ *An embarrassing blunder nearly blighted his career before it got off the ground.* 一度の大失敗で彼はこれからというときにキャリアを台無しにするところだった. □ *...thousands of families whose lives were blighted by unemployment.* 失業で生活が困窮した何千もの家庭. **3** N-UNCOUNT 不可算名詞 **Blight** is a disease which makes plants dry up and die. 胴枯れ病, 葉枯れ病 □ *All you can do to prevent potato blight is keep an eye on your crops.* ジャガイモの葉枯れ病を防ぐには注意深く観察するしかない.

blind /blaɪnd/ (**blinds, blinding, blinded**) **1** ADJ 形容詞 Someone who is **blind** is unable to see because their eyes are damaged. 目の見えない □ *I started helping him run the business when he went blind.* 私が彼の事業を手伝いだしたのは彼が視力を失ったときだった. ●N-PLURAL 複数名詞 **The blind** are people who are blind. 目の不自由な人 □ *He was a teacher of the blind.* 彼は盲学校の教師だ. ●**blind|ness** N-UNCOUNT 不可算名詞 失明 □ *Early diagnosis and treatment can usually prevent blindness.* 失明は通常, 早期の診断と治療で防げる. **2** V-T 他動詞 If something **blinds** you, it makes you unable to see, either for a short time or permanently. 目を見えなくする [他動詞] □ *The sun hit the windshield, momentarily blinding him.* フロントガラスがまぶしくて, 彼は一瞬目が見えなくなった. **3** ADJ 形容詞 [v-link ADJ, usu ADJ 'with' n] If you are **blind with** something such as tears or a bright light, you are unable to see for a short time because of the tears or light. で目が見えない □ *Her mother groped for the back of the chair, her eyes blind with tears.* 彼女の母は涙で見えなくなっていすの背もたれをまさぐった. ●**blind|ly** ADV 副詞 手探りで □ *Lettie groped blindly for the glass.* レティーは手探りでグラスを捜した. **4** ADJ 形容詞 [v-link ADJ 'to' n] If you say that someone is **blind to** a fact or a situation, you mean that they ignore it or are unaware of it, although you

think that they should take notice of it or be aware of it. が見えていない [DISAPPROVAL 不賛成] □ *David's good looks and impeccable manners had always made her blind to his faults.* デイビッドはハンサムで身のこなしもよく, 彼女はずっと彼の欠点が目に入らなかった. ●**blind|ness** N-UNCOUNT 不可算名詞 気づかないこと □ *...blindness in government policy to the very existence of the unemployed.* 失業者の存在そのものを視野に入れていない政策. **5** V-T 他動詞 If something **blinds** you to the real situation, it prevents you from realizing that it exists or from understanding it properly. 見えなくさせる [他動詞] □ *He never allowed his love of Australia to blind him to his countrymen's faults.* 彼はオーストラリアを愛しているからといって同国人の欠点に目をつぶることはなかった. **6** ADJ 形容詞 You can describe someone's beliefs or actions as **blind** when you think that they seem to take no notice of important facts or behave in an unreasonable way. 盲目的な [DISAPPROVAL 不賛成] □ *...her blind faith in the wisdom of the church.* 彼女の教会からの知識への盲目的な信心. **7** N-COUNT 可算名詞 A **blind** is a roll of cloth or paper which you can pull down over a window as a covering. ブラインド □ *Pulling the blinds up, she let some of the bright sunlight in.* 彼女はブラインドを上げ, 明るい日ざしが入るようにした. **8** → see also **blinding, blindly** **9** PHRASE 句 If you say that someone is **turning a blind eye to** something bad or illegal that is happening, you mean that you think that they are pretending not to notice that it is happening so that they will not have to do anything about it. 見て見ぬふりをする [DISAPPROVAL 不賛成] □ *Teachers are turning a blind eye to pupils smoking at school, a report reveals today.* 教師は生徒の喫煙を黙認する傾向にあるとの調査結果が今日発表された.

→ see **disability**

<table>
<tr><td colspan="2">**Word Partnership** blind は次の語句と使われる:</td></tr>
<tr><td>ADJ.</td><td>blind **and deaf** **1**</td></tr>
<tr><td>ADV.</td><td>**legally** blind, **partially** blind **1**</td></tr>
<tr><td>N.</td><td>blind **person** **1**
blind **faith** **6**</td></tr>
</table>

blind|fold /blaɪndfoʊld/ (**blindfolds, blindfolding, blindfolded**) **1** N-COUNT 可算名詞 A **blindfold** is a strip of cloth that is tied over someone's eyes so that they cannot see. 目隠し **2** V-T 他動詞 If you **blindfold** someone, you tie a blindfold over their eyes. 目隠しをする [他動詞] □ *His abductors blindfolded him and drove him to an apartment in southern Beirut.* 誘拐犯は彼に目隠しをして車でベイルート南部のアパートに連れて行った.

blind|ing /blaɪndɪŋ/ **1** ADJ 形容詞 A **blinding** light is extremely bright. まばゆい □ *The doctor worked busily beneath the blinding lights of the delivery room.* 医師は分娩室のまばゆいライトの下で忙しく立ち働いた. **2** ADJ 形容詞 You use **blinding** to emphasize that something is very obvious. きわめて明らかな [EMPHASIS 強調] [ADJ n] □ *The miseries I went through made me suddenly realize with a blinding flash what life was all about.* 不幸な経験を重ね, 人生とは何かを突然悟った. **3** ADJ 形容詞 **Blinding** pain is very strong pain. (痛みが) 非常に強い □ *There was a pain then, a quick, blinding agony that jumped down Danlo's spine.* 一度痛みを感じた後, 目のくらむような苦痛がさっとダンロの背中を走った.

blind|ly /blaɪndli/ **1** ADV 副詞 If you say that someone does something **blindly**, you mean that they do it without having enough information, or without thinking about it. よく考えずに [DISAPPROVAL 不賛成] □ *Don't just blindly follow what the banker says.* 銀行の言うことをうのみにしてはいけない. □ *Without adequate information, many students choose a college almost blindly.* 多くの学生は十分な情報を持たずに短絡的に大学を選ぶ. **2** → see also **blind**

blind trust (**blind trusts**) N-COUNT 可算名詞 A **blind trust** is a financial arrangement in which someone's investments are managed without the person knowing where the money is invested. **Blind trusts** are used especially by people in public office, so that they cannot be accused of using their position to make money unfairly. 資産を第三者に委託する制度. 特に公職につく人が不正の疑いを受けないよう利用する. □ *Yang transferred the shares into a blind trust earlier this week.* 今週, ヤンは株式をブラインド・トラストに移した. [BUSINESS 実業]

bling /blɪŋ/ also **bling-bling** N-UNCOUNT Some people refer to expensive or fancy jewelry or clothes as **bling** or **bling-bling**. 派手なアクセサリー [INFORMAL] □ *Big-name jewelers are battling it out to get celebrities to wear their bling.* 有名な宝石商は有名人に自分たちのアクセサリーを着けてもらおうとしのぎを削っている. □ *...gangsta rap's love of bling-bling.* 不良ラッパーの派手なアクセサリー好き.

blink /blɪŋk/ (**blinks, blinking, blinked**) **1** V-T/V-I 他動詞/自動詞 When you **blink** or when you **blink** your eyes, you shut your eyes and very quickly open them again. 目をしばたたく [他動詞], まばたきする [自動詞] □ *Kathryn blinked and forced a smile.* キャサリンは目をしばたたいて, 作り笑いをした. □ *She was blinking her eyes rapidly.* 彼女はすばやく瞬きを繰り返した. ●N-COUNT 可算名詞 **Blink** is also a noun. まばたき □ *He kept giving quick blinks.* かれは短くまばたきをして合図し続けた. **2** V-I 自動詞 When a light **blinks**, it flashes on and off. 点滅する [自動詞] □ *Green and yellow lights blinked on the*

surface of the harbor. 入り江の水面には黄色と緑のライトがキラキラ と反射していた. ❏ *The plane was flying normally for about 15 minutes before a warning light blinked on.* 飛行機は警告灯が点灯するまで約15分間は正常に飛行していた.

bliss /blɪs/ N-UNCOUNT 不可算名詞 **Bliss** is a state of complete happiness. 至福 ❏ *It was a scene of such domestic bliss.* それはまさに幸福な家庭の光景だった.

bliss|ful /blɪsfəl/ **1** ADJ 形容詞 A **blissful** situation or period of time is one in which you are extremely happy. とても幸福な ❏ *We spent a blissful week together.* 私たちはとても幸せな1週間を一緒にすごした. ● **bliss|ful|ly** /blɪsfəli/ ADV 副詞 とても幸福に ❏ *We're blissfully happy.* 私たちは最高に幸せです. **2** ADJ 形容詞 [ADJ n] If someone is in **blissful** ignorance of something unpleasant or serious, they are totally unaware of it. 幸いーを知らない ❏ *Many country towns were still living in blissful ignorance of the post-war crime wave.* 多くの田舎町は幸いにも戦後の急増する犯罪とは無縁のままであった. ● **bliss|ful|ly** ADV 副詞 幸いーを知らないで ❏ *At first, he was blissfully unaware of the conspiracy against him.* 彼は, 当初おめでたいことに自分への陰謀に気づいていなかった.

blis|ter /blɪstər/ (blisters, blistering, blistered) **1** N-COUNT 可算名詞 A **blister** is a painful swelling on the surface of your skin. Blisters contain a clear liquid and are usually caused by heat or by something repeatedly rubbing your skin. 水ぶくれ **2** V-T/V-I 他動詞/自動詞 When your skin **blisters** or when something **blisters** it, blisters appear on it. 水ぶくれにする [他動詞], 水ぶくれになる [自動詞] ❏ *The affected skin turns red and may blister.* 罹(り)患した皮膚は赤くなり, 水疱ができる可能性もある. ❏ *The sap of this plant blisters the skin.* この植物の樹液に触れると水疱ができる.

blis|ter|ing /blɪstərɪŋ/ **1** ADJ 形容詞 **Blistering** heat is very great heat. 焼けつくように熱い ❏ *...a blistering summer day.* 焼けつくような夏の日. **2** ADJ 形容詞 A **blistering** remark expresses great anger or dislike. 辛らつな ❏ *The president responded to this with a blistering attack on his critics.* 大統領は自分への批判に辛らつな言葉で応酬した. **3** ADJ 形容詞 **Blistering** is used to describe actions in sports to emphasize that they are done with great speed or force. 猛烈な [JOURNALISM ジャーナリズム, EMPHASIS 強調] [ADJ n] ❏ *Sharon Wild set a blistering pace to take the lead.* シャロン・ワイルドはリードを奪おうと猛烈にペースを上げた.

blithe /blaɪð/ ADJ 形容詞 You use **blithe** to indicate that something is done casually, without serious or careful thought. 軽率な [DISAPPROVAL 不賛成] ❏ *Acts of trespass and petty theft often grew out of the blithe disregard that boys had for private property.* 少年たちが私有地に軽率に入っているうちに不法侵入やこそ泥を働くようになることが多い. ● **blithe|ly** ADV 副詞 軽率に ❏ *Your editorial blithely ignores the hard facts.* 貴殿の社説は不注意にも事実を把握していない.

blitz /blɪts/ (blitzes, blitzing, blitzed) **1** N-COUNT 可算名詞 If you have a **blitz on** something, you make a big effort to deal with it or to improve it. 多大な努力 [INFORMAL くだけた] ❏ *Regional accents are still acceptable but there is to be a blitz on incorrect grammar.* なまりはまだ許されますが, 誤った文法は努力して直すべきです. **2** N-PROPER 固有名詞 The heavy bombing of British cities by German aircraft in 1940 and 1941 is referred to as **the Blitz**. (ドイツ空軍による1940～41年の) 英国大空襲 **3** V-T 他動詞 If a city or building **is blitzed** during a war, it is attacked by bombs dropped by enemy aircraft. 空襲する [他動詞] ❏ *In the autumn of 1940 London was blitzed by an average of two hundred aircraft a night.* 1940年秋, ロンドンは一晩に平均200機の空襲を受けた.

bliz|zard /blɪzərd/ (blizzards) N-COUNT 可算名詞 A **blizzard** is a very bad snowstorm with strong winds. 猛吹雪
→ see **storm, weather**

bloat|ed /bloʊtɪd/ **1** ADJ 形容詞 If someone's body or a part of their body is **bloated**, it is much larger than normal, usually because it has a lot of liquid or gas inside it. ふくれた ❏ *...the bloated body of a dead bullock.* 去勢牛のふくれた死体. **2** ADJ 形容詞 If you feel **bloated** after eating a large meal, you feel very full and uncomfortable. 食べ過ぎでくるしい [v-link ADJ] ❏ *Diners do not want to leave the table feeling bloated.* 食事客は, 席を立つとき苦しくなるまで食べようとは思わない.

blob /blɒb/ (blobs) **1** N-COUNT 可算名詞 A **blob of** thick or sticky liquid is a small, often round, amount of it. (どろっとした液体の) 小さな塊 [INFORMAL くだけた] ❏ *...a blob of chocolate mousse.* チョコムースの小さな塊. **2** N-COUNT 可算名詞 You can use **blob** to refer to something that you cannot see very clearly, for example because it is in the distance. おぼろげなもの [INFORMAL くだけた] ❏ *You could just see vague blobs of faces.* 人々の顔がおぼろげに見えるでしょう.

bloc /blɒk/ (blocs) N-COUNT 可算名詞 A **bloc** is a group of countries that have similar political aims and interests and that act together over some issues. 連合, 一圏 ❏ *...the former Soviet bloc.* 旧ソ連圏.

block /blɒk/ (blocks, blocking, blocked) **1** N-COUNT 可算名詞 A **block of** a substance is a large rectangular piece of it. 直方体 A **block of** a substance is a large rectangular piece of it. 直方

体の塊 ❏ *...a block of ice.* 氷の塊. **2** N-COUNT 可算名詞 A **block of** apartments or offices is a large building containing them. (住居や事務所からなる) ひと棟の建物・ひと棟・白い外壁のアパート棟. **3** N-COUNT 可算名詞 A **block** in a town or city is an area of land with streets on all its sides, or the area or distance between such streets. 街区 ❏ *He walked around the block three times.* 彼はその街区を3回歩いて回った. ❏ *She walked four blocks down High Street.* 彼女はハイ・ストリートを4ブロック歩いた. **4** N-COUNT 可算名詞 **Blocks** are wooden or plastic cubes, such as those used as toys by children. (おもちゃの) ブロック **5** V-T 他動詞 To **block** a road, channel, or pipe means to put an object across it or in it so that nothing can pass through it or along it. ふさぐ ❏ *Some students today blocked a highway that cuts through the center of the city.* 今日, 学生が町の中央を通るハイウェイを封鎖した. **6** V-T 他動詞 If something **blocks** your view, it prevents you from seeing something because it is between you and that thing. 見えなくする ❏ *...a row of spruce trees that blocked his view of the long north slope of the mountain.* 北側の長い斜面への彼の視界を遮断していたトウヒの並木. **7** V-T 他動詞 If you **block** someone's way, you prevent them from going somewhere or entering a place by standing in front of them. 遮る [他動詞] ❏ *I started to move around him, but he blocked my way.* 私は彼の周りで動き出したが, 彼に遮られた. **8** V-T 他動詞 If you **block** something that is being arranged, you prevent it from being done. 阻止する ❏ *For years the country has tried to block imports of various cheap foreign products.* その国は何年もさまざまな安い外国製品の輸入を阻止してきた. **9** N-COUNT 可算名詞 A **block of** something such as tickets or shares is a large quantity of them, especially when they are all sold at the same time and are in a particular sequence or order. ひとまとめ [usu N 'of' n] ❏ *Those booking a block of seats get them at reduced rates.* 座席をまとめて予約すると割引を受けられる. **10** N-COUNT 可算名詞 If you have a **mental block** or a **block**, you are temporarily unable to do something that you can normally do which involves using, thinking about, or remembering something. 思考停止 ❏ *I cannot do math. I've got a mental block about it.* 数学ができないよ. 頭がとまっちゃうんだ. **11** → see also **stumbling block**

▸ **block out** **1** PHRASAL VERB 句動詞 If someone **blocks out** a thought, they try not to think about it. 考えないようにする ❏ *She accuses me of having blocked out the past.* 過去を顧みなかったことで彼女は私を責めた. **2** PHRASAL VERB 句動詞 Something that **blocks out** light prevents it from reaching a place. 遮光する ❏ *He pulled down the shades, blocking out the bright sunlight.* 彼はまぶしい光を遮ろうと日よけを下ろした.

block|ade /blɒkeɪd/ (blockades, blockading, blockaded) **1** N-COUNT 可算名詞 A **blockade** of a place is an action that is taken to prevent goods or people from entering or leaving it. 封鎖 ❏ *It's not yet clear who will actually enforce the blockade.* だれが封鎖を実施するのかはまだ明らかでない. **2** V-T 他動詞 If a group of people **blockade** a place, they stop goods or people from reaching that place. If they **blockade** a road or a port, they stop people from using that road or port. 封鎖する ❏ *About 50,000 people are trapped in the town, which has been blockaded for more than 40 days.* 40日以上封鎖が続き, 町にはまだ約5万人が閉じ込められています.

block|age /blɒkɪdʒ/ (blockages) N-COUNT 可算名詞 A **blockage** in a pipe, tube, or tunnel is an object which blocks it, or the state of being blocked. 障害物 ❏ *The logical treatment is to remove this blockage.* 合理的な処置はこの障害物を除去することだ.

block|bust|er /blɒkbʌstər/ (blockbusters) N-COUNT 可算名詞 A **blockbuster** is a movie or book that is very popular and successful, usually because it is very exciting. 大ヒット [INFORMAL くだけた] ❏ *...the latest Hollywood blockbuster.* ハリウッドの最新大ヒット作品.

blog /blɒg/ (blogs) N-COUNT A **blog** is a website containing a diary or journal on a particular subject. ブログ [COMPUTING] ❏ *When Barbieux started his blog, his aspirations were small; he simply hoped to communicate with a few people.* バービオがブログを始めた時, 大きな目標は持っていなかった. 何人かの人とやり取りできればと思っただけだった. ● **blog|ger** N-COUNT (bloggers ❏ *While most bloggers comment on news reported elsewhere, some do their own reporting.* 大半のブロガーは他で報告されたニュースにコメントをするが, 中には独自のレポートをする者もある. ● **blog|ging** N-UNCOUNT ❏ *...the explosion in the popularity of blogging.* ブログの人気爆発
→ see Word Web: **blog**

blogo|sphere /blɒgəsfɪər/ also **blogsphere** /blɒgsfɪər/ N-SING In computer technology, **the blogosphere** or **the blogsphere** is all the weblogs on the Internet, considered collectively. ブロゴスフィア (すべてのブログとそのつながりを総称する) ❏ *Consequently, even as the blogosphere continues to expand, only a few blogs are likely to emerge as focal points.* その結果, ブログ同士のネットワークは拡大し続けるが, その中心となるものはほんの少数となるだろう. ['the' n] ❏ *The blogsphere has changed a lot in the past few years.* ここ数年, ブログ同士のつながりは大きく変化した.

Word Web   blog

The word **blog** is a combination of the words **web** and **log**. It is a **website** containing a series of dated **entries**. A blog can focus on a single subject of interest. Most blogs are written by individuals. But sometimes a political committee, corporation, or other group maintains a blog. Many blogs invite readers to leave comments on the site. This often results in a community of **bloggers** who write back and forth to each other. The total group of web logs is the **blogosphere**. A blogstorm occurs when there is a lot of blog activity on a certain topic.

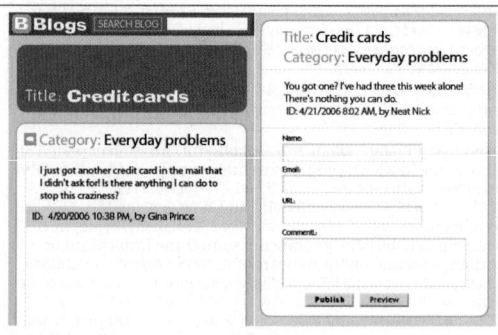

blonde /blɒnd/ (blondes, blonder, blondest)

The form **blonde** is usually used to refer to women, and **blond** to refer to men.

blonde 形は通常女性を指すのに使われ, **blond** が男性を指すのに使われる.

■ COLOR 色彩語 A woman who has **blonde** hair has pale-colored hair. Blonde hair can be very light brown or light yellow. The form **blond** is used when describing men. ブロンド色の □...*a little girl with blonde hair.* 金髪の少女. ■ ADJ 形容詞 Someone who is **blonde** has blonde hair. 金髪の □ *He was blonder than his brother.* 彼は弟より明るい金髪をしていた. ■ N-COUNT 可算名詞 A **blonde** is a woman who has blonde hair. 金髪の女性 □...*a stunning blonde in her early thirties.* 30代前半の金髪美女.

blood /blʌd/ ■ N-UNCOUNT 不可算名詞 **Blood** is the red liquid that flows inside your body, which you can see if you cut yourself. 血液 □ *His shirt was covered in blood.* 彼のシャツは血だらけだった. ■ N-UNCOUNT 不可算名詞 You can use **blood** to refer to the race or social class of someone's parents or ancestors. 血筋 □ *There was Greek blood in his veins: his ancestors originally bore the name Karajannis.* 彼にはギリシャ人の血が流れていた. 先祖が元はカラヤニスという名前だった. ■ N-COUNT 可算名詞 If you say that there is **bad blood between** people, you mean that they have argued about something and dislike each other. 敵意 □ *There is, it seems, some bad blood between Mills and the Baldwins.* ミルズ家とボールドウィン家はお互いに敵意を持っているようだ. ■ PHRASE 句 If something violent and cruel is done in **cold blood**, it is done deliberately and in an unemotional way. 冷酷に [DISAPPROVAL 不賛成] □ *The crime had been committed in cold blood.* 犯行手口は冷酷なものだった. ■ → see also **cold-blooded** ■ PHRASE 句 If you say that someone has a person's **blood** on their **hands**, you mean that they are responsible for that person's death. ~の死に責任がある □ *He has my son's blood on his hands. I hope it haunts him for the rest of his days.* 私の息子が死んだのは彼のせいだ. そのことを生涯悔やむがよい. ■ PHRASE 句 If a quality or talent is in your **blood**, it is part of your nature, and other members of your family have it too. 親譲りの □ *Diplomacy was in his blood: his ancestors were feudal lords.* 彼の外交手腕は親譲りだった. 彼の祖先は代々領主だったのだ. ■ PHRASE 句 You can use the expressions **new blood, fresh blood**, or **young blood** to refer to people who are brought into an organization to improve it by thinking of new ideas or new ways of doing things. 新勢力 □ *There's been a major reshuffle of the cabinet to bring in new blood.* 新風を吹き込むため内閣大改造が行われた. ■ **flesh and blood →** see **flesh** ⯑ **own flesh and blood →** see **flesh**
→ see **donor**

Word Partnership   *blood* は次の語句と使われる:

N.	(red/white) blood **cells**, blood **clot**, blood **disease**, blood **loss**, **pool of** blood, blood **sample**, blood **stream**, blood **supply**, blood **test**, blood **transfusion** ■
V.	**donate/give** blood ■
ADJ.	**covered in** blood, blood **stained** ■ **related by** blood ■ **bad** blood ■
PREP.	**in** *someone's* blood ■ ■

blood pres|sure N-UNCOUNT 不可算名詞 Your **blood pressure** is the amount of force with which your blood flows around your body. 血圧 □ *Your doctor will monitor your blood pressure.* 先生があとで血圧を測りますよ.
→ see **diagnosis**

blood|shed /blʌdʃed/ N-UNCOUNT 不可算名詞 **Bloodshed** is violence in which people are killed or wounded. 流血の惨事 □ *The government must increase the pace of reforms to avoid further bloodshed.* 政府はこれ以上の流血の惨事を防ぐため改革スピードをあげる必要がある.

blood|stream /blʌdstrim/ (bloodstreams) N-COUNT 可算名詞 Your **bloodstream** is the blood that flows around your body. 血流 □ *The disease releases toxins into the bloodstream.* その病気では血中に毒素が放出される.

blood test (blood tests) N-COUNT 可算名詞 A **blood test** is a medical examination of a small amount of your blood. 血液検査

blood ves|sel (blood vessels) N-COUNT 可算名詞 **Blood vessels** are the narrow tubes through which your blood flows. 血管

bloody /blʌdi/ (bloodier, bloodiest, bloodies, bloodying, bloodied) ■ ADJ 形容詞 If you describe a situation or event as **bloody**, you mean that it is very violent and a lot of people are killed. 血なまぐさい □ *Forty-three demonstrators were killed in bloody clashes.* デモ参加者43人が血なまぐさい衝突で死亡した. ■ ADJ 形容詞 You can describe something or someone as **bloody** if they are covered in a lot of blood. 血まみれの □ *He was arrested last October still carrying a bloody knife.* 彼はまだ血だらけのナイフを持ったまま, 10月に逮捕された. ■ V-T 他動詞 If you have **bloodied** part of your body, there is blood on it, usually because you have had an accident or you have been attacked. 出血させる □ *One of our children fell and bloodied his knee.* 子供の1人が転倒し, ひざから出血した.

bloom /blum/ (blooms, blooming, bloomed) ■ N-COUNT 可算名詞 A **bloom** is the flower on a plant. 花 [LITERARY 文語的の] □ *The sweet fragrance of the white blooms makes this climber a favorite.* このツル植物は白い花の甘い香りで人気がある. ■ PHRASE 句 A plant or tree that is **in bloom** has flowers on it. 開花している □...*a pink climbing rose in full bloom.* ピンクに咲くつるバラ. ■ V-I 自動詞 When a plant or tree **blooms**, it produces flowers. When a flower **blooms**, it opens. 開花する □ *This plant blooms between May and June.* この植物は5月から6月に開花する. ■ V-I 自動詞 If someone or something **blooms**, they develop good, attractive, or successful qualities. 栄える □ *Not many economies bloomed in 1990, least of all gold exporters like Australia.* 1990年に繁栄していた経済は多くなかった. 特にオーストラリアのような金輸出国はすべて不振だった. ■ N-UNCOUNT 不可算名詞 If something such as someone's skin has a **bloom**, it has a fresh and healthy appearance. (ほおや肌の) 健康な色つや [also 'a' N] □ *The skin loses its youthful bloom.* その肌は若々しいつやを失う.

blos|som /blɒsəm/ (blossoms, blossoming, blossomed) ■ N-VAR 可変性名詞 **Blossom** is the flowers that appear on a tree before the fruit. 花 □ *The cherry blossom came out early in Washington this year.* 今年は, ワシントンの桜の開花は早かった. ■ V-I 自動詞 If someone or something **blossoms**, they develop good, attractive, or successful qualities. (比ゆ的に) 花開く □ *Why do some people take longer than others to blossom?* なぜ遅咲きの人がいるのだろう. □ *What began as a local festival has blossomed into an international event.* 地方のお祭りが国際イベントに発展した. ■ V-I 自動詞 When a tree **blossoms**, it produces blossom. 花を咲かせる □ *Rain begins to fall and peach trees blossom.* 雨が降り始め, 桃の花が咲く.

blot /blɒt/ (blots, blotting, blotted) ■ N-COUNT 可算名詞 If something is a **blot on** a person's or thing's reputation, it spoils their reputation. 汚点 □...*a blot on the reputation of the architectural profession.* 建築家という職業の評判を汚す汚点. ■ N-COUNT 可算名詞 A **blot** is a drop of liquid that has fallen on to a surface and has dried. しみ □...*an ink blot.* インクのしみ. ■ V-T 他動詞 If you **blot** a surface, you remove liquid from it by pressing a piece of soft paper or cloth onto it. 吸い取る [他動詞] □ *Before applying makeup, blot the face with a tissue to remove any excess oils.* メークをする前に顔にティッシュをおしつけて余分な油を吸い取る.

▶ **blot out** ■ PHRASAL VERB 句動詞 If one thing **blots out** another thing, it is in front of the other thing and prevents it from being seen. 覆い隠す □ *About the time the three climbers were halfway down, clouds blotted out the sun.* 3人が半分くらい下山したところで, 雲が

太陽を覆い隠した。 **2** PHRASAL VERB 句動詞 If you try to **blot out** a memory, you try to forget it. If one thought or memory **blots out** other thoughts or memories, it becomes the only one that you can think about. （記憶などを）消し去る □*Are you saying that she's trying to blot out all memory of the incident?* 彼女がその記憶をすべて消し去ろうとしているっていうのかい。 □*The boy has gaps in his mind about it. He is blotting certain things out.* 少年の記憶には空白部分がある。何かを忘却しているようだ。

blotch /blɒtʃ/ (**blotches**) N-COUNT 可算名詞 A **blotch** is a small unpleasant-looking area of color, for example, on someone's skin. しみ □*His face was covered in red blotches, seemingly a nasty case of acne.* 彼は顔中に赤いしみがある。おそらくたちの悪いにきびだろう。

blouse /blaʊs/ (**blouses**) N-COUNT 可算名詞 A **blouse** is a kind of shirt worn by a girl or woman. ブラウス
→ see **clothing**

blow

❶ VERB USES
❷ NOUN USES

❶ blow /bloʊ/ (**blows, blowing, blew, blown**)
⇨ Please look at category **12** to see if the expression you are looking for is shown under another headword. **1** V-I 自動詞 When a wind or breeze **blows**, the air moves. 吹く □*A chill wind blew at the top of the hill.* 丘の上では冷たい風が吹いていた。 **2** V-T/V-I 他動詞/自動詞 If the wind **blows** something somewhere or if it **blows** there, the wind moves it there. 吹きつける □*The wind blew her hair back from her forehead.* 風が彼女の髪を後ろに吹き流した。 □*Sand blew in our eyes.* 風で砂が目に入った。 **3** V-I 自動詞 If you **blow**, you send out a stream of air from your mouth. 息を吹く □*Danny rubbed his arms and blew on his fingers to warm them.* 彼は腕をこすり、指を暖めようと息を吹きかけた。 **4** V-T 他動詞 If you **blow** something somewhere, you move it by sending out a stream of air from your mouth. 吹き払う □*He picked up his mug and blew off the steam.* 彼はマグカップを持ち上げ、湯気をフーっと吹いた。 **5** V-T 他動詞 If you **blow** bubbles or smoke rings, you make them by blowing air out of your mouth through liquid or smoke. 吹き出してーの形にする □*He blew a ring of blue smoke.* 彼は青い煙の輪を吐き出した。 **6** V-T/V-I 他動詞/自動詞 When a whistle or horn **blows** or someone **blows** it, they make a sound by blowing into it. 吹き鳴らす[他動詞]、鳴る[自動詞] □*The whistle blew and the train slid forward.* 警笛が鳴り、電車は滑らかに前進した。 **7** V-T 他動詞 When you **blow** your nose, you force air out of it through your nostrils in order to clear it. （鼻を）かむ □*He took out a handkerchief and blew his nose.* 彼はハンカチを取り出して鼻をかんだ。 **8** V-T 他動詞 To **blow** something **out, off,** or **away** means to remove or destroy it violently with an explosion. （爆発で）吹き飛ばす □*The can exploded, wrecking the kitchen and bathroom and blowing out windows.* 缶が爆発し、台所と風呂場が壊れ、窓ガラスが吹き飛んだ。 **9** V-T 他動詞 If you **blow** a chance or attempt to do something, you make a mistake which wastes the chance or causes the attempt to fail. ふいにする □*One careless word could blow the whole deal.* 不用意な一言でその取引が台なしになった。 [INFORMAL くだけた] □*Oh you fool! You've blown it!* なんて馬鹿なんだい。ふいにしたぞ。 **10** V-T 他動詞 If you say that something **blows** an event, situation, or argument into a particular extreme state, especially an uncertain or unpleasant state, you mean that it causes it to be in that state. ある状態にする □*Someone took an inappropriate use of words on my part and tried to blow it into a major controversy.* 私の方で誰かが言葉を不適当に使って、大論争を引き起こそうとした。 **11** V-T 他動詞 If you **blow** a large amount of money, you spend it quickly on luxuries. 浪費する □*My brother lent me some money and I went and blew it all.* 兄がお金を貸してくれたが、全部使ってしまった。 [INFORMAL くだけた] **12** → see also **full-blown** **13** to **blow hot and cold** → see **hot** **14** to **blow a kiss** → see **kiss** **15** to **blow the whistle** → see **whistle**
→ see **glass, wind**

▶ **blow away** PHRASAL VERB 句動詞 If you say that you **are blown away** by something, or if it **blows** you **away**, you mean that you are very impressed by it. 圧倒する [INFORMAL くだけた] □*I was blown away by the tone and the quality of the voice.* 私はその物語のトーンと質に圧倒された。 □*Everyone I met overwhelmed me and kind of blew me away.* 出会った人はみんな僕を圧倒してね、ぶっ飛ばされたっていうかね。

▶ **blow off** PHRASAL VERB 句動詞 If you **blow** something **off**, you ignore it or choose not to deal with it. 無視する [AM 米国英語, INFORMAL くだけた] □*I don't think we can afford just to blow this off.* これを無視するわけにはいかないと思うよ。

▶ **blow out** PHRASAL VERB 句動詞 If you **blow out** a flame or a candle, you blow at it so that it stops burning. 吹き消す □*I blew out the candle.* 私はろうそくを吹き消した。

▶ **blow over** PHRASAL VERB 句動詞 If something such as trouble or an argument **blows over**, it ends without any serious consequences. 立ち消える □*Wait, and it'll all blow over.* 待ってよ。

そのうち収まるさ。

▶ **blow up** **1** PHRASAL VERB 句動詞 If someone **blows** something **up** or if it **blows up**, it is destroyed by an explosion. 吹き飛ばす □*He was jailed for 45 years for trying to blow up a plane.* 彼は航空機爆破未遂で45年間投獄された。 **2** PHRASAL VERB 句動詞 If you **blow up** something such as a balloon or a tire, you fill it with air. 膨らませる □*Other than blowing up a tire I hadn't done any car maintenance.* 私の車の手入れといえば、タイヤに空気を入れるくらいだった。 **3** PHRASAL VERB 句動詞 If a wind or a storm **blows up**, the weather becomes very windy or stormy. 吹き荒れる □*A storm blew up over the mountains.* 山で嵐が吹き荒れた。 **4** PHRASAL VERB 句動詞 If you **blow up at** someone, you lose your temper and shout at them. 激怒する [INFORMAL くだけた] □*I'm sorry I blew up at you.* かっとしてごめんなさい。 **5** PHRASAL VERB 句動詞 If someone **blows** an incident **up** or if it **blows up**, it is made to seem more serious or important than it really is. 誇張する □*Newspapers blew up the story.* 新聞は誇張した記事を載せた。 □*The media may be blowing it up out of proportion.* メディアは大げさに伝えようとしているようだ。 **6** PHRASAL VERB 句動詞 If a photographic image **is blown up**, a large copy is made of it. 引き伸ばす □*The image is blown up on a large screen.* 映像はスクリーンに大きく映し出された。

Word Partnership		*blow* は次の語句と使われる:
ADV.	blow **away** ❶ 2 8	
N.	blow **bubbles, blow smoke** ❶ 5	
	blow **a whistle** ❶ 6	
	blow **your nose** ❶ 7	
V.	**deliver/strike a** blow ❷ 1	
	cushion/soften a blow, **suffer a** blow ❷ 1 2	
ADJ.	**crushing/devastating/heavy** blow ❷ 1 2	
PREP.	blow **to the head** ❷ 1	
	blow **to someone** ❷ 2	

❷ blow /bloʊ/ (**blows**) **1** N-COUNT 可算名詞 If someone receives a **blow**, they are hit with a fist or weapon. 一撃 □*He went to the hospital after a blow to the face.* 彼は顔を一発なぐられ、病院に行った。 **2** N-COUNT 可算名詞 If something that happens is a **blow to** someone or something, it is very upsetting, disappointing, or damaging to them. 打撃 □*That ruling comes as a blow to environmentalists.* その決定は環境保護主義者には打撃です。

bludgeon /blʌdʒən/ (**bludgeons, bludgeoning, bludgeoned**) V-T 他動詞 To **bludgeon** someone means to hit them several times with a heavy object. 殴打する [他動詞] □*He broke into the old man's house and bludgeoned him with a hammer.* 家に押し入った男が老人をハンマーで殴打した。

blue /blu/ (**bluer, bluest, blues**) **1** COLOR 色彩語 Something that is **blue** is the color of the sky on a sunny day. 青い □*There were swallows in the cloudless blue sky.* 雲一つない青空をつばめが飛んでいた。 □*She fixed her pale blue eyes on her father's.* 彼女は淡いブルーの瞳で父の目をじっと見つめた。 **2** N-PLURAL 複数名詞 **The blues** is a type of music which was developed by African American musicians in the southern United States. It is characterized by a slow tempo and a strong rhythm. ブルース □*Can white girls sing the blues?* 白人の女がブルースを歌えるのかい。 **3** ADJ 形容詞 If you are feeling **blue**, you are feeling sad or depressed, often when there is no particular reason. ゆううつな [v-link ADJ] □*There's no earthly reason for me to feel so blue.* なぜこんなにゆううつなのか、まったく分からないのよ。 **4** ADJ 形容詞 If a U.S. state is described as **blue**, it means that the majority of its residents vote for the Democratic Party in elections, especially in the presidential elections. 民主党支持者が多数の □*This issue could drive an even bigger wedge between the red and blue states.* この問題は民主党支持州と共和党支持州の溝をさらに深めるかもしれません。
→ see **color, rainbow**

blueberry /bluberi/ (**blueberries**) N-COUNT 可算名詞 A **blueberry** is a small dark blue fruit that is found in North America. ブルーベリー

blue chip (**blue chips**) N-COUNT 可算名詞 **Blue chip** stocks and shares are an investment which are considered fairly safe to invest in while also being profitable. 優良株 [BUSINESS 実業] □*Blue chip issues were sharply higher, but the rest of the market actually declined slightly by the end of the day.* 優良株は急な上昇を見せたが、その他の銘柄は引けにかけてやや値を下げた。

blue-collar ADJ 形容詞 **Blue-collar** workers work in industry, doing physical work, rather than in offices. 肉体労働の [ADJ n] □*It wasn't just the blue-collar workers who lost their jobs, it was everyone.* 肉体労働者だけじゃなく、誰だって失業した。

blueprint /bluprɪnt/ (**blueprints**) **1** N-COUNT 可算名詞 A **blueprint for** something is a plan or set of proposals that shows how it is expected to work. 青写真 □*The president will offer delegates his blueprint for the country's future.* 大統領は代議員に国の将来の青写真を示すだろう。 **2** N-COUNT 可算名詞 A **blueprint** of an architect's building plans or a designer's pattern is a photographic print

consisting of white lines on a blue background. Blueprints contain all of the information that is needed to build or make something. 設計図 ❑ ...a blueprint of the whole place, complete with heating ducts and wiring. 暖房用ダクトと配線を記載した全体設計図. ❑ N-COUNT 可算名詞 A **blueprint** is a pattern that is contained within all living cells. This pattern decides how the organism develops and what it looks like. (遺伝的な) 青写真 ❑ The offspring contain a mixture of the genetic blueprint of each parent. 子供は両親それぞれから遺伝の青写真を受け継ぎます.

→ see copy

bluff /blʌf/ (bluffs, bluffing, bluffed) ❶ N-VAR 可変性名詞 A **bluff** is an attempt to make someone believe that you will do something when you do not really intend to do it. はったり ❑ The letter was a bluff. その手紙ははったりだった. ❑ It is essential to build up the military option and show that this is not a bluff. 武力行使の道を強化し、それが単なるこけおどしではないことを示すことが不可欠だ. ❷ PHRASE 句 If you **call** someone's **bluff**, you tell them to do what they have been threatening to do, because you are sure that they will not really do it. (人のこけおどしやはったりに) 挑戦する ❑ The socialists have decided to call the opposition's bluff. 社会党は野党のこけおどしに乗らないことを決めた. ❸ V-T/V-I 他動詞/自動詞 If you **bluff**, you make someone believe that you will do something when you do not really intend to do it, or that you know something when you do not really know it. こけおどす [他動詞]、虚勢を張る [自動詞] ❑ Either side, or both, could be bluffing. 片方もしくは両方が虚勢を張っているのでしょう. ❑ In each case the hijackers bluffed the crew using fake grenades. いずれの犯行も、ハイジャック犯が乗務員を偽の手りゅう弾でおどした.

blun|der /blʌndər/ (blunders, blundering, blundered) ❶ N-COUNT 可算名詞 A **blunder** is a stupid or careless mistake. 大失敗 ❑ I think he made a tactical blunder by announcing it so far ahead of time. かなり前に公表するくらいだから、彼は駆け引きのためへまをしたと私は思う. ❷ V-I 自動詞 If you **blunder**, you make a stupid or careless mistake. へまをする ❑ No doubt I had blundered again. 今度もへまをしたってことは間違いなかった. ❸ V-I 自動詞 If you **blunder into** a dangerous or difficult situation, you get involved in it by mistake. うっかり入り込む ❑ People wanted to know how they had blundered into war, and how to avoid it in the future. 人々は、自分たちが戦争に至った経緯と、今後どうしたら戦争を回避できるのかを知りたかった. ❹ V-I 自動詞 If you **blunder** somewhere, you move there in a clumsy and careless way. うっかりぶつかる ❑ He had blundered into the table, upsetting the flowers. 彼はうっかりテーブルにぶつかり、花をひっくり返した.

blunt /blʌnt/ (blunter, bluntest, blunts, blunting, blunted) ❶ ADJ 形容詞 If you are **blunt**, you say exactly what you think without trying to be polite. 単刀直入な ❑ She is blunt about her personal life. 彼女は私生活をありのままに話します. ● **blunt|ly** ADV 副詞 [ADV with v] 単刀直入に ❑ "I don't believe you!" Jeanne said bluntly. ジーンは「あなたの言うことなんて信じないわ」とあからさまに言った. ● **blunt|ness** N-UNCOUNT 不可算名詞 無愛想さ ❑ His bluntness got him into trouble. 彼は無愛想なため面倒に巻き込まれた. ❷ ADJ 形容詞 A **blunt** object has a rounded or flat end rather than a sharp one. とがっていない ❑ One of them had been struck 13 times over the head with a blunt object. 彼らの1人は鈍器で13回も頭を殴られた. ❸ ADJ 形容詞 A **blunt** knife or blade is no longer sharp and does not cut well. 切れ味の悪い ❑ The edge is as blunt as an old butter knife. 切れ味は古いバターナイフのような鈍さだ. ❹ V-T 他動詞 If something **blunts** an emotion, a feeling or a need, it weakens it. 鈍らせる ❑ The constant repetition of violence has blunted the human response to it. 暴力が常に繰り返され、人々はそれに鈍感になった.

blur /blɜr/ (blurs, blurring, blurred) ❶ N-COUNT 可算名詞 A **blur** is a shape or area which you cannot see clearly because it has no distinct outline or because it is moving very fast. 不鮮明 ❑ Out of the corner of my eye I saw a blur of movement on the other side of the glass. ガラスの向こうでぼんやりした何かが動くのがチラッと見えた. ❷ V-T/V-I 他動詞/自動詞 When a thing **blurs** or when something **blurs** it, you cannot see it clearly because its edges are no longer distinct. 不鮮明にする [他動詞]、ぼやける [自動詞] ❑ This creates a spectrum of colors at the edges of objects which blurs the image. このため物体のふちにスペクトルができ、像がぼやける. ● **blurred** ADJ 形容詞 不鮮明な ❑ ...blurred black and white photographs. 不鮮明な白黒写真. ❸ V-T 他動詞 If something **blurs** an idea or a distinction between things, that idea or distinction no longer seems clear. あいまいにする ❑ ...her belief that scientists are trying to blur the distinction between "how" and "why" questions. 科学者が「どのように」型と「どうして」型の問いの差異をあいまいにしようとしているという彼女の確信. ● **blurred** ADJ 形容詞 あいまいな ❑ The line between fact and fiction is becoming blurred. 事実とフィクションの線引きがあいまいになりつつある. ❹ V-T/V-I 他動詞/自動詞 If your vision **blurs**, or if something **blurs** it, you cannot see things clearly. 曇らせる [他動詞]、曇る [自動詞] ❑ Her eyes, behind her glasses, began to blur. めがねの奥の彼女の目は曇り始めた. ● **blurred** ADJ 形容詞 かすんだ ❑ ...visual disturbances like eye-strain and blurred vision. 眼精疲労やかすみ目などの視覚障害.

blurt /blɜrt/ (blurts, blurting, blurted) V-T 他動詞 If someone **blurts** something, they say it suddenly, after trying hard to keep quiet or to keep it secret. 口走る ❑ "I was looking for Sally," he blurted, and his eyes filled with tears. 彼は「サリーを探していたんだ」と漏らして、目に涙を浮かべた. ▶ **blurt out** PHRASAL VERB 句動詞 If someone **blurts** something **out**, they blurt it. うっかり口走る [INFORMAL くだけた] ❑ "You're mad," the driver blurted out. 「あんたはいかれている」と運転手は思わず言った.

blush /blʌʃ/ (blushes, blushing, blushed) V-I 自動詞 When you **blush**, your face becomes redder than usual because you are ashamed or embarrassed. 赤面する ❑ "Hello, Maria," he said, and she blushed again. 「こんにちは、マリア」と彼が声をかけると、マリアは再び頬を染めた. ● N-COUNT 可算名詞 **Blush** is also a noun. 紅潮 ❑ "The most important thing is to be honest," she says, without the trace of a blush. 彼女は少しも顔を赤らめることなく「何より大事なのは、正直であることです」と言う.

Thesaurus	blush また次を参照:
v.	redden, turn red

boar /bɔr/ (boars)

The plural **boar** can also be used for meaning ❶.

複数の **boar** は ❶ の意味にも使える.

❶ N-COUNT 可算名詞 A **boar** or a **wild boar** is a wild pig. イノシシ ❑ Wild boar are numerous in the valleys. その谷間にはイノシシが多く息している. ❷ N-COUNT 可算名詞 A **boar** is a male pig. 雄豚

board /bɔrd/ (boards, boarding, boarded) ❶ N-COUNT 可算名詞 A **board** is a flat, thin, rectangular piece of wood or plastic which is used for a particular purpose. 板 ❑ ...a cutting board. まな板. ❷ N-COUNT 可算名詞 A **board** is a square piece of wood or stiff cardboard that you use for playing games such as chess. 盤 ❑ ...a checkers board. チェッカーボード. ❸ N-COUNT 可算名詞 You can refer to a blackboard or a bulletin board as a **board**. 一板 ❑ He wrote a few more notes on the board. 彼は黒板にいくつか書き足した. ❹ N-COUNT 可算名詞 **Boards** are long flat pieces of wood which are used, for example, to make floors or walls. 板 ❑ The floor was drafty bare boards. 床はすき間だらけの裸板だった. ❺ N-COUNT 可算名詞 The **board** of a company or organization is the group of people who control it and direct it. 取締役会 [BUSINESS 実業] ❑ Arthur has made a recommendation, which he wants her to put before the board at a special meeting scheduled for tomorrow afternoon. アーサーは提言書を書き上げた. 彼女に明日午後の特別会議で取締役会に提出してもらうつもりだ. ❻ → see also **board of directors** ❼ N-COUNT 可算名詞 **Board** is used in the names of various organizations which are involved in dealing with a particular kind of activity. 委員会、部局 ❑ The Scottish tourist board said 33,000 Japanese visited Scotland last year. スコットランド観光局は昨年の日本人観光客数は3万3千人だったと発表した. ❽ V-T 他動詞 When you **board** a train, ship, or aircraft, you get on it in order to travel somewhere. 乗り込む ❑ I boarded the plane bound for Boston. ボストン行きの飛行機に乗った. [FORMAL 形式ばった] ❾ N-UNCOUNT 不可算名詞 **Board** is the food which is provided when you stay somewhere, for example in a hotel. 食事 ❑ Free room and board are provided for all hotel staff. ホテルの従業員は部屋と賄いつきです. ❿ PHRASE 句 If a policy or a situation applies **across the board**, it affects everything or everyone in a particular group. 全体にわたり ❑ There are hefty charges across the board for one-way rental. 片道レンタルはどこでも高い料金を取られます. ⓫ PHRASE 句 If something **goes by the board**, it is rejected or ignored, or is no longer possible. 顧みられない ❑ It's a case of not what you know but who you know in this world today and qualifications quite go by the board. 今の世の中、ものを言うのは知識ではなく人脈だね. 資格なんて忘れられてるよ. ⓬ PHRASE 句 When you are **on board** a train, ship, or aircraft, you are on it or in it. 〜に乗って ❑ All 269 people on board the plane were killed. 飛行機に乗っていた269人全員が死亡した. ⓭ PHRASE 句 If someone **sweeps the board** in a competition or election, they win nearly everything that it is possible to win. 圧勝する ❑ Spain swept the board in boys' team competitions. 男子団体はスペインの圧勝に終わった. ⓮ PHRASE 句 If you **take on board** an idea or a problem, you begin to accept it or understand it. 理解する ❑ You may have to accept their point of view, but hope that they will take on board some of what you have said. きみは彼らの見方を受け入れる必要があるかもしれないが、彼らもきみの意見を少しは理解してくれることを期待できるね.

▶ **board up** PHRASAL VERB 句動詞 If you **board up** a door or window, you fix pieces of wood over it so that it is covered up. 板でふさぐ ❑ Shopkeepers have boarded up their windows. 店の人たちは窓を板でふさいだ.

Word Partnership   board は次の語句と使われる:

N.   **cutting** board, **diving** board **1**
board **game** **2**
bulletin board, **message** board **3**
chair/member of the board, board **of directors**,
board **meeting** **5 6**
board **a flight/plane/ship 7**
room and board **8**

board|ing card → see **boarding pass**

board|ing pass (**boarding passes**) N-COUNT 可算名詞 A
boarding pass is a card that a passenger must have when
boarding a plane or a boat. 搭乗券

board|ing school (**boarding schools**) also **boarding-school**
N-VAR 可変性名詞 A **boarding school** is a school that some or all of
the students live in during the school term. Compare **day school**.
全寮制の学校

board of di|rec|tors (**boards of directors**) N-COUNT 可算名詞 A
company's **board of directors** is the group of people elected by its
shareholders to manage the company. 取締役会 [BUSINESS 実業]
❑ The board of directors has approved the decision unanimously. 取締役会
は満場一致でその決定を承認した.

board|room /bɔrdrum/ (**boardrooms**) also **board room**
N-COUNT 可算名詞 The **boardroom** is a room where the board of a
company meets. 役員会議室 [BUSINESS 実業] ❑ Everyone had already
assembled in the boardroom for the 9:00 a.m. session. 9時からの会議の
参加者全員がすでに役員会議室に集まっていた.

boast /boʊst/ (**boasts, boasting, boasted**) **1** V-T/V-I 他動詞/
自動詞 If someone **boasts** about something that they have done
or that they own, they talk about it very proudly, in a way that
other people may find irritating or offensive. 自慢する ❑ Witnesses
said Furci boasted that he took part in killing them. ファルチは殺し
に加担したことを自慢したと証人は語った. [DISAPPROVAL 不賛
成] ❑ Carol boasted about her costume. キャロルは自分の衣装を自慢
した. ● N-COUNT 可算名詞 Boast is also a noun. 自慢 ❑ It is the
charity's proud boast that it has never yet turned anyone away. その慈善
事業の一番の誇りは，これまで誰にも門前払いをしたことがないこと
だ. **2** V-T 他動詞 If someone or something can **boast** a particular
achievement or possession, they have achieved or possess that
thing. (誇らしいものを) 有する ❑ The houses will boast the latest
energy-saving technology. 家には最新の省エネ技術を駆使した設備が
付く.

boat /boʊt/ (**boats**) **1** N-COUNT 可算名詞 A **boat** is something
in which people can travel across water. 船 [also 'by' N] ❑ One of
the best ways to see the area is in a small boat. お勧めは小型船での観光
です. **2** N-COUNT 可算名詞 You can refer to a passenger ship as a
boat. 客船 ❑ When the boat reached Cape Town, we said goodbye. 客船
がケープタウンに到着し，私たちはお別れを言った. **3** PHRASE 句 If
you say that someone has **missed the boat**, you mean that they
have missed an opportunity and may not get another. 機会を逃が
す ❑ If you don't want to miss the boat, the auction is scheduled for 2:30
p.m. on June 26. オークションは6月26日午後2時半からです. お見逃し
なく.
→ see Word Web: **boat**
→ see **ship**

Thesaurus   boat また次を参照:

N.   craft, ship, vessel **1 2**

boat|ing /boʊtɪŋ/ N-UNCOUNT 不可算名詞 **Boating** is traveling
on a lake or river in a small boat for pleasure. ボート遊び ❑ You can
go boating or play tennis. ボート遊びやテニスなどができます.

bob /bɒb/ (**bobs, bobbing, bobbed**) **1** V-I 自動詞 If something
bobs, it moves up and down, like something does when it is
floating on water. 上下に動く ❑ Huge balloons bobbed about in the
sky above. 大きな気球が空をフワフワと上下していた. **2** V-I 自動
詞 If you **bob** somewhere, you move there quickly so that you
disappear from view or come into view. 急に動く ❑ She handed over
a form, then bobbed down again behind a typewriter. 彼女は書類を手渡

し，またスッとタイプライターの向こうに座った.

bob|by pin /bɒbi pɪn/ (**bobby pins**) N-COUNT 可算名詞 A **bobby
pin** is a small piece of metal or plastic bent back on itself that
someone uses to hold their hair in position. ヘアピン [AM 米国
英語]

bode /boʊd/ (**bodes, boding, boded**) V-I 自動詞 If something
bodes ill, it makes you think that something bad will happen
in the future. If something **bodes** well, it makes you think that
something good will happen. 前兆となる ❑ She says the way the bill
was passed bodes ill for democracy. 彼女は，あのように法案が通った
のは民主主義へのよからぬ前兆だと言う. [FORMAL 形式ばった]

bod|i|ly /bɒdɪli/ **1** ADJ 形容詞 Your **bodily** needs and
functions are the needs and functions of your body. 体の [ADJ
n] ❑ ...descriptions of natural bodily functions. 自然の肉体機能につい
ての説明. **2** ADV 副詞 You use **bodily** to indicate that an action
involves the whole of someone's body. 体ごと [ADV with v] ❑ I was
hurled bodily to the deck. 私は体ごとデッキに投げ出された.

body /bɒdi/ (**bodies**) **1** N-COUNT 可算名詞 Your **body** is all your
physical parts, including your head, arms, and legs. 身体 ❑ The
largest organ in the body is the liver. 体の中で最も大きな器官は肝臓で
す. **2** N-COUNT 可算名詞 You can also refer to the main part of
your body, except for your arms, head, and legs, as your **body**. 胴
体 ❑ Lying flat on the floor, twist your body on to one hip and cross your
upper leg over your body. 床に寝て，一方の腰を下にして体をねじり，上
になった足を胴の前方に倒す. **3** N-COUNT 可算名詞 You can refer to
a person's dead body as a **body**. 死体 ❑ Officials said they had found
no traces of violence on the body of the politician. 公式発表によると，政
治家の遺体には暴行された形跡はなかったとのことです. **4** N-COUNT
可算名詞 A **body** is an organized group of people who deal with
something officially. 組織体 ❑ She was elected student body president
at the University of North Carolina. 彼女はノースカロライナ大学の
学生会長に選ばれた. **5** N-COUNT 可算名詞 A **body of** people is a
group of people who are together or who are connected in some
way. 団体 ❑ ...that large body of people which teaches other people how
to teach. 指導法の教授の大きな団体. **6** N-SING 単数名詞 The **body
of** something such as a building or a document is the main part
of it or the largest part of it. 主要部 ❑ The main body of the church
had been turned into a massive television studio. 教会の主要部は大きな
テレビスタジオに変わっていた. **7** N-COUNT 可算名詞 The **body** of
a car or airplane is the main part of it, not including its engine,
wheels, or wings. 車体 ❑ The only shade was under the body of the
plane. 影になっているのは機体の下だけだった. **8** N-COUNT 可算名詞
A **body of** water is a large area of water, such as a lake or an ocean.
水域 ❑ It is probably the most polluted body of water in the world. そこ
は世界で最も汚染された水域だろう. **9** N-COUNT 可算名詞 A **body
of** information is a large amount of it. 大量の ❑ An increasing body
of evidence suggests that all of us have cancer cells in our bodies at times
during our lives. 誰でも生存中に時折，体内にがん細胞ができるという
多数の証拠が集まっている. **10** N-UNCOUNT 不可算名詞 If you say
that an alcoholic drink has **body**, you mean that it has a full and
strong flavor. こく ❑ ...a dry wine with good body. しっかりとしたこ
くのある辛口のワイン.
→ see Picture Dictionary: **body**

body|guard /bɒdigard/ (**bodyguards**) N-COUNT 可算名詞 A
bodyguard is a person or a group of people employed to protect
someone. ボディーガード ❑ Three of his bodyguards were injured in the
attack. その襲撃で彼のボディーガード3人が負傷した.

body lan|guage N-UNCOUNT 不可算名詞 Your **body language**
is the way in which you show your feelings or thoughts to other
people by means of the position or movements of your body,
rather than with words. ボディーランゲージ，身振り ❑ I can tell by
your body language that you're happy with the decision. あなたの身振り
からその決定を喜んでいるのが伝わってくる.

bog /bɒg/ (**bogs**) N-COUNT 可算名詞 A **bog** is an area of land
that is very wet and muddy. 湿地
→ see **wetland**

bogged down ADJ 形容詞 If you get **bogged down in**
something, it prevents you from making progress or getting
something done. 行き詰った ❑ But why get bogged down in legal
details? なぜ法律面の細かいことで動きが取れなくなったんだろう.

Word Web   boat

People once used **boats** only for transportation. But today they are a favorite form of
recreation for millions. Weekend **captains** enjoy quietly **sailing** their skiffs along the shore.
However, other boaters prefer to ride around in **motorboats**. Any rowboat can become a
motorboat just by attaching an outboard **motor** to the back. Inboard motors are quieter, but
they're more expensive. Fishermen usually prefer using a rowboat with **oars**. That way they
don't scare the fish. For an even more peaceful ride, some people **paddle** around in **canoes**.
But really adventurous folks like the thrill of white-water **rafting**.

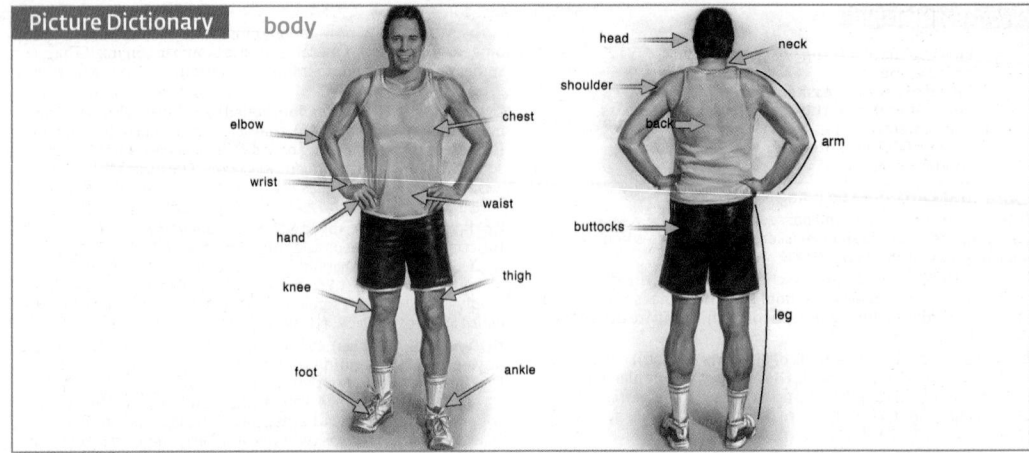

Picture Dictionary — body

head, neck, shoulder, back, arm, buttocks, leg

elbow, chest, wrist, waist, hand, knee, thigh, foot, ankle

---

bog|gle /bɒgᵊl/ (boggles, boggling, boggled) V-T/V-I 他動詞/自動詞 If you say that the mind **boggles at** something, or that something **boggles** the mind, you mean that it is so strange or amazing that it is difficult to imagine or understand. 驚いてひるませる [他動詞], 驚いてひるむ [自動詞] ❑ *The mind boggles at the possibilities that could be in store for us.* 自分たちの可能性を考えるとひるんでしまう.

bo|gus /boʊgəs/ ADJ 形容詞 If you describe something as **bogus**, you mean that it is not genuine. 偽の ❑ *...their bogus insurance claim.* 彼らによる架空の保険金請求.

boil /bɔɪl/ (boils, boiling, boiled) **1** V-T/V-I 他動詞/自動詞 When a hot liquid **boils** or when you **boil** it, bubbles appear in it and it starts to change into steam or vapor. 沸かす [他動詞], 沸騰する [自動詞] ❑ *I stood in the kitchen, waiting for the water to boil.* 台所で立ったままお湯が沸くのを待ってたの. ❑ *Boil the water in the saucepan and add the sage.* なべで湯を沸かし, セージを入れる. **2** V-T/V-I 他動詞/自動詞 When you **boil** a pot or a kettle, or put it on to **boil**, you heat the water inside it until it boils. 沸かす [他動詞], 沸く [自動詞] ❑ *He had nothing to do but boil the kettle and make the tea.* やかんで湯を沸かしてお茶を入れるほかに彼がすることがなかった. **3** V-I 自動詞 When a pot **is boiling**, the water inside it has reached boiling point. 沸騰する [自動詞] ❑ *The pot was boiling.* ポットは沸騰していた. [only cont] **4** V-T/V-I 他動詞/自動詞 When you **boil** food, or when it **boils**, it is cooked in boiling water. 煮える [自動詞] ❑ *Boil the chickpeas, add garlic and lemon juice.* ひよこ豆をゆで, にんにくとレモン汁を加えてください. ❑ *I'd peel potatoes and put them on to boil.* 私がジャガイモをむいてゆでましょう. **5** V-I 自動詞 If you **are boiling with** anger, you are very angry. 激怒する [自動詞] ❑ *I used to be all sweetness and light on the outside, but inside I would be boiling with rage.* ご機嫌なそぶりを見せていたのに, 内心は怒りに震えていたものでした. [usu cont] **6** N-COUNT 可算名詞 A **boil** is a red, painful swelling on your skin that contains a thick yellow liquid called pus. おでき **7** → see also **boiling** **8** PHRASE 句 When you **bring** a liquid **to a boil**, you heat it until it boils. When it **comes to a boil**, it begins to boil. 沸騰させる, 沸騰する ❑ *Put water, butter and lard into a saucepan and bring slowly to the boil.* なべに水, バター, ラードを入れ, それをゆっくりと沸騰させます.

▶ **boil down to** PHRASAL VERB 句動詞 If you say that a situation or problem **boils down to** a particular thing or can be **boiled down to** a particular thing, you mean that this is the most important or the most basic aspect of it. 要約する ❑ *What they want boils down to just one thing. It is land.* 彼らが欲しいのは, つまるところただ一つ. 土地だ.

▶ **boil over** **1** PHRASAL VERB 句動詞 When a liquid that is being heated **boils over**, it rises and flows over the edge of the container. 噴きこぼれる ❑ *Heat the liquid in a large, wide container rather than a high narrow one, or it can boil over.* 液体は, 細長い容器ではなく, 口の広いもので加熱すること. そうしないと噴きこぼれる恐れがある. **2** PHRASAL VERB 句動詞 When someone's feelings **boil over**, they lose their temper or become violent. 憤慨する ❑ *Sometimes frustration and anger can boil over into direct and violent action.* イライラや怒りが頂点に達したちすると, ときに直接的な暴力的な行為に発展することがある.
→ see **cook, egg**

boil|er /bɔɪlər/ (boilers) N-COUNT 可算名詞 A **boiler** is a device that burns gas, oil, electricity, or coal in order to provide hot water, especially for the central heating in a building. ボイラー

boil|ing /bɔɪlɪŋ/ **1** ADJ 形容詞 Something that is **boiling** or **boiling hot** is very hot. 煮えるように暑い ❑ *"It's boiling in here,"*

complained Miriam. 「ここは熱すぎるよ」とミリアムはこぼした. **2** ADJ 形容詞 If you say that you are **boiling** or **boiling hot**, you mean that you feel very hot, usually unpleasantly hot. うだるように熱い [v-link ADJ] ❑ *When everybody else is boiling hot, I'm freezing!* みんなとても暑がっているのに, 私は凍えるように寒いんだ.

In informal English, if you want to emphasize how hot the weather is, you can say that it is **boiling** or **scorching**. In winter, if the temperature is above average, you can say that it is **mild**. In general, **hot** suggests a higher temperature than **warm**, and **warm** things are usually pleasant. ❑ *...a warm evening.*

bois|ter|ous /bɔɪstərəs, -strəs/ ADJ 形容詞 Someone who is **boisterous** is noisy, lively, and full of energy. にぎやかな ❑ *...a boisterous but good-natured crowd.* にぎやかだが気のいい人たち.

bold /boʊld/ (bolder, boldest) **1** ADJ 形容詞 Someone who is **bold** is not afraid to do things that involve risk or danger. 大胆な ❑ *Amrita becomes a bold, daring rebel.* アムリタは大胆不敵な反逆者になる. ❑ *In 1960 this was a bold move.* 1960年だと, これは大胆な動きでした. ● **bold|ly** ADV 副詞 [ADV with v] 大胆に ❑ *You must act boldly and confidently.* 大胆かつ自信をもって行動すべきです. ● **bold|ness** N-UNCOUNT 不可算名詞 大胆さ ❑ *Don't forget the boldness of his economic program.* 彼が作った経済計画の大胆さを忘れるな. **2** ADJ 形容詞 Someone who is **bold** is not shy or embarrassed in the company of other people. ずぶとい ❑ *I don't feel I'm being bold, because it's always been natural for me to just speak out about whatever disturbs me.* 自分がずぶといとは思わない. どんな妨害があっても, それについて声をあげることが僕にとってはいつも自然だったからだ. ● **bold|ly** ADV 副詞 大胆に ❑ *"You should do it," the girl said, boldly.* 「やるべきよ」と少女がきっぱり言った. **3** ADJ 形容詞 A **bold** color or pattern is very bright and noticeable. 派手な ❑ *...bold flowers in various shades of red, blue or white.* 赤や青, 白など様々な色調で際立つ花々. **4** ADJ 形容詞 **Bold** lines or designs are drawn in a clear, strong way. くっきりとした ❑ *Each picture is shown in color on one page and as a bold outline on the opposite page.* それぞれの写真はカラーで片側 1 ページに, 反対側のページにはその輪郭をくっきりとした線で掲載している. **5** N-UNCOUNT 不可算名詞 **Bold** is print which is thicker and looks blacker than ordinary printed letters. ボールド体 (太い字体) [TECHNICAL 技術的] ❑ *When a candidate is elected his or her name will be highlighted in bold.* 候補者の当選が決まると, 名前が太字体で表示される.

bol|ster /boʊlstər/ (bolsters, bolstering, bolstered) **1** V-T 他動詞 If you **bolster** something such as someone's confidence or courage, you increase it. 強める ❑ *Hopes of an early cut in interest rates bolstered confidence.* 早期利下げへの期待感が経済信頼感を高めた. **2** V-T 他動詞 If someone tries to **bolster** their position in a situation, they try to strengthen it. 強化する ❑ *The country is free to adopt policies to bolster its economy.* 国は経済を強化する施策は何でも採択できる. **3** N-COUNT 可算名詞 A **bolster** is a firm pillow shaped like a long tube which is sometimes put across a bed instead of pillows, or under the ordinary pillows. 長枕

bolt /boʊlt/ (bolts, bolting, bolted) **1** N-COUNT 可算名詞 A **bolt** is a long metal object that screws into a nut and is used to fasten things together. ボルト **2** V-T 他動詞 When you **bolt** one thing to another, you fasten them firmly together, using a bolt. ボルトで固定する ❑ *The safety belt is easy to fit as there's no need to bolt it to seat belt anchorage points.* この安全ベルトはシートベルトの固定部へのボルトづけが不要なので取り付けが簡単だ. ❑ *Bolt the components together.* 部品をボルトで組み立てなさい. **3** N-COUNT 可算名詞 A **bolt** on a door or window is a metal bar that you can slide across

in order to fasten the door or window. かんぬき □I heard the sound of a bolt being slowly and reluctantly slid open. かんぬきがゆっくり、ぎしぎしと引き抜かれるのが聞こえた. **4** V-T 他動詞 When you **bolt** a door or window, you slide the bolt across to fasten it. かんぬきをかける □He reminded her that he would have to lock and bolt the kitchen door after her. 彼は彼女のあとにきは自分で錠前とかんぬきをかけることになると注意した. **5** V-I 自動詞 If a person or animal **bolts**, they suddenly start to run very fast, often because something has frightened them. (何かに驚いて) 急に駆け出す □The pig rose squealing and bolted. 豚はキーッと鳴いて駆け出した. **6** V-T 他動詞 If you **bolt** your food, you eat it so quickly that you hardly chew it or taste it. うのみにする □Being under stress can cause you to miss meals, eat on the move, or bolt your food. 緊張状態におかれると、食事をしなかったり、移動しながら食べたり、よくかまずに食べたりすることがある. ● PHRASAL VERB 句動詞 **Bolt down** means the same as **bolt**. かまずに飲み込む □I like to think back to high school, when I could bolt down three or four burgers and a pile of French fries. 高校時代はよかった. ハンバーガー3、4個と大盛りのフライドポテトを一瞬で平らげられたもんだ. **7** N-COUNT 可算名詞 A **bolt of** lightning is a flash of lightning that is seen as a white line in the sky. 電光 □Suddenly a bolt of lightning crackled through the sky. 突然稲妻が空を走った. **8** PHRASE 句 If someone is sitting or standing **bolt upright**, they are sitting or standing very straight. まっすぐに □When I pushed her door open, Trevor was sitting bolt upright in bed. トレバーの部屋のドアをあけたとき、彼はベッドでしゃんと座っていた.

→ see **lightning**

bomb /bɒm/ (bombs, bombing, bombed) **1** N-COUNT 可算名詞 A **bomb** is a device that explodes and damages or destroys a large area. 爆弾 □Bombs went off at two London train stations. ロンドンの2つの鉄道駅で爆発が爆発した. □It's not known who planted the bomb. 誰が爆弾を仕掛けたかは不明だ. **2** N-SING 単数名詞 Nuclear weapons are sometimes referred to as **the bomb**. 核爆弾 □They are generally thought to have the bomb. 彼らは核を所持していると一般に考えられている. **3** V-T 他動詞 When people **bomb** a place, they attack it with bombs. 爆撃する □Air force jets bombed the airport. 空軍戦闘機が空港を爆撃した. ● **bomb**|**ing** N-VAR 可変性名詞 (bombings) 爆撃 □Aerial bombing of rebel positions is continuing. 反乱軍拠点への空爆が続いている.

Word Partnership	*bomb*は次の語句と使われる:
N.	bomb **blast**, car bomb, **pipe** bomb, bomb **shelter**, bomb **squad**, bomb **threat** **1**
V.	**drop/plant a** bomb, **set off a** bomb **1**
ADJ.	**atomic/nuclear** bomb, **live** bomb **1 2**

bom|**bard** /bɒmbɑrd/ (bombards, bombarding, bombarded) **1** V-T 他動詞 If you **bombard** someone with something, you make them face a great deal of it. For example, if you **bombard** them **with** questions or criticism, you keep asking them a lot of questions or you keep criticizing them. 攻めたてる □He bombarded Catherine with questions to which he should have known the answers. 彼はキャサリンを質問攻めにしたが、彼はその答えを知っているはずだった. **2** V-T 他動詞 When soldiers **bombard** a place, they attack it with continuous heavy gunfire or bombs. 砲撃する □Rebel artillery units have regularly bombarded the airport. 反乱軍の砲兵隊は定期的に空港を爆撃してきた.

bom|**bard**|**ment** /bɒmbɑrdmənt/ (bombardments) **1** N-VAR 可変性名詞 A **bombardment** is a strong and continuous attack of gunfire or bombing. その街は激しい爆撃で壊滅状態になった. □The city has been flattened by heavy artillery bombardments. その街は激しい爆撃で壊滅状態になった. **2** N-VAR 可変性名詞 A **bombardment of** ideas, demands, questions, or criticisms is an aggressive and exhausting stream of them. (要求、質問や批判などが) 次々に浴びせかけられること □...the constant bombardment of images urging that work was important. 働くことは大事だと矢つぎばやに訴える映像

bomb|**er** /bɒmər/ (bombers) **1** N-COUNT 可算名詞 **Bombers** are people who cause bombs to explode in public places. 爆撃犯 □Detectives hunting the bombers will be eager to interview him. 爆撃犯を追っている刑事たちは彼らの事情徴収を切望するだろう. **2** N-COUNT 可算名詞 A **bomber** is a military aircraft which drops bombs. 爆撃機 □...a high-speed bomber with twin engines. 双発の高速爆撃機

bomb|**shell** /bɒmʃɛl/ (bombshells) **1** N-COUNT 可算名詞 A **bombshell** is a sudden piece of bad or unexpected news. 寝耳に水の知らせ □His resignation is a political bombshell. 彼の辞任は政界の突然事件だった. **2** PHRASE 句 If someone **drops a bombshell**, they give you a sudden piece of bad or unexpected news. 不意打ちをくらわす

bo|**nan**|**za** /bənænzə/ (bonanzas) N-COUNT 可算名詞 You can refer to a sudden great increase in wealth, success, or luck as a **bonanza**. 大当たり □The expected sales bonanza hadn't materialized. 予想された巨額の売り上げは実現していなかった.

bond /bɒnd/ (bonds, bonding, bonded) **1** N-COUNT 可算名詞 A **bond between** people is a strong feeling of friendship, love, or shared beliefs and experiences that unites them. きずな □The experience created a very special bond between us. その経験は私たちの間にとても特別なきずなを築いた. **2** V-RECIP 相互動詞 When people **bond with** each other, they form a relationship based on love or shared beliefs and experiences. You can also say that people **bond** or that something **bonds** them. つなぐ [他動詞]、つながる、関係を築く [自動詞] □Belinda was having difficulty bonding with the baby. ベリンダは赤ちゃんとうまくつきあえなかった. □They all bonded while writing graffiti together. 彼らは一緒に落書きをしている間に仲が良くなった. **3** N-COUNT 可算名詞 A **bond between** people or groups is a close connection that they have with each other, for example because they have a special agreement. 結束 □...the strong bond between church and nation. 教会と国家との強い結束 **4** N-COUNT 可算名詞 A **bond between** two things is the way in which they stick to one another or are joined in some way. 接着 □If you experience difficulty with the superglue not creating a bond with dry wood, moisten the surfaces with water. 接着剤で乾いた木材を接着しにくい場合は、表面を水で湿らせて下さい. **5** V-RECIP 相互動詞 When one thing **bonds with** another, it sticks to it or becomes joined to it in some way. You can also say that two things **bond together**, or that something **bonds** them **together**. 接合させる [他動詞]、接合する [自動詞] □In graphite sheets, carbon atoms bond together in rings. グラファイト板の中では炭素原子が環状につながっている. **6** N-COUNT 可算名詞 When a government or company issues a **bond**, it borrows money from investors. The certificate that is issued to investors who lend money is also called a **bond**. 国債、社債 [BUSINESS 実業] □Most of it will be financed by government bonds. そのほとんどが国債でまかなわれることになる. **7** → see also **junk bond**

→ see **love**

bond|**age** /bɒndɪdʒ/ **1** N-UNCOUNT 不可算名詞 **Bondage** is the condition of being someone's property and having to work for them. 奴隷の身 □Masters sometimes allowed their slaves to buy their way out of bondage. 主人たちは奴隷が金を払って自由の身になることを許すことがあった. **2** N-UNCOUNT 不可算名詞 **Bondage** is the condition of not being free because you are strongly influenced by something or someone. とらわれの身 [FORMAL 形式ばった] □All people, she said, lived their lives in bondage to hunger, pain and lust. 人はすべて飢えと痛みと肉欲にとらわれて人生を過ごす、と彼女は述べた.

bond|**ed** /bɒndɪd/ ADJ 形容詞 A **bonded** company has entered into a legal agreement that offers its customers some protection if the company does not fulfill its contract with them. 保証契約を結んだ [BUSINESS 実業] □They are a fully bonded and licensed company. 完全な保証契約を結び認可を受けた会社だ.

bond|**hold**|**er** /bɒndhoʊldər/ (bondholders) also bond holder N-COUNT 可算名詞 A **bondholder** is a person who owns one or more investment bonds. 債権者 [BUSINESS 実業]

bone /boʊn/ (bones, boning, boned) **1** N-VAR 可変性名詞 Your **bones** are the hard parts inside your body that together form your skeleton. 骨 □Many passengers suffered broken bones. 多くの乗客が骨折した. □The body is made up primarily of bone, muscle, and fat. 体は主に骨と筋肉と脂肪でできている. **2** V-T 他動詞 If you **bone** a piece of meat or fish, you remove the bones from it before cooking it. 骨を抜く □Make sure that you do not pierce the skin when boning the chicken thighs. 鶏のもも肉の骨を取り除く時、皮に穴を開けないようにして下さい. **3** ADJ 形容詞 A **bone** tool or ornament is made of bone. 骨や象牙でできた [ADJ n] □...a small, expensive pocketknife with a bone handle. 骨の柄がついた小型の高価なポケットナイフ **4** PHRASE 句 The **bare bones of** something are its most basic parts or details. 必要最小限のもの、骨子 □There are not even the bare bones of a garden here - I've got nothing. この庭には必要最小限のものさえない. 私には何もない. **5** → see also **bare-bones** **6** PHRASE 句 If something such as costs are cut **to the bone**, they are reduced to the minimum possible. ぎりぎりまで □It has survived by cutting its costs to the bone. それは経費をぎりぎりまで切り詰めて生き残ってきた.

▶ **bone up on** PHRASAL VERB 句動詞 If you **bone up on** a subject, you try to find out about it or remind yourself what you have already learned about it. 勉強する、勉強し直す □I had spent the last few months boning up on neurology. 私はその数か月を神経学の勉強に費やしていた.

→ see **skeleton**

bone of con|**ten**|**tion** (bones of contention) N-COUNT 可算名詞 If a particular matter or issue is a **bone of contention**, it is the subject of a disagreement or argument. 論点 □The main bone of contention is the temperature level of the air-conditioners. 言い争いのおおもとはエアコンの設定温度だ.

bon|**fire** /bɒnfaɪər/ (bonfires) N-COUNT 可算名詞 A **bonfire** is a fire that is made outdoors, usually to burn waste. Bonfires are also sometimes lit as part of a celebration. たき火、(祝い事の) 大かがり火 □With bonfires outlawed in urban areas, gardeners must cart their refuse to a dump. 都市部のたき火禁止令のため、庭師は廃棄物をご み捨て場まで運ばなくてはならない.

bon|**net** /bɒnɪt/ (bonnets) **1** N-COUNT 可算名詞 A **bonnet** is a

B

hat with ribbons that are tied under the chin. Bonnets are now worn by babies. In the past, they were also worn by women. 婦人や幼児用の帽子 **2** N-COUNT 可算名詞 The **bonnet** of a car is the metal cover over the engine at the front. （車の）ボンネット [BRIT 英国英語; AM **hood** 米国英語 **hood**]

bo|nus /b**ou**nəs/ (**bonuses**) **1** N-COUNT 可算名詞 A **bonus** is an extra amount of money that is added to someone's pay, usually because they have worked very hard. ボーナス, 特別賞与 □ *Workers in big firms receive a substantial part of their pay in the form of bonuses and overtime.* 大企業の社員は俸給の大部分をボーナスや残業代として受け取っている. □ *...a $60 bonus.* 60ドルのボーナス **2** N-COUNT 可算名詞 A **bonus** is something good that you get in addition to something else, and which you would not usually expect. 御の字, 思いがけない嬉しいおまけ □ *We felt we might finish third. Any better would be a bonus.* 私たちは3位に入れるかもしれないと思った. それ以上だったら御の字だ.

bony /b**ou**ni/ **1** ADJ 形容詞 Someone who has a **bony** face or **bony** hands, for example, has a very thin face or very thin hands, with very little flesh covering their bones. やせた □ *...an old man with a bony face and white hair.* やせた顔と白髪の老人 **2** ADJ 形容詞 The **bony** parts of a person's or animal's body are the parts made of bone. 骨でできた □ *...the bony ridge of the eye socket.* 眼窩（がんか）の上の骨の突き出た所

boo /b**u**/ (**boos, booing, booed**) **1** V-T/V-I 他動詞/自動詞 If you **boo** a speaker or performer, you shout "boo" or make other loud sounds to indicate that you do not like them, their opinions, or their performance. （非難や不賛成を表して）ブーという, ブーイングする □ *People were booing and throwing things at them.* 人々は彼らにブーイングし, 物を投げていた. □ *Demonstrators booed and jeered him.* デモ参加者は彼に非難の声とやじを浴びせた. ● N-COUNT 可算名詞 **Boo** is also a noun. ブーという声 □ *She was greeted with boos and hisses.* 彼女は非難のやじに迎えられた. ● **boo|ing** N-UNCOUNT 不可算名詞 ブーイング □ *The fans are entitled to their opinion but booing doesn't help anyone.* ファンには意見を述べる権利があるが, ブーイングは何の役にも立たない. **2** EXCLAM 感嘆詞 You say "**Boo!**" loudly and suddenly when you want to surprise someone who does not know that you are there. （相手に存在を知らせるための）ばあ！

book /b**u**k/ (**books, booking, booked**) **1** N-COUNT 可算名詞 A **book** is a number of pieces of paper, usually with words printed on them, which are fastened together and fixed inside a cover of stronger paper or cardboard. Books contain information, stories, or poetry, for example. 本 □ *His eighth book came out earlier this year and was an instant best-seller.* 彼の8冊目の本が今年の初めに出版され, すぐにベストセラーとなった. □ *...the author of a book on politics.* 政治に関する本の筆者 □ *...a new book by Rosella Brown.* ロゼッラ・ブラウンの新刊書 **2** N-COUNT 可算名詞 A **book of** something such as stamps, matches, or tickets is a small number of them fastened together between thin cardboard covers. つづり □ *Can I have a book of first class stamps please?* ファーストクラスの切手を1つづり下さい. **3** V-T 他動詞 When you **book** something such as a hotel room or a ticket, you arrange to have it or use it at a particular time. 予約する □ *American officials have booked hotel rooms for the women and children.* 米当局者が女性や子供たちのためにホテルに部屋を予約した. □ *Laurie booked herself a flight home.* ローリーは帰国便を予約した. **4** N-PLURAL 複数名詞 A company's or organization's **books** are its records of money that has been spent and earned or of the names of people who belong to it. 帳簿 [BUSINESS 実業] □ *For the most part he left the books to his managers and accountants.* 彼は帳簿をほとんど管理者と会計士らに任せていた. **5** V-T 他動詞 When a police officer **books** someone, he or she officially records their name and the offense that they may be charged with. 警察の記録に載せる □ *They took him to the station and booked him for assault with a deadly weapon.* 彼らは彼を署に連れて行き, 凶器による暴行罪で記録をとった. **6** N-COUNT 可算名詞 In a very long written work such as the Bible, a **book** is one of the sections into which it is divided. （聖書など長編の書物の）巻 書 □ *...the last book of the Bible.*

聖書の最後の書 **7** → see also **booking, checkbook, phone book** **8** PHRASE 句 If you say that someone or something is a **closed book**, you mean that you do not know anything about them. 得体の知れない人, 不可解なこと □ *Frank Spriggs was a very able man but something of a closed book.* フランク・スプリッグズは才能にあふれた人だったが, どこか得体の知れないところがあった. **9** PHRASE 句 If transportation or a hotel, restaurant, or theater is **booked up**, **fully booked**, or **booked solid**, it has no tickets, rooms, or tables left for a particular time or date. 満席の, 満室の □ *The car ferries from the mainland are often fully booked by February.* 本土からのカー・フェリーは, 2月までに予約で一杯になることが多い.

→ see Word Web: **book**

→ see **concert, library**

N.	**address** book, book **award**, **children's** book, book **club**, **comic** book, **copy of a** book, book **cover**, **library** book, **phone** book, book **review**, **subject of a** book, **title of a** book **1**
ADJ.	**latest/new/recent** book **1**
V.	**publish a** book, **read a** book, **write a** book **1**

book|case /b**u**kkeɪs/ (**bookcases**) N-COUNT 可算名詞 A **bookcase** is a piece of furniture with shelves that you keep books on. 本箱

book|ing /b**u**kɪŋ/ (**bookings**) N-COUNT 可算名詞 A **booking** is the arrangement that you make when you book something such as a hotel room, a table at a restaurant, or a theater seat. 予約 □ *There was a mistake over his booking.* 彼の予約に手違いがあった.

book|keeper /b**u**kkiːpər/ (**bookkeepers**) also **book-keeper** N-COUNT 可算名詞 A **bookkeeper** is a person whose job is to keep an accurate record of the money that is spent and received by a business or other organization. 簿記係 [BUSINESS 実業]

book|keeping /b**u**kkiːpɪŋ/ also **book-keeping** N-UNCOUNT 不可算名詞 **Bookkeeping** is the job or activity of keeping an accurate record of the money that is spent and received by a business or other organization. 経理 [BUSINESS 実業]

book|let /b**u**klɪt/ (**booklets**) N-COUNT 可算名詞 A **booklet** is a very thin book that has a paper cover and that gives you information about something. 小冊子 □ *...a 48-page booklet of notes for the completion of the form.* その用紙に記入するための注意事項が書かれた48ページの小冊子

book|mark /b**u**kmark/ (**bookmarks, bookmarking, bookmarked**) **1** N-COUNT 可算名詞 A **bookmark** is a narrow piece of card or leather that you put between the pages of a book so that you can find a particular page easily. しおり **2** N-COUNT 可算名詞 In computing, a **bookmark** is the address of an Internet site that you put into a list on your computer so that you can return to it easily. （インターネットの）「お気に入り」や「ブックマーク」 [COMPUTING コンピューティング] □ *This makes it extremely simple to save what you find with an electronic bookmark so you can return to it later.* これであなたが見つけたページを「お気に入り」にとても簡単に保存でき, 後でそのページに戻ることができる. V-T 他動詞 ● **Bookmark** is also a verb. 「お気に入り」や「ブックマーク」に加える [COMPUTING コンピューティング] □ *This site is definitely worth bookmarking.* このサイトは絶対「お気に入り」に加える価値がある.

book|store /b**u**kstor/ (**bookstores**) N-COUNT 可算名詞 A **bookstore** is a store where books are sold. 書店 [mainly AM 主に米国英語]

book value (**book values**) N-COUNT 可算名詞 In business, the

Word Web book

Before the invention of the book in first century Rome, **literary works** were recorded on **scrolls**. The earliest examples of bookbinding used sheets of parchment. Workers folded them in half and then sewed through the fold. Scribes copied books by hand until the invention of the **printing press** in the fifteenth century. Today, most books come from factories. High-speed presses print thousands of pages every hour. The pages are then folded into signatures* and trimmed to size. Finally, machines sew or glue the signatures onto the cover. Today's **e-books** provide pages on a computer screen instead of paper.

signature: a group of pages.

b

book value of an asset is the value it is given in the account books of the company that owns it. 帳簿価格 [BUSINESS 実業] ❏ *The insured value of the airplane was greater than its book value.* その飛行機の保険価格は帳簿価格よりも多かった.

boom /buːm/ (booms, booming, boomed) **1** N-COUNT 可算名詞 If there is a **boom** in the economy, there is an increase in economic activity, for example, in the number of things that are being bought and sold. 急上昇 ❏ *An economic boom followed, especially in housing and construction.* その後, 特に住宅と建築業で好景気が始まった. ❏ *The 1980s were indeed boom years.* 1980年代はまさしく好況の時代だった. **2** N-COUNT 可算名詞 A **boom in** something is an increase in its amount, frequency, or success. ブーム ❏ *The boom in the sport's popularity has meant more calls for stricter safety regulations.* スポーツブームによって, さらに厳しい安全規定の必要性が増した. **3** V-I 自動詞 If the economy or a business **is booming**, the number of things being bought or sold is increasing. 景気づく ❏ *By 1988 the economy was booming.* 1988年には経済が大活況だった. ❏ *Sales are booming.* 売り上げが好調だ. **4** V-T/V-I 他動詞/自動詞 When something such as someone's voice, a cannon, or a big drum **booms**, it makes a loud, deep sound that lasts for several seconds. とどろき渡る ❏ *"Ladies," boomed Helena, without a microphone, "we all know why we're here tonight."* 「女性の皆さん」とヘレナの声がマイクなしで響き渡った. 「私たちが今夜何のためにここに集まったか皆さんご承知の通りです」. ❏ *Thunder boomed over Crooked Mountain.* まがり山に雷鳴がとどろいた. ● PHRASAL VERB 句動詞 **Boom out** means the same as **boom**. とどろき渡る ❏ *Music boomed out from loudspeakers.* 音楽がスピーカーから大音響で鳴った. ❏ *A megaphone boomed out, "this is the police."* 「こちらは警察です」と拡声器の声が響き渡った. ● N-COUNT; SOUND 可算名詞, 音声語 **Boom** is also a noun. とどろき ❏ *The stillness of the night was broken by the boom of a cannon.* 夜の静けさが大砲のドーンという大音響で破られた.

Thesaurus boom また次を参照:

V.	flourish, prosper, succeed, thrive; (ant.) fail **3**
N.	explosion, roar **4**

boom-bust cy|cle (boom-bust cycles) N-COUNT 可算名詞 A **boom-bust cycle** is a series of events in which a rapid increase in business activity in the economy is followed by a rapid decrease in business activity, and this process is repeated again and again. 景気循環 [BUSINESS 実業] ❏ *We must avoid the damaging boom-bust cycles which characterized the 1980s.* 1980年代の特徴だった有害な波のある景気循環を避けなければいけない.

boon /buːn/ (boons) N-COUNT 可算名詞 You can describe something as a **boon** when it makes life better or easier for someone. 恩恵 ❏ *It is for this reason that television proves such a boon to so many people.* こうした理由から, テレビは多くの人々に大きな恩恵をもたらしている.

boost /buːst/ (boosts, boosting, boosted) **1** V-T 他動詞 If one thing **boosts** another, it causes it to increase, improve, or be more successful. 押し上げる, 後援する ❏ *Lower interest rates can boost the economy by reducing borrowing costs for consumers and businesses.* 金利が下がると消費者や企業の融資コストを引き下げることで, 経済を押し上げる可能性がある. ● N-COUNT 可算名詞 **Boost** is also a noun. ❏ *It would get the economy going and give us the boost that we need.* それは経済を動かし, 必要な刺激を与える. **2** V-T 他動詞 If something **boosts** your confidence or morale, it improves it. (自信や志気を) 高める ❏ *We need a big win to boost our confidence.* 私たちが自信をつけるためには大勝利が必要だ. ● N-COUNT 可算名詞 **Boost** is also a noun. 励まし ❏ *It did give me a boost to win such a big event.* あんな大きな試合に勝てたことは確かに私の自信となった. **3** N-COUNT 可算名詞 If you give someone a **boost**, you push or lift them from behind so that they can reach something. 押し上げ [usu sing] ❏ *He cupped his hands and gave her a boost up to the ledge.* 彼は手の平をお椀型にして彼女を棚に押し上げた.

boot /buːt/ (boots, booting, booted) **1** N-COUNT 可算名詞 **Boots** are shoes that cover your whole foot and part of your leg. ブーツ, 長靴 ❏ *He sat in a kitchen chair, reached down and pulled off his boots.* 彼は台所の椅子に座り, 下に手を伸ばしてブーツを脱いだ. **2** N-COUNT 可算名詞 **Boots** are strong, heavy shoes that cover your ankle and that have thick soles. You wear them to protect your feet, for example, when you are walking or taking part in sports. 頑丈な厚底の靴 ❏ *The soldiers' boots resounded in the street.* 軍靴が通りに鳴り響いた. **3** V-T 他動詞 To **boot** an illegally parked car means to fit a device to one of its wheels so that it cannot be driven away. (駐車違反の車に) 車輪止めをつける [AM 米国英語] ❏ *Though the city will no longer boot cars, illegally parked vehicles will be towed.* その市では車輪止めをもう使わないが, 駐車違反の車はレッカー移動されることになる. **4** V-T/V-I 他動詞/自動詞 If a computer **boots** or you **boot** it, it is made ready to use by putting in the instructions it needs in order to start working. (コンピュータが) 起動する [COMPUTING コンピューティング][自動詞], 起動させる [他動詞] ❏ *The computer won't boot.* コンピュータが起動しない. ❏ *Put*

the CD into the drive and boot the machine.* CDをドライブに入れて, コンピュータを立ち上げて下さい. ● PHRASAL VERB 句動詞 **Boot up** means the same as **boot**. ❏ *Go over to your PC and boot it up.* (コンピュータを) 起動する [自動詞], 起動させる [他動詞] **5** N-COUNT 可算名詞 The **boot** of a car is the same as the **trunk**. (自動車の) トランク [BRIT 英国英語] **6** PHRASE 句 If you **get the boot** or **are given the boot**, you are told that you are not wanted anymore, either in your job or by someone you are having a relationship with. 首になる, ふられる [INFORMAL くだけた] ❏ *She was a disruptive influence, and after a year or two she got the boot.* 彼女は和を乱したので, 1, 2年後に首になった.

→ see **clothing**

booth /buːθ/ (booths) **1** N-COUNT 可算名詞 A **booth** is a small area separated from a larger public area by screens or thin walls where, for example, people can make a telephone call or vote in private. (仕切りや壁で区切られた) ブース ❏ *I called her from a public phone booth near the entrance to the bar.* 私はバーの入り口付近の電話ボックスから彼女に電話をかけた. **2** N-COUNT 可算名詞 A **booth** in a restaurant or café consists of a table with long fixed seats on two or sometimes three sides of it. (レストランやバーの) 仕切り席, ボックス席 ❏ *They sat in a corner booth, away from other diners.* 彼らは他の食事客から離れて, 隅の仕切り席に座った.

booze /buːz/ (boozes, boozing, boozed) **1** N-UNCOUNT 不可算名詞 **Booze** is alcoholic drink. 酒, アルコール飲料 [INFORMAL くだけた] [also 'the' N] ❏ *...booze and cigarettes.* 酒とたばこ **2** V-I 自動詞 If people **booze**, they drink alcohol. 酒を飲む [INFORMAL くだけた] ❏ *...a load of drunken businessmen who had been boozing all afternoon.* 午後ずっと酒を飲んでいた大勢の酔っ払いビジネスマン

bor|der /bɔːrdər/ (borders, bordering, bordered) **1** N-COUNT 可算名詞 The **border** between two countries or regions is the dividing line between them. Sometimes **the border** also refers to the land close to this line. 境界 ❏ *They fled across the border.* 彼らは国境を超えて逃げた. ❏ *Soldiers had temporarily closed the border between the two countries.* 兵士たちは両国間の国境を一時的に封鎖していた. **2** V-T 他動詞 A country that **borders** another country, a sea, or a river is next to it. 隣接する ❏ *...the European and Arab countries bordering the Mediterranean.* 地中海に接するヨーロッパとアラブの国々 ● PHRASAL VERB 句動詞 **Border on** means the same as **border**. 隣接する ❏ *Both republics border on the Black Sea.* どちらの共和国も黒海に隣接している. **3** N-COUNT 可算名詞 A **border** is a strip or band around the edge of something. 縁, 端 ❏ *...pillowcases trimmed with a hand-crocheted border.* 手編みの縁飾りがついた枕カバー **4** N-COUNT 可算名詞 In a garden, a **border** is a long strip of ground planted with flowers, along the edge of a path or lawn. 庭の小道や芝生の縁に沿った花の植え込み ❏ *...a lawn flanked by wide herbaceous borders.* 幅広い草の植え込みで縁どられた芝生 **5** V-T 他動詞 If something **is bordered** by another thing, the other thing forms a line along the edge of it. 縁取る ❏ *...the mile of white sand beach bordered by palm trees and tropical flowers.* やしの木と南国の花々に縁取られた1マイルの白い砂浜

Thesaurus border また次を参照:

V.	abut, surround, touch **2** **5**
N.	boundary, end, extremity, perimeter; (ant.) center, inside, middle **3**

bor|der|line /bɔːrdərlaɪn/ (borderlines) **1** N-COUNT 可算名詞 The **borderline between** two different or opposite things is the division between them. 境界線 ❏ *...a task which involves exploring the borderline between painting and photography.* 絵画と写真の境界線の探求を伴う仕事 **2** ADJ 形容詞 Something that is **borderline** is only just acceptable as a member of a class or group. 境界線上の ❏ *Some were obviously unsuitable and could be ruled out at once. Others were borderline cases.* 明らかに不適切で, ただちに除外できるものもあった. 判断の難しいケースもあった.

bore /bɔːr/ (bores, boring, bored) **1** V-T 他動詞 If someone or something **bores** you, you find them dull and uninteresting. 退屈させる ❏ *Dickie bored him all through the meal with stories of the navy.* ディッキーは食事中ずっと海軍の話をして彼をうんざりさせた. **2** PHRASE 句 If someone or something **bores** you **to tears**, **bores** you **to death**, or **bores** you **stiff**, they bore you very much. ひどく退屈させる [INFORMAL くだけた, EMPHASIS 強調] ❏ *Monuments and museums bore him to tears.* 記念碑や博物館は彼には死ぬほど退屈だ. **3** N-COUNT 可算名詞 You describe someone as a **bore** when you think that they talk in a very uninteresting way. 退屈な人 ❏ *There is every reason why I shouldn't enjoy his company – he's a bore and a fool.* 私が彼との付き合いを楽しめないのにはすべて理由がある. かれは退屈な上にばかだ. **4** N-SING 単数名詞 You can describe a situation as a **bore** when you find it annoying. 不快な事 ❏ *It's a bore to be sick, and the novelty of lying in bed all day wears off quickly.* 病気になるのは嫌なものだ. 一日中寝ていることの珍しさもすぐに消えてしまう. **5** V-T 他動詞 If you **bore** a hole in something, you make a deep round hole in it using a special tool. (道具を使って) 穴をあける ❏ *Get the special drill bit to bore the correct size hole for the job.* この

仕事に合った大きさの穴をあけるために特殊なドリルのビットを持って来てくれ。 **6** Bore is the past tense of **bear**. bearの過去形 **7** → see also **bored, boring**

bored /bɔːrd/ ADJ 形容詞 If you are **bored**, you feel tired and impatient because you have lost interest in something or because you have nothing to do. 退屈した ❏ *I am getting very bored with this entire business.* この仕事全体にとてもうんざりしてきている。

Word Link dom ≈ state of being : bore**dom**, free**dom**, wis**dom**

---

bore|dom /bɔːrdəm/ N-UNCOUNT 不可算名詞 **Boredom** is the state of being bored. 退屈 ❏ *He had given up attending lectures out of sheer boredom.* 講義が本当につまらなかったので、彼は出席するのをやめていた。

bor|ing /bɔːrɪŋ/ ADJ 形容詞 Someone or something **boring** is so dull and uninteresting that they make people tired and impatient. 退屈な ❏ *Not only are mothers not paid but also most of their boring or difficult work is unnoticed.* 母親たちは報酬を受けていないばかりか、退屈な困難な仕事のほとんどが見過ごされている。

Thesaurus boring また次を参照:

ADJ. dull, tedious, unexciting, uninteresting; (ant.) exciting, fun, interesting, lively

---

born /bɔːrn/ **1** V-T PASSIVE 受動態他動詞 When a baby **is born**, it comes out of its mother's body at the beginning of its life. In formal English, if you say that someone **is born of** someone or **to** someone, you mean that person is their parent. 生まれる ❏ *She was born in Milan on April 29, 1923.* 彼女は1923年4月29日にミラノで生まれた。 ❏ *He was born of German parents and lived most of his life abroad.* 彼はドイツ人の両親の下に生まれ、その生涯のほとんどを外国で過ごした。 **2** V-T PASSIVE 受動態他動詞 If someone **is born with** a particular disease, problem, or characteristic, they have it from the time they are born. もって生まれた [no cont] ❏ *He was born with only one lung.* 彼は生まれつき片肺しかなかった。 ❏ *Some people are born brainy.* 生まれつき頭のいい人もいる。 **3** V-T PASSIVE 受動態他動詞 You can use **be born** in front of a particular name to show that a person was given this name at birth, although they may be better known by another name. 本名、旧姓 [FORMAL 形式ばった] [no cont] ❏ *She was born Jenny Harvey on June 11, 1946.* 彼女は1946年6月11日にジェニー・ハービーとして生まれた。 **4** ADJ 形容詞 You use **born** to describe someone who has a natural ability to do a particular activity or job. For example, if you are a **born** cook, you have a natural ability to cook well. 生まれながらの [ADJ n] ❏ *Jack was a born teacher.* ジャックは天性の教師だった。 **5** V-T PASSIVE 受動態他動詞 When an idea or organization **is born**, it comes into existence. If something **is born of** a particular emotion or activity, it exists as a result of that emotion or activity. （考えや組織が）生まれる [FORMAL 形式ばった] ❏ *The idea for the show was born in his hospital room.* 舞台のアイデアは彼の病室で生まれた。 ❏ *Congress passed the National Security Act, and the CIA was born.* 米下院が国家安全保障法を承認し、CIAが設立された。 **6** → see also **newborn**

borne /bɔːrn/ **Borne** is the past participle of **bear**. bearの過去分詞形

bor|ough /bɜːroʊ/ (boroughs) N-COUNT 可算名詞 A **borough** is a town, or a district within a large city, which has its own council, government, or local services. （行政単位としての）区 市 ❏ *...the New York City borough of Brooklyn.* ニューヨーク市ブルックリン区

bor|row /bɒroʊ/ (borrows, borrowing, borrowed) **1** V-T 他動詞 If you **borrow** something that belongs to someone else, you take it or use it for a period of time, usually with their permission. 借りる ❏ *Can I borrow a pen please?* ペンを貸してもらえますか？ **2** V-T/V-I 他動詞/自動詞 If you **borrow** money **from** someone or **from** a bank, they give it to you and you agree to pay it back at some time in the future. 借金する ❏ *Morgan borrowed $5,000 from his father to form the company 20 years ago.* モーガンは20年前に会社を設立するため父親から5千ドルを借りた。 ❏ *It's so expensive to borrow from finance companies.* 金融会社に借金をするのはとても高くつく。 **3** V-T 他動詞 If you **borrow** a book **from** a library, you take it away for a fixed period of time. （図書館から本を）借りる ❏ *I couldn't afford to buy any, so I borrowed them from the library.* 一冊も買う余裕がなかったので、図書館から借りた。 **4** V-T 他動詞 If you **borrow** something such as a word or an idea from another language or from another person's work, you use it in your own language or work. 借用する ❏ *I borrowed his words for my book's title.* 私は彼の言葉を自著の書名に採り入れた。
→ see **bank, library**

Do not confuse **borrow** and **lend**. You say that you **borrow** something **from** another person. However, if you allow someone to **borrow** something that belongs to you, you say that you **lend** it to them. **Lend** is often followed by two objects. ❏ *Betty lent him some blankets... He lent Tim the money.* Both **borrow** and **lend** can be used without objects. ❏ *The poor had to borrow from the rich... Banks will not lend to them.* The noun related to **lend** is **loan**. ❏ *...a government loan of $3m.* **Loan** can also be used as a verb in the same way as **lend**, especially in American English. ❏ *I'll loan you fifty dollars.*

Word Partnership borrow は次の語句と使われる:

V.	forced to borrow **1 2**
PREP.	borrow from **1** – **4**
	borrow against *something* **2**
ADV.	borrow heavily **2 4**
N.	ability to borrow, borrow cash/funds/money **2**
	borrow a phrase **4**

---

bor|row|er /bɒroʊər/ (borrowers) N-COUNT 可算名詞 A **borrower** is a person or organization that borrows money. 借り手、負債主 ❏ *Borrowers with a big mortgage should go for a fixed rate.* 多額の融資を受けている人は固定利率を選ぶべきだ。
→ see **bank, interest**

bor|row|ing /bɒroʊɪŋ/ (borrowings) N-UNCOUNT 不可算名詞 **Borrowing** is the activity of borrowing money. 借金 [also N in pl] ❏ *We have allowed spending and borrowing to rise in this recession.* 私たちはこの景気後退の中で支出と借入れの増大を許してきた。

bos|om /bʊzəm/ (bosoms) **1** N-COUNT 可算名詞 A woman's breasts are sometimes referred to as her **bosom** or her bosoms. 胸 [OLD-FASHIONED 古風な] ❏ *...a young mother with a baby resting against her ample bosom.* 豊かな胸に赤ちゃんを眠らせる若い母親 **2** ADJ 形容詞 A **bosom** buddy is a friend who you know very well and like very much. 親しい [ADJ n] ❏ *They were bosom buddies.* 彼らは親友同士だった。

boss /bɒs/ (bosses, bossing, bossed) **1** N-COUNT 可算名詞 Your **boss** is the person in charge of the organization or department where you work. 上司、（組織や部署の）長 ❏ *He cannot stand his boss.* 彼は上司に我慢がならない。 **2** N-COUNT 可算名詞 If you are **the boss** in a group or relationship, you are the person who makes all the decisions. 親分、（グループや人間関係の中で）決定権を持つ者 [INFORMAL くだけた] ❏ *He thinks he's the boss.* 彼は自分が親分だと思っている。 **3** V-T 他動詞 If you say that someone **bosses** you, you mean that they keep telling you what to do in a way that is irritating. ボス面をする、命令する ❏ *We cannot boss them into doing more.* あれ以上やるよう無理には言えないよ。 ● PHRASAL VERB 句動詞 **Boss around** means the same as **boss**. bossに同じ ❏ *He started bossing people around.* 彼はみんなに威張り散らし始めた。

Thesaurus boss また次を参照:

N. chief, director, employer, foreman, manager, owner; (ant.) superintendent, supervisor **1 2**

---

bossy /bɒsi/ ADJ 形容詞 If you describe someone as **bossy**, you mean that they enjoy telling people what to do. 偉そうな、威張って [DISAPPROVAL 不賛成] ❏ *She remembers being a rather bossy little girl.* 彼女は、かなり威張っていた少女時代を覚えている。

Word Link botan ≈ plant : botanical, botanist, botany

---

bo|tani|cal /bətænɪkəl/ ADJ 形容詞 **Botanical** books, research, and activities relate to the scientific study of plants. 植物学の [ADJ n] ❏ *The area is of great botanical interest.* この地方は植物学的にとても興味深い。

bota|nist /bɒtənɪst/ (botanists) N-COUNT 可算名詞 A **botanist** is a scientist who studies plants. 植物学者

bota|ny /bɒtəni/ N-UNCOUNT 不可算名詞 **Botany** is the scientific study of plants. 植物学

botch /bɒtʃ/ (botches, botching, botched) **1** V-T 他動詞 If you **botch** something that you are doing, you do it badly or clumsily. 下手な仕事をする [INFORMAL くだけた] ❏ *...a botched job.* おざなりな仕事 ● PHRASAL VERB 句動詞 **Botch up** means the same as **botch**. botchに同じ ❏ *I hate having builders botch up repairs on my house.* 私は建築業者が家に下手な修繕を加えるのが大嫌いだ。 **2** N-COUNT 可算名詞 If you **make a botch** of something that you are doing, you botch it. やり損なう [INFORMAL くだけた]

both /boʊθ/ **1** DET 限定詞 You use **both** when you are referring to two people or things and saying that something is true about each of them. 両方の ❏ *She cried out in fear and flung both arms up to protect her face.* 彼女は恐怖の叫び声を上げ、両腕で顔をかばった。 ● QUANT 数量詞 **Both** is also a quantifier. 両方 [QUANT 'of' pl-n] ❏ *Both of these women have strong memories of the Vietnam War.* 女性は2人ともベトナム戦争の強烈な記憶がある。 ● PRON 代名詞 **Both**

is also a pronoun. （代名詞として）両方、2人 ❑ *Miss Brown and her friend, both from Brooklyn, were arrested on the 8th of June.* ブラウン嬢と彼女の友人はどちらもブルックリン出身で、6月8日に逮捕された。 ● PRON-EMPH 強調的代名詞 **Both** is also an emphasizing pronoun. どちらも [N PRON] ❑ *He visited the Institute of Neurology in Havana where they both worked.* 彼は彼ら二人ともが勤務するハバナの神経学研究所を訪ねた。 PREDET 前限定詞 ● **Both** is also a predeterminer. 両方 [EMPHASIS 強調] [PREDET det pl-n] ❑ *Both the horses were out, tacked up and ready to ride.* 馬は2頭とも外で馬具をつけられ、乗る準備が整っていた。 ② CONJ 接続詞 You use the structure **both...and** when you are giving two facts or alternatives and emphasizing that each of them is true or possible. 一も一も両方 ❑ *Now women work both before and after having their children.* 今日では女性は子供を産む前も後も仕事をする。

Notice that all these sentences mean the same thing: "**Both boys have been ill**," "**Both the boys have been ill**," "**Both of the boys have been ill**," "**The boys have both been ill**." You cannot say "**Both of boys have been ill**," although when a pronoun is used, you can say "**Both of them have been ill**." See also note at **all**.

both|er /bɒðər/ (bothers, bothering, bothered) ① V-T/V-I 他動詞/自動詞 If you do not **bother** to do something or if you do not **bother** with it, you do not do it, consider it, or use it because you think it is unnecessary or because you are too lazy. （わざわざ）する [with brd-neg] ❑ *Lots of people don't bother to go through a marriage ceremony these days.* 最近はわざわざ結婚式を挙げない人が多い。 ❑ *Nothing I do makes any difference anyway, so why bother?* 私が何をやっても変わらないのなら、わざわざしなくてもいいでしょ？ ② N-UNCOUNT 不可算名詞 **Bother** means trouble or difficulty. You can also use **bother** to refer to an activity which causes this, especially when you would prefer not to do it or get involved with it. 面倒 [also 'a' N] ❑ *I usually buy sliced bread – it's less bother.* 普段、私はスライスしたパンを買う。その方が手がかからない。 ❑ *The courts take too long and going to the police is a bother.* 裁判は時間がかかり過ぎるし、警察に行くのは面倒だ。 ③ V-T/V-I 他動詞/自動詞 If something **bothers** you, or if you bother about it, it worries, annoys, or upsets you. 心配させる、悩ませる [他動詞]、心配する、悩む [自動詞] ❑ *Is something bothering you?* 何か心配事があるの？ ❑ *It bothered me that boys weren't interested in me.* 男の子たちが私に興味ないのが悩みの種だった。 ● **both|ered** ADJ 形容詞 [v-link ADJ] 気にして ❑ *I was bothered about the blister on my hand.* 私は手の水ぶくれが気になった。 ④ V-T 他動詞 If someone **bothers** you, they talk to you when you want to be left alone or interrupt you when you are busy. わずらわせる ❑ *We are playing a trick on a man who keeps bothering me.* 私たちはいつも私をわずらわせる男にいたずらしているの。 ⑤ PHRASE 句 If you say that you **can't be bothered to** do something, you mean that you are not going to do it because you think it is unnecessary or because you are too lazy. （わざわざ）したくない、する気になれない ❑ *I just can't be bothered to look after the house.* 私はとても家の手入れをする気になれない。 ⑥ **hot and bothered** → see **hot**

bot|tle /bɒtəl/ (bottles, bottling, bottled) ① N-COUNT 可算名詞 A **bottle** is a glass or plastic container in which drinks and other liquids are kept. Bottles are usually round with straight sides and a narrow top. （酒や液体の）瓶 ❑ *There were two empty beer bottles on the table.* テーブルの上には空のビール瓶が2本あった。 ❑ *He was pulling the cork from a bottle of wine.* 彼はワインボトルのコルクを抜いていた。 ② N-COUNT 可算名詞 You can use **bottle** to refer to a bottle and its contents, or to the contents only. 瓶の中身 ❑ *She had drunk half a bottle of whiskey.* 彼女はウィスキーボトルの半分を飲んでいた。 ③ V-T 他動詞 To **bottle** a drink or other liquid means to put it into bottles after it has been made. 瓶に詰める ❑ *This is a large truck which has equipment to automatically bottle the wine.* これはワインを自動で瓶詰めする機械を乗せた大型トラックだ。 ④ N-COUNT 可算名詞 A **bottle** is a drinking container used by babies. It has a special rubber part at the top through which they can suck their drink. 哺乳瓶 ❑ *Gary was holding a bottle to the baby's lips.* ゲーリーは赤ちゃんの唇にほ乳瓶を含ませていた。 ⑤ → see also **bottled** → see **glass**

bot|tled /bɒtəld/ ADJ 形容詞 **Bottled** gas is kept under pressure in special metal cylinders which can be moved from one place to another. ボンベに詰めた

bot|tom /bɒtəm/ (bottoms) ① N-COUNT 可算名詞 The **bottom** of something is the lowest or deepest part of it. 最下部 ❑ *He sat at the bottom of the stairs.* 彼は階段の一番下に座った。 ❑ *Answers can be found at the bottom of page 8.* 答えは8ページの下にある。 ② ADJ 形容詞 The **bottom** thing or layer in a series of things or layers is the lowest one. 最下部の [ADJ n] ❑ *There's an extra duvet in the bottom drawer of the cupboard.* 戸棚の一番下の引き出しに余分の布団が入っている。 ③ N-COUNT 可算名詞 The **bottom of** an object is the flat surface at its lowest point. You can also refer to the inside or outside of this surface as the **bottom**. 底 ❑ *Spread the onion slices on the bottom of the dish.* 深皿に玉ねぎの薄切りを広げ

る。 ❑ *...the bottom of their shoes.* 靴の中底 ④ N-SING 単数名詞 If you say that **the bottom** has dropped or fallen out of a market or industry, you mean that people have stopped buying the products it sells. 景気循環の底 [BUSINESS, JOURNALISM 実業、ジャーナリズム] ❑ *The bottom had fallen out of the city's property market.* その都市の不動産市場は底をついた。 ⑤ N-SING 単数名詞 The **bottom of** an organization or career structure is the lowest level in it, where new employees often start. 下っぱ ['the' N, oft N 'of' n] ❑ *He had worked in the theater for many years, starting at the bottom.* 彼は下っぱから始めて、長年その劇場で働いていた。 ⑥ N-SING 単数名詞 If someone is **bottom** or at the **bottom** in a survey, test, or league, their performance is worse than that of all the other people involved. （成績が）最下位 ['the' N, also no det] ❑ *He was always bottom of the class.* 彼はいつもクラスで最下位だった。 ⑦ N-COUNT 可算名詞 The lower part of a swimsuit, tracksuit, or pair of pajamas can be referred to as the **bottoms** or the **bottom**. （ビキニの）パンツ、（パジャマやトレーニングウェアなどの）ズボン ❑ *She wore blue tracksuit bottoms.* 彼女は青いトレーニングパンツをはいていた。 ⑧ N-SING 単数名詞 The **bottom of** a street or yard is the end farthest away from you or from your house. （通りや庭の）いちばん奥 [mainly BRIT 主に英国英語; AM usually **end** 米国英語では通常 **end**] ⑨ N-SING 単数名詞 The **bottom of** a table is the end farthest away from where you are sitting. The **bottom of** a bed is the end where you usually rest your feet. 末席、（ベッドの）足元 [mainly BRIT 主に英国英語; AM usually **end** 米国英語では通常 **end**] ⑩ N-COUNT 可算名詞 Your **bottom** is the part of your body that you sit on. 尻 [mainly BRIT 主に英国英語; AM usually **behind** 米国英語では通常 **behind**] ⑪ → see also **rock bottom** ⑫ PHRASE 句 You use **at bottom** to emphasize that you are stating what you think is the real nature of something or the real truth about a situation. 基本的に、根本的に [EMPHASIS 強調] ❑ *The two systems are, at bottom, conceptual models.* その2つのシステムは基本的に概念モデルだ。 ⑬ PHRASE 句 If something is **at the bottom of** a problem or an unpleasant situation, it is the real cause of it. 一の根底に ❑ *Often I find that anger and resentment are at the bottom of the problem.* 私は問題の根底には怒りと憤りがあるとしばしば感じる。 ⑭ PHRASE 句 If you want to **get to the bottom of** a problem, you want to solve it by finding out its real cause. 真相を極める ❑ *I have to get to the bottom of this.* 私はこのことの真相を追及しなくてはならない。

Thesaurus **bottom** また次を参照：

| N. | base, floor, foundation, ground; (ant.) peak, top ② |

Word Partnership **bottom** は次の語句と使われる：

V.	reach the bottom, sink to the bottom ①
N.	bottom of a hill, bottom of the page/screen ① bottom drawer, bottom of the sea, bottom of the pool, river bottom ① ② bottom lip, bottom rung ② ③
PREP.	along the bottom, on the bottom ① ② at/near the bottom ① – ③ ⑤ ⑧

bot|tom line (bottom lines) ① N-COUNT 可算名詞 The **bottom line** in a decision or situation is the most important factor that you have to consider. 最重要事項 ❑ *The bottom line is that it's not profitable.* 要点はそれが利益にならないことだ。 ② N-COUNT 可算名詞 The **bottom line** in a business deal is the least a person is willing to accept. 最低値 ❑ *She says $95,000 is her bottom line.* 彼女の最低ラインは9万5千ドルだそうだ。 ③ N-COUNT 可算名詞 The **bottom line** is the total amount of money that a company has made or lost over a particular period of time. 企業決算での利益または損失 [BUSINESS 実業] ❑ *...to force chief executives to look beyond the next quarter's bottom line.* 最高経営責任者に次の四半期決算のさらに先の見通しをさせる

bought /bɔt/ **Bought** is the past tense and past participle of **buy**. buy の過去形、過去分詞形

boul|der /boʊldər/ (boulders) N-COUNT 可算名詞 A **boulder** is a large rounded rock. 大きな丸石 ❑ *It is thought that the train hit a boulder that had fallen down a cliff on to the track.* 電車は崖から線路に落ちていた巨石にぶつかったものと思われる。

boule|vard /bʊləvɑrd/ (boulevards) N-COUNT 可算名詞 A **boulevard** is a wide street in a city, usually with trees along each side. 広い並木道 ❑ *...Lenton Boulevard.* レントン大通り

bounce /baʊns/ (bounces, bouncing, bounced) ① V-T/V-I 他動詞/自動詞 When an object such as a ball **bounces** or when you **bounce** it, it moves upward from a surface or away from it immediately after hitting it. 跳ねる、跳ね返る [自動詞]、弾ませる、跳ね返す [他動詞] ❑ *My father would burst into the kitchen bouncing a tennis ball.* 私の父はよくテニスボールを弾ませながら台所に駆け込んできたものだ。 ❑ *...a falling pebble, bouncing down the eroded cliff.* 侵食された崖を跳ね返りながら落ちる小石 ● N-COUNT 可算名詞 **Bounce** is also a noun. はずみ、跳ね返り ❑ *The wheelchair tennis player is allowed two bounces of the ball.* 車椅子のテニスプレー

B

ヤーはボールが2回バウンドしてもかまわない. **2** V-T/V-I 他動詞/自動詞 If sound or light **bounces off** a surface or **is bounced off** it, it reaches the surface and is reflected back. 反射させる [他動詞], (光や音が) 反射する [自動詞] □ *Your arms and legs need protection from light bouncing off glass.* ガラスに反射した光からあなたの手足を守るものが必要だ. **3** V-T/V-I 他動詞/自動詞 If something **bounces** or if something **bounces** it, it swings or moves up and down. 上下に揺らす [他動詞], 上下に揺れる [自動詞] □ *Her long black hair bounced as she walked.* 彼女が歩くと長い黒髪が揺れた. □ *The car was bouncing up and down as if someone were jumping on it.* 車は誰かが上で飛び跳ねているかのように上下に揺れていた. **4** V-I 自動詞 If you **bounce** on a soft surface, you jump up and down on it repeatedly. 上下に飛び跳ねる □ *She lets us do anything, even bounce on our beds.* 彼女は私たちに何でもやらせてくれた. ベッドの上で飛び跳ねることさえ. **5** V-I 自動詞 If someone **bounces** somewhere, they move there in an energetic way, because they are feeling happy. (嬉しくて) 勢いよく動く □ *Moira bounced into the office.* モイラは, はつらつと事務所に入ってきた. **6** V-T 他動詞 If you **bounce** your ideas **off** someone, you tell them to that person, in order to find out what they think about them. (意見などを) 投げかける □ *It was good to bounce ideas off another mind.* アイデアを別の人にぶつけてよかった. **7** V-T/V-I 他動詞/自動詞 If a check **bounces** or if someone **bounces** it, the bank refuses to accept it and pay out the money, because the person who wrote it does not have enough money in their account. (小切手が) 不渡りで返ってくる □ *Our only complaint would be if the check bounced.* 私たちが困るのは小切手が不渡りで戻ってくる場合だけだ. **8** V-I 自動詞 If an e-mail or other electronic message **bounces**, it is returned to the person who sent it because the address was wrong or because of a problem with one of the computers involved in sending it. (電子メールが) 宛て先不明で戻ってくる [COMPUTING コンピューティング] □ *...a message saying that your mail has bounced or was unable to be delivered.* メールの返送もしくは不達を伝えるメッセージ
▶ **bounce back** PHRASAL VERB 句動詞 If you **bounce back** after a bad experience, you return very quickly to your previous level of success, enthusiasm, or activity. すぐに立ち直る □ *We lost two or three early games but we bounced back.* 私たちは初めの方の2, 3試合で負けたが, すぐに立ち直った. □ *He is young enough to bounce back from this disappointment.* 彼は若いからすぐこの失意から立ち直るよ.

Word Partnership　bounce は次の語句と使われる:
ADJ.	a big/high/little bounce **1**
N.	bounce a ball **1**
	bounce a check **7**
	bounce ideas off someone **6**
ADV.	bounce off **1** **2** **6**
	bounce along **1** **3**
	bounce around **1** **3** **5**

bounc|er /baʊnsər/ (**bouncers**) N-COUNT 可算名詞 A **bouncer** is someone who stands at the door of a club, prevents unwanted people from coming in, and makes people leave if they cause trouble. (クラブなどの) 警備員, 用心棒

bouncy /baʊnsi/ **1** ADJ 形容詞 Someone or something that is **bouncy** is very lively. 快活な □ *She was bouncy and full of energy.* 彼女は快活で元気いっぱいだった. **2** ADJ 形容詞 A **bouncy** thing can bounce very well or makes other things bounce well. よく弾む, 弾力性のある □ *...a children's paradise filled with bouncy toys.* よく弾むおもちゃがいっぱいある子供の楽園

bound
❶ BE BOUND
❷ OTHER USES

❶ bound /baʊnd/ **1** **Bound** is the past tense and past participle of **bind**. bindの過去形および過去分詞形 **2** PHRASE 句 If you say that something **is bound to** happen, you mean that you are sure it will happen, because it is a natural consequence of something that is already known or exists. (現在の状況から推測して) 一するに違いない □ *There are bound to be price increases next year.* 来年は物価が上がるに違いない. **3** PHRASE 句 If you say that something **is bound to** happen or be true, you feel confident and certain of it, although you have no definite knowledge or evidence. きっと一のはずだ [SPOKEN 口語] □ *I'll show it to Benjamin. He's bound to know.* それをベンジャミンに見せよう. 彼ならきっと知っているはずだ. **4** ADJ 形容詞 If one person, thing, or situation is **bound to** another, they are closely associated with each other, and it is difficult for them to be separated or to escape from each other. 縛られた [v-link ADJ 'to' n] □ *We are as tightly bound to the people we dislike as to the people we love.* 私たちは愛する人たちと同様に, 嫌いな人たちにも固く縛られている. **5** ADJ 形容詞 If a vehicle or person is **bound for** a particular place, they are traveling toward it. 一行きの [v-link ADJ 'for' n] □ *The ship was bound for Italy.* その船はイタリア行きだった. ● COMB IN ADJ 形容詞の複合 **Bound** is also a combining form. (連結形で)

一行きの □ *...a Texas-bound oil freighter.* テキサス州行きの油送船

Word Partnership　bound は次の語句と使われる:
V.	bound and gagged **❶** **1**
	bound to fail **❶** **2** **3**
N.	feet/hands/wrists bound, leather bound spiral bound, bound with tape **❶** **1**
	a flight/plane/ship/train bound for **❶** **5**
PREP.	bound together, bound up with **❶** **4**
N.	bound by duty **❷** **1**
ADV.	legally bound, tightly bound **❷** **1**

❷ bound /baʊnd/ (**bounds, bounding, bounded**) **1** N-PLURAL 複数名詞 **Bounds** are limits which normally restrict what can happen or what people can do. 限界 □ *Changes in temperature occur slowly and are constrained within relatively tight bounds.* 気温の変化はゆっくりと生じ, 比較的狭い範囲内に限られている. □ *...a forceful personality willing to go beyond the bounds of convention.* 因習の限界を飛び越えようとする力強い個性 **2** V-T 他動詞 If an area of land is **bounded by** something, that thing is situated around its edge. 隣接する, 境界をなす □ *Kirgizia is bounded by Uzbekistan, Kazakhstan and Tajikistan.* キルギジアはウズベキスタンとカザフスタンおよびタジキスタンに隣接している. □ *...the trees that bounded the parking lot.* 駐車場の境目をなしていた木々 **3** V-T PASSIVE 受動態他動詞 If someone's life or situation **is bounded by** certain things, those are its most important aspects and it is limited or restricted by them. 制限する □ *Our lives are bounded by work, family and television.* 私たちの生活は仕事と家族とテレビに制約される. **4** V-I 自動詞 If a person or animal **bounds** in a particular direction, they move quickly with large steps or jumps. 跳び上がる □ *He bounded up the steps and pushed the bell of the door.* 彼は階段を駆け上り, 扉の呼び鈴を鳴らした. **5** N-COUNT 可算名詞 A **bound** is a long or high jump. 跳躍 [LITERARY 文語的] □ *With one bound Jack was free.* 一度大きく跳び上がると, ジャックは自由になった. **6** V-I 自動詞 If the quantity or performance of something **bounds** ahead, it increases or improves quickly and suddenly. 急上昇する, 急に好転する □ *Shares in the company bounded ahead by almost 3 percent.* その会社の株式はほぼ3パーセント急上昇した. **7** PHRASE 句 If a place is **out of bounds**, people are not allowed to go there. 立ち入り禁止の □ *For the last few days the area has been out of bounds to foreign journalists.* ここ数日, 外国人記者はその地区への立ち入りを禁止されている. **8** PHRASE 句 If something is **out of bounds**, people are not allowed to do it, use it, see it, or know about it. (行為や使用が) 禁止されて □ *American parents may soon be able to rule violent TV programs out of bounds.* アメリカの親たちは間もなく暴力的なテレビ番組を制限できるかもしれない.

bound|a|ry /baʊndəri/ (**boundaries**) **1** N-COUNT 可算名詞 The **boundary of** an area of land is an imaginary line that separates it from other areas. (土地の) 境界線 □ *The Bow Brook forms the western boundary of the wood.* ボウ・ブルックという小川がその森の西の境界線となっている. **2** N-COUNT 可算名詞 The **boundaries of** something such as a subject or activity are the limits that people think that it has. 境界, 限界 □ *The boundaries between history and storytelling are always being blurred and muddled.* 歴史と物語の境界線はいつもはっきりせず混同されている.

Word Partnership　boundary は次の語句と使われる:
N.	boundary dispute, boundary line **1**
PREP.	boundary around places/things, boundary between places/things, beyond a boundary, boundary of someplace/something, **1** **2**
V.	cross a boundary, mark/set a boundary **1** **2**

boun|ty /baʊnti/ (**bounties**) **1** N-VAR 可変性名詞 You can refer to something that is provided in large amounts as **bounty**. 恵み深さ [LITERARY 文語的] □ *...autumn's bounty of fruits, seeds and berries.* 果実や種, ベリーといった秋の恵み **2** N-COUNT 可算名詞 A **bounty** is money that is offered as a reward for doing something, especially for finding or killing a particular person. 賞金 □ *A bounty of $50,000 was put on Dr. Alvarez's head.* アルバレス博士の首に5万ドルの賞金がかけられた.

bou|quet /boʊkeɪ, bu-/ (**bouquets**) **1** N-COUNT 可算名詞 A **bouquet** is a bunch of flowers which is attractively arranged. 花束, ブーケ □ *The woman carried a bouquet of dried violets.* その女性はドライフラワーのすみれの束を抱えていた. **2** N-VAR 可変性名詞 The **bouquet** of something, especially wine, is the pleasant smell that it has. (ワインなどの) 良い香り □ *...a Sicilian wine with a light red color and a bouquet of cloves.* 薄赤色でクローブの香りがするシチリアワイン

bour|geois /bʊərʒwɑ/ ADJ 形容詞 If you describe people, their way of life, or their attitudes as **bourgeois**, you disapprove of them because you consider them typical of conventional middle-class people. 中産階級の, ブルジョワの [DISAPPROVAL 不賛成] □ *He's accusing them of having a bourgeois and limited vision.* 彼は彼ら

ものの見方が中産階級的で狭いと非難した.

bout /baʊt/ (**bouts**) **1** N-COUNT 可算名詞 If you have a **bout** of an illness or of an unpleasant feeling, you have it for a short period. 発病中の期間 ❑ *He was recovering from a severe bout of flu.* 彼はインフルエンザの大変な時期から回復しつつあった. **2** N-COUNT 可算名詞 A **bout of** something that is unpleasant is a short time during which it occurs a great deal. (不快な出来事の) いっとき ❑ *The latest bout of violence has claimed twenty four lives.* 先の武力衝突中に24人の命が失われた. **3** N-COUNT 可算名詞 A **bout** is a boxing or wrestling match. (ボクシングやレスリングの) 試合 ❑ *This will be his eighth title bout in 19 months.* これは19か月で彼の8回目のタイトルマッチになる.

bou|tique /butik/ (**boutiques**) N-COUNT 可算名詞 A **boutique** is a small store that sells fashionable clothes, shoes, or jewelry. ブティック, 洋装店

bow
❶ BENDING OR SUBMITTING
❷ PART OF A SHIP
❸ OBJECTS

❶ bow /baʊ/ (**bows, bowing, bowed**) **1** V-I 自動詞 When you **bow** to someone, you briefly bend your body toward them as a formal way of greeting them or showing respect. おじぎをする ❑ *They bowed low to Louis and hastened out of his way.* 彼らはルイに深々とおじぎをし, 急いで道を空けた. ● N-COUNT 可算名詞 **Bow** is also a noun. おじぎ ❑ *I gave a theatrical bow and waved.* 私は芝居がかったおじぎをして手を振った. **2** V T 他動詞 If you **bow** your head, you bend it downward so that you are looking toward the ground, for example, because you want to show respect or because you are thinking deeply about something. (頭を) 下げる, 垂れる ❑ *The Colonel bowed his head and whispered a prayer of thanksgiving.* 大佐は頭を垂れ, ささやくように感謝の祈りを捧げた. **3** V-I 自動詞 If you **bow to** pressure or to someone's wishes, you agree to do what they want you to do. 屈服する ❑ *Some stores are bowing to consumer pressure and stocking organically grown vegetables.* 消費者からの圧力に負けて, 有機栽培の野菜を置く店もある.

▸ **bow out** PHRASAL VERB 句動詞 If you **bow out** of something, you stop taking part in it. 身を引く [WRITTEN 書き言葉] ❑ *He had bowed out gracefully when his successor had been appointed.* 後継者が任命されると彼は潔く身を引いた.

❷ bow /baʊ/ (**bows**) N-COUNT 可算名詞 The front part of a ship is called **the bow** or **the bows**. The plural **bows** can be used to refer either to one or to more than one of these parts. 船首 ❑ *The waves were about five feet high now, and the bow of the boat was leaping up and down.* 波の高さは5フィートほどになり, 船首は上下に激しく揺れていた.

❸ bow /boʊ/ (**bows**) **1** N-COUNT 可算名詞 A **bow** is a knot with two loops and two loose ends that is used in tying shoelaces and ribbons. ちょう結び ❑ *Add a length of ribbon tied in a bow.* ちょう結びにしたリボンを付ける. **2** N-COUNT 可算名詞 A **bow** is a weapon for shooting arrows that consists of a long piece of curved wood with a string attached to both its ends. 弓 ❑ *Some of the raiders were armed with bows and arrows.* 侵略者の中には弓と矢で武装した者もいた. **3** N-COUNT 可算名詞 The **bow** of a violin or other stringed instrument is a long thin piece of wood with fibers stretched along it that you move across the strings of the instrument in order to play it. (バイオリンの) 弓

bowed

Pronounced /boʊd/ for meaning **1**, and /baʊd/ for meaning **2**.
1 の意味では/boʊd/ と, **2** の意味では /baʊd/ と発音される.

1 ADJ 形容詞 Something that is **bowed** is curved. (物が) 曲がった ❑ *...an old lady with bowed legs.* 足の曲がったおばあさん **2** ADJ 形容詞 If a person's body is **bowed**, it is bent forward. (体を前に) 曲げた ❑ *He walked aimlessly along the street, head down and shoulders bowed.* 彼はうつむき背中を丸めて通りを当てもなく歩いた.

bow|el /baʊəl/ (**bowels**) N-COUNT 可算名詞 Your **bowels** are the tubes in your body through which digested food passes from your stomach to your anus. 腸 ❑ *Symptoms such as stomach pains and irritable bowels can be signs of bowel cancer.* 腹痛や過敏性腸といった症状は腸がんの兆候である可能性がある.

bowl /boʊl/ (**bowls, bowling, bowled**) **1** N-COUNT 可算名詞 A **bowl** is a round container with a wide uncovered top. Some kinds of bowl are used, for example, for serving or eating food from, or in cooking, while other larger kinds are used for washing or cleaning. (調理用の) ボウル, 鉢, 洗面器 ❑ *Put all the ingredients into a large bowl.* すべての材料を大きなボウルに入れる. **2** N-COUNT 可算名詞 The contents of a bowl can be referred to as a **bowl of** something. (鉢やボウルに) 一杯分 ❑ *...a bowl of soup.* 椀一杯のスープ **3** N-COUNT 可算名詞 You can refer to the hollow rounded part of an object as its **bowl**. 丸い空洞部分 ❑ *He smacked the bowl*

of his pipe into his hand. 彼はパイプの火皿を自分の手の平に打ちつけた. **4** V-T 他動詞 In a sport such as bowling or lawn bowling, when a bowler **bowls** a ball, he or she rolls it down a narrow track or field of grass. (ボウリングで) ボールを投げる ❑ *Neither finalist bowled a particularly strong game.* 決勝戦出場者はどちらも特に見事なボウリングの試合ぶりではなかった. **5** V-T/V-I 他動詞/自動詞 In a sport such as cricket, when a bowler **bowls** a ball, he or she throws it down the field toward a batsman. (クリケットなどで) 投球する ❑ *I can't see the point of bowling a ball like that.* あんなふうにボールを投げる目的が私には分からない. **6** V-I 自動詞 If you **bowl along** in a car or on a boat, you move along very quickly, especially when you are enjoying yourself. なめらかに進む ❑ *Veronica looked at him, smiling, as they bowled along.* 車は滑らかに進み, ベロニカはほほえみを浮かべて彼を見た. **7** → see also **bowling** → see **dish**

bow|ler /boʊlər/ (**bowlers**) **1** N-COUNT 可算名詞 A **bowler** is someone who plays bowls or goes bowling. ボウリングをする人, クリケットの投手 **2** N-COUNT 可算名詞 The **bowler** in a sport such as cricket is the player who is bowling the ball. (クリケットで) 投球している人

bowl|ing /boʊlɪŋ/ **1** N-UNCOUNT 不可算名詞 **Bowling** is a game in which you roll a heavy ball down a narrow track toward a group of wooden objects and try to knock down as many of them as possible. ボウリング ❑ *I go bowling for relaxation.* 私は息抜きにボウリングに出かける. **2** N-UNCOUNT 不可算名詞 In a sport such as cricket, **bowling** is the action or activity of bowling the ball toward the batsman. クリケットの投球 ❑ *Much of the bowling today will be done by Phil Tufnell.* 今日はほとんどフィル・タフネルが投球する.

box /bɒks/ (**boxes, boxing, boxed**) **1** N-COUNT 可算名詞 A **box** is a square or rectangular container with hard or stiff sides. Boxes often have lids. 箱 ❑ *He reached into the cardboard box beside him.* 彼は近くにあった段ボール箱に手を伸ばした. ❑ *They sat on wooden boxes.* 彼らは木箱の上に座った. **2** N-COUNT 可算名詞 You can use **box** to refer to a box and its contents, or to the contents only. 箱の中身 ❑ *She ate two boxes of chocolates.* 彼女はチョコレートを2箱食べた. **3** N-COUNT 可算名詞 A **box** is a square or rectangle that is printed or drawn on a piece of paper, a road, or on some other surface. 四角い枠 ❑ *For more information, just check the box and send us the form.* 詳細をご希望の方は, 記入欄に印を入れて用紙をお送り下さい. **4** N-COUNT 可算名詞 A **box** is a small separate area in a theater or at a sports arena or stadium, where a small number of people can sit to watch the performance or game. ボックス席 ❑ *Jim watched the game from a private box.* ジムはその試合を専用のボックス席で観戦した. **5** N-COUNT 可算名詞 **Box** is used before a number as a mailing address by people or organizations that rent a post office box. 私書箱 ❑ *...Country Crafts, Box 111, Landisville.* ランディスビル, 私書箱111, カントリー・クラフツ **6** N-UNCOUNT 不可算名詞 **Box** is a small evergreen tree with dark leaves that is often used to form hedges. ツゲ (ツゲ科の常緑樹.) [oft N n] ❑ *...box hedges.* ツゲの生け垣 **7** V-I 自動詞 To **box** means to fight someone according to the rules of boxing. ボクシングをする ❑ *At school I boxed and played rugby.* 私は学校でボクシングとラグビーをした. **8** → see also **boxing, post office box**

▸ **box in 1** PHRASAL VERB 句動詞 If you **are boxed in**, you are unable to move from a particular place because you are surrounded by other people or cars. 進路をふさぐ ❑ *The cabs cut in front of them, trying to box them in.* 複数のタクシーが彼らの行く手をふさごうと前に割り込んできた. **2** PHRASAL VERB 句動詞 If something **boxes** you **in**, it puts you in a situation where you have very little choice about what you can do. 封じ込める ❑ *We are not trying to box anybody in, we are trying to find a satisfactory way forward.* 我々は誰かを封じ込めようとしているのではなく, 納得できる前進策を見つけようとしているのだ.

box|er /bɒksər/ (**boxers**) N-COUNT 可算名詞 A **boxer** is someone who takes part in the sport of boxing. ボクサー

box|ing /bɒksɪŋ/ N-UNCOUNT 不可算名詞 **Boxing** is a sport in which two people wearing large padded gloves fight according to special rules. ボクシング

box lunch (**box lunches**) N-COUNT 可算名詞 A **box lunch** is food packed in a box, for example a sandwich, that you buy and eat as your lunch. 弁当 [AM 米国英語] ❑ *Box lunches can be arranged to take with you on day trips into the valley.* 谷への遠足に持っていくお弁当を用意できます.

box num|ber (**box numbers**) N-COUNT 可算名詞 A **box number** is a number used as an address, for example one given by a newspaper for replies to a private advertisement, or one used by an organization for the letters sent to it. 広告番号 ❑ *He produced 1000 leaflets tagged with his phone number and a post office box number.* 彼は自分の電話番号と私書箱の番号を書いたちらしを1千部作った.

box of|fice (**box offices**) also **box-office 1** N-COUNT 可算名詞 The **box office** in a theater or concert hall is the place where the tickets are sold. (劇場やコンサートホールの) チケット売り場

...*the long line of people outside the box-office.* チケット売り場の外にできた長蛇の列 **2** N-SING 単数名詞 When people talk about **the box office**, they are referring to the degree of success of a film or play in terms of the number of people who go to watch it or the amount of money it makes. （映画や舞台の）興行成績，（映画や舞台の）（収入） □ *The film has taken $180 million at the box office.* その映画は1億8万ドルの収益を上げた.

boy /bɔɪ/ (**boys**) **1** N-COUNT 可算名詞 A **boy** is a child who will grow up to be a man. 男の子 □ *He was still just a boy.* 彼はまだほんの子供だった. **2** N-COUNT 可算名詞 You can refer to a young man as a **boy**, especially when talking about relationships between boys and girls. 男子 □ ...*the age when girls get interested in boys.* 女子が男子に興味を持ち始める年頃 **3** N-COUNT 可算名詞 Someone's **boy** is their son. 息子 [INFORMAL くだけた] □ *Eric was my cousin Edward's boy.* エリックは私のいとこエドワードの息子だった. **4** N-COUNT 可算名詞 You can refer to a man as a **boy**, especially when you are talking about him in an affectionate way. 成人男子に対する親しみを込めた呼び方 □ ...*the local boy who made president.* 大統領となった地元出身の男 [INFORMAL くだけた, FEELINGS 感情] **5** EXCLAM 感嘆詞 Some people say "**boy**" or "**oh boy**" in order to express feelings of excitement or admiration. （興奮や感嘆を込めて）わあ，まあ [mainly AM 主に米国英語, INFORMAL くだけた, FEELINGS 感情] □ *Oh boy! what resourceful children I have.* まあ！私の子供たちはなんて機知に富んでいるのでしょう.

boy|cott /bɔɪkɒt/ (**boycotts, boycotting, boycotted**) V-T 他動詞 If a country, group, or person **boycotts** a country, organization, or activity, they refuse to be involved with it in any way because they disapprove of it. ボイコットする，参加を拒否する □ *The main opposition parties are boycotting the elections.* 主要野党各党は選挙をボイコットしている. ● N-COUNT 可算名詞 **Boycott** is also a noun. ボイコット，参加拒否 □ *Opposition leaders had called for a boycott of the vote.* 反対派の指導者たちは投票を拒否するよう呼びかけていた.

boy|friend /bɔɪfrɛnd/ (**boyfriends**) N-COUNT 可算名詞 Someone's **boyfriend** is a man or boy with whom they are having a romantic or sexual relationship. （男性または男子の）恋人 □ ...*Brenda and her boyfriend Anthony.* ブレンダとその恋人アントニー

> A **boyfriend** is the male person in a romantic relationship. It is not used to describe friendship between men. This is different from **girlfriend**, which can describe either a friendship or a romance.

boy|hood /bɔɪhʊd/ N-UNCOUNT 不可算名詞 **Boyhood** is the period of a male person's life during which he is a boy. 少年時代 □ *They are rivals who have known each other since boyhood.* 彼らは少年時代からお互いを知っている好敵手だ.

boy|ish /bɔɪɪʃ/ ADJ 形容詞 If you describe a man as **boyish**, you mean that he is like a boy in his appearance or behavior, and you find this characteristic quite attractive. 少年のような [APPROVAL 賛成] □ *She was relieved to see his face light up with a boyish grin.* 彼女は彼の顔に少年のような笑みが浮かぶのを見てホッとした. ● **boy|ish|ly** ADV 副詞 少年のように □ *John grinned boyishly.* 彼は少年のようににっこりほほえんだ.

bps /bi pi ɛs/ **bps** is a measurement of the speed at which computer data is transferred, for example, by a modem. **bps** is an abbreviation for "bits per second." ビット/秒（データ転送速度の単位）[COMPUTING コンピューティング] □ *A minimum 28,800 bps modem is probably the slowest you'll want to put up with.* 最低でも28,800 bpsのモデムがおそらく我慢できる限界の遅さだろう.

bra /brɑː/ (**bras**) N-COUNT 可算名詞 A **bra** is a piece of underwear that women wear to support their breasts. ブラジャー

brace /breɪs/ (**braces, bracing, braced**) **1** V-T 他動詞 If you **brace yourself for** something unpleasant or difficult, you prepare yourself for it. （困難や不快な事に）備える □ *He braced himself for the icy plunge into the black water.* 彼は冷たく暗い水に飛び込むため身構えた. **2** V-T 他動詞 If you **brace yourself against** something or **brace** part of your body **against** it, you press against something in order to steady your body or to avoid falling. （体を）支える □ *Elaine braced herself against the dresser and looked in the mirror.* イレインは化粧台にもたれて鏡をのぞき込んだ. **3** V-T 他動詞 If you **brace** your shoulders or knees, you keep them stiffly in a particular position. （肩に）力を入れる，踏ん張る □ *He braced his shoulders defiantly as another squall of wet snow slashed across his face.* 湿った雪を含む突風がまた彼の顔に打ち付けたとき，彼は挑戦するように肩に力を入れた. **4** V-T 他動詞 To **brace** something means to strengthen or support it with something else. （他の物を使って）支える，補強する □ *Overhead, the lights showed the old timbers, used to brace the roof.* 頭上で明かりが，かつて屋根を支えていた古いはりを照らし出した. **5** N-COUNT 可算名詞 A **brace** is a device attached to a part of a person's body, for example, to a weak leg, in order to strengthen or support it. 装具，（体の弱い部分を支える）コルセット □ *He wore leg braces after he had polio in childhood.* 彼は子供の時にポリオを患ってから下肢装具を着けていた. **6** N-PLURAL 複数名詞 **Braces** are a metal device that can be fastened to a person's

teeth in order to help them grow straight. 歯列矯正器 □ *I used to have to wear braces.* 私は以前，歯列矯正器をつけなくてはならなかった. **7** N-COUNT 可算名詞 **Braces** are a pair of written marks {} that you place around words, numbers, or parts of a computer code, for example, to indicate that they are connected in some way or are separate from other parts of the writing or code. 中かっこ [AM 米国英語] **8** N-PLURAL 複数名詞 **Braces** are a pair of straps that pass over your shoulders and fasten to your pants at the front and back in order to stop them from falling down. （ズボンがずり落ちないようにする）サスペンダー [BRIT 英国英語; AM suspenders 米国英語 **suspenders**]
→ see **teeth**

brace|let /breɪslɪt/ (**bracelets**) N-COUNT 可算名詞 A **bracelet** is a chain or band, usually made of metal, that you wear around your wrist as jewelry. ブレスレット，腕輪
→ see **jewelry**

brac|ing /breɪsɪŋ/ ADJ 形容詞 If you describe something, especially a place, climate, or activity as **bracing**, you mean that it makes you feel fresh and full of energy. すがすがしい □ ...*a bracing walk.* すがすがしい散歩

brack|et /brækɪt/ (**brackets, bracketing, bracketed**) **1** N-COUNT 可算名詞 If you say that someone or something is in a particular **bracket**, you mean that they come within a particular range, for example, a range of incomes, ages, or prices. （所得，年齢，価格などの）階層，（所得，年齢，価格などの）部類 □ ...*a 33% top tax rate on everyone in these high-income brackets.* これらの所得階層の全員にかかる33%の最高税率 **2** N-COUNT 可算名詞 **Brackets** are pieces of metal, wood, or plastic that are fastened to a wall in order to support something such as a shelf. （棚などを支える）腕木，（棚などを支える）ブラケット □ *Fix the beam with the brackets and screws.* はりをブラケットとねじで修理しなさい. **3** V-T 他動詞 If two or more people or things **are bracketed together**, they are considered to be similar or related in some way. 分類する，同類と見なす □ *The Magi, Brahmins, and Druids were bracketed together as men of wisdom.* マギ，バラモン，ドルイドは賢人としてひとまとめにされた. **4** N-COUNT 可算名詞 **Brackets** are pair of marks ( ) that are placed around a series of symbols in a mathematical expression to indicate that those symbols function as one item within the expression. かっこ（数式で（ ）の記号を用いる）**5** N-COUNT 可算名詞 **Brackets** are a pair of written marks ( ) that you place around a word, expression, or sentence in order to indicate that you are giving extra information. かっこ（文中で（ ）の記号を用いる）[BRIT 英国英語; AM parentheses 米国英語 **parentheses**]

brag /bræg/ (**brags, bragging, bragged**) V-T/V-I 他動詞/自動詞 If you **brag**, you say in a very proud way that you have something or have done something. 自慢する [DISAPPROVAL 不賛成] □ *He's always bragging that he's a great martial artist.* 彼はいつも自分が素晴らしい武道家だと自慢している. □ *He'll probably go around bragging to his friends.* 彼は恐らく友たちに自慢して回るだろう. □ *Winn bragged that he had spies in the department.* ウィンはその部署にスパイがいると自慢した.

braid /breɪd/ (**braids, braiding, braided**) **1** N-UNCOUNT 不可算名詞 **Braid** is a narrow piece of decorated cloth or twisted threads, which is used to decorate clothes or curtains. 組みひも □ ...*a plum-colored uniform with lots of gold braid.* たくさんの金の組みひもで飾られた濃い紫色の制服 **2** V-T 他動詞 If you **braid** hair or a group of threads, you twist three or more lengths of the hair or threads over and under each other to make one thick length. 三つ編みにする [AM 米国英語] □ *She had almost finished braiding Louisa's hair.* 彼女はもう少しでルイーザの髪を三つ編みにし終えるところだった. **3** N-COUNT 可算名詞 A **braid** is a length of hair that has been divided into three or more lengths and then braided. 三つ編み [AM 米国英語] □ ...*a short, energetic woman with her hair in braids.* 髪が三つ編みで背が低く活発な女性

brain /breɪn/ (**brains**) **1** N-COUNT 可算名詞 Your **brain** is the organ inside your head that controls your body's activities and enables you to think and to feel things such as heat and pain. 脳 □ *Her father died of a brain tumor.* 彼女の父親は脳しゅようのため死亡した. **2** N-COUNT 可算名詞 Your **brain** is your mind and the way that you think. 頭脳，頭 □ *Once you stop using your brain you soon go stale.* 頭を使うのを止めるとすぐに生気がなくなるだろう. **3** N-COUNT 可算名詞 If someone has **brains** or a good **brain**, they have the ability to learn and understand things quickly, to solve problems, and to make good decisions. 頭脳，（明晰な）知力 □ *They were not the only ones to have brains and ambition.* 頭脳明晰で野心を抱いているのは彼らだけではなかった. **4** N-COUNT 可算名詞 If someone is **the brains** behind an idea or an organization, he or she had that idea or makes the important decisions about how that organization is managed. 知的な指導者，ブレーン [INFORMAL くだけた] □ *Mr. White was the brains behind the scheme.* ホワイト氏がこの計画の知的指導者だった. **5** to **rack** your **brains** → see **rack**
→ see Word Web: **brain**
→ see **nervous system**

Word Web   brain

The human **brain** weighs about three pounds. It contains seven distinct sections. The largest are the cerebrum, the cerebellum, and the medulla oblongata. The cerebrum wraps around the outside of the brain. It handles **learning**, **communication**, and voluntary **movement**. The cerebellum controls **balance**, **posture**, and movement. The medulla oblongata links the **spinal cord** with other parts of the brain. This part of the brain controls automatic actions such as breathing, heartbeat, and swallowing. It also tells us when we are hungry and when we need to sleep.

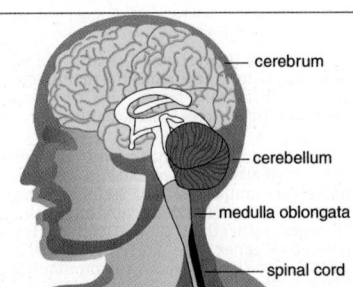

cerebrum

cerebellum

medulla oblongata

spinal cord

brain|child /breɪntʃaɪld/ N-SING 単数名詞 Someone's **brainchild** is an idea or invention that they have thought up or created. 独創的な考え, 頭脳の産物 ❑ *The record was the brainchild of rock star Bob Geldof.* そのレコードはロックスターのボブ・ゲルドフの案出物だった.

brain|storm /breɪnstɔrm/ (**brainstorms, brainstorming, brainstormed**) **1** N-COUNT 可算名詞 If you have a **brainstorm**, you suddenly have a clever idea. 突然の名案, ひらめき [AM 米国英語] ❑ *"Look," she said, getting a brainstorm, "why don't you invite them here?"* 「ねえ」突然ひらめいたように彼女が言った. 「彼らをここに呼んだらどう. 」 **2** V-T/V-I 他動詞/自動詞 If a group of people **brainstorm**, they have a meeting in which they all put forward as many ideas and suggestions as they can think of. ブレーンストーミングをする ❑ *The women meet twice a month to brainstorm and set business goals for each other.* その女性たちはブレーンストーミングをするために毎月2回ミーティングをし, お互いのビジネスの目標を立てる. ❑ *She brainstormed the possible approaches she might take.* 彼女は自分がとる可能性のある方法についてブレーンストーミングをした. ● **brain|storming** N-UNCOUNT 不可算名詞 ブレーンストーミング ❑ *Hundreds of other ideas had been tried and discarded during two years of brainstorming.* 2年間のブレーンストーミングで何百もの案が試され, 放棄された.

brain|wash /breɪnwɒʃ/ (**brainwashes, brainwashing, brainwashed**) V-T 他動詞 If you **brainwash** someone, you force them to believe something by continually telling them that it is true, and preventing them from thinking about it properly. 洗脳する ❑ *They brainwash people into giving up all their money.* 彼らは全財産を寄付するように人々を洗脳する.

brain|wave /breɪnweɪv/ (**brainwaves**) N-COUNT 可算名詞 If you have a **brainwave**, you suddenly have a clever idea. ひらめき [BRIT 英国英語; AM **brainstorm** 米国英語 **brainstorm**]

brake /breɪk/ (**brakes, braking, braked**) **1** N-COUNT 可算名詞 **Brakes** are devices in a vehicle that make it go slower or stop. ブレーキ ❑ *A seagull swooped down in front of her car, causing her to slam on the brakes.* かもめが車の前に舞い降りたので, 彼女は急ブレーキをかけた. **2** V-T/V-I 他動詞/自動詞 When a vehicle or its driver **brakes**, or when a driver **brakes** a vehicle, the driver makes it slow down or stop by using the brakes. ブレーキをかける [他動詞], ブレーキがかかる [自動詞] ❑ *He heard tires squeal as the car braked to avoid a collision.* 衝突を避けるために車がブレーキをかけた際, 彼にはタイヤがキキーッとなるのが聞こえた. ❑ *He braked the car slightly.* 彼は車のブレーキをゆるくかけた. **3** N-COUNT 可算名詞 You can use **brake** in a number of expressions to indicate that something has slowed down or stopped. 歯止め ❑ *Illness had put a brake on his progress.* 病気が彼の進歩に歯止めをかけた.

bran /bræn/ N-UNCOUNT 不可算名詞 **Bran** is the outer skin of grain that is left when the grain has been used to make flour. ふすま, ぬか ❑ *...oat bran.* オート麦ぬか

branch /bræntʃ/ (**branches, branching, branched**) **1** N-COUNT 可算名詞 The **branches** of a tree are the parts that grow out from its trunk and have leaves, flowers, or fruit growing on them. 枝 ❑ *...the upper branches of a row of pines.* 松並木の上部の枝 **2** N-COUNT 可算名詞 A **branch of** a business or other organization is one of the offices, stores, or groups which belong to it and which are located in different places. 支店, 支所 ❑ *The local branch of Bank of America is handling the accounts.* 地域のバンクオブアメリカの支店が口座を取り扱っている. **3** N-COUNT 可算名詞 A **branch of** an organization such as the government or the police force is a department that has a particular function. (組織・制度などの) 部門, (組織・制度などの) 分課 ❑ *Senate employees could take their employment grievances to another branch of government.* 上院従業員は雇用に関する苦情を政府の他の部門に申し立てることができる. ❑ *He had a fascination for submarines and joined this branch of the service.* 彼は潜水艦に魅力を感じ, 軍のこの部門に入った. **4** N-COUNT 可算名詞 A **branch of** a subject is a part or type of it. (研究・学問分野などの) 部門, (研究・学問分野などの) 課 ❑ *Whole branches of science may not receive any grants.* 科学の全部門が助成金を受けない可能性がある. **5** N-COUNT 可算名詞 A **branch of** your family is a group of its members who

are descended from one particular person. 血筋 ❑ *This is one of the branches of the Roosevelt family.* こちらはルーズベルト家の血筋です.

▶ **branch off** PHRASAL VERB 句動詞 A road or path that **branches off** from another one starts from it and goes in a slightly different direction. If you **branch off** somewhere, you change the direction in which you are going. (道路などが) 分かれる, (話題などが) それる ❑ *After a few miles, a small road branched off to the right.* 数マイル行くと, 細い道が右に分岐していた.

▶ **branch out** PHRASAL VERB 句動詞 If a person or an organization **branches out**, they do something that is different from their normal activities or work. 新分野に乗り出す ❑ *I continued studying moths, and branched out to other insects.* 私は蛾(が)の研究を続けながら他の昆虫にも手を広げた.

brand /brænd/ (**brands, branding, branded**) **1** N-COUNT 可算名詞 A **brand** of a product is the version of it that is made by one particular manufacturer. ブランド, 銘柄 ❑ *Winston is a brand of cigarette.* ウィンストンはタバコの銘柄だ. ❑ *I bought one of the leading brands.* 私は一流ブランドを買った. **2** N-COUNT 可算名詞 A **brand of** something such as a way of thinking or behaving is a particular kind of it. 独特の ❑ *Joel Hatch brings his own unique brand of humor to the role.* ジョエル・ハッチは独特のユーモアをその役に生かしている. **3** V-T 他動詞 If someone **is branded** as something bad, people think they are that thing. 決めつける, 烙印(らくいん) を押す ❑ *I was instantly branded as a rebel.* 私は早速, 反抗者としての烙印を押された. ❑ *The company has been branded racist by some of its own staff.* 会社は従業員の一部から人種差別主義者という烙印を押された. **4** V-T 他動詞 When you **brand** an animal, you put a permanent mark on its skin in order to show who it belongs to, usually by burning a mark onto its skin. (家畜に) 焼印を押す ❑ *The owner couldn't be bothered to brand the cattle.* 牧場主はわざわざ牛に焼印は押さなかった. ● N-COUNT 可算名詞 **Brand** is also a noun. (家畜に押す) 焼印 ❑ *A brand was a mark of ownership burned into the hide of an animal with a hot iron.* 焼印とは所有を示すために熱い鉄で家畜の皮を焼いて付ける印だった.

The **brand** of a product such as jeans, tea, or soap is its name, which can also be the name of the company that makes or sells it. The **make** of a car or electrical appliance such as a radio or washing machine is the name of the company that produces it. If you talk about what **type** of product or service you want, you are talking about its quality and what features it should have. You can also talk about **types** of people or of abstract things. ❑ *...which type of coffeemaker to choose. ...a new type of bank account. ...looking for a certain type of actor.* A **model** of car or of some other devices is a name that is given to a particular **type**, for example, a Ford Escort. Note that **type** can also be used informally to mean either **make** or **model**. For example, if someone asks what **type** of car you have got, you could reply "an SUV," "a Ford," or perhaps "an Escort."

brand|ed /brændɪd/ ADJ 形容詞 A **branded** product is one that is made by a well-known manufacturer and has the manufacturer's label on it. (有名) ブランドの [BUSINESS 実業] [ADJ] N ❑ *Supermarket lines are often cheaper than branded goods.* スーパーの商品はブランド物より安いことが多い.

brand im|age (**brand images**) N-COUNT 可算名詞 The **brand image** of a particular brand of a product is the image or impression that people have of it, usually created by advertising. ブランドイメージ [BUSINESS 実業] ❑ *Few products have brand images anywhere near as strong as Levi's.* リーバイスほどブランドイメージが高い商品はほとんどない.

bran|dish /brændɪʃ/ (**brandishes, brandishing, brandished**) V-T 他動詞 If you **brandish** something, especially a weapon, you hold it in a threatening way. (武器などを威嚇するために) 振りかざす ❑ *He appeared in the lounge brandishing a knife.* 彼はナイフを振りかざして居間に現れた.

brand lead|er (**brand leaders**) N-COUNT 可算名詞 The **brand leader** of a particular product is the brand of it that most people choose to buy, or the manufacturer that makes that brand. 代表

ブランド, 人気ブランド [BUSINESS 実業] ❏ *In office supplies, we're the brand leader.* 事務用品では当社が代表ブランドだ.

brand name (**brand names**) N-COUNT 可算名詞 The **brand name** of a product is the name the manufacturer gives it and under which it is sold. 商標名, ブランド名 [BUSINESS 実業] ❏ *The drug is marketed under the brand name Viramune.* その薬品はビラミューンという商品名で市販されている.

> The maker of a product may come to be identified so closely with it that all products of that sort are called by the same name. For example, tissue paper for blowing your nose is branded as Kleenex and so people often call all brands of tissue "Kleenex" rather than "tissue." "My nose is running. Please give me a Kleenex." The "Trademark" label in this dictionary will show you brands which are commonly used in this way.

brand-name prod|uct (**brand-name products**) N-COUNT 可算名詞 A **brand-name product** is one which is made by a well-known manufacturer and has the manufacturer's label on it. ブランド商品 [BUSINESS 実業] ❏ *In buying footwear, 66% prefer brand-name products.* 靴を買う人の66%がブランド商品を好む.

brand-new ADJ 形容詞 A **brand-new** object is completely new. 新品の ❏ *Yesterday he went off to buy himself a brand-new car.* 昨日, 彼は新車を買いにいった.

bran|dy /brǽndi/ (**brandies**) ■ N-MASS 質量名詞 **Brandy** is a strong alcoholic drink. It is often drunk after a meal. ブランデー ■ N-COUNT 可算名詞 A **brandy** is a glass of brandy. ブランデー1杯 ❏ *After a couple of brandies Michael started telling me his life story.* ブランデーを2杯飲んだ後, マイケルは身の上話を始めた.

brash /brǽʃ/ (**brasher, brashest**) ADJ 形容詞 If you describe someone or their behavior as **brash**, you disapprove of them because you think that they are too confident and aggressive. 厚かましい [DISAPPROVAL 不賛成] ❏ *On stage she seems hard, brash and uncompromising.* ステージでは彼女はきつく, 厚かましく, 頑固にみえる. ● **brash|ly** ADV 副詞 厚かましく ❏ *I brashly announced to the group that NATO needed to be turned around.* 私は厚かましくも北大西洋条約機構は方向転換をする必要があるとグループに宣言した.

brass /brǽs/ ■ N-UNCOUNT 不可算名詞 **Brass** is a yellow-colored metal made from copper and zinc. It is used especially for making ornaments and musical instruments. 真鍮（ちゅう）, 黄銅 ❏ *The instrument is beautifully made in brass.* その楽器は真鍮で精巧に作られている. ■ N-SING 単数名詞 The **brass** is the section of an orchestra which consists of brass wind instruments such as trumpets and horns. 金管楽器 ❏ *Consequently even this vast chorus was occasionally overwhelmed by the brass.* したがって, この大合唱でさえ, ときに金管楽器に圧倒された.
→ see **orchestra**

brat /brǽt/ (**brats**) N-COUNT 可算名詞 If you call someone, especially a child, a **brat**, you mean that he or she behaves badly or annoys you. がき [INFORMAL くだけた, DISAPPROVAL 不賛成] ❏ *He's a spoiled brat.* 彼はわがままながきだ.

bra|va|do /brəvɑ́doʊ/ N-UNCOUNT 不可算名詞 **Bravado** is an appearance of courage or confidence that someone shows in order to impress other people. 虚勢, 空いばり ❏ *"You won't get away with this," he said with unexpected bravado.* 「このままでは済まないぞ」と彼は意外にも空いばりをして言った.

brave /breɪv/ (**braver, bravest, braves, braving, braved**) ■ ADJ 形容詞 Someone who is **brave** is willing to do things that are dangerous, and does not show fear in difficult or dangerous situations. 勇気がある, 勇敢な ❏ *He was not brave enough to report the loss of the documents.* 彼は書類の紛失を報告する勇気がなかった. ● **brave|ly** ADV 副詞 勇敢に ❏ *Our men wiped them out, but the enemy fought bravely and well.* 当軍が圧倒的勝利を収めたが, 敵も勇敢によく戦った. ■ V-T 他動詞 If you **brave** unpleasant or dangerous conditions, you deliberately expose yourself to them, usually in order to achieve something. 立ち向かう [WRITTEN 書き言葉] ❏ *Thousands have braved icy rain to demonstrate their support.* 数千人が凍りつくような雨の中をものともせずに支持を示威した.
→ see **hero**

Thesaurus	*brave* また次を参照:
ADJ.	courageous, fearless, unafraid; (*ant.*) afraid, cowardly ■
V.	dare, endure, risk ■

brav|ery /breɪvəri/ N-UNCOUNT 不可算名詞 **Bravery** is brave behavior or the quality of being brave. 勇気, 勇敢さ ❏ *He deserves the highest praise for his bravery.* 彼の勇敢さは最大の称賛に値する.

brawl /brɔ́l/ (**brawls, brawling, brawled**) ■ N-COUNT 可算名詞 A **brawl** is a rough or violent fight. 騒々しいけんか, 乱闘 ❏ *He had been in a drunken street brawl.* 彼は路上での酔っ払いのけんかに巻き込まれました. ■ V-RECIP 相互動詞 If someone **brawls**, they fight in a very rough or violent way. 騒々しいけんかをする, 乱闘する ❏ *He was suspended for a year from the university after brawling with police*

over a speeding ticket. 彼はスピード違反について警察と激しいけんかをした後, 大学から1年停学処分を受けた.

bra|zen /breɪzⁿn/ ADJ 形容詞 If you describe a person or their behavior as **brazen**, you mean that they are very bold and do not care what other people think about them or their behavior. ずうずうしい, 恥知らずな ❏ *They're quite brazen about their bisexuality, it doesn't worry them.* 彼らは同性愛者であることには平然としていて, 気にしていない. ● **bra|zen|ly** ADV 副詞 厚かましく, 平然と ❏ *He was brazenly running a $400,000-a-month drug operation from the prison.* 彼は月々40万ドル相当の麻薬取引を平然と刑務所から行っていた.

breach /bríʧ/ (**breaches, breaching, breached**) ■ V-T 他動詞 If you **breach** an agreement, a law, or a promise, you break it. （協定・法律などに）違反する, （約束などを）破る ❏ *The newspaper breached the code of conduct on privacy.* その新聞はプライバシーに関する行動規範に違反した. ■ N-VAR 可変名詞 A **breach** of an agreement, a law, or a promise is an act of breaking it. （協定・法律・約束などの）違反, （協定・法律・約束などの）不履行 ❏ *The congressman was accused of a breach of secrecy rules.* その国会議員は秘密規定違反で告発された. ■ N-COUNT 可算名詞 A **breach in** a relationship is a serious disagreement which often results in the relationship ending. 不和 [FORMAL 形式ばった] ❏ *Their actions threatened a serious breach in relations between the two countries.* 彼らの行動により2国間の関係に深刻な亀裂が生じる恐れが生じた. ■ V-T 他動詞 If someone or something **breaches** a barrier, they make an opening in it, usually leaving it weakened or destroyed. 破る, 裂く [FORMAL 形式ばった] ❏ *The limestone is sufficiently fissured for tree roots to have breached the roof of the cave.* 洞くつの天井の石灰岩には木の根がそれを破るほどの亀裂があった. ■ V-T 他動詞 If you **breach** someone's security or their defenses, you manage to get through and attack an area that is heavily guarded and protected. （警備・防衛などを）抜ける, （警備・防衛などを）突破する ❏ *The bomber had breached security by hurling his dynamite from a roof overlooking the building.* 爆破犯人は建物を見下ろすところにある屋根からダイナマイトを投げて警備を突破した. ● N-COUNT 可算名詞 **Breach** is also a noun. （警備・防衛などの）突破 ❏ *...serious breaches of security at Camp Delta.* キャンプ・デルタでの深刻な安全侵害

bread /brɛ́d/ (**breads**) N-MASS 質量名詞 **Bread** is a very common food made from flour, water, and usually yeast. パン ❏ *...a loaf of bread.* パン1斤 ❏ *...bread and butter.* バターつきのパン

breadth /brɛ́tθ/ ■ N-UNCOUNT 不可算名詞 The **breadth** of something is the distance between its two sides. 幅, 横幅 ❏ *The breadth of the whole camp was 400 paces.* 収容所全体の横幅は, 400歩分だ. ■ N-UNCOUNT 不可算名詞 The **breadth** of something is its quality of consisting of or involving many different things. 幅広さ ❏ *Older people have a tremendous breadth of experience.* 年配者には素晴らしい経験の幅広さがある.

bread|winner /brɛ́dwɪnər/ (**breadwinners**) also **bread-winner** N-COUNT 可算名詞 The **breadwinner** in a family is the person in it who earns the money that the family needs for essential things. 一家の稼ぎ手 ❏ *I've always paid the bills and been the breadwinner.* 私はいつも一家の大黒柱として家計を支えてきた.

break
❶ DAMAGE OR DESTROY
❷ STOP OR CHANGE SOMETHING
❸ OTHER USES
❹ PHRASAL VERBS

❶ **break** /breɪk/ (**breaks, breaking, broke, broken**) ■ V-T/V-I 他動詞/自動詞 When an object **breaks** or when you **break** it, it suddenly separates into two or more pieces, often because it has been hit or dropped. 壊す, 割る [他動詞], 壊れる, 割れる [自動詞] ❏ *He fell through the window, breaking the glass.* 彼は窓ガラスを割って, 窓から落ちた. ❏ *The plate broke.* お皿が割れた. ❏ *The plane broke into three pieces.* 飛行機が3つに分解した. ■ V-T/V-I 他動詞/自動詞 If you **break** a part of your body such as your leg, your arm, or your nose, or if a bone **breaks**, you are injured because a bone cracks or splits. 折る [他動詞], 骨折する, ひびが入る [自動詞] ❏ *She broke a leg in a skiing accident.* 彼女はスキー事故で足を折った. ❏ *Old bones break easily.* お年寄りは骨折しやすい. ● N-COUNT 可算名詞 **Break** is also a noun. 骨折 ❏ *It has caused a bad break to Gabriella's leg.* それが原因でガブリエルの足はひどい骨折をした. ■ V-T/V-I 他動詞/自動詞 If a surface, cover, or seal **breaks** or if something **breaks** it, a hole or tear is made in it, so that a substance can pass through. 破る [他動詞], 破れる [自動詞] ❏ *Once you've broken the seal of a bottle there's no way you can put it back together again.* 一度瓶の封印を破ると, 二度と元に戻せない. ❏ *The bandage must be put on when the blister breaks.* 水ぶくれが破れたら, 包帯を巻かなければいけない. ■ V-T/V-I 他動詞/自動詞 When a tool or piece of machinery **breaks** or when you **break** it, it is damaged and no longer works. （機械などを）壊す [他動詞], （機械などが）壊れる, （機械などが）故障する [自動詞] ❏ *When the clutch broke, the car was locked into second*

gear. クラッチが故障したとき，車のギアはセカンドに入ったまま動かなかった.

→ see **crash**, **factory**

Word Partnership	*break* は次の語句と使われる:
N.	break **a bone**, break **your arm/leg/neck** ❶ ❷
	break **the silence** ❷ ❷
	break **a habit** ❷ ❹
	coffee/lunch break ❷ ❻
	break **the law**, break **a promise**, break **a rule** ❸ ❶
	break **a record** ❸ ❼
V.	**need a** break, **take a** break ❷ ❻

❷ **break** /breɪk/ (breaks, breaking, broke, broken) ❶ V-T 他動詞 If someone **breaks** something, especially a difficult or unpleasant situation that has existed for some time, they end it or change it. 打開する，断ち切る ❑ *We need to break the vicious cycle of violence and counterviolence.* 暴力と報復の悪循環を断ち切る必要がある. ❑ *New proposals have been put forward to break the deadlock among rival factions.* 対抗する派閥間での膠着(こうちゃく)状態を打開するために新提案が提出された. ●N-COUNT 可算名詞 **Break** is also a noun. 打開 ❑ *Nothing that might lead to a break in the deadlock has been discussed yet.* 膠着(こうちゃく)状態打開に向けての協議は全く行われなかった. ❷ V-T 他動詞 If someone or something **breaks** a silence, they say something or make a noise after a long period of silence. (沈黙などを) 破る ❑ *Hugh broke the silence. "Is she always late?" he asked.* ヒューが沈黙を破った. 「彼女はいつも遅いのかい?」と彼は尋ねた. ❸ V-T/V-I 他動詞/自動詞 If you **break with** a group of people or a traditional way of doing things, or you **break** your connection with them, you stop being involved with that group or stop doing things in that way. (伝統などを) 破る，(人との) 関係を絶つ ❑ *In 1959, Akihito broke with imperial tradition by marrying a commoner.* 1959年に明仁皇太子は民間人と結婚し皇室の伝統を破る決意だった. ❑ *They were determined to break from precedent.* 彼らは慣習を破る決意だった. ●N-COUNT 可算名詞 **Break** is also a noun. 決別，断絶 ❑ *Making a completely clean break with the past, the couple got rid of all their old furniture.* 過去を清算するために，その夫婦は古い家具を全て処分した. ❹ V-T 他動詞 If you **break** a habit or if someone **breaks** you **of** it, you no longer have that habit. (癖・習慣などを) 止める ❑ *If you continue to smoke, keep trying to break the habit.* タバコを吸いつづける人は習慣を断ち切る努力を続けるべきだ. ❺ V-I 自動詞 If someone **breaks for** a short period of time, they rest or change from what they are doing for a short period. 休憩する ❑ *They broke for lunch.* 彼らは昼休みを取りました. ❻ N-COUNT 可算名詞 A **break** is a short period of time when you have a rest or a change from what you are doing, especially if you are working or if you are in a boring or unpleasant situation. 休憩 ❑ *They may be able to help with childcare so that you can have a break.* あなたが休憩できるように彼らが子供の面倒を見てくれるかもしれません. ❑ *I thought a 15-minute break from his work would do him good.* 私は，彼が15分休憩を取ったほうがいいだろうと思った. ❼ N-COUNT 可算名詞 A **break** is a short vacation. 短期旅行 ❑ *They are currently taking a short break in Spain.* 彼らは現在スペインで短期休暇を取っている. ❽ V-T 他動詞 If you **break** your journey somewhere, you stop there for a short time so that you can have a rest. (旅の途中で) 休憩する，(旅の途中で) 立ち寄る ❑ *We broke our journey at a small country hotel.* 私たちは旅の途中で小さな田舎のホテルに立ち寄った.

→ see **factory**

❸ **break** /breɪk/ (breaks, breaking, broke, broken) ❶ V-T 他動詞 If you **break** a rule, promise, or agreement, you do something that you should not do according to that rule, promise, or agreement. (規則・約束・協定を) 破る ❑ *We didn't know we were breaking the law.* 我々は法律を犯しているとは知らずにいた. ❑ *The company has consistently denied it had knowingly broken arms embargoes.* その会社は故意に武器禁輸に違反したことを一貫して否定した. ❷ V-I 自動詞 If you **break** free or loose, you free yourself from something or escape from it. 逃げ出す，脱出する ❑ *She broke free by thrusting her elbow into his chest.* 彼女はひじを彼の胸にグイと突いて逃げ出した. ❸ V-T 他動詞 To **break** the force of something such as a blow or fall means to weaken its effect, for example, by getting in the way of it. 効果を弱める ❑ *He sustained serious neck injuries after he broke someone's fall.* 彼は人が落ちるのを受け止めて首に重傷を負った. ❹ V-I 自動詞 When a piece of news **breaks**, people hear about it from the newspapers, television, or radio. (ニュースなどが) 明るみに出る ❑ *The news broke that Montgomery was under investigation.* モントゴメリが取り調べを受けているというニュースが流れた. ❺ V-T 他動詞 When you **break** a piece of bad news to someone, you tell it to them, usually in a kind way. 打ち明ける，切り出す ❑ *Then Louise broke the news that she was leaving me.* そのときルイーズが別れ話を切り出した. ❻ N-COUNT 可算名詞 A **break** is a lucky opportunity that someone gets to achieve something. チャンス [INFORMAL くだけた] ❑ *Her first break came when she was chosen out of 100 guitarists auditioning for a spot on Michael Jackson's tour.* 彼女に最初のチャンスが訪れたのはマイケル・ジャクソンのツアーのメンバー募集のオーディ

ションで100人のギターリストの中から選考されたときだった. ❼ V-T 他動詞 If you **break** a record, you beat the previous record for a particular achievement. (記録などを) 破る，(記録などを) 更新する ❑ *Carl Lewis has broken the world record in the 100 meters.* カール・ルイスは100メートル走で世界記録を更新した. ❽ V-I 自動詞 When day or dawn **breaks**, it starts to grow light after the night has ended. (夜が) 明ける ❑ *They continued the search as dawn broke.* 夜が明けるとともに捜索を再開した. ❾ V-I 自動詞 When a wave **breaks**, it passes its highest point and turns downward, for example, when it reaches the shore. (波が) 砕ける ❑ *Danny listened to the waves breaking against the shore.* ダニーは波が海岸に砕ける音を聞いていた. ❿ V-T 自動詞 If you **break** a secret code, you work out how to understand it. (暗号を) 解読する ❑ *It was feared they could break the Allies' codes.* 彼らが連合国の暗号を解読する恐れがあった. ⓫ V-I 自動詞 If someone's voice **breaks** when they are speaking, it changes its sound, for example, because they are sad or afraid. (感情により声が) 上ずる ❑ *Godfrey's voice broke, and halted.* ゴドフリーの声が上ずり，言葉に詰まった. ⓬ V-I 自動詞 When a boy's voice **breaks**, it becomes deeper and sounds more like a man's voice. 声変わりする ❑ *He sings with the strained discomfort of someone whose voice hasn't quite broken.* 彼は声変わりが済んでいないのを無理しながら歌う. ⓭ V-I 自動詞 If the weather **breaks** or a storm **breaks**, it suddenly becomes rainy or stormy after a period of sunshine. (天候が) 崩れる ❑ *I've been waiting for the weather to break.* 天候が崩れるのをずっと待っていた. ⓮ → see also **broke**, **broken**, **heartbreak**, **heartbreaking**, **heartbroken**, **outbreak** ⓯ to break even → see **even** ⓰ to break new ground → see **ground** ⓱ to break someone's heart → see **heart** ⓲ all hell breaks loose → see **hell** ⓳ to break the ice → see **ice** ⓴ to break ranks → see **rank** ㉑ to break wind → see **wind**

❹ **break** /breɪk/ (breaks, breaking, broke, broken)

▶ **break down** ❶ PHRASAL VERB 句動詞 If a machine or a vehicle **breaks down**, it stops working. 故障する ❑ *Their car broke down.* 彼らの自動車が故障した. ❷ PHRASAL VERB 句動詞 If a discussion, relationship, or system **breaks down**, it fails because of a problem or disagreement. (話し合いが) 決裂する (関係・体制が) 破綻(はたん)する ❑ *Talks with business leaders broke down last night.* 昨夜，財界首脳との話し合いは決裂に終わった. ❸ PHRASAL VERB 句動詞 To **break down** something such as an idea or statement means to separate it into smaller parts in order to make it easier to understand or deal with. 分割する，分ける ❑ *The report breaks down the results region by region.* 報告書は結果を地域ごとに分割している. ❹ PHRASAL VERB 句動詞 When a substance **breaks down** or when something **breaks** it **down**, a biological or chemical process causes it to separate into the substances which make it up. (化学的に) 分解する ❑ *Over time, the protein in the eggshell breaks down into its constituent amino acids.* 時がたてば，卵殻のたんぱく質は構成アミノ酸に分解する. ❺ PHRASAL VERB 句動詞 If someone **breaks down**, they lose control of themselves and start crying. 取り乱す ❑ *Because he was being so kind and concerned, I broke down and cried.* 彼があまりにも優しくて気遣ってくれたので，私は泣き崩れてしまった. ❻ PHRASAL VERB 句動詞 If you **break down** a door or barrier, you hit it so hard that it falls to the ground. (ドアなどを) たたき壊す ❑ *An unruly mob broke down police barricades and stormed the courtroom.* 暴徒の集まりが警察バリケードを打ち破って法廷を襲撃した. ❼ PHRASAL VERB 句動詞 To **break down** barriers or prejudices that separate people or restrict their freedom means to change people's attitudes so that the barriers or prejudices no longer exist. (障害や偏見を) 取り除く [APPROVAL 賛成] ❑ *Women's sports are breaking down the barriers in previously male-dominated domains.* 女性スポーツは以前は男性が中心だった分野で障壁を取り除いている. ❽ → see also **breakdown**

▶ **break in** ❶ PHRASAL VERB 句動詞 If someone, usually a thief, **breaks in**, they get into a building by force. 乱入する ❑ *Masked robbers broke in and made off with $8,000.* 覆面強盗が乱入し，8千ドルを持ち去った. ❷ → see also **break-in** ❸ PHRASAL VERB 句動詞 If you **break in** on someone's conversation or activity, you interrupt them. 割り込む，口を挟む ❑ *O'Leary broke in on his thoughts.* 彼が考えごとをしているときにオーリアリーがじゃまをした. ❑ *Mrs. Southern listened keenly, occasionally breaking in with pertinent questions.* サザン夫人は熱心に聞きながら，たまに適切な質問をして話に割り込んだ. ❹ PHRASAL VERB 句動詞 If you **break** someone **in**, you get them used to a new job or situation. (新しい仕事・状況に) 慣れさせる ❑ *The band is breaking in a new backing vocalist, who sounds great.* バンドはいい声の新しいバッキング・ボーカリストの慣らしをしている. ❺ PHRASAL VERB 句動詞 If you **break in** something new, you gradually use or wear it for longer and longer periods until it is ready to be used or worn all the time. 新しいものを徐々に使用しながら慣らす ❑ *When breaking in an engine, you should refrain from high speeds for the first thousand miles.* エンジンの慣らし運転では，最初の1000マイルでは高速運転を控えるべきだ.

▶ **break into** ❶ PHRASAL VERB 句動詞 If someone **breaks into** a building, they get into it by force. 乱入する ❑ *There was no one nearby who might see him trying to break into the house.* 彼がその家に侵入しようとするのを見るような人は近くにいなかった.

B

② PHRASAL VERB 句動詞 If someone **breaks into** something they suddenly start doing it. For example, if someone **breaks into** a run they suddenly start running, and if they **break into** song they suddenly start singing. 突然—し始める ❑ *The moment she was out of sight she broke into a run.* 彼女は見えなくなった途端に走り出した. ③ PHRASAL VERB 句動詞 If you **break into** a profession or area of business, especially one that is difficult to succeed in, you manage to have some success in it. (新事業などに）参入する ❑ *She finally broke into films after an acclaimed stage career.* 彼女は高い評価を得た舞台生活の末、映画の世界に入った.

▶ **break off** ❶ PHRASAL VERB 句動詞 If part of something **breaks off** or if you **break it off**, it comes off or is removed by force. もぎ取る ❑ *The two wings of the aircraft broke off on impact.* 飛行機の両翼が衝撃でもぎ取られた. ❑ *Grace broke off a large piece of the clay.* グレースは粘土を大きくもぎ取った. ❷ PHRASAL VERB 句動詞 If you **break off** when you are doing or saying something, you suddenly stop doing it or saying it. 急に止める, 急に黙る ❑ *Barry broke off in mid-sentence.* バリーは文の途中で急に黙った. ❸ PHRASAL VERB 句動詞 If someone **breaks off** a relationship, they end it. (関係を）解消する ❑ *The two West African states had broken off relations two years ago.* 西アフリカの2国は2年前に外交関係を絶っていた.

▶ **break out** ❶ PHRASAL VERB 句動詞 If something such as war, fighting, or disease **breaks out**, it begins suddenly. (ぼっぱつ）勃発（ぼっぱつ）する（戦争が）（病気が）発生する ❑ *He was 29 when war broke out.* 戦争が勃発したとき, 彼は29歳だった. ❷ PHRASAL VERB 句動詞 If a prisoner **breaks out of** a prison, they escape from it. 脱獄する ❑ *The two men broke out of their cells and cut through a perimeter fence.* 2人の男が独房から脱出し、外周フェンスを通り抜けた. ❸ → see also **breakout** ❹ PHRASAL VERB 句動詞 If you **break out of** a dull situation or routine, you manage to change it or escape from it. (退屈な状況から）抜け出す ❑ *It's taken a long time to break out of my own conventional training.* 私は自分の型にはまった練習から抜け出すのに長い時間がかかった. ❺ PHRASAL VERB 句動詞 If you **break out in** a rash or a sweat, a rash or sweat appears on your skin. (湿疹・吹き出物・汗が）ふきでる ❑ *A person who is allergic to cashews may break out in a rash when he consumes these nuts.* カシューにアレルギーがある人はこれらのナッツを食べると発疹が出る可能性がある.

▶ **break through** ❶ PHRASAL VERB 句動詞 If you **break through** a barrier, you succeed in forcing your way through it. 力づくで通り抜ける, 打ち破る ❑ *Protesters tried to break through a police cordon.* 抗議グループが警察の非常線を突き抜けようとした. ❷ PHRASAL VERB 句動詞 If you **break through**, you achieve success even though there are difficulties and obstacles. 大前進する ❑ *There is still scope for new writers to break through.* まだ新しい作家が突破口を開く余地がある. ❸ → see also **breakthrough**

▶ **break up** ❶ PHRASAL VERB 句動詞 When something **breaks up** or when you **break it up**, it separates or is divided into smaller parts. ばらばらになる, ばらばらにする, 崩壊する ❑ *Civil war could come if the country breaks up.* 国が崩壊すると内戦が始まる可能性がある. ❑ *Break up the chocolate and melt it.* チョコレートを小さく割って溶かしなさい. ❷ PHRASAL VERB 句動詞 If you **break up with** your boyfriend, girlfriend, husband, or wife, your relationship with that person ends. (恋人・夫婦が）別れる ❑ *My girlfriend has broken up with me.* 彼女に振られた. ❑ *He felt appalled by the idea of marriage so we broke up.* 彼は結婚という考えにぞく然としたので私たちは別れた. ❸ PHRASAL VERB 句動詞 If a marriage or romantic relationship **breaks up** or if someone **breaks it up**, it ends and the partners separate. (結婚・恋愛関係が）破綻（結婚・恋愛関係が）する（はたん）❑ *His first marriage broke up.* 彼の最初の結婚は破綻した. ❹ PHRASAL VERB 句動詞 When a meeting or gathering **breaks up** or when someone **breaks it up**, it is brought to an end and the people involved in it leave. (会議・集まりが）終わる, (会議・集まりが）お開きになる ❑ *A neighbor asked for the music to be turned down and the party broke up.* 隣人が音楽の音量を下げるよう頼んできて, パーティはお開きとなった. ❑ *Police used tear gas to break up a demonstration.* 警察はデモを解散させるために催涙ガスを使用した.

break|away /breɪkəweɪ/ ADJ 形容詞 A **breakaway** group is a group of people who have separated from a larger group, for example, because of a disagreement. (団体などから）離脱した, (団体などから）分離した [ADJ n] ❑ *A breakaway faction of the rebel group has claimed responsibility for the killing.* 反抗勢力の分派が殺害の犯行声明を出した.

break|down /breɪkdaʊn/ (breakdowns) ❶ N-COUNT 可算名詞 The **breakdown** of something such as a relationship, plan, or discussion is its failure or ending. 断絶, 決裂 ❑ *the breakdown of talks between the U.S. and E.U. officials.* 米国とEUの関係者間の話し合いの決裂 ❑ *...the irretrievable breakdown of a marriage.* 修復不可能な結婚の破綻 ❷ N-COUNT 可算名詞 If you have a **breakdown**, you become very depressed, so that you are unable to cope with your life. 神経衰弱 ❑ *My personal life was terrible. My mother had died, and a couple of years later I had a breakdown.* 私の私生活は最悪だった. 母が死亡し, その二年後に私は神経が参ってしまった. ❸ → see also

nervous breakdown ❹ N-COUNT 可算名詞 If a car or a piece of machinery has a **breakdown**, it stops working. 故障 ❑ *Her old car was unreliable, so the trip was plagued by breakdowns.* 彼女の古い車は当てにならず, 旅行は故障続きでさんざんだった. ❺ N-COUNT 可算名詞 A **breakdown** of something is a list of its separate parts. 内訳 ❑ *The organizers were given a breakdown of the costs.* 主催者には経費の内訳が報告された.
→ see **traffic**

break|fast /brɛkfəst/ (breakfasts, breakfasting, breakfasted) ❶ N-VAR 可変性名詞 **Breakfast** is the first meal of the day. It is usually eaten in the early part of the morning. 朝食, 朝ごはん ❑ *What's for breakfast?* 朝ごはんは何？ ❷ → see also **bed and breakfast** ❸ V-I 自動詞 When you **breakfast**, you have breakfast. 朝食をとる [FORMAL 形式ばった] ❑ *All the ladies breakfasted in their rooms.* 女性は全員各自の部屋で朝食をとりました.
→ see **meal**

break-in (break-ins) N-COUNT 可算名詞 If there has been a **break-in**, someone has got into a building by force. 乱入 ❑ *The break-in had occurred just before midnight.* 押し入られたのは夜中の12時直前だった.

break|ing point N-UNCOUNT 不可算名詞 If something or someone has reached **breaking point**, they have so many problems or difficulties that they can no longer cope with them, and may soon collapse or be unable to continue. (忍耐などの）限界点 [also 'the/a' N] ❑ *The report on the riot exposed a prison system stretched to breaking point.* 暴動についての報告で刑務所制度が限界点にたちていることが明らかになった.

break|neck /breɪknɛk/ ADJ 形容詞 If you say that something happens or travels at **breakneck** speed, you mean that it happens or travels very fast. (スピードが）無謀な [ADJ n] ❑ *Jack drove to the hospital at breakneck speed.* ジャックは無謀なスピードで病院に車を走らせた.

break|out /breɪkaʊt/ (breakouts) N-COUNT 可算名詞 If there has been a **breakout**, someone has escaped from prison. 脱走, 脱獄 ❑ *He is thought to have planned a prison breakout of militants suspected of the July bombing.* 彼が7月の爆破事件の容疑者である過激派の脱獄を計画したとみなされている.

break|through /breɪkθru/ (breakthroughs) N-COUNT 可算名詞 A **breakthrough** is an important development or achievement. 飛躍的進歩 ❑ *The company looks poised to make a significant breakthrough in China.* その会社は中国で飛躍的な進歩を遂げる体制が整っているようだ.

break|up /breɪkʌp/ (breakups) ❶ N-COUNT 可算名詞 The **breakup** of a marriage, relationship, or association is the act of it finishing or coming to an end because the people involved decide that it is not working successfully. (結婚・恋愛関係）破局, (連合などの）分裂 ❑ *...the acrimonious breakup of the meeting's first session.* 一回目の会議の大分裂 ❷ N-COUNT 可算名詞 The **breakup** of an organization or a country is the act of it separating or dividing into several parts. (組織・国家の）解体 ❑ *The Justice Department advocated a breakup of Microsoft.* 司法省がマイクロソフト社の解体を提唱した.

breast /brɛst/ (breasts) ❶ N-COUNT 可算名詞 A woman's **breasts** are the two soft, round parts on her chest that can produce milk to feed a baby. 乳房, 乳 ❑ *She wears a low-cut dress which reveals her breasts.* 彼女は乳房が見えるほど襟ぐりの深いドレスを着ている. ❷ N-COUNT 可算名詞 A person's **breast** is the upper part of his or her chest. 胸 [LITERARY 文語的] ❑ *He struck his breast in a dramatic gesture.* 彼は大げさなしぐさで胸をたたいた. ❸ N-COUNT 可算名詞 A bird's **breast** is the front part of its body. (鳥類の）胸部 ❑ *The cock's breast is tinged with chestnut.* その雄鶏の胸部はかすかにくり色がかっている. ❹ N-SING 単数名詞 The **breast** of a shirt, jacket, or coat is the part which covers the top part of the chest. (シャツ・ジャケット・コートなどの）胸部 ❺ N-VAR 可変性名詞 You can refer to a piece of meat that is cut from the front of a bird or lamb as **breast**. (鳥の）胸肉 ❑ *...a chicken breast with vegetables.* 鳥の胸肉と野菜の添えもの

breast|stroke /brɛststroʊk, brɛststroʊk/ N-UNCOUNT 不可算名詞 **Breaststroke** is a swimming stroke that you do lying on your front, moving your arms and legs horizontally in a circular motion. 平泳ぎ [also 'the' N] ❑ *I do not yet know how to swim breaststroke effectively.* 私はまだ平泳ぎの効果的な泳ぎ方が分からない.

breath /brɛθ/ (breaths) ❶ N-VAR 可変性名詞 Your **breath** is the air that you let out through your mouth when you breathe. If someone has **bad breath**, their breath smells unpleasant. (吐く）息 ❑ *I could smell the whiskey on his breath.* 彼の息がウィスキー臭かった. ❷ N-VAR 可変性名詞 When you take a **breath**, you breathe in once. (take a）息 ❑ *He took a deep breath, and began to climb the stairs.* 彼は深く息を吸って階段を上り始めた. ❑ *Gasping for breath, she leaned against the door.* 苦しそうにあえぎながら, 彼女はドアにもたれかかった. ❸ PHRASE 句 If you go outside **for a breath of fresh air** or **for a breath of air**, you go outside because it

is unpleasantly warm indoors. 新鮮な空気を吸うために ❑ *I had to step outside for a breath of fresh air.* 私は新鮮な空気を吸うために外に出なければならなかった. ◀ PHRASE 句 If you describe something new or different as **a breath of fresh air**, you mean that it makes a situation or subject more interesting or exciting. 新風を吹き込むもの [APPROVAL 賛成] ❑ *Her brisk treatment of an almost taboo subject was a breath of fresh air.* 彼女がタブーぎりぎりの話題を小気味よく扱ったのは新鮮だった. ⑤ PHRASE 句 When you **get** your **breath back** after doing something energetic, you start breathing normally again. 呼吸を整える ❑ *I reached out a hand to steady myself against the house while I got my breath back.* 呼吸を整えながら, 私は手を伸ばして家と体の支えにした. ⑥ PHRASE 句 If you are **out of breath**, you are breathing very quickly and with difficulty because you have been doing something energetic. (運動などで) 息を切らして ❑ *She was slightly out of breath from running.* 彼女は走って少し息を切らしていた. ⑦ PHRASE 句 You can use **in the same breath** or **in the next breath** to indicate that someone says two very different or contradictory things, especially when you are criticizing them. (相反することを) 同時に [DISAPPROVAL 不賛成] ❑ *He hailed this week's arms agreement but in the same breath expressed suspicion about the motivations of the United States.* 彼は今週の武器協定を称賛する一方で, 同時に米国の動機に関して不信感を表明した. ⑧ PHRASE 句 If you are **short of breath**, you find it difficult to breathe properly, for example, because you are ill. You can also say that someone suffers from **shortness of breath**. (不健康で) 息切れをして ❑ *She felt short of breath and flushed.* 彼女は息が切れて顔が紅潮する感じだった. ⑨ PHRASE 句 If you say something **under** your **breath**, you say it in a very quiet voice, often because you do not want other people to hear what you are saying. 小声で ❑ *Walsh muttered something under his breath.* ウォルシュは小声で何かつぶやいた.

Word Partnership breath は次の語句と使われる:

ADJ.	**bad** breath, **fresh** breath ❶
	deep breath ❷
V.	**hold** *your* breath ❶
	gasp for breath, **take a** breath ❷
	catch *your* breath ❺

breatha\|lyze /brɛθəlaɪz/ (**breathalyzes, breathalyzing, breathalyzed**) V-T 他動詞 If the driver of a car **is breathalyzed** by the police, they ask him or her to breathe into a special bag or device in order to test whether he or she has drunk too much alcohol. 飲酒検査をする [usu passive] ❑ *She was breathalyzed and found to be over the limit.* 彼女は飲酒検査を受けて基準値以上飲んでいたことが見つかった.

Breatha\|lyz\|er /brɛθəlaɪzər/ (**Breathalyzers**) N-COUNT 可算名詞 商標 A **Breathalyzer** is a bag or electronic device that the police use to test whether a driver has drunk too much alcohol. 飲酒検知器 [TRADEMARK] ❑ *Luckily I was never stopped for a Breathalyzer.* 幸運にも私は飲酒検査で停められたことがなかった.

breathe /brið/ (**breathes, breathing, breathed**) ❶ V-T/V-I 他動詞/自動詞 When people or animals **breathe**, they take air into their lungs and let it out again. When they **breathe** smoke or a particular kind of air, they take it into their lungs and let it out again as they breathe. 呼吸する, 息する ❑ *He stood there breathing deeply and evenly.* 彼はそこに立ち, むらなく深呼吸をした. ❑ *No American should have to drive out of town to breathe clean air.* アメリカ人は誰もきれいな空気を吸うために車で郊外に出かけなくてもいいはずだ. ● **breath\|ing** N-UNCOUNT 不可算名詞 呼吸 ❑ *Her breathing became slow and heavy.* 彼女の呼吸が遅く荒くなった. ❷ **to be breathing down** someone's **neck** → see **neck** ❸ **to breathe a sigh of relief** → see **sigh**

→ see **respiratory**

▶ **breathe in** PHRASAL VERB 句動詞 When you **breathe in**, you take some air into your lungs. 息を吸う ❑ *She breathed in deeply.* 彼女は深く息を吸った.

▶ **breathe out** PHRASAL VERB 句動詞 When you **breathe out**, you send air out of your lungs through your nose or mouth. 息を吐く ❑ *Breathe out and ease your knees in toward your chest.* 息を吐き, ひざを楽にして胸のほうに動かしなさい.

breath\|er /briðər/ (**breathers**) N-COUNT 可算名詞 If you take a **breather**, you stop what you are doing for a short time in order to rest. 一休み, 一息 [INFORMAL くだけた] ❑ *Relax and take a breather whenever you feel that you need one.* いつでも必要だと思ったらリラックスして一息つきなさい.

breath\|ing space (**breathing spaces**) N-VAR 可変性名詞 A **breathing space** is a short period of time between two activities in which you can recover from the first activity and prepare for the second one. 息をつく時間 ❑ *Firms need a breathing space if they are to recover.* 会社が回復するには息をつく余裕が必要だ.

breath\|less /brɛθlɪs/ ADJ 形容詞 If you are **breathless**, you have difficulty in breathing properly, for example, because you have been running or because you are afraid or excited. 息を切らした ❑ *I was a little breathless and my heartbeat was bumpy and fast.* 私は少

し息切れをして, 胸の鼓動が荒く速くなっていた. ● **breath\|less\|ly** ADV 副詞 息を切らして ❑ *"I'll go in," he said breathlessly.* 「入るよ」と彼は息を切らしながら言った. ● **breath\|less\|ness** N-UNCOUNT 不可算名詞 息切れ ❑ *Asthma causes wheezing and breathlessness.* ぜんそくになると息がゼーゼーし, 息切れがする.

breath\|taking /brɛθteɪkɪŋ/ also **breath-taking** ADJ 形容詞 If you say that something is **breathtaking**, you are emphasizing that it is extremely beautiful or amazing. はっとするような [EMPHASIS 強調] ❑ *The house has breathtaking views from every room.* 家のどの部屋からも, はっとするような素晴らしい景色が見えた. ❑ *Some of their football was breathtaking, a delight to watch.* はっとするようなサッカーの試合ぶりもあり, 楽しませてくれた.

breed /brid/ (**breeds, breeding, bred**) ❶ N-COUNT 可算名詞 A **breed** of a pet animal or farm animal is a particular type of it. For example, terriers are a breed of dog. 品種 ❑ *...rare breeds of cattle.* 牛の珍しい品種 ❷ V-T 他動詞 If you **breed** animals or plants, you keep them for the purpose of producing more animals or plants with particular qualities, in a controlled way. (動植物を) 繁殖させる, (動植物を) 飼育・栽培する ❑ *He lived alone, breeding horses and dogs.* 彼は馬や犬を繁殖させながら一人暮らしをしていた. ❑ *He used to breed dogs for the police.* 彼は以前警察犬の飼育をしていた. ● **breed\|ing** N-UNCOUNT 不可算名詞 ❑ *There is potential for selective breeding for better yields.* 収穫高を上げるために選択的栽培の可能性がある. ❸ V-I 自動詞 When animals **breed**, they have babies. 繁殖する ❑ *Frogs will usually breed in any convenient pond.* カエルは普通どこの池でも繁殖する. ● **breed\|ing** N-UNCOUNT 不可算名詞 繁殖 ❑ *During the breeding season the birds come ashore.* 鳥は繁殖期に陸地にやってくる. ❹ V-T 他動詞 If you say that something **breeds** bad feeling or bad behavior, you mean that it causes bad feeling or bad behavior to develop. (否定的感情や行動を) 引き起こす ❑ *If they are unemployed it's bound to breed resentment.* 失業中ならきっと恨みを抱き始めるよ. ❺ → see also **breeding**

→ see **gene**

breed\|er /bridər/ (**breeders**) N-COUNT 可算名詞 **Breeders** are people who breed animals or plants. 畜産家, 栽培者 ❑ *Her father was a well-known racehorse breeder.* 彼女の父親は有名な競争馬の飼育家だ.

breed\|ing /bridɪŋ/ ❶ N-UNCOUNT 不可算名詞 If someone says that a person has **breeding**, they mean that they think the person is from a good social background and has good manners. 教養, よい育ち ❑ *It's a sign of good breeding to know the names of all your staff.* 職員の名前を全員知っているというのは家柄のよさの表れだ. ❷ → see also **breed**

→ see **zoo**

breeze /briz/ (**breezes, breezing, breezed**) ❶ N-COUNT 可算名詞 A **breeze** is a gentle wind. そよ風, 微風 ❑ *...a cool summer breeze.* 涼しい夏のそよ風 ❷ V-I 自動詞 If you **breeze** into a position, you enter it in a very casual or relaxed manner. なんなく入る ❑ *Lopez breezed into the quarter-finals of the tournament.* ロペスはトーナメントの準々決勝戦に楽々と勝ち進んだ. ❸ V-I 自動詞 If you **breeze through** something such as a game or test, you cope with it easily. 楽々とこなす ❑ *John seems to breeze effortlessly through his many commitments at work.* ジョンは職場での多くの義務を楽々とこなしているようだ.

→ see **wind**

breezy /brizi/ ADJ 形容詞 If you describe someone as **breezy**, you mean that they behave in a casual, cheerful, and confident manner. 快活な ❑ *...his bright and breezy personality.* 彼の明るく快活な性格

breth\|ren /brɛðrɪn/ N-PLURAL 複数名詞 You can refer to the members of a particular organization or group, especially a religious group, as **brethren**. 仲間 [OLD-FASHIONED 古風な] ❑ *We must help our brethren, it is our duty.* 我々の仲間を助けなければならない. それが我々の義務だ.

brew /bru/ (**brews, brewing, brewed**) ❶ V-T 他動詞 If you **brew** tea or coffee, you make it by pouring hot water over tea leaves or ground coffee. (お茶・コーヒーを) いれる ❑ *He brewed a pot of coffee.* 彼はポット1杯のコーヒーを入れた. ❷ N-COUNT 可算名詞 A **brew** is a particular kind of tea or coffee. It can also be a particular pot of tea or coffee. 特定の種類の茶・コーヒー ❑ *She swallowed a mouthful of the hot strong brew, and wiped her eyes.* 彼女は熱くて濃いお茶を一口飲んで, 目をふいた. ❸ V-T 他動詞 If a person or company **brews** beer, they make it. 醸造する ❑ *I brew my own beer.* 私はビールを自家醸造している. ❹ V-I 自動詞 If a storm **is brewing**, large clouds are beginning to form and the sky is becoming dark because there is going to be a storm. (嵐などが) 起ころうとしている [usu cont] ❑ *We'd seen the storm brewing when we were out in the boat.* ボートに乗っているとき嵐がやってくるのが見えた. ❺ V-I 自動詞 If an unpleasant or difficult situation **is brewing**, it is starting to develop. (不快なことや困難な状況が) 起ころうとしている [usu cont] ❑ *At home a crisis was brewing.* 本国では危機が起ころうとしていた.

→ see **coffee, tea**

brew|er /brúər/ (brewers) N-COUNT 可算名詞 Brewers are people or companies who make beer. ビール醸造業者, ビール醸造会社

brew|ery /brúəri/ (breweries) N-COUNT 可算名詞 A brewery is a place where beer is made. ビール醸造所

bribe /braɪb/ (bribes, bribing, bribed) **1** N-COUNT 可算名詞 A bribe is a sum of money or something valuable that one person offers or gives to another in order to persuade him or her to do something. わいろ □ He was being investigated for receiving bribes. 彼は収賄で取調べを受けていた. **2** V-T 他動詞 If one person bribes another, they give them a bribe. わいろを贈る, 買収する □ He was accused of bribing a senior bank official. 彼は銀行の重役を買収した罪で告発された.

brib|ery /braɪbəri/ N-UNCOUNT 不可算名詞 Bribery is the act of offering someone money or something valuable in order to persuade them to do something to help you. 贈賄 □ He was jailed on charges of bribery. 彼は贈賄の罪で投獄された.

brick /brɪk/ (bricks) **1** N-VAR 可変性名詞 Bricks are rectangular blocks of baked clay used for building walls, which are usually red or brown. Brick is the material made up of these blocks. れんが □ She built bookshelves out of bricks and planks. 彼女はれんがと厚板で本棚を作った. **2** PHRASE 句 If you hit a brick wall or come up against a brick wall, you are unable to continue or make progress because something stops you. 壁に突き当たる, 行き詰まる [INFORMAL くだけた] □ After that my career just seemed to hit a brick wall. そのあと私の仕事は壁に突き当たったようだった.

brid|al /braɪdᵊl/ ADJ 形容詞 Bridal is used to describe something that belongs or relates to a bride, or to both a bride and her bridegroom. 花嫁の, 婚礼の [ADJ n] □ She wore a floor-length bridal gown. 彼女はすそが床まで届く花嫁衣裳を着ていた.

bride /braɪd/ (brides) N-COUNT 可算名詞 A bride is a woman who is getting married or who has just gotten married. 花嫁, 新婦 □ Guests toasted the bride and groom with champagne. 招待客は新郎新婦にシャンパンで乾杯をした.

→ see **wedding**

bride|groom /braɪdgrum/ (bridegrooms) N-COUNT 可算名詞 A bridegroom is a man who is getting married. 花婿, 新郎

brides|maid /braɪdzmeɪd/ (bridesmaids) N-COUNT 可算名詞 A bridesmaid is a woman or a girl who helps and accompanies a bride on her wedding day. 花嫁の介添えの女性

→ see **wedding**

bridge /brɪdʒ/ (bridges, bridging, bridged) **1** N-COUNT 可算名詞 A bridge is a structure that is built over a railroad, river, or road so that people or vehicles can cross from one side to the other. 橋 □ He walked back over the railroad bridge. 彼は鉄橋を歩いて渡って帰った. **2** N-COUNT 可算名詞 A bridge between two places is a piece of land that joins or connects them. （２つの場所を結ぶ）細長い土地 □ ...a land bridge linking Serbian territories. セルビア領土同士を橋のように結ぶ土地 **3** V-T 他動詞 To bridge the gap between two people or things means to reduce it or get rid of it. （隔たりを）なくす □ It is unlikely that the two sides will be able to bridge their differences. 両者が互いの相違を乗り越える可能性は低い. **4** V-T 他動詞 Something that bridges the gap between two very different things has some of the qualities of each of these things. 異なる２つのものの両方の特性を持つ □ ...the singer who bridged the gap between pop music and opera. ポップミュージックとオペラという異なる世界を融合させた歌手 **5** N-COUNT 可算名詞 If something or someone acts as a bridge between two people, groups, or things, they connect them. 橋渡し □ We hope this book will act as a bridge between doctor and patient. 我々はこの本が医者と患者の橋渡し役となることを願っています. **6** N-COUNT 可算名詞 The bridge is the place on a ship from which it is steered. 船橋 □ Captain Ronald Warwick was on the bridge when the wave hit. 波にぶつかったときロナルド・ウォリック船長が船橋にいた. **7** N-COUNT 可算名詞 The bridge of your nose is the thin top part of it, between your eyes. 鼻柱 □ On the bridge of his hooked nose was a pair of gold rimless spectacles. 彼のわし鼻の鼻柱

には金の縁なし眼鏡がのっていた. **8** N-COUNT 可算名詞 The bridge of a pair of glasses is the part that rests on your nose. （眼鏡の）ブリッジ **9** N-COUNT 可算名詞 The bridge of a violin, guitar, or other stringed instrument is the small piece of wood under the strings that holds them up. （弦楽器の）駒 **10** N-UNCOUNT 不可算名詞 Bridge is a card game for four players in which the players begin by declaring how many tricks they expect to win. （トランプの）ブリッジ

→ see Word Web: **bridge**
→ see **ship**

bridge loan (bridge loans) N-COUNT 可算名詞 A bridge loan is money that a bank lends you for a short time, for example, so that you can buy a new house before you have sold the one you already own. つなぎ融資 [AM 米国英語]

bri|dle /braɪdᵊl/ (bridles) N-COUNT 可算名詞 A bridle is a set of straps that is put around a horse's head and mouth so that the person riding or driving the horse can control it. 馬ろく

→ see **horse**

brief /brif/ (briefer, briefest, briefs, briefing, briefed) **1** ADJ 形容詞 Something that is brief lasts for only a short time. 短期間の, 短時間の □ She once made a brief appearance on television. 彼女はかつて少しだけテレビに出た. **2** ADJ 形容詞 A brief speech or piece of writing does not contain too many words or details. 簡潔な □ In a brief statement, he concentrated entirely on international affairs. 簡潔な声明の中で, 彼はもっぱら国際情勢に争点を当てた. **3** ADJ 形容詞 If you are brief, you say what you want to say in as few words as possible. 手短な [v-link ADJ] □ Now please be brief – my time is valuable. さて手短にお願いします. 私の時間は貴重です. **4** ADJ 形容詞 You can describe a period of time as brief if you want to emphasize that it is very short. 時間が短かいことを強調して □ For a few brief minutes we forgot the anxiety and anguish. ほんの少しの間, 私たちは心配事や苦悩を忘れた. [EMPHASIS 強調] **5** N-PLURAL 複数名詞 Men's or women's underpants can be referred to as briefs. （男性・女性の下着）パンツ, （男性・女性の下着）ブリーフ, （男性・女性の下着）パンティ [also 'a pair of' N] □ A bra and a pair of briefs lay on the floor. ブラとパンティが床に落ちていた. **6** V-T 他動詞 If someone briefs you, especially about a piece of work or a serious matter, they give you information that you need before you do it or consider it. 前もって指示を与える, 概要を説明する □ A Defense Department spokesman briefed reporters. 国防省報道官が記者に概要を説明した. **7** N-COUNT 可算名詞 A brief is a document containing all the information relating to a particular legal case, which is used by a lawyer to defend his or her client in court. 訴訟事件摘要書 □ Griffith's expertise is in writing legal briefs. グリフィスの専門は訴訟事件摘要書の作成だ. **8** N-COUNT 可算名詞 If someone gives you a brief, they officially give you responsibility and instructions for dealing with a particular thing. 任務 [mainly BRIT 主に英国英語, FORMAL 形式ばった] □ ...customs officials with a brief to stop foreign porn coming into Britain. 外国のポルノ商品が英国に輸入されるのを阻止する任務を与えられた税関職員 **9** → see also **briefing** **10** PHRASE 句 You can say in brief to indicate that you are about to say something in as few words as possible or to give a summary of what you have just said. 要するに □ In brief, take no risks. 要するに危険を冒すな.

Word Partnership briefは次の語句と使われる:

N. brief **appearance**, brief **conversation**, brief **pause** **1**
    brief **description**, brief **explanation**, brief **history**,
    brief **speech**, brief **statement** **2**

brief|case /brifkeɪs/ (briefcases) N-COUNT 可算名詞 A briefcase is a case used for carrying documents in. ブリーフケース, 書類かばん

brief|ing /brifɪŋ/ (briefings) **1** N-VAR 可変性名詞 A briefing is a meeting at which information or instructions are given to people, especially before they do something. 説明会 □ They're holding a press briefing tomorrow. 明日記者に対する説明会が開かれ

Word Web bridge

The world's longest and tallest **suspension bridge** is the Akashi Kaikyo Bridge. It is 12,828 feet long and almost 1,000 feet tall. It can withstand an 8.5 magnitude earthquake. Another famous **span**, the Brooklyn Bridge in New York City, dates from 1883. It was the first suspension bridge to use **steel** for its **cable** wire. Over 120,000 vehicles still use the bridge every day. The Evergreen Point Floating Bridge near Seattle, Washington, floats on pontoons. It's more than a mile long. During windy weather the drawbridge in the middle must remain open. This prevents damage to the **span**.

b

る． **2** → see also brief

brief|ly /bríːfli/ **1** ADV 副詞 Something that happens or is done **briefly** happens or is done for a very short period of time. 少しの間 [ADV with v] □ *He smiled briefly.* 彼はしばらく微笑んだ． **2** ADV 副詞 If you say or write something **briefly**, you use very few words or give very few details. 簡潔に [ADV with v] □ *There are four basic alternatives; they are described briefly below.* 4つの基本的な代案がある．概略は以下の通り． **3** ADV 副詞 You can say **briefly** to indicate that you are about to say something in as few words as possible. 要するに [ADV with cl] □ *Briefly, no less than nine of our agents have passed information to us.* 要するに，当方の情報部員9人以上が私たちに情報をもたらした．

bri|gade /brɪɡéɪd/ (brigades) N-COUNT-COLL 集合可算名詞 A **brigade** is one of the groups which an army is divided into. 旅団，（軍隊編成の）団体 □ *...the soldiers of the 173rd Airborne Brigade.* 第173空挺旅団の兵士

bright /bráɪt/ (brights, brighter, brightest) **1** ADJ 形容詞 A **bright** color is strong and noticeable, and not dark. （色が）明るい，鮮やかな □ *...a bright red dress.* 鮮やかな赤色のドレス ● **bright|ly** ADV 副詞 （色が）明るく，鮮やかに □ *...a display of brightly colored flowers.* 色鮮やかな花々の陳列 ● **bright|ness** N-UNCOUNT 不可算名詞 明るさ，（色の）鮮やかさ □ *You'll be impressed with the brightness and the beauty of the colors.* その色の鮮やかさと美しさに感動することでしょう． **2** ADJ 形容詞 A **bright** light, object, or place is shining strongly or is full of light. （光，物，場所などが）明るい □ *...a bright October day.* よく晴れた10月の日 ● **bright|ly** ADV 副詞 [ADV with v]（光，物，場所などが）明るく，輝いて □ *...a warm, brightly lit room.* 暖かく明るい部屋 ● **bright|ness** N-UNCOUNT 不可算名詞 明るさ，輝き □ *An astronomer can determine the brightness of each star.* 天文学者はそれぞれの星の明るさを測定できる． **3** ADJ 形容詞 If you describe someone as **bright**, you mean that they are quick at learning things. 頭がいい，賢い □ *I was convinced that he was brighter than average.* 私は彼の頭のよさが平均以上だと確信した． **4** ADJ 形容詞 A **bright** idea is clever and original. 素晴らしい □ *There are lots of books crammed with bright ideas.* 名案がぎっしり詰まった本がたくさんある． **5** ADJ 形容詞 If someone looks or sounds **bright**, they look or sound cheerful and lively. （人の）見た目や声が）明るい □ *The boy was so bright and animated.* その少年は明るく生き生きとしていた． ● **bright|ly** ADV 副詞 [ADV with v] 明るく □ *He smiled brightly as Ben approached.* ベンが近づくと彼は明るく微笑んだ． **6** ADJ 形容詞 If the future is **bright**, it is likely to be pleasant or successful. （将来が）明るい，（将来が）有望だ □ *Both had successful careers and the future looked bright.* 2人ともキャリアがあって将来有望に見えた． **7** N-PLURAL 複数形名詞 The **brights** on a vehicle are its headlights when they are set to shine their brightest. （自動車の一番明るい）ヘッドライト [AM 米国英語] □ *...a Bronco with its brights on, parked in the middle of the street.* ヘッドライトをあかあかとつけて通りの真ん中に停められたブロンコ．

bright|en /bráɪtᵊn/ (brightens, brightening, brightened) **1** V-I 自動詞 If someone **brightens** or their face **brightens**, they suddenly look happier. 表情が明るく見える □ *Seeing him, she seemed to brighten a little.* 彼を見て，彼女の表情が少し明るくなったようだった． ● PHRASAL VERB 句動詞 **Brighten up** means the same as **brighten**. 表情が明るく見える □ *He brightened up a bit.* 彼の顔がちょっと明るくなった． **2** V-I 自動詞 If your eyes **brighten**, you suddenly look interested or excited. 輝く □ *His eyes brightened and he laughed.* 彼の目が輝き，そして笑い声を立てた． **3** V-T 他動詞 If someone or something **brightens** a place, they make it more colorful and attractive. 華やかにする □ *Tubs planted with flowers brightened the area outside the door.* 鉢植えの花が戸口を出たあたりを華やかにした． ● PHRASAL VERB 句動詞 **Brighten up** means the same as **brighten**. 華やかにする □ *David spotted the pink silk lampshade in a shop and thought it would brighten up the room.* デイビッドはピンクのシルク製ランプ傘を店で見かけ，それで部屋が華やかになるだろうと思った． **4** V-T/V-I 他動詞/自動詞 If someone or something **brightens** a situation or the situation **brightens**, it becomes more pleasant, enjoyable, or favorable. （状況など）明るくする [他動詞]，（状況などが）明るくなる [自動詞] □ *That does not do much to brighten the prospects of kids in the city.* それが都会の子供の前途をそれほど明るくするわけではない． **5** V-T/V-I 他動詞/自動詞 When a light **brightens** a place or when a place **brightens**, it becomes brighter or lighter. （場所を）明るくする [他動詞]，（場所が）明るくなる [自動詞] □ *The sky above the ridge of mountains brightened.* 尾根の上の空が明るくなった． **6** V-I 自動詞 If the weather **brightens**, it becomes less cloudy or rainy, and the sun starts to shine. 晴れる □ *By early afternoon the weather had brightened.* お昼過ぎには天気がよくなった．

bril|liant /bríljᵊnt/ **1** ADJ 形容詞 A **brilliant** person, idea, or performance is extremely clever or skillful. 優れた，優秀な □ *She had a brilliant mind.* 彼女は優れた知性を持っていた． ● **bril|liant|ly** ADV 副詞 素晴らしく □ *It is a very high quality production, brilliantly written and acted.* それは非常に質の高い作品だ．台本も演技も素晴らしい． ● **bril|liance** N-UNCOUNT 不可算名詞 素晴らしい才能 □ *He was a deeply serious musician who had shown his brilliance*

very early. 彼はとても早くから才能の素晴らしさを示した極めて本格派の音楽家だった． **2** ADJ 形容詞 A **brilliant** career or success is very successful. （経歴・成功などが）輝かしい □ *He served four years in prison, emerging to find his brilliant career in ruins.* 彼は刑務所で4年間過ごして，輝かしいキャリアがめちゃくちゃになっていたことが分かった． ● **bril|liant|ly** ADV 副詞 輝かしく □ *The strategy worked brilliantly.* 戦略は素晴らしい成功を収めた． **3** ADJ 形容詞 [ADJ n] A **brilliant** color is extremely bright. （色が）鮮やかな □ *The woman had brilliant green eyes.* その女性は鮮やかな緑の眼をしていた． ● **bril|liant|ly** ADV 副詞 [ADV adj.-ed] 鮮やかに □ *Many of the patterns show brilliantly colored flowers.* 鮮やかな色の花模様が多い． ● **bril|liance** N-UNCOUNT 不可算名詞 鮮やかさ □ *...an iridescent blue butterfly in all its brilliance.* 虹のように鮮やかに輝く青い蝶 **4** ADJ 形容詞 You describe light, or something that reflects light, as **brilliant** when it shines very brightly. きらきら光る □ *The event was held in brilliant sunshine.* その行事はまぶしく輝く太陽の下で開かれた． ● **bril|liant|ly** ADV 副詞 きらきら光って □ *It's a brilliantly sunny morning.* 太陽がきらきらと光り輝く朝です． ● **bril|liance** N-UNCOUNT 不可算名詞 光の輝き □ *His eyes became accustomed to the dark after the brilliance of the sun outside.* 外の陽の光のまぶしさから，彼の目は暗さに慣れた． **5** ADJ 形容詞 You can say that something is **brilliant** when you are very pleased about it or think that it is very good. すごくいい，すごい [mainly BRIT 主に英国英語，INFORMAL, SPOKEN くだけた，口語] □ *If you get a chance to see the show, do go – it's brilliant.* そのショーを見に行く機会があれば，行くべきだよ．すごいよ．

brim /brím/ (brims, brimming, brimmed) **1** N-COUNT 可算名詞 The **brim** of a hat is the wide part that sticks outward at the bottom. つば □ *Rain dripped from the brim of his baseball cap.* 雨が彼の野球帽のつばからぽたぽた落ちた． **2** V-I 自動詞 If someone or something is **brimming with** a particular quality, they are full of that quality. ～にあふれる [usu cont] □ *The team is brimming with confidence after two straight wins in the tournament.* そのチームはトーナメントで2連勝して2勝し，自信満々だ． **3** V-I 自動詞 When your eyes **are brimming with** tears, they are full of fluid because you are upset, although you are not actually crying. （液体で）一杯になる □ *Michael looked at him imploringly, eyes brimming with tears.* マイケルは目を涙で一杯にして哀願するように彼を見た． **4** PHRASE 句 If something, especially a container, is **filled to the brim** or **full to the brim** with something, it is filled right up to the top. 縁まで一杯に □ *Her glass was filled right up to the brim.* 彼女のグラスはなみなみとつがれていた．

bring /bríŋ/ (brings, bringing, brought) **1** V-T 他動詞 If you **bring** someone or something **with** you when you come to a place, they come with you or you have them with you. 持参する □ *Remember to bring an apron or an old shirt to protect your clothes.* 衣服を守るためにエプロンまたは古いシャツを忘れずに持って来なさい． □ *Someone went upstairs and brought down a huge kettle.* 誰かが上階に行き，巨大なヤカンを持ってきた． **2** V-T 他動詞 If you **bring** something somewhere, you move it there. 動かす □ *Reaching into her pocket, she brought out a cigarette.* 彼女はポケットから1本のタバコを取り出した． **3** V-T 他動詞 If you **bring** something that someone wants or needs, you get it for them or carry it to them. 持っていく □ *He went and poured a brandy for Dena and brought it to her.* 彼はブランデーを注ぎ，ディーナのところに持ってきた． **4** V-T 他動詞 To **bring** something or someone to a place or a position means to cause them to come to the place or move into that position. 来させる □ *I told you about what brought me here.* 私がここに来た理由は説明した． □ *The shock of her husband's arrival brought her to her feet.* 夫が到着したショックで彼女は立ち上がった．

> **Bring** and **take** are both used to talk about carrying something or accompanying someone somewhere, but **bring** is used to suggest movement toward the speaker and **take** is used to suggest movement away from the speaker. □ *Bring your calculator to every lesson...Anna took the book to school with her.* In the first sentence, **bring** suggests that the person and the calculator should come to the place where the speaker is. In the second sentence, □ *took* suggests that Anna left the speaker when she went to school. You could also say "take your calculator to every lesson" to suggest that the speaker will not be present at the lesson, and "Anna brought the book to school with her" to suggest that Anna and the speaker were both at school.

5 V-T 他動詞 If you **bring** something new **to** a place or group of people, you introduce it to that place or cause those people to hear or know about it. もたらす □ *...the drive to bring art to the public.* 芸術を一般に紹介する動き **6** V-T 他動詞 To **bring** someone or something into a particular state or condition means to cause them to be in that state or condition. （ある状態に）至らせる □ *He brought the car to a stop in front of the square.* 彼は広場の前で車を止めた． □ *They have brought down income taxes.* 彼らは所得税を引き下げた． **7** V-T 他動詞 If something **brings** a particular feeling, situation, or quality, it makes people experience it or have it. もたらす □ *He called on the United States to play a more effective role in*

bringing peace to the region. 彼は地域に平和をもたらすため米国により効果的な役割を果たすことを求めた. ❑ Her three children brought her joy. 3人の子供は彼女に喜びをもたらした. **8** V-T 他動詞 If a period of time **brings** a particular thing, it happens during that time. 〜になると〜が起こる ❑ For Sandro, the new year brought disaster. サンドロの場合、新年になると災いが降りかかった. **9** V-T 他動詞 When you are talking, you can say that something **brings** you **to** a particular point in order to indicate that you have now reached that point and are going to talk about a new subject. 至らせる ❑ And that brings us to the end of this special report from Germany. ドイツからの特別レポートはこれで終わりです. **10** V-T 他動詞 If you cannot **bring yourself to** do something, you cannot do it because you find it too upsetting, embarrassing, or disgusting. する気にさせる [with brd-neg] ❑ It is all very tragic and I am afraid I just cannot bring myself to talk about it at the moment. あまりに悲惨で今は話す気になれない. **11** to **bring** something **alive** → see **alive** **12** to bring the house down → see house **13** to bring up the rear → see rear

> Do not confuse the verbs **bring up** and **grow up**. Bring up is a transitive verb, and describes the process of looking after and socializing a child. ❑ ...we both felt the town was the perfect place to bring up a family. **Grow up** is an intransitive verb, and describes the process of becoming an adult. ❑ I grew up in rural southern Colorado. Note then, that parents do not "grow up" their children, they "bring them up." See also note at **educate**.

▶ **bring about** PHRASAL VERB 句動詞 To **bring** something **about** means to cause it to happen. 成し遂げる ❑ The only way they can bring about political change is by putting pressure on the country. 政治的変化を成し遂げる唯一の方法はその国に圧力をかけることだ.
▶ **bring along** PHRASAL VERB 句動詞 If you **bring** someone or something **along**, you bring them with you when you come to a place. 携行する ❑ They brought baby Michael along in a carrier. 彼らは赤ちゃんのマイケルを携帯ベッドに入れて連れてきた.
▶ **bring back** PHRASAL VERB 句動詞 Something that **brings back** a memory makes you think about it. 思い出させる ❑ Your article brought back sad memories for me. あなたの記事を読んで悲しい思い出がよみがえってきた. **2** PHRASAL VERB 句動詞 When people **bring back** a practice or fashion that existed at an earlier time, they introduce it again. 復活させる ❑ Pennsylvania brought back the death penalty in 1978. ペンシルバニア州は1978年に死刑制度を復活させた.
▶ **bring down** **1** PHRASAL VERB 句動詞 When people or events **bring down** a government or ruler, they cause the government or ruler to lose power. 倒す ❑ They were threatening to bring down the government by withdrawing from the ruling coalition. 彼らは与党連立から脱退することによって政府を倒すと脅かしていた. **2** PHRASAL VERB 句動詞 If someone or something **brings down** a person or airplane, they cause them to fall, usually by shooting them. 墜落させる ❑ Military historians may never know what brought down the jet. 軍事歴史家はジェット機墜落の原因を永遠に究明できないかもしれない.
▶ **bring forward** PHRASAL VERB 句動詞 If you **bring forward** a meeting or event, you arrange for it to take place at an earlier date or time than had been planned. 繰り上げる ❑ He had to bring forward an 11 o'clock meeting so that he could get to the funeral on time. 彼は時間通りに葬式に出席できるように11時の打合せを早めた.
▶ **bring in** **1** PHRASAL VERB 句動詞 When a government or organization **brings in** a new law or system, they introduce it. 導入する ❑ The government brought in a controversial law under which it could take any land it wanted. 政府は問題となる法律を導入し、自由に土地収用ができるようになった. **2** PHRASAL VERB 句動詞 Someone or something that **brings in** money makes it or earns it. 稼ぐ ❑ I have three part-time jobs, which bring in about $24,000 a year. 私は3種類のアルバイトを掛け持ちしており、年収は2万4千ドルだ. **3** PHRASAL VERB 句動詞 If you **bring in** someone from outside a team or organization, you invite them to do a job or join in an activity or discussion. 迎え入れる ❑ The firm decided to bring in a new management team. 会社は新しい経営陣を迎え入れることに決めた.
▶ **bring out** **1** PHRASAL VERB 句動詞 When a person or company **brings out** a new product, especially a new book or CD, they produce it and put it on sale. 売り出す ❑ A journalist all his life, he's now brought out a book. 生涯ジャーナリストの彼が今度本を出版した. **2** PHRASAL VERB 句動詞 Something that **brings out** a particular kind of behavior or feeling in you causes you to show it, especially when it is something you do not normally show. 引き出す ❑ He is totally dedicated and brings out the best in his pupils. 彼は非常に献身的で生徒の能力を最大限に引き出す.
▶ **bring up** **1** PHRASAL VERB 句動詞 When someone **brings up** a child, they look after it until it is an adult. If someone has **been brought up** in a certain place or with certain attitudes, they grew up in that place or were taught those attitudes when they were growing up. 育てる ❑ She brought up four children. 彼女は4人の子供を育てた. ❑ He was brought up in Nebraska. 彼はネブラスカ州で育った. **2** PHRASAL VERB 句動詞 If you **bring up** a particular subject, you introduce it into a discussion or conversation. 持ち出す ❑ He

brought up a subject rarely raised during the course of this campaign. 彼はこの運動中にほとんど提起されなかった問題を持ち出した.

Thesaurus   bring また次を参照:
v.   accompany, bear, carry, take; (ant.) drop, leave **1**
     move, take, transfer **2**

Word Partnership   bring は次の語句と使われる:
N.   bring bad/good luck **1**
     bring to a boil, bring to life, bring together **6**
     bring something/someone home, bring to someone's attention, bring to justice, bring to mind **7**

brink /brɪŋk/ N-SING 単数名詞 If you are **on the brink of** something, usually something important, terrible, or exciting, you are just about to do it or experience it. 〜の寸前で ❑ Their economy is teetering on the brink of collapse. 経済は崩壊の危機にひんしている.

brisk /brɪsk/ (brisker, briskest) **1** ADJ 形容詞 A **brisk** activity or action is done quickly and in an energetic way. 元気のよい ❑ Taking a brisk walk can often induce a feeling of well-being. 元気よく歩くとしばしば満足感が得られる. ●**brisk|ly** ADV 副詞 [ADV with v] きびきびと ❑ Eve walked briskly down the corridor to her son's room. イーヴは息子の部屋に向かって廊下をきびきびした足取りで歩いた. **2** ADJ 形容詞 If trade or business is **brisk**, things are being sold very quickly and a lot of money is being made. 活況の ❑ Vendors were doing a brisk trade in souvenirs. 記念品の売れ行きは活発だった. ●**brisk|ly** ADV 副詞 [ADV after v] 活発に ❑ A trader said gold sold briskly on the local market. トレーダーは地元市場の金の売れ行きは好調だと述べた. **3** ADJ 形容詞 If the weather is **brisk**, it is cold and fresh. 身の引き締まるような ❑ ...a typically brisk winter's day on the south coast. 南海岸での身の引き締まるような典型的な冬のある日 **4** ADJ 形容詞 Someone who is **brisk** behaves in a busy, confident way which shows that they want to get things done quickly. てきぱきした ❑ The Chief summoned me downstairs. He was brisk and businesslike. チーフは私に階下に来るよう命じた. 彼はてきぱきして事務的だった. ●**brisk|ly** ADV 副詞 [ADV with v] きびきびと ❑ "Anyhow," she added briskly, "it's none of my business." 「とにかく、それは私には関係ないことよ」と彼女はきびきびとした態度で付け加えた.

bris|tle /brɪsəl/ (bristles) **1** N-COUNT 可算名詞 **Bristles** are the short hairs that grow on a man's face after he has shaved. The hairs on the top of a man's head can also be called **bristles** when they are cut very short. 短く硬い毛 ❑ ...two days' growth of bristles. 2日間剃(そ)らなかった無精ひげ **2** N-COUNT 可算名詞 The **bristles** of a brush are the thick hairs or hairlike pieces of plastic which are attached to it. (ブラシなどの)毛 ❑ As soon as the bristles on your toothbrush begin to wear, throw it out. 歯ブラシの毛が磨り減り始めたらすぐに捨てなさい. **3** N-COUNT 可算名詞 **Bristles** are thick, strong animal hairs that feel hard and rough. 剛毛 ❑ It has a short stumpy tail covered with bristles. それは剛毛でおおわれた太くて短い尻尾がある.

Brit|on /brɪtən/ (Britons) N-COUNT 可算名詞 A **Briton** is a British citizen, or a person of British origin. 英国人 [FORMAL 形式ばった] ❑ The role is played by seventeen-year-old Briton Jane March. その役を演じるのは17歳の英国人、ジェイン・マーチだ.

brit|tle /brɪtəl/ ADJ 形容詞 An object or substance that is **brittle** is hard but easily broken. 硬いがもろい ❑ Pine is brittle and breaks. 松材は砕けて割れやすい.

broach /broʊtʃ/ (broaches, broaching, broached) V-T 他動詞 When you **broach** a subject, especially a sensitive one, you mention it in order to start a discussion on it. 切り出す ❑ Eventually I broached the subject of her early life. ついに私は彼女の若い頃の話を切り出した.

broad /brɔd/ (broader, broadest) **1** ADJ 形容詞 Something that is **broad** is wide. 幅広い ❑ His shoulders were broad and his waist narrow. 彼は肩幅が広く、ウエストが細い. ❑ The hills rise green and sheer above the broad river. 丘陵は幅広い川をみおろす緑色にそそり立っている. **2** ADJ 形容詞 A **broad** smile is one in which your mouth is stretched very wide because you are very pleased or amused. にこにこした ❑ He greeted them with a wave and a broad smile. 彼は手を振り、にこにこ微笑みながら彼らを迎えた. ●**broad|ly** ADV 副詞 広く ❑ Charles grinned broadly. チャールズは大きく口をあけて笑った. **3** ADJ 形容詞 You use **broad** to describe something that includes a large number of different things or people. 範囲の広い ❑ A broad range of issues was discussed. 広範な問題が討議された. ●**broad|ly** ADV 副詞 [ADV with v] 広く ❑ Such policies will do little to resolve long-standing problems more broadly affecting America's global competitiveness. そのような政策は、米国の国際競争力にさらに幅広く影響する積年の問題を解決することにはほとんどならない. **4** ADJ 形容詞 You use **broad** to describe a word or meaning which covers or refers to a wide range of different things. 一般の ❑ ...restructuring in the broad sense of the word. 広義のリストラ ●**broad|ly** ADV 副詞

[ADV with v] 広範囲に □*We define education very broadly and students can study any aspect of its consequences for society.* 私たちは教育を非常に広範囲に定義しており, 学生は教育の社会的意義のあらゆる側面を研究することができる. **5** ADJ 形容詞 You use **broad** to describe a feeling or opinion that is shared by many people, or by people of many different kinds. 広範囲に及ぶ [ADJ n] □*The agreement won broad support in the U.S. Congress.* その協定は米国の議会で広範囲に及ぶ支持を得た. ● **broad|ly** ADV 副詞 [ADV with v] あまねく □*The new law has been broadly welcomed by road safety organizations.* 新しい法律は交通安全団体によってあまねく歓迎された. **6** in broad daylight → see daylight

N. broad **expanse**, broad **shoulders 1**
broad **smile 2**
broad **range**, broad **spectrum 3**
broad **definition**, broad **strokes**, broad **view 5**

broad|band /brɒdbænd/ N-UNCOUNT 不可算名詞 **Broadband** is a method of sending many electronic messages at the same time by using a wide range of frequencies. 広帯域の [COMPUTING コンピューティング] [oft N n] □*A recent study shows many broadband services lack basic security features.* 最近の調査によると, ブロードバンドサービスの多くは基本的なセキュリティ機能が欠如していることが示された.

broad|cast /brɒdkæst/ (broadcasts, broadcasting)

The form **broadcast** is used in the present tense and is the past tense and past participle of the verb.

broadcast 形は現在形に使われ, 動詞の過去形と過去分詞でもある.

1 N-COUNT 可算名詞 A **broadcast** is a program, performance, or speech on the radio or on television. 放送 □*In a broadcast on state radio the government announced that it was willing to resume peace negotiations.* 政府は国営ラジオ放送で和平交渉を再開する意志があると発表した. **2** V-T/V-I 他動詞/自動詞 To **broadcast** a program means to send it out by radio waves, wires, or satellites so that it can be heard on the radio or seen on television. 放送する □*The concert will be broadcast live on television and radio.* そのコンサートはテレビとラジオで生放送される. □*CNN also broadcasts in Europe.* CNNはヨーロッパでも放送している.

broad|cast|er /brɒdkæstər/ (broadcasters) N-COUNT 可算名詞 A **broadcaster** is someone who gives talks or takes part in interviews and discussions on radio or television programs. 放送者 □*...the prominent naturalist and broadcaster, Sir David Attenborough.* 著名な博物学者で放送者のサー・デイビッド・アッテンボロー

broad|cast|ing /brɒdkæstɪŋ/ N-UNCOUNT 不可算名詞 **Broadcasting** is the making and sending out of television and radio programs. 放送 □*If this happens it will change the face of religious broadcasting.* これが起こったら宗教番組放送の様相が変わるだろう.

broad|en /brɒdᵊn/ (broadens, broadening, broadened) **1** V-I 自動詞 When something **broadens**, it becomes wider. 広くなる □*The trails broadened into roads.* 小道は広くなり道路となった. **2** V-T/V-I 他動詞/自動詞 When you **broaden** something such as your experience or popularity, or when it **broadens**, the number of things or people that it includes becomes greater. 広げる □*We must broaden our appeal.* 私たちの訴えを広げる必要がある. □*I thought you wanted to broaden your horizons.* あなたは視野を広げたいのだと思っていた.

broad|ly /brɒdli/ **1** ADV 副詞 You can use **broadly** to indicate that something is generally true. 概して [ADV with cl] □*The president broadly got what he wanted out of his meeting.* 会談の決末は概して大統領の意向に沿うものだった. **2** → see also **broad**

broad|sheet /brɒdʃit/ (broadsheets) N-COUNT 可算名詞 A **broadsheet** is a newspaper that is printed on large sheets of paper. Broadsheets are generally considered to be more serious than other newspapers. Compare **tabloid**. 大判の新聞 [mainly BRIT 主に英国英語] □*Even the broadsheets made it their lead story.* 高級紙ですらトップニュースに取り上げた.

broc|co|li /brɒkəli/ N-UNCOUNT 不可算名詞 **Broccoli** is a vegetable with green stalks and green or purple tops. ブロッコリー → see **vegetable**

bro|chure /broʊʃʊr/ (brochures) N-COUNT 可算名詞 A **brochure** is a thin magazine with pictures that gives you information about a product or service. パンフレット □*...travel brochures.* 旅行パンフレット

broil /brɔɪl/ (broils, broiling, broiled) V-T 他動詞 When you **broil** food, you cook it using very strong heat directly above it. あぶり焼く [AM 米国英語] □*I'll broil the lobster.* ロブスターを焼くつもりだ. → see **cook**

broil|er /brɔɪlər/ (broilers) **1** N-COUNT 可算名詞 A **broiler** is a part of an oven that produces strong heat and cooks food placed underneath it. 焼肉器 [AM 米国英語] □*Remove from heat and finish off under the broiler until cheese melts.* 火からおろし, 焼肉器でチーズが溶けるまで仕上げ焼きする. **2** N-COUNT 可算名詞 A **broiler** or a **broiler chicken** is a young chicken that is suitable for broiling, roasting, or frying. ブロイラー [AM 米国英語]

broke /broʊk/ **1** **Broke** is the past tense of **break**. breakの過去形 **2** ADJ 形容詞 If you are **broke**, you have no money. 無一文の [INFORMAL くだけた] [v-link ADJ] □*What do you mean, I've got enough money? I'm as broke as you are.* 僕がお金を十分持っているってどういう意味だ. 僕もきみと同じくらい一文無しだ. **3** PHRASE 句 If a company or person **goes broke**, they lose money and are unable to continue in business or to pay their debts. 破産する [INFORMAL くだけた] □*Balton went broke twice in his career.* ボルトンの事業は2度破産した.

ADJ. bankrupt, destitute, impoverished, penniless, poor; (ant.) rich, wealthy, well-to-do **2**

bro|ken /broʊkən/ **1** **Broken** is the past participle of **break**. breakの過去分詞形 **2** ADJ 形容詞 A **broken** line is not continuous but has gaps or spaces in it. 断続的な [ADJ n] □*A broken blue line means the course of a waterless valley.* 破線 **3** ADJ 形容詞 You can use **broken** to describe a marriage that has ended in divorce, or a home in which the parents of the family are divorced, when you think this is a sad or bad thing. 破綻した [DISAPPROVAL 不賛成] [ADJ n] □*She spoke for the first time about the traumas of a broken marriage.* 彼女は破綻した結婚の精神的衝撃について初めて語った. **4** ADJ 形容詞 If someone talks in **broken** English, for example, or in **broken** French, they speak slowly and make a lot of mistakes because they do not know the language very well. たどたどしい [ADJ n] □*Eric could only respond in broken English.* エリックはあやしげな英語でしか対応できなかった.

bro|ker /broʊkər/ (brokers, brokering, brokered) **1** N-COUNT 可算名詞 A **broker** is a person whose job is to buy and sell securities, foreign money, real estate, or goods for other people. 仲買人 [BUSINESS 実業] **2** V-T 他動詞 If a country or government **brokers** an agreement, a ceasefire, or a round of talks, they try to negotiate or arrange it. 仲介する □*The United Nations brokered a peace in Mogadishu at the end of March.* 国連は3月末にモガディシオで和平調停を行った.

bro|ker|age /broʊkərɪdʒ/ (brokerages) N-COUNT 可算名詞 A **brokerage** or a **brokerage** firm is a company of brokers. 証券会社 [BUSINESS 実業] □*...Japan's four biggest brokerages.* 日本の4大証券会社 □*...the nation's largest brokerage firms.* 国内最大の証券会社

Bronx cheer /brɒnks tʃɪər/ (Bronx cheers) N-COUNT 可算名詞 A **Bronx cheer** is a sound that people make by vibrating their lips in order to express disapproval or contempt. 野卑なあざけり [AM 米国英語 くだけた]

bronze /brɒnz/ **1** N-UNCOUNT 不可算名詞 **Bronze** is a yellowish-brown metal which is a mixture of copper and tin. 青銅 □*...a bronze statue of Giorgi Dimitrov.* ジョージ・ディミトロフのブロンズ像 **2** COLOR 色彩語 Something that is **bronze** is yellowish-brown in color. ブロンズ色 □*Her hair shone bronze and gold.* 彼女の髪はブロンズと金の色に輝いた.

bronze med|al (bronze medals) N-COUNT 可算名詞 A **bronze medal** is a medal made of bronze or bronze-colored metal that is given as a prize to the person who comes third in a competition, especially a sports contest. 銅メダル

brooch /broʊtʃ/ (brooches) N-COUNT 可算名詞 A **brooch** is a piece of jewelry that has a pin at the back so it can be fastened on a dress, blouse, or coat. ブローチ → see **jewelry**

brood /brud/ (broods, brooding, brooded) **1** N-COUNT 可算名詞 A **brood** is a group of baby birds that were born at the same time to the same mother. 一かえりのひな □*...a hungry brood of fledglings.* お腹を空かした一かえりのひな **2** N-COUNT 可算名詞 You can refer to someone's young children as their **brood** when you want to emphasize that there are a lot of them. 子供たち [EMPHASIS 強調] □*...a large brood of children.* 大勢の子供たち **3** V-I 自動詞 If someone **broods** over something, they think about it a lot, seriously. 気に病む □*She constantly broods about her family.* 彼女はひっきりなしに家族のことを気に病んでいる.

brood|ing /brudɪŋ/ ADJ 形容詞 **Brooding** is used to describe an atmosphere or feeling that makes you feel anxious or slightly afraid. 気がめいっている [LITERARY 文語的] □*The same heavy, brooding silence descended on them.* あの重苦しく陰鬱(いんうつ)な沈黙が彼らを襲った.

broom /brum/ (brooms) **1** N-COUNT 可算名詞 A **broom** is a kind of brush with a long handle. You use a broom for sweeping

the floor. ほうき **2** N-UNCOUNT 不可算名詞 **Broom** is a wild bush with a lot of tiny yellow flowers. エニシダ

Bros. **Bros.** is a written abbreviation for **brothers**. It is usually used as part of the name of a company. brothersの略 [BUSINESS 実業]

broth /brɔθ/ (broths) N-VAR 可変性名詞 **Broth** is a kind of soup made by boiling meat or vegetables. ブロス

broth|el /brɒθ°l/ (brothels) N-COUNT 可算名詞 A **brothel** is a building where men can go to pay to have sex with prostitutes. 売春宿

broth|er /brʌðər/ (brothers)

The old-fashioned form **brethren** is still sometimes used as the plural for meanings **3** and **4**.

古風な **brethren** 形はまだ時々 **3** と **4** の意味を表す複数に使われる.

1 N-COUNT 可算名詞 Your **brother** is a boy or a man who has the same parents as you. 兄弟 ❑ Oh, so you're Peter's younger brother. じゃあきみはピーターの弟なんだ. **2** → see also **half brother, stepbrother 3** N-COUNT 可算名詞 You can describe a man as your **brother** if he belongs to the same race, religion, country, or profession as you, or if he has similar ideas to you. 同胞 ❑ He told reporters he'd come to be with his Latvian brothers. 彼は記者にラトビア人の同胞と会うために来たと語った. **4** N-TITLE; N-COUNT; N-VOC 称号名詞, 可算名詞, 呼格名詞 **Brother** is a title given to a man who belongs to a religious community such as a monastery. 修道僧 ❑ ...Brother Otto. ブラザー・オットー. **5** N-IN-NAMES 名称中の名詞 **Brothers** is used in the names of some companies and stores. 兄弟社 ❑ ...the movie company Warner Brothers. 映画会社のワーナーブラザーズ

→ see **family**

brother|hood /brʌðərhʊd/ (brotherhoods) **1** N-UNCOUNT 不可算名詞 **Brotherhood** is the affection and loyalty that you feel for people who you have something in common with. 兄弟の縁 ❑ People threw flowers into the river between the two countries as a symbolic act of brotherhood. 人々は同胞愛を象徴する行為として両国間を流れる川に花を投げた. **2** N-COUNT 可算名詞 A **brotherhood** is an organization whose members all have the same political aims and beliefs or the same job or profession. 同業組合など ❑ ...the Brotherhood of Locomotive Engineers. 機関手組合

brother-in-law (brothers-in-law) N-COUNT 可算名詞 Someone's **brother-in-law** is the brother of their husband or wife, or the man who is married to their sister. 義理の兄弟

→ see **family**

brought /brɔt/ **Brought** is the past tense and past participle of **bring**. bringの過去・過去分詞形

brow /braʊ/ (brows) **1** N-COUNT 可算名詞 Your **brow** is your forehead. 額 ❑ He wiped his brow with the back of his hand. 彼は手の甲で額をぬぐった. **2** N-COUNT 可算名詞 Your **brows** are your eyebrows. まゆ毛 [usu pl] ❑ He had thick brown hair and shaggy brows. 彼は茶色の濃い髪ともじゃもじゃのまゆ毛の持ち主だった. **3** N-COUNT 可算名詞 The **brow** of a hill is the top part of it. 丘の頂上 ❑ He was on the lookout just below the brow of the hill. 彼は丘の頂上のすぐ下で見張りをしていた.

brown /braʊn/ (browner, brownest, browns, browning, browned) **1** COLOR 色彩語 Something that is **brown** is the color of earth or of wood. 茶色 ❑ ...her deep brown eyes. 彼女の濃い茶色の目 **2** ADJ 形容詞 You can describe a white-skinned person as **brown** when they have been sitting in the sun until their skin has become darker than usual. 日焼けした **3** ADJ 形容詞 **Brown** is used to describe grains that have not had their outer layers removed, and foods made from these grains. 全粒状の ❑ ...brown bread. 全粒粉パン ❑ ...spicy tomato sauce served over a bed of brown rice. 玄米の上にかけたぴりっと辛いトマトソース **4** V-T/V-I 他動詞/自動詞 When food **browns** or when you **brown** food, you cook it, usually for a short time on a high flame. きつね色に焼く ❑ Cook for ten minutes until the sugar browns. 砂糖が茶色になるまで10分間加熱する.

brown|field /braʊnfild/ ADJ 形容詞 **Brownfield** land is land in a town or city where houses or factories have been built in the past, but which is not being used at the present time. 商工業施設として利用されなくなった [ADJ n]

browse /braʊz/ (browses, browsing, browsed) **1** V-I 自動詞 If you **browse** in a store, you look at things in a fairly casual way, in the hope that you might find something you like. 商品をざっと見る ❑ I stopped in several bookstores to browse. 私はいくつかの書店に立ち寄り, ひやかした. ❑ She browsed in an upscale antiques shop. 彼女は高級アンティーク店の品物を眺めた. ●N-COUNT 可算名詞 **Browse** is also a noun. 見て回ること ❑ ...a browse around the shops. 店々をひやかし歩く **2** V-I 自動詞 If you **browse through** a book or magazine, you look through it in a fairly casual way. ざっと目を通す ❑ ...sitting on the sofa browsing through the TV pages of the paper. ソ

ファーに座って新聞のテレビ欄にざっと目を通す **3** V-I 自動詞 If you **browse** on a computer, you search for information in computer files or on the Internet, especially on the World Wide Web. 閲覧する [COMPUTING コンピューティング] ❑ Try browsing around in the network bulletin boards. ネットワークの掲示板を閲覧してみたら. **4** V-T/V-I 他動詞/自動詞 When animals **browse**, they feed on plants. 草などを食べる ❑ ...three red deer stags browsing on the fringes of the forest. 森の端っこで草を食べているアカシカの雄3匹

brows|er /braʊzər/ (browsers) N-COUNT 可算名詞 A **browser** is a piece of computer software that you use to search for information on the Internet, especially on the World Wide Web. ブラウザー [COMPUTING コンピューティング] ❑ You need an up-to-date Web browser. あなたは最新版のブラウザーが必要だ.

bruise /bruz/ (bruises, bruising, bruised) **1** N-COUNT 可算名詞 A **bruise** is an injury that appears as a purple mark on your body, although the skin is not broken. 打撲傷 ❑ How did you get that bruise on your cheek? あなたの頬の傷はどうやってできたのか. **2** V-T/V-I 他動詞/自動詞 If you **bruise** a part of your body, a bruise appears on it, for example, because something hits you. If you **bruise** easily, bruises appear when something hits you only slightly. 傷つける [他動詞], 傷ができる [自動詞] ❑ I bruised my knee. ひざに傷を作っただけよ. ●bruised ADJ 形容詞 傷がついた ❑ I escaped with severely bruised legs. 足にひどい傷を負いながら逃げた. **3** V-T/V-I 他動詞/自動詞 If a fruit, vegetable, or plant **bruises** or is **bruised**, it is damaged by being handled roughly, making a mark on the skin. 傷める [他動詞], 傷む [自動詞] ❑ Choose a warm, dry day to cut them off the plants, being careful not to bruise them. 暖かく晴れた日に傷めないように気をつけて木から切りとりなさい. ❑ ...bruised tomatoes and cucumbers. 傷物のトマトときゅうり ●N-COUNT 可算名詞 **Bruise** is also a noun. 傷 ❑ ...bruises on the fruit's skin. 果物の傷 **4** V-T 他動詞 [usu passive] If you **are bruised** by an unpleasant experience, it makes you feel unhappy or upset. 傷つく ❑ The government will be severely bruised by yesterday's events. 政府は昨日の出来事でひどく傷つくだろう.

brunt /brʌnt/ PHRASE 句 To **bear the brunt** or **take the brunt** of something unpleasant means to suffer the main part or force of it. 矢面に立つ ❑ Young people are bearing the brunt of unemployment. 若者は失業の矢面に立たされている.

brush /brʌʃ/ (brushes, brushing, brushed) **1** N-COUNT 可算名詞 A **brush** is an object that has a large number of bristles or hairs fixed to it. You use brushes for painting, for cleaning things, and for making your hair neat. ブラシ ❑ We gave him paint and brushes. 私たちは彼にペンキとブラシを与えた. ❑ Stains are removed with buckets of soapy water and scrubbing brushes. しみはバケツ何杯ものせっけん水と洗いブラシで取る. **2** V-T 他動詞 If you **brush** something or **brush** something such as dirt off it, you clean it or make it neat using a brush. ブラシをかける ❑ Have you brushed your teeth? 歯を磨いたか. ❑ She brushed the powder out of her hair. 彼女は髪についた粉をブラシで落とした. ●N-SING 単数名詞 **Brush** is also a noun. ブラシをかけること ❑ I gave it a quick brush with my hairbrush. 私はヘアブラシで軽く髪をといた. **3** V-T 他動詞 If you **brush** something **with** a liquid, you apply a layer of that liquid using a brush. 塗る ❑ Brush the dough with beaten egg yolk. パン生地にといた卵の黄身を塗る. **4** V-T 他動詞 If you **brush** something somewhere, you remove it with quick light movements of your hands. 払いのける ❑ He brushed his hair back with both hands. 彼は両手で髪を後ろへかき上げた. ❑ She brushed away tears as she spoke of him. 彼女は彼の話をしながら涙を手でぬぐった. **5** V-T/V-I 他動詞/自動詞 If one thing **brushes against** another or if you **brush** on one thing **against** another, the first thing touches the second thing lightly while passing it. 軽く触れる ❑ Something brushed against her leg. 何かが彼の足にすっと触れた. ❑ I felt her dark brown hair brushing the back of my shoulder. 彼女のこげ茶色の髪が肩に触れるのを感じた. **6** N-COUNT 可算名詞 If you have a **brush with** a particular situation, usually an unpleasant one, you almost experience it. あぶないところ ❑ ...the trauma of a brush with death. 死にそうになった経験のトラウマ **7** N-UNCOUNT 不可算名詞 **Brush** is an area of rough open land covered with small bushes and trees. You also use **brush** to refer to the bushes and trees on this land. 低木 (の茂み) ❑ ...the brush fire that destroyed nearly 500 acres. 500エーカー近くを破壊した低木地帯の火事

▶ **brush aside** or **brush away** PHRASAL VERB 句動詞 If you **brush aside** or **brush away** an idea, remark, or feeling, you refuse to consider it because you think it is not important or useful, even though it may be. 軽くあしらう ❑ Perhaps you shouldn't brush the idea aside too hastily. そのアイデアを軽くあしらうのは早計じゃないか.

▶ **brush off** PHRASAL VERB 句動詞 If someone **brushes** you **off** when you speak to them, they refuse to talk to you or be nice to you. 相手にしない ❑ When I tried to talk to her about it she just brushed me off. それについて話そうとしたら彼女は私を相手にしてくれなかった.

▶ **brush up** or **brush up on** PHRASAL VERB 句動詞 If you **brush up** something or **brush up on** it, you practice it or improve your

knowledge of it. 磨きをかける ❑ I had hoped to brush up my Spanish. スペイン語に磨きをかけたいと思っていた.
→ see **hair, teeth**

brusque /brʌsk/ ADJ 形容詞 If you describe a person or their behavior as **brusque**, you mean that they deal with things, or say things, quickly and shortly, so that they seem to be rude. ぞんざいな ❑ The doctors are brusque and busy. 医者たちはぞんざいで忙しい.

brus|sels sprout /brʌsəlz spraʊt/ (**brussels sprouts**) also **Brussels sprout** N-COUNT 可算名詞 **Brussels sprouts** are vegetables that look like tiny cabbages. 芽キャベツ

bru|tal /brut°l/ **1** ADJ 形容詞 A **brutal** act or person is cruel and violent. 残酷な ❑ He was the victim of a very brutal murder. 彼は非常に残酷な方法で殺された ❑ ...the brutal suppression of anti-government protests. 反政府抗議への粗暴な鎮圧 ● **bru|tal|ly** ADV 副詞 残忍な方法で ❑ Her real parents had been brutally murdered. 彼女の実の両親は残忍な方法で殺された. **2** ADJ 形容詞 If someone expresses something unpleasant with **brutal** honesty or frankness, they express it in a clear and accurate way, without attempting to disguise its unpleasantness. 情け容赦のない ❑ It was refreshing to talk about themselves and their feelings with brutal honesty. 彼ら自身のことや感じていることをあからさまに話してすっきりした. ● **bru|tal|ly** ADV 副詞 情け容赦なく ❑ The talks had been brutally frank. 話し合いは洗いざらい率直だった.

bru|tal|ity /brutæliti/ (**brutalities**) N-VAR 可変性名詞 **Brutality** is cruel and violent treatment or behavior. A **brutality** is an instance of cruel and violent treatment or behavior. 残忍性 ❑ Her experience of men was of domination and brutality. 彼女が男について経験したのは支配的で残忍だということだった. ❑ ...police brutality. 警察の残虐行為

brute /brut/ (**brutes**) N-COUNT 可算名詞 If you call someone, usually a man, a **brute**, you mean that they are rough, violent, and insensitive. 人でなし [DISAPPROVAL 不賛成] ❑ Custer was an idiot and a brute and he deserved his fate. カスターは馬鹿で嫌な男で, その運命を受けて当然だった.

BSE /bi ɛs i/ N-UNCOUNT 不可算名詞 **BSE** is a disease that affects the nervous system of cattle and kills them. **BSE** is an abbreviation for "bovine spongiform encephalopathy." 牛海綿状脳症 ❑ ...meat from cattle infected with BSE, or mad cow disease. 牛海綿状脳症, 通称狂牛病に感染した牛の肉

BTW **BTW** is the written abbreviation for "by the way," often used in e-mail. by the wayの略 ❑ BTW, the machine is simply amazing. ところであの機械はすごいね.

bub|ble /bʌb°l/ (**bubbles, bubbling, bubbled**) **1** N-COUNT 可算名詞 **Bubbles** are small balls of air or gas in a liquid. 泡 ❑ Ink particles attach themselves to air bubbles and rise to the surface. インク粒子は気泡に付着し, 表面に浮かび上がる. **2** N-COUNT 可算名詞 A **bubble** is a hollow ball of soapy liquid that is floating in the air or standing on a surface. シャボン玉 ❑ With soap and water, bubbles and boats, children love bathtime. せっけんと水, シャボン玉と船があるお風呂の時間で子供たちは大好きだ. **3** N-COUNT 可算名詞 In a cartoon, a speech **bubble** is the shape which surrounds the words which a character is thinking or saying. (漫画の)吹き出し ❑ All that was missing were speech bubbles saying, "Golly!" and "Wow!" 欠けているのは「おや！」と「うわー！」という吹き出しだけだった. **4** V-I 自動詞 When a liquid **bubbles**, bubbles move in it, for example, because it is boiling or moving quickly. 沸騰する ❑ Heat the seasoned stock until it is bubbling. 味付けしたスープストックを沸騰するまで煮る. ❑ The fermenting wine had bubbled up and over the top. 発酵中のワインは上面でぶくぶく音を立てた. **5** V-I 自動詞 A feeling, influence, or activity that is **bubbling** away continues to occur. 煮えたぎる [usu cont] ❑ ...political tensions that have been bubbling away for years. 長年にわたり煮えたぎってきた政治的緊張
→ see **soap**

bub|bly /bʌbli/ **1** ADJ 形容詞 Someone who is **bubbly** is very lively and cheerful and talks a lot. 陽気な [APPROVAL 賛成] ❑ ...a bubbly girl who loves to laugh. 笑うのが大好きな陽気な女の子 **2** ADJ 形容詞 If something is **bubbly**, it has a lot of bubbles in it. 泡状の ❑ Melt the butter over a medium-low heat. When it is melted and bubbly, put in the flour. バターを中～弱火で溶かす. 溶けて泡がたってきたら小麦粉を入れる.

buck /bʌk/ (**bucks, bucking, bucked**) **1** N-COUNT 可算名詞 A **buck** is a U.S. or Australian dollar. ドル [INFORMAL くだけた] ❑ That would probably cost you about fifty bucks. それは50ドルくらいするだろう. ❑ Why can't you spend a few bucks on a coat? 少しくらいのお金をコートに使えないの？ **2** N-COUNT 可算名詞 A **buck** is the male of various animals, including the deer, antelope, rabbit, and kangaroo. 雄 **3** ADJ 形容詞 If someone has **buck** teeth, their upper front teeth stick forward out of their mouth. 出っ歯 [ADJ n] **4** V-I 自動詞 If a horse **bucks**, it kicks both of its back legs wildly into the air, or jumps into the air wildly with all four feet off the ground. はね上がる ❑ The stallion bucked as he fought against the reins holding him tightly in. その種馬はきつい手綱に逆らおうとして, 急に背を曲げてはね上がった. **5** V-T 他動詞 If you **buck** the trend, you

obtain different results from others in the same area. If you **buck** the system, you get what you want by breaking or ignoring the rules. 逆らう ❑ While other newspapers are losing circulation, we are bucking the trend. 他の新聞は発行部数が減っているのに本紙は動向に逆らっている. ❑ He wants to be the tough rebel who bucks the system. 彼は体制に逆らう屈強な反抗者になりたがっている. **6** PHRASE 句 If you **pass the buck**, you refuse to accept responsibility for something, and say that someone else is responsible. 責任をなすりつける [INFORMAL くだけた] ❑ David says the responsibility is Mr. Smith's and it's no good trying to pass the buck. デイビッドは, スミス氏に責任があり, 人になすりつけようとしても無駄だと言っている.

buck|et /bʌkɪt/ (**buckets**) **1** N-COUNT 可算名詞 A **bucket** is a round metal or plastic container with a handle attached to its sides. Buckets are often used for holding and carrying water. バケツ ❑ We drew water in a bucket from the well outside the door. 私たちは出入り口の外にある井戸からつるべで水をくんだ. **2** N-COUNT 可算名詞 A **bucket of** something such as water is the amount of it that is contained in a bucket. バケツ一杯の ❑ She threw a bucket of water over them. 彼女は彼らにバケツ一杯の水をかけた.

buck|le /bʌk°l/ (**buckles, buckling, buckled**) **1** N-COUNT 可算名詞 A **buckle** is a piece of metal or plastic attached to one end of a belt or strap, which is used to fasten it. バックル ❑ He wore a belt with a large brass buckle. 彼は大きな真ちゅう製のバックルのついたベルトを身に着けた. **2** V-T 他動詞 When you **buckle** a belt or strap, you fasten it. 締める ❑ A door slammed in the house and a man came out buckling his belt. 家のドアがバタンと閉まり, 男がベルトを締めながら出てきた. **3** V-T/V-I 他動詞/自動詞 If an object **buckles** or if something **buckles** it, it becomes bent as a result of very great heat or force. 曲げる [他動詞], 曲がる [自動詞] ❑ The door was beginning to buckle from the intense heat. 床は強い熱のため曲がり始めていた. **4** V-I 自動詞 If your legs or knees **buckle**, they bend because they have become very weak or tired. がくがくする ❑ Mcanally's knees buckled and he crumpled down onto the floor. マコーナリーは膝ががくがくして崩れるように床に倒れた.
→ see **crash**

▶ **buckle up** PHRASAL VERB 句動詞 When you **buckle up** in a car or airplane, you fasten your seat belt. ベルトを締める [INFORMAL くだけた] ❑ A sign just ahead of me said, "Buckle Up. It's the Law in Illinois." 前方の標識には「シートベルトを締めよ. イリノイ州の法律です.」と書いてあった.

bud /bʌd/ (**buds**) **1** N-COUNT 可算名詞 A **bud** is a small pointed lump that appears on a tree or plant and develops into a leaf or flower. 芽 ❑ Rosanna's favorite time is early summer, just before the buds open. ロザンナが好きなのは初夏, つぼみが開く前の季節だ. **2** → see also **budding** **3** PHRASE 句 If you **nip** something such as bad behavior **in the bud**, you stop it before it can develop very far. 初期に食い止める [INFORMAL くだけた] ❑ It is important to recognize jealousy and to nip it in the bud before it gets out of hand. しっとを認識し, 手に負えなくなる前に食い止めることが大事だ.
→ see **taste**

Bud|dhism /bʊdɪzəm, bʊd-/ N-UNCOUNT 不可算名詞 **Buddhism** is a religion which teaches that the way to end suffering is by overcoming your desires. 仏教
→ see **religion**

Bud|dhist /bʊdɪst, bʊd-/ (**Buddhists**) **1** N-COUNT 可算名詞 A **Buddhist** is a person whose religion is Buddhism. 仏教徒 **2** ADJ 形容詞 **Buddhist** means relating or referring to Buddhism. 仏教の ❑ ...Buddhist monks. 仏教僧

bud|ding /bʌdɪŋ/ **1** ADJ 形容詞 If you describe someone as, for example, a **budding** businessman or a **budding** artist, you mean that they are starting to succeed or become interested in business or art. 新進の [ADJ n] ❑ The forum is now open to all budding entrepreneurs. このフォーラムは現在全ての新進起業家に開かれている. **2** ADJ 形容詞 You use **budding** to describe a situation that is just beginning. 芽生えた [ADJ n] ❑ Our budding romance was over. 私たちの芽生えた恋は終わった.

bud|dy /bʌdi/ (**buddies**) N-COUNT 可算名詞 A **buddy** is a close friend, usually a male friend of a man. 男の親しい友人 [mainly AM 主に米国英語] ❑ We became great buddies. 僕たちは親友になった.

budge /bʌdʒ/ (**budges, budging, budged**) **1** V-T/V-I 他動詞/自動詞 If someone will not **budge** on a matter, or if nothing **budges** them, they refuse to change their mind or to come to an agreement. 意見を変える [with brd-neg] ❑ The Americans will not budge on this point. アメリカ人はこの点について意見を変えないだろう. **2** V-T/V-I 他動詞/自動詞 If someone or something will not **budge**, they will not move. If you cannot **budge** them, you cannot make them move. 動かす [他動詞], 動く [自動詞] ❑ Her mother refused to budge from Omaha. 彼女の母親はオマハから動くのを拒否した. [with brd-neg] ❑ The window refused to budge. 窓はびくともしなかった.

budg|et /bʌdʒɪt/ (**budgets, budgeting, budgeted**) **1** N-COUNT 可算名詞 Your **budget** is the amount of money that you have available to spend. The **budget** for something is the amount of

money that a person, organization, or country has available to spend on it. 予算 [BUSINESS 実業] ❑ *She will design a fantastic new kitchen for you – and all within your budget.* 彼女はあなたの予算内で素晴らしいキッチンを設計するだろう. ❑ *Someone had furnished the place on a tight budget.* 誰かが厳しい予算でその場所に家具を取り付けた. **2** N-COUNT 可算名詞 The **budget** of an organization or country is its financial situation, considered as the difference between the money it receives and the money it spends. 収支 [BUSINESS 実業] ❑ *The hospital obviously has to balance the budget each year.* 病院は言うまでもなく毎年収支の均衡をはかる必要がある. **3** V-T/V-I 他動詞/自動詞 If you **budget** certain amounts of money for particular things, you decide that you can afford to spend those amounts on those things. 予算を立てる ❑ *The company has budgeted $10 million for advertising.* その会社は1千万ドルの広告費予算を立てた. ❑ *The movie is only budgeted at $10 million.* 映画の予算は1千万ドルだけである. ❑ *I'm learning how to budget.* 私は予算を立てる方法を学んでいるところだ. ● **budg|et|ing** N-UNCOUNT 不可算名詞 予算を立てること ❑ *We have continued to exercise caution in our budgeting for the current year.* 我々は本年度の資金計画で引き続き慎重さを実行している. **4** ADJ 形容詞 [ADJ n] **Budget** is used in advertising to suggest that something is being sold cheaply. 格安の ❑ *Cheap flights are available from budget travel agents from $240.* 格安旅行代理店では240ドルから始まる安い航空券が手に入る. ▸ **budget for** PHRASAL VERB 句動詞 If you **budget for** something, you take account of it when you are deciding how much you can afford to spend on different things. 予算に組入れる ❑ *The authorities had budgeted for some non-payment.* 当局は未納を予算に組入れていた.

budg|et|ary /bʌdʒiteri/ ADJ 形容詞 A **budgetary** matter or policy is concerned with the amount of money that is available to a country or organization, and how it is to be spent. 予算上の [FORMAL 形式ばった] [ADJ n] ❑ *There are huge budgetary pressures on all governments in Europe to reduce their armed forces.* ヨーロッパの全ての国の政府は、軍削減に向け非常に大きな予算的圧力を受けている.

buff /bʌf/ (buffs) **1** COLOR 色彩語 Something that is **buff** is pale brown in color. 淡黄色の ❑ *He took a largish buff envelope from his pocket.* 彼はポケットから大きめの淡黄色の封筒を取り出した. **2** N-COUNT 可算名詞 You use **buff** to describe someone who knows a lot about a particular subject. For example, if you describe someone as a movie **buff**, you mean that they know a lot about movies. 通 [INFORMAL くだけた] ❑ *Judge Lanier is a real movie buff.* ラニエ判事は真の映画通だ.

buf|fa|lo /bʌfəlou/ (buffalo)

The plural can be either **buffaloes** or **buffalo**.

複数は **buffaloes** か **buffalo** のいずれかである.

N-COUNT 可算名詞 A **buffalo** is a wild animal like a large cow with horns that curve upwards. Buffalo are usually found in southern and eastern Africa. 水牛

buff|er /bʌfər/ (buffers, buffering, buffered) **1** N-COUNT 可算名詞 A **buffer** is something that prevents something else from being harmed or that prevents two things from harming each other. 緩衝物 ❑ *Keep savings as a buffer against unexpected cash needs.* 突然現金が必要になった場合の蓄えとして貯金を続けなさい. **2** V-T 他動詞 If something **is buffered**, it is protected from harm. 保護される ❑ *The company is buffered by long-term contracts with growers.* その会社は栽培者との長期契約によって保護されている. **3** N-COUNT 可算名詞 A **buffer** is an area in a computer's memory where information can be stored for a short time. バッファー [COMPUTING コンピューティング]

buf|fet (buffets, buffeting, buffeted)

Pronounced /bufeɪ/ for meanings **1** and **2**, and /bʌfɪt/ for meaning **3**.

1 と **2** の意味では /bufeɪ/ と発音され、**3** の意味では /bʌfɪt/ と発音される.

1 N-COUNT 可算名詞 A **buffet** is a meal of food that is displayed on a long table at a party or public occasion. Guests usually serve themselves. ビュッフェ式の食事 ❑ *...a buffet lunch.* ビュッフェ式のランチ. **2** N-COUNT 可算名詞 A **buffet** is a café, usually in a hotel or station. 堂 ❑ *We sat in the station buffet sipping tea.* 私たちは駅の軽食堂に入りお茶を飲んだ. **3** V-T 他動詞 If something **is buffeted** by strong winds or by stormy seas, it is repeatedly struck or blown around by them. もまれる ❑ *Their plane had been severely buffeted by*

storms. 彼らの飛行機は嵐のためにひどく揺れた.

bug /bʌg/ (bugs, bugging, bugged) **1** N-COUNT 可算名詞 A **bug** is an insect or similar small creature. 虫 [INFORMAL くだけた] ❑ *We noticed tiny bugs that were all over the walls.* 私たちは壁全体に小さな虫がはっているのに気付いた. **2** N-COUNT 可算名詞 A **bug** is an illness which is caused by small organisms such as bacteria. 病原菌による病気 [INFORMAL くだけた] ❑ *I think I've got a bit of a stomach bug.* ちょっと胃がやられたみたいだ. **3** N-COUNT 可算名詞 If there is a **bug** in a computer program, there is a mistake in it. 不具合 [COMPUTING コンピューティング] ❑ *There is a bug in the software.* ソフトウェアにバグがある. **4** N-COUNT 可算名詞 A **bug** is a tiny hidden microphone that transmits what people are saying. 隠しマイク ❑ *There was a bug on the phone.* 電話機に隠しマイクがついていた. **5** V-T 他動詞 If someone **bugs** a place, they hide tiny microphones in it that transmit what people are saying. 隠しマイクを取り付ける ❑ *He heard that they were planning to bug his office.* 彼は、彼らが自分の執務室に盗聴器をつける計画だと聞いた. **6** V-T 他動詞 If someone or something **bugs** you, they worry or annoy you. いらだたせる [INFORMAL くだけた] ❑ *I only did it to bug my parents.* 私は両親を悩ますためにそれをしただけだ.

build /bɪld/ (builds, building, built) **1** V-T 他動詞 If you **build** something, you make it by joining things together. 建てる ❑ *Developers are now proposing to build a hotel on the site.* 開発業者は現在その敷地にホテルを建てることを提案中だ. ❑ *The house was built in the early 19th century.* その家は19世紀初期に建てられた. ● **build|ing** N-UNCOUNT 不可算名詞 建築 ❑ *In Japan, the building of Kansai airport continues.* 日本では関西空港の建築工事が続く. ● **built** ADJ 形容詞 [adv ADJ, ADJ 'for' n, ADJ to-inf] 建築された ❑ *Even newly built houses can need repairs.* 新築の家ですら修理が必要なことがある. ❑ *It's a product built for safety.* それは安全のために造られた製品だ. **2** V-T 他動詞 If you **build** something **into** a wall or object, you make it in such a way that it is in the wall or object, or is part of it. 作りつけにする ❑ *If the TV was built into the ceiling, you could lie there while watching your favorite program.* テレビが天井にはめ込まれていれば寝転がって好きな番組を観ることができるのに. **3** V-T 他動詞 If people **build** an organization, a society, or a relationship, they gradually form it. 築き上げる ❑ *He and a partner set up on their own and built a successful fashion company.* 彼とパートナーは繁盛しているファッション会社を築き上げた. ❑ *Their purpose is to build a fair society and a strong economy.* 彼らが目指すのは公正な社会と強い経済を築き上げることだ. ● **build|ing** N-UNCOUNT 不可算名詞 建築 ❑ *...the building of the great civilizations of the ancient world.* 古代世界の偉大な文明の建築 **4** V-T 他動詞 If you **build** an organization, system, or product **on** something, you base it on it. 基礎にして構築する ❑ *We will then have a firmer foundation of fact on which to build theories.* 我々はその後、理論を構築するための一層確実な事実的基盤を得るだろう. **5** V-T 他動詞 If you **build** something into a policy, system, or product, you make it part of it. 中に組み込む ❑ *We have to build computers into the school curriculum.* コンピューターを学校のカリキュラムに組み込む必要がある. **6** V-T 他動詞 To **build** someone's confidence or trust means to increase it gradually. 徐々に築き上げる ❑ *Diplomats hope the meetings will build mutual trust.* 外交官はその会合を通して相互の信頼が築き上げられることを望んでいる. ● PHRASAL VERB 句動詞 **Build up** means the same as **build**. 築き上げる ❑ *The delegations had begun to build up some trust in one another.* 代表団は相互間の信頼を築き上げ始めていた. **7** V-I 自動詞 If you **build on** the success of something, you take advantage of this success in order to make further progress. 基にことを進める ❑ *The new regime has no successful economic reforms on which to build.* 新政権が基盤とすべき成果ある経済改革は存在しない. **8** V-I 自動詞 If pressure, speed, sound, or excitement **builds**, it gradually becomes greater. 徐々に高まる ❑ *Pressure built yesterday for postponement of the ceremony.* 昨日は式典延期への圧力が高まった. ● PHRASAL VERB 句動詞 **Build up** means the same as **build**. 徐々に高まる ❑ *We can build up the speed gradually and safely.* スピードを徐々に安全に上げることができる. **9** N-VAR 可変性名詞 Someone's **build** is the shape that their bones and muscles give to their body. 体格 ❑ *He's described as around thirty years old, six feet tall and of medium build.* 彼は30歳前後で、身長6フィートで普通の体格だ. **10** → see also **building**, **built**
▸ **build up 1** PHRASAL VERB 句動詞 If you **build up** something or if it **builds up**, it gradually becomes bigger, for example, because more is added to it. 築き上げる ❑ *The regime built up the largest army in Africa.* その政権はアフリカ最大の軍隊を築き上げた. ❑ *The collection has been built up over the last seventeen years.* そのコレクションは過去17年間で集められた. **2** PHRASAL VERB 句動詞 If you **build** someone **up**, you help them to feel stronger or more confident, especially when they have had a bad experience or have been ill. 自信をつけさせる ❑ *Build her up with kindness and a sympathetic ear.* 親切に親身になって話を聞いて彼女に自信をつけさせる. **3** PHRASAL VERB 句動

詞 If you **build** someone or something **up**, you make them seem important or exciting, for example, by talking about them a lot. 誇張する ❑ *The media will report on it and the tabloids will build it up.* メディアはそれについて報告し，タブロイド紙はそれを誇張して伝える。 ❑ *The soccer community built him up as the savior of the sport.* サッカー界はサッカーの救世主として彼を売り込んだ。 **4** → see also **build 6, 8, build-up, built-up**
→ see **muscle**

Thesaurus   *build* また次を参照：

V.	assemble, make, manufacture, produce, put together, set up; (*ant.*) demolish, destroy, knock down **1**

Word Partnership   *build* は次の語句と使われる：

V.	**plan to** build **1**
N.	build **bridges**, build **roads**, build **schools** **1** build **confidence** **6** build **momentum** **8**
ADJ.	**athletic** build, **slender** build, **strong** build **9**

build|er /bɪldər/ (**builders**) N-COUNT 可算名詞 A **builder** is a person whose job is to build or repair houses and other buildings. 建築業者 ❑ *The builders have finished the roof.* 建築業者は屋根を仕上げた。

build|ing /bɪldɪŋ/ (**buildings**) N-COUNT 可算名詞 A **building** is a structure that has a roof and walls, for example, a house or a factory. 建物 ❑ *They were on the upper floor of the building.* 彼らはその建物の上の階にいた。
→ see **architecture, skyscraper**

build-up (**build-ups**) also **buildup** or **build up** **1** N-COUNT 可算名詞 A **build-up** is a gradual increase in something. 増強 ❑ *There has been a build-up of troops on both sides of the border.* 国境の両側で兵力が増強された。 **2** N-COUNT 可算名詞 The **build-up** to an event is the way that journalists, advertisers, or other people talk about it a lot in the period of time immediately before it, and try to make it seem important and exciting. 盛り上がり ❑ *The exams came, almost an anticlimax after the build-up that the students had given them.* 試験がやってきた。学生たちが大いに盛り上がった後で，拍子抜け同然だった。

built /bɪlt/ **1 Built** is the past tense and past participle of **build**. build の過去・過去分詞形 **2** ADJ 形容詞 If you say that someone is **built** in a particular way, you are describing the kind of body they have. 体格の ❑ *...a strong, powerfully-built man of 60.* 頑健な体格をした60歳の男 **3** → see also **well-built**

built-in ADJ 形容詞 **Built-in** devices or features are included in something as a part of it, rather than being separate. 作り付けの [ADJ n] ❑ *...modern cameras with built-in flash units.* フラッシュユニットを内蔵した近代的カメラ

built-up ADJ 形容詞 A **built-up** area is an area such as a town or city which has a lot of buildings in it. 家が建て込んだ ❑ *A speed limit of 30 mph was introduced in built-up areas.* 住宅密集地区では時速30マイルの最高速度が導入された。

bulb /bʌlb/ (**bulbs**) **1** N-COUNT 可算名詞 A **bulb** is the glass part of an electric light or lamp, which gives out light when electricity passes through it. 電球 ❑ *The stairwell was lit by a single bulb.* 階段の照明は電球一つだった。 **2** N-COUNT 可算名詞 A **bulb** is a root shaped like an onion that grows into a flower or plant. 球根 ❑ *...tulip bulbs.* チューリップの球根

bulge /bʌldʒ/ (**bulges, bulging, bulged**) **1** V-I 自動詞 If something such as a person's stomach **bulges**, it sticks out. 突き出る ❑ *Jiro waddled closer, his belly bulging and distended.* 次郎はよたよた歩いてきた。彼のお腹は出っ張りふくらんでいた。 ❑ *He bulges out of his black T-shirt.* 彼の体は黒のTシャツから膨れ出ている。 **2** V-I 自動詞 If someone's eyes or veins **are bulging**, they seem to stick out a lot, often because the person is making a strong physical effort or is experiencing a strong emotion. 膨れ上がる ❑ *He shouted at his brother, his neck veins bulging.* 彼は首の静脈を膨張させながら弟に向かって怒鳴った。 **3** V-I 自動詞 If you say that something is **bulging with** things, you are emphasizing that it is full of them. いっぱい詰まっている [EMPHASIS 強調] [oft cont] ❑ *They returned home with the car bulging with boxes.* 彼らは車に箱をいっぱい詰めて家に帰ってきた。 **4** N-COUNT 可算名詞 **Bulges** are lumps that stick out from a surface which is otherwise flat or smooth. 膨らんだ部分 ❑ *Why won't those bulges on your hips and thighs go?* あなたのおしりと太ももの贅肉はなぜ消えないのか。 **5** N-COUNT 可算名詞 If there is a **bulge in** something, there is a sudden large increase in it. 急増 ❑ *...a bulge in aircraft sales.* 航空機売上高の急増

bu|limia /bulimiə, -lɪm-/ N-UNCOUNT 不可算名詞 **Bulimia** or **bulimia nervosa** is an illness in which a person has a very great fear of becoming fat, and so they make themselves vomit after eating. 過食症

bu|limic /bulɪmɪk, -lɪm-/ (**bulimics**) ADJ 形容詞 If someone is

bulimic, they are suffering from bulimia. 過食症の ❑ *...bulimic patients.* 過食症の患者 ● N-COUNT 可算名詞 A **bulimic** is someone who is bulimic. 過食症の人 ❑ *...a former bulimic.* 過食症だった人

bulk /bʌlk/ (**bulks, bulking, bulked**) **1** N-SING 単数名詞 You can refer to something's **bulk** when you want to emphasize that it is very large. 巨大さ [WRITTEN 書き言葉, EMPHASIS 強調] ❑ *The truck pulled out of the lot, its bulk unnerving against the dawn.* きょうとするほど巨大なトラックが夜明けに駐車場から出てきた。 **2** N-SING 単数名詞 You can refer to a large person's body or to their weight or size as their **bulk**. 巨体 ❑ *Bannol lowered his bulk carefully into the chair.* バノルはその巨体を注意深く椅子に下ろした。 **3** QUANT 数量詞 The **bulk of** something is most of it. 大部分 [QUANT 'of' def-n] ❑ *The bulk of the text is essentially a review of these original documents.* 文章の大部分は基本的には原文書の批評だ。 ● PRON 代名詞 **Bulk** is also a pronoun. 大半 ❑ *They come from all over the world, though the bulk is from the Indian subcontinent.* 大半はインド亜大陸の出身だが世界各国から集まっている。 **4** PHRASE 句 If you buy or sell something in **bulk**, you buy or sell it in large quantities. 大量に ❑ *Buying in bulk is more economical than shopping for small quantities.* 大量買入れは少量を買うより経済的だ。

▶ **bulk up** PHRASAL VERB 句動詞 If someone **bulks up** or if they **bulk up** their body, they put on weight in the form of extra muscle. 筋肉をつける ❑ *They feel I need to bulk up, and to improve my upper body strength.* 彼らは，私が筋肉をつけ，上半身を鍛える必要があると感じている。 ❑ *My friend is obsessed with going to the gym and has really bulked up her arms.* 私の友人はジム通いに夢中で，腕にかなり筋肉がついた。

bulky /bʌlki/ (**bulkier, bulkiest**) ADJ 形容詞 Something that is **bulky** is large and heavy. Bulky things are often difficult to move or deal with. かさばった ❑ *...bulky items like lawnmowers.* 芝刈り機などのかさばった品目

bull /bʊl/ (**bulls**) **1** N-COUNT 可算名詞 A **bull** is a male animal of the cow family. 雄牛 **2** N-COUNT 可算名詞 Some other male animals, including elephants and whales, are called **bulls**. （象や鯨などの）雄 ❑ *Suddenly a massive bull elephant with huge tusks charged us.* 突然，巨大なきばを持った大きな雄の象が私たちの方に突進してきた。 **3** N-COUNT 可算名詞 In the stock market, **bulls** are people who buy shares in expectation of a price rise, in order to make a profit by selling the shares again after a short time. Compare **bear**. 強気の買い手 [BUSINESS 実業] ❑ *The bulls argue stock prices are low and there are bargains to be had.* 強気の買い手は株価が低く割安株があると主張する。 **4** N-COUNT 可算名詞 In the Roman Catholic church, a papal **bull** is an official statement on a particular subject that is issued by the pope. （ローマ教皇の）大勅書 **5** N-UNCOUNT 不可算名詞 If you say that something is **bull** or a load of **bull**, you mean that it is complete nonsense or absolutely untrue. ほら話 [INFORMAL くだけた] ❑ *I think it's a load of bull.* それは大ぼらだと思う。

bull|doze /bʊldoʊz/ (**bulldozes, bulldozing, bulldozed**) **1** V-T 他動詞 If people **bulldoze** something such as a building, they knock it down using a bulldozer. ブルドーザーで解体する ❑ *She defeated developers who wanted to bulldoze her home to build a supermarket.* 彼女は，スーパーマーケットの建設のため自分の家をブルドーザーで解体しようとした開発業者に打ち負かした。 **2** V-T 他動詞 If people **bulldoze** earth, stone, or other heavy material, they move it using a bulldozer. ブルドーザーでならす ❑ *They have been cutting down the trees and bulldozing the land.* 彼らは木を切り倒とし，ブルドーザーで整地してきた。 **3** V-T 他動詞 If someone **bulldozes** a plan **through** or **bulldozes** another person **into** doing something, they get what they want in an unpleasantly forceful way. 強制する [DISAPPROVAL 不賛成] ❑ *Dropping all pretense of reason, they began to bulldoze through the democratic reforms.* 彼らは見せかけの理性を捨て去って，民主的改革を強行し始めた。 ❑ *...to sway public opinion and bulldoze them into adopting uneconomic practices.* 国民の意見を動かし，無理やり非経済的な慣行を採用させる。

bull|doz|er /bʊldoʊzər/ (**bulldozers**) N-COUNT 可算名詞 A **bulldozer** is a large vehicle with a broad metal blade at the front, which is used for knocking down buildings or moving large amounts of earth. ブルドーザー

bul|let /bʊlɪt/ (**bullets**) **1** N-COUNT 可算名詞 A **bullet** is a small piece of metal with a pointed or rounded end, which is fired out of a gun. 弾丸 ❑ *Two of the police fired 16 bullets each.* 2人の警官はそれぞれ16発の弾丸を発砲した。 **2** PHRASE 句 If someone **bites the bullet**, they accept that they have to do something unpleasant but necessary. つらい仕事を我慢してやる [JOURNALISM ジャーナリズム] ❑ *Tour operators may be forced to bite the bullet and cut prices.* 旅行業者にはつらいところだが値引きせざるを得なくなるかもしれない。

bul|letin /bʊlɪtɪn/ (**bulletins**) **1** N-COUNT 可算名詞 A **bulletin** is a short news report on the radio or television. 短いニュース ❑ *...the early morning news bulletin.* 早朝の定時ニュース **2** N-COUNT 可算名詞 A **bulletin** is a short official announcement made publicly to inform people about an important matter. 告示 ❑ *At 3:30 p.m. a bulletin was released announcing that the president was out*

B

of immediate danger. 午後3時30分に大統領が危篤状態を脱したと発表する公報が発表された. **3** N-COUNT 可算名詞 A **bulletin** is a regular newspaper or leaflet that is produced by an organization or group such as a school or church. 会報

bul|letin board (**bulletin boards**) **1** N-COUNT 可算名詞 A **bulletin board** is a board that is usually attached to a wall in order to display notices giving information about something. 掲示板 [mainly AM 主に米国英語] **2** N-COUNT 可算名詞 In computing, a **bulletin board** is a system that enables users to send and receive messages of general interest. 電子掲示板 ❏ *The Internet is the largest computer bulletin board in the world, and it's growing.* インターネットは世界最大のコンピュータ掲示板で, 拡大を続けている.

bul|let point (**bullet points**) N-COUNT 可算名詞 A **bullet point** is one of a series of important items for discussion or action in a document, usually marked by a square or round symbol. 箇条書き ❏ *Use bold type for headings and bullet points for noteworthy achievements.* 注目に値する成果の見出しと箇条書きには太字を使用する.

bullet|proof /ˈbʊlɪtpruːf/ also **bullet-proof** ADJ 形容詞 Something that is **bulletproof** is made of a strong material that bullets cannot pass through. 防弾の ❏ *...bulletproof glass.* 防弾ガラス
→ see **glass**

bull|horn /ˈbʊlhɔrn/ (**bullhorns**) N-COUNT 可算名詞 A **bullhorn** is a device for making your voice sound louder in the open air. ハンドマイク [AM 米国英語] ❏ *A bullhorn blared warnings of a bomb scare.* 拡声器が爆破予告警告をがなりたてた.

bul|lion /ˈbʊliən/ N-UNCOUNT 不可算名詞 **Bullion** is gold or silver, usually in the form of bars. 金塊, 銀塊 ❏ *The Japanese are busy buying up gold bullion.* 日本人は金塊を忙しく買い占めている.

bull|ish /ˈbʊlɪʃ/ ADJ 形容詞 In the stock market, if there is a **bullish** mood, prices are expected to rise. Compare **bearish**. 強気の [BUSINESS 実業] ❏ *The market opened in a bullish mood.* 相場は強気なムードで始まった.

bull mar|ket (**bull markets**) N-COUNT 可算名詞 A **bull market** is a situation in the stock market when people are buying a lot of shares because they expect the shares will increase in value and they will be able to make a profit by selling them again after a short time. Compare **bear market**. 強気相場 [BUSINESS 実業] ❏ *...the decline in prices after the bull market peaked in April 2000.* 買い相場が2000年4月にピークにたちして以来の値下がり

bull|ock /ˈbʊlək/ (**bullocks**) N-COUNT 可算名詞 A **bullock** is a young bull that has been castrated. 去勢牛

bul|ly /ˈbʊli/ (**bullies, bullying, bullied**) **1** N-COUNT 可算名詞 A **bully** is someone who uses their strength or power to hurt or frighten other people. 弱い者いじめ ❏ *I fell victim to the office bully.* 私はオフィスでいじめにあった. **2** V-T 他動詞 If someone **bullies** you, they use their strength or power to hurt or frighten you. いじめる ❏ *I wasn't going to let him bully me.* 私は彼に威張らせてなどつもりはない. ● **bul|ly|ing** N-UNCOUNT 不可算名詞 いじめ ❏ *...schoolchildren who were victims of bullying.* いじめの的となった児童 **3** V-T 他動詞 If someone **bullies** you **into** something, they make you do it by using force or threats. 脅す ❏ *We think an attempt to bully them into submission would be counterproductive.* 彼らを脅して服従させようとするのは逆効果だと思う. ❏ *She used to bully me into doing my schoolwork.* 私は彼女に脅されて学校の勉強をしたものだった.

bum /bʌm/ (**bums, bumming, bummed**) **1** N-COUNT 可算名詞 A **bum** is a person who has no permanent home or job and who gets money by working occasionally or by asking people for money. 浮浪者 [AM 米国英語, INFORMAL くだけた] ❏ *...the bums on the corner fighting over beers.* ビールの取り合いをしている, 失業中の飲んだくれ **2** N-COUNT 可算名詞 If someone refers to another person as a **bum**, they think that person is worthless or irresponsible. 甲斐性なし [INFORMAL くだけた, DISAPPROVAL 不賛成] ❏ *You're all a bunch of bums.* おまえたちは皆くずだ. **3** ADJ 形容詞 Some people use **bum** to describe a situation that they find unpleasant or annoying. ひどい [INFORMAL くだけた] [ADJ n] ❏ *He knows you're getting a bum deal.* きみがひどい目にあっているのを彼は知っている. **4** V-T 他動詞 If you **bum** something off someone, you ask them for it and they give it to you. ねだる [INFORMAL くだけた] ❏ *Mind if I bum a cigarette?* たばこをねだってもいいかな. **5** a **bum rap** → see **rap**

bump /bʌmp/ (**bumps, bumping, bumped**) **1** V-T/V-I 他動詞/自動詞 If you **bump** into something or someone, you accidentally hit them while you are moving. ぶつかる [自動詞] つける [他動詞] ❏ *They stopped walking and he almost bumped into them.* 彼らが突然立ち止まったので, 彼は彼らにぶつかりそうになった. ❏ *She bumped her head against a low branch.* 彼女は低い枝に頭をぶつけた. ● N-COUNT 可算名詞 **Bump** is also a noun. 衝突 ❏ *Small children often cry after a minor bump.* 小さな子供はちょっとぶつかるくらいですぐ泣くものだ. **2** N-COUNT 可算名詞 A **bump** is the action or the

dull sound of two heavy objects hitting each other. ドスン ❏ *I felt a little bump and I knew instantly what had happened.* 私はわずかな衝撃を感じ, 一瞬にして何が起こったかを理解した. **3** N-COUNT 可算名詞 A **bump** is a minor injury or swelling that you get if you bump into something or if something hits you. こぶ ❏ *She fell against our coffee table and got a large bump on her forehead.* 彼女はコーヒーテーブルの上に倒れて, 額に大きなこぶをつくった. **4** N-COUNT 可算名詞 A **bump** on a road is a raised, uneven part. 隆起 ❏ *The truck hit a bump and bounced.* トラックは段差に乗り上げ大きく弾んだ. **5** V-I 自動詞 If a vehicle **bumps over** a surface, it travels in a rough, bouncing way because the surface is very uneven. ガタガタ揺れて通る ❏ *We left the road, and again bumped over the mountainside.* 私たちは道路を出て, 再び山腹をガタガタと走った.
▸ **bump into** PHRASAL VERB 句動詞 If you **bump into** someone you know, you meet them unexpectedly. ばったり出会う [INFORMAL くだけた] ❏ *I happened to bump into Mervyn Johns in the hallway.* 廊下でマーヴィン・ジョンズにばったり出会った.

bump|er /ˈbʌmpər/ (**bumpers**) **1** N-COUNT 可算名詞 **Bumpers** are bars at the front and back of a vehicle that protect it if it bumps into something. バンパー ❏ *What stickers do you have on the bumper or the back windshield?* バンパーやリアガラスにどんなシールを貼っていますか. **2** ADJ 形容詞 A **bumper** crop or harvest is one that is larger than usual. 豊作の [ADJ n] ❏ *...a bumper crop of rice.* 米の豊作 **3** ADJ 形容詞 If you say that something is **bumper** size, you mean that it is very large. 非常に大きな [ADJ n] ❏ *...bumper profits.* 大もうけ **4** PHRASE 句 If traffic is **bumper-to-bumper**, the vehicles are so close to one another that they are almost touching and are moving very slowly. 縦にぎっしりと並んだ ❏ *...bumper-to-bumper rush-hour traffic.* ぎっしり詰まったラッシュアワーの交通渋滞

bumpy /ˈbʌmpi/ (**bumpier, bumpiest**) **1** ADJ 形容詞 A **bumpy** road or path has a lot of bumps on it. 凸凹のある ❏ *...bumpy cobbled streets.* 車がガタガタとはねる, 丸石を敷いた通り **2** ADJ 形容詞 A **bumpy** ride is uncomfortable and rough, usually because you are traveling over an uneven surface. がたつく ❏ *...a hot and bumpy ride across the desert.* 暑くて揺れるひどい砂漠の旅

bun /bʌn/ (**buns**) **1** N-COUNT 可算名詞 **Buns** are small bread rolls. They are sometimes sweet and may contain dried fruit or spices. 柔らかい菓子パン ❏ *...a currant bun.* 干しぶどう入りのロールパン **2** N-COUNT 可算名詞 If a woman has her hair in a **bun**, she has fastened it tightly on top of her head or at the back of her head in the shape of a ball. 束髪 **3** N-PLURAL 複数名詞 Your **buns** are your buttocks. しり [mainly AM 主に米国英語, INFORMAL くだけた] ❏ *I'd pinch his buns and kiss his neck.* 彼のしりをつまんで, 首にキスしたい.

bunch /bʌntʃ/ (**bunches, bunching, bunched**) **1** N-COUNT 可算名詞 A **bunch of** people is a group of people who share one or more characteristics or who are doing something together. 一団, 連中 [INFORMAL くだけた] ❏ *My neighbors are a bunch of busybodies.* 私の隣人はお節介焼きがそろっている. ❏ *We were a pretty inexperienced bunch of people really.* 私たちは皆確かに非常に未経験だった. **2** N-COUNT 可算名詞 A **bunch of** flowers is a number of flowers with their stalks held or tied together. 束 ❏ *He had left a huge bunch of flowers in her hotel room.* 彼は, 彼女のホテルの部屋に巨大な花束を残した. **3** N-COUNT 可算名詞 A **bunch of** bananas or grapes is a group of them growing on the same stem. 房 ❏ *Lili had fallen asleep clutching a fat bunch of grapes.* リリーはぶどうの大きな房をしっかり握って眠りに落ちた. **4** N-COUNT 可算名詞 A **bunch of** keys is a set of keys kept together on a metal ring. 一束 ❏ *George took out a bunch of keys and went to work on the complicated lock.* ジョージは一束の鍵を取り出して, 複雑な錠前の解除に取りかかった.
▸ **bunch up** or **bunch together** PHRASAL VERB 句動詞 If people or things **bunch up** or if you **bunch** them up, they move close to each other so that they form a small tight group. **Bunch together** means the same as **bunch up**. 一団に集める ❏ *They were bunching up, almost stepping on each other's heels.* 彼らはお互いのかかとを踏むほどぎゅうぎゅうに一か所に集まっていた. ❏ *People were bunched up at all the exits.* 人々はあらゆる出口につめかけていた.

bun|dle /ˈbʌndəl/ (**bundles, bundling, bundled**) **1** N-COUNT 可算名詞 A **bundle of** things is a number of them that are tied together or wrapped in a cloth or bag so that they can be carried or stored. 束, 包み ❏ *Lance pulled a bundle of papers out of a folder.* ランスはフォルダから紙の束を引っ張り出した. ❏ *He gathered the bundles of clothing into his arms.* 彼は一包みの衣服を腕の中にかき集めた. **2** N-SING 単数名詞 If you describe someone as, for example, a **bundle of** fun, you are emphasizing that they are full of fun. If you describe someone as a **bundle of** nerves, you are emphasizing that they are very nervous. 大量 [EMPHASIS 強調] ❏ *I remember Mickey as a bundle of fun, great to have around.* ミッキーはお茶目で一緒にいるのが楽しいやつだったなあ. ❏ *Life at high school wasn't a bundle of laughs.* 高校生活は笑いにあふれていたわけではない. **3** V-T 他動詞 If someone **is bundled** somewhere, someone pushes them there in a rough and hurried way. ごちゃごちゃに投げ込む ❏ *He was bundled into a car and driven 50 miles to a police station.* 彼は車の中に投げ込まれ, 警察署まで50マイル運ばれた. **4** V-T 他動詞 To **bundle**

software means to sell it together with a computer, or with other hardware or software, as part of a set. バンドルする [COMPUTING コンピューティング] ❑ *It's cheaper to buy software bundled with a PC than separately.* ソフトウェアは個別に買うより、PCと抱き合わせのほうが安い.

bun|ga|low /bʌ́ŋgəloʊ/ (bungalows) N-COUNT 可算名詞 A **bungalow** is a house that has only one level, and no stairs. バンガロー

bun|gle /bʌ́ŋgªl/ (bungles, bungling, bungled) V-T 他動詞 If you **bungle** something, you fail to do it properly, because you make mistakes or are clumsy. しくじる ❑ *Two prisoners bungled an escape bid after running either side of a lamppost while handcuffed.* 2人の囚人は逃亡を企てたが、お互いが手錠でつながれたまま街灯柱の別々の側を走ろうとしてしくじった. ● N-COUNT 可算名詞 **Bungle** is also a noun. しくじり ❑ *...an appalling administrative bungle.* 驚くばかりの行政の不手際 ● **bun|gling** ADJ 形容詞 へまな ❑ *...a bungling burglar.* へまな泥棒

bunk /bʌ́ŋk/ (bunks) N-COUNT 可算名詞 A **bunk** is a narrow bed that is usually attached to a wall, especially in a ship. 寝棚 ❑ *He left his bunk and went up on deck again.* 彼は寝棚を抜け出してもう一度デッキに上がった.

bun|ker /bʌ́ŋkər/ (bunkers) ◼ N-COUNT 可算名詞 A **bunker** is a place, usually underground, that has been built with strong walls to protect it against heavy gunfire and bombing. 掩蔽（えんぺい）壕 ❑ *...an extensive network of fortified underground bunkers.* 要塞化された地下掩蔽壕の大規模ネットワーク ◻ N-COUNT 可算名詞 A **bunker** is a container for coal or other fuel. 燃料庫 ◼ N-COUNT 可算名詞 On a golf course, a **bunker** is a large area filled with sand that is deliberately put there so that golfers must try to avoid. バンカー ❑ *He put his second shot in a bunker to the left of the green.* 彼は第2打目をグリーンの左側にあるバンカーに打ち込んだ.

bun|ny /bʌ́ni/ (bunnies) N-COUNT 可算名詞 A **bunny** or a **bunny rabbit** is a child's word for a rabbit. ウサちゃん [INFORMAL くだけた]

buoy /búi/ (buoys, buoying, buoyed) ◼ N-COUNT 可算名詞 A **buoy** is a floating object that is used to show ships and boats where they can go and to warn them of danger. ブイ ◻ V-T 他動詞 If someone in a difficult situation **is buoyed** by something, it makes them feel more cheerful and optimistic. 元気づける ❑ *In May they danced in the streets, buoyed by their victory.* 5月には、彼らは勝利に浮かれて通りで踊った. ● PHRASAL VERB 句動詞 **Buoy up** means the same as **buoy**. 浮かす ❑ *They are buoyed up by a sense of hope.* 彼らは期待感で浮かれた.

buoy|an|cy /bɔ́iənsi/ ◼ N-UNCOUNT 不可算名詞 **Buoyancy** is the ability that something has to float on a liquid or in the air. 浮力 ❑ *Air can be pumped into the diving suit to increase buoyancy.* 潜水服は、空気を送り込んで浮力を増すことができる. ◻ N-UNCOUNT 不可算名詞 **Buoyancy** is a feeling of cheerfulness. 快活さ ❑ *...a mood of buoyancy and optimism.* 明るく楽観的なムード ◼ N-UNCOUNT 不可算名詞 There is economic **buoyancy** when the economy is growing. 上がり傾向 ❑ *The likelihood is that the slump will be followed by a period of buoyancy.* 不景気の後には回復傾向の期間が訪れる可能性が高い.

buoy|ant /bɔ́iənt/ ◼ ADJ 形容詞 If you are in a **buoyant** mood, you feel cheerful and behave in a lively way. 楽天的な ❑ *You will feel more buoyant and optimistic about the future than you have for a long time.* きみは、これまでの長い期間とは異なり、これからは将来をより明るく楽観視するようになるだろう. ◻ ADJ 形容詞 A **buoyant** economy is a successful one in which there is a lot of trade and economic activity. 上がりぎみの ❑ *We have a buoyant economy and unemployment is considerably lower than the regional average.* 我々の景気は上り調子で、失業率も地域平均よりもかなり低い. ◼ ADJ 形容詞 A **buoyant** object floats on a liquid. 浮遊性のある ❑ *While there is still moisture trapped in the container to keep it buoyant, it will float.* コンテナは、内部に閉じ込められた空気の量が浮力の保持に十分である限りは浮くだろう.

bur|den /bɜ́rdªn/ (burdens, burdening, burdened) ◼ N-COUNT 可算名詞 If you describe a problem or a responsibility as a **burden**, you mean that it causes someone a lot of difficulty, worry, or hard work. 負担、苦しみ、難渋 ❑ *The developing countries bear the burden of an enormous external debt.* 開発途上国は、莫大な海外債務の負担を負っている. ❑ *Her death will be an impossible burden on Paul.* 彼女の死はポールにとって途方もない苦しみだろう. ◻ N-COUNT 可算名詞 A **burden** is a heavy load that is difficult to carry. 重荷 [FORMAL 形式ばった] ❑ *...African women carrying burdens on their heads.* 荷物を頭に載せて運ぶアフリカの女性 ◼ V-T 他動詞 If someone **burdens** you with something that is likely to worry you, for example, a problem or a difficult decision, they tell you about it. 苦しめる ❑ *We decided not to burden him with the news.* 私たちは彼を苦しめないよう、ニュースを聞かせないことにした.

bur|dened /bɜ́rdªnd/ ◼ ADJ 形容詞 If you are **burdened** with something, it causes you a lot of worry or hard work. 悩ます、荷を負わせる [v-link ADJ 'with/by' n] ❑ *Nicaragua was burdened with a foreign debt of $11 billion.* ニカラグアは110億ドルの対外債務に苦しん

でいた. ◻ ADJ 形容詞 If you describe someone as **burdened** with a heavy load, you are emphasizing that it is very heavy and that they are holding it or carrying it with difficulty. 重荷を背負った [EMPHASIS 強調] [v-link ADJ 'with/by' n] ❑ *Anna arrived burdened by bags and food baskets.* アナは大量の袋や食料品を抱えてやってきた.

bu|reau /byʊ́əroʊ/ (bureaus) ◼ N-COUNT; N-IN-NAMES 可算名詞、名称中の名詞 A **bureau** is an office, organization, or government department that collects and distributes information. 局、部 ❑ *...the Federal Bureau of Investigation.* 連邦捜査局 ◻ N-COUNT 可算名詞 A **bureau** is an office of a company or organization that has its main office in another city or country. 営業所 [mainly AM 主に米国英語 BUSINESS 実業] ❑ *...the Wall Street Journal's Washington bureau.* 『ウォール・ストリート・ジャーナル』のワシントン営業所 ◼ N-COUNT 可算名詞 A **bureau** is a chest of drawers. 衣類だんす [AM 米国英語] ◼ N-COUNT 可算名詞 A **bureau** is a writing desk with shelves and drawers and a lid that opens to form the writing surface. 引き出し付き事務机 [BRIT 英国英語]

Word Link	cracy ≈ rule by : aristocracy, bureaucracy, democracy

bu|reau|cra|cy /byʊrɒ́krəsi/ (bureaucracies) ◼ N-COUNT 可算名詞 A **bureaucracy** is an administrative system operated by a large number of officials. 官僚制度 ❑ *State bureaucracies can tend to stifle enterprise and initiative.* 州の官僚制度は進取の気性およびイニシアチブを抑圧する傾向がある. ◻ N-UNCOUNT 不可算名詞 **Bureaucracy** refers to all the rules and procedures followed by government departments and similar organizations, especially when you think that these are complicated and cause long delays. 官僚式の煩雑な手続き [DISAPPROVAL 不賛成] ❑ *People usually complain about too much bureaucracy.* 国民はあまりに煩雑な手続きに関する不満を常に漏らしている.

Word Link	crat ≈ power : aristocrat, bureaucrat, democrat

bu|reau|crat /byʊ́ərəkræt/ (bureaucrats) N-COUNT 可算名詞 **Bureaucrats** are officials who work in a large administrative system. You can refer to officials as bureaucrats especially if you disapprove of them because they seem to follow rules and procedures too strictly. 官僚、官僚主義者 [DISAPPROVAL 不賛成] ❑ *The economy is still controlled by bureaucrats.* 経済はいまだに官僚主義者によって制御されている.

bu|reau|crat|ic /byʊ̀ərəkrǽtik/ ADJ 形容詞 **Bureaucratic** means involving complicated rules and procedures which can cause long delays. 手続きの煩雑な [DISAPPROVAL 不賛成] ❑ *Bureaucratic delays are inevitable.* 官僚的な遅れは避けられない.

bur|geon /bɜ́rdʒªn/ (burgeons, burgeoning, burgeoned) V-I 自動詞 If something **burgeons**, it grows or develops rapidly. 急に発展する [LITERARY 文語的] ❑ *Plants burgeon from every available space.* 植物はありとあらゆる場所から芽を出す. ❑ *My confidence began to burgeon later in life.* 私は後年になって自信がつき始めた.

burg|er /bɜ́rgər/ (burgers) N-COUNT 可算名詞 A **burger** is a flat round mass of ground meat or minced vegetables that is fried and often eaten in a bread roll. ハンバーガー ❑ *...burger and fries.* ハンバーガーとフライドポテト

bur|glar /bɜ́rglər/ (burglars) N-COUNT 可算名詞 A **burglar** is a thief who enters a house or other building by force. 住宅侵入者 ❑ *Burglars broke into their home.* 彼らの家に強盗が入った.

bur|glar|ize /bɜ́rgləraɪz/ (burglarizes, burglarizing, burglarized) V-T 他動詞 If a building **is burglarized**, a thief enters it by force and steals things. 強盗に入る [AM 米国英語] [usu passive] ❑ *Her home was burglarized.* 彼女の家は強盗に入られた.

bur|gla|ry /bɜ́rgləri/ (burglaries) N-VAR 可変性名詞 If someone commits a **burglary**, they enter a building by force and steal things. **Burglary** is the act of doing this. 住宅侵入 ❑ *An 11-year-old boy committed a burglary.* 11歳の少年は夜盗を働いた.

bur|gle /bɜ́rgªl/ (burgles, burgling, burgled) V-T 他動詞 If a building **is burgled**, a thief enters it by force and steals things. 強盗を働く [BRIT 英国英語; AM burglarize 米国英語 burglarize] ❑ *I thought we had been burgled.* 強盗に入られたかと思った.

bur|ial /bɛ́riəl/ (burials) N-VAR 可変性名詞 A **burial** is the act or ceremony of putting a dead body into a grave in the ground. 埋葬 ❑ *The priest prepared the body for burial.* 牧師は遺体に葬式の支度をさせた.

bur|ly /bɜ́rli/ (burlier, burliest) ADJ 形容詞 A **burly** man has a broad body and strong muscles. 太くたくましい ❑ *He was a big, burly man.* 彼は頑丈な大男だ.

burn /bɜ́rn/ (burns, burning, burned or burnt) ◼ V-I 自動詞 If there is a fire or a flame somewhere, you say that there is a fire or flame **burning** there. 燃える ❑ *Fires were burning out of control in the center of the city.* 市の中心で手のつけようのない火事が燃え広がっていた. ❑ *There was a fire burning in the fireplace.* 暖炉では火が燃え立っている. ◻ V-I 自動詞 If something **is burning**, it is on fire. 燃える ❑ *When I arrived one of the vehicles was still burning.* 私が到着した

B

時, 車の内1台はまだ燃えていた. ❏ *The building housed 1,500 refugees and it burned for hours.* その建物は1500人の難民を収容しており, 何時間も燃え続けた. ● **burn|ing** N-UNCOUNT 不可算名詞 燃焼 ❏ *When we arrived in our village there was a terrible smell of burning.* 私たちが村に戻った時, 何かが焼き焦げるひどい匂いがした. **3** V-T 他動詞 If you **burn** something, you destroy or damage it with fire. 燃やす ❏ *Protesters set cars on fire and burned a building.* 抗議者らは車に火を点け, 建物を燃やした. ❏ *Incineration plants should be built to burn household waste.* 家庭廃棄物を燃却する焼却工場を建設する必要がある. ● **burn|ing** N-UNCOUNT 不可算名詞 燃焼 ❏ *The French government has criticized the burning of a U.S. flag outside the American embassy.* フランス政府は, アメリカ大使館外部で行われた米国国旗の焼き捨てを非難した. **4** V-T/V-I 他動詞/自動詞 If you **burn** a fuel or if it **burns**, it is used to produce heat, light, or energy. 燃やす [他動詞] 燃える [自動詞] ❏ *The power stations burn coal from the Ruhr region.* 発電所はルール地方産の石炭を燃やす. **5** V-T/V-I 他動詞/自動詞 If you **burn** something that you are cooking or if it **burns**, you spoil it by using too much heat or cooking it for too long. 焦がす [他動詞] 焦げる [自動詞] ❏ *I burned the toast.* トーストを焦がしてしまった. ● **burnt** ADJ 形容詞 焦げた ❏ *...the smell of burnt toast.* 焦げたトーストの匂い **6** V-T 他動詞 If you **burn** part of your body, **burn yourself,** or **are burned** or **burnt,** you are injured by fire or by something very hot. やけどする ❏ *Take care not to burn your fingers.* 指にやけどしないように気をつけなさい. ● N-COUNT 可算名詞 **Burn** is also a noun. やけど ❏ *She suffered appalling burns to her back.* 彼女は背中にひどいやけどを負った. **7** V-T 他動詞 [usu passive] If someone **is burned** or **burned** to death, they are killed by fire. 焼死する ❏ *Women were burned as witches in the Middle Ages.* 中世には魔女だとして女性が火あぶりにされた. **8** V-I 自動詞 If a light **is burning,** it is shining. 輝く [LITERARY 文語的] ❏ *The building was darkened except for a single light burning in a third-story window.* 3階の窓に輝くただ1つの光以外, その建物は暗くされた. **9** V-T/V-I 他動詞/自動詞 If you **burn** or get **burned** in the sun, the sun makes your skin become red and sore. 日焼けさせる [他動詞] 日焼けする [自動詞] ❏ *Build up your tan slowly and don't allow your skin to burn.* 肌は徐々に小麦色に焼き, やけどさせてはならない. **10** V-T/V-I 他動詞/自動詞 If a part of your body **burns** or if something **burns** it, it has a painful hot or stinging feeling. ひりひりさせる [他動詞] 燃えるように感じる, ひりひりする [自動詞] ❏ *My eyes burn from staring at the needle.* 針をじっとみていたので目が焼けるように痛い. ❏ *His face was burning with cold.* 彼の顔は寒さでひりひりしていた. **11** V-T 他動詞 To **burn** a CD means to write or copy data onto it. 書き込む, 焼く [COMPUTING コンピューティング] ❏ *You can use this software to burn custom compilations of your favorite tunes.* このソフトウェアを使用すると, お気に入りの歌を独自に編集してCDに書き込むことができる. **12** → see also **burning** **13** to **burn** something **to the ground** → see **ground** **14** to **burn the midnight oil** → see **midnight** **15** to **have money to burn** → see **money**
▶ **burn down** PHRASAL VERB 句動詞 If a building **burns down** or if someone **burns** it **down,** it is completely destroyed by fire. 全焼する, 焼き尽くす ❏ *Six months after Bud died, the house burned down.* バドが死んでから6か月後に家が全焼した.
→ see **calorie, fire**

<table>
<tr><td colspan="2">**Thesaurus**   *burn* また次を参照:</td></tr>
<tr><td>V.</td><td>ignite, incinerate, kindle, scorch, singe; (ant.) extinguish, put out **1** – **6**</td></tr>
</table>

<table>
<tr><td colspan="2">**Word Partnership**   *burn* は次の語句と使われる:</td></tr>
<tr><td>N.</td><td>fires burn **1**
burn **calories,** burn **coal,** burn **fat,** burn **fuel,** burn **oil** **4**
burn **victim** **6**
burn a **CD** **11**</td></tr>
<tr><td>V.</td><td>watch *something* burn **1** **2**</td></tr>
<tr><td>ADJ.</td><td>**first/second/third degree** burn **6**</td></tr>
</table>

burned-out also **burnt-out** **1** ADJ 形容詞 **Burned-out** vehicles or buildings have been so badly damaged by fire that they can no longer be used. 燃え尽きた ❏ *...a burned-out car.* 黒焦げになった車 **2** ADJ 形容詞 If someone is **burned-out,** they exhaust themselves at an early stage in their life or career because they have achieved too much too quickly. 疲れきった, 燃え尽きた [INFORMAL くだけた] ❏ *Everyone I know who kept it up at that intensity is burned-out.* あの激しさを持続した私の知人はすべて疲れきっている.

burn|er /bɜ́rnər/ (**burners**) N-COUNT 可算名詞 A **burner** is a device which produces heat or a flame, especially as part of a stove or heater. バーナー ❏ *He put the frying pan on the gas burner.* 彼はガスバーナーにフライパンを置いた.

burn|ing /bɜ́rnɪŋ/ **1** ADJ 形容詞 You use **burning** to describe something that is extremely hot. 燃えるような ❏ *...the burning desert of central Asia.* 中央アジアの灼熱の砂漠 ● ADV 副詞 **Burning** is also an adverb. 燃えるように ❏ *He touched the boy's*

forehead. It was burning hot. 彼は赤ちゃんの額に手を当てた. それは燃えるように熱かった. **2** ADJ 形容詞 If you have a **burning** interest in something or a **burning** desire to do something, you are extremely interested in it or want to do it very much. 強烈な [ADJ n] ❏ *I had a burning ambition to become a journalist.* 僕はジャーナリストになるという強烈な野心を持っていた. **3** ADJ 形容詞 A **burning** issue or question is a very important or urgent one that people feel very strongly about. 目下の, 緊急の [ADJ n] ❏ *The burning question in this year's debate over the federal budget is: whose taxes should be raised?* 今年の連邦予算をめぐる論議における緊急課題は, 誰の税を増やすかである.

burnt /bɜ́rnt/ **Burnt** is a past tense and past participle of **burn.** *burn*の過去・過去分詞

burnt-out → see **burned-out**

bur|row /bɜ́roʊ/ (**burrows, burrowing, burrowed**) **1** N-COUNT 可算名詞 A **burrow** is a tunnel or hole in the ground that is dug by an animal such as a rabbit. (うさぎなどの動物の) 穴 ❏ *Normally timid, they rarely stray far from their burrows.* 通常は臆病なので, 隠れ穴から遠くに離れることはまれである. **2** V-I 自動詞 If an animal **burrows** into the ground or into a surface, it moves through it by making a tunnel or hole. 穴を掘る ❏ *The larvae burrow into cracks in the floor.* 幼虫は床の割れ目から穴を掘る. **3** V-I 自動詞 If you **burrow** in a container or pile of things, you search there for something using your hands. 突っ込んで調べる ❏ *...the enthusiasm with which he burrowed through old records in search of facts.* 事実を探すために古い記録をあさる彼の熱意 **4** V-I 自動詞 If you **burrow** into something, you move underneath it or press against it, usually in order to feel warmer or safer. 潜り込む, すり寄せる ❏ *She turned her face away from him, burrowing into her heap of covers.* 彼女は彼から顔を背けて山になったカバーの下に潜り込んだ.

burst /bɜ́rst/ (**bursts, bursting**)

The form **burst** is used in the present tense and is the past tense and past participle.

burst 形は現在形に使われ, 過去形と過去分詞でもある.

1 V-T/V-I 他動詞/自動詞 If something **bursts** or if you **burst** it, it suddenly breaks open or splits open and the air or other substance inside it comes out. 破裂させる [他動詞] 破裂する [自動詞] ❏ *The driver lost control when a tire burst.* タイヤが破裂して, ドライバーはコントロールを失った. ❏ *It is not a good idea to burst a blister.* まめをつぶしてはいけません. **2** V-T/V-I 他動詞/自動詞 If a dam **bursts,** or if something **bursts** it, it breaks apart because the force of the river is too great. どっと流れ出す [他動詞] 噴き出る [自動詞] ❏ *A dam burst and flooded their villages.* ダムが炸裂し, その村は水浸しになった. **3** V-T 他動詞 If a river **bursts** its banks, the water rises and goes on to the land. はんらんする ❏ *Monsoons caused the river to burst its banks.* 季節風により, 川が河防を越えてはんらんした. **4** V-I 自動詞 When a door or lid **bursts** open, it opens very suddenly and violently because someone pushes it or there is great pressure behind it. 勢いよく開く ❏ *The door burst open and an angry young nurse appeared.* 扉がバッと開いて, 怒った若い看護師が現れた. **5** V-I 自動詞 To **burst into** or **out** of a place means to enter or leave it suddenly with a lot of energy or force. 乱入する, 飛び出す ❏ *Gunmen burst into his home and opened fire.* ガンマンは彼の自宅に乱入して発砲した. **6** V-I 自動詞 If you say that something **bursts** onto the scene, you mean that it suddenly starts or becomes active, usually after developing quietly for some time. 突然現れる [JOURNALISM ジャーナリズム] ❏ *He burst onto the fashion scene in the early 1980s.* 彼は1980年代初期のファッションシーンに突然現れた. **7** N-COUNT 可算名詞 A **burst of** something is a sudden short period of it. 一気 ❏ *...a burst of machine-gun fire.* 連続機銃掃射
▶ **burst into** **1** PHRASAL VERB 句動詞 If you **burst into** tears, laughter, or song, you suddenly begin to cry, laugh, or sing. 突然しだす ❏ *She burst into tears and ran from the kitchen.* 彼女は突然ワッ泣き出して台所から走り去った. **2** PHRASAL VERB 句動詞 If you say that something **bursts into** a particular situation or state, you mean that it suddenly changes into that situation or state. 突入する ❏ *This weekend's fighting is threatening to burst into full-scale war.* 今週末の戦いは全面戦争に突入するのではないかと危惧 (ぐ) されている. **3** to **burst into flames** → see **flame**
▶ **burst out** PHRASAL VERB 句動詞 If someone **bursts out** laughing, crying, or making another noise, they suddenly start making that noise. You can also say that a noise **bursts out.** 突然しだす, 突発する ❏ *The class burst out laughing.* クラスはドッと笑い出した. ❏ *Then the applause burst out.* そして, 拍手喝采が沸き起こった.
→ see **crash, cry, laugh**

<table>
<tr><td colspan="2">**Thesaurus**   *burst* また次を参照:</td></tr>
<tr><td>V.</td><td>blow, explode, pop, rupture **1**</td></tr>
</table>

b

Word Partnership	*burst* は次の語句と使われる:
N.	burst **appendix**, **bubble** burst, **pipe** burst **1**
	burst **of air**, burst **of energy**, burst **of laughter 7**
ADJ.	**ready to** burst **1**
	sudden burst **7**

burst|ing /bɜrstɪŋ/ **1** ADJ 形容詞 If a place is **bursting with** people or things, it is full of them. いっぱいになって、超満員で [v-link ADJ] ❑ *The place appears to be bursting with women directors.* ここは女性の重役であふれているようだ。**2** ADJ 形容詞 If you say that someone is **bursting with** a feeling or quality, you mean that they have a great deal of it. はちきれそう [v-link ADJ 'with' n] ❑ *I was bursting with curiosity.* 僕は興味津々だった。**3** → see also **burst**

bury /bɛri/ (buries, burying, buried) **1** V-T 他動詞 To **bury** something means to put it into a hole in the ground and cover it up with earth. 埋める ❑ *They make the charcoal by burying wood in the ground and then slowly burning it.* 彼らは、木材を地中に埋めてゆっくり燃焼させて木炭を製造する。❑ *...squirrels who bury nuts and seeds.* 木の実や種を埋めるりす **2** V-T 他動詞 To **bury** a dead person means to put their body into a grave and cover it with earth. 葬る ❑ *Soldiers helped to bury the dead in large communal graves.* 兵士は大規模な共同墓地に死者を葬るのを手伝った。❑ *I was horrified that people would think I was dead and bury me alive.* 死んでいるものと思い込まれて生き埋めにされるのではないかと思いぞっとした。**3** V-T 他動詞 If someone says they **have buried** one of their relatives, they mean that one of their relatives has died. 埋葬する ❑ *He had buried his wife some two years before he retired.* 彼は退職の2年前に妻に先立たれた。**4** V-T 他動詞 If you **bury** something under a large quantity of things, you put it there, often in order to hide it. 埋蔵する ❑ *She buried it under some leaves.* 彼女は葉っぱの下にそれを埋めた。**5** V-T 他動詞 If something **buries** a place or person, it falls on top of them so that it completely covers them and often harms them in some way. 最新の報告によると、村全体が土砂崩れで流された。❑ *Latest reports say that mud slides buried entire villages.* 最新の報告によると、村全体が土砂崩れで流された。❑ *Their house was buried by a landslide.* 彼らの家は地滑りでつぶされた。**6** V-T 他動詞 If you **bury** your head or face in something, you press your head or face against it, often because you are unhappy. うずめる ❑ *She buried her face in the pillows.* 彼女は枕に顔をうずめた。**7** V-T 他動詞 If something **buries itself** somewhere, or if you **bury** it there, it is pushed very deeply into there. 深く入れる ❑ *The missile buried itself deep in the grassy hillside.* ミサイルは草の茂った丘の斜面に深く突入した。**8** to **bury the hatchet**→see **hatchet**

bus /bʌs/ (buses, busing, bused)

The spellings **busses, bussing, bussed** are also used for the verb.

つづりの **busses, bussing, bussed** は動詞にも使われる。

1 N-COUNT 可算名詞 A **bus** is a large motor vehicle that carries passengers from one place to another. Buses drive along particular routes, and you usually have to pay to travel in them. バス [also 'by' n] ❑ *He missed his last bus home.* 彼は最終バスに間に合わなかった。**2** V-T/V-I 他動詞/自動詞 When someone is **bused** to a particular place or when they **bus** there, they travel there on a bus. バスで行く [自動詞] バスで運ぶ [他動詞] ❑ *On May Day hundreds of thousands used to be bused in to parade through East Berlin.* メーデーには、何十万人もの人がバスで東ベルリンのパレードに参加した。❑ *To get our Colombian visas we bused back to Medellín.* コロンビアビザを取得するため、私たちはバスでメデジンに戻った。**3** V-T 他動詞 To **bus** tables means to clear away dirty dishes and reset the tables. テーブルを整えたり、食器を下げたりする [AM 米国英語] ❑ *As a fundraiser, police officers will don aprons, take orders and bus tables today.* 今日警官が、資金調達者としてエプロンを着け、注文をとったり、テーブルを整えたり食器を下げたりする。

→ see **transportation**

bush /bʊʃ/ (bushes) **1** N-COUNT 可算名詞 A **bush** is a large plant which is smaller than a tree and has a lot of branches. 低木 ❑ *Trees and bushes grew down to the water's edge.* 木や低木は水際まで育成した。**2** N-SING 単数名詞 The wild, uncultivated parts of some hot countries are referred to as **the bush**. 未開墾地 ❑ *They walked through the dense Mozambican bush for thirty-six hours.* 彼らはモザンビークのうっそうとした未開墾地を36時間歩きまわった。

bushy /bʊʃi/ (bushier, bushiest) **1** ADJ 形容詞 **Bushy** hair or fur is very thick. ふさふさした ❑ *...bushy eyebrows.* ぼうぼうとしたまゆ毛 **2** ADJ 形容詞 A **bushy** plant has a lot of leaves very close together. 繁茂した ❑ *...strong, sturdy, bushy plants.* 繁茂する強く頑丈な植物

busi|ly /bɪzɪli/ ADV 副詞 If you do something **busily**, you do it in a very active way. 精を出して [ADV with v] ❑ *The two saleswomen were busily trying to keep up with the demand.* 2人の女性販売員は需要に追いつこうとせっせと働いた。

busi|ness /bɪznɪs/ (businesses) **1** N-UNCOUNT 不可算名詞 **Business** is work relating to the production, buying, and selling of goods or services. 業務 ❑ *Jennifer has an impressive*

academic and business background. ジェニファーの学歴と職歴は印象的だ。❑ *...Harvard Business School.* ハーバード大学大学院経営学研究科 **2** N-UNCOUNT 不可算名詞 **Business** is used when talking about how many products or services a company is able to sell. If **business** is good, a lot of products or services are being sold and if **business** is bad, few of them are being sold. 商売 ❑ *They worried that German companies would lose business.* ドイツの会社が商売を逃すのではないかと彼らは心配した。**3** N-COUNT 可算名詞 A **business** is an organization that produces and sells goods or that provides a service. 商業企業体 ❑ *The company was a family business.* その会社は家族経営だった。❑ *The majority of small businesses fail within the first twenty-four months.* 零細企業のほとんどは最初の24か月以内に倒産する。**4** N-UNCOUNT 不可算名詞 **Business** is work or some other activity that you do as part of your job and not for pleasure. 職務 ❑ *I'm here on business.* 商用で来ています。❑ *You can't mix business with pleasure.* 仕事と遊びを混同させてはなりません。**5** N-SING 単数名詞 You can use **business** to refer to a particular area of work or activity in which the aim is to make a profit. 職業 ❑ *May I ask you what business you're in?* お仕事は何か伺ってもよろしいですか。**6** N-SING 単数名詞 You can use **business** to refer to something that you are doing or concerning yourself with. やるべき仕事 ❑ *...recording Ben as he goes about his business.* ベンの私的生活を記録する。**7** N-UNCOUNT 不可算名詞 You can use **business** to refer to important matters that you have to deal with. 用件 ❑ *The most important business was left to the last.* 最も重要な用件は最後にまわされた。**8** N-UNCOUNT 不可算名詞 If you say that something is your **business**, you mean that it concerns you personally and that other people have no right to ask questions about it or disagree with it. 関心事、関係・干渉する権利 [poss N] ❑ *My sex life is my business.* 私の性生活は私の問題だ。❑ *If she doesn't want the police involved, that's her business.* 警察を巻き込みたくないのなら、それは彼女が決めることだ。**9** N-SING 単数名詞 You can use **business** to refer in a general way to an event, situation, or activity. For example, you can say something is a "wretched business" or you can refer to "this assassination business." 事件、事柄 ❑ *We have sorted out this wretched business at last.* 僕たちはこのひどい問題をようやく解決した。**10** → see also **big business**, **show business 11** PHRASE 句 If two people or companies **do business with** each other, one sells goods or services to the other. 取引する ❑ *I was fascinated by the different people who did business with me.* 私は様々な取引先の人たちに魅了された。**12** PHRASE 句 If you say that someone **has no business to** be in a place or **to** do something, you mean that they have no right to be there or to do it. 権利がない ❑ *Really I had no business to be there at all.* 実際のところ、私にはそこにいる権利は全くない。**13** PHRASE 句 A company that is **in business** is operating and trading. 商売を行って ❑ *You can't stay in business without cash.* 現金なしで事業を継続することはできない。**14** PHRASE 句 If a store or company goes **out of business** or is put **out of business**, it has to stop trading because it is not making enough money. 廃業して ❑ *Thousands of firms could go out of business.* 何千もの会社が廃業に追い込まれる可能性があった。**15** PHRASE 句 In a difficult situation, if you say it is **business as usual**, you mean that people will continue doing what they normally do. 変わりばえしない日常生活 ❑ *For the time being it's business as usual for consumers.* 差し当たり、顧客に対する業務は平常どおりである。

→ see **city**

Thesaurus	*business* また次を参照：
N.	company, corporation, firm, organization **3**

Word Partnership	*business* は次の語句と使われる:
ADJ.	business **casual**, **family** business, **online** business, **small** business **1**
	your own business **1 6 - 8**
	unfinished business **7**
N.	**close of** business, business **opportunity**, business **school 1 2**
	business **administration**, business **decision**, business **expenses**, business **hours**, business **owner**, business **partner**, business **practices 1 - 5**
V.	**go out of** business, **run a** business **3 5**

busi|ness card (business cards) N-COUNT 可算名詞 A person's **business card** or their **card** is a small card that they give to other people, and that has their name and details of their job and company printed on it. 名刺 ❑ *When we met, he gave me his business card.* 出会ったとき、彼は私に名刺をくれた。

busi|ness class ADJ 形容詞 **Business class** seating on an airplane costs less than first class but more than economy class. ビジネスクラス [ADJ n] ❑ *You can pay to be upgraded to a business class seat.* 料金を支払えばビジネスクラスの席に変えてもらうことができる。● ADV 副詞 **Business class** is also an adverb. ビジネスクラスを使って [ADV after v] ❑ *They flew business class.* 彼らはビジネスクラスで飛

B

んだ. ● N-UNCOUNT 不可算名詞 **Business class** is the business class seating on an airplane. （飛行機の座席の）ビジネスクラス ❑ The Australian team will be seated in business class. オーストラリアチームはビジネスクラスに座ることになっている.

busi|ness hours N-PLURAL 複数名詞 **Business hours** are the hours of the day in which a store or a company is open for business. 営業時間 ❑ All showrooms are staffed during business hours. 営業時間内は, どのショールームでも職員が働いている.

business|like /bíznəslaɪk/ ADJ 形容詞 If you describe someone as **businesslike**, you mean that they deal with things in an efficient way without wasting time. 能率的な ❑ Mr. Penn sounds quite businesslike. ペン氏は非常に事務的な人のようだ.

business|man /bíznəsmæn/ (businessmen) N-COUNT 可算名詞 A **businessman** is a man who works in business. 実業家 ❑ ...a wealthy businessman who owns a printing business in Orlando. オーランドに印刷会社を持つ裕福な実業家

business|person /bíznəspɜrsən/ (businesspeople) also **business person** N-COUNT 可算名詞 **Businesspeople** are people who work in business. 実業家 ❑ ...businesspeople who serve or supply the security forces. 保安部隊にサービスや物資を供給する実業家

busi|ness plan (business plans) N-COUNT 可算名詞 A **business plan** is a detailed plan for setting up or developing a business, especially one that is written in order to borrow money. 経営計画 ❑ She learned how to write a business plan for the catering business she wanted to launch. 彼女は夢だった仕出し屋の事業計画の作成方法を習った.

busi|ness school (business schools) N-COUNT 可算名詞 A **business school** is a school or college which teaches business subjects such as economics and management. 経営学大学院

business|woman /bíznəswʊmən/ (businesswomen) N-COUNT 可算名詞 A **businesswoman** is a woman who works in business. 女性実業家 ❑ ...a successful businesswoman who runs her own international cosmetics company. 独自の国際的化粧品会社を経営するやり手の女性実業家

bust /bʌst/ (busts, busting, busted)

The form **bust** is used as the present tense of the verb, and can also be used as the past tense and past participle.

bust 形は動詞の現在形として使われ, 過去形と過去分詞としても使える.

1 V-T 他動詞 If you **bust** something, you break or damage it so badly that it cannot be used. 破裂させる [INFORMAL くだけた] ❑ They will have to bust the door to get him out. 彼を救出するためには扉を爆破する必要があるだろう. **2** V-T 他動詞 If someone **is busted**, the police arrest them. 逮捕する [INFORMAL くだけた] [usu passive] ❑ They were busted for possession of cannabis. 彼らは大麻所持で逮捕された. **3** V-T 他動詞 If police **bust** a place, they go to it in order to arrest people who are doing something illegal. 手入れする [INFORMAL くだけた] ❑ Police busted an underground network of illegal sports gambling. 警察は不法なスポーツ賭博の地下組織網を手に入れた. ● N-COUNT 可算名詞 **Bust** is also a noun. 手入れ ❑ Six tons of cocaine were seized last week in Panama's biggest drug bust. 先週, パナマにおける最も大掛かりな麻薬の押収で6トンのコカインが没収された. **4** ADJ 形容詞 A company or fund that is **bust** has no money left and has been forced to close down. 破産した [INFORMAL くだけた] ❑ It is taxpayers who will pay most of the bill for bailing out bust banks. 破産した銀行の救済費のほとんどを支払うのは納税者となるであろう. **5** PHRASE 句 If a company **goes bust**, it loses so much money that it is forced to close down. 倒産する [INFORMAL くだけた] ❑ ...a Swiss company which went bust last May. 昨年5月に破産したスイスの会社 **6** N-COUNT 可算名詞 A **bust** is a statue of the head and shoulders of a person. 胸像 ❑ ...a bronze bust of Thomas Jefferson. トーマス・ジェファーソンの胸像 **7** N-COUNT 可算名詞 You can use **bust** to refer to a woman's breasts, especially when you are describing their size. バスト ❑ Good posture helps your bust look bigger. 良い姿勢は胸を大きく見せる.

bus|tle /bʌsəl/ (bustles, bustling, bustled) **1** V-I 自動詞 If someone **bustles** somewhere, they move there in a hurried way, often because they are very busy. せわしく動く ❑ My mother bustled around the kitchen. 母は台所でせっせと働いた. **2** V-I 自動詞 A place that is **bustling** or **bustling with** people or activity is full of people who are very busy or lively. 活気のある ❑ The sidewalks are bustling with people. 歩道は多くの人出でにぎやかである. **3** N-UNCOUNT 不可算名詞 **Bustle** is busy, noisy activity. 大騒動 ❑ ...the hustle and bustle of modern life. 現代生活の喧（けん）騒

busy /bízi/ (busier, busiest, busies, busying, busied) **1** ADJ 形容詞 When you are **busy**, you are working hard or concentrating on a task, so that you are not free to do anything else. 忙しい ❑ What is it? I'm busy. 何か用? 今忙しいのよ. ❑ They are busy preparing for a hectic day's activity on Saturday. 彼らは土曜日の慌ただしい活動の準備に追われている. **2** ADJ 形容詞 A **busy** time is a period of time during which you have a lot of things to do. 多忙な ❑ It'll have to

wait. This is our busiest time. 今は最も忙しい時期なので, それは後回しだ. ❑ Even with her busy schedule she finds time to watch TV. 彼女は多忙なスケジュールの合間をぬってテレビを見た. **3** ADJ 形容詞 If you say that someone is **busy** thinking or worrying about something, you mean that it is taking all their attention, often to such an extent that they are unable to think about anything else. ふさがっている, 余念がない [v-link ADJ] ❑ Companies are so busy analyzing the financial implications that they overlook the effect on workers. 会社は財政予測の分析にかまけて, 従業員の効果を見落とした. **4** V-T 他動詞 If you **busy yourself** with something, you occupy yourself by dealing with it. 忙しくする ❑ He busied himself with the camera. 彼はせっせとカメラ撮影をした. ❑ She busied herself getting towels ready. 彼女はタオルの準備に忙しく働いた. **5** ADJ 形容詞 A **busy** place is full of people who are doing things or moving around. 繁華な ❑ ...a busy commercial street. にぎやかな商業街 **6** ADJ 形容詞 When a telephone line is **busy**, you cannot make your call because the line is already being used by someone else. 話し中の [mainly AM 主に米国英語] ❑ I tried to reach him, but the line was busy. 彼に電話をしたが, 話し中だった. **7** → see also **busily**

but /bət, STRONG bʌt/ **1** CONJ 接続詞 You use **but** to introduce something that contrasts with what you have just said, or to introduce something that adds to what you have just said. しかし ❑ "You said you'd stay till tomorrow."—"I know, Bel, but I think I would rather go back." 「明日までここにいるって言ったじゃないの.」「わかってるよ, ベル, でも帰ったほうがいいと思うんだ.」 **2** Place the saucepan over moderate heat until the cider is very hot but not boiling. ソースパンを中火にかけて, リンゴジュースが沸騰直前になるまで熱します. **2** CONJ 接続詞 You use **but** when you are about to add something further in a discussion or to change the subject. ところで, さて ❑ After three weeks, they gradually reduced their sleep to about eight hours. But another interesting thing happened. 3週間後, 彼らは睡眠時間を徐々に8時間まで減らした. すると, 他にもおもしろいことが起こった. **3** CONJ 接続詞 You use **but** after you have made an excuse or apologized for what you are just about to say. が ❑ Please excuse me, but there is something I must say. すみませんが, 一言いわせてください. ❑ I'm sorry, but it's nothing to do with you. ごめんなさい, あなたには関係ないのよ. **4** CONJ 接続詞 You use **but** to introduce a reply to someone when you want to indicate surprise, disbelief, refusal, or protest. （驚き・反対・抗議などの意味で）でも [FEELINGS 感情] だが ❑ "I don't think I should stay in this house."—"But why?" 「この家にいるべきじゃないと思う.」「でも, どうして.」 **5** PREP 前置詞 **But** is used to mean "except." を除いては [n PREP n] ❑ Europe will be represented in all but two of the seven races. ヨーロッパはレースの内2つを除いてすべてのレースに出場している. ❑ He didn't speak anything but Greek. 彼はギリシャ語しか話さなかった. **6** ADV 副詞 **But** is used to mean "only." ただ [FORMAL 形式ばった] ❑ Zach insists that he is but one among many who are fighting for equality. ザックは平等のために戦う多くの者の1人に過ぎないと主張している. **7** PHRASE 句 You use **but for** to introduce the only factor that causes a particular thing not to happen or not to be completely true. を別にすれば ❑ ...the small square below, empty but for a dirty white van and a clump of palm trees. 下方に見える, 汚れた白いライトバンとやしの木々の茂みがあるだけの小さな広場 **8** PHRASE 句 You use **but then** or **but then again** before a remark which slightly contradicts what you have just said. しかしまた, その反面 ❑ My husband spends hours in the bathroom, but then again so do I. 主人はトイレに何時間も費やすが, 私だってそうだ. **9** PHRASE 句 You use **but then** before a remark which suggests that what you have just said should not be regarded as surprising. しかしその場合 ❑ He was a fine young man, but then so had his father been. 彼はハンサムな青年だったが, 彼の父親もそうだった. **10** **all but** → see **all** **11** **anything but** → see **anything**

butch|er /bʊtʃər/ (butchers, butchering, butchered) **1** N-COUNT 可算名詞 A **butcher** is a storekeeper who cuts up and sells meat. Some butchers also kill animals for meat and make foods such as sausages and meat pies. 食肉処理業者 **2** N-COUNT 可算名詞 A **butcher** or a **butcher's** is a store where meat is sold. 肉屋 [mainly BRIT 主に英国英語] ❑ He worked in a butcher's. 彼は肉屋で働いた. [AM usually **butcher shop** 米国英語では通常 **butcher shop**] **3** V-T 他動詞 To **butcher** an animal means to kill it and cut it up for meat. ❑ Pigs were butchered, hams were hung to dry from the ceiling. 食物用に（動物を）屠殺する **4** V-T 他動詞 You can say that someone **has butchered** people when they have killed a lot of people in a very cruel way, and you want to express your horror and disgust. 大量に殺す [DISAPPROVAL 不賛成] ❑ ...rebels who butchered eight tourists in Bwindi national park. ブウィンディ国立公園で8人の旅行者を惨殺した反逆者たち

but|ler /bʌtlər/ (butlers) N-COUNT 可算名詞 A **butler** is the most important male servant in a wealthy house. 使用人頭 ❑ I called for the butler to clear up the broken crockery. 私はバトラーを呼んで壊れた陶器を片付けさせた.

butt /bʌt/ (butts, butting, butted) **1** N-COUNT 可算名詞 Someone's **butt** is their bottom. しり [AM 米国英語, INFORMAL くだけた] ❑ Frieda grinned, pinching him on the butt. フリーダは, 彼の

おしりをつねってニヤッと笑った. **2** N-COUNT 可算名詞 The **butt** or the **butt end of** a weapon or tool is the thick end of its handle. (道具や武器の) 太いほうの端 □ Troops used tear gas and rifle butts to break up the protests. 兵士たちは催涙ガスとライフルの台尻を使って抗議をやめさせた. **3** N-COUNT 可算名詞 The **butt of** a cigarette or cigar is the small part of it that is left when someone has finished smoking it. (たばこの) 吸いさし □ He dropped his cigarette butt into the street below. 彼はたばこの吸いさしを眼下の通りに落とした. **4** N-COUNT 可算名詞 A **butt** is a large barrel used for collecting or storing liquid. 大酒たる □ Make sure your water butt has a top to exclude sunlight. 必ず水槽にふたをして太陽光線を防ぎなさい. **5** N-SING 単数名詞 If someone or something is **the butt of** jokes or criticism, people often make fun of them or criticize them. (あざけりや批評などの) 的 □ He is still the butt of cruel jokes about his humble origins. 彼は生まれが卑しいために今でもきついジョークの種になっている. **6** V-T 他動詞 If a person or animal **butts** you, they hit you with the top of their head. (頭・角で) 突く □ Lawrence kept on butting me but the referee did not warn him. ローレンスはおれに頭突きを浴びせかけたが, レフェリーは警告を与えなかった.

▶ **butt in** PHRASAL VERB 句動詞 If you say that someone **is butting in**, you are criticizing the fact that they are joining in a conversation or activity without being asked to. でしゃばる, 干渉する [DISAPPROVAL 不賛成] □ Sorry, I don't mean to butt in. ごめん, 余計なお世話だったね.

but|ter /bʌtər/ (**butters, buttering, buttered**) **1** N-MASS 質量名詞 **Butter** is a soft yellow substance made from cream. You spread it on bread or use it in cooking. バター □ ...bread and butter. パンとバター. **2** V-T 他動詞 If you **butter** something such as bread or toast, you spread butter on it. バターを塗る □ She spread pieces of bread on the counter and began buttering them. 彼女は何切れもパンを調理台に並べてバターを塗り始めた.

→ see **dish**

butter|fly /bʌtərflaɪ/ (**butterflies**) N-COUNT 可算名詞 A **butterfly** is an insect with large colorful wings and a thin body. ちょう □ Butterflies and moths are attracted to the wild flowers. ちょうとがは野草に引き寄せられる.

→ see **flower**

but|tock /bʌtək/ (**buttocks**) N-COUNT 可算名詞 Your **buttocks** are the two rounded fleshy parts of your body that you sit on. しり □ There were marks on his buttocks I hadn't seen before. 彼のおしりには私の見たことのないあとがついていた.

→ see **body**

but|ton /bʌtᵊn/ (**buttons, buttoning, buttoned**) **1** N-COUNT 可算名詞 **Buttons** are small hard objects sewn onto shirts, coats, or other pieces of clothing. You fasten the clothing by pushing the buttons through holes called buttonholes. ボタン □ ...a coat with brass buttons. しんちゅうのボタンのついたコート **2** V-T 他動詞 If you **button** a shirt, coat, or other piece of clothing, you fasten it by pushing its buttons through the buttonholes. ボタンをかける □ Ferguson stood up and buttoned his coat. ファーガソンは立ち上がってコートのボタンをかけた. ● PHRASAL VERB 句動詞 **Button up** means the same as **button**. ボタンをかける □ I buttoned up my coat; it was chilly. 寒かったので, 私はコートのボタンをしっかりかけた. □ The young man slipped on the shirt and buttoned it up. その若者は素早くシャツを着て肩のボタンをかけた. **3** N-COUNT 可算名詞 A **button** is a small object on a machine or electrical device that you press in order to operate it. ボタン □ He reached for the remote control and pressed the "play" button. 彼はリモートコントロールに手を伸ばして「再生」ボタンを押した. **4** N-COUNT 可算名詞 A **button** is a small piece of metal or plastic that you wear in order to show that you support a particular movement, organization, or person. You fasten a button to your clothes with a pin. バッジ [AM 米国英語] □ Wear a campaign button to show support for mothers in prison. 服役中の母親を応援する構えを示すキャンペーンバッジをつける.

▶ **button up** → see **button 2**

button は次の語句と使われる:

V.	**sew on** a button **1**
	press a button, **push** a button **3**
N.	**shirt** button **1**
PREP.	button **up something 2**

button|hole /bʌtᵊnhoʊl/ (**buttonholes**) N-COUNT 可算名詞 A **buttonhole** is a hole that you push a button through in order to fasten a shirt, coat, or other piece of clothing. ボタン穴

but|tress /bʌtrɪs/ (**buttresses**) N-COUNT 可算名詞 **Buttresses** are supports, usually made of stone or brick, that support a wall. 控え壁 □ ...the neo-Gothic buttresses of Riverside Church in Manhattan. マンハッタンにあるリバーサイド教会のネオゴシックバットレス

buy /baɪ/ (**buys, buying, bought**) **1** V-T 他動詞 If you **buy** something, you obtain it by paying money for it. 買う □ Lizzie bought herself a mountain bike. リジーは自分のマウンテンバイクを買った. **2** V-T 他動詞 If you talk about the quantity or standard of

goods an amount of money **buys**, you are referring to the price of the goods or the value of the money. 金で買える □ About $70,000 buys a habitable house. 住むのに適した家はおよそ7万ドルで買える. **3** V-T 他動詞 If you **buy** something like time, freedom, or victory, you obtain it but only by offering or giving up something in return. 犠牲を払って獲得する □ It was a risky operation, but might buy more time. これは危険を伴う手術だったが, もう少し時間が稼げるかもしれない. **4** V-T 他動詞 If you say that a person can **be bought**, you are criticizing the fact that they will give their help or loyalty to someone in return for money. 買収する [DISAPPROVAL 不賛成] [usu passive] □ Any number of our military and government officials can be bought. 軍隊および政府高官に何人でも買収できる. **5** V-T 他動詞 If you **buy** an idea or a theory, you believe and accept it. 賛成する [INFORMAL くだけた] (意見や理論を) 受け入れる □ I'm not buying any of that nonsense. そんなばかなことは信じられない. ● PHRASAL VERB 句動詞 **Buy into** means the same as **buy**. 受け入れる □ I bought into the popular myth that when I got the new car or the next house, I'd finally be happy. 私は, 新しい車または次の家を買うとやっと幸せになれるという一般に流布している作り話を信じた. **6** N-COUNT 可算名詞 If something is a good **buy**, it is of good quality and not very expensive. 買い得品 □ This was still a good buy even at the higher price. これは高価であっても掘り出し物だった.

> Do not confuse **buy** and **pay**. If you **buy** something, you obtain it by paying money for it. □ Gary's bought a bicycle. If you **pay** someone, **pay** them money, or **pay** for something, you give someone money for something they are selling to you. □ I paid the taxi driver ... I need some money to pay the window cleaner ... Some people are forced to pay for their own health insurance. If you **pay** a bill or debt, you pay the amount of money that is owed. □ He paid his bill and left...We were paying $50 for a single room.

▶ **buy into** **1** PHRASAL VERB 句動詞 If you **buy into** a company or an organization, you buy part of it, often in order to gain some control of it. 株主になる [BUSINESS 実業] □ Other companies could buy into the firm. 他の会社がその企業の株主になることも可能だった. **2** → see also **buy 5**

▶ **buy out** **1** PHRASAL VERB 句動詞 If you **buy** someone **out**, you buy their share of something such as a company or piece of property that you previously owned together. (個人の株・権利などを) 買い取る [BUSINESS 実業] □ The bank had to pay to buy out most of the 200 former partners. その銀行は, お金を支払って, 元パートナー200社のほとんどを買い取る必要があった. **2** → see also **buyout**

▶ **buy up** PHRASAL VERB 句動詞 If you **buy up** land, property, or a commodity, you buy large amounts of it, or all that is available. できるだけ買い得る, 買い占める □ The mention of price increases sent citizens out to buy up as much as they could. 物価騰貴のニュースを聞いて, 市民は買い占めに走った.

buy また次を参照:

V.	acquire, bargain, barter, get, obtain, pay, purchase **1**

buy は次の語句と使われる:

V.	**afford** to buy, buy **and/or sell 1**
N.	buy **in bulk**, buy **a condo/house**, buy **clothes**, buy **food**, buy **shares/stocks**, buy **tickets 1**
ADV.	buy **direct**, buy **online**, buy **retail**, buy **secondhand**, buy **wholesale 1**

buy-back (**buy-backs**) N-COUNT 可算名詞 A **buy-back** is a situation in which a company buys shares back from its investors. 買い戻し [BUSINESS 実業] □ ...a share buy-back plan. 自社株買い計画

ar, er ≈ one who acts as : **buyer, liar, seller**

buy|er /baɪər/ (**buyers**) **1** N-COUNT 可算名詞 A **buyer** is a person who is buying something or who intends to buy it. 買い手 □ Car buyers are more interested in safety and reliability than speed. 車の買い手は速度よりも安全性と信頼性に関心がある. **2** N-COUNT 可算名詞 A **buyer** is a person who works for a large store deciding what goods will be bought from manufacturers to be sold in the store. 仕入係 □ Diana is a buyer for a chain of furniture stores. ダイアナはチェーン家具店の仕入係だ.

buy|er's mar|ket N-SING 単数名詞 When there is a **buyer's market** for a particular product, there are more of the products for sale than there are people who want to buy them, so buyers have a lot of choice and can make prices come down. 買い手市場 [BUSINESS 実業] □ Real estate remains a buyer's market. 不動産は買い手市場で推移している.

buy|out /baɪaʊt/ (**buyouts**) **1** N-COUNT 可算名詞 A **buyout** is the buying of a company, especially by its managers or employees. 買収 [BUSINESS 実業] □ It is thought that a management buyout is one option. マネジメントバイアウトも選択肢の1つと考えられる. **2** → see also **MBO**

buzz /bʌz/ (buzzes, buzzing, buzzed) 1 v-i 自動詞 If something **buzzes** or buzzes somewhere, it makes a long continuous sound, like the noise a bee makes when it is flying. ブンブンいう □*The intercom buzzed and he pressed down the appropriate switch.* インターホンが鳴ったので彼は対応するスイッチを押した。 ● N-COUNT; SOUND 可算名詞，音声語 **Buzz** is also a noun. ブンブンいう唸り … □*the irritating buzz of an insect.* イライラさせる虫のうなり声 2 v-i 自動詞 If people **are buzzing around**, they are moving around quickly and busily. 忙しく動き回る[WRITTEN 書き言葉] □*A few tourists were buzzing around.* 活動的に動き回っている旅行客は少なかった。 3 v-i 自動詞 If questions or ideas **are buzzing around** your head, or if your head **is buzzing with** questions or ideas, you are thinking about a lot of things, often in a confused way. 飛び交う □*Many more questions were buzzing around in my head.* それ以外にも多くの質問が私の頭の中を駆け巡っていた。 4 v-i 自動詞 If a place **is buzzing with** activity or conversation, there is a lot of activity or conversation there, especially because something important or exciting is about to happen. ざわつく[usu cont] □*The rehearsal studio is buzzing with lunchtime activity.* リハーサルスタジオは昼食時で活気にあふれていた。 5 N-SING 単数名詞 You can use **buzz** to refer to a long continuous sound, usually caused by lots of people talking at once. ガヤガヤいう声 □*A buzz of excitement filled the courtroom as the defendant was led in.* 原告が入廷すると，法廷は興奮したざわめきで満たされた。 6 ADJ 形容詞 You can use **buzz** to refer to a word, idea, or activity which has recently become extremely popular. 流行の[ADJ n] □*…the latest buzz phrase in garden design circles.* 造園仲間の間で最近流行している言葉 7 N-SING 単数名詞 If a place or event has a **buzz** around it, it has a lively, interesting, and modern atmosphere. 活気['a' n] □*There is a real buzz around the place. Everyone is really excited.* この場所は本当に活気がある。誰もがすごく興奮している。 8 v-T 他動詞 If an aircraft **buzzes** a place, it flies low over it, usually in a threatening way. 上空をすれすれに飛ぶ □*American fighter planes buzzed the city.* アメリカの戦闘機が町の上空をすれすれに飛んだ。

buzz|er /bʌzər/ (buzzers) N-COUNT 可算名詞 A **buzzer** is an electrical device that is used to make a buzzing sound, for example, to attract someone's attention. ブザー □*She rang a buzzer at the information desk.* 彼女は案内所のブザーを鳴らした。

buzz|word /bʌzwɜrd/ (buzzwords) also **buzz word** N-COUNT 可算名詞 A **buzzword** is a word or expression that has become fashionable in a particular field and is being used a lot by the media. 専門的流行語 □*Biodiversity was the buzzword of the Rio Earth Summit.* 生物学的多様性はリオ地球サミットにおけるスローガンだった。

---

by

1 WHO DOES SOMETHING OR HOW IT IS DONE
2 POSITION OR PLACE
3 TIMES AND AMOUNTS

---

1 **by** 1 PREP 前置詞 If something is done **by** a person or thing, that person or thing does it. (行為者に) よって □*The feast was served by his mother and sisters.* 彼の母と姉妹がごちそうを出した。 □*I was amazed by their discourtesy and lack of professionalism.* 彼らの無礼とプロ意識の欠如に私はびっくりさせられた。 2 PREP 前置詞 If you say that something such as a book, a piece of music, or a painting is **by** a particular person, you mean that this person wrote it or created it. 作 □*A painting by Van Gogh has been sold in New York for more than eighty-two million dollars.* ヴァン・ゴッホ作の絵画が，ニューヨークで，8千2百万ドル以上で売られた。

> When you are talking about the author of a book or play, the composer of a piece of music, or the painter of a painting, you say that the piece of work is written or painted **by** him or her. □*… three books by Michael Moorcock … a collection of piano pieces by Mozart.* When you are talking about the person who has written you a letter or sent a message to you, you say that the letter or message is **from** that person. □*He received a message from Vito Corleone.*

3 PREP 前置詞 If you do something **by** a particular means, you do it using that thing. (手段を) 用いて □*If you're traveling by car, ask whether there are parking facilities nearby.* 車で旅行するなら，近くに駐車施設があるかどうか聞きなさい。 4 PREP 前置詞 If you achieve one thing **by** doing another thing, your action enables you to achieve the first thing. (原因に) よって □*Make the sauce by boiling the cream and stock together in a pan.* なべでクリームとブイヨンを一緒に沸騰させてソースを作る。 □*The all-female yacht crew made history by becoming the first to sail around the world.* 女性のみで構成されるヨットクルーは，世界一周の船旅を初めて成功させるという，歴史的な偉業を成し遂げた。 5 PREP 前置詞 You use **by** in phrases such as "by chance" or "by accident" to indicate whether or not an event was planned. (意思とは異なる状況) で □*I met him by chance out*

---

walking yesterday. 昨日散歩中，彼にばったり出会った。 □*He opened Ingrid's letter by mistake.* 彼は間違ってイングリッドの手紙を開封した。 6 PREP 前置詞 If someone is a particular type of person **by** nature, **by** profession, or **by** birth, they are that type of person because of their nature, their profession, or the family they were born into. (生まれ，職業，家族などの) 点では[adj/adv PREP n] □*I am certainly lucky to have a kind wife who is loving by nature.* 生まれつき愛情に満ちた優しい妻を持ってもちろん幸運だ。 □*She's a nurse by profession and now runs a counseling service for women.* 彼女の職業は看護婦で，現在女性を対象としたカウンセリング業を経営している。 7 PREP 前置詞 If something must be done **by** law, it happens according to the law. If something is the case **by** law, it is the case according to the standards. (判断の根拠に) 基づいて □*Pharmacists are required by law to give the medicine prescribed by the doctor.* 医師によって処方された薬を与えるために，法律により薬剤師が必要とされている。 8 PREP 前置詞 If you say what someone means **by** a particular word or expression, you are saying what they intend the word or expression to refer to. (言葉・表現に) よって □*Stella knew what he meant by "start again."* 「やり直そう」という彼の言葉の意味をステラは知っていた。 9 PREP 前置詞 If you hold someone or something **by** a particular part of them, you hold that part. (体の部分を) 用いて □*He caught her by the shoulder and turned her around.* 彼は彼女の肩をつかんで振り向かせた。 □*She was led by the arm to a small room at the far end of the corridor.* 彼女は腕を引かれて，廊下の向こう側にある小部屋に案内された。 10 PHRASE 句 If you are **by yourself**, you are alone. ひとりで □*…a dark-haired man sitting by himself in a corner.* 角にひとりで座っている黒髪の男 11 PHRASE 句 If you do something **by yourself**, you succeed in doing it without anyone helping you. 他人の助力なしで □*I didn't know if I could raise a child by myself.* 他人の助けなしに子供を育てられるかわからなかった。

2 **by** 1 PREP 前置詞 Someone or something that is **by** something else is beside it and close to it. 〜のそばに □*Judith was sitting in a rocking chair by the window.* ジュディスは窓際の揺りいすに座っていた。 □*Felicity Maxwell stood by the bar and ordered a glass of wine.* フェリシティ・マックスウェルはカウンターのそばに立ち，ワインを1杯注文した。 ● ADV 副詞 **By** is also an adverb. そばに[ADV after v] □*Large numbers of security police stood by.* 大勢の治安警察官が待機していた。 2 PREP 前置詞 If a person or vehicle goes **by** you, they move past you without stopping. 〜のそばを通って[v PREP n] □*A few cars passed close by me.* 何台かの自動車が私のすぐそばを通り過ぎた。 ● ADV 副詞 **By** is also an adverb. 通って[ADV after v] □*The bomb went off as a police patrol went by.* 警察のパトロール隊が通り過ぎたとき，爆弾が爆発した。 3 PREP 前置詞 If you stop **by** a place, you visit it for a short time. 〜に立ち寄って □*We had made arrangements to stop by her house in Pacific Grove.* 我々はパシフィック・グローブの彼女の家に立ち寄る手はずを整えた。 ● ADV 副詞 **By** is also an adverb. 立ち寄って[ADV after v] □*I'll stop by after dinner and we'll have that talk.* 私が夕食後に立ち寄るから，その話をしよう。

3 **by** /baɪ/ 1 PREP 前置詞 If something happens **by** a particular time, it happens at or before that time. 〜までに □*By eight o'clock he had arrived at my hotel.* 彼は8時までに私のホテルに到着していた。 2 PREP 前置詞 If you do something **by** day, you do it during the day. If you do it **by** night, you do it during the night. 〜の間に □*By day a woman could safely walk the streets.* 日中は女性が安全に通りを歩くことができた。 3 PREP 前置詞 In arithmetic, you use **by** before the second number in a multiplication or division sum. 〜によって[PREP num] □*an annual rate of 22.8 percent (1.9 multiplied by 12).* 年率22.8パーセント（1.9の12倍） 4 PREP 前置詞 You use **by** to talk about measurements of area. For example, if a room is twenty feet **by** fourteen feet, it measures twenty feet in one direction and fourteen feet in the other direction. 〜で[PREP num] □*Three prisoners were sharing one small cell 3 meters by 2½ meters.* 3人の囚人が縦3メートル横2.5メートルの小部屋に一緒にいた。 5 PREP 前置詞 If something increases or decreases **by** a particular amount, that amount is gained or lost. 〜だけ[PREP amount] □*Violent crime has increased by 10 percent since last year.* 昨年以来，暴力的な犯罪が10パーセント増加した。 6 PREP 前置詞 Things that are made or sold **by** the million or **by** the dozen are made or sold in those quantities. 〜ごとに[PREP 'the' n] □*Packages arrived by the dozen from America.* 小包は1ダースごとにアメリカから届いた。 7 PREP 前置詞 You use **by** in expressions such as "minute by minute" and "drop by drop" to talk about things that happen gradually, not all at once. ずつ[n PREP n] □*His father began to lose his memory bit by bit, becoming increasingly forgetful.* 彼の父親は少しずつ記憶を失い始め，物忘れがますますひどくなってきた。

> In addition to the uses shown here, **by** is used in phrasal verbs such as "abide by," "put by," and "stand by."

> The preposition is pronounced /baɪ/. The adverb is pronounced /baɪ/.

bye /baɪ/ also **bye-bye** CONVENTION 慣習表現 **Bye** and bye-bye are informal ways of saying goodbye. じゃあね □*Bye, Daddy.* 父さん，またね。

by-election (**by-elections**) N-COUNT 可算名詞 A **by-election** is an election that is held to choose a new member of parliament or another legislature when a member has resigned or died. 補欠選挙 [mainly BRIT 主に英国英語]

by|gone /baɪgɔn/ ADJ 形容詞 **Bygone** means happening or existing a very long time ago. 過去の [ADJ n] ❑ *The book recalls other memories of a bygone age.* その本は過ぎ去った時代の別の記憶を呼び起こす.

by|pass /baɪpæs/ (**bypasses, bypassing, bypassed**) ■ V-T 他動詞 If you **bypass** someone or something that you would normally have to get involved with, you ignore them, often because you want to achieve something more quickly. 無視する ❑ *A growing number of employers are trying to bypass the unions altogether.* 労働組合を完全に無視しようとする雇い主が増えている. ② N-COUNT 可算名詞 A **bypass** is a surgical operation performed on or near the heart, in which the flow of blood is redirected so that it does not flow through a part of the heart that is diseased or blocked. 側管, バイパス ❑ *...heart bypass surgery.* 心臓バイパス手術 ③ N-COUNT 可算名詞 A **bypass** is a main road that takes traffic around the edge of a town or city rather than through its center. う回路, バイパス ❑ *A new bypass around the city is being built.* その市の周囲に新し

いバイパスを建設中だ. ④ V-T 他動詞 If a road **bypasses** a place, it goes around it rather than through it. う回する ❑ *...money for new roads to bypass cities.* 都市部を避ける新しい道路の資金 ⑤ V-T 他動詞 If you **bypass** a place when you are traveling, you avoid going through it. 避ける ❑ *The rebel forces simply bypassed the town on their way further south.* 反乱軍はさらなる南下の途中その町をただ避けて通った.

by|product /baɪprɒdʌkt/ (**byproducts**) also **by-product** N-COUNT 可算名詞 A **byproduct** is something that is produced during the manufacture or processing of another product. 副産物 ❑ *The raw material for the tire is a byproduct of gasoline refining.* タイヤの原材料はガソリン精製の副産物だ.

by|stander /baɪstændər/ (**bystanders**) N-COUNT 可算名詞 A **bystander** is a person who is present when something happens and who sees it but does not take part in it. 傍観者 ❑ *It looks like an innocent bystander was killed instead of you.* あなたの代わりに罪のない傍観者が殺されたようだ.

byte /baɪt/ (**bytes**) N-COUNT 可算名詞 In computing, a **byte** is a unit of storage approximately equivalent to one printed character. バイト ❑ *...two million bytes of data.* 200万バイトのデータ

b

Cc

C also **c** /siː/ (**C's, c's**) **1** N-VAR 可変性名詞 **C** is the third letter of the English alphabet. 英語アルファベットの第3字 **2** N-VAR 可変性名詞 In music, **C** is the first note in the scale of C major. ハ音、ドの音 **3** N-VAR 可変性名詞 If you get a **C** as a mark for a piece of work or in an exam, your work is average. 可、C **4** **c.** is written in front of a date or number to indicate that it is approximate. **c.** is an abbreviation for "circa." およそ □ ...the museum's re-creation of a New York dining room (c. 1825-35). ニューヨークの食堂（およそ1825-35年）の博物館による再現 **5** **C** or **c** is used as an abbreviation for words beginning with c, such as "copyright" or "Celsius." Cから始まる語の略 □ Heat the oven to 180°C. オーブンを摂氏180度に熱しなさい。 **6** → see also **C-in-C, c/o**

cab /kæb/ (**cabs**) **1** N-COUNT 可算名詞 A **cab** is a taxi. タクシー □ Could I use your phone to call a cab? タクシーを呼ぶので電話をお借りできますか。 **2** N-COUNT 可算名詞 The **cab** of a truck or train is the front part in which the driver sits. 運転室 □ The van has additional load space over the driver's cab. その小型トラックは運転席の上にさらに収納場所を備えている.

caba|ret /kæbəreɪ/ N-UNCOUNT 不可算名詞 **Cabaret** is live entertainment consisting of dancing, singing, or comedy acts that are performed in the evening in restaurants or nightclubs. キャバレーのショー [oft N N] □ Helen made a successful career in cabaret. ヘレンはキャバレーのショーで成功した.

cab|bage /kæbɪdʒ/ (**cabbages**) N-VAR 可変性名詞 A **cabbage** is a round vegetable with white, green, or purple leaves that is usually eaten cooked. キャベツ
→ see **vegetable**

cab|in /kæbɪn/ (**cabins**) **1** N-COUNT 可算名詞 A **cabin** is a small wooden house, especially one in an area of forests or mountains. (木造の) 小屋 □ ...a log cabin. 丸太小屋 **2** N-COUNT 可算名詞 A **cabin** is a small room in a ship or boat. 船室 □ He showed her to a small cabin. 彼は彼女に小さな船室を見せた. **3** N-COUNT 可算名詞 A **cabin** is one of the areas inside a plane. 機室 □ He sat quietly in the first class cabin of the flight looking tired. 彼はその便のファーストクラスの席に静かに座り、疲れて見えた.

cabi|net /kæbɪnɪt/ (**cabinets**) **1** N-COUNT 可算名詞 A **cabinet** is a cupboard used for storing things such as medicine or alcoholic drinks or for displaying decorative things in. 戸棚 □ She looked in the medicine cabinet and found some aspirin. 彼女は薬の戸棚を覗き、アスピリンを見つけた. **2** N-COUNT 可算名詞 The **cabinet** is a group of the most senior advisers or ministers in a government, who meet regularly to discuss policies. 内閣 □ The announcement came after a three-hour cabinet meeting. その声明は3時間の閣議の後に出された.

ca|ble /keɪbəl/ (**cables**) **1** N-VAR 可変性名詞 A **cable** is a kind of very strong, thick rope, made of wires twisted together. 太い綱 □ The miners rode a conveyance attached to a cable made of braided steel wire. 鉱夫たちは鉄線を編んだケーブルに取り付けられた貨車に乗った. **2** N-VAR 可変性名詞 A **cable** is a thick wire, or a group of wires inside a rubber or plastic covering, which is used to carry electricity or electronic signals. 被覆電線 □ ...overhead power cables. 架空送電線 **3** N-UNCOUNT 不可算名詞 **Cable** is used to refer to television systems in which the signals are sent along underground wires rather than by radio waves. ケーブルテレビ □ They ran commercials on cable systems across the country. 彼らは国中のケーブルテレビによって広告放送を流した.
→ see **bridge, laser, television**

cache /kæʃ/ (**caches**) **1** N-COUNT 可算名詞 A **cache** is a quantity of things such as weapons that have been hidden. 隠匿物 □ A huge arms cache was discovered by police. 警察によって大量の隠匿武器類が発見された. **2** N-COUNT 可算名詞 A **cache** or **cache memory** is an area of computer memory that is used for temporary storage of data and can be accessed more quickly than the main memory. キャッシュ [COMPUTING コンピューティング] □ In your Web browser's cache are the most recent Web files that you have downloaded. あなたのウェブ・ブラウザのキャッシュにはあなたがダウンロードした最新のウェブ・ファイルがある.

cac|tus /kæktəs/ (**cactuses** or **cacti** /kæktaɪ/) N-COUNT 可算名詞 A **cactus** is a thick, fleshy plant that grows in many hot, dry parts of the world. Cacti have no leaves and many of them are covered in prickles. サボテン
→ see **desert**

CAD /kæd/ N-UNCOUNT 不可算名詞 **CAD** refers to the use of computer software in the design of things such as cars, buildings, and machines. **CAD** is an abbreviation for "computer aided design." コンピュータ援用設計 [COMPUTING コンピューティング] □ ...CAD software. CADソフト

ca|det /kədet/ (**cadets**) N-COUNT 可算名詞 A **cadet** is a young man or woman who is being trained in the armed services or the police force. 士官候補生、警察学校の生徒 □ ...army cadets. 陸軍士官候補生

caf|eteria /kæfɪtɪəriə/ (**cafeterias**) N-COUNT 可算名詞 A **cafeteria** is a restaurant where you choose your food from a counter and take it to your table after paying for it. Cafeterias are usually found in public buildings such as hospitals, colleges, and offices. セルフサービスの食堂
→ see **restaurant**

caf|feine /kæfiːn/ N-UNCOUNT 名詞 **Caffeine** is a chemical substance found in coffee, tea, and cocoa, which affects your brain and body and makes you more active. カフェイン
→ see **coffee**

cage /keɪdʒ/ (**cages**) N-COUNT 可算名詞 A **cage** is a structure of wire or metal bars in which birds or animals are kept. おり、かご □ I hate to see birds in cages. 私はかごの中の鳥を見るのは嫌だ.

caged /keɪdʒd/ ADJ 形容詞 A **caged** bird or animal is inside a cage. (おりなどに) 閉じ込められた □ Mark was still pacing like a caged animal. マークはまだおりのなかの動物のようにゆっくりと歩いていた.

ca|jole /kədʒoʊl/ (**cajoles, cajoling, cajoled**) V-T 他動詞 If you **cajole** someone **into** doing something, you get them to do it after persuading them for some time. 甘言でつる、丸め込む □ It was he who had cajoled Garland into doing the film. その映画を撮るようガーランドを丸め込んだのは彼だった.

cake /keɪk/ (**cakes**) **1** N-VAR 可変性名詞 A **cake** is a sweet food made by baking a mixture of flour, eggs, sugar, and fat in an oven. Cakes may be large and cut into slices or small and intended for one person only. ケーキ □ ...a piece of cake. ケーキ1つ □ Would you like some chocolate cake? チョコレートケーキはいかがですか。 □ ...a birthday cake. バースデー・ケーキ **2** N-COUNT 可算名詞 Food that is formed into flat round shapes before it is cooked can be referred to as **cakes**. 調理前に平たく丸い形にした食料 □ ...fish cakes. フィッシュケーキ **3** N-COUNT 可算名詞 A **cake of soap** is a small block of it. 塊 □ ...a small cake of lime-scented soap. ライムの香りの小さな石鹸ひとつ **4** PHRASE 句 If someone has done something very stupid, rude, or selfish, you can say that they **take the cake** or that what they have done **takes the cake**, to emphasize your surprise at their behavior. まったくあきれる [AM 米国英語, EMPHASIS 強調] **5** the icing on the cake → see **icing**
→ see **dessert**

cake pan (**cake pans**) N-COUNT 可算名詞 A **cake pan** is a metal container that you bake a cake in. ケーキを焼くための金属容器 □ Lightly grease and flour a 13-by-9-inch cake pan. 縦13インチ横9インチのケーキパンに薄く油を塗り、粉を敷きなさい。 [AM 米国英語]

ca|lam|ity /kəlæmɪti/ (**calamities**) N-VAR 可変性名詞 A **calamity** is an event that causes a great deal of damage, destruction, or personal distress. 災難、災害 [FORMAL 形式ばった] □ He described drugs as the greatest calamity of the age. 彼は麻薬をこの時代の最大の災害と表現した.

cal|cium /kælsiəm/ N-UNCOUNT 不可算名詞 **Calcium** is a soft white chemical element which is found in bones and teeth, and also in limestone, chalk, and marble. カルシウム

cal|cu|late /kælkjəleɪt/ (**calculates, calculating, calculated**) **1** V-T 他動詞 If you **calculate** a number or amount, you discover it from information that you already have, by using arithmetic, mathematics, or a special machine. 計算する □ From this you can calculate the total mass in the Galaxy. このことから銀河系全体の全質量を算出することができる。 □ We calculate that the average size farm in Lancaster County is 65 acres. 我々の算出によると、ランキャスター郡の平均規模の農場は65エーカーである。 **2** V-T 他動詞 If you **calculate** the effects of something, especially a possible course of action, you think about them in order to form an opinion or decide what to do. 策定する □ I believe I am capable of calculating the political

consequences accurately. 私は自分が政治的結果を正確に予測することができると信じている.

cal|cu|lat|ed /ˈkælkyəleɪtɪd/ ■ ADJ 形容詞 If something is **calculated** to have a particular effect, it is specially done or arranged in order to have that effect. 意図されて [v-link ADJ to-inf] ❑ *Their movements through the region were calculated to terrify landowners into abandoning their holdings.* その地域じゅうでの彼らの作戦行動は、地主がおびえて土地を手放すように意図したものであった. ❷ ADJ 形容詞 If you say that something is not **calculated to** have a particular effect, you mean that it is unlikely to have that effect. しそうな [with brd-neg, v-link ADJ to-inf] ❑ *The liberal agenda is not calculated to help minority groups.* その自由主義的な行動指針では少数民族の人たちを救えそうもない. ❸ ADJ 形容詞 You can describe a clever or dishonest action as **calculated** when it is very carefully planned or arranged. 計算された ❑ *Irene's use of the mop had been a calculated attempt to cover up her crime.* イレーヌがモップを使ったのは、自分の犯罪を隠蔽するための計画的行動だった. ❹ ADJ 形容詞 If you take a **calculated** risk, you do something which you think might be successful, although you have fully considered the possible bad consequences of your action. 予測される [ADJ n] ❑ *The president took a calculated political risk in throwing his full support behind the rebels.* 大統領は予測される政治的危険を覚悟の上で反乱軍を全面的に支援した.

cal|cu|lat|ing /ˈkælkyəleɪtɪŋ/ ADJ 形容詞 If you describe someone as **calculating**, you disapprove of the fact that they deliberately plan to get what they want, often by hurting or harming other people. 打算的な [DISAPPROVAL 不賛成] ❑ *Northbridge is a cool, calculating, and clever criminal who could strike again.* ノースブリッジは冷たく打算的で抜け目のない犯罪者で、再び事を起こしかねない.

cal|cu|la|tion /ˌkælkyəˈleɪʃ°n/ (**calculations**) N-VAR 可変名詞 A **calculation** is something that you think about and work out mathematically. **Calculation** is the process of working something out mathematically. 計算 ❑ *Leonard made a rapid calculation: he'd never make it in time.* レナードは急いで計算した. とても間に合わないだろうと.

→ see **mathematics**

cal|cu|la|tor /ˈkælkyəleɪtər/ (**calculators**) N-COUNT 可算名詞 A **calculator** is a small electronic device that you use for making mathematical calculations. 計算機 ❑ *...a pocket calculator.* 電卓

→ see **office**

cal|en|dar /ˈkælɪndər/ (**calendars**) ■ N-COUNT 可算名詞 A **calendar** is a chart or device which displays the date and the day of the week, and often the whole of a particular year divided up into months, weeks, and days. カレンダー、暦 ❑ *There was a calendar on the wall above, with large squares around the dates.* 壁の上のほうにカレンダーがあり、日付は大きな四角形で囲まれていた. ❷ N-COUNT 可算名詞 A **calendar** is a particular system for dividing time into periods such as years, months, and weeks, often starting from a particular point in history. 暦 ❑ *The Christian calendar was originally based on the Julian calendar of the Romans.* キリスト教の暦はもともとローマのユリウス暦を基にして作られた. ❸ N-COUNT 可算名詞 You can use **calendar** to refer to a series or list of events and activities which take place on particular dates, and which are important for a particular organization, community, or person. 日程 ❑ *It is one of the hottest tickets on Washington's social calendar.* それはワシントンの社交行事日程の中で最重要の行事の1つである.

→ see **year**

cal|en|dar year (**calendar years**) N-COUNT 可算名詞 A **calendar year** is a period of twelve months from January 1 to December 31. **Calendar year** is often used in business to compare with the **fiscal year**. 暦年 ❑ *In the last calendar year the company had a turnover of $426m.* 昨暦年度はその会社の売り上げ高は4億2千6百万ドルであった.

calf /ˈkæf/ (**calves** /ˈkævz/) ■ N-COUNT 可算名詞 A **calf** is a young cow. 子牛 ❷ N-COUNT 可算名詞 Some other young animals, including elephants and whales, are called **calves**. (ゾウ、クジラなどの) 子 ❸ N-COUNT 可算名詞 Your **calf** is the thick part at the back of your leg, between your ankle and your knee. ふくらはぎ ❑ *...a calf injury.* ふくらはぎの負傷

cali|ber /ˈkælɪbər/ ■ N-UNCOUNT 不可算名詞 The **caliber of** a person is the quality or standard of their ability or intelligence, especially when this is high. 器量、力量 ❑ *I was impressed by the high caliber of the researchers and analysts.* 私は研究者と分析者たちの高い能力に感銘を受けた. ❷ N-UNCOUNT 不可算名詞 The **caliber of** something is its quality, especially when it is good. 質 ❑ *The caliber of teaching was very high.* 教育の質はとても高い. ❸ N-COUNT 可算名詞 The **caliber** of a gun is the width of the inside of its barrel. 口径 [TECHNICAL 技術的] ❑ *...a small-caliber rifle.* 小口径のライフル銃 ❹ N-COUNT 可算名詞 The **caliber** of a bullet is its diameter. 弾径 [TECHNICAL 技術的] ❑ *She was hit in the head by a .22-caliber bullet.* 彼女は弾径22の弾丸で頭を撃たれた.

cali|brate /ˈkælɪbreɪt/ (**calibrates, calibrating, calibrated**) V-T 他動詞 If you **calibrate** an instrument or tool, you mark or adjust it so that you can use it to measure something accurately. 目盛りを調整する [TECHNICAL 技術的] ❑ *...instructions on how to calibrate a thermometer.* 温度計の較正(こうせい)方法についての指示

cali|bre /ˈkælɪbər/ → see **caliber**

---

call

❶ NAMING
❷ DECLARING, ANNOUNCING, AND DEMANDING
❸ TELEPHONING AND VISITING
❹ PHRASAL VERBS

---

❶ **call** /ˈkɔl/ (**calls, calling, called**) ■ V-T 他動詞 If you **call** someone or something **by** a particular name or title, you give them that name or title. 呼ぶ ❑ *I always wanted to call the dog Mufty for some reason.* 私はいつもその犬をなんとなくマフティと呼びたかった. ❑ *"Doctor..."—"Will you please call me Sarah?"* 「先生」「サラと呼んでくださいませんか」 ❷ V-T 他動詞 If you **call** someone or something a particular thing, you suggest they are that thing or describe them as that thing. 見なす ❑ *The speech was interrupted by members of the Republican Party, who called him a traitor.* 演説は共和党員たちによって中断されたが、彼らは彼を裏切り者と呼んでいた. ❑ *She calls me lazy and selfish.* 彼女は私を怠け者でわがままだと見なしている. ❸ → see also **so-called** ❹ to **call** something your **own** → see **own** ❺ to **call it quits** → see **quit**

❷ **call** /ˈkɔl/ (**calls, calling, called**) ■ V-T 他動詞 If you **call** something, you say it in a loud voice, because you are trying to attract someone's attention. 呼びかける ❑ *He could hear the others downstairs calling his name.* 彼は他の人たちが階下で自分の名前を呼んでいるのが聞こえた. ● PHRASAL VERB 句動詞 **Call out** means the same as **call**. 呼びかける ❑ *The butcher's son called out a greeting.* 肉屋の息子が声を出して挨拶した. ❷ V-T 他動詞 If you **call** someone, you ask them to come to you by shouting to them. 呼びつける ❑ *She called her young son: "Here, Stephen, come and look at this!"* 彼女は幼い息子が声を呼んだ. 「ほら、スティーヴン、こっちに来てこれを見てごらん」 ❸ V-T 他動詞 If you **call** someone such as a doctor or the police, you ask them to come to you, usually by telephoning them. 呼び寄せる ❑ *He screamed for his wife to call an ambulance.* 彼は妻に向かって救急車を呼ぶようにと叫んだ. ❹ V-T 他動詞 If someone in authority **calls** something such as a meeting, rehearsal, or election, they arrange for it to take place at a particular time. 召集する ❑ *We're going to call a meeting and discuss how we can work with other groups.* 我々は会合を開き、他集団との協働のありかたについて討議するつもりだ. ❺ V-T 他動詞 If someone **is called** before a court or committee, they are ordered to appear there, usually to give evidence. 召喚する [usu passive] ❑ *The child waited two hours before she was called to give evidence.* その子供は証言するために呼び出される前に2時間待った. ❻ V-T 他動詞 To **call** a game or sporting event means to cancel it, for example because of rain or bad light. 中止する [AM 米国英語] ❑ *We called the next game.* 我々は次の試合を中止した.

If you **cancel** or **call off** an arrangement or an appointment, you stop it from happening. ❑ *His failing health forced him to cancel the meeting... The European Community has threatened to call off peace talks.* If you **postpone** or **put off** an arrangement or an appointment, you make another arrangement for it to happen at a later time. ❑ *Elections have been postponed until next year... The senate put off a vote on the nomination for one week.* If you **delay** something that has been arranged, you make it happen later than planned. ❑ *Space agency managers decided to delay the launch of the space shuttle.* If something **delays** you or **holds** you **up**, you start or finish what you are doing later than you planned. ❑ *He was delayed in traffic... Delivery of equipment had been held up by delays and disputes.*

Thesaurus | *call* また次を参照:
v. | cry, holler, scream, shout ❷ ■ ❷

---

❼ N-COUNT 可算名詞 If there is a **call for** something, someone demands that it should happen. 要求 ❑ *There have been calls for a new kind of security arrangement.* 新しい警備体制を求める声が上がっている. ❽ N-COUNT 可算名詞 The **call** of a particular bird or animal is the characteristic sound that it makes. 鳴き声 ❑ *...a wide range of animal noises and bird calls.* さまざまな動物の鳴き声や小鳥のさえずり ❾ N-UNCOUNT 不可算名詞 If there is little or no **call for** something, very few people want it to be done or provided. 需要 ❑ *"Have you got just plain chocolate?"—"No, I'm afraid there's not much call for that."* 「生チョコレートがありますか」「ありません. それはあまり人気がないんです」 ❿ N-SING 単数名詞 The **call of** something such as a place is the way it attracts or interests you

strongly. 魅力 ❑*But the call of the wild was simply too strong and so he set off once more.* しかし野生の魅力は全くあまりに強力で，だから彼はもう1度出かけたのだ． **11 PHRASE 句** *If someone is on call,* they are ready to go to work at any time if they are needed, especially if there is an emergency. 待機して ❑*In theory I'm on call day and night.* 理論的には，私は昼も夜も待機している． **12 to call** someone's **bluff** → see **bluff 13 to call a halt** → see **halt 14 to call** something **into question** → see **question 15 to call the tune** → see **tune**

Word Partnership *call* は次の語句と使われる:

N.	call someone names ❶ 2
	call an ambulance, call a doctor, call the police ❷ 3
	call a meeting 3
	conference call, emergency call, a number to call, (tele)phone call ❸ 4
ADJ.	collect call ❸ 4
V.	make a call, receive a call, return a call, take a call, wait for a call ❸ 4

---

❸ **call** /kɔl/ (calls, calling, called) **11 V-T 他動詞** *If you call* someone, you telephone them. 電話する ❑*Would you call me as soon as you find out? My number's in the phone book.* わかったらすぐに電話をいただけますか．私の番号は電話帳にあります． ❑*A friend of mine gave me this number to call.* 友人が私にこの電話番号をくれた． **2 V-I 自動詞** *If you call* somewhere, you make a short visit there. 訪問する ❑*A market researcher called at the house where my uncle was living.* 市場調査員が私のおじの住んでいる家を訪ねた． ● **N-COUNT 可算名詞 Call** is also a noun. 訪問 ❑*He decided to pay a call on Tommy Cummings.* 彼はトミー・カミングスを訪ねることにした． **3 V-I 自動詞** *When a train, bus, or ship calls* somewhere, it stops there for a short time to allow people to get on or off. 停車する ❑*The steamer calls at several palm-fringed ports along the way.* 途中，汽船はやしの木で飾られたいくつかの港に立ち寄った． **4 N-COUNT 可算名詞** *When you make a telephone call,* you telephone someone. 通話 ❑*I made a phone call to the United States to talk to a friend.* 私は友人と話すため米国に電話をかけた． ❑*I've had hundreds of calls from other victims.* 私は他の被害者から何百もの電話を受けた．

❹ **call** /kɔl/ (calls, calling, called)
▶ **call around PHRASAL VERB 句動詞** *If you call around,* you phone several people, usually when you are trying to organize something or to find some information. 方々に電話をかける [mainly AM 主に米国英語] ❑*Call around to find the best bargains.* 一番の掘り出し物を求めて方々に電話をかけよ．
▶ **call back PHRASAL VERB 句動詞** *If you call* someone **back,** you telephone them again or in return for a telephone call that they have made to you. （相手に電話を）かけなおす ❑*If we're not around, she'll take a message and we'll call you back.* 私たちが不在の場合，彼女がメッセージを承り，後ほどかけなおさせていただきます．
▶ **call for 11 PHRASAL VERB 句動詞** *If something calls for* a particular action or quality, it needs it or makes it necessary. 要求する ❑*It's a situation that calls for a blend of delicacy and force.* これは繊細さと迫力を共に必要とする状況だ． **2 PHRASAL VERB 句動詞** *If you call for* someone, you go to the building where they are, so that you can both go somewhere. 呼びに行く，迎えに行く ❑*I'll call for you at seven o'clock.* 7時に迎えに行くよ． **3 PHRASAL VERB 句動詞** *If you call for* something, you demand that it should happen. 要求する ❑*They angrily called for Robinson's resignation.* 彼らは怒ってロビンソンの辞職を要求した．
▶ **call in PHRASAL VERB 句動詞** *If you call* someone **in,** you ask them to come and help you or do something for you. 手助けを求める ❑*Call in an architect or engineer to oversee the work.* その仕事を監督するために建築家か技師の援助を求めよ． **2 PHRASAL VERB 句動詞** *If you call in,* you phone a place, such as the place where you work, or a radio or TV station. 電話を入れる ❑*She reached for the phone to call in sick.* 彼女は病欠の電話を入れるために手を伸ばした． ❑*24 million viewers called in to cast their final votes last night.* 昨夜2400万人の視聴者が最終投票のために電話を入れた． **3 →** see also **call-in 4 PHRASAL VERB 句動詞** *If you call in* somewhere, you make a short visit there. 立ち寄る ❑*He just calls in occasionally.* 彼はときおり立ち寄るだけだ．
▶ **call off PHRASAL VERB 句動詞** *If you call off* an event that has been planned, you cancel it. 中止する ❑*He has called off the trip.* 彼は旅行を中止した．
▶ **call on or call upon 11 PHRASAL VERB 句動詞** *If you call on* someone **to** do something or **call upon** them **to** do it, you say publicly that you want them to do it. 依頼する ❑*One of Kenya's leading churchmen has called on the government to resign.* ケニアの指導的な聖職者の1人が政府の辞職を求めた． **2 PHRASAL VERB 句動詞** *If you call on* someone or **call upon** someone, you pay them a short visit. ❑*Sofia was intending to call on Miss Kitts.* ソフィアはキッツさんのところに立ち寄るつもりだった．
▶ **call out 11 PHRASAL VERB 句動詞** *If you call* someone **out,** you order or request that they come to help, especially in an emergency. 呼び出す ❑*Colombia has called out the army and imposed*

emergency measures. コロンビアは軍を召集し，応急対策を課した． **2 →** see also **call ❷1**
▶ **call up 11 PHRASAL VERB 句動詞** *If you call* someone **up,** you telephone them. 電話をかける [mainly AM 主に米国英語] ❑*When I'm in Pittsburgh, I call him up.* ピッツバーグにいるとき私は彼に電話をかける． ❑*He called up the museum.* 彼は博物館に電話をかけた． **2 PHRASAL VERB 句動詞** *If someone is called up,* they are ordered to join the army, navy, or air force. 召集する ❑*The United States has called up some 150,000 military reservists.* 米国は約15万人の予備兵を招集した．
▶ **call upon →** see **call on**

call cen|ter (call centers) N-COUNT 可算名詞 A **call center** is an office where people work answering or making telephone calls for a particular company. 顧客電話窓口

call|er /kɔlər/ (callers) **11 N-COUNT 可算名詞** A **caller** is a person who is making a telephone call. 電話をかける人 ❑*An anonymous caller told police what had happened.* 匿名の電話が警察に一部始終を伝えた． **2 N-COUNT 可算名詞** A **caller** is a person who comes to see you for a short visit. 訪問者 ❑*She ushered her callers into a cluttered living room.* 彼女は散らかった居間に訪問者を通した．

call-in (call-ins) N-COUNT 可算名詞 A **call-in** is a program on radio or television in which people telephone with questions or opinions and their calls are broadcast. 視聴者参加番組 [AM 米国英語] ❑*...a call-in show on Los Angeles radio station KABC.* ロサンゼルスのラジオ局KABCの視聴者参加番組

call|ing card (calling cards) 11 N-COUNT 可算名詞 A **calling card** is a small card with personal information about you on it, such as your name and address, which you can give to people when you go to visit them. 名刺 [mainly AM 主に米国英語, OLD-FASHIONED 古風な] ❑*Don't forget to give your calling card to those you'd like to see again.* もう1度会いたい人に名刺を渡すのを忘れないことだ． **2 N-COUNT 可算名詞** *If you say that someone has left a calling card,* you mean that they have left evidence that shows they have been in a particular place, especially at the scene of a crime. 形跡 ❑*John was studying the medallion in the evidence bag – the killer's calling card.* ジョンは証拠品の鞄のなかにあった大メダルを調べていた．それが殺人犯の痕跡（こんせき）だった．

cal|lous /kæləs/ **ADJ 形容詞** A **callous** person or action is very cruel and shows no concern for other people or their feelings. 冷淡な，無情な ❑*...his callous disregard for human life.* 彼の冷淡な人命軽視 ● **cal|lous|ness N-UNCOUNT 不可算名詞** 冷淡さ ❑*...the callousness of Raymond's murder.* レイモンド殺害の冷酷さ ● **cal|lous|ly ADV 副詞 [ADV with v]** 冷淡に ❑*He is accused of callously ill-treating his wife.* 彼は妻への無情な虐待で告訴されている．

call wait|ing N-UNCOUNT 不可算名詞 Call waiting is a telephone service that sends you a signal if another call arrives while you are already on the phone. 通話中着信 ❑*The service includes caller ID, voice mail, and call waiting.* このサービスには発信電話番号通知，音声メール，通話中着信が含まれている．

calm /kɑm/ (calmer, calmest, calms, calming, calmed) **11 ADJ 形容詞** A **calm** person does not show or feel any worry, anger, or excitement. 冷静な ❑*She is usually a calm and diplomatic woman.* 彼女はいつも冷静で如才ない女性だ． ❑*Try to keep calm and just tell me what happened.* 気持ちを落ち着けて，何が起こったかを話してくれ． ● **N-UNCOUNT 不可算名詞 Calm** is also a noun. 冷静 [also "a" N] ❑*He felt a sudden sense of calm, of contentment.* 彼は突然，平穏と安らぎを感じた． ● **calm|ly ADV 副詞** 冷静に ❑*Alan looked at him and said calmly, "I don't believe you."* アランは彼を見つめ，「君の言うことは信じない」と冷静に言った． **2 ADJ 形容詞** *If someone says that a place is calm,* they mean that it is free from fighting or public disorder, when trouble has recently occurred there or had been expected.* 穏やかな [JOURNALISM ジャーナリズム] ❑*The city of Sarajevo appears relatively calm today.* 今日，サラエボ市は比較的落ち着いているようだ． ● **N-UNCOUNT 不可算名詞 Calm** is also a noun. 平穏 ❑*Community and church leaders have appealed for calm and no retaliation.* 地域と教会の指導者たちは，冷静を保ち報復を控えるよう訴えている． **3 ADJ 形容詞** *If the sea or a lake is calm,* the water is not moving very much and there are no big waves. 穏やかな ❑*...the safe, calm waters protected by an offshore reef.* 沖合いの岩礁に守られた安全で穏やかな水域 **4 ADJ 形容詞 Calm weather** is pleasant weather with little or no wind. 静かな ❑*Tuesday was a fine, clear and calm day.* 火曜日は好天で，空は晴れ，風はなかった． **5 N-UNCOUNT 不可算名詞 Calm** is used to refer to a quiet, still, or peaceful atmosphere in a place. 閑静な ❑*The house projects an atmosphere of calm and order.* その家は閑静で整然とした雰囲気をかもしている． **6 V-T 他動詞** *If you calm* someone, you do something to make them feel less angry, worried, or excited. なだめる ❑*The ruling party's veterans know how to calm their critics.* 与党の古参は批判者のあしらい方を知っている． ❑*She was breathing quickly and tried to calm herself.* 彼女は速い息づかいをしていたが，気持ちを落ち着けようとした． ● **calm|ing ADJ 形容詞** 落ち着かせる ❑*...a fresh, cool fragrance which produces a very calming effect on the mind.* 気持ちを落ち着かせるのにとても効果的な新鮮でさわやかな香り **7 V-T 他動**

詞 To **calm** a situation means to reduce the amount of trouble, violence, or panic there is. 静める ❑*Officials hoped admitting fewer foreigners would calm the situation.* 当局は外国人の受け入れを減らすことでその事態を沈静化できると思った. **3** V-I 自動詞 When the sea **calms**, it becomes still because the wind stops blowing strongly. When the wind calms, it stops blowing strongly. 静まる ❑*Dawn came, the sea calmed but the cold was as bitter as ever.* 夜明けが訪れ, 海は静まったが, 冷え込みは相変わらず厳しかった.

▶ **calm down** **1** PHRASAL VERB 句動詞 If you **calm down**, or if someone **calms** you **down**, you become less angry, upset, or excited. 落ち着く, 落ち着かせる ❑*Calm down for a minute and listen to me.* 少しの間落ち着いて私の話を聞いてよ. ❑*I'll try a herbal remedy to calm him down.* 彼を落ち着かせるため薬草を使ってみよう. **2** PHRASAL VERB 句動詞 If things **calm down**, or someone or something **calms** things **down**, the amount of activity, trouble, or panic is reduced. 静まる, 静める ❑*We will go back to normal when things calm down.* 我々は事態が静まったときに平常に戻るだろう.
→ see **hypnosis**

Thesaurus　　　calm また次を参照：

ADJ.　cool-headed, laid-back, relaxed; (*ant.*) excited, upset **1**
　　　mild, peaceful, placid, serene, tranquil;
　　　(*ant.*) rough **1** – **4**

Word Link　　cal, caul ≈ hot, heat : calorie, cauldron, scald

calo|rie /kǽləri/ (**calories**) N-COUNT 可算名詞 **Calories** are units used to measure the energy value of food. People who are on diets try to eat food that does not contain many calories. カロリー ❑*Sweetened drinks contain a lot of calories.* 甘味料を加えた飲料はカロリーが高い.
→ see Word Web: **calories**
→ see **diet**

cam|cord|er /kǽmkɔrdər/ (**camcorders**) N-COUNT 可算名詞 A **camcorder** is a portable video camera which records both pictures and sound. ビデオカメラ

came /kéɪm/ **Came** is the past tense of **come**. comeの過去形

cam|el /kǽməl/ (**camels**) **1** N-COUNT 可算名詞 A **camel** is a large animal that lives in deserts and is used for carrying goods and people. Camels have long necks and one or two lumps on their backs called humps. ラクダ **2** **the straw that broke the camel's back** → see **straw**

cameo /kǽmioʊ/ (**cameos**) **1** N-COUNT 可算名詞 A **cameo** is a short description or piece of acting which expresses cleverly and neatly the nature of a situation, event, or person's character. さわり, 名場面 ❑*...a succession of memorable cameos of American history.* アメリカ史の記憶に残る名場面の連続 **2** N-COUNT 可算名詞 A **cameo** is a piece of jewelry, usually oval in shape, consisting of a raised stone figure or design fixed on to a flat stone of another color. カメオ ❑*...a cameo brooch.* カメオのブローチ

cam|era /kǽmrə/ (**cameras**) **1** N-COUNT 可算名詞 A **camera** is a piece of equipment that is used for taking photographs, making movies, or producing television pictures. カメラ, 写真機, 撮影機 ❑*Her grandmother lent her a camera for a school trip to Venice and Egypt.* 祖母が彼女にヴェニスとエジプトへの修学旅行のためにカメラを貸してくれた. **2** PHRASE 句 If someone or something is **on camera**, they are being filmed. 撮影中 ❑*Fay was so impressive on camera that a special part was written in for her.* カメラの前のフェイはとても魅力的だったので, 彼女のために特別の役が書き込まれた. **3** PHRASE 句 If you do something or if something happens **off camera**, you do it or it happens when not being filmed. 撮影されていない ❑*They were anything but friendly off camera, refusing even to take the same elevator.* 撮影外では彼らは親密どころではなく, 同じエレベーターに乗ることすら避けていた. **4** PHRASE 句 If a trial is held **in camera**, the public and the press are not allowed to attend. 非公開で [FORMAL 形式ばった] ❑*This morning's appeal was held in camera.* 今朝の控訴審は非公開で開かれた.
→ see **photography**

camera|man /kǽmrəmæn/ (**cameramen**) N-COUNT 可算名詞 A **cameraman** is a person who operates a camera for television or movies. カメラマン, 撮影技師

camou|flage /kǽməflɑ:ʒ/ (**camouflages, camouflaging, camouflaged**) **1** N-UNCOUNT 不可算名詞 **Camouflage** consists of things such as leaves, branches, or brown and green paint, which are used to make it difficult for an enemy to see military forces and equipment. 擬装 [also "a" N, oft N N] ❑*They were dressed in camouflage and carried automatic rifles.* 彼らは擬装をして, 自動ライフルを携行した. ❑*...a camouflage jacket.* 迷彩服 **2** N-UNCOUNT 不可算名詞 **Camouflage** is the way in which some animals are colored and shaped so that they cannot easily be seen in their natural surroundings. 擬態 [also "a" N] ❑*Confident in its camouflage, being the same color as the rocks, the lizard stands still when it feels danger.* 岩の同じ色である擬態に自信を持ち, トカゲは危険を察知するとじっとしている. **3** V-T 他動詞 If military buildings or vehicles **are camouflaged**, things such as leaves, branches, or brown and green paint are used to make it difficult for an enemy to see them. 擬装する [usu passive] ❑*The entrance was camouflaged with bricks and dirt.* 入り口はれんがと泥で擬装されていた. **4** V-T 他動詞 If you **camouflage** something such as a feeling or a situation, you hide it or make it appear to be something different. ごまかす, 隠す ❑*He has never camouflaged his desire to better himself.* 彼は出世したいという願望を隠すことは決してなかった. ● N-UNCOUNT 不可算名詞 **Camouflage** is also a noun. ごまかし [also "a" N] ❑*There was much laughter – a perfect camouflage for the anxiety of waiting for the verdict in the trial.* たくさんの笑い声が聞こえたが, それは裁判の評決を待つ不安を完全に隠そうとするものであった.

camp /kǽmp/ (**camps, camping, camped**) **1** N-COUNT 可算名詞 A **camp** is a collection of huts and other buildings that is provided for a particular group of people, such as refugees, prisoners, or soldiers, as a place to live or stay. 駐留地, 野営地 ❑*...a refugee camp.* 避難民居住地 **2** N-COUNT 可算名詞 You can refer to a group of people who all support a particular person, policy, or idea as a particular **camp**. 陣営 ❑*The press release provoked furious protests from the Gore camp and other top Democrats.* その新開発表はゴア陣営および他の民主党上層部の怒りに満ちた抗議を引き起こした. **3** N-VAR 可変性名詞 A **camp** is an outdoor area with cabins, tents, or trailers where people stay on vacation. キャンプ場, 野営地 **4** N-VAR 可変性名詞 A **camp** is a collection of tents or trailers where people are living or staying, usually temporarily while they are traveling. テント集団 ❑*...gypsy camps.* ジプシーのテント村 **5** V-I 自動詞 If you **camp** somewhere, you stay or live there for a short time in a tent or trailer, in the open air. 野営する ❑*We camped near the beach.* 我々は浜辺の近くに野営した. ● PHRASAL VERB 句動詞 **Camp out** means the same as **camp**. 野営する ❑*For six months they camped out in a meadow at the back of the house.* 6ヶ月間彼らは家の裏の牧草地に野営した. ● **camp|ing** N-UNCOUNT 不可算名詞 野営 ❑*They went camping in the wild.* 彼らは野生地に野営に行った. **6** ADJ 形容詞 If you describe someone's behavior, performance, or style of dress as **camp**, you mean that it is exaggerated and amusing, often in a way that is thought to be typical of some male homosexuals. 大げさでわざとらしい [INFORMAL くだけた] ❑*James Barron turns in a delightfully camp performance.* ジェームス・バロンは楽しいほどに仰々しい演技をやってのける. **7** → see also **concentration camp**

cam|paign /kæmpéɪn/ (**campaigns, campaigning, campaigned**) **1** N-COUNT 可算名詞 A **campaign** is a planned set of activities that people carry out over a period of time in order to achieve something such as social or political change. (社会的) 運動 ❑*During his election campaign he promised to put the economy back on its feet.* 選挙戦の間, 彼は経済を復興させることを約束した. ❑*...a campaign to improve the training of staff.* 職員の養成を改善する運動 **2** N-COUNT 可算名詞 In a war, a **campaign** is a series of planned movements carried out by armed forces. 軍事行動 ❑*The allies are intensifying their air campaign.* 同盟諸国は空爆作戦を強化している. **3** V-I 自動詞 If someone **campaigns for** something, they carry out a planned set of activities over a period of time in order

---

Word Web　　calories

Calories are a measure of **energy**. One calorie of heat raises the **temperature** of 1 gram of water by 1°C*. However, we usually think of calories in relation to food and exercise. A person eating a cup of vanilla ice cream **takes in** 270 calories. Walking a mile **burns** 66 calories. Different types of foods store different amounts of energy. **Proteins** and **carbohydrates** contain 4 calories per gram. However **fat** contains 9 calories per gram. Our bodies store extra calories in the form of fat. For every 3,500 excess calories we take in, we gain a pound of fat.

0°Celsius = 32° Fahrenheit

to achieve their aim. 運動する □*We are campaigning for law reform.* 我々は法改正のために運動している. ◢ → see also **ad campaign** → see **army, election**

Word Partnership *campaign* は次の語句と使われる:

N.	**election** campaign, campaign **slogan** ◢
	advertising/marketing campaign ◢ ◢
PREP.	campaign **against** *someone/something*, campaign **for** *something* ◢

cam|paign|er /kæmpeɪnər/ (**campaigners**) N-COUNT 可算名詞 A **campaigner** is a person who campaigns for social or political change. 運動家 □*...anti-war campaigners.* 反戦運動家

camp|er /kæmpər/ (**campers**) ◢ N-COUNT 可算名詞 A **camper** is someone who is camping somewhere. 野営する人 □*My fellow campers were already packing up their tents.* 野営の仲間はすでにテントの荷造りを始めていた. ◢ N-COUNT 可算名詞 A **camper** is a motor vehicle which is equipped with beds and cooking equipment so that you can live, cook, and sleep in it. キャンプ用自動車, キャンピングカー [mainly AM 主に米国英語]

Word Link *site, situ ≈ position, location : camp*site, *situ*ation, *web*site

camp|site /kæmpsaɪt/ (**campsites**) N-COUNT 可算名詞 A **campsite** is a place where people who are on vacation can stay in tents. 野営場, キャンプ場

cam|pus /kæmpəs/ (**campuses**) N-COUNT 可算名詞 A **campus** is an area of land that contains the main buildings of a university or college. 構内, キャンパス [also prep N] □*...during a rally at the campus.* 構内での集会の間に

---

can

❶ MODAL USES
❷ CONTAINER

---

❶ **can** /kən, STRONG kæn/

Can is a modal verb. It is used with the base form of a verb. The form **cannot** is used in negative statements. The usual spoken form of **cannot** is **can't**, pronounced /kænt/.

Can は法動詞であり, 動詞の原型とともに用いられる. **cannot** 形は否定陳述文に用いられる. **cannot** の通常の話し言葉の形態は **can't** で, /kænt/ と発音される.

◢ MODAL 法動詞 You use **can** when you are mentioning a quality or fact about something which people may make use of if they want to. できる □*Tickets can be purchased at the Madstone Theater box office.* 入場券はマッドストーン劇場の窓口で購入できる. □*A central reservation number can direct you to accommodations that best suit your needs.* 予約センターに電話すれば, 自分の要求に最も合う宿泊施設を教えてもらえる. ◢ MODAL 法動詞 You use **can** to indicate that someone has the ability or opportunity to do something. できる □*Don't worry yourself about me, I can take care of myself.* 私のことは心配しないで. 私は自分のことは自分でできるよ. □*I can't give you details because I don't actually have any details.* 実は詳しいことは知らないので, 詳細については申し上げられません. □*The United States will do whatever it can to help Greece.* 米国はギリシアの支援のためにはできることは何でもするだろう. ◢ MODAL 法動詞 You use **cannot** to indicate that someone is not able to do something because circumstances make it impossible for them to do it. できない □*We cannot buy food and clothes and pay for rent and utilities on $20 a week.* 週に20ドルでは食糧と衣類を買い, 家賃と光熱費を支払うことはできません. ◢ MODAL 法動詞 You use **can** to indicate that something is true sometimes or is true in some circumstances. ありえる □*...long-term therapy that can last five years or more.* 5年かそれ以上続く可能性のある長期治療 □*Exercising alone can be boring.* 1人でする運動は退屈かもしれません. ◢ MODAL 法動詞 You use **cannot** and **can't** to state that you are certain that something is not the case or will not happen. ありえない □*From her knowledge of Douglas's habits, she feels sure that that person can't have been Douglas.* 彼女がダグラスの習慣について知っているかぎりでは, その人物がダグラスであったはずがないと感じている. □*Things can't be that bad.* 事態がそこまで悪いはずがない. ◢ MODAL 法動詞 You use **can** to indicate that someone is allowed to do something. You use **cannot** or **can't** to indicate that someone is not allowed to do something. してもよい □*Can I really have your jeans when you go?* 君が去るとき, 本当に君のジーンズをもらっていいのかい. □*We can't answer any questions, I'm afraid.* 申し訳ありませんが, 質問には一切答えられません. ◢ MODAL 法動詞 You use **cannot** or **can't** when you think it is very important that something should not happen or that someone should not do something. してはならない, ありえない [EMPHASIS 強調] □*It is an intolerable situation and it can't be allowed to go on.* それは耐え難い状況であり, その状態が続くことを許して

はならない. ◢ MODAL 法動詞 You use **can**, usually in questions, in order to make suggestions or to offer to do something. できる □*What can I do around here?* ここで私に何ができるでしょうか. □*This elderly woman was struggling out of the train and I said, "Oh, can I help you?"* この老女が列車から降りようともがいていたので, 「ああ, お手伝いしましょうか」と私は言った. ◢ MODAL 法動詞 You use **can** in questions in order to make polite requests. You use **can't** in questions in order to request strongly that someone does something. してもらう, させていただく [POLITENESS 丁寧さ] □*Can I have a look at that?* それを見せてもらってもいいですか. □*Why can't you leave me alone?* なぜほっといてくれないのか. ◢ MODAL 法動詞 You use **can** as a polite way of interrupting someone or of introducing what you are going to say next. させていただく [FORMAL, SPOKEN 形式ばった, 口語] □*Can I interrupt you just for a minute?* 少しお時間を頂いてもかまいませんか. □*But if I can interrupt, Joe, I don't think anybody here is personally blaming you.* しかし, ジョー, 口を挟むようで申し訳ないけれど, 私はここにいる者は誰も個人的に君を非難していないと思うよ. ◢ MODAL 法動詞 You use **can** with verbs such as "imagine," "think," and "believe" in order to emphasize how you feel about a particular situation. できる, はず [INFORMAL OR SPOKEN くだけた, または口語, EMPHASIS 強調] □*You can imagine he was terribly upset.* 彼がひどく動転したことは想像がつくはずだ. □*You can't think how glad I was to see them all go.* 彼らがみんな出て行くのを見て私がどんなに嬉しかったか, あなたには思いも及ばないでしょう. ◢ MODAL 法動詞 You use **can** in questions with "how" to indicate that you feel strongly about something. できる [SPOKEN 口語, EMPHASIS 強調] □*How can millions of dollars go astray?* どうすれば何百万ドルも行方不明になるのだ. □*How can you say such a thing?* 君はどうしてそんなことが言えるんだ.

Can, **could**, and **be able to** are all used to talk about a person's ability to do something. They are followed by the infinitive form of a verb. You use **can** or a present form of **be able to** to refer to the present, although **can** is more common. □*They can all read and write... The snake is able to catch small mammals.* You use **could** or a past form of **be able to** to refer to the past, and "will" or "shall" with **be able to** to refer to the future. **Be able to** is used if you want refer to doing something at a particular time. □*After treatment he was able to return to work.* **Can** and **could** are used to talk about possibility. **Could** refers to a particular occasion and **can** to more general situations. □*Many jobs could be lost... Too much salt can be harmful.* When talking about the past, you use **could have** and a past participle. □*It could have been much worse.* You also use **can** for the present and **could** for the past to talk about rules or what people are allowed to do. □*They can leave at any time.* Note that when making requests either **can** or **could** may be used. □*Can I have a drink?... Could we put the fire on?* However, **could** is always used for suggestions. □*You could phone her and ask.*

❷ **can** /kæn/ (**cans, canning, canned**) ◢ N-COUNT 可算名詞 A **can** is a metal container in which something such as food, drink, or paint is put. The container is usually sealed to keep the contents fresh. 缶 □*Several young men were kicking a tin can along the middle of the road.* 数人の若者が道の真ん中でブリキ缶を蹴っていた. □*...empty beer cans.* ビールの空き缶 ◢ N-COUNT 可算名詞 You can use **can** to refer to a can and its contents, or to the contents only. 缶 □*She grabbed a can of soda out of the refrigerator.* 彼女はソーダを1缶ひっつかんで冷蔵庫から取り出した. ◢ V-T 他動詞 When food or drink **is canned**, it is put into a metal container and sealed so that it will remain fresh. 缶詰にする [usu passive] □*...fruits and vegetables that will be canned, skinned, diced, or otherwise processed.* 缶詰にする, 皮をむく, 角切りにする, あるいは他の方法で加工する果物と野菜 ◢ V-T 他動詞 If you **are canned**, you are dismissed from your job. 首にする [AM 米国英語, INFORMAL くだけた] □*The extremists prevailed, and the security chief was canned.* 過激派がはびこり, 治安責任者が首になった. ◢ N-SING 単数名詞 **The can** is the toilet. 便所 [AM 米国英語, INFORMAL くだけた] → see Word Web: **can**

ca|nal /kənæl/ (**canals**) ◢ N-COUNT 可算名詞 A **canal** is a long, narrow stretch of water that has been made for boats to travel along or to bring water to a particular area. 運河 □*...the Grand Union Canal.* グランドユニオン運河 ◢ N-COUNT 可算名詞 A **canal** is a narrow tube inside your body for carrying food, air, or other substances. 管 □*...delaying its progress through the alimentary canal.* それが消化管を通るのを遅らせて

can|cel /kænsᵊl/ (**cancels, canceling** or **cancelling, canceled** or **cancelled**) ◢ V-T/V-I 他動詞/自動詞 If you **cancel** something that has been arranged, you stop it from happening. If you **cancel** an order for goods or services, you tell the person or organization supplying them that you no longer wish to receive them. 中止する [他動詞/自動詞] □*The Russian foreign minister yesterday canceled his visit to Washington.* ロシアの外相は昨日ワシントン訪問を中止した. □*Many trains have been cancelled and a limited service is operating on other lines.* 多くの列車が運行中止となっていて, 他の路線で限定

Word Web can

A Frenchman named Nicholas Appert* invented the process of canning in 1795. First he pre-**cooked** the **food**. Then he placed it in glass **jars** with cork **lids** to make an **airtight seal**. The final step was a boiling water bath to kill **bacteria**. Food **preserved** in this way lasted for at least a year. In 1804, Appert opened the world's first factory to produce **vacuum-packed** foods. In 1810, an Englishman, Peter Durance, began to use **metal containers** to can food. Today's canning factories use steel cans covered with a thin coating of **tin**.

Nicholas Appert (1750-1840): a confectioner.

PEARS
25% SUGAR SYRUP
CHOICE QUALITY

C

的な運行がなされている. ❏ *The customer called to cancel.* その顧客が取り消しの電話を入れてきた. ●**can|cel|la|tion** /kænsəleɪʃⁿn/ (**cancellations**) N-VAR 可変性名詞 取り消し ❏ *Outbursts of violence forced the cancellation of Haiti's first free elections in 1987.* 暴動の激発により1987年のハイチでの初の自由選挙は中止を余儀なくされた.

If you **cancel** or **call off** an arrangement or an appointment, you stop it from happening. ❏ *His failing health forced him to cancel the meeting... The European Community has threatened to call off peace talks.* If you **postpone** or **put off** an arrangement or an appointment, you make another arrangement for it to happen at a later time. ❏ *Elections have been postponed until next year... The senate put off a vote on the nomination for one week.* If you **delay** something that has been arranged, you make it happen later than planned. ❏ *Space agency managers decided to delay the launch of the space shuttle.* If something **delays** you or **holds** you **up**, you start or finish what you are doing later than you planned. ❏ *He was delayed in traffic... Delivery of equipment had been held up by delays and disputes.*

② V-T 他動詞 If someone in authority **cancels** a document, an insurance policy, or a debt, they officially declare that it is no longer valid or no longer legally exists. 無効にする ❏ *He intends to try to leave the country, in spite of a government order canceling his passport.* 政府はパスポートの失効を命じたが, 彼は出国しようとしている. ●**can|cel|la|tion** N-UNCOUNT 不可算名詞 取り消し ❏ *...a march by groups calling for cancellation of Third World debt.* 第3世界の負債の帳消しを要求する団体の行進 ③ V-T 他動詞 To **cancel** a stamp or a check means to mark it to show that it has already been used and cannot be used again. 消印を押す ❏ *The new device can also cancel the check after the transaction is complete.* 新しい装置は取引の完了後小切手を無効にすることもできる.

▶ **cancel out** PHRASAL VERB 句動詞 If one thing **cancels out** another thing, the two things have opposite effects, so that when they are combined no real effect is produced. 相殺する ❏ *He wonders if the different influences might not cancel each other out.* 彼は違った影響が相殺作用を起こさないかしらと思っている.

Thesaurus cancel また次を参照:

V. annul, break, call off, scrap, trash, undo ①

can|cer /kænsər/ (**cancers**) N-VAR 可変性名詞 **Cancer** is a serious disease in which cells in a person's body increase rapidly in an uncontrolled way, producing abnormal growths. がん ❏ *Her mother died of breast cancer.* 彼女の母は乳がんで死んだ. ❏ *Jane was just 25 when she learned she had cancer.* 自分のがんを知ったとき, ジェーンはほんの25歳だった.
→ see Word Web: **cancer**

can|cer|ous /kænsərəs/ ADJ 形容詞 **Cancerous** cells or growths are cells or growths that are the result of cancer. がんの ❏ *The production of these cancerous cells suppresses the production of normal white blood cells.* こうしたがん細胞の形成が正常な白血球の形成を抑制する.

can|did /kændɪd/ ❶ ADJ 形容詞 When you are **candid** about something or with someone, you speak honestly. 率直な ❏ *Natalie is candid about the problems she is having with Steve.* ナタリーはスティーブとの間の問題について率直だ. ❏ *I haven't been completely candid with him.* 私は彼に対して完全に心を開いたことはない. ❷ ADJ 形容

詞 A **candid** photograph of someone is one that was taken when the person did not know they were being photographed. 気取らない [ADJ n] ❏ *...candid snaps of off-duty film stars.* 仕事から離れた映画俳優のスナップ写真

can|di|da|cy /kændɪdəsi/ (**candidacies**) N-VAR 可変性名詞 Someone's **candidacy** is their position of being a candidate in an election. 立候補 ❏ *Today he is formally announcing his candidacy for president.* 今日彼は正式に大統領選への立候補を表明することになっている.

can|di|date /kændɪdeɪt/ (**candidates**) ❶ N-COUNT 可算名詞 A **candidate** is someone who is being considered for a position, for example someone who is running in an election or applying for a job. 候補者 ❏ *The Democratic candidate is still leading in the polls.* その民主党候補は世論調査でまだ優位に立っている. ❏ *He is a candidate for the office of governor.* 彼は知事選の候補者だ. ❷ N-COUNT 可算名詞 A **candidate** is someone who is studying for a degree at a college. 学位取得希望者 [AM 米国英語] ❏ *He is now a candidate for a Master's degree in social work at San Francisco State University.* 彼はサンフランシスコ州立大学で社会福祉事業に関する修士号を取得しようとしている. ❸ N-COUNT 可算名詞 A **candidate** is a person or thing that is regarded as being suitable for a particular purpose or as being likely to do or be a particular thing. なりそうな物, なりそうな人 ❏ *Those who are overweight or indulge in high-salt diets are candidates for hypertension.* 肥満あるいは塩分過多の食事を取る者は高血圧症の予備軍である.
→ see **election, vote**

can|dle /kænd³l/ (**candles**) N-COUNT 可算名詞 A **candle** is a stick of hard wax with a piece of string called a wick through the middle. You light the wick in order to give a steady flame that provides light. ろうそく ❏ *The bedroom was lit by a single candle.* 寝室は1本のろうそくで照らされていた.

can|dor /kændər/ N-UNCOUNT 不可算名詞 **Candor** is the quality of speaking honestly and openly about things. 率直さ ❏ *...a brash, forceful man, noted both for his candor and his quick temper.* 率直さと短気の両面で知られた生意気で強引な男

can|dy /kændi/ (**candies**) N-VAR 可変性名詞 **Candy** is sweet foods such as chocolate or taffy. 甘い菓子類 ❏ *...a piece of candy.* ひとつのキャンディー [AM 米国英語]

can|dy apple (**candy apples**) N-COUNT 可算名詞 A **candy apple** is an apple coated with hard red sugar syrup and fixed on a stick. りんごあめ [AM 米国英語]

candy cane (**candy canes**) N-COUNT 可算名詞 A **candy cane** is a stick of red and white candy with a curve at one end. つえの形をした紅白のあめ

cane /keɪn/ (**canes**) ❶ N-VAR 可変性名詞 **Cane** is used to refer to the long, hollow, hard stems of plants such as bamboo. Strips of cane are often used to make furniture, and some types of cane can be crushed and processed to make sugar. 茎, 籐(とう) ❏ *...cane furniture.* 籐家具 ❏ *...cane sugar.* かんしょ糖 ❷ N-COUNT 可算名詞 A **cane** is a long thin stick with a curved or round top which you can use to support yourself when you are walking, or which in the past was fashionable to carry with you. つえ ❏ *He wore a gray suit and leaned heavily on his cane.* 彼は灰色の背広を着て, ひどくつえにすがっていた.
→ see **disability, sugar**

ca|nine /keɪnaɪn/ ADJ 形容詞 **Canine** means relating to dogs. イ

Word Web cancer

The traditional **treatments** for **cancer** are **surgery**, **radiation therapy**, and chemotherapy. However, a new type of treatment called targeted therapy has emerged in the past few years. This treatment uses new drugs that target specific types of cancer cells. Targeted therapy also eliminates many of the **toxic** effects on healthy **tissue** that often result from traditional chemotherapy. One of these drugs helps prevent blood vessels that feed a tumor from growing. Another drug kills cancer cells.

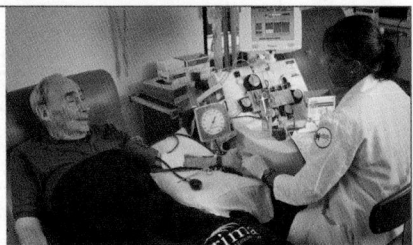

ヌ科の [ADJ n] ❑ ...*research into canine diseases.* 犬の病気の研究

can|is|ter /kǽnɪstər/ (**canisters**) **1** N-COUNT 可算名詞 A **canister** is a strong, metal container. It is used to hold gases or chemical substances. 丈夫な金属製容器 ❑ *Riot police hurled tear gas canisters and smoke bombs into the crowd.* 機動隊は催涙弾と発炎筒を群衆の中に投げ込んだ. **2** N-COUNT 可算名詞 A **canister** is a metal, plastic, or china container with a lid. It is used for storing food such as sugar and flour. 缶 ❑ ...*a canister of tea.* お茶の缶

can|na|bis /kǽnəbɪs/ N-UNCOUNT 不可算名詞 **Cannabis** is the hemp plant when it is used as a drug. 大麻 ❑ ...*cannabis smokers.* 大麻使用者

canned /kǽnd/ **1** ADJ 形容詞 **Canned** music, laughter, or applause on a television or radio program has been recorded beforehand and is added to the program to make it sound as if there is a live audience. 録音された [usu ADJ n] ❑ *However, the temptation is always there to add canned laughter in the editing.* しかし編集の際に録音された笑い声を使いたいという誘惑は常にある. **2** → see also **can**

can|ni|bal /kǽnɪbəl/ (**cannibals**) N-COUNT 可算名詞 **Cannibals** are people who eat the flesh of other human beings. 人食い人種 ❑ ...*a tropical island inhabited by cannibals.* 人食い人種の住む熱帯の島

can|ni|bal|ism /kǽnɪbəlɪzəm/ N-UNCOUNT 不可算名詞 If a group of people practice **cannibalism**, they eat the flesh of other people. 人食いの風習 ❑ *They were forced to practice cannibalism in order to survive.* 彼らは生き残るために人食いをすることを余儀なくされた.

can|non /kǽnən/ (**cannons**) **1** N-COUNT 可算名詞 A **cannon** is a large gun, usually on wheels, which used to be used in battles. 大砲 ❑ *The cannons boom, the band plays.* 大砲がとどろき, 楽団が演奏する. **2** N-COUNT 可算名詞 A **cannon** is a heavy automatic gun, especially one that is fired from an aircraft. 機関砲 ❑ *Others carried huge cannons plundered from Russian aircraft.* 他の者たちはロシアの航空機から略奪した巨大な機関砲を運んでいた. **3** PHRASE 句 If someone is a **loose cannon**, they do whatever they want and nobody can predict what they are going to do. 勝手で気まぐれな行動をする人 ❑ *Max is a loose cannon politically.* 政治の面ではマックスの言動は気ままで予測できない.

can|not /kǽnɒt, kənɒt/ **Cannot** is the negative form of **can**. can の否定形

ca|noe /kənúː/ (**canoes**) N-COUNT 可算名詞 A **canoe** is a small, narrow boat that you move through the water using a stick with a wide end called a paddle. カヌー, 丸木舟
→ see **boat**

can|on /kǽnən/ (**canons**) **1** N-COUNT 可算名詞 A **canon** is a member of the clergy who is on the staff of a cathedral. 司教座聖堂参事会員 **2** N-COUNT 可算名詞 A **canon** of texts is a list of them that is accepted as genuine or important. 真作品リスト [FORMAL 形式ばった] [oft N of n] ❑ ...*a canon of accepted literary texts.* 確立した文学作品のリスト ❑ ...*the Irish literary canon.* アイルランド文学の代表的作品

cano|py /kǽnəpi/ (**canopies**) **1** N-COUNT 可算名詞 A **canopy** is a decorated cover, often made of cloth, which is placed above something such as a bed or a seat. 天蓋 (てんがい) **2** N-COUNT 可算名詞 A **canopy** is a layer of something that spreads out and covers an area, for example the branches and leaves that spread out at the top of trees in a forest. 上部を覆うもの ❑ *The trees formed such a dense canopy that all beneath was a deep carpet of pine needles.* 木々が非常に密集した天蓋を形成していたので, その下にはずっと松葉のじゅうたんが広がっていた.
→ see **bed**

can't /kǽnt/ **Can't** is the usual spoken form of "cannot." 口語で用いられる cannot の短縮形

can|teen /kæntíːn/ (**canteens**) **1** N-COUNT 可算名詞 A **canteen** is a place in a factory or military base where meals or snacks are served to the people who work there. (工場, 基地などの) 食堂 ❑ *Rennie had eaten his supper in the canteen.* レニーは食堂で夕食を食べた. **2** N-COUNT 可算名詞 A **canteen** is a small metal or plastic bottle for carrying water and other drinks. Canteens are used by soldiers. 水筒 ❑ ...*a full canteen of water.* 水筒に満杯の水

can|ter /kǽntər/ (**canters, cantering, cantered**) V-I 自動詞 When a horse **canters**, it moves at a speed that is slower than a gallop but faster than a trot. 普通駆け足で駆ける ❑ *The competitors cantered into the arena to conclude the closing ceremony.* 出場選手たちが閉会式を締めくくるため普通駆け足で競技場に入ってきた. ● N-COUNT 可算名詞 **Canter** is also a noun. 普通駆け足 ❑ *Carnac set off at a canter.* カーナックは普通駆け足で出発した.

can|vas /kǽnvəs/ (**canvases**) **1** N-UNCOUNT 不可算名詞 **Canvas** is a strong, heavy cloth that is used for making things such as tents, sails, and bags. 帆布 ❑ ...*a canvas bag.* 帆布の鞄 **2** N-VAR 可変性名詞 A **canvas** is a piece of canvas or similar material on which an oil painting can be done. 画布, カンバス **3** N-COUNT 可算名詞 A **canvas** is a painting that has been done

on canvas. 油絵, カンバスに描いた絵 ❑ *The show includes canvases by masters like Carpaccio, Canaletto and Guardi.* 展覧会はカルパッチオ, カナレット, グアルディなどの巨匠の油彩画が入っている.
→ see **painting**

can|vass /kǽnvəs/ (**canvasses, canvassing, canvassed**) **1** V-I 自動詞 If you **canvass for** a particular person or political party, you go around an area trying to persuade people to vote for that person or party. 投票の依頼に回る ❑ *I'm canvassing for the Republican Party.* 私は共和党のために選挙運動をしている. **2** V-T 他動詞 If you **canvass** public opinion, you find out how people feel about a particular subject. (世論などを) 調査する ❑ *Members of Congress are spending the weekend canvassing opinion in their constituencies.* 国会議員は週末を自分の選挙区の世論の動向を調べるのに費やしている.

can|yon /kǽnyən/ (**canyons**) N-COUNT 可算名詞, N-IN-NAMES 名称中の名詞 A **canyon** is a long, narrow valley with very steep sides. 渓谷 ❑ ...*the Grand Canyon.* グランドキャニオン

cap /kǽp/ (**caps, capping, capped**) **1** N-COUNT 可算名詞 A **cap** is a soft, flat hat with a curved part at the front which is called a visor. (縁なしの) 帽子 ❑ ...*a dark blue baseball cap.* 紺の野球帽 **2** N-COUNT 可算名詞 A **cap** is a special hat which is worn as part of a uniform. 制帽 ❑ ...*a border guard in olive gray uniform and a cap.* 灰色がかった薄緑の制服と制帽に身を包んだ国境警備隊員 **3** N-COUNT 可算名詞 The **cap** of a bottle is its lid. ふた ❑ *She unscrewed the cap of her water bottle and gave him a drink.* 彼女は自分の水筒のふたを開け, 彼に飲ませた. **4** V-T 他動詞 If someone says that a good or bad event **caps** a series of events, they mean it is the final event in the series, and the other events were also good or bad. 締めくくる [JOURNALISM ジャーナリズム] ❑ *The unrest capped a weekend of right-wing attacks on foreigners.* 右翼による外国人襲撃で始まった週末は最後には不穏な情勢になった.

ca|pa|bil|ity /kéɪpəbɪ́lɪti/ (**capabilities**) **1** N-VAR 可変性名詞 If you have the **capability** or the **capabilities** to do something, you have the ability or the qualities that are necessary to do it. 能力 ❑ *People experience differences in physical and mental capability depending on the time of day.* 人は肉体的あるいは精神的能力が1日の時間帯によって違うことを経験する. **2** N-VAR 可変性名詞 A country's military **capability** is its ability to fight in a war. 軍力 ❑ *Their military capability has gone down because their air force has proved not to be an effective force.* 空軍がそれほど有力でないことが証明されたので, 彼らの軍事力は低下した.

Do not confuse **capability** with **ability** and **capacity**. A person's **capability** is the amount of work they can do and how well they can do it. ❑ ...*a job that was beyond the capability of one man. ...the director's ideas of the capability of the actor.* You often use **ability** to say that someone can do something well. ❑ *He had remarkable ability as a musician. ...the ability to bear hardship.* If someone has a particular **capacity**, a **capacity** for something, or a **capacity** to do something, they have the qualities required to do it. **Capacity** is a more formal word than **ability**. ❑ ...*their capacity for hard work. ...his capacity to see the other person's point of view.*

ca|pable /kéɪpəbəl/ **1** ADJ 形容詞 If a person or thing is **capable of** doing something, they have the ability to do it. 能力がある [v-link ADJ "of" -ing/n] ❑ *He appeared hardly capable of conducting a coherent conversation.* 彼は筋の通った会話をすることがほとんどできないように見えた. ❑ *The kitchen is capable of serving several hundred people.* その厨房 (ちゅうぼう) は数百人の食事を用意することができる. **2** ADJ 形容詞 Someone who is **capable** has the skill or qualities necessary to do a particular thing well, or is able to do most things well. 有能な ❑ *She's a very capable speaker.* 彼女はとても話すのがうまい. ● **ca|pably** /kéɪpəbli/ ADV 副詞 [ADV with v] 有能に ❑ *It was all dealt with very capably by the police and security people.* それはすべて警察と警備員によってとてもうまく処理された.

Note that **capable** and **able** are both used to say that someone can do something. When you say that someone is **able** to do something, you mean that they can do it either because of their knowledge or skill, or because it is possible. ❑ *He wondered if he would be able to climb over the rail... They were able to use their profits for new investments.* Note that if you use a past tense, you are saying that someone has actually done something. ❑ *We were able to reduce costs.* When you say that someone is **capable** of doing something, you mean either that they have the knowledge and skill to do it, or that they are likely to do it. ❑ *The workers are perfectly capable of running the organization themselves... She was quite capable of falling asleep.* You can say that someone is **capable of** a particular feeling or action. ❑ *He's capable of loyalty... Bowman could not believe him capable of murder.* You can also use **capable of** when talking about what something such as a car or machine can do. ❑ *The car was capable of 110 miles per hour.* If you describe someone as **able** or **capable**, you mean that they do things well. ❑ *He's certainly a capable gardener.*

Thesaurus *capable* また次を参照：

ADJ. able, competent, skillful, talented; (ant.) incapable, incompetent ②

ca|pac|ity /kəpæsɪti/ (capacities) ■ N-VAR 可変性名詞 Your **capacity for** something is your ability to do it, or the amount of it that you are able to do. 能力，容量 ❑ *Our capacity for giving care, love, and attention is limited.* 相手を思いやり，愛し，気づかうための我々の能力には限界がある。❑ *Her mental capacity and temperament are as remarkable as his.* 彼女の精神的能力および気性は彼と同じくらい素晴らしい。

> Do not confuse **capacity** with **ability** and **capability**. If someone has a particular **capacity**, a **capacity** for something, or a **capacity** to do something, they have the qualities required to do it. **Capacity** is a more formal word than **ability**. ❑ *...their capacity for hard work. ...his capacity to see the other person's point of view.* You often use **ability** to say that someone can do something well. ❑ *He had remarkable ability as a musician. ...the ability to bear hardship.* A person's **capability** is the amount of work they can do and how well they can do it. ❑ *...a job that was beyond the capability of one man. ...the director's ideas of the capability of the actor.*

② N-VAR 可変性名詞 The **capacity** of a container is its volume, or the amount of liquid it can hold, measured in units such as quarts or gallons. 容量 ❑ *...containers with a maximum capacity of 200 gallons of water.* 最大200ガロンの水を貯蔵する容量を備えた容器 ③ N-UNCOUNT 不可算名詞 The **capacity** of something such as a factory, industry, or region is the quantity of things that it can produce or deliver with the equipment or resources that are available. 生産能力 ❑ *...the amount of spare capacity in the economy.* その経済圏での予備生産能力の総量 ❑ *Bread factories are working at full capacity.* パン工場は最大生産能力で稼動している。④ N-COUNT 可算名詞 The **capacity** of a piece of equipment is its size or power, often measured in particular units. 能力 ❑ *...an aircraft with a bomb-carrying capacity of 1000 pounds.* 1000ポンドの爆弾搭載能力を備えた航空機 ⑤ N-COUNT 可算名詞 If you do something **in a** particular **capacity**, you do it as part of a particular job or duty, or because you are representing a particular organization or person. 資格 [WRITTEN 書き言葉] ❑ *Ms. Halliwell visited the Philippines in her capacity as a Special Representative of UNICEF.* ハリウェルさんはユニセフの特別代表の立場でフィリピンを訪問した。⑥ N-SING 単数名詞 The **capacity** of a building, place, or vehicle is the number of people or things that it can hold. 収容能力 [also no det, oft "to" N] ❑ *Each stadium had a seating capacity of about 50,000.* それぞれの競技場が5万人の観客収容能力を持っていた。⑦ ADJ 形容詞 A **capacity** crowd or audience completely fills a theater, sports stadium, or other place. 収容力いっぱいの，満員の [ADJ n] ❑ *A capacity crowd of 76,000 people was at the stadium for the event.* 満員の7万6千人がこの催しのため競技場に詰めかけていた。

cape /keɪp/ (capes) ■ N-COUNT; N-IN-NAMES 可算名詞，名称中の名詞 A **cape** is a large piece of land that sticks out into the sea from the coast. 岬 ❑ *Naomi James became the first woman to sail solo around the world via Cape Horn.* ナオミ・ジェームズはケープ岬経由で単独世界一周航海を果たした最初の女性となった。② N-COUNT 可算名詞 A **cape** is a short cloak. 婦人用の袖なしの外とう ❑ *...a woolen cape.* ウールのケープ

Word Link cap ≈ head : capital, capitulate, captain

capi|tal /kæpɪtᵊl/ (capitals) ■ N-UNCOUNT 不可算名詞 **Capital** is a large sum of money which you use to start a business, or which you invest in order to make money. 資金 [BUSINESS 実業] ❑ *Companies are having difficulty in raising capital.* 会社は資金調達難に陥っている。② N-UNCOUNT 不可算名詞 You can use **capital** to refer to buildings or machinery which are necessary to produce goods or to make companies more efficient, but which do not make money directly. 資本 [BUSINESS 実業] ❑ *...capital equipment that could have served to increase production.* 生産量を増やすのに役立つはずだった資本設備 ③ N-UNCOUNT 不可算名詞 **Capital** is the part of an amount of money borrowed or invested which does not include interest. 元本 [BUSINESS 実業] ❑ *With a conventional mortgage, the payments consist of both capital and interest.* 通常の住宅ローンでは，支払いは元本と利息の両方となっている。④ N-COUNT 可算名詞 The **capital** of a country is the city or town where its government or legislature meets. 首都 ❑ *...Kathmandu, the capital of Nepal.* ネパールの首都のカトマンドゥー ⑤ N-COUNT 可算名詞 If a place is **the capital** of a particular industry or activity, it is the place that is most famous for it, because it happens in that place more than anywhere else. 中心地 ❑ *Colmar has long been considered the capital of the wine trade.* 長年にわたり，コルマールはワイン取引の中心地と見なされてきた。⑥ N-COUNT 可算名詞 **Capitals** or **capital letters** are written or printed letters in the form which is

used at the beginning of sentences or names. "T," "B," and "F" are capitals. 大文字 ❑ *The name and address are written in capitals.* 名前と住所は大文字で書かれる。

> Note that you must always use a capital letter with days of the week, months of the year, and festivals. ❑ *...on Monday the 13th of January. ...at Christmas.* Names of seasons, however, usually begin with a small letter. ❑ *...in spring.* Capitals must also be used with the names of countries and other places, as well with the adjectives and nouns derived from them, such as those which refer to their inhabitants or languages. ❑ *...in Portugal. ...the Swiss police. ...thousands of Germans... He spoke fluent Arabic.*

⑦ ADJ 形容詞 A **capital** offense is one that is so serious that the person who commits it can be punished by death. 極刑の [ADJ n] ❑ *Espionage is a capital offense in this country.* この国ではスパイ行為は極刑に値する罪である。⑧ PHRASE 句 If you say that someone **is making capital out of** a situation, you disapprove of the way they are gaining an advantage for themselves through other people's efforts or bad luck. つけこむ [FORMAL 形式ばった, DISAPPROVAL 不賛成] ❑ *He rebuked the president for trying to make political capital out of the hostage situation.* 人質の状況を政治的に利用しようとしたとして，彼は大統領を非難した。⑨ → see also **working capital**
→ see **city, country, economics, stock market**

capi|tal ac|count (capital accounts) ■ N-COUNT 可算名詞 A country's **capital account** is the part of its balance of payments that is concerned with the movement of capital. 資本勘定 ❑ *...restrictions that affect the capital account of a country's balance of payments.* 国家の国際収支の資本勘定に影響を及ぼす制約 ② N-COUNT 可算名詞 A **capital account** is a financial statement showing the capital value of a company on a particular date. 資本勘定 [BUSINESS 実業] ❑ *No business can survive without a capital account.* 資本勘定なきでやっていける企業はない。

capi|tal gains N-PLURAL 複数名詞 **Capital gains** are the profits that you make when you buy something and then sell it again at a higher price. 資本利得 [BUSINESS 実業] ❑ *He called for the reform of capital gains tax.* 彼は資本利得税の改革を要求した。

capi|tal goods N-PLURAL 複数名詞 **Capital goods** are used to make other products. Compare **consumer goods**. 資本財 [BUSINESS 実業] ❑ *Most imports into Korea are raw materials and capital goods.* 韓国のたいていの輸入品は，原材料および資本財である。

capital-intensive ADJ 形容詞 **Capital-intensive** industries and businesses need the investment of large sums of money. Compare **labor-intensive**. 資本集約的な [BUSINESS 実業] ❑ *...highly capital-intensive industries like auto manufacturing or petrochemicals.* 自動車製造や石油化学産業のように高度に資本集約的な産業

capi|tal|ise /kæpɪtᵊlaɪz/ → see **capitalize**

capi|tal|ism /kæpɪtᵊlɪzəm/ N-UNCOUNT 不可算名詞 **Capitalism** is an economic and political system in which property, business, and industry are owned by private individuals and not by the state. 資本主義 ❑ *...the two fundamentally opposed social systems, capitalism and socialism.* 資本主義と社会主義という2つの根本的に対立する社会制度

capi|tal|ist /kæpɪtᵊlɪst/ (capitalists) ■ ADJ 形容詞 A **capitalist** country or system supports or is based on the principles of capitalism. 資本家 ❑ *China has pledged to retain Hong Kong's capitalist system for 50 years.* 中国は香港の資本主義体制を50年間維持することを誓約している。② N-COUNT 可算名詞 A **capitalist** is someone who believes in and supports the principles of capitalism. 資本主義者 ❑ *Lenin had hoped to even have a working relationship with the capitalists.* レーニンは資本主義者と共に働く関係を築くことすら希望していた。③ N-COUNT 可算名詞 A **capitalist** is someone who owns a business which they run in order to make a profit for themselves. 資本家 ❑ *They argue that only private capitalists can remake Poland's economy.* 彼らは民間の資本家のみがポーランド経済を再建できると主張している。

capi|tal|ize /kæpɪtᵊlaɪz/ (capitalizes, capitalizing, capitalized) ■ V-I 自動詞 If you **capitalize on** a situation, you use it to gain some advantage for yourself. つけ込む ❑ *The rebels seem to be trying to capitalize on the public's discontent with the government.* 反体制派は政府に対する国民の不満に乗じようとしているようだ。② V-T 他動詞 In business, if you **capitalize** something that belongs to you, you sell it in order to make money. 資本化する [BUSINESS 実業] ❑ *Our intention is to capitalize the company by any means we can.* 何としてもその会社を売却して資金を得るつもりだ。③ V-T 他動詞 If you **capitalize** a letter, you write it as a capital letter. If you **capitalize** a word, you spell it in capital letters, or with the first letter as a capital letter. 大文字にする；大文字で始める ❑ *Capitalize all proper nouns but not the articles (a, an) that precede them.* 固有名詞はすべて大文字で始めるが，その前に来る冠詞(a，an)は大文字にしないこと。

capi|tal pun|ish|ment N-UNCOUNT 不可算名詞 **Capital punishment** is punishment which involves the legal killing of a

person who has committed a serious crime such as murder. 極刑, 死刑 □*Most democracies have abolished capital punishment.* 民主国家の ほとんどが死刑を廃止している.

ca|pitu|late /kəpɪtʃəleɪt/ (**capitulates, capitulating, capitulated**) V-I 自動詞 If you **capitulate**, you stop resisting and do what someone else wants you to do. 降伏する, 抵抗をやめる □*The club eventually capitulated and now grants equal rights to women.* クラブはようやく要求を受け入れ今では女性にも同じ権利を与えている.

cap|size /kæpsaɪz/ (**capsizes, capsizing, capsized**) V-T/V-I 他 動詞/自動詞 If you **capsize** a boat or if it **capsizes**, it turns upside down in the water. 転覆させる[他動詞], 転覆する[自動詞] □*The sea got very rough and the boat capsized.* 海が大荒れになって船は転覆した.

cap|sule /kæps³l/ (**capsules**) **1** N-COUNT 可算名詞 A **capsule** is a very small tube containing powdered or liquid medicine, which you swallow. カプセル剤 □*...cod liver oil capsules.* タラ肝油カプセル. **2** N-COUNT 可算名詞 A **capsule** is a small container with a drug or other substance inside it, which is used for medical or scientific purposes. 小型の容器 □*They first implanted capsules into the animals' brains.* まず動物の脳にカプセルを埋め込んだ. **3** N-COUNT 可算名詞 A space **capsule** is the part of a spacecraft in which people travel, and which often separates from the main rocket. 宇宙カプセル □*A Russian space capsule is currently orbiting the Earth.* ロシアの宇宙カプセルは現在地球を周回中である. **4** N-COUNT 可算名詞 A time **capsule** is a container into which people put typical everyday objects from their lives. The container is buried so that people in the future can dig it up, and find out about what life was like in the past. タイムカプセル □*Twenty-five years ago they filled a time capsule and buried it.* 25年前にタイムカプセルを作って埋めたんだ.

cap|tain /kæptɪn/ (**captains, captaining, captained**) **1** N-TITLE; N-COUNT; N-VOC 称号名詞, 可算名詞, 呼格名詞 In the army, navy, and some other armed forces, a **captain** is an officer of middle rank. (陸空軍の) 大尉; (海軍の) 大佐 □*...Captain Mark Phillips.* マーク・フィリップス大尉. □*...a captain in the army.* 陸軍大尉. **2** N-COUNT 可算名詞 The **captain of** a sports team is the player in charge of it. キャプテン, 主将 □*...Mickey Thomas, the captain of the tennis team.* テニスチームの主将ミッキー・トマス. **3** N-COUNT 可算名詞 The **captain** of a ship is the sailor in charge of it. 船長 □*...the captain of an excursion boat.* 遊覧船の船長. **4** N-COUNT; N-TITLE 可算名詞, 称号名詞 The **captain** of an airplane is the pilot in charge of it. 機長 **5** N-COUNT; N-TITLE 可算名詞, 称号名詞 In the United States and some other countries, a **captain** is a police officer or firefighter of fairly senior rank. 警部; (消防署の) 分署長 □*...a former Honolulu police captain.* ホノルル警察の元警部. **6** V-T 他動詞 If you **captain** a team or a ship, you are the captain of it. キャプテンを務める; 船長を務める □*He captained the winning team in 1991.* 彼は1991年の優勝チームのキャプテンだった.
→ see **boat, ship**

cap|tain|cy /kæptɪnsi/ N-UNCOUNT 不可算名詞 The **captaincy** of a team is the position of being captain. キャプテンの地位 □*His captaincy of the team was ended by mild eye trouble.* 軽い目の不調に見舞われ彼はチームの主将の地位を退いた.

cap|tion /kæpʃ³n/ (**captions**) N-COUNT 可算名詞 A **caption** is the words printed underneath a picture or cartoon which explain what it is about. 説明 □*The local paper featured me standing on a stepladder with a caption, "Wendy climbs the ladder to success."* 地元紙は脚立にあがっている私の写真を取り上げて, それを「成功の階段をのぼるウェンディー」と銘打った.

cap|ti|vate /kæptɪveɪt/ (**captivates, captivating, captivated**) V-T 他動詞 If you **are captivated** by someone or something, you

find them fascinating and attractive. とりこになる, 心を奪われる [usu passive] □*I was captivated by her brilliant mind.* 彼女の頭のよさにほれぼれした.

cap|tive /kæptɪv/ (**captives**) **1** ADJ 形容詞 A **captive** person or animal is being kept imprisoned or enclosed. 捕らわれの [LITERARY 文語的] □*Her heart had begun to pound inside her chest like a captive animal.* 捕らえられた動物のように, 彼女の心臓は胸の中で高鳴り始めていた. ● N-COUNT 可算名詞 A **captive** is someone who is captive. 捕虜 □*He described the difficulties of surviving for four months as a captive.* 彼は4ヵ月にわたる過酷な捕虜生活について語った. **2** ADJ 形容詞 A **captive** audience is a group of people who are not free to leave a certain place and so have to watch or listen. A **captive** market is a group of people who cannot choose whether or where to buy things. 嫌が上でも開かされる聴衆; 特定の商品を買うしかない消費者 [ADJ n] □*We all performed action songs, sketches, and dances before a captive audience of parents and patrons.* 私達みんなが歌ったり劇をしたり踊ったりするのを両親や保護者たちはじっと見ていてくれた. **3** PHRASE 句 If you **take** someone **captive** or **hold** someone **captive**, you take or keep them as a prisoner. 捕虜にする □*Richard was finally released on February 4, one year and six weeks after he'd been taken captive.* リチャードは2月4日にようやく解放された. 捕虜となって1年6週間後のことだった.

cap|tiv|ity /kæptɪvɪti/ N-UNCOUNT 不可算名詞 **Captivity** is the state of being kept imprisoned or enclosed. 監禁状態 □*The great majority of barn owls are reared in captivity.* メンフクロウは大半がケージで飼育されている.

cap|ture /kæptʃər/ (**captures, capturing, captured**) **1** V-T 他動詞 If you **capture** someone or something, you catch them, especially in a war. 捕虜にする; 占領する □*The guerrillas shot down one airplane and captured the pilot.* ゲリラ軍は飛行機を一機撃墜しパイロットを捕虜にした. □*The Russians now appear ready to capture more territory from the Chechens.* ロシア軍はチェチェンの領土をさらに攻略する勢いだ. ● N-UNCOUNT 不可算名詞 **Capture** is also a noun. 占領 □*...the final battles which led to the army's capture of the town.* 陸軍がその町を占領することになった最後の戦い. **2** V-T 他動詞 If something or someone **captures** a particular quality, feeling, or atmosphere, they represent or express it successfully. 見事に表す [no cont] □*Chef Idris Caldora offers an inspired menu that captures the spirit of the Mediterranean.* コック長イドリス・カルドラが作る料理は地中海人の気質を見事に表現している. **3** V-T 他動詞 If something **captures** your attention or imagination, you begin to be interested or excited by it. If someone or something **captures** your heart, you begin to love them or like them very much. 引きつける; 心を捉える □*...the great names of the past who usually capture the historian's attention.* たいていの歴史家が関心を抱く過去の偉人たち. **4** V-T 他動詞 If an event **is captured** in a photograph or on film, it is photographed or filmed. 撮影される [usu passive] □*The incident was captured on videotape.* その事件はビデオに撮られていました.

car /kɑr/ (**cars**) **1** N-COUNT 可算名詞 A **car** is a motor vehicle with room for a small number of passengers. 自動車, 乗用車 [also "by" N] □*He had left his tickets in his car.* 彼は切符を車に置き忘れていた. **2** N-COUNT 可算名詞 A **car** is one of the separate, long sections of a train that carries passengers. 車両 [mainly AM 主に米国英語] □*The company manufactured elegant railroad cars.* この会社は豪華な車両を製造していた. **3** N-COUNT 可算名詞 The separate sections of a train are called **cars** when they are used for a particular purpose. 一車 □*He made his way into the dining car for breakfast.* 彼は朝食をとろうと食堂車に向かった.
→ see Word Web: **car**
→ see **train, transportation**

The first mass-produced **automobile** in the U.S. was the Model T. In 1909, Ford sold over 10,000 of these **vehicles**. They all had the same basic **engine** and **chassis**. For years the only color choice was black. Three different bodies were available—roadster, **sedan**, and coupe. Today manufacturers offer many more options. These include **convertibles, sports cars, station wagons, vans, pickups,** and **SUVs**. Laws now require devices such as **seat belts** and **airbags** to make **driving** safer. Some car makers now offer **hybrid** vehicles. They combine an electrical engine with an **internal combustion engine** to improve **fuel** economy.

car alarm (car alarms) N-COUNT 可算名詞 A **car alarm** is a device in a car which makes a loud noise if anyone tries to break into the vehicle. 自動車盗難警報装置 ❑ He returned to the airport to find his car alarm going off. 空港に戻ると車の警報装置が鳴っていた.

cara|mel /kærəmɛl, -məl, kɑrməl/ (caramels) **1** N-VAR 可変性名詞 A **caramel** is a chewy sweet food made from sugar, butter, and milk. キャラメル **2** N-UNCOUNT 不可算名詞 **Caramel** is burnt sugar used for coloring and flavoring food. カラメル

car|at /kærət/ (carats) **1** N-COUNT 可算名詞 A **carat** is a unit for measuring the weight of diamonds and other precious stones. It is equal to 0.2 grams. カラット（宝石類の重さの単位）❑ The gemstone is 28.6 millimeters high and weighs 139.43 carats. その原石は28.6ミリの大きさで139.43カラットの重さがある. **2** COMB IN ADJ 形容詞の複合 **Carat** is the same as **karat**. カラット（金の純度の単位）[BRIT 英国英語]
→ see **diamond**

cara|van /kærəvæn/ (caravans) **1** N-COUNT 可算名詞 A **caravan** is a group of people and animals or vehicles who travel together. 隊商、キャラバン ❑ ...the old caravan routes from Central Asia to China. 中央アジアから中国に至る古くからの隊商ルート. **2** N-COUNT 可算名詞 A **caravan** is the same as a **trailer**. トレーラーハウス [BRIT 英国英語] → see **trailer 2**

cara|van site (caravan sites) N-COUNT 可算名詞 A **caravan site** is the same as a **trailer park**. トレーラーハウス駐車区域 [BRIT 英国英語]

car|bo|hy|drate /kɑrbouhaɪdreɪt/ (carbohydrates) N-VAR 可変性名詞 **Carbohydrates** are substances, found in certain kinds of food, that provide you with energy. Foods such as sugar and bread that contain these substances can also be referred to as **carbohydrates**. 炭水化物 ❑ ...carbohydrates such as bread, pasta, or potatoes. パンやパスタやジャガイモなどの炭水化物.
→ see **calorie, diet**

car|bon /kɑrbən/ N-UNCOUNT 不可算名詞 **Carbon** is a chemical element that diamonds and coal are made up of. 炭素
→ see **diamond**

car|bon|at|ed /kɑrbəneɪtɪd/ ADJ 形容詞 **Carbonated** drinks are drinks that contain small bubbles of carbon dioxide. 炭酸入りの [usu ADJ n] ❑ ...colas and other carbonated soft drinks. コーラなどの炭酸飲料.

car|bon di|ox|ide /kɑrbən daɪɒksaɪd/ N-UNCOUNT 不可算名詞 **Carbon dioxide** is a gas. It is produced by animals and people breathing out, and by chemical reactions. 二酸化炭素
→ see **air, dry-cleaning, greenhouse, respiratory**

car|bon mon|ox|ide /kɑrbən mənɒksaɪd/ N-UNCOUNT 不可算名詞 **Carbon monoxide** is a poisonous gas that is produced especially by the engines of vehicles. 一酸化炭素 ❑ The limit for carbon monoxide is 4.5 per cent of the exhaust gas. 排気ガス中の一酸化炭素の許容限度は4.5%となっている.

car|cass /kɑrkəs/ (carcasses) N-COUNT 可算名詞 A **carcass** is the body of a dead animal. 死骸 ❑ A cluster of vultures crouched on the carcass of a dead buffalo. ハゲワシが水牛の死骸に群がっていた.

card /kɑrd/ (cards) **1** N-COUNT 可算名詞 A **card** is a piece of stiff paper or thin cardboard on which something is written or printed. 札、券 ❑ Check the numbers below against the numbers on your card. 下記の番号とお手持ちの札の番号を照合してください. **2** N-COUNT 可算名詞 A **card** is a piece of cardboard or plastic, or a small document, which shows information about you and which you carry with you, for example to prove your identity. カード ❑ ...they check my bag and press card. 彼らはかばんと取材許可証を調べる. ❑ ...her membership card. 彼女の会員券. **3** N-COUNT 可算名詞 A **card** is a rectangular piece of plastic, issued by a bank, company, or store, which you can use to buy things or obtain money. キャッシュカード、クレジットカード ❑ He paid the whole bill with an American Express card. 彼は勘定をすべてアメリカンエキスプレスカードで支払った. **4** N-COUNT 可算名詞 A **card** is a folded piece of stiff paper with a picture and sometimes a message printed on it, which you send to someone on a special occasion. （お祝いなどの）カード ❑ She sends me a card on my birthday. 誕生日になると彼女はカードを送ってきます. **5** N-COUNT 可算名詞 A **card** is the same as a **postcard**. はがき ❑ Send your details on a card to the following address. 詳細を書いて以下のあて先までお送りください. **6** N-COUNT 可算名詞 A **card** is a piece of thin cardboard carried by someone such as a businessperson in order to give it to other people. A card shows the name, address, telephone number, and other details of the person who carries it. 名刺 [BUSINESS 実業] ❑ Here's my card. You may need me. 私、こういう者です. 今後ともよろしくお願いします. **7** N-COUNT 可算名詞 **Cards** are thin pieces of cardboard with numbers or pictures printed on them which are used to play various games. トランプ ❑ ...a deck of cards. トランプ一組. **8** N-UNCOUNT 不可算名詞 If you are playing **cards**, you are playing a game using cards. トランプをす

る ❑ They enjoy themselves drinking wine, smoking, and playing cards. 彼らの楽しみはワインを飲んだりたばこを吸ったりトランプをしたりすることだ. **9** N-UNCOUNT 不可算名詞 **Card** is strong, stiff paper or thin cardboard. 厚紙 ❑ She put the pieces of card in her pocket. 彼女は切った厚紙をポケットに入れた. **10** → see also **bank card, business card, calling card, credit card, debit card, gold card, greeting card, identity card, playing card, smart card, wild card** **11** PHRASE 句 If you say that something is **in the cards**, you mean that it is very likely to happen. 多分ありそうな ❑ Last summer she began telling friends that a New Year marriage was in the cards. 年が明けたら多分結婚すると、彼女は去年の夏から友達に話し始めた. **12** PHRASE 句 If you **have** your **cards read**, you have your fortune told by someone who uses playing cards or tarot cards to tell you about yourself and predict your future. トランプやタロットで占ってもらう ❑ The shop had a sign in the window: "Have your cards read here, $25." 店の窓には「タロット占い. 1回25ドル」という看板がさがっていた.

card|board /kɑrdbɔrd/ N-UNCOUNT 不可算名詞 **Cardboard** is thick, stiff paper that is used, for example, to make boxes and models. 段ボール ❑ ...a cardboard box. 段ボール箱.

car|di|ac /kɑrdiæk/ ADJ 形容詞 **Cardiac** means relating to the heart. 心臓の [MEDICAL 医学の] [ADJ n] ❑ The man was suffering from cardiac weakness. その人は心臓が弱っていた.
→ see **muscle**

car|di|gan /kɑrdɪgən/ (cardigans) N-COUNT 可算名詞 A **cardigan** is a knitted woolen sweater that you can fasten at the front with buttons or a zipper. カーディガン

car|di|nal /kɑrdɪnəl/ (cardinals) **1** N-COUNT; N-TITLE 可算名詞、称号名詞 A **cardinal** is a high-ranking priest in the Catholic church. 枢機卿（すうききょう）❑ In 1448, Nicholas was appointed a cardinal. 1448年ニコラスは枢機卿に任命された. **2** ADJ 形容詞 A **cardinal** rule or quality is the one that is considered to be the most important. 最も重要な [FORMAL 形式ばった] [ADJ n] ❑ As a salesman, your cardinal rule is to do everything you can to satisfy a customer. 販売員として最も大切なことはお客様に満足していただけるように最大限の努力をすることです. **3** N-COUNT 可算名詞 A **cardinal** is a common North American bird. The male has bright red feathers. ショウジョウコウカンチョウ

card in|dex (card indexes) N-COUNT 可算名詞 A **card index** is a number of cards with information written on them which are arranged in a particular order, usually alphabetical, so that you can find the information you want easily. カードファイル ❑ Then he turned to the card index and tore out the entry for Matthew Holmwood. それから彼はカードホルダーを調べ、そこからマシュー・ホルムウッドのカードを引きちぎった.

care /kɛər/ (cares, caring, cared) **1** V-T/V-I 他動詞/自動詞 If you **care** about something, you feel that it is important and are concerned about it. 大切だと思う、心配する [no cont] ❑ ...a company that cares about the environment. 環境に配慮している会社. ❑ ...young men who did not care whether they lived or died. 生きてても しょうがないと感じていた若者たち. **2** V-I 自動詞 If you **care for** someone, you feel a lot of affection for them. 好む [APPROVAL 賛成] [no cont] ❑ He wanted me to know that he still cared for me. 彼は私のことが今でも好きだということを分かってほしいと思っている.
● **caring** N-UNCOUNT 不可算名詞 優しさ ❑ ...the "feminine" traits of caring and compassion. 優しさや思いやりといった女性らしさに結びつけられる特徴. **3** V-I 自動詞 If you **care for** someone or something, you look after them and keep them in a good state or condition. 世話する；監督する ❑ They hired a nurse to care for her. 彼らは看護婦を雇って彼女の世話をさせた. ❑ ...these distinctive cars, lovingly cared for by private owners. 所有者の愛情が注がれたこれらの風変わりな車. ● N-UNCOUNT 不可算名詞 **Care** is also a noun. 世話 ❑ Most of the staff specialize in the care of children. 職員のほとんどが育児を専門としている. ❑ ...sensitive teeth which need special care. 特に注意が必要な悪くなりやすい歯. **4** V-T/V-I 他動詞/自動詞 [no cont] You can ask someone if they would **care for** something or if they would **care to** do something as a polite way of asking if they would like to have or do something. いかがですか [POLITENESS 丁寧さ] ❑ Would you care for some orange juice? オレンジジュースはいかがですか. **5** N-UNCOUNT 不可算名詞 If you do something **with care**, you give careful attention to it because you do not want to make any mistakes or cause any damage. 注意して ❑ Condoms are an effective method of birth control if used with care. 注意して使いさえすれば、コンドームは効果的な避妊法である. **6** N-COUNT 可算名詞 Your **cares** are your worries, anxieties, or fears. 心配 ❑ Lean back in a hot bath and forget all the cares of the day. 温かいお風呂にゆっくり入って一日の疲れを癒しましょう. **7** → see also **caring, day care, intensive care** **8** PHRASE 句 You can use **for all I care** to emphasize that it does not matter at all to you what someone does. ～にはどうでもいいことだ [EMPHASIS 強調] ❑ You can go right now for all I care. 今すぐ行けばよい. こっちはちっともかまやしないさ. **9** PHRASE 句 If you say that you **couldn't care less about** someone or something, you are emphasizing that you are not interested in them or worried

about them. You can also say that you **could care less**, with the same meaning. 少しも気にしない[EMPHASIS 強調] ❑ I couldn't care less about the woman. あんな女のことなどどうでもいい。 ❑ I don't care if they respect me. I could care less. 彼らから尊敬されているかなんてかまやしないさ。知ったことか。 ⑩ PHRASE 句 If someone sends you a letter or package **care of** or **in care of** a particular person or place, they send it to that person or place, and it is then passed on to you. 一気付、一方 ❑ Please write to me care of the publishers. 手紙は出版社宛にてお願いします。 ❑ He wrote to me in care of my publisher. 彼は勤務先の出版社のほうに便りをくれた。 ⑪ PHRASE 句 If you **take care of** someone or something, you look after them and prevent them from being harmed or damaged. 世話をする; 監督する ❑ There was no one else to take care of their children. ほかには誰も子供たちの世話をする者がいなかったのです。 ⑫ PHRASE 句 If you **take care to** do something, you make sure that you do it. 気をつける ❑ Foley followed Albert through the gate, taking care to close the latch. フォーリーはアルバートの後から門を出るときちんと掛け金をかけておいた。 ⑬ PHRASE 句 To **take care of** a problem, task, or situation means to deal with it. 対処する ❑ They leave it to the system to try and take care of the problem. 彼らはこの問題の対処を部署のほうに任せている。 ⑭ PHRASE 句 You can say "**Who cares?**" to emphasize that something does not matter to you at all. 誰がかまうものか [EMPHASIS 強調] ❑ "But we might ruin the stove." — "Who cares?" 「でもコンロがつぶれるかもよ」「かまやしないよ」

Word Partnership care は次の語句と使われる:

| ADJ. | good care, loving care ③ |
| V. | provide care, receive care ③ |

ca|reer /kərɪər/ (careers, careering, careered) ❶ N-COUNT 可算名詞 A **career** is the job or profession that someone does for a long period of their life. 一生の仕事 ❑ She is now concentrating on a career as a fashion designer. 彼女は今ファッションデザイナーとしての仕事に打ち込んでいる。 ❑ ...a career in journalism. ジャーナリズムでの経験。 ❷ N-COUNT 可算名詞 Your **career** is the part of your life that you spend working. 現役時代 ❑ During his career, he wrote more than fifty plays. 彼がその生涯に書いた戯曲は50作品を超える。 ❸ ADJ 形容詞 **Career** advice or guidance consists of information about different jobs and help with deciding what kind of job you want to do. 就職に関する [ADJ n] ❑ She received very little career guidance when young. 若いころ彼女は就職指導をほとんど受けなかった。 ❹ V-I 自動詞 If a person or vehicle **careers** somewhere, they move fast and in an uncontrolled way. 暴走する [oft cont] ❑ His car careered into a river. 車は暴走して川に突っ込んだ。

Thesaurus career また次を参照:

| N. | field, job, profession, specialty, vocation, work ① |

Word Partnership career は次の語句と使われる:

N.	career advancement, career goals, career opportunities, career path ① ②
ADJ.	political career, professional career ① ②
V.	pursue a career ① ②

ca|reer wom|an (career women) N-COUNT 可算名詞 A **career woman** is a woman with a career who is interested in working and progressing in her job, rather than staying at home taking care of the house and children. キャリアウーマン

Word Link free ≈ without : care**free**, duty-**free**, tax-**free**

care|free /kɛərfri/ ADJ 形容詞 A **carefree** person or period of time doesn't have or involve any problems, worries, or responsibilities. のんきな; 気ままな ❑ Chantal remembered carefree summers at the beach. シャンタルは浜辺で過ごした気ままな夏のことを思い出した。

Word Link ful ≈ filled with : beauti**ful**, care**ful**, dread**ful**

care|ful /kɛərfəl/ ❶ ADJ 形容詞 If you are **careful**, you give serious attention to what you are doing, in order to avoid harm, damage, or mistakes. If you are **careful to** do something, you make sure that you do it. 気をつける ❑ Be very careful with this stuff, it can be dangerous if it isn't handled properly. この取り扱いには十分注意してください。使い方を間違えると危険です。 ❑ Careful on those stairs! その階段、気をつけて! ● **care|ful|ly** ADV 副詞 [ADV with v] 気をつけて ❑ Have a nice time, dear, and drive carefully. 楽しんでらっしゃい、運転には気をつけてね。 ❷ ADJ 形容詞 **Careful** work, thought, or examination is thorough and shows a concern for details. 入念な ❑ He has decided to prosecute her after careful consideration of all the relevant facts. 彼は関連のあるすべての事実を入念に検討したうえで彼女の起訴に踏み切った。 ● **care|ful|ly** ADV 副詞 [ADV with v] 入念に ❑ ...a vast series of deliberate and carefully planned thefts. 次から次へと起こる用意周到な窃盗事件。 ❸ ADJ 形容詞 If you tell someone to be **careful about** doing something, you think that what they intend

to do is probably wrong, and that they should think seriously before they do it. 一することに注意する [v-link ADJ "about/of" -ing] ❑ I think you should be careful about talking of the rebels as heroes. 反体制派を英雄扱いするような発言は気をつけたほうがいいと思う。 ● **care|ful|ly** ADV 副詞 [ADV after v] 慎重に ❑ He should think carefully about actions like this which play into the hands of his opponents. 敵を有利にしてしまうような行動を彼は慎んだほうがよい。 ❹ ADJ 形容詞 If you are **careful with** something such as money or resources, you use or spend only what is necessary. 無駄にしない ❑ Industries should be more careful with natural resources. 産業界は資源の無駄をなくすべきだ。

Word Partnership careful は次の語句と使われる:

ADV.	better be careful ❶
	extremely careful, very careful ❷ ❸ ❹
N.	careful attention, careful consideration, careful observation, careful planning ❷

care|giv|er /kɛərgɪvər/ (caregivers) N-COUNT 可算名詞 A **caregiver** is someone who is responsible for taking care of another person, for example, a person who is disabled, ill, or very young. 介護者 [mainly AM 主に米国英語] ❑ It is always women who are the primary caregivers. 主に介護するのはきまって女性のほうだ。

care|less /kɛərlɪs/ ❶ ADJ 形容詞 If you are **careless**, you do not pay enough attention to what you are doing, and so you make mistakes, or cause harm or damage. 不注意な ❑ I'm sorry. How careless of me. ごめんね、そそっかしくって。 ❑ Some parents are accused of being careless with their children's health. 子供の健康に対する配慮が足りないと子供の親は非難されている。 ● **care|less|ly** ADV 副詞 [ADV with v] 不注意に ❑ She was fined $200 for driving carelessly. 彼女は不注意な運転で200ドルの罰金を科された。 ● **care|less|ness** N-UNCOUNT 不可算名詞 不注意 ❑ Errors are sometimes made from simple carelessness. ほんの不注意から間違いが起こることがある。 ❷ ADJ 形容詞 If you say that someone is **careless of** something such as their health or appearance, you mean that they do not seem to be concerned about it, or do nothing to keep it in a good condition. 気にかけない ❑ He had shown himself careless of personal safety where the life of his colleagues might be at risk. 仲間の生命が危険にさらされたとき、彼は我が身の危険を顧みないほどの勇気を示した。

Thesaurus careless また次を参照:

| ADJ. | absent-minded, forgetful, irresponsible, reckless, sloppy; (ant.) attentive, careful, cautious ❶ |

car|er /kɛərər/ (carers) N-COUNT 可算名詞 A **carer** is the same as a **caregiver**. 介護者 [BRIT 英国英語]

ca|ress /kərɛs/ (caresses, caressing, caressed) V-T 他動詞 If you **caress** someone or something, you stroke them gently and affectionately. 優しくなでる [WRITTEN 書き言葉] ❑ He was gently caressing her golden hair. 彼は彼女の金髪を優しくなでていた。 ● N-COUNT 可算名詞 **Caress** is also a noun. 愛撫(あいぶ)抱擁 ❑ Margaret took me to one side, holding my arm in a gentle caress. マーガレットは私の腕を優しくつかんでわきへ連れてきた。

care|tak|er /kɛərteɪkər/ (caretakers) ❶ N-COUNT 可算名詞 A **caretaker** is a person whose job it is to take care of a house or property when the owner is not there. 留守番 ❑ Slater remained at the house, acting as the family was not in residence. スレイターは家族が不在のときは留守番として家に残った。 ❷ N-COUNT 可算名詞 A **caretaker** is someone who is responsible for looking after another person, for example, a person who is disabled, ill, or very young. 世話をする人 [mainly AM 主に米国英語] ❑ His caretakers labeled him severely disabled. 介護者たちは彼を重度障害者だと決めつけた。 ❸ N-COUNT 可算名詞 A **caretaker** is a person whose job it is to take care of a large building such as a school or an apartment house, and deal with small repairs to it. 管理人 [BRIT 英国英語; AM janitor 米国英語] ❹ ADJ 形容詞 A **caretaker** government or leader is in charge temporarily until a new government or leader is appointed. 暫定的な [ADJ n] ❑ The military intends to hand over power to a caretaker government and hold elections within six months. 軍部は暫定政府に権力を移譲し半年以内に選挙を実施する方針です。

car|go /kɑrgoʊ/ (cargoes) N-VAR 可変性名詞 The **cargo** of a ship or plane is the goods that it is carrying. 貨物 ❑ The boat calls at the main port to load its regular cargo of bananas. 船は大きな港に立ち寄っていつもどおりバナナの貨物を積み込む。
→ see **ship**

Car|ib|bean /kærəbiən, kərɪbiən/ (Caribbeans) ❶ N-PROPER 固有名詞 The **Caribbean** is the sea which is between the West Indies, Central America and the north coast of South America. カリブ海 ❷ ADJ 形容詞 **Caribbean** means belonging or relating to the Caribbean Sea and its islands, or to its people. カリブ海の; カリブ人の ❑ ...the Caribbean island of St. Thomas. カリブ海に浮かぶセントトマス島。 ● N-COUNT 可算名詞 A **Caribbean** is a person from a

Caribbean island. カリブ人

car|ca|ture /kǽrɪkətʃər, -tʃʊər/ (**caricatures, caricaturing, caricatured**) **1** N-COUNT 可算名詞 A **caricature** of someone is a drawing or description of them that exaggerates their appearance or behavior in a humorous or critical way. カリカチュア, 風刺漫画 ❏ The poster showed a caricature of Hitler with a devil's horns and tail. ポスターには悪魔の角としっぽが生えているヒットラーの風刺画が描かれていた。 **2** N-COUNT 可算名詞 If you describe something as a **caricature of** an event or situation, you mean that it is a very exaggerated account of it. 風刺 [DISAPPROVAL 不賛成] ❏ Hall is angry at what he sees as a caricature of the training offered to modern-day social workers. ホールが腹を立てているのは, 現在のソーシャルワーカーに対する研修をこきおろしているせいだ。 **3** V-T 他動詞 If you **caricature** someone, you draw or describe them in an exaggerated way in order to be humorous or critical. 風刺する ❏ Her political career has been caricatured in the headlines. 彼女の政治歴がマスコミからさんざん揶揄(やゆ)された。

car|ing /kέərɪŋ/ **1** ADJ 形容詞 If someone is **caring**, they are affectionate, helpful, and sympathetic. 思いやりのある ❏ He is a lovely boy, very gentle and caring. かわいい子で, とても優しく思いやりがある。 **2** ADJ 形容詞 The **caring** professions are those such as nursing and social work that are involved with looking after people who are ill or who need help in coping with their lives. 福祉の [ADJ n] ❏ The course is also suitable for those in the caring professions. このコースは福祉関係の方にも適しています。

Word Link carn = flesh : **carn**age, in**carn**ation, reincarn**ation**

car|nage /kάrnɪdʒ/ N-UNCOUNT 不可算名詞 **Carnage** is the violent killing of large numbers of people, especially in a war. 大虐殺, (さつりく)殺戮 [LITERARY 文語的] ❏ …his strategy for stopping the carnage in Kosovo. コソボでの殺戮(さつりく)をやめさせる彼の方策。

car|na|tion /kɑrnéɪʃ⁰n/ (**carnations**) N-COUNT 可算名詞 A **carnation** is a plant with white, pink, or red flowers. カーネーション

car|ni|val /kάrnɪv⁰l/ (**carnivals**) **1** N-COUNT 可算名詞 A **carnival** is a public festival during which people play music and sometimes dance in the streets. カーニバル, お祭り **2** N-COUNT 可算名詞 A **carnival** is a traveling show which is held in a park or field and at which there are machines to ride on, entertainments, and games. 移動遊園地 [AM 米国英語]

car|ol /kάr⁰l/ (**carols**) N-COUNT 可算名詞 **Carols** are Christian religious songs that are sung at Christmas. クリスマスキャロル ❏ The singing of Christmas carols is a custom derived from early dance routines of pagan origin. クリスマスキャロルを歌う習慣は異教徒に由来する古い踊りから生れた。

carou|sel /kǽrəsέl/ (**carousels**) **1** N-COUNT 可算名詞 At an airport, a **carousel** is a moving surface from which passengers can collect their luggage. ターンテーブル **2** N-COUNT 可算名詞 A **carousel** is a large, circular machine with seats, often in the shape of animals or cars. People can sit on it and go around and around for fun. メリーゴーランド, 回転木馬
→ see **park**

car park (**car parks**) also **carpark** N-COUNT 可算名詞 A **car park** is an area or building where people can leave their cars. 駐車場 [BRIT 英国英語; AM **parking lot, parking garage** 米国英語 **parking lot, parking garage**]

car|pen|ter /kάrpɪntər/ (**carpenters**) N-COUNT 可算名詞 A **carpenter** is a person whose job is making and repairing wooden things. 大工

car|pet /kάrpɪt/ (**carpets, carpeting, carpeted**) **1** N-VAR 可変性名詞 A **carpet** is a thick covering of soft material which is laid over a floor or a staircase. じゅうたん ❏ They put down wooden boards, and laid new carpets on top. 木の板を敷いてからその上に新しいじゅうたんを敷いた。 **2** V-T 他動詞 If a floor or a room **is carpeted**, a carpet is laid on the floor. じゅうたんを敷く [usu passive] ❏ The room had been carpeted and the windows glazed with colored glass. 以前その部屋にはじゅうたんが敷かれ窓には色ガラスがはめてあった。

car phone (**car phones**) N-COUNT 可算名詞 A **car phone** is a cellular phone which is designed to be used in a car. 自動車電話

car|pool /kάrpul/ (**carpools, carpooling, carpooled**) also **car pool** or **car-pool** **1** N-COUNT 可算名詞 A **carpool** is an arrangement where a group of people take turns driving each other to work, or driving each other's children to school. A **carpool** also refers to the people traveling together in a car. 車の相乗り; 車を相乗りする人 ❏ His wife stays home to drive the children to school in the carpool. 彼の妻は家にいて子供たちを交代で学校まで車で送っている。 **2** N-COUNT 可算名詞 A **carpool** is a number of cars that are owned by a company or organization for the use of its employees or members. 社用車, 団体所有車 [BUSINESS 実業] **3** V-I 自動詞 If a group of people **carpool**, they take turns driving each other to work, or driving each other's children to school. 相乗りを

する [mainly AM OR AUSTRALIAN 主に米国英語, またはオーストラリア英語] ❏ The government says fewer Americans are carpooling to work. 政府によると相乗り通勤をするアメリカ人は減っている。

car|riage /kǽrɪdʒ/ (**carriages**) **1** N-COUNT 可算名詞 A **carriage** is an old-fashioned vehicle, usually for a small number of passengers, which is pulled by horses. 馬車 ❏ The president-elect followed in an open carriage drawn by six beautiful gray horses. その後には次期大統領が6頭の美しい灰色の馬が引く無蓋(むがい)馬車に乗って現れた。 **2** N-COUNT 可算名詞 A **carriage** is the same as a **car**. 車両 [mainly BRIT 主に英国英語] → see **car 2** **3** N-UNCOUNT 不可算名詞 **Carriage** is the same as a **delivery charge**. 送料 [BRIT 英国英語]

car|ri|er /kǽriər/ (**carriers**) **1** N-COUNT 可算名詞 A **carrier** is a vehicle that is used for carrying people, especially soldiers, or things. 輸送車両 ❏ There were armored personnel carriers and tanks on the streets. 市街地には装甲兵員輸送車や戦車が出ていた。 **2** N-COUNT 可算名詞 A **carrier** is a company that provides telecommunications services, such as telephone and Internet services. 通信事業会社 ❏ …Japan's top wireless carrier. 日本最大の無線通信会社。 ❏ Regional carriers get paid for calls that pass through their switches. 地域の電話会社は交換機を通過する通話料に応じて支払いを受ける。 **3** N-COUNT 可算名詞 A **carrier** is a passenger airline. 航空会社 ❏ American Airlines is the third-largest carrier at Denver International Airport. アメリカン航空はデンバー国際空港で第3位の航空会社である。 **4** N-COUNT 可算名詞 A **carrier** is a company that transports goods from one place to another by truck. 運送会社 ❏ The Colorado Motor Carriers Association represents 450 trucking companies across the state. コロラドトラック運送会社協会は州内のトラック運送会社450社を擁する。 **5** N-COUNT 可算名詞 A **carrier** is a person or an animal that is infected with a disease and so can make other people or animals ill. 保菌者 ❏ …an AIDS carrier. エイズ感染者。
→ see **ship**

car|rot /kǽrət/ (**carrots**) N-VAR 可変性名詞 **Carrots** are long, thin, orange-colored vegetables. They grow under the ground, and have green shoots above the ground. ニンジン **2** N-COUNT 可算名詞 Something that is offered to people in order to persuade them to do something can be referred to as a **carrot**. Something that is meant to persuade people not to do something can be referred to in the same sentence as a "stick." ご褒美 ❏ Why the new emphasis on sticks instead of diplomatic carrots? 最近, 外交において懐柔策より強硬策に重点が置かれるようになったのはどうしてでしょうか。
→ see **vegetable**

car|ry /kǽri/ (**carries, carrying, carried**) **1** V-T 他動詞 If you **carry** something, you take it with you, holding it so that it does not touch the ground. 持っていく ❏ He was carrying a briefcase. 彼は書類かばんを持っていた。 ❏ She carried her son to the car. 彼女は息子を車まで抱いていった。 **2** V-T 他動詞 If you **carry** something, you have it with you wherever you go. 携帯する ❏ You have to carry a pager so that they can call you in at any time. いつでも呼び出しを受けられるようにポケットベルを携帯しなければならない。

> Do not confuse **carry** and **lift**. When you **carry** something, you move it from one place to another without letting it touch the ground. When you **lift** something, you move it upwards using your hands or a machine. After you have lifted it, you may **carry** it to a different place.

3 V-T 他動詞 If something **carries** a person or thing somewhere, it takes them there. 運ぶ ❏ Flowers are designed to attract insects which then carry the pollen from plant to plant. 花は昆虫を誘い寄せるようにできている。 そうして集まってきた昆虫が花粉を花から花へ運んでくれる。 ❏ The delegation was carrying a message of thanks to President Mubarak. 代表団はムバラク大統領への感謝の意を伝える親書を携えていた。 **4** V-T 他動詞 If a person or animal **is carrying** a disease, they are infected with it and can pass it on to other people or animals. 媒介する ❏ The test could be used to screen healthy people to see if they are carrying the virus. この検査法を利用すれば, 健常者がウィルスの保菌者かどうか検査することができる。 **5** V-T 他動詞 If an action or situation has a particular quality or consequence, you can say that it **carries** it. 伴う, 生じる [no passive, no cont] ❏ Check that any medication you're taking carries no risk for your developing baby. 使用中の薬は全て調べてお腹の子に影響がないか確認しましょう。 **6** V-T 他動詞 If a quality or advantage **carries** someone into a particular position or through a difficult situation, it helps them to achieve that position or deal with that situation. 至らせる ❏ He had the ruthless streak necessary to carry him into the cabinet. 彼には閣僚入りを果たすためなら他人には目もくれないところがあった。 **7** V-T 他動詞 If you **carry** an idea or a method to a particular extent, you use or develop it to that extent. 発展させる ❏ It's not such a new idea, but I carried it to extremes. そんなに新しい考えじゃなくて, 僕はただ極端にやったまでだよ。 **8** V-T 他動詞 If a newspaper or poster **carries** a picture or a piece of writing, it contains it or displays it. 載せる, 報道する ❏ Several papers carry the photograph of Mr. Anderson. ア

ンダーソン氏のこの写真を掲載した新聞は数紙あります。 **9** V-T 他動詞 In a debate, if a proposal or motion **is carried**, a majority of people vote in favor of it. 通過する [usu passive] ❑ *A motion backing its economic policy was carried by 322 votes to 296.* その経済政策を支持する動議は322票対296票で可決された。 **10** V-T 他動詞 If a crime **carries** a particular punishment, a person who is found guilty of that crime will receive that punishment. 伴う [no cont] ❑ *It was a crime of espionage and carried the death penalty.* スパイ罪で死刑は免れなかった。 **11** V-I 自動詞 If a sound **carries**, it can be heard a long way away. 届く，伝わる ❑ *Even in this stillness Leaphorn doubted if the sound would carry far.* これほど静かでもその音が遠くまで届くのかリープホーンには疑わしかった。 **12** V-T 他動詞 If you **carry yourself** in a particular way, you walk and move in that way. ふるまう ❑ *They carried themselves with great pride and dignity.* 彼らの態度は誇りに満ちて堂々としていた。 **13** PHRASE 句 If you **get carried away** or **are carried away**, you are so eager or excited about something that you do something hasty or foolish. 我を忘れる ❑ *I got completely carried away and almost cried.* 夢中になりすぎて泣きそうになった。 **14** to **carry weight** → see **weight**

▶ **carry off** PHRASAL VERB 句動詞 If you **carry** something **off**, you do it successfully. やってのける ❑ *He's got the experience and the authority to carry it off.* 彼には経験もあるし権限もあるからうまくやってのけるだろう。

▶ **carry on** **1** PHRASAL VERB 句動詞 If you **carry on** doing something, you continue to do it. 続ける ❑ *The assistant carried on talking.* 店員はしゃべり続けた。 ❑ *Her bravery has given him the will to carry on with his life and his work.* 彼女の勇敢な態度に打たれて彼は人生と仕事に対する意欲を取り戻した。 ❑ *His eldest son Joseph carried on his father's traditions.* 長男のジョゼフが父から伝統を受け継いだ。 **2** PHRASAL VERB 句動詞 If you **carry on** an activity, you do it or take part in it for a period of time. 続ける ❑ *The consulate will carry on a political dialogue with Indonesia.* 領事は今後もインドネシアとの政治的対話を継続する。

▶ **carry out** PHRASAL VERB 句動詞 If you **carry out** a threat, task, or instruction, you do it or act according to it. 実行する ❑ *The Social Democrats could still carry out their threat to leave the government.* 社会民主党は政権を離脱するという脅しを実行に移す可能性が残っています。 ❑ *Police say they believe the attacks were carried out by nationalists.* 警察は今回の襲撃をナショナリストの仕業だと見ています。

▶ **carry through** PHRASAL VERB 句動詞 If you **carry** something **through**, you do it or complete it, often in spite of difficulties. 成し遂げる ❑ *We don't have the confidence that the U.N. will carry through a sustained program.* 国連が持続的な計画を遂行できるのか確信がもてません。

Thesaurus	*carry* また次を参照：
v.	bear, bring, cart, haul, lug, move, tote, truck **1**

carry|all /kǽriɔl/ (**carryalls**) N-COUNT 可算名詞 A **carryall** is a large bag made of nylon, canvas, or leather, which you use to carry your clothes and other possessions, for example when you are traveling. 大型のかばん [mainly AM 主に米国英語] ❑ *He shivered, humping his canvas carryall higher onto his shoulder.* 彼はキャンバス地の大きなかばんを肩に担ぎながら身震いした。

car|ry|over /kǽriouvər/ (**carryovers**) N-COUNT 可算名詞 If something is a **carryover** from an earlier time, it began during an earlier time but still exists or happens now. 以前からの影響 [AM 米国英語] [usu sing] ❑ *Her love of these sandwiches was a carryover from the Depression, when she sometimes had nothing else to eat.* 彼女がこのサンドイッチを大好きになったのは大恐慌のとき以来で，当時はこれ以外に食べる物がなかったことがあった。

cart /kɑ́rt/ (**carts, carting, carted**) **1** N-COUNT 可算名詞 A **cart** is an old-fashioned wooden vehicle that is used for transporting goods or people. Some carts are pulled by animals. 荷車 ❑ *...a country where horse-drawn carts far outnumber cars.* 車より荷馬車の数のほうがずっと多い国。 **2** N-COUNT 可算名詞 A **cart** is a small vehicle with a motor. カート [AM 米国英語] ❑ *Cars are prohibited, so transportation is by electric cart or by horse and buggy.* 自動車は禁止されているので，交通手段といえば電気カートか馬か軽装馬車ぐらいである。 **3** N-COUNT 可算名詞 A **cart** or a **shopping cart** is a large metal basket on wheels which is provided by stores such as supermarkets for customers to use while they are in the store. ショッピングカート [AM 米国英語] **4** V-T 他動詞 If you **cart** things or people somewhere, you carry or transport them there, often with difficulty. 運ぶ [INFORMAL くだけた] ❑ *After their parents died, one of their father's relatives carted off the entire contents of the house.* 彼らの両親が亡くなると，父方の親戚の一人が家財道具を一切運び出した。 ❑ *...a neat tote bag for carting around your child's books or toys.* 子供の本やおもちゃを持ち運ぶのにうってつけのトートバッグ。

→ see **golf, hotel**

carte blanche /kɑ́rt blɑ́nʃ/ N-UNCOUNT 不可算名詞 If someone gives you **carte blanche**, they give you the authority to do whatever you think is right. 白紙委任 ❑ *They gave him carte blanche to make decisions.* 彼らは彼に一切の決定権を与えた。

car|tel /kɑrtél/ (**cartels**) N-COUNT 可算名詞 A **cartel** is an association of similar companies or businesses that have grouped together in order to prevent competition and to control prices. カルテル [BUSINESS 実業] ❑ *...a drug cartel.* 麻薬カルテル。

car|ti|lage /kɑ́rtɪlɪdʒ/ (**cartilages**) N-VAR 可変性名詞 **Cartilage** is a strong, flexible substance in your body, especially around your joints and in your nose. 軟骨 ❑ *Andre Agassi has pulled out of next week's Grand Slam Cup after tearing a cartilage in his chest.* アンドレ・アガシは胸の軟骨剥離（はくり）のため来週のグランドスラムカップの出場を取りやめた。

→ see **shark**

car|ton /kɑ́rtʰn/ (**cartons**) **1** N-COUNT 可算名詞 A **carton** is a plastic or cardboard container in which food or drink is sold. カートン ❑ *A quart carton of milk is cheaper than two single pints.* 牛乳1クオート入りパック1個のほうが1パイント入りパック2個より安い。 **2** N-COUNT 可算名詞 You can use **carton** to refer to the carton and its contents, or to the contents only. カートンの中身 ❑ *He went to the store for a carton of milk.* 彼は牛乳を1パック買いに店まで出かけた。 **3** N-COUNT 可算名詞 A **carton** is a large, strong cardboard box in which goods are stored and transported. 段ボール箱 [AM 米国英語] ❑ *Those cartons contain the archives of The New Yorker for the years 1925 to 1980.* その段ボール箱には1925年ー80年までのニューヨーカー誌が保管されています。

car|toon /kɑrtún/ (**cartoons**) **1** N-COUNT 可算名詞 A **cartoon** is a humorous drawing or series of drawings in a newspaper or magazine. 漫画 ❑ *Mickey Mouse, Donald Duck, and other Disney cartoon characters gave endless delight to millions of children.* ミッキーマウスやドナルドダックなどのディズニーの漫画キャラクターは数多くの子供たちに楽しみを与え続けた。 **2** N-COUNT 可算名詞 A **cartoon** is a film in which all the characters and scenes are drawn rather than being real people or objects. アニメ ❑ *...a TV set blares out a cartoon comedy.* コミカルなアニメの大きな音がテレビから鳴り響く。

→ see **animation**

car|toon|ist /kɑrtúnɪst/ (**cartoonists**) N-COUNT 可算名詞 A **cartoonist** is a person whose job is to draw cartoons for newspapers and magazines. 漫画家

car|tridge /kɑ́rtrɪdʒ/ (**cartridges**) **1** N-COUNT 可算名詞 A **cartridge** is a metal or cardboard tube containing a bullet and an explosive substance. Cartridges are used in guns. 装弾 ❑ *Only four of the five spent cartridges were recovered by police.* 警察が発見したのは5発の薬莢（やっきょう）のうちの4発だけだった。 **2** N-COUNT 可算名詞 A **cartridge** is part of a machine or device that can be easily removed and replaced when it is worn out or empty. カートリッジ ❑ *Change the filter cartridge as instructed by the manufacturer.* フィルターカートリッジはメーカーが指示する期間ごとに交換してください。

carve /kɑ́rv/ (**carves, carving, carved**) **1** V-T/V-I 他動詞/自動詞 If you **carve** an object, you make it by cutting it out of a substance such as wood or stone. If you **carve** something such as wood or stone into an object, you make the object by cutting it out. 彫る ❑ *One of the prisoners has carved a beautiful wooden chess set.* 囚人の一人が見事な木彫のチェスセットを作った。 ❑ *I picked up a piece of wood and started carving.* 私は木材を1本取り上げて彫刻を始めた。 **2** → see also **carving 3** V-T 他動詞 If you **carve** writing or a design **on** an object, you cut it into the surface of the object. 刻む ❑ *He carved his name on his desk.* 彼は自分の名前を自分の机に刻み込んだ。 **4** V-T 他動詞 If you **carve** a piece of cooked meat, you cut slices from it so that you can eat it. 切り分ける ❑ *Andrew began to carve the chicken.* アンドリューはとり肉を切り分け始めた。

▶ **carve out** PHRASAL VERB 句動詞 If you **carve out** a niche or a career, you succeed in getting the position or the career that you want by your own efforts. 自ら切り開く ❑ *Vick carved out his niche as the fastest quarterback in football.* ビックはアメフトで最も俊足のクオーターバックとして自分の地位を築いた。

▶ **carve up** PHRASAL VERB 句動詞 If you say that someone **carves** something **up**, you disapprove of the way they have divided it into small parts. 分割する [DISAPPROVAL 不賛成] ❑ *He has set about carving up the company which Hammer created from almost nothing.* 彼はハマーがほとんどゼロから築き上げた会社の分割に着手した。

carv|ing /kɑ́rvɪŋ/ (**carvings**) **1** N-COUNT 可算名詞 A **carving** is an object or a design that has been cut out of a material such as stone or wood. 彫刻作品 ❑ *...a wood carving of a human hand.* 人の手を彫った木彫。 **2** N-UNCOUNT 不可算名詞 **Carving** is the art of carving objects, or of carving designs or writing on objects. 彫刻術 ❑ *I found wood carving satisfying, and painting fun.* 木彫には満足を感じ絵画には楽しみを感じた。

cas|cade /kæskéɪd/ (**cascades, cascading, cascaded**) **1** N-COUNT 可算名詞 If you refer to a **cascade** of something, you mean that there is a large amount of it. 滝状のもの [LITERARY 文語的] ❑ *The women have lustrous cascades of black hair.* その女たちはつややかで流れるような黒髪をしている。 **2** V-I 自動詞 If water **cascades** somewhere, it pours or flows downward very fast and in large quantities. 滝のように落ちる ❑ *She hung on as the freezing, rushing*

water cascaded past her. 凍てつくような激流のなかで彼女は必死にしがみつった.

case

❶ INSTANCES AND OTHER ABSTRACT MEANINGS
❷ CONTAINERS
❸ GRAMMAR TERM

❶ **case** /keɪs/ (**cases**) **1** N-COUNT 可算名詞 A particular **case** is a particular situation or incident, especially one that you are using as an individual example or instance of something. 場合 ❏ *Surgical training takes at least nine years, or 11 in the case of obstetrics.* 外科の研修には最低でも9年, 産科なら11年かかる. ❏ *In extreme cases, insurance companies can prosecute for fraud.* 悪質なケースでは保険会社は保険金詐欺に対し損害賠償請求訴訟を起こすことがある. **2** N-COUNT 可算名詞 A **case** is a person or their particular problem that a doctor, social worker, or other professional is dealing with. 症例, 事例 ❏ *Dr. Thomas Bracken describes the case of a 45-year-old Catholic priest much given to prayer whose left knee became painful.* トマス・ブラッケン医師は45歳のカトリックの司祭が祈り過ぎて左膝を痛めた症例について述べる. ❏ *Some cases of arthritis respond to a gluten-free diet.* 関節炎では症例によってグルテン除去食で効果が見られる場合がある. **3** N-COUNT 可算名詞 If you say that someone is a sad **case** or a hopeless **case**, you mean that they are in a sad situation or a hopeless situation. 悪い状況に置かれた人 ❏ *I knew I was going to make it – that I wasn't a hopeless case.* 自分がうまくやれることは分かっていたよ. 自分が駄目人間じゃないっていうことはね. **4** → see also **basket case 5** N-COUNT 可算名詞 A **case** is a crime or mystery that the police are investigating. 事件 ❏ *The police have several suspects in the case of five murders committed in Gainesville, Florida.* フロリダ州ゲインズビルで起こった5件の殺人事件について, 警察は容疑者を数名に絞り込んでいる. **6** N-COUNT 可算名詞 The **case for** or **against** a plan or idea consists of the facts and reasons used to support it or oppose it. 言い分, 主張 ❏ *He sat there while I made the case for his dismissal.* 私が解雇の理由を説明している間, 彼はそこに座っていた. ❏ *Both these facts strengthen the case against hanging.* これらの事実は共に絞首刑に反対する主張を補強するものです. **7** N-COUNT 可算名詞 In law, a **case** is a trial or other legal inquiry. 訴訟 ❏ *It can be difficult for public figures to win a libel case.* 有名人が名誉毀損裁判で勝訴するのは難しいことがある. **8** → see also **test case 9** PHRASE 句 You say **in any case** when you are adding something which is more important than what you have just said, but which supports or corrects it. いずれにしても [EMPHASIS 強調] ❏ *The concert was sold out, and in any case, most of the people gathered in the square could not afford the price of a ticket.* コンサートのチケットは売り切れだったし, いずれにしても広場に集まった人たちの大半はチケット1枚すら買う余裕がなかった. **10** PHRASE 句 If you do something **in case** or **just in case** a particular thing happens, you do it because that thing might happen. 万一に備えて ❏ *In case anyone was following me, I made an elaborate detour.* 万が一誰かにつけられているといけないので私はわざと回り道をした. **11** PHRASE 句 If you do something or have something **in case of** a particular thing, you do it or have it because that thing might happen or be true. 一の場合に備えて ❏ *Many stores along the route have been boarded up in case of trouble.* 路沿いの商店の多くは板を打ち付けて万一の暴動に備えた. **12** PHRASE 句 You use **in case** in expressions like "in case you didn't know" or "in case you've forgotten" when you are telling someone in a rather irritated way something that you think is either obvious or none of their business. 一かもしれないけれども [FEELINGS 感情] ❏ *She's nervous about something, in case you didn't notice.* 気づいてないかもしれないけど, 彼女は気をもんでいることがあるの. **13** PHRASE 句 You say **in that case** or **in which case** to indicate that what you are going to say is true if the possible situation that has just been mentioned actually exists. そうだとしたら ❏ *Perhaps you've some doubts about the attack. In that case it may interest you to know that Miss Woods witnessed it.* ひょっとして暴行があったことを目撃したのかも. そうだとしたら, ウッズさんが目撃したことを知ったら気が変わらない? **14** PHRASE 句 You can say that you are doing something **just in case** to refer vaguely to the possibility that a thing might happen or be true, without saying exactly what it is. 念のため ❏ *I guess we've already talked about this but I'll ask you again just in case.* これについてはもうお話ししたと思いますが, 念のためもう一度お聞きします. **15** PHRASE 句 If you say that a task or situation is **a case of** a particular thing, you mean that it consists of that thing or can be described as that thing. 一という問題 ❏ *It's not a case of whether anyone would notice or not.* 誰かが気づくとかとか気づかないとかいう問題ではないよ. **16** PHRASE 句 If you say that something **is the case**, you mean that it is true or correct. 事実である ❏ *You'll probably notice her having difficulty swallowing. If this is the case, give her plenty of liquids.* 彼女がのみ込みに苦労をしていたらすぐに分かりますから, そのときは十分な水分をあげてください.
→ see **hospital**

❷ **case** /keɪs/ (**cases**) **1** N-COUNT 可算名詞 A **case** is a container that is specially designed to hold or protect something. ケース ❏ *...a black case for his glasses.* 彼の黒い眼鏡ケース. **2** → see also **bookcase, briefcase**

❸ **case** /keɪs/ (**cases**) **1** N-COUNT 可算名詞 In the grammar of many languages, the **case** of a group such as a noun group or adjective group is the form it has which shows its relationship to other groups in the sentence. 格 **2** → see also **lowercase, uppercase**

case study (**case studies**) N-COUNT 可算名詞 A **case study** is a written account that gives detailed information about a person, group, or thing and their development over a period of time. 事例研究 ❏ *...a large case study of malaria in West African children.* 西アフリカの児童を対象にした大規模なマラリアの症例研究.

cash /kæʃ/ (**cashes, cashing, cashed**) **1** N-UNCOUNT 不可算名詞 **Cash** is money in the form of bills and coins rather than checks. 現金 ❏ *...two thousand dollars in cash.* 現金2000ドル. **2** → see also **hard cash, petty cash 3** N-UNCOUNT 不可算名詞 **Cash** means the same as money, especially money which is immediately available. 即金 [INFORMAL くだけた] ❏ *...a state-owned financial-services group with plenty of cash.* 資金力のある国営の総合金融グループ. **4** V-T 他動詞 If you **cash** a check, you exchange it at a bank for the amount of money that it is worth. 現金化する ❏ *There are similar charges if you want to cash a check or withdraw money at a branch other than your own.* 口座のある店舗以外での小切手の現金化や現金の引き出しにも同様の手数料がかかる.

▶ **cash in 1** PHRASAL VERB 句動詞 If you say that someone **cashes in on** a situation, you are criticizing them for using it to gain an advantage, often in an unfair or dishonest way. つけこむ [DISAPPROVAL 不賛成] ❏ *Residents said local gang leaders had cashed in on the violence to seize valuable land.* 住民によれば, 地元のギャングの幹部が力ずくで大切な土地を奪い取ったという. **2** PHRASAL VERB 句動詞 If you **cash in** something such as an insurance policy, you exchange it for money. 換金する ❏ *Avoid cashing in a policy early as you could lose out heavily.* 大きな損をすることがあるので保険の中途解約はやめたほうがよい.

cash bar (**cash bars**) N-COUNT 可算名詞 A **cash bar** is a bar at a party or similar event where guests can buy drinks. キャッシュバー ❏ *At 6 p.m. there will be a reception and cash bar.* レセプションは午後6時から始まります. お飲み物は有料となっております.

cash cow (**cash cows**) N-COUNT 可算名詞 In business, a **cash cow** is a product or investment that steadily continues to be profitable. ドル箱 [BUSINESS 実業] ❏ *The retail division is BT's cash cow.* 小売部門はBT社のドル箱である.

cash dis|pens|er (**cash dispensers**) N-COUNT 可算名詞 A **cash dispenser** is a machine built into the wall of a bank or other building, which allows people to take out money from their bank account using a special card. 現金自動支払機 [BRIT 英国英語; AM 米国英語 **ATM**]

cash flow also **cash-flow** N-UNCOUNT 不可算名詞 The **cash flow** of a firm or business is the movement of money into and out of it. 資金繰り [BUSINESS 実業] ❏ *The company ran into cash-flow problems and faced liquidation.* その会社は資金繰りに行き詰まり破産に直面した.

cash|ier /kæʃɪər/ (**cashiers**) N-COUNT 可算名詞 A **cashier** is a person who customers pay money to or get money from in places such as stores or banks. レジ係; 窓口係

cash|ier's desk (**cashier's desks**) N-COUNT 可算名詞 A **cashier's desk** is a place in a large store where you pay for the things you want to buy. レジ台 [AM 米国英語]

cash|mere /kæʒmɪər/ N-UNCOUNT 不可算名詞 **Cashmere** is a kind of very fine, soft wool. カシミア ❏ *...a big, soft cashmere sweater.* ゆったりとした柔らかなカシミアのセーター.

cash|point /kæʃpɔɪnt/ (**cashpoints**) N-COUNT 可算名詞 A **cashpoint** is the same as a **cash dispenser**. 現金自動支払機 [BRIT 英国英語]

cash reg|is|ter (**cash registers**) N-COUNT 可算名詞 A **cash register** is a machine in a store, bar, or restaurant that is used to add up and record how much money people pay, and in which the money is kept. レジ

cash-starved ADJ 形容詞 A **cash-starved** company or

organization does not have enough money to operate properly, usually because another organization, such as the government, is not giving them the money that they need. 財政難の [BUSINESS, JOURNALISM 実業, ジャーナリズム] ❏*We are heading for a crisis, with cash-starved councils forced to cut back on vital community services.* 財政難の地方議会は市民に不可欠なサービスの縮小を余儀なくされており, 危機的状況に向かっている.

ca|si|no /kəsiːnoʊ/ (**casinos**) N-COUNT 可算名詞 A **casino** is a building or room where people play gambling games such as roulette. カジノ

cas|se|role /kæsəroʊl/ (**casseroles**) **1** N-COUNT 可算名詞 A **casserole** is a dish made of meat and vegetables that have been cooked slowly in a liquid. キャセロール ❏*...a huge beef casserole, full of herbs, vegetables, and wine.* ハーブや野菜やワインをふんだんに使った大量のビーフキャセロール **2** N-COUNT 可算名詞 A **casserole** or a **casserole dish** is a large heavy container with a lid. You cook casseroles and other dishes in it. キャセロールなべ ❏*Place all the chopped vegetables into a casserole dish.* 刻んだ野菜をすべてキャセロールなべに入れます.

cas|sette /kəsɛt/ (**cassettes**) N-COUNT 可算名詞 A **cassette** is a small, flat, rectangular plastic case containing magnetic tape which is used for recording and playing back sound or film. カセット [also "on" N] ❏*His two albums released on cassette have sold 10 million copies.* 2枚のアルバムを収録した彼のカセットは1千万本売れました.

cast /kæst/ (**casts, casting**)

> The form **cast** is used in the present tense and is the past tense and past participle.
>
> **cast** 形は現在時制に使われ, 過去時制や過去分詞でもある.

1 N-COUNT-COLL 集合可算名詞 The **cast** of a play or movie is all the people who act in it. 配役 ❏*The show is very amusing and the cast is very good.* そのショーはとても面白いし配役も素晴らしい. **2** V-T 他動詞 To **cast** an actor in a play or film means to choose them to act a particular role in it. 役を割り当てる ❏*The world premiere of Harold Pinter's new play casts Ian Holm in the lead role.* ハロルド・ピンターの新作の世界初演ではイアン・ホルムが主役を演じる. ❏*He was cast as a college professor.* 彼は大学教授の役を演じることになった. **3** V-T 他動詞 If you **cast** your eyes or **cast** a look in a particular direction, you look quickly in that direction. 目を向ける [WRITTEN 書き言葉] ❏*He cast a stern glance at the two men.* 彼は2人の男たちを厳しい目つきでちらっと見た. ❏*I cast my eyes down briefly.* ちょっと下を向いた. **4** V-T 他動詞 If something **casts** a light or shadow somewhere, it causes it to appear there. 投げかける [WRITTEN 書き言葉] ❏*The moon cast a bright light over the yard.* 月の光が明るく庭を照らしていた. **5** V-T 他動詞 To **cast** doubt **on** something means to cause people to be unsure about it. 投げかける ❏*Last night a top criminal psychologist cast doubt on the theory.* 第一線の犯罪心理学者が昨夜その説に疑問を投げかけた. **6** V-T 他動詞 When you **cast** your vote in an election, you vote. 投票する ❏*About ninety-five per cent of those who cast their votes approve the new constitution.* 投票者の約95%が新憲法に賛成した. **7** V-T 他動詞 To **cast** an object means to make it by pouring a liquid such as hot metal into a specially shaped container and leaving it there until it becomes hard. 鋳造する ❏*Our door knocker is cast in solid brass.* うちのドアノッカーは真鍮(しんちゅう)で鋳造されている. **8** N-COUNT 可算名詞 A **cast** is a model that has been made by pouring a liquid such as plaster or hot metal onto something or into something, so that when it hardens it has the same shape as that thing. 鋳型 ❏*An orthodontist took a cast of the inside of Billy's mouth to make a dental plate.* 矯正医が義歯床を作るためにビリーの口の型を取った. **9** N-COUNT 可算名詞 A **cast** is the same as a **plaster cast**. ギプス **10** to **cast** your **mind** back → see **mind**
→ see **election, vote**

▸ **cast aside** PHRASAL VERB 句動詞 If you **cast aside** someone or something, you get rid of them because they are no longer necessary or useful to you. 関係を切る; 捨て去る ❏*We need to cast aside outdated policies.* 時代遅れの政策は廃止する必要がある.

caste /kæst/ (**castes**) **1** N-COUNT 可算名詞 A **caste** is one of the traditional social classes into which people are divided in a Hindu society. カースト ❏*Most of the upper castes worship the goddess Kali.* 高いカーストの人たちの多くが女神カーリーを崇拝しています. **2** N-UNCOUNT 不可算名詞 **Caste** is the system of dividing people in a society into different social classes. 階級制度 ❏*Caste is defined primarily by social honor attained through personal lifestyle.* 個人の生き方を通して獲得していく社会的な信用こそが, 何よりも階級を決定するのである.

cas|ti|gate /kæstɪgeɪt/ (**castigates, castigating, castigated**) V-T 他動詞 If you **castigate** someone or something, you speak to them angrily or criticize them severely. 酷評する [FORMAL 形式ばった] ❏*Marx never lost an opportunity to castigate colonialism.* マルクスはことあるたびに植民地主義を痛烈に批判した.

cast|ing vote (**casting votes**) N-COUNT 可算名詞 When a committee has given an equal number of votes for and against a proposal, the chairperson can give a **casting vote**. This vote decides whether or not the proposal will be passed. 決定票 ❏*The vote was tied and a union leader used his casting vote in favor of the return to work.* 投票は賛否が同数に分かれ, 組合長の決定票により職場復帰が決定しました.

cast iron **1** N-UNCOUNT 不可算名詞 **Cast iron** is iron which contains a small amount of carbon. It is hard and cannot be bent so it has to be made into objects by casting. 鋳鉄 ❏*Made from cast iron, it is finished in graphite enamel.* 鋳鉄製で黒鉛エナメル仕上げになっている. **2** ADJ 形容詞 A **cast-iron** guarantee or alibi is one that is absolutely certain to be effective and will not fail you. 確固たる ❏*They would have to offer cast-iron guarantees to invest in long-term projects.* 彼らは長期プロジェクトへの投資を確実に保証する必要があるだろう.
→ see **pan**

cas|tle /kæsəl/ (**castles**) N-COUNT 可算名詞 A **castle** is a large building with thick, high walls. Castles were built by important people, such as kings, in former times, especially for protection during wars and battles. 城

cas|trate /kæstreɪt/ (**castrates, castrating, castrated**) V-T 他動詞 To **castrate** a male animal or a man means to remove his testicles. 去勢する ❏*In the ancient world, it was probably rare to castrate a dog or cat.* 古代世界ではイヌやネコを去勢するのはおそらくまれなことだった. ● **cas|tra|tion** /kæstreɪʃən/ (**castrations**) N-VAR 可変性名詞 去勢 ❏*...the castration of male farm animals.* 家畜のオスの去勢

cas|ual /kæʒuəl/ **1** ADJ 形容詞 If you are **casual**, you are, or you pretend to be, relaxed and not very concerned about what is happening or what you are doing. 深く考えない, 何気ない ❏*It's difficult for me to be casual about anything.* 私にはどんなことでもなかなか簡単に済ませることができない. ● **casu|al|ly** ADV [ADV with V] 何気なく ❏*"No need to hurry," Ben said casually.* 「急がなくていいよ」とベンは何の気なしに言った. **2** ADJ 形容詞 A **casual** event or situation happens by chance or without planning. 偶然の, 思いがけない [ADJ n] ❏*What you mean as a casual remark could be misinterpreted.* 何気なく言ったことが誤解につながるなるおそれがある. **3** ADJ 形容詞 **Casual** clothes are ones that you normally wear at home or on vacation, and not on formal occasions. ふだんの [ADJ n] ❏*I also bought some casual clothes for the weekend.* 週末に着るふだん着も買った. ● **casu|al|ly** ADV 副詞 ふだん着で ❏*They were casually dressed.* 彼らはふだん着姿だった. **4** ADJ 形容詞 **Casual** work is done for short periods and not on a permanent or regular basis. 臨時の [mainly BRIT 主に英国英語; AM **temporary** 米国英語 **temporary**]

casu|al|ty /kæʒuəlti/ (**casualties**) **1** N-COUNT 可算名詞 A **casualty** is a person who is injured or killed in a war or in an accident. 死傷者 ❏*Troops fired on the demonstrators causing many casualties.* 軍がデモの参加者に向かって発砲し多くの死傷者が出ました. **2** N-COUNT 可算名詞 A **casualty** of a particular event or situation is a person or a thing that has suffered badly as a result of that event or situation. 被害者 ❏*The car industry has been one of the greatest casualties of the recession.* 自動車業界は不況の影響が最も深刻な業界の1つだ. **3** N-UNCOUNT 不可算名詞 **Casualty** is the part of a hospital where people who have severe injuries or sudden illnesses are taken for emergency treatment. 救急部門 [BRIT 英国英語; AM **emergency room** 米国英語 **emergency room**]

cat /kæt/ (**cats**) **1** N-COUNT 可算名詞 A **cat** is a furry animal that has a long tail and sharp claws. Cats are often kept as pets. ネコ **2** N-COUNT 可算名詞 **Cats** are lions, tigers, and other wild animals in the same family. ネコ科の動物 ❏*The lion is perhaps the most famous member of the cat family.* ライオンがネコ科で最も知られた動物じゃないかな. **3** → see also **fat cat**
→ see **pet**

cata|log /kætəlɒg/ (**catalogs**) also **catalogue** **1** N-COUNT 可算名詞 A **catalog** is a list of things such as the goods you can buy from a particular company, the objects in a museum, or the books in a library. カタログ, 目録 ❏*...the world's biggest seed catalog.* 種子を扱った世界最大のカタログ. **2** N-COUNT 可算名詞 A **catalog** of similar things, especially bad things, is a number of them considered or discussed one after another. 一の連続 ❏*His story is a catalog of misfortune.* 彼の物語は不幸な出来事の連続だ.
→ see **library**

cata|lyst /kætəlɪst/ (**catalysts**) **1** N-COUNT 可算名詞 You can describe a person or thing that causes a change or event to happen as a **catalyst**. きっかけ ❏*I very much hope that this case will prove to be a catalyst for change.* 今回の件が変化をもたらすきっかけになればと強く願っています. **2** N-COUNT 可算名詞 In chemistry, a **catalyst** is a substance that causes a chemical reaction to take place more quickly. 触媒

cata|pult /kætəpʌlt/ (**catapults, catapulting, catapulted**) **1** V-T/V-I 他動詞/自動詞 If someone or something **catapults** or is **catapulted** through the air, they are thrown very suddenly,

quickly, and violently through it. 勢いよく放つ ❑*We've all seen enough dummies catapulting through windshields in TV warnings to know the dangers of not wearing seat belts.* ダミー人形がフロントガラスを突き破って放り出されるテレビの衝撃的な映像を何度も目にしているので、シートベルトを着用しないとどれほど危険であるかよく分かっている. **2** V-T/V-I 他動詞/自動詞 If something **catapults** you into a particular state or situation, or if you **catapult** there, you are suddenly and unexpectedly caused to be in that state or situation. 突然〜の状態にする [他動詞], 突然〜の状態になる [自動詞] ❑*"Basic Instinct" catapulted her to top status Hollywood.* 映画『氷の微笑』で彼女はハリウッドのトップの座に躍り出た.

cata|ract /kǽtərækt/ (**cataracts**) N-COUNT 可算名詞 **Cataracts** are layers over a person's eyes that prevent them from seeing properly. Cataracts usually develop because of old age or illness. 白内障 ❑*In one study, light smokers were found to be more than twice as likely to get cataracts as non-smokers.* ある研究によると、たばこを少しでも吸うと吸わない人に比べて白内障に2倍以上かかりやすいことが分かった.

cata|stro|phe /kətǽstrəfi/ (**catastrophes**) N-COUNT 可算名詞 A **catastrophe** is an unexpected event that causes great suffering or damage. 大惨事 ❑*From all points of view, war would be a catastrophe.* どのように考えてみても戦争は大惨事であろう.

cata|stroph|ic /kætəstrɒfɪk/ **1** ADJ 形容詞 Something that is **catastrophic** involves or causes a sudden terrible disaster. 壊滅的な ❑*A tidal wave caused by the earthquake hit the coast causing catastrophic damage.* 地震による津波が海岸を襲い壊滅的な被害を引き起こした. ❑*The water shortage in this country is potentially catastrophic.* この国の水不足は大問題に発展するおそれがある. **2** ADJ 形容詞 If you describe something as **catastrophic**, you mean that it is very bad or unsuccessful. 大失敗 ❑*...another catastrophic attempt to arrest control from a rival Christian militia.* 敵のキリスト教武装集団から支配権を奪おうとしましたが、またしても大失敗に終わりました.

---

catch

❶ HOLD OR TOUCH
❷ MANAGE TO SEE, HEAR, OR TALK TO
❸ OTHER USES
❹ PHRASAL VERBS

---

❶ **catch** /kǽtʃ/ (**catches, catching, caught**) **1** V-T 他動詞 If you **catch** a person or animal, you capture them after chasing them, or by using a trap, net, or other device. 捕まえる ❑*Police say they are confident of catching the gunman.* 警察はその拳銃強盗を捕まえる自信があると言っている. ❑*Where did you catch the fish?* どこでその魚をとったのか. **2** V-T 他動詞 If you **catch** an object that is moving through the air, you seize it with your hands. 捕る ❑*I jumped up to catch a ball and fell over.* 私はボールを捕ろうとして飛び上がり、転んだ. ●N-COUNT 可算名詞 **Catch** is also a noun. 捕ること ❑*He missed the catch and the game was lost.* 彼はボールを捕り損ね、試合に敗れた. **3** V-T 他動詞 If you **catch** a part of someone's body, you take or seize it with your hand, often in order to stop them from going somewhere. つかむ ❑*Liz caught his arm.* リズは彼の腕をつかんだ. ❑*He knelt beside her and caught her hand in both of his.* 彼は彼女のそばにひざまずき、両手で彼女の手を握った. **4** V-T 他動詞 If one thing **catches** another, it hits it accidentally or manages to hit it. 当たる ❑*The stinging slap almost caught his face.* 彼はもう少しで顔にその痛い平手打ちを食うところだった. ❑*I may have caught him with my elbow but it was just an accident.* ひじが彼に当たったかもしれないが、わざとしたのではなかった. **5** V-I 自動詞 If something **catches on** or **in** an object, it accidentally becomes attached to the object or stuck in it. 引っかかる ❑*Her ankle caught on a root, and she almost lost her balance.* 足首が根に引っかかり、彼女はバランスを失いかけた. **6** to **catch hold of** something → see **hold**

Thesaurus catch また次を参照:

v.	apprehend, arrest, capture, grab, nab, seize, snatch, trap; (ant.) free, let go, let off, release ❶ **1** **2**

Word Partnership catch は次の語句と使われる:

N.	catch **a fish** ❶ **1**
	catch **a ball** ❶ **2**
	catch **a bus/flight/plane/train** ❷ **1**
	catch **a thief** ❷ **1**
	catch **your attention**, catch **your eye** ❸ **1**
v.	play catch ❶ **2**
PREP.	catch **on** something ❶ **5**

---

❷ **catch** /kǽtʃ/ (**catches, catching, caught**) **1** V-T 他動詞 When you **catch** a bus, train, or plane, you get on it in order to travel somewhere. 乗る ❑*We were in plenty of time for Anthony to catch*

---

the ferry. 我々はアンソニーがフェリー船に乗るのに十分間に合った. **2** V-T 他動詞 If you **catch** someone doing something wrong, you see or find them doing it. 見つける ❑*He caught a youth breaking into a car.* 彼は若者が車上荒らしをしようとしているのを見つけた. ❑*I don't want to catch you pushing yourself into the picture to get some personal publicity.* あなたが個人的な注目を得るためにその映画に自分を売り込んでいる姿は見たくない. **3** V-T 他動詞 If you **catch yourself** doing something, especially something surprising, you suddenly become aware that you are doing it. 気づく ❑*I caught myself feeling almost sorry for poor Mr. Laurence.* 私は哀れなローレンス氏にほとんど気の毒な感じを抱いているのにふと気づいた. **4** V-T 他動詞 If you **catch** something or **catch** a glimpse of it, you notice it or manage to see it briefly. ちらっと見る ❑*As she turned back she caught the puzzled look on her mother's face.* 彼女が引き返す際に母親の当惑した顔つきがちらっと見えた. **5** V-T 他動詞 If you **catch** something that someone has said, you manage to hear it. 聞き取る ❑*His ears caught a faint cry.* 彼はかすかな泣き声を聞いた. ❑*I do not believe I caught your name.* あなたの名前が聞き取れませんでした. **6** V-T 他動詞 If you **catch** a TV or radio program or an event, you manage to see or listen to it. 見る、聞く ❑*Bill turns on the radio to catch the local news.* ビルは地方ニュースを聞くためにラジオをつける. **7** V-T 他動詞 If you **catch** someone, you manage to contact or meet them to talk to them, especially when they are just about to go somewhere else. つかまえる ❑*I dialed Elizabeth's number thinking I might catch her before she left for work.* エリザベスが出勤する前につかまえられるかもしれないと思って、私は彼女に電話した. **8** V-T 他動詞 If something or someone **catches** you by surprise or at a bad time, you were not expecting them or do not feel able to deal with them. 不意を突く ❑*She looked as if the photographer had caught her by surprise.* 彼女はその写真家に不意を突かれたように見える. ❑*I'm sorry but I just cannot say anything. You've caught me at a bad time.* 悪いけれど何も言えません. 間の悪い時に私に不意打ちをかけました. **9** to **catch sight of** something → see **sight**

---

❸ **catch** /kǽtʃ/ (**catches, catching, caught**) **1** V-T 他動詞 If something **catches** your attention or your eye, you notice it or become interested in it. 引きつける ❑*My shoes caught his attention.* 私の靴が彼の注意を引いた. **2** V-T 他動詞 If you **catch** a cold or a disease, you become ill with it. かかる ❑*The more stress you are under, the more likely you are to catch a cold.* ストレスが大きければ大きいほど風邪を引きやすい. **3** V-T 他動詞 If something **catches** the light or if the light **catches** it, it reflects the light and looks bright or shiny. 受ける ❑*They saw the ship's guns, catching the light of the moon.* 彼らはその船の大砲が月の明かりを受けているのを見た. **4** V-T PASSIVE 受動態他動詞 If you **are caught** in a storm or other unpleasant situation, it happens when you cannot avoid its effects. あう ❑*When he was fishing off the island he was caught in a storm and almost drowned.* 彼はその島の沖で魚釣り中に嵐にあい、おぼれ死にかけた. **5** V-T PASSIVE 受動態他動詞 If you **are caught between** two alternatives or two people, you do not know which one to choose or follow. 間にはさまる ❑*The Jordanian leader is caught between both sides in the dispute.* ヨルダンの指導者はその紛争で両者の板ばさみになっている. **6** N-COUNT 可算名詞 A **catch** on a window, door, or container is a device that fastens it. 留め金 ❑*She fiddled with the catch of her bag.* 彼女はハンドバッグの留め金をいじくった. **7** N-COUNT 可算名詞 A **catch** is a hidden problem or difficulty in a plan or an offer that seems surprisingly good. 思わぬ欠点 ❑*The catch is that you work for your supper, and the food and accommodations can be very basic.* その食事や宿泊施設がお粗末なものかもしれないということが欠点. **8** to **catch fire** → see **fire**

---

❹ **catch** /kǽtʃ/ (**catches, catching, caught**) ▶ **catch on** **1** PHRASAL VERB 句動詞 If you **catch on to** something, you understand it, or realize that it is happening. 理解する ❑*He got what he could out of me before I caught on to the kind of person he'd turned into.* 彼がどんな人物になったかを理解する前に彼は僕から取れるだけのものを取った. **2** PHRASAL VERB 句動詞 If something **catches on**, it becomes popular. 人気を得る ❑*The idea has been around for ages without catching on.* その発想は長年あるが、はやったことはない.

▶ **catch up** **1** PHRASAL VERB 句動詞 If you **catch up with** someone who is in front of you, you reach them by walking faster than they are walking. 追いつく ❑*I stopped and waited for her to catch up.* 私は立ち止まり、彼女が追いつくのを待った. **2** PHRASAL VERB 句動詞 To **catch up with** someone means to reach the same standard, stage, or level that they have reached. 追いつく ❑*Most late developers will catch up with their friends.* 成長の遅れた生徒の大半は同級生に追いつくだろう. ❑*John began the season better than me but I have fought to catch up.* 今シーズンのスタートは私よりもジョンの方が好調だったが、私は苦闘して追いついた. **3** PHRASAL VERB 句動詞 If you **catch up on** an activity that you have not had much time to do recently, you spend time doing it. 遅れを取り戻す ❑*I was catching up on a bit of reading.* 私はちょっと読書の遅れを取り戻していたところだ. **4** PHRASAL VERB 句動詞 If you **catch up on** friends who you have not seen for some time or on their lives, you talk

to them and find out what has happened in their lives since you last talked together. 久しぶりに語り合う ❑ *The ladies spent some time catching up on each other's health and families.* 女性たちはお互いの健康状態や家族について久しぶりに語り合ってしばらく時間を過ごした。 ᠍⃟ PHRASAL VERB 句動詞 If you **are caught up in** something, you are involved in it, usually unwillingly. 巻き込まれる ❑ *The people themselves weren't part of the conflict; they were just caught up in it.* その人たちは紛争とは関係なかった．彼らは巻き添えになっただけだった。

▶ **catch up with** ᠍⃟ PHRASAL VERB 句動詞 When people **catch up with** someone who has done something wrong, they succeed in finding them in order to arrest or punish them. 逮捕する，処罰する ❑ *The law caught up with him yesterday.* 昨日彼は法の下で処罰を受けた。 ᠎⃟ PHRASAL VERB 句動詞 If something **catches up with** you, you are forced to deal with something unpleasant that happened or that you did in the past, which you have been able to avoid until now. 悪い結果をもたらす ❑ *Although he subsequently became a successful businessman, his criminal past caught up with him.* 彼はその後事業家として成功したけれども，結局罪を犯した過去のつけが彼に回ってきた。

catch|word /kǽtʃwɜrd/ (**catchwords**) N-COUNT 可算名詞 A **catchword** is a word or phrase that becomes popular or well-known, for example, because it is associated with a political campaign. スローガン ❑ *The catchword he and his supporters have been using is "consolidation."* 彼が支援者と共に使ってきたスローガンは「強化」である。

catchy /kǽtʃi/ (**catchier, catchiest**) ADJ 形容詞 If you describe a tune, name, or advertisement as **catchy**, you mean that it is attractive and easy to remember. 楽しくて覚えやすい ❑ *The songs were both catchy and cutting.* それらの歌は覚えやすくまた痛烈なものだった。

cat|egori|cal /kætɪɡɔ́rɪkəl/ ADJ 形容詞 If you are **categorical** about something, you state your views very definitely and firmly. 絶対的な ❑ *...his categorical denial of the charges of sexual harassment.* 性的嫌がらせの嫌疑に対する彼の全面的な否定 ● **cat|egori|cal|ly** /kætɪɡɔ́rɪkli/ ADV 副詞 [ADV with v] 絶対的に ❑ *They totally and categorically deny the charges.* 彼らは必ず完全かつ明確に嫌疑を否定する。

cat|ego|rize /kǽtɪɡəraɪz/ (**categorizes, categorizing, categorized**) V-T 他動詞 If you **categorize** people or things, you divide them into sets or you say which set they belong to. 分類する ❑ *Lindsay, like his films, is hard to categorize.* リンゼイは彼の映画同様に類別するのが難しい。 ❑ *Make a list of your child's toys and then categorize them as sociable or antisocial.* 子供のおもちゃのリストを作り，社交的なものと反社会的なものに分類せよ。 ● **cat|ego|ri|za|tion** /kætɪɡərɪzéɪʃən/ N-VAR 可変性名詞 分類 ❑ *Her first novel defies easy categorization.* 彼女の最初の小説は容易に分類できるものではない。

cat|ego|ry /kǽtɪɡɔri/ (**categories**) N-COUNT 可算名詞 If people or things are divided into **categories**, they are divided into groups in such a way that the members of each group are similar to each other in some way. 部類 ❑ *This book clearly falls into the category of fictionalized autobiography.* この本は明らかに小説化された自伝の部類に入る。

Thesaurus	*category* また次を参照：
N.	class, classification, grouping, kind, rank, sort, type

ca|ter /kéɪtər/ (**caters, catering, catered**) ᠍⃟ V-I 自動詞 To **cater to** a group of people means to provide all the things that they need or want. 要求を満たす ❑ *We cater to an exclusive clientele.* 我々は上流の顧客相手に商売する。 ᠎⃟ V-I 自動詞 To **cater to** something means to take it into account. 考慮に入れる ❑ *Exercise classes cater to all levels of fitness.* 運動クラスはあらゆるレベルのフィットネスを考慮に入れている。 ❑ *...shops that cater to the needs of men.* 男性のニーズを考慮した店 ᠏⃟ V-T 他動詞 If a person or company **caters** an occasion such as a wedding or a party, they provide food and drink for all the people there. 料理を提供する ❑ *...a full-service restaurant equipped to cater large events.* 大規模な行事向けの料理を提供する設備のあるフルサービスのレストラン ● → see also **catering**

ca|ter|er /kéɪtərər/ (**caterers**) N-COUNT 可算名詞 **Caterers** are people or companies that provide food and drink for a place such as an office or for special occasions such as weddings and parties. 料理の仕出屋，配膳業者 ❑ *The caterers were already laying out the tables for lunch.* 料理の仕出屋は既にランチのためにテーブルの準備をしていた。

ca|ter|ing /kéɪtərɪŋ/ N-UNCOUNT 不可算名詞 **Catering** is the activity of providing food and drink for a large number of people, for example, at weddings and parties. 配膳業 [also "the" N, oft N n] ❑ *His catering business made him a millionaire at 41.* 彼は配膳業で成功し，41歳で百万長者になった。

cat|er|pil|lar /kǽtərpɪlər/ (**caterpillars**) N-COUNT 可算名詞 A **caterpillar** is a small, worm-like animal that feeds on plants and eventually develops into a butterfly or moth. 芋虫

ca|thedral /kəθíːdrəl/ (**cathedrals**) N-COUNT 可算名詞 A **cathedral** is a very large and important church which has a bishop in charge of it. 大聖堂 ❑ *...St. Paul's Cathedral.* セントポール大聖堂

Catho|lic /kǽθlɪk/ (**Catholics**) ᠍⃟ ADJ 形容詞 The **Catholic** Church is the branch of the Christian Church that accepts the Pope as its leader and is based in the Vatican in Rome. カトリック教会の ❑ *...the Catholic Church.* カトリック教会 ❑ *...Catholic priests.* カトリック教会の司祭 ᠎⃟ ADJ 形容詞 If you describe a collection of things or people as **catholic**, you are emphasizing that they are very varied. 広範囲にわたる ❑ *He was a man of catholic tastes, a lover of grand opera, history, and the fine arts.* オペラ，歴史，美術と，彼は広範囲な趣味を持つ男だった。 ᠏⃟ N-COUNT 可算名詞 A **Catholic** is a member of the Catholic Church. カトリック教徒 ❑ *At least nine out of ten Mexicans are baptized Catholics.* メキシコ人は少なくとも10人のうち9人が洗礼を受けたカトリック教徒だ。

Ca|tholi|cism /kəθɔ́lɪsɪzəm/ N-UNCOUNT 不可算名詞 **Catholicism** is the traditions, the behavior, and the set of Christian beliefs that are held by Catholics. カトリック主義 ❑ *...her conversion to Catholicism.* 彼女のカトリック主義への改宗

cat|nip /kǽtnɪp/ N-UNCOUNT 不可算名詞 **Catnip** is an herb with scented leaves, which cats are fond of. イヌハッカ，チクマハッカ ❑ *Catnip grows wild in much of the United States.* イヌハッカは米国の多くの地域で自生する。

cat|tle /kǽtəl/ N-PLURAL 複数名詞 **Cattle** are cows and bulls. 牛 ❑ *...the finest herd of beef cattle for two hundred miles.* 200マイルにわたり最上の肉牛の群れ
→ see **dairy**

cat|walk /kǽtwɔk/ (**catwalks**) ᠍⃟ N-COUNT 可算名詞 At a fashion show, the **catwalk** is a narrow platform that models walk along to display clothes. キャットウォーク（客席に突き出た細長い舞台） ❑ *On the catwalk the models stomped around in thigh-high leather boots.* ももまで届く革のブーツをはいたモデルたちは，キャットウォークを力強い足取りで歩き回った。 ᠎⃟ N-COUNT 可算名詞 A **catwalk** is a narrow bridge high in the air, for example between two parts of a tall building, on the outside of a large structure, or over a stage. （ビル間などの空中の）連絡通路 ❑ *...a catwalk overlooking a vast room.* 巨大な部屋を見下ろす連絡通路

Cau|ca|sian /kɔkéɪʒən/ (**Caucasians**) ADJ 形容詞 A **Caucasian** person is a white person. 白人の [FORMAL 形式ばった] ❑ *...a 25-year-old Caucasian male.* 25歳の白人の男性 ● N-COUNT 可算名詞 A **Caucasian** is someone who is Caucasian. 白人 ❑ *Ann Hamilton was a Caucasian from New England.* アン・ハミルトンはニューイングランド出身の白人だった。

cau|cus /kɔ́kəs/ (**caucuses**) N-COUNT 可算名詞 A **caucus** is a group of people within an organization who share similar aims and interests or who have a lot of influence. 会派，幹部会 [FORMAL 形式ばった] ❑ *...the Black Caucus of minority congressmen.* 少数民会議員の黒人会派

caught /kɔt/ **Caught** is the past tense and past participle of **catch**. catchの過去・過去分詞

Word Link	*cal, caul* ≈ *hot, heat : calorie, cauldron, scald*

caul|dron /kɔ́ldrən/ (**cauldrons**) N-COUNT 可算名詞 A **cauldron** is a very large, round metal pot used for cooking over a fire. 大がま [LITERARY 文語的] ❑ *...a witch's cauldron.* 魔女の大がま

cau|li|flow|er /kɔ́lɪflaʊər/ (**cauliflowers**) N-VAR 可変性名詞 **Cauliflower** is a large, round vegetable that has a hard, white center surrounded by green leaves. カリフラワー

cause /kɔz/ (**causes, causing, caused**) ᠍⃟ N-COUNT 可算名詞 The **cause of** an event, usually a bad event, is the thing that makes it happen. 原因 ❑ *Smoking is the biggest preventable cause of death and disease.* 喫煙は防止できる死亡と病気の最大の原因である。 ᠎⃟ N-COUNT 可算名詞 A **cause** is an aim or principle which a group of people supports or is fighting for. 目標，主義 ❑ *Refusing to have one leader has not helped the cause.* 1人の指導者を持つことを拒否したことはその目標のためにならなかった。 ᠏⃟ V-T 他動詞 To **cause** something, usually something bad, means to make it happen. 引き起こす ❑ *The insecticide used on weeds can cause health problems.* 一部の雑草に使われる殺虫剤は健康上の問題を引き起こすことがある。 ❑ *This was a genuine mistake, but it did cause me some worry.* これは本当の間違いだったが，私は多少心配させられた。 ᠐⃟ N-UNCOUNT 不可算名詞 If you have **cause for** a particular feeling or action, you have good reasons for feeling it or doing it. 正当な理由 ❑ *Only a few people can find any cause for celebration.* お祝いをする何らかの正当な理由を見出せる人はほとんどいない。 ᠑⃟ PHRASE 句 If you say that something is **for a good cause**, you mean that it is worth doing or giving to because it will help other people, for example by raising money for charity. 大義のために，よい目的のために ❑ *The Raleigh International Bike Ride is open to anyone who wants to raise money for a good cause.* ローリー国際バイクライドは慈善のために募金をしたい人なら誰でも参加できる。

cause

v.   generate, make, produce, provoke; *(ant.)* deter, prevent, stop **3**

v.   **determine the** cause **1**
     support a cause **2**
N.   cause **of death 1**
     cause **an accident,** cause **cancer,** cause **problems,** cause **a reaction 3**
     cause **for concern 4**

'cause /kʌz, kɔz/ also **cause** CONJ 接続詞 **'Cause** is an informal way of saying **because.** becauseの口語 [SPOKEN 口語] ❑ *Hopefully everybody's well-rested 'cause it could be a long day.* 長い1日となるかもしれないので、全員が十分休憩を取ったことを望む.

cau|tion /kɔʃ⁰n/ (cautions, cautioning, cautioned) **1** N-UNCOUNT 不可算名詞 **Caution** is great care which you take in order to avoid possible danger. 注意 ❑ *Extreme caution should be exercised when buying used tires.* 中古のタイヤを買う際は細心の注意を払うべきだ. **2** V-T/V-I 他動詞/自動詞 If someone **cautions** you, they warn you about problems or danger. 警告する ❑ *Tony cautioned against misrepresenting the situation.* トニーは状況を不正確に伝えないようにと警告した. ❑ *The statement clearly was intended to caution Seoul against attempting to block the council's action again.* その声明は明らかに韓国政府に評議会の行動を再度妨害しようとしないように警告するためのものだった. ● N-UNCOUNT 不可算名詞 **Caution** is also a noun. 警告 ❑ *There was a note of caution for the treasury in the figures.* その数字には国庫に対する警告のしるしが含まれていた. **3** to **err on the side of** caution → see **err**

cau|tion|ary /kɔʃəneri/ ADJ 形容詞 A **cautionary** story or a **cautionary** note to a story is one that is intended to give a warning to people. 戒めの ❑ *Barely fifteen months later, it has become a cautionary tale of the pitfalls of international mergers and acquisitions.* 15ヶ月も経つか経たないうちに、それは国際合併・買収の落とし穴の教訓物語となった.

cau|tious /kɔʃəs/ ADJ 形容詞 Someone who is **cautious** acts very carefully in order to avoid possible danger. 慎重な ❑ *The scientists are cautious about using enzyme therapy on humans.* 科学者は人間に酵素療法を行うことについて慎重である. ● **cau|tious|ly** ADV 副詞 注意深く ❑ *David moved cautiously forward and looked over the edge.* デイビッドは注意深く前方に進み、縁を見渡した.

ADJ.   alert, careful, guarded, watchful; *(ant.)* careless, rash, reckless

cava|lier /kævəlɪər/ ADJ 形容詞 If you describe a person or their behavior as **cavalier,** you are criticizing them because you think that they do not consider other people's feelings or take account of the seriousness of a situation. むとんじゃくな、おうような [DISAPPROVAL 不賛成] ❑ *The editor takes a cavalier attitude to the concept of fact checking.* 編集長は事実確認という考え方にむとんじゃくな態度を取る.

cav|al|ry /kævᵊlri/ **1** N-SING 単数名詞 **The cavalry** is the part of an army that uses armored vehicles for fighting. 機甲隊 ❑ *The 3rd Cavalry went on the offensive.* 第3機甲隊は攻撃に出た. **2** N-SING 単数名詞 **The cavalry** is the group of soldiers in an army who ride horses. 騎兵隊 ❑ *...a young cavalry officer.* 若い騎兵将校

cave /keɪv/ (caves, caving, caved) N-COUNT 可算名詞 A **cave** is a large hole in the side of a cliff or hill, or one that is under the ground. 洞窟(どうくつ) ❑ *Outside the cave mouth the blackness of night was like a curtain.* 洞窟の入り口の外は夜の闇が幕を張ったようだった.

▶ **cave in 1** PHRASAL VERB 句動詞 If something such as a roof or a ceiling **caves in,** it collapses inward. 陥没する ❑ *Part of the roof has caved in.* 屋根の一部が陥没した. **2** PHRASAL VERB 句動詞 If you **cave in,** you suddenly stop arguing or resisting, especially when people put pressure on you to stop. 屈服する ❑ *After a ruinous strike, the union caved in.* 破滅的なストライキの後、組合は屈服した. ❑ *The judge has caved in to political pressure.* 判事は政治的圧力に屈服した.

cav|ern /kævərn/ (caverns) N-COUNT 可算名詞 A **cavern** is a large, deep cave. 大洞窟(どうくつ)

cav|ern|ous /kævərnəs/ ADJ 形容詞 A **cavernous** room or building is very large inside, and so it reminds you of a cave. 洞穴のような ❑ *Climbing steep stairs to the choir gallery you peer into a*

cavernous interior. 急な階段をつたい聖歌隊席に登ると、洞穴のような室内が見える.

cavi|ar /kæviɑr/ (caviars) also **caviare** N-MASS 質量名詞 **Caviar** is the salted eggs of a fish called a sturgeon. キャビア

cav|ity /kæviti/ (cavities) **1** N-COUNT 可算名詞 A **cavity** is a space or hole in something such as a solid object or a person's body. 空洞; 腔(こう) [FORMAL 形式ばった] ❑ *...a cavity in the roof.* 屋根の空洞 **2** N-COUNT 可算名詞 In dentistry, a **cavity** is a hole in a tooth, caused by decay. 虫歯の穴 [TECHNICAL 技術的]
→ see **smell, teeth**

cc /si si/ **1** You use **cc** when referring to the volume or capacity of something such as the size of a car engine. **cc** is an abbreviation for "cubic centimeters." cubic centimetersの略 ❑ *...1,500 cc sports cars.* 1500ccのスポーツカー **2** **cc** is used in e-mail headers or at the end of a business letter to indicate that a copy is being sent to another person. cc (電子メールなどで本来の宛先以外にコピーを送付する機能) [BUSINESS 実業] ❑ *...cc j.jones@ harpercollins.co.uk.* j. jones@harpercollins. co. ukにコピーを送信 ❑ *...cc J. Chater, S. Cooper.* J. Chater, S. Cooperにコピーを送信

CCTV /si si ti vi/ N-UNCOUNT 不可算名詞 **CCTV** is an abbreviation for "closed-circuit television." closed-circuit televisionの略 ❑ *...a CCTV camera.* CCTVカメラ

CD /si di/ (CDs) N-COUNT 可算名詞 **CDs** are small plastic discs on which sound, especially music, is recorded. **CDs** can also be used to store information which can be read by a computer. **CD** is an abbreviation for "compact disc." compact discの略 ❑ *The Beatles' Red and Blue compilations are issued on CD for the first time next month.* ビートルズの「レッド」と「ブルー」の編集版が来月CDで初めて発売される.
→ see **DVD, laser**

CD burn|er (CD burners) N-COUNT 可算名詞 A **CD burner** is a piece of computer equipment that you use for copying data from a computer onto a CD. CDバーナー [COMPUTING コンピューティング] ❑ *Users can download MP3 music files and record them directly onto a CD audio disc using a PC CD burner.* 利用者はMP3音楽ファイルをダウンロードし、パソコンのCDバーナーを使ってCDオーディオディスクに直接録音できる.

CD play|er (CD players) N-COUNT 可算名詞 A **CD player** is a machine on which you can play CDs. CDプレイヤー

CD-ROM /si di rɒm/ (CD-ROMs) N-COUNT 可算名詞 A **CD-ROM** is a CD on which a very large amount of information can be stored and then read using a computer. **CD-ROM** is an abbreviation for "compact disc read-only memory." compact disc read-only memoryの略 [COMPUTING コンピューティング] ❑ *A single CD-ROM can hold more than 500 megabytes of data.* たった1枚のCD-ROMに500メガバイトのデータを保管できる.

CD-ROM drive /si di rɒm draɪv/ (CD-ROM drives) N-COUNT 可算名詞 A **CD-ROM drive** is the device that you use with a computer to play CD-ROMs. CD-ROMドライブ

CD writ|er (CD writers) N-COUNT 可算名詞 A **CD writer** is the same as a **CD burner.** CDライター [COMPUTING コンピューティング]

cease /sis/ (ceases, ceasing, ceased) **1** V-I 自動詞 If something **ceases,** it stops happening or existing. やめる [FORMAL 形式ばった] ❑ *At one o'clock the rain had ceased.* 1時に雨が降り止んだ. **2** V-T 他動詞 If you **cease** to do something, you stop doing it. やめる [FORMAL 形式ばった] ❑ *The secrecy about the president's condition had ceased to matter.* 大統領の病状に関する秘密厳守は問題ではなくなっていた. **3** V-T 他動詞 If you **cease** something, you stop it happening or working. しなくなる [FORMAL 形式ばった] ❑ *The Tundra Times, a weekly newspaper in Alaska, ceased publication this week.* アラスカの週報「ツンドラ・タイムズ」は今週廃刊になった.

v.   end, finish, halt, quit, shut down, stop; *(ant.)* begin, continue, start **1**

cease|fire /sisfaɪər/ (ceasefires) N-COUNT 可算名詞 A **ceasefire** is an arrangement in which countries or groups of people that are fighting each other agree to stop fighting. 停戦 ❑ *They have agreed to a ceasefire after three years of conflict.* 彼らは3年間続いた戦闘の後、停戦に合意した.

ce|dar /sidər/ (cedars) N-COUNT 可算名詞 A **cedar** is a large evergreen tree with wide branches and small, thin leaves called needles. ヒマラヤスギ ● N-UNCOUNT 不可算名詞 **Cedar** is the wood of this tree. ヒマラヤスギ材 ❑ *The yacht is built of cedar strip planking.* ヨットはヒマラヤスギの細長い張り板でできている.

cede /sid/ (cedes, ceding, ceded) V-T 他動詞 If someone in a position of authority **cedes** land or power to someone else, they let them have the land or power, often as a result of military or political pressure. 譲る、割譲する [FORMAL 形式ばった] ❑ *Only a short campaign took place in Puerto Rico, but after the war Spain ceded the island to America.* プエルトリコでの戦闘は短期間だったが、スペイ

C

Word Web   cellphone

The word **"cell"** does not refer to something inside the **cellular phone** itself. It describes the area around a **wireless transmitter**. The electrical system and **battery** in today's **mobile** phones are tiny. This makes their electronic **signals** weak. They can't travel very far. Therefore today's **cellular** phone systems need a lot of closely-spaced cells. When you make a call, your phone connects to the transmitter with the strongest signal. Then it chooses a **channel** and connects you to the number you dialed. If you are in a car, **stations** in several different cells may handle your call.

ンはアメリカに同島を割譲した.

ceil|ing /síːlɪŋ/ (**ceilings**) **1** N-COUNT 名詞 A **ceiling** is the horizontal surface that forms the top part or roof inside a room. 天井 □ *The rooms were spacious, with tall windows and high ceilings.* それらの部屋は大きな窓と高い天井があり広々としていた. **2** N-COUNT 可算名詞 A **ceiling on** something such as prices or wages is an official upper limit that cannot be broken. 上限 □ *...an informal agreement to put a ceiling on salaries.* 給料に上限を設ける非公式の取り決め. **3** → see also **glass ceiling**

cel|ebrate /sélɪbreɪt/ (**celebrates, celebrating, celebrated**) **1** V-T/V-I 他動詞/自動詞 If you **celebrate** an occasion or if you **celebrate**, you do something enjoyable because of a special occasion or to mark someone's success. 祝う □ *I was in a mood to celebrate.* 私はお祝いをする気分だった. □ *Dick celebrated his 60th birthday Monday.* ディックは月曜に還暦を祝った. **2** V-T 他動詞 If an organization or country **is celebrating** an anniversary, it has existed for that length of time and is doing something special because of it. (周年祭などを) 挙行する □ *The society is celebrating its tenth anniversary this year.* その協会は今年設立10周年の祝賀行事を行なう予定だ. **3** V-T 他動詞 When priests **celebrate** Holy Communion or Mass, they officially perform the actions and ceremonies that are involved. (宗教的儀式を) 行う □ *Pope John Paul celebrated mass today in a city in central Poland.* ヨハネパウロ教皇はポーランド中心部にある都市で今日ミサを行なった.

cel|ebrat|ed /sélɪbreɪtɪd/ ADJ 形容詞 A **celebrated** person or thing is famous and much admired. 著名な □ *He was soon one of the most celebrated young painters in England.* 彼はまもなくイギリスで最も著名な若い画家の1人となった.

Word Link   ation ≈ state of: celebration, elevation, relaxation

cel|ebra|tion /sélɪbreɪʃⁿn/ (**celebrations**) **1** N-COUNT 可算名詞 A **celebration** is a special enjoyable event that people organize because something pleasant has happened or because it is someone's birthday or anniversary. 祝賀会 □ *I can tell you, there was a celebration in our house that night.* 私たちの家ではその晩祝賀会があったのよ. **2** N-SING 単数名詞 The **celebration of** something is praise and appreciation which is given to it. 賞賛 □ *This was not a memorial service but a celebration of his life.* これは追悼会ではなく彼の人生の賛美だった.

ce|leb|rity /sɪlébrɪti/ (**celebrities**) **1** N-COUNT 可算名詞 A **celebrity** is someone who is famous, especially in areas of entertainment such as movies, music, writing, or sports. 有名人 □ *In 1944, at the age of 30, Hersey suddenly became a celebrity.* ハーシーは1944年に30歳で突然有名人になった. **2** N-UNCOUNT 不可算名詞 If a person or thing achieves **celebrity**, they become famous, especially in areas of entertainment such as movies, music, writing, or sports. 名声 □ *He achieved celebrity as a sports commentator.* 彼はスポーツ解説者として名声を得た.

cel|ery /séləri/ N-UNCOUNT 不可算名詞 **Celery** is a vegetable with long, pale green stalks. It is eaten raw in salads. セロリ □ *...a stick of celery.* 1本のセロリ

ce|les|tial /sɪléstʃəl/ ADJ 形容詞 **Celestial** is used to describe things relating to heaven or to the sky. 天空の [LITERARY 文語的] □ *...the clusters of celestial bodies in the ever-expanding universe.* 常に拡張し続ける宇宙の天体の群れ
→ see **astronomer**

celi|ba|cy /sélɪbəsi/ N-UNCOUNT 不可算名詞 **Celibacy** is the state of being celibate. 独身主義 □ *...priests who violate their vows of celibacy.* 独身主義の誓いに背く聖職者

celi|bate /sélɪbɪt/ (**celibates**) **1** ADJ 形容詞 Someone who is **celibate** does not marry or have sex, because of their religious beliefs. 独身主義の □ *The Pope bluntly told the world's priests yesterday to stay celibate.* 教皇は昨日, 世界の聖職者に独身を守るようはっきりと指示した. ● N-COUNT 可算名詞 A **celibate** is someone who is celibate. 独身主義者 □ *...the U.S.A.'s biggest group of celibates.* 米国最大の独身主義者の集団 **2** ADJ 形容詞 Someone who is **celibate** does not have sex during a particular period of their life. 禁欲している □ *I was celibate for two years.* 私は2年間禁欲生活を送った.

cell /sél/ (**cells**) **1** N-COUNT 可算名詞 A **cell** is the smallest part

of an animal or plant that is able to function independently. Every animal or plant is made up of millions of cells. 細胞 □ *Those cells divide and give many other different types of cells.* そうした細胞は分裂し, 多くの異なるタイプの細胞を産み出す. □ *...blood cells.* 血液細胞 **2** N-COUNT 可算名詞 A **cell** is a small room in which a prisoner is locked. A **cell** is also a small room in which a monk or nun lives. 独房 □ *Do you recall how many prisoners were placed in each cell?* 各独房には何人の囚人が入れられたか覚えていますか.
→ see **cellphone, clone, skin**

cel|lar /sélər/ (**cellars**) **1** N-COUNT 可算名詞 A **cellar** is a room underneath a building, which is often used for storing things in. 地下室 □ *The box of papers had been stored in a cellar at the family home.* 書類の箱が家の地下室に保管されていた. **2** N-COUNT 可算名詞 A person's or restaurant's **cellar** is the collection of different wines that they have. ワインの貯え □ *Choose a superb wine to complement your meal from our extensive wine cellar.* 当店の豊富なワインコレクションからお食事を引き立てる素晴らしいワインをお選びください.

cel|list /tʃélɪst/ (**cellists**) N-COUNT 可算名詞 A **cellist** is someone who plays the cello. チェロ奏者

cel|lo /tʃéloʊ/ (**cellos**) N-VAR 可変性名詞 A **cello** is a musical instrument with four strings that looks like a large violin. You play the cello with a bow while sitting down and holding it upright between your legs. チェロ
→ see **orchestra, string**

cell|phone /sélfoʊn/ (**cellphones**) N-COUNT 可算名詞 A **cellphone** is the same as a **cellular phone**. 携帯電話 [mainly AM 主に米国英語]
→ see Word Web: **cellphone**

cel|lu|lar /sélyələr/ ADJ 形容詞 **Cellular** means relating to the cells of animals or plants. 細胞の □ *Many toxic effects can be studied at the cellular level.* 多くの中毒作用は細胞レベルで研究できる.
→ see **cellphone**

cel|lu|lar phone (**cellular phones**) N-COUNT 可算名詞 A **cellular phone** or **cellular telephone** is a type of telephone which does not need wires to connect it to a telephone system. 携帯電話 [mainly AM 主に米国英語]
→ see **cellphone**

cel|lu|lite /sélyəlaɪt/ N-UNCOUNT 不可算名詞 **Cellulite** is lumpy fat which people may get under their skin, especially on their thighs. セルライト □ *...an Italian-made product that is said to eradicate cellulite within weeks.* 数週間のうちにセルライトをなくすと言われるイタリア製の製品

Cel|sius /sélsiəs/ ADJ 形容詞 **Celsius** is a scale for measuring temperature, in which water freezes at 0 degrees and boils at 100 degrees. It is represented by the symbol °C. 摂氏の [n/num ADJ] □ *Highest temperatures 11° Celsius, that's 52° Fahrenheit.* 最高気温はセ氏11度, それはカ氏52度. ● N-UNCOUNT 不可算名詞 **Celsius** is also a noun. セ氏 □ *The thermometer shows the temperature in Celsius and Fahrenheit.* 温度計はセ氏とカ氏の温度を示す.

ce|ment /sɪmént/ (**cements, cementing, cemented**) **1** N-UNCOUNT 不可算名詞 **Cement** is a gray powder which is mixed with sand and water in order to make concrete. セメント □ *Builders have trouble getting the right amount of cement into their concrete.* 建設業者はコンクリートに適量のセメントを入れるのに苦労している. **2** N-UNCOUNT 不可算名詞 **Cement** is the same as **concrete**. コンクリート □ *...the hard, cold cement floor.* 硬く冷たいコンクリートの床 **3** N-UNCOUNT 不可算名詞 Glue that is made for sticking particular substances together is sometimes called **cement**. 接合剤 □ *Stick the pieces on with tile cement.* タイル用接合剤でタイルを貼り付けなさい. **4** V-T 他動詞 Something that **cements** a relationship or agreement makes it stronger. 固める □ *Nothing cements a friendship between countries so much as trade.* 貿易ほど相手国間の友好を強化するものはない. **5** V-T 他動詞 If things **are cemented** together, they are stuck or fastened together. 結合する [usu passive] □ *Most artificial joints are cemented into place.* 大半の人工関節は正しく結合されている.

cem|etery /sémətéri/ (**cemeteries**) N-COUNT 可算名詞 A **cemetery** is a place where dead people's bodies or their ashes are buried. 共同墓地

cen|sor /sɛnsər/ (**censors**, **censoring**, **censored**) **1** V-T 他動詞 If someone in authority **censors** letters or the media, they officially examine them and cut out any information that is regarded as secret. 検閲する □ *The military-backed government has heavily censored the news.* 軍部の支援を受けた政権はニュースを大幅に検閲した。 **2** V-T 他動詞 If someone in authority **censors** a book, play, or movie, they officially examine it and cut out any parts that are considered to be immoral or inappropriate. 検閲して削除する □ *The Late Show censored the band's live version of "Bullet in the Head."* レイトショーはそのバンドの「頭に弾を」のライブ版を検閲して削除した。 **3** N-COUNT 可算名詞 A **censor** is a person who has been officially appointed to examine letters or the media and to cut out any parts that are regarded as secret. 検閲官 □ *The report was cleared by the American military censors.* その報道はアメリカの軍事検閲官の許可を受けた。 **4** N-COUNT 可算名詞 A **censor** is a person who has been officially appointed to examine plays, movies, and books and to cut out any parts that are considered to be immoral. 検閲官 □ *The movie had to be cut before the board of censors accepted it.* その映画は検閲委員会の承認を受ける前に一部カットする必要があった。

cen|sor|ship /sɛnsərʃɪp/ N-UNCOUNT 不可算名詞 **Censorship** is the censoring of books, plays, movies, or reports, especially by government officials, because they are considered immoral or secret in some way. 検閲 □ *The government today announced that press censorship was being lifted.* 政府は今日報道の検閲を廃止すると発表した。

cen|sure /sɛnʃər/ (**censures**, **censuring**, **censured**) V-T 他動詞 If you **censure** someone **for** something that they have done, you tell them that you strongly disapprove of it. 非難する [FORMAL 形式ばった] □ *The ethics committee may take a decision to admonish him or to censure him.* 倫理委員会は彼に勧告もしくは非難することを決定するかもしれない。 ● N-UNCOUNT 不可算名詞 **Censure** is also a noun. 非難 □ *It is a controversial policy which has attracted international censure.* それは国際的非難を招いている問題のある政策だ。

cen|sus /sɛnsəs/ (**censuses**) N-COUNT 可算名詞 A **census** is an official survey of the population of a country that is carried out in order to find out how many people live there and to obtain details of such things as people's ages and jobs. 国勢調査 □ *The detailed assessment of the latest census will be ready in three months.* 最新の国勢調査の詳しい評価は3ヵ月後に出る予定だ。
→ see Word Web: **census**

cent /sɛnt/ (**cents**) N-COUNT 可算名詞 A **cent** is a small unit of money worth one hundredth of some currencies, for example the dollar and the euro. セント □ *A cup of rice which cost thirty cents a few weeks ago is now being sold for up to one dollar.* 数週間前まで30セントだった1杯の米は現在1ドルもする。

cen|te|nary /sɛntɛnəri/ (**centenaries**) N-COUNT 可算名詞 A **centenary** is the same as a **centennial**. 百周年 [mainly BRIT 主に英国英語]

cen|ten|nial /sɛntɛniəl/ N-SING 単数名詞 The **centennial of** an event such as someone's birth is the 100th anniversary of that event. 百周年 [mainly AM 主に米国英語] [oft N n] □ *The centennial Olympics was in Atlanta, Georgia.* 百周年記念のオリンピックはジョージア州アトランタで開催された。

cen|ter /sɛntər/ (**centers**, **centering**, **centered**) **1** N-COUNT 可算名詞 The **center** of something is the middle of it. 中心 □ *A large, wooden table dominates the center of the room.* 部屋の中央には大きな

木のテーブルがある。 **2** N-COUNT 可算名詞 A **center** is a building where people have meetings, take part in a particular activity, or get help of some kind. センター □ *She now also does pottery classes at a community center.* 彼女は現在コミュニティセンターの陶芸教室にも出ている。 **3** N-COUNT 可算名詞 If an area or town is a **center** for an industry or activity, that industry or activity is very important there. 中心地 □ *New York is also a major international financial center.* ニューヨークは国際金融の主要な中心でもある。 **4** N-COUNT 可算名詞 The **center** of a town or city is the part where there are the most stores and businesses and where a lot of people come from other areas to work or shop. 中心部 □ *...the city center.* 市の中心部 **5** N-COUNT 可算名詞 If someone or something is at the **center of** a situation, they are the most important thing or person involved. 中核 □ *...the man at the center of the controversy.* 論争の中核となっている男 **6** N-COUNT 可算名詞 If someone or something is the **center of** attention or interest, people are giving them a lot of attention. 的 □ *The rest of the cast was used to her being the center of attention.* 他の出演者たちは彼女が注目の的であるのに慣れていた。 **7** N-SING 単数名詞 In politics, **the center** refers to groups and their beliefs, when they are considered to be neither left-wing nor right-wing. 中道派 □ *The Democrats have become a party of the center.* 民主党は中道派の政党になった。 **8** V-T/V-I 他動詞/自動詞 If something **centers** or **is centered on** a particular thing or person, that thing or person is the main subject of attention. 集中させる [他動詞]、中心となる [自動詞] □ *...the improvement was the result of a plan which centered on academic achievement and personal motivation.* その向上は学業の達成と個人のやる気を中心にした計画の結果だった。 □ *All his concerns were centered around himself rather than Rachel.* 彼の関心は全てレイチェルよりむしろ彼自身に向けられていた。 ● **-centered** COMB IN ADJ 形容詞の複合 一中心の □ *...a child-centered approach to teaching.* 子供中心の教育アプローチ **9** V-T/V-I 他動詞/自動詞 If an industry or event **is centered** in a place, or if it **centers** there, it takes place to the greatest extent there. 集中する □ *The fighting has been centered around the town of Vucovar.* 戦闘はヴコヴァーの町の周辺に集中していた。 □ *The disturbances have centered around the two main university areas.* 騒動は2つの主な大学地域に集中した。 **10** → see also **community center**, **shopping center**
→ see **soccer**

-centered /-sɛntərd/ **1** COMB IN ADJ 形容詞の複合 **-centered** can be added to adjectives and nouns to indicate what kind of a center something has. 中央にある □ *...lemon-centered white chocolates.* 真ん中にレモンのあるホワイトチョコレート **2** → see also **center**, **self-centered**

center|piece /sɛntərpis/ (**centerpieces**) **1** N-COUNT 可算名詞 The **centerpiece** of something is the best or most interesting part of it. 主眼となる点 □ *The centerpiece of the plan is the idea of regular referendums, initiated by voters.* その計画の主眼は有権者が始めた定期的な住民投票という考えだ。 **2** N-COUNT 可算名詞 A **centerpiece** is an ornament which you put in the middle of something, especially a dinner table. センターピース □ *He was arranging floral centerpieces in the banquet hall.* 彼は宴会場でセンターピースの生花を活けていた。

cen|ti|grade /sɛntɪgreɪd/ ADJ 形容詞 **Centigrade** is a scale for measuring temperature, in which water freezes at 0 degrees and boils at 100 degrees. It is represented by the symbol ºC. セ氏 □ *...daytime temperatures of up to forty degrees centigrade.* 最高40℃の日中の気温 ● N-UNCOUNT 不可算名詞 **Centigrade** is also a noun. セ氏温度計 □ *The number at the bottom is the recommended water*

Every 10 years the U.S. government conducts a **census**. This **survey counts** the number of people and provides details about the way they live. It determines how many delegates each state sends to the House of Representatives. It also affects how the federal government spends its money. The census takes months to complete. In March, the Census Bureau* mails out around 100 million **questionnaires**. Government employees also deliver about 22 million more forms in person. In April, census workers visit people who haven't returned their forms. All the information must be pulled together by December 31 of that year.

Census Bureau: a part of the government that collects and reports data about the population and economy.

temperature in centigrade. 下の数字はセ氏温度計での推奨水温だ.

cen|ti|me|ter /sɛntɪmiːtər/ (**centimeters**) N-COUNT 可算名詞 A **centimeter** is a unit of length in the metric system equal to ten millimeters or one-hundredth of a meter. センチメートル ❑ *...a tiny fossil plant, only a few centimeters high.* 高さがわずか数センチの小さな化石化した植物

Word Link	centr ≈ middle : central, concentrated, decentralized

cen|tral /sɛntrəl/ 🚹 ADJ 形容詞 Something that is **central** is in the middle of a place or area. 中央の ❑ *...Central America's Caribbean coast.* 中央アメリカのカリブ海の海岸 ❑ *The disruption has now spread and is affecting a large part of central Liberia.* 今や騒動は広がり, リベリアの中部地方の大半が影響を受けている. ● **cen|tral|ly** ADV 副詞 中央に ❑ *The main cabin has its full-sized double bed centrally placed with plenty of room around it.* 主船室の中央にはフルサイズのダブルベッドが置かれ, 周りには十分な空間がある. 🚺 ADJ 形容詞 A place that is **central** is easy to reach because it is in the center of a city, town, or particular area. 中心にある ❑ *...a central location in the capital.* 首都の中心部の位置 ● **cen|tral|ly** ADV 副詞 中心部に ❑ *...this centrally located hotel, situated on the banks of the river.* その川の岸辺にあって, 中心部に立地するこのホテル 🚼 ADJ 形容詞 [ADJ n] A **central** group or organization makes all the important decisions that are followed throughout a larger organization or a country. 中心的な, 中央の ❑ *There is a lack of trust toward the central government in Rome.* ローマの中央政府に対する信頼が欠けている. ● **cen|tral|ly** ADV 副詞 中央で ❑ *This is a centrally planned economy.* これは中央で計画された経済である. 🚽 ADJ 形容詞 The **central** person or thing in a particular situation is the most important one. 主要な ❑ *Black dance music has been central to mainstream pop since the early '60s.* 黒人のダンス音楽は60年代初期からポップミュージックの主流の中枢をなしてきた.

Word Partnership	central は次の語句と使われる:
N.	central **location** 🚺 central **government** 🚼

cen|tral heat|ing N-UNCOUNT 不可算名詞 **Central heating** is a heating system for buildings. Air or water is heated in one place and travels around a building through pipes and radiators. セントラルヒーティング ❑ *I am thinking of installing central heating.* 私はセントラルヒーティングを取り付けることを考慮中だ.

cen|tral|ize /sɛntrəlaɪz/ (**centralizes, centralizing, centralized**) V-T 他動詞 To **centralize** a country, state, or organization means to create a system in which one central group of people gives instructions to regional groups. 中央に集める ❑ *In the mass production era, multinational firms tended to centralize their operations.* 大量生産の時代には多国籍企業は経営を1点に集中させる傾向がある. ● **cen|tral|iza|tion** /sɛntrəlɪzeɪʃⁿn/ N-UNCOUNT 不可算名詞 集中化 ❑ *...public hostility to central banks and the centralization of power.* 中央銀行と権力の集中化への国民の敵意

cen|tre /sɛntər/ → see **center**

Word Link	cent ≈ hundred : cent, century, percent

cen|tu|ry /sɛntʃəri/ (**centuries**) 🚹 N-COUNT 可算名詞 A **century** is a period of a hundred years that is used when stating a date. For example, the 19th century was the period from 1801 to 1900. 世紀 ❑ *The material position of the Church had been declining since the late eighteenth century.* 教会の世俗的な地位は18世紀後期から衰退しつつあった. 🚺 N-COUNT 可算名詞 A **century** is any period of a hundred years. 百年 ❑ *The drought there is the worst in a century.* そこの干ばつは百年間で最悪である.

CEO /siː iː oʊ/ (**CEOs**) N-COUNT 可算名詞 **CEO** is an abbreviation for **chief executive officer**. chief executive officerの略

ce|ram|ic /sɪræmɪk/ (**ceramics**) 🚹 N-MASS 質量名詞 **Ceramic** is clay that has been heated to a very high temperature so that it becomes hard. 陶磁器 ❑ *...ceramic tiles.* 陶磁器のタイル 🚺 N-COUNT 可算名詞 **Ceramics** are ceramic ornaments or objects. 陶磁器製品 [usu pl] ❑ *...a collection of Chinese ceramics.* 中国陶磁器の収集品 🚼 N-UNCOUNT 不可算名詞 **Ceramics** is the art of making artistic objects out of clay. 陶芸 ❑ *...a degree in ceramics.* 陶芸の学位
→ see **pottery**

ce|real /sɪəriəl/ (**cereals**) 🚹 N-MASS 質量名詞 **Cereal** or **breakfast cereal** is a food made from grain. It is mixed with milk and eaten for breakfast. シーリアル ❑ *I have a bowl of cereal every morning.* 私は毎朝どんぶり1杯のシーリアルを食べる. 🚺 N-COUNT 可算名詞 **Cereals** are plants such as wheat, corn, or rice that produce grain. 穀物 ❑ *...the cereal-growing districts of the Midwest.* 中西部の穀物栽培地域

cere|bral /səribrəl/ 🚹 ADJ 形容詞 If you describe someone or something as **cerebral**, you mean that they are intellectual rather than emotional. 知的な [FORMAL 形式ばった] ❑ *Washington struck me as a precarious place from which to publish such a cerebral newspaper.* ワシントンはそのように知的な新聞を発行するには不安定な場所に思えた. 🚺 ADJ 形容詞 **Cerebral** means relating to the brain. 脳の [MEDICAL 医学の] [ADJ n] ❑ *...a cerebral hemorrhage.* 脳出血

cer|emo|nial /sɛrɪmoʊniəl/ 🚹 ADJ 形容詞 Something that is **ceremonial** relates to a ceremony or is used in a ceremony. 儀式上の [ADJ n] ❑ *He represented the nation on ceremonial occasions.* 彼は国を代表して儀式的行事に出席した. 🚺 ADJ 形容詞 A position, function, or event that is **ceremonial** is considered to be representative of an institution, but has very little authority or influence. 儀式的な ❑ *Up to now the post of president has been largely ceremonial.* 現在まで大統領の職は主に儀式的だった.
→ see **funeral**

Word Link	mony ≈ resulting state : ceremony, harmony, testimony

cer|emo|ny /sɛrɪmoʊni/ (**ceremonies**) 🚹 N-COUNT 可算名詞 A **ceremony** is a formal event such as a wedding. 儀式 ❑ *...his grandmother's funeral, a private ceremony attended only by the family.* 家族のみが出席した内輪の儀式だった彼の祖母の葬式 🚺 N-UNCOUNT 不可算名詞 **Ceremony** consists of the special things that are said and done on very formal occasions. 仰々しさ ❑ *The republic was proclaimed with great ceremony.* 共和国の樹立がいとも厳粛に宣言された.
→ see **graduation, wedding**

certain

❶ BEING SURE
❷ REFERRING TO AND INDICATING AMOUNT

❶ **cer|tain** /sɜrtⁿn/ 🚹 ADJ 形容詞 If you are **certain** about something, you firmly believe it is true and have no doubt about it. If you are not **certain** about something, you do not have definite knowledge about it. 確信して [v-link ADJ] ❑ *She's absolutely certain she's going to make it in the world.* 彼女は自分が世に出ることをすっかり確信している. ❑ *We are not certain whether the appendix had already burst or not.* 盲腸が既に破れたのかどうか不確かだ. 🚺 ADJ 形容詞 If you say that something is **certain** to happen, you mean that it will definitely happen. 確かな ❑ *However, the scheme is certain to meet opposition from fishermen's leaders.* しかしその計画は漁師の指導者たちの反対に遭うことは確かだ. ❑ *It's not certain they'll accept that candidate if he wins.* あの候補者が勝っても, 彼らに受け入れられるかどうか確かではない. ❑ *The prime minister is heading for certain defeat if he forces a vote.* 首相が無理やり投票に持ち込めば負けることは確かだ. 🚼 ADJ 形容詞 If you say that something is **certain**, you firmly believe that it is true, or have definite knowledge about it. 確実で [v-link ADJ] ❑ *One thing is certain, both have the utmost respect for each other.* 1つのことは確実だ, つまり両人ともお互いを最高に尊敬しているのだ. 🚽 PHRASE 句 If you know something **for certain**, you have no doubt at all about it. 確かに ❑ *She couldn't know what time he'd go, or even for certain that he'd go at all.* 彼女は彼が何時に出発するのか分からなかったし, 出発するかどうかすら確かには分からなかった. 🚾 PHRASE 句 If you **make certain that** something is the way you want or expect it to be, you take action to ensure that it is. 確かめる, 確実にする ❑ *Parents should make certain that the children spend enough time doing homework.* 親は確実に子供が十分な時間をかけて宿題をするように気を配るべきである.

Thesaurus	certain また次を参照:
ADJ.	definite, known, positive, sure, true, unmistakable ❶ 🚹

❷ **cer|tain** /sɜrtⁿn/ 🚹 ADJ 形容詞 You use **certain** to indicate that you are referring to one particular thing, person, or group, although you are not saying exactly which it is. ある― [det ADJ, ADJ n] ❑ *There will be certain people who'll say "I told you so!"* 「ほら言ったでしょ」と言うような人たちが出るでしょう. ❑ *You owe a certain person a sum of money.* あなたはさる人物に借金がある. 🚺 ADJ 形容詞 You use **a certain** to indicate that something such as a quality or condition exists, and often to suggest that it is not great in amount or degree. ある程度の ❑ *That was the very reason why he felt a certain bitterness.* 彼がある程度の苦々しさを感じたのは正にそれが理由だった. 🚼 QUANT 数量詞 When you refer to **certain of** a group of people or things, you are referring to some particular members of that group. (―のうちの) いくらか [FORMAL 形式ばった] [QUANT "of" def-pl-n] ❑ *They'll have to give up completely on certain of their studies.* 彼らは研究の一部を完全にあきらめなければならないだろう.

cer|tain|ly /sɜrtⁿnli/ 🚹 ADV 副詞 You use **certainly** to emphasize what you are saying when you are making a statement. 確実に [EMPHASIS 強調] [ADV with cl/group] ❑ *The public is certainly getting tired of hearing about it.* 国民は間違いなくその話にうんざりしてきている. ❑ *The bombs are almost certainly part of a*

much bigger conspiracy. それらの爆弾はほぼ間違いなくもっと大きい陰謀の一部だ. **2** ADV 副詞 You use **certainly** when you are agreeing with what someone has said. もちろん [ADV as reply] □*"In any case you remained friends."—"Certainly."* 「いずれにせよ、君たちの交友関係は続いた」「もちろんだ」 **3** ADV 副詞 You say **certainly not** to say "no" in a strong way. とんでもない [EMPHASIS 強調] [ADV as reply] □*"Perhaps it would be better if I withdrew altogether."—"Certainly not!"* 「私が完全に退いた方がいいのかもしれない」「とんでもない」

> You use **certainly** to emphasize that what you say is definitely true. □*His death was certainly not an accident.* You use **surely** to express disagreement or surprise. □*Surely you care about what happens to her.* Both British and American speakers use **certainly** to agree with requests and statements. Note that American speakers also use **surely** in this way. □*"Can I have a drink?"—"Why, surely."*

cer|tain|ty /sɜrtᵊnti/ (**certainties**) **1** N-UNCOUNT 不可算名詞 **Certainty** is the state of being definite or of having no doubts at all about something. 確信 □*I have told them with absolute certainty there'll be no change of policy.* 私は完全な確信をもって政策の変更はないと彼らに伝えた. **2** N-UNCOUNT 不可算名詞 **Certainty** is the fact that something is certain to happen. 確実 [also "a" N] □*A general election became a certainty last week.* 先週総選挙は確実なものとなった. □*...the certainty of more violence and bloodshed.* 暴力と流血が確実に続く見込み **3** N-COUNT 可算名詞 **Certainties** are things that nobody has any doubts about. 確実なもの [usu pl] □*There are no certainties in modern Europe.* 現代のヨーロッパでは確実なものは何もない.

cer|tif|i|cate /sərtɪfɪkɪt/ (**certificates**) **1** N-COUNT 可算名詞 A **certificate** is an official document stating that particular facts are true. 証明書 □*...birth certificates.* 出生証明書 **2** N-COUNT 可算名詞 A **certificate** is an official document that you receive when you have completed a course of study or training. The qualification that you receive is sometimes also called a **certificate**. 修業証書, 免許状 □*To the right of the fireplace are various framed certificates.* 暖炉の右側には額縁入りの様々な修業証書がある.
→ see **wedding**

cer|ti|fy /sɜrtɪfaɪ/ (**certifies, certifying, certified**) **1** V-T 他動詞 If someone in an official position **certifies** something, they officially state that it is true. 認証する □*The president certified that the project would receive at least $650m from overseas sources.* 大統領はそのプロジェクトに海外から少なくとも6億5千万ドルが投入されることを認証した. □*The National Election Council is supposed to certify the results of the election.* 全国選挙協議会は選挙結果を認証することになっている. ● **cer|ti|fi|ca|tion** /sɜrtɪfɪkeɪʃᵊn/ (**certifications**) N-VAR 可変性名詞 証明, 証明書 □*An employer can demand written certification that the relative is really ill.* 雇用主は親族が実際に病気であるという証明書を要求することができる. **2** V-T 他動詞 [usu passive] If someone **is certified as** a particular kind of worker, they are given a certificate stating that they have successfully completed a course of training in their profession. 認定する □*They wanted to get certified as divers.* 彼らは公認のダイバーになりたかった. □*...a certified public accountant.* 公認会計士 ● **cer|ti|fi|ca|tion** N-UNCOUNT 不可算名詞 認定 □*Students would be offered on-the-job training leading to the certification of their skill in a particular field.* 学生は特定の分野における技能認定につながる職場内訓練を勧められるだろう.

cer|vi|cal /sɜrvɪkᵊl/ **1** ADJ 形容詞 **Cervical** means relating to the cervix. 子宮頸(けい)の [MEDICAL 医学の] [ADJ n] □*Doctors aim to cut the number of women dying from cervical cancer by half this decade.* 医者はこの10年間に子宮頸がんの死亡率を半減させることを目指している. **2** ADJ 形容詞 **Cervical** means relating to the neck. 首に関する [MEDICAL 医学の] [ADJ n] □*...injury to the cervical spine from motor vehicle collisions.* 自動車の衝突による頸椎(けいつい)の負傷

cer|vix /sɜrvɪks/ (**cervixes** or **cervices** /sɜrvaɪsiz, sɜrvɪsiz/) N-COUNT 可算名詞 The **cervix** is the entrance to the womb. 子宮頸(けい) [MEDICAL 医学の]

cf. **cf.** is used in writing to introduce something that should be considered in connection with the subject you are discussing. —を参照 □*For the more salient remarks on the matter, cf. "Isis Unveiled," Vol. I.* 本問題に関するより顕著な所見については『ベールをはがされたイシス』第1巻を参照.

CFC /si ɛf si/ (**CFCs**) N-COUNT 可算名詞 **CFCs** are gases that are used in things such as aerosols and refrigerators and can cause damage to the ozone layer. **CFC** is an abbreviation for "chlorofluorocarbon." フロン □*...the continued drop in CFC emissions.* フロン排出の継続的減少

chain /tʃeɪn/ (**chains, chaining, chained**) **1** N-COUNT 可算名詞 A **chain** consists of metal rings connected together in a line. 首飾り □*His open shirt revealed a fat gold chain.* 彼の開襟シャツからは大きな金の首飾りが見えた. **2** N-COUNT 可算名詞 A **chain of** things

is a group of them existing or arranged in a line. ひと続き □*...a chain of islands known as the Windward Islands.* ウィンワード諸島と呼ばれる列島 **3** N-COUNT 可算名詞 A **chain of** stores, hotels, or other businesses is a number of them owned by the same person or company. チェーン組織 □*...a large supermarket chain.* 大きなスーパーマーケット・チェーン **4** N-PLURAL 複数名詞 If prisoners are **in chains**, they have thick rings of metal around their wrists or ankles to prevent them from escaping. 鎖 □*He'd spent four and a half years in windowless cells, much of the time in chains.* 彼は窓のない独房で、4年半過ごし、その大半を鎖につながれていた. **5** V-T 他動詞 If a person or thing **is chained to** something, they are fastened to it with a chain. 鎖でつなぐ □*The dogs were chained to a fence.* 犬は鎖で塀につながれていた. □*We were sitting together in our cell, chained to the wall.* 我々は鎖で壁につながれ, 独房に一緒に座っていた. ● PHRASAL VERB 句動詞 **Chain up** means the same as **chain**. 鎖でつなぐ □*They kept me chained up every night and released me each day.* 彼らは毎晩私を鎖でつないでおき, 日中は毎日私を鎖から放した. **6** N-SING 単数名詞 A **chain of** events is a series of them happening one after another. 連鎖 □*...the bizarre chain of events that led to his departure in January 1938.* 1938年1月の彼の退去につながった一連の奇怪な出来事
→ see **food**

chair /tʃɛər/ (**chairs, chairing, chaired**) **1** N-COUNT 可算名詞 A **chair** is a piece of furniture for one person to sit on, with a back and four legs. 椅子 □*He rose from his chair and walked to the window.* 彼は椅子から立ち上がり窓の方に歩いて行った. **2** N-COUNT 可算名詞 At a university, a **chair** is the position or job of professor. 教授の職 □*He has been appointed to the chair of sociology.* 彼は社会学の教授に任命された. **3** N-COUNT 可算名詞 The person who is the **chair of** a committee or meeting is the person in charge of it. 委員長, 議長 □*She is the chair of the Defense Advisory Committee on Women in the Military.* 彼女は軍隊の女性に関する防衛諮問委員会の委員長だ. **4** V-T 他動詞 If you **chair** a meeting or a committee, you are the person in charge of it. 議長を務める □*He was about to chair a meeting in Venice of E.U. foreign ministers.* 彼はヴェニスでのEU外相会議の議長を務めようとしていた. **5** N-SING 単数名詞 The **chair** is the same as the **electric chair**. 電気椅子

chair|man /tʃɛərmən/ (**chairmen**) **1** N-COUNT 可算名詞 The **chairman** of a committee, organization, or company is the head of it. 委員長, 会長 □*Glyn Ford is chairman of the committee which produced the report.* グレン・フォードはその報告書を作成した委員会の委員長である. **2** N-COUNT; N-VOC 可算名詞, 呼格名詞 The **chairman** of a meeting or debate is the person in charge, who decides when each person is allowed to speak. 議長 □*The chairman declared the meeting open.* 議長は会議の開会を宣言した.

chair|man|ship /tʃɛərmənʃɪp/ (**chairmanships**) N-VAR 可変性名詞 The **chairmanship** of a committee or organization is the fact of being its chairperson. Someone's **chairmanship** can also mean the period during which they are chairperson. chairmanの地位, 期間 □*The government has set up a committee under the chairmanship of Professor Roy Goode.* 政府はロイ・グッド教授を委員長とする委員会を設立した.

chair|per|son /tʃɛərpɜrsᵊn/ (**chairpersons**) N-COUNT 可算名詞 The **chairperson** of a meeting, committee, or organization is the person in charge of it. 委員長, 議長 □*She's the chairperson of the safety committee.* 彼女は安全委員会の委員長だ.

chair|woman /tʃɛərwʊmən/ (**chairwomen**) N-COUNT 可算名詞 The **chairwoman** of a meeting, committee, or organization is the woman in charge of it. 女性の委員長 □*Primakov was in Japan meeting with the chairwoman of the Socialist Party there.* プリマコフは訪日中で, 日本の社会党の女性委員長と会っていた.

cha|let /ʃæleɪ/ (**chalets**) N-COUNT 可算名詞 A **chalet** is a small wooden house, especially in a mountain area. 山小屋 □*...Swiss ski chalets.* スイスのスキー小屋

chalk /tʃɔk/ (**chalks, chalking, chalked**) **1** N-UNCOUNT 不可算名詞 **Chalk** is a type of soft, white rock. You can use small pieces of it for writing or drawing with. 白亜 □*...white cliffs made of chalk.* 白亜の白い崖(がけ) **2** N-UNCOUNT 不可算名詞 **Chalk** is small sticks of chalk, or a substance similar to chalk, used for writing or drawing with. チョーク [also N in pl] □*...somebody writing with a piece of chalk.* 1本のチョークで書いている誰か **3** V-T 他動詞 If you **chalk** something, you draw or write it using a piece of chalk. チョークで書く □*He chalked the message on the blackboard.* 彼は黒板に伝言をチョークで書いた.
▶ **chalk up** PHRASAL VERB 句動詞 If you **chalk up** a success, a victory, or a number of points in a game, you achieve it. 達成す

る ❑ *For almost 11 months, the Bosnian army chalked up one victory after another.* ボスニア軍は11か月近く次々と勝利をあげた.

chalk|board /tʃɔːkbɔːd/ (**chalkboards**) N-COUNT 可算名詞 A **chalkboard** is a dark-colored board that you can write on with chalk. Chalkboards are often used by teachers in the classroom. 黒板 [mainly AM 主に米国英語] ❑ *The menu was on a chalkboard.* メニューは黒板に書いてあった.

chal|lenge /tʃælɪndʒ/ (**challenges, challenging, challenged**) **1** N-VAR 可変性名詞 A **challenge** is something new and difficult which requires great effort and determination. 難題 ❑ *The new government's first challenge is the economy.* 新政府の最初の難題は経済である. **2** N-VAR 可変性名詞 A **challenge to** something is a questioning of its truth or value. A **challenge to** someone is a questioning of their authority. 異議 ❑ *The demonstrators have now made a direct challenge to the authority of the government.* デモ行進者たちは今や政府の権力に直接挑戦している. **3** PHRASE 句 If someone **rises to the challenge**, they act in response to a difficult situation which is new to them and are successful. 難局に立派に対処する ❑ *The new Germany must rise to the challenge of its enhanced responsibilities.* 新しいドイツは責任の増大という試練に立派に対処しなくてはならない. **4** V-T 他動詞 If you **challenge** ideas or people, you question their truth, value, or authority. 異議を唱える ❑ *Democratic leaders have challenged the president to sign the bill.* 民主党の指導者たちは大統領がその法案に署名するのに異議を唱えた. ❑ *The move was immediately challenged by two of the republics.* その動きは直ちに共和国のうちの2か国の異議申し立てに遭った. **5** V-T 他動詞 If you **challenge** someone, you invite them to fight or compete with you in some way. 挑戦する ❑ *Marsyas thought he could play the flute better than Apollo and challenged the god to a contest.* マルシュアースはアポロより上手にフルートを演奏できると思い, その神との競争に挑んだ. ❑ *He left a note at the scene of the crime, challenging detectives to catch him.* 彼は犯行現場にメモを残し, 捕えてみろと刑事に挑んだ. ● N-COUNT 可算名詞 **Challenge** is also a noun. 挑戦 ❑ *A third presidential candidate emerged to mount a serious challenge and throw the campaign wide open.* 3人目の大統領候補者が現われて, 本格的な挑戦を始め, 選挙戦をすっかりオープンなものにした. **6** → see also **challenging**

Word Partnership	challenge は次の語句と使われる:
V.	accept a challenge, present a challenge **1 3 5** dare to challenge **4 5**
ADJ.	biggest challenge, new challenge **1 3 5** legal challenge **5**

chal|leng|er /tʃælɪndʒər/ (**challengers**) N-COUNT 可算名詞 A **challenger** is someone who competes with you for a position or title that you already have, for example being a sports champion or a political leader. 挑戦者 ❑ *The strongest challenger, Texas Democrat Martin Frost, has withdrawn from the race.* 最強の挑戦者であるテキサスの民主党員マーティン・フロストは選挙戦から撤退した.

chal|leng|ing /tʃælɪndʒɪŋ/ **1** ADJ 形容詞 A **challenging** task or job requires great effort and determination. やりがいのある ❑ *Mike found a challenging job as a computer programmer.* マイクはコンピュータプログラマーというやりがいのある仕事を見つけた. **2** ADJ 形容詞 If you do something in a **challenging** way, you seem to be inviting people to argue with you or compete against you in some way. 挑発的な ❑ *Mona gave him a challenging look.* モナは挑発的な顔つきで彼を見た.

cham|ber /tʃeɪmbər/ (**chambers**) **1** N-COUNT 可算名詞 A **chamber** is a large room, especially one that is used for formal meetings. 大きな部屋 ❑ *We are going to be in the council chamber every time he speaks.* 私達は彼が話すたびに会議室にいる予定だ. **2** N-COUNT 可算名詞 You can refer to a country's legislature or to one section of it as a **chamber**. 議院 ❑ *More than 80 parties are contesting seats in the two-chamber parliament.* 80以上の政党が2院制の議会で議席を争い合っている. **3** N-COUNT 可算名詞 A **chamber** is a room designed and equipped for a particular purpose. (特定の目的のための) 部屋 ❑ *For many, the dentist's office remains a torture chamber.* 多くの人々にとって歯科医院は今でも拷問部屋だ.

cham|ber of com|merce (**chambers of commerce**) N-COUNT 可算名詞 A **chamber of commerce** is an organization of businesspeople that promotes local commercial interests. 商工会議所 [BUSINESS 実業]

champ /tʃæmp/ (**champs**) N-COUNT 可算名詞 A **champ** is the same as a **champion**. チャンピオン [INFORMAL くだけた] [oft n N] ❑ *...boxing champ Mike Tyson.* ボクシングのチャンピオン, マイク・タイソン.

cham|pagne /ʃæmpeɪn/ (**champagnes**) N-MASS 質量名詞 Champagne is an expensive French white wine with bubbles in. It is often drunk to celebrate something. シャンパン

cham|pi|on /tʃæmpiən/ (**champions, championing, championed**) **1** N-COUNT 可算名詞 A **champion** is someone who has won the first prize in a competition, contest, or fight. 優勝者, チャンピオン ❑ *...a former Olympic champion.* 元オリンピック優勝者 ❑ *Kasparov became world champion.* カスパロフは世界チャンピオンとなった. **2** N-COUNT 可算名詞 If you are a **champion of** a person, a cause, or a principle, you support or defend them. 擁護者 ❑ *He received acclaim as a champion of the oppressed.* 彼はしいたげられた人々の擁護者としての称賛を浴びた. **3** V-T 他動詞 If you **champion** a person, a cause, or a principle, you support or defend them. 擁護する ❑ *He passionately championed the poor.* 彼は貧困者たちを熱烈に擁護した.

Word Partnership	champion は次の語句と使われる:
ADJ.	defending champion, former champion, reigning champion, world champion **1**
N.	champion a cause **3**

cham|pi|on|ship /tʃæmpiənʃɪp/ (**championships**) **1** N-COUNT 可算名詞 A **championship** is a competition to find the best player or team in a particular sport. 選手権大会 ❑ *...the world chess championship.* 世界チェス選手権大会 **2** N-SING 単数名詞 The **championship** refers to the title or status of being a sports champion. 選手権 ❑ *He went on to take the championship.* 彼は次に選手権を取った.

chance /tʃæns/ (**chances, chancing, chanced**) **1** N-VAR 可変性名詞 If there is a **chance of** something happening, it is possible that it will happen. 見込み ❑ *Do you think they have a chance of beating Australia?* 彼らがオーストラリアに勝つ見込みがあると思うか. ❑ *There was really very little chance that Ben would ever have led a normal life.* そもそもベンが普通の生活をすることがあっただろうという可能性はほとんどなかった. **2** N-SING 単数名詞 If you have a **chance to** do something, you have the opportunity to do it. 機会 ❑ *The electoral council announced that all eligible people would get a chance to vote.* 選挙評議会は有権者は全員投票の機会を得るだろうと発表した. ❑ *Most refugee doctors never get the chance to practice medicine in our hospitals.* 難民の医者の大半はわが国の病院で医療に携わる機会は全くない. **3** ADJ 形容詞 A **chance** meeting or event is one that is not planned or expected. 偶然の [ADJ n] ❑ *...a chance meeting.* 偶然の出会い ● N-UNCOUNT 不可算名詞 **Chance** is also a noun. 偶然, 運 ❑ *...a victim of chance and circumstance.* 運と境遇の犠牲者 **4** V-T 他動詞 If you **chance** something, you do it even though there is a risk that you may not succeed or that something bad may happen. 思い切ってやってみる ❑ *Andy knew the risks. I cannot believe he would have chanced it.* アンディはその危険を知っていた. 彼がそれを思い切ってやったなんて信じられない. **5** PHRASE 句 Something that happens **by chance** was not planned by anyone. 偶然に ❑ *He had met Mr. Maude by chance.* 彼は偶然モード氏に出会った. **6** PHRASE 句 You can use **by any chance** when you are asking questions in order to find out whether something that you think might be true is actually true. ひょっとして ❑ *Are they by any chance related?* 彼らはひょっとして親戚関係か. **7** PHRASE 句 If you say that someone **stands a chance of** achieving something, you mean that they are likely to achieve it. If you say that someone doesn't **stand a chance of** achieving something, you mean that they cannot possibly achieve it. 見込みがある ❑ *Being very good at science subjects, I stood a good chance of gaining high grades.* 私は理科系の科目が得意なので優秀な成績を取る見込みが十分にあった. **8** PHRASE 句 When you **take a chance**, you try to do something although there is a large risk of danger or failure. 運を任せる ❑ *You take a chance on the weather if you vacation in Maine.* メイン州で休暇を過ごす場合は天候を運に任せることになる. ❑ *Retailers are taking no chances on unknown brands.* 小売業者は有名でないブランドに賭けたりしてはいない.

Word Partnership	chance は次の語句と使われる:
N.	chance of success, chance of survival, chance of winning **1** chance encounter, chance meeting **3**
ADJ.	fair chance, good chance, slight chance **1 2**
V.	give someone/something a chance, have a chance, miss a chance **1 2** get a chance **2**

chan|cel|lor /tʃænsələr, -slər/ (**chancellors**) **1** N-TITLE; N-COUNT 称号名詞, 可算名詞 **Chancellor** is the title of the head of government in Germany and Austria. 首相 ❑ *...Chancellor Gerhard Schrder of Germany.* ツのゲアハルト・シュレーダー首相 **2** N-COUNT 可算名詞 The head of some American universities is called **the chancellor**. 大学総長 **3** N-COUNT 可算名詞 In Britain, the **chancellor** is the chancellor of the exchequer. 財務大臣

chan|cel|lor of the ex|cheq|uer (**chancellors of the exchequer**) N-COUNT 可算名詞 The **chancellor of the exchequer** is the minister in the British government who makes decisions about finance and taxes. 財務大臣

chan|de|lier /ʃændəliər/ (**chandeliers**) N-COUNT 可算名詞 A

C

chandelier is a large, decorative frame which holds light bulbs or candles and hangs from the ceiling. シャンデリア □*A crystal chandelier lit the room.* クリスタルガラスのシャンデリアで部屋が照らされていた。

change /tʃeɪndʒ/ (changes, changing, changed) **1** N-VAR 可変性名詞 If there is a **change in** something, it becomes different. 変化 □*The ambassador appealed for a change in U.S. policy.* 大使は米国の政策変更を訴えた。 □*There are going to have to be some drastic changes.* 何らかの抜本的な変化が必要となるだろう。 **2** → see also **sea change 3** N-SING 単数名詞 If you say that something is a **change** or **makes a change**, you mean that it is enjoyable because it is different from what you are used to. 気分転換 [APPROVAL 賛成] □*It is a complex system, but it certainly makes a change.* それは複雑なシステムだが、確かに気分転換になる。 **4** V-I 自動詞 If you **change from** one thing to another, you stop using or doing the first one and start using or doing the second. 変える □*His physician modified the dosage but did not change to a different medication.* 彼の主治医は服用量を減らしたが、薬を変えはしなかった。 **5** V-T/V-I 他動詞/自動詞 When something **changes** or when you **change** it, it becomes different. 変える [他動詞]、変わる [自動詞] □*We are trying to detect and understand how the climates change.* 我々は気候がどのように変化するかを探知し、理解しようとしている。 □*In the union office, the mood gradually changed from resignation to rage.* 組合事務所では雰囲気は次第にあきらめから激怒に変っていった。 □*She has now changed into a happy, self-confident woman.* 彼女は今や幸せで自信のある女性に変わった。 □*They should change the law to make it illegal to own replica weapons.* 彼らは法律を変え、武器の複製を所持することを違法にすべきだ。 **6** V-T 他動詞 To **change** something means to replace it with something new or different. 取り替える □*I paid $80 to have my car radio fixed and I bet all they did was change a fuse.* 車のラジオの修理代に80ドル支払ったが、ヒューズを取り替えただけだと思う。 ●N-COUNT 可算名詞 **Change** is also a noun. 取り替え □*A change of leadership alone will not be enough.* 指導者の交替だけでは不十分だ。 **7** V-T/V-I 他動詞/自動詞 When you **change** your clothes or **change**, you take some or all of your clothes off and put on different ones. 着替える □*Ben had merely changed his shirt.* ベンはシャツを着替えただけだった。 □*They had allowed her to shower and change.* 彼らは彼女がシャワーを浴びて着替えをするのを許していた。 **8** V-T 他動詞 When you **change** a bed or **change** the sheets, you take off the dirty sheets and put on clean ones. シーツを取り替える □*After changing the bed, I would fall asleep quickly.* ベッドのシーツを取り替えると、私はすぐに眠ってしまったものです。 **9** V-T 他動詞 When you **change** a baby or **change** its diaper, you take off the dirty one and put on a clean one. おむつを替える □*She criticizes me for the way I feed or change him.* 彼女は私の授乳の仕方やおむつの替え方を批判する。 **10** V-T/V-I 他動詞/自動詞 When you **change** buses, trains, or planes or **change**, you get off one bus, train, or plane and get on to another in order to continue your journey. 乗り換える □*At Glasgow I changed trains for Greenock.* グラスゴーで私はグリーノック行きの列車に乗り換えた。 **11** V-T/V-I 他動詞/自動詞 When you **change** gear or **change** into another gear, you move the gear lever on a car, bicycle, or other vehicle in order to use a different gear. ギアを入れ替える [mainly BRIT 主に英国英語; AM usually **shift** 米国英語では通常 **shift**] **12** V-T 他動詞 When you **change** money, you exchange it for the same amount of money in a different currency, or in smaller bills or coins. 両替する □*You can expect to pay the bank a fee of around 1% to 2% every time you change money.* 銀行で両替する場合には毎回約1～2%の手数料がかかる。 **13** N-COUNT 可算名詞 A **change of** clothes is an extra set of clothes that you take with you when you go to stay somewhere or to take part in an activity. 着替え [N "of" n] □*He stuffed a bag with a few changes of clothing.* 彼はかばんに数枚の着替えを詰め込んだ。 **14** N-UNCOUNT 不可算名詞 Your **change** is the money that you receive when you pay for something with more money than it costs because you do not have exactly the right amount of money. つり銭 □*"There's your change."—"Thanks very much."* 「おつりです」「どうもありがとう」 **15** N-UNCOUNT 不可算名詞 **Change** is coins, rather than paper money. 小銭 □*Thieves ransacked the office, taking a sack of loose change.* 泥棒たちは事務所をくまなく探し、ばら銭を盗んで行った。 **16** N-UNCOUNT 不可算名詞 If you have **change for** larger bills or coins, you have the same value in smaller bills or coins, which you can give to someone in exchange. つり銭、くずした金 □*The courier had change for a $10 bill.* 配送業者は10ドル札に対するつり銭を持っていた。 PHRASE 句 ● If you **make change**, you give someone smaller bills or coins, in exchange for the same value of larger ones. つり銭を渡す [AM 米国英語] **17** PHRASE 句 If you say that you are doing something or something is happening **for a change**, you mean that you do not usually do it or it does not usually happen, and you are happy to be doing it or that it is happening. 目先を変えて □*Now let me ask you a question, for a change.* 今度は目先を変えて私にご質問させてください。 **18** to **change for the better** → see **better 19** to **change hands** → see **hand 20** a **change of heart** → see **heart 21** to **change** your **mind** → see **mind 22** to **change places** → see **place 23** to **change the subject** → see **subject 24** to **change tack** → see **tack 25** to **change** your **tune** → see **tune**

26 to **change for the worse** → see **worse**
▶ **change over** PHRASAL VERB 句動詞 If you **change over from** one thing **to** another, you stop doing one thing and start doing the other. 変更する □*We are gradually changing over to a completely metric system.* 我々は徐々に完全なメートル法に切り替えているところだ。

Thesaurus change また次を参照:
N.	adjustment, alteration **1**
V.	adapt, modify, transform, vary **4**

Word Partnership change は次の語句と使われる:
V.	adapt to change, resist change **1**
	make a change **1 2**
N.	policy change **1**
	change of pace **3**
	change direction **4**
	change of address, change color, change the subject **5**
	change clothes **6**
ADJ.	gradual change, social change, sudden change **1**
	loose change, spare change **14**

change purse (change purses) N-COUNT 可算名詞 A **change purse** is a very small bag that people, especially women, keep their coins in. 小銭入れ [AM 米国英語] □*Eve searched her change purse and found thirty cents.* イブは小銭入れを探って30セントを見つけた。

chan|nel /tʃænʲl/ (channels, channeling or channelling, channeled or channelled) **1** N-COUNT; N-IN-NAMES 可算名詞, 名称中の名詞 A **channel** is a television station. テレビ局 □*...the only serious current affairs program on either channel.* 両方のテレビ局で唯一の真面目な時事問題番組 □*...the proliferating number of television channels in America.* アメリカで急増するテレビ局数 **2** N-COUNT 可算名詞 A **channel** is a band of radio waves on which radio messages can be sent and received. 周波数帯、チャンネル □*The radio channels were filled with the excited, jabbering voices of men going to war.* ラジオの周波数帯はどれも参戦する男たちが興奮気味の早口にしゃべる声でいっぱいであった。 **3** N-COUNT 可算名詞 If you do something through a particular **channel**, or particular **channels**, that is the system or organization that you use to achieve your aims or to communicate. ルート □*The government will surely use the diplomatic channels available.* 政府が利用できる外交ルートを使うことは間違いないだろう。 □*The Americans recognize that the U.N. can be the channel for greater diplomatic activity.* アメリカ人は国連がより大きな外交活動のルートになりうることを認識している。 **4** N-COUNT 可算名詞 A **channel** is a passage along which water flows. 水路、水管 □*Keep the drainage channel clear.* 排水溝がふさがれないようにしなさい。 **5** N-COUNT 可算名詞 A **channel** is a route used by boats. 可航水路 □*...the busy shipping channels of the harbor.* 港の活気のある輸送水路 **6** V-T 他動詞 If you **channel** money or resources into something, you arrange for them to be used for that thing, rather than for a wider range of things. 当てる □*Jacques Delors wants a system set up to channel help to the poor countries.* ジャック・ドロールは貧しい国々に資金を投入する制度の設立を望んでいる。 **7** V-T 他動詞 If you **channel** your energies or emotions **into** something, you concentrate on or do that one thing, rather than a range of things. 向ける □*Stephen is channeling his energies into a novel called Blue.* スティーブンは『青』という題名の小説に精力を傾けている。
→ see **cellphone**

chant /tʃænt/ (chants, chanting, chanted) **1** N-COUNT 可算名詞 A **chant** is a word or group of words that is repeated over and over again. 繰り返す叫び声、シュプレヒコール □*He was greeted by the chant of "Judas! Judas!"* 彼は「ユダ、ユダ」というシュプレヒコールで迎えられた。 **2** N-COUNT 可算名詞 A **chant** is a religious song or prayer that is sung on only a few notes. 聖歌 □*...a Gregorian chant.* グレゴリオ聖歌 **3** V-T/V-I 他動詞/自動詞 If you **chant** something or if you **chant**, you repeat the same words over and over again. 繰り返し叫ぶ、シュプレヒコールする □*Demonstrators chanted slogans.* デモ隊員たちはスローガンをシュプレヒコールした。 □*The crowd chanted "We are with you."* 群集は「我々はあなたを応援している」とシュプレヒコールした。 ● **chant|ing** N-UNCOUNT 不可算名詞 繰り返し叫ぶこと □*A lot of the chanting was in support of the deputy prime minister.* シュプレヒコールの多くは副首相を支持するものだった。 **4** V-T/V-I 他動詞/自動詞 If you **chant** or if you **chant** something, you sing a religious song or prayer. 詠唱する □*Muslims chanted and prayed.* イスラム教徒は詠唱し祈った。 ● **chant|ing** N-UNCOUNT 不可算名詞 詠唱すること □*The chanting inside the temple stopped.* 寺院内の詠唱が止まった。

cha|os /keɪɒs/ N-UNCOUNT 不可算名詞 **Chaos** is a state of complete disorder and confusion. 混乱状態 □*The world's first transatlantic balloon race ended in chaos last night.* 世界初の気球による大西洋横断レースは昨夜混乱状態で終わった。

C

cha|ot|ic /keɪɒtɪk/ ADJ 形容詞 Something that is **chaotic** is in a state of complete disorder and confusion. 無秩序な □*My own house feels as filthy and chaotic as a bus terminal.* 私自身の家はバスターミナルのように汚れて雑然とした感じだ.

chap /tʃæp/ (**chaps**) ■ N-COUNT 可算名詞 A **chap** is a man or boy. 男 [mainly BRIT 主に英国英語, INFORMAL くだけた] □*"I am a very lucky chap," he commented. "The doctors were surprised that I was not paralysed."* 「僕は本当にラッキーな男だ. 医者たちは僕がまひ状態でないのに驚いていた」と彼は述べた. ■ → see also **chapped**

chap|el /tʃæpᵊl/ (**chapels**) ■ N-COUNT 可算名詞 A **chapel** is a part of a church which has its own altar and which is used for private prayer. 礼拝所 □*...the chapel of the Virgin Mary.* 聖母マリアの礼拝所 ■ N-COUNT 可算名詞 A **chapel** is a small church attached to a hospital, school, or prison. 礼拝堂, チャペル □*We married in the college chapel.* 私達は大学の礼拝堂で結婚した. ■ N-VAR 可変性名詞 A **chapel** is a building used for worship by members of some Christian churches. **Chapel** refers to the religious services that take place there. 礼拝堂, 礼拝 □*...a Methodist chapel.* メソディスト派の礼拝堂

chap|lain /tʃæplɪn/ (**chaplains**) N-COUNT 可算名詞 A **chaplain** is a member of the Christian clergy who does religious work in a place such as a hospital, school, prison, or in the armed forces. 礼拝堂付き牧師 □*He joined the 40th Division as an army chaplain.* 彼は従軍牧師として第40師団に加わった.

chapped /tʃæpt/ ADJ 形容詞 If your skin is **chapped**, it is dry, cracked, and sore. 荒れた, ひびの切れた □*...chapped hands.* ひびの切れた手

chap|ter /tʃæptər/ (**chapters**) ■ N-COUNT 可算名詞 A **chapter** is one of the parts that a book is divided into. Each chapter has a number, and sometimes a title. 章 [also N num] □*Chromium supplements were used successfully in the treatment of diabetes (see Chapter 4).* クロムのサプリメントは糖尿病の治療に使われ効果を挙げた（第4章参照）. ■ N-COUNT 可算名詞 A **chapter in** someone's life or in history is a period of time during which a major event or series of related events takes place. 重要な1区切り [WRITTEN 書き言葉] □*This had been a particularly difficult chapter in Lebanon's recent history.* これはレバノンの最近の歴史で特に困難な時期だった.

char|ac|ter /kærɪktər/ (**characters**) ■ N-COUNT 可算名詞 The **character** of a person or place consists of all the qualities they have that make them distinct from other people or places. 性格, 特質 □*Perhaps there is a negative side to his character that you haven't seen yet.* 多分彼の性格にはあなたがまだ気づいていないマイナスの面があるでしょう. ■ N-COUNT 可算名詞 You use **character** to say what kind of person someone is. For example, if you say that someone is a strange **character**, you mean they are strange. 人物 □*It's that kind of courage and determination that makes him such a remarkable character.* 彼があんなに非凡な人物なのは, そうした類の勇気と決断力を持っているからだ. ■ N-COUNT 可算名詞 The **characters** in a movie, book, or play are the people that it is about. 登場人物 □*The film is autobiographical and the central character is played by Collard himself.* その映画は自伝的で, 主役はコラード自身が演じている. ■ N-COUNT 可算名詞 A **character** is a letter, number, or other symbol that is written or printed. 文字 □*...a shopping list written in Chinese characters.* 漢字で書かれた買い物リスト ■ N-SING 単数名詞 If something has a particular **character**, it has a particular quality. 性質 [usu supp N, also "in" N] □*The financial concessions were of a precarious character.* 経済的譲歩は不安定な性質のものだった. ■ N-SING 単数名詞 You can use **character** to refer to the qualities that people from a particular place are believed to have. 気質, 国民性 □*Individuality is a valued and inherent part of the British character.* 個性は英国の国民性の持ち前の大切な部分である. ■ N-VAR 可変性名詞 Your **character** is your personality, especially how reliable and honest you are. If someone is **of good character**, they are reliable and honest. If they are **of bad character**, they are unreliable and dishonest. 人格 □*He's begun a series of personal attacks on my character.* 彼は私の人格について一連の個人攻撃を始めた. ■ N-UNCOUNT 不可算名詞 If you say that someone has **character**, you mean that they have the ability to deal effectively with difficult, unpleasant, or dangerous situations. 気骨 [APPROVAL 賛成] □*She showed real character in her attempts to win over the crowd.* 彼女は群集を説得しようとする試みで真の気骨を示した. ■ N-UNCOUNT 不可算名詞 If you say that a place has **character**, you mean that it has an interesting or unusual quality which makes you notice it and like it. 特色 [APPROVAL 賛成] □*A soulless shopping center stands across from one of the few buildings with character, the town hall.* 味気ないショッピングセンターは特色ある数少ない建物の1つである市役所の向かい側にある. ■ N-COUNT 可算名詞

詞 If you say that someone is a **character**, you mean that they are interesting, unusual, or amusing. 面白い人物 □*He's a nut, a real character.* 彼は変わり者で, 本当に面白いやつだ.
→ see **printing**, **theater**

char|ac|ter|is|tic /kærɪktərɪstɪk/ (**characteristics**) ■ N-COUNT 可算名詞 The **characteristics** of a person or thing are the qualities or features that belong to them and make them recognizable. 特徴, 特性 □*Genes determine the characteristics of every living thing.* 遺伝子は全ての生き物の特徴を決める. ■ ADJ 形容詞 A quality or feature that is **characteristic of** someone or something is one which is often seen in them and seems typical of them. 特徴的な, 特有な □*...the absence of strife between the generations that was so characteristic of such societies.* そうした社会に大変特有な世代間闘争の欠如 □*Windmills are a characteristic feature of the Mallorcan landscape.* 風車はマヨルカ島の風景の典型的な特徴だ. ● **char|ac|ter|is|ti|cal|ly** /kærɪktərɪstɪkli/ ADV 副詞 特徴的に □*He replied in characteristically robust style.* 彼はいかにも彼らしく元気に応えた.
→ see **gene**

char|ac|teri|za|tion /kærɪktəraɪzeɪʃᵊn/ (**characterizations**) N-VAR 可変性名詞 **Characterization** is the way an author or an actor describes or shows what a character is like. 性格描写 □*As a writer, I am interested in characterization.* 私は作家として性格描写に関心がある.

char|ac|ter|ize /kærɪktəraɪz/ (**characterizes, characterizing, characterized**) ■ V-T 他動詞 If something is **characterized by** a particular feature or quality, that feature or quality is an obvious part of it. 特徴づける [FORMAL 形式ばった] [usu passive] □*This election campaign has been characterized by violence.* この選挙戦の特徴は暴力だった. ■ V-T 他動詞 If you **characterize** someone or something **as** a particular thing, you describe them as that thing. みなす [FORMAL 形式ばった] □*Both companies have characterized the relationship as friendly.* 両社はその関係を友好的とみなしてきた.

char|ac|ter rec|og|ni|tion N-UNCOUNT 不可算名詞 **Character recognition** is a process which allows computers to recognize written or printed characters such as numbers or letters and to change them into a form that the computer can use. 文字認識 [COMPUTING コンピューティング] □*...optical character recognition software that allows you to convert a scanned document to an electronic file.* スキャンした文書を電子ファイルに転換できる光学式文字認識ソフト

cha|rade /ʃəreɪd/ (**charades**) ■ N-COUNT 可算名詞 If you describe someone's actions as a **charade**, you mean that their actions are so obviously false that they do not convince anyone. 見え透いたごまかし [DISAPPROVAL 不賛成] □*I wondered why he had gone through the elaborate charade.* 私は彼がなぜ手の込んだ見せかけをしたのかと不審に思った. ■ N-UNCOUNT 不可算名詞 **Charades** is a game for teams of players in which one team acts a word or phrase, syllable by syllable, until other players guess the whole word or phrase. シャレード（言葉当て遊び） □*We are all going to play charades in the library.* 私たちはみんなで図書室でシャレードをして遊ぶつもりだ.

char|coal /tʃɑrkoʊl/ N-UNCOUNT 不可算名詞 **Charcoal** is a black substance obtained by burning wood without much air. It can be burned as a fuel, and small sticks of it are used for drawing. 炭
→ see **drawing**, **firework**

charge /tʃɑrdʒ/ (**charges, charging, charged**) ■ V-T/V-I 他動詞/自動詞 If you **charge** someone an amount of money, you ask them to pay that amount for something that you have sold to them or done for them. 請求する □*Even local nurseries charge $150 a week.* 地元の保育園ですら週150ドルかかる. □*Some banks charge if you access your account to determine your balance.* 残高照会のために口座にアクセスしても手数料を取る銀行もある. □*The architect charged us a fee of seven hundred and fifty dollars.* その建築家は750ドルの料金を請求した. ■ V-T 他動詞 To **charge** something **to** a person or organization means to tell the people providing it to send the bill to that person or organization. To **charge** something **to** someone's account means to add it to their account so they can pay for it later. 負担させる, つけにする □*Go out and buy a pair of glasses, and charge it to us.* メガネを買いに行って, 私たちも持ちにしなさい. ■ V-T 他動詞 When the police **charge** someone, they formally accuse them of having done something illegal. 告発する □*They have the evidence to charge him.* 彼らには彼を告発する証拠がある. ■ V-I 自動詞 If you **charge** toward someone or something, you move

quickly and aggressively toward them. 突進する □*He charged through the door to my mother's office.* 彼はそのドアを通って私の母の事務所に突進した。*He ordered us to charge.* 彼は我々に突撃の指示を与えた。● N-COUNT 可算名詞 **Charge** is also a noun. 突撃 □*...a bayonet charge.* 銃剣突撃 ⑤ V-T 他動詞 To **charge** a battery means to pass an electrical current through it in order to make it more powerful or to make it last longer. 充電する □*Alex had forgotten to charge the battery.* アレックスはバッテリーに充電するのを忘れていた。● PHRASAL VERB 句動詞 **Charge up** means the same as **charge**. 充電する □*There was nothing in the brochure about having to drive it every day to charge up the battery.* パンフレットには電池を充電するために毎日それを運転しなければならないことについては何も書いてなかった。⑥ N-COUNT 可算名詞 A **charge** is an amount of money that you have to pay for a service. 料金 □*We can arrange this for a small charge.* わずかな料金でこれを手配することができる。⑦ → see also **service charge** ⑧ N-COUNT 可算名詞 A **charge** is a formal accusation that someone has committed a crime. 告発 □*He may still face criminal charges.* 彼はまだ刑事告発を受けるかもしれない。⑨ N-COUNT 可算名詞 If you describe someone as your **charge**, they have been given to you to be taken care of and you are responsible for them. 預かった人 □*The coach tried to get his charges motivated.* コーチは託された人々のやる気を引き出そうとした。⑩ N-COUNT 可算名詞 An electrical **charge** is an amount of electricity that is held in or carried by something. 電荷 [TECHNICAL 技術的] ⑪ N-UNCOUNT 不可算名詞 If you take **charge of** someone or something, you make yourself responsible for them and take control over them. If someone or something is in your **charge**, you are responsible for them. 管理、委託 □*A few years ago Bacryl took charge of the company.* 数年前バクリルはその会社の経営を引き受けた。□*I have been given charge of this class.* 私はこのクラスの担任をしている。⑫ PHRASE 句 If you are in **charge** in a particular situation, you are the most senior person and have control over something or someone. 指揮している □*Who's in charge here?* ここの指揮者は誰か。⑬ PHRASE 句 If something is **free of charge**, it does not cost anything. 無料で □*The leaflet is available free of charge from post offices.* その小冊子は郵便局から無料で入手できる。

→ see **lightning, magnet, trial**

charge|able /tʃɑrdʒəbᵊl/ ❶ ADJ 形容詞 If something is **chargeable**, you have to pay a sum of money for it. 支払われるべきで [FORMAL 形式ばった] □*The day of discharge is not chargeable if rooms are vacated by 12:00 noon.* 12時までに部屋を引き払えば、退院日の費用は負担しなくてよい。❷ ADJ 形容詞 If something is **chargeable**, you have to pay tax on it. 課されるべきで [BRIT 英国英語, FORMAL 形式ばった] □*...the taxpayer's chargeable gain.* 納税者の課税対象の利益

charge card (**charge cards**) ❶ N-COUNT 可算名詞 A **charge card** is a plastic card that you use to buy goods on credit from a particular store or group of stores. （特定の店の）クレジットカード ❷ N-COUNT 可算名詞 A **charge card** is the same as a **credit card**. クレジットカード [AM 米国英語]

charg|er /tʃɑrdʒər/ (**chargers**) N-COUNT 算名詞 A **charger** is a device used for charging or recharging batteries. 充電器 □*He forgot the charger for his mobile phone.* 彼は携帯電話の充電器を忘れた。

cha|ris|ma /kərɪzmə/ N-UNCOUNT 不可算名詞 You say that someone has **charisma** when they can attract, influence, and inspire people by their personal qualities. カリスマ □*He has neither the policies nor the personal charisma to inspire people.* 彼には人々を鼓舞する政策も個人的なカリスマもない。

char|is|mat|ic /kærɪzmætɪk/ ADJ 形容詞 A **charismatic** person attracts, influences, and inspires people by their personal qualities. カリスマ的な □*With her striking looks and charismatic personality, she was noticed far and wide.* 人目を引く容貌とカリスマ的な性格のため、彼女はあまねく注目された。

chari|table /tʃærɪtəbᵊl/ ❶ ADJ 形容詞 A **charitable** organization or activity helps and supports people who are ill, disabled, or very poor. 慈善の □*...charitable work for the handicapped.* 身体障害者のための慈善事業 ❷ ADJ 形容詞 Someone who is **charitable** to people is kind or understanding toward them. 思いやりがある □*They were less than charitable toward the referee.* 彼らは審判員に対して少しも思いやりがなかった。

char|ity /tʃærɪti/ (**charities**) ❶ N-COUNT 可算名詞 A **charity** is an organization which raises money in order to help people who are ill, disabled, or very poor. 慈善団体 □*...an AIDS charity.* エイズの慈善団体 ❷ N-UNCOUNT 不可算名詞 If you give money to

charity, you give it to one or more charitable organizations. If you do something **for charity**, you do it in order to raise money for one or more charitable organizations. 慈善 □*He made substantial donations to charity.* 彼は慈善のために多額の寄付をした。□*Gooch will be raising money for charity.* グーチは慈善のために募金をする予定だ。❸ N-UNCOUNT 不可算名詞 People who live on **charity** live on money or goods which other people give them because they are poor. 施し □*Her husband is unemployed and the family depends on charity.* 彼女の夫は失業中で、家族は施しに頼っている。

charm /tʃɑrm/ (**charms, charming, charmed**) ❶ N-VAR 可変性名詞 **Charm** is the quality of being pleasant or attractive. 魅力 □*"Snow White and the Seven Dwarfs," the 1937 Disney classic, has lost none of its original charm.* 1937年のディズニーの名作「白雪姫と7人の小人」はその元来の魅力を全く失っていない。❷ N-UNCOUNT 不可算名詞 Someone who has **charm** behaves in a friendly, pleasant way that makes people like them. 魅力 □*He was a man of great charm and distinction.* 彼は魅力いっぱいの傑出した男だった。❸ V-T 他動詞 If you **charm** someone, you please them, especially by using your charm. 魅了する □*He even charmed Mrs. Prichard, carrying her groceries and flirting with her, though she's 83.* 食料品の買い物を運んでやったりいちゃついたりして、彼は83歳になるプリチャード夫人ですら魅了した。❹ N-COUNT 可算名詞 A **charm** is a small ornament that is fixed to a bracelet or necklace. 飾り物 □*Inside was a gold charm bracelet, with one charm on it - a star.* 中には星の飾り物が1つついた金の腕輪があった。❺ N-COUNT 可算名詞 A **charm** is an act, saying, or object that is believed to have magic powers. まじない □*They cross their fingers and spit over their shoulders as charms against the evil eye.* 彼らは人差し指と中指を交差させ、凶眼に対するまじないとして肩越しにつばを吐いた。

→ see **jewelry**

charm|ing /tʃɑrmɪŋ/ ❶ ADJ 形容詞 If you say that something is **charming**, you mean that it is very pleasant or attractive. 魅力的な □*...a charming little fishing village.* うっとりするような小さな漁村 ● **charm|ing|ly** ADV 副詞 魅力的に □*There's something charmingly old-fashioned about his brand of entertainment.* 彼流の演芸には魅力的に古風なものがある。❷ ADJ 形容詞 If you describe someone as **charming**, you mean they behave in a friendly, pleasant way that makes people like them. 感じのよい □*...a charming young man.* 感じのよい若者 □*He found her as smart and beautiful as she is charming.* 彼は彼女が感じよいばかりでなく賢明で美しいと思った。● **charm|ing|ly** ADV 副詞 [ADV after v] 魅力的に □*Calder smiled charmingly and put out his hand. "A pleasure, Mrs. Talbot."* コールダーは魅力的にほほ笑み、手を差し出した。「こちらこそ、タルボット夫人」

charred /tʃɑrd/ ADJ 形容詞 **Charred** plants, buildings, or vehicles have been badly burned and have become black because of fire. 黒焦げになった □*...the charred remains of a tank.* 黒焦げになった戦車の残骸

chart /tʃɑrt/ (**charts, charting, charted**) ❶ N-COUNT 可算名詞 A **chart** is a diagram, picture, or graph which is intended to make information easier to understand. 図表 □*Male unemployment was 14.2%, compared with 5.8% for women (see chart on next page).* 男性の失業率は女性の5.8%に対して14.2%だった（次ページの表参照）。❷ → see also **bar chart, flow chart, pie chart** ❸ N-COUNT 可算名詞 A **chart** is a map of the sea or stars. 海図 □*...charts of Greek waters.* ギリシャ海域の海図 ❹ V-T 他動詞 If you **chart** an area of land, sea, or sky, or a feature in that area, you make a map of the area or show the feature in it. 地図を作る □*Ptolemy charted more than 1,000 stars in 48 constellations.* トレミーは48の星座の1000以上の星図を作った。❺ V-T 他動詞 If you **chart** the development or progress of something, you observe it and record or show it. You can also say that a report or graph **charts** the development or progress of something. 記録する □*One doctor has charted a dramatic rise in local childhood asthma since the road was built.* 1人の医者がその道路が建設されてから地元の子供のぜんそくが激増したことを記録して示した。

char|ter /tʃɑrtər/ (**charters, chartering, chartered**) ❶ N-COUNT 可算名詞 A **charter** is a formal document describing the rights, aims, or principles of an organization or group of people. 宣言書、憲章 □*...Article 50 of the United Nations Charter.* 国連合憲章の第50条 ❷ ADJ 形容詞 A **charter** plane or boat is one which is rented for use by a particular person or group and which is not part of a regular service. 借り上げの [ADJ n] □*...the last charter plane carrying out foreign nationals.* 外国人を国外へ運ぶ最後のチャーター機 ❸ V-T 他動詞 If a person or organization **charters** a plane, boat, or other vehicle, they rent it for their own use. 借り上げる □*He chartered*

a jet to fly her home from California to Switzerland. 彼女は彼女をカリフォルニアからスイスの自宅に飛行機で送るためにジェット機をチャーターした.

char|tered /tʃɑ̃rtərd/ ADJ 形容詞 **Chartered** is used to indicate that someone, such as an accountant or a surveyor, has formally qualified in their profession. 公認の [BRIT 英国英語; AM **certified** 米国英語 **certified**]

chase /tʃeɪs/ (chases, chasing, chased) **1** V-T/V-I 他動詞/自動詞 If you **chase** someone, or **chase after** them, you run after them or follow them quickly in order to catch or reach them. 追いかける □ *She chased the thief for 100 yards.* 彼女は100ヤード泥棒を追いかけた. ● N-COUNT 可算名詞 **Chase** is also a noun. 追跡 □ *He was reluctant to give up the chase.* 彼は追跡するのをあきらめたくなかった. **2** V-T/V-I 他動詞/自動詞 If you are **chasing** something you want, such as work or money, or are **chasing after** it, you are trying hard to get it. 追い求める □ *In some areas, 14 people are chasing every job.* 1部の地域では1つの職につき14人の求職者がいる. □ *There are too many schools chasing after too few students.* 少なすぎる学生を確保しようとしている学校の数が多すぎる. ● N-SING 単数名詞 **Chase** is also a noun. 追求 [N "for" n] □ *They took an invincible lead in the chase for the championship.* 彼らは選手権の追求で無敵の優位に立った. **3** V-T/V-I 他動詞/自動詞 If someone **chases** someone that they are attracted to, or **chases after** them, they try hard to persuade them to have a sexual relationship with them. 追い回す □ *Women also have another reason for not chasing men too hard, of course.* もちろん女が男をそれ程熱心に追い回さないのには別の理由もある. ● N-SING 単数名詞 **Chase** is also a noun. 追い回すこと □ *The chase is always much more exciting than the conquest anyway.* とにかく追い回すことは常に征服することよりずっといっそう刺激的だ. **4** V-T 他動詞 If someone **chases** you from a place, they force you to leave by using threats or violence. 追い払う □ *Many farmers will then chase you off their land quite aggressively.* それから多くの農民があなた方を彼らの土地から全く攻撃的に追い払おうとするだろう. **5** V-T 他動詞 To **chase** someone **from** a job or a position or **from** power means to force them to leave it. 追い出す □ *In the '70s he had been chased out of his job.* 彼は70年代に辞職を余儀なくされていた. **6** V-I 自動詞 If you **chase** somewhere, you run or rush there. 急ぐ □ *They chased down the stairs into the narrow, dirty street.* 彼らは階段を急いで降り、細くて汚い通りに入った. **7** PHRASE 句 If someone **cuts to the chase**, they start talking about or dealing with what is important, instead of less important things. 本題に入る □ *Hi everyone, we all know why we are here today, so let's cut to the chase.* 皆さんこんにちわ. 今日ここにいる理由は全員が知っていますので、本題に入りましょう.

chasm /kæzəm/ (chasms) **1** N-COUNT 可算名詞 A **chasm** is a very deep crack in rock, earth, or ice. 大きく開いた割れ目 □ *...a yawning fourteen-foot-deep chasm which inexplicably had opened up in the riverbed.* 川底になぜか開いた深さ14フィートの口を大きく開けた割れ目 **2** N-COUNT 可算名詞 If you say that there is a **chasm** between two things or between two groups of people, you mean that there is a very large difference between them. 隔たり、相違 □ *...the chasm that divides the worlds of university and industry.* 大学と産業界の世界を分かつみぞ

chas|sis /tʃæsi, ʃæsi/ (chassis)

Chassis /tʃæsiz, ʃæsiz/ is also the plural form.

Chassis /tʃæsiz, ʃæsiz/は複数形でもある.

N-COUNT 可算名詞 A **chassis** is the framework that a vehicle is built on. 車台、シャシー
→ see car

chat /tʃæt/ (chats, chatting, chatted) V-RECIP 相互動詞 When people **chat**, they talk to each other in an informal and friendly way. 雑談する □ *The women were chatting.* 女たちはおしゃべりをしていた. □ *I was chatting to him the other day.* 私は先日彼と雑談していた. ● N-COUNT 可算名詞 **Chat** is also a noun. 雑談 □ *I had a chat with John.* 私はジョンと雑談した.

chat room (chat rooms) also **chatroom** N-COUNT 詞 A **chat room** is a site on the Internet where people can exchange messages about a particular subject. チャットルーム [COMPUTING コンピューティング] □ *...a woman I met in a chat room.* チャットルームで知り合った女性

chat show (chat shows) N-COUNT 可算名詞 A **chat show** is the same as a **talk show**. トークショー [BRIT 英国英語]

chat|ter /tʃætər/ (chatters, chattering, chattered) **1** V-I 自動詞 If you **chatter**, you talk quickly and continuously, usually about things which are not important. ぺちゃくちゃしゃべる □ *Everyone's chattering away in different languages.* 皆それぞれの言語でしゃべっている. □ *Erica was friendly and chattered about Andrew's children.* エリカは人なつっこくて、アンドリューの子供たちについてぺちゃくちゃしゃべった. ● N-UNCOUNT 不可算名詞 **Chatter** is also a noun. くだらないおしゃべり. 無駄話 **2** V-I 自動詞 If your teeth **chatter**, they keep knocking together because you are very cold or very nervous. ガチガチ鳴る □ *She was so cold her teeth chattered.* 彼女は非常に寒くて歯がガチガチ鳴った. **3** V-I 自動詞 When birds or animals **chatter**, they make high-pitched noises. けたたましく鳴く [LITERARY 文語的] □ *Birds were chattering somewhere, and occasionally he could hear a vehicle pass by.* どこかで鳥がやかましくさえずり、時々車が通る音が彼に聞えた. ● N-UNCOUNT 不可算名詞 **Chatter** is also a noun. けたたましい鳴き声 □ *...almond trees vibrating with the chatter of crickets.* コオロギの鳴き声で反響しているアーモンドの木

chauf|feur /ʃoʊfər, ʃoʊfɜr/ (chauffeurs, chauffeuring, chauffeured) **1** N-COUNT 可算名詞 The **chauffeur** of a rich or important person is the man or woman who is employed to take care of their car and drive them around in it. お抱え運転手 **2** V-T 他動詞 If you **chauffeur** someone somewhere, you drive them there in a car, usually as part of your job. 車で連れて行く □ *It was certainly useful to have her there to chauffeur him around.* 彼女を車で案内するために彼女にそこにいてもらうのは確かに便利だった.

chau|vin|ism /ʃoʊvɪnɪzəm/ N-UNCOUNT 不可算名詞 **Chauvinism** is a strong, unreasonable belief that your own country, sex, race, or religion, is better and more important than any other. 狂信的愛国主義 [DISAPPROVAL 不賛成] □ *...it may also appeal to the latent chauvinism of many ordinary people.* それは多くの普通の人々の隠れた狂信的愛国主義にも受けるかもしれない. ● **chau|vin|ist** (chauvinists) N-COUNT 可算名詞 狂信的愛国主義者 □ *He is arrogant and a bit of a chauvinist.* 彼は傲慢でちょっと狂信的愛国主義者のところがある.

cheap /tʃip/ (cheaper, cheapest) **1** ADJ 形容詞 Goods or services that are **cheap** cost less money than usual or than you expected. 安い □ *I'm going to live somewhere off campus if I can find somewhere cheap enough.* 私は十分に安い場所が見つかればキャンパス外に住むつもりだ. □ *Operating costs are coming down because of cheaper fuel.* 操業費により安い燃料が原因で下がってきている. ● **cheap|ly** ADV 副詞 [ADV after v] 安く □ *It will produce electricity more cheaply than a nuclear plant.* それは原子力発電所より安く電気を発生させるだろう. **2** ADJ 形容詞 If you describe goods as **cheap**, you mean they cost less money than similar products but their quality is poor. 安っぽい [ADJ n] □ *Don't resort to cheap imitations; save up for the real thing.* 安物のイミテーションに頼らず、本物を手に入れるために貯金しなさい. **3** ADJ 形容詞 If you describe someone's remarks or actions as **cheap**, you mean they are unkindly or insincerely using a situation to benefit themselves or to harm someone else. 軽蔑に値する [DISAPPROVAL 不賛成] [ADJ n] □ *These tests will inevitably be used by politicians to make cheap political points.* こうしたテストが政治家によってつまらない政治的主張のために利用されるのは避けられないだろう. **4** ADJ 形容詞 If you describe someone as **cheap**, you are criticizing them for being unwilling to spend money. けちな [AM 米国英語, DISAPPROVAL 不賛成] □ *Oh, please, Dad, just this once don't be cheap.* ねえお父さん、どうか今回だけはけちるのをやめて.

cheat /tʃit/ (cheats, cheating, cheated) **1** V-I 自動詞 When someone **cheats**, they do not obey a set of rules which they should be obeying, for example in a game or exam. ごまかしをする □ *Students may be tempted to cheat in order to get into top schools.* 学生は上位校に入学するためについカンニングしてしまうかもしれない. ● **cheat|ing** N-UNCOUNT 不可算名詞 不正 □ *In an election in 1988, he was accused of cheating by his opponent.* 1988年の選挙で彼は対立候補者から不正をしていると非難された. **2** V-T 他動詞 If someone **cheats** you **out of** something, they get it from you by behaving dishonestly. だまし取る □ *The company engaged in a deliberate effort to cheat them out of their pensions.* その会社は計画的に彼らをだまして年金を取ろうとした. **3** N-COUNT 可算名詞 Someone who is a **cheat** does not obey a set of rules which they should be obeying. 不正をする者 □ *Cheats will be disqualified.* ルールに従わない者は失格するでしょう.

▶ **cheat on** **1** PHRASAL VERB 句動詞 If someone **cheats on** their

husband, wife, or partner, they have a sexual relationship with another person. 浮気をする [INFORMAL くだけた] ❑ *I'd found Philippe was cheating on me and I was angry and hurt.* 私はフィリップの浮気を知り, 腹が立ち傷ついた. ② PHRASAL VERB 句動詞 If someone **cheats on** something such as an agreement or their taxes, they do not do what they should do under a set of rules. 違反する [mainly AM 主に米国英語] ❑ *Their job is to check that none of the signatory countries is cheating on the agreement.* 彼らの仕事は加盟国が条約違反をしていないことを確認することだ.

check /tʃɛk/ (checks, checking, checked) ① V-T/V-I 他動詞/自動詞 If you **check** something such as a piece of information or a document, you make sure that it is correct or satisfactory. 確かめる ❑ *Check the accuracy of everything in your résumé.* 履歴書に間違いが1つもないことを確かめなさい. ❑ *I think there is an age limit, but I'd have to check.* 私は年齢制限があると思うが, 確認する必要がある. ❑ *She hadn't checked whether she had a clean, ironed shirt.* 彼女は洗い立てのアイロンをかけたシャツがあるかどうか確かめていなかった. ● N-COUNT 可算名詞 **Check** is also a noun. 検査 ❑ *He is being constantly monitored with regular checks on his blood pressure.* 彼は定期的な血圧検査により絶え間なく監視されている. ② V-I 自動詞 If you **check on** someone or something, you make sure they are in a safe or satisfactory condition. 安全を確かめる ❑ *Stephen checked on her several times during the night.* スティーブンは夜中に数回彼女の状態を確かめた. ③ V-T 他動詞 If you **check** something that is written on a piece of paper, you put a mark, like a V with the right side extended, next to it to show that something is correct or has been selected or dealt with. (照合・選択などの) 印をつける [mainly AM 主に米国英語] ❑ *To request your free gift, please check the appropriate box below.* 無料のギフトがほしい方は, 下の適切な欄に印をつけてください. ④ V-T 他動詞 To **check** something, usually something bad, means to stop it from spreading or continuing. 食い止める ❑ *Sex education is also expected to help check the spread of AIDS.* 性教育はエイズの蔓延 (まんえん) を食い止めることに役立つことも期待されている. ⑤ V-T 他動詞 When you **check** your luggage at an airport, you give it to an official so that it can be taken on to your plane. 預ける [AM 米国英語] ❑ *We arrived at the airport, checked our baggage and wandered around the gift shops.* 我々は空港に到着し, 手荷物を預けてみやげ物店を見て回った. ● PHRASAL VERB 句動詞 To **check in** your luggage means the same as to **check** it. 預ける ❑ *They checked in their luggage and found seats in the departure loange.* 彼らは手荷物を預け, 出発ラウンジで座るいすを見つけた. ⑥ N-COUNT 可算名詞 The **check** in a restaurant is a piece of paper on which the price of your meal is written and which you are given before you pay. 勘定書 [mainly AM 主に米国英語] ❑ *After coffee, Gastler asked for the check.* コーヒーを飲んでからギャスラーは勘定書を頼んだ. ⑦ N-COUNT 可算名詞 A pattern of squares, usually of two colors, can be referred to as **checks** or a **check**. 格子じま, チェック ❑ *Styles include stripes and checks.* 様式にはストライプとチェックがある. ⑧ N-COUNT 可算名詞 A **check** is a printed form on which you write an amount of money and who it is to be paid to. Your bank then pays the money to that person from your account. 小切手 ❑ *He handed me an envelope with a check for $1,500.* 彼は1500ドルの小切手入りの封筒を私に手渡した. ⑨ → see also **blank check, traveler's check** ⑩ PHRASE 句 If something or someone is **held in check** or is **kept in check**, they are controlled and prevented from becoming too great or powerful. 抑制する ❑ *Life on Earth will become unsustainable unless population growth is held in check.* 地球上の生命が, 人口増加を抑えない限り持続できないようになるだろう. ⑪ → see also **double-check, rain check**

→ see **bank, hotel**

▶ **check in** ① PHRASAL VERB 句動詞 When you **check in** or check **into** a hotel or clinic, or if someone **checks** you in, you arrive and go through the necessary procedures before you stay there. 記帳する, チェックインする ❑ *I'll call the hotel. I'll tell them we'll check in tomorrow.* 私がホテルに電話します. 私たちが明日チェックインすると伝えましょう. ❑ *He has checked into an alcohol treatment center.* 彼はアルコール治療センターの入院手続きをした. ② PHRASAL VERB 句動詞 When you **check in** at an airport, you arrive and show your ticket before going on a flight. 搭乗手続きをする ❑ *He had checked in at Amsterdam's Schiphol airport for a flight to Atlanta.* 彼はアトランタ行きの便に乗るためにアムステルダムのスキポール空港で搭乗手続きをしていた. ③ → see also **check-in, check 5**

→ see **hotel**

▶ **check off** PHRASAL VERB 句動詞 When you **check** things **off**, you check or count them while referring to a list of them, to make sure you have considered all of them. 照合済みの印をつける ❑ *Once you've checked off the items you ordered, put this record in your file.* 注文した品目を照合し終えたら, この記録をあなたのファイルに保管しなさい. ❑ *I haven't checked them off but I would say that's about the number.* 私はそれを照合し終えていないが, 大体その数だと思う.

▶ **check out** ① PHRASAL VERB 句動詞 When you **check out of** a hotel or clinic where you have been staying, or if someone **checks** you **out**, you pay the bill and leave. 勘定を払って出る, チェックアウトする ❑ *They packed and checked out of the hotel.* 彼は荷

造りし, ホテルをチェックアウトした. ❑ *I was disappointed to miss Bryan, who had just checked out.* 私はブライアンに会いそこねてがっかりした. 彼はチェックアウトしたばかりだったから. ② PHRASAL VERB 句動詞 If you **check out** something or someone, you find out information about them to make sure that everything is correct or satisfactory. 調べて確認する ❑ *Maybe we ought to go down to the library and check it out.* たぶん我々は図書館に行ってそのことを調べるべきだろう. ❑ *We ought to check him out on the computer.* 我々はコンピュータで彼のことを調べるべきだ. ③ PHRASAL VERB 句動詞 If something **checks out**, it is correct or satisfactory. 符合する ❑ *She was in San Diego the weekend Jensen got killed. Her alibi checked out.* 彼女はジェンセンが殺された週末にサンディエゴにいた. 彼女のアリバイは成立した. ④ PHRASAL VERB 句動詞 If you **check out** a library book, you borrow it for a fixed period of time. 手続きをして借り出す ❑ *No books can be checked out after 6 p.m. tomorrow.* 明日午後6時以降は本の貸し出し手続きはできません. ⑤ → see also **checkout**

▶ **check up** ① PHRASAL VERB 句動詞 If you **check up on** something, you find out information about it. 調べる ❑ *It is certainly worth checking up on your benefit entitlements.* 給付金を受ける権利は確かに調べる価値がある. ② → see also **checkup** ③ PHRASAL VERB 句動詞 If you **check up on** someone, you obtain information about them, usually secretly. 動きを追う ❑ *I'm sure he knew I was checking up on him.* 私が彼の動きを追っていたことを彼は知っていたことは確かだ.

Thesaurus   check また次を参照:

V.   confirm, find out, make sure, verify; *(ant.)* ignore, overlook ①

Word Partnership   check は次の語句と使われる:

PREP.   check **for/that** *something*, check **with** *someone* ①
N.   **background** check, **credit** check, **security** check ②
       check **your baggage/luggage** ⑤
V.   **cash** a check, **deposit** a check, **pay with** a check, **write** a check ⑧

check|book /tʃɛkbʊk/ (checkbooks) N-COUNT 可算名詞 A **checkbook** is a book of checks which your bank gives you so that you can pay for things by check. 小切手帳 [AM 米国英語] ❑ *The woman took out her checkbook and quickly made out four checks.* その女性は小切手帳を取り出し, 素早く4枚の小切手を切った.

checked /tʃɛkt/ ADJ 形容詞 Something that is **checked** has a pattern of small squares, usually of two colors. 格子じまの ❑ *He was wearing blue jeans and a checked shirt.* 彼は紺のジーンズとチェックのシャツを着ていた.

check|er /tʃɛkər/ (checkers) ① N-UNCOUNT 不可算名詞 **Checkers** is a game for two people, played with 24 round pieces on a board. チェッカー [AM 米国英語] ❑ *...a game of checkers.* チェッカーのひと勝負. ② N-COUNT 可算名詞 A **checker** is a person or machine that has the job of checking something. チェックする人, チェックする装置 ❑ *Modern word processors usually have spelling checkers and even grammar checkers.* 近頃のワードプロセッサには普通つづりのチェック, 文法のチェック機能すらある.

check-in (check-ins) N-COUNT 可算名詞 At an airport, a **check-in** is the counter or desk where you check in. 搭乗手続きカウンター ❑ *The line at the check-in was already dispersing.* 搭乗手続きカウンターの列に並んでいた人々は既に散りかけていた.

check|ing ac|count (checking accounts) N-COUNT 可算名詞 A **checking account** is a personal bank account which you can take money out of at any time using your check book or bank card. 当座預金口座 [mainly AM 主に米国英語] ❑ *...Commonwealth Bank, where he has his checking account.* 彼が当座預金口座を持っているコモンウェルス銀行

→ see **bank**

check|out /tʃɛkaʊt/ (checkouts) N-COUNT 可算名詞 In a supermarket, a **checkout** is a counter where you pay for things you are buying. レジ ❑ *...the supermarket checkout counter.* スーパーマーケットのレジ

check|point /tʃɛkpɔɪnt/ (checkpoints) N-COUNT 可算名詞 A **checkpoint** is a place where traffic is stopped so that it can be checked. 検問所 ❑ *...a bomb explosion close to an army checkpoint.* 軍の検問所近くの爆発

check|up /tʃɛkʌp/ (checkups) N-COUNT 可算名詞 A **checkup** is a medical examination by your doctor or dentist to make sure that there is nothing wrong with your health. 健康診断 ❑ *The disease was detected during a routine checkup.* その病気は定期的な健康診断中に発見された.

cheek /tʃik/ (cheeks) ① N-COUNT 可算名詞 Your **cheeks** are the sides of your face below your eyes. ほお ❑ *Tears were running down her cheeks.* 涙が彼女のほおを流れていた. ② N-COUNT 可算名詞 Your **cheeks** are your buttocks. 尻 (しり) [usu pl] ❑ *My butt cheeks are sore from sitting on this bench too long.* このベンチに長く座りすぎてお尻が

痛い。 **3** N-SING 単数名詞 You say that someone has **cheek** when you are annoyed or shocked at something unreasonable that they have done. ずうずうしさ [mainly BRIT 主に英国英語, INFORMAL くだけた] [also no det] *I'm amazed they had the cheek to ask in the first place.* そもそも彼らがずうずうしく聞いたことに私は驚いている。
→ see **face, kiss**

cheek|bone /tʃikboʊn/ (cheekbones) N-COUNT 可算名詞 Your **cheekbones** are the two bones in your face just below your eyes. ほお骨 *She was very beautiful, with high cheekbones.* 彼女はほお骨が高く、非常に美しかった。

cheeky /tʃiki/ (cheekier, cheekiest) ADJ 形容詞 If you describe a person or their behavior as **cheeky**, you think that they are slightly rude or disrespectful but in a charming or amusing way. 生意気な [mainly BRIT 主に英国英語] *The boy was cheeky and casual.* その少年は生意気でぶっきらぼうだった。

cheer /tʃɪər/ (cheers, cheering, cheered) **1** V-T/V-I 他動詞/自動詞 When people **cheer**, they shout loudly to show their approval or to encourage someone who is doing something such as taking part in a game. 声援する *The crowd cheered as she went up the steps to the bandstand.* 彼女が野外ステージへの階段を登っていくと群集は歓声を上げた。 *Hundreds of thousands of jubilant Americans cheered him on his return.* 何十万人もの大喜びのアメリカ人は帰ってきた彼を歓呼の声で迎えた。 ● N-COUNT 可算名詞 **Cheer** is also a noun. 歓呼 *The colonel was rewarded with a resounding cheer from the men.* 大佐は兵士の鳴り響く歓迎を受けた。 **2** V-T 他動詞 If you **are cheered** **by** something, it makes you happier or less worried. 元気づける *Stephen noticed that the people around him looked cheered by his presence.* スティーブンは彼がいることで周囲の人々が元気づけられたように見えることに気づいた。 ● **cheer|ing** ADJ 形容詞 励ましになる *...very cheering news.* 大変喜ばしい知らせ **3** CONVENTION 慣習表現 People sometimes say "**Cheers**" to each other just before they drink an alcoholic drink. 乾杯 [mainly BRIT 主に英国英語]
▶ **cheer on** PHRASAL VERB 句動詞 When you **cheer** someone **on**, you shout loudly in order to encourage them, for example when they are taking part in a game. 声援する *A thousand supporters packed into the stadium to cheer them on.* 1千人のサポーターが彼らに声援を送るためにスタジアムに詰めかけた。
▶ **cheer up** PHRASAL VERB 句動詞 When you **cheers** up or when something **cheers** you **up**, you stop feeling depressed and become more cheerful. 元気づく, 元気づける *I think he misses her terribly. You might cheer him up.* 彼は彼女をひどく恋しがっているようだ。 彼を元気づけてくれないか。 *I wrote that song just to cheer myself up.* 私は自分自身を元気づけるためにあの歌を作った。

cheer|ful /tʃɪərfəl/ **1** ADJ 形容詞 Someone who is **cheerful** is happy and shows this in their behavior. 朗らかな *Paddy was always cheerful and jolly.* パディはいつも朗らかで陽気だった。 ● **cheer|ful|ly** ADV 副詞 [ADV with v] 陽気に *"We've come with good news," Pat said cheerfully.* 「いい知らせだ」とパットは上機嫌で言った。 ● **cheer|ful|ness** N-UNCOUNT 不可算名詞 快活さ *I remember this extraordinary man with particular affection for his unfailing cheerfulness.* 私はこの並外れた男のことを特にそのいつも変らぬ朗らかさに愛着を感じながら思い出す。 **2** ADJ 形容詞 Something that is **cheerful** is pleasant and makes you feel happy. 楽しい *The nursery is bright and cheerful, with plenty of toys.* その保育所はおもちゃが沢山あり、明るく楽しい。 **3** ADJ 形容詞 [usu ADJ n] If you describe someone's attitude as **cheerful**, you mean they are not worried about something, and you think that they should be. 楽観的な *There is little evidence to support his cheerful assumptions.* 彼の楽観的な仮説を裏付ける証拠はほとんどない。 ● **cheer|ful|ly** ADV 副詞 [ADV before v] 楽観的に *He cheerfully ignored medical advice which could have prolonged his life.* 彼は彼の余命を引き伸ばしたかもしれない医者の意見を楽観的に無視した。

cheery /tʃɪəri/ (cheerier, cheeriest) ADJ 形容詞 If you describe a person or their behavior as **cheery**, you mean that they are cheerful and happy. 楽しそうな *She was cheery and talked to them about their problems.* 彼女は上機嫌で彼らの問題について彼らと話し合った。 ● **cheer|ily** ADV 副詞 明るく *"Come on in," she said cheerily.* 「お入りなさい」と彼女は上機嫌で言った。

cheese /tʃiz/ (cheeses) N-MASS 質量名詞 **Cheese** is a solid food made from milk. It is usually white or yellow. チーズ *...bread and cheese.* パンとチーズ *...delicious French cheeses.* おいしいフランス製のチーズ

cheese|burg|er /tʃizbɜrgər/ (cheeseburgers) N-COUNT 可算名詞 A **cheeseburger** is a hamburger with a slice of cheese on top, served on a bun. チーズバーガー

chef /ʃɛf/ (chefs) N-COUNT 可算名詞 A **chef** is a cook in a restaurant or hotel. コック *...some of Australia's leading chefs.* オーストラリアの一流コックの1部

Word Link chem ≈ chemical : biochemist, chemical, chemistry

chemi|cal /kɛmɪkəl/ (chemicals) **1** ADJ 形容詞 **Chemical** means involving or resulting from a reaction between two or more substances, or relating to the substances that something

consists of. 化学の [ADJ n] *...chemical reactions that cause ozone destruction.* オゾン破壊を引き起こす化学反応 *...the chemical composition of the ocean.* 海洋の化学構成 ● **chemi|cal|ly** /kɛmɪkli/ ADV 副詞 化学的に *...chemically treated foods.* 化学的に処理された食品 **2** N-COUNT 可算名詞 **Chemicals** are substances that are used in a chemical process or made by a chemical process. 化学物質 *The whole food chain is affected by the overuse of chemicals in agriculture.* 全食物連鎖は農業における化学物質の使いすぎの影響を受けている。 *...a chemical company.* 化学製品会社
→ see **dry-cleaning, farm, firework, war**

Word Link ist ≈ one who practices : artist, chemist, pharmacist

chem|ist /kɛmɪst/ (chemists) **1** N-COUNT 可算名詞 A **chemist** is a person who does research connected with chemistry or who studies chemistry. 化学者 *She worked as a research chemist.* 彼女は化学研究員として働いた。 **2** N-COUNT 可算名詞 A **chemist** or a **chemist's** is the same as a **drugstore** or a **pharmacy**. 薬局 [BRIT 英国英語]

In American English, the usual way of referring to a store where medicines are sold is a **drugstore**. *She went into a drugstore and bought some aspirin.* **Pharmacy** refers specifically to a part of the drugstore where you get prescription medicines. Pharmacies are often located in stores that mainly sell other merchandise, such as supermarkets and discount centers. In Britain, the nearest equivalent of a drugstore is a **chemist's**.

3 N-COUNT 可算名詞 A **chemist** is the same as a **druggist** or a **pharmacist**. 薬剤師, 薬屋 [BRIT 英国英語]

chem|is|try /kɛmɪstri/ **1** N-UNCOUNT 不可算名詞 **Chemistry** is the scientific study of the structure of substances and of the way that they react with other substances. 化学 **2** N-UNCOUNT 不可算名詞 The **chemistry** of an organism or a material is the chemical substances that make it up and the chemical reactions that go on inside it. 化学的性質 *We have literally altered the chemistry of our planet's atmosphere.* 我々は我々の惑星の大気の化学的性質を文字通り変えてしまった。 **3** N-UNCOUNT 不可算名詞 If you say that there is **chemistry** between two people, you mean that it is obvious they are attracted to each other or like each other very much. 相性 *...the extraordinary chemistry between Ingrid and Bogart.* イングリッドとボガート間の並外れた相性

cher|ish /tʃɛrɪʃ/ (cherishes, cherishing, cherished) **1** V-T 他動詞 If you **cherish** something such as a hope or a pleasant memory, you keep it in your mind for a long period of time. 忘れずにいる *The president will cherish the memory of this visit to Ohio.* 大統領は今回のオハイオ州訪問の思い出を忘れないだろう。 ● **cher|ished** ADJ 形容詞 [ADJ n] 心に抱いた *...the cherished dream of a world without wars.* 戦争のない世界という胸に秘めた夢 **2** V-T 他動詞 If you **cherish** someone or something, you take good care of them because you love them. 大事にする *He genuinely loved and cherished her.* 彼は彼女を心から愛し、大事にした。 ● **cher|ished** ADJ 形容詞 [ADJ n] 大事な *He described the picture as his most cherished possession.* 彼はその絵を最も大事な持ち物と説明した。 **3** V-T 他動詞 If you **cherish** a right, a privilege, or a principle, you regard it as important and try hard to keep it. 重んじる *Chinese people cherish their independence and sovereignty.* 中国人は彼らの独立と主権を重んじる。 ● **cher|ished** ADJ 形容詞 [ADJ n] 重視された *Freud called into question some deeply cherished beliefs.* フロイトはいくつかの深く信じられていた考えに異議を唱えた。

cher|ry /tʃɛri/ (cherries) **1** N-COUNT 可算名詞 **Cherries** are small, round fruit with red skins. サクランボ **2** N-COUNT 可算名詞 A **cherry** or a **cherry tree** is a tree that cherries grow on. 桜の木

cherry-pick (cherry-picks, cherry-picking, cherry-picked) V-T 他動詞 If someone **cherry-picks** people or things, they choose the best ones from a group of them, often in a way that other people consider unfair. 慎重に選び取る *The team is in debt while others are lining up to cherry-pick their best players.* 他のチームが最優秀の選手を獲得する準備をしているのに、そのチームには借金がある。

chess /tʃɛs/ N-UNCOUNT 不可算名詞 **Chess** is a game for two people, played on a chessboard. Each player has 16 pieces, including a king. Your aim is to move your pieces so that your opponent's king cannot escape being taken. チェス *He was playing chess with his uncle.* 彼はおじとチェスをしていた。
→ see **Word Web: chess**

chest /tʃɛst/ (chests) **1** N-COUNT 可算名詞 Your **chest** is the top part of the front of your body where your ribs, lungs, and heart are. 胸 *He crossed his arms over his chest.* 彼は胸の上で腕を組んだ。 *He was shot in the chest.* 彼は胸を撃たれた。 **2** N-COUNT 可算名詞 A **chest** is a large, heavy box used for storing things. 収納箱 *At the very bottom of the chest were his carving tools.* その収納箱の1番下には彼の彫刻道具があった。 *...a treasure chest.* 秘蔵品入れ
→ see **body**

chest|nut /tʃɛsnʌt, -nət/ (chestnuts) **1** N-COUNT 可算名詞 A **chestnut** or **chestnut tree** is a tall tree with broad leaves. クリの木

Word Web   chess

Scholars disagree on the origin of **chess**. Some say it started in China around 570 AD. Others say it was invented in India sometime later. In early versions of the **game**, the **king** was the most powerful **chess piece**. But when the game was brought to Europe in the Middle Ages, a new form appeared. It was called Queen's Chess. Modern chess is based on this game. The king is the most important piece, but the **queen** is the most powerful. Chess **players** use **rooks**, **bishops**, **knights**, and **pawns** to protect their king and to put their **opponent** in checkmate.

2 N-COUNT 可算名詞 **Chestnuts** are the reddish brown nuts that grow on chestnut trees. You can eat chestnuts. クリ **3** COLOR 色彩語 Something that is **chestnut** is dark reddish brown in color. 赤茶色 ❏ ...chestnut hair. 赤茶色の髪

chew /tʃuː/ (**chews, chewing, chewed**) **1** V-T/V-I 他動詞/自動詞 When you **chew** food, you use your teeth to break it up in your mouth so that it becomes easier to swallow. かむ ❏ Be certain to eat slowly and chew your food extremely well. 食べ物を十分によくかんで、ゆっくりと食べるようにしなさい. ❏ Daniel leaned back on the sofa, still chewing on his apple. ダニエルはソファーにもたれて、まだリンゴをかじっていた. **2** V-T 他動詞 If you **chew** gum or tobacco, you keep biting it and moving it around your mouth to taste the flavor of it. You do not swallow it. かむ ❏ One girl was chewing gum. 1人の少女がガムをかんでいた. **3** V-T 他動詞 If you **chew** your lips or your fingernails, you keep biting them because you are nervous. かむ ❏ He chewed his lower lip nervously. 彼は下唇を神経質そうにかんだ. **4** V-T/V-I 他動詞/自動詞 If a person or animal **chews** an object or **chews on** it, they bite it with their teeth. かむ ❏ They pause and chew their pencils. 彼らは中断し、鉛筆をかむ. ❏ She chewed through the tape that bound her. 彼女は彼女を縛り付けたテープをかみ切った.

chic /ʃiːk/ **1** ADJ 形容詞 Something or someone that is **chic** is fashionable and sophisticated. 上品な、いきな ❏ Her gown was very French and chic. 彼女のガウンはとてもフランス風でとても上品だった. **2** N-UNCOUNT 不可算名詞 **Chic** is used to refer to a particular style or to the quality of being chic. 一風、上品さ ❏ ...French designer chic. フランスのデザイナー風

chick /tʃɪk/ (**chicks**) **1** N-COUNT 可算名詞 A **chick** is a baby bird. ひな (鳥の) ❏ ...newly-hatched chicks. ふ化したばかりのひな **2** N-COUNT 可算名詞 Some men refer to women as **chicks**. This use could cause offense. 女 [INFORMAL くだけた] ❏ I'm madly in love with this hot biker chick. おれはこのセクシーな女ライダーに夢中さ.

chick|en /tʃɪkɪn/ (**chickens, chickening, chickened**) **1** N-COUNT 可算名詞 **Chickens** are birds which are kept on a farm for their eggs and for their meat. 鶏 ❏ Lionel built a coop so that they could raise chickens and have a supply of fresh eggs. ライオネルは彼らが鶏を飼って新鮮な卵を得られるように鶏小屋を作った. **2** N-UNCOUNT 不可算名詞 **Chicken** is the flesh of this bird eaten as food. 鶏肉 ❏ ...roast chicken with wild mushrooms. 野生きのこを添えたローストチキン **2** N-COUNT 可算名詞 If someone calls you a **chicken**, they mean that you are afraid to do something. 臆病者 [INFORMAL くだけた, DISAPPROVAL 不賛成] ❏ I'm scared of the dark. I'm a big chicken. ぼくは暗やみが怖い. ぼくはとても弱虫なんだ. ● ADJ 形容詞 **Chicken** is also an adjective. 臆病な [v-link ADJ] ❏ Why are you so chicken, Gregory? グレゴリー、どうしてお前はそんなに怖がりなんだ? **3** PHRASE 句 If you say that someone **is counting** their **chickens**, you mean that they are assuming that they will be successful or get something, when this is not certain. 皮算用をする ❏ I don't want to count my chickens before they are hatched. 私は取らぬたぬきの皮算用をしたくない. **4 chickens come home to roost** → see **roost**
▶ **chicken out** PHRASAL VERB 句動詞 If someone **chickens out** of something they were intending to do, they decide not to do it because they are afraid. おじけづく [INFORMAL くだけた] ❏ I had never ridden on a motor-cycle before. But it was too late to chicken out. 私はそれまでオートバイに乗ったことがなかった. でもしり込みするには遅すぎた.
→ see **meat**

chide /tʃaɪd/ (**chides, chiding, chided**) V-T 他動詞 If you **chide** someone, you speak to them angrily because they have done something bad or foolish. しかる [OLD-FASHIONED 古風な] ❏ Jack chided himself for worrying. ジャックはくよくよしている自分を叱った (しった) した.

chief /tʃiːf/ (**chiefs**) **1** N-COUNT 可算名詞 The **chief** of an organization is the person who is in charge of it. (組織の) 長 ❏ ...a commission appointed by the police chief. 警察署長から与えられた任務 **2** N-COUNT; N-TITLE 可算名詞, 称号名詞 The **chief** of a tribe is its leader. (部族の) 首長 ❏ ...Sitting Bull, chief of the Sioux tribes of the Great Plains. 大平原のスー族の首長、シッティング・ブル **3** ADJ 形容詞 **Chief** is used in the job titles of the most senior worker or workers of a particular kind in an organization. 最高位の [ADJ n] ❏ ...the chief test pilot. 一等試験操縦士 **4** ADJ 形容詞 The **chief** cause, part, or member of something is the most important one. 主な [ADJ n] ❏ Financial stress is well established as a chief reason for divorce. 金銭的なストレスが離婚の主な理由であることは十分に証明されている.

Thesaurus   chief また次を参照:

| N. | boss, director, head, leader **1** |
| ADJ. | key, main, major; (ant.) minor, unimportant **4** |

chief ex|ecu|tive of|fi|cer (**chief executive officers**) N-COUNT 可算名詞 The **chief executive officer** of a company is the person who has overall responsibility for the management of that company. The abbreviation **CEO** is often used. 最高経営責任者 [BUSINESS 実業]

chief jus|tice (**chief justices**) N-COUNT; N-TITLE 可算名詞, 称号名詞 A **chief justice** is the most important judge in a court of law, especially a supreme court. 裁判長、最高裁判所長官

chief|ly /tʃiːfli/ ADV 副詞 You use **chiefly** to indicate that a particular reason, emotion, method, or feature is the main or most important one. 主に ❏ He joined the consular service in China, chiefly because this was one of the few job vacancies. 彼は在中領事館に就職した. その主な理由はこれが数少ない求人の1つだったからだ.

chief of staff (**chiefs of staff**) N-COUNT 可算名詞 The **chiefs of staff** are the highest-ranking officers of each service of the armed forces. 参謀長

chif|fon /ʃɪfɒn/ (**chiffons**) N-MASS 質量名詞 **Chiffon** is a kind of very thin silk or nylon cloth that you can see through. シフォン (絹やナイロン製の薄く透けて見える布) ❏ ...floaty chiffon skirts. ふわっとしたシフォンのスカート

child /tʃaɪld/ (**children**) **1** N-COUNT 可算名詞 A **child** is a human being who is not yet an adult. 子供 ❏ When I was a child I lived in a country village. 私は子供の頃、田舎の村に住んでいた. ❏ ...a child of six. 6歳の子供 **2** N-COUNT 可算名詞 Someone's **children** are their sons and daughters of any age. (親に対して) 子 ❏ How are the children? 子供たちは元気? ❏ His children have left home. 彼の子供たちは家を出ている.
→ see Word Web: **child**
→ see **age**

Word Partnership   child は次の語句と使われる:

N.	child abuse, child care **1**
V.	adopt a child, have a child, raise a child **1**
ADJ.	difficult child, happy child, small/young child, unborn child **1**

child|birth /tʃaɪldbɜːrθ/ N-UNCOUNT 不可算名詞 **Childbirth** is the act of giving birth to a child. 出産 ❏ She died in childbirth. 彼女はお産で亡くなった.

child|care /tʃaɪldkɛər/ N-UNCOUNT 不可算名詞 **Childcare** refers to taking care of children, and to the facilities which help parents to do so. 育児、保育所 ❏ Both partners shared childcare. 夫婦で育児を分担した.

Word Web   child

In the Middle Ages, only **infants** and **toddlers** enjoyed the freedoms of **childhood**. A **child** of seven or eight was important to the survival of the family. In the countryside, **sons** started working on the family's farm. **Daughters** did essential housework. In cities, children became laborers and worked along with adults. Today **parents** treat children with special care. The toys **babies** play with help them learn. There are educational programs for preschoolers. The idea of **adolescence** as a separate phase of life appeared about 100 years ago. Today **teenagers** often have part-time jobs while they go to school.

Word Link   hood ≈ state, condition : adulthood, childhood, manhood

child|hood /tʃaɪldhʊd/ (**childhoods**) N-VAR 可変性名詞 A person's **childhood** is the period of their life when they are a child. 子供時代 ❑ She had a happy childhood. 彼女は幸せな子供時代を過ごした。 ❑ He was remembering a story heard in childhood. 彼は子供の頃に聞いた話を思い出していた。
→ see **child**

child|ish /tʃaɪldɪʃ/ ❶ ADJ 形容詞 **Childish** means relating to or typical of a child. 子供らしい ❑ ...childish enthusiasm. 子供らしいひたむきさ ❷ ADJ 形容詞 If you describe someone, especially an adult, as **childish**, you disapprove of them because they behave in an immature way. 子供じみた [DISAPPROVAL 不賛成] ❑ ...Penny's selfish and childish behavior. ペニーの自分勝手で子供じみた行動

child|less /tʃaɪldlɪs/ ADJ 形容詞 Someone who is **childless** has no children. 子供のいない ❑ ...childless couples. 子供のいない夫婦

Word Link   like ≈ similar : alike, childlike, likeness

child|like /tʃaɪldlaɪk/ ADJ 形容詞 You describe someone as **childlike** when they seem like a child in their character, appearance, or behavior. 子供のような ❑ His most enduring quality is his childlike innocence. 彼の最も永続的な資質はその子供のような純真さだ。

chil|dren /tʃɪldrən/ **Children** is the plural of **child**. 子供たち

chili /tʃɪli/ (**chilies** or **chilis**) ❶ N-VAR 可変性名詞 **Chilies** are small, red or green peppers. They have a very hot taste and are used in cooking. とうがらし ❷ N-UNCOUNT 不可算名詞 **Chili** is a dish made from meat or beans, or sometimes both, with a thick sauce of tomatoes, and powdered or fresh chilies. チリ（肉や豆をトマトソース、とうがらしで煮込んだ料理）
→ see **spice**

chill /tʃɪl/ (**chills, chilling, chilled**) ❶ V-T/V-I 他動詞/自動詞 When you **chill** something or when it **chills**, you lower its temperature so that it becomes colder but does not freeze. 冷やす [他動詞]、冷える [自動詞] ❑ Chill the fruit salad until serving time. 食卓に出すまでフルーツサラダを冷やしておきなさい。 ❑ These doughs can be rolled out while you wait for the pastry to chill. ペストリーが冷めるのを待っている間に、これらの生地を伸ばすこともできます。 ❷ V-T 他動詞 When cold weather or something cold **chills** a person or a place, it makes that person or that place feel very cold. 冷やす ❑ The marble floor was beginning to chill me. 私は大理石の床の上で寒くなってきた。 ❑ Wade placed his chilled hands on the radiator and warmed them. ウェイドは冷えた両手を暖房器の上に置いて温めた。 ❸ N-COUNT 可算名詞 If something sends a **chill** through you, it gives you a sudden feeling of fear or anxiety. おじけ ❑ The violence used against the students sent a chill through Indonesia. その学生たちに加えられた暴行はインドネシア中をぞっとさせた。 ❹ N-COUNT 可算名詞 A **chill** is a mild illness which can give you a slight fever and headache. 悪寒、風邪 ❑ He caught a chill while performing at a rain-soaked open-air venue. 彼は雨でびしょ濡れの野外会場で公演している間に風邪を引いた。 ❺ ADJ 形容詞 **Chill** weather is cold and unpleasant. 肌寒い [ADJ n] ❑ ...chill winds, rain and choppy seas. 冷たい風、雨と荒れる海 ● N-SING 単数名詞 **Chill** is also a noun. 肌寒さ ❑ September is here, bringing with it a chill in the mornings. 当地は9月になり、朝方が肌寒くなってきた。
→ see **illness, refrigerator**

▶ **chill out** PHRASAL VERB 句動詞 To **chill out** means to relax after you have done something tiring or stressful. 落ち着く [INFORMAL くだけた] ❑ After school, we used to chill out in each others' bedrooms. 放課後に私たちはお互いの寝室に入ってくつろいだものだった。

chil|li /tʃɪli/ (**chillies** or **chillis**) → see **chili**

chill|ing /tʃɪlɪŋ/ ADJ 形容詞 If you describe something as **chilling**, you mean it is frightening. ぞっとさせる ❑ He described in chilling detail how he attacked her. 彼は彼女を襲った時のぞっとするような話を詳細に語った。 ● **chill|ing|ly** ADV 副詞 ぞっとするほど

❑ ...the murder of a Chicago teenager in chillingly similar circumstances in February. 2月に起こった状況がぞっとするほど似ているシカゴの10代の若者の殺人事件

chil|ly /tʃɪli/ (**chillier, chilliest**) ❶ ADJ 形容詞 Something that is **chilly** is unpleasantly cold. (寒さで) ぞくぞくする ❑ It was a chilly afternoon. それはぞくぞくするほど寒い午後だった。 ❷ ADJ 形容詞 If you feel **chilly**, you feel rather cold. 肌寒い [v-link ADJ] ❑ I'm a bit chilly. ちょっと肌寒いわ。

> If you want to emphasize how cold the weather is, you can say that it is **freezing**, especially in winter when there is ice or frost. In summer, if the temperature is below average, you can say that it is **cool**. In general, **cold** suggests a lower temperature than **cool**, and **cool** things may be pleasant or refreshing. ❑ A cool breeze swept off the ocean; it was pleasant out there. If it is very **cool** or too **cool**, you can also say that it is **chilly**.

chime /tʃaɪm/ (**chimes, chiming, chimed**) ❶ V-T/V-I 他動詞/自動詞 When a bell or a clock **chimes**, it makes ringing sounds. (時計やベルを) 鳴らす 他動詞 鳴る 自動詞 ❑ He heard the front doorbell chime. 彼は玄関の呼び鈴が鳴るのを聞いた。 ❑ ...as the town hall clock chimed three o'clock. 市役所の時計が3時を知らせると ❷ N-COUNT 可算名詞 A **chime** is a ringing sound made by a bell, especially when it is part of a clock. (玄関や時計の) チャイム ❑ At that moment a chime sounded from the front of the house. その時、玄関からチャイムが聞こえてきた。 ❸ N-PLURAL 複数名詞 **Chimes** are a set of small objects which make a ringing sound when they are blown by the wind. 風鈴 ❑ ...the haunting sound of the wind chimes. あの風鈴の忘れられない音

▶ **chime in** PHRASAL VERB 句動詞 If you **chime in**, you say something just after someone else has spoken. (人の話に) 割って入る ❑ "Why?" Pete asked impatiently. — "Yes, why?" Bob chimed in. "It seems like a good idea to me." 「どうして？」ピートがいらいらして聞いた。「そうだよ。どうして？」とボブが割って入ってきた。「ぼくには名案のように思えるよ」

chim|ney /tʃɪmni/ (**chimneys**) N-COUNT 可算名詞 A **chimney** is a pipe through which smoke goes up into the air, usually through the roof of a building. 煙突 ❑ Thick, yellow smoke pours constantly out of the chimneys at the steel plant in Katowice. カトヴィツェの製鋼所の煙突からはいつも黄色の煙がもうもうと立ち上っている。

chim|pan|zee /tʃɪmpænzi/ (**chimpanzees**) N-COUNT 可算名詞 A **chimpanzee** is a kind of small African ape. チンパンジー
→ see **primate, zoo**

chin /tʃɪn/ (**chins**) N-COUNT 可算名詞 Your **chin** is the part of your face that is below your mouth and above your neck. あご ❑ ...a double chin. 二重あご

chi|na /tʃaɪnə/ ❶ N-UNCOUNT 不可算名詞 **China** is a hard white substance made from clay. It is used to make things such as cups, bowls, plates, and ornaments. 磁器 ❑ ...a small bowl made of china. 磁器の小さな鉢 ❷ N-UNCOUNT 不可算名詞 Cups, bowls, plates, and ornaments made of china are referred to as **china**. 陶磁器 ❑ Judy collects blue and white china. ジュディは染付けの陶磁器を収集している。
→ see **pottery**

chink /tʃɪŋk/ (**chinks**) ❶ N-COUNT 可算名詞 A **chink** in a surface is a very narrow crack or opening in it. 割れ目 ❑ ...a chink in the wall. 壁のすき間 ❷ N-COUNT 可算名詞 A **chink of** light is a small patch of light that shines through a small opening in something. ひとすじ ❑ I noticed a chink of light at the end of the corridor. 廊下の突き当りに1条の光がさしているのに気づいた。

chip /tʃɪp/ (**chips, chipping, chipped**) ❶ N-COUNT 可算名詞 **Chips** or **potato chips** are very thin slices of fried potato that are eaten as a snack. ポテトチップス [AM 米国英語] ❑ ...a package of onion-flavored potato chips. たまねぎ風味のポテトチップス1袋 ❷ N-COUNT 可算名詞 **Chips** are long, thin pieces of potato fried in oil or fat and eaten hot, usually with a meal. フライドポテト [BRIT 英国英語; AM **French fries** 米国英語 French

fries] **3** N-COUNT 可算名詞 A silicon **chip** is a very small piece of silicon with electronic circuits on it which is part of a computer or other piece of machinery. (コンピューターなどの) チップ ❑ ...an electronic card containing a chip. チップを埋め込んだICカード **4** N-COUNT 可算名詞 A **chip** is a small piece of something or a small piece which has been broken off something. かけら、片 ❑ It contains real chocolate chips. それには本物のチョコレートチップスが入っている. **5** N-COUNT 可算名詞 A **chip** in something such as a piece of china or furniture is where a small piece has been broken off it. 欠け ❑ The cup had a small chip. そのカップは少し欠けていた. **6** N-COUNT 可算名詞 **Chips** are plastic counters used in gambling to represent money. (賭博用の) チップ ❑ He put the pile of chips in the center of the table and drew a card. 彼はテーブルの真ん中にチップを積み上げ、カードを引いた. **7** V-T/V-I 他動詞/自動詞 If you **chip** something or if it **chips**, a small piece is broken off it. 欠く [他動詞]、欠ける [自動詞] ❑ The blow chipped the woman's tooth. その一撃で女性の歯が欠けた. ● **chipped** ADJ 形容詞 欠けて、はげて ❑ The wagon's paint was badly chipped on the outside. そのワゴン車の外側は塗料がひどくはげていた. **8** → see also **bargaining chip, blue chip**

▶ **chip in** PHRASAL VERB 句動詞 When a number of people **chip in**, each person gives some money so that they can pay for something together. 金を出し合う [INFORMAL くだけた] ❑ They chip in for the gas. 彼らはガソリン代を出し合った.

→ see **computer**

chis|el /tʃɪzªl/ (**chisels**, **chiseling** or **chiselling**, **chiseled** or **chiselled**) **1** N-COUNT 可算名詞 A **chisel** is a tool that has a long metal blade with a sharp edge at the end. It is used for cutting and shaping wood and stone. のみ ❑ ...a hammer and chisel. 金づちとのみ **2** V-T 他動詞 If you **chisel** wood or stone, you cut and shape it using a chisel. のみで彫る ❑ He set out to chisel a dog out of sandstone. 彼は砂岩に犬を彫り始めた.

chlo|rine /klɔrin/ N-UNCOUNT 不可算名詞 **Chlorine** is a strong-smelling gas that is used to clean water and to make cleaning products. 塩素

choco|late /tʃɔkəlɪt, tʃɔklɪt/ (**chocolates**) **1** N-MASS 質量名詞 **Chocolate** is a sweet, hard food made from cacao. It is usually brown in color and is eaten as a candy. チョコレート ❑ a bar of chocolate. 板チョコ1つ ❑ Do you want some chocolate? チョコレートが欲しいですか? **2** N-UNCOUNT 不可算名詞 **Chocolate** or **hot chocolate** is a drink made from a powder containing chocolate. It is usually made with hot milk. ココア、ホット・チョコレート ❑ ...a small cafeteria where the visitors can buy tea, coffee and chocolate. 客が紅茶、コーヒー、ココアを買える小さなセルフサービス式食堂 **3** N-COUNT 可算名詞 **Chocolates** are small candies or nuts covered with a layer of chocolate. They are usually sold in a box. チョコレート・キャンディ ❑ ...a box of chocolates. チョコレート・キャンディ1箱 **4** COLOR 色彩語 **Chocolate** is used to describe things that are dark brown in color. 赤褐色の ❑ The curtains and the bedspread were chocolate velvet. カーテンとベッドカバーは赤褐色のビロードだった.

→ see **dessert**

choice /tʃɔɪs/ (**choices**, **choicer**, **choicest**) **1** N-COUNT 可算名詞 If there is a **choice of** things, there are several of them and you can choose the one you want. (豊富な) 品ぞろえ、選択肢 ❑ It's available in a choice of colors. それは豊富な色の品ぞろえがあります. ❑ At lunchtime, there's a choice between the buffet or the set menu. 昼食はビュッフェ式食事か定食を選べます. **2** N-COUNT 可算名詞 Your **choice** is someone or something that you choose from a range of things. 選択 ❑ Although he was only grumbling, his choice of words made Rodney angry. 彼はただブツブツ不平を言っていただけだったが、その言葉にロドニーはカチンと来た. **3** ADJ 形容詞 **Choice** means of very high quality. 厳選の、極上の [FORMAL 形式ばった] [ADJ n] ❑ ...a box of their choicest chocolates. 彼らの極上のチョコレート1箱 **4** PHRASE 句 If you **have no choice but** to do something or **have little choice but** to do it, you cannot avoid doing it. 選択の余地がない ❑ They had little choice but to agree to what he suggested. 彼らは彼の提案に同意せざるをえなかった. **5** PHRASE 句 The thing or person of your choice is the one that you choose. 〜が選んだ、〜の好みの ❑ ...tickets to see the football team of your choice. あなたの好きなフットボールチームの試合を見る入場券 **6** PHRASE 句 The item of choice is the one that most people prefer. 一般に好まれるもの ❑ The drug is set to become the treatment of choice for asthma worldwide. その薬は世界中でぜんそくに対する一般的な治療薬となろうとしている.

Word Partnership *choice* は次の語句と使われる:

ADJ.	**best/good** choice, **wide** choice **1**
N.	**freedom of** choice, choice **of** *something* **1**
V.	**given a** choice, **have a** choice, **make a** choice **1 2**

choir /kwaɪər/ (**choirs**) N-COUNT 可算名詞 A **choir** is a group of people who sing together, for example in a church or school. 合唱団 ❑ He has been singing in his church choir since he was six. 彼は6歳の時

から教会の聖歌隊で歌っている.

choke /tʃoʊk/ (**chokes**, **choking**, **choked**) **1** V-T/V-I 他動詞/自動詞 When you **choke** or when something **chokes** you, you cannot breathe properly or get enough air into your lungs. 窒息させる [他動詞]、窒息する [自動詞] ❑ Dense smoke swirled and billowed, its rank fumes choking her. 濃い煙が渦巻きながら押し寄せ、その悪臭のある煙霧に彼女は息が詰まった. ❑ The girl choked to death after breathing in smoke. その少女は煙を吸って窒息死した. **2** V-T 他動詞 To **choke** someone means to squeeze their neck until they are dead. 絞め殺す ❑ The men pushed him into the entrance of a nearby building, where they choked him with his tie. その男たちは彼を近くのビルの入り口まで追い詰め、そこで彼のネクタイで絞め殺した. **3** V-T 他動詞 If a place **is choked with** things or people, it is full of them and they prevent movement in it. すし詰めにする [usu passive] ❑ The village's roads are choked with traffic. その村の道路は車が大渋滞している. **4** N-COUNT 可算名詞 The **choke** in a car, truck, or other vehicle is a device that reduces the amount of air going into the engine and makes it easier to start. チョーク (自動車のエンジン発動を助ける装置) ❑ It is like driving your car with the choke out all the time. それはチョークをずっと引っ張ったまま車を運転しているみたいだ.

Word Partnership *choke* は次の語句と使われる:

N.	choke **on** *something* **1**
	choke *someone* **2**
V.	**make** *someone* choke **1 2**

chol|era /kɒlərə/ N-UNCOUNT 不可算名詞 **Cholera** is a serious disease that often kills people. It is caused by drinking infected water or by eating infected food. コレラ ❑ ...a cholera epidemic. コレラの流行

cho|les|ter|ol /kəlɛstərɔl/ N-UNCOUNT 不可算名詞 **Cholesterol** is a substance that exists in the fat, tissues, and blood of all animals. Too much cholesterol in a person's blood can cause heart disease. コレステロール ❑ ...a dangerously high cholesterol level. 危険なほど高いコレステロール値

choose /tʃuz/ (**chooses**, **choosing**, **chose**, **chosen**) **1** V-T/V-I 他動詞/自動詞 If you **choose** someone or something **from** several people or things that are available, you decide which person or thing you want to have. 選ぶ [他動詞/自動詞] ❑ They will be able to choose their own leaders in democratic elections. 彼らは自分たちの指導者たちを民主的選挙で選べるようになるだろう. ❑ There are several patchwork cushions to choose from. いくつかのパッチワーク・クッションの中から選べる. **2** V-T/V-I 他動詞/自動詞 If you **choose to** do something, you do it because you want to or because you feel that it is right. (〜することを) 選ぶ [他動詞]、選ぶ [自動詞] ❑ They knew that discrimination was going on, but chose to ignore it. 彼らは差別が続いていることを知っていたが、それを無視することにした. ❑ You have the right to remain silent if you choose. 黙っていたいなら、あなたには黙秘権があります.

Thesaurus *choose* また次を参照:

V.	decide on, opt for, prefer, settle on; (ant.) pass over, refuse, reject **1**

chop /tʃɒp/ (**chops**, **chopping**, **chopped**) **1** V-T 他動詞 If you **chop** something, you cut it into pieces with strong, downward movements of a knife or an ax. (ナイフやおので) たたき割る ❑ Chop the butter into small pieces. バターを小さく切り刻みなさい. ❑ Visitors were set to work chopping wood. 来訪者たちはまき割りをするよう指示された. **2** N-COUNT 可算名詞 A **chop** is a small piece of meat cut from the ribs of a sheep or pig. (羊や豚の) あばら骨付きの切り身 チョップ ❑ ...grilled lamb chops. 網焼きにした子羊のあばら肉

→ see **cut**

▶ **chop down** PHRASAL VERB 句動詞 If you **chop down** a tree, you cut through its trunk with an ax so that it falls to the ground. 切り倒す ❑ Sometimes they have to chop down a tree for firewood. 彼らは時々まき用に木を切り倒す必要がある.

▶ **chop off** PHRASAL VERB 句動詞 To **chop off** something such as a part of someone's body means to cut it off. 切り落とす ❑ She chopped off her golden, waist-length hair. 彼女は腰まであった金髪をばっさり切った.

▶ **chop up** PHRASAL VERB 句動詞 If you **chop** something **up**, you chop it into small pieces. 細かく切る ❑ Chop up three firm tomatoes. 固めのトマトを3つ細かく切りなさい.

→ see **cut**

chop|per /tʃɒpər/ (**choppers**) N-COUNT 可算名詞 A **chopper** is a helicopter. ヘリコプター [INFORMAL くだけた] ❑ Overhead, the chopper roared and the big blades churned the air. 頭上でヘリコプターがごう音を立て、巨大なプロペラの羽根が空気を激しくかき乱した.

cho|ral /kɔrəl/ ADJ 形容詞 **Choral** music is sung by a choir. 合唱の ❑ His collection of choral music from around the world is called

"Voices." 彼が世界中から集めた合唱曲のコレクションは『歌声』と呼ばれている.

chord /kɔrd/ (**chords**) **1** N-COUNT 可算名詞 A **chord** is a number of musical notes played or sung at the same time with a pleasing effect. 和音, コード ❑ *I could play a few chords on the guitar and sing a song.* 私は少しギターのコードを弾きながら歌を歌うことができた. **2** PHRASE 句 If something **strikes a chord with** you, it makes you feel sympathy or enthusiasm. 心の琴線に触れる, 共感を得る ❑ *Mr. Jenkins's arguments for stability struck a chord with Europe's two most powerful politicians.* ジェンキンズ氏の安定性を訴える主張は, ヨーロッパで最も有力な2人の政治家の共感を得た.

chore /tʃɔr/ (**chores**) N-COUNT 可算名詞 A **chore** is a task that you must do but that you find unpleasant or boring. いやな仕事, 雑用 ❑ *She sees exercise primarily as an unavoidable chore.* 彼女はまず練習を避けられない面倒と思っている.

cho|reo|graph /kɔriəgræf/ (**choreographs, choreographing, choreographed**) V-T/V-I 他動詞/自動詞 When someone **choreographs** a ballet or other dance, they invent the steps and movements and tell the dancers how to perform them. 振り付けをする ❑ *Achim had choreographed the dance in Act II himself.* アキムは第2幕のダンスを自分で振り付けていた.

cho|reog|ra|phy /kɔriɒgrəfi/ N-UNCOUNT 不可算名詞 **Choreography** is the inventing of steps and movements for ballets and other dances. 振り付け ❑ *The choreography of Eric Hawkins is considered radical by ballet audiences.* エリック・ホーキンズの振り付けはバレエの観客から過激だとみなされている.

cho|rus /kɔrəs/ (**choruses, chorusing, chorused**) **1** N-COUNT 可算名詞 A **chorus** is a part of a song which is repeated after each verse. (歌の) 繰り返しの部分 ❑ *Caroline sang two verses and the chorus of her song.* キャロラインは彼女の歌の2番までとその繰り返し部分を歌った. **2** N-COUNT 可算名詞 A **chorus** is a large group of people who sing together. 合唱団 ❑ *The chorus was singing "The Ode to Joy."* その合唱団は『歓喜の歌』を歌っていた. **3** N-COUNT 可算名詞 A **chorus** is a piece of music written to be sung by a large group of people. 合唱曲 **4** N-COUNT 可算名詞 A **chorus** is a group of singers or dancers who perform together in a show, in contrast to the soloists. コーラス, 合唱舞踏団 ❑ *Students played the lesser parts and sang in the chorus.* 学生たちは小さい役を演じ, コーラスで歌った. **5** N-COUNT-COLL 集合可算名詞 In drama, a **chorus** is an actor or a group of actors who comment on the action of the play. (演劇の) 語り手 ❑ *He decides to sort out her life for her, while a pushy Greek chorus dispenses advice from the sidelines.* 厚かましいギリシャ人の語り手が横から口出ししている間に, 彼は彼女の人生をよくしてやろうと決心する. ❑ *...commanding performances from Joe Savino as the chorus and Stephen Brennan as the ghost.* 語り手のジョー・サビーノと亡霊役のスティーブン・ブレナンの堂々とした演技 **6** N-COUNT 可算名詞 When there is a **chorus** of criticism, disapproval, or praise, that attitude is expressed by a lot of people at the same time. (批判や不満, または賞賛などを) 一斉に発する声 ❑ *The government is defending its economic policies against a growing chorus of criticism.* 政府は高まりつつある一斉批判に対し, その経済政策の弁護している. **7** V-T 他動詞 When people **chorus** something, they say it or sing it together. 声をそろえて言う, 合唱する [WRITTEN 書き言葉] ❑ *"Hi," they chorused.* 「やあ」と彼らは声をそろえて言った.

chose /tʃouz/ **Chose** is the past tense of **choose**. chooseの過去形

cho|sen /tʃouzⁿn/ **Chosen** is the past participle of **choose**. chooseの過去分詞

Christ /kraɪst/ N-PROPER 固有名詞 **Christ** is one of the names of Jesus, whom Christians believe to be the son of God and whose teachings are the basis of Christianity. キリスト ❑ *...the teachings of Christ.* キリストの教え

chris|ten /krɪsⁿn/ (**christens, christening, christened**) V-T 他動詞 When a baby **is christened**, he or she is given a name during the Christian ceremony of baptism. Compare **baptize**. 洗礼を施す, 洗礼を施して命名する [usu passive] ❑ *She was born in March and christened in June.* 彼女は3月に生まれ, 6月に洗礼を受けた.

chris|ten|ing /krɪsⁿnɪŋ/ (**christenings**) N-COUNT 可算名詞 A **christening** is a Christian ceremony in which a baby is made a member of the Christian church and is officially given his or her name. Compare **baptism**. 洗礼, 命名式 ❑ *...my granddaughter's christening.* 私の孫娘の洗礼式

Christian /krɪstʃən/ (**Christians**) **1** N-COUNT 可算名詞 A **Christian** is someone who follows the teachings of Jesus Christ. キリスト教徒 ❑ *He was a devout Christian.* 彼は信心深いキリスト教徒だった. **2** ADJ 形容詞 **Christian** means relating to Christianity or Christians. キリスト教の, キリスト教徒の ❑ *...the Christian Church.* キリスト教会 ❑ *Most of my friends are Christian.* 私の友人のほとんどはキリスト教徒だ.

→ see **religion**

Chris|ti|an|ity /krɪstʃiænɪti/ N-UNCOUNT 不可算名詞 **Christianity** is a religion that is based on the teachings of Jesus Christ and the belief that he was the son of God. キリスト教 ❑ *I converted to Christianity that day.* 私はその日にキリスト教に改宗した.

Christian name (**Christian names**) N-COUNT 可算名詞 Some people refer to their first names as their **Christian names**. 洗礼名 ❑ *Despite my attempts to get him to call me by my Christian name, he insisted on addressing me as "Mr. Kennedy."* 私なら洗礼名で呼ばせようとしたのに, 彼は私を「ケネディさん」と呼んで譲らなかった.

Christ|mas /krɪsməs/ (**Christmases**) **1** N-VAR 可変性名詞 **Christmas** is a Christian festival when the birth of Jesus Christ is celebrated. Christmas is celebrated on the 25th of December. クリスマス ❑ *The day after Christmas is generally a busy one for retailers.* 通常, 小売店にとってクリスマスの翌日は忙しい. **2** N-VAR 可変性名詞 **Christmas** is the period of several days around and including Christmas Day. クリスマスの季節 ❑ *During the Christmas holidays there's a tremendous amount of traffic between the Northeast and Florida.* クリスマス休暇中は北東部とフロリダ州の交通量がすさまじい.

Christ|mas Day N-UNCOUNT 不可算名詞 **Christmas Day** is the 25th of December, when Christmas is celebrated. クリスマス降誕日

Christ|mas Eve N-UNCOUNT 不可算名詞 **Christmas Eve** is the 24th of December, the day before Christmas Day. クリスマスイブ

chrome /kroum/ N-UNCOUNT 不可算名詞 **Chrome** is metal plated with chromium. クロムめっきした金属 ❑ *...old-fashioned chrome taps.* 旧式なクロムめっきの蛇口

chro|mium /kroumiəm/ N-UNCOUNT 不可算名詞 **Chromium** is a hard, shiny, metallic element, used to make steel alloys and to coat other metals. クロム (特殊鋼の製造や, めっきに使用) ❑ *...chromium-plated fire accessories.* クロムめっきされた暖房器具の付属品

chro|mo|some /kroumasoum/ (**chromosomes**) N-COUNT 可算名詞 A **chromosome** is a part of a cell in an animal or plant. It contains genes which determine what characteristics the animal or plant will have. 染色体 ❑ *Each cell of our bodies contains 46 chromosomes.* 我々の体の各細胞には46の染色体が入っている.

chron|ic /krɒnɪk/ **1** ADJ 形容詞 A **chronic** illness or disability lasts for a very long time. Compare **acute**. 慢性の ❑ *...chronic back pain.* 慢性の腰痛 ● **chroni|cal|ly** /krɒnɪkli/ ADV 副詞 [ADV adj/-ed] 慢性的に ❑ *Most of them were chronically ill.* 彼らのほとんどは慢性的な病気を抱えていた. **2** ADJ 形容詞 You can describe someone's bad habits or behavior as **chronic** when they have behaved like that for a long time and do not seem to be able to stop themselves. 常習的な [ADJ n] ❑ *...a chronic worrier.* いつも心配ばかりしている人 **3** ADJ 形容詞 A **chronic** situation or problem is very severe and unpleasant. (状況や問題が) ひどい ❑ *One cause of the artist's suicide seems to have been chronic poverty.* その芸術家の自殺の原因の1つはひどい貧困だったようだ. ● **chroni|cal|ly** ADV 副詞 [ADV adj/-ed] ひどく ❑ *Research and technology are said to be chronically underfunded.* 研究と科学技術は深刻な資金不足だと言われている.

chron|i|cle /krɒnɪkⁿl/ (**chronicles, chronicling, chronicled**) **1** V-T 他動詞 To **chronicle** a series of events means to write about them or show them in broadcasts in the order in which they happened. 年代順に記録する ❑ *The series chronicles the everyday adventures of two eternal bachelors.* そのシリーズは生涯独身男性2人の日々の冒険を記録している. **2** N-COUNT 可算名詞 A **chronicle** is an account or record of a series of events. 年代記 ❑ *...this vast chronicle of Napoleonic times.* ナポレオン時代のこのぼう大な年代記 **3** N-IN-NAMES 名称中の名詞 **Chronicle** is sometimes used as part of the name of a newspaper. 一新聞 ❑ *...the San Francisco Chronicle.* サンフランシスコ新聞

→ see **diary**

chrono|logi|cal /krɒnⁿlɒdʒɪkⁿl/ ADJ 形容詞 If things are described or shown in **chronological** order, they are described or shown in the order in which they happened. 年代順の ❑ *I have arranged these stories in chronological order.* 私はこれらの話を年代順に編纂(へんさん)した. ● **chrono|logi|cal|ly** ADV 副詞 年代順に ❑ *The exhibition is organized chronologically.* この展示会は年代順にまとめられている.

chub|by /tʃʌbi/ (**chubbier, chubbiest**) ADJ 形容詞 A **chubby** person is somewhat fat. 小太りの ❑ *Do you think I'm too chubby?* あなたは私が太り気味だと思う?

chuck /tʃʌk/ (**chucks, chucking, chucked**) **1** V-T 他動詞 When you **chuck** something somewhere, you throw it there in a casual or careless way. 放り投げる [INFORMAL くだけた] ❑ *I took a great dislike to the clock, so I chucked it in the trash.* 私はその時計が大嫌いになったので, ゴミ箱に放り込んだ. **2** V-T 他動詞 If you **chuck** your job or some other activity, you stop doing it. やめる [INFORMAL く

だけた] ❑ *Last summer, he chucked his 10-year career as a stockbroker and headed for the mountains.* 去年の夏、彼は株式仲買人として の10年のキャリアを捨てて山岳地帯に向かった. **3** PHRASE 句 If someone **chucks it all**, they stop doing their job, and usually move somewhere else. すべてを投げ出す ❑ *Sometimes I'd like to chuck it all and go fishing.* 私は時々すべてを投げ出して田舎へ出かけ たくなる. **4** N-COUNT 可算名詞 A **chuck** is a device for holding a tool in a machine such as a drill. （ドリルなどの）チャック、つかみ **5** N-UNCOUNT 不可算名詞 **Chuck** is a cut of beef. 牛肩ロース

chuck|le /tʃʌkᵊl/ (**chuckles**, **chuckling**, **chuckled**) V-I 自動詞 When you **chuckle**, you laugh quietly. 含み笑いをする ❑ *The banker chuckled and said, "Of course not."* その銀行家は含み笑いをして、「と んでもない」と言った. **2** N-COUNT 可算名詞 **Chuckle** is also a noun. 含み笑い ❑ *He gave a little chuckle.* 彼は小さく含み笑いをした.

chug /tʃʌg/ (**chugs**, **chugging**, **chugged**) **1** V-I 自動詞 When a vehicle **chugs** somewhere, it goes there slowly, noisily, and with difficulty. シュッシュッ（ポッポッ）と音を立てて進む ❑ *The train chugs down the track.* その汽車はシュッシュッと音を立てて線路を走 る. **2** V-T 他動詞 If you **chug** something, you drink it very quickly without stopping. 一気に飲む [AM 米国英語, INFORMAL くだけた] ❑ *Nadine chugs her beer and orders another.* ナディーンがビールを一気 に飲み干し、お代わりを注文する.

chunk /tʃʌŋk/ (**chunks**) **1** N-COUNT 可算名詞 **Chunks of** something are thick, solid pieces of it. 大きな塊 ❑ *They had to be careful of floating chunks of ice.* 彼らは巨大な流氷に気をつけなければ ならなかった. ❑ *...a chunk of meat.* 大きな肉の塊 **2** N-COUNT 可算 名詞 A **chunk of** something is a large amount or large part of it. 大量、大部分 [INFORMAL くだけた] ❑ *The company owns a chunk of farmland near the airport.* その会社は空港の近くに広大な農地を所有 している.

chunky /tʃʌŋki/ (**chunkier**, **chunkiest**) **1** ADJ 形容詞 A **chunky** person is broad and heavy. がっしりした ❑ *The soprano was a chunky girl from California.* そのソプラノ歌手はカリフォルニア州出身のずん ぐりした女の子だった. **2** ADJ 形容詞 A **chunky** object is large and thick. 分厚い ❑ *Her taste in fiction was for chunky historical romances.* 彼女は小説では分厚い歴史ものが好きだった. ❑ *...a chunky sweater.* 厚手のセーター

church /tʃɜrtʃ/ (**churches**) **1** N-VAR 可変性名詞 A **church** is a building in which Christians worship. You usually refer to this place as **church** when you are talking about the time that people spend there. 教会 ❑ *...one of the country's most historic churches.* その国で最も由緒ある教会の1つ ❑ *St Helen's Church.* 聖ヘレン教 会 ❑ *The family had gone to church.* その一家は教会に行ってしまっ ていた. **2** N-COUNT 可算名詞 A **Church** is one of the groups of people within the Christian religion, for example Catholics or Methodists, that have their own beliefs, clergy, and forms of worship. （キリスト教の）教会 ❑ *...cooperation with the Catholic Church.* カトリック教会との協調 ❑ *Church leaders said he was welcome to return.* 教会の指導者たちは彼が戻って来るなら喜んで迎え ると述べた.

churn /tʃɜrn/ (**churns**, **churning**, **churned**) **1** N-COUNT 可算 名詞 A **churn** is a container which is used for making butter. （ バターを作るときに使う）大型牛乳缶 **2** V-T 他動詞 If something **churns** water, mud, or dust, it moves it about violently. 激しくか き回す ❑ *...dirt roads now churned into mud by the annual rains.* 例年 の雨にかき乱されてぬかるみとなった未舗装の道路 ● PHRASAL VERB 句動詞 **Churn up** means the same as **churn**. 激しくかき回す ❑ *The recent rain had churned up the waterfall into a muddy whirlpool.* 最近の 雨にかき乱されて滝が濁流の渦と化していた. ❑ *Occasionally dolphins slap the water with their tails or churn it up in play.* イルカたちは時おり 尾で水をたたいたり、ふざけて水をはね上げたりする. **3** V-T/V-I 他 動詞/自動詞 If you say that your stomach **is churning**, you mean that you feel sick. You can also say that something **churns** your stomach. 胃がむかつく ❑ *My stomach churned as I stood up.* 立ち上が ると胃がむかついた.

▶ **churn out** PHRASAL VERB 句動詞 To **churn out** something means to produce large quantities of it very quickly. 大量生産する [INFORMAL くだけた] ❑ *He began to churn out literary compositions in English.* 彼は英語で文学作品を次々と書き始めた.

▶ **churn up** → see **churn 2**

chute /ʃut/ (**chutes**) **1** N-COUNT 可算名詞 A **chute** is a steep, narrow slope down which people or things can slide. 滑降斜 面路、シュート ❑ *Passengers escaped from the plane's front exits by sliding down emergency chutes.* 乗客は飛行機の前方出口から緊急脱出 シュートを滑り降りて避難した. **2** N-COUNT 可算名詞 A **chute** is a parachute. パラシュート [INFORMAL くだけた] ❑ *You can release the chute with either hand, but it is easier to do it with the left.* どちらの手で もパラシュートを開けるが、左手で行う方がやりやすい.

chut|ney /tʃʌtni/ (**chutneys**) N-MASS 質量名詞 **Chutney** is a cold sauce made from fruit, vinegar, sugar, and spices. It is sold in jars and you eat it with meat or cheese. チャツネ（調味料） ❑ *...mango chutney.* マンゴー・チャツネ

ci|der /saɪdər/ (**ciders**) N-MASS 質量名詞 **Cider** is a drink made

from apples. **Cider** does not usually contain alcohol, and if it does contain alcohol, it is usually called **hard cider**. In Britain, **cider** usually contains alcohol. りんごジュース（米国）りんご酒（英国） ● N-COUNT 可算名詞 A glass of cider can be referred to as a **cider**. り んごジュース ❑ *At the bar he ordered a cider.* バーで彼はりんごジュース を1杯注文した.

ci|gar /sɪgɑr/ (**cigars**) N-COUNT 可算名詞 **Cigars** are rolls of dried tobacco leaves which people smoke. 葉巻 ❑ *He was smoking a big cigar.* 彼は大きな葉巻を吸っていた.

Word Link ette ≈ small : cigar**ette**, disk**ette**, ros**ette**

ciga|rette /sɪgərɛt/ (**cigarettes**) N-COUNT 可算名詞 **Cigarettes** are small tubes of paper containing tobacco which people smoke. 紙巻きたばこ ❑ *He went out to buy a packet of cigarettes.* 彼はたばこを 1箱買いに外へ出た.

cin|ema /sɪnɪmə/ (**cinemas**) **1** N-UNCOUNT 不可算名詞 **Cinema** is the business and art of making movies. 映画産業 ❑ *Contemporary African cinema has much to offer.* 現代のアフリカ映 画産業は優れた作品が多い. **2** N-COUNT 可算名詞 A **cinema** is a place where people go to watch movies for entertainment. 映画 館 [mainly BRIT 主に英国英語; AM usually **movie theater**, **movie house** 米国英語では通常 **movie theater**, **movie house**] **3** N-SING 単数名詞 You can talk about the **cinema** when you are talking about seeing a movie. 映画 [mainly BRIT 主に英国英語; AM usually **the movies** 米国英語では通常 **the movies**]

cin|emat|ic /sɪnəmætɪk/ ADJ 形容詞 **Cinematic** means relating to movies made for movie theaters. 映画の ❑ *...a cinematic masterpiece.* 映画の傑作

cin|na|mon /sɪnəmən/ N-UNCOUNT 不可算名詞 **Cinnamon** is a sweet spice used for flavoring food. シナモン
→ see **spice**

cir|ca /sɜrkə/ PREP 前置詞 **Circa** is used in front of a particular year to say that this is the approximate date when something happened or was made. 一頃、およそ [FORMAL 形式ばった] ❑ *The story tells of a runaway slave girl in Louisiana, circa 1850.* その話は1850年 頃ルイジアナ州で逃亡した奴隷少女について伝えている.

Word Link circ ≈ around : **circ**le, **circ**uit, **circ**ulate

cir|cle /sɜrkᵊl/ (**circles**, **circling**, **circled**) **1** N-COUNT 可算名 詞 A **circle** is a shape consisting of a curved line completely surrounding an area. Every part of the line is the same distance from the center of the area. 円、丸 ❑ *The flag was red, with a large white circle in the center.* その旗は赤地で中央に大きな白丸がついて いた. **2** N-COUNT 可算名詞 A **circle of** something is a round, flat piece or area of it. 円形のもの ❑ *Cut out 4 circles of pastry.* 生地を 丸く4つに切り抜く. **3** N-COUNT 可算名詞 A **circle of** objects or people is a group of them arranged in the shape of a circle. 輪 ❑ *...a circle of gigantic stones.* 巨石群の輪 **4** N-COUNT 可算名詞 You can refer to a group of people as a **circle** when they meet each other regularly because they are friends or because they belong to the same profession or share the same interests. 仲間 ❑ *He has a small circle of friends.* 彼は交際範囲が狭い. **5** V-T/V-I 他動詞/自動 詞 If something **circles** an object or a place, or **circles around** it, it forms a circle around it. 周りを囲む ❑ *This is the road that circles the city.* これがその街を囲む道路だ. **6** V-T/V-I 他動詞/自動詞 If an aircraft or a bird **circles** or **circles** something, it moves around in a circle in the air. 旋回する ❑ *The plane circled, awaiting permission to land.* 飛行機は旋回して着陸の許可を待っていた. ❑ *There were two helicopters circling around.* 2機のヘリコプターがあちこち旋回してい た. **7** V-T 他動詞 If you **circle** something on a piece of paper, you draw a circle around it. 丸で囲む ❑ *Circle the words on this list that you recognize.* この一覧に載っている言葉で知っているものに丸をつけ なさい. **8** → see also **inner circle**, **vicious circle**
→ see **globe**, **shape**, **soccer**

Word Partnership circle は次の語句と使われる:

V. **draw** a circle **1 2**
   form a circle, **make** a circle **1 – 3**
ADV. circle **around 1 – 3**
ADJ. **big/large/small** circle **1 – 4**
PREP. **inside/outside/within** a circle **1 – 4**
   circle **around 5**

cir|cuit /sɜrkɪt/ (**circuits**) **1** N-COUNT 可算名詞 An electrical **circuit** is a complete route which an electric current can flow around. 回路 ❑ *Any attempts to cut through the cabling will break the electrical circuit.* どんな方法でそのケーブル布線を切断しても、電気回 路が遮断されるだろう. **2** → see also **closed-circuit** **3** N-COUNT 可 算名詞 A **circuit** is a series of places that are visited regularly by a person or group, especially as a part of their job. 巡回、巡業 ❑ *It's a common problem, the one I'm asked about most when I'm on the lecture circuit.* それはよくある問題だ. 私が講演活動中に最も頻繁に質問され るものだ.

cir|cu|lar /sɜ̃rkyələr/ (**circulars**) **1** ADJ 形容詞 Something that is **circular** is shaped like a circle. 円形の ☐ ...a circular hole twelve feet wide and two feet deep. 幅12フィート，深さ2フィートの丸い穴 **2** ADJ 形容詞 A **circular** journey or route is one in which you go to a place and return by a different route. 回遊の ☐ Both sides of the river can be explored on this circular walk. この循環遊歩道で川の両岸を見て回ることができる． **3** N-COUNT 可算名詞 A **circular** is an official letter or advertisement that is sent to a large number of people at the same time. 回状，ちらし ☐ The proposal has been widely publicized in press information circulars sent to 1,800 newspapers. その提案は報道資料の回状で1,800の新聞社に送られて広く公にされている．
→ see **circle**

Word Link	circ ≈ around : circle, circuit, circulate

cir|cu|late /sɜ̃rkyəleɪt/ (**circulates, circulating, circulated**) **1** V-T/V-I 他動詞/自動詞 If a piece of writing **circulates** or is **circulated**, copies of it are passed around among a group of people. 配布する，流布する 他動詞，流布される 自動詞 ☐ The document was previously circulated in New York at the United Nations. その文書は以前にニューヨークの国際連合で流布されていた． ☐ Public employees, teachers and liberals are circulating a petition for his recall. 公務員，教師，自由主義者たちが彼のリコールを求める請願書を配布している． ●**cir|cu|la|tion** /sɜ̃rkyəleɪʃ⁰n/ N-UNCOUNT 不可算名詞 配布，流布 ☐ ...an inquiry into the circulation of "unacceptable literature." 「容認できない文学」の流布に対する調査 **2** V-T/V-I 他動詞/自動詞 If something such as a rumor **circulates** or is **circulated**, the people in a place tell it to each other. (うわさなどを) 広める [他動詞]，広まる [自動詞] ☐ Rumors were already beginning to circulate that the project might have to be abandoned. その企画を断念しなければならないかもしれないといううわさが，すでに広まり始めていた． **3** V-I 自動詞 When something **circulates**, it moves easily and freely within a closed place or system. 循環する ☐ ...a virus which circulates via the bloodstream and causes ill health in a variety of organs. 血流によって循環して，さまざまな臓器で病気を引き起こすウィルス ●**cir|cu|la|tion** N-UNCOUNT 不可算名詞 循環 ☐ The north pole is warmer than the south and the circulation of air around it is less well contained. 北極は南極よりも温かく，周辺の空気の循環が自由である． **4** V-I 自動詞 If you **circulate** at a party, you move among the guests and talk to different people. (パーティーで) いろんな人に話しかける ☐ If you'll excuse me, I really must circulate. すみませんが失礼して，皆さんに挨拶して回らなくてはなりません．

cir|cu|la|tion /sɜ̃rkyəleɪʃ⁰n/ (**circulations**) **1** N-COUNT 可算名詞 The **circulation** of a newspaper or magazine is the number of copies that are sold each time it is produced. 販売部数 ☐ The Daily News once had the highest circulation of any daily in the country. かつてデイリー・ニュースは全国の日刊紙の中で最も販売部数が多かった． **2** N-UNCOUNT 不可算名詞 Your **circulation** is the movement of blood through your body. 血液循環 ☐ Anyone with heart, lung, or circulation problems should seek medical advice before flying. 心臓，肺，血液循環に問題のある人は飛行の前に医師に相談してください． **3** → see also **circulate** **4** PHRASE 句 If something such as money is **in circulation**, it is being used by the public. If something is **out of circulation** or has been **withdrawn from circulation**, it is no longer available for use by the public. 流通して/流通していない ☐ The supply of money in circulation was drastically reduced overnight. 流通貨幣の供給が1晩で大幅に減らされた． ☐ ...a society like America, with perhaps 180 million guns in circulation. おそらく1億8千万丁の銃が出回っているアメリカのような社会

Word Link	circum ≈ around : circumcise, circumference, circumstance

cir|cum|cise /sɜ̃rkəmsaɪz/ (**circumcises, circumcising, circumcised**) **1** V-T 他動詞 If a boy or man is **circumcised**, the loose skin at the end of his penis is cut off. (男子の陰茎の包皮を切り取る) 割礼を施す [usu passive] ☐ He had been circumcised within eight days of birth as required by Jewish law. 彼はユダヤ教のおきてが定めるところにより，生後8日以内に割礼を受けていた． ●**cir|cum|ci|sion** /sɜ̃rkəmsɪʒ⁰n/ N-UNCOUNT 不可算名詞 [also "a" N] 割礼 ☐ Jews and Moslems practice circumcision for religious reasons. ユダヤ教徒とイスラム教徒は宗教上の理由で割礼を施す． **2** V-T 他動詞 In some cultures, if a girl or woman is **circumcised**, her clitoris is cut or cut off. (女子の陰核を切り取る) 割礼を施す [usu passive] ☐ An estimated number of 90 to 100 million women around the world living today have been circumcised. 今日生存する世界の女性のうち推定9千万人から1億人が割礼を施された． ●**cir|cum|ci|sion** N-UNCOUNT 不可算名詞 割礼 ☐ ...a campaigner against female circumcision. 女性の割礼に反対する活動家

cir|cum|fer|ence /sərkʌmfrəns/ **1** N-UNCOUNT 不可算名詞 The **circumference** of a circle, place, or round object is the distance around its edge. 円周 ☐ ...a scientist calculating the Earth's circumference. 地球の円周を計算している科学者 **2** N-UNCOUNT 不可算名詞 The **circumference** of a circle, place, or round object is

its edge. 外周 ☐ Cut the salmon into long strips and wrap it round the circumference of the bread. さけを縦長に切り，それをパンの外側に巻きつけなさい．
→ see **area**

cir|cum|stance /sɜ̃rkəmstæns/ (**circumstances**) **1** N-COUNT 可算名詞 The **circumstances** of a particular situation are the conditions which affect what happens. 状況，状態 ☐ Recent opinion polls show that 60 percent favor abortion under certain circumstances. 最近の世論調査によると，60パーセントの人が一定の状況下での堕胎を支持している． ☐ The strategy was too dangerous in the explosive circumstances of the times. 当時の一触即発の状況の中で，その対策は危険すぎた． **2** N-PLURAL 複数名詞 The **circumstances** of an event are the way it happened or the causes of it. 状況，原因 ☐ I'm making inquiries about the circumstances of Mary Dean's murder. 私はメアリー・ディーン殺害の状況を調査している． **3** N-PLURAL 複数名詞 Your **circumstances** are the conditions of your life, especially the amount of money that you have. (特に経済的な) 生活状態 ☐ ...help and support for the single mother, whatever her circumstances. 生活状態のいかんに関わらず，未婚の母に対する支援と援助 **4** N-UNCOUNT 不可算名詞 Events and situations which cannot be controlled are sometimes referred to as **circumstance**. どうしようもない事情 ☐ There are those, you know, who, by circumstance, end up homeless. ほら，やむを得ない事情でホームレスになる人たちがいるでしょう． **5** PHRASE 句 You can emphasize that something must not or will not happen by saying that it must not or will not happen **under any circumstances**. いかなる場合でも [EMPHASIS 強調] ☐ Racism is wholly unacceptable under any circumstances. いかなる場合でも人種差別は決して許されない． **6** PHRASE 句 You can use **in the circumstances** or **under the circumstances** before or after a statement to indicate that you have considered the conditions affecting the situation before making the statement. そのような状況の下で ☐ In the circumstances, Paisley's plans looked highly appropriate. その状況下では，ペイズリーの案が極めて適切のように思えた．

Word Partnership	circumstances は次の語句と使われる：

PREP.	**under the** circumstances **1 2**
ADJ.	**certain** circumstances, **different/similar** circumstances, **difficult** circumstances, **exceptional** circumstances **1 – 3**

cir|cus /sɜ̃rkəs/ (**circuses**) **1** N-COUNT 可算名詞 A **circus** is a group that consists of clowns, acrobats, and animals that travels around to different places and performs shows. サーカス ☐ My real ambition was to work in a circus. 私の本当の念願はサーカスで働くことだった． ●N-SING 単数名詞 The **circus** is the show performed by these people. 曲芸 ☐ My dad took me to the circus. お父さんが私をサーカスに連れて行ってくれた． **2** N-SING 単数名詞 If you describe a group of people or an event as a **circus**, you disapprove of them because they attract a lot of attention to but do not achieve anything useful. ばか騒ぎする人，ばか騒ぎ [DISAPPROVAL 不賛成] ☐ It could well turn into some kind of a media circus. それはある種の報道合戦になる可能性が高い．

ci|ta|tion /saɪteɪʃ⁰n/ (**citations**) **1** N-COUNT 名詞 A **citation** is an official document or speech which praises a person for something brave or special that they have done. 表彰状，表彰 ☐ His citation says he showed outstanding and exemplary courage. 彼の表彰状には，彼が際立った模範となる勇気を示したと書かれている． **2** N-COUNT 可算名詞 A **citation** from a book or other piece of writing is a passage or phrase from it. 引用 [FORMAL 形式ばった] ☐ ...a 50-minute manifesto with citations from the Koran. コーランを引用した50分にわたる声明 **3** N-COUNT 可算名詞 A **citation** is the same as a **summons**. 召喚状 [AM 米国英語] ☐ The court could issue a citation and fine Ms. Robbins. 裁判所はロビンズさんに召喚状を発行し，罰金を課すことができるであろう． **4** N-COUNT 可算名詞 A **citation** is an official piece of paper which orders you to pay a fine or to appear in court because you have committed a traffic offense. 交通違反切符 [AM 米国英語] ☐ The Highway Patrol this year issued 1,018 speeding citations. ハイウェイパトロールは今年1,018件の速度違反切符を発行した．

cite /saɪt/ (**cites, citing, cited**) **1** V-T 他動詞 If you **cite** something, you quote it or mention it, especially as an example or proof of what you are saying. 引用する，言及する [FORMAL 形式ばった] ☐ She cites a favorite poem by George Herbert. 彼女はお気に入りのジョージ・ハーバートの詩を引用する． ☐ Domestic interest rates are often cited as a major factor affecting exchange rates. 国内利率はしばしば為替相場に影響を与える重要な要因の1つとして挙げられる． **2** V-T 他動詞 To **cite** a person means to officially name them in a legal case. To **cite** a reason or cause means to state it as the official reason for your case. (法廷で名前・理由を) 挙げる ☐ They cited Alex's refusal to return to the marital home. 彼らはアレックスが結婚生活に戻ることを拒んでいることを申し立てた． **3** V-T 他動詞 If someone is **cited**, they are officially ordered to appear before a court. 召喚する [AM 米国英語 LEGAL 法律的] [usu passive] ☐ He is the owner of a restaurant chain that was cited for violations of child labor laws. 彼が

Word Web city

For the past 6,000 years people have been moving from the **countryside** to **urban** centers. The world's oldest **capital** is Damascus, Syria. People have lived there for over 2,500 years. Cities are usually economic, commercial, cultural, political, social, and transportation centers. **Tourists** travel to cities for shopping and **sightseeing**. In some big cities, **skyscrapers** contain **apartments, businesses, restaurants, theaters,** and **retail stores**. People never have to leave their building. Sometimes cities become overpopulated and **crime rates** soar. Then people move to the **suburbs**. In recent decades this trend has been reversed in some places and **inner cities** are being rebuilt.

児童労働法違反の容疑で召喚されたレストランのチェーン店の所有者だ. **4** V-T 他動詞 If a judge **cites** someone, he or she officially names them in a critical way in court. (裁判官が法廷で) 非難する [AM 米国英語 LEGAL 法律的] ❑ *The judge ruled a mistrial and cited the prosecutors for outrageous misconduct.* その裁判官は無効審理の判決を下し, 検察当局の甚だしい不手際を非難した.

citi|zen /sɪtɪzⁿn/ (citizens) **1** N-COUNT 可算名詞 Someone who is a **citizen** of a particular country is legally accepted as belonging to that country. 国民 ❑ *...American citizens.* アメリカ国民 **2** N-COUNT 可算名詞 The **citizens** of a town or city are the people who live there. 市民, 住民 ❑ *...the citizens of Buenos Aires.* ブエノスアイレスの市民 **3** → see also senior citizen
→ see election

Word Link ship ≈ condition or state : censorship, citizenship, friendship

citi|zen|ship /sɪtɪzⁿnʃɪp/ **1** N-UNCOUNT 不可算名詞 If you have **citizenship** of a country, you are legally accepted as belonging to it. 市民権 ❑ *After 15 years in the U.S., he has finally decided to apply for American citizenship.* 米国に15年住んだ後, 彼はついに米国の市民権を申請することにした. **2** N-UNCOUNT 不可算名詞 **Citizenship** is the fact of belonging to a community because you live in it, and the duties and responsibilities that this brings. 市民であること, 市民の義務と責任 ❑ *Their German peers had a more developed sense of citizenship.* 彼らのドイツ人の同輩たちは市民の義務と責任についてより高い自覚を持っていた.

cit|rus /sɪtrəs/ ADJ 形容詞 A **citrus** fruit is a juicy fruit with a sharp taste such as an orange, lemon, or grapefruit. 柑橘 (かんきつ) 類の [ADJ n] ❑ *...citrus groves.* 柑橘類の果樹園

city /sɪti/ (cities) N-COUNT 可算名詞 A **city** is a large town. 市, 都市 ❑ *...the city of Bologna.* ボローニャ市
→ see Word Web: city
→ see skyscraper

Word Link civ ≈ citizen : civic, civil, civilian

civ|ic /sɪvɪk/ **1** ADJ 形容詞 You use **civic** to describe people or things that have an official status in a town or city. 市の, 市の [ADJ n] ❑ *...the businessmen and civic leaders of Manchester.* マンチェスター市の実業家と市の指導者たち **2** ADJ 形容詞 You use **civic** to describe the duties or feelings that people have because they belong to a particular community. 市民としての [ADJ n] ❑ *...a sense of civic pride.* 市民としての誇り

civ|il /sɪvⁿl/ **1** ADJ 形容詞 You use **civil** to describe events that happen within a country and that involve the different groups of people in it. 国家の [ADJ n] ❑ *...civil unrest.* 国情不安 **2** ADJ 形容詞 You use **civil** to describe people or things in a country that are not connected with its armed forces. 民間の ❑ *...the U.S. civil aviation industry.* 米国の民間航空産業 **3** ADJ 形容詞 You use **civil** to describe things that are connected with the state rather than with a religion. 世俗の, 民事の [ADJ n] ❑ *They were married on August 9 in a civil ceremony in Venice.* 彼らは8月9日にヴェネスにて民事婚で結婚した. **4** ADJ 形容詞 You use **civil** to describe the rights that people have within a society. 市民の [ADJ n] ❑ *...a United Nations covenant on civil and political rights.* 国際連合の市民的および政治的権利に関する規約 **5** ADJ 形容詞 Someone who is **civil** is polite in a formal way, but not particularly friendly. 礼儀正しい [FORMAL 形式ばった] ❑ *As visitors, the least we can do is be civil to the people in their own land.* 訪問者として私たちにできる最低限の事は, その国の人々に礼儀正しくすることだ. ● **ci|vil|ity** /sɪvɪlɪti/ N-UNCOUNT 不可算名詞 礼儀正しさ ❑ *...civility to underlings.* 下の者に対する礼儀正しさ

Word Partnership civil は次の語句と使われる:

N.	civil **disobedience**, civil **unrest** **1**
	civil **liberties/rights** **1** **4**
	civil **court (law)suit/trial** **3**

ci|vil|ian /sɪvɪlyən/ (civilians) **1** N-COUNT 可算名詞 In a military situation, a **civilian** is anyone who is not a member of the armed forces. 一般市民 ❑ *The safety of civilians caught up in the fighting must be guaranteed.* 戦闘に巻き込まれた民間人の安全は保障されなければならない. **2** ADJ 形容詞 In a military situation, **civilian** is used to describe people or things that are not military. 民間の ❑ *...the country's civilian population.* その国の一般市民 ❑ *...civilian casualties.* 民間人の犠牲者
→ see war

ci|vil|ity /sɪvɪlɪti/ → see civil

civi|li|za|tion /sɪvɪlɪzeɪʃⁿn/ (civilizations) **1** N-VAR 可変性名詞 A **civilization** is a human society with its own social organization and culture. 文明 ❑ *The ancient civilizations of Central and Latin America were founded upon corn.* 中南米諸国の古代文明はとうもろこしの生産で成り立っていた. **2** N-UNCOUNT 不可算名詞 **Civilization** is the state of having an advanced level of social organization and a comfortable way of life. 文明化 ❑ *...our advanced state of civilization.* 我々の高度に文明化された状態
→ see history

civi|lize /sɪvɪlaɪz/ (civilizes, civilizing, civilized) V-T 他動詞 To **civilize** a person or society means to educate them and improve their way of life. 教化する ❑ *...a comedy about a man who tries to civilize a woman – but she ends up civilizing him.* 女を教化しようとするが, 結局その女に教化されるはめになる男についての喜劇

civi|lized /sɪvɪlaɪzd/ **1** ADJ 形容詞 If you describe a society as **civilized**, you mean that it is advanced and has established laws and customs. 文明化した [APPROVAL 賛成] ❑ *I believed that in civilized countries, torture had ended long ago.* 私は文明の進んだ国々では拷問はとっくの昔に廃止されていると信じ込んでいた. **2** ADJ 形容詞 If you describe a person or their behavior as **civilized**, you mean that they are polite and reasonable. 礼儀正しい ❑ *I wrote to my ex-wife last week. She was very civilized about it.* 先週, 私は別れた妻に手紙を書いた. それに対し彼女はとても礼儀正しかった.

civ|il rights N-PLURAL 複数形名詞 **Civil rights** are the rights that people have in a society to equal treatment and equal opportunities, whatever their race, sex, or religion. 公民権 ❑ *...the civil rights movement.* 公民権運動

civ|il serv|ant (civil servants) N-COUNT 可算名詞 A **civil servant** is a person who works for the local, state, or federal government in the United States, or in the civil service in Britain and some other countries. 公務員 ❑ *...two senior civil servants.* 2人の上級公務員

civ|il ser|vice N-SING 単数名詞 The **civil service** of a country consists of its government departments and all the people who work in them. In many countries, the departments concerned with military and judicial affairs are not part of the civil service. 政府官庁, 公務員 ❑ *...a job in the civil service.* 公務員の職

civ|il war (civil wars) N-COUNT 可算名詞 A **civil war** is a war which is fought between different groups of people who live in the same country. 内戦 ❑ *...the American Civil War.* アメリカ南北戦争

CJD /si dʒeɪ di/ N-UNCOUNT 不可算名詞 **CJD** is an incurable brain disease that affects human beings and is believed to be caused by eating beef from cows infected with BSE. **CJD** is an abbreviation for "Creutzfeldt-Jakob disease." クロイツフェルト・ヤコブ病 (記憶障害や運動障害を起こす難病の神経疾患)

clad /klæd/ **1** ADJ 形容詞 If you are **clad in** particular clothes, you are wearing them. 着て [LITERARY 文語的] ❑ *...the figure of a woman, clad in black.* 黒い服を着た女性の姿 ❑ *Johnson was clad casually in slacks and a light blue golf shirt.* ジョンソンはズボンと水色のゴルフシャツをさりげなく着ていた. ● COMB IN ADJ 形容詞の複合 **Clad** is also a combining form. 〜を着た ❑ *...the leather-clad biker.* 革の服を着たバイク乗り **2** ADJ 形容詞 A building, part of a building, or mountain that is **clad with** something is covered with that thing. 覆われた [LITERARY 文語的] [v-link ADJ "in/with" n] ❑ *The walls and floors are clad with ceramic tiles.* その壁と床は陶磁器のタイルが張られている. ● COMB IN ADJ 形容詞の複合 **Clad** is also a

combining form. ～で覆われた ❑ *...the distant shapes of snow-clad mountains.* 遠くに見える雪に覆われた山々の形状

claim /kleɪm/ (**claims, claiming, claimed**) **1** V-T 他動詞 If you say that someone **claims that** something is true, you mean they say that it is true but you are not sure whether or not they are telling the truth. (証拠なしに本当であると) 主張する ❑ *He claimed that it was all a conspiracy against him.* 彼はそれがすべて彼に対する陰謀だと主張した. ❑ *A man claiming to be a journalist threatened to reveal details about her private life.* 新聞記者と自称する男が彼女に私生活の詳細を暴露すると脅迫した. **2** V-T 他動詞 If you say that someone **claims** responsibility or credit for something, you mean they say that they are responsible for it, but you are not sure whether or not they are telling the truth. (根拠なしに) 宣言する ❑ *An underground organization has claimed responsibility for the bomb explosion.* ある地下組織がその爆発事件について犯行声明を出している. **3** V-T 他動詞 If you **claim** something, you try to get it because you think you have a right to it. (所有権を) 主張する ❑ *Now they are returning to claim what was theirs.* 現在, 彼らは自分たちの物だった物を取り返しに戻ってこようとしている. **4** V-T 他動詞 If someone **claims** a record, title, or prize, they gain or win it. 獲得する [JOURNALISM ジャーナリズム] ❑ *Zhuang claimed the record in 54.64 seconds.* チュアンは54.64秒の記録を打ち立てた. **5** V-T 他動詞 If something or someone **claims** your attention, they need you to spend your time and effort on them. (人の注意を) 引く ❑ *There is already a long list of people claiming her attention.* 彼女の助けを借りようとする人は以前から多い. **6** V-T/V-I 他動詞/自動詞 If you **claim** money from the government, an insurance company, or another organization, you officially apply to them for it, because you think you are entitled to it according to their rules. (規則に定められた権利として) 請求する ❑ *Some 25 percent of the people who are entitled to claim benefits do not do so.* 給付金を請求する資格がある人たちの約25パーセントが請求していない. ❑ *John had taken out insurance but when he tried to claim, the insurance company refused to pay.* ジョンは保険に加入していたにもかかわらず, いざ請求しようとすると, その保険会社は支払いを拒否した. ● N-COUNT 可算名詞 **Claim** is also a noun. 請求 ❑ *Last time we made a claim on our insurance, they paid up really quickly.* この前私たちが保険の請求をしたら, 保険会社はとても迅速に全額を支払ってくれた. **7** V-T 他動詞 If you **claim** money or other benefits from your employers, you demand them because you think you deserve or need them. (受けるに値すると思い) 要求する ❑ *The union claimed a raise worth four times the rate of inflation.* その労働組合はインフレ率の4倍に相当する賃上げを要求した. ● N-COUNT 可算名詞 **Claim** is also a noun. 要求 ❑ *They are making substantial claims for improved working conditions.* 彼らは労働条件改善のため, 相当な要求をしている. **8** V-T 他動詞 If you say that a war, disease, or accident **claims** someone's life, you mean that they are killed in it or by it. (命を) 奪う [FORMAL 形式ばった] ❑ *The civil war claimed the life of a U.N. interpreter yesterday.* 昨日その内戦で国連の通訳官が1人死亡した. **9** N-COUNT 可算名詞 A **claim** is something which someone says which they cannot prove and which may be false. (証拠の伴わない) 主張 ❑ *He repeated his claim that the people of Trinidad and Tobago backed his action.* 彼はトリニダード・トバゴの国民が彼の活動を支持しているという主張を繰り返した. **10** N-COUNT 可算名詞 A **claim** is a demand for something that you think you have a right to. (所有権があるとした) 主張 ❑ *Rival claims to Macedonian territory caused conflict in the Balkans.* マケドニアの領土の取り合いで, バルカン半島諸国の間に対立が起こった. **11** N-COUNT 可算名詞 If you have a **claim on** someone or their attention, you have the right to demand things from them or to demand their attention. 要求する権利 ❑ *She had no claims on him now.* 彼女には彼に要求する権利はもうなかった. **12** to **stake a claim** → see **stake**

claim|ant /kleɪmənt/ (**claimants**) N-COUNT 可算名詞 A **claimant** is someone who asks to be given something which they think they are entitled to. 要求者, 原告 ❑ *The claimants allege that manufacturers failed to warn doctors that their drugs should be used only in limited circumstances.* 原告たちは, 製薬会社が薬は限られた状況にのみ使用されるべきであると医者に警告しなかったと主張している.

claims ad|just|er (**claims adjusters**) also **claims adjustor** N-COUNT 可算名詞 A **claims adjuster** is someone who is employed by an insurance company to decide how much money a person making a claim should receive. 保険査定員 [AM 米国英語 BUSINESS 実業]

clair|voy|ant /kleərvɔɪənt/ ADJ 形容詞 Someone who is believed to be **clairvoyant** is believed to know about future events or to be able to communicate with dead people. 千里眼の; 霊媒の ❑ *...clairvoyant powers.* 透視能力

clam /klæm/ (**clams**) N-COUNT 可算名詞 **Clams** are a kind of shellfish which can be eaten. 二枚貝

clam|ber /klæmbər/ (**clambers, clambering, clambered**) V-I 自動詞 If you **clamber** somewhere, you climb there with difficulty, usually using your hands as well as your feet. よじ登る ❑ *They clambered up the stone walls of a steeply terraced olive grove.* 彼らは急勾配のオリーブの段々畑の石垣をいくつもよじ登っていった.

Word Link   **claim, clam ≈ shouting : ac**claim, clamor, ex**claim

clam|or /klæmər/ (**clamors, clamoring, clamored**) V-I 自動詞 If people **are clamoring for** something, they are demanding it in a noisy or angry way. 騒々しく要求する [JOURNALISM ジャーナリズム] ❑ *...competing parties clamoring for the attention of the voter.* 投票者の関心を得ようとやかましく張り合っている政党

clamp /klæmp/ (**clamps, clamping, clamped**) **1** N-COUNT 可算名詞 A **clamp** is a device that holds two things firmly together. 留め金 ❑ *Many openers have a magnet or set of clamps to grip the open lid.* 多くの缶切りには開けたふたをつかむ磁石や1組の留め金がついている. **2** N-COUNT 可算名詞 A **clamp** is the same as a **Denver boot**. (駐車違反の車を固定する) 車輪止め [mainly BRIT 主に英国英語] **3** V-T 他動詞 When you **clamp** one thing **to** another, you fasten the two things together with a clamp. 留め金で固定する ❑ *Somebody forgot to bring along the U-bolts to clamp the microphones to the pole.* マイク立てにマイクを留めるU字形ボルトを持ってくるのを誰かが忘れた. **4** V-T 他動詞 To **clamp** something in a particular place means to put it or hold it there firmly and tightly. ぎゅっと押さえる ❑ *Simon finished dialing and clamped the phone to his ear.* サイモンはダイヤルを回して終えて, 受話器を耳に押し当てた. ❑ *He clamped his lips together.* 彼は口をぎゅっと結んだ. **5** V-T 他動詞 To **clamp** a car means the same as to **boot** a car. 車輪止めをつける [BRIT 英国英語]

▶ **clamp down** PHRASAL VERB 句動詞 To **clamp down on** people or activities means to take strong official action to stop or control them. 取り締まる [JOURNALISM ジャーナリズム] ❑ *If the government clamps down on the movement, that will only serve to strengthen it in the long run.* もし政府がこの運動を弾圧したら, 結局はその運動を強化するのに役立つだけだろう.

clan /klæn/ (**clans**) **1** N-COUNT 可算名詞 A **clan** is a group which consists of families that are related to each other. 氏族 ❑ *...rival clans.* 敵同士の氏族 **2** N-COUNT 可算名詞 You can refer to a group of people with the same interests as a **clan**. 仲間 [INFORMAL くだけた] ❑ *...a powerful clan of industrialists from Monterrey.* モンテレー市出身の勢力のある実業家仲間
→ see **society**

clan|des|tine /klændestɪn/ ADJ 形容詞 Something that is **clandestine** is hidden or kept secret, often because it is illegal. (悪だくみなどの) 秘密の [FORMAL 形式ばった] ❑ *...their clandestine meetings.* 彼らの秘密の会合

clap /klæp/ (**claps, clapping, clapped**) **1** V-T/V-I 他動詞/自動詞 When you **clap**, you hit your hands together to express appreciation or attract attention. 手をたたく ❑ *The men danced and the women clapped.* 男たちは踊り, 女たちは手で拍子をとった. ❑ *Midge clapped her hands, calling them back to order.* ミッジは手をたたいて, 彼らに静粛にするように求めた. **2** V-T 他動詞 If you **clap** your hand or an object onto something, you put it there quickly and firmly. さっと置く ❑ *I clapped a hand over her mouth.* 私は彼女の口を手でさっと押さえた. **3** N-COUNT 可算名詞 A **clap of thunder** is a sudden and loud noise of thunder. (雷鳴の) ゴロゴロいう音

Word Link   **clar ≈ clear : clar**ify, **clar**ity, de**clar**e

Word Link   **ify ≈ making : clar**ify, divers**ify**, intens**ify**

clari|fy /klærɪfaɪ/ (**clarifies, clarifying, clarified**) V-T 他動詞 To **clarify** something means to make it easier to understand, usually by explaining it in more detail. 明白にする [FORMAL 形式ばった] ❑ *Thank you for writing and allowing me to clarify the present position.* お手紙くださり現状を明白に説明する機会をいただき感謝いたします. ● clari|fi|ca|tion /klærɪfɪkeɪᵊn/ (**clarifications**) N-VAR 可変性名詞 明らかにすること ❑ *The union has written to Detroit asking for clarification of the situation.* 状況を明確にしてほしいと組合がデトロイトに手紙を書いた.

clari|net /klærɪnet/ (**clarinets**) N-VAR 可変性名詞 A **clarinet** is a musical instrument in the shape of a pipe. You play the clarinet by blowing into it and covering and uncovering the holes with your fingers. クラリネット
→ see **orchestra**

clar|ity /klærɪti/ **1** N-UNCOUNT 不可算名詞 The **clarity** of something such as a book or argument is its quality of being well explained and easy to understand. 明快さ ❑ *...the ease and clarity with which the author explains difficult technical and scientific subjects.* 著者が難しい技術や科学の話題を平易で明快に説明していること **2** N-UNCOUNT 不可算名詞 **Clarity** is the ability to think clearly. 明晰(めいせき) ❑ *In business circles he is noted for his flair and clarity of vision.* 実業界では彼は直観力と明晰な先見力で注目されている. **3** N-UNCOUNT 不可算名詞 **Clarity** is the quality of being clear in outline or sound. 明瞭; 明澄 ❑ *This remarkable technology provides far greater clarity than conventional x-rays.* この優れた技術では従来のX線よりもはるかに明瞭なものが得られます.

clash /klæʃ/ (**clashes, clashing, clashed**) **1** V-RECIP 相互動詞 When people **clash**, they fight, argue, or disagree with each

other. 衝突する [JOURNALISM ジャーナリズム] □ *A group of 400 demonstrators ripped down the front gate and clashed with police.* 400人のデモ隊が正門を引き倒し警官隊と衝突した. ● *Behind the scenes, Parsons clashed with almost everyone on the show.* 舞台裏でパーソンズはショー関係者のほとんど全員と意見が衝突した. ● N-COUNT 可算名詞 **Clash** is also a noun. 衝突 [oft n "between/with" n] □ *There have been a number of clashes between police in riot gear and demonstrators.* 機動隊とデモ隊間で何度も衝突が起きている. **2** V-RECIP 相互動詞 Beliefs, ideas, or qualities that **clash with** each other are very different from each other and therefore are opposed. 対立する □ *Don't make any policy decisions which clash with official company thinking.* 社是と対立するような方針決定はするな. ● N-COUNT 可算名詞 **Clash** is also a noun. 対立 □ *Inside government, there was a clash of views.* 政府内では見解の対立があった. **3** V-RECIP 相互動詞 If one color or style **clashes with** another, the colors or styles look ugly together. You can also say that two colors or styles **clash**. つり合わない □ *The red door clashed with the soft, natural tones of the stone walls.* 赤い色のドアは石壁のやわらかで自然な色調とつり合っていなかった. **4** V-I 自動詞 If one event **clashes with** another, the two events happen at the same time so that you cannot attend both of them. かち合う [BRIT 英国英語; AM 米国英語 **conflict** 米国英語 **conflict**]

clasp /klǽsp/ (clasps, clasping, clasped) **1** V-T 他動詞 If you **clasp** someone or something, you hold them tightly in your hands or arms. 握りしめる; 抱きしめる □ *She clasped the children to her.* 彼女は子供たちを抱きしめた. **2** N-COUNT 可算名詞 A **clasp** is a small device that fastens something. 留め金 □ *...the clasp of her handbag.* 彼女のハンドバッグの留め金

class /klǽs/ (classes, classing, classed) **1** N-COUNT 可算名詞 A **class** is a group of students who are taught together. 学級 □ *He had to spend about six months in a class with younger students.* 彼は年下の学生たちと6ヵ月ほど同じ学級にいなければならなかった. **2** N-COUNT 可算名詞 A **class** is a course of teaching in a particular subject. 授業 □ *He acquired a law degree by taking classes at night.* 夜学に通って法律の学位を取得した. **3** N-COUNT 可算名詞 A **class of** things is a group of them with similar characteristics. 部類 □ *Harbor staff noticed that measurements given for the same class of boats often varied.* 港湾職員は同じ等級の船に関する測定値がしばしばまちまちであることに気がついた. **4** N-UNCOUNT 不可算名詞 If you do something **in class**, you do it during a lesson in school. 授業中に □ *There's lots of reading in class.* 授業では読み方がたくさんある. **5** N-UNCOUNT 不可算名詞 If you say that someone or something has **class**, you mean that they are elegant and sophisticated. 気品 [INFORMAL くだけた, APPROVAL 賛成] □ *The most elegant woman I've ever met – she had class in every sense of the word.* いままでに会った女性の中でも最も優雅な女性である彼女はあらゆる点で気品があった. **6** N-SING 単数名詞 The students in a school or college who finish their course in a particular year are often referred to as the **class of** that year. 同期卒業生 □ *These two members of Yale's Class of '57 never miss a reunion.* エール大学1957年度卒業生であるこの2人は同窓会を絶対見逃さない. **7** N-VAR 可変性名詞 **Class** refers to the division of people in a society into groups according to their social status. 社会階級 □ *...the relationship between social classes.* 社会階級間の関係 □ *What it will do is create a whole new ruling class.* それがしようとしていることは、まるまる新しい支配階級をつくることだ. **8** → see also **middle class, upper class, working class** **9** V-T 他動詞 If someone or something is **classed as** a particular thing, they are regarded as belonging to that group of things. 分類する □ *Since they can and do successfully inter-breed, they cannot be classed as different species.* それらの交配は可能であるし、実際問題なく交配しているので、別々の種に分類することはできない. □ *I class myself as an ordinary working person.* 私は自分が普通の労働者の部類に入ると思っている. **10** → see also **business class, first-class, second-class, world-class**

clas|sic /klǽsik/ (classics) **1** ADJ 形容詞 A **classic** example of a thing or situation has all the features which you expect such a thing or situation to have. 典型的な □ *The debate in the press has been a classic example of hypocrisy.* 報道界のその議論は典型的な偽善の例であった. ● N-COUNT 可算名詞 **Classic** is also a noun. 典型 □ *It was a classic of interrogation: first the bully, then the kind one who offers sympathy.* それは最初にいじめる人、次に同情する優しい人が出てくるという尋問の典型的な方法であった. **2** ADJ 形容詞 A **classic** movie, piece of writing, or piece of music is of very high quality and has become a standard against which similar things are judged. 一流の, 傑作の [ADJ n] □ *...the classic children's film Huckleberry Finn.* 子供映画の名作である『ハックルベリー・フィン』. ● N-COUNT 可算名詞

Classic is also a noun. 傑作 □ *The record won a gold award and remains one of the classics of modern popular music.* そのレコードは金賞を受賞し, 今も依然として現代流行歌の傑作の1つである. **3** N-COUNT 可算名詞 A **classic** is a book which is well-known and considered to be of a high literary standard. You can refer to such books generally as the **classics**. 古典 □ *As I grow older, I like to reread the classics regularly.* だんだん年をとるにしたがい, 私は定期的に古典を読み直すのが好きになる. **4** N-UNCOUNT 不可算名詞 **Classics** is the study of the ancient Greek and Roman civilizations, especially their languages, literature, and philosophy. 古典学 (古代ギリシャおよびローマ文明の研究) □ *...a Classics degree.* 古典学の学位

clas|si|cal /klǽsikᵊl/ **1** ADJ 形容詞 You use **classical** to describe something that is traditional in form, style, or content. 伝統的な □ *Fokine did not change the steps of classical ballet; instead he found new ways of using them.* フォーキンは伝統的なバレーのステップを変えたのではなく, 代わりにそのステップの新しい使い方を見つけたのだ. **2** ADJ 形容詞 **Classical** music is music that is considered to be serious and of lasting value. 古典派の □ *...a classical composer like Beethoven.* ベートーベンのようなクラシック作曲家 **3** ADJ 形容詞 **Classical** is used to describe things which relate to the ancient Greek or Roman civilizations. 古代ギリシャ・ローマの □ *...the healers of ancient Egypt and classical Greece.* 古代エジプトや古代ギリシャの神霊治療者

→ see **genre**

clas|si|cal|ly /klǽsikli/ **1** ADV 副詞 Someone who has been **classically** trained in something such as art, music, or ballet has learned the traditional skills and methods of that subject. 古典的に [ADV -ed] □ *Peter is a classically trained pianist.* ピーターは正統派教育を受けたピアノ演奏家だ. **2** ADV 副詞 **Classically** is used to indicate that something is based on or reminds people of the culture of ancient Greece and Rome. 古代ギリシャ・ローマ風に [ADV adj/-ed] □ *...the classically inspired church of S. Francesco.* 古代ギリシャ・ローマ様式の聖フランチェスコ教会

clas|si|fi|ca|tion /klǽsɪfɪkeɪʃᵊn/ (classifications) **1** N-COUNT 可算名詞 A **classification** is a division or category in a system which divides things into groups or types. 分類 □ *The government uses a classification system that includes both race and ethnicity.* 政府は人種と民族性の両方を含む分類体制を使用している. **2** → see also **classify**

clas|si|fied /klǽsɪfaɪd/ ADJ 形容詞 **Classified** information or documents are officially secret. 機密扱いの □ *He has a security clearance that allows him access to classified information.* 彼は機密情報にアクセスできる機密委任許可証を持っている.

clas|si|fied ad (classified ads) N-COUNT 可算名詞 **Classified ads** or **classified advertisements** are small advertisements in a newspaper or magazine. They are usually from a person or company. 項目別広告

clas|si|fieds /klǽsɪfaɪdz/ N-PLURAL 複数名詞 The **classifieds** are the same as **classified ads**. 項目別広告 □ *It's common for companies to post job openings on their websites and in newspaper classifieds.* 会社が仕事の空きをウェブサイトや新聞の項目別広告に掲示するのは普通だ.

clas|si|fy /klǽsɪfaɪ/ (classifies, classifying, classified) V-T 他動詞 To **classify** things means to divide them into groups or types so that things with similar characteristics are in the same group. 分類する □ *It is necessary initially to classify the headaches into certain types.* 最初に頭痛をあるいくつかのタイプに分類することが必要である. ● **clas|si|fi|ca|tion** /klǽsɪfɪkeɪʃᵊn/ N-VAR 可変性名詞 分類 □ *...the arbitrary classification of knowledge into fields of study.* 知識の研究分野への恣意 (しい) 的な分類

class|less /klǽslɪs/ ADJ 形容詞 When politicians talk about a **classless** society, they mean a society in which people are not affected by social status. 階級差別のない [APPROVAL 賛成] □ *...the new prime minister's vision of a classless society.* 階級差別のない社会についての新首相の展望

class|mate /klǽsmeɪt/ (classmates) N-COUNT 可算名詞 Your **classmates** are students who are in the same class as you at school or college. 同級生

class|room /klǽsrum/ (classrooms) N-COUNT 可算名詞 A **classroom** is a room in a school where lessons take place. 教室

class sched|ule (class schedules) N-COUNT 可算名詞 In a school or college, a **class schedule** is a list that shows the times in the week at which particular subjects are taught. You can also refer to the range of subjects that a student learns or the classes that a teacher teaches as their **class schedule**. 授業の時間割 [AM 米国英語] □ *They had to be back at their colleges this week to enroll and work out class schedules for the new term.* 彼らは今週大学に戻って, 新学期の登録をして授業時間割を作成しなければならなかった.

classy /klǽsi/ (classier, classiest) ADJ 形容詞 If you describe someone or something as **classy**, you mean they are stylish and sophisticated. しゃれた [INFORMAL くだけた] □ *The German star put in a classy performance.* そのドイツ人スターは素敵な演技をした.

clat|ter /klǽtər/ (**clatters, clattering, clattered**) V-I 自動詞 If you say that people or things **clatter** somewhere, you mean that they move there noisily. がやがや音を立てて進む □He turned and clattered down the stairs. 彼は向きを変えて階段をドタドタと降りていった.

clause /klɔ́z/ (**clauses**) **1** N-COUNT 可算名詞 A **clause** is a section of a legal document. 条項 □He has a clause in his contract which entitles him to a percentage of the profits. 契約書には彼は利潤の何パーセントかを得る権利があるという条項がある. □a compromise document sprinkled with escape clauses. 免責条項があちこちにある妥協文書 **2** N-COUNT 可算名詞 In grammar, a **clause** is a group of words containing a verb. Sentences contain one or more clauses. 節

claw /klɔ́/ (**claws, clawing, clawed**) **1** N-COUNT 可算名詞 The **claws** of a bird or animal are the thin, hard, curved nails at the end of its feet. かぎつめ □The cat tried to cling to the edge by its claws. その猫はつめで端にしがみつこうとした. **2** N-COUNT 可算名詞 The **claws** of a lobster, crab, or scorpion are the two pointed parts at the end of its legs which are used for holding things. はさみ **3** V-I 自動詞 If an animal **claws at** something, it scratches or damages it with its claws. つめで引っかく □The wolf clawed at the tree and howled the whole night. その狼は夜通し木を引っかき, 夜通し鳴き続けた. **4** V-I 自動詞 To **claw at** something mean to try very hard to get hold of it. つかまえようとする □His fingers clawed at Blake's wrist. 彼の指がブレイクの手首をつかまえようとした. **5** V-T 他動詞 If you **claw** your **way** somewhere, you move there with great difficulty, trying desperately to find things to hold on to. 苦労して少しずつ進む □From the flooded depths of the ship, some did manage to claw their way up iron ladders to the safety of the upper deck. 浸水した船の奥底から, 何人かは必死に鉄はしごをよじ登って安全な上部甲板まではいあがってきた.

→ see **bird**

clay /kléɪ/ (**clays**) **1** N-MASS 質量名詞 **Clay** is a kind of earth that is soft when it is wet and hard when it is dry. Clay is shaped and baked to make things such as pots and bricks. 粘土 □...the heavy clay soils of Georgia. ジョージア州の重い粘土質の土壌 □As the wheel turned, the potter shaped and squeezed the lump of clay into a graceful shape. ろくろが回るにつれて, 陶工は粘土の塊を形取り, しぼって優雅な形に仕上げていった. **2** N-UNCOUNT 不可算名詞 In tennis, matches played on **clay** are played on courts whose surface is covered with finely crushed stones or brick. クレーコート □Most tennis is played on hard courts, but a substantial amount is played on clay. ほとんどのテニスはハードコートで行われるが, かなりの数がクレーコートで行われる.

→ see **pottery**

clean /klín/ (**cleaner, cleanest, cleans, cleaning, cleaned**) **1** ADJ 形容詞 Something that is **clean** is free from dirt or unwanted marks. 清潔な □The subway is efficient and spotlessly clean. 地下鉄は能率良く, 1点の汚れもないほどきれいである. □Tiled kitchen floors are easy to keep clean. タイル張りのキッチンの床は清潔に保ちやすい. **2** ADJ 形容詞 You say that people or animals are **clean** when they keep themselves or their surroundings clean. きれい好きな □We like pigs, they're very clean. 私たちは豚が好きだ. 大変きれい好きな動物だから. **3** ADJ 形容詞 A **clean** fuel or chemical process does not create many harmful or polluting substances. 汚染しない □Fans of electric cars say they are clean, quiet, and economical. 電気自動車の公告を起こさないし, 静かで経済的だとその支持者は言う. **4** ADJ 形容詞 If you describe something such as a book, joke, or lifestyle as **clean**, you think that they are not sexually immoral or offensive. わいせつでない [APPROVAL 賛成] □They're trying to show clean, wholesome, decent movies. 彼らはわいせつでなく健全で上品な映画を見せようと努力している. □Flirting is good clean fun. 恋のたわむれはみだらでないよい遊びだ. **5** ADJ 形容詞 If someone has a **clean** reputation or record, they have never done anything illegal or wrong. 潔白な □Accusations of tax evasion have tarnished his clean image. 脱税の告発によって彼のクリーンなイメージに傷がついてしまった. **6** ADJ 形容詞 A **clean** game or fight is carried out fairly, according to the rules. 公明正大な □He called for a clean fight in the election and an end to "negative campaigning." 彼は選挙での公明正大な戦いと「非難合戦」の終止を求めた. ● **clean|ly** ADV 副詞 正々堂々と □The game had been cleanly fought. 試合は正々堂々と戦われた. **7** ADJ 形容詞 A **clean** sheet of paper has no writing or drawing on it. 何も書いてない □Take a clean sheet of paper and down the left-hand side make a list. 白紙を用意してその左側の下にリストを作りなさい. **8** V-T/V-I 他動詞/自動詞 If you **clean** something or **clean** dirt off it, you make it free from dirt and unwanted marks, for example by washing or wiping it. If something **cleans** easily, it is easy to clean. きれいにする, きれいになる □Her father cleaned his glasses with a paper napkin. 彼女の父親は紙ナプキンで眼鏡をきれいに拭いた. □It took half an hour to clean the orange powder off the bathtub. 浴槽に付いたオレンジ色の粉をきれいにするのに半時間かかった. ● **clean|ing** N-UNCOUNT 不可算名詞 掃除 □The windows will have to be given a thorough cleaning. 窓を十二分に掃除する必要があるだろう. **9** V-T/V-I 他動詞/自動詞 If you **clean** a room or house,

you make the inside of it and the furniture in it free from dirt and dust. 掃除する □Mary cooked and cleaned for them. メアリーは彼らのために料理をし掃除をした. ● **clean|ing** N-UNCOUNT 不可算名詞 掃除 □I do the cleaning myself. 私は自分で掃除する. **10** ADV 副詞 **Clean** is used to emphasize that something was done completely. すっかり [INFORMAL くだけた, EMPHASIS 強調] □It burned clean through the seat of my overalls. 私の上っ張りの尻の部分がすっかり焼けてなくなった. □The thief got clean away with the money. 泥棒は金を取ってまんまと逃げた. **11** to **clean up** your **act** → see **act** **12** to **keep** your **nose clean** → see **nose** **13** a **clean slate** → see **slate** **14** a **clean sweep** → see **sweep** **15** **clean as a whistle** → see **whistle** → see **dry-cleaning, soap**

▶ **clean out** PHRASAL VERB 句動詞 If you **clean out** something such as a closet, room, or container, you take everything out of it and clean the inside of it thoroughly. 内部をきれいにする □Mr. Wall asked if I would help him clean out the barrels. たるの中をきれいにするのを手伝ってくれるか, とウォールさんは僕に尋ねた.

▶ **clean up** **1** PHRASAL VERB 句動詞 If you **clean up** a mess or **clean up** a place where there is a mess, you make things neat and free of dirt again. すっかりきれいに掃除する □Police in the city have been cleaning up the debris left by a day of violent confrontation. 市の警察は激しい衝突の1日が残した瓦礫（がれき）を片付けているところだ. **2** PHRASAL VERB 句動詞 To **clean up** something such as the environment or an industrial process means to make it free from substances or processes that cause pollution. 片付ける; 浄化する □Under pressure from the public, many regional governments cleaned up their beaches. 公衆の圧力を受けて多数の地方自治体が砂浜をきれいに片付けた. **3** PHRASAL VERB 句動詞 If the police or authorities **clean up** a place or area of activity, they make it free from crime, corruption, and other unacceptable forms of behavior. 浄化する □After years of neglect and decline, the city was cleaning itself up. 怠慢や堕落が何年も続いた後, 市は自らを浄化しようとしていた. **4** PHRASAL VERB 句動詞 If you go and **clean up**, you make yourself clean and neat, especially after doing something that has made you dirty. 身ぎれいにする □Johnny, go inside and get cleaned up. ジョニー, 中に入って身ぎれいにしなさい.

Thesaurus　　　　clean また次を参照:

ADJ. 　neat, pure; (ant.) dirty, filthy **1**
V. 　launder, rinse, wash; (ant.) dirty, soil, stain **8**

clean|er /klínər/ (**cleaners**) **1** N-COUNT 可算名詞 A **cleaner** is someone who is employed to clean the rooms and furniture inside a building. 掃除係 □...the prison hospital where Sid worked as a cleaner. シドが掃除夫として働いた刑務所病院 **2** N-COUNT 可算名詞 A **cleaner** is someone whose job is to clean a particular type of thing. 清掃作業員 □He was a window cleaner. 彼は窓磨きだった. **3** N-COUNT 可算名詞 A **cleaner** is a device used for cleaning things. 洗浄器具 □...an air cleaner. 空気洗浄器 **4** → see also **vacuum cleaner** **5** N-COUNT 可算名詞 A **cleaner** or a **cleaner's** is a store where things such as clothes are dry-cleaned. クリーニング屋 □Did you pick up my suit from the cleaner's? クリーニング店に僕のスーツを取りに行ってくれたかい? **6** N-MASS 質量名詞 A **cleaner** is a substance used for cleaning things. 洗剤 □...oven cleaner. オーブン用洗剤

Word Link　　**ness ≈ state, condition : cleanliness, conscious**ness, kindness

clean|li|ness /klɛ́nlinɪs/ N-UNCOUNT 不可算名詞 **Cleanliness** is the degree to which people keep themselves and their surroundings clean. 清潔さ □Many of the state's beaches fail to meet minimum standards of cleanliness. 同州の砂浜の多くが清浄度の最低基準を満たしていない.

cleanse /klɛ́nz/ (**cleanses, cleansing, cleansed**) **1** V-T 他動詞 To **cleanse** a place, person, or organization **of** something dirty, unpleasant, or evil means to make them free from it. 清潔にする; 浄化する □Right after your last cigarette, your body will begin to cleanse itself of tobacco toxins. あなたがタバコを吸い終わった直後に, 体がタバコの毒素を取り除き始めるでしょう. **2** V-T 他動詞 If you **cleanse** your skin or a wound, you clean it. 清潔にする □Kathryn demonstrated the proper way to cleanse the face. キャサリンは正しい洗顔方法を実演して見せた. **3** → see also **ethnic cleansing**

cleans|er /klɛ́nzər/ (**cleansers**) **1** N-MASS 質量名詞 A **cleanser** is a liquid or cream that you use to clean your skin. 洗顔料 □...an extremely effective cleanser for dry and sensitive skins. 乾燥して敏感な肌に大変効果のあるスキンクリーム **2** N-MASS 質量名詞 A **cleanser** is a liquid or powder that you use in cleaning kitchens and bathrooms. クレンザー [mainly AM 主に米国英語] □...a certain kind of bathroom cleanser. ある種の浴室用クレンザー

clear

① FREE FROM CONFUSION
② FREE FROM PHYSICAL OBSTACLES
③ MORALLY OR LEGALLY RIGHT, POSSIBLE, OR PERMITTED
④ PHRASAL VERBS

① clear /klɪər/ (clearer, clearest, clears, clearing, cleared) **1** ADJ 形容詞 Something that is **clear** is easy to understand, see, or hear. わかりやすい；はっきりした ❑ The book is clear, readable, and adequately illustrated. その本はわかりやすいし、おもしろく、挿絵も適切だ。 ❑ The space telescope has taken the clearest pictures ever of Pluto. 宇宙望遠鏡はいままでの中で最もはっきりした冥王星の写真を撮った。 ● **clear|ly** ADV 副詞 わかりやすく；はっきりと ❑ Whales journey up the coast of California, clearly visible from the beach. クジラは浜辺からはっきり見える、カリフォルニア海岸を北上するが、浜辺からはっきり見える。 **2** ADJ 形容詞 Something that is **clear** is obvious and impossible to be mistaken about. 明白な ❑ It was a clear case of homicide. それは明白な殺人事件だった。 ❑ It became clear that I hadn't been able to convince Mike. 私がマイクを説得できなかったことがはっきりした。 ● **clear|ly** ADV 副詞 [ADV with cl/group] 明白に ❑ Clearly, the police cannot break the law in order to enforce it. 明らかに、警察は法律を強制執行するわけにはいかない。 **3** ADJ 形容詞 If you are **clear about** something, you understand it completely. はっきりわかっている ❑ It is important to be clear about what Chomsky is doing here. チョムスキーがここで何をしているのかをはっきり理解していることが重要である。 ❑ He is not entirely clear on how he will go about it. 彼はそれをどのように進めるのか完全にはわかっていない。 **4** ADJ 形容詞 If your mind or your way of thinking is **clear**, you are able to think sensibly and reasonably, and you are not affected by confusion or by a drug such as alcohol. 明晰（めいせき）な ❑ She needed a clear head to carry out her instructions. 彼女は指示を実行するためにはさえた頭が必要だった。 ● **clear|ly** ADV 副詞 [ADV after v] 明晰（めいせき）に ❑ The only time I can think clearly is when I'm alone. 私が明晰に考えることができる時は、独りでいるときだけである。 **5** V-T 他動詞 To **clear** your mind or your head means to free it from confused thoughts or from the effects of a drug such as alcohol. すっきりさせる ❑ He walked up Fifth Avenue to clear his head. 頭をすっきりさせるために5番街を歩いた。 **6** CONVENTION 慣習表現 You can say "**Is that clear?**" or "**Do I make myself clear?**" after you have told someone your wishes or instructions, to make sure that they have understood you, and to emphasize your authority. 今言ったことがわかったか。 ❑ We're only going for half an hour, and you're not going to buy anything. Is that clear? 30分行くだけだから、何も買うんじゃありませんよ、わかった？ **7** PHRASE 句 If you **make** something **clear**, you say something in a way that makes it impossible for there to be any doubt about your meaning, wishes, or intentions. はっきりさせる ❑ Mr. O'Friel made it clear that further insults of this kind would not be tolerated. オフリール氏は、このような侮辱はこれから先我慢するつもりはないとはっきり述べた。

② clear /klɪər/ (clearer, clearest, clears, clearing, cleared) **1** ADJ 形容詞 A **clear** substance is one which you can see through and which has no color, like clean water. 透明な ❑ ...a clear glass panel. 透明なガラス板 ❑ ...a clear gel. 透明なゼリー状物質 **2** ADJ 形容詞 If a surface, place, or view is **clear**, it is free of unwanted objects or obstacles. じゃまがない ❑ The runway is clear - go ahead and land. 滑走路は空いています。どうぞ着陸してください。 ❑ Caroline prefers her countertops to be clear of clutter. キャロラインはカウンター上に物が何もないほうが好きだ。 **3** ADJ 形容詞 If it is a **clear** day or if the sky is **clear**, there is no mist, rain, or cloud. 晴れた ❑ On a clear day you can see the coast. 晴れた日には海岸が見える。 **4** ADJ 形容詞 **Clear** eyes look healthy, attractive, and shining. 澄んだ ❑ ...clear blue eyes. 澄んだ青い目 **5** ADJ 形容詞 If your skin is **clear**, it is healthy and free from blemishes. しみのない ❑ No amount of cleansing or mineral water consumption can guarantee a clear skin. 洗顔化粧水や天然鉱水を多量に使ったからといって、きれいな肌を保証することはできない。 **6** ADJ 形容詞 If something or someone is **clear of** something else, it is not touching it or is a safe distance away from it. 離れた ❑ As soon as he was clear of the terminal building, he looked around. 彼はターミナルビルから離れたらすぐにあたりを見まわした。 **7** V-T 他動詞 When you **clear** an area or place or **clear** something **from** it, you remove things from it that you do not want to be there. 取り除く ❑ To clear the land and harvest the bananas, they decided they needed a male workforce. 土地を開墾してバナナを収穫するには、彼らは男の労働力が必要だと判断した。 ❑ Workers could not clear the tunnels of smoke. 作業者たちは坑道から煙を取り除くことができなかった。 **8** V-I 自動詞 When fog or mist **clears**, it gradually disappears. 晴れる ❑ The early morning mist had cleared. 早朝のもやが晴れていた。 **9** to **clear the air** → see **air** **10** to **clear** your **throat** → see **throat** → see also **clearing, crystal clear**

Thesaurus *clear* また次を参照：

ADJ. obvious, plain, straightforward ① **1**
bright, cloudless, sunny ② **3**

③ clear /klɪər/ (clearer, clearest, clears, clearing, cleared) **1** ADJ 形容詞 If you say that your conscience is **clear**, you mean you do not think you have done anything wrong. 潔白な ❑ Mr. Garcia said his conscience was clear over the jail incidents. ガルシア氏は拘置所の事件に関しては自分の良心にやましいところはないと述べた。 **2** V-T/V-I 他動詞／自動詞 When a bank **clears** a check or when a check **clears**, the bank agrees to pay the sum of money mentioned on it. 現金化する ❑ Banks can still take two or three weeks to clear a check. 小切手を現金化するのに銀行はまだ2, 3週間かかることがある。 **3** V-T 他動詞 If something or someone **clears** the way or the path **for** something to happen, they make it possible. 障害を取り去る ❑ The prime minister resigned today, clearing the way for the formation of a new government. 首相は本日退陣し、新政府の成立に道を開いた。 **4** V-T 他動詞 If a course of action is **cleared**, people in authority give permission for it to happen. 許可する [usu passive] ❑ Linda Gradstein has this report from Jerusalem, which was cleared by an Israeli censor. イスラエル検閲官の認可済みであるとのニュースを、エルサレムからリンダ・グラドシュタインが報告しています。 **5** V-T 他動詞 If someone is **cleared**, they are proved to be not guilty of a crime or mistake. 疑いを晴らす ❑ She was cleared of murder and jailed for just five years for manslaughter. 彼女は謀殺の疑いが晴れ、故殺罪としての5年間の懲役となった。 **6** PHRASE 句 If someone is **in the clear**, they are not in danger, or are not blamed or suspected of anything. 危険を脱して；疑いが晴れて ❑ It would be stupid to do anything until we know we're in the clear. 我々が危険を脱したとわかるまでは何かするのは愚かなことだろう。

Word Partnership *clear* は次の語句と使われる：

V. be clear, **make** it clear, **seem** clear ① **1** **2**
N. clear **goals/purpose**, clear **picture** ① **1** **2**
clear **idea**, clear **understanding** ① **1** **2**
clear **someone's head** ① **5**
clear **the way** ③ **3**
ADJ. **crystal** clear ① **1** - **3** ② **1** - **3**

④ clear /klɪər/ (clears, clearing, cleared)
▶ **clear away** PHRASAL VERB 句動詞 When you **clear** things **away** or **clear away**, you put away the things that you have been using, especially for eating or cooking. 片づける ❑ The waitress had cleared away the plates and brought coffee. ウエートレスが皿を下げて、コーヒーを持ってきた。
▶ **clear out 1** PHRASAL VERB 句動詞 If you tell someone to **clear out of** a place or to **clear out**, you are telling them rather rudely to leave the place. 立ち去る [INFORMAL くだけた, DISAPPROVAL 不賛成] ❑ She turned to the others in the room. "The rest of you clear out of here." 彼女は部屋の中にいる他の人たちの方を向いた。「あなたたちもここを出ていってよ」 **2** PHRASAL VERB 句動詞 If you **clear out** a container, room, or house, you make it neat and throw away the things in it that you no longer want. 不要なものを捨てる ❑ I took the precaution of clearing out my desk before I left. 私は立ち去る前にデスクを片づけて空にする用心をした。
▶ **clear up 1** PHRASAL VERB 句動詞 When you **clear up** or **clear** a place **up**, you make things neat and put them away. きれいに片づける ❑ After breakfast they played while I cleared up. 朝食後私が片づけている間彼らは遊んでいた。 **2** PHRASAL VERB 句動詞 To **clear up** a problem, misunderstanding, or mystery means to settle it or find a satisfactory explanation for it. 解決する ❑ There should be someone to whom you can turn for any advice or to clear up any problems. あなたに問題を解決したり、助言してもらったりするのに誰か頼れる人がいるべきだ。 **3** PHRASAL VERB 句動詞 To **clear up** a medical problem, infection, or disease means to cure it or get rid of it. If a medical problem **clears up**, it goes away. 治す、治る ❑ Antibiotics should be used to clear up the infection. その感染症を治すために抗生物質を使用すべきだ。 **4** PHRASAL VERB 句動詞 When the weather **clears up**, it stops raining or being cloudy. 晴上がる ❑ It all depends on the weather clearing up. それはすべて天気が晴れ上がるかにかかっている。

clear|ance /klɪərəns/ (clearances) **1** N-VAR 可変性名詞 **Clearance** is the removal of old buildings, trees, or other things that are not wanted from an area. 除去 ❑ ...a slum clearance operation in Nairobi. ナイロビ市のスラム街一掃計画 ❑ The U.N. pledged to help supervise the clearance of mines. 国連は地雷除去を指揮することを援助すると約束した。 **2** N-VAR 可変性名詞 If you get **clearance to** do or have something, you get official approval or permission to do or have it. 許可 ❑ Thai Airways said the plane had been given clearance to land. タイ航空会社はその飛行機は着陸許可を得ていたと述べた。

clear-cut also **clear cut** ADJ 形容詞 Something that is **clear-cut** is easy to recognize and quite distinct. はっきりした ❑ This was a clear-cut case of the original land owner being in the right. これは最初の

地主が正しいという明白な事例であった.

clear|ing /klɪərɪŋ/ (**clearings**) N-COUNT 可算名詞 A **clearing** is a small area in a forest where there are no trees or bushes. 森の空き 地 □A helicopter landed in a clearing in the dense jungle. ヘリコプターが 密生したジャングルの中の空き地に降りた.

clearing|house /klɪərɪŋhaʊs/ (**clearinghouses**) **1** N-COUNT 可算名詞 If an organization acts as a **clearinghouse**, it collects, sorts, and distributes specialized information. 情報センター □The center will act as a clearinghouse for research projects for former nuclear scientists. このセンターは以前の原子核科学者たちのための研究プロ ジェクト用情報センターとしての役割を果たすでしょう. **2** N-COUNT 可算名詞 A **clearinghouse** is a central bank which deals with all business among the banks that use its services. 手形交換所 [BUSINESS 実業]

clench /klɛntʃ/ (**clenches, clenching, clenched**) **1** V-T/V-I 他 動詞/自動詞 When you **clench** your fist or your fist **clenches**, you curl your fingers up tightly, usually because you are very angry. 固く握る □Alex clenched her fists and gritted her teeth. アレックスはこ ぶしを固く握り,歯をくいしばった. □She pulled at his sleeve and he turned on her, fists clenching again before he saw who it was. 彼女は彼の 袖を引っ張った. 彼はそれが誰なのか気がつく前に再びこぶしを固めて 彼女に向かっていった. **2** V-T/V-I 他動詞/自動詞 When you **clench** your teeth or they **clench**, you squeeze your teeth together firmly, usually because you are angry or upset. (歯を) 食いしばる □Patsy had to clench her jaw to suppress her anger. パツィーは怒りを抑えるた めに口を固く結ばなければならなかった. **3** V-T 他動詞 If you **clench** something in your hand or in your teeth, you hold it tightly with your hand or your teeth. 握り締める □I clenched the arms of my chair. 私は椅子のひじかけを握り締めた.

cler|gy /klɜːrdʒi/ N-PLURAL 複数名詞 The **clergy** are the official leaders of the religious activities of a particular group of believers. 聖職者 □Stalin deported Catholic clergy to Siberia. スターリ ンはカトリック教の聖職者たちをシベリアに追放した.

clergy|man /klɜːrdʒimən/ (**clergymen**) N-COUNT 可算名詞 A **clergyman** is a male member of the clergy. 聖職者

cler|ic /klɛrɪk/ (**clerics**) N-COUNT 可算名詞 A **cleric** is a member of the clergy. 聖職者 □His grandfather was a Muslim cleric. 彼の祖父は イスラム教の聖職者だった.

cleri|cal /klɛrɪkəl/ **1** ADJ 形容詞 **Clerical** jobs, skills, and workers are concerned with routine work that is done in an office. 事務の [ADJ n] □...a strike by clerical staff in all government departments. 政府の全部門における事務職員のストライキ **2** ADJ 形容 詞 **Clerical** means relating to the clergy. 聖職者の [ADJ n] □...Iran's clerical leadership. イランの聖職者の首脳陣

clerk /klɜːrk/ (**clerks, clerking, clerked**) **1** N-COUNT 可算名 詞 A **clerk** is a person who works in an office, bank, or law court and whose job is to keep the records or accounts. 事務員 □She was offered a job as a clerk with a travel agency. 彼女は旅行代理店の事 務員としての採用通知があった. **2** N-COUNT 可算名詞 In a hotel, office, or hospital, a **clerk** is the person whose job is to answer the telephone and deal with people when they arrive. 受付係 [mainly AM 主に米国英語] □...a hotel clerk. ホテルのフロント係 **3** N-COUNT 可算名詞 A **clerk** is someone who sells things to customers in a store. 店員 [AM 米国英語] □Now Thomas was working as a clerk in a shop that sold leather goods. さて,トマスは革製品を売る店の店員とし て働いていた. **4** V-I 自動詞 To **clerk** means to work as a clerk. 事務 員として働く [mainly AM 主に米国英語] □Gene clerked at the auction. ジーンはその競売で事務員として働いた.

→ see **hotel**

clev|er /klɛvər/ (**cleverer, cleverest**) **1** ADJ 形容詞 Someone who is **clever** is intelligent and able to understand things easily or plan things well. 賢い □He's a very clever man. 彼は大変頭がい い男だ. ● **clev|er|ly** ADV 副詞 賢く □She would cleverly pick up on what I said. 彼女はよく私が言うことを如才なく察知したものだった. ● **clev|er|ness** N-UNCOUNT 不可算名詞 賢さ □Her cleverness seems to get in the way of her emotions. 彼女の利口さが感情の邪魔になって いるように思える. **2** ADJ 形容詞 A **clever** idea, book, or invention is extremely effective and shows the skill of the people involved. 巧 みな □It is a clever and gripping novel, yet something is missing from its heart. それは巧みで実におもしろい小説だが,その本質にはまだ何か が欠けている. ● **clev|er|ly** ADV 副詞 [ADV -ed] 巧妙に □...a cleverly designed swimsuit. 巧みなデザインの水着

Thesaurus	clever また次を参照:
ADJ.	bright, ingenious, smart; (ant.) dumb, stupid **1** **2**

click /klɪk/ (**clicks, clicking, clicked**) **1** V-T/V-I 他動詞/自動詞 If something **clicks** or if you **click** it, it makes a short, sharp sound. カチッと音がする □The applause rose to a crescendo and cameras clicked. 拍手は次第に大きくなり,カメラがパチリ,パチリと音を 立てた. □He clicked off the radio. 彼はラジオをカチリと消した. ● N-COUNT 可算名詞 **Click** is also a noun. カチリという音 □The telephone rang three times before I heard a click and then her recorded voice. 電話は3回鳴ってカチッと音がし,録音した彼女の声が聞こえ た. **2** V-T/V-I 他動詞/自動詞 If you **click** on an area of a computer screen, you point the cursor at that area and press one of the buttons on the mouse in order to make something happen. クリ ックする [COMPUTING コンピューティング] [no passive] □I clicked on a link and recent reviews of the production came up. 私がリンクをク リックしたら,その上演作品の最近の論評が出てきた. □Click the link and see what happens. リンクをクリックして,次はどうなるか見てく ださい. ● N-COUNT 可算名詞 **Click** is also a noun. クリックすること □You can check your e-mail with a click of your mouse. マウスをクリッ クすることで電子メールの確認ができます. **3** V-I 自動詞 When you suddenly understand something, you can say that it **clicks**. ぴん とくる [INFORMAL くだけた] □When I saw the television report, it all clicked. 私はテレビ報道を見たときに全てがぴんときた. **4** to **click into place** → see **place**

click|able /klɪkəbəl/ ADJ 形容詞 A **clickable** image on a computer screen is one that you can point the cursor at and click on, in order to make something happen. クリックすることがで きる [COMPUTING コンピューティング] □...a website with clickable maps showing hotel locations. ホテルの所在地を示すクリック可能な地 図があるウェブサイト

cli|ent /klaɪənt/ (**clients**) N-COUNT 可算名詞 A **client** of a professional person or organization is a person or company that receives a service from them in return for payment. 顧客 [BUSINESS 実業] □...a lawyer and his client. 弁護士と依頼人
→ see **trial**

If you use the professional services of someone such as a lawyer or an accountant, you are one of their **clients**. When you buy goods from a particular shop or company, you are one of its **customers**. Doctors and hospitals have **patients**, while hotels have **guests**. People who travel on public transportation are referred to as **passengers**.

cli|en|tele /klaɪəntɛl, kliɒn-/ N-SING-COLL 集合的単数名詞 The **clientele** of a place or organization are its customers or clients. 顧 客 □This pub had a mixed clientele. この酒場はいろいろな客が混ざっ ていた.

cliff /klɪf/ (**cliffs**) N-COUNT 可算名詞 A **cliff** is a high area of land with a very steep side, especially one next to the sea. がけ □The car rolled over the edge of a cliff. その車はがけっぷちを越えて転がり落 ちた.

→ see **mountain**

cli|mate /klaɪmɪt/ (**climates**) **1** N-VAR 可変性名詞 The **climate** of a place is the general weather conditions that are typical of it. 気候 □...the hot and humid climate of Florida. フロリダ州の高温多 湿の気候 **2** N-COUNT 可算名詞 You can use **climate** to refer to the general atmosphere or situation somewhere. 情勢 □The economic climate remains uncertain. 経済情勢が不安定のままである. □...the existing climate of violence and intimidation. 暴力と脅迫が現存する情勢
→ see Word Web: **climate**

cli|max /klaɪmæks/ (**climaxes, climaxing, climaxed**) **1** N-COUNT 可算名詞 The **climax of** something is the most exciting or important moment in it, usually near the end. 最高 潮 □For Pritchard, reaching the Olympics was the climax of her career. プ リチャードにとって,オリンピック出場が生涯の絶頂であった. □It was the climax to 24 hours of growing anxiety. それは不安がつのってい った24時間の山場であった. **2** V-T/V-I 他動詞/自動詞 The event that **climaxes** a sequence of events is an exciting or important event that comes at the end. You can also say that a sequence of events **climaxes with** a particular event. 絶頂に到達する [JOURNALISM ジ ャーナリズム] □The demonstration climaxed two weeks of strikes. 2週間 続いたストライキはデモ行進で絶頂に達した.

climb /klaɪm/ (**climbs, climbing, climbed**) **1** V-T/V-I 他動詞/自 動詞 If you **climb** something such as a tree, mountain, or ladder, or **climb up** it, you move toward the top of it. If you **climb down** it, you move toward the bottom of it. 登る, 上る; 降りる □Climbing the first hill took half an hour. 最初の丘を登るのに半時間かかった. □I told her about him climbing up the drainpipe. 私は彼女に彼が排水管を上 って行ったと伝えた. ● N-COUNT 可算名詞 **Climb** is also a noun. 登 ること □...an hour's leisurely climb through olive groves and vineyards. オリーブ園やぶどう畑を通って行く1時間ほどのゆっくりした登り **2** V-I 自動詞 If you **climb** somewhere, you move there carefully, for example because you are moving into a small space or trying to avoid falling. よじ登る; (車などに) 乗り込む □The girls hurried outside, climbed into the car, and drove off. 少女たちは急いで外に出て, 車に乗り込んで走り去った. □He must have climbed out of his bed. 彼 はベッドを抜け出たに違いない. **3** V-I 自動詞 When something such as an airplane climbs, it moves upward to a higher position. When the sun **climbs**, it moves higher in the sky. 上る, 昇る □The plane took off for L.A., lost an engine as it climbed, and crashed just off the runway. その飛行機はロサンジェルスに向かって離陸したが,上昇中 にエンジンが1つ止まり,滑走路を過ぎたところで墜落した. **4** V-I 自 動詞 When something **climbs**, it increases in value or amount.

Word Web climate

During the past 100 years, the surface air **temperature** of the earth has increased by about 1° **Fahrenheit** (F). Alaska has warmed by about 4°F. At the same time, precipitation over the northern hemisphere increased by 10%. The global sea level also rose 4-8 inches. The years 1998, 2001, and 2002 were the three hottest ever recorded. This warm period followed what some scientists call the "Little Ice Age." Researchers found that from the 1400s to the 1800s the Earth cooled by about 6°F. Air and water temperatures were lower, **glaciers** grew quickly, and **ice** floes came further south than usual.

St. Mark's Square in Venice flooded 111 times in 2002.

上昇する ❑ *The nation's unemployment rate has been climbing steadily since last June.* 全国の失業率は去る6月以来着実に上昇している. ❑ *Prices have climbed by 21% since the beginning of the year.* 物価は年初め以来21％上昇している. **5** → see also **climbing 6 a mountain to climb** → see **mountain**

Word Partnership   climb は次の語句と使われる:

PREP.	climb **down/up**, climb **in/on** 1
N.	climb **the stairs** 2
	prices climb 4
V.	**begin/continue to** climb 3 4

climb|er /klaɪmər/ (**climbers**) **1** N-COUNT 可算名詞 A **climber** is someone who climbs rocks or mountains as a sport or a hobby. 登山家 ❑ *She was an experienced climber, who had climbed several of the world's tallest mountains.* 彼女は経験豊かな登山家であって、世界でも最高の山々をいくつも登ったことがあった. **2** N-COUNT 可算名詞 A **climber** is a plant that grows upward by attaching itself to other plants or objects. つる性植物 ❑ *All good garden centers carry a selection of climbers.* よい園芸用品店はどこでもつる性植物を取り揃えている.

climb|ing /klaɪmɪŋ/ N-UNCOUNT 不可算名詞 **Climbing** is the activity of climbing rocks or mountains. 登山 ❑ *I had done no skiing, no climbing, and no hiking.* 私はスキーも登山もハイキングもしたことがなかった.

clinch /klɪntʃ/ (**clinches, clinching, clinched**) **1** V-T 他動詞 If you **clinch** something you are trying to achieve, such as a business deal or victory in a contest, you succeed in obtaining it. まとめる、決着をつける ❑ *Her second-place finish in the final race was enough to clinch the overall victory.* 最後の競技における2位のゴールは、彼女が総合優勝を決するに充分だった. **2** V-T 他動詞 The thing that **clinches** an uncertain matter settles it or provides a definite answer. 決着をつける ❑ *Evidently this information clinched the matter.* 明らかにこの情報がその問題の片をつけた.

cling /klɪŋ/ (**clings, clinging, clung**) **1** V-I 自動詞 If you **cling** to someone or something, you hold onto them tightly. しがみつく ❑ *Another man was rescued as he clung to the riverbank.* もう1人の男は川の土手にしがみついているところを救助された. ❑ *She had to cling onto the door handle until the pain passed.* 彼女は痛みが去るまでドアの取っ手にすがりついていなければならなかった. **2** V-I 自動詞 If someone **clings to** a position or a possession they have, they do everything they can to keep it even though this may be very difficult. 執着する ❑ *Instead, he appears determined to cling to power.* それどころか彼は権力にしがみついて絶対離さないように見える. ❑ *Another congressman clung on with a majority of only 18.* もう1人の国会議員は、わずか18票の得票差で辛うじてしがみついていた.

clin|ic /klɪnɪk/ (**clinics**) N-COUNT 可算名詞 A **clinic** is a building where people go to receive medical advice or treatment. 診療所 ❑ *...a family planning clinic.* 家族計画診療所

Word Partnership   clinic は次の語句と使われる:

| N. | **abortion/family planning** clinic, **fertility** clinic |
| ADJ. | **free** clinic, **medical** clinic |

clini|cal /klɪnɪkᵊl/ **1** ADJ 形容詞 **Clinical** means involving or relating to the direct medical treatment or testing of patients. 臨床の ❑ *The first clinical trials were expected to begin next year.* 初回の臨床試験は来年開始されると予想されていた. [MEDICAL 医学の] [ADJ n] ●**clini|cal|ly** /klɪnɪkli/ ADV 副詞 臨床的に ❑ *She was diagnosed as being clinically depressed.* 臨床的にうつ病であると診断された. **2** ADJ 形容詞 You use **clinical** to describe thought or behavior that is very

logical and does not involve any emotion. 客観的な [DISAPPROVAL 不賛成] ❑ *All this questioning is so clinical – it kills romance.* まったくこんな質問はとても冷静で、ロマンチックな雰囲気を壊してしまう.

clip /klɪp/ (**clips, clipping, clipped**) **1** N-COUNT 可算名詞 A **clip** is a small device, usually made of metal or plastic, that is specially shaped for holding things together. クリップ ❑ *She took the clip out of her hair.* 彼女は髪の毛から髪留めを外した. **2** N-COUNT 可算名詞 A **clip** from a movie or a radio or television program is a short piece of it that is broadcast separately. 録音録画の1場面 ❑ *...an historical film clip of Lenin speaking.* レーニンが演説している映画の歴史的な1場面 **3** V-T/V-I 他動詞/自動詞 When you **clip** things together or when things **clip** together, you fasten them together using a clip or clips. クリップで留める、クリップで留められる ❑ *He clipped his safety belt to a fitting on the deck.* 彼は安全ベルトのクリップを甲板の金具にしっかり留めた. **4** V-T 他動詞 If you **clip** something, you cut small pieces from it, especially in order to shape it. 刈り込む ❑ *I saw an old man out clipping his hedge.* 私は老人が外で生垣を刈り込んでいるのを見た. **5** V-T 他動詞 If you **clip** something out of a newspaper or magazine, you cut it out. 切り取る ❑ *Kids in his neighborhood clipped his picture from the newspaper and carried it around.* 彼の近所の子供たちは、新聞から彼の写真を切り取って持ち歩いた. **6** V-T 他動詞 If something **clips** something else, it hits it accidentally at an angle before moving off in a different direction. ぶつかってそれる ❑ *The truck clipped the rear of a tanker and then crashed into a second truck.* そのトラックはタンク車の後部にぶつかってそれて、それから別のトラックに衝突した. **7** → see also **clipped, clipping, paper clip**

Word Partnership   clip は次の語句と使われる:

V.	**play a** clip 2
N.	**audio/film/movie/music/video** clip, **a** clip **from a tape** 2
	clip **coupons** 5

clip|board /klɪpbɔrd/ (**clipboards**) **1** N-COUNT 可算名詞 A **clipboard** is a board with a clip at the top. It is used to hold together pieces of paper that you need to carry around, and provides a firm base for writing. 紙ばさみ付き筆記板 **2** N-COUNT 可算名詞 In computing, a **clipboard** is a place where you can temporarily store text or images from one document until you are ready to use them again. クリップボード [COMPUTING コンピューティング]

clipped /klɪpt/ **1** ADJ 形容詞 **Clipped** means neatly cut. 刈り込んだ ❑ *...a quiet street of clipped hedges and flowering gardens.* 刈り込んだ生垣や花が咲いている庭のある静かな通り **2** ADJ 形容詞 If you say that someone has a **clipped** way of speaking, you mean they speak with quick, short sounds, and usually that they sound upper-class. 早口で歯切れのいい ❑ *Her clipped tones crackled over the telephone line.* 彼女の歯切れのよい口調が電話でパリパリと音を立てて聞こえた.

clip|ping /klɪpɪŋ/ (**clippings**) **1** N-COUNT 可算名詞 A **clipping** is an article, picture, or advertisement that has been cut from a newspaper or magazine. 切り抜き ❑ *...bulletin boards crowded with newspaper clippings.* 新聞の切り抜きでぎっしり詰まった掲示板 **2** N-PLURAL 複数名詞 **Clippings** are small pieces of something that have been cut from something larger. 切り取ったもの ❑ *Having mown the lawn, there are all those grass clippings to get rid of.* 芝を刈ったので、捨てなければならない刈り取った芝がこんなにあります.

clique /klik, klɪk/ (**cliques**) N-COUNT 可算名詞 If you describe a group of people as a **clique**, you mean that they spend a lot of time together and seem unfriendly towards people who are not

Word Web   clone

Clones have always existed. For example, plant propagation using a leaf cutting produces an **identical** new plant. Identical **twins** are also natural clones of each other. Recently however, scientists have started using **genetic engineering** to produce artificial clones of animals. The first step involves removing the **DNA** from a **cell**. Next, a technician places this genetic information into an egg cell. The egg then matures into a **copy** of the donor animal. The first animal experiments in the 1970s involved tadpoles. In 1997 a sheep named Dolly became the first successfully cloned mammal.

in the group. 徒党 [DISAPPROVAL 不賛成] ❑ *He was accepted into the most popular clique on campus.* 彼は大学で最も人気のある派閥に受け入れられた.

cloak /kloʊk/ (**cloaks**) **1** N-COUNT 可算名詞 A **cloak** is a long, loose, sleeveless piece of clothing which people used to wear over their other clothes when they went out. マント **2** N-SING 単数名詞 A **cloak** of something such as mist or snow completely covers and hides something. 覆い隠すもの ❑ *Today most of New England will be under a cloak of thick mist.* 今日はニューイングランドのほとんどの地域は深い霧に覆われるでしょう. **3** N-SING 単数名詞 If you refer to something as a **cloak**, you mean that it is intended to hide the truth about something. 隠れみの ❑ *Preparations for the wedding were made under a cloak of secrecy.* 結婚準備は極秘裏のうちに行われた.

cloak|room /kloʊkrum/ (**cloakrooms**) N-COUNT 可算名詞 A **cloakroom** is the same as a **coat check**. 携帯品一時預かり所 [OLD-FASHIONED 古風な] ❑ *...a cloakroom attendant.* クローク係

clock /klɒk/ (**clocks, clocking, clocked**) **1** N-COUNT 可算名詞 A **clock** is an instrument that shows what time of day it is. 時計 ❑ *He was conscious of a clock ticking.* 彼は時計がカチカチと音を立てているのを意識していた. ❑ *...a digital clock.* デジタル時計 **2** N-COUNT 可算名詞 A time **clock** in a factory or office is a device that is used to record the hours that people work. Each worker puts a special card into the device when they arrive and leave, and the times are recorded on the card. 計器 ❑ *Government workers were made to punch time clocks morning, noon and night.* 政府機関の職員は朝、正午、夜とタイムレコーダーにパンチさせられた. **3** V-T 他動詞 To **clock** a particular time or speed in a race means to reach that time or speed. 記録する ❑ *Elliott clocked the fastest time this year for the 800 meters.* 800メートル競走でエリオットは今年の最速時間を記録した. **4** V-T 他動詞 If something or someone **is clocked at** a particular time or speed, their time or speed is measured at that level. 記録を出す [usu passive] ❑ *He has been clocked at 11 seconds for 100 meters.* 彼は100メートルで11秒の記録を出している. **5** → see also **alarm clock, o'clock** **6** PHRASE 句 If you are doing something **against the clock**, you are doing it in a great hurry, because there is very little time. 時間と競争で ❑ *The emergency services were working against the clock as the tide began to rise.* 潮が満ち始めてきたので、救助隊は時間とにらめっこで仕事をしていた. **7** PHRASE 句 If something is done **around the clock** or **round the clock**, it is done all day and all night without stopping. 昼夜兼行で ❑ *Rescue services have been working round the clock to free stranded motorists.* 立ち往生したドライバーたちを救出するために、救助隊は昼夜兼行で作業を進めている.

▶ **clock in** PHRASAL VERB 句動詞 When you **clock in** at work, you arrive there or put a special card into a device to show what time you arrived. 出勤する; 出勤時間を記録する ❑ *I have to clock in by eight.* 私は8時までに出勤しなければならない.

▶ **clock off** PHRASAL VERB 句動詞 When you **clock off** at work, you leave work or put a special card into a device to show what time you left. 退社する; 退社時間の記録をする ❑ *The night duty officer was ready to clock off.* その夜勤職員は退社する準備ができていた.

▶ **clock on** PHRASAL VERB 句動詞 When workers **clock on** at a factory or office, they put a special card into a device to show what time they arrived. 出勤時間を記録する ❑ *They arrived to clock on and found the factory gates locked.* 彼らは出勤してきたが、工場の門は鍵がかかっていることがわかった.

▶ **clock out** PHRASAL VERB 句動詞 **Clock out** means the same as **clock off**. 退社時間を記録する ❑ *She had clocked out of her bank at 5:02pm using her plastic card.* 彼女はプラスティックのカードを使って午後5時2分に退社記録をして銀行を出た.

▶ **clock up** PHRASAL VERB 句動詞 If you **clock up** a large number or total of things, you reach that number or total. 記録を出す; 達成する [BRIT 英国英語; AM chalk up 米国英語 **chalk up**]
→ see **time**

Word Partnership   *clock は次の語句と使われる:*

V.	look at a clock, put/turn the clock back/forward, set a clock, clock **strikes**, clock **ticks** **1**
N.	clock **radio**, hands of a clock **1**

Word Link   *wise ≈ in the direction or manner of : clock*wise, like*wise, other*wise

clock|wise /klɒkwaɪz/ ADV 副詞 When something is moving **clockwise**, it is moving in a circle in the same direction as the hands on a clock. 時計回りに [ADV after v] ❑ *He told the children to start moving clockwise around the room.* 彼は子供たちに部屋でぐるっと時計回りにまわり始めるように言った. ● ADJ 形容詞 **Clockwise** is also an adjective. 時計回りの [ADJ n] ❑ *Gently swing your right arm in a clockwise direction.* 右腕をゆっくり時計回りの方向にまわしてください.

clock|work /klɒkwɜrk/ **1** ADJ 形容詞 A **clockwork** toy or device has machinery inside it which makes it move or operate when it is wound up with a key. ぜんまい仕掛けの [ADJ n] ❑ *...a clockwork train set.* ぜんまい仕掛けの汽車のセット **2** PHRASE 句 If you say that something happens **like clockwork**, you mean that it happens without any problems or delays, or happens regularly. 支障なく; 規則正しく ❑ *The president's trip is arranged to go like clockwork, everything pre-planned to the minute.* 大統領の旅行は全て前もって分刻みで計画され、支障なくいくように手配されている.

clog /klɒg/ (**clogs, clogging, clogged**) **1** V-T 他動詞 When something **clogs** a hole or place, it blocks it so that nothing can pass through. 詰まらせる ❑ *Dirt clogs the pores, causing blemishes.* 汚れで毛穴が詰り、しみとなる. **2** N-COUNT 可算名詞 **Clogs** are heavy leather or wooden shoes with thick, wooden soles. 木靴

clone /kloʊn/ (**clones, cloning, cloned**) **1** N-COUNT 可算名詞 If someone or something is a **clone** of another person or thing, they are so similar to this person or thing that they seem to be exactly the same as them. そっくりの物や人 ❑ *Tom was in some ways a younger clone of his handsome father.* トムはいくつかの点でハンサムな父親を若くしたようなものだった. **2** N-COUNT 可算名詞 A **clone** is an animal or plant that has been produced artificially, for example in a laboratory, from the cells of another animal or plant. A clone is exactly the same as the original animal or plant. クローン ❑ *...the world's first human clone.* 世界初の人クローン **3** V-T 他動詞 To **clone** an animal or plant means to produce it as a clone. クローンとして発生させる ❑ *The idea of cloning extinct life forms still belongs to science fiction.* 絶滅した生物形態をクローンさせるのはまだ空想科学小説の世界だ.
→ see Word Web: **clone**

close
❶ SHUTTING OR COMPLETING
❷ NEARNESS; ADJECTIVE USES
❸ NEARNESS; VERB USES

❶ close /kloʊz/ (**closes, closing, closed**)
⇨ **Please look at meaning 11 to see if the expression you are looking for is shown under another headword.** **1** V-T/V-I 他動詞/自動詞 When you **close** something such as a door or lid or when it **closes**, it moves so that a hole, gap, or opening is covered. 閉める [他動詞]、閉まる [自動詞] ❑ *If you are cold, close the window.* 寒いなら窓を閉めなさい. ❑ *Zacharias heard the door close.* ザカリアスはドアが閉まるのを聞いた. **2** V-T 他動詞 When you **close** something such as an open book or umbrella, you move the different parts of it together. 閉じる; たたむ ❑ *Slowly he closed the book.* 彼はゆっくりと本を閉じた. **3** V-T 他動詞 If you **close** something such as a computer file or window, you give the computer an instruction to remove it from the screen. 閉じる、終了する [COMPUTING コンピューティング] ❑ *To close your document, press CTRL+W on your keyboard.* 文書を閉じるには、キーボードのCRT+Wを押しなさい. **4** V-T/V-I 他動詞/自動詞 When you **close** your eyes or your eyes **close**, your eyelids move downward, so that you can no longer see. 閉じる ❑ *Bess closed her eyes and fell asleep.* ベスは目を閉じて眠りについた. **5** V-T/V-I 他動詞/自動詞 When a place **closes** or **is closed**, work or activity stops there for a short period. 閉める [他動詞]、閉まる [自動詞] ❑ *Shops close only on Christmas Day and New Year's Day.* 店はクリスマスと元旦のみ閉店する. ❑ *Government troops closed the airport.* 政府軍が空港を封鎖した. **6** V-T/V-I 他動詞/自動詞 If a place such as a factory, store, or school **closes**, or if it **is closed**, all work

or activity stops there permanently. （永久的に）閉鎖する □*Many enterprises will be forced to close.* 多数の企業が廃業を余儀なくされるだろう. ● PHRASAL VERB 句動詞 **Close down** means the same as **close**. （永久的に）閉鎖する □*Minford closed down the business and went into politics.* ミンフォードは事業を廃業して政治の道に入った. ● **clos|ing** N-SING 単数名詞 閉鎖 □*...since the closing of the steel mill in 1984.* その製鋼所を1984年に閉鎖して以来 **7** V-T 他動詞 To **close** a road or border means to block it in order to prevent people from using it. 通行止めにする □*They were cut off from the West in 1948 when their government closed that border crossing.* 彼らは政府が越境地点を通行止めにした1948年に西側から切り離された. **8** V-T 他動詞 To **close** a conversation, event, or matter means to bring it to an end or to complete it. 終える □*Judge Isabel Oliva said last night: "I have closed the case. There was no foul play."* 昨夜イザベル・オリバ裁判官は「訴訟裁判を終結しました. 不正な行為はありませんでした」と述べた. □*The governor is said to now consider the matter closed.* その件は終結したと州知事は現在考えていることが伝えられている. **9** V-T 他動詞 If you **close** a bank account, you take all your money out of it and inform the bank that you will no longer be using the account. 閉める □*He had closed his account with the bank five years earlier.* 彼は5年早くその銀行の口座を閉めた. **10** V-I 自動詞 On the stock market or the currency markets, if a share price or a currency **closes** at a particular value, that is its value at the end of the day's business. 引ける, 終わり値である [BUSINESS 実業] □*The U.S. dollar closed higher in Tokyo today.* 米ドルは本日東京では高目の終わり値でした. **11** → see also **closing** **12** to **close** your **eyes** to something → see **eye** **13** to **close ranks** → see **rank**
▶ **close down** → see **close ❶** 6
▶ **close up** **1** PHRASAL VERB 句動詞 If someone **closes up** a building, they shut it completely and securely, often because they are going away. すっかり閉める □*Just close up the shop.* ともかく店を閉め切ってしまいなさい. □*The summer house had been closed up all year.* そのあずま屋は年中閉め切られていた. **2** PHRASAL VERB 句動詞 If an opening, gap, or something hollow **closes up**, or if you **close** it **up**, it becomes closed or covered. すっかりふさぐ[他動詞], すっかりふさがる[自動詞] □*Don't use cold water as it shocks the blood vessels into closing up.* 衝撃で血管が収縮するので冷水は使うな.

Thesaurus

close また次を参照:

V.	fasten, shut, slam, seal; (*ant.*) open **❶ 1**

Word Partnership

close は次の語句と使われる:

N.	close a door **❶ 1** close your eyes **❶ 1** close friend, close to someone **❷ 2** close family/relative **❷ 2 3** close attention/scrutiny **❷ 7** close election, close race **❷ 9**
ADV.	close enough, so/too/very close **❷ 1 9 12 13**

---

❷ close /klo͟ʊs/ (closer, closest)

↪ Please look at meaning **15** to see if the expression you are looking for is shown under another headword. **1** ADJ 形容詞 If one thing or person is **close** to another, there is only a very small distance between them. 近い □*Her lips were close to his head and her breath tickled his ear.* 彼女の唇は彼の頭の近くにあり, 息が彼の耳をくすぐった. □*The man moved closer, lowering his voice.* その男はさらに近寄り声を落とした. ● **close|ly** ADV 副詞 近く □*They crowded more closely around the stretcher.* 彼らは担架のまわりにさらに近づいて群がった. **2** ADJ 形容詞 You say that people are **close to** each other when they like each other very much and know each other very well. 親密な □*She and Linda became very close.* 彼女とリンダは大変親しくなった. □*I shared a house with a close friend from school.* 私は学校の親友と共同で1軒の家を借りた. ● **close|ness** N-UNCOUNT 不可算名詞 □*I asked whether her closeness to her mother ever posed any problems.* 彼女が母親と仲がいいかでいつまでに何か問題が起こったことがあるかどうか私は尋ねた. **3** ADJ 形容詞 [ADJ n] Your **close** relatives are the members of your family who are most directly related to you, for example your parents and your brothers or sisters. （親族関係が）近い □*...large changes such as the birth of a child or death of a close relative.* 子供の誕生や近親の死去などの大きな変化 **4** ADJ 形容詞 A **close** ally or partner of someone knows them well and is very involved in their work. 密接な □*He was once regarded as one of Mr. Brown's closest political advisers.* 彼はかつてブラウン氏の最も密接な政治顧問の1人とみなされていた. **5** ADJ 形容詞 **Close** contact or cooperation involves seeing or communicating with someone often. 緊密な [ADJ n] □*Both nations are seeking closer links with the West.* 両国とも西側とのいっそう緊密なつながりを求めている. ● **close|ly** ADV 副詞 [ADV after v] 緊密に □*Our agencies work closely with local groups in developing countries.* 私どもの代理店は発展途上国の現地グループと緊密に仕事をしています. **6** ADJ 形容詞 If there is a **close** connection or resemblance between two things, they are strongly connected or are very similar. 強い; 似通った □*There is a close connection between pain and tension.* 苦痛と

緊張は強いつながりがある. ● **close|ly** ADV 副詞 強く; 似通って □*...a pattern closely resembling a cross.* 十字によく似た模様 **7** ADJ 形容詞 **Close** inspection or observation of something is careful and thorough. 綿密な □*He discovered, on closer inspection, that the rocks contained gold.* 彼が注意深く調べてみると, 岩石には金が含まれていることがわかった. ● **close|ly** ADV 副詞 [ADV with v] 綿密に □*If you look closely at many of the problems in society, you'll see evidence of racial discrimination.* 社会での問題の多くを綿密に調べれば, 人種差別を示す証拠が見えてくるだろう. **8** ADJ 形容詞 A **close** competition or election is won or seems likely to be won by only a small amount. 互角の □*It is still a close contest between two leading opposition parties.* 2つの有力な野党間でいまだ接戦中である. ● **close|ly** ADV 副詞 互角に □*This will be a closely fought race.* この競走は激しい接戦となるだろう. **9** ADJ 形容詞 [v-link ADJ, usu ADJ "to" n/-ing] If you are **close** to something, you are likely to do it soon. 間近い □*If you are **close to** doing something, you are likely to do it soon.* 間近い □*She sounded close to tears.* 彼女はいまにも泣き出しそうに思えた □*A senior White House official said the agreement is close.* 米国政府のある高官が合意は間近だと述べた. **10** ADJ 形容詞 If something is **close** or comes **close** to something else, it almost is, does, or experiences that thing. もう少しで―しそうになる [v-link ADJ, usu ADJ "to" n] □*An airliner came close to disaster while approaching Kennedy Airport.* 旅客機がケネディー空港に近づいているとき, もう少しで大惨事になるところだった. **11** ADJ 形容詞 If the atmosphere somewhere is **close**, it is unpleasantly warm with not enough air. 蒸し暑い **12** PHRASE 句 Something that is **close by** or **close at hand** is near to you. すぐ近くに □*Did a new hair salon open close by?* 新しい美容院が近所に開店したか? **13** PHRASE 句 **Close to** a particular amount or distance means slightly less than that amount or distance. ほぼ □*Sisulu spent close to 30 years in prison.* シスルはほぼ30年近く刑務所に入っていた. **14** PHRASE 句 If you look at something **close up**, you look at it when you are very near to it. すぐ近くで □*They always look smaller close up.* すぐ近くでは, それらはいついつも小さく見える. **15** → see also **close-up** **16** at **close quarters** → see **quarter** **17** at **close range** → see **range**

❸ close /klo͟ʊz/ (closes, closing, closed) V-I 自動詞 If you are **closing on** someone or something that you are following, you are getting nearer and nearer to them. 迫る [自動詞] □*I was within 15 seconds of the guy in second place and closing on him.* 私は2位の人まで15秒以内で, さらに差が縮まりつつあった.
▶ **close in** PHRASAL VERB 句動詞 If a group of people **close in on** a person or place, they come nearer and nearer to them and gradually surround them. だんだんと迫る □*Hitler himself committed suicide as Soviet forces were closing in on Berlin.* ソ連軍のベルリン包囲網が迫りつつあったとき, ヒトラーは自殺した.

closed-circuit ADJ 形容詞 A **closed-circuit** television or video system is one that operates within a limited area such as a building. 閉回路の [ADJ n] □*There's a closed-circuit television camera in the reception area.* 受付には監視カメラが設置されている.

closed shop (closed shops) N-COUNT 可算名詞 If a factory, store, or other business is a **closed shop**, the employees must be members of a particular trade union. クローズドショップ（労働組合員だけを雇用する事業所）[BUSINESS 実業] □*...the trade union which they are required to join under the closed shop agreement.* クローズドショップ協定により彼らが加入しなければならない労働組合.

clos|et /klɒ̱zɪt/ (closets) N-COUNT 可算名詞 A **closet** is a very small room for storing things, especially one without windows. クローゼット [mainly AM 主に米国英語]
→ see **house**

close-up /klo͟ʊsʌp/ (close-ups) N-COUNT 可算名詞 A **close-up** is a photograph or a picture in a film that shows a lot of detail because it is taken very near to the subject. クローズアップ（接写）□*...a close-up of Harvey's face.* ハービーの顔のクローズアップ. ● PHRASE 句 If you see something **in close-up**, you see it in great detail in a photograph or piece of film which has been taken very near to the subject. クローズアップで

clos|ing /klo͟ʊzɪŋ/ (closings) **1** ADJ 形容詞 The **closing** part of an activity or period of time is the final part of it. 終わりの [ADJ n] □*He entered the army in the closing stages of the war.* 彼は戦争の末期に軍に入隊した. **2** N-COUNT 可算名詞 A **closing** is the final meeting between the buyer and seller of a property. 所有権譲渡のための不動産売買の最終会合

clos|ing price (closing prices) N-COUNT 可算名詞 On the stock exchange, the **closing price** of a share is its price at the end of a day's business. 終値 [BUSINESS 実業] □*The price is slightly above yesterday's closing price.* 昨日の終値より少し値をあげている.

clo|sure /klo͟ʊʒər/ (closures) **1** N-VAR 可変性名詞 The **closure** of a place such as a business or factory is the permanent ending of the work or activity there. 閉鎖 □*...the closure of the steel mill.* 製鉄所の閉鎖. □*...protests against the proposed pit closures.* 炭坑閉鎖案に対する抗議. **2** N-COUNT 可算名詞 The **closure** of a road or border is the blocking of it in order to prevent people from using it. 封鎖

❏ *Overnight storms left many streets underwater and forced the closure of road tunnels in the city.* 昨夜の嵐で多くの通りが冠水し，市内の道路トンネルは通行止めになった． ❸ N-UNCOUNT 不可算名詞 If someone achieves **closure**, they succeed in accepting something bad that has happened to them. 気持の整理 [mainly AM 主に米国英語] ❏ *I asked McKean if the reunion was meant to achieve closure.* 再会は気持の整理をつけるためだったのか，と私はマッキーンに尋ねた．

clot /klɒt/ (clots, clotting, clotted) ❶ N-COUNT 可算名詞 A **clot** is a sticky lump that forms when blood dries up or becomes thick. 血の塊 ❏ *He needed emergency surgery to remove a blood clot from his brain.* 彼は脳の血栓を除去する緊急手術が必要だった． ❷ V-I 自動詞 When blood **clots**, it becomes thick and forms a lump. 凝固する [自動詞] ❏ *The patient's blood refused to clot.* 患者の血液はどうしても凝固しなかった．

cloth /klɔθ/ (cloths) ❶ N-MASS 質量名詞 **Cloth** is fabric which is made by weaving or knitting a substance such as cotton, wool, silk, or nylon. Cloth is used especially for making clothes. 布地 ❏ *She began cleaning the wound with a piece of cloth.* 彼女は布で傷口をふき始めた． ❷ N-COUNT 可算名詞 A **cloth** is a piece of cloth which you use for a particular purpose, such as cleaning something or covering something. （特定の用途の）布 ❏ *Clean the surface with a damp cloth.* 表面は湿らせたふきんでふきなさい．

clothed /kloʊðd/ ADJ 形容詞 If you are **clothed in** a certain way, you are dressed in that way. 服を着た ❏ *He lay down on the bed fully clothed.* 彼は服を着たままベッドに横たわっていた． ❏ *She was clothed in a flowered dress.* 彼女は花柄のドレスを身に着けていた．

clothes /kloʊz, kloʊðz/ N-PLURAL 複数名詞 **Clothes** are the things that people wear, such as shirts, coats, pants, and dresses. 衣服 ❏ *Moira walked upstairs to change her clothes.* モイラは服を着替えに上の階に上がった．

> Note that there is no singular form of **clothes**, so you cannot talk about "a clothe." In informal English, you can talk about a **garment**. **Clothing** is a more formal word that is used to refer to a person's clothes. ❏ *He took off his wet clothing. ...prison clothing.* You can refer to a **garment** less formally as a **piece of clothing**, an **article of clothing**, or an **item of clothing**, but in ordinary conversation you usually just name the piece of clothing you are talking about. **Cloth** is material made from something such as cotton, wool, or nylon. A **cloth** is a piece of **cloth** that is used, for example, for cleaning or wiping things. Note that the plural, **cloths**, is used only for this sense. For the different verbs associated with clothes, see the note at **wear**.

clothes|pin /kloʊzpɪn, kloʊðz-/ (clothespins) N-COUNT 可算名詞 A **clothespin** is a small device which you use to fasten clothes to a clothesline. 洗濯ばさみ [AM 米国英語]

cloth|ing /kloʊðɪŋ/ N-UNCOUNT 不可算名詞 **Clothing** is the things that people wear. 衣料品 ❏ *Some locals offered food and clothing to the refugees.* 難民に食糧や衣料品を差し入れる地元民もいる． ❏ *...the clothing industry.* 衣料品産業．
→ see Picture Dictionary: **clothing**
→ see dry-cleaning

cloud /klaʊd/ (clouds, clouding, clouded) ❶ N-VAR 可変性名詞 A **cloud** is a mass of water vapor that floats in the sky. Clouds are usually white or gray in color. 雲 ❏ *...the varied shapes of the clouds.* さまざまな形をした雲． ❏ *...a black mass of cloud.* 黒い大きな雲． ❷ N-COUNT 可算名詞 A **cloud** of something such as smoke or dust is a mass of it floating in the air. 雲状のもの ❏ *The hens darted away on all sides, raising a cloud of dust.* めんどりが四方八方に駆け出し，砂ぼこりが上がった． ❸ V-T 他動詞 If you say that something **clouds** your view of a situation, you mean that it makes you unable to understand the situation or judge it properly. 曇らせる [他動詞] ❏ *Perhaps anger had clouded his vision, perhaps his judgment had been faulty.* ひょっとして怒りのため洞察力が鈍っていたのかもしれないし，彼の判断に問題があったのかもしれない． ❹ V-T 他動詞 If you say that something **clouds** a situation, you mean that it makes it unpleasant. 暗くする [他動詞] ❏ *The atmosphere has already been clouded by the party's anger at the media.* メディアに対する党の怒り

で，すでに暗い空気が漂っている． ❺ V-T/V-I 他動詞/自動詞 If glass **clouds** or if moisture **clouds** it, tiny drops of water cover the glass, making it difficult to see through. 曇らせる [他動詞], 曇る [自動詞] ❏ *The mirror clouded beside her cheek.* 彼女の頬の側の鏡が曇った．
→ see water

Word Partnership   *cloud* は次の語句と使われる：

| ADJ. | **black/dark** cloud, **white** cloud ❶ |
| N. | cloud **of dust**, cloud **of smoke** ❷ |

cloudy /klaʊdi/ (cloudier, cloudiest) ❶ ADJ 形容詞 If it is **cloudy**, there are a lot of clouds in the sky. 曇りの ❏ *...a windy, cloudy day.* 風の強い，曇った日． ❷ ADJ 形容詞 A **cloudy** liquid is less clear than it should be. 濁った ❏ *If the water's cloudy like that, it'll be hard to see anyone underwater.* 水がそんな具合に濁っていたら，水中に人がいても見えにくいだろう．

clout /klaʊt/ (clouts, clouting, clouted) ❶ V-T 他動詞 If you **clout** someone, you hit them. 殴る [他動詞] ❏ *Rachel clouted him.* レイチェルは彼をたたいた． [INFORMAL くだけた] ● N-COUNT 可算名詞 **Clout** is also a noun. 殴打 ❏ *I was half tempted to give one of them a clout myself.* 私はそのうちの1人を自ら殴りそうになった． ❷ N-UNCOUNT 不可算名詞 A person or institution that has **clout** has influence and power. 影響力 [INFORMAL くだけた] ❏ *Mr. Sutherland may have the clout needed to push the two trading giants into a deal.* サザーランド氏には貿易大手2社の合意を成立させるのに必要な影響力があるかもしれない．

clove /kloʊv/ (cloves) ❶ N-VAR 可変性名詞 **Cloves** are small dried flower buds used as a spice. クローブ ❏ *...chicken soup with cloves.* クローブ入りのチキンスープ． ❷ N-COUNT 可算名詞 A **clove of** garlic is one of the sections of a garlic bulb. （ニンニクの）1片

clown /klaʊn/ (clowns, clowning, clowned) ❶ N-COUNT 可算名詞 A **clown** is a performer in a circus who wears funny clothes and bright makeup, and does silly things in order to make people laugh. 道化師 ❷ N-COUNT 可算名詞 If you say that someone is a **clown**, you mean that they say funny things or do silly things to amuse people. 道化役 ❏ *Chapman was the family clown, with a knack for making a joke out of any situation.* チャップマンは家族のおどけ役で，どんな場面でもジョークを言うコツを心得ていた． ❸ V-I 自動詞 If you **clown**, you do silly things in order to make people laugh. 道化役をする [自動詞] ❏ *He clowned with John Belushi and Bill Murray in National Lampoon shows.* 彼は『ナショナル・ランプーン』の番組でジョン・ベルーシやビル・マレーと一緒に馬鹿をやっていた． ● PHRASAL VERB 句動詞 **Clown around** means the same as **clown**. 道化役をする ❏ *Bev made her laugh, the way she was always clowning around.* ベブはいつもおどけてみせるやり方で，彼女を笑わせた．

club /klʌb/ (clubs, clubbing, clubbed) ❶ N-COUNT 可算名詞 A **club** is an organization of people interested in a particular activity or subject who usually meet on a regular basis. クラブ ❏ *...the Young Republicans Club.* 共和党青年部． ❏ *...a youth club.* 青少年クラブ． ❷ N-COUNT 可算名詞 A **club** is a place where the members of a club meet. クラブ（会館）❏ *I stopped in at the club for a drink.* 私は一杯飲みたくてクラブに立ち寄った． ❸ N-COUNT 可算名詞 A **club** is a team which competes in sports competitions. （スポーツの）チーム ❏ *...the New York Yankees baseball club.* ニューヨーク・ヤンキース球団 ❹ N-COUNT 可算名詞 A **club** is the same as a **nightclub**. ナイトクラブ ❏ *It's a big dance hit in the clubs.* クラブでビッグなダンスヒット音楽だ． ❺ N-COUNT 可算名詞 A **club** is a long, thin, metal stick with a piece of wood or metal at one end that you use to hit the ball in golf. ゴルフクラブ ❏ *...a six-iron club.* 6番アイアン． ❻ N-COUNT 可算名詞 A **club** is a thick, heavy stick that can be used as a weapon. こん棒 ❏ *Men armed with knives and clubs attacked his home.* ナイフやこん棒を所持した男達が彼の家を襲撃した． ❼ V-T 他動詞 To **club** a person or animal means to hit them hard with a thick heavy stick or a similar weapon. 打つ [他動詞] ❏ *Two thugs clubbed him with baseball bats.* 暴漢2人が彼をバットで殴打した． ❽ N-UNCOUNT-COLL 集合的不可算名詞 **Clubs** is one of the four suits in a pack of playing cards. Each card in the

---

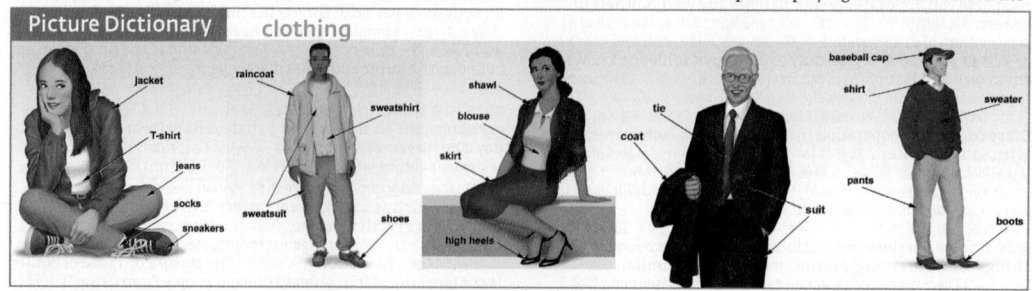

Picture Dictionary   clothing

jacket, T-shirt, jeans, socks, sneakers, raincoat, sweatshirt, black, sweatsuit, shoes, shawl, blouse, skirt, high heels, tie, coat, shirt, sweater, pants, boots, baseball cap, suit

suit is marked with one or more black symbols: Đ. (トランプの) クラブ札 □…the ace of clubs. クラブの1（エース）●N-COUNT 可算名詞 A **club** is a playing card of this suit. (トランプの) クラブ □The next player discarded a club. 次のプレーヤーはクラブを捨てた.
→ see **golf**

club|house /klʌbhaʊs/ (**clubhouses**) N-COUNT 可算名詞 A **clubhouse** is a place where the members of a club, especially a sports club, meet. クラブハウス

clue /klu/ (**clues**) **1** N-COUNT 可算名詞 A **clue to** a problem or mystery is something that helps you to find the answer to it. 糸口 □Geneticists in Canada have discovered a clue to the puzzle of why our cells get old and die. ヒトの細胞はなぜ老化し死ぬのかという謎を解く糸口をカナダの遺伝学研究チームが発見した. **2** N-COUNT 可算名詞 A **clue** is an object or piece of information that helps someone solve a crime. 手掛かり □The vital clue to the killer's identity was his nickname, Peanuts. 殺人者の身元を解く重要な手掛かりは, 彼のニックネームのピーナッツだった. **3** N-COUNT 可算名詞 A **clue** in a crossword or game is information which is given to help you to find the answer to a question. ヒント □Give me a clue. What's it begin with? ヒントをちょうだい. 最初の文字は何なの. **4** PHRASE 句 If you **haven't a clue** about something, you do not know anything about it or you have no idea what to do about it. 見当がつかない [INFORMAL くだけた] □I haven't a clue what I'll give Carl for his birthday next year. 来年のカールの誕生日プレゼントを何にしたらいいのか, 全然見当がつかないわ.

clump /klʌmp/ (**clumps**) **1** N-COUNT 可算名詞 A **clump of** things such as trees or plants is a small group of them growing together. 木立, やぶ □…a clump of trees bordering a side road. 側道を縁どる木立. **2** N-COUNT 可算名詞 A **clump** of things such as wires or hair is a group of them collected together in one place. ひとまとまり □I was combing my hair and it was just falling out in clumps. 髪をといていたら, ごそっと抜けたのね.

clum|sy /klʌmzi/ (**clumsier, clumsiest**) **1** ADJ 形容詞 A **clumsy** person moves or handles things in a careless, awkward way, often so that things are knocked over or broken. 不器用な □I'd never seen a clumsier, less coordinated boxer. これほど不器用で不器用なボクサーは見たことがなかった. ●**clum|si|ly** /klʌmzɪli/ ADV 副詞 [ADV with v] ぎこちなく □In the sudden pitch darkness, she scrambled clumsily toward the ladder. 暗闇の中, 彼女はぎこちなくはしごの方にはって行った. ●**clum|si|ness** N-UNCOUNT 不可算名詞 ぎこちなさ □His clumsiness and ineptitude with the wooden sticks did not embarrass him. ばちさばきが下手でもぎこちなくても彼はどぎまぎしなかった. **2** ADJ 形容詞 A **clumsy** action or statement is not skillful or is likely to upset people. 気の利かない □The action seemed a clumsy attempt to topple the government. その行動は政府を打倒するには下手な試みに思われた. ●**clum|si|ly** ADV 副詞 要領悪く □If the matter were handled clumsily, it could cost Miriam her life. 事の扱いを誤ると, ミリアムの命を失いかねない. ●**clum|si|ness** N-UNCOUNT 不可算名詞 不手際 □I was ashamed at my clumsiness and insensitivity. 私は自分の不手際と配慮のなさを恥じた.

clung /klʌŋ/ **Clung** is the past tense and past participle of **cling**. cling の過去形, 過去分詞形

clus|ter /klʌstər/ (**clusters, clustering, clustered**) **1** N-COUNT 可算名詞 A **cluster of** people or things is a small group of them close together. 集団 □…clusters of men in formal clothes. 正装をした男性の集団. **2** V-I 自動詞 If people **cluster together**, they gather together in a small group. 集まる [自動詞] □The passengers clustered together in small groups. 乗客らはいくつかの集団になった.

clutch /klʌtʃ/ (**clutches, clutching, clutched**) **1** V-T/V-I 他動詞/自動詞 If you **clutch at** something or **clutch** something, you hold it tightly, usually because you are afraid or anxious. しっかりつかむ [他動詞] [自動詞] □I staggered and had to clutch at a chair for support. 私はふらついて, いすにつかまって支えにした. **2** N-PLURAL 複数名詞 If someone is in another person's **clutches**, that person has captured them or has power over them. 手中 □Tony fell into the clutches of an attractive American who introduced him to drugs. トニーは自分に麻薬を覚えさせた魅力的なアメリカ人の手中に落ちた. **3** N-COUNT 可算名詞 In a vehicle, the **clutch** is the pedal that you press before you change gear. クラッチ □Laura let out the clutch and pulled slowly away down the drive. ローラはクラッチから足をはずし, ゆっくりと車道を進み始めた. **4** to **clutch at straws** → see **straw**

clut|ter /klʌtər/ (**clutters, cluttering, cluttered**) **1** N-UNCOUNT 不可算名詞 **Clutter** is a lot of things in a messy state, especially things that are not useful or necessary. 散乱物 □Caroline prefers her countertops to be clear of clutter. キャロラインはカウンターの上が乱雑でないきれいな状態を好む. **2** V-T 他動詞 If things or people **clutter** a place, they fill it in a messy way. 取り散らかす [他動詞] □Empty soft-drink cans lie everywhere. They clutter the desks and are strewn across the floor. 飲み物の空き缶があちこちにある. 机の上に散らかり, 床中にころがっている. ●PHRASAL VERB 句動詞 **Clutter up** means the same as **clutter**. 取り散らかす □The vehicles cluttered up the parking lot. 車は駐車場を雑然と埋めつくした.

cm cm is the written abbreviation for **centimeter** or **centimeters**. センチメートルの略号 □His height had increased by 2.5 cm. 彼は2.5センチ背が伸びていた.

c/o You write **c/o** before an address on an envelope when you are sending it to someone who is staying or working at that address, often for only a short time. **c/o** is an abbreviation for "care of." 一様方

Co. Co. is used as an abbreviation for **company** when it is part of the name of an organization. 社名の一部として使われる略号で『一会社』を意味する □…the Blue Star Amusement Co. ブルー・スター・アミューズメント会社. [BUSINESS 実業]

coach /koʊtʃ/ (**coaches, coaching, coached**) **1** N-COUNT 可算名詞 A **coach** is someone who trains a person or team of people in a particular sport. コーチ □Tony Woodcock has joined the team as coach. トニー・ウッドコックはコーチとしてチームに加入した. **2** N-COUNT 可算名詞 A **coach** is a person who is in charge of a sports team. 監督 [mainly AM 主に米国英語] □…the women's soccer coach at Rowan University. ローワン大学の女子サッカー部監督 **3** N-COUNT 可算名詞 A **coach** is someone who gives people special teaching in a particular subject, especially in order to prepare them for an examination. 指導者, 家庭教師 □What you need is a drama coach. あなたに必要なのは演劇の先生です. **4** N-COUNT 可算名詞 A **coach** is an enclosed vehicle with four wheels which is pulled by horses, and in which people used to travel. Coaches are still used for ceremonial events in some countries, such as Britain. 4輪馬車 □…a coach pulled by six black horses. 6頭の黒馬がひく馬車 **5** N-COUNT 可算名詞 A **coach** is a large, comfortable bus that carries passengers on long trips. 長距離バス [BRIT 英国英語] [also "by" N] [AM **bus** 米国英語 **bus**] **6** N-COUNT 可算名詞 A **coach** is one of the separate sections of a train that carries passengers. 客車 [BRIT 英国英語; AM **car, train car** 米国英語 **car, train car**] **7** V-T 他動詞 When someone **coaches** a person or a team, they help them to become better at a particular sport. コーチする [他動詞] □After her pro playing career, she coached a golf team in San Jose. プロ生活の後, 彼女はサンノゼのゴルフチームのコーチを務めていた. **8** V-T 他動詞 If you **coach** someone, you give them special teaching in a particular subject, especially in order to prepare them for an examination. 指導する, 家庭教師をする [他動詞] □He gently coached me in French. 彼はやさしくフランス語を指導してくれた.

coal /koʊl/ (**coals**) **1** N-UNCOUNT 不可算名詞 **Coal** is a hard, black substance that is extracted from the ground and burned as fuel. 石炭 □Gas is cheaper than coal. ガスは石炭より安い. **2** N-PLURAL 複数名詞 **Coals** are burning pieces of coal. 炭火 □The iron teakettle was hissing splendidly over live coals. 炭火にかけられたやかんがシューシューと激しく沸騰していた.
→ see **energy**

coa|li|tion /koʊəlɪʃən/ (**coalitions**) **1** N-COUNT 可算名詞 A **coalition** is a government consisting of people from two or more political parties. 連立政権 □Since June the country has had a coalition government. その国には6月から連立政権が存在する. **2** N-COUNT 可算名詞 A **coalition** is a group consisting of people from different political or social groups who are cooperating to achieve a particular aim. 連合 □He had been opposed by a coalition of about 50 civil rights, women's, and Latino organizations. 彼は, 公民権運動, 女性, ヒスパニック系など約50の団体から成る連合組織から反対を受けていた.

coarse /kɔrs/ (**coarser, coarsest**) **1** ADJ 形容詞 **Coarse** things have a rough texture because they consist of thick threads or large pieces. きめの粗い □…a jacket made of very coarse cloth. きめの粗い生地で仕立てたジャケット. ●**coarse|ly** ADV 副詞 粗く □…coarsely ground black pepper. 粗びきの黒こしょう. **2** ADJ 形容詞 If you describe someone as **coarse**, you mean that he or she talks and behaves in a rude and offensive way. 粗野な [DISAPPROVAL 不賛成] □The soldiers did not bother to moderate their coarse humor in her presence. 彼女がいるからといって兵士たちは下品なユーモアを控えるようなことはしなかった. ●**coarse|ly** ADV 副詞 [ADV with v] 粗野に □The women laughed coarsely at some vulgar joke. 女性たちは低俗な冗談で下品に笑った.
→ see **coffee**

coast /koʊst/ (**coasts, coasting, coasted**) **1** N-COUNT 可算名詞 The **coast** is an area of land that is next to the sea. 海岸 □Campsites are usually situated along the coast, close to beaches. キャンプ場は海水浴場付近の海岸近くにある場合が多い.

You can use **beach, coast,** and **shore** to talk about the piece of land beside a stretch of water. The **coast** is the area of land that lies alongside the ocean. You may be referring just to the land close to the ocean, or to a wider area that extends further inland. A **beach** is a flat area of sand or pebbles next to the ocean. The **shore** is the area of land along the edge of the ocean, a lake, or a wide river.

2 V-I 自動詞 If a vehicle **coasts** somewhere, it continues to move there with the motor switched off, or without being pushed or

pedaled. 惰性で進む[自動詞] ❑He pushed in the clutch and coasted to a halt. 彼はクラッチを踏んで、止まるまで勢いで走った.
→ see **beach**

coast|al /koʊstᵊl/ ADJ 形容詞 **Coastal** is used to refer to things that are in the sea or on the land near a coast. 沿岸の[ADJ n] ❑Local radio stations serving coastal areas often broadcast forecasts for yachtsmen. 沿岸地方に放送するローカルラジオ局は、ヨット愛好家向けの天気予報をよく放送する.

coast guard (**coast guards**) also **Coast Guard** or **coastguard** N-COUNT 可算名詞 The **coast guard** is a part of a country's military forces and is responsible for protecting the coast, carrying out rescues, and doing police work along the coast. 沿岸警備隊[AM 米国英語] ❑The U.S. Coast Guard says it rescued more than 100 Haitian refugees. 米国沿岸警備隊によると、100人以上のハイチ難民を救助したとのことだ. N-COUNT 可算名詞 A **coast guard** is a member of the coast guard. 沿岸警備隊員[● AM 米国英語] ❑The boat was intercepted by U.S. Coast Guards. 船は米国沿岸警備隊員によってだ捕された.

coast|line /koʊstlaɪn/ (**coastlines**) N-VAR 可変性名詞 A country's **coastline** is the outline of its coast. 海岸線 ❑This is some of the most exposed coastline in the world. ここは世界で最も波風にさらされる海岸線の一つです.

coat /koʊt/ (**coats, coating, coated**) ■ N-COUNT 可算名詞 A **coat** is a piece of clothing with long sleeves which you wear over your other clothes when you go outside. コート ❑He turned off the television, put on his coat, and walked out. 彼はテレビを消し、コートを着て出て行った. ■ N-COUNT 可算名詞 An animal's **coat** is the fur or hair on its body. (動物の) 毛 ❑Vitamin B6 is great for improving the condition of dogs' and horses' coats. ビタミンB6は犬や馬の毛づやの改善に優れた効果を発揮する. ■ N-COUNT 可算名詞 A **coat of** paint or varnish is a thin layer of it on a surface. 表面塗装 ❑The front door needs a new coat of paint. 玄関のドアにペンキを塗り直す必要がある. ■ V-T 他動詞 If you **coat** something **with** a substance or **in** a substance, you cover it with a thin layer of the substance. 表面を覆う[他動詞] ❑Coat the fish with seasoned flour. 魚に味付けした小麦粉をまぶしてください.
→ see **clothing, painting**

-coated /koʊtɪd/ ■ COMB IN ADJ 形容詞の複 **-coated** combines with color adjectives such as "white" and "red," or words for types of coat like "fur," to form adjectives that describe someone as wearing a certain sort of coat. 一の上着を着た[ADJ n] ❑At the top of the stairs stood the white-coated doctors. 階段の上には白衣を着た医者たちが立っていた. ■ COMB IN ADJ 形容詞の複合 **-coated** combines with names of substances such as "sugar" and "plastic" to form adjectives that describe something as being covered with a thin layer of that substance. 一でコーティングされた ❑...chocolate-coated strawberries. チョコレートでコーティングされたいちご.

coat hang|er (**coat hangers**) N-COUNT 可算名詞 A **coat hanger** is a curved piece of wood, metal, or plastic that you hang a piece of clothing on. ハンガー

coat|ing /koʊtɪŋ/ (**coatings**) N-COUNT 可算名詞 A **coating of** a substance is a thin layer of it spread over a surface. 一の覆い ❑Under the coating of dust and cobwebs, he discovered a fine French Louis XVI clock. 彼は、ほこりやくもの巣に埋もれたルイ16世の美しい時計を見つけた.

coax /koʊks/ (**coaxes, coaxing, coaxed**) ■ V-T 他動詞 If you **coax** someone **into** doing something, you gently try to persuade them to do it. 説得する[他動詞] ❑After lunch, she watched, listened and coaxed Bobby into talking about himself. 昼食後、彼女はボビーの様子をみて、耳を傾けて、自分のことを話すよう促した. ■ V-T 他動詞 If you **coax** something such as information out of someone, you gently persuade them to give it to you. 引き出す[他動詞] ❑The officer spoke yesterday of her role in trying to coax vital information from the young victim. 警官は昨日、若い被害者から重要な情報を引き出そうとして自分の役割について語った.

cob|ble /kɒbᵊl/ (**cobbles, cobbling, cobbled**) N-COUNT 可算名詞 **Cobbles** are the same as **cobblestones**. (鉄道や道路用の) 玉石 [mainly BRIT 主に英国英語]
▶ **cobble together** PHRASAL VERB 句動詞 If you say that someone has **cobbled** something **together**, you mean that they have made or produced it roughly or quickly. 急ごしらえをする[DISAPPROVAL 不賛成] ❑The group had cobbled together a few decent songs. グループはまずまずの曲を数曲、なんとかつくった.

cobble|stone /kɒbᵊlstoʊn/ (**cobblestones**) N-COUNT 可算名詞 **Cobblestones** are stones with a rounded upper surface which used to be used for making streets. 左岸の狭い、石畳の道 ❑...the narrow, cobblestone streets of the Left Bank.

co|bra /koʊbrə/ (**cobras**) N-COUNT 可算名詞 A **cobra** is a kind of poisonous snake that can make the skin on the back of its neck into a hood. コブラ

cob|web /kɒbwɛb/ (**cobwebs**) N-COUNT 可算名詞 A **cobweb** is the net which a spider makes for catching insects. くもの巣 ❑The windows are cracked and covered in cobwebs. 窓はひび割れ、くもの巣が張っている.

co|caine /koʊkeɪn/ N-UNCOUNT 不可算名詞 **Cocaine** is a powerful drug which some people take for pleasure, but which they can become addicted to. コカイン

cock /kɒk/ (**cocks**) N-COUNT 可算名詞 A **cock** is an adult male chicken. おんどり[mainly BRIT 主に英国英語; AM **rooster** 米国英語 **rooster**]

cock|a|ma|mie /kɒkəmeɪmi/ ADJ 形容詞 If you describe something as **cockamamie**, you mean that it is ridiculous or silly. ばかばかしい[AM 米国英語, INFORMAL くだけた] [usu ADJ n] ❑...some cockamamie story about being late. 遅刻に対するばかばかしい言い訳.

cock|pit /kɒkpɪt/ (**cockpits**) N-COUNT 可算名詞 In an airplane or racing car, the **cockpit** is the part where the pilot or driver sits. 操縦室、操縦席

cock|roach /kɒkroʊtʃ/ (**cockroaches**) N-COUNT 可算名詞 A **cockroach** is a large brown insect that is sometimes found in warm places or where food is kept. ゴキブリ

cock|tail /kɒkteɪl/ (**cocktails**) ■ N-COUNT 可算名詞 A **cocktail** is an alcoholic drink which contains several ingredients. カクテル ❑On arrival, guests are offered wine or a champagne cocktail. 到着されましたら、ワインかシャンパンカクテルをお召し上がりいただけます. ■ N-COUNT 可算名詞 A **cocktail** is a mixture of a number of different things, especially ones that do not go together well. 混合物 ❑The court was told she had taken a cocktail of drugs and alcohol. 裁判では、彼女が薬物とアルコールを混ぜて飲んでいたとの証言があった.

cocky /kɒki/ (**cockier, cockiest**) ADJ 形容詞 Someone who is **cocky** is so confident and sure of their abilities that they annoy other people. うぬぼれた[INFORMAL くだけた, DISAPPROVAL 不賛成] ❑He was a little bit cocky when he was about 11 because he was winning everything. 彼は11歳のころ何においても右に出るものがなかったため、うぬぼれぎみだった.

co|coa /koʊkoʊ/ ■ N-UNCOUNT 不可算名詞 **Cocoa** is a brown powder made from the seeds of a tropical tree. It is used in making chocolate. カカオ ❑The Ivory Coast became the world's leading cocoa producer. コートジボワールは世界有数のカカオの産地になった. ■ N-UNCOUNT 不可算名詞 **Cocoa** is a hot drink made from cocoa powder and milk or water. ココア ❑...a cup of cocoa. 1杯のココア.

coco|nut /koʊkənʌt/ (**coconuts**) ■ N-COUNT 可算名詞 A **coconut** is a very large nut with a hairy shell, which has white flesh and milky juice inside it. ココナツ ❑...the smell of roasted meats mingled with spices, coconut oil, and ripe tropical fruits. スパイス、ココナツ油、熟したトロピカルフルーツと一体になった焼肉の香り. ■ N-UNCOUNT 不可算名詞 **Coconut** is the white flesh of a coconut. ココナツの果肉 ❑Put 2 cups of grated coconut into a blender or food processor. すりおろしたココナツの果肉2カップをミキサーかフードプロセッサーに入れます.

co|coon /kəkuːn/ (**cocoons, cocooning, cocooned**) ■ N-COUNT 可算名詞 A **cocoon** is a covering of silky threads that the larvae of moths and other insects make for themselves before they grow into adults. 繭 ❑...like a butterfly emerging from a cocoon. 繭から出てくるちょうのように. ■ N-COUNT 可算名詞 If you are in a **cocoon** of something, you are wrapped up in it or surrounded by it. 覆い ❑He stood there in a cocoon of golden light. 彼は金色の光に包まれてそこに立っていた. ■ N-COUNT 可算名詞 If you are living in a **cocoon**, you are in an environment in which you feel protected and safe, and sometimes isolated from everyday life. 居心地がよく安全だと感じる状態や場所のこと ❑...her innocent desire to envelop her beloved in a cocoon of love. 最愛の人を愛で包みたいという彼女の無邪気な願い. ■ V-T 他動詞 If something **cocoons** you from something, it protects you or isolates you from it. 守る[他動詞] ❑There is nowhere to hide when things go wrong, no organization to cocoon you from blame. 何か悪いことが起きても逃げ場はないし、あなたを非難から守ってくれる組織もない.

cod /kɒd/ (**cod**)

The plural can be either **cod** or **cods**.

複数は **cod** か **cods** のいずれかである.

N-VAR 可変性名詞 **Cod** are a type of large edible fish. タラ ● N-UNCOUNT 不可算名詞 **Cod** is this fish eaten as food. 食べ物としてのタラ ❑A Catalan speciality is to serve salt cod cold. カタロニアの名物料理は塩漬けタラの冷製です.
→ see **fish**

Word Link   cod ≈ writing : **cod**e, en**cod**e, de**cod**e

code /koʊd/ (**codes, coding, coded**) ■ N-COUNT 可算名詞 A **code** is a set of rules about how people should behave or about how something must be done. 規則 ❑...Article 159 of the state's

penal code. 州刑法第159条. **2** N-COUNT 可算名詞 A **code** is a system of replacing the words in a message with other words or symbols, so that nobody can understand it unless they know the system. 暗号 [also "in" N] ❑ *They used elaborate secret codes, as when the names of trees stood for letters.* 彼らは、木の名前が文字を表すといった手のこんだ暗号を使っていた. **3** N-COUNT 可算名詞 A **code** is a group of numbers or letters which is used to identify something, such as a mailing address or part of a telephone system. 符号 ❑ *Callers dialing the wrong area code will not get through.* 市外局番を間違えるとつながらない. **4** N-COUNT 可算名詞 A **code** is any system of signs or symbols that has a meaning. コード ❑ *It will need other chips to reconvert the digital code back into normal TV signals.* デジタルコードを通常のテレビ信号に再変換するには別のチップが必要でしょう. **5** N-COUNT 可算名詞 The genetic **code** of a person, animal, or plant is the information contained in DNA which determines the structure and function of cells, and the inherited characteristics of all living things. コード ❑ *Scientists provided the key to understanding the genetic code that determines every bodily feature.* 科学者はあらゆる身体的特徴を決定する遺伝子コードを理解するかぎを提供した. **6** V-T 他動詞 To **code** something means to give it a code or to mark it with its code. コード化する [他動詞] ❑ *He devised a way of coding every statement uniquely.* 彼はどの文も固有のコードに変換する方法を考案した. **7** N-UNCOUNT 不可算名詞 Computer **code** is a system or language for expressing information and instructions in a form which can be understood by a computer. コード [COMPUTING コンピューティング] ❑ *She began writing software code at the age of nine.* 彼女は9歳でコンピュータソフトのコードを書き始めた. **8** → see also **bar code, postcode, zip code**

Word Partnership	code は次の語句と使われる：
N.	code of conduct, dress code, code of ethics **1**
	code name, code word **2**
ADJ.	secret code **2**

cod|ed /koʊdɪd/ **1** ADJ 形容詞 **Coded** messages have words or symbols which represent other words, so that the message is secret unless you know the system behind the code. 暗号化された ❑ *In a coded telephone warning, the police were told four bombs had been planted in the area.* 暗号による電話警告で地区に4つの爆弾が仕掛けられたと警察は通報を受けた. **2** ADJ 形容詞 If someone is using **coded** language, they are expressing their opinion in an indirect way, usually because that opinion is likely to offend people. 婉曲な ❑ *They have sent barely coded messages to the secretary of education endorsing this criticism.* 彼らはこの批判を支持して遠回しとは言えないメッセージを教育相に送った. **3** ADJ 形容詞 **Coded** electronic signals use a binary system of digits which can be decoded by an appropriate machine. コード化された [TECHNICAL 技術的] [ADJ n] ❑ *The coded signal is received by satellite dishes.* コード化された信号は衛星アンテナが受信する.

cod|ing /koʊdɪŋ/ N-UNCOUNT 不可算名詞 **Coding** is a method of making something easy to recognize or distinct, for example by coloring it. コード付加 ❑ *...a color coding that will ensure easy reference for potential users.* ユーザーが容易に参照できるようにカラーコードをつける.

co|erce /koʊɜrs/ (**coerces, coercing, coerced**) V-T 他動詞 If you **coerce** someone **into** doing something, you make them do it, although they do not want to. 強要する [他動詞] ❑ *Potter had argued that the government coerced him into pleading guilty.* ポッターは、政府が彼に有罪を認めるよう強要したと主張した. [FORMAL 形式ばった]

co|er|cion /koʊɜrʃ³n/ N-UNCOUNT 不可算名詞 **Coercion** is the act or process of persuading someone forcefully to do something that they do not want to do. 強制 ❑ *It was vital that the elections should be free of coercion or intimidation.* 選挙は強制や脅迫が行われないことが絶対条件だ.

cof|fee /kɔfi/ (**coffees**) **1** N-UNCOUNT 不可算名詞 **Coffee** is a hot drink made with water and ground or powdered coffee beans. コーヒー ❑ *Would you like some coffee?* コーヒーはいかがですか. ● N-COUNT 可算名詞 A **coffee** is a cup of coffee. (カップ1杯分の) コーヒー ❑ *I made a coffee.* コーヒーを1杯入れました. **2** N-MASS 質量名詞 **Coffee** is the roasted beans or powder from which the drink is made. コーヒー (豆、豆をひいた粉) ❑ *Brazil harvested 28 million bags of coffee in 1991, the biggest crop for four years.* 1991年のブラジルのコーヒー豆の収穫高は2800万袋で、4年間で最大だった.
→ see Word Web: **coffee**

cof|fee shop (**coffee shops**) N-COUNT 可算名詞 A **coffee shop** is an informal restaurant that sells food and drink, but not normally alcoholic drinks. 喫茶軽食店
→ see **restaurant**

cof|fin /kɔfɪn/ (**coffins**) **1** N-COUNT 可算名詞 A **coffin** is a box in which a dead body is buried or cremated. ひつぎ **2** PHRASE 句 If you say that one thing is **a nail in the coffin of** another thing, you mean that it will help bring about its end or failure. とどめを刺す ❑ *A fine would be the final nail in the coffin of the airline.* 罰金が果せられればその航空会社には致命傷になるだろう.

cog|nac /koʊnyæk/ (**cognacs**) also **Cognac** N-MASS 質量名詞 **Cognac** is a type of brandy made in the southwest of France. コニャック ❑ *...a bottle of Cognac.* 1本のコニャック ● N-COUNT 可算名詞 A **cognac** is a glass of cognac. (グラス1杯分の) コニャック ❑ *Phillips ordered a cognac.* フィリップはコニャックを1杯注文した.

Word Link	cogn ≈ knowing : *cognitive, recognize, unrecognizable*

cog|ni|tive /kɒgnɪtɪv/ ADJ 形容詞 **Cognitive** means relating to the mental process involved in knowing, learning, and understanding things. 認識の [FORMAL 形式ばった] [ADJ n] ❑ *As children grow older, their cognitive processes become sharper.* 子供は成長するにつれ、認識力が高まっていく.

co|her|ence /koʊhɪərəns, -hɛrəns/ N-UNCOUNT 不可算名詞 **Coherence** is a state or situation in which all the parts or ideas fit together well so that they form a united whole. 一貫性 ❑ *The anthology has a surprising sense of coherence.* その詩集は驚くほど統一がとれている.

Word Link	co ≈ together : *coherent, collaborate, cooperate*

co|her|ent /koʊhɪərənt, -hɛrənt/ **1** ADJ 形容詞 If something is **coherent**, it is well planned, so that it is clear and sensible and all its parts go well with each other. 首尾一貫した ❑ *He has failed to work out a coherent strategy for modernizing the service.* 彼はサービスを近代化する首尾一貫した戦略を立てることに失敗した. ● **co|her|ence** N-UNCOUNT 不可算名詞 首尾一貫性 ❑ *The campaign was widely criticized for making tactical mistakes and for a lack of coherence.* そのキャンペーンは戦略がまずく首尾一貫性がないと大いに批判された. **2** ADJ 形容詞 [v-link ADJ] If someone is **coherent**, they express their thoughts in a clear and calm way, so that other people can understand what they are saying. 理路整然とした ❑ *He's so calm when he answers questions in interviews. I wish I could be that coherent.* 彼は面接でとても沈着冷静に対応する. 私もあのように理路整然としていられればいいのに. ● **co|her|ence** N-UNCOUNT 不可算名詞 理路整然としていること ❑ *This was debated eagerly at first, but with diminishing coherence as the champagne took hold.* この件は、最初は熱心に議論されていたが、シャンパンの酔いが回るにつれ論理性が失われていった.

co|he|sion /koʊhiʒ³n/ N-UNCOUNT 不可算名詞 If there is **cohesion** within a society, organization, or group, the different members fit together well and form a united whole. 結束 ❑ *By 1990, it was clear that the cohesion of the armed forces was rapidly breaking down.* 1990年までに軍の結束力が急速に弱まっていったことは明らかだった.

co|he|sive /koʊhisɪv/ ADJ 形容詞 Something that is **cohesive** consists of parts that fit together well and form a united whole. 結束性のある ❑ *"Daring Adventures" from '86 is a far more cohesive and successful album.* 86年のアルバムでは、『恐れを知らぬ冒険』がとてもよくまとまっていて、できがいい.

coil /kɔɪl/ (**coils**) **1** N-COUNT 可算名詞 A **coil of** rope or wire is

Word Web	coffee

Coffee plants produce a bright red fruit. Inside each fruit is a single coffee **bean**. Workers pick the beans and dry them in the sun. Then the beans are roasted at 550°F* to bring out the true coffee flavor. Next the coffee is **ground**. It can be either **coarse** or **fine**. Many people **brew** coffee by putting it in a **filter** and **pouring** boiling water over it. Some people add **cream** or **sugar**, while others like it **black**. Many people drink coffee in the morning because the **caffeine** in it wakes them up. Others drink **decaffeinated** coffee, or decaf, which has little or no caffeine.

550°F=287.8°C

a length of it that has been wound into a series of loops. （ロープや針金の）輪 □ *Tod shook his head angrily and slung the coil of rope over his shoulder.* トッドは腹立たしげに頭を振り、輪にしたロープを肩にかけた。 **2** N-COUNT 可算名詞 A **coil** is one loop in a series of loops. 一巻き □ *Pythons kill by tightening their coils so that their victim cannot breathe.* ニシキヘビは相手に体を巻きつけて窒息死させる。 **3** N-COUNT 可算名詞 A **coil** is a thick spiral of wire through which an electrical current passes. コイル

coin /kɔɪn/ (**coins, coining, coined**) **1** N-COUNT 可算名詞 A **coin** is a small piece of metal which is used as money. 硬貨 □ *...a few loose coins.* 数枚の小銭。 **2** V-T 他動詞 If you **coin** a word or a phrase, you are the first person to say it. （新しい言葉を）作り出す ［他動詞］ □ *Jaron Lanier coined the term "virtual reality" and pioneered its early development.* ジャロン・ラニアーは「バーチャルリアリティ」という語を生み出し、発展期の草分けとなった。 **3** PHRASE 句 You say **"to coin a phrase"** to show that you realize you are making a pun or using a cliché. 言い方をすれば（しゃれなどを使うときの前置き） □ *Fifty local musicians have, to coin a phrase, banded together to form the Jazz Umbrella.* 50人の地元のミュージシャンが、斬新な表現を使えば、ジャズ・アンブレラを組織した。 **4** PHRASE 句 You use **the other side of the coin** to mention a different aspect of a situation. 逆の見方をすれば □ *On the other side of the coin, there'll be tax incentives for small businesses.* 逆の見方をすれば、小規模企業に対する税制優遇措置が採られるようだ。

→ see **English, money**

coin|age /kɔɪnɪdʒ/ **1** N-UNCOUNT 不可算名詞 **Coinage** is the coins which are used in a country. （集合的に）硬貨 □ *The city produced its own coinage from 1325 to 1864.* 市は独自の硬貨を1325年から1864年に造っていた。 **2** N-UNCOUNT 不可算名詞 **Coinage** is the system of money used in a country. 貨幣制度 □ *In 1783 he secured the adoption of the decimal coinage in Congress.* 1783年に彼は議会で10進貨幣制を採用させた。

co|in|cide /kɔʊɪnsaɪd/ (**coincides, coinciding, coincided**) **1** V-RECIP 相互動詞 If one event **coincides with** another, they happen at the same time. 同時に起こる □ *The exhibition coincides with the 50th anniversary of his death.* 展覧会の日程は彼の没後50年と重なっている。 **2** V-RECIP 相互動詞 If the ideas or interests of two or more people **coincide**, they are the same. 一致する □ *The kids' views on life don't always coincide, but they're not afraid of voicing their opinions.* 子供はみんな同じ人生観を持つとは限らないが、自分の意見を口に出すことを恐れない。

co|in|ci|dence /kɔʊɪnsɪdəns/ (**coincidences**) N-VAR 可変性名詞 A **coincidence** is when two or more similar or related events occur at the same time by chance and without any planning. 偶然の一致 □ *Mr. Berry said the timing was a coincidence and that his decision was unrelated to Mr. Roman's departure.* ベリー氏は、時期が一致したのは偶然で、自分の決定がローマン氏の離脱とは無関係だと述べた。

co|in|ci|den|tal /kɔʊɪnsɪdɛntˀl/ ADJ 形容詞 Something that is **coincidental** is the result of a coincidence and has not been deliberately arranged. 偶然に一致した □ *Any resemblance to actual persons, places, or events is purely coincidental.* 実在の人物、場所、出来事とのいかなる類似も全くの偶然によるものです。

co|in|ci|den|tal|ly /kɔʊɪnsɪdɛntli/ ADV 副詞 You use **coincidentally** when you want to draw attention to a coincidence. 偶然にも □ *Coincidentally, I had once found myself in a similar situation.* 偶然にも、私はかつて同じような状況に置かれたことがあった。

coke /koʊk/ **1** N-UNCOUNT 不可算名詞 **Coke** is a solid, black substance that is produced from coal and is burned as a fuel. コークス □ *...a coke-burning stove.* コークス（を燃料とする）ストーブ。 **2** N-UNCOUNT 不可算名詞 **Coke** is the same as **cocaine**. コカイン ［INFORMAL くだけた］

cola /koʊlə/ (**colas**) N-MASS 質量名詞 **Cola** is a sweet, brown, nonalcoholic carbonated drink. コーラ □ *...a can of cola.* 缶コーラ

Word Link er ≈ more : colder, higher, larger

Word Link est ≈ most : coldest, highest, largest

cold /koʊld/ (**colder, coldest, colds**) **1** ADJ 形容詞 Something that is **cold** has a very low temperature or a lower temperature than is normal or acceptable. 冷たい □ *Rinse the vegetables under cold running water.* 野菜を冷たい流水で洗ってください。 □ *He likes his tea neither too hot nor too cold.* 彼は熱すぎず、冷たすぎない紅茶が好みだ。 ● **cold|ness** N-UNCOUNT 不可算名詞 □ *She complained about the coldness of his hands.* 彼女は彼の手が冷たいと文句を言った。 **2** ADJ 形容詞 If it is **cold**, or if a place is **cold**, the temperature of the air is very low. 寒い □ *It was bitterly cold.* 身を切るような寒さだった。 □ *The house is cold because I can't afford to turn the heat on.* 家が寒いのはヒーターをつける財布の余裕がないからだ。 ● **cold|ness** N-UNCOUNT 不可算名詞 寒さ □ *Within a quarter of an hour, the coldness of the night had gone.* 15分もすると夜の寒さはどこかに消えた。

If you want to emphasize how cold the weather is, you can say that it is **freezing**, especially in winter when there is ice or frost. In summer, if the temperature is below average, you can say that it is **cool**. In general, **cold** suggests a lower temperature than **cool**, and **cool** things may be pleasant or refreshing. □ *A cool breeze swept off the ocean; it was pleasant out there.* If it is very **cold** or too **cool**, you can also say that it is **chilly**.

3 ADJ 形容詞 If you are **cold**, your body is at an unpleasantly low temperature. 寒い □ *I was freezing cold.* 寒くて凍えそうだった。 **4** ADJ 形容詞 **Cold** colors or **cold** light give an impression of coldness. 寒色の □ *Generally, warm colors advance in painting and cold colors recede.* 一般に、絵では暖色系は進出色、寒色系は後退色になります。 **5** ADJ 形容詞 A **cold** person does not show much emotion, especially affection, and therefore seems unfriendly and unsympathetic. If someone's voice is **cold**, they speak in an unfriendly, unsympathetic way. 冷淡な ［DISAPPROVAL 不賛成］ □ *I saw a cold, unfeeling woman she was.* 冷ややかで冷淡で、無情な人なのでしょう。 ● **cold|ly** ADV 副詞 冷淡に □ *"I'll see you in the morning," Hugh said coldly.* 「では朝にお会いしましょう」とヒューは冷たく言った。 ● **His coldness angered her.** 彼の冷淡さに彼女は腹が立った。 **6** N-UNCOUNT 不可算名詞 ［also "the" N］ Cold weather or low temperatures can be referred to as **the cold**. □ *He must have come inside to get out of the cold.* 彼は寒さから逃れるために中に入ってきたに違いない。 **7** in **cold blood** → see **blood** **8** to get **cold feet** → see **foot** **9** to blow **hot and cold** → see **hot** **10** to **pour cold water** on something → see **water** **11** N-COUNT 可算名詞 If you have a **cold**, you have a mild, very common illness which makes you sneeze a lot and gives you a sore throat or a cough. 風邪 □ *I had a pretty bad cold.* かなり悪い風邪をひいた。 **12** PHRASE 句 If you **catch cold**, or **catch a cold**, you become ill with a cold. 風邪をひく □ *Let's dry our hair so we don't catch cold.* 風邪をひかないように髪をかわかそう。 **13** PHRASE 句 If someone is **out cold**, they are unconscious or sleeping very heavily. 意識を失って □ *She was out cold but still breathing.* 彼女は意識はなかったが呼吸はしていた。

Thesaurus   cold また次を参照：

ADJ.   bitter, chilly, cool, freezing, frozen, raw; (ant.) hot, warm **1 2**
       cool, distant; (ant.) friendly, warm **5**

Word Partnership   cold は次の語句と使われる：

N.   cold **air**, **dark and** cold, cold **night**, cold **rain**, cold **water**, cold **weather**, cold **wind 1 2**
ADV. **bitterly** cold **1 2**
      freezing cold **1 - 3**
V.   **feel** cold, **get** cold **1 - 3**
      catch/get a cold **8**

cold-blooded 1 ADJ 形容詞 Someone who is **cold-blooded** does not show any pity or emotion. 冷血な ［DISAPPROVAL 不賛成］ □ *...a cold-blooded murderer.* 冷血な殺人犯。 **2** ADJ 形容詞 **Cold-blooded** animals have a body temperature that changes according to the surrounding temperature. Reptiles, for example, are cold-blooded. 変温の（動物）

cold call (**cold calls, cold calling, cold called**) **1** N-COUNT 可算名詞 If someone makes a **cold call**, they telephone or visit someone they have never contacted, without making an appointment, in order to try and sell something. 勧誘電話、勧誘訪問 □ *She had worked as a call center operator making cold calls for time-share vacations.* 彼女はコールセンターで、休暇施設の共同所有を電話で勧誘する仕事をしていたことがある。 **2** V-T/V-I 他動詞/自動詞 To **cold-call** means to make a cold call. 勧誘電話をかける、勧誘訪問をする ［他動詞］［自動詞］ □ *You should refuse to meet anyone who cold-calls you with an offer of financial advice.* 金融相談をもちかける勧誘訪問は門前払いをするべきです。 ● **cold-calling** N-UNCOUNT 不可算名詞 勧誘訪問をすること、勧誘電話をかけること □ *We will adhere to strict sales ethics, with none of the cold-calling that has given the industry such a bad name.* 我々は厳しいセールス倫理を厳守し、業界の評判をおとしめた勧誘活動は一切しない。

Word Link co ≈ together : coherent, collaborate, cooperate

Word Link labor ≈ working : collaborate, elaborate, laboratory

col|labo|rate /kəlæbəreɪt/ (**collaborates, collaborating, collaborated**) **1** V-RECIP 相互動詞 When one person or group **collaborates with** another, they work together, especially on a book or on some research. 共同して働く □ *Much later he collaborated with his son Michael on the English translation of a text on food production.* 彼はずっと後に息子のマイケルと共同で食糧生産に関するテキストを英訳した。 □ *He turned his country house into a place where professionals and amateurs collaborated in the making of music.* 彼は自

分の別荘をプロとアマチュアの音楽家が共同で作曲できる場所にしつらえた. **2** V-I 自動詞 If someone **collaborates with** an enemy that is occupying their country during a war, they help them. (敵側に)協力する [DISAPPROVAL 不賛成] [自動詞] □ He was accused of having collaborated with the Communist secret police. 彼は共産党秘密警察に協力したかどで告発された.

col|labo|ra|tion /kəlæbəreɪʃ^ən/ (**collaborations**) **1** N-VAR 可変性名詞 **Collaboration** is the act of working together to produce a piece of work, especially a book or some research. 協力 □ There is substantial collaboration with neighboring departments. 近隣領域とは相当の協力関係がある. □ ...scientific collaborations. 科学協力 **2** N-COUNT 可算名詞 A **collaboration** is a piece of work that has been produced as the result of people or groups working together. 共同作品 □ He was also a writer of beautiful stories, some of which are collaborations with his fiance. 美しい物語を書く作家でもある. 婚約者との共著もある. **3** N-UNCOUNT 不可算名詞 **Collaboration** is the act of helping an enemy who is occupying your country during a war. (敵への) 協力 [DISAPPROVAL 不賛成] □ ...rumors of his collaboration with the occupying forces during the war. 戦時中に彼が占領軍に協力したといううわさ

col|labo|ra|tive /kəlæbəreɪtɪv, -ərətɪv/ ADJ 形容詞 A **collaborative** piece of work is done by two or more people or groups working together. 共同の [FORMAL 形式ばった] [ADJ n] □ ...a collaborative research project. 共同研究プロジェクト

col|labo|ra|tor /kəlæbəreɪtər/ (**collaborators**) **1** N-COUNT 可算名詞 A **collaborator** is someone that you work with to produce a piece of work, especially a book or some research. 共同制作者, 共同研究者 □ The Irvine group and their collaborators are testing whether lasers do the job better. アービングループと共同研究者たちはレーザーの方が結果がいいかどうかを確認する試験を行っている. **2** N-COUNT 可算名詞 A **collaborator** is someone who helps an enemy who is occupying their country during a war. (敵への) 協力者 [DISAPPROVAL 不賛成] □ Two alleged collaborators were shot dead by masked activists. 敵に協力したとの嫌疑を受けた2人は, 覆面をした活動家に射殺された.

col|lage /kəlɑʒ/ (**collages**) **1** N-COUNT 可算名詞 A **collage** is a picture that has been made by sticking pieces of colored paper and cloth onto paper. コラージュ作品 □ ...a collage of words and pictures from magazines. 雑誌の言葉や写真を切り貼りしたコラージュ作品. **2** N-UNCOUNT 不可算名詞 **Collage** is the method of making pictures by sticking pieces of colored paper and cloth onto paper. コラージュ □ The illustrations make use of collage, watercolor, and other media. それらのイラストにはコラージュや水彩, その他の媒体が用いられている.

Word Link	lapse ≈ falling : collapse, elapse, lapse

col|lapse /kəlæps/ (**collapses, collapsing, collapsed**) **1** V-I 自動詞 If a building or other structure **collapses**, it falls down very suddenly. 崩壊する [自動詞] □ A section of the Bay Bridge had collapsed. ベイブリッジの一部が崩れ落ちた. ● N-UNCOUNT 不可算名詞 **Collapse** is also a noun. 倒壊 □ The governor called for an inquiry into the freeway's collapse. 知事がフリーウェイ倒壊の調査を要請した. **2** V-I 自動詞 If something, for example a system or institution, **collapses**, it fails or comes to an end completely and suddenly. (はたん) 破綻する [自動詞] □ His business empire collapsed under a massive burden of debt. 彼の企業帝国は巨額の負債により破綻した. ● N-UNCOUNT 不可算名詞 **Collapse** is also a noun. 破綻 (はたん) □ The coup's collapse has speeded up the drive to independence. クーデターの破綻により独立運動が加速した. **3** V-I 自動詞 If you **collapse**, you suddenly faint or fall down because you are very ill or weak. 倒れる [自動詞] □ He collapsed following a vigorous exercise session at his home. 彼は自宅で激しい運動をした後に倒れた. ● N-UNCOUNT 不可算名詞 **Collapse** is also a noun. 倒れること □ A few days after his collapse he was sitting up in bed. 彼は倒れてから数日後にベッドで起き上がっていた. **4** V-I 自動詞 If you **collapse** onto something, you sit or lie down suddenly because you are very tired. 倒れこむ [自動詞] □ She arrived home exhausted and barely capable of showering before collapsing on her bed. 彼女は疲れきって帰宅し, まともにシャワーも浴びることができないままベッドに倒れこんだ.

col|lar /kɒlər/ (**collars**) **1** N-COUNT 可算名詞 The **collar** of a shirt or coat is the part which fits around the neck and is usually folded over. 襟 □ His tie was pulled loose and his collar hung open. ネクタイは緩められ, 彼の襟元は開いたままだった. **2** → see also **blue-collar, white-collar** **3** N-COUNT 可算名詞 A **collar** is a band of leather or plastic which is put around the neck of a dog or cat. 首輪

collar|bone /kɒlərboʊn/ (**collarbones**) N-COUNT 可算名詞 Your **collarbones** are the two long bones which run from throat to your shoulders. 鎖骨 □ Harold had a broken collarbone. ハロルドは鎖骨を骨折していた.

col|late /kəleɪt/ (**collates, collating, collated**) V-T 他動詞 When you **collate** pieces of information, you gather them all together and examine them. (情報を集めて) 分析する [他動詞]

□ Roberts has spent much of his working life collating the data on which the study was based. ロバーツの仕事の大半は, その研究の基礎データの分析だった. **2** V-T 他動詞 If someone, or something such as a photocopier, **collates** pieces of paper, they put them together in the correct order. ページ順に並べる [他動詞] □ They took sheets of paper off piles, collated them and put them into envelopes. 彼らは紙の山から紙を取り出し, ページ順に並べ替えて封筒に入れた.

col|lat|er|al /kəlætərəl/ N-UNCOUNT 不可算名詞 **Collateral** is money or property which is used as a guarantee that someone will repay a loan. 担保 [FORMAL 形式ばった] □ Many people use personal assets as collateral for small business loans. 個人資産を小規模事業融資の担保にするのは一般的だ.

col|lat|er|al dam|age N-UNCOUNT 不可算名詞 **Collateral damage** is accidental injury to nonmilitary people or damage to nonmilitary buildings which occurs during a military operation. 軍事行動によって民間人が受ける人的および物的被害 □ To minimize collateral damage, maximum precision in bombing was required. 巻き添え被害を最小限にとどめるには爆撃を最大限に正確に行う必要があった.

col|league /kɒliːg/ (**colleagues**) N-COUNT 可算名詞 Your **colleagues** are the people you work with, especially in a professional job. 同僚 □ Without consulting his colleagues, he flew from Los Angeles to Chicago. 彼は同僚には相談せず, ロサンゼルスからシカゴに飛んだ.

col|lect /kəlɛkt/ (**collects, collecting, collected**) **1** V-T 他動詞 If you **collect** a number of things, you bring them together from several places or from several people. 集める [他動詞] □ Two young girls were collecting firewood. 2人の少女はまきを集めていた. □ Elizabeth had been collecting snails for a school project. エリザベスが学校の課題のため巻貝を集めていた. **2** V-T 他動詞 If you **collect** things, such as stamps or books, as a hobby, you get a large number of them over a period of time because they interest you. 収集する [他動詞] □ I used to collect stamps. 以前は切手を収集していました. ● **col|lect|ing** N-UNCOUNT 不可算名詞 一の収集 □ ...hobbies like stamp collecting and fishing. 切手の収集や釣りなどの趣味. **3** V-T/V-I 他動詞/自動詞 If a substance **collects** somewhere, or if something **collects** it, it keeps arriving over a period of time and is held in that place or thing. ためる [他動詞], たまる [自動詞] □ Methane gas does collect in the mines around here. メタンガスは確かにこの辺りの鉱山にたまっている. **4** V-T 他動詞 If something **collects** light, energy, or heat, it attracts it. 吸収する [他動詞] □ Like a telescope, it has a curved mirror to collect the sunlight. 望遠鏡と同様に, それには太陽光を集める曲面鏡がついている. **5** V-T/V-I 他動詞/自動詞 If you **collect for** a charity or **for** a present for someone, you ask people to give you money for it. (寄付を) 募る [他動詞] [自動詞] □ Are you collecting for charity? 慈善目的の募金ですか. □ The organization has collected $2.5 million for the relief effort. その組織は救援目的で250万ドルの募金を集めました. **6** V-T 他動詞 When you **collect** someone or something, you go and get them from the place where they are waiting for you or have been left for you. 迎えに行く [他動詞] [AM usually **pick up** 米国英語では通常 **pick up**]

Thesaurus	collect また次を参照:
v.	accumulate, compile, gather; (ant.) scatter **1**

col|lect call (**collect calls**) N-COUNT 可算名詞 A **collect call** is a telephone call which is paid for by the person who receives the call, rather than the person who makes the call. コレクトコール [AM 米国英語] □ "I want to make a collect call," she said as soon as a voice came on the line. 彼女は電話で声がするやいなや「コレクトコールをお願いします」と言った. PHRASE 句 ● If you **call collect** when you make a telephone call, the person who you are phoning pays the cost of the call and not you. コレクトコールをかける [AM 米国英語]

col|lec|tion /kəlɛkʃ^ən/ (**collections**) **1** N-COUNT 可算名詞 A **collection of** things is a group of similar things that you have deliberately acquired, usually over a period of time. コレクション □ Robert's collection of prints and paintings has been bought over the years. ロバートの版画と絵画のコレクションは何年にもわたって買い集められたものだ. □ The Art Gallery of Ontario has the world's largest collection of sculptures by Henry Moore. オンタリオ美術館は世界最大のヘンリー・ムーアの彫刻コレクションを誇っている. **2** N-COUNT 可算名詞 A **collection of** stories, poems, or articles is a number of them published in one book. 作品集 □ Two years ago he published a collection of short stories called "Facing The Music." 2年前, 彼は短編集『報いを受けて』を出版した. **3** N-COUNT 可算名詞 A **collection of** things is a group of things. 一の集まり □ ...a collection of modern glass office buildings. 近代的なガラス張りのビル群. **4** N-COUNT 可算名詞 A fashion designer's new **collection** consists of the new clothes they have designed for the next season. コレクション □ Her spring/summer collection for this year deliberately uses both simple and rich fabrics. 彼女の今年の春・夏コレクションはシンプルな布地とリッチな布地の両方を意図的に使った. **5** N-COUNT 可算名詞 If you organize a **collection** for charity, you collect money from people

C

to give to charity. 募金活動 ❑ *I asked my principal if he could arrange a collection for a refugee charity.* 私は校長に難民救済募金の取り計らいをしてもらえないかと尋ねた。 ❻ N-COUNT 可算名詞 A **collection** is money that is given by people in church during some Christian services. 献金 ❼ N-UNCOUNT 不可算名詞 **Collection** is the act of collecting something from a place or from people. 回収 ❑ *Money can be sent to any one of 22,000 agents worldwide for collection.* 世界中に2万2千の代理店のどこに送金しても受け取りができます。 ❑ *...computer systems to speed up collection of information.* 情報収集をスピードアップさせるコンピュータシステム。

col|lec|tive /kəlɛktɪv/ (collectives) ❶ ADJ 形容詞 **Collective** actions, situations, or feelings involve or are shared by every member of a group of people. 集団の [ADJ n] ❑ *It was a collective decision.* それは団体としての決定だった。 ● col|lec|tive|ly ADV 副詞 ❑ *They collectively decided to recognize the changed situation.* 彼らは事態の変化を認識することを総意として決定した。 ❷ ADJ 形容詞 [ADJ n] A **collective** amount of something is the total obtained by adding together the amounts that each person or thing in a group has. 全体の ❑ *Their collective volume wasn't very large.* それらの全体量はそれほど大きくない。 ● col|lec|tive|ly ADV 副詞 [ADV with v] ❑ *In 1968 the states collectively spent $2 billion on it.* 1968年に各州はそれに合計で20億ドルを費した。 ❸ ADJ 形容詞 The **collective** term for two or more types of thing is a general word or expression which refers to all of them. 総称 [ADJ n] ❑ *Social science is a collective name, covering a series of individual sciences.* 社会科学は科学諸分野の一系統に対する総称です。 ● col|lec|tive|ly ADV 副詞 [ADV with v] 総称として ❑ *...other sorts of cells (known collectively as white corpuscles).* その他の種類の細胞（白血球という総称で知られている）。 ❹ N-COUNT 可算名詞 A **collective** is a business or farm which is run, and often owned, by a group of people. 組合 [BUSINESS 実業] ❑ *He will see that he is participating in all the decisions of the collective.* 彼は自分が組合のすべての決定に関与していることを理解するだろう。

col|lec|tive bar|gain|ing N-UNCOUNT 不可算名詞 When a labor union engages in **collective bargaining**, it has talks with an employer about its members' pay and working conditions. 団体交渉 [BUSINESS 実業] ❑ *...a new collective-bargaining agreement.* 新しい団体協約。

→ see **union**

col|lec|tor /kəlɛktər/ (collectors) ❶ N-COUNT 可算名詞 A **collector** is a person who collects things of a particular type as a hobby. 収集家 ❑ *...a stamp collector.* 切手の収集家 ❑ *...a respected collector of Indian art.* 一目置かれているインド美術の収集家 ❷ N-COUNT 可算名詞 You can use **collector** to refer to someone whose job is to take something such as money, tickets, or garbage from people. For example, a rent **collector** collects rent from people. 回収する人 ❑ *He earned his living as a tax collector.* 彼は収税官として生計を立てた。

→ see **gallery**

col|lege /kɒlɪdʒ/ (colleges) ❶ N-VAR; N-IN-NAMES 可変性名詞，名称中の名詞 A **college** is an institution where students study after they have left secondary school. 大学 ❑ *Their daughter Joanna is taking business courses at a local college.* 彼らの娘のジョアンナは地元の大学で経営を学んでいる。 ❑ *Stephanie took up making jewelry after leaving art college this summer.* ステファニーはこの夏に美術大学を出て宝飾品の製作を始めた。 ❷ N-COUNT; N-IN-NAMES 可算名詞，名称中の名詞 At some universities in the United States, **colleges** are divisions which offer degrees in particular subjects. 学部 ❑ *...a professor at the University of Florida College of Law.* フロリダ大学の法学部教授

In North American education, students who have finished secondary school may go on to **college, university,** or **technical school.** College and university both offer baccalaureate degrees. Universities also have graduate schools for post-graduate education. Technical school provides training in a very specific area. In everyday speech a person will say they **go to college** regardless of which type of institution they attend.

❸ N-COUNT 可算名詞 A **college** is one of the institutions which some British universities are divided into. 学寮 ❑ *He was educated at Balliol College, Oxford.* 彼はオックスフォード大学ベイリオル校で学んだ。

→ see **graduation**

col|lide /kəlaɪd/ (collides, colliding, collided) ❶ V-RECIP 相互動詞 If two or more moving people or objects **collide**, they crash into one another. If a moving person or object **collides with** a person or object that is not moving, they crash into them. 衝突する ❑ *Two trains collided head-on in Ohio early this morning.* 今朝早くオハイオ州で列車同士の正面衝突事故が起きた。 ❑ *Racing up the stairs, he almost collided with Daisy.* 急いで階段を上がっていた彼は、デイジーとぶつかりそうになった。 ❷ V-RECIP 相互動詞 If the aims, opinions, or interests of one person or group **collide with** those of another person or group, they are very different from each other and are therefore opposed. ぶつかる ❑ *The aims of the negotiators in New York again seem likely to collide with the aims of the warriors in the field.* ニュ

ーヨークの交渉者と戦場の戦士の目的は再びぶつかりそうだ。

col|li|sion /kəlɪʒn/ (collisions) ❶ N-VAR 可変性名詞 A **collision** occurs when a moving object crashes into something. 衝突 ❑ *They were on their way to the airport when their van was involved in a collision with a car.* 彼らはバンで空港に向かっている途中、乗用車との衝突事故に巻き込まれた。 ❷ N-COUNT 可算名詞 A **collision** of cultures or ideas occurs when two very different cultures or people meet and conflict. 対立 ❑ *The play represents the collision of three generations.* この劇は、3世代の対立を描いている。

col|lo|quial /kəloʊkwiəl/ ADJ 形容詞 **Colloquial** words and phrases are informal and are used mainly in conversation. 口語の ❑ *...a colloquial expression.* 口語表現

col|lude /kəlud/ (colludes, colluding, colluded) V-RECIP 相互動詞 If one person **colludes with** another, they cooperate with them secretly or illegally. 結託する [DISAPPROVAL 不賛成] ❑ *Several local officials are in jail on charges of colluding with the Mafia.* マフィアと癒着していた容疑で地元の公務員数人が収監されている。 ❑ *We all colluded in the myth of him as the swanky businessman.* 私たち全員で結託して彼が粋なビジネスマンだという神話を仕立て上げた。

col|lu|sion /kəluʒn/ N-UNCOUNT 不可算名詞 **Collusion** is secret or illegal cooperation, especially between countries or organizations. 癒着 [FORMAL 形式ばった, DISAPPROVAL 不賛成] [usu N "between" pl-n, N "with" n,"in" n] ❑ *He found no evidence of collusion between record companies and retailers.* 彼はレコード会社と小売業者が癒着しているという証拠を発見できなかった。

co|lon /koʊlən/ (colons) ❶ N-COUNT 可算名詞 A **colon** is the punctuation mark : which you can use in several ways. For example, you can put it before a list of things or before reported speech. コロン ❷ N-COUNT 可算名詞 Your **colon** is the part of your intestine above your rectum. 結腸，大腸 ❑ *In the U.S., there are 60,000 deaths a year from colon cancer.* 米国では年間6万人が大腸がんで死亡する。

colo|nel /kɜrnəl/ (colonels) N-COUNT; N-TITLE; N-VOC 可算名詞，称号名詞，呼格名詞 A **colonel** is a senior officer in an army, air force, or the marines. 大佐 ❑ *This particular place was run by an ex-Army colonel.* この特定の場所は元陸軍大佐によって運営されていた。

co|lo|nial /kəloʊniəl/ ❶ ADJ 形容詞 **Colonial** means relating to countries that are colonies, or to colonialism. 植民地の [ADJ n] ❑ *...the 31st anniversary of Jamaica's independence from British colonial rule.* 英国植民地支配からのジャマイカの独立31周年 ❷ ADJ 形容詞 A **Colonial** building or piece of furniture was built or made in a style that was popular in America in the 17th and 18th centuries. コロニアル風の [mainly AM 主に米国英語] ❑ *...the white colonial houses on the north side of the campus.* キャンパスの北側に建つ白いコロニアル風の家

co|lo|ni|al|ism /kəloʊniəlɪzəm/ N-UNCOUNT 不可算名詞 **Colonialism** is the practice by which a powerful country directly controls less powerful countries and uses their resources to increase its own power and wealth. 植民地主義 ❑ *...the bitter oppression of slavery and colonialism.* 奴隷制と植民地政策の苦痛の抑圧

colo|nist /kɒlənɪst/ (colonists) N-COUNT 可算名詞 **Colonists** are the people who start a colony or the people who are among the first to live in a particular colony. 入植者 ❑ *The apple was brought over here by the colonists when they came.* リンゴは入植者の到来時にこの地にもたらされた。

colo|nize /kɒlənaɪz/ (colonizes, colonizing, colonized) ❶ V-T 他動詞 If people **colonize** a foreign country, they go to live there and take control of it. 植民地にする [他動詞] ❑ *The first British attempt to colonize Ireland was in the twelfth century.* イギリスによるアイルランド植民地化の最初の企ては12世紀のことだった。 ❑ *Liberia was never colonized by the European powers.* リベリアは一度もヨーロッパ勢力の植民地にはならなかった。 ❷ V-T 他動詞 When large numbers of animals **colonize** a place, they go to live there and make it their home. コロニーをつくる [他動詞] ❑ *Toads are colonizing the whole place.* ヒキガエルはその場所全体に住みついている。 ❸ V-T 他動詞 When an area **is colonized by** a type of plant, the plant grows there in large amounts. 群生する [他動詞] ❑ *The area was then colonized by scrub.* その一帯には雑木が群生していた。 [usu passive]

colo|ny /kɒləni/ (colonies) ❶ N-COUNT 可算名詞 A **colony** is a country which is controlled by a more powerful country. 植民地 ❑ *In France's former North African colonies, anti-French feeling is growing.* フランスの旧北アフリカ植民地で、反仏感情が高まっている。 ❷ N-COUNT 可算名詞 You can refer to a place where a particular group of people lives as a particular kind of **colony.** 居

留地 ❏ *In 1932, he established a school and artists' colony in Stone City, Iowa.* 1932年に彼はアイオワ州ストーンシティで学校と芸術家村を設立した. ❏ *...a penal colony.* 流刑地, 囚人植民地 ❸ N-COUNT 可算名詞 A **colony of** birds, insects, or animals is a group of them that live together. 個体群 ❏ *The islands are famed for their colonies of sea birds.* その諸島は海鳥の群生地として名高い.

col|or /kʌlər/ (**colors, coloring, colored**) ❶ N-COUNT 可算名詞 The **color** of something is the appearance that it has as a result of the way in which it reflects light. Red, blue, and green are colors. 色彩 ❏ *"What color is the car?" — "Red."* 「その自動車は何色なんだい」 – 「赤です」 ❏ *Judi's favourite color is pink.* ジュディの好きな色は桃色だ. ❷ N-COUNT 可算名詞 Someone's **color** is the color of their skin. People often use **color** in this way to refer to a person's race. (人種を示す肌の) 色 [POLITENESS 丁寧な] ❏ *I don't care what color she is.* 彼女の肌の色など気にしない. ❸ N-VAR 可変名詞 A **color** is a substance that you use to give something a particular color. Dyes and makeup are sometimes referred to as **colors**. 色をつけるもの ❏ *It is better to avoid all food colors.* 着色料はすべて避けたほうがいい. ❏ *Her nail color was coordinated with her lipstick.* 彼女の爪の色は口紅と合わせてあった. ❹ V-T 他動詞 If you **color** something, you use something such as dyes or paint to change its color. 着色する [他動詞] ❏ *Many women begin coloring their hair in their mid-30s.* 多くの女性が30代半ばで髪を染め始める. ❏ *We'd been making cakes and coloring the posters.* 我々はケーキを作り, ポスターに色を塗っていた. ● **col|or|ing** N-UNCOUNT 不可算名詞 着色 ❏ *They could not afford to spoil those maps by careless coloring.* 彼らは不注意に色をつけて地図を駄目にするわけにはいかなかった. ❺ V-I 自動詞 If someone **colors**, their face becomes redder than it normally is, usually because they are embarrassed. 赤面する [自動詞] ❏ *Andrew couldn't help noticing that she colored slightly.* アンドリューは彼女の顔が少し赤くなったのに気づかずにはいられなかった. ❻ V-T 他動詞 If something **colors** your opinion, it affects the way that you think about something. 影響を与える [他動詞] ❏ *All too often it is only the negative images of Ireland that are portrayed, coloring opinions and hiding the true nature of the country.* アイルランドの描写はややもすれば負のイメージばかりになり, 評価に影響を能え, 国の本質を隠す. ❼ ADJ 形容詞 A **color** television, photograph, or picture is one that shows things in all their colors, and not just in black, white, and gray. 色つきの ❏ *In Japan 99 per cent of all households now have a color television set.* 今, 日本では全家庭の99パーセントがカラーテレビを所有している. ❽ N-UNCOUNT 不可算名詞 **Color** is a quality that makes something especially interesting or exciting. 彩り ❏ *She had resumed the travel necessary to add depth and color to her novels.* 彼女は自分の小説に深みと彩りを与えるのに必要な旅を再開した. ❾ N-PLURAL 複数名詞 A country's national **colors** are the colors of its national flag. 国旗の色 ❏ *The Opera House is decorated with the Hungarian national colors: green, red, and white.* オペラハウスはハンガリー国旗の緑, 赤, 白で飾られた. ❿ N-PLURAL 複数名詞 People sometimes refer to the flag of a particular part of an army, navy, or air force, or the flag of a particular country as its

colors. 旗 ❏ *Troops raised the country's colors in a special ceremony.* 軍隊は特別の儀式で国旗を掲げた. ⓫ N-PLURAL 複数名詞 A sports team's **colors** are the colors of the clothes they wear when they play. 制服の色 ❏ *I was wearing the team's colors.* 私はチームのユニホームを着ていた. ⓬ → see also **colored, coloring** ⓭ PHRASE 句 If a movie or television program is **in color**, it has been made so that you see the picture in all its colors, and not just in black, white, or gray. 色つきの ❏ *Was he going to show the movie? Was it in color?* 彼はその映画を見せるつもりだったのか. それはカラー作品だったのか. ⓮ PHRASE 句 People **of color** are people who belong to a race with dark skins. 有色人種の [POLITENESS 丁寧な] ❏ *Black communities spoke up to defend the rights of all people of color.* 黒人社会がすべての有色人種の権利を守るために声を上げた.
▶ **color in** PHRASAL VERB 句動詞 If you **color in** a drawing, you give it different colors using crayons or paints. 色を加える ❏ *Someone had colored in all the black and white pictures.* 白と黒のみの絵に誰かが色を加えた.
→ see Picture Dictionary: color
→ see **flower, painting**

Word Partnership	*color* は次の語句と使われる:
ADJ.	**bright** color, **favorite** color ❶
N.	color **blind, eye/hair** color ❶
	skin color ❷
	color **film/photograph**, color **television** ❼ ⓭
PREP.	**in** color ⓭

col|ored /kʌlərd/ ❶ ADJ 形容詞 Something that is **colored** a particular color is that color. 着色した ❏ *The illustration shows a cluster of five roses colored apricot orange.* その挿絵はアプリコット・オレンジ色のバラ5本の寄せ集めを描いている. ❷ ADJ 形容詞 Something that is **colored** is a particular color or combination of colors, rather than being just white, black, and the color that it is naturally. 色つきの ❏ *You can often choose between plain white or colored and patterned scarves.* 多くの場合, 真っ白, 色つき, あるいは柄の入ったスカーフを選ぶことができる. ❸ ADJ 形容詞 A **colored** person belongs to a race of people with dark skins. 有色人種の [OFFENSIVE, OLD-FASHIONED 無礼な, 古風な]

col|or|ful /kʌlərfəl/ ❶ ADJ 形容詞 Something that is **colorful** has bright colors or a lot of different colors. 色彩に富んだ ❏ *The flowers were colorful and the scenery magnificent.* 色とりどりの花が咲き, 風景は壮麗だった. ❷ ADJ 形容詞 A **colorful** story is full of exciting details. 多彩な ❏ *The story she told was certainly colorful, and extended over her life in England, Germany, and Spain.* 彼女の話は実に多彩で, イングランド, ドイツ, スペインでの彼女の生活にまで及んだ. ❸ ADJ 形容詞 A **colorful** character is a person who behaves in an interesting and amusing way. 華やかな ❏ *Casey Stengel was probably the most colorful character in baseball.* ケーシー・ステンゲルはおそらく球界で最も華やかな人物であった.
→ see **flower**

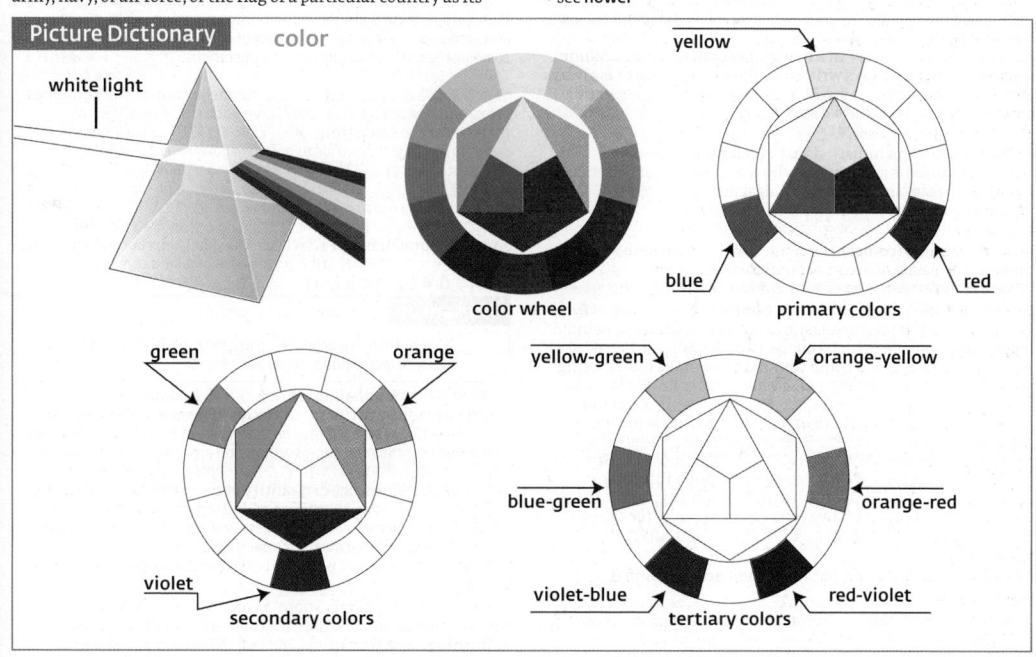

Picture Dictionary color

white light

color wheel

yellow

blue   red

primary colors

green   orange

violet

secondary colors

yellow-green   orange-yellow

blue-green   orange-red

violet-blue   red-violet

tertiary colors

c

Thesaurus   *colorful* また次を参照：

ADJ.   bright, lively, vibrant, vivid; (ant.) bland, colorless, dull **1**
    animated, dramatic, interesting **2**

col|or|ing /kʌlərɪŋ/ **1** N-UNCOUNT 不可算名詞 The **coloring** of something is the color or colors that it is. 彩色 ❑ *Other countries vary the coloring of their bank notes as well as their size.* 他の国では 紙幣の大きさも、色合いも変えている。 **2** N-UNCOUNT 不可算名詞 Someone's **coloring** is the color of their hair, skin, and eyes. (髪、肌、目の) 色 ❑ *None of them had their father's dark coloring.* 彼らの中に色黒の父親に似た者はいなかった。 **3** N-UNCOUNT 不可算名詞 **Coloring** is a substance that is used to give color to food. 着色料 ❑ *A few drops of green food coloring were added.* 数滴の緑色着色料が加えられた。 **4** → see also **color**

col|or|less /kʌlərlɪs/ **1** ADJ 形容詞 Something that is **colorless** has no color at all. 無色の ❑ *...a colorless, almost odorless liquid.* 無色でほとんど無臭の液体。 **2** ADJ 形容詞 If someone's face is **colorless**, it is very pale, usually because they are frightened, shocked, or ill. 血の気の引いた ❑ *Her face was colorless, and she was shaking.* 彼女は顔面蒼白（そうはく）で震えていた。 **3** ADJ 形容詞 **Colorless** people or places are dull and uninteresting. 精彩を欠いた ❑ *...the much more experienced but colorless general.* 経験では大幅に勝るが、精彩を欠いた将軍

col|or line (color lines) N-COUNT 可算名詞 A **color line** is the set of social, economic or political barriers that exist between different racial groups. 人種間の境界線 [usu sing] ❑ *...one of the first black players to break the color line in the deep South.* 深南部で最初に人種間の壁を打ち破った黒人選手の一人

co|los|sal /kəlɒsəl/ ADJ 形容詞 If you describe something as **colossal**, you are emphasizing that it is very large. 巨大な [EMPHASIS 強調] ❑ *There has been a colossal waste of public money.* 莫大な公共資金が無駄にされてきた。

col|our /kʌlər/ → see **color**

colt /koʊlt/ (colts) N-COUNT 可算名詞 A **colt** is a young male horse. 雄の子馬

col|umn /kɒləm/ (columns) **1** N-COUNT 可算名詞 A **column** is a tall, often decorated cylinder of stone which is built to honor someone or forms part of a building. 円柱 ❑ *Seven massive columns rise up from a marble floor.* 大理石の床にそびえ立つ7本の巨大な円柱 **2** N-COUNT 可算名詞 A **column** is something that has a tall, narrow shape. 柱 ❑ *The explosion sent a column of smoke thousands of feet into the air.* 爆発で空中数千フィートの高さまで煙の柱が立ち上った。 **3** N-COUNT 可算名詞 A **column** is a group of people or animals which moves in a long line. 行列 ❑ *There were reports of columns of military vehicles appearing on the streets.* 街路には軍用車の隊列があったと報告された。 **4** N-COUNT 可算名詞 On a printed page such as a page of a dictionary, newspaper, or printed chart, a **column** is one of two or more vertical sections which are read downward. (新聞、雑誌などの) 縦の欄 ❑ *We had stupidly been looking at the wrong column of figures.* 我々は愚かにも別の数字の列をみていたのだった。 **5** N-COUNT 可算名詞 In a newspaper or magazine, a **column** is a section that is always written by the same person or is always about the same topic. コラム記事 ❑ *His name features frequently in the social columns of the tabloid newspapers.* 彼はタブロイド版新聞の社会コラムでよく主要記事を書いている。

col|um|nist /kɒləmnɪst, -əmɪst/ (columnists) N-COUNT 可算名詞 A **columnist** is a journalist who regularly writes a particular kind of article in a newspaper or magazine. コラム記事執筆者 ❑ *Clarence Page is a columnist for the Chicago Tribune.* クラレンス・ペイジはシカゴ・トリビューンでコラム記事を書いている。

coma /koʊmə/ (comas) N-COUNT 可算名詞 Someone who is in a **coma** is in a state of deep unconsciousness. 昏睡（こんすい） ❑ *She was in a coma for seven weeks.* 彼女は7週間、昏睡状態だった。

comb /koʊm/ (combs, combing, combed) **1** N-COUNT 可算名詞 A **comb** is a flat piece of plastic or metal with narrow, pointed teeth along one side, which you use to make your hair neat. くし **2** V-T 他動詞 When you **comb** your hair, you make it neat using a comb. くしでとかす [他動詞] ❑ *Salvatore combed his hair carefully.* サルバトーレは注意深く髪をといた。 **3** V-T 他動詞 If you **comb** a place, you search everywhere in it in order to find someone or something. 徹底的に捜索する [他動詞] ❑ *Officers combed the woods for the murder weapon.* 警察は殺人に用いた凶器を求め、その森を徹底的に捜索した。 **4** V-I 自動詞 If you **comb through** information, you look at it very carefully in order to find something. 入念に調査する ❑ *Eight policemen then spent two years combing through the evidence.* それから8名の警官が2年を費やし、その証拠品を入念に調査した。
→ see **hair**

com|bat (combats, combating or combatting, combated or combatted)

The noun is pronounced /kɒmbæt/. The verb is pronounced /kəmbæt/.

名詞は /kɒmbæt/ と発音される。動詞は /kəmbæt/ と発音される。

1 N-UNCOUNT 不可算名詞 **Combat** is fighting that takes place in a war. 戦闘 ❑ *Over 16 million men had died in combat.* 1600万人以上が戦闘で死んだ。 ❑ *Yesterday saw hand-to-hand combat in the city.* 昨日、その都市で白兵戦があった。 **2** N-COUNT 可算名詞 A **combat** is a battle, or a fight between two people. 闘争 ❑ *It was the end of a long combat. それは長い戦いの終わりだった。* **3** V-T 他動詞 If people in authority **combat** something, they try to stop it from happening. 戦う [他動詞] ❑ *Congress has criticized new government measures to combat crime.* 議会は犯罪と戦うための新しい政府案を批判した。
→ see **war**

Word Partnership   *combat* は次の語句と使われる：

N.	combat **forces/troops/units**, combat **gear 1**
	combat **crime**, combat **disease**, combat **terrorism 3**
ADJ.	**hand-to-hand** combat, **heavy** combat **1**

com|bat|ant /kɒmbætᵊnt/ (combatants) N-COUNT 可算名詞 A **combatant** is a person, group, or country that takes part in the fighting in a war. 戦闘員 ❑ *I have never suggested that U.N. forces could physically separate the combatants in the region.* 私は地域で国連軍が戦闘員を物理的に分離できるとの示唆は一切していない。

com|bat|ive /kəmbætɪv/ ADJ 形容詞 A person who is **combative** is aggressive and eager to fight or argue. 戦闘的な ❑ *He conducted the meeting yesterday in his usual combative style, refusing to admit any mistakes.* 昨日、彼はいつもの戦闘的なやり方で会議を取り仕切り、いかなる失敗を認めることも拒んだ。

com|bi|na|tion /kɒmbɪneɪʃᵊn/ (combinations) N-COUNT 可算名詞 A **combination of** things is a mixture of them. 組み合わせ ❑ *...a fantastic combination of colors.* 色彩の組み合わせの妙

Word Link   com ≈ with, together : **combine, compact, companion**

com|bine /kəmbaɪn/ (combines, combining, combined) **1** V-RECIP 相互動詞 If you **combine** two or more things or if they **combine**, they exist together. 結合する ❑ *The Church has something to say on how to combine freedom with responsibility.* 教会には自由と責任を結びつけるやり方について言うべきことがある。 ❑ *Relief workers say it's worse than ever as disease and starvation combine to kill thousands.* 援助関係者らによると、事態は最悪になり病気と飢餓の複合により数千人の死者がでているとのことだ。 **2** V-RECIP 相互動詞 If you **combine** two or more things or if they **combine**, they join together to make a single thing. 結びつける ❑ *David Jacobs was given the job of combining the data from these 19 studies into one giant study.* デヴィッド・ジェイコブズは、これら19件の研究から得られたデータをまとめ、ひとつの大型研究となす仕事を与えられた。 ❑ *Combine the flour with 3 tablespoons water to make a paste.* 小麦粉を茶さじ3杯の水と混ぜ、練り粉にする。 **3** V-RECIP 相互動詞 If two or more groups or organizations **combine** or if someone **combines** them, they join to form a single group or organization. 合併する ❑ *...an announcement by Steetley and Tarmac of a joint venture that would combine their brick, tile, and concrete operations.* スティートレイ社およびターマック社によるブロック、タイル、コンクリート事業を統合する合弁事業の発表 **4** V-T 他動詞 If someone or something **combines** two qualities or features, they have both those qualities or features at the same time. 兼ね備える [他動詞] ❑ *Their system seems to combine the two ideals of strong government and proportional representation.* 彼らの制度は強い政府と比例代表制という二つの理想を兼ね備えているように思われる。 ❑ *...a clever, far-sighted lawyer who combines legal expertise with social concern.* 法律の専門知識と社会問題への関心の両方を持つ賢く先見の明のある法律家 **5** V-T 他動詞 If someone **combines** two activities, they do them both at the same time. 兼務する [他動詞] ❑ *It is possible to combine a career with being a mother.* 仕事を持つことと母親であることの両立は可能だ。

Thesaurus   *combine* また次を参照：

V.	blend, fuse, incorporate, join, mix, unite; (ant.) detach, disconnect, divide, separate **1** – **3**

com|bined /kəmbaɪnd/ **1** ADJ 形容詞 A **combined** effort or attack is made by two or more groups of people at the same time. 合同の [ADJ n] ❑ *These refugees are taken care of by the combined efforts of the host countries and non-governmental organizations.* 難民は、受け入れ国と非政府組織の合同の取り組みで援助を受ける。 **2** ADJ 形容詞 The **combined** size or quantity of two or more things is the total of their sizes or quantities added together. 一体とした [ADJ n] ❑ *Such a merger would be the largest in U.S. banking history, giving the two banks combined assets of some $146 billion.* 2行が合併すればアメリカの銀行史上最大のものとなり、資産額はあわせて約1460億ドルになる。

com|bus|tion /kəmbʌstʃən/ N-UNCOUNT 不可算名詞 **Combustion** is the act of burning something or the process of burning. 燃焼 [TECHNICAL 技術的の] ❑ *The energy is released by*

combustion on the application of a match. マッチを燃焼させること でエネルギーが放出する.

→ see **engine**

---

come

❶ ARRIVE AT A PLACE
❷ OTHER USES
❸ PHRASAL VERBS

---

❶ **come** /kʌm/ (comes, coming, came)

The form **come** is used in the present tense and is the past participle.

come 形は現在時制に使われ，過去分詞でもある.

1 V-I 自動詞 When a person or thing **comes** to a particular place, especially to a place where you are, they move there. 来る [自動詞] ❑ *Two police officers came into the hall.* 二人の警官が集会所に来た. ❑ *Come here, Tom.* こっちにおいで，トム. ❑ *We heard the train coming.* 列車が近づいてくるのが聞こえた. ❑ *The impact blew out some of the windows and the sea came rushing in.* その衝撃で何枚かの窓が吹き飛び，海水が入りこんだ. **2** V-T 他動詞 When someone **comes** to do something, they move to the place where someone else is in order to do it, and they do it. Someone can also **come** do something and **come and** do something. However, you always say that someone **came and** did something. するために来る [他動詞] ❑ *Eleanor had come to see her.* エレノアは彼女に会いに来た. ❑ *I want you to come visit me.* 私はあなたに訪ねてきて欲しい. **3** V-I 自動詞 When you **come to** a place, you reach it. 到着する [自動詞] ❑ *He came to a door that led into a passageway.* 彼は通路に続く扉にたどり着いた. **4** V-I 自動詞 If something **comes up to** a particular point or **down to** it, it is tall enough, deep enough, or long enough to reach that point. 達する [自動詞] ❑ *The water came up to my chest.* 水位は私の胸の高さに達した.

---

❷ **come** /kʌm/ (comes, coming, came)

The form **come** is used in the present tense and is the past participle.

come 形は現在時制に使われ，過去分詞でもある.

1 V-I 自動詞 If something **comes apart** or **comes to pieces**, it breaks into pieces. If something **comes off** or **comes away**, it becomes detached from something else. ばらばらになる，はずれる [自動詞] ❑ *The lid won't come off.* ふたが外れない. ❑ *The pistol came to pieces, easily and quickly.* 拳銃は容易に手早く分解した. **2** V-T 他動詞 If someone **comes to** do something, they do it at the end of a long process or period of time. するようになる [他動詞] ❑ *She said it so many times that she came to believe it.* 彼女は自分がそれを信じるようになったと何度も言った. **3** V-T 他動詞 You can ask how something **came to** happen when you want to know what caused it to happen or made it possible. するようになる [他動詞] ❑ *How did you come to meet him?* どんなふうにして彼と会うようになったんだい? **4** V-I 自動詞 When a particular event or time **comes**, it arrives or happens. 到来する [他動詞]，到来する [自動詞] ❑ *The announcement came after a meeting at the White House.* ホワイトハウスでの会合の後，その発表があった. ❑ *There will come a time when they will have to negotiate.* 彼らが交渉せねばならないときが来るだろう. ● **com|ing** N-SING 単数名詞 到来 ❑ *Most of my patients welcome the coming of summer.* 私の患者のほとんどが夏の到来を歓迎する. **5** V-I 自動詞 If a thought, idea, or memory **comes to** you, you suddenly think of it or remember it. 思い浮かぶ [自動詞] ❑ *He was about to shut the door when an idea came to him.* 考えを思いついたとき，彼は扉を閉めるところだった. **6** V-I 自動詞 If money or property is going to **come to** you, you are going to inherit or receive it. 懐に入る [自動詞] ❑ *He did have retirement money coming to him when the factory shut down.* 工場が閉鎖したとき彼は退職金を受け取った. **7** V-I 自動詞 If a case **comes before** a court or tribunal or **comes to** court, it is presented there so that the court or tribunal can examine it. 審議される [自動詞] ❑ *The membership application came before the committee in September.* 会員申し込みは9月の委員会で審査された. **8** V-I 自動詞 If something **comes to** a particular number or amount, it adds up to it. 合計が～になる [自動詞] ❑ *Lunch came to $80.* 昼食代はあわせて80ドルになった. **9** V-I 自動詞 If someone or something **comes from** a particular place or thing, that place or thing is their origin, source, or starting point. 由来する [自動詞] ❑ *Nearly half the students come from overseas.* 半分近くの学生が留学生だ. ❑ *Chocolate comes from the cacao tree.* チョコレートの原料はカカオの木からとれる. **10** V-I 自動詞 Something that **comes from** something else or **comes of** it is the result of it. もたらされる [自動詞] ❑ *There is a feeling of power that comes from driving fast.* 自動車をとばせば自分に力があると感じる. ❑ *Some good might come of all this gloomy business.* こんな陰鬱なことからも，なにかいい結果がでてくるかもしれない. **11** V-T 他動詞 If someone or something **comes** first, next, or last, they are first, next, or last in a series, list, or competition.

(ある順位に) なる [他動詞] ❑ *The two countries have been unable to agree which step should come next.* 両国が次の段階についての合意に達することは不可能だった. ❑ *The alphabet might be more rational if all the vowels came first.* すべての母音が最初にきたなら，アルファベットはもっと合理的だったかもしれない. **12** V-I 自動詞 If a type of thing **comes in** a particular range of colors, forms, styles, or sizes, it can have any of those colors, forms, styles, or sizes. の色，形，スタイル，大きさなどがある [自動詞] ❑ *Bikes come in all shapes and sizes.* 自転車はあらゆる形と大きさがそろっている. **13** V-I 自動詞 The next subject in a discussion that you **come to** is the one that you talk about next. 話題にする [自動詞] ❑ *Finally, I come to the subject of genetic engineering.* 最後に遺伝子工学の話です. **14** V-LINK 連結動詞 You use **come** in expressions such as **come to an end** and **come into operation** to indicate that someone or something enters or reaches a particular state or situation. 特定の状態や状況になる ❑ *The summer came to an end.* 夏が終わった. ❑ *Their worst fears may be coming true.* 彼らの最悪の恐れが現実になりつつあるのかもしれない. **15** PREP 前置詞 You can use **come** before a date, time, or event to mean when it arrives. For example, you can say **come spring** to mean "when the spring arrives." が来れば ❑ *Come the election on the 20th of May, we will have to decide.* 5月20日の選挙が来たときには，我々は決定せねばならない.

---

❸ **come** /kʌm/ (comes, coming, came)

The form **come** is used in the present tense and is the past participle.

come 形は現在時制に使われ，過去分詞でもある.

1 PHRASE 句 You can use the expression **when it comes down to it** or **when you come down to it** for emphasis, when you are giving a general statement or conclusion. 要は [EMPHASIS 強調] ❑ *When you come down to it, however, the basic problems of life have not changed.* 人生の基本問題というものは概して変わっていない. **2** PHRASE 句 You use the expression **come to think of it** to indicate that you have suddenly realized something, often something obvious. 考えてみると ❑ *He was his distant relative, as was everyone else on the island, come to think of it.* 彼は彼の遠縁だった. そういえば島の人はみんなそうだったが. **3** PHRASE 句 When you refer to a time or an event **to come** or one that is still **to come**, you are referring to a future time or event. 来たるべき ❑ *I hope in years to come he will reflect on his decision.* 私は彼が今後数年，自分の決断を熟考することを望む. **4** PHRASE 句 You can use expressions like **I know where you're coming from** or **you can see where she's coming from** to say that you understand someone's attitude or point of view. その人の態度や物の見方 ❑ *To understand why they are doing it, it is necessary to know where they are coming from.* 彼らがなぜそうしているのかを理解するには，彼らの考え方を知る必要がある. **5** → see also **coming**

▶ **come about** PHRASAL VERB 句動詞 When you say how or when something **came about**, you say how or when it happened. 生じる ❑ *The peace agreement came about through intense pressure by the international community.* 和平合意は国際社会の強力な圧力によってもたらされた. ❑ *That came about when we went to New York last year.* あのことは昨年，我々がニューヨークに行ったときに起こった.

▶ **come across 1** PHRASAL VERB 句動詞 If you **come across** something or someone, you find them or meet them by chance. 出くわす ❑ *He came across the jawbone of a 4.5 million-year-old marsupial.* 彼は450万年前の有袋類のあごの骨に遭遇した. **2** PHRASAL VERB 句動詞 If someone or what they are saying **comes across** in a particular way, they make that impression on people who meet them or are listening to them. 印象を与える ❑ *When sober, he can come across as an extremely pleasant and charming young man.* しらふのときの彼は，とびきり面白くて魅力的な若者である印象を与えることがある.

▶ **come along 1** PHRASAL VERB 句動詞 You tell someone to **come along** to encourage them in a friendly way to do something, especially to attend something. 参加する ❑ *There's a barbecue tonight and you're very welcome to come along.* 今晩，バーベキューを開催しますので，ぜひお越しください. **2** PHRASAL VERB 句動詞 When something or someone **comes along**, they occur or arrive by chance. 偶然現れる ❑ *I waited a long time until a script came along that I thought was genuinely funny.* 私は自分が本当に愉快だと思える台本が出現するのを長い間待った. **3** PHRASAL VERB 句動詞 If something **is coming along**, it is developing or making progress. 進展する ❑ *Pentagon spokesman Williams says those talks are coming along quite well.* 国防総省のウィリアムズ報道官は，会談はとても順調に進展していると述べた.

▶ **come around 1** PHRASAL VERB 句動詞 If someone **comes around to** your house, they come there to see you. 会いにくる ❑ *Beth came around, this morning to apologize.* 今朝，ベスは謝罪に訪れた. **2** PHRASAL VERB 句動詞 If you **come around to** an idea, you eventually change your mind and accept it or agree with it. (意見，態度などを) 変えて同意する ❑ *It looks like they're coming around to our way of thinking.* 彼らは我々の考え方にあわせ考えを変えているよう

だ. ❸ PHRASAL VERB 句動詞 When something **comes around**, it happens as a regular or predictable event. 巡り来る ❑I hope to be fit when the World Championship comes around next year. 来年の世界選手権開催時には万全な体調であることを望む. ❹ PHRASAL VERB 句動詞 When someone who is unconscious **comes around**, they become conscious again. 意識を取り戻す ❑When I came around I was on the kitchen floor. 意識を回復した時, 私は台所の床の上にいた.

▶ **come at** PHRASAL VERB 句動詞 If a person or animal **comes at** you, they move towards you in a threatening way and try to attack you. とびかかる ❑He maintained that he was protecting himself from Mr. Cox, who came at him with an ax. 彼は, 斧で襲いかかってきたコックス氏から自分の身を守っていたのだと主張した.

▶ **come back** ❶ PHRASAL VERB 句動詞 If someone comes back to a place, they return to it. 戻る ❑He wanted to come back to Washington. 彼はワシントンに戻りたかった. ❑She just wanted to go home and not come back. 彼女は家に帰ったら, 戻ってきたくなかった. ❷ PHRASAL VERB 句動詞 If something that you had forgotten **comes back** to you, you remember it. 思い出す ❑I'll think of his name in a moment when it comes back to me. もうすぐ彼の名前を思い出すから, それについて考えるよ. ❸ PHRASAL VERB 句動詞 When something **comes back**, it becomes fashionable again. 再流行する ❑I'm glad hats are coming back. 帽子がまた流行りはじめて嬉しい. ❹ → see also comeback

▶ **come between** PHRASAL VERB 句動詞 If someone or something **comes between** two people, or **comes between** a person and a thing, they make the relationship or connection between them less close or happy. 仲を裂く ❑I don't want this misunderstanding to come between us. この誤解で我々の関係を悪化させたくない.

▶ **come by** PHRASAL VERB 句動詞 To **come by** something means to obtain it or find it. 手に入れる ❑How did you come by that check? その小切手をどうやって手に入れたんだい.

▶ **come down** ❶ PHRASAL VERB 句動詞 If the cost, level, or amount of something **comes down**, it becomes less than it was before. 下がる ❑Interest rates should come down. 金利は下がるはずだ. ❑If you buy three bottles, the bottle price comes down to $10. 3本買えば, 1本あたりの値段は10ドルまで下がる. ❷ PHRASAL VERB 句動詞 If something **comes down**, it falls to the ground. 落ちる ❑The cold rain came down for hours. 冷たい雨が何時間も降った.

▶ **come down on** ❶ PHRASAL VERB 句動詞 If you **come down on** one side of an argument, you declare that you support that side. 支持する ❑He clearly and decisively came down on the side of the president. 彼は明確に決然と大統領の立場を支持した. ❷ PHRASAL VERB 句動詞 If you **come down on** someone, you criticize them severely or treat them strictly. 食ってかかる ❑If Douglas came down hard enough on him, Dale would rebel. ダグラスが彼を厳しく攻撃するなら, デールは反抗するだろう.

▶ **come down to** PHRASAL VERB 句動詞 If a problem, decision, or question **comes down** to a particular thing, that thing is the most important factor involved. 帰結する ❑The problem comes down to money. 結局, 問題は金だ. ❑I think that it comes down to the fact that people do feel very dependent on their automobiles. つまるところ人々が自動車に頼り切っていると感じていることが問題なのだと思う.

▶ **come down with** PHRASAL VERB 句動詞 If you **come down with** an illness, you get it. (病気に) かかる ❑Thomas came down with the chickenpox. トーマスは水ぼうそうにかかった.

▶ **come for** PHRASAL VERB 句動詞 If people such as soldiers or police **come for** you, they come to find you, usually in order to harm you or take you away, for example to prison. 連行や危害を加える目的で来る ❑Tanya was getting ready to fight if they came for her. ターニャは, 彼らが襲いに来るなら戦う覚悟をしていた.

▶ **come forward** PHRASAL VERB 句動詞 If someone **comes forward**, they make themselves known and offer to help. 名乗り出る ❑A vital witness came forward to say that she saw Tanner wearing the boots. 重要な証人が名乗り出て, タナーがブーツを履いているのを見たと言った.

▶ **come in** ❶ PHRASAL VERB 句動詞 If information, a report, or a telephone call **comes in**, it is received. (電話, 報告などが) 入ってくる ❑Reports are now coming in of trouble at yet another jail. さらに別の刑務所の騒動についての報告も入っているところだ. ❷ PHRASAL VERB 句動詞 If you have some money **coming in**, you receive it regularly as your income. 収入として入る ❑She had no money coming in and no funds. 彼女は収入も蓄えもなかった. ❸ PHRASAL VERB 句動詞 If someone **comes in** on a discussion, arrangement, or task, they join it. 参加する ❑Can I come in here too, on both points? 両方の点について私も発言に参加してもいいですか. ❹ PHRASAL VERB 句動詞 When a new idea, fashion, or product **comes in**, it becomes popular or available. 一般的になる ❑It was just when attitudes were really beginning to change and lots of new ideas were coming in. それはちょうど態度が本当に変わりはじめ, 多くの新しい考えが普及しようとしているだった. ❺ PHRASAL VERB 句動詞 If you ask where something or someone **comes in**, you are asking what their role is in a particular matter. 役割を担う ❑Rose asked again, "But where do we come in, Henry?" ローズはまた訊ねた. 「でも, ヘンリー, 私たちの

役割は何なの」 ❻ PHRASAL VERB 句動詞 When the tide **comes in**, the water in the sea gradually moves so that it covers more of the land. 満ちる [V P] ❑She became trapped as the tide came in. 潮が満ち, 彼女はどこにもいけなくなった.

▶ **come in for** PHRASAL VERB 句動詞 If someone or something **comes in for** criticism or blame, they receive it. (非難などを) 受ける ❑The plans have already come in for fierce criticism. 計画はすでに厳しい非難を受けている.

▶ **come into** ❶ PHRASAL VERB 句動詞 If someone **comes into** some money, some property, or a title, they inherit it. 相続する [no passive] ❑My father has just come into a fortune in diamonds. 父はちょうどダイヤモンドで巨額の資産を相続したところだ. ❷ PHRASAL VERB 句動詞 If someone or something **comes into** a situation, they have a role in it. 参加する [no passive] ❑We don't really know where Hortense comes into all this, Inspector. ホーテンスがどこでこのことにかかわってくるのか, 私たちには全然わかりません.

▶ **come off** ❶ PHRASAL VERB 句動詞 If something **comes off**, it is successful or effective. うまくいく ❑It was a good try but it didn't really come off. 試みとしてはよかったが, 実際にはうまくいかなかった. ❷ PHRASAL VERB 句動詞 If someone **comes off** worst in a contest or conflict, they are in the worst position after it. If they **come off** best, they are in the best position. (争いなどの結果が) 〜になる ❑Some Democrats still have bitter memories of how they came off worst during the investigation. 民主党員の一部は調査の間, いかに最悪の結果となったかについて苦い記憶をいまだに持っている. ❸ CONVENTION 慣習表現 You say **"come off it"** to someone to show them that you think what they are saying is untrue or wrong. やめてくれ

▶ **come on** ❶ CONVENTION 慣習表現 You say **"Come on"** to someone to encourage him to do something they do not want to do. しっかり, さあ [SPOKEN 口語] ❑Come on Doreen, let's dance. さあ, ドリーン, 踊ろうよ. ❷ CONVENTION 慣習表現 You say **"Come on"** to someone to encourage them to hurry up. 急ぎましょう, あなた, 遅れるわ [SPOKEN 口語] ❑Come on, darling, we'll be late. 急ぎましょう, あなた, 遅れるわ. ❸ PHRASAL VERB 句動詞 If you have an illness or a headache **coming on**, you can feel it starting. (病気や熱が) 出てくる ❑Tiredness and fever are much more likely to be a sign of the flu coming on. 倦怠感と発熱はインフルエンザの兆候である可能性が高い. ❹ PHRASAL VERB 句動詞 If something or someone **is coming on** well, they are developing well or making good progress. 良くなる ❑Leah is coming on very well now and it's a matter of deciding how to fit her into the team. リアは調子が上々だから, 彼女をチームにどうフィットさせるかだ. ❺ PHRASAL VERB 句動詞 When something such as a machine or system **comes on**, it starts working or functioning. 動き始める ❑The central heating was coming on and the ancient wooden boards creaked. セントラルヒーティングが効きはじめて, 古びた木の板がきしんだ.

▶ **come on to** PHRASAL VERB 句動詞 If someone **comes on to** you, they show that they are interested in starting a sexual relationship with you. 言い寄る [INFORMAL くだけた] ❑I met a guy at a party and he came on to me real hard. パーティーである男と出会ったんだけど, その人がしつこく言い寄って来たんだ.

▶ **come out** ❶ PHRASAL VERB 句動詞 When a new product such as a book or CD **comes out**, it becomes available to the public. 売り出される ❑The book comes out this week. その本は今週発売だ. ❷ PHRASAL VERB 句動詞 If a fact **comes out**, it becomes known to people. 知られる ❑The truth is beginning to come out about what happened. できごとの真相が世に知られ始めた. ❸ PHRASAL VERB 句動詞 When a gay person **comes out**, they let people know that they are gay. 同性愛者であることを公言する ❑...the few gay men there who dare to come out. あえて同性愛者であることを公言する男性はほとんどいない. ❹ PHRASAL VERB 句動詞 To **come out** in a particular way means to be in the position or state described at the end of a process or event. (最終的に) 〜になる ❑In this grim little episode of recent American history, few people come out well. アメリカ現代史のこの残酷で小さな出来事の結果では, うまくいく人はほとんどいない. ❑So what makes a good marriage? Faithfulness comes out top of the list. ではいい結婚の条件とはなんなのか. 最も大切なのは忠誠だとの結果だ. ❺ PHRASAL VERB 句動詞 If you **come out for** something, you declare that you support it. If you **come out against** something, you declare that you do not support it. 立場を表明する ❑Its members had come out virtually unanimously against the tests. メンバー全員がほぼ満場一致で試験に反対を表明していた. ❻ PHRASAL VERB 句動詞 When the sun, moon, or stars **come out**, they appear in the sky. 姿をあらわす ❑Oh, look! The sun's coming out! おや. お陽さまが顔を出してるよ. ❼ PHRASAL VERB 句動詞 When a group of workers **comes out** on strike, they go on strike. ストライキをする [BRIT 英国英語; AM **go on strike** 米国英語 **go on strike**]

▶ **come over** ❶ PHRASAL VERB 句動詞 If a feeling or desire, especially a strange or surprising one, **comes over** you, it affects you strongly. 襲う [no passive] ❑As I entered the hallway which led to my room that eerie feeling came over me. 私の部屋に続く廊下に出たとき, あの不気味な感情に襲われた. ❷ PHRASAL VERB 句動詞 If someone or what they are saying **comes over** in a particular way,

they make that impression on people who meet them or are listening to them. 印象を与える ❑ *You come over as a capable and amusing companion.* あなたは有能で面白い仲間だという印象を与える。 **3** PHRASAL VERB 句動詞 If someone **comes over** to your house or another place, they visit you there. 立ち寄る ❑ *Maybe I could come over to your house before the party?* たぶんパーティーの前にあなたの家に寄れるかもしれないけれど。

▶ **come round** → see **come around**

▶ **come through** **1** PHRASAL VERB 句動詞 To **come through** a dangerous or difficult situation means to survive it and recover from it. 切り抜ける [no passive] ❑ *The city had faced racial crisis and come through it.* 市は人種危機に直面したが、それを切り抜けた。 **2** PHRASAL VERB 句動詞 If a feeling or message **comes through**, it is clearly shown in what is said or done. 感情や知らせが伝わる ❑ *The message that comes through is that taxes will have to be raised.* 増税が必要になるとの意図が伝達された。 **3** PHRASAL VERB 句動詞 If something **comes through**, it arrives, especially after some procedure has been carried out. 到着する ❑ *The father of the baby was waiting for his divorce to come through.* その赤ん坊の父親は離婚手続きの完了を待っていた。 **4** PHRASAL VERB 句動詞 If you **come through** with what is expected or needed from you, you succeed in doing or providing it. 期待に応える ❑ *He puts his administration at risk if he doesn't come through on these promises for reform.* もしこうした改革の公約を果たせなければ、彼は政権を危険にさらすことになる。

▶ **come to** PHRASAL VERB 句動詞 When someone who is unconscious **comes to**, they become conscious. 意識を取り戻す ❑ *When he came to and raised his head, he saw Barney.* 彼が意識を取り戻し、頭を起こしたとき、バーニーが見えた。

▶ **come under** **1** PHRASAL VERB 句動詞 If you **come under** attack or pressure, people attack you or put pressure on you. (攻撃、圧迫などを) 受ける [no passive] ❑ *The police came under attack from angry crowds.* 警察は怒れる群集からの攻撃を受けた。 **2** PHRASAL VERB 句動詞 If something **comes under** a particular authority, it is managed or controlled by that authority. 支配される、監督される [no passive] ❑ *They were neglected before because they did not come under NATO.* 彼らは北大西洋条約機構の管轄ではなかったので、以前は無視されていた。 **3** PHRASAL VERB 句動詞 If something **comes under** a particular heading, it is in the category mentioned. 分類される [no passive] ❑ *Her articles come under the heading of human interest.* 彼女の記事は、人間的興味という項目に分類されている。

▶ **come up** **1** PHRASAL VERB 句動詞 If someone **comes up** or **comes up to** you, they approach you until they are standing close to you. やってくる ❑ *Her cat came up and rubbed itself against my legs.* 彼女の猫がやってきて、彼らの足に体をこすりつけた。 **2** PHRASAL VERB 句動詞 If something **comes up** in a conversation or meeting, it is mentioned or discussed. 話題に上る ❑ *The subject came up at work.* 仕事中にそのことが話題になって。 **3** PHRASAL VERB 句動詞 If something **is coming up**, it is about to happen or take place. 起きる ❑ *We do have elections coming up.* 実際、もうすぐ選挙がある。 **4** PHRASAL VERB 句動詞 If something **comes up**, it happens unexpectedly. 生じる ❑ *I was delayed – something came up at home.* 私は遅れたんだ。 - 家でちょっとあってね。 **5** PHRASAL VERB 句動詞 If a job **comes up** or if something **comes up for** sale, it becomes available. (仕事が) ある、売り出される ❑ *A research fellowship came up and I applied for it and got it.* 研究奨学金給費生の募集があり、私はそれに応募し、採用された。 **6** PHRASAL VERB 句動詞 When the sun or moon **comes up**, it rises. 昇る ❑ *It will be so great watching the sun come up.* 日が昇るのを見るのはとても素晴らしいだろう。 **7** PHRASAL VERB 句動詞 In law, when a case **comes up**, it is heard in a court of law. 審理される ❑ *He is one of the reservists who will plead not guilty when their cases come up.* 彼はその件の審理に際し無罪を主張するはずの在郷軍人の一人だ。

▶ **come up against** PHRASAL VERB 句動詞 If you **come up against** a problem or difficulty, you are faced with it and have to deal with it. 直面する ❑ *We came up against a great deal of resistance in dealing with the case.* 我々はこの事態の収拾にあたり多大な抵抗に直面した。

Come is used in a large number of expressions which are explained under other words in this dictionary. For example, the expression "to come to terms with something" is explained at "term."

come|back (**comebacks**) **1** N-COUNT 可算名詞 If someone such as an entertainer or sports personality makes a **comeback**, they return to their profession or sport after a period away. 復帰 ❑ *Sixties singing star Petula Clark is making a comeback.* 60年代の人気歌手ペチュラ・クラークが復活しようとしている。 **2** N-COUNT 可算名詞 If something makes a **comeback**, it becomes fashionable again. 再流行 ❑ *Tight fitting T-shirts are making a comeback.* 体に密着するTシャツが再流行している。

co|median /kəmiːdiən/ (**comedians**) N-COUNT 可算名詞 A **comedian** is an entertainer whose job is to make people laugh, by telling jokes or funny stories. お笑い芸人 ❑ *...a stand-up comedian.* 漫談師

com|edy /kɒmədi/ (**comedies**) **1** N-UNCOUNT 不可算名詞 **Comedy** consists of types of entertainment, such as plays and movies, or particular scenes in them, that are intended to make people laugh. お笑い ❑ *Actor Dom Deluise talks about his career in comedy.* 俳優ドム・デルーイズが自身のお笑いの芸歴を語る。 **2** N-COUNT 可算名詞 A **comedy** is a play, movie, or television program that is intended to make people laugh. 喜劇 ❑ *The movie is a romantic comedy.* その映画は恋愛喜劇だ。

→ see **genre**, **theater**

com|et /kɒmɪt/ (**comets**) N-COUNT 可算名詞 A **comet** is a bright object with a long tail that travels around the sun. 彗星 ❑ *Halley's Comet is going to come back in 2061.* ハレー彗星は2061年に戻ってくる。

→ see **solar**

com|fort /kʌmfərt/ (**comforts, comforting, comforted**) **1** N-UNCOUNT 不可算名詞 If you are doing something **in comfort**, you are physically relaxed and contented, and are not feeling any pain or other unpleasant sensations. 快適 ❑ *This will enable the audience to sit in comfort while watching the shows.* これにより観客はショーを見ている間、快適に座っていることができるだろう。 **2** N-UNCOUNT 不可算名詞 **Comfort** is a style of life in which you have enough money to have everything you need. 安楽 ❑ *Surely there is some way of ordering our busy lives so that we can live in comfort and find spiritual harmony too.* 当然、安楽に暮らし精神的調和を得るためにも、忙しい生活を調整する方法はいくつかある。 **3** N-UNCOUNT 不可算名詞 **Comfort** is what you feel when worries or unhappiness stop. 安楽 ❑ *He welcomed the truce, but pointed out that there was of little comfort to families spending Christmas without a loved one.* 彼は停戦を歓迎したが、愛する人のいないクリスマスを過ごす家族のやすらぎにはほとんどならないと指摘した。 ❑ *They will be able to take some comfort from inflation figures due on Friday.* 彼らは金曜に発表されるインフレデータを見ていくらかの安堵 (あんど) を得ることができるだろう。 **4** N-COUNT 可算名詞 If you refer to a person, thing, or idea as a **comfort**, you mean that it helps you to stop worrying or makes you feel less unhappy. 慰め ❑ *It's a comfort talking to you.* 君と話すと気持ちが安らぐ。 **5** N-COUNT 可算名詞 **Comforts** are things which make your life easier and more pleasant, such as electrical devices you have in your home. 生活を快適にするもの ❑ *She enjoys the material comforts married life has brought her.* 彼女は結婚によって実現した物質的に快適な暮らしを楽しんでいる。 **6** V-T 他動詞 If you **comfort** someone, you make them feel less worried, unhappy, or upset, for example by saying kind things to them. 慰める [他動詞] ❑ *Ned put his arm around her, trying to comfort her.* ネッドは彼女の体に腕を回し、彼女を慰めようとした。 **7** PHRASE 句 If you say that something is, for example, **too close for comfort**, you mean that you are worried because it is closer than you would like it to be. 不安なほど近い ❑ *The bombs fell in the sea, many too close for comfort.* 爆弾が海に落ちたが、多くは距離が近すぎて不安だ。

Word Partnership	comfort は次の語句と使われる:
V.	find/take comfort, give/offer/provide comfort **3**
N.	comfort level/zone **3**
	source of comfort **4**
	comfort *someone* **6**

com|fort|able /kʌmftəbᵊl, -fərtəbᵊl/ **1** ADJ 形容詞 If a piece of furniture or an item of clothing is **comfortable**, it makes you feel physically relaxed when you use it, for example because it is soft. 快適な ❑ *...a comfortable fireside chair.* 快適な炉端のいす **2** ADJ 形容詞 If a building or room is **comfortable**, it makes you feel physically relaxed when you spend time in it, for example because it is warm and has nice furniture. 快適な ❑ *A home should be comfortable and friendly.* 家庭は心地よく暖もりのある場所であるべきだ。 ● **com|fort|ably** ADV 副詞 快適に ❑ *...the comfortably furnished living room.* 快適な家具をそろえた居間 **3** ADJ 形容詞 If you are **comfortable**, you are physically relaxed because of the place or position you are sitting or lying in. 快適な ❑ *Lie down on your bed and make yourself comfortable.* 自分のベッドに横になり、楽にしてください。 ● **com|fort|ably** ADV 副詞 [ADV with v] 快適に ❑ *Are you sitting comfortably?* 座り心地はいいですか。 **4** ADJ 形容詞 If you say that someone is **comfortable**, you mean that they have enough money to be able to live without financial problems. 経済的に余裕のある ❑ *"Is he rich?"— "He's comfortable."* 「彼は金持ちかい」 - 「余裕がある」 ● **com|fort|ably** ADV 副詞 経済的余裕がある ❑ *Cayton describes himself as comfortably well-off.* ケイトンは自分の暮らしを余裕があると表現した。 **5** ADJ 形容詞 [ADJ n] In a race, competition, or election, if you have a **comfortable** lead, you are likely to win it easily. If you gain a **comfortable** victory or majority, you win easily. 大差の ❑ *By half distance we held a comfortable two-lap lead.* 半分の距離で我々は2周分の大差でリードしていた。 ● **com|fort|ably** ADV 副詞 [ADV with v] 余裕で ❑ *...the Los Angeles Raiders, who comfortably beat the Bears earlier in the season.* シーズンに入ってベアーズを大差で破ったロスアンジェルス・レイダーズ

C

6 ADJ 形容詞 If you feel **comfortable with** a particular situation or person, you feel confident and relaxed with them. 安心した [v-link ADJ] ❑ Nervous politicians might well feel more comfortable with a step-by-step approach. 神経を尖らせた政治家たちが段階的な手段の方を安心と感じるのは当然だ. ❑ He liked me and I felt comfortable with him. 彼は私を好きだったし、私は彼といると居心地がよかった. ● **com|fort|ably** ADV 副詞 ❑ They talked comfortably of their plans. 彼らは自分たちの計画を自信ありげに語った. **7** ADJ 形容詞 When a sick or injured person is said to be **comfortable**, they are without pain. 安楽な ❑ He was described as comfortable in the hospital last night. 昨夜、病院で彼は苦痛のない状態だったと説明された.

> **Thesaurus** _comfortable_ また次を参照:
>
> ADV. comfy, cozy, soft; (ant.) uncomfortable **1**
> relaxed, untroubled **3**
> well-off **4**

com|fort|ably /kʌmftəbli, -fərtəbli/ **1** ADV 副詞 If you manage to do something **comfortably**, you do it easily. 楽に [ADV with v] ❑ Only take upon yourself those things that you know you can manage comfortably. 自分で楽にできることだとわかっていることだけを引き受けなさい. **2** → see also **comfortable**

com|fort|er /kʌmfərtər/ (**comforters**) **1** N-COUNT 可算名詞 A **comforter** is a person or thing that comforts you. 慰める人 ❑ He became Vivien Leigh's devoted friend and comforter. 彼はヴィヴィアン・リーの献身的な友人で慰め相手となった. **2** N-COUNT 可算名詞 A **comforter** is a large cover filled with feathers or similar material that you use like a blanket. 羽根布団 [AM 米国英語]

com|fort|ing /kʌmfərtɪŋ/ ADJ 形容詞 If you say that something is **comforting**, you mean it makes you feel less worried or unhappy. 慰めとなる ❑ My mother had just died and I found the book very comforting. 母が死んだばかりで、その本が私の大きな慰めになった.

com|fy /kʌmfi/ (**comfier, comfiest**) ADJ 形容詞 A **comfy** item of clothing, piece of furniture, room, or position is a comfortable one. 快適な [INFORMAL くだけた] ❑ ...a comfy chair. 心地よいいす

com|ic /kɒmɪk/ (**comics**) **1** ADJ 形容詞 If you describe something as **comic**, you mean that it makes you laugh, and is often intended to make you laugh. 喜劇的な ❑ The novel is comic and tragic. その小説は喜劇的かつ悲劇的だ. **2** ADJ 形容詞 **Comic** is used to describe funny entertainment, and the actors and entertainers who perform it. お笑い [ADJ n] ❑ Grodin is a fine comic actor. グローディンは喜劇の名優だ. **3** N-COUNT 可算名詞 A **comic** is an entertainer who tells jokes in order to make people laugh. お笑い芸人 ❑ ...the funniest comic in America. アメリカ一おかしな芸人 **4** N-SING 単数名詞 The **comics** is the part of a newspaper that contains the comic strips. 漫画 ❑ She read the comics in the Philadelphia Inquirer. 彼女はフィラデルフィア・インクワイアラー紙の漫画を読んだ. **5** N-COUNT 可算名詞 A **comic** is a magazine that contains stories told in pictures. 漫画雑誌 [mainly BRIT 主に英国英語; AM usually **comic book** 米国英語では通常 comic book]

comi|cal /kɒmɪkəl/ ADJ 形容詞 If you describe something as **comical**, you mean that it makes you laugh because it is funny or silly. こっけいな ❑ Her expression is almost comical. 彼女の表現はこっけいなほどだ.

com|ic book (**comic books**) N-COUNT 可算名詞 A **comic book** is a magazine that contains stories told in pictures. 漫画雑誌 [mainly AM 主に米国英語] ❑ ...comic book heroes such as Spider Man. スパイダーマンのような漫画雑誌の英雄

com|ing /kʌmɪŋ/ **1** ADJ 形容詞 A **coming** event or time is an event or time that will happen soon. 来たるべき、次の [ADJ n] ❑ This obviously depends on the weather in the coming months. これは明らかにここ数か月の天気に左右される. **2** → see also **come**

com|ma /kɒmə/ (**commas**) N-COUNT 可算名詞 A **comma** is the punctuation mark, which is used to separate parts of a sentence or items in a list. コンマ 読点

com|mand /kəmænd/ (**commands, commanding, commanded**) **1** V-T 他動詞 If someone in authority **commands** you to do something, they tell you that you must do it. 命じる [他動詞] ❑ He commanded his troops to attack. 彼は自分の部隊に攻撃を命じた. [mainly WRITTEN 主に書き言葉] ❑ "Get in your car and follow me," she commanded. 「クルマに乗り込んでついてきなさい」彼女は命令した. ● N-VAR 可変性名詞 **Command** is also a noun. 命令 ❑ The tanker failed to respond to a command to stop. タンカーは停止命令に応じ損ねた. ❑ I closed my eyes at his command. 私は彼の命令に従って目を閉じた. **2** V-T 他動詞 If you **command** something such as respect or obedience, you obtain it because you are popular, famous, or important. 値する [他動詞] ❑ ...an excellent physician who commanded the respect of all her colleagues. 同僚全員の尊敬を集めた優れた物理学者 [no cont] **3** V-T 他動詞 If an army or country **commands** a place, they have total control over it. 支配する [他動詞] ❑ Yemen commands the strait at the southern end of the Red Sea. イ

エメンは紅海南端の海峡の支配権をもつ. ● N-UNCOUNT 不可算名詞 **Command** is also a noun. 支配 ❑ ...the struggle for command of the air. 制空権をめぐる争い **4** V-T 他動詞 An officer who **commands** part of an army, navy, or air force is responsible for controlling and organizing it. 指揮する [他動詞] ❑ ...the French general who commands the U.N. troops in the region. その地域で国連軍を指揮するフランス人司令官 ● N-UNCOUNT 不可算名詞 **Command** is also a noun. 指揮 ❑ ...a small garrison under the command of Major James Craig. ジェームズ・クレイグ少佐指揮下の小さな駐屯軍 **5** N-COUNT-COLL 集合可算名詞 In the armed forces, a **command** is a group of officers who are responsible for organizing and controlling part of an army, navy, or air force. 司令部 ❑ He had authorization from the military command to retaliate. 彼は軍司令部から報復を行う許可を得た. **6** N-COUNT 可算名詞 In computing, a **command** is an instruction that you give to a computer. コンピューターの命令 ❑ I entered the command into my navigational computer. 私は航法コンピューターにコマンドを入力した. **7** N-UNCOUNT 不可算名詞 If someone has **command** of a situation, they have control of it because they have, or seem to have, power or authority. 指揮権 ❑ Mr. Baker would take command of the campaign. ベーカー氏は選挙運動の指揮を執るだろう. **8** N-UNCOUNT 不可算名詞 Your **command** of something, such as a foreign language, is your knowledge of it and your ability to use this knowledge. 運用力 ❑ His command of English was excellent. 彼が英語を駆使する力は見事だ. **9** PHRASE 句 If you have a particular skill or particular resources **at** your **command**, you have them and can use them fully. 自由に使えて ❑ The country should have the right to defend itself with all legal means at its command. 国はあらゆる法的手段を自由に使って自らを守る権利を有するべきだ.

com|man|dant /kɒməndænt/ (**commandants**) N-COUNT; N-TITLE 可算名詞, 称号名詞 A **commandant** is an army officer in charge of a particular place or group of people. 司令官

com|mand econo|my (**command economies**) N-COUNT 可算名詞 In a **command economy**, business activities and the use of resources are decided by the government, and not by market forces. 計画経済 [BUSINESS 実業] ❑ ...the Czech Republic's transition from a command economy to a market system. チェコ共和国の計画経済から市場経済への移行

com|mand|er /kəmændər/ (**commanders**) **1** N-COUNT; N-TITLE; N-VOC 可算名詞, 称号名詞, 呼格名詞 A **commander** is an officer in charge of a military operation or organization. 司令官 ❑ The commander and some of the men had been released. 司令官と兵士の一部が解放された. **2** N-COUNT; N-TITLE; N-VOC 可算名詞, 称号名詞, 呼格名詞 A **commander** is an officer in the U.S. Navy or the Royal Navy. 海軍中佐

com|mand|ing /kəmændɪŋ/ **1** ADJ 形容詞 If you are in a **commanding** position or situation, you are in a strong or powerful position or situation. 支配的な ❑ Right now you're in a more commanding position than you have been for ages. 今、あなたはこれまでの長い間にくらべ支配力のある位置に置かれている. **2** ADJ 形容詞 If you describe someone as **commanding**, you mean that they are powerful and confident. 堂々とした [APPROVAL 賛成] ❑ Lovett was a tall, commanding man with a waxed gray mustache. ロベットは背が高く堂々とした男で、ろうを塗った灰色のひげをたくわえていた. **3** → see also **command**

com|man|do /kəmændoʊ/ (**commandos** or **commandoes**) **1** N-COUNT 可算名詞 A **commando** is a group of soldiers who have been specially trained to carry out surprise attacks. 奇襲部隊 ❑ ...a small commando of marines. 海軍の小規模な奇襲部隊 **2** N-COUNT 可算名詞 A **commando** is a soldier who is a member of a commando. 奇襲部隊員 ❑ ...small groups of American commandos. アメリカ奇襲部隊員の小集団

> **Word Link** _memor ≈ memory_ : com**memor**ate, **memor**ial, **memor**y

com|memo|rate /kəmɛməreɪt/ (**commemorates, commemorating, commemorated**) V-T 他動詞 To **commemorate** an important event or person means to remember them by means of a special action, ceremony, or specially created object. 記念する [他動詞] ❑ One room contained a gallery of paintings commemorating great moments in baseball history. ひとつの部屋の中には野球史の偉大な瞬間を記念する絵を飾ったギャラリーがあった. ● **com|memo|ra|tion** /kəmɛməreɪʃən/ (**commemorations**) N-VAR 可変性名詞 記念 ❑ ...a march in commemoration of Malcolm X. マルコムXを記念する行進

com|memo|ra|tive /kəmɛmərətɪv, -əreɪtɪv/ ADJ 形容詞 A **commemorative** object or event is intended to make people remember a particular event or person. 記念の [ADJ n] ❑ A commemorative stamp will be issued October 15. 10月15日に記念切手が発行される.

com|mence /kəmɛns/ (**commences, commencing, commenced**) V-T/V-I 他動詞/自動詞 When something **commences** or you **commence** it, it begins. 開始する [他動詞] 開

始する [自動詞] ❑ *The academic year commences at the beginning of October.* 新学年は10月初旬にはじまる． [FORMAL 形式ばった] ❑ *They commenced a systematic search.* 彼らは系統立てた調査を開始した．

Commence, start, and begin all have a similar meaning, although commence is more formal and is not normally used in conversation. ❑ *The meeting is ready to begin... He tore the list up and started a fresh one... an alternative to commencing the process of European integration.* Note that begin, start, and commence can all be followed by an "-ing form" or a noun, but only begin and start can be followed by a "to" infinitive.

---

com|mence|ment /kəmɛnsmənt/ (commencements)
1 N-UNCOUNT 不可算名詞 The **commencement** of something is its beginning. 開始 [FORMAL 形式ばった] ❑ *All applicants should be at least 16 years of age at the commencement of this course.* 申込者は，課程の開始時に満16歳に達していることが必要 **2** N-VAR 可変性名詞 **Commencement** is a ceremony at a university, college, or high school at which students formally receive their degrees or diplomas. 卒業式 [AM 米国英語] ❑ *President Bush gave the commencement address today at the University of Notre Dame.* ブッシュ大統領はノートルダム大学の卒業式で演説を行った．

com|mend /kəmɛnd/ (commends, commending, commended) **1** V-T 他動詞 If you **commend** someone or something, you praise them formally. 賞讃する [他動詞] ❑ *I commended her for that action.* 私は彼女の行為をたたえた． [FORMAL 形式ばった] ❑ *The reports commend her bravery.* その報告で彼女の勇気が賞賛された． ● **com|men|da|tion** /kɒməndeɪʃⁿn/ (commendations) N-COUNT 可算名詞 賞賛 ❑ *Clare won a commendation for bravery in 1998 after risking his life at the scene of a gas blast.* クレアはガス爆発の現場で生命を危険にさらした勇気をたたえられ，1998年に表彰された． **2** V-T 他動詞 If someone **commends** a person or thing **to** you, they tell you that you will find them good or useful. 推薦する [他動詞] ❑ *I can commend it to him as a realistic course of action.* 現実的行為として私は彼にそれを薦めることができる． [FORMAL 形式ばった]

com|mend|able /kəmɛndəbⁿl/ ADJ 形容詞 If you describe someone's behavior as **commendable**, you approve of it or are praising it. 賞賛に値する [FORMAL 形式ばった, APPROVAL 賛成] ❑ *He has acted with commendable speed.* 彼は賞賛に値する速さで行動した．

com|ment /kɒmɛnt/ (comments, commenting, commented) **1** V-T/V-I 他動詞/自動詞 If you **comment on** something, you give your opinion about it or you give an explanation for it. 論評する [他動詞], 論評する [自動詞] ❑ *So far, Mr. Cook has not commented on these reports.* これまでクック氏はこれらの報告について意見を述べていない． ❑ *You really can't comment until you know the facts.* あなたは真相を知るまで本当に意見を述べることはできない． ❑ *One student commented that she preferred literature to social science.* ある学生が社会科学よりも文学を好むとの考えを述べた．

If you **comment** on a situation, or make a **comment** about it, you give your opinion on it. ❑ *Mr. Cook has not commented on these reports... I was wondering whether you had any comments.* If you **mention** something, you say it, but only briefly, especially when you have not talked about it before. ❑ *He mentioned that he might go to New York.* If you **remark** on something, or make a **remark** about it, you say what you think or what you have noticed, often in a casual way. ❑ *Visitors remark on how well the children look... General Sutton's remarks about the conflict.*

---

2 N-VAR 可変性名詞 A **comment** is something that you say which expresses your opinion of something or which gives an explanation of it. 論評 ❑ *He made his comments at a news conference in Amsterdam.* 彼はアムステルダムの記者会見で考えを述べた． ❑ *There's been no comment so far from police about the allegations.* これまでその嫌疑に関して警察からの見解はない． **3** CONVENTION 慣習表現 People say **"no comment"** as a way of refusing to answer a question, usually when it is asked by a journalist. ノーコメント ❑ *No comment. I don't know anything.* ノーコメントです．何も知らないんです．

com|men|tary /kɒmənteri/ (commentaries) **1** N-VAR 可変性名詞 A **commentary** is a description of an event that is broadcast on radio or television while the event is taking place. 解説 ❑ *He gave the listening crowd a running commentary.* 彼は聴衆に向けて実況放送を行った． **2** N-COUNT 可算名詞 A **commentary** is an article or book which explains or discusses something. 解説 ❑ *Ms. Rich will be writing a twice-weekly commentary on American society and culture.*

リッチ氏は週2回，アメリカ社会および文化に関する解説を書いているだろう． **3** N-UNCOUNT 不可算名詞 **Commentary** is discussion or criticism of something. 批評 [also "a", with supp] ❑ *The show mixed comedy with social commentary.* お笑いと社会批評を織り交ぜた番組

com|men|tate /kɒmənteɪt/ (commentates, commentating, commentated) V-I 自動詞 To **commentate** means to give a radio or television commentary on an event. 解説する [自動詞] ❑ *They are in New Hampshire to commentate on the ice hockey.* 彼らはアイスホッケーの解説のためニューハンプシャーにいる．

com|men|ta|tor /kɒmənteɪtər/ (commentators) **1** N-COUNT 可算名詞 A **commentator** is a broadcaster who gives a radio or television commentary on an event. 解説者 ❑ *...a sports commentator.* スポーツ解説者 **2** N-COUNT 可算名詞 A **commentator** is also someone who often writes or broadcasts about a particular subject. 解説者 ❑ *...a political commentator.* 政治解説者

Word Link merc ≈ trading : commerce, merchandise, merchant

---

com|merce /kɒmɜrs/ **1** N-UNCOUNT 不可算名詞 **Commerce** is the activities and procedures involved in buying and selling things. 商業 ❑ *They have made their fortunes from industry and commerce.* 彼らはその富を商工業によって築いた． **2** → see also **chamber of commerce**
→ see **stock market**

com|mer|cial /kəmɜrʃⁿl/ (commercials) **1** ADJ 形容詞 **Commercial** means involving or relating to the buying and selling of goods. 商業の ❑ *Baltimore in its heyday was a major center of industrial and commercial activity.* 最盛期のボルティモアは商工業活動の重要拠点だった． **2** ADJ 形容詞 **Commercial** organizations and activities are concerned with making money or profits, rather than, for example, with scientific research or providing a public service. 営利目的の ❑ *The company has indeed become more commercial over the past decade.* 確かにその会社はこの10年で利益追及の度合が高まった． ❑ *Conservationists in Chile are concerned over the effect of commercial exploitation of forests.* チリの環境保護主義者は森林の営利的利用の影響を懸念している． ● **com|mer|cial|ly** ADV 副詞 商業的に ❑ *The plane will be commercially viable if 400 can be sold.* その飛行機は400機が売れればビジネスとして成り立つ． **3** ADJ 形容詞 A **commercial** product is made to be sold to the public. 市販用の ❑ *They are the leading manufacturer in both defense and commercial products.* その会社は防衛用，民生用どちらの製品でも代表メーカーだ． ● **com|mer|cial|ly** ADV 副詞 市販用に ❑ *It was the first commercially available machine to employ artificial intelligence.* それは人工知能を用いた最初の市販機であった． **4** ADJ 形容詞 A **commercial** vehicle is a vehicle used for carrying goods, or passengers who pay. 商用の ❑ *The route is used every day by many hundreds of commercial vehicles.* そのルートは，毎日，何百台もの商用車が利用する． **5** ADJ 形容詞 **Commercial** television and radio are paid for by the broadcasting of advertisements, rather than by the government. 民間の ❑ *There were no commercial radio stations until 1920.* 1920年まで民間のラジオ局はなかった． **6** ADJ 形容詞 **Commercial** is used to describe something such as a movie or a type of music that it is intended to be popular with the public, and is not very original or of high quality. 営利本位の ❑ *There's a feeling among a lot of people that music has become too commercial.* 音楽が営利本位になりすぎたと感じる人が多い． **7** N-COUNT 可算名詞 A **commercial** is an advertisement that is broadcast on television or radio. 宣伝 ❑ *Turn the channel – there are too many commercials.* チャンネルを変えてくれ． - 宣伝が多すぎる．
→ see **advertising**

A **commercial** is a form of advertising done on the radio or television. **Advertisements** that appear in newspapers, magazines or on the internet are not called commercials. Newspapers allow individuals to post notices for selling items or announcing job vacancies. These are called **classified ads** or (in the U.S. only) **want ads**.

---

com|mer|cial bank (commercial banks) N-COUNT 可算名詞 A **commercial bank** is a bank whose main customers are businesses. 商業銀行 [BUSINESS 実業]

com|mer|cial break (commercial breaks) N-COUNT 可算名詞 A **commercial break** is the interval during a commercial television program, or between programs, during which advertisements are shown. コマーシャル ❑ *The movie was aired without commercial breaks.* 映画はコマーシャルなしで放映された．

com|mer|cial|ism /kəmɜrʃəlɪzəm/ N-UNCOUNT 不可算名詞 **Commercialism** is the practice of making a lot of money from things without caring about their quality. 商業主義，もうけ主義 [DISAPPROVAL 不賛成] ❑ *Koons has engrossed himself in a world of commercialism that most modern artists disdain.* クーンズはほとんどの現代の芸術家が見向きもしない金もうけの世界にはまり込んでいる．

com|mer|cial|ize /kəmɜrʃəlaɪz/ (**commercializes, commercializing, commercialized**) V-T 他動詞 If something **is commercialized**, it is used or changed in such a way that it makes money or profits, often in a way that people disapprove of. 金もうけの手段にする [DISAPPROVAL 不賛成] [usu passive] ❑ It seems such a pity that a distinguished and honored name should be commercialized in this way. 著名で栄誉ある名がこのように金もうけの手段にされるのはとても残念に思われる. ● **com|mer|cial|ized** ADJ 形容詞 金もうけの手段になった ❑ Rock'n'roll has become so commercialized and safe since punk. パンクロック以降、ロックンロールは商業主義によって堕落し無害になってしまった. ● **com|mer|ciali|za|tion** /kəmɜrʃəlaɪzeɪʃ°n/ N-UNCOUNT 不可算名詞 商業化 ❑...the commercialization of Christmas. クリスマスの商業化.

com|mis|sion /kəmɪʃ°n/ (**commissions, commissioning, commissioned**) **1** V-T 他動詞 If you **commission** something or **commission** someone **to** do something, you formally arrange for someone to do a piece of work for you. 委託する ❑ The Department of Agriculture commissioned a study into organic farming. 農務省は有機農法の研究を委託した. ● N-VAR 可変性名詞 **Commission** is also a noun. 委託 ❑ Our china can be bought off the shelf by commission. 当社の陶器は店頭または受注にて販売しております. **2** N-COUNT 可算名詞 A **commission** is a piece of work that someone is asked to do and is paid for. 任務 ❑ Just a few days ago, I finished a commission. ほんの数日前に任務を完了したばかりです. **3** N-VAR 可変性名詞 **Commission** is a sum of money paid to a salesperson for every sale that he or she makes. If a salesperson is paid **on commission**, the amount they receive depends on the amount they sell. 歩合 ❑ The salespeople work on commission only. 販売員は歩合給のみで働いている. **4** N-UNCOUNT 不可算名詞 If a bank or other company charges **commission**, they charge a fee for providing a service, for example for exchanging money or issuing an insurance policy. 手数料 [BUSINESS 実業] ❑ Travel agents charge 1 per cent commission on tickets. 旅行代理店の手数料としてチケット代金の1パーセントがかかる. **5** N-COUNT-COLL 集合可算名詞 A **commission** is a group of people who have been appointed to find out about something or to control something. 委員会 ❑ The government has set up a commission to look into those crimes. 政府はこうした犯罪を調査するための委員会を設置しました. **6** N-COUNT 可算名詞 If a member of the armed forces receives a **commission**, he or she becomes an officer. 任官辞令 ❑ He accepted a commission as a naval officer. 彼は海軍士官に任命された.

com|mis|sion|er /kəmɪʃənər/ (**commissioners**) also **Commissioner** N-COUNT 可算名詞 A **commissioner** is an important official in a government department or other organization. 長官；理事 ❑...Alaska's commissioner of education. アラスカ州教育庁長官.

com|mit /kəmɪt/ (**commits, committing, committed**) **1** V-T 他動詞 If someone **commits** a crime or a sin, they do something illegal or bad. 犯す ❑ I have never committed any crime. 私はどんな犯罪も犯したことはない. ❑ This is a man who has committed murder. こいつは人殺しだ. **2** V-T 他動詞 If someone **commits** suicide, they deliberately kill themselves. 自殺する ❑ There are unconfirmed reports he tried to commit suicide. 未確認ですが、彼は自殺を図ったということです. **3** V-T 他動詞 If you **commit** money or resources **to** something, you decide to use them for a particular purpose. 投じる ❑ They called on Western nations to commit more money to the poorest nations. 彼らは最貧国への拠出金を増やすように欧米諸国に呼びかけた. ❑ The company had committed thousands of dollars for a plan to reduce mercury emissions. その会社では水銀の排出を削減する計画に数千ドルを投じてきました. **4** V-T/V-I 他動詞/自動詞 If you **commit yourself to** something, you say that you will definitely do it. If you **commit yourself to** someone, you decide that you want to have a long-term relationship with them. 堅く誓う；一と一緒にやっていくことを心に決める ❑ I would advise people to think very carefully about committing themselves to working Sundays. 私なら日曜の勤務については十分考えてから約束するように言うでしょうね. ❑ I'd like a friendship that might lead to something deeper, but I wouldn't want to commit myself too soon. 仲よくなれる友人ができればと思いますが、今すぐそうしたいというわけではないんです. ❑ He won't commit. 彼にはそのつもりはない. **5** V-T 他動詞 If you do not want to **commit yourself** on something, you do not want to say what you really think about it or what you are going to do. 明言を避ける [with brd-neg] ❑ It isn't their diplomatic style to commit themselves on such a delicate issue. このような微妙な問題に対して明確な態度を示すのは彼らの外交スタイルではありません. **6** V-T 他動詞 If someone **is committed to** a mental hospital, prison, or other institution, they are officially sent there for a period of time. 収容される [usu passive] ❑ Arthur's drinking caused him to be committed to a psychiatric hospital. 飲酒が原因でアーサーは精神病院に収容されることになった. **7** V-T 他動詞 If you **commit** something to paper or **to** writing, you record it by writing it down. If you **commit** something to memory, you learn it so that you will remember it. 書き留める；記憶する ❑ She had not committed anything to paper about it. 彼女はそのことは何も書き留めていなかった.

Word Partnership *commit* は次の語句と使われる:

N.	commit **a crime** [1]
	commit **suicide** [2]
	commit **resources** [3]
	commit **to** *something* [4]
	commit **to memory** [7]

com|mit|ment /kəmɪtmənt/ (**commitments**) **1** N-UNCOUNT 不可算名詞 **Commitment** is a strong belief in an idea or system. 強い信念 ❑...commitment to the ideals of democracy. 民主主義の理想に対する強い信念. **2** N-COUNT 可算名詞 A **commitment** is something which regularly takes up some of your time because of an agreement you have made or because of responsibilities that you have. 必ずやらなければならないこと ❑ I've got a lot of commitments. やるべきことが山ほどある. **3** N-COUNT 可算名詞 If you make a **commitment to** do something, you promise that you will do it. 約束 ❑ We made a commitment to keep working together. 今後も協力し合っていくことを約束した. **4** N-VAR 可変性名詞 **Commitment** is the process of officially sending someone to a prison or a hospital. 収容 [AM 米国英語] ❑ State law allows involuntary commitment for psychiatric evaluation. 州法は本人の同意なしに精神鑑定を行うことを認めている.

Word Partnership *commitment* は次の語句と使われる:

ADJ.	**deep/firm/strong** commitment [1]
	long-term commitment, **prior** commitment [3]
N.	*someone's* commitment [1] [2] [3]
PREP.	commitment **to** *someone/something* [2] [3]
V.	**make a** commitment [3]

com|mit|tee /kəmɪti/ (**committees**) N-COUNT-COLL 集合可算名詞 A **committee** is a group of people who meet to make decisions or plans for a larger group or organization that they represent. 委員会 ❑...the school yearbook committee. 卒業記念アルバム制作委員会.

com|mod|ity /kəmɒdɪti/ (**commodities**) N-COUNT 可算名詞 A **commodity** is something that is sold for money. 商品 [BUSINESS 実業] ❑ Prices went up on several basic commodities like bread and meat. パンや肉などの生活必需品数点が値上がりしました.

→ see **economics, stock market**

com|mon /kɒmən/ (**commons**) **1** ADJ 形容詞 If something is **common**, it is found in large numbers or it happens often. 一般の ❑ His name was Hansen, a common name in Norway. 彼はハンセンという名字で、ノルウェーではよくある名前だった. ❑ Oil pollution is the most common cause of death for seabirds. 油汚染は海鳥の最も一般的な死因である. ● **com|mon|ly** ADV 副詞 [ADV with v] ❑ Parsley is one of the most commonly used herbs. パセリは最もよく使われるハーブの1つである. **2** ADJ 形容詞 If something is **common to** two or more people or groups, it is done, possessed, or used by them all. 共通の ❑ Moldavians and Romanians share a common language. モルダビア人とルーマニア人は同じ言語を使用しています. **3** ADJ 形容詞 When there are more animals or plants of a particular species than there are of related species, then the first species is called **common**. 普通の、よく見かける [ADJ n] ❑...the common house fly. 普通よく見かけるイエバエ. **4** ADJ 形容詞 **Common** is used to indicate that someone or something is of the ordinary kind and not special in any way. ごく一般的な [ADJ n] ❑ Democracy might elevate the common man to a position of political superiority. 民主主義においては一般市民が政治的に優位に立つこともある. **5** ADJ 形容詞 **Common** decency or **common** courtesy is the decency or courtesy which most people have. You usually talk about this when someone has not shown these characteristics in their behavior to show your disapproval of them. 常識的な [DISAPPROVAL 不賛成] ❑ It is common decency to give your seat to anyone in greater need. 体のつらそうな人に席を譲るのは当たり前である. **6** ADJ 形容詞 You can use **common** to describe knowledge, an opinion, or a feeling that is shared by people in general. 共有している [ADJ n] ❑ It is common knowledge that swimming is one of the best forms of exercise. 水泳が特に優れた運動であることは誰もが知っている. ● **com|mon|ly** ADV 副詞 [ADV -ed] 一般に ❑ A little adolescent rebellion is commonly believed to be healthy. ふつう思春期に少々反抗的になるのは当たり前のことだと考えられている. **7** ADJ 形容詞 If you describe someone or their behavior as **common**, you mean that they show a lack of taste, education, and good manners. 低俗な [mainly BRIT 主に英国英語, DISAPPROVAL 不賛成] ❑ She might be a little common at times, but she was certainly not boring. 彼女はちょっと品のないところがあるが、まず人を飽きさせることはなかった. **8** N-COUNT; N-IN-NAMES 可算名詞、名称中の名詞 A **common** is an area of grassy land, usually in or near a village or small town, where the public is allowed to go. 共有地 ❑ We are warning women not to go out on to the common alone. 女性が一人でその共有地に行かないように注意を呼びかけている. **9** PHRASE 句 If two or more things have something **in common**, they have the same

characteristic or feature. 共通の ❑ *The oboe and the clarinet have certain features in common.* オーボエとクラリネットにはある共通した特徴がある. **10** PHRASE 句 If two or more people have something **in common**, they share the same interests or experiences. 共通の ❑ *He had very little in common with his sister.* 彼は妹とほとんど共通点がない. **11 common ground** → see **ground**

Thesaurus   common また次を参照:

ADJ.   frequent, typical, usual **1**
     commonplace, everyday; (ant.) special **4**
     accepted, standard, universal **6**

Word Partnership   common は次の語句と使われる:

N.   common **belief**, common **language**, common **practice**, common **problem** **1**
ADV.   **fairly/increasingly/more/most** common **1**
V.   **have** *something* in common **9 10**

---

com|mon law **1** N-UNCOUNT 不可算名詞 **Common law** is the system of law which is based on judges' decisions and on custom rather than on written laws. 慣習法 ❑ *Canadian libel law is based on English common law.* カナダの文書誹毀(ひき)法はイギリスのコモンローが下敷きとなっている. **2** ADJ 形容詞 A **common law** relationship is regarded as a marriage because it has lasted a long time, although no official marriage contract has been signed. 内縁の [ADJ n] ❑ *...his common law wife.* 彼の内縁の妻.

com|mon noun (common nouns) N-COUNT 可算名詞 A **common noun** is a noun such as "tree," "water," or "beauty" that is not the name of one particular person or thing. Compare **proper noun**. 普通名詞

com|mon|place /kɒmənpleɪs/ ADJ 形容詞 If something is **commonplace**, it happens often or is often found, and is therefore not surprising. 平凡な ❑ *Inter-racial marriages have become commonplace.* もはや異人種間の結婚は珍しくなくなった.

com|mon sense also **commonsense** N-UNCOUNT 不可算名詞 Your **common sense** is your natural ability to make good judgments and to behave in a practical and sensible way. 常識 ❑ *Use your common sense.* 自らの良識をもって判断せよ. ❑ *She always had a lot of common sense.* 彼女はいつも常識をわきまえていた.

com|mon stock **1** N-UNCOUNT 不可算名詞 **Common stock** refers to the shares in a company that are owned by people who have a right to vote at the company's meetings and to receive part of the company's profits after the holders of preferred stock have been paid. 普通株式 [AM 米国英語 BUSINESS 実業] ❑ *The company priced its offering of 2.7 million shares of common stock at 20 cents a share.* 会社は普通株式270万株の発行価格を1株20セントにした. **2** → see also **preferred stock**

common|wealth /kɒmənwelθ/ **1** N-PROPER 固有名詞 The **commonwealth** is an organization consisting of the United Kingdom and most of the countries that were previously under its rule. イギリス連邦 ❑ *...the Asian, Caribbean and African members of the commonwealth.* アジア, カリブ海, アフリカのイギリス連邦加盟国. **2** N-IN-NAMES 名称中の名詞 **Commonwealth** is used in the official names of some countries, groups of countries, or parts of countries. 共和国; 連邦; 州 ❑ *...the Commonwealth of Australia.* オーストラリア連邦.

com|mo|tion /kəmoʊʃⁿn/ **(commotions)** N-VAR 可変性名詞 A **commotion** is a lot of noise, confusion, and excitement. 騒動 ❑ *He heard a commotion outside.* 彼は外で騒ぎ声がするのを耳にした.

com|mu|nal /kəmjʊnⁿl/ **1** ADJ 形容詞 **Communal** means relating to particular groups in a country or society. 共同体の, コミュニティーの [ADJ n] ❑ *Communal violence broke out in different parts of the country.* 国の各地で暴動が発生しました. **2** ADJ 形容詞 You use **communal** to describe something that is shared by a group of people. 公共の, 共同の ❑ *The inmates ate in a communal dining room.* 受刑者は共同食堂で食事をとった.

com|mune /kɒmjʊn/ **(communes)** N-COUNT 可算名詞 A **commune** is a group of people who live together and share many of their possessions and responsibilities. コミューン ❑ *Mack lived in a commune.* マックはコミューンで共同生活を送った.

Word Link   commun ≈ sharing : communicate, communism, community

---

com|mu|ni|cate /kəmjʊnɪkeɪt/ **(communicates, communicating, communicated)** **1** V-RECIP 相互動詞 If you **communicate with** someone, you share or exchange information with them, for example by speaking, writing, or using equipment. You can also say that two people **communicate**. 情報交換する ❑ *My birth mother has never communicated with me.* 生みの母からは一度だって連絡はありません. ❑ *Officials of the CIA depend heavily on e-mail to communicate with each other.* CIAでは互い

の連絡をほとんど電子メールに頼っている. ● **com|mu|ni|ca|tion** N-UNCOUNT 不可算名詞 [oft N "with/between" n] 情報交換 ❑ *Lithuania hasn't had any direct communication with Moscow.* リトアニアはまだモスクワと直接交渉していません. ❑ *...use of the radio telephone for communication between controllers and pilots.* 管制官とパイロットの通信手段としての無線電話の利用. **2** V-RECIP 相互動詞 If one person **communicates** with another, they successfully make each other aware of their feelings and ideas. You can also say that two people **communicate**. 意思疎通する ❑ *He was never good at communicating with the players.* 彼は選手との意思疎通がいつも苦手だった. ❑ *Family therapy showed us how to communicate with each other.* 家族療法を通して互いに意思疎通する方法を学ぶことができた. ● **com|mu|ni|ca|tion** N-UNCOUNT 不可算名詞 意思疎通 ❑ *There was a tremendous lack of communication between us.* 私たちにはほとんど全く意思疎通がなかった. ❑ *Good communication with people around you could prove difficult.* 周りの人とうまく意思疎通しようとしても難しいことがあるだろう. **3** V-T 他動詞 If you **communicate** information, a feeling, or an idea **to** someone, you let them know about it. 伝える ❑ *They successfully communicate their knowledge to others.* 彼らは自分たちの知識を周りに伝えるのがうまい.

com|mu|ni|ca|tion /kəmjʊnɪkeɪʃⁿn/ **(communications)** **1** N-PLURAL 複数名詞 **Communications** are the systems and processes that are used to communicate or broadcast information, especially by means of electricity or radio waves. 通信 ❑ *...a communications satellite.* 通信衛星. **2** N-COUNT 可算名詞 A **communication** is a message. 伝言 [FORMAL 形式ばった] ❑ *The ambassador has brought with him a communication from the president.* 大使は大統領の親書を携えてきました. **3** → see also **communicate** → see **brain**, **radio**

com|mun|ion /kəmjʊnyən/ **1** N-UNCOUNT 不可算名詞 **Communion** with nature or with a person is the feeling that you are sharing thoughts or feelings with them. 親交 [also "a" N, oft n "with" n] ❑ *...communion with nature.* 自然との深いかかわり. **2** N-UNCOUNT 不可算名詞 **Communion** is the Christian ceremony in which people eat bread and drink wine in memory of Christ's death. 聖餐(せいさん)式 ❑ *Most villagers took communion only at Easter.* 大方の村人は復活祭のときだけ聖体を拝領した.

Word Link   ism ≈ action or state : communism, optimism, patriotism

---

com|mun|ism /kɒmyənɪzəm/ also **Communism** N-UNCOUNT 可算名詞 **Communism** is the political belief that all people are equal, that there should be no private ownership and that workers should control the means of producing things. 共産主義 ❑ *...the ultimate triumph of communism in the world.* 全世界における共産主義の究極的な勝利.

com|mun|ist /kɒmyənɪst/ **(communists)** also **Communist** **1** N-COUNT 可算名詞 A **communist** is someone who believes in communism. 共産主義者 ❑ *Her family fled Czechoslovakia when the communists seized power in 1947.* 1947年に共産党が権力を掌握すると, 彼女は家族とともにチェコスロバキアを脱出した. **2** ADJ 形容詞 **Communist** means relating to communism. 共産主義の ❑ *...the Communist Party.* 共産党

com|mu|ni|ty /kəmjʊniti/ **(communities)** **1** N-SING-COLL 集合的単数名詞 The **community** is all the people who live in a particular area or place. 地域住民 ❑ *He's well liked by people in the community.* 彼は地元で人気がある. **2** N-COUNT-COLL 集合可算名詞 A particular **community** is a group of people who are similar in some way. 一社会 ❑ *The police haven't really done anything for the black community in particular.* 警察は黒人社会に対して特に対策を講じていません. **3** N-UNCOUNT 不可算名詞 **Community** is friendship between different people or groups, and a sense of having something in common. 連帯感 ❑ *Two of our greatest strengths are diversity and community.* 我々の最大の強みといえば, 多様性と連帯感である.

Thesaurus   community また次を参照:

N.   neighborhood, public, society **1**

---

com|mu|ni|ty cen|ter (community centers) N-COUNT 可算名詞 A **community center** is a place that is specially provided for the people, groups, and organizations in a particular area, where they can go in order to meet one another and do things. 市民センター

com|mu|ni|ty ser|vice **1** N-UNCOUNT 不可算名詞 **Community service** is unpaid work that criminals sometimes do as a punishment instead of being sent to prison. 地域奉仕 ❑ *He was sentenced to 140 hours' community service for drunk driving.* 彼は飲酒運転で地域奉仕140時間の判決を受けた. **2** N-UNCOUNT 不可算名詞 **Community service** is unpaid voluntary work that a person performs for the benefit of his or her local community. 地域でのボランティア活動 ❑ *I have been doing community service work in Oakland for the past several years.* 私はここ数年オークランドでボランティア活動を行っています.

> **Word Link**   mut ≈ changing : com**mute**, **mut**ate, **mut**ilate

com|mute /kəmyut/ (commutes, commuting, commuted) **1** V-I 自動詞 If you **commute**, you travel a long distance every day between your home and your place of work. 通勤する ❑ *Mike commutes to Miami every day.* マイクは毎日マイアミまで通勤している. ❑ *McLaren began commuting between Philadelphia and New York.* マクラーレンはフィラデルフィアとニューヨークの間を通い始めた. ●**com|mut|er** (commuters) N-COUNT 可算名詞 通勤者 ❑ *There are significant numbers of commuters using our streets.* この辺りの通りを利用する通勤者はかなりいます. **2** N-COUNT 可算名詞 A **commute** is the journey that you make when you commute. 通勤 ❑ *The average Los Angeles commute is over 60 miles a day.* ロサンゼルスの通勤者は一日平均60マイル以上移動している.
→ see **traffic, transportation**

com|mut|er belt (commuter belts) N-COUNT 可算名詞 A **commuter belt** is the area surrounding a large city, where many people who work in the city live. ベッドタウン ❑ *…people who live in the commuter belt around the capital.* 首都圏のベッドタウンに住む人々.

> **Word Link**   com ≈ with, together : **com**bine, **com**pact, **com**panion

com|pact /kəmpækt/ (compacts) **1** ADJ 形容詞 **Compact** things are small or take up very little space. You use this word when you think this is a good quality. 小型の [APPROVAL 賛成] ❑ *…my compact office in Washington.* ワシントンのこじんまりした私のオフィス. **2** ADJ 形容詞 A **compact** person is small but looks strong. 小柄でがっちりした ❑ *He was compact, probably no taller than me.* 彼は小柄でがっちりした人で, 確か身長は私と同じくらいだった. **3** N-COUNT 可算名詞 A **compact** or a **compact car** is a car that is smaller than the average car, and that is economical to run. 小型の

com|pact disc (compact discs) also **compact disk** N-COUNT 可算名詞 **Compact discs** are small shiny discs that contain music or computer information. The abbreviation **CD** is also used. CD [also "on" N]
→ see **DVD**

com|pan|ion /kəmpænyən/ (companions) N-COUNT 可算名詞 A **companion** is someone who you spend time with or who you are traveling with. 仲間; 連れ ❑ *Fred had been her constant companion for the last six years of her life.* フレッドはここ6年間ずっと彼女に連れ添ってきました.
→ see **pet**

com|pan|ion|ship /kəmpænyənʃɪp/ N-UNCOUNT 不可算名詞 **Companionship** is having someone you know and like with you, instead of being on your own. 友達づきあい ❑ *I depended on his companionship and on his judgment.* 私にとって彼は頼みの綱で, 彼の意見は貴重だった.

com|pa|ny /kʌmpəni/ (companies) **1** N-COUNT-COLL; N-IN-NAMES 集合可算名詞, 名称中の名詞 A **company** is a business organization that makes money by selling goods or services. 会社 ❑ *Sheila found some work as a secretary in an insurance company.* シーラは保険会社で秘書の仕事を見つけた. **2** N-COUNT-COLL; N-IN-NAMES 集合可算名詞, 名称中の名詞 A **company** is a group of opera singers, dancers, or actors who work together. 一座, 劇団 ❑ *…the Phoenix Dance Company.* フェニックスダンスカンパニー. **3** N-COUNT; N-IN-NAMES 可算名詞, 名称中の名詞 A **company** is a group of soldiers that is usually part of a battalion or regiment, and that is divided into two or more platoons. 中隊 ❑ *The division will consist of two tank companies and one infantry company.* 師団は2個タンク中隊と1個歩兵中隊で編成されます. **4** N-UNCOUNT 不可算名詞 **Company** is having another person or other people with you, usually when this is pleasant or stops you feeling lonely. 付き合い ❑ *"I won't stay long." — "No, please. I need the company."* 「長居はできないよ」「そんなこといわないで, 一緒にいて」 ❑ *Ross had always enjoyed the company of women.* ロスはいつも女たちといるのが楽しかった. **5** → see also **joint-stock company, public company** **6** PHRASE 句 If you **have company**, you have a visitor or friend with you. 客

が来ている; 友達といる ❑ *He didn't say he had company.* 彼は連れがいるとは言ってなかった. **7** PHRASE 句 If you **keep someone company**, you spend time with them and stop them from feeling lonely or bored. 一の相手をする ❑ *Why don't you stay here and keep Emma company?* ここにいてエマの相手をしてくれない?
→ see Word Web: **company**
→ see **electricity**

> **Word Partnership**   company は次の語句と使われる:
>
> | | |
> |---|---|
> | ADJ. | **foreign** company, **parent** company **1** |
> | V. | **buy/own/sell/start** a company, company **employs**, company **makes 1** |
> | | **have** company, **keep** company, **part** company **6 7** |

com|pa|ny car (company cars) N-COUNT 可算名詞 A **company car** is a car which an employer gives to an employee to use as their own, usually as a benefit of having a particular job, or because their job involves a lot of driving. 会社からの貸与車 [BUSINESS 実業] ❑ *…changes to tax laws for company cars.* 貸与車に関する税法改正

com|pa|rable /kɒmpərəbəl/ **1** ADJ 形容詞 Something that is **comparable** to something else is roughly similar, for example in amount or importance. 匹敵する ❑ *…paying the same wages to men and women for work of comparable value.* 同程度の仕事に対しては男女同一の賃金を支払う ❑ *Farmers were supposed to get an income comparable to that of townspeople.* 農業従事者は都会の人たちと同程度の収入を得ていると思われていた. **2** ADJ 形容詞 If two or more things are **comparable**, they are of the same kind or are in the same situation, and so they can reasonably be compared. 類似した, 同様の ❑ *In other comparable countries, real wages increased much more rapidly.* 同じ水準の国々では実質賃金が急上昇した. ❑ *By contrast, the comparable figure for Canada is 16 percent.* それとは対照的に, カナダの同様の値は16%である.

com|para|tive /kəmpærətɪv/ (comparatives) **1** ADJ 形容詞 You use **comparative** to show that you are judging something against a previous or different situation. For example, **comparative** calm is a situation which is calmer than before or calmer than the situation in other places. 比較的 [ADJ n] ❑ *The task was accomplished with comparative ease.* その仕事はわりと簡単に片付いた. ●**com|para|tive|ly** ADV 副詞 [ADV adj/adv] 比較的に ❑ *…a comparatively small nation.* 比較的小さな国 **2** ADJ 形容詞 A **comparative** study is a study that involves the comparison of two or more things of the same kind. 比較の [ADJ n] ❑ *…a comparative study of the dietary practices of people from various regions of India.* インド各地の食習慣の比較研究 **3** ADJ 形容詞 In grammar, the **comparative** form of an adjective or adverb shows that something has more of a quality than something else has. For example, "bigger" is the comparative form of "big," and "more quickly" is the comparative form of "quickly." Compare **superlative**. 比較級の [ADJ n] ●N-COUNT 可算名詞 **Comparative** is also a noun. 比較級 ❑ *The comparative of "pretty" is "prettier."* prettyの比較級はprettierである.

> **Word Link**   par ≈ equal : com**pare**, dis**par**ate, **par**t

com|pare /kəmpɛər/ (compares, comparing, compared) **1** V-T 他動詞 When you **compare** things, you consider them and discover the differences or similarities between them. 比較する ❑ *Compare the two illustrations in Figure 60.* 図60にある2つの例を比較してみよう. ❑ *Managers analyze their company's data and compare it with data on their competitors.* 経営者は自社のデータの分析結果をライバル企業のデータと比較する. **2** V-T 他動詞 If you **compare** one person or thing **to** another, you say that they are like the other person or thing. たとえる ❑ *Some commentators compared his work to that of James Joyce.* 彼の作品をジェイムズ・ジョイスの作品になぞらえる批評家もいました. **3** V-I 自動詞 If you say that something does not **compare with** something else, you mean that it is much worse. 一にはるかに劣る [usu with neg] ❑ *The flowers here do not compare with those at home.* ここに咲いている花はうちの花には全く及ばない. **4** V-I 自動詞 If one thing **compares** favorably

---

> **Word Web**   **company**
>
> In the United States most **companies** are **privately held corporations**. All of the **stock** in the company goes to the people who organized it. All the **profits** go to the same people. Some companies have publicly **traded stock**. This means that some or all of the start-up money came from **shares** of stock sold to the public. Such shares are **traded** on the **stock market**. People who own stock in a company receive **dividends**. They usually also have voting rights. This allows them to play a role in guiding the corporation.

with another, it is better than the other thing. If it **compares** unfavorably, it is worse than the other thing. 一に勝っている；一に劣っている □ *Our road safety record compares favorably with that of other countries.* 交通安全の実績では我が国は他国を上回っています. 5 → see also **compared**

Thesaurus *compare* また次を参照：

v. analyze, consider, contrast, examine 1
equate, match 2

com|pared /kəmpεərd/ 1 PHRASE 句 If you say, for example, that one thing is large or small **compared with** another or **compared to** another, you mean that it is larger or smaller than the other thing. 一に比べて □ *The room was light and lofty compared to the basement.* 地下室に比べその部屋は明るく天井も高かった. 2 PHRASE 句 You talk about one situation or thing **compared with** another or **compared to** another when contrasting the two situations or things. 一に対して □ *In 1800 Ireland's population was nine million, compared to Britain's 16 million.* 1800年当時のアイルランドの人口は900万人，対するイギリスの人口は1600万人だった.

com|pari|son /kəmpǽrɪsən/ (comparisons) 1 N-VAR 可変性名詞 When you make a **comparison**, you consider two or more things and discover the differences between them. 比較 □ *...a comparison of the Mexican and Guatemalan economies.* メキシコ経済とグアテマラ経済の比較. □ *Its recommendations are based on detailed comparisons between the public and private sectors.* その勧告は公共部門と民間部門を詳細に比較した調査結果に基づいている. 2 N-COUNT 可算名詞 When you make a **comparison**, you say that one thing is like another in some way. 類似 □ *It is demonstrably an unfair comparison.* 明らかに不公平な比較である. 3 PHRASE 句 If you say, for example, that something is large or small **in comparison with**, **in comparison to**, or **by comparison with** something else, you mean that it is larger or smaller than the other thing. 一と比較して □ *The amount of carbon dioxide released by human activities such as burning coal and oil is small in comparison.* 化石燃料の利用などの人間活動によって放出される二酸化炭素量のほうがむしろ少ないのです.

Word Partnership *comparison* は次の語句と使われる：

PREP. comparison **between/of/with** *something* 1 2
by/in comparison, **in** comparison 3

com|part|ment /kəmpɑrtmənt/ (compartments) 1 N-COUNT 可算名詞 A **compartment** is one of the separate parts of an object that is used for keeping things in. 区画 □ *The fire started in the baggage compartment.* 火の手は手荷物室から上がった. 2 → see also **glove compartment** 3 N-COUNT 可算名詞 A **compartment** is one of the separate spaces into which a railroad car is divided. 個室 □ *On the way home we shared our first class compartment with a group of businessmen.* 帰りの一等車では経営者の一行と一緒だった.

com|pass /kʌmpəs/ (compasses) N-COUNT 可算名詞 A **compass** is an instrument that you use for finding directions. It has a dial and a magnetic needle that always points to the north. 方位磁石 □ *We had to rely on a compass and a lot of luck to get here.* 方位磁石と運だけを頼りにしてここまでたどり着いた.
→ see **magnet**, **navigation**

com|pas|sion /kəmpǽʃ°n/ N-UNCOUNT 不可算名詞 **Compassion** is a feeling of pity, sympathy, and understanding for someone who is suffering. 同情，思いやり □ *Elderly people need time and compassion from their physicians.* 高齢者に対しては，時間をかけた思いやりのある医療が求められる.

Word Link *ate* ≈ filled with : affection*ate*, compassion*ate*, consider*ate*

com|pas|sion|ate /kəmpǽʃ°nɪt/ ADJ 形容詞 If you describe someone or something as **compassionate**, you mean that they feel or show pity, sympathy, and understanding for people who are suffering. 情け深い，思いやりのある [APPROVAL 賛成] □ *My father was a deeply compassionate man.* 父はとても慈悲深い人だった. □ *She has a wise, compassionate face.* 彼女の表情には賢明さと思いやりがうかがえる.

com|pas|sion|ate leave N-UNCOUNT 不可算名詞 **Compassionate leave** is time away from your work that your employer allows you for personal reasons, especially when a member of your family dies or is seriously ill. 忌引休暇；介護休暇 [BRIT 英国英語 BUSINESS 実業] [AM leave of absence 米国英語 **leave of absence**]

com|pat|ible /kəmpǽtɪb°l/ 1 ADJ 形容詞 If things, for example systems, ideas, and beliefs, are **compatible**, they work well together or can exist together successfully. 共存する □ *Free enterprise, he argued, was compatible with Russian values and traditions.* 彼によれば，自由競争はロシアの価値観や伝統に矛盾するものではないといいます. ● **com|pat|ibil|ity** /kəmpǽtɪbɪliti/ N-UNCOUNT

不可算名詞 両立すること，共存すること □ *...the issue of Islam and its compatibility with democracy.* イスラム教の問題とイスラム教と民主主義が両立するかという問題. 2 ADJ 形容詞 If you say that you are **compatible** with someone, you mean that you have a good relationship with them because you have similar opinions and interests. 相性がよい □ *Mildred and I are very compatible. She's interested in the things that interest me.* ミルドレッドと僕はとても相性がいいんだ. 僕が関心のあることは彼女も興味を示すんだ. ● **com|pat|ibil|ity** N-UNCOUNT 不可算名詞 相性のよさ □ *As a result of their compatibility, Haig and Fraser were able to bring about wide-ranging reforms.* ヘイグとフレイザーの相性がよかったので，2人は広範にわたる改革を実現できた. 3 ADJ 形容詞 If one brand of computer or computer equipment is **compatible with** another brand, they can be used together and can use the same software. 互換性がある □ *Fujitsu took over another American firm, Amdal, to help make and sell machines compatible with IBM in the United States.* 富士通は新たにアメリカのアムダル社を子会社化し，アメリカ市場でのIBM互換機の製造・販売に乗り出した.

com|pat|ri|ot /kəmpeɪtriət/ (compatriots) N-COUNT 可算名詞 Your **compatriots** are people from your own country. 同国人，同胞 □ *Chris Robertson of Australia beat his compatriot Chris Dittmar in the final.* オーストラリアのクリス・ロバートソンは，決勝戦で同じオーストラリアのクリス・ディットマーを破りました.

Word Link *pel* ≈ driving, forcing : com*pel*, ex*pel*, pro*pel*

com|pel /kəmpέl/ (compels, compelling, compelled) 1 V-T 他動詞 If a situation, a rule, or a person **compels** you to do something, they force you to do it. 強いる □ *...the introduction of legislation to compel cyclists to wear a helmet.* 自転車でのヘルメット着用を義務化する法律の導入. 2 PHRASE 句 If you **feel compelled to** do something, you feel that you must do it, because it is the right thing to do. 一せざるをえない □ *Dickens felt compelled to return to the stage for a final goodbye.* ディケンズはやむなくステージに戻り最後のあいさつをした.

com|pel|ling /kəmpέlɪŋ/ 1 ADJ 形容詞 A **compelling** argument or reason is one that convinces you that something is true or that something should be done. 説得力のある □ *Factual and forensic evidence makes a suicide verdict the most compelling answer to the mystery of his death.* 具体的事実と科学捜査の証拠からすれば，自殺という評決が彼の死の謎を解き明かす上で最も説得力のある答えになる. 2 ADJ 形容詞 If you describe something such as a movie or book, or someone's appearance, as **compelling**, you mean you want to keep looking at it or reading it because you find it so interesting. 面白くてたまらない，気になってしようがない □ *...a frighteningly violent yet compelling movie.* ぞっとするほど暴力的なのに思わず引き込まれてしまう映画.

com|pen|sate /kɒmpənseɪt/ (compensates, compensating, compensated) 1 V-T 他動詞 To **compensate** someone **for** money or things that they have lost, means to pay them money or give them something to replace those things. 補償する □ *The damages are designed to compensate victims for their direct losses.* 損害賠償金は被害者の直接被害を補償するためのものである. 2 V-I 自動詞 If you **compensate for** a lack of something or **for** something you have done wrong, you do something to make the situation better. 埋め合わせる □ *The company agreed to keep up high levels of output in order to compensate for supplies lost.* 会社は高い稼働率を維持して供給減を補うことに同意しました. 3 V-I 自動詞 Something that **compensates for** something else balances it or reduces its effects. 一の効果をなくす □ *Senators say it is crucial that a mechanism is found to compensate for inflation.* 上院ではインフレを抑制する施策を見出すことが何よりも重要だといわれています. 4 V-I 自動詞 If you try to **compensate for** something that is wrong or missing in your life, you try to do something that removes or reduces the harmful effects. 補う □ *Their sense of humor and ability to get along with people are two characteristics that compensate for their lack of experience.* ユーモアのセンスと人付き合いの才能，この2つの取り柄が彼らの経験不足を補っている.

com|pen|sa|tion /kɒmpənseɪʃ°n/ (compensations) 1 N-UNCOUNT 不可算名詞 **Compensation** is money that someone who has experienced loss or suffering claims from the person or organization responsible, or from the state. 補償金 □ *He received one year's salary as compensation for loss of office.* 彼は失業補償金として1年分の給料を受け取った. □ *They want $20,000 in compensation for each of about 500 claimants.* 約500人いる原告1人につき2万ドルの補償金を求めている. 2 N-VAR 可変性名詞 If something is some **compensation for** something bad that has happened, it makes you feel better. 埋め合わせ □ *Helen gained some compensation for her earlier defeat by winning the final open class.* ヘレンはオープンクラス最終戦で勝利し，前戦での雪辱を果たした.

com|pete /kəmpit/ (competes, competing, competed) 1 V-RECIP 詞 When one firm or country **competes with** another, it tries to get people to buy its own goods in preference to those of the other firm or country. You can also say that two firms or

countries **compete**. 競争する □ *The banks have long competed with American Express's charge cards and various store cards.* 銀行はアメリカンエキスプレスカードなどのカード会社と長年にわたって競争してきた. □ *Hardware stores are competing fiercely for business.* ホームセンターは激しい商戦を繰り広げている. **2** V-RECIP 相互動詞 If you **compete with** someone **for** something, you try to get it for yourself and stop the other person from getting it. You can also say that two people **compete for** something. 競い合う □ *Kangaroos compete with sheep and cattle for sparse supplies of food and water.* カンガルーは羊や牛と乏しい食料と水をめぐって争っている. □ *Young men compete with each other for membership in these societies and fraternities.* 若者はこうした協会や団体の入会資格をめぐって互いにしのぎを削っている. **3** V-I 自動詞 If you **compete** in a contest or a game, you take part in it. 参加する □ *He will be competing in the 100-meter race.* 彼は今度の100m走に出場することになるだろう.

com|pe|tence /kɒmpɪtəns/ N-UNCOUNT 不可算名詞 **Competence** is the ability to do something well or effectively. 能力 □ *Many people have testified to his competence.* 彼の優れた能力は多くの人が認めるところだ.

com|pe|tent /kɒmpɪtənt/ **1** ADJ 形容詞 Someone who is **competent** is efficient and effective. 有能な □ *He was a loyal, distinguished and very competent civil servant.* 彼は忠実で信頼が厚く非常に有能な公務員でした. ●**com|pe|tent|ly** ADV 副詞 うまく □ *The government performed competently in the face of multiple challenges.* 多くの問題に直面しながらも, 政府はうまく舵(かじ)を取ってきた. **2** ADJ 形容詞 If you are **competent to** do something, you have the skills, abilities, or experience necessary to do it well. できる □ *Most adults do not feel competent to deal with a medical emergency involving a child.* 子供の救急措置にはほとんどの大人が自信がないと感じている.

com|pe|ti|tion /kɒmpɪtɪʃ°n/ (competitions) **1** N-UNCOUNT 不可算名詞 **Competition** is a situation in which two or more people or groups are trying to get something which not everyone can have. 競争 □ *There's been some fierce competition for the title.* タイトルをめぐって熾烈(しれつ)な競争が繰り広げられています. **2** N-UNCOUNT 不可算名詞 **Competition** is an activity involving two or more companies, in which each company tries to get people to buy its own goods in preference to the other companies' goods. 競争 □ *The deal would have reduced competition in the commuter-aircraft market.* 取引が成立していたら, 通勤用航空機市場は緩和されていただろう. □ *The farmers have been seeking higher prices as better protection from foreign competition.* 農業従事者は海外からの競争に対する保護策としてずっと値上げを求めています. **3** N-UNCOUNT 不可算名詞 The **competition** is the goods or services that a rival organization is selling. 競合する商品・サービス □ *The American aerospace industry has been challenged by some stiff competition.* アメリカの航空宇宙産業は一部から厳しい競争を受けている. **4** N-SING 単数名詞 The **competition** is the person or people you are competing with. 競争相手 □ *I have to change my approach, the competition is too good now.* 敵が強くなった今, 私はこれまでの戦術を変えなければならない. **5** N-VAR 可変性名詞 A **competition** is an event in which many people take part in order to find out who is best at a particular activity. 競技会 □ *...a surfing competition.* サーフィン競技会.

com|peti|tive /kəmpɛtɪtɪv/ **1** ADJ 形容詞 **Competitive** is used to describe situations or activities in which people or companies compete with each other. 競争の □ *Only by keeping down costs will America maintain its competitive advantage over other countries.* アメリカが国際競争力を維持するにはコスト削減しか手がない. □ *Japan is a highly competitive market system.* 日本市場は非常に競争が激しい. ●**com|peti|tive|ly** ADV 副詞 [ADV after v] 競争して □ *He's now back up on the slopes again, skiing competitively in events for the disabled.* 今では彼はゲレンデに復帰し, 障害者のスキー大会で活躍している. **2** ADJ 形容詞 A **competitive** person is eager to be more successful than other people. 競争心が強い □ *He has always been ambitious and fiercely competitive.* 彼はいつも野心的で競争心が旺盛だ. ●**com|peti|tive|ly** ADV 副詞 [ADV after v] 競争して □ *They worked hard together, competitively and under pressure.* 互いに対する対抗意識や重圧を感じながらも, 彼らは力を合わせてがんばった. ●**com|peti|tive|ness** N-UNCOUNT 不可算名詞 競争 □ *I can't stand the pace, I suppose, and the competitiveness, and the unfriendliness.* どうも私には, このテンポや競争や敵対心が我慢ならないんです. **3** ADJ 形容詞 Goods or services that are at a **competitive** price or rate are likely to be bought, because they are less expensive than other goods of the same kind. 割安な □ *Only those homes offered for sale at competitive prices will secure interest from serious purchasers.* 真剣に家

探しをしている人の目に留まるのは, 割安な価格で提供されるそうした住宅だけだろう. ●**com|peti|tive|ly** ADV 副詞 割安に □ *...a number of early Martin and Gibson guitars, which were competitively priced.* 数多くの初期のマーチンギターやギブソンギター, しかも価格も割安だ. ●**com|peti|tive|ness** N-UNCOUNT 不可算名詞 競争力 □ *It is only on the world market that we can prove the competitiveness and quality of our software.* 世界市場に進出して初めて当社のソフトウェアの競争力と品質が証明されることになる.

com|peti|tor /kəmpɛtɪtər/ (competitors) **1** N-COUNT 可算名詞 A company's **competitors** are companies who are trying to sell similar goods or services to the same people. ライバル企業 □ *The bank isn't performing as well as some of its competitors.* その銀行よりも業績のよいライバル行がある. **2** N-COUNT 可算名詞 A **competitor** is a person who takes part in a competition or contest. 出場者, 参加者 □ *One of the oldest competitors won the individual silver medal.* 最高齢の出場者の1人が個人競技で銀メダルを獲得した.

com|pi|la|tion /kɒmpɪleɪʃ°n/ (compilations) N-COUNT 可算名詞 A **compilation** is a book, CD, or program that contains many different items that have been gathered together, usually ones which have already appeared in other places. 選集, 一集 □ *His latest CD is a compilation of his jazz works over the past decade.* 最新のCDはこの10年間のジャズの演奏が集められている.

com|pile /kəmpaɪl/ (compiles, compiling, compiled) V-T 他動詞 When you **compile** something such as a report, book, or program, you produce it by collecting and putting together many pieces of information. 編集する □ *The book took 10 years to compile.* この本の編集には10年を要した.

com|pla|cen|cy /kəmpleɪs³nsi/ N-UNCOUNT 不可算名詞 **Complacency** is being complacent about a situation. 無頓着 [DISAPPROVAL 不賛成] □ *...a worrying level of complacency about the risks of infection from AIDS.* エイズ感染の危険性を軽視する風潮が憂慮すべき段階に達していること.

com|pla|cent /kəmpleɪs³nt/ ADJ 形容詞 A **complacent** person is very pleased with themselves or feels that they do not need to do anything about a situation, even though the situation may be uncertain or dangerous. 無頓着な [DISAPPROVAL 不賛成] □ *We cannot afford to be complacent about our health.* 誰もが自分の健康に無関心ではいられない.

com|plain /kəmpleɪn/ (complains, complaining, complained) **1** V-T/V-I 他動詞/自動詞 If you **complain about** a situation, you say that you are not satisfied with it. 不満を言う □ *Miners have complained bitterly that the government did not fulfill their promises.* 政府は約束を果たしていないと, 炭鉱労働者は不満をあらわにしました. □ *The couple complained about the high cost of visiting Europe.* ヨーロッパ旅行はお金がかかると夫婦は不満を漏らした. □ *I shouldn't complain, I've got a good job to go back to.* 文句は言えないよね. いい仕事に戻れるんだから. □ *"I wish someone would do something about it," he complained.* 「誰か何とかしてくれないのか」と彼は不満を口にした. **2** V-I 自動詞 If you **complain of** pain or illness, you say that you are feeling pain or feeling ill. 訴える □ *He complained of a headache.* 彼は頭痛を訴えた.

com|plaint /kəmpleɪnt/ (complaints) **1** N-VAR 可変性名詞 A **complaint** is a statement in which you express your dissatisfaction with a situation. 苦情 □ *There's been a record number of complaints about the standard of service.* サービスの質に対する苦情がこれまでで最も多く寄せられています. □ *People have been reluctant to make formal complaints to the police.* 警察に正式に苦情を申し出ることについては市民は消極的である. **2** N-COUNT 可算名詞 A **complaint** is a reason for complaining. 不平の種 □ *My main complaint is that we can't go out on the racecourse anymore.* 特に不満なのはもう二度とコースに戻れないことなんだ. **3** N-COUNT 可算名詞 You can refer to an illness as a **complaint**, especially if it is not very serious. 軽い病気 □ *Eczema is a common skin complaint which often runs in families.* 湿疹はよく見られる皮膚病で, 家族に感染することがよくあります.

Word Link ple ≈ filling : complement, complete, deplete

com|ple|ment (complements, complementing, complemented)

The verb is pronounced /kɒmplɪmɛnt/. The noun is pronounced /kɒmplɪmənt/.

動詞は /kɒmplɪment/ と発音される. 名詞は /kɒmplɪmənt/ と発音される.

1 V-T 他動詞 If one thing **complements** another, it goes well with the other thing and makes its good qualities more noticeable. 補完する ❏ Nutmeg, parsley and cider all complement the flavor of these beans well. ナツメグやパセリやりんごジュースはどれも豆の風味を引き立てます. **2** V-T 他動詞 If people or things **complement** each other, they are different or do something different, which makes them a good combination. 補い合う ❏ There will be a written examination to complement the practical test. 実技試験に加えて筆記試験が行われる. **3** N-COUNT 可算名詞 Something that is a **complement** to something else complements it. 補完するもの ❏ The green wallpaper is the perfect complement to the old pine of the dresser. その緑色の壁紙にすると，古びた松材のドレッサーととてもマッチする.

com|ple|men|tary /kɒmplɪmɛntəri, -mɛntri/ **1** ADJ 形容詞 **Complementary** things are different from each other but make a good combination. 補完的な [FORMAL 形式ばった] ❏ To improve the quality of life through work, two complementary strategies are necessary. 仕事を通じて生活の質を向上させるには，2つの方法を補完させる必要がある. ❏ He has done experiments complementary to those of Eigen. 彼はアイゲンの実験を補完する実験を行った. **2** ADJ 形容詞 **Complementary** medicine refers to ways of treating patients which are different from the ones used by most Western doctors, for example acupuncture and homeopathy. 補完医療 [ADJ n] ❏ ...combining orthodox treatment with a wide range of complementary therapies. 従来の治療法にさまざまな補完医療を組み合わせること.

com|plete /kəmplit/ (completes, completing, completed) **1** ADJ 形容詞 You use **complete** to emphasize that something is as great in extent, degree, or amount as it possibly can be. 完全な [EMPHASIS 強調] ❏ The house is a complete mess. 家中がちらかっている. ❏ The rebels had taken complete control. 反体制派が完全に実権を掌握していた. ❏ The resignation came as a complete surprise. 辞任は青天の霹靂（へきれき）でした. ● **com|plete|ly** ADV 副詞 完全に ❏ Dozens of homes had been completely destroyed. 数十軒の家屋が倒壊しました. ❏ Make sure that you defrost it completely. しっかりと解凍します. ● **com|plete|ness** [ADJ n] You can use **complete** to emphasize that you are referring to the whole of something and not just part of it. 全体の [EMPHASIS 強調] ❏ A complete apartment complex was burned to the ground. アパートが1棟全焼した. **3** ADJ 形容詞 If something is **complete**, it contains all the parts that it should contain. 完全な ❏ The list may not be complete. リストには漏れがあるかも知れません. ❏ a complete dinner service. ディナーセット一式. **4** ADJ 形容詞 The **complete** works of a writer are all their books or poems published together in one book or as a set of books. 全集 [v-link ADJ] ❏ ...the Complete Works of William Shakespeare. 『ウィリアム・シェイクスピア全集』 **5** ADJ 形容詞 If something is **complete**, it has been finished. 完成した [v-link ADJ] ❏ The work of restoring the farmhouse is complete. 農家の修復作業は完了した. **6** V-T 他動詞 To **complete** a set or group means to provide the last item that is needed to make it a full set or group. 全部揃える [no cont] ❏ Children don't complete their set of 20 baby teeth until they are two to three years old. 20本の乳歯が全て生え揃うのは2－3歳である. **7** V-T 他動詞 If you **complete** something, you finish doing, making, or producing it. 完成させる ❏ Peter Mayle has just completed his first novel. ピーター・メイルは初めての小説を書き上げたばかりだ. ● **com|ple|tion** /kəmpliʃ°n/ (completions) N-VAR 可変性名詞 完成 ❏ The project is nearing completion. プロジェクトの完成も間近だ. **8** V-T 他動詞 [no cont] If you **complete** something, you do all of it. 終える ❏ She completed her degree in two years. 彼女は2年間で学位を取得した. **9** V-T 他動詞 If you **complete** a form or questionnaire, you write the answers or information asked for in it. 記入する ❏ Simply complete part 1 of the application. 最初の申込書にだけご記入ください. **10** PHRASE 句 If one thing comes **complete with** another, it has that thing as an extra or additional part. 一付きの ❏ The diary comes complete with a gold ballpoint pen. その日記には金色のボールペンが付いてくる.

Thesaurus complete また次を参照:

ADJ. total, utter **1**
entire, whole; (ant.) partial **2**
unabridged; (ant.) abridged, selected **4**

com|plex (complexes)

The adjective is pronounced /kəmplɛks/ or sometimes /kɒmplɛks/. The noun is pronounced /kɒmplɛks/.

形容詞は /kəmplɛks/，あるいは時々 /kɒmplɛks/ と発音される. 名詞は /kɒmplɛks/ と発音される.

1 ADJ 形容詞 Something that is **complex** has many different parts, and is therefore often difficult to understand. 複雑な ❏ ...in-depth coverage of today's complex issues. 今起きている複雑な問題を徹底取材. ❏ ...a complex system of voting. 複雑な投票方式. **2** N-COUNT 可算名詞 A **complex** is a group of buildings designed for a particular purpose, or one large building divided into several smaller parts. 一施設 ❏ ...a low-cost apartment complex. 低価格のマンション.

Thesaurus complex また次を参照:

ADJ. complicated, intricate, involved; (ant.) obvious, plain, simple **1**

Word Partnership complex は次の語句と使われる:

N. complex **issues**, complex **personality**, complex **problem/situation**, complex **process**, complex **system** **1**

com|plex|ion /kəmplɛkʃ°n/ (complexions) N-COUNT 可算名詞 When you refer to someone's **complexion**, you are referring to the natural color or condition of the skin on their face. 顔色, 顔のつや ❏ She had short brown hair and a pale complexion. 短い茶色い髪で，顔は青白かった.
→ see makeup

com|plex|ities /kəmplɛksɪtiz/ N-PLURAL 複数名詞 The **complexities** of something are the many complicated factors involved in it. 複雑なもの ❏ ...those who find it hardest to cope with the complexities of modern life. 錯綜（さくそう）した現代生活にはついていけないと感じている人たち.

com|plex|ity /kəmplɛksɪti/ N-UNCOUNT 不可算名詞 **Complexity** is the state of having many different parts connected or related to each other in a complicated way. 複雑さ ❏ ...a diplomatic tangle of great complexity. 複雑に錯綜（さくそう）した外交問題.

com|pli|ance /kəmplaɪəns/ N-UNCOUNT 不可算名詞 **Compliance with** something, for example a law, treaty, or agreement, means doing what you are required or expected to do. 遵守 [FORMAL 形式ばった] ❏ Inspectors were sent to visit nuclear sites and verify compliance with the treaty. 原子力施設に査察官を派遣して，条約が遵守されているかどうか確認することになった.

Word Link ate ≈ causing to be : complicate, humiliate, motivate

com|pli|cate /kɒmplɪkeɪt/ (complicates, complicating, complicated) V-T 他動詞 To **complicate** something means to make it more difficult to understand or deal with. 複雑にする ❏ What complicates the issue is the burden of history. これまでの経緯がこの問題をさらに複雑にしています. ❏ The day's events, he said, would only complicate the task of the peacekeeping forces. その日の出来事は一層平和維持活動を困難にするだけだろうと，彼は語りました.

com|pli|cat|ed /kɒmplɪkeɪtɪd/ ADJ 形容詞 If you say that something is **complicated**, you mean it has so many parts or aspects that it is difficult to understand or deal with. 困難な ❏ The situation in Lebanon is very complicated. レバノンは非常に難しい局面にあります.

com|pli|ca|tion /kɒmplɪkeɪʃ°n/ (complications) **1** N-COUNT 可算名詞 A **complication** is a problem or difficulty that makes a situation harder to deal with. さらなる問題. ❏ The age difference was a complication to the relationship. 年齢差がさらに関係を難しいものにしました. ❏ There are too many complications to explain now. 問題は山ほどあって今ここで説明し尽くすことはできない. **2** N-COUNT 可算名詞 A **complication** is a medical problem that occurs as a result of another illness or disease. 合併症 ❏ Blindness is a common complication of diabetes. 失明は糖尿病によく見られる合併症である.

com|plic|ity /kəmplɪsɪti/ N-UNCOUNT 不可算名詞 **Complicity** is involvement with other people in an illegal activity or plan. 共謀 [FORMAL 形式ばった] ❏ Recently a number of policemen were sentenced to death for their complicity in the murder. 近年，殺人共謀罪で死刑判決を受ける警察官が相次いでいる.

com|pli|ment (compliments, complimenting, complimented)

The verb is pronounced /kɒmplɪmɛnt/. The noun is pronounced /kɒmplɪmənt/.

動詞は /kɒmplɪment/ と発音される. 名詞は /kɒmplɪmənt/ と発音される.

1 N-COUNT 可算名詞 A **compliment** is a polite remark that you make to someone to show that you like their appearance, appreciate their qualities, or approve of what they have done. ほめ言葉 ❏ You can do no harm by paying a woman compliments. 女性をほ

めたところで害はない. **2** V-T 他動詞 If you **compliment** someone, you give them a compliment. ほめる □ *They complimented me on the way I looked each time they saw me.* 彼らは会うたびに私の身なりをほめてくれた.

com|pli|men|tary /kɒmplɪmɛntəri, -mɛntri/ **1** ADJ 形容詞 If you are **complimentary** about something, you express admiration for it. ほめて □ *The staff have been very complimentary, and so have the customers.* とても愛想のいいスタッフで, 客もまた愛想がいい. **2** ADJ 形容詞 A **complimentary** seat, ticket, or book is given to you free. 無料の □ *He had complimentary tickets to take his wife to see the movie.* 妻と二人で見に行くつもりでその映画の招待券をもらった.

com|ply /kəmplaɪ/ (**complies, complying, complied**) V-I 自動詞 If someone or something **complies with** an order or set of rules, they do what is required or expected. 従う □ *The commander said that the army would comply with the ceasefire.* 軍は停戦に応じることになるだろうと, 司令官は語りました. □ *Some beaches had failed to comply with environmental regulations.* 環境基準を満たしていない海岸がありました.

com|po|nent /kəmpoʊnənt/ (**components**) **1** N-COUNT 可算名詞 The **components** of something are the parts that it is made of. 成分 □ *Enriched uranium is a key component of a nuclear weapon.* 濃縮ウランは核兵器の主な原料です. □ *The management plan has four main components.* この経営計画は4つの柱からなる. **2** ADJ 形容詞 The **component** parts of something are the parts that make it up. 構成する [ADJ n] □ *Gorbachev failed to keep the component parts of the Soviet Union together.* ゴルバチョフはソ連の構成国の独立を阻止できなかった.

→ see **mass production**

Word Partnership	component は次の語句と使われる:
ADJ.	**key** component, **main** components, **separate** components **1**
N.	component **parts** **2**

com|pose /kəmpoʊz/ (**composes, composing, composed**) **1** V-T 他動詞 The things that something **is composed of** are its parts or members. The separate things that **compose** something are the parts or members that form it. 構成される □ *The force would be composed of troops from NATO countries.* 部隊はNATO諸国の軍隊で編成されることになるだろう. □ *Protein molecules compose all the complex working parts of living cells.* 生体細胞の複雑な構成要素はすべてタンパク質でできています. **2** V-T/V-I 他動詞/自動詞 When someone **composes** a piece of music or **composes**, they write music. 作曲する □ *Vivaldi composed a large number of very fine concertos.* ビバルディは多くの優れた協奏曲を作曲した. **3** V-T 他動詞 If you **compose** something such as a letter, poem, or speech, you write it, often using a lot of concentration or skill. 書く [FORMAL 形式ばった] □ *He started at once to compose a reply to Anna.* 彼はすぐにアナへの返事を書き始めた.

→ see **music**

com|pos|er /kəmpoʊzər/ (**composers**) N-COUNT 可算名詞 A **composer** is a person who writes music, especially classical music. 作曲家 □ *...music by Strauss, Mozart, Beethoven, and other great composers.* ストラウス, モーツァルト, ベートーベンなどの偉大な作曲家たちの音楽.

→ see **music**

com|pos|ite /kəmpɒzɪt/ (**composites**) ADJ 形容詞 A **composite** object or item is made up of several different things, parts, or substances. 複数の部分からなる □ *Galton devised a method of creating composite pictures in which the features of different faces were superimposed over one another.* ガルトンは, 顔の様々な特徴を重ね合わせた合成写真を作る方法を編み出した. ●**Composite** is also a noun. 合成物, 複合物 [usu sing, oft N "of" n] □ *Cuba is a composite of diverse traditions and people.* キューバは多様な伝統と人種から成る.

com|po|si|tion /kɒmpəzɪʃ⁰n/ (**compositions**) **1** N-UNCOUNT 不可算名詞 When you talk about the **composition** of something, you are referring to the way in which its various parts are put together and arranged. 構成 □ *Television has transformed the size and social composition of the audience at great sporting occasions.* テレビのおかげで, 大きなスポーツ大会の観戦者の人数や階層は様変わりした. **2** N-COUNT 可算名詞 The **compositions** of a composer, painter, or other artist are the works of art that they have produced. 作品 □ *Mozart's compositions are undoubtedly among the world's greatest.* モーツァルトの作品はまさしく古今の最高傑作に数えられる. **3** N-COUNT 可算名詞 A **composition** is a piece of written work that children write at school. 作文 □ *We had to write a composition on the subject "My Pet."* 「私のペット」というテーマで作文を書かされた.

→ see **orchestra**

com|post /kɒmpoʊst/ (**composts, composting, composted**) **1** N-UNCOUNT 不可算名詞 **Compost** is a mixture of decayed plants

and vegetable waste which is added to the soil to help plants grow. 堆肥 □ *...a small compost heap.* 小さな堆肥の山. **2** N-MASS 質量名詞 **Compost** is specially treated soil that you buy and use to grow seeds and plants in pots. 培養土 □ *...a 75-pound bag of compost.* 75ポンド入りの培養土1袋. **3** V-T 他動詞 To **compost** things such as unwanted bits of plants means to make them into compost. 堆肥にする

→ see **dump**

com|po|sure /kəmpoʊʒər/ N-UNCOUNT 不可算名詞 **Composure** is the appearance or feeling of calm and the ability to control your feelings. 落ち着き, 平静 [FORMAL 形式ばった] □ *She was a little nervous at first but she soon regained her composure.* 彼女は初め緊張ぎみだったが, すぐに緊張はほぐれてきた.

com|pound
/kɒmpaʊnd/ (**compounds, compounding, compounded**)

> The noun is pronounced /kɒmpaʊnd/. The verb is pronounced /kəmpaʊnd/.
>
> 名詞は /kɒmpaʊnd/ と発音される. 動詞は /kəmpaʊnd/ と発音される.

1 N-COUNT 可算名詞 A **compound** is an enclosed area of land that is used for a particular purpose. 構内 □ *They took refuge in the embassy compound.* 彼らは大使館構内に駆け込んで亡命を求めました. □ *...a military compound.* 軍事基地 **2** N-COUNT 可算名詞 In chemistry, a **compound** is a substance that consists of two or more elements. 化合物 □ *Organic compounds contain carbon in their molecules.* 有機化合物の分子には炭素が含まれる. **3** N-COUNT 可算名詞 If something is a **compound** of different things, it consists of those things. 複合物 [FORMAL 形式ばった] □ *Honey is basically a compound of water, two types of sugar, vitamins and enzymes.* はちみつに含まれる基本成分は, 水, 2種類の糖, ビタミン, 酵素などです. **4** ADJ 形容詞 **Compound** is used to indicate that something consists of two or more parts or things. 複数の要素からなる [ADJ n] □ *...the big compound eyes of dragonflies.* とんぼの大きな複眼. **5** V-T 他動詞 To **compound** a problem, difficulty, or mistake means to make it worse by adding to it. 悪化させる □ *Additional loss of life will only compound the tragedy.* これ以上の人命の損失はさらに悲劇を拡大するだけです. □ *The problem is compounded by the medical system here.* 現地の医療制度がさらに問題を深刻化している. **6** ADJ 形容詞 In grammar, a **compound** noun, adjective, or verb is one that is made up of two or more words, for example "fire engine," "bottle-green," and "firelight." 複合語 [ADJ n]

→ see **element, rock**

com|pound in|ter|est N-UNCOUNT 不可算名詞 **Compound interest** is interest that is calculated both on an original sum of money and on interest which has previously been added to the sum. 複利 [BUSINESS 実業] Compare **simple interest**.

com|pre|hend /kɒmprɪhɛnd/ (**comprehends, comprehending, comprehended**) V-T/V-I 他動詞/自動詞 If you cannot **comprehend** something, you cannot understand it. 理解できない [FORMAL 形式ばった] [with brd-neg] □ *I just cannot comprehend your attitude.* 君の態度は理解に苦しむ.

com|pre|hen|sion /kɒmprɪhɛnʃ⁰n/ **1** N-UNCOUNT 不可算名詞 **Comprehension** is the ability to understand something. 理解力 [FORMAL 形式ばった] □ *This was utterly beyond her comprehension.* これは彼女の理解を全く超えていた. **2** N-UNCOUNT 不可算名詞 **Comprehension** is full knowledge and understanding of the meaning of something. 理解 [FORMAL 形式ばった] □ *They turned to one another with the same expression of dawning comprehension, surprise, and relief.* みんなは同じ表情でお互いの顔を見た. ようやく分かったという表情が驚きに変わると, 最後は安堵 (ど) に変わった.

com|pre|hen|sive /kɒmprɪhɛnsɪv/ ADJ 形容詞 Something that is **comprehensive** includes everything that is needed or relevant. 包括的な □ *The Rough Guide to Nepal is a comprehensive guide to the region.* 『ネパールのラフガイド』はネパールの総合的なガイドブックである.

com|pre|hen|sive|ly /kɒmprɪhɛnsɪvli/ ADV 副詞 Something that is done **comprehensively** is done thoroughly. 徹底的に □ *She was comprehensively outplayed by Coetzer.* 彼女はクッツァーに完敗した.

com|press /kəmprɛs/ (**compresses, compressing, compressed**) **1** V-T/V-I 他動詞/自動詞 When you **compress** something or when it **compresses**, it is pressed or squeezed so that it takes up less space. 圧縮する [他動詞], 圧縮される [自動詞] □ *Poor posture, sitting or walking slouched over, compresses the body's organs.* 前かがみで座ったり歩いたりして悪い姿勢をしていると内臓が圧迫される. ●**com|pres|sion** /kəmprɛʃ⁰n/ N-UNCOUNT 不可算名詞 圧縮 □ *The compression of the wood is easily achieved.* 木材の圧縮は簡単にできる. **2** V-T 他動詞 If you **compress** something such as a piece of writing or a description, you make it shorter. 要約する □ *He never understood how to organize or compress large masses of material.* 大量の資料をどうやった整理し要約したらよいのか, いつも彼は途方に暮れた. **3** V-T 他動詞 [usu passive] If an event **is compressed into** a

c

Word Web · computer

Computers have revolutionized the way we live. Particularly exciting are the advances in the field of medicine. Computer **chips** allow deaf people to hear. Doctors recently placed an implant in the brain of a paralyzed man who could not speak. Soon he learned to move a **cursor** on a computer **screen** just by thinking. By pointing to letters and icons, he was able to express his ideas. Voice recognition **software** allows handicapped people to use a computer without a **keyboard**. Scientists are now experimenting with **devices** that will permit blind people to see.

monitor
keyboard
mouse

---

short space of time, it is given less time to happen than normal or previously. 短縮される ❑ *The four debates will be compressed into an eight-day period.* 4回の討論会は8日間に短縮して行われる.

com|prise /kəmpraɪz/ (comprises, comprising, comprised) V-T 他動詞 If you say that something **comprises** or **is comprised of** a number of things or people, you mean it has them as its parts or members. ～から成る [FORMAL 形式ばった] ❑ *The special cabinet committee comprises Mr. Brown, Mr. Mandelson, and Mr. Straw.* 特別内閣委員会のメンバーは，ブラウン氏，マンデルソン氏，ストロー氏である. ❑ *The task force is comprised of congressional leaders, cabinet heads and administration officials.* 特別委員会は有力議員，閣僚，政府高官で構成されます.

com|pro|mise /kɒmprəmaɪz/ (compromises, compromising, compromised) **1** N-VAR 可変性名詞 A **compromise** is a situation in which people accept something slightly different from what they really want, because of circumstances or because they are considering the wishes of other people. 妥協 ❑ *Encourage your child to reach a compromise between what he wants and what you want.* 自分がやりたいことと親がこうしなさいということのどこで折り合いをつけるのか，子供自身に考えさせるようにしなさい. **2** V-RECIP 相互動詞 If you **compromise with** someone, you reach an agreement with them in which you both give up something that you originally wanted. You can also say that two people or groups **compromise**. 歩み寄る ❑ *The government has compromised with its critics over monetary policies.* 政府は金融政策の批判を受けて妥協した. ❑ *"Nine," I said. "Nine thirty," he replied. We compromised on 9:15.* こっちが「9時がいい」と言うと，相手は「9時半がいい」と言ったので，間をとって9時15分にした. **3** V-T 他動詞 If someone **compromises** themselves or **compromises** their beliefs, they do something which damages their reputation for honesty, loyalty, or high moral principles. 自らの信用を傷つける [DISAPPROVAL 不賛成] ❑ *...members of the government who have compromised themselves by accepting bribes.* わいろを受け取って信用を失った政治家たち.

Word Partnership · compromise は次の語句と使われる:

V.	**reach a** compromise **1**
	to be **willing to** compromise **2**
PREP.	compromise **between** *someone* and *someone* **else 1 2**
	compromise **with** *someone* **2**

com|pro|mis|ing /kɒmprəmaɪzɪŋ/ ADJ 形容詞 If you describe information or a situation as **compromising**, you mean that it reveals an embarrassing or guilty secret about someone. 疑惑を招くような ❑ *How had this compromising picture come into the possession of the press?* このような恥ずべき写真がなぜマスコミの手に渡ったのか.

comp|trol|ler /kəntroʊlər, kɒmp-/ (comptrollers) N-COUNT 可算名詞 A **comptroller** is someone who is in charge of the accounts of a business or a government department; used mainly in official titles. 監査役; 会計検査官 [BUSINESS 実業] ❑ *...Robert Clarke, U.S. Comptroller of the Currency.* アメリカ通貨監査官局長ロバート・クラーク

Word Link · puls ≈ driving, pushing : compulsion, expulsion, impulse

com|pul|sion /kəmpʌlʃən/ (compulsions) **1** N-COUNT 可算名詞 A **compulsion** is a strong desire to do something, which you find difficult to control. 衝動 ❑ *He felt a sudden compulsion to drop the bucket and run.* 彼は突然バケツを捨てて走りたい衝動にかられた. **2** N-UNCOUNT 不可算名詞 If someone uses **compulsion** in order to get you to do something, they force you to do it, for example by threatening to punish you if you do not do it. 強制 ❑ *Many universities argued that students learned more when they were in classes out of choice rather than compulsion.* 多くの大学関係者の話では，強制するより主体性を重んじたほうが学生はよく勉強したという.

com|pul|sive /kəmpʌlsɪv/ **1** ADJ 形容詞 You use **compulsive** to describe people or their behavior when they cannot stop doing

something wrong, harmful, or unnecessary. ～せずにはいられない [ADJ n] ❑ *...a compulsive liar.* 虚言癖のある人 ❑ *He was a compulsive gambler and often heavily in debt.* ギャンブルにのめり込み，大きな借金を抱えることがたびたびだった. **2** ADJ 形容詞 If a book or television program is **compulsive**, it is so interesting that you do not want to stop reading or watching it. 人の心を捕らえて離さない ❑ *Her new series is compulsive viewing.* 今度の彼女のシリーズものは目が離せない.

com|pul|so|ry /kəmpʌlsəri/ ADJ 形容詞 If something is **compulsory**, you must do it or accept it, because it is the law or because someone in a position of authority says you must. 義務的な ❑ *In East Germany learning Russian was compulsory.* 東ドイツではロシア語が必修科目でした.

com|pu|ta|tion|al /kɒmpyʊteɪʃənˀl/ ADJ 形容詞 **Computational** means using computers. コンピューターを利用した ❑ *Students may pursue research in any aspect of computational linguistics.* コンピューター言語学はどのような視点からでも研究を進めることができます.

Word Link · put ≈ thinking : computer, dispute, indisputable

com|put|er /kəmpyutər/ (computers) **1** N-COUNT 可算名詞 A **computer** is an electronic machine that can store and deal with large amounts of information. コンピューター [also "by/on" N] ❑ *The data are then fed into a computer.* 次にデータをコンピューターに入力する. ❑ *The company installed a $650,000 computer system.* その会社は65万ドルのコンピューターシステムを導入した. **2** → see also **personal computer**
→ see Word Web: **computer**
→ see **office**

com|put|er game (computer games) N-COUNT 可算名詞 A **computer game** is a game that you play on a computer or on a small piece of electronic equipment. コンピューターゲーム

com|put|er|ize /kəmpyutəraɪz/ (computerizes, computerizing, computerized) V-T 他動詞 To **computerize** a system, process, or type of work means to arrange for a lot of the work to be done by computer. コンピューターで処理する ❑ *I'm trying to make a spreadsheet up to computerize everything that's done by hand at the moment.* これまで手作業でしてきた仕事をすべてコンピュータでやろうと思い，今スプレッドシートでやってみようとしているところなんです.

com|put|er|ized /kəmpyutəraɪzd/ **1** ADJ 形容詞 A **computerized** system, process, or business is one in which the work is done by computer. コンピュータ化された ❑ *The National Cancer Institute now has a computerized system that can quickly provide information.* 国立ガン研究所には現在素早く情報を提供できるコンピュータ化されたシステムがある. **2** ADJ 形容詞 **Computerized** information is stored on a computer. コンピュータに蓄積された ❑ *Computerized databases are proliferating fast.* 電子データベースは急増している.

computer-literate ADJ 形容詞 If someone is **computer-literate**, they have enough skill and knowledge to be able to use a computer. コンピュータを使いこなせる ❑ *We look for applicants who are good with numbers, computer-literate, and energetic self-starters.* 我々は数字に強く，コンピュータが使いこなせ，エネルギッシュで自発的な応募者を求めている.

com|put|ing /kəmpyutɪŋ/ **1** N-UNCOUNT 不可算名詞 **Computing** is the activity of using a computer and writing programs for it. コンピュータ利用 ❑ *Courses range from cooking to computing.* コースは料理からコンピュータ利用まで多岐にわたる. **2** ADJ 形容詞 **Computing** means relating to computers and their use. コンピュータ関連の [ADJ n] ❑ *Many graduates are employed in the electronics and computing industries.* 卒業生は電子工学とコンピュータ関連産業に従事している者が多い.

com|rade /kɒmræd/ (comrades) N-COUNT 可算名詞 Your **comrades** are your friends, especially friends that you share a difficult or dangerous situation with. 仲間 [LITERARY 文語的] ❑ *Unlike so many of his comrades, he survived the war.* 戦友の非常に多くの者とは異なり，彼は戦争で生き残った.

con /kɒn/ (**cons, conning, conned**) **1** V-T 他動詞 If someone **cons** you, they persuade you to do something or believe something by telling you things that are not true. だます [INFORMAL くだけた] *He claimed that the businessman had conned him of $10,000.* 彼はその実業家に1万ドルだまし取られたと主張した. *White conned his way into a job as a warehouseman with Dutch airline, KLM.* ホワイトはオランダの航空会社KLMをだまして倉庫係の職に就いた. **2** N-COUNT 可算名詞 A **con** is a trick in which someone deceives you by telling you something that is not true. ぺてん [INFORMAL くだけた] *Snacks that offer miraculous weight loss are a con.* 奇跡的な減量をうたう軽食はぺてんだ. **3** pros and cons → see **pro**

con|ceal /kənsiːl/ (**conceals, concealing, concealed**) **1** V-T 他動詞 If you **conceal** something, you cover it or hide it carefully. 隠す *Frances decided to conceal the machine behind a hinged panel.* フランシスは開き戸の後ろにその機器を隠すことに決めた. **2** V-T 他動詞 If you **conceal** a piece of information or a feeling, you do not let other people know about it. 秘密にする *Robert could not conceal his relief.* ロバートは安堵(あんど)の念を隠すことができなかった. **3** V-T 他動詞 If something **conceals** something else, it covers it and prevents it from being seen. 見えないようにする *...a pair of carved Indian doors which concealed a built-in cupboard.* 作り付けの戸棚を隠している1対のインド製の木彫りのドア

con|ceal|ment /kənsiːlmənt/ N-UNCOUNT 不可算名詞 **Concealment** is the state of being hidden or the act of hiding something. 隠すこと, 隠されていること *The criminals vainly sought concealment from the searchlight.* 犯罪者たちはサーチライトから隠れようとしたが無駄だった.

con|cede /kənsiːd/ (**concedes, conceding, conceded**) **1** V-T 他動詞 If you **concede** something, you admit, often unwillingly, that it is true or correct. 認める *Bess finally conceded that Nancy was right.* ベスはナンシーが正しいことをようやく認めた. *"Well," he conceded, "I do sometimes mumble a bit."* 「そうだね. 僕が時々ちょっとロごもるのは確かだ」と彼は認めた. **2** V-T 他動詞 If you **concede** to someone, you allow them to have it as a right or privilege. (権利・特権として) 与える *Poland's Communist government conceded the right to establish independent trade unions.* ポーランドの共産党政府は独立した労働組合を設立する権利を認めた. **3** V-T 他動詞 If you **concede** something, you give it to the person who has been trying to get it from you. 与える *The strike by bank employees ended after employers conceded some of their demands.* 銀行職員によるストライキは雇用主側が彼らの要求の一部に応じて終わった. **4** V-T 他動詞 If you **concede** a game, contest, or argument, you end it by admitting that you can no longer win. 相手の勝利を認める *Reiner, 56, has all but conceded the race to his rival.* レイナー (56歳) はそのレースでライバルの勝利を事実上認めた. **5** V-T 他動詞 If you **concede** defeat, you accept that you have lost a struggle. (敗北を) 認める *She has conceded defeat in her bid for the Democratic Party's nomination for governor.* 彼女は民主党の州知事候補指名を求める試みで敗北を認めた.

con|ceiv|able /kənsiːvəbəl/ ADJ 形容詞 If something is **conceivable**, you can imagine it or believe it. 考えられる *Without their support, the project would not have been conceivable.* そのプロジェクトは彼らの支援なしには考えられなかっただろう.

con|ceive /kənsiːv/ (**conceives, conceiving, conceived**) **1** V-T/V-I 他動詞/自動詞 If you cannot **conceive of** something, you cannot imagine it or believe it. 想像する [usu with brd-neg] *I just can't even conceive of that quantity of money.* 私はあのような金額はちょっと想像すらできない. *We could not conceive that he might soon be dead.* 私たちは彼がまもなく死ぬかもしれないとは想像できなかった. **2** V-T/V-I 他動詞/自動詞 If you **conceive** something **as** a particular thing, you consider it to be that thing. 考える *The ancients conceived the earth as afloat in water.* 古代人は地球が水上に浮かんでいると考えた. *We conceive of the family as being in a constant state of change.* 私たちは家族が常に変化する状態にあると考える. **3** V-T 他動詞 If you **conceive** a plan or idea, you think of it and work out how it can be done. 考え出す *She had conceived the idea of a series of novels, each of which would reveal some aspect of Chinese life.* 彼女は一連の小説の案を考え出したが, その各々が中国人の生活のある側面を現すことになるものだった. **4** V-T/V-I 他動詞/自動詞 When a woman **conceives** a child or **conceives**, she becomes pregnant. 身ごもる *Women, he says, should give up alcohol before they plan to conceive.* 女性は妊娠しようとする前に断酒すべきだと彼は言う.

con|cen|trate /kɒnsəntreɪt/ (**concentrates, concentrating, concentrated**) **1** V-T/V-I 他動詞/自動詞 If you **concentrate on** something, or **concentrate** your mind **on** it, you give all your attention to it. 集中する *It was up to him to concentrate on his studies and make something of himself.* 学業に専念して成功するのは彼次第だった. *At work you need to be able to concentrate.* 職場では集中できなければならない. **2** V-T 他動詞 If something **is concentrated** in an area, it is all there rather than being spread around. 集中する [usu passive] *Italy's industrial districts are concentrated in its*

north-central and northeastern regions. イタリアの産業地域は北中部地方と北東地方に集中している.

Word Link	centr ≈ middle : **central, concentrated, decentralized**

con|cen|trat|ed /kɒnsəntreɪtɪd/ **1** ADJ 形容詞 A **concentrated** liquid has been increased in strength by having water removed from it. 濃縮した *Sweeten dishes sparingly with honey, or concentrated apple or pear juice.* はちみつまたはリンゴか梨の濃縮ジュースで控えめに料理に甘みを加えなさい. **2** ADJ 形容詞 A **concentrated** activity is directed with great intensity in one place. 集中した *...a more concentrated effort to reach out to troubled kids.* 困っている子供たちに援助の手を差し伸べるいっそうの集中的努力

con|cen|tra|tion /kɒnsəntreɪʃən/ (**concentrations**) **1** N-UNCOUNT 不可算名詞 **Concentration** on something involves giving all your attention to it. 集中 *Neal kept interrupting, breaking my concentration.* ニールは邪魔し続け, 私が集中するのを妨げた. **2** N-VAR 可変性名詞 A **concentration** of something is a large amount of it or large numbers of it in a small area. 集結 *The area has one of the world's greatest concentrations of wildlife.* その地域には世界最大の野生生物の集団の1つがある. **3** N-VAR 可変性名詞 The **concentration** of a substance is the proportion of essential ingredients or substances in it. 濃度 *pH is a measure of the concentration of free hydrogen atoms in a solution.* pHは溶液における遊離水素原子の濃度の尺度である.

con|cen|tra|tion camp (**concentration camps**) N-COUNT 可算名詞 A **concentration camp** is a prison in which large numbers of ordinary people are kept in very bad conditions, usually during a war. 強制収容所 *...the ruins of the Nazi concentration camp at Buchenwald.* ブーヘンワルトのナチ強制収容所の廃墟

con|cept /kɒnsɛpt/ (**concepts**) N-COUNT 可算名詞 A **concept** is an idea or abstract principle. 概念 *She added that the concept of arranged marriages is misunderstood in the west.* 彼女は見合い結婚という概念は西欧諸国で誤解されていると付け加えた.

con|cep|tion /kənsɛpʃən/ (**conceptions**) **1** N-VAR 可変性名詞 A **conception** of something is an idea that you have of it in your mind. 考え *My conception of a garden was based on gardens I had visited in England.* 庭園に関する私の考えはイングランドで訪れた庭園に基づいていた. **2** N-VAR 可変性名詞 **Conception** is the process in which the egg in a woman is fertilized and she becomes pregnant. 受胎 *Six weeks after conception, your baby is the size of your little fingernail.* 受胎後6週間であなたの赤ちゃんは小指のつめの大きさになる.

con|cern /kənsɜːrn/ (**concerns, concerning, concerned**) **1** N-UNCOUNT 不可算名詞 **Concern** is worry about a situation. 懸念 *The group has expressed concern about reports of political violence in Africa.* その団体はアフリカの政治的暴力行為の報道についての懸念を表明している. *The move follows growing public concern over the spread of the disease.* その措置はその病気の蔓(まん)延についての国民の懸念の高まりの結果である. **2** V-T 他動詞 If something **concerns** you, it worries you. 心配させる [no cont] *The growing number of people seeking refuge in Thailand is beginning to concern Western aid agencies.* タイで避難する人々の数が増えていることは西欧の援助機関の懸念の種となり始めている. ● **con|cerned** ADJ 形容詞 心配して *Academics and employers are concerned that students are not sufficiently prepared for college courses.* 大学教師や企業主は学生が大学の授業を受ける学力が十分についていないことを案じている. **3** V-T 他動詞 If you **concern yourself with** something, you give it attention because you think that it is important. 関心を持つ *I didn't concern myself with politics.* 私は政治には関心がなかった. ● **con|cerned** ADJ 形容詞 [v-link ADJ "with" n] 関心のある *The agency is more concerned with making arty ads than understanding its clients' businesses.* その代理店は依頼主の事業を理解するよりも凝った広告を作ることに関心がある. **4** V-T 他動詞 If something such as a book or a piece of information **concerns** a particular subject, it is about that subject. 関係する [no cont] *The bulk of the book concerns Sandy's two middle-aged children.* その本の大半はサンディの2人の中年の子供に関するものだ. ● **con|cerned** ADJ 形容詞 [v-link ADJ "with" n] 関係して *Randolph's work was exclusively concerned with the effects of pollution on health.* ランドルフの仕事は専ら公害が健康に与える影響に関するものだった. **5** V-T 他動詞 If a situation, event, or activity **concerns** you, it affects or involves you. かかわる [no cont] *It was just a little unfinished business from my past, and it doesn't concern you at all.* それは私の過去から引き続いている小さなことで, あなたとは全然関係ない. ● **con|cerned** ADJ 形容詞 [n ADJ, v-link ADJ "in/with" n] 関与している *It's a very stressful situation for everyone concerned.* それは関係者全員にとって非常にストレスの多い状況だ. **6** N-COUNT 可算名詞 A **concern** is a fact or situation that worries you. 心配事 *His concern was that people would know that he was responsible.* 彼は自分に責任があると人々に知られることを心配していた. **7** N-COUNT 可算名詞 You can refer to a company or business as a **concern**, usually when you are describing what type of company or business it is. 事業 [FORMAL 形式ばった

Word Web   concert

A **rock concert** is much more than a group of **musicians** playing **music** on a **stage**. It is a full-scale **performance**. Each **band** must have a **manager** and an **agent** who **books** the **venue** and promotes the **show**. Roadies set up the stage, test the **microphones**, and tune the **instruments**. **Sound engineers** make sure the band sounds as good as possible. There's always **lighting** to **spotlight** the lead **singer** and **backup** singers. The bright, moving lights help to build excitement. The **fans** scream and yell when they hear their favorite **songs**. The **audience** never wants the show to end.

BUSINESS 実業] ❏ *If not a large concern, the Potomac Nursery was at least a successful one.* ポトマック園芸農場は大規模な事業とまではいかないが、少なくとも成功している事業だった。 **⑧** N-VAR 可変性名詞 **Concern for** someone is a feeling that you want them to be happy, safe, and well. If you do something out of **concern** for someone, you do it because you want them to be happy, safe, and well. 気遣い ❏ *Without her care and concern, he had no chance at all.* 彼女の世話と気遣いなしでは、彼には成算は全くなかった。 **⑨** N-SING 単数名詞 If a situation or problem is your **concern**, it is something that you have a duty or responsibility to be involved with. 任務 ❏ *The technical aspects were the concern of the Army.* 技術面は陸軍の役目だった。 **⑩** PHRASE 句 If a company is a **going concern**, it is actually doing business, rather than having stopped trading or not yet having started trading. 営業中の企業 [BUSINESS 実業] ❏ *The receivers will always prefer to sell a business as a going concern.* 管財人は常に事業を営業中の企業として売却することを好む。

Word Partnership   concern は次の語句と使われる:

N.   **cause for** concern **⑧**
    health/safety concern **⑥**
V.   **express** concern **⑧ ⑥ ⑧**

con|cerned /kənsɜrnd/ **①** → see concern **②** ADJ 形容詞 If you are **concerned to** do something, you want to do it because you think it is important. 願って [v-link ADJ to-inf] ❏ *We are deeply concerned to get out of this problematic situation.* 私どもはこの問題のある状況から抜け出すことを切望している。

Word Partnership   concerned は次の語句と使われる:

PREP.   concerned **about** *something*, concerned **for** *something*,
       concerned **with** *someone*, concerned **with** *something* **①**

con|cern|ing /kənsɜrnɪŋ/ **①** PREP 前置詞 You use **concerning** to indicate what a question or piece of information is about. ～に関する [FORMAL 形式ばった] ❏ *For more information concerning the club, contact Mr. Coldwell.* 当クラブに関する詳細についてはコールドウェル氏に連絡してください。 **②** ADJ 形容詞 If something is **concerning**, it causes you to feel concerned about it. 気がかりな [usu "it" v-link ADJ "that"] ❏ *It is particularly concerning that he is working for foreign companies while advising on foreign policy.* 彼が外交政策について助言する一方で外国の企業のために働いていることは特に気がかりなことだ。

con|cert /kɒnsərt/ (**concerts**) **①** N-COUNT 可算名詞 A **concert** is a performance of music. 演奏会 ❏ *...a short concert of piano music.* ピアノ音楽の短い演奏会 ❏ *I've been to plenty of live rock concerts.* 私はロックのライブ公演に何度も行ったことがある。 **②** PHRASE 句 If a musician or group of musicians appears **in concert**, they are giving a live performance. ライブ公演で ❏ *I want people to remember Elvis in concert.* 私は人々がエルビスのライブ公演を思い出してほしい。
→ see Word Web: concert

con|cert|ed /kənsɜrtɪd/ **①** ADJ 形容詞 A **concerted** action is done by several people or groups working together. 協同の [ADJ n] ❏ *Martin Parry, author of the report, says it's time for concerted action by world leaders.* そのリポートの著者であるマーティン・パリーは、世界の指導者が一致協力した行動を取る時が来たと述べている。 **②** ADJ 形容詞 If you make a **concerted** effort to do something, you try very hard to do it. 非常な [ADJ n] ❏ *He made a concerted effort to win me away from my steady, sweet but boring boyfriend.* 彼はステディの関係にある優しいが退屈なボーイフレンドから引き離して私の心をつかもうと非常な努力をした。

con|cer|to /kəntʃɛərtoʊ/ (**concertos**) N-COUNT 可算名詞 A **concerto** is a piece of music written for one or more solo instruments and an orchestra. 協奏曲 ❏ *...Tchaikovsky's First Piano Concerto.* チャイコフスキーの最初のピアノ協奏曲
→ see music

con|ces|sion /kənsɛʃⁿn/ (**concessions**) **①** N-COUNT 可算名詞 If you make a **concession to** someone, you agree to let them do or have something, especially in order to end an argument or conflict. 譲歩 ❏ *We made too many concessions and we got too little*

in return. 我々は譲歩をしすぎ、その代わりに得たものは少なすぎた。 **②** N-COUNT 可算名詞 A **concession** is a special right or privilege that is given to someone. 特許 ❏ *Farmers were granted concessions from the government to develop the farms.* 農場経営者たちは農場を開発するための特許を政府から与えられた。 **③** N-COUNT 可算名詞 A **concession** is an arrangement where someone is given the right to sell a product or to run a business, especially in a building belonging to another business. 営業許可権 [mainly AM 主に米国英語 BUSINESS 実業] ❏ *...the man who ran the catering concession at the Rob Roy Links in Palominas.* パロミナスのロブロイゴルフ場で食堂を経営していた男

Word Partnership   concession は次の語句と使われる:

V.   **make a** concession **①~②**
PREP.   concessions **for** *someone* **① — ②**
N.   **tax** concessions **②**

con|ces|sion|aire /kənsɛʃənɛər/ (**concessionaires**) N-COUNT 可算名詞 A **concessionaire** is a person or company that has the right to sell a product or to run a business, especially in a building belonging to another business. 営業権保有者 [AM 米国英語 BUSINESS 実業] ❏ *Concessionaires and shop owners report retail sales are up.* 営業権保有者と店舗所有者によると、小売の売上高が増加している。

con|cili|ation /kənsɪlieɪʃⁿn/ N-UNCOUNT 不可算名詞 **Conciliation** is willingness to end a disagreement or the process of ending a disagreement. 和解 ❏ *Resolving the dispute will require a mood of conciliation on both sides.* 紛争を解決するためには両当事者に和解の心構えが必要だろう。

con|cilia|tory /kənsɪliətɔri/ ADJ 形容詞 When you are **conciliatory** in your actions or behavior, you show that you are willing to end a disagreement with someone. 懐柔的な ❏ *The next time he spoke, he used a more conciliatory tone.* 次に話した際には彼は前よりなだめるような口の利き方をした。

con|cise /kənsaɪs/ **①** ADJ 形容詞 Something that is **concise** says everything that is necessary without using any unnecessary words. 簡潔な ❏ *Burton's text is concise and informative.* バートンの本文は簡潔で有益だ。 ● **con|cise|ly** ADV 副詞 [ADV with v] 簡潔に ❏ *He'd delivered his report clearly and concisely.* 彼は報告を明瞭かつ簡潔に発表した。 **②** ADJ 形容詞 A **concise** edition of a book, especially a dictionary, is shorter than the original edition. 簡略化した [ADJ n] ❏ *...Sotheby's Concise Encyclopedia of Porcelain.* サザビーの磁器コンサイス百科事典

con|clude /kənklud/ (**concludes, concluding, concluded**) **①** V-T 他動詞 If you **conclude that** something is true, you decide that it is true using the facts you know as a basis. 推断する ❏ *Larry had concluded that he had no choice but to accept Paul's words as the truth.* ラリーはポールの言葉を真実だと受け入れざるを得ないとの結論を下した。 ❏ *So what can we conclude from this debate?* ではこの討論から我々はどんな結論を下せるのか。 **②** V-T/V-I 他動詞/自動詞 When you **conclude**, you say the last thing that you are going to say. 結びとして言う [FORMAL 形式ばった] ❏ *"It's a waste of time,"* *he concluded.* 「それは時間の無駄だ」と彼は結んだ。 **③** V-T/V-I 他動詞/自動詞 When something **concludes**, or when you **conclude** it, you end it. 終える [他動詞]、終わる [自動詞] ❏ *The evening concluded with dinner and speeches.* 夜会はディナーとスピーチで締めくくられた。 [FORMAL 形式ばった] **④** V-T 他動詞 If one person or group **concludes** an agreement, such as a treaty or business deal, **with** another, they arrange it. You can also say that two people or groups **conclude** an agreement. 締結する [FORMAL 形式ばった] ❏ *Mexico and the Philippines have both concluded agreements with their commercial bank creditors.* メキシコとフィリピンは両国共に民間銀行の債権者と協定を結んだ。

Word Partnership   conclude は次の語句と使われる:

N.   conclude *something*, conclude that *something* **① ④**
    conclude **a deal** **④**
PRON.   **he/she** concluded **③**

con|clu|sion /kənkluːʒ³n/ (conclusions) **1** N-COUNT 可算名詞 When you come to a **conclusion**, you decide that something is true after you have thought about it carefully and have considered all the relevant facts. 結論 □ Over the years I've come to the conclusion that she's a very great musician. 長年の間に私は彼女が非常に偉大な音楽家であるという結論に達した. **2** N-SING 単数名詞 The **conclusion** of something is its ending. 終わり □ At the conclusion of the program, I asked the children if they had any questions they wanted to ask me. プログラムの終わりに私は子供たちに私に聞きたい質問があるかどうか尋ねた. **3** N-SING 単数名詞 The **conclusion** of a treaty or a business deal is the act of arranging it or agreeing on it. 締結 □ ...the expected conclusion of a free-trade agreement between Mexico and the United States. メキシコと米国間の自由貿易協定の予定されている締結 **4** PHRASE 句 You say "**in conclusion**" to indicate that what you are about to say is the last thing that you want to say. 最後に □ In conclusion, walking is a cheap, safe, enjoyable, and readily available form of exercise. 終わりに、散歩は安上がりで安全かつ楽しくたやすくできる運動だ.

Word Partnership   conclusion は次の語句と使われる:

V.	**come to a** conclusion, **draw a** conclusion, **reach a** conclusion **1**
N.	conclusion **of** something **1** – **3**
PREP.	**in** conclusion **4**

con|clu|sive /kənkluːsɪv/ ADJ 形容詞 **Conclusive** evidence shows that something is certainly true. 決定的な □ Her attorneys claim there is no conclusive evidence that any murders took place. 彼女の弁護側は殺人が起こった決定的な証拠は何もないと主張した.

con|coct /kənkɒkt/ (concocts, concocting, concocted) **1** V-T 他動詞 If you **concoct** an excuse or explanation, you invent one that is not true. でっち上げる □ Mr. Ferguson said the prisoner concocted the story to get a lighter sentence. ファーガソン氏はその被告人がより軽い判決を受けるためにその話をでっち上げたと述べた. **2** V-T 他動詞 If you **concoct** something, especially something unusual, you make it by mixing several things together. 混ぜ合わせて作る □ Eugene was concocting Rossini Cocktails from champagne and pureed raspberries. ユージーンはシャンパンとピューレにしたラズベリーからローシーニ・カクテルを作っていた.

con|coc|tion /kənkɒkʃ³n/ (concoctions) N-COUNT 可算名詞 A **concoction** is something that has been made out of several things mixed together. 混合物 □ ...a concoction of honey, yogurt, oats, and apples. はちみつ、ヨーグルト、オート麦、リンゴを混ぜ合わせた料理

con|crete /kɒnkriːt/ (concretes, concreting, concreted) **1** N-UNCOUNT 不可算名詞 **Concrete** is a substance used for building which is made by mixing together cement, sand, small stones, and water. コンクリート □ We sat on the concrete floor. 我々はコンクリートの床に座った. **2** V-T 他動詞 When you **concrete** something such as a path, you cover it with concrete. コンクリートで固める □ He merely cleared and concreted the floors. 彼は床を片付け、コンクリートで固めただけだった. **3** ADJ 形容詞 You use **concrete** to indicate that something is definite and specific. 具体的な □ I had no concrete evidence. 私には具体的な証拠は何もなかった. □ There were no concrete proposals on the table. 検討中の具体的な提案は何もなかった. **4** ADJ 形容詞 A **concrete** object is a real, physical object. 具体的な □ ...using concrete objects to teach addition and subtraction. 足し算と引き算を教えるために具体的な物を使うこと **5** ADJ 形容詞 A **concrete** noun is a noun that refers to a physical object rather than to a quality or idea. 具象の [ADJ n]

con|cur /kənkɜr/ (concurs, concurring, concurred) V-RECIP 相互動詞 If one person **concurs** with another person, the two people agree. You can also say that two people **concur**. 同意見である [FORMAL 形式ばった] □ Local feeling does not necessarily concur with the press. 地元の意見は報道陣と同じとは限らない. □ Daniels and Franklin concurred in an investigator's suggestion that the police be commended. ダニエルズとフランクリンは警察を推賞しようという1人の捜査官の提案に同意した.

Word Link   curr, curs ≈ running, flowing : con**cur**rent, **cur**rent, **curs**or

con|cur|rent /kənkɜrənt/ ADJ 形容詞 **Concurrent** events or situations happen at the same time. 同時発生の □ Galerie St. Etienne is holding three concurrent exhibitions. サンテティエンヌ現代美術館は3種類の展覧会を同時に開催中である. □ He will actually be serving three concurrent five-year sentences. 彼はなんと5年間の刑期を3つ同時に服することになっている. ● **con|cur|rent|ly** ADV 副詞 [ADV with v] 同時に □ He was jailed for 33 months to run concurrently with a sentence he is already serving for burglary. 彼は33か月間投獄されたが、これは押し込み罪ですでに服役中の刑期と同時に行われた.

con|cus|sion /kənkʌʃ³n/ (concussions) N-VAR 可変性名詞 If you suffer a **concussion** after a blow to your head, you lose consciousness or feel sick or confused. 震盪(しんとう) □ Nicky was rushed to the hospital with a concussion. ニッキーは震盪で病院にかつぎ込まれた.

Word Link   damn, demn ≈ harm, loss : con**demn**, **damn**ing, in**demn**ify

con|dem /kəndem/ (condemns, condemning, condemned) **1** V-T 他動詞 If you **condemn** something, you say that it is very bad and unacceptable. 非難する □ Political leaders united yesterday to condemn the latest wave of violence. 政治指導者たちは昨日結束して最近の暴力の高まりを非難した. □ Graham was right to condemn his players for lack of ability, attitude, and application. グレアムが選手達の能力、心構え、そして努力の不足を非難したのは正しかった. **2** V-T 他動詞 If someone **is condemned** to a punishment, they are given this punishment. 刑を宣告される [usu passive] □ He was condemned to life imprisonment. 彼は終身懲役刑を申し渡された. **3** V-T 他動詞 If circumstances **condemn** you to an unpleasant situation, they make it certain that you will suffer in that way. 運命づける □ Their lack of qualifications condemned them to a lifetime of boring, usually poorly-paid work. 彼らは資格を持っていなかったので、生涯退職で通常低賃金の職につかなければならなかった. **4** V-T 他動詞 If authorities **condemn** a building, they officially decide that it is not safe and must be pulled down or repaired. 廃棄処分に決める □ The court's ruling clears the way to condemn buildings in the area. 法廷の裁定はその地域の建物を取り壊す道を切り開く. **5** → see also **condemned**

con|dem|na|tion /kɒndemneɪʃ³n/ (condemnations) N-VAR 可変性名詞 **Condemnation** is the act of saying that something or someone is very bad and unacceptable. 非難 □ There was widespread condemnation of Saturday's killings. 土曜日の殺害事件は広範囲に及ぶ非難を受けた.

con|demned /kəndemd/ ADJ 形容詞 A **condemned** man or woman is going to be executed. 死刑を宣告された □ ...prison officers who had sat with the condemned man during his last days. 残された日々の間その死刑囚の世話をした刑務官たち

con|dense /kəndens/ (condenses, condensing, condensed) **1** V-T 他動詞 If you **condense** something, especially a piece of writing or a speech, you make it shorter, usually by including only the most important parts. 圧縮する □ When you summarize, you condense an extended idea or argument into a sentence or more in your own words. 要約する際には、詳述された発想や議論を自分の言葉で1文にまとめ以上の文に縮約する. **2** V-T/V-I 他動詞/自動詞 When a gas or vapor **condenses**, or **is condensed**, it changes into a liquid. 凝縮する、液化する □ Water vapor condenses to form clouds. 水蒸気は凝縮して雲となる.

→ see **matter, water**

Word Link   scend ≈ climbing : a**scend**, conde**scend**, de**scend**

con|de|scend /kɒndɪsend/ (condescends, condescending, condescended) **1** V-T 他動詞 If someone **condescends to** do something, they agree to do it, but in a way which shows that they think they are better than other people and should not have to do it. もったいぶった態度を取る [DISAPPROVAL 不賛成] □ When he condescended to speak, he contradicted himself three or four times in the space of half an hour. 彼がもったいぶった態度で話した時、30分の間に3~4回も矛盾することを言った. **2** V-I 自動詞 If you say that someone **condescends** to other people, you are showing your disapproval of the fact that they behave in a way which shows that they think they are superior to other people. 見下したような振る舞いをする [DISAPPROVAL 不賛成] □ Don't condescend to me. 私を見下すような態度を取らないでくれ.

con|de|scend|ing /kɒndɪsendɪŋ/ ADJ 形容詞 If you say that someone **is condescending**, you are showing your disapproval of the fact that they talk or behave in a way which shows that they think they are superior to other people. 相手を見下すような [DISAPPROVAL 不賛成] □ I'm fed up with your money and your whole condescending attitude. 私はあなたの金や相手を見下すような態度の全てにうんざりしている.

con|di|tion /kəndɪʃ³n/ (conditions, conditioning, conditioned) **1** N-SING 単数名詞 If you talk about the **condition** of a person or thing, you are talking about the state that they are in, especially how good or bad their physical state is. 状態 [also no det] □ He remains in a critical condition in a California hospital. 彼はカリフォルニアの病院で重体のままだ. □ I received several compliments on the condition of my skin. 私は肌の状態を何回かほめられた. □ The two-bedroom chalet is in good condition. 寝室が2つある山小屋はいい状態だ. **2** N-PLURAL 複数名詞 The **conditions** under which something is done or happens are all the factors or circumstances which directly affect it. 状態 □ It's easy to make a wrong turn here even under ideal weather conditions. たとえ理想的な天候でもここは方向を間違いやすい. **3** N-PLURAL 複数名詞 The **conditions** in which people live or work are the factors which affect their comfort, safety, or health. 状況 □ People are living in appalling conditions. 人々はひどい生活をしている. □ I could not work in these conditions any longer. 私

はこのような状況ではもう働くことはできなかった. **4** N-COUNT 可算名詞 A **condition** is something which must happen or be done in order for something else to be possible, especially when this is written into a contract or law. 条件 ❑*Argentina failed to hit the economic targets set as a condition for loan payments.* アルゼンチンは融資支払いの条件として設定された経済目標を達成できなかった. ❑*...terms and conditions of employment.* 雇用条件 **5** N-COUNT 可算名詞 It someone has a particular **condition**, they have an illness or other medical problem. 健康状態 ❑*Doctors suspect he may have a heart condition.* 医者は彼が心臓病に罹(かか)っている可能性を疑っている. **6** V-T 他動詞 If someone **is conditioned** by their experiences or environment, they are influenced by them over a period of time so that they do certain things or think in a particular way. 決定する [usu passive] ❑*We are all conditioned by early impressions and experiences.* 我々は皆幼児期の印象や経験の影響を受けている. ❑*I just feel women are conditioned into doing housework.* 私は女は家事をするように仕込まれていると感じているだけよ. ● con|di|tion|ing N-UNCOUNT 不可算名詞 条件付け ❑*Because of social conditioning, men don't expect to be managed by women.* 社会的な条件づけにより，男は女の上司を持つことを期待しない. **7** PHRASE 句 When you agree to do something **on condition that** something else happens, you mean that you will only do it if this other thing also happens. 〜という条件で ❑*He agreed to speak to reporters on condition that he was not identified.* 彼は身元を明かさないという条件で取材記者に話すことに同意した.

→ see **factory**

con|di|tion|al /kəndɪʃənˀl/ **1** ADJ 形容詞 If a situation or agreement is **conditional on** something, it will only happen or continue if this thing happens. 条件付きの ❑*Their support is conditional on his proposals meeting their approval.* 彼らの支援は彼の提案が彼らの承認を得ることを条件としている. ❑*...a conditional offer.* 条件付きの申し出 **2** ADJ 形容詞 In grammar, a **conditional** clause is a subordinate clause which refers to a situation which may exist or happen. Most conditional clauses begin with "if" or "unless," for example "If that happens, we'll be in big trouble" and "You don't have to come unless you want to." 条件を表す [ADJ n]

con|do|lence /kəndoʊləns/ (condolences) **1** N-UNCOUNT 不可算名詞 A message of **condolence** is a message in which you express your sympathy for someone because one of their friends or relatives has died recently. 悔やみ ❑*Neil sent him a letter of condolence.* ニールは彼に悔やみ状を送った. **2** N-PLURAL 複数名詞 When you offer or express your **condolences** to someone, you express your sympathy for them because one of their friends or relatives has died recently. 弔詞 ❑*He expressed his condolences to the families of the people who died in the incident.* 彼は事故で亡くなった人々の家族に哀悼の言葉を述べた.

con|dom /kɒndəm/ (condoms) N-COUNT 可算名詞 A **condom** is a covering made of thin rubber which a man can wear on his penis as a contraceptive or as protection against disease during sexual intercourse. コンドーム

con|done /kəndoʊn/ (condones, condoning, condoned) V-T 他動詞 If someone **condones** behavior that is morally wrong, they accept it and allow it to happen. 大目に見る [oft with brd-neg] ❑*I have never encouraged nor condoned violence.* 私は決して暴力を奨励したことも大目に見たこともない.

con|du|cive /kəndusɪv/ ADJ 形容詞 If one thing is **conducive** to another thing, it makes the other thing likely to happen. 助けとなる ❑*Make your bedroom as conducive to sleep as possible.* 寝室をできるだけ睡眠に役立つようにしなさい.

con|duct (conducts, conducting, conducted)

The verb is pronounced /kəndʌkt/. The noun is pronounced /kɒndʌkt/.

動詞は /kəndʌkt/ と発音される. 名詞は /kɒndʌkt/ と発音される.

1 V-T 他動詞 When you **conduct** an activity or task, you organize it and do it. 行なう ❑*I decided to conduct an experiment.* 私は実験を行なうことに決めた. **2** V-T 他動詞 If you **conduct** yourself in a particular way, you behave in that way. 振舞う ❑*The way he conducts himself reflects on the family.* 彼の振舞い方は家族に影響する. **3** V-T/V-I 他動詞/自動詞 When someone **conducts** an orchestra or choir, they stand in front of it and direct its performance. 指揮する ❑*Dennis had recently begun a successful career conducting opera.* デニスは最近オペラの指揮者として首尾よくスタートを切っていた. ❑*Solti continued to conduct here and abroad.* ソルティは引き続き国内や国外で指揮者を務めた. **4** V-T 他動詞 If something **conducts** heat or electricity, it allows heat or electricity to pass

through it or along it. 伝導する [no cont] ❑*Water conducts heat faster than air.* 水は空気より速く熱を伝える. **5** N-SING 単数名詞 The **conduct** of a task or activity is the way in which it is organized and carried out. 遂行 ❑*Also up for discussion will be the conduct of free and fair elections.* また自由で公正な選挙の遂行も議題となる予定だ. **6** N-UNCOUNT 不可算名詞 Someone's **conduct** is the way they behave in particular situations. 振舞い ❑*For Europeans, the law is a statement of basic principles of civilized conduct.* ヨーロッパの人々にとって法律は礼儀正しい振舞いの基本的原則を述べたものである.

con|duc|tor /kəndʌktər/ (conductors) **1** N-COUNT 可算名詞 A **conductor** is a person who stands in front of an orchestra or choir and directs its performance. 指揮者 **2** N-COUNT 可算名詞 On a train, a **conductor** is a person whose job is to travel on the train in order to help passengers and check tickets. 車掌 [AM 米国英語] **3** N-COUNT 可算名詞 On a streetcar or bus, the **conductor** is the person whose job is to sell tickets to the passengers. 車掌 **4** N-COUNT 可算名詞 A **conductor** is a substance that heat or electricity can pass through or along. 伝導体 ❑*Graphite is a highly efficient conductor of electricity.* 石墨は電気の非常に効率的な伝導体である. **5** → see also **semiconductor**

→ see **metal**

cone /koʊn/ (cones) **1** N-COUNT 可算名詞 A **cone** is a shape with a circular base ending in a point at the top. 円錐(えんすい)形 ❑*...orange traffic cones.* オレンジ色の円錐形の交通標識 ❑*...the streetlight's yellow cone of light.* 街灯の黄色い円錐形の照明 **2** N-COUNT 可算名詞 A **cone** is the fruit of a tree such as a pine or fir. 球果 ❑*...a bowl of fir cones.* ボウル1杯のモミのまつかさ **3** N-COUNT 可算名詞 A **cone** is a thin, cone-shaped cookie that is used for holding ice cream. You can also refer to ice cream that you eat in this way as a **cone**. (アイスクリームの) コーン ❑*She stopped by the ice-cream shop and had a chocolate cone.* 彼女はアイスクリーム店に立ち寄り，チョコレートアイスクリームを食べた.

→ see **solid, volcano, volume**

con|fec|tion|ers' sug|ar N-UNCOUNT 不可算名詞 **Confectioners' sugar** is very fine white sugar that is used for making frosting and candy. 精製粉末糖 [AM 米国英語]

con|fed|era|tion /kənfedəreɪʃˀn/ (confederations) N-COUNT; N-IN-NAMES 可算名詞; 名称中の名詞 A **confederation** is an organization or group consisting of smaller groups or states, especially one that exists for business or political purposes. 同盟; 連邦 ❑*...the Confederation of Indian Industry.* インド産業同盟

con|fer /kənfɜr/ (confers, conferring, conferred) **1** V-RECIP 相互動詞 When you **confer with** someone, you discuss something with them in order to make a decision. You can also say that two people **confer**. 相談する ❑*He conferred with Hill and the others in his office.* 彼はヒルや事務所の他の者と相談した. **2** V-T 他動詞 To **confer** something such as power or an honor on someone means to give it to them. 与える [FORMAL 形式ばった] ❑*The constitution also confers large powers on Brazil's 25 constituent states.* 憲法はまたブラジルを構成する25の州に大きな権限を与えている.

con|fer|ence /kɒnfərəns, -frəns/ (conferences) **1** N-COUNT 可算名詞 A **conference** is a meeting, often lasting a few days, which is organized on a particular subject or to bring together people who have a common interest. 会議，大会 ❑*The president took the unprecedented step of summoning all the state governors to a conference on education.* 大統領は教育に関する会議に全ての州知事を招集するという前例のない手段を取った. ❑*...the Alternative Energy conference.* 代替エネルギー会議 **2** N-COUNT 可算名詞 A **conference** is a meeting at which formal discussions take place. 協議 [also "in" N] ❑*They sat down at the dinner table for a conference.* 彼らは打ち合わせを行なうために食卓に着いた. **3** → see also **press conference**

con|fer|ence call (conference calls) N-COUNT 可算名詞 A **conference call** is a phone call in which more than two people take part. 電話会議 [BUSINESS 実業] ❑*There are daily conference calls with Washington.* ワシントンと毎日電話会議が行なわれる.

con|fess /kənfes/ (confesses, confessing, confessed) **1** V-T/V-I 他動詞/自動詞 If someone **confesses** to doing something wrong, they admit that they did it. 告白する ❑*He had confessed to seventeen murders.* 彼は17の殺人を犯したと告白した. ❑*I had expected her to confess that she only wrote these books for the money.* 私は彼女が金銭的な理由のみでこうした本を書いたと告白することを期待していた. ❑*Ray changed his mind, claiming that he had been forced into confessing.* レイは心変わりし，告白することを強要されたと主張した. **2** V-T/V-I

C

他動詞/自動詞 If someone **confesses** or **confesses** their sins, they tell God or a priest about their sins so that they can be forgiven. 告解する ❏ *You just go to the church and confess your sins.* あなたはちょっと教会に行き、罪を告解しなさい。

con|fes|sion /kənfɛʃ⁰n/ (**confessions**) **1** N-COUNT 可算名詞 A **confession** is a signed statement by someone in which they admit that they have committed a particular crime. 供述書 ❏ *They forced him to sign a confession.* 彼らは彼に供述書に署名することを強要した。 **2** N-VAR 可変性名詞 **Confession** is the act of admitting that you have done something that you are ashamed of or embarrassed about. 白状 ❏ *I have a confession to make.* 私は白状したいことがある。 ❏ *The diaries are a mixture of confession and observation.* それらの日記には告白と観察が交じり合っている。 **3** N-VAR 可変性名詞 If you make a **confession of** your beliefs or feelings, you publicly tell people that this is what you believe or feel. 告白 ❏ *...Tatyana's confession of love.* タチアナの愛の告白 **4** N-VAR 可変性名詞 In the Catholic church and in some other churches, if you go to **confession**, you privately tell a priest about your sins and ask for forgiveness. 告解 ❏ *He never went to Father Porter for confession again.* 彼がポーター神父に告解しに行くことは2度となかった。

con|fide /kənfaɪd/ (**confides, confiding, confided**) V-T/V-I 他動詞/自動詞 If you **confide in** someone, you tell them a secret. 秘密を打ち明ける ❏ *I knew she had some fundamental problems in her marriage because she had confided in me a year earlier.* 私は1年前に打ち明けられていたので、彼女の結婚に根本的な問題が若干あることは知っていた。 ❏ *He confided to me that he felt like he was being punished.* 彼は処罰されているように感じたと私に打ち明けた。

con|fi|dence /kɒnfɪdəns/ **1** N-UNCOUNT 不可算名詞 If you have **confidence in** someone, you feel that you can trust them. 信頼 ❏ *I have every confidence in you.* 私はあなたを全面的に信頼している。 ❏ *This has contributed to the lack of confidence in the FDA.* これがFDAが信頼されないことの1因となっている。 **2** N-UNCOUNT 不可算名詞 If you have **confidence**, you feel sure about your abilities, qualities, or ideas. 自信 ❏ *The band is in excellent form and brimming with confidence.* そのバンドは調子が良く、自信満々だ。 **3** N-UNCOUNT 不可算名詞 If you can say something **with confidence**, you feel certain it is correct. 確信 ❏ *I can say with confidence that such rumors were totally groundless.* 私はそのようなうわさは全く事実無根だったと確信を持って言える。 **4** N-UNCOUNT 不可算名詞 If you tell someone something **in confidence**, you tell them a secret. 秘密 ❏ *We told you all these things in confidence.* 我々にこうした事柄をすべて内緒であなたに伝えた。 ❏ *Even telling Lois seemed a betrayal of confidence.* ロイスに伝えることすら秘密の裏切りのように思えた。 ● PHRASE 句 If you **take** someone **into** your **confidence**, you tell them a secret. 人に秘密を打ち明ける → see **stock market**

con|fi|dent /kɒnfɪdənt/ **1** ADJ 形容詞 If you are **confident** about something, you are certain that it will happen in the way you want it to. 確信して ❏ *I am confident that everything will come out right in time.* 私はそのうち全てがうまく行くことを確信している。 ❏ *Mr. Ryan is confident of success.* ライアン氏は成功を確信している。 ● **con|fi|dent|ly** ADV 副詞 [ADV with v] 確信を持って ❏ *I can confidently promise that this year is going to be very different.* 私は今年は非常に違う年になることを確かに約束できる。 **2** ADJ 形容詞 If a person or their manner is **confident**, they feel sure about their own abilities, qualities, or ideas. 自信に満ちた ❏ *In time he became more confident and relaxed.* やがて彼はより自信が出てきて、リラックスした。 ● **con|fi|dent|ly** ADV 副詞 自信に満ちて ❏ *She walked confidently across the hall.* 彼女は自信に満ちた調子でホールを横切って歩いた。 **3** ADJ 形容詞 If you are **confident that** something is true, you are sure that it is true. A **confident** statement is one that the speaker is sure is true. 確信して ❏ *She is confident that everybody is on her side.* 彼女は全員が彼女を支持していることを確信している。 ● **con|fi|dent|ly** ADV 副詞 [ADV with v] 自信を持って ❏ *I can confidently say that none of them were or are racist.* 彼らの中には人種差別主義者であったか、現在そうである人物はいないと私は自信を持って言える。

con|fi|den|tial /kɒnfɪdɛnʃ⁰l/ **1** ADJ 形容詞 Information that is **confidential** is meant to be kept secret or private. 秘密の ❏ *She accused them of leaking confidential information about her private life.* 彼女は彼らが彼女の私的生活についての秘密の情報を漏らしたことを非難した。 ● **con|fi|den|tial|ly** ADV 副詞 内密に ❏ *People can phone in, knowing that any information they give will be treated confidentially.* 人々は提供する情報は全て内密に扱われることを知った上で、電話することができる。 ● **con|fi|den|ti|al|ity** /kɒnfɪdɛnʃiæliti/ N-UNCOUNT 不可算名詞 秘密性 ❏ *...the confidentiality of the client-attorney relationship.* 依頼人と弁護士の関係の秘密性 **2** ADJ 形容詞 If you talk to someone in a **confidential** way, you talk to them quietly because what you are saying is secret or private. 内緒話をするような ❏ *"Look," he said in a confidential tone, "I want you to know that me and Joey are cops."* 「いいかい、僕とジョーイは警官だということを君に知ってもらいたい」と彼は内緒話をするような口調で言った。 ● **con|fi|den|tial|ly** ADV 副詞 内緒話をするように ❏ *Nash hadn't*

raised his voice, still spoke rather softly, **confidentially**. ナッシュは声を荒げず、依然として内緒話をするようにかなり穏やかな声で話した。

con|fi|den|tial|ly /kɒnfɪdɛnʃəli/ **1** ADV 副詞 **Confidentially** is used to say that what you are telling someone is a secret and should not be discussed with anyone else. 内密に [ADV with cl] ❏ *Confidentially, I am not sure that it wasn't above their heads.* ここだけの話だが、それを彼らが理解できたのか確かでない。 **2** → see also **confidential**

con|figu|ra|tion /kənfɪgyəreɪʃ⁰n/ (**configurations**) **1** N-COUNT 可算名詞 A **configuration** is an arrangement of a group of things. 配置 [FORMAL 形式ばった] ❏ *...Stonehenge, in southwestern England, an ancient configuration of giant stones.* イングランド南西部にある、大昔からの巨大石の配列であるストーンヘンジ **2** N-UNCOUNT 不可算名詞 The **configuration** of a computer system is the way in which all its parts, such as the hardware and software, are connected together in order for the computer to work. コンフィギュレーション [COMPUTING コンピューティング] ❏ *Prices range from $119 to $199, depending on the particular configuration.* 価格は個々のコンフィギュレーションによって119ドルから199ドルまでさまざまだ。

Word Link   *fig ≈ form, shape : configure, disfigure, figurative*

con|fig|ure /kənfɪgyər/ (**configures, configuring, configured**) V-T 他動詞 If you **configure** a piece of computer equipment, you set it up so that it is ready for use. （コンピュータの）コンフィギュレーションを行なう [COMPUTING コンピューティング] ❏ *How easy was it to configure the software?* そのソフトのコンフィギュレーションはどの程度簡単でしたか。

con|fine /kənfaɪn/ (**confines, confining, confined**) **1** V-T 他動詞 To **confine** something **to** a particular place or group means to prevent it from spreading beyond that place or group. （一定の範囲に）限る ❏ *Health officials have successfully confined the epidemic to the Tabatinga area.* 保健局員たちは伝染病をタバテンガ地域にとどめることに成功した。 **2** V-T 他動詞 If you **confine** somebody or something, you prevent them from leaving or escaping. 閉じ込める ❏ *He was confined in an internment camp in Utah.* 彼はユタ州の収容所に監禁された。 ❏ *They decided not to let their new dog run loose, confining it to a fenced enclosure during the day.* 彼らは新しい犬を放し飼いにしないことに決め、日中は柵で囲われた場所に閉じ込めた。 **3** V-T 他動詞 If you **confine yourself** or your activities to something, you do only that thing and are involved with nothing else. 限定する ❏ *He did not confine himself to the one language.* 彼はその1つの言語だけに絞らなかった。

con|fined /kənfaɪnd/ **1** ADJ 形容詞 If something is **confined to** a particular place, it exists only in that place. If it is **confined to** a particular group, only members of that group have it. 限られた [v-link ADJ "to" n] ❏ *The problem is not confined to Georgia.* その問題はジョージア州だけに限られていない。 **2** ADJ 形容詞 A **confined** space or area is small and enclosed by walls. 狭い ❏ *His long legs bent up in the confined space.* 彼の長い足は狭い場所では曲がった。 **3** ADJ 形容詞 If someone is **confined to** a wheelchair, bed, or house, they have to stay there, because they are disabled or ill. （病気・障害で）閉じ込められた [v-link ADJ "to" n] ❏ *He had been confined to a wheelchair since childhood.* 彼は幼年時代から車椅子生活を送っていた。

con|fine|ment /kənfaɪnmənt/ N-UNCOUNT 不可算名詞 **Confinement** is the state of being forced to stay in a prison or another place which you cannot leave. 監禁状態 ❏ *She had been held in solitary confinement for four months.* 彼女は4か月間独りで監禁されていた。

Word Link   *firm ≈ making strong : affirm, confirm, infirm*

con|firm /kənfɜrm/ (**confirms, confirming, confirmed**) **1** V-T 他動詞 If something **confirms** what you believe, suspect, or fear, it shows that it is definitely true. 確証する [no cont] ❏ *X-rays have confirmed that he has not broken any bones.* レントゲン撮影の結果、彼は骨が折れていないことが確証された。 ● **con|fir|ma|tion** /kɒnfərmeɪʃ⁰n/ N-UNCOUNT 不可算名詞 確証 ❏ *They took her resignation as confirmation of their suspicions.* 彼らは彼女が辞任したことで彼らの疑念が確証されたと考えた。 **2** V-T 他動詞 If you **confirm** something that has been stated or suggested, you say that it is true because you know about it. 確認する ❏ *The spokesman confirmed that the area was now in rebel hands.* スポークスマンはその地域が現在反乱軍の支配下にあることを確認した。 ● **con|fir|ma|tion** N-UNCOUNT 不可算名詞 確認 ❏ *She glanced over at James for confirmation.* 彼女は確認のためにジェームスの方をちらっと見た。 **3** V-T 他動詞 If you **confirm** an arrangement or appointment, you say that it is definite, usually in a letter or on the telephone. 確認する ❏ *You make the reservation, and I'll confirm it in writing.* あなたが予約してくれれば、私が確認の手紙を

出します。 ●con|fir|ma|tion N-UNCOUNT 不可算名詞 確認 ❏ *Travel arrangements are subject to confirmation by the head office.* 旅行の手配は本社の確認が必要です。 ❹ V-T 他動詞 [usu passive] *If someone is* **confirmed**, they are formally accepted as a member of a Christian church during a ceremony in which they say they believe what the church teaches. 堅信礼を施す ❏ *He was confirmed as a member of the Methodist Church.* 彼はメソジスト教会の1員として堅信礼を受けた。 ●con|fir|ma|tion (confirmations) N-VAR 可変性名詞 堅信礼 ❏ *...when I was being prepared for Confirmation.* 私が堅信礼の準備を受けていた時 ❺ V-T 他動詞 [no cont] *If something* **confirms** *you in your decision, belief, or opinion,* it makes you think that you are definitely right. 強める ❏ *It has confirmed me in my decision not to become a nun.* それで修道女にはならないという私の決意はますます強固になった。 ❻ V-T 他動詞 *If something* **confirms** *you as something,* it shows that you definitely deserve a name, role, or position. 確証する ❏ *Her new role could confirm her as one of our leading actors.* 彼女の新しい役で彼女は当社の一流女優の1人としての地位を確実なものにするかもしれない。

con|fis|cate /kɒnfɪskeɪt/ (confiscates, confiscating, confiscated) V-T 他動詞 *If you* **confiscate** *something from someone,* you take it away from them, usually as a punishment. 没収する ❏ *The law has been used to confiscate assets from people who have committed minor offenses.* その法律はちょっとした違法行為を犯した人々から資産を没収するのに利用されてきた。 ●con|fis|ca|tion /kɒnfɪskeɪʃⁿn/ (confiscations) N-VAR 可変性名詞 ❏ *The new laws allow the confiscation of assets purchased with proceeds of the drugs trade.* 新しい法律は麻薬取引の利益で購入した資産の没収を認めている。

Word Link *flict ≈ striking : affliction, conflict, inflict*

con|flict (conflicts, conflicting, conflicted)

The noun is pronounced /kɒnflɪkt/. The verb is pronounced /kənflɪkt/.

名詞は /kɒnflɪkt/ と発音される。 動詞は /kənflɪkt/ と発音される。

❶ N-UNCOUNT 不可算名詞 **Conflict** is serious disagreement and argument about something important. *If two people or groups are* **in conflict**, they have had a serious disagreement or argument and have not yet reached agreement. 争い [oft "in/into" N] ❏ *Try to keep any conflict between you and your ex-partner to a minimum.* あなたと別れたパートナーとの間の対立は最小限にとどめるようにしなさい。 ❷ N-UNCOUNT 不可算名詞 **Conflict** is a state of mind in which you find it impossible to make a decision. 葛藤（かっとう）❏ *...the anguish of his own inner conflict.* 彼自身の内心の葛藤の苦悩 ❸ N-VAR 可変性名詞 **Conflict** is fighting between countries or groups of people. 戦い，紛争 [WRITTEN 書き言葉] ❏ *...talks aimed at ending four decades of conflict.* 40年間にわたる紛争を終結させるための会談 ❹ N-VAR 可変性名詞 *A* **conflict** is a serious difference between two or more beliefs, ideas, or interests. *If two beliefs, ideas, or interests are* **in conflict**, they are very different. 対立 ❏ *There is a conflict between what they are doing and what you want.* 彼らのしていることとあなたの望むことには対立がある。 ❺ V-RECIP 相互動詞 *If ideas, beliefs, or accounts* **conflict**, they are very different from each other and it seems impossible for them to exist together or to each be true. 対立する ❏ *Personal ethics and professional ethics sometimes conflict.* 個人的倫理と職業上の倫理は時に相容れないことがある。 ❏ *He held firm opinions which usually conflicted with mine.* 彼は私の意見と通常対立する強い意見を持っていた。
→ see war

Word Partnership *conflict* は次の語句と使われる:

N.	conflict **resolution, source of** conflict ❶
V.	**end/resolve/settle a** conflict ❶ ❸
	avoid conflict ❶ ❸ ❹
ADJ.	**military** conflict ❸

con|form /kənfɔrm/ (conforms, conforming, conformed) ❶ V-I 自動詞 *If something* **conforms to** *something such as a law or someone's wishes,* it is of the required type or quality. 従う ❏ *The lamp has been designed to conform to new safety standards.* そのランプは新しい安全基準に準拠するように設計されている。 ❷ V-I 自動詞 *If you* **conform**, you behave in the way that you are expected or supposed to behave. 順応する ❏ *Many children who can't or don't conform are bullied.* 周りに順応できないか，順応しない子供の多くはいじめの対象となる。

con|form|ity /kənfɔrmiti/ ❶ N-UNCOUNT 不可算名詞 *If something happens* **in conformity with** *something such as a law or someone's wishes,* it happens as the law says it should, or as the person wants it to. 準拠して ❏ *The prime minister is, in conformity with their constitution, chosen by the president.* 首相は憲法に準拠して大統領によって選ばれる。 ❷ N-UNCOUNT 不可算名詞 **Conformity** means behaving in the same way as most other people. (慣行に) 順応，服従 ❏ *Excessive conformity is usually caused by fear of*

disapproval. 過度の順応は通常非難を恐れることに起因している。

con|found /kənfaʊnd/ (confounds, confounding, confounded) V-T 他動詞 *If someone or something* **confounds** *you,* they make you feel surprised or confused, often by showing you that your opinions or expectations of them were wrong. 困惑させる ❏ *He momentarily confounded his critics by his cool handling of the hostage crisis.* 彼は人質事件の危機に対する冷静な対処で批判的な人たちを一時的にまごつかせた。

con|front /kənfrʌnt/ (confronts, confronting, confronted) ❶ V-T 他動詞 *If you* **are confronted** *with a problem, task, or difficulty,* you have to deal with it. 立ちはだかる ❏ *She was confronted with severe money problems.* 彼女は深刻な金銭問題に直面した。 ❷ V-T 他動詞 *If you* **confront** *a difficult situation or issue,* you accept the fact that it exists and try to deal with it. 直面する ❏ *We are learning how to confront death.* 我々はいかに死と直面するかを学んでいるところだ。 ❸ V-T 他動詞 *If you* **are confronted** *by something that you find threatening or difficult to deal with,* it is there in front of you. 向かい合う [usu passive] ❏ *I was confronted with an array of knobs, levers, and switches.* 私はずらりと並んだノブ，レバー，スイッチに出くわした。 ❹ V-T 他動詞 *If you* **confront** *someone,* you stand or sit in front of them, especially when you are going to fight, argue, or compete with them. 対決する ❏ *She pushed her way through the mob and confronted him face to face.* 彼女は暴徒の中を押し進み，彼と面と向かって対決した。 ❏ *They don't hesitate to open fire when confronted by police.* 彼らは警察が向かってきたら発砲することをためらわない。 ❺ V-T 他動詞 *If you* **confront** *someone* **with** *something,* you present them facts or evidence to them in order to accuse them of something or force them to deal with a situation. 突きつける ❏ *She had decided to confront Kathryn with the truth.* 彼女はキャサリンに真実を告げることに決めた。 ❏ *I could not bring myself to confront him about it.* 私はどうしてもそれについて彼を責める気になれなかった。

con|fron|ta|tion /kɒnfrʌnteɪʃⁿn/ (confrontations) N-VAR 可変性名詞 *A* **confrontation** is a dispute, fight, or battle between two groups of people. 対決 ❏ *The commission remains so weak that it will continue to avoid confrontation with governments.* その委員会はまだ非常に弱いので諸国の政府との対決を回避し続けるだろう。

con|fron|ta|tion|al /kɒnfrʌnteɪʃənⁿl/ ADJ 形容詞 *If you describe the way that someone behaves as* **confrontational**, you are showing your disapproval of the fact that they are aggressive and likely to cause an argument or dispute. 対立的な [DISAPPROVAL 不賛成] ❏ *The committee's confrontational style of campaigning has made it unpopular.* キャンペーンのやり方が対立的なため，委員会は人気がなくなっている。

con|fuse /kənfyuz/ (confuses, confusing, confused) ❶ V-T 他動詞 *If you* **confuse** *two things,* you get them mixed up, so that you think one is the other one. 混同する ❏ *I always confuse my left with my right.* 私はいつも右と左の区別がつかない。 ●con|fu|sion /kənfyuʒⁿn/ N-UNCOUNT 不可算名詞 混同 ❏ *Use different colors of felt pen on your sketch to avoid confusion.* 混同を避けるためスケッチにはいろいろな色のフェルトペンを使いなさい。 ❷ V-T 他動詞 *To* **confuse** *someone means to make it difficult for them to know exactly what is happening or what to do.* 混乱させる ❏ *My words surprised and confused him.* 私の言葉は彼を驚かせ，混乱させた。 ❸ V-T 他動詞 *To* **confuse** *a situation means to make it complicated or difficult to understand.* 複雑にする ❏ *To further confuse the issue, there is an enormous variation in the amount of sleep people feel happy with.* 問題をさらに複雑にすることに，人々が満足する睡眠時間には大幅な差がある。

con|fused /kənfyuzd/ ❶ ADJ 形容詞 *If you are* **confused**, you do not know exactly what is happening or what to do. 混乱した ❏ *A survey showed people were confused about what they should eat to stay healthy.* ある調査は，人々は健康でいるために何を食べるべきかについて困惑していることを示した。 ❷ ADJ 形容詞 *Something that is* **confused** *does not have any order or pattern and is difficult to understand.* 不明瞭な ❏ *The situation remains confused as both sides claim success.* 双方が成功だと言い張っているため，状況は不明瞭なままである。

con|fus|ing /kənfyuzɪŋ/ ADJ 形容詞 *Something that is* **confusing** *makes it difficult for people to know exactly what is happening or what to do.* 曖昧（あいまい）な ❏ *The statement is really confusing.* その声明は本当に曖昧だ。

con|fu|sion /kənfyuʒⁿn/ (confusions) ❶ N-VAR 可変性名詞 *If there is* **confusion** *about something,* it is not clear what the true situation is, especially because people believe different things. 不明瞭（ふめいりょう）❏ *There's still confusion about the number of students.* 学生数はまだ不明瞭だ。 ❷ N-UNCOUNT 不可算名詞 **Confusion** is a situation in which everything is in disorder, especially because there are lots of things happening at the same time. 混乱状態 ❏ *There was confusion when a man fired shots.* 1人の男が発砲した時に混乱状態が起こった。 ❸ → see also **confuse**

con|gen|ial /kəndʒinyəl/ ADJ 形容詞 *A* **congenial** *person, place, or environment is pleasant.* 心地よい，感じのよい [FORMAL 形式ば

った] ❏*He is back in more congenial company.* 彼はもっと気の合った仲間のところに戻っている.

con|gest|ed /kəndʒɛstɪd/ ADJ 形容詞 A **congested** road or area is extremely crowded and blocked with traffic or people. 混雑した ❏*He promised to clear the city's congested roads.* 彼は同市の道路の渋滞をなくすことを約束した.

con|ges|tion /kəndʒɛstʃən/ ■ N-UNCOUNT 不可算名詞 If there is **congestion** in a place, the place is extremely crowded and blocked with traffic or people. 混雑 ❏*The problems of traffic congestion will not disappear in a hurry.* 交通渋滞の問題はすぐになくなるものではないだろう. ② N-UNCOUNT 不可算名詞 **Congestion** in a part of the body is a medical condition in which the part becomes blocked. 充血, つまり ❏*...nasal congestion.* 鼻づまり
→ see **traffic**

con|glom|er|ate /kənglɒmərɪt/ (**conglomerates**) N-COUNT 可算名詞 A **conglomerate** is a large business firm consisting of several different companies. 複合企業 [BUSINESS 実業] ❏*...the world's second-largest media conglomerate.* 世界で2番目に規模の大きいメディア・コングロマリット

Word Link	grat ≈ pleasing : congratulate, gratify, gratitude

con|gratu|late /kəngrætʃəleɪt/ (**congratulates, congratulating, congratulated**) ■ V-T 他動詞 If you **congratulate** someone, you say something to show you are pleased that something nice has happened to them. 祝う ❏*She congratulated him on the birth of his son.* 彼女は彼に息子の誕生のお祝いを言った. ● **con|gratu|la|tion** /kəngrætʃəleɪʃən/ N-UNCOUNT 不可算名詞 祝い ❏*We have received many letters of congratulation.* 私どもは数多くのお祝いの手紙を受け取った. ② V-T 他動詞 If you **congratulate** someone, you praise them for something good that they have done. ほめる ❏*I really must congratulate the organizers for a well run and enjoyable event.* これはうまく運営された楽しいイベントに関して本当に主催者の方々に賛辞を呈さなければなりません.

con|gratu|la|tions /kəngrætʃəleɪʃənz/ ■ CONVENTION 慣習表現 You say "**Congratulations**" to someone in order to congratulate them on something nice that has happened to them or something good that they have done. おめでとう ❏*Congratulations, you have a healthy baby girl.* おめでとう. 健やかな女の赤ちゃんです. ❏*Congratulations on your interesting article.* 興味深い記事おめでとう. ② N-PLURAL 複数名詞 If you offer someone your **congratulations**, you congratulate them on something nice that has happened to them or on something good that they have done. 祝辞 ❏*The club also offers its congratulations to D. Brown on her appointment as president.* クラブはまたD・ブラウンに会長に任命されたことに対して祝辞を呈する.

con|gre|gate /kɒngrɪgeɪt/ (**congregates, congregating, congregated**) V-I 自動詞 When people **congregate**, they gather together and form a group. 集まる ❏*Visitors congregated on Sunday afternoons to view public exhibitions.* 一般展示を見るために参観者が日曜の午後に集まった.

con|gre|ga|tion /kɒngrɪgeɪʃən/ N-COUNT-COLL 集合可算名詞 The people who are attending a religious service or who regularly attend a religious service are referred to as the **congregation**. (礼拝に集まる) 会衆 ❏*Most members of the congregation begin arriving a few minutes before services.* 会衆のほとんどは礼拝が始まる数分前に到着し始める.

con|gress /kɒngrɪs/ (**congresses**) N-COUNT-COLL 集合可算名詞 A **congress** is a large meeting that is held to discuss ideas and policies. 大会 ❏*A lot has changed after the party congress.* 党大会後に大いに変った.

Con|gress N-PROPER-COLL 集合的固有名詞 **Congress** is the elected group of politicians that is responsible for making laws in the United States. It consists of two parts: the House of Representatives and the Senate. (米国の) 議会 ❏*We want to cooperate with both the administration and Congress.* 我々は政府と議会の両方と協力したい.

con|gres|sion|al /kəngrɛʃənəl/ also **Congressional** ADJ 形容詞 A **congressional** policy, action, or person relates to the U.S. Congress. 米国議会の [ADJ n] ❏*The president explained his plans to congressional leaders.* 大統領は議会の指導者たちに彼の計画を説明した.

congress|man /kɒngrɪsmən/ (**congressmen**) N-COUNT; N-TITLE 可算名詞, 称号名詞 A **congressman** is a male member of the U.S. Congress, especially of the House of Representatives. (米国の) 連邦議会議員; (特に) 下院議員

congress|woman /kɒngrɪswʊmən/ (**congresswomen**) N-COUNT; N-TITLE 可算名詞, 称号名詞 A **congresswoman** is a female member of the U.S. Congress, especially of the House of Representatives. (米国の) 女性の連邦議会議員; (特に) 女性の下院議員

con|jec|ture /kəndʒɛktʃər/ (**conjectures, conjecturing, conjectured**) ■ N-VAR 可変性名詞 A **conjecture** is a conclusion that is based on information that is not certain or complete. 推測 [FORMAL 形式ばった] ❏*That was a conjecture, not a fact.* それは事実ではなく推測だった. ❏*There are several conjectures.* いくつかの推測がある. ② V-T/V-I 他動詞/自動詞 When you **conjecture**, you form an opinion or reach a conclusion on the basis of information that is not certain or complete. 推測する [FORMAL 形式ばった] ❏*He conjectured that some individuals may be able to detect major calamities.* 彼は一部の人物には大規模な災難を探知する能力があるかもしれないと推測した.

con|junc|tion /kəndʒʌŋkʃən/ (**conjunctions**) ■ N-COUNT 可算名詞 A **conjunction of** two or more things is the occurrence of them at the same time or place. 同時発生 [FORMAL 形式ばった] ❏*...the conjunction of two events.* 2つの行事の同時開催 ② N-COUNT 可算名詞 In grammar, a **conjunction** is a word or group of words that joins together words, groups, or clauses. In English, there are coordinating conjunctions such as "and" and "but," and subordinating conjunctions such as "although," "because," and "when." 接続詞 ③ PHRASE 句 If one thing is done **in conjunction with** another, the two things are done or used together. 一と関連して [usu PHR "with" n] ❏*Textbooks are designed to be used in conjunction with classroom teaching.* 教科書は教室の授業と共に使用されるように作られている.

con|jure /kɒndʒər/ (**conjures, conjuring, conjured**) V-T 他動詞 If you **conjure** something out of nothing, you make it appear as if by magic. 魔法をかけたようにーを引き起こす ❏*Thirteen years ago she found herself having to conjure a career from thin air.* 彼女は13年前に魔法のように無から身を立てなければならないのに気づいた. ● PHRASAL VERB 句動詞 **Conjure up** means the same as **conjure**. 魔法のように出現させる ❏*Every day a different chef will be conjuring up delicious dishes in the restaurant.* そのレストランでは毎日違うコックが美味しい料理を魔法のように作り出す予定だ.
▶ **conjure up** ■ PHRASAL VERB 句動詞 If you **conjure up** a memory, picture, or idea, you create it in your mind. 心に思い起こす ❏*When he closed his eyes, he could conjure up in exact color almost every event of his life.* 目を閉じると, 彼は人生のほとんど全ての出来事を正確な色彩で思い出すことができた. ② → see **conjure**

con|nect /kənɛkt/ (**connects, connecting, connected**) ■ V-RECIP 相互動詞 If something or someone **connects** one thing **to** another, or if one thing **connects to** another, or if two things **connect**, the two things are joined together. 接続する ❏*You can connect the speakers to your CD player.* スピーカーをCDプレイヤーに接続できる. ❏*I connected the wires for the transformer.* 私は変圧器向けに電線を接続した. ② V-RECIP 相互動詞 If two things or places **connect** or if something **connects**, they are joined and people or things can pass between them. 結ぶ ❏*...the long hallway that connects the rooms.* 部屋を結ぶ長い廊下 ❏*A pedestrian bridge now connects the parking garage with the mall.* 今は歩道橋が駐車場をモールと結んでいる. ③ V-I 自動詞 If one train or plane, for example, **connects with** another, it arrives at a time which allows passengers to change to the other one in order to continue their trip. 連絡する ❏*...a train connecting with a ferry to Ireland.* アイルランド行きのフェリーと連絡する列車 ④ V-T 他動詞 If a piece of equipment or a place **is connected to** a source of power or water, it is joined to that source so that it has power or water. 接続する [usu passive] ❏*These appliances should not be connected to power supplies.* こうした機器は電源に接続されるべきではない. ● PHRASAL VERB 句動詞 **Connect up** means the same as **connect**. 接続する ❏*The shower is easy to install - it needs only to be connected up to the hot and cold water supply.* シャワーを取り付けるのは簡単だ. 湯と水の導管につなぐだけだ. ⑤ V-T 他動詞 If you **connect** a person or thing **with** something, you realize that there is a link or relationship between them. 結びつけて考える ❏*I hoped he would not connect me with that now-embarrassing review I'd written seven years earlier.* 私は彼が私を7年前に書いた今では恥ずかしくなるような批評記事と結び付けて考えないことを願った. ⑥ V-T 他動詞 Something that **connects** a person or thing **with** something else shows or provides a link or relationship between them. 関係づける ❏*A search of Brady's house revealed nothing that could connect him with the robberies.* ブレーディの家宅捜査では彼を一連の強盗事件と関連づけられるものは何も発見されなかった.

con|nect|ed /kənɛktɪd/ ■ ADJ 形容詞 If one thing is **connected with** another, there is a link or relationship between them. 関係のある ❏*Have you ever had any skin problems connected with exposure to the sun?* あなたは日光を浴びることと関係のある皮膚病にかかったことはありますか? ❏*The dispute is not directly connected to the negotiations.* その紛争は交渉とは直接関係していない. ② → see also **connect, well-connected**

con|nec|tion /kənɛkʃən/ (**connections**) ■ N-VAR 可変性名詞 A **connection** is a relationship between two things, people, or groups. 関係 ❏*There was no evidence of a connection between BSE and the brain diseases recently confirmed in cats.* 狂牛病と最近猫に確認された脳の病気の間に関係があるという証拠はなかった. ❏*I felt a strong connection between us.* 私は私たちの間に強いつながりを感じた. ② N-COUNT 可算名詞 A **connection** is a joint where two

wires or pipes are joined together. 連結部 ❑ *Check all radiators for small leaks, especially round pipework connections.* わずかな漏れがないか、全てのラジエーターに、特に丸い導管の連結部をチェックしなさい. **3** N-COUNT 可算名詞 If a place has good road, rail, or air **connections**, many places can be directly reached from there by car, train, or plane. 連絡 ❑ *Mexico City has excellent air and rail connections to the rest of the country.* メキシコ市は全国各地への飛行機や列車の連絡が大変いい. **4** N-COUNT 可算名詞 If you get a **connection** at a station or airport, you catch a train, bus, or plane, after getting off another train, bus, or plane, in order to continue your trip. 連絡便 ❑ *My flight was late and I missed the connection.* 飛行機の便が遅れ、私は連絡列車に乗り遅れた.

con|nec|tiv|ity /kɒnɛktɪvəti/ N-UNCOUNT 不可算名詞 **Connectivity** is the ability of a computing device to connect to other computers or to the Internet. 接続性 [COMPUTING コンピューティング] ❑ *...a DVD video and CD player with Internet connectivity.* インターネットに接続できるDVDビデオとCDプレーヤー

con|nois|seur /kɒnəsɜr, -sʊər/ (**connoisseurs**) N-COUNT 可算名詞 A **connoisseur** is someone who knows a lot about the arts, food, drink, or some other subject. (美術品などの) 鑑定家、目利き ❑ *Sarah tells me you're something of an art connoisseur.* あなたは美術に通じているとサラから聞いています.

con|no|ta|tion /kɒnəteɪʃən/ (**connotations**) N-COUNT 可算名詞 The **connotations** of a particular word or name are the ideas or qualities which it makes you think of. 言外の意味 ❑ *It's just one of those words that's got so many negative connotations.* それはまさに非常に多くの否定的な意味を含む語の1つだ.

con|quer /kɒŋkər/ (**conquers, conquering, conquered**) **1** V-T 他動詞 If one country or group of people **conquers** another, they take complete control of their land. 征服する ❑ *During 1936, Mussolini conquered Abyssinia.* 1936年内にムッソリーニはアビシニアを制圧した. **2** V-T 他動詞 If you **conquer** something such as a problem, you succeed in ending it or dealing with it successfully. 克服する、打破する ❑ *I was certain that love was quite enough to conquer our differences.* 私は愛があれば2人の違いを十分に乗り越えられると確信していた. ❑ *He has never conquered his addiction to smoking.* 彼は喫煙を決してやめられないでいる.
→ see **army, empire**

con|quer|or /kɒŋkərər/ (**conquerors**) N-COUNT 可算名詞 The **conquerors** of a country or group of people are the people who have taken complete control of that country or group's land. 征服者 ❑ *The people of an oppressed country obey their conquerors because they want to go on living.* 抑圧された国の国民は生き延びたいがために征服者に従う.

con|quest /kɒŋkwɛst/ (**conquests**) **1** N-UNCOUNT 不可算名詞 **Conquest** is the act of conquering a country or group of people. 征服 [also N in pl, oft N "of" n] ❑ *He had led the conquest of southern Poland in 1939.* 彼は1939年の南部のポーランド征服を指揮していた. ❑ *...the Spanish conquest of Mexico.* スペインによるメキシコ征服 **2** N-SING 単数名詞 The **conquest of** something such as a problem is success in ending it or dealing with it. 克服 ❑ *The conquest of inflation has been the Government's overriding economic priority for nearly 15 years.* 15年近くインフレーションの克服が政府の最優先の重要な経済問題となっている.

<table><tr><td>**Word Link**</td><td>sci ≈ knowing : con**sci**ence, **sci**ence, uncon**sci**ous</td></tr></table>

con|science /kɒnʃəns/ (**consciences**) **1** N-COUNT 可算名詞 Your **conscience** is the part of your mind that tells you whether what you are doing is right or wrong. If you have a **guilty conscience**, you feel guilty about something because you know it was wrong. If you have a **clear conscience**, you do not feel guilty because you know you have done nothing wrong. 良心 ❑ *I have battled with my conscience over whether I should really send this letter.* 私はこの手紙を本当に送るべきか、心の中で葛藤している. ❑ *What if he got a guilty conscience and brought it back?* もし彼が罪悪感を感じて、それを返しに来たらどうする? **2** N-UNCOUNT 不可算名詞 **Conscience** is doing what you believe is right even though it might be unpopular, difficult, or dangerous. 良心に従うこと ❑ *He refused for reasons of conscience to eat meat.* 彼は良心に従い、肉を食べることを拒否した. **3** N-UNCOUNT 不可算名詞 **Conscience** is a feeling of guilt because you know you have done something that is wrong. 罪悪感 ❑ *I'm so glad he had a pang of conscience.* 彼は良心がとがめたなんて本当に嬉しいわ. **4** PHRASE 句 If you have something **on** your **conscience**, you feel guilty because you know you have done something wrong. 罪悪感を持って ❑ *The drunk driver has two deaths on his conscience.* その酔っ払い運転手は2人を死亡させたことに罪悪感を持っている.

con|sci|en|tious /kɒnʃiɛnʃəs/ ADJ 形容詞 Someone who is **conscientious** is very careful to do their work properly. 良心的な ❑ *We are generally very conscientious about our work.* 私たちは大体とても良心的に仕事をしている. ● **con|sci|en|tious|ly** ADV 副詞 良心的に ❑ *He studied conscientiously and enthusiastically.* 彼はまじめに熱心に勉強した.

con|scious /kɒnʃəs/ **1** ADJ 形容詞 If you are **conscious of** something, you notice it or realize that it is happening. 意識して、自覚して [v-link ADJ] ❑ *He was conscious of the faint, musky aroma of aftershave.* 彼はひげ剃り後のローションのかすかなじゃこうの香りを意識していた. ❑ *She was very conscious of Max studying her.* 彼女はマックスが自分を観察していることを強く意識していた. **2** ADJ 形容詞 If you are **conscious of** something, you think about it a lot, especially because you are unhappy about it or because you think it is important. 気になって [v-link ADJ] ❑ *I'm very conscious of my weight.* 私は体重がとても気になっている. **3** ADJ 形容詞 A **conscious** decision or action is made or done deliberately with you giving your full attention to it. 意図的な ❑ *I don't think we ever made a conscious decision to have a big family.* 私たちは決して意図的に大家族となったわけではないと思う. ● **con|scious|ly** ADV 副詞 [ADV with v] ❑ *Sophie was not consciously seeking a replacement after her father died.* ソフィーは父親が亡くなった後、意識的にその代わりを探していたわけではない. **4** ADJ 形容詞 Someone who is **conscious** is awake rather than asleep or unconscious. 意識のある、目覚めて ❑ *She was fully conscious throughout the surgery and knew what was going on.* 彼女は手術の間中はっきり意識があり、何が起こっているかを知っていた. **5** ADJ 形容詞 **Conscious** memories or thoughts are ones that you are aware of. 自覚した [ADJ n] ❑ *He had no conscious memory of his four-week stay in the hospital.* 彼は病院に入院していた4週間のことをまったく覚えていなかった. ● **con|scious|ly** ADV 副詞 意識的に ❑ *Most people cannot consciously remember much before the ages of 3 to 5 years.* ほとんどの人は3歳から5歳より前のことをあまり意識的に思い出せないものだ.
→ see **hypnosis**

<table><tr><td>**Thesaurus**</td><td>conscious また次を参照:</td></tr><tr><td>ADJ.</td><td>calculated, deliberate, intentional, rational **3** awake, aware, responsive; (*ant.*) unaware, unconscious **4**</td></tr></table>

-conscious /kɒnʃəs/ COMB IN ADJ 形容詞の複合 **-conscious** combines with words such as "health," "fashion," "politically," and "environmentally" to form adjectives which describe someone who believes that the aspect of life indicated is important. ーを意識して ❑ *We're all becoming increasingly health-conscious these days.* 最近私たちはみんな健康に対する意識がますます高まりつつある.

<table><tr><td>**Word Link**</td><td>ness ≈ state, condition : cleanli**ness**, conscious**ness**, kind**ness**</td></tr></table>

con|scious|ness /kɒnʃəsnɪs/ (**consciousnesses**) **1** N-COUNT 可算名詞 Your **consciousness** is your mind and your thoughts. 意識、心 ❑ *That idea has been creeping into our consciousness for some time.* ここしばらくその考えが私たちの心に忍び込みつつある. **2** N-UNCOUNT 不可算名詞 The **consciousness** of a group of people is their set of ideas, attitudes, and beliefs. (集団の) 意識 ❑ *The Green Party is attempting to shift the American consciousness.* 緑の党はアメリカ人の意識を変えようと試みている. **3** N-UNCOUNT 不可算名詞 You use **consciousness** to refer to an interest in and knowledge of a particular subject or idea. 意識、関心 ❑ *Her political consciousness sprang from her upbringing when her father's illness left the family short of money.* 彼女の政治への関心は父が病死で家族が金に困った生い立ちから来た. **4** N-UNCOUNT 不可算名詞 **Consciousness** is the state of being awake rather than being asleep or unconscious. If someone **loses consciousness**, they become unconscious, and if they **regain consciousness**, they become conscious after being unconscious. 意識がある状態 ❑ *She banged her head and lost consciousness.* 彼女は頭をぶつけて意識を失った.

con|script (**conscripts, conscripting, conscripted**)

The noun is pronounced /kɒnskrɪpt/. The verb is pronounced /kənskrɪpt/.

名詞は /kɒnskrɪpt/ と発音される. 動詞は /kənskrɪpt/ と発音される.

1 N-COUNT 可算名詞 A **conscript** is a person who has been made to join the armed forces of a country. 徴集兵 ❑ *Most of the soldiers are reluctant conscripts.* その兵士たちはほとんどがしぶしぶ徴集された者だ. **2** V-T 他動詞 If someone **is conscripted**, they are officially made to join the armed forces of a country. 徴兵する [usu passive] ❑ *He was conscripted into the U.S. army.* 彼は米陸軍に徴兵された.

con|scrip|tion /kənskrɪpʃən/ N-UNCOUNT 不可算名詞 **Conscription** is officially making people in a particular country join the armed forces. 徴兵 [FORMAL 形式ばった] ❑ *All adult males will be liable for conscription.* すべての成人男子が徴兵の義務を負うようになる.

con|se|crate /kɒnsɪkreɪt/ (**consecrates, consecrating, consecrated**) V-T 他動詞 When a building, place, or object **is consecrated**, it is officially declared to be holy. When a person **is**

consecrated, they are officially declared to be a bishop. 神聖化する □ *The church was consecrated in 1234.* その教会は1234年に聖別された.

con|secu|tive /kənsɛkyətɪv/ ADJ 形容詞 **Consecutive** periods of time or events happen one after the other without interruption. 連続した □ *The Cup was won for the third consecutive year by the Toronto Maple Leafs.* トロント・メープル・リーフスが3年連続で優勝杯を手にした.

Word Link con ≈ together, with : consensus, contemporary, convene

con|sen|sus /kənsɛnsəs/ N-SING 単数名詞 A **consensus** is general agreement among a group of people. (大多数の) 意見の一致 [also no det] □ *The consensus among the world's scientists is that the world is likely to warm up over the next few decades.* 世界は今後数十年で温暖化するだろうというのが世界の科学者たちの一致した意見だ.

con|sent /kənsɛnt/ (consents, consenting, consented)
■ N-UNCOUNT 不可算名詞 If you give your **consent to** something, you give someone permission to do it. 承諾 [FORMAL 形式ばった] □ *At approximately 11:30 p.m., Pollard finally gave his consent to the search.* 午後11時30分ごろ、やっとポラードがその捜査に同意した. ■ V-T/V-I 他動詞/自動詞 If you **consent to** something, you agree to do it or to allow it to be done. 同意する、許可する [FORMAL 形式ばった] □ *He finally consented to go.* 彼はやっと行くことに同意した. □ *He asked Ginny if she would consent to a small celebration after the christening.* 彼は洗礼の後ささやかなお祝いをすることに同意するかジニーに聞いた. ■ → see also **age of consent**

Word Link sequ ≈ following : consequence, sequel, sequence

con|se|quence /kɒnsɪkwɛns, -kwəns/ (consequences)
■ N-COUNT 可算名詞 The **consequences of** something are the results or effects of it. 結果 □ *Her lawyer said she understood the consequences of her actions and was prepared to go to jail.* 彼女の弁護士は、彼女がその行動の結果どうなるかを理解しており、刑務所に行く覚悟でいると述べた. ■ PHRASE 句 If one thing happens and then another thing happens **in consequence** or **as a consequence**, the second thing happens as a result of the first. その結果 □ *His death was totally unexpected and, in consequence, no plans had been made for his replacement.* 彼の死はまったく予期せぬことだった。そのため彼の後任については何の案も立てられていなかった. □ *Maternity services were to be reduced as a consequence of falling birth rates.* 出産率の低下のため、産院施設が縮小されようとしていた.

Word Partnership consequence は次の語句と使われる:

ADJ.	**disastrous** consequence, **unfortunate** consequence ■
PREP.	consequence **for/of** *something* ■
V.	**suffer the** consequence ■

con|se|quent /kɒnsɪkwənt, -kwənt/ ADJ 形容詞 **Consequent** means happening as a direct result of an event or situation. 結果として起こる [FORMAL 形式ばった] □ *The warming of the Earth and the consequent climatic changes affect us all.* 地球温暖化とその結果起こる気候の変化は我々すべてに影響を与える.

con|se|quent|ly /kɒnsɪkwɛntli, -kwəntli/ ADV 副詞 **Consequently** means as a result. その結果として [FORMAL 形式ばった] [ADV with cl] □ *Grandfather had sustained a broken back while working in the mines. Consequently, he spent the rest of his life in a wheelchair.* 祖父は炭鉱で働いている時に背骨を怪我した。そのため、彼はその後の人生を車椅子で過ごした.

con|ser|va|tion /kɒnsərveɪʃən/ ■ N-UNCOUNT 不可算名詞 **Conservation** is saving and protecting the environment. 保護 □ *...a four-nation regional meeting on elephant conservation.* 象の保護に関する4か国の地域会議 ■ N-UNCOUNT 不可算名詞 **Conservation** is saving and protecting historical objects or works of art such as paintings, sculptures, or buildings. 保存 □ *Then he began his most famous work, the conservation and rebinding of the Book of Kells.* そして彼は彼の最もよく知られた仕事に取りかかった。それは「ケルズの書」を保存し製本し直すことだった. ■ N-UNCOUNT 不可算名詞 The **conservation** of a supply of something is the careful use of it so that it lasts for a long time. 節約 □ *...projects aimed at promoting energy conservation.* 省エネルギーを促進するための事業計画

con|ser|va|tion|ist /kɒnsərveɪʃənɪst/ (conservationists)
N-COUNT 可算名詞 A **conservationist** is someone who cares very much about the conservation of the environment and who works to protect it. 自然保護論者 □ *Conservationists say the law must be strengthened.* 自然保護論者は法律の強化が絶対必要だと述べている.

con|ser|va|tism /kənsɜrvətɪzəm/ ■ N-UNCOUNT 不可算名詞 **Conservatism** is a political philosophy which believes that if changes need to be made to society, they should be made gradually. You can also refer to the political beliefs of a conservative party in a particular country as **conservatism**. 保守主義 □ *...the philosophy of modern conservatism.* 近代保守主義の哲

学 ■ N-UNCOUNT 不可算名詞 **Conservatism** is unwillingness to accept changes and new ideas. 保守性 □ *The conservatism of the literary establishment in this country is astounding.* この国の既成文壇の保守的な姿勢には全く驚かされる.

con|serva|tive /kənsɜrvətɪv/ (conservatives)

The spelling **Conservative** is also used for meaning ⑤.

つづりの **Conservative** は ⑤ の意味にも使われる.

■ ADJ 形容詞 Someone who is **conservative** has views that are toward the political right. In the U.S. the Republicans are more conservative than the Democrats, who are more liberal. 保守主義の、保守派の □ *...counties whose citizens invariably support the most conservative candidate in any election.* 市民がどの選挙でも常に最も保守的な候補者を支持する郡 ● N-COUNT 可算名詞 **Conservative** is also a noun. 保守派 □ *The new judge is 50-year-old David Suitor who's regarded as a conservative.* 新しい裁判官は50歳のデイビッド・スーター氏で、保守派と目されている. ■ ADJ 形容詞 Someone who is **conservative** or has **conservative** ideas is unwilling to accept changes and new ideas. 保守的な □ *People tend to be more liberal when they're young and more conservative as they get older.* 人は若い時には新しいことにより積極的で、年を取るにつれてより保守的になりがちだ. ■ ADJ 形容詞 If someone dresses in a **conservative** way, their clothes are conventional in style. 古風な、地味な □ *The girl was well dressed, as usual, though in a more conservative style.* その少女は比較的地味ながら、いつものようにきちんとした身なりをしていた. ● con|ser|va|tive|ly ADV 副詞 [ADV with v] 古風に、地味に □ *She was always very conservatively dressed when we went out.* 彼女は私とつき合っていた頃、いつも地味な服を着ていた. ■ ADJ 形容詞 A **conservative** estimate or guess is one in which you are cautious and estimate or guess a low amount which is probably less that the real amount. 控えめな、慎重な □ *The average fan spends $25 – a conservative estimate based on ticket price and souvenirs.* 普通のファンは、チケット代とお土産代を基に、控えめに見積もっても25ドルを費やす. ● con|ser|va|tive|ly ADV 副詞 [ADV with v] 控えめに □ *The bequest is conservatively estimated at $30 million.* 遺産は控えめな見積もりで3千万ドルになる. ⑤ ADJ 形容詞 A **Conservative** politician or voter is a member of or votes for the Conservative Party in Britain and in various other countries. 保守党の □ *Most Conservative MPs appear happy with the government's reassurances.* 大半の保守党議員は政府の再保証に満足そうだ. ● N-COUNT 可算名詞 **Conservative** is also a noun. 保守党員 □ *In 1951 the Conservatives were returned to power.* 1951年に保守党が政権に返り咲いた.

Thesaurus conservative また次を参照:

ADJ.	right-wing; (ant.) left-wing, liberal, radical ■ conventional, traditional ■

Word Link ory ≈ place where something happens : conservatory, factory, observatory

con|serva|tory /kənsɜrvətɔri/ (conservatories) ■ N-COUNT; N-IN-NAMES 可算名詞、名称中の名詞 A **conservatory** is an institution where musicians are trained. 音楽学校 □ *...the New England Conservatory of Music.* ニューイングランド音楽院 ■ N-COUNT 可算名詞 A **conservatory** is a room with glass walls and a glass roof, which is attached to a house. People often grow plants in a conservatory. サンルーム、温室

Word Link serv ≈ keeping : conserve, observe, preserve

con|serve /kənsɜrv/ (conserves, conserving, conserved) ■ V-T 他動詞 If you **conserve** a supply of something, you use it carefully so that it lasts for a long time. 節約して使う □ *The factories have closed for the weekend to conserve energy.* 工場はエネルギー節約のため、その週末は閉められている. ■ V-T 他動詞 To **conserve** something means to protect it from harm, loss, or change. 保護する □ *...a big increase in U.S. aid to help developing countries conserve their forests.* 発展途上国の森林保護を支援するための米国の援助の大幅増加

con|sid|er /kənsɪdər/ (considers, considering, considered) ■ V-T 他動詞 If you **consider** a person or thing **to** be something, you have the opinion that this is what they are. 考える、見なす □ *We don't consider our customers to be mere consumers; we consider them to be our friends.* 私たちは顧客をただの顧客とは思っていない。顧客を私たちの友人だと考えている. □ *I had always considered myself a strong, competent woman.* 私はいつも自分を強くて仕事のできる女性だと思っていた.

Note that when you are using the verb **consider** with a "that" -clause in order to state a negative opinion or belief, you normally make **consider** negative, rather than the verb in the "that" -clause. For instance, it is more usual to say "I don't consider that you kept your promise." than "I consider that you didn't keep your promise." The same pattern applies to other verbs with a similar meaning, such as **believe**, **suppose**, and **think**.

2 V-T 他動詞 If you **consider** something, you think about it carefully. 熟考する ❏ *The administration continues to consider ways to resolve the situation.* 政府はその状況の解決策を引き続き熟考する. ❏ *You do have to consider the feelings of those around you.* あなたは周りの人の気持ちをよく考えないといけませんよ. **3** V-T 他動詞 If you **are considering** doing something, you intend to do it, but have not yet made a final decision whether to do it. 検討する ❏ *I had seriously considered telling the story from the point of view of the wives.* 私は妻たちの視点からその話をしようと真剣に考えていた. **4** → see also **considering**

Thesaurus   *consider* また次を参照:

v.   contemplate, examine, study, think about, think over;   (ant.) dismiss, forget, ignore **2**

con|sid|er|able /kənsɪdərəbəl/ ADJ 形容詞 **Considerable** means great in amount or degree. かなりの [FORMAL 形式ばった] ❏ *To be without Pearce would be a considerable blow.* ピアス抜きというのはかなりの痛手になるだろう. ❏ *Doing it properly makes considerable demands on our time.* それをきちんとやるにはかなりの時間が必要だ. ● **con|sid|er|ably** ADV 副詞 かなり ❏ *Children vary considerably in the rate at which they learn these lessons.* 子供たちがこれらの学課を学ぶペースにはかなり個人差がある.

Word Link   ate ≈ filled with : affection*ate*, compassion*ate*, consider*ate*

con|sid|er|ate /kənsɪdərɪt/ ADJ 形容詞 Someone who is **considerate** pays attention to the needs, wishes, or feelings of other people. 思いやりのある [APPROVAL 賛成] ❏ *I think he's the most charming, most considerate man I've ever known.* 彼は私がこれまで知っている人の中で最も魅力的で最も思いやりがある人だと思う.

con|sid|era|tion /kənsɪdəreɪʃən/ (**considerations**) **1** N-UNCOUNT 不可算名詞 **Consideration** is careful thought about something. 熟考, 配慮 ❏ *There should be careful consideration about the use of such toxic chemicals.* そのような有害化学物質の使用に関しては慎重な配慮が必要だ. **2** N-UNCOUNT 不可算名詞 If something is **under consideration**, it is being discussed. 検討 ❏ *Several proposals are under consideration by the state assembly.* いくつかの提案が州議会で検討されている. **3** N-UNCOUNT 不可算名詞 If you show **consideration**, you pay attention to the needs, wishes, or feelings of other people. 思いやり ❏ *Show consideration for your neighbors.* 近所の人に思いやりを示しなさい. **4** N-COUNT 可算名詞 A **consideration** is something that should be thought about, especially when you are planning or deciding something. 考慮すべき事柄 ❏ *Price has become a more important consideration for shoppers in choosing which store to visit than it was before the recession.* 不況前と比べると, 値段は買い物客が店を選ぶ際により重要な考慮の対象となっている. **5** PHRASE 句 If you **take** something **into consideration**, you think about it because it is relevant to what you are doing. 考慮する ❏ *Safe driving is good driving because it takes into consideration the lives of other people.* 安全運転は他人の命を考慮に入れているからよい運転だ.

Word Partnership   *consideration* は次の語句と使われる:

ADJ.	**careful** consideration, **an important** consideration **1**
PREP.	**in** consideration of **1**
	under consideration **2**
V.	**show** consideration **3**
	take into consideration **5**

con|sid|er|ing /kənsɪdərɪŋ/ **1** PREP 前置詞 You use **considering** to indicate that you are thinking about a particular fact when making a judgment or giving an opinion. 〜を考えると ❏ *He must be hoping, but considering the situation in June he may hoping for too much too soon.* 彼は期待しているに違いないが, 6月の状況を考えると, 性急に多くを望みすぎているかもしれない. **2** CONJ 接続詞 You use **considering that** to indicate that you are thinking about a particular fact when making a judgment or giving an opinion. 〜であることを考えると ❏ *Considering that you are no longer involved with this man, your response is a little extreme.* あなたがもうこの男性とつきあっていないことを考えると, あなたの反応の仕方はちょっと行き過ぎだよ. **3** ADV 副詞 When you are giving an opinion or making a judgment, you can use **considering** to suggest that you have thought about all the circumstances, and often that something

has succeeded in spite of these circumstances. すべてを考慮すると, その割りに安全だと思う. [SPOKEN 口語] [cl ADV] ❏ *I think you're pretty safe, considering.* その割に, 君はかなり安全だと思うよ.

con|sign /kənsaɪn/ (**consigns**, **consigning**, **consigned**) V-T 他動詞 To **consign** something or someone **to** a place where they will be forgotten about, or **to** an unpleasant situation or place, means to put them there. (不快な状況や場所に) ゆだねる [FORMAL 形式ばった] ❏ *For decades, many of Malevich's works were consigned to the basements of Soviet museums.* 何十年もの間マレーヴィチの多くの作品はソ連の美術館の地下室に放置されていた.

con|sign|ment /kənsaɪnmənt/ (**consignments**) **1** N-COUNT 可算名詞 A **consignment** of goods is a load that is being delivered to a place or person. 配送荷物 ❏ *The first consignment of food was flown in yesterday.* 昨日最初の食糧の荷が空輸されてきた. **2** PHRASE 句 If goods are sold **on consignment**, the owner is given a percentage of the price once they are sold. 委託販売で ❏ *She sold clothes on consignment to benefit homeless people.* 彼女はホームレスの人のために委託販売で服を売った.

con|sist /kənsɪst/ (**consists**, **consisting**, **consisted**) **1** V-I 自動詞 Something that **consists of** particular things or people is formed from them. (〜より) 成る ❏ *My diet consisted almost exclusively of chocolate-covered cookies and glasses of milk.* 私の食事はほぼもっぱらチョコレートのかかったクッキーと何杯かの牛乳より成っていた. **2** V-I 自動詞 Something that **consists in** something else has that thing as its main or only part. (〜に) ある ❏ *His work as a consultant consisted in advising foreign companies on the siting of new factories.* 彼のコンサルタントとしての仕事は, 外資系企業に新しい工場地について助言することだった.

con|sist|en|cy /kənsɪstənsi/ **1** N-UNCOUNT 不可算名詞 **Consistency** is the quality or condition of being consistent. 一貫性, 堅実さ ❏ *She scores goals with remarkable consistency.* 彼女の得点の決め方は驚くほど堅実だ. **2** N-UNCOUNT 不可算名詞 The **consistency** of a substance is how thick or smooth it is. 濃度 ❏ *Dilute the paint with water until it is the consistency of milk.* ペンキが牛乳くらいの濃度になるまで水で薄めなさい.

con|sist|ent /kənsɪstənt/ **1** ADJ 形容詞 Someone who is **consistent** always behaves in the same way, has the same attitudes towards people or things, or achieves the same level of success in something. 堅実な, 一貫性のある ❏ *Becker was never the most consistent of players anyway.* どちらにしてもベッカーは最も堅実な選手では決してなかった. ● **con|sist|ent|ly** ADV 副詞 一貫して ❏ *It's something I have consistently denied.* それは私が一貫して否定してきたことだ. **2** ADJ 形容詞 [v-link ADJ, usu ADJ "with" n] If one fact or idea is **consistent with** another, they do not contradict each other. 一致した ❏ *This result is consistent with the findings of Garnett & Tobin.* この結果はガーネットとトビンの研究結果と一致している. **3** ADJ 形容詞 An argument or set of ideas that is **consistent** is one in which no part contradicts or conflicts with any other part. つじつまが合う ❏ *A theory should be internally consistent.* 学説は内部的につじつまが合っていなくてはならない.

con|sole (**consoles**, **consoling**, **consoled**)

The verb is pronounced /kənsoʊl/. The noun is pronounced /kɒnsoʊl/.

動詞は /kənsoʊl/ と発音される. 名詞は /kɒnsoʊl/ と発音される.

1 V-T 他動詞 If you **console** someone who is unhappy about something, you try to make them feel more cheerful. 慰める ❏ *"Never mind, Ned," he consoled me.* 「気にするなよ, ネッド」と彼は私を慰めた. ❏ *I can console myself with the fact that I'm not alone.* 私は独りではないという事実で自分を慰めることができる. ● **con|so|la|tion** /kɒnsəleɪʃən/ (**consolations**) N-VAR 可変性名詞 慰め ❏ *The only consolation for the baseball team is that they look likely to get another chance.* その野球チームにとっての唯一の慰めは, もう1度チャンスがありそうなことだ. **2** N-COUNT 可算名詞 A **console** is a panel with a number of switches or knobs that is used to operate a machine. 操作盤 ❏ *Several nurses sat before a console of flickering lights and bleeping monitors.* 看護師が数人, ランプが点滅しモニターが鳴っている操作盤の前に座った.

con|soli|date /kənsɒlɪdeɪt/ (**consolidates**, **consolidating**, **consolidated**) **1** V-T 他動詞 If you **consolidate** something that you have, for example power or success, you strengthen it so that it becomes more effective or secure. 強化する ❏ *The question is: will the junta consolidate its power by force?* 問題は, 軍事政権が強引に権力を強化するか, ということだ. **2** V-T 他動詞 To **consolidate** a number of small groups or companies means to make them into one large organization. 合併する ❏ *Judge Charles Schwartz is giving the state 60 days to disband and consolidate Louisiana's four higher education boards.* チャールズ・シュワルツ裁判官は, ルイジアナ州の4つの高等教育委員会を解散・合併するために州に60日の期間を与えている.

con|so|nant /kɒnsənənt/ (**consonants**) N-COUNT 可算名詞 A **consonant** is a sound such as "p," "f," "n," or "t" which you pronounce by stopping the air flowing freely through your

mouth. Compare **vowel**. 子音

con|sor|tium /kənsɔrʃiəm, -ti-/ (**consortia** /kənsɔrʃiə, -ti-/ or **consortiums**) N-COUNT-COLL 集合可算名詞 A **consortium** is a group of people or firms who have agreed to cooperate with each other. 合弁企業 [FORMAL 形式ばった] ❑ *The consortium includes some of the biggest building contractors in North America.* その合弁企業には北米で最大の建設業者がいくつか含まれている.

con|spicu|ous /kənspɪkyuəs/ ADJ 形容詞 If someone or something is **conspicuous**, people can see or notice them very easily. よく見える, 人目を引く ❑ *Most people don't want to be too conspicuous.* ほとんどの人はあまり目立ちたがらない. ● **con|spicu|ous|ly** ADV 副詞 目立って ❑ *Britain continues to follow U.S. policy in this and other areas where American policies have most conspicuously failed.* 英国は米国が最も顕著に失敗したこの分野や他の分野で米国の政策に従い続けている.

con|spira|cy /kənspɪrəsi/ (**conspiracies**) ■ N-VAR 可変性名詞 **Conspiracy** is secret planning by a group of people to do something illegal. 陰謀 ❑ *Seven men, all from North Carolina, admitted conspiracy to commit arson.* 皆ノースカロライナ州出身である7人の男が放火をたくらんでいたことを認めた. ■ N-COUNT 可算名詞 A **conspiracy** is an agreement between a group of people which other people think is wrong or is likely to be harmful. 共同謀議 ❑ *It's all part of a conspiracy to dispense with the town center all together and move everything out to the suburbs.* それはすべて, 町の中心地を一切廃棄し, すべてを郊外へ移そうという共同謀議の一環だ.

con|spira|tor /kənspɪrətər/ (**conspirators**) N-COUNT 可算名詞 A **conspirator** is a person who joins a conspiracy. 共謀者 ❑ *Julius Caesar was murdered by a group of conspirators famously headed by Marcus Junius Brutus.* ジュリアス・シーザーは, 周知の通りマルクス・ユニウス・ブルータス率いる共謀者の1団に殺害された.

con|spire /kənspaɪər/ (**conspires, conspiring, conspired**) ■ V-RECIP 相互動詞 If two or more people or groups **conspire to** do something illegal or harmful, they make a secret agreement to do it. 共謀する ❑ *They'd conspired to overthrow the government.* 彼らは政府を打倒しようと共謀した. ❑ *...a defendant accused of conspiring with his brother to commit robberies.* 弟と共謀し強盗を企てた罪で告訴されている被告 ■ V-T/V-I 他動詞/自動詞 If events **conspire to** produce a particular result, they seem to work together to cause this result. (事態が) 重なってーするに至る ❑ *History and geography have conspired to bring the country to a moment of decision.* 歴史的要素と地理的要素が重なり, その国は決断の時を迎えている.

con|sta|ble /kʌnstəbºl, kɒn-/ (**constables**) ■ N-COUNT; N-TITLE 可算名詞, 称号名詞 In the United States, a **constable** is an official who helps keep the peace in a town. They are lower in rank than a sheriff. 副保安官 ❑ *Courts and magistrates may be set up but they cannot function without sheriffs and constables.* 裁判所や治安判事を置くことはできても, 保安官や副保安官官らもなくしてそれらは機能しない. ■ N-COUNT; N-TITLE; N-VOC 可算名詞, 称号名詞, 呼格名詞 In Britain and some other countries, a **constable** is a police officer of the lowest rank. 巡査

con|stant /kɒnstənt/ ■ ADJ 形容詞 You use **constant** to describe something that happens all the time or is always there. 絶え間ない ❑ *She suggests that women are under constant pressure to be abnormally thin.* 女性は異常なほど細身であるべきというプレッシャーを常に感じている, と彼女は示唆する. ❑ *Inflation is a constant threat.* インフレーションは絶え間ない脅威となっている. ● **con|stant|ly** ADV 副詞 常に, 絶えず ❑ *The direction of the wind is constantly changing.* 風の向きが絶えず変わり続けている. ■ ADJ 形容詞 If an amount or level is **constant**, it stays the same over a particular period of time. 一定の ❑ *The body feels hot and the temperature remains more or less constant at the new elevated level.* 身体が熱っぽく, 体温は高くなった状態のままほとんど変わらない.

> You can use **constant, continual,** and **continuous** to describe things that happen or exist without stopping. You describe something as **constant** when it happens all the time or never goes away. ❑ *He was in constant pain. ...Eva's constant criticism.* **Continual** is usually used to describe something that happens often over a period of time, especially something undesirable. ❑ *...his continual drinking. ...continual demands to cut costs.* If something is **continuous**, it happens all the time without stopping, or seems to do so. ❑ *...days of continuous rain. ...a continuous background noise.*

> **Thesaurus**   **constant** また次を参照:
>
> ADJ.   continual, continuous, uninterrupted; (ant.) occasional ■
>   consistent, permanent, stable; (ant.) changeable, variable ■

con|stel|la|tion /kɒnstəleɪʃºn/ (**constellations**) N-COUNT 可算名詞 A **constellation** is a group of stars which form a pattern and have a name. 星座 ❑ *...a planet orbiting a star in the constellation of*

Cepheus. ケフェウス座の星の1つの周りを回っている惑星 → see **star**

con|ster|na|tion /kɒnstərneɪʃºn/ N-UNCOUNT 不可算名詞 **Consternation** is a feeling of anxiety or fear. 非常な驚き, 仰天 [FORMAL 形式ばった] ❑ *His decision caused consternation in the art photography community.* 彼の決断に芸術写真界は仰天した.

con|sti|pa|tion /kɒnstɪpeɪʃºn/ N-UNCOUNT 不可算名詞 **Constipation** is a medical condition which causes people to have difficulty getting rid of solid waste from their body. 便秘 ❑ *Do you suffer from constipation?* あなたは便秘症ですか?

con|stitu|en|cy /kənstɪtʃuənsi/ (**constituencies**) ■ N-COUNT 可算名詞 A particular **constituency** is a section of society that may give political support to a particular party or politician. 選挙民, 支持者 ❑ *In Iowa, farmers are a powerful political constituency.* アイオワ州では農場経営者たちが強力な政治的支持層だ. ■ N-COUNT 可算名詞 A **constituency** is an area for which someone is elected as the representative in a legislature or government. 選挙区 ❑ *Voters in 17 constituencies are going back to the polls today.* 今日17の選挙区の有権者は再投票する.

con|stitu|ent /kənstɪtʃuənt/ (**constituents**) ■ N-COUNT 可算名詞 A **constituent** is someone who lives in a particular constituency, especially someone who is able to vote in an election. 選挙区民, 有権者 ❑ *He told his constituents that he would continue to represent them to the best of his ability.* 彼は力の及ぶ限り選挙区民の代表を務め続けると彼らに述べた. ■ N-COUNT 可算名詞 A **constituent** of a mixture, substance, or system is one of the things from which it is formed. 構成物質 [FORMAL 形式ばった] ❑ *Caffeine is the active constituent of drinks such as tea and coffee.* カフェインは紅茶やコーヒーといった飲み物の有効成分である. ■ ADJ 形容詞 The **constituent** parts of something are the things from which it is formed. 構成する [FORMAL 形式ばった] [ADJ n] ❑ *...a plan to split the company into its constituent parts and sell them separately.* その会社を構成部門ごとに分け, 別々に売却しようとする計画

con|sti|tute /kɒnstɪtut/ (**constitutes, constituting, constituted**) ■ V-LINK 連結動詞 If something **constitutes** a particular thing, it can be regarded as being that thing. 構成する, なる [no cont] ❑ *Testing patients without their consent would constitute a professional and legal offense.* 患者の同意なしに検査を行うことは, 職業上および法律上の罪になるであろう. ■ V-LINK 連結動詞 If a number of things or people **constitute** something, they are the parts or members that form it. 構成要素となる [no cont] ❑ *China's ethnic minorities constitute less than 7 percent of its total population.* 中国の少数民族は総人口の7パーセント以下だ.

con|sti|tu|tion /kɒnstɪtuʃºn/ (**constitutions**) ■ N-COUNT 可算名詞 The **constitution** of a country or organization is the system of laws which formally states people's rights and duties. 憲法, 規約 ❑ *The king was forced to adopt a new constitution which reduced his powers.* 国王は彼の権力を縮小する新しい憲法を強制されて採用した. ■ N-COUNT 可算名詞 Your **constitution** is your health. 健康, 体質 ❑ *He must have an extremely strong constitution.* 彼はとても強い体質をしているに違いない.

con|sti|tu|tion|al /kɒnstɪtuʃºnəl/ ADJ 形容詞 **Constitutional** means relating to the constitution of a particular country or organization. 憲法の ❑ *The issue is one of constitutional and civil rights.* その問題は憲法で認められた公民権の一つだ.

con|strain /kənstreɪn/ (**constrains, constraining, constrained**) V-T 他動詞 To **constrain** someone or something means to limit their development or force them to behave in a particular way. 抑制する, 強いる [FORMAL 形式ばった] ❑ *Women are too often constrained by family commitments and by low expectations.* 女性は家庭の仕事や低い期待に制約されることが多すぎる.

con|straint /kənstreɪnt/ (**constraints**) ■ N-COUNT 可算名詞 A **constraint** is something that limits or controls what you can do. 制約 ❑ *Their decision to abandon the trip was made because of financial constraints.* 彼らが旅行を取りやめたのは金銭的に厳しかったからだ. ■ N-UNCOUNT 不可算名詞 **Constraint** is control over the way you behave which prevents you from doing what you want to do. 束縛 ❑ *Journalists were given the freedom to visit, investigate, and report without constraint.* 記者たちは束縛されずに訪問し, 調査し, 報道する自由を与えられた.

con|strict /kənstrɪkt/ (**constricts, constricting, constricted**) ■ V-T/V-I 他動詞/自動詞 If a part of your body, especially your throat, **is constricted** or if it **constricts**, something causes it to become narrower. 締め付ける [他動詞], 収縮する [自動詞] ❑ *Severe migraines can be treated with a drug that constricts the blood vessels.* ひどい偏頭痛は血管を収縮させる薬で治療できる. ■ V-T 他動詞 If something **constricts** you, it limits your actions so that you cannot do what you want to do. 抑制する ❑ *She objects to the constant testing because it constricts her teaching style.* 彼女は自分の授業の進め方が束縛されるという理由で, ひっきりなしのテストに反対している.

Word Link   struct ≈ building : *con*struct, *de*struct*ive*, *in*struct

con|struct /kənstrʌkt/ (constructs, constructing, constructed) ■ V-T 他動詞 If you **construct** something such as a building, road, or machine, you build it or make it. 建設する □*His company recently constructed an office building in downtown Denver.* 彼の会社は最近デンバーの中心街に事務所ビルを建設した. □*The boxes should be constructed from rough-sawn timber.* それらの箱は粗くこぎり引きした木材で作るべきだ. ■ V-T 他動詞 If you **construct** something such as an idea, a piece of writing, or a system, you create it by putting different parts together. 組み立てる，構成する □*He eventually constructed a huge business empire.* 彼はついに巨大な企業帝国を築き上げた. □*The novel is constructed from a series of on-the-spot reports.* その小説は一連の現地報告から構成されている.

con|struc|tion /kənstrʌkʃⁿ/ (constructions) ■ N-UNCOUNT 不可算名詞 **Construction** is the building of things such as houses, factories, roads, and bridges. 建設 □*He'd already started construction on a hunting lodge.* 彼は既に狩猟小屋を建て始めていた. □...*the downturn in the construction industry.* 建設業界の低迷 □*Jim now works in construction.* ジムは今建設の仕事をしている. ■ N-UNCOUNT 不可算名詞 The **construction** of something such as a vehicle or machine is the making of it. 製造 □...*companies who have long experience in the construction of those types of equipment.* その種の機器の製造に長年の経験を持つ会社 ■ N-UNCOUNT 不可算名詞 The **construction** of something such as a system is the creation of it. (建物の) 構築 □...*the construction of a just system of criminal justice.* 刑事裁判の公正な制度の構築 ■ N-UNCOUNT 不可算名詞 You use **construction** to refer to the structure of something and the way it has been built or made. (建物の) 造り □*The Shakers believed that furniture should be plain, simple, useful, practical, and of sound construction.* シェーカー教徒は，家具は飾りのない簡素なもので使いやすく実用的また造りのしっかりしたものであるべきと考えていた. ■ N-COUNT 可算名詞 You can refer to an object that has been built or made as a **construction**. 建築物 □...*an impressive steel and glass construction.* 鋼鉄とガラスの素晴らしい建築物 ■ N-COUNT 可算名詞 A grammatical **construction** is a particular arrangement of words in a sentence, clause, or phrase. 構文 □*Avoid complex verbal constructions.* 複雑な動詞構文を避けよ.

→ see **skyscraper**

con|struc|tive /kənstrʌktɪv/ ADJ 形容詞 A **constructive** discussion, comment, or approach is useful and helpful rather than negative and unhelpful. 建設的な □*She welcomes constructive criticism.* 彼女は建設的な批判を歓迎する. □*After their meeting, both men described the talks as frank, friendly and constructive.* 会合の後，双方の男性はその話し合いが率直で友好的かつ建設的だったと述べた.

con|strue /kənstru/ (construes, construing, construed) V-T 他動詞 If something is **construed** in a particular way, its nature or meaning is interpreted in that way. 解釈する [FORMAL 形式ばった] □*What may seem helpful behavior to you can be construed as interference by others.* あなたには手助けと思える行為でも，他の人には干渉と受け取られることがある. □*He may construe the approach as a hostile act.* 彼はそのやり方を敵意のある行為ととるかもしれない.

con|sul /kɒnsⁿl/ (consuls) N-COUNT; N-TITLE 可算名詞，称号名詞 A **consul** is an official who is sent by his or her government to live in a foreign city in order to help other citizens from his or her country who are in that foreign city. 領事 □...*Stephanie Sweet, the British Consul in Tangier.* 在タンジール英国領事であるステファニー・スウィート

con|su|lar /kɒnsələr/ ADJ 形容詞 **Consular** means involving or relating to a consul or the work of a consul. 領事の [ADJ n] □*U.S. consular officials have visited the men, although they have not yet had access to lawyers.* その男たちはまだ弁護士と連絡が取れないでいるが，米国領事館員が彼らを訪れていた.

con|su|late /kɒnsəlɪt/ (consulates) N-COUNT 可算名詞 A **consulate** is the place where a consul works. 領事館 □...*the Canadian consulate in Seattle.* シアトル市のカナダ領事館

con|sult /kənsʌlt/ (consults, consulting, consulted) ■ V-T/V-I 他動詞/自動詞 If you **consult** an expert or someone senior to you or **consult with** them, you ask them for their opinion, advice, or permission. (専門家に) 相談する，助言を求める □*Consult your doctor about how much exercise you should get.* どのくらい運動すればいいかは医師に聞いてください. □*He needed to consult with an attorney.* 彼は弁護士に相談する必要があった. ■ V-T 他動詞 If you **consult** a book or a map, you look in it or look at it in order to find some information. 調べる □*Consult the chart on page 44 for the correct cooking times.* 44ページの図表で正しい調理時間を調べてください. ■ V-RECIP 相互動詞 If a person or group of people **consults with** other people or **consults** them, or if two people or groups **consult**, they talk and exchange ideas and opinions about what they might decide to do. 相談する，話し合う □*After consulting with her daughter and manager, she decided to take on the part, on her terms.* 娘やマネージャーと話し合った後，彼女は自分の提示した条件でその役を引き受けることにした. □*The two countries will have to consult their*

allies. 両国はそれぞれの同盟国と協議する必要があるだろう.

con|sul|tan|cy /kənsʌltənsi/ (consultancies) ■ N-COUNT 可算名詞 A **consultancy** is a company that gives expert advice on a particular subject. コンサルタント会社 □*A survey of 57 hospitals by Newchurch, a consultancy, reveals striking improvements.* コンサルタント会社ニューチャーチによる57の病院を対象にした調査では，著しい改善が見られる. ■ N-UNCOUNT 不可算名詞 **Consultancy** is expert advice on a particular subject which a person or group is paid to provide to a company or organization. 専門家の助言 [mainly BRIT 主に英国英語]

con|sul|tant /kənsʌltənt/ (consultants) ■ N-COUNT 可算名詞 A **consultant** is a person who gives expert advice to a person or organization on a particular subject. コンサルタント，顧問 □*She is a consultant to the government.* 彼女は政府顧問である. ■ N-COUNT 可算名詞 A **consultant** is an experienced doctor with a high position, who specializes in one area of medicine. (病院の) 上級専門医 [BRIT 英国英語; AM usually **specialist** 米国英語では通常 **specialist**]

con|sul|ta|tion /kɒnsəlteɪʃⁿn/ (consultations) ■ N-VAR 可変性名詞 A **consultation** is a meeting to discuss something. **Consultation** is discussion about something. 会議，相談 □*Next week he'll be in Florida for consultations with President Vicente Fox.* 来週彼はビンセンテ・フォックス大統領との会談のためフロリダ州にいる. ■ N-VAR 可変性名詞 A **consultation with** a doctor or other expert is a meeting with them to discuss a particular problem and get their advice. **Consultation** is the process of getting advice from a doctor or other expert. (医師や専門家との) 相談 診察 □*A personal diet plan is devised after a consultation with a nutritionist.* 個人の食事療法計画は栄養士と話し合ってから作成される. ■ N-COUNT 可算名詞 A **consultation** is a meeting where several doctors discuss a patient and his or her condition and treatment. (患者の症状や治療について医師の) 協議会 [AM 米国英語]

con|sul|ta|tive /kənsʌltətɪv/ ADJ 形容詞 A **consultative** committee or document gives advice or makes proposals about a particular problem or subject. 諮問の □...*the consultative committee on local government finance.* 地方財政に関する諮問委員会

con|sum|able /kənsuməbⁿl/ (consumables) ADJ 形容詞 **Consumable** goods are items which are intended to be bought, used, and then replaced. 消費できる □...*demand for consumable articles.* 消耗品の需要 ● N-COUNT 可算名詞 **Consumable** is also a noun. 消耗品 □*Suppliers add computer consumables, office equipment and furniture to their product range.* 業者は彼らの製品の種類にコンピュータの消耗品，事務機器，家具を追加する.

Word Link   sume ≈ taking : *as*sume, *con*sume, *pre*sume

con|sume /kənsum/ (consumes, consuming, consumed) ■ V-T 他動詞 If you **consume** something, you eat or drink it. 飲食する [FORMAL 形式ばった] □*Martha would consume nearly a pound of cheese per day.* マーサは1日約1ポンドのチーズを食べていたものだ. ■ V-T 他動詞 To **consume** an amount of fuel, energy, or time means to use it up. 消費する □*Some of the most efficient refrigerators consume 70 percent less electricity than traditional models.* 最も効率の良い冷蔵庫のいくつかは，電力消費が従来の型より70パーセント少ない. ■ → see also **consuming**

con|sum|er /kənsumər/ (consumers) N-COUNT 可算名詞 A **consumer** is a person who buys things or uses services. 消費者 □...*claims that tobacco companies failed to warn consumers about the dangers of smoking.* たばこ会社が消費者に喫煙の危険性を警告しなかったという主張

→ see **advertising**

con|sum|er cred|it N-UNCOUNT 不可算名詞 **Consumer credit** is money that is lent to people by organizations such as banks and stores so that they can buy things. 消費者金融 □*New consumer credit fell to $3.7 billion in August.* 新しい消費者金融は8月に37億ドルまで下がった.

con|sum|er du|rable (consumer durables) N-COUNT 可算名詞 **Consumer durables** are goods which are expected to last a long time, and are bought infrequently. 耐久消費財 [BRIT 英国英語 BUSINESS 実業] [AM **durable goods** 米国英語 **durable goods**]

con|sum|er goods N-PLURAL 複数名詞 **Consumer goods** are items bought by people for their own use, rather than by businesses. Compare **capital goods**. 消費財 [BUSINESS 実業] □*The choice of consumer goods available in local shops is small.* 地元商店で手に入る商品の選択肢は限られている.

con|sum|er so|ci|ety (consumer societies) N-COUNT 可算名詞 You can use **consumer society** to refer to a society where people think that spending money on goods and services is very important. 消費者社会 □*We live in a consumer society in which money is a massive preoccupation.* 私たちはお金がすごく大きな関心事である消費者社会に生きている.

con|sum|ing /kənsumɪŋ/ ■ ADJ 形容詞 A **consuming** passion or interest is more important to you than anything else. 熱烈な

❑ *He has developed a consuming passion for chess.* 彼はチェスに夢中になっている. ❷ → see also **consume, time-consuming**

Word Link | summ ≈ highest point : con**summ**ate, **summ**ary, **summ**it

con|sum|mate (**consummates, consummating, consummated**)

The adjective is pronounced /kɒnsəmɪt, kənsʌmɪt/. The verb is pronounced /kɒnsəmeɪt/.

形容詞は /kɒnsəmɪt, kənsʌmɪt/ と発音される. 動詞は /kɒnsəmeɪt/ と発音される.

❶ ADJ 形容詞 You use **consummate** to describe someone who is extremely skillful. 完璧な, 熟練した [FORMAL 形式ばった] ❑ *He acted the part with consummate skill.* 彼はその役を完璧な技量で演じた. ❷ V-T 他動詞 If two people **consummate** a marriage or relationship, they make it complete by having sex. (セックスで) 結婚を完成する [FORMAL 形式ばった] ❑ *His wife divorced him for failing to consummate their marriage.* 彼の妻は彼が結婚の性生活を満たせないという理由で離婚した.

Word Link | sumpt ≈ taking : as**sumpt**ion, con**sumpt**ion, pre**sumpt**ion

con|sump|tion /kənsʌmpʃⁿn/ ❶ N-UNCOUNT 不可算名詞 The **consumption** of fuel or natural resources is the act of using them or the amount used. (ガソリンや天然資源の) 消費 消費量 ❑ *The laws have led to a reduction in fuel consumption in the U.S.* それらの法律により米国内の燃料消費量が減少した. ❷ N-UNCOUNT 不可算名詞 The **consumption** of food or drink is the act of eating or drinking something, or the amount eaten or drunk. 飲食, 飲食の量 [FORMAL 形式ばった] ❑ *Most of the wine was unfit for human consumption.* そのワインのほとんどが飲用に適さなかった. ❸ N-UNCOUNT 不可算名詞 **Consumption** is the act of buying and using things. (物品の) 消費 ❑ *They were prepared to put people out of work and reduce consumption by strangling the whole economy.* 彼らは経済全体を締めつけることで人々を失業させ消費を減らすつもりだった.

cont. Cont. is an abbreviation for "continued," which is used at the bottom of a page to indicate that a letter or text continues on another page. 「続く」の略

con|tact /kɒntækt/ (**contacts, contacting, contacted**) ❶ N-UNCOUNT 不可算名詞 **Contact** involves meeting or communicating with someone, especially regularly. (人との) 接触 連絡 [also N in pl, oft N "with/between" n] ❑ *Opposition leaders are denying any contact with the government in Kabul.* 野党の指導者たちはカブールの政府と接触したことをまったく否定している. ❷ N-UNCOUNT 不可算名詞 If you come **into contact with** someone or something, you meet that person or thing in the course of your work or other activities. 接触 ❑ *Doctors I came into contact with voiced their concern.* 私が接した医師たちは彼らの懸念を口にした. ❸ N-UNCOUNT 不可算名詞 When people or things are in **contact**, they are touching each other. 接触, 触れること ❑ *They compared how these organisms behaved when left in contact with different materials.* 彼らはこれらの生物が違う材料に触れたままにされるとどう反応するかを比較した. ❑ *The cry occurs when air is brought into contact with the baby's larynx.* 吸い込んだ空気が赤ちゃんの喉頭に触れると泣き声が出る. ❹ ADJ 形容詞 Your **contact** details or number are information such as a telephone number where you can be contacted. 連絡先の [ADJ n] ❑ *You must leave your full name and contact details when you phone.* 電話をかける時はあなたの氏名と連絡先を残さないといけない. ❺ PHRASE 句 If you are in **contact** with someone, you regularly meet them or communicate with them. (人と) 接触して, 連絡して ❑ *He was in direct contact with the kidnappers.* 彼は誘拐犯たちと直接連絡を取っていた. ❻ PHRASE 句 If you **make contact with** someone, you find out where they are and talk or write to them. (人と) 連絡を取る ❑ *How did you make contact with the author?* どうやってその著者に連絡を取ったの? ❼ PHRASE 句 If you **lose contact with** someone who you have been friendly with, you no longer see them, speak to them, or write to them. (人と) 連絡をしなくなる ❑ *Though they all live nearby, I lost contact with them really quickly.* 彼らがみな近くに住んでいるにもかかわらず, 私と彼らとのつきあいはあっという間に途絶えた. ❽ V-T 他動詞 If you **contact** someone, you telephone them, write to them, or go to see them in order to tell or ask them something. 連絡を取る ❑ *Contact the Women's Alliance for further details.* 詳しくは女性同盟にご連絡ください. ❾ N-COUNT 可算名詞 A **contact** is someone you know in an organization or profession who helps you or gives you information. つて, 連絡相手 ❑ *Their contact at the United States embassy was Phillip Norton.* 米国大使館での彼ら窓口はフィリップ・ノートンだった.

con|tact lens (**contact lenses**) N-COUNT 可算名詞 **Contact lenses** are small plastic lenses that you put on the surface of your eyes to help you see better, instead of wearing glasses. コンタクトレンズ
→ see **eye**

con|ta|gious /kənteɪdʒəs/ ❶ ADJ 形容詞 A disease that is **contagious** can be caught by touching people or things that are infected with it. Compare **infectious**. (接触) 感染性の ❑ *...a highly contagious disease of the lungs.* 感染力の強い肺の病気 ❷ ADJ 形容詞 A feeling or attitude that is **contagious** spreads quickly among a group of people. うつりやすい ❑ *Laughing is contagious.* 笑いは伝染する.

con|tain /kənteɪn/ (**contains, containing, contained**) ❶ V-T 他動詞 If something such as a box, bag, room, or place **contains** things, those things are inside it. (入れ物や場所に) 含む, 入っている [no cont] ❑ *The envelope contained a Christmas card.* その封筒にはクリスマスカードが入っていた. ❑ *The first two floors of the building contain retail space and a restaurant.* そのビルの1階と2階には小売店用のスペースとレストランが1軒ある. ❷ V-T 他動詞 If a substance **contains** something, that thing is a part of it. (物質を) 含む [no cont] ❑ *Watermelon contains vitamins and also potassium.* すいかはビタミン類やカリウムを含んでいる. ❸ V-T 他動詞 If writing, speech, or film **contains** particular information, ideas, or images, it includes them. 収録する [no cont] ❑ *This sheet contained a list of problems a patient might like to raise with the doctor.* この用紙には患者が医師に提起したい問題の一覧が載っていた. ❹ V-T 他動詞 If a group or organization **contains** a certain number of people, those are the people that are in it. (組織などが) 成る [no cont] ❑ *The committee contains 11 Democrats and nine Republicans.* その委員会は11人の民主党員と9人の共和党員から成る. ❺ V-T 他動詞 If you **contain** something, you control it and prevent it from spreading or increasing. (災害や病気を) 抑制する ❑ *More than a hundred firemen are still trying to contain the fire at the plant.* 100人を超える消防士がまだその工場の火事を食い止めようとしている. ❻ → see also **self-contained**

con|tain|er /kənteɪnər/ (**containers**) ❶ N-COUNT 可算名詞 A **container** is something such as a box or bottle that is used to hold or store things in. 入れ物 ❑ *...the plastic containers in which fish are stored and sold.* 魚を入れて販売するためのプラスチック容器 ❷ N-COUNT 可算名詞 A **container** is a large metal or wooden box used for transporting goods so that they can be loaded easily onto ships and trucks. (輸送用の) コンテナ ❑ *The train, carrying loaded containers on flatcars, was 1.2 miles long.* 平台型貨車で荷物を積んだコンテナを運ぶその列車は全長1.2マイルだった.
→ see **can, ship**

con|tami|nate /kəntæmɪneɪt/ (**contaminates, contaminating, contaminated**) V-T 他動詞 If something **is contaminated by** dirt, chemicals, or radiation, they make it dirty or harmful. 汚染する ❑ *Have any fish been contaminated in the Arctic Ocean?* 北極海で魚が汚染されているのか. ● **con|tami|na|tion** /kəntæmɪneɪʃⁿn/ N-UNCOUNT 不可算名詞 汚染 ❑ *The contamination of the ocean around Puget Sound may be just the beginning.* ピュージェット湾の海洋汚染はまだ始まったばかりかもしれない.

con|tem|plate /kɒntəmpleɪt/ (**contemplates, contemplating, contemplated**) ❶ V-T 他動詞 If you **contemplate** an action, you think about whether to do it or not. 考える ❑ *For a time he contemplated a career as an army medical doctor.* 一時は彼は軍医として働くことを考えた. ❷ V-T 他動詞 If you **contemplate** an idea or subject, you think about it carefully for a long time. 熟考する ❑ *As he lay in his hospital bed that night, he cried as he contemplated his future.* その夜病院のベッドで横になっていたとき, 彼は自分の将来のことをじっと考え続けた. ● **con|tem|pla|tion** /kɒntəmpleɪʃⁿn/ N-UNCOUNT 不可算名詞 熟考 ❑ *It is a place of quiet contemplation.* それは黙想の場所だ. ❸ V-T 他動詞 If you **contemplate** something or someone, you look at them for a long time. 凝視する ❑ *He contemplated his hands, still frowning.* 彼はまだしかめ面のまま自分の両手を凝視した. ● **con|tem|pla|tion** N-UNCOUNT 不可算名詞 凝視 ❑ *He was lost in the contemplation of the landscape for a while.* 彼はしばらく我を忘れてその景色をじっと見つめていた.

Word Link | con ≈ together, with : **con**sensus, **con**temporary, **con**vene

Word Link | tempo ≈ time : con**tempo**rary, **tempo**ral, **tempo**rary

con|tem|po|rary /kəntɛmpəreri/ (**contemporaries**) ❶ ADJ 形容詞 **Contemporary** things are modern and relate to the present time. 現代の ❑ *She writes a lot of contemporary music for people like Whitney Houston.* 彼女はホイットニー・ヒューストンのような人のために多くの現代音楽を作曲している. ❷ ADJ 形容詞 **Contemporary** people or things were alive or happened at the same time as something else you are talking about. 同時代の ❑ *...drawing upon official records and the reports of contemporary witnesses.* 公式記録と同時代の目撃者の報告書を参考にして ❸ N-COUNT 可算名詞 Someone's **contemporary** is a person who is or was alive at the same time as them. 同年代の ❑ *Like most of my contemporaries, I*

grew up in a vastly different world. 私は同年代のほとんどの人たちのように非常に違った世界で育った.

con|tempt /kəntɛmpt/ N-UNCOUNT 不可算名詞 If you have **contempt** for someone or something, you have no respect for them or think that they are unimportant. 軽蔑 □ *He has contempt for those beyond his immediate family circle.* 彼は身内以外の人たちを軽蔑している.

con|temp|tu|ous /kəntɛmptʃuəs/ ADJ 形容詞 If you are **contemptuous of** someone or something, you do not like or respect them at all. 軽蔑した □ *He's openly contemptuous of all the major political parties.* 彼は主要政党のすべてをおおっぴらに軽蔑している.

con|tend /kəntɛnd/ (contends, contending, contended) **1** V-I 自動詞 If you have to **contend** with a problem or difficulty, you have to deal with it or overcome it. (問題や困難に) 戦う □ *It is time, once again, to contend with racism.* もう1度人種差別と戦う時が来た. **2** V-T 他動詞 If you **contend** that something is true, you state or argue that it is true. 主張する [FORMAL 形式ばった] □ *The government contends that he is fundamentalist.* 政府は彼が原理主義者であると主張している. **3** V-RECIP 相互動詞 If you **contend with** someone **for** something such as power, you compete with them to try to get it. 争う □ *...the two main groups contending for power.* 権力争いをしている2つの主力グループ □ *Small-market clubs such as the Kansas City Royals have had trouble contending with richer teams for championships.* カンザスシティ・ロイヤルズのような小規模なクラブは, より豊かなチームと優勝を争うのに苦労してきた.

con|tend|er /kəntɛndər/ (contenders) N-COUNT 可算名詞 A **contender** is someone who takes part in a competition. 競技の参加者 [JOURNALISM ジャーナリズム] □ *Her trainer said yesterday that she would be a strong contender for a place on the Olympic team.* 彼女のコーチは昨日彼女がオリンピック・チーム参加の有力候補になるだろうと述べた.

---

content

❶ NOUN USES
❷ ADJECTIVE USES

---

❶ con|tent /kɒntɛnt/ (contents) **1** N-PLURAL 複数名詞 The **contents** of a container such as a bottle, box, or room are the things that are inside it. 中身 □ *Empty the contents of the pan into the sieve.* フライパンの中身をザルに空けなさい. **2** N-PLURAL 複数名詞 The **contents** of a book are its different chapters and sections, usually shown in a list at the beginning of the book. 目次 □ *There is no Table of Contents.* 目次がない. **3** N-UNCOUNT 不可算名詞 If you refer to the **content** or **contents** of something such as a book, television program, or website, you are referring to the subject that it deals with, the story that it tells, or the ideas that it expresses. (本やテレビなどの) 内容 [also N in pl, usu N "of" n] □ *She is reluctant to discuss the content of the play.* 彼女はその芝居の内容について話したがらない. □ *Stricter controls were placed on the content of videos.* ビデオの内容にさらに厳しい規制が敷かれた. **4** N-UNCOUNT 不可算名詞 The **content** of something such as an educational course or a program of action is the elements that it consists of. (授業や計画の) 内容 □ *Previous students have had nothing but praise for the course content and staff.* 以前の学生たちはそのコースの内容と担当者をただただ称賛している. **5** N-SING 単数名詞 You can use **content** to refer to the amount or proportion of something that a substance contains. 含有量 □ *Sunflower margarine has the same fat content as butter.* ヒマワリのマーガリンはバターと同量の脂肪を含んでいる.

❷ con|tent /kəntɛnt/ **1** ADJ 形容詞 If you are **content with** something, you are willing to accept it, rather than wanting something more or something better. 満足した [v-link ADJ] □ *I am content to admire the mountains from below.* 私は下からその山々に見とれるだけで満足している. □ *I'm perfectly content with the way the campaign was run.* 私はキャンペーンの成り行きにまったく満足している. **2** ADJ 形容詞 If you are **content**, you are fairly happy or satisfied. 満足して, 幸せな [v-link ADJ] □ *He says his daughter is quite content.* 彼は娘はかなり満足していると言っている. **3 to** your **heart's content** → see **heart**

con|tent|ed /kəntɛntɪd/ ADJ 形容詞 If you are **contented**, you are satisfied with your life or the situation you are in. 満足した □ *Whenever he returns to this place, he is happy and contented.* 彼はこの場所に帰って来る度に, 幸せで満ち足りた気持ちだ.

con|ten|tion /kəntɛnʃən/ (contentions) **1** N-COUNT 可算名詞 Someone's **contention** is the idea or opinion that they are expressing in an argument or discussion. 主張 □ *It is my contention that death and murder always lurk as potentials in violent relationships.* 暴力的な関係にはいつも死や殺人の可能性が潜んでいるというのが私の考えだ. **2** N-UNCOUNT 不可算名詞 If something is a cause **of contention**, it is a cause of disagreement or argument. 争い, 口論 □ *His case has become a source of contention between civil liberties activists and the government.* 彼の事件は市民的自由を求める

活動家と政府との間で争いの元となっている. **3** → see also **bone of contention**

con|ten|tious /kəntɛnʃəs/ ADJ 形容詞 A **contentious** issue causes a lot of disagreement or arguments. 議論を呼ぶ [FORMAL 形式ばった] □ *Sanctions are expected to be among the most contentious issues.* 制裁措置は最も議論を呼ぶ問題の1つとなるはずだ.

con|tent|ment /kəntɛntmənt/ N-UNCOUNT 不可算名詞 **Contentment** is a feeling of quiet happiness and satisfaction. 満足 □ *I cannot describe the feeling of contentment that was with me at that time.* 私がその時感じた満足感は言葉に表せない.

con|test (contests, contesting, contested)

The noun is pronounced /kɒntɛst/. The verb is pronounced /kəntɛst/.

名詞は /kɒntɛst/ と発音される. 動詞は /kəntɛst/ と発音される.

1 N-COUNT 可算名詞 A **contest** is a competition or game that people try to win. 競技会, コンクール □ *Few contests in the recent history of boxing have been as thrilling.* 近年のボクシング史の中で, これほどぞくぞくするような試合はほとんどなかった. **2** N-COUNT 可算名詞 A **contest** is a struggle to win power or control. 争い, 抗争 □ *The state election in November will be the last such ballot before next year's presidential contest.* 11月の州議会選挙は来年の大統領選挙戦前のその種の最後の投票になるであろう. **3** V-T 他動詞 If you **contest** a statement or decision, you object to it formally because you think it is wrong or unreasonable. 異議を唱える □ *Your former employer has to reply within 14 days in order to contest the case.* あなたの元雇用主は, この訴訟に異議を申し立てるためには, 14日以内に返事を出さなければならない. **4** V-T 他動詞 If someone **contests** an election or competition, they take part in it and try to win it. 争う [BRIT 英国英語] □ *He quickly won his party's nomination to contest the elections.* 彼はその党から選挙に出馬する候補者の座をすぐ勝ち取った.

Thesaurus	*contest* また次を参照:
N.	competition, game, match **1**
	fight, struggle **2**

con|test|ant /kəntɛstənt/ (contestants) N-COUNT 可算名詞 A **contestant** in a competition or game show is a person who takes part in it. (競技の) 出場者 □ *Later he applied to be a contestant on the television show.* 後で彼はテレビ番組の出場者に応募した.

con|text /kɒntɛkst/ (contexts) **1** N-VAR 可変性名詞 The **context** of an idea or event is the general situation that relates to it, and which helps it to be understood. (考えや出来事の) 背景 □ *We are doing this work in the context of reforms in the economic, social and cultural spheres.* 私たちは, 経済・社会・文化の分野の改革と関連して, この仕事をしている. □ *It helps to understand the historical context in which Chaucer wrote.* それはチョーサーが執筆した歴史的背景を理解するのに役立つ. **2** N-VAR 可変性名詞 The **context** of a word, sentence, or text consists of the words, sentences, or text before and after it which help to make its meaning clear. (言葉や文の) 前後関係, 文脈 □ *Without a context, I would have assumed it was written by a man.* 前後関係がなかったら, 私は男の人がそれを書いたと思っただろう. **3** PHRASE 句 If something is seen **in context** or if it is put **into context**, it is considered together with all the factors that relate to it. 文脈において □ *Taxation is not popular in principle, merely acceptable in context.* 課税は基本的に歓迎されないもので, ただ状況を勘案して受け入れられるだけのことだ. **4** PHRASE 句 If a statement or remark is quoted **out of context**, the circumstances in which it was said are not correctly reported, so that it seems to mean something different from the meaning that was intended. 脈絡がない □ *Thomas says that he has been quoted out of context.* トマスは, 自分の言ったことが文脈を無視して引用されていると言っている.

con|ti|nent /kɒntɪnənt/ (continents) **1** N-COUNT 可算名詞 A **continent** is a very large area of land, such as Africa or Asia, that consists of several countries. 大陸 □ *She loved the African continent.* 彼女はアフリカ大陸が大好きだった. **2** N-PROPER 固有名詞 People sometimes use **the Continent** to refer to the continent of Europe except for Britain. ヨーロッパ大陸 [mainly BRIT 主に英国英語] □ *Its shops are among the most stylish on the Continent.* その店はヨーロッパ大陸の中でも最もおしゃれな店に入っている.

→ see Word Web: **continents**
→ see **earth**

con|ti|nen|tal /kɒntɪnɛntəl/ (continentals) **1** ADJ 形容詞 **Continental** is used to refer to something that belongs to or relates to a continent. 大陸の [ADJ n] □ *The most ancient parts of the continental crust are 4000 million years old.* その大陸地殻のもっとも古い部分は40億年前のものだ. **2** ADJ 形容詞 The **continental** United States consists of all the states which are situated on the continent of North America, as opposed to Hawaii and territories such as the Virgin Islands. 米国本土の [mainly AM 主に米国英語] □ *Shipping is included on orders sent within the continental U.S.* 米国本土内に発送される注文は送料込みです. **3** ADJ 形容詞 **Continental**

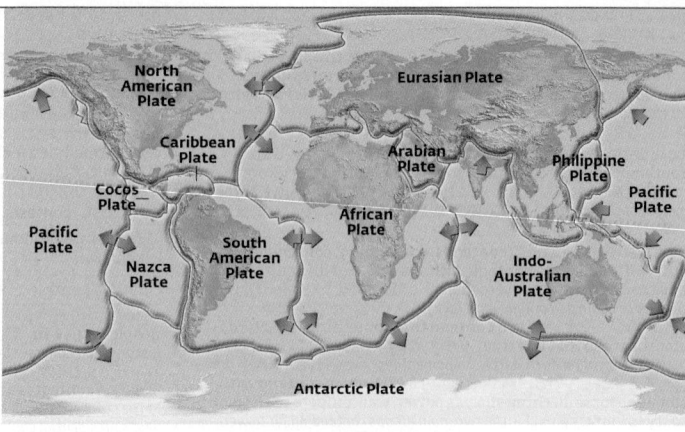

Word Web continents

In 1912, Alfred Wegener* made an important discovery. The shapes of the various **continents** seemed to fit together like the pieces of a puzzle. He decided they had once been a single **land mass** which he called Pangaea. He thought the continents had slowly moved apart. Wegener called this theory **continental drift**. He said the earth's **crust** is not a single, solid piece. It's full of cracks which allow huge pieces to move around on the earth's mantle. The movement of these tectonic **plates** increases the distance between Europe and North America by about 20 millimeters every year.

Alfred Wegener (1880-1930): a German scientist.

Major Plates of the Earth's Crust

---

means existing or happening in the American colonies during the American Revolution. 米国植民地の [AM 米国英語] [usu ADJ n] □...*George Washington, Commander of the Continental Army.* 大陸軍の司令官であるジョージ・ワシントン ◳ ADJ 形容詞 **Continental** means situated on or belonging to the continent of Europe except for Britain. (アメリカ独立戦争で戦った) ヨーロッパ大陸の [mainly BRIT 主に英国英語] [ADJ n] □ *He sees no signs of improvement in the U.K. and continental economy.* 彼は英国にもヨーロッパ大陸にも経済回復の兆しを見出せない。 ◳ N-COUNT 可算名詞 **Continentals** were soldiers who fought in the Continental Army against the British in the American Revolution. (アメリカ独立戦争で戦った) 米国兵 [AM 米国英語]
→ see **continent**

con|tin|gen|cy /kəntɪndʒ³nsi/ (**contingencies**) ◱ N-VAR 可変性名詞 A **contingency** is something that might happen in the future. 将来起こりえること [FORMAL 形式ばった] □ *I need to examine all possible contingencies.* 私は起こりえるすべての可能性を検証する必要がある。 ◲ ADJ 形容詞 A **contingency** plan or measure is one that is intended to be used if a possible situation actually occurs. 不測の事態の [FORMAL 形式ばった] [ADJ n] □ *We have contingency plans.* 私たちには非常事態計画がある。

con|tin|gent /kəntɪndʒ³nt/ (**contingents**) ◱ N-COUNT 可算名詞 A **contingent of** police, soldiers, or military vehicles is a group of them. (警察や軍隊の) 派遣団 □ *Nigeria provided a large contingent of troops to the West African Peacekeeping Force.* ナイジェリアは西アフリカの平和維持部隊に大規模な部隊を送り込んだ。 ◲ N-COUNT 可算名詞 A **contingent** is a group of people representing a country or organization at a meeting or other event. 代表団 [FORMAL 形式ばった] □ *The American contingent will stay overnight in London.* 米国代表団はロンドンに1夜滞在する。

con|tin|ual /kəntɪnyuəl/ ◱ ADJ 形容詞 A **continual** process or situation happens or exists without stopping. 絶え間のない [ADJ n] □ *The school has been in continual use since 1883.* その校舎は1883年以来休みなく利用されている。 □ *They felt continual pressure to perform well.* 彼らはよい試合をしないといけないというプレッシャーを常に感じた。 ●**con|tin|ual|ly** ADV 副詞 絶え間なく □ *She cried almost continually and threw temper tantrums.* 彼女はほとんどずっと泣きっぱなしで、かんしゃくを起こした。 ◲ ADJ 形容詞 [ADJ n] **Continual** events happen again and again. 繰り返し起こる □ ...*the government's continual demands for cash to finance its chronic deficit.* その政府の慢性的な赤字に融資するための資金のひんぱんな要求 ●**con|tin|ual|ly** ADV 副詞 頻繁に □ *Malcolm was continually changing his mind.* マルコムの考えはしょっちゅう変わっていた。

> You can use **continual**, **continuous**, and **constant** to describe things that happen or exist without stopping. **Continual** is usually used to describe something that happens often over a period of time, especially something undesirable. □ ...*his continual drinking. ...continual demands to cut costs.* If something is **continuous**, it happens all the time without stopping, or seems to do so. □ ...*days of continuous rain. ...a continuous background noise.* You describe something as **constant** when it happens all the time or never goes away. □ *He was in constant pain. ...Eva's constant criticism.*

Thesaurus
continual また次を参照:

ADJ. ongoing, repeated, constant, unending ◱ ◲

---

con|tinu|ation /kəntɪnyueɪ³n/ (**continuations**) ◱ N-VAR 可変性名詞 The **continuation of** something is the fact that it continues, instead of stopping. 継続 □ *It's the coalition forces who are to blame for the continuation of the war.* 戦争が終わらないのはそれら多国籍軍のせいだ。 ◲ N-COUNT 可算名詞 Something that is a **continuation of** something else is closely connected with it or forms part of it. 続編 □ *This chapter is a continuation of Chapter 8.* この章は第8章の続きだ。

con|tinue /kəntɪnyu/ (**continues, continuing, continued**) ◱ V-T/V-I 他動詞/自動詞 If someone or something **continues to** do something, they keep doing it and do not stop. 続ける [他動詞], 続く [自動詞] □ *I hope they continue to fight for equal justice after I'm gone.* 私が去った後も彼らが公正のために戦い続けてくれることを願う。 □ *Diana and Roy Jarvis are determined to continue working when they reach retirement age.* ダイアナとロイ・ジャービスは定年が来ても断固働き続けるつもりだ。 ◲ V-T/V-I 他動詞/自動詞 If something **continues** or if you **continue** it, it does not stop. 続ける [他動詞], 続く [自動詞] □ *He insisted that the conflict would continue until conditions were met for a ceasefire.* 停戦の条件がそろわない限り、その紛争は止まないと彼は主張した。 □ *Outside the building people continue their vigil, huddling around bonfires.* その建物の外では、たき火を囲んで人々が寝ずの番を続けている。 ◳ V-T/V-I 他動詞/自動詞 If you **continue** something or **continue** with something, you start doing it again after a break or interruption. (中断後) 継続する □ *I went up to my room to continue with my packing.* 私は荷造りを再開するため自分の部屋へ上がった。 □ *She looked up for a minute and then continued drawing.* 彼女はしばらく上を見上げ、そしてまた絵を描き始めた。 ◴ V-T/V-I 他動詞/自動詞 If something **continues** or if you **continue** it, it starts again after a break or interruption. 再開する [他動詞], 再開される [自動詞] □ *He denies 18 charges. The trial continues today.* 彼は18の容疑を否定している。本日裁判が再開される。 ◵ V-T/V-I 他動詞/自動詞 If you **continue**, you begin speaking again after a pause or interruption. (話を) 続ける □ *"You have no right to intimidate this man," Alison continued.* 「あなたにはこの男性を脅迫する権利はまったくありません」とアリソンは続けた。 □ *Tony drank some coffee before he continued.* トニーは話を続ける前にコーヒーを飲んだ。 ◶ V-I 自動詞 If you **continue as** something or **continue** in a particular state, you remain in a particular job or state. (仕事や状態に) 留まる [自動詞] □ *He had hoped to continue as a full-time career officer.* 彼は常勤の職業軍人として働き続けることを希望していた。 ◷ V-I 自動詞 If you **continue** in a particular direction, you keep walking or traveling in that direction. (ある方向に) 歩き続ける □ *He continued rapidly up the path, not pausing until he neared the Chapter House.* 彼は参事会館に近づくまで立ち止まらずに、小道を急いで上り続けた。

Thesaurus
continue また次を参照:

v. go on, persist; (*ant.*) stop ◱
carry on, resume ◳

con|tinu|ing edu|ca|tion N-UNCOUNT 不可算名詞 **Continuing education** is education for adults in a variety of subjects. 成人教育

con|ti|nu|ity /kɒntɪnuiti/ (**continuities**) N-VAR 可変性名詞 **Continuity** is the fact that something continues to happen or exist, with no great changes or interruptions. 連続, 継続 □ ...*a tank designed to ensure continuity of fuel supply during aerobatics.* 曲芸飛行中に継続した燃料供給を確保するために設計されたタンク

con|tinu|ous /kəntɪnyuəs/ ◱ ADJ 形容詞 A **continuous** process

or event continues for a period of time without stopping. 連続的な, 継続的な □ *Residents report that they heard continuous gunfire.* 住民は連続的な発砲が聞こえたと通報している。 ● con|tinu|ous|ly ADV 副詞 連続して, 継続して □ *The civil war has raged almost continuously since 1976.* 内戦が1976年以来ほぼ継続的に激しく続いている。

> You can use **continual**, **continuous**, and **constant** to describe things that happen or exist without stopping. **Continual** is usually used to describe something that happens often over a period of time, especially something undesirable. □ *…his continual drinking. …continual demands to cut costs.* If something is **continuous**, it happens all the time without stopping, or seems to do so. □ *…days of continuous rain. …a continuous background noise.* You describe something as **constant** when it happens all the time or never goes away. □ *He was in constant pain. …Eva's constant criticism.*

2 ADJ 形容詞 A **continuous** line or surface has no gaps or holes in it. 切れ目なく続いた □ *…a continuous line of boats.* 途切れなく並んだボート **3** ADJ 形容詞 In English grammar, **continuous** verb groups are formed using the auxiliary "be" and the present participle of a verb, as in "I'm feeling a bit tired" and "She had been watching them for some time." Continuous verb groups are used especially when you are focusing on a particular moment. Compare **simple**. (文法用語で) 進行形の

con|tort /kəntɔrt/ (contorts, contorting, contorted) V-T/V-I 他動詞/自動詞 If someone's face or body **contorts** or **is contorted**, it moves into an unnatural and unattractive shape or position. (体を) よじる (顔を) ゆがめる [他動詞], (体が) よじれる (顔が) ゆがむ [自動詞] □ *His face contorts as he screams out the lyrics.* 彼がその歌詞を大声で歌うときに顔がゆがむ。 □ *The gentlest of her caresses would contort his already tense body.* 彼女がとても優しく愛撫をするだけでも, 彼のすでに緊張している体がよじれるだろう。

con|tour /kɒntʊər/ (contours) **1** N-COUNT 可算名詞 You can refer to the general shape or outline of an object as its **contours**. 輪郭 [LITERARY 文語的] □ *…the texture and color of the skin, contours of the body.* 肌触りと肌の色, そして体の曲線 **2** N-COUNT 可算名詞 A **contour** on a map is a line joining points of equal height and indicating hills, valleys, and the steepness of slopes. 等高線 □ *…a contour map showing two hills and this large mountain in the middle.* 中心に2つの丘とこの大きな山が見える等高線地図

Word Link contra ≈ against : contraception, contradict, contrary

contra|cep|tion /kɒntrəsɛpʃən/ N-UNCOUNT 不可算名詞 **Contraception** refers to methods of preventing pregnancy. 避妊 □ *Use a reliable method of contraception.* 信頼できる避妊法を用いなさい。

contra|cep|tive /kɒntrəsɛptɪv/ (contraceptives) **1** ADJ 形容詞 A **contraceptive** method or device is used to prevent pregnancy. 避妊の [ADJ n] □ *…the contraceptive pill.* ピル, 経口避妊薬 **2** N-COUNT 可算名詞 A **contraceptive** is a device or drug that prevents a woman from becoming pregnant. 避妊具, 避妊薬 □ *…oral contraceptives.* ピル, 経口避妊薬

Word Link tract ≈ dragging, drawing : contract, subtract, tractor

con|tract (contracts, contracting, contracted)

> The noun is pronounced /kɒntrækt/. The verb is pronounced /kəntrækt/.
>
> 名詞は /kɒntrækt/ と発音される。動詞は /kəntrækt/ と発音される。

1 N-COUNT 可算名詞 A **contract** is a legal agreement, usually between two companies or between an employer and employee, which involves doing work for a stated sum of money. 契約 □ *The company won a hefty contract for work on Chicago's tallest building.* その会社はシカゴで1番高いビルの建設に関する多額の契約を獲得した。 □ *Have you read the contract?* 契約書を読みましたか。 **2** V-T 他動詞 If you **contract with** someone to do something, you legally agree to do it for them or for them to do it for you. 契約を結ぶ [FORMAL 形式ばった] □ *You can contract with us to deliver your cargo.* 貴社の貨物を運搬する契約を当社と結ぶことができます。 **3** V-T/V-I 他動詞/自動詞 When something **contracts** or when something **contracts** it, it becomes smaller or shorter. 縮める [他動詞], 縮む [自動詞] □ *Blood is only expelled from the heart when it contracts.* 心臓が収縮するときにのみ血液が送り出される。 ● con|trac|tion /kəntrækʃən/ (contractions) N-VAR 可変性名詞 可変性の □ *…the contraction and expansion of blood vessels.* 血管の収縮と拡張 **4** V-I 自動詞 When something such as an economy or market **contracts**, it becomes smaller. (経済・市場が) 縮小する □ *The manufacturing economy contracted in October for the sixth consecutive month.* 製造業界の景気は10月で6か月間続いて下降した。 **5** V-T 他動詞 [no cont] If you **contract** a serious illness, you become ill with it. (病気に) かかる [FORMAL 形式ばった] □ *He contracted AIDS from a blood transfusion.* 彼は輸血によりエイズに感染した。 **6** PHRASE 句 If you are **under**

contract to someone, you have signed a contract agreeing to work for them, and for no one else, during a fixed period of time. 契約中で, 契約をしている □ *The director wanted Olivia de Havilland, then under contract to Warner Brothers.* 監督は当時ワーナー・ブラザーズと契約中だったオリビア・デ・ハビランドの出演を望んだ。

▶ **contract out** PHRASAL VERB 句動詞 If a company **contracts out** work, they employ other companies to do it. 外注に出す, 委託する [BUSINESS 実業] □ *Firms can contract out work to one another.* 会社は相互に業務を委託することができる。 □ *When the bank contracted out its cleaning, the new company was cheaper.* 銀行が清掃を外注に出したら, 新しい会社のほうが安かった。

→ see **illness, muscle**

Word Partnership contract は次の語句と使われる:

V.	**sign a** contract **1**
N.	**terms of a** contract **1**
	contract **a disease 5**
PREP.	contract **with** someone **2**

con|trac|tion /kəntrækʃən/ (contractions) **1** N-COUNT 可算名詞 When a woman who is about to give birth has **contractions**, she experiences a very strong, painful tightening of the muscles of her womb. 陣痛 □ *The contractions were getting stronger.* 陣痛がだんだん強くなってきた。 **2** N-COUNT 可算名詞 A **contraction** is a shortened form of a word or words. (語句の) 短縮形 □ *"It's" (with an apostrophe) can be used as a contraction for "it is."* It's (アポストロフィーのついた) はit is の短縮形として用いることができる。 **3** → see also **contract**

con|trac|tor /kɒntræktər, kəntræk-/ (contractors) N-COUNT 可算名詞 A **contractor** is a person or company that does work for other people or organizations. 請負人, 請負業者 [BUSINESS 実業] □ *We told the building contractor that we wanted a garage big enough for two cars.* 私たちは建築請負業者に自動車が2台入る大きさのガレージが欲しいと言った。

con|trac|tual /kəntræktʃuəl/ ADJ 形容詞 A **contractual** arrangement or relationship involves a legal agreement between people. 契約上の [FORMAL 形式ばった] □ *The company has not fulfilled certain contractual obligations.* その会社はいくつかの契約上の義務を果たしておりません。 ● con|trac|tu|al|ly ADV 副詞 契約によって □ *He is contractually bound to another year in Los Angeles.* 彼は契約上ロサンゼルスにあと1年滞在する義務がある。

Word Link dict ≈ speaking : contradict, dictate, predict

contra|dict /kɒntrədɪkt/ (contradicts, contradicting, contradicted) **1** V-T 他動詞 If you **contradict** someone, you tell them that what they have just said is wrong, or suggest that it is wrong by saying something different. 反論する □ *She dared not contradict him.* 彼女はあえて彼に逆らわなかった。 □ *His comments appeared to contradict remarks made earlier in the day by the chairman.* 彼のコメントは会長がその日に先に発言したことに反論しているようだった。 **2** V-T 他動詞 If one statement or piece of evidence **contradicts** another, the first one makes the second one appear to be wrong. 矛盾する □ *Her version contradicted her daughter's.* 彼女の話は娘の話と矛盾する。

contra|dic|tion /kɒntrədɪkʃən/ (contradictions) N-COUNT 可算名詞 If you describe an aspect of a situation as a **contradiction**, you mean that it is completely different from other aspects, and so makes the situation confused or difficult to understand. 矛盾 □ *The militants see no contradiction in using violence to bring about a religious state.* 過激派は宗教国家の建設のために暴力を使うことに何の矛盾も感じていません。

Word Link ory ≈ relating to : advisory, contradictory, predatory

contra|dic|tory /kɒntrədɪktəri/ ADJ 形容詞 If two or more facts, ideas, or statements are **contradictory**, they state or imply that opposite things are true. 矛盾した □ *Customs officials have made a series of contradictory statements about the equipment.* 税関職員はその装置について一連の矛盾した説明を行った。

con|tra|ry /kɒntrɛri/ **1** ADJ 形容詞 Ideas, attitudes, or reactions that are **contrary** to each other are completely different from each other. (考え・態度・反応などが) 反対の □ *This view is contrary to the aims of critical social research for a number of reasons.* この見解はいくつかの理由で批判的な社会調査の目的と相反している。 **2** PHRASE 句 If you say that something is **contrary to** other people's beliefs or opinions, you are emphasizing that it is true and that they are wrong. 一に反して [EMPHASIS 強調] □ *Contrary to popular belief, moderate exercise actually decreases your appetite.* 社会通念に反して, 適度な運動をすると実は食欲が減退する。 **3** PHRASE 句 You use **on the contrary** when you have just said or implied that something is not true and are going to say that the opposite is true. それどころか □ *It is not an idea around which the community can unite. On the contrary, I see it as one that will divide us.* それは地域住民が1つにまとまるようなアイデアではありませ

ん．それどころか我々を2分化するものだと私は考えます．**4** PHRASE
句 You can use **on the contrary** when you are disagreeing
strongly with something that has just been said or implied, or
are making a strong negative reply. とんでもない[EMPHASIS 強調]
❑ *"People just don't do things like that."* — *"On the contrary, they do them
all the time."* 「人々はただそんな風にはしないよ．」「とんでもない常
にそういうことをしているんだ．」

Do not confuse **on the contrary** with **on the other hand**. **On
the contrary** is used to contradict someone, to say that they
are wrong. **On the other hand** is used to state a different,
often contrasting aspect of the situation you are considering.
❑ *Prices of other foods and consumer goods fell. Wages on the other hand
increased.*

5 PHRASE 句 When a particular idea is being considered,
evidence or statements **to the contrary** suggest that this idea
is not true or that the opposite is true. 反対に ❑ *He continued to
maintain that he did nothing wrong, despite clear evidence to the contrary.*
反対のはっきりとした証拠があるにも関わらず，彼は何も悪いことはし
ていないと言い続けた．

con|trast (contrasts, contrasting, contrasted)

The noun is pronounced /kɒntræst/. The verb is pronounced
/kəntræst/.

名詞は /kɒntræst/ と発音される．動詞は /kəntræst/ と発音される．

1 N-VAR 可変性名詞 A **contrast** is a great difference between two
or more things which is clear when you compare them. 対照，
相違 ❑ *...the contrast between town and country.* 都会と田舎の相違
点 ❑ *The two visitors provided a startling contrast in appearance.* その
2人の訪問者は外見が驚くほど異なっていた．**2** PHRASE 句 You say
by contrast or **in contrast**, or **in contrast to** something, to show
that you are mentioning a very different situation from the one
you have just mentioned. 対照的に ❑ *The private sector, by contrast,
has plenty of money to spend.* 民間企業は対照的に十分な資本があ
る．❑ *In contrast, the lives of girls in well-to-do families were often very
sheltered.* 対照的に，裕福な家庭の女の子はしばしば過保護に育てられ
た．**3** PHRASE 句 If one thing is **in contrast** to another, it is very
different from it. 対照をなして，大違いで ❑ *His public statements
have always been in marked contrast to those of his son.* 彼の公式声明は
常に彼の息子のものとは際立った対照が見られます．**4** V-T 他動詞 If
you **contrast** one thing **with** another, you point out or consider
the differences between those things. 対比する ❑ *She contrasted
the situation then with the present crisis.* 彼女はその状況を現在
の危機と対比しました．❑ *Contrast that approach with what goes on
in most organizations.* そのやり方とほとんどの組織で行われている方
法を比べなさい．**5** V-RECIP 相互動詞 If one thing **contrasts with**
another, it is very different from it. 対照を成す ❑ *Johnson's easy
charm contrasted sharply with the prickliness of his boss.* ジョンソンの
気さくな魅力は彼の上司のとげとげしい態度とは明確な対照を成してい
た．**6** N-UNCOUNT 不可算名詞 **Contrast** is the degree of difference
between the darker and lighter parts of a photograph, television
picture, or painting. (写真・テレビ画面・絵などの) コントラスト
❑ *...a television with brighter colors, better contrast, and digital sound.*
今までより高輝度，高コントラスト，それにデジタル音声を実現した
テレビ

contra|vene /kɒntrəvin/ (contravenes, contravening, contravened) V-T 他動詞 To **contravene** a law or rule means
to do something that is forbidden by the law or rule. 違反する
[FORMAL 形式ばった] ❑ *The board has banned the film on the grounds
that it contravenes criminal libel laws.* 委員会は名誉棄損法に反するとい
う理由でその映画を禁止した．● **contra|ven|tion** /kɒntrəvenʃⁿ/
(contraventions) N-VAR 可変性名詞 違反 ❑ *The government has lent
millions of dollars to debt-ridden banks in contravention of local banking
laws.* 政府は地方銀行法に違反して負債を抱えた銀行に数百万ドルの
融資をした．

Word Link tribute ≈ giving : at**tribute**, con**tribute**, dis**tribute**

con|trib|ute /kəntrɪbyut/ (contributes, contributing, contributed) **1** V-I 自動詞 If you **contribute to** something, you
say or do things to help make it successful. 貢献する ❑ *The
three sons also contribute to the family business.* その3人の息子も家業
に役立っている．❑ *I believe that each of us can contribute to the future
of the world.* 私は我々1人1人が世界の未来に貢献できると信じてい
る．**2** V-T/V-I 他動詞/自動詞 To **contribute** money or resources
to something means to give money or resources to help pay for
something or to help achieve a particular purpose. 寄付する
❑ *The U.S. is contributing $4 billion in loans, credits, and grants.* 米国
は融資，借款 (しゃっかん)，補助金の形で40億ドル拠出しています．
❑ *Local businesses have agreed to contribute.* 地元の企業が寄付するこ
とに合意した．● **con|trib|u|tor** (contributors) N-COUNT 可算名詞
寄付者 ❑ *Candidates for Congress received 53 percent of their funds from
individual contributors.* 連邦議会議員の候補者たちは資金の53%を個人
の寄付者から受け取った．**3** V-I 自動詞 If something **contributes to**
an event or situation, it is one of the causes of it. 1因となる ❑ *The*

report says design faults in both the vessels contributed to the tragedy. 報
告書によると，両方の船の設計上の欠陥が悲劇の1因となったとのこ
とです．

Thesaurus contribute また次を参照：

v.   aid, assist, chip in, commit, donate, give, grant, help,
      support; (*ant.*) neglect, take away **2**

con|tri|bu|tion /kɒntrɪbyuʃⁿ/ (contributions) **1** N-COUNT
可算名詞 If you make a **contribution** to something, you do
something to help make it successful or to produce it. 貢献
❑ *American economists have made important contributions to the field
of financial and corporate economics.* アメリカ人経済学者は金融と企
業経済学の分野で重要な貢献をしました．**2** N-COUNT 可算名詞 A
contribution is a sum of money that you give in order to help
pay for something. 寄付 ❑ *This list ranked companies that make
charitable contributions of a half million dollars or more.* このリストには
50万ドル以上の慈善寄付をした会社がランク付けされていた．

Word Partnership contribution は次の語句と使われる：

ADJ.	**important** contribution, **significant** contribution **1** **2**
v.	**make a** contribution, **send a** contribution **1** **2**

con|tribu|tor /kəntrɪbyətər/ (contributors) **1** N-COUNT 可
算名詞 You can use **contributor** to refer to one of the causes of
an event or situation, especially if that event or situation is an
unpleasant one. 1因 ❑ *Old buses are major contributors to pollution
in cities.* 年代物のバスは都市の大気汚染の主な原因となってい
る．**2** → see also **contribute**

con|trive /kəntraɪv/ (contrives, contriving, contrived) V-T 他
動詞 If you **contrive** an event or situation, you succeed in making
it happen, often by tricking someone. 企てる，もくろむ [FORMAL
形式ばった] ❑ *The oil companies were accused of contriving a shortage of
gasoline to justify price increases.* それらの石油会社は石油価格上昇を正
当化するためにガソリン不足を企てたことで非難されました．

con|trived /kəntraɪvd/ ADJ 形容詞 If you say that something
someone says or does is **contrived**, you think it is false and
deliberate, rather than natural and not planned. わざとらしい
[DISAPPROVAL 不賛成] ❑ *There was nothing contrived about what he
said.* 彼が言ったことに不自然な点は何もなかった．

con|trol /kəntroʊl/ (controls, controlling, controlled)
1 N-UNCOUNT 不可算名詞 **Control of** an organization, place, or
system is the power to make all the important decisions about
the way that it is run. 支配権 ❑ *The restructuring involves Mr.
Ronson giving up control of the company.* そのリストラにはロンソン
氏が会社の支配権を引き渡すことも含まれている．● PHRASE 句 If
you are **in control** of something, you have the power to make all
the important decisions about the way it is run. 支配権を握っ
て ❑ *Nobody knows who is in control of the club.* だれがそのクラブの
支配権を握っているのかを知っている者はいない．● PHRASE 句 If
something is **under** your **control**, you have the power to make all
the important decisions about the way that it is run. 一の支配下に
ある ❑ *All the newspapers are under government control.* 全ての新聞は
政府の管理下にある．**2** N-UNCOUNT 不可算名詞 If you have **control**
of something or someone, you are able to make them do what you
want them to do. 規制，制御 [oft N "of/over" n] ❑ *He lost control
of his car.* 彼は自分の車の制御ができなくなった．● **con|trolled**
ADJ 形容詞 制御された ❑ *...a controlled experiment.* 制御下の実
験 **3** N-UNCOUNT 不可算名詞 If you show **control**, you prevent
yourself behaving in an angry or emotional way. (感情の) 抑
制，自制 ❑ *He had a terrible temper, and sometimes he would completely
lose control.* 彼は気性が激しく，時折完全に自制心を失うことがあ
った．**4** V-T 他動詞 The people who **control** an organization or
place have the power to make all the important decisions about
the way that it is run. 支配する ❑ *He now controls the largest retail
development empire in southern California.* 彼は今やカリフォルニア
州南部で最大の小売開発企業集団の支配者である．**5** V-T 他動詞 To
control a piece of equipment, process, or system means to make
it work in the way that you want it to work. (装置などを) 制御す
る，コントロールする ❑ *...a computerized system to control the gates.*
門の開閉を制御するコンピュータシステム ❑ *Scientists would soon be
able to manipulate human genes to control the aging process.* 科学者は
まもなく老齢化の過程を制御するために人の遺伝子を操作するこ
とができるようになるだろう．**6** V-T 他動詞 When a government
controls prices, wages, or the activity of a particular group, it uses
its power to restrict them. (価格・団体活動などを) 規制する ❑ *The
federal government tried to control rising health-care costs.* 連邦政府は上
昇する医療費を抑制しようとした．● N-UNCOUNT 不可算名詞 **Control**
is also a noun. 規制 ❑ *Control of inflation remains the government's
absolute priority.* インフレ抑制が依然として政府の絶対優先事項であ
る．**7** V-T 他動詞 If you **control yourself**, or if you **control** your
feelings, voice, or expression, you make yourself behave calmly
even though you are feeling angry, excited, or upset. (感情などを)

抑える ❏*Jo was advised to learn to control herself.* ジョーは自制することを学ぶように忠告された. ●**con|trolled** ADJ 形容詞 感情を抑えた ❏*Her manner was quiet and very controlled.* 彼女の態度は静かでとても落ち着いていた. **8** V-T 他動詞 To **control** something dangerous means to prevent it from becoming worse or from spreading. 食い止める, 抑制する ❏*...the need to control environmental pollution.* 環境汚染を抑制する必要 **9** N-COUNT 可算名詞 A **control** is a device such as a switch or lever which you use in order to operate a machine or other piece of equipment. 制御装置 ❏*I practiced operating the controls.* 私はその制御装置の操作を練習した. **10** N-VAR 可変性名詞 **Controls** are the methods that a government uses to restrict increases, for example in prices, wages, or weapons. (価格などの) 規制 ❏*Critics question whether price controls would do any good.* 評論家は価格規制に何の効果があるのかとの疑問を投げかけました. **11** N-VAR 可変性名詞 **Control** is used to refer to a place where your documents or luggage are officially checked when you enter a foreign country. 入国審査所 ❏*He went straight through Passport Control without incident.* 彼は問題なく旅券審査所を通過した.

You do not use **control** as a verb to talk about inspecting documents. The verb you use is **check**. ❏*Police were searching cars and checking identity documents.* However, at an airport or port, the place where passports are checked is called **passport control**.

12 → see also **birth control, quality control, remote control, stock control** **13** PHRASE 句 If something is **out of control**, no one has any power over it. 制御できなくて ❏*The fire is burning out of control.* その火事は手がつけられなく燃えています. **14** PHRASE 句 If something harmful is **under control**, it is being dealt with successfully and is unlikely to cause any more harm. 制御されて ❏*The situation is under control.* 事態は収拾しています.

con|trol|ler /kəntroʊlər/ (**controllers**) **1** N-COUNT 可算名詞 A **controller** is a person who has responsibility for a particular organization or for a particular part of an organization. 管理者 [mainly BRIT 主に英国英語] ❏*...the job of controller of BBC1.* BBC1の管理者という職 **2** → see also **air traffic controller 3** N-COUNT 可算名詞 A **controller** is the same as a **comptroller**. 会計監査役

con|tro|ver|sial /kɒntrəvɜrʃ⁰l/ ADJ 形容詞 If you describe something or someone as **controversial**, you mean that they are the subject of intense public argument, disagreement, or disapproval. 論争の的になる, 意見が分かれる ❏*Immigration is a controversial issue in many countries.* 入国移民は多くの国で論争を呼ぶ問題だ.

con|tro|ver|sy /kɒntrəvɜrsi/ (**controversies**) N-VAR 可変性名詞 **Controversy** is a lot of discussion and argument about something, often involving strong feelings of anger or disapproval. 論争, 議論 ❏*The proposed cuts have caused considerable controversy.* その削減案は相当大きな議論を引き起こした.

con|va|lesce /kɒnvəlɛs/ (**convalesces, convalescing, convalesced**) V-I 自動詞 If you **are convalescing**, you are resting and getting your health back after an illness or operation. 健康を回復する [FORMAL 形式ばった] ❏*After two weeks, I was allowed home, where I convalesced for three months.* 2週間後に私は帰宅を許され, 3か月間自宅療養した.

con|va|les|cence /kɒnvəlɛs⁰ns/ N-UNCOUNT 不可算名詞 **Convalescence** is the period or process of becoming healthy and well again after an illness or operation. 回復期, 療養 [FORMAL 形式ばった] ❏*Also thanks to Lucy and Guthrie Scott for inviting me to stay with them during my convalescence.* またスコット夫妻が療養期間中にご自宅に滞在するように勧めてくださったことに感謝しております.

con|vene /kənvin/ (**convenes, convening, convened**) V-T/V-I 他動詞/自動詞 If someone **convenes** a meeting or conference, they arrange for it to take place. You can also say that people **convene** or that a meeting **convenes**. (会議を) 召集する [FORMAL 形式ばった] [他動詞], (会議が) 開催される (人が) 会合する [自動詞] ❏*Last August he convened a meeting of his closest advisers at Camp David.* 去る8月に彼は側近の顧問の会議をキャンプ・デービッドで開いた.

con|veni|ence /kənvinyəns/ (**conveniences**) **1** N-UNCOUNT 不可算名詞 If something is done for your **convenience**, it is done in a way that is useful or suitable for you. 好都合, 便宜 ❏*He was happy to make a detour for her convenience.* 彼は彼女の都合に合わせて喜んで遠回りをした. **2** N-COUNT 可算名詞 If you describe something as a **convenience**, you mean that it is very useful. 便利 ❏*Mail order is a convenience for buyers who are too busy to shop.* 通信販売は忙しくて買い物をする時間がない消費者にとって便利だ. **3** N-COUNT 可算名詞 **Conveniences** are pieces of equipment designed to make your life easier. 便利品 ❏*...an apartment with all the modern conveniences.* 現代の利器をすべて備えたアパート **4** → see also **convenient**

con|veni|ent /kənvinyənt/ **1** ADJ 形容詞 If a way of doing something is **convenient**, it is easy, or very useful or suitable for a particular purpose. 便利な ❏*...a flexible and convenient way of paying for business expenses.* 融通がきき便利なビジネス経費支払い法 ●**con|veni|ence** N-UNCOUNT 不可算名詞 便利さ ❏*They may use a credit card for convenience.* 彼らはクレジットカードを便宜上使用するかもしれない. ●**con|veni|ent|ly** ADV 副詞 便利よく ❏*The body spray slips conveniently into your sports bag for freshening up after a game.* そのボディースプレーは試合のあとのリフレッシュ用にスポーツバッグに都合よくすっと入る. **2** ADJ 形容詞 If you describe a place as **convenient**, you are pleased because it is near to where you are, or because you can reach another place from there quickly and easily. (場所が) 便利な [APPROVAL 賛成] ❏*The town is well placed for easy access to Washington D.C. and convenient for Dulles Airport.* その町はワシントン市への交通の便がよいところに位置し, またダレス空港にも便利です. ●**con|veni|ent|ly** ADV 副詞 便利な場所に ❏*It was conveniently situated just across the road from the City Reference Library.* それは市立参考図書館の向かい側でとても便利な場所に位置しています. **3** ADJ 形容詞 A **convenient** time to do something, for example to meet someone, is a time when you are free to do it or would like to do it. 都合のよい ❏*She will try to arrange a mutually convenient time and place for an interview.* インタビューには双方にとって便利な時間と場所を彼女が取り計らいます.

con|vent /kɒnvɛnt, -vⁿnt/ (**convents**) N-COUNT 可算名詞 A **convent** is a building in which a community of nuns live. (女性の) 修道院

con|ven|tion /kənvɛnʃⁿn/ (**conventions**) **1** N-VAR 可変性名詞 A **convention** is a way of behaving that is considered to be correct or polite by most people in a society. しきたり, 慣習 ❏*It's just a social convention that men don't wear skirts.* 男性がスカートをはかないというのは社会的な慣習にすぎない. **2** N-COUNT 可算名詞 In art, literature, or the theater, a **convention** is a traditional method or style. (芸術などの) 伝統的な手法・様式 ❏*We go offstage and come back for the convention of the encore.* 私たちは舞台裏に行き, お決まりのアンコールに応えるのに戻る. **3** N-COUNT 可算名詞 A **convention** is an official agreement between countries or groups of people. (国家・団体間の) 協定 ❏*...the U.N. convention on climate change.* 気候変動に関する国連協定 **4** N-COUNT 可算名詞 A **convention** is a large meeting of an organization or political group. (組織・政治団体などの) 大会 ❏*...the annual convention of the Society of Professional Journalists.* プロジャーナリスト協会の年次大会

con|ven|tion|al /kənvɛnʃⁿnⁿl/ **1** ADJ 形容詞 Someone who is **conventional** has behavior or opinions that are ordinary and normal. 月並みな, 平凡な ❏*...a respectable married woman with conventional opinions.* 一般的な考え方をする品のよい既婚女性 ●**con|ven|tion|al|ly** ADV 副詞 月並みに, 平凡に ❏*Men still wear their hair short and dressed conventionally.* 男性はまだ短髪で月並みな服装をしていた. **2** ADJ 形容詞 A **conventional** method or product is one that is usually used or that has been in use for a long time. (方法・製品などが) 従来の, 慣習的な ❏*...the risks and drawbacks of conventional family planning methods.* 従来の家族計画方法の危険と欠点 ●**con|ven|tion|al|ly** ADV 副詞 [ADV with v] 従来の方式で ❏*Organically grown produce does not differ greatly in appearance from conventionally grown crops.* 有機栽培の農産物は従来の方式で栽培された作物と外見上たいして変わらない. **3** ADJ 形容詞 **Conventional** weapons and wars do not involve nuclear explosives. (核兵器を用いない) 通常の ❏*We must reduce the danger of war by controlling nuclear, chemical, and conventional arms.* 我々は核兵器, 化学兵器, 通常兵器を抑制することにより戦争の危険度を軽減しなければならない.

Word Link

verg, vert ≈ turning : converge, di**verge,** sub**vert**

con|verge /kənv3rdʒ/ (**converges, converging, converged**)
1 V-I 自動詞 If people or vehicles **converge** on a place, they move toward it from different directions. 集結する □*Hundreds of tractors will converge on the capital.* 数百台のトラクターが首都に集結する。 **2** V-I 自動詞 If roads or lines **converge**, they meet or join at a particular place. (道路・線などが) 合流する [FORMAL 形式ばった] □*As they flow south, the five rivers converge.* その5つの川は南下して流れぬおる合流する。

con|ver|gence /kənv3rdʒ³ns/ (**convergences**) N-VAR 可変性名詞 The **convergence** of different ideas, groups, or societies is the process by which they stop being different and become more similar. (異なる意見・団体・社会などの) 一致すること、一体化 [FORMAL 形式ばった] □*...the need to move towards greater economic convergence.* さらに大規模な経済の一体化へ向かう必要性

con|ver|sa|tion /kɒnvərseɪʃ³n/ (**conversations**) N-COUNT 可算名詞 If you have a **conversation with** someone, you talk with them, usually in an informal situation. 会話 □*He's a talkative guy, and I struck up a conversation with him.* 彼は話し好きな男で、私は彼と話し始めた。

con|ver|sa|tion|al /kɒnvərseɪʃən³l/ ADJ 形容詞 **Conversational** means relating to, or similar to, casual and informal talk. 会話に関する、会話調の □*What is refreshing is the author's easy, conversational style.* 新鮮なのは著者の平易で会話調のスタイルだ。

con|verse (**converses, conversing, conversed**)

The verb is pronounced /kənv3rs/. The noun is pronounced /kɒnv3rs/.

動詞は /kənv3rs/ と発音される。名詞は /kɒnv3rs/ と発音される。

1 V-RECIP 相互動詞 If you **converse with** someone, you talk to them. You can also say that two people **converse**. 話し合う [FORMAL 形式ばった] □*Luke sat directly behind the pilot and conversed with him.* ルークはパイロットの真後ろに座り、彼と会話をした。 **2** N-SING 単数名詞 The **converse** of a statement is its opposite or reverse. 正反対、逆 [FORMAL 形式ばった] □*What you do for a living is critical to where you settle and how you live – and the converse is also true.* 職業により住む場所および暮らし向きが大きく左右される。また逆もしかり。

con|verse|ly /kɒnv3rsli, kənv3rs-/ ADV 副詞 You say **conversely** to indicate that the situation you are about to describe is the opposite or reverse of the one you have just described. 反対に、逆に [FORMAL 形式ばった] [ADV with cl] □*Malaysia and Indonesia rely on open markets for forest and fishery products. Conversely, some Asian countries are highly protectionist.* マレーシアとインドネシアは森林・漁業生産物の自由市場に依存している。逆に、アジア諸国でも非常に保護主義的な国もある。

con|ver|sion /kənv3rʒ³n/ (**conversions**) **1** N-VAR 可変性名詞 **Conversion** is the act or process of changing something into a different state or form. 変換、改造 □*...the conversion of disused rail lines into cycle routes.* 廃線跡をサイクリング専用道路に転用 **2** N-VAR 可変性名詞 Someone's **conversion** is the change of their religion or beliefs. 改宗、転向 □*...his conversion to Christianity.* 彼のキリスト教への改宗

Word Link

vert ≈ turning : convert, **in**vert, **re**vert

con|vert (**converts, converting, converted**)

The verb is pronounced /kənv3rt/. The noun is pronounced /kɒnv3rt/.

動詞は /kənv3rt/ と発音される。名詞は /kɒnv3rt/ と発音される。

1 V-T/V-I 他動詞/自動詞 If one thing **is converted** or **converts into** another, it is changed into a different form. 変える、転換する [他動詞]、変わる、転換する [自動詞] □*...naturally occurring substances which the body can convert into vitamins.* 身体がビタミンに変換できる自然に発生する物質 **2** V-T 他動詞 If someone **converts** a room or building, they alter it in order to use it for a different purpose. 改造する □*By converting the attic, they were able to have extra bedrooms.* 彼らは屋根裏部屋を改造して寝室を2部屋増やすことができた。 □*...the entrepreneur who wants to convert County Hall into a hotel.* 都役所の建物をホテルに改築希望している企業家 **3** V-T 他動詞 If you **convert** a vehicle or piece of equipment, you change it so that it can use a different fuel. (車・機器などを) 改造する、変換する □*Save money by converting your car to run on used vegetable oil.* 自家用車を使用済みの野菜油で走行できるように改造しお金を節約しなさい。 **4** V-T 他動詞 If you **convert** a quantity **from** one system of measurement **to** another, you calculate what the quantity is in the second system. (測量法を) 変換する □*Converting metric measurements to U.S. equivalents is easy.* メートル法を米国式に変換するのはたやすい。 **5** V-T/V-I 他動詞/自動詞 If someone **converts** you, they persuade you to change your religious or political

beliefs. You can also say that someone **converts to** a different religion. 転向させる、改宗させる [他動詞]、転向する、改宗する [自動詞] □*If you try to convert him, you could find he just walks away.* もし彼を転向させようとしても、彼はただ立ち去っていくだけだろう。 □*He was a major influence in converting Godwin to political radicalism.* 彼がゴドウィンを政治的急進主義に転向させるのに重要な影響を及ぼした1人だ。 **6** N-COUNT 可算名詞 A **convert** is someone who has changed their religious or political beliefs. 改宗者、転向者 [oft N "to" n] □*She, too, was a convert to Roman Catholicism.* 彼女もローマカトリック教への改宗者だった。 **7** N-COUNT 可算名詞 If you describe someone as a **convert to** something, you mean that they have recently become very enthusiastic about it. (なりたての) 転向者 [usu N "to" n] □*As recent converts to vegetarianism and animal rights, they now live with a menagerie of stray animals.* 彼らは菜食主義および動物愛好家に最近転向したばかりで、現在迷子の動物の群れと一緒に暮らしている。

Thesaurus

convert また次を参照:

v.　　adapt, alter, change, modify, transform **1**

con|vert|ible /kənv3rtɪb³l/ (**convertibles**) **1** N-COUNT 可算名詞 A **convertible** is a car with a soft roof that can be folded down or removed. オープンカー、コンバーチブル □*Her own car is a convertible VW.* 彼女の自家用車はフォルクスワーゲンのオープンカーだ。 **2** ADJ 形容詞 In finance, **convertible** investments or money can be easily exchanged for other forms of investments or money. 転換可能な、兌換 (だかん) 可能な [BUSINESS 実業] □*...the introduction of a convertible currency.* 兌換通貨の導入 ● **con|vert|ibil|ity** /kənv3rtɪbɪlɪti/ N-UNCOUNT 不可算名詞 交換可能性、兌換可能性 □*...the convertibility of the peso.* ペソの兌換可能性 → see **car**

con|vey /kənveɪ/ (**conveys, conveying, conveyed**) V-T 他動詞 To **convey** information or feelings means to cause them to be known or understood by someone. (情報・感情などを) 伝える □*When I returned home, I tried to convey the wonder of this machine to my husband.* 家に帰ったとき、私は夫にこの機械の素晴らしさを伝えようとした。 □*In every one of her pictures she conveys a sense of immediacy.* 彼女の写真1枚1枚に緊迫感が表れている。

con|vey|or belt /kənveɪər belt/ (**conveyor belts**) N-COUNT 可算名詞 A **conveyor belt** or a **conveyor** is a continuously moving strip of rubber or metal which is used in factories for moving objects along so that they can be dealt with as quickly as possible. ベルトコンベヤー □*The damp bricks went along a conveyor belt into another shed to dry.* 水気のあるれんがはベルトコンベヤーで乾燥用の倉庫に運ばれた。

Word Link

vict, vinc ≈ conquering : convict, **con**vince, **in**vincible

con|vict (**convicts, convicting, convicted**)

The verb is pronounced /kənvɪkt/. The noun is pronounced /kɒnvɪkt/.

動詞は /kənvɪkt/ と発音される。名詞は /kɒnvɪkt/ と発音される。

1 V-T 他動詞 If someone **is convicted of** a crime, they are found guilty of that crime in a court of law. 有罪判決を出す □*In 1977 he was convicted of murder and sentenced to life imprisonment.* 1977年に彼は殺人罪で有罪となり、終身刑を宣告された。 □*There was insufficient evidence to convict him.* 彼に有罪判決を出すには証拠不十分でした。 **2** N-COUNT 可算名詞 A **convict** is someone who is in prison. 囚人、受刑者 [JOURNALISM ジャーナリズム] □*...Neil Jordan's tale of two escaped convicts who get mistaken for priests.* 2人の脱走囚人が聖職者に間違われるというニール・ジョーダンの物語

con|vic|tion /kənvɪkʃ³n/ (**convictions**) **1** N-COUNT 可算名詞 A **conviction** is a strong belief or opinion. 信念 [usu N that] □*It is our firm conviction that a step forward has been taken.* 1歩前進したと我々は確信しています。 **2** N-COUNT 可算名詞 If someone has a **conviction**, they have been found guilty of a crime in a court of law. 有罪判決 □*He will appeal against his conviction.* 彼は有罪判決に対して上訴します。 **3** N-UNCOUNT 不可算名詞 If you have **conviction**, you have great confidence in your beliefs or opinions. 確信 □*"We shall, sir," said Thorne, with conviction.* 「かしこまりました。」と確信を持ってソーンは言った。

con|vince /kənvɪns/ (**convinces, convincing, convinced**) **1** V-T 他動詞 If someone or something **convinces** you **to** do something, they persuade you to do it. 説得する □*That weekend in Plattsburgh, he convinced her to go ahead and marry Bud.* その週末にプラッツバーグで彼は彼女がバッドと結婚に踏み切るよう説得した。 **2** V-T 他動詞 If someone or something **convinces** you of something, they make you believe that it is true or that it exists. 納得させる □*Although I soon convinced him of my innocence, I think he still has serious doubts about my sanity.* まもなく彼に私が無罪であることを納得してもらったが、彼は今でも私の正気をひどく疑っていると思う。

Picture Dictionary cook

boil · steam · roast · fry · stir fry · bake · microwave · toast · barbecue · broil

Thesaurus convince また次を参照:

v. argue, brainwash, persuade, sell, talk into, win, over; (ant.) discourage ① ②

con|vinced /kənvɪnst/ ADJ 形容詞 If you are **convinced that** something is true, you feel sure that it is true. 確信して □ He was convinced that I was part of the problem. 私がその問題の一部であると彼は確信していた。□ He became convinced of the need for cheap editions of good quality writing. 彼は質のよい本の廉価版が必要であると確信するようになった。

con|vinc|ing /kənvɪnsɪŋ/ ADJ 形容詞 If you describe someone or something as **convincing**, you mean that they make you believe that a particular thing is true, correct, or genuine. 説得力がある，納得のいく □ Scientists say there is no convincing evidence that power lines have anything to do with cancer. 電線とがんとの関連性を示す確かな証拠はないと科学者は言っている。● **con|vinc|ing|ly** ADV 副詞 説得力を持って，納得のいくように □ He argued forcefully and convincingly that they were likely to bankrupt the budget. それらは予算を上回る可能性が高いと彼は力強く説得力を持って主張した。

con|voy /kɒnvɔɪ/ (convoys) N-COUNT 可算名詞 A **convoy** is a group of vehicles or ships traveling together. 輸送車隊，輸送船団 [also "in" N] □ ...a U.N. convoy carrying food and medical supplies. 食糧や医薬品を輸送する国連の輸送車隊 □ ...humanitarian relief convoys. 人道援助物資の輸送車隊

con|vul|sion /kənvʌlʃⁿn/ (convulsions) N-COUNT 可算名詞 If someone has **convulsions**, they suffer uncontrollable movements of their muscles. けいれん，ひきつけ □ Thirteen per cent said they became unconscious at night and 5 per cent suffered convulsions. 13%が夜に意識不明になったと言い，5%がけいれんを起こした。

cook /kʊk/ (cooks, cooking, cooked) ① V-T/V-I 他動詞/自動詞 When you **cook** a meal, you prepare food for eating by heating it. (食事を) 作る，料理する [他動詞]，料理を作る [自動詞] □ I have to go and cook dinner. 帰ってご飯を作らなくっちゃ。□ Chefs at the restaurant once cooked for President Kennedy. そのレストランのコックたちはかつてケネディ大統領のために料理を作ったことがある。● **cook|ing** N-UNCOUNT 不可算名詞 料理をすること，調理 □ Her hobbies include music, dancing, sport, and cooking. 彼女の趣味は音楽，ダンス，スポーツ，料理などだ。② V-T/V-I 他動詞/自動詞 When you **cook** food, or when food **cooks**, it is heated until it is ready to be eaten. 調理する [他動詞]，(食材が) 調理される [自動詞] □ ...some basic instructions on how to cook a turkey. 七面鳥の調理法についてのいくつかの基本的な指示 □ Let the vegetables cook gently for about 10 minutes. 野菜を弱火で約10分煮てください。

You often use a more specific verb instead of **cook** when you are talking about preparing food using heat. For example, you **roast** meat in an oven, but you **bake** bread and cakes. You can **boil** vegetables in hot water, or you can **steam** them over a pan of boiling water. You can **fry** meat and vegetables in oil or fat. You can also **broil** or, in British English, **grill** them directly under or over a flame. You do not normally talk about **grilling** bread. Instead, you **toast** it.

③ N-COUNT 可算名詞 A **cook** is a person whose job is to prepare and cook food, especially in someone's home or in an institution. コック，料理人 □ They had a butler, a cook, and a maid. 彼らの家には執事，コック，そしてお手伝いがいた。④ N-COUNT 可算名詞 If you say that someone is a good **cook**, you mean they are good at preparing and cooking food. 料理する人 □ I'm a lousy cook. 私は料理が下手だ。

▶ **cook up** ① PHRASAL VERB 句動詞 If someone **cooks up** a

dishonest scheme, they plan it. たくらむ [INFORMAL くだけた] □ He must have cooked up his scheme on the spur of the moment. 彼は衝動的にその計画をたくらんだに違いない。② PHRASAL VERB 句動詞 If someone **cooks up** an explanation or a story, they make it up. でっち上げる [INFORMAL くだけた] □ She'll cook up a convincing explanation. 彼女はもっともらしい言い訳をでっち上げるだろう。
→ see Picture Dictionary: cook
→ see can

Thesaurus cook また次を参照:

v. heat up, make, prepare ①
n. chef ③

cook|book /kʊkbʊk/ (cookbooks) N-COUNT 可算名詞 A **cookbook** is a book that contains recipes for preparing food. 料理の本

cook|er /kʊkər/ (cookers) N-COUNT 可算名詞 A **cooker** is a large metal device for cooking food using gas or electricity. A cooker usually consists of an oven, a broiler, and some gas burners or electric rings. レンジ [BRIT 英国英語; AM stove 米国英語 stove]

cook|ery /kʊkəri/ N-UNCOUNT 不可算名詞 **Cookery** is the activity of preparing and cooking food. 料理，料理法 □ The school runs cookery classes throughout the year. その学校は年間を通して料理のクラスを開いています。

cookie /kʊki/ (cookies) ① N-COUNT 可算名詞 A **cookie** is a small sweet cake. クッキー [mainly AM 主に米国英語] ② N-COUNT 可算名詞 A **cookie** is a piece of computer software which enables a website you have visited to recognize you if you visit it again. (ウェブサイト閲覧の) クッキー [COMPUTING コンピューティング]
→ see dessert

cook|ing /kʊkɪŋ/ ① N-UNCOUNT 不可算名詞 **Cooking** is food which has been cooked. 料理 (した食べ物) □ The menu is based on classic French cooking. そのメニューは伝統的なフラン料理に基づいている。② N-UNCOUNT 不可算名詞 **Cooking** is the activity of preparing food. 料理 (すること) □ He did the cooking, cleaning, laundry, and home repairs. 彼は料理，掃除，洗濯，家の修理をした。③ ADJ 形容詞 **Cooking** ingredients or equipment are used in cookery. 調理用の [ADJ n] □ Finely slice the cooking apples. 調理用のリンゴを薄く切りなさい。④ → see also cook
→ see Word Web: cooking

cool /kul/ (cooler, coolest, cools, cooling, cooled) ① ADJ 形容詞 Something that is **cool** has a temperature which is low but not very low. 涼しい，ひんやりする □ I felt a current of cool air. 私は涼しい空気の流れを感じた。□ The water was slightly cooler than a child's bath. その水は子供用の風呂よりややぬるかった。② ADJ 形容詞 If it is **cool**, or if a place is **cool**, the temperature of the air is low but not very low. 涼しい，ひんやりする □ Thank goodness it's cool in here. ありがたい，ここは涼しい。□ Store grains and cereals in a cool, dry place. 穀物とシリアルは冷温で乾燥した場所に保管しなさい。● N-SING 単数名詞 **Cool** is also a noun. 涼しさ □ She walked into the cool of the hallway. 彼女は涼しい廊下へ歩いて入った。

If you want to emphasize how cold the weather is, you can say that it is **freezing**, especially in winter when there is ice or frost. In summer, if the temperature is below average, you can say that it is **cool**. In general, **cold** suggests a lower temperature than **cool**, and **cool** things may be pleasant or refreshing. □ A cool breeze swept off the ocean; it was pleasant out there. If it is very **cool** or too **cool**, you can also say that it is **chilly**.

③ ADJ 形容詞 Clothing that is **cool** is made of thin material

Word Web   cooking

Anthropologists believe our ancestors began to experiment with **cooking** about 1.5 million years ago. Cooking made some toxic or **inedible** plants safe to **eat**. It made tough meat **tender** and easier to **digest**. It also improved the flavor of the food they ate. **Heating up food** to a high **temperature** killed dangerous bacteria. **Cooked** food could be stored longer. This all helped increase the amount of food available to our ancestors.

so that you do not become too hot in hot weather. （服の生地が）涼しげな □*In warm weather, you should wear clothing that is cool and comfortable.* 暖かい日には涼しくて着心地のいい服装をすべきだ. **4** ADJ 形容詞 **Cool** colors are light colors which give an impression of coolness. 冷たい感じの, 寒色の [ADJ n] □*Choose a cool color such as cream.* クリーム色のような淡い色を選びなさい. **5** ADJ 形容詞 If you say that a person or their behavior is **cool**, you mean that they are calm and unemotional, especially in a difficult situation. 冷静な [APPROVAL 賛成] □*He was marvelously cool again, smiling as if nothing had happened.* 彼はまたしても驚くほど冷静で, 何事もなかったかのように微笑んでいた. ● **cool|ly** ADV 副詞 冷静に □*Everyone must think this situation through calmly and coolly.* 全員が落ち着いて冷静にこの状況をよく考えなければなりません. **6** ADJ 形容詞 If you say that a person or their behavior is **cool**, you mean that they are unfriendly or not enthusiastic. 冷淡な □*I didn't like him at all. I thought he was cool, aloof, and arrogant.* 私は彼がぜんぜん好きじゃなかった. 冷淡で, よそよそしく, 横柄な人だと思った. ● **cool|ly** ADV 副詞 冷淡に □*"It's your choice, Nina," David said coolly.* 「君が決めるんだよ, ニーナ.」とデービッドは冷淡に言った. **7** ADJ 形容詞 If you say that a person or thing is **cool**, you mean that they are fashionable and attractive. すてきな, かっこいい [INFORMAL くだけた, APPROVAL 賛成] □*He was trying to be really cool and trendy.* 彼は本当にかっこよくて流行の先端を行くように努力していた. □*That's a cool hat.* あれはかっこいい帽子だね. **8** V-T/V-I 他動詞/自動詞 When something **cools** or when you **cool** it, it becomes lower in temperature. 冷やす [他動詞], 冷える [自動詞] □*Drain the meat and allow it to cool.* 肉の脂切りをして冷ましなさい. □*Huge fans will have to cool the concrete floor to keep it below 150 degrees.* コンクリートの床を150度未満に保つためには, 大型の扇風機で冷却しなければならないだろう. ● PHRASAL VERB 句動詞 To **cool down** means the same as to **cool**. 冷却する □*Avoid putting your car away until the engine has cooled down.* エンジンが冷却するまで自動車をしまうのを避けなさい. **9** V-T/V-I 他動詞/自動詞 When a feeling or emotion **cools**, or when you **cool** it, it becomes less powerful. (感情を) 冷ます [他動詞], (感情が) 冷める [自動詞] □*Within a few minutes tempers had cooled.* 数分のうちに腹立ちがおさまっていた. **10** ADJ 形容詞 [v-link ADJ] If you say that someone is **cool about** something, you mean that they accept it and are not angry or upset about it. (気持ちよく) 受け入れて [INFORMAL くだけた, APPROVAL 賛成] □*Bev was really cool about it all.* ベブはそのことを全然怒っていなかった. **11** ADJ 形容詞 If you say that something or someone is **cool**, you think they are excellent in some way. 素敵だ, かっこいい [INFORMAL くだけた] □*Kathleen gave me a really cool dress.* キャスリーンは私にとても素敵なドレスをくれた. □*He's such a cool guy.* 彼はとってもかっこいいやつだ.

▶ **cool down** **1** PHRASAL VERB 句動詞 → see **cool 8** **2** PHRASAL VERB 句動詞 If someone **cools down** or if you **cool** them **down**, they become less angry than they were. 頭を冷やす, 気を落ち着ける □*He has had time to cool down and look at what happened more objectively.* 彼は気を落ち着けて, もう少し客観的に何が起こったかを考える時間がありました.

▶ **cool off** **1** PHRASAL VERB 句動詞 If someone or something **cools off**, or if you **cool** them **off**, they become cooler after having been hot. 冷やす, 涼しくなる □*Maybe he's trying to cool off out there in the rain.* たぶん彼はあそこで雨に打たれて体を冷やそうとしているのでしょう. □*She made a fanning motion, pretending to cool herself off.* 彼女は涼を取るふりをして自分をあおいだ. **2** PHRASAL VERB 句動詞 If someone **cools off**, they become less angry than they were. 頭を冷やす □*We've got to give him some time to cool off.* 彼に頭を冷やす時間を与えないといけない.

→ see **refrigerator**

Thesaurus   *cool* また次を参照:

ADJ.	chilly, cold, nippy; (ant.) warm **1**
	easygoing, serene, tranquil **5**
	distant, unfriendly **6**

Word Partnership   *cool* は次の語句と使われる:

N.	cool **air**, cool **breeze** **1 2**
V.	**play it** cool, **stay** cool **5 10 11**

Word Link   co ≈ together : coherent, collaborate, cooperate

Word Link   oper ≈ work : cooperate, opera, operation

co|oper|ate /koʊɒpəreɪt/ (**cooperates, cooperating, cooperated**) **1** V-RECIP 相互動詞 If you **cooperate with** someone, you work with them or help them for a particular purpose. You can also say that two people **cooperate**. (特定の目的に) 協力する □*The U.N. had been cooperating with the State Department on a plan to find countries willing to take the refugees.* 国連は難民を受け入れる国を探す計画で国務省と協力してきている. ● **co|opera|tion** /koʊɒpəreɪʃᵊn/ N-UNCOUNT 不可算名詞 協力 □*A deal with Japan could open the door to economic cooperation with East Asia.* 日本と取引することによって東アジアとの経済協力への道が開けるかもしれない. **2** V-I 自動詞 If you **cooperate**, you do what someone has asked or told you to do. (言われた通りに) 協力する □*He agreed to cooperate with the police investigation.* 彼は警察の取調べに協力することに同意しました. ● **co|opera|tion** N-UNCOUNT 不可算名詞 協力 □*The police underlined the importance of the public's cooperation in the hunt for the bombers.* 警察は爆破犯の捜索に関して一般人の協力が重要であることを強調した.

Word Partnership   *cooperate* は次の語句と使われる:

V.	**agree to** cooperate, **continue to** cooperate, **fail to** cooperate, **refuse to** cooperate **1 2**
ADV.	cooperate **fully 1 2**
N.	**willingness to** cooperate **1 2**

Word Partnership   *cooperation* は次の語句と使われる:

ADJ.	**close** cooperation, **full** cooperation **1 2**
N.	**lack of** cooperation **1 2**

co|opera|tive /koʊɒpərətɪv/ (**cooperatives**) **1** N-COUNT 可算名詞 A **cooperative** is a business or organization run by the people who work for it, or owned by the people who use it. These people share its benefits and profits. 協同組合 [BUSINESS 実業] □*They decided a housing cooperative was the way to regenerate the area.* 彼らは住宅協同組合が地域再生への道であると決定した. **2** ADJ 形容詞 A **cooperative** activity is done by people working together. 協力的な, 共同の □*He was transferred to FBI custody in a smooth cooperative effort between Egyptian and U.S. authorities.* エジプト当局と米国当局間の円滑な協力的努力により, 彼の身柄は連邦捜査局に引き渡された. ● **co|opera|tive|ly** ADV 副詞 [ADV after v] 協力的に □*They agreed to work cooperatively to ease tensions wherever possible.* 彼らは緊張を緩和するためにできる限り協力的に取り組むことに合意しました. **3** ADJ 形容詞 If you say that someone is **cooperative**, you mean that they do what you ask them to without complaining or arguing. 協力的な □*I made every effort to be cooperative.* 私はできる限り協力的に行った.

Thesaurus   *cooperative* また次を参照:

ADJ.	combined, shared, united; (ant.) independent, private, separate **2**
	accommodating; (ant.) uncooperative **3**

co|or|di|nate (**coordinates, coordinating, coordinated**)

The verb is pronounced /koʊɔrdᵊneɪt/. The noun is pronounced /koʊɔrdᵊnət/.

動詞は /koʊɔrdᵊneɪt/ と発音される. 名詞は /koʊɔrdᵊnət/ と発音される.

1 V-T 他動詞 If you **coordinate** an activity, you organize the various people and things involved in it. 調整する, 取りまとめる □*Government officials visited the earthquake zone on Thursday morning to coordinate the relief effort.* 政府の役人が木曜日の午前に救援活動の調整のために地震地帯を視察しました. ● **co|or|di|nated** ADJ 形容詞 調整した, 協調した □*Coalition forces were planning a coordinated effort to attack the drug trade.* 多国籍軍は麻薬取引を攻撃する協調作戦を計画していました. □*...a well-coordinated surprise attack.* うまく協調した奇襲攻撃. ● **co|or|di|na|tor** (**coordinators**) N-COUNT 可算名詞 調整役 □*...the party's campaign coordinator, Mr. Peter Mandelson.*

C

党の選挙活動調整役であるピーター・マンデルソン氏 **2** V-T 他動詞 If you **coordinate** the different parts of your body, you make them work together efficiently to perform particular movements. (体の各部を) 協調させて動かす ❑ *You need to coordinate legs, arms, and breathing for the front crawl.* クロールで泳ぐには脚, 腕, 呼吸を協調させなければならない. **3** V-RECIP 相互動詞 If you **coordinate** clothes or furnishings that are used together, or if they **coordinate**, they are similar in some way and look nice together. (服・家具などを) コーディネートする, (服・家具などを) 合わせる ❑ *She'll show you how to coordinate pattern and colors.* 彼女があなたに柄と色の合わせ方をお見せします. ❑ *Tie it with fabric bows that coordinate with other furnishings.* それを他の服飾品と合う生地でちょう結びをしなさい. **4** N-COUNT 可算名詞 The **coordinates** of a point on a map or graph are the two sets of numbers or letters that you need in order to find that point. 座標, (緯度・経度などによる) 位置 [TECHNICAL 技術的] ❑ *Can you give me your coordinates?* あなたの地図上の位置をお知らせください.

Thesaurus *coordinate* また次を参照:

v. direct, manage, organize **1**

---

co|or|di|na|tion /koʊˈɔrd³neɪʃⁿn/ **1** N-UNCOUNT 不可算名詞 **Coordination** means organizing the activities of two or more groups so that they work together efficiently and know what the others are doing. 協調, 連携 ❑ *...the lack of coordination between the civilian and military authorities.* 文民当局と軍当局の間の協調性の欠落 ❑ *...the coordination of economic policy.* 経済政策の調整 ● PHRASE 句 If you do something **in coordination with** someone else, you both organize your activities so that you work together efficiently. 一と協調して **2** N-UNCOUNT 不可算名詞 **Coordination** is the ability to use the different parts of your body efficiently. (体の各部の) 同調 ❑ *...clumsiness and lack of coordination.* 不器用さと体の同調作用の欠落

cop /kɒp/ (cops, copping, copped) N-COUNT 可算名詞 A **cop** is a policeman or policewoman. お巡り, 警官 [INFORMAL くだけた] ❑ *Frank didn't like having the cops know where to find him.* フランクはお巡りに居所がばれるのがいやだった.

▶ **cop out** PHRASAL VERB 句動詞 If you say that someone **is copping out**, you mean that they are avoiding doing something they should do. 責任逃れをする [INFORMAL くだけた] ❑ *The soldiers' families accused the government of copping out.* 兵士たちの家族は政府を責任逃れのかどで非難した.

▶ **cop to** PHRASAL VERB 句動詞 If you **cop to** something bad or wrong that you have done, you admit that you have done it. 白状する [AM 米国英語, INFORMAL くだけた] ❑ *I left, but you told me to. I'd appreciate it if you'd cop to that.* 私は立ち去ったけど, あなたがそうしろと言ったからですよ. そのことを認めてくれるとありがたいわ.

cope /koʊp/ (copes, coping, coped) **1** V-I 自動詞 If you **cope with** a problem or task, you deal with it successfully. うまく対処する, 切り抜ける ❑ *It was amazing how my mother coped with bringing up three children on less than thirty dollars a week.* 母が週30ドル足らずで3人の子供を無事に育てたのは驚くべきことだった. **2** V-I 自動詞 If you have to **cope with** an unpleasant situation, you have to accept it or bear it. 対処する ❑ *Never before has the industry had to cope with war and recession at the same time.* これまでに産業界が戦争と不況に同時に対処しなければならないようなことは決してなかった. **3** V-I 自動詞 If a machine or a system can **cope with** something, it is large enough or complex enough to deal with it satisfactorily. (機会・システムなどが) 処理する ❑ *A giant washing machine copes with the mountain of laundry created by their nine boys and five girls.* 巨大な洗濯機のおかげで9人の男の子と5人の女の子が出す山のような洗濯物を処理できる.

Word Partnership *cope* は次の語句と使われる:

ADV. **how to** cope **1 2**
V. **learn to** cope, **manage to** cope **1 2**
ADJ. **unable to** cope **1** – **3**
N. **ability to** cope **1** – **3**
  cope **with loss 2**

---

co|pi|ous /koʊpiəs/ ADJ 形容詞 A **copious** amount of something is a large amount of it. 大量の ❑ *I went out for dinner last night and drank copious amounts of red wine.* 私は昨夜夕食に出かけて, 大量の赤ワインを飲んだ. ● co|pi|ous|ly ADV 副詞 ❑ *The victims were bleeding copiously.* 被害者たちは血をおびただしく流していた.

cop|per /kɒpər/ (coppers) **1** N-UNCOUNT 不可算名詞 **Copper** is reddish brown metal that is used to make things such as coins and electrical wires. 銅 ❑ *Chile is the world's largest producer of copper.* チリが世界最大の銅生産国だ. **2** ADJ 形容詞 **Copper** is sometimes used to describe things that are reddish-brown in color. 赤褐色の, 銅色の [LITERARY 文語的] ❑ *His hair has reverted back to its original copper hue.* 彼の髪は元の赤褐色に戻った.
→ see **metal, mineral, pan, plumbing**

copy /kɒpi/ (copies, copying, copied) **1** N-COUNT 可算名詞 If you make a **copy of** something, you produce something that looks like the original thing. コピー, 複写 ❑ *The reporter apparently obtained a copy of Steve's resignation letter.* その記者はスティーブの辞表のコピーを入手していたようだ. **2** N-COUNT 可算名詞 A **copy** of a book, newspaper, or CD is one of many that are exactly the same. (本・新聞・CDなど) 冊, 部, 枚 ❑ *I bought a copy of "USA Today" from a street-corner machine.* 私は街頭の自動販売機で『USA トゥディー』を買った. **3** V-T 他動詞 If you **copy** something, you produce something that looks like the original thing. 複製する ❑ *...lawsuits against companies who have unlawfully copied computer programs.* 不法にコンピュータープログラムを複製した会社に対する訴訟 ❑ *He copied the chart from a book.* 彼は図を本から写した. **4** V-T/V-I 他動詞/自動詞 If you **copy**, or **copy** a piece of writing, you write it again exactly. 書き写す [他動詞/自動詞] ❑ *He copied the data into a notebook.* 彼はそのデータをノートに書き写した. ❑ *We're copying from textbooks because we don't have enough to go round.* 私たちは教科書から写しているのは, 全員に行き渡るだけないからだ. ● PHRASAL VERB 句動詞 **Copy out** means the same as **copy**. 書き写す ❑ *He wrote the title on the blackboard, then copied out the text, sentence by sentence.* 彼は題名を黒板に書き, そして本文を1文ずつ書き写した. **5** V-T 他動詞 If you **copy** a letter, document, or e-mail to someone, you send them a copy of a letter or document that you have sent to someone else. 写しを送る ❑ *He fired off a letter and copied it to the president.* 彼は手紙を急送し, 大統領にも写しを送った. **6** V-T 他動詞 If you **copy** someone's answer, you look at what that person has written and write the same thing yourself, in order to cheat in a test or exam. カンニングする ❑ *He would allow John slyly to copy his answers to impossibly difficult algebra questions.* 彼は途方もなく難解な代数の問題の答えをジョンにこっそり書き写させてやったものだ. **7** V-T 他動詞 If you **copy** a person or what they do, you try to do what they do or try to be like them, usually because you admire them or what they have done. まねをする, 模倣する ❑ *Children can be seen to copy the behavior of others whom they admire or identify with.* 子供は尊敬する人や共感する人のふるまいをまねるのが見られる. ❑ *He can claim to have been defeated by opponents copying his own tactics.* 彼は自身の作戦を相手が模倣したために敗れたと主張できる. **8** → see also **hard copy**
→ see Word Web: **copy**
→ see **clone**

▶ **copy in** PHRASAL VERB 句動詞 If you **copy** someone **in on** something, you send them a copy of something you have written to someone else. 写しを送る [BRIT 英国英語]

Thesaurus *copy* また次を参照:

N. likeness, photocopy, replica, reprint; (*ant.*) master, original **1**
V. replicate, reproduce; (*ant.*) originate **3**
  imitate, mimic **7**

---

copy|right /kɒpiraɪt/ (copyrights) N-VAR 可変性名詞 If someone has the **copyright** on a piece of writing or music, it is illegal to reproduce or perform it without their permission. 著作権 ❑ *Who owns the copyright on this movie?* この映画の著作権は誰が所有していますか?

Word Web copy

Making **copies** used to be difficult. Typists used sheets of carbon **paper** to make **multiple** copies. But the process was messy and the copies weren't very clear. Architects made photographic **blueprints**. But it was complicated and expensive. Modern **photocopiers** are completely different. You place your **document** on the glass and press a button. A bright light helps transfer the **image** from the paper onto a drum. Toner is spread over the drum. It sticks only to the image on the drum, not the blank spaces. A sheet of paper then passes over the drum and picks up the image.

C

Picture Dictionary

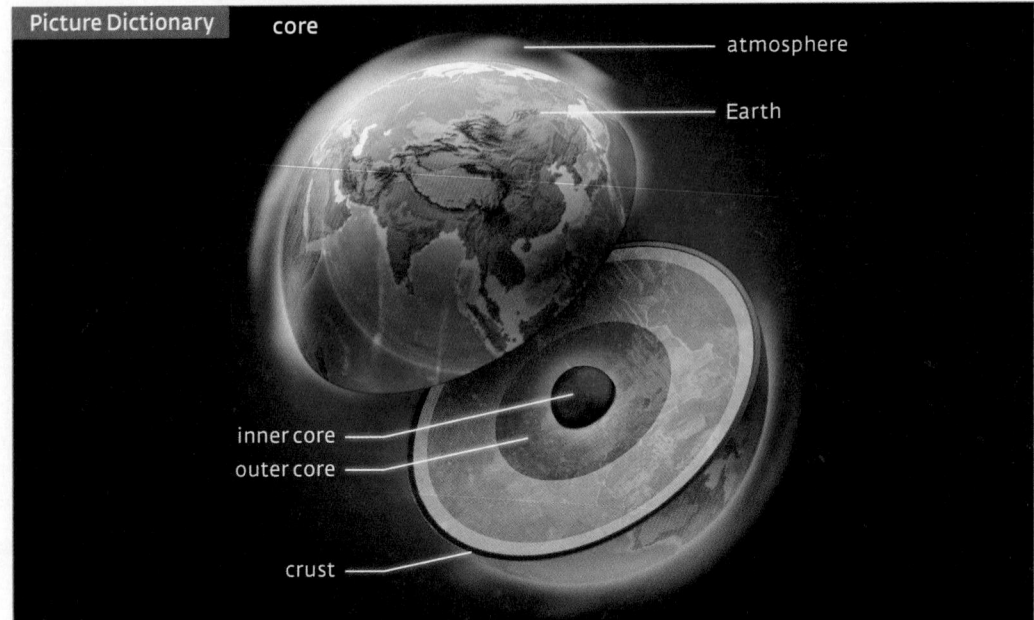

core

atmosphere

Earth

inner core

outer core

crust

cor|al /kɔrəl/ (corals) **1** N-VAR 可変性名詞 **Coral** is a hard substance formed from the bones of very small sea animals. It is often used to make jewelry. サンゴ ❑ *The women have elaborate necklaces of turquoise and pink coral.* その女性たちはトルコ石とピンク色のサンゴで作られた凝ったネックレスをしている. **2** N-COUNT 可算名詞 **Corals** are very small sea animals. サンゴ虫 ❑ *The seas around Bermuda are full of colorful corals and fantastic fish.* バミューダ周辺の海には色鮮やかなサンゴや素晴らしい魚で一杯だ. **3** COLOR 色彩語 Something that is **coral** is dark orangey-pink in color. サンゴ色 ❑ *...coral lipstick.* サンゴ色の口紅

cord /kɔrd/ (cords) **1** N-VAR 可変性名詞 **Cord** is strong, thick string. ひも, 綱 ❑ *The door had been tied shut with a length of nylon cord.* そのドアは長いナイロンのひもで縛られ閉まっていた. **2** N-VAR 可変性名詞 **Cord** is wire covered in rubber or plastic which connects electrical equipment to an electricity supply. コード ❑ *...electrical cord.* 電気コード ❑ *...an extension cord.* 延長コード → see **nervous system, rope**

cor|dial /kɔrdʒəl/ ADJ 形容詞 **Cordial** means friendly. 友好的な, 心の温かい [FORMAL 形式ばった] ❑ *He had never known him to be so chatty and cordial.* 彼がそれほどおしゃべりで心の温かい人だとは知らなかった. ● **cor|di|al|ly** ADV 副詞 [ADV with v] 心から ❑ *They all greeted me very cordially and were eager to talk about the new project.* 彼らは皆とても温かく私を迎えてくれ, 新しい企画についてしきり話したがった.

cor|don /kɔrdᵊn/ (cordons, cordoning, cordoned) N-COUNT 可算名詞 A **cordon** is a line or ring of police, soldiers, or vehicles preventing people from entering or leaving an area. 非常線 ❑ *Police formed a cordon between the two crowds.* 警察は2つの群衆の間に非常線を張った. ▶ **cordon off** PHRASAL VERB 句動詞 If police or soldiers **cordon off** an area, they prevent people from entering or leaving an area. 非常線を張る ❑ *Police cordoned off part of the city center.* 警察は市の中心部の一部に非常線を張った. ❑ *The police cordoned everything off.* 警察は全面的に交通遮断した.

core /kɔr/ (cores, coring, cored) **1** N-COUNT 可算名詞 The **core** of a fruit is the central part of it that contains seeds. (果物の) しん ❑ *Someone threw an apple core.* だれかがリンゴのしんを投げた. **2** N-COUNT 可算名詞 The **core** of an object, building, or city is the central part of it. (物・建物・町などの) 中心, 中心部 [usu with poss] ❑ *...the Earth's core.* 地球の中心核 **3** V-T 他動詞 If you **core** a fruit, you remove its core. (果物の) しんを取る ❑ *...machines for peeling and coring apples.* リンゴの皮をむきしんを取る機械 **4** N-SING 単数名詞 The **core of** something such as a problem or an issue is the part of it that has to be understood or accepted before the whole thing can be understood or dealt with. (問題・争点などの) 核心 ❑ *...the ability to get straight to the core of a problem.* 問題の核心をつかむ能力 **5** ADJ 形容詞 A **core** team or a **core** group is a group of people who do the main part of a job or piece of work. Other people may also help, but only for limited periods of time. 中核と

なる (チーム・団体など) ❑ *We already have our core team in place.* 我々はすでに中核チームの準備が整っている. **6** ADJ 形容詞 In a school or college, **core** subjects are a group of subjects that have to be studied. (科目が) 必修の ❑ *The core subjects are English, mathematics and science.* 必修科目は英語, 数学, 理科だ. ❑ *I'm not opposed to a core curriculum in principle, but I think requiring a foreign language is unrealistic.* 私は原則的には必修カリキュラムに反対していないが, 外国語の義務化は非現実的だと思う. **7** N-SING 単数名詞 The **core** businesses or the **core** activities of a company or organization are their most important ones. (ビジネス・活動などの) 中核となる ❑ *The core activities of social workers were reorganized.* 社会福祉相談員の中心的活動が再編成された. → see Picture Dictionary: **core**

cork /kɔrk/ (corks) **1** N-UNCOUNT 不可算名詞 **Cork** is a soft, light substance which forms the bark of a type of Mediterranean tree. コルク ❑ *...cork floors.* コルク製の床 **2** N-COUNT 可算名詞 A **cork** is a piece of cork or plastic that is pushed into the opening of a bottle to close it. コルク栓 ❑ *He popped the cork and the champagne fizzed out over the bottle.* 彼がコルク栓をぽんと抜くと, シャンパンの泡が瓶から吹き出てきた.

cork|screw /kɔrkskru/ (corkscrews) N-COUNT 可算名詞 A **corkscrew** is a device for pulling corks out of bottles. コルク栓抜き

corn /kɔrn/ **1** N-UNCOUNT 不可算名詞 **Corn** is a tall plant which produces long vegetables covered with yellow seeds. It can also be used to refer to the yellow seeds. トウモロコシ ❑ *...rows of corn in an Iowa field.* アイオワ州の畑に育つトウモロコシの列 ❑ *We're having corn-on-the-cob for lunch.* 私たちは軸付きトウモロコシを昼食に食べている. **2** N-UNCOUNT 不可算名詞 **Corn** is used to refer to crops such as wheat and barley. It can also be used to refer to the seeds from these plants. 穀物 [BRIT 英国英語; AM **grain** 米国英語 **grain**] **3** → see also **popcorn, sweetcorn** → see **grain**

cor|ner /kɔrnər/ (corners, cornering, cornered) **1** N-COUNT 可算名詞 A **corner** is a point or an area where two or more edges, sides, or surfaces of something join. 角 ❑ *He saw the corner of a magazine sticking out from under the blanket.* 彼には雑誌の角が毛布の下から突き出ているのが見えた. **2** N-COUNT 可算名詞 The **corner** of a room, box, or similar space is the area inside it where its edges or walls meet. 隅 ❑ *...a card table in the corner of the living room.* 居

間の隅にあるトランプ台 ❑ *The ball hurtled into the far corner of the net.* ボールがネットの向こうの隅にビューンと入った. ❸ N-COUNT 可算名詞 The **corner of** your mouth or eye is the side of it. (口・目など の) 端 ❑ *She flicked a crumb off the corner of her mouth.* 口の端 からパンくずを払いのけた. ❹ N-COUNT 可算名詞 The **corner of** a street is the place where one of its sides ends as it joins another street. (通りの) 角 ❑ *She would spend the day hanging around street corners.* 彼女は町をうろうろしながら日を過ごしたものだ. ❑ *We can't have police officers on every corner.* 全ての街角に警官を配置すること はできません. ❺ N-COUNT 可算名詞 A **corner** is a bend in a road. 曲がり, カーブ ❑ *...a sharp corner.* 急カーブ ❻ N-COUNT 可算名詞 In soccer, hockey, and some other sports, a **corner** is a free shot or kick taken from the corner of the field. コーナーキック, コー ナーヒット ❑ *McPherson took the corner and James crashed his header off the crossbar and over the line.* マックファーソンがコーナーキック をし, ジェームズがヘディングシュートしてクロスバーをそらし, ゴールした. ❼ V-T 他動詞 If you **corner** a person or animal, you force them into a place they cannot escape from. 追い詰める ❑ *A police motorcycle chased his car twelve miles, and cornered him near Gainsborough.* 白バイが彼の車を12マイル追跡し, ゲインズバラ付近で 追い詰めた. ❽ V-T 他動詞 If you **corner** someone, you force them to speak to you when they have been trying to avoid you. 問い詰 める, 無理に話させる ❑ *Thomas managed to corner the young producer-director for an interview.* トマスは若いプロデューサ兼ディレクターの インタビューに何とかこぎつけた. ❾ V-T 他動詞 If a company or place **corners** an area of trade, they gain control over it so that no one else can have any success in that area. 独占する [BUSINESS 実 業] ❑ *Sony has cornered the market in chic-looking MP3 players.* ソニー 社はシックなデザインのMP3プレーヤーで市場を独占した. ❿ V-I 自 動詞 If a car, or the person driving it, **corners** in a particular way, the car goes around bends in roads in this way. カーブを曲がる ❑ *Peter drove jerkily, cornering too fast and fumbling the gears.* ピータ ーはカーブでスピードを出しすぎたり, 不器用なギアチェンジをした りでガタガタ運転した. ⓫ PHRASE 句 If you say that something is **around the corner**, you mean that it will happen very soon. もう すぐ ❑ *Economic recovery is just around the corner.* 景気回復はもう間 近である. ⓬ PHRASE 句 If you say that something is **around the corner**, you mean that it is very near. すぐ近くに ❑ *My new place is just around the corner.* 私の新しい住まいはすぐ近くだ. ⓭ PHRASE 句 If you **cut corners**, you do something quickly by doing it in a less thorough way than you should. 手抜きをする [DISAPPROVAL 不 賛成] ❑ *Take your time, don't cut corners, and follow instructions to the letter.* 時間をかけ, 手抜きをしないで, 文字通り指示に従いなさい.

Word Partnership　corner は次の語句と使われる:

ADJ.	**far** corner ❶ ❷ ❹
	sharp corner ❶ ❹ ❺ ❻
V.	**sit in a** corner ❷
	round/turn a corner ❷ ❹ ❺
PREP.	**in a** corner ❷
	around the corner ❷ ❹ ❺ ⓫
N.	corner **of a room** ❷
	street corner ❹ ❺

corner|stone /kɔrnərstoʊn/ (**cornerstones**) N-COUNT 可算名 詞 The **cornerstone of** something is the basic part of it on which its existence, success, or truth depends. 基礎 [FORMAL 形式ばっ た] ❑ *Research is the cornerstone of the profession.* 研究がその職業の 基盤である.

corny /kɔrni/ (**cornier, corniest**) ADJ 形容詞 If you describe something as **corny**, you mean that it is obvious or sentimental and not at all original. 古くさい, 感傷的な [DISAPPROVAL 不賛成] ❑ *I know it sounds corny, but I'm really not motivated by money.* 陳腐に 聞こえるだろうが, 私は本当に金に左右されないんだ. ❑ *...a corny slapstick movie.* 陳腐などたばた映画

coro|nary /kɔrənɛri/ (**coronaries**) ❶ ADJ 形容詞 **Coronary** means belonging or relating to the heart. 心臓の [MEDICAL 医 学の] [ADJ n] ❑ *If all the coronary arteries are free of significant obstructions, all parts of the heart will receive equal amounts of oxygen.* 全ての冠状動脈に問題になるような塞栓 (そくせん) がなければ, 心臓全 体に同量の酸素が行き渡る. ❷ N-COUNT 可算名詞 If someone has a **coronary**, they collapse because the flow of blood to their heart is blocked by a large lump of blood called a clot. 冠状動脈血栓症

coro|na|tion /kɔrəneɪʃ°n/ (**coronations**) N-COUNT 可算名詞 A **coronation** is the ceremony at which a king or queen is crowned. 戴冠 (たいかん) 式

coro|ner /kɔrənər/ (**coroners**) N-COUNT 可算名詞 A **coroner** is an official who is responsible for investigating the deaths of people who have died in a sudden, violent, or unusual way. 検死 官 ❑ *The coroner recorded a verdict of accidental death.* 検死官は事故死 という判定を記録した.

Corp. **Corp.** is a written abbreviation for **corporation**. corporationの略 [BUSINESS 実業] ❑ *...Sony Corp. of Japan.* 日本のソ

ニー (株)

Word Link　corp ≈ body : corporal, corpse, incorporate

cor|po|ral /kɔrpərəl, -prəl/ (**corporals**) N-COUNT; N-TITLE 可算 名詞, 称号名詞 A **corporal** is a noncommissioned officer in the army or United States Marines. 伍長 ❑ *The corporal shouted an order at the men.* 伍長は兵士たちに対して大声で命令を出した.

cor|po|ral pun|ish|ment N-UNCOUNT 不可算名詞 **Corporal punishment** is the punishment of people by hitting them. 体罰 ❑ *Corporal punishment in public schools is forbidden.* 公立学校における 体罰は禁じられている.

cor|po|rate /kɔrpərɪt, -prɪt/ ADJ 形容詞 **Corporate** means relating to business corporations or to a particular business corporation. 法人の, 会社の [BUSINESS 実業] [ADJ n] ❑ *...top U.S. corporate executives.* 米国のトップクラスの企業経営者 ❑ *...a corporate lawyer.* 会社の顧問弁護士

Word Partnership　corporate は次の語句と使われる:

N.	corporate **clients**, corporate **culture**, corporate **hospitality**, corporate **image**, corporate **lawyer**, corporate **sector**, corporate **structure**

cor|po|rate raid|er (**corporate raiders**) N-COUNT 可算名詞 A **corporate raider** is a person or organization that tries to take control of a company by buying a large number of its shares. 企 業乗っ取り屋 [BUSINESS 実業] ❑ *Your present company could be taken over by corporate raiders.* あなたの今の会社は企業乗っ取り屋に乗っ取 られかねない.

cor|po|ra|tion /kɔrpəreɪʃ°n/ (**corporations**) N-COUNT; N-IN-NAMES 可算名詞, 名称中の名詞 A **corporation** is a large business or company with special rights and powers. 法人, 会社 [BUSINESS 実業] ❑ *...multinational corporations.* 多国籍企業 ❑ *Many voters resented the power of big corporations.* 多くの有権者は大企業の 権力に憤慨していた.

cor|po|ra|tion tax N-UNCOUNT 不可算名詞 **Corporation tax** is a tax that companies have to pay on the profits they make. 法人 税 [BUSINESS 実業]

corps /kɔr/ (**corps**)

Corps is both the singular and the plural form.

Corps は単数形でも複数形でもある.

❶ N-COUNT; N-IN-NAMES 可算名詞, 名称中の名詞 A **corps** is a part of the army which has special duties. (特殊任務を持った) 部隊 ❑ *...the Army Medical Corps.* 陸軍医療隊 ❷ N-COUNT 可算名詞 The **Corps** is the United States Marine Corps. アメリカ海兵隊 [AM 米 国英語] ❑ *...seventy-five men, all combat veterans, all members of The Corps' most exclusive unit.* 全員が戦闘のヴェテラン兵士で, かつ全員が 海兵隊の最も選りすぐりの部隊の隊員である75人の男たち ❸ N-COUNT 可算名詞 A **corps** is a small group of people who do a special job. 団体 ❑ *...the diplomatic corps.* 外交団

corpse /kɔrps/ (**corpses**) N-COUNT 可算名詞 A **corpse** is a dead body, especially the body of a human being. (特に人間の) 死体 ❑ *Detectives placed the corpse in a body bag.* 刑事たちは死体を遺体袋 に入れた.

Word Link　rect ≈ right, straight : correct, rectangle, rectify

cor|rect /kərɛkt/ (**corrects, correcting, corrected**) ❶ ADJ 形容 詞 If something is **correct**, it is right and true. 正しい ❑ *The correct answers can be found at the bottom of page 8.* 正解は8ページの下部にあ る. ❑ *The following information was correct at time of going to press.* 下 記の情報は印刷時点では正しいものであった. ● **cor|rect|ly** 副詞 [ADV with v] 正しく ❑ *Did I pronounce your name correctly?* 私はあなた の名前を正しく発音したでしょうか. ● **cor|rect|ness** N-UNCOUNT 不 可算名詞 正確さ ❑ *Ask the investor to check the correctness of what he has written.* その投資家に彼が書いた内容が正しいかどうかを確認する ように頼みなさい. ❷ ADJ 形容詞 [v-link ADJ] If someone is **correct**, what they have said or thought is true. 正しい [FORMAL 形式ば った] ❑ *You are absolutely correct. The leaves are from a bay tree.* 全く そのとおりです. これは月桂樹の葉です. ❸ ADJ 形容詞 The **correct** thing or method is the thing or method that is required or is most suitable in a particular situation. 適切な [ADJ n] ❑ *The use of the correct materials was crucial.* 適切な材料の使用は極めて重大であった. ❑ *White was in no doubt the referee made the correct decision.* レフェリ ーが適切な判断を下したことをホワイトは疑わなかった. ● **cor|rect|ly** ADV 副詞 [ADV with v] 適切に ❑ *If correctly executed, this shot will give them a better chance of getting the ball close to the hole.* このショ ットをきちんとやれば, 彼らがボールをホールに近づける可能性が より高いだろう. ❹ ADJ 形容詞 If you say that someone is **correct in** doing something, you approve of their action. 当を得た ❑ *You are perfectly correct in trying to steer your mother toward increased independence.* 君が母親をより子離れするよう仕向けているのは全く当 を得たことだ. ● **cor|rect|ly** ADV 副詞 [ADV with cl] 正しく ❑ *I think*

the police commission acted correctly. 警察の委員会は適切な行動をしたと私は思う. **5** ADJ 形容詞 If a person or their behavior is **correct**, their behavior is in accordance with social or other rules. 礼儀正しい，品行方正な □ *He was very polite and very correct.* 彼は非常に丁寧で，非常に礼儀正しい. ● **cor|rect|ly** ADV 副詞 [ADV with v] 礼儀正しく □ *She began speaking politely, even correctly.* 彼女は丁寧に，いやそれどころか礼儀正しく話し始めた. ● **cor|rect|ness** N-UNCOUNT 不可算名詞 礼儀正しさ □ *...his stiff-legged gait and formal correctness.* 彼のこわばった歩き方とかしこまった礼儀正しさ **6** V-T 他動詞 If you **correct** a problem, mistake, or fault, you do something which puts it right. 直す □ *He may need surgery to correct the problem.* 彼の障害を矯正するには外科手術が必要かもしれない. ● **cor|rec|tion** /kərˈekʃən/ (**corrections**) N-VAR 可変性名詞 訂正 □ *...legislation to require the correction of factual errors.* 事実誤認の訂正を命じる法律 **7** V-T 他動詞 If you **correct** someone, you say something which you think is more accurate or appropriate than what they have just said. 誤りを指摘する □ *"Actually, that isn't what happened,"* *George corrects me.* 「実は，実際に起こったことはそれとは違う」とジョージは私の誤りを指摘する. **8** V-T 他動詞 When someone **corrects** a piece of writing, they look at it and mark the mistakes in it. 添削する □ *It took an extraordinary effort to focus on preparing his classes or correcting his students' work.* 彼が授業の準備と生徒の作文の添削に集中するには異常な努力を要した.

Thesaurus **correct** また次を参照:

ADJ.	accurate, legitimate, precise, right, true; (ant.) false, inaccurate, incorrect, wrong **1**
V.	fix, rectify, repair; (ant.) damage, hurt **6**

Word Partnership **correct** は次の語句と使われる:

N.	correct **answer**, correct **response** **1** **2**
	correct **a situation** **6**
	correct **a mistake** **6** **8**
	correct **someone** **7**

cor|rec|tion /kərˈekʃən/ (**corrections**) **1** N-COUNT 可算名詞 **Corrections** are marks or comments made on a piece of work, especially school work, which indicate where there are mistakes and what are the right answers. 訂正，添削 □ *In a group, compare your corrections to Exercise 2A.* グループ内で，演習問題2Aに対する訂正を比較しなさい. **2** N-UNCOUNT 不可算名詞 **Correction** is the punishment of criminals. 罰 [mainly AM 主に米国英語] □ *...jails and other parts of the correction system.* 刑務所およびその他の矯正施設 **3** → see also **correct**

cor|rec|tive /kərˈektɪv/ (**correctives**) **1** ADJ 形容詞 **Corrective** measures or techniques are intended to put right something that is wrong. 矯正的な □ *Scientific institutions have been reluctant to take corrective action.* 科学の学術機関はこれまで是正措置を取りたがらなかった. **2** N-COUNT 可算名詞 If something is a **corrective to** a particular view or account, it gives a more accurate or fairer picture than there would have been without it. 矯正策 [FORMAL 形式ばった] □ *...a useful corrective to the mistaken view that all psychologists are behaviorists.* 精神分析医すべてが行動主義者であるという誤った見方に対する有益な矯正策

Word Link **cor ≈ with** : **cor**relate, **cor**respond, **cor**roborate

cor|re|late /kɔrəleɪt/ (**correlates, correlating, correlated**) **1** V-RECIP 相互動詞 If one thing **correlates with** another, there is a close similarity or connection between them, often because one thing causes the other. You can also say that two things **correlate**. 相関する [FORMAL 形式ばった] □ *Obesity correlates with increased risk for hypertension and stroke.* 肥満は高血圧および発作のリスクの上昇と相関関係がある. □ *The political opinions of spouses correlate more closely than their heights.* 配偶者間では，身長よりも政見がいっそう密接な相関関係がある. **2** V-T 他動詞 If you **correlate** things, you work out the way in which they are connected or the way they influence each other. 相関させる [FORMAL 形式ばった] □ *Attempts to correlate specific language functions with particular parts of the brain have not advanced very far.* 特定の言語機能を脳の特定部分と関連付ける試みはあまり進展していない.

cor|re|la|tion /kɔrəleɪʃən/ (**correlations**) N-COUNT 可算名詞 A **correlation between** things is a connection or link between them. 相関 [FORMAL 形式ばった] □ *...the correlation between smoking and disease.* 喫煙と疾病の相関関係

Word Partnership **correlation** は次の語句と使われる:

V.	**find a** correlation
ADJ.	**direct** correlation, **negative** correlation, **significant** correlation, **strong** correlation

cor|re|spond /kɔrɪspɒnd/ (**corresponds, corresponding, corresponded**) **1** V-RECIP 相互動詞 If one thing **corresponds to**

another, there is a close similarity or connection between them. You can also say that two things **correspond**. 相当する，対応する □ *Racegoers will be given a number which will correspond to a horse running in a race.* 競馬のファンはレースで走る馬に対応する番号を与えられる. □ *The two maps of the Rockies correspond closely.* これら2枚のロッキー山脈の地図はよく一致している. ● **cor|re|spond|ing** ADJ 形容詞 [ADJ n] 相当する □ *The rise in interest rates was not reflected in a corresponding rise in the dollar.* 金利の上昇はそれに相当するドルの上昇に反映されなかった. **2** V-RECIP 相互動詞 If you **correspond with** someone, you write letters to them. You can also say that two people **correspond**. 文通する □ *She still corresponds with friends she met in Majorca nine years ago.* 彼女は9年前にマヨルカ島で会った友人たちといまだに文通している.

cor|re|spond|ence /kɔrɪspɒndəns/ (**correspondences**) **1** N-UNCOUNT 不可算名詞 **Correspondence** is the act of writing letters to someone. 文通 [also "a" N, oft N "with" n] □ *The judges' decision is final and no correspondence will be entered into.* 裁判官の判決は最終的であり，いかなる通信連絡もできないであろう. **2** N-UNCOUNT 不可算名詞 Someone's **correspondence** is the letters that they receive or send. 書状 □ *He always replied to his correspondence.* 彼は手紙には常に返事を書いた. **3** N-COUNT 可算名詞 If there is a **correspondence** between two things, there is a close similarity or connection between them. 一致 □ *In African languages there is a close correspondence between sounds and letters.* アフリカの言語では音声と文字は密接に対応している.

cor|re|spond|ence course (**correspondence courses**) N-COUNT 可算名詞 A **correspondence course** is a course in which you study at home, receiving your work by mail and sending it back by mail. 通信教育 □ *I took a correspondence course in computing.* 私はコンピューティングの通信講座を取った.

cor|re|spond|ent /kɔrɪspɒndənt/ (**correspondents**) N-COUNT 可算名詞 A **correspondent** is a newspaper or television journalist, especially one who specializes in a particular type of news. 特派員 □ *As our Diplomatic Correspondent Mark Brayne reports, the president was given a sympathetic hearing.* 我が社の外交特派員であるマーク・ブレインの報告によると，大統領は同情的な発言の機会を与えられた.

cor|re|spond|ing|ly /kɔrɪspɒndɪŋli/ ADV 副詞 You use **correspondingly** when describing a situation which is closely connected with one you have just mentioned or is similar to it. 相応して，一致して □ *As his political stature has shrunk, he has grown correspondingly more dependent on the army.* 彼は政治的威信が下がるにつれて，それに相応してますます軍に頼るようになった.

cor|ri|dor /kɔrɪdər, -dɔr/ (**corridors**) **1** N-COUNT 可算名詞 A **corridor** is a long passage in a building, with doors and rooms on one or both sides. 廊下 [mainly BRIT 主に英国英語] □ *There were doors on both sides of the corridor.* 廊下の両側に扉があった. **2** N-COUNT 可算名詞 A **corridor** is a strip of land that connects one country to another or gives it a route to the sea through another country. 回廊地帯 □ *East Prussia and the rest of Germany were separated, in 1919, by the Polish corridor.* 東プロシアとドイツの他の地域は，1919年にポーランド回廊で分離された. **3** N-COUNT 可算名詞 A **corridor** is an area of land between 2 large cities. 回廊地帯 □ *...the Northeast corridor.* 北東部回廊線

cor|robo|rate /kərɒbəreɪt/ (**corroborates, corroborating, corroborated**) V-T 他動詞 To **corroborate** something that has been said or reported means to provide evidence or information that supports it. 確証を与える [FORMAL 形式ばった] □ *I had access to a wide range of documents which corroborated the story.* 私はその話を確証する広範な文書を入手することができた. ● **cor|robo|ra|tion** /kərɒbəreɪʃən/ N-UNCOUNT 不可算名詞 確証 □ *He could not get a single witness to establish independent corroboration of his version of the accident.* 彼は事故についての彼の言い分を独自に裏付けられる証人を1人として得ることができなかった.

cor|rode /kəroʊd/ (**corrodes, corroding, corroded**) V-T/V-I 他動詞/自動詞 If metal or stone **corrodes**, or **is corroded**, it is gradually destroyed by a chemical or by rust. 腐食する [他動詞] 腐食させる [自動詞] □ *He has devised a process for making gold wires which neither corrode nor oxidize.* 彼は腐食も酸化もしない金線を製造する方法を考案した. □ *Engineers found the structure had been corroded by moisture.* 技師たちはその建造物が湿気によって侵食されていることを発見した. ● **cor|rod|ed** ADJ 形容詞 腐食した □ *The investigators found that the underground pipes were badly corroded.* 調査員たちは埋設管がひどく腐食していることを発見した.

cor|ro|sion /kəroʊʒən/ N-UNCOUNT 不可算名詞 **Corrosion** is the damage that is caused when something is corroded. 腐食 □ *Zinc is used to protect other metals from corrosion.* 亜鉛は他の金属を腐食から保護するのに使われる.

cor|ru|gat|ed /kɔrəgeɪtɪd/ ADJ 形容詞 **Corrugated** metal or cardboard has been folded into a series of small parallel folds to make it stronger. 波形の □ *...a hut with a corrugated iron roof.* トタン屋根の小屋

cor|rupt /kərʌpt/ (**corrupts, corrupting, corrupted**) **1** ADJ 形容詞 Someone who is **corrupt** behaves in a way that is morally

wrong, especially by doing dishonest or illegal things in return for money or power. 腐敗した ❑ ...to save the nation from corrupt politicians of both parties. 両党の腐敗した政治家から国を救うために ◪ V-T/V-I 他動詞/自動詞 If someone **is corrupted by** something, it causes them to become dishonest and unjust and unable to be trusted. 腐敗させる [他動詞], 腐敗する [自動詞] ❑ It is sad to see a man so corrupted by the desire for money and power. 金と権力への欲望によってここまで腐敗した男を見るのは悲しい. ❑ Power tends to corrupt. 権力は腐敗しやすい. ◪ V-T 他動詞 To **corrupt** someone means to cause them to stop caring about moral standards. 堕落させる ❑ ...warning that television will corrupt us all. テレビは我々すべてを堕落させるだろうという警告

cor|rup|tion /kərʌpʃ°n/ N-UNCOUNT 不可算名詞 **Corruption** is dishonesty and illegal behavior by people in positions of authority or power. 汚職 ❑ The president faces 54 charges of corruption and tax evasion. 大統領は54件の汚職と脱税の容疑を受けている.

'cos /kəz, STRONG kʌz/ also COS CONJ **'Cos** is an informal way of saying **because**. becauseの省略形 [BRIT 英国英語, SPOKEN 口語] [AM cuz 米国英語 cuz]

cos|met|ic /kɒzmɛtɪk/ (**cosmetics**) ◪ N-COUNT 可算名詞 **Cosmetics** are substances such as lipstick or powder, which people put on their face to make themselves look more attractive. 化粧品 ❑ ...the cosmetics counter of a department store. 百貨店の化粧品カウンター ◪ ADJ 形容詞 If you describe measures or changes as **cosmetic**, you mean they improve the appearance of a situation or thing but do not change its basic nature, and you are usually implying that they are inadequate. 外見を取りつくろった [DISAPPROVAL 不賛成] ❑ It is a cosmetic measure which will do nothing to help the situation long term. それは長期的には状況を全く改善することのない, きれいごとの対策だ.
→ see **makeup**

cos|met|ic sur|gery N-UNCOUNT 不可算名詞 **Cosmetic surgery** is surgery done to make a person look more attractive. 美容外科 ❑ She is rumored to have had cosmetic surgery on nine different parts of her body. 彼女は体の9か所に美容整形をしているとうわさされている.

cos|mic /kɒzmɪk/ ◪ ADJ 形容詞 **Cosmic** means occurring in, or coming from, the part of space that lies outside Earth and its atmosphere. 宇宙の ❑ ...cosmic radiation. 宇宙線 ◪ ADJ 形容詞 **Cosmic** means belonging or relating to the universe. 宇宙的な ❑ ...the cosmic laws governing our world. 我々の世界を支配する宇宙の法則

cos|mo|poli|tan /kɒzməpɒlɪtən/ ◪ ADJ 形容詞 A **cosmopolitan** place or society is full of people from many different countries and cultures. 多民族が住む, 国際的な [APPROVAL 賛成] ❑ ...a cosmopolitan city. 国際都市 ◪ ADJ 形容詞 Someone who is **cosmopolitan** has had a lot of contact with people and things from many different countries and as a result is very open to different ideas and ways of doing things. 世界主義的な [APPROVAL 賛成] ❑ The family is rich, and extremely sophisticated and cosmopolitan. この家族は裕福であり, 非常に教養があり, かつ国際的である.

cos|mos /kɒzməs, -moʊs/ N-SING 単数名詞 **The cosmos** is the universe. 宇宙 [LITERARY 文語的] ❑ ...the natural laws of the cosmos. 宇宙の自然法則

cost /kɔst/ (**costs, costing**)

> The form **cost** is used in the present tense, and is also the past tense and participle, except for meaning ◪, where the form **costed** is used.
>
> **cost** 形は現在時制に使われ, ◪ の意味の場合以外は, 過去時制と分詞でもある. その意味の場合は **costed** 形が使われる.

◪ N-COUNT 可算名詞 The **cost** of something is the amount of money that is needed in order to buy, do, or make it. 費用, 原価 ❑ The cost of a loaf of bread has increased five-fold. パン1個の原価は5倍にまで膨れ上がった. ❑ In 1989 the price of coffee fell so low that in many countries it did not even cover the cost of production. 1989年にはコーヒーの価格が暴落し, 多くの国において生産原価さえも賄うことができなくなった. ◪ V-T 他動詞 If something **costs** a particular amount of money, you can buy, do, or make it for that amount. (費用が) かかる ❑ This course is limited to 12 people and costs $150. このコースは12人に限られており, 授業料は150ドルです. ❑ Painted walls look much more interesting and don't cost much. 壁にペンキを塗るとずっと面白く見えるし, 費用もあまりかからない. ◪ V-T 他動詞 When something that you plan to do or make **is costed**, the amount of money you need is calculated in advance. 費用を見積もる [usu passive] ❑ The building work has not been fully costed but runs into millions of dollars. その建築工事はまだ完全には見積もられていないが, 数百万ドルに上る. ◪ V-T 他動詞 If an event or mistake **costs** you something, you lose that thing as the result of it. 犠牲にさせる ❑ ...a six-year-old boy whose life was saved by an operation that cost him his sight. 手術で生命は取り留めたが視力を失った6歳の男の子 ◪ N-PLURAL 複数名詞 Your **costs** are the total amount of money that you must spend on

running your home or business. 経費 ❑ Costs have been cut by 30 to 50 percent. 出費は30から50パーセント削減された.

> Do not confuse **cost** and **costs**. The **cost** of something is the amount of money that you need in order to buy it, do it, or make it. ❑ ...the cost of the telephone call. ...the total cost was over a million pounds. The **costs** of a business or a home are the sums of money that have to be spent on running it. They include money spent on electricity, repairs, and taxes. ❑ ...attempts to cut costs and boost profits. See also note at **price**.

◪ N-PLURAL 複数名詞 If someone is ordered by a court of law to pay **costs**, they have to pay a sum of money toward the expenses of a court case they are involved in. 訴訟費用 ❑ He was jailed for 18 months and ordered to pay $550 costs. 彼は18か月投獄され, 訴訟費用550ドルを支払うよう命じられた. ◪ N-UNCOUNT 不可算名詞 If something is sold **at cost**, it is sold for the same price as it cost the seller to buy it. 仕入れ値段で ❑ ...a store that provided cigarettes and candy bars at cost. たばことキャンディーバーを仕入値段で売っていた店 ◪ N-SING 単数名詞 The **cost of** something is the loss, damage, or injury that is involved in trying to achieve it. 損失, 犠牲 ❑ In March Mr. Salinas shut down the city's oil refinery at a cost of $500 million and 5,000 jobs. 3月にサリナス氏は5億ドルと5千の職を犠牲にして, その市の石油精製所を閉鎖した. ◪ PHRASE 句 If you say that something must be avoided **at all costs**, you are emphasizing that it must not be allowed to happen under any circumstances. ぜひとも [EMPHASIS 強調] ❑ They told Jacques Delors a disastrous world trade war must be avoided at all costs. 彼らはジャック・デロアに, 悲惨な世界貿易戦争はなんとしても避けなければならないと言った. ◪ PHRASE 句 If you say that something must be done **at any cost**, you are emphasizing that it must be done, even if this requires a lot of effort or money. どんな犠牲を払っても [EMPHASIS 強調] ❑ This book is of such importance that it must be published at any cost. この本は非常に重要なものでどんなに費用がかかろうとも出版する必要がある.

> **Thesaurus**　　cost また次を参照:
>
> N.　　fee, price ◪
> 　　　harm, loss, sacrifice ◪

> **Word Partnership**　　cost は次の語句と使われる:
>
> ADJ.　　**additional** costs ◪
> N.　　cost **of living** ◪
> V.　　**cover the** cost, **cut** costs, **keep** costs **down** ◪ ◪ ◪

cost ac|count|ing N-UNCOUNT 不可算名詞 **Cost accounting** is the recording and analysis of all the various costs of running a business. 原価会計 [BUSINESS 実業] ❑ But full cost accounting will be introduced without delay. しかし, 完全な原価会計は遅滞なく取り入れられるだろう.

co|star /koʊstɑr/ (**costars, costarring, costarred**) ◪ N-COUNT 可算名詞 An actor's **costars** are the other actors who also have one of the main parts in a particular movie. 共演者 ❑ During the filming, Curtis fell in love with his costar, Christine Kaufmann. 映画撮影の間に, カーティスは共演者のクリスティーヌ・カウフマンと恋に落ちた. ◪ V-T 他動詞 If a movie **costars** particular actors, they have the main parts in it. 共演させる ❑ Produced by Oliver Stone, "Wild Palms" costars Dana Delaney, Jim Belushi and Angie Dickinson. オリバー・ストーン制作の『野生のしゅろ』ではダナ・デラニー, ジム・ベルーシおよびアンジー・ディッキンソンが共演している.

cost-effective ADJ 形容詞 Something that is **cost-effective** saves or makes a lot of money in comparison with the costs involved. 費用効果が大きい ❑ The bank must be run in a cost-effective way. 銀行は費用効果の大きい方法で経営する必要がある. ● **cost-effectively** ADV 副詞 費用効果よく ❑ The management tries to produce the magazine as cost-effectively as possible. 経営陣はその雑誌をできる限り低コストで制作しようとする. ● **cost-effectiveness** N-UNCOUNT 不可算名詞 費用効果 ❑ A report has raised doubts about the cost-effectiveness of the proposals. ある報告書がそれらの提案の費用効果に関して疑念を提起した.

cost|ly /kɔstli/ (**costlier, costliest**) ADJ 形容詞 If you say that something is **costly**, you mean that it costs a lot of money, often more than you would want to pay. 高価な ❑ Having professionally made curtains can be costly, so why not make your own? プロが作ったカーテンは高くつくだろうから, 自分独自のものを作ってはどうだろうか.

cost of liv|ing N-SING 単数名詞 The **cost of living** is the average amount of money that people in a particular place need in order to be able to afford basic food, housing, and clothing. 生計費 ❑ The cost of living has increased dramatically. 生計費は大幅に増加した.

cost-plus ADJ 形容詞 A **cost-plus** basis for a contract for work to be done is one in which the buyer agrees to pay the seller or contractor all the cost plus a profit. コストプラス方式の [ADJ n] ❑ All vessels were to be built on a cost-plus basis. 全船舶はコストプラス

Word Web   cotton

Some historians believe that **cotton** was first used in Egypt around 12,000 BC. Pieces of **fabric** containing a mixture of cotton and fur have been found in Mexico. They date back to about 5000 BC. Today's cotton **crop** in the U.S. totals about 20 billion dollars a year. The **textile industry** uses most of this cotton to make things like **denim** clothing, T-shirts, and bed sheets. However, many other products contain some cotton. For example, cotton fiber is used to make coffee filters, tents, stationery, and even U.S. currency.

方式で建造される予定だった.

cos|tume /kɒstum/ (**costumes**) **1** N-VAR 可変性名詞 An actor's or performer's **costume** is the set of clothes they wear while they are performing. 衣裳 ❑ *Even from a distance, the effect of his fox costume was stunning.* 彼のキツネの衣裳の効果は遠くからでもとても見事だった. ❑ *The performers, in costume and makeup, were walking up and down backstage.* 衣裳を着てメーキャップをした役者たちが舞台裏を行ったり来たりしていた. **2** N-UNCOUNT 不可算名詞 The clothes worn by people at a particular time in history, or in a particular country, are referred to as a particular type of **costume**. (時代・国などに特有の) 服装 ❑ ...*men and women in eighteenth-century costume.* 18世紀の服装をした男女 **3** ADJ 形容詞 A **costume** drama is one which is set in the past and in which the actors wear the type of clothes that were worn in that period. 時代衣装を身につけた [ADJ n] ❑ ...*a lavish costume drama set in Ireland and the U.S. in the 1890s.* 1890代のアイルランドとアメリカを舞台にした豪華な時代劇
→ see **theater**

cosy /kouzi/ → see **cozy**

cot /kɒt/ (**cots**) **1** N-COUNT 可算名詞 A **cot** is a narrow bed, usually made from canvas fitted over a frame which can be folded up. (カンバスを張った) 簡易寝台 [AM 米国英語] **2** N-COUNT 可算名詞 A **cot** is a bed for a baby. 小児用ベッド [BRIT 英国英語; AM 米国英語 **crib**]

cot|tage /kɒtɪdʒ/ (**cottages**) N-COUNT; N-IN-NAMES 可算名詞, 名称中の名詞 A **cottage** is a small house, usually in the country. 田舎家 ❑ *They used to have a cottage in N.W. Scotland.* 彼らは以前スコットランド北西部に小さな家を持っていた.

cot|tage in|dus|try (**cottage industries**) N-COUNT 可算名詞 A **cottage industry** is a small business that is run from someone's home, especially one that involves a craft such as knitting or pottery. 家内工業 [BUSINESS 実業] ❑ *Bookbinding is largely a cottage industry.* 製本は大部分家内工業で行われる.

cot|ton /kɒtⁿn/ (**cottons**) **1** N-MASS 質量名詞 **Cotton** is a type of cloth made from soft fibers from a particular plant. 綿布 ❑ ...*a cotton shirt.* 木綿のシャツ **2** N-UNCOUNT 不可算名詞 **Cotton** is a plant which is grown in warm countries and which produces soft fibers used in making cotton cloth. 綿 ❑ ...*a large cotton plantation in Tennessee.* テネシー州の大規模な綿花農園 **3** N-UNCOUNT 不可算名詞 **Cotton** or **absorbent cotton** is a soft mass of cotton, used especially for applying liquids or creams to your skin. 脱脂綿 [AM 米国英語] ❑ ...*cotton balls.* 綿ボール **4** N-MASS 質量名詞 **Cotton** is thread that is used for sewing, especially thread that is made from cotton. 綿糸 [BRIT 英国英語; AM 米国英語 **thread**]
→ see **Word Web: cotton**

cot|ton can|dy N-UNCOUNT 不可算名詞 **Cotton candy** is a large pink or white mass of sugar threads that is eaten from a stick. It is sold at fairs or other outdoor events. 綿菓子 [AM 米国英語]

cot|ton wool N-UNCOUNT 不可算名詞 **Cotton wool** is a soft mass of cotton, used especially for applying liquids or creams to your skin. 脱脂綿 ❑

couch /kaʊtʃ/ (**couches**) **1** N-COUNT 可算名詞 A **couch** is a long, comfortable seat for two or three people. ソファー **2** N-COUNT 可算名詞 A **couch** is a narrow bed which patients lie on while they are being treated by a psychoanalyst. (精神分析を受ける患者の) 寝台 ❑ *Between films he often winds up spending every single morning on his psychiatrist's couch.* 映画制作の合間, 彼は往々にして精神科医の寝台で毎朝を過ごす結果になる.

cough /kɔf/ (**coughs, coughing, coughed**) **1** V-I 自動詞 When you **cough**, you force air out of your throat with a sudden, harsh noise. You often cough when you are ill, or when you are nervous or want to attract someone's attention. せきをする ❑ *Graham began to cough violently.* グラハムは激しくせき込み始めた. ● N-COUNT 可算名詞 **Cough** is also a noun. せき ❑ *Coughs and sneezes spread infections much faster in a warm atmosphere.* 暖かい空気ではせきとくしゃみが伝染病をいっそう速く広める. ● **cough|ing** N-UNCOUNT 不可算名詞 せきこみ ❑ *He was then overcome by a terrible fit of coughing.* 彼はその時ひどいせきの発作に襲われた. **2** V-T 他動詞 If you **cough**

blood or mucus, it comes up out of your throat or mouth when you **cough**. せきをして吐き出す ❑ *I started coughing blood so they transferred me to a hospital.* 私がせきをして血を吐き始めたので, 彼らは私を病院に送った. ● PHRASAL VERB 句動詞 **Cough up** means the same as **cough**. せきをして吐き出す ❑ *On the chilly seas, Keats became feverish, continually coughing up blood.* 冷えびえとした海上で, キーツは発熱して, 喀血し続けた. **3** N-COUNT 可算名詞 A **cough** is an illness in which you cough often and your chest or throat hurts. せきの出る病気 ❑ *I had a persistent cough for over a month.* 私は1か月以上もしつこいせきに悩まされた.
→ see **illness**

▶ **cough up** PHRASAL VERB 句動詞 If you **cough up** an amount of money, you pay or spend that amount, usually when you would prefer not to. しぶしぶ支払う ❑ *I'll have to cough up $10,000 a year for tuition.* 私は授業料を年1万ドルをいやでも支払わねばならないだろう. → see also **cough 2**

could /kəd, STRONG kʊd/

Could is a modal verb. It is used with the base form of a verb. **Could** is sometimes considered to be the past form of **can**, but in this dictionary the two words are dealt with separately.

Could は法動詞であり, 動詞の原型とともに用いられる. **Could** は時々 **can** の過去形であると考えられているが, 本辞書では両語は別々に取り扱われている.

1 MODAL 法動詞 You use **could** to indicate that someone had the ability to do something. You use **could not** or **couldn't** to say that someone was unable to do something. することができた ❑ *I could see that something was terribly wrong.* 私は何かがとても間違っていることがわかった. ❑ *When I left school at 16, I couldn't read or write.* 16歳で学校を出たとき, 私は読むことも書くこともできなかった. **2** MODAL 法動詞 You use **could** to indicate that something sometimes happened. あり得た ❑ *Though he had a temper and could be nasty, it never lasted.* 彼は怒りっぽくて, 意地悪になることもあったが, それが長続きすることは決してなかった. **3** MODAL 法動詞 You use **could have** to indicate that something was a possibility in the past, although it did not actually happen. 可能性があった ❑ *He could have made a fortune as a lawyer.* 彼は弁護士として富を成すことができただろうに. ❑ *You could have been killed!* 君は殺されていたかも知れないんだぞ. **4** MODAL 法動詞 You use **could** to indicate that something is possibly true, or that it may possibly happen. かもしれない ❑ *Doctors told him the disease could have been caused by years of working in smokey clubs.* 病気はたばこの煙が立ち込めるクラブで長年にわたって働いたせいかもしれないと医師は告げた. ❑ *An improvement in living standards could be years away.* 生活水準の改善は何年も先かもしれない. **5** MODAL 法動詞 You use **could not** or **couldn't** to indicate that it is not possible that something is true. ありえない ❑ *They argued all the time and thought it couldn't be good for the baby.* 彼らは常に言い争いをしていたが, それが赤ちゃんにとって良いはずはないと思った. ❑ *Anne couldn't be expected to understand the situation.* アンが状況を理解することは期待できないでしょう. **6** MODAL 法動詞 You use **could** to talk about a possibility, ability, or opportunity that depends on other conditions. (条件が合えば) 可能性がある ❑ *Their hope was that a new and better East Germany could be born.* 彼らはより良い新生東ドイツの誕生を望んでいた. **7** MODAL 法動詞 You use **could** when you are saying that one thing or situation resembles another. —しているみたいだ ❑ *The charming characters she draws look like they could have walked out of the 1920s.* 彼女が描くチャーミングな人物は, あたかも1920年代から飛び出てきたかのようだ. **8** MODAL 法動詞 You use **could**, or **couldn't** in questions, when you are making offers and suggestions. しませんか ❑ *I could call the local doctor.* 地元の医者を呼びましょうか. ❑ *You could look for a career abroad where environmental jobs are better paid and more secure.* 環境保護の仕事がもっと給料がよくて, より安定している海外で職を探したらいかがですか. ❑ *Couldn't we call a special meeting?* 臨時会議を招集しましょうか. **9** MODAL 法動詞 You use **could** in questions when you are making a polite request or asking for permission to do something. Speakers sometimes use **couldn't** instead of "could" to show that they realize that their request may be refused. してもよいでしょうか [POLITENESS 丁寧

さ] ❑*Could I stay tonight?* 今夜泊まってもよいでしょうか。 ❑*He asked if he could have a cup of coffee.* 彼はコーヒーを1杯いただけませんかと尋ねた。 ❑*Couldn't I watch you do it?* あなたがそれをするのを見ていてもよいでしょうか。

Can, **could**, and **be able to** are all used to talk about a person's ability to do something. They are followed by the infinitive form of a verb. You use **can** or a present form of **be able to** to refer to the present, although **can** is more common. ❑*They can all read and write…The snake is able to catch small mammals.* You use **could** or a past form of **be able to** to refer to the past, and "will" or "shall" with **be able to** to refer to the future. **Be able to** is used if you want refer to doing something at a particular time. ❑*After treatment he was able to return to work.* **Can** and **could** are used to talk about possibility. **Could** refers to a particular occasion and **can** to more general situations. ❑*Many jobs could be lost…Too much salt can be harmful.* When talking about the past, you use **could have** and a past participle. ❑*It could have been much worse.* You also use **can** for the present and **could** for the past to talk about rules or what people are allowed to do. ❑*They can leave at any time.* Note that when making requests either **can** or **could** may be used. ❑*Can I have a drink?… Could we put the fire on?* However, **could** is always used for suggestions. ❑*You could phone her and ask.*

---

10 MODAL 法助詞 You use **could** to say emphatically that someone ought to do the thing mentioned, especially when you are annoyed because they have not done it. You use **why couldn't** in questions to express your surprise or annoyance that someone has not done something. してもよさそうなものだ [EMPHASIS 強調] ❑*We've come to see you, so you could at least stand and greet us properly.* 私たちはあなたに会いに来たのですから、少なくとも立ち上がって、きちんと挨拶してくださってもよいのではないですか。 ❑*Why couldn't she have said something?* どうして彼女は何も言わなかったのですか。 **11** MODAL 法動詞 You use **could** when you are expressing strong feelings about something by saying that you feel as if you want to do the thing mentioned, although you do not do it. できるならーしたい [EMPHASIS 強調] ❑*I could kill you! I swear I could!* できるならあなたを殺してやりたい。それは断言するわ。 ❑*"Welcome back" was all they said. I could have kissed them!* 彼らは「ようこそお帰り」としか言わなかった。私はどんなに彼らにキスしたことか。 **12** MODAL 法動詞 You use **could** after "if" when talking about something that you do not have the ability or opportunity to do, but which you are imagining in order to consider what the likely consequences might be. できるなら ❑*If I could afford it, I'd have four television sets.* 私にお金があったらテレビを4台買いたい。 **13** MODAL 法動詞 You use **could not** or **couldn't** with comparatives to emphasize that someone or something has as much as is possible of a particular quality. For example, if you say "I couldn't be happier," you mean that you are extremely happy. 最高である [EMPHASIS 強調] ❑*The rest of the players are great and I couldn't be happier.* 他の選手はみんなすばらしいので、私はこんなにうれしいことはない。 **14** MODAL 法動詞 In speech, you use **how could** in questions to emphasize that you feel strongly about something bad that has happened. どうしてーできたのか [EMPHASIS 強調] ❑*How could you allow him to do something like that?* どうして彼にそんなことをさせたのか。 ❑*How could I have been so stupid?* どうして私はあんなばかなことをしてしまったのか。 **15** **could do with** → see **do**

couldn't /kʊdˀnt/ **Couldn't** is the usual spoken form of "could not." could not の短縮形

could've /kʊdəv/ **Could've** is the usual spoken form of "could have," when "have" is an auxiliary verb. could have の短縮形

coun|cil /kaʊnsˀl/ (councils) **1** N-COUNT-COLL; N-IN-NAMES 集合可算名詞、名称中の名詞 A **council** is a group of people who are elected to govern a local area such as a city. 地方議会 ❑*The city council has voted almost unanimously in favor.* 市議会はほとんど満場一致で賛成に投票した。 **2** N-COUNT-COLL 集合可算名詞 **Council** is used in the names of some organizations. 評議会 ❑*…the National Council for Civil Liberties.* 市民的自由に関する全国評議会 ❑*…the Arts Council.* 芸術評議会 **3** N-COUNT-COLL 集合可算名詞 In some organizations, the **council** is the group of people that controls or governs it. 評議員会 ❑*The permanent council of the Organization of American States meets today here in Washington.* 米州機構の常設評議員会が本日ここワシントンで開かれる。 **4** N-COUNT 可算名詞 A **council** is a specially organized, formal meeting that is attended by a particular group of people. 会議 ❑*President Najibullah said he would call a grand council of all Afghans.* ナジブラ大統領は、全アフガニスタン人の大会議を招集すると言った。

coun|ci|lor /kaʊnsələr/ (councilors) N-COUNT; N-TITLE 可算名詞、称号名詞 A **councilor** is a member of a local council. (地方議会の) 議員 ❑*…Councilor Michael Poulter.* マイケル・ポウルター議員

coun|sel /kaʊnsˀl/ (counsels, counseling or counselling, counseled or counselled) **1** N-UNCOUNT 不可算名詞 **Counsel** is advice. 助言 [FORMAL 形式ばった] ❑*He had always been able to count on her wise counsel.* 彼はいつも彼女の賢明な忠告を当てにすることが

できた。 **2** V-T 他動詞 If you **counsel** someone **to** take a course of action, or if you **counsel** a course of action, you advise that course of action. 忠告する、勧める [FORMAL 形式ばった] ❑*My advisers counseled me to do nothing.* 私の助言者は私に何もしないように忠告した。 **3** V-T 他動詞 If you **counsel** people, you give them advice about their problems. 助言する ❑*…a psychologist who counsels people with eating disorders.* 摂食障害に悩む患者に助言を与える心理学者 **4** N-COUNT 可算名詞 Someone's **counsel** is the lawyer who gives them advice on a legal case and speaks on their behalf in court. 弁護士 ❑*Singleton's counsel said after the trial that he would appeal.* 裁判の後でシングルトンの弁護士は上訴すると言った。

coun|sel|ing /kaʊnsəlɪŋ/ also **counselling** N-UNCOUNT 不可算名詞 **Counseling** is advice which a therapist or other expert gives to someone about a particular problem. カウンセリング ❑*She will need medical help and counseling to overcome the tragedy.* 彼女が悲劇的な事件を乗り越えるためには医療とカウンセリングが必要であろう。

coun|se|lor /kaʊnsələr/ (counselors) also **counsellor** **1** N-COUNT 可算名詞 A **counselor** is a person whose job is to give advice to people who need it, especially advice on their personal problems. カウンセラー ❑*Children who have suffered like this should see a counselor experienced in bereavement.* このようなひどい経験をした子供たちは、死別問題の経験を積んだカウンセラーにかかるべきだ。 **2** N-COUNT 可算名詞 A **counselor** is a young person who supervises children at a summer camp. (キャンプ生活の) 指導員 ❑*Hicks worked with children as a camp counselor.* ヒックスはキャンプ生活の指導員として子供たちの手助けをした。

count /kaʊnt/ (counts, counting, counted) **1** V-I 自動詞 When you **count**, you say all the numbers one after another up to a particular number. 数を数える ❑*He was counting slowly under his breath.* 彼は声をひそめてゆっくりと数を数えていた。 **2** V-T 他動詞 If you **count** all the things in a group, you add them up in order to find how many there are. 数える ❑*I counted the money. It was more than five hundred dollars.* 私はその金を数えた。500ドル以上あった。 ❑*I counted 34 wild goats grazing.* 草を食べている野生のやぎが合計34頭いた。 ● PHRASAL VERB 句動詞 **Count up** means the same as **count**. 数え上げる ❑*Couldn't we just count up our ballots and bring them to the courthouse?* ただ票を数え上げて郡庁舎に持っていくことはできないのですか。 **3** V-I 自動詞 If something or someone **counts for** something or **counts**, they are important or valuable. 重要である ❑*Surely it doesn't matter where charities get their money from: what counts is what they do with it.* もちろん慈善事業の資金源は問題ではない。重要なのはその使用目的である。 **4** V-T-V/V-I 他動詞/自動詞 If something **counts** or **is counted** as a particular thing, it is regarded as being that thing, especially in particular circumstances or under particular rules. みなす [他動詞]、みなされる [自動詞] ❑*No one agrees on what counts as a desert.* 何が砂漠とみなされるかについてだれも意見が一致しない。 **5** V-T 他動詞 If you **count** something when you are making a calculation, you include it in that calculation. 勘定に入れる ❑*It's under 7 percent only because statistics don't count the people who aren't qualified to be in the work force.* 統計では労働人口に含められる資格のない人々は数えられないので、それはわずか7パーセント未満である。 **6** N-COUNT 可算名詞 A **count** is the action of counting a particular set of things, or the number that you get when you have counted them. 計算、集計 ❑*The final count in last month's referendum showed 56.7 per cent in favor.* 先月行われた住民投票の最終集計では、賛成が56.7パーセントを示した。 **7** N-COUNT 可算名詞 You use **count** when referring to the level or amount of something that someone or something has. 総計、総数 ❑*A glass or two of wine will not significantly add to the calorie count.* ワインの1、2杯でカロリー摂取量が著しく増えることはないだろう。 **8** N-COUNT 可算名詞 In law, a **count** is one of a number of charges brought against someone in court. 訴因 ❑*He was indicted by a grand jury on two counts of murder.* 彼は大陪審により2件の殺人罪で起訴された。 **9** N-COUNT; N-TITLE; N-VOC 可算名詞、称号名詞、呼格名詞 A **count** is a European nobleman. 伯爵 ❑*Her father was a Polish count.* 彼女の父親はポーランドの伯爵だった。 **10** PHRASE 句 If you **keep count of** a number of things, you note or keep a record of how many have occurred. If you **lose count of** a number of things, you cannot remember how many have occurred. 数を覚えている、数を忘れる ❑*The authorities say they are not able to keep count of the bodies still being found as bulldozers clear the rubble.* 当局は、死体は今もなお、ブルドーザーががれきを除去するにつれて発見されており、その数は数えられないと言う。

▶ **count against** PHRASAL VERB 句動詞 If something **counts against** you, it may cause you to be rejected or punished, or cause people to have a lower opinion of you. 不利となる ❑*He is highly regarded, but his youth might count against him.* 彼は高く評価されているが、彼の青年時代が彼にとって不利になる恐れがある。

▶ **count on** or **count upon** PHRASAL VERB 句動詞 If you **count on** something or **count upon** it, you expect it to happen and include it in your plans. 期待する、当てにする ❑*What they did not know was how much support they could count on from Democrats.* 民主党員からのどのくらいの支持を期待できるかについては、彼らは何もわ

からなかった. ② PHRASAL VERB 句動詞 If you **count on** someone or **count upon** them, you rely on them to support you or help you. 頼る ❑ *Don't count on Lillian.* リリアンを当てにするな.

▶ **count out** PHRASAL VERB 句動詞 If you **count out** a sum of money, you count the bills or coins as you put them in a pile one by one. 数えて出す ❑ *Mr. Rohmbauer counted out the money and put it in an envelope.* ロームバウアー氏は金を数えて出し, 封筒に入れた.

▶ **count up** → see **count 2**
▶ **count upon** → see **count on**
→ see **census**, **mathematics**, **zero**

count|able noun /kaʊntəbᵊl naʊn/ (**countable nouns**) N-COUNT 可算名詞 A **countable noun** is the same as a **count noun**. 可算名詞

count|down /kaʊntdaʊn/ N-SING 単数名詞 A **countdown** is the counting aloud of numbers in reverse order before something happens, especially before a spacecraft is launched. 秒読み [also no det] ❑ *The countdown has begun for the launch of the space shuttle.* スペースシャトル打ち上げの秒読みが開始された.

coun|te|nance /kaʊntɪnəns/ (**countenances, countenancing, countenanced**) ① V-T 他動詞 If someone will not **countenance** something, they do not agree with it and will not allow it to happen. 認める [FORMAL 形式ばった] [usu with brd-neg] ❑ *Jake would not countenance Janis's marrying while still a student.* ジェイクはジャニスが学生結婚することをどうしても認めようとしなかった. ② N-COUNT 可算名詞 Someone's **countenance** is their face. 顔つき [FORMAL 形式ばった]

coun|ter /kaʊntər/ (**counters, countering, countered**) ① N-COUNT 可算名詞 In a place such as a store or café, a **counter** is a long narrow table or flat surface at which customers are served. ター ❑ *...those guys we see working behind the counter at our local video rental store.* 地元のビデオレンタル店の店員として働いているのを見かける男たち ② N-COUNT 可算名詞 A **counter** is a mechanical or electronic device which keeps a count of something and displays the total. カウンター ❑ *The new answering machine has a call counter.* この新型留守番電話にはコールカウンターが搭載されている. ③ N-COUNT 可算名詞 A **counter** is a small, flat, round object used in board games. チップ ❑ *...a versatile book which provides boards and counters for fifteen different games.* 15種のゲーム用の盤とチップを備えた多目的な本 ④ V-T/V-I 他動詞/自動詞 If you do something to **counter** a particular action or process, you do something which has an opposite effect to it or makes it less effective. 逆らう, 押しとどめる ❑ *The leadership discussed a plan of economic measures to counter the effects of such a blockade.* 指導者たちはそのような封鎖の効果に対抗する経済的措置の計画を討議した. ❑ *Sears countered by filing an antitrust lawsuit.* シアーズ社は反トラスト訴訟を起こして対抗した. ⑤ N-SING 単数名詞 Something that is **a counter to** something else has an opposite effect to it or makes it less effective. 逆, 対抗力 ❑ *...NATO's traditional role as a counter to the military might of the Warsaw pact.* ワルシャワ条約機構の軍事力に対するNATOの伝統的な役割 ⑥ PHRASE 句 If a medicine can be bought **over the counter**, you do not need a prescription to buy it. 処方せんなしで ❑ *Are you taking any other medicines whether on prescription or bought over the counter?* 処方せんの有無にかかわらず, 他の薬を何か服用していますか. ❑ *...over-the-counter medicines.* 市販薬 ⑦ PHRASE 句 **Over-the-counter** shares are bought and sold directly rather than on a stock exchange. 店頭で [BUSINESS 実業] ❑ *In national over-the-counter trading yesterday, Clarcor shares tumbled $35.625 to close at $35.625.* 昨日の国内店頭取引で, クラコア社の株が6.125ドル急落し, 35.625ドルの終値で取り引きされた.

Word Partnership *counter* は次の語句と使われる:

PREP.	**behind the** counter, **on the** counter ①
	over the counter ⑥
N.	counter **an argument** ④

---

counter|act /kaʊntərækt/ (**counteracts, counteracting, counteracted**) V-T 他動詞 To **counteract** something means to reduce its effect by doing something that produces an opposite effect. 打ち消す ❑ *My husband has to take several pills to counteract high blood pressure.* 私の夫は高血圧を下げるために錠剤を数種飲まなければならない.

counter|at|tack /kaʊntərətæk/ (**counterattacks, counterattacking, counterattacked**) V-I 自動詞 If you **counterattack**, you attack someone who has attacked you. 逆襲する ❑ *The security forces counterattacked the following day and quelled the unrest.* 治安部隊は翌日逆襲に出て騒乱を鎮圧した. ● N-COUNT 可算名詞 **Counterattack** is also a noun. 逆襲 ❑ *The army began its counterattack this morning.* 軍が今朝逆襲を開始した.

counter|clock|wise /kaʊntərklɒkwaɪz/ ADV 副詞 If something is moving **counterclockwise**, it is moving in the opposite direction to the direction in which the hands of a clock move. 時計の針と反対に [AM 米国英語] [ADV after v] ❑ *Rotate the*

head clockwise and counterclockwise. 頭を左右に回しなさい. ● ADJ 形容詞 **Counterclockwise** is also an adjective. 時計の針と反対の [ADJ n] ❑ *The dance moves in a counterclockwise direction.* ダンスは左回りの方向に進む.

counter|feit /kaʊntərfɪt/ (**counterfeits, counterfeiting, counterfeited**) ① ADJ 形容詞 **Counterfeit** money, goods, or documents are not genuine, but have been made to look exactly like genuine ones in order to deceive people. 偽造の ❑ *He admitted possessing and delivering counterfeit currency.* 彼は偽造通貨を所持し運んだことを認めた. ● N-COUNT 可算名詞 **Counterfeit** is also a noun. 偽造物 ❑ *Levi Strauss says counterfeits of the company's jeans are flooding Europe.* リーバイ・ストラウスは, 欧州ではリーバイスジーンズの模造品で溢れていると述べた. ② V-T 他動詞 If someone **counterfeits** something, they make a version of it that is not genuine but made to look genuine in order to deceive people. 偽造する ❑ *...the coins Davies is alleged to have counterfeited.* デイビスが偽造したとされる硬貨

counter|part /kaʊntərpɑrt/ (**counterparts**) N-COUNT 可算名詞 Someone's or something's **counterpart** is another person or thing that has a similar function or position in a different place. 相当する人, 相当する物 ❑ *As soon as he heard what was afoot, he telephoned his German and Italian counterparts to protest.* 何が起きているかを聞くや否や, 彼はドイツとイタリアの対応する人物に電話で抗議した.

counter|pro|duc|tive /kaʊntərprədʌktɪv/ ADJ 形容詞 Something that is **counterproductive** achieves the opposite result from the one that you want to achieve. 逆効果の ❑ *In practice, however, such an attitude is counterproductive.* しかしながら, こういった態度は実際には逆効果だ.

counter|top /kaʊntərtɒp/ (**countertops**) N-COUNT 可算名詞 A **countertop** is a flat surface in a kitchen which is easily cleaned and on which you can prepare food. 台所用カウンター [AM 米国英語] ❑ *She reached for a cloth and began scouring the countertop.* 彼女は手を伸ばして布を取り, 台所用カウンターをごしごし磨き始めた.

count|less /kaʊntlɪs/ ADJ 形容詞 **Countless** means very many. 無数の [ADJ n] ❑ *She brought joy to countless people through her music.* 彼女はその音楽によって無数の人たちに喜びをもたらした.

count noun (**count nouns**) N-COUNT 可算名詞 A **count noun** is a noun such as "bird," "chair," or "year" which has a singular and a plural form and is always used after a determiner in the singular. 可算名詞

coun|try /kʌntri/ (**countries**) ① N-COUNT 可算名詞 A **country** is one of the political units which the world is divided into, covering a particular area of land. 国 ❑ *Indonesia is the fifth most populous country in the world.* インドネシアは人口が世界で5番目に大きい国である. ❑ *...the boundary between the two countries.* 両国間の境界線

Country is the most usual word to use when you are talking about the major political units that the world is divided into. **State** is used when you are talking about politics or government institutions. ❑ *...the new German state created by the unification process...Italy's state-controlled telecommunications company.* **State** can also refer to a political unit within a particular country. ❑ *...the state of California.* **Nation** is often used when you are talking about a country's inhabitants, and their cultural or ethnic background. ❑ *Wales is a proud nation with its own traditions...A senior government spokesman will address the nation.* **Land** is a less precise and more literary word, which you can use, for example, to talk about the feelings you have for a particular country. ❑ *She was fascinated to learn about this strange land at the edge of Europe.*

---

② N-SING 単数名詞 The people who live in a particular country can be referred to as **the country**. 国民 ❑ *Finally the country got some much-needed good news.* 国民はようやく切望していた朗報を聞いた. ③ N-SING 単数名詞 The **country** consists of places such as farms, open fields, and villages which are away from towns and cities. 田舎 ❑ *...a healthy life in the country.* 田舎での健康的な生活 ❑ *She was cycling along a country road near Compigne.* コンピエーニュ付近の田舎道を自転車で走っていた. ④ N-UNCOUNT 不可算名詞 A particular kind of **country** is an area of land which has particular characteristics or is connected with a particular well-known person. 地域 ❑ *Varese Ligure is a small town in mountainous country east of Genoa.* ヴァレーゼ・リグレはジェノバの東にある山国にある小さな町だ. ⑤ N-UNCOUNT 不可算名詞 **Country** music is popular music from the southern United States. カントリー ❑ *For a long time I just wanted to play country music.* 長い間私のしたいことはカントリーミュージックを演奏することだけだった.
→ see Word Web: **country**

country|man /kʌntrimən/ (**countrymen**) ① N-COUNT 可算名詞 Your **countrymen** are people from your own country. 同国人 ❑ *He beat his fellow countryman, Andre Agassi, 6-4, 6-3, 6-2.* 彼は同国人のアンドレ・アガシを6-4, 6-3, 6-2で破った. ② N-COUNT 可算名詞

Word Web — country

The largest **country** in the world geographically is Russia. It has an area of 9.5 million square kilometres and a **population** of more than 142 million people. Russia is a federal state with a republican form of **government**. The government is based in Russia's **capital** city, Moscow.

One of the smallest countries in the world is Nauru. This tiny island **nation** in the South Pacific Ocean is 8.1 square kilometres in size. Many of Nauru's more than 13,000 **residents** live in Yaren, which is the largest city, but not the capital. The Republic of Nauru is the only nation in the world without an official capital.

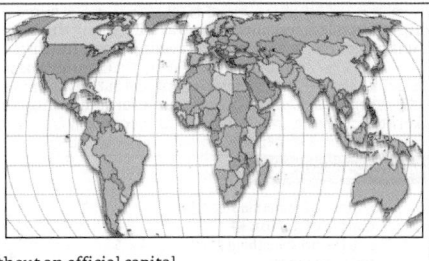

A **countryman** is a person who lives in the country rather than in a city or a town. 田舎者 ❑ *He had the red face of a countryman.* 彼は田舎者特有の赤ら顔をしていた.

country|side /kʌntrisaɪd/ N-UNCOUNT 不可算名詞 The **countryside** is land which is away from towns and cities. 田舎, 地方 ❑ *I've always loved the English countryside.* 私はいつも英国の田舎が大好きだった.
→ see **city**

> Do not confuse **countryside**, **scenery**, **landscape**, and **nature**.
> **Countryside** is land which is away from towns and cities.
> ❑ *...3,500 acres of mostly flat countryside.* With **landscape**, the emphasis is on the physical features of the land, while **scenery** includes everything you can see when you look out over an area of land. ❑ *...the landscape of steep woods and distant mountains. ... unattractive urban scenery.* **Nature** includes the landscape, the weather, animals, and plants. ❑ *These creatures roamed the Earth as the finest and rarest wonders of nature.*

coun|ty /kaʊnti/ (**counties**) N-COUNT 可算名詞 A **county** is a region of the U.S., Britain, or Ireland, which has its own local government. 郡, 州 ❑ *He arrived at the Palm Beach County courthouse with his mother.* 彼は母親と共にパームビーチ郡庁舎に到着した.

coup /ku/ (**coups**) ■ N-COUNT 可算名詞 When there is a **coup**, a group of people seize power in a country. クーデター ❑ *...a military coup.* 軍事クーデター ■ N-COUNT 可算名詞 A **coup** is an achievement which is thought to be especially good because it was very difficult. 大成功 ❑ *The sale is a big coup for the auction house.* オークション会社にとって, その販売は大成功である.

Word Partnership coup は次の語句と使われる:

N.	**coup attempt**, **leader of the** coup ■
V.	**plot a** coup, **support the** coup ■
ADJ.	**bloodless** coup, **military** coup ■ **big** coup ■

coup d'état /ku deɪtɑ/ (**coups d'état**) N-COUNT 名詞 When there is a **coup d'état**, a group of people seize power in a country. クーデター

cou|ple /kʌpᵊl/ (**couples, coupling, coupled**) ■ QUANT 数量詞 If you refer to a **couple of** people or things, you mean two or approximately two of them, although the exact number is not important or you are not sure of it. 2, 3の [QUANT "of" pl-n] ❑ *Across the street from me there are a couple of police officers standing guard.* 通りの向こう側では, 2, 3人の警官が見張りをしている. ❑ *I think the trouble will clear up in a couple of days.* 問題は2, 3日で解決されると思う. ● DET 限定詞 **Couple** is also a determiner in spoken American English, and is often used before "more" and "less." 2, 3の ❑ *...a couple weeks before the election.* 選挙の2, 3週間前 ● PRON 代名詞 **Couple** is also a pronoun. 2, 3人, 2, 3個 ❑ *I've got a couple that don't look too bad.* 私は結構いけるのを2, 3個持っている. ■ N-COUNT-COLL 集合可算名詞 A **couple** is two people who are married, living together, or having a sexual relationship. 夫婦, 恋人同士 ❑ *The couple have no children.* その夫婦には子供がいない. ❑ *Burglars ransacked an elderly couple's home.* 泥棒は老夫婦の家をくまなく探した. ■ N-COUNT-COLL 集合可算名詞 A **couple** is two people that you see together on a particular occasion or that have some association. カップル, 男女1組 ❑ *...as the four couples began the opening dance.* 4組のカップルが開幕のダンスを開始すると ■ V-T 他動詞 If you say that one thing produces a particular effect when it **is coupled with** another, you mean that the two things combine to produce that effect. 結びつける [usu passive] ❑ *...a problem that is coupled with lower demand for the machines themselves.* その機械の需要が下がったのと相まった問題

cou|pon /kupɒn, kyu-/ (**coupons**) ■ N-COUNT 可算名詞 A **coupon** is a piece of printed paper which allows you to pay less money than usual for a product, or to get it free. クーポン ❑ *...a money-saving coupon.* 金を節約するクーポン ■ N-COUNT 可算名詞 A **coupon** is a small form, for example, in a newspaper or magazine, which you send off to ask for information, to order something, or to enter a competition. 申込用紙, 請求券 ❑ *Mail this coupon with your check or money order.* 小切手または為替とともにこの申込用紙を郵送してください.

Word Link age ≈ state of, related to : courage, marriage, patronage

cour|age /kɜrɪdʒ/ ■ N-UNCOUNT 不可算名詞 **Courage** is the quality shown by someone who decides to do something difficult or dangerous, even though they may be afraid. 勇気 ❑ *General Lewis Mackenzie has impressed everyone with his authority and personal courage.* ルイス・マッケンジー将軍の威信と個人的勇気はすべての人に感銘を与えた. ■ to **pluck up the courage** → see **pluck**

Word Partnership courage は次の語句と使われる:

V.	courage **to do** *something*, **find the** courage, **have the** courage, **show** courage ■
ADJ.	**great** courage ■

cou|ra|geous /kəreɪdʒəs/ ADJ 形容詞 Someone who is **courageous** shows courage. 勇敢な ❑ *The children were very courageous.* 子供たちは大変勇敢だった.

cour|gette /kʊrʒɛt/ (**courgettes**) N-VAR 可変性名詞 **Courgettes** are long thin vegetables with dark green skin. ズッキーニ [BRIT 英国英語; AM zucchini 米国英語 **zucchini**]

cou|ri|er /kʊəriər, kɜr-/ (**couriers, couriering, couriered**) ■ N-COUNT 可算名詞 A **courier** is a person who is paid to take letters and packages direct from one place to another. 宅配便配達人 ❑ *...a motorcycle courier.* オートバイに乗った宅配便配達人 ■ V-T 他動詞 If you **courier** something somewhere, you send it there by courier. 宅配便で送る ❑ *I couriered it to Darren in New York.* 私はそれをニューヨークのダレンに宅配便で送った.

course /kɔrs/ (**courses**) ■ N-COUNT 可算名詞 **Course** is often used in the expression "of course," or instead of "of course" in informal spoken English. See **of course**. (of courseの形で) 当然; of course の省略形 ■ N-UNCOUNT 不可算名詞 The **course** of a vehicle, especially a ship or aircraft, is the route along which it is traveling. 進路 [also "a" N] ❑ *Aircraft can avoid each other by altering course to left or right.* 航空機は飛行方向を左右に変更することによりお互いを避けることができる. ■ N-COUNT 可算名詞 A **course of action** is an action or a series of actions that you can do in a particular situation. (行動の) 方針 ❑ *My best course of action was to help Gill by being sympathetic.* 私の取れる最善の方策は, 思いやりを持ってジルを助けることだった. ■ N-COUNT 可算名詞 A **course** is a series of lessons or lectures on a particular subject. コース, 科目 ❑ *...a course in business administration.* 経営学のコース ■ → see **correspondence course**, **refresher course** ■ N-COUNT 可算名詞 A **course of** medical treatment is a series of treatments that a doctor gives someone. ひと続き, クール ❑ *He had a course of antibiotics to kill the bacterium.* 彼はその細菌を殺す一連の抗生物質治療を受けた. ■ N-COUNT 可算名詞 A **course** is one part of a meal. (コース料理の) 1皿 ❑ *The lunch was excellent, especially the first course.* 昼食は特に最初の料理がすばらしかった. ■ N-COUNT 可算名詞 In sports, a **course** is an area of land where races are held or golf is played, or the land over which a race takes place. コース, 競馬場 ❑ *Only 12 seconds separated the first three riders on the course.* 競馬場でトップを走る3騎手の差はたった12秒だった. ■ N-COUNT 可算名詞 The **course** of a river is the channel along which it flows. 水路 ❑ *Romantic castles overlook the river's twisting course.* ロマンチックな城からその川の曲がりくねった流れが見渡せる. ■ **in due course** → see **due** ■ PHRASE 句 If something happens in the **course of** a particular period of time, it happens during that period of time. ～の過程で ❑ *In the course of the 1930s steel production approximately doubled.* 1930年代には鉄鋼生産量がおよそ2倍になった. ■ PHRASE 句 If you do something **as a matter of course**, you do it as part of your normal work or way of life. 当然のこととして ❑ *If police are carrying arms as a matter of course, then doesn't it encourage criminals to carry them?* 警察が当然のこととして武器を携行している

と，犯罪者の武器の携行が助長されないだろうか. **13 PHRASE** 句 If a ship or aircraft is **on course**, it is traveling along the correct route. If it is **off course**, it is no longer traveling along the correct route. 正しい進路を進んで，正しい進路から外れて ❑ *The ship was sent off course into shallow waters.* その船は航路を外れて浅い水域に入りこんだ. **14 PHRASE** 句 If you are **on course for** something, you are likely to achieve it. コースに乗って ❑ *The company is on course for profits of $20m.* その会社は2千万ドルの利益を達成しそうだ.

Word Partnership　　course は次の語句と使われる:

N.	course of *something* ② ③ ⑤
	course **of action** ③
	course on *something* ④
	golf course ⑦
ADJ.	full-time course ④
	main course ⑥

course book (**course books**) also **coursebook** N-COUNT 可算名詞 A **course book** is a textbook that students and teachers use as the basis of a course. 教科書

course work also **coursework** N-UNCOUNT 不可算名詞 **Course work** is work that students do during a course, rather than in exams, especially work that counts toward a student's final grade. コースワーク ❑ *Some 20 percent of grades are awarded for coursework.* コースワークは成績評価の約20％を占める.

court
❶ NOUN USES
❷ VERB USES

❶ court /kɔrt/ (**courts**) **1** N-COUNT 可算名詞 A **court** is a place where legal matters are decided by a judge and jury or by a magistrate. 裁判所 [oft in N, N n, also "in/at" N] ❑ *At this rate, we could find ourselves in the divorce courts!* こんな調子では，私たちは離婚裁判所で争うことになりかねないわ. ❑ *...a county court judge.* 郡裁判所の裁判官 **2** N-COUNT 可算名詞 You can refer to the people in a court, especially the judge, jury, or magistrates, as a **court**. 法廷 ❑ *A court at Tampa, Florida has convicted five officials on charges of handling millions of dollars earned from illegal drug deals.* フロリダ州タンパの法廷は，違法薬物取引で得た数百万ドルを処理した罪で公務員5人に有罪を宣告した. **3** N-COUNT 可算名詞 A **court** is an area in which you play a game such as tennis, basketball, badminton, or squash. コート [usu supp N, also "on/off" N] ❑ *The hotel has several tennis and squash courts.* そのホテルにはテニスやスカッシュのコートがいくつかある. **4** N-COUNT 可算名詞 The **court** of a king or queen is the place where he or she lives and carries out ceremonial and administrative duties. 宮廷 ❑ *She came to visit England, where she was presented at the court of James I.* 彼女は英国を訪問し，ジェームズ1世の宮廷で謁見（えっけん）を賜った. **5** PHRASE 句 If you **go to court** or **take** someone **to court**, you take legal action against them. 裁判ざたにする ❑ *They have received at least twenty thousand dollars each but went to court to demand more.* 彼らはそれぞれ少なくとも2万ドルを受け取っているが，それ以上を要求するために訴訟を起こした. **6** PHRASE 句 If a legal matter is decided or settled **out of court**, it is decided without legal action being taken in a court of law. 法廷外で ❑ *The Government is anxious to keep the whole case out of court.* 政府はしきりに事件全体を法廷外にとどめようとしている.
→ see park

Word Partnership　　court は次の語句と使われる:

| V. | appear in court, hold court ❶ **1** |
| | go to court ❶ **1** **5** |

❷ court /kɔrt/ (**courts, courting, courted**) **1** V-T 他動詞 To **court** a particular person, group, or country means to try to please them or improve your relations with them, often so that they will do something that you want them to do. 機嫌を伺う [JOURNALISM ジャーナリズム] ❑ *Both Democratic and Republican parties are courting former supporters of Ross Perot.* 民主党も共和党もロス・ペローのかつての支持者のご機嫌を伺っている. **2** V-T 他動詞 If you **court** something such as publicity or popularity, you try to attract it. 得ようと努める ❑ *Having spent a lifetime avidly courting publicity, Paul has suddenly become secretive.* ポールは貪欲に名声に努めて一生を送った後，突然口を閉ざしてしまった. **3** V-T 他動詞 If you **court** something unpleasant such as disaster or unpopularity, you act in a way that makes it likely to happen. 招く ❑ *If he thinks he can remain in power by force, he is courting disaster.* 力ずくで政権を維持できると思うなら，彼は災難を自ら招いていることになる. **4** V-RECIP 相互動詞 If you **are courting** someone of the opposite sex, you spend a lot of time with them, because you are intending to get married. You can also say that a man and a woman **are courting**. （結婚を前提に）交際する [OLD-FASHIONED 古風な] ❑ *I was courting Billy at 19 and married him when I was 21.* 私は19歳の時にはビリーと交際しており，21歳の時に彼と結婚した.

cour|teous /kɜrtiəs/ ADJ 形容詞 Someone who is **courteous** is polite and respectful to other people. 礼儀正しい ❑ *He was a kind and courteous man.* 彼は親切で礼儀正しい男だった. ● **cour|teous|ly** ADV 副詞 礼儀正しく ❑ *Then he nodded courteously to me and walked off to perform his unpleasant duty.* そして彼は私に丁重に会釈して，不愉快な任務を行うために立ち去った.

cour|tesy /kɜrtisi/ **1** N-UNCOUNT 不可算名詞 **Courtesy** is politeness, respect, and consideration for others. 礼儀 [FORMAL 形式ばった] ❑ *...a gentleman who behaves with the utmost courtesy towards ladies.* 女性に対しこの上ない礼儀を持ってふるまう紳士 **2** N-SING 単数名詞 If you refer to **the courtesy of** doing something, you are referring to a polite action. 丁重な行為 [FORMAL 形式ばった] ❑ *By extending the courtesy of a phone call to my clients, I was building a personal relationship with them.* 顧客に丁重な電話をかけることにより，私は彼らとの個人的関係を築いていた. **3** ADJ 形容詞 **Courtesy** is used to describe services that are provided free of charge by an organization to its customers, or to the general public. 優待の [ADJ n] ❑ *A courtesy shuttle bus operates between the hotel and the town.* 送迎シャトルバスがホテルと町の間を運行している. **4** ADJ 形容詞 A **courtesy** call or a **courtesy** visit is a formal visit that you pay someone as a way of showing them politeness or respect. 儀礼の ❑ *The president paid a courtesy call on Emperor Akihito.* 大統領は天皇陛下に儀礼訪問を行った. **5** PHRASE 句 If something is provided **courtesy of** someone or **by courtesy of** someone, they provide it. You often use this expression in order to thank them. 好意によって ❑ *The waitress brings over some congratulatory glasses of champagne, courtesy of the restaurant.* ウエイトレスが，レストランからのサービスで，お祝いのシャンペンを何杯か運んでくる.

court|house /kɔrthaʊs/ (**courthouses**) **1** N-COUNT 可算名詞 A **courthouse** is a building in which a court of law meets. 裁判所 [AM 米国英語] ❑ *The two were tried in the same courthouse at the same time, on separate floors.* その2人は同じ裁判所で同時に裁判にかけられた. **2** N-COUNT 可算名詞 A **courthouse** is a building used by the government of a county. 郡庁舎 [AM 米国英語] ❑ *They were married at the Los Angeles County Courthouse.* 彼らはロスアンゼルス郡庁舎で結婚した.

court|i|er /kɔrtiər/ (**courtiers**) N-COUNT 可算名詞 **Courtiers** were noblemen and women who spent a lot of time at the court of a king or queen. 廷臣

court mar|tial (**court martials, court martialing** or **court martialling, court martialed** or **court martialled**) also **court-martial**

Courts martial is also used as a plural form for the noun.

Courts martial は名詞の複数形としても使われる

1 N-VAR 可変性名詞 A **court martial** is a trial in a military court of a member of the armed forces who is charged with breaking a military law. 軍法会議 ❑ *He is due to face a court martial on drugs charges.* 彼は薬物容疑で軍法会議にかけられることになっている. **2** V-T 他動詞 If a member of the armed forces is **court martialed**, he or she is tried in a military court. 軍法会議にかける [usu passive] ❑ *I was court martialed and sentenced to six months in a military prison.* 私は軍法会議にかけられ，陸軍刑務所における懲役6ヶ月の判決を受けた.

court|room /kɔrtrum/ (**courtrooms**) N-COUNT 可算名詞 A **courtroom** is a room in which a legal court meets. 法廷

court|yard /kɔrtyɑrd/ (**courtyards**) N-COUNT 可算名詞 A **courtyard** is an open area of ground which is surrounded by buildings or walls. 中庭 ❑ *They walked together through the arch and into the cobbled courtyard.* 彼らは一緒に歩いてアーチをくぐって，丸石で舗装された中庭に入った.

cous|in /kʌzºn/ (**cousins**) N-COUNT 可算名詞 Your **cousin** is the child of your uncle or aunt. いとこ ❑ *My cousin Mark helped me to bring in the bags.* いとこのマークが私がバッグを運び入れるのを手伝ってくれた.

cove /koʊv/ (**coves**) N-COUNT; N-IN-NAMES 可算名詞，名称中の名詞 A **cove** is a part of a coast where the land curves inward so that the sea is partly enclosed. 入り江 ❑ *The house is situated on a hillside overlooking Fairview Cove.* その家はフェアビュー入り江が見渡せる丘の中腹に位置している.

cov|enant /kʌvənənt/ (**covenants**) **1** N-COUNT 可算名詞 A **covenant** is a formal written agreement between two or more people or groups of people which is recognized in law. 契約 ❑ *...the International Covenant on Civil and Political Rights.* 市民的および政治的権利に関する国際規約 **2** N-COUNT 可算名詞 A **covenant** is a formal written promise to pay a sum of money each year for a fixed period, especially to a charity. （寄付金などの）支払い契約書 [mainly BRIT 主に英国英語] [also "by" N] [AM usually **pledge** 米国英語では通常 **pledge**]

cover

❶ VERB USES
❷ NOUN USES

❶ cov|er /kʌvər/ (covers, covering, covered) **1** V-T 他動詞 If you **cover** something, you place something else over it in order to protect it, hide it, or close it. 覆う ❑ *Cover the casserole with a tight-fitting lid.* キャセロールをぴったりと閉まるふたで覆いなさい. ❑ *He whimpered and covered his face.* 彼はすすり泣いて顔を覆った. **2** V-T 他動詞 If one thing **covers** another, it has been placed over it in order to protect it, hide it, or close it. ふさぐ ❑ *His finger went up to touch the black patch which covered his left eye.* 彼は指を上げて左目を覆う黒い眼帯に触った. **3** V-T 他動詞 If one thing **covers** another, it forms a layer over its surface. かぶさる ❑ *The clouds had spread and covered the entire sky.* 雲は広がって空全体を覆っていた. **4** V-T 他動詞 To **cover** something **with** or **in** something else means to put a layer of the second thing over its surface. 覆いをする ❑ *The desk was covered with papers.* 机は書類だらけだった. **5** V-T 他動詞 If you **cover** a particular distance, you travel that distance. (ある距離を) 行く ❑ *It would not be easy to cover ten miles on that amount of gas.* あのガソリンの量で10マイルを走るのは容易ではないだろう. **6** V-T 他動詞 An insurance policy that **covers** a person or thing guarantees that money will be paid by the insurance company in relation to that person or thing. 保険をかける ❑ *Their insurer paid the $900 bill, even though the policy did not strictly cover it.* 彼らの保険会社は、保険では厳密にはカバーされていなかったけれども、900ドルの請求書を支払った. **7** V-T 他動詞 If a law **covers** a particular set of people, things, or situations, it applies to them. 対象とする ❑ *The law covers four categories of experiments.* その法律は4種類の実験に適用される. **8** V-T 他動詞 If you **cover** a particular topic, you discuss it in a lecture, course, or book. 取り扱う ❑ *Introduction to Chemistry aims to cover important topics in organic chemistry.* 化学入門では有機化学の重要な題目を扱うことを目的としている. **9** V-T 他動詞 If a sum of money **covers** something, it is enough to pay for it. まかなう ❑ *Send it to the address given with $2.50 to cover postage and administration.* 送料と処理費をまかなうために2.50ドルを添えて、それを所定の宛先に送りなさい. **10** V-I 自動詞 If you **cover** for someone who is doing something secret or illegal, you give false information or do not give all the information you have, in order to protect them. かばう ❑ *Why would she cover for someone who was trying to kill her?* 彼女は自分を殺そうとしていた者をどうしてかばうのか. **11** V-I 自動詞 If you **cover for** someone who is ill or away, you do their work for them while they are not there. 代わりをつとめる ❑ *She did not have enough nurses to cover for those who were sick.* 彼女には病気の看護師の代わりをする看護師が十分いなかった. **12** PHRASE 句 If you **cover your ass** or **cover your butt**, you do something in order to protect yourself, for example against criticism or against accusations of doing something wrong. 言い訳を用意する [INFORMAL, VULGAR くだけた、下品な]

▶ **cover up** **1** PHRASAL VERB 句動詞 If you **cover** something or someone **up**, you put something over them in order to protect or hide them. 覆う ❑ *He fell asleep in the front room so I covered him up with a duvet.* 彼は居間で眠ってしまったので、私は掛け布団をかけてあげた. **2** PHRASAL VERB 句動詞 If you **cover up** something that you do not want people to know about, you hide the truth about it. かばって隠す ❑ *He suspects there's a conspiracy to cover up the crime.* 彼はその犯罪を隠蔽 (いんぺい) する陰謀があるのではと疑っている. ❑ *They knew they had done terribly wrong and lied to cover it up.* 彼らは恐ろしくまずいことをしたのがわかっており、それを隠蔽するために嘘をついた. **3** → see also **cover-up**

Thesaurus   cover また次を参照:

V.   conceal, drape, hide, screen; (ant.) uncover ❶ **1** – **3**
     guard, insure, protect ❶ **6**

❷ cov|er /kʌvər/ (covers) **1** N-COUNT 可算名詞 A **cover** is something which is put over an object, usually in order to protect it. 覆い ❑ *...a sofa with washable covers.* 洗濯できるカバーをかけたソファー **2** N-COUNT 可算名詞 The **cover** of a book or a magazine is the outside part of it. 表紙 ❑ *...a small book with a green cover.* 緑の表紙の小さな本 **3** N-UNCOUNT 不可算名詞 **Cover** is protection from enemy attack that is provided for troops or ships carrying out a particular operation, for example, by aircraft. 援護 ❑ *They could not provide adequate air cover for ground operations.* 彼らは地上作戦のための十分な上空援護を送ることができなかった. **4** N-UNCOUNT 不可算名詞 **Cover** is trees, rocks, or other places where you shelter from the weather or from an attack, or hide from someone. 避難場所 ❑ *Charles lit the fuses and they ran for cover.* チャールズは導火線に着火し、彼らは避難所に走った. **5** N-UNCOUNT 不可算名詞 Insurance **cover** is a guarantee from an insurance company that money will be paid by them if it is needed. 保険の保障額 ❑ *Make sure that the firm's insurance cover is adequate.* その会社の保険保障が十分かどうかを確認すること. **6** N-COUNT 可算名詞 Something that is a **cover** for secret or illegal activities seems respectable or

normal, and is intended to hide the activities. 隠蔽 (いんぺい) するもの ❑ *He ran a construction company as a cover for drug dealing.* 彼は麻薬取引の隠れみのとして建設会社を運営した. **7** N-PLURAL 複数名詞 The **covers** on your bed are the things such as sheets and blankets that you have on top of you. 寝具 ❑ *She set her glass down and slid under the covers.* 彼女はグラスを置き、寝具にもぐりこんだ. **8** → see also **covering** **9** PHRASE 句 If you **take cover**, you shelter from gunfire, bombs, or the weather. 避難する ❑ *Shoppers took cover behind cars as the gunman fired.* 銃を持った男が発砲すると、買い物たちは自動車の後ろに隠れた. **10** PHRASE 句 If you do something **under cover of** a particular situation, you are able to do it without being noticed because of that situation. 隠れて ❑ *They move under cover of darkness.* 彼らは暗闇にまぎれて移動する.

Word Partnership	cover は次の語句と使われる:
N.	cover **your face** ❶ **1** **2**
PREP.	covered **in** *something* ❶ **4**
	under cover ❷ **10**
V.	**run for** cover ❷ **4**
	take cover ❷ **9**

cov|er|age /kʌvərɪdʒ/ N-UNCOUNT 不可算名詞 The **coverage** of something in the news is the reporting of it. 報道 ❑ *Now a special TV network gives live coverage of most races.* 今では専門のテレビ局がたいていのレースの実況放送を行っている.

cov|er|ing /kʌvərɪŋ/ (coverings) N-COUNT 可算名詞 A **covering** is a layer of something that protects or hides something else. 覆う物 ❑ *Leave a thin covering of fat.* 脂肪の薄い覆いを残しておきなさい.

cov|er|ing let|ter → see **cover letter**

cov|er let|ter (cover letters) N-COUNT 可算名詞 A **cover letter** is a letter that you send with a package or with another letter in order to provide extra information. 添え状 [AM 米国英語] ❑ *Your cover letter creates the employer's first impression of you.* 添え状はあなたについて雇い主がいだく第1印象を作り出します.

cov|ert /koʊvərt, kʌvərt/ ADJ 形容詞 **Covert** activities or situations are secret or hidden. 秘密の [FORMAL 形式ばった] ❑ *They have been supplying covert military aid to the rebels.* 彼らは反乱軍に秘密の軍事援助を行ってきた. ● **cov|ert|ly** ADV 副詞 密かに ❑ *They covertly observed Lauren, who was sitting between Ned and Algie at a nearby table.* 彼らは近くのテーブルでネッドとアルジーの間に座っていたローレンを密かに観察した.

cover-up (cover-ups) also **coverup** N-COUNT 可算名詞 A **cover-up** is an attempt to hide a crime or mistake. もみ消し ❑ *General Schwarzkopf denied there'd been any cover-up.* シュワルツコフ大将は、いかなるもみ消し工作の存在も否定した.

cov|et /kʌvɪt/ (covets, coveting, coveted) V-T 他動詞 If you **covet** something, you strongly want to have it for yourself. 切望する [FORMAL 形式ばった] ❑ *She coveted his job so openly that their conversations were tense.* 彼女があからさまに彼の仕事を欲しがったので、会話は緊張した.

cov|et|ed /kʌvɪtɪd/ ADJ 形容詞 You use **coveted** to describe something that very many people would like to have. 熱望された ❑ *Allan Little from Radio 4 took the coveted title of reporter of the year.* ラジオ4のアラン・リトルが、あこがれの年間最優秀リポーターの称号を手にした. ❑ *...one of sport's most coveted trophies.* 最も切望されているスポーツのトロフィーの1つ

cow /kaʊ/ (cows, cowing, cowed) **1** N-COUNT 可算名詞 A **cow** is a large female animal that is kept on farms for its milk. People sometimes refer to male and female animals of this species as **cows**. 雌牛 ❑ *He kept a few dairy cows.* 彼は乳牛を何頭か飼っていた. ❑ *Dad went out to milk the cows.* お父さんは牛の乳を搾りに出て行った. **2** N-COUNT 可算名詞 Some female animals, including elephants and whales, are called **cows**. 雌 ❑ *...a cow elephant.* 雌のゾウ **3** V-T 他動詞 If someone **is cowed**, they are made afraid, or made to behave in a particular way because they have been frightened or badly treated. 脅す [FORMAL 形式ばった] [usu passive] ❑ *The government, far from being cowed by these threats, vowed to continue its policy.* 政府は、これらの脅迫におびえるどころか、その政策の継続を誓っている. ● **cowed** ADJ 形容詞 脅えた ❑ *By this time she was so cowed by the beatings that she meekly obeyed.* このごろでは彼女はたたかれてひどく怯えていたので、おとなしく従った.

→ see **barn, dairy, meat**

cow|ard /kaʊərd/ (cowards) N-COUNT 可算名詞 If you call someone a **coward**, you disapprove of them because they are easily frightened and avoid dangerous or difficult situations. 臆病者 [DISAPPROVAL 不賛成] ❑ *She accused her husband of being a coward.* 彼女は夫を臆病者と非難した.

cow|ard|ice /kaʊərdɪs/ N-UNCOUNT 不可算名詞 **Cowardice** is cowardly behavior. 臆病 ❑ *He openly accused his opponents of cowardice.* 彼は公然と反対者たちを臆病だと非難した.

cow|ard|ly /ka͟ʊərdli/ ADJ 形容詞 If you describe someone as **cowardly**, you disapprove of them because they are easily frightened and avoid doing dangerous and difficult things. 憶病な [DISAPPROVAL 不賛成] ❑ I was too cowardly to complain. 私は憶病すぎて不満を言えなかった.

cow|boy /ka͟ʊbɔɪ/ (**cowboys**) ■ N-COUNT 可算名詞 A **cowboy** is a male character in a western. カウボーイ ❑ Boys used to play at cowboys and Indians. 男の子はカウボーイとインディアンになって遊んだものだ. ❷ N-COUNT 可算名詞 A **cowboy** is a man employed to look after cattle in North America, especially in former times. 牧童 ❑ In his twenties Roosevelt had sought work as a cowboy on a ranch in the Dakota Territory. 20代の頃, ルーズベルトはダコタ準州の牧場で牧童の仕事を探した.
→ see **horse**

coy /kɔ͟ɪ/ ■ ADJ 形容詞 A **coy** person is shy, or pretends to be shy, about love and sex. はにかみ屋の, 恥ずかしがるふりをする ❑ I was sickened by the way Carol charmed all the men by turning coy. 私はキャロルが純情ぶってあらゆる男の気をひくやり方にはうんざりした. ● **coy|ly** ADV 副詞 [ADV with v] はにかんで ❑ She smiled coyly at Algie as he took her hand and raised it to his lips. アルジーが彼女の手を取り自分の唇まで持ち上げたとき, 彼女ははにかんで彼に微笑んだ. ❷ ADJ 形容詞 If someone is being **coy**, they are unwilling to talk about something that they feel guilty or embarrassed about. 口が重い ❑ Mr. Alexander is not the slightest bit coy about his ambitions. アレクサンダー氏は自らの野心を語ることについて, まったくはばかるところがない. ● **coy|ly** ADV 副詞 [ADV with v] 重い口ぶりで ❑ The administration coyly refused to put a firm figure on the war's costs. 政府はその戦争の費用の確かな数字を示すことを遠慮がちに拒んだ.

cozy /ko͟ʊzi/ (**cozies, cozier, coziest**) ■ ADJ 形容詞 A house or room that is **cozy** is comfortable and warm. 居心地よい ❑ Downstairs there's a breakfast room and guests can relax in the cozy bar. 階下に朝食の食堂があり, 客は居心地のよいバーでくつろげる. ❷ ADJ 形容詞 If you are **cozy**, you are comfortable and warm. 心地よい [v-link ADJ] ❑ They like to make sure their guests are comfortable and cozy. 彼らは必ず客が快適に心地よく過ごせるようにするのが好きだ. ❸ ADJ 形容詞 You use **cozy** to describe activities that are pleasant and friendly, and involve people who know each other well. くつろいだ ❑ ...a cozy chat between friends. 友だち同士のくつろいだおしゃべり ❹ N-COUNT 可算名詞 A **cozy** or a **tea cozy** is a soft knitted or fabric cover which you put over a teapot in order to keep the tea hot. 保温カバー ❑ ...unusual miniature tea sets, elegant tea accessories, colorful cozies. 独特のミニチュア紅茶セット, 上品な紅茶用小道具, 色とりどりの保温カバー. ❑ ...a whimsical tea cozy printed with a bright scene of the Tower of London. ロンドン塔の明るい風景を印刷した風変わりな紅茶用保温カバー

CPU /si͟ pi yu͟/ (**CPUs**) N-COUNT 可算名詞 In a computer, the **CPU** is the part that processes all the data and makes the computer work. **CPU** is an abbreviation for "central processing unit." 中央処理装置 [COMPUTING コンピューティング]

crab /kræ͟b/ (**crabs**) N-COUNT 可算名詞 A **crab** is a sea creature with a flat round body covered by a shell, and five pairs of legs with large claws on the front pair. Crabs usually move sideways. カニ ● N-UNCOUNT 不可算名詞 **Crab** is the flesh of this creature eaten as food. カニ肉 ❑ I can't remember when I last had crab. 私は最後にいつカニを食べたのか思い出せない.

---

crack

❶ VERB USES
❷ NOUN AND ADJECTIVE USES

---

❶ crack /kræ͟k/ (**cracks, cracking, cracked**) ■ V-T/V-I 他動詞/自動詞 If something hard **cracks**, or if you **crack** it, it becomes slightly damaged, with lines appearing on its surface. ひびを入れる [他動詞], ひびが入る [自動詞] ❑ A gas main had cracked under my neighbor's garage and gas had seeped into our homes. 私の隣の家の車庫の下でガス本管にひびが入り, ガスが漏れて私たちの家に入っていた. ❷ V-T/V-I 他動詞/自動詞 If something **cracks**, or if you **crack** it, it makes a sharp sound like the sound of a piece of wood breaking. 鋭い音を鳴らす [他動詞], 鋭い音が鳴る [自動詞] ❑ Thunder cracked in the sky. 空で雷鳴がとどろいた. ❸ V-T 他動詞 If you **crack** a hard part of your body, such as your knee or your head, you hurt it by accidentally hitting it hard against something. 強くぶつける ❑ He cracked his head on the pavement and was knocked cold. 彼は舗道に頭を強く打ちつけ, 失神した. ❹ V-T 他動詞 When you **crack** something that has a shell, such as an egg or a nut, you break the shell in order to reach the inside part. 割る ❑ Crack the eggs into a bowl. 小鉢に卵を割る. ❺ V-T 他動詞 If you **crack** a problem or a code, you solve it, especially after a lot of thought. 解決する, 解読する ❑ He has finally cracked the system after years of painstaking research. 何年にもわたる骨の折れる研究の末, 彼はついにそのシステムの解読に成功した. ❻ V-I 自動詞 If someone **cracks**, they lose control of their emotions or actions because they are under a lot of pressure. 神経が参る [INFORMAL くだけた] ❑ She's calm and strong, and she is just not going to crack. 彼女は冷静で強く, けっして参ってしまうことはない. ❼ V-I 自動詞 If your voice **cracks** when you are speaking or singing, it changes in pitch because you are feeling a strong emotion. うわずる ❑ Her voice cracked and she began to cry. 彼女の声はうわずり, 彼女は泣き始めた. ❽ V-T 他動詞 If you **crack a joke**, you tell it. 口にする ❑ He drove a Volkswagen, cracked jokes, and talked about beer and girls. 彼はフォルクスワーゲンを運転し, 冗談を飛ばし, ビールと女の話をした.

▶ **crack down** ■ PHRASAL VERB 句動詞 If people in authority **crack down on** a group of people, they become stricter in making the group obey rules or laws. 取り締まる ❑ The government has cracked down hard on those campaigning for greater democracy. 政府は民主主義の拡大を求めて運動している人々をきびしく取り締まった. ❷ → see also **crackdown**

▶ **crack up** ■ PHRASAL VERB 句動詞 If someone **cracks up**, they are under such a lot of emotional strain that they become mentally ill. くじける [INFORMAL くだけた] ❑ She would have cracked up if she hadn't allowed herself some fun. 多少の楽しみにふけっていなかったら, 彼女は参っていたかもしれない. ❷ PHRASAL VERB 句動詞 If you **crack up** or if someone or something **cracks** you **up**, you laugh a lot. 笑い転げる [INFORMAL くだけた] ❑ She told stories that cracked me up and I swore to write them down so you could enjoy them too. 彼女の話に私は笑い転げ, 私は君も楽しめるようにその話を書き留めることを約束した.
→ see **crash**

❷ crack /kræ͟k/ (**cracks**) ■ N-COUNT 可算名詞 A **crack** is a very narrow gap between two things, or between two parts of a thing. すき間 ❑ Kathryn had seen him through a crack in the curtains. キャスリンはカーテンのすき間から彼を見ていた. ❷ N-COUNT 可算名詞 A **crack** is a line that appears on the surface of something when it is slightly damaged. ひび ❑ The plate had a crack in it. その皿はひびが入っていた. ❸ N-SING 単数名詞 If you open something such as a door, window, or curtain a **crack**, you open it only a small amount. わずかなすき間, ちょっと ❑ He went to the door, opened it a crack, and listened. 彼はドアに行き, ほんの少しだけ開き, 耳を澄ました. ❹ N-COUNT; SOUND 音声部 A **crack** is a sharp sound, like the sound of a piece of wood breaking. 鋭い音 ❑ Suddenly there was a loud crack and glass flew into the car. 突然激しい音が聞こえ, 割れたガラスが車に入ってきた. ❺ N-UNCOUNT 不可算名詞 **Crack** is a very pure form of the drug cocaine. 高純度のコカイン ❻ ADJ 形容詞 A **crack** soldier or sportsman is highly trained and very skillful. 一流の [ADJ n] ❑ ...a crack undercover police officer. 優秀な秘密警察官 ❼ N-COUNT 可算名詞 A **crack** is a slightly rude or cruel joke. 皮肉な冗談 ❑ Tell Tracy you're sorry for that crack about her weight. トレーシーに彼女の体重について悪い冗談を言ったことを誤りなさい.

Word Partnership		crack は次の語句と使われる:
ADJ.	crack **open** ❶ ■ ❹	
N.	crack **a code**, crack **the system** ❶ ❺	
	crack **jokes** ❶ ❽	
V.	**have a** crack ❷ ■ ❷	
ADJ.	**deep** crack ❷ ■ ❷	

crack|down /kræ͟kdaʊn/ (**crackdowns**) N-COUNT 可算名詞 A **crackdown** is strong official action that is taken to punish people who break laws. 取り締まり ❑ ...anti-government unrest that ended with the violent army crackdown. 軍の激しい弾圧で終息した不穏な反政府運動

crack|er /kræ͟kər/ (**crackers**) N-COUNT 可算名詞 A **cracker** is a thin, crisp piece of baked bread which is often eaten with cheese. クラッカー

crack|le /kræ͟kᵊl/ (**crackles, crackling, crackled**) V-I 自動詞 If something **crackles**, it makes a rapid series of short, harsh noises. ぱちぱちと音を立てる ❑ The radio crackled again. またラジオがぱりりと鳴り始めた. ● N-COUNT 可算名詞 **Crackle** is also a noun. ぱちぱちという音 ❑ ...the crackle of flames and gunfire. 炎と砲撃の音

cra|dle /kre͟ɪdᵊl/ (**cradles, cradling, cradled**) ■ N-COUNT 可算名詞 A **cradle** is a baby's bed with high sides. Cradles often have curved bases so that they rock from side to side. 揺りかご ❷ V-T 他動詞 If you **cradle** someone or something in your arms or hands, you hold them carefully and gently. 両腕で抱える ❑ I cradled her in my arms. 私は両腕で彼女を包み込んだ.

craft /kræ͟ft/ (**crafts, crafting, crafted**)

Craft is both the singular and the plural form for meaning ■.

Craft は ■ を意味するための単数形でも複数形でもある.

■ N-COUNT 可算名詞 You can refer to a boat, a spacecraft, or an aircraft as a **craft**. 船舶, 航空機 ❑ With great difficulty, the fisherman maneuvered his small craft close to the reef. ひどく苦労の末, 漁師は小船を岩礁の近くに寄せた. ❷ N-COUNT 可算名詞 A **craft** is an activity such as weaving, carving, or pottery that involves making things skillfully with your hands. 工芸 ❑ ...the arts and

crafts of the North American Indians. 北米インディアンの美術品と工芸品 **3** N-COUNT 可算名詞 You can use **craft** to refer to any activity or job that involves doing something skillfully. 技巧を要する仕事 ❏ _...the craft of writing._ ものを書く技巧 **4** V-T 他動詞 If something **is crafted**, it is made skillfully. 巧みに作る [usu passive] ❏ _The windows would probably have been crafted in the latter part of the Middle Ages._ その窓はおそらく中世の後半に巧みに制作されたものだろう. ❏ _...original, hand-crafted bags at affordable prices._ 手ごろな価格の独自の手工芸鞄

→ see **fly, ship**

crafts|man /krǽftsmən/ (**craftsmen**) N-COUNT 可算名詞 A **craftsman** is a man who makes things skillfully with his hands. 工芸家 ❏ _The table in the kitchen was made by a local craftsman._ 台所の食卓は地元の工芸家によって作られた.

crafts|man|ship /krǽftsmənʃɪp/ N-UNCOUNT 不可算名詞 **Craftsmanship** is the skill that someone uses when they make beautiful things with their hands. 技能 ❏ _It is easy to appreciate the craftsmanship of Armani._ アルマーニの職人技のよさを理解するのは易しい.

crafty /krǽfti/ (**craftier, craftiest**) ADJ 形容詞 If you describe someone as **crafty**, you mean that they achieve what they want in a clever way, often by deceiving people. 巧妙な, ずる賢い ❏ _...a crafty, lying character who enjoys plotting against others._ 他人を陥れることを楽しむずる賢くて嘘つきの人物 ❏ _A crafty look came to his eyes._ 彼はずる賢そうな目つきをした.

cram /kræm/ (**crams, cramming, crammed**) **1** V-T 他動詞 If you **cram** things or people **into** a container or place, you put them into it, although there is hardly enough room for them. 詰め込む ❏ _Terry crammed the dirty clothes into his bag._ テリーは汚れた衣服を鞄に詰め込んだ. ❏ _She crammed her mouth with caviar._ 彼女はキャビアを口に詰め込んだ. **2** V-T/V-I 他動詞/自動詞 If people **cram into** a place or vehicle or **cram** a place or vehicle, so many of them enter it at one time that it is completely full. 詰め込む [他動詞], 詰めかける [自動詞] ❏ _We crammed into my car and set off._ 私たちは私の車に乗り込んで出発した. **3** V-I 自動詞 If you **are cramming** for an examination, you are learning as much as possible in a short time just before you take the examination. 頭に詰め込む ❏ _She was cramming for her Economics exam._ 彼女は経済学の試験のために詰め込み勉強をしていた. ● **cram|ming** N-UNCOUNT 不可算名詞 詰め込み ❏ _It would take two or three months of cramming to prepare for Vermont's bar exam._ バーモント州の弁護士試験の準備には2, 3か月の詰め込みが必要だろう.

crammed /kræmd/ **1** ADJ 形容詞 If a place is **crammed with** things or people, it is full of them, so that there is hardly room for anything or anyone else. いっぱいの ❏ _The house is crammed with priceless furniture and works of art._ その家は値段のつけられないほど貴重な家具や美術品でいっぱいだ. **2** ADJ 形容詞 If people or things are **crammed into** a place or vehicle, it is full of them. ぎっしり詰められた [v-link ADJ] ❏ _Between two and three thousand refugees were crammed into the church buildings._ 2千人から3千人の避難民が教会の建物にひしめいていた.

cramp /kræmp/ (**cramps, cramping, cramped**) **1** N-VAR 可変性名詞 A **cramp** is a sudden strong pain caused by a muscle suddenly contracting. You sometimes get cramps in a muscle after you have been making a physical effort over a long period of time. けいれん [also N in pl] ❏ _Hillsden was complaining of a cramp in his calf muscles._ ヒルズデンはふくらはぎの筋肉のけいれんを訴えていた. ❏ _...muscle cramps._ 筋けいれん **2** PHRASE 句 If someone or something **cramps** your **style**, their presence or existence restricts your behavior in some way. 人の行動を妨げる [INFORMAL くだけた] ❏ _Like more and more women, she believes wedlock would cramp her style._ 結婚のせいで自分の思うようにできないと考える女性が増えており, 彼女もその1人だ.

cramped /kræmpt/ ADJ 形容詞 A **cramped** room or building is not big enough for the people or things in it. 窮屈な ❏ _There are hundreds of families living in cramped conditions on the floor of the airport lounge._ 空港の待合室の床で何百もの家族がひしめきあって過ごしている.

crane /kreɪn/ (**cranes, craning, craned**) **1** N-COUNT 可算名詞 A **crane** is a large machine that moves heavy things by lifting them in the air. 起重機 ❏ _The little prefabricated hut was lifted away by a huge crane._ その小さな組み立て式の小屋は巨大な起重機に持ち上げられ撤去された. **2** N-COUNT 可算名詞 A **crane** is a kind of large bird with a long neck and long legs. ツル **3** V-T/V-I 他動詞/自動詞 If you **crane** your neck or head, you stretch your neck in a particular direction in order to see or hear something better. 伸ばす [他動詞], 身を乗り出す [自動詞] ❏ _She craned her neck to get a better view._ 彼女はもっとよく見えるように首を伸ばした. ❏ _Children craned to get close to him._ 子供たちは彼に近づこうと身を乗り出した.

crank /kræŋk/ (**cranks, cranking, cranked**) **1** N-COUNT 可算名詞 If you call someone a **crank**, you think their ideas or behavior are strange. 変人 [INFORMAL くだけた, DISAPPROVAL 不賛成] ❏ _The man with a new idea is a crank until the idea succeeds._ 新しい発想を持

った人は, その発想で成功するまでは変人だ. **2** N-COUNT 可算名詞 A **crank** is a device that you turn in order to make something move. クランク, 曲がり柄 ❏ _He was idly turning a crank on a strange mechanism strapped to his chest._ 彼は自分の胸につるした奇妙な装置のクランクをいたずらに回していた. **3** V-T 他動詞 If you **crank** an engine or machine, you make it move or function, especially by turning a handle. クランクを回して始動させる ❏ _The chauffeur got out to crank the motor._ 専属の運転手がモーターを始動させるため出て行った.

▶ **crank out** PHRASAL VERB 句動詞 If you say that a company or person **cranks out** a quantity of similar things, you mean they produce them quickly, in the same way, and are usually implying that the things are not original or are of poor quality. 量産する ❏ _In 1933 the studio cranked out fifty-five feature films._ 1933年にその撮影所は55本もの特作映画を次々と作り出した. ❏ _The writer must have cranked it out in his lunch-hour._ その作家は昼食時にそれをでっち上げたにちがいない.

▶ **crank up** PHRASAL VERB 句動詞 If you **crank up** a machine or device, you turn it on higher. 強さを増す ❏ _May's warm weather caused Americans to crank up their air conditioners._ 5月の暖かい気候のせいでアメリカ人は冷房を強くした.

crap /kræp/ **1** ADJ 形容詞 If you describe something as **crap**, you think that it is wrong or of very poor quality. ひどい [INFORMAL, VULGAR くだけた, 下品な, DISAPPROVAL 不賛成] ❏ _She later said the book was "crap."_ のちに彼女はその本は「くず」だと言った. ● N-UNCOUNT 不可算名詞 **Crap** is also a noun. くず, くだらないこと ❏ _It is a tedious, humorless load of crap._ それは退屈で面白みのないくずの山だ. **2** N-UNCOUNT 不可算名詞 **Crap** is sometimes used to refer to feces. くそ [INFORMAL, VULGAR くだけた, 下品な] ❏ _I look down and I'm standing next to a pile of crap!_ 私は下を見ると, 何とその山の隣に立っているんだ. **3** N-UNCOUNT 不可算名詞 **Craps** or **crap** is a gambling game, played mainly in North America, in which you throw two dice and bet what the total will be. クラップス ❏ _I'll shoot some craps or play some blackjack._ 私はクラップスかブラックジャックをしよう.

crash /kræʃ/ (**crashes, crashing, crashed**) **1** N-COUNT 可算名詞 A **crash** is an accident in which a moving vehicle hits something and is damaged or destroyed. 衝突 ❏ _His elder son was killed in a car crash a few years ago._ 彼の上の息子は数年前に自動車事故で死んだ. **2** N-COUNT 可算名詞 A **crash** is a sudden, loud noise. すさまじい音 ❏ _Two people recalled hearing a loud crash about 1:30 a.m._ 2人が午前1時30分ごろのすさまじい音を聞いたのを思い出した. **3** V-T/V-I 他動詞/自動詞 If a moving vehicle **crashes** or if the driver **crashes** it, it hits something and is damaged or destroyed. 衝突させる [他動詞], 衝突する [自動詞] ❏ _The plane crashed mysteriously near the island of Ustica._ その飛行機はウスティカ島の近くで謎の墜落をした. ❏ _Her car crashed into the rear of a van._ 彼女の車はバンの後ろに追突した. **4** V-I 自動詞 If something **crashes** somewhere, it moves and hits something else violently, making a loud noise. 衝突する ❏ _The door swung inwards to crash against a chest of drawers behind it._ 扉は内側に揺れ動き, 裏側にあった整理だんすに激しくぶつかった. ❏ _My words were lost as the walls above us crashed down, filling the cellar with brick dust._ 頭上の壁が崩れ落ちて私の声は聞こえなくなり, 地下室はレンガのがれきで満たされた. **5** V-I 自動詞 If a business or financial system **crashes**, it fails suddenly, often with serious effects. つぶれる [BUSINESS 実業] ❏ _When the market crashed, they assumed the deal would be cancelled._ 市場が崩壊したときは, 取引は取り消されると想定された. ● N-COUNT 可算名詞 **Crash** is also a noun. 崩壊 ❏ _He predicted correctly that there was going to be a stock market crash._ 彼は株式市場が崩壊するだろうと正確に予測した. **6** V-I 自動詞 If a computer or a computer program **crashes**, it fails suddenly. 故障する ❏ _The computer crashed for the second time in 10 days._ そのコンピュータは10日間で2度目の故障を起こした.

→ see **Word Web: crash**

→ see **stock market**

Thesaurus			_crash_ また次を参照:
N.	collision, wreck **1**		
	bang **2**		
V.	collide, hit, smash **3**		
	fail **5 6**		

crass /kræs/ (**crasser, crassest**) ADJ 形容詞 **Crass** behavior is stupid and does not show consideration for other people. 粗野な ❏ _The government has behaved with crass insensitivity._ 政府は愚かで無神経に行動してきた.

crate /kreɪt/ (**crates, crating, crated**) **1** N-COUNT 可算名詞 A **crate** is a large box used for transporting or storing things. 木枠 ❏ _...a pile of wooden crates._ 木箱の山 **2** N-COUNT 可算名詞 A **crate** is a plastic or wire box divided into sections that is used for carrying bottles. 枠箱 **3** N-COUNT 可算名詞 You can use **crate** to refer to a crate and its contents, or to the contents only. 木箱 ❏ _...a crate of oranges._ 1箱のみかん **4** V-T 他動詞 If something **is crated** or **crated up**, it is packed in a crate so that it can be transported or stored

Word Web crash

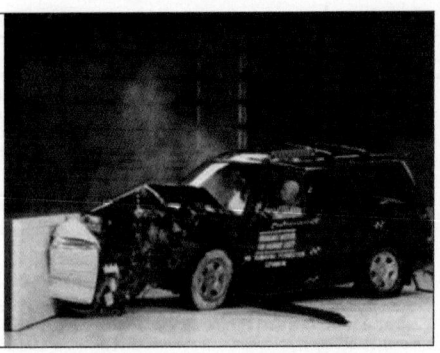

Every year the National Highway Traffic Safety Administration* conducts crash tests on new cars. They evaluate exactly what happens during an accident. How fast do you have to be going to **buckle** a bumper during a collision? Does the gas tank **rupture**? Do the tires **burst**? What happens when the windshield **breaks**? Does it **crack**, or does it **shatter** into a thousand pieces? Does the force of the **impact crush** the front of the car completely? This is actually a good thing. It means that the engine and hood would protect the passengers during the crash.

National Highway Traffic Safety Administration: a U.S. government agency that sets safety standards.

---

somewhere safely. 木箱に詰める [usu passive] ❑*Equipment and office supplies were crated and shipped.* 設備と事務用品が箱詰めされ出荷された.

cra|ter /kréɪtər/ (craters) N-COUNT 可算名詞 A **crater** is a very large hole in the ground, which has been caused by something hitting it or by an explosion. 噴火口, 爆弾の跡 ❑*The explosion, believed to be a car bomb, left a ten-foot crater in the street.* 自動車爆弾と考えられる爆発により, 街路に10フィートの穴ができた.
→ see **astronomer, lake, meteor, moon, solar system**

crave /kréɪv/ (craves, craving, craved) V-T 他動詞 If you **crave** something, you want to have it very much. 切望する ❑*There may be certain times of day when smokers crave their cigarette.* 喫煙者は1日に何度かたばこが欲しくてたまらなくなる時があるかもしれない. ● **crav|ing** (cravings) N-COUNT 可算名詞 切望 ❑*...a craving for sugar.* 砂糖への渇望

crawl /krɔ́l/ (crawls, crawling, crawled) ■ V-I 自動詞 When you **crawl**, you move forward on your hands and knees. はう ❑*Don't worry if your baby seems a little reluctant to crawl or walk.* 赤ちゃんがはったり歩いたりするのを少し嫌がっているように見えても心配しないでください. ❑*I began to crawl on my hands and knees toward the door.* 私は四つんばいになって扉のほうにはい始めた. ■ V-I 自動詞 When an insect **crawls** somewhere, it moves there quite slowly. はう ❑*I watched the moth crawl up the outside of the lampshade.* 私はランプのかさの外側を蛾がはい上がるのをじっと見た. ■ V-I 自動詞 If someone or something **crawls** somewhere, they move or progress slowly or with great difficulty. はう ❑*I crawled out of bed at nine-thirty.* 私は9時半に寝床からはい出た. ● N-SING 単数名詞 **Crawl** is also a noun. はうこと ["a" N] ❑*The traffic on the off-ramp slowed to a crawl.* 出口車線の交通は速度が落ち, 徐行になった. ■ V-I 自動詞 If you say that a place **is crawling with** people or animals, you are emphasizing that it is full of them. いっぱいである [INFORMAL くだけた, EMPHASIS 強調] [only cont] ❑*This place is crawling with police.* この場所には警官がうようよしている. ■ N-SING 単数名詞 **The crawl** is a kind of swimming stroke which you do lying on your front, swinging one arm over your head, and then the other arm. クロール ❑*I expected him to do 50 lengths of the crawl.* 私は彼にクロール25往復を求めた.

cray|on /kréɪɒn/ (crayons) N-COUNT 可算名詞 A **crayon** is a rod of colored wax used for drawing. クレヨン

craze /kréɪz/ (crazes) N-COUNT 可算名詞 If there is a **craze** for something, it is very popular for a short time. 熱狂 ❑*...the craze for Mutant Ninja Turtles.* ミュータント・ニンジャ・タートルの熱狂的な嵐

crazed /kréɪzd/ ADJ 形容詞 **Crazed** people are wild and uncontrolled, and perhaps insane. 狂った [WRITTEN 書き言葉] ❑*A crazed gunman slaughtered five people last night.* 昨夜, 正気をなくした銃撃犯が5人を殺害した.

cra|zy /kréɪzi/ (crazier, craziest, crazies) ■ ADJ 形容詞 If you describe someone or something as **crazy**, you think they are very foolish or strange. 狂った [INFORMAL くだけた, DISAPPROVAL 不賛成] ❑*People thought they were all crazy to try to make money from manufacturing.* 人々は, 製造業で金をもうけようとするなんて, 彼らはみんな頭がおかしいと思った. ● **cra|zily** ADV 副詞 狂気のように ❑*The teenagers shook their long, black hair and gesticulated crazily.* 10代の若者たちは長い黒髪を振り乱し, 狂ったような身振りをした. ■ ADJ 形容詞 Someone who is **crazy** is insane. 狂気の [INFORMAL くだけた] ❑*If I sat home and worried about all this stuff, I'd go crazy.* 私は家にいてこのことばかり心配していたら, 頭がおかしくなるだろう. ● N-COUNT 可算名詞 **Crazy** is also a noun. 狂気 ❑*Outside, mumbling, was one of New York's ever-present crazies.* 往来のよく聞き取れない声は, ニューヨークでは絶え間なく付きまとう狂気のひとつだ. ■ ADJ 形容詞 [v-link ADJ "about" n] If you are **crazy about** something, you are very enthusiastic about it. If you are **not crazy about** something, you do not like it. 熱を上げる [INFORMAL くだけた] ❑*He's still crazy about both his work and his hobbies.* 彼はまだ仕事

と趣味の両方に熱を上げている. ● COMB IN ADJ 形容詞の複合 **Crazy** is also a combining form. 一狂の ❑*Sports-crazy Coloradans will buy tickets to anything.* スポーツ狂のコロラド州の住民はどんな入場券でも買うだろう. ■ ADJ 形容詞 If you are **crazy about** someone, you are deeply in love with them. 恋焦がれる [INFORMAL くだけた] [v-link ADJ "about" n] ❑*We're crazy about each other.* 私たちはお互いのことを好きでたまらない.

creak /krík/ (creaks, creaking, creaked) V-I 自動詞 If something **creaks**, it makes a short, high-pitched sound when it moves. きしる ❑*The bed-springs creaked.* ベッドのばねがきしんだ. ❑*The door creaked open.* 扉がきしみながら開いた. ● N-COUNT 可算名詞 **Creak** is also a noun. きしり ❑*The door was pulled open with a creak.* 扉が引かれ, きしりながら開いた.

cream /krím/ (creams, creaming, creamed) ■ N-UNCOUNT 不可算名詞 **Cream** is a thick yellowish-white liquid taken from milk. You can use it in cooking or put it on fruit or desserts. クリーム ❑*...strawberries and cream.* イチゴとクリーム ■ N-UNCOUNT 不可算名詞 **Cream** is used in the names of soups that contain cream or milk. クリーム ❑*...cream of mushroom soup.* きのこのクリームスープ [N "of" n] ■ N-VAR 可変名詞 A **cream** is a substance that you rub into your skin, for example, to keep it soft or to heal or protect it. クリーム 乳脂 ❑*Gently apply the cream to the affected areas.* 症状の現れた場所に優しくクリームを塗りなさい. ■ COLOR 色彩語 Something that is **cream** is yellowish-white in color. クリーム色 ❑*...cream silk stockings.* クリーム色の絹のストッキング ■ → see also **ice cream**
▸ **cream off** ■ PHRASAL VERB 句動詞 To **cream off** part of a group of people means to take them away and treat them in a special way, because they are better than the others. 選抜する [DISAPPROVAL 不賛成] ❑*The private schools cream off many of the best pupils.* 私立学校は最も優秀な生徒の多くを選抜する. ■ PHRASAL VERB 句動詞 If a person or organization **creams off** a large amount of money, they take it and use it for themselves. かすめ取る [INFORMAL くだけた, DISAPPROVAL 不賛成] ❑*This means smaller banks can cream off big profits during lending booms.* つまり小規模な銀行は貸し出し景気の間に巨額の利益を荒稼ぎできるのだ.
→ see **coffee**

creamy /krími/ (creamier, creamiest) ■ ADJ 形容詞 Food or drink that is **creamy** contains a lot of cream or milk. クリームを多く含んだ ❑*...rich, creamy coffee.* 豊かな味わいのクリームたっぷりのコーヒー ■ ADJ 形容詞 Food that is **creamy** has a soft smooth texture and appearance. クリーム状の ❑*...creamy mashed potato.* クリームのようなマッシュポテト

crease /krís/ (creases, creasing, creased) ■ N-COUNT 可算名詞 **Creases** are lines that are made in cloth or paper when it is crushed or folded. 折り目 ❑*She stood up, frowning at the creases in her silk dress.* 彼女は立ち上がり, 自分の絹のドレスについたしわに眉をひそめた. ❑*...cream-colored pants with sharp creases.* きちんと折り目のついたクリーム色のパンツ ■ N-COUNT 可算名詞 **Creases** in someone's skin are lines which form where their skin folds when they move. しわ ❑*...the tiny creases at the corners of his eyes.* 彼の目じりの小さなしわ ● **creased** ADJ 形容詞 しわのついた ❑*Sweat poured down her deeply creased face.* 深いしわの刻まれた彼女の顔を汗が流れ落ちた. ■ V-T/V-I 他動詞/自動詞 If cloth or paper **creases** or if you **crease** it, lines form in it when it is crushed or folded. 折り目をつける [他動詞], 折り目がつく [自動詞] ❑*Most outfits crease a bit when you are traveling.* 旅行中にはたいていの衣装に多少のしわがつく. ● **creased** ADJ 形容詞 折り目のついた ❑*His clothes were creased, as if he had slept in them.* 彼の服にはまるでそのまま寝ていたかのようにしわができていた.

cre|ate /kriéɪt/ (creates, creating, created) ■ V-T 他動詞 To **create** something means to cause it to happen or exist. 創り出す [他動詞] ❑*We set business free to create more jobs.* 企業の規制をはずして雇用を創出させた. ❑*She could create a fight out of anything.* 彼女はどんなものからでも争いを引き起こしかねない. ● **crea|tion**

/krieɪʃ°n/ N-UNCOUNT 不可算名詞 創造 ❑ *These businesses stimulate the creation of local jobs.* こうした企業が地域の雇用創出を刺激する. **2** V-T 他動詞 When someone **creates** a new product or process, they invent it or design it. 創作する, 考案する ❑ *It is really great for a radio producer to create a show like this.* ラジオ番組の制作者にとって、こんな番組を創ることは本当に素晴らしいことだ.

Thesaurus create また次を参照:

v. make, produce; *(ant.)* destroy **1**
compose, craft, design, invent **2**

Word Link creat ≈ making : creation, creature, recreate

crea|tion /krieɪʃ°n/ (creations) **1** N-UNCOUNT 不可算名詞 In many religions, **creation** is the making of the universe, earth, and creatures by God. 天地創造 [also "the" N] ❑ *...the Creation of the universe as told in Genesis Chapter One.* 創世記第1章で語られた天地創造 **2** N-UNCOUNT 不可算名詞 People sometimes refer to the whole universe as **creation**. 宇宙, 万物 [LITERARY 文語的] ❑ *The whole of creation is made up of energy.* 宇宙全体がエネルギーでできている. **3** N-COUNT 可算名詞 You can refer to something that someone has made as a **creation**, especially if it shows skill, imagination, or artistic ability. 創作 ❑ *The bathroom is entirely my own creation.* その浴室は完全に私自身の手になるものだ. **4** → see also **create**

crea|tive /krieɪtɪv/ **1** ADJ 形容詞 A **creative** person has the ability to invent and develop original ideas, especially in the arts. 創造力のある ❑ *Like so many creative people, he was never satisfied.* 非常に多くの創造的な人々と同じように、彼は決して満足することがなかった ● **crea|tiv|ity** /kriːeɪtɪvɪti/ N-UNCOUNT 不可算名詞 創造性 ❑ *American art reached a peak of creativity in the '50s and 60s.* アメリカ美術は50年代および60年代にその創造性の頂点に達した. **2** ADJ 形容詞 **Creative** activities involve the inventing and making of new kinds of things. 創造的な ❑ *...creative writing.* 文芸創作 [の授業] ❑ *...creative arts.* 創造的芸術 **3** ADJ 形容詞 If you use something in a **creative** way, you use it in a new way that produces interesting and unusual results. 独創的な ❑ *...his creative use of words.* 彼の独創的な言葉づかい

crea|tive ac|count|ing N-UNCOUNT 不可算名詞 **Creative accounting** is when companies present or organize their accounts in such a way that they gain money for themselves or give a false impression of their profits. 粉飾決算 [DISAPPROVAL 不賛成] ❑ *Much of the apparent growth in profits in the 1980s was the result of creative accounting.* 1980年代の見かけの利益成長の多くの部分は粉飾決算によるものだった.

Word Link ator ≈ one who does : creator, innovator, spectator

crea|tor /krieɪtər/ (creators) **1** N-COUNT 可算名詞 The **creator** of something is the person who made it or invented it. 創案者 ❑ *...Ian Fleming, the creator of James Bond.* ジェームズ・ボンドの産みの親、イアン・フレミング **2** N-PROPER 固有名詞 God is sometimes referred to as **the Creator**. 創造主 ❑ *This was the first object placed in the heavens by the Creator.* これが創造主によって天におかれた最初の物であった.

crea|ture /kriːtʃər/ (creatures) N-COUNT 可算名詞 You can refer to any living thing that is not a plant as a **creature**, especially when it is of an unknown or unfamiliar kind. People also refer to imaginary animals and beings as **creatures**. 生き物 ❑ *Alaskan Eskimos believe that every living creature possesses a spirit.* アラスカのエスキモーはすべての生き物は霊魂を持っていると信じている.

crèche /krɛʃ/ (crèches) also **creche** N-COUNT 可算名詞 A **crèche** is a place where small children can be left to be cared for while their parents are doing something else. 所 [BRIT 英国英語] AM **day care center** 米国英語 **day care center**]

cre|dence /kriːd°ns/ **1** N-UNCOUNT 不可算名詞 If something lends or gives **credence to** a theory or story, it makes it easier to believe. 信用 [FORMAL 形式ばった] ❑ *Good studies are needed to lend credence to the notion that genuine progress can be made in this important field.* この重要な分野で本物の発展が可能だという考えを信用させてくれるようなよい研究が必要である. **2** N-UNCOUNT 不可算名詞 If you give **credence to** a theory or story, you believe it. 信用 [FORMAL 形式ばった] ❑ *You're surely not giving any credence to this story of Hythe's?* 君は本当にこのハイズの話をまったく信じないのかい.

Word Link cred ≈ to believe : credentials, credibility, incredible

cre|den|tials /krɪdɛnʃ°lz/ **1** N-PLURAL 複数名詞 Someone's **credentials** are their previous achievements, training, and general background, which indicate that they are qualified to do something. 信用証明, 資格 ❑ *...her credentials as a Bach specialist.* 彼女がバッハの専門家であることを証明するもの **2** N-PLURAL 複数名詞 Someone's **credentials** are a letter or certificate that proves their identity or qualifications. 人物証明書, 信任状 ❑ *The new*

ambassador to Lebanon has presented his **credentials** to the president. 新しいレバノン駐在大使は大統領に信任状を提出した.

cred|ibil|ity /krɛdɪbɪlɪti/ N-UNCOUNT 不可算名詞 If someone or something has **credibility**, people believe in them and trust them. 信用性 ❑ *The police have lost their credibility.* 警察は信頼をなくした.

cred|ible /krɛdɪb°l/ **1** ADJ 形容詞 **Credible** means able to be trusted or believed. 信用できる ❑ *Her claims seem credible to many.* 彼女の主張を信用できると思っている人が多い. **2** ADJ 形容詞 A **credible** candidate, policy, or system, for example, is one that appears to have a chance of being successful. 有望な ❑ *Mr. Robertson would be a credible candidate.* ロバートソン氏は有望候補だろう.

cred|it /krɛdɪt/ (credits, crediting, credited) **1** N-UNCOUNT 不可算名詞 If you are given **credit**, you are allowed to pay for goods or services several weeks or months after you have received them. 掛売り ❑ *The group can't get credit to buy farming machinery.* その集団は農機の購入にあたって掛売りが認められない. **2** N-UNCOUNT 不可算名詞 If you get **the credit for** something good, people praise you because you are responsible for it, or are thought to be responsible for it. 賞賛, 評価 ❑ *We don't mind who gets the credit so long as we don't get the blame.* 我々が非難を受けないかぎり, 我々は誰が賞賛されるかは気にしない. ❑ *It would be wrong for us to take all the credit.* 我々が功績を独り占めするのは良くないだろう. **3** V-T 他動詞 When a sum of money **is credited to** an account, the bank adds that sum of money to the total in the account. 貸し方に記入する ❑ *She noticed that only $80,000 had been credited to her account.* 彼女は自分の口座に8万ドルしか振り込まれていないのに気づいた. ❑ *Midland decided to change the way it credited payments to accounts.* ミッドランド銀行は口座振り込み方法の変更を決めた. **4** V-T 他動詞 If people **credit** someone **with** an achievement or if it **is credited to** them, people say or believe that they were responsible for it. 功績を認める ❑ *The staff are crediting him with having saved Hythe's life.* 職員たちはハイズの命を救った功績は彼のものだと言っている. ❑ *The 74-year-old mayor is credited with helping make Los Angeles the financial capital of the West Coast.* 74歳の市長はロサンゼルスを西海岸の金融中心都市とするのに一役買ったと功績を認められている. **5** N-COUNT 可算名詞 A **credit** is a sum of money which is added to an account. 預金残高 ❑ *The statement of total debits and credits is known as a balance.* 貸し方と借り方全部の計算書は差引残高として知られている. **6** N-COUNT 可算名詞 A **credit** is an amount of money that is given to someone. 給付金額, 控除 ❑ *Senator Bill Bradley outlined his own tax cut, giving families $350 in tax credits per child.* ビル・ブラッドリー上院議員は自らの減税案について説明して, 家庭に子供1人当たり350ドルの税額控除を与えると言った. **7** N-PLURAL 複数名詞 The list of people who helped to make a movie, a CD, or a television program is called the **credits**. 制作に関わった人々の名前 ❑ *It was fantastic seeing my name in the credits.* クレジットに自分の名前を見つけるのは素晴らしいことだった. **8** N-COUNT 可算名詞 A **credit** is a successfully completed part of a higher education course, representing about one hour of instruction a week. At universities and colleges you need a certain number of credits to be awarded a degree. 単位 ❑ *Through the AP program students can earn college credits in high school.* 飛び級制度により, 学生は高校で大学の単位を取得することができる. **9** N-SING 単数名詞 If you say that someone is **a credit to** someone or something, you mean that their qualities or achievements will make people have a good opinion of the person or thing mentioned. 誉れ ❑ *He is one of the greatest players of recent times and is a credit to his profession.* 彼は近年最高の選手の1人であり, その職業にとっての誉れでもある. **10** PHRASE 句 To **give** someone **credit for** a good quality means to believe that they have it. (人がある特質を) 持っていると認める ❑ *Bratbakk had more ability than the media gave him credit for.* ブラットバックは報道機関が認める以上の能力を持っていた. **11** PHRASE 句 If something is **to** someone's **credit**, they deserve praise for it. 〜の名誉として ❑ *She had managed to pull herself together and, to her credit, continued to look upon life as a positive experience.* 彼女はなんとか気を取り直して, 偉いことに人生を肯定的な経験と見なし続けた.

Word Partnership credit は次の語句と使われる:

N.	credit **history** **1**
	letter of credit **1** **5** **6**
	credit **an account** **3**
ADJ.	**personal** credit **1** **2** **6**
V.	**provide** credit **1** **5** **6**
	deserve credit, **take** credit **2**

cred|it|able /krɛdɪtəb°l/ **1** ADJ 形容詞 A **creditable** performance or achievement is of a reasonably high standard. 立派な ❑ *They turned out a quite creditable performance.* 彼らはまったく見事な演奏をした. **2** ADJ 形容詞 If you describe someone's actions or aims as **creditable**, you mean that they are morally good. 賞賛に値する ❑ *Not a very creditable attitude, I'm afraid.* あまりほめられた態度ではないですね.

cred|it card (credit cards) N-COUNT 可算名詞 A credit card is a plastic card that you use to buy goods on credit. Compare **charge card**. クレジットカード

cred|i|tor /krɛdɪtər/ (creditors) N-COUNT 可算名詞 Your **creditors** are the people who you owe money to. 債権者 ❑ The company said it would pay in full all its creditors except Credit Suisse. その会社はクレディ・スイス銀行以外のすべての債権者に対し満額支払うと言った。

cred|it rat|ing N-SING 単数名詞 Your **credit rating** is a judgment of how likely you are to pay money back if you borrow it or buy things on credit. 信用格付け ❑ But Cahoot's overdraft rate depends on your credit rating. しかしカフートの超過引出し額は利用者の信用格付けによる。

cred|it slip (credit slips) **1** N-COUNT 可算名詞 A **credit slip** is a piece of paper that a shop gives you when you return goods that you have bought from it. It states that you are entitled to take goods of the same value without paying for them. 商品引き換え券 [AM 米国英語] **2** N-COUNT 可算名詞 A **credit slip** is a piece of paper which shows that your account has been credited. 預金伝票

cred|it trans|fer (credit transfers) N-COUNT 可算名詞 A **credit transfer** is a direct payment of money from one bank account into another. 銀行口座振替 [BRIT 英国英語; AM **money transfer** 米国英語 **money transfer**]

Word Link worthy ≈ deserving, suitable : credit**worthy**, trust**worthy**, un**worthy**

credit|worthy /krɛdɪtwɜrði/ also credit-worthy ADJ 形容詞 A **creditworthy** person or organization is one who can safely be lent money or allowed to have goods on credit, for example, because in the past they have always paid back what they owe. 信用できる ❑ The Fed wants banks to continue to lend to creditworthy borrowers. 連邦準備制度理事会は銀行が信用のできる借り手に貸し続けることを望んでいる。 ● **credit|worthi|ness** N-UNCOUNT 不可算名詞 信用力 ❑ They now take extra steps to verify the creditworthiness of customers. 彼らは今すぐに顧客の信用力を確認するために追加の処置をとる。

creed /krid/ (creeds) **1** N-COUNT 可算名詞 A **creed** is a set of beliefs, principles, or opinions that strongly influence the way people live or work. 信条 [FORMAL 形式ばった] ❑ …their devotion to their creed of self-help. 自助努力の信条への彼らの傾向 **2** N-COUNT 可算名詞 A **creed** is a religion. 宗教 [FORMAL 形式ばった] ❑ The center is open to all, no matter what race or creed. その施設は、どんな人種や宗教であろうとも、すべての人に開放されている。

creek /krik/ (creeks) N-COUNT 可算名詞 A **creek** is a small stream or river. 小川 [AM 米国英語] ❑ Follow Austin Creek for a few miles. オースティン川に沿って数マイル進みなさい。

creep /krip/ (creeps, creeping, crept) **1** V-I 自動詞 When people or animals **creep** somewhere, they move quietly and slowly. はう ❑ Back I go to the hotel and creep up to my room. 私はホテルに戻り、自分の部屋にこっそり上がる。 **2** V-I 自動詞 If something **creeps** somewhere, it moves very slowly. はう ❑ Mist had crept in again from the sea. また海から霧が入りこんできた。 **3** V-I 自動詞 If something **creeps** in or **creeps** back, it begins to occur or becomes part of something without people realizing or without them wanting it. 忍び寄る ❑ Insecurity might creep in. 不安感が忍び寄るかもしれない。 ❑ An increasing ratio of mistakes, perhaps induced by tiredness, crept into her game. おそらくは疲れのせいで、彼女の試合はいつの間にか失敗の比率が高くなった。 **4** V-I 自動詞 If a rate or number **creeps up** to a higher level, it gradually reaches that level. 徐々に増す ❑ The inflation rate has been creeping up to 9.5 per cent. インフレ率が9.5パーセントまで徐々に上昇してきた。 **5** to **make** someone's **flesh creep** → see **flesh**

Word Partnership creep は次の語句と使われる:

PREP.	creep **toward 1 2**
	creep **into 1** - **3**
	creep **in 2 4**
	creep **up 2 4**
V.	**give someone the creeps 5**

creepy /kripi/ (creepier, creepiest) ADJ 形容詞 If you say that something or someone is **creepy**, you mean they make you feel very nervous or frightened. 身の毛がよだつ [INFORMAL くだけた] ❑ There were certain places that were really creepy at night. 夜には本当に不気味な場所がいくつかあった。

cre|mate /krimeɪt/ (cremates, cremating, cremated) V-T 他動詞 When someone **is cremated**, their dead body is burned, usually as part of a funeral service. 火葬にする [usu passive] ❑ She wants Chris to be cremated. 彼女はクリスを火葬にすることを望んでいる。 ● **cre|ma|tion** /krimeɪʃ°n/ (cremations) N-VAR 可変性名詞 火葬 ❑ At Miss Garbo's request, there was a cremation after a private ceremony. ガルボさんの要望で密葬の後で火葬が行われた。

crept /krɛpt/ **Crept** is the past tense and past participle of **creep**. creepの過去・過去分詞

cre|scen|do /krɪʃɛndoʊ/ (crescendos) **1** N-COUNT 可算名詞 A **crescendo** is a noise that gets louder and louder. Some people also use **crescendo** to refer to the point when a noise is at its loudest. 漸強音 ❑ She spoke in a crescendo: "You are a bad girl! You are a wicked girl! You are evil!" 彼女の声は次第に大きくなった。「悪い子よ。あなたは意地の悪い女の子よ。最悪だわ」 **2** N-COUNT 可算名詞 People sometimes describe an increase in the intensity of something, or its most intense point, as a **crescendo**. 最高潮 [JOURNALISM ジャーナリズム] ❑ There was a crescendo of press criticism. 報道機関の批判が頂点に達していた。

Word Link cresc, creas ≈ growing : **cresc**ent, de**creas**e, in**creas**e

cres|cent /krɛs°nt/ (crescents) **1** N-COUNT 可算名詞 A **crescent** is a curved shape that is wider in the middle than at its ends, like the shape of the moon during its first and last quarters. It is the most important symbol of the Islamic faith. 三日月形 ❑ A glittering Islamic crescent tops the mosque. きらきら輝くイスラムの三日月飾りがモスクのてっぺんにある。 ❑ …a narrow crescent of sand dunes. 砂丘の細長い三日月形 **2** N-IN-NAMES 名称中の名詞 **Crescent** is sometimes used as part of the name of a street or row of houses that is usually built in a curve. 三日月形の通りや家並み ❑ The address is 44 Colville Crescent. 住所はコルヴィル・クレセント44番地です。

crest /krɛst/ (crests) **1** N-COUNT 可算名詞 The **crest** of a hill or a wave is the top of it. 頂上 ● PHRASE 句 If you say that you are **on the crest of a wave**, you mean that you are feeling very happy and confident because things are going well for you. 得意の絶頂で ❑ The band is riding on the crest of a wave with the worldwide success of their number-one-selling single. そのバンドは売り上げ第1位のシングル版の世界的成功により得意の絶頂にある。 **2** N-COUNT 可算名詞 A bird's **crest** is a group of upright feathers on the top of its head. とさか ❑ Both birds had a dark blue crest. その鳥は両方とも濃い青のとさかを持っていた。 **3** N-COUNT 可算名詞 A **crest** is a design that is the symbol of a noble family, a town, or an organization. 紋章 ❑ On the wall is the family crest. 壁に家紋がかかっている。 → see **sound**

crev|ice /krɛvɪs/ (crevices) N-COUNT 可算名詞 A **crevice** is a narrow crack or gap, especially in a rock. 割れ目 ❑ …a huge boulder with rare ferns growing in every crevice. 割れ目のいたるところに希少なシダの生えている巨大な岩

crew /kru/ (crews, crewing, crewed) **1** N-COUNT-COLL 集合可算名詞 The **crew** of a ship, an aircraft, or a spacecraft is the people who work on and operate it. 乗組員 ❑ The mission for the crew of the space shuttle is essentially over. スペースシャトルの乗組員の任務は基本的に終了した。 ❑ Despite their size, these vessels carry small crews, usually of around twenty men. 大きさのわりに、これらの船舶は通常20名程度のわずかな乗組員しか乗せていない。 **2** N-COUNT 可算名詞 A **crew** is a group of people with special technical skills who work together on a task or project. 一団 ❑ …a two-man film crew making a documentary. 記録映画を制作している2名からなる撮影班 **3** V-T/V-I 他動詞/自動詞 If you **crew** a boat, you work on it as part of the crew. 乗組員として働く [他動詞]、乗組員として働く [自動詞] ❑ This neighbor crewed on a ferryboat. この隣人はフェリーで乗務員として働いた。 ❑ There were to be five teams of three crewing the boat. 3人ずつの5つのチームがボートに乗っている予定だった。

crib /krɪb/ (cribs) N-COUNT 可算名詞 A **crib** is a bed for a baby. ベビーベッド [mainly AM 主に米国英語]

crick|et /krɪkɪt/ (crickets) **1** N-UNCOUNT 不可算名詞 **Cricket** is an outdoor game played between two teams. Players try to score points, called runs, by hitting a ball with a wooden bat. クリケット ❑ During the summer term we would play cricket at the village ground. 夏学期の間には私たちは村の広場でクリケットをしたものだ。 **2** N-COUNT 可算名詞 A **cricket** is a small jumping insect that produces short, loud sounds by rubbing its wings together. コオロギ

crick|et|er /krɪkɪtər/ (cricketers) N-COUNT 可算名詞 A **cricketer** is a person who plays cricket. クリケットの選手

crime /kraɪm/ (crimes) **1** N-VAR 可変性名詞 A **crime** is an illegal action or activity for which a person can be punished by law. 犯罪 ❑ He and Lieutenant Cassidy were checking the scene of the crime. 彼とカシディー中尉は犯罪現場を調べていた。 ❑ …the growing problem of organized crime. 増加する組織犯罪の問題 **2** N-COUNT 可算名詞 If you say that doing something is a **crime**, you think it is very wrong or a serious mistake. あってはならないこと [DISAPPROVAL 不賛成] ❑ It would be a crime to travel all the way to Australia and not stop in Sydney. はるばるオーストラリアまで旅行をしてシドニーに立ち寄らないなんてとんでもないことだ。 → see **city**

	Word Partnership	*crime* は次の語句と使われる:
V.	commit a crime, fight against crime **1**	
ADJ.	organized crime, terrible crime, violent crime **1**	
N.	crime prevention, crime scene, crime wave **1** partner in crime **1** **2**	

crim|i|nal /krɪmɪnªl/ (criminals) **1** N-COUNT 可算名詞 A **criminal** is a person who has committed a crime. 犯罪者 [A *group of gunmen attacked a prison and set free nine criminals.* 銃撃犯の集団が刑務所を襲い，9名の犯罪者を解放した. **2** ADJ 形容詞 **Criminal** means connected with crime. 犯罪の □*Her husband faces various criminal charges.* 彼女の夫はさまざまな刑事責任を問われる. **3** ADJ 形容詞 If you describe an action as **criminal**, you think it is very wrong or a serious mistake. とんでもない [DISAPPROVAL 不賛成] □*He said a full-scale dispute involving strikes would be criminal.* 彼はストライキを伴う全面的な争議などはもってのほかであろうと言った.

crim|son /krɪmzªn/ (crimsons) COLOR 色彩語 Something that is **crimson** is deep red in color. 深紅色 □*...a mass of crimson flowers.* たくさんの深紅色の花々

cringe /krɪndʒ/ (cringes, cringing, cringed) V-I 自動詞 If you **cringe at** something, you feel embarrassed or disgusted, and perhaps show this feeling in your expression or by making a slight movement. すくむ □*Molly had cringed when Ann started picking up the guitar.* アンがギターを習い始めたとき，モリーはしり込みしていた. □*Chris had cringed at the thought of using her own family for publicity.* クリスは彼女自身の家族を宣伝に使うという考えにしり込みしていた.

crip|ple /krɪpªl/ (cripples, crippling, crippled) **1** N-COUNT 可算名詞 A person with a physical disability or a serious permanent injury is sometimes referred to as a **cripple**. 障害者 [OFFENSIVE 無礼な] □*She has gone from being a healthy, fit, and sporty young woman to being a cripple.* 彼女は健康で元気な運動好きの若い女性から障害者になってしまった. **2** V-T 他動詞 If someone **is crippled** by an injury, it is so serious that they can never move their body properly again. 障害を与える □*Mr. Easton was crippled in an accident and had to leave his job.* イーストン氏は事故で障害を負い，仕事を辞めねばならなかった. □*He had been warned that another bad fall could cripple him for life.* 彼はもう1度ひどく転落すれば，一生体が不自由になりかねないと警告を受けていた.

crip|pling /krɪplɪŋ/ **1** ADJ 形容詞 A **crippling** illness or disability is one that severely damages your health or your body. 身体障害を引き起こす [ADJ n] □*Arthritis and rheumatism are prominent crippling diseases.* 関節炎とリウマチは体の自由を奪う病気として際立っている. **2** ADJ 形容詞 If you say that an action, policy, or situation has a **crippling** effect on something, you mean it has a very serious, harmful effect. ひどい損害を与える □*The high cost of capital has a crippling effect on many small firms.* 資本のコスト高は多くの小企業にひどい悪影響を与える.

cri|sis /kraɪsɪs/ (crises /kraɪsiz/) N-VAR 可変性名詞 A **crisis** is a situation in which something or someone is affected by one or more very serious problems. 危機 □*Natural disasters have obviously contributed to the continent's economic crisis.* 自然災害が明らかにヨーロッパ大陸の経済危機の1因になっている. □*...someone to turn to in moments of crisis.* いざというときに頼りになる誰か

	Word Partnership	*crisis* は次の語句と使われる:
N.	housing crisis, crisis management, solution to a crisis	
ADJ.	major crisis, political crisis	
V.	solve a crisis	

crisp /krɪsp/ (crisper, crispest, crisps, crisping, crisped) **1** ADJ 形容詞 Food that is **crisp** is pleasantly hard, or has a pleasantly hard surface. パリパリした [APPROVAL 賛成] □*Bake the potatoes for 15 minutes, till they're nice and crisp.* ジャガイモがよい具合にパリパリになるまで15分焼きなさい. □*...crisp bacon.* かりっとしたベーコン **2** ADJ 形容詞 Weather that is pleasantly fresh, cold, and dry can be described as **crisp**. さわやかな [APPROVAL 賛成] □*...a crisp autumn day.* さわやかな秋の日 **3** ADJ 形容詞 **Crisp** cloth or paper is clean and has no creases in it. ぱりっとした，手の切れるような □*He wore a panama hat and a crisp white suit.* 彼はパナマ帽をかぶり，ぱりっとした白い背広を着ていた. □*I slipped between the crisp clean sheets.* 私はしわひとつない清潔なシーツの間にするっと入った. **4** V-T/V-I 他動詞/自動詞 If food **crisps** or if you **crisp** it, it becomes pleasantly hard, for example, because you have heated it at a high temperature. パリパリにする [他動詞]，パリパリになる [自動詞] □*Cook the bacon until it begins to crisp.* かりっとし始めるまでベーコンに火を通しなさい. **5** N-COUNT 可算名詞 **Crisps** are very thin slices of fried potato that are eaten cold as a snack. ポテトチップス [BRIT 英国英語; AM **chips, potato chips** 米国英語 **chips, potato chips**]

criss-cross /krɪs krɔs/ (criss-crosses, criss-crossing, criss-

crossed) also **crisscross** **1** V-T 他動詞 If a person or thing **criss-crosses** an area, they travel from one side to the other and back again many times, following different routes. If a number of things **criss-cross** an area, they cross it, and cross over each other. 縦横に動く □*They criss-crossed the country by bus.* 彼らはバスでその国を縦横に移動した. **2** V-RECIP 相互動詞 If two sets of lines or things **criss-cross**, they cross over each other. 交差する □*Wires criss-cross between the tops of the poles, forming a grid.* 電線は電柱の上端の間で交差し，格子状になっている. **3** ADJ 形容詞 A **criss-cross** pattern or design consists of lines crossing each other. 十文字の [ADJ n] □*Slash the tops of the loaves with a serrated knife in a criss-cross pattern.* ぎざぎざのナイフでパンの塊の上に十文字の切込みを入れなさい.

cri|teri|on /kraɪtɪəriən/ (criteria /kraɪtɪəriə/) N-COUNT 可算名詞 A **criterion** is a factor on which you judge or decide something. 基準 □*The most important criterion for entry is that applicants must design and make their own work.* 参加登録のための最も重要な基準は，申込者が自分で作品を設計し，制作しなければならないことである.

Word Link	crit ≈ to judge : critic, critical, criticize

crit|ic /krɪtɪk/ (critics) **1** N-COUNT 可算名詞 A **critic** is a person who writes about and expresses opinions about things such as books, movies, music, or art. 批評家，評論家 □*Mather was film critic for many years.* マザーは長年にわたって映画評論家だった. **2** N-COUNT 可算名詞 Someone who is a **critic** of a person or system disapproves of them and criticizes them publicly. 批判する人 □*The newspaper has been one of the most consistent critics ever of the government.* その新聞は最も首尾一貫して政府を批判してきたものの1つである.

criti|cal /krɪtɪkªl/ **1** ADJ 形容詞 A **critical** time, factor, or situation is extremely important. 決定的な □*The incident happened at a critical point in the campaign.* その出来事は選挙戦の重大な時期に起こった. □*He says setting priorities is of critical importance.* 彼は優先順位の設定が極めて重要であると言う. ●**criti|cal|ly** /krɪtɪkli/ ADV 副詞 決定的に □*Economic prosperity depends critically on an open world trading system.* 経済的繁栄は開かれた世界貿易機構に決定的に依存する. **2** ADJ 形容詞 A **critical** situation is very serious and dangerous. 危機的な □*The German authorities are considering an airlift if the situation becomes critical.* ドイツ当局は状況が危機的になれば，空輸を検討している. ●**criti|cal|ly** ADV 副詞 危機的に □*Moscow is running critically low on food supplies.* モスクワでは食糧の蓄えが危機的にひっぱくしている. **3** ADJ 形容詞 If a person is **critical** or in a **critical** condition in a hospital, they are seriously ill. 危篤の □*Ten of the injured are said to be in critical condition.* 負傷者のうち10名が危篤状態にあると言われている. ●**criti|cal|ly** ADV 副詞 危篤状態で □*She was critically ill.* 彼女は危篤だった. **4** ADJ 形容詞 To be **critical** of someone or something means to criticize them. 批判的な □*His report is highly critical of the trial judge.* 彼の報道はその公判裁判官に対して非常に批判的だ. □*She spoke critically of Lara.* 彼女はローラのことを批判的に語った. **5** ADJ 形容詞 A **critical** approach to something involves examining and judging it carefully. 批評力のある □*We need to become critical text-readers.* 我々は批評眼のある本文読解者になる必要がある. ●**criti|cal|ly** ADV 副詞 批判的に □*Wyman watched them critically.* ワイマンは彼らを批評的な目で眺めた. **6** ADJ 形容詞 If something or someone receives **critical** acclaim, critics say that they are very good. 批評家の □*The film met with considerable critical and public acclaim.* その映画は批評家および一般客からかなりの賞賛を得た.

	Word Partnership	*critical* は次の語句と使われる:
N.	critical issue, critical role **1** critical state **1** – **3** critical condition **3** critical acclaim **6**	
V.	become critical **1** **2**	
PREP.	critical of *someone*, critical of *something* **4**	

criti|cism /krɪtɪsɪzəm/ (criticisms) **1** N-VAR 可変性名詞 **Criticism** is the action of expressing disapproval of something or someone. A **criticism** is a statement that expresses disapproval. 批判 □*This policy had repeatedly come under strong criticism on Capitol Hill.* この政策は米国会で繰り返し強い批判にさらされていた. **2** N-UNCOUNT 不可算名詞 **Criticism** is a serious examination and judgment of something such as a book or play. 批評 □*She has published more than 20 books including novels, poetry and literary criticism.* 彼女は小説，詩，文芸批評など20冊以上の書籍を出版している.

	Thesaurus	*criticism* また次を参照:
N.	disapproval, judgment, put-down; (*ant.*) approval, flattery, praise **1** commentary, critique, evaluation, review **2**	

Word Partnership *criticism* は次の語句と使われる:

PREP.	criticism **against** *something*, criticism **from** *something*, criticism **of** *something* 1
ADJ.	**constructive** criticism, **open to** criticism 1 2
N.	**public** criticism 1 2
	literary criticism 2

Word Link crit ≈ to judge : critic, critical, criticize

criti|cize /krɪtɪsaɪz/ (criticizes, criticizing, criticized) V-T 他動詞 If you **criticize** someone or something, you express your disapproval of them by saying what you think is wrong with them. 批判する ❑ *His mother had rarely criticized him or any of her other children.* 彼の母は彼や他の子供たちの誰をもめったに批判しなかった.

Word Partnership *criticize* は次の語句と使われる:

N.	criticize **the government**
PREP.	**be** criticized **about/by/for**

cri|tique /krɪtik/ (critiques) N-COUNT 可算名詞 A **critique** is a written examination and judgment of a situation or of a person's work or ideas. 批評 [FORMAL 形式ばった] ❑ *She had brought a book, a feminist critique of Victorian lady novelists.* 彼女はビクトリア朝の女性小説家に関するフェミニズム的批評の本を買っていた.

croak /kroʊk/ (croaks, croaking, croaked) 1 V-I 自動詞 When a frog or bird **croaks**, it makes a harsh, low sound. ガーガー鳴く ❑ *Thousands of frogs croaked in the reeds by the riverbank.* 数千匹のカエルが川岸のアシの茂みで鳴いた. ● N-COUNT 可算名詞 **Croak** is also a noun. ガーガーいう鳴き声 ❑ *...the guttural croak of the frogs.* カエルのゲロゲロ声の鳴き声 2 V-T 他動詞 If someone **croaks** something, they say it in a low, rough voice. 低い声で言う ❑ *Tiller moaned and managed to croak, "Help me."* ティラーはうめき, しわがれた声を絞り出した. 「助けてくれ」 ● N-COUNT 可算名詞 **Croak** is also a noun. しわがれ声 ❑ *His voice was just a croak.* 彼の声はほとんどかすれていた. 3 V-I 自動詞 When someone **croaks**, they die. くたばる [INFORMAL くだけた] ❑ *I think the doctors were worried that I was going to croak on their watch.* 医者たちは私が自分たちの目の前で死ぬのではないかと心配していたと思う.

crock|ery /krɒkəri/ N-UNCOUNT 不可算名詞 **Crockery** is the plates, cups, saucers, and dishes that you use at meals. 陶器類 [mainly BRIT 主に英国英語]

croco|dile /krɒkədaɪl/ (crocodiles) N-COUNT 可算名詞 A **crocodile** is a large reptile with a long body and strong jaws. Crocodiles live in rivers and eat meat. ワニ

crois|sant /krwɑsɒn, krəsɒnt/ (croissants) N-VAR 可変性名詞 **Croissants** are bread rolls in the shape of a crescent that are eaten for breakfast. クロワッサン ❑ *...coffee and croissants.* コーヒーとクロワッサン.

cro|ny /kroʊni/ (cronies) N-COUNT 可算名詞 You can refer to friends that someone spends a lot of time with as their **cronies**, especially when you disapprove of them. 悪友 [INFORMAL くだけた, DISAPPROVAL 不賛成] ❑ *...lunchtime drinking sessions with his business cronies.* ランチタイムに仕事仲間と一杯.

crook /krʊk/ (crooks, crooking, crooked) 1 N-COUNT 可算名詞 A **crook** is a dishonest person or a criminal. 不正直な人, 悪人 [INFORMAL くだけた] ❑ *The man is a crook and a liar.* その男はとんでもない嘘つきだ. 2 N-COUNT 可算名詞 The **crook of** your arm or leg is the soft inside part where you bend your elbow or knee. (ひじやひざの) 内側 ❑ *She hid her face in the crook of her arm.* 彼女はひじで顔を隠した. 3 N-COUNT 可算名詞 A **crook** is a long pole with a large hook at the end. A crook is carried by a bishop in religious ceremonies, or by a shepherd. 柄の曲がった杖 (つえ) 4 V-T 他動詞 If you **crook** your arm or finger, you bend it. 曲げる ❑ *He crooked his finger: "Come forward," he said.* 彼は指を曲げて合図し, 「前に出ろ」と言った.

crook|ed /krʊkɪd/ 1 ADJ 形容詞 If you describe something as **crooked**, especially something that is usually straight, you mean that it is bent or twisted. 屈曲した ❑ *...the crooked line of his broken nose.* 折れて曲がった彼の鼻筋. 2 ADJ 形容詞 A **crooked** smile is uneven and bigger on one side than the other. ゆがんだ ❑ *Polly gave her a crooked grin.* ポリーはゆがんだ笑顔を見せた. 3 ADJ 形容詞 If you describe a person or an activity as **crooked**, you mean that they are dishonest or criminal. 不正な [INFORMAL くだけた] ❑ *...a crooked cop.* 悪徳警官.

croon /krun/ (croons, crooning, crooned) 1 V-T/V-I 他動詞/自動詞 If you **croon**, you sing or hum quietly and gently. ささやき声で歌う ❑ *He would much rather have been crooning in a smoky bar.* それよりずっと彼は紫煙たなびくバーで甘い歌声を聞かせたかっただろう. 2 V-T/V-I 他動詞/自動詞 If one person talks to another in a soft gentle voice, you can describe them as **crooning**, especially if you think they are being sentimental or insincere. 優しく声をか

ける; 甘い声をかける ❑ *"Dear boy," she crooned, hugging him heartily.* 彼女は男の子をぎゅっと抱きしめて「いい子ね」と優しく言った.

crop /krɒp/ (crops, cropping, cropped) 1 N-COUNT 可算名詞 **Crops** are plants such as wheat and potatoes that are grown in large quantities for food. 農作物 ❑ *Rice farmers here still plant and harvest their crops by hand.* ここでは今でも手作業で田植えと稲刈りをしています. 2 N-COUNT 可算名詞 The plants or fruits that are collected at harvest time are referred to as a **crop**. 収穫高 ❑ *Each year it produces a fine crop of fruit.* 毎年見事な実がなる. ❑ *The U.S. government says that this year's corn crop should be about 8 percent more than last year.* アメリカ政府は, 今年のトウモロコシの作柄を前年比8%増と予想しています. 3 N-COUNT 可算名詞 A **crop** is a short hairstyle. 短く刈った頭 ❑ *She had her long hair cut into a boyish crop.* 彼女は長かった髪を男の子のように短く刈った. 4 N-SING 単数名詞 You can refer to a group of people or things that have appeared together as a **crop of** people or things. 一の続出 [INFORMAL くだけた] ❑ *The present crop of books and documentaries about Marilyn Monroe exploit the thirtieth anniversary of her death.* マリリン・モンロー没後30年を当て込んだ出版物や番組が相次いでいる. 5 V-I 自動詞 When a plant **crops**, it produces fruits or parts which people want. (作物が) できる ❑ *Although these vegetables adapt well to our temperate climate, they tend to crop poorly.* これらの野菜はこの辺りの穏やかな気候に適しているが, なりは悪いことが多い. 6 V-T 他動詞 To **crop** someone's hair means to cut it short. 刈り込む ❑ *She cropped her hair and dyed it blonde.* 彼女は髪を短く刈ってブロンドに染めた. 7 V-T 他動詞 If you **crop** a photograph, you cut part of it off, in order to get rid of part of the picture or to be able to frame it. トリミングする ❑ *I decided to crop the picture just above the water line.* 写真を水面のちょうど上の部分で切り取ることにした.

▶ **crop up** PHRASAL VERB 句動詞 If something **crops up**, it appears or happens, usually unexpectedly. 不意に現れる ❑ *His name has cropped up at every selection meeting this season.* 今季の選出会議では予想に反して毎回彼の名前が持ち上がった.

→ see **cotton, farm, grain, photography**

cro|quet /kroʊkeɪ/ N-UNCOUNT 不可算名詞 **Croquet** is a game played on grass in which the players use long wooden sticks called mallets to hit balls through metal arches. クローケー (日本のゲートボールのもとになったスポーツ)

cross

1 MOVING ACROSS
2 ANGRY

1 **cross** /krɒs/ (crosses, crossing, crossed)
↪ Please look at meaning 12 to see if the expression you are looking for is shown under another headword.

1 V-T/V-I 他動詞/自動詞 If you **cross** something such as a room, a road, or an area of land or water, you move or travel to the other side of it. If you **cross to** a place, you move or travel over a room, road, or area of land or water in order to reach that place. 横切る ❑ *She was partly to blame for failing to look as she crossed the road.* 道路を渡るときによく見ていなかったので, 彼女の側にも落ち度がある. ❑ *Egan crossed to the drinks cabinet and poured a Scotch.* イーガンは酒棚に行ってスコッチを注いだ. 2 V-T 他動詞 A road, railroad, or bridge that **crosses** an area of land or water passes over it. 越える, 渡る; 架かる ❑ *The road crosses the river half a mile outside the town.* その道は町から半マイル行ったところで川を越える. 3 V-T 他動詞 If someone or something **crosses** a limit or boundary, for example, the limit of acceptable behavior, they go beyond it. 越える (一線を) ❑ *I normally never write into magazines but Mr. Stubbs has finally crossed the line.* 私はまず雑誌に書くことはないが, スタッブズ氏はついにその一線を越えてしまった. 4 V-T 他動詞 If an expression **crosses** someone's face, it appears briefly on their face. (表情が) よぎる [WRITTEN 書き言葉] ❑ *Berg tilts his head and a mischievous look crosses his face.* バーグは首をかしげて一瞬いたずらっぽい表情をした. 5 V-T 他動詞 If you **cross** your arms, legs, or fingers, you put one of them on top of the other. 交差させる ❑ *Jill crossed her legs and rested her chin on one fist, as if lost in deep thought.* ジルは足を組んでこぶしであごを支え, 深い物思いにふけっているかのようだった. 6 V-RECIP 相互動詞 Lines or roads that **cross** meet and go across each other. 交差する ❑ *...the intersection where Main and Center streets cross.* メイン通りとセンター通りの交差点. 7 N-COUNT 可算名詞 A **cross** is a shape that consists of a vertical line or piece with a shorter horizontal line or piece across it. It is the most important Christian symbol. 十字形; 十字架 ❑ *Around her neck was a cross on a silver chain.* 彼女は首に銀の十字のネックレスをしていた. 8 N-COUNT 可算名詞 A **cross** is a written mark in the shape of an X. You can use it, for example, to indicate that an answer to a question is wrong, to mark the position of something on a map, or to indicate your vote on a ballot. バツ印 ❑ *Put a cross next to those activities you like.* やりたいと思うものに×をつけてください. 9 N-COUNT 可算名詞 In some team sports such as soccer and hockey, a **cross** is the passing of the ball from the side of the field to a player in the center, usually in front of the goal. クロ

スパス ❑*Johnson hit an accurate cross to Groves.* ジョンソンはグローブズに正確なクロスパスを送った. ⑩ N-SING 単数名詞 Something that is **a cross between** two things is neither one thing nor the other, but a mixture of both. 中間のもの ❑*"Ha!" It was a cross between a laugh and a bark.* 「ハー！」それは笑い声とも叫び声ともつかなかった. ⑪ ADJ 形容詞 A **cross** street is a road that crosses another more important road. 幹線道路に交差する [AM 米国英語] [ADJ n] ❑*The Army boys had personnel carriers blockading the cross streets.* 横這は兵士たちの乗る兵員輸送車でふさがれていた. ⑫ → see also **crossing** ⑬ to **cross** your **fingers** → see **finger** ⑭ **cross** my **heart** → see **heart** ⑮ to **cross** your **mind** → see **mind** ⑯ to **cross swords** → see **sword**

▶ **cross out** PHRASAL VERB 句動詞 If you **cross out** words on a page, you draw a line through them, because they are wrong or because you want to change them. 打ち消し線を引く ❑*He crossed out "fellow subjects," and instead inserted "fellow citizens."* 彼は「同国の臣民」を消し「同国の市民」に直した.

N.	cross **a street** ❶ ⓵ ❷
	cross **someone** ❶ ⓷
	cross **your legs** ❶ ⓹
	cross **someone's mind** ❶ ⑫

❷ **cross** /krɔs/ (crosser, crossest) ADJ 形容詞 Someone who is **cross** is angry or irritated. いらいらした ❑*The women are cross and bored.* 女性たちは腹を立てうんざりしている. ❑*I'm terribly cross with him.* あいつには無性に腹が立つ. ● **cross**|**ly** ADV 副詞 [ADV with v] いらいらして ❑*"No, no, no," Morris said crossly.* モリスはむしゃくしゃして「だめ、だめ、だめ」と繰り返した.

cross-country ⓵ N-UNCOUNT 不可算名詞 **Cross-country** is the sport of running, riding, or skiing across open countryside rather than along roads or around a running track. クロスカントリー ❑*She finished third in the world cross-country championships in Antwerp.* アントワープで開かれた世界クロスカントリー選手権で彼女は3位にゴールした. ⓶ ADJ 形容詞 A **cross-country** trip takes you from one side of a country to the other. 国土を横断する [ADJ n] ❑*...cross-country rail services.* 国土を結ぶ鉄道網. ● ADV 副詞 **Cross-country** is also an adverb. 国土を横断して [ADV after v] ❑*I drove cross-country in his van.* 私は彼のライトバンで国土を横断した.

cross-examine (cross-examines, cross-examining, cross-examined) V-T 他動詞 When a lawyer **cross-examines** someone during a trial or hearing, he or she questions them about the evidence that they have already given. 反対尋問する ❑*The accused's lawyers will get a chance to cross-examine him.* 被告人弁護団は被告に対する反対尋問が与えられる. ● **cross-examination** (cross-examinations) N-VAR 可変性名詞 反対尋問 ❑*...the cross-examination of a witness in a murder case.* 殺人事件における証人への反対尋問.
→ see **trial**

cross|**ing** /krɔsɪŋ/ (crossings) ⓵ N-COUNT 可算名詞 A **crossing** is a journey by boat or ship to a place on the other side of an ocean, river, or lake. 船で渡ること ❑*He made the crossing from Cape Town to Sydney in just over twenty-six days.* 彼はケープタウンからシドニーまでをわずか26日余りで航海しました. ⓶ N-COUNT 可算名詞 A **crossing** is a place where two roads, paths, or lines cross. 交差点 ❑*She sighed and squatted down next to the crossing of the two trails.* 彼女はため息をつくと四つ辻のそばにしゃがみ込んだ. ⓷ N-COUNT 可算名詞 A **crossing** is the same as a **grade crossing** or a **level crossing**. 踏切

cross|**over** /krɔsoʊvər/ (crossovers) ⓵ N-VAR 可変性名詞 A **crossover** of one style and another, especially in music or fashion, is a combination of the two different styles. クロスオーバー ❑*...the contemporary crossover of pop, jazz and funk.* ポップスとジャズとファンクが融合した現代のクロスオーバー. ⓶ N-SING 単数名詞 In music or fashion, if someone makes a **crossover from** one style **to** another, they become successful outside the style they were originally known for. 転向 ❑*I told her the crossover from actress to singer is easier than from singer to actress.* 歌手が女優になるよりも女優が歌手になるほうが簡単なのよ、と私は彼女に言った.

cross-reference (cross-references) N-COUNT 可算名詞 A **cross-reference** is a note in a book which tells you that there is relevant or more detailed information in another part of the book. 参照箇所を示す注 ❑*It concludes with a very useful summary of key points, with cross-references to where each key point is dealt with in the book.* 巻末には要点のまとめがあり、それぞれ本文の参照ページが示されていてとても使いやすい.

cross|**roads** /krɔsroʊdz/ (crossroads)

Crossroads is both the singular and the plural form.

Crossroads は単数形でも複数形でもある.

⓵ N-COUNT 可算名詞 A **crossroads** is a place where two roads meet and cross each other. 十字路 ❑*Turn right at the first crossroads.* 最初の交差点を右に曲がってください. ⓶ N-SING 単数名詞 If you say that something is **at a crossroads**, you mean that it has reached a very important stage in its development where it could go one way or another. 岐路 ❑*The company was clearly at a crossroads.* 間違いなく会社は岐路に立たされていた.

cross-section (cross-sections) also **cross section** ⓵ N-COUNT 可算名詞 If you refer to a **cross-section** of particular things or people, you mean a group of them that you think is typical or representative of all of them. 代表例 ❑*I was surprised at the cross-section of people there.* そこの人たちの平均的な姿には驚かされた. ⓶ N-COUNT 可算名詞 A **cross-section** of an object is what you would see if you could cut straight through the middle of it. 断面図 [also "in" n] ❑*...a cross-section of an airplane.* 飛行機の断面図.

cross|**word** /krɔswɜrd/ (crosswords) N-COUNT 可算名詞 A **crossword** or **crossword puzzle** is a word game in which you work out the answers and write them in the white squares of a pattern of small black and white squares. クロスワード ❑*He could do the Times crossword in 15 minutes.* 彼ならタイムズ紙のクロスワードを15分で解いてしまうだろう.

crotch /krɒtʃ/ (crotches) ⓵ N-COUNT 可算名詞 Your **crotch** is the part of your body between the tops of your legs. (人の) 股 (また) ❑*Glover kicked him hard in the crotch.* グローバーは彼のまたぐらを思い切り蹴った. ⓶ N-COUNT 可算名詞 The **crotch** of something such as a pair of pants is the part that covers the area between the tops of your legs. (ズボンの) 股 (また) ❑*They were too long in the crotch.* それは股上が深すぎた.

crouch /kraʊtʃ/ (crouches, crouching, crouched) V-I 自動詞 If you **are crouching**, your legs are bent under you so that you are close to the ground and leaning forward slightly. しゃがみ込む ❑*We were crouching in the bushes.* 私たちは茂みにしゃがみ込んでいた. ❑*I crouched on the ground.* 私は地面にうずくまった. ● N-SING 単数名詞 **Crouch** is also a noun. しゃがむこと ❑*They walked in a crouch, each bent over close to the ground.* 彼らはそれぞれ地面にかがむようにして進んでいった. ● PHRASAL VERB 句動詞 **Crouch down** means the same as **crouch**. しゃがむ ❑*He crouched down and reached under the mattress.* 彼はしゃがみ込んでマットレスの下に手を伸ばした.

crow /kroʊ/ (crows, crowing, crowed) ⓵ N-COUNT 可算名詞 A **crow** is a large black bird which makes a loud, harsh noise. カラス ❑*The crows roosted in Fonsa's Tower.* カラスたちはフォンサ塔をねぐらにしていた. ⓶ V-I 自動詞 When a cock **crows**, it makes a loud sound, often early in the morning. 鳴く ❑*The cock crows and the dawn chorus begins.* ニワトリが鳴き声を告げると、小鳥たちもさえずり出す. ⓷ PHRASE 句 If someone **eats crow**, they admit they have been wrong and apologize, especially in situations where this is humiliating or embarrassing for them. しぶしぶ誤りを認める [AM 米国英語] ❑*He wanted to make his critics eat crow.* 彼は批判した連中に頭を下げさせたい気分だった.

crowd /kraʊd/ (crowds, crowding, crowded) ⓵ N-COUNT-COLL 集合可算名詞 A **crowd** is a large group of people who have gathered together, for example, to watch or listen to something interesting, or to protest about something. 群衆 ❑*A huge crowd gathered in a square outside the Kremlin walls.* クレムリン宮殿の城外広場に大群衆が集結しました. ❑*It took some two hours before the crowd was fully dispersed.* 群衆がすっかりいなくなるのに2時間ほどかかりました. ⓶ N-COUNT 可算名詞 A particular **crowd** is a group of friends, or a set of people who share the same interests or job. 一の仲間 [INFORMAL くだけた] ❑*The old friends have all come out for this occasion.* この集まりに昔の仲間がみな顔を揃えた. ⓷ V-I 自動詞 When people **crowd around** someone or something, they gather closely together around them. 群がる ❑*The hungry refugees crowded around the tractors.* 空腹の難民たちはトラクターを取り囲みました. ⓸ V-T/V-I 他動詞/自動詞 If people **crowd into** a place or **are crowded into** a place, large numbers of them enter it so that it becomes very full. 押し寄せる ❑*Hundreds of thousands of people have crowded into the center of the Lithuanian capital, Vilnius.* 数十万もの人々がリトアニア首都ビリニュスの中心に押し寄せてきました. ❑*One group of journalists were crowded into a minibus.* 記者の一団がマイクロバスに詰め込まれた. ⓹ V-T 他動詞 If a group of people **crowd** a place, there are so many of them there that it is full. いっぱいにする ❑*Thousands of demonstrators crowded the streets shouting slogans.* 何千人ものデモ参加者が通りを埋め尽くしてスローガンを叫びました.

V.	attract **a crowd**, avoid **the crowd**, crowd **gathers** ⓵
ADJ.	enthusiastic **crowd**, small **crowd** ⓵
PREP.	crowd **around something** ⓷
	crowd **into something** ⓸

crowd|**ed** /kraʊdɪd/ ⓵ ADJ 形容詞 If a place is **crowded**, it is full of people. 人でいっぱいの ❑*He peered slowly around the small crowded room.* 彼は混雑した小さな部屋をゆっくりと見渡した. ⓶ ADJ 形容詞 If a place is **crowded**, a lot of people live there. 人口の多い ❑*...a crowded city of 2 million.* 人口2百万の混雑した大都市. ⓷ ADJ 形

容詞 If your schedule, your life, or your mind is **crowded**, it is full of events, activities, or thoughts. ぎっしり詰まった ❑ *Never before has a summit had such a crowded agenda.* これほど議題が多いサミットはこれまでになかった.

crown /kraʊn/ (crowns, crowning, crowned) **1** N-COUNT 可算名詞 A **crown** is a circular ornament, usually made of gold and jewels, which a king or queen wears on their head at official ceremonies. You can also use **crown** to refer to anything circular that is worn on someone's head. 冠 ❑ *...a crown of flowers.* 花の冠. **2** N-COUNT 可算名詞 Your **crown** is the top part of your head, at the back. 頭頂部 ❑ *He laid his hand gently on the crown of her head.* 彼は彼女の頭の上にそっと手を置いた. **3** N-COUNT 可算名詞 A **crown** is an artificial top piece fixed over a broken or decayed tooth. 人工歯冠 ❑ *How long does it take to have crowns fitted?* 歯冠をかぶせてもらうのにどのくらい時間がかかりますか. **4** N-PROPER 固有名詞 The government of a country that has a king or queen is sometimes referred to as **the Crown**. 君主国の政府 ❑ *She says the sovereignty of the Crown must be preserved.* 君主制は継続すべきだと彼女は言います. ❑ *...a minister of the Crown.* 閣内相. **5** V-T 他動詞 When a king or queen **is crowned**, a crown is placed on their head as part of a ceremony in which they are officially made king or queen. 王位につく [usu passive] ❑ *Two days later, Juan Carlos was crowned king.* 2日後にファン・カルロスが王位についた.
→ see **teeth**

Word Link cruc ≈ cross : *crucial, crucifixion, crucify*

cru|cial /kruʃ⁰l/ ADJ 形容詞 If you describe something as **crucial**, you mean it is extremely important. 重大な ❑ *He had administrators under him but made the crucial decisions himself.* 彼の下には管理職がいたが, 重大な決定は自ら下した. ● **cru|cial|ly** ADV 副詞 きわめて ❑ *Chewing properly is crucially important.* きちんとかむことは特に大切に.

Word Partnership *crucial* は次の語句と使われる:

N.	crucial **decision**, crucial **development**, crucial **role**, crucial **skill**, crucial **stage**, crucial **to something**

cru|ci|fix|ion /kruːsɪfɪkʃ⁰n/ (crucifixions) **1** N-VAR 可変性名詞 **Crucifixion** is a way of killing people which was common in the Roman Empire, in which they were tied or nailed to a cross and left to die. はりつけ ❑ *...her historical novel about the crucifixion of Christians in Rome.* 古代ローマでのキリスト教徒の磔刑 (たくけい) をテーマにした彼女の歴史小説. **2** N-PROPER 固有名詞 **The Crucifixion** is the crucifixion of Christ. キリストのはりつけ ❑ *...the central message of the Crucifixion.* キリストの処刑がもつ最も重要なメッセージ.

cru|ci|fy /kruːsɪfaɪ/ (crucifies, crucifying, crucified) **1** V-T 他動詞 If someone **is crucified**, they are killed by being tied or nailed to a cross and left to die. はりつけの刑に処せられる [usu passive] ❑ *...the day that Christ was crucified.* キリストがはりつけにされた日. **2** V-T 他動詞 To **crucify** someone means to criticize or punish them severely. さんざん言う; 恐ろしい目にあわせる [INFORMAL くだけた] ❑ *She'll crucify me if she finds you still here.* まだ君がここにいるのが知れたら, 彼女からどんな目にあわされるか.

crude /kruːd/ (cruder, crudest) **1** ADJ 形容詞 A **crude** method or measurement is not exact or detailed, but may be useful or correct in a rough, general way. 大まかな ❑ *Standard measurements of blood pressure are an important but crude way of assessing the risk of heart disease or strokes.* 心疾患や脳卒中のリスクを判断する上で, 一般的な血圧測定は重要ではあるが大雑把な与えるものに過ぎない. ● **crude|ly** ADV 副詞 大まかに ❑ *The donors can be split – a little crudely – into two groups.* やや大ざっぱだが, ドナーは次の2つに分類することができる. **2** ADJ 形容詞 If you describe an object that someone has made as **crude**, you mean that it has been made in a very simple way or from very simple parts. 粗雑な ❑ *...crude wooden boxes.* 粗作りの木箱. ● **crude|ly** ADV 副詞 粗く ❑ *...a crudely carved wooden form.* 粗削りの木型. **3** ADJ 形容詞 If you describe someone as **crude**, you disapprove of them because they speak or behave in a rude, offensive, or unsophisticated way. 無作法な [DISAPPROVAL 不賛成] ❑ *Must you be quite so crude?* あなたって人はどうしてそんなに下品なのかしら. ● **crude|ly** ADV 副詞 無作法に ❑ *He hated it when she spoke so crudely.* 彼は彼女がそのような下品な話し方をするのが大嫌いだった. **4** ADJ 形容詞 [ADJ n] **Crude** substances are in a natural or unrefined state, and have not yet been used in manufacturing processes. 未加工の **5** N-MASS 質量名詞 **Crude** is the same as **crude oil**. 原油
→ see **oil**

crude oil N-UNCOUNT 不可算名詞 **Crude oil** is oil in its natural state before it has been processed or refined. 原油 ❑ *A thousand tons of crude oil has spilled into the sea from an oil tanker.* タンカーから千トンの原油が海に流出しました.

cru|el /kruːəl/ (crueler or crueller, cruelest or cruellest) **1** ADJ 形容詞 Someone who is **cruel** deliberately causes pain or distress to

people or animals. 残酷な ❑ *Children can be so cruel.* 子供はときに残酷になる. ● **cru|el|ly** ADV 副詞 [ADV with v] 残酷に ❑ *Douglas was often cruelly tormented by jealous siblings.* 彼は嫉妬深い兄弟にひどくいじめられることがよくあった. **2** ADJ 形容詞 A situation or event that is **cruel** is very harsh and causes people distress. 過酷な ❑ *...struggling to survive in a cruel world with which they cannot cope.* 耐え切れないほど過酷な世界で必死に生き残る. ● **cru|el|ly** ADV 副詞 過酷にも ❑ *His life was cruelly shattered by an event not of his own making.* 何の関係のない事件に巻き込まれ, 彼は人生をめちゃくちゃにされた.

Thesaurus *cruel* また次を参照:

ADJ.	harsh, heartless, mean, nasty, unkind; (ant.) gentle, kind **1**
	grim, severe **2**

cru|el|ty /kruːəlti/ (cruelties) N-VAR 可変性名詞 **Cruelty** is behavior that deliberately causes pain or distress to people or animals. 残忍な行為 ❑ *Britain had laws against cruelty to animals but none to protect children.* イギリスには動物虐待を防止する法律はあったが, 児童虐待を防止する法律はなかった.

cruise /kruːz/ (cruises, cruising, cruised) **1** N-COUNT 可算名詞 A **cruise** is a vacation during which you travel on a ship or boat and visit a number of places. 船旅 ❑ *He and his wife were planning to go on a world cruise.* 彼は妻と世界一周の船旅を計画していた. **2** V-T/V-I 他動詞/自動詞 If you **cruise** an ocean, river, or canal, you travel around it or along it on a cruise. 船で巡る ❑ *She wants to cruise the canals of France in a barge.* 彼女はフランスの運河を船で巡ってみたいと思っている. ❑ *...a vacation cruising around the Caribbean.* カリブ海周遊のバカンスの旅. **3** V-I 自動詞 If a car, ship, or aircraft **cruises** somewhere, it moves there at a steady comfortable speed. 巡回する, 巡航する ❑ *A black and white police car cruised past.* 巡回中の白黒のパトカーが通り過ぎていった.
→ see **ship**

cruis|er /kruːzər/ (cruisers) **1** N-COUNT 可算名詞 A **cruiser** is a motorboat which has an area for people to live or sleep. クルーザー ❑ *...a three-hour journey in a small cruiser with indoor and outdoor seating.* 室内と甲板にベンチシートがある小型クルーザーでの3時間の旅. **2** N-COUNT 可算名詞 A **cruiser** is a large fast warship. 巡洋艦 ❑ *Italy had lost three cruisers and two destroyers.* イタリアは巡洋艦3隻と駆逐艦2隻を失っていた. **3** N-COUNT 可算名詞 A **cruiser** is a police car. パトカー [AM 米国英語] ❑ *Police cruisers surrounded the bank throughout the day.* 一日中パトカーがその銀行を包囲した.

crumb /krʌm/ (crumbs) N-COUNT 可算名詞 **Crumbs** are tiny pieces that fall from bread, cookies, or cake when you cut it or eat it. くず, かけら ❑ *I stood up, brushing crumbs from my pants.* 私は立ち上がって, ズボンについたパンくずを払い落とした.

crum|ble /krʌmb⁰l/ (crumbles, crumbling, crumbled) **1** V-T/V-I 他動詞/自動詞 If something **crumbles**, or if you **crumble** it, it breaks into a lot of small pieces. 砕く [他動詞], 砕ける [自動詞] ❑ *Under the pressure, the flint crumbled into fragments.* 圧力がかかると火打ち石は粉々に砕けた. **2** V-I 自動詞 If an old building or piece of land **is crumbling**, parts of it keep breaking off. ぼろぼろと崩れる ❑ *The high and low-rise apartment blocks built in the 1960s are crumbling.* 1960年代に建築された高層や低層のアパートが一部崩れてきています. ● PHRASAL VERB 句動詞 **Crumble away** means the same as **crumble**. 崩れる ❑ *Much of the coastline is crumbling away.* 多くの海岸線が失われている. **3** V-I 自動詞 If something such as a system, relationship, or hope **crumbles**, it comes to an end. 崩れてなくなる ❑ *Their economy crumbled under the weight of United Nations sanctions.* 国連制裁の影響でその国の経済は破綻 (はたん) した. ● PHRASAL VERB 句動詞 **Crumble away** means the same as **crumble**. ❑ *Opposition more or less crumbled away.* 反対の声はほとんどなくなった.

crum|bly /krʌmbli/ (crumblier, crumbliest) ADJ 形容詞 Something that is **crumbly** is easily broken into a lot of little pieces. もろい ❑ *...crumbly cheese.* 砕けやすいチーズ.

crum|ple /krʌmp⁰l/ (crumples, crumpling, crumpled) V-T/V-I 他動詞/自動詞 If you **crumple** something such as paper or cloth, or if it **crumples**, it is squashed and becomes full of untidy creases and folds. しわくちゃにする [他動詞], しわくちゃになる [自動詞] ❑ *She crumpled the paper in her hand.* 彼女は手で紙をくしゃっと丸めた. ● PHRASAL VERB 句動詞 **Crumple up** means the same as **crumple**. しわくちゃにする ❑ *She crumpled up her coffee cup.* 彼女は紙コップをくしゃっとつぶした. ● **crum|pled** ADJ 形容詞 しわくちゃの ❑ *His uniform was crumpled and untidy.* 彼の制服はしわくちゃで汚らしかった.

crunch /krʌntʃ/ (crunches, crunching, crunched) **1** V-T/V-I 他動詞/自動詞 If you **crunch** something hard, such as a piece of candy, or if it **crunches**, you crush it noisily between your teeth. バリバリとかむ [他動詞], バリバリと音を立てる [自動詞] ❑ *She sucked an ice cube into her mouth, and crunched it loudly.* 彼女は氷を口に含むと, ガリガリと音を立ててかみ砕いた. **2** V-T/V-I 他動詞/自動詞 If

something **crunches** or if you **crunch** it, it makes a breaking or crushing noise, for example, when you step on it. 砕ける [自動詞], 砕く [他動詞] ▢ *A piece of china crunched under my foot.* 磁器が足の下でパリッと砕けた. ●N-COUNT 可算名詞 **Crunch** is also a noun. ものが砕ける音 ▢ *She heard the crunch of tires on the gravel driveway.* 彼女は砂利道を進んでくる車の音を聞いた. ③ V-I 自動詞 If you **crunch** across a surface made of very small stones, you move across it causing it to make a crunching noise. ザクザクと音を立てる ▢ *I crunched across the gravel.* 私は砂利道をザクザクと音を立てながら歩いた. ④ V-T 他動詞 To **crunch** numbers means to do a lot of calculations using a calculator or computer. （大量のデータを）処理する ▢ *I pored over the books with great enthusiasm, often crunching the numbers until 1:00 a.m.* 帳簿を隅々まで精査したので, 計算が深夜1時までかかることもよくあった. ⑤ N-SING 単数名詞 You can refer to an important time or event, for example, when an important decision has to be made, as **the crunch**. 重大な局面 ▢ *He can rely on my support when the crunch comes.* 彼が重大な決断をしなければならないときは力になってやれると思います. ⑥ N-COUNT 可算名詞 A situation in which a business or economy has very little money can be referred to as a **crunch**. 資金の逼迫（ひっぱく）[BUSINESS 実業] ▢ *The U.N. is facing a cash crunch.* 国連は財政危機に直面しています.

crunchy /krʌntʃi/ (**crunchier, crunchiest**) ADJ 形容詞 Food that is **crunchy** is pleasantly hard or crisp so that it makes a noise when you eat it. しゃきしゃきした [APPROVAL 賛成] ▢ *...fresh, crunchy vegetables.* しゃきっとした新鮮な野菜

cru|sade /kruseɪd/ (**crusades, crusading, crusaded**) ① N-COUNT 可算名詞 A **crusade** is a long and determined attempt to achieve something for a cause that you feel strongly about. 熱心な活動 ▢ *He made it his crusade to teach children to love books.* 子供たちが本を好きになるように彼は熱心に活動した. ② V-I 自動詞 If you **crusade** for a particular cause, you make a long and determined effort to achieve something for it. 熱心に活動する [自動詞] ▢ *...a newspaper that has crusaded against the country's cocaine traffickers.* 国内のコカインを撲滅する運動に力を注いできた新聞社

cru|sad|er /kruseɪdər/ (**crusaders**) N-COUNT 可算名詞 A **crusader** for a cause is someone who does a lot in support of it. 運動家 ▢ *He set himself up as a crusader for higher press and broadcasting standards.* 彼は新聞や放送の報道の質を向上させるための活動に取り組んでいくことにした.

crush /krʌʃ/ (**crushes, crushing, crushed**) ① V-T 他動詞 To **crush** something means to press it very hard so that its shape is destroyed or so that it breaks into pieces. 押しつぶす, 粉々にする ▢ *Andrew crushed his empty can.* アンドリューは空き缶を押しつぶした. ▢ *...crushed ice.* クラッシュアイス ② V-T 他動詞 To **crush** a protest or movement, or a group of opponents, means to defeat it completely, usually by force. 鎮圧する, 壊滅させる ▢ *The military operation was the first step in a plan to crush the uprising.* その軍事行動は反乱を鎮圧する計画の第一段階でした. ●**crush|ing** N-UNCOUNT 不可算名詞 ▢ *...the violent crushing of anti-government demonstrations.* 反政府デモに対する力による鎮圧 ③ V-T 他動詞 [usu passive] If you **are crushed** by something, it upsets you a great deal. 打ちひしがれる ▢ *Listen to criticism but don't be crushed by it.* 批判に耳を傾けなさい. でも批判に打ちひしがれてはならない. ④ V-T 他動詞 If you **are crushed** against someone or something, you are pushed or pressed against them. 押しつけられる [usu passive] ▢ *We were at the front, crushed against the stage.* 最前列にいた私たちは舞台の壁に押しつけられた. ⑤ N-COUNT 可算名詞 A **crush** is a crowd of people close together, in which it is difficult to move. 人込み ▢ *His thirteen-year-old son somehow got separated in the crush.* 人込みの中で彼の13歳になる息子がなぜかはぐれてしまった. ⑥ N-COUNT 可算名詞 If you have a **crush on** someone, you are in love with them but do not have a relationship with them. 一目ぼれする [INFORMAL くだけた] ▢ *She had a crush on you, you know.* あの子はお前に一目ぼれだろ.
→ see **crash**

crush|ing /krʌʃɪŋ/ ADJ 形容詞 A **crushing** defeat, burden, or disappointment is a very great or severe one. 決定的な, 圧倒的な [EMPHASIS 強調] [ADJ n] ▢ *...since their crushing defeat in the local elections.* 地方選挙で大敗を喫してからは

crust /krʌst/ (**crusts**) ① N-COUNT 可算名詞 The **crust** on a loaf of bread is the outside part. パンの皮, パンの耳 ▢ *Cut the crusts off the bread and soak the bread in the milk.* 耳を切ったパンをミルクに浸します. ② N-COUNT 可算名詞 A pie's **crust** is its cooked pastry. パイ皮 ▢ *The Key lime pie was bursting with flavor. Good crust, too.* そのキーライムパイはとても風味が豊かで, パイ皮もおいしかった. ③ N-COUNT 可算名詞 A **crust** is a hard layer of something, especially on top of a softer or wetter substance. 硬くなった表面 ▢ *As the water evaporates, a crust of salt is left on the surface of the soil.* 水が蒸発した地表には塩の層ができる. ④ N-COUNT 可算名詞 The Earth's **crust** is its outer layer. 地殻 ▢ *Earthquakes leave scars in the Earth's crust.* 地震が起こると地殻に痕跡が残る.
→ see **continent, core, earthquake**

crusty /krʌsti/ (**crustier, crustiest**) ADJ 形容詞 **Crusty** bread has a hard, crisp outside. （パンなどの）皮がパリパリした ▢ *...crusty French loaves.* パリッとした皮のフランスパン

crutch /krʌtʃ/ (**crutches**) ① N-COUNT 可算名詞 A **crutch** is a stick whose top fits around or under the user's arm, which someone with an injured foot or leg uses to support their weight when walking. つえ ▢ *I can walk without the aid of crutches.* つえがなくても歩けます. ② N-SING 単数名詞 If you refer to someone or something as a **crutch**, you mean that they give you help or support. 支え ▢ *He gave up the crutch of alcohol.* 彼は酒に頼るのをやめた.

crux /krʌks/ N-SING 単数名詞 The **crux of** a problem or argument is the most important or difficult part of it which affects everything else. 一の核心 ▢ *He said the crux of the matter was economic policy.* 問題の核心は経済政策だと彼は述べた.

cry /kraɪ/ (**cries, crying, cried**) ① V-I 自動詞 When you **cry**, tears come from your eyes, usually because you are unhappy or hurt. 泣く ▢ *I hung up the phone and started to cry.* 電話を切ったら泣けてきた. ▢ *He cried with anger and frustration.* 彼は怒りと失望のあまり泣いた. ●N-SING 単数名詞 **Cry** is also a noun. 泣くこと ▢ *A nurse patted me on the shoulder and said, "You have a good cry, dear."* 看護師が私の肩を軽くたたき, 「思い切り泣いていいのよ」と言ってくれた. ●**cry|ing** N-UNCOUNT 不可算名詞 泣くこと ▢ *She had been unable to sleep for three days because of her 13-week-old son's crying.* 生後13週になる息子が夜泣きするので彼女は3日間眠れなかった. ② V-T 他動詞 If you **cry** something, you shout it or say it loudly. 叫ぶ ▢ *"Nancy Drew," she cried, "you're under arrest!"* 「ナンシー・ドルー, お前を逮捕する」と彼女は叫んだ. ●PHRASAL VERB 句動詞 **Cry out** means the same as **cry**. 叫ぶ ▢ *"You're wrong, quite wrong!" Henry cried out, suddenly excited.* 彼は急に興奮して「それは違う, 全く違う」と叫んだ. ③ N-COUNT 可算名詞 A **cry** is a loud, high sound that you make when you feel a strong emotion such as fear, pain, or pleasure. 叫び声 ▢ *A cry of horror broke from me.* 恐怖のあまり叫び声を上げた. ④ N-COUNT 可算名詞 A **cry** is a shouted word or phrase, usually one that is intended to attract someone's attention. 大声 ▢ *Thousands of Ukrainians burst into cries of "bravo."* 何千人ものウクライナ人が突然「ブラボー」と叫び出しました. ⑤ N-COUNT 可算名詞 You can refer to a public protest about something or an appeal for something as a **cry** of some kind. 声 [JOURNALISM ジャーナリズム] ▢ *There have been cries of outrage about this expenditure.* この支出に対して怒りの声が上がっています. ⑥ N-COUNT 可算名詞 A bird's or an animal's **cry** is the loud, high sound that it makes. 鳴き声 ▢ *...the cry of a seagull.* カモメの鳴き声 ⑦ → see also **crying** ⑧ to **cry** your **eyes out** → see **eye** ⑨ a **shoulder** to **cry** on → see **shoulder**
→ see Word Web: **cry**

▶ **cry out** ① PHRASAL VERB 句動詞 If you **cry out**, you call out loudly because you are frightened, unhappy, or in pain. 大声で叫ぶ ▢ *He was crying out in pain when the ambulance arrived.* 救急車が到着したとき, 彼は痛みのあまり叫び声を上げていた. ② → see also **cry 2**

▶ **cry out for** PHRASAL VERB 句動詞 If you say that something **cries out for** a particular thing or action, you mean that it needs that thing or action very much. 一を強く求める ▢ *This is a disgraceful state of affairs and cries out for a thorough investigation.* これは恥ずべき事態であり, ぜひとも徹底した調査が必要である.

Word Web   cry

Have you ever seen someone **burst into tears** when something wonderful happened to them? We expect people to **cry** when they are **sad** or upset. But why do people sometimes **weep** when they are happy? Scientists have found there are three different types of **tears**. Basal tears lubricate the **eyes**. Reflex tears clear the eyes of dirt or smoke. The third type, emotional tears, contain high levels of manganese and prolactin. Decreasing the amount of these chemicals in the body helps us feel better. When people experience strong feelings, negative or positive, **shedding tears** may help restore emotional balance.

c

Thesaurus   *cry* また次を参照：

V.	sob, weep **1**
	call, shout, yell **2**
N.	howl, moan, shriek **3**

Word Partnership   *cry* は次の語句と使われる：

V.	**begin to** cry, **start to** cry **1**
N.	cry **with anger 1 – 4**
	cry **for help**, cry **of horror**, cry **with joy**, cry **of pain 2 – 4**

cry|ing /krɑɪɪŋ/ PHRASE 句 If you say that there is **a crying need** for something, you mean that there is a very great need for it. 一の差し迫った必要性 ❑ *There is a crying need for more magistrates from the ethnic minority communities.* マイノリティー出身の判事を増やすことが急務である。 **2** → see also **cry**

cryp|tic /krɪptɪk/ ADJ 形容詞 A **cryptic** remark or message contains a hidden meaning or is difficult to understand. 謎めいた、不可解な ❑ *He has issued a short, cryptic statement denying the spying charges.* 彼は自らのスパイ容疑を否定する謎めいた短いコメントを出しました。 ● **cryp|ti|cal|ly** ADV 副詞 [ADV with v] 謎めいて ❑ *"Not necessarily," she says cryptically.* 「必ずしもそうではない」と彼女はあいまいに答える。

crys|tal /krɪstᵊl/ (**crystals**) **1** N-COUNT 可算名詞 A **crystal** is a small piece of a substance that has formed naturally into a regular symmetrical shape. 結晶 ❑ *...salt crystals.* 塩の結晶。 ❑ *...ice crystals.* 氷の結晶。 **2** N-VAR 可変性名詞 **Crystal** is a transparent rock that is used to make jewelry and ornaments. 水晶 ❑ *She was wearing a strand of crystal beads.* 彼女は水晶玉のネックレスをしていた。 **3** N-UNCOUNT 不可算名詞 **Crystal** is a high quality glass, usually with patterns cut into its surface. クリスタルガラス ❑ *Some of the finest drinking glasses are made from lead crystal.* 最高級のグラスの中には、鉛クリスタル製のグラスがあります。
→ see Word Web: **crystal**
→ see **rock, sugar**

crys|tal clear **1** ADJ 形容詞 Water that is **crystal clear** is absolutely clear and transparent like glass. 澄み切った ❑ *The cliffs, lapped by a crystal-clear sea, remind me of Capri.* 透き通った海に臨むその崖 (がけ) を見ると、彼女はカプリのことを思い出す。 **2** ADJ 形容詞 If you say that a message or statement is **crystal clear**, you are emphasizing that it is very easy to understand. 明快な [EMPHASIS 強調] ❑ *The message is crystal clear – if you lose weight, you will have a happier, healthier, better life.* もう言うまでもないが、体重を落すだけで今より幸福で健康的で快適な生活が送れるようになる。

crys|tal|lize /krɪstᵊlɑɪz/ (**crystallizes, crystallizing, crystallized**) **1** V-T/V-I 他動詞/自動詞 If you **crystallize** an opinion or idea, or if it **crystallizes**, it becomes fixed and definite in someone's mind. 具体化させる [他動詞]、具体化する [自動詞] ❑ *He has managed to crystallize the feelings of millions of ordinary Russians.* 彼は数多くのロシア民衆の声を活かすことに成功してきた。 **2** V-T/V-I 他動詞/自動詞 If a substance **crystallizes**, or something **crystallizes** it, it turns into crystals. 結晶化させる [他動詞]、結晶化する [自動詞] ❑ *Don't stir or the sugar will crystallize.* 砂糖が固まるのでかき混ぜないようにします。

cub /kʌb/ (**cubs**) N-COUNT 可算名詞 A **cub** is a young wild animal such as a lion, wolf, or bear. 動物の子 ❑ *...three five-week-old lion cubs.* 生後5週間になる3匹のライオンの赤ちゃん。

cube /kyub/ (**cubes, cubing, cubed**) **1** N-COUNT 可算名詞 A **cube** is a solid object with six square surfaces which are all the same size. 立方体 ❑ *...cold water with ice cubes in it.* 角氷の入った冷水 ❑ *...a box of sugar cubes.* 角砂糖1箱 **2** N-COUNT 可算名詞 The **cube of** a number is another number that is produced by multiplying the first number by itself twice. For example, the cube of 2 is 8. 3乗 **3** V-T 他動詞 When you **cube** food, you cut it into cube-shaped pieces. 角切りにする ❑ *Remove the seeds and*

stones and cube the flesh. 種や核をとってから果肉をさいの目に切ります。
→ see **solid, volume**

cu|bic /kyubɪk/ ADJ 形容詞 **Cubic** is used in front of units of length to form units of volume such as "cubic meter" and "cubic foot." 立方の [ADJ n] ❑ *...3 billion cubic meters of soil.* 30億立方メートルの土。

Word Link   cle ≈ small : article, **cubicle**, particle

cu|bi|cle /kyubɪkᵊl/ (**cubicles**) **1** N-COUNT 可算名詞 A **cubicle** is a very small enclosed area, for example, one where you can take a shower or change your clothes. 小さく仕切った部屋 ❑ *...a separate shower cubicle.* 仕切られたシャワー室 **2** N-COUNT 可算名詞 A **cubicle** is an area in an office that is separated from the rest of the room by thin walls. ブース ❑ *I'm not the kind of person to sit in a cubicle behind a desk.* 私はブースの机に座っているようなタイプの人間じゃないんです。
→ see **office**

cuckoo /kuku, kuku/ (**cuckoos**) N-COUNT 可算名詞 A **cuckoo** is a bird that has a call of two quick notes, and lays its eggs in other birds' nests. カッコウ

cu|cum|ber /kyukʌmbər/ (**cucumbers**) N-VAR 可変性名詞 A **cucumber** is a long thin vegetable with a hard green skin and wet transparent flesh. It is eaten raw in salads. きゅうり ❑ *...a cheese and cucumber sandwich.* チーズときゅうりのサンドイッチ

cud|dle /kʌdᵊl/ (**cuddles, cuddling, cuddled**) V-T 他動詞 If you **cuddle** someone, you put your arms around them and hold them close as a way of showing your affection. 抱きしめる ❑ *He cuddled the newborn girl.* 彼は生まれたばかりの女の赤ちゃんを抱きしめた。 ● N-COUNT 可算名詞 **Cuddle** is also a noun. 抱擁 ❑ *It would have been nice to give him a cuddle and a kiss but there wasn't time.* 彼を抱きしめてキスできたらよかったんだけど、そんな暇などなかった。

cud|dly /kʌdli/ (**cuddlier, cuddliest**) **1** ADJ 形容詞 A **cuddly** person or animal makes you want to cuddle them. 抱きしめたくなるような [APPROVAL 賛成] ❑ *He is a small, cuddly man with spectacles.* 彼は眼鏡をかけた小柄で愛すべき男だ。 **2** ADJ 形容詞 **Cuddly** toys are soft toys that look like animals. 動物のぬいぐるみの [ADJ n]

cue /kyu/ (**cues, cueing, cued**) **1** N-COUNT 可算名詞 In the theater or in a musical performance, a performer's **cue** is something another performer says or does that is a signal for them to begin speaking, playing, or doing something. キュー (合図となるせりふやしぐさ) ❑ *The actors not performing sit at the side of the stage in full view, waiting for their cues.* 出番を待つ役者たちは、ステージを見渡せる舞台のそでに座ってキューが出るのを待ちます。 **2** N-COUNT 可算名詞 If you say that something that happens is a **cue for** an action, you mean that people start doing that action when it happens. それがきっかけとなって ❑ *That was the cue for several months of intense bargaining.* それがきっかけとなって、数ヶ月にわたる真剣な交渉が始まった。 **3** N-COUNT 可算名詞 A **cue** is a long, thin wooden stick that is used to hit the ball in games such as billiards, pool, and snooker. (ビリヤードの) キュー **4** V-T 他動詞 If one performer **cues** another, they say or do something which is a signal for the second performer to begin speaking, playing, or doing something. キューを出す ❑ *He read the scene, with Seaton cueing him.* シートンがキューを出したので、彼は情景を朗読し始めた。

cuff /kʌf/ (**cuffs**) **1** N-COUNT 可算名詞 The **cuffs** of a shirt or dress are the parts at the ends of the sleeves, which are thicker than the rest of the sleeve. そで口 ❑ *...a pale blue shirt with white collar and cuffs.* 白い襟とそで口のついた水色のシャツ **2** N-COUNT 可算名詞 The **cuffs** on a pair of pants are the parts at the ends of the legs, which are folded up. (ズボンの) 折り返し [AM 米国英語] [usu pl] **3** PHRASE 句 An **off-the-cuff** remark is made without being prepared or thought about in advance. 即席の ❑ *I didn't mean any offense. It was a flippant, off-the-cuff remark.* 悪気はなかったんです。軽率で不用意な発言でした。
→ see **diagnosis**

cui|sine /kwɪzin/ (**cuisines**) N-VAR 可変性名詞 The **cuisine** of a country or district is the style of cooking that is characteristic of

Word Web   *crystal*

The outsides of **crystals** have smooth flat planes. These surfaces form because of the repeating patterns of atoms, molecules, or ions inside the crystal. Evaporation, temperature changes, and pressure can all help to form crystals. Crystals grow when sea water evaporates and leaves behind **salt**. When water freezes, **ice** crystals form. When magma cools, it becomes **rock** with a crystalline structure. Pressure can also create one of the hardest, most beautiful crystals—the **diamond**.

Word Web   culture

Each **society** has its own **culture** which influences how people live their lives. Culture includes **customs, language, art**, and other shared **traits**. When people move from one culture to another, the result is often cultural **diffusion**. For example, European artists first saw Japanese art about 150 years ago. This caused a change in their painting style. That new approach was called Impressionism. **Assimilation** also occurs when people enter a new culture. For instance, **immigrants** may adopt American customs when they move to the U.S. People whose ideas differ from **mainstream** society may also form **subcultures** within the society.

that place. お国料理；郷土料理 ❑ *The cuisine of Japan is low in fat.* 日本料理は脂肪分が少ない.
→ see **restaurant**

cul|i|nary /kyu̱ləneri, kʌ̱lə-/ ADJ 形容詞 **Culinary** means concerned with cooking. 料理の [FORMAL 形式ばった] [ADJ n] ❑ *...advanced culinary skills.* 料理の見事な腕前

cull /kʌ̱l/ (**culls, culling, culled**) **1** V-T 他動詞 If items or ideas **are culled from** a particular source or number of sources, they are taken and gathered together. 選び抜かれる [usu passive] ❑ *All this, needless to say, had been culled second-hand from radio reports.* もちろん，これは全てラジオの報道からの選び抜かれたものだった. **2** V-T 他動詞 To **cull** animals means to kill the weaker animals in a group in order to reduce their numbers. 間引く ❑ *To save remaining herds and habitat, the national parks department is planning to cull 2000 elephants.* 残された群れとその生息地を保護しようと，国立公園局は2千頭の象の処分を計画している. ● N-COUNT 可算名詞 **Cull** is also a noun. 間引き ❑ *In the reserves of Zimbabwe and South Africa, annual culls are already routine.* ジンバブエと南アフリカの保護区では，毎年の捕殺がすでに恒常化している. ● **cull|ing** N-UNCOUNT 不可算名詞 間引くこと ❑ *The culling of seal cubs has led to an outcry from environmental groups.* 子アザラシの捕殺は環境団体からの激しい抗議に遭った.

cul|mi|nate /kʌ̱lmɪneɪt/ (**culminates, culminating, culminated**) V-I 自動詞 If you say that an activity, process, or series of events **culminates in** or **with** a particular event, you mean that event happens at the end of it. 最後は―で終わる ❑ *They had an argument, which culminated in Tom getting drunk.* 2人は言い合いを始めたが，結局トムが酔っ払っておしまいになった.

cul|mi|na|tion /kʌ̱lmɪneɪʃ*ə*n/ N-SING 単数名詞 Something, especially something important, that is the **culmination of** an activity, process, or series of events happens at the end of it. 結末 ❑ *Their arrest was the culmination of an operation in which 120 other people were detained.* 作戦では他に120人が拘束されたが，彼らの逮捕で幕を閉じた.

cul|prit /kʌ̱lprɪt/ (**culprits**) **1** N-COUNT 可算名詞 When you are talking about a crime or something wrong that has been done, you can refer to the person who did it as **the culprit**. 犯人 ❑ *All the men were being deported even though the real culprits in the fight have not been identified.* 容疑者は全員国外退去処分を受けましたが，攻撃の首謀者は依然特定されていません. **2** N-COUNT 可算名詞 When you are talking about a problem or bad situation, you can refer to its cause as **the culprit**. 原因 ❑ *About 10% of Japanese teenagers are overweight. Nutritionists say the main culprit is increasing reliance on Western fast food.* 日本の10代の子供たちの約1割が太りすぎである. 最大の原因で栄養学者が挙げるのは，欧米のファーストフードに偏った食事である.

cult /kʌ̱lt/ (**cults**) **1** N-COUNT 可算名詞 A **cult** is a fairly small religious group, especially one which is considered strange. カルト ❑ *The teenager may have been abducted by a religious cult.* その若者はカルト教団に誘拐された恐れがある. **2** N-COUNT 可算名詞 The **cult** of something is a situation in which people regard that thing as very important or special. 崇拝，称賛 [DISAPPROVAL 不賛成] ❑ *...the cult of youth that recently gripped publishing.* 近年の出版界を席巻した若者ブーム **3** ADJ 形容詞 **Cult** is used to describe things that are very popular or fashionable among a particular group of people. 崇拝の [ADJ n] ❑ *Since her death, she has become a cult figure.* 彼女は亡くなると伝説の人になった. **4** N-SING 単数名詞 Someone or something that is a **cult** has become very popular or fashionable among a particular group of people. 流行 ❑ *Violence has become a cult among some young men.* 一部の若者の間では暴力がもてはやされるようになった.

cul|ti|vate /kʌ̱ltɪveɪt/ (**cultivates, cultivating, cultivated**) **1** V-T 他動詞 If you **cultivate** land or crops, you prepare land and grow crops on it. 耕作する ❑ *She also cultivated a small garden of her own.* 彼女も自分の小さな菜園で作物を作った. ● **cul|ti|va|tion**

/kʌ̱ltɪveɪʃ*ə*n/ N-UNCOUNT 不可算名詞 耕作；栽培 ❑ *...the cultivation of fruits and vegetables.* 果物と野菜の栽培 **2** V-T 他動詞 If you **cultivate** an attitude, image, or skill, you try hard to develop it and make it stronger or better. 養う，磨く ❑ *He has written eight books and has cultivated the image of an elder statesman.* 彼はこれまで8冊の著書を手がけ，政界の長老というイメージを築き上げてきた. ● **cul|ti|va|tion** N-UNCOUNT 不可算名詞 養うこと ❑ *...the cultivation of a positive approach to life and health.* 生活や健康に対して前向きに努力すること **3** V-T 他動詞 If you **cultivate** someone or **cultivate** a friendship with them, you try hard to develop a friendship with them. はぐくむ ❑ *Howe carefully cultivated Daniel C. Roper, the Assistant Postmaster General.* ハウは郵政副長官だったダニエル・C・ローパーを特にかわいがった.
→ see **farm, grain**

Thesaurus   *cultivate* また次を参照:
V.	farm, grow, tend **1**
	develop, refine **2**

cul|ti|vat|ed /kʌ̱ltɪveɪtɪd/ **1** ADJ 形容詞 If you describe someone as **cultivated**, you mean they are well educated and have good manners. 教養のある [FORMAL 形式ばった] ❑ *His mother was an elegant, cultivated woman.* 彼の母は上品で教養のある女性だった. **2** ADJ 形容詞 **Cultivated** plants have been developed for growing on farms or in gardens. 栽培用の [ADJ n] ❑ *...a mixture of wild and cultivated varieties.* 野生種と栽培種の交雑

cul|tur|al /kʌ̱ltʃərəl/ **1** ADJ 形容詞 **Cultural** means relating to a particular society and its ideas, customs, and art. 文化の ❑ *...a deep sense of personal honor which was part of his cultural heritage.* 彼が文化的伝統として受け継いだものの一つである強い自尊心 ● **cul|tur|al|ly** ADV 副詞 文化的に ❑ *...an informed guide to culturally and historically significant sites.* 主要な文化財や史跡が詳しく載っているガイド **2** ADJ 形容詞 [ADJ n] **Cultural** means involving or concerning the arts. 芸術の ❑ *...the sponsorship of sports and cultural events by tobacco companies.* たばこ会社によるスポーツ大会や文化行事の後援 ● **cul|tur|al|ly** ADV 副詞 芸術的に ❑ *...one of our better-governed, culturally active regional centers.* 運営管理に優れ文化活動が盛んな地域センターの一つ

cul|ture /kʌ̱ltʃər/ (**cultures**) **1** N-UNCOUNT 不可算名詞 **Culture** consists of activities such as the arts and philosophy, which are considered to be important for the development of civilization and of people's minds. 文化 ❑ *There is just not enough fun and frivolity in culture today.* 今の文化には面白みや遊び心が欠落している. ❑ *...aspects of popular culture.* 大衆文化の様々な側面 **2** N-COUNT 可算名詞 A **culture** is a particular society or civilization, especially considered in relation to its beliefs, way of life, or art. 一文化；一文明 ❑ *...people from different cultures.* 文化の異なる人々 **3** N-COUNT 可算名詞 The **culture** of a particular organization or group consists of the habits of the people in it and the way they generally behave. 風土；風潮 ❑ *But social workers say that this has created a culture of dependency, particularly in urban areas.* しかしソーシャルワーカーの話では，このような依存的な風潮を生み出し，そうした傾向は都市部で顕著であるということです. **4** N-COUNT 可算名詞 In science, a **culture** is a group of bacteria or cells which are grown, usually in a laboratory as part of an experiment. 培養物 [TECHNICAL 技術的] ❑ *...a culture of human cells.* ヒトの培養細胞
→ see Word Web: **culture**
→ see **myth**

Word Partnership   *culture* は次の語句と使われる:
ADJ.	ancient culture, popular culture **1**
N.	culture and religion, society and culture **1**
	culture shock, richness of culture **1 2**

cul|tured /kʌ̱ltʃərd/ ADJ 形容詞 If you describe someone as

cultured, you mean that they have good manners, are well educated, and know a lot about the arts. 教養のある，芸術に造詣の深い □ *He is a cultured man with a wide circle of friends.* 彼は教養があって交友関係も広い.

-cum- /-kʌm-/ COMB IN N-COUNT 可算名詞の複合 **-cum-** is put between two nouns to form a noun referring to something or someone that is partly one thing and partly another. 一兼一 □ *...a dining-room-cum-study.* ダイニングルーム兼勉強部屋

cum|ber|some /kʌmbərsəm/ **1** ADJ 形容詞 Something that is **cumbersome** is large and heavy and therefore difficult to carry, wear, or handle. 扱いにくい □ *Although the machine looks cumbersome, it is actually easy to use.* その機械は見た目は扱いにくそうだが，実際は使いやすい. **2** ADJ 形容詞 A **cumbersome** system or process is very complicated and inefficient. 面倒な □ *...an old and cumbersome computer system.* 旧式で面倒なコンピューターシステム

cu|mu|la|tive /kyuːmyələtɪv/ ADJ 形容詞 If a series of events have a **cumulative** effect, each event makes the effect greater. 累積する □ *It is simple pleasures, such as a walk on a sunny day, which have a cumulative effect on our mood.* 晴れた日の散歩など，ちょっとした楽しみをいろいろ見つけていくと，だんだん気分がすっきりしてくる.

cun|ning /kʌnɪŋ/ **1** ADJ 形容詞 Someone who is **cunning** has the ability to achieve things in a clever way, often by deceiving other people. ずる賢い □ *These disturbed kids can be cunning.* こうした情緒障害の子供はときに悪賢くなることがある. ● **cun|ning|ly** ADV 副詞 ずる賢く □ *They were cunningly disguised in golf clothes.* 彼らはゴルフウェアで巧妙に変装していた. **2** N-UNCOUNT 不可算名詞 **Cunning** is the ability to achieve things in a clever way, often by deceiving other people. ずる賢さ □ *...one more example of the cunning of today's art thieves.* 近頃の美術品窃盗犯のもう一つの巧妙な手口

cup /kʌp/ (**cups, cupping, cupped**) **1** N-COUNT 可算名詞 A **cup** is a small round container that you drink from. Cups usually have handles and are made from china or plastic. カップ □ *...cups and saucers.* ソーサー付きカップ **2** N-COUNT 可算名詞 You can use **cup** to refer to the cup and its contents, or to the contents only. カップ1杯分 □ *...a cup of coffee.* 1杯のコーヒー **3** N-COUNT 可算名詞 A **cup** is a unit of measurement used in cooking. It is equal to 16 tablespoons or 8 fluid ounces. 計量カップ1杯分 □ *Gradually add 1 cup of milk, stirring until the liquid is absorbed.* 牛乳1カップを少しずつ加え，完全に混ざるまでかきまぜます. □ *...half a cup of sugar.* 砂糖半カップ **4** N-COUNT 可算名詞 Things, or parts of things, that are small, round, and hollow in shape can be referred to as **cups**. カップ状のもの □ *...the brass cups of the small chandelier.* 小さなシャンデリアの真鍮（しんちゅう）のカップ **5** N-COUNT 可算名詞 A **cup** is a large metal cup with two handles that is given to the winner of a game or competition. 優勝杯 □ *The Stars won the Stanley Cup in 1999.* スターズは1999年のスタンリーカップ杯を手中に収めた. **6** N-IN-NAMES 名称中の名詞 **Cup** is used in the names of some sports competitions in which the prize is a cup. 一杯, 一カップ □ *Sri Lanka's cricket team will play India in the final of the Asia Cup.* クリケットのアジアカップ決勝戦でスリランカはインドと対戦します. **7** V-T 他動詞 If you **cup your hands**, you make them into a curved shape like a cup. 手のひらをおわんの形にする □ *He cupped his hands around his mouth and called out for Diane.* 彼は両手を口元に当て大声でダイアンを呼んだ. □ *David knelt, cupped his hands and splashed river water on to his face.* デイビッドはひざまずくと，丸めた手で川の水をすくい顔に浴びせかけた. **8** V-T 他動詞 If you **cup** something in your hands, you make your hands into a curved dish-like shape and support it or hold it gently. （丸くした手のひらで）支える □ *He cupped her chin in the palm of his hand.* 彼は片方の手のひらでそっとあごを押さえた.

→ see **dish, tea**

cup|board /kʌbərd/ (**cupboards**) N-COUNT 可算名詞 A **cupboard** is a piece of furniture that has one or two doors, usually contains shelves, and is used to store things. 戸棚 □ *The kitchen cupboard was stocked with cans of soup and food.* 台所の食器棚にはスープや食品類の缶詰が入っていた.

cur|able /kyʊərəbəl/ ADJ 形容詞 If a disease or illness is **curable**, it can be cured. 治療できる □ *Most skin cancers are completely curable if detected in the early stages.* 早期に発見すれば皮膚がんはほとんどの場合治します.

Word Link cur ≈ caring : **curate, curator, manicure**

---

cu|rate (**curates, curating, curated**)

The noun is pronounced /kyʊərɪt/. The verb is pronounced /kyʊreɪt/.

名詞は /kyʊərɪt/ と発音される. 動詞は /kyʊreɪt/ と発音される.

1 N-COUNT 可算名詞 A **curate** is a clergyman in the Anglican Church who helps the priest. 副牧師, 牧師補 **2** V-T 他動詞 If an exhibition **is curated** by someone, they organize it. 企画される [usu passive] □ *The Hayward exhibition has been curated by the artist*

Bernard Luthi. ヘイワード美術館展は芸術家バーナード・ルティが企画監修してきた.

cu|ra|tor /kyʊreɪtər, kyʊəreɪtər/ (**curators**) N-COUNT 可算名詞 A **curator** is someone who is in charge of the objects or works of art in a museum or art gallery. キュレーター（日本の学芸員より大きな権限をもつ）□ *Peter Forey is curator of fossil fishes at the Natural History Museum.* ピーター・フォレーは自然史博物館の魚類化石部門のキュレーターである.

curb /kɜrb/ (**curbs, curbing, curbed**) **1** V-T 他動詞 If you **curb** something, you control it and keep it within limits. 抑える, 制限する □ *...advertisements aimed at curbing the spread of AIDS.* エイズの蔓延（まんえん）防止を狙った広告. ● N-COUNT 可算名詞 **Curb** is also a noun. 抑制, 抑止 □ *He called for much stricter curbs on immigration.* 彼は移民をさらに厳しく制限するように求めた. **2** V-T 他動詞 If you **curb** an emotion or your behavior, you keep it under control. 抑える □ *He curbed his temper.* 彼は怒りを抑えた. **3** N-COUNT 可算名詞 **The curb** is the raised edge of a sidewalk which separates it from the road. 縁石 [AM 米国英語] □ *I pulled over to the curb.* 私は車を縁石に寄せて止めた.

cure /kyʊər/ (**cures, curing, cured**) **1** V-T 他動詞 If doctors or medical treatments **cure** an illness or injury, they cause it to end or disappear. 治す □ *An operation finally cured his shin injury.* すねに負ったけがは手術でようやく完治した. **2** V-T 他動詞 If doctors or medical treatments **cure** a person, they make the person well again after an illness or injury. 治療する □ *It is an effective treatment and could cure all the leprosy sufferers worldwide.* これは有効な治療法で，世界の全てのハンセン病患者を治療できる可能性があります. □ *Almost overnight I was cured.* ほぼ一晩で回復した. **3** V-T 他動詞 If someone or something **cures** a problem, they bring it to an end. 解決する □ *Private firms are willing to make large scale investments to help cure Russia's economic troubles.* 民間企業は積極的に大型投資を進めることで混乱したロシア経済の建て直しに一役買うつもりである. **4** V-T 他動詞 When food, tobacco, or animal skin **is cured**, it is dried, smoked, or salted so that it will last for a long time. 長期保存できるようにする [usu passive] □ *Legs of pork were cured and smoked over the fire.* 豚の脚の肉は塩漬けにしてから薫製した. **5** N-COUNT 可算名詞 A **cure for** an illness is a medicine or other treatment that cures the illness. 治療法 □ *There is still no cure for a cold.* 風邪の治療法はいまだにない. **6** N-COUNT 可算名詞 A **cure for** a problem is something that will bring it to an end. 解決法 □ *The magic cure for inflation does not exist.* インフレを退治する特効薬は存在しません.

cur|few /kɜrfyu/ (**curfews**) **1** N-VAR 可変性名詞 A **curfew** is a law stating that people must stay inside their houses after a particular time at night, for example, during a war. 夜間外出禁止令 □ *The village was placed under curfew.* その村に夜間外出禁止令が出された. **2** N-VAR 可変性名詞 **Curfew** or a **curfew** is the time after which a child or student will be punished if they are found outside their home or dormitory. 門限 □ *They raced back to the dormitory before the nine o'clock curfew.* 9時の門限に間に合うように彼らは大急ぎで寮に戻った.

cu|ri|os|ity /kyʊəriɒsɪti/ (**curiosities**) **1** N-UNCOUNT 不可算名詞 **Curiosity** is a desire to know about something. 好奇心 □ *Ryle accepted more out of curiosity than anything else.* ライルが承諾したのは何よりも好奇心のせいだった. □ *...enthusiasm and genuine curiosity about the past.* 過去に対する強い関心と純粋な好奇心. **2** N-COUNT 可算名詞 A **curiosity** is something that is unusual, interesting, and fairly rare. 珍品 □ *There is much to see in the way of castles, curiosities, and museums.* 城，資料館，博物館など見どころは多い.

cu|ri|ous /kyʊəriəs/ **1** ADJ 形容詞 If you are **curious about** something, you are interested in it and want to know more about it. 一に興味をひかれて □ *Steve was intensely curious about the world I came from.* スティーブは私の生まれ育った世界のことをすごく知りたがった. ● **cu|ri|ous|ly** ADV 副詞 [ADV after v] 興味ありげに □ *The woman in the shop had looked at them curiously.* 店にいた女はもの珍しそうに彼らを見ていた. **2** ADJ 形容詞 If you describe something as **curious**, you mean that it is unusual or difficult to understand. 珍しい □ *The pageant promises to be a curious mixture of the ancient and modern.* その野外劇は古代と現代が錯綜（さくそう）する一風変わった劇になりそうです. ● **cu|ri|ous|ly** ADV 副詞 珍しく □ *Harry was curiously silent through all this.* その間ずっとハリーは妙に静かだった.

Word Partnership *curious* は次の語句と使われる：

N.	curious **expression**, curious **gaze**, curious **glance** **1 2**
	curious **mixture of** *something* **2**

---

curl /kɜrl/ (**curls, curling, curled**) **1** N-COUNT 可算名詞 If you have **curls**, your hair is in the form of tight curves and spirals. 巻き毛 □ *...the little girl with blonde curls.* ブロンドで巻き毛の女の子. **2** N-COUNT 可算名詞 A **curl of** something is a piece or quantity of it that is curved or spiral in shape. 渦巻き状のもの □ *A thin curl of smoke rose from a rusty stove.* 一筋の煙が渦を巻きながらさ

ぴたコンロから立ち昇った. **3** N-UNCOUNT 不可算名詞 If your hair has **curl**, it is full of curls. 巻き髪, カール ❑ Dry curly hair naturally for maximum curl and shine. つやのある美しいカールが出るように自然に乾燥させます. **4** V-T/V-I 他動詞/自動詞 If your hair **curls** or if you **curl** it, it is full of curls. カールさせる [他動詞], カールする [自動詞] ❑ She has hair that refuses to curl. 彼女の髪はどうしてもカールがつかない. ❑ Maria had curled her hair for the event. マリアはその催しのために髪をカールした. **5** V-T/V-I 他動詞/自動詞 If your toes, fingers, or other parts of your body **curl**, or if you **curl** them, they form a curved or round shape. 曲げる [他動詞], 曲がる [自動詞] ❑ His fingers curled gently around her wrist. 彼の指が優しく彼女の手首を包みこんだ. ❑ Raise one foot, curl the toes and point the foot downwards. 片足を上げ, つま先を曲げて足を下に向けてください. **6** V-T/V-I 他動詞/自動詞 If something **curls** somewhere, or if you **curl** it there, it moves there in a spiral or curve. らせん状に動かす [他動詞], らせん状に動く [自動詞] ❑ Smoke was curling up the chimney. 煙が煙突からららせん状に立ち昇っていた. **7** V-I 自動詞 If a person or animal **curls** into a ball, they move into a position in which their body makes a rounded shape. 体を丸める ❑ He wanted to curl into a tiny ball. 彼は体をぎゅっと小さく丸めたかった. ● PHRASAL VERB 句動詞 **Curl up** means the same as **curl**. ❑ In colder weather, your cat will curl up into a tight, heat-conserving ball. 寒い時期になれば, お宅の猫も体温を逃さないようにぎゅっと丸まりますよ. **8** V-I 自動詞 When a leaf, a piece of paper, or another flat object **curls**, its edges bend toward the center. 反り返る ❑ The rose leaves have curled because of an attack by grubs. 地虫にやられてバラの葉が反り返ってしまった. ● PHRASAL VERB 句動詞 **Curl up** means the same as **curl**. 反り返る ❑ The corners of the rug were curling up. カーペットの角が反り返ってきていた.

▶ **curl up** → see **curl 7, 8**

curly /kɜːrli/ (curlier, curliest) **1** ADJ 形容詞 **Curly** hair is full of curls. 巻き毛の ❑ I've got naturally curly hair. 私は生まれつき巻き毛だ. **2** ADJ 形容詞 **Curly** is sometimes used to describe things that are curved or spiral in shape. 巻いた ❑ ...cauliflowers with extra-long curly leaves. 長くて巻いた葉が普通よりたくさんついたカリフラワー.

cur|ren|cy /kɜːrənsi/ (currencies) N-VAR 可変性名詞 The money used in a particular country is referred to as its **currency**. 通貨 ❑ Tourism is the country's top earner of foreign currency. 観光がその国の最大の外貨収入源です. ❑ More people favor a single European currency than oppose it. 欧州単一通貨については反対より支持のほうが多い.

→ see **money**

Word Link | curr, curs ≈ running, flowing : con**curr**ent, **curr**ent, **curs**or
---

cur|rent /kɜːrənt/ (currents) **1** N-COUNT 可算名詞 A **current** is a steady and continuous flowing movement of some of the water in a river, lake, or ocean. 水流 ❑ Under normal conditions, the ocean currents of the tropical Pacific travel from east to west. 通常の条件では, 熱帯太平洋の海流は東から西に流れる. **2** N-COUNT 可算名詞 A **current** is a steady flowing movement of air. 気流 ❑ I felt a current of cool air blowing in my face. 涼しい風が顔にあたるのを感じた. **3** N-COUNT 可算名詞 An electric **current** is a flow of electricity through a wire or circuit. 電流 ❑ A powerful electric current is passed through a piece of graphite. 非常に強い電流が黒鉛に流れています. **4** N-COUNT 可算名詞 A particular **current** is a particular feeling, idea, or quality that exists within a group of people. 風潮 ❑ Each party represents a distinct current of thought. 各党とも独自の考え方を打ち出している. **5** ADJ 形容詞 **Current** means happening, being used, or being done at the present time. 現在の ❑ The current situation is very different to that in 1990. 現在の状況は1990年当時とは全く違っている. ● **cur|rent|ly** ADV 副詞 [ADV before v] 現在のところ ❑ Twelve potential vaccines are currently being tested on human volunteers. 現在のところ, ワクチン候補12種類について, ボランティアによる臨床試験行われている. **6** ADJ 形容詞 Ideas and customs that are **current** are generally accepted and used by most people. 一般に受け入れられている ❑ Current thinking suggests that toxins only have a small part to play in the build-up of cellulite. 一般的には, 毒素が皮下脂肪の蓄積の原因となることはほとんどないと考えられている.

→ see **beach, erosion, ocean, tide**

cur|rent ac|count (current accounts) N-COUNT 可算名詞 A **current account** is a personal bank account which you can take money out of at any time using your checkbook or ATM card. 当座預金 [BRIT 英国英語; AM **checking account** 米国英語 **checking account**]

cur|rent af|fairs also current events N-PLURAL 複数名詞 If you refer to **current affairs**, you are referring to political events and problems in society which are discussed in newspapers, and on television and radio. 時事問題 ❑ I am ill-informed on current affairs. 私は時事問題には疎い.

cur|ricu|lum /kərɪkyələm/ (curriculums or curricula /kərɪkyələ/) **1** N-COUNT 可算名詞 A **curriculum** is all the different courses of study that are taught in a school, college, or university. カリキュラム, 教育課程 ❑ Teachers incorporated business skills into the regular school curriculum. 教師は通常のカリキュラムに実務技能を導入した. **2** N-COUNT 可算名詞 A particular **curriculum** is one particular course of study that is taught in a school, college, or university. 教科課程, 学科課程 ❑ ...the history curriculum. 歴史のカリキュラム.

Outside of the required school classes in the **curriculum**, students may participate in a variety of **extracurricular** (non-compulsory) activities that develop their interests and skills. In North American high schools there are sports clubs and teams, newspapers, future scientists' clubs and drama or music groups to name a few. Students who participate in these groups use their experience as an advantage when they apply for university. Such activities are also found on college campuses.
---

cur|ricu|lum vitae /kərɪkyələm vaːtiː/ N-SING 単数名詞 A **curriculum vitae** is the same as a **CV**. 履歴書

cur|ry /kɜːri/ (curries, currying, curried) **1** N-VAR 可変性名詞 **Curry** is a dish composed of meat and vegetables, or just vegetables, in a sauce containing hot spices. It is usually eaten with rice and is one of the main dishes of India. カレー ❑ ...vegetable curry. 野菜カレー. **2** PHRASE 句 If one person tries to **curry favor with** another, they do things in order to try to gain their support or cooperation. 一の機嫌をとる ❑ Politicians are eager to promote their "happy family" image to curry favor with voters. 政治家たちは有権者の心を・つかもうと, 「幸せな家庭」のイメージの売り込みに躍起になっている.

curse /kɜːrs/ (curses, cursing, cursed) **1** V-I 自動詞 If you **curse**, you use very impolite or offensive language, usually because you are angry about something. ののしる [WRITTEN 書き言葉] ❑ I cursed and hobbled to my feet. 悪態をついて足を引きずって歩いた. ● N-COUNT 可算名詞 **Curse** is also a noun. ののしり言葉 ❑ He shot her an angry look and a curse. 彼は彼女に怒りのまなざしを向けてのろった. **2** V-T 他動詞 If you **curse** someone, you say insulting things to them because you are angry with them. ののしる ❑ Grandma protested, but he cursed her and rudely pushed her aside. おばあちゃんは反対したが, 彼はののしって乱暴に押しのけた. **3** V-T 他動詞 If you **curse** something, you complain angrily about it, especially using very impolite language. 悪口を言う ❑ So we set off again, cursing the delay, toward the west. 遅れたことに不満をぶちまけながら, 再び西に向かって出発した. **4** N-COUNT 可算名詞 If you say that there is a **curse on** someone, you mean that there seems to be a supernatural power causing unpleasant things to happen to them. のろい ❑ Maybe there is a curse on my family. 家族に対する呪いなのかも知れない. **5** N-COUNT 可算名詞 You can refer to something that causes a great deal of trouble or harm as a **curse**. 災い ❑ Apathy is the long-standing curse of democracy. 政治に対する無関心は民主主義が長年抱えてきた厄介な問題である.

cur|sor /kɜːrsər/ (cursors) N-COUNT 可算名詞 On a computer screen, the **cursor** is a small shape that indicates where anything that is typed by the user will appear. カーソル [COMPUTING コンピューティング] ❑ He moves the cursor, clicks the mouse. 彼はカーソルを動かしてマウスをクリックする.

→ see **computer**

curt /kɜːrt/ ADJ 形容詞 If you describe someone as **curt**, you mean that they speak or reply in a brief and rather rude way. ぶっきらぼうな ❑ Her tone of voice was curt. 彼女の口調はそっけなかった. ● **curt|ly** ADV 副詞 [ADV with v] ぶっきらぼうに ❑ "I'm leaving," she said curtly. 「行くわ」と彼女はそっけなく言った.

cur|tail /kɜːrteɪl/ (curtails, curtailing, curtailed) V-T 他動詞 If you **curtail** something, you reduce or limit it. 縮小する [FORMAL 形式ばった] ❑ NATO plans to curtail the number of troops being sent to the region. NATOはその地域での兵力削減を検討している.

cur|tain /kɜːrtən/ (curtains) **1** N-COUNT 可算名詞 **Curtains** are pieces of material which you hang from the top of a window. カーテン ❑ Her bedroom curtains were drawn. 彼女の寝室のカーテンは閉まっていた. **2** N-SING 単数名詞 In a theater, **the curtain** is the large piece of material that hangs in front of the stage until a performance begins. 舞台の幕 ❑ The curtain rises toward the end of the Prelude. 前奏曲の終わりが近づくと幕が上がり出す.

curve /kɜːrv/ (curves, curving, curved) **1** N-COUNT 可算名詞 A **curve** is a smooth, gradually bending line, for example, part of the edge of a circle. 曲線 ❑ ...the curve of his lips. 彼の唇の形. **2** N-COUNT 可算名詞 You can refer to a change in something as a particular **curve**, especially when it is represented on a graph. 曲線 ❑ Youth crime overall is on a slow but steady downward curve. 全般的に少年犯罪は緩やかだが確実に減少してきている. **3** → see also **learning curve** **4** V-T/V-I 他動詞/自動詞 If something **curves**, or if someone or something **curves** it, it has the shape of a curve. 曲げる [他動詞] 曲がる [自動詞] ❑ Her spine curved. 彼女の背中は曲がっていた. ❑ ...a knife with a slightly curving

blade. 刃がわずかにカーブしたナイフ． **5** V-I 自動詞 If something **curves**, it moves in a curve, for example, through the air. カーブする □ *The ball curved strangely in the air.* 球は空中で奇妙なカーブを描いた． **6** PHRASE 句 If someone **throws** you **a curve** or **throws** you **a curve ball**, they surprise you by doing something that you do not expect. 一の意表をつく [mainly AM 主に米国英語] □ *At the last minute, I threw them a curve ball by saying, "We're going to bring spouses."* 最後の最後になって「連れ合いと来るからね」と言って意表をついてやった．

curved /kɜrvd/ ADJ 形容詞 A **curved** object has the shape of a curve or has a smoothly bending surface. 曲線状の □ *...the curved lines of the chairs.* 椅子のカーブしたライン．
→ see **flight**

cush|ion /kʊʃ⁰n/ (**cushions, cushioning, cushioned**)
1 N-COUNT 可算名詞 A **cushion** is a fabric case filled with soft material, which you put on a seat to make it more comfortable. クッション □ *...a velvet cushion.* ベルベットのクッション． **2** N-COUNT 可算名詞 A **cushion** is a soft pad or barrier, especially one that protects something. 緩衝材 □ *The company provides a styrofoam cushion to protect the tablets during shipping.* その会社では，輸送中に銘板が破損しないように発泡スチロールの緩衝材を使用している． **3** N-COUNT 可算名詞 Something that is a **cushion against** something unpleasant reduces its effect. 和らげるもの □ *Welfare provides a cushion against hardship.* 生活保護によって苦しい生活は少しは楽になる． **4** V-T 他動詞 Something that **cushions** an object when it hits something protects it by reducing the force of the impact. 衝撃から守る □ *There is also a new steering wheel with an energy-absorbing rim to cushion the driver's head in the worst impacts.* 衝撃を吸収する新型のハンドルも装備されており，非常に強い衝撃でもドライバーの頭部を保護することができる． **5** V-T 他動詞 To **cushion** the effect of something unpleasant means to reduce it. 和らげる □ *They said Western aid was needed to cushion the blows of vital reform.* 彼らによれば，きわめて重要な改革の痛みを和らげるためには欧米の援助が必要だということです．

cus|tard /kʌstərd/ (**custards**) **1** N-VAR 可変性名詞 **Custard** is a baked dessert made of milk, eggs, and sugar. カスタード □ *...a custard with a caramel sauce.* カラメルソースをのせたカスタードプリン． **2** N-MASS 質量名詞 **Custard** is a sweet yellow sauce made from milk and eggs or from milk and a powder. It is eaten with fruit and puddings. カスタードソース □ *...bananas and custard.* バナナカスタード．
→ see **dessert**

Word Link | custod ≈ guarding : custodial, custodian, custody

cus|to|dial /kʌstoudiəl/ **1** ADJ 形容詞 If a child's parents are divorced or separated, the **custodial** parent is the parent who has custody of the child. 養育権のある [LEGAL 法律的] [ADJ n] □ *...all the general expenses that come with being the custodial parent.* 普通子育てするのに親権者にかかってくる全ての費用． **2** ADJ 形容詞 **Custodial care** is help with basic personal needs, such as washing, dressing, and eating. 日常生活の [usu ADJ n] □ *In the event that you are mentally or physically disabled, who will provide custodial care and who will pay for it?* 精神的または身体的な障害を負った場合，誰が日常生活の介護を提供し，誰がその費用を負担するのか．

cus|to|dian /kʌstoudiən/ (**custodians**) **1** N-COUNT 可算名詞 The **custodian** of an official building, a company's assets, or something else valuable is the person who is officially in charge of it. 管理者 □ *...the custodian of the holy shrines in Mecca and Medina.* メッカとメジナの聖堂の管理者． **2** N-COUNT 可算名詞 The **custodian** of a large building such as an office or a school is responsible for cleaning and maintaining it. 用務員 [AM 米国英語] □ *Augustine Hancock served as an elementary-school custodian for 20 years.* オーガスティン・ハンコックは小学校の用務員として20年間勤めた．

cus|to|dy /kʌstədi/ **1** N-UNCOUNT 不可算名詞 **Custody** is the legal right to keep and take care of a child, especially the right given to a child's mother or father when they get divorced. 養育権 □ *I'm going to go to court to get custody of the children.* 子供たちの親権を得るために裁判するつもりです． □ *Child custody is normally granted to the mother.* 子供の親権は母親に与えられるのが普通である． **2** N-UNCOUNT 不可算名詞 If someone is being held in a particular type of **custody**, they are being kept in a place that is similar to a prison. 拘留 □ *The youngster got nine months' youth custody.* 少年は9ヵ月間少年院に収容されることになった． **3** PHRASE 句 Someone who is **in custody** or has been taken **into custody** has been arrested and is being kept in prison until they can be tried in a court. 拘留されて □ *Three people appeared in court and two of them were remanded in custody.* 裁判には3人が出廷し，うち2人は再拘留となりました．

cus|tom /kʌstəm/ (**customs**) **1** N-VAR 可変性名詞 A **custom** is an activity, a way of behaving, or an event which is usual or traditional in a particular society or in particular circumstances. 慣習 □ *The custom of lighting the Olympic flame goes back centuries.* 慣

オリンピック聖火を聖火台に点火する伝統はずっと昔にさかのぼる． **2** N-SING 単数名詞 If it is your **custom to** do something, you usually do it in particular circumstances. 習慣 □ *It was his custom to approach every problem cautiously.* どんな問題に対しても彼はいつも慎重に臨んだ． **3** → see also **customs**
→ see **culture, society**

cus|tom|ary /kʌstəmeri/ **1** ADJ 形容詞 **Customary** is used to describe things that people usually do in a particular society or in particular circumstances. 慣習的な [FORMAL 形式ばった] □ *It is customary to offer a drink on a snack to guests.* 客が来たら飲み物や軽食を出すのが普通だ． **2** ADJ 形容詞 **Customary** is used to describe something that a particular person usually does or has. 習慣的な [ADJ n] □ *Yvonne took her customary seat behind her desk.* イボンはいつもの机に座った．

cus|tom|er /kʌstəmər/ (**customers**) N-COUNT 可算名詞 A **customer** is someone who buys goods or services, especially from a store. 客 □ *...a satisfied customer.* 満足した客． □ *The quality of customer service is extremely important.* 質の高い顧客サービスは特に重要である．

When you buy goods from a particular shop or company, you are one of its **customers**. If you use the professional services of someone such as a lawyer or an accountant, you are one of their **clients**. Doctors and hospitals have **patients**, while hotels have **guests**. People who travel on public transportation are referred to as **passengers**.

Word Partnership customer は次の語句と使われる：

| N. | customer **account**, customer **loyalty**, customer **satisfaction** |
| V. | **greet** customers, **satisfy a** customer |

cus|tom|ize /kʌstəmaɪz/ (**customizes, customizing, customized**) V-T 他動詞 If you **customize** something, you change its appearance or features to suit your tastes or needs. 変更する □ *...a control that allows photographers to customize the camera's basic settings.* カメラの基本設定を変更できる機能．

cus|toms /kʌstəmz/ **1** N-PROPER 固有名詞 **Customs** is the official organization responsible for collecting taxes on goods coming into a country and preventing illegal goods from being brought in. 税関局 □ *What right does Customs have to search my car?* 税関はどんな権限があって私の車を検査するのか． **2** N-UNCOUNT 不可算名詞 **Customs** is the place where people arriving from a foreign country have to declare goods that they bring with them. 税関 □ *He walked through customs.* 彼は税関は通過しました． **3** ADJ 形容詞 **Customs** duties are taxes that people pay for importing and exporting goods. 関税 [ADJ n] □ *Personal property which is to be re-exported at the end of your visit is not subject to customs duties.* 入国時に持ち込んだ物については，出国の際に関税の対象になりません． **4** → see also **custom**

	cut
1	PHYSICAL ACTION
2	SHORTEN OR REDUCE AMOUNT
3	OTHER USES
4	PHRASAL VERBS

❶ cut /kʌt/ (**cuts, cutting**)

The form **cut** is used in the present tense and is the past tense and past participle.

cut 形は現在時制に使われ，過去時制と過去分詞でもある．

1 V-T/V-I 他動詞/自動詞 If you **cut** something, you use a knife or a similar tool to divide it into pieces, or to mark it or damage it. If you **cut** a shape or a hole in something, you make the shape or hole by using a knife or similar tool. 切る；刻む；穴を開ける □ *Mrs. Haines stood nearby, holding scissors to cut a ribbon.* ヘインズさんはリボンを切ろうとはさみを持って近くに立っていました． □ *Cut the tomatoes in half vertically.* トマトを縦に半分に切ります． □ *The thieves cut a hole in the fence.* 泥棒は塀に穴を開けた． □ *This little knife cuts really well.* この小型ナイフはとてもよく切れる． ● N-COUNT 可算名詞 **Cut** is also a noun. 切り口 □ *Carefully make a cut in the shell with a small serrated knife.* 刃がぎざぎざになった小型ナイフでゆっくりと貝に切り込みを入れます． **2** V-T 他動詞 If you **cut yourself** or **cut** a part of your body, you accidentally injure yourself on a sharp object so that you bleed. (体の一部を) 切る □ *Johnson cut himself shaving.* ジョンソンはひげをそっていて顔を切った． □ *I started to cry because I cut my finger.* 指を切ったので泣き始めた． ● N-COUNT 可算名詞 **Cut** is also a noun. 泥棒は塀に □ *He had sustained a cut on his left eyebrow.* 左の眉 (まゆ) に切り傷を負った． **3** V-T 他動詞 If you **cut** something such as grass, your hair, or your fingernails, you shorten them using scissors or another tool. 短く切る，刈る □ *The most recent tenants hadn't even cut the grass.* つい最近越してきた入居

Picture Dictionary

cut

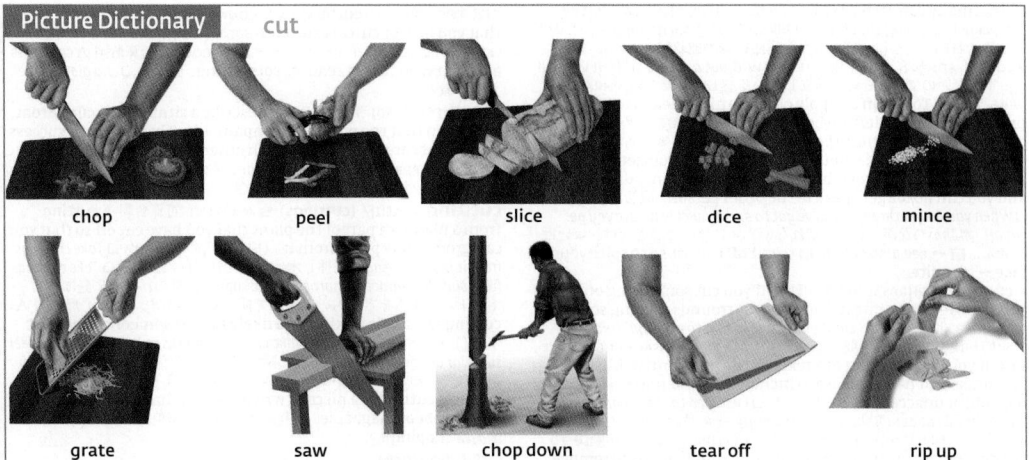

chop   peel   slice   dice   mince

grate   saw   chop down   tear off   rip up

者は草も刈っていなかった．□*You've had your hair cut, it looks great.* 散髪したのね，すてきよ．●N-SING 単数名詞 **Cut** is also a noun. 短く切ること □*Prices vary from salon to salon, starting at $30 for a cut and blow-dry.* 料金は美容院によって違うが，カットとブロードライの場合，安いところで30ドルである．**4** V-T 他動詞 The way that clothes **are cut** is the way they are designed and made. 裁断された，仕立てられた [usu passive] □*...badly cut blue suits.* 仕立ての悪い青のスーツ．

→ see Picture Dictionary: **cut**

❷ cut /kʌt/ (**cuts, cutting**)

> The form **cut** is used in the present tense and is the past tense and past participle.

> **cut** 形は現在時制に使われ，過去時制と過去分詞でもある.

1 V-T 他動詞 If you **cut** something, you reduce it. 切り詰める □*The first priority is to cut costs.* まずやるべきことはコストの削減である．□*The U.N. force is to be cut by 90%.* 国連軍は兵力を90%削減する予定である．●N-COUNT 可算名詞 **Cut** is also a noun. 削減 [with supp, oft N "in" n] □*The economy needs an immediate 2 percent cut in interest rates.* 経済の現状からすれば，すぐにでも利率を2%切り下げる必要がある．**2** V-T 他動詞 If you **cut** a text, broadcast, or performance, you shorten it. If you **cut** a part of a text, broadcast, or performance, you do not publish, broadcast, or perform that part. 短縮する □*Branagh has cut the play judiciously.* ブラナーはうまく劇を短くまとめた．●N-COUNT 可算名詞 **Cut** is also a noun. 短縮 □*It has been found necessary to make some cuts in the text.* 本文を一部削除する必要のあることが分かった．**3** V-I 自動詞 If you **cut across** or **through** a place, you go through it because it is the shortest route to another place. 横切って近道する □*Jesse cut across the parking lot and strolled through the main entrance.* ジェスは駐車場をまっすぐ横切って，正門入口をぶらぶらと歩いて通り抜けた．**4** → see also **shortcut 5** V-I 自動詞 If you **cut** in front of someone, you move in front of them and take their place. 割り込む □*Somebody tried to cut in line and a fight broke out.* 行列に割り込もうとした者がいて，けんかが始まった．**6** V-T 他動詞 To **cut** a supply of something means to stop providing it or stop it from being provided. 供給を止める □*Winds have knocked down power lines, cutting electricity to thousands of people.* 強風で送電線が切れ，数千世帯が停電した．●N-COUNT 可算名詞 **Cut** is also a noun. 供給停止 [with supp, usu N "in" n] □*The strike had already led to cuts in electricity and water supplies in many areas.* すでにストライキの影響で多くの地域で電気や水道の供給が止まっていた．**7** to cut something **to the bone** → see **bone 8** to cut corners → see **corner**

Thesaurus

cut また次を参照：

N.	incision, slit **❶ 1**
	gash, nick, wound **❶ 2**
V.	carve, slice, trim **❶ 1**
	graze, nick, stab **❶ 2**
	mow, shave, trim **❶ 3**
	decrease, reduce, lower; (*ant.*) increase **❷ 1**

❸ cut /kʌt/ (**cuts, cutting**)

> The form **cut** is used in the present tense and is the past tense and past participle.

> **cut** 形は現在時制に使われ，過去時制と過去分詞でもある.

1 V-T 他動詞 If you **cut** a deck of playing cards, you divide it into two. 2組に分ける □*Place the cards face down on the table and cut them.* トランプを裏向きにして2つの山を作ります．**2** V-T 他動詞 If you tell someone to **cut** something, you are telling them in an irritated way to stop it. やめる [mainly AM 主に米国英語, INFORMAL くだけた, FEELINGS 感情] □*"Cut the euphemisms, Daniel,"* Brenda snapped. 「そういうもって回った言い方はやめてよ，ダニエル」とブレンダはぴしゃりと言った．**3** CONVENTION 慣習表現 When the director of a movie says "cut," they want the actors and the camera crew to stop filming. カットする **4** N-COUNT 可算名詞 A **cut** of meat is a piece or type of meat which is cut in a particular way from the animal, or from a particular part of it. 切った肉 □*Use a cheap cut such as spare rib chops.* スペアリブのような安い肉を使います．**5** N-SING 単数名詞 Someone's **cut** of the profits or winnings from something, especially ones that have been obtained dishonestly, is their share. 分け前 [INFORMAL くだけた] □*The agency is expected to take a cut of the money awarded to its client.* 仲介者は依頼主が手にした金額の一部を報酬として受け取るはずである．**6** N-COUNT 可算名詞 A **cut** is a narrow valley which has been cut through a hill so that a road or railroad track can pass through. 谷合い [AM 米国英語] **7** → see also **cutting 8** to cut the **mustard** → see **mustard**

❹ cut /kʌt/ (**cuts, cutting**)

> The form **cut** is used in the present tense and is the past tense and past participle.

> **cut** 形は現在時制に使われ，過去時制と過去分詞でもある.

▸ **cut across** PHRASAL VERB 句動詞 If an issue or problem **cuts across** the division between two or more groups of people, it affects or matters to people in all the groups. 一に及ぶ □*The problem cuts across all socioeconomic lines and affects all age groups.* この問題は社会的あるいは経済的な階層の違いを超えて，あらゆる年齢層に影響を及ぼしている．

▸ **cut back 1** PHRASAL VERB 句動詞 If you **cut back** something such as expenditure or **cut back on** it, you reduce it. 切り詰める □*Customers have cut back spending because of the economic slowdown.* 景気が後退しているせいで顧客は出費を控えている．□*The Government has cut back on defense spending.* 政府は防衛費を削減している．**2** → see also **cutback**

▸ **cut down 1** PHRASAL VERB 句動詞 If you **cut down on** something or **cut down** something, you use or do less of it. 量を減らす □*He cut down on coffee and cigarettes, and ate a balanced diet.* 彼はコーヒーとタバコの量を減らしバランスのとれた食事にした．□*Car owners were asked to cut down travel.* ドライバーは車の運転を控えるように求められた．**2** PHRASAL VERB 句動詞 If you **cut down** a tree, you cut through its trunk so that it falls to the ground. 切り倒す □*A vandal with a chainsaw cut down a tree.* チェーンソーをもった心無い者が木を切り倒しました．

▸ **cut in** PHRASAL VERB 句動詞 If you **cut in on** someone, you interrupt them when they are speaking. 話しをさえぎる □*Immediately, Daniel cut in on Joanne's attempts at reassurance.* ジョアンが励まそうとするのをすぐさまダニエルはさえぎった．□*"Not true,"* the Duchess cut in. 「本当じゃないわ」と公爵夫人がさえぎった．

▸ **cut off 1** PHRASAL VERB 句動詞 If you **cut** something **off**, you remove it with a knife or a similar tool. 切り取る □*Mrs. Johnson cut off a generous piece of the meat.* ジョンソンさんは肉の塊から分厚い1枚を切った．□*He threatened to cut my hair off.* 彼は髪を切ってしまうぞと私を脅した．**2** PHRASAL VERB 句動詞 To **cut** someone or something **off** means to separate them from things that they

are normally connected with. 切り離す □ *One of the goals of the campaign is to cut off the elite Republican Guard from its supplies.* この軍事作戦の目的の一つは、精鋭の共和国防衛隊の補給路を断つことです. ● **cut off** ADJ 形容詞 切り離されて □ *Without a car we still felt very cut off.* 車がないので依然として孤立している感じがした. **3** PHRASAL VERB 句動詞 To **cut off** a supply of something means to stop providing it or stop it from being provided. 供給を止める □ *The rebels have cut off electricity from the capital.* 反政府軍は首都への電力供給を止めている. **4** PHRASAL VERB 句動詞 If you get **cut off** when you are on the telephone, the line is suddenly disconnected and you can no longer speak to the other person. 電話が切れる □ *When you do get through, you've got to speak quickly before you get cut off.* 電話がつながったら、切れないうちに急いで話さなければいけません. **5** → see also **cutoff** **6** to **cut off** your **nose to spite** your **face** → see **spite**

▶ **cut out 1** PHRASAL VERB 句動詞 If you **cut** something **out**, you remove or separate it from what surrounds it by using scissors or a knife. 切り抜く □ *I cut it out and pinned it to my studio wall.* それを切り抜いて仕事場の壁にピンで留めた. **2** PHRASAL VERB 句動詞 If you **cut out** a part of a text, you do not print, publish, or broadcast that part, because to include it would make the text too long or unacceptable. 削除する □ *I listened to the program and found they'd cut out all the interesting stuff.* その番組を聞いたけど、面白いところはすっかり削られてた. **3** PHRASAL VERB 句動詞 To **cut out** something unnecessary or unwanted means to remove it completely from a situation. For example, if you **cut out** a particular type of food, you stop eating it, usually because it is bad for you. やめる □ *I've simply cut egg yolks out entirely.* 卵の黄身をまったく食べないようにしているだけです. **4** PHRASAL VERB 句動詞 If an object **cuts out** the light, it is between you and the light so that you are in the dark. 遮る □ *The curtains were half drawn to cut out the sunlight.* 光を遮るためにカーテンは半分だけ閉められていた. **5** PHRASAL VERB 句動詞 If an engine **cuts out**, it suddenly stops working. 急に止まる □ *The helicopter crash landed when one of its two engines cut out.* 2基のエンジンのうちの1基が止まり、ヘリコプターは不時着した. **6** → see also **cut out**

▶ **cut up** PHRASAL VERB 句動詞 If you **cut** something **up**, you cut it into several pieces. 切り分ける □ *Halve the tomatoes, then cut them up coarsely.* トマトはまず半分にしてから大きめに切っていきます.
→ see also **cut up**

cut|back /kʌtbæk/ (**cutbacks**) N-COUNT 可算名詞 A **cutback** is a reduction that is made in something. 縮小 □ *The region has also been hit hard by cutbacks in defense spending, which has left thousands out of work.* その地域では国防費削減による大きな打撃も受け、数多くの失業者が出ている.

cute /kyut/ (**cuter, cutest**) **1** ADJ 形容詞 Something or someone that is **cute** is very pretty or attractive, or is intended to appear pretty or attractive. かわいい □ *Oh, look at that dog! He's so cute.* ほら、あの犬！すごくかわいい. **2** ADJ 形容詞 If you describe someone as **cute**, you think they are sexually attractive. かわいい [mainly AM 主に米国英語, INFORMAL くだけた] □ *There was this girl, and I thought she was really cute.* この子がいてさ、すごくかわいいと思ったんだ. **3** ADJ 形容詞 If you describe someone as **cute**, you mean that they deal with things cleverly. 抜け目のない [AM 米国英語] □ *That's a cute trick.* 利口なやり方です.

Thesaurus	*cute* また次を参照:
ADJ.	adorable, charming, pretty; (*ant.*) homely, ugly **1**

cut|lery /kʌtləri/ **1** N-UNCOUNT 不可算名詞 You can refer to knives and tools used for cutting as **cutlery**. 刃物類 [AM 米国英語] □ *The first catalog featured specialty shavers, accessories, and cutlery.* 最初のカタログで特集されたのは、特製のひげそり用具やアクセサリーや刃物類だった. **2** N-UNCOUNT 不可算名詞 **Cutlery** consists of the knives, forks, and spoons that you eat your food with. カトラリー [mainly BRIT 主に英国英語; AM usually **silverware, flatware** 米国英語では通常 **silverware, flatware**]

cut|off /kʌtɔf/ (**cutoffs**) **1** N-COUNT 可算名詞 A **cutoff** or a **cutoff** point is the level or limit at which you decide that something should stop happening. 期限、限度 □ *The cutoff date for registering is yet to be announced.* 登録の締切日はまだ発表されていない. **2** N-COUNT 可算名詞 The **cutoff** of a supply or service is the complete stopping of the supply or service. 供給停止 □ *A total cutoff of supplies would cripple the country's economy.* 全く供給が止まってしまえば、国の経済は麻痺(まひ)するでしょう.

cut out ADJ 形容詞 If you are not **cut out for** a particular type of work, you do not have the qualities that are needed to be able to do it well. 一に向いていない □ *I left medicine anyway. I wasn't really cut out for it.* ともかく医学の道には進まなかったんです. 医学にはあまり向いてなかったんです.

cut-rate ADJ 形容詞 **Cut-rate** goods or services are cheaper than usual. 特価の [ADJ n] □ *...cut-rate auto insurance.* 割引価格の自動車保険

cut|ter /kʌtər/ (**cutters**) **1** N-COUNT 可算名詞 A **cutter** is a tool that you use for cutting through something. カッター、裁断機 □ *...wire cutters.* ワイヤーカッター **2** N-COUNT 可算名詞 A **cutter** is a person who cuts or reduces something. 切る人 □ *...a glass cutter.* ガラス職人

cut-throat ADJ 形容詞 If you describe a situation as **cut-throat**, you mean that the people or companies involved all want success and do not care if they harm each other in getting it. 熾烈(しれつ)な [DISAPPROVAL 不賛成] □ *...the cut-throat competition in personal computers.* パソコン業界の熾烈な競争

cut|ting /kʌtɪŋ/ (**cuttings**) **1** N-COUNT 可算名詞 A **cutting** from a plant is a part of the plant that you have cut off so that you can grow a new plant from it. 挿し木、挿し穂 □ *Take cuttings from it in July or August.* 挿し木は7月か8月に行います. □ *Take cuttings from suitable garden tomatoes in late summer.* 夏の終わりに庭にあるトマトからよさそうなものを選んで挿し木にします. **2** ADJ 形容詞 A **cutting** remark is unkind and likely to hurt someone's feelings. 辛辣(しんらつ)な □ *People make cutting remarks to help themselves feel superior or powerful.* 人は辛辣に話すことがあるが、それは自分のほうが優れているとか能力があると思いたいからである. **3** N-COUNT 可算名詞 A **cutting** is a piece of writing which has been cut from a newspaper or magazine. 切り抜き [BRIT 英国英語; AM **clipping** 米国英語 **clipping**]

cut|ting edge

The spelling **cutting-edge** is used for meaning **2**.
つづりの **cutting-edge** は **2** を意味するのに使われる.

1 N-SING 単数名詞 If you are **at the cutting edge of** a particular field of activity, you are involved in its most important or most exciting developments. 最先端 □ *This shipyard is at the cutting edge of world shipbuilding technology.* この造船所は世界最先端の造船技術を誇る. **2** ADJ 形容詞 **Cutting-edge** techniques or equipment are the most advanced that there are in a particular field. 最先端の □ *What we are planning is cutting-edge technology never seen in Australia before.* 計画中のものはオーストラリア初の最先端技術である
→ see **technology**

CV /si vi/ (**CVs**) N-COUNT 可算名詞 Your **CV** is a written account of your personal details, your education, and the jobs you have had. **CV** is an abbreviation for "curriculum vitae." 履歴書 [mainly BRIT 主に英国英語; AM usually **résumé** 米国英語では通常 **résumé**]

cya|nide /saɪənaɪd/ N-UNCOUNT 不可算名詞 **Cyanide** is a highly poisonous substance. シアン化物 □ *His death has all the signs of cyanide poisoning.* 彼の死には青酸中毒に見られる全ての症状が現れている.

cy|ber|café /saɪbərkæfeɪ/ (**cybercafés**) N-COUNT 可算名詞 A **cybercafé** is a café where people can pay to use the Internet. ネットカフェ

cy|ber|sex /saɪbərsɛks/ N-UNCOUNT 名詞 **Cybersex** involves using the Internet for sexual purposes, especially by exchanging sexual messages with another person. サイバーセックス □ *It's a place where you can role-play and have cybersex.* そのサイトでは、ロールプレイングゲームをしながらサイバーセックスができる.

cy|ber|space /saɪbərspeɪs/ N-UNCOUNT 不可算名詞 In computer technology, **cyberspace** refers to data banks and networks, considered as a place. サイバースペース [COMPUTING コンピューティング] □ *...a report circulating in cyberspace.* サイバースペースで流れているうわさ

Word Link	*cycl ≈ circle : bicycle, cycle, cyclical*

cy|cle /saɪkəl/ (**cycles, cycling, cycled**) **1** N-COUNT 可算名詞 A **cycle** is a series of events or processes that is repeated again and again, always in the same order. 周期、循環 □ *...the life cycle of the plant.* 植物のライフサイクル. **2** N-COUNT 可算名詞 A **cycle** is a single complete series of movements in an electrical, electronic, or mechanical process. サイクル □ *...10 cycles per second.* 1秒当たり10サイクル. **3** N-COUNT 可算名詞 A **cycle** is a bicycle. 自転車 □ *We supply the travel ticket for you and your cycle.* 自転車持込用の乗車券を用意しています. **4** V-I 自動詞 If you **cycle**, you ride a bicycle. 自転車に乗る □ *He cycled to Ingwold.* 彼はイングウォールドまで自転車で行った. ● **cy|cling** N-UNCOUNT 不可算名詞 サイクリング □ *The quiet country roads are ideal for cycling.* 静かな田舎道はサイクリングにうってつけだ.

cy|cli|cal /sɪklɪkəl, saɪk-/ ADJ 形容詞 A **cyclical** process is one in which a series of events happens again and again in the same order. 周期的な □ *...the cyclical nature of the airline business.* 航空業界の景気循環的な特性

cy|clist /saɪklɪst/ (**cyclists**) N-COUNT 可算名詞 A **cyclist** is someone who rides a bicycle, or is riding a bicycle. 自転車乗り、サイクリスト □ *...better protection for pedestrians and cyclists.* 歩行者や自転車の一層の保護
→ see **park**

cy|clone /saɪkloʊn/ (**cyclones**) N-COUNT 可算名詞 A **cyclone** is a violent tropical storm in which the air goes around and around. サイクロン（インド洋に発生する熱帯性低気圧）❑ *The race was called off as a cyclone struck.* サイクロンの襲来でレースは中止された.
→ see **hurricane**

cyl|in|der /sɪlɪndər/ (**cylinders**) ■ N-COUNT 可算名詞 A **cylinder** is an object with flat circular ends and long straight sides. 円筒 ❑ *It was recorded on a wax cylinder.* それはろう管に記録されました. ■ N-COUNT 可算名詞 A gas **cylinder** is a cylinder-shaped container in which gas is kept under pressure. ボンベ ❑ *...oxygen cylinders.* 酸素ボンベ ■ N-COUNT 可算名詞 In an engine, a **cylinder** is a cylinder-shaped part in which a piston moves backward and forward. シリンダー ❑ *...a four-cylinder engine.* 4気筒エンジン
→ see **engine, solid, volume**

cyn|ic /sɪnɪk/ (**cynics**) N-COUNT 可算名詞 A **cynic** is someone who believes that people always act selfishly. 人間不信の人，世をすねた人 ❑ *I have come to be very much of a cynic in these matters.* このことに私は相当不信感を募らせている.

cyni|cal /sɪnɪkəl/ ■ ADJ 形容詞 If you describe someone as **cynical**, you mean they believe that people always act selfishly. 冷笑的な ❑ *...his cynical view of the world.* 世の中に対する彼の冷ややかな目 ● **cyni|cal|ly** ADV 副詞 [ADV with v] 冷ややかに ❑ *The fast-food industry cynically continues to target children.* ファーストフード業界は依然として子供たちを食いものにしている. ■ ADJ 形容詞 If you are **cynical about** something, you do not believe that it can be successful or that the people involved are honest. 不信感を抱いた ❑ *It's hard not to be cynical about reform.* 改革には不信感を抱かざるを得ません.

cyni|cism /sɪnɪsɪzəm/ ■ N-UNCOUNT 不可算名詞 **Cynicism** is the belief that people always act selfishly. 人間不信 ❑ *I found Ben's cynicism wearing at times.* ベンの世をすねたようなところにはときどきうんざりした. ■ N-UNCOUNT 不可算名詞 **Cynicism about** something is the belief that it cannot be successful or that the people involved are not honorable. 悲観，不信感 ❑ *In an era of growing cynicism about politicians, Mr. Mandela is a model of dignity and integrity.* 政治家に対する不信が高まる時代にあって，謹厳実直なマンデラ氏はまさに政治家の鑑（かがみ）である.

cyst /sɪst/ (**cysts**) N-COUNT 可算名詞 A **cyst** is a growth containing liquid that appears inside your body or under your skin. 嚢胞（のうほう）❑ *He had a minor operation to remove a cyst.* 彼は嚢胞を切除する簡単な手術を受けた.

Dd

D also **d** /diː/ (**D's, d's**) N-VAR 可変性名詞 **D** is the fourth letter of the English alphabet. 英語アルファベットの第4字

dab /dæb/ (**dabs, dabbing, dabbed**) ■ V-T/V-I 他動詞/自動詞 If you **dab** something, you touch it several times using quick, light movements. If you **dab** a substance onto a surface, you put it there using quick, light movements. 軽くたたく ❑ *She arrived weeping, dabbing her eyes with a tissue.* 彼女はティッシュで目を押さえつつ，泣きながらやって来た. ❑ *She dabbed iodine on the cuts on her forehead.* 彼女は額の切り傷にヨードチンキを塗った. ■ N-COUNT 可算名詞 A **dab of** something is a small amount of it that is put onto a surface. 少量 [INFORMAL くだけた] ❑ *...a dab of glue.* 少量の接着剤

dab|ble /dæbᵊl/ (**dabbles, dabbling, dabbled**) V-I 自動詞 If you **dabble in** something, you take part in it but not very seriously. (興味半分に) 手を出す ❑ *He dabbled in business.* 彼は商売にちょっと手を出した.

dad /dæd/ (**dads**) N-FAMILY 家族名詞 Your **dad** is your father. お父さん [INFORMAL くだけた] ❑ *How do you feel, Dad?* 気分はどう，お父さん?

dad|dy /dædi/ (**daddies**) N-FAMILY 家族名詞 Children often call their father **daddy**. お父ちゃん (子供がよく使う) [INFORMAL くだけた] ❑ *Look at me, Daddy!* お父ちゃん，見て!

daf|fo|dil /dæfədɪl/ (**daffodils**) N-COUNT 可算名詞 A **daffodil** is a yellow spring flower with a central part shaped like a tube and a long stem. ラッパズイセン

dag|ger /dægər/ (**daggers**) N-COUNT 可算名詞 A **dagger** is a weapon like a knife with two sharp edges. 短剣

dai|ly /deɪli/ ■ ADV 副詞 If something happens **daily**, it happens every day. 毎日 [ADV after v] ❑ *Cathay Pacific flies daily nonstop to Hong Kong.* キャセイ・パシフィックの香港直行便は毎日飛んでいる. ● ADJ 形容詞 **Daily** is also an adjective. 毎日の [ADJ n] ❑ *They held daily press briefings.* 彼らは毎日，記者会見を開いた. ■ ADJ 形容詞 **Daily** quantities or rates relate to a period of one day. 1日の [ADJ n] ❑ *...a diet containing adequate daily amounts of fresh fruit.* 新鮮な果物の1日の適量を含む食事 ■ PHRASE 句 Your **daily life** is the things that you do every day as part of your normal life. 日常生活 ❑ *All of us in our daily life react favorably to people who take us*

and our views seriously. 日常生活の中で私たちはみな，自分自身や自分の意見を真剣に受け止めてくれる人々に好意的にふるまう.

dain|ty /deɪnti/ (**daintier, daintiest**) ADJ 形容詞 If you describe a movement, person, or object as **dainty**, you mean that they are small, delicate, and pretty. 繊細な ❑ *The girls were dainty and feminine.* その女の子たちはかれんで女らしかった. ● **dain|ti|ly** ADV 副詞 繊細に ❑ *She walked daintily down the steps.* 彼女は優美に階段を下りてきた.

dairy /deəri/ (**dairies**) ■ N-COUNT 可算名詞 A **dairy** is a company that sells milk and food made from milk, such as butter, cream, and cheese. 乳製品販売店 ❑ *In my childhood, local dairies bought milk from local farmers.* 私が子供の頃は地元の乳製品販売店が地元の農家から牛乳を買っていた. ■ ADJ 形容詞 **Dairy** is used to refer to foods such as butter and cheese that are made from milk. 乳製品の [ADJ n] ❑ *He avoids all meat and dairy products.* 彼は肉と乳製品をすべて避けている. ■ ADJ 形容詞 **Dairy** is used to refer to the use of cattle to produce milk rather than meat. 酪農の [ADJ n] ❑ *...a small vegetable and dairy farm.* 野菜と酪農の小さな農場
→ see Word Web: **dairy**

dai|sy /deɪzi/ (**daisies**) N-COUNT 可算名詞 A **daisy** is a small wildflower with a yellow center and white petals. ヒナギク
→ see **plant**

dam /dæm/ (**dams**) N-COUNT 可算名詞 A **dam** is a wall that is built across a river in order to stop the water from flowing and to make a lake. ダム ❑ *Before the dam was built, Campbell River used to flood in the spring.* そのダムが建設されるまで，キャンベルリバーは春になると氾濫していた.
→ see Word Web: **dam**

dam|age /dæmɪdʒ/ (**damages, damaging, damaged**) ■ V-T 他動詞 To **damage** an object means to break it, spoil it physically, or stop it from working properly. 壊す，損害を与える ❑ *He maliciously damaged a car with a baseball bat.* 彼は悪意をもって野球のバットで車を壊した. ■ V-T 他動詞 To **damage** something means to cause it to become less good, pleasant, or successful. (評判などを) 傷つける，損なう ❑ *...the electoral chaos that damaged Florida's reputation.* フロリダ州の評判を落とした選挙の混乱 ● **dam|ag|ing** ADJ 形容詞 損害を与える ❑ *The weakened currency could have damaging effects for the*

economy. 弱含みの通貨はその国の経済に不利な効果をもたらす可能性がある. **3** N-UNCOUNT 不可算名詞 **Damage** is physical harm that is caused to an object. 損害 ❑ *The blast had serious effects with quite extensive damage to the house.* 爆風はその家に非常に大きな被害を与え, 深刻な結果をもたらした. **4** N-UNCOUNT 不可算名詞 **Damage** consists of the unpleasant effects that something has on a person, situation, or type of activity. （否定的な）影響 ❑ *Incidents of this type cause irreparable damage to relations with the community.* この手の事件はその地域社会との関係に取り返しのつかない影響を与える. **5** N-PLURAL 複数名詞 If a court of law awards **damages** to someone, it orders money to be paid to them by a person who has damaged their reputation or property, or who has injured them. 損害賠償 ❑ *She is seeking more than $75,000 in damages.* 彼女は7万5千ドル以上の損害賠償を要求している.
→ see **disaster**

Thesaurus	*damage* また次を参照:
V.	break, harm, hurt **1**
	ruin, wreck **2**
N.	harm, loss **3**

Word Partnership	*damage* は次の語句と使われる:
N.	damage to *someone's* reputation **2**
	damage to *someone's* health, damage to the
	environment **4**
V.	damage caused by/to *something* **3** **4**
ADJ.	extensive damage, permanent damage **3** **4**

dam|age con|trol N-UNCOUNT 不可算名詞 **Damage control** is action that is taken to make the bad results of something as small as possible, when it is impossible to avoid bad results completely. 被害対策 [AM 米国英語] ❑ *But Broomfield argues that the long-running case is now an exercise in damage control for the Los Angeles police.* しかしブルームフィールドは, その長期におよぶ訴訟でロサンゼルス警察が今や評判に傷がつくのを最小限にとどめようと躍起になっている, と主張している.

damn /dǽm/ (**damns, damning, damned**) **1** EXCLAM 感嘆詞 **Damn, damn it,** and **dammit** are used by some people to express anger or impatience. くそっ！, しまった！ [INFORMAL, VULGAR くだけた, 下品な, FEELINGS 感情] ❑ *Don't be flippant, damn it! This is serious.* くそっ, ふざけるなよ！これは深刻な事態なんだぞ. **2** ADJ 形容詞 **Damn** is used by some people to emphasize what they are saying. （強調して）まったく [INFORMAL, VULGAR くだけた, 下品な, EMPHASIS 強調] [ADJ n] ❑ *There's not a damn thing you can do about it now.* それについて今お前にできることはまったく何もないよ. ● ADV 副詞 **Damn** is also an adverb. まったく, ひどく [ADV adj/adv] ❑ *As it turned out, I was damn right.* 結局, おれが本当に正しかったのさ. **3** V-T 他動詞 If you say that a person or a news report **damns** something such as a policy or action, you mean that they are very critical of it. ひどく非難する ❑ *...a sensational book in which she damns the ultraright party.* 彼女がその極右政党を厳しく非難している衝撃的な本. **4** → see also **damned, damning** **5** PHRASE 句 If you say that someone **does not give a damn** about something, you are emphasizing that they do not care about it at all. 一切気にしない [INFORMAL, VULGAR くだけた, 下品な, EMPHASIS 強調] ❑ *I don't give a damn about the money, Nicole.* ニコル, ぼくはその金のことなんてぜんぜん気にしちゃいないよ.

damned /dǽmd/ **1** ADJ 形容詞 **Damned** is used by some people to emphasize what they are saying, especially when they are angry or frustrated. ひどい, とんでもない [INFORMAL, VULGAR くだけた, 下品な, EMPHASIS 強調] [ADJ n] ❑ *They're a damned nuisance most of the time.* 大体, やつらはとんでもない厄介者だ. ● ADV 副詞 **Damned** is also an adverb. とても, ひどく [ADV adj/adv] ❑ *We are making a damned good profit, I tell you that.* おれたちのもうけはすごいんだぜ, ほんとに. **2** PHRASE 句 If someone says "**I'm damned if I'm** going to do it" or "**I'll be damned if I'll do it,**" they are emphasizing that they do not intend to do something and think it is unreasonable for anyone to expect them to do it. 絶対にしない [INFORMAL, VULGAR くだけた, 下品な, EMPHASIS 強調] ❑ *I was damned if I was going to ask for an explanation and beg to keep my job.* おれが説明を求めて首にしないように頼むことなどしたわけがない.

Word Link	*damn, demn* ≈ *harm, loss* : con**demn**, **damn**ing, in**demn**ify

damn|ing /dǽmɪŋ/ ADJ 形容詞 If you describe evidence or a report as **damning**, you mean that it suggests very strongly that someone is guilty of a crime or has made a serious mistake. （証拠などが）とても不利な 批判的な ❑ *...a damning report on safety standards at US space agency NASA.* 米国航空宇宙局NASAの安全基準に対する手厳しい報告

damp /dǽmp/ (**damper, dampest, damps, damping, damped**) **1** ADJ 形容詞 Something that is **damp** is slightly wet. 湿っ

た ❑ *Her hair was still damp.* 彼女の髪はまだ生乾きだった. ❑ *...the damp, cold air.* 湿った冷たい空気 **2** N-UNCOUNT 不可算名詞 **Damp** is moisture on the inside walls of a house or in the air. 湿気 ❑ *There was damp everywhere and the entire building was in need of rewiring.* いたるところが湿気っていて, その建物全体の配線を取り替える必要があった.
→ see **weather**

▶ **damp down** PHRASAL VERB 句動詞 To **damp down** something such as a strong emotion, an argument, or a crisis means to make it calmer or less intense. （感情や危機などを）静める ❑ *His hand moved to his mouth as he tried to damp down the panic.* 彼が恐怖を静めようとすると手が口元に行った.

damp|en /dǽmpən/ (**dampens, dampening, dampened**) V-T 他動詞 To **dampen** something such as someone's enthusiasm or excitement means to make it less lively or intense. （熱意や興奮を）そぐ ❑ *Nothing seems to dampen his perpetual enthusiasm.* 彼の果てしない熱意は何事にもそがれそうにない. ● PHRASAL VERB 句動詞 To **dampen** something **down** means the same as to **dampen** it. そぐ ❑ *The new penalties were aimed at dampening down consumer spending.* 新しい罰金制度には消費者の支出を抑えるねらいがあった.

damp|ness /dǽmpnɪs/ N-UNCOUNT 不可算名詞 **Dampness** is moisture in the air, or on the surface of something. 湿気 ❑ *It was cooler here, and there was dampness in the air.* ここは他よりも涼しく, 空気が湿っぽかった.

dance /dǽns/ (**dances, dancing, danced**) **1** V-I 自動詞 When you **dance**, you move your body and feet in a way which follows a rhythm, usually in time to music. 踊る ❑ *Polly had never learned to dance.* ポリーは1度もダンスを習ったことがなかった. **2** V-T 他動詞 If you **dance** a particular kind of dance, you do it or perform it. （特定のダンスを）踊る ❑ *Then we put the music on, and we all danced the Charleston.* そして私たちは音楽をかけ, みんなでチャールストンを踊った. **3** V-I 自動詞 If you **dance** somewhere, you move there lightly and quickly, usually because you are happy or excited. 小躍りする [LITERARY 文語的] ❑ *He danced off down the road.* 彼は道路を小躍りして行った. **4** V-I 自動詞 If you say that something **dances**, you mean that it moves around, or seems to move around, lightly and quickly. 跳ね回る [LITERARY 文語的] ❑ *Patterns of light, reflected by the river, dance along the base of the cliffs.* 川に反射した光の模様ががけのふもとに沿って躍動する. **5** N-COUNT 可算名詞 A **dance** is a particular series of graceful movements of your body and feet, which you usually do in time to music. ダンス, 踊り ❑ *Sometimes the people doing this dance hold brightly colored scarves.* この踊りを踊る人たちは色鮮やかなスカーフを手に持つことがある. **6** N-COUNT 可算名詞 A **dance** is a social event where people dance with each other. ダンスパーティー ❑ *At the school dance he sat and talked to her all evening.* 学校のダンスパーティーでは, 彼はその夜ずっと彼女と隣で話をしていた. **7** V-RECIP 相互動詞 When you **dance with** someone, the two of you take part in a dance together, as partners. You can also say that two people **dance**. 踊る ❑ *It's a terrible thing when nobody wants to dance with you.* 誰もあなたと踊りたがらなかったらとんでもないことだ. ❑ *Shall we dance?* 踊りましょうか? ● N-COUNT 可算名詞 **Dance** is also a noun. 踊り ❑ *Come and have a dance with me.* 来て私と一緒に踊りましょう. **8** N-UNCOUNT 不可算名詞 **Dance** is the activity of performing dances, as a public entertainment or an art form. 舞踊 ❑ *Their contribution to international dance, drama and music is inestimable.* 彼らの国際的な舞踊・演劇・音楽への貢献は計り知れない.

Word Partnership	*dance* は次の語句と使われる:
V.	learn to dance **1** **7**
	let's dance **1** **6**
	choreograph a dance **5**
N.	dance music, dance partner **6**
	dance class, dance moves **5**

dance floor (**dance floors**) N-COUNT 可算名詞 In a restaurant or night club, the **dance floor** is the area where people can dance. ダンスフロア, 踊り場 ❑ *Everybody is on the dance floor with the men forming a circle around the women.* みんなダンスフロアにいて, 男性が女性を丸く囲んでいる.

danc|er /dǽnsər/ (**dancers**) **1** N-COUNT 可算名詞 A **dancer** is a person who earns money by dancing, or a person who is dancing. ダンサー, 踊り子 ❑ *His girlfriend was a dancer with the New York City Ballet.* 彼の恋人はニューヨーク市バレエ団のダンサーだった. **2** N-COUNT 可算名詞 If you say that someone is a good **dancer** or a bad **dancer**, you are saying how well or badly they can dance. （上手な, または下手な）踊り手 ❑ *He was the best dancer in LA.* 彼はロサンゼルスで1番の踊り手だった.

danc|ing /dǽnsɪŋ/ N-UNCOUNT 不可算名詞 When people dance for enjoyment or to entertain others, you can refer to this activity as **dancing**. （娯楽的な）踊り ❑ *All the schools have music and dancing as part of the curriculum.* 全ての学校が音楽とダンスを教育課程の一部にしている. ❑ *Let's go dancing tonight.* 今夜, 踊りに行こう.

dan|de|lion /dǽndɪlaɪən/ (dandelions) N-COUNT 可算名詞 A **dandelion** is a wild plant which has yellow flowers with lots of thin petals. When the petals of each flower drop off, a fluffy white ball of seeds grows. タンポポ

dan|druff /dǽndrəf/ N-UNCOUNT 不可算名詞 **Dandruff** is small white pieces of dead skin in someone's hair, or fallen from someone's hair. ふけ ❑ He has very bad dandruff. 彼はふけがひどい.

dan|ger /déɪndʒər/ (dangers) ■ N-UNCOUNT 不可算名詞 **Danger** is the possibility that someone may be harmed or killed. 危険 ❑ My friends endured tremendous danger in order to help me. 友人たちは私を助けるためにとてつもない危険に耐え抜いた. ② N-COUNT 可算名詞 A **danger** is something or someone that can hurt or harm you. 危険なもの, 危険な人 ❑ ...the dangers of smoking. 喫煙の害 ③ N-SING 単数名詞 If there is a **danger that** something unpleasant will happen, it is possible that it will happen. 危険性 ❑ There is a real danger that some people will no longer be able to afford insurance. 一部の人々がもはや保険に入る余裕がなくなるという真の危険性がある. ❑ There was no danger that any of these groups would be elected to power. これらのグループのどれかが選ばれて政権を取る危険性はまったくなかった. ④ PHRASE 句 If someone who has been seriously ill is **out of danger**, they are still ill, but they are not expected to die. 危機を脱して ❑ There is some risk of the lung collapsing again, but he is out of danger. 肺がまた虚脱する危険性はいくらかあるが, 彼は危機を脱した.

→ see **hero**

Word Link   ous ≈ having the qualities of : danger**ous**, fabul**ous**, glamor**ous**

dan|ger|ous /déɪndʒərəs, déɪndʒrəs/ ADJ 形容詞 If something is **dangerous**, it is able or likely to hurt or harm you. 危険な ❑ It's a dangerous stretch of road. その長く伸びた道路は危険だ. ❑ ...dangerous drugs. 危険な薬物 ● **dan|ger|ous|ly** ADV 副詞 危険なほど ❑ He is dangerously ill. 彼は重態だ.

Thesaurus   dangerous また次を参照 :

ADJ.   risky, threatening, unsafe

Word Partnership   dangerous は次の語句と使われる :

N.   dangerous **area**, dangerous **criminal**, dangerous **driving**, dangerous **man**, dangerous **situation**

ADV.   **potentially** dangerous

dan|gle /dǽŋgəl/ (dangles, dangling, dangled) ■ V-T/V-I 他動詞/自動詞 If something **dangles from** somewhere or if you **dangle** it somewhere, it hangs or swings loosely. ぶら下げる [他動詞], ぶら下がる [自動詞] ❑ A gold bracelet dangled from his left wrist. 金のブレスレットが彼の左手首から垂れ下がっていた. ② V-T 他動詞 If you say that someone **is dangling** something attractive **before** you, you mean they are offering it to you in order to try to influence you in some way. ちらつかせる ❑ They dangle hope in front of our eyes, then snatch it clear away. 彼らは私たちの目の前に希望をちらつかせ, それからそれをすっかり取り去る.

dare /déər/ (dares, daring, dared)

Dare sometimes behaves like an ordinary verb, for example, "He dared to speak" and "He doesn't dare to speak" and sometimes like a modal, for example, "He dare not speak."

Dare は時々普通動詞のように振る舞う, 例えば, **He dared to speak** や **He doesn't dare to speak**. そして時々法動詞のように振る舞う, 例えば, **He dare not speak**.

■ V-T 他動詞 If you do not **dare to** do something, you do not have enough courage to do it, or you do not want to do it because you fear the consequences. If you **dare to** do something, you do something which requires a lot of courage. あえて~する ❑ Most people hate Harry but they don't dare to say so. ほとんどの人はハリーを嫌っているが, みんなそれを口にする勇気がない. ● MODAL 法動詞 **Dare** is also a modal. (法動詞) あえて~する ❑ Dare she risk staying where she was? 彼女はあえてそこに居続ける勇気を冒すか? ❑ The yen is weakening. But Tokyo dare not raise its interest rates again. 円安が進んでいる. しかし東京はあえて金利を再び引き上げない.

You can leave out the word **to** after **dare**. ❑ Nobody dared complain. The form **dares** is never used in a question or in a negative statement. You use **dare** instead. ❑ Dare he tell him?... He dare not enter.

② V-T 他動詞 If you **dare** someone **to** do something, you challenge them to prove that they are not frightened of doing it. (人に何かをするよう) 挑発する ❑ Over coffee, she lit a cigarette, her eyes daring him to comment. コーヒーを飲みながら, 彼女は彼に文句があるなら言ってみようと言わんばかりの目つきで, たばこに火をつけた. ③ N-COUNT 可算名詞 A **dare** is a challenge which one person

gives to another to do something dangerous or frightening. 挑戦 ❑ Jones broke into a military base on a dare. ジョーンズは挑戦されて軍用基地に押し入った. ④ PHRASE 句 If you say to someone "**don't you dare**" do something, you are telling them not to do it and letting them know that you are angry. (怒りを込めて) ~したら承知しない [SPOKEN 口語, FEELINGS 感情] ❑ Allen, don't you dare go anywhere else, you hear? アレン, どこか他の所に行ったら承知しないよ. 分かった? ⑤ PHRASE 句 You say "**how dare you**" when you are very shocked and angry about something that someone has done. (怒りやショックを込めて) よくも~したな [SPOKEN 口語, FEELINGS 感情] ❑ How dare you pick up the phone and listen in on my conversations! よくも受話器を取って私の会話を盗み聞きしたわね! ⑥ PHRASE 句 You can use "**I daresay**" or "**I dare say**" before or after a statement to indicate that you believe it is probably true. 多分~だろう ❑ I daresay that the computer would provide a clear answer to that. 多分そのコンピュータならそれに対するはっきりした答えを出すだろう.

dar|ing /déərɪŋ/ ■ ADJ 形容詞 People who are **daring** are willing to do or say things which are new or which might shock or anger other people. 大胆不敵な ❑ Bergit was probably more daring than I was. バージットはおそらく私よりも大胆だった. ② ADJ 形容詞 A **daring** person is willing to do things that might be dangerous. 勇敢な ❑ His daring rescue saved the lives of the youngsters. 彼の勇気ある救出が子供たちの命を救った. ③ N-UNCOUNT 不可算名詞 **Daring** is the courage to do things which might be dangerous or which might shock or anger other people. 勇気, 向こう見ず ❑ His daring may have cost him his life. その向こう見ずさのせいで彼は命を落としたのかもしれない.

dark /dɑ́rk/ (darker, darkest) ■ ADJ 形容詞 When it is **dark**, there is not enough light to see properly, for example, because it is night. 暗い ❑ It was too dark inside to see much. 中はとても暗かったので, あまり見えなかった. ❑ People usually draw the curtains once it gets dark. 普通, 暗くなるとカーテンを閉める. ● **dark|ness** N-UNCOUNT 不可算名詞 暗闇 ❑ The light went out, and the room was plunged into darkness. 明かりが消え, 部屋が急に真っ暗になった. ● **dark|ly** ADV 副詞 [ADV -ed] 暗く, ぼんやりと ❑ In a darkly lit, seedy dance hall, hundreds of men lounge around small tables. 薄暗くて怪しげなダンスホールでは, 何百人もの男が小さなテーブルについてぶらぶらしていた. ② ADJ 形容詞 If you describe something as **dark**, you mean that it is black in color, or a shade that is close to black. 黒い, 黒っぽい ❑ He wore a dark suit and carried a black attaché case. 黒っぽいスーツを着て, 黒いアタッシュケースを持っていた. ● **dark|ly** ADV 副詞 黒ずんで ❑ The freckles on Joanne's face suddenly stood out darkly against her pale skin. ジョアンの顔のそばかすが突然白い肌に対照的に黒ずんで浮かび上がった. ③ ADJ 形容詞 If someone has **dark** hair, eyes, or skin, they have brown or black hair, eyes, or skin. (髪や目などが) 黒い, こげ茶色の ❑ He had dark, curly hair. 彼は黒い巻き毛をしていた. ④ ADJ 形容詞 A **dark** period of time is unpleasant or frightening. 暗い ❑ There's talk of very dark days ahead. 前途は暗たんたる時代だという話が再び起こっている. ⑤ ADJ 形容詞 [ADJ n] A **dark** place or area is mysterious and not fully known about. 不明な ❑ The spacecraft would enable scientists to study some dark corners of the solar system. その宇宙船で科学者たちは太陽系の未知の部分を調査できるようになるだろう. ⑥ ADJ 形容詞 **Dark** thoughts are sad, and show that you are expecting something unpleasant to happen. (考えが) 悲観的な [LITERARY 文語的] ❑ Troy's endless happy chatter kept me from thinking dark thoughts. トロイの延々と続く明るいおしゃべりのおかげで, 私は悲観的な考えにとらわれずにすんだ. ● **dark|ly** ADV 副詞 [ADV with v] 悲観的に ❑ She hinted darkly that she might have to resign. 彼女は辞任しなくてはいけないかもしれないと悲観的にほのめかした. ⑦ ADJ 形容詞 If you describe something as **dark**, you mean that it is related to things that are serious or unpleasant, rather than lighthearted. 陰険な, 陰うつな ❑ There's plenty of dark humor in the movie. その映画にはブラックユーモアがたくさん盛り込まれている. ● **dark|ly** ADV 副詞 [ADV adj] 陰険に ❑ The atmosphere after Wednesday's debut was as darkly comic as the movie itself. 水曜日の初公開後の雰囲気は, その映画自体のようにブラックユーモアの陰険なものだった. ⑧ N-SING 単数名詞 The **dark** is the lack of light in a place. 暗い場所 ❑ I've always been afraid of the dark. いつも私は暗い場所が怖いんだ. ⑨ COMB IN COLOR 色彩語の複合 When you use **dark** to describe a color, you are referring to a shade of that color which is close to black, or seems to have some black in it. 濃い, 黒に近い ❑ She was wearing a dark blue dress. 彼女は濃紺のドレスを着ていた. ⑩ PHRASE 句 If you do something **after dark**, you do it when the sun has set and night has begun. 暗くなってから ❑ They avoid going out alone after dark. 彼らは暗くなってから1人で外出するのを避けている. ⑪ PHRASE 句 If you do something **before dark**, you do it before the sun sets and night begins. 暗くなる前に ❑ They'll be back well before dark. 彼らは暗くなるだいぶ前に帰ってくるだろう. ⑫ PHRASE 句 If you are **in the dark** about something, you do not know anything about it. 見当がつかないで ❑ The investigators admit that they are completely in the dark about the killing. 捜査官たちはまったくその殺人事件の見当がつかないことを認めている.

Word Partnership *dark* は次の語句と使われる:

v.	**get** dark ▪ ▪
	afraid of the dark, **scared of the** dark ▪
N.	dark **clouds**, dark **suit** ▪ ▪

dark|en /dɑrkən/ (darkens, darkening, darkened) ▪ V-T/V-I 他動詞/自動詞 If something **darkens** or if a person or thing **darkens** it, it becomes darker. 暗くする [他動詞], 暗くなる [自動詞] □ *The sky darkened abruptly.* 急に空が暗くなった. ▪ V-T/V-I 他動詞/自動詞 If someone's mood **darkens** or if something **darkens** their mood, they suddenly become unhappy. 憂うつにする [他動詞], 憂うつにな る [自動詞] □ *My sunny mood suddenly darkened.* 私の明るい気分が突然暗く沈んだ. [LITERARY 文語的]

dark|room /dɑrkrum/ (darkrooms) N-COUNT 可算名詞 A **darkroom** is a room which can be sealed off from natural light and is lit only by red light. It is used for developing photographs. 暗室

dar|ling /dɑrlɪŋ/ (darlings) ▪ N-VOC 呼格名詞 You call someone **darling** if you love them or like them very much. 最愛の人 [FEELINGS 感情] □ *Thank you, darling.* ありがとう, あなた. ▪ ADJ 形容詞 Some people use **darling** to describe someone or something that they love or like very much. 最愛の [INFORMAL くだけた] [ADJ n] □ *To have a darling baby boy was the greatest gift I could imagine.* かわいい男の子を授かるなんて, 私の想像できる限り最も素敵な贈り物だった. ▪ N-COUNT 可算名詞 If you describe someone as a **darling**, you are fond of them and think that they are nice. 素敵な人 [INFORMAL くだけた] □ *He's such a darling.* 彼はほんとに素敵なのよ.

darn /dɑrn/ (darns, darning, darned) ▪ V-T 他動詞 If you **darn** something knitted or made of cloth, you repair a hole in it by sewing stitches across the hole and then weaving stitches in and out of them. 繕う □ *Aunt Emilie darned old socks.* エミリー叔母さんは古い靴下を繕った. ▪ ADJ 形容詞 People sometimes use **darn** or **darned** to emphasize what they are saying, often when they are annoyed. (強調して) まさにその [INFORMAL くだけた, EMPHASIS 強調] [ADJ n] □ *There's not a darn thing he can do about it.* それについて彼にできる事なんてまったくないのさ. ● ADV 副詞 **Darn** is also an adverb. [ADV adj/adv] □ *...the desire to be free to do just as we darn well please.* 私たちがまったくしたいようにする自由への願望 ▪ PHRASE 句 You can say **I'll be darned** to show that you are very surprised about something. びっくりした [AM 米国英語, INFORMAL くだけた, FEELINGS 感情] □ *"A talking pig!" he exclaimed. "Well, I'll be darned."* 「言葉を話す豚！」と彼は叫んだ. 「へえ, こりゃたまげた」.

dart /dɑrt/ (darts, darting, darted) ▪ V-I 自動詞 If a person or animal **darts** somewhere, they move there suddenly and quickly. すばやく動く [WRITTEN 書き言葉] □ *Ingrid darted across the deserted street.* イングリッドは人けのない通りを素早く横切った. ▪ V-T/V-I 他動詞/自動詞 If you **dart** a look **at** someone or something, or if your eyes **dart to** them, you look at them very quickly. 向ける [LITERARY 文語的] □ *She darted a sly sideways glance at Bramwell.* 彼女はブラムウェルをずるそうな横目でちらっと見た. ▪ N-COUNT 可算名詞 A **dart** is a small, narrow object with a sharp point which can be thrown or shot. (武器の) 投げ矢, 吹き矢 □ *Markov died after being struck by a poison dart.* マルコフは毒を塗った吹き矢に当たって死亡した. ▪ N-UNCOUNT 不可算名詞 **Darts** is a game in which you throw darts at a round board which has numbers on it. ダーツ (室内ゲーム) □ *I started playing darts at 15.* 私は15歳でダーツを始めた.

dash /dæʃ/ (dashes, dashing, dashed) ▪ V-I 自動詞 If you **dash** somewhere, you run or go there quickly and suddenly. 突然駆け出す □ *Suddenly she dashed down to the cellar.* 彼女は突然地下室に駆け下りた. ● N-SING 単数名詞 **Dash** is also a noun. 突進 □ *...a 160-mile dash to the hospital.* 160マイル離れた病院への突進 ▪ V-I 自動詞 If you say that you have to **dash**, you mean that you are in a hurry and have to leave immediately. 急いで出かける [INFORMAL くだけた] [no cont] □ *Oh, Tim! I'm sorry but I have to dash.* あら, ティム！悪いけど, 私急いで出かけなくちゃならないの. ▪ V-T 他動詞 If you **dash** something **against** a wall or other surface, you throw or push it violently, often so hard that it breaks. 投げつける [LITERARY 文語的] □ *She seized the doll and dashed it against the stone wall with tremendous force.* 彼女は人形をつかむと, それをすごい勢いで石垣に投げつけた. ▪ V-T 他動詞 If an event or person **dashes** someone's hopes or expectations, it destroys them by making it impossible that the thing that is hoped for or expected will ever happen. (希望を) 打ち砕く [LITERARY 文語的 JOURNALISM ジャーナリズム] □ *Renewed fighting has dashed hopes for a United Nations-organized interim government.* 戦闘の再開で, 国連が組織する暫定政府の樹立への希望は粉々に打ち砕かれた. ▪ N-COUNT 可算名詞 A **dash of** something is a small quantity of it which you add when you are preparing food or mixing a drink. (調味料など) 少量 □ *Pour over olive oil and a dash of balsamic vinegar to accentuate the sweetness.* オリーブオイルを注ぎ入れ, 甘みを際立たせるためバルサミコ酢を少々入れなさい. ▪ N-COUNT 可算名詞 A **dash of** a quality is a small amount of it that is found in something and often makes it more interesting or distinctive. (特質などの) わずかな徴候 □ *...a story with a dash of mystery thrown in.* 推理小説の要素が少しに盛り込まれた小説 ▪ N-COUNT 可算名詞 A **dash** is a straight, horizontal line used in writing, for example, to separate two main clauses whose meanings are closely connected. ダッシュ記号 (文中に挿入する '−' の記号) □ *...the dash between the birth date and death date.* 生年と死亡年の間のダッシュ記号 ▪ N-COUNT 可算名詞 The **dash** of a car is its **dashboard**. (車の) ダッシュボード ▪ PHRASE 句 If you **make a dash for** a place, you run there very quickly, for example, to escape from someone or something. 全力疾走する □ *I made a dash for the front door but he got there before me.* 私は玄関に向かって思いきり走ったが, 彼は私よりも先にそこに着いた.

▸ **dash off** ▪ PHRASAL VERB 句動詞 If you **dash off to** a place, you go there very quickly. 急いで行く □ *He dashed off to lunch at the Hard Rock Cafe.* 彼は急いでハードロック・カフェへ昼食を取りに行った. ▪ PHRASAL VERB 句動詞 If you **dash off** a piece of writing, you write or compose it very quickly, without thinking about it very much. 一気に書き上げる □ *He dashed off a couple of novels.* 彼は2つの小説を一気に書き上げた.

dash|board /dæʃbɔrd/ (dashboards) N-COUNT 可算名詞 The **dashboard** in a car is the panel facing the driver's seat where most of the instruments and switches are. 計器盤, ダッシュボード □ *The clock on the dashboard said it was five to two.* ダッシュボードの時計は2時5分前を指していた.

dash|ing /dæʃɪŋ/ ADJ 形容詞 A **dashing** person or thing is very stylish and attractive. [OLD-FASHIONED 古風な] □ *He was the very model of the dashing Air Force pilot.* 彼はまさにさっそうとした空軍パイロットの見本だった.

da|ta /deɪtə, dætə/ ▪ N-PLURAL 複数名詞 N-UNCOUNT 不可算名詞 You can refer to information as **data**, especially when it is in the form of facts or statistics that you can analyze. 資料 □ *The study was based on data from 2,100 women.* その研究は2, 100人の女性からの資料を元にしていた. ▪ N-UNCOUNT 不可算名詞 **Data** is information that can be stored and used by a computer program. (コンピュータ・プログラムで使う) データ [COMPUTING コンピューティング] □ *This system uses powerful microchips to compress huge amounts of data onto a CD-ROM.* このシステムは大量のデータをCD-ROM上に圧縮する高性能のマイクロチップを使用している.

→ see forecast

Thesaurus *data* また次を参照:

N.	facts, figures, information, results, statistics ▪

da|ta bank (data banks) also **databank** N-COUNT 可算名詞 A **data bank** is the same as a **database**. データベース

data|base /deɪtəbeɪs, dætə-/ (databases) also **data base** N-COUNT 可算名詞 A **database** is a collection of data that is stored in a computer and that can easily be used and added to. データベース, 情報の集まり □ *The state maintains a database of names of people allowed to vote.* その州は投票できる人の名前をデータベースに保存している.

da|ta pro|cess|ing N-UNCOUNT 不可算名詞 **Data processing** is the series of operations that are carried out on data, especially by computers, in order to present, interpret, or obtain information. データ処理 □ *Taylor's company makes data-processing systems.* テイラーの会社はデータ処理システムを構築している.

date /deɪt/ (dates, dating, dated) ▪ N-COUNT 可算名詞 A **date** is a specific time that can be named, for example, a particular day or a particular year. 日付 □ *What's the date today?* 今日は何日ですか. ▪ N-COUNT 可算名詞 A **date** is an appointment to meet someone or go out with them, especially someone with whom you are having, or may soon have, a romantic relationship. デート □ *I have a date with Bob.* 私はボブとデートするの. ▪ V-RECIP 相互動詞 If you **are dating** someone, you go out with them regularly because you are having, or may soon have, a romantic relationship with them. You can also say that two people **are dating**. (男性と女性が) 交際する □ *For a year I dated a woman who was a research assistant.* 私は研究助手をしていた女性と1年つきあった. ▪ N-COUNT 可算名詞 If you have a **date** with someone with whom you are having, or may soon have, a romantic relationship, you can refer to that person as your **date**. 恋人 □ *He lied to Essie, saying his date was one of the girls in the show.* 彼はエッシーに, デートの相手はショーに出ていた女の1人だと言って嘘をついた. ▪ N-COUNT 可算名詞 A **date** is a small, dark-brown, sticky fruit with a stone inside. Dates grow on palm trees in hot countries. ナツメヤシ ▪ V-T 他動詞 If you **date** something, you give or discover the date when it was made or when it began. (作品や出来事の) 年代を定める □ *I think we can date the decline of Western Civilization quite precisely.* 我々は西洋文明の衰退の年代を全く正確に割り出すことができるだろう. ▪ V-T 他動詞 When you **date**

something such as a letter or a check, you write that day's date on it. 日付を書く ❑ *Once the decision is reached, he can date and sign the sheet.* いったん決定が下されると、彼はその用紙に日付を書き入れサインすることができる。 ⑥ V-I 自動詞 If something **dates**, it goes out of fashion and becomes unacceptable to modern tastes. 時代遅れになる ❑ *Blue and white is the classic color combination for bathrooms. It always looks smart and will never date.* 青と白は浴室の昔ながらの色の組み合わせだ。それはいつでもおしゃれに見え、流行り廃りがない。 ⑨ → see also **dated, out of date** ⑩ PHRASE 句 **To date** means up until the present time. 今まで ❑ *"Dottie" is by far his best novel to date.* 今までで『ドッティ』が間違いなく彼の最高の小説だ。 ▶ **date back** PHRASAL VERB 句動詞 If something **dates back to** a particular time, it started or was made at that time. さかのぼる ❑ *The issue is not a new one. It dates back to the 1930s at least.* この問題は新しいものではない。少なくとも1930年代にさかのぼる。

Word Partnership	*date* は次の語句と使われる:
N.	**birth** date, **cut-off** date, **due** date, **expiration** date ①
V.	**set a** date ①
	date **and sign** ⑦

dat|ed /déɪtɪd/ ADJ 形容詞 **Dated** things or ideas seem old-fashioned, although they may once have been fashionable or modern. 時代遅れの ❑ *Many of his ideas have value, but some are dated and others are plain wrong.* 彼の考えの多くは貴重なのだが、いくつかは時代遅れでその他は明らかに間違っている。

date of birth (dates of birth) N-COUNT 可算名詞 Your **date of birth** is the exact date on which you were born, including the year. 生年月日 ❑ *The registration form showed his date of birth as August 2, 1979.* その登録票には彼の生年月日が1979年8月2日と書かれていた。

daub /dɔ́b/ (daubs, daubing, daubed) V-T 他動詞 When you **daub** a substance such as mud or paint on something, you spread it on that thing in a rough or careless way. 塗りたくる ❑ *The makeup woman had been daubing mock blood on Jeremy Fox when last he'd seen her.* 彼がメーキャップ担当の女性を最後に見た時、彼女はジェレミー・フォックスに偽の血のりを塗りたくっていた。

daugh|ter /dɔ́tər/ (daughters) N-COUNT 可算名詞 Someone's **daughter** is their female child. 娘 ❑ *...Flora and her daughter Catherine.* フローラと彼女の娘キャサリン ❑ *...the daughter of a university professor.* 大学教授の娘
→ see **child**

daughter-in-law (daughters-in-law) N-COUNT 可算名詞 Someone's **daughter-in-law** is the wife of their son. 義理の娘 (息子の妻)

daunt /dɔ́nt/ (daunts, daunting, daunted) V-T 他動詞 If something **daunts** you, it makes you feel slightly afraid or worried about dealing with it. ひるませる ❑ *...a grueling trip that would have daunted a woman half her age.* 彼女の半分の年齢の女性でもおじけづいただろう厳しい旅 ● **daunt|ed** ADJ 形容詞 [v-link ADJ] おじけづいて ❑ *It is hard to pick up such a book and not to feel a little daunted.* そんな本を選んで少しもひるまないのは難しい。

daunt|ing /dɔ́ntɪŋ/ ADJ 形容詞 Something that is **daunting** makes you feel slightly afraid or worried about dealing with it. (人の) 気力をくじく ❑ *He and his wife Jane were faced with the daunting task of restoring the gardens to their former splendor.* 彼と妻はそれらの庭を元の見事な状態に戻すという骨の折れる作業に直面した。

dawn /dɔ́n/ (dawns, dawning, dawned) ① N-VAR 可変性名詞 **Dawn** is the time of day when light first appears in the sky, just before the sun rises. 夜明け ❑ *Nancy woke at dawn.* ナンシーは夜明けに目覚めた。 ② N-SING 単数名詞 The **dawn** of a period of time or a situation is the beginning of it. 始まり [LITERARY 文語的] ❑ *...the dawn of the radio age.* ラジオ時代の幕開け ③ V-I 自動詞 If something **is dawning**, it is beginning to develop or come into existence. 発達し始める、現れ始める [WRITTEN 書き言葉] ❑ *A new century was dawning.* 新しい世紀が始まりかけていた。 ● **dawn|ing** N-SING 単数名詞 出現 ❑ *...the dawning of the space age.* 宇宙時代の始まり ▶ **dawn on** or **dawn upon** PHRASAL VERB 句動詞 If a fact or idea **dawns on** you, you realize it. わかり始める ❑ *It gradually dawned on me that I still had talent and ought to run again.* 私にはまだ才能があり、再びレースに出るべきだということがだんだんわかってきた。

dawn raid (dawn raids) N-COUNT 可算名詞 If police officers carry out a **dawn raid**, they go to someone's house very early in the morning to search it or arrest them. 早朝の家宅捜査 ❑ *The dawn raids Tuesday were carried out by about 170 policemen.* 火曜日の早朝に行われた家宅捜査は約170人の警官が直面した。

day /déɪ/ (days) ① N-COUNT 可算名詞 A **day** is one of the seven twenty-four hour periods of time in a week. 1日 ❑ *And it has snowed almost every day for the past week.* そしてここ1週間はほとんど毎日雪が降っている。 ② N-COUNT 可算名詞 You can refer to a particular period in history as a particular **day** or as particular **days**. 時代 ❑ *He began to talk about the Ukraine of his uncle's day.* 彼は叔父の時代のウクライナについて語り始めた。 ❑ *...his early days*

of struggle and deep poverty. 彼の苦闘とひどい貧乏の駆け出し時代 ③ **it is early days** → see **early** ④ **at the end of the day** → see **end** ⑤ **the good old days** → see **old** ⑥ N-VAR 可変性名詞 **Day** is the time when it is light, or the time when you are up and doing things. 日中 ❑ *Twenty-seven million working days are lost each year due to work accidents and sickness.* 毎年、2700万日分の労働時間が仕事中の事故と病気のために失われている。 ❑ *She gives herself one day a week off, on Thursdays.* 彼女は毎週木曜日の1日を休日に充てている。 ⑦ PHRASE 句 If something happens **day after day**, it happens every day without stopping. 来る日も来る日も ❑ *The newspaper job had me doing the same thing day after day.* 私はその新聞の仕事で毎日同じことをしていた。 ⑧ PHRASE 句 If something happens **day in, day out** or **day in and day out**, you mean that it happens regularly over a long period of time. 明けても暮れても [V PHR] ❑ *I used to drink coffee day in, day out.* 明けても暮れてもコーヒーを飲んでいた。 ⑨ PHRASE 句 **In this day and age** means in modern times. 現代では ❑ *Even in this day and age the old attitudes persist.* 現代でもその古い考え方が残っている。 ⑩ PHRASE 句 If you say that something **has seen better days**, you mean that it is old and in poor condition. もっと良い時があった、全盛期を過ぎた ❑ *The tweed jacket she wore had seen better days.* 彼女が着ていたツィードの上着はすっかり着古されていた。 ⑪ PHRASE 句 If you **call it a day**, you decide to stop what you are doing because you are tired of it or because it is not successful. 切り上げる ❑ *Faced with mounting debts, the decision to call it a day was inevitable.* かさむ借金を目の前にし、それをやめる決断は避けられなかった。 ⑫ PHRASE 句 If something **makes your day**, it makes you feel very happy. 幸せな気分にする [INFORMAL くだけた] ❑ *Come on, Bill. Send Tom a card and make his day.* さあ、ビル。トムにカードを送って喜ばせてやれよ。 ⑬ PHRASE 句 **One day** or **some day** or **one of these days** means at some time in the future. いつか ❑ *I too dreamed of living in Dallas one day.* 私もいつかダラスに住もうと夢見たわ。 ❑ *I hope some day you will find the woman who will make you happy.* いつかあなたを幸せにしてくれる女性が見つかることを願っている。 ⑭ PHRASE 句 If you say that something happened **the other day**, you mean that it happened a few days ago. 先日 ❑ *I phoned your office the other day.* 先日あなたの職場に電話したのよ。 ⑮ PHRASE 句 If someone or something **saves the day** in a situation which seems likely to fail, they manage to make it successful. 窮地を救う ❑ *...this story about how he saved the day at his daughter's birthday party.* 彼がどうやって娘の誕生パーティーをピンチから救ったかというこの話 ⑯ PHRASE 句 If something happens **from day to day** or **day by day**, it happens each day. 日ごとに ❑ *Your needs can differ from day to day.* あなたに必要な物はその日その日で変わることがある。 ⑰ PHRASE 句 If it is a month or a year or **a day** since a particular thing happened, it is exactly a month or a year since it happened. (年月が) ちょうど ❑ *It was January 19, a year to the day since he had arrived in Singapore.* それは彼がシンガポールに着いてからちょうど1年目の1月19日だった。 ⑱ PHRASE 句 **To this day** means up until and including the present time. 今日に至るまで ❑ *The controversy continues to this day.* その論争は今も続いている。 ⑲ PHRASE 句 If you say that a task is **all in a day's work** for someone, you mean that they do not mind doing it although it may be difficult, because it is part of their job or because they often do it. (困難ながら) よくあることだ ❑ *For war reporters, dodging snipers' bullets is all in a day's work.* 従軍記者にとって、狙撃兵の弾丸をよけるのは日常茶飯事だ。 ⑳ your **day in court** → see **court**
→ see **year**

day care also **daycare** N-UNCOUNT 不可算名詞 **Day care** is care that is provided during the day for people who cannot take care of themselves, such as small children, old people, or people who are ill. Day care is provided by paid workers. 保育、デイケア ❑ *She had to contend with day care for her 2-year-old twins being canceled.* 彼女は2歳の双子の保育が取り消されたことに対処しなければならなかった。 ❑ *...a daycare center for elderly people.* 高齢者のデイケアセンター

day|dream /déɪdriːm/ (daydreams, daydreaming, daydreamed) ① V-I 自動詞 If you **daydream**, you think about pleasant things for a period of time, usually about things that you would like to happen. 空想にふける ❑ *Do you work hard for success rather than daydream about it?* あなたは成功を夢見るより、むしろそれに向かって一生懸命に努力しますか？ ❑ *He daydreams of being a famous journalist.* 彼は有名な新聞記者になることを夢見ている。 ② N-COUNT 可算名詞 A **daydream** is a series of pleasant thoughts, usually about things that you would like to happen. 空想、白昼夢 ❑ *He learned to escape into daydreams of handsome men and beautiful women.* 彼は美男美女の夢想の世界に逃げ込むようになった。

Word Link	*light ≈ shining : daylight, enlighten, light*

day|light /déɪlaɪt/ ① N-UNCOUNT 不可算名詞 **Daylight** is the natural light that there is during the day, before it gets dark. 日中の光 ❑ *Lack of daylight can make people feel depressed.* 日光不足で人は気がめいることもある。 ② N-UNCOUNT 不可算名詞 **Daylight** is the time of day when it begins to get light. 夜明け ❑ *Quinn returned shortly after daylight yesterday morning.* クインは昨日の朝、夜が明

けて間もなく帰って来た. **3** PHRASE 句 If you say that a crime is committed **in broad daylight**, you are expressing your surprise that it is done during the day when people can see it, rather than at night. 白昼公然と [EMPHASIS 強調] ❑*A girl was attacked on a train in broad daylight.* 女の子が真昼間に電車の中で襲われた.

> Clocks are set one hour fast in the spring and in the fall returned to the standard time so that residents have more convenient use of daylight hours. The saying "spring ahead, fall back" is used to remember which way to turn the clocks. This is not practiced uniformly across the United States. Some local areas have decided not to participate, often out of economic consideration for neighboring communities.

day off (days off) N-COUNT 可算名詞 A **day off** is a day when you do not go to work, even though it is usually a working day. 休日, 非番の日 ❑*It was Mrs. Dearden's day off, and Paul was on duty in her place.* それはディアデン夫人の休日で, ポールが代わりに勤務中だった.

day school (day schools) N-COUNT 可算名詞 A **day school** is a school where the students go home every evening and do not live at the school. Compare **boarding school**. (全寮制の学校に対し) 通学学校

day|time /déɪtaɪm/ **1** N-SING 単数名詞 The **daytime** is the part of a day between the time when it gets light and the time when it gets dark. 昼間 ['the' N, also no det] ❑*In the daytime he stayed up in his room, sleeping, or listening to music.* 昼間は彼は自分の部屋に閉じこもって寝たり音楽を聴いたりしていた. **2** ADJ 形容詞 **Daytime** television and radio is broadcast during the morning and afternoon on weekdays. 昼間の [ADJ n] ❑*She took on the role as host of a daytime TV show.* 彼女は昼間のテレビ番組の司会役を引き受けた.

day-to-day ADJ 形容詞 **Day-to-day** things or activities exist or happen every day as part of ordinary life. 毎日の [ADJ n] ❑*I am a vegetarian and use a lot of lentils in my day-to-day cooking.* 私は菜食主義者で, 毎日の料理にたくさんのレンズマメを使う.

day trad|er (day traders) N-COUNT 可算名詞 In the stock market, **day traders** are traders who buy and sell particular securities on the same day. デイトレーダー (同日内に売買する株式投資家) [BUSINESS 実業] ❑*Unlike the day traders, they tended to hold on to stocks for days and weeks, sometimes even months.* デイトレーダーとは異なり, 彼らは株を何日も何週間も, 時には何か月も手放さない傾向があった.

daze /deɪz/ N-SING 単数名詞 If someone is **in a daze**, they are feeling confused and unable to think clearly, often because they have had a shock or surprise. ぼう然とした状態 ❑*For an hour I was walking around in a daze.* 私は1時間, ぼう然と歩き回っていた.

dazed /deɪzd/ ADJ 形容詞 If someone is **dazed**, they are confused and unable to think clearly, often because of shock or a blow to the head. ぼう然として ❑*At the end of the interview I was dazed and exhausted.* 面接の終わりには私は放心状態で疲れ切っていた.

daz|zle /dǽzᵊl/ (dazzles, dazzling, dazzled) **1** V-T 他動詞 If someone or something **dazzles** you, you are extremely impressed by their skill, qualities, or beauty. 感銘を与える ❑*George dazzled her with his knowledge of the world.* 世界に関するジョージの知識は彼女を感嘆させた. **2** V-T 他動詞 If a bright light **dazzles** you, it makes you unable to see properly for a short time. 目をくらませる ❑*The sun, glinting from the pool, dazzled me.* プールに反射した太陽の光に私は目がくらんだ. **3** N-SING 単数名詞 The **dazzle of** something is a quality it has, such as beauty or skill, which is impressive and attractive. 見事さ ❑*The dazzle of stardom and status attracts them.* スターの地位の華やかさが彼らを魅了する.

dazz|ling /dǽzlɪŋ/ **1** ADJ 形容詞 Something that is **dazzling** is very impressive or beautiful. 素晴らしい ❑*He gave Alberg a dazzling smile.* 彼はアルバーグにまばゆい笑顔を見せた. ● **dazz|ling|ly** ADV 副詞 見事に ❑*The view was dazzlingly beautiful.* その眺めは見事なほど美しかった. **2** ADJ 形容詞 A **dazzling** light is very bright and makes you unable to see properly for a short time. まぶしい ❑*He shielded his eyes against the dazzling declining sun.* 彼は西に傾いてきたまぶしい太陽の光に手をかざして目を守った. ● **dazz|ling|ly** ADV 副詞 [ADV adj] 目もくらむほど ❑*The loading bay seemed dazzlingly bright.* 船積みする湾は目がくらむほどまぶしく見えた.

dead /dɛd/ **1** ADJ 形容詞 A person, animal, or plant that is **dead** is no longer living. 死んだ *"You're a widow?"* — *"Yes. My husband's been dead a year now."* 「あなたは未亡人ですか?」, 「はい. 夫が亡くなってもう1年になります」. ❑*The group had shot dead another hostage.* そのグループはもう1人の人質を射殺していた. ● N-PLURAL 複数名詞 **The dead** are people who are dead. 死者 ❑*Two American soldiers were among the dead.* 死者の中には米兵が2人いた.

> Do not confuse **dead** with **died**. **Died** is the past tense and past participle of the verb **die**, and thus indicates the action of dying. ❑*She died in 1934... Two men have died since the rioting broke out.* You do not use **died** as an adjective. You use **dead** instead. ❑*More than 2,200 dead birds have been found.*

2 ADJ 形容詞 If you describe a place or a period of time as **dead**, you do not like it because there is very little activity taking place in it. 活気のない [DISAPPROVAL 不賛成] ❑*...some dead little town where the liveliest thing is the flies.* 1番元気なのはハエだというほどさびれたある小さな町 **3** ADJ 形容詞 Something that is **dead** is no longer being used or is finished. ❑*The dead cigarette was still between his fingers.* 彼は火の消えたたばこをまだ指にはさんでいた. **4** ADJ 形容詞 If you say that an idea, plan, or subject is **dead**, you mean that people are no longer interested in it or willing to develop it any further. 興味の失せた ❑*It's a dead issue, Baxter.* もうそれは済んだ問題だよ, バクスター. **5** ADJ 形容詞 A telephone or piece of electrical equipment that is **dead** is no longer functioning, for example, because it is no longer has any electrical power. (電話が) 通じない, (電気が) 通っていない ❑*On another occasion I answered the phone and the line went dead.* またある時は私が電話に出ると, 電話が切れた. **6** ADJ 形容詞 **Dead** is used to mean "complete" or "absolute," especially before the words "center," "silence," and "stop." 完全な [EMPHASIS 強調] [ADJ n] ❑*They hurried about in dead silence, with anxious faces.* 彼らは不安そうな顔で完全な沈黙してあちこちに急いだ. **7** ADV 副詞 **Dead** means "precisely" or "exactly." 正確に [EMPHASIS 強調] [ADV prep/adv/adj] ❑*Mars was visible, dead in the center of the telescope.* 火星が望遠鏡のちょうど真ん中に見えた. **8** CONVENTION 慣習表現 If you reply "**Over my dead body**" when a plan or action has been suggested, you are emphasizing that you dislike it, and will do everything you can to prevent it. そんなことは絶対させない [INFORMAL くだけた, EMPHASIS 強調] ❑*"Let's invite her to dinner."* — *"Over my dead body!"* 「彼女を食事に招待しようよ」, 「絶対だめだ!」. **9** PHRASE 句 If you say that a person or animal **dropped dead** or **dropped down dead**, you mean that they died very suddenly and unexpectedly. 急死する ❑*He dropped dead of a heart attack.* 彼は心臓発作で急死した. **10** PHRASE 句 If you say that you **feel dead** or **are half dead**, you mean that you feel very tired or ill and very weak. 疲れ切った [INFORMAL くだけた, EMPHASIS 強調] ❑*I thought you looked half dead at dinner, and who could blame you after that trip.* 君は食事の時にとても疲れていたみたいだけど, あの旅行の後じゃあ仕方がないね. **11** PHRASE 句 If something happens **in the dead of night**, **at dead of night**, or **in the dead of winter**, it happens in the middle part of the night or the winter, when it is darkest or coldest. 真夜中に, 真冬に [LITERARY 文語的] ❑*All three incidents occurred in the dead of night.* 3つの事件はすべて真夜中に起きた. **12** PHRASE 句 If you say that you wouldn't **be seen dead** or **be caught dead** in particular clothes, places, or situations, you are expressing strong dislike or disapproval of them. 〜なら死んだ方がまし [INFORMAL くだけた, EMPHASIS 強調] ❑*I wouldn't be seen dead in a straw hat.* 麦わら帽子なんて死んでも嫌だ. **13** PHRASE 句 To **stop dead** means to suddenly stop happening or moving. To **stop** someone or something **dead** means to cause them to suddenly stop happening or moving. 急に止まる, 急に止める ❑*We all stopped dead and looked at it.* 私たちみんなは急に止まり, それを見た. **14** to **stop dead in** your **tracks** → see **track** → see **funeral**

Thesaurus | *dead* また次を参照:

ADJ. deceased, lifeless; (ant.) alive, living **1**

dead end (dead ends) **1** N-COUNT 可算名詞 If a street is a **dead end**, there is no way out at one end of it. 行き止まり ❑*There was another alleyway which came to a dead end just behind the house.* その家のすぐ後ろにもう1つ行き止まりの路地があった. **2** N-COUNT 可算名詞 A **dead-end** job or course of action is one that you think is bad because it does not lead to further developments or progress. 将来性のない ❑*Waitressing was a dead-end job.* ウェイトレスは将来性のない仕事だった.

dead|line /dɛ́dlaɪn/ (deadlines) N-COUNT 可算名詞 A **deadline** is a time or date before which a particular task must be finished or a particular thing must be done. 締め切り ❑*We were not able to meet the deadline because of manufacturing delays.* 製造の遅れで私たちは締め切りに間に合わなかった.

dead|lock /dɛ́dlɒk/ (deadlocks) N-VAR 可変性名詞 If a dispute or series of negotiations reaches **deadlock**, neither side is willing to give in at all and no agreement can be made. こう着状態 ❑*They called for a compromise on all sides to break the deadlock in the world trade talks.* 彼らは国際貿易交渉のこう着状態を打開するため関係国全に歩み寄りを呼びかけた.

dead|ly /dɛ́dli/ (deadlier, deadliest) **1** ADJ 形容詞 If something is **deadly**, it is likely or able to cause someone's death, or has already caused someone's death. 致命的な ❑*He was acquitted on*

charges of assault with a deadly weapon. 彼は凶器による暴行の容疑に
対し無罪になった. □...a deadly disease currently affecting dolphins.
目下いるかを冒している致死的な病気 ② ADJ 形容詞 If you describe
a person or their behavior as **deadly**, you mean that they will do
or say anything to get what they want, without caring about
other people. 執念深い [DISAPPROVAL 不賛成] □ The Duchess leveled
a deadly look at Nikko. 公爵夫人はニッコーに執念深そうな視線を向け
た. ③ ADJ 形容詞 A **deadly** situation has unpleasant or dangerous
consequences. ひどい □...the deadly combination of low expectations
and low achievement. 低い期待と低い成果のひどい組み合わせ ④ ADV
副詞 You can use **deadly** to emphasize that something has a
particular quality, especially an unpleasant or undesirable
quality. うんざりするほど [EMPHASIS 強調] [ADV adj] □ Broadcast
news was accurate and reliable but deadly dull. 放送されたニュースは正
確で信頼できるものではなかったが, 死ぬほど退屈だった.

deaf /dɛf/ (deafer, deafest) ① ADJ 形容詞 Someone who is **deaf**
is unable to hear anything or is unable to hear very well. 耳が聞こ
えない, 耳が遠い □ She is now profoundly deaf. 現在彼女はひどく耳が
遠い. ● N-PLURAL 複数名詞 The **deaf** are people who are deaf. 聴覚
障害者, 難聴者 □ Many regular TV programs are captioned for the deaf.
多くのテレビのレギュラー番組には聴覚障害者のために字幕が付いて
いる. ● **deaf|ness** N-UNCOUNT 不可算名詞 □ Because of
her deafness she was hard to make conversation with. 彼女は耳が遠いの
で, 彼女と話をするのは難しかった. ② to **fall on deaf ears** → see ear
③ to **turn a deaf ear** → see ear
→ see **disability**

deaf|en /dɛfən/ (deafens, deafening, deafened) ① V-T 他動詞
If a noise **deafens** you, it is so loud that you cannot hear anything
else at the same time. (騒音が) 耳を聞こえなくする □ The noise of
the typewriters deafened her. タイプライターの騒音で彼女には何も聞こ
えなかった. ② If you **are deafened** by something, you
are made deaf by it, or are unable to hear for some time. 耳を聞
こえなくする [usu passive] □ He was deafened by the noise from the gun.
銃の音で彼は耳が聞こえなくなった. ③ → see also **deafening**

deaf|en|ing /dɛfənɪŋ/ ① ADJ 形容詞 A **deafening** noise is
a very loud noise. 耳をつんざくような □...the deafening roar of
fighter jets taking off. 離陸するジェット戦闘機の耳をつんざくよう
なごう音 ② ADJ 形容詞 If you say there was a **deafening silence**,
you are emphasizing that there was no reaction or response
to something that was said or done. 水を打ったような (沈黙)
[EMPHASIS 強調] □ What was truly despicable was the deafening silence
maintained by the candidates concerning the riots. まったく見下げ果
てたことは, 候補者たちがその暴動について押し黙ったままだったこ
とだ.

---

deal
❶ QUANTIFIER USES
❷ VERB AND NOUN USES

---

❶ **deal** /diːl/ QUANT 数量詞 If you say that you need or have
a great deal of or **a good deal of** a particular thing, you are
emphasizing that you need or have a lot of it. 多量 [EMPHASIS 強
調] □...a great deal of money. 大金 ● **Deal** is also an adverb.
大いに □ As a relationship becomes more established, it also becomes a
good deal more complex. 関係が築かれていくにつれ, それはより複雑に
もなる. ● PRON 代名詞 **Deal** is also a pronoun. 多量 □ Although he
had never met Geoffrey Hardcastle, he knew a good deal about him. 彼は
ジェフリー・ハードキャッスルに1度も会ったことはなかったが, 彼に
ついていろいろ知っていた.

❷ **deal** /diːl/ (deals, dealing, dealt)
▷ Please look at meaning ❻ to see if the expression you are
looking for is shown under another headword. ① N-COUNT 可
算名詞 If you **make a deal**, **do a deal**, or **cut a deal**, you complete
an agreement or an arrangement with someone, especially in
business. 取引 [BUSINESS 実業] □ He made a deal to testify against
the others and wasn't charged. 彼は他の人たちに不利な証言をする取
引をし, 告訴を免れた. □ Japan will have to do a deal with the U.S. on
rice imports. 日本は米国と米の輸入に関して取引をせざるを得なく
なるだろう ② N-COUNT 可算名詞 If someone has had a **bad deal**,
they have been unfortunate or have been treated unfairly. 扱い
□ The people of Hartford have had a bad deal for many, many years. ハー
トフォードの人々は長年に渡り, 不当な扱いを受けている. ③ V-I 自
動詞 If a person, company, or store **deals in** a particular type of
goods, their business involves buying or selling those goods. (商
品を) 扱う [BUSINESS 実業] □ They deal in antiques. 彼らは骨董品を
扱っている. ④ V-T 他動詞 If someone **deals** illegal drugs, they sell
them. (麻薬を) 売る □ I certainly don't deal drugs. ぼくは絶対に麻
薬を売ったりしない. ⑤ V-T 他動詞 If you **deal** playing cards, you
give them out to the players in a game of cards. (トランプを) 配
る □ The croupier dealt each player a card, face down. 胴元が各プレー
ヤーにカードを1枚ずつ裏向けて配った. ● PHRASAL VERB 句動詞 **Deal
out** means the same as **deal**. (トランプを) 配る □ Dalton dealt out
five cards to each player. ダルトンは各プレーヤーにカードを5枚ずつ配
った. ❻ → see also **dealings, wheel and deal**

Word Partnership　　deal は次の語句と使われる:

ADJ.	**better** deal, **big** deal ❷ ❶
V.	**close** a deal, **seal** a deal, **strike** a deal ❷ ❶
N.	**business** deal, **peace** deal ❷ ❶
	deal **drugs** ❷ ❹

▶ **deal out** ① PHRASAL VERB 句動詞 If someone **deals out** a
punishment or harmful action, they punish or harm someone.
(罰を) 与える, (危害を) 加える [WRITTEN 書き言葉] □...a failure by
the governments of established states to deal out effective punishment to
aggressors. 支配的国家の政府が侵略者に有効な処罰を与えることに失
敗したこと ② → see also **deal** ❷ 5
▶ **deal with** ① PHRASAL VERB 句動詞 When you **deal with**
something or someone that needs attention, you give your
attention to them, and often solve a problem or make a decision
concerning them. 〜に対処する, 〜に対応する □...the way that
banks deal with complaints. 苦情に対する銀行の対処方法 ② PHRASAL
VERB 句動詞 If you **deal with** an unpleasant emotion or an
emotionally difficult situation, you recognize it, and remain
calm and in control of yourself in spite of it. 冷静に向き合う □ She
saw a psychiatrist who used hypnotism to help her deal with her fear. 彼
女は催眠術によって彼女の恐怖心の克服を助けてくれる精神分析医に
見てもらった. ③ PHRASAL VERB 句動詞 If a book, speech, or movie
deals with a particular thing, it has that thing as its subject or
is concerned with it. 〜を扱う □...the parts of his book which deal
with contemporary Paris. 彼の本の中で現代のパリを題材にした部分
④ PHRASAL VERB 句動詞 If you **deal with** a particular person or
organization, you have business relations with them. 〜と取引す
る □ When I worked in Florida I dealt with tourists all the time. 私がフロ
リダ州で仕事をしていた時は, ずっと観光客を相手にしていた.

deal|er /diːlər/ (dealers) ① N-COUNT 可算名詞 A **dealer** is a
person whose business involves buying and selling things. 販売
業者 [BUSINESS 実業] □...an antique dealer. 古美術商 ② N-COUNT 可
算名詞 A **dealer** is someone who buys and sells illegal drugs. (麻
薬の) 売人 □ They will stay on the job for as long as it takes to clear every
dealer from the street. 彼らは通りから麻薬の密売人を一掃するまで, そ
の仕事にとどまるつもりだ.

deal|er|ship /diːlərʃɪp/ (dealerships) N-COUNT 可算名詞 A
dealership is a company that sells cars, usually for one car
company. 販売代理店 [BUSINESS 実業] □...a car dealership. 車の販
売代理店

deal|ings /diːlɪŋz/ N-PLURAL 複数名詞 Someone's **dealings with**
a person or organization are the relations that they have with
them or the business that they do with them. 取引関係, 取引 □ He
has learned little in his dealings with the international community. 彼は国
際社会との取引の中でほとんど何も学んでこなかった.

dealt /dɛlt/ **Dealt** is the past tense and past participle of **deal**.
deal の過去・過去分詞

dean /diːn/ (deans) ① N-COUNT 可算名詞 A **dean** is an
important official at a university or college. 学部長 □ She was
dean of the University of Washington's Graduate School. 彼女はワシント
ン大学大学院の研究科長だった. ② N-COUNT 可算名詞 A **dean** is a
priest who is the main administrator of a large church. 首席司祭
□...Bob Gregg, dean of the Chapel, Stanford Memorial Church. スタンフ
ォード・メモリアル教会の礼拝堂首席司祭であるボブ・グレッグ

dear /dɪər/ (dearer, dearest, dears) ① ADJ 形容詞 You use **dear**
to describe someone or something that you feel affection for. 親
愛な [ADJ n] □ Mrs. Cavendish is a dear friend of mine. キャベンディッシ
ュ夫人は私の親友の1人です. ② ADJ 形容詞 If something is **dear** to
you or **dear** to your **heart**, you care deeply about it. 大切な [v-link
ADJ 'to' n] □ This is a subject very dear to the hearts of academics up
and down the country. これは国中の大学人にとって非常に大事な主題
です. ③ ADJ 形容詞 **Dear** is written at the beginning of a letter,
followed by the name or title of the person you are writing to. (手
紙の書き出しで) 親愛なる [ADJ n] □ Dear Peter, I have been thinking
about you so much during the past few days. 親愛なるピーター, 私は
ここ数日ずっとあなたのことを大変考えています. ④ CONVENTION
慣習表現 You begin formal letters with "**Dear Sir**" or "**Dear
Madam**." You can also begin them with "**Sir**" or "**Madam**." 拝啓
[WRITTEN 書き言葉] □ "Dear Sir," she began. 「拝啓」 と彼女は書き始
めた. ⑤ N-VOC 呼格名詞 You can call someone **dear** as a sign of
affection. (呼びかけ語として) あなた [FEELINGS 感情] □ You're a
lot like me, dear. あなたはとても私に似ているわ. ⑥ EXCLAM 感嘆詞
You can use **dear** in expressions such as "**oh dear**," "**dear me**," and
"**dear, dear**" when you are sad, disappointed, or surprised about
something. (驚きや失望を込めて) あらまあ, おやおや [FEELINGS
感情] □ "Oh dear, oh dear." McKinnon sighed. "You, too." 「おやおや」 と
マッキノンはため息をついた. 「あなたもなのね」.

dear|est /dɪərɪst/ ADJ 形容詞 When you are writing to someone
you are very fond of, you can use **dearest** at the beginning of
the letter before the person's name or the word you are using to
address them. 最愛の [ADJ n] □ Dearest Maria, Aren't I terrible, not

coming back like I promised? 最愛なるマリア，約束どおり帰って来ない なんて，ぼくはひどいよね？

dear|ly /dɪ̯ərli/ **1** ADV 副詞 If you love someone **dearly**, you love them very much. 心から [FORMAL 形式ばった, EMPHASIS 強調] [ADV with v] ❑ She loved her father dearly. 彼女は父を心から敬愛してい た. **2** ADV 副詞 If you would **dearly** like to do or have something, you would very much like to do it or have it. 非常に [FORMAL 形式 ばった, EMPHASIS 強調] [ADV before v] ❑ I would dearly love to marry. 私は本当に結婚したいの. **3** PHRASE 句 If you **pay dearly** for doing something or if it **costs** you **dearly**, you suffer a lot as a result. 高 くつく [FORMAL 形式ばった] ❑ He drank too much and is paying dearly for the pleasure. 彼は酒を飲みすぎ，その快楽のために高いつけを払っ ている.

death /dɛθ/ (deaths) **1** N-VAR 可変性名詞 **Death** is the permanent end of the life of a person or animal. 死 ❑ 1.5 million people are in immediate danger of death from starvation. 1500万人の人が 差し迫った餓死の危険にさらされている. ❑ ...the thirtieth anniversary of Judy Garland's death. ジュディ・ガーランドの没後30周年 **2** N-SING 単数名詞 **The death of** something is the permanent end of it. 終 わり ❑ It meant the death of everything he had ever been or ever hoped to be. それは彼がこれまで達成してきたもの，またこれから達成しよう としたものすべての終わりを意味していた. **3** PHRASE 句 If you say that someone is **at death's door**, you mean they are very ill and likely to die. 危篤状態で [INFORMAL くだけた] ❑ He told his boss a tale about his mother being at death's door. 彼は上司に母親が危篤だと嘘 をついた. **4** PHRASE 句 If you say that you will **fight to the death** for something, you are emphasizing that you will do anything to achieve or protect it, even if you suffer as a consequence. (一つの めなら) 何でもする [EMPHASIS 強調] ❑ She'd have fought to the death for that child. 彼女はその子のためなら何でもしただろう. **5** PHRASE 句 If you say that something is a matter of **life and death**, you are emphasizing that it is extremely important, often because someone may die or suffer great harm if people do not act immediately. 生死 (にかかわる問題) [EMPHASIS 強調] ❑ Well, never mind, John, it's not a matter of life and death. まあ，気にするなよ，ジョ ン．それは死ぬか生きるかの問題じゃないんだから. **6** PHRASE 句 If someone **is put to death**, they are executed. 処刑にする [FORMAL 形式ばった] ❑ Those put to death by firing squad included three generals. 銃殺隊に処刑された者の中には3人の将軍もいた. **7** PHRASE 句 You use **to death** after an adjective or a verb to emphasize the action, state, or feeling mentioned. For example, if you are **frightened to death** or **bored to death**, you are extremely frightened or bored. 死ぬほど [EMPHASIS 強調] ❑ He scares teams to death with his pace and power. 彼のペースとパワーにどのチームも死ぬほどおびえた.

Word Partnership   death は次の語句と使われる：

ADJ.	**accidental** death, **violent** death **1** **sudden** death **1** **2**
N.	**brush with** death, death **threat**, *someone's* death **1** **cause of** death **1** **2**

death|ly /dɛθli/ **1** ADV 副詞 If you say that someone is **deathly** pale or **deathly** still, you are emphasizing that they are very pale or still, like a dead person. 死人のような [LITERARY 文語的, EMPHASIS 強調] [ADV adj] ❑ Bernadette turned deathly pale. バーナ デットは死人のように真っ青になった. **2** ADJ 形容詞 If you say that there is a **deathly** silence or a **deathly** hush, you are emphasizing that it is very quiet. はなはだしい [LITERARY 文語的, EMPHASIS 強 調] [ADJ n] ❑ A deathly silence hung over the square. 広場には水を打った ような静寂が立ち込めていた.

death pen|al|ty N-SING 単数名詞 **The death penalty** is the punishment of death used in some countries for people who have committed very serious crimes. 死刑 ❑ If convicted for murder, both men could face the death penalty. 殺人の有罪判決を受けると，男は2人 とも死刑に直面するかもしれない.

death rate (death rates) N-COUNT 可算名詞 The **death rate** is the number of people per thousand who die in a particular area during a particular period of time. 死亡率 ❑ By the turn of the century, Pittsburgh had the highest death rate in the United States. 世紀 の変わり目まで，米国で最も死亡率の高いのはピッツバーグだった.
→ see **population**

death row /dɛθroʊ/ N-UNCOUNT 不可算名詞 If someone is **on death row**, they are in the part of a prison which contains the cells for criminals who have been sentenced to death. 死刑囚監房 [AM 米国英語] ❑ He has been on death row for 11 years. 彼は11年間死刑 囚監房にいる.

death sen|tence (death sentences) N-COUNT 可算名詞 A **death sentence** is a punishment of death given by a judge to someone who has been found guilty of a serious crime such as murder. 死刑宣告 ❑ His original death sentence was commuted to life in prison. 彼は最初死刑宣告されたが，終身刑に減刑された.

death toll (death tolls) also **death-toll** N-COUNT 可算名詞 The **death toll** of an accident, disaster, or war is the number of

people who die in it. 死亡者数 ❑ The death toll continues to rise from yesterday's earthquake. 昨日の地震の犠牲者数は増え続けている.

death|trap /dɛθtræp/ (deathtraps) N-COUNT 可算名詞 If you say that a place or vehicle is a **deathtrap**, you mean it is in such bad condition that it might cause someone's death. 死のわな [INFORMAL くだけた] ❑ Badly built cars can be deathtraps. 造りの悪い 車は人命に係わる恐れがある.

de|ba|cle /dɪbɑkᵊl, -bækᵊl/ (debacles) N-COUNT 可算名詞 A **debacle** is an event or attempt that is a complete failure. 大失敗 ❑ People believed it was a privilege to die for your country, but after the debacle of the war they never felt the same again. 人々は自国のために死 ぬのは名誉だと信じていたが，その戦争の大失敗後は同じように考える 人は皆無になった.

de|bat|able /dɪbeɪtəbᵊl/ ADJ 形容詞 If you say that something is **debatable**, you mean that it is not certain. 疑問の余地のあ る ❑ It is debatable whether or not the shareholders were ever properly compensated. 株主がかつて適切な補償を受けたことがあるか否かにつ いては異論がある.

de|bate /dɪbeɪt/ (debates, debating, debated) **1** N-VAR 可変 性名詞 A **debate** is a discussion about a subject on which people have different views. 論争 ❑ An intense debate is going on within the Israeli government. イスラエル政府内では激しい議論が行われている. ❑ There has been a lot of debate among scholars about this. これに関して は学者たちが大いに論争してきた. **2** N-COUNT 可算名詞 A **debate** is a formal discussion, for example, in a parliament or institution, in which people express different opinions about a particular subject and then vote on it. 討論会 ❑ He is expected to force a debate in Congress on his immigration reform. 彼は連邦議会で彼の移民改革案 に関する討論を強行する期待される. **3** V-RECIP 相互動詞 If people **debate** a topic, they discuss it fairly formally, putting forward different views. You can also say that one person **debates** a topic **with** another person. 討論する ❑ The United Nations Security Council will debate the issue today. 国連安全保障理事会は本日その問題を討論 することになっている. ❑ Scientists were debating whether an asteroid was about to hit the Earth. 科学者たちは，小惑星が地球に衝突しようと しているかどうかについて討議していた. **4** V-T 他動詞 If you **debate** whether to do something or what to do, you think or talk about possible courses of action before deciding exactly what you are going to do. 熟慮する [他動詞] ❑ Taggart debated whether to have yet another double vodka. タガートはダブルのウオッカをもう一杯飲むか どうかを思案した.
→ see **election**

Word Partnership   debate は次の語句と使われる：

V.	**open to** debate **1** **2**
ADJ.	**major** debate, **ongoing** debate, **televised** debate **1** **2** **political** debate, **presidential** debate **2**
N.	debate **over** *something*, debate **the issue** **3** **4**

de|ben|ture /dɪbɛntʃər/ (debentures) N-COUNT 可算名詞 A **debenture** is a type of savings bond which offers a fixed rate of interest over a long period. Debentures are usually issued by a company or a government agency. 無担保社債，債務証書 [BUSINESS 実業]

deb|it /dɛbɪt/ (debits, debiting, debited) **1** V-T 他動詞 When your bank **debits** your account, money is taken from it and paid to someone else. 借方に記入する ❑ We will always confirm the revised amount to you in writing before debiting your account. 私どもは，口座 の借方に記入する前に必ず，改定額を書面であなたに確認いたします. **2** N-COUNT 可算名詞 A **debit** is a record of the money taken from your bank account, for example, when you write a check. 借方記 入 ❑ The total of debits must balance the total of credits. 借方合計額と貸 方合計額の帳尻は合わなくてはならない.

deb|it card (debit cards) N-COUNT 可算名詞 A **debit card** is a bank card that you can use to pay for things. When you use it the money is taken out of your bank account immediately. デビット カード

de|bris /dɛɪbri/ N-UNCOUNT 不可算名詞 **Debris** is pieces from something that has been destroyed or pieces of trash or unwanted material that are spread around. 破壊物の破片，くず ❑ A number of people were killed by flying debris. 多くの人々が飛び散っ た破片に当たって死亡した.

debt /dɛt/ (debts) **1** N-VAR 可変性名詞 A **debt** is a sum of money that you owe someone. 借金 ❑ Three years later, he is still paying off his debts. 3年後の今も彼は借金を返済している. **2** → see also **bad debt** **3** N-UNCOUNT 不可算名詞 **Debt** is the state of owing money. 借金している状態，負債 ❑ ...a monthly report on the amount of debt owed by consumers. 消費者が負う負債額に関する月報 ● PHRASE 句 If you are **in debt** or **get into debt**, you owe money. If you are **out of debt** or **get out of debt**, you succeed in paying all the money that you owe. 借金がある，借金がない ❑ He was already deeply in debt through gambling losses. 彼はすでにギャンブルの損失 でひどい借金を抱えていた. **4** N-COUNT 可算名詞 You use **debt** in

expressions such as **I owe you a debt** or **I am in your debt** when you are expressing gratitude for something that someone has done for you. 恩義 [FORMAL 形式ばった, FEELINGS 感情] ❑ *He was so good to me that I can never repay the debt I owe him.* 彼は私に非常によくしてくれたので、いつになっても彼の恩義に報いきることはできない. ❑ *I owe a debt of thanks to Joyce Thompson, whose careful and able research was of great help.* 私は、慎重かつ有能な研究で多大な力添えをいただいたジョイス・トンプソンに感謝しなければならない.

Word Partnership *debt* は次の語句と使われる:

V.	**incur** debt, **pay off a** debt, **reduce** debt, **repay a** debt 1
ADV.	**deeply in** debt 2

---

debt bur|den (debt burdens) N-COUNT 可算名詞 A **debt burden** is a large amount of money that one country or organization owes to another and which they find very difficult to repay. 債務負担 ❑ *The massive debt burden of the Third World has become a crucial issue for many leaders of poorer countries.* 第3世界が抱える巨額の債務負担は、貧困国の指導者の多くにとって極めて重要な問題になっている.

debt|or /dɛtər/ (debtors) N-COUNT 可算名詞 A **debtor** is a country, organization, or person who owes money. 負債者 ❑ *...important improvements in the situation of debtor countries.* 債務国の状況における重要な改善

de|bug /dibʌg/ (debugs, debugging, debugged) V-T 他動詞 When someone **debugs** a computer program, they look for the problems in it and correct them so that it will run properly. デバッグする [COMPUTING コンピューティング] ❑ *The production lines ground to a halt for hours while technicians tried to debug software.* 技術者がソフトウェアのバグを修正しようと努めている間、生産ラインは何時間も停止状態になった.

de|but /deɪbju/ (debuts) N-COUNT 可算名詞 The **debut** of a performer or sports player is their first public performance, appearance, or recording. デビュー ❑ *She made her debut in a 1937 production of "Hamlet".* 彼女は1937年の『ハムレット』の上演でデビューした.

Dec. Dec. is a written abbreviation for **December**. December の省略形

Word Link *dec ≈ ten : decade, decathlon, decimal*

dec|ade /dɛkeɪd/ (decades) N-COUNT 可算名詞 A **decade** is a period of ten years, especially one that begins with a year ending in 0, for example, 1980 to 1989. 10年間 ❑ *...the last decade of the nineteenth century.* 19世紀の最後の10年間

deca|dent /dɛkədənt/ ADJ 形容詞 If you say that a person or society is **decadent**, you think that they have low moral standards and are interested mainly in pleasure. 退廃的な [DISAPPROVAL 不賛成] ❑ *...the excesses and stresses of their decadent rock 'n' roll lifestyles.* 彼らの退廃的なロックンロール風生き方の行き過ぎとそれに起因するストレス ● **deca|dence** N-UNCOUNT 不可算名詞 頽廃, 衰微 ❑ *The empire had for years been falling into decadence.* 帝国は何年も衰微し続けていた.

de|caf|fein|at|ed /dikæfɪneɪtɪd, -kæfiə-/ ADJ 形容詞 **Decaffeinated** coffee or tea has had most of the caffeine removed from it. カフェインを除いた
→ see **coffee**

de|capi|tate /dɪkæpɪteɪt/ (decapitates, decapitating, decapitated) V-T 他動詞 If someone **is decapitated**, their head is cut off. 首を切る [FORMAL 形式ばった] ❑ *There were nine corpses. Two of them had been decapitated.* 死体は9体あり、そのうちの2体は断頭されていた.

de|cath|lon /dɪkæθlɒn/ (decathlons) N-COUNT 可算名詞 The **decathlon** is a competition in which athletes compete in 10 different sports events. 十種競技

de|cay /dɪkeɪ/ (decays, decaying, decayed) 1 V-I 自動詞 When something such as a dead body, a dead plant, or a tooth **decays**, it is gradually destroyed by a natural process. 腐敗する ❑ *The bodies buried in the fine ash slowly decayed.* 細かい灰に埋められた死体はゆっくり腐敗した. ● N-UNCOUNT 不可算名詞 腐敗 ❑ *When not removed, plaque causes tooth decay and gum disease.* 歯垢は取り除かないと、虫歯や歯周病の原因になる. ● **de|cayed** ADJ 形容詞 腐食した ❑ *Even young children have teeth so decayed they need to be pulled.* 小さい子供にさえ、ぼろぼろで抜かなければならないほどの虫歯がある. 2 V-I 自動詞 If something such as a society, system, or institution **decays**, it gradually becomes weaker or its condition gets worse. 衰退する ❑ *In practice, the agency system has decayed. Most "agents" now sell only to themselves or their immediate family.* 実際には代理店組織は衰退してしまった. 今ではほとんどの「代理店」は自分のみまたは近縁にのみ販売を行っている. ● N-UNCOUNT 不可算名詞 Decay is also a noun. 衰退 ❑ *There are problems of urban decay and gang violence.* 都市の衰退と犯罪組織による暴力の問題がある.
→ see **teeth**

---

de|ceased /dɪsist/ (deceased)

> **Deceased** is both the singular and the plural form.

> **Deceased** は単数形でも複数形でもある.

1 N-COUNT 可算名詞 **The deceased** is used to refer to a particular person or to particular people who have recently died. 故人 [LEGAL 法律的] ❑ *The navy is notifying next of kin now that the identities of the deceased have been determined.* 故人の身元が明らかになってきたので、海軍は近親者への連絡をしている. 2 ADJ 形容詞 A **deceased** person is one who has recently died. 死去した [FORMAL 形式ばった] ❑ *...his recently deceased mother.* 彼の最近亡くなった母
→ see **funeral**

de|ceit /dɪsit/ (deceits) N-VAR 可変性名詞 **Deceit** is behavior that is deliberately intended to make people believe something which is not true. 欺くこと ❑ *He was living a secret life of deceit and unfaithfulness.* 彼は欺瞞と不誠実に満ちた秘密の生活を送っていた.

de|ceit|ful /dɪsitfəl/ ADJ 形容詞 If you say that someone is **deceitful**, you mean that they behave in a dishonest way by making other people believe something that is not true. 人をだます ❑ *The ambassador called the report deceitful and misleading.* 大使は、報告は虚偽で、誤解を招く恐れがあると思った.

de|ceive /dɪsiv/ (deceives, deceiving, deceived) 1 V-T 他動詞 If you **deceive** someone, you make them believe something that is not true, usually in order to get some advantage for yourself. 欺く ❑ *He has deceived and disillusioned us all.* 彼は我々皆を欺き幻滅させた. 2 V-T 他動詞 If something **deceives** you, it gives you a wrong impression and makes you believe something that is not true. 惑わす ❑ *Do not be deceived by claims on food labels like "light" or "low fat".* 「低カロリー」、「低脂肪」といった食品表示に惑わされてはならない.

De|cem|ber /dɪsɛmbər/ (Decembers) N-VAR 可変性名詞 **December** is the twelfth and last month of the year in the Western calendar. 12月 ❑ *...a bright morning in mid-December.* 12月半ばの明るく晴れた朝

de|cen|cy /dis⁰nsi/ 1 N-UNCOUNT 不可算名詞 **Decency** is the quality of following accepted moral standards. 礼儀正しさ, 良識 ❑ *His sense of decency forced him to resign.* 彼は自分の良識が許さず辞任した. 2 PHRASE 句 If you say that someone **did not have the decency to** do something, you are criticizing them because there was a particular action which they did not do but which you believe they ought to have done. 礼儀をわきまえている [DISAPPROVAL 不賛成] ❑ *He didn't even have the decency to tell them in person.* 彼は彼らに直接言うだけの礼儀さえもわきまえていなかった.

de|cent /dis⁰nt/ 1 ADJ 形容詞 **Decent** is used to describe something which is considered to be of an acceptable standard or quality. きちんとした ❑ *He didn't get a decent explanation.* 彼はまともな説明をしてもらえなかった. 2 ADJ 形容詞 **Decent** is used to describe something which is morally correct or acceptable. ふさわしい ❑ *But, after a decent interval, trade relations began to return to normal.* しかし、ほどよい期間が過ぎると、貿易関係は通常に戻り始めた. ● **de|cent|ly** ADV 副詞 ふさわしく ❑ *And can't you dress more decently – people will think you're a tramp.* それから、もっと見苦しくない格好はできないの. これじゃ浮浪者かと思われるわよ. 3 ADJ 形容詞 **Decent** people are honest and behave in a way that most people approve of. たしなみのよい, ちゃんとした ❑ *The majority of people around here are decent people.* ここら辺りの人たちの大多数はきちんとした人だ.

● **de|cent|ly** ADV 副詞 適切に ❑ *The allies say they will treat their prisoners decently.* 同盟諸国は捕虜を適切に扱うと言っている.

Thesaurus *decent* また次を参照 :

ADJ.	acceptable, adequate, passable, reasonable; (ant.) satisfactory 1
	honorable, respectable 2 3

Word Link *centr ≈ middle : central, concentrated, decentralized*

de|cen|tral|ize /disɛntrəlaɪz/ (decentralizes, decentralizing, decentralized) V-T/V-I 他動詞/自動詞 To **decentralize** government or a large organization means to move some departments away from the main administrative area, or to give more power to local departments. 分散化する [自動詞] 分散させる [他動詞] ❑ *...the need to decentralize and devolve power to regional governments.* 行政権を地方自治体に分散し、委譲する必要性 ● **de|cen|tral|i|za|tion** /disɛntrəlaɪzeɪʃ⁰n/ N-UNCOUNT 不可算名詞 分散, 地方分権 ❑ *He seems set against the idea of increased decentralization and greater powers for regional authorities.* 集中排除を高め、地方分権を強めるという考えに彼は反対しているようだ.

de|cep|tion /dɪsɛpʃ⁰n/ (deceptions) N-VAR 可変性名詞 **Deception** is the act of deceiving someone or the state of being deceived by someone. 欺くこと, 欺かれること ❑ *He admitted conspiring to obtain property by deception.* 彼は詐欺により財産を手に入れようと共謀したことを認めた.

de|cep|tive /dɪsɛptɪv/ ADJ 形容詞 If something is **deceptive**, it encourages you to believe something which is not true. 人を欺き

やすい □*Johnston isn't tired of Las Vegas yet, it seems, but appearances can be deceptive.* ジョンストンはラスベガスにはまだ飽きていないようだが、外見は当てにならない。●*The storyline is deceptively simple.* ストーリー展開は一見簡単にみえる.

deci|bel /dɛsɪbəl/ (**decibels**) N-COUNT 可算名詞 A **decibel** is a unit of measurement which is used to indicate how loud a sound is. デシベル □*Continuous exposure to sound above 80 decibels could be harmful.* 80デシベル以上の音に継続的にさらされると害がある可能性がある.

de|cide /dɪsaɪd/ (**decides, deciding, decided**) ■ V-T/V-I 他動詞/自動詞 If you **decide** to do something, you choose to do it, usually after you have thought carefully about the other possibilities. 決心する [他動詞]、決心する [自動詞] □*She decided to take a course in philosophy.* 彼女は哲学の講義を取ることに決めた. □*Think about it very carefully before you decide.* そのことについて慎重に考えてから決めなさい. ■ V-T 他動詞 If a person or group of people **decides** something, they choose what something should be like or how a particular problem should be solved. 決定する □*She was still young, he said, and that would be taken into account when deciding her sentence.* 彼女はまだ若いので、判決を決める際にはそれが考慮されるだろうと彼は言った. ■ V-T 他動詞 If an event or fact **decides** something, it makes it certain that a particular choice will be made or that there will be a particular result. 決める □*What happens next could decide their destiny.* 彼らの運命は次に何が起こるかによって決まるろう. □*The election will decide if either party controls both houses of Congress.* どちらの党が議会の両院を支配するかはその選挙で決まる. ■ V-T 他動詞 If you **decide** that something is true, you form that opinion about it after considering the facts. 判断する □*He decided Franklin must be suffering from a bad cold.* フランクリンはひどい風邪にかかっているに違いないと彼は判断した.

▶ **decide on** PHRASAL VERB 句動詞 If you **decide on** something or **decide upon** something, you choose it from two or more possibilities. 決める □*Denikin held a staff meeting to decide on the next strategic objective.* デニキンはスタッフ会議を開いて、次の戦略目標を決めた.

Thesaurus	*decide* また次を参照:
V.	choose, elect, pick, select ■ ■

Word Partnership	*decide* は次の語句と使われる:
V.	try to decide ■ ■
	help (to) decide, let *someone* decide ■ – ■
ADJ.	unable to decide ■ ■

de|cid|ed /dɪsaɪdɪd/ ADJ 形容詞 **Decided** means clear and definite. 確固たる [ADJ n] □*They got involved in a long and exhausting struggle and were at a decided disadvantage in the afternoon.* 彼らは長時間の精根尽きるような争いに巻き込まれ、午後には決定的に不利な立場に立たされた.

de|cid|ed|ly /dɪsaɪdɪdli/ ADV 副詞 **Decidedly** means to a great extent and in a way that is very obvious. はっきりと [ADV group] □*He admits there will be moments when he's decidedly uncomfortable at what he sees on the screen.* 彼は画面で見るものに明らかに不愉快を感じる時があるだろうと認めている.

Word Link	*dec ≈ ten : decade, decathlon, decimal*

deci|mal /dɛsɪməl/ (**decimals**) ■ ADJ 形容詞 A **decimal** system involves counting in units of ten. 十進法の [ADJ n] □*The mathematics of ancient Egypt were based on a decimal system.* 古代エジプトの数学は十進法に基づいていた. ■ N-COUNT 可算名詞 A **decimal** is a fraction that is written in the form of a dot followed by one or more numbers which represent tenths, hundredths, and so on: for example, .5, .51, .517. 小数 □*...simple math concepts, such as decimals and fractions.* 小数や分数といった単純な数学の概念

deci|mal point (**decimal points**) N-COUNT 可算名詞 A **decimal point** is the dot in front of a decimal fraction. 小数点 □*A waiter omitted the decimal point in the $13.09 bill.* ウェイターは13.09ドルの勘定書きの小数点を書き落とした.

deci|mate /dɛsɪmeɪt/ (**decimates, decimating, decimated**) ■ V-T 他動詞 To **decimate** something such as a group of people or animals means to destroy a very large number of them. 多くを殺す □*The pollution could decimate the river's thriving population of kingfishers.* その川で繁殖しているカワセミの数が汚染により激減するかもしれない. ■ V-T 他動詞 To **decimate** a system or organization means to reduce its size and effectiveness greatly. 大打撃を与える □*...a recession which decimated the nation's manufacturing industry.* 国の製造業界に大打撃を与えた景気後退

de|ci|pher /dɪsaɪfər/ (**deciphers, deciphering, deciphered**) V-T 他動詞 If you **decipher** a piece of writing or a message, you work out what it says, even though it is very difficult to read or understand. 解読する □*I'm still no closer to deciphering the code.* この暗号はまだ少しも解読できない.

de|ci|sion /dɪsɪʒən/ (**decisions**) ■ N-COUNT 可算名詞 When you make a **decision**, you choose what should be done or which is the best of various possible actions. 決断 □*I don't want to make the wrong decision and regret it later.* 間違った決断をして後で後悔したくない. ■ N-UNCOUNT 不可算名詞 **Decision** is the act of deciding something or the need to decide something. 決定 □*The growing pressures of the crisis may mean that the moment of decision can't be too long delayed.* 危機の圧力が増大しているということは、決定の時はもうあまり長く遅らせないということこそだろう. ■ N-UNCOUNT 不可算名詞 **Decision** is the ability to decide quickly and definitely what to do. 決断力 □*He is very quick-thinking and very much a man of decision.* 彼は機転が利くし、たいそう果断の人だ.

Word Partnership	*decision* は次の語句と使われる:
ADJ.	**final** decision, **right** decision, **wise** decision, **wrong** decision, **difficult** decision, **important** decision ■
V.	**make a** decision, **arrive at a** decision, **postpone a** decision, **reach a** decision ■

de|ci|sive /dɪsaɪsɪv/ ■ ADJ 形容詞 If a fact, action, or event is **decisive**, it makes certain a particular result. 決定的な □*...his decisive victory in the presidential elections.* 大統領選挙における彼の決定的勝利 ● **de|ci|sive|ly** ADV 副詞 決定的に □*The plan was decisively rejected by Congress three weeks ago.* その計画は3週間前に議会によって断固として却下された. ■ ADJ 形容詞 If someone is **decisive**, they have or show an ability to make quick decisions in a difficult or complicated situation. 決断力のある □*He should give way to a younger, more decisive leader.* 彼はもっと若くてもっと決断力のある指導者に位を譲るべきだ. ● **de|ci|sive|ly** ADV 副詞 決断力を持って □*"I'll call for you at ten," she said decisively.* 「10時に迎えに行くわ」と彼女は断言した. ● **de|ci|sive|ness** N-UNCOUNT 不可算名詞 果断さ □*His supporters admire his decisiveness.* 彼の支援者は彼の果断さを賞賛する.

deck /dɛk/ (**decks**) ■ N-COUNT 可算名詞 A **deck** on a vehicle such as a bus or ship is a lower or upper area of it. 床、甲板 □*...a luxury liner with five passenger decks.* 客室甲板が5つある豪華定期船 ■ N-COUNT 可算名詞 The **deck** of a ship is the top part of it that forms a floor in the open air which you can walk on. 甲板 [also 'on' N] □*She stood on the deck and waved her hand to them as the steamer moved off.* 蒸気船が立ち去る際、彼女は甲板に立って彼らに手を振った. ■ N-COUNT 可算名詞 A **deck** is a flat wooden area next to a house, where people can sit and relax or eat. テラス □*A natural timber deck leads into the main room of the home.* 自然木材でできたテラスがその家の主室に通じている. ■ N-COUNT 可算名詞 A **deck** of cards is a complete set of playing cards. トランプの1組 [mainly AM 主に米国英語] □*Matt picked up the cards and shuffled the deck.* マットはトランプを取り上げ、その1組をシャッフルした.
→ see **ship**

dec|la|ra|tion /dɛkləreɪʃən/ (**declarations**) ■ N-COUNT 可算名詞 A **declaration** is an official announcement or statement. 布告、発表 □*The opening speeches sounded more like declarations of war than offerings of peace.* 開幕の辞は、和平の申し出というよりも宣戦布告のように聞こえた. ■ N-COUNT 可算名詞 A **declaration** is a firm, emphatic statement which shows that you have no doubts about what you are saying. 宣言 □*...declarations of undying love.* 不滅の愛の誓い ■ N-COUNT 可算名詞 A **declaration** is a written statement about something which you have signed and which can be used as evidence in a court of law. 申告書、供述書 □*On the customs declaration, the sender labeled the freight as agricultural machinery.* 税関申告では送り主はその貨物を農機具としていた.

Word Link	*clar ≈ clear : clarify, clarity, declare*

de|clare /dɪklɛər/ (**declares, declaring, declared**) ■ V-T 他動詞 If you **declare** that something is true, you say that it is true in a firm, deliberate way. You can also **declare** an attitude or intention. 断言する [WRITTEN 書き言葉] □*He declared he would not run for a second term as president.* 彼は大統領として2期目に立候補する気はないと断言した. □*He declared his intention to become the best golfer in the world.* 彼は世界で最高のゴルファーになるつもりだと明言した. ■ V-T 他動詞 If you **declare** something, you state officially and formally that it exists or is the case. 宣言する □*The government is ready to declare a permanent ceasefire.* 政府は恒久的停戦を宣言する用意がある. □*His lawyers are confident that the judges will declare Mr. Stevens innocent.* 判事がスティーヴンス氏の無罪を宣言することに彼の弁護団は確信を持っている. ■ V-T 他動詞 If you **declare** goods that you have bought in another country or money that you have earned, you say how much you have bought or earned so that you can pay tax on it. (課税品、所得額を) 申告する □*Declaring the wrong income by mistake will no longer lead to an automatic fine.* 誤って間違った所得を申告しても、自動的に罰金が課されることはなくなるであろう.
→ see **war**

Word Link | clin = leaning : decline, incline, recline

de|cline /dɪklaɪn/ (declines, declining, declined) **1** V-I 自動詞 If something **declines**, it becomes less in quantity, importance, or strength. 減退する ❑ The number of staff has declined from 217,000 to 114,000. 従業員数は21万7千人から11万4千人まで減少した. ❑ Hourly output by workers declined 1.3% in the first quarter. 第1四半期には、労働者の時間当たりの生産高は1.3%減少した. **2** V-T/V-I 他動詞/自動詞 If you **decline** something or **decline to** do something, you politely refuse to accept it or do it. 丁重に断る ❑ He declined their invitation. 彼は彼らの招待を丁重に断った. [FORMAL 形式ばった] ❑ He offered the boys some coffee. They declined politely. 彼は少年たちにコーヒーを勧めたが、彼らは丁重に断った. **3** N-VAR 可変性名詞 If there is a **decline in** something, it becomes less in quantity, importance, or quality. 減退, 低下 ❑ Official figures show a sharp decline in the number of foreign tourists. 公式の数字は外国人観光客数の劇的な減少を示している. **4** PHRASE 句 If something is **in decline** or **on the decline**, it is gradually decreasing in importance, quality, or power. 衰えて ❑ Thankfully the smoking of cigarettes is on the decline. ありがたいことに、喫煙は下降線をたどっている. **5** PHRASE 句 If something **goes** or **falls into decline**, it begins to gradually decrease in importance, quality, or power. 衰微して ❑ Libraries are an investment for the future and they should not be allowed to fall into decline. 図書館は将来のための投資であり、衰微させてはならない.

Word Partnership | decline は次の語句と使われる:

ADJ. | **economic** decline, **gradual** decline, **rapid** decline, **steady** decline **3**

Word Link | cod = writing : code, encode, decode

de|code /dikoʊd/ (decodes, decoding, decoded) **1** V-T 他動詞 If you **decode** a message that has been written or spoken in a code, you change it into ordinary language. 解読する ❑ All he had to do was decode it and pass it over. 彼はそれを解読して引き渡すだけでよかった. **2** V-T 他動詞 A device that **decodes** a broadcast signal changes it into a form that can be displayed on a television screen. 復調する ❑ About 60,000 subscribers have special adapters to receive and decode the signals. 約6万の加入者が信号を受信して復調する特別なアダプタを持つ.

de|com|pose /dikəmpoʊz/ (decomposes, decomposing, decomposed) V-T/V-I 他動詞/自動詞 When things such as dead plants or animals **decompose**, or when something **decomposes** them, they change chemically and begin to decay. 分解する ❑ ...a dead body found decomposing in the woods. 森で発見された腐敗死体 ❑ The debris slowly decomposes into compost. くずはゆっくりと分解して堆肥になる.

de|cor /deɪkɔr/ N-UNCOUNT 不可算名詞 The **decor** of a house or room is its style of furnishing and decoration. 装飾様式 ❑ The decor is simple – black lacquer panels on white walls. その装飾様式は、白の壁に黒漆塗りのパネルといったシンプルなものである.

deco|rate /dɛkəreɪt/ (decorates, decorating, decorated) **1** V-T 他動詞 If you **decorate** something, you make it more attractive by adding things to it. 装飾を施す ❑ He decorated his room with pictures of all his favorite sports figures. 彼はお気に入りのスポーツ選手全員の写真で部屋を飾った. **2** V-T/V-I 他動詞/自動詞 If you **decorate** a room or the inside of a building, you put new paint or wallpaper on the walls and ceiling, and paint the woodwork. ペンキを塗る, 壁紙を貼る ❑ When they came to decorate the rear bedroom, it was Jemma who had the final say. 裏の寝室の内装となると、最終決定権を持ったのはジェンマであった. ❑ The boys are planning to decorate when they get the time. 少年たちは時間があればペンキを塗ろうと計画している. ●**deco|rat|ing** N-UNCOUNT 不可算名詞 ペンキを塗ること, 壁紙を張ること ❑ I did a lot of the decorating myself. その内装はかなり自分でやった. ●**deco|ra|tion** N-UNCOUNT 不可算名詞 ❑ The renovation and decoration took four months. 改築と内装には4か月かかった.

deco|ra|tion /dɛkəreɪʃⁿn/ (decorations) **1** N-UNCOUNT 不可算名詞 The **decoration** of a room is its furniture, wallpaper, and ornaments. 装飾物 ❑ The decoration and furnishings had to be practical enough for a family home. 家族用住宅の場合、装飾物と備品は十分実用的である必要があった. **2** N-VAR 可変性名詞 **Decorations** are features that are added to something in order to make it look more attractive. 飾りつけ ❑ The only wall decorations are candles and a single mirror. 壁の飾りつけはろうそくとたった1つの鏡だけである. **3** N-COUNT 可算名詞 **Decorations** are brightly colored objects such as pieces of paper and balloons, which you put up in a room on special occasions to make it look more attractive. 飾り物 ❑ Colorful streamers and paper decorations had been hung from the ceiling. 色とりどりの飾りリボンや紙の飾り物が天井から下がっていた. **4** → see also **decorate**

deco|ra|tive /dɛkərətɪv, -əreɪtɪv/ ADJ 形容詞 Something that is **decorative** is intended to look pretty or attractive. 装飾の ❑ The curtains are for purely decorative purposes and do not open or close. その

カーテンは純粋に装飾目的のみで、開閉しない.

deco|ra|tor /dɛkəreɪtər/ (decorators) **1** N-COUNT 可算名詞 A **decorator** is a person who is employed to design and decorate the inside of people's houses. 室内装飾家 [AM 米国英語] ❑ ...Bloomberg's private palace, with its intricate interior design by decorator Jamie Drake. 装飾家ジェイミー・ドレイクによる複雑なインテリアデザインのブルームバーグの大邸宅 **2** → see also **interior decorator**

de|coy /dikɔɪ/ (decoys) N-COUNT 可算名詞 If you refer to something or someone as a **decoy**, you mean that they are intended to attract people's attention and deceive them, for example, by leading them into a trap or away from a particular place. おとり ❑ A plane was waiting at the airport with its engines running but this was just one of the decoys. 飛行機が1機エンジンをかけたまま空港で待機していたが、これはおとりの1つに過ぎなかった.

Word Link | cresc, creas ≈ growing : crescent, decrease, increase

de|crease (decreases, decreasing, decreased)

The verb is pronounced /dɪkris/. The noun is pronounced /dikris/ or /dɪkris/.

動詞は /dɪkris/ と発音される. 名詞は /dikris/ か /dɪkris/ と発音される.

1 V-T/V-I 他動詞/自動詞 When something **decreases** or when you **decrease** it, it becomes less in quantity, size, or intensity. 減少させる [他動詞], 減少する [自動詞] ❑ Population growth is decreasing by 1.4% each year. 人口成長率は毎年1.4%低下している. ❑ The number of independent firms decreased from 198 to 96. 独立した会社の数は196から96に減少した. ❑ Since 1945 air forces have decreased in size. 1945年以来、空軍は規模が縮小している. **2** N-COUNT 可算名詞 A **decrease in** the quantity, size, or intensity of something is a reduction in it. 減少 ❑ In Spain and Portugal there has been a decrease in the number of young people out of work. スペインとポルトガルでは無職の若者の数が減少している.

Thesaurus | decrease また次を参照:

V. | decline, diminish, go down; (ant.) increase **1**

de|cree /dɪkri/ (decrees, decreeing, decreed) **1** N-COUNT 可算名詞 A **decree** is an official order or decision, especially one made by the ruler of a country. 法令, 布告 [also 'by' N] ❑ In July he issued a decree ordering all unofficial armed groups in the country to disband. 7月、彼は国内の非公式武装集団すべてに解散を命じる法令を発布した. **2** N-COUNT 可算名詞 A **decree** is a judgment made by a law court. (裁判所の) 判決 [mainly AM 主に米国英語] ❑ ...court decrees. 裁判所の決定 **3** V-T 他動詞 If someone in authority **decrees** that something must happen, they decide or state this officially. 法令で定める ❑ The government decreed that all who wanted to live and work in Kenya must hold Kenyan passports. 政府はケニアで生活し働きたいものは全員ケニアの旅券を所持していなければならないと法令で定めた.

dedi|cate /dɛdɪkeɪt/ (dedicates, dedicating, dedicated) **1** V-T 他動詞 If you say that someone **has dedicated** themselves **to** something, you approve of the fact that they have decided to give a lot of time and effort to it because they think that it is important. (時間や労力を) ささげる [APPROVAL 賛成] ❑ For the next few years, she dedicated herself to her work. その後数年間彼女は仕事に専念した. ●**dedi|cat|ed** ADJ 形容詞 献身的な ❑ He's quite dedicated to his students. 彼は学生のために非常に尽くしている. ●**dedi|ca|tion** N-UNCOUNT 不可算名詞 献身 ❑ We admire her courage, compassion, and dedication to the cause of humanity, justice, and peace. 私たちは彼女の勇気、思いやり、そして人道、正義および平和の大義への献身ぶりに敬服している. **2** V-T 他動詞 If someone **dedicates** something such as a book, play, or piece of music **to** you, they mention your name, for example, in the front of a book or when a piece of music is performed, as a way of showing affection or respect for you. ささげる ❑ She dedicated her first album to Woody Allen, who she says understands her obsession. 彼女は自分の執念を理解してくれていると言って、ウッディ・アレンに最初のアルバムをささげた.

dedi|cat|ed /dɛdɪkeɪtɪd/ **1** ADJ 形容詞 You use **dedicated** to describe someone who enjoys a particular activity very much and spends a lot of time doing it. 打ち込んだ ❑ Her great-grandfather had clearly been a dedicated and stoical traveler. 彼女の曽祖父は明らかに、熱心でストイックな旅行者だった. **2** ADJ 形容詞 You use **dedicated** to describe something that is made, built, or designed for one particular purpose or thing. 特定の用途向きの ❑ Such areas should also be served by dedicated cycle routes. こういった地域は自転車専用道路の便も整備されるべきだ. ❑ ...the world's first museum dedicated to ecology. 世界初の生態学専門博物館 **3** → see also **dedicate**

de|duce /dɪdus/ (deduces, deducing, deduced) V-T 他動詞 If you **deduce** something or **deduce** that something is true, you reach that conclusion because of other things that you know to be true. 論理的に推理する ❑ Alison cleverly deduced that I was the

author of the letter. アリソンは賢明にも私が手紙の筆者であることを推論した. ❑ *The date of the document can be deduced from references to the Civil War.* その文書の年代は南北戦争への言及から推察することができる.

de|duct /dɪdˈʌkt/ (deducts, deducting, deducted) V-T 他動詞 When you **deduct** an amount from a total, you subtract it from the total. 差し引く ❑ *The company deducted this payment from his compensation.* 会社はこの支払額を彼の補償額から差し引いた.

de|duc|tion /dɪdˈʌkʃən/ (deductions) **1** N-COUNT 可算名詞 A **deduction** is an amount that has been subtracted from a total. 差し引き額 ❑ *Most homeowners can get a federal income tax deduction on interest payments to a home equity loan.* 大多数の住宅所有者は, 住宅担保ローンの利子支払いに連邦所得税控除が受けられる. **2** N-COUNT 可算名詞 A **deduction** is a conclusion that you have reached about something because of other things that you know to be true. 結論, 推論 ❑ *It was a pretty astute deduction.* それはかなり明敏な結論だった. **3** N-UNCOUNT 不可算名詞 **Deduction** is the process of reaching a conclusion about something because of other things that you know to be true. 推定 ❑ *Miss Allan beamed at him. "You are clever to guess. I'm sure I don't know how you did it." — "Deduction," James said.* アラン嬢は彼に微笑んだ. 「よく言い当てたわね. でもどうやってしたのかわからないわ」「推理さ」とジェームズは言った.
→ see **science**

deed /dˈiːd/ (deeds) **1** N-COUNT 可算名詞 A **deed** is something that is done, especially something that is very good or very bad. 行為 [LITERARY 文語的] ❑ *The perpetrators of this evil deed must be brought to justice.* この邪悪な行為の犯人たちは法に基づいて裁かれるべきだ. **2** N-COUNT 可算名詞 A **deed** is a document containing the terms of an agreement, especially an agreement concerning the ownership of land or a building. 証書 [LEGAL 法律的] ❑ *He asked if I had the deeds to his father's property.* 彼は私が父の資産の証書を持っているかと聞いた.

deem /dˈiːm/ (deems, deeming, deemed) V-T 他動詞 If something is **deemed** to have a particular quality or **to** do a particular thing, it is considered to have that quality or do that thing. 考える [FORMAL 形式ばった] ❑ *French and German were deemed essential.* フランス語とドイツ語は必須であると考えられた. ❑ *He says he would support the use of force if the UN deemed it necessary.* 国連が必要と考えるのであれば, 彼は武力行使を支持するだろうと言っている.

deep /dˈiːp/ (deeper, deepest) **1** ADJ 形容詞 If something is **deep**, it extends a long way down from the ground or from the top surface of something. 深い ❑ *The water is very deep and mysterious looking.* 水は非常に深く, 神秘的に見えた. ❑ *Den had dug a deep hole in the center of the garden.* デンは庭の真ん中に深い穴を掘った. ● ADV 副詞 **Deep** is also an adverb. 深く ❑ *Gingerly, she put her hand in deeper, to the bottom.* 彼女は極めて慎重に手をさらに深く入れ, 底に触れた. ● **deep|ly** ADV 副詞 深く ❑ *There isn't time to dig deeply and put in manure or compost.* 深く掘って, 肥料や堆肥を入れる時間はない. **2** ADJ 形容詞 A **deep** container, such as a closet, extends or measures a long distance from front to back. 奥行のある ❑ *The wardrobe was very deep.* 洋服ダンスはかなり奥行があった. **3** ADJ 形容詞 You use **deep** to emphasize the seriousness, strength, importance, or degree of something. (程度が) 強い [EMPHASIS 強調] ❑ *I had a deep admiration for Sartre.* 私はサルトルに強く感服していた. ❑ *He wants to express his deep sympathy to the family.* 彼はその家族に対して深い同情の念を表明したい. ● **deep|ly** ADV 副詞 深く ❑ *He loved his brother deeply.* 彼は弟を深く愛していた. **4** ADJ 形容詞 [ADJ n] If you are in a **deep** sleep, you are sleeping peacefully and it is difficult to wake you. 深い ❑ *Una soon fell into a deep sleep.* ウーナはじきに深い眠りに落ちた. ● **deep|ly** ADV 副詞 [ADV after v] 深く ❑ *She slept deeply but woke early.* 彼女の眠りは深かったが, 寝覚めは早かった. **5** ADJ 形容詞 If you are **deep in** thought or **deep in** conversation, you are concentrating very hard on what you are thinking or saying and are not aware of the things that are happening around you. 深く没頭して [v-link ADJ 'in' n] ❑ *Before long, we were deep in conversation.* やがて私たちは会話に夢中になっていた. **6** ADJ 形容詞 A **deep** breath or sigh uses or fills the whole of your lungs. 深い [ADJ n] ❑ *Cal took a long, deep breath, struggling to control his own emotions.* キャルは長く深く呼吸して必死で自分の感情を制御しようとした. ● **deep|ly** ADV 副詞 [ADV after v] ❑ *She sighed deeply and covered her face with her hands.* 彼女は深いため息をついて, 両手で顔を覆った. **7** ADJ 形容詞 A **deep** sound is low in pitch. 太く低い ❑ *His voice was deep and mellow.* 彼の声は太く低く, 心地よかった. **8** ADJ 形容詞 If you describe something such as a problem or a piece of writing as **deep**, you mean that it is important, serious, or complicated. 深遠な ❑ *They're written as adventure stories. They're not intended to be deep.* それらは冒険小説として書かれており, 深遠なものを意図したものではない. **9** ADV 副詞 **deep** in an area means a long way inside in. 奥深くへ ❑ *Picking up his bag the giant strode off deep into the forest.* バッグを手に取って, 巨人は森の奥深くへ大またに歩き去った. **10** ADV 副詞 If you experience or feel something **deep inside** you or **deep down**, you feel it very strongly even though you do not necessarily show it.

(考えを表さずに) 奥深く ❑ *Deep down, she supported her husband's involvement in the organization.* 心の奥底では, 彼女は夫がその団体に関与することを支持していた. **11** ADV 副詞 If you are **deep in** debt, you have a lot of debts. 過度に [ADV 'in/into' n] ❑ *He is so deep in debt and desperate for money that he's apparently willing to say anything.* 彼は借金で首が回らず, よくよく金に困っているので, 彼はどうも何でも進んで言いそうだ. ● **deep|ly** ADV 副詞 [ADV 'in/into' n] ひどく ❑ *Because of her medical and her legal bills, she is now penniless and deeply in debt.* 医療費と弁護料で, 彼女は現在1文なしで, ひどく借金している. **12** COMB IN COLOR 色彩語の複合 You use **deep** to describe colors that are strong and fairly dark. 濃い ❑ *The sky was peach colored in the east, deep blue and starry in the west.* 東には桃色の空, 西には濃紺色の星空が広がっていた. ● ADJ 形容詞 **Deep** is also an adjective. 濃い ❑ *These Amish cushions in traditional deep colors are available in two sizes.* これらの伝統的な濃い色のアーミッシュクッションは2サイズでお求めになれます. **13** PHRASE 句 If you say that something **goes deep** or **runs deep**, you mean that it is very serious or strong and is hard to change. 根深い ❑ *His anger and anguish clearly went deep.* 彼の怒りと苦悩は明らかに根深いものになった. **14** **in at the deep end →** see **end** **15** **in deep water →** see **water**

deep|en /dˈiːpən/ (deepens, deepening, deepened) **1** V-T/V-I 他動詞/自動詞 If a situation or emotion **deepens** or if something **deepens** it, it becomes stronger and more intense. 深刻にする [他動詞], 深刻になる [自動詞] ❑ *If this is not stopped, the financial crisis will deepen.* これが止められない場合, 財政危機は深刻になるだろう. **2** V-T 他動詞 If you **deepen** your knowledge or understanding of a subject, you learn more about it and become more interested in it. 深める ❑ *The course is an exciting opportunity for anyone wishing to deepen their understanding of themselves and other people.* この講義は, 自己および他人をより深く理解したいと思っている者にとって刺激的な機会である. **3** V-T/V-I 他動詞/自動詞 When a sound **deepens** or **is deepened**, it becomes lower in tone. 低くする [他動詞], 低くなる [自動詞] ❑ *The music room had been made to reflect and deepen sounds.* 音楽室は音を反射し低くするように作られていた. **4** V-T 他動詞 If people **deepen** something, they increase its depth by digging out its lower surface. 深くする ❑ *The project would deepen the river from 40 to 45 feet, to allow for larger ships.* そのプロジェクトは河を40フィートから45フィートまで深くし, 従来より大型の船舶の通過を可能にするであろう.

deep-seated ADJ 形容詞 A **deep-seated** problem, feeling, or belief is difficult to change because its causes have been there for a long time. 根深い ❑ *The country is still suffering from deep-seated economic problems.* その国はいまだに根深い経済問題に悩まされている.

deer /dˈɪər/ (deer)

Deer is both the singular and the plural form.

Deer は単数形でも複数形でもある.

N-COUNT 可算名詞 A **deer** is a large wild animal that eats grass and leaves. A male deer usually has large, branching horns. シカ

de|face /dɪfˈeɪs/ (defaces, defacing, defaced) V-T 他動詞 If someone **defaces** something such as a wall or a notice, they spoil it by writing or drawing things on it. 外観を汚損する ❑ *It's illegal to deface property.* 不動産への落書き行為は違法である.

de|fault /dɪfˈɔːlt/ (defaults, defaulting, defaulted) **1** V-I 自動詞 If a person, company, or country **defaults on** something that they have legally agreed to do, such as paying some money or doing a piece of work before a particular time, they fail to do it. (債務などを) 履行しない [LEGAL 法律的] ❑ *The credit card business is down, and more borrowers are defaulting on loans.* クレジットカードビジネスは下向きで, ローン支払いを怠る借り主が増えている. ● N-UNCOUNT 不可算名詞 **Default** is also a noun. 不履行 ❑ *The corporation may be charged with default on its contract with the government.* その企業は政府との契約の不履行で起訴されるかもしれない. **2** ADJ 形容詞 A **default** situation is what exists or happens unless someone or something changes it. 既定の [ADJ n] ❑ *He appeared unimpressed; but then, unimpressed was his default state.* 彼は感動していないようだったが, それでも彼はいつもそうなのだからしかたがない. **3** N-UNCOUNT 不可算名詞 In computing, the **default** is a particular set of instructions which the computer always uses unless the person using the computer gives other instructions. 初期値, デフォルト [COMPUTING コンピューティング] ❑ *The default setting on Windows Explorer will not show these files.* Windows Explorer の初期設定ではこれらのファイルは表示されない. **4** PHRASE 句 If something happens **by default**, it happens only because something else which might have prevented it or changed it has not happened. 不履行によって [FORMAL 形式ばった] ❑ *I would rather pay the individuals than let the money go to the State by default.* 私は何もしないでその金を州に渡してしまうよりも, 個人に支払いたい.

de|feat /dɪfˈiːt/ (defeats, defeating, defeated) **1** V-T 他動詞 If you **defeat** someone, you win a victory over them in a battle, game, or contest. 負かす ❑ *His guerrillas defeated the colonial army in 1954.* 彼のゲリラ兵は1954年に植民地軍を破った. **2** V-T 他動詞 If

d

a proposal or motion in a debate **is defeated**, more people vote against it than for it. 否決する [usu passive] ❏ *The bill was defeated with support from only two congressmen.* 支持した下院議員はたった2人であったため法案は否決された. ■ V-T 他動詞 If a task or a problem **defeats** you, it is so difficult that you cannot do it or solve it. （人を）挫折させる ❏ *The book he most wanted to write was the one which nearly defeated him.* 彼の最も書きたかった本は，彼が挫折しかけたものだった. ■ V-T 他動詞 To **defeat** an action or plan means to cause it to fail. （行動，計画などを）挫折させる ❏ *The navy played a limited but significant role in defeating the rebellion.* 海軍はその反乱の鎮圧に，限られたものではあるが重要な役割を果たした. ■ N-VAR 可変性名詞 **Defeat** is the experience of being beaten in a battle, game, or contest, or of failing to achieve what you wanted to. 敗北 ❏ *The most important thing is not to admit defeat until you really have to.* 最も重要なことは，本当に負けを認めなければならなくなるまであきらめないことだ. ❏ *...the Sonics' 31-point defeat at Sacramento on Sunday.* 日曜日のサクラメント市におけるソニックスの31ポイントの敗北

de|fect (defects, defecting, defected)

> The noun is pronounced /dífɛkt/. The verb is pronounced /dɪfɛkt/.
>
> 名詞は /dífɛkt/ と発音される. 動詞は /dɪfɛkt/ と発音される.

■ N-COUNT 可算名詞 A **defect** is a fault or imperfection in a person or thing. 欠陥 ❏ *He was born with a hearing defect.* 彼は生まれつき難聴である. ❏ *A report has pointed out the defects of the present system.* ある報告書が現在のシステムの欠陥を指摘している. ■ V-I 自動詞 If you **defect**, you leave your country, political party, or other group, and join an opposing country, party, or group. 自分の国（党，グループなど）を捨てる ❏ *a KGB officer who defected in 1963.* 1963年に亡命したKGBの役人 ● **de|fec|tion** /dɪfɛkʃən/ (defections) N-VAR 可変性名詞 離脱 ❏ *...the defection of at least sixteen parliamentary deputies.* 少なくとも16人の国会議員の脱会

de|fec|tive /dɪfɛktɪv/ ADJ 形容詞 If something is **defective**, there is something wrong with it and it does not work properly. 欠陥のある ❏ *Retailers can return defective merchandise.* 小売店は欠陥商品を返品することができる.

de|fence /dɪfɛns/ → see defense

de|fence|less /dɪfɛnslɪs/ → see defenseless

Word Link fend ≈ striking : defend, fender, offend

de|fend /dɪfɛnd/ (defends, defending, defended) ■ V-T 他動詞 If you **defend** someone or something, you take action in order to protect them. 守る ❏ *His courage in defending religious and civil rights inspired many outside the church.* 宗教上の権利と市民権を擁護する彼の勇気は，教会外部の多くの人たちを鼓舞した. ■ V-T 他動詞 If you **defend** someone or something when they have been criticized, you argue in support of them. 擁護する ❏ *He defended his administration's response to the disaster against critics who charge the federal government is moving too slowly.* 連邦政府の動きがあまりにも鈍いと非難する批判者たちに対して，彼は惨事に対する自分の政権の対応を擁護した. ■ V-T 他動詞 When a lawyer **defends** a person who has been accused of something, the lawyer argues on their behalf in a court of law that the charges are not true. 弁護する ❏ *...a lawyer who defended political prisoners during the military regime.* 軍事政権の時代に政治犯を弁護した弁護士 ❏ *He has hired a lawyer to defend him against the allegation.* 彼はその主張に対して自分の弁護を担当する弁護士を雇った. ■ V-T 他動詞 When a sports player plays in the tournament which they won the previous time it was held, you can say that they **are defending** their title. 防衛する [JOURNALISM ジャーナリズム] ❏ *Torrence expects to defend her title successfully in the next Olympics.* トレンスは次回のオリンピックで首尾よくタイトルを守りぬくものつもりである.

→ see hero

Thesaurus defend また次を参照：

| v. | protect ■ |
| | back, support ■ |

Word Link ant ≈ one who does, has : defendant, deodorant, occupant

de|fend|ant /dɪfɛndənt/ (defendants) N-COUNT 可算名詞 A **defendant** is a person who has been accused of breaking the law and is being tried in court. 被告 ❏ *The defendant pleaded guilty and was fined $500.* 被告は罪状を認め，500ドルの罰金を科された.

→ see trial

de|fend|er /dɪfɛndər/ (defenders) ■ N-COUNT 可算名詞 If someone is a **defender of** a particular thing or person that has been criticized, they argue or act in support of that thing or person. 擁護者 ❏ *...the most ardent defenders of conventional family values.* 昔ながらの家庭の価値観を最も熱心に擁護する人たち ■ N-COUNT 可算名詞 A **defender** in a game such as soccer or

hockey is a player whose main task is to try and stop the other side from scoring. 守備の選手 ❏ *Lewis was the NFL's top defender in the 2000 season.* ルイスは2000年シーズンにおいてNFLの最優秀ディフェンダーだった.

de|fense /dɪfɛns/ (defenses)

> **Defense** in meaning ■ is pronounced /díːfɛns/.
>
> **Defense** の意味の ■ は /díːfɛns/ と発音される.

■ N-UNCOUNT 不可算名詞 **Defense** is action that is taken to protect someone or something against attack. 防御 ❏ *The land was flat, giving no scope for defense.* その土地は平坦で，防御の見込みはない. ■ N-UNCOUNT 不可算名詞 **Defense** is the organization of a country's armies and weapons, and their use to protect the country or its interests. 国防 ❏ *Twenty-eight percent of the federal budget is spent on defense.* 連邦予算の28パーセントが国防に費やされる. ❏ *...U.S. Defense Secretary Donald Rumsfeld.* ドナルド・ラムズフェルド米国防長官 ■ N-PLURAL 複数名詞 The **defenses** of a country or region are all its armed forces and weapons. 防衛力 ❏ *He emphasized the need to maintain Britain's defenses at a level sufficient to deal with the unexpected.* 彼は英国が予期せぬ事態に対応するために十分なレベルの防衛力を維持することの必要性を強調した. ■ N-COUNT 可算名詞 A **defense** is something that people or animals can use or do to protect themselves. 防御手段 ❏ *Despite anything the science of medicine may have achieved, the immune system is our main defense against disease.* 医学が何を達成したとしても，疾病に対する我々の主要な防御手段は免疫系である. ■ N-COUNT 可算名詞 A **defense** is something that you say or write which supports ideas or actions that have been criticized or questioned. 擁護のための弁論 [oft N 'of' n, also 'in' n] ❏ *Chomsky's defense of his approach goes further.* チョムスキーが自分の研究法を擁護する弁論はさらに進む. ■ N-SING 単数名詞 The **defense** is the case that is presented by a lawyer in a trial for the person who has been accused of a crime. You can also refer to this person's lawyers as **the defense**. 抗弁，被告弁護士 ❏ *The defense was that the records of the interviews were fabricated by the police.* 抗弁は，インタビューの記録は警察によってねつ造されたというものだった. ■ N-SING-COLL 集合的単数名詞 In games such as soccer or hockey, the **defense** is the group of players in a team who try to stop the opposing players from scoring a goal or a point. 守備勢 [oft poss N, also 'in' N] ❏ *Their defense, so strong last season, has now conceded 12 goals in six games.* 昨シーズン非常に強かった彼らのディフェンスは，今では6試合で12の得点を許してしまった. ■ PHRASE 句 If you come **to** someone's **defense**, you help them by doing or saying something to protect them. 擁護に回って ❏ *He realized none of his schoolmates would come to his defense.* 彼は学校の友だちは誰も彼の擁護に回ってはくれないことが分かった.

de|fense|less /dɪfɛnslɪs/ ADJ 形容詞 If someone or something is **defenseless**, they are weak and unable to defend themselves properly. 無防備の ❏ *...a savage attack on a defenseless young girl.* 無防備の若い女性に対する残忍な暴行

de|fen|sive /dɪfɛnsɪv/ ■ ADJ 形容詞 You use **defensive** to describe things that are intended to protect someone or something. 防御用の ❏ *The Government hastily organized defensive measures, deploying searchlights and antiaircraft guns around the target cities.* 政府はあわてて防衛策を準備し，標的となる都市の回りにサーチライトと高射砲を配備した. ■ ADJ 形容詞 Someone who is **defensive** is behaving in a way that shows they feel unsure or threatened. 守勢の ❏ *Like their children, parents are often defensive about their private lives.* 子供と同じように，親も私生活は守りたがるものだ. ● **de|fen|sive|ly** ADV 副詞 防衛的に ❏ *"Oh, I know, I know," said Kate, defensively.* 「ええ，わかってますとも」とケイトは言い訳がましく言った. ■ ADJ 形容詞 In sports, **defensive** play is play that is intended to prevent your opponent from scoring points against you. 守備の ❏ *I'd always played a defensive game, waiting for my opponent to make a mistake.* 私は常に相手が間違いを犯すのを待つような受身のゲームをしてきた. ● **de|fen|sive|ly** ADV 副詞 [ADV after v] 守勢的に ❏ *We didn't play well defensively in the first half.* 私たちは前半，守勢的にはよいプレーをしなかった. ■ PHRASE 句 If someone is **on the defensive**, they are trying to protect themselves or their interests because they feel unsure or threatened. 守勢に立って ❏ *The administration has been on the defensive about the war.* 政権はその戦争に関しては守勢に立たされている.

de|fer /dɪfɜr/ (defers, deferring, deferred) ■ V-T 他動詞 If you **defer** an event or action, you arrange for it to happen at a later date, rather than immediately or at the previously planned time. 延期する ❏ *Customers often defer payment for as long as possible.* 顧客は往々にしてできる限り支払いを延期する. ■ V-I 自動詞 If you **defer to** someone, you accept their opinion or do what they want you to do, even when you do not agree with it yourself, because you respect them or their authority. 譲歩する ❏ *Doctors are encouraged to defer to experts.* 医師は専門家には譲歩するよう奨励されている.

def|er|ence /dɛfərəns/ N-UNCOUNT 不可算名詞 **Deference** is a polite and respectful attitude toward someone, especially because they have an important position. 敬意，服従 ❏ *...the older*

political tradition of deference to great leaders. 偉大な指導者には服従するという古くからの政治的伝統

de|fi|ance /dɪfaɪəns/ N-UNCOUNT 不可算名詞 **Defiance** is behavior or an attitude which shows that you are not willing to obey someone. 反抗的態度 [oft N 'of' n] □ ...his courageous defiance of the government. 政府に対する彼の勇気ある抵抗

de|fi|ant /dɪfaɪənt/ ADJ 形容詞 If you say that someone is **defiant**, you mean they show aggression or independence by refusing to obey someone. 反抗的な, 挑戦的な □ The players are in a defiant mood as they prepare for tomorrow's game. 選手たちは明日の試合に備えて, 挑戦的な気分である. ● **de|fi|ant|ly** ADV 副詞 挑戦的に □ They defiantly rejected any talk of a compromise. 彼らは妥協点を探る話し合いはすべて傲然と拒否した.

de|fi|cien|cy /dɪfɪʃənsi/ (deficiencies) N-VAR 可変性名詞 **Deficiency** in something, especially something that your body needs, is not having enough of it. 不足 □ They did blood tests on him for signs of vitamin deficiency. 彼はビタミン不足の兆候があるために, 血液検査を受けた. ② N-VAR 可変性名詞 A **deficiency** that someone or something has is a weakness or imperfection in them. 欠陥 [FORMAL 形式ばった] □ The most serious deficiency in NATO's air defense is the lack of an identification system to distinguish friend from foe. NATOの防空体制で最も深刻な欠陥は, 敵と味方を区別する識別システムの欠如である.

de|fi|cient /dɪfɪʃənt/ ADJ 形容詞 If someone or something is **deficient in** a particular thing, they do not have the full amount of it that they need in order to function normally or work properly. 不足した [FORMAL 形式ばった] □ ...a diet deficient in vitamin B. ビタミンBが不足した食事

defi|cit /dɛfəsɪt/ (deficits) N-COUNT 可算名詞 A **deficit** is the amount by which something is less than what is required or expected, especially the amount by which the total money received is less than the total money spent. 不足 □ They're ready to cut the federal budget deficit for the next fiscal year. 彼らは来年度の国家予算赤字を削減する用意がある. □ ...a deficit of five billion dollars. 50億ドルの不足額 ● PHRASE 句 If an account or organization is in **deficit**, more money has been spent than has been received. 赤字の

de|fine /dɪfaɪn/ (defines, defining, defined) V-T 他動詞 If you **define** something, you show, describe, or state clearly what it is and what its limits are, or what it is like. 定義する □ The Convention Against Torture defines torture as any act that inflicts severe pain or suffering, physical or mental. 拷問禁止条約は, 拷問を肉体的または精神的な激痛または苦痛を加える行為と定義している.

defi|nite /dɛfɪnɪt/ ① ADJ 形容詞 If something such as a decision or an arrangement is **definite**, it is firm and clear, and unlikely to be changed. 確定的な □ It's too soon to give a definite answer. 確答をするには早すぎる. □ She made no definite plans for her future. 彼女は将来について何も確かな計画をしなかった. ② ADJ 形容詞 **Definite** evidence or information is true, rather than being someone's opinion or guess. 確実な □ We didn't have any definite proof. 私たちには確かな証拠が何もなかった. ③ ADJ 形容詞 You use **definite** to emphasize the strength of your opinion or belief. 明確な [EMPHASIS 強調] [ADJ n] □ There has already been a definite improvement. すでに明らかな改善が見られた. ④ ADJ 形容詞 Someone who is **definite** behaves or talks in a firm, confident way. 確信して □ Mary is very definite about this. メアリーはこれについて非常に確信がある.

defi|nite ar|ti|cle (definite articles) N-COUNT 可算名詞 The word "the" is sometimes called **the definite article**. 定冠詞

defi|nite|ly /dɛfɪnɪtli/ ① ADV 副詞 You use **definitely** to emphasize that something is the case, or to emphasize the strength of your intention or opinion. 確かに [EMPHASIS 強調] □ I'm definitely going to get in touch with these people. 私はもちろんこれらの人たちと連絡を取っているつもりだ. ② ADV 副詞 If something has been **definitely** decided, the decision will not be changed. 決定的に [ADV before v] □ She had definitely decided that she wanted to continue working with women in prison. 彼女は刑務所の女性たちのところで働き続けたいと最終的に決心した.

defi|ni|tion /dɛfɪnɪʃən/ (definitions) ① N-COUNT 可算名詞 A **definition** is a statement giving the meaning of a word or expression, especially in a dictionary. 定義 □ There is no general agreement on a standard definition of intelligence. 知能の標準的な定義について一般的に一致した意見はない. ● PHRASE 句 If you say that something has a particular quality **by definition**, you mean

that it has this quality simply because of what it is. 定義上, 当然 ② N-UNCOUNT 不可算名詞 **Definition** is the quality of being clear and distinct. 明確さ □ The first speakers at the conference criticized Prof. Johnson's new program for lack of definition. 会議の最初のスピーカーたちは, ジョンソン教授の新しいプログラムを明確さに欠けると批判した.

de|fini|tive /dɪfɪnɪtɪv/ ① ADJ 形容詞 Something that is **definitive** provides a firm conclusion that cannot be questioned. 最終的な □ No one has come up with a definitive answer as to why this should be so これがなぜそうなのかについて最終的な解答を見つけ出した人はまだいない. ● **de|fini|tive|ly** ADV 副詞 最終的に □ Law enforcement officials had definitively identified Blanco as a potential suspect. 捜査当局者は最終的に容疑者の可能性のある人物としてブランコを特定した. ② ADJ 形容詞 A **definitive** book or performance is thought to be the best of its kind that has ever been done or that will ever be done. 最も権威のある □ ...Ian Macdonald's definitive book on The Beatles. イアン・マクドナルドによる, ビートルズに関する本の決定版

de|flate /dɪfleɪt/ (deflates, deflating, deflated) ① V-T 他動詞 If you **deflate** someone or something, you take away their confidence or make them seem less important. (自信などを) くじく, 減ずる □ I hate to deflate your ego, but you seem to have an exaggerated idea of your importance to me. 君の自尊心をくじきたくはないが, 君は僕に対する自分の重要性について過信しているようだね. ● **de|flat|ed** ADJ 形容詞 自信をなくした □ When she refused I felt deflated. 彼女に拒否されて, 僕は自信をなくした. ② V-T/V-I 自動詞 When something such as a tire or balloon **deflates**, or when you **deflate** it, all the air comes out of it. (空気が抜けて) しぼむ □ We drove a few miles until the tire deflated and we had to stop the car. 数マイル運転したらタイヤの空気が抜けたので, 車を止めなければならなかった.

de|fla|tion /dɪfleɪʃən/ N-UNCOUNT 不可算名詞 **Deflation** is a reduction in economic activity that leads to lower levels of industrial output, employment, investment, trade, profits, and prices. デフレーション [BUSINESS 実業] □ Deflation is beginning to take hold in the clothing industry. デフレは衣料品産業に押し寄せ始めている.

de|fla|tion|ary /dɪfleɪʃənɛri/ ADJ 形容詞 A **deflationary** economic policy or measure is one that is intended to or likely to cause deflation. デフレの [BUSINESS 実業] □ ...the government's refusal to implement deflationary measures. 政府によるデフレ政策実行の拒否

de|flect /dɪflɛkt/ (deflects, deflecting, deflected) ① V-T 他動詞 If you **deflect** something such as criticism or attention, you act in a way that prevents it from being directed toward you or affecting you. かわす □ Cage changed his name to deflect accusations of nepotism. ケイジは縁故採用の非難をかわすために名前を変えた. ② V-T 他動詞 To **deflect** someone **from** a course of action means to make them decide not to continue with it by putting pressure on them or by offering them something desirable. 転向させる □ The war did not deflect him from the path he had long ago taken. 彼がずっと以前に取った道は, 戦争によってゆがめられることはなかった. ③ V-T 他動詞 If you **deflect** something that is moving, you make it go in a slightly different direction, for example, by hitting or blocking it. そらす □ My forearm deflected the first punch. 私は最初のパンチを前腕でそらした.

de|for|est /dɪfɔrɪst/ (deforests, deforesting, deforested) V-T 他動詞 If an area is **deforested**, all the trees there are cut down or destroyed. 樹木を切り払う [usu passive] □ ...the 400,000 square kilometers of the Amazon basin that have already been deforested. アマゾン盆地のすでに切り開かれた40万平方キロメートルの土地 ● **de|for|esta|tion** /dɪfɔrɪsteɪʃən/ N-UNCOUNT 不可算名詞 森林伐採 □ One percent of Brazil's total forest cover is being lost every year to deforestation. 毎年, ブラジルの全森林被膜の1パーセントが森林伐採のために失われている.
→ see greenhouse

de|form /dɪfɔrm/ (deforms, deforming, deformed) V-T/V-I 他動詞/自動詞 If something **deforms** a person's body or something else, it causes it to have an unnatural shape. In technical English, you can also say that the second thing **deforms** when it changes to an unnatural shape. 変形させる [他動詞] 変形する [自動詞] □ Bad rheumatoid arthritis deforms limbs. 関節リウマチが重症になると手足が変形する. ● **de|formed** ADJ 形容詞 変形した □ He was born with a deformed right leg. 彼は生まれつき右足が不自由だ.

de|form|ity /dɪfɔrmɪti/ (deformities) ① N-COUNT 可算名詞 A **deformity** is a part of someone's body which is not the normal shape because of injury or illness, or because they were born this way. 奇形部分, 変形部分 □ ...facial deformities in babies. 赤ちゃんに見られる顔面奇形 ② N-UNCOUNT 不可算名詞 **Deformity** is the condition of having a deformity. 奇形 □ The object of these movements is to prevent stiffness or deformity of joints. これらの動作の

目的は関節のこわばりや奇形を防ぐことである.

de|fraud /dɪfrɔd/ (**defrauds, defrauding, defrauded**) v-т 他動詞 If someone **defrauds** you, they take something away from you or stop you from getting what belongs to you by means of tricks and lies. だまし取る □ *He pleaded guilty to charges of conspiracy to defraud the government.* 彼は政府から詐取しようとした共同謀議の罪を認めた.

deft /dɛft/ (**defter, deftest**) ADJ 形容詞 A **deft** action is skillful and often quick. 器用な [WRITTEN 書き言葉] □ *With a deft flick of his wrist, he extinguished the match.* 彼は手首を巧みに振ってマッチの火を消した. ● **deft|ly** ADV 副詞 器用に □ *One of the waiting servants deftly caught him as he fell.* 侍っている使用人の1人が倒れかけた彼をすばやくとらえた.

de|funct /dɪfʌŋkt/ ADJ 形容詞 If something is **defunct**, it no longer exists or has stopped functioning or operating. 消滅した, 廃止された □ *...the leader of the now defunct Social Democratic Party.* 今ではつぶれてしまった社会民主党の指導者

de|fuse /dɪfyuz/ (**defuses, defusing, defused**) ① v-т 他動詞 If you **defuse** a dangerous or tense situation, you calm it. 緩和する □ *Police administrators credited the organization with helping defuse potentially violent situations.* 警察の幹部たちは暴動になる可能性のあった状況が緩和されたのは, その組織の力添えがあったからだと言った. ② v-т 他動詞 If someone **defuses** a bomb, they remove the fuse so that it cannot explode. (爆弾の) 信管をはずす □ *Police have defused a bomb found in a downtown building.* 警察は繁華街のビルで見つかった爆弾の信管をはずした.

defy /dɪfaɪ/ (**defies, defying, defied**) ① v-т 他動詞 If you **defy** someone or something that is trying to make you behave in a particular way, you refuse to obey them and behave in that way. 反抗する □ *This was the first (and last) time that I dared to defy my mother.* 私が母にあえて反抗したのはこれが最初で最後であった. ② v-т 他動詞 If you **defy** someone to do something, you challenge them to do it when you think that they will be unable to do it or too frightened to do it. (人に不可能なことをしろと) 挑む □ *I defy you to come up with one major accomplishment of the current president.* できるものなら現大統領の主要な業績を1つでもあげてみなさい. ③ v-т 他動詞 If something **defies** description or understanding, it is so strange, extreme, or surprising that it is almost impossible to understand or explain. (物事が説明や理解を) 許さない [no passive, no cont] □ *It's a devastating and barbaric act that defies all comprehension.* それは理解を絶する壊滅的かつ野蛮な行為だ.

de|gen|er|ate (**degenerates, degenerating, degenerated**)

The verb is pronounced /dɪdʒɛnəreɪt/. The adjective is pronounced /dɪdʒɛnərɪt/.

動詞は /dɪdʒɛnəreɪt/ と発音される. 形容詞は /dɪdʒɛnərɪt/ と発音される.

① v-ı 自動詞 If you say that someone or something **degenerates**, you mean that they become worse in some way, for example, weaker, lower in quality, or more dangerous. 悪化する □ *Inactivity can make your joints stiff, and the bones may begin to degenerate.* 活動しないと関節がこわばって, 骨が退化し始めることがある. ● **de|gen|era|tion** /dɪdʒɛnəreɪʃən/ N-UNCOUNT 不可算名詞 退化 □ *...various forms of physical and mental degeneration.* 様々な種類の肉体的および精神的退化 ② ADJ 形容詞 If you describe a person or their behavior as **degenerate**, you disapprove of them because you think they have low standards of behavior or morality. 堕落した [DISAPPROVAL 不賛成] □ *...a group of degenerate computer hackers.* 1群の堕落したコンピューターハッカーたち

deg|ra|da|tion /dɛgrədeɪʃən/ (**degradations**) ① N-VAR 可変性名詞 You use **degradation** to refer to a situation, condition, or experience which you consider shameful and disgusting, especially one which involves poverty or immorality. 退廃, 堕落 [DISAPPROVAL 不賛成] □ *They were sickened by the scenes of misery and degradation they found.* 彼らは出くわした窮乏と退廃の光景に気分が悪くなった. ② N-UNCOUNT 不可算名詞 **Degradation** is the process of something becoming worse or weaker, or being made worse or weaker. 下落 □ *...air pollution, traffic congestion, and the steady degradation of our quality of life.* 空気汚染, 交通混雑, および我々の生活の質の着実な低落

de|grade /dɪgreɪd/ (**degrades, degrading, degraded**) ① v-т 他動詞 Something that **degrades** someone causes people to have less respect for them. 品位を落とす □ *...the notion that pornography degrades women.* ポルノは女性を侮辱するものだという考え ● **de|grad|ing** ADJ 形容詞 屈辱的な □ *Mr. Porter was subjected to a degrading strip search.* ポーター氏は屈辱的な全裸での身体検査をされた. ② v-т 他動詞 To **degrade** something means to cause it to get worse. 悪化させる [FORMAL 形式ばった] □ *...the ability to meet human needs indefinitely without degrading the environment.* 環境を悪化させずに人類の要望を無期限に満たす能力

de|gree /dɪgri/ (**degrees**) ① N-COUNT 可算名詞 You use **degree**

to indicate the extent to which something happens or is the case, or the amount which something is felt. 程度 □ *These man-made barriers will ensure a very high degree of protection for several hundred years.* この人工柵は数百年にわたり非常に高いレベルの防護を保証するであろう. □ *Recent presidents have used television, as well as radio, with varying degrees of success.* 近頃の大統領はラジオだけでなくテレビも利用し, さまざまな程度の成功を収めている. ● PHRASE 句 If something has **a degree of** a particular quality, it has a small but significant amount of that quality. ある程度の ② N-COUNT 可算名詞 A **degree** is a unit of measurement that is used to measure temperatures. It is often written as °, for example, 23°. 度 (温度の単位) □ *It's over 80 degrees outside.* 外の気温は80度を超えています. ③ N-COUNT 可算名詞 A **degree** is a unit of measurement that is used to measure angles, and also longitude and latitude. It is often written as °, for example, 23°. 度 (角度・緯度・経度の単位) □ *It was pointing outward at an angle of 45 degrees.* それは外向きに45度の角度を指していた. ④ N-COUNT 可算名詞 A **degree** is a title or rank given by a university or college when you have completed a course of study there. It can also be given as an honorary title. 学位 □ *...an engineering degree.* 工学の学位 ⑤ PHRASE 句 You use expressions such as **to some degree, to a large degree**, or **to a certain degree** in order to indicate that something is partly true, but not entirely true. ある程度は, いくぶんは [VAGUENESS あいまいさ] □ *These statements are, to some degree, all correct.* これらの陳述はある程度まですべて正しい.

Word Partnership	*degree* は次の語句と使われる:
N.	degree **of certainty**, degree **of difficulty** ① **45/90** degree **angle** ③ **bachelor's/master's** degree, **college** degree, degree **program** ④
ADJ.	**high** degree ① **honorary** degree ④

Word Link	*hydr = water : dehydrate, hydraulic, hydrologic cycle*

de|hy|drate /dihaɪdreɪt/ (**dehydrates, dehydrating, dehydrated**) ① v-т 他動詞 When something such as food **is dehydrated**, all the water is removed from it, often in order to preserve it. 乾燥させる [usu passive] □ *Normally specimens have to be dehydrated.* ふつう標本にするには乾燥させなければならない. ② v-т/v-ı 他動詞/自動詞 If you **dehydrate** or if something **dehydrates** you, you lose too much water from your body so that you feel weak or ill. 脱水状態にする [他動詞], 脱水状態になる [自動詞] □ *People can dehydrate in weather like this.* このような天候では脱水症状を起こす可能性がある. ● **de|hy|dra|tion** /dihaɪdreɪʃən/ N-UNCOUNT 不可算名詞 脱水, 脱水症状 □ *...a child who's got diarrhea and is suffering from dehydration.* 下痢になり脱水症状を起こしている子供
→ see **sweat**

de|ity /diɪti/ (**deities**) N-COUNT 可算名詞 A **deity** is a god or goddess. 神, 女神 [FORMAL 形式ばった] □ *...a deity revered by thousands of Hindus and Buddhists.* 無数のヒンズー教徒や仏教徒に崇拝されている神
→ see **religion**

de|lay /dɪleɪ/ (**delays, delaying, delayed**) ① v-т/v-ı 他動詞/自動詞 If you **delay** doing something, you do not do it immediately or at the planned or expected time, but you leave it until later. 遅らせる, 延期する □ *For sentimental reasons I wanted to delay my departure until June 1980.* 感傷的な理由で私は出発を1980年6月まで遅らせたかった. □ *They had delayed having children, for the usual reason, to establish their careers.* 彼らはキャリアを築くというよくある理由のために子作りを遅らせた.

If you **cancel** or **call off** an arrangement or an appointment, you stop it from happening. □ *His failing health forced him to cancel the meeting... The European Community has threatened to call off peace talks.* If you **postpone** or **put off** an arrangement or an appointment, you make another arrangement for it to happen at a later time. □ *Elections have been postponed until next year... The senate put off a vote on the nomination for one week.* If you **delay** something that has been arranged, you make it happen later than planned. □ *Space agency managers decided to delay the launch of the space shuttle.* If something **delays** you or **holds** you **up**, you start or finish what you are doing later than you planned. □ *He was delayed in traffic... Delivery of equipment had been held up by delays and disputes.*

② v-т 他動詞 To **delay** someone or something means to make them late or to slow them down. 遅らせる □ *Can you delay him in some way?* 何とかして彼を遅らせることができませんか. □ *Various setbacks and problems delayed production.* さまざまな障害や問題のために生産が遅れた. ③ v-ı 自動詞 If you **delay**, you deliberately take longer than necessary to do something. ぐずぐずする □ *If he delayed any longer, the sun would be up.* 彼があと少しでも手間取ったら, 太陽が昇るよ. ④ N-VAR 可変性名詞 If there is a **delay**,

something does not happen until later than planned or expected. 遅延 ❏ *They claimed that such a delay wouldn't hurt anyone.* 彼らはその ような遅延は誰にも差し障りないだろうと主張した. **5** N-UNCOUNT 不可算名詞 **Delay** is a failure to do something immediately or in the required or usual time. 遅れ ❏ *We'll send you a quote without delay.* すぐに見積もりを送ります.

de|lay|er|ing /diːleɪərɪŋ/ N-UNCOUNT 不可算名詞 **Delayering** is the process of simplifying the administrative structure of a large organization in order to make it more efficient. 管理階層削減, ディ レイアリング [BUSINESS 実業] ❏ *...downsizing, delayering, and other cost cutting measures.* 人員削減, 管理階層削減, またその他の経費削 減対策

del|egate (delegates, delegating, delegated)

> The noun is pronounced /delɪgɪt/. The verb is pronounced / delɪgeɪt/.
>
> 名詞は /delɪgɪt/ と発音される. 動詞は /delɪgeɪt/ と発音される.

1 N-COUNT 可算名詞 A **delegate** is a person who is chosen to vote or make decisions on behalf of a group of other people, especially at a conference or a meeting. 代表 ❏ *The Canadian delegate offered no reply.* カナダ代表は返答しなかった. **2** V-T/V-I 他動詞/自動詞 If you **delegate** duties, responsibilities, or power **to** someone, you give them those duties, those responsibilities, or that power so that they can act on your behalf. 委任する ❏ *He talks of traveling less, and delegating more authority to his deputies.* 彼は出張を減らし, 彼の代理にさらに権限を譲ることを口にしている. ● **del|ega|tion** N-UNCOUNT 不可算名詞 委任 ❏ *A key factor in running a business is the delegation of responsibility.* 事業経営のかぎとなる要素は責任の 委譲だ. **3** V-T 他動詞 [usu passive] If you **are delegated to** do something, you are given the duty of acting on someone else's behalf by making decisions, voting, or doing some particular work. 委任する ❏ *Officials have now been delegated to start work on a draft settlement.* 官僚たちは今解決案の草案に取り掛かるよう委任さ れました.

del|ega|tion /delɪgeɪʃən/ (delegations) **1** N-COUNT 可算名詞 A **delegation** is a group of people who have been sent somewhere to have talks with other people on behalf of a larger group of people. 代表団 ❏ *...the Chinese delegation to the UN talks in New York.* ニューヨ ーク市での国連会議に派遣された中国代表団 **2** → see also **delegate**

de|lete /diːliːt/ (deletes, deleting, deleted) V-T 他動詞 If you **delete** something that has been written down or stored in a computer, you cross it out or remove it. 削除する, 消去する ❏ *He also deleted files from the computer system.* 彼はコンピュータシステム からファイル削除もした.

deli /deli/ (delis) N-COUNT 可算名詞 A **deli** is a **delicatessen**. デ リカテッセンの略語

de|lib|er|ate (deliberates, deliberating, deliberated)

> The adjective is pronounced /dɪlɪbərɪt/. The verb is pronounced /dɪlɪbəreɪt/.
>
> 形容詞は /dɪlɪbərɪt/ と発音される. 動詞は /dɪlɪbəreɪt/ と発音さ れる.

1 ADJ 形容詞 If you do something that is **deliberate**, you planned or decided to do it beforehand, and so it happens on purpose rather than by chance. 意図的な, 計画的な ❏ *Witnesses say the firing was deliberate and sustained.* 目撃者の証言では発砲は意図的で連続的 だった. ● **de|lib|er|ate|ly** ADV 副詞 わざと, 意図的に ❏ *It looks as if the blaze was started deliberately.* その火災は意図的な放火のようで す. **2** ADJ 形容詞 If a movement or action is **deliberate**, it is done slowly and carefully. 慎重な ❏ *...stepping with deliberate slowness up the steep paths.* 急な上り坂を慎重な足取りで上って ● **de|lib|er|ate|ly** ADV 副詞 [ADV after v] 慎重に ❏ *The Japanese have acted calmly and deliberately.* 日本人は落ち着いて慎重に行動した. **3** V-T/V-I 他動詞/ 自動詞 If you **deliberate**, you think about something carefully, especially before making a very important decision. 熟考する ❏ *She deliberated over the decision for a good few years before she finally made up her mind.* 彼女は最終的に決心するまでにたっぷり数年その 決断について熟慮した. → see **trial**

de|lib|era|tion /dɪlɪbəreɪʃən/ (deliberations) **1** N-UNCOUNT 不 可算名詞 **Deliberation** is the long and careful consideration of a subject. 熟慮 ❏ *In this house nothing is there by chance: it is always the result of great deliberation.* この家の中にはたまたま置かれているものは

ない. 全てが大検討の結果だ. **2** N-PLURAL 複数名詞 **Deliberations** are formal discussions where an issue is considered carefully. 審 議 ❏ *Their deliberations were rather inconclusive.* その審議は十分に結論 に到達しなかった.

deli|ca|cy /delɪkəsi/ (delicacies) **1** N-UNCOUNT 不可算名詞 **Delicacy** is the quality of being easy to break or harm, and refers especially to people or things that are attractive or graceful. 繊細 さ ❏ *...the delicacy of a rose.* バラの繊細な美しさ **2** N-UNCOUNT 不可 算名詞 If you say that a situation or problem is of **some delicacy**, you mean that it is difficult to handle and needs careful and sensitive treatment. 扱いにくさ, デリケートさ ❏ *There was a matter of some delicacy on which he would be grateful for her advice.* 彼が彼女に アドバイスを求めたいような多少微妙な問題があった. **3** N-UNCOUNT 不可算名詞 If someone handles a difficult situation **with delicacy**, they handle it very carefully, making sure that nobody is offended. 慎重さ ❏ *Both countries are behaving with rare delicacy.* 両国はまれなほど慎重にふるまっている. **4** N-COUNT 可算名詞 A **delicacy** is a rare or expensive food that is considered especially nice to eat. 珍味 ❏ *Smoked salmon was considered an expensive delicacy.* 燻製(くんせい)のサケは高価な珍味とみなされていた.

deli|cate /delɪkɪt/ **1** ADJ 形容詞 Something that is **delicate** is small and beautifully shaped. きゃしゃな ❏ *He had delicate hands.* 彼はきゃしゃな手をしていた. ● **deli|cate|ly** ADV 副詞 [ADV adj/-ed] きゃしゃに ❏ *She was a shy, delicately pretty girl with enormous blue eyes.* 彼女は大変大きな青い目をした恥ずかしがり屋できゃしゃなかわ いい女の子でした. **2** ADJ 形容詞 Something that is **delicate** has a color, taste, or smell which is pleasant and not strong or intense. (色合いが)柔らかい, (味が)あっさりしておいしい, (香りが)ほ のかな ❏ *Young haricot beans have a tender texture and a delicate, subtle flavor.* 若いインゲン豆は歯ごたえが柔らかく, あっさりとした微妙な 味がする. ● **deli|cate|ly** ADV 副詞 [ADV -ed/adj] ほのかに ❏ *...a soup delicately flavored with nutmeg.* ほのかにナツメグの風味がある スープ **3** ADJ 形容詞 If something is **delicate**, it is easy to harm, damage, or break, and needs to be handled or treated carefully. 壊 れやすい, 繊細な ❏ *Although the coral looks hard, it is very delicate.* さ んごは硬く見えるが, とてももろい. **4** ADJ 形容詞 Someone who is **delicate** is not healthy and strong, and becomes ill easily. 虚 弱な ❏ *She was physically delicate and psychologically unstable.* 彼女は 体が弱く, 精神的に不安定だった. **5** ADJ 形容詞 You use **delicate** to describe a situation, problem, matter, or discussion that needs to be dealt with carefully and sensitively in order to avoid upsetting things or offending people. 慎重を要する, (状況・ 問題・論議などが)デリケートな ❏ *Ottawa and Washington have to find a delicate balance between the free flow of commerce and legitimate security concerns.* カナダと米国の両政府は自由な商取引と合法的な 安全保障問題の間の微妙なバランスをとらなければならなません. ● **deli|cate|ly** ADV 副詞 [ADV with v] 慎重に, 微妙に ❏ *Clearly, the situation remains delicately poised.* 明らかに, 状況はまだ予断を許さ ない状態だ. **6** ADJ 形容詞 A **delicate** task, movement, action, or product needs or shows great skill and attention to detail. ちみ つな, 精巧な ❏ *...a long and delicate operation carried out at a hospital in Pittsburgh.* ピッツバーグ市内の病院で行われた長時間にわたるち みつな手術 ● **deli|cate|ly** ADV 副詞 [ADV with v] ちみつに, 精巧に ❏ *...the delicately embroidered sheets.* 精巧な刺しゅう入りのシーツ

deli|ca|tes|sen /delɪkətesⁿn/ (delicatessens) N-COUNT 可算 名詞 A **delicatessen** is a store that sells cold cuts, cheeses, salads, and often a selection of imported foods. デリカテッセン

de|li|cious /dɪlɪʃəs/ ADJ 形容詞 Food that is **delicious** has a very pleasant taste. とてもおいしい ❏ *There's always a wide selection of delicious meals to choose from.* いつもおいしい料理の豊富なメニューが あって選ぶにはうれしい. ● **de|li|cious|ly** ADV 副詞 [ADV adj/-ed] お いしく ❏ *This yogurt has a deliciously creamy flavor.* このヨーグルトは とてもクリームのような風味がする.

de|light /dɪlaɪt/ (delights, delighting, delighted) **1** N-UNCOUNT 不可算名詞 **Delight** is a feeling of very great pleasure. 大喜び ❏ *Throughout the house, the views are a constant source of surprise and delight.* 家中のどこからでも見える景色が次 々と驚きと歓喜をもたらす. ❏ *Andrew roared with delight when he heard Rachel's nickname for the baby.* アンドリューは, レイチェルが 赤ちゃんにつけた愛称を聞いたとき, うれしさのあまり大声を出し た. **2** PHRASE 句 If someone **takes delight** or **takes a delight in** something, they get a lot of pleasure from it. 一に喜びを感じる ❏ *Haig took obvious delight in proving his critics wrong.* ヘイグは彼の批 判者たちが間違っていると証明できて明らかに喜んだ. **3** N-COUNT 可算名詞 You can refer to someone or something that gives you great pleasure or enjoyment as a **delight**. 楽しみ [APPROVAL 賛成] ❏ *The aircraft was a delight to fly.* その飛行機の操縦はとても楽しかっ た. **4** V-T 他動詞 If something **delights** you, it gives you a lot of pleasure. 大いに楽しませる ❏ *She has created a style of music that has delighted audiences all over the world.* 彼女は世界中の聴衆を大いに楽し

ませている音楽のスタイルを創り出した.

de|light|ed /dɪlaɪtɪd/ ① ADJ 形容詞 If you are **delighted**, you are extremely pleased and excited about something. とてもうれしい ❑ *I know Frank will be delighted to see you.* 私はフランクがあなたに会えると大喜びすることを知っている. ● **de|light|ed|ly** ADV 副詞 [ADV with v] 大喜びして ❑ *"There!" Jackson exclaimed delightedly.* 「よしよし！」とジャクソンは大喜びして叫んだ. ② ADJ 形容詞 If someone invites or asks you to do something, you can say that you would be **delighted** to do it, as a way of showing that you are very willing to do it. 喜んで～します [FEELINGS 感情] ❑ *"You have to come to Todd's graduation party." — "I'd be delighted."* 「ぜひトッドの卒業パーティに来てください」「喜んで伺います」

de|light|ful /dɪlaɪtfəl/ ADJ 形容詞 If you describe something or someone as **delightful**, you mean they are very pleasant. 愉快な, 素晴らしい ❑ *It was the most delightful garden I had ever seen.* 私が今までに見た中で最も素晴らしい庭でした. ● **de|light|ful|ly** ADV 副詞 [ADV adj/-ed] とても, 素晴らしく ❑ *This delightfully refreshing cologne can be splashed on liberally.* この素晴らしくさっぱりしたオーデコロンはたっぷり振りかけてもいい.

de|lin|quen|cy /dɪlɪŋkwənsi/ (**delinquencies**) N-UNCOUNT 不可算名詞 **Delinquency** is criminal behavior, especially that of young people. 犯罪, 非行 ❑ *He had no history of delinquency.* 彼には非行の経歴がありませんでした.

de|lin|quent /dɪlɪŋkwənt/ (**delinquents**) ① ADJ 形容詞 Someone, usually a young person, who is **delinquent** repeatedly commits minor crimes. 非行の, 非行に走った ❑ *...homes for delinquent children.* 非行児童のための矯正施設 ● N-COUNT 可算名詞 **Delinquent** is also a noun. 非行少年 ❑ *...a nine-year-old delinquent.* 9歳の非行少年 ② ADJ 形容詞 A **delinquent** borrower or taxpayer is someone who has failed to pay their debts or taxes. 滞納している [AM 米国英語] ❑ *...a legal shortcut to take homes from delinquent borrowers.* 債務不履行の借り手から自宅を取り上げる法的な近道

de|liri|ous /dɪlɪəriəs/ ① ADJ 形容詞 Someone who is **delirious** is unable to think or speak in a sensible and reasonable way, usually because they are very ill and have a fever. 精神の錯乱した, うわごとを言う ❑ *I was delirious and blacked out several times.* 私はうわごとを言い, 何度か失神した. ② ADJ 形容詞 Someone who is **delirious** is extremely excited and happy. 有頂天になった ❑ *A raucous crowd of 25,000 delirious fans greeted the team at Grand Central Station.* 熱狂した2万5千人のファンが群がって大騒ぎしながらグランドセントラル駅でチームを迎えた. ● **de|liri|ous|ly** ADV 副詞 有頂天になって ❑ *Dora returned from her honeymoon deliriously happy.* ドーラは最高に幸せそうに新婚旅行から帰ってきた.

de|list /dɪlɪst/ (**delists, delisting, delisted**) V-T 他動詞 If a company **delists** or if its shares **are delisted**, its shares are removed from the official list of shares that can be traded on the stock market. 上場廃止にする [BUSINESS 実業] ❑ *The company's stock was delisted from the Nasdaq market in July 2000.* その会社の株はナズダック市場から2000年7月に上場廃止になった.

de|liv|er /dɪlɪvər/ (**delivers, delivering, delivered**) ① V-T 他動詞 If you **deliver** something somewhere, you take it there. 配達する ❑ *The Canadians plan to deliver more food to southern Somalia.* カナダ政府はソマリア南部への食料の配送を増やすことを計画しています. ② V-T/V-I 他動詞/自動詞 If you **deliver** something that you have promised to do, make, or produce, you do, make, or produce it. やり遂げる, 果たす ❑ *They have yet to show that they can really deliver working technologies.* 彼らはさらに実際に実用的な技術を達成できることを示さなければならない. ❑ *The question is, can he deliver?* 問題は, 彼がやり遂げられるかということです. ③ V-T 他動詞 If you **deliver** a lecture or speech, you give it in public. (講義・スピーチを) する [FORMAL 形式ばった] ❑ *The president will deliver a speech about schools.* 大統領が学校についての演説をする予定です. ④ V-T 他動詞 When someone **delivers** a baby, they help the woman who is giving birth to the baby. (赤ん坊を) 取り上げる ❑ *Although we'd planned to have our baby at home, we never expected to deliver her ourselves!* 自宅出産を計画していたのもの自分たちで赤ちゃんを取り上げることになるとは予想もしなかった. ⑤ V-T 他動詞 If someone **delivers** a blow to someone else, they hit them. (打撃を) 与える [WRITTEN 書き言葉] ❑ *Those blows to the head could have been delivered by a woman.* この頭部への打撃は女性によって与えられたものかもしれない.

Thesaurus   *deliver* また次を参照:

V.	bring, give, hand over, transfer; (ant.) hold, keep, retain ①

Word Partnership   *deliver* は次の語句と使われる:

N.	deliver **a letter**, deliver **mail**, deliver **a message**, deliver **news**, deliver **a package** ① deliver **a service** ② deliver **a lecture**, deliver **a speech** ③ deliver **a baby** ④ deliver **a blow** ⑤

de|liv|ery /dɪlɪvəri/ (**deliveries**) ① N-VAR 可変名詞 **Delivery** or a **delivery** is the bringing of letters, packages, or other goods to someone's house or to another place where they want them. 配達 ❑ *Please allow 28 days for delivery.* 配達には28日かかります. ❑ *The uprising is threatening the delivery of humanitarian supplies of food and medicine.* その暴動は食料・薬品などの人道的救援物資の配送を脅かしています. ② N-VAR 可変名詞 **Delivery** is the process of giving birth to a baby. 出産, 分娩 ❑ *In the end, it was an easy delivery: a fine baby boy.* 結果的には安産だった. 元気な男の子だ. ③ N-COUNT 可算名詞 A **delivery** of something is the goods that are delivered. 配達 (の品物) ❑ *I got a delivery of fresh eggs this morning.* 今朝私に新鮮な卵の配達があった. ④ ADJ 形容詞 A **delivery** person or service delivers things to a place. 配達の [ADJ n] ❑ *...a pizza delivery man.* ピザ配達員 ⑤ N-UNCOUNT 不可算名詞 You talk about someone's **delivery** when you are referring to the way in which they give a speech or lecture. 演説・講義のしかた ❑ *His speeches were magnificently written but his delivery was hopeless.* 彼の演説は見事に書かれていたが, 演説のしかたはひどかった.

de|liv|ery charge (**delivery charges**) N-COUNT 可算名詞 A **delivery charge** is the cost of transporting or delivering goods. 配送料 [AM 米国英語, FORMAL 形式ばった] ❑ *Buyers need to check if delivery charges are included in the price.* 同様に, 購入者は配送料が価格に含まれているかを確認する必要がある.

del|ta /dɛltə/ (**deltas**) N-COUNT 可算名詞 A **delta** is an area of low, flat land shaped like a triangle, where a river splits and spreads out into several branches before entering the sea. 三角州, デルタ地帯 ❑ *...the Mississippi delta.* ミシシッピ河のデルタ地帯 → see **river**

de|lude /dɪlud/ (**deludes, deluding, deluded**) ① V-T 他動詞 If you **delude yourself**, you let yourself believe that something is true, even though it is not true. 思い込ませる ❑ *The president was deluding himself if he thought he was safe from such action.* 大統領がそのような行動から自分は安全だと思っていたのなら, 思い違いをしていたことになります. ❑ *We delude ourselves that we are in control.* 我々は自分たちが支配権を握っていると思い込んでいる. ② V-T 他動詞 To **delude** someone **into** thinking something means to make them believe what is not true. だます, (真実でないことを) 信じ込ませる ❑ *Television deludes you into thinking you have experienced reality, when you haven't.* テレビを見ることで, 実際には体験していないのにあたかも体験したかのように勘違いすることがあります.

del|uge /dɛlyudʒ/ (**deluges, deluging, deluged**) ① N-COUNT 可算名詞 A **deluge of** things is a large number of them which arrive or happen at the same time. 殺到 ❑ *There was a deluge of requests for interviews and statements.* 会見や声明を求める要求が殺到した. ② V-T 他動詞 If a place or person **is deluged with** things, a large number of them arrive or happen at the same time. 殺到させる [usu passive] ❑ *During 1933, Papen's office was deluged with complaints.* 1933年の間じゅうパーペンの事務所には苦情が殺到した.

de|lu|sion /dɪluʒ³n/ (**delusions**) ① N-COUNT 可算名詞 A **delusion** is a false idea. 錯覚, 思い違い ❑ *I was under the delusion that he intended to marry me.* 私は彼が私と結婚する気でいると勘違いしていた. ② N-UNCOUNT 不可算名詞 **Delusion** is the state of believing things that are not true. 妄想 ❑ *Insinuations about her mental state, about her capacity for delusion, were being made.* 彼女の精神状態, つまり妄想能力がほのめかされていました.

deluxe /dɪlʌks/ ADJ 形容詞 **Deluxe** goods or services are better in quality and more expensive than ordinary ones. 高級な, デラックスな [ADJ n, n ADJ] ❑ *...a rare, highly prized deluxe wine.* 珍しくて評価の高い高級ワイン

delve /dɛlv/ (**delves, delving, delved**) V-I 自動詞 If you **delve into** something, you try to discover new information about it. 探求する ❑ *Tormented by her ignorance, Jenny delves into her mother's past.* 自分の無知にさいなまれ, ジェニーは母の過去をせんさくする.

de|mand /dɪmænd/ (**demands, demanding, demanded**) ① V-T 他動詞 If you **demand** something such as information or action, you ask for it in a very forceful way. 要求する ❑ *Human rights groups are demanding an investigation into the shooting.* 人権擁護団体がその襲撃事件の調査を要求しています. ❑ *Russia demanded that UNITA send a delegation to the peace talks.* ロシアはアンゴラ全面独立民族同盟が和平交渉に代表団を送ることを要求した. ② V-T 他動詞 If one thing **demands** another, the first needs the second in order to happen or be dealt with successfully. 要する ❑ *He said the task of reconstruction would demand much patience, hard work, and sacrifice.* 復興作業にはかなりの忍耐力, 大変な努力そして犠牲を要

すると彼は言いました. ❸ N-COUNT 可算名詞 A **demand** is a firm request for something. 要求 □ *There have been demands for services from tenants up there.* あそこの間借り人たちから修理を求める要求が出ています. ❹ N-UNCOUNT 不可算名詞 If you refer to **demand**, or to the **demand for** something, you are referring to how many people want to have it, do it, or buy it. 需要 □ *Another flight would be arranged on Saturday if sufficient demand arose.* 十分な需要があれば, 土曜日にもう1便手配されます. ❺ N-PLURAL 複数名詞 The **demands** of something or its **demands** on you are the things which it needs or the things which you have to do for it. 負担 □ *...the demands and challenges of a new job.* 新しい仕事の負担とやりが い ❻ PHRASE 句 If someone or something is **in demand** or **in great demand**, they are very popular and a lot of people want them. 需要が(大いに)あって □ *He was much in demand as a lecturer in the U.S., as well as at universities all over Europe.* 彼は講演者としてヨーロッパ中の大学だけでなく米国でも引っ張りだこだった. ❼ PHRASE 句 If something is available or happens **on demand**, you can have it or it happens whenever you want it or ask for it. 要求に応じて □ *...a new entertainment system that offers 25 movies on demand.* 要求に応じて映画を25本提供する新しい娯楽システム
→ see **economics**

| **Thesaurus** | *demand* また次を参照: |

V.	command, insist on, order; (ant.) give, grant, offer ❶
	necessitate, need, require; (ant.) give, supply ❷

de|mand|ing /dɪmǽndɪŋ/ ❶ ADJ 形容詞 A **demanding** job or task requires a lot of your time, energy, or attention. 負担が大きい □ *He tried to return to work, but found he could no longer cope with his demanding job.* 彼は仕事に復帰しようとしたが, もはや自分のきつい仕事に耐えられないことに気づいた. ❷ ADJ 形容詞 People who are **demanding** are not easily satisfied or pleased. 要求の厳しい □ *Ricky was a very demanding child.* リッキーはとても手がかかる子供だ.

de|mean /dɪmíːn/ (**demeans, demeaning, demeaned**) V-T 他動詞 To **demean** someone or something means to make people have less respect for them. 品位を落とす □ *Some groups say that pornography demeans women and incites rape.* ポルノは女性の品位を傷つけレイプをあおると言っている団体もある.

de|mean|ing /dɪmíːnɪŋ/ ADJ 形容詞 Something that is **demeaning** makes people have less respect for the person who is treated in that way, or who does that thing. 屈辱的な □ *...making demeaning sexist comments.* 屈辱的な性差別発言をして

de|mean|or /dɪmíːnər/ N-UNCOUNT 不可算名詞 Your **demeanor** is the way you behave, which gives people an impression of your character and feelings. ふるまい, 品行 [FORMAL 形式ばった] □ *...her calm and cheerful demeanor.* 彼女の落ち着いて朗らかな態度

Word Link	ment ≈ mind : de**ment**ia, **ment**al, **ment**ality

de|men|tia /dɪmɛ́nʃə/ (**dementias**) N-VAR 可変性名詞 **Dementia** is a serious illness of the mind. 認知症, 痴呆 [MEDICAL 医学の] □ *...a treatment for mental conditions such as dementia and Alzheimer's disease.* 認知症やアルツハイマー病などの精神状態に対する治療

Word Link	milit ≈ soldier : de**milit**arize, **milit**ary, **milit**ia

de|mili|ta|rize /dɪmílɪtəraɪz/ (**demilitarizes, demilitarizing, demilitarized**) V-T 他動詞 To **demilitarize** an area means to ensure that all military forces are removed from it. 非武装化する □ *He said the UN had made remarkable progress in demilitarizing the region.* 国連はその地域の非武装化を目覚ましく進展させたと彼は述べた.

de|mise /dɪmáɪz/ N-SING 単数名詞 The **demise** of something or someone is their end or death. 終焉(しゅうえん) [FORMAL 形式ばった] □ *...the demise of the reform movement.* 改革運動の終焉(しゅうえん)

demo /dɛ́moʊ/ (**demos**) ❶ N-COUNT 可算名詞 A **demo** is a CD or tape with a sample of someone's music recorded on it. 試聴盤, 試聴用テープ [INFORMAL くだけた] □ *He arranged for Reba to record her first demo tape.* 彼はリーバが最初の試聴用テープに吹き込むように手配した. ❷ N-COUNT 可算名詞 A **demo** is a demonstration of something. 実演販売, デモ版 [INFORMAL くだけた] □ *Download free demos of our newest products and upgrades.* 当社の最新製品とアップグレード用の無料デモ版をダウンロードしよう.

de|mo|bi|lize /dɪmóʊbɪlaɪz/ (**demobilizes, demobilizing, demobilized**) V-T/V-I 他動詞/自動詞 If a country or armed force **demobilizes** its troops, or if its troops **demobilize**, its troops are released from service and allowed to go home. (部隊の)動員を解く [他動詞], 解散する [自動詞] □ *Dos Santos has demanded that UNITA sign a cease-fire and demobilize its troops.* ドスサントス大統領は, アンゴラ全面独立民族同盟が停戦命令に署名してその部隊を解除することを要求しました. ●**de|mo|bi|li|za|tion** /dɪmóʊbɪlɪzeɪʃən/ N-UNCOUNT 不可算名詞 動員解除, 部隊の解散 □ *The government had*

previously been opposed to the demobilization of its 100,000 strong army. 政府は以前は10万人の兵士を有する軍隊の動員解除に反対していた.

Word Link	cracy ≈ rule by : aristo**cracy**, bureau**cracy**, demo**cracy**

Word Link	demo ≈ people : **demo**cracy, **demo**graphic, un**demo**cratic

de|moc|ra|cy /dɪmɑ́krəsi/ (**democracies**) ❶ N-UNCOUNT 不可算名詞 **Democracy** is a system of government in which people choose their rulers by voting for them in elections. 民主主義 □ *The spread of democracy in Eastern Europe appears to have had negative as well as positive consequences.* 東ヨーロッパにおける民主主義の拡大は, 肯定的な結果だけでなく否定的な結果も招いたようです. ❷ N-COUNT 可算名詞 A **democracy** is a country in which the people choose their government by voting for it. 民主主義国家 □ *The new democracies face tough challenges.* 新しい民主主義国家は厳しい難題に直面しています.
→ see **vote**

Word Link	crat ≈ power : aristo**crat**, bureau**crat**, demo**crat**

demo|crat /dɛ́məkræt/ (**democrats**) ❶ N-COUNT 可算名詞 A **Democrat** is a member or supporter of a particular political party which has the word "democrat" or "democratic" in its title, for example, the Democratic Party in the United States. 民主党員, 民主党支持者 □ *Murray has joined other Senate Democrats in blocking the legislation.* マレーはその立法を妨げるために他の民主党上院議員に加わった. ❷ N-COUNT 可算名詞 A **democrat** is a person who believes in the ideals of democracy, personal freedom, and equality. 民主主義者 □ *This is the time for democrats and not dictators.* 現在は独裁者ではなく民主主義者の時代です.

demo|crat|ic /dɛ̀məkrǽtɪk/ ❶ ADJ 形容詞 A **democratic** country, government, or political system is governed by representatives who are elected by the people. 民主主義の □ *Bolivia returned to democratic rule in 1982, after a series of military governments.* ボリビアは一連の軍事政権のあと, 1982年に民主政治に戻った. ●**demo|crati|cal|ly** /dɛ̀məkrǽtɪkli/ ADV 副詞 民主的に □ *That June, Yeltsin became Russia's first democratically elected president.* その6月にエルツィンがロシア初の民主的に選ばれた大統領となった. ❷ ADJ 形容詞 Something that is **democratic** is based on the idea that everyone should have equal rights and should be involved in making important decisions. 民主的な □ *Education is the basis of a democratic society.* 教育は民主的社会の基本だ. ●**demo|crati|cal|ly** ADV 副詞 民主的に □ *This committee will enable decisions to be made democratically.* この委員会は民主的に決定を下すことができるだろう.

Word Link	demo ≈ people : **demo**cracy, **demo**graphic, un**demo**cratic

de|mo|graph|ic /dɛ̀məɡrǽfɪk/ (**demographics**) ❶ N-PLURAL 複数名詞 The **demographics** of a place or society are the statistics relating to the people who live there. 人口統計 □ *...the changing demographics of the United States.* アメリカ合衆国の人口統計の変化 ❷ N-SING 単数名詞 In business, a **demographic** is a group of people in a society, especially people in a particular age group. 年齢層 [BUSINESS 実業] □ *The station has won more listeners in the 25-39 demographic.* その放送局は25〜39歳の年齢層の視聴率上昇に成功した.

de|mol|ish /dɪmɑ́lɪʃ/ (**demolishes, demolishing, demolished**) ❶ V-T 他動詞 To **demolish** something such as a building means to destroy it completely. 破壊する □ *A storm moved directly over the island, demolishing buildings and flooding streets.* 嵐がその島を直撃し, 建物が破壊され市街は洪水に襲われました. ❷ V-T 他動詞 If you **demolish** someone's ideas or arguments, you prove that they are completely wrong or unreasonable. くつがえす □ *Our intention was quite the opposite – to demolish rumors that have surrounded him since he took office.* 我々の意図は全く逆で, 彼が就任してから彼にまつわるうわさを一掃することだった.

demo|li|tion /dɛ̀məlíʃən/ (**demolitions**) N-VAR 可変性名詞 The **demolition** of a structure, for example, a building, is the act of deliberately destroying it, often in order to build something else in its place. (建物などの)取り壊し, 解体 □ *The project required the total demolition of the old bridge.* その計画はその古い橋の全面取り壊しを必要とした.

de|mon /díːmən/ (**demons**) also **daemon** ❶ N-COUNT 可算名詞 A **demon** is an evil spirit. 悪霊, 悪鬼 □ *...a woman possessed by demons.* 悪鬼に取りつかれた女性 ❷ N-COUNT 可算名詞 If you approve of someone because they are very skilled at what they do or because they do it energetically, you can say that they do it like a **demon**. 達人, 〜の鬼 [APPROVAL 賛成] □ *She worked like a demon and expected everybody else to do the same.* 彼女は仕事の鬼となって働き, ほかの人も同様に働くことを求めた. □ *He is a demon organizer.* 彼は組織作りの天才だ.

de|mon|ic /dɪmɒnɪk/ ADJ 形容詞 **Demonic** means coming from or belonging to a demon or being like a demon. 悪霊の, 悪魔のような 口 *a demonic grin.* 悪魔のような笑み

dem|on|strate /dɛmənstreɪt/ (**demonstrates, demonstrating, demonstrated**) ■ V-T 他動詞 To **demonstrate** a fact means to make it clear to people. 証明する 口 *The study also demonstrated a direct link between obesity and mortality.* その研究は肥満と死亡率の直接的な関連も証明した. 口 *They are anxious to demonstrate to the voters that they have practical policies.* 彼らは有権者に現実的な政策があることを証明することを切望している. ☑ V-T 他動詞 If you **demonstrate** a particular skill, quality, or feeling, you show by your actions that you have it. 示す 口 *Have they, for example, demonstrated a commitment to democracy?* 彼らは例えば, 民主主義への献身を行動で示したか. ☑ V-I 自動詞 When people **demonstrate**, they march or gather somewhere to show their opposition to something or their support for something. デモを行う 口 *Some 30,000 angry farmers arrived in Brussels yesterday to demonstrate against possible cuts in subsidies.* 約3万人の怒りに満ちた農民が昨日ブリュッセル市に到着し, 予想される補助金削減反対のデモを行った. 口 *In the cities vast crowds have been demonstrating for change.* 都市では大勢の群衆が変化を求めてデモを行っている. ☑ V-T 他動詞 If you **demonstrate** something, you show people how it works or how to do it. 実演する 口 *A selection of cosmetic companies will be there to demonstrate their new products.* えり抜きの化粧品会社がそこに出店して新製品の実演をすることになっている.

Thesaurus	*demonstrate* また次を参照:
v.	describe, illustrate, prove, show ■ ☑
	march, picket, protest ☑

dem|on|stra|tion /dɛmənstreɪʃ(ə)n/ (**demonstrations**) ■ N-COUNT 可算名詞 A **demonstration** is a march or gathering which people take part in to show their opposition to something or their support for something. デモ行進, デモ集会 口 *Riot police used tear gas to break up the demonstration.* 機動隊がデモを解散させるために催涙ガスを使用しました. ☑ N-COUNT 可算名詞 A **demonstration** of something is a talk by someone which shows you how to do it or how it works. 実演, デモンストレーション 口 *...a cooking demonstration.* 料理の実演 ☑ N-COUNT 可算名詞 A **demonstration** of a fact or situation is a clear proof of it. 実証するもの 口 *It was an unprecedented demonstration of people power by the citizens of Moscow.* それはモスクワ市民による民衆の力を実証する空前の出来事だった. ☑ N-COUNT 可算名詞 A **demonstration** of a quality or feeling is an expression of it. 表明, 表現 口 *There's been no public demonstration of opposition to the president.* 大統領に対して一般からの反対表明は出ておりません.

de|mon|stra|tor /dɛmənstreɪtər/ (**demonstrators**) ■ N-COUNT 可算名詞 **Demonstrators** are people who are marching or gathering somewhere to show their opposition to something or their support for something. デモの参加者 口 *I saw the police using tear gas to try and break up a crowd of demonstrators.* 私は警察が1群のデモ隊を解散させようとして催涙ガスを使っているのを見ました. ☑ N-COUNT 可算名詞 A **demonstrator** is a person who shows people how something works or how to do something. デモンストレーター, 実演する人 口 *...a demonstrator in a department store.* 百貨店のデモンストレーター

de|mor|al|ize /dɪmɒrəlaɪz/ (**demoralizes, demoralizing, demoralized**) V-T 他動詞 If something **demoralizes** someone, it makes them lose so much confidence in what they are doing that they want to give up. やる気を喪失させる 口 *Clearly, one of the objectives is to demoralize the enemy troops in any way they can.* 明らかに, その目標の1つはいかなる方法であっても敵軍の士気を低下させることだ. ● **de|mor|al|ized** ADJ 形容詞 やる気をなくした 口 *The Bismarck could now move only at a crawl and her crew were exhausted, hopeless, and utterly demoralized.* ビスマルクはもはやのろのろとしか進むことができず, 乗組員は疲れ果て, 絶望し, 完全に意気消沈していた.

de|mor|al|iz|ing /dɪmɒrəlaɪzɪŋ/ ADJ 形容詞 If something is **demoralizing**, it makes you lose so much confidence in what you are doing that you want to give up. 自信をなくすような 口 *Losing their star player was another demoralizing blow for the team.* 花形選手を失うことは, チームにとってしても士気を下げるような打撃った.

de|mote /dɪmoʊt/ (**demotes, demoting, demoted**) V-T 他動詞 If someone **demotes** you, they give you a lower rank or a less important position than you already have, often as a punishment. 降格する 口 *It's very difficult to demote somebody who has been filling in during maternity leave.* 産休の代理を務めてきた者を降格するのは大変難しい. ● **de|mo|tion** /dɪmoʊʃ(ə)n/ (**demotions**) N-VAR 可変性名詞 降格 口 *He is seeking redress for what he alleges was an unfair demotion.* 彼は降格が不当であると主張し是正を求めている.

de|mu|tu|al|ize /dɪmjuːtʃuəlaɪz/ (**demutualizes, demutualizing, demutualized**) V-I 自動詞 If a savings and loan association or an insurance company **demutualizes**, it abandons its mutual status and becomes a different kind of company. (相互会社を) 株式会社に変更する [BUSINESS 実業] 口 *The group won the support of 97 percent of its members for plans to demutualize.* その団体は株式会社への移行計画に対して会員の97%の支持を獲得した. ● **de|mu|tu|al|iza|tion** /dɪmjuːtʃuəlɪzeɪʃ(ə)n/ 不可算名詞 非相互会社化, 株式会社化 口 *The 503,000 policyholders who voted for demutualization should be represented.* 株式会社化に賛成票を入れた50万3千人の保険契約者は代表が参加すべきだ.

den /dɛn/ (**dens**) ■ N-COUNT 可算名詞 A **den** is the home of certain types of wild animals such as lions or foxes. (野生動物の) 住みか ☑ N-COUNT 可算名詞 Your **den** is a quiet room in your house where you can go to study, work, or relax without being disturbed. 書斎, 自室 [AM 米国英語] 口 *The silver-haired retiree sits in his den surrounded by photos of sailing boats.* その銀髪の退職者はヨットの写真に囲まれた自室に座る. ☑ N-COUNT 可算名詞 A **den** is a secret place where people meet, usually for a dishonest purpose. 隠れ家 口 *I could provide you with the addresses of at least three illegal drinking dens.* 少なくとも3つの不法酒場の所在地を教えられないこともないよ. ☑ N-COUNT 可算名詞 If you describe a place as a **den** of a particular type of bad or illegal behavior, you mean that a lot of that type of behavior goes on there. (ひゆ的に) 巣窟 (そうくつ) 口 *...this den of iniquity called New York City.* ニューヨーク市と呼ばれるこの邪悪の巣窟 (そうくつ)
→ see **house**

de|ni|al /dɪnaɪəl/ (**denials**) ■ N-VAR 可変性名詞 A **denial** of something is a statement that it is not true, does not exist, or did not happen. 否定 口 *It seems clear that despite official denials, differences of opinion lay behind the ambassador's decision to quit.* 公式の否定にもかかわらず, 大使が辞任を決断した裏にはさまざまな意見の相違があったのは明らかなようだ. ☑ N-UNCOUNT 不可算名詞 The **denial of** something to someone is the act of refusing to let them have it. 拒絶, 却下 [FORMAL 形式ばった] 口 *...the denial of visas to international relief workers.* 国際救援活動家へのビザの却下 ☑ N-UNCOUNT 不可算名詞 In psychology, **denial** is when a person cannot or will not accept an unpleasant truth. 否認 口 *With major life traumas, like losing a loved one, for instance, the mind's first reaction is denial.* 例えば愛する人を失うというような人生における大きな心的外傷に対して, 心の最初の反応は否認です.

den|im /dɛnɪm/ N-UNCOUNT 不可算名詞 **Denim** is a thick cotton cloth, usually blue, which is used to make clothes. Jeans are made from denim. デニム 口 *...a light blue denim jacket.* 淡い青色のデニムジャケット
→ see **cotton**

Word Link *nom ≈ name : de**nom**ination, **nom**inal, **nom**inee*

de|nomi|na|tion /dɪnɒmɪneɪʃ(ə)n/ (**denominations**) ■ N-COUNT 可算名詞 A particular **denomination** is a particular religious group which has slightly different beliefs from other groups within the same faith. 宗派 口 *Acceptance of women preachers varies greatly from denomination to denomination.* 女性説教師の容認は宗派によって大きな違いがあります. ☑ N-COUNT 可算名詞 The **denomination** of a banknote or coin is its official value. 額面金額 口 *She paid in cash, in bills of large denominations.* 彼女は現金, しかも高額紙幣で支払いをした.

de|note /dɪnoʊt/ (**denotes, denoting, denoted**) ■ V-T 他動詞 If one thing **denotes** another, it is a sign or indication of it. 示す [FORMAL 形式ばった] 口 *Red eyes denote strain and fatigue.* 充血した目はストレスと疲労を示す. ☑ V-T 他動詞 What a symbol **denotes** is what it represents. 表す [FORMAL 形式ばった] 口 *X denotes those not voting.* Xの印は不投票者を表す.

Word Link *nounce ≈ reporting : an**nounce**, de**nounce**, pro**nounce***

de|nounce /dɪnaʊns/ (**denounces, denouncing, denounced**) ■ V-T 他動詞 If you **denounce** a person or an action, you criticize them severely and publicly because you feel strongly that they are wrong or evil. 糾弾する, 公然と非難する 口 *German leaders all took the opportunity to denounce the attacks and plead for tolerance.* ドイツの指導者全員が機会をとらえてその攻撃を公然と非難し, 寛容な態度を取るように要請した. ☑ V-T 他動詞 If you **denounce** someone who has broken a rule or law, you report them to the authorities. 告発する, 通報する 口 *They were at the mercy of informers who might at any moment denounce them.* 彼らはいつ何時彼らを通報するかもしれない密告者たちのなすがままだった.

dense /dɛns/ (**denser, densest**) ■ ADJ 形容詞 Something that is **dense** contains a lot of things or people in a small area. 密集した 口 *Where Bucharest now stands, there once was a large, dense forest.* 現在のブカレスト市がある場所にはかつては大きな密林があった. ● **dense|ly** ADV 副詞 密集して 口 *Java is a densely populated island.* ジャワ島は人口が密集した島である. ☑ ADJ 形容詞 **Dense** fog or smoke is difficult to see through because it is very heavy and dark. 濃い 口 *A dense column of smoke rose several miles into the air.* もうもうとした煙の柱が空中に数マイルも立ち上った. ☑ ADJ 形

容詞 In science, a **dense** substance is very heavy in relation to its volume. 高密度の [TECHNICAL 技術的] ❑ *...a small dense star.* 小さく高密度の星

den|sity /dɛnsɪti/ (**densities**) **1** N-VAR 可変性名詞 **Density** is the extent to which something is filled or covered with people or things. 密集度 ❑ *The region has a very high population density.* その地域は人口密度が非常に高い。 **2** N-VAR 可変性名詞 In science, the **density** of a substance or object is the relation of its mass or weight to its volume. 密度 [TECHNICAL 技術的] ❑ *Jupiter's moon Io, whose density is 3.5 grams per cubic centimeter, is all rock.* 木星の衛星イオは密度が1立方センチ当たり3.5gで、全てが岩で形成されている。

dent /dɛnt/ (**dents, denting, dented**) **1** V-T 他動詞 If you **dent** the surface of something, you make a hollow area in it by hitting or pressing it. へこませる ❑ *Its brass feet dented the carpet's thick pile.* その真ちゅうの足でカーペットの厚いけばがへこんだ。 **2** V-T 他動詞 If something **dents** your confidence or your pride, it makes you realize that you are not as good or successful as you thought. (自信を) 無くす、(自尊心を) 傷つける ❑ *Record oil prices have dented consumer confidence.* 記録的な石油価格のため消費意欲が低下した。 **3** N-COUNT 可算名詞 A **dent** is a hollow in the surface of something which has been caused by hitting or pressing it. へこみ、くぼみ ❑ *I was convinced there was a dent in the hood which hadn't been there before.* 私はボンネットに前にはなかったへこみがあると確信していた。

> **Word Link** **dent** ≈ *tooth* : **dent**al, **dent**ist, **dent**ures

den|tal /dɛntᵊl/ ADJ 形容詞 **Dental** is used to describe things that relate to teeth or to the care and treatment of teeth. 歯の、歯科の [ADJ n] ❑ *Good oral hygiene and regular dental care are important, whatever your age.* 年齢に関わらず、口腔(こうくう)衛生に気をつけ定期的に歯の治療をすることが大切だ。

den|tist /dɛntɪst/ (**dentists**) N-COUNT 可算名詞 A **dentist** is a medical practitioner who is qualified to examine and treat people's teeth. 歯科医 ❑ *Visit your dentist twice a year for a checkup.* 歯の検査のために年2回、歯医者に行きなさい。 ● N-SING 単数名詞 The **dentist** or **the dentist's** is used to refer to the office or clinic where a dentist works. 歯科医院 ❑ *It's worse than being at the dentist's.* それなら歯医者に行くほうがましだよ。

→ see **teeth**

den|tist's of|fice (**dentist's offices**) N-COUNT 可算名詞 A **dentist's office** is the room or house where a dentist works. 歯科医院 [AM 米国英語]

den|tures /dɛntʃərz/

> The form **denture** is used as a modifier.

> **denture** 形は修飾語として使われる。

N-PLURAL 複数名詞 **Dentures** are artificial teeth worn by people who no longer have all their own teeth. 総義歯、総入れ歯 ❑ *People who wear dentures may sleep better if they leave them in overnight.* 総義歯を入れている人は、夜は入れたままのほうがよく眠れるかもしれない。

→ see **teeth**

de|nun|cia|tion /dɪnʌnsieɪʃᵊn/ (**denunciations**) **1** N-VAR 可変性名詞 **Denunciation** of someone or something is severe public criticism of them. 公式の非難 ❑ *On September 24, he wrote a stinging denunciation of his critics.* 彼は9月24日に彼の批判者に対して痛烈な非難文を書いた。 **2** N-VAR 可変性名詞 **Denunciation** is the act of reporting someone who has broken a rule or law to the authorities. 告発、密告 ❑ *...memories of the denunciation of French Jews to the Nazis during the Second World War.* 第2次世界大戦中にフランス系ユダヤ人をナチスに密告した記憶

Den|ver boot /dɛnvər bʊt/ (**Denver boots**) N-COUNT 可算名詞 A **Denver boot** is a large metal device which is attached to the wheel of an illegally parked car or other vehicle in order to prevent it from being driven away. The driver has to pay to have the device removed. (駐車違反対策で使用する) 車輪止め [AM 米国英語] ❑ *I watched a couple of cops clap a Denver boot on a green Mercedes.* 私は2人組みの警官が緑色のメルセデスベンツに車輪止めを取り付けるのをじっと見ていた。

deny /dɪnaɪ/ (**denies, denying, denied**) **1** V-T 他動詞 When you **deny** something, you state that it is not true. 否定する ❑ *She denied both accusations.* 彼女は両方の罪状を否定した。 ❑ *The government has denied that the authorities have uncovered a plot to assassinate the president.* 政府は当局が大統領暗殺の陰謀を摘発したということを否定した。 **2** V-T 他動詞 If you **deny** someone something that they need or want, you refuse to let them have it. 拒む、認めない ❑ *Two federal courts ruled that the military cannot deny prisoners access to lawyers.* 2つの連邦裁判所は、軍が囚人の弁護士接見を拒むことはできないと判決を下した。

Do not confuse **deny** and **refuse**. If you **deny** something, you say that it is not true. ❑ *The allegation was denied by government spokesmen.* If someone **denies** you something, they do not allow you to have it. ❑ *I never denied her anything.* If you **refuse** to do something, you deliberately do not do it, or you say firmly that you will not do it. ❑ *...people who refuse to change their opinions... He refused to condemn them.* You can **refuse** something that someone offers you. ❑ *The patient has the right to refuse treatment.* If someone does not allow you to have something you ask for, or to do something you have asked to do, you can say that they **refuse** you. ❑ *He can run to Dad for money if I refuse him.*

> **Word Partnership** **deny** は次の語句と使われる：
> V. confirm or deny **1**
> N. deny a charge, officials deny **1**
>   deny access, deny entry, deny a request **2**

> **Word Link** **ant** ≈ *one who does, has* : defend**ant**, deodor**ant**, occup**ant**

de|odor|ant /dioʊdərənt/ (**deodorants**) N-MASS 質量名詞 **Deodorant** is a substance that you can use on your body to hide or prevent the smell of sweat. 消臭剤、デオドラント

de|part /dɪpɑrt/ (**departs, departing, departed**) **1** V-T/V-I 他動詞/自動詞 When something or someone **departs from** a place, they leave it and start a trip to another place. You can also say that someone **departs** a place. 出発する ❑ *Flight 43 will depart from Denver at 11:45 a.m. and arrive in Honolulu at 4:12 p.m.* フライト43便は午前11時45分にデンバーを出発し、午後4時12分にホノルルに到着する予定である。 ❑ *In the morning Mr. McDonald departed for Sydney.* 午前中にマクドナルド氏はシドニーに向けて出発しました。 **2** V-I 自動詞 If you **depart from** a traditional, accepted, or agreed way of doing something, you do it in a different or unexpected way. それる、はずれる ❑ *Why is it in this country that we have departed from good educational sense?* どうしてこの国では教育の良識から外れたのでしょうか。

de|part|ment /dɪpɑrtmənt/ (**departments**) N-COUNT 可算名詞 A **department** is one of the sections in an organization such as a government, business, or university. A department is also one of the sections in a large store. (政府の) 省、(企業などの) 部門、(大学の) 学科、(大型店舗の) 売り場 ❑ *...the U.S. Department of Health and Human Services.* 米国保健社会福祉省 ❑ *He moved to the sales department.* 彼は営業部に異動した。

de|part|men|tal /dɪpɑrtmɛntᵊl/ ADJ 形容詞 **Departmental** is used to describe the activities, responsibilities, or possessions of a department in a government, company, or other organization. 部門の [ADJ n] ❑ *The Secretary of Education is right to seek a bigger departmental budget.* 教育省長官が同省の予算の増加を求めるのは正しい。

de|part|ment store (**department stores**) N-COUNT 可算名詞 A **department store** is a large store which sells many different kinds of goods. 百貨店、デパート ❑ *...the dazzling window displays of world-famous department stores such as Macy's and Bloomingdale's.* メーシー百貨店やブルーミングデイルズ百貨店のような世界的に有名な百貨店の人の目を奪うショーウィンドー

de|par|ture /dɪpɑrtʃər/ (**departures**) **1** N-VAR 可変性名詞 **Departure** or a **departure** is the act of going away from somewhere. 出発 ❑ *...the president's departure for Helsinki.* 大統領のヘルシンキへの出発 ❑ *They hoped this would lead to the departure of all foreign forces from the country.* 彼らはこれにより外国の軍隊が同国から全面撤退することになるのを期待した。 **2** N-COUNT 可算名詞 If someone does something different or unusual, you can refer to their action as a **departure**. 離脱、逸脱 ❑ *Such a move would have been a startling departure from tradition.* そのような動きは伝統からの驚くべき逸脱になったことだろう。

de|par|ture lounge (**departure lounges**) N-COUNT 可算名詞 In an airport, the **departure lounge** is the place where passengers wait before they get onto their plane. 出発ロビー

> **Word Link** **pend** ≈ *hanging* : ap**pend**ix, de**pend**, **pend**ant

de|pend /dɪpɛnd/ (**depends, depending, depended**) **1** V-I 自動詞 If you say that one thing **depends on** another, you mean that the first thing will be affected or determined by the second. 一次第である ❑ *The cooking time needed depends on the size of the potato.* 必要な調理時間はジャガイモの大きさによる。 **2** V-I 自動詞 If you **depend on** someone or something, you need them in order to be able to survive physically, financially, or emotionally. 頼る、依存する ❑ *He depended on his writing for his income.* 彼は収入源を文筆に頼っていた。 **3** V-I 自動詞 If you can **depend on** a person, organization, or law, you know that they will support you or help you when you need them. 信頼する、当てにする ❑ *"You can depend on me," Cross assured him.* 「僕に頼っていいよ。」とクロスは彼

D

を安心させた. **4** V-I 自動詞 You use **depend** in expressions such as **it depends** to indicate that you cannot give a clear answer to a question because the answer will be affected or determined by other factors. 状況次第である ❏ "But how long can you stay in the house?" — "I don't know. It depends." 「でもどのくらいその家に滞在できるの」「わからないよ. 状況次第だね」 **5** PHRASE 句 You use **depending on** when you are saying that something varies according to the circumstances mentioned. 一によって ❏ I tend to have a different answer, depending on the family. 私は家族によって違う答えを出すようだ.

Word Partnership depend は次の語句と使われる:

N.	depend **on circumstances, outcome will** depend, **survival will/may** depend, depend **on the weather** **1**
ADV.	depend **largely** **1**
PREP.	depend **on** someone/something **1** – **3**

---

de|pend|able /dɪpɛndəb³l/ ADJ 形容詞 If you say that someone or something is **dependable**, you approve of them because you feel that you can be sure that they will always act consistently or sensibly, or do what you need them to do. 当てになる, 頼りになる [APPROVAL 賛成] ❏ He was a good friend, a dependable companion. 彼はいい友人で, 頼りになる仲間だった.

de|pend|ant /dɪpɛndənt/ → see **dependent**

Word Link ence ≈ state, condition : depend**ence**, excell**ence**, independ**ence**

---

de|pend|ence /dɪpɛndəns/ **1** N-UNCOUNT 不可算名詞 Your **dependence on** something or someone is your need for them in order to succeed or be able to survive. 依存, 頼ること ❏ ...the city's traditional dependence on tourism. その市が従来通り観光事業に依存していること **2** N-UNCOUNT 不可算名詞 If you talk about drug **dependence** or alcohol **dependence**, you are referring to a situation where someone is addicted to drugs or is an alcoholic. 依存症, 中毒 ❏ French doctors tend to regard drug dependence as a form of deep-rooted psychological disorder. フランス人の医者は麻薬中毒を1種の根深い心理的障害であるとみなす傾向がある. **3** N-UNCOUNT 不可算名詞 You talk about the **dependence** of one thing **on** another when the first thing will be affected or determined by the second. 依存 ❏ ...the dependence of politicians on rich donors to fund their increasingly expensive campaigns. 選挙活動費の資金を出してくれる政治家が依存している状態

de|pend|en|cy /dɪpɛndənsi/ (**dependencies**) **1** N-COUNT 可算名詞 A **dependency** is a country which is controlled by another country. 保護領, 属国 ❏ ...the tiny British dependency of Montserrat in the eastern Caribbean. 東カリブ海の小さな英領モントセラット **2** N-UNCOUNT 不可算名詞 You talk about someone's **dependency** when they have a deep emotional, physical, or financial need for a particular person or thing, especially one that you consider excessive or undesirable. (精神的・肉体的・経済的に) 依存 ❏ We saw his dependency on his mother and worried that he might not survive long if anything happened to her. 私たちは彼が母親に頼りきっているのを見て, もし母親に何かがあれば彼は長くは生き延びれないのではないかと心配した. **3** N-VAR 可変性名詞 If you talk about alcohol **dependency** or chemical **dependency**, you are referring to a situation where someone is an alcoholic or is addicted to drugs. 中毒 [mainly AM 主に米国英語] ❏ In 1985, he began to show signs of alcohol and drug dependency. 1985年に彼はアルコールと薬物の中毒症の兆しを見せ始めた.

Word Link ent ≈ one who does, has : depend**ent**, resid**ent**, superintend**ent**

---

de|pend|ent /dɪpɛndənt/ (**dependents**) also **dependant** **1** ADJ 形容詞 To be **dependent on** something or someone means to need them in order to succeed or be able to survive. 依存して ❏ The local economy is overwhelmingly dependent on oil and gas extraction. その地方の経済は石油とガスの産出に圧倒的に依存している. **2** ADJ 形容詞 If one thing is **dependent on** another, the first thing will be affected or determined by the second. 一によって決まる, 一次第である [v-link ADJ 'on/upon' n] ❏ ...companies whose earnings are largely dependent on the performance of the Chinese economy. 企業利益が中国経済の業績に大きく左右される会社 **3** N-COUNT 可算名詞 Your **dependents** are the people you support financially, such as your children. 扶扶養者, 扶養家族 [FORMAL 形式ばった] ❏ Companies with 200 or more workers must offer health benefits to employees and their dependents. 雇用者数が200人以上の会社は, 従業員とその扶養家族に健康保健を用意する義務がある.

Word Link pict ≈ painting : de**pict**, **pict**ure, **pict**uresque

---

de|pict /dɪpɪkt/ (**depicts, depicting, depicted**) V-T 他動詞 To **depict** someone or something means to show or represent them in a work of art such as a drawing or painting. 描写する ❏ ...a gallery of pictures depicting Lee's most famous battles. リー将軍の最も有名な戦いを描いた絵画の展示室

Word Link ple ≈ filling : com**ple**ment, com**ple**te, de**ple**te

---

de|plete /dɪplit/ (**depletes, depleting, depleted**) V-T 他動詞 To **deplete** a stock or amount of something means to reduce it. 減らす, 消耗させる [FORMAL 形式ばった] ❏ ...substances that deplete the ozone layer. オゾン層を激減させる物質 ● **de|plet|ed** ADJ 形容詞 劣化した ❏ ...Lee's worn and depleted army. リー将軍の疲弊し消耗した陸軍 ● **de|ple|tion** /dɪpliʃⁿ/ N-UNCOUNT 不可算名詞 減少, 消耗 ❏ ...the depletion of underground water supplies. 地下水供給量の減少

de|plor|able /dɪplɔrəb³l/ ADJ 形容詞 If you say that something is **deplorable**, you think that it is very bad and unacceptable. 悲惨な, 許しがたい [FORMAL 形式ばった] ❏ Many of them live under deplorable conditions. 彼らの多くが悲惨な状況で暮らしています.

de|plore /dɪplɔr/ (**deplores, deploring, deplored**) V-T 他動詞 If you say that you **deplore** something, you think it is very wrong or immoral. 遺憾に思う, 非難する [FORMAL 形式ばった] ❏ Muslim and Jewish leaders have issued statements deploring the violence and urging the United Nations to take action. イスラム教徒とユダヤ人の指導者は暴力を非難し, 国連に措置を取るように求める表明を出しました.

de|ploy /dɪplɔɪ/ (**deploys, deploying, deployed**) V-T 他動詞 To **deploy** troops or military resources means to organize or position them so that they are ready to be used. 配置する, 展開する ❏ The president said he had no intention of deploying ground troops. 大統領は地上部隊を展開する意思はないと述べた.
→ see **army**

de|ploy|ment /dɪplɔɪmənt/ (**deployments**) N-VAR 可変性名詞 The **deployment** of troops, resources, or equipment is the organization and positioning of them so that they are ready for quick action. 配置, 展開 ❏ ...the deployment of troops into townships. 非白人居住地区に部隊を展開

de|port /dɪpɔrt/ (**deports, deporting, deported**) V-T 他動詞 If a government **deports** someone, usually someone who is not a citizen of that country, it sends them out of the country because they have committed a crime or because it believes they do not have the right to be there. 本国に強制送還する ❏ ...a government decision earlier this month to deport all illegal immigrants. 今月初めに下された不法移住者全員を強制送還するという政府の決定 ● **de|por|ta|tion** /dɪpɔrteɪʃⁿn/ (**deportations**) N-VAR 可変性名詞 強制送還 ❏ ...thousands of migrants facing deportation. 強制送還に直面している数千人の移住者

de|pose /dɪpoʊz/ (**deposes, deposing, deposed**) V-T 他動詞 If a ruler or political leader **is deposed**, they are forced to give up their position. 退陣させる [usu passive] ❏ Mr. Ben Bella was deposed in a coup in 1965. ベン・ベラ氏は1965年のクーデターで失脚した.

Word Link pos ≈ placing : de**pos**it, **pos**ition, re**pos**itory

---

de|pos|it /dɪpɒzɪt/ (**deposits, depositing, deposited**) **1** N-COUNT 可算名詞 A **deposit** is a sum of money which is part of the full price of something, and which you pay when you agree to buy it. 手付金, 頭金 ❏ The initial deposit required to open an account is a minimum 100 dollars. 口座を開くために必要な最初の預金額は最低100ドルです. **2** N-COUNT 可算名詞 A **deposit** is a sum of money which is in a bank account or savings account, especially a sum which will be left there for some time. 貯蓄高 **3** N-COUNT 可算名詞 A **deposit** is an amount of a substance that has been left somewhere as a result of a chemical or geological process. 堆積物, 鉱床 ❏ ...underground deposits of gold and diamonds. 金とダイアモンドの地下鉱床 **4** N-COUNT 可算名詞 A **deposit** is a sum of money which you pay when you start renting something. The money is returned to you if you do not damage what you have rented. 保証金, 敷金 [usu sing] ❏ I put down a $500 security deposit for another apartment. 私は別のアパートに保証金を500ドル払った. **5** N-COUNT 可算名詞 A **deposit** is a sum of money which you put into a bank account. 預金 ❏ She told me I should make a deposit every week and they'd stamp my book. 毎週積み立てすることを勧め, 通帳に印を押してくれると彼女は私に言った. **6** V-T 他動詞 If you **deposit** a sum of money, you put it into a bank account or savings account. 預け入る, 預金する ❏ The customer has to deposit a minimum of $100 monthly. 顧客は毎月最低100ドルの預金をしなければならない. **7** V-T 他動詞 To **deposit** someone or something somewhere means to put them or leave them there. 置く ❏ Mr. Crenshaw deposited the boys and their suitcases on Mr. Peck's lawn. クレンショー氏は少年たちと彼らのスーツケースをペック氏の庭に降ろした. **8** V-T 他動詞 If you **deposit** something somewhere, you put it where it will be safe until it is needed again. 預ける ❏ You are advised to deposit valuables in the hotel safe. ホテルの金庫に貴重品を預けることをお勧めする.
→ see **bank**

de|pos|it ac|count (**deposit accounts**) N-COUNT 可算名詞 A **deposit account** is the same as a **savings account**. 預金口座 [BRIT 英国英語]

depo|si|tion /dɛpəzɪʃⁿn/ (depositions) N-COUNT 可算名詞 A **deposition** is a formal written statement, made for example, by a witness to a crime, which can be used in a court of law if the witness cannot be present. 宣誓供述書, 証言録取書 ❑ *The material would be checked against the depositions from other witnesses.* 資料は他の証人からの宣誓供述書と照合されるでしょう.

de|pot /diːpoʊ/ (depots) ◻ N-COUNT 可算名詞 A **depot** is a bus station or train station. バス発着所 (鉄道の), 駅 [AM 米国英語] ❑ *She was reunited with her boyfriend in the depot of Ozark, Alabama.* 彼女はアラバマ州のオザークのバス発着所で恋人に再会した. ◻ N-COUNT 可算名詞 A **depot** is a place where large amounts of raw materials, equipment, arms, or other supplies are kept until they are needed. 貯蔵所, 倉庫 ❑ *...food depots.* 食物貯蔵庫

de|pre|ci|ate /dɪpriːʃieɪt/ (depreciates, depreciating, depreciated) V-T/V-I 他動詞/自動詞 If something such as a currency **depreciates** or if something **depreciates**, it loses some of its original value. 価値が下がる [自動詞], 価値を下げる [他動詞] ❑ *Inflation is rising rapidly; the yuan is depreciating.* インフレが急騰しており, 元の価値は低下している. ❑ *The demand for foreign currency depreciates the real value of local currencies.* 外国通貨に対する需要が国内通貨の実質価値を下げる. ● **de|pre|ci|a|tion** /dɪpriːʃieɪʃⁿn/ (depreciations) N-VAR 可変性名詞 価値下落, 価値低下 ❑ *...miscellaneous costs, including machinery depreciation and wages.* 機械装置の減価償却費や給料などを含めたさまざまな経費

de|press /dɪprɛs/ (depresses, depressing, depressed) ◻ V-T 他動詞 If someone or something **depresses** you, they make you feel sad and disappointed. 落ち込ませる ❑ *I must admit the state of the country depresses me.* 正直なところこの国の状態を思うと気が滅入るよ. ◻ V-T 他動詞 If something **depresses** prices, wages, or figures, it causes them to become less. 下落させる ❑ *The stronger U.S. dollar depressed sales.* ドル高で売り上げが減少した.

de|pressed /dɪprɛst/ ◻ ADJ 形容詞 If you are **depressed**, you are sad and feel that you cannot enjoy anything, because your situation is so difficult and unpleasant. 落ち込んだ, 気が滅いった ❑ *She's been very depressed and upset about this whole situation.* 彼女はこの状況全体のことでかなり落ち込んで動揺している. ◻ ADJ 形容詞 A **depressed** place or industry does not have enough business or employment to be successful. 不景気な ❑ *Many states already have enterprise zones and legislation that encourage investment in depressed areas.* 多くの州が衰退地域への投資を推進するための企業誘致地区や法律をすでに設けている.

de|press|ing /dɪprɛsɪŋ/ ADJ 形容詞 Something that is **depressing** makes you feel sad and disappointed. 気がめいるような, 重苦しい ❑ *Yesterday's unemployment figures were as depressing as those of the previous 22 months.* 昨日発表された失業者数は過去22ヶ月間の数字と同様にゆううつな数字だ. ● **de|press|ing|ly** ADV 副詞 気がめいるほど ❑ *It all sounded depressingly familiar to Janet.* それはすべてジャネットにとってうっとうしいほど聞き覚えがあった.

de|pres|sion /dɪprɛʃⁿn/ (depressions) ◻ N-VAR 可変性名詞 **Depression** is a mental state in which you are sad and feel that you cannot enjoy anything, because your situation is so difficult and unpleasant. うつ病 ❑ *Mr. Thomas was suffering from depression.* トマス氏はうつ病にかかっていた. ◻ N-COUNT 可算名詞 A **depression** is a time when there is very little economic activity, which causes a lot of unemployment and poverty. 不況 ❑ *He never forgot the hardships he witnessed during the Great Depression of the 1930s.* 彼は1930年代の大恐慌時代に経験した苦難を決して忘れなかった. ◻ N-COUNT 可算名詞 A **depression** in a surface is an area which is lower than the parts surrounding it. くぼみ ❑ *...an area pockmarked by rain-filled depressions.* 雨水のくぼみでぼこぼこになった地域 ◻ N-COUNT 可算名詞 A **depression** is a mass of air that has a low pressure and that often causes rain. 低気圧 ❑ *To the northwest lies a depression with clouds and rain.* 北西に雲と雨を伴った低気圧がある.
→ see **hurricane**

dep|ri|va|tion /dɛprɪveɪʃⁿn/ (deprivations) N-VAR 可変性名詞 If you suffer **deprivation**, you do not have or are prevented from having something that you want or need. 欠乏 ❑ *Millions more suffer from serious sleep deprivation caused by long work hours.* さらに数百万人が長時間労働による深刻な睡眠不足で苦しんでいる.

de|prive /dɪpraɪv/ (deprives, depriving, deprived) V-T 他動詞 If you **deprive** someone of something that they want or need, you take it away from them, or you prevent them from having it. 奪う ❑ *They've been deprived of the fuel necessary to heat their homes.* 彼らは家の暖房に必要な燃料を奪われました.

de|prived /dɪpraɪvd/ ADJ 形容詞 **Deprived** people or people from **deprived** areas do not have the things that people consider to be essential in life, for example, acceptable living conditions or education. 困窮している, 貧困な ❑ *...probably the most severely deprived children in the country.* その国でおそらく最も困窮している子供たち

dept. (depts.) **Dept.** is used as a written abbreviation for **department**, usually in the name of a particular department. department の略語 ❑ *...the Philadelphia Police Dept.* フィラデルフィア警察署

depth /dɛpθ/ (depths) ◻ N-VAR 可変性名詞 The **depth** of something such as a river or hole is the distance downward from its top surface, or between its upper and lower surfaces. 深さ ❑ *The depth of the shaft is 520 yards.* 縦坑の深さは520ヤードだ. ❑ *The smaller lake ranges from five to fourteen feet in depth.* 小さい方の湖は深さ5フィートから14フィートに及ぶ. ❑ *The depth of a standard straight valance is usually about 12 inches.* 標準サイズのストレートのたれ布の長さはふつう12インチくらいだ. ◻ N-VAR 可変性名詞 The **depth** of something such as a closet or drawer is the distance between its front surface and its back. 奥行き ◻ N-VAR 可変性名詞 If an emotion is very strongly or intensely felt, you can talk about its **depth**. (感情の) 深さ ❑ *I am well aware of the depth of feeling that exists in Ontario.* 私はオンタリオ州に存在する深い感情について十分承知している. ◻ N-UNCOUNT 不可算名詞 The **depth** of a situation is its extent and seriousness. 重大さ ❑ *The country's leadership had underestimated the depth of the crisis.* その国の指導者たちは危機の深刻さを過小評価していた. ◻ N-UNCOUNT 不可算名詞 The **depth** of someone's knowledge is the great amount that they know. (知識の) 深さ ❑ *We felt at home with her and were impressed with the depth of her knowledge.* 私たちは彼女と一緒にいてくつろげ, また彼女の知識の深さに感心した. ◻ N-PLURAL 複数名詞 The **depths** are places that are a long way below the surface of the sea or earth. 深海, 深部 [LITERARY 文語的] ❑ *Leaves, brown with long immersion, rose to the surface and vanished back into the depths.* 長い間沈んでい茶色くなった葉が表面に上がってきて, そしてまた深みに消えていった. ◻ N-PLURAL 複数名詞 If you talk about the **depths of** an area, you mean the parts of it which are very far from the edge. 奥地 ❑ *...the depths of the countryside.* 田舎の奥地 ◻ N-PLURAL 複数名詞 If you are in the **depths of** an unpleasant emotion, you feel that emotion very strongly. どん底で ❑ *I was in the depths of despair when the baby was terribly sick every day, and was losing weight.* 赤ん坊が毎日ひどく加減が悪く体重が減っていったときに, 私は絶望のどん底にいた. ◻ PHRASE 句 If you deal with a subject in **depth**, you deal with it very thoroughly and consider all the aspects of it. 徹底的に ❑ *We will discuss these three areas in depth.* 私たちはこの3つの分野について徹底的に議論するつもりだ. ◻ → see also **in-depth** ◻ PHRASE 句 If you say that someone is **out of** their **depth**, you mean that they are in a situation that is much too difficult for them to be able to cope with it. ついていけない ❑ *Mr. Gibson is clearly intellectually out of his depth.* ギブソン氏の頭では明らかに理解できない. ◻ PHRASE 句 If you are **out of** your **depth**, you are in water that is deeper than you are tall, with the result that you cannot stand up with your head above water. 背が立たない深さに ❑ *Somehow I got out of my depth in the pool.* どういうわけか私はプールで背が立たない場所に行ってしまった.

depu|ty /dɛpyəti/ (deputies) ◻ N-COUNT 可算名詞 A **deputy** is the second most important person in an organization such as a business or government department. Someone's deputy often acts on their behalf when they are not there. 副... ❑ *Jack Lang, France's minister for culture, and his deputy, Catherine Tasca.* フランスジャック・ラング文化大臣とカトリーヌ・タスカ副大臣 ◻ N-COUNT 可算名詞 In some legislatures, the elected members are called **deputies**. 代議士 ❑ *The president appealed to deputies to approve the plan quickly.* 大統領は代議士たちに計画の速やかな承認を訴えた. ◻ N-COUNT 可算名詞 A **deputy** is a police officer. 保安官代理 [AM 米国英語] ❑ *Robyn asked the deputy on duty if she could speak with Sheriff Adkins.* ロビンは当直の保安官代理にアドキンス保安官と話すことができるか尋ねた. ◻ N-COUNT 可算名詞 A **deputy** is a person appointed to act on another person's behalf. 代理人 ❑ *His brother was acting as his deputy in America.* 彼の兄弟はアメリカで彼の代理人を務めていた.

de|rail /diːreɪl/ (derails, derailing, derailed) ◻ V-T 他動詞 To **derail** something such as a plan or a series of negotiations means to prevent it from continuing as planned. 脱線させる [JOURNALISM ジャーナリズム] ❑ *The present wave of political killings is the work of people trying to derail peace talks.* 現在の政治的な殺害の波は平和会談を脱線させようとする人々の仕業だ. ◻ V-T/V-I 他動詞/自動詞 If a train **is derailed** or if it **derails**, it comes off the track on which it is running. 脱線させる [他動詞], 脱線する [自動詞] ❑ *At least six people were killed and about twenty injured when a train was derailed in an isolated mountain region.* 人里離れた山間部で列車が脱線し, 少なくとも6人が死亡し, 20人がけがをした.

de|ranged /diːreɪndʒd/ ADJ 形容詞 Someone who is **deranged** behaves in a wild and uncontrolled way, often as a result of mental illness. 錯乱した ❑ *Three years ago today a deranged man shot and killed 14 people in the main square.* 3年前の今日, 中央広場で錯乱した男が発砲し, 14名が死亡した.

de|regu|late /diːrɛgyəleɪt/ (deregulates, deregulating, deregulated) V-T 他動詞 To **deregulate** something means to remove controls and regulations from it. 規制緩和する ❑ *...the need to deregulate the U.S. airline industry.* 米航空業界の規制緩和の必要性

de|reg|u|la|tion /di:rɛgyəleɪʃ³n/ N-UNCOUNT 不可算名詞 **Deregulation** is the removal of controls and restrictions in a particular area of business or trade. 規制緩和 [BUSINESS 実業] ❑ *Since deregulation, banks are permitted to set their own interest rates.* 規制緩和以降、銀行は独自の利率を設定することを許されている.

der|elict /dɛrɪlɪkt/ (**derelicts**) **1** ADJ 形容詞 A place or building that is **derelict** is empty and in a bad state of repair because it has not been used or lived in for a long time. 見捨てられた ❑ *Her body was found dumped in a derelict warehouse less than a mile from her home.* 彼女の遺体は自宅から1マイルたらずの場所にある荒廃した倉庫に捨てられているのを発見された. **2** N-COUNT 可算名詞 A **derelict** is a person who has no home or job and who has to live on the streets. 浮浪者 [FORMAL 形式ばった] ❑ *I had never seen so many derelicts in one place.* ひとつの場所でこれほど多くの浮浪者をみたことがなかった.

Word Link rid, ris ≈ laughing : deride, derision, ridicule

de|ride /dɪraɪd/ (**derides, deriding, derided**) V-T 他動詞 If you **deride** someone or something, you say that they are stupid or have no value. あざける [FORMAL 形式ばった] ❑ *Critics derided the move as too little, too late.* 処置を批判する人は、量的に不十分でタイミングを逸したものだとあざけった.

de|ri|sion /dɪrɪʒ³n/ N-UNCOUNT 不可算名詞 If you treat someone or something with **derision**, you express contempt for them. あざけり ❑ *He tried to calm them, but was greeted with shouts of derision.* 彼は彼らをなだめようとしたが、あざけりの叫びで迎えられた.

de|ri|sive /dɪraɪsɪv/ ADJ 形容詞 A **derisive** noise, expression, or remark expresses contempt. あざけりの ❑ *There was a short, derisive laugh.* 短い嘲笑 (ちょうしょう) があった.

de|riva|tive /dɪrɪvətɪv/ (**derivatives**) N-COUNT 可算名詞 A **derivative** is something which has been developed or obtained from something else. 派生物 ❑ *...a poppy-seed derivative similar to heroin.* ヘロインと類似したケシの実の派生物

de|rive /dɪraɪv/ (**derives, deriving, derived**) **1** V-T 他動詞 If you **derive** something such as pleasure or benefit **from** a person or from something, you get it from them. 引き出す [FORMAL 形式ばった] ❑ *Mr. Ying is one of those happy people who derive pleasure from helping others.* イン氏も人助けから喜びを得られるような幸せな人だ. **2** V-T/V-I 他動詞/自動詞 If you say that something such as a word or feeling **derives** or **is derived from** something else, you mean that it comes from that thing. 由来する ❑ *The name Anastasia is derived from a Greek word meaning "of the resurrection."* アナスタシアという名前は「復活」を意味するギリシャ語に由来する.

de|roga|tory /dɪrɒgətɔri/ ADJ 形容詞 If you make a **derogatory** remark or comment about someone or something, you express your low opinion of them. けいべつ的な ❑ *He refused to withdraw derogatory remarks made about his boss.* 彼は上司に対する軽蔑的な発言の撤回を拒否した.

Word Link de ≈ from, down, away : deflate, descend, detach

Word Link scend ≈ climbing : ascend, condescend, descend

de|scend /dɪsɛnd/ (**descends, descending, descended**) **1** V-T/V-I 他動詞/自動詞 If you **descend** or if you **descend** a staircase, you move downward from a higher to a lower level. 降りる [FORMAL 形式ばった] ❑ *Things are cooler and more damp as we descend to the cellar.* 地下室に下りるにつれ、だんだん涼しくじめじめしてくる. **2** V-I 自動詞 If a large group of people arrive to see you, especially if their visit is unexpected or causes you a lot of work, you can say that they **have descended on** you. 急襲する ❑ *Some 3,000 city officials will descend on Capitol Hill on Tuesday to lobby for more money.* およそ3千人の市の役人が資金追加の陳情のため火曜日に米国議会に押しかける. **3** V-I 自動詞 When you want to emphasize that the situation that someone is entering is very bad, you can say that they **are descending into** that situation. 陥る [EMPHASIS 強調] ❑ *He was ultimately overthrown and the country descended into chaos.* 彼は結局は打倒され、国は混乱に陥った. **4** V-I 自動詞 If you say that someone **descends to** behavior which you consider unacceptable, you are expressing your disapproval of the fact that they do it. 身を落とす [DISAPPROVAL 不賛成] ❑ *We're not going to descend to such methods.* 我々はそんな手を使うようなまねはしない.

de|scend|ant /dɪsɛndənt/ (**descendants**) also **descendent** **1** N-COUNT 可算名詞 Someone's **descendants** are the people in later generations who are related to them. 子孫 ❑ *They are descendants of the original English and Scottish settlers.* 彼らはもともとイングランドとスコットランドからの移民の子孫だ. **2** N-COUNT 可算名詞 Something modern which developed from an older thing can be called a **descendant** of it. 派生物 ❑ *His design was a descendant of a 1956 device.* 彼の設計は1956年の装置の系譜をひくものだ.

de|scend|ed /dɪsɛndɪd/ ADJ 形容詞 A person who is **descended from** someone who lived a long time ago is directly related to

them. 子孫の [v-link ADJ 'from' n] ❑ *Anna is descended from pioneers who settled in Colorado in 1898.* アンナは1898年にコロラド州に移民した開拓者の子孫だ.

de|scend|ent /dɪsɛndənt/ → see **descendant**

de|scent /dɪsɛnt/ (**descents**) **1** N-VAR 可変性名詞 A **descent** is a movement from a higher to a lower level or position. 降下 ❑ *Sixteen of the youngsters set off for help, but during the descent three collapsed in the cold and rain.* 16人の若者が救助のために出発したが、降下の際、3名が寒さと雨のため倒れた. **2** N-COUNT 可算名詞 A **descent** is a surface that slopes downward, for example, the side of a steep hill. 下り坂 ❑ *On the descents, cyclists spin past cars, freewheeling downhill at tremendous speed.* 下り坂で自転車選手たちは車を追い抜き疾走し、下りの勢いにのって猛烈な速度で飛ばす. **3** N-SING 単数名詞 When you want to emphasize that a situation becomes very bad, you can talk about someone's or something's **descent** into that situation. 転落 [EMPHASIS 強調] ❑ *...his swift descent from respected academic to struggling small businessman.* 尊敬を受ける学者から苦労の絶えない、しがない実業家へのあっけない彼の没落. **4** N-UNCOUNT 不可算名詞 You use **descent** to talk about a person's family background, for example, their nationality or social status. 家系 [FORMAL 形式ばった] ❑ *All the contributors were of African descent.* 貢献した者はみなアフリカ系の人々だった.

de|scribe /dɪskraɪb/ (**describes, describing, described**) **1** V-T 他動詞 If you **describe** a person, object, event, or situation, you say what they are like or what happened. 描写する ❑ *We asked her to describe what kind of things she did in her spare time.* 我々は余暇に何をしたかを彼女に説明するよう求めた. ❑ *She read a poem by Carver which describes their life together.* 彼女は彼らの同居生活を描写するカーバーの詩を読んだ. **2** V-T 他動詞 If a person **describes** someone or something **as** a particular thing, he or she believes that they are that thing and says so. 評する ❑ *He described it as an extraordinarily tangled and complicated tale.* 彼はそれを極めて複雑で入り組んだ話だと表現した. ❑ *Even his closest allies describe him as forceful, aggressive, and determined.* 最も近い味方でさえ、彼のことを押しが強く攻撃的で頑固だと評する.

> When you use **describe** with an indirect object, you must put **to** in front of the indirect object. ❑ *He later described to me what he had found... Could you describe the man to the police?* You do not say, for example, "He described me what he had found."

de|scrip|tion /dɪskrɪpʃ³n/ (**descriptions**) **1** N-VAR 可変性名詞 A **description** of someone or something is an account which explains what they are or what they look like. 描写 ❑ *Police have issued a description of the man who was aged between fifty and sixty.* 警察は年齢50歳から60歳のその男の人物像を公表した. ❑ *The paper provides a detailed description of how to create human embryos by cloning.* 新聞はクローン技術によるヒト胚の製法の詳述を掲載する. **2** N-SING 単数名詞 If something is **of** a particular **description**, it belongs to the general class of items that are mentioned. 種類 ❑ *Events of this description occurred daily.* この種の出来事は毎日起こった. **3** N-UNCOUNT 不可算名詞 You can say that something is **beyond description**, or that it **defies description**, to emphasize that it is very unusual, impressive, terrible, or extreme. 筆舌に尽くしがたい [EMPHASIS 強調] ❑ *His face is weary beyond description.* 彼の顔は言いようのないほど疲れている.

Thesaurus description また次を参照 :

| N. | account, characterization, summary **1** category, class, kind, type **2** |

Word Partnership description は次の語句と使われる :

| ADJ. | accurate description, brief description, detailed description, physical description, vague description **1** |
| V. | fit a description, give a description, match a description **1** |

de|scrip|tive /dɪskrɪptɪv/ ADJ 形容詞 **Descriptive** language or writing indicates what someone or something is like. 記述的 ❑ *The group adopted the simpler, more descriptive title of Angina Support Group.* 団体は単純に活動をよく表現する方の名称「狭心症支援団体」を採用した.

des|e|crate /dɛsɪkreɪt/ (**desecrates, desecrating, desecrated**) V-T 他動詞 If someone **desecrates** something which is considered to be holy or very special, they deliberately damage or insult it. ぼうとくする ❑ *She shouldn't have desecrated the picture of a religious leader.* 彼女は宗教的指導者の写真をぼうとくすべきではなかった. ● **des|e|cra|tion** /dɛsɪkreɪʃ³n/ N-UNCOUNT 不可算名詞 ぼうとく ❑ *The whole area has been shocked by the desecration of the cemetery.* 地域全体が墓地のぼうとく行為に衝撃を受けている.

des|ert (deserts, deserting, deserted)

> The noun is usually pronounced /dɛzərt/. The verb and the noun in meaning ⑥ are pronounced /dɪzɜrt/ and are hyphenated de|sert.
>
> 名詞は通常 /dɛzərt/ と発音される. ⑥ の意味の場合の動詞と名詞は /dɪzɜrt/ と発音され, de|sert とハイフンで結ばれる.

1 N-VAR 可変性名詞 A **desert** is a large area of land, usually in a hot region, where there is almost no water, rain, trees, or plants. 砂漠 ❑ ...the Sahara Desert. サハラ砂漠 **2** V-T 他動詞 If people or animals **desert** a place, they leave it and it becomes empty. 見捨てる ❑ Poor farmers are deserting their parched farm fields and coming here looking for jobs. 貧しい農民たちは干上がった農地を捨て, ここに仕事探しに来ている. ●**de|sert|ed** ADJ 形容詞 見捨てられた ❑ She led them into a deserted sidestreet. 彼女は彼らを人気のない横道に連れ込んだ. **3** V-T 他動詞 If someone **deserts** you, they go away and leave you, and no longer help or support you. 見捨てる ❑ Mrs. Roding's husband deserted her years ago. 数年前, ロディング夫人は夫を見限った. ●**de|ser|tion** /dɪzɜrʃ⁰n/ (**desertions**) N-VAR 可変性名詞 放棄 ❑ It was a long time since she'd referred to her father's desertion. 彼女が自分の父に捨てられたことを話してから長い時間がたった. **4** V-T/V-I 他動詞/自動詞 If you **desert** something that you support, use, or are involved with, you stop supporting it, using it, or being involved with it. 放棄する ❑ The sport is being written off as boring and predictable and the fans are deserting in droves. そのスポーツは, 退屈で結果が見え透いており, ファンが愛想を尽かしていると書かれている. ❑ He was pained to see many youngsters deserting kibbutz life. 彼は多くの若者がキブツの生活を捨てるのを目にして胸を痛めた. ●**de|ser|tion** N-VAR 可変性名詞 放棄 ❑ They blamed his proposal for much of the mass desertion by the Republican electorate. 彼らは支持者多数の共和党離れを主に彼の提案のせいにした. **5** V-T/V-I 他動詞/自動詞 If someone **deserts**, or **deserts** a job, especially a job in the armed forces, they leave that job without permission. 職務放棄する ❑ He deserted from army intelligence last month. 彼は先月, 陸軍の諜報機関から逃亡した. **6** PHRASE 句 If you say that someone got their **just deserts**, you mean that they deserved the unpleasant things that happened to them, because they did something bad. 報いを受ける [FEELINGS 感情] ❑ At the end of the book the child's true identity is discovered, and the bad guys get their just deserts. その本の最後で子供の正体が明らかになり, 悪党どもは報いを受ける.

→ see Picture Dictionary: **desert**

de|sert|er /dɪzɜrtər/ (**deserters**) N-COUNT 可算名詞 A **deserter** is someone who leaves their job in the armed forces without permission. 脱走兵 ❑ Peters had two deserters followed and shot. ピーターズは二人の脱走兵を追跡, 銃撃させた.

de|serve /dɪzɜrv/ (**deserves, deserving, deserved**) V-T 他動詞 If you say that a person or thing **deserves** something, you mean that they should have it or receive it because of their actions or qualities. 値する ❑ Government officials clearly deserve some of the blame as well. 政府高官も明らかになんらかの非難を受けて当然だ. ❑ These people deserve to make more than the minimum wage. こうした人々は最低賃金以上の収入があってもよい.

<table>
<tr><td colspan="2">**Word Partnership**   deserve は次の語句と使われる:</td></tr>
<tr><td>N.</td><td>deserve **a chance**, deserve **credit**, deserve **recognition**, deserve **respect**</td></tr>
<tr><td>V.</td><td>**don't** deserve, deserve **to know**</td></tr>
</table>

de|serv|ing /dɪzɜrvɪŋ/ ADJ 形容詞 If you describe a person, organization, or cause as **deserving**, you mean that you think they should be helped. 値する ❑ The money saved could be used for more deserving causes. お金はもっと価値のある目的に使うことができた.

de|sign /dɪzaɪn/ (**designs, designing, designed**) **1** V-T 他動詞 When someone **designs** a garment, building, machine, or other object, they plan it and make a detailed drawing of it from which it can be built or made. 設計する ❑ They wanted to design a machine that was both attractive and practical. 彼らは魅力と実用性をともに備えた機械を設計したかった. **2** V-T 他動詞 When someone **designs** a survey, policy, or system, they plan and prepare it, and decide on all the details of it. 計画する ❑ We may be able to design a course to suit your particular needs. 我々はあなたがたの個別の必要性にあわせ課程を計画することができるかもしれない. **3** N-UNCOUNT 不可算名詞 **Design** is the process and art of planning and making detailed drawings of something. 意匠術 ❑ He was a born mechanic with a flair for design. 彼は生まれつきの技師で意匠の才能を備えていた. **4** N-UNCOUNT 不可算名詞 The **design** of something is the way in which it has been planned and made. 設計 ❑ ...a new design of clock. 時計の新しい設計 **5** N-COUNT 可算名詞 A **design** is a drawing which someone produces to show how they would like something to be built or made. 設計図 ❑ When Bernardello asked them to build him a home, they drew up the design in a week. ベルナル

Picture Dictionary   desert

cactus

palm tree

sand dune

oasis

lizard

snake

sand

D

デロが家を建てるように頼んだとき，彼らは一週間で設計図を描いた．**6** N-COUNT 可算名詞 A **design** is a pattern of lines, flowers, or shapes which is used to decorate something. 模様 □ *Many pictures have been based on simple geometric designs.* 多くの絵が単純な幾何学模様を基にしてきた．**7** V-T PASSIVE 受動態他動詞 If something **is designed** for a particular purpose, it is intended for that purpose. 特定の目的のため計画されている □ *This project is designed to help homeless people.* この計画はホームレス救済を目的としている．

→ see **architecture, quilt**

des|ig|nate (designates, designating, designated)

> The verb is pronounced /dɛzɪgneɪt/. The adjective is pronounced /dɛzɪgnɪt/.
>
> 動詞は /dɛzɪgneɪt/ と発音される．形容詞は /dɛzɪgnɪt/ と発音される．

1 V-T 他動詞 When you **designate** someone or something **as** a particular thing, you formally give them that description or name. 称する □ *…a man interviewed in one of our studies whom we shall designate as E.* 我々の研究で面談したEと称する男性 □ *There are efforts under way to designate the bridge a historic landmark.* その橋を歴史的名所として指定するための取り組みがある．**2** V-T 他動詞 If something **is designated for** a particular purpose, it is set aside for that purpose. 指定する [usu passive] □ *Some of the rooms were designated as offices.* いくつかの部屋が事務所に指定されていた．**3** V-T 他動詞 When you **designate** someone **as** something, you formally choose them to do that particular job. 任命する □ *Designate someone as the spokesperson.* 誰かを報道官に任命せよ．**4** ADJ 形容詞 **Designate** is used to describe someone who has been formally chosen to do a particular job, but has not yet started doing it. 指名された [n ADJ] □ *Japan's prime minister-designate is completing his cabinet today.* 今日，日本の次期首相が組閣を終えようとしている．

de|sign|er /dɪzaɪnər/ (designers) **1** N-COUNT 可算名詞 A **designer** is a person whose job is to design things by making drawings of them. デザイナー 設計士 □ *Carolyne is a fashion designer.* キャロラインは服飾デザイナーだ．**2** ADJ 形容詞 **Designer** clothes or **designer** labels are expensive, fashionable clothes made by a famous designer, rather than being made in large quantities in a factory. デザイナーの [n ADJ] □ *He wears designer clothes and drives an antique car.* 彼は有名デザイナーものの服を着て年代物の車に乗っている．**3** ADJ 形容詞 You can use **designer** to describe things that are worn or bought because they are fashionable. 流行の [INFORMAL くだけた] [n ADJ] □ *She sat up and removed her designer sunglasses.* 彼女は背筋を伸ばして座り，流行のサングラスをはずした．

de|sign|er baby (designer babies) also **designer child** N-COUNT 可算名詞 People sometimes refer to a baby that has developed from an embryo with certain desired characteristics as a **designer baby**. 望ましい形質を得るため遺伝子操作で生まれた子供 □ *A couple with a terminally ill child want to have a designer baby that could save the boy's life.* 不治の病にかかる息子を持つ夫婦がその命を救うためデザイナーベビーをつくることを望んでいる．[MAINLY JOURNALISM 主にジャーナリズム]

de|sir|able /dɪzaɪərəbəl/ ADJ 形容詞 Something that is **desirable** is worth having or doing because it is useful, necessary, or popular. 望ましい □ *Prolonged negotiation was not desirable.* 交渉が長引くことは望ましくなかった．●**de|sir|abil|ity** /dɪzaɪərəbɪlɪti/ N-UNCOUNT 不可算名詞 望ましさ □ *…the desirability of democratic reform.* 民主改革が望ましいこと **2** ADJ 形容詞 Someone who is **desirable** is considered to be sexually attractive. 性的魅力のある □ *…the young women of his own age whom his classmates thought most desirable.* 彼の級友が最も魅力的だとみなした彼と同い年の若い女たち ●**de|sir|abil|ity** N-UNCOUNT 不可算名詞 性的魅力 □ *He had not at all overrated Veronica's desirability.* 彼はベロニカの魅力をまったく過大評価していなかった．

de|sire /dɪzaɪər/ (desires, desiring, desired) **1** N-COUNT 可算名詞 A **desire** is a strong wish to do or have something. 欲望 □ *I had a strong desire to help and care for people.* 私は人々を助け世話したいという強い欲求を持っていた．**2** V-T 他動詞 If you **desire** something, you want it. 欲する [FORMAL 形式ばった] [no cont] □ *She had remarried and desired a child with her new husband.* 彼女は再婚しており，新しい夫と子供を持ちたいと望んでいた．●**de|sired** ADJ 形容詞 [ADJ n] 望まれた □ *You may find that just threatening this course of action will produce the desired effect.* この手順を危険にさらすことだけで望みどおりの結果につながることが分かるかもしれない．**3** N-UNCOUNT 不可算名詞 **Desire** for someone is a strong feeling of wanting to have sex with them. 性欲 □ *It's common to lose your sexual desire when you have your first child.* 最初の子供ができて性欲をなくすのはよくあることだ．

desk /dɛsk/ (desks) **1** N-COUNT 可算名詞 A **desk** is a table, often with drawers, which you sit at to write or work. 机 **2** N-SING 単数名詞 The place in a hotel, hospital, airport, or other building where you check in or obtain information is referred to as a particular **desk**. 受付 □ *I told the girl at the reception desk that I was terribly sorry, but I was half an hour late.* 私は受付嬢に，大変申し訳ないが30分遅れたと言った．**3** N-SING 単数名詞 A particular department of a broadcasting company, or of a newspaper or magazine company, can be referred to as a particular **desk**. 部局 □ *Let our news desk know as quickly as possible.* できるだけ早く報道部に知らせて．

→ see **office**

desk clerk (desk clerks) N-COUNT 可算名詞 A **desk clerk** is someone who works at the main desk in a hotel. 受付係 [AM 米国英語]

de|skill /diːskɪl/ (deskills, deskilling, deskilled) V-T 他動詞 If workers **are deskilled**, they no longer need special skills to do their work, especially because of modern methods of production. 単純作業化する [oft passive] □ *Administrative staff may be deskilled through increased automation and efficiency.* 管理スタッフの仕事は自動化と効率化の進展により技能不要になる可能性がある．

desk|top /dɛsktɒp/ (desktops) also **desk-top** **1** ADJ 形容詞 **Desktop** computers are a convenient size for using on a desk or table, but are not designed to be portable. デスクトップ型の [ADJ n] □ *When launched, the Macintosh was the smallest desktop computer ever produced.* 発売当時，マッキントッシュは史上最小のデスクトップ型コンピュータだった．**2** N-COUNT 可算名詞 A **desktop** is a desktop computer. デスクトップ型コンピュータ □ *We have stopped making desktops because no one is making money from them.* 霊の利益にもならないので，我々はデスクトップの製造をやめた．**3** N-COUNT 可算名詞 The **desktop** of a computer is the display of icons that you see on the screen when the computer is ready to use. デスクトップ □ *A dramatic full-sized lightning bolt will then fill your screen's desktop.* するとドラマチックな稲妻がスクリーンのデスクトップいっぱいに表示される．

desk|top pub|lish|ing N-UNCOUNT 不可算名詞 **Desktop publishing** is the production of printed materials such as newspapers and magazines using a desktop computer and a laser printer, rather than using conventional printing methods. The abbreviation **DTP** is also used. デスクトップ・パブリッシング

deso|late /dɛsəlɪt/ **1** ADJ 形容詞 A **desolate** place is empty of people and lacking in comfort. 荒廃した □ *…a desolate landscape of flat green fields.* 平坦な緑の野の荒廃した風景 **2** ADJ 形容詞 If someone is **desolate**, they feel very sad, alone, and without hope. 惨めな [LITERARY 文語的] □ *He was desolate without her.* 彼は彼女を失くし打ちひしがれていた．

deso|la|tion /dɛsəleɪʃən/ **1** N-UNCOUNT 不可算名詞 **Desolation** is a feeling of great unhappiness and hopelessness. 絶望 □ *Kozelek expresses his sense of desolation absolutely without self-pity.* コゼレックはまったく自分を憐れにみせずに絶望感を表現する．**2** N-UNCOUNT 不可算名詞 If you refer to **desolation** in a place, you mean that it is empty and frightening, for example, because it has been destroyed by a violent force or army. 荒廃 [DISAPPROVAL 不賛成] □ *We looked out upon a scene of desolation and ruin.* 注意すると荒れ果て破壊された光景が目にはいった．

des|pair /dɪspɛər/ (despairs, despairing, despaired) **1** N-UNCOUNT 不可算名詞 **Despair** is the feeling that everything is wrong and that nothing will improve. 絶望 □ *I looked at my wife in despair.* 私は絶望して妻を見た．**2** V-I 自動詞 If you **despair**, you feel that everything is wrong and that nothing will improve. 絶望する □ *"Oh, I despair sometimes," he says in mock sorrow.* 「ああ，ときどき絶望するよ」彼は悲しいふりをして言った．**3** V-I 自動詞 If you **despair** of something, you feel that there is no hope that it will happen or improve. If you **despair** of someone, you feel that there is no hope that they will improve. 断念する □ *He wished to earn a living through writing but despaired of doing so.* 彼は文筆で身を立てたいが，見込みはないとあきらめていた．

des|patch /dɪspætʃ/ → see **dispatch**

Word Link sper ≈ hope : **desperate, exasperate, prosperity**

des|per|ate /dɛspərɪt/ **1** ADJ 形容詞 If you are **desperate**, you are in such a bad situation that you are willing to try anything to change it. 絶望的な □ *Troops are needed to help get food into Kosovo where people are in desperate need.* 絶望的な困窮状態のコソボへの

Picture Dictionary   dessert

ice cream   cake   pie   cookies

custard   Jell-O™   chocolate mousse   fruit salad

食糧供給のために部隊が必要だ. ●**des|per|ate|ly** ADV 副詞 [ADV with v] 必死になって ❏*Thousands are desperately trying to leave their battered homes and villages.* 数千人が必死になって，壊滅した家や村を去ろうとしている. **2** ADJ 形容詞 If you are **desperate for** something or **desperate to** do something, you want or need it very much indeed. 切望している [v-link ADJ] ❏*They'd been married nearly four years and June was desperate to start a family.* 彼らは結婚してもうすぐ4年になり，ジューンは子供が欲しくてたまらなかった. ●**des|per|ate|ly** ADV 副詞 [ADV with v] 死に物狂いで ❏*He was a boy who desperately needed affection.* 彼は狂おしいほど愛情を求める少年だった. **3** ADJ 形容詞 A **desperate** situation is very difficult, serious, or dangerous. 絶望的な ❏*India's United Nations ambassador said the situation is desperate.* インドの国連大使は，状況は絶望的だと述べた.

Word Partnership   desperate は次の語句と使われる:

V.	**sound** desperate **1**
	grow desperate **1** – **3**
N.	desperate **act**, desperate **attempt**, desperate **measures**, desperate **need**, desperate **struggle** **1**
	desperate **situation** **3**

des|pera|tion /dɛspəreɪˌʃ⁰n/ N-UNCOUNT 不可算名詞 **Desperation** is the feeling that you have when you are in such a bad situation that you will try anything to change it. 絶望 ❏*This feeling of desperation and helplessness was common to most of the refugees.* この絶望感と無力感は避難民の大半に共通していた.

des|pic|able /dɛspɪkəbºl/ ADJ 形容詞 If you say that a person or action is **despicable**, you are emphasizing that they are extremely nasty, cruel, or evil. 卑劣な [EMPHASIS 強調] ❏*The minister, who visited the scene a few hours after the explosion, said it was a despicable crime.* 爆発の数時間後に現場を訪れた大臣が，それは卑劣な犯罪だと言った.

des|pise /dɪspaɪz/ (**despises, despising, despised**) V-T 他動詞 If you **despise** something or someone, you dislike them and have a very low opinion of them. けいべつする ❏*I can never, ever forgive him. I despise him.* なんとしても彼を許すことはできない. 私は彼をけいべつする.

de|spite /dɪspaɪt/ **1** PREP 前置詞 You use **despite** to introduce a fact which makes the other part of the sentence surprising. にもかかわらず [PREP n/-ing] ❏*She has been under house arrest for most of the past decade, despite efforts by the United Nations to have her released.* 国連による解放のための努力にもかかわらず，彼女は過去10年間の大半を自宅軟禁状態で過ごしてきた. **2** PREP 前置詞 You use **despite** to introduce an idea that appears to contradict your main statement, without suggesting that this idea is true or that you believe it. ～に反して ❏*She told friends she will stand by husband, despite reports that he sent another woman love notes.* 彼が他の女に愛の言葉を送ったという報告に反して，彼女は夫を支持するつもりだと語った.

de|spond|ent /dɪspɒndənt/ ADJ 形容詞 If you are **despondent**, you are very unhappy because you have been experiencing difficulties that you think you will not be able to overcome. 落胆した ❏*He was despondent over the breakup of his marriage.* 彼は結婚の破局でがっくりきていた.

des|sert /dɪzɜrt/ (**desserts**) N-MASS 質量名詞 **Dessert** is something sweet, such as fruit, pastry, or ice cream, that you eat at the end of a meal. デザート ❏*She had homemade ice cream for dessert.* 彼女はデザートに手作りのアイスクリームを食べた. → see Picture Dictionary: **dessert**

Word Link   *stab* ≈ *steady* : *de*stabilize, *e*stablish, *in*stability

de|sta|bi|lize /disteɪbəlaɪz/ (**destabilizes, destabilizing, destabilized**) V-T 他動詞 To **destabilize** something such as a country or government means to create a situation which reduces its power or influence. 不安定にさせる ❏*Their sole aim is to destabilize the Indian government.* 彼らの唯一の目的はインド政府の不安定化だ.

des|ti|na|tion /dɛstɪneɪˌʃ⁰n/ (**destinations**) N-COUNT 可算名詞 The **destination** of someone or something is the place to which they are going or being sent. 目的地 ❏*Ellis Island has become one of America's most popular tourist destinations.* エリス島はアメリカでも特に人気のある観光地となった.

des|tined /dɛstɪnd/ **1** ADJ 形容詞 If something is **destined to** happen or if someone is **destined to** behave in a particular way, that thing seems certain to happen or be done. 前もって定められた ❏*Any economic strategy based on a weak dollar is destined to fail.* ドル安を前提とした経済戦略はすべて失敗する運命にある. **2** ADJ 形容詞 If someone is **destined for** a particular place, or if goods are **destined for** a particular place, they are traveling toward that place or will be sent to that place. 一行きの [v-link ADJ 'for' n] ❏*...products destined for Saudi Arabia.* サウジアラビア向け製品

des|ti|ny /dɛstɪni/ (**destinies**) **1** N-COUNT 可算名詞 A person's **destiny** is everything that happens to them during their life, including what will happen in the future, especially when it is considered to be controlled by someone or something else. 運命 ❏*We are masters of our own destiny.* 私たちは自分の運命を支配できる. **2** N-UNCOUNT 不可算名詞 **Destiny** is the force which some people believe controls the things that happen to you in your life. 運命 ❏*Is it destiny that brings people together, or is it accident?* 人の出会いは運命なのか，それとも偶然なのか.

des|ti|tute /dɛstɪtut/ ADJ 形容詞 Someone who is **destitute** has no money or possessions. 困窮した [FORMAL 形式ばった] ❏*...destitute children who live on the streets.* 路上で暮らす極めて貧しい子供たち

de|stroy /dɪstrɔɪ/ (**destroys, destroying, destroyed**) **1** V-T 他動詞 To **destroy** something means to cause so much damage to it that it is completely ruined or does not exist any more. 破壊する ❏*That's a sure recipe for destroying the economy and creating chaos.* それは経済を壊滅させ混乱を招く条件がそろっている. **2** V-T 他動詞 To **destroy** someone means to ruin their life or to make their situation impossible to bear. 破滅させる ❏*If I was younger or more naive, the criticism would have destroyed me.* 私がもっと若く世間知らずであれば，その批判に打ちのめされていただろう. **3** V-T 他動詞 If an animal **is destroyed**, it is killed, either because it is ill or because it is dangerous. 殺す [usu passive] ❏*Lindsay was unhurt but the horse had to be destroyed.* リンゼイは無傷だったが，馬は処分された.

Thesaurus destroy また次を参照:

v. annihilate, crush, demolish, eradicate, ruin, wipe out; (ant.) build, construct, create, repair **1**

de|struc|tion /dɪstrʌkʃ°n/ N-UNCOUNT 不可算名詞 **Destruction** is the act of destroying something, or the state of being destroyed. 破壊 ❏...an international agreement aimed at halting the destruction of the ozone layer. オゾン層の破壊を食い止めるための国際合意

Word Link struct ≈ building : construct, destructive, instruct

de|struc|tive /dɪstrʌktɪv/ ADJ 形容詞 Something that is **destructive** causes or is capable of causing great damage, harm, or injury. 破壊的な ❏...the awesome destructive power of nuclear weapons. 核兵器の恐ろしい破壊力

Word Link de ≈ from, down, away : deflate, descend, detach

de|tach /dɪtætʃ/ (detaches, detaching, detached) **1** V-T/V-I 他動詞/自動詞 If you **detach** one thing **from** another that it is attached to, you remove it. If one thing **detaches from** another, it becomes separated from it. 取り外す [FORMAL 形式ばった] ❏ Detach the white part of the application form and keep it for reference only. 申込み用紙の白い部分を取り外し、控えとして保存してください。❏ They clambered back under the falls to detach the raft from a jagged rock. 彼らはゴツゴツした岩からいかだを引き離すため滝の下からよじ登って戻った。**2** V-T 他動詞 If you **detach yourself from** something, you become less involved in it or less concerned about it than you used to be. 距離を置く ❏ It helps them detach themselves from their problems and become more objective. そのおかげで彼らは自分たちの問題と距離を置き、客観性を高めることができる。

de|tached /dɪtætʃt/ **1** ADJ 形容詞 Someone who is **detached** is not personally involved in something or has no emotional interest in it. 距離を置いた ❏ He tries to remain emotionally detached from the prisoners, but fails. 彼は囚人たちから感情的に距離を置こうと努めているが、そうできない。**2** ADJ 形容詞 A **detached** building is one that is not joined to any other building. 一戸建ての ❏...a house on the corner with a detached garage. 別棟の車庫がある角の家

de|tach|ment /dɪtætʃmənt/ N-UNCOUNT 不可算名詞 **Detachment** is the feeling that you have of not being personally involved in something or of having no emotional interest in it. 無関心、公平 ❏ She did not care for the idea of socializing with her clients. It would detract from her professional detachment. 彼女は客と親密になることを好まなかった。そうなれば彼女の職業的な公平を損なうだろう。

de|tail /diteɪl/ (details, detailing, detailed)

The pronunciation /dɪteɪl/ is also used for the noun.

名詞では /dɪteɪl/ とも発音される。

1 N-COUNT 可算名詞 The **details of** something are its individual features or elements. 詳細 ❏ The details of the plan are still being worked out. その計画の詳細はまだ検討中である。❏ No details of the discussions have been given. 議論の詳細は知らされていない。**2** N-COUNT 可算名詞 A **detail** is a minor point or aspect of something, as opposed to the central ones. 些事 (さじ) ❏ Only minor details now remain to be settled. 細かい点だけが未解決のままだ。**3** N-PLURAL 複数名詞 **Details** about someone or something are facts or pieces of information about them. 詳細 ❏ See the bottom of this page for details of how to apply for this exciting offer. このすばらしいご提供への申込み方法の詳細はこのページの下部をご覧ください。**4** N-UNCOUNT 不可算名詞 You can refer to the small features of something which are often not noticed as **detail**. 細部 ❏ We like his attention to detail and his enthusiasm. 我々は彼の細部への気配りと彼の情熱が好きだ。**5** V-T 他動詞 If you **detail** things, you list them or give information about them. 詳述する ❏ The report detailed the human rights abuses committed during the war. その報告書は戦争中の人権侵害について詳述していた。**6** N-COUNT 可算名詞 A **detail** of people such as soldiers or prisoners is a small group of them who have been given a special task to carry out. 特務班 [oft N 'of' n] ❏...a sergeant with a detail of four men. 四人の特務員を持つ軍曹 **7** PHRASE 句 If someone does not **go into detail** about a subject, or does not **go into the details**, they mention it without explaining it fully or properly. 詳細に述べる ❏ He doesn't wish to go into detail about all the events of those days. 彼は当時のすべての出来事について詳しく語りたくないと思っている。**8** PHRASE 句 If you examine or discuss something **in detail**, you do it thoroughly and carefully. 詳しく ❏ We examine the wording in detail before deciding on the final text. 最終文書に関して決定を下す前に我々は文言を詳細に検討する。

Thesaurus detail また次を参照:

N. component, element, feature, point **1** **3**; fact, information **3**
v. depict, describe, specify; (ant.) approximate, generalize **5**

de|tailed /diteɪld/ ADJ 形容詞 A **detailed** report or plan contains a lot of details. 詳細な ❏ Yesterday's letter contains a detailed account of the decisions. 昨日の手紙には決定に関する詳しい説明が含まれている。

Word Partnership detailed は次の語句と使われる:

N. detailed **account**, detailed **analysis**, detailed **description**, detailed **instructions**, detailed **plan**, detailed **record**

de|tain /dɪteɪn/ (detains, detaining, detained) **1** V-T 他動詞 When people such as the police **detain** someone, they keep them in a place under their control. 拘束する [FORMAL 形式ばった] ❏ Police have detained two suspects in connection with the attack. 警察はその襲撃に関わりのある二人の容疑者を拘留した。**2** V-T 他動詞 To **detain** someone means to delay them, for example, by talking to them. 引き止める [FORMAL 形式ばった] ❏ Millson stood up. "Thank you. We won't detain you any further, Mrs. Stebbing." ミルソンは立ち上がった。「ありがとうございます。これ以上あなたをお止めいたしません、ステビングさん」

de|tain|ee /diteɪni/ (detainees) N-COUNT 可算名詞 A **detainee** is someone who is held prisoner by a government because of his or her political views or activities. 抑留者 ❏ Earlier this year, Amnesty International called for the release of more than 100 political detainees. 今年の初め、アムネスティ・インターナショナルは100名以上の政治拘留者の解放を要求した。

Word Link tect ≈ covering : detect, protect, protective

de|tect /dɪtɛkt/ (detects, detecting, detected) **1** V-T 他動詞 To **detect** something means to find it or discover that it is present somewhere by using equipment or making an investigation. 探知する ❏...a sensitive piece of equipment used to detect radiation. 放射能探知に使われる高感度の装置 **2** V-T 他動詞 If you **detect** something, you notice it or sense it, even though it is not very obvious. 察知する ❏ Arnold could detect a certain sadness in the old man's face. アーノルドは老人の顔のある種の悲哀に気づいた。

de|tec|tion /dɪtɛkʃ°n/ N-UNCOUNT 不可算名詞 **Detection** is the act of noticing or sensing something. 探知 ❏...the early detection of breast cancer. 乳がんの早期発見

de|tec|tive /dɪtɛktɪv/ (detectives) **1** N-COUNT 可算名詞 A **detective** is someone whose job is to discover what has happened in a crime or other situation and to find the people involved. Some detectives work in the police force and others work privately. 探偵 ❏ Now detectives are appealing for witnesses who may have seen anything suspicious last night. 今、探偵たちは昨晩なにか疑わしいものを見たかもしれない目撃者の協力を求めている。**2** ADJ 形容詞 A **detective** novel or story is one in which a detective tries to solve a crime. 探偵の [ADJ n] ❏...Arthur Conan Doyle's classic detective novel. アーサー・コナン・ドイルの古典的探偵小説

de|tec|tor /dɪtɛktər/ (detectors) N-COUNT 可算名詞 A **detector** is an instrument which is used to discover that something is present somewhere, or to measure how much of something there is. 探知機 ❏...a metal detector. 金属探知機

de|ten|tion /dɪtɛnʃ°n/ (detentions) **1** N-UNCOUNT 算名詞 **Detention** is when someone is arrested or put into prison. 拘留 [also N in pl] ❏...the detention without trial of government critics. 政府批判者の裁判なしでの拘留 **2** N-VAR 可変性名詞 **Detention** is a punishment for students who misbehave, who are made to stay at school after the other students have gone home. 居残り ❏ The teacher kept the boys in detention after school. 教師は少年たちに放課後の居残りをさせた。

de|ter /dɪtɜr/ (deters, deterring, deterred) V-T 他動詞 To **deter** someone **from** doing something means to make them not want to do it or continue doing it. 妨げる ❏ Supporters of the death penalty argue that it would deter criminals from carrying guns. 死刑肯定論者は、死刑が犯罪者の銃携行を抑制すると主張する。

de|ter|gent /dɪtɜrdʒ°nt/ (detergents) N-MASS 質量名詞 **Detergent** is a chemical substance, usually in the form of a powder or liquid, which is used for washing things such as clothes or dishes. 洗剤 ❏...a brand of detergent. 洗剤の銘柄 → see soap

de|terio|rate /dɪtɪəriəreɪt/ (deteriorates, deteriorating, deteriorated) V-I 自動詞 If something **deteriorates**, it becomes worse in some way. 悪化する ❏ There are fears that the situation might deteriorate into full-scale war. 状況が悪化し全面戦争になる恐れ

がある. ●de|terio|ra|tion /dɪtɪəriəreɪʃ°n/ N-UNCOUNT 不可算名詞 悪化 ❏ …concern about the rapid deterioration in relations between the two countries. 二国間関係の急速な悪化に関する懸念

de|ter|mi|na|tion /dɪtɜrmɪneɪʃ°n/ ■ N-UNCOUNT 不可算名詞 Determination is the quality that you show when you have decided to do something and you will not let anything stop you. 決意 ❏ Everyone concerned acted with great courage and determination. 関係者の誰もが偉大な勇気と決意をもって行動した. ❷ → see also determine

Word Partnership   determination は次の語句と使われる:

N.	courage and determination, strength and determination
ADJ.	fierce determination

Word Link   term, termin ≈ limit, end : determine, terminal, terminate

de|ter|mine /dɪtɜrmɪn/ (determines, determining, determined) ■ V-T 他動詞 If a particular factor determines the nature of a thing or event, it causes it to be of a particular kind. 決定する [FORMAL 形式ばった] ❏ The size of the chicken pieces will determine the cooking time. 鶏肉の切り身の大きさで調理時間が決まる. ●de|ter|mi|na|tion N-UNCOUNT 不可算名詞 決定 ❏ …the gene which is responsible for male sex determination. 男性の性決定に関わる遺伝子 ❷ V-T 他動詞 To determine a fact means to discover it as a result of investigation. 見つけ出す [FORMAL 形式ばった] ❏ The investigation will determine what really happened. 調査により現実に起こったことが究明されるだろう. ❏ Experts say testing needs to be done on each contaminant to determine the long-term effects on humans. 専門家は, 人体に対する長期的影響を確定するためそれぞれの汚染物質の試験が必要だと言う. ❸ V-T 他動詞 If you determine something, you decide about it or settle it. 決定する ❏ The Baltic people have a right to determine their own future. バルト海沿岸地域の人々は自らの未来を決定する権利を持っている. ●de|ter|mi|na|tion N-COUNT 可算名詞 決定 ❏ We must take into our own hands the determination of our future. 我々は自らの判断で将来を決定せねばならない. ❹ V-T 他動詞 If you determine to do something, you make a firm decision to do it. 決意する [FORMAL 形式ばった] ❏ He determined to rescue his two countrymen. 彼は二人の同国人の救出を決意した.

de|ter|mined /dɪtɜrmɪnd/ ADJ 形容詞 If you are determined to do something, you have made a firm decision to do it and will not let anything stop you. 決然とした ❏ His enemies are determined to ruin him. 敵は断固として彼を破滅させる気だ. ●de|ter|mined|ly ADV 副詞 決然と ❏ She shook her head, determinedly. 彼女は決然と頭を振った.

de|ter|min|er /dɪtɜrmɪnər/ (determiners) N-COUNT 可算名詞 In grammar, a determiner is a word which is used at the beginning of a noun group to indicate, for example, which thing you are referring to or whether you are referring to one thing or several. Common English determiners are "a," "the," "some," "this," and "each." 限定詞

de|ter|rence /dɪtɜrəns/ N-UNCOUNT 不可算名詞 Deterrence is the prevention of something, especially war or crime, by having something such as weapons or punishment to use as a threat. 抑止 ❏ …policies of nuclear deterrence. 核抑止政策

de|ter|rent /dɪtɜrənt/ (deterrents) ■ N-COUNT 可算名詞 A deterrent is something that prevents people from doing something by making them afraid of what will happen to them if they do it. 抑止するもの ❏ They seriously believe that capital punishment is a deterrent. 彼らは本気で極刑が抑止力になると信じている. ❷ N-COUNT 可算名詞 A deterrent is a weapon or set of weapons designed to prevent enemies from attacking by making them afraid to do so. 抑止兵器 ❏ The idea of building a nuclear deterrent is completely off the political agenda. 核抑止力の構築構想は政治の検討項目から完全に外れている.

de|test /dɪtɛst/ (detests, detesting, detested) V-T 他動詞 If you detest someone or something, you dislike them very much. 嫌悪する ❏ My mother detested him. 私の母は彼を毛嫌いしていた.

deto|nate /dɛtəneɪt/ (detonates, detonating, detonated) V-T/V-I 他動詞/自動詞 If someone detonates a device such as a bomb, or if it detonates, it explodes. 爆発させる ❏ France is expected to detonate its first nuclear device in the next few days. フランスは数日中に最初の核装置を爆発させると予測されている.

de|tour /ditʊər/ (detours) ■ N-COUNT 可算名詞 If you make a detour on a trip, you go by a route which is not the shortest way, because you want to avoid something such as a traffic jam, or because there is something you want to do on the way. 回り道 ❏ He did not take the direct route to his home, but made a detour around the outskirts of the city. 彼は自宅に直接帰る道筋をとらず, 町の郊外に回り道をした. ❷ N-COUNT 可算名詞 A detour is a special route for

traffic to follow when the normal route is blocked, for example, because it is being repaired. 迂回路 (うかいろ) [AM 米国英語] ❏ A slight detour in the road is causing major headaches for businesses along El Camino Real. エル・カミノ・レアルの沿線企業にとって, 少しの迂回路が設けられただけで大きな頭痛の種となっている.

de|tract /dɪtrækt/ (detracts, detracting, detracted) V-T/V-I 他動詞/自動詞 If one thing detracts from another, it makes it seem less good or impressive. 損なう ❏ They feared that the publicity surrounding him would detract from their own election campaigns. 彼らは彼の状況が公になって, 自分達自身の選挙戦が損なわれることを恐れていた.

det|ri|ment /dɛtrɪmənt/ ■ PHRASE 句 If something happens to the detriment of something or to a person's detriment, it causes harm or damage to them. 有害 [FORMAL 形式ばった] ❏ These tests will give too much importance to written exams to the detriment of other skills. こうした試験は, 記述式偏重で, 他の技能にとって有害になろう. ❷ PHRASE 句 If something happens without detriment to a person or thing, it does not harm or damage them. を損ねることなく [FORMAL 形式ばった] ❏ These difficulties have been overcome without detriment to performance. これらの問題は業績を損ねることなく克服された.

det|ri|men|tal /dɛtrɪmɛnt°l/ ADJ 形容詞 Something that is detrimental to something else has a harmful or damaging effect on it. 有害な ❏ Many foods are suspected of being detrimental to health because of the chemicals and additives they contain. 多くの食品が, 含有化学物質や添加物のため, 健康への害を疑われている.

de|value /divælyu/ (devalues, devaluing, devalued) ■ V-T 他動詞 To devalue something means to cause it to be thought less impressive or less deserving of respect. 価値を減じる ❏ They spread tales about her in an attempt to devalue her work. 彼らは彼女についてのうわさ話を広めて仕事への評価を下ようとする. ❷ V-T 他動詞 To devalue the currency of a country means to reduce its value in relation to other currencies. 平価を切り下げる ❏ India has devalued the rupee by about eleven percent. インドは約11パーセントのルピー切り下げを行った. ●de|valu|ation /divælyueɪʃ°n/ (devaluations) N-VAR 可変性名詞 平価切下げ ❏ It will lead to devaluation of a number of currencies. それは多くの通貨の平価切り下げを招くだろう.

dev|as|tate /dɛvəsteɪt/ (devastates, devastating, devastated) V-T 他動詞 If something devastates an area or a place, it damages it very badly or destroys it totally. 荒廃させる ❏ The tsunami devastated parts of Indonesia and other countries in the region. 津波はインドネシアや周辺国の諸地域を壊滅させた.

dev|as|tat|ed /dɛvəsteɪtɪd/ ADJ 形容詞 If you are devastated by something, you are very shocked and upset by it. 打ちひしがれた [V-link ADJ] ❏ Teresa was devastated, her dreams shattered. テリーザは打ちひしがれ, 彼女の夢は砕かれた.

dev|as|tat|ing /dɛvəsteɪtɪŋ/ ■ ADJ 形容詞 If you describe something as devastating, you are emphasizing that it is very harmful or damaging. 破壊的な [EMPHASIS 強調] ❏ Affairs do have a devastating effect on marriages. 情事は結婚に対して壊滅的な影響を与える. ❷ ADJ 形容詞 You can use devastating to emphasize that something is very shocking, upsetting, or terrible. 衝撃的な [EMPHASIS 強調] ❏ The diagnosis was devastating. She had cancer. 診断は衝撃的だった. 彼女はがんだった. ❸ ADJ 形容詞 You can use devastating to emphasize that something or someone is very impressive. 圧倒的な [EMPHASIS 強調] ❏ He returned to his best with a devastating display of galloping and jumping. 馬はギャロップとジャンプで圧倒的な演技を見せ最高の状態に復活した.

dev|as|ta|tion /dɛvəsteɪʃ°n/ N-UNCOUNT 不可算名詞 Devastation is severe and widespread destruction or damage. 壊滅 ❏ The war brought massive devastation and loss of life to the region. 戦争はその地域に大規模な破壊と人命損失をもたらした.

de|vel|op /dɪvɛləp/ (develops, developing, developed) ■ V-I 自動詞 When something develops, it grows or changes over a period of time and usually becomes more advanced, complete, or severe. 発展する ❏ It's hard to say at this stage how the market will develop. この段階で市場がどのように発展するかを述べることは難しい. ❏ These clashes could develop into open warfare. こうした衝突が限りのない戦争に発展することもありうる. ●de|vel|oped ADJ 形容詞 発展した ❏ Their bodies were well developed and super fit. 彼らの肉体はよく発達し極めて壮健だった. ❷ V-I 自動詞 If a problem or difficulty develops, it begins to occur. 発現する ❏ The space agency says a problem has developed with an experiment aboard the space shuttle. 宇宙局によるとスペースシャトルの実験で問題が生じたとのことだ. ❸ V-I 自動詞 If you say that a country develops, you mean that it changes from being a poor agricultural country to being a rich industrial country. 発展する ❏ All countries, it was predicted, would develop and develop fast. すべての国が発展し, しかも急速に発展すると予測されていた. ❹ → see also developed, developing ❺ V-T/V-I 他動詞/自動詞 If you develop a business or industry, or if it develops, it becomes bigger and more successful. 発展させる [他動詞], 発展する [自動詞] ❏ An amateur hatmaker has won a scholarship to pursue her dreams of developing her own business. 帽子づ

くりのアマチュアが，自分の事業を発展させる夢を追求するため奨学金を勝ち取った． [BUSINESS 実業] ● de|vel|oped ADJ 形容詞 発展した □ ...the countries that have suffered the most from the absence of more developed financial systems. 発達した金融制度を持てなかったため最も苦しんできた国々 ⑤ V-T 他動詞 To **develop** land or property means to make it more profitable, by building houses or factories or by improving the existing buildings. 開発する □ Local entrepreneurs developed fashionable restaurants, bars and discotheques in the area. 地元起業家が活躍して，おしゃれなレストランやバー，ディスコを開発した． ● de|vel|oped ADJ 形容詞 開発された □ Developed land was to grow from 5.3% to 6.9%. 開発された土地は5.3%から6.9%に増加するはずだった． ⑥ V-T 他動詞 If you **develop** a habit, reputation, or belief, you start to have it and it then becomes stronger or more noticeable. 持ち始める □ Mr. Robinson has developed the reputation of a ruthless cost-cutter. ロビンソン氏は非常な経費削減男との評判を得た． ⑦ V-T/V-I 他動詞/自動詞 If you **develop** a skill, quality, or relationship, or if it **develops**, it becomes better or stronger. 発達させる [他動詞]，発達する [自動詞] □ Now you have a good opportunity to develop a greater understanding of each other. 今，お互いの理解をさらに育むのにいい機会がある． ● de|vel|oped ADJ 形容詞 発達した □ ...a highly developed instinct for self-preservation. 高度に発達した自己保存本能 ⑧ V-T 他動詞 If a piece of equipment **develops** a fault, it starts to have the fault. 来す □ The aircraft made an unscheduled landing at Logan after developing an electrical fault. 飛行機は電気系統の故障を来たし，ローガンで予定外の着陸を行った． ⑩ V-T 他動詞 If someone **develops** a new product, they design it and produce it. つくり上げる □ He claims that several countries have developed nuclear weapons secretly. 彼はいくつかの国が秘密裏に核兵器を開発したと主張する． ⑪ V-T/V-I 他動詞/自動詞 If you **develop** an idea, theory, story, or theme, or if it **develops**, it gradually becomes more detailed, advanced, or complex. 展開する □ I would like to thank them for allowing me to develop their original idea. 彼らがもともと考えついたアイデアを私に展開させてくれたことに感謝したい． ⑫ V-T 他動詞 To **develop** photographs means to make negatives or prints from a photographic film. 現像する □ ...after developing one roll of film. フィルム1本の現像後

→ see **photography**

de|vel|oped /dɪvɛləpt/ ADJ 形容詞 If you talk about **developed** countries or the **developed** world, you mean the countries or the parts of the world that are wealthy and have many industries. 発展した □ This scarcity is inevitable in less developed countries. こうした欠乏は発展が進んでいない国では避けがたい．

de|vel|op|er /dɪvɛləpər/ (**developers**) ① N-COUNT 可算名詞 A **developer** is a person or a company that buys land and builds houses, offices, stores, or factories on it, or buys existing buildings and makes them more modern. 開発事業者 [BUSINESS 実業] □ ...common land which would have a high commercial value if sold to developers. 開発事業者に売却すれば高い商業価値を持つはずの共有地 ② N-COUNT 可算名詞 A **developer** is someone who develops something such as an idea, a design, or a product. 開発者 □ John Bardeen was also co-developer of the theory of superconductivity. ジョン・バーディーンは超伝導理論を共同で展開させた人でもあった．

→ see **skyscraper**

de|vel|op|ing /dɪvɛləpɪŋ/ ADJ 形容詞 If you talk about **developing** countries or the **developing** world, you mean the countries or the parts of the world that are poor and have few industries. 発展途上の [ADJ n] □ In the developing world cigarette consumption is increasing. 発展途上地域でのたばこ消費が増加している．

de|vel|op|ment /dɪvɛləpmənt/ (**developments**) ① N-UNCOUNT 不可算名詞 **Development** is the gradual growth or formation of something. 発達 □ ...an ideal system for studying the development of the embryo. 胚の発達を研究するための理想的なシステム ② N-UNCOUNT 不可算名詞 **Development** is the growth of something such as a business or an industry. 発展 [BUSINESS 実業] □ He firmly believes that education and a country's economic development are key factors to progress. 教育と国の経済発展が進歩の重要要素であると彼は固く信じている． ③ N-UNCOUNT 不可算名詞 **Development** is the process of making an area of land or water more useful or profitable. 開発 □ The talks will focus on economic development of the region. その会談では地域の経済開発が焦点となるだろう． ④ N-VAR 可変性名詞 **Development** is the process or result of making a basic design gradually better and more advanced. 発展 □ It is spending $850M on research and development to get to the market place as soon as possible with faster microprocessors. 速度の速いマイクロプロセッサーをできるだけ早く市場に投入するため研究開発に8億5千万ドルを投資している． ⑤ N-COUNT 可算名詞 A **development** is an event or incident which has recently happened and is likely to have an effect on the present situation. 進展 □ The police spokesman said: "We believe there has been a significant development in the case." 警察の広報担当者は「私たちはこの事件に関する重要な新展開があったと考えている」と述べた． ⑥ N-COUNT 可算名詞 A **development** is an area of houses or buildings which have been built by property developers. 開発地 □ ...a 16-house development

planned by Everlast Enterprises. エバーラスト・エンタープライズ社の計画する住宅16戸の開発地

de|vel|op|ment bank (**development banks**) N-COUNT 可算名詞 A **development bank** is a bank that provides money for projects in poor countries or areas. 開発銀行

de|vi|ant /diviənt/ ADJ 形容詞 **Deviant** behavior or thinking is different from what people normally consider to be acceptable. 逸脱した □ ...the social reactions to deviant and criminal behavior. 異常犯罪行為に対する社会的反応 ● de|vi|ance /diviəns/ N-UNCOUNT 不可算名詞 □ ...sexual deviance, including the abuse of children. 児童虐待を含む性的逸脱

de|vi|ate /diviert/ (**deviates, deviating, deviated**) V-I 自動詞 To **deviate from** something means to start doing something different or not planned, especially in a way that causes problems for others. 逸脱する □ They stopped you as soon as you deviated from the script. 台本から外れると彼らはすぐにあなたを止めた．

de|via|tion /diviʃn/ (**deviations**) N-VAR 可変性名詞 **Deviation** means doing something that is different from what people consider to be normal or acceptable. 逸脱 □ Deviation from the norm is not tolerated. 基準からの逸脱は容認されない．

de|vice /dɪvaɪs/ (**devices**) N-COUNT 可算名詞 A **device** is an object that has been invented for a particular purpose, for example, for recording or measuring something. 装置 □ ...the electronic device that tells the starter when an athlete has moved from his blocks prematurely. 選手がブロックから早まって動いた際，出走係に知らせる電子装置

→ see **computer**

dev|il /dɛvl/ (**devils**) ① N-PROPER 固有名詞 In Judaism, Christianity, and Islam, **the Devil** is the most powerful evil spirit. 悪魔 ② N-COUNT 可算名詞 A **devil** is an evil spirit. 悪魔 □ ...the idea of angels with wings and devils with horns and hoofs. 羽を持った天使と角とひづめの悪魔という考え

de|vi|ous /diviəs/ ADJ 形容詞 If you describe someone as **devious** you do not like them because you think they are dishonest and like to keep things secret, often in a complicated way. ひねくれた [DISAPPROVAL 不賛成] □ Newman was certainly devious, prepared to say one thing in print and something quite different in private. ニューマンは確かにずる賢く，活字になる場合と非公式な場とではまったく違うことを言えた．

de|vise /dɪvaɪz/ (**devises, devising, devised**) V-T 他動詞 If you **devise** a plan, system, or machine, you have the idea for it and design it. 考案する □ We devised a scheme to help him. 我々は彼を助けるための案を出した．

Word Partnership	devise は次の語句と使われる:
N.	devise **new ways**, devise **a plan**, devise **a system**, devise **a strategy**

de|void /dɪvoɪd/ ADJ 形容詞 If you say that someone or something is **devoid of** a quality or thing, you are emphasizing that they have none of it. 欠いている [FORMAL 形式ばった, EMPHASIS 強調] [v-link ADJ 'of' n] □ I have never looked on a face that was so devoid of feeling. これほど感情の欠落した顔を見たことは今までにない．

de|vo|lu|tion /divəluʃn, dɛv-/ N-UNCOUNT 不可算名詞 **Devolution** is the transfer of some authority or power from a central organization or government to smaller organizations or government departments. 権限委譲 □ ...the devolution of power to the regions. 地域への権限委譲

de|volve /dɪvɒlv/ (**devolves, devolving, devolved**) V-T/V-I 他動詞/自動詞 If you **devolve** power, authority, or responsibility **to** a less powerful person or group, or if it **devolves upon** them, it is transferred to them. 権限委譲する □ ...the need to decentralize and devolve power to regional governments. 権限分散と地方分権の必要性 □ The best companies are those that devolve responsibility as far as they can. 最良の企業とは可能な限り責任を委譲する企業である．

de|vote /dɪvoʊt/ (**devotes, devoting, devoted**) ① V-T 他動詞 If you **devote** yourself, your time, or your energy **to** something, you spend all or most of your time or energy on it. ささげる □ He decided to devote the rest of his life to scientific investigation. 彼は残りの人生を科学調査にささげることを決意した． □ Considerable resources have been devoted to proving him a liar. 彼が嘘つきであることを証明するため相当の資金が当てられてきた． ② V-T 他動詞 If you **devote** a particular proportion of a piece of writing or a speech **to** a particular subject, you deal with the subject in that amount of space or time. 充てる □ He devoted a major section of his massive report to an analysis of U.S. aircraft design. 彼は大部の報告書の主要部分を米国の航空機設計の分析に充てた．

de|vot|ed /dɪvoʊtɪd/ ① ADJ 形容詞 Someone who is **devoted to** a person loves that person very much. 献身的な [ADJ n, v-link ADJ 'to' n] □ ...a loving and devoted husband. 愛情に満ち献身的な夫 ② ADJ 形容詞 If you are **devoted to** something, you care about it a lot

and are very enthusiastic about it. 傾倒する [v-link ADJ 'to' n, ADJ n] ❑ *I have personally been devoted to this cause for many years.* 私は何年もの間この大義に個人的に奉じてきた. ❸ ADJ 形容詞 Something that is **devoted** to a particular thing deals only with that thing or contains only that thing. 割かれる [v-link ADJ 'to' n] ❑ *A large part of the Internet is now devoted to weblogs.* 今、インターネットのかなりの部分がブログに費やされている.

de|vo|tion /dɪvoʊʃⁿn/ ❶ N-UNCOUNT 不可算名詞 **Devotion** is great love, affection, or admiration for someone. 献身的愛情 ❑ *At first she was flattered by his devotion.* 最初、彼女は彼の無私の愛にほだされた. ❷ N-UNCOUNT 不可算名詞 **Devotion** is commitment to a particular activity. 献身 ❑ *...devotion to the cause of the people and to socialism.* 国民の大義と社会主義への献身

de|vour /dɪvaʊər/ (devours, devouring, devoured) ❶ V-T 他動詞 If a person or animal **devours** something, they eat it quickly and eagerly. むさぼる ❑ *A medium-sized dog will devour at least one can of food plus biscuits per day.* 中型犬なら1日に少なくとも1缶のドッグフードとビスケットを平らげる. ❷ V-T 他動詞 If you **devour** a book or magazine, for example, you read it quickly and with great enthusiasm. むさぼり読む ❑ *She began buying and devouring newspapers when she was only 12.* 彼女はまだ12歳のときに新聞を買い、むさぼり読むようになった.

de|vout /dɪvaʊt/ ❶ ADJ 形容詞 A **devout** person has deep religious beliefs. 信心深い ❑ *She was a devout Christian.* 彼女は敬虔なキリスト教徒だった. ● N-PLURAL 複数名詞 The **devout** are people who are devout. 敬虔な人 ❑ *...priests instructing the devout.* 敬虔な信徒を指導する司祭 ❷ ADJ 形容詞 If you describe someone as a **devout** supporter or a **devout** opponent of something, you mean that they support it enthusiastically or oppose it strongly. 熱烈な [ADJ n] ❑ *Devout Marxists believed fascism was the "last stand of the bourgeoisie."* 熱烈なマルクス主義者はファシズムを「ブルジョワジーの最後の抵抗」だと信じていた.

dew /dju/ N-UNCOUNT 不可算名詞 **Dew** is small drops of water that form on the ground and other surfaces outdoors during the night. 露 ❑ *The dew gathered on the leaves.* 露が葉っぱについた.

dia|be|tes /daɪəbiːtɪs, -tiz/ N-UNCOUNT 不可算名詞 **Diabetes** is a medical condition in which someone has too much sugar in their blood. 糖尿病
→ see **sugar**

dia|bet|ic /daɪəbɛtɪk/ (diabetics) ❶ N-COUNT 可算名詞 A **diabetic** is a person who suffers from diabetes. 糖尿病患者 ❑ *...an insulin-dependent diabetic.* インシュリンに頼る糖尿病患者 ● ADJ 形容詞 **Diabetic** is also an adjective. 糖尿病の ❑ *...diabetic patients.* 糖尿病患者 ❷ ADJ 形容詞 **Diabetic** means relating to diabetes. 糖尿病の [ADJ n] ❑ *He found her in a diabetic coma.* 彼は彼女は糖尿病による昏睡状態だと気づいた.

Word Link   dia ≈ across, through : diagnose, diagonal, dialogue

di|ag|nose /daɪəgnoʊs/ (diagnoses, diagnosing, diagnosed) V-T 他動詞 If someone or something **is diagnosed as** having a particular illness or problem, their illness or problem is identified. If an illness or problem **is diagnosed**, it is identified. 診断する ❑ *The soldiers were diagnosed as having flu.* 兵士たちはインフルエンザと診断された. ❑ *Susan had a mental breakdown and was diagnosed with schizophrenia.* スーザンは神経衰弱にかかっており、統合失調症と診断された.
→ see **diagnosis, illness**

di|ag|no|sis /daɪəgnoʊsɪs/ (diagnoses) N-VAR 可変性名詞 **Diagnosis** is the discovery and naming of what is wrong with someone who is ill or with something that is not working properly. 診断 ❑ *I need to have a second test to confirm the diagnosis.* 私は診断の確認のため2度目の検査を受ける必要がある.
→ see Word Web: **diagnosis**

di|ag|nos|tic /daɪəgnɒstɪk/ ADJ 形容詞 **Diagnostic** equipment, methods, or systems are used for discovering what is wrong with people who are ill or with things that do not work properly. 診断の [ADJ n] ❑ *...X-rays and other diagnostic tools.* X線などの診断手段

di|ag|o|nal /daɪægənⁿl, -ægnⁿl/ ADJ 形容詞 A **diagonal** line or movement goes in a sloping direction, for example, from one corner of a square across to the opposite corner. 斜め線の ❑ *...a*

pattern of diagonal lines. 斜め線の模様 ● di|ag|o|nal|ly ADV 副詞 斜めに ❑ *Vaulting the stile, he headed diagonally across the paddock.* 彼は踏み越え段を飛び越え、パドックを斜めに横切った.

Word Link   gram ≈ writing : diagram, program, telegram

dia|gram /daɪəgræm/ (diagrams) N-COUNT 可算名詞 A **diagram** is a simple drawing which consists mainly of lines and is used, for example, to explain how a machine works. 図 ❑ *...a circuit diagram.* 回路図

Thesaurus   diagram また次を参照:

N.   blueprint, chart, design, illustration, plan

dial /daɪəl/ (dials, dialing, dialed) ❶ N-COUNT 可算名詞 A **dial** is the part of a machine or instrument such as a clock or watch which shows you the time or a measurement that has been recorded. 文字盤 ❑ *The luminous dial on the clock showed five minutes to seven.* 時計の蛍光文字盤が7時5分前を示していた. ❷ N-COUNT 可算名詞 A **dial** is a control on a device or piece of equipment which you can move in order to adjust the setting, for example, to select or change the frequency on a radio or the temperature of a heater. ダイヤル ❑ *He turned the dial on the radio.* 彼はラジオのダイヤルを回した. ❸ V-T/V-I 他動詞/自動詞 If you **dial** or if you **dial** a number, you turn the dial or press the buttons on a telephone in order to phone someone. ダイヤルを回す ❑ *He lifted the phone and dialed her number.* 彼は電話を手に取り、彼女の番号にかけた.

dia|lect /daɪəlɛkt/ (dialects) N-COUNT 可算名詞 A **dialect** is a form of a language that is spoken in a particular area. 方言 [also 'in' N] ❑ *It is often appropriate to use the local dialect to communicate your message.* 言いたいことを伝えるために土地の方言を使うのが適切であることは多い.
→ see **English**

dial|ling code (dialling codes) N-COUNT 可算名詞 A **dialling code** for a particular city or region is the series of numbers that you have to dial before a particular telephone number if you are making a call to that place from a different area. 市外局番 [mainly BRIT 主に英国英語; AM **area code** 米国英語 **area code**]

dial|ling tone (dialling tones) N-COUNT 可算名詞 The **dialling tone** is the same as the **dial tone**. 発信音 [BRIT 英国英語]

dia|log box (dialog boxes) N-COUNT 可算名詞 A **dialog box** is a small area containing information or questions that appears on a computer screen when you are performing particular operations. ダイアログボックス ❑ *You should now see a dialog box listing all of the print queues on your network.* さてネットワーク上の印刷待ちの一覧ダイアログボックスが表示されているはずです. [COMPUTING コンピューティング]

Word Link   log ≈ reason, speech : apology, dialogue, logic

dia|logue /daɪəlɒg/ (dialogues) also dialog ❶ N-VAR 可変性名詞 **Dialogue** is communication or discussion between people or groups of people such as governments or political parties. 対話 ❑ *People of all social standings should be given equal opportunities for dialogue.* あらゆる社会的立場の人々に平等な対話の機会が与えられるべきだ. ❷ N-VAR 可変性名詞 A **dialogue** is a conversation between two people in a book, film, or play. せりふ ❑ *Although the dialogue is sharp, the actors move too awkwardly around the stage.* せりふは鋭かったが、舞台での役者たちの演技はあまりにも無様だ.

dial tone (dial tones) N-COUNT 可算名詞 The **dial tone** is the noise which you hear when you pick up a telephone receiver and which means that you can dial the number you want. 発信音 ❑ *It was only as she tried for the second time that she realized that there was no dial tone.* 2度目の試みでようやく彼女は発信音がないことに気づいた.

di|am|eter /daɪæmɪtər/ (diameters) N-COUNT 名詞 The **diameter** of a round object is the length of a straight line that can be drawn across it, passing through the middle of it. 直径 [also 'in' N] ❑ *...a tube less than a fifth of the diameter of a human hair.* 人間の髪の5分の1以下の直径しかない管
→ see **area, circle**

Word Web   diagnosis

Many doctors recommend that their **patients** get a routine **physical examination** once a year—even if they're feeling perfectly well. This enables the **physician** to detect **symptoms** and **diagnose** possible **diseases** at an early stage. The doctor may begin by using a **tongue depressor** to look down the patient's throat for possible **infections**. Then he or she may use a stethoscope to listen to subtle sounds in the heart, lungs, and stomach. A **blood pressure** reading is always part of the exam and involves the use of a **blood pressure cuff**.

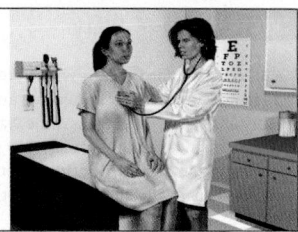

D

Word Web   diamond

Diamonds are made of pure **carbon**. They are the hardest **mineral** to form and develop deep inside the earth. To create a diamond, the pressure must reach almost half a million pounds per square inch. The temperature must be at least 400°C*. Many of today's diamonds formed millions of years ago. They reach the surface of the earth through a process similar to a volcanic eruption. Then the diamonds are **mined**. A diamond is not beautiful until someone cuts it and exposes its many **facets**. **Jewelers** give the weight of a diamond in **carats**. One carat is about 200 milligrams.

400°C=*about 752°F.*

dia|mond /daɪmənd, daɪə-/ (**diamonds**) **1** N-VAR 可変性名詞 A **diamond** is a hard, bright, precious stone which is clear and colorless. Diamonds are used in jewelry and for cutting very hard substances. ダイヤモンド ❑ ...*a pair of diamond earrings.* ダイヤモンドのイヤリング1組 **2** N-COUNT 可算名詞 A **diamond** is a shape with four straight sides of equal length where the opposite angles are the same, but none of the angles is equal to 90° ひし形 ❑ ...*forming his hands into the shape of a diamond.* 彼の手をひし形に組み合わせる **3** N-UNCOUNT-COLL 集合的不可算名詞 **Diamonds** is one of the four suits of cards in a pack of playing cards. Each card in the suit is marked with one or more red symbols in the shape of a diamond. トランプダイヤ ❑ *He drew the seven of diamonds.* 彼はダイヤの7を引いた. ● N-COUNT 可算名詞 A **diamond** is a playing card of this suit. ❑ ...*win the ace of clubs and play a diamond.* クラブのエースを取り、ダイヤを1枚出す. **4** N-COUNT 可算名詞 In baseball, the **diamond** is the square formed by the four bases, or the whole of the playing area. 内野 [usu 'the' N] ❑ *Just drive around the city and see all the empty baseball diamonds there are.* 町のなかを車で回って、野球場がどこも空っぽなのを見てください.
→ see Word Web: **diamond**
→ see **baseball, crystal**

dia|per /daɪpər, daɪə-/ (**diapers**) N-COUNT 可算名詞 A **diaper** is a piece of soft towel or paper, which you fasten around a baby's bottom in order to contain its urine and feces. おむつ [AM 米国英語] ❑ *He never changed her diapers, never bathed her.* 彼は彼女のおしめを取り替えたことも、風呂に入れたこともなかった.

dia|phragm /daɪəfræm/ (**diaphragms**) **1** N-COUNT 可算名詞 Your **diaphragm** is a muscle between your lungs and your stomach. It is used when you breathe. 隔膜 ❑ ...*the skill of breathing from the diaphragm.* 隔膜から息をする技 **2** N-COUNT 可算名詞 A **diaphragm** is a circular rubber contraceptive device that a woman places inside her vagina. ペッサリー
→ see **respiration**

di|ar|rhea /daɪəriə/ N-UNCOUNT 不可算名詞 If someone has **diarrhea**, a lot of liquid feces comes out of their body because they are ill. 下痢 ❑ *But the food itself was barely digestible, and many team members suffered from diarrhea or constipation.* だが食べ物自体はほとんど消化できないもので、チームメンバーの多くは下痢や便秘に悩まされた.

dia|ry /daɪəri/ (**diaries**) N-COUNT 可算名詞 A **diary** is a book which has a separate space for each day of the year. You use a diary to write down things you plan to do, or to record what happens in your life day by day. 日記 ❑ *I had earlier read the entry from Harold Nicholson's diary for July 10, 1940.* 私は以前ハロルド・ニコルソンの1940年7月10日の日記を読んだことがあった.
→ see Word Web: **diary**
→ see **history**

dice /daɪs/ (**dices, dicing, diced**) **1** N-COUNT 可算名詞 A **dice** is a small cube which has between one and six spots or numbers on its sides, and which is used in games to provide random numbers. In old-fashioned English, "dice" was used only as a plural form, and the singular was **die**, but now "dice" is used as both the singular and the plural form. さいころ ❑ *I throw both dice and get double 6.* 私は両方のさいころを投げ、ダブル6を得る. **2** V-T 他動詞 If you **dice** food, you cut it into small cubes. さいの目に切る ❑ *Dice the onion and boil in the water for about fifteen minutes.* たまねぎ

をさいの目に切り、15分ほど煮る. **3** PHRASE 句 If you are trying to achieve something and you say that it's **no dice**, you mean that you are having no success or luck with it. If someone asks you for something and you reply **no dice**, you are refusing to do what they ask. 駄目だ、嫌だ ❑ *If there'd been a halfway decent house for rent on this island, I would have taken it. But it was no dice.* この島に多少ともまともな貸家があればそこに住んでいたと思う。だが駄目だった. ❑ *If the Republicans were to say "no dice," the Democrats would think they have a campaign issue.* もし共和党が「駄目だ」と言うとしたら民主党側はキャンペーンに問題があると見るだろう.
→ see **cut**

Word Link   dict ≈ speaking : contra**dict**, **dict**ate, pre**dict**

dic|tate (**dictates, dictating, dictated**)

The verb is pronounced /dɪkteɪt, dɪkteɪt/. The noun is pronounced /dɪkteɪt/.

動詞は /dɪkteɪt, dɪkteɪt/ と発音される。名詞は /dɪkteɪt/ と発音される.

1 V-T 他動詞 If you **dictate** something, you say or read it aloud for someone else to write down. 口述する ❑ *Sheldon writes every day of the week, dictating his novels in the morning.* シェルドンは1週間毎日原稿を書く。午前中は小説を口述する. **2** V-T 他動詞 If someone **dictates** to someone else, they tell them what they should do or can do. 指図する ❑ *What right has one country to dictate the environmental standards of another?* どこかの国に他国の環境基準を設定する権限があるだろうか. ❑ *What gives them the right to dictate to us what we should eat?* 彼らに我々が食べるものを指図するどんな権利があるというのか. **3** V-T 他動詞 If one thing **dictates** another, the first thing causes or influences the second thing. 規定する ❑ *The film's budget dictated a tough schedule.* 映画は予算のために厳しい日程となった. ❑ *Of course, a number of factors will dictate how long an apple tree can survive.* リンゴの木の寿命はもちろん複数の要因に左右されるだろう. **4** V-T 他動詞 You say that logic or common sense **dictates that** a particular thing is the case when you believe strongly that it is the case and that logic or common sense will cause other people to agree. 規定する ❑ *Logic dictates that our ancestors could not have held a yearly festival until they figured what a year was.* 我々の祖先は1年という概念を理解するまで毎年の祭りを催すことはできなかったことは論理にかなっている. **5** N-COUNT 可算名詞 **Dictates** are principles or rules which you consider to be extremely important. (良心・理性などの) 命じるところ ❑ *We have followed the dictates of our consciences and have done our duty.* 我々は良心の命に従い、義務を果たした.

Word Partnership   dictate は次の語句と使われる:

N.	dictate **terms 2**
	rules dictate **2 3**
	circumstances dictate, **factors** dictate **3**

dic|ta|tion /dɪkteɪʃ³n/ N-UNCOUNT 不可算名詞 **Dictation** is the speaking or reading aloud of words for someone else to write down. 口述 ❑ ...*taking dictation from the dean of the graduate school.* 大学院の学生監の口述を書き取ること

dic|ta|tor /dɪkteɪtər/ (**dictators**) N-COUNT 可算名詞 A **dictator** is a ruler who has complete power in a country, especially power

Word Web   diary

A **diary** is an informal daily written **record** of the events in someone's life. Most diaries are private **documents**. But sometimes an important diary is published. One such example is *The Diary of a Young Girl*. This is Anne Frank's World War II **chronicle** of her family's unsuccessful attempt to hide from the Nazis. They were eventually arrested, and later Anne died in a concentration camp. This **primary source** document offers us a personal view. It is full of rich details that are often missing from other historical **texts**. The book is now available in 60 different languages.

Word Web diet

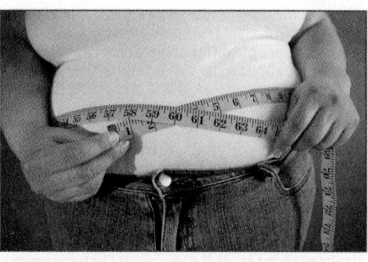

Recent U.S. government reports show that about 64% of American adults are **overweight** or **obese**. The number of people on **weight loss diets** is at an all-time high. And **fad** diets are everywhere. One diet advises people to eat mostly **protein**—meat, fish, and cheese—and very few **carbohydrates**. However, another diet recommends eating at least 40% carbohydrates. But when a weight-loss diet works, it's for one simple reason. When you burn more **calories** than you take in, you lose weight. Most doctors agree that a balanced diet with plenty of exercise is best.

---

which was obtained by force and is used unfairly or cruelly. 独裁者 ❑ *…foreign dictators who contravene humanitarian conventions.* 人道主義の協定に違反する外国の独裁者

dic|ta|to|rial /dɪktətɔriəl/ ADJ 形容詞 If you describe someone's behavior as **dictatorial**, you do not like the fact that they tell people what to do in a forceful and unfair way. 独裁的な [DISAPPROVAL 不賛成] ❑ *…his dictatorial management style.* 独裁的な経営方法

dic|ta|tor|ship /dɪkteɪtərʃɪp/ (**dictatorships**) ■ N-VAR 可変性名詞 **Dictatorship** is government by a dictator. 独裁政治 ❑ *…a new era of democracy after a long period of military dictatorship in the country.* その国での長期間の軍事独裁制の後の民主主義の新時代 ■ N-COUNT 可算名詞 A **dictatorship** is a country which is ruled by a dictator or by a very strict and harsh government. 独裁国 ❑ *Every country in the region was a military dictatorship.* 地域のあらゆる国は軍事独裁国だった.

dic|tion|ary /dɪkʃəneri/ (**dictionaries**) N-COUNT 可算名詞 A **dictionary** is a book in which the words and phrases of a language are listed alphabetically, together with their meanings or their translations in another language. 辞書 ❑ *…a Spanish-English dictionary.* 西英辞典

did /dɪd/ **Did** is the past tense of **do**. do の過去形

didn't /dɪdənt/ **Didn't** is the usual spoken form of "did not." 口語で用いられる did not の短縮形

die /daɪ/ (**dies, dying, died**) ■ V-T/V-I 他動詞/自動詞 When people, animals, and plants **die**, they stop living. 死ぬ [no passive] ❑ *A year later my dog died.* 1年後私の犬が死んだ. ❑ *Sadly, both he and my mother died of cancer.* 悲しいことに彼も私の母もガンで死んだ. ❑ *I would die a very happy person if I could stay in music my whole life.* 一生音楽を続けられたら大変幸福に死ねるだろう.

Do not confuse **dead** with **died**. **Died** is the past tense and past participle of the verb **die**, and thus indicates the action of dying. ❑ *She died in 1934… Two men have died since the rioting broke out.* You do not use **died** as an adjective. You use **dead** instead. ❑ *More than 2,200 dead birds have been found.*

■ V-I 自動詞 If a machine or device **dies**, it stops completely, especially after a period of working more and more slowly or inefficiently. 動かなくなる [WRITTEN 書き言葉] ❑ *Then suddenly, the engine coughed, spluttered, and died.* それから突然エンジンが咳込むような音を出し, 動かなくなった. ■ V-I 自動詞 You can say that you **are dying of** thirst, hunger, boredom, or curiosity to emphasize that you are very thirsty, hungry, bored, or curious. ひどく感じる [INFORMAL くだけた, EMPHASIS 強調] [only cont] ❑ *Order me a soda water. I'm dying of thirst.* ソーダ水を注文してくれ. 喉がからからだ. ■ V-T/V-I 他動詞/自動詞 You can say that you **are dying for** something or **are dying to** do something to emphasize that you very much want to have it or do it. ほしくてたまらない (〜したくて) たまらない [INFORMAL くだけた, EMPHASIS 強調] [only cont] ❑ *I'm dying for a breath of fresh air.* 新鮮な空気が吸いたくてたまらない. ■ V-T/V-I 他動詞/自動詞 You can use **die** in expressions such as "**I almost died**" or "**I'd die if anything happened**" where you are emphasizing your feelings about a situation, for example, to say that it is very shocking, upsetting, embarrassing, or amusing. 死にそうなほど感じる [INFORMAL, mainly SPOKEN くだけた, 主に口語, EMPHASIS 強調] ❑ *I nearly died when I read what she'd written about me.* 彼女が私について書いたことを読んだ時は死にそうな気がした. ❑ *I nearly died of shame.* 私は恥ずかしくて死にそうだった. ❑ *I thought I'd die laughing.* 笑いすぎて死ぬかと思ったほどだ. ■ → see also **dying** ■ PHRASE 句 If you say that something is **to die for**, you mean that you want it or like it very much. すてきな [INFORMAL くだけた] ❑ *It may be that your property has a stunning view, or perhaps it has a kitchen or bathroom to die for.* あなたの家には素晴らしい眺めがあるかもしれないし, ひょっとしたらすごく素敵なキッチンかバスルームでもあるのかもしれない. ■ PHRASE 句 If you say that habits or attitudes **die hard**, you mean that they take a very long time to disappear or change, so that it may not be possible to get rid of them completely. なかなか消えない ❑ *Old habits die hard.* 古い習慣はなかなかなくならない.

▸ **die out** ■ PHRASAL VERB 句動詞 If something **dies out**, it

becomes less and less common and eventually disappears completely. 廃れる ❑ *We used to believe that capitalism would soon die out.* 我々は資本主義がまもなく廃れるだろうと信じたものだ. ■ PHRASAL VERB 句動詞 If something such as a fire or wind **dies out**, it gradually stops burning or blowing. 消える [AM 米国英語] ❑ *Once the fire has died out, the salvage team will move in.* 一旦火が消えたら救助団が入っていくだろう.

Thesaurus die また次を参照:

V.	pass away; (*ant.*) live ■
	break down, fail ■

Word Partnership die は次の語句と使われる:

V.	**deserve to** die, **going to** die, **live or** die, **sentenced to** die, **want to** die, **would rather** die ■
N.	**right to** die ■

die|sel /diːzəl/ (**diesels**) ■ N-MASS 質量名詞 **Diesel** or **diesel oil** is the heavy fuel used in a diesel engine. ディーゼル油 ■ N-COUNT 可算名詞 A **diesel** is a vehicle which has a diesel engine. ディーゼル車 ❑ *I keep hearing that diesels are better now than ever before.* ディーゼル車は以前よりずっとよくなったという話ばかり聞いている.

die|sel en|gine (**diesel engines**) N-COUNT 可算名詞 A **diesel engine** is an internal combustion engine in which oil is burned by very hot air. Diesel engines are used in buses and trucks, and in some trains and cars. ディーゼルエンジン

diet /daɪət/ (**diets, dieting, dieted**) ■ N-VAR 可変性名詞 Your **diet** is the type and variety of food that you regularly eat. 日常の飲食物 ❑ *It's never too late to improve your diet.* 食生活の改善が遅すぎると言うことは決してない. ■ N-VAR 可変性名詞 If you are on a **diet**, you eat special kinds of food or you eat less food than usual because you are trying to lose weight. ダイエット ❑ *Have you been on a diet? You've lost a lot of weight.* ダイエットしてたのか, 随分痩せたね. ■ N-COUNT 可算名詞 If a doctor puts someone on a **diet**, he or she makes them eat a special type or variety of foods in order to improve their health. 規定食 ❑ *Certain chronic conditions, such as diabetes, require special diets that should be monitored by your physician.* 糖尿病などの慢性疾患は主治医の監督下での規定食が必要となるものがある. ■ N-COUNT 可算名詞 If you are fed on a **diet of** something, especially something unpleasant or of poor quality, you receive or experience a very large amount of it. いつも与えられるもの ❑ *The radio had fed him a diet of pop songs.* 彼は常にラジオから流れるポピュラー音楽ばかりを聴いていた. ■ V-I 自動詞 If you **are dieting**, you eat special kinds of food or you eat less food than usual because you are trying to lose weight. ダイエットする ❑ *I've been dieting ever since the birth of my fourth child.* 私は4人目の子供が生まれてからずっとダイエットをしている. ■ ADJ 形容詞 **Diet** drinks or foods have been specially produced so that they do not contain many calories. 低カロリーの [ADJ n] ❑ *…sugar-free diet drinks.* 砂糖なしの低カロリー飲料
→ see Word Web: **diet**
→ see **vegetarian**

Word Partnership diet は次の語句と使われる:

ADJ.	**balanced** diet, **healthy** diet, **proper** diet, **vegetarian** diet ■
	strict diet ■
N.	diet **and exercise** ■ – ■
	diet **pills**, diet **supplements** ■
	diet **soda** ■
PREP.	**on a** diet ■

di|etary /daɪəteri/ ADJ 形容詞 You can use **dietary** to describe anything that concerns a person's diet. 食べ物の ❑ *Dr. Susan Hankinson has studied the dietary habits of more than 50,000 women.* スーザン・ハンキンソン先生は5万人以上の女性の食習慣を調査した.

dif|fer /dɪfər/ (**differs, differing, differed**) ■ V-RECIP 相互動詞 If two or more things **differ**, they are unlike each other in some way.

D

異なる ❑ *The story he told police differed from the one he told his mother.* 彼が警察に伝えた話は母親に伝えた話と異なる内容だった. **2** V-RECIP 相互動詞 If people **differ** about something, they do not agree with each other about it. 意見が異なる ❑ *The two leaders had differed on the issue of sanctions.* 2人の指導者は制裁措置の問題に関して異なる意見を持っていた. ❑ *That is where we differ.* それが我々の意見が異なる点だ. **3** to **agree to differ** → see **agree**

dif|fer|ence /dɪfərəns, dɪfrəns/ (**differences**) **1** N-COUNT 可算名詞 The **difference** between two things is the way in which they are unlike each other. 違い ❑ *That is the fundamental difference between the two societies.* それが2つの社会の根本的な違いだ. ❑ *...the vast difference in size.* 規模の大きな違い **2** N-COUNT 可算名詞 If people have their **differences** about something, they disagree about it. 意見の不一致 ❑ *The two communities are learning how to resolve their differences.* 2つのコミュニティは意見の不一致をいかに解決するかを学んでいるところだ. **3** N-SING 単数名詞 A **difference** between two quantities is the amount by which one quantity is less than the other. 差 ❑ *The difference is 8532.* 差は8532だ. **4** PHRASE 句 If something **makes a difference** or **makes a lot of difference**, it affects you and helps you in what you are doing. If something **makes no difference**, it does not have any effect on what you are doing. 大きく影響する, 全く影響しない ❑ *Where you live can make such a difference to the way you feel.* 住む場所は感情に大きく影響することがある. **5** PHRASE 句 If there is a **difference of opinion** between two or more people or groups, they disagree about something. 意見の不一致 ❑ *Was there a difference of opinion over what to do with the Nobel Prize money?* ノーベル賞の賞金を何に使うかについて意見の不一致があったのか.

Word Partnership   *difference* は次の語句と使われる:

ADJ.	**big/major** difference **1**
V.	**know the** difference, **notice a** difference, **tell the** difference **1**
	settle a difference **2**
	pay the difference **3**
	make a difference **4**
N.	difference **in age**, difference **in price 3**
	difference **of opinion 5**

dif|fer|ent /dɪfərənt, dɪfrənt/ **1** ADJ 形容詞 If two people or things are **different**, they are not like each other in one or more ways. 違う ❑ *London was different from most European capitals.* ロンドンは他の欧州諸国の首都の大部分と違っていた. ❑ *If he'd attended music school, how might things have been different?* もし彼が音楽学校に通っていたとしたら状況はどのように違っていただろうか. ADJ 形容詞 People sometimes say that one thing is **different than** another. This use is acceptable in American English, but is often considered incorrect in British English. 違って [v-link ADJ 'than' n/cl] ❑ *We're not really any different than they are.* 私達は彼らとそれほど違わない. ●**dif|fer|ent|ly** ADV 副詞 違った方法で ❑ *Every individual learns differently.* 学習方法は1人1人違う. **2** ADJ 形容詞 [ADJ n] You use **different** to indicate that you are talking about two or more separate and distinct things of the same kind. 別の ❑ *Different countries specialized in different products.* 国によって得意とする製品は違る. **3** ADJ 形容詞 You can describe something as **different** when it is unusual and not like others of the same kind. 特別な [v-link ADJ] ❑ *The result is interesting and different, but do not attempt the recipe if time is short.* 興味深く特別なものができあがるが, 時間がない時にはこの調理法を試みないように.

Thesaurus   *different* また次を参照:

| ADJ. | dissimilar, mismatched, unalike **1** |
| | distinct, odd, offbeat, peculiar, unique **3** |

dif|fer|en|tial /dɪfərénʃəl/ (**differentials**) N-COUNT 可算名詞 In mathematics and economics, a **differential** is a difference between two values in a scale. 差 ❑ *...the wage differential between blue-collar and white-collar workers.* ブルーカラーとホワイトカラー労働者の賃金格差

dif|fer|en|ti|ate /dɪfərénʃieɪt/ (**differentiates, differentiating, differentiated**) **1** V-T/V-I 他動詞/自動詞 If you **differentiate between** things or if you **differentiate** one thing **from** another, you recognize or show the difference between them. 区別する ❑ *A child may not differentiate between his imagination and the real world.* 子供は想像の世界と現実を区別できないことがある. **2** V-T 他動詞 A quality or feature that **differentiates** one thing **from** another makes the two things different. 分化する ❑ *...distinctive policies that differentiate them from the other parties.* 他政党と差別化する独自政策 ●**dif|fer|en|tia|tion** /dɪfərénʃiéɪʃən/ N-UNCOUNT 不可算名詞 区別 ❑ *For about six or seven weeks after conception, there is no differentiation between male and female.* 受胎後の約6〜7週間では男と女の区別はない.

dif|fi|cult /dɪfɪkʌlt, -kəlt/ **1** ADJ 形容詞 Something that is **difficult** is not easy to do, understand, or deal with. 難しい ❑ *The*

lack of childcare provisions made it difficult for single mothers to get jobs.* 保育支援の不備により未婚の母が職を得るのは難しかった. ❑ *It was a very difficult decision to make.* それは非常に困難な決定だった. **2** ADJ 形容詞 Someone who is **difficult** behaves in an unreasonable and unhelpful way. 扱いにくい ❑ *I had a feeling you were going to be difficult about this.* 私はあなたがこの件に関して頑固な態度を取るような気がした.

Thesaurus   *difficult* また次を参照:

| ADJ. | challenging, demanding, hard, tough; (ant.) easy, simple, uncomplicated **1** |
| | disagreeable, irritable, uncooperative; (ant.) accommodating, cooperative **2** |

dif|fi|cul|ty /dɪfɪkʌlti, -kəlti/ (**difficulties**) **1** N-COUNT 可算名詞 A **difficulty** is a problem. 困難 ❑ *...the difficulty of getting accurate information.* 正確な情報を得ることの難しさ **2** N-UNCOUNT 不可算名詞 If you have **difficulty** doing something, you are not able to do it easily. 難事 ❑ *Do you have difficulty getting up?* あなたは起き上がるのに苦労するか. **3** PHRASE 句 If someone or something is **in difficulty**, they are having a lot of problems. 困っている ❑ *The city's film industry is in difficulty.* 市の映画産業は難題を抱えている.

Thesaurus   *difficulty* また次を参照:

| N. | dilemma, problem, trouble **1** |

dif|fi|dent /dɪfɪdənt/ ADJ 形容詞 Someone who is **diffident** is rather shy and does not enjoy talking about themselves or being noticed by other people. 内気な ❑ *John was as bouncy and ebullient as Helen was diffident and reserved.* ジョンは活発で威勢がよかったが, ヘレンは内気で引っ込み思案だった. ●**dif|fi|dence** /dɪfɪdəns/ N-UNCOUNT 不可算名詞 遠慮 ❑ *He tapped on the door, opened it, and entered with a certain diffidence.* 彼は軽くノックしてからドアを開け, 遠慮がちに中に入った.

dif|fuse /dɪfyúz/ (**diffuses, diffusing, diffused**) **1** V-T/V-I 他動詞/自動詞 If something such as knowledge or information is **diffused**, or if it **diffuses** somewhere, it is made known over a wide area or to a lot of people. 広める, 広まる [WRITTEN 書き言葉] ❑ *Over time, however, the technology is diffused and adopted by other countries.* しかし時間が経てば技術は広まり, 他国にも取り入れられる. ❑ *...to diffuse new ideas obtained from elsewhere.* 他から入手した新しい発想を広める ●**dif|fu|sion** /dɪfyúʒ°n/ N-UNCOUNT 不可算名詞 普及 ❑ *...the development and diffusion of ideas.* アイデアの開発と普及 **2** V-T 他動詞 To **diffuse** a feeling, especially an undesirable one, means to cause it to weaken and lose its power to affect people. 消散させる ❑ *The presidents will meet to try and diffuse the tensions that threaten to reignite the conflict.* 大統領は紛争を再燃させそうな緊張を消散させるための会合を行なう予定だ. **3** V-T 他動詞 If something **diffuses** light, it causes the light to spread weakly in different directions. 散乱させる ❑ *Diffusing a light also reduces its power.* 光を散乱させると電力の削減にもなる. **4** V-I 自動詞 To **diffuse** or be **diffused** through something means to move and spread through it. 拡散する, 拡散される ❑ *It allows nicotine to diffuse slowly and steadily into the bloodstream.* それはニコチンがゆっくり着実に血流に拡散するのを可能にする. ●**dif|fu|sion** N-UNCOUNT 不可算名詞 拡散 ❑ *There are data on the rates of diffusion of molecules.* 分子の拡散率についてのデータがある.

→ see **culture**

dig /dɪg/ (**digs, digging, dug**) **1** V-T/V-I 他動詞/自動詞 If people or animals **dig**, they make a hole in the ground or in a pile of earth, stones, or trash. 掘る ❑ *I grabbed the spade and started digging.* 私はすきを取り, 掘り始めた. ❑ *Dig a large hole and drive the stake in first.* まず大きな穴を掘り, 杭 (くい) を打ち込みなさい. **2** V-I 自動詞 If you **dig into** something such as a deep container, you put your hand in it to search for something. 手を入れる ❑ *Do you have difficulty getting up?* 彼はコートのポケットに手を突っ込み鍵を探した. **3** V-T/V-I 他動詞/自動詞 If you **dig** one thing **into** another or if one thing **digs into** another, the first thing is pushed hard into the second, or presses hard into it. 突き立てる ❑ *She digs the serving spoon into the moussaka.* 彼女は給仕用のスプーンをムサカに突き立てる. **4** V-I 自動詞 If you **dig into** a subject or a store of information, you study it very carefully in order to discover or check facts. 探求する ❑ *...as a special congressional enquiry digs deeper into the alleged financial misdeeds of his government.* 彼の政府の財務不正疑惑に対して議会の特別調査の追求が進むにつれ ❑ *He has been digging into the local archives.* 彼は地元の古文書を念入りに調べてきた. **5** V-T 他動詞 If you **dig yourself out of** a difficult or unpleasant situation, especially one which you caused yourself, you manage to get out of it. 脱する ❑ *He's taken these measures to try and dig himself out of a hole.* 彼は苦境から脱するためにこうした措置を取った. **6** N-COUNT 可算名詞 If you have a **dig at** someone, you say something which is intended to make fun of them or upset them. 当てこすり ❑ *She couldn't resist a dig at Dave after his unfortunate performance.* デイブの出来があいにくだったので, 彼女はつい皮肉を言ってしまった.

7 N-COUNT 可算名詞 If you give someone a **dig** in a part of their body, you push them with your finger or your elbow, usually as a warning or as a joke. つつくこと □ *Cassandra silenced him with a sharp dig in the small of the back.* カサンドラは彼の腰のくびれた部分を小突いて黙らせた. **8** to **dig** one's **heels in** → see **heel**

▶ **dig out** PHRASAL VERB 句動詞 If you **dig** someone or something **out of** a place, you get them out by digging or by forcing them from the things surrounding them. 掘り出す □ *...digging minerals out of the Earth.* 地球から鉱物を掘り出すこと **2** PHRASAL VERB 句動詞 If you **dig** something **out**, you find it after it has been stored, hidden, or forgotten for a long time. 探し出す [INFORMAL くだけた] □ *Recently, I dug out Barstow's novel and read it again.* 最近私はバーストウの小説を掘り起こしてきて再読した. → see **tunnel**

di|gest (**digests**, **digesting**, **digested**)

The verb is pronounced /dɪdʒɛst/. The noun is pronounced /daɪdʒɛst/.
動詞は /dɪdʒɛst/ と発音される. 名詞は /daɪdʒɛst/ と発音される.

1 V-T/V-I 他動詞/自動詞 When food **digests** or when you **digest** it, it passes through your body to your stomach. Your stomach removes the substances that your body needs and gets rid of the rest. 消化する □ *Do not undertake strenuous exercise for a few hours after a meal to allow food to digest.* 食べ物が消化できるように食後数時間は激しい運動をしてはならない. □ *She couldn't digest food properly.* 彼女は食べ物をきちんと消化できなかった. **2** V-T 他動詞 If you **digest** information, you think about it carefully so that you understand it. 熟慮理解する □ *They learn well but seem to need time to digest information.* 彼らはよく学ぶが情報を理解する時間が必要なようだ. **3** V-T 他動詞 If you **digest** some unpleasant news, you think about it until you are able to accept it and know how to deal with it. こなす □ *All this has upset me. I need time to digest it all.* このこと全体に私は動揺した. こなしきるのに時間が必要だ. **4** N-COUNT 可算名詞 A **digest** is a collection of pieces of writing. They are published together in a shorter form than they were originally published. ダイジェスト □ *...the Middle East Economic Digest.* 中東経済ダイジェスト → see **cooking**

di|ges|tion /daɪdʒɛstʃən/ (**digestions**) **1** N-UNCOUNT 不可算名詞 **Digestion** is the process of digesting food. 消化 □ *No liquids are served with meals because they interfere with digestion.* 飲み物は消化を妨げるので食事と一緒には出しません. **2** N-COUNT 可算名詞 Your **digestion** is the system in your body which digests your food. 消化機能 □ *Keep your digestion working well by eating plenty of fiber.* 繊維分を沢山取ることによって消化機能を向上させるよう務めなさい.

di|ges|tive /daɪdʒɛstɪv/ ADJ 形容詞 You can describe things that are related to the digestion of food as **digestive**. 消化の [ADJ n] □ *...digestive juices that normally work on breaking down our food.* 通常食べ物を分解する効果のある消化液

digi|cam /dɪdʒɪkæm/ (**digicams**) N-COUNT 可算名詞 A **digicam** is the same as a **digital camera**. デジカメ □ *Filmmaking was transformed by digital editing, digital f/x, and digicams.* 映画制作はデジタル編集, デジタル効果そしてデジタルカメラによって変貌した.

dig|it /dɪdʒɪt/ (**digits**) N-COUNT 可算名詞 A **digit** is a written symbol for any of the ten numbers from 0 to 9. ディジット □ *Her telephone number differs from mine by one digit.* 彼の電話番号は私のと数字が1つだけ違う.

digi|tal /dɪdʒɪtⁿl/ **1** ADJ 形容詞 **Digital** systems record or transmit information in the form of thousands of very small signals. デジタルの □ *The new digital technology would allow a rapid expansion in the number of TV channels.* 新しいデジタル技術はテレビのチャンネル数の急増を可能にするだろう. **2** ADJ 形容詞 **Digital** devices such as watches or clocks give information by displaying numbers rather than by having a pointer which moves round a dial. Compare **analog**. 数字表示の [ADJ n] □ *...a digital display.* デジタル式表示 **3** PHRASE 句 People sometimes refer to poorer people's lack of access to the latest computer technology as **the digital divide**. デジタル・デバイド [MAINLY JOURNALISM 主にジャーナリズム] ['the/a' PHR] □ *...an attempt to reduce the "digital divide" between poor students who have no computers and those from well-off families who do.* パソコンを持っていない貧しい学生と持っている裕福な家族のデジタルデバイドを低減する試み → see **DVD**, **technology**, **television**

digi|tal cam|era (**digital cameras**) N-COUNT 可算名詞 A **digital camera** is a camera that produces digital images that can be stored on a computer, displayed on a screen, and printed. デジタルカメラ □ *The speed with which digital cameras can take, process, and transmit an image is phenomenal.* デジタルカメラで映像は撮影・処理・送信できる速度は驚異的だ.

digi|tal ra|dio (**digital radios**) **1** N-UNCOUNT 不可算名詞 **Digital radio** is radio in which the signals are transmitted in digital form and decoded by the radio receiver. デジタルラジオ □ *...those with access to digital radio, satellite TV, or the Internet.* デジ

タルラジオ, 衛星テレビもしくはインターネットにアクセスできる人々 **2** N-COUNT 可算名詞 A **digital radio** is a radio that can receive digital signals. デジタルラジオ □ *Manufacturers are working on a new generation of cheaper digital radios.* メーカーは新しい世代の安いデジタルラジオを開発中だ.

digi|tal tele|vi|sion (**digital televisions**) **1** N-UNCOUNT 不可算名詞 **Digital television** is television in which the signals are transmitted in digital form and decoded by the television receiver. デジタルテレビ □ *At present only 31 percent of the population has access to digital television.* 現在デジタルテレビを利用できるのは人口の31%だけだ. **2** N-COUNT 可算名詞 A **digital television** is a television that can receive digital signals. デジタルテレビ受像機 □ *Other new technology products are also doing well, such as digital cameras and wide screen digital televisions.* デジタルカメラやワイドスクリーンのデジタルテレビなど他の新技術製品も好調だ.

digi|tal TV (**digital TVs**) **1** N-UNCOUNT 不可算名詞 **Digital TV** is the same as **digital television**. デジタルテレビ **2** N-COUNT 可算名詞 A **digital TV** is the same as a **digital television**. デジタルテレビ受像機

Word Link **dign** ≈ proper, worthy : **dign**ified, **dign**itary, in**dign**ant

dig|ni|fied /dɪgnɪfaɪd/ ADJ 形容詞 If you say that someone or something is **dignified**, you mean they are calm, impressive, and deserve respect. 威厳のある □ *He seemed a very dignified and charming man.* 彼は大変威厳があり魅力的な男性のようだった.

dig|ni|tary /dɪgnɪtɛri/ (**dignitaries**) N-COUNT 可算名詞 **Dignitaries** are people who are considered to be important because they have a high rank in government or in a church. 高位の人 □ *...an office fund used to entertain visiting dignitaries.* 来賓をもてなすために使われる事務関係資金

dig|nity /dɪgnɪti/ **1** N-UNCOUNT 不可算名詞 If someone behaves or moves with **dignity**, they are calm, controlled, and admirable. 威厳 □ *...her extraordinary dignity and composure.* 彼女の並外れた威厳と落ち着き **2** N-UNCOUNT 不可算名詞 If you talk about the **dignity** of people or their lives or activities, you mean that they are valuable and worthy of respect. 尊厳 □ *...the sense of human dignity.* 人間的尊厳という間隔 **3** N-UNCOUNT 不可算名詞 Your **dignity** is the sense that you have of your own importance and value, and other people's respect for you. 自尊心 □ *She still has her dignity.* 彼女はまだ自尊心をもっている.

dike /daɪk/ (**dikes**) **1** N-COUNT 可算名詞 A **dike** is a thick wall that is built to stop water flooding onto very low-lying land from a river or from the ocean. 防壁 **2** → see **dyke**

di|lapi|dat|ed /dɪlæpɪdeɪtɪd/ ADJ 形容詞 A building that is **dilapidated** is old and in a generally bad condition. 荒廃した □ *...an old dilapidated barn.* 古い荒廃した納屋

di|late /daɪleɪt/ (**dilates**, **dilating**, **dilated**) V-T/V-I 他動詞/自動詞 When things such as blood vessels or the pupils of your eyes **dilate** or when something **dilates** them, they become wider or bigger. 広げる, 広がる □ *At night, the pupils dilate to allow in more light.* ひとみは夜になると広がって多くの光を通す. ● **di|lat|ed** ADJ 形容詞 □ *His eyes seemed slightly dilated.* 彼の目は少し見開いているようだった.

Word Link **di** ≈ two : **di**lemma, **di**verge, **di**vision

di|lem|ma /dɪlɛmə/ (**dilemmas**) N-COUNT 可算名詞 A **dilemma** is a difficult situation in which you have to choose between two or more alternatives. ジレンマ □ *He was faced with the dilemma of whether or not to return to his country.* 彼は母国に戻るかどうかのジレンマに直面していた.

dili|gent /dɪlɪdʒⁿnt/ ADJ 形容詞 Someone who is **diligent** works hard in a careful and thorough way. 勤勉な □ *Meyers is a diligent and prolific worker.* メイヤーズは勤勉でたくさん仕事をする労働者だ. ● **dili|gence** /dɪlɪdʒⁿns/ N-UNCOUNT 不可算名詞 勤勉 □ *The police are pursuing their inquiries with great diligence.* 警察は精を出して捜査を続けている. ● **dili|gent|ly** ADV 副詞 [ADV with v] 精励して □ *The two sides are now working diligently to resolve their differences.* 両者は現在, 精通して意見の不一致を解決する努力をしている.

di|lute /daɪlut/ (**dilutes**, **diluting**, **diluted**) **1** V-T/V-I 他動詞/自動詞 If a liquid **is diluted** or **dilutes**, it is added to or mixes with water or another liquid, and becomes weaker. 薄める □ *If you give your baby juice, dilute it well with cooled, boiled water.* 乳飲み子にジュースをやるときには冷やしたお湯で薄めなさい. □ *The liquid is then diluted.* 液体はそれから薄められる. **2** V-T 他動詞 If someone or something **dilutes** a belief, quality, or value, they make it weaker and less effective. 弱める □ *There was a clear intention to dilute black voting power.* 黒人の投票力を弱める明らかな意図があった. **3** ADJ 形容詞 A **dilute** liquid is very thin and weak, usually because it has had water added to it. 希釈の □ *...a dilute solution of bleach.* 漂白剤の希釈液

dim /dɪm/ (**dimmer**, **dimmest**, **dims**, **dimming**, **dimmed**) **1** ADJ 形容詞 **Dim** light is not bright. 薄暗い □ *She stood waiting in the dim*

D

light. 彼女は薄暗い所で立って待っていた. ● **dim|ly** ADV 副詞 薄暗く ❑ *Two lamps burned dimly.* ２つのランプがかすかに燃えた. **2** ADJ 形容詞 A **dim** place is rather dark because there is not much light in it. 薄暗い ❑ *The room was dim and cool and quiet.* その部屋は薄暗く涼しく静かだった. **3** ADJ 形容詞 A **dim** figure or object is not very easy to see, either because it is in shadow or darkness, or because it is far away. ぼやけた ❑ *Pete's flashlight picked out the dim figures of Bob and Chang.* ピートの懐中電灯でボブとチャンの姿がぼやけて見えた. ● **dim|ly** ADV 副詞 ぼんやりと ❑ *The shoreline could be dimly seen.* 海岸線がぼんやりと見えた. **4** ADJ 形容詞 If you have a **dim** memory or understanding of something, it is difficult to remember or is unclear in your mind. ぼんやりした ❑ *It seems that the '60s era of social activism is all but a dim memory.* 60年代の社会行動主義はおぼろげな思い出でしかないようだ. ● **dim|ly** ADV 副詞 おぼろげに ❑ *Christina dimly recalled the procedure.* クリスティーナは手順をおぼろげに思い出した. **5** ADJ 形容詞 If the future of something is **dim**, you have no reason to feel hopeful or positive about it. 見込み薄の ❑ *The prospects for a peaceful solution are dim.* 平和的解決の見込みは薄い. **6** ADJ 形容詞 If you describe someone as **dim**, you think that they are stupid. まぬけな [INFORMAL くだけた] ❑ *Sometimes he thought George was a bit dim.* 彼はジョージが少し鈍いと思うことがあった. **7** V-T/V-I 他動詞/自動詞 If you **dim** a light or if it **dims**, it becomes less bright. 薄暗くする, 薄暗くなる ❑ *Dim the lighting – it is unpleasant to lie with a bright light shining in your eyes.* 照明を弱めて. あかあかとして光が目に入ったまま横たわるのは不快だ. **8** V-T/V-I 他動詞/自動詞 If your future, hopes, or emotions **dim** or if something **dims** them, they become less good or less strong. 弱まる, 弱める ❑ *Their economic prospects have dimmed.* 彼らの経済的展望は悪化した. **9** V-T/V-I 他動詞/自動詞 If your memories **dim** or if something **dims** them, they become less clear in your mind. あいまいにする, あいまいになる ❑ *Their memory of what happened has dimmed.* 出来事についての彼らの記憶はあいまいになった.

dime /daɪm/ (**dimes**) N-COUNT 可算名詞 A **dime** is a U.S. coin worth ten cents. ダイム ❑ *The penny meters are slowly being replaced by electronic ones that take nickels, dimes, and quarters.* 1セント硬貨用計器は5セント, 10セント, 25セント硬貨が使える電子式のものに徐々に交換されつつある.

di|men|sion /dɪmenʃən, daɪ-/ (**dimensions**) **1** N-COUNT 可算名詞 A particular **dimension** of something is a particular aspect of it. 特徴 ❑ *There is a political dimension to the accusations.* その非難には政治的一面がある. **2** N-COUNT 可算名詞 A **dimension** is a measurement such as length, width, or height. If you talk about the **dimensions** of an object or place, you are referring to its size and proportions. 寸法 ❑ *Drilling will continue on the site to assess the dimensions of the new oilfield.* 新しい油田の規模を見極めるために当地の掘削作業は続く予定である. **3** N-PLURAL 複数名詞 If you talk about the **dimensions** of a situation or problem, you are talking about its extent and size. 規模 ❑ *The dimensions of the market collapse, in terms of turnover and price, were certainly not anticipated.* 出来高と株価に関する市場崩壊の規模は確かに予測されていなかった.

di|min|ish /dɪmɪnɪʃ/ (**diminishes, diminishing, diminished**) **1** V-T/V-I 他動詞/自動詞 When something **diminishes**, or when something **diminishes** it, it becomes reduced in size, importance, or intensity. 減少させる, 減少する ❑ *The threat of nuclear war has diminished.* 核戦争の脅威は減少した. ❑ *Federalism is intended to diminish the power of the central state.* 連邦主義は中央国家の権力を減少させるものである. **2** V-T 他動詞 If you **diminish** someone or something, you talk about them or treat them in a way that makes them appear less important than they really are. けなす ❑ *He never put her down or diminished her.* 彼は彼女をけなしたり, 非難したことは一度もなかった.

di|minu|tive /dɪmɪnyətɪv/ ADJ 形容詞 A **diminutive** person or object is very small. 小さい ❑ *Her eyes scanned the room until they came to rest on a diminutive figure standing at the entrance.* 彼女は部屋を見渡し, 入り口に立っている小柄な人物に目がとまった.

din /dɪn/ N-SING 単数名詞 A **din** is a very loud and unpleasant noise that lasts for some time. 騒音 ❑ *They tried to make themselves heard over the din of the crowd.* 彼らは群集の騒音に負けないように大声で叫んだ.

dine /daɪn/ (**dines, dining, dined**) V-I 自動詞 When you **dine**, you have dinner. 食事をする [FORMAL 形式ばった] [no passive] ❑ *He dines alone most nights.* 彼はほとんど毎晩1人で食事をする.

din|er /daɪnər/ (**diners**) **1** N-COUNT 可算名詞 A **diner** is a small cheap restaurant that is often open all day. 簡易食堂 [AM 米国英語] **2** N-COUNT 可算名詞 The people who are having dinner in a restaurant can be referred to as **diners**. 食事をする人 ❑ *They sat in*

a corner, away from other diners. 彼らは他の食事客から離れて隅に座った.

din|ghy /dɪŋi/ (**dinghies**) N-COUNT 可算名詞 A **dinghy** is a small open boat that you sail or row. ディンギー ❑ *...a rubber dinghy.* ゴム製のディンギー

din|gy /dɪndʒi/ (**dingier, dingiest**) **1** ADJ 形容詞 A **dingy** building or place is dark and depressing, and perhaps dirty. みすぼらしい ❑ *Shaw took me to his dingy office.* ショーは私を彼のみすぼらしい事務所に連れて行った. **2** ADJ 形容詞 **Dingy** clothes, curtains, or furnishings look dirty or dull. 薄汚れた ❑ *...wallpaper with stripes of dingy yellow.* 黒ずんだ黄色のストライプの壁紙

din|ing room (**dining rooms**) N-COUNT 可算名詞 The **dining room** is the room in a house where people have their meals, or a room in a hotel where meals are served. 食堂
→ see **house**

din|ner /dɪnər/ (**dinners**) **1** N-VAR 可変性名詞 **Dinner** is the main meal of the day, usually served in the early part of the evening. 正餐 ❑ *She invited us to her house for dinner.* 彼女は私達を食事のため家に招待してくれた. ❑ *Would you like to stay and have dinner?* 食事を召し上がって行きませんか. **2** N-VAR 可変性名詞 Any meal you eat in the middle of the day can be referred to as **dinner**. 昼食 **3** N-COUNT 可算名詞 A **dinner** is a formal social event at which a meal is served. It is held in the evening. 薄汚れた ❑ *...a series of official lunches and dinners.* 一連の公式の昼食会と晩餐会
→ see **dish, meal**

din|ner jack|et (**dinner jackets**) also **dinner-jacket** N-COUNT 可算名詞 A **dinner jacket** is a jacket, usually black, worn by men for formal social events. ディナージャケット

di|no|saur /daɪnəsɔr/ (**dinosaurs**) **1** N-COUNT 可算名詞 **Dinosaurs** were large reptiles which lived in prehistoric times. 恐竜 **2** N-COUNT 可算名詞 If you refer to an organization as a **dinosaur**, you mean that it is large, inefficient, and out of date. 巨大で扱いにくいもの [DISAPPROVAL 不賛成] ❑ *...industrial dinosaurs.* 時代遅れの企業

dip /dɪp/ (**dips, dipping, dipped**) **1** V-T 他動詞 If you **dip** something **in** a liquid, you put it into the liquid for a short time, so that only part of it is covered, and take it out again. ちょっと浸す ❑ *Dip each apple in the syrup until thickly coated.* りんごを厚いころもがつきるまでシロップにちょっと浸す. ● **Dip** is also a noun. ちょっと浸すこと ❑ *...a quick dip of his toe into the water.* 彼の足指を水にちょっと浸すこと **2** V-T/V-I 他動詞/自動詞 If you **dip** something **into** a container or **dip into** the container, you put your hand into it in order to take something out of it. 突っ込む ❑ *She dipped a hand into the jar of candies and pulled one out.* 彼女はキャンディの瓶に手を突っ込んで, 1つ取り出した. ❑ *Nancy dipped into the bowl of popcorn that Hannah had made for them.* ナンシーはハンナが彼らのために作ったポップコーンの深皿に手を突っ込んだ. **3** V-I 自動詞 If something **dips**, it makes a downward movement, usually quickly. ひょいと下がる ❑ *Blake jumped in expertly; the boat dipped slightly under his weight.* ブレイクは上手に飛び乗り, ボートは彼の重みでわずかに沈んだ. ● N-COUNT 可算名詞 **Dip** is also a noun. ちょっと浸すこと ❑ *I noticed little things, a dip of the head, a twitch in the shoulder.* 頭がひょいと下がること, 肩の痙攣 (けいれん) などの些細なことに気づいた. **4** V-I 自動詞 If an area of land, a road, or a path **dips**, it goes down quite suddenly to a lower level. 急に下がる ❑ *The road dipped and rose again as it neared the top of Parker Mountain.* 道路はパーカー山の頂上に近づくにつれて急に下り坂になった後再び上り坂になった. ● N-COUNT 可算名詞 **Dip** is also a noun. 沈下 ❑ *Where the road makes a dip, soon after a small vineyard on the right, turn right.* 右側の小さなぶどう園を過ぎた後まもなくして道路が下り坂になった場所で右折しなさい. **5** V-I 自動詞 If the amount or level of something **dips**, it becomes smaller or lower, usually only for a short period of time. 下がる ❑ *Unemployment dipped to 6.9 percent last month.* 失業率は先月6.9%に低下した. ● N-COUNT 可算名詞 **Dip** is also a noun. 減少 ❑ *...the current dip in farm spending.* 農業支出の現在の減少 **6** V-I 自動詞 If you **dip into** a book, you take a brief look at it without reading or studying it seriously. 軽く目を通す ❑ *...a chance to dip into a wide selection of books on Tibetan Buddhism.* チベットの仏教に関するさまざまな本に軽く目を通す機会 **7** V-I 自動詞 If you **dip into** a sum of money that you had intended to save, you use some of it to buy something or pay for something. 使い込む (貯金・資金などを) ❑ *Just when she was ready to dip into her savings, Greg hastened to her rescue.* グレッグは彼女が貯金を使い込もうとしている時に急いで助けた. **8** N-COUNT 可算名詞 If you have or take a **dip**, you go for a quick swim in the ocean, a lake, a river, or a swimming pool. 一泳ぎ ❑ *She flicked through a romantic paperback between occasional dips in the pool.* 彼女は時おりプールで一泳ぎする合間に恋愛小説をすばやく読んだ.

di|plo|ma /dɪploʊmə/ (**diplomas**) N-COUNT 可算名詞 A **diploma** is a document which may be awarded to a student who has completed a course of study by a university or college, or by a high school in the United States. 修了証書 ❑ *...a new two-year course leading to a diploma in social work.* ソーシャルワークの修了証書を取得

できる新しい2年間のコース
→ see **graduation**

di|plo|ma|cy /dɪplo͟ʊməsi/ **1** N-UNCOUNT 不可算名詞 **Diplomacy** is the activity or profession of managing relations between the governments of different countries. 外交 □ *Today's Security Council resolution will be a significant success for American diplomacy.* 今日の安全保障理事会の決議は米国外交にとって大成果となるだろう。**2** N-UNCOUNT 不可算名詞 **Diplomacy** is the skill of being careful to say or do things which will not offend people. 如才なさ □ *He stormed off in a fury, and it took all Minnelli's powers of diplomacy to get him to return.* 彼は激怒して飛び出し、戻らせるにはミネリがその社交術をありったけ利用した。

dip|lo|mat /dɪpləmæt/ (**diplomats**) N-COUNT 可算名詞 A **diplomat** is a senior official who discusses affairs with another country on behalf of his or her own country, usually working as a member of an embassy. 外交官 □ *a Western diplomat with long experience in Asia.* アジアで長い経験を持つ西側の外交官

dip|lo|mat|ic /dɪpləmæ͟tɪk/ **1** ADJ 形容詞 **Diplomatic** means relating to diplomacy and diplomats. 外交に関する □ *...before the two countries resume full diplomatic relations.* 両国が完全な外交関係を再開する前に ● **dip|lo|mati|cal|ly** /dɪpləmæ͟tɪkli/ ADV 副詞 外交的に □ *...a growing sense of doubt that the conflict can be resolved diplomatically.* 紛争を外交的に解決する可能性への高まりつつある疑い **2** ADJ 形容詞 Someone who is **diplomatic** is careful to say or do things without offending people. そつのない □ *She is very direct. I tend to be more diplomatic, I suppose.* 彼女は非常に率直だ。私はもっと如才ない方だと思う。● **dip|lo|mati|cal|ly** ADV 副詞 [ADV with v] 如才なく □ *"I really like their sound, although I'm not crazy about their lyrics," he says, diplomatically.* 「歌詞は大したことないが曲は大変いい」と彼は如才なく言った。

N.	diplomatic **activity**, diplomatic **immunity**, diplomatic **mission**, diplomatic **relations**, diplomatic **skills**, diplomatic **solution**, diplomatic **ties** **1**

dip|lo|mat|ic corps (**diplomatic corps**)
Diplomatic corps is both the singular and the plural form.
Diplomatic corps は単数形でも複数形でもある。
N-COUNT-COLL 集合可算名詞 **The diplomatic corps** is the group of all the diplomats who work in one city or country. 外交団

dire /da͟ɪər/ **1** ADJ 形容詞 **Dire** is used to emphasize how serious or terrible a situation or event is. 悲惨な [EMPHASIS 強調] □ *The government looked as if it would split apart, with dire consequences for domestic peace.* 政府は分裂するかのように見えた。もしそうなったら国内の和平に悲惨な結果をもたらす。**2** ADJ 形容詞 If you describe something as **dire**, you are emphasizing that it is of very low quality. ひどく質の悪い [INFORMAL くだけた, EMPHASIS 強調] □ *...a book of children's verse, which ranged from the barely tolerable to the utterly dire.* まあまあなものから全くひどいものまで多岐にわたる子供の書いた詩の本

di|rect /dɪre͟kt, da͟ɪ-/ (**directs, directing, directed**) **1** ADJ 形容詞 **Direct** means moving toward a place or object, without changing direction and without stopping, for example, in a trip. まっすぐな □ *They'd come on a direct flight from Athens.* 彼らはアテネから直行便で来た。● **di|rect** ADV 副詞 **Direct** is also an adverb. まっすぐに [ADV after v] □ *You can fly direct from Seattle to Europe.* シアトルからヨーロッパへの直行便がある。● **di|rect|ly** ADV 副詞 [ADV after v] まっすぐに □ *On arriving in New York, Dylan went directly to Greenwich Village.* ニューヨークに着いてからディランはグリニッチ・ビレッジに直行した。**2** ADJ 形容詞 If something is in **direct** heat or light, it is strongly affected by the heat or light, because there is nothing between it and the source of heat or light to protect it. 直射の [ADJ n] □ *All medicines should be stored away from moisture, direct sunlight, and heat.* 医薬品は全て湿気、直射日光、熱から離れた場所に貯蔵すべきである。**3** ADJ 形容詞 You use **direct** to describe an experience, activity, or system which only involves the people, actions, or things that are necessary to make it happen. 直の □ *He has direct experience of the process of privatization.* 彼は民営化プロセスに関して直接の経験がある。● ADV 副詞 **Direct** is also an adverb. 直接に [ADV after v] □ *More farms are selling direct to consumers.* 消費者に直接販売する農場が増えている。● **di|rect|ly** ADV 副詞 [ADV with v] 直接に □ *We cannot measure pain directly. It can only be estimated.* 我々は直接に痛みを測定できない。推定することしかできない。**4** ADJ 形容詞 You use **direct** to emphasize the closeness of a connection between two things. 直接の [EMPHASIS 強調] □ *They were unable to prove that the unfortunate lady had died as a direct result of his injection.* 彼の行った注射が不運な女性の直接の死因だったと証明できなかった。**5** ADJ 形容詞 If you describe a person or their behavior as **direct**, you mean that they are honest and open, and say exactly what they mean. 率直な □ *He avoided giving a direct answer.* 彼は

率直に答えるのを避けた。● **di|rect|ly** ADV 副詞 [ADV after v] 率直に □ *At your first meeting, explain simply and directly what you hope to achieve.* 最初の面談であなたが達成したいことを簡潔かつ率直に説明しなさい。● **di|rect|ness** N-UNCOUNT 不可算名詞 率直 □ *Using "I" ensures clarity and directness, and it adds warmth to a piece of writing.* 「私」を使うことは明瞭さと率直さを確実にし、作品に温かみを加える。**6** → see also **direction**, **directly 7** V-T 他動詞 If you **direct** something **at** a particular thing, you aim or point it at that thing. 向ける □ *I reached the cockpit and directed the extinguisher at the fire without effect.* 私はコックピットに到達し、火をめがけて消火器を使ったが効果はなかった。**8** V-T 他動詞 If your attention, emotions, or actions **are directed at** a particular person or thing, you are focusing them on that person or thing. 向ける □ *The learner's attention needs to be directed to the significant features.* 学習者の注意を重要な特徴に向ける必要がある。**9** V-T 他動詞 If a remark or look **is directed at** you, someone says something to you or looks at you. 向けられた □ *She could hardly believe the question was directed toward her.* 彼女はその質問が自分に向けられたことがとても信じられなかった。□ *The abuse was directed at the TV crews.* 悪態はテレビ取材班に向けられた。**10** V-T 他動詞 If you **direct** someone somewhere, you tell them how to get there. 道を教える □ *Could you direct them to Dr. Lamont's office, please?* 彼らにラモント先生の事務所への行き方を教えてますか。**11** V-T 他動詞 When someone **directs** a project or a group of people, they are responsible for organizing the people and activities that are involved. 指揮する □ *Christopher will direct day-to-day operations.* クリストファーは日々の事業を管理することになる。● **di|rec|tion** /dɪre͟kʃən, da͟ɪ-/ N-UNCOUNT 不可算名詞 指揮 □ *Organizations need clear direction, set priorities and performance standards, and clear controls.* 組織は明確な指揮、規定された優先事項と業績水準、明確な管理が必要だ。**12** V-T/V-I 他動詞/自動詞 When someone **directs** a movie, play, or television program, they are responsible for the way in which it is performed and for telling the actors and assistants what to do. 演出する □ *He directed various TV shows.* 彼はテレビ番組を演出した。

ADJ.	nonstop, straight	**1**
	firsthand, personal	**3**
	candid, frank, plain	**5**

di|rect dis|course N-UNCOUNT 不可算名詞 In grammar, **direct discourse** is speech which is reported by using the exact words that the speaker used. 直接話法 [mainly AM 主に米国英語]

di|rec|tion /dɪre͟kʃən, da͟ɪ-/ (**directions**) **1** N-VAR 可変性名詞 A **direction** is the general line that someone or something is moving or pointing in. 方向 □ *St. Andrews was ten miles in the opposite direction.* セントアンドルースは反対方向に10マイル行ったところにあった。□ *He got into Margie's car and swung out onto the road in the direction of Larry's shop.* 彼はマージーの車に乗り、ラリーの店の方向に走り去った。**2** N-VAR 可変性名詞 A **direction** is the general way in which something develops or progresses. 方針 □ *They threatened to lead a mass walk-out if the party did not sharply change direction.* 彼らは党が方針を大きく変えない場合には集団ストライキを統率すると脅した。**3** N-PLURAL 複数名詞 **Directions** are instructions that tell you what to do, how to do something, or how to get somewhere. 手引き □ *I should know by now not to throw away the directions until we've finished cooking.* 料理ができるまで作り方を捨てるべきでないことはもうわかっている。**4** → see also **direct**

N.	**sense of** direction **1**
ADJ.	**opposite** direction, **right** direction, **wrong** direction **1**
	general direction **1 2**
V.	**change** direction, **move in a** direction **1 2**
	lack direction, **take** direction **2**

di|rec|tive /dɪre͟ktɪv, da͟ɪ-/ (**directives**) N-COUNT 可算名詞 A **directive** is an official instruction that is given by someone in authority. 指令 □ *Thanks to a new directive, food labeling will be more specific.* 新しい指令のおかげで食品の表示はより明確になるだろう。

di|rect|ly /dɪre͟ktli, da͟ɪ-/ **1** ADV 副詞 If something is **directly** above, below, or in front of something, it is in exactly that position. じかに [ADV prep/adv] □ *The second rainbow will be bigger than the first, and directly above it.* 2番目の虹は1番目より大きく、その真上にできるだろう。**2** ADV 副詞 If you do one action **directly after** another, you do the second action as soon as the first one is finished. すぐに [ADV prep/adv] □ *Most guests left directly after the wake.* 大半の客は通夜の後すぐに帰った。**3** → see also **direct**

di|rect mail N-UNCOUNT 不可算名詞 **Direct mail** is a method of marketing which involves companies sending advertising material directly to people who they think may be interested in their products. ダイレクトメール [BUSINESS 実業] □ *...efforts to*

D

solicit new customers by direct mail and television advertising. ダイレクトメールとテレビにより新しい顧客を勧誘する努力

di|rect mar|ket|ing N-UNCOUNT 不可算名詞 **Direct marketing** is the same as **direct mail**. ダイレクト・マーケティング [BUSINESS 実業] □ *The direct marketing industry has become adept at packaging special offers.* ダイレクト・マーケティング業界はセット販売がうまくなった.

di|rect ob|ject (direct objects) N-COUNT 可算名詞 In grammar, the **direct object** of a transitive verb is the noun group which refers to someone or something directly affected by or involved in the action performed by the subject. For example, in "I saw him yesterday," "him" is the direct object. Compare **indirect object**. 直接目的語

di|rec|tor /dɪrɛktər, daɪ-/ (directors) ■ N-COUNT 可算名詞 The **director** of a play, movie, or television program is the person who decides how it will appear on stage or screen, and who tells the actors and technical staff what to do. 演出家 □ "Cut!" the director yelled. "That was perfect." 「カット」と演出家は大声で言った. 「完璧だったよ」 ■ N-COUNT 可算名詞 In some organizations and public authorities, the person in charge is referred to as the **director**. 理事 □ ...the director of the intensive care unit at Buffalo General Hospital. バッファロー総合病院の集中治療室の室長 ■ N-COUNT 可算名詞 The **directors** of a company are its most senior managers, who meet regularly to make important decisions about how it will be run. 取締役 [BUSINESS 実業] □ He served on the board of directors of a local bank. 彼は地元銀行の取締役会のメンバーだった. ■ N-COUNT 可算名詞 The **director** of a choir is the person who is conducting it. 指揮者 [AM 米国英語]

di|rec|to|rate /dɪrɛktərɪt, daɪ-/ (directorates) ■ N-COUNT 可算名詞 A **directorate** is a board of directors in a company or organization. 取締役会 [BUSINESS 実業] □ The bank will be managed by a directorate of around five professional bankers. その銀行は約5名のプロの銀行家から成る取締役会が運営する予定だ. ■ N-COUNT 可算名詞 A **directorate** is a part of a government department which is responsible for one particular thing. 局 □ ...the CIA's intelligence directorate. CIAの情報局

di|rec|tor gen|er|al (directors general) N-COUNT 可算名詞 The **director general** of a large organization is the person who is in charge of it. 長官, 事務総長 [BUSINESS 実業]

di|rec|tor|ship /dɪrɛktərʃɪp, daɪ-/ (directorships) N-COUNT 可算名詞 A **directorship** is the job or position of a company director. 管理者の職 [BUSINESS 実業] □ Barry resigned his directorship in December 1973. バリーは1973年12月に管理職を辞めた.

di|rec|tory /dɪrɛktəri, daɪ-/ (directories) ■ N-COUNT 可算名詞 A **directory** is a book which gives lists of facts, for example, people's names, addresses, and telephone numbers, or the names and addresses of business companies, usually arranged in alphabetical order. 住所氏名録 □ ...a telephone directory. 電話帳 ■ N-COUNT 可算名詞 A **directory** is an area of a computer disk which contains one or more files or other directories. ディレクトリー [COMPUTING コンピューティング] □ This option lets you search your current directory for files by date, contents, and document summary. これを選択すると, 日付, 内容, 文書要約でカレントディレクトリーを検索できる. ■ N-COUNT 可算名詞 On the World Wide Web, a **directory** is one of the subjects that you can find information on. ディレクトリー [COMPUTING コンピューティング] □ Yahoo is the oldest and best-known Web directory service. ヤフーは最も古くて有名なインターネット上のディレクトリーサービスである.

di|rec|tory as|sis|tance N-UNCOUNT 不可算名詞 **Directory assistance** is a service which you can telephone to find out someone's telephone number. 電話番号案内 [AM 米国英語] □ He dialed directory assistance. 彼は電話番号案内をダイアルした.

di|rect speech N-UNCOUNT 不可算名詞 In grammar, **direct speech** is speech which is reported by using the exact words that the speaker used. 直接話法 [mainly BRIT 主に英国英語; AM also **direct discourse** 米国英語, また **direct discourse**]

di|rect tax (direct taxes) N-COUNT 可算名詞 A **direct tax** is a tax which a person or organization pays directly to the government, for example, income tax. 直接税 [BUSINESS 実業] □ What people had to pay in direct and indirect taxes had not gone up since 1979. 直接税と間接税は1979年以来引き上げられていない.

dirt /dɜrt/ ■ N-UNCOUNT 不可算名詞 If there is **dirt** on something, there is dust, mud, or a stain on it. 汚れ □ I started to scrub off the dirt. 私は汚れをごしごしこすって洗い落とし始めた. ■ N-UNCOUNT 不可算名詞 You can refer to the earth on the ground as **dirt**, especially when it is dusty. 土 □ They all sit on the dirt in the dappled shade of a tree. 彼らは全員まだらになった木陰の土の上に座った. ■ ADJ 形容詞 A **dirt** road or track is made from hard earth. A **dirt** floor is made from earth without any cement, stone, or wood laid on it. 土の [ADJ n] □ I drove along the dirt road. 私は土道で車を運転した. ■ N-SING 単数名詞 If you say that you have the **dirt on** someone, you mean you have information that could

harm their reputation or career. 汚点 [INFORMAL くだけた] □ ...a sleazy reporter assigned to dig up dirt on Jack. ジャックの恥部暴露の命を受けた低俗なリポーター ■ PHRASE 句 If you say that someone **treats** you **like dirt**, you are angry with them because you think that they treat you unfairly and with no respect. 汚らわしい物のように扱う [DISAPPROVAL 不賛成] □ People think they can treat me like dirt! 世間は私を汚らわしい物のように扱ってもいいと思っているんだ.
→ see **erosion**

dirty /dɜrti/ (dirtier, dirtiest, dirties, dirtying, dirtied) ■ ADJ 形容詞 If something is **dirty**, it is marked or covered with stains, spots, or mud, and needs to be cleaned. 汚い □ She still did not like the woman who had dirty fingernails. 彼女は指の爪の汚い女が未だに好きでなかった. ■ ADJ 形容詞 If you describe an action as **dirty**, you disapprove of it and consider it unfair, immoral, or dishonest. 卑劣な [DISAPPROVAL 不賛成] □ The gunman had been hired by a rival Mafia family to do the dirty deed. ガンマンは卑劣な行為をするためにライバルのマフィア一族に雇われた. ● ADV 副詞 **Dirty** is also an adverb. 卑劣に [ADV after v] □ Jim Browne is the kind of fellow who can fight dirty, but make you like it. ジム・ブラウンは卑劣に戦っても, 君に嫌われないような奴だ. ■ ADJ 形容詞 If you describe something such as a joke, a book, or someone's language as **dirty**, you mean that it refers to sex in a way that some people find offensive. みだらな □ He laughed at their dirty jokes and sang their raucous ballads. 彼は彼らのみだらな冗談に笑い, 耳障りなバラードを歌った. ● ADV 副詞 **Dirty** is also an adverb. みだらに [ADV after v] □ I'm often asked whether the men talk dirty to me. The answer is no. 私に男たちがみだらな話をするかとよく聞かれるが, 答えはノーだ. ■ V-T 他動詞 To **dirty** something means to cause it to become dirty. 汚す □ He was afraid the dog's hairs might dirty the seats. 彼は犬の毛が座席を汚すことを心配した. ■ PHRASE 句 If someone gives you a **dirty look**, they look at you in a way which shows that they are angry with you. 非難の目 [INFORMAL くだけた] □ Jack was being a real pain. Michael gave him a dirty look and walked out. ジャックは本当に嫌なやつだった. マイケルは彼を非難するような目で見てから部屋を出て行った. ■ PHRASE 句 To **do** someone's **dirty work** means to do a task for them that is dishonest or unpleasant and which they do not want to do themselves. 人の嫌がることをする □ As a member of an elite army hit squad, the army would send us out to do their dirty work for them. 陸軍は精鋭の陸軍狙撃隊を構成する我々を派遣して汚い仕事をさせるだろう. ■ PHRASE 句 If you say that an expression is **a dirty word** in a particular group of people, you mean it refers to an idea that they strongly dislike or disagree with. 禁句 □ Marketing became a dirty word at the company. マーケティングはその会社で禁句となった. ■ PHRASE 句 If you say that someone **airs** their **dirty laundry in public**, you disapprove of their discussing or arguing about unpleasant or private things in front of other people. There are several other forms of this expression, for example **wash** your **dirty linen in public**, or **wash** your **dirty laundry in public**. 人前で恥をさらす [DISAPPROVAL 不賛成] □ The captain refuses to air the team's dirty laundry in public. キャプテンはチーム内の恥をさらすのを拒否した.

Word Partnership	dirty は次の語句と使われる:
V.	**get** dirty ■
	talk dirty ■
N.	dirty **diapers**, dirty **dishes**, dirty **laundry** ■
	dirty **joke** ■
	dirty **your hands** ■
	dirty **look** ■
	dirty **job** ■
	dirty **word** ■

dis|abil|ity /dɪsəbɪliti/ (disabilities) ■ N-COUNT 可算名詞 A **disability** is a permanent injury, illness, or physical or mental condition that tends to restrict the way that someone can live their life. 障害 □ Facilities for people with disabilities are still insufficient. 障害者向けの施設はまだ不十分だ. ■ N-UNCOUNT 不可算名詞 **Disability** is the state of being disabled. 障害があること □ Disability can make extra demands on financial resources because the disabled need extra care. 障害者は余分のケアを必要とするため, 障害は財源に特別の要求を行うことがある.
→ see Word Web: **disability**

dis|able /dɪseɪbªl/ (disables, disabling, disabled) ■ V-T 他動詞 If an injury or illness **disables** someone, it affects them so badly that it restricts the way that they can live their life. 障害を与える □ She did all this tendon damage and it really disabled her. 彼女はあれだけ腱を傷めたため, 体が不自由になった. ■ V-T 他動詞 If someone or something **disables** a system or mechanism, they stop it from working, usually temporarily. 機能しなくする □ ...if you need to disable a car alarm. 車の盗難防止アラームを鳴らないようにする必要がある場合は

dis|abled /dɪseɪbªld/ ADJ 形容詞 Someone who is **disabled** has an illness, injury, or condition that tends to restrict the way that they can live their life, especially by making it difficult for

Word Web   disability

Careful planning is making public places more **accessible** for people with **disabilities**. For hundreds of years **wheelchairs** have helped **paralyzed** people move around their homes. Today, **ramps** help these people cross the street, enter buildings, and get to work. Extra-wide doorways allow them to use public restrooms. **Blind** people are also more active and independent. **Seeing Eye dogs, canes**, and beeping crosswalks all help them get around town safely. Some movie theaters rent headsets for the **hearing-impaired**. **Hearing dogs** help **deaf** people stay connected. And sign language allows people who are deaf or **dumb** to communicate.

them to move about. 体の不自由な □ …an insight into the practical problems encountered by disabled people in the workplace. 身体障害者が職場で直面する実用的な問題への洞察 ● N-PLURAL 複数名詞 People who are disabled are sometimes referred to as **the disabled**. 身体障害者 □ There are toilet facilities for the disabled. 身体障害者用のトイレがある.

In the United States there are many laws giving **disabled** people the same rights and benefits as other people. The adjectives **disabled, physically challenged** and **differently abled** are terms more in favor now than **handicapped**. The most sensitive ways of referring to people with a restricting physical condition are to call them **people with disabilities** or **people with special needs**.

dis|ad|van|tage /dɪsədvæntɪdʒ/ (**disadvantages**) ■ N-COUNT 可算名詞 A **disadvantage** is a factor which makes someone or something less useful, acceptable, or successful than other people or things. 不利 □ His two main rivals suffer the disadvantage of having been long-term political exiles. 彼の2人の主なライバルは長期間にわたり政治的亡命者であったという不利な立場にある. ■ PHRASE 句 If you are **at a disadvantage**, you have a problem or difficulty that many other people do not have, which makes it harder for you to be successful. 不利な立場 □ The children from poor families were at a distinct disadvantage. 貧しい家庭の子供は明らかに不利な立場に立たされた. ■ PHRASE 句 If something is **to your disadvantage** or works **to your disadvantage**, it creates difficulties for you. 不利な条件で □ We need a rethink of the present law which works so greatly to the disadvantage of women. 我々は女性にとって非常に不利に働く現在の法律を再考する必要がある.

dis|ad|van|taged /dɪsədvæntɪdʒd/ ADJ 形容詞 People who are **disadvantaged** or live in **disadvantaged** areas live in bad conditions and tend not to get a good education or have a reasonable standard of living. 不利な境遇にある □ …the educational problems of disadvantaged children. 不利な境遇にある子供の教育問題

dis|af|fect|ed /dɪsəfɛktɪd/ ADJ 形容詞 **Disaffected** people no longer fully support something such as an organization or political ideal which they previously supported. 不満を抱いている □ He attracts disaffected voters. 彼は離反した有権者に人気がある.

Word Link   dis = negative, not : disagree, discomfort, disrespect

dis|agree /dɪsəgri/ (**disagrees, disagreeing, disagreed**) ■ V-RECIP 相互動詞 If you **disagree with** someone or **disagree with** what they say, you do not accept that what they say is true or correct. You can also say that two people **disagree**. 意見が合わない □ You must continue to see them no matter how much you may disagree with them. どんなに意見が合わなくとも彼らと会い続ける必要がある. □ They can communicate even when they strongly disagree. 彼らはたとえ意見が大きく食い違うときでも意思の疎通ができる. ■ V-I 自動詞 If you **disagree with** a particular action or proposal, you disapprove of it and believe that it is wrong. 異議がある □ I respect the president but I disagree with his decision. 私は大統領を尊敬するが彼の決定には異議がある.

dis|agree|ment /dɪsəgrimənt/ (**disagreements**) ■ N-UNCOUNT 不可算名詞 **Disagreement** means objecting to something such as a proposal. 異議のあること □ Britain and France have expressed some disagreement with the proposal. 英国とフランスはその提案に多少の異議を唱えた. ■ N-VAR 可変性名詞 When there is **disagreement** about something, people disagree or argue about what should be done. 意見の相違 □ The United States Congress and the president are still locked in disagreement over proposals to reduce the massive budget deficit. 米国下院と大統領はまだ巨大な財政赤字の削減提案についてまだ意見が違ったままだ.

dis|al|low /dɪsəlaʊ/ (**disallows, disallowing, disallowed**) V-T 他動詞 If something **is disallowed**, it is not allowed or accepted officially, because it has not been done correctly. 認可しない □ The goal was disallowed. ゴールは認められなかった.

dis|ap|pear /dɪsəpɪər/ (**disappears, disappearing,**

disappeared) ■ V-I 自動詞 If you say that someone or something **disappears**, you mean that you can no longer see them, usually because you or they have changed position. 見えなくなる □ The black car drove away from them and disappeared. 黒い車は彼らの前を走り去り見えなくなった. ■ V-I 自動詞 If someone or something **disappears**, they go away or are taken away somewhere where nobody can find them. 消息を絶つ □ …a Japanese woman who disappeared thirteen years ago. 13年前に消息を絶った日本人女性 ■ V-I 自動詞 If something **disappears**, it stops existing or happening. 存在しなくなる □ The immediate threat of the past has disappeared and the security situation in Europe has significantly improved. 過去の差し迫った脅威はなくなり、ヨーロッパの安全保障は大幅に改善した.

Word Partnership   disappear は次の語句と使われる:

V.	make something/someone disappear ■ – ■
ADV.	disappear completely, quickly disappear ■ – ■
	mysteriously disappear ■
	disappear forever ■ ■

dis|ap|pear|ance /dɪsəpɪərəns/ (**disappearances**) ■ N-VAR 可変性名詞 If you refer to someone's **disappearance**, you are referring to the fact that nobody knows where they have gone. 失踪(しっそう) □ Her disappearance has baffled police. 彼女の失踪(しっそう)に警察は困惑した. ■ N-COUNT 可算名詞 If you refer to the **disappearance** of an object, you are referring to the fact that it has been lost or stolen. 紛失 □ Police are investigating the disappearance of key files on the killers. 警察は殺人者の主なファイルの紛失を調査中である. ■ N-UNCOUNT 不可算名詞 The **disappearance** of a type of thing, person, or animal is a process in which it becomes less common and finally no longer exists. 消滅 □ …the virtual disappearance of common dolphins from the western Mediterranean in recent years. 西地中海から近年イルカが事実上消滅したこと

dis|ap|point /dɪsəpɔɪnt/ (**disappoints, disappointing, disappointed**) V-T 他動詞 If things or people **disappoint** you, they are not as good as you had hoped, or do not do what you hoped they would do. 失望させる □ She would do anything she could to please him, but she knew that she was fated to disappoint him. 彼女は彼を喜ばせるためには何でもするが、彼を失望させる運命にあることを知っていた.

dis|ap|point|ed /dɪsəpɔɪntɪd/ ■ ADJ 形容詞 If you are **disappointed**, you are sad because something has not happened or because something is not as good as you had hoped. 失望した □ Adamski says he was very disappointed with the mayor's decision. 市長の決定には大変失望したとアダムスキーは言う. □ I was disappointed that John was not there. ジョンがいなくて私はがっかりした. ■ ADJ 形容詞 If you are **disappointed** in someone, you are sad because they have not behaved as well as you expected them to. 当て外れの [v-link ADJ 'in' 句] □ You should have accepted that. I'm disappointed in you. それは受け入れるべきだったよ. 君にはがっかりした.

dis|ap|point|ing /dɪsəpɔɪntɪŋ/ ADJ 形容詞 Something that is **disappointing** is not as good or as large as you hoped it would be. 期待外れの □ The wine was excellent, but the meat was overdone and the vegetables disappointing. ワインは素晴らしかったけど肉は焼き過ぎで野菜は期待外れだった. ● **dis|ap|point|ing|ly** ADV 副詞 がっかりするほど □ Progress is disappointingly slow. 進行はがっかりするほど遅い.

dis|ap|point|ment /dɪsəpɔɪntmənt/ (**disappointments**) ■ N-UNCOUNT 不可算名詞 **Disappointment** is the state of feeling disappointed. 失望 □ Despite winning the title, their last campaign ended in great disappointment. タイトルは獲得したものの彼らの最後の試合は期待外れに終わった. ■ N-COUNT 可算名詞 Something or someone that is a **disappointment** is not as good as you had hoped. 期待外れ □ For many, their long-awaited homecoming was a bitter disappointment. 大多数にとって彼らの待ちに待った帰郷はひどく期待外れであった.

dis|ap|prov|al /dɪsəpruvᵊl/ N-UNCOUNT 不可算名詞 If you feel or show **disapproval** of something or someone, you feel or show

that you do not approve of them. 不可とすること □*His action had been greeted with almost universal disapproval.* 彼の行為はほとんど全員の非難を受けていた.

dis|ap|prove /dɪsəprúːv/ (**disapproves, disapproving, disapproved**) V-I 自動詞 If you **disapprove of** something or someone, you feel or show that you do not like them or do not approve of them. 不可とする □*Most people disapprove of such violent tactics.* ほとんどの人がそのような暴力的な策略は認めない.

dis|ap|prov|ing /dɪsəprúːvɪŋ/ ADJ 形容詞 A **disapproving** action or expression shows that you do not approve of something or someone. 非難するような □*Janet gave him a disapproving look.* ジャネットは非難の目で彼を見た. ● **dis|ap|prov|ing|ly** ADV 副詞 [ADV after v] 非難するように □*Antonio looked at him disapprovingly.* アントニオは非難するように彼を見た.

dis|arm /dɪsɑ́ːrm/ (**disarms, disarming, disarmed**) **1** V-T 他動詞 To **disarm** a person or group means to take away all their weapons. 武装解除する □*We will agree to disarming troops and leaving their weapons at military positions.* われわれは軍隊の武装を解除して軍の陣地に兵器を捨ておくことに合意するだろう. **2** V-I 自動詞 If a country or group **disarms**, it gives up the use of weapons, especially nuclear weapons. 軍備を縮小する □*There has also been a suggestion that the forces in Lebanon should disarm.* レバノン軍は軍備縮小すべきだと示唆もある. **3** V-T 他動詞 If a person or their behavior **disarms** you, they cause you to feel less angry, hostile, or critical toward them. 敵意を除く □*His unease disarmed her.* 彼の困惑した様子が彼女の気持ちを和らげた.

dis|arma|ment /dɪsɑ́ːrməmənt/ N-UNCOUNT 不可算名詞 **Disarmament** is the act of reducing the number of weapons, especially nuclear weapons, that a country has. 軍備縮小 □*The goal would be to increase political stability in the region and accelerate the pace of nuclear disarmament.* 目標は地域の政治的安定を増大させ核軍縮の歩調を速めることであろう.

dis|arm|ing /dɪsɑ́ːrmɪŋ/ ADJ 形容詞 If someone or something is **disarming**, they make you feel less angry or hostile. 人を安心させる □*Leonard approached with a disarming smile.* レオナルドは人懐っこい微笑を浮かべながら近づいてきた. ● **dis|arm|ing|ly** ADV 副詞 人を安心させるほどに □*He is, as ever, business-like, and disarmingly honest.* 彼は相変わらずてきぱきして人を安心させるほどに誠実だ.

dis|ar|ray /dɪsəréɪ/ **1** N-UNCOUNT 不可算名詞 If people or things are **in disarray**, they are disorganized and confused. 混乱 □*The nation is in disarray following rioting led by the military.* 軍の率いる暴動の後で国は混乱している. **2** N-UNCOUNT 不可算名詞 If things or places are **in disarray**, they are in a very disorganized state. 乱れた状態 □*She was left lying on her side and her clothes were in disarray.* 彼女は横に寝た状態で放置され, 衣服が乱れていた.

dis|as|ter /dɪzǽstər/ (**disasters**) **1** N-COUNT 可算名詞 A **disaster** is a very bad accident such as an earthquake or a plane crash, especially one in which a lot of people are killed. 災難 □*It was the second air disaster in the region in less than two months.* それは地域でこの2か月に起こった2件目の航空機事故であった. **2** N-COUNT 可算名詞 If you refer to something as a **disaster**, you are emphasizing that you think it is extremely bad or unacceptable. 大失敗 [EMPHASIS 強調] □*The whole production was just a disaster!* この上演は完全に大失敗だった！ **3** N-UNCOUNT 不可算名詞 **Disaster** is something which has very bad consequences for you. 大難 □*The government brought itself to the brink of fiscal disaster.* 政府は財政破綻の一歩手前だった. **4** PHRASE 句 If you say that something is **a recipe for disaster**, you mean that it is very likely to have unpleasant consequences. 災いのもと □*You give them a gun, and it's a recipe for disaster.* 彼らに銃を与えてごらん, 災いのもとになるよ.

→ see Word Web: **disaster**

dis|as|trous /dɪzǽstrəs/ **1** ADJ 形容詞 A **disastrous** event has extremely bad consequences and effects. 壊滅的な □*...the recent, disastrous earthquake.* 最近起きた壊滅的な地震 ● **dis|as|trous|ly** ADV 副詞 壊滅的に □*The vegetable harvest is disastrously behind schedule.* 野菜の収穫が壊滅的に遅れている. **2** ADJ 形容詞 If you describe something as **disastrous**, you mean that it was very unsuccessful. 悲惨な □*...after their disastrous performance in the election.* 選挙での悲

惨な結果の後 ● **dis|as|trous|ly** ADV 副詞 悲惨に □*...debts resulting from the company's disastrously timed venture into property development.* 会社がタイミング悪く不動産開発に投機したための負債

dis|band /dɪsbǽnd/ (**disbands, disbanding, disbanded**) V-T/V-I 他動詞/自動詞 If someone **disbands** a group of people, or if the group **disbands**, it stops operating as a single unit. 解散する □*All the armed groups will be disbanded.* 武装グループは全て解体されるであろう.

dis|be|lief /dɪsbɪlíːf/ N-UNCOUNT 不可算名詞 **Disbelief** is not believing that something is true or real. 不信 □*She looked at him in disbelief.* 彼女は彼を信じられない様子で見た.

disc /dɪsk/ → see **disk**
→ see DVD

dis|card /dɪskɑ́ːrd/ (**discards, discarding, discarded**) V-T 他動詞 If you **discard** something, you get rid of it because you no longer want it or need it. 捨てる □*Read the manufacturer's guidelines before discarding the box.* 箱を捨てる前にメーカーのガイドラインを読むこと.

dis|cern /dɪsɜ́ːrn/ (**discerns, discerning, discerned**) **1** V-T 他動詞 If you can **discern** something, you are aware of it and know what it is. 認識する [FORMAL 形式ばった] □*You need a long series of data to be able to discern such a trend.* このような傾向を認識するためには長期にわたるデータが必要である. **2** V-T 他動詞 If you can **discern** something, you can just see it, but not clearly. 見分ける [FORMAL 形式ばった] □*Below the bridge we could just discern a narrow, weedy ditch.* 橋の下に細くて雑草だらけの溝があるのがなんとか分かった.

dis|cern|ible /dɪsɜ́ːrnəbəl/ ADJ 形容詞 If something is **discernible**, you can see it or recognize that it exists. 認められる [FORMAL 形式ばった] □*Far away the outline of the island is just discernible.* はるかかなたに島の輪郭がやっと分かる.

dis|cern|ing /dɪsɜ́ːrnɪŋ/ ADJ 形容詞 If you describe someone as **discerning**, you mean that they are able to judge which things of a particular kind are good and which are bad. 眼力のある [APPROVAL 賛成] □*Even the most accomplished writers show their work-in-progress to discerning readers.* 名人級の作家でさえ書きかけの原稿を読んで違いのわかる人に見てもらうものだ.

dis|charge (**discharges, discharging, discharged**)

> The verb is pronounced /dɪstʃɑ́ːrdʒ/. The noun is pronounced /dɪstʃɑːrdʒ/.
>
> 動詞は /dɪstʃɑ́ːrdʒ/ と発音される. 名詞は /dɪstʃɑːrdʒ/ と発音される.

1 V-T 他動詞 When someone **is discharged from** a hospital, prison, or one of the armed services, they are officially allowed to leave, or told that they must leave. (病院から) 退院させる, (刑務所から) 釈放する, (軍部から) 除隊させる, 解任する □*He has a broken nose but may be discharged today.* 彼は鼻の骨を折ったが今日中に退院するかもしれない. ● N-VAR 可変性名詞 **Discharge** is also a noun. 退院, 釈放, 除隊, 解任 □*He was given a conditional discharge and ordered to pay Miss Smith $500 compensation.* 彼は条件付で釈放されスミスさんに500ドルの賠償金を支払うように命じられた. **2** V-T 他動詞 If someone **discharges** their duties or responsibilities, they do everything that needs to be done in order to complete them. 履行する [FORMAL 形式ばった] □*...the quiet competence with which he discharged his many duties.* 彼がたくさんの責務を履行するのに用いた秘めた能力 **3** V-T 他動詞 If something **is discharged from** inside a place, it comes out. 排出する [FORMAL 形式ばった] □*The resulting salty water will be discharged at sea.* その結果できた塩水は海に排出される. **4** N-VAR 可変性名詞 When there is a **discharge** of a substance, the substance comes out from inside somewhere. 分泌物 [FORMAL 形式ばった] □*They develop a fever and a watery discharge from their eyes.* 熱が出て目から水っぽい分泌物が出る.
→ see **lightning**

dis|ci|ple /dɪsáɪpəl/ (**disciples**) N-COUNT 可算名詞 If you are someone's **disciple**, you are influenced by their teachings and try to follow their example. 弟子 □*...a major intellectual figure with disciples throughout Europe.* 欧州の至るところに弟子のいる偉大な知識人

dis|ci|pli|nary /dɪsɪplɪneri/ ADJ 形容詞 **Disciplinary** bodies or

Word Web   disaster

We are learning more about nature's cycles. But natural **disasters** remain a big challenge. Some, such as **hurricanes** and **floods**, are predictable. However, we still can't avoid the **damage** they do. Each year **monsoons** strike southern Asia. Monsoons are a combination of **typhoons**, **tropical storms**, and heavy **rains**. In addition to the damage caused by flooding, **landslides** and **mudslides** add to the problem. In 2005 more than 90 million people were affected in China alone. Over 700 people died there and millions of acres of crops were destroyed. The **economic loss** totaled nearly 6 billion dollars.

actions are concerned with making sure that people obey rules or regulations and that they are punished if they do not. 懲戒の [ADJ n] ❑ *He will now face a disciplinary hearing for having an affair.* 彼は不倫について懲戒審問を受けることになっている.

dis|ci|pline /dɪsɪplɪn/ (**disciplines, disciplining, disciplined**)
■ N-UNCOUNT 不可算名詞 **Discipline** is the practice of making people obey rules or standards of behavior, and punishing them when they do not. 規律 ❑ *Order and discipline have been placed in the hands of governing bodies.* 秩序と規律は統治組織の手にゆだねられた. ■ N-UNCOUNT 不可算名詞 **Discipline** is the quality of being able to behave and work in a controlled way which involves obeying particular rules or standards. 自制 ❑ *It was that image of calm, control, and discipline that appealed to millions of voters.* 多くの有権者に訴えたのは, あの落ち着き, 自律, 自制を持つ印象だった. ■ N-VAR 可変性名詞 If you refer to an activity or situation as a **discipline**, you mean that, in order to be successful in it, you need to behave in a strictly controlled way and obey particular rules or standards. 訓練 ❑ *The discipline of studying music can help children develop good work habits and improve self-esteem.* 子供にみっちり音楽を学ばせれば, よい勉強のくせをつけ自尊心を向上させることができる. ■ V-T 他動詞 If someone **is disciplined** for something that they have done wrong, they are punished for it. 懲戒する ❑ *The workman was disciplined by his company but not dismissed.* その労働者は彼の会社から懲戒されたが解雇はされなかった. ■ V-T 他動詞 If you **discipline yourself** to do something, you train yourself to behave and work in a strictly controlled and regular way. しつける ❑ *Discipline yourself to check your messages once a day every couple of days.* 毎日1回あるいは1日置きにメッセージを確認するように自分をしつけなさい. ■ N-COUNT 可算名詞 A **discipline** is a particular area of study, especially a subject of study in a college or university. 学問分野 [FORMAL 形式ばった] ❑ *We're looking for people from a wide range of disciplines.* 広い範囲の学問分野から人材を探している.

dis|ci|plined /dɪsɪplɪnd/ ADJ 形容詞 Someone who is **disciplined** behaves or works in a controlled way. 規律正しい ❑ *For me it meant being very disciplined about how I run my life.* 私にとってそれはとても規則正しく生活の仕方を守ることを意味した.

disc jock|ey (**disc jockeys**) also **disk jockey** N-COUNT 可算名詞 A **disc jockey** is someone who plays and introduces music on the radio or at a disco. ディスクジョッキー

dis|claim|er /dɪskleɪmər/ (**disclaimers**) N-COUNT 可算名詞 A **disclaimer** is a statement in which a person says that they did not know about something or that they are not responsible for something. 免責条項 [FORMAL 形式ばった] ❑ *The company asserts in a disclaimer that it won't be held responsible for the accuracy of information.* その会社は免責条項の中で情報の正確さに関しては責任を持たないと主張している.

dis|close /dɪskl00z/ (**discloses, disclosing, disclosed**) V-T 他動詞 If you **disclose** new or secret information, you tell people about it. 発表する ❑ *Neither side would disclose details of the transaction.* 両者とも取引の詳細は発表しないであろう.

dis|clo|sure /dɪskl00ʒər/ (**disclosures**) N-VAR 可変性名詞 **Disclosure** is the act of giving people new or secret information. 公開 ❑ *...insufficient disclosure of negative information about the company.* 会社について否定的な情報の不十分な開示

dis|co /dɪsk00/ (**discos**) N-COUNT 可算名詞 A **disco** is a place or event at which people dance to pop music. ディスコ ❑ *Fridays and Saturdays are regular disco nights.* 金曜と土曜の夜に決まってディスコに行く.

Word Link   dis ≈ negative, not : disagree, discomfort, disrespect

dis|com|fort /dɪskʌmfərt/ (**discomforts**) ■ N-UNCOUNT 不可算名詞 **Discomfort** is a painful feeling in part of your body when you have been hurt slightly or when you have been uncomfortable for a long time. 不快感 ❑ *Steve had some discomfort, but no real pain.* スティーブはある程度の不快感があったが実際の痛みはなかった. ■ N-UNCOUNT 不可算名詞 **Discomfort** is a feeling of worry caused by shame or embarrassment. 不安 ❑ *She hears the discomfort in his voice.* 彼女は彼の声に不安を聞き取った. ■ N-COUNT 可算名詞 **Discomforts** are conditions which cause you to feel physically uncomfortable. 不便さ ❑ *...the discomforts of camping.* キャンプ生活の不便さ

dis|con|cert|ing /dɪskənsɜrtɪŋ/ ADJ 形容詞 If you say that something is **disconcerting**, you mean that it makes you feel anxious, confused, or embarrassed. まごつかせる ❑ *The reception desk is not at street level, which is a little disconcerting.* 同じ階にはなく少しまごつかされる. ● **dis|con|cert|ing|ly** ADV 副詞 まごつくほど ❑ *She looks disconcertingly like a familiar aunt or grandmother.* 彼女は親しい叔母や祖母にまごつくほど似ている.

dis|con|nect /dɪskənekt/ (**disconnects, disconnecting, disconnected**) ■ V-T 他動詞 To **disconnect** a piece of equipment means to separate it from its source of power or to break a connection that it needs in order to work. 切断する ❑ *The device automatically disconnects the ignition when the engine is switched off.*

この装置はエンジンが切れると自動的に点火装置を切断する. ■ V-T 他動詞 If you **are disconnected** by a gas, electricity, water, or telephone company, they turn off the connection to your house, usually because you have not paid the bill. サービスを打ち切る [usu passive] ❑ *You are likely to be given almost three months – until the time of your next bill – before you are disconnected.* サービス停止まで, ほぼ3か月間つまり次の請求書の時まで猶予があるだろう. ■ V-T 他動詞 If you **disconnect** something **from** something else, you separate the two things. 分離する ❑ *He disconnected the IV bottle from the overhead hook and carried it beside the moving cart.* 彼は点滴用の瓶を頭上のフックから外し移動カートのそばに持っていった.

dis|con|nect|ed /dɪskənektɪd/ ADJ 形容詞 **Disconnected** things are not linked in any way. つながりのない ❑ *...sequences of utterly disconnected events.* 全くつながりのない出来事の連続

dis|con|tent /dɪskəntent/ (**discontents**) N-UNCOUNT 不可算名詞 **Discontent** is the feeling that you have when you are not satisfied with your situation. 不満 [also N in pl] ❑ *There are reports of widespread discontent in the capital.* 首都では不満が広がっているという報告がある.

dis|con|tinue /dɪskəntɪnyu/ (**discontinues, discontinuing, discontinued**) ■ V-T 他動詞 If you **discontinue** something that you have been doing regularly, you stop doing it. 中止する [FORMAL 形式ばった] ❑ *Do not discontinue the treatment without consulting your doctor.* 医者に相談せずに治療を中止しないように. ■ V-T 他動詞 If a product **is discontinued**, the manufacturer stops making it. 製造中止する [usu passive] ❑ *The Leica M2 was discontinued in 1967.* ライカM2は1967年に製造中止となった.

dis|count (**discounts, discounting, discounted**)

Pronounced /dɪskaʊnt/ for meanings ■ and ■, and /dɪskaʊnt/ for meaning ■.
と■■ の意味では /dɪskaʊnt/ と発音され, ■ の意味では /dɪskaʊnt/と発音される.

■ N-COUNT 可算名詞 A **discount** is a reduction in the usual price of something. 割引 ❑ *They are often available at a discount.* これらはしばしば割引されている. ❑ *All full-time staff get a 20 percent discount.* 常勤の全社員に20パーセントの割引がある. ■ V-T 他動詞 If a store or company **discounts** an amount or percentage from something that they are selling, they take the amount or percentage off the usual price. 値引く ❑ *This has forced airlines to discount fares heavily in order to spur demand.* このため航空会社は料金を大く値引きして需要を刺激しなければならなかった. ■ V-T 他動詞 If you **discount** an idea, fact, or theory, you consider that it is not true, not important, or not relevant. 無視する ❑ *However, traders tended to discount the rumor.* しかしトレーダーたちは噂を無視しがちだった.

dis|cour|age /dɪskɜrɪdʒ/ (**discourages, discouraging, discouraged**) ■ V-T 他動詞 If someone or something **discourages** you, they cause you to lose your enthusiasm about your actions. やる気を失わせる ❑ *It may be difficult to do at first. Don't let this discourage you.* 最初は難しいかもしれない. それでもやる気を失わないように. ● **dis|cour|aged** ADJ 形容詞 がっかりした ❑ *She was determined not to be too discouraged.* 彼女はあくまでも落胆しすぎないようにした. ● **dis|cour|ag|ing** ADJ 形容詞 思わしくない ❑ *Today's report is extremely discouraging for the economy.* 本日の報告は経済にとって極めて思わしくないものである. ■ V-T 他動詞 To **discourage** an action or to **discourage** someone **from** doing it means to make them not want to do it. 思いとどませる ❑ *...typhoons that discouraged shopping and leisure activities.* 買い物やレジャー活動を思いとどませた台風

dis|cour|age|ment /dɪskɜrɪdʒmənt/ N-UNCOUNT 不可算名詞 **Discouragement** is the act of trying to make someone not want to do something. 邪魔 ❑ *He persevered in the face of active discouragement from those around him.* 彼は回りの人が思いとどまらせようとするのを物ともせずやり抜いた.

dis|course /dɪskɔrs/ (**discourses**) ■ N-UNCOUNT 不可算名詞 **Discourse** is spoken or written communication between people, especially serious discussion of a particular subject. 会話 ❑ *...a tradition of political discourse.* 政治の会話の伝統 ■ → see also **direct discourse, indirect discourse**

dis|cov|er /dɪskʌvər/ (**discovers, discovering, discovered**) ■ V-T 他動詞 If you **discover** something that you did not know about before, you become aware of it or learn of it. 分かる ❑ *She discovered that they'd escaped.* 彼女は彼らが逃げたことに気づいた. ❑ *It was difficult for the inspectors to discover which documents were important and which were not.* どの書類が重要でどれがそうでないかを見分けるのは刑事たちには困難であった.

D

You can use **discover**, **find**, or **find out** to talk about learning that something is the case. ❑ *He discovered the whole school knew about it… The young child finds that noise attracts attention…We found out that she was wrong.* **Discover** is a slightly more formal word than **find**, and is often used to talk about scientific research or formal investigations. For example, you can **discover** a cure for a particular disease. You can also use **discover** when you find something by accident. ❑ *This well-known flower was discovered in 1903.* If you cannot see something you are looking for, you say that you cannot **find** it. You do not use "discover" or 'find out' in this way. ❑ *I'm lost – I can't find the bridge.* You can say that someone **finds out** facts when this is easy to do, but you cannot use "discover" or 'find' in this way. ❑ *I found out the train times.*

2 V-T 他動詞 If a person or thing **is discovered**, someone finds them, either by accident or because they have been looking for them. 見つける ❑ *A few days later his badly beaten body was discovered on a roadside outside the city.* 数日後，ひどく殴られた彼の死体が市外の道端で発見された. **3** V-T 他動詞 When someone **discovers** a new place, substance, scientific fact, or scientific technique, they are the first person to find it or become aware of it. 発見する ❑ *…the first European to discover America.* アメリカ大陸を初めて発見したヨーロッパ人 **4** V-T 他動詞 When a actor, musician, or other performer who is not well known **is discovered**, someone recognizes that they have talent and helps them in their career. 見いだす [usu passive] ❑ *The Beatles were discovered in the early 1960s.* ビートルズは1960年代初期に見いだされた.

Thesaurus　　discover また次を参照:

V.　　come upon, detect, find out, learn, uncover; *(ant.)* ignore, miss, overlook **1**

dis|cov|ery /dɪskʌvəri/ (**discoveries**) **1** N-VAR 可変性名詞 If someone makes a **discovery**, they become aware of something that they did not know about before. 発見 ❑ *I felt I'd made an incredible discovery.* 私は驚くべき発見をしたのだと自覚した. **2** N-VAR 可変性名詞 If someone makes a **discovery**, they are the first person to find or become aware of a place, substance, or scientific fact that no one knew about before. 発見したもの ❑ *In that year, two momentous discoveries were made.* その年二つの重大な発見があった. **3** N-VAR 可変性名詞 When the **discovery** of people or objects happens, someone finds them, either by accident or as a result of looking for them. 発見すること ❑ *…the discovery and destruction by soldiers of millions of marijuana plants.* 数百万株の大麻が兵士たちにより発見, 処分されたこと

dis|cred|it /dɪskrɛdɪt/ (**discredits, discrediting, discredited**) V-T 他動詞 To **discredit** someone or something means to cause them to lose people's respect or trust. 信用を傷つける ❑ *…a secret unit within the company that had been set up to discredit its major rival.* 主要な競合相手の評判を悪くする目的で社内に設けられた秘密部門 ● **dis|cred|it|ed** ADJ 形容詞 信用を落とした ❑ *The previous government is, by now, thoroughly discredited.* 前政府は今ではまったく信用されていない.

dis|creet /dɪskrit/ **1** ADJ 形容詞 If you are **discreet**, you are polite and careful in what you do or say, because you want to avoid embarrassing or offending someone. 思慮深い ❑ *They were gossipy and not always discreet.* 彼らはうわさ好きで，いつも控えめなわけではなかった. ● **dis|creet|ly** ADV 副詞 目立たずに ❑ *I took the phone, and she went discreetly into the living room.* 私が電話に出ると彼女は目立たないようにそっと居間に行った. **2** ADJ 形容詞 If you are **discreet about** something you are doing, you do not tell other people about it, in order to avoid being embarrassed or to gain an advantage. 慎重な ❑ *We were very discreet about the romance.* 私たちは恋愛について，とても口をつつしんでいた. ● **dis|creet|ly** ADV 副詞 控えめに ❑ *Everyone worked to make him welcome, and, more discreetly, to find out about him.* みんなは彼を歓迎するように努力し，そしてもっと目立たないところで彼について知ろうとした. **3** ADJ 形容詞 If you describe something as **discreet**, you approve of it because it is small in size or degree, or not easily noticed. 控えめな [APPROVAL 賛成] ❑ *She is wearing a noticeably stylish, feminine dress, plus discreet jewellery.* 彼女はきわめておしゃれで女性的なドレスを着て，控えめな装身具をつけていた. ● **dis|creet|ly** ADV 副詞 [ADV -ed/adj] 目立たないように ❑ *…stately houses, discreetly hidden behind great avenues of sturdy trees.* がっしりとした木がならぶ並木道に目立たぬように隠れている大邸宅

dis|crep|an|cy /dɪskrɛpənsi/ (**discrepancies**) N-VAR 可変性名詞 If there is a **discrepancy between** two things that ought to be the same, there is a noticeable difference between them. 食い違い ❑ *…the discrepancy between press and radio reports.* 新聞とラジオの報道の食い違い

dis|cre|tion /dɪskrɛʃ°n/ **1** N-UNCOUNT 不可算名詞 **Discretion** is the quality of behaving in a quiet and controlled way without drawing attention to yourself or giving away personal or private information. 慎重さ [FORMAL 形式ばった] ❑ *Larsson sometimes*

joined in the fun, but with more discretion. ラーソンは時々遊びに加わったがより慎重であった. **2** N-UNCOUNT 不可算名詞 If someone in a position of authority uses their **discretion** or has the **discretion** to do something in a particular situation, they have the freedom and authority to decide what to do. 自由裁量権, 行動の自由 [FORMAL 形式ばった] ❑ *This committee may want to exercise its discretion to look into those charges.* それらの嫌疑について本委員会の裁量で調査をおこなう可能性がある. **3** PHRASE 句 If something happens **at** someone's **discretion**, it can happen only if they decide to do it or give their permission. 自由裁量で [FORMAL 形式ばった] ❑ *We may vary the limit at our discretion and will notify you of any change.* 私たちの判断で限度を変更する場合があり，変更した場合にはあなたに通知します.

dis|cre|tion|ary /dɪskrɛʃənɛri/ ADJ 形容詞 **Discretionary** things are not fixed by rules but are decided on by people in authority, who consider each individual case. 自由裁量の ❑ *Magistrates were given wider discretionary powers.* 治安判事の自由裁量権が拡大された.

dis|crimi|nate /dɪskrɪmɪneɪt/ (**discriminates, discriminating, discriminated**) **1** V-I 自動詞 If you can **discriminate between** two things, you can recognize that they are different. 区別する ❑ *He is incapable of discriminating between a good idea and a terrible one.* 彼はいいアイデアとひどいアイデアを区別することができない. **2** V-I 自動詞 To **discriminate against** a group of people or **in favor of** a group of people means to unfairly treat them worse or better than other groups. 差別する ❑ *They believe the law discriminates against women.* その法律が女性を冷遇していると彼らは思っている. ❑ *…legislation which would discriminate in favor of racial minorities.* 人種的少数派を優遇する法規

dis|crimi|na|tion /dɪskrɪmɪneɪʃ°n/ **1** N-UNCOUNT 不可算名詞 **Discrimination** is the practice of treating one person or group of people less fairly or less well than other people or groups. 差別 ❑ *She is exempt from sex discrimination laws.* 彼女は性差別禁止法の適用から除外されている. **2** N-UNCOUNT 不可算名詞 **Discrimination** is knowing what is good or of high quality. 識別 ❑ *They cooked without skill and ate without discrimination.* 彼らは技術を使わずに料理して何でもかまわずに食べた. **3** N-UNCOUNT 不可算名詞 **Discrimination** is the ability to recognize and understand the differences between two things. 識別力 ❑ *We will then have an objective measure of how color discrimination and visual acuity develop at the level of the brain.* そうして色の識別能と視力がどのようにその水準の脳で発達するのかをはかる客観的な指標を得ることになる.

dis|crimi|na|tory /dɪskrɪmɪnətɔri/ ADJ 形容詞 **Discriminatory** laws or practices are unfair because they treat one group of people worse than other groups. 差別的な ❑ *These reforms will abolish racially discriminatory laws.* これらの改革により人種差別的な法律がなくなるであろう.

dis|cur|sive /dɪskɜrsɪv/ ADJ 形容詞 If a style of writing is **discursive**, it includes a lot of facts or opinions that are not necessarily relevant. とりとめのない [FORMAL 形式ばった] ❑ *…a livelier, more candid and more discursive treatment of the subject.* もっと活発で，もっと率直で，もっととりとめのない主題の扱い方

dis|cuss /dɪskʌs/ (**discusses, discussing, discussed**) **1** V-T 他動詞 If people **discuss** something, they talk about it, often in order to reach a decision. 話し合う ❑ *I will be discussing the situation with colleagues tomorrow.* あした同僚とその状況について話し合う予定だ. **2** V-T 他動詞 If you **discuss** something, you write or talk about it in detail. 論じる ❑ *I will discuss the role of diet in cancer prevention in Chapter 7.* 第7章でガン予防における食事の役割について論じます.

Note that **discuss** is never used as an intransitive verb. You cannot say, for example, "They discussed," "I discussed with him," or "They discussed about politics." Instead, you can say that you **have a discussion** with someone about something. ❑ *I had a long discussion about all this with Stephen.* You can also add an object and say that you **discuss** something **with** someone. If the discussion is less formal, you can simply use the verb **talk**. ❑ *They come here and sit for hours talking about politics…We talked all night long.*

Word Partnership　　discuss は次の語句と使われる:

V.　　meet to discuss, refuse to discuss **1**
N.　　discuss **options**, discuss **problems** **1**
　　　discuss **an issue**, discuss **a matter**, discuss **plans** **1** **2**

dis|cus|sion /dɪskʌʃ°n/ (**discussions**) **1** N-VAR 可変性名詞 If there is **discussion** about something, people talk about it, in order to reach a decision. 論議, 話し合い ❑ *There was a lot of discussion about the wording of the report.* 報告書の表現についてたくさん論議された. ❑ *Board members are due to have informal discussions later on today.* 役員は今日この後で非公式な意見の交換をする予定である. ● PHRASE 句 If something is **under discussion**, it is still being

talked about and a final decision has not yet been reached. 検討中 **2** N-COUNT 可算名詞 A **discussion of** a subject is a piece of writing or a lecture in which someone talks about it in detail. 考察 ❑ *For a discussion of biology and sexual politics, see chapter 4.* 生物学と性的政治に関する考察は第4章を参照のこと. **3** ADJ 形容詞 A **discussion** document or paper is one that contains information and usually proposals for people to discuss. 検討用の [ADJ n] ❑…*a NASA discussion paper on long-duration ballooning.* 気球の長期飛行に関するアメリカ航空宇宙局の検討論文

Thesaurus *discussion* また次を参照:

N. conference, conversation, debate, talk **1**

dis|dain /dɪsdeɪn/ (disdains, disdaining, disdained) **1** N-UNCOUNT 不可算名詞 If you feel **disdain for** someone or something, you dislike them because you think that they are inferior or unimportant. 軽蔑 ❑ *Janet looked at him with disdain.* ジャネットは彼を軽蔑の目で見た. **2** V-T 他動詞 If you **disdain** someone or something, you regard them with disdain. 軽蔑する ❑ *Jackie disdained the servants that her millions could buy.* 彼女の富で買収できる使用人を軽蔑した.

dis|ease /dɪziz/ (diseases) N-VAR 可変性名詞 A **disease** is an illness which affects people, animals, or plants, for example, one which is caused by bacteria or infection. 病気 ❑…*the rapid spread of disease in the area.* その地域における疾病の急速な広がり方
→ see **diagnosis, medicine**

Word Partnership *disease* は次の語句と使われる:

V.	**cause** disease, **cure a** disease, **spread** disease, **treat a** disease
ADJ.	**contagious** disease, **fatal** disease, **infectious** disease, **rare** disease, **sexually transmitted** disease
N.	**death and** disease, **gum** disease, **heart** disease, **symptoms of** disease

dis|eased /dɪzizd/ ADJ 形容詞 Something that is **diseased** is affected by a disease. 病気にかかった ❑ *The arteries are diseased and a transplant is the only hope.* 動脈が病んでおり移植が唯一の望みである.

dis|en|chant|ed /dɪsɪntʃæntɪd/ ADJ 形容詞 If you are **disenchanted with** something, you are disappointed with it and no longer believe that it is good or worthwhile. 幻滅した ❑ *The electorate had grown disenchanted with politics.* 有権者は政治に幻滅していた.

dis|en|chant|ment /dɪsɪntʃæntmənt/ N-UNCOUNT 不可算名詞 **Disenchantment** is the feeling of being disappointed with something, and no longer believing that it is good or worthwhile. 幻滅 ❑ *There is growing public disenchantment with the educational system.* 教育制度に対する国民の幻滅感が広がってきている.

dis|en|fran|chise /dɪsɪnfræntʃaɪz/ (disenfranchises, disenfranchising, disenfranchised) V-T 他動詞 To **disenfranchise** a group of people means to take away their right to vote or other rights that most other people have. 公民権を剥奪(はくだつ)する ❑…*fears of an organized attempt to disenfranchise supporters of Father Aristide.* アリスティド神父の支持者から公民権を剥奪(はくだつ)する組織的試みの懸念
→ see **vote**

dis|en|gage /dɪsɪngeɪdʒ/ (disengages, disengaging, disengaged) V-T/V-I 他動詞/自動詞 If you **disengage** something, or if it **disengages**, it becomes separate from something which it has been attached to. 外す, 離れる ❑ *She disengaged the film advance mechanism on the camera.* 彼女はカメラのフィルム巻上げ装置を外した. ❑ *John gently disengaged himself from his sister's tearful embrace.* ジョンは彼の妹の涙ながらの抱擁から徐々に身を解いた.

Word Link *fig ≈ form, shape : con*figure*, dis*figure*,* figurative

dis|fig|ure /dɪsfɪɡyər/ (disfigures, disfiguring, disfigured) V-T 他動詞 If someone **is disfigured**, their appearance is spoiled. 外観を損じる [usu passive] ❑ *Many of the wounded had been badly disfigured.* 負傷者の多くは体がひどく傷つけられていた. ● **dis|fig|ured** ADJ 形容詞 醜くなった ❑ *She tried not to look at the scarred, disfigured face.* 彼女は傷跡の残る醜くなった顔を見ないようにした.

Word Link *grac ≈ pleasing : dis*grace*,* grace*,* graceful

dis|grace /dɪsɡreɪs/ (disgraces, disgracing, disgraced) **1** N-UNCOUNT 不可算名詞 If you say that someone is **in disgrace**, you are emphasizing that other people disapprove of them and do not respect them because of something that they have done. 不面目 [EMPHASIS 強調] ❑ *His vice president also had to resign in disgrace.* 彼を補佐する副大統領も恥辱の中で辞任しなければならなかった. **2** N-SING 単数名詞 If you say that something is **a disgrace**, you are emphasizing that it is very bad or wrong, and that you find it

completely unacceptable. 恥 [EMPHASIS 強調] ❑ *The way the sales were handled was a disgrace.* 販売のしかたは全く恥ずべきものだった. **3** N-SING 単数名詞 You say that someone is a **disgrace to** someone else when you want to emphasize that their behavior causes the other person to feel ashamed. 面汚し [EMPHASIS 強調] ❑ *Republican leaders called him a disgrace to the party.* 共和党の指導者たちは彼を党の面汚しと呼んだ. **4** V-T 他動詞 If you say that someone **disgraces** someone else, you are emphasizing that their behavior causes the other person to feel ashamed. 辱める [EMPHASIS 強調] ❑ *I have disgraced my family's name.* 私は私の家の名を汚した.

dis|graced /dɪsɡreɪst/ ADJ 形容詞 You use **disgraced** to describe someone whose bad behavior has caused them to lose the approval and respect of the public or of people in authority. 屈辱を受けた ❑…*the disgraced leader of the coup.* 面目を失ったクーデター の指導者

dis|grace|ful /dɪsɡreɪsfəl/ ADJ 形容詞 If you say that something such as behavior or a situation is **disgraceful**, you disapprove of it strongly, and feel that the person or people responsible should be ashamed of it. 恥ずべき [DISAPPROVAL 不賛成] ❑ *It's disgraceful that they have detained him for so long.* こんなに長く彼を勾留(こうりゅう)したのは恥ずべき事だ. ● **dis|grace|ful|ly** ADV 副詞 みっともなく ❑ *He felt that his brother had behaved disgracefully.* 彼は彼の兄はみっともないふるまいをしたと思った.

dis|grun|tled /dɪsɡrʌntᵊld/ ADJ 形容詞 If you are **disgruntled**, you are angry and dissatisfied because things have not happened the way that you wanted them to happen. 不満を抱いた ❑ *Disgruntled employees recently called for his resignation.* 不満を抱く従業員が最近彼の辞職を求めた.

dis|guise /dɪsɡaɪz/ (disguises, disguising, disguised) **1** N-VAR 可変性名詞 If you are **in disguise**, you are not wearing your usual clothes or you have altered your appearance in other ways, so that people will not recognize you. 変装 ❑ *You'll have to travel in disguise.* あなたは変装して移動しなければならないだろう. **2** V-T 他動詞 If you **disguise yourself**, you put on clothes which make you look like someone else or alter your appearance in other ways, so that people will not recognize you. 変装する ❑ *She disguised herself as a man so she could fight on the battlefield.* 彼女は戦地で戦えるように男装した. ● **dis|guised** ADJ 形容詞 変装した ❑ *The extremists entered the building disguised as medical workers.* 過激派は医療従事者に変装し建物の中に入った. **3** V-T 他動詞 To **disguise** something means to hide it or make it appear different so that people will not know about it or will not recognize it. 隠す ❑ *He made no attempt to disguise his agitation.* 彼は動揺の色を隠そうとしなかった. ● **dis|guised** ADJ 形容詞 隠した ❑ *The proposal is a thinly disguised effort to revive the price controls of the 1970s.* この提案は1970年代の価格統制を復活させようとしているのがみえみえだ.

dis|gust /dɪsɡʌst/ (disgusts, disgusting, disgusted) **1** N-UNCOUNT 不可算名詞 **Disgust** is a feeling of very strong dislike or disapproval. いやけ ❑ *He spoke of his disgust at the incident.* 彼はその出来事に対する嫌悪感について話した. **2** V-T 他動詞 To **disgust** someone means to make them feel a strong sense of dislike and disapproval. うんざりさせる ❑ *He disgusted many with his boorish behavior.* 彼はその粗野なふるまいで多くの人をうんざりさせた.

dis|gust|ed /dɪsɡʌstɪd/ ADJ 形容詞 If you are **disgusted**, you feel a strong sense of dislike and disapproval at something. うんざりした ❑ *I'm disgusted with the way that he was treated.* 彼が受けた扱いに腹が立っている. ● **dis|gust|ed|ly** ADV 副詞 [ADV with v] それをつかして ❑ *"It's a little late for that," Ritter said disgustedly.* 「それにはちょっと間に合わなかったね」とリッターは嫌気がさした感じで言った.

dis|gust|ing /dɪsɡʌstɪŋ/ **1** ADJ 形容詞 If you say that something is **disgusting**, you are criticizing it because it is extremely unpleasant. 胸が悪くなるような ❑ *It tasted disgusting.* それはひどい味がした. **2** ADJ 形容詞 If you say that something is **disgusting**, you mean that you find it completely unacceptable. 実にいやな ❑ *It's disgusting that all this damage has been caused by mindless vandalism.* この破損がすべて心ない破壊行為により生じたのは実に不愉快である.

dish /dɪʃ/ (dishes, dishing, dished) **1** N-COUNT 可算名詞 A **dish** is a shallow container with a wide uncovered top. You eat and serve food from dishes and cook food in them. 皿 ❑…*plastic bowls and dishes.* プラスティックのおわんと皿 **2** N-COUNT 可算名詞 Food that is prepared in a particular style or combination can be referred to as a **dish**. 料理 ❑ *There are plenty of vegetarian dishes to choose from.* 菜食料理の種類がよりどりだ. **3** N-COUNT 可算名詞 You can use **dish** to refer to anything that is round and hollow in shape with a wide uncovered top. 皿状のもの, パラボラアンテナ ❑…*a dish used to receive satellite broadcasts.* 衛星放送受信用のアンテナ **4** N-PLURAL 複数名詞 All the objects that have been used to cook, serve, and eat a meal can be referred to as **the dishes**. 食器類 ❑ *He'd cooked dinner and washed the dishes.* 彼は食事を用意し, 皿

D

Picture Dictionary | **dish**

cup & saucer

butter dish

jug

sugar bowl

mug

dinner plate | salad plate | bread plate | bowl | platter

を洗った. **5** → see also **satellite dish** **6** PHRASE 句 If you **do the dishes**, you wash the dishes. 皿洗いをする ❏ I hate doing the dishes. 私はお皿を洗うのが大嫌い.

▸ **dish out** **1** PHRASAL VERB 句動詞 If you **dish out** something, you distribute it among a number of people. 供給する [INFORMAL くだけた] ❏ Doctors, not pharmacists, are responsible for dishing out drugs. 薬剤師ではなく医師に薬を供する責任がある. **2** PHRASAL VERB 句動詞 If someone **dishes out** criticism or punishment, they give it to someone. 与える [INFORMAL くだけた] ❏ Do you usually dish out criticism to someone who's doing you a favor? あなたは普通、世話になっている人を非難する? **3** PHRASAL VERB 句動詞 If you **dish out** food, you serve it to people at the beginning of each course of a meal. 皿に盛る [INFORMAL くだけた] ❏ Here the cooks dish out sweet and sour pork. ここで料理人が豚を盛り付ける.

▸ **dish up** PHRASAL VERB 句動詞 If you **dish up** food, you serve it. (食べ物を) 出す [INFORMAL くだけた] ❏ They dished up a superb meal. 素晴らしい食事が出た.
→ see Picture Dictionary: **dish**
→ see **pottery**

dis|heart|ened /dɪshɑ́rtʲnd/ ADJ 形容詞 If you are **disheartened**, you feel disappointed about something and have less confidence or less hope about it than you did before. 気落ちする ❏ He was disheartened by their hostile reaction. 彼らの敵意に満ちた反応に彼はがっかりした.

dis|heart|en|ing /dɪshɑ́rtʲnɪŋ/ ADJ 形容詞 If something is **disheartening**, it makes you feel disappointed and less confident or less hopeful. がっかりさせる ❏ The news was disheartening for investors. ニュースは投資家たちをがっかりさせるものだった.

di|shev|eled /dɪʃɛ́vʲld/ ADJ 形容詞 If you describe someone's hair, clothes, or appearance as **disheveled**, you mean that it is very untidy. 取り乱した ❏ She arrived flushed and disheveled. 彼女は赤い顔をして取り乱した身なりで到着した.

dis|hon|est /dɪsɒ́nɪst/ ADJ 形容詞 If you say that a person or their behavior is **dishonest**, you mean that they are not truthful or honest and that you cannot trust them. 不正直な ❏ It would be dishonest to mislead people and not to present the data as fairly as possible. 人の誤解を招き不当に限り公正にデータを示さないのは不正直である. ● **dis|hon|est|ly** ADV 副詞 不正直に ❏ The key issue was whether the four defendants acted dishonestly. 重要な点は4人の被告が不正直にふるまったかどうかだった.

dis|hon|es|ty /dɪsɒ́nɪsti/ N-UNCOUNT 不可算名詞 **Dishonesty** is dishonest behavior. 不正直 ❏ She accused the government of dishonesty and incompetence. 彼女は政府を不正直で無能であると非難した.

dish|wash|er /dɪ́ʃwɒʃər/ (dishwashers) **1** N-COUNT 可算名詞 A **dishwasher** is an electrically operated machine that washes and dries dishes, pans and flatware. 皿洗い機 **2** N-COUNT 可算名詞 A **dishwasher** is a person who is employed to wash dishes, for example at a restaurant, or who usually washes the dishes at home. 皿洗い人 ❏ I was a short-order cook and a dishwasher. 私は即席料理を作って皿も洗った.

dis|il|lu|sion /dɪsɪluʒʲn/ (disillusions, disillusioning, disillusioned) **1** V-T 他動詞 If a person or thing **disillusions** you, they make you realize that something is not as good as you thought. 幻滅させる ❏ I'd hate to be the one to disillusion him. 私が彼を幻滅させる役はいやだ. **2** N-UNCOUNT 不可算名詞 **Disillusion** is the same as **disillusionment**. 幻滅感 ❏ There is disillusion with established political parties. 既存の政党への幻滅感がある.

dis|il|lu|sioned /dɪsɪluʒʲnd/ ADJ 形容詞 If you are **disillusioned with** something, you are disappointed, because it is not as good as you had expected or thought. 幻滅した ❏ I've become very disillusioned with politics. 政治にはすっかり幻滅してしまった.

dis|il|lu|sion|ment /dɪsɪluʒʲnmənt/ N-UNCOUNT 不可算名詞 **Disillusionment** is the disappointment that you feel when you discover that something is not as good as you had expected or thought. 幻滅感 ❏ Polls have charted growing disillusionment with the campaign. 世論調査は選挙戦で増大しつつある幻滅感を示した.

dis|in|fect /dɪsɪnfɛ́kt/ (disinfects, disinfecting, disinfected) V-T 他動詞 If you **disinfect** something, you clean it using a substance that kills germs. 消毒する ❏ Chlorine is used to disinfect water. 塩素は水を消毒するのに使われる.

dis|in|fect|ant /dɪsɪnfɛ́ktənt/ (disinfectants) N-MASS 質量名詞 **Disinfectant** is a substance that kills germs. It is used, for example, for cleaning kitchens and bathrooms. 消毒剤 ❏ Effluent from the sedimentation tank is dosed with disinfectant to kill any harmful organisms. 沈殿槽からの廃液には有害な微生物を殺す消毒剤が投与されている.

dis|in|fla|tion /dɪsɪnfleɪʃʲn/ N-UNCOUNT 不可算名詞 **Disinflation** is a reduction in the rate of inflation, especially as a result of government policies. ディスインフレ (ディフレにならない程度にインフレを抑えること) ❏ The 1990s was a period of disinflation, when companies lost much of their power to raise prices. 1990年代はディスインフレの期間で企業は値上げする力をほとんど失った.

dis|in|te|grate /dɪsɪ́ntɪɡreɪt/ (disintegrates, disintegrating, disintegrated) **1** V-I 自動詞 If something **disintegrates**, it becomes seriously weakened, and is divided or destroyed. 分裂する ❏ During October 1918 the Austro-Hungarian Empire began to disintegrate. 1918年の10月にオーストリア・ハンガリー帝国は分裂し始めた. ● **dis|in|te|gra|tion** /dɪsɪntɪɡreɪʃʲn/ N-UNCOUNT 不可算名詞 分裂 ❏ ...the violent disintegration of Yugoslavia. ユーゴスラビアの激しい分裂 **2** V-I 自動詞 If an object or substance **disintegrates**, it breaks into many small pieces or parts and is destroyed. 分解する ❏ At 420 mph the windshield disintegrated. 時速420マイルで風防がバラバラに壊れた. ● **dis|in|te|gra|tion** N-UNCOUNT 不可算名詞 分解 ❏ The report describes the catastrophic disintegration of the aircraft after the explosion. 報告書は爆発後に航空機が壊滅的に分解した様子を描写している.

dis|in|ter|est /dɪsɪ́ntərɪst, -ɪntrɪst/ N-UNCOUNT 不可算名詞 If there is **disinterest in** something, people are not interested in it. 無関心 ❏ The fact that Liberia has no oil seems to explain foreign disinterest in its internal affairs. リベリアが非産油国であることで、外国が内政に無関心なことを説明できそうだ.

dis|in|ter|est|ed /dɪsɪ́ntərɪstɪd, -ɪ́ntrɪstɪd/ **1** ADJ 形容詞 Someone who is **disinterested** is not involved in a particular situation or not likely to benefit from it and is therefore able to act in a fair and unselfish way. 公平無私な ❏ The current sole superpower is far from being a disinterested observer. 現在の唯一の超大国は公平無私な監視役とはとても言えたものではない. **2** ADJ 形容詞 If you are **disinterested in** something, you are not interested in it. Some users of English believe that it is not correct to use **disinterested** with this meaning. 興味のない ❏ Lili had clearly regained her appetite but Doran was disinterested in food. リリーは明らかに食欲を取り戻したがドランは食べ物に興味を示さなかった.

dis|joint|ed /dɪsdʒɔ́ɪntɪd/ ADJ 形容詞 **Disjointed** words, thoughts, or ideas are not presented in a smooth or logical way

and are therefore difficult to understand. 筋道のたたない □*Sally was used to hearing his complaints, usually in the form of disjointed, drunken ramblings.* サリーは、大抵は支離滅裂で酔ってしゃべりまくる彼の不平を聞くのに慣れていた.

disk /dɪsk/ (disks) also disc **1** N-COUNT 可算名詞 A **disk** is a flat, circular shape or object. 円盤 □*The food processor has thin, medium, and thick slicing disks.* そのフードプロセッサーには薄め, 中間, 厚めのスライス用円盤がある. **2** N-COUNT 可算名詞 A **disk** is one of the thin, circular pieces of cartilage which separates the bones in your back. つい間板 □*I had slipped a disk and was frozen in a spasm of pain.* 私はぎっくり腰になり痛みの発作で動けなかった. **3** N-COUNT 可算名詞 In a computer, the **disk** is the part where information is stored. データ保存用ディスク □*The program takes up 2.5 megabytes of disk space and can be run on a standard personal computer.* プログラムは2.5メガバイトのディスクスペースを取る標準仕様のパソコンで動作する. **4** N-COUNT 可算名詞 A **disk** is the same as a **compact disk**. コンパクトディスク **5** → see also **disk drive, floppy disk, hard disk**

disk drive (disk drives) N-COUNT 可算名詞 The **disk drive** on a computer is the part that contains the disk or into which a disk can be inserted. The disk drive allows you to read information from the disk and store information on the disk. ディスクドライブ

Word Link ette ≈ small : cigarette, diskette, rosette

disk|ette /dɪskɛt/ (diskettes) N-COUNT 可算名詞 A **diskette** is the same as a **floppy disk**. フロッピーディスク

dis|like /dɪslaɪk/ (dislikes, disliking, disliked) **1** V-T 他動詞 If you **dislike** someone or something, you consider them to be unpleasant and do not like them. 嫌う □*Liver is a great favorite of his and we don't serve it often because so many people dislike it.* レバーは彼の大好物で, とても多くの人が嫌うのでいつもは出さない. **2** N-UNCOUNT 不可算名詞 **Dislike** is the feeling that you do not like someone or something. 嫌い □*My dislike of thunder and even small earthquakes was due to Mother.* 私が雷そして小さな地震でも嫌うのは母のせいであった. **3** N-COUNT 可算名詞 Your **dislikes** are the things that you do not like. きらい □*Consider what your likes and dislikes are about your job.* あなたの仕事で好きな点ときらいな点は何か考えてください. **4** PHRASE 句 If you **take a dislike to** someone or something, you decide that you do not like them. 嫌いになる □*He may suddenly take a dislike to foods that he's previously enjoyed.* 彼は以前楽しんでいた食べ物を突然嫌うかもしれない.

Thesaurus dislike また次を参照:

V.	disapprove of, object to **1**
N.	aversion to **2**

dis|lo|cate /dɪsloʊkeɪt, dɪsloʊkeɪt/ (dislocates, dislocating, dislocated) **1** V-T 他動詞 If you **dislocate** a bone or joint in your body, or in someone else's body, it moves out of its proper position in relation to other bones, usually in an accident. 脱臼する □*Harrison dislocated a finger.* ハリソンは指の関節を脱臼した. **2** V-T 他動詞 To **dislocate** something such as a system, process, or way of life means to disturb it greatly or prevent it from continuing as normal. 混乱させる □*It would help to end illiteracy and disease, but it would also dislocate a traditional way of life.* これは文盲と疾病をなくするのに役立つであろうが, 伝統的な生活様式を混乱させることにもなろう.

dis|lodge /dɪslɒdʒ/ (dislodges, dislodging, dislodged) **1** V-T 他動詞 To **dislodge** something means to remove it from where it was fixed or held. 移動させる □*Rainfall from a tropical storm dislodged the debris from the slopes of the volcano.* 熱帯性の嵐に伴う雨は火山の斜面から岩屑 (がんせつ) を押し流した. **2** V-T 他動詞 To **dislodge** a person from a position or job means to remove them from it. 取り除く □*Congress had sought to dislodge him from the post.* 議会はその座から彼を引きずり降ろそうとした.

dis|loy|al /dɪslɔɪəl/ ADJ 形容詞 Someone who is **disloyal to** their friends, family, or country does not support them or does things that could harm them. 不実な □*She was so disloyal to her deputy she made his position untenable.* 彼女は副官の立場を失わせるほど彼に不誠実だった.

dis|loy|al|ty /dɪslɔɪəlti/ N-UNCOUNT 不可算名詞 **Disloyalty** is disloyal behavior. 不信行為 □*Charges had already been made against certain officials suspected of disloyalty.* 不信行為の嫌疑を受けた一部の担当官はすでに告訴されていた.

dis|mal /dɪzməl/ **1** ADJ 形容詞 Something that is **dismal** is bad in a sad or depressing way. 情けない □*...Israel's dismal record in the Olympics.* オリンピックでのイスラエルの情けない成績 **2** ADJ 形容詞 Something that is **dismal** is sad and depressing, especially in appearance. 陰気な □*The main part of the hospital is pretty dismal but the children's ward is really lively.* 病院の主要部分はかなり陰気だが小児病棟は本当に活気がある.

dis|man|tle /dɪsmæntəl/ (dismantles, dismantling, dismantled) **1** V-T 他動詞 If you **dismantle** a machine or structure, you carefully separate it into its different parts. 分解

する □*He asked for immediate help from the United States to dismantle the warheads.* 彼は米国にただちに弾頭廃棄の支援を提供するよう求めた. **2** V-T 他動詞 To **dismantle** an organization or system means to cause it to stop functioning by gradually reducing its power or purpose. 解体する □*Public services of all kinds are being dismantled.* あらゆる種類の公益事業体が解体されつつある.

dis|may /dɪsmeɪ/ (dismays, dismaying, dismayed) **1** N-UNCOUNT 不可算名詞 **Dismay** is a strong feeling of fear, worry, or sadness that is caused by something unpleasant and unexpected. うろたえ [FORMAL 形式ばった] □*Local politicians have reacted with dismay and indignation.* 地元の政治家たちはうろたえ憤慨した反応を示した. **2** V-T 他動詞 If you **are dismayed** by something, it makes you feel afraid, worried, or sad. うろたえさせる [FORMAL 形式ばった] □*The committee was dismayed by what it had been told.* 委員会はその話にうろたえた. ● **dis|mayed** ADJ 形容詞 うろたえた □*He was dismayed at the cynicism of the youngsters.* 彼は若者たちが冷笑的なのでうろたえた.

Word Link miss ≈ sending : dismiss, missile, missionary

dis|miss /dɪsmɪs/ (dismisses, dismissing, dismissed) **1** V-T 他動詞 If you **dismiss** something, you decide or say that it is not important enough for you to think about or consider. 退ける □*Mr. Wakeham dismissed the reports as speculation.* ウェイカム氏は報道を憶測として退けた. **2** V-T 他動詞 If you **dismiss** something **from** your mind, you stop thinking about it. 払いのける □*I dismissed the problem from my mind.* 私はその問題を念頭から払いのけた. **3** V-T 他動詞 When an employer **dismisses** an employee, the employer tells the employee that they are no longer needed to do the job that they have been doing. 解雇する □*...the power to dismiss civil servants who refuse to work.* 仕事を拒む公務員を解雇する権限 **4** V-T 他動詞 If you **are dismissed** by someone in authority, they tell you that you can go away from them. 退出させる □*Two more witnesses were called, heard, and dismissed.* 証人があと二人呼ばれ, 審問され, 退廷した. **5** V-T 他動詞 When a judge **dismisses** a case against someone, he or she formally states that there is no need for a trial, usually because there is not enough evidence for the case to continue. 棄却する □*A federal judge dismissed the charges against the doctor yesterday.* 昨日, 米国連邦の裁判官は, 医者に対する訴えを棄却した.

Word Partnership dismiss は次の語句と使われる:

ADJ.	easy to dismiss **1**
N.	dismiss **an idea**, dismiss **a possibility** **1**
	dismiss **an employee** **3**
	dismiss **a case**, dismiss **charges** **5**

dis|mis|sal /dɪsmɪsəl/ (dismissals) **1** N-VAR 可変性名詞 When an employee is dismissed from their job, you can refer to their **dismissal**. 解雇 □*...Mr. Low's dismissal from his post at the head of the commission.* ロウ氏の委員長職からの免職 **2** N-UNCOUNT 不可算名詞 **Dismissal** of something means deciding or saying that it is not important. 重要でないと片付けること □*...bureaucratic indifference to people's rights and needs, and high-handed dismissal of public opinion.* 国民の権利と要求に対する官僚的無関心と高圧的な世論の無視

dis|mis|sive /dɪsmɪsɪv/ ADJ 形容詞 If you are **dismissive of** someone or something, you say or show that you think they are not important or have no value. 拒否するような □*Mr. Jones was dismissive of the report, saying it was riddled with inaccuracies.* ジョーンズ氏はその報告書は不正確な部分ばかりだと否定的に言った. ● **dis|mis|sive|ly** ADV 副詞 拒否するように □*"Critical acclaim from people who don't know what they're talking about is meaningless," he claims dismissively.* 「わけも分からぬものを言う人から批評で称賛されても無意味だ」と彼は拒否するように主張する.

dis|obe|di|ence /dɪsəbidiəns/ N-UNCOUNT 不可算名詞 **Disobedience** is deliberately not doing what someone tells you to do, or what a rule or law says that you should do. 不服従 □*A single act of rebellion or disobedience was often enough to seal a woman's fate.* たった一度の反抗や不服従で女性の運命は大決まってしまった.

dis|obey /dɪsəbeɪ/ (disobeys, disobeying, disobeyed) V-T/V-I 他動詞/自動詞 When someone **disobeys** a person or an order, they deliberately do not do what they have been told to do. 服従しない □*...a naughty boy who often disobeyed his mother and father.* お母さんやお父さんの言うことをしばしば聞かないわんぱくな男の子

dis|or|der /dɪsɔrdər/ (disorders) **1** N-VAR 可変性名詞 A **disorder** is a problem or illness which affects someone's mind or body. 障害 □*...a rare nerve disorder that can cause paralysis of the arms.* 腕が麻痺する可能性のある, まれな神経障害 **2** N-VAR 可変性名詞 **Disorder** is violence or rioting in public. 無秩序 □*Six months ago America's worst civil disorder in more than 100 years erupted in the city of Los Angeles.* 6か月前に, 米国で100年以上もなかったような最悪の市民暴動がロサンゼルス市で勃発した. **3** N-UNCOUNT 不可算名詞 **Disorder** is a state of being untidy, badly prepared, or badly organized. 混乱 □*The emergency room was in disorder.* 救急治療室は

混乱していた.

dis|or|der|ly /dɪsɔ́rdərli/ ■ ADJ 形容詞 If you describe something as **disorderly**, you mean that it is messy, irregular, or disorganized. [FORMAL 形式ばった] □ *There were young men and women working away at tables all over the large and disorderly room.* 広く散らかった部屋のあちこちにある机に向かってせっせと働く若い男女がいた. ② ADJ 形容詞 If you describe someone as **disorderly**, you mean that they are behaving in a noisy, rude, or violent way in public. You can also describe a place or event as **disorderly** if the people there behave in this way. 混乱した, 無秩序の [FORMAL 形式ばった] □ *She was jailed for being drunk and disorderly.* 彼女は酔って暴れて留置所に入れられた.

dis|or|gani|za|tion /dɪsɔ̀rgənɪzéɪʃ°n/ N-UNCOUNT 不可算名詞 If something is in a state of **disorganization**, it is disorganized. 混乱 □ *The military, he says, is now in a state of disorganization.* 彼は現在, 軍は混乱状態だと言う.

dis|or|gan|ized /dɪsɔ́rgənaɪzd/ ■ ADJ 形容詞 Something that is **disorganized** is in a confused state or is badly planned or managed. まとまりのない □ *A report by the state prosecutor described the police action as confused and disorganized.* 国の検察官による報告書は, 警察の行動は混乱していて組織だっていないと述べた. ② ADJ 形容詞 Someone who is **disorganized** is very bad at organizing things in their life. きちょうめんでない □ *My boss is completely disorganized and leaves the most important items until very late.* 私の上司は計画性が全然なくて一番大切なことを最後までほったらかしにする.

dis|or|ent /dɪsɔ́riɛnt/ (disorients, disorienting, disoriented) V-T 他動詞 If something **disorients** you, you lose your sense of direction, or you generally feel lost and uncertain, for example, because you are in an unfamiliar environment. 方角を分からなくさせる, まごつかせる □ *An overnight stay at a friend's house disorients me.* 友達の家に泊まると調子が狂う. ● **dis|ori|ent|ed** ADJ 形容詞 混乱した □ *I feel dizzy and disoriented.* 目まいがして混乱した感じがする. ● **dis|ori|en|ta|tion** /dɪsɔ̀riɛntéɪʃ°n/ N-UNCOUNT 不可算名詞 見当識 (時, 場所, 周囲の状況を正しく理解する能力) の喪失 □ *Morris was so stunned by this that he experienced a moment of total disorientation.* モリスは瞬間的に完全に見当識を失った経験にとてもびっくりした.

dis|ori|en|tate /dɪsɔ́riɛnteɪt/ (disorientates, disorientating, disorientated) → see disorient

dis|own /dɪsóʊn/ (disowns, disowning, disowned) V-T 他動詞 If you **disown** someone or something, you say or show that you no longer want to have any connection with them or any responsibility for them. 自分のものと認めない □ *The man who murdered the girl is no son of mine. I disown him.* あの少女を殺した男は私の息子などではない. 彼とは縁切りだ.

dis|par|age /dɪspǽrɪdʒ/ (disparages, disparaging, disparaged) V-T 他動詞 If you **disparage** someone or something, you speak about them in a way which shows that you do not have a good opinion of them. 軽蔑する [FORMAL 形式ばった] □ *...Larkin's tendency to disparage literature.* ラーキンの文学を軽視する傾向

dis|par|ag|ing /dɪspǽrɪdʒɪŋ/ ADJ 形容詞 If you are **disparaging** about someone or something, or make **disparaging** comments about them, you say things which show that you do not have a good opinion of them. 軽蔑の □ *He was critical of the people, disparaging of their crude manners.* 彼はその人たちに批判的で, がさつな態度をさげすんでいた.

Word Link	par ≈ equal : compare, disparate, part

dis|par|ate /dɪspǽrɪt/ ■ ADJ 形容詞 **Disparate** things are clearly different from each other in quality or type. 本質的に異なる [FORMAL 形式ばった] □ *Scientists are trying to pull together disparate ideas in astronomy.* 科学者たちは天文学での異種の考え方をまとめようとしている. ② ADJ 形容詞 A **disparate** thing is made up of very different elements. 種々の要素から成る [FORMAL 形式ばった] □ *...a very disparate nation, with enormous regional differences.* 大きな地域差があり共通点のとても少ない国家

dis|par|ity /dɪspǽriti/ (disparities) N-VAR 可変性名詞 If there is a **disparity between** two or more things, there is a noticeable difference between them. 相違 [FORMAL 形式ばった] □ *...the health disparities between ethnic and socioeconomic groups in the U.S.* 米国における民族及び社会経済的グループ間の健康格差

dis|patch /dɪspǽtʃ/ (dispatches, dispatching, dispatched) ■ V-T 他動詞 If you **dispatch** someone to a place, you send them there for a particular reason. 派遣する [FORMAL 形式ばった] □ *He had been continually dispatching scouts ahead.* 彼は絶えず偵察を前方に送っていた. ● N-UNCOUNT 不可算名詞 **Dispatch** is also a noun. 派遣 □ *The dispatch of the task force is purely a contingency measure.* 機動部隊の派遣は単なる不測の事態に備えての措置である. ② V-T 他動詞 If you **dispatch** a message, letter, or parcel, you send it to a particular person or destination. 発送する [FORMAL 形式ばった] □ *The victory inspired him to dispatch a gleeful telegram to Roosevelt.* その勝利は彼を大喜びの電報をルーズベルト宛に打つ気にさせた.

● N-UNCOUNT 不可算名詞 **Dispatch** is also a noun. 発送 □ *We have 125 cases ready for dispatch.* 125箱発送の準備ができています.

dis|pel /dɪspɛ́l/ (dispels, dispelling, dispelled) V-T 他動詞 To **dispel** an idea or feeling that people have means to stop them having it. 払いのける □ *The president is attempting to dispel the notion that he has neglected the economy.* 大統領は経済をなおざりにしたという意見を払いのけようとしている.

dis|pen|sable /dɪspɛ́nsəb°l/ ADJ 形容詞 If someone or something is **dispensable** they are not really needed. なくても済む □ *All those people in the middle are dispensable.* この真ん中にいる人たちは全て不要だ.

dis|pense /dɪspɛ́ns/ (dispenses, dispensing, dispensed) ■ V-T 他動詞 If someone **dispenses** something that they own or control, they give or provide it to a number of people. 分配する [FORMAL 形式ばった] □ *The union had already dispensed $60,000 in grants.* 組合は既に6万ドルを助成金として支給していた. ② V-T 他動詞 If you obtain a product by getting it out of a machine, you can say that the machine **dispenses** the product. (自動販売機などが商品を) 販売する □ *For two weeks, the cash machine spewed out receipts apologizing for its inability to dispense money.* 2週間にわたり現金支払い機は引き出しができなかったことを謝罪する明細書を出し続けた. ③ V-T 他動詞 When a pharmacist **dispenses** medicine, he or she prepares it, and gives or sells it to the patient or customer. (薬剤師が薬を調剤して) 出す □ *Health officials hope to begin dispensing anti-retroviral drugs on a wide scale at the beginning of next year.* 保健当局は抗レトロウイルス剤の本格供給を来年の初めに開始したいと考えている.

▶ **dispense with** PHRASAL VERB 句動詞 If you **dispense with** something, you stop using it or get rid of it completely, especially because you no longer need it. なしで済ませる □ *More modern heating systems dispense with the need for a tank.* 新式の暖房装置はタンクが不要になった.

dis|pens|er /dɪspɛ́nsər/ (dispensers) N-COUNT 可算名詞 A **dispenser** is a machine or container designed so that you can get an item or quantity of something from it in an easy and convenient way. ディスペンサー □ *...cash dispensers.* 現金支払い機

dis|perse /dɪspɜ́rs/ (disperses, dispersing, dispersed) ■ V-T/V-I 他動詞/自動詞 When something **disperses** or when you disperse it, it spreads over a wide area. 散らす, 散る □ *The oil appeared to be dispersing.* 油は分散しつつあるようだ. ② V-T/V-I 他動詞/自動詞 When a group of people **disperses** or when someone disperses them, the group splits up and the people leave in different directions. 解散する [自動詞], 解散させる [他動詞] □ *Police fired shots and used tear gas to disperse the demonstrators.* 警察はデモ参加者を解散させるため発砲し催涙ガスも使った.

dis|place /dɪspléɪs/ (displaces, displacing, displaced) ■ V-T 他動詞 If one thing **displaces** another, it forces the other thing out of its place, position, or role, and then occupies that place, position, or role itself. 取って代わる □ *These factories have displaced tourism as the country's largest source of foreign exchange.* 最大の外貨収入源として工場が観光に取って代わった. ② V-T 他動詞 If a person or group of people **is displaced**, they are forced to move away from the area where they live. 立ち退かせる [usu passive] □ *More than 600,000 people were displaced by the tsunami.* 津波により60万人以上が住む場所を失った.

dis|placed per|son (displaced people, displaced persons) N-COUNT 可算名詞 A **displaced person** is someone who has been forced to leave the place where they live, especially because of a war. 避難民 □ *There is an urgent need for food and shelter for these displaced people.* これらの避難民のための食料と避難所が大至急必要だ.

dis|place|ment /dɪspléɪsmənt/ ■ N-UNCOUNT 不可算名詞 **Displacement** is the removal of something from its usual place or position by something which then occupies that place or position. 置き換え [FORMAL 形式ばった] □ *...the displacement of traditional agriculture by industrial crops.* 伝統的農業が工業作物に置き換えられること ② N-UNCOUNT 不可算名詞 **Displacement** is the forcing of people away from the area or country where they live. 立ち退き □ *...the gradual displacement of the American Indian.* 段階的なアメリカインディアンの強制的退去

dis|play /dɪspléɪ/ (displays, displaying, displayed) ■ V-T 他動詞 If you **display** something that you want people to see, you put it in a particular place, so that people can see it easily. 展示する □ *Among the protesters and war veterans proudly displaying their medals was Aubrey Rose.* 抗議者と誇らしげに勲章をつけた退役軍人たちの中にオーブリー・ローズがいた. ● N-UNCOUNT 不可算名詞 **Display** is also a noun. 展示 □ *Most of the other artists whose work is on display were his pupils or colleagues.* 展示中のほかの芸術家の作品の作者の大多数は彼の門下生や仲間だった. ② V-T 他動詞 If you **display** something, you show it to people. 見せる □ *She displayed her wound to the twelve gentlemen of the jury.* 彼女は傷を12人の陪審員に見せた. ③ V-T 他動詞 If you **display** a characteristic, quality, or emotion, you behave in a way which shows that you have it. 表

に出す □ *It was unlike Gordon to display his feelings.* 感情を表に出す のはゴードンらしくないことだった。 ● N-VAR 可変性名詞 **Display** is also a noun. 表現 □ *Normally, such an outward display of affection is reserved for his mother.* 普通こんなに愛情を表に出すのは彼の母親だけ であった。 ◢ V-T 他動詞 When a computer **displays** information, it shows it on a screen. 表示する □ *They started out by looking at the computer screens which display the images.* 彼らはそれらの画像を表示 しているコンピューターの展示を調べることから始めた。 ◢ N-COUNT 可算名詞 A **display** is an arrangement of things that have been put in a particular place, so that people can see them easily. 展示 □ *...a display of your work.* あなたの作品の展示。 ◢ N-COUNT 可算 名詞 A **display** is a public performance or other event which is intended to entertain people. 見せ物 □ *...the fireworks display.* 花 火大会 ◢ N-COUNT 可算名詞 The **display** on a computer screen is the information that is shown there. The screen itself can also be referred to as the **display**. 表示、ディスプレイ □ *A hard copy of the screen display can also be obtained from a printer.* 画面表示のハードコピ ーはプリンターからも得られる。

dis|pleas|ure /dɪsplɛʒər/ N-UNCOUNT 不可算名詞 Someone's **displeasure** is a feeling of annoyance that they have about something that has happened. 不満 □ *The population has already begun to show its displeasure at the slow pace of change.* 変化の歩みが遅 いことに住民はすでに不満の色を示し始めている。

dis|pos|able /dɪspoʊzəbᵊl/ (**disposables**) ◢ ADJ 形容詞 A **disposable** product is designed to be thrown away after it has been used. 使い捨ての □ *...disposable diapers suitable for babies up to 8lbs.* 体重8ポンドまでの乳児用の使い捨ておむつ ● N-COUNT 可算名 詞 Disposable products can be referred to as **disposables**. 使い捨て のもの □ *Currently, disposables account for about 80% to 85% of the $3 billion-plus annual diaper market.* 現在のところ年間30億ドル以上のお むつ市場の80から85パーセントを使い捨ての製品が占める。 ◢ ADJ 形 容詞 Your **disposable** income is the amount of income you have left after you have paid bills and taxes. 可処分の [ADJ n] □ *Gerald had little disposable income.* ジェラルドにはほとんど可処分所得がな かった。

dis|pos|al /dɪspoʊzᵊl/ ◢ PHRASE 句 If you have something **at your disposal**, you are able to use it whenever you want, and for whatever purpose you want. If you say that you are **at** someone's **disposal**, you mean that you are willing to help them in any way you can. 思い通りにできる □ *Do you have this information at your disposal?* あなたはこの情報を自由に使えますか。 ◢ N-UNCOUNT 不 可算名詞 Disposal is the act of getting rid of something that is no longer wanted or needed. 処分 □ *...methods for the permanent disposal of radioactive wastes.* 放射性物質の恒久処分法

dis|pose /dɪspoʊz/ (**disposes, disposing, disposed**) ▶ **dispose of** PHRASAL VERB 句動詞 If you **dispose of** something that you no longer want or need, you throw it away. ーを捨てる □ *...the safest means of disposing of nuclear waste.* 放射性廃棄物を処分 する最も安全な方法。

dis|posed /dɪspoʊzd/ ◢ ADJ 形容詞 If you are **disposed to** do something, you are willing or eager to do it. ーをする気があっ て、ーしたいと思って [FORMAL 形式ばった] [v-link ADJ to-inf] □ *We passed one or two dwellings, but were not disposed to stop.* 1、2軒の家の 前を通り過ぎたが、立ち止まるつもりはなかった。 ◢ ADJ 形容詞 You can use **disposed** when you are talking about someone's general attitude or opinion. For example, if you are well or favorably **disposed to** or **toward** someone or something, you like them or approve of them. ー的な [FORMAL 形式ばった] □ *I saw that the publishers were well disposed toward my book.* 出版社が私の本にと ても乗り気なのが分かった。

dis|po|si|tion /dɪspəzɪʃᵊn/ (**dispositions**) N-COUNT 可算名詞 Someone's **disposition** is the way that they tend to behave or feel. 性格、気質 □ *The rides are unsuitable for people of a nervous disposition.* その乗り物は臆病な人には向いていない。

dis|pro|por|tion|ate /dɪsprəpɔrʃənɪt/ ADJ 形容詞 Something that is **disproportionate** is surprising or unreasonable in amount or size, compared with something else. 不釣合いな、極端な □ *A disproportionate amount of time was devoted to one topic.* 一つの話題に あまりにも多くの時間が割かれた。 ● **dis|pro|por|tion|ate|ly** ADV 副詞 不釣り合いに、極端に □ *There is a disproportionately high suicide rate among prisoners facing very long sentences.* 刑期がとても長い服役者の 自殺率は突出している。

dis|prove /dɪspruv/ (**disproves, disproving, disproved, disproven**) V-T 他動詞 To **disprove** an idea, belief, or theory means to show that it is not true. 誤りを証明する □ *The statistics to prove or disprove his hypothesis will take years to collect.* 彼の仮説が正し いかどうかを証明するには、何年にもわたり統計データを収集する必 要があるだろう。
→ see **science**

Word Link put ≈ thinking : com**put**er, dis**put**e, indis**put**able

dis|pute /dɪspyut/ (**disputes, disputing, disputed**) ◢ N-VAR 可変性名詞 A **dispute** is an argument or disagreement between

people or groups. 論争、紛争 □ *They have won previous pay disputes with the government.* 政府との前回の賃金闘争では彼らは勝利を収めて いる。

Do not confuse **dispute** and **argument**. A **dispute** is a serious argument that can last for a long time. **Disputes** generally occur between organizations, political parties, or countries. □ *...a 10-year-old dispute over crude oil.* An **argument** is a disagreement between people who may or may not know each other. □ *She had an argument with her father about practicing the piano...Travis got in an argument with another motorist.*

◢ V-T 他動詞 If you **dispute** a fact, statement, or theory, you say that it is incorrect or untrue. 反論する □ *He disputed the allegations.* 彼は陳述に対し異議を唱えた。 □ *Nobody disputed that Davey was clever.* デイビーが利口であることは誰もが認めていた。 ◢ V-RECIP 相 互動詞 When people **dispute** something, they fight for control or ownership of it. You can also say that one group of people **dispute** something with another group. ーをめぐって争う □ *Russia and Ukraine have been disputing the ownership of the fleet.* ロシアとウクラ イナはその艦隊の所有権をめぐってずっと争っています。 ◢ PHRASE 句 If two or more people or groups are **in dispute**, they are arguing or disagreeing about something. 論争して □ *The two countries are in dispute over the boundaries of their coastal waters.* 両国は沿岸水域 の境界線をめぐって争っています。 ◢ PHRASE 句 If something is **in dispute**, people are questioning it or arguing about it. 議論され て □ *The schedule for the talks has been agreed, but the location is still in dispute.* 会議の日程については合意に至ったが、場所については検 討中だ。

dis|quali|fy /dɪskwɒlɪfaɪ/ (**disqualifies, disqualifying, disqualified**) V-T 他動詞 When someone **is disqualified**, they are officially stopped from taking part in a particular event, activity, or competition, usually because they have done something wrong. 失格になる；資格を剥奪(はくだつ)される □ *Thomson was disqualified from the 400 meter freestyle.* トムソンは400メートル自 由形で失格になった。 ● **dis|quali|fi|ca|tion** /dɪskwɒlɪfɪkeɪʃᵊn/ (**disqualifications**) N-VAR 可変性名詞 失格；資格剥奪 □ *Livingston faces a four-year disqualification from athletics.* リビングストンは4年 間、陸上競技に出場できないことになる。

dis|qui|et /dɪskwaɪɪt/ N-UNCOUNT 不可算名詞 Disquiet is a feeling of worry or anxiety. 心配、不安 [FORMAL 形式ばった] □ *There is growing public disquiet about the cost of such policing.* そうし た取り締まりにどれほどの費用がかかるのか、人々の間で懸念が広が っている。

dis|re|gard /dɪsrɪgɑrd/ (**disregards, disregarding, disregarded**) V-T 他動詞 If you **disregard** something, you ignore it or do not take account of it. 無視する □ *He disregarded the advice of his executives.* 彼は重役の忠告を無視した。 ● N-UNCOUNT 不可算名詞 Disregard is also a noun. 無視 □ *Whoever planted the bomb showed a total disregard for the safety of the public.* 誰がその爆弾を仕掛けたにせよ、それは民間 人の安全を全く無視したものだ。

dis|re|pute /dɪsrɪpyut/ PHRASE 句 If something is **brought into disrepute** or **falls into disrepute**, it loses its good reputation, because it is connected with activities that people do not approve of. 信頼を失って □ *It is a disgrace that such people should bring our profession into disrepute.* こうした連中のせいで我々の仕事に対する信 頼が失われてしまうのは不名誉なことだ。

Word Link dis ≈ negative, not : **dis**agree, **dis**comfort, **dis**respect

dis|re|spect /dɪsrɪspɛkt/ N-UNCOUNT 不可算名詞 If someone shows **disrespect**, they speak or behave in a way that shows lack of respect for a person, law, or custom. 無礼 □ *...young people with attitudes and complete disrespect for authority.* 権威に対して横柄で全く 礼を欠く若者たち。

Word Link rupt ≈ breaking : dis**rupt**, e**rupt**, inter**rupt**

dis|rupt /dɪsrʌpt/ (**disrupts, disrupting, disrupted**) V-T 他 動詞 If someone or something **disrupts** an event, system, or process, they cause difficulties that prevent it from continuing or operating in a normal way. 混乱させる、中断させる □ *Anti-war protesters disrupted the debate.* 反戦活動家たちが討論を妨害しまし た。

dis|rup|tion /dɪsrʌpʃᵊn/ (**disruptions**) N-VAR 可変性名詞 When there is **disruption** of an event, system, or process, it is prevented from continuing or operating in a normal way. 混乱、中断 □ *The plan was designed to ensure disruption to business was kept to a minimum.* できる限り事業が滞りなく進むように計画が立てられた。

dis|rup|tive /dɪsrʌptɪv/ ADJ 形容詞 To be **disruptive** means to prevent something from continuing or operating in a normal way. 混乱を招く、支障をきたす □ *Alcohol can produce violent, disruptive behavior.* アルコールが原因で暴力や問題行動を起こすこと がある。

d

Word Link sat, satis ≈ enough : dissatisfaction, insatiable, satisfy

dis|sat|is|fac|tion /dɪsˌsætɪsfækʃᵊn/ (dissatisfactions) N-VAR 可変性名詞 If you feel **dissatisfaction with** something, you are not contented or pleased with it. 不満 ❑ *She has already expressed her dissatisfaction with this aspect of the policy.* 政策のこの点に対して彼女はすでに不満を明らかにしている.

dis|sat|is|fied /dɪsˌsætɪsfaɪd/ ADJ 形容詞 If you are **dissatisfied with** something, you are not contented or pleased with it. 一に不満で ❑ *Eighty-two percent of voters are dissatisfied with the way their country is being governed.* 国の統治のあり方については有権者の82%が不満を感じている.

Word Link sect ≈ cutting : dissect, intersect, section

dis|sect /dɪsɛkt, daɪ-/ (dissects, dissecting, dissected) ■ V-T 他動詞 If someone **dissects** the body of a dead person or animal, they carefully cut it up in order to examine it scientifically. 解剖する ❑ *We dissected a frog in biology class.* 生物の授業でカエルを解剖した. ● **dis|sec|tion** /dɪsɛkʃᵊn, daɪ-/ (dissections) N-VAR 可変性名詞 解剖 ❑ *Researchers need a growing supply of corpses for dissection.* 研究者の間で解剖用遺体の需要が高まっている. ❷ V-T 他動詞 If someone **dissects** something such as a theory, a situation, or a piece of writing, they consider and talk about each detail of it. 詳細に検討する ❑ *People want to dissect his work and question his motives.* 人々は彼の作品を詳細に分析することでその真意に迫ろうとしている. ● **dis|sec|tion** N-VAR 可変性名詞 (dissections) 分析 ❑ *...her calm, condescending dissection of my proposals.* 私の提案に対する彼女のこちらを見下すような冷徹な分析.

dis|semi|nate /dɪsɛmɪneɪt/ (disseminates, disseminating, disseminated) V-T 他動詞 To **disseminate** information or knowledge means to distribute it so that it reaches many people or organizations. 広める, 普及させる [FORMAL 形式ばった] ❑ *They disseminated anti-French propaganda.* 彼らは反仏のプロパガンダを流した. ● **dis|semi|na|tion** /dɪsɛmɪneɪʃᵊn/ N-UNCOUNT 不可算名詞 普及 ❑ *He actively promoted the dissemination of scientific ideas about matters such as morality.* 彼が精力を傾けて普及させようとしたのは, 道徳のような問題を科学的に捉えることだった.

dis|sent /dɪsɛnt/ (dissents, dissenting, dissented) ■ N-UNCOUNT 不可算名詞 **Dissent** is strong disagreement or dissatisfaction with a decision or opinion, especially one that is supported by most people or by people in authority. 異議, 反対 ❑ *He is the toughest military ruler yet and has responded harshly to any dissent.* 彼はどれほど厳しい軍事独裁者ともこれまでなく, 反対意見は容赦なく排除してきました. ❷ V-I 自動詞 If you **dissent**, you express disagreement with a decision or opinion, especially one that is supported by most people or by people in authority. 異議を唱える [FORMAL 形式ばった] ❑ *Just one of the 10 members dissented.* 10人のうち1人だけが反対しました.

dis|sent|er /dɪsɛntər/ (dissenters) N-COUNT 可算名詞 **Dissenters** are people who say that they do not agree with something that other people agree with or that is official policy. 反体制派 ❑ *The party does not tolerate dissenters in its ranks.* 党は党内の反対者を容認しない.

dis|ser|ta|tion /dɪsərteɪʃᵊn/ (dissertations) N-COUNT 可算名詞 A **dissertation** is a long formal piece of writing on a particular subject, especially for an advanced university degree. 修士論文; 博士論文 ❑ *He is currently writing a dissertation on the Somali civil war.* 現在彼はソマリア内戦について論文を書いている.

dis|si|dent /dɪsɪdᵊnt/ (dissidents) ■ N-COUNT 可算名詞 **Dissidents** are people who disagree with and criticize their government, especially because it is undemocratic. 反体制派 ❑ *...political dissidents.* 政治的反体制派. ❷ ADJ 形容詞 **Dissident** people disagree with or criticize their government or a powerful organization they belong to. 反体制の [ADJ n] ❑ *...a dissident Russian novelist.* ロシアの反体制作家.

Word Link simil ≈ similar : assimilate, dissimilar, similarity

dis|simi|lar /dɪsɪmɪlər/ ADJ 形容詞 If one thing is **dissimilar to** another, or if two things are **dissimilar**, they are very different from each other. 全く異なる ❑ *His methods were not dissimilar to those used by Freud.* 彼の方法はフロイトが用いた方法と大差ありませんでした. ❑ *It would be difficult to find two men who were more dissimilar.* これほど正反対の2人を探し出すのは難しいだろう.

dis|si|pate /dɪsɪpeɪt/ (dissipates, dissipating, dissipated) ■ V-T/V-I 他動詞/自動詞 When something **dissipates** or when you **dissipate** it, it becomes less or becomes less strong until it disappears or goes away completely. 消し去る [他動詞], 消える [自動詞] ❑ *The tension in the room had dissipated.* 部屋に漂っていた緊張は消え去っていった. [FORMAL 形式ばった] ❷ V-T 他動詞 When someone **dissipates** money, time, or effort, they waste it in a foolish way. 浪費する [FORMAL 形式ばった] ❑ *He needs someone who can keep him from dissipating his time and energy on too many different things.* 彼は時間と精力をつぎ込む対象があまりに多く, それをくい止めてくれる人が必要なのです.

dis|so|ci|ate /dɪsoʊʃieɪt, -sieɪt/ (dissociates, dissociating, dissociated) ■ V-T 他動詞 If you **dissociate yourself from** something or someone, you say or show that you are not connected with them, usually in order to avoid trouble or blame. 関係を絶つ ❑ *It seems harder and harder for the president to dissociate himself from the scandals that surround Mr. Galdos.* 大統領はガルドス氏をめぐるスキャンダルとの関係を否定しているものの, 状況は大統領にとってますます不利になってきているようだ. ❷ V-T 他動詞 If you **dissociate** one thing **from** another, you consider the two things as separate from each other, or you separate them. 区別する [FORMAL 形式ばった] ❑ *Almost the first lesson they learn is how to dissociate emotion from reason.* 彼らが最初に学ぶことは, 感情と理性を区別する方法である.

dis|so|lu|tion /dɪsəluʃᵊn/ ■ N-UNCOUNT 不可算名詞 **Dissolution** is the act of breaking up officially an organization or institution, or of formally ending a parliament. 解散 [FORMAL 形式ばった] [also 'a' N, oft N 'of' n] ❑ *He stayed on until the dissolution of the firm in 1948.* 彼は1948年の解散まで会社にとどまった. ❷ N-UNCOUNT 不可算名詞 **Dissolution** is the act of officially ending a formal agreement, for example, a marriage or a business arrangement. 解消 [FORMAL 形式ばった] ❑ *...the statutory requirement for granting dissolution of a marriage.* 婚姻解消を認める際の法的な要件.

dis|solve /dɪzɒlv/ (dissolves, dissolving, dissolved) ■ V-T/V-I 他動詞/自動詞 If a substance **dissolves** in liquid or if you **dissolve** it, it becomes mixed with the liquid and disappears. 溶かす [他動詞], 溶ける [自動詞] ❑ *Heat gently until the sugar dissolves.* 砂糖が溶けるまで弱火で温めます. ❷ V-T 他動詞 When an organization or institution **is dissolved**, it is officially ended or broken up. 解散させる ❑ *The committee has been dissolved.* 委員会は解散した. ❸ V-T 他動詞 When a parliament **is dissolved**, it is formally ended, so that elections for a new parliament can be held. 解散させる ❑ *The present assembly will be dissolved on April 30th.* 今の議会は4月30日に解散する. ❹ V-T 他動詞 When a marriage or business arrangement **is dissolved**, it is officially ended. 解消する [usu passive] ❑ *The marriage was dissolved in 1976.* 婚姻を解消したのは1976年だった. ❺ V-T/V-I 他動詞/自動詞 If something such as a problem or feeling **dissolves** or **is dissolved**, it becomes weaker and disappears. 消える, なくなる ❑ *His new-found optimism dissolved.* 最近になって彼は気楽に構えるようになっていたが, そうした気分も消えうせてしまった.

Word Link suad, suas ≈ urging : dissuade, persuade, persuasive

dis|suade /dɪsweɪd/ (dissuades, dissuading, dissuaded) V-T 他動詞 If you **dissuade** someone **from** doing or believing something, you persuade them not to do or believe it. 思いとどまらせる [FORMAL 形式ばった] ❑ *Doctors had tried to dissuade patients from smoking.* 医師は患者に禁煙するように説得していました. ❑ *She steadfastly maintained that her grandsons were innocent, and nothing could dissuade her from that belief.* 彼女は孫息子の無実をひたすら主張し, 決してその信念を曲げることはなかった.

dis|tance /dɪstəns/ (distances, distancing, distanced) ■ N-VAR 可変性名詞 The **distance between** two points or places is the amount of space between them. 距離, 道のり ❑ *...the distance between the island and the nearby shore.* 島から近くの岸までの距離. ❷ N-UNCOUNT 不可算名詞 When two things are very far apart, you talk about the **distance** between them. 遠距離 ❑ *The distance wouldn't be a problem.* 距離が離れていても問題にはならないだろう. ❸ N-UNCOUNT 不可算名詞 When you want to emphasize that two people or things do not have a close relationship or are not the same, you can refer to the **distance between** them. 隔たり [EMPHASIS 強調] ❑ *There was a vast distance between psychological clues and concrete proof.* 頭で思いついた手掛かりと具体的な証拠の間には大きな隔たりがあった. ❹ N-UNCOUNT 不可算名詞 **Distance** is coolness or unfriendliness in the way that someone behaves toward you. 冷淡さ, よそよそしさ [FORMAL 形式ばった] ❑ *There were periods of sulking, of pronounced distance, of coldness.* 気分屋らしくよそよそしく不機嫌で冷淡な時期が幾度かあった. ❺ ADJ 形容詞 **Distance** learning or **distance** education involves studying at home and sending your work to a college or university, rather than attending the college or university in person. 遠隔教育, 通信教育 [ADJ n] ❑ *The Internet is often used as a resource and as a tool for distance learning.* インターネットは通信教育の教材や資料としてよく活用されている. ❻ N-SING 単数名詞 If you can see something **in the distance**, you can see it, far away from you. 遠くに ['in/into the' n] ❑ *We suddenly saw her in the distance.* 突然, 遠くに彼女を姿を見つけた. ❼ V-T 他動詞 If you **distance yourself from** a person or thing, or if something **distances** you **from** them, you feel less friendly or positive toward them, or become less involved with them. 距離を置く ❑ *The author distanced himself from some of the comments in his book.* その作家は著書で述べた一部の見解について明

言を避けました. ●**dis|tanced** ADJ 形容詞 [v-link ADJ] 距離を置いて ❑*Clough felt he'd become too distanced from his fans.* クラフはファンとの距離が大きくなりすぎたように感じた. **8** PHRASE 句 If you are **at a distance** from something, or if you see it or remember it **from a distance**, you are a long way away from it in space or time. 離れて, 遠くから ❑*The only way I can cope with my mother is at a distance.* 母とうまくやろうと思えば, 距離を置くしかない. **9** PHRASE 句 If you **keep** your **distance** from someone or something or **keep** them **at a distance**, you do not become involved with them. 距離を置く ❑*Jay had always tended to keep his girlfriends at a distance.* ジェイはこれまで恋人ができても深入りすることはなかった.

ADJ.	**safe** distance, **short** distance **1**
PREP.	**within walking** distance **1**
	distance **between 1 – 3**
	in the distance **6**
	at a distance, **from a** distance **8**

Word Partnership distance は次の語句と使われる:

dis|tant /dɪstənt/ **1** ADJ 形容詞 **Distant** means very far away. 遠い ❑*The mountains rolled away to a distant horizon.* 山々は起伏しながらはるか地平線まで続いていた. **2** ADJ 形容詞 You use **distant** to describe a time or event that is very far away in the future or in the past. 遠い ❑*There is little doubt, however, that things will improve in the not too distant future.* とはいえ, そう遠くない将来に状況が改善することはまず間違いないだろう. **3** ADJ 形容詞 A **distant** relative is one who you are not closely related to. 遠縁の ❑*He's a distant relative of the mayor.* 彼は市長の遠い親戚だ. ●**dis|tant|ly** ADV 副詞 離れて ❑*The O'Shea girls are distantly related to our family.* オシェ家の娘たちはうちの遠縁にあたる. **4** ADJ 形容詞 [v-link ADJ] If you describe someone as **distant**, you mean that you find them cold and unfriendly. よそよそしい ❑*He found her cold, icelike, and distant.* 彼女が氷のように冷淡でよそよそしい女だと彼は知った. **5** ADJ 形容詞 If you describe someone as **distant**, you mean that they are not concentrating on what they are doing because they are thinking about other things. ぼんやりとした ❑*There was a distant look in her eyes from time to time, her thoughts elsewhere.* 時折別のことを考えているのか, 彼女はぼんやりとした目つきになった.

Thesaurus distant また次を参照:

| ADJ. | faraway, remote; (ant.) close, near **1** |
| | aloof, cool, unfriendly **4** |

dis|tant|ly /dɪstəntli/ **1** ADV 副詞 **Distantly** means very far away. 遠くに [LITERARY 文語的] ❑*Distantly, to her right, she could make out the town of Chiffa.* 右手の遠方にかすかにチフアの町が見えた. **2** ADV 副詞 If you are **distantly** aware of something or if you **distantly** remember it, you are aware of it or remember it, but not very strongly. ぼんやりと, かすかに ❑*She became distantly aware that the light had grown strangely brighter and was flickering gently.* 光が異様な度を増しながらゆらゆらと揺らめいているのに, 彼女はぼんやりと気づいた. **3** → see also **distant**

dis|taste /dɪsteɪst/ N-UNCOUNT 不可算名詞 If you feel **distaste** for someone or something, you dislike them and consider them to be unpleasant, disgusting, or immoral. 嫌悪 ❑*He professed a violent distaste for everything related to commerce, production, and money.* 商売, 大量生産, 金儲けに関するものはみな大嫌いだと, 彼ははっきり言った.

dis|taste|ful /dɪsteɪstfʊl/ ADJ 形容詞 If something is **distasteful to** you, you think it is unpleasant, disgusting, or immoral. 不快な ❑*He found it distasteful to be offered a cold buffet and drinks before witnessing the execution.* 彼がけしからんと思ったのは, 死刑執行の立ち会いの前に冷たい軽食と飲み物が出されたことである.

dis|till /dɪstɪl/ (distills, distilling, distilled) **1** V-T 他動詞 If a liquid such as whiskey or water **is distilled**, it is heated until it changes into steam or vapor and then cooled until it becomes liquid again. This is usually done in order to make it pure. 蒸留する ❑*The whiskey had been distilled in 1926 and sat quietly maturing until 1987.* そのウィスキーは1926年に蒸留し, 1987年までじっくりわねかせて熟成させたものだ. ●**dis|til|la|tion** /dɪstɪleɪʃ°n/ N-UNCOUNT 不可算名詞 蒸留 ❑*Any faults in the original cider stood out sharply after distillation.* 元のシードルに問題があると, 蒸留後にはっきりと現れた. **2** V-T 他動詞 If an oil or liquid **is distilled from** a plant, it is produced by a process which extracts the most essential part of the plant. To **distill** a plant means to produce an oil or liquid from it by this process. 抽出される ❑*The oil is distilled from the berries of this small tree.* その油はこの小さな木の果実から抽出したものである. ●**dis|til|la|tion** N-UNCOUNT 不可算名詞 抽出 ❑*The distillation of rose petals to produce rosewater almost certainly originated in Ancient Persia.* バラの花びらを蒸留してローズ水が作られるようになったのは古代ペルシャがおそらく最初である. **3** V-T 他動詞 If a thought or idea **is distilled from** previous thoughts, ideas, or experiences, it comes from them. If **it is distilled into** something, it becomes part of that thing. 〜から引き出す; 〜にまとめ上げる ❑*Reviews*

are distilled from articles previously published in the main column. 論評は過去に掲載したメインコラムの記事から精選したものである. **4** V-T 他動詞 If something **is distilled into** the natural beauty of a balmy night. やがて情熱は浄化されて, かぐわしき夜の自然美にその姿を変えた. ●**dis|til|la|tion** N-SING 単数名詞 要旨, 精髄 ❑*The material below is a distillation of his work.* 以下の内容は彼の作品を要約したものである.

dis|tinct /dɪstɪŋkt/ **1** ADJ 形容詞 If something is **distinct from** something else of the same type, it is different or separate from it. 異なる ❑*Engineering and technology are disciplines distinct from one another and from science.* 工学と科学技術は互いに異なる分野であり, また両者は自然科学とも異なる. ●**dis|tinct|ly** ADV 副詞 [ADV adj] 区別して ❑*...a banking industry with two distinctly different sectors.* 全く異なる2つの部門からなる銀行業. **2** ADJ 形容詞 If something is **distinct**, you can hear, see, or taste it clearly. はっきりとした ❑*...to impart a distinct flavor with a minimum of cooking fat.* ほんのわずか調理油を加えて独特の風味を添えること. ●**dis|tinct|ly** ADV 副詞 [ADV with v] はっきりと ❑*I distinctly heard the loudspeaker calling passengers for the Washington-Miami flight.* ワシントン-マイアミ便の搭乗客に呼びかける場内放送をはっきりと聞いた. **3** ADJ 形容詞 If an idea, thought, or intention is **distinct**, it is clear and definite. 明確な ❑*Now that Tony was no longer present, there was a distinct change in her attitude.* トニーがいなくなると, 明らかに彼女の態度は変化した. ●**dis|tinct|ly** ADV 副詞 [ADV with v] 明確に ❑*I distinctly remember wishing I had not gotten involved.* 巻き込まれなかったらよかったのにと思ったことをはっきりと記憶している. **4** ADJ 形容詞 You can use **distinct** to emphasize that something is great enough in amount or degree to be noticeable or important. 際立った [EMPHASIS 強調] [ADJ n] ❑*Being 6ft 3in tall has some distinct disadvantages!* 身長が6フィート3インチであることは明らかに不利である. ●**dis|tinct|ly** ADV 副詞 [ADV adj/-ed] 際立って ❑*His government is looking distinctly shaky.* 彼の政権は目立って弱体化してきています. **5** PHRASE 句 If you say that you are talking about one thing **as distinct from** another, you are indicating exactly which thing you mean. 〜とは違って ❑*There's a lot of evidence that oily fish, as distinct from fatty meat, has a beneficial effect.* 脂身の多い肉とは違い, 脂ののった魚に健康効果があることは確かである.

dis|tinc|tion /dɪstɪŋkʃ°n/ (distinctions) **1** N-COUNT 可算名詞 A **distinction between** similar things is a difference. 違い ❑*There are obvious distinctions between the two wine-making areas.* 2つのワイン醸造地には明らかな差がある. ❑*The distinction between craft and fine art is more controversial.* 工芸と芸術の違いになると, さらに意見が食い違ってくる. ●PHRASE 句 If you **draw a distinction** or **make a distinction**, you say that two things are different. 区別する **2** N-COUNT 可算名詞 A **distinction** is a special award or honor that is given to someone because of their very high level of achievement. 栄誉のしるし ❑*The award was established in 1902 as a special distinction for eminent men and women.* その賞は優れた人物を表彰する目的で1902年に創設された. **3** N-UNCOUNT 不可算名詞 **Distinction** is the quality of being very good or better than other things of the same type. 卓越 [FORMAL 形式ばった] ❑*Lewis emerges as a composer of distinction and sensitivity.* ルイスは感性の豊かな卓越した作曲家として知られている. **4** N-SING 単数名詞 If you say that someone or something has **the distinction of** being something, you are drawing attention to the fact that they have the special quality of being that thing. **Distinction** is normally used to refer to good qualities, but can sometimes also be used to refer to bad qualities. 傑出 ❑*He has the distinction of being regarded as the Federal Republic's greatest living writer.* 彼はその国で生存している最大の作家としてその名を馳せている.

dis|tinc|tive /dɪstɪŋktɪv/ ADJ 形容詞 Something that is **distinctive** has a special quality or feature which makes it easily recognizable and different from other things of the same type. 独特な, 特有の ❑*...the distinctive odor of chlorine.* 塩素特有の臭い. ●**dis|tinc|tive|ly** ADV 副詞 [ADV adj/-ed] 独特に ❑*...the distinctively fragrant taste of elderflowers.* ニワトコの花の独特な風味.

dis|tin|guish /dɪstɪŋgwɪʃ/ (distinguishes, distinguishing, distinguished) **1** V-T/V-I 他動詞/自動詞 If you can **distinguish** one thing **from** another or **distinguish between** two things, you can see or understand how they are different. 見分ける, 区別する ❑*Could he distinguish right from wrong?* 彼は善悪の判断ができたのか. ❑*Research suggests that babies learn to see by distinguishing between areas of light and dark.* 研究によれば, 乳児は明暗を区別することでものを見ることができるようになるという. **2** V-T 他動詞 A feature or quality that **distinguishes** one thing **from** another causes the two things to be regarded as different, because only the first thing has the feature or quality. ❑*There is something about music that distinguishes it from all other art forms.* 音楽には他の芸術には見られない特徴がある. **3** V-T 他動詞 If you can **distinguish** something, you can see, hear, or taste it although it is very difficult to detect. 違いが分かる [FORMAL 形式ばった] ❑*There were cries, calls. He could distinguish voices.* 泣き叫ぶ声の中に何か話している声を彼は聞き取った. **4** V-T 他動詞 If you **distinguish yourself**, you do something that makes you famous or important.

名をあげる □*Over the next few years he distinguished himself as a leading constitutional scholar.* それから数年のうちに、彼は一流の憲法学者としてその名をほしいままにした.

dis|tin|guished /dɪstɪŋgwɪʃt/ ■ ADJ 形容詞 If you describe a person or their work as **distinguished**, you mean that they have been very successful in their career and have a good reputation. 優れた, 著名な □*...a distinguished academic family.* 著名な学者一家. ② ADJ 形容詞 If you describe someone as **distinguished**, you mean that they look very noble and respectable. 気品のある □*His suit was immaculately cut and he looked very distinguished.* 仕立てのよいぴったりのスーツに身をつつんだ彼は気品にあふれていた.

dis|tort /dɪstɔːt/ (distorts, distorting, distorted) ■ V-T 他動詞 If you **distort** a statement, fact, or idea, you report or represent it in an untrue way. ゆがめる □*The media distorts reality; it categorizes people as all good or all bad.* メディアによって現実はゆがめられる. 例えば, 人は善人か悪人かのどちらかに分けられてしまう. ●**dis|tort|ed** ADJ 形容詞 ゆがんだ □*These figures give a distorted view of the significance for the local economy.* これらの数値を見ると地域経済の重要性について誤解を招いてしまう. ② V-T/V-I 他動詞/自動詞 If something you can see or hear **is distorted** or **distorts**, its appearance or sound is changed so that it seems unclear. ひずむ □*A painter may exaggerate or distort shapes and forms.* 画家は姿や形を誇張したりデフォルメしたりすることがある. ●**dis|tort|ed** ADJ 形容詞 ひずんだ □*Sound was becoming more and more distorted through the use of hearing aids.* 補聴器を使うと, 音のひずみがますますひどくなりました.

dis|tor|tion /dɪstɔːʃ(ə)n/ (distortions) ■ N-VAR 可変性名詞 **Distortion** is the changing of something into something that is not true or not acceptable. 歪(わい)曲 [DISAPPROVAL 不賛成] □*I think it would be a gross distortion of reality to say that they were motivated by self-interest.* 彼らが私利私欲でやったというのは, とんでもない事実の歪曲だと思います. ② N-VAR 可変性名詞 **Distortion** is the changing of the appearance or sound of something in a way that makes it seem strange or unclear. ひずみ □*He demonstrated how audio signals could be transmitted along cables without distortion.* 音声信号をケーブルに伝送するときのひずみを防ぐ方法を彼は実演してみせた.

dis|tract /dɪstrækt/ (distracts, distracting, distracted) V-T 他動詞 If something **distracts** you or your attention **from** something, it takes your attention away from it. 気を散らす, 注意をそらす □*Tom admits that playing video games sometimes distracts him from his homework.* テレビゲームのせいでときどき宿題が手につかなくなることをトムは認めている. □*Don't let yourself be distracted by fashionable theories.* 流行の学説に目移りしてはいけない.

dis|tract|ed /dɪstræktɪd/ ADJ 形容詞 If you are **distracted**, you are not concentrating on something because you are worried or are thinking about something else. 気が散った □*She had seemed curiously distracted.* 彼女は妙に落ち着かない様子だった. ●**dis|tract|ed|ly** ADV 副詞 [ADV with v] 気が散って □*He looked up distractedly. "Be with you in a second."* 彼はうわのそらで顔を上げ, 「いますぐ行くよ」と言った.

dis|tract|ing /dɪstræktɪŋ/ ADJ 形容詞 If you say that something is **distracting**, you mean that it makes it difficult for you to concentrate properly on what you are doing. 気を散らせる □*I find it slightly distracting to have someone watching me while I work.* 仕事をしているところを誰かに見られるとちょっと気になります.

dis|trac|tion /dɪstrækʃ(ə)n/ (distractions) N-VAR 可変性名詞 A **distraction** is something that turns your attention away from something you want to concentrate on. 気を散らすもの □*Total concentration is required with no distractions.* 気を散らさずに完全に集中することが必要だ.

dis|traught /dɪstrɔːt/ ADJ 形容詞 If someone is **distraught**, they are so upset and worried that they cannot think clearly. 取り乱した, 気が動転した □*Mr. Barker's distraught parents were last night being comforted by relatives.* 昨夜はバーカー氏の両親はひどく動揺し, 親類から慰めを受けていた.

dis|tress /dɪstres/ (distresses, distressing, distressed) ■ N-UNCOUNT 不可算名詞 **Distress** is a state of extreme sorrow, suffering, or pain. 悲嘆, 苦悩 □*Jealousy causes distress and painful emotions.* 嫉妬すると, つらくて悲しい思いをする. ② N-UNCOUNT 不可算名詞 **Distress** is the state of being in extreme danger and needing urgent help. 窮地 □*He expressed concern that the ship might be in distress.* 船は遭難している可能性があると彼は懸念を示した. ③ V-T 他動詞 If someone or something **distresses** you, they cause you to be upset or worried. 悩ませる □*The idea of Toni being in danger distresses him enormously.* トニーが危険な状態にあることを思うと, 彼はひどく心が痛んだ.

dis|tressed /dɪstrest/ ADJ 形容詞 If someone is **distressed**, they are upset or worried. 悲嘆にくれて, 苦悩して □*I feel very alone and distressed about my problem.* 私は強い孤独感に感じながら, そのことに深く悩んでいた.

dis|tress|ing /dɪstresɪŋ/ ADJ 形容詞 If something is

distressing, it upsets you or worries you. つらい □*It is very distressing to see your baby attached to tubes and monitors.* チューブやモニターにつながれているわが子の姿を見るのはとてもつらいものである. ●**dis|tress|ing|ly** ADV 副詞 痛ましいほど □*A distressingly large number of firms have been breaking the rules.* 多くの企業がルール違反をしてきたことは全く嘆かわしい.

Word Link　　tribute ≈ giving : at**tribute**, con**tribute**, dis**tribute**

dis|trib|ute /dɪstrɪbjuːt/ (distributes, distributing, distributed) ■ V-T 他動詞 If you **distribute** things, you hand them or deliver them to a number of people. 配布する; 配達する □*Students shouted slogans and distributed leaflets.* 学生たちはスローガンを叫びながらチラシを配りました. ② V-T 他動詞 When a company **distributes** goods, it supplies them to the stores or businesses that sell them. 流通させる [BUSINESS 実業] □*We didn't understand how difficult it was to distribute a national paper.* どれほど全国紙を流通させるのが難しいことか, 我々は理解していませんでした. ③ V-T 他動詞 To **distribute** a substance **over** something means to scatter it over it. まき散らす [FORMAL 形式ばった] □*Distribute the topping evenly over the fruit.* フルーツの上に均等にトッピングをのせます.

dis|tri|bu|tion /dɪstrɪbjuːʃ(ə)n/ (distributions) ■ N-UNCOUNT 不可算名詞 The **distribution** of things involves giving or delivering them to a number of people or places. 配布; 配達 □*...the council which controls the distribution of foreign aid.* 海外からの援助物資の配給を管理する評議会. ② N-VAR 可変性名詞 The **distribution** of something is how much of it there is in each place or at each time, or how much of it each person has. 配分 □*Mr. Roh's economic planners sought to achieve a more equitable distribution of wealth.* ロー氏の経済政策立案者はより公正な富の分配を実現しようとしていた.

dis|tribu|tor /dɪstrɪbjətər/ (distributors) N-COUNT 可算名詞 A **distributor** is a company that supplies goods to stores or other businesses. 卸売業者, 流通業者 [BUSINESS 実業] □*...Spain's largest distributor of petroleum products.* スペイン最大の石油製品卸売会社.

dis|tribu|tor|ship /dɪstrɪbjətərʃɪp/ (distributorships) N-COUNT 可算名詞 A **distributorship** is a company that supplies goods to stores or other businesses, or the right to supply goods to stores and businesses. 卸売業者, 流通業者; 販売権 [BUSINESS 実業] □*...the general manager of an automobile distributorship.* 自動車販売代理店のゼネラルマネジャー.

dis|trict /dɪstrɪkt/ (districts) N-COUNT 可算名詞 A **district** is a particular area of a town or country. 地域, 地方 □*I drove around the business district.* オフィス街を車で回った.

dis|trust /dɪstrʌst/ (distrusts, distrusting, distrusted) ■ V-T 他動詞 If you **distrust** someone or something, you think they are not honest, reliable, or safe. 信用しない □*I don't have any particular reason to distrust them.* 彼らを信用しない特別な理由があるわけではない. ② N-UNCOUNT 不可算名詞 **Distrust** is the feeling of doubt that you have toward someone or something you distrust. 不信 [also 'a' N, oft N 'of' n] □*What he saw there left him with a profound distrust of all political authority.* そこで目にしたものが, 彼があらゆる政治権力に対して深い不信感を抱く原因となりました.

dis|turb /dɪstɜːb/ (disturbs, disturbing, disturbed) ■ V-T 他動詞 If you **disturb** someone, you interrupt what they are doing and upset them. 邪魔する □*Did you sleep well? I didn't want to disturb you. You looked so peaceful.* よく眠れた？ お休みのところを邪魔したくなかったの. それは気持ちよさそうに寝てたわよ. ② V-T 他動詞 If something **disturbs** you, it makes you feel upset or worried. 動揺させる, 不安にする □*I dream about him, dreams so vivid that they disturb me for days.* 彼の夢を見る. その鮮明な夢のせいで何日も不安に悩まされる. ③ V-T 他動詞 If something **disturbs** something, its position or shape is changed. 場所を移す □*He'd placed his notes in the brown envelope. They hadn't been disturbed.* 彼は茶封筒にメモを入れていた. メモはずっとそこに入れられたままだった. ④ V-T 他動詞 If something **disturbs** a situation or atmosphere, it spoils it or causes trouble. かき乱す □*What could possibly disturb such tranquility?* こうした平安を乱しかねないものとは一体何なのか.

Word Partnership　　disturb は次の語句と使われる:

V.	do not disturb ■
	be sorry to disturb ■ ② ④
	be careful not to disturb ■ ③
N.	disturb the neighbors ■ ②
	disturb the peace ④

dis|turb|ance /dɪstɜːb(ə)ns/ (disturbances) ■ N-COUNT 可算名詞 A **disturbance** is an incident in which people behave violently in public. 騒動 □*During the disturbance which followed, three Englishmen were hurt.* その後の騒ぎでイングランド人の男性3人が負傷した. ② N-UNCOUNT 不可算名詞 **Disturbance** means upsetting or disorganizing something which was previously in a calm and well-ordered state. 混乱, 迷惑 □*Successful breeding requires quiet, peaceful conditions with as little disturbance as possible.* 繁殖を成功させるには, 静かで落ち着いた環境をできる限り乱さな

いようにすることが必要である. 🔳 N-VAR 可変性名詞 You can use **disturbance** to refer to a medical or psychological problem, when someone's body or mind is not working in the normal way. 精神障害 ❑ *Poor educational performance is related to emotional disturbance.* 学業の不振は情緒障害と関係がある.

dis|turbed /dɪstɜ́rbd/ 🔝 ADJ 形容詞 A **disturbed** person is very upset emotionally, and often needs special care or treatment. 情緒が不安定な, 情緒障害の ❑ *...working with severely emotionally disturbed children.* 重度の情緒障害のある子供たちとかかわった. 🔼 ADJ 形容詞 You can say that someone is **disturbed** when they are very worried or anxious. 気が動転して, 不安に駆られた ❑ *Doctors were disturbed that less than 30 percent of the patients were women.* 医師たちが強く不安を感じたのは, 女性患者が30パーセントに満たないということでした. 🔳 ADJ 形容詞 If you describe a situation or period of time as **disturbed**, you mean that it is unhappy and full of problems. 問題を抱えた ❑ *...women from disturbed backgrounds.* 過去に問題を抱えた女性たち.

dis|turb|ing /dɪstɜ́rbɪŋ/ ADJ 形容詞 Something that is **disturbing** makes you feel worried or upset. 不安にさせる ❑ *There was something about him she found disturbing.* 彼にはどこか彼女を不安にさせるところがあった. ●**dis|turb|ing|ly** ADV 副詞 不安になるほど ❑ *The government has itself recognized the disturbingly high frequency of racial attacks.* 人種差別による襲撃が多発し, 憂慮すべき状況にあることは政府も認めている.

dis|used /dɪsjúːzd/ ADJ 形容詞 A **disused** place or building is empty and is no longer used. もはや使われていない ❑ *...a disused air field near the village of Ive.* アイブ村の近くにある閉鎖された飛行場.

ditch /dɪtʃ/ (ditches, ditching, ditched) 🔝 N-COUNT 可算名詞 A **ditch** is a long narrow channel cut into the ground at the side of a road or field. 溝 ❑ *Both vehicles ended up in a ditch.* 結局, 車は2台とも側溝に脱輪した. 🔼 V-T 他動詞 If you **ditch** something that you have or are responsible for, you abandon it or get rid of it, because you no longer want it. 捨てる [INFORMAL くだけた] ❑ *I decided to ditch the sofa bed.* 私はソファベッドを捨てることにした. 🔳 V-T 他動詞 If someone **ditches** someone, they end a relationship with that person. 関係を絶つ [INFORMAL くだけた] ❑ *I can't bring myself to ditch him and start again.* 彼を見捨ててやり直す気になれない. 🔳 V-T/V-I 他動詞/自動詞 If a pilot **ditches** an aircraft or if it **ditches**, the pilot makes an emergency landing. 緊急着陸させる [他動詞], 緊急着陸する [自動詞] ❑ *One American pilot was forced to ditch his jet in the Gulf.* 米軍のジェット戦闘機一機がペルシャ湾に緊急着水しました. 🔳 V-T 他動詞 If someone **ditches** school or work, they decide not to go to school or work, although they are supposed to go there. さぼる [AM 米国英語, INFORMAL くだけた] ❑ *What do you say we ditch school and go to the mall?* 学校をさぼってショッピングモールに行こうよ. ●see also **last-ditch**

dith|er /dɪ́ðər/ (dithers, dithering, dithered) V-I 自動詞 When someone **dithers**, they hesitate because they are unable to make a quick decision about something. 拘泥(ちゅうでい)する ❑ *We've been living together for five years, and we're still dithering over whether to marry.* 5年も一緒に暮らしているけど, いまだに結婚するかどうか迷っている.

dit|to /dɪ́toʊ/ In informal English, you can use **ditto** to represent a word or phrase that you have just used in order to avoid repeating it. In written lists, **ditto** can be represented by ditto marks - the symbol "- underneath the word that you want to repeat. 前に同じ, 同上 ❑ *Lister's dead. Ditto three Miami drug dealers and a lady.* リスターは死んだ. マイアミの麻薬密売人3人と女性1人も死んだ.

dive /daɪv/ (dives, diving, dived, dove, dived) 🔝 V-I 自動詞 If you **dive into** some water, you jump in head first with your arms held straight above your head. 飛び込む ❑ *He tried to escape by diving into a river.* 彼は川に飛び込んで逃げようとした. ❑ *She was standing by a pool, about to dive in.* 彼女はプールのそばに立ち, これから飛び込もうとしていた. ●N-COUNT 可算名詞 **Dive** is also a noun. 飛び込み ❑ *Pat had earlier made a dive of 80 feet from the Chasm Bridge.* パットは以前に渓谷橋からの80フィートのダイビングに挑戦していた. 🔼 V-I 自動詞 If you **dive**, you go under the surface of the sea or a lake, using special breathing equipment. ダイビングする ❑ *Bezanik is diving to collect marine organisms.* ベザニックは海に潜って海洋物を採集している. ●N-COUNT 可算名詞 **Dive** is also a noun. ダイビング ❑ *This sighting occurred during my dive to a sunken wreck off Sardinia.* 目撃したのはサルジニア島沖の沈没船に潜っているときだった. 🔳 V-I 自動詞 When birds and animals **dive**, they go quickly downward, head first, through water. 急降下する ❑ *...a pelican which had just dived for a fish.* ちょうど魚を捕まえるために急降下したペリカン. 🔳 V-I 自動詞 If you **dive** in a particular direction or into a particular place, you jump or move there quickly. 突進する, 駆け込む ❑ *They dived into a taxi.* 彼らはタクシーに飛び乗った. ●N-COUNT 可算名詞 **Dive** is also a noun. 突進 ❑ *He made a sudden dive for Uncle Jim's legs to try to trip him up.* 突然彼はジムおじさんの足に飛びついてつまずかせようとした. 🔳 V-I 自動

詞 If shares, profits, or figures **dive**, their value falls suddenly and by a large amount. 急落する [JOURNALISM ジャーナリズム] ❑ *They feared the stock could dive after its first day of trading.* 取引初日以降に株価が急落するのではないかと彼らは心配した. ❑ *Profits have dived from $7.7m to $7.1m.* 収益は770万ドルから710万ドルに激減した. ●N-COUNT 可算名詞 **Dive** is also a noun. 急落 ❑ *Stock prices took a dive.* 株価が暴落しました. 🔳 N-COUNT 可算名詞 If you describe a bar or club as a **dive**, you mean it is dirty and dark, and not very respectable. いかがわしい店 [INFORMAL くだけた, DISAPPROVAL 不賛成] ❑ *We've played in all the little clubs and dives around Philadelphia.* フィラデルフィア周辺の小さなクラブや怪しげなバーはすべて回った.

div|er /daɪvər/ (divers) N-COUNT 可算名詞 A **diver** is a person who swims under water using special breathing equipment. ダイバー, 潜水士 ❑ *Police divers have recovered the body of a sixteen year old boy.* 警察のダイバーが16歳の少年の遺体を収容しました.
→ see **scuba diving**

| **Word Link** | di ≈ two : di**lemma**, di**verge**, di**vision** |

| **Word Link** | verg, vert ≈ turning : con**verge**, di**verge**, sub**vert** |

di|verge /daɪvɜ́rdʒ/ (diverges, diverging, diverged) 🔝 V-RECIP 相互動詞 If one thing **diverges from** another similar thing, the first thing becomes different from the second or develops differently from it. You can also say that two things **diverge**. 分化する ❑ *His interests increasingly diverged from those of his colleagues.* 彼の関心事は同僚たち関心事からどんどんかけ離れていった. 🔼 V-RECIP 相互動詞 If one opinion or idea **diverges from** another, they contradict each other or are different. You can also say that two opinions or ideas **diverge**. 異なる, 分かれる [no cont] ❑ *The view of the Estonian government does not diverge that far from Lipmaa's thinking.* エストニア政府の考えはリプマー氏の考えとさほど違いません.

di|ver|gence /daɪvɜ́rdʒəns/ (divergences) N-VAR 可変性名詞 A **divergence** is a difference between two or more things, attitudes, or opinions. 相違 [FORMAL 形式ばった] ❑ *There's a substantial divergence of opinion within the party.* 党内の意見の隔たりはかなり大きい.

di|ver|gent /daɪvɜ́rdʒənt/ ADJ 形容詞 **Divergent** things are different from each other. 異なる [FORMAL 形式ばった] ❑ *Two people who have divergent views on this question are George Watt and Bob Marr.* この問題に対する見解が異なるのはジョージ・ワットとボブ・マールの2人です.

di|verse /daɪvɜ́rs/ 🔝 ADJ 形容詞 If a group of things is **diverse**, it is made up of a wide variety of things. 多様な ❑ *The building houses a wide and diverse variety of antiques.* その建物は多種多様な骨董(こっとう)品が収蔵されている. 🔼 ADJ 形容詞 **Diverse** people or things are very different from each other. 全く異なった ❑ *Albert Jones' new style will inevitably put him in touch with a much more diverse and perhaps younger audience.* 間違いなくアルバート・ジョーンズの新しいスタイルはこれまで以上に広い層のファンに受け入れられるだろう. ひょっとしたら若いファンを獲得するかも知れない.

| **Word Link** | ify ≈ making : clar**ify**, divers**ify**, intens**ify** |

di|ver|si|fy /daɪvɜ́rsɪfaɪ/ (diversifies, diversifying, diversified) V-T/V-I 他動詞/自動詞 When an organization or person **diversifies** into other things, or **diversifies** their product line, they increase the variety of things that they do or make. 多様化する ❑ *The company's troubles started only when it diversified into new products.* 会社が問題を抱えるようになったのは新製品の開発に乗り出してからだった. ❑ *As demand has increased, so manufacturers have been encouraged to diversify and improve quality.* 需要が高まるにつれ, メーカーはさらに商品の多様化と品質の向上にしのぎを削っている. ●**di|ver|si|fi|ca|tion** /daɪvɜ́rsɪfɪkeɪʃən/ (diversifications) N-VAR 可変性名詞 多様化; 多角化 ❑ *The seminar was to discuss diversification of agriculture.* セミナーでは農業の多角化について討議されました.

di|ver|sion /dɪvɜ́rʒən/ (diversions) 🔝 N-COUNT 可算名詞 A **diversion** is an action or event that attracts your attention away from what you are doing or concentrating on. 注意をそらすもの ❑ *...armed robbers who escaped after throwing smoke bombs to create a diversion.* 発煙筒を投げつけたそのすきを狙って逃走した武装強盗団. 🔼 N-COUNT 可算名詞 A **diversion** is a special route arranged for traffic to follow when the normal route cannot be used. 迂回(うかい)路 [BRIT 英国英語; AM 米国英語 **detour** 米国英語 detour] 🔳 N-UNCOUNT 不可算名詞 The **diversion** of something involves changing its course or destination. 流用, 転用 ❑ *...the illegal diversion of profits from secret arms sales.* 武器の密売によって得た利益の違法な転用.

di|ver|sion|ary /dɪvɜ́rʒəneri/ ADJ 形容詞 A **diversionary** activity is one intended to attract people's attention away from something which you do not want them to think about, know about, or deal with. 注意をそらせる ❑ *It's thought the fires were started by the prisoners as a diversionary tactic.* その火災は受刑者が注意をそらす目的で起こしたものと見られます.

di|ver|sity /dɪvɜ́rsɪti/ (diversities) 🔝 N-VAR 可変性名詞 The

diversity of something is the fact that it contains many very different elements. 多様性 □ …*the cultural diversity of Latin America.* ラテンアメリカ文化の多様性。 **2** N-SING 単数名詞 A **diversity** of things is a range of things which are very different from each other. 多種多様な □ *Forslan's object is to gather as great a diversity of genetic material as possible.* フォースランの目的はできる限り多種多様な遺伝物質を収集することです。

→ see **zoo**

divert /dɪvɜrt, daɪ-/ (**diverts, diverting, diverted**) **1** V-T/V-I 他動詞/自動詞 To **divert** vehicles or travelers means to make them follow a different route or go to a different destination than they originally intended. You can also say that someone or something **diverts from** a particular route or **to** a particular place. 進路を変更する □ *We diverted a plane to rescue 100 passengers.* 乗客100人を救うために飛行機の進路を変更した。 □ *Abington Memorial Hospital has been diverting trauma patients to other hospitals because it does not have enough surgeons.* アビントン記念病院では外科医が不足しているため、外傷患者は他の病院に回している。 **2** V-T 他動詞 To **divert** money or resources means to cause them to be used for a different purpose. 転用する，流用する □ *A wave of deadly bombings has forced the United States to divert funds from reconstruction to security.* 急増する爆破テロの影響で，アメリカは復興資金を治安に回さざるを得なくなっている。 **3** V-T 他動詞 To **divert** a phone call means to send it to a different number or place from the one that was dialed by the person making the call. 転送する □ *He instructed the switchboard staff to divert all Laura's calls to him.* 彼は交換士に頼んでローラにかかってくる電話はすべて自分に転送させた。 **4** V-T 他動詞 If you say that someone **diverts** your attention from something important or serious, you disapprove of them behaving or talking in a way that stops you thinking about it. 注意をそらす [DISAPPROVAL 不賛成] □ *They want to divert the attention of the people from the real issues.* 彼らのねらいは人々の関心を真の問題からそらしてしまうことです。

divide /dɪvaɪd/ (**divides, dividing, divided**) **1** V-T/V-I 他動詞/自動詞 When people or things **are divided** or **divide into** smaller groups or parts, they become separated into smaller parts. 〜に分かれる □ *The physical benefits of exercise can be divided into three factors.* 運動が身体に及ぼす効果は3つに分けられる。 □ *Divide the pastry in half and roll out each piece.* 生地を2つに分け，それぞれをめん棒で伸ばします。 **2** V-T 他動詞 If you **divide** something **among** people or things, you separate it into several parts or quantities which you distribute to the people or things. 〜の間で分ける □ *Divide the sauce among 4 bowls.* ソースをボウル4つに分けます。 **3** V-T 他動詞 If you **divide** a larger number **by** a smaller number or **divide** a smaller number **into** a larger number, you calculate how many times the smaller number can fit exactly into the larger number. 割る □ *Measure the floor area of the greenhouse and divide it by six.* 温室の床面積を求め，それを6で割ります。 **4** V-T 他動詞 If a border or line **divides** two areas or **divides** an area into two, it keeps the two areas separate from each other. 仕切る □ …*remote border areas dividing Tamil and Muslim settlements.* タミル族とイスラム教徒の集落を隔てる辺境地域。 **5** V-T/V-I 他動詞/自動詞 If people **divide** over something or if something **divides** them, it causes strong disagreement between them. 対立させる [他動詞]，対立する [自動詞] □ …*the major issues that divided the country.* 国を二分した重大な問題。 **6** N-COUNT 可算名詞 A **divide** is a significant distinction between two groups, often one that causes conflict. 対立点 □ …*a deliberate attempt to create a Hindu-Muslim divide in India.* インド国内のヒンドゥー教徒とイスラム教徒を敵対させようとする企て。

▸ **divide up** **1** PHRASAL VERB 句動詞 If you **divide** something **up**, you separate it into smaller or more useful groups. 分ける □ *The idea is to divide up the country into four sectors.* 計画では国を4つの地域に分割することが考えられている。 **2** PHRASAL VERB 句動詞 If you **divide** something **up**, you share it out among a number of people or groups in approximately equal parts. 分配する □ *The aim was to divide up the business, give everyone an equal stake in its future.* その目的は事業を分割して，全ての人たちに公平に恩恵が行き渡るようにすることであった。

Thesaurus　　　*divide* また次を参照:

V.　　categorize, group, segregate, separate, split **1** part, separate, split; (*ant.*) unite **5**

Word Partnership　　*divide* は次の語句と使われる:

PREP.　divide **into** **1**
　　　　divide **among** **2**
　　　　divide **between**, divide **by** **3**
N.　　 divide **in half**, divide *your* **time** **3**

divided highway (**divided highways**) N-COUNT 可算名詞 A **divided highway** is a road which has two lanes of traffic traveling in each direction with a strip of grass or concrete down the middle to separate the traffic. 中央分離帯のある上下2車線の幹線道路。 [AM 米国英語]

dividend /dɪvɪdɛnd/ (**dividends**) **1** N-COUNT 可算名詞 A **dividend** is the part of a company's profits which is paid to people who own shares in the company. 配当 [BUSINESS 実業] □ *The first quarter dividend has been increased by nearly 4 percent.* 第1四半期の配当は4%近く増加している。 **2** PHRASE 句 If something **pays dividends**, it brings advantages at a later date. 実を結ぶ □ *Steps taken now to maximize your health will pay dividends later on.* 今から何でも健康によいことをしておけば，あとでやってよかったと思うときがくる。

→ see **company**

divine /dɪvaɪn/ **1** ADJ 形容詞 You use **divine** to describe something that is provided by or relates to a god or goddess. 神による □ *He suggested that the civil war had been a divine punishment.* 内戦は天罰だったというようなことを彼は言いました。 ● **divinely** ADV 副詞 神のように，神の力で □ *The law was divinely ordained.* 法は神が与えたもうた。 **2** ADJ 形容詞 People use **divine** to express their pleasure or enjoyment of something. すてきな □ *Her carrot cake is divine.* 彼女のキャロットケーキは絶品だわ。

→ see **religion**

diving /daɪvɪŋ/ **1** N-UNCOUNT 不可算名詞 **Diving** is the activity of working or looking around underwater, using special breathing equipment. ダイビング □ …*equipment and accessories for diving.* ダイビング器材と備品。 **2** N-UNCOUNT 不可算名詞 **Diving** is the sport or activity in which you jump into water head first with your arms held straight above your head, usually from a diving board. 飛び込み □ *Weight is crucial in diving because the aim is to cause the smallest splash possible.* 飛び込みでは水しぶきを上げないように着水するため，体重移動が重要な鍵となる。

Word Link　　*di ≈ two : dilemma, diverge, division*

division /dɪvɪʒ³n/ (**divisions**) **1** N-UNCOUNT 不可算名詞 The **division of** a large unit **into** two or more distinct parts is the act of separating it into these parts. 分割 □ …*the unification of Germany, after its division into two states at the end of World War Two.* 第2次世界大戦後に東西に分割された両ドイツの統一。 **2** N-UNCOUNT 不可算名詞 The **division of** something among people or things is its separation into parts which are distributed among the people or things. 分配 □ *The current division of labor between workers and management will alter.* 労働を労使関係として捉える今のあり方は変わっていくだろう。 **3** N-UNCOUNT 不可算名詞 **Division** is the arithmetical process of dividing one number into another number. 割り算 □ *I taught my daughter how to do division at the age of six.* 娘に割り算のしかたを教えたのは6歳のときだった。 **4** N-VAR 可変性名詞 A **division** is a significant distinction or argument between two groups, which causes the two groups to be considered as very different and separate. 格差，対立 □ *The division between the prosperous west and the impoverished east remains.* 豊かな西と貧しい東の格差は今も続いています。 **5** N-COUNT 可算名詞 In a large organization, a **division** is a group of departments whose work is done in the same place or is connected with similar tasks. 課，部門 □ …*the bank's Latin American division.* 銀行のラテンアメリカ部門。 **6** N-COUNT 可算名詞 A **division** is a group of military units which fight as a single unit. 師団 □ *Several armoured divisions are being moved from Germany.* 機甲師団数個がドイツからの撤収を進めている。 **7** N-COUNT 可算名詞 In some sports, such as soccer, baseball, and basketball, a **division** is one of the groups of teams which make up a league. The teams in each division are of the same level, and they all play against each other during the season. リーグの部 □ *Chico State reached the NCAA Division II national finals last season.* カリフォルニア州立大学チコ校は昨シーズン，NCAA 2部リーグの全国決勝まで勝ち進んだ。

→ see **mathematics**

Word Partnership　　*division* は次の語句と使われる:

N.　　division **of labor** **2**
　　　multiplication and division **3**
　　　division **head** **5**
　　　infantry division **6**
ADJ.　armored division **6**

divisive /dɪvaɪsɪv/ ADJ 形容詞 Something that is **divisive** causes unfriendliness and argument between people. 対立を招く □ *Abortion has always been a divisive issue.* 妊娠中絶についてはこれまでずっと意見が対立してきました。

divorce /dɪvɔrs/ (**divorces, divorcing, divorced**) **1** N-VAR 可変性名詞 A **divorce** is the formal ending of a marriage by law. 離婚 □ *Numerous marriages now end in divorce.* 今では結婚したものの離婚に終わるケースが数多い。 **2** V-RECIP 相互動詞 If a man and woman **divorce** or if one of them **divorces** the other, their marriage is legally ended. 離婚する □ *He and Lillian had got divorced.* 彼とリリアンは離婚していた。 □ *I am absolutely furious that he divorced me to marry her.* 彼が彼女と結婚するために私と離婚したなんて絶対に許せな

い． **3** N-SING 単数名詞 A **divorce of** one thing **from** another, or a divorce **between** two things is a separation between them which is permanent or is likely to be permanent. 分離 □ …*this divorce of Christian culture from the roots of faith.* このようにキリスト教文化が根底にある信仰から乖離（かいり）してしまったこと． **4** V-T 他動詞 If you say that one thing cannot be **divorced from** another, you mean that the two things cannot be considered as different and separate things. 切り離すことはできない □ *Good management in the police cannot be divorced from accountability.* 健全な警察活動は説明責任と切っても切り離せない． □ *Democracy cannot be divorced from social and economic progress.* 民主主義は社会や経済の発展と切っても切れない関係にある．

Word Partnership	*divorce* は次の語句と使われる：
N.	divorce **court**, divorce **lawyer**, divorce **papers**, divorce **rate**, divorce **settlement** **1**
V.	**file for** divorce, **get a** divorce, **want a** divorce **1**

di|vorced /dɪvɔ́rst/ **1** ADJ Someone who **is divorced** from their former husband or wife has separated from them and is no longer legally married to them. 離婚した □ *He is divorced, with a young son.* 彼は離婚して，幼い息子が1人いる． **2** ADJ 形容詞 If you say that one thing **is divorced from** another, you mean that the two things are very different and separate from each other. 一からかけ離れた [v-link ADJ 'from' n] □ …*speculative theories divorced from political reality.* 現実の政治からかけ離れた空論．

di|vor|cee /dɪvɔ́rseɪ, -sí/ (**divorcees**) N-COUNT 可算名詞 A **divorcee** is a person, especially a woman, who is divorced. 離婚した人 [mainly BRIT 主に英国英語] □ *In 1939 he married Clare Hollway, a divorcee 13 years his senior.* 彼は1939年に13歳年上の離婚歴のあるクレア・ホルウェイと結婚した．

di|vulge /dɪvʌ́ldʒ/ (**divulges, divulging, divulged**) V-T 詞 If you **divulge** a piece of secret or private information, you tell it to someone. 暴露する [FORMAL 形式ばった] □ *Officials refuse to divulge details of the negotiations.* 交渉の詳しい内容について当局者は堅く口を閉ざしている．

DIY /dí aɪ waɪ/ N-UNCOUNT 不可算名詞 **DIY** is the activity of making or repairing things yourself, especially in your home. **DIY** is an abbreviation for **do-it-yourself**. 日曜大工 [mainly BRIT 主に英国英語] □ *He's useless at DIY. He won't even put up a shelf.* 彼に日曜大工を頼んでも無駄．棚1つ作れないだろうから．

diz|zy /dɪ́zi/ (**dizzier, dizziest**) **1** ADJ 形容詞 If you feel **dizzy**, you feel that you are losing your balance and are about to fall. 目まいがする □ *Her head still hurt, and she felt slightly dizzy and disoriented.* 彼女の頭痛は相変わらず続き，少しふらついて意識がもうろうとしていた． ● **diz|zi|ness** N-UNCOUNT 不可算名詞 目まい □ *His head injury causes dizziness and nausea.* 頭部に負った傷のせいで彼は目まいと吐き気に悩まされている． **2** ADJ 形容詞 You can use **dizzy** to describe a woman who is careless and forgets things, but is easy to like. そっかしい，おっちょこちょいの [mainly BRIT 主に英国英語] □ *She is famed for playing dizzy blondes.* 彼女はブロンドのそそっかし屋さんを演じることで知られている． **3** PHRASE 句 If you say that someone has reached **the dizzy heights** of something, you are emphasizing that they have reached a very high level by achieving it. 目もくらむような高み [HUMOROUS ユーモアのある，EMPHASIS 強調] □ *I escalated to the dizzy heights of director's secretary.* 取締役の秘書という目もくらむような地位に昇進した．

DJ /dí dʒéɪ/ (**DJs**) also **D.J.** or **dj** N-COUNT 可算名詞 A **DJ** is the same as a **disc jockey**. ディスクジョッキー

DNA /dí en éɪ/ N-UNCOUNT 不可算名詞 **DNA** is an acid in the chromosomes in the center of the cells of living things. DNA determines the particular structure and functions of every cell and is responsible for characteristics being passed on from parents to their children. **DNA** is an abbreviation for "deoxyribonucleic acid." DNA，デオキシリボ核酸 □ *A routine DNA sample was taken.* いつものようにDNAサンプルが採取された．
→ see **clone, gene**

do
❶ AUXILIARY VERB USES
❷ OTHER VERB USES
❸ NOUN USES

❶ **do** /də, STRONG du/ (**does, doing, did, done**)

Do is used as an auxiliary with the simple present tense. Did is used as an auxiliary with the simple past tense. In spoken English, negative forms of **do** are often shortened, for example, **do not** is shortened to **don't** and **did not** is shortened to **didn't**.

Do は単純現在時制と共に助動詞として用いられる．Did は単純過去時制と共に助動詞として用いられる．口語英語では **do** の否定形はしばしば短縮される．例えば，**do not** は **don't** に短縮され，**did not** は **didn't** に短縮される．

1 AUX 助動詞 **Do** is used to form the negative of main verbs, by putting "not" after "do" and before the main verb in its infinitive form, that is the form without "to." 否定文でnotとともに用いる． □ *They don't want to work.* 彼らは働くつもりなどないのです． □ *I did not know Jamie had a knife.* ジェーミーがナイフを所持していたことを知らなかった． **2** AUX 助動詞 **Do** is used to form questions, by putting the subject after "do" and before the main verb in its infinitive form, that is the form without "to." 疑問文でdoとともに用いる． □ *Do you like music?* 音楽は好き？ □ *What did he say?* 彼，何て言ってた？ **3** AUX 助動詞 **Do** is used in question tags. 付加疑問で用いる． □ *You know about Andy, don't you?* ねえ，アンディーのことを知っているんでしょう？ **4** AUX 助動詞 You use **do** when you are confirming or contradicting a statement containing "do," or giving a negative or positive answer to a question. 質問に対する応答文で用いる． □ *"Did he think there was anything suspicious going on?"* ―*"Yes, he did."* 「彼は不可解なことが起こっているのに気づいていたのか」「ああ，気づいてた」 **5** V-T/V-I 他動詞/自動詞 **Do** can be used to refer back to another verb group when you are comparing or contrasting two things, or saying that they are the same. 比較の文などで動詞の反復を避けて用いる． □ *I make more money than he does.* 私のほうが彼より稼ぎがよい． □ *I had fantasies, as do all mothers, about how life would be when my girls were grown.* 母親なら誰でもするように，娘たちが大きくなった頃には人生はどんなふうになっているのだろうと私も想像をめぐらした． **6** V-T 他動詞 You use **do** after "so" and "nor" to say that the same statement is true for two people or groups. ―も同じ；―も―ない □ *You know that's true, and so do I.* きみがそれが本当だと分かっているように，僕も分かっている．

❷ **do** /du/ (**does, doing, did, done**)

Do is used in a large number of expressions which are explained under other words in the dictionary. For example, the expression "easier said than done" is explained at "easy."

Do は本辞書の他の単語のもとで説明されている多数の表現に使われる．例えば，表現 **easier said than done** は **easy** のところで説明されている．

1 V-T 他動詞 When you **do** something, you take some action or perform an activity or task. **Do** is often used instead of a more specific verb, to talk about a common action involving a particular thing. For example you can say "do your hair" instead of "brush your hair." する（日常的に行われる動作について話す場合に特定の動詞よりもよく用いられる．） □ *I was trying to do some work.* ちょっと仕事をしかけてたんだ． □ *After lunch Elizabeth and I did the dishes.* お昼が済むと，エリザベスと私は一緒に皿を洗った． **2** V-T 他動詞 **Do** can be used to stand for any verb group, or to refer back to another verb group, including one that was in a previous sentence. する（前述の動詞など他の動詞の意味を受けて用いられる．） □ *What are you doing?* 何してるの？ **3** V-T 他動詞 You can use **do** in a clause at the beginning of a sentence after words like "what" and "all," to give special emphasis to the information that comes at the end of the sentence. する（what，allなどの語の後で用いられ強調を表す．） [EMPHASIS 強調] □ *All she does is complain.* 彼女は口を開けば文句ばかりだ． **4** V-T 他動詞 If you **do** a particular thing **with** something, you use it in that particular way. ―を―に使う □ *I was allowed to do whatever I wanted with my life.* 私は人生で何でもやりたいことをやらせてもらえた． **5** V-T 他動詞 If you **do** something about a problem, you take action to try to solve it. 何とかする □ *They refuse to do anything about the real cause of crime: poverty.* 犯罪の真の原因である貧困の問題に彼らは手をつけようとしない． **6** V-T 他動詞 If an action or event **does** a particular thing, such as harm or good, it has that result or effect. もたらす □ *A few bombs can do a lot of damage.* 数発の爆弾でも甚大な被害を及ぼすことがある． **7** V-T 他動詞 If you ask someone what they **do**, you want to know what their job or profession is. （仕事を）する □ *"What does your father do?"* ― *"Well, he's a civil servant."* 「お父さんの仕事は？」「うーん，公務員だよ」 **8** V-T 他動詞 If you **are doing** something, you are busy or active in some way, or have planned an activity for some time in the future. する（ことがある） □ *Are you doing anything tomorrow night?* 明日の夜は何か予定あるの？ **9** V-I 自動詞 If you say that someone or something does well or badly, you are talking about how successful or unsuccessful they are. うまくいく；うまくいかない □ *Connie did well at school and graduated with honors.* コニーは学業に優れ，優等で卒業した． **10** V-T 他動詞 You can use **do** when referring to the speed or rate that something or someone achieves or is able to achieve. 出す □ *They were doing 70 miles an hour.* 彼らは時速70マイルで走っていた． **11** V-T 他動詞 If someone **does** drugs, they take illegal drugs. （麻薬を）やる □ *I don't do drugs.* 麻薬はやらないよ． **12** V-T/V-I 他動詞/自動詞 If you say that something **will do** or **will do** you, you mean that there is enough of it or that it is of good enough quality to

meet your requirements or to satisfy you. 十分である，間に合う □*Anything to create a scene and attract attention will do.* 騒ぎを起こして注目を集められれば何でも構わない． **13** V-T 他動詞 If you **do** a subject, author, or book, you study them at school or college. 勉強する；専攻する [mainly BRIT 主に英国英語, SPOKEN 口語] □*She planned to do math at night school.* 彼女は夜間学校で数学を勉強するつもりだった． **14** PHRASE 句 If you say that you **could do with** something, you mean that you need it or would benefit from it. 必要である，あればありがたい □*I could do with a cup of tea.* お茶が1杯欲しいなあ． **15** PHRASE 句 You can ask someone **what** they **did with** something as another way of asking them where they put it. 一はどこにやったのか □*What did you do with that notebook?* あのノート，どこにやったの？ **16** PHRASE 句 If you ask **what** someone or something **is doing** in a particular place, you are asking why they are there. 一体なぜ一にいるのか，一体なぜ一にあるのか □*"Dr. Campbell," he said, clearly surprised. "What are you doing here?"* 「キャンベル先生」と彼は明らかに驚いた様子だった．「どうしてこんなところにいらっしゃるんですか？」 **17** PHRASE 句 If you say that one thing **has** something **to do with** or is something **to do with** another thing, you mean that the two things are connected or that the first thing is about the second thing. 一と関係がある □*Mr. Butterfield denies having anything to do with the episode.* バターフィールド氏はそのことには関係ないと否定した．

▶ **do away with** **1** PHRASAL VERB 句動詞 To **do away with** something means to remove it completely or put an end to it. 処分する，廃止する □*The long-range goal must be to do away with nuclear weapons altogether.* 将来的には核兵器の廃絶を目指さなければならない． **2** PHRASAL VERB 句動詞 If one person **does away with** another, the first murders the second. If you **do away with** yourself, you kill yourself. 始末する，やる [INFORMAL くだけた] □*...a woman whose husband had made several attempts to do away with her.* 夫から何度も殺されかけた女性．

▶ **do in** PHRASAL VERB 句動詞 To **do** someone **in** means to kill them. 始末する，やる [INFORMAL くだけた] □*Whoever did him in removed a man who was brave as well as ruthless.* 彼をやったのが霊にせよ，毅然としてしかも勇敢な一人の男がこの世から姿を消した．

▶ **do up** **1** PHRASAL VERB 句動詞 If you **do** something **up**, you fasten it. 留める，締める □*Mari did up the buttons.* マーリはボタンを留めた． **2** PHRASAL VERB 句動詞 If you say that a person or room **is done up** in a particular way, you mean they are dressed or decorated in that way, often a way that is rather ridiculous or extreme. 着飾る；模様替えする □*...a small salon done up in saffron silks and plum velvet cushions.* 部屋のアクセントにサフラン色のシルクとプラム色のベルベットのクッションを置いた小さな応接間．

▶ **do without** **1** PHRASAL VERB 句動詞 If you **do without** something you need, want, or usually have, you are able to survive, continue, or succeed although you do not have it. 一なしで何とかする □*We can't do without the help of your organization.* あなたがた団体の支援がないとやっていけません． **2** PHRASAL VERB 句動詞 If you say that you could **do without** something, you mean that you would prefer not to have it or it is of no benefit to you. 一などいらない [INFORMAL くだけた] □*He could do without her rhetorical questions at five o'clock in the morning.* 彼にしたら早朝の5時に彼女から問いつめられるなんてまっぴら御免だった．

❸ **do** /duː/ (**dos**) PHRASE 句 If someone tells you the **dos and don'ts** of a particular situation, they advise you what you should and should not do in that situation. 心得 □*Please advise me on the most suitable color print film and some dos and don'ts.* 最も適したカラーフィルムと注意事項について教えてください．

dock /dɒk/ (**docks, docking, docked**) **1** N-COUNT 可算名詞 A **dock** is an enclosed area in a harbor where ships go to be loaded, unloaded, and repaired. 埠頭 (ふとう)，波止場；ドック [also 'in/into' N] □*She headed for the docks, thinking that Ricardo might be hiding in one of the boats.* リカルドがどれかのボートに潜んでいるかも知れないと思いながら，彼女は港に向かった． **2** N-COUNT 可算名詞 A **dock** is a platform for loading vehicles or trains. 積み下ろし用プラットホーム [AM 米国英語] □*The truck left the loading dock with hoses still attached.* トラックはホースを付けたまま積み下ろし用のプラットホームを出ました． **3** N-COUNT 可算名詞 A **dock** is a small structure at the edge of water where boats can tie up, especially one that is privately owned. 桟橋，船着場 [AM 米国英語] □*He had a house there and a dock and a little aluminum boat.* 彼はそこに家を持ち，船着場には小型のアルミのボートがあった． **4** V-T/V-I 他動詞/自動詞 When a ship **docks** or **is docked**, it is brought into a dock. 埠頭につく；ドックに入る □*The crash happened as the ferry attempted to dock on Staten Island.* フェリーがスタテン島の港に入るときに衝突事故が起こった． **5** V-T 他動詞 If you **dock** someone's pay or money, you take some of the money away. 差し引く □*He threatens to dock her fee.* 彼は報酬から差し引くぞと彼女を脅す． **6** V-T 他動詞 If you **dock** someone points in a contest, you take away some of the points that they have. 減点する **7** V-RECIP 相互動詞 When one spacecraft **docks** or **is docked with** another, the two crafts join together in space. ドッキングする □*The space shuttle Atlantis is scheduled to dock with Russia's Mir space station.* スペースシャトル・ア

トランティス号はロシアのミール宇宙ステーションとドッキングする予定です． **8** N-SING 単数名詞 In a law court, the **dock** is where the person accused of a crime stands or sits. 被告席 □*What about the odd chance that you do put an innocent man in the dock?* ごくまれだろうが，無実の人を被告人席に座らせているという可能性はないのか．

doc|tor /dɒktər/ (**doctors, doctoring, doctored**) **1** N-COUNT; N-TITLE; N-VOC 可算名詞，称号名詞，呼格名詞 A **doctor** is someone who has a degree in medicine and treats people who are sick or injured. 医者，医師 □*Do not discontinue the treatment without consulting your doctor.* 治療を中止するときは必ず医師に相談してください． **2** N-COUNT; N-TITLE; N-VOC 可算名詞，称号名詞，呼格名詞 A **dentist** or **veterinarian** can also be called **doctor**. 歯科医；獣医 [AM 米国英語] **3** N-COUNT 可算名詞 The **doctor's** is used to refer to the office where a doctor works. 病院，診療所 □*I have an appointment at the doctor's.* 病院の予約があります． **4** N-COUNT; N-TITLE 可算名詞，称号名詞 A **doctor** is someone who has been awarded the highest academic or honorary degree by a university. 博士 □*He is a doctor of philosophy.* 彼は博士号を持っている． **5** V-T 他動詞 If someone **doctors** something, they change it in order to deceive people. 改ざんする □*They doctored the prints, deepening the lines to make her look as awful as possible.* 彼らはしわが深くなるように写真に手を加えて，なるだけ彼女がひどく見えるようにした．

doc|tor|ate /dɒktərɪt/ (**doctorates**) N-COUNT 可算名詞 A **doctorate** is the highest degree awarded by a university. 博士号 □*Professor Lanphier obtained his doctorate in social psychology from the University of Michigan.* ランフィア教授はミシガン大学で社会心理学の博士号を取得した．

doc|tor's of|fice (**doctor's offices**) N-COUNT 可算名詞 A **doctor's office** is the room or clinic where a doctor works. 診察室，医院 [AM 米国英語] □*Some people made it as far as a doctor's office, only to pass out and die within minutes.* 遠くの診療所にようやくたどり着いたかと思うと，何分も経たないうちに意識を失って亡くなる人もいます．

doc|tor's sur|gery (**doctor's surgeries**) N-COUNT 可算名詞 A **doctor's surgery** is the same as a **doctor's office**. 診察室，医院 [BRIT 英国英語]

doc|tri|nal /dɒktrɪnᵊl/ ADJ 形容詞 **Doctrinal** means relating to doctrines. 教義上の [FORMAL 形式ばった] □*Doctrinal differences were vigorously debated among religious leaders.* 教義の違いについて宗教指導者の間で白熱した議論が交わされた．

doc|trine /dɒktrɪn/ (**doctrines**) N-VAR 可変性名詞 A **doctrine** is a set of principles or beliefs, especially religious ones. 教義，信条 □*...the Marxist doctrine of perpetual revolution.* マルクスの永久革命論．

docu|ment (**documents, documenting, documented**)

The noun is pronounced /dɒkyəmənt/. The verb is pronounced /dɒkyəmɛnt/.

名詞は /dɒkyəmənt/ と発音される．動詞は /dɒkyəmɛnt/ と発音される．

1 N-COUNT 可算名詞 A **document** is one or more official pieces of paper with writing on them. 文書，書類 □*She produces legal documents for a downtown Seattle law firm.* 彼女はシアトル都心の法律事務所で法律書類を作成している． **2** N-COUNT 可算名詞 A **document** is a piece of text or graphics, for example, a letter, that is stored as a file on a computer and that you can access in order to read it or change it. 文書，ドキュメント [COMPUTING コンピューティング] □*When you are finished typing, remember to save your document.* 入力が終わったら，忘れずに文書を保存しましょう． **3** V-T 他動詞 If you **document** something, you make a detailed record of it in writing or on film or tape. 記録する □*He wrote a book documenting his prison experiences.* 彼は獄中での生活を記録した本を書いた．

→ see copy, diary, history, printing

docu|men|tary /dɒkyəmɛntəri, -tri/ (**documentaries**) **1** N-COUNT 可算名詞 A **documentary** is a television or radio program, or a movie, which shows real events or provides information about a particular subject. ドキュメンタリー □*...a TV documentary on homelessness.* ホームレスをテーマにしたドキュメンタリー番組． **2** ADJ 形容詞 **Documentary** evidence consists of things that are written down. 記録された，文書になった [ADJ n] □*The government says it has documentary evidence that the two countries were planning military action.* 政府によれば，両国が軍事行動を計画していたことを示す証拠文書があるとのことです．

docu|men|ta|tion /dɒkyəmɛnteɪᵊn/ N-UNCOUNT 不可算名詞 **Documentation** consists of documents which provide proof or evidence of something, or are a record of something. 証拠資料 □*Passengers must carry proper documentation.* 乗客は適正な証明書を所持していなければならない．

dodge /dɒdʒ/ (**dodges, dodging, dodged**) **1** V-I 自動詞 If you **dodge**, you move suddenly, often to avoid being hit, caught, or seen. 身をかわす □*I dodged back into the alley and waited a minute.*

再び路地に身を隠してしばらく待った． **2** V-T 他動詞 If you **dodge** something, you avoid it by quickly moving aside or out of reach so that it cannot hit or reach you. さっとよける □ *He desperately dodged a speeding car trying to run him down.* 彼は猛スピードではねようとする車から必死に逃れた． **3** V-T 他動詞 If you **dodge** something, you deliberately avoid thinking about it or dealing with it, often by being deceitful. 逃れる □ *He boasts of dodging military service by feigning illness.* 彼は病気を装って兵役を逃れたことを自慢している． ● N-COUNT 可算名詞 **Dodge** is also a noun. 逃れること □ *This was not just a tax dodge.* これは単なる税金逃れではなかった．

does /dəz, STRONG dʌz/ **Does** is the third person singular in the present tense of **do.** do の 3 人称単数現在形

doesn't /dʌzªnt/ **Doesn't** is the usual spoken form of "does not." 口語で用いられる does not の短縮形

dog /dɒg/ (**dogs, dogging, dogged**) **1** N-COUNT 可算名詞 A **dog** is a very common four-legged animal that is often kept by people as a pet or to guard or hunt. There are many different breeds of dog. 犬 □ *The British are renowned as a nation of dog lovers.* イギリス人は犬好きの国民として知られています． **2** N-COUNT 可算名詞 People use **dog** to refer to something that they consider unsatisfactory or of poor quality. くだらない [AM 米国英語, INFORMAL くだけた, DISAPPROVAL 不賛成] □ *It's a real dog.* 実につまらない． **3** V-T 他動詞 If problems or injuries **dog** you, they are with you all the time. 付きまとう □ *His career has been dogged by bad luck.* 彼は仕事の面では不運の連続だった． **4** → see also **dogged 5** PHRASE 句 You use **dog eat dog** to express your disapproval of a situation where everyone wants to succeed and is willing to harm other people in order to do so. 食うか食われるかの争い [DISAPPROVAL 不賛成] □ *It is very much dog eat dog out there.* まさにそこは食うか食われるかの世界だ． **6** PHRASE 句 If you say that something **is going to the dogs,** you mean that it is becoming weaker and worse in quality. 落ちぶれる [INFORMAL くだけた, DISAPPROVAL 不賛成] □ *They sit doing nothing while the country goes to the dogs.* 国が傾いているというのに彼らは何もせずただじっとしている．

→ see **pet**

dog|ged /dɒgɪd/ ADJ 形容詞 If you describe someone's actions as **dogged,** you mean that they are determined to continue with something even if it becomes difficult or dangerous. 根気強い [ADJ n] □ *They have, through sheer dogged determination, slowly gained respect for their efforts.* 彼らの努力はその粘り強さによって次第に認められるようになった． ● **dog|ged|ly** ADV 副詞 根気強く □ *She would fight doggedly for her rights as the children's mother.* 彼女はその子供たちの母親としての権利のために粘り強く戦うだろう． ● **dog|ged|ness** N-UNCOUNT 不可算名詞 根気強さ □ *Most of my accomplishments came as the result of sheer doggedness rather than talent.* 私の業績のほとんどが才能よりもむしろ地道な努力の賜物である．

dog|house /dɒghaʊs/ (**doghouses**) **1** N-COUNT 可算名詞 A **doghouse** is a small building made especially for a dog to sleep in. 犬小屋 [AM 米国英語] **2** PHRASE 句 If you are **in the doghouse,** people are annoyed or angry with you. 不興をかって [INFORMAL くだけた] □ *Her husband was in the doghouse for leaving her to cope on her own.* 任せっきりにしたので夫は妻からにらまれた．

dog|ma /dɒgmə/ (**dogmas**) N-VAR 可変性名詞 If you refer to a belief or a system of beliefs as a **dogma,** you disapprove of it because people are expected to accept that it is true, without questioning it. 教条, ドグマ [DISAPPROVAL 不賛成] □ *Their political dogma has blinded them to the real needs of the country.* その独断的な政治信念のせいで, 彼らはその国にとって何が本当に必要なのかを見失ってしまっている．

dog|mat|ic /dɒgmætɪk/ ADJ 形容詞 If you say that someone is **dogmatic,** you are critical of them because they are convinced that they are right, and refuse to consider that other opinions might also be justified. 独断的な [DISAPPROVAL 不賛成] □ *Many writers at this time held rigidly dogmatic views.* この頃は作家の多くが視野の狭い見方をしていた． ● **dog|mati|cal|ly** /dɒgmætɪkli/ ADV 副詞 [ADV with v] 独断的に □ *Bennett had wanted this list of books to be dogmatically imposed on the nation's universities.* ベネットはこの書籍リストを国内の大学に押し付けようとしていた．

dog|ma|tism /dɒgmətɪzəm/ N-UNCOUNT 不可算名詞 If you refer to an opinion as **dogmatism,** you are criticizing it for being strongly stated without considering all the relevant facts or other people's opinions. 独断的意見 [DISAPPROVAL 不賛成] □ *We cannot allow dogmatism to stand in the way of progress.* 一方的な主張によって進展が妨げられるようなことがあってはならない．

do-it-yourself N-UNCOUNT 不可算名詞 **Do-it-yourself** is the same as DIY. 日曜大工

dol|drums /dɒuldrəmz/ PHRASE 句 If an activity or situation is **in the doldrums,** it is very quiet and nothing new or exciting is happening. 停滞して □ *The economy is in the doldrums.* 経済は低迷している．

dole /dɒul/ **1** N-UNCOUNT 不可算名詞 The **dole** or **dole** is money

that is given regularly by the government to people who are unemployed. 失業手当 [mainly BRIT 主に英国英語; AM usually **welfare** 米国英語では通常 **welfare**] **2** PHRASE 句 Someone who is **on the dole** is registered as unemployed and receives money from the government. 失業手当を受けて [mainly BRIT 主に英国英語; AM usually **on welfare** 米国英語では通常 **on welfare**]

doll /dɒl/ (**dolls**) N-COUNT 可算名詞 A **doll** is a child's toy which looks like a small person or baby. 人形

dol|lar /dɒlər/ (**dollars**) N-COUNT 可算名詞 The **dollar** is the unit of money used in the U.S., Canada, Australia, and some other countries. It is represented by the symbol $, the dollar sign. A dollar is divided into one hundred smaller units called cents. ドル □ *She gets paid seven dollars an hour.* 彼女の時給は 7 ドルです． ● N-SING 単数名詞 The **dollar** is also used to refer to the American currency system. 米ドル □ *In early trading in Tokyo, the dollar fell sharply against the yen.* 前場の東京市場では, 米ドルは円に対して急落した．

dol|phin /dɒlfɪn/ (**dolphins**) N-COUNT 可算名詞 A **dolphin** is a mammal which lives in the sea and looks like a large fish with a pointed mouth. イルカ

→ see **whale**

Word Link   dom, domin ≈ rule, master : do**main**, **domin**ate, pre**domin**ant

do|main /dɒumeɪn/ (**domains**) **1** N-COUNT 可算名詞 A **domain** is a particular field of thought, activity, or interest, especially one over which someone has control, influence, or rights. 分野, 一界 [FORMAL 形式ばった] □ *...the great experimenters in the domain of art.* 芸術界における偉大なる実験者たち． **2** N-COUNT 可算名詞 On the Internet, a **domain** is a set of addresses that shows, for example, the category or geographical area that an Internet address belongs to. ドメイン [COMPUTING コンピューティング] □ *An Internet society spokeswoman said .org domain users will not experience any disruptions during the transition.* インターネットソサエティの女性広報官によると, 移行期間中も org ドメイン利用者に支障が及ぶことはないという．

do|main name (**domain names**) N-COUNT 可算名詞 A **domain name** is the name of a person's or an organization's website on the Internet, for example, "collins.co.uk." ドメイン名 [COMPUTING コンピューティング] □ *Users need to find out if a domain name is already registered or is still available.* ユーザーはドメイン名が登録済みかどうかを調べなければならない．

dome /dɒum/ (**domes**) **1** N-COUNT 可算名詞 A **dome** is a round roof. 丸屋根, ドーム □ *...the dome of the Capitol.* 連邦議会議事堂のドーム． **2** N-COUNT 可算名詞 A **dome** is any object that has a similar shape to a dome. 半球状のもの □ *...the dome of the hill.* 丘の頂上．

do|mes|tic /dəmestɪk/ **1** ADJ 形容詞 **Domestic** political activities, events, and situations happen or exist within one particular country. 国内の □ *...over 100 domestic flights a day to 30 leading U.S. destinations.* アメリカの主要な 30 都市を結ぶ 1 日 100 便を超える国内便． **2** → see also **gross domestic product 3** ADJ 形容詞 **Domestic** duties and activities are concerned with the running of a home and family. 家庭の; 家事の [ADJ n] □ *...a plan for sharing domestic chores.* 家事を分担する計画． **4** ADJ 形容詞 **Domestic** items and services are intended to be used in people's homes rather than in factories or offices. 家庭用の [ADJ n] □ *...domestic appliances.* 家電製品． **5** ADJ 形容詞 A **domestic** situation or atmosphere is one which involves a family and their home. 家庭的な □ *It was a scene of such domestic bliss.* まさに幸せな家庭の一場面だった． **6** ADJ 形容詞 A **domestic** animal is one that is not wild and is kept either on a farm to produce food or in someone's home as a pet. 飼育された, 飼いならされた □ *...a domestic cat.* 飼い猫．

domi|nance /dɒmɪnəns/ N-UNCOUNT 不可算名詞 The **dominance** of a particular person or thing is the fact that they are more powerful, successful, or important than other people or things. 優勢, 優越 □ *The latest fighting appears to be an attempt by each group to establish dominance over the other.* 最近の戦闘は各派による勢力争いと見られます．

Thesaurus   dominance また次を参照:

N.   authority, control, supremacy, upper hand

domi|nant /dɒmɪnənt/ ADJ 形容詞 Someone or something that is **dominant** is more powerful, successful, influential, or noticeable than other people or things. 優勢な □ *...a change which would maintain his party's dominant position in Scotland.* スコットランドにおいて彼の党の優位を維持するような変更．

→ see **gene**

domi|nate /dɒmɪneɪt/ (**dominates, dominating, dominated**) **1** V-T/V-I 他動詞/自動詞 To **dominate** a situation means to be

the most powerful or important person or thing in it. 優勢である，優位を占める ❑ *The book is expected to dominate the best-seller lists.* その本はベストセラーの座を奪いそうだ．❑ *...countries where life is dominated by war.* 生活が戦争に巻き込まれた国々．❑ *Selling could continue to dominate as investors play it safe.* ● **dom|i|na|tion** /dɒmɪneɪʃ⁰n/ N-UNCOUNT 不可算名詞 投資家がリスクを避けて，売りが続く可能性がある．❑ *...the domination of the market by a small number of organizations.* 少数の組織による市場支配． **2** V-T 他動詞 If one country or person **dominates** another, they have power over them. 支配する ❑ *He denied that his country wants to dominate Europe.* 自国がヨーロッパを支配しようとしている点について彼は否定しました．❑ *Women are no longer dominated by the men in their relationships.* もはや恋愛において女性は男性に支配されることはなくなった． ● **dom|i|na|tion** N-UNCOUNT 不可算名詞 ❑ *They had five centuries of domination by the Romans.* 彼らは5世紀にわたってローマの支配を受けた． **3** V-T 他動詞 If a building, mountain, or other object **dominates** an area, it is so large or impressive that you cannot avoid seeing it. 見下ろす，そびえ立つ ❑ *It's one of the biggest buildings in this area, and it really dominates this whole place.* この地域最大の建築物の1つで，あたり一帯を見下ろすようにそびえています．

domi|nat|ing /dɒmɪneɪtɪŋ/ ADJ 形容詞 A **dominating** person has a very strong personality and influences the people around them. 強烈な個性を持つ，絶大な影響力を持つ ❑ *She certainly was a dominating figure, a leader who gave her name to a political philosophy.* 確かに彼女は絶大な影響力を持ち，独自の政治哲学を残した指導者でした．

Word Link   dom, domin ≈ rule, master : domain, dominate, predominant

do|min|ion /dəmɪnyən/ (**dominions**) N-COUNT 可算名詞 A **dominion** is an area of land that is controlled by a ruler. 領地 ❑ *The republic is a dominion of the Brazilian people.* 共和国はブラジル領である．

domi|no /dɒmɪnoʊ/ (**dominoes**) **1** N-COUNT 可算名詞 **Dominoes** are small rectangular blocks marked with two groups of spots on one side. They are used for playing various games. ドミノ牌（はい） **2** N-UNCOUNT 不可算名詞 **Dominoes** is a game in which players put dominoes onto a table in turn. ドミノ ❑ *I used to play dominoes there.* 昔よくそこでドミノをした．

domi|no ef|fect N-SING 単数名詞 If one event causes another similar event, which in turn causes another event, and so on, you can refer to this as a **domino effect**. ドミノ効果 ❑ *The timetable for trains is so tight that if one is a bit late, the domino effect is enormous.* 過密ダイヤのせいで1本の電車が少しでも遅れると，他の電車にも次々と遅れが生じて大きな影響が出てしまう．

Word Link   don ≈ giving : donate, donor, pardon

do|nate /doʊneɪt/ (**donates, donating, donated**) **1** V-T 他動詞 If you **donate** something to a charity or other organization, you give it to them. 寄付する ❑ *He frequently donates large sums to charity.* 彼はよく慈善団体に高額の寄付をしている． ● **do|na|tion** /doʊneɪʃ⁰n/ N-UNCOUNT 不可算名詞 ❑ *...the donation of his collection to the art gallery.* 彼のコレクションを美術館に寄付． **2** V-T 他動詞 If you **donate** your blood or a part of your body, you allow doctors to use it to help someone who is ill. 献血する；臓器提供する ❑ *...people who are willing to donate their organs for use after death.* 死亡時の臓器提供の意思を示している者． ● **do|na|tion** N-UNCOUNT 不可算名詞 臓器提供 ❑ *...measures aimed at encouraging organ donation.* 臓器提供の普及に向けた施策．

do|na|tion /doʊneɪʃ⁰n/ (**donations**) **1** N-COUNT 可算名詞 A **donation** is something which someone gives to a charity or other organization. 寄付金，寄贈品 ❑ *Employees make regular donations to charity.* 従業員は定期的に慈善団体に寄付している． **2** → see also **donate**
→ see **donor**

Word Partnership   donation は次の語句と使われる：

V.	**accept** a donation, **make** a donation, **receive** a donation
ADJ.	**charitable** donation, **generous** donation, **suggested** donation

done /dʌn/ **1** **Done** is the past participle of **do**. **2** ADJ 形容詞 A task or activity that is **done** has been completed successfully. 済んだ，うまくいった [v-link ADJ] ❑ *When her deal is done, the client emerges with her purchase.* 取引が終わると，客は買ったものを手にして姿を現す． **3** ADJ 形容詞 When something that you are cooking is **done**, it has been cooked long enough and is ready. 調理できた [v-link ADJ] ❑ *As soon as the cake is done, remove it from the oven.* ケーキが焼けたらすぐにオーブンから出します． **4** CONVENTION 慣習表現 You say "**Done**" when you are accepting a deal, arrangement, or bet that someone has offered to make with you. 了解，よし，わかった [SPOKEN 口語, FORMULAE 決まり文句] ❑ *"You lead and we'll look for it."—"Done."* 「前を行ってくれますか．私たちが探しますから」「了解」

don|key /dɒŋki/ (**donkeys**) N-COUNT 可算名詞 A **donkey** is an animal which is like a horse but which is smaller and has longer ears. ロバ

do|nor /doʊnər/ (**donors**) **1** N-COUNT 可算名詞 A **donor** is someone who gives a part of their body or some of their blood to be used by doctors to help a person who is ill. 献血者；臓器提供者，ドナー ❑ *Doctors removed the healthy kidney from the donor.* 医師はドナーから健康な腎臓を摘出しました． **2** N-COUNT 可算名詞 A **donor** is a person or organization who gives something, especially money, to a charity, organization, or country that needs it. 献金者，寄贈者 ❑ *Donor countries are becoming more choosy about which countries they are prepared to help.* どの国ならば援助してもよいか，援助国のえり好みは激しくなっている． **3** ADJ 形容詞 **Donor** organs or parts are organs or parts of the body which people allow doctors to use to help people who are ill. 移植用の [ADJ n] ❑ *...the severe shortage of donor organs.* 深刻な臓器不足．
→ see Word Web: **donor**

don't /doʊnt/ **Don't** is the usual spoken form of "do not."

do|nut /doʊnʌt, -nət/ (**donuts**) → see **doughnut**

doo|dle /dud⁰l/ (**doodles, doodling, doodled**) **1** N-COUNT 可算名詞 A **doodle** is a pattern or picture that you draw when you are bored or thinking about something else. いたずら書き ❑ *Dillworthy was staring into space, with a scrawl of doodles on the pad in front of him.* ディルワージーは宙を見つめて，目の前にあるパッドにいたずら書きをしていた． **2** V-I 自動詞 When someone **doodles**, they draw doodles. いたずら書きをする ❑ *He looked across at Jackson, doodling on his notebook.* 彼はノートにいたずら書きをしながらジャクソンを遠巻きに見た．

doom /dum/ (**dooms, dooming, doomed**) **1** N-UNCOUNT 不可算名詞 **Doom** is a terrible future state or event which you cannot prevent. 避けられない未来，宿命 ❑ *...his warnings of impending doom.* 恐ろしい未来が迫っているという彼の警告． **2** N-UNCOUNT 不可算名詞 If you have a sense or feeling of **doom**, you feel that things are going very badly and are likely to get even worse. 不吉 ❑ *Why are people so full of gloom and doom?* どうして人々はそんなに悲観的なのでしょうか． **3** V-T 他動詞 If a fact or event **dooms** someone or something **to** a particular fate, it makes certain that they are going to suffer in some way. 運命づける ❑ *That argument was the turning point for their marriage, and the one which doomed it to failure.* その口論がもとで二人の結婚生活にひびが入り，やがて破綻することになった．

doomed /dumd/ **1** ADJ 形容詞 If something **is doomed to** happen, or if you **are doomed to** a particular state, something unpleasant is certain to happen, and you can do nothing to prevent it. 運命にある [v-link ADJ] ❑ *Their plans seemed doomed to failure.* 彼らの計画は確実に失敗するかのように思われた． **2** ADJ 形容詞 Someone or something that is **doomed** is certain to fail or be destroyed. 失敗するに決まっている ❑ *I used to pour time and energy into projects that were doomed from the start.* 最初から全く見込みのな

Word Web   donor

Many people **give donations**. They like to **help** others. They **donate money,** clothes, food, or their time. Some people even give parts of themselves. Doctors performed the first successful human **organ transplants** in the 1950s. Today this type of operation is a relatively routine procedure. The problem now is finding enough **donors** to meet the needs of potential **recipients**. Organs such as the **kidney** often come from a living donor. **Hearts, lungs,** and other vital organs come from deceased donors. Of course our health care system relies on **blood** donors. They help save lives every day.

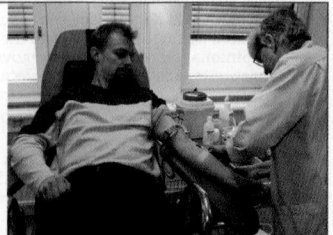

いような計画に，私はいつも時間とエネルギーを注ぎ込んでいた.

door /dɔːr/ (doors) **1** N-COUNT 可算名詞 A **door** is a piece of wood, glass, or metal, which is moved to open and close the entrance to a building, room, closet, or vehicle. ドア, 戸 ❏ *I was knocking at the front door but there was no answer.* 玄関をノックしたが応答がなかった. **2** N-COUNT 可算名詞 A **door** is the space in a wall when a door is open. 出入り口, 戸口 ❏ *She looked through the door of the kitchen. Her daughter was at the stove.* 彼女が勝手口からのぞき込むと，娘がコンロのところにいた. **3** N-PLURAL 複数名詞 **Doors** is used in expressions such as **a few doors down** or **three doors up** to refer to a place that is a particular number of buildings away from where you are. 一軒先 [INFORMAL くだけた] [amount n 'down/up'] ❏ *Mrs. Cade's house was only a few doors down from her daughter's apartment.* ケイドさんの家は彼女の娘のアパートからほんの数軒先だった. **4** → see also **next door** **5** PHRASE 句 When you **answer the door**, you go and open the door because a visitor has knocked on it or rung the bell. 玄関に出る ❏ *Carol answered the door as soon as I knocked.* 玄関をノックするとすぐにキャロルが出てきた. **6** PHRASE 句 If you say that someone gets or does something **by the back door** or **through the back door**, you are criticizing them for doing it secretly and unofficially. 裏口で [DISAPPROVAL 不賛成] ❏ *The government would not allow anyone to sneak in by the back door and seize power by force.* 政府は，密かに入国する者や暴力によって権力を手にしようとする者には容赦しない構えです. **7** PHRASE 句 If people have talks and discussions **behind closed doors**, they have them in private because they want them to be kept secret. 秘密裏で ❏ *...decisions taken in secret behind closed doors.* 秘密裏になされた決定. **8** PHRASE 句 If someone goes **from door to door** or goes **door to door**, they go along a street calling at each house in turn, for example, selling something. 一軒一軒，戸別に ❏ *They are going from door to door collecting money from civilians.* 彼らは一軒一軒訪ねて一般の人たちから寄付金を集めている. **9** PHRASE 句 If you talk about a distance or trip **from door to door** or **door to door**, you are talking about the distance from the place where the trip starts to the place where it finishes. ドアツードアで，出発地から目的地まで ❏ *...tickets covering the whole trip from door to door.* 出発地から目的地までの全行程の切符. **10** PHRASE 句 If you say that something helps someone to get their **foot in the door**, you mean that it gives them an opportunity to start doing something new, usually in an area that is difficult to succeed in. 足がかり ❏ *If we can get our foot in the door, that can help us build our market.* 足がかりさえ得られれば，我々の市場を開拓することができるだろう. **11** PHRASE 句 If someone **shuts the door in** your **face** or **slams the door in** your **face**, they refuse to talk to you or give you any information. 一切口を聞かない，門前払いする ❏ *Did you say anything to me just now or just shut the door in his face?* 彼に何か言ったの．それともただ門前払いをしたの. **12** PHRASE 句 If you **lay** something **at** someone's **door**, you blame them for an unpleasant event or situation. 一を一のせいにする ❏ *Much of the blame for the long delay could be laid at the door of the manufacturer.* かなりの遅れが出た責任の多くはメーカー側にあるだろう. **13** PHRASE 句 When you are **out of doors**, you are not inside a building, but in the open air. 屋外で ❏ *The weather was fine enough for working out of doors.* 外で作業ができるぐらい天気がよかった. **14** PHRASE 句 If you **see** someone **to the door**, you go to the door with a visitor when they leave. 玄関で見送る ❏ *Politely she saw her to the door and opened it for her.* 彼は丁寧に彼女を玄関まで見送ってドアを開けた. **15** PHRASE 句 If someone **shows** you **the door**, they ask you to leave because they are angry with you. 追い払う ❏ *Would they forgive and forget – or show him the door?* 彼らは彼を許して忘れてくれるのか，それとも追い払ってしまうのか. **16 at death's door** → see **death**

door|man /dɔːrmæn, -mən/ (doormen) **1** N-COUNT 可算名詞 A **doorman** is a person, usually a uniformed employee, who stands at the door of a building such as a hotel or apartment and helps people who are going in or out. ドアマン，守衛 **2** N-COUNT 可算名詞 A **doorman** is the same as a **bouncer**. 用心棒 [BRIT 英国英語]

door|step /dɔːrstɛp/ (doorsteps) **1** N-COUNT 可算名詞 A **doorstep** is a step in front of a door on the outside of a building. 戸口の上がり段 ❏ *...a youth who was sitting on a doorstep, drinking.* ドアステップに座って酒を飲んでいた若者. **2** PHRASE 句 If a place is **on** your **doorstep**, it is very near to where you live. If something happens **on** your **doorstep**, it happens very close to where you live. 家のすぐ近くで，ごく身近なところで ❏ *It is easy to lose sight of what is happening on our own doorstep.* ごく身近で起こっていることは見逃としやすい.

door|way /dɔːrweɪ/ (doorways) **1** N-COUNT 可算名詞 A **doorway** is a space in a wall where a door opens and closes. 戸口，入口 ❏ *Hannah looked up to see David and another man standing in the doorway.* ハンナが見上げると，デイビッドともう1人の男が玄関に立っていた. **2** N-COUNT 可算名詞 A **doorway** is a covered space just outside the door of a building. 戸口のすぐ外側 ❏ *...homeless people sleeping in doorways.* 出入り口の前で眠っているホームレス.

dope /doʊp/ (dopes, doping, doped) **1** N-UNCOUNT 不可算名詞 **Dope** is a drug, usually an illegal drug such as marijuana or cocaine. 麻薬，ヤク [INFORMAL くだけた] ❏ *A man asked them if they wanted to buy some dope.* 男が彼らにヤクを買わないかと尋ねた. **2** V-T 他動詞 If someone **dopes** an animal or **dopes** their food, they put drugs into their food or force them to take drugs. 薬を混ぜる ❏ *Anyone could have got in and doped the wine.* 誰かが侵入してワインに薬を混ぜたのかもしれない. ❏ *I'd been doped with Somnolin.* 睡眠薬のソムノリンを飲まされていた. **3** N-COUNT 可算名詞 If someone calls a person a **dope**, they think that the person is stupid. ばか [INFORMAL くだけた, DISAPPROVAL 不賛成] ❏ *I'm more comfortable with them. I don't feel I'm such a dope.* 彼らと一緒でも楽な気分になって，もう自分がばかだとは感じなくなった.

dor|mant /dɔːrmənt/ ADJ 形容詞 Something that is **dormant** is not active, growing, or being used at the present time but is capable of becoming active later on. 休止状態にある ❏ *...when the long dormant volcano of Mount St. Helens erupted in 1980.* 長い間活動していなかったセント・ヘレンズ山が1980年に噴火した.
→ see **plant**

dor|mi|tory /dɔːrmɪtɔːri/ (dormitories) **1** N-COUNT 可算名詞 A **dormitory** is a building at a college or university where students live. 寮 [AM 米国英語] ❏ *She lived in a college dormitory.* 彼女は大学の寮で暮らしていた. **2** N-COUNT 可算名詞 A **dormitory** is a large bedroom where several people sleep, for example, in a boarding school. 共同寝室 ❏ *...the boys' dormitory.* 男子用の共同寝室.

> A college **dormitory** usually provides both a place to sleep and meals, called **room and board**. Some students choose to live in privately rented accommodation outside the college, which is owned by a **landlord**. A landlord only provides the room(s) and the renter must supply his or her own food.

DOS /dɒs/ N-UNCOUNT 不可算名詞 商標 **DOS** is the part of a computer operating system that controls and manages files and programs stored on disk. **DOS** is an abbreviation for "disk operating system." DOS (ドス) [COMPUTING コンピューティング, TRADEMARK] ❏ *Where do I find the instructions to load DOS programs from Windows 98?* Windows98からDOSプログラムを起動する方法はどこに書かれていますか.

dos|age /doʊsɪdʒ/ (dosages) N-COUNT 可算名詞 A **dosage** is the amount of a medicine or drug that someone takes or should take. 服用量，投薬量 ❏ *He was put on a high dosage of vitamin C.* 彼はビタミンCを大量投与されていた.

dose /doʊs/ (doses, dosing, dosed) **1** N-COUNT 可算名詞 A **dose of** medicine or a drug is a measured amount of it which is intended to be taken at one time. 1回の服用量 ❏ *One dose of penicillin can wipe out the infection.* ペニシリンの1回の投与で感染症は完治します. **2** V-T 他動詞 If you **dose** a person or animal **with** medicine, you give them an amount of it. 投薬する ❏ *The doctor fixed the rib, dosed him heavily with drugs, and said he would probably get better.* 医者はろっ骨を治療してから大量の薬を投与し，きっとよくなるだろうと言った. ● PHRASAL VERB 句動詞 **Dose up** means the same as **dose**. 投薬する ❏ *I dosed him up with Valium.* 彼に精神安定剤のバリウムを投与した.

dos|si|er /dɒsieɪ/ (dossiers) N-COUNT 可算名詞 A **dossier** is a collection of papers containing information on a particular event, or on a person such as a criminal or a spy. 調査書類，一件書類 ❏ *The company is compiling a dossier of evidence to back its allegations.* 会社は申し立てを裏付ける証拠書類をまとめている.

dot /dɒt/ (dots, dotting, dotted) **1** N-COUNT 可算名詞 A **dot** is a very small round mark, for example, one that is used as the top part of the letter "i," as a period, or in the names of websites. 点 ❏ *...a system of painting using small dots of color.* 色のついた小さなドットを利用した描画方式. **2** V-T 他動詞 When things **dot** a place or an area, they are scattered or spread all over it. 点在する ❏ *Small coastal towns dot the landscape.* そこから見渡すと海岸沿いに小さな町が点在しています. **3** → see also **dotted** **4** PHRASE 句 If you arrive somewhere or do something **on the dot**, you arrive there or do it at exactly the time that you were supposed to. 時間どおりに ❏ *They appeared on the dot of 9:50 p.m. as always.* 彼らはいつも通り午後9時50分ぴったりに姿を現した.

dot-com (dot-coms) also **dotcom** N-COUNT 可算名詞 A **dot-com** is a company that does all or most of its business on the Internet. ネット企業 ❏ *In 1999, dot-coms spent more than $1 billion on TV spots.* ネット企業は1999年にテレビCMに10億ドル以上をつぎ込んだ.

dote /doʊt/ (dotes, doting, doted) V-I 自動詞 If you say that someone **dotes on** a person or a thing, you mean that they love or care about them very much and ignore any faults they may have. やたらかわいがる ❏ *He dotes on his nine-year-old son.* 彼は9歳の息子がかわいくてしかたがない.

dot|ing /doʊtɪŋ/ ADJ 形容詞 If you say that someone is, for example, a **doting** mother, husband, or friend, you mean that they show a lot of love for someone. 世話を焼き過ぎる，至れり尽くせりの ❏ *His doting parents bought him his first racing bike at 13.* 息子が13歳のとき，過保護な両親はレース用自転車を初めて買ってやった.

dot|ted /dɒtɪd/ **1** ADJ 形容詞 A **dotted** line is a line which is made of a row of dots. 点線 ◻ *Cut along the dotted line.* 点線に沿って切ります. ● PHRASE 句 If you **sign on the dotted line**, you formally agree to something by signing an official document. 署名欄にサインする, 正式に承認する **2** ADJ 形容詞 If a place or object is **dotted with** things, it has many of those things scattered over its surface. 一が点在して [v-link ADJ 'with' n] ◻ *The maps were dotted with the names of small towns.* 地図には小さな町の名前が点在していた. **3** ADJ 形容詞 If things are **dotted around** a place, they can be found in many different parts of that place. 一に点在している [v-link ADJ prep] ◻ *Many pieces of sculpture are dotted around the house.* 多くの彫刻が家のあちらこちらにある. **4** → see also **dot**

dou|ble /dʌbəl/ (**doubles, doubling, doubled**) **1** ADJ 形容詞 You use **double** to indicate that something includes or is made of two things of the same kind. 2つの部分からなる, 二重の [ADJ n] ◻ *...a pair of double doors into the room from the new entrance hall.* その部屋から新しい玄関ホールにつながる両開きのドア. **2** ADJ 形容詞 You use **double** before a singular noun to refer to two things of the same type that occur together, or that are connected in some way. 連続の [ADJ n] ◻ *...an extremely nasty double murder.* 極めて凶悪な連続殺人. **3** ADJ 形容詞 You use **double** to describe something which is twice the normal size or can hold twice the normal quantity of something. 倍の, 2倍の ◻ *...a double helping of ice cream.* ダブルのアイスクリーム. **4** ADJ 形容詞 A **double** room is a room intended for two people, usually a couple, to stay or live in. ダブル一 [ADJ n] ◻ *...bed and breakfast for $180 for two people in a double room.* 朝食付きのダブルで1部屋180ドル. ● N-COUNT 可算名詞 **Double** is also a noun. ダブル ◻ *The Great Western Hotel is ideal, costing around £90 a night for a double.* グレートウェスタンホテルはダブルで1泊90ポンド前後と申し分ない. **5** ADJ 形容詞 A **double** bed is a bed that is wide enough for two people to sleep in. ダブルベッド [ADJ n] ◻ *One bedroom had a double bed and the other had single beds for the boys.* 1つの寝室にはダブルベッドがあり, もう1つには男の子たちのシングルベッドが置いてあった. **6** ADJ 形容詞 You use **double** to describe a drink that is twice the normal measure. ダブルの [ADJ n] ◻ *He was drinking his double whiskey too fast and scowling.* 彼はしかめ面をしながらダブルのウイスキーを一気に飲んでいた. ● N-COUNT 可算名詞 **Double** is also a noun. ダブル ◻ *"Give me a whiskey," Debilly said to Francis. "Make it a double."* 「ウィスキーをくれ」とドゥビリーがフランシスに言った.「ダブルにしてくれ」 **7** PREDET 前限定詞 If something is **double** the amount or size of another thing, it is twice as large. 2倍の [PREDET 'the' n] ◻ *The offer was to start a new research laboratory at double the salary he was then getting.* その申し出は, 彼が当時稼いでいた倍の給料で新しい研究所を始めないかというものだった. ● PRON 代名詞 **Double** is also a pronoun. 2倍 ◻ *On average doctors write just over seven prescriptions each year per patient; in Germany it is double.* 患者1人当たりに出す年間の処方せんの数は7回あまりで, ドイツではその2倍ある. **8** V-T/V-I 他動詞/自動詞 When something **doubles** or when you **double** it, it becomes twice as great in number, amount, or size. 倍にする [他動詞], 倍になる [自動詞] ◻ *The number of managers must double to 100 within 3 years.* むこう3年間でマネージャーを倍増して100名にしなければならない. **9** V-I 自動詞 If a person or thing **doubles as** someone or something else, they have a second job or purpose as well as their main one. 兼ねる ◻ *Lots of homes in town double as businesses.* 町の多くの家が店をやっている. ● PHRASAL VERB 句動詞 **Double up** means the same as **double**. 兼ねる ◻ *The lids of the casserole dishes are designed to double up as baking dishes.* キャセロール鍋のふたはベーキング皿としても使えるようになっている. **10** N-COUNT 可算名詞 If you refer to someone as a person's **double**, you mean that they look exactly like them. そっくりな人 ◻ *Your mother sees you as her double.* お母さんはあなたが自分にそっくりだと思っている. **11** N-UNCOUNT 不可算名詞 In tennis or badminton, when people play **doubles**, two teams consisting of two players on each team play against each other on the same court. ダブルス ◻ *In the doubles, the pair beat Hungary's Renata Csay and Kornelia Szanda.* ダブルスでは, そのペアがハンガリーのレナータ・セイとコーネリア・ザンダを破った. **12** PHRASE 句 If you do something **on the double**, you do it very quickly or immediately. 急いで, 直ちに [INFORMAL くだけた] ◻ *I need a copy of the police report on the double.* 今すぐ警察の証明書が1通いる. **13** PHRASE 句 If you are **bent double**, the top half of your body is bent downward so that your head is close to your knees. 前かがみになる ◻ *I was bent double in agony.* 私は苦しくて前かがみになっていた. **14** PHRASE 句 If you are **seeing double**, there is something wrong with your eyes, and you can see two images instead of one. ものが二重に見える ◻ *For 35 minutes I was walking around in a daze. I was dizzy, seeing double.* ぼう然として35分間歩き回っていた. ふらついてものがダブって見えた. **15** in **double figures** → see **figure**

▸ **double up** PHRASAL VERB 句動詞 If something **doubles** you **up**, or if you **double up**, you bend your body quickly or violently, for example, because you are laughing a lot or because you are feeling a lot of pain. 腹をかかえる; 身をよじる ◻ *...a savage blow which doubled him up.* 彼を身もだえさせた強烈な一発. ● PHRASAL VERB 句動詞 **Double over** means the same as **double up**. 腹をかか

える; 身をよじる ◻ *Everyone was doubled over in laughter.* みんな腹を抱えて笑った.
→ see **hotel, tennis**

dou|ble bass /dʌbəl beɪs/ (**double basses**) also **double-bass** N-VAR 可変性名詞 A **double bass** is the largest instrument in the violin family. コントラバス
→ see **orchestra, string**

double-check (**double-checks, double-checking, double-checked**) V-T/V-I 他動詞/自動詞 If you **double-check** something, you examine or test it a second time to make sure that it is completely correct or safe. 再確認する ◻ *Check and double-check spelling and punctuation.* スペルや句読点は二度確認しなさい. ◻ *Double-check that the ladder is secure.* はしごが安全かどうかもう一度確認します.

double-click (**double-clicks, double-clicking, double-clicked**) V-T 他動詞 If you **double-click on** an area of a computer screen, you point the cursor at that area and press one of the buttons on the mouse twice quickly in order to make something happen. ダブルクリックする [COMPUTING] [no passive] ◻ *Go to Control Panel and double-click on Sounds for a list of sounds.* コントロール・パネルに行ってサウンドをダブルクリックしサウンド一覧を表示させる.

double-decker (**double-deckers**) N-COUNT 可算名詞 A **double-decker** or a **double-decker bus** is a bus that has two levels, so that passengers can sit upstairs or downstairs. 二階建てバス

double-edged **1** ADJ 形容詞 If you say that a comment is **double-edged**, you mean that it has two meanings, so that you are not sure whether the person who said it is being critical or is giving praise. どちらにもとれる ◻ *Even his praise is double-edged.* 彼のほめ言葉も聞きようでは反対にとれる. **2** ADJ 形容詞 If you say that something is **double-edged**, you mean that its positive effects are balanced by its negative effects, or that its negative effects are greater. 長short相半ばする ◻ *But tourism is double-edged, for although it's boosting the country's economy, the Reef could be damaged.* しかし観光には長short両面があります. 国の経済を活性化する一方で, サンゴ礁を破壊する危険性があるからです. **3** a **double-edged sword** → see **sword**

dou|bly /dʌbli/ **1** ADV 副詞 You use **doubly** to indicate that there are two aspects or features that are having an influence on a particular situation. 二重に ◻ *Employees choosing to move with a relocating company benefit doubly from employer-related housing assistance and lower house prices.* 会社の移転にあわせて引越しすれば, 従業員は会社からの住宅手当と安い住宅価格という二重の恩恵が受けられる. **2** ADV 副詞 You use **doubly** to emphasize that something exists or happens to a greater degree than usual. いっそう [EMPHASIS 強調] [ADV adj/adv] ◻ *In pregnancy a high fiber diet is doubly important.* 妊娠中はふだんにも増して高繊維食が大切だ.

doubt /daʊt/ (**doubts, doubting, doubted**) **1** N-VAR 可変性名詞 If you have **doubt** or **doubts** about something, you feel uncertain about it and do not know whether it is true or possible. If you have **no doubt** about it, you mean that you are certain it is true. 疑い ◻ *This raises doubts about the point of advertising.* このことから広告が適切なのかという疑問が湧いてくる. ◻ *There is little doubt that man has had an impact on the Earth's climate.* 人類が地球の気候に影響を及ぼしてきたことはほぼ間違いない. **2** V-T 他動詞 If you **doubt** whether something is true or possible, you believe that it is probably not true or possible. 一かどうか疑う ◻ *Others doubted whether that would happen.* そうしたことが起こるのか疑問視する者もいた. ◻ *He doubted if he would learn anything new from Marie.* 彼はマリーから新しく学ぶことなどあるのだろうかと思った. **3** V-T 他動詞 If you **doubt** something, you believe that it might not be true or genuine. 疑う ◻ *No one doubted his ability.* 彼の能力を疑う者はなかった. **4** V-T 他動詞 If you **doubt** someone or **doubt** their word, you think that they may not be telling the truth. 一の言うことを信用しない ◻ *No one directly involved with the case doubted him.* その事件に直接関わった者は誰も彼を疑わなかった. **5** PHRASE 句 You say that something is **beyond doubt** or **beyond reasonable doubt** when you are certain that it is true and it cannot be contradicted or disproved. 疑いの余地がなく [EMPHASIS 強調] ◻ *A referendum showed beyond doubt that voters wanted independence.* 国民投票の結果から有権者が独立を求めていることは確かめて明白だった. **6** PHRASE 句 If you are **in doubt** about something, you feel unsure or uncertain about it. 疑って ◻ *He is in no doubt as to what is needed.* 何が必要なのか, 彼にははっきり分かっていた. **7** PHRASE 句 If you say that something is **in doubt** or **open to doubt**, you consider it to be uncertain or unreliable. 疑わしい, 信用できない ◻ *The outcome was still in doubt.* 結果はまだはっきりしない. **8** PHRASE 句 You use **no doubt** to emphasize that something seems certain or very likely to you. きっと [EMPHASIS 強調] ◻ *The contract for this will no doubt be widely advertised.* 間違いなく今回の契約は大きく宣伝されるだろう. **9** PHRASE 句 You use **no doubt** to indicate that you accept the truth of a particular point, but that you do not think it is important or contradicts the rest of what you are saying. 確かに一だが ◻ *No doubt many will regard these as harsh words, but regrettably*

they are true. 確かにこうした言い方をすると手厳しいと感じる向きは多いだろうか，残念ながらこれが事実なのだ． **10** PHRASE 句 If you say that something is true **without doubt** or **without a doubt**, you are emphasizing that it is definitely true. 間違いなく [EMPHASIS 強調] ❑ *This was without doubt the most interesting situation that Amanda had ever found herself in.* 間違いなくこれはアマンダがこれまでに遭遇したうちで最も興味深い状況だった． **11** CONVENTION 慣習表現 You say **I doubt it** as a response to a question or statement about something that you think is untrue or unlikely. そうは思わない ❑ *"Somebody would have seen her." — "I doubt it, not on Monday."* 「彼女を見かけた者がいたかも知れないぞ」「そうは思わないな．月曜だったしな」 **12 the benefit of the doubt** → see **benefit** **13 a shadow of a doubt** → see **shadow**

Thesaurus	doubt また次を参照：

N.	misgivings, reservations, uncertainty **1**
V.	discredit, distrust **2** – **4**

Word Partnership	doubt は次の語句と使われる：

V.	have doubt, express doubt, raise doubt, cast doubt **1**
ADJ.	little doubt, reasonable doubt **1**

doubt|ful /dautfəl/ **1** ADJ 形容詞 If it is **doubtful that** something will happen, it seems unlikely to happen or you are uncertain whether it will happen. ーするか疑わしい ❑ *For a time it seemed doubtful that he would move at all.* 一時は彼が動くかどうかさえ疑わしかった． **2** ADJ 形容詞 If you are **doubtful about** something, you feel unsure or uncertain about it. 疑って ❑ *I was still very doubtful about the chances for success.* 依然として成功する見込みについてかなりの疑問を抱いていた． ● **doubt|ful|ly** ADV 副詞 [ADV after v] 疑わしそうに ❑ *Keeton shook his head doubtfully.* キートンは疑わしそうに首を横に振った． **3** ADJ 形容詞 If you say that something is **of doubtful** quality or value, you mean that it is of low quality or value. 品質が悪い，値打ちのない [DISAPPROVAL 不賛成] ❑ *...selling something that is overpriced or of doubtful quality.* 法外な値をつけて売ったり粗悪品を売ったりすること． **4** ADJ 形容詞 If a sports player is **doubtful for** a match or event, he or she seems unlikely to play, usually because of injury. 出場が危ぶまれる [JOURNALISM ジャーナリズム] ❑ *Forsyth is doubtful for tonight's game with a badly bruised leg.* フォーサイスは足の打撲傷により今晩の試合の出場は難しいだろう．

Do not confuse **doubtful**, **dubious**, and **suspicious**. If you feel **doubtful** about something, you are unsure about it or about whether it will happen or be successful. ❑ *Do you feel insecure and doubtful about your ability?... It was doubtful he would ever see her again.* If you are **dubious** about something, you are not sure whether it is the right thing to do. ❑ *Alison sounded very dubious... The men in charge were a bit dubious about taking him on.* If you describe something as **dubious**, you think it is not completely honest, safe, or reliable. ❑ *...his dubious abilities as a teacher.* If you are **suspicious** of a person, you do not trust them and think they might be involved in something dishonest or illegal. ❑ *I am suspicious of his intentions... Miss Lenaut had grown suspicious.* If you describe something as **suspicious**, it suggests behavior that is dishonest, illegal, or dangerous. ❑ *He listened for any suspicious sounds.*

doubt|less /dautlɪs/ ADV 副詞 If you say that something is **doubtless** the case, you mean that you think it is probably or almost certainly the case. 間違いなく [ADV with cl/group] ❑ *He will doubtless try and persuade his colleagues to change their minds.* きっと彼は同僚たちに対して考え直すよう説得することでしょう．

dough /dou/ (**doughs**) **1** N-MASS 質量名詞 **Dough** is a fairly firm mixture of flour, water, and sometimes also fat and sugar. It can be cooked to make bread or pastry. 生地 ❑ *Roll out the dough into one large circle.* 生地をめん棒で大きく丸く伸ばします． **2** N-UNCOUNT 不可算名詞 You can refer to money as **dough**. 現なま [INFORMAL くだけた] ❑ *He worked hard for his dough.* 彼は金のために必死に働いた．

dough|nut /dounʌt, -nət/ (**doughnuts**) also **donut** N-COUNT 可算名詞 A **doughnut** is a breadlike cake, often in the shape of a ring, made from sweet dough that has been cooked in hot fat. ドーナツ

dour /duər, dauər/ ADJ 形容詞 If you describe someone as **dour**, you mean that they are very serious and unfriendly. 気難しい，むっつりした ❑ *...a dour, taciturn man.* 気難しくて無口な男．

douse /daus/ (**douses, dousing, doused**) also **dowse** **1** V-T 他動詞 If you **douse** a fire, you stop it from burning by pouring a lot of water over it. 水をかけて消火する ❑ *The pumps were started and the crew began to douse the fire with water.* ポンプが作動し始め，消防隊員は水で消火し始めた． **2** V-T 他動詞 If you **douse** someone or something **with** a liquid, you throw a lot of that liquid over them. ぶっかける，浴びせかける ❑ *They hurled abuse at their victim as they*

doused him with gasoline. 彼らは被害者の男性に暴言を吐き，ガソリンを浴びせかけた．

dove (**doves**)

Pronounced /dʌv/ for meanings **1** and **2**, and /douv/ for meaning **3**.

1 と **2** の意味では /dʌv/ と発音され，**3** の意味では /douv/ と発音される．

1 N-COUNT 可算名詞 A **dove** is a bird that looks like a pigeon but is smaller and lighter in color. Doves are often used as a symbol of peace. ハト **2** N-COUNT 可算名詞 In politics, you can refer to people who support the use of peaceful methods to solve difficult situations as **doves**. Compare **hawk**. ハト派 ❑ *A clear split over tactics appears to be emerging between doves and hawks in the party.* 戦術については党内のタカ派とハト派の間で意見がはっきり分かれています． **3 Dove** is sometimes used as the past tense of **dive**.

down
❶ PREPOSITION AND ADVERB USES
❷ ADJECTIVE USES
❸ VERB USES
❹ NOUN USES

❶ down /daun/

Down is often used with verbs of movement, such as "fall" and "pull," and also in phrasal verbs such as "bring down" and "calm down."

Down はしばしば fall や pull のような移動の動詞と共に用いられ，また **bring down** や **calm down** のような句動詞にも用いられる．

⇨ Please look at meaning **12** to see if the expression you are looking for is shown under another headword. **1** PREP 前置詞 To go **down** something such as a slope or a pipe means to go toward the ground or to a lower level. 下に向かって ❑ *We're going down a mountain.* 私たちは山を下っている． ❑ *A man came down the stairs to meet them.* 男が階段から降りてきて彼らを出迎えた． ● ADV 副詞 **Down** is also an adverb. 下へ [ADV after v] ❑ *She went down to the kitchen again.* 彼女はまた台所へ降りてきた． **2** PREP 前置詞 If you are a particular distance **down** something, you are that distance below the top or surface of it. ーから下で [amount PREP n] ❑ *He managed to cling on to a ledge 40 feet down the rock face.* 彼は岩壁の上から40フィートのところの足場にどうにかしがみついた． ● ADV 副詞 **Down** is also an adverb. 下に [amount ADV] ❑ *At the bottom of the pit, some 1,300 feet down, are huge heaps of ore.* 地下約1300フィートの深さにある採掘場の底には，巨大な鉱石の山がいくつもある． **3** PREP 前置詞 If you go or look **down** something such as a road or river, you go or look along it. If you are **down** a road or river, you are somewhere along it. ーに沿って；ーを下って ❑ *They set off at a jog up one street and down another.* 彼らはジョギングを始め，辺りの通りを往復した． **4** ADV 副詞 You use **down** to say that you are looking or facing in a direction that is toward the ground or toward a lower level. 下方に，地面のほうに [ADV after v] ❑ *She was still looking down at her papers.* 相変わらず彼女はうつむいたまま書類を見ていた． **5** ADV 副詞 If you put something **down**, you put it onto a surface. 地面へ，床へ（ーの）表面へ [ADV after v] ❑ *Danny put down his glass.* ダニーはグラスを置いた． **6** ADV 副詞 If an amount of something goes **down**, it decreases. If an amount of something is **down**, it has decreased and is at a lower level than it was. 下がって ❑ *Interest rates came down today.* 利子が今日下がりました． ❑ *Inflation will be down to three percent.* インフレは3%まで下がる見通しだ． **7** PHRASE 句 **Down to** a particular detail means including everything, even that detail. **Down to** a particular person means including everyone, even that person. ーの細部に至るまで，ーまでみんな含めて ❑ *The bedroom was an exact replica of the original, perfect right down to the patterns on the wallpaper and the hairbrushes on the dressing table.* 寝室は，壁紙の模様や化粧台の上のヘアブラシなどの細部に至るまで，実物を忠実に再現したものだった． **8** PHRASE 句 If you are **down to** a certain amount of something, you have only that amount left. ーしか残っていない ❑ *The poor man's down to his last $5.* 気の毒に男は5ドルしか持ってなかった． **9** PHRASE 句 If someone or something is **down for** a particular thing, it has been arranged that they will do that thing, or that thing will happen. ーを準備して，ーを予定して ❑ *Mark had told me that he was down for an interview.* マークは面接の予定が入っていると言っていた． **10** PHRASE 句 If you pay money **down** on something, you pay part of the money you owe for it. 頭金として [mainly AM 主に米国英語] ❑ *He had a simple, conventional deal and paid 20 percent down at settlement.* 彼はごく一般的な契約を結んで，20%の頭金を支払った． **11** → see also **put down** **12** PHRASE 句 If people shout "**down with**" something or someone, they are saying that they dislike them and want to get rid of them. ーを打倒せよ [SPOKEN 口語, DISAPPROVAL 不賛成] ❑ *Demonstrators chanted "down with the rebels."* デモ参加者は「反逆者を打倒せよ」とシュプレ

ヒコールをあげました. **13** up and down → see up

❷ **down** /daʊn/ **1** ADJ 形容詞 If you are feeling **down**, you are feeling unhappy or depressed. 落ち込んだ [INFORMAL くだけた] [v-link ADJ] ❑ *The old man sounded really down.* 老人はとても落ち込んでいる様子だった. **2** ADJ 形容詞 If something is **down on** paper, it has been written on the paper. 記録して, 書き留めて [v-link ADJ] ❑ *That date wasn't down on our news sheet.* その日程は広報には載っていなかった. **3** ADJ 形容詞 If a piece of equipment, especially a computer system, is **down**, it is temporarily not working. Compare up. ダウンして, ダウンした [v-link ADJ] ❑ *The computer's down again.* コンピュータがまたダウンした.

❸ **down** /daʊn/ (downs, downing, downed) **1** V-T 他動詞 If you say that someone **downs** food or a drink, you mean that they eat or drink it. 食べる, 飲む ❑ *We downed bottles of local wine.* 地元のワインを何本も飲み干した. **2** V-T 他動詞 If something or someone is **downed**, they fall to the ground because they have been hurt or damaged in some way. 地面に落ちる [JOURNALISM ジャーナリズム] ❑ *A couple of jet fighters were downed during the five-week rebellion.* 5週間に及ぶ反乱でジェット戦闘機2機が撃墜された.

❹ **down** /daʊn/ **1** N-UNCOUNT 不可算名詞 **Down** consists of the small, soft feathers on young birds. **Down** is used to make bed-covers and pillows. 羽毛, ダウン ❑ *...goose down.* グースダウン. **2** N-UNCOUNT 不可算名詞 **Down** is very fine hair. 綿毛 産毛 ❑ *The whole plant is covered with fine down.* 植物全体が綿毛で覆われている.

down-and-out ADJ 形容詞 If you describe someone as **down-and-out**, you mean that they have no job and nowhere to live, and they have no real hope of improving their situation. 落ちぶれた ❑ *...a short story about a down-and-out advertising copywriter.* 落ちぶれたコピーライターを描いた短編.

Word Link **down** ≈ below, lower : down**fall**, down**hill**, down**stairs**

---

down|fall /daʊnfɔl/ (downfalls) **1** N-COUNT 可算名詞 The **downfall** of a successful or powerful person or institution is their loss of success or power. 転落, 没落, 失脚 ❑ *His lack of experience had led to his downfall.* 経験不足が彼を失脚に追いやったのだった. **2** N-COUNT 可算名詞 The thing that was a person's **downfall** caused them to fail or lose power. 破滅のもと ❑ *Jeremy's honesty had been his downfall.* ジェレミーの正直さがかえってあだとなった.

down|grade /daʊngreɪd/ (downgrades, downgrading, downgraded) **1** V-T 他動詞 If something **is downgraded**, it is given less importance than it used to have or than you think it should have. 格下げされる [usu passive] ❑ *The boy's condition has been downgraded from critical to serious.* 少年は生命の危険を脱したが, 依然として重体である. **2** V-T 他動詞 If someone **is downgraded**, their job or status is changed so that they become less important or receive less money. 降格される ❑ *There was no criticism of her work until after she was downgraded.* 降格されるまでは彼女の仕事に対する批判はなかった.

down|hill /daʊnhɪl/ **1** ADV 副詞 If something or someone is moving **downhill** or is **downhill**, they are moving down a slope or are located toward the bottom of a hill. 坂を下って, ふもとの方へ ❑ *He headed downhill toward the river.* 彼は坂を下って川のほうへ向かった. ● ADJ 形容詞 **Downhill** is also an adjective. 下り坂の [ADJ n] ❑ *...downhill ski runs.* ダウンヒルのスキーコース. **2** ADV 副詞 If you say that something is **going downhill**, you mean that it is becoming worse or less successful. 悪くなる, うまくいかなくなる ❑ *Since I started to work longer hours things have gone steadily downhill.* 勤務時間が延びてからというもの, 状況は悪くなる一方だ. **3** ADJ 形容詞 If you say that a task or situation is **downhill** after a particular stage or time, you mean that it is easy to deal with after that stage or time. 楽な [v-link ADJ] ❑ *Well, I guess it's all downhill from here.* まあ, あとは簡単なんじゃないかな.

down|load /daʊnloʊd/ (downloads, downloading, downloaded) V-T 他動詞 To **download** data means to transfer it to or from a computer along a line such as a telephone line, a radio link, or a computer network. ダウンロードする ❑ *Users can download their material to a desktop PC back in the office.* ユーザーは会社のデスクトップパソコンにデータをダウンロードできる.

down|load|able /daʊnloʊdəbəl/ ADJ 形容詞 If a computer file or program is **downloadable**, it can be downloaded to another computer. ダウンロード可能な [COMPUTING] [usu ADJ n] ❑ *...downloadable computer games.* ダウンロード可能なコンピュータゲーム

down|market /daʊnmɑrkɪt/ also **down-market** ADJ 形容詞 **Downmarket** means the same as **downscale**. 低価格の [BRIT 英国英語]

down pay|ment (down payments) also **downpayment** N-COUNT 可算名詞 If you make a **down payment** on something, you pay only a percentage of the total cost when you buy it. You then finish paying for it later, usually by paying a certain amount every month. 頭金 ❑ *Celeste asked for the money as a down payment*

on an old farmhouse. セレストは古い農家の頭金を支払ってほしいと要求した.

down|pour /daʊnpɔr/ (downpours) N-COUNT 可算名詞 A **downpour** is a sudden and unexpected heavy fall of rain. どしゃ降り, 大雨 ❑ *...sheltering from a sudden downpour of rain.* 突然降り出した雨に雨宿りしながら.

down|right /daʊnraɪt/ ADV 副詞 You use **downright** to emphasize unpleasant or bad qualities or behavior. 全く [EMPHASIS 強調] [ADV adj] ❑ *...ideas that would have been downright dangerous if put into practice.* もし実行に移されていたら無謀としか言いようのない計画. ● **Downright** is also an adjective. 全くの [ADJ n] ❑ *...downright bad manners.* ひどい礼儀知らず.

down|side /daʊnsaɪd/ N-SING 単数名詞 The **downside** of a situation is the aspect of it which is less positive, pleasant, or useful than its other aspects. マイナス面 ❑ *The downside of this approach is a lack of clear leadership.* このやり方の問題点は明確なリーダーシップの欠如である.

down|size /daʊnsaɪz/ (downsizes, downsizing, downsized) V-T/V-I 他動詞/自動詞 To **downsize** something such as a business or industry means to make it smaller. 規模を縮小する [BUSINESS 実業] ❑ *American manufacturing organizations have been downsizing their factories.* アメリカの製造業界は工場の合理化を進めている. ❑ *...today's downsized economy.* 今日の縮小経済. ● **down|siz|ing** N-UNCOUNT 不可算名詞 ❑ *a trend toward downsizing in the personal computer market.* パソコン市場におけるダウンサイジングの傾向.

down|stairs /daʊnstɛərz/ **1** ADV 副詞 If you go **downstairs** in a building, you go down a staircase toward the ground floor. 1階へ [ADV after v] ❑ *Denise went downstairs and made some tea.* デニーズは1階に下りてお茶を入れた. **2** ADV 副詞 If something or someone is **downstairs** in a building, they are on the ground floor or on a lower floor than you. 階下に ❑ *The telephone was downstairs in the entrance hall.* 電話は1階の玄関ホールにあった. **3** ADJ 形容詞 **Downstairs** means situated on the ground floor of a building or on a lower floor than you are. 階下の [ADJ n] ❑ *She repainted the downstairs rooms and closed off the second floor.* 彼女は階下の部屋のペンキを塗り直して, 2階を閉鎖した. **4** N-SING 単数名詞 The **downstairs** of a building is its lower floor or floors. 階下 ❑ *The downstairs of the two little houses had been entirely refashioned.* 2軒の小さな家は1階部分の内装を全てやり変えた.

down|stream /daʊnstrim/ ADV 副詞 Something that is moving **downstream** is moving toward the mouth of a river, from a point further up the river. Something that is **downstream** is further toward the mouth of a river than where you are. 下流に ❑ *We had drifted downstream.* 私たちは下流に流されていた. ● ADJ 形容詞 **Downstream** is also an adjective. 下流の ❑ *Breaking the dam could submerge downstream cities such as Wuhan.* ダムが決壊すると下流にあるウーハンなどの都市が水没する危険がある.

down|swing /daʊnswɪŋ/ (downswings) N-COUNT 可算名詞 A **downswing** is a sudden downward movement in something such as an economy, that had previously been improving. 落ち込み ❑ *Industry may disappear if the manufacturing economy remains on a downswing.* このまま製造業の衰退が続けば, 産業が消滅してしまう恐れがある.

down|time /daʊntaɪm/ **1** N-UNCOUNT 不可算名詞 In industry, **downtime** is the time during which machinery or equipment is not operating. 休止時間 ❑ *On the production line, downtime has been reduced from 55% to 26%.* 生産ラインでは, 休止時間が55%から26%まで短縮された. **2** N-UNCOUNT 不可算名詞 In computing, **downtime** is time when a computer is not working. 停止時間 ❑ *Downtime due to worm removal from networks cost close to $450 million.* ネットワークからワームを除去するためにシステムを停止したことで, ほぼ4億5千万ドルもの被害が出た. **3** N-UNCOUNT 不可算名詞 **Downtime** is time when people are relaxing or not working. 休憩時間 [mainly AM 主に米国英語] ❑ *Downtime in Hollywood can cost a lot of money.* ハリウッドでは休養するにも大金がいる.

down-to-earth ADJ 形容詞 If you say that someone is **down-to-earth**, you approve of the fact that they concern themselves with practical things and actions, rather than with abstract theories. 現実的な [APPROVAL 賛成] ❑ *Gloria is probably the most down-to-earth person I've ever met.* 今まで出会った人の中で, おそらくグロリアが最も現実的なものを考える人はいなかった.

down|town /daʊntaʊn/ ADJ 形容詞 **Downtown** places are in or toward the center of a large town or city, where the stores and places of business are. 中心街の [mainly AM 主に米国英語] [ADJ n] ❑ *...an office in downtown Chicago.* シカゴの中心にあるオフィス. ● ADV 副詞 **Downtown** is also an adverb. 中心街で ❑ *By day he worked downtown for American Standard.* 昼間, 彼はオフィス街にあるアメリカン・スタンダードで勤務した. ● N-UNCOUNT 不可算名詞 **Downtown** is also a noun. 中心街 [oft 'the' N] ❑ *...in a large vacant area of the downtown.* ダウンタウンにある大きな空き地.

down|trend /daʊntrɛnd/ N-SING 単数名詞 A **downtrend** is a

general downward movement in something such as a company's profits or the economy. 下降傾向 □ *The increase slowed to 0.4 percent, possibly indicating the start of a downtrend.* 上昇率は0.4%まで減速し、後退局面に入った可能性をうかがわせる。

down|turn /daʊntɜrn/ (**downturns**) N-COUNT 可算名詞 If there is a **downturn** in the economy or in a company or industry, it becomes worse or less successful than it had been. 下降 □ *They predicted a severe economic downturn.* 彼らは深刻な不況が来ると予測しました。

down|ward /daʊnwərd/

The form **downwards** is also used for the adverb.

downwards 形は副詞にも使われる。

■ ADJ 形容詞 A **downward** movement or look is directed toward a lower place or a lower level. 下向きの [ADJ n] □ *...a firm downward movement of the hands.* 手をしっかりと下に動かすこと。 ■ ADJ 形容詞 If you refer to a **downward** trend, you mean that something is decreasing or that a situation is getting worse. 下降傾向の [ADJ n] □ *The downward trend in home ownership is likely to continue.* 住宅保有率の下降傾向はこのまま続くだろう。 ■ ADV 副詞 If you move or look **downward**, you move or look toward the ground or a lower level. 下向きに □ *Benedict pointed downward again with his stick.* ベネディクトは棒で再び下のほうを指した。 ■ ADV 副詞 If an amount or rate moves **downward**, it decreases. 減少して [ADV after v] □ *Inflation is moving firmly downward.* インフレ率は着実に下降している。 ■ ADV 副詞 If you want to emphasize that a statement applies to everyone in an organization, you can say that it applies from its leader **downward**. 一以下全ての人に [EMPHASIS 強調] ['from' n ADV] □ *...from the president downward.* 大統領以下全ての。

dowse /daʊs/ (**dowses, dowsing, dowsed**) → see **douse**

doze /doʊz/ (**dozes, dozing, dozed**) V-I 自動詞 When you **doze**, you sleep lightly or for a short period, especially during the daytime. うとうとする □ *For a while she dozed fitfully.* しばらくの間彼女はうつらうつらした。

▶ **doze off** PHRASAL VERB 句動詞 If you **doze off**, you fall into a light sleep, especially during the daytime. 居眠りする □ *I closed my eyes for a minute and must have dozed off.* 私はしばらく目を閉じていたが、きっと居眠りしていたのだろう。

→ see **sleep**

doz|en /dʌzⁿn/ (**dozens**)

The plural form is **dozen** after a number, or after a word or expression referring to a number, such as "several" or "a few."

数字、あるいは **a few** や **several** のような数を示す語のあとでは **dozen** が複数形として用いられる。

■ NUM 数詞 If you have **a dozen** things, you have twelve of them. ダース □ *You will be able to take ten dozen bottles free of duty through customs.* 10ダースの持ち出しなら免税になるだろう。 ■ NUM 数詞 You can refer to a group of approximately twelve things or people as **a dozen**. You can refer to a group of approximately six things or people as **half a dozen**. 約12個の、約12人の □ *In half a dozen words, he had explained the bond that linked them.* 彼は互いのきずなについて言葉少なに語った。 ■ QUANT 数量詞 If you refer to **dozens of** things or people, you are emphasizing that there are very many of them. 多くの [EMPHASIS 強調] [QUANT 'of' pl-n] □ *...a storm which destroyed dozens of homes and buildings.* 多くの家屋や建物を破壊した暴風雨。 ● PRON 代名詞 You can also use **dozens** as a pronoun. 多く □ *Just as revealing are Mr. Johnson's portraits, of which there are dozens.* 同様に興味深いのはジョンソン氏の肖像画で、数多くを所蔵している。

Dr. (**Drs.**) **Dr.** is a written abbreviation for **Doctor.** 一博士 □ *...Dr. John Hardy of St. Mary's Medical School.* セントメアリー医学校のジョン・ハーディ博士。

drab /dræb/ (**drabber, drabbest**) ADJ 形容詞 If you describe something as **drab**, you think that it is dull and boring to look at or experience. 単調な、つまらない □ *...his drab little office.* 彼の殺風景で狭いオフィス。 ● **drab|ness** N-UNCOUNT 不可算名詞 単調さ □ *...the dusty drabness of nearby villages.* 近隣の村々の単調で活気のない様子。

dra|co|nian /dreɪkoʊniən, drə-/ ADJ 形容詞 **Draconian** laws or measures are extremely harsh and severe. 過酷な [FORMAL 形式ばった] □ *...indications that there would be no draconian measures to lower U.S. health care costs.* 米国の医療費を削減するために厳格な措置は取られないという指摘

draft /dræft/ (**drafts, drafting, drafted**) ■ N-COUNT 可算名詞 A **draft** is an early version of a letter, book, or speech. 草稿 □ *I rewrote his rough draft, which was published under my name.* 私は、私の名前で出版された彼の草稿を書き直した。 □ *I faxed a first draft of this article to him.* 私は、この記事の原案を彼にファックスした。 ■ N-COUNT 可算名詞 A **draft** is a written order for payment of money by a bank, especially from one bank to another. 支払命令書 □ *Payments must be made in U.S. dollars by a bank draft drawn to the order of the United Nations Postal Administration.* 国連郵政の指図によ

り、支払いは米ドルの銀行為替手形引き落としでなされなければならない。 ■ N-COUNT 可算名詞 A **draft** is a current of air that comes into a place in an undesirable way. 隙間風 [AM 米国英語] □ *Block drafts around doors and windows.* 扉や窓付近からの隙間風を遮りなさい。 ■ V-T 他動詞 When you **draft** a letter, book, or speech, you write the first version of it. 起草する □ *He drafted a letter to the editors.* 彼は編集者への手紙の文案を練った。 ■ V-T 他動詞 If you **are drafted**, you are ordered to serve in the armed forces, usually for a limited period of time. 徴兵する [mainly AM 主に米国英語] [usu passive] □ *During the Second World War, he was drafted into the U.S. Army.* 第二次世界大戦中、彼は米陸軍に徴兵された。 ■ V-T 他動詞 If people **are drafted** to do something, they are asked to do a particular job. 選抜する □ *She hoped that Fox could be drafted to run the organization.* 彼女はフォックスが組織を運営する選ばれることを望んだ。 ■ N-SING 単数名詞 **The draft** is the practice of ordering people to serve in the armed forces, usually for a limited period of time. 徴兵 [mainly AM 主に米国英語] □ *...his effort to avoid the draft.* 徴兵を逃れるための彼の試み

Word Partnership	**draft** は次の語句と使われる:
ADJ.	**final** draft, **rough** draft ■
V.	**revise a** draft, **write a** draft ■
	feel a draft ■
	dodge the draft ■
N.	**bank** draft ■
	draft **a letter**, draft **a speech** ■

drag /dræg/ (**drags, dragging, dragged**) ■ V-T 他動詞 If you **drag** something, you pull it along the ground, often with difficulty. (重いものを) 引っ張る □ *He got up and dragged his chair toward the table.* 彼は立ち上がっていすをテーブルの方へ引きずった。 ■ V-T 他動詞 To **drag** a computer image means to use the mouse to move the position of the image on the screen, or to change its size or shape. ドラッグする [COMPUTING コンピューティング] □ *Use your mouse to drag the pictures to their new size.* マウスドラッグで画像のサイズを変更します。 ■ V-T 他動詞 If someone **drags** you somewhere, they pull you there, or force you to go there by physically threatening you. 引っ張っていく □ *The vigilantes dragged the men out of the vehicles.* 自警団員は車両から男たちを引きずり出した。 ■ V-T 他動詞 If someone **drags** you somewhere you do not want to go, they make you go there. 強引に引っ張っていく □ *When you can drag him away from his work, he can also be a devoted father.* 仕事から引き離すことができれば、彼はよい父親でもある。 ■ V-T 他動詞 If you say that you **drag yourself** somewhere, you are emphasizing that you have to make a very great effort to go there. 骨折って行く [EMPHASIS 強調] □ *I find it really hard to drag myself out and exercise regularly.* 自分を励まし運動するよう仕向けるのは非常に難しいことがわかった。 ■ V-T 他動詞 If you **drag** your foot or your leg behind you, you walk with great difficulty because your foot or leg is injured in some way. (足を) 引きずる □ *He was barely able to drag his poisoned leg behind him.* 彼は、毒にやられた脚をかろうじて引きずった。 ■ V-T 他動詞 If the police **drag** a river or lake, they pull nets or hooks across the bottom of it in order to look for something. (川や湖を) さらう □ *Police are planning to drag the pond later this morning.* 警察は、今朝後ほど、池をさらう計画である。 ■ V-I 自動詞 If a period of time or an event **drags**, it is very boring and seems to last a long time. だらだら長引く [自動詞] □ *The minutes dragged past.* 非常に長く感じられた時間 ■ N-SING 単数名詞 If something is **a drag on** the development or progress of something, it slows it down or makes it more difficult. じゃま物 □ *The satellite acts as a drag on the shuttle.* 衛星はシャトルのじゃまになる。 ■ N-SING 単数名詞 If you say that something is **a drag**, you mean that it is unpleasant or very dull. うんざりする物 [INFORMAL くだけた, DISAPPROVAL 不賛成] □ *As far as shopping for clothes goes, it is a drag.* 衣類の買い物はうんざりする物以外の何物でもない。 ■ N-COUNT 可算名詞 If you take a **drag on** a cigarette or pipe that you are smoking, you take in air through it. たばこの一服 [INFORMAL くだけた] □ *He took a drag on his cigarette, and exhaled the smoke.* 彼はたばこを吸って、煙を吐き出した。 ■ N-UNCOUNT 不可算名詞 **Drag** is the wearing of women's clothes by a male entertainer. 女装 □ *Drag has been with us since the birth of comedy, because it's funny to see a man pretending to be a woman.* 男が女のふりをするのをみるのはおかしいので、女装は喜劇の誕生時から楽しまれてきた。 ● PHRASE 句 If a man is **in drag**, he is wearing women's clothes. 女装して [PHRASE 句] ■ PHRASE 句 If you **drag** your **feet** or **drag** your **heels**, you delay doing something or do it very slowly because you do not want to do it. 故意にぐずぐずする □ *The government was dragging its feet, and this was threatening moves toward peace.* 政府がすぐに腰をあげなかったことは、平和に対する脅威となった。

→ see **flight**

▶ **drag out** ■ PHRASAL VERB 句動詞 If you **drag** something **out**, you make it last for longer than is necessary. 長引かせる □ *...a company that was willing and able to drag out the proceedings for years.* 手続きを何年も長引かせる用意があり、またその能力もある会社

2 PHRASAL VERB 句動詞 If you **drag** something **out of** a person, you persuade them to tell you something that they do not want to tell you. 聞き出す □ The families soon discovered that every piece of information had to be dragged out of the authorities. 家族は、あらゆる情報を当局から聞き出さなければならないことにすぐに気づいた.

drag|on /drǽgən/ (**dragons**) N-COUNT 可算名詞 In stories and legends, a **dragon** is an animal like a big lizard. It has wings and claws, and breathes out fire. 竜
→ see **fantasy**

dragon|fly /drǽgənflaɪ/ (**dragonflies**) N-COUNT 可算名詞 **Dragonflies** are brightly colored insects with long, thin bodies and two sets of wings. Dragonflies are often found near slow-moving water. トンボ

drain /dreɪn/ (**drains, draining, drained**) **1** V-T/V-I 他動詞/自動詞 If you **drain** a liquid from a place or object, you remove the liquid by causing it to flow somewhere else. If a liquid **drains** somewhere, it flows there. 排水する [他動詞] 流出する [自動詞] □ Miners built the tunnel to drain water out of the mines. 鉱山労働者は鉱業場から水を排出するためにトンネルを掘った. □ Now the focus is on draining the water. 現在，焦点は排水に当てられている. **2** V-T/V-I 他動詞/自動詞 If you **drain** a place or object, you dry it by causing water to flow out of it. If a place or object **drains**, water flows out of it until it is dry. 水気をかわかす [他動詞] 水がはける [自動詞] □ The authorities have mobilized vast numbers of people to drain flooded land and build or repair dikes. 当局は，洪水で没した土地を干拓し注防を補修するために，多数の人員を動員した. **3** V-T/V-I 他動詞/自動詞 If you **drain** food or if food **drains**, you remove the liquid that it has been in, especially after it has been cooked or soaked in water. 水気を切る [他動詞] 水がはける [自動詞] □ Drain the pasta well, arrange on four plates and pour over the sauce. パスタの水をよく切って4皿に取り分け，ソースをかける. **4** V-T/V-I 他動詞/自動詞 If the color or the blood **drains** or is **drained from** someone's face, they become very pale. You can also say that someone's face **drains** or is **drained of** color. 血の気が引く，顔面蒼白になる [LITERARY 文語的] □ Harry felt the color drain from his face. ハリーは自分の顔が蒼白になるのを感じた. **5** V-T 他動詞 If something **drains** you, it leaves you feeling physically and emotionally exhausted. (資源や財源を) 消耗させる [他動詞] □ My emotional turmoil had drained me. 私は情緒不安で消耗した. ● **drained** ADJ 形容詞 消耗した □ I began to suffer from headaches, which left me feeling completely drained. 私は頭痛に悩まされ始め，完全に疲れ果ててしまった. ● **drain|ing** ADJ 形容詞 消耗させる □ This work is physically exhausting and emotionally draining. この仕事は心身を極度に疲労させる. **6** V-T 他動詞 If you say that a country's or a company's resources or finances **are drained**, you mean that they are used or spent completely. (資源や財源を) 枯渇させる [他動詞] □ The state's finances have been drained by drought and civil disorder. 国家財政は，干ばつと騒擾で枯渇した. **7** N-COUNT 可算名詞 A **drain** is a pipe that carries water or sewage away from a place, or an opening in a surface that leads to the pipe. 排水管 □ Tony built his own house and laid his own drains. トニーは自分で自分の家を建てて，自分の排水管を設置した. **8** N-SING 単数名詞 If you say that something is **a drain on** an organization's finances or resources, you mean that it costs the organization a large amount of money, and you do not think that it is worth it. 乱費 □ ...an ultramodern printing plant, which has been a big drain on resources. 資源の深刻な枯渇をもたらした最先端の印刷工場 **9** PHRASE 句 If you say that something is **going down the drain**, you mean that it is being destroyed or wasted. 無駄になって [INFORMAL くだけた] □ They were aware that their public image was rapidly going down the drain. 彼らは自分の大衆イメージが急速に失墜しつつあることに気づいていた.
→ see **plumbing**

drain|age /dreɪnɪdʒ/ N-UNCOUNT 不可算名詞 **Drainage** is the system or process by which water or other liquids are drained from a place. 排水 □ Line the pots with pebbles to ensure good drainage. 排水をよくするために，鉢に小石を並べる.
→ see **farm**

dra|ma /dráːmə, drǽmə/ (**dramas**) **1** N-COUNT 可算名詞 A **drama** is a serious play for the theater, television, or radio, or a serious movie. 劇 □ He acted in radio dramas. 彼はラジオ放送劇に出演した. □ The movie is a drama about a woman searching for her children. この映画は，子供を探す女性についてのドラマだ. **2** N-UNCOUNT 不可算名詞 You use **drama** to refer to plays in general or to work that is connected with plays and the theater, such as acting or producing. 演劇 □ He knew nothing of Greek drama. 彼はギリシャ戯曲について何も知識を持たなかった. **3** N-VAR 可変性名詞 You can refer to a real situation which is exciting or distressing as **drama**. 劇的事件 □ There was none of the drama and relief of a hostage release. 人質解放の劇的状況も安堵もなかった.
→ see **genre**

dra|mat|ic /drəmǽtɪk/ **1** ADJ 形容詞 A **dramatic** change or event happens suddenly and is very noticeable and surprising. 劇的な □ A fifth year of drought is expected to have dramatic effects on the California economy. 5年目の干ばつはカリフォルニア経済に劇的な影響

を及ぼすと予想される. ● **dra|mat|i|cal|ly** /drəmǽtɪkli/ ADV 副詞 劇的に □ At speeds above 50 mph, serious injuries dramatically increase. 50 mphを超える速度では，重傷が劇的に増加する. **2** ADJ 形容詞 A **dramatic** action, event, or situation is exciting and impressive. 印象的な □ He witnessed many dramatic escapes as people jumped from as high as the fourth floor. 彼は，人々が4階もの高さから飛び降りる脱出劇を何度も目撃した. ● **dra|mat|i|cal|ly** ADV 副詞 顕著に □ He tipped his head to one side and sighed dramatically. 彼は頭をかしげて，大げさにため息をついた. **3** ADJ 形容詞 [ADJ n] You use **dramatic** to describe things connected with or relating to the theater, drama, or plays. 演劇の □ ...a dramatic arts major in college. 大学の劇芸術専攻

dra|ma|tist /drǽmətɪst/ (**dramatists**) N-COUNT 可算名詞 A **dramatist** is someone who writes plays. 劇作家

dra|ma|tize /drǽmətaɪz/ (**dramatizes, dramatizing, dramatized**) **1** V-T 他動詞 If a book or story **is dramatized**, it is written or presented as a play, movie, or television drama. (本，物語を) 劇化する [usu passive] [他動詞] □ ...an incident later dramatized in the movie "The Right Stuff." 後に『ライトスタッフ』で映画化された事件 ● **dra|ma|ti|za|tion** /drǽmətɪzeɪʃn/ (**dramatizations**) N-COUNT 可算名詞 劇化 □ ...a dramatization of D. H. Lawrence's novel, "Lady Chatterley's Lover." D. H. ローレンスの小説『チャタレイ夫人の恋人』の劇化 **2** V-T 他動詞 If you say that someone **dramatizes** a situation or event, you mean that they try to make it seem more serious, more important, or more exciting than it really is. (事件，イベントを) 脚色する [DISAPPROVAL 不賛成] □ They have a capacity to show off, to dramatize almost every situation. 彼らには，ほとんどの状況を劇的に表現して誇示する傾向がある.

drank /drǽŋk/ **Drank** is the past tense of **drink**. drinkの過去形

drape /dreɪp/ (**drapes, draping, draped**) **1** V-T 他動詞 If you **drape** a piece of cloth somewhere, you place it there so that it hangs down in a casual and graceful way. 無造作に掛ける □ Natasha took the coat and draped it over her shoulders. ナターシャはコートを取り，肩にまとった. **2** V-T 他動詞 If someone or something **is draped in** a piece of cloth, they are loosely covered by it. (衣類などで) おおう □ ...a casket draped in the Virginia flag. バージニア州の旗で飾られた棺 **3** N-COUNT 可算名詞 **Drapes** are long heavy curtains. カーテン [AM 米国英語] □ He pulled the drapes shut, locked the door behind him. 彼はカーテンを引いて閉じ，背後のドアをロックした.

dras|tic /drǽstɪk/ **1** ADJ 形容詞 If you have to take **drastic** action in order to solve a problem, you have to do something extreme to solve it. 思い切った □ Drastic measures are needed to clean up the profession. 同業者連を浄化するには抜本策が必要だ. **2** ADJ 形容詞 A **drastic** change is a very great change. 激烈な □ Foreign food aid has led to a drastic reduction in the numbers of people dying of starvation. 外国による食糧援助により飢餓による死亡者数は大幅に削減された. ● **dras|ti|cal|ly** ADV 副詞 [ADV with v] 激烈に □ As a result, services have been drastically reduced. その結果，サービスは大幅に削減された.

draughts /drǽfts/ N-UNCOUNT 不可算名詞 **Draughts** is the same as **checkers**. チェッカー [BRIT 英国英語]

draw
❶ MAKE A PICTURE
❷ MOVE, PULL, OR TAKE
❸ OTHER USES AND PHRASAL VERBS

❶ draw /drɔː/ (**draws, drawing, drew, drawn**) **1** V-T/V-I 他動詞/自動詞 When you **draw**, or when you **draw** something, you use a pencil or pen to produce a picture, pattern, or diagram. 描く □ She would sit there drawing with the pencil stub. 彼女はそこに座ってちびた鉛筆で絵を描くだろう. ● **draw|ing** N-UNCOUNT 不可算名詞 素描 □ I like dancing, singing, and drawing. 私は踊り，歌それとスケッチが好きだ. **2** to **draw the line** → see **line**
→ see **animation, drawing**

❷ draw /drɔː/ (**draws, drawing, drew, drawn**) **1** V-I 自動詞 If you **draw** somewhere, you move there slowly. 近寄る [WRITTEN 書き言葉] □ She drew away and did not smile. 彼女はあとずさりし，微笑みを見せなかった. **2** V-T 他動詞 If you **draw** something or someone in a particular direction, you move them in that direction, usually by pulling them gently. 引く [WRITTEN 書き言葉] □ He drew his chair nearer the fire. 彼はいすを火の近くに引き寄せた. □ He put his arm around Caroline's shoulders and drew her close to him. 彼はキャロラインの肩に腕を回して引き寄せた. **3** V-T 他動詞 When you **draw** a curtain or blind, you pull it across a window, either to cover or to uncover it. (カーテン，ブラインドを) 引く □ After drawing the curtains, she lit a candle. カーテンを閉めたあと，彼女はろうそくに火をつけた. **4** V-T 他動詞 If someone **draws** a gun, knife, or other weapon, they pull it out of its container and threaten you with it. (ピストル，刀剣などを) 抜く □ He drew his dagger and turned to face his pursuers. 彼は短剣を抜いて，追手を振り返った. **5** V-I 自動詞 When a vehicle **draws** somewhere, it moves there smoothly

Word Web   drawing

The first thing **art** students must learn is how to **draw**. They often carry **sketchbooks** and soft **graphite pencils** around with them. You'll see them sitting and **sketching** everyday objects and **scenes**. Many famous **works of art** began as simple **pen and ink drawings**. For example, Leonardo da Vinci* did several **sketches** before he started painting "The Last Supper"*. Other sketching materials include **charcoal sticks** and **pastels**. They allow greater shading. However, they require fixative to prevent **smudging**.

Leonardo da Vinci (1452-1519): an Italian artist.
"The Last Supper": a famous painting.

and steadily. 近づく [自動詞] □*Claire had seen the taxi drawing away.* クレアはタクシーが静かに走り去るのを見た. ⑥ V-T 他動詞 If you **draw** a deep breath, you breathe in deeply once. （息を）吸い込む □*He paused, drawing a deep breath.* 彼は言葉を切って，息を深く吸い込んだ. ⑦ V-I 自動詞 If you **draw on** a cigarette, you breathe the smoke from it into your mouth or lungs. （たばこを）吸う [自動詞] □*He drew on an American cigarette.* 彼はアメリカ製のたばこを吸った. ⑧ V-T 他動詞 To **draw** something such as water or energy **from** a natural source means to take it from that source. 採取する □*Villagers still have to draw their water from wells.* 村民は今でも井戸から水をくみ上げなければならない. ⑨ V-T 他動詞 If something that hits you or presses part of your body **draws** blood, it cuts your skin so that it bleeds. （血などを）出させる [他動詞] □*Any practice that draws blood could increase the risk of getting the virus.* 出血を伴う治療はすべて，ウイルス感染の危険性を高める可能性がある. ⑩ V-T 他動詞 If you **draw** money out of a bank account, you get it from the account so that you can use it. （お金を）引き出す [他動詞] □*She was drawing out cash from an ATM.* 彼女はATMから現金を引き出していた. ⑪ V-T 他動詞 To **draw** something means to choose it or to be given it, as part of a competition, game, or lottery. （くじなどを）引く □*He put the pile of chips in the center of the table and drew a card.* 彼はテーブルの中央にチップの山を置き，カードを取った. ●N-COUNT 可算名詞 **Draw** is also a noun. 抽選 □*...the final draw for all prize winners takes place on March 17.* ご受賞者すべての最終抽選は3月17日に行われる. ⑫ V-T 他動詞 To **draw** something from a particular thing or place means to take or get it from that thing or place. 得る □*I draw strength from the millions of women who have faced this challenge successfully.* 私は，この難関に立ち向かい成功した何百万もの女性から強さをもらった. ⑬ V-T 他動詞 If something such as a movie or an event **draws** a lot of people, it is so interesting or entertaining that a lot of people go to it. （人を）引きつける [他動詞] □*The game is currently drawing huge crowds.* 試合には現在ものすごい人気がある. ⑭ V-T 他動詞 If someone or something **draws** you, it attracts you very strongly. （人を）引きつける □*In no sense did he draw and enthral her as Alex had done.* 彼が，アクセルほど彼女を引きつけ，魅了することはありえなかった. ⑮ to **draw** lots → see lot

❸ draw /drɔ/ (**draws, drawing, drew, drawn**) ❶ V-T 他動詞 If you **draw** a particular conclusion, you decide that that conclusion is true. （結論を）引き出す □*He draws two conclusions from this.* 彼は，これから2つの結論を引き出した. ❷ V-T 他動詞 If you **draw** a comparison, parallel, or distinction, you compare or contrast two different ideas, systems, or other things. （比較，区別を）設ける，類似点を示す □*...literary critics drawing comparisons between George Sand and George Eliot.* ジョージ・サンドとジョージ・エリオットを比較する文芸評論家 ❸ V-T 他動詞 If you **draw** someone's attention to something, you make them aware of it or make them think about it. （注意を）ひきつける □*He was waving his arms to draw their attention.* 彼は彼らの注意をひきつけるために大きく手を振っていた. ❹ V-T 他動詞 If someone or something **draws** a particular reaction, people react to it in that way. （反応を）引き出す □*Such a policy would inevitably draw fierce resistance from farmers.* そういった方針は必然的に農民の激しい反抗を招くであろう. ❺ V-RECIP 相互動詞 In a game or competition, if one person or team **draws with** another one, or if two people or teams **draw**, they have the same number of points or goals at the end of the game. 引き分けにする [mainly BRIT 主に英国英語; AM usually **tie** 米国英語では通常 **tie**] □*Holland and the Republic of Ireland drew one-one.* オランダとアイルランドは1対1で引き分けた. □*We drew with Ireland in the first game.* 前半戦，我々はアイルランドと引き分けた. ●N-COUNT 可算名詞 **Draw** is also a noun. 引分け ❻ → see also **drawing** ❼ PHRASE 句 When an event or period of time **draws to a close** or **draws to an end**, it finishes. 終わりに近づく □*Another celebration had drawn to its close.* もう1つの式典が終わった. ❽ PHRASE 句 If an event or period of time **is drawing closer** or **is drawing nearer**, it is approaching. 近づく □*Next spring's elections are drawing closer.* 来年春の選挙がだんだん近づいている.

Thesaurus   draw また次を参照：

v.   illustrate, sketch, trace ❶ ⑤
      bring out, pull out, take out ❷ ⑫
      inhale ❷ ⑥ ⑦
      extract, take ❷ ⑧
      conclude, decide, make a decision, settle on ❸ ❶

▶ **draw in** PHRASAL VERB 句動詞 If you **draw** someone **in** or **draw** them **into** something you are involved with, you cause them to become involved with it. 引き込む，ひきずり込む □*It won't be easy for you to draw him in.* 彼を誘い込むのは君にとって容易ではないだろう.

▶ **draw on** PHRASAL VERB 句動詞 If you **draw on** or **draw upon** something such as your skill or experience, you make use of it in order to do something. 利用する □*He drew on his experience as a yachtsman to make a documentary program.* 彼はヨット操縦者としての経験を生かしてドキュメンタリーを制作した.

▶ **draw up** PHRASAL VERB 句動詞 If you **draw up** a document, list, or plan, you prepare it and write it out. 作成する □*They agreed to establish a working party to draw up a formal agreement.* 彼らは作業班を設立して，正式協定を作成することで一致した.

▶ **draw upon** → see **draw on**

draw|back /drɔbæk/ (**drawbacks**) N-COUNT 可算名詞 A **drawback** is an aspect of something or someone that makes them less acceptable than they would otherwise be. 欠点 □*He felt the apartment's only drawback was that it was too small.* 彼は，そのアパートは小さすぎる以外問題ないと思った.

drawer /drɔr/ (**drawers**) N-COUNT 可算名詞 A **drawer** is part of a desk, chest, or other piece of furniture that is shaped like a box and is designed for putting things in. You pull it toward you to open it. 引き出し □*She opened her desk drawer and took out the manual.* 彼女は机の引き出しを開けて，取扱説明書を取り出した.

draw|ing /drɔɪŋ/ (**drawings**) ❶ N-COUNT 可算名詞 A **drawing** is a picture made with a pencil or pen. 線画 □*She did a drawing of me.* 彼女は私の絵を描いた. ❷ → see also **draw** 1
→ see Word Web: **drawing**

draw|ing pin (**drawing pins**) also **drawing-pin** N-COUNT 可算名詞 A **drawing pin** is the same as a **thumbtack**. 画鋲 [BRIT 英国英語]

draw|ing room (**drawing rooms**) N-COUNT 可算名詞 A **drawing room** is a room, especially a large room in a large house, where people sit and relax, or entertain guests. 客間 [mainly BRIT 主に英国英語, OLD-FASHIONED 古風な]

drawl /drɔl/ (**drawls, drawling, drawled**) V-T/V-I 他動詞/自動詞 If someone **drawls**, they speak slowly and not very clearly, with long vowel sounds. のろのろ話す □*"I guess you guys don't mind if I smoke?" he drawled.* 「たばこをすってもいいよな」と彼はのろのろと聞いた. ●N-COUNT 可算名詞 **Drawl** is also a noun. のろのろとした話しぶり □*Jack's southern drawl had become more pronounced as they'd traveled southward.* ジャックの米国南部人特有のゆっくりした話し方は南に進むにつれて顕著になった.

drawn /drɔn/ ❶ **Drawn** is the past participle of **draw**. drawの過去分詞 ❷ ADJ 形容詞 If someone or their face looks **drawn**, their face is thin and they look very tired, ill, worried, or unhappy. やつれた □*She looked drawn and tired when she turned toward me.* 彼女はこちらを見たとき，やつれ疲れて見えた.

drawn-out ADJ 形容詞 You can describe something as **drawn-out** when it lasts or takes longer than you would like it to. 長引いた □*The road to peace will be long and drawn-out.* 平和への道は長くて長期にわたるだろう.

dread /drɛd/ (**dreads, dreading, dreaded**) ❶ V-T 他動詞 If you **dread** something which may happen, you feel very anxious and unhappy about it because you think it will be unpleasant or upsetting. 恐れる □*I'm dreading Christmas this year.* 今年のクリ

スマスは気が進まない. ❑*I dreaded coming back, to be honest.* 正直に いうと、帰るのが怖かったんだ. **2** N-UNCOUNT 不可算名詞 **Dread** is a feeling of great anxiety and fear about something that may happen. 恐怖 ❑*She thought with dread of the cold winters to come.* 彼女は来るべき寒い冬を恐れた. **3** → see also **dreaded** **4** PHRASE 句 If you say that you **dread to think** what might happen, you mean that you are anxious about it because it is likely to be very unpleasant. 恐ろしくて考えられない ❑*I dread to think what will happen in the case of a major emergency.* 大緊急事態には何が起こるのか考えただけで恐ろしい.

dread|ed /drɛdɪd/ **1** ADJ 形容詞 **Dreaded** means terrible and greatly feared. こわい、非常に恐れられる [ADJ n] ❑*No one knew how to treat this dreaded disease.* この恐ろしい病気の治療法を知るものはいなかった. **2** ADJ 形容詞 You can use **the dreaded** to describe something that you, or a particular group of people, find annoying, inconvenient, or undesirable. 非常に恐れられる [INFORMAL くだけた, FEELINGS 感情] [ADJ n] ❑*She's a victim of the dreaded hay fever.* 彼女は案じられた花粉症にかかっている.

dread|ful /drɛdfəl/ **1** ADJ 形容詞 If you say that something is **dreadful**, you mean that it is very bad or unpleasant, or very poor in quality. まったくひどい ❑*They told us the dreadful news.* 彼らは実に不快なニュースを我々に伝えた. ● **dread|fully** ADV 副詞 [ADV with v] ❑*You behaved dreadfully.* 君の振る舞いはまったくひどかった. **2** ADJ 形容詞 **Dreadful** is used to emphasize the degree or extent of something bad. ものすごい [EMPHASIS 強調] [ADJ n] ❑*We've made a dreadful mistake.* 我々は恐ろしい間違いを犯した. ● **dread|fully** ADV 副詞 ものすごく ❑*He looks dreadfully ill.* 彼はひどく気分が悪そうだ.

dream /driːm/ (dreams, dreaming, dreamed or dreamt) **1** N-COUNT 可算名詞 A **dream** is a series of events that you experience only in your mind while you are asleep. 夢 ❑*He had a dream about Claire.* 彼はクララの夢を見た. **2** N-COUNT 可算名詞 You can refer to a situation or event as a **dream** if you often think about it because you would like it to happen. 夢 ❑*He had finally accomplished his dream of becoming a pilot.* 彼はパイロットになる夢をついに達成した. **3** N-COUNT 可算名詞 You can refer to a situation or event that does not seem real as a **dream**, especially if it is very strange or unpleasant. 夢うつつ ❑*When the right woman comes along, this bad dream will be over.* ぴったりの女性が現れたら、この悪夢は終わるだろう. **4** V-T/V-I 他動詞/自動詞 When you **dream**, you experience events in your mind while you are asleep. 夢を見る ❑*Ivor dreamed that he was on a bus.* アイヴァーはバスに乗っている夢を見た. ❑*She dreamed about her baby.* 彼女は自分の赤ちゃんの夢を見た. **5** V-T/V-I 他動詞/自動詞 If you often think about something that you would very much like to happen or have, you can say that you **dream of** it. 夢に見る ❑*As a schoolgirl, she had dreamed of becoming an actress.* 学生のころ、彼女は女優になることを夢見た. ❑*For most of us, a brand new designer kitchen is something we can only dream about.* 我々の多くにとって、真新しいデザイナーキッチンは夢でしかない. ❑*I dream that my son will attend college.* 私は息子が大学に行くことを夢見ている. **6** V-I 自動詞 If you say that you **would not dream of** doing something, you are emphasizing that you would never do it because you think it is wrong or is not possible or suitable for you. 夢にも思わない [EMPHASIS 強調] [with neg] ❑*I wouldn't dream of making fun of you.* 君をばかにしようなんて夢にも思っていない. **7** V-T/V-I 他動詞/自動詞 If you say that you **never dreamed that** something would happen, you are emphasizing that you did not think that it would happen because it seemed very unlikely. 夢にも思わない [EMPHASIS 強調] [with brd-neg] ❑*I never dreamed that I would be able to afford a home here.* この地に家を持てるとは夢にも思わなかった. **8** ADJ 形容詞 You can use **dream** to describe something that you think is ideal or perfect, especially

if it is something that you thought you would never be able to have or experience. 夢の [ADJ n] ❑*...a dream holiday to Jamaica.* ジャマイカへの夢の休日 **9** N-SING 単数名詞 If you describe something as **a particular person's dream**, you think that it would be ideal for that person and that he or she would like it very much. 理想 ❑*Greece is said to be a botanist's dream.* ギリシャは植物学者の夢といわれている. **10** PHRASE 句 If you say that someone does something **like a dream**, you think that they do it very well. If you say that something happens **like a dream**, you mean that it happens successfully without any problems. 不思議に ❑*She cooked like a dream.* 彼女はみごとな料理をした. **11** PHRASE 句 If you describe someone or something as **the person or thing of your dreams**, you mean that you consider them to be ideal or perfect. 夢のようにすばらしい ❑*This could be the man of my dreams.* この人が私の理想の男性かも知れない. **12** PHRASE 句 If you say that you could not imagine a particular thing **in your wildest dreams**, you are emphasizing that you think it is extremely strange or unlikely. 夢にも思わない [EMPHASIS 強調] ❑*"Never in my wildest dreams did I think I'd ever accomplish this," said Toni.* 「これが達成できるなんて夢にも思わなかった」とトニーは言った. **13** PHRASE 句 If you describe something as being **beyond your wildest dreams**, you are emphasizing that it is better than you could have imagined or hoped for. 夢想だにしない [EMPHASIS 強調] ❑*She had already achieved success beyond her wildest dreams.* 彼女は、すでに、信じられないほどのすばらしい成功を収めていた.
→ see Word Web: **dream**

▶ **dream up** PHRASAL VERB 句動詞 If you **dream up** a plan or idea, you work it out or create it in your mind. 考え出す ❑*I dreamed up a plan to solve both problems at once.* 私は両方の問題を同時に解決する計画を思いついた.

dream|er /driːmər/ (dreamers) N-COUNT 可算名詞 If you describe someone as a **dreamer**, you mean that they spend a lot of time thinking about and planning for things that they would like to happen but which are improbable or impractical. 空想家 ❑*Far from being a dreamer, she's a level-headed pragmatist.* 彼女は決して空想家ではなく、冷静な現実主義者だ.

dreamy /driːmi/ (dreamier, dreamiest) **1** ADJ 形容詞 If you say that someone has a **dreamy** expression, you mean that they are not paying attention to things around them and look as if they are thinking about something pleasant. 夢見るような ❑*His face assumed a sort of dreamy expression.* 彼は夢でも見ているような表情をした. **2** ADJ 形容詞 If you describe something as **dreamy**, you mean that you like it and that it seems gentle and soft, like something in a dream. 夢のような [APPROVAL 賛成] ❑*...dreamy shots of beautiful sunsets.* 夢のような美しい夕日の写真

dreary /drɪəri/ (drearier, dreariest) ADJ 形容詞 If you describe something as **dreary**, you mean that it is dull and depressing. 陰鬱な ❑*...a dreary little town in the Midwest.* 中西部の荒涼とした小さな町

dredge /drɛdʒ/ (dredges, dredging, dredged) V-T 他動詞 When people **dredge** a harbor, river, or other area of water, they remove

Dreams appear to happen most frequently during REM **sleep**. During these periods, the eyes move around quickly, the heart rate goes up, and respiration becomes more rapid. Seventy percent to 90 percent of people **awakened** during REM sleep report dreams. Only 10 percent to 15 percent of people **roused** during non-REM sleep remember dreaming. One of the most common dreams reported is of the person flying. Some people look for meaning in their dreams. They try to **interpret** the sights, sounds, and sensations of the dream. Some psychoanalysts say dreams show us the **unconscious** mind. Some later researchers argue that dreams are just random electrical impulses in the brain.

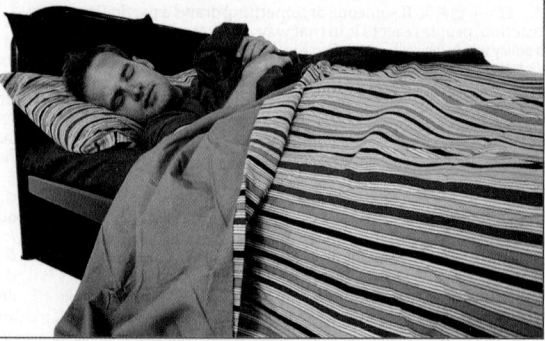

mud and unwanted material from the bottom with a special machine in order to make it deeper or to look for something. (港湾，川などを）浚渫（しゅんせつ）する，[他動詞] □*Police have spent weeks dredging the lake but have not found his body.* 警察は何週間にもわたって湖をしゅんせつしたが，彼の死体は見つからなかった．

▶ **dredge up** PHRASAL VERB 句動詞 If someone **dredges up** a piece of information they learned a long time ago, or if they **dredge up** a distant memory, they manage to remember it. 掘り起こす □*...an American trying to dredge up some French or German learned in high school.* 高校で学んだフランス語とドイツ語を掘り起こそうとしているアメリカ人 **2** PHRASAL VERB 句動詞 If someone **dredges up** a damaging or upsetting fact about your past, they remind you of it or tell other people about it. （過去のことを）思い起こさせる □*She dredges up a minor misdemeanor: "You didn't give me money for the school trip."* 彼女は，「遠足のお金をくれなかった」と些細な事を蒸し返した．

drench /drɛntʃ/ (**drenches, drenching, drenched**) V-T 他動詞 To **drench** something or someone means to make them completely wet. びしょぬれにする □*They turned fire hoses on the people and drenched them.* 彼らは消防ホースを人々に向けてびしょぬれにした． □*...the idea of spending two whole days hanging on to a raft and getting drenched by icy water.* いかだにしがみついて，氷混じりの水に浸されながら丸2日間を過ごすという着想

dress /drɛs/ (**dresses, dressing, dressed**) **1** N-COUNT 可算名詞 A **dress** is a piece of clothing worn by a woman or girl. It covers her body and part of her legs. ドレス □*She was wearing a black dress.* 彼女は黒いドレスを着ていた． **2** N-UNCOUNT 不可算名詞 You can refer to clothes worn by men or women as **dress**. 衣服 □*He wore formal evening dress.* 彼はフォーマルな夜会服を着た． **3** V-T/V-I 他動詞/自動詞 When you **dress** or **dress yourself**, you put on clothes. 服を着る □*He told Sarah to wait while he dressed.* 彼は，身支度をする間待つようサラに告げた． **4** V-T 他動詞 If you **dress** someone, for example, a child, you put clothes on them. 服を着せる □*She bathed her and dressed her in clean clothes.* 彼女は，彼女を風呂に入れ，清潔な衣服を着せた． **5** V-I 自動詞 If someone **dresses** in a particular way, they wear clothes of a particular style or color. 盛装する [自動詞] □*He dresses in a way that lets everyone know he's got authority.* 彼は誰が見ても権威者とわかるよう盛装した． **6** V-I 自動詞 If you **dress for** something, you put on special clothes for it. 正装する [自動詞] □*We don't dress for dinner here.* ここでは晩餐会に特別の服装をしない． **7** V-T 他動詞 When someone **dresses** a wound, they clean it and cover it. 手当てをする □*The poor child never cried or protested while I was dressing her wounds.* 哀れな子供は私が傷の手当てをする間，全く泣いたり叫んだりしなかった． **8** → see also **dressing, dressed**

▶ **dress down** PHRASAL VERB 句動詞 If you **dress down**, you wear clothes that are less formal than usual. 控えめな服装をする □*She dresses down in dark glasses and baggy clothes to avoid hordes of admirers.* 彼女は，多数のファンを避けるため，黒の眼鏡とだぶだぶの洋服という地味な服装をしている．

▶ **dress up 1** PHRASAL VERB 句動詞 If you **dress up** or **dress yourself up**, you put on different clothes, in order to make yourself look more formal than usual or to disguise yourself. 盛装する，扮装する □*You do not need to dress up for dinner.* 夕食に盛装する必要はありません． □*I just love the fun of dressing up in another era's clothing.* 私は別の時代の衣服で着飾るのが楽しくて大好きだ． **2** PHRASAL VERB 句動詞 If you **dress** someone **up**, you give them special clothes to wear, in order to make them look more formal or to disguise them. 盛装させる，扮装させる □*Mother loved to dress me up.* 母は私を着飾らせるのが大好きだった． **3** PHRASAL VERB 句動詞 If you **dress** something **up**, you try to make it seem more attractive, acceptable, or interesting than it really is. よく見せる □*Politicians are happier to dress up their ruthless ambition as a necessary pursuit of the public good.* 政治家は，公共利益の追求に必要として，冷酷な野望を喜んで粉飾する．

Word Partnership   dress は次の語句と使われる：

V.	put on a dress, wear a dress **1**
ADJ.	casual dress, formal dress, traditional dress **2**
ADV.	dress appropriately, dress casually, dress well **5**

dressed /drɛst/ **1** ADJ 形容詞 If you are **dressed**, you are wearing clothes rather than being naked or wearing your nightclothes. If you **get dressed**, you put on your clothes. 服を着た □*He was fully dressed, including shoes.* 彼は靴を含めきちんと正装していた． **2** ADJ 形容詞 If you are **dressed** in a particular way, you are wearing clothes of a particular color or kind. 服装をして [v-link ADJ] □*...a tall thin woman dressed in black.* 黒い服を着た背の高いやせた婦人 **3** → see also **well-dressed 4 dressed to the nines** → see **nine**

dress|er /drɛsər/ (**dressers**) **1** N-COUNT 可算名詞 A **dresser** is a chest of drawers, sometimes with a mirror on the top. ドレッサー [mainly AM 主に米国英語] **2** N-COUNT 可算名詞 You can use **dresser** to refer to the kind of clothes that a person wears. For example, if you say that someone is a **casual dresser**, you mean that they wear casual clothes. 着こなしが（カジュアル）な人 □*Mr.*

Jorgensen was an immaculate dresser. ヨーエンセン氏は着こなしが完璧な人だった．

dress|ing /drɛsɪŋ/ (**dressings**) **1** N-MASS 質量名詞 A salad **dressing** is a mixture of oil, vinegar, and flavorings, which you pour over salad. ドレッシング □*Mix the ingredients for the dressing in a bowl.* ドレッシングの材料をボールで混ぜ合わせます． **2** N-COUNT 可算名詞 A **dressing** is a covering that is put on a wound to protect it while it heals. 包帯 □*Miss Finkelstein will put a dressing on your thumb.* フィンケルスタインさんがあなたの親指に包帯を巻いてくれます． **3** N-MASS 質量名詞 **Dressing** is a mixture of food that is cooked and then put inside a bird such as a turkey before it is eaten. （鳥料理の）詰め物 [AM 米国英語] □*...cornbread dressing for the first Thanksgiving she cooked at home.* 彼女が初めて自宅で作った感謝祭のコーンブレッドドレッシング

dress|ing gown (**dressing gowns**) also **dressing-gown** N-COUNT 可算名詞 A **dressing gown** is a long, loose garment which you wear over your nightclothes when you are not in bed. 化粧着

dress re|hears|al (**dress rehearsals**) **1** N-COUNT 可算名詞 The **dress rehearsal** of a play, opera, or show is the final rehearsal before it is performed, in which the performers wear their costumes and the lights and scenery are all used as they will be in the performance. 本稽古 □*We went to all the dress rehearsals together.* 私達はすべての本稽古に一緒に行った． **2** N-COUNT 可算名詞 You can describe an event as a **dress rehearsal** for a later, more important event when it indicates how the later event will be. 試演 □*Yesterday's NEA event looked like a dress rehearsal for the Democratic convention.* 昨日のNEAイベントは民主党大会の試演のようだった．

drew /dru/ **Drew** is the past tense of **draw**. draw の過去形

drib|ble /drɪbəl/ (**dribbles, dribbling, dribbled**) **1** V-T/V-I 他動詞/自動詞 If a liquid **dribbles** somewhere, or if you **dribble** it, it drops down slowly or flows in a thin stream. したたらせる [他動詞] したたる [自動詞] □*Sweat dribbled down Hart's face.* ハートの顔を汗がぼたぼたたれた． **2** V-T/V-I 他動詞/自動詞 When players **dribble** the ball in a game such as basketball or soccer, they keep kicking or tapping it quickly in order to keep it moving. ドリブルする □*He dribbled the ball toward Ferris.* 彼はフェリスのいる方向にボールをドリブルした． □*He dribbled past four defenders.* 彼はドリブルして防御者4人を通り抜けた． **3** V-I 自動詞 If a person **dribbles**, saliva drops slowly from their mouth. よだれをたらす [自動詞] □*...to protect sheets when the baby dribbles.* 赤ちゃんがよだれをたらした際にシーツを保護する ために

dried /draɪd/ **1** ADJ 形容詞 **Dried** food or milk has had all the water removed from it so that it will last for a long time. 乾燥した [ADJ n] □*...an infusion which may be prepared from the fresh plant or the dried herb.* 新鮮な植物または乾燥ハーブから調合される煎じ薬 **2** → see also **dry**

dri|er /draɪər/ → see **dry, dryer**

drift /drɪft/ (**drifts, drifting, drifted**) **1** V-I 自動詞 When something **drifts** somewhere, it is carried there by the movement of wind or water. 吹き流される，漂流する □*We proceeded to drift on up the river.* 私達はそのまま川の流れに逆らわなかった． **2** V-I 自動詞 If someone or something **drifts into** a situation, they get into that situation in a way that is not planned or controlled. 知らぬ間にずるずると陥る □*We need to offer young people drifting into crime an alternative set of values.* 我々は，ずるずると犯罪に巻き込まれていく若者に別の価値体系を提供する必要がある． **3** V-I 自動詞 If you say that someone **drifts** around, you mean that they travel from place to place without a plan or settled way of life. 放浪する [DISAPPROVAL 不賛成] □*You've been drifting from job to job without any real commitment.* 君は現実に深く関与することなく仕事を転々としてきた． **4** V-I 自動詞 To **drift** somewhere means to move there slowly or gradually. ゆっくり移動する □*As rural factories lay off workers, people drift toward the cities.* 地方の工場による労働者の一時解雇に伴い，人口は次第に都市部に移っていった． **5** V-I 自動詞 If sounds **drift** somewhere, they can be heard but they are not very loud. 漂う □*Cool summer dance sounds are drifting from the stereo indoors.* 涼しい夏の踊りの音楽が室内のステレオから漂っている． **6** V-I 自動詞 If snow **drifts**, it builds up into piles as a result of the movement of the wind. （雪などが）吹き寄せられて積もる □*The snow, except where it drifted, was only calf-deep.* 吹き寄せられて積もった場所を除いて，雪はひざまでの深さしかなかった． **7** N-COUNT 可算名詞 A **drift** is a movement away from somewhere or something, or a movement toward somewhere or something different. 移動 □*...the drift toward the cities.* 都市への移動 **8** N-COUNT 可算名詞 A **drift** is a mass of snow that has built up into a pile as a result of the movement of wind. 吹き溜まり □*A nine-year-old boy was trapped in a snow drift.* 9歳の男の子が雪の吹き溜まりに閉じ込められた． **9** N-SING 単数名詞 The **drift** of an argument or speech is the general point that is being made in it. 主意 □*Grace was beginning to get his drift.* グレースは彼の主意を理解し始めていた．

▶ **drift off** PHRASAL VERB 句動詞 If you **drift off** to sleep, you

gradually **fall asleep**. 知らない間に眠る □*It was only when he finally drifted off to sleep that the headaches eased.* 頭痛は，彼がとうとう知らぬ間に眠りに落ちるまで和らぐことがなかった.

→ see **continent**

drill /drɪl/ (**drills, drilling, drilled**) **1** N-COUNT 可算名詞 A **drill** is a tool or machine that you use for making holes. ドリル □*...a dentist's drill.* 歯科医のドリル **2** N-COUNT 可算名詞 A **drill** is a routine exercise or activity, in which people practice what they should do in dangerous situations. きびしい訓練 □*...a fire drill.* 消防訓練 **3** V-T/V-I 他動詞/自動詞 When you **drill** something or **drill** a hole in something, you make a hole in it using a drill. 穴をあける □*He drilled into the wall of Lili's bedroom.* 彼は，リリーの寝室の壁に穴をあけた. **4** V-I 自動詞 When people **drill for** oil or water, they search for it by drilling deep holes in the ground or in the bottom of the sea. 掘る [自動詞] □*There have been proposals to drill for more oil.* さらに多くの油田を掘る提案がされていた. **5** N-VAR 可変性名詞 A **drill** is repeated training for a group of people, especially soldiers, so that they can do something quickly and efficiently. 教練 □*The Marines carried out landing exercises in a drill that includes 18 ships and 90 aircraft.* 海兵隊員は18隻の船舶と90機の飛行機を含む軍事訓練で着陸の練習を行った.

→ see **oil, tool**

drink /drɪŋk/ (**drinks, drinking, drank, drunk**) **1** V-T/V-I 他動詞/自動詞 When you **drink** a liquid, you take it into your mouth and swallow it. 飲む □*He drank his cup of tea.* 彼はお茶を飲んだ. □*He drank thirstily.* 彼はのどの渇きを癒すかのように飲んだ. **2** V-I 自動詞 To **drink** means to drink alcohol. （酒などアルコール類を）飲む □*By his own admission, he was smoking and drinking too much.* 自分で認めるところでは，彼は吸いすぎ飲みすぎであった. ●**drink|ing** N-UNCOUNT 不可算名詞 飲酒 □*She had left him because of his drinking.* 彼女は彼の飲酒が原因で彼と別れた. **3** N-COUNT 可算名詞 A **drink** is an amount of a liquid which you drink. 一飲み □*I'll get you a drink of water.* 水を一杯持ってきてあげるよ. **4** N-COUNT 可算名詞 A **drink** is an alcoholic drink. 一杯 □*She felt like a drink after a hard day.* 忙しい一日のあと，彼女は一杯やりたかった. **5** N-UNCOUNT 不可算名詞 **Drink** is alcohol, such as beer, wine, or whiskey. 酒類 [mainly BRIT 主に英国英語] □*Too much drink is bad for your health.* 飲み過ぎは健康に悪い.

▶ **drink to** PHRASAL VERB 句動詞 When people **drink to** someone or something, they wish them success, good luck, or good health before having an alcoholic drink. 祝杯を挙げる □*Let's drink to his memory, eh?* 彼の思い出に乾杯しようか.

Thesaurus		*drink* また次を参照:
v.	gulp, sip **1**	
N.	beer, liquor, spirit, wine **4**	

drink-driving N-UNCOUNT 不可算名詞 **Drink-driving** is the same as **drunk driving**. 飲酒運転 [BRIT 英国英語]

drink|er /drɪŋkər/ (**drinkers**) **1** N-COUNT 可算名詞 If someone is a tea **drinker** or a beer **drinker**, for example, they regularly drink tea or beer. 飲む人 □*Sherry drinkers far outnumber wine drinkers or whiskey drinkers.* シェリーを飲む人は，ワインやウイスキーを飲む人よりもはるかに多い. **2** N-COUNT 可算名詞 If you describe someone as a **drinker**, you mean that they drink alcohol, especially in large quantities. 酒飲み □*I'm not a heavy drinker.* 私は大酒飲みではない.

drip /drɪp/ (**drips, dripping, dripped**) **1** V-I 他動詞/自動詞 When liquid **drips** somewhere, or you **drip** it somewhere, it falls in individual small drops. （液が）したたる [自動詞] 滴にしてたらす [他動詞] □*Blood dripped from the corner of his mouth.* 彼の口角から血がポタリポタリと落ちた. □*Amid the trees the sea mist was dripping and moisture formed on Tom's glasses.* 木々に囲まれ，トムの眼鏡には，海霧がしたたり，水滴が凝結した. **2** V-I 自動詞 When something **drips**, drops of liquid fall from it. 滴をたらす □*A faucet in the kitchen was dripping.* 台所の蛇口は漏れている. □*Lou was dripping with perspiration.* ルーはしたたるほど汗をかいていた. **3** V-I 自動詞 If you say that something **is dripping with** a particular thing, you mean that it contains a lot of that thing. こぼれんばかりである [LITERARY 文語的] [usu cont] □*They were dazed by window displays dripping with diamonds and furs.* 彼らはダイヤモンドや毛皮がこぼれんばかりのウィンドウディスプレイに目がくらんだ. **4** N-COUNT 可算名詞 A **drip** is a small individual drop of a liquid. 滴 □*Drips of water rolled down the trousers of his uniform.* 水滴が彼のユニフォームのズボンを転げ落ちた. **5** N-COUNT 可算名詞 A **drip** is a piece of medical equipment by which a liquid is slowly passed through a tube into a patient's blood. 点滴 □*He was put on intravenous drip to treat his dehydration.* 彼は脱水症を治療するために点滴を施された.

drive /draɪv/ (**drives, driving, drove, driven**) **1** V-T/V-I 他動詞/自動詞 When you **drive** somewhere, you operate a car or other vehicle and control its movement and direction. 運転する □*I drove into town and went to a restaurant for dinner.* 私は車で町に入り，レストランで夕食を食べた. □*She never learned to drive.* 彼女は運転を習うことはなかった. □*We drove the car down to Richmond for the weekend.* 私

たちは週末リッチモンドまで車で行った. ●**driv|ing** N-UNCOUNT 不可算名詞 運転 □*...a qualified driving instructor.* 有資格の，自動車教習所の教官 **2** V-T 他動詞 If you **drive** someone somewhere, you take them there in a car or other vehicle. 車で送る □*His daughter Carly drove him to the train station.* 彼の娘カーリーが彼を駅まで車で送った. **3** V-T 他動詞 If something **drives** a machine, it supplies the power that makes it work. 動かす [他動詞] □*The current flows into electric motors that drive the wheels.* 電流が電気モーターに流れ，車輪を動かす. **4** V-T 他動詞 If you **drive** something such as a nail **into** something else, you push it in or hammer it in using a lot of effort. 打ち込む □*I had to use our sledgehammer to drive the pegs into the side of the path.* 道端にくいを打ち込むのには大ハンマーが必要だった. **5** V-I 自動詞 If the wind, rain, or snow **drives** in a particular direction, it moves with great force in that direction. 吹きつける □*Rain drove against the window.* 雨が激しく窓を叩きつけた. ●**driv|ing** ADJ 形容詞 [ADJ n] 猛烈な □*He crashed into a tree in driving rain.* 土砂降りの雨の中，彼は木に衝突した. **6** V-T 他動詞 If you **drive** people or animals somewhere, you make them go to or from that place. 追い立てる □*The last offensive drove thousands of people into Thailand.* 最後の攻撃は何千人もの人々をタイに追い立てた. **7** V-T 他動詞 To **drive** someone **into** a particular state or situation means to force them into that state or situation. 無理にさせる [他動詞] □*The recession and hospital bills drove them into bankruptcy.* 不景気と病院からの請求書が彼らを破産させた. **8** V-T 他動詞 The desire or feeling that **drives** a person to do something, especially something extreme, is the desire or feeling that causes them to do it. 駆り立てる [他動詞] □*More than once, depression drove him to attempt suicide.* 鬱病は何度も彼を自殺未遂に追い込んだ. □*Jealousy drives people to murder.* しっとは人々を殺人に駆り立てる. **9** N-COUNT 可算名詞 A **drive** is a trip in a car or other vehicle. ドライブ □*I thought we might go for a drive on Sunday.* 日曜日には一緒にドライブに行こうかと思ったのだが. **10** N-COUNT 可算名詞 A **drive** is a wide piece of hard ground, or sometimes a private road, that leads from the road to a person's house. 車道 □*The boys followed Eleanor up the drive to the house.* 少年たちは家の車道までエレノアについて来た. **11** N-COUNT 可算名詞 You use **drive** to refer to the mechanical part of a computer which reads the data on disks and tapes, or writes data onto them. ドライブ □*The firm specialized in supplying pieces of equipment, such as terminals, tape drives, or printers.* その会社は，ターミナル，テープドライブやプリンタといった機器の供給を専門としている. **12** → see also **disk drive** **13** N-COUNT 可算名詞 A **drive** is a very strong need or desire in human beings that makes them act in particular ways. 衝動 □*...compelling, dynamic sex drives.* 抑えきれない強い性的欲求 **14** N-UNCOUNT 不可算名詞 If you say that someone has **drive**, you mean they have energy and determination. 意欲 □*John will be best remembered for his drive and enthusiasm.* ジョンはその意欲と情熱で最もよく覚えられるだろう. **15** N-SING 単数名詞 A **drive** is a special effort made by a group of people for a particular purpose. 大がかりな運動 □*The ANC is about to launch a nationwide recruitment drive.* ANCは全国的な採用キャンペーンを開始しようとしている. **16** N-IN-NAMES 名称中の名詞 **Drive** is used in the names of some streets. ドライブ □*...3091 North Beverly Hills Drive, Beverly Hills, CA.* カリフォルニア州，ビバリーヒルズ，ノースビバリーヒルズドライブ3091 **17** → see also **driving**

▶ **drive away** PHRASAL VERB 句動詞 To **drive** people **away** means to make them want to stay away, usually by being unpleasant. 追い払う □*Patrick's rudeness soon drove Monica's friends away.* パトリックが無礼だったためにモニカの友人はやがて遠ざかってしまった.

drive-by ADJ 形容詞 A **drive-by** shooting or a **drive-by** murder involves shooting someone from a moving car. 走行中の自動車内から行う犯罪 [ADJ n] □*He was killed by three shots to the head in a drive-by shooting.* 彼は走行中の車からの射撃を頭部に3か所に受けて殺された.

drive-in (**drive-ins**) N-COUNT 可算名詞 A **drive-in** is a restaurant, movie theater, or other commercial place which is specially designed so that customers can use the services provided while staying in their cars. ドライブイン □*...a small neat town, uncluttered by stores, gas stations, or fast food drive-ins.* 店，ガソリンスタンドやドライブインファストフードレストランによる混乱のない，こぎれいな小さな町

driv|en /drɪvᵊn/ **Driven** is the past participle of **drive**. driveの過去分詞

driv|er /draɪvər/ (**drivers**) **1** N-COUNT 可算名詞 The **driver** of a vehicle is the person who is driving it. 運転者 □*The driver got out of his van.* 運転者はトラックから降りた. **2** N-COUNT 可算名詞 A **driver** is a computer program that controls a device such as a printer. ドライバ [COMPUTING コンピューティング] □*Printer driver software includes standard features such as print layout and fit-to-page printing.* プリンタドライバソフトウェアには，印刷レイアウトや用紙に合わせた印刷といった標準機能が含まれている.

driv|er's li|cense (**driver's licenses**) N-COUNT 可算名詞 A **driver's license** is a card showing that you are qualified to drive because you have passed a driving test. 運転免許証 [AM 米国英語]

drive-through (**drive-throughs**) also **drive-thru** ADJ 形容詞 A **drive-through** store, bank, or restaurant is one where you can be served without leaving your car. ドライブスルーの [ADJ n] □ ...a drive-through burger bar. ドライブスルーのバーガーバー ● N-COUNT 可算名詞 **Drive-through** is also a noun. ドライブスルー □ I got some dinner at a drive-through and headed home. 私はドライブスルーで夕食を買って帰った.

drive-thru (**drive-thrus**) → see **drive-through**

drive|way /dráɪvweɪ/ (**driveways**) N-COUNT 可算名詞 A **driveway** is a piece of hard ground that leads from the road to the front of a house, garage, or other building. 車道 □ I was running down the driveway to the car and I lost my balance. 私は車に乗るためにドライブウェイを走っているときにバランスを崩した.

driv|ing /dráɪvɪŋ/ ■ ADJ 形容詞 The **driving** force or idea behind something that happens or is done is the main thing that has a strong effect on it and makes it happen or be done in a particular way. 推進の [ADJ n] □ Consumer spending was the driving force behind the economic growth in the summer. 個人消費がこの夏の経済成長の推進力だった. ② → see also **drive**
→ see **car**

driv|ing li|cence (**driving licences**) N-COUNT 可算名詞 A **driving licence** is the same as a **driver's license**. 運転免許証 [BRIT 英国英語]

driz|zle /drɪzəl/ (**drizzles, drizzling, drizzled**) ■ N-UNCOUNT 不可算名詞 **Drizzle** is light rain falling in fine drops. 霧雨 [also 'a' N] □ The drizzle had now stopped and the sun was breaking through. 霧雨はもう止んで, 太陽が雲間から現れていた. ② V-I 自動詞 If it is **drizzling**, it is raining very lightly. 霧雨が降る □ Clouds had come down and it was starting to drizzle. 雲が立ち込め, 霧雨が降り始めていた.

drone /dróʊn/ (**drones, droning, droned**) ■ V-I 自動詞 If something **drones**, it makes a low, continuous, dull noise. ブーンとうなる □ Above an invisible plane droned through the night sky. 夜空の上空では, 夜空で目に見えない飛行機がブーンとうなり声を上げていた. ● N-SING 単数名詞 **Drone** is also a noun. ブーンとうなる音 □ I hear the drone of an airplane as it banks across the bay. 飛行機が湾を横切り機体を傾ける際にブーンとうなる音が聞こえる. ② V-I 自動詞 If you say that someone **drones**, you mean that they keep talking about something in a boring way. ものうげに話す [DISAPPROVAL 不賛成] □ Chambers' voice droned, maddening as an insect around his head. 頭の周りを飛ぶ虫のようにだらだらと単調な判事室の声に彼はいらいらさせられた. ● N-SING 単数名詞 **Drone** is also a noun. 単調音 □ The minister's voice was a relentless drone. 大臣は絶え間なく単調な低音で話した. ● PHRASAL VERB 句動詞 **Drone on** means the same as **drone**. 単調にしゃべり続ける □ Aunt Maimie's voice droned on. マイミーおばさんはものうげにしゃべり続けた.

drool /drúːl/ (**drools, drooling, drooled**) ■ V-I 自動詞 To **drool over** someone or something means to look at them with great pleasure, perhaps in an exaggerated or ridiculous way. やたらに喜ぶ [DISAPPROVAL 不賛成] [自動詞] □ Fashion editors drooled over every item. ファッションエディターはそれぞれのアイテムをやたらと喜んだ. ② V-I 自動詞 If a person or animal **drools**, saliva drools slowly from their mouth. よだれをたらす □ My dog Jacques is drooling on my shoulder. 私の犬ジャックは私の肩によだれをたらしている.

droop /drúːp/ (**droops, drooping, drooped**) V-I 自動詞 If something **droops**, it hangs or leans downward with no strength or firmness. うなだれる □ Crook's eyelids drooped and he yawned. クルックは伏し目になり, あくびをした. ● N-SING 単数名詞 **Droop** is also a noun. うなだれること □ ...the droop of his shoulders. うなだれた彼の肩

drop /drɒp/ (**drops, dropping, dropped**) ■ V-T/V-I 他動詞/自動詞 If a level or amount **drops** or if someone or something **drops** it, it quickly becomes less. 低下する □ Temperatures can drop to freezing at night. 夜には温度が氷点下まで下がることもある. □ His blood pressure had dropped severely. 彼の血圧はひどく低下した. ● N-COUNT 可算名詞 **Drop** is also a noun. 降下 □ He was prepared to take a drop in wages. 彼には賃金の下落を受け入れる用意があった. ② V-T 他動詞 If you **drop** something, you accidentally let it fall. 落とす [他動詞] □ I dropped my glasses and broke them. 私は眼鏡を落として壊してしまった. ③ V-I 自動詞 If something **drops onto** something else, it falls onto that thing. If something **drops from** somewhere, it falls from that place. 落ちる [自動詞] □ He felt hot tears dropping onto his fingers. 彼は熱い涙が指に落ちるのを感じた. ④ V-T/V-I 他動詞/自動詞 If you **drop** something somewhere or if it **drops** there, you deliberately let it fall there. 落下させる [他動詞] 落下する [自動詞] □ Drop the noodles into the water. 水に麺を投入する □ ...television footage of bombs dropping on the city. 都市への爆弾落下のテレビ映像 ● **drop|ping** N-UNCOUNT 不可算名詞 [usu N 'of' n] 落下 □ ...the dropping of the first atomic bomb. 最初の原子爆弾の落下 ⑤ V-T/V-I 他動詞/自動詞 If a person or a part of their body **drops** to a lower position, or if they **drop** a part of their body to a lower position, they move to that position, often in a tired and lifeless way. 落とす [他動詞] 下がる [自動詞] □ Nancy dropped into a nearby chair. ナン

シーは近くのいすに崩れ落ちた. □ She let her head drop. 彼女は頭を下げた. ⑥ V-I 自動詞 To **drop** is used in expressions such as to **be about to drop** and to **dance until you drop** to emphasize that you are exhausted and can no longer continue doing something. 倒れる [EMPHASIS 強調] [no cont] [自動詞] □ She looked about to drop. 彼女は倒れそうだった. ⑦ V-T/V-I 他動詞/自動詞 If your voice **drops** or if you **drop** your voice, you speak more quietly. 落とす [他動詞] 下がる [自動詞] □ Her voice will drop to a dismissive whisper. 彼女は声を落とし, 見下すようにささやくだろう. ⑧ V-T 他動詞 If you **drop** someone or something somewhere, you take them somewhere and leave them there, usually in a car or other vehicle. 降ろす [他動詞] □ He dropped me outside the hotel. 彼はホテルの外で私を降ろした. ● PHRASAL VERB 句動詞 **Drop off** means the same as **drop**. 降ろす □ Just drop me off at the airport. 空港で降ろしてくれれば結構です. ⑨ V-T 他動詞 If you **drop** an idea, course of action, or habit, you do not continue with it. やめる □ He was told to drop the idea. 彼はそのアイデアは捨てろと言われた. ● **drop|ping** N-UNCOUNT 不可算名詞 中止 □ This was one of the factors that led to President Suharto's dropping of his previous objections. これはスハルト大統領が以前の異議を捨てるにいたった要因の1つである. ⑩ V-T 他動詞 [usu passive] If someone **is dropped** by a sports team or organization, they are no longer included in that team or employed by that organization. 解雇する □ Alexander has been dropped from his multimillion-dollar-a-year job as spokesman for the company. アレキサンダーはその会社のスポークスマンとしての年収数百万ドルの職から解雇された. ⑪ V-I 自動詞 If you **drop** to a lower position in a sports competition, you move to that position. 落後する [自動詞] □ She has dropped to third in the world ranking. 彼女は世界ランキングで3位まで落ちた. ⑫ N-COUNT 可算名詞 A **drop** of a liquid is a very small amount of it shaped like a little ball. In informal English, you can also use **drop** when you are referring to a very small amount of something such as a drink. しずく, 少量 □ ...a drop of blue ink. 1滴の青インク ⑬ N-COUNT 可算名詞 You use **drop** to talk about vertical distances. For example, a thirty-foot **drop** is a distance of thirty feet between the top of a cliff or wall and the bottom of it. 落下距離 □ There was a sheer drop just outside my window. 私の窓のすぐ外に, 切り立つ急斜面があった. ⑭ N-PLURAL 複数名詞 **Drops** are a kind of medicine which you put drop by drop into your ears, eyes, or nose. 点滴 □ And he had to have these drops in his eyes as well. そして彼は目にも点滴薬を入れなければならなかった.

Do not confuse **drop** and **fall**. Although things can **drop** or **fall** by accident, note that **fall** is not followed by an object, so you cannot say that someone "falls" something. However, you can say that they **drop** something, or that something **drops**. □ Leaves were falling to the ground... He dropped his cigar... Plate after plate dropped from his fingers. You say that a person **drops** when they jump straight down from something, for example, when someone jumps from a plane using a parachute. If someone **falls**, it is usually because of an accident. □ He stumbled and fell. **Drop** and **fall** are also nouns. A **drop** is the height of something when you imagine falling off it. □ Sixteen hundred feet is a considerable drop. A **fall** is what happens when someone has an accident. □ I had been badly bruised by the fall.

---

⑮ PHRASE 句 If you **drop a hint**, you give a hint or say something in a casual way. ヒントを与える, ちょっとほのめかす □ Jerry dropped hints that he and Julie were talking about getting married. ジェリーは彼とジュリーが結婚を考えていることをほのめかした. ⑯ PHRASE 句 If you want someone to **drop the subject**, **drop it**, or **let it drop**, you want them to stop talking about something, often because you are annoyed that they keep talking about it. 話題を打ち切る □ Mary Ann wished he would just drop it. メリー・アンは彼がその話題をやめてくれればいいのにと願った. ⑰ to **drop dead** → see **dead** ⑱ at the drop of a hat → see **hat** ⑲ a drop in the ocean → see **ocean**

▶ **drop by** PHRASAL VERB 句動詞 If you **drop by**, you visit someone informally. ひょっこり立ち寄る □ She and Danny will drop by later. 彼女とダニーは後で顔を出すだろう.

▶ **drop in** PHRASAL VERB 句動詞 If you **drop in on** someone, you visit them informally, usually without having arranged it. 不意に訪れる □ Why not drop in for a chat? 話をしに立ち寄ってよ.

▶ **drop off** ■ → see **drop 8** ② PHRASAL VERB 句動詞 If you **drop off** to sleep, you go to sleep. 眠りに落ちる [INFORMAL くだけた] □ I must have dropped off to sleep. うとうとしてしまったようだ. ③ PHRASAL VERB 句動詞 If the level of something **drops off**, it becomes less. 低下する □ Two years later, earnings from the stocks had dropped off by nearly 50%. 2年後, 株からの収入は50%近く低下した.

▶ **drop out** PHRASAL VERB 句動詞 If someone **drops out of** college or a race, for example, they leave it without finishing what they started. 中途退学する □ He'd dropped out of high school at the age of 16. 彼は16歳のとき高校を中途退学した. → see also **dropout**

D

N.	drop **in sales** 1
	drop **a ball** 2
	drop **a bomb** 4
	drop **of blood, tear** drop, drop **of water** 12
	drop **a hint** 15
ADJ.	**sudden** drop 1
	steep drop 13

drop-down menu (drop-down menus) N-COUNT 可算名詞 On a computer screen, a **drop-down menu** is a list of choices that appears when you give the computer a command. ドロップダウン・メニュー ❏ In the drop-down menu with all your Favorites, right-click on any individual item. ドロップダウン・メニューで表示されたお気に入りのうちどれかひとつを選んで右クリックする.

drop|let /drɒplɪt/ (droplets) N-COUNT 可算名詞 A **droplet** is a very small drop of liquid. 小滴 ❏ Droplets of sweat were welling up on his forehead. 彼の額に汗が玉になって噴き出してきた.

drop|out /drɒpaʊt/ (dropouts) also drop-out   1 N-COUNT 可算名詞 If you describe someone as a **dropout**, you disapprove of the fact that they have rejected the accepted ways of society, for example, by not having a regular job. 脱落者 [DISAPPROVAL 不賛成] ❏ …long-haired, dope-smoking dropouts. 長髪でマリファナを吸っている落ちこぼれ.   2 N-COUNT 可算名詞 A **dropout** is someone who has left school or college before they have finished their studies. 中退者 ❏ …high-school dropouts. 高校中退者.   3 ADJ 形容詞 If you refer to the **dropout** rate, you are referring to the number of people who leave a school or college early, or leave a course or other activity before they have finished it. 中退者の [ADJ n] ❏ The dropout rate among students is currently one in three. 学生の中退率は今のところ3人に1人である.

drought /draʊt/ (droughts) N-VAR 可変性名詞 A **drought** is a long period of time during which no rain falls. 干ばつ ❏ …a country where drought and famines have killed up to two million people during the last eighteen years. 干ばつや凶作による死者がここ18年間で200万人に上った国.
→ see **dam**

drove /droʊv/ **Drove** is the past tense of **drive**. drive の過去形

drown /draʊn/ (drowns, drowning, drowned)   1 V-T/V-I 他動詞/自動詞 When someone **drowns** or **is drowned**, they die because they have gone or been pushed under water and cannot breathe. 溺死 (できし) させる [他動詞], おぼれ死ぬ [自動詞] ❏ A child can drown in only a few inches of water. 子供は深さが数インチしかなくてもおぼれる可能性がある. ❏ Last night a boy was drowned in the river. 昨晩男の子が川で溺死 (できし) する事故がありました.   2 V-I 自動詞 If you say that a person or thing **is drowning** in something, you are emphasizing that they have a very large amount of it, or are completely covered in it. どっぷりつかる [自動詞] ❏ …people who gradually find themselves drowning in debt. 借金にどっぷりはまっていると徐々にわかってきた人々. [EMPHASIS 強調]   3 V-T 他動詞 If something **drowns** a sound, it is so loud that you cannot hear that sound properly. かき消す ❏ Clapping drowned the speaker's words for a moment. 少しの間, 拍手で講演者の話が聞こえなかった. ● PHRASAL VERB 句動詞 **Drown out** means the same as **drown**. かき消す ❏ Their cheers drowned out the protests of demonstrators. 彼らの歓声がデモ隊の抗議の声をかき消しました.   4 PHRASE 句 If you say that someone **is drowning** their **sorrows**, you mean that they are drinking alcohol in order to forget something sad or upsetting that has happened to them. お酒で悲しみを紛らわす ❏ Carly drowned her sorrows in vodka cocktails at a South Beach nightclub. カーリーは悲しみを紛らわそうと, サウスビーチのナイトクラブでウォッカのカクテルを飲みふけっていた.

drowsy /draʊzi/ (drowsier, drowsiest) ADJ 形容詞 If you feel **drowsy**, you feel sleepy and cannot think clearly. 眠い ❏ He felt pleasantly drowsy and had to fight off the urge to sleep. 彼は心地よい眠気を催し, その強い眠気と戦わねばならなかった. ● **drowsi|ness** N-UNCOUNT 不可算名詞 眠気 ❏ Big meals during the day cause

drowsiness. 日中に食べ過ぎると眠くなるものだ.

drug /drʌg/ (drugs, drugging, drugged)   1 N-COUNT 可算名詞 A **drug** is a chemical which is given to people in order to treat or prevent an illness or disease. 薬 ❏ The drug will be useful to hundreds of thousands of infected people. その薬は多数の感染症患者に有効だとされている.   2 N-COUNT 可算名詞 **Drugs** are substances that some people take because of their pleasant effects, but which are usually illegal. 薬物, 麻薬 ❏ His mother was on drugs, on cocaine. 彼女の母親はコカインの薬物常用者である.   3 V-T 他動詞 If you **drug** a person or animal, you give them a chemical substance in order to make them sleepy or unconscious. 薬で眠らせる ❏ She was drugged and robbed. 彼女は薬で眠らされ, 所持品を盗まれた.   4 V-T 他動詞 If food or drink **is drugged**, a chemical substance is added to it in order to make someone sleepy or unconscious when they eat or drink it. 薬を盛る ❏ I wonder now if that drink had been drugged. 今思うと, あの飲み物には薬が盛られていたのではないか.

ADJ.	**generic** drug 1
	dangerous drug, **experimental** drug 1 2
	illegal drug 2
N.	drug **abuse, effect of a** drug 1 2
	drug **dealer**, drug **money**, drug **overdose**, drug **problem**, drug **smuggling**, drug **test**, drug **use** 2

drug ad|dict (drug addicts) N-COUNT 可算名詞 A **drug addict** is someone who is addicted to illegal drugs. 麻薬中毒

drug|gist /drʌgɪst/ (druggists)   1 N-COUNT 可算名詞 A **druggist** is the same as a **pharmacist**. 薬剤師 [AM 米国英語]   2 N-COUNT 可算名詞 A **druggist** or a **druggist's** is the same as a **pharmacy**. 薬屋 [AM 米国英語] [oft 'the' N]

drug|store /drʌgstɔr/ (drugstores) N-COUNT 可算名詞 A **drugstore** is a store where drugs and medicines are sold, and where you can buy cosmetics, some household goods, and also drinks and snacks. ドラッグストア [AM 米国英語]

In American English, the usual way of referring to a store where medicines are sold is a **drugstore**. ❏ She went into a drugstore and bought some aspirin. **Pharmacy** refers specifically to a part of the drugstore where you get prescription medicines. Pharmacies are often located in stores that mainly sell other merchandise, such as supermarkets and discount centers. In Britain, the nearest equivalent of a drugstore is a **chemist's**.

drum /drʌm/ (drums, drumming, drummed)   1 N-COUNT 可算名詞 A **drum** is a musical instrument consisting of a skin stretched tightly over a round frame. You play a drum by beating it with sticks or with your hands. 太鼓 ❏ …a worker who died after collapsing while beating a drum during a demonstration. デモで太鼓をたたいていて気を失い, その後死亡した労働者.   2 N-COUNT 可算名詞 A **drum** is a large cylindrical container which is used to store fuel or other substances. ドラム缶 ❏ …an oil drum. 石油缶.   3 V-T/V-I 他動詞/自動詞 If something **drums** on a surface, or if you **drum** something **on** a surface, it hits it regularly, making a continuous beating sound. (一定のリズムで) たたく ❏ He drummed his fingers on the leather top of his desk. 彼は机の皮の表面を指でトントンとたたいた.
→ see Word Web: **drum**

▶ **drum into** PHRASAL VERB 句動詞 If you **drum** something **into** someone, you keep saying it to them until they understand it or remember it. たたき込む ❏ Standard examples were drummed into students' heads. 標準的な例題は生徒の頭にたたき込まれた.

▶ **drum up** PHRASAL VERB 句動詞 If you **drum up** support or business, you try to get it. 獲得する ❏ It is to be hoped that he is merely drumming up business. 彼は単に事業を起こそうとしているだけだと願いたいものだ.

drum|mer /drʌmər/ (drummers) N-COUNT 可算名詞 A **drummer** is a person who plays a drum or drums in a band or group. ドラマー ❏ He was a drummer in a rock band. 彼はロックバンドのドラマーだった.
→ see **drum**

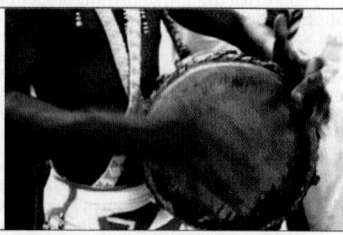

The "talking **drum**" has been common in central Africa for centuries. People use it to communicate between villages up to five miles apart. **Drummers** can **beat** a wide variety of sounds and **rhythms** on these **percussion instruments**. The languages in this part of the world are tonal. This means that different parts of a sentence are spoken at higher or lower pitches. The **tone** and the **beat** of the drum duplicate the sounds of the language very closely. This allows listeners to interpret a **drummer's** playing almost as if it were spoken language.

Word Web dry-cleaning

Dry-cleaning is not actually dry at all. It **cleans clothes** with liquid **chemicals** instead of water. The first dry-cleaning **solvent** was **kerosene**. A Frenchman named Jolly discovered dry-cleaning by accident in 1855. He had spilled kerosene from a lamp on a tablecloth. He noticed the **stains** came out when the kerosene **washed** over them. Soon Jolly opened the first dry-cleaning **service**. Since then, cleaners have also used **gasoline** and other dangerous chemicals. Recently, a company developed a safer dry-cleaning system using **carbon dioxide**. The washer is pressurized which turns the CO_2 gas into a liquid.

drunk /drʌŋk/ (**drunks**) **1** ADJ 形容詞 Someone who is **drunk** has drunk so much alcohol that they cannot speak clearly or behave sensibly. 酔って □*I got drunk and had to be carried home.* 私は酔っ払い、家に担がれて帰るはめになった. **2** N-COUNT 可算名詞 A **drunk** is someone who is drunk or frequently gets drunk. 酔っ払い □*A drunk lay in the alley.* 酔っ払いが路地に寝ていた. **3** **Drunk** is the past participle of **drink**. drinkの過去分詞

drunk driv|ing N-UNCOUNT 不可算名詞 **Drunk driving** is the offense of driving a vehicle after you have drunk more than the amount of alcohol that is legally allowed. 飲酒運転 [mainly AM 主に米国英語] □*He was arrested for drunk driving.* 彼は飲酒運転で捕まった. ● **drunk driv|er** (**drunk drivers**) N-UNCOUNT 不可算名詞 飲酒運転者 □*...a car accident caused by a drunk driver.* 飲酒運転者が起こした自動車事故.

drunk|en /drʌŋkən/ **1** ADJ 形容詞 **Drunken** is used to describe events and situations that involve people who are drunk. 酔った上での [ADJ n] □*The pain roused him from his drunken stupor.* 痛みで彼は泥酔状態から覚めた. **2** ADJ 形容詞 A **drunken** person is drunk or is frequently drunk. 酒に酔った [ADJ n] □*Groups of drunken hooligans smashed windows and threw stones.* 酔ったフーリガンの集団が窓を割り投石を働く事件が起きました. ● **drunk|en|ly** ADV 副詞 [ADV with v] 酔って □*Once Bob stormed drunkenly into her house and smashed some chairs.* ボブは酔って彼女の家に押し入り、いすを数脚壊したことがある. ● **drunk|en|ness** N-UNCOUNT 不可算名詞 めいてい □*He was arrested for drunkenness.* 彼は泥酔で捕まった.

dry /draɪ/ (**drier** or **dryer**, **driest**, **dries**, **drying**, **dried**) **1** ADJ 形容詞 If something is **dry**, there is no water or moisture on it or in it. 乾いた □*Clean the metal with a soft dry cloth.* その金属は乾いた柔らかい布でふいてください. □*Pat it dry with a soft towel.* 柔らかなタオルで軽くたたいて水分を吸い取ってください. ● **dry|ness** N-UNCOUNT 不可算名詞 乾燥 □*...the parched dryness of the air.* カラカラに乾いた空気. **2** ADJ 形容詞 If you say that your skin or hair is **dry**, you mean that it is less oily than, or not as oily as, normal. 乾燥性の □*Nothing looks worse than dry, cracked lips.* パサパサでひび割れた唇が一番顔色を悪く見せる. ● **dry|ness** N-UNCOUNT 不可算名詞 *Dryness of the skin can also be caused by living in centrally heated homes and offices.* 乾燥肌の原因として、セントラルヒーティングの家やオフィスで長時間過ごすことも挙げられます. **3** ADJ 形容詞 If the weather or a period of time is **dry**, there is no rain or there is much less rain than average. 雨の降らない、雨の少ない □*Exceptionally dry weather over the past year had cut agricultural production.* この1年は記録的に降水量が少なく農作物の収穫量が低下しました. **4** ADJ 形容詞 A **dry** place or climate is one that gets very little rainfall. 雨の少ない □*It was one of the driest and dustiest places in Africa.* そこはアフリカで最も雨が少なく、ほこりっぽい土地の一つでした. ● **dry|ness** N-UNCOUNT 不可算名詞 雨が少ないこと □*He was advised to spend time in the warmth and dryness of Italy.* 彼は、暖かく雨の少ないイタリアで過ごすよう助言された. **5** ADJ 形容詞 If a river, lake, or well is **dry**, it is empty of water, usually because of hot weather and lack of rain. 干上がった □*The aquifer which had once fed the wells was pronounced dry.* その帯水層は、かつては井戸の水源であったが、干上がっていることが確認された. **6** ADJ 形容詞 If an oil well is **dry**, it is no longer producing any oil. 枯渇した □*To harvest oil and gas profitably from the North Sea, we must focus on the exploitation of small reserves as the big wells run dry.* 北海の石油やガス採掘で採算を上げるには、大きな井戸は枯渇するので小規模埋蔵箇所の開拓に力をいれなければならない. **7** ADJ 形容詞 If your mouth or throat is **dry**, it has little or no saliva in it, and so feels very unpleasant, perhaps because you are tense or ill. （口やのどが）渇いた □*His mouth was still dry, he would certainly be glad of a drink.* 彼はまだ口が渇くようでしたが、飲み物ならきっと喜ばれますよ. ● **dry|ness** N-UNCOUNT 不可算名詞 渇くこと □*Symptoms included frequent dryness in the mouth.* 何度も口が渇く、などの症状. **8** ADJ 形容詞 If someone has **dry** eyes, there are no tears in their eyes; often used with negatives or in contexts where you are expressing surprise that they are not crying. 涙を流さない □*There were few dry eyes in the house when I finished.* 私が話し終えたとき、ほとんどの聴衆が涙を流していた. **9** ADJ 形容詞 **Dry** humor is very amusing, but in a subtle and clever way. （ユーモアが）さりげなく巧みな [APPROVAL 賛成] □*Though the pressure Fulton is under*

must be considerable, he has retained his dry humor. フルトンは相当なプレッシャーを受けているにちがいないが、彼は平然とユーモアを言い続けている. ● **dry|ness** N-UNCOUNT 不可算名詞 □*It has a wry dryness you won't recognize.* あなたには恐らくわからないでしょうが、そこには皮肉たっぷりのユーモアがかくされているのです. **10** ADJ 形容詞 If you describe something such as a book, play, or activity as **dry**, you mean that it is dull and uninteresting. 無味乾燥な [DISAPPROVAL 不賛成] □*My eyelids were drooping over the dry, academic phrases.* 話があまりに退屈で小難しくて、うつらうつらしていました. **11** ADJ 形容詞 **Dry** sherry or wine does not have a sweet taste. 辛口の □*...a glass of chilled, dry white wine.* 冷えた辛口の白ワイン1杯. **12** V-T/V-I 他動詞/自動詞 When something **dries** or when you **dry** it, it becomes dry. 乾かす [他動詞]、乾く [自動詞] □*I let your hair dry naturally whenever possible.* 可能な限り髪は自然に乾かしてください. **13** V-T 他動詞 When you **dry** the dishes after a meal, you wipe the water off the plates, cups, knives, pans, and other things when they have been washed, using a cloth. （水分などを）ふく □*Mrs. Madrigal picked up a towel and began drying dishes next to her daughter.* マドリガル夫人はタオルを手に取り、娘と並んでお皿をふき始めた. **14** **high and dry** → see **high** **15** **home and dry** → see **home**

▶ **dry out** **1** PHRASAL VERB 句動詞 If something **dries out** or is **dried out**, it loses all the moisture that was in it and becomes hard. 水分がすっかり抜ける □*If the soil is allowed to dry out the tree could die.* もし土がすっかり乾いてしまったら、木は枯れるかもしれません. **2** PHRASAL VERB 句動詞 If someone **dries out** or is **dried out**, they stop drinking alcohol. お酒を断つ [INFORMAL くだけた] □*He checked into Cedars Sinai Hospital to dry out.* 彼はアルコール依存症の治療のためシーダーズ・シナイ病院に入院した.

▶ **dry up** **1** PHRASAL VERB 句動詞 If something **dries up** or if something **dries up**, it loses all its moisture and becomes completely dry and shriveled or hard. カラカラに乾く □*As the day goes on, the pollen dries up and becomes hard.* 日がたつにつれ、花粉は水分をすっかり失って硬くなる. **2** PHRASAL VERB 句動詞 If a river, lake, or well **dries up**, it becomes empty of water, usually because of hot weather and a lack of rain. 干上がる □*Reservoirs are drying up and farmers have begun to leave their land in search of water.* 貯水池が干上がりつつあり、農家は水源を求めて土地を離れ始めました. **3** PHRASAL VERB 句動詞 If a supply of something **dries up**, it stops. なくなる □*The main source of income, tourism, is expected to dry up completely this summer.* 重要な収入源である観光収入がこの夏は完全になくなってしまうと予測されています. **4** PHRASAL VERB 句動詞 If you **dry up** when you are speaking, you stop in the middle of what you were saying, because you cannot think what to say next. 話すことができなくなる □*When he turned around and saw her, his conversation dried up.* 彼が振り返って彼女を見たとき、彼の会話は止まってしまった.

→ see **weather**

dry-clean (**dry-cleans**, **dry-cleaning**, **dry-cleaned**) V-T 他動詞 When things such as clothes **are dry-cleaned**, they are cleaned with a liquid chemical rather than with water. ドライクリーニングする [usu passive] □*Natural-filled duvets must be dry-cleaned by a professional.* 天然羽毛布団のドライクリーニングは専門家に任せるべきです.

→ see Word Web: **dry cleaning**

dry|er /draɪər/ (**dryers**) also **drier** **1** N-COUNT 可算名詞 A **dryer** is a machine for drying things. There are different kinds of dryers, for example, ones designed for drying clothes, crops, or people's hair or hands. ドライヤー、乾燥機 □*...hot air electric hand dryers.* 電気温風ハンドドライヤー. **2** → see also **dry**, **tumble dryer**

dry run (**dry runs**) N-COUNT 可算名詞 If you have a **dry run**, you practice something to make sure that you are ready to do it properly. 予行演習 □*The competition is planned as a dry run for the World Cup finals.* その大会はワールドカップ本大会の予行演習として企画されている.

DTP /di ti pi/ **DTP** is an abbreviation for **desktop publishing**. デスクトップ・パブリッシング（電子編集システム）の略

Word Link du ≈ two: dual, duopoly, duplicate

dual /duəl/ ADJ 形容詞 **Dual** means having two parts, functions, or aspects. 2部分からなる、2重の [ADJ n] □*...his dual role as head of the party and head of state.* 彼の党首と国家元首としての2重責務.

dub /dʌb/ (dubs, dubbing, dubbed) **1** V-T 他動詞 If someone or something **is dubbed** a particular thing, they are given that description or name. 〜と呼ぶ [JOURNALISM ジャーナリズム] ❑ Today's session has been widely dubbed as a "make or break" meeting. 本日の会議は広く「成否を左右する」会議と称されてきました. **2** V-T 他動詞 If a movie or soundtrack in a foreign language **is dubbed**, a new soundtrack is added with actors giving a translation. 吹き替える [usu passive] ❑ It was dubbed into Spanish for Mexican audiences. それはメキシコの視聴者向けにスペイン語に吹き替えられた.

du|bi|ous /dˈubiəs/ **1** ADJ 形容詞 If you describe something as **dubious**, you mean that you do not consider it to be completely honest, safe, or reliable. 疑わしい ❑ This claim seems to us to be rather dubious. この申し立ては我々には多少疑わしく思えます. ● **du|bi|ous|ly** ADV 副詞 疑わしく ❑ Carter was dubiously convicted of shooting three white men in a bar. カーターはバーで3名の白人男性を撃ったかどで、疑わしくも有罪となった. **2** ADJ 形容詞 [v-link ADJ] If you are **dubious about** something, you are not completely sure about it and have not yet made up your mind about it. 半信半疑の ❑ My parents were a bit dubious about it all at first but we soon convinced them. 初め両親は少しためらっていたが、私たちに諭されてすぐに納得した. ● **du|bi|ous|ly** ADV 副詞 半信半疑で ❑ He eyed Coyne dubiously. 彼は半信半疑でコインを見た.

> Do not confuse **dubious**, **doubtful**, and **suspicious**. If you are **dubious** about something, you are not sure whether it is the right thing to do. Alison sounded very dubious…The men in charge were a bit dubious about taking him on. If you describe something as **dubious**, you think it is not completely honest, safe, or reliable. ❑ …his dubious abilities as a teacher. If you feel **doubtful** about something, you are unsure about it or about whether it will happen or be successful. ❑ Do you feel insecure and doubtful about your ability?… It was doubtful he would ever see her again. If you are **suspicious** of a person, you do not trust them and think they might be involved in something dishonest or illegal. ❑ I am suspicious of his intentions… Miss Lenaut had grown suspicious. If you describe something as **suspicious**, it suggests behavior that is dishonest, illegal, or dangerous. ❑ He listened for any suspicious sounds.

duch|ess /dˈʌtʃɪs/ (duchesses) N-COUNT 可算名詞 A **duchess** is a woman who has the same rank as a duke, or who is a duke's wife or widow. 公爵夫人 ❑ …the Duchess of Kent. ケント公夫人.

duck /dʌk/ (ducks, ducking, ducked) **1** N-VAR 可変性名詞 A **duck** is a common water bird with short legs, a short neck, and a large flat beak. カモ ❑ Chickens and ducks scratch around the outbuildings. ニワトリやカモが小屋の周りをひっかき回していた. ● N-UNCOUNT 不可算名詞 **Duck** is the flesh of this bird when it is eaten as food. カモ肉 ❑ …honey roasted duck. ハニーローストしたカモ肉. **2** V-I 自動詞 If you **duck**, you move your head or the top half of your body quickly downward to avoid something that might hit you, to avoid being seen, or to make the expression on your face. 身をかがめる、頭をよける ❑ He ducked in time to save his head from a blow from the poker. 彼はさっと身をかがめ、棒による攻撃からかろうじて頭を守った. **3** V-T 他動詞 If you **duck** something such as a blow, you avoid it by moving your head or body quickly downward. かわす ❑ Hans deftly ducked their blows. ハンスはたくみに彼らの攻撃をかわした. **4** V-T 他動詞 If you **duck** your head, you move your head quickly downward to hide the expression on your face. (顔を) 伏せる ❑ He ducked his head to hide his admiration. 彼は感心したことを知られないように顔を伏せた. **5** V-T 他動詞 You say that someone **ducks** a duty or responsibility when you disapprove of the fact that they avoid it. 逃れる [INFORMAL くだけた、DISAPPROVAL 不賛成] ❑ The defense secretary ducked the question of whether the United States was winning the war. 国防長官は、アメリカは戦争に勝利しつつあるのかという質問から逃れた. **6** PHRASE 句 You say that criticism is **like water off a duck's back** or **water off a duck's back** to emphasize that it is not having any effect on the person being criticized. カエルの面に水 [EMPHASIS 強調] ❑ All the criticism is water off a duck's back to me. どんな批判も私にはカエルの面に水だ. **7** PHRASE 句 If you **take to** something **like a duck to water**, you discover that you are naturally good at it or that you find it very easy to do. すんなりとーになじむ ❑ Some mothers take to breastfeeding like a duck to water, while others find they need some help to get started. 母乳をすんなり授乳できる母親もいれば、最初は助けが必要な人もいる.

▶ **duck out** PHRASAL VERB 句動詞 If you **duck out of** something that you are supposed to do, you avoid doing it. 〜から逃れる [INFORMAL くだけた] ❑ George ducked out of his forced marriage to a cousin. ジョージはむりやりいとこと結婚させられそうになったが逃れた.

duct /dʌkt/ (ducts) N-COUNT 可算名詞 A **duct** is a pipe, tube, or channel which carries a liquid or gas. ダクト ❑ …a big air duct in the ceiling. 天井の大きな空気ダクト.

dud /dʌd/ (duds) ADJ 形容詞 **Dud** means not working properly or not successful. だめな [INFORMAL くだけた] [ADJ n] ❑ He replaced

a dud valve. 彼は不良なバルブを取り替えた. ● N-COUNT 可算名詞 **Dud** is also a noun. だめな物 ❑ The mine was a dud. その地雷は不発だった.

dude /dud/ (dudes) N-COUNT 可算名詞 A **dude** is a man. In very informal situations, **dude** is sometimes used as a greeting or form of address to a man. 男、おい (男性に対する呼びかけ) [AM 米国英語、INFORMAL くだけた] ❑ My doctor is a real cool dude. 私の主治医はとても素敵な男性です.

due /du/ **1** PHRASE 句 If an event is **due to** something, it happens or exists as a direct result of that thing. 〜が原因で ❑ The country's economic problems are largely due to the weakness of the recovery. その国の経済上の問題は主として景気回復力の弱さに起因しています. **2** PHRASE 句 You can say **due to** to introduce the reason for something happening. Some speakers of English believe that it is not correct to use **due to** in this way. 〜のために ❑ Due to the large volume of letters he receives Dave regrets he is unable to answer queries personally. あまりにも多くの手紙が届いたために、デイブは自分で質問に答えられないことを残念に思っている. **3** PHRASE 句 If you say that something will happen or take place **in due course**, you mean that you cannot make it happen any quicker and it will happen when the time is right for it. やがて ❑ In due course the baby was born. やがて赤ちゃんが生まれました. **4** PHRASE 句 You can say "**to give** him his **due**," or "**giving** him his **due**," when you are admitting that there are some good things about someone, even though there are things that you do not like about them. (いやな人に対しても) 認めるべきところは認める ❑ To give Linda her due, she had tried to encourage John in his school work. リンダについて認めるべきは、ジョンの学業を奨励しようとしたことだ. **5** PHRASE 句 You can say "**with due respect**" when you are about to disagree politely with someone. お言葉を返すようですがー [POLITENESS 丁寧さ] ❑ With all due respect I submit to you that you're asking the wrong question. お言葉はごもっともですが、あなたが不適切なことをお尋ねだということを言わせていただきます. **6** ADJ 形容詞 If something is **due** at a particular time, it is expected to happen, be done, or arrive at that time. 〜することになっている ❑ The results are due at the end of the month. その結果は月末に出ることになっている. ❑ Mr. Carter is due in Washington on Monday. カーター氏は、月曜日はワシントンに滞在予定です. **7** ADJ 形容詞 **Due** attention or consideration is the proper, reasonable, or deserved amount of it under the circumstances. しかるべき [ADJ n] ❑ After due consideration it was decided to send him away to live with foster parents. しかるべき検討がなされ、里親と暮らせるように彼を送り出すことが決定された. **8** ADJ 形容詞 Something that is **due**, or that is **due** to someone, is owed to them, either as a debt or because they have a right to it. 〜に支払うべき、〜が受けるべき [v-link ADJ] ❑ I was sent a check and advised that no further pension was due. 小切手と、これが最後の支払年金である旨の通知が送られてきた. **9** ADJ 形容詞 If someone is **due for** something, that thing is planned to happen or be given to them now, or very soon, often after they have been waiting for it for a long time. 〜するはずの [v-link ADJ 'for' n] ❑ Although not due for release until 2001, he was let out of his low-security prison to spend a weekend with his wife. 2001年まで釈放される予定ではなかったが、彼は妻と週末をすごすために警備のゆるやかな刑務所から出所することを許された.

duel /dˈuəl/ (duels) N-COUNT 可算名詞 A **duel** is a formal fight between two people in which they use guns or swords in order to settle a quarrel. 決闘 ❑ He killed a man in one duel and was himself wounded in another. 彼は決闘で相手を殺したこともあるし、自分が負傷したこともある.

duet /dˈuɛt/ (duets) N-COUNT 可算名詞 A **duet** is a piece of music sung or played by two people. デュエット ❑ Tonight she sings a duet with first husband Maurice Gibb. 今夜彼女は最初の夫、モーリス・ギブとデュエットする.

dug /dʌg/ **Dug** is the past tense and past participle of **dig**. dig の過去・過去分詞
→ see **tunnel**

duke /duk/ (dukes) N-COUNT 可算名詞 A **duke** is a man with a very high social rank in the nobility of some countries. 公爵 ❑ …the Queen and the Duke of Edinburgh. 女王とエディンバラ公爵.

dull /dʌl/ (duller, dullest, dulls, dulling, dulled) **1** ADJ 形容詞 If you describe someone or something as **dull**, you mean they are not interesting or exciting. 退屈な [DISAPPROVAL 不賛成] ❑ I felt she found me boring and dull. 彼女は私が退屈で面白くない人間だと思っているようだった. ● **dull|ness** N-UNCOUNT 不可算名詞 退屈なこと ❑ They enjoy anything that breaks the dullness of their routine life. 彼らは退屈な日常生活を打ち破れることなら何だっていいのさ. **2** ADJ 形容詞 Someone or something that is **dull** is not very lively or energetic. 活力のない ❑ The body's natural rhythms mean we all feel dull and sleepy between 1 and 3 pm. 体内時計によって誰でも午後1時から3時付近にだるさを感じます. ● **dul|ly** ADV 副詞 [ADV after v] 不活発に ❑ His giant face had a rough growth of stubble, his eyes looked dully ahead. 彼の大きな顔にはまだらに無精ひげが生え、目はうつろに前を向いていた. ● **dull|ness** N-UNCOUNT 不可算名詞 不活発さ ❑ Did

you notice any unusual depression or dullness of mind? いつもは感じないいゆううつさやだるさを感じましたか。 ③ ADJ 形容詞 A **dull** color or light is not bright. くすんだ □*The stamp was a dark, dull blue color with a heavy black postmark.* 切手は暗くくすんだ青色で濃い消印がついていた。 ● **dul|ly** ADV 副詞 [ADV with v] ぼんやりと □*The street lamps gleamed dully through the night's mist.* 街灯が夜霧の中でぼんやりと光っていた。 ④ ADJ 形容詞 You say the weather is **dull** when it is very cloudy. どんよりと曇った □*It's always dull and raining.* いつもどんよりして雨が降る。 ⑤ ADJ 形容詞 **Dull** sounds are not very clear or loud. はっきりしない □*The coffin closed with a dull thud.* 棺は鈍い音をたてて閉まった。 ● **dul|ly** ADV 副詞 [ADV after v] 鈍く □*He heard his heart thudding dully but more quickly.* 彼は自分の心臓が鈍いけれど、より早く鼓動するのを感じた。 ⑥ ADJ 形容詞 **Dull** feelings are weak and not intense. 鈍い [ADJ n] □*The pain, usually a dull ache, gets worse with exercise.* 普段は鈍い痛みが、運動するにつれどんどん激しくなる。 ⑦ V-T/V-I 他動詞/自動詞 If something **dulls** or if it is **dulled**, it becomes less intense, bright, or lively. 鈍くする [他動詞], 鈍くなる [自動詞] □*Her eyes dulled and she gazed blankly.* 彼女はうつろな目でぼんやりと眺めていた。

Thesaurus **dull** また次を参照：

ADJ. dingy, drab, faded, plain ③

---

duly /djúːli/ ① ADV 副詞 If you say that something **duly** happened or was done, you mean that it was expected to happen or was requested, and it did happen or it was done. しかるべく [ADV before v] □*Westcott appealed to Waite for an apology, which he duly received.* ウェストコットはウェイトに謝罪を求めたが、それは正当な要求だった。 ② ADV 副詞 If something is **duly** done, it is done in the correct way. 正式に [FORMAL 形式ばった] [ADV before v] □*He is a duly elected president of the country and we're going to be giving him all the support we can.* 彼は正式に選任された大統領ですから、私たちは全力で彼をサポートするつもりです。

dumb /dʌm/ (dumber, dumbest, dumbs, dumbing, dumbed) ① ADJ 形容詞 Someone who is **dumb** is completely unable to speak. 口のきけない人 □*...a young deaf and dumb man.* 耳が聞こえず、口もきけない若い男性。 ② ADJ 形容詞 If someone is **dumb** on a particular occasion, they cannot speak because they are angry, shocked, or surprised. あぜんとした [LITERARY 文語的] [v-link ADJ] □*We were all struck dumb for a minute.* 我々はしばらくあぜんとしていた。 ③ ADJ 形容詞 If you call a person **dumb**, you mean that they are stupid or foolish. 愚かな [INFORMAL くだけた, DISAPPROVAL 不賛成] □*The questions were set up to make him look dumb.* 質問は彼女を愚かに見せるよう構成されていた。 ④ ADJ 形容詞 If you say that something is **dumb**, you think that it is silly and annoying. くだらない [AM 米国英語, INFORMAL くだけた, DISAPPROVAL 不賛成] □*I came up with this dumb idea.* 私はこのくだらない考えを思いついた。

→ see **disability**

▶ **dumb down** PHRASAL VERB 句動詞 If you **dumb down** something, you make it easier for people to understand, especially when this spoils it. (内容をやさしくするために) 〜のレベルを下げる □*This sounded like a case for dumbing down the magazine, which no one favored.* この案こそ雑誌のレベルが低下しかねないし、誰も賛成しないよ。

dum|my /dʌ́mi/ (dummies) ① N-COUNT 可算名詞 A **dummy** is the same as a **mannequin**. マネキン ② N-COUNT 可算名詞 You can use **dummy** to refer to things that are not real, but have been made to look or behave as if they are real. にせの □*Dummy patrol cars will be set up beside highways to frighten speeding motorists.* スピード違反を抑制するために、ダミーのパトカーがハイウェイ沿いに配置される予定だ。 ③ N-COUNT 可算名詞 If you call a person a **dummy**, you mean that they are stupid or foolish. ばか [AM 米国英語, INFORMAL くだけた, DISAPPROVAL 不賛成] ④ N-COUNT 可算名詞 A baby's **dummy** is the same as a **pacifier**. おしゃぶり [BRIT 英国英語]

dump /dʌmp/ (dumps, dumping, dumped) ① V-T 他動詞 If

you **dump** something somewhere, you put it or unload it there quickly and carelessly. どさっと下ろす [INFORMAL くだけた] □*We dumped our bags at the nearby Grand Hotel and hurried toward the market.* 私たちは荷物をすぐ近くのグランドホテルに下ろし、マーケットに急いだ。 ② V-T 他動詞 If something **is dumped** somewhere, it is put or left there because it is no longer wanted or needed. 捨てる [INFORMAL くだけた] □*The getaway car was dumped near the freeway.* 逃走車はハイウェイ近くに乗り捨てられた。 ● **dump|ing** N-UNCOUNT 不可算名詞 投棄 □*German law forbids the dumping of hazardous waste on German soil.* ドイツでは国内に有害廃棄物を投棄することは法律で禁じられている。 ③ V-T 他動詞 To **dump** something such as an idea, policy, or practice means to stop supporting or using it. 捨てる [INFORMAL くだけた] □*The party dumped the policy of nationalization in favor of the free market.* 党は自由市場を支持して国有化政策を捨てた。 ④ V-T 他動詞 If a firm or company **dumps** goods, it sells large quantities of them at prices far below their real value, usually in another country, in order to gain a bigger market share or to keep prices high in the home market. ダンピングする [BUSINESS 実業] □*It produces more than it needs, then dumps its surplus onto the world market.* 過剰生産で余剰品の世界市場向けダンピングを生む。 ⑤ V-T 他動詞 If you **dump** someone, you end your relationship with them. (恋人などを) 捨てる [INFORMAL くだけた] □*My heart sank because I thought he was going to dump me for another girl.* 彼が私を捨てて他の女のところに行くと思うと心が沈んだ。 ⑥ V-T 他動詞 To **dump** computer data or memory means to copy it from one storage system onto another, such as from disk to magnetic tape. ダンプする (コンピュータの記憶装置の内容を出力すること) [COMPUTING コンピューティング] □*All the data is then dumped into the main computer.* そうすると全データはメインコンピュータにダンプされる。 ⑦ N-COUNT 可算名詞 A **dump** is a place where garbage and waste material are left, for example, on open ground outside a town. ごみ収集場 □*...companies that bring their trash straight to the dump.* 自社のごみを直接収集場に運ぶ会社。 ⑧ N-COUNT 可算名詞 If you say that a place is a **dump**, you think it is ugly and unpleasant to live in or visit. みすぼらしい場所 [INFORMAL くだけた, DISAPPROVAL 不賛成] □*"What a dump!" Christabel said, standing in the doorway of the youth hostel.* クリスタベルはユースホステルの入り口に立ち「なんてきたない所なの」と言った。 ⑨ N-COUNT 可算名詞 A **dump** is a list of the data that is stored in a computer's memory at a particular time. **Dumps** are often used by computer programmers to find out what is causing a problem with a program. ダンプ (コンピュータの記憶領域の内容の出力) [COMPUTING コンピューティング] □*...print it out and it'll do a screen dump of what's there.* それを印字するとメモリ内容を紙面上に出力してくれますよ.

→ see Word Web: **dump**

Dump|ster /dʌ́mpstər/ (Dumpsters) N-COUNT 可算名詞 商標 A **Dumpster** is a large metal container for holding trash. 大型のごみ容器 [AM 米国英語, TRADEMARK]

dune /djúːn/ (dunes) N-COUNT 可算名詞 A **dune** is a hill of sand near the ocean or in a desert. 砂丘 □*Large dunes make access to the beach difficult in places.* 大きな砂丘があり、所々でビーチへのアクセスが悪くなっている。

→ see **beach**, **desert**

dung /dʌŋ/ N-UNCOUNT 不可算名詞 **Dung** is feces from animals, especially from large animals such as cattle and horses. ふん □*Workers at Sydney's harborside Taronga zoo are refusing to collect animal dung in a protest over wages.* シドニー湾地区、タロンガ動物公園の従業員が、賃金を不服として動物のふんの回収を拒否しています。

dun|ga|rees /dʌ̀ŋgəríːz/ ① N-PLURAL 複数名詞 **Dungarees** are the same as **jeans**. デニムパンツ [AM 米国英語] [also 'a pair of' N] ② N-PLURAL 複数名詞 **Dungarees** are a one-piece garment consisting of pants, a piece of cloth which covers your chest, and straps which go over your shoulders. オーバーオール [BRIT 英国英語] [also 'a pair of' N] [AM **overalls** 米国英語 **overalls**]

dun|geon /dʌ́ndʒən/ (dungeons) N-COUNT 可算名詞 A **dungeon** is a dark underground prison in a castle. 地下牢 (ちかろう)

Word Web **dump**

Most communities used to dispose of **solid waste** in **dumps**. However, more **environmentally friendly** methods are common today. There are alternatives to dumping **refuse** in a **landfill**. **Reduction** means creating less waste. For example, using washable napkins instead of paper napkins. Reuse involves finding a second use for something without processing it. For instance, giving old clothing to a charity. **Recycling** and **composting** involve finding a new use for something by processing it—using food scraps to fertilize a garden. **Incineration** involves burning solid waste and using the heat for another useful purpose.

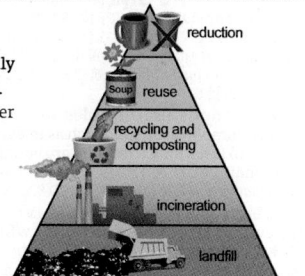

reduction
reuse
recycling and composting
incineration
landfill

dun|no /dʌnoʊ/ **Dunno** is sometimes used in written English to represent an informal way of saying "don't know." don't know の非公式な表記方法 ❑ "How on earth did she get it?" — "I dunno." 「いったい彼女はどうやってそれを手に入れたんだ?」「知らないね」

duo /djuːoʊ/ (**duos**) **1** N-COUNT 可算名詞 A **duo** is two musicians, singers, or other performers who perform together as a pair. デュオ ❑ ...a famous dancing and singing duo. 歌と踊りの有名なデュオ. **2** N-COUNT 可算名詞 You can refer to two people together as a **duo**, especially when they have something in common. 2人組 [MAINLY JOURNALISM 主にジャーナリズム] ❑ The Giants are led by the scoring duo of Adam Courchaine and Gilbert Brule. ジャイアンツは得点の2枚看板, アダム・クーチェインとギルバート・ブリュレの活躍でリードしています.

| **Word Link** | duo ≈ two : dual, duopoly, duplicate |

duo|poly /djuːpəli/ (**duopolies**) **1** N-VAR 可変性名詞 If two companies or people have a **duopoly** on something such as an industry, they share complete control over it and it is impossible for others to become involved in it. 〜への複占 [BUSINESS 実業] ❑ ...they are no longer part of a duopoly on overseas routes. 彼らはもはや海外ルートの複占を担っていない. **2** N-COUNT 可算名詞 A **duopoly** is a group of two companies which are the only ones which provide a particular product or service, and which therefore have complete control over an industry. 複占 [BUSINESS 実業] ❑ Their smaller rival is battling to end their duopoly. ライバル企業が彼らの複占を崩そうと努力している.

dupe /djuːp/ (**dupes, duping, duped**) **1** V-T 他動詞 If a person **dupes** you, they trick you into doing something or into believing something which is not true. だます ❑ ...a plot to dupe stamp collectors into buying fake rarities. 切手収集家をだまし, 偽の珍品を買わせようとする計画. **2** N-COUNT 可算名詞 A **dupe** is someone who is tricked by someone else. だまされた人 ❑ He was accused of being a dupe of the communists. 彼は共産主義者の手先だと非難された.

du|pli|cate (**duplicates, duplicating, duplicated**)

The verb is pronounced /djuːplɪkeɪt/. The noun and adjective are pronounced /djuːplɪkɪt/.

動詞は /djuːplɪkeɪt/ と発音される. 名詞と形容詞は /djuːplɪkɪt/ と発音される.

1 V-T 他動詞 If you **duplicate** something that has already been done, you repeat or copy it. 再現する ❑ His task will be to duplicate his success overseas here at home. 彼の役目は, 海外での成功を国内で再現することだろう. ● N-COUNT 可算名詞 **Duplicate** is also a noun. 再現 ❑ The tight race is almost a duplicate of the elections in Georgia and South Dakota last month that pitted a Republican challenger against a Democratic incumbent. 選挙戦は, 先月行われたジョージア州とサウスダコタ州の民主党現職と共和党候補との接戦を再現するかのようです. **2** V-T 他動詞 To **duplicate** something which has been written, drawn, or recorded onto tape means to make exact copies of it. 複製する ❑ ...a business which duplicates video tapes for the movie makers. 映画制作会社向けにビデオテープを複製する企業. ● N-COUNT 可算名詞 **Duplicate** is also a noun. [also 'in' n] ❑ I'm on my way to Switzerland, but I've lost my card. I've got to get a duplicate. スイスへ向かっているところで, カードを紛失してしまいました. 再発行してもらわないといけません. **3** ADJ 形容詞 **Duplicate** is used to describe things that have been made as an exact copy of other things, usually in order to serve the same purpose. 複製の [ADJ n] ❑ He let himself in with a duplicate key. 彼は合鍵で中に入った.

du|pli|ca|tion /djuːplɪkeɪʃ°n/ N-UNCOUNT 不可算名詞 If you say that there has been **duplication** of something, you mean that someone has done a task unnecessarily because it has already been done before. 重複 ❑ There could be a serious loss of efficiency through unnecessary duplication of resources. 不必要に人手が重なると効率がひどく低下しかねない.

du|rable /djʊərəb°l/ ADJ 形容詞 Something that is **durable** is strong and lasts a long time without breaking or becoming weaker. 耐久性のある ❑ Fine bone china is eminently practical, since it is strong and durable. 上質な骨灰磁器は丈夫で耐久性があるため, ファイン・ボーン・チャイナはとても実用的です. ● **du|rabil|ity** /djʊərəbɪlɪti/ N-UNCOUNT 不可算名詞 耐久性 ❑ Airlines recommend hard-sided cases for durability. 航空会社は耐久性のある硬い材質のスーツケースを推奨しています.

du|rable goods also **durables** N-PLURAL 複数名詞 **Durable goods** or **durables** are goods such as televisions or cars which are expected to last a long time, and are bought infrequently. 耐久消費財 [mainly AM 主に米国英語] ❑ ...a 2.6% rise in orders for durable goods in January. 1月度は耐久消費財の発注数が2.6パーセント上昇.

du|ra|tion /djʊəreɪʃ°n/ N-UNCOUNT 不可算名詞 The **duration** of an event or state is the time during which it happens or exists. 〜の期間 ❑ He was given the task of protecting her for the duration of the trial. 彼は裁判の期間中彼女を保護する任務を与えられた. **2** PHRASE 句 If you say that something will happen **for the duration**, you

mean that it will happen for as long as a particular situation continues. 〜の期間中 ❑ His wounds knocked him out of combat for the duration. 戦いは負傷している間, 戦列に加われなかった.

dur|ing /djʊərɪŋ/ **1** PREP 前置詞 If something happens **during** a period of time or an event, it happens continuously, or happens several times between the beginning and end of that period or event. 〜の間に ❑ Sandstorms are common during the Saudi Arabian winter. サウジアラビアでは冬に砂あらしがよく発生する. **2** PREP 前置詞 If something develops **during** a period of time, it develops gradually from the beginning to the end of that period. 〜の間にわたって ❑ Wages have fallen by more than twenty percent during the past two months. この2か月間で賃金水準は20パーセント以上下落した. **3** PREP 前置詞 An event that happens **during** a period of time happens at some point or moment in that period. 〜中に ❑ During his visit, the Pope will also bless the new hospital. 訪問中, ローマ教皇はその新設病院の祝福も行う予定です.

You do not use **during** to say how long something lasts. You use **for**. You do not say, for example, "I went to Florida during two weeks." You say "**I went to Florida for two weeks.**"

dusk /dʌsk/ N-UNCOUNT 不可算名詞 **Dusk** is the time just before night when the daylight has almost gone but when it is not completely dark. たそがれ ❑ We arrived home at dusk. 私たちはたそがれ時に帰宅した.

dust /dʌst/ (**dusts, dusting, dusted**) **1** N-UNCOUNT 不可算名詞 **Dust** is very small dry particles of earth or sand. 砂ぼこり ❑ Tanks raise huge trails of dust when they move. タンク車が動くとものすごい砂ぼこりが上がる. **2** N-UNCOUNT 不可算名詞 **Dust** is the very small pieces of dirt which you find inside buildings, for example, on furniture, floors, or lights. ほこり ❑ I could see a thick layer of dust on the stairs. 階段にほこりがうず高く積もっているのが見えていた. **3** N-UNCOUNT 不可算名詞 **Dust** is a fine powder which consists of very small particles of a substance such as gold, wood, or coal. 粉末 ❑ The air is so black with diesel fumes and coal dust, I can barely see. ディーゼルの排気ガスや石炭の粉で暗くなっていて, ほとんどなにも見えません. **4** V-T/V-I 他動詞/自動詞 When you **dust** something such as furniture, you remove dust from it, usually using a cloth. ほこりを払う ❑ I vacuumed and dusted and polished the living room. リビングルームに掃除機をかけ, ほこりを払い, 床を磨いた. **5** V-T/V-I 他動詞/自動詞 If you **dust** something **with** a fine substance such as powder or if you **dust** a fine substance **onto** something, you cover it lightly with that substance. まぶす ❑ Lightly dust the fish with flour. 魚に薄く小麦粉をまぶしてください. **6** PHRASE 句 If you say that something **has bitten the dust**, you are emphasizing that it no longer exists or that it has failed. だめになる [HUMOROUS, INFORMAL ユーモアのある, くだけた, EMPHASIS 強調] ❑ In the last 30 years many cherished values have bitten the dust. この30年間で長くあたためられてきた多くの価値観が覆された. **7** PHRASE 句 If you say that something will happen when **the dust settles**, you mean that a situation will be clearer after it has calmed down. If you let **the dust settle** before doing something, you let a situation calm down before you try to do anything else. 事態が収まる [INFORMAL くだけた] ❑ Once the dust had settled Beck defended his decision. 事態が収まると, ベックは彼の決定を弁護した. **8** PHRASE 句 If you say that something **is gathering dust**, you mean that it has been left somewhere and nobody is using it or doing anything with it. 長い間放置される ❑ Many of the machines are gathering dust in basements. 機械の多くは地下室で放置されていた.

dust|bin /dʌstbɪn/ (**dustbins**) N-COUNT 可算名詞 A **dustbin** is the same as a **garbage can**. ごみ入れ [BRIT 英国英語]

dusty /dʌsti/ (**dustier, dustiest**) **1** ADJ 形容詞 If places, roads, or other things outside are **dusty**, they are covered with tiny bits of earth or sand, usually because it has not rained for a long time. ほこりっぽい ❑ They started strolling down the dusty road in the moonlight. 彼らは月明かりの中, ほこりっぽい道をぶらぶらと歩き始めた. **2** ADJ 形容詞 If a room, house, or object is **dusty**, it is covered with very small pieces of dirt. ほこりだらけの ❑ ...a dusty attic. ほこりだらけの屋根裏部屋.

du|ti|ful /djuːtɪfəl/ ADJ 形容詞 If you say that someone is **dutiful**, you mean that they do everything that they are expected to do. 忠実な ❑ The days of the dutiful wife, who sacrifices her career for her husband, are over. 妻が自分のキャリアを犠牲にして忠実に夫に仕えるような時代は終わった. ● **du|ti|ful|ly** ADV 副詞 [ADV with v] 忠実に ❑ The inspector dutifully recorded the date in a large red book. 調査官は赤い大きな台帳に日付を忠実に記録した.

duty /djuːti/ (**duties**) **1** N-UNCOUNT 不可算名詞 **Duty** is work that you have to do for your job. 任務 ❑ Staff must report for duty at their normal place of work. スタッフはいつもの仕事場に出勤しなければなりません. **2** N-PLURAL 複数名詞 Your **duties** are tasks which you have to do because they are part of your job. 職務 ❑ I carried out my duties conscientiously. 私は自分の職務を忠実に実行した. **3** N-SING 単数名詞 If you say that something is your **duty**, you

believe that you ought to do it because it is your responsibility. 義務 ❑ *I consider it my duty to write to you and thank you.* あなたにお礼状をしたためなければならないと思っています. ◨ N-VAR 可変性名詞 **Duties** are taxes which you pay to the government on goods that you buy. 税金 ❑ *Import duties still average 30%.* 輸入税は依然として平均30パーセントです. ◨ PHRASE 句 If someone such as a police officer or a nurse is **off duty**, they are not working. If someone is **on duty**, they are working. 非番で, 勤務中で ❑ *I'm off duty.* 私は非番です.

duty-free ADJ 形容詞 **Duty-free** goods are sold at airports or on planes or ships at a cheaper price than usual because you do not have to pay import tax on them. 免税の ❑ *...duty-free cigarettes.* 免税のたばこ.

duty-free shop (**duty-free shops**) N-COUNT 可算名詞 A **duty-free shop** is a shop, for example, at an airport, where you can buy goods at a cheaper price than usual, because no tax is paid on them. 免税店

du|vet /duveɪ/ (**duvets**) N-COUNT 可算名詞 A **duvet** is the same as a **comforter**. 羽毛布団 [mainly BRIT 主に英国英語]

DVD /di vi di/ (**DVDs**) N-COUNT 可算名詞 A **DVD** is a disk on which a movie or music is recorded. DVD disks are similar to compact disks but hold a lot more information. **DVD** is an abbreviation for "digital video disk" or "digital versatile disk." DVD ❑ *...a DVD player.* DVDプレーヤー.
→ see Word Web: DVD
→ see **laser**

DVT /di vi ti/ (**DVTs**) N-VAR 可変性名詞 **DVT** is a serious medical condition caused by blood clots in the legs moving up to the lungs. **DVT** is an abbreviation for **deep vein thrombosis**. DVT（深部静脈血栓症） [MEDICAL 医学の]

dwarf /dwɔrf/ (**dwarves, dwarfs, dwarfing, dwarfed**)

> The spellings **dwarves** or **dwarfs** are used for the plural form of the noun.

> つづりの **dwarves** または **dwarfs** は名詞の複数形に使われる.

◨ V-T 他動詞 If one person or thing **is dwarfed** by another, the second is so much bigger than the first that it makes them look very small. 小さく見せる ❑ *His figure is dwarfed by the huge red McDonald's sign.* 彼の姿はマクドナルドの赤い巨大な看板で小さく見える. ◨ ADJ 形容詞 **Dwarf** is used to describe varieties or species of plants and animals which are much smaller than the usual size for their kind. わい小動物, わい小植物 [ADJ n] ❑ *...dwarf shrubs.* わい性の低木. ◨ N-COUNT 可算名詞 In children's stories, a **dwarf** is an imaginary creature that is like a small man. Dwarfs often have magical powers. （童話にでてくる想像上の）小人 ◨ N-COUNT 可算名詞 In former times, people who were much smaller than normal were called **dwarves**. （小さい人に対する蔑称（べっしょう））小人 [OFFENSIVE, OLD-FASHIONED 無礼な, 古風な]

dwell /dwɛl/ (**dwells, dwelling, dwelt** or **dwelled**) ◨ V-I 自動詞 If you **dwell on** something, especially something unpleasant, you think, speak, or write about it a lot or for quite a long time. くよくよ考える ❑ *"I'd rather not dwell on the past," he told me.* 「過去を引きずりたくないんだ」と彼は私に言った. ◨ → see also **dwelling**

dwell|er /dwɛlər/ (**dwellers**) N-COUNT 可算名詞 A city **dweller** or slum **dweller**, for example, is a person who lives in the kind of place or house indicated. 住人 ❑ *The number of city dwellers is growing.* 都市部の人口は増加傾向にある.

dwell|ing /dwɛlɪŋ/ (**dwellings**) N-COUNT 可算名詞 A **dwelling** or a **dwelling place** is a place where someone lives. 居所 [FORMAL 形式ばった] ❑ *Some 3,500 new dwellings are planned for the area.* その地区には3500件の住居が建設される予定だ.

dwelt /dwɛlt/ **Dwelt** is the past tense and past participle of **dwell**. dwell の過去・過去分詞

dwin|dle /dwɪndªl/ (**dwindles, dwindling, dwindled**) V-I 自動詞 If something **dwindles**, it becomes smaller, weaker, or less in number. 次第に小さくなる, 次第に弱くなる ❑ *The factory's workforce has dwindled from over 4,000 to a few hundred.* 4000名を越えていた工員数は減少を続け, 数百人になった.

dye /daɪ/ (**dyes, dyeing, dyed**) ◨ V-T 他動詞 If you **dye** something such as hair or cloth, you change its color by soaking it in a special liquid. 染める ❑ *The women prepared, spun, and dyed the wool.* 女性たちは羊毛の下処理, 紡糸, 染色を行った. ◨ N-MASS 質量名詞 **Dye** is a substance made from plants or chemicals which is mixed into a liquid and used to change the color of something such as cloth or hair. 染料 ❑ *...bottles of hair dye.* 毛髪染料のボトル.
→ see **hair**

dy|ing /daɪɪŋ/ ◨ **Dying** is the present participle of **die**. die の現在分詞 ◨ ADJ 形容詞 A **dying** person or animal is very ill and likely to die soon. 瀕死（ひんし）の [ADJ n] ❑ *...a dying man.* 瀕死（ひんし）の男性. ● N-PLURAL 複数名詞 **The dying** are people who are dying. 死にゆく人々 ❑ *By the time our officers arrived, the dead and the dying were everywhere.* 将校が到着したときには, 死者や瀕死（ひんし）の人々であふれていた. ◨ ADJ 形容詞 You use **dying** to describe something which happens at the time when someone dies, or is connected with that time. 最期の [ADJ n] ❑ *It'll stay in my mind till my dying day.* それは私の最期の日まで心に残っていることでしょう. ◨ ADJ 形容詞 The **dying** days or **dying** minutes of a state of affairs or an activity are its last days or minutes. 最後の [ADJ n] ❑ *...a story of love and war in the dying days of the Ottoman Empire.* オスマン帝国末期の恋と戦いの物語. ◨ ADJ 形容詞 A **dying** tradition or industry is becoming less important and is likely to disappear completely. 消えつつある [ADJ n] ❑ *Shipbuilding is a dying business.* 造船業は斜陽産業だ.

dyke /daɪk/ (**dykes**) ◨ N-COUNT 可算名詞 A **dyke** is a lesbian. レズビアン [INFORMAL, OFFENSIVE くだけた, 無礼な] ◨ → see **dike** 1

dy|nam|ic /daɪnæmɪk/ (**dynamics**) ◨ ADJ 形容詞 If you describe someone as **dynamic**, you approve of them because they are full of energy or full of new and exciting ideas. 活力に満ちた [APPROVAL 賛成] ❑ *He seemed a dynamic and energetic leader.* 彼は活力とエネルギーあふれるリーダーに思えた. ● **dy|nam|i|cal|ly** /daɪnæmɪkli/ ADV 副詞 生き生きと ❑ *He's one of the most dynamically imaginative jazz pianists of our time.* 彼は最も生き生きと想像力に富んだ演奏をする現代ジャズピアニストの1人だ. ◨ ADJ 形容詞 If you describe something as **dynamic**, you approve of it because it is very active and energetic. 活発な [APPROVAL 賛成] ❑ *South Asia continues to be the most dynamic economic region in the world.* 南アジアは世界で最も経済が活発な地区の地位を維持している. ◨ ADJ 形容詞 A **dynamic** process is one that constantly changes and progresses. 動的な ❑ *...a dynamic, evolving worldwide epidemic.* 世界中で発生し広がりつつある伝染病 ◨ N-COUNT 可算名詞 The **dynamic** of a system or process is the force that causes it to change or progress. 活力 ❑ *The dynamic of the market demands constant change and adjustment.* 市場の活性化には継続的な変化と調整が求められる. ◨ N-PLURAL 複数名詞 The **dynamics** of a situation or group of people are the opposing forces within it that cause it to change. 動態 ❑ *What is needed is insight into the dynamics of the social system.* 求められるのは社会システム動態の洞察力である.

dy|na|mism /daɪnəmɪzəm/ ◨ N-UNCOUNT 不可算名詞 If you say that someone or something has **dynamism**, you are

expressing approval of the fact that they are full of energy or full of new and exciting ideas. 活力があること [APPROVAL 賛成] ❏ *...a situation that calls for dynamism and new thinking.* 活力と新しい考え方が要求される状況. **2** N-UNCOUNT 不可算名詞 If you refer to the **dynamism** of a situation or system, you are referring to the fact that it is changing in an exciting and dramatic way. 活発さ [APPROVAL 賛成] ❏ *Such changes are also indicators of economic dynamism and demographic expansion.* そういった変化は経済的活力と人口拡大の指標にもなる.

Word Link   dyn ≈ power : dyn**amic**, dyn**amite**, dyn**amo**

---

dy|na|mite /daɪnəmaɪt/ **1** N-UNCOUNT 不可算名詞 **Dynamite** is a type of explosive that contains nitroglycerin. ダイナマイト ❏ *Fifty yards of track was blown up with dynamite.* ダイナマイトで線路が50ヤード爆破されました. **2** N-UNCOUNT 不可算名詞 If you describe a piece of information as **dynamite**, you think that people will react strongly to it. 衝撃を与えるもの [INFORMAL くだけた] ❏ *The book is dynamite, and if she publishes it, there will be no hiding place for her.* その本の衝撃は大きいため、出版すれば彼女は身を隠す場所を失うだろう. **3** N-UNCOUNT 不可算名詞 If you describe someone or something as **dynamite**, you think that they are exciting. 刺激的な人、刺激的なもの [INFORMAL くだけた, APPROVAL 賛成] ❏ *The first kiss is dynamite.* 初めてのキスは刺激的だ.

dy|na|mo /daɪnəmoʊ/ (**dynamos**) **1** N-COUNT 可算名詞 A **dynamo** is a device that uses the movement of a machine or vehicle to produce electricity. 発電機 ❏ *...a bicycle with a dynamo.* 発電機がついた自転車. **2** N-COUNT 可算名詞 If you describe someone as a **dynamo**, you mean that they are very energetic and are always busy and active. 元気あふれる人 ❏ *Myles is a human dynamo.* マイルズは疲れを知らない人だ.

dyn|as|ty /daɪnəsti/ (**dynasties**) **1** N-COUNT 可算名詞 A **dynasty** is a series of rulers of a country who all belong to the same family. 王朝 ❏ *The Seljuk dynasty of Syria was founded in 1094.* シリアのセルジュク王朝は1094年に誕生した. **2** N-COUNT 可算名詞 A **dynasty** is a period of time during which a country is ruled by members of the same family. 王朝時代 ❏ *...carvings dating back to the Ming dynasty.* 明王朝時代の彫刻. **3** N-COUNT 可算名詞 A **dynasty** is a family which has members from two or more generations who are important in a particular field of activity, for example, in business or politics. 名門 ❏ *This is a family-owned company – the current president is the fourth in this dynasty.* この会社は同族企業で、現社長は4代目です.

dys|lexia /dɪslɛksiə/ N-UNCOUNT 不可算名詞 If someone suffers from **dyslexia**, they have difficulty with reading because of a slight disorder of their brain. 失読症 [TECHNICAL 技術的]

Ee

E also **e** /iː/ (**E's, e's**) N-VAR 可変性名詞 **E** is the fifth letter of the English alphabet. アルファベットの5番目の字

each /iːtʃ/ **1** DET 限定詞 If you refer to **each** thing or **each** person in a group, you are referring to every member of the group and considering them as individuals. おのおの ❑ *Each book is beautifully illustrated.* それぞれの本に美しい挿絵が施されている. ❑ *Each year, hundreds of animals are killed in this way.* 毎年, 数百匹の動物がこの方法で殺されている. ● PRON 代名詞 **Each** is also a pronoun. おのおの ❑ *...two bedrooms, each with three beds.* 二つの寝室, それぞれに三つのベッド ● PRON-EMPH 強調的代名詞 **Each** is also an emphasizing pronoun. それぞれ ❑ *We each have different needs and interests.* 我々一人一人が異なった要求と興味を持っている. ● ADV 副詞 **Each** is also an adverb. それぞれ [amount ADV] ❑ *The children were given one each, handed to them or placed on their plates.* 子供たちは手のひらか皿の上にひとつずつ受け取った. ● QUANT 数量詞 **Each** is also a quantifier. それぞれ [QUANT 'of' def-pl-n] ❑ *He handed each of them a page of photos.* 彼は一人一人に1ページの写真を渡した. ❑ *Each of these exercises takes one or two minutes to do.* こうした練習のそれぞれに1分あるいは2分かかる. **2** QUANT 数量詞 If you refer to **each one** of the members of a group, you are emphasizing that something applies to every one of them. それぞれ [EMPHASIS 強調] [QUANT 'of' def-pl-n] ❑ *He picked up forty of these publications and read each one of them.* 彼はこれら40部の出版物を取り上げ, それぞれをすべて読んだ. **3** PHRASE 句 You can refer to **each and every** member **of** a group to emphasize that you mean all the members of that group. それぞれすべて [EMPHASIS 強調] ❑ *My goal was that each and every person responsible for Yankel's murder be brought to justice.* 私の目標はヤンケルの殺害に関わったすべての人間を残らず法の裁きにかけることだった. **4** PRON-RECIP 相互代名詞 You use **each other** when you are saying that each member of a group does something to the others or has a particular connection with the others. お互い [V PRON, prep PRON] ❑ *We looked at each other in silence, each equally shocked.* 我々は黙ってお互いを見た. それぞれ同じように衝撃を受けていた. ❑ *Both sides are willing to make allowances for each other's political sensitivities.* 両陣営がお互いの政治的感応性をすすんで考慮している.

> You use **each** to refer to every person or thing in a group when you are thinking about them as individuals. You use **every** to refer to all the members of a group that has more than two members. ❑ *He listened to every news bulletin. ...an equal chance for every child.* Note that **each** can be used to refer to both members of a pair. ❑ *Each apartment has two bedrooms...We each carried a suitcase.* Note that **each** and **every** are only used with singular nouns.

eager /iːgər/ **1** ADJ 形容詞 If you are **eager** to do or have something, you want to do it or have it very much. 熱望する ❑ *Robert was eager to talk about life in the Army.* ロバートは軍隊の生活を話したがった. ❑ *When my own son was five years old, I became eager for another baby.* 私自身の息子が5歳の頃, もう一人子供が欲しくてたまらなかった. ● **eager|ness** N-UNCOUNT 不可算名詞 熱望 ❑ *...an eagerness to learn.* 学習への熱望 **2** ADJ 形容詞 If you look or sound **eager**, you look or sound as if you expect something interesting or enjoyable to happen. 切望している ❑ *Arty sneered at the crowd of eager faces around him.* アーティーは彼の周りで物欲しげな表情を浮かべる群衆を冷笑した. ● **eager|ly** ADV 副詞 熱望して ❑ *"So what do you think will happen?" he asked eagerly.* 「それでなにが起こると思うんだい」彼は熱心に尋ねた. ● **eager|ness** N-UNCOUNT 不可算名詞 熱

望 ❑ *It was the voice of a woman speaking with breathless eagerness.* それは息もつかぬほど熱心に話す女性の声だった.

eagle /iːgəl/ (**eagles**) N-COUNT 可算名詞 An **eagle** is a large bird that lives by eating small animals. ワシ

ear /ɪər/ (**ears**) **1** N-COUNT 可算名詞 Your **ears** are the two parts of your body, one on each side of your head, with which you hear sounds. 耳 ❑ *He whispered something in her ear.* 彼は彼女の耳に何かをささやいた. **2** N-SING 単数名詞 If you have **an ear for** music or language, you are able to hear its sounds accurately and to interpret them or reproduce them well. 聞き分ける能力 ❑ *Moby certainly has a fine ear for a tune.* モビーは確かに音楽に関するよい耳を持っている. **3** N-COUNT 可算名詞 **Ear** is often used to refer to people's willingness to listen to what someone is saying. 聞く意思 ❑ *What would cause the masses to give him a far more sympathetic ear?* どうすれば今よりもはるかに思いやりを持って話を聞く耳を彼に持たせることができるだろうか. **4** N-COUNT 可算名詞 The **ears** of a cereal plant such as corn or barley are the parts at the top of the stem that contain the seeds or grains. 穂 ❑ *American farmers use machines to pick the ears of corn from the plants.* アメリカの農夫はトウモロコシの穂を茎から刈り取るのに機械を使う. **5** PHRASE 句 If a request **falls on deaf ears** or if the person to whom the request is made **turns a deaf ear to** it, they take no notice of it. 無視される ❑ *I hope that our appeals will not fall on deaf ears.* 我々の訴えが無視されないことを望む. **6** PHRASE 句 If you **play by ear** or **play** a piece of music **by ear**, you play music by relying on your memory rather than by reading printed music. 聴き覚えで演奏する ❑ *Neil sat at the piano and began playing, by ear, the music he'd heard his older sister practicing.* ニールはピアノの前に座り, 姉の練習していた曲を聞き覚えで演奏しはじめた. **7** PHRASE 句 If you say that someone **has a tin ear** for something, you mean that they do not have any natural ability for it and cannot appreciate or understand it fully. 理解力のない [usu PHR 'for' n] ❑ *Worst of all, for a playwright specializing in characters who use the vernacular, he has a tin ear for dialogue.* なによりもまずいことに, 土地の言葉で話す登場人物を使う劇作家でありながら, 彼は方言を理解する能力に欠けていた. **8** **music to** your **ears** → see music → see face

ear|ache /ɪəreɪk/ (**earaches**) N-COUNT 可算名詞 An **earache** is a pain in the inside part of your ear. 耳の痛み ❑ *He had an earache and a fever.* 彼は耳が痛み, 熱があった.

ear|drum /ɪərdrʌm/ (**eardrums**) also **ear drum** N-COUNT 可算名詞 Your **eardrums** are the thin pieces of tightly stretched skin inside each ear that vibrate when sound waves reach them. 鼓膜 ❑ *The blast burst Ollie Williams' eardrum.* その爆音でオリー・ウィリアムズの鼓膜が破れた. → see ear

earl /ɜːrl/ (**earls**) N-COUNT 可算名詞 An **earl** is a British nobleman. 伯爵 ❑ *...the first Earl of Birkenhead.* 初代バーケンヘッド伯爵

ear|li|er /ɜːrliər/ **1** Earlier is the comparative of **early**. earlyの比較級 **2** ADV 副詞 **Earlier** is used to refer to a point or period in time before the present or before the one you are talking about. 前に ❑ *As mentioned earlier, the university supplements this information with an interview.* 前に述べたとおり, 大学は面接でこの情報を補う. ❑ *...political reforms announced by the president earlier this year.* 今年の早い時期に大統領が発表した政治改革 ● ADJ 形容詞 **Earlier** is also

Word Web　　ear

The **ear** collects **sound waves** and sends them to the brain. First the **external ear** picks up sound waves. Then these sound **vibrations** travel along the **ear canal** and strike the **eardrum**. The eardrum pushes against a series of tiny bones. These bones carry the vibrations into the **inner ear**. There they are picked up by the hair cells in the cochlea. At that point, the vibrations turn into electronic impulses. The cochlea is connected to the hearing **nerve**. It sends the electronic impulses to the brain.

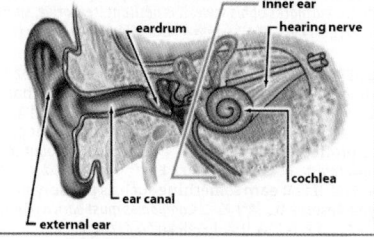

E

an adjective. 前の [ADJ n] ❑ *Earlier reports of gunshots have not been substantiated.* 銃撃に関する以前の報告はまだ実証されていない.

ear|li|est /ˈɜːrliɪst/ ■ **Earliest** is the superlative of **early**. early の最上級 ② PHRASE 句 **At the earliest** means not before the date or time mentioned. 最も早くて ❑ *The first official results are not expected until Tuesday at the earliest.* 最初の公式結果は最も早い場合でも火曜日までは出てこない.

ear|lobe /ˈɪərloʊb/ **(earlobes)** also **ear lobe** N-COUNT 可算名詞 Your **earlobes** are the soft parts at the bottom of your ears. 耳たぶ ❑ *...the holes in her earlobes.* 彼女の耳たぶに開いた穴

ear|ly /ˈɜːrli/ **(earlier, earliest)** ■ ADV 副詞 **Early** means before the usual time that a particular event or activity happens. 早く [ADV after v] ❑ *I knew I had to get up early.* 早く起きねばならないことはわかっていた. ● ADJ 形容詞 **Early** is also an adjective. [ADJ n] ❑ *I decided that I was going to take early retirement.* 私は早期退職することを決めた. ② ADJ 形容詞 **Early** means near the beginning of a day, week, year, or other period of time. 早く [ADJ n] ❑ *...in the 1970s and the early 1980s.* 1970年代および1980年代初期に ❑ *She was in her early teens.* 彼女は10代前半だった. ● ADV 副詞 **Early** is also an adverb. 早く ❑ *We'll hope to see you some time early next week.* 来週の早い時期にお会いできればと思います. ③ ADV 副詞 **Early** means before the time that was arranged or expected. 早い時間に [ADV after v] ❑ *She arrived early to get a place at the front.* 彼女は一番前の場所を取るために早く到着した. ● ADJ 形容詞 **Early** is also an adjective. 早い時間の ❑ *I'm always early.* 私はいつも早めだ. ④ ADJ 形容詞 **Early** means near the beginning of a period in history, or in the history of something such as the world, a society, or an activity. 初期の [ADJ n] ❑ *...the early stages of pregnancy.* 妊娠初期 ❑ *...Fassbinder's early films.* ファスビンダーの初期の映画 ⑤ ADJ 形容詞 **Early** means near the beginning of something such as a piece of work or a process. 初期の [ADJ n] ❑ *...the book's early chapters.* この本の始めのほうの章 ● ADV 副詞 **Early** is also an adverb. 初期に ❑ *...an incident that occurred much earlier in the game.* 試合のずっと早い時期に起きた事件 ⑥ ADJ 形容詞 **Early** refers to plants that flower or crop before or at the beginning of the main season. はしりの [ADJ n] ❑ *...these early cabbages and cauliflowers.* わせのキャベツとカリフラワー ● ADV 副詞 **Early** is also an adverb. 早めに [ADV with v] ❑ *This early flowering gladiolus is not very hardy.* この早咲きのグラジオラスはあまり丈夫ではない. ⑦ ADJ 形容詞 **Early** reports or indications of something are the first reports or indications about it. 初期の [FORMAL 形式ばった] [ADJ n] ❑ *The early indications look encouraging.* 初期兆候は希望が持てそうだ. ⑧ PHRASE 句 You can use **as early as** to emphasize that a particular time or period is surprisingly early. 早くも [EMPHASIS 強調] ❑ *Inflation could fall back into single figures as early as this month.* インフレーションは早くも今月に一桁の数値に落ち着くかもしれない.

ear|ly bird (early birds) ■ N-COUNT 可算名詞 An **early bird** is someone who does something or goes somewhere very early, especially very early in the morning. 早めに行動する人 ❑ *We've always been early birds, getting up at 5:30 or 6 a.m.* 我々はいつも早起きで, 5時半か6時には起床してきた. ② ADJ 形容詞 An **early bird** deal or special is one that is available at a reduced price, but that you must buy earlier than you would normally. 早朝の [ADJ n] ❑ *Early bird discounts are usually available at the beginning of the season.* 早朝割引は, 通常, 季節の初めに実施される.

ear|mark /ˈɪərmɑːrk/ **(earmarks, earmarking, earmarked)** ■ V-T 他動詞 If resources such as money **are earmarked for** a particular purpose, they are reserved for that purpose. 取っておく ❑ *...the extra money being earmarked for the new projects.* 新しい計画のために充てられる余剰資金 ❑ *China has earmarked more than $20 billion for oil exploration.* 中国は石油調査のため200億ドル以上を充ててきた. ② V-T 他動詞 If something **has been earmarked for** closure or disposal, for example, people have decided that it will be closed or got rid of. 指定する [usu passive] ❑ *Their support meant that he was not forced to sell the business which was earmarked for disposal last year.* 彼の支援は, 彼が昨年処分の決定を受けた会社の売却を強いられていたのではないことを意味していた. ③ N-COUNT 可算名詞 The **earmark** of something or someone is their most typical quality or feature. 特徴 [AM 米国英語] [with poss] ❑ *Davis's solo work exhibits all the earmarks of his style: it is hesitant, tentative, spare.* デイビスの個人の仕事は彼の様式の特徴をすべて現している. それはためらいがちで, つかの間のもので, 閑散としている.

earn /ɜːrn/ **(earns, earning, earned)** ■ V-T 他動詞 If you **earn** money, you receive money in return for work that you do. 稼ぐ ❑ *What a lovely way to earn a living.* なんと素敵な生計の立て方だろう. ② V-T 他動詞 If something **earns** money, it produces money as profit or interest. もたらす ❑ *...a bank account that earns little or no interest.* ほとんどあるいはまったく利子のつかない銀行口座 ③ V-T 他動詞 If you **earn** something such as praise, you get it because you deserve it. 値する ❑ *Companies must earn a reputation for honesty.* 企業は誠実さにより名声を得なばならない.

| **Thesaurus** | *earn* また次を参照: |

v. | bring in, make, take in ■

ear|nest /ˈɜːrnɪst/ ■ PHRASE 句 If something is done or happens **in earnest**, it happens to a much greater extent and more seriously than before. 本格的に ❑ *Campaigning will begin in earnest tomorrow.* 運動は明日から本格的に始まる. ② ADJ 形容詞 **Earnest** people are very serious and sincere in what they say or do, because they think that their actions and beliefs are important. まじめな ❑ *Catherine was a pious, earnest woman.* キャサリンは敬虔でまじめな女性だった.

ear|nest|ly /ˈɜːrnɪstli/ ■ ADV 副詞 If you say something **earnestly**, you say it very seriously, often because you believe that it is important or you are trying to persuade someone else to believe it. 真剣に [ADV with v] ❑ *"Did you?" she asked earnestly.* 「やったの」彼女は真剣に尋ねた. ② ADV 副詞 If you do something **earnestly**, you do it in a thorough and serious way, intending to succeed. 真剣に ❑ *She always listened earnestly as if this might help her to understand.* 彼女はいつもまるでそうすることが理解に役立つかのようにまじめに話を聞いた.

earn|ings /ˈɜːrnɪŋz/ N-PLURAL 複数名詞 Your **earnings** are the sums of money that you earn by working. 収益 ❑ *Average weekly earnings rose by 1.5% in July.* 7月の週間平均収益は1．5%に上昇した.

ear|phone /ˈɪərfoʊn/ **(earphones)** N-COUNT 可算名詞 **Earphones** are a small piece of equipment that you wear over or inside your ears so that you can listen to a radio or recorded music without anyone else hearing. イヤホン

ear|ring /ˈɪərɪŋ/ **(earrings)** N-COUNT 可算名詞 **Earrings** are pieces of jewelry that you attach to your ears. 耳飾り ❑ *...a pair of diamond earrings.* 一組のダイヤモンドの耳飾り
→ see **jewelry**

ear|shot /ˈɪərʃɒt/ PHRASE 句 If you are **within earshot of** someone or something, you are close enough to be able to hear them. If you are **out of earshot**, you are too far away to hear them. すぐ近くで ❑ *It is within earshot of a main road.* それは主要道からすぐ近くだ.

earth /ɜːrθ/ ■ N-PROPER 固有名詞 **Earth** or **the Earth** is the planet on which we live. People usually say **Earth** when they are referring to the planet as part of the universe, and **the Earth** when they are talking about the planet as the place where we live. 地球 ❑ *The space shuttle Atlantis returned safely to Earth today.* スペースシャトル・アトランティスは, 今日, 無事に地球に戻ってきた. ② N-SING 単数名詞 **The earth** is the land surface on which we live and move around. 地面 ❑ *The earth shook and swayed and the walls of neighboring houses fell around them.* 地面が揺れ動き, 隣接する家々の壁が落ちた. ③ N-UNCOUNT 不可算名詞 **Earth** is the substance on the land surface of the earth, for example clay or sand, in which plants grow. 地表 ❑ *The road winds for miles through parched earth, scrub and cactus.* その道路は焼けついた地表, 雑木, サボテンの間を何マイルも曲がりくねっている. ④ N-SING 単数名詞 The **earth** in an electric plug or piece of electrical equipment is the same as the **ground**. 接地線, アース [BRIT 英国英語] ⑤ → see also **down-to-earth** ⑥ PHRASE 句 **On earth** is used for emphasis in questions that begin with words such as "how," "why," "what," or "where." It is often used to suggest that there is no obvious or easy answer to the question being asked. 一体 [EMPHASIS 強調] ❑ *How on earth did that happen?* 一体どんなふうにそれが起こったんだ. ⑦ PHRASE 句 **On earth** is used for emphasis after some negative noun groups, for example "no reason." まったく [EMPHASIS 強調] ❑ *There was no reason on earth why she couldn't have moved in with us.* 彼女が私たちと一緒に引っ越せない理由はまったくなかった. ⑧ PHRASE 句 If you come **down to earth** or **back to earth**, you have to face the reality of everyday life after a period of great excitement. 現実に戻る ❑ *When he came down to earth after his win he admitted: "It was an amazing feeling."* 勝利のあとで現実に戻り, 彼は認めた. 「それは驚くような感覚だった」
→ see Word Web: **earth**
→ see **core, eclipse, erosion**

earth|ly /ˈɜːrθli/ ■ ADJ 形容詞 **Earthly** means happening in the material world of our life on earth and not in any spiritual life or life after death. この世の [ADJ n] ❑ *...the need to confront evil during the earthly life.* 現実生活のなかで悪を抑える必要性 ② ADJ 形容詞 **Earthly** is used for emphasis in phrases such as **no earthly reason**. If you say that there is **no earthly reason why** something should happen, you are emphasizing that there is no reason at all why it should happen. 少しも [EMPHASIS 強調] [ADJ n] ❑ *There is no earthly reason why they should ever change.* 彼らが変わらねばならない理由はまったくない.

earth|quake /ˈɜːrθkweɪk/ **(earthquakes)** N-COUNT 可算名詞 An **earthquake** is a shaking of the ground caused by movement of the Earth's crust. 地震 ❑ *...the San Francisco earthquake of 1906.* 1906年のサンフランシスコ地震
→ see Word Web: **earthquake**

Word Web   earth

The **earth** is made of material left over when the **sun** formed. In the beginning, about 4 billion years ago, the earth was liquid **rock**. During its first million years, it cooled into solid rock. **Life**, in the form of bacteria, began in the **oceans** about 3.5 billion years ago. During the next billion years, the **continents** formed. At the same time, the level of **oxygen** in the **atmosphere** increased. **Life forms evolved**, and some of them began to use oxygen. **Evolution** allowed **plants** and **animals** to move from the oceans onto the **land**.

earthy /ɜrθi/ (**earthier, earthiest**) ◼ ADJ 形容詞 If you describe someone as **earthy**, you mean that they are open and direct, and talk about subjects that other people avoid or feel ashamed about. 粗野な [APPROVAL 賛成] ❑…*his extremely earthy humor.* 彼のとんでもなく野卑なユーモア ◻ ADJ 形容詞 If you describe something as **earthy**, you mean it looks, smells, or feels like earth. 土のような ❑*I'm attracted to warm, earthy colors.* 私は温かい土の色に惹かれる.

earwig /ɪərwɪɡ/ (**earwigs**) N-COUNT 可算名詞 An **earwig** is a small, thin, brown insect that has a pair of claws at the back end of its body. ハサミムシ

ease /iz/ (**eases, easing, eased**) ◼ PHRASE 句 If you do something **with ease**, you do it easily, without difficulty or effort. たやすく ❑*Anne was intelligent and capable of passing her exams with ease.* アンは聡明で簡単に試験に合格することができた. ◻ N-UNCOUNT 不可算名詞 If you talk about the **ease** of a particular activity, you are referring to the way that it has been made easier to do, or to the fact that it is already easy to do. たやすさ ❑*For ease of reference, only the relevant extracts of the regulations are included.* 参照を容易にするため、規則のうちから関連する抜粋のみが含まれている. ◼ N-UNCOUNT 不可算名詞 **Ease** is the state of being very comfortable and able to live as you want, without any worries or problems. 安らぎ ❑*She lived a life of ease.* 彼女は気楽な生活を送った. ◼ V-T/V-I 他動詞/自動詞 If something unpleasant **eases** or if you **ease** it, it is reduced in degree, speed, or intensity. 和らげる [他動詞]、和らぐ [自動詞] ❑*Tensions had eased.* 緊張は緩んでいた. ❑*I gave him some brandy to ease the pain.* 私は痛みを和らげるため彼にブランデーを与えた. ◼ V-T/V-I 他動詞/自動詞 If you **ease** your **way** somewhere or **ease** somewhere, you move there slowly, carefully, and gently. If you **ease** something somewhere, you move it there slowly, carefully, and gently. ゆっくり動かす [他動詞]、ゆっくり動く [自動詞] ❑*I eased my way toward the door.* 私は扉のほうにゆっくりと動いた. ❑*He eased his foot off the accelerator.* 彼はアクセルからゆっくりと足を離した. ◼ PHRASE 句 If you are **at ease**, you are feeling confident and relaxed, and are able to talk to people without feeling nervous or anxious. If you put someone **at ease**, you make them feel at ease. くつろいで ❑*It is essential to feel at ease with your therapist.* 治療士の前ではくつろぐことが大切です. ◼ PHRASE 句 If you are **ill at ease**, you feel somewhat uncomfortable, anxious, or worried. 落ち着かない ❑*He appeared embarrassed and ill at ease with the sustained applause that greeted him.* 鳴りやまぬ歓迎の拍手に彼は戸惑い落ち着かないように見えた.
▶**ease up** ◼ PHRASAL VERB 句動詞 If something **eases up**, it is reduced in degree, speed, or intensity. 治まる ❑*The rain had eased up.* 雨足が弱まっていた. ◻ PHRASAL VERB 句動詞 If you **ease up**, you start to make less effort. 気を抜く ❑*He told supporters not to ease up even though he's leading in the presidential race.* 彼は支持者に、たとえ彼が大統領選において優位に立っているとは言え、気を緩めないようにと語った.

easel /iz³l/ (**easels**) N-COUNT 可算名詞 An **easel** is a frame that supports a picture which an artist is painting or drawing. 画架 → see **painting**

easi|ly /izɪli/ ◼ ADV 副詞 You use **easily** to emphasize that something is very likely to happen, or is very likely to be true. 多分に [EMPHASIS 強調] ❑*It could easily be another year before the economy starts to show some improvement.* 経済が何がしかの回復を示し始めるのが来年になることは大いにありえる. ◻ ADV 副詞 You use **easily** to say that something happens more quickly or more often than is usual or normal. すぐに [ADV after v] ❑*He had always cried very easily.* 彼はいつもほんのちょっとしたことで泣き出していた. ◼ → see also **easy**

Thesaurus   easily また次を参照:

ADV. quickly, readily ◻

east /ist/ also **East** ◼ N-UNCOUNT 不可算名詞 The **east** is the direction where the sun rises. 東 [also 'the' N] ❑*…the vast swamps that lie to the east of the River Nile.* ナイル川の東に広がる広大な沼地 ◻ N-SING 単数名詞 The **east of** a place, country, or region is the part which is in the east. 東部 ❑*…a village in the east of the country.* 国の東部の村 ◼ ADV 副詞 If you go **east**, you travel toward the east. 東方 [ADV after v] ❑*To drive, go east on Route 9.* 9号線で東方に車を運転する. ◼ ADV 副詞 Something that is **east of** a place is positioned to the east of it. 東側 ❑*…just east of the center of town.* 町の中心のちょうど東側 ◼ ADJ 形容詞 The **east** edge, corner, or part of a place or country is the part toward the east. 東の [ADJ n] ❑*…a low line of hills running along the east coast.* 東海岸に沿って連なる丘の低い線 ◼ ADJ 形容詞 **East** is used in the names of some countries, states, and regions in the east of a larger area. 東の [ADJ n] ❑*He had been on safari in East Africa with his son.* 彼は息子と共に東アフリカでの狩猟旅行に行ったことがあった. ◼ ADJ 形容詞 An **east** wind is a wind that blows from the east. 東の ❑*…a bitter east wind.* 厳しい東風 ◼ N-SING 単数名詞 **The East** is used to refer to the southern and eastern part of Asia, including India, China, and Japan. 東洋 ❑*Every so often, a new martial art arrives from the East.* たびたび新しい武術が東洋からもたらされる. ◼ → see also **Middle East, Far East**

East|er /istər/ (**Easters**) N-VAR 可変性名詞 **Easter** is a Christian festival when Jesus Christ's return to life is celebrated. It is celebrated on a Sunday in March or April. 復活祭 [oft N n] ❑*"Happy Easter," he yelled.* 「ご復活おめでとう」彼は叫んだ.

east|er|ly /istərli/ ◼ ADJ 形容詞 An **easterly** point, area, or direction is to the east or toward the east. 東方の ❑*He progressed slowly along the coast in an easterly direction.* 彼は海岸沿いを東の方向にゆっくりと進んだ. ◻ ADJ 形容詞 An **easterly** wind is a wind that blows from the east. 東からの ❑*It was a beautiful September day, with stiff easterly winds.* それは美しい9月の日で、強い風が東から吹いていた.

Word Web   earthquake

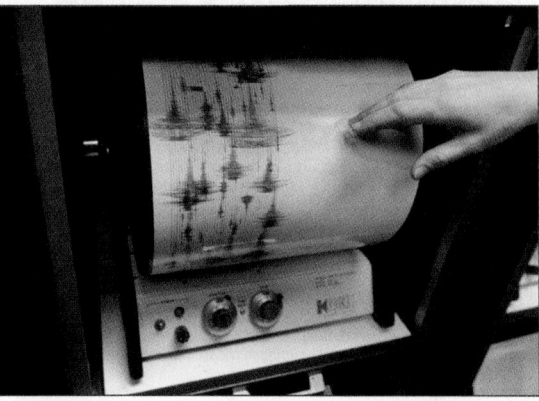

Earthquakes occur when two tectonic **plates** meet and start to slide past each other. This meeting point is called the focus. It may be located anywhere from a few hundred meters to a few hundred kilometers below the surface. The resulting pressure causes a split in the earth's **crust** called a **fault**. Vibrations travel out from the focus in all directions. These **seismic waves** cause little damage until they reach the surface. The **epicenter**, directly above the focus, receives the greatest damage. Seismologists use seismographs to measure the amount of ground movement during an earthquake.

A seismograph recording a major earthquake.

east|ern /ístərn/ **1** ADJ 形容詞 **Eastern** means in or from the east of a region, state, or country. 東の [ADJ n] ☐ ...Eastern Europe. 東欧 **2** ADJ 形容詞 **Eastern** means coming from or associated with the people or countries of the East, such as India, China, or Japan. 東洋の [ADJ n] ☐ In many Eastern countries massage was and is a part of everyday life. 東洋の国の多くでは、マッサージが日常生活の一部であったし、今もそうである。

east|ward /ístwərd/

The form **eastwards** is also used.

eastwards 形も使われる。

ADV 副詞 **Eastward** or **eastwards** means toward the east. 東方に [ADV after v] ☐ A powerful snow storm is moving eastward. 強力な吹雪が東へ進んでいる。● ADJ 形容詞 **Eastward** is also an adjective. 東方への ☐ ...the eastward expansion of the city. 都市の東方への拡大

easy /ízi/ (**easier, easiest**) **1** ADJ 形容詞 If a job or action is **easy**, you can do it without difficulty or effort, because it is not complicated and causes no problems. 容易な ☐ This is not an easy task. これは簡単な仕事ではない。● **easi|ly** ADV 副詞 容易に ☐ Dress your child in layers of clothes you can remove easily. 簡単に脱がせやすいように子供には重ね着で服を着させること。**2** ADJ 形容詞 If you describe an action or activity as **easy**, you mean that it is done in a confident, relaxed way. If someone is **easy about** something, they feel relaxed and confident about it. 気楽な ☐ He was an easy person to talk to. 彼は気楽に話しかけられる人物だった。● **easi|ly** ADV 副詞 [ADV with v] ☐ They talked amiably and easily about a range of topics. 彼らは愛想よく気楽にさまざまな話題について話した。**3** ADJ 形容詞 If you say that someone has an **easy** life, you mean that they live comfortably without any problems or worries. 安楽な ☐ She has not had an easy life. 彼女は安楽に暮らしたことがない。**4** ADJ 形容詞 If you say that something is **easy** or too **easy**, you are criticizing someone because they have done the most obvious or least difficult thing, and have not considered the situation carefully enough. 安直な [DISAPPROVAL 不賛成] ☐ That's easy for you to say. 言うのは簡単だ。**5** PHRASE 句 If you tell someone to **go easy on** something, you are telling them to use only a small amount of it. 少なめにする [INFORMAL くだけた] ☐ Go easy on the alcohol. アルコールを控えるように。**6** PHRASE 句 If you tell someone to **go easy on**, or **be easy on**, a particular person, you are telling them not to punish or treat that person very severely. 寛大に扱う [INFORMAL くだけた] ☐ "Go easy on him," Sam repeated, opening the door. 「大目に見てやれ」サムは繰り返し、扉を開いた。**7** PHRASE 句 If someone tells you to **take it easy** or **take things easy**, they mean that you should relax and not do very much at all. 気楽にやる [INFORMAL くだけた] ☐ It is best to take things easy for a week or two. 1, 2週間、気楽にやるのが一番だ。**8** → see also **easily**

easy|going /ízigoʊɪŋ/ ADJ 形容詞 If you describe someone as **easygoing**, you mean that they are not easily annoyed, worried, or upset, and you think this is a good quality. のんびりした [APPROVAL 賛成] ☐ He was easygoing and good-natured. 彼はのんびりしていて気立てがよかった。

eat /ít/ (**eats, eating, ate, eaten**) **1** V-T/V-I 他動詞/自動詞 When you **eat** something, you put it into your mouth, chew it, and swallow it. 食べる ☐ She was eating a sandwich. 彼女はサンドイッチを食べていた。**2** V-I 自動詞 If you **eat** sensibly or healthily, you eat food that is good for you. 食事をする ☐ ...a campaign to persuade people to eat more healthily. より健康な食生活を推奨するための運動 **3** V-T/V-I 他動詞/自動詞 If you **eat**, you have a meal. 食べる [他動詞], 食事する [自動詞] ☐ Let's go out to eat. 外に食べに行こう。☐ We ate lunch together every day. 我々は毎日一緒に昼食をとった。**4** V-T 他動詞 If something is **eating** you, it is annoying or worrying you. むしばむ [INFORMAL くだけた] [only cont] ☐ "What the hell's eating you?" he demanded. 「一体なにがそんなに大変なんだい」彼は尋ねた。**5** **dog eat dog** → see **dog** **6** **eat crow** → see **crow**

▶ **eat away** PHRASAL VERB 句動詞 If one thing **eats away** another or **eats away at** another, it gradually destroys or uses it up. 侵食する、次第になくなる ☐ Water pours through the roof, encouraging rot to eat away the interior of the house. 屋根から水が入り込み、屋内の腐敗浸食を早めた。

▶ **eat into 1** PHRASAL VERB 句動詞 If something **eats into** your time or your resources, it uses them, when they should be used for other things. 食い込む ☐ Responsibilities at home and work eat into his time. 家庭と仕事での責任が時間を侵食する。**2** PHRASAL VERB 句動詞 If a substance such as acid or rust **eats into** something, it destroys or damages its surface. 侵食する ☐ Ulcers occur when the stomach's natural acids eat into the lining of the stomach. 胃の内側を自然の胃酸が侵食したときかいようができる。

→ see **cooking, food**

eat|er /ítər/ (**eaters**) N-COUNT 可算名詞 You use **eater** to refer to someone who eats in a particular way or who eats particular kinds of food. 食べる人 ☐ I've never been a fussy eater. 私は食べ物についてとやかく言ったことがない。

eaves /ívz/ N-PLURAL 複数名詞 The **eaves** of a house are the lower edges of its roof. ひさし ☐ There were icicles hanging from the eaves. ひさしからつららが下がっていた。

eaves|drop /ívzdrɒp/ (**eavesdrops, eavesdropping, eavesdropped**) V-I 自動詞 If you **eavesdrop on** someone, you listen secretly to what they are saying. 盗み聞きする ☐ The government illegally eavesdropped on his telephone conversations. 政府は法を侵し彼の電話での会話を盗聴した。

ebb /ɛb/ (**ebbs, ebbing, ebbed**) **1** V-I 自動詞 When the tide or the sea **ebbs**, its level gradually falls. 潮が引く ☐ When the tide ebbs, you can paddle out for a mile and barely get your ankles wet. 潮が引くと1マイル歩いて出てもくるぶしのあたりまで濡れるくらいだ。**2** N-COUNT 可算名詞 The **ebb** or the **ebb** tide is one of the regular periods, usually two per day, when the sea gradually falls to a lower level as the tide moves away from the land. 引き潮 ☐ ...the spring ebb tide. 春の引き潮 **3** V-I 自動詞 If someone's life, support, or feeling **ebbs**, it becomes weaker and gradually disappears. 衰退する [FORMAL 形式ばった] ☐ Were there occasions when enthusiasm ebbed? 熱狂が収まったときに好機があったのか。● PHRASAL VERB 句動詞 **Ebb away** means the same as **ebb**. 衰退する ☐ His little girl's life ebbed away. 彼の幼い娘の命は衰えた。**4** PHRASE 句 If someone or something is **at a low ebb** or at their **lowest ebb**, they are not very successful or profitable. 衰退しきって ☐ ...a time when everyone is tired and at a low ebb. 皆が疲れ沈みきっているとき

→ see **ocean, tide**

e-book (**e-books**) N-COUNT 可算名詞 An **e-book** is a book which is produced for reading on a computer screen. **E-book** is an abbreviation for **electronic book**. 電子書籍 ☐ In addition to the classics, the new e-books will include a host of Rough Guide titles. 古典に加え、新しい電子書籍にはラフガイド社の出版物も多く含まれる。

→ see **book**

ebul|lient /ɪbʌliənt, -bʊl-/ ADJ 形容詞 If you describe someone as **ebullient**, you mean that they are lively and full of enthusiasm or excitement about something. 活気のある [FORMAL 形式ばった] ☐ ...the ebullient Russian president. 活力にあふれるロシアの大統領 ● **ebul|lience** /ɪbʌliəns, -bʊl-/ N-UNCOUNT 不可算名詞 ほとばしり ☐ His natural ebullience began to return. 彼の自然の活力が戻り始めた。

e-business (**e-businesses**) **1** N-COUNT 可算名詞 An **e-business** is a business that uses the Internet to sell goods or services, especially one that does not also have stores or offices that people can visit or phone. 電子取引企業 [BUSINESS 実業] ☐ ...JSL Trading, an e-business in Vancouver. バンクーバーの電子ビジネス企業、JSLトレーディング社 **2** N-UNCOUNT 不可算名詞 **E-business** is the buying, selling, and ordering of goods and services using the Internet. 電子取引 [BUSINESS 実業] ☐ ...proven e-business solutions. 試験済みの電子取引手段

ec|cen|tric /ɪksɛntrɪk/ (**eccentrics**) ADJ 形容詞 If you say that someone is **eccentric**, you mean that they behave in a strange way, and have habits or opinions that are different from those of most people. 風変わりな ☐ He is an eccentric character who likes wearing a beret and dark glasses. 彼はベレー帽をかぶり色の濃いサングラスをかけるのが好きな変わり者だ。● N-COUNT 可算名詞 An **eccentric** is an eccentric person. 変人 ☐ Askew used several names, and had a reputation as an eccentric. アスキューはいくつかの名前を使い、変人との評判を得ていた。

ec|cen|tri|city /ɛksɛntrɪsiti/ (**eccentricities**) **1** N-UNCOUNT 不可算名詞 **Eccentricity** is unusual behavior that other people consider strange. 奇行 ☐ She is unusual to the point of eccentricity. 彼女は奇癖を持っているという点で変わっていた。**2** N-COUNT 可算名詞 **Eccentricities** are ways of behaving that people think are strange, or habits or opinions that are different from those of

Word Web — echo

We can learn a lot from studying **echoes**. Geologists use **sound reflection** to predict how earthquake waves will travel through the earth. They also use echolocation to find underground oil reservoirs. Oceanographers use sonar to explore the ocean. Marine mammals, bats, and humans also use sonar for navigation. Architects study building materials and surfaces to understand how they absorb or **reflect** sound **waves**. They may use hard reflective surfaces to help create a noisy, exciting atmosphere in a restaurant. They may suggest soft drapes and carpeting to create a quiet, calm library.

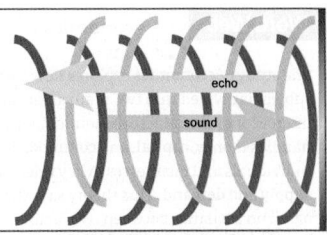

most people. 変わった点 □*We all have our eccentricities.* 我々は誰でも変わって点を持っている.

ec|cle|si|as|ti|cal /ɪkl,iziˈæstɪkəl/ ADJ 形容詞 **Ecclesiastical** means belonging to or connected with the Christian Church. キリスト教教会の □*My ambition was to travel upwards in the ecclesiastical hierarchy.* 私の野望は教会の身分階層を上まで昇ることだった.

eche|lon /ˈɛʃəlɒn/ (**echelons**) N-COUNT 可算名詞 An **echelon** in an organization or society is a level or rank in it. 階層 [FORMAL 形式ばった] □*...the lower echelons of society.* 社会の下層

echo /ˈɛkoʊ/ (**echoes, echoing, echoed**) **1** N-COUNT 可算名詞 An **echo** is a sound caused by a noise being reflected off a surface such as a wall. 反響 □*He listened and heard nothing but the echoes of his own voice in the cave.* 洞窟の中で彼は自分の声のこだましか耳にしなかった. **2** V-I 自動詞 If a sound **echoes**, it is reflected off a surface and can be heard again after the original sound has stopped. 反響 □*His feet echoed on the hardwood floor.* 彼の足音が硬い木の床で反響した. **3** V-I 自動詞 In a place that **echoes**, a sound is reflected off a surface, and is repeated after the original sound has stopped. 反響する □*The room echoed.* 部屋で音が反響した. □*The corridor echoed with the barking of a dozen dogs.* 多くの犬のほえる声が廊下にこだました. **4** V-T 他動詞 If you **echo** someone's words, you repeat them or express agreement with their attitude or opinion. 同調する □*Their views often echo each other.* 彼らの見解はしばしば互いに共鳴しあう. **5** N-COUNT 可算名詞 A detail or feature that reminds you of something else can be referred to as an **echo**. 名残 □*The accident has echoes of past disasters.* その事故は過去の災難の名残を引きずっている. **6** V-T 他動詞 If one thing **echoes** another, the first is a copy of a particular detail or feature of the other. 反映する □*Pinks and beiges were chosen to echo the colors of the ceiling.* 天井の色にあわせて桃色と肌色が選ばれた. **7** V-I 自動詞 If something **echoes**, it continues to be discussed and remains important or influential in a particular situation or among a particular group of people. 影響しつづける □*The old fable continues to echo down the centuries.* 古い寓話が数世紀にわたり影響を残し続ける.
→ see Word Web: **echo**
→ see **sound**

Word Link — ec ≈ away, from, out : eccentric, eclectic, ecstatic

ec|lec|tic /ɪklˈɛktɪk/ ADJ 詞 An **eclectic** collection of objects, ideas, or beliefs is wide-ranging and comes from many different sources. 多方面の [FORMAL 形式ばった] □*...an eclectic collection of paintings, drawings, and prints.* 絵画, デッサン, 版画の多種多様な収集品

eclipse /ɪklˈips/ (**eclipses, eclipsing, eclipsed**) **1** N-COUNT 可算名詞 An **eclipse** of the sun is an occasion when the moon is between the earth and the sun, so that for a short time you cannot see part or all of the sun. An **eclipse** of the moon is an occasion when the earth is between the sun and the moon, so that for a short time you cannot see part or all of the moon. (天体の) 食 □*...an eclipse of the sun.* 日食 □*...the solar eclipse on May 21.* 5月21日の日食 **2** V-T 他動詞 If one thing **is eclipsed by** a second thing that is bigger, newer, or more important than it, the first thing is no longer noticed because the second thing gets all the attention. 影を投げる □*...the space program has been eclipsed by other pressing needs.* 宇宙計画は他の切迫した案件の影となってきた.
→ see Word Web: **eclipse**

eco-friendly ADJ 形容詞 **Eco-friendly** products or services are less harmful to the environment than other similar products or services. 環境に優しい □*...eco-friendly laundry detergent.* 環境に優しい洗濯洗剤

eco|logi|cal /ˌɛkəlˈɒdʒɪkəl, iːk-/ ADJ 形容詞 **Ecological** means involved with or concerning ecology. 環境学の [ADJ n] □*Large dams have harmed Siberia's delicate ecological balance.* 大型ダムがシベリアの繊細な自然環境の釣り合いを損ねてきた. ● **eco|logi|cal|ly** /ˌɛkəlˈɒdʒɪkliː, iːk-/ ADV 副詞 環境学的に □*It is economical to run and ecologically sound.* それは経済的に実行できるし, 環境面でも健全だ.

ecol|ogist /ɪkˈɒlədʒɪst/ (**ecologists**) N-COUNT 可算名詞 An **ecologist** is a person who studies ecology. 環境学者 □*Ecologists argue that the benefits of treating sewage with disinfectants are doubtful.* 環境学者は消毒薬を使って沼を整備することの利点は疑わしいと論じる.

ecol|ogy /ɪkˈɒlədʒi/ (**ecologies**) **1** N-UNCOUNT 不可算名詞 **Ecology** is the study of the relationships between plants, animals, people, and their environment, and the balances between these relationships. 環境学 □*...a professor in ecology.* 環境学の教授 **2** N-VAR 可変性名詞 When you talk about the **ecology** of a place, you are referring to the pattern and balance of relationships between plants, animals, people, and the environment in that place. 生態系 □*...the ecology of the rocky Negev desert in Israel.* イスラエルの岩がちなネゲフ砂漠の生態系

Word Link — e ≈ electronic : e-book, e-commerce, e-mail

e-commerce N-UNCOUNT 不可算名詞 **E-commerce** is the same as **e-business**. 電子取引 [BUSINESS 実業] □*...the anticipated explosion of e-commerce.* 予想通りの電子取引の爆発的増加

eco|nom|ic /ˌɛkəˈnɒmɪk, iːk-/ **1** ADJ 形容詞 **Economic** means concerned with the organization of the money, industry, and trade of a country, region, or society. 経済の □*...Poland's radical economic reforms.* ポーランドの根本的な経済改革 ● **eco|nomi|cal|ly** /ˌɛkəˈnɒmɪkli, iːk-/ ADV 副詞 経済的に □*...an economically depressed area.* 経済の落ち込んだ地域 **2** ADJ 形容詞 If something is **economic**, it produces a profit. 利益の出る □*Critics say that the new system may be more economic but will lead to a decline in program quality.* 批評家は, 新しい制度は利潤を増やすかもしれないが, 計画の質を落とすだろうと言う.

eco|nomi|cal /ˌɛkəˈnɒmɪkəl, iːk-/ **1** ADJ 形容詞 Something that is **economical** does not require a lot of money to operate. For example, a car that only uses a small amount of gasoline is **economical**. 費用のかからない □*...plans to trade in their car for something smaller and more economical.* 彼らの車を下取りに出し, より小さくて経済的なものに変えるという計画 ● **eco|nomi|cal|ly** ADV 副詞 [ADV after v] 経済的に □*Services could be operated more efficiently and economically.* もっと効率的かつ経済的に業務の運営をできるかもしれない. **2** ADJ 形容詞 Someone who is **economical** spends money sensibly and does not want to waste it on things that are unnecessary. A way of life that is **economical** does not require a lot of money. 費用のかからない □*...ideas for economical housekeeping.* 経済的な家事の案 **3** ADJ 形容詞 **Economical** means using the minimum amount of time, effort, or language that is necessary. 経済的な □*His gestures were economical, his words generally mild.* 彼の仕草は最小限のものに絞られ, 言葉は概して穏やかだった.

Thesaurus — economical また次を参照:

ADJ.	cost-effective, inexpensive **1**
	careful, frugal, practical, thrifty **2**

Word Web — eclipse

When the **earth** passes between the **sun** and the **moon**, we see a lunar eclipse. When the moon passes between the sun and the earth, we see a solar eclipse. A total eclipse of the sun happens when the moon covers it completely. In the past, people were frightened of eclipses. Leaders of some civilizations understood eclipses. They pretended to control the sun in order to gain the respect of their people. On July 22, 2009, a total eclipse of the sun will be visible in North America.

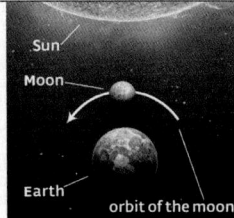

Word Web   economics

The study of **economics** explores how a society distributes its **wealth**. This subject is divided into two main areas: macroeconomics and microeconomics. Macroeconomics looks at how a society as a whole handles money, **capital**, and **commodities**. Microeconomics focuses on individuals and businesses. A key microeconomic principle is the law of **supply and demand**. This theory says that prices of **goods** and **services** are based on a balance between two factors. The first is how much of something is available (supply). The second is how much people are willing to pay for it (demand).

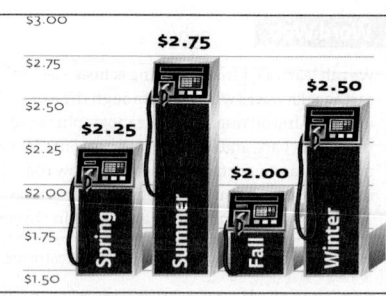

eco|nom|ics /ɛkənɒmɪks, ik-/ N-UNCOUNT 不可算名詞
Economics is the study of the way in which money, industry, and commerce are organized in a society. 経済学 ❑ *His younger sister is studying economics.* 彼の妹は経済学を学んでいる.
→ see Word Web: **economics**

econo|mies of scale N-PLURAL 複数名詞 **Economies of scale** are the financial advantages that a company gains when it produces large quantities of products. 規模の経済性 [BUSINESS 実業] ❑ *Some companies are simply trying to get bigger to achieve economies of scale.* 企業のなかには規模の経済を達成するため大きくなろうとするだけのものもある.

econo|mist /ɪkɒnəmɪst/ (**economists**) N-COUNT 可算名詞
An **economist** is a person who studies, teaches, or writes about economics. 経済学者, 経済の専門家

econo|mize /ɪkɒnəmaɪz/ (**economizes, economizing, economized**) V-I 自動詞 If you **economize**, you save money by spending it very carefully. 節約する ❑ *We're going to have to economize from now on.* 我々はこれから節約せねばならない.

econo|my /ɪkɒnəmi/ (**economies**) ❶ N-COUNT 可算名詞 An **economy** is the system according to which the money, industry, and commerce of a country or region are organized. 経済 ❑ *Zimbabwe boasts Africa's most industrialized economy.* ジンバブエはアフリカで最も工業化した経済圏であることを誇っている. ❷ N-COUNT 可算名詞 A country's **economy** is the wealth that it gets from business and industry. 経済 ❑ *The Japanese economy grew at an annual rate of more than 10 percent.* 日本経済は年率10パーセント以上で成長した. ❸ N-UNCOUNT 不可算名詞 **Economy** is the use of the minimum amount of money, time, or other resources needed to achieve something, so that nothing is wasted. 経済性 ❑ *...improvements in the fuel economy of cars.* 自動車の燃費向上 ❹ ADJ 形容詞 **Economy** services such as travel are cheap and have no luxuries or extras. 安価な [ADJ n] ❑ *...the limitations that come with economy travel.* 格安旅行に付随する制約 → see **economy class** ❺ ADJ 形容詞 **Economy** is used to describe large packs of products that are cheaper than normal sized packs. 買い得な [ADJ n] ❑ *...an economy pack containing 150 assorted screws.* 150個入りのお買い得な詰め合わせ ❻ PHRASE 句 If you describe an attempt to save money as a **false economy**, you mean that you have not saved any money as you will have to spend a lot more later. 見せかけの経済性 ❑ *A cheap bed can be a false economy, so spend as much as you can afford.* 安いベッドは高い買い物につくかもしれないので, できるだけ高価なものを選ぶべきだ.

econo|my class ADJ 形容詞 On an airplane, an **economy class** ticket or seat is the cheapest available. エコノミークラス ❑ *The price includes two economy class airfares from Brisbane to Los Angeles.* ブリスベーンからロサンジェルスまでのエコノミークラス二人分を含む値段. [ADJ n]

eco|sys|tem /ɛkoʊsɪstəm, ik-/ (**ecosystems**) N-COUNT 可算名詞 An **ecosystem** is all the plants and animals that live in a particular area together with the complex relationship that exists between them and their environment. 生態系 [TECHNICAL 技術的] ❑ *...the forest ecosystem.* 森林の生態系

eco|tour|ism /ɛkoʊtʊərɪzəm, ik-/ N-UNCOUNT 不可算名詞 **Ecotourism** is the business of providing vacations and related services that are not harmful to the environment of the area. 環境を大事にする観光 ● **eco|tour|ist** /ɛkoʊtʊərɪst, ik-/ (**ecotourists**) N-COUNT 可算名詞 環境を考えて観光する人 ❑ *...an environmentally sensitive project to cater to ecotourists.* 環境を考える旅行者に食事を提供する環境に配慮した計画 [BUSINESS 実業]

ec|sta|sy /ɛkstəsi/ (**ecstasies**) ❶ N-VAR 可変性名詞 **Ecstasy** is a feeling of very great happiness. 法悦 ❑ *...a state of almost religious ecstasy.* ほとんど宗教的な法悦に近い状態 ❷ N-UNCOUNT 不可算名詞 **Ecstasy** is an illegal drug that makes people feel happy and energetic. エクスタシー ❑ *The teenager died after taking ecstasy on her birthday.* 十代の少女が誕生日にエクスタシーを使い死亡した.

Word Link   ec ≈ away, from, out : eccentric, eclectic, ecstatic

ec|stat|ic /ɛkstætɪk/ ❶ ADJ 形容詞 If you are **ecstatic**, you feel very happy and full of excitement. 有頂天の ❑ *His wife gave birth to their first child, and he was ecstatic about it.* 妻が最初の子を産み, 彼は有頂天になった. ● **ec|stati|cal|ly** /ɛkstætɪkli/ ADV 副詞 有頂天で ❑ *We are both ecstatically happy.* 我々は両方とも有頂天になるほど幸福だ. ❷ ADJ 形容詞 [ADJ n] You can use **ecstatic** to describe reactions that are very enthusiastic and excited. For example, if someone receives an **ecstatic** reception or an **ecstatic** welcome, they are greeted with great enthusiasm and excitement. 熱狂的な ❑ *They gave an ecstatic reception to the speech.* 彼らはその演説を熱狂的に歓迎した.

ec|ze|ma /ɛksəmə, ɛgzə-, ɪgzi-/ N-UNCOUNT 不可算名詞 **Eczema** is a skin condition that makes your skin itch and become sore, rough, and broken. 湿しん

edge /ɛdʒ/ (**edges, edging, edged**) ❶ N-COUNT 可算名詞 The **edge** of something is the place or line where it stops, or the part of it that is farthest from the middle. 端 ❑ *We were on a hill, right on the edge of town.* 我々は町のちょうど端にある丘の上にいた. ❑ *She was standing at the water's edge.* 彼女は水際に立っていた. ❷ N-COUNT 可算名詞 The **edge** of something sharp such as a knife or an ax is its sharp or narrow side. 刃 ❑ *...the sharp edge of the sword.* 剣の鋭い刃 ❸ V-I 自動詞 If someone or something **edges** somewhere, they move very slowly in that direction. じりじり進む ❑ *He edged closer to the telephone, ready to grab it.* 彼は電話のほうにじりじりと進み, 受話器をつかむ体勢をとった. ❹ N-SING 単数名詞 The **edge** of something, especially something bad, is the point at which it may start to happen. 間際 ❑ *They have driven the rhino to the edge of extinction.* 彼らはサイを絶滅の間際まで追いやった. ❺ N-SING 単数名詞 If someone or something has an **edge**, they have an advantage that makes them stronger or more likely to be successful than another thing or person. 優越 ❑ *The three days Uruguay have to prepare could give them the edge over Brazil.* ウルグアイが三日の準備期間を持てたことは, ブラジルに対する彼らの優位につながったかもしれない. ❻ N-SING 単数名詞 If you say that someone or something has an **edge**, you mean that they have a powerful quality. 力強さ ❑ *Featuring new bands gives the show an edge.* 新しい楽団を使うことで出し物に迫力が出る. ❼ N-SING 単数名詞 If someone's voice has an **edge to** it, it has a sharp, bitter, or emotional quality. 鋭さ ❑ *But underneath the humor is an edge of bitterness.* しかしこっけい味の裏には辛らつな鋭さがある. ❽ → see also **cutting edge, leading edge** ❾ PHRASE 句 If you or your nerves are **on edge**, you are tense, nervous, and unable to relax. 興奮している ❑ *My nerves were constantly on edge.* 私の神経は常に張り詰めていた. ❿ PHRASE 句 If something **takes the edge off** an unpleasant situation, it weakens its effect or intensity. 鈍らせる ❑ *Poor health took the edge off her performance.* 体調の悪さが彼女の演技を鈍らせた.

▶ **edge out** PHRASAL VERB 句動詞 If someone **edges out** someone else, they just manage to beat them or get in front of them in a game, race, or contest. 辛勝する ❑ *In the second race, the American competitor edged out the Ethiopian runner by less than a second.* 第2レースでアメリカの選手がエチオピアの走者に2秒足らずの差で辛勝した.

Thesaurus   edge また次を参照:

N.   border, boundary, rim; (ant.) center, middle ❶
      advantage ❺

edged /ɛdʒd/ ADJ 形容詞 If something is **edged with** a particular thing, that thing forms a border around it. 縁取った [v-link ADJ 'with/in' n] ❑ *...a large lawn edged with flowers and shrubs.* 花と低木で縁取られた広い芝生 ● COMB IN ADJ 形容詞の複合 **Edged** is also a combining form. 縁取りの ❑ *...clutching a lace-edged handkerchief.* レースで縁取ったハンカチを握り締め

edgy /ɛdʒi/ (**edgier, edgiest**) ADJ 形容詞 If someone is **edgy**, they are nervous and anxious, and seem likely to lose control of themselves. いらいらした [INFORMAL くだけた] ❑ *She was nervous and edgy, still chain-smoking.* 彼女は神経質でいらいらしており，相変わらず次々とたばこを吸っていた．

ed|ible /ɛdɪbəl/ ADJ 形容詞 If something is **edible**, it is safe to eat and not poisonous. 食用の ❑ *...edible fungi.* 食用キノコ類

edict /idɪkt/ (**edicts**) N-COUNT 可算名詞 An **edict** is a command or instruction given by someone in authority. 指令 [FORMAL 形式ばった] ❑ *He issued an edict that none of his writings be destroyed.* 彼は自分の著作は一切破損してはならないとの指令を発した．

edi|fice /ɛdɪfɪs/ (**edifices**) N-COUNT 可算名詞 An **edifice** is a large and impressive building. 大建築 [FORMAL 形式ばった] ❑ *The taxi driver reeled off a list of historic edifices they must not fail to visit.* タクシーの運転手は彼らが必ず訪問すべき歴史的大建築の一覧をひもといて見せた．

edit /ɛdɪt/ (**edits, editing, edited**) ■ V-T 他動詞 If you **edit** a text such as an article or a book, you correct and adapt it so that it is suitable for publishing. 校定する ❑ *The majority of contracts give the publisher the right to edit a book after it's done.* 大半の契約で，出版後，出版社に書籍校定の権利がある． ② V-T 他動詞 If you **edit** a book or a series of books, you collect several pieces of writing by different authors and prepare them for publishing. 編集する ❑ *This collection of essays is edited by Ellen Knight.* この随筆集はエレン・ナイトによって編集された． ❑ *He edits the literary journal, Murmur.* 彼は文芸誌『マーマー』を編集している． ③ V-T 他動詞 If you **edit** a movie or a television or radio program, you choose some of what has been filmed or recorded and arrange it in a particular order. 編集する ❑ *He taught me to edit and splice film.* 彼は私に映画を編集しつなぎ合わせることを教えた． ④ V-T 他動詞 Someone who **edits** a newspaper, magazine, or journal is in charge of it. 編集する ❑ *I used to edit the college paper in the old days.* 昔，私は大学新聞の編集をしていた．

edi|tion /idɪʃən/ (**editions**) ■ N-COUNT 可算名詞 An **edition** is a particular version of a book, magazine, or newspaper that is printed at one time. 版 ② N-COUNT 可算名詞 An **edition** is the total number of copies of a particular book or newspaper that are printed at one time. 版 ❑ *The second edition was published only in Canada.* 第2版はカナダのみで出版された． ③ N-COUNT 可算名詞 An **edition** is a single television or radio program that is one of a series about a particular subject. 一回分の放送 ❑ *...an interview featured on last week's edition of "60 Minutes."* 先週の『60ミニッツ』の特集となった会見

Word Partnership	*edition* は次の語句と使われる:
N.	**collector's** edition, **paperback** edition ■ ②
ADJ.	**new** edition, **special** edition ■ - ③
	limited edition, **revised** edition ②

edi|tor /ɛdɪtər/ (**editors**) ■ N-COUNT 可算名詞 An **editor** is the person who is in charge of a newspaper or magazine and who decides what will be published in each edition of it. 編集者 ❑ *Her father was the former editor of the Saturday Review.* 彼女の父は『サタデーレビュー』誌の元編集者だった． ② N-COUNT 可算名詞 An **editor** is a journalist who is responsible for a particular section of a newspaper or magazine. 部長 ❑ *Mike later became the sports editor for The Beacon.* マイクはのちに『ザ・ビーコン』紙の運動部長となった． ③ N-COUNT 可算名詞 An **editor** is a person who checks and corrects texts before they are published. 編集者 ❑ *Your role as editor is important, for you can look at a piece of writing objectively.* 編集者としてのあなたの役割は重要だ．あなたは客観的にその著作を見ることができるのだから． ④ N-COUNT 可算名詞 An **editor** is a radio or television journalist who reports on a particular type of news. 編集者 ❑ *...our economics editor, Tom Goldberg.* 当局の経済担当編集者，トム・ゴールドバーグ ⑤ N-COUNT 可算名詞 An **editor** is a person who prepares a movie, or a radio or television program, by selecting some of what has been filmed or recorded and putting it in a particular order. 編集者 ❑ *A few years earlier, she had worked at 20th Century Fox as a film editor.* 数年後，彼女は映画編集者として20世紀フォックス社で働いていた． ⑥ N-COUNT 可算名詞 An **editor** is a person who collects pieces of writing by different authors and prepares them for publication in a book or a series of books. 編集者 ❑ *Michael Rosen is the editor of the anthology.* マイケル・ローゼンはこの作品集の編集者だ． ⑦ N-COUNT 可算名詞 An **editor** is a computer program that enables you to change and correct stored data. エディタ ❑ *To edit it, you need to run the built-in Windows Registry editor.* その変更にはウィンドウズに組み込まれたレジストリ・エディタを起動する必要がある． [COMPUTING コンピューティング]

edi|to|rial /ɛdɪtɔriəl/ (**editorials**) ■ ADJ 形容詞 **Editorial** means involved in preparing a newspaper, magazine, or book for publication. 編集に関する [ADJ n] ❑ *I went to the editorial board meetings when I had the time.* 時間のあるときには編集役員会議に行った． ② ADJ 形容詞 **Editorial** means involving the attitudes, opinions, and contents of something such as a newspaper, magazine, or television program. 論説の [ADJ n] ❑ *We are not about to change our editorial policy.* 我々は論説の方針を変えるつもりはない． ③ N-COUNT 可算名詞 An **editorial** is an article in a newspaper that gives the opinion of the editor or owner on a topic or item of news. 論説 ❑ *In an editorial, The New York Times suggests the victory could turn nasty.* 論説記事で，『ニューヨーク・タイムズ』紙は勝利が汚点になるかもしれないと示唆している．
→ see **newspaper**

edu|cate /ɛdʒʊkeɪt/ (**educates, educating, educated**) ■ V-T 他動詞 When someone, especially a child, **is educated**, he or she is taught at a school or college. 教育する [usu passive] ❑ *He was educated at Yale and Stanford.* 彼はエール大学とスタンフォード大学で教育を受けた． ② V-T 他動詞 To **educate** people means to teach them better ways of doing something or a better way of living. 教える ❑ *...World AIDS Day, an event designed to educate people about AIDS.* 人々にエイズについて伝えることを目的とした催し，世界エイズデー

Note that you do not use **educate** or **education** to talk about the way parents look after their children and teach them about good behavior and life in general. Instead, you should use the verb **bring up** or the noun **upbringing.** ❑ *His parents brought him up to be polite and courteous.*

Thesaurus	*educate* また次を参照:
V.	coach, instruct, teach, train ②

edu|cat|ed /ɛdʒʊkeɪtɪd/ ADJ 形容詞 Someone who is **educated** has a high standard of learning. 学識ある ❑ *The new CEO is an educated, amiable, and decent man.* 新しい最高経営責任者は，学識が高く，気立てがよく，上品な男だ．

edu|ca|tion /ɛdʒʊkeɪʃən/ (**educations**) ■ N-VAR 可変性名詞 **Education** involves teaching people various subjects, usually at a school or college, or being taught. 教育 ❑ *They're cutting funds for education.* 彼らは教育資金を削減した． ② N-UNCOUNT 不可算名詞 **Education** of a particular kind involves teaching the public about a particular issue. 教育 ❑ *...better health education.* よりよい健康教育 ③ → see also **further education, higher education**

edu|ca|tion|al /ɛdʒʊkeɪʃənəl/ ■ ADJ 形容詞 **Educational** matters or institutions are concerned with or relate to education. 教育的な ❑ *...the Japanese educational system.* 日本の教育制度 ② ADJ 形容詞 An **educational** experience teaches you something. ためになる ❑ *The staff should make sure the kids have an enjoyable and educational day.* 職員は子供たちが楽しくてためになる1日を過ごしていることを確認すること．

eel /il/ (**eels**) N-VAR 可変性名詞 An **eel** is a long, thin fish that looks like a snake. ウナギ ● N-UNCOUNT 不可算名詞 **Eel** is the flesh of this fish eaten as food. ウナギは食べ物になるこの魚の身です． ❑ *...smoked eel.* ウナギの薫製

eerie /ɪəri/ (**eerier, eeriest**) ADJ 形容詞 If you describe something as **eerie**, you mean that it seems strange and frightening, and makes you feel nervous. 不気味な ❑ *I walked down the eerie dark path.* 私は不気味な暗い小路を歩いた． ● **eeri|ly** /ɪərili/ ADV 副詞 ぞっとするほど ❑ *Monrovia after the fighting is eerily quiet.* 戦闘の後のモンロビアは不気味なほど静かだ．

ef|fect /ɪfɛkt/ (**effects, effecting, effected**) ■ N-VAR 可変性名詞 The **effect of** one thing **on** another is the change that the first thing causes in the second thing. 影響 ❑ *Parents worry about the effect of music on their adolescent's behavior.* 親たちは彼らの青年期の行動に対する音楽の影響について心配している． ② N-COUNT 可算名詞 An **effect** is an impression that someone creates deliberately, for example in a place or in a piece of writing. 効果 ❑ *The whole effect is cool, light, and airy.* 全体の印象は涼しげで明るく空気のようだ． ③ N-PLURAL 複数名詞 A person's **effects** are the things that they have with them at a particular time, for example when they are arrested or admitted to a hospital, or the things that they owned when they died. 動産 [FORMAL 形式ばった] ❑ *His daughters were collecting his effects.* 彼の娘が彼の個人資産を集めていた． ④ N-PLURAL 複数名詞 The **effects** in a movie are the specially created sounds and scenery. 効果 ❑ *It's got a gripping story, great acting, superb sets, and stunning effects.* それは，人をひきつける筋書き，素晴らしい演技，最高の舞台装置，さらに驚くような効果を具えている． ⑤ V-T 他動詞 If you **effect** something that you are trying to achieve, you succeed in causing it to happen. もたらす [FORMAL 形式ばった] ❑ *Prospects for effecting real political change seemed to have taken a major step backwards.* 実際の政治的変化をもたらす見込みは大きく後退したように思われた． ⑥ → see also **greenhouse effect, side-effect, special effect**

Note that the verb **affect** is connected with the noun **effect**. You can say that something **affects** you. ❑ *Noise affects different people in different ways.* You can also say that something has an **effect** on you ❑ *...the effect that noise has on people in factories.*

7 PHRASE 句 If you say that someone is doing something **for effect**, you mean that they are doing it in order to impress people and to draw attention to themselves. 効果をねらって ❑ *The southern accent was put on for effect.* 効果をねらって南部なまりが使われた. **8** PHRASE 句 You add **in effect** to a statement or opinion that is not precisely accurate, but that you feel is a reasonable description or summary of a particular situation. 事実上 [VAGUENESS あいまいさ] ❑ *That deal would create, in effect, the world's biggest airline.* その取引は, 事実上, 世界最大の航空会社を作り出すかもしれない. **9** PHRASE 句 If you **put, bring**, or **carry a plan or idea into effect**, you cause it to happen in practice. 実施する ❑ *These and other such measures ought to have been put into effect in 1985.* あれやこれやのこうした方策は1985年に実施されているべきだった. **10** PHRASE 句 If a law or policy **takes effect** or **comes into effect** at a particular time, it officially begins to apply or be valid from that time. If it **remains in effect**, it still applies or is still valid. 発効する ❑ *...the ban on new logging permits which will take effect in July.* 7月に発効する新たな伐木搬出許可の禁止 **11** PHRASE 句 You can say that something **takes effect** when it starts to produce the results that are intended. 効果を生じる ❑ *The second injection should only have been given once the first drug had taken effect.* 最初の薬が効果を現した場合のみ, 二度目の注射を打つこと. **12** PHRASE 句 You use **effect** in expressions such as **to good effect** and **to no effect** in order to indicate how successful or impressive an action is. 効果的に ❑ *Mr. Morris feels the museum is using advertising to good effect.* モリス氏はその博物館が効果的に広告を使用していると感じている. **13** PHRASE 句 You use **to this effect, to that effect**, or **to the effect that** to indicate that you have given or are giving a summary of something that was said or written, and not the actual words used. この趣旨で, その趣旨で ❑ *I understand that a circular to this effect will be issued in the next few weeks.* この趣旨の回覧状が2, 3週間で発行されると理解しました.

Word Partnership   *effect* は次の語句と使われる:

ADJ.	**adverse** effect, **negative/positive** effect **1**
	desired effect, **immediate** effect, **lasting** effect **1 2**
V.	**have an** effect **1**
	produce an effect **2**
	take effect **11**
N.	effect **a change** **5**

ef|fec|tive /ɪfɛktɪv/ **1** ADJ 形容詞 Something that is **effective** works well and produces the results that were intended. 効果的な ❑ *The project looks at how we could be more effective in encouraging students to enter teacher training.* その計画は, より効果的に学生を教員養成に送り込む方法について調べている. ❑ *Simple antibiotics are effective against this organism.* 簡単な抗生物質がこの菌に対して有効だ. ●**ef|fec|tive|ly** ADV 副詞 ❑ *Services need to be organized more effectively than they are at present.* 業務が現在よりもより効果的に組織される必要がある. ●**ef|fec|tive|ness** N-UNCOUNT 不可算名詞 ❑ *...the effectiveness of computers as an educational tool.* 教育の道具としてのコンピューターの有効性 **2** ADJ 形容詞 [ADJ n] **Effective** means having a particular role or result in practice, though not officially or in theory. 事実上の ❑ *They have had effective control of the area since the security forces left.* 保安軍撤退後, 彼らがその地域の事実上の支配権を握ってきた. **3** ADJ 形容詞 When something such as a law or an agreement becomes **effective**, it begins officially to apply or be valid. 実効力のある [v-link ADJ] ❑ *The new rules will become effective in the next few days.* ここ数日で新しい規則が発効する.

Word Partnership   *effective* は次の語句と使われる:

N.	effective **means**, effective **method**, effective **treatment**, effective **use** **1**
ADV.	**highly** effective **1**
	effective **immediately** **3**

ef|fec|tive|ly /ɪfɛktɪvli/ ADV 副詞 You use **effectively** with a statement or opinion to indicate that it is not accurate in every detail, but that you feel it is a reasonable description or summary of a particular situation. 事実上 ❑ *The region was effectively independent.* その地域は事実上独立していた.

ef|fi|ca|cy /ɛfɪkəsi/ N-UNCOUNT 不可算名詞 If you talk about the **efficacy** of something, you are talking about its effectiveness and its ability to do what it is supposed to. 有効性 [FORMAL 形式ばった] ❑ *Recent medical studies confirm the efficacy of a healthier lifestyle.* より健康的な生活習慣の有効性が最近の医学研究により確かめられている.

ef|fi|cien|cy /ɪfɪʃnsi/ N-UNCOUNT 不可算名詞 **Efficiency** is the quality of being able to do a task successfully, without wasting time or energy. 効率性 ❑ *There are many ways to increase agricultural efficiency in the poorer areas of the world.* 世界のより貧しい地域では農業の効率性を高めるための多くの手段がある.

ef|fi|cient /ɪfɪʃ^ənt/ ADJ 形容詞 If something or someone is **efficient**, they are able to do tasks successfully, without wasting time or energy. 効率的な ❑ *With today's more efficient contraception women can plan their families and careers.* 今日のより効率的な避妊法により, 女性は家族と仕事について計画することができる. ●**ef|fi|cient|ly** ADV 副詞 効率的に ❑ *I work very efficiently and am decisive, and accurate in my judgement.* 私はとても効率的に働く, 決断力もあり, 判断は正確だ.

Word Partnership   *efficient* は次の語句と使われる:

N.	**energy** efficient, **fuel** efficient, efficient **method**, efficient **system**, efficient **use of something**
ADV.	**highly** efficient

ef|fort /ɛfərt/ (efforts) **1** N-VAR 可変性名詞 If you make an **effort to** do something, you try very hard to do it. 努力 ❑ *He made no effort to hide his disappointment.* 彼は自分の失望を隠すための努力をしなかった. ❑ *Finding a cure requires considerable time and effort.* 治療法を見つけるにはかなりの時間と努力が必要だ. **2** N-UNCOUNT 不可算名詞 If you say that someone did something **with effort** or **with an effort**, you mean it was difficult for them to do. 苦労 [WRITTEN 書き言葉] [usu 'with' N, also 'a' N] ❑ *She took a deep breath and sat up slowly and with great effort.* 彼女は深々と呼吸し, ゆっくりと大変な苦労をして座りなおした. **3** N-COUNT 可算名詞 An **effort** is a particular series of activities that is organized by a group of people in order to achieve something. 取り組み ❑ *...a famine relief effort in Angola.* アンゴラの飢餓救済の取り組み **4** N-SING 単数名詞 If you say that something is an **effort**, you mean that an unusual amount of physical or mental energy is needed to do it. 奮闘 ❑ *Even carrying the camcorder while hiking in the forest was an effort.* 森林の歩行では録画装置の運搬でさえも奮闘になった. **5** PHRASE 句 If you **make the effort to** do something, you do it, even though you need extra energy to do it or you do not really want to. 努力する ❑ *I don't get lonely now because I make the effort to see people.* 人と会う努力をするので, 今, 私は寂しくならない.

Thesaurus   *effort* また次を参照:

N.	attempt **1**
	exertion, labor, work **4**

ef|fort|less /ɛfərtlɪs/ **1** ADJ 形容詞 Something that is **effortless** is done easily and well. 簡単な ❑ *...effortless and elegant Italian cooking.* 簡単で洗練されたイタリア料理 ●**ef|fort|less|ly** ADV 副詞 楽に ❑ *Her son Peter adapted effortlessly to his new surroundings.* 彼女の息子のピーターは新しい環境に難なく順応した. **2** ADJ 形容詞 You use **effortless** to describe a quality that someone has naturally and does not have to learn. 巧まない ❑ *She liked him above all for his effortless charm.* 彼女は彼のさりげない魅力が何よりも好きだった.

EFL /i ɛf ɛl/ N-UNCOUNT 不可算名詞 **EFL** is the teaching of English to people whose first language is not English. **EFL** is an abbreviation for "English as a Foreign Language." English as a Foreign Languageの略. 外国語としての英語 [oft N n] ❑ *...an EFL teacher.* EFLの教師

e.g. /i dʒi/ **e.g.** is an abbreviation that means "for example." It is used before a noun, or to introduce another sentence. 例えば ❑ *We need helpers of all types, e.g., geologists and teachers.* 我々には, 例えば地質学者や教師などのあらゆるタイプの助力が必要だ.

egg /ɛg/ (eggs, egging, egged) **1** N-COUNT 可算名詞 An **egg** is an oval object that is produced by a female bird and contains a baby bird. Other animals such as reptiles and fish also lay eggs. 卵 ❑ *...a baby bird hatching from its egg.* 卵から孵化(ふか)するひな **2** N-VAR 可変性名詞 In many countries, **eggs** often means hen's eggs, eaten as food. 鶏卵 ❑ *Break the eggs into a shallow bowl and beat them lightly.* 浅いボウルに卵を割り, 軽くかき混ぜます. **3** N-COUNT 可算名詞 **Egg** is used to refer to an object in the shape of a hen's egg. 卵形のもの ❑ *...a chocolate egg.* 卵形のチョコレート **4** N-COUNT 可算名詞 An **egg** is a cell that is produced in the bodies of female animals and humans. If it is fertilized by a sperm, a baby develops from it. 卵子 ❑ *It only takes one sperm to fertilize an egg.* 卵子を受精させるには精子が1つしか要らない. **5** PHRASE 句 If someone puts **all** their **eggs in one basket**, they put all their effort or resources into doing one thing so that, if it fails, they have no alternatives left. 1つのことに全てをかける ❑ *The key word here is diversify; don't put all your eggs in one basket.* ここでのキイワードは多角化だ. 1つの事業に全財産を投資してはならない. **6** PHRASE 句 If someone has **egg on** their **face** or has **egg all over** their **face**, they have been made to look foolish. 恥をさらす ❑ *If*

Picture Dictionary

egg

fried egg   scrambled eggs   hard-boiled egg   soft-boiled egg   omelet

they take this game lightly they could end up with egg on their faces. この試合を軽く見るなら、彼らは最後に面目を失う可能性がある.

▶ **egg on** PHRASAL VERB 句動詞 If you **egg** a person **on**, you encourage them to do something, especially something dangerous or foolish. そそのかす □ He was lifting up handfuls of leaves and throwing them at her. She was laughing and egging him on. 彼は落ち葉をひとつかみ拾って彼女に投げつけていた. 彼女は笑ってけしかけていた.

→ see Picture Dictionary: **egg**
→ see bird

egg|plant /ɛgplænt/ (**eggplants**) N-VAR 可変性名詞 An **eggplant** is a vegetable with a smooth, dark purple skin. ナス [AM 米国英語]

ego /iɡoʊ, ɛɡoʊ/ (**egos**) N-VAR 可変性名詞 Someone's **ego** is their sense of their own worth. For example, if someone has a large **ego**, they think they are very important and valuable. 自尊心 □ He had a massive ego, never would he admit he was wrong. 彼は自尊心が強く、絶対に自分が間違っていると認めようとしなかった.

Word Partnership ego は次の語句と使われる:

ADJ. **big** ego
V. **boost** *someone's* ego

eh /eɪ/ CONVENTION 慣習表現 **Eh** is used in writing to represent a noise that people make as a response in conversation, for example to express agreement or to ask for something to be explained or repeated. (同意して、説明を求めて) えっ!、でしょう? □ Let's talk all about it outside, eh? それについては全て外で話そうか.

eight /eɪt/ (**eights**) NUM 数詞 **Eight** is the number 8. (基数の) 8 □ So far eight workers have been killed. これまでに8名の作業員が死亡した.

Word Link teen ≈ plus ten, from 13-19 : eigh*teen*, seven*teen*, *teen*ager

eight|een /eɪtin/ NUM 数詞 **Eighteen** is the number 18. (基数の) 18 □ He was employed by them for eighteen years. 彼は18年間彼らに雇われていた.

eight|eenth /eɪtinθ/ ORD 序数詞 The **eighteenth** item in a series is the one that you count as number eighteen. 第18番目の □ The siege is now in its eighteenth day. 包囲攻撃は現在18日目である.

eighth /eɪtθ/ (**eighths**) **1** ORD 序数詞 The **eighth** item in a series is the one that you count as number eight. 第8番目の □ ...the eighth prime minister of India. インドの第8代目首相 **2** FRACTION 端数 An **eighth** is one of eight equal parts of something. 8分の1 □ The Kuban produces an eighth of Russia's grain, meat, and milk. クバン地方はロシアの穀物、肉、牛乳の8分の1を産出する.

eighti|eth /eɪtiəθ/ ORD 序数詞 The **eightieth** item in a series is the one that you count as number eighty. 第80番目 □ Mr. Stevens recently celebrated his eightieth birthday. スティーブンズ氏は最近80歳の誕生日を祝った.

eighty /eɪti/ (**eighties**) **1** NUM 数詞 **Eighty** is the number 80. (基数の) 80 □ Eighty horses trotted up. 80頭の馬が駆け上った. **2** N-PLURAL 複数名詞 When you talk about the **eighties**, you are referring to numbers between 80 and 89. For example, if you are **in** your **eighties**, you are aged between 80 and 89. If the temperature is **in the eighties**, the temperature is between 80 and 89 degrees. 80から89までの数、(年齢の) 80代 □ He was in his late eighties and had become the country's most respected elder statesman. 彼は80代後半でその国で最も尊敬される元老となっていた. **3** N-PLURAL 複数名詞 The **eighties** is the decade between 1980 and 1989. 1980年代 □ He ran a property development business in the eighties. 彼は80年代に不動産開発業を営んだ.

either /iðər, aɪðər/ **1** CONJ 接続詞 You use **either** in front of the first of two or more alternatives, when you are stating the only possibilities or choices that there are. The other alternatives are introduced by "or." かまたは―か □ Sightseeing is best done either by tour bus or by bicycles. 観光は観光バスか自転車でするのが

一番よい. □ The former president was demanding that he should be either put on trial or set free. 前大統領は裁判にかけられるか、または釈放されるかのいずれかを要求していた. **2** CONJ 接続詞 You use **either** in a negative statement in front of the first of two alternatives to indicate that the negative statement refers to both the alternatives. どちらの―も □ There had been no indication of either breathlessness or any loss of mental faculties right until his death. 彼には死の直前まで呼吸困難も精神機能の喪失の兆候も見られなかった. **3** PRON 代名詞 You can use **either** to refer to one of two things, people, or situations, when you want to say that they are both possible and it does not matter which one is chosen or considered. どちらも □ There were glasses of iced champagne and cigars. Unfortunately not many of either were consumed. グラスに入った冷やしたシャンパンと葉巻があった. 残念ながらどちらもかなり残っていた. ● QUANT 数量詞 **Either** is also a quantifier. どちらか一方 [QUANT 'of' def-pl-n] □ Do either of you smoke or drink heavily? 君たちのどちらかはヘビースモーカーまたは大酒のみか. ● DET 限定詞 **Either** is also a determiner. どちらかの □ ...a special Indian drug police that would have the authority to pursue suspects into either country. どちらの国へも容疑者を追跡する権限を持つインドの特別麻薬警察 **4** PRON 代名詞 You use **either** in a negative statement to refer to each of two things, people, or situations to indicate that the negative statement includes both of them. どちらも [with brd-neg] □ She warned me that I'd never marry or have children. — "I don't want either." 彼女は私が結婚もしなければ子供を生むこともないだろうと警告した. 「私はどちらも望んでいない」 ● QUANT 数量詞 **Either** is also a quantifier. どちらも □ There are no simple answers to either of those questions. そうした質問のどちらにも簡単な答えはない. ● DET 限定詞 **Either** is also a determiner. どちらの □ He sometimes couldn't remember either man's name. 彼はどちらの男の名前も思い出せないことがあった. **5** ADV 副詞 You use **either** by itself in negative statements to indicate that there is a similarity or connection with a person or thing that you have just mentioned. もまた―ない [ADV after v, with brd-neg] □ He did not even say anything to her, and she did not speak to him either. 彼は彼女にはひと言も口を利かず、彼女も彼に話しかけなかった. **6** ADV 副詞 When one negative statement follows another, you can use **either** at the end of the second one to indicate that you are adding an extra piece of information, and to emphasize that both are equally important. …と言っても [ADV after v] □ Don't agree, but don't argue either. 同意するな、と言っても文句も言ってはならない. **7** DET 限定詞 You can use **either** to introduce a noun that refers to each of two things when you are talking about both of them. 両方の □ The basketball nets hung down from the ceiling at either end of the gymnasium. バスケットボールのネットは体育館の両端の天井から垂れ下がっていた.

Word Link e ≈ away, out : eject, emigrate, emit

eject /ɪdʒɛkt/ (**ejects, ejecting, ejected**) **1** V-T 他動詞 If you **eject** someone **from** a place, you force them to leave. 追い出す □ Officials used guard dogs to eject the protesters. 役人は番犬を使って抗議者たちを追い払った. ● ejec|tion /ɪdʒɛkʃ⁰n/ (**ejections**) N-VAR 可変性名詞 追い出し □ ...the ejection and manhandling of hecklers at the meeting. 集会で野次を飛ばす連中の追い出しと手荒い扱い **2** V-T 他動詞 To **eject** something means to remove it or push it out forcefully. 吐き出す □ He aimed his rifle, fired a single shot, then ejected the spent cartridge. 彼はライフルの的を定め、一発発射し、それから使用済みの弾薬筒をはき出した. **3** V-I 自動詞 When a pilot **ejects from** an aircraft, he or she leaves the aircraft quickly using an ejector seat, usually because the plane is about to crash. 脱出する □ The pilot ejected from the plane and escaped injury. パイロットは飛行機から脱出し、けがを負わずにすんだ.

Word Link labor ≈ working : collabor*ate*, elabor*ate*, *labor*atory

elabo|rate (**elaborates, elaborating, elaborated**)

The adjective is pronounced /ɪlæbərɪt/. The verb is pronounced /ɪlæbəreɪt/.

形容詞は /ɪlæbərɪt/ と発音される. 動詞は /ɪlæbəreɪt/ と発音される.

1 ADJ 形容詞 You use **elaborate** to describe something that is

very complex because it has a lot of different parts. 複雑な ☐...*an elaborate research project.* 複雑な研究計画 **2** ADJ 形容詞 **Elaborate** plans, systems, and procedures are complicated because they have been planned in very great detail, sometimes too much detail. 入念な ☐...*elaborate efforts at the highest level to conceal the problem.* 問題を頭べいしようとするトップレベルによる入念な試み ● **ela|bo|rate|ly** ADV 副詞 入念に ☐*It was clearly an elaborately planned operation.* それは明らかに入念に計画された作戦だった。 **3** ADJ 形容詞 **Elaborate** clothing or material is made with a lot of detailed artistic designs. 手のこんだ ☐*He is known for his elaborate costumes.* 彼は手のこんだコスチュームで知られている。 **4** V-T 他動詞 If you **elaborate** a plan or theory, you develop it by making it more complicated and more effective. 練り上げる ☐*His task was to elaborate policies that would make a market economy compatible with a clean environment.* 彼の仕事は市場経済を環境保護と両立させる政策を練り上げることだった。 ● **elabo|ra|tion** /ɪlæbəreɪʃən/ N-UNCOUNT 不可算名詞 練り上げること ☐...*the elaboration of specific policies and mechanisms.* 特定の政策と仕組みを練り上げること **5** V-I 自動詞 If you **elaborate** on something that has been said, you say more about it, or give more details. 詳しく述べる ☐*A spokesman declined to elaborate on a statement released late yesterday.* スポークスマンは昨日遅く発表された声明について詳しく述べることを拒否した。

elapse /ɪlæps/ (**elapses, elapsing, elapsed**) V-I 自動詞 When time **elapses**, it passes. 経過する [FORMAL 形式ばった] ☐*Forty-eight hours have elapsed since his arrest.* 彼が逮捕されてから48時間が経過した。

elas|tic /ɪlæstɪk/ **1** N-UNCOUNT 不可算名詞 **Elastic** is a rubber material that stretches when you pull it and returns to its original size and shape when you let it go. Elastic is often used in clothes to make them fit tightly, for example, around the waist. ゴムひも ☐*Make a mask with long ears and attach a piece of elastic to go around the back of the head.* 長い耳のついた仮面を作り，1本のゴムひもを頭の後ろに回るように付けなさい。 **2** ADJ 形容詞 Something that is **elastic** is able to stretch easily and then return to its original size and shape. 弾力のある ☐*Beat it until the dough is slightly elastic.* 生地に弾力性が出るまで強くかき混ぜます。

elas|tic band (**elastic bands**) N-COUNT 可算名詞 An **elastic band** is a thin circle of very stretchy rubber that you can put around things in order to hold them together. ゴムバンド [mainly BRIT 主に英国英語; AM **rubber band** 米国英語 **rubber band**]

elas|tic|ity /ɪlæstɪsɪti, iːlæst-/ N-UNCOUNT 不可算名詞 The **elasticity** of a material or substance is its ability to return to its original shape, size, and condition after it has been stretched. 弾力性 ☐*Daily facial exercises help to retain the skin's elasticity.* 毎日の顔のエクササイズは肌の弾力性を保つのに役立つ。

elat|ed /ɪleɪtɪd/ ADJ 形容詞 If you are **elated**, you are extremely happy and excited because of something that has happened. 大喜びの ☐*I was elated that my recent second bypass had been successful.* 最近受けた2回目のバイパス手術が成功したので私は有頂天だった。

ela|tion /ɪleɪʃən/ N-UNCOUNT 不可算名詞 **Elation** is a feeling of great happiness and excitement about something that has happened. 意気揚々 ☐*His supporters have reacted to the news with elation.* 彼の支援者はその知らせに大喜びした。
→ see **emotion**

el|bow /ɛlboʊ/ (**elbows, elbowing, elbowed**) **1** N-COUNT 可算名詞 Your **elbow** is the part of your arm where the upper and lower halves are joined. ひじ ☐*He slipped and fell, badly bruising an elbow.* 彼は滑って転び，片方のひじにひどい打撲傷を負った。 **2** V-T 他動詞 If you **elbow** people **aside** or **elbow** your **way** somewhere, you push people with your elbows in order to move somewhere. 押しのけて進む ☐*They also claim that the security team elbowed aside a steward.* 彼らは保安チームが客室係をひじで押しのけたとも主張している。 **3** V-T 他動詞 If someone or something **elbows** their **way** somewhere, or **elbows** other people or things **out of the way**, they achieve success by being aggressive and determined. 押し分けて進む ☐*Non-state firms gradually elbow aside the inefficient state-owned*

ones. 非国営企業が徐々に非効率な国営企業を押しのける。 **4** to **rub elbows with** → see **rub**
→ see **body**

el|der /ɛldər/ (**elders**) **1** ADJ 形容詞 The **elder of** two people is the one who was born first. 年長の [ADJ n, 'the' ADJ, 'the' ADJ 'of' n] ☐...*his elder brother.* 彼の兄 **2** N-COUNT 可算名詞 A person's **elder** is someone who is older than them, especially someone quite a lot older. 年長者 [FORMAL 形式ばった] ☐*They have no respect for their elders.* 彼らには年長者に対する敬意は全くない。 **3** N-COUNT 可算名詞 In some societies, an **elder** is one of the respected older people who have influence and authority. 長老 ☐...*a meeting of political figures and tribal elders.* 政治家と部族の長老との会合

> The adjective **elder** means "older" when it is followed by brother, sister, son, daughter, or other terms for relatives that are in your generation or younger. You use **older** to talk about the age of other people or things. **Elder** cannot be followed by "than" but **older** can be. ☐*I've got a sister who is older than me.* Do not confuse **elder** and **elderly**. If you describe someone as **elderly**, you mean that they are old, but this is a slightly more polite word than **old**. The **elderly** are elderly people.

el|der|ly /ɛldərli/ ADJ 形容詞 You use **elderly** as a polite way of saying that someone is old. 初老の [POLITENESS 丁寧さ] ☐*There was an elderly couple on the terrace.* テラスには初老の夫婦がいた ● N-PLURAL 複数名詞 The **elderly** are people who are old. 年配者たち ☐*The elderly are a formidable force in any election.* 年配者たちはどの選挙でも手ごわい勢力だ。
→ see **age**

eld|est /ɛldɪst/ ADJ 形容詞 The **eldest** person in a group is the one who was born before all the others. 最年長の ☐*The eldest child was a daughter called Fatiha.* 長子はファティハという名前の娘だった。

elect /ɪlɛkt/ (**elects, electing, elected**) **1** V-T 他動詞 When people **elect** someone, they choose that person to represent them, by voting for them. 選挙する ☐*The people of the Philippines have voted to elect a new president.* フィリピンの国民は新しい大統領を選出するために投票した。 ☐*The University of Washington elected him dean in 1956.* ワシントン大学は1956年に彼を学部長に選任した。 **2** V-T 他動詞 If you **elect** to do something, you choose to do it. (~することを)決める [FORMAL 形式ばった] ☐*Those electing to smoke will be seated at the rear.* 喫煙したい人は後ろの座席に座ってください。 **3** ADJ 形容詞 **Elect** is added after words such as "president" or "governor" to indicate that a person has been elected to the post but has not officially started to carry out the duties involved. 選挙された [FORMAL 形式ばった] [n ADJ] ☐...*the date when the president-elect takes office.* 大統領当選者の就任日
→ see **election**

elec|tion /ɪlɛkʃən/ (**elections**) **1** N-VAR 可変性名詞 An **election** is a process in which people vote to choose a person or group of people to hold an official position. 選挙 ☐...*Poland's first fully free elections for more than fifty years.* 50数年振りに行われたポーランドの完全に自由な選挙 ☐*In his election campaign he promised to put the economy back on its feet.* 彼は選挙運動中に景気を回復させることを約束した。 **2** N-UNCOUNT 不可算名詞 The **election** of a particular person or group of people is their success in winning an election. 当選 [usu with poss] ☐...*the election of the Democrat candidate last year.* 昨年の民主党候補者の当選 ☐...*Vaclav Havel's election as president of Czechoslovakia.* チェコスロバキアの大統領にヴァーツラフ・ハヴェルが当選したこと
→ see Word Web: **election**

elec|tor /ɪlɛktər/ (**electors**) N-COUNT 可算名詞 An **elector** is a person who has the right to vote in an election. 選挙人 ☐*There are*

Presidential candidates spend millions of dollars on their **campaigns**. They give **speeches**, appear on TV, and **debate** each other. On election day, **voters cast** their **votes** at local **polling places**. **Citizens** living outside of the US mail in **absentee ballots**. But voters don't directly **elect** their **president**. States send representatives to the **electoral college**. There, representatives from all but two states must cast all their votes for one candidate—even if 49% of the people wanted the other candidate. Four times a candidate has **won** the popular vote and lost the election. This happened when George W. Bush won in 2000.

now 117 cardinals who can be cardinal electors, that is, eligible to enter the secret conclave that will choose the next pope. 選挙人枢機卿 (すうききょう) になりうる, つまり次の教皇を選出するための秘密のコンクラーベに参加できる枢機卿は現在117名いる.

elec|tor|al /ɪlɛktərəl/ ADJ 形容詞 **Electoral** is used to describe things that are connected with elections. 選挙の [ADJ n] □ The Mongolian Democratic Party is campaigning for electoral reform. モンゴル民主党は選挙改革運動をしている. ● **elec|tor|al|ly** ADV 副詞 選挙的に □ He believed that the policies were both wrong and electorally disastrous. 彼はその政策は間違っており選挙に破滅的な影響を与えると信じていた.

elec|tor|ate /ɪlɛktərɪt/ (**electorates**) N-COUNT-COLL 集合可算名詞 The **electorate** of a country or area is all the people in it who have the right to vote in an election. 有権者 □ He has the backing of almost a quarter of the electorate. 彼は有権者の4分の1近くの支持を得ている.

elec|tric /ɪlɛktrɪk/ ◼ ADJ 形容詞 An **electric** device or machine works by means of electricity, rather than using some other source of power. 電気で動く □ ...her electric guitar. 彼女のエレキギター ◼ ADJ 形容詞 An **electric** current, voltage, or charge is one that is produced by electricity. 電気から生じる [ADJ n] ◼ ADJ 形容詞 **Electric** plugs, sockets, or power lines are designed to carry electricity. 電気を伝える [ADJ n] □ More people are deciding that electric power lines could present a health risk. 電力線は健康に危険にさらす可能性があると考える人々が増えつつある. ◼ ADJ 形容詞 **Electric** is used to refer to the supply of electricity. 電気の [INFORMAL くだけた] [ADJ n] □ An average electric bill might go up $2 or $3 per month. 電気代は平均して毎月2ドルか3ドル値上がりするかもしれない. ◼ ADJ 形容詞 If you describe the atmosphere of a place or event as **electric**, you mean that people are in a state of great excitement. 電撃的な, わくわくさせる □ The mood in the hall was electric. 会場のムードは熱狂的だった.
→ see **keyboard**

elec|tri|cal /ɪlɛktrɪkᵊl/ ◼ ADJ 形容詞 **Electrical** goods, equipment, or appliances work by means of electricity. 電気を用いた □ ...shipments of electrical equipment. 電気機器の輸送 ● **elec|tri|cal|ly** ADV 副詞 [ADV -ed] 電気を用いて □ ...electrically powered vehicles. 電動車 ◼ ADJ 形容詞 **Electrical** systems or parts supply or use electricity. 電気に関する □ ...lighting and other electrical systems on the new runway. 新滑走路の照明や他の電気関係システム ◼ ADJ 形容詞 **Electrical** energy is energy in the form of electricity. 電気による □ ...brief pulses of electrical energy. 電気エネルギーの短いパルス ● **elec|tri|cal|ly** ADV 副詞 電気により □ ...electrically charged particles. 荷電粒子 ◼ ADJ 形容詞 [ADJ n] **Electrical** industries, engineers, or workers are involved in the production and supply of electricity or electrical products. 電気に関する □ ...company representatives from the electrical industry. 電気業界の会社の代表者たち
→ see **electricity**

elec|tric chair (**electric chairs**) N-COUNT 可算名詞 The **electric chair** is a rarely-used method for killing criminals, in which a person is strapped to a special chair and killed by a powerful electric current. 電気椅子 □ Murderer Walter Kemmler was the first man to die in the electric chair. 殺人犯のウォルター・ケムラーは電気椅子で処刑された最初の男であった.

Word Link	electr ≈ electric : electrician, electricity, electron

Word Link	ician ≈ person who works at : electrician, musician, physician

elec|tri|cian /ɪlɛktrɪʃᵊn, ilɛk-/ (**electricians**) N-COUNT 可算名詞 An **electrician** is a person whose job is to install and repair electrical equipment. 電気技師

Word Link	electr ≈ electric : electrician, electricity, electron

elec|tric|ity /ɪlɛktrɪsiti, ilɛk-/ N-UNCOUNT 不可算名詞 **Electricity** is a form of energy that can be carried by wires and is used for heating and lighting, and to provide power for machines. 電気 □ We moved into a cabin with electricity but no running water. 我々は電気はあるが水道のない小屋に移った.
→ see Word Web: **electricity**
→ see **energy, light**

elec|tric shock (**electric shocks**) N-COUNT 可算名詞 If you get an **electric shock**, you get a sudden painful feeling when you touch something connected to a supply of electricity. 感電

elec|tri|fi|ca|tion /ɪlɛktrɪfɪkeɪʃᵊn/ N-UNCOUNT 不可算名詞 The **electrification** of a house, town, or area is the connecting of that place to a supply of electricity. 電力供給, 電化 □ ...rural electrification. 田舎の電化

elec|tri|fy /ɪlɛktrɪfaɪ/ (**electrifies, electrifying, electrified**) ◼ V-T 他動詞 If people **are electrified by** an event or experience, it makes them feel very excited and surprised. 感激させる [usu passive] □ The world was electrified by his courage and resistance. 世界は彼の勇気と抵抗に感動した. ● **elec|tri|fy|ing** ADJ 形容詞 感動的な □ He gave an electrifying performance. 彼は感動的な演技をした. ◼ V-T 他動詞 [usu passive] When a rail system or rail line **is electrified**, electric cables are put over the tracks, or electric rails are put beside them, so that the trains can be powered by electricity. 電化する □ The railroad line was electrified as long ago as 1974. その鉄道線はずっと前の1974年に電化された.

elec|tro|cute /ɪlɛktrəkyut/ (**electrocutes, electrocuting, electrocuted**) ◼ V-T 他動詞 If someone **is electrocuted**, they are accidentally killed or badly injured when they touch something connected to a source of electricity. 感電させる □ Three people were electrocuted by falling power lines. 落下した電線に3名が感電死した. ◼ V-T 他動詞 If a criminal **is electrocuted**, he or she is executed using electricity. 電気死刑にする [usu passive] □ He was electrocuted for a murder committed when he was 17. 彼は17歳の時に犯した殺人罪で電気処刑された. ● **elec|tro|cu|tion** /ɪlɛktrəkyuʃᵊn/ (**electrocutions**) N-VAR 可変性名詞 (**electrocutions**) 電気死刑 □ The court pronounced him guilty and sentenced him to death by electrocution. 法廷は彼に有罪を宣告し, 電気死刑の判決を下した.

elec|trode /ɪlɛktroʊd/ (**electrodes**) N-COUNT 可算名詞 An **electrode** is a small piece of metal or other substance that is used to take an electric current to or from a source of power, a piece of equipment, or a living body. 電極棒 □ Two electrodes that measure changes in the body's surface moisture are attached to the palms of your hands. 身体の表面の湿気の変化を測定する電極棒が, あなたの両手の手のひらに取り付けられる.

elec|tron /ɪlɛktrɒn/ (**electrons**) N-COUNT 可算名詞 An **electron** is a tiny particle of matter that is smaller than an atom and has a negative electrical charge. 電子 [TECHNICAL 技術的] □ Most things are balanced - with equal numbers of electrons and protons. 大半のものは等しい数の電子と陽子で釣り合っている.
→ see **television**

elec|tron|ic /ɪlɛktrɒnɪk, i-/ ◼ ADJ 形容詞 An **electronic** device has transistors or silicon chips that control and change the electric current passing through the device. 電子の [ADJ n] □ ...expensive electronic equipment. 高価な電子機器 ◼ ADJ 形容詞 An **electronic** process or activity involves the use of electronic devices. 電子の □ ...electronic music. 電子音楽 ● **elec|troni|cal|ly** ADV 副詞 [ADV with v] 電子的に □ Data is transmitted electronically. データは電子的に送信される.

elec|tron|ic book (**electronic books**) N-COUNT 可算名詞 An **electronic book** is the same as an **e-book**. 電子ブック [COMPUTING コンピューティング]

elec|tron|ic mail N-SING 単数名詞 **Electronic mail** is the same as **e-mail**. 電子メール

elec|tron|ic pub|lish|ing N-UNCOUNT 不可算名詞 **Electronic publishing** is the publishing of documents in a form that can be read on a computer, for example, as a CD-ROM. 電子出版

Word Link	ics ≈ system, knowledge : economics, electronics, ethics

elec|tron|ics /ɪlɛktrɒnɪks, i-/ N-UNCOUNT 不可算名詞 **Electronics** is the technology of using transistors and silicon chips, especially in devices such as radios, televisions, and

---

Word Web　　electricity

Demand for **electrical** power in the U.S. will likely rise by 35 percent over the next 20 years. **Power companies** are moving quickly to meet this need. At the heart of every **power station** are electrical **generators**. Traditionally, they ran on hydroelectric power or **fossil fuel**. However, today new sources of **energy** are available. On **wind farms**, wind **turbines** use the power of moving air to run generators. Seaside tidal power stations make use of rising and falling tides to turn turbines. And in sunny climates, **photovoltaic cells** produce electrical power from the sun's rays.

e

computers. 電子工学 ❑ ...*Ohio's three main electronics companies*. オハイオ州の3つの主な電子工学会社

el|egant /ˈɛlɪgənt/ **1** ADJ 形容詞 If you describe a person or thing as **elegant**, you mean that they are pleasing and graceful in appearance or style. 優雅な ❑ *Patricia looked beautiful and elegant as always.* パトリシアはいつものように美しく優雅だった。 ● **el|egance** N-UNCOUNT 不可算名詞 優雅 ❑ *The furniture managed to combine practicality with elegance.* その家具は実用性と優雅さがうまく組み合わせられていた。 ● **el|egant|ly** ADV 副詞 優雅に ❑ ...*a tall, elegantly dressed man with a mustache.* 長身で上品な服装をした口ひげのある男 **2** ADJ 形容詞 If you describe a piece of writing, an idea, or a plan as **elegant**, you mean that it is simple, clear, and clever. 明快な ❑ *The document impressed me with its elegant simplicity.* 私はその文書の明快な簡潔さに感心した。 ● **el|egant|ly** ADV 副詞 すっきりして ❑ ...*an elegantly simple idea.* すっきりした簡潔な考え

Thesaurus　　　　　elegant また次を参照:

ADJ.　chic, exquisite, luxurious, stylish; (*ant.*) inelegant, unsophisticated **1**

el|ement /ˈɛlɪmənt/ (**elements**) **1** N-COUNT 可算名詞 The different **elements** of something are the different parts it contains. 構成部分 ❑ *The exchange of prisoners of war was one of the key elements of the UN's peace plan.* 捕虜の交換は国連の和平案の主要な構成部分の1つだった。 **2** N-COUNT 可算名詞 A particular **element** of a situation, activity, or process is an important quality or feature that it has or needs. 要素 ❑ *Physical fitness has now become an important element in our lives.* 身体的健康は今や我々の生活の重要な要素となっている。 **3** N-COUNT 可算名詞 When you talk about **elements** within a society or organization, you are referring to groups of people who have similar aims, beliefs, or habits. 集団 ❑ *The government must weed out criminal elements from within the security forces.* 政府は警備隊内部から犯罪分子を排除しなければならない。 **4** N-COUNT 可算名詞 If something has an **element** of a particular quality or emotion, it has a certain amount of this quality or emotion. 多少 ❑ *These reports clearly contain elements of propaganda.* これらの報告書には明らかに宣伝が多少含まれている。 **5** N-COUNT 可算名詞 An **element** is a substance such as gold, oxygen, or carbon that consists of only one type of atom. 元素 **6** N-COUNT 可算名詞 The **element** in an electric or water heater is the metal part that changes the electric current into heat. 電熱線 **7** N-PLURAL 複数名詞 You can refer to the weather, especially wind and rain, as **the elements**. 天気, 風雨 ❑ *The area where most refugees are waiting is exposed to the elements.* 大半の避難民が待機している地区は悪天候にさらされている。 **8** PHRASE 句 If you say that someone is **in their element**, you mean that they are in a situation they enjoy. 本領を発揮して ❑ *My stepmother was in her element, organizing everything.* 私のまま母は何でも切り盛りし, 本領を発揮していた。

→ see Word Web: **element**

→ see **rock**

el|emen|ta|ry /ˌɛlɪˈmɛntəri, -tri/ ADJ 形容詞 Something that is **elementary** is very simple and basic. 初歩的な ❑ *Literacy now includes elementary computer skills.* 識字能力には現在, 初歩的なコンピュータ技能が含まれている。

el|emen|ta|ry school (**elementary schools**) N-VAR 可変性名詞 An **elementary school** is a school where children are taught for the first six or seven years of their education. 小学校 [mainly AM 主に米国英語] ❑ *The move from elementary school to middle school or junior high can be difficult.* 小学校から中等学校あるいは中学校への進学が困難なことがある。

el|ephant /ˈɛlɪfənt/ (**elephants**) N-COUNT 可算名詞 An **elephant** is a very large animal with a long, flexible nose called a trunk, which it uses to pick up things. Elephants live in India and Africa. 象

el|evate /ˈɛlɪveɪt/ (**elevates, elevating, elevated**) **1** V-T 他動詞 When someone or something achieves a more important rank or status, you can say that they **are elevated to** it. 昇進させる [FORMAL 形式ばった] [usu passive] ❑ *He was elevated to the post of president.* 彼は社長の地位に昇進した。 ● **el|eva|tion** /ˌɛlɪˈveɪʃən/ N-UNCOUNT 不可算名詞 昇進 ❑ *The elevation of the assistant coach to the head coaching position within only 9 months was a surprise.* たったの9ヶ月でコーチ助手からヘッドコーチの地位に昇進したことは意外だった。 **2** V-T 他動詞 If you **elevate** something **to** a higher status, you consider it to be better or more important than it really is. 高める ❑ *Don't elevate your superiors to superstar status.* 上司をスーパースターの地位に高めるな。 **3** V-T 他動詞 To **elevate** something means to increase it in amount or intensity. 上昇させる [FORMAL 形式ばった] ❑ *Emotional stress can elevate blood pressure.* 感情面のストレスは血圧を上昇させる。 **4** V-T 他動詞 If you **elevate** something, you raise it higher. 高く持ち上げる ❑ *A few times a day, elevate feet above heart level.* 1日に数回は両足を心臓より高い位置に上げなさい。 ❑ *I built a platform to elevate the bed.* 私はベッドを高くするために壇を作った。

Word Link　　ation ≈ state of : celebration, elevation, relaxation

el|eva|tion /ˌɛlɪˈveɪʃən/ (**elevations**) **1** N-COUNT 可算名詞 The **elevation** of a place is its height above sea level. 海抜 ❑ *We're probably at an elevation of about 13,000 feet above sea level.* 我々はおそらく海抜1万3000フィート位の高さにいると思われる。 **2** N-COUNT 可算名詞 An **elevation** is a piece of ground that is higher than the area around it. 高台 ❑ ...*the monument was on an elevation, which could be seen from the church.* その記念碑は高台にあり, 教会から見えた。

el|eva|tor /ˈɛlɪveɪtər/ (**elevators**) N-COUNT 可算名詞 An **elevator** is a device that carries people or goods up and down inside tall buildings. エレベーター [AM 米国英語] ❑ *We took the elevator to the fourteenth floor.* 我々は14階までエレベーターに乗って行った。

→ see **skyscraper**

elev|en /ɪˈlɛvən/ (**elevens**) NUM 数詞 **Eleven** is the number 11. (基数の) 11 ❑ ...*the Princess and her eleven friends.* 王女と11人の友だち

elev|enth /ɪˈlɛvənθ/ ORD 序数詞 The **eleventh** item in a series is the one that you count as number eleven. 第11番目の ❑ *We were working on the eleventh floor.* 我々は11階で働いていた。

elic|it /ɪˈlɪsɪt/ (**elicits, eliciting, elicited**) **1** V-T 他動詞 If you **elicit** a response or a reaction, you do or say something that makes other people respond or react. 引き出す ❑ *Mr. Norris said he was hopeful that his request would elicit a positive response.* ノリス氏は彼の要求に対して前向きの応えが得られることを期待していると述べた。 **2** V-T 他動詞 If you **elicit** a piece of information, you get it by asking the right questions. 聞き出す [FORMAL 形式ばった] ❑ *My letters to her have elicited no response.* 私は彼女に手紙を何通か出したが返事はない。

eli|gible /ˈɛlɪdʒɪbəl/ **1** ADJ 形容詞 Someone who is **eligible to** do something is qualified or able to do it, for example, because they are old enough. 資格のある ❑ *Almost half the population are eligible to vote in today's election.* 人口の半数近くは今日の選挙で投票する資格がある。 ● **eli|gibil|ity** /ˌɛlɪdʒəˈbɪlɪti/ N-UNCOUNT 不可算名詞 適格性 ❑ *The rules covering eligibility for benefits changed in the 1980s.* 給付金をもらう資格に関する規則は1980年代に変った。 **2** ADJ 形容詞 An **eligible** man or woman is not yet married and is thought by many people to be a suitable partner. 結婚の相手に望ましい ❑ *He's the most eligible bachelor in Japan.* 彼は日本で最も結婚相手にしたい独身男性だ。

elimi|nate /ɪˈlɪmɪneɪt/ (**eliminates, eliminating, eliminated**) **1** V-T 他動詞 To **eliminate** something, especially something you do not want or need, means to remove it completely. 排除する [FORMAL 形式ばった] ❑ *Recent measures have not eliminated discrimination in employment.* 最近の対策にもかかわらず, 雇用の差別は残っている。 ● **elimi|na|tion** N-UNCOUNT 不可算名詞 排除 ❑ ...*the prohibition and elimination of chemical weapons.* 化学兵器の禁止と排除

Word Web　　　element

Elements—like copper, sodium, and oxygen—are made from only one type of **atom**. Each element has its own unique **properties**. For instance, oxygen is a gas at room temperature and copper is a solid. Often elements come together with other types of elements to make **compounds**. When the atoms in a compound bind together, they form a **molecule**. One of the best known molecules is H_2O. It is made up of two hydrogen atoms and one oxygen atom. This molecule is also known as water. The periodic table is a complete listing of all the elements.

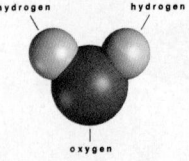

hydrogen　hydrogen

oxygen

The Periodic Table of Elements

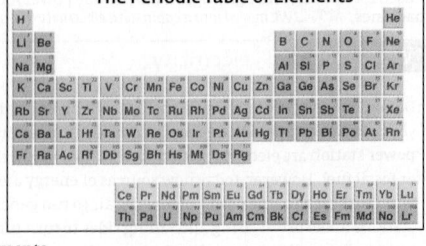

2 V-T PASSIVE 受動態他動詞 When a person or team **is eliminated from** a competition, they are defeated and so stop participating in the competition. ふるい落とす ❑ *I was eliminated from the 400 meters in the semi-finals.* 私は400メートルの準決勝で敗退した. **3** V-T 他動詞 If someone says that they **have eliminated** an enemy, they mean that they have killed them. By using the word "eliminate," they are trying to make the action sound more positive than if they used the word "kill." 消す, 殺す ❑ *He declared war on the government and urged right-wingers to eliminate their opponents.* 彼は政府に宣戦布告し, 右翼勢力に敵対者を消すよう強く促した.

Thesaurus		eliminate また次を参照:
v.	dispose of, erase, expel, knock out; *(ant.)* choose, include **1**	

elimi|na|tion /ɪlɪmɪneɪʃ³n/ **1** N-UNCOUNT 不可算名詞 **Elimination** is the process of getting rid of waste products from your body by going to the bathroom. 排泄 (はいせつ) [FORMAL 形式ばった] ❑ *Breast-feeding is as natural as sex or elimination or any other bodily function.* 母乳養育は性交や排泄やその他の肉体的機能と変らず自然なことだ. **2** → see **eliminate 1**

elite /ɪlit, eɪ-/ (**elites**) **1** N-COUNT 可算名詞 You can refer to the most powerful, rich, or talented people within a particular group, place, or society as the **elite**. エリート ❑ *...a government comprised mainly of the elite.* 主にエリート層から成る政府. **2** ADJ 形容詞 **Elite** people or organizations are considered to be the best of their kind. えり抜きの [ADJ n] ❑ *...the elite troops of the president's bodyguard.* 大統領の護衛のえり抜きの部隊

elit|ism /ɪlitɪzəm, eɪ-/ N-UNCOUNT 不可算名詞 **Elitism** is the quality or practice of being elitist. エリート主義 ❑ *It became difficult to promote conventional ideas of excellence without being instantly accused of elitism.* ただちにエリート主義だと非難されずに, 卓越性という伝統的な概念を促進するのは難しくなった.

elit|ist /ɪlitɪst, eɪ-/ (**elitists**) **1** ADJ 形容詞 **Elitist** systems, practices, or ideas favor the most powerful, rich, or talented people within a group, place, or society. エリート主義の [DISAPPROVAL 不賛成] ❑ *He worries about a time when college athletics become even more elitist than they are now.* 彼は大学の運動競技が今以上にエリート主義になる時を心配している. **2** N-COUNT 可算名詞 An **elitist** is someone who has elitist ideas or is part of an elite. エリート主義者, エリート [DISAPPROVAL 不賛成] ❑ *He was an elitist who had no time for the masses.* 彼は一般大衆のことを意に介さないエリート主義者だった.

elm /ɛlm/ (**elms**) N-VAR 可変性名詞 An **elm** is a tree that has broad leaves which it loses in winter. ニレ ❑ N-UNCOUNT 不可算名詞 **Elm** is the wood of this tree. ニレ材 ❑ *It was a good table too, sturdily constructed of elm.* それはニレ材でしっかりと作られた立派なテーブルでもあった.

elo|quent /ɛləkwənt/ **1** ADJ 形容詞 Speech or writing that is **eloquent** is well expressed and effective in persuading people. 説得力のある ❑ *I heard him make a very eloquent speech at that dinner.* 私は彼があの夕食会で非常に説得力のある演説をするのを聞いた. ●**elo|quence** N-UNCOUNT 不可算名詞 巧みさ ❑ *...the eloquence of his prose.* 彼の散文の巧みさ ●**elo|quent|ly** ADV 副詞 ❑ *Juanita speaks eloquently about her art.* ワニータは自分の芸術について巧みに語る. **2** ADJ 形容詞 A person who is **eloquent** is good at speaking and able to persuade people. 雄弁な [APPROVAL 賛成] ❑ *He was eloquent about his love of books.* 彼は書物をいかに愛しているかを雄弁に語った. ●**elo|quence** N-UNCOUNT 不可算名詞 雄弁さ ❑ *She can speak with an eloquence that is almost inspirational.* 彼女はほとんど霊感を与えるほどの雄弁さで話すことができる.

else /ɛls/ **1** ADJ 形容詞 You use **else** after words such as "anywhere," "someone," and "what" to refer in a vague way to another person, place, or thing. その他の ❑ *If I can't make a living at painting, at least I can teach someone else to paint.* 私は絵で生計が立てられなくとも, 少なくとも誰か他の人に絵をかくことを教えられる. ❑ *We had nothing else to do on those long trips.* 我々はそうした長い旅で他に何もすることがなかった. ●ADV 副詞 **Else** is also an adverb. その他に [adv ADV] ❑ *I never wanted to live anywhere else.* 私は他のどの場所にも決して住みたくなかった. **2** ADJ 形容詞 You use **else** after words such as "everyone," "everything," and "everywhere" to refer in a vague way to all the other people, things, or places except the one you are talking about. (すべての) 他の [pron-indef ADJ] ❑ *As I try to be truthful, I expect everyone else to be truthful.* 私は嘘を言わないよう努力しているのだから, 他のすべての人も嘘をつかないでほしいと思う. ●ADV 副詞 **Else** is also an adverb. 他に [adv ADV] ❑ *Cleveland seems so much dirtier than everywhere else.* クリーブランド市は他のどの場所よりもひどく汚いように見える. **3** PHRASE 句 You use **or else** after stating a logical conclusion, to indicate that what you are about to say is evidence for that conclusion. でなければ ❑ *Evidently no lessons have been learned or else the government would not have handled the problem so badly.* 明らかに何の教訓にもなっていなかった. そうでなければ政府はその問題をあれほどひどく処理

4 PHRASE 句 You use **or else** to introduce a statement that indicates the unpleasant results that will occur if someone does or does not do something. さもないと ❑ *This time we really need to succeed or else people will start giving us funny looks.* 今回こそは本当に成功する必要がある. さもないと人々は我々を変な目で見始めるだろう. **5** PHRASE 句 You use **or else** to introduce the second of two possibilities when you do not know which one is true. でなければ ❑ *You are either a total genius or else you must be totally crazy.* あなたは完全な天才か, でもなければ全くの狂人のどちらかだ. **6** PHRASE 句 **Above all else** is used to emphasize that a particular thing is more important than other things. とりわけ [EMPHASIS 強調] ❑ *Above all else I hate the cold.* 私は寒いのが何にもまして嫌いだ. **7** PHRASE 句 You can say "**if nothing else**" to indicate that what you are mentioning is, in your opinion, the only good thing in a particular situation. ともかく ❑ *If nothing else, you'll really enjoy meeting them.* いずれにせよ, 君は彼らに会って本当によかったと思うだろう. **8** PHRASE 句 You say "**or else**" after a command to warn someone that if they do not obey, you will be angry and may harm or punish them. さもないと [SPOKEN 口語] ❑ *Behave, or else!* 行儀よくしなさい. さもないとひどいぞ.

else|where /ɛlswɛər/ ADV 副詞 **Elsewhere** means in other places or to another place. どこかよそで ❑ *Almost 80 percent of the state's residents were born elsewhere.* その州の居住者の8割近くが他の場所で生まれている. ❑ *They were living well, in comparison with people elsewhere in the world.* 彼らの生活水準は世界の他の地域の人々と比べると悪くなかった.

elude /ɪlud/ (**eludes, eluding, eluded**) **1** V-T 他動詞 If something that you want **eludes** you, you fail to obtain it. すり抜ける [no passive] ❑ *Sleep eluded her.* 彼女は眠れなかった. **2** V-T 他動詞 If you **elude** someone or something, you avoid them or escape from them. 逃れる ❑ *He eluded the police for 13 years.* 彼は13年間警察を逃れてきた. **3** V-T 他動詞 If a fact or idea **eludes** you, you do not succeed in understanding it, realizing it, or remembering it. 理解できない, 思い出せない [no passive] ❑ *The appropriate word eluded him.* 彼には適切な語がどうも出てこなかった.

elu|sive /ɪlusɪv/ ADJ 形容詞 Something or someone that is **elusive** is difficult to find, describe, remember, or achieve. 入手しにくい ❑ *In Denver late-night taxis are elusive and far from cheap.* デンバー市では深夜のタクシーは見つけにくく, なかなかどうして安くはない.

'em /əm, STRONG ɛm/ PRON 代名詞 **'em** is an informal way of saying or writing **them**. themのくだけた言い方 ❑ *There was also two other men there with 'em too.* 彼らと一緒にそこには他の2人の男がいた.

Word Link		e ≈ electronic : *e-book, e-commerce, e-mail*

e-mail (**e-mails, e-mailing, e-mailed**) also **E-mail** or **email** **1** N-VAR 可変性名詞 **E-mail** is a system of sending written messages electronically from one computer to another. **E-mail** is an abbreviation of **electronic mail**. 電子メール ❑ *You can contact us by e-mail.* 私たちに電子メールで連絡できます. ❑ *Do you want to send an E-mail?* あなたは電子メールを送信したいですか. **2** V-T 他動詞 If you **e-mail** someone, you send them an e-mail. 電子メールを送信する ❑ *Jamie e-mailed me to say he couldn't come.* ジェイミーは来られないことを伝える電子メールを私に送ってきた.
→ see **Internet**

ema|nate /ɛməneɪt/ (**emanates, emanating, emanated**) **1** V-T/V-I 他動詞/自動詞 If a quality **emanates from** you, or if you **emanate** a quality, you give people a strong sense that you have that quality. 発散させる, 発散する [FORMAL 形式ばった] ❑ *Intelligence and cunning emanated from him.* 聡明さと抜け目なさが彼からにじみ出ていた. **2** V-I 自動詞 If something **emanates from** somewhere, it comes from there. 発する [FORMAL 形式ばった] ❑ *The heady aroma of wood smoke emanated from the stove.* まきの煙の猛烈な匂いがストーブから発散した.

Word Link		man ≈ hand : *emancipate, manicure, manipulate*

eman|ci|pate /ɪmænsɪpeɪt/ (**emancipates, emancipating, emancipated**) V-T 他動詞 If people **are emancipated**, they are freed from unpleasant or unfair social, political, or legal restrictions. 解放する [FORMAL 形式ばった] ❑ *Catholics were emancipated in 1792.* カトリック教徒は1792年に解放された. ❑ *That war preserved the Union and emancipated the slaves.* あの戦争で合衆国が維持され, 奴隷が解放された. ●**eman|ci|pa|tion** /ɪmænsɪpeɪʃ³n/ N-UNCOUNT 不可算名詞 [oft N 'of' n] 解放 ❑ *...the emancipation of women.* 女性の解放

em|bank|ment /ɪmbæŋkmənt/ (**embankments**) N-COUNT 可算名詞 An **embankment** is a thick wall of earth that is built to carry a road or railroad track over an area of low ground, or to prevent water from a river or the sea from flooding the area. 注 ❑ *They climbed a steep embankment.* 彼らは急な注防を上った. ❑ *...a railroad embankment.* 鉄道の土手

em|bar|go /ɪmbɑrgoʊ/ (**embargoes, embargoing, embargoed**) **1** N-COUNT 可算名詞 If one country or group of countries imposes

an **embargo** against another, it forbids trade with that country. 通商停止 □ *The United Nations imposed an arms embargo against the country.* 国連は某の国に対して武器の通商停止を課した. **2** V-T 他動詞 If goods of a particular kind **are embargoed**, people are not allowed to import them from a particular country or export them to a particular country. (通商を) 禁止する □ *The fruit was embargoed.* 果物の通商は禁止された. □ *They embargoed oil shipments to the U.S.* 彼らは米国向けの石油の輸送を禁止した.

em|bark /ɪmbɑːɹk/ (**embarks, embarking, embarked**) **1** V-I 自動詞 If you **embark on** something new, difficult, or exciting, you start doing it. 始める □ *He's embarking on a new career as a writer.* 彼は作家としての新しい仕事を始めている. **2** V-I 自動詞 When someone **embarks on** a ship, they go on board before the start of a journey. 乗船する □ *They embarked on a ship bound for Europe.* 彼らはヨーロッパ行きの船に乗り込んだ.

em|bar|rass /ɪmbæɹəs/ (**embarrasses, embarrassing, embarrassed**) **1** V-T 他動詞 If something or someone **embarrasses** you, they make you feel shy or ashamed. 恥ずかしい思いをさせる □ *His clumsiness embarrassed him.* 彼は自分の不器用さを恥ずかしく思った. **2** V-T 他動詞 If something **embarrasses** a public figure such as a politician or an organization such as a political party, it causes problems for them. 困らせる □ *Aides spoke of disposing of records that would embarrass the governor.* 補佐官らは知事を困らせることになるような記録を処分することを口にした.

em|bar|rassed /ɪmbæɹəst/ ADJ 形容詞 A person who is **embarrassed** feels shy, ashamed, or guilty about something. きまり悪い思いをして □ *He looked a bit embarrassed.* 彼はややきまり悪がっているように見えた.

em|bar|rass|ing /ɪmbæɹəsɪŋ/ **1** ADJ 形容詞 Something that is **embarrassing** makes you feel shy or ashamed. 当惑させるような □ *That was an embarrassing situation for me.* それは私にとってきまり悪い状態だった. ● **em|bar|rass|ing|ly** ADV 副詞 まごつかせるほどに □ *The lyrics of the song are embarrassingly banal.* その歌の歌詞はあきれるほどに陳腐だった. **2** ADJ 形容詞 Something that is **embarrassing to** a public figure such as a politician or an organization such as a political party causes problems for them. 厄介な □ *He has put the administration in an embarrassing position.* 彼によって政府は厄介な立場に追い込まれた.

em|bar|rass|ment /ɪmbæɹəsmənt/ (**embarrassments**) **1** N-VAR 可変性名詞 **Embarrassment** is the feeling you have when you are embarrassed. きまり悪さ □ *I think I would have died of embarrassment.* 私は恥ずかしくて死にそうだったと思う. □ *We apologize for any embarrassment this may have caused.* このためにきまり悪い思いをした方々にお詫びします. **2** N-COUNT 可算名詞 An **embarrassment** is an action, event, or situation that causes problems for a politician, political party, government, or other public group. 困惑させるもの □ *The poverty figures were undoubtedly an embarrassment to the president.* 貧困の統計は疑いなく大統領にとって困惑の種だった. **3** N-SING 単数名詞 If you refer to a person as **an embarrassment**, you mean that you disapprove of them but cannot avoid your connection with them. やっかい者 [DISAPPROVAL 不賛成] □ *You have been an embarrassment to us from the day Doug married you.* ダグがあなたと結婚した日から, あなたは私たちにとってやっかい者だった.

em|bas|sy /ɛmbəsi/ (**embassies**) N-COUNT 可算名詞 An **embassy** is a group of government officials, headed by an ambassador, who represent their government in a foreign country. The building in which they work is also called an **embassy**. 大使館 □ *The American embassy has already complained.* 米国大使館はすでに苦情を言った.

Word Link   *em ≈ making, putting : embed, embellish, empower*

---

em|bed /ɪmbɛd/ (**embeds, embedding, embedded**) **1** V-T 他動詞 If an object **embeds itself** in a substance or thing, it becomes fixed there firmly and deeply. はめ込む □ *One of the bullets passed through Andrea's chest before embedding itself in a wall.* 弾丸の1つは壁に食い込む前にアンドレアの胸を貫通した. ● **em|bed|ded** ADJ 形容詞 はまり込んだ □ *The fossils at Dinosaur Cove are embedded in hard sandstone.* 恐竜の入り江の化石は硬質の砂岩の中に埋まっている. **2** V-T 他動詞 [usu passive] If something such as an attitude or feeling **is embedded in** a society or system, or in someone's personality, it becomes a permanent and noticeable feature of it. 刻み込む □ *This agreement will be embedded in a state treaty to be signed soon.* この取り決めはまもなく署名される国家条約に組み込まれる予定だ. ● **em|bed|ded** ADJ 形容詞 刻み込まれた □ *I think that hatred of the other is deeply embedded in our society.* 他人に対する憎悪感は我々の社会に深く根ざしていると思う.

em|bel|lish /ɪmbɛlɪʃ/ (**embellishes, embellishing, embellished**) **1** V-T 他動詞 If something **is embellished** with decorative features or patterns, it has those features or patterns on it and they make it look more attractive. 装飾する □ *The boat was embellished with carvings in red and blue.* そのボートは赤と青の彫り物で飾られていた. □ *Ivy leaves embellish the front of the dresser.* 食器棚

の正面にはツタの葉の飾りがある. **2** V-T 他動詞 If you **embellish** a story, you make it more interesting by adding details that may be untrue. (話・物語などを) 潤色する □ *I launched into the parable, embellishing the story with invented dialogue and extra details.* 私はでっち上げた対話や余分な細部で話を潤色しながら, たとえ話を始めた.

em|bez|zle /ɪmbɛzəl/ (**embezzles, embezzling, embezzled**) V-T 他動詞 If someone **embezzles** money that their organization or company has placed in their care, they take it and use it illegally for their own purposes. 横領する □ *One former director embezzled $34 million in company funds.* ある元取締役は3400万ドルの会社資金を横領した.

em|bez|zle|ment /ɪmbɛzəlmənt/ N-UNCOUNT 不可算名詞 **Embezzlement** is the crime of embezzling money. 横領 □ *He was later charged with embezzlement.* 彼は後に横領罪で起訴された.

em|blem /ɛmbləm/ (**emblems**) **1** N-COUNT 可算名詞 An **emblem** is a design representing a country or organization. 紋章, 記章 □ *...the emblem of the Soviet Union.* ソ連の国章 **2** N-COUNT 可算名詞 An **emblem** is something that represents a quality or idea. 象徴 □ *The eagle was an emblem of strength and courage.* ワシは強さと勇気の象徴だった.

em|bodi|ment /ɪmbɒdimənt/ N-SING 単数名詞 If you say that someone or something is **the embodiment of** a quality or idea, you mean that that is their most noticeable characteristic or the basis of all they do. 体現, 具象 [FORMAL 形式ばった] □ *A baby is the embodiment of vulnerability.* 赤ん坊は傷つきやすさの具象だ.

em|body /ɪmbɒdi/ (**embodies, embodying, embodied**) **1** V-T 他動詞 To **embody** an idea or quality means to be a symbol or expression of that idea or quality. 具体的に表現する □ *Jack Kennedy embodied all the hopes of the 1960s.* ジャック・ケネディは1960年代の希望の全てを体現していた. □ *For twenty-nine years, Checkpoint Charlie embodied the Cold War.* チャーリー検問所は29年間にわたって冷戦を具現していた. **2** V-T 他動詞 If something **is embodied in** a particular thing, the second thing contains or consists of the first. 盛り込む □ *The proposal has been embodied in a draft resolution.* その提案は決議案の草案に盛り込まれた.

em|brace /ɪmbreɪs/ (**embraces, embracing, embraced**) **1** V-RECIP 相互動詞 If you **embrace** someone, you put your arms around them and hold them tightly, usually in order to show your love or affection for them. You can also say that two people **embrace**. 抱きしめる □ *Penelope came forward and embraced her sister.* ペネロペは進み出て妹を抱きしめた. □ *At first people were sort of crying for joy and embracing each other.* 最初は人々はちょっとうれし泣きし, 抱き合っていた. ● N-COUNT 可算名詞 **Embrace** is also a noun. 抱擁 □ *...a young couple locked in an embrace.* 抱き合った若いカップル **2** V-T 他動詞 If you **embrace** a change, political system, or idea, you accept it and start supporting it or believing in it. 受け入れる [FORMAL 形式ばった] □ *He embraces the new information age.* 彼は新しい情報時代を受け入れている. ● N-SING 単数名詞 **Embrace** is also a noun. 受け入れ □ *The marriage signaled James's embrace of the Catholic faith.* その結婚はジェイムズがカトリック教を受け入れる表れであった. **3** V-T 他動詞 If something **embraces** a group of people, things, or ideas, it includes them in a larger group or category. 包含する [FORMAL 形式ばった] □ *...a theory that would embrace the whole field of human endeavor.* 人間活動の全分野を包含するような理論

em|broi|der /ɪmbrɔɪdəɹ/ (**embroiders, embroidering, embroidered**) **1** V-T/V-I 他動詞/自動詞 If something such as clothing or cloth **is embroidered with** a design, the design is stitched into it. 刺繍(ししゅう)する □ *The collar was embroidered with very small red strawberries.* 襟には非常に小さな赤いイチゴの刺繍があった. □ *I have a pillow with my name embroidered on it.* 私は自分の名前が縫いこまれた枕を持っている. **2** V-T/V-I 他動詞/自動詞 If you **embroider** a story or account of something, or if you **embroider** on it, you try to make it more interesting by adding details that may be untrue. 潤色する □ *He told some lies and sometimes just embroidered the truth.* 彼は多少嘘をついたり, 時には真実を誇張することがあった.

em|broi|dery /ɪmbrɔɪdəri/ (**embroideries**) **1** N-VAR 可変性名詞 **Embroidery** consists of designs stitched into cloth. 刺繍(ししゅう) □ *The shorts had blue embroidery over the pockets.* そのショートパンツは両ポケットに青の刺繍がある. **2** N-UNCOUNT 不可算名詞 **Embroidery** is the activity of stitching designs onto cloth. 刺繍(ししゅう) □ *She learned sewing, knitting, and embroidery.* 彼女は裁縫, 編み物, 刺繍を学んだ.

→ see **quilt**

em|broiled /ɪmbrɔɪld/ ADJ 形容詞 If you become **embroiled in** a fight or argument, you become deeply involved in it. 巻き込まれて [V-link ADJ] □ *The government insisted that troops would not become embroiled in battles in Bosnia.* 政府はボスニアで部隊が戦闘に巻き込まれることはないだろうと主張した.

em|bryo /ɛmbrioʊ/ (**embryos**) **1** N-COUNT 可算名詞 An **embryo** is an unborn animal or human being in the very early stages of development. 胎芽(たいが) □ *There are 24,000 frozen embryos in clinics across the country.* 全国の診療所には2万4千の凍結

胎芽が保管されている. **2** ADJ 形容詞 An **embryo** idea, system, or organization is in the very early stages of development, but is expected to grow stronger. 初期の [ADJ n] ❑ *They are an embryo party of government.* 彼らは未発達の政党である.

em|bry|on|ic /ɛmbriɒnɪk/ ADJ 形容詞 An **embryonic** process, idea, organization, or organism is one at a very early stage in its development. 未発達の [FORMAL 形式ばった] ❑ *...Romania's embryonic democracy.* ルーマニアのできたばかりの民主主義 ❑ *At the time, he was trying to recruit members for his embryonic resistance group.* 当時彼は作ったばかりの抵抗運動グループに新メンバーを集めようとしていた.

em|er|ald /ɛmərəld, ɛmrəld/ (**emeralds**) **1** N-COUNT 可算名詞 An **emerald** is a precious stone that is clear and bright green. エメラルド **2** COLOR 色彩語 Something that is **emerald** is bright green in color. エメラルド色の ❑ *...an emerald valley.* 鮮やかな緑の渓谷

emerge /ɪmɜrdʒ/ (**emerges, emerging, emerged**) **1** V-I 自動詞 To **emerge** means to come out from an enclosed or dark space such as a room or a vehicle, or from a position where you could not be seen. 現われる ❑ *Richard was waiting outside the door as she emerged.* リチャードは彼女が現われた時にドアの外で待っていた. ❑ *She then emerged from the courthouse to thank her supporters.* 彼女はそれから裁判所から姿を現して, 支援者に礼を言った. **2** V-I 自動詞 If you **emerge** from a difficult or bad experience, you come to the end of it. 抜け出す ❑ *There is growing evidence that the economy is at last emerging from recession.* 経済はやっと景気後退から脱却しつつある証拠が増えている. **3** V-T/V-I 他動詞/自動詞 If a fact or result **emerges** from a period of thought, discussion, or investigation, it becomes known as a result of it. 明らかになる ❑ *...the growing corruption that has emerged in the past few years.* 過去数年間に明らかになった増大する腐敗 ❑ *It soon emerged that neither the July nor August mortgage payment had been collected.* 7月と8月の住宅ローン支払いが徴収されなかったことがまもなく判明した. **4** V-I 自動詞 If someone or something **emerges as** a particular thing, they become recognized as that thing. 出現する [JOURNALISM ジャーナリズム] ❑ *Vietnam has emerged as the world's third-biggest rice exporter.* ベトナムは世界第3位の米の輸出国としてのし上がってきた. **5** V-I 自動詞 When something such as an organization or an industry **emerges**, it comes into existence. 生まれる [JOURNALISM ジャーナリズム] ❑ *...the new republic that emerged in October 1917.* 1917年に誕生した新しい共和国

Thesaurus emerge また次を参照:

V. appear, come out; *(ant.)* disappear **1**

emer|gence /ɪmɜrdʒ³ns/ N-UNCOUNT 不可算名詞 The **emergence of** something is the process or event of its coming into existence. 出現, 発生 ❑ *...the emergence of new democracies in Latin America.* 中南米における新しい民主主義国家の誕生

emer|gen|cy /ɪmɜrdʒ³nsi/ (**emergencies**) **1** N-COUNT 可算名詞 An **emergency** is an unexpected and difficult or dangerous situation, especially an accident, that happens suddenly and that requires quick action to deal with it. 緊急事態 ❑ *He deals with emergencies promptly.* 彼は緊急事態にすばやく対処する. **2** ADJ 形容詞 An **emergency** action is one that is done or arranged quickly and not in the normal way, because an emergency has occurred. 緊急の [ADJ n] ❑ *Yesterday, the center's board held an emergency meeting.* 昨日センターの理事会は緊急会議を開いた. **3** ADJ 形容詞 **Emergency** equipment or supplies are those intended for use in an emergency. 非常用の [ADJ n] ❑ *The plane is carrying emergency supplies for refugees.* その飛行機は避難民のための非常用物資を運んでいた.

→ see **hospital**

Word Partnership emergency は次の語句と使われる:

ADJ. **major** emergency, **medical** emergency, **minor** emergency **1**

N. **state of** emergency **1**
emergency **care**, emergency **surgery 2**
emergency **supplies**, emergency **vehicle 3**

emer|gen|cy brake (**emergency brakes**) N-COUNT 可算名詞 In a vehicle, the **emergency brake** is a brake that the driver operates with his or her hand or foot, and uses, for example, in emergencies or when parking. サイドブレーキ [mainly AM 主に米国英語] ❑ *He stopped just as his truck tilted down the steep incline, put on the emergency brake, and stepped out.* 彼は彼のトラックが丁度急な坂を下ったところで停車し, サイドブレーキをかけ, 車から出てきた.

emer|gen|cy room (**emergency rooms**) N-COUNT 可算名詞 The **emergency room** is the room or department in a hospital where people who have severe injuries or sudden illnesses are taken for emergency treatment. The abbreviation **ER** is often used. 救急処置室 [mainly AM 主に米国英語] ❑ *She began hyperventilating and was rushed to the emergency room.* 彼女は呼吸亢進をし始めて, 救急処置室に担ぎ込まれた.

emer|gen|cy ser|vices N-PLURAL 複数名詞 The **emergency services** are the public organizations whose job is to take quick action to deal with emergencies when they occur, especially the fire department, the police, and the ambulance service. 緊急隊 ❑ *...members of the emergency services.* 緊急隊員

emi|grant /ɛmɪgrənt/ (**emigrants**) N-COUNT 可算名詞 An **emigrant** is a person who has left their own country to live in another country. Compare **immigrant**. 移住者 ❑ *...Irish emigrants to America.* アメリカに移住したアイルランド人

emi|grate /ɛmɪgreɪt/ (**emigrates, emigrating, emigrated**) V-I 自動詞 If you **emigrate**, you leave your own country to live in another country. 移住する ❑ *He emigrated to Belgium.* 彼はベルギーに移住した. ● **emi|gra|tion** /ɛmɪgreɪʃ³n/ N-UNCOUNT 不可算名詞 移住 ❑ *...the huge emigration of workers to the West.* 西欧への大量の労働者の移住

emi|nence /ɛmɪnəns/ N-UNCOUNT 不可算名詞 **Eminence** is the quality of being very well-known and highly respected. 高名, 著名 ❑ *Many of the pilots were to achieve eminence in the aeronautical world.* そのパイロットたちの多くは航空界で名をなす運命にあった.

emi|nent /ɛmɪnənt/ ADJ 形容詞 An **eminent** person is well-known and respected, especially because they are good at their profession. 著名な ❑ *...an eminent scientist.* 著名な科学者

emi|nent|ly /ɛmɪnəntli/ ADV 副詞 You use **eminently** in front of an adjective describing a positive quality in order to emphasize the quality expressed by that adjective. 非常に [EMPHASIS 強調] [ADV adj/-ed] ❑ *His books on diplomatic history were eminently readable.* 外交の歴史に関する彼の著作は非常に読みやすい.

emis|sion /ɪmɪʃ³n/ (**emissions**) N-VAR 可変性名詞 An **emission** of something such as gas or radiation is the release of it into the atmosphere. 排出 [FORMAL 形式ばった] ❑ *The emission of gases such as carbon dioxide should be stabilized at their present level.* 二酸化炭素などのガスの排出は現在のレベルで固定されるべきだ.

→ see **pollution**

emit /ɪmɪt/ (**emits, emitting, emitted**) **1** V-T 他動詞 If something **emits** heat, light, gas, or a smell, it produces it and sends it out by means of a physical or chemical process. 放つ [FORMAL 形式ばった] ❑ *The new device emits a powerful circular column of light.* 新しい装置は強力な環状の光を発する. **2** V-T 他動詞 To **emit** a sound or noise means to produce it. 出す [FORMAL 形式ばった] ❑ *Whitney blinked and emitted a long, low whistle.* ウィットニーはまばたきして, 長く低い口笛を吹いた.

→ see **light**

emo|ti|con /ɪmoʊtɪkɒn/ (**emoticons**) N-COUNT 可算名詞 An **emoticon** is a symbol used in e-mail to show how someone is feeling. :-) is an emoticon showing happiness. 顔文字 [COMPUTING コンピューティング]

emo|tion /ɪmoʊʃ³n/ (**emotions**) **1** N-VAR 可変性名詞 An **emotion** is a feeling such as happiness, love, fear, anger, or hatred, which can be caused by the situation that you are in or the people you are with. 感情 ❑ *Happiness was an emotion that Jerry was having to relearn.* 幸福はジェリーが学びなおさなければならなくなっている感情だった. **2** N-UNCOUNT 不可算名詞 **Emotion** is the part of a person's character that consists of their feelings, as opposed to their thoughts. 感情, 情緒 ❑ *...the split between reason and emotion.* 理性と感情間の分裂

→ see Word Web: **emotion**

emo|tion|al /ɪmoʊʃ³n³l/ **1** ADJ 形容詞 **Emotional** means concerned with emotions and feelings. 感情的な ❑ *I needed this man's love, and the emotional support he was giving me.* 私はこの男の愛と, それに彼が私に与えている情緒的な支援が必要だった. ● **emo|tion|al|ly** ADV 副詞 [ADV adj/-ed] 感情的に ❑ *Are you saying that you're becoming emotionally involved with me?* あなたは私に感情的に夢中になりかけていると言っているんですか. **2** ADJ 形容詞 An **emotional** situation or issue is one that causes people to have strong feelings. 感情に訴える ❑ *Abortion is a very emotional issue.* 妊娠中絶は感情に強く訴える問題だ. ● **emo|tion|al|ly** ADV 副詞 [ADV adj/-ed] 感情に訴えて ❑ *In an emotionally charged speech, he said he was resigning.* 感情に訴えたスピーチで彼は辞任するつもりだと述べ

E

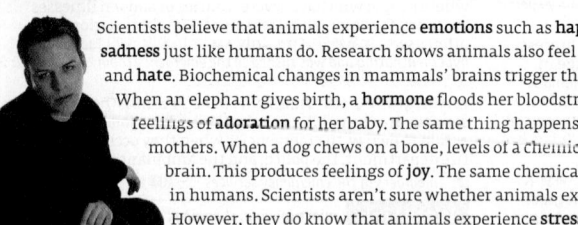

Scientists believe that animals experience **emotions** such as **happiness** and **sadness** just like humans do. Research shows animals also feel **anger**, **fear**, **love**, and **hate**. Biochemical changes in mammals' brains trigger these emotions. When an elephant gives birth, a **hormone** floods her bloodstream. This causes feelings of **adoration** for her baby. The same thing happens to human mothers. When a dog chews on a bone, levels of a chemical increase in its brain. This produces feelings of **joy**. The same chemical produces **elation** in humans. Scientists aren't sure whether animals experience **shame**. However, they do know that animals experience **stress**.

た。 ❸ ADJ 形容詞 If someone is or becomes **emotional**, they show their feelings very openly, especially because they are upset. 感情 に動かされやすい，情にもろい ❑ *He is a very emotional man.* 彼は非常 に情にもろい男だ。

emo|tive /ɪmoʊtɪv/ ADJ 形容詞 An **emotive** situation or issue is likely to make people feel strong emotions. 感情に訴える ❑ *Embryo research is an emotive issue.* 胎芽の研究は感情に訴える問題だ。

em|pa|thy /ɛmpəθi/ N-UNCOUNT 不可算名詞 **Empathy** is the ability to share another person's feelings and emotions as if they were your own. 共感 ❑ *Having begun my life in a children's home, I have great empathy with the little ones.* 児童施設で育った私は子供たちに大きく共感する。

em|per|or /ɛmpərər/ (**emperors**) N-COUNT; N-TITLE 可算名詞，称号名詞 An **emperor** is a man who rules an empire or is the head of state in an empire. 皇帝 ❑ *...the emperor of Japan.* 日本の天皇
→ see **empire**

em|pha|sis /ɛmfəsɪs/ (**emphases** /ɛmfəsiz/) ❶ N-VAR 可変性名詞 **Emphasis** is special or extra importance that is given to an activity or to a part or aspect of something. 重要性 ❑ *Too much emphasis is placed on research.* 調査に重きが置かれすぎている。 ❷ N-VAR 可変性名詞 **Emphasis** is extra force that you put on a syllable, word, or phrase when you are speaking in order to make it seem more important. 強調 ❑ *The emphasis is on the first syllable of the last word.* 最後の単語の最初の音節を強調する。

em|pha|size /ɛmfəsaɪz/ (**emphasizes, emphasizing, emphasized**) V-T 他動詞 To **emphasize** something means to indicate that it is particularly important or true, or to draw special attention to it. 強調する ❑ *But it's also been emphasized that no major policy changes can be expected to come out of the meeting.* しかし，その会議で方針の大幅な変更が打ち出される見込みがないことも強調されている。

em|phat|ic /ɪmfætɪk/ ❶ ADJ 形容詞 An **emphatic** response or statement is one made in a forceful way, because the speaker feels very strongly about what they are saying. 断固とした ❑ *His response was immediate and emphatic.* 彼はすぐにきっぱりと応答した。 ❷ ADJ 形容詞 If you are **emphatic about** something, you use forceful language that shows you feel very strongly about what you are saying. 強調する [v-link ADJ] ❑ *The rebels are emphatic that this is not a surrender.* 反乱者たちはこれが降伏ではないことを強調している。 ❸ ADJ 形容詞 An **emphatic** win or victory is one in which the winner has won by a large amount or distance. (勝利の度合が) 際立った ❑ *Yesterday's emphatic victory was their fifth in succession.*

昨日の彼らの大勝利は連続5回目だった。

em|phati|cal|ly /ɪmfætɪkli/ ❶ ADV 副詞 If you say something **emphatically**, you say it in a forceful way that shows you feel very strongly about what you are saying. 断固として [ADV with v] ❑ *"No fast food," she said emphatically.* 「ファーストフードはいやよ」と彼女はきっぱり言った。 ❷ ADV 副詞 You use **emphatically** to emphasize the statement you are making. まったく [EMPHASIS 強調] [ADV with cl/group] ❑ *Making people feel foolish is emphatically not my strategy.* 人を愚か者だという気持ちにさせることは，決して私のやり方ではない。

em|pire /ɛmpaɪər/ (**empires**) ❶ N-COUNT 可算名詞 An **empire** is a number of individual nations that are all controlled by the government or ruler of one particular country. 帝国 ❑ *...the Roman Empire.* ローマ帝国 ❷ N-COUNT 可算名詞 You can refer to a group of companies controlled by one person as an **empire**. 企業集団，企業帝国 ❑ *...the global Murdoch media empire.* 世界的なマードック・メディア帝国
→ see Word Web: **empire**
→ see **history**

em|piri|cal /ɪmpɪrɪkᵊl/ ADJ 形容詞 **Empirical** evidence or study relies on practical experience rather than theories. 実験による，経験による ❑ *There is no empirical evidence to support his thesis.* 彼の論文を支える実験に基づく証拠は何もない。 ● **em|piri|cal|ly** ADV 副詞 実験的に，経験的に ❑ *They approached this part of their task empirically.* 彼らは課題のこの部分を実証的に取り組んだ。
→ see **science**

em|ploy /ɪmplɔɪ/ (**employs, employing, employed**) ❶ V-T 他動詞 If a person or company **employs** you, they pay you to work for them. 雇う ❑ *The company employs 18 workers.* その会社には18人の従業員がいる。 ❑ *More than 3,000 local workers are employed in the tourism industry.* 3千人以上の現地労働者が観光業に携わっている。 ❷ V-T 他動詞 If you **employ** certain methods, materials, or expressions, you use them. (手段や材料などを) 用いる ❑ *The group will employ a mix of tactics to achieve its aim.* そのグループは目的を達成するためさまざまな作戦を用いるだろう。 ❸ V-T 他動詞 If your time **is employed in** doing something, you are using the time you have to do that thing. (時間を) 費やす [usu passive] ❑ *Your time could be usefully employed in attending night classes.* あなたの時間を夜間クラスに出席して有益に使うこともできるでしょう。

em|ployee /ɪmplɔɪi/ (**employees**) N-COUNT 可算名詞 An **employee** is a person who is paid to work for an organization or for another person. 従業員 ❑ *He is an employee of Fuji Bank.* 彼は富士

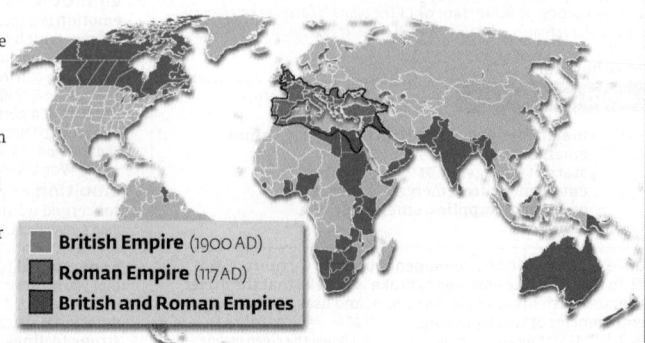

An **empire** is formed when a strong nation-state **conquers** other states and creates a larger **political union**. An early example is the Roman Empire which began in 31 BC. The Roman **emperor** Augustus Caesar* ruled a vast area from the Mediterranean Sea* to Western Europe. Later, the British Empire flourished from about 1600 to 1900 AD. Queen Victoria's* empire spread across oceans and continents. One of her many titles was **Empress** of India. Both of these empires spread their political influence as well as their language and culture over large areas.

Augustus Caesar: the first emperor of Rome.
Mediterranean Sea: between Europe and Africa.
Queen Victoria (1819-1901): queen of the United Kingdom.

British Empire (1900 AD)
Roman Empire (117 AD)
British and Roman Empires

銀行に勤めている.
→ see **factory**, **union**

em|ploy|er /ɪmplɔɪər/ (**employers**) N-COUNT 可算名詞 Your **employer** is the person or organization that you work for. 雇用者 ❑ *He had been sent to Rome by his employer.* 彼は社長の命でローマに派遣されていた.

em|ploy|ment /ɪmplɔɪmənt/ **1** N-UNCOUNT 不可算名詞 **Employment** is the fact of having a paid job. 就職 ❑ *She was unable to find employment.* 彼女は仕事を見つけられなかった. **2** N-UNCOUNT 不可算名詞 **Employment** is the fact of employing someone. 雇用 ❑ *...the employment of children under nine.* 9歳未満の児童の雇用 **3** N-UNCOUNT 不可算名詞 **Employment** is the work that is available in a country or area. 職, 勤め口 ❑ *...economic policies designed to secure full employment.* 完全雇用を保障するための経済政策

em|ploy|ment agen|cy (**employment agencies**) N-COUNT 可算名詞 An **employment agency** is a company whose business is to help people to find work and help employers to find the workers they need. 職業紹介会社, 人材派遣会社 [BUSINESS 実業]

em|power /ɪmpaʊər/ (**empowers, empowering, empowered**) **1** V-T 他動詞 If someone **is empowered to** do something, they have the authority or power to do it. 権限を与える [FORMAL 形式ばった] ❑ *The army is now empowered to operate on a shoot-to-kill basis.* 軍は今や射殺を原則に行動する権限を与えられている. **2** V-T 他動詞 To **empower** someone means to give them the means to achieve something, for example, to become stronger or more successful. (目標達成に必要な) 手段を与える ❑ *You must delegate effectively and empower people to carry out their roles with your full support.* あなたは効果的に権限を委譲して, 人々がそれぞれの役割を果たせるよう全面的に支援しなければならない.

em|pow|er|ment /ɪmpaʊərmənt/ N-UNCOUNT 不可算名詞 The **empowerment** of a person or group of people is the process of giving them power and status in a particular situation. 権限を与えること ❑ *This government believes very strongly in the empowerment of women.* この政府は女性の地位向上の大切さを非常に強く信じている.

em|press /ɛmprɪs/ (**empresses**) N-COUNT; N-TITLE 可算名詞, 称号名詞 An **empress** is a woman who rules an empire or who is the wife of an emperor. 女帝, 皇后 ❑ *...Catherine II, Empress of Russia.* ロシアの女帝であるエカテリーナ2世
→ see **empire**

emp|ti|ness /ɛmptɪnɪs/ **1** N-UNCOUNT 不可算名詞 A feeling of **emptiness** is an unhappy or frightening feeling that nothing is worthwhile, especially when you are very tired or have just experienced something upsetting. (心の) むなしさ ❑ *The result later in life may be feelings of emptiness and depression.* 人生の晩年の成り行きはむなしさやうつ状態に陥ることかもしれない. **2** N-UNCOUNT 不可算名詞 The **emptiness** of a place is the fact that there is nothing in it. (場所が) 空虚 ❑ *...the emptiness of the desert.* その砂漠の空虚さ

emp|ty /ɛmpti/ (**emptier, emptiest, empties, emptying, emptied**) **1** ADJ 形容詞 An **empty** place, vehicle, or container is one that has no people or things in it. 空の ❑ *The room was bare and empty.* その部屋は家具がなく空っぽだった. ❑ *...empty cans of beer.* ビールの空き缶 **2** ADJ 形容詞 An **empty** gesture, threat, or relationship has no real value or meaning. 中身のない, 意味のない ❑ *His father had threatened disinheritance, but both men had known it was an empty threat.* 彼の父は遺産相続権を取り消すと脅していたが, 2人ともそれがただの脅しに過ぎないことを知っていた. **3** ADJ 形容詞 If you describe a person's life or a period of time as **empty**, you mean that nothing interesting or valuable happens in it. つまらない ❑ *My life was very hectic but empty before I met him.* 彼に出会う以前は私の人生はとても忙しかったが, つまらなかった. **4** ADJ 形容詞 If you **feel empty**, you feel unhappy and have no energy, usually because you are very tired or have just experienced something upsetting. むなしい ❑ *I feel so empty, my life just doesn't seem worth living any more.* とてもむなしい. 私の人生なんてこれ以上生きている価値がないような気がする. **5** V-T 他動詞 If you **empty** a container, or **empty** something out of it, you remove its contents, especially by tipping it up. 空にする, 中身を空ける ❑ *I emptied the ashtray.* 私は灰皿を空にした. ❑ *Empty the noodles and liquid into a serving bowl.* めんとつゆをどんぶりに空けなさい. **6** V-T/V-I 他動詞/自動詞 If someone **empties** a room or place, or if it **empties**, everyone in it goes away. 空ける (部屋や場所を) [他動詞], 空になる [自動詞] ❑ *The stadium emptied at the end of the first day of games.* 試合の初日の終わりに競技場は空になった. **7** V-I 自動詞 A river or canal that **empties into** a lake, river, or sea flows into it. (川が湖・海などに) 流れ込む ❑ *The Milwaukee River empties into Lake Michigan near that pipe.* ミルウォーキー川はあの導管付近でミシガン湖に流れ込んでいる. **8** N-COUNT 可算名詞 **Empties** are bottles or containers that no longer have anything in them. 空にした入れ物 ❑ *After breakfast we'll take the empties down in the sack.* 朝食が終わったら, みんなで空き缶をその袋に入れて持って下りるわよ.

ADJ.	uninhabited, unoccupied, vacant; (*ant.*) full, occupied **1**
	meaningless, without substance **2 3**
V.	drain out, pour out **5 7**
	evacuate, go out, leave **6**

N.	empty **bottle**, empty **box**, empty **building**, empty **room**, empty **seat**, empty **space**, empty **stomach 1** empty **promise**, empty **threat 2** empty **the trash 5**
V.	feel empty **4**

empty-handed ADJ 形容詞 If you come away from somewhere **empty-handed**, you have failed to get what you wanted. 手ぶらの [ADJ after v] ❑ *Delegates from the warring sides held a new round of peace talks but went away empty-handed.* 交戦中の両国の代表が新たな和平交渉を持ったが, 何の収穫もなく別れた.

emu|late /ɛmyʊleɪt/ (**emulates, emulating, emulated**) V-T 他動詞 If you **emulate** something or someone, you imitate them because you admire them a great deal. まねる [FORMAL 形式ばった] ❑ *Sons are traditionally expected to emulate their fathers.* 息子たちは昔から父親をまねるものと思われている.

en|able /ɪneɪbᵊl/ (**enables, enabling, enabled**) **1** V-T 他動詞 If someone or something **enables** you **to** do a particular thing, they give you the opportunity to do it. 機会を与える ❑ *The new test should enable doctors to detect the disease early.* その新しい検査できっと医師たちがその病気を早期発見できるようになるはずだ. **2** V-T 他動詞 To **enable** something **to** happen means to make it possible for it to happen. 可能にする ❑ *The hot sun enables the grapes to reach optimum ripeness.* 暑い日ざしのおかげでそれらのぶどうが最適に成熟できる. **3** V-T 他動詞 To **enable** someone **to** do something means to give them permission or the right to do it. 許可する ❑ *...legislation which enables young people to do a form of alternative service.* 若者が1種の代わりの奉仕活動をすることを認める法律

V.	facilitate, permit; (*ant.*) prevent **1** – **3** allow, approve, authorize; (*ant.*) block, disallow, forbid **2 3**

en|act /ɪnækt/ (**enacts, enacting, enacted**) **1** V-T 他動詞 When a government or authority **enacts** a proposal, they make it into a law. 法律にする, 立法化する [TECHNICAL 技術的] ❑ *The authorities have failed so far to enact a law allowing unrestricted emigration.* 当局は今のところ自由な移住を許可する法律を制定できないでいる. **2** V-T 他動詞 If people **enact** a story or play, they perform it by acting. 上演する ❑ *She often enacted the stories told to her by her father.* 彼女は父親が語ってくれた物語をよく上演した. **3** V-T 他動詞 If a particular event or situation **is enacted**, it happens; used especially to talk about something that has happened before. (出来事などを繰り返し) 起こす [JOURNALISM ジャーナリズム] [usu passive] ❑ *It was a scene enacted month after month for eight years.* それは毎月毎月, 8年間にわたって繰り返された光景だった.

en|act|ment /ɪnæktmənt/ (**enactments**) N-VAR 可変性名詞 The **enactment of** a law is the process in a legislature by which the law is agreed upon and made official. (法律の) 制定 [TECHNICAL 技術的] ❑ *We support the call for the enactment of a Bill of Rights.* 我々は権利章典制定の要求を支持する.

enam|el /ɪnæmᵊl/ (**enamels**) **1** N-MASS 質量名詞 **Enamel** is a substance like glass that can be heated and put onto metal, glass, or pottery in order to decorate or protect it. エナメル, ほうろう ❑ *...a white enamel saucepan.* 白いほうろうの片手鍋 **2** N-MASS 質量名詞 **Enamel** is a hard, shiny paint that is used especially for painting metal and wood. エナメル塗料 ❑ *...enamel polymer paints.* エナメルポリマー塗料 **3** N-UNCOUNT 不可算名詞 **Enamel** is the hard white substance that forms the outer part of a tooth. (歯の) エナメル質

en|am|ored /ɪnæmərd/ ADJ 形容詞 If you are **enamored of** something, you like or admire it a lot. If you are not **enamored of** something, you dislike or disapprove of it. 夢中になって [LITERARY 文語的] ❑ *I became totally enamored of the wildflowers there.* 私はそこの野草の花にすっかり心を奪われた.

en|cap|su|late /ɪnkæpsəleɪt, -syu-/ (**encapsulates, encapsulating, encapsulated**) V-T 他動詞 To **encapsulate** particular facts or ideas means to represent all their most important aspects in a very small space or in a single object or event. 要約する ❑ *A Wall Street Journal editorial encapsulated the views*

of many conservatives. ウォールストリートジャーナル紙の社説は多くの保守派の意見を要約していた.

Word Link cas ≈ box, hold : case, encase, suitcase

en|case /ɪnkeɪs/ (encases, encasing, encased) V-T 他動詞 If a person or an object **is encased in** something, they are completely covered or surrounded by it. 入れる，包む □ *When nuclear fuel is manufactured it is encased in metal cans.* 核物質が製造される時，それは金属缶に詰められる. □ *These weapons also had a heavy brass guard which encased almost the whole hand.* これらの武器にも手をほぼすっぽり覆う重い真ちゅうの防御装置が付いていた.

en|chant /ɪntʃænt/ (enchants, enchanting, enchanted) **1** V-T 他動詞 If you **are enchanted by** someone or something, they cause you to have feelings of great delight or pleasure. 魅了する □ *Dena was enchanted by the house.* ディーナはその家にうっとりとなった. **2** V-T 他動詞 In fairy tales and legends, to **enchant** someone or something means to put a magic spell on them. 魔法をかける □ *...Celtic stories of cauldrons and enchanted vessels.* ケルト族に伝わる大釜と魔法のかかった器の話

en|chant|ing /ɪntʃæntɪŋ/ ADJ 形容詞 If you describe someone or something as **enchanting**, you mean that they are very attractive or charming. 魅力的な □ *She's an absolutely enchanting child.* 彼女はほれぼれするほどかわいらしい子だ.

en|cir|cle /ɪnsɜrkᵊl/ (encircles, encircling, encircled) V-T 他動詞 To **encircle** something or someone means to surround or enclose them, or to go around them. 取り囲む；周りを回る □ *A forty-foot-high concrete wall encircles the jail.* 40フィートの高さのコンクリート塀がその刑務所を囲んでいる.

en|clave /ɛnkleɪv, ɒn-/ (enclaves) N-COUNT 可算名詞 An **enclave** is an area within a country or a city where people live who have a different nationality or culture from the people living in the surrounding country or city. 少数民族居住地 □ *Nagorno-Karabakh is an Armenian enclave inside Azerbaijan.* ナゴルノ・カラバフはアゼルバイジャン内のアルメニア人居住地だ.

en|close /ɪnkloʊz/ (encloses, enclosing, enclosed) **1** V-T 他動詞 If a place or object **is enclosed by** something, the place or object is inside that thing or completely surrounded by it. 取り囲む，入れる □ *The rules state that samples must be enclosed in two watertight containers.* 規則には，見本を2つの密封容器に入れなければならないと書いてある. □ *Enclose the flower in a small muslin bag.* その花をモスリンの小さな袋に入れなさい. **2** V-T 他動詞 If you **enclose** something with a letter, you put it in the same envelope as the letter. 同封する □ *I have enclosed a check for $100.* 私は100ドルの小切手を同封している.

en|clo|sure /ɪnkloʊʒər/ (enclosures) N-COUNT 可算名詞 An **enclosure** is an area of land that is surrounded by a wall or fence and that is used for a particular purpose. 囲い地 □ *This enclosure was so vast that the outermost wall could hardly be seen.* この囲い地は非常に広かったので，一番外側の塀はほとんど見えなかった.

Word Link cod ≈ writing : code, encode, decode

Word Link en ≈ making, putting : enable, enact, encode

en|code /ɪnkoʊd/ (encodes, encoding, encoded) V-T 他動詞 If you **encode** a message or some information, you put it into a code or express it in a different form or system of language. 記号化する □ *The two parties encode confidential data in a form that is not directly readable by the other party.* その両者は機密データを相手方がそのまま読めないよう暗号化している.

en|com|pass /ɪnkʌmpəs/ (encompasses, encompassing, encompassed) **1** V-T 他動詞 If something **encompasses** particular things, it includes them. 含む □ *His repertoire encompassed everything from Bach to Schoenberg.* 彼のレパートリーにはバッハからシェーンベルクまですべて含まれていた. **2** V-T 他動詞 To **encompass** a place means to completely surround or cover it. 包囲する，すっぽり覆う □ *The map shows the rest of the western region, encompassing nine states.* その地図には9州にわたる西側地域の残りすべてが載っている.

en|core /ɒŋkɔr, -kɔr/ (encores) N-COUNT 可算名詞 An **encore** is a short extra performance at the end of a longer one, that an entertainer gives because the audience asks for it. アンコール □ *Lang's final encore last night was "Barefoot."* 昨夜，ラングの最後のアンコール曲は『ベアフット』だった.

en|coun|ter /ɪnkaʊntər/ (encounters, encountering, encountered) **1** V-T 他動詞 If you **encounter** problems or difficulties, you experience them. (問題・困難に) 直面する □ *Every day of our lives we encounter major and minor stresses of one kind or another.* 私たちは生活の中で，毎日大なり小なり何らかのストレスを受けている. **2** V-T 他動詞 If you **encounter** someone, you meet them, usually unexpectedly. (思いがけなく) 出会う [FORMAL 形式ばった] □ *Did you encounter anyone in the building?* あなたはその建物の中で誰かに出会った？ **3** N-COUNT 可算名詞 An **encounter**

with someone is a meeting with them, particularly one that is unexpected or significant. (思いがけない) 出会い □ *The author tells of a remarkable encounter with a group of South Vietnamese soldiers.* 著者は南ベトナム人兵士の1団との驚くべき出会いについて語る. **4** N-COUNT 可算名詞 An **encounter** is a particular type of experience. 経験 □ *...a sexual encounter.* 性体験

Thesaurus encounter また次を参照：

v. bump into, come across, run into; (ant.) avoid, miss **1 2**

en|cour|age /ɪnkɜrɪdʒ/ (encourages, encouraging, encouraged) **1** V-T 他動詞 If you **encourage** someone, you give them confidence, for example by letting them know that what they are doing is good and telling them that they should continue to do it. 励ます，勇気づける □ *When things aren't going well, he encourages me, telling me not to give up.* 物事がうまく行かない時，彼は私にあきらめるなと言って私を励ましてくれる. **2** V-T 他動詞 If someone **is encouraged by** something that happens, it gives them hope or confidence. 希望を与える，自信を与える [usu passive] □ *Investors were encouraged by the news.* 投資家たちはその知らせに希望を持った. ● **en|cour|aged** ADJ 形容詞 [v-link ADJ] 希望を与えられて，自信を与えられて □ *We were very encouraged after over 17,000 pictures were submitted.* 1万7千点以上の写真が寄せられて，私たちはとても勇気づけられた. **3** V-T 他動詞 If you **encourage** someone **to** do something, you try to persuade them to do it, for example, by telling them that it would be a pleasant thing to do, or by trying to make it easier for them to do it. You can also **encourage** an activity. (一するよう) 奨励する，勧める □ *Herbie Hancock was encouraged by his family to learn music at a young age.* ハービー・ハンコックは幼少の頃に家族から音楽を習うよう勧められた. **4** V-T 他動詞 If something **encourages** a particular activity or state, it causes it to happen or increase. 促進する □ *...a natural substance that encourages cell growth.* 細胞の成長を促進する自然物質

en|cour|age|ment /ɪnkɜrɪdʒmənt/ (encouragements) N-VAR 可変性名詞 **Encouragement** is the activity of encouraging someone, or something that is said or done in order to encourage them. 激励，励まし □ *Friends gave me a great deal of encouragement.* 友人たちが私を大変励ましてくれた.

en|cour|ag|ing /ɪnkɜrɪdʒɪŋ/ ADJ 形容詞 Something that is **encouraging** gives people hope or confidence. 希望や自信を与える，心強い □ *There are encouraging signs of an artistic revival.* 芸術の復興という明るい兆し □ *The results have been encouraging.* 有望な結果が出ている. ● **en|cour|ag|ing|ly** ADV 副詞 勇気づけるように □ *The people at the next table watched me eat and smiled encouragingly.* 隣のテーブルの人たちは私が食べるのをじっと見て，勇気づけるようにほほえんだ.

en|croach /ɪnkroʊtʃ/ (encroaches, encroaching, encroached) **1** V-I 自動詞 If one thing **encroaches on** another, the first thing spreads or becomes stronger, and slowly begins to restrict the power, range, or effectiveness of the second thing. (他人の権利などを) 侵害する [FORMAL 形式ばった, DISAPPROVAL 不賛成] □ *The new institutions do not encroach on political power.* その新しい制度は政治権力を侵害するものではない. **2** V-I 自動詞 If something **encroaches on** a place, it spreads and takes over more and more of that place. (土地などを) 侵食する [FORMAL 形式ばった] □ *The shrubs encroached ever more on the twisting drive.* それらの低木は曲がりくねった車道にさらに一層はみ出ていた.

en|croach|ment /ɪnkroʊtʃmənt/ (encroachments) N-VAR 可変性名詞 You can describe the action or process of encroaching on something as **encroachment**. 侵害 [FORMAL 形式ばった, DISAPPROVAL 不賛成] □ *It's a sign of the encroachment of commercialism in medicine.* それは医学における営利主義の侵害の表れだ.

en|cy|clo|pedia /ɪnsaɪkləpidiə/ (encyclopedias) also encyclopaedia N-COUNT 可算名詞 An **encyclopedia** is a book or set of books in which facts about many different subjects or about one particular subject are arranged for reference, usually in alphabetical order. 百科事典

end
❶ NOUN USES
❷ VERB USES
❸ PHRASAL VERBS

❶ end /ɛnd/ (ends) **1** N-SING 単数名詞 The **end of** something such as a period of time, an event, a book, or a movie is the last part of it or the final point in it. 終わり □ *The report is expected by the end of the year.* その年の終わりまでに報告書ができあがると見込まれている. □ *...families who settled in the region at the end of the 17th century.* 17世紀末にその地域に定住した家族 **2** N-COUNT 可算名詞 An **end to** something or the **end of** it is the act or result of stopping it so that it does not continue any longer. 終結 □ *The*

government today called for an end to the violence. 政府は本日暴力行為の終結を呼びかけた. ❏ I was worried she would walk out or bring the interview to an end. 私は彼女が退席するか会見を切り上げるのではないかと心配した. **4** N-COUNT 可算名詞 The two **ends** of something long and narrow are the two points or parts of it that are farthest away from each other. 両端 ❏ The company is planning to place surveillance equipment at both ends of the tunnel. その会社はトンネルの両端に監視装置を設置することを計画している. **4** N-COUNT 可算名詞 The **end** of a long, narrow object such as a finger or a pencil is the tip or smallest edge of it, usually the part that is furthest away from you. 先端 ❏ He tapped the ends of his fingers together. 彼は両手の指先をトントンと打ち合わせた. **5** N-COUNT 可算名詞 **End** is used to refer to either of the two extreme points of a scale, or of something that you are considering as a scale. (対極的な立場の) 片方 ❏ At the other end of the social scale was the grocer. 社会階級の対極的なもう一方が食料雑貨商だった. **6** N-COUNT 可算名詞 The **other end** is one of two places that are connected because people are communicating with each other by telephone or writing, or are traveling from one place to the other. (電話や手紙などの) 相手方 ❏ When he answered the phone, Fred was at the other end. 彼が電話に出るとフレッドからだった. **7** N-COUNT 可算名詞 If you refer to a particular **end** of a project or piece of work, you mean a part or aspect of it, such as a part of it that is done by a particular person or in a particular place. (計画や作業の) 受け持ち [SPOKEN 口語] ❏ You take care of your end, kid, I'll take care of mine. きみは自分の分をやってくれ, おれはおれの分をやる. **8** N-COUNT 可算名詞 An **end** is the purpose for which something is done or toward which you are working. 目的 ❏ The police force is being manipulated for political ends. 警察は政治的な目的にあやつられている. **9** PHRASE 句 If something is **at an end**, it has finished and will not continue. 終わって ❏ The recession is definitely at an end. 不況は間違いなく終わった. **10** PHRASE 句 If something **comes to an end**, it stops. 終わる ❏ The cold war came to an end. 冷戦が終わった. **11** PHRASE 句 You say **at the end of the day** when you are talking about what happens after a long series of events or what appears to be the case after you have considered the relevant facts. 結局のところ, 要するに [INFORMAL くだけた] ❏ At the end of the day it's up to them to decide. 要するに彼らが決めることだ. **12** PHRASE 句 You say **in the end** when you are saying what is the final result of a series of events, or what is your final conclusion after considering all the relevant facts. 結局, 最後に ❏ I toyed with the idea of calling the police, but in the end I didn't. 私は警察に電話しようかと思ったが, 結局そうしなかった. **13** PHRASE 句 If you find it difficult to **make ends meet**, you cannot manage very well financially because you hardly have enough money for the things you need. 収支を合わせる ❏ With Betty's salary they barely made ends meet. ベティーの給料で彼らはかろうじてやりくりできた. **14** PHRASE 句 **No end** means a lot. 大いに, たくさん [INFORMAL くだけた] ❏ Teachers inform me that Todd's behavior has improved no end. 先生方から私までの連絡ではトッドの態度がとても良くなったということだ. **15** PHRASE 句 When something happens for hours, days, weeks, or years **on end**, it happens continuously and without stopping for the amount of time that is mentioned. 続けて ❏ He is a wonderful companion and we can talk for hours on end. 彼は素晴らしい仲間で, 私たちは何時間でも話し続けられる. **16** PHRASE 句 Something that is **on end** is upright, instead of in its normal or natural position, for example, lying down, flat, or on its longest side. 直立して ❏ Wet books should be placed on end with their pages kept apart. ぬれた本はページを別々に離して縦に置かないといけない. **17** PHRASE 句 To **put an end to** something means to cause it to stop. 終止符を打つ, 終わらせる ❏ Only a political solution could put an end to the violence. 政治的解決だけがその暴動を鎮めるであろう. **18** PHRASE 句 If a process or person has reached **the end of the road**, they are unable to progress any further. 行き詰まり, 限界 ❏ Given the results of the vote, is this the end of the road for the hardliners in Congress? 投票の結果を考えると, これが議会内強硬派にとって限界だろうか? **19** PHRASE 句 If you say that something bad is **not the end of the world**, you are trying to stop yourself or someone else being so upset by it, by suggesting that it is not the worst thing that could happen. この世の終わりではない (慰めや励ましの言葉) ❏ Obviously I'd be disappointed if we don't make it, but it wouldn't be the end of the world. もしそれが無理ならもちろん私はがっかりするだろうけど, それがこの世の終わりではもちろんない. **20** The **end of your tether** → see **tether** **21** to **make** your **hair stand on end** → see **hair** **22** to **be on the receiving end** → see **receive** **23** to **get the wrong end of the stick** → see **stick**

❷ end /end/ (**ends, ending, ended**) **1** V-T/V-I 他動詞/自動詞 When a situation, process, or activity **ends**, or when something or someone **ends** it, it reaches its final point and stops. 終える [他動詞], 終わる [自動詞] ❏ The meeting quickly ended and Steve and I left the room. その会議はすぐに終わって, スティーブと私は部屋を出た. ●**ending** N-SING 単数名詞 終わり ❏ The ending of a marriage by death is different in many ways from an ending caused by divorce. 死別による結婚生活の終わりは離婚による終わりといろんな点で違う. **2** V-T/V-I 他

動詞/自動詞 If you say that someone or something **ends** a period of time in a particular way, you are indicating what the final situation was like. You can also say that a period of time **ends** in a particular way. 終わりを〜にする [他動詞], 終わりが〜になる [自動詞] ❏ The markets ended the week on a quiet note. その週の市場は動きが少ない状態で終わった. **3** V-I 自動詞 If a period of time **ends**, it reaches its final point. (期間が) 終わる ❏ Reports on usually come out about three weeks after each month ends. 予定されている報告書は通常, 毎月月末から約3週間後に発表される. **4** V-T/V-I 他動詞/自動詞 If something such as a book, speech, or performance **ends with** a particular thing or the writer or performer **ends** it **with** that thing, its final part consists of the thing mentioned. (本やスピーチなどを〜で) 締めくくる [他動詞], 締めくくられる [自動詞] ❏ His statement ended with the words: "Pray for me." 彼の声明は次の言葉で締めくくられていた. 「私のために祈ってください」 ❏ The book ends on a lengthy description of Hawaii. その本はハワイの長い描写で終結していた. **5** V-I 自動詞 If a situation or event **ends** in a particular way, it has that particular result. (〜という) 結果になる ❏ The incident could have ended in tragedy. その出来事は惨事になっていたかもしれなかった. ❏ Our conversations ended with him saying he would try to be more understanding. 私たちの話し合いの結果, 彼はもっと理解ある人間になるよう努力すると言った. **6** V-I 自動詞 If an object **ends with** or **in** a particular thing, it has that thing on its tip or point, or as its last part. (末端に) 〜ついている ❏ It has three pairs of legs, each ending in a large claw. それには3対の足があり, それぞれの足の先には大きなかぎ爪がついている. **7** V-I 自動詞 A journey, road, or river that **ends** at a particular place stops there and no further. (旅・道路・川などが) 終わる 途切れる ❏ The highway ended at an intersection. その幹線道路は交差点のところで終わっていた. **8** V-I 自動詞 If you say that something **ends** at a particular point, you mean that it is applied or exists up to that point, and no further. (類似点がある点で) 終わる ❏ Heather is also 25 and from Boston, but the similarity ends there. ヘザーも25歳でボストン出身だが, 似ているのはそこまでだった. **9** V-I 自動詞 If you **end by** doing something or **end** in a particular state, you do that thing or get into that state even though you did not originally intend to. (〜することで) 終わる (結果として) なる ❏ They ended by making themselves miserable. 彼らは結局惨めな状態になった. **10** PHRASE 句 If someone **ends it all**, they kill themselves. 自殺する ❏ He grew suicidal, thinking up ways to end it all. 彼は自殺願望を持つようになり, 自殺する方法を考え出していた.

Thesaurus end また次を参照:

N. close, conclusion, finale, finish, stop;
(ant.) beginning ❶ **1** **2**
V. conclude, finish, wrap up ❷ **1**

❸ end /end/ (**ends, ending, ended**)
▶ **end up** **1** PHRASAL VERB 句動詞 If someone or something **ends up** somewhere, they eventually arrive there, usually by accident. 最後に〜へたどり着く ❏ She fled with her children, moving from neighbor to neighbor and ending up in a friend's basement. 彼女は子供たちと一緒に逃げ出して, 隣家を転々とした後, 最後に友だちの家の地下室に落ち着いた. **2** PHRASAL VERB 句動詞 If you **end up** doing something or **end up** in a particular state, you do that thing or get into that state even though you did not originally intend to. 結局〜になる, 最後は〜することになる ❏ If you don't know what you want, you might end up getting something you don't want. 自分の欲しいものが分からないと, 結局欲しくない物をもらう羽目になるよ. ❏ Every time they went dancing they ended up in a bad mood. 彼らは踊りに出かけるたび, 最後には不機嫌になっていた.

en|dan|ger /ɪndeɪndʒər/ (**endangers, endangering, endangered**) V-T 他動詞 To **endanger** something or someone means to put them in a situation where they might be harmed or destroyed completely. 危険にさらす ❏ The debate could endanger the proposed Mideast peace talks. その議論は中東和平会談案を危機にさらしかねないであろう.

en|dear /ɪndɪər/ (**endears, endearing, endeared**) V-T 他動詞 If something **endears** you **to** someone or if you **endear yourself to** them, you become popular with them and well liked by them. 慕わせる, 人気者にする ❏ Their taste for gambling has endeared them to Las Vegas casino owners. 彼らはかけごとが好きなため, ラスベガスのカジノ経営者の間で人気がある.

en|dear|ing /ɪndɪərɪŋ/ ADJ 形容詞 If you describe someone's behavior as **endearing**, you mean that it causes you to feel very fond of them. 人の心を引きつける [v-link ADJ] ❏ She has such an endearing personality. 彼女は本当に人を引きつける性格をしている.

en|deav|or /ɪndɛvər/ (**endeavors, endeavoring, endeavored**) **1** V-T 他動詞 If you **endeavor to** do something, you try very hard to do it. 努力する [FORMAL 形式ばった] ❏ They are endeavoring to protect labor union rights. 彼らは労働組合の権利を守ろうと手を尽くしている. **2** N-VAR 可変性名詞 An **endeavor** is an attempt to do something, especially something new or original. 試み [FORMAL 形式ばった] ❏ The company's creative endeavors are thriving. その会社

E

の独創的な試みが成功している. ❑*Extracting information about the large-scale composition of a planet from a sample weighing a millionth of a gram was a fascinating example of scientific endeavor.* 惑星の大規模な組成に関する情報を1グラムの100万分の1の重さのサンプルから引き出すことは, 科学的試みの非常に興味深い例だった.

en|dem|ic /ɛndɛmɪk/ **1** ADJ 形容詞 If a disease or illness is **endemic** in a place, it is frequently found among the people who live there. (病気が) 特有の, 風土性の [TECHNICAL 技術的] ❑*Polio was then endemic among children my age.* ポリオはその頃私の年齢の子供たちに特有の病気だった. **2** ADJ 形容詞 If you say that a condition or problem is **endemic**, you mean that it is very common and strong, and cannot be dealt with easily. 根強い [WRITTEN 書き言葉] ❑*Discrimination against Catholics is endemic in Northern Ireland's institutions.* カトリック教徒に対する差別は北アイルランドの慣行の中に根強く残っている.

end|ing /ɛndɪŋ/ (**endings**) **1** N-COUNT 可算名詞 You can refer to the last part of a book, story, play, or movie as the **ending**, especially when you are considering the way that the story ends. (本・映画などの) 結末, 終わり ❑*The film has a Hollywood happy ending.* その映画はハリウッドらしいハッピーエンドで終わる. **2** N-COUNT 可算名詞 The **ending** of a word is the last part of it. 末尾 ❑*...common word endings, like "ing" in walking.* walkingの 'ing' のような, よくある語尾 **3** → see also **end**

end|less /ɛndlɪs/ ADJ 形容詞 If you say that something is **endless**, you mean that it is very large or lasts for a very long time, and it seems as if it will never stop. 終わりのない, きりがない ❑*...the endless hours I spent on homework.* 私が宿題に費やした膨大な時間 ●**end|less|ly** ADV 副詞 延々と, 果てしなく ❑*They talk about it endlessly.* 彼らは延々とそれについて語る.

en|dorse /ɪndɔrs/ (**endorses, endorsing, endorsed**) **1** V-T 他動詞 If you **endorse** someone or something, you say publicly that you support or approve of them. 承認する, 支持する ❑*I can endorse their opinion wholeheartedly.* 私は彼らの意見を心から支持することができる. **2** V-T 他動詞 If you **endorse** a product or company, you appear in advertisements for it. 薦める, 宣伝する ❑*The twins endorsed a line of household cleaning products.* その双子は一連の家庭用洗剤の宣伝をした.

en|dorse|ment /ɪndɔrsmənt/ (**endorsements**) **1** N-COUNT 可算名詞 An **endorsement** is a statement or action that shows you support or approve of something or someone. 承認, 推薦 ❑*This is a powerful endorsement for his softer style of government.* これは彼のより柔軟な施政に対する強力な支持だ. **2** N-COUNT 可算名詞 An **endorsement for** a product or company involves appearing in advertisements for it or showing support for it. 広告出演 ❑*His commercial endorsements for everything from running shoes to breakfast cereals will take his earnings to more than ten million dollars a year.* 運動靴から朝食用シリアルまであらゆるコマーシャルに出演して, 彼は年間1千万ドル以上の収入を得るだろう.

en|dow /ɪndaʊ/ (**endows, endowing, endowed**) **1** V-T 他動詞 You say that someone **is endowed with** a particular desirable ability, characteristic, or possession when they have it by chance or by birth. (財産・才能などを) 授ける [usu passive] ❑*You are endowed with wealth, good health and a lively intellect.* あなたは生まれながら財産と健康と活発な知性に恵まれている. **2** V-T 他動詞 If you **endow** something **with** a particular feature or quality, you provide it with that feature or quality. (特徴や性質を) 与える ❑*Herbs have been used for centuries to endow a whole range of foods with subtle flavors.* ハーブ類はあらゆる食べ物にほのかな風味を加えるため, 何世紀にもわたって使われてきた. **3** V-T 他動詞 If someone **endows** an institution, scholarship, or project, they provide a large amount of money that will produce the income needed to pay for it. (施設・事業などに) 基金を寄付する ❑*The ambassador has endowed a $1 million public-service fellowships program.* 大使は100万ドルの公益事業研究奨学生プログラムの基金を寄付した.

en|dow|ment /ɪndaʊmənt/ (**endowments**) N-COUNT 可算名詞 An **endowment** is a gift of money that is made to an institution or community in order to provide it with an annual income. 寄付, 基金 ❑*...the National Endowment for the Arts.* 全米芸術基金

end prod|uct (**end products**) N-COUNT 可算名詞 The **end product** of something is the thing that is produced or achieved by means of it. 最終製品 [oft N 'of' n] ❑*It is the end product of exhaustive research and development.* それは徹底的な研究開発の最終製品だ.

end re|sult (**end results**) N-COUNT 可算名詞 The **end result** of an activity or a process is the final result that it produces. 最終結果 ❑*The end result is very good and very successful.* 最終結果は大変良好で大成功だ.

en|dur|ance /ɪndʊrəns/ N-UNCOUNT 不可算名詞 **Endurance** is the ability to continue with an unpleasant or difficult situation, experience, or activity over a long period of time. 忍耐 ❑*The exercise obviously will improve strength and endurance.* その運動はきっと体力と忍耐力を向上させるだろう.

en|dure /ɪndʊər/ (**endures, enduring, endured**) **1** V-T 他動詞

If you **endure** a painful or difficult situation, you experience it and do not avoid it or give up, usually because you cannot. 耐える ❑*The company endured heavy financial losses.* その会社は財務上の大きな損失に持ちこたえた. **2** V-I 自動詞 If something **endures**, it continues to exist without any loss in quality or importance. 持続する ❑*Somehow the language endures and continues to survive.* どういうわけかその言語は絶えることなく存在し続けている. ●**en|dur|ing** ADJ 形容詞 永続的な ❑*This chance meeting was the start of an enduring friendship.* この偶然の出会いが, その後長く続く友情の始まりだった.

end user (**end users**) N-COUNT 可算名詞 The **end user** of a piece of equipment is the user that it has been designed for, rather than the person who installs or maintains it. エンドユーザー [COMPUTING コンピューティング] ❑*You have to be able to describe things in a form that the end user can understand.* あなたはエンドユーザーが理解できるように物事を説明できなければならない.

en|emy /ɛnəmi/ (**enemies**) **1** N-COUNT 可算名詞 If someone is your **enemy**, they hate you or want to harm you. 敵, かたき ❑*Imagine loving your enemy and doing good to those who hated you.* あなたの敵を愛し, あなたを嫌った人たちに親切にすることを想像してごらん. **2** N-COUNT 可算名詞 If someone is your **enemy**, they are opposed to you and to what you think or do. 反対者 ❑*Her political enemies were quick to pick up on this series of disasters.* 彼女の政敵は早くもこの一連の大失態に気づいた. **3** N-SING-COLL 集合的単数名詞 The **enemy** is an army or other force that is opposed to you in a war, or a country with which your country is at war. 敵軍 ['the' N, N n] ❑*The enemy were pursued for two miles.* 敵軍を2マイル追跡した. **4** N-COUNT 可算名詞 If one thing is the **enemy of** another thing, the second thing cannot happen or succeed because of the first thing. 妨害するもの [FORMAL 形式ばった] ❑*Reform, as we know, is the enemy of revolution.* ご存知のとおり改革は革命を妨げる.

Word Partnership	enemy は次の語句と使われる:
V.	**make an** enemy **1**
	defeat an enemy **3**
N.	enemy **attack**, enemy **position**, enemy **territory**, enemy **troops 3**

en|er|get|ic /ɛnərdʒɛtɪk/ **1** ADJ 形容詞 If you are **energetic** in what you do, you have a lot of enthusiasm and determination. 精力的な, 情熱的な ❑*Ibrahim is 59, strong looking, enormously energetic and accomplished.* イブラヒムは59歳, せいかんな面つきで非常に精力的であり教養がある. ●**en|er|geti|cal|ly** /ɛnərdʒɛtɪkli/ ADV 副詞 [ADV with v] 精力的に ❑*He had worked energetically all day on his new book.* 彼は新しい本の執筆に1日中精力的に取り組んでいた. **2** ADJ 形容詞 An **energetic** person is very active and does not feel at all tired. An **energetic** activity involves a lot of physical movement and power. 活発な, 力強い ❑*Ten year-olds are incredibly energetic.* 10歳の子供たちは信じられないほど元気だ. ●**en|er|geti|cal|ly** ADV 副詞 [ADV with v] 活発に ❑*David chewed energetically on the gristly steak.* デイビッドは筋の多いステーキを力強くかんで食べた.

en|er|gy /ɛnərdʒi/ (**energies**) **1** N-UNCOUNT 不可算名詞 **Energy** is the ability and strength to do active physical things and the feeling that you are full of physical power and life. 活力 ❑*He was saving his energy for next week's race in Tuscon.* 彼は来週トゥーソンで行われる競技のために活力を蓄えていた. **2** N-UNCOUNT 不可算名詞 **Energy** is determination and enthusiasm about doing things. 意気込み [APPROVAL 賛成] ❑*You have drive and energy for those things you are interested in.* あなたは興味のあることには気力と熱意がある. **3** N-COUNT 可算名詞 Your **energies** are the efforts and attention that you can direct toward a particular aim. 努力, 尽力 ❑*She had started to devote her energies to teaching rather than performing.* 彼女は自分で演じるよりも指導に当たることに力を注ぎ始めていた. **4** N-UNCOUNT 不可算名詞 **Energy** is the power from sources such as electricity and coal that makes machines work or provides heat. エネルギー, エネルギー源 ❑*...those who favor nuclear energy.* 原子力エネルギーに賛成する者
→ see Word Web: **energy**
→ see **calorie, electricity, food, solar system**

Word Partnership	energy は次の語句と使われる:
ADJ.	**physical** energy, **sexual** energy **1**
	full of energy **1 2**
	atomic energy, **nuclear** energy, **solar** energy **4**
V.	**focus** energy **1 2**
	conserve/save energy **4**

en|force /ɪnfɔrs/ (**enforces, enforcing, enforced**) **1** V-T 他動詞 If people in authority **enforce** a law or a rule, they make sure that it is obeyed, usually by punishing people who do not obey it. 守らせる, 施行する ❑*Boulder was one of the first cities in the nation to enforce a ban on smoking.* ボールダーは喫煙禁止を実施した国内で最初の都市の1つだった. **2** V-T 他動詞 To **enforce** something means to force or cause it to be done or to happen. 強制する ❑*They struggled*

Word Web   energy

Wood was the primary **energy** source for American settlers. Then, as industry developed, factories began to use **coal**. Coal was also used to **generate** most of the **electrical power** in the early 1900s. However, widespread automobile use soon made **petroleum** the most important **fuel**. **Natural gas** remains popular for home heating and industrial use. Hydroelectric power isn't a major source of energy in the U.S. It requires too much land and water to produce. Some companies built **nuclear** power plants to make **electricity** in the 1970s. Today **solar** panels convert sunlight and giant wind farms convert wind into electricity.

to limit the cost by enforcing a low-tech specification. 彼らは低い技術規格を強制することで原価を抑えようと苦しんだ.

en|force|ment /ɪnfɔ́rsmənt/ N-UNCOUNT 不可算名詞 If someone carries out the **enforcement of** an act or rule, they enforce it. 施行 □ *The doctors want stricter enforcement of existing laws.* 医師たちは現行の法律をいっそう厳格に施行することを望んでいる.

en|gage /ɪngéɪdʒ/ (**engages, engaging, engaged**) **1** V-I 自動詞 If you **engage in** an activity, you do it or are actively involved with it. 行う, 従事する [FORMAL 形式ばった] □ *I have never engaged in drug trafficking.* 私は麻薬密売をしたことなど1度もない. **2** V-T 他動詞 If something **engages** you or your attention or interest, it keeps you interested in it and thinking about it. (注意・関心を) 引きつける □ *They never learned skills to engage the attention of the others.* 彼らは他人の注意を引きつける技を習ったことはなかった. **3** V-T 他動詞 If you **engage** someone **in** conversation, you have a conversation with them. (会話に) 引き込む □ *They tried to engage him in conversation.* 彼らは彼を会話に引き入れようとした. **4** V-I 自動詞 If you **engage with** something or **with** a group of people, you get involved with that thing or group and feel that you are connected with it or have real contact with it. (人・物に) かかわる □ *She found it hard to engage with office life.* 彼女は事務員生活に適応するのが難しかった. ● **en|gage|ment** N-UNCOUNT 不可算名詞 かかわり合い □ *...the candidate's apparent lack of engagement with younger voters.* その候補者の若い有権者に対する明らかな取り組み不足 **5** V-T 他動詞 If you **engage** someone to do a particular job, you appoint them to do it. (人を) 雇う [FORMAL 形式ばった] □ *We engaged the services of a famous engineer.* 私たちは有名な技師を雇って仕事をしてもらった. **6** → see also **engaged, engaging**

en|gaged /ɪngéɪdʒd/ **1** ADJ 形容詞 Someone who is **engaged** in a particular activity is doing that thing. 携わって [FORMAL 形式ばった] [v-link ADJ 'in/on'] □ *...the various projects he was engaged in.* 彼がかかわっていたさまざまな事業 **2** ADJ 形容詞 When two people are **engaged**, they have agreed to marry each other. 婚約して □ *We got engaged on my eighteenth birthday.* 私たちは私の18歳の誕生日に婚約した. **3** ADJ 形容詞 If a telephone or a telephone line is **engaged**, it is already being used by someone else so that you are unable to speak to the person you are phoning. (電話が) 話し中の [BRIT 英国英語; AM 米国英語 **busy**] **4** ADJ 形容詞 If a public toilet is **engaged**, it is already being used by someone else. 使用中の [mainly BRIT 主に英国英語; AM usually **occupied** 米国英語では通常 **occupied**]

en|gaged tone → see **busy signal**

en|gage|ment /ɪngéɪdʒmənt/ (**engagements**) **1** N-COUNT 可算名詞 An **engagement** is an arrangement that you have made to do something at a particular time. 約束 [FORMAL 形式ばった] □ *He had an engagement at a restaurant at eight.* 彼はレストランに8時に行く約束をしていた. **2** N-COUNT 可算名詞 An **engagement** is an agreement that two people have made with each other to get married. 婚約 □ *I've broken off my engagement to Arthur.* 私はア

ーサーとの婚約を解消した. **3** N-COUNT 可算名詞 You can refer to the period of time during which two people are engaged as their **engagement**. 婚約期間 □ *We spoke every night during our engagement.* 婚約期間中, 私たちは毎晩話をした. **4** N-VAR 可変性名詞 A military **engagement** is an armed conflict between two enemies. 交戦 □ *The constitution prohibits them from military engagement on foreign soil.* その憲法は彼らが国外地域で交戦することを禁止している. **5** → see also **engage**

en|gag|ing /ɪngéɪdʒɪŋ/ ADJ 形容詞 An **engaging** person or thing is pleasant, interesting, and entertaining. 人を引き付ける □ *...one of her most engaging and least known novels.* 彼女の最も興味深く, また最も世に知られていない小説の1つ

en|gen|der /ɪndʒéndər/ (**engenders, engendering, engendered**) V-T 他動詞 If someone or something **engenders** a particular feeling, atmosphere, or situation, they cause it to occur. (感情・雰囲気を) 生み出す 引き起こす [FORMAL 形式ばった] □ *It helps engender a sense of common humanity.* それは一般の博愛心を呼び起こすのに役立っている.

en|gine /éndʒɪn/ (**engines**) **1** N-COUNT 可算名詞 The **engine** of a car or other vehicle is the part that produces the power which makes the vehicle move. エンジン □ *He got into the driving seat and started the engine.* 彼は運転席に乗り, エンジンをかけた. **2** N-COUNT 可算名詞 An **engine** is also the large vehicle that pulls a train. 機関車 □ *In 1941, the train would have been pulled by a steam engine.* 1941年には, その列車は蒸気機関車で引っ張られていただろう.
→ see Word Web: **engine**
→ see **car**

en|gi|neer /éndʒɪníər/ (**engineers, engineering, engineered**) **1** N-COUNT 可算名詞 An **engineer** is a person who uses scientific knowledge to design, construct, and maintain engines and machines or structures such as roads, railroads, and bridges. 技術者 **2** N-COUNT 可算名詞 An **engineer** is a person who repairs mechanical or electrical devices. 修理工 □ *They send a service engineer to fix the disk drive.* 彼らはディスクドライブを修理するのに修理工を派遣する. **3** N-COUNT 可算名詞 An **engineer** is a person who is responsible for maintaining the engine of a ship while it is at sea. (船の) 機関士 **4** V-T 他動詞 When a vehicle, bridge, or building **is engineered**, it is planned and constructed using scientific methods. 設計する [usu passive] □ *Its spaceship was engineered by Bert Rutan, renowned for designing the Voyager.* その宇宙船はボイジャーの設計で名高いバート・ルータンによって設計された. **5** V-T 他動詞 If you **engineer** an event or situation, you arrange for it to happen, in a clever or indirect way. 巧みに手配する □ *Some people believe that his murder was engineered by Stalin.* 彼の殺害はスターリンによって画策されたと信じる人もいる.

Thesaurus	engineer また次を参照:
v.	arrange, concoct, create, devise, originate, plan; (*ant.*) set up **5**

Word Web   engine

In the **internal combustion engine** found in most cars, there are four, six, or eight **cylinders**. To produce an engine stroke, the **intake valve** opens and a small amount of **fuel** enters the **combustion** chamber of the cylinder. A **spark plug** ignites the fuel and air mixture, causing it to explode. This **combustion** moves the **cylinder head**, which causes the crankshaft to turn. Next, the **exhaust valve** opens and the burned gases are drawn out. As the cylinder head returns to its original position, it compresses the new gas and air mixture and the process repeats itself.

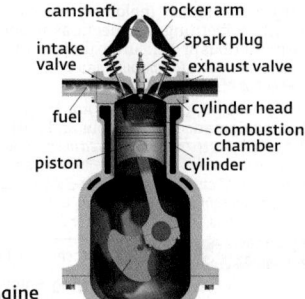

internal combustion engine

E

Word Web · English

The **English language** has more **words** than any other language. Early English grew out of a Germanic language. Much of its **grammar** and basic **vocabulary** came from that language. But in 1066, England was conquered by the Normans. Norman French became the language of the rulers. Therefore many French and Latin words came into the English language. The playwright Shakespeare* **coined** over 1,600 new words in his plays. English has become an international language with many regional **dialects**.

William Shakespeare (1564-1616): an English playwright and poet.

---

en|gi|neer|ing /ɛndʒɪnɪərɪŋ/ ■ N-UNCOUNT 不可算名詞 **Engineering** is the work involved in designing and constructing engines and machinery or structures such as roads and bridges. **Engineering** is also the subject studied by people who want to do this work. 工学技術, 工学 □ *...graduates with degrees in engineering.* 工学の学位を持った卒業生 ② → see also **genetic engineering**

Eng|lish /ɪŋglɪʃ/ ■ N-UNCOUNT 不可算名詞 **English** is the language spoken by people who live in Great Britain and Ireland, the United States, Canada, Australia, and many other countries. 英語 ② ADJ 形容詞 **English** means belonging or relating to England, or to its people or language. It is also often used to mean belonging or relating to Great Britain, although many people object to this. イングランドの, 英国の □ *...the English way of life.* イングランドの生活様式 ● N-PLURAL 複数名詞 **The English** are English people. イングランド人, 英国人 □ *It is often said that the English are reserved.* よく英国人は控えめだと言われている.
→ see Word Web: **English**

en|graved /ɪŋgreɪvd/ ADJ 形容詞 If you say that something is **engraved on** your mind or memory or **on** your heart, you are emphasizing that you will never forget it, because it has made a very strong impression on you. (心・記憶に) 深く刻み込まれた [EMPHASIS 強調] [v-link ADJ 'in/on/upon' n] □ *Her image is engraved upon my heart.* 彼女の面影は私の心に深く刻まれている.

en|grossed /ɪŋgroʊst/ ADJ 形容詞 If you are **engrossed in** something, it holds your attention completely. 夢中になって □ *Tony didn't notice because he was too engrossed in his work.* トニーは仕事にとても没頭していたので気づかなかった.

en|gulf /ɪŋgʌlf/ (**engulfs, engulfing, engulfed**) ■ V-T 他動詞 If one thing **engulfs** another, it completely covers or hides it, often in a sudden and unexpected way. 飲み込む, 巻き込む □ *A seven-year-old boy was found dead after a landslide engulfed an apartment block.* 共同住宅団地が地滑りに飲み込まれた後, 7歳の少年が死体で発見された. ② V-T 他動詞 If a feeling or emotion **engulfs** you, you are strongly affected by it. (感情などに) 圧倒される □ *...the pain that engulfed him.* 彼を襲った痛み

en|hance /ɪnhæns/ (**enhances, enhancing, enhanced**) V-T 他動詞 To **enhance** something means to improve its value, quality, or attractiveness. (価値・質などを) 高める □ *The White House is eager to protect and enhance that reputation.* ホワイトハウスはなんとかその評判を守り高めようとしている.

Thesaurus · enhance また次を参照:

V.	boost, complement, improve; (ant.) decrease, diminish

en|hance|ment /ɪnhænsmənt/ (**enhancements**) N-VAR 可変性名詞 The **enhancement of** something is the improvement of it in relation to its value, quality, or attractiveness. (価値・質の) 強化 増強 [FORMAL 形式ばった] □ *Music is merely an enhancement to the power of her words.* 音楽は彼女の言葉の力をただ補強しているに過ぎない.

enig|ma /ɪnɪgmə/ (**enigmas**) N-COUNT 可算名詞 If you describe something or someone as an **enigma**, you mean they are mysterious or difficult to understand. なぞ [usu sing] □ *Iran remains an enigma for the outside world.* イランは外部の世界にとってなぞのままだ.

enig|mat|ic /ɛnɪgmætɪk/ ADJ 形容詞 Someone or something that is **enigmatic** is mysterious and difficult to understand. なぞめいた, 不思議な □ *She starred in one of Welles's most enigmatic films.* 彼女はウェルズの最もなぞめいた映画の1つに主演した. ● **enig|mati|cal|ly** ADV 副詞 □ *"Corbiere didn't deserve this," she said enigmatically.* 「コルビエールはこれを受けるに値しなかった」と彼女はなぞめかして言った.

Word Link · joy ≈ being glad : enjoy, joyful, joyous

en|joy /ɪndʒɔɪ/ (**enjoys, enjoying, enjoyed**) ■ V-T 他動詞 If you **enjoy** something, you find pleasure and satisfaction in doing it or experiencing it. 楽しむ □ *Ross had always enjoyed the company of women.* ロスはいつも女性の相手をするのが好きだった. □ *He was*

---

a guy who enjoyed life to the full. 彼は人生を最大限に楽しんだ男だった. ② V-T 他動詞 If you **enjoy yourself**, you do something that you like doing or you take pleasure in the situation that you are in. 楽しく過ごす □ *I am really enjoying myself at the moment.* 今とっても楽しいです. ■ V-T 他動詞 If you **enjoy** something such as a right, benefit, or privilege, you have it. (権利・利益などを) 享受する [FORMAL 形式ばった] □ *The average German will enjoy 40 days' paid holiday this year.* 今年, 平均的なドイツ人は40日間の有給休暇が取れるだろう.

Word Partnership · enjoy は次の語句と使われる:

N.	enjoy *someone's* **company**, enjoy **life**, enjoy **a meal** ■ enjoy **privileges**, enjoy **success** ■

en|joy|able /ɪndʒɔɪəbəl/ ADJ 形容詞 Something that is **enjoyable** gives you pleasure. 楽しい □ *It was much more enjoyable than I had expected.* それは私の期待以上にとても楽しかった.

en|joy|ment /ɪndʒɔɪmənt/ N-UNCOUNT 不可算名詞 **Enjoyment** is the feeling of pleasure and satisfaction that you have when you do or experience something that you like. 喜び, 楽しみ □ *I apologize if your enjoyment of the movie was spoiled.* あなたが映画を楽しんでいたのが台なしになったらごめんなさい.

en|large /ɪnlɑrdʒ/ (**enlarges, enlarging, enlarged**) ■ V-T/V-I 他動詞/自動詞 When you **enlarge** something or when it **enlarges**, it becomes bigger. 大きくする, 大きくなる □ *The college has announced its intention to enlarge its stadium.* その大学は付属の競技場を拡張する意向を発表している. ② V-I 自動詞 If you **enlarge on** something that has been mentioned, you give more details about it. 詳しく述べる [FORMAL 形式ばった] □ *He didn't enlarge on the form that the interim government and assembly would take.* 彼は暫定政府と議会がどのような形になるかについて詳しく語らなかった.
→ see **photography**

en|large|ment /ɪnlɑrdʒmənt/ (**enlargements**) ■ N-UNCOUNT 不可算名詞 The **enlargement of** something is the process or result of making it bigger. 拡大 □ *There is insufficient space for enlargement of the buildings.* それらの建物を拡張するには十分なスペースがない. ② N-COUNT 可算名詞 An **enlargement** is a photograph that has been made bigger. (写真の) 引き伸ばし □ *Ordering reprints and enlargements is easier than ever.* 焼き増しと引き伸ばしを注文するのはこれまでになく簡単だ.

Word Link · light ≈ shining : daylight, enlighten, light

en|light|en /ɪnlaɪtən/ (**enlightens, enlightening, enlightened**) V-T 他動詞 To **enlighten** someone means to give them more knowledge and greater understanding about something. 啓発する, 教える [FORMAL 形式ばった] [no cont] □ *A few dedicated doctors have fought for years to enlighten the profession.* 少数の献身的な医師が同業の医師たちを啓発しようと長年格闘してきた. ● **en|light|en|ing** ADJ 形容詞 啓発的な □ *...an enlightening talk on the work done at the zoo.* その動物園で行われた研究についての啓発的な話

en|light|ened /ɪnlaɪtənd/ ADJ 形容詞 If you describe someone or their attitudes as **enlightened**, you mean that they have sensible, modern attitudes and ways of dealing with things. (考え方が) 開けた 賢明な [APPROVAL 賛成] □ *...an enlightened policy.* 開けた政策

en|list /ɪnlɪst/ (**enlists, enlisting, enlisted**) ■ V-T/V-I 他動詞/自動詞 If someone **enlists** or **is enlisted**, they join the army, navy, marines, or air force. 軍隊に入れる [他動詞], 入隊する [自動詞] □ *He enlisted in the 82nd Airborne 20 years ago.* 彼は20年前に第82空挺師団に入隊した. □ *He enlisted as a private in the Mexican War.* 彼はメキシコ戦争時に兵卒として入隊した. ② V-T 他動詞 If you **enlist** the help of someone, you persuade them to help or support you in doing something. (助け・支持を) 得る □ *I had to cut down a tree and enlist the help of seven neighbors to get it out of the yard!* 私は木を切り倒し, それを庭から運び出すのに近所の7人の手を借りなければならなかった.

en|liv|en /ɪnlaɪvən/ (**enlivens, enlivening, enlivened**) V-T 他動詞 To **enliven** events, situations, or people means to make them

more lively or cheerful. 活気づける □Even the most boring meeting was enlivened by Dan's presence. ダンが出席していると1番退屈な会議でさえ活気づけられた.

en masse /ɒn mæs/ ADV 副詞 If a group of people do something **en masse**, they do it all together and at the same time. 一緒に，一斉に □The people marched en masse. 人々は一団となって行進した.

en|mity /ɛnmɪti/ (enmities) N-VAR 可変性名詞 **Enmity** is a feeling of hatred toward someone that lasts for a long time. 敵意，憎悪 □I think there is an historic enmity between them. 私は彼らの間には歴史に由来する敵対意識があると思う.

enor|mity /ɪnɔrmɪti/ ■ N-UNCOUNT 不可算名詞 If you refer to the **enormity** of something that you consider to be a problem or difficulty, you are referring to its very great size, extent, or seriousness. (問題などの) 重大さ 巨大さ □I was numbed by the enormity of the responsibility. 私はその責任の重大さにぼう然となった. ■ N-UNCOUNT 不可算名詞 If you refer to **the enormity of** an event, you are emphasizing that it is terrible and frightening. 深刻さ，極悪さ [EMPHASIS 強調] □...the enormity of the disaster. その惨事のひどさ

enor|mous /ɪnɔrməs/ ■ ADJ 形容詞 Something that is **enormous** is extremely large in size or amount. 巨大な，莫大な □The main bedroom is enormous. その主寝室は並外れて大きい. ■ ADJ 形容詞 You can use **enormous** to emphasize the great degree or extent of something. (程度や範囲が) 桁はずれの [EMPHASIS 強調] □It was an enormous disappointment. それにはすごくがっかりした. ● **enor|mous|ly** ADV 副詞 非常に □This book was enormously influential. この本はすごく大きな影響力を持っていた.

> **Thesaurus** enormous また次を参照:
>
> ADJ. colossal, gigantic, huge, immense, massive, tremendous; (ant.) minute, tiny ■ ■

enough /ɪnʌf/ ■ DET 限定詞 **Enough** means as much as you need or as much as is necessary. 必要なだけの □They had enough cash for a one-way ticket. 彼らは片道切符が買えるだけのお金を持っていた. ● ADV 副詞 **Enough** is also an adverb. 十分に □I was old enough to work and earn money. 私は十分に働いてお金を稼げる年齢だった. □Do you believe that sentences for criminals are tough enough at present? あなたは犯罪者に対する判決が現在十分に厳しいと思いますか？ ● PRON 代名詞 **Enough** is also a pronoun. 十分 □Although the police say efforts are being made, they are not doing enough. 警察は努力をしていると言っているが，十分にはやっていない. ● QUANT 数量詞 **Enough** is also a quantifier. 十分な量 [QUANT 'of' def-n] □All parents worry about whether their child is getting enough of the right foods. 親たちはみな自分の子供が体に良い食べ物を十分取っているかどうか心配している. ● ADJ 形容詞 **Enough** is also an adjective. 十分な [n ADJ] □Her disappearance and death would give proof enough of Charles's guilt. 彼女の失踪と死は，チャールズの犯罪の十分な証拠となるだろう. ■ PRON 代名詞 If you say that something is **enough**, you mean that you do not want it to continue any longer or get any worse. もうたくさん □I met him only the once, and that was enough. 私は彼に1度だけ会ったが，もうたくさんだった. □I think I have said enough. 私は言うだけのことは言ったと思う. ● QUANT 数量詞 **Enough** is also a quantifier. うんざりする量 [QUANT 'of' def-n] □Ann had heard enough of this. アンはこれについてうんざりするほど聞かされていた. ● DET 限定詞 **Enough** is also a determiner. うんざりするほどの □Would you shut up, please! I'm having enough trouble with these children! ちょっと黙ってよ！この子供たちのことでてんてこ舞いしているんだから！ ● ADV 副詞 **Enough** is also an adverb. いやになるほど [adj ADV] □I'm serious, things are difficult enough as they are. 私は真剣なのよ．今でさえいろんな事がすごく大変なんだから. ■ ADV 副詞 You can use **enough** to say that something is the case to a moderate or fairly large degree. まあまあ [adj/adv ADV] □Winters is a common enough surname. ウィンターズというのは割とよくある名字だ. ■ ADV 副詞 You use **enough** in expressions such as **strangely enough** and **interestingly enough** to indicate that you think a fact is strange or interesting. 一な ことに □Strangely enough, the last thing he thought of was his beloved Tanya. 不思議なことに，彼の念頭で1番最後に浮かんだのが最愛のターニャのことだった. ■ PHRASE 句 If you say that you **have had enough**, you mean that you are unhappy with a situation and you want it to stop. もうたくさんだ □I had had enough of other people for one night. 1晩にこれ以上他の人が来るのは勘弁してほしかった. ■ **fair enough → see fair** ■ **sure enough → see sure**

> **Thesaurus** enough また次を参照:
>
> ADJ. adequate, complete, satisfactory, sufficient; (ant.) deficient, inadequate, insufficient ■

en|quire /ɪnkwaɪər/ → see **inquire**

en|quiry /ɪnkwaɪəri/ → see **inquiry**

en|rage /ɪnreɪdʒ/ (enrages, enraging, enraged) V-T 他動詞 If you **are enraged** by something, it makes you extremely angry. 激怒させる □Many were enraged by the discriminatory practice. 多くの人がその差別的な慣習に激怒していた.

en|rich /ɪnrɪtʃ/ (enriches, enriching, enriched) ■ V-T 他動詞 To **enrich** something means to improve its quality, usually by adding something to it. 質を高める，充実させる □It is important to enrich the soil prior to planting. 植え付けの前に土を肥やしておくことは大切だ. ■ V-T 他動詞 To **enrich** someone means to increase the amount of money that they have. 富ませる，豊かにする □He will drain, rather than enrich, the country. 彼は国を豊かにするどころか消耗させてしまうだろう.

en|rich|ment /ɪnrɪtʃmənt/ N-UNCOUNT 不可算名詞 **Enrichment** is the act of enriching someone or something or the state of being enriched. 豊かにすること □...the enrichment of society. 社会の向上

en|roll /ɪnroʊl/ (enrolls, enrolling, enrolled) V-T/V-I 他動詞/自動詞 If you **enroll** or **are enrolled** at an institution or in a class, you officially join it. 入学させる，入会させる [他動詞]，入学する，入会する [自動詞] □Cherny was enrolled at the University in 1945. チャーニーは1945年にその大学に入学した.

en|roll|ment /ɪnroʊlmənt/ ■ N-UNCOUNT 不可算名詞 **Enrollment** is the act of enrolling at an institution or in a class. 入学，登録 □A fee is charged for each year of study and is payable at enrollment. 授業料は1学年ごとに請求され，登録の際に支払わなければならない. ■ N-UNCOUNT 不可算名詞 **Enrollment** is the total number of students enrolled. 入学者数 □The district's enrollment is expected to stabilize in 2006-07 at 10,200 students. その地域の2006年から2007年の入学者数は1万200人で安定すると見込まれている.

en route /ɒn rut/ → see **route**

en|sem|ble /ɒnsɒmbəl/ (ensembles) N-COUNT 可算名詞 An **ensemble** is a group of musicians, actors, or dancers who regularly perform together. 合奏団，合唱団 (その他，俳優やダンサーなどのグループ) □...an ensemble of young musicians. 若い音楽家たちの合奏団

en|sue /ɪnsu/ (ensues, ensuing, ensued) V-I 自動詞 If something **ensues**, it happens immediately after another event, usually as a result of it. 続いて起こる [no cont] □If the Europeans did not reduce subsidies, a trade war would ensue. もし欧州諸国が助成金を減らさなければ，貿易戦争となるだろう.

en|su|ing /ɪnsuɪŋ/ ■ ADJ 形容詞 **Ensuing** events happen immediately after other events. 続いて起こる [ADJ n] □The ensuing argument had been bitter. その後に起こった口論は激しいものであった. ■ ADJ 形容詞 **Ensuing** hours, months, or years follow the time you are talking about. 次の [det ADJ] □The two companies grew tenfold in the ensuing ten years. その2社は次の10年で10倍に成長した.

en suite /ɒn swit/ ADJ 形容詞 An **en suite** bathroom is next to a bedroom and can only be reached by a door in the bedroom. An **en suite** bedroom has an en suite bathroom. (浴室が) 寝室に隣接する (寝室の) 浴室つきの [BRIT 英国英語] [ADJ n] [AM **private bathroom** 米国英語 **private bathroom**]

en|sure /ɪnʃʊər/ (ensures, ensuring, ensured) V-T 他動詞 To **ensure** something, or to **ensure that** something happens, means to make certain that it happens. 保証する [FORMAL 形式ばった] □We must ensure that all patients have access to high quality care. 我々は患者全員が手厚い看護を受けられることを保証しなければならない.

en|tail /ɪnteɪl/ (entails, entailing, entailed) V-T 他動詞 If one thing **entails** another, it involves it or causes it. 伴う，引き起こす [FORMAL 形式ばった] □Such a decision would entail a huge political risk in the midst of the presidential campaign. 大統領選挙戦の真っ最中にそんな決定をするのは，大きな政治的危険を伴うだろう.

> **Word Link** tang ≈ touching : entangle, intangible, tangible

en|tan|gle /ɪntæŋgəl/ (entangles, entangling, entangled) ■ V-T 他動詞 If one thing **entangles itself with** another, the two things become caught together very tightly. もつれさせる □The blade of the oar had entangled itself with the strap of her bag. 櫂 (かい) の先が彼女のバッグのひもにからまっていた. ■ V-T 他動詞 If something **entangles** you in problems or difficulties, it causes you to become involved in problems or difficulties from which it is hard to escape. (問題などに) 巻き込む □Bureaucracy can entangle applications for months. 煩雑なお役所手続きは申請を何か月も遅らせる可能性がある.

en|tan|gled /ɪntæŋgəld/ ■ ADJ 形容詞 If something is **entangled in** something such as a rope, wire, or net, it is caught in it very firmly. もつれた，からまった □Divers battled for hours to try to free a whale entangled in crab nets. 潜水夫たちはかに網にからまった鯨を解き放そうと何時間も格闘した. ■ ADJ 形容詞 If you become **entangled in** problems or difficulties, you become involved in problems or difficulties from which it is hard to escape. (問題に) 巻き込まれて [v-link ADJ] □This case was bound to get entangled in international politics. この1件が国際政治問題になってくるのは必至だった.

E

en|tan|gle|ment /ɪntæŋgᵊlmənt/ (entanglements) **1** N-COUNT 可算名詞 An **entanglement** is a complicated or difficult relationship or situation. 複雑な関係、困難な状況 ❑ ...a military and political entanglement the president probably doesn't want. おそらく大統領の望まない軍事的かつ政治的もつれ **2** N-VAR 可変性名詞 If things become entangled, you can refer to this as **entanglement**. もつれ ❑ Many dolphins are accidentally killed through entanglement with fishing equipment. たくさんのいるかが誤って魚網に引っかかり死んでいる.

en|ter /ɛntər/ (enters, entering, entered) **1** V-T/V-I 他動詞/自動詞 When you **enter** a place such as a room or building, you go into it or come into it. (部屋・建物に) 入る [FORMAL 形式ばった] ❑ He entered the room briskly and stood near the door. 彼は元気よく部屋に入り, 扉の近くに立った. ❑ When Spinks entered they all turned to look at him. スピンクスが入ると, 彼らは全員が振り返って彼を見た. **2** V-T 他動詞 If you **enter** an organization or institution, you start to work there or become a member of it. (組織などに) 入る ❑ He entered the firm as a junior associate. 彼はその会社に下級社員として入社した. **3** V-T 他動詞 If something new **enters** your mind, you suddenly think about it. (考えなどが) 頭に浮かぶ 思いつく ❑ Dreadful doubts began to enter my mind. 恐ろしい疑惑が私の心に浮かび始めた. **4** V-T 他動詞 If it does not **enter** your head to do, think, or say something, you do not think of doing that thing although you should have. (頭に) 入る [with brd-neg] ❑ It never enters his mind that anyone is better than him. 誰かが彼よりも優れているなんて彼は考えたこともない. **5** V-T 他動詞 If someone or something **enters** a particular situation or period of time, they start to be in it or part of it. (状況・期間に) 入り込む 加わる ❑ The war has entered its second month. その戦争は2か月目に入っている. ❑ A million young people enter the labor market each year. 毎年100万人の若者が労働市場に参入している. **6** V-T 他動詞 If you **enter** a competition, race, or examination, you officially state that you will compete or take part in it. (競技・試験などに) 出場する 参加する ❑ I run so well I'm planning to enter some races. 私は足が非常に速いから, いくつかの競走に出るつもりだ. ❑ As a boy soprano he entered many competitions, winning several gold medals. 彼はボーイソプラノとして多くのコンクールに出場し, いくつもの金メダルを獲得した. **7** V-T 他動詞 If you **enter** someone **for** a race or competition, you officially state that they will compete or take part in it. (競技などに) 出場させる ❑ His wife Marie secretly entered him for the championship. 彼の妻のマリーはこっそり彼の選手権参加を申し込んだ. **8** V-T 他動詞 If you **enter** something in a notebook, register, or financial account, you write it down. (ノート・帳簿などに) 記入する 記録する ❑ Each week she meticulously entered in her notebooks all sums received. 毎週彼女は受け取った金額をノートに細かく記録した. **9** V-T 他動詞 To **enter** information **into** a computer or database means to record it there by typing it on a keyboard. (コンピュータに) 入力する ❑ When a baby is born, they enter that baby's name into the computer. 赤ちゃんが生まれると, 彼らはその名前をコンピュータに入力する.
▸ **enter into** PHRASAL VERB 句動詞 If you **enter into** something such as an agreement, discussion, or relationship, you become involved in it. You can also say that two people **enter into** something. (協定・関係などを) 結ぶ (議論に) 参加する [FORMAL 形式ばった] ❑ I have not entered into any financial agreements with them. 私は彼らとなんの金融協定も結んでいない. ❑ The United States and Canada may enter into an agreement that would allow easier access to jobs across the border. 米国とカナダは国境を越えた就職をよりいっそう容易にする協定を結ぶかもしれない.

Thesaurus enter また次を参照:
V. come in **1**
   join **5**

en|ter|prise /ɛntərpraɪz/ (enterprises) **1** N-COUNT 可算名詞 An **enterprise** is a company or business. 企業, 会社 [BUSINESS 実業] ❑ There are plenty of small industrial enterprises. 小規模産業企業は多数存在する. **2** N-COUNT 可算名詞 An **enterprise** is something new, difficult, or important that you do or try to do. (新しい, 困難または重要な) 事業 ❑ Horse breeding is indeed a risky enterprise. 馬の飼育は実にリスクを伴う事業だ. **3** N-UNCOUNT 不可算名詞 **Enterprise** is the activity of managing companies and businesses and starting new ones. 企業経営, 起業 [BUSINESS 実業] ❑ He is still involved in voluntary work promoting local enterprise. 彼は今でも現地起業を促進する自主活動に従事している. **4** N-UNCOUNT 不可算名詞 **Enterprise** is the ability to think of new and effective things to do, together with an eagerness to do them. 進取の気性 [APPROVAL 賛成] ❑ ...the spirit of enterprise worthy of a free and industrious people. 自由で勤勉な国民にふさわしい進取の気性.

en|ter|pris|ing /ɛntərpraɪzɪŋ/ ADJ 形容詞 An **enterprising** person is willing to try out new, unusual ways of doing or achieving something. 進取的な ❑ Some enterprising members found ways of reducing their expenses or raising their incomes. 進取的なメンバー何名かが費用削減または増収の方法を見つけた.

en|ter|tain /ɛntərteɪn/ (entertains, entertaining, entertained) **1** V-T/V-I 他動詞/自動詞 If a performer, performance, or activity **entertains** you, it amuses you, interests you, or gives you pleasure. 楽しませる [他動詞・自動詞] ❑ They were entertained by top singers, dancers and celebrities. トップクラスの歌手, ダンサーおよび有名人が彼らを歓待した. ● **en|ter|tain|ing** ADJ 形容詞 おもしろい ❑ To generate new money the sport needs to be more entertaining. 新しい収益を生み出すには, そのスポーツはもっと面白くなくてはならない. **2** V-T/V-I 他動詞/自動詞 If you **entertain**, or **entertain** people, you provide food and drink for them, for example, when you have invited them to your house. もてなす [他動詞・自動詞] ❑ I don't like to entertain guests anymore. 私はもう客をもてなしたくない. ❑ He loves to entertain. 彼は人をもてなすのが好きだ. ● **en|ter|tain|ing** N-UNCOUNT 不可算名詞 もてなし ❑ ...a cozy area for entertaining and relaxing. もてなしやくつろぎのために居心地のよい場所 **3** V-T 他動詞 If you **entertain** an idea or suggestion, you allow yourself to consider it as possible or as worth thinking about seriously. (考え・意見などを) 抱く [FORMAL 形式ばった] ❑ How foolish I am to entertain doubts. 疑いを抱くとはなんて私はばかなんだろう.

en|ter|tain|er /ɛntərteɪnər/ (entertainers) N-COUNT 可算名詞 An **entertainer** is a person whose job is to entertain audiences, for example, by telling jokes, singing, or dancing. 芸人 ❑ Some have called him the greatest entertainer of the twentieth century. 彼を20世紀の最も偉大な芸人と称する人もいる.

en|ter|tain|ment /ɛntərteɪnmənt/ (entertainments) N-VAR 可変性名詞 **Entertainment** consists of performances of plays and movies, and activities such as reading and watching television, that give people pleasure. 娯楽 ❑ ...the world of entertainment and international stardom. 娯楽の世界と国際的スターの座
→ see **radio**

en|thrall /ɪnθrɔl/ (enthralls, enthralling, enthralled) V-T 他動詞 If you **are enthralled by** something, you enjoy it and give it your complete attention and interest. 魅了する ❑ The passengers were enthralled by the scenery. 乗客は景色に魅了された.

en|thuse /ɪnθuz/ (enthuses, enthusing, enthused) **1** V-I 自動詞 If you **enthuse about** something, you talk about it in a way that shows how excited you are about it. 感激する ❑ Elizabeth David enthuses about the taste, fragrance and character of Provencal cuisine. エリザベス・デイヴィドはプロバンス料理の味, 香りおよび特性に夢中になっている. **2** V-T 他動詞 If you **are enthused by** something, it makes you feel excited and enthusiastic. 熱狂させる ❑ I was immediately enthused. 私は即座に熱中した.

en|thu|si|asm /ɪnθuziæzəm/ (enthusiasms) **1** N-VAR 可変性名詞 **Enthusiasm** is great eagerness to be involved in a particular activity that you like and enjoy or that you think is important. 熱中, 熱意 ❑ Their skill and enthusiasm has gotten them on the team. 彼らはその腕と熱意でチームに加えられた. **2** N-COUNT 可算名詞 An **enthusiasm** is an activity or subject that interests you very much and that you spend a lot of time on. 熱狂の対象 ❑ Draw him out about his current enthusiasms and future plans. 彼から現在熱中しているものと将来の計画を聞き出せ.

Thesaurus enthusiasm また次を参照:
N. eagerness, energy, excitement, passion, zest; (ant.) apathy, indifference **1**

en|thu|si|ast /ɪnθuziæst/ (enthusiasts) N-COUNT 可算名詞 An **enthusiast** is a person who is very interested in a particular activity or subject and who spends a lot of time on it. 熱狂者 ❑ He is a great sports enthusiast. 彼はスポーツの大ファンだ.

en|thu|si|as|tic /ɪnθuziæstɪk/ ADJ 形容詞 If you are **enthusiastic about** something, you show how much you like or enjoy it by the way that you behave and talk. 熱狂的な ❑ Tom was very enthusiastic about the place. トムはその場所にとても夢中になっていた. ● **en|thu|si|as|ti|cal|ly** /ɪnθuziæstɪkli/ ADV 副詞 熱狂的に ❑ The announcement was greeted enthusiastically. その発表は熱烈に歓迎された.

en|tice /ɪntaɪs/ (entices, enticing, enticed) V-T 他動詞 To **entice** someone **to** go somewhere or **to** do something means to try to persuade them to go to that place or to do that thing. 誘う ❑ They'll entice thousands of doctors to move from the cities to the rural areas by paying them better salaries. 彼らはより良い給与を支払うことにより, 都市から農村部に移動するように何千人もの医師を勧誘する予定である. ❑ Retailers have tried almost everything, from cheap credit to free flights, to entice shoppers through their doors. 小売商人たちは買い物客の来店を誘うため, 低利掛売りから無料航空便までほとんどあらゆる策を講じている.

en|tic|ing /ɪntaɪsɪŋ/ ADJ 形容詞 Something that is **enticing** is extremely attractive and makes you want to get it or to become involved with it. 誘惑的な ❑ A prospective premium of about 30 percent on their initial investment is enticing. 初期投資額に対して見込まれるプレミアムが約30%というのは魅力的だ.

en|tire /ɪntaɪər/ ADJ 形容詞 You use **entire** when you want to emphasize that you are referring to the whole of something, for example, the whole of a place, time, or population. 全体の [EMPHASIS 強調] [det ADJ] ❑ *He had spent his entire life in China as a doctor.* 彼は全生涯を医師として中国で過ごした. ❑ *There are only 60 swimming pools in the entire country.* 水泳プールは全国で60しかない.

Thesaurus　　entire また次を参照：

ADJ.　absolute, complete, total, whole; (ant.) incomplete, limited, partial

en|tire|ly /ɪntaɪərli/ **1** ADV 副詞 **Entirely** means completely and not just partly. 完全に ❑ *...an entirely new approach.* 全く新しい研究法 ❑ *Their price depended almost entirely on their scarcity.* それらの値段はほとんど完全に希少性に依存していた. ❑ *This administration is not entirely free of suspicion.* 当該経営陣には全く疑惑がないというわけではない. **2** ADV 副詞 **Entirely** is also used to emphasize what you are saying. すっかり [EMPHASIS 強調] ❑ *I agree entirely.* 私は完全に同意だ.

en|tire|ty /ɪntaɪərti, -taɪrɪti/ PHRASE 句 If something is used or affected **in its entirety**, the whole of it is used or affected. 全体 ❑ *The peace plan has not been accepted in its entirety by all parties.* その和平計画はすべての関係国が完全に承認したわけではない.

en|ti|tle /ɪntaɪtᵊl/ (entitles, entitling, entitled) **1** V-T 他動詞 If you are **entitled to** something, you have the right to have it or do it. 権利を与える ❑ *If the warranty is limited, the terms may entitle you to a replacement or refund.* 保証が限られている場合, 条件により交換または返金してもらえるかもしれない. ❑ *They are entitled to first class travel.* 彼らはファーストクラスで旅行する資格がある. **2** V-T 他動詞 If the title of something such as a book, movie, or painting is, for example, "Sunrise," you can say that it is **entitled** "Sunrise." (本・映画などに) 表題をつける [usu passive] ❑ *...a performance entitled "United States."* 『アメリカ合衆国』と題された公演

en|ti|tle|ment /ɪntaɪtᵊlmənt/ (entitlements) N-VAR 可変性名詞 An **entitlement to** something is the right to have it or do it. 権利 [FORMAL 形式ばった] ❑ *They lose their entitlement to welfare when they start work.* 彼らは働き始めると生活保護を受ける権利を失う.

en|tity /ɛntɪti/ (entities) N-COUNT 可算名詞 An **entity** is something that exists separately from other things and has a clear identity of its own. 実在物 [FORMAL 形式ばった] ❑ *...the earth as a living entity.* 生きた存在としての地球

en|tou|rage /ɒntʊrɑːʒ/ (entourages) N-COUNT 可算名詞 A famous or important person's **entourage** is the group of assistants, servants, or other people who travel with them. 側近, 随員たち ❑ *Rachel was quickly whisked away by her entourage.* レイチェルは彼女の取り巻きに急いで連れ去られた.

---

entrance

❶ NOUN USES
❷ VERB USE

---

❶ en|trance /ɛntrəns/ (entrances) **1** N-COUNT 可算名詞 The **entrance to** a place is the way into it, for example, a door or gate. 入り口 ❑ *Beside the entrance to the church, turn right.* 教会への入り口のそばで右に曲がりなさい. ❑ *He was driven out of a side entrance with his hand covering his face.* 彼は手で顔を覆った格好で通用口から追い出された. **2** N-COUNT 可算名詞 You can refer to someone's arrival in a place as their **entrance**, especially when you think that they are trying to be noticed and admired. 入場 ❑ *If she had noticed her father's entrance, she gave no indication.* 父親が入ってきたことに気づいていたとしても, 彼女はそのそぶりも見せなかった. **3** N-COUNT 可算名詞 When a performer makes his or her **entrance** onto the stage, he or she comes onto the stage. 登場 ❑ *When he made his entrance on stage there was uproar.* 彼が舞台に登場すると, 大騒ぎが起こった. **4** N-UNCOUNT 不可算名詞 If you gain **entrance to** a particular place, you manage to get in there. 入り込むこと [FORMAL 形式ばった] ❑ *Hewitt had gained entrance to the Hall by pretending to be a heating engineer.* ヒューイットは暖房技師の振りをしてホールに入り込んでいた. **5** N-UNCOUNT 不可算名詞 If you gain **entrance to** a particular profession, society, or institution, you are accepted as a member of it. 入会 ❑ *Many students have insufficient science and mathematics background to gain entrance to engineering school.* 多くの学生が工学部に入学するのに十分な科学と数学の基礎知識を持っていない. **6** N-SING 単数名詞 If you make an **entrance into** a particular activity or system, you succeed in becoming involved in it. 参入 ❑ *The acquisition helped BCCI make its initial entrance into the U.S. market.* その買収はBCCI銀行が初めて米国市場に参入するのに役立った.

Thesaurus　　entrance また次を参照：

N.　doorway, entry; (ant.) exit ❶ **1**
　　appearance, approach, debut ❶ **2** **3**

---

❷ en|trance /ɪntrɑːns/ (entrances, entrancing, entranced) V-T 他動詞 If something or someone **entrances** you, they cause you to feel delight and wonder, often so that all your attention is taken up and you cannot think about anything else. (喜び・驚嘆など で) 我を忘れさせる ❑ *As soon as I met Dick, he entranced me because he has a lovely voice.* ディックの声はすてきだったので, 私は会うなりすっかり魅了された. ● **en|tranced** ADJ 形容詞 うっとりさせる ❑ *He is entranced by the kindness of her smile.* 彼は彼女の微笑みの優しさにうっとりした.

en|trance hall (entrance halls) N-COUNT 可算名詞 The **entrance hall** of a large house, hotel, or other large building, is the area just inside the main door. 玄関の広間

en|trant /ɛntrənt/ (entrants) **1** N-COUNT 可算名詞 An **entrant** is a person who is taking part in a competition. 競技参加者 ❑ *All items entered for the competition must be the entrant's own work.* コンテストに出される品目すべては参加者の自作でなければならない. **2** N-COUNT 可算名詞 An **entrant** is a person or company who has recently become a member of an institution or market. 新入者 ❑ *...the company that made a name for itself as an early entrant in the digital video-recorder market.* デジタルビデオレコーダー市場への早期参入業者として名を成した会社

en|trench /ɪntrɛntʃ/ (entrenches, entrenching, entrenched) V-T 他動詞 If something such as power, a custom, or an idea is **entrenched**, it is firmly established, so that it would be difficult to change it. 定着させる ❑ *...a series of measures designed to entrench democracy and the rule of law.* 民主主義と法の支配の定着を狙った一連の施策 ● **en|trenched** ADJ 形容詞 定着した ❑ *The recession remains deeply entrenched.* 不況は深く根付いたままである.

Word Link　　eur ≈ one who does : amateur, chauffeur, entrepreneur

en|tre|pre|neur /ɒntrəprənɜr, -nʊər/ (entrepreneurs) N-COUNT 可算名詞 An **entrepreneur** is a person who sets up businesses and business deals. 企業家 [BUSINESS 実業]

en|tre|pre|neur|ial /ɒntrəprənɜriəl, -nʊər-/ ADJ 形容詞 **Entrepreneurial** means having the qualities that are needed to succeed as an entrepreneur. 企業家的な [BUSINESS 実業] ❑ *...her prodigious entrepreneurial flair.* 彼女の並外れた企業家的能力

en|trust /ɪntrʌst/ (entrusts, entrusting, entrusted) V-T 他動詞 If you **entrust** something important to someone or **entrust** them **with** it, you make them responsible for looking after it or dealing with it. ゆだねる ❑ *He entrusted his cash to a business partner for investment in a series of projects.* 彼は一連の計画に投資するために, 現金をビジネスパートナーに預けた. ❑ *They can be entrusted to solve major national problems.* 彼らには主要な国家的問題の解決を任せられる.

en|try /ɛntri/ (entries) **1** N-UNCOUNT 不可算名詞 If you gain **entry to** a particular place, you are able to go in. 入ること ❑ *You can gain entry to the club only through a member.* クラブには会員を通してのみ入ることが許される. ❑ *Entry to the museum is free.* その博物館は入場無料だ. ● PHRASE 句 **No Entry** is used on signs to indicate that you are not allowed to go into a particular area or go through a particular door or gate. 立ち入り禁止 **2** N-COUNT 可算名詞 You can refer to someone's arrival in a place as their **entry**, especially when you think that they are trying to be noticed and admired. 入場 ❑ *He made his triumphal entry into Mexico City.* 彼は意気揚々とメキシコ市に入った. **3** N-UNCOUNT 不可算名詞 Someone's **entry** into a particular society or group is their joining of it. 加入 ❑ *...China's entry into the World Trade Organization.* 世界貿易機構への中国の加入 **4** N-COUNT 可算名詞 An **entry** in a diary, account book, computer file, or reference book is a short piece of writing in it. 記載事項 ❑ *Violet's diary entry for April 20, 1917 records Brigit admitting to the affair.* 1917年4月20日のバイオレットの日記には, ブリジットが不倫を認めたことが記録されている. **5** N-COUNT 可算名詞 An **entry for** a competition is a piece of work, a story or drawing, or the answers to a set of questions, which you complete in order to take part in the competition. 出品物 ❑ *The closing date for entries is December 31.* 出品は12月31日に締め切られる. **6** N-SING 単数名詞 Journalists sometimes use **entry** to refer to the total number of people taking part in an event or competition. For example, if a competition has an **entry** of twenty people, twenty people take part in it. 参加者数 ❑ *Our competition has attracted a huge entry.* 我々のコンテストは膨大な参加者を引き付けた. **7** N-UNCOUNT 不可算名詞 **Entry** in a competition is the act of taking part in it. 参加, 出場 ❑ *Entry to this competition is by invitation only.* このコンテストには招待者のみが参加できる. **8** N-COUNT 可算名詞 The **entry to** a place is the way into it, for example a door or gate. 入り口 ❑ *...the towering marble archway that marked the entry to the Pelican Point development.* ペリカンポイント開発地への入口を示す, 高くそびえる大理石のアーチ形の門

→ see **blog**

entry-level **1** ADJ 形容詞 **Entry-level** is used to describe basic low-cost versions of products such as cars or computers that are suitable for people who have no previous experience

or knowledge of them. 初心者向けの [BUSINESS 実業] ❑ *Several companies are offering new, entry-level models in hopes of attracting more buyers.* より多くの買い手を期待して，数社が新しい初心者用機種を提供している. ❷ ADJ 形容詞 **Entry-level** jobs are suitable for people who do not have previous experience or qualifications in a particular area of work. 初心者の [BUSINESS 実業] ❑ *Many entry-level jobs were filled by high school grads.* 多くの初心者レベルの仕事は高卒によって埋められていた.

en|vel|op /ɪnvɛləp/ (**envelops, enveloping, enveloped**) V-T 他動詞 If one thing **envelops** another, it covers or surrounds it completely. 包む ❑ *That lovely, rich fragrant smell of the forest enveloped us.* あの森林の心地よい，豊かな高い香りが私たちを包んだ.

en|ve|lope /ɛnvəloʊp, ɒn-/ (**envelopes**) ❶ N-COUNT 可算名詞 An **envelope** is the rectangular paper cover in which you send a letter to someone through the mail. 封筒 ❷ PHRASE 句 If someone **pushes the envelope**, they do something to a greater degree or in a more extreme way than it has ever been done before. 限界に挑む ❑ *There's a valuable place for fashion and design that pushes the envelope a bit.* 少し今までより高いレベルを追求する，ファッションとデザインの貴重な場がある.

→ see **office**

en|vi|able /ɛnviəbᵊl/ ADJ 形容詞 You describe something such as a quality as **enviable** when someone else has it and you wish that you had it too. うらやましい ❑ *Japan, unlike other big economies, is in the enviable position of having a budget surplus.* 他の経済大国と異なり，日本は財政が黒字といううらやましい立場にある.

en|vi|ous /ɛnviəs/ ADJ 形容詞 If you are **envious of** someone, you want something that they have. うらやましがる ❑ *I don't think I'm envious of your success.* 私は君の成功をうらやましいとは思わない. ❑ *Do I sound envious? I pity them, actually.* 僕がうらやましそうに聞こえるかい. それどころか，彼らには同情しているんだ. ●**en|vi|ous|ly** ADV 副詞 [ADV with v] うらやましそうに ❑ *"You haven't changed," I am often enviously told.* 私はよく「変わってないね」とうらやましげに言われる.

en|vi|ron|ment /ɪnvaɪrənmənt, -vaɪərn-/ (**environments**) ❶ N-VAR 可変性名詞 Someone's **environment** is all the circumstances, people, things, and events around them that influence their life. 周囲を取り巻くもの，環境 ❑ *Students in our schools are taught in a safe, secure environment.* 我が校の生徒は安全で危険の心配のない環境で学んでいる. ❑ *The moral characters of men are formed not by heredity but by environment.* 人の徳性は遺伝ではなく，環境によって形成される. ❷ N-COUNT 可算名詞 Your **environment** consists of the particular natural surroundings in which you live or exist, considered in relation to their physical characteristics or weather conditions. 環境 ❑ *...a safe environment for marine mammals.* 海洋哺乳類にとって安全な環境 ❸ N-SING 単数名詞 The **environment** is the natural world of land, sea, air, plants, and animals. 自然環境 ❑ *...persuading people to respect the environment.* 環境を尊重するよう人々を説得して

→ see **pollution**

Word Partnership	*environment* は次の語句と使われる:
ADJ.	**hostile** environment, **safe** environment, **supportive** environment, **unhealthy** environment ❶ **natural** environment ❷
V.	**damage** the environment, **protect** the environment ❸

en|vi|ron|men|tal /ɪnvaɪrənmɛntᵊl, -vaɪərn-/ ❶ ADJ 形容詞 **Environmental** means concerned with the protection of the natural world of land, sea, air, plants, and animals. 環境保護の [ADJ n] ❑ *Environmental groups plan to stage public protests during the conference.* 環境保護団体は，会議期間中に，公開抗議行動を計画している. ●**en|vi|ron|men|tal|ly** ADV 副詞 [ADV adj] 環境的に ❑ *...the high price of environmentally friendly goods.* 環境に優しい商品の高値 ❷ ADJ 形容詞 **Environmental** means relating to or caused by the surroundings in which someone lives or something exists. 周囲の，環境の [ADJ n] ❑ *It protects against environmental hazards such as wind and sun.* 風や日光といった環境危険から保護する.

en|vi|ron|men|tal|ist /ɪnvaɪrənmɛntəlɪst, -vaɪərn-/ (**environmentalists**) N-COUNT 可算名詞 An **environmentalist** is a person who is concerned with protecting and preserving the natural environment, for example, by preventing pollution. 環境保護論者

en|vis|age /ɪnvɪzɪdʒ/ (**envisages, envisaging, envisaged**) V-T 他動詞 If you **envisage** something, you imagine that it is true, real, or likely to happen. 心に描く，想像する ❑ *He envisages the possibility of establishing direct diplomatic relations in the future.* 彼は将来直接の外交関係を確立する可能性を予見している.

en|vi|sion /ɪnvɪʒᵊn/ (**envisions, envisioning, envisioned**) V-T 他動詞 If you **envision** something, you envisage it. 心に描く，想像する [AM 米国英語] ❑ *In the future we envision a federation of companies.* 将来我々は企業連合を構想している. ❑ *Alana never envisioned her*

college career ending like this. アラナは大学生活がこんな形で終わるとは全く予測しなかった.

en|voy /ɛnvɔɪ, ɒn-/ (**envoys**) ❶ N-COUNT 可算名詞 An **envoy** is someone who is sent as a representative from one government or political group to another. 使節 ❑ *A U.S. envoy is expected in the region this month to collect responses to the proposal.* 米国使節がその提案に対する反応を収集する目的で，今月その地に入ると予想されている. ❷ N-COUNT 可算名詞 An **envoy** is a diplomat in an embassy who is immediately below the ambassador in rank. 公使

en|vy /ɛnvi/ (**envies, envying, envied**) ❶ N-UNCOUNT 不可算名詞 **Envy** is the feeling you have when you wish you could have the same thing or quality that someone else has. うらやみ ❑ *Gradually he began to acknowledge his feelings of envy towards his mother.* 彼は母親に対してうらやましい気持ちを持っていることを次第に認識し始めた. ❷ V-T 他動詞 If you **envy** someone, you wish that you had the same things or qualities that they have. うらやむ ❑ *I don't envy the young ones who've become TV superstars and know no other world.* 私はテレビの大スターになって別の世界を知らない若者たちをうらやましいとは思わない. ❸ N-SING 単数名詞 If a thing or quality is **the envy of** someone, they wish very much that they could have or achieve it. 羨望（せんぼう）の的 ❑ *Their economy is the envy of the developing world.* 彼らの経済は発展途上地域の羨望の的だ.

en|zyme /ɛnzaɪm/ (**enzymes**) N-COUNT 可算名詞 An **enzyme** is a chemical substance found in living creatures that produces changes in other substances without being changed itself. 酵素 [TECHNICAL 技術的]

epic /ɛpɪk/ (**epics**) ❶ N-COUNT 可算名詞 An **epic** is a long book, poem, or movie whose story extends over a long period of time or tells of great events. 叙事詩，叙事詩的な長編作品 ❑ *...the Middle High German epic, "Nibelungenlied," written about 1200.* 1200年ごろに書かれた中高ドイツ語の叙事詩『ニーベルンゲンの歌』 ● ADJ 形容詞 **Epic** is also an adjective. 叙事詩の ❑ *...epic narrative poems.* 叙事詩的な物語詩 ❷ ADJ 形容詞 Something that is **epic** is very large and impressive. 雄壮な ❑ *...Columbus's epic voyage of discovery.* コロンブスによる新世界発見の大航海

→ see **hero**

epi|dem|ic /ɛpɪdɛmɪk/ (**epidemics**) ❶ N-COUNT 可算名詞 If there is an **epidemic of** a particular disease somewhere, it affects a very large number of people there and spreads quickly to other areas. 伝染病の流行 ❑ *A flu epidemic is sweeping through Moscow.* インフルエンザはモスクワで大流行している. ❷ N-COUNT 可算名詞 If an activity that you disapprove of is increasing or spreading rapidly, you can refer to this as an **epidemic of** that activity. はやり，流行 [DISAPPROVAL 不賛成] ❑ *...an epidemic of serial killings.* 連続殺人のはやり

→ see **illness**

epi|lep|sy /ɛpɪlɛpsi/ N-UNCOUNT 不可算名詞 **Epilepsy** is a brain condition that causes a person to suddenly lose consciousness and sometimes to have seizures. てんかん ❑ *Shawna suffers from epilepsy.* ショーナはてんかん持ちだ.

epi|lep|tic /ɛpɪlɛptɪk/ (**epileptics**) ❶ ADJ 形容詞 Someone who is **epileptic** suffers from epilepsy. てんかんの ❑ *He was epileptic and refused to take medication for his condition.* 彼はてんかんにかかっていたが，薬剤投与を受けることを拒否した. ● N-COUNT 可算名詞 An **epileptic** is someone who is epileptic. てんかん患者 ❑ *His wife is an epileptic.* 彼の妻はてんかん持ちだ. ❷ ADJ 形容詞 An **epileptic** seizure is caused by epilepsy. てんかん性の [ADJ n] ❑ *He suffered an epileptic seizure.* 彼はてんかん性の発作にかかった.

epi|sode /ɛpɪsoʊd/ (**episodes**) ❶ N-COUNT 可算名詞 You can refer to an event or a short period of time as an **episode** if you want to suggest that it is important or unusual, or has some particular quality. 挿話 ❑ *This episode is bound to be a deep embarrassment for Washington.* このエピソードは米国政府にとって非常にきまり悪いものとなるであろう. ❷ N-COUNT 可算名詞 An **episode** of something such as a series on television or a story in a magazine is one of the separate parts in which it is broadcast or published. (続き物の) 放送番組などの) 1回分 ❑ *The final episode will be shown next Sunday.* 最終回は次の日曜日に放送される.

→ see **animation**

epito|me /ɪpɪtəmi/ N-SING 単数名詞 If you say that a person or thing is **the epitome of** something, you are emphasizing that they are the best possible example of it. 典型 [FORMAL 形式ばった, EMPHASIS 強調] ❑ *Maureen was the epitome of sophistication.* モーリーンは洗練そのものだった.

epito|mize /ɪpɪtəmaɪz/ (**epitomizes, epitomizing, epitomized**) V-T 他動詞 If you say that something or someone **epitomizes** a particular thing, you mean that they are a perfect example of it. 典型である ❑ *Seafood is a regional specialty epitomized by Captain Anderson's Restaurant.* シーフードはアンダーソン船長のレストランに代表される地域の自慢料理である.

epoch /ɛpək/ (**epochs**) N-COUNT 可算名詞 If you refer to a long period of time as an **epoch**, you mean that important events or

great changes took place during it. (画期的な) 時代 ❑ *The birth of Christ was the beginning of a major epoch of world history.* キリストの誕生は世界史における主要な時代の始まりであった.

equal /íːkwəl/ (**equals, equaling, equaled**) ■ ADJ 形容詞 If two things are **equal** or if one thing is **equal to** another, they are the same in size, number, standard, or value. 等しい ❑ *Investors can borrow an amount equal to the property's purchase price.* 投資者はその不動産の購入価格と同額を借りることができる. ❑ *…in a population having equal numbers of men and women.* 男性と女性の数が等しい母集団 ■ ADJ 形容詞 If different groups of people have **equal** rights or are given **equal** treatment, they have the same rights or are treated the same as each other, however different they are. 均等の, 平等の ❑ *We will be demanding equal rights at work.* 私たちは職場での平等の権利を要求するであろう. ❑ *…the commitment to equal opportunities.* 機会均等への献身 ■ ADJ 形容詞 If you say that people are **equal**, you mean that they have or should have the same rights and opportunities as each other. 平等の [v-link ADJ] ❑ *We are equal in every way.* 私たちはあらゆる点で平等だ. ■ N-COUNT 可算名詞 Someone who is your **equal** has the same ability, status, or rights as you have. 匹敵者 ❑ *She was one of the boys, their equal.* 彼女はその少年たちの仲間であり, 彼らと互角だった. ■ ADJ 形容詞 If someone is **equal to** a particular job or situation, they have the necessary ability, strength, or courage to deal successfully with it. 匹敵する, 対処できる [v-link ADJ 'to' n] ❑ *She was determined that she would be equal to any test the corporation put to them.* 彼女は会社が彼らに与えるどんな試練でもやってのけようと決心していた. ■ V-LINK 連結動詞 If something **equals** a particular number or amount, it is the same as that amount or the equivalent of that amount. 等しい ❑ *9 percent interest less 7 percent inflation equals 2 percent.* 9パーセントの利子から7パーセントのインフレを差し引くと2パーセントである. ■ V-T 他動詞 To **equal** something or someone means to be as good or as great as them. 匹敵する ❑ *The victory equaled the team's best in history.* その勝利はチーム史上最高に匹敵した. ■ PHRASE 句 If you say **"other things being equal"** or **"all things being equal"** when talking about a possible situation, you mean if nothing unexpected happens or if there are no other factors that affect the situation. 他の条件が同じなら, すべての条件が同じなら ❑ *It appears reasonable to assume that, other things being equal, most hostel tenants would prefer single to shared rooms.* 他の条件が同じなら, ユースホステルの合宿者のほとんどは相部屋よりシングルを好むと仮定してもよいだろう.

Word Partnership   equal は次の語句と使われる:

N.   equal **importance**, equal **number**, equal **parts**, equal **pay**, equal **share** ■
   equal **rights**, equal **treatment** ■

---

equal|ity /ɪkwɒ́lɪti/ N-UNCOUNT 不可算名詞 **Equality** is the same status, rights, and responsibilities for all the members of a society, group, or family. 平等 ❑ *…equality of the sexes.* 男女平等

equal|ize /íːkwəlaɪz/ (**equalizes, equalizing, equalized**) V-T 他動詞 To **equalize** a situation means to give everyone the same rights or opportunities, for example, in education, wealth, or social status. 平等にする ❑ *Such measures are needed to equalize wage rates between countries.* 国家間の賃金率を同等にするためにはこういった施策が必要である. ● **equali|za|tion** /ìːkwəlaɪzéɪʃⁿn/ N-UNCOUNT 不可算名詞 平等化 ❑ *…the equalization of parenting responsibilities between men and women.* 男女間の子育ての責任の平等化

equal|ly /íːkwəli/ ■ ADV 副詞 **Equally** means in sections, amounts, or spaces that are the same size as each other. 等しく ❑ *Try to get into the habit of eating at least three small meals a day, at equally spaced intervals.* 1日に軽い食事を少なくとも3回, 等しく時間間隔をおいて食べる習慣をつけるよう努めなさい. ■ ADV 副詞 **Equally** means to the same degree or extent. 同じ程度に ❑ *All these techniques are equally effective.* これらの技術はすべて同じ位効果的だ. ■ ADV 副詞 **Equally** is used to introduce another comment on the same topic, that balances or contrasts with the previous comment. 同時に ❑ *Subscribers should be allowed call-blocking services, but equally, they should be able to choose whether to accept calls from blocked numbers.* 加入者はコールブロックサービスを受けられるべきだが, 同時にブロックされたメンバーからの電話を受けるか否かも選択できるべきである.

equal op|por|tu|ni|ty em|ploy|er (**equal opportunity employers**) N-COUNT 可算名詞 An **equal opportunity employer** is an employer who gives people the same opportunities for employment, pay, and promotion, without discrimination against anyone. 機会均等雇用者 [BUSINESS 実業] ❑ *The police force is committed to being an equal opportunity employer.* 警察は機会均等雇用者であることを明言している.

equal sign (**equal signs**) N-COUNT 可算名詞 An **equal sign** is the sign _oo3D_, which is used in arithmetic to indicate that two numbers or sets of numbers are equal. 等号

equate /ɪkwéɪt/ (**equates, equating, equated**) V-T/V-I 他動詞/

自動詞 If you **equate** one thing **with** another, or if you say that one thing **equates with** another, you believe that they are strongly connected. 同一視する [他動詞・自動詞] ❑ *I'm always wary of men wearing suits, as I equate this with power and authority.* 私は男性のスーツ着用は, 権力と権威を表すものと考え, 常に警戒している. ❑ *The author doesn't equate liberalism and conservatism.* 著者は自由主義と保守主義を同等とは考えていない. ● **equa|tion** N-UNCOUNT 不可算名詞 同一視 ❑ *The equation of gangsterism with business in general in Coppola's film was intended to be subversive.* コッポラの映画でギャング行為をビジネス一般と同等に扱っているのは, 反体制的なものを意図していたのだ.

equa|tion /ɪkwéɪʒⁿn/ (**equations**) ■ N-COUNT 可算名詞 An **equation** is a mathematical statement saying that two amounts or values are the same, for example 6x4_oo3D_12x2. 等式 ■ N-COUNT 可算名詞 An **equation** is a situation in which two or more parts have to be considered together so that the whole situation can be understood or explained. 釣り合い, 均衡 ❑ *The equation is simple: research breeds new products.* その釣り合いは簡単だ. つまり研究は新製品を生み出す. ❑ *The party fears the equation between higher spending and higher taxes.* その政党は支出の増加につれて税金が増加するという均衡を恐れた.

equa|tor /ɪkwéɪtər/ N-SING 単数名詞 The **equator** is an imaginary line around the middle of the earth at an equal distance from the North Pole and the South Pole. 赤道 → see **globe**

eques|trian /ɪkwéstriən/ ADJ 形容詞 **Equestrian** means connected with the activity of riding horses. 馬の ❑ *…his equestrian skills.* 彼の馬術の腕

Word Link   equi ≈ equal : *equilibrium, equitable, equivalent*

---

equi|lib|rium /ìːkwɪlíbriəm/ (**equilibria**) ■ N-VAR 可変性名詞 **Equilibrium** is a balance between several different influences or aspects of a situation. 釣り合い, 均衡 [FORMAL 形式ばった] ❑ *Stocks seesawed ever lower until prices found some new level of equilibrium.* 株価は, 新たな均衡レベルに達するまで, いっそう低く変動した. ■ N-UNCOUNT 不可算名詞 Someone's **equilibrium** is their normal calm state of mind. 平静 ❑ *I paused in the hall to take three deep breaths to restore my equilibrium.* 私は玄関の広間で立ち止まり, 3度深く息を吸って平静を取り戻した.

equip /ɪkwíp/ (**equips, equipping, equipped**) ■ V-T 他動詞 If you **equip** a person or thing with something, you give them the tools or equipment that are needed. 装備する ❑ *They try to equip their vehicles with gadgets to deal with every possible contingency.* 彼らは起こりうるあらゆる不慮の事故に対処する装置を車に備え付けようとする. ❑ *Owners of restaurants have to equip them to admit disabled people.* レストランの所有者は身体障害者を受け入れるために必要な設備を備え付けなければならない. ■ V-T 他動詞 If something **equips** you for a particular task or occasion, it gives you the skills and attitudes you need for it, especially by educating you in a particular way. 身につけさせる ❑ *Relative poverty, however, did not prevent Martin from equipping himself with an excellent education.* 比較的貧しかったことは, しかしながら, マーチンが優れた教育を受けることの妨げにならなかった.

Thesaurus   equip また次を参照:

V.   prepare, provide with, stock, supply ■

---

equip|ment /ɪkwípmənt/ N-UNCOUNT 不可算名詞 **Equipment** consists of the things that are used for a particular purpose, such as a hobby or job. 装置 ❑ *…computers, electronic equipment and machine tools.* コンピューター, 電子装置および工作機械

Thesaurus   equipment また次を参照:

N.   accessories, facilities, gear, machinery, supplies; (*ant.*) tools, utensils

---

equi|table /ékwɪtəbⁿl/ ADJ 形容詞 Something that is **equitable** is fair and reasonable in a way that gives equal treatment to everyone. 公正な ❑ *He has urged them to come to an equitable compromise that gives Hughes his proper due.* 彼は, ヒューズを適切に扱う公正な妥協点を見出すように, 彼らを熱心に説得した.

equi|ties /ékwɪtiz/ ■ N-PLURAL 複数名詞 **Equities** are shares in a company that are owned by people who have a right to vote at the company's meetings and to receive part of the company's profits after the holders of preference shares have been paid. 普通株 [BUSINESS 実業] ❑ *Investors have poured money into U.S. equities.* 投資家は米国の普通株に金をつぎ込んできた. ■ → see also **preference shares**

equi|ty /ékwɪti/ N-UNCOUNT 不可算名詞 In finance, your **equity** is the sum of your assets, for example the value of your house, once your debts have been subtracted from it. 純資産額 [BUSINESS 実業] ❑ *To capture his equity, Murphy must either sell or refinance.* 純資金額を確保するには, マーフィーは売るか借り換えをするしかない.

Word Link   equi ≈ equal : equilibrium, equitable, equivalent

equiva|lent /ɪkwɪvələnt/ (**equivalents**) **1** N-SING 単数名詞 If one amount or value is **the equivalent of** another, they are the same. 同等なもの ❑ *Mr. Li's pay is the equivalent of about $80 a month.* リ氏の給料は月額80ドルに相当する。● ADJ 形容詞 **Equivalent** is also an adjective. 同等の ❑ *If they want to change an item in the budget, they will have to propose equivalent cuts elsewhere.* もし彼らが予算のある品目を変更したい場合は、どこか他で同額の削減を捻出しなければならない。 **2** N-COUNT 可算名詞 The **equivalent** of someone or something is a person or thing that has the same function in a different place, time, or system. 相当する人、相当する物 ❑ *...the Red Cross emblem, and its equivalent in Muslim countries, the Red Crescent.* 赤十字の記章と、回教国でそれに相当する赤い三日月 ● ADJ 形容詞 **Equivalent** is also an adjective. 相当する ❑ *...a decrease of 10% in property investment compared with the equivalent period in 1991.* 1991年の同期と比較して、10%の不動産投資の減少 **3** N-SING 単数名詞 You can use **equivalent** to emphasize the great or severe effect of something. 匹敵する [EMPHASIS 強調] ❑ *His party has just suffered the equivalent of a near-fatal heart attack.* 彼の党は危うく命を落とすような心臓発作に匹敵する損害をこうむったところだ。

Thesaurus   equivalent また次を参照:

N.	counterpart, match, parallel, peer, substitute **2**
ADJ.	equal, similar; (ant.) different, dissimilar, unequal **2**

er /ɜr/ **Er** is used in writing to represent the sound that people make when they hesitate, especially while they decide what to say next. えー ❑ *People that are addicted to drugs get, er, help from the government one way or another.* 薬物中毒者は、えー、あれやこれやと政府の援助を受けます。

ER /i ɑr/ (**ERs**) N-COUNT 可算名詞 The **ER** is the part of a hospital where people who have severe injuries or sudden illnesses are taken for emergency treatment. 救急治療室, emergency roomの略 [AM 米国英語] ❑ *...people who come to the ER thinking they're having heart attacks.* 心臓発作が起こっていると思って救急治療室に来る人たち

era /ɪərə/ (**eras**) N-COUNT 可算名詞 You can refer to a period of history or a long period of time as an **era** when you want to draw attention to a particular feature or quality that it has. 時代 ❑ *...the nuclear era.* 原子力時代 ❑ *...the Reagan-Bush era.* レーガンからブッシュの時代

eradi|cate /ɪrædɪkeɪt/ (**eradicates, eradicating, eradicated**) V-T 他動詞 To **eradicate** something means to get rid of it completely. 根絶する [FORMAL 形式ばった] ❑ *They are already battling to eradicate illnesses such as malaria and tetanus.* 彼らはすでにマラリヤや破傷風といった疾病を根絶するために闘っている。 ● **eradi|ca|tion** /ɪrædɪkeɪʃən/ N-UNCOUNT 不可算名詞 根絶 ❑ *...a significant contribution toward the eradication of corruption.* 汚職の根絶への顕著な貢献

erase /ɪreɪs/ (**erases, erasing, erased**) **1** V-T 他動詞 If you **erase** a thought or feeling, you destroy it completely so that you can no longer remember something or no longer feel a particular emotion. ぬぐい去る、忘れる ❑ *They are desperate to erase the memory of that last defeat.* 彼らはあの最後の敗北の記憶をぬぐい去ろうと必死である。 **2** V-T 他動詞 If you **erase** sound that has been recorded on a tape or information which has been stored in a computer, you completely remove or destroy it. 消去する ❑ *An intruder broke into the campaign headquarters and managed to erase 17,000 names from computer files.* 侵入者が選挙事務所に押し入り、まんまとコンピューターファイルから1万7千の名前を消去した。 **3** V-T 他動詞 If you **erase** something such as writing or a mark, you remove it, usually by rubbing it with a cloth. こすって消す ❑ *It was unfortunate that she had erased the message.* 彼女がその伝言を消してしまったのは残念だった。

eras|er /ɪreɪsər/ (**erasers**) N-COUNT 可算名詞 An **eraser** is an object, for example, a piece of rubber or a felt pad, that is used for removing something that has been written using a pencil or chalk. 消しゴム [AM 米国英語]

erect /ɪrɛkt/ (**erects, erecting, erected**) **1** V-T 他動詞 If people **erect** something such as a building, bridge, or barrier, they build it or create it. 建設する [FORMAL 形式ばった] ❑ *Opposition demonstrators have erected barricades in roads leading to the parliament building.* 反政府示威運動者たちは、国会議事堂につながる道にバリケードを構築した。 ❑ *The building was erected in 1900-1901.* その建物は1900年から1901年にかけて建設された。 **2** V-T 他動詞 If you **erect** a system, a theory, or an institution, you create it. 組み立てる ❑ *Japanese proprietors are erecting a complex infrastructure of political influence throughout America.* 日本の経営者たちはアメリカ全土にわたって複雑な政治的影響力基盤を構築している。 **3** ADJ 形容詞 People or things that are **erect** are straight and upright. 直立した ❑ *Stand reasonably erect, your arms hanging naturally.* 腕を自然に下げて、無理なく真っ直ぐ立ってください。

erec|tion /ɪrɛkʃən/ (**erections**) **1** N-COUNT 可算名詞 If a man has an **erection**, his penis is stiff, swollen, and sticking up because he is sexually aroused. 勃起 **2** N-UNCOUNT 不可算名詞 The **erection of** something is the act of building it or placing it in an upright position. 建設 ❑ *...the erection of temporary fencing to protect hedges.* 生垣を保護するために仮の柵を作ること

erode /ɪroʊd/ (**erodes, eroding, eroded**) **1** V-T/V-I 他動詞/自動詞 If rock or soil **erodes** or **is eroded** by the weather, sea, or wind, it cracks and breaks so that it is gradually destroyed. 浸食する [他動詞] 浸食される [自動詞] ❑ *The storm washed away buildings and roads and eroded beaches.* 暴風雨は建物や道路を洗い流し、海岸を浸食した。 **2** V-T/V-I 他動詞/自動詞 If someone's authority, right, or confidence **erodes** or **is eroded**, it is gradually destroyed or removed. 衰退させる [FORMAL 形式ばった] [他動詞] 衰退する [自動詞] ❑ *His critics say his fumbling on the issue of reform has eroded his authority.* 彼を批判する人たちは改革問題での不手際が彼の権威を損なったと言う。 **3** V-T/V-I 他動詞/自動詞 If the value of something **erodes** or **is eroded** by something such as inflation or age, its value decreases. 減退させる [他動詞] 減退する [自動詞] ❑ *Competition in the financial marketplace has eroded profits.* 金融市場における競争で利益が減少した。
→ see **beach, rock**

ero|sion /ɪroʊʒən/ **1** N-UNCOUNT 不可算名詞 **Erosion** is the gradual destruction and removal of rock or soil in a particular area by rivers, the sea, or the weather. 浸食 ❑ *...erosion of the river valleys.* 川の流域の浸食 **2** N-UNCOUNT 不可算名詞 The **erosion of** a person's authority, rights, or confidence is the gradual destruction or removal of them. 衰退 ❑ *...the erosion of confidence in world financial markets.* 世界金融市場に対する信頼感の低下 **3** N-UNCOUNT 不可算名詞 The **erosion of** support, values, or money is a gradual decrease in its level or standard. 減退 ❑ *...the erosion of moral standards.* 道徳的基準の下落
→ see **Word Web: erosion**
→ see **beach**

Word Link   otic ≈ affecting, causing : erotic, neurotic, patriotic

erot|ic /ɪrɒtɪk/ ADJ 形容詞 If you describe something as **erotic**, you mean that it involves sexual feelings or arouses sexual desire. 性愛の、性欲をかきたてる ❑ *It might sound like a fantasy, but it wasn't an erotic experience at all.* 空想のように聞こえるかもしれないが、それは全くエロティックな経験ではなかった。

err /ɜr, ɛr/ (**errs, erring, erred**) **1** V-I 自動詞 If you **err**, you make a mistake. 誤る [FORMAL 形式ばった] ❑ *It criticises the main contractor for seriously erring in its estimates.* それは元請業者が見積もりで大きな誤りを犯したことを批判している。 **2** PHRASE 句 If you **err on the side of** caution, for example, you decide to act in a cautious way, rather than take risks. 一に失する ❑ *They may be wise to err on the side of caution.* 彼らは慎重過ぎるぐらいが賢明かもしれない。

er|rand /ɛrənd/ (**errands**) **1** N-COUNT 可算名詞 An **errand** is a short trip that you make in order to do a job, for example, when you go to a store to buy something. 使い走り ❑ *She went off on some errand.* 彼女は何かの使いに行った。 **2** PHRASE 句 If you **run an errand for** someone, you do or get something for them, usually by making a short trip somewhere. 使いに行く ❑ *Run an errand for me,*

There are two main causes of **soil erosion**—**water** and **wind**. **Rainfall**, especially heavy **thunderstorms**, breaks down **dirt**. Small particles of **earth**, **sand**, and **silt** are then carried away by the water. The run off may form **gullies** on hillsides. Heavy rain sometimes even causes a large, flat soil surface to wash away all at once. This is called sheet erosion. When the soil contains too much water, **mudslides** occur. Strong **currents** of **air** cause wind erosion. There are two major ways to prevent this damage. Permanent **vegetation** anchors the soil and **windbreaks** reduce the force of the wind.

will you? Go find Roger for me. 私の使いに行ってくれないか. ロジャーを探してきてくれ.

er|rat|ic /ɪrætɪk/ ADJ 形容詞 Something that is **erratic** does not follow a regular pattern, but happens at unexpected times or moves along in an irregular way. 不規則な □ Argentina's erratic inflation rate threatens to upset the plans. アルゼンチンの不安定なインフレ率により, 計画が狂う恐れがある. ● **er|rati|cal|ly** /ɪrætɪkli/ ADV 副詞 不規則に □ Police stopped him for driving erratically. 彼は常軌を逸した運転をして警察に止められた.

er|ro|neous /ɪroʊniəs/ ADJ 形容詞 Beliefs, opinions, or methods that are **erroneous** are incorrect or only partly correct. 誤った □ Some people have the erroneous notion that one can contract AIDS by giving blood. 献血をすることがエイズに感染する可能性があるという間違った考えを持っている人もいる. ● **er|ro|neous|ly** ADV 副詞 [ADV with v] 誤って □ It had been widely and erroneously reported that Armstrong had refused to give evidence. アームストロングが証言するのを拒否したと広く間違って報道されていた.

er|ror /ɛrər/ (errors) **1** N-VAR 可変性名詞 An **error** is something you have done that is considered to be incorrect or wrong, or that should not have been done. 誤り □ NASA discovered a mathematical error in its calculations. NASAは計算に数学的間違いを発見した. **2** PHRASE 句 If you do something **in error** or if it happens **in error**, you do it or it happens because you have made a mistake, especially in your judgment. 間違って □ The plane was shot down in error by a NATO missile. その飛行機はNATOのミサイルにより誤って撃ち落された. **3** PHRASE 句 If someone sees **the error of** their **ways**, they realize or admit that they have made a mistake or behaved badly. 自分のやり方の間違いに気づく □ I wanted an opportunity to talk some sense into him and try to make him see the error of his ways. 私は彼に筋の通った話をして, 自分の行いの誤りに気づかせる機会が欲しかった.

erupt /ɪrʌpt/ (erupts, erupting, erupted) **1** V-I 自動詞 When a volcano **erupts**, it throws out a lot of hot, melted rock called lava, as well as ash and steam. 噴火する □ The volcano erupted in 1980, devastating a large area of Washington state. その火山は1980年に噴火し, ワシントン州の広域を荒廃させた. ● **erup|tion** /ɪrʌpʃⁿ/ (eruptions) N-VAR 可変性名詞 噴火 □ ...the volcanic eruption of Tambora in 1815. 1815年のタンボラの火山噴火 **2** V-I 自動詞 If violence or fighting **erupts**, it suddenly begins or gets worse in an unexpected, violent way. 勃発する [JOURNALISM ジャーナリズム] □ Heavy fighting erupted there today after a two-day cease-fire. 2日間の休戦後, 本日そこで激しい戦闘が勃発した. ● **erup|tion** N-COUNT 可算名詞 勃発 □ ...this sudden eruption of violence. この突然の暴動の勃発 **3** V-I 自動詞 When people in a place suddenly become angry or violent, you can say that they **erupt** or that the place **erupts**. (怒りなどを) 爆発させる [JOURNALISM ジャーナリズム] □ In Los Angeles, the neighborhood known as Watts erupted into riots. ロスアンゼルスでは, ワッツとして知られる地区で暴動が起こった. **4** V-I 自動詞 You say that someone **erupts** when they suddenly have a change in mood, usually becoming quite noisy. (感情などが) 突発する □ Then, without warning, she erupts into laughter. そして突然に彼女がドッと笑い出す. ● **erup|tion** N-COUNT 可算名詞 爆発 □ ...an eruption of despair. 絶望感の爆発
→ see **rock, volcano**

es|ca|late /ɛskəleɪt/ (escalates, escalating, escalated) V-T/V-I 他動詞/自動詞 If a bad situation **escalates** or if someone or something **escalates** it, it becomes greater in size, seriousness, or intensity. 漸増する [JOURNALISM ジャーナリズム] [他動詞・自動詞] □ Both unions and management fear the dispute could escalate. 組合と経営陣の両方が, 争議がエスカレートするのではないかと懸念している. □ The protests escalated into five days of rioting. 抗議は5日間におよぶ暴動に拡大した. ● **es|ca|la|tion** /ɛskəleɪʃⁿn/ (escalations) N-VAR 可変性名詞 漸増 □ The threat of nuclear escalation remains. 核戦争にエスカレートする恐れは依然としてある.

es|ca|la|tor /ɛskəleɪtər/ (escalators) N-COUNT 可算名詞 An **escalator** is a moving staircase on which people can go from one level of a building to another. エスカレーター □ Take the escalator to the third floor and it's the last office on the left. エスカレーターで3階に行くと, 左側の最後の事務室です.

es|cape /ɪskeɪp/ (escapes, escaping, escaped) **1** V-I 自動詞 If you **escape from** a place, you succeed in getting away from it. 逃げる [no passive] □ They are reported to have escaped to the other side of the border. 彼らは国境の反対側に逃亡したと報告されてい

る. **2** N-COUNT 可算名詞 Someone's **escape** is the act of escaping from a particular place or situation. 逃亡 □ The man made his escape. その男は首尾よく逃走した. **3** V-T/V-I 他動詞/自動詞 You can say that you **escape** when you survive something such as an accident. 逃れる [他動詞・自動詞] □ The two officers were extremely lucky to escape serious injury. その将校2人は幸運にも運よく重傷を免れた. □ The man's girlfriend managed to escape unhurt. その男性の恋人は何とか無傷で逃れた. ● N-COUNT 可算名詞 **Escape** is also a noun. 回避 □ I hear you had a very narrow escape on the bridge. 君があの橋で九死に一生を得たと聞きました. **4** N-COUNT 可算名詞 If something is an **escape**, it is a way of avoiding difficulties or responsibilities. 逃避 □ But for me television is an escape. しかし私にとってはテレビが現実逃避です. **5** ADJ 形容詞 You can use **escape** to describe things that allow you to avoid difficulties or problems. For example, an **escape route** is an activity or opportunity that lets you improve your situation. An **escape clause** is part of an agreement that allows you to avoid having to do something that you do not want to do. 逃避の [ADJ n] □ We all need the occasional escape route from the boring, routine aspects of our lives. 我々は皆, 退屈で平凡な生活からの逃げ道が時として必要だ. **6** V-T 他動詞 If something **escapes** you or **escapes** your attention, you do not know about it, do not remember it, or do not notice it. (ものが人の注意などを) 免れる □ It was an actor whose name escapes me for the moment. それは, 今, 名前をちょっと思い出せない俳優だった. **7** V-I 自動詞 When gas, liquid, or heat **escapes**, it comes out from a pipe, container, or place. 漏れ出る □ Leave a vent open to let some moist air escape. 湿った空気を逃がすために通気孔を開けておきなさい. **8** → see also **fire escape**

es|cap|ism /ɪskeɪpɪzəm/ N-UNCOUNT 不可算名詞 If you describe an activity or type of entertainment as **escapism**, you mean that it makes people think about pleasant things instead of the uninteresting or unpleasant aspects of their life. 現実逃避 □ Horoscopes are merely harmless escapism. 星占いは罪のない現実逃避に過ぎない.

es|cap|ist /ɪskeɪpɪst/ ADJ 形容詞 **Escapist** ideas, activities, or types of entertainment make people think about pleasant or unlikely things instead of the uninteresting or unpleasant aspects of their life. 現実逃避の □ ...a little escapist fantasy. ちょっとした現実逃避のための空想

es|cort (escorts, escorting, escorted)

The noun is pronounced /ɛskɔrt/. The verb is pronounced /ɪskɔrt/.

名詞は /ɛskɔrt/ と発音される. 動詞は /ɪskɔrt/ と発音される.

1 V-T 他動詞 If you **escort** someone somewhere, you accompany them there, usually in order to make sure that they leave a place or get to their destination. 護衛する □ I escorted him to the door. 私は戸口まで彼に付き添った. **2** N-COUNT 可算名詞 An **escort** is a person who travels with someone in order to protect or guard them. 護衛 □ He arrived with a police escort shortly before half past nine. 彼は1人の警官に警護されて9時半少し前に到着した. ● PHRASE 句 If someone is taken somewhere **under escort**, they are accompanied by guards, either because they have been arrested or because they need to be protected. 護衛付きで **3** N-COUNT 可算名詞 An **escort** is a person who accompanies another person of the opposite sex to a social event. Sometimes people are paid to be escorts. 付き添い, エスコート □ My sister needed an escort for a company dinner. 私の妹は会社の晩餐 (ばんさん) 会に行くのにエスコートが必要だった.

ESL /i ɛs ɛl/ **ESL** is taught to people whose native language is not English but who live in a society in which English is the main language or one of the main languages. **ESL** is an abbreviation for "English as a second language." English as a second languageの略, 第2言語としての英語

eso|ter|ic /ɛsətɛrɪk/ ADJ 形容詞 If you describe something as **esoteric**, you mean it is known, understood, or appreciated by only a small number of people. 常人には理解できがたい, 秘伝の [FORMAL 形式ばった] □ ...esoteric knowledge. 奥伝の知識

es|pe|cial|ly /ɪspɛʃ°li/ **1** ADV 副詞 You use **especially** to emphasize that what you are saying applies more to one person,

thing, time, or area than to any others. 特に [EMPHASIS 強調] [ADV with cl/group] □Millions of wild flowers color the valleys, especially in April and May. 特に4月と5月には、何百万もの野草の花が谷間を彩る. ◻️ ADV 副詞 You use **especially** to emphasize a characteristic or quality. ことのほか [EMPHASIS 強調] [ADV adj/adv] □Babies lose heat much faster than adults, and are especially vulnerable to the cold in their first month. 赤子は大人よりもずっと速く熱を失い、生後最初の月はことのほか風邪を引き易い.

Thesaurus   especially また次を参照:

ADV.	exclusively, only, solely ◻️
	extraordinarily, particularly ◻️

es|pio|nage /ɛspiənɑʒ/ N-UNCOUNT 不可算名詞 **Espionage** is the activity of finding out the political, military, or industrial secrets of your enemies or rivals by using spies. スパイ活動 [FORMAL 形式ばった] □The authorities have arrested several people suspected of espionage. 当局はスパイ活動容疑で数人を逮捕した.

es|pouse /ɪspauz/ (**espouses, espousing, espoused**) V-T 他動詞 If you **espouse** a particular policy, cause, or belief, you become very interested in it and give your support to it. 信奉する [FORMAL 形式ばった] □She ran away with him to Mexico and espoused the revolutionary cause. 彼女は彼とメキシコに逃亡し、革命運動を支持した.

es|say /ɛseɪ/ (**essays**) ◻️ N-COUNT 可算名詞 An **essay** is a short piece of writing on a particular subject written by a student. 小論文、作文 □We asked Jason to write an essay about his hometown. 私たちはジェイソンに故郷の町について作文を書くように頼んだ. ◻️ N-COUNT 可算名詞 An **essay** is a short piece of writing on a particular subject that is written by a writer for publication. 評論、随筆 □...Thomas Malthus's essay on population. トマス・マルサスの人口に関する評論

es|sence /ɛsᵊns/ (**essences**) ◻️ N-UNCOUNT 不可算名詞 The **essence of** something is its basic and most important characteristic that gives it its individual identity. 本質 □The essence of consultation is to listen to, and take account of, the views of those consulted. 相談の真髄は相談された者の考えに耳を傾け、それを考慮に入れることである. PHRASE 句 ●You use **in essence** to emphasize that you are talking about the most important or central aspect of an idea, situation, or event. 本質において [FORMAL 形式ばった, EMPHASIS 強調] □Though complicated in detail, local taxes are in essence simple. 詳細は複雑ではあるが、地方税は本質的にわかりやすい. PHRASE 句 ●If you say that something **is of the essence**, you mean that it is absolutely necessary in order for a particular action to be successful. 絶対に欠かせない [FORMAL 形式ばった] □Speed was of the essence in a project of this type. この種の計画ではスピードが最も重要であった. ◻️ N-MASS 質量名詞 **Essence** is a very concentrated liquid that is used for flavoring food or for its smell. エキス □...a few drops of vanilla essence. 数滴のバニラエッセンス

es|sen|tial /ɪsɛnʃᵊl/ (**essentials**) ◻️ ADJ 形容詞 Something that is **essential** is extremely important or absolutely necessary to a particular subject, situation, or activity. 必須の □It was absolutely essential to separate crops from the areas that animals used as pasture. 動物の牧草地として使った区画から農作物を分離することは絶対的に必要であった. □As they must also sprint over short distances, speed is essential. 彼らは短距離も全速力で走らなければならないので、スピードが欠かせない. ◻️ N-COUNT 可算名詞 The **essentials** are the things that are absolutely necessary for the situation you are in or for the task you are doing. 不可欠なもの □The apartment contained the basic essentials for bachelor life. そのアパートには独身生活に基本的に必須なものが備わっていた. ◻️ ADJ 形容詞 The **essential** aspects of something are its most basic or important aspects. 最も基本的な □Most authorities agree that play is an essential part of a child's development. 遊びが子供の発育において極めて基本的な役割を果たすことはほとんどの権威者が同意している. ◻️ N-PLURAL 複数名詞 The **essentials** are the most important principles, ideas, or facts of a particular subject. 根本的な要素 □...the essentials of everyday life, such as eating and exercise. 食事や運動といった日常生活の基本的要素

Word Partnership   essential は次の語句と使われる:

N.	essential **personnel**, essential **services** ◻️
	essential **information**, essential **ingredients** ◻️ ◻️
	essential **element**, essential **function**, essential **nutrients**, essential **oils** ◻️

es|sen|tial|ly /ɪsɛnʃəli/ ◻️ ADV 副詞 You use **essentially** to emphasize a quality that someone or something has, and to say that it is their most important or basic quality. 根本的に、本質的に [FORMAL 形式ばった, EMPHASIS 強調] [ADV with cl/group] □It's been believed for centuries that great writers, composers, and scientists are essentially quite different from ordinary people. 偉大な作家、作曲

家、科学者は本質的に凡人とは全く異なるものと何世紀にもわたって信じられてきた. ◻️ ADV 副詞 You use **essentially** to indicate that what you are saying is mainly true, although some parts of it are wrong or more complicated than has been stated. 基本的に [FORMAL 形式ばった, VAGUENESS あいまいさ] □His analysis of urban use of agricultural land has been proved essentially correct. 都市における農地の利用に関する彼の分析は基本的に正しいことが証明された.

Word Link   stab ≈ steady : de**stab**ilize, e**stab**lish, in**stab**ility

es|tab|lish /ɪstæblɪʃ/ (**establishes, establishing, established**) ◻️ V-T 他動詞 If someone **establishes** something such as an organization, a type of activity, or a set of rules, they create it and introduce it in such a way that it is likely to last for a long time. 設立する、制定する □The UN has established detailed criteria for who should be allowed to vote. 国連は投票権が与えられるべき対象を詳細な規準を制定した. ◻️ V-RECIP 相互動詞 If you **establish** contact with someone, you start to have contact with them. You can also say that two people, groups, or countries **establish** contact. (連絡を) 取る [FORMAL 形式ばった] □We had already established contact with the museum. 私たちはすでに博物館に接触していた. ◻️ V-T 他動詞 If you **establish** that something is true, you discover facts that show that it is definitely true. 確認する [FORMAL 形式ばった] □Medical tests established that she was not their own child. 医学的検査により、彼女は彼らの子供ではないことが立証された. □It will be essential to establish how the money is being spent. その金の使い道を確認することは不可欠だろう. ●**es|tab|lished** ADJ 形容詞 確立した □That link is an established medical fact. その繋がりは動かし難い医学的事実だ. ◻️ V-T 他動詞 If you **establish yourself**, your reputation, or a good quality that you have, you succeed in doing something, and achieve respect or a secure position as a result of this. 確立する □This is going to be the show where up-and-coming comedians will establish themselves. これは有望なコメディアンが地位を確立するショーになるだろう. □He has established himself as a pivotal figure in state politics. 彼は国政の中枢人物としての地位を確立した.

Word Partnership   establish は次の語句と使われる:

N.	establish **control**, establish **independence**, establish **rules** ◻️
	establish **contact**, establish **relations** ◻️
	establish **someone's identity** ◻️
	establish **credibility**, establish **a reputation** ◻️

es|tab|lished /ɪstæblɪʃt/ ADJ 形容詞 If you use **established** to describe something such as an organization, you mean that it is well known because it has existed for a long time. 確立した □These range from established companies to start-ups. これらは既存企業から新規企業にまで及ぶ.

es|tab|lish|ment /ɪstæblɪʃmənt/ (**establishments**) ◻️ N-SING 単数名詞 The **establishment of** an organization or system is the act of creating it or beginning it. 創立 [FORMAL 形式ばった] □The establishment of the regional government in 1980 did not end terrorism. 1980年における地域政府の樹立によりテロリズムが終わることはなかった. ◻️ N-COUNT 可算名詞 An **establishment** is a store, business, or organization occupying a particular building or place. 施設 [FORMAL 形式ばった] □...a scientific research establishment. 科学研究施設 ◻️ N-SING 単数名詞 You refer to the people who have power and influence in the running of a country, society, or organization as the **establishment**. 支配層 □While scientists were once considered cranks and outsiders to the system, we are now part of the establishment. 科学者はかつて変人で体制の部外者と考えられていたが、今では権力機構の1部だ.

es|tate /ɪsteɪt/ (**estates**) ◻️ N-COUNT 可算名詞 An **estate** is a large area of land in the country which is owned by a person, family, or organization. 地所 □He spent holidays at the 300-acre estate of his aunt and uncle. 彼は休日を伯父と伯母の300エーカーの地所で過ごした. ◻️ N-COUNT 可算名詞 Someone's **estate** is all the money and property that they leave behind when they die. 財産 [LEGAL 法律的] □His estate was valued at $150,000. 彼の資産は15万ドルと評価された. ◻️ → see also **real estate**

es|tate agen|cy (**estate agencies**) N-COUNT 可算名詞 An **estate agency** is a company that sells houses and land for people. 不動産会社 [BRIT 英国英語; AM **real estate agency** 米国英語 **real estate agency**]

es|tate agent (**estate agents**) N-COUNT 可算名詞 An **estate agent** is someone who works for a company that sells houses and land for people. 不動産仲買業者 [BRIT 英国英語; AM **Realtor, real estate agent** 米国英語 **Realtor, real estate agent**]

es|teem /ɪstim/ N-UNCOUNT 不可算名詞 **Esteem** is the admiration and respect that you feel toward another person. 尊敬 [FORMAL 形式ばった] □He is held in high esteem by colleagues in the construction industry. 彼は建設業界の同業者から高く尊敬されている. ◻️ → see also **self-esteem**

es|thet|ic /ɛsθɛtɪk/ → see **aesthetic**

es|ti|mate (estimates, estimating, estimated)

> The verb is pronounced /ɛstɪmeɪt/. The noun is pronounced /ɛstɪmɪt/.
>
> 動詞は /ɛstɪmeɪt/ と発音される。名詞は /ɛstɪmɪt/ と発音される。

1 V-T 他動詞 If you **estimate** a quantity or value, you make an approximate judgment or calculation of it. 評価する □ *Try to estimate how many steps it will take to get to a close object.* 近くの目標物に到着するために何歩必要か見積もってみなさい。□ *I estimate that total cost for treatment will go from $9,000 to $12,500.* 私は治療の合計費用が9000ドルから1万2500ドルになるだろうと見ている。● **es|ti|mat|ed** ADJ 形容詞 推測の □ *There are an estimated 90,000 gangsters in the country.* この国には推定9万の暴力団員がいる。**2** N-COUNT 可算名詞 An **estimate** is an approximate calculation of a quantity or value. 見積もり □ *...the official estimate of the election result.* 選挙結果の公式推計 **3** N-COUNT 可算名詞 An **estimate** is a judgment about a person or situation that you make based on the available evidence. 評価 □ *I hadn't been far wrong in my estimate of his grandson's capabilities.* 孫の係の能力に関する私の評価はそれほど間違っていなかった。**4** N-COUNT 可算名詞 An **estimate** from someone who you employ to do a job for you, such as a builder or a plumber, is a written statement of how much the job is likely to cost. 見積書 □ *Quotes and estimates can be prepared by computer on the spot.* 見積書などはコンピューターで即座に作成できる。

> **Thesaurus** estimate また次を参照:
>
> | | |
> |---|---|
> | v. | appraise, gauge, guess, judge; (ant.) calculate **1** |
> | n. | appraisal, guess, valuation **2** |
> | | appraisal, evaluation **3** |
> | | appraisal, valuation **4** |

> **Word Partnership** estimate は次の語句と使われる:
>
> | | |
> |---|---|
> | ADJ. | **best** estimate, **conservative** estimate, **rough** estimate **2** |
> | | **original** estimate **2 4** |
> | v. | **make an** estimate **2 4** |

es|ti|ma|tion /ɛstɪmeɪʃᵊn/ (estimations) **1** N-SING 単数名詞 Your **estimation** of a person or situation is the opinion or impression that you have formed about them. 評価 [FORMAL 形式ばった] □ *He has gone down considerably in my estimation.* 彼に対する私の評価はかなり下落した。**2** N-COUNT 可算名詞 An **estimation** is an approximate calculation of a quantity or value. 概算 □ *...estimations of pre-tax profits of 12.25 million.* 1225万ドルの推定税引前利益

es|tranged /ɪstreɪndʒd/ **1** ADJ 形容詞 An **estranged** wife or husband is no longer living with their husband or wife. 別居している □ *...his estranged wife.* 別居した妻 **2** ADJ 形容詞 If you are **estranged from** your family or friends, you have quarreled with them and are not communicating with them. 疎遠になった [FORMAL 形式ばった] □ *Joanna spent most of her twenties virtually estranged from her father.* ジョアンナは20歳台を父親にほとんど会わずに過ごした。**3** ADJ 形容詞 If you describe someone as **estranged from** something such as society or their profession, you mean that they no longer seem involved in it. 遠ざかった [FORMAL 形式ばった] [v-link ADJ] □ *Arran became increasingly estranged from the mainstream of Hollywood.* アランはますますハリウッドの主流から遠ざかっていった。

es|tu|ary /ɛstʃueri/ (estuaries) N-COUNT; N-IN-NAMES 可算名詞, 名称中の名詞 An **estuary** is the wide part of a river where it joins the sea. 河口 □ *Sturgeon fishing has been pretty good in the estuary.* その河口ではチョウザメがかなりよく釣れている。

e-tailer /iteɪlər/ (e-tailers) also **etailer** N-COUNT 可算名詞 An **e-tailer** is a person or company that sells products on the Internet. Eテイラー [COMPUTING コンピューティング] □ *This company is the biggest wine e-tailer in California.* この会社はカリフォルニア州最大のワインのEテイラーだ。

e-tailing /iteɪlɪŋ/ also **etailing** N-UNCOUNT 不可算名詞 **E-tailing** is the business of selling products on the Internet. Eテーリング [COMPUTING コンピューティング] □ *Electronic retailing has predictably become known as e-tailing.* 電子小売りは予想通りEテーリングとして知られるようになった。

et al. /ɛt æl, -ɑl/ **et al.** is used after a name or a list of names to indicate that other people are also involved. It is used especially when referring to books or articles that were written by more than two people. およびその他 □ *...Blough et al.* ブラフ他

etc. /ɛt sɛtərə, -sɛtrə/ **etc.** is used at the end of a list to indicate that you have mentioned only some of the items involved and have not given a full list. **etc.** is a written abbreviation for "etcetera." など、etceteraの略 □ *She knew all about my schoolwork, my hospital work, etc.* 彼女は私の学業、病院勤めなどすべてを把握していた。

etch /ɛtʃ/ (etches, etching, etched) **1** V-T 他動詞 If a line or pattern **is etched into** a surface, it is cut into the surface by means of acid or a sharp tool. You can also say that a surface **is etched with** a line or pattern. エッチングで（絵や模様を）つくる □ *Crosses were etched into the walls.* 十字架が壁に刻み込まれていた。□ *Windows are etched with the vehicle identification number.* 窓には車両識別番号が食刻されている。**2** V-T PASSIVE 受動態他動詞 If something **is etched on** your memory, you remember it very clearly, usually because it has some special importance for you. 刻み込む [LITERARY 文語的] □ *The ugly scene in the study was still etched on her mind.* その書斎の忌まわしい光景はまだ彼女の心に刻み込まれていた。

etch|ing /ɛtʃɪŋ/ (etchings) N-COUNT 可算名詞 An **etching** is a picture printed from a metal plate that has had a design cut into it with acid. エッチング

eter|nal /ɪtɜrnᵊl/ **1** ADJ 形容詞 Something that is **eternal** lasts forever. 永遠の □ *...the quest for eternal youth.* 不老の探求 ● **eter|nal|ly** ADV 副詞 永久に □ *She is eternally grateful to her family for their support.* 彼女は家族の支えに対しいつまでも感謝の気持ちを抱いている。**2** ADJ 形容詞 If you describe something as **eternal**, you mean that it seems to last forever, often because you think it is boring or annoying. 果てしない □ *In the background was that eternal hum.* 背景ではあのブンブンという音が絶え間なく聞こえていた。

eter|nity /ɪtɜrnɪti/ **1** N-UNCOUNT 不可算名詞 **Eternity** is time without an end or a state of existence outside time, especially the state that some people believe they will pass into after they have died. 永遠 □ *I have always found the thought of eternity terrifying.* 私は永遠という考えに常に恐怖を覚えた。**2** N-SING 単数名詞 If you say that a situation lasted for **an eternity**, you mean that it seemed to last an extremely long time, usually because it was boring or unpleasant. 際限なく思われる時間 □ *The war continued for an eternity.* 戦争は果てしなく続いた。

ethe|real /ɪθɪəriəl/ ADJ 形容詞 Someone or something that is **ethereal** has a delicate beauty. 優美な [FORMAL 形式ばった] □ *She's the prettiest, most ethereal romantic heroine in the movies.* 彼女は映画の中で、最もかれんで、最も優美でロマンチックなヒロインだ。

> **Word Link** ics ≈ system, knowledge : economics, electronics, ethics

eth|ic /ɛθɪk/ (ethics) **1** N-PLURAL 複数名詞 **Ethics** are moral beliefs and rules about right and wrong. 道徳 □ *Refugee workers said such action was a violation of medical ethics.* そういった行為は医療倫理に反すると難民労働者は言った。**2** N-PLURAL 複数名詞 Someone's **ethics** are the moral principles about right and wrong behavior that they believe in. 倫理 □ *He told the police that he had thought honestly about the ethics of what he was doing.* 彼は自分の行為の善し悪しを誠実に考えたと警察に話した。**3** N-UNCOUNT 不可算名詞 **Ethics** is the study of questions about what is morally right and wrong. 倫理学 □ *...the teaching of ethics and moral philosophy.* 倫理学と道徳哲学の授業 **4** N-SING 単数名詞 An **ethic** of a particular kind is an idea or moral belief that influences the behavior, attitudes, and philosophy of a group of people. 道徳律 □ *...the ethic of public service.* 公務員としての職務の倫理

ethi|cal /ɛθɪkᵊl/ **1** ADJ 形容詞 **Ethical** means relating to beliefs about right and wrong. 倫理の □ *...the medical, nursing and ethical issues surrounding terminally-ill people.* 末期患者を取り巻く医療、介護および倫理問題 ● **ethi|cal|ly** /ɛθɪkli/ ADV 副詞 倫理的に □ *Attorneys are ethically and legally bound to absolute confidentiality.* 弁護士には倫理的および法的に絶対的な守秘義務がある。**2** ADJ 形容詞 If you describe something as **ethical**, you mean that it is morally right or morally acceptable. 倫理にかなった □ *The trade association promotes ethical business practices.* 商業組合は倫理にかなった商慣行を促進する。● **ethi|cal|ly** ADV 副詞 [ADV after v] 倫理的に □ *Mayors want local companies to behave ethically.* 市長たちは地元の会社が倫理にかなった行動を取ることを望んでいる。

eth|nic /ɛθnɪk/ **1** ADJ 形容詞 **Ethnic** means connected with or relating to different racial or cultural groups of people. 民族の □ *...a survey of Britain's ethnic minorities.* 英国の少数民族についての調査 ● **eth|ni|cal|ly** /ɛθnɪkli/ ADV 副詞 民族的に □ *...a predominantly young, ethnically mixed audience.* 大多数が若者で、民族的には多様な聴衆 **2** ADJ 形容詞 [ADJ n] You can use **ethnic** to describe people who belong to a particular racial or cultural group but who, usually, do not live in the country where most members of that group live. 少数民族の □ *There are still several million ethnic Germans in Russia.* 今でもロシアには数百万人のドイツ系民族がいます。● **eth|ni|cal|ly** ADV 副詞 [ADV adj] 民族的には □ *...a large ethnically Albanian population.* 多数のアルバニア系住民 **3** ADJ 形容詞 **Ethnic** clothing, music, or food is characteristic of the traditions of a particular ethnic group, and different from what is usually found in modern Western culture. 少数民族特有の □ *...a magnificent range of ethnic fabrics.* 素晴らしい種類のエスニック風の織物

eth|nic cleans|ing N-UNCOUNT 不可算名詞 **Ethnic cleansing** is the process of using violent methods to force certain groups of people out of a particular area or country. 民族浄化 [DISAPPROVAL 不賛成] ❑ In late May, government forces began the "ethnic cleansing" of the area around the town. 5月の下旬に政府軍はその町の周辺地域の「民族浄化」を始めた.

ethos /íθɒs/ N-SING 単数名詞 An **ethos** is the set of ideas and attitudes that is associated with a particular group of people or a particular type of activity. 気風, 精神 [FORMAL 形式ばった] ❑ The whole ethos of the hotel is effortless service. そのホテルの全体的な気風はさりげないサービスだ.

eti|quette /étɪkət, -ket/ N-UNCOUNT 不可算名詞 **Etiquette** is a set of customs and rules for polite behavior, especially among a particular class of people or in a particular profession. エチケット, 礼儀作法 ❑ This was such a great breach of etiquette, he hardly knew what to do. これはあまりにも無作法だったので, 彼はどうしたらいいかほとんど分からなかった.

EU /íː júː/ N-PROPER 固有名詞 The **EU** is an organization of European countries that have joint policies on matters such as trade, agriculture, and finance. **EU** is an abbreviation for **European Union**. 欧州連合, European Union の略 ❑ ...the ten new EU members. 新たにEUに加盟した10か国

euphemism /júːfəmɪzəm/ (**euphemisms**) N-COUNT 可算名詞 A **euphemism** is a polite word or expression that is used to refer to things that people may find upsetting or embarrassing to talk about, for example sex, the human body, or death. 婉曲(えんきょく)表現, 遠回しな言い方 ❑ The term "early retirement" is nearly always a euphemism for layoffs nowadays. early retirement (早期退職) というのは言葉は, 最近ではたいてい layoffs (レイオフ) の婉曲表現だ.

euphemis|tic /júːfəmɪstɪk/ ADJ 形容詞 **Euphemistic** language uses polite, pleasant, or neutral words and expressions to refer to things that people may find unpleasant, upsetting, or embarrassing to talk about, for example, sex, the human body, or death. 婉曲(えんきょく)な, 遠回しの ❑ ...a euphemistic way of saying that someone has been lying. 誰かがうそをついているという遠回しの言い方. ● **euphemis|ti|cal|ly** /júːfəmɪstɪkli/ ADV 副詞 [ADV with v] 婉曲に, 遠回しに ❑ ...political prisons, called euphemistically "reeducation camps." 婉曲的に「再教育収容所」と呼ばれる政治犯刑務所

eupho|ria /juːfɔ́riə/ N-UNCOUNT 不可算名詞 **Euphoria** is a feeling of intense happiness and excitement. 幸福感, 高揚感 ❑ There was euphoria after the election. 選挙後は高揚感がありました.

euphor|ic /juːfɔ́rɪk/ ADJ 形容詞 If you are **euphoric**, you feel intense happiness and excitement. 幸福感にあふれた, 高揚した ❑ The war had received euphoric support from the public. その戦争は一般から陶酔的な支持を得ていた.

euro /jʊ́əroʊ/ (**euros**) N-COUNT 可算名詞 The **euro** is a unit of currency that is used by several member countries of the European Union. ユーロ ❑ Millions of words have been written about the introduction of the euro. ユーロ導入に関して非常にたくさんの記事が書かれた.

Euro|pean /jʊ́ərəpíən/ (**Europeans**) ❶ ADJ 形容詞 **European** means belonging or relating to, or coming from Europe. ヨーロッパの ❑ ...in some other European countries. ヨーロッパのいくつかの他の国では ❷ N-COUNT 可算名詞 A **European** is a person who comes from Europe. ヨーロッパ人 ❑ Three-quarters of working-age Americans work, compared with roughly 60% of Europeans. アメリカ人の労働人口のうちの4分の3が職に就いているが, ヨーロッパ人の場合は約60%だ.

Euro|pean Un|ion N-PROPER 固有名詞 The **European Union** is an organization of European countries that have joint policies on matters such as commerce, agriculture, and finance. 欧州連合

eutha|na|sia /jùːθənéɪʒə/ N-UNCOUNT 不可算名詞 **Euthanasia** is the practice of killing someone who is very ill and will never get better in order to end their suffering, usually done at their request or with their consent. 安楽死 ❑ ...those in favor of voluntary euthanasia. 自発的な安楽死に賛成している人々

Word Link	vac ≈ empty : *evacuate, vacant, vacate*

evacu|ate /ɪvǽkjueɪt/ (**evacuates, evacuating, evacuated**) ❶ V-T 他動詞 To **evacuate** someone means to send them to a place of safety, away from a dangerous building, town, or area. (人を) 避難させる ❑ They were planning to evacuate the seventy American officials still in the country. 彼らはまだその国にいる70名のアメリカ人職員を避難させる計画をしていた. ● **evacu|ation** /ɪvækjueɪʃ⁰n/ (**evacuations**) N-VAR 可変性名詞 避難 ❑ ...the evacuation of the sick and wounded. 病人とけが人の避難 ❑ An evacuation of the city's four-million inhabitants is planned for later this week. 同市の400万人の住民の避難が今週の後半に予定されています. ❷ V-T 他動詞 If people **evacuate** a place, they move out of it for a period of time, especially because it is dangerous. (場所から) 避難する ❑ The fire is threatening about sixty homes, and residents have evacuated the area.

その火事は約60軒の家を脅かしており, 住民はその付近から避難した. ● **evacu|ation** N-VAR 可変性名詞 (**evacuations**) 避難 ❑ ...the mass evacuation of the Bosnian town of Srebrenica. ボスニアの町, スレブレニカからの大規模な退避

evac|uee /ɪvækjuíː/ (**evacuees**) N-COUNT 可算名詞 An **evacuee** is someone who has been sent away from a dangerous place to somewhere safe, especially during a war. 避難民, 疎開者

evade /ɪvéɪd/ (**evades, evading, evaded**) ❶ V-T 他動詞 If you **evade** something, you find a way of not doing something that you really ought to do. 逃れる ❑ By his own admission, he evaded paying taxes as a Florida real-estate speculator. 彼が自分で認めたところによると, 彼はフロリダ州の不動産投機家として脱税をした. ❷ V-T 他動詞 If you **evade** a question or a topic, you avoid talking about it or dealing with it. はぐらかす, (質問・話題を) 避ける ❑ Too many companies, she says, are avoiding the issue. あまりにも多くの会社が, 彼女の話では, その問題を避けています. ❸ V-T 他動詞 If you **evade** someone or something, you move so that you can avoid meeting them or avoid being touched or hit. (人・ものを) 避ける ❑ She turned and gazed at the river, evading his eyes. 彼女は向きを変えて川を見つめて, 彼の視線を避けた.

evalu|ate /ɪvǽljueɪt/ (**evaluates, evaluating, evaluated**) V-T 他動詞 If you **evaluate** something or someone, you consider them in order to make a judgment about them, for example about how good or bad they are. 評価する ❑ The market situation is difficult to evaluate. 市場の状況は評価が難しい. ● **evalu|ation** /ɪvæljueɪʃ⁰n/ (**evaluations**) N-VAR 可変性名詞 評価 ❑ ...the opinions and evaluations of college supervisors. 大学の指導教官の意見と評価

evapo|rate /ɪvǽpəreɪt/ (**evaporates, evaporating, evaporated**) ❶ V-T/V-I 他動詞/自動詞 When a liquid **evaporates**, or **is evaporated**, it changes from a liquid state to a gas, because its temperature has increased. 蒸発させる [他動詞], 蒸発する [自動詞] ❑ Moisture is drawn to the surface of the fabric so that it evaporates. 水分が繊維の表面に引きつけられ蒸発する. ❑ The water is evaporated by the sun. その水は日光で蒸発する. ● **evapo|ra|tion** /ɪvæpəreɪʃ⁰n/ N-UNCOUNT 不可算名詞 蒸発 ❑ The soothing, cooling effect is caused by the evaporation of the sweat on the skin. 肌の汗が蒸発することで気を静め体を冷やす効果がある. ❷ V-I 自動詞 If a feeling, plan, or activity **evaporates**, it gradually becomes weaker and eventually disappears completely. 消える ❑ My anger evaporated and I wanted to cry. 私は怒りが消えて, 泣きたくなった.

→ see **matter, sweat, water**

eva|sion /ɪvéɪʒ⁰n/ (**evasions**) ❶ N-VAR 可変性名詞 **Evasion** means deliberately avoiding something that you are supposed to do or deal with. 回避 ❑ He was arrested for tax evasion. 彼は脱税で逮捕された. ❷ N-VAR 可変性名詞 If you accuse someone of **evasion** when they have been asked a question, you mean that they are deliberately avoiding giving a clear direct answer. 言い逃れ ❑ We want straight answers. No evasions. 私たちははっきりとした答えを求めている. 言い逃れはお断りだ.

eva|sive /ɪvéɪsɪv/ ❶ ADJ 形容詞 If you describe someone as **evasive**, you mean that they deliberately avoid giving clear direct answers to questions. 回避的な, はぐらかすような ❑ He was evasive about the circumstances of his first meeting with Stanley Dean. 彼はスタンリー・ディーンと始めてあった状況についてはぐらかした. ● **eva|sive|ly** ADV 副詞 [ADV with v] はぐらかすように ❑ "Until I can speak to your husband I can't come to any conclusion about that," Manuel said evasively. 「ご主人さんとお話があるまでは, それについての結論は出せません」とマニュエルは, はぐらかすように言った. ❷ PHRASE 句 If you **take evasive action**, you deliberately move away from someone or something in order to avoid meeting them or being hit by them. 回避行動をとる ❑ At least four high-flying warplanes had to take evasive action. 少なくとも4機の高空飛行中の軍用機が回避行動をとらざるをえなかった.

eve /íːv/ (**eves**) ❶ N-COUNT 可算名詞 The **eve of** a particular event or occasion is the day before it, or the period of time just before it. 前夜 ❑ ...on the eve of his 27th birthday. 彼の27回目の誕生日の前夜 ❷ → see also **Christmas Eve, New Year's Eve**

even
❶ DISCOURSE USES
❷ ADJECTIVE USES
❸ PHRASAL VERB USES

❶ **even** /íːv⁰n/ ❶ ADV 副詞 You use **even** to suggest that what comes just after or just before it in the sentence is rather surprising. 〜でさえ ❑ He kept calling me for years, even after he got married. 彼は何年も, 結婚後でさえも, 私に電話をし続けた. ❑ Even dark-skinned women should use sunscreens. 肌黒の女性でさえ日焼け止めクリームを使用するべきだ. ❷ ADV 副詞 You use **even** with comparative adjectives and adverbs to emphasize a quality that someone or something has. (形容詞・副詞の比較級を強調して) さらに [EMPHASIS 強調] [ADV compar] ❑ On television he made an even stronger impact as an interviewer. テレビで彼は会見記者としてさらに

いっそう強い影響を与えた. **3** PHRASE 句 You use **even if** or **even though** to indicate that a particular fact does not make the rest of your statement untrue. たとえ～でも ❏ *Cynthia is not ashamed of what she does, even if she ends up doing something wrong.* シンシアはたとえ最終的に何か間違ったことをすることになっても, 自分のすることを恥じていない. **4** PHRASE 句 You use **even so** to introduce a surprising fact that relates to what you have just said. たとえそうでも, それにしても [SPOKEN 口語] ❏ *The bus was only half full. Even so, a young man asked Nina if the seat next to her was taken.* バスの席は半分ほど埋まっているだけだ. それでも, 若者がニーナに彼女の隣の席は空いているかと尋ねた. **5** PHRASE 句 You use **even then** to say that something is the case in spite of what has just been stated or whatever the circumstances may be. それでも ❏ *Peace could come only gradually, in carefully measured steps. Even then, it sounds almost impossible to achieve.* 平和は慎重な足取りで徐々にしか訪れないだろう. それでさえ達成がほぼ不可能なようだ.

❷ **even** /iːvᵊn/
↪ Please look at meaning **8** to see if the expression you are looking for is shown under another headword. **1** ADJ 形容詞 An **even** measurement or rate stays at about the same level. 一定の ❏ *How important is it to have an even temperature when you're working?* 作業中に一定の温度を保つことはどのくらい重要ですか. ● **even|ly** ADV 副詞 一定で ❏ *He looked at Ellen, breathing evenly in her sleep.* 彼は睡眠中安定した呼吸をしているエレンを眺めた. **2** ADJ 形容詞 An **even** surface is smooth and flat. 平らな ❏ *The tables are fitted with a glass top to provide an even surface.* テーブルの上面はガラス張りになっていて表面が平らだ. **3** ADJ 形容詞 If there is an **even** distribution or division of something, each person, group, or area involved has an equal amount. 均等な ❏ *Divide the dough into 12 even pieces and shape each piece into a ball.* 生地を12等分し, それぞれをボール形に丸めなさい. ● **even|ly** ADV 副詞 ❏ *The meat is divided evenly and boiled in a stew.* 肉を等分に切り分け, シチューで煮る. **4** ADJ 形容詞 An **even** contest or competition is equally balanced between the two sides who are taking part. 互角の ❏ *It was an even game.* それは互角の試合だった. ● **even|ly** ADV 副詞 [ADV -ed] 互角で ❏ *They must choose between two evenly matched candidates for governor.* 彼らは知事に実力が伯仲した2人の候補者から選ばなければならない. **5** ADJ 形容詞 An **even** number can be divided exactly by the number two. 偶数の **6** ADJ 形容詞 If there is an **even** chance that something will happen, the chances that it will or will not happen are equal. 五分五分の [ADJ n] ❏ *They have a more than even chance of winning the next election.* 次の選挙で当選する可能性は五分五分以上だ. **7** PHRASE 句 When a company or a person running a business **breaks even**, they make neither a profit nor a loss. 損得なしになる, 収支が合う [BUSINESS 実業] ❏ *The airline hopes to break even next year and return to profit the following year.* その航空会社は来年には収支が合い, 再来年には再び利益が出ることを願っている. **8** to be on an even keel → see keel

❸ **even** /iːvᵊn/ (evens, evening, evened)
▸ **even out** PHRASAL VERB 句動詞 If something **evens out**, or if you **even** it **out**, the differences between the different parts of it are reduced. 差をなくす, 差がなくなる ❏ *The power-balance has evened out in the interim government.* 暫定政権で権力のバランスが安定した.

eve|ning /iːvnɪŋ/ (evenings) N-VAR 可変性名詞 The **evening** is the part of each day between the end of the afternoon and the time when you go to bed. 夕方, 晩 ❏ *All he did that evening was sit around the house.* その晩彼は家でごろごろしただけだった. ❏ *Supper is from 5:00 to 6:00 in the evening.* 夕食は夕方の5時から6時までだ.

eve|ning class (evening classes) N-COUNT 可算名詞 An **evening class** is a class for adults that is taught in the evening rather than during the day. 夜間講座 ❏ *He's trying to learn English fast with evening classes twice a week.* 彼は週に2回夜間クラスに通って英語を早く習得しようとしている.

event /ɪvɛnt/ (events) **1** N-COUNT 可算名詞 An **event** is something that happens, especially when it is unusual or important. You can use **events** to describe all the things that are happening in a particular situation. 出来事 ❏ *A new inquiry into the events of the day was opened in 2002.* その日の出来事についての新しい調査が2002年に開始された. **2** N-COUNT 可算名詞 An **event** is a planned and organized occasion, for example a social gathering or a sports tournament. 行事 ❏ *...major sporting events.* 重要なスポーツ大会 **3** N-COUNT 可算名詞 An **event** is one of the races or competitions that are part of an organized occasion such as a sports tournament. 種目 ❏ *The main events start at 1 p.m.* 主な種目は午後1時に始まる. **4** PHRASE 句 You use **in the event of, in the event that,** and **in that event** when you are talking about a possible future situation, especially when you are planning what to do if it occurs. ～という場合には ❏ *The bank has agreed to give an immediate refund in the event of an error being made.* 銀行は万が一誤りがあった場合には即時返金することに同意した. **5** PHRASE 句 You say **in any event** after you have been discussing a situation, in order to indicate that what you are saying is true or possible, in spite of anything that has happened or may happen. とにかく

❏ *In any event, the bowling alley restaurant proved quite acceptable.* とにかくそのボーリング場のレストランは大変よかった.
→ see history

Thesaurus   event また次を参照:

N.   happening, occasion, occurrence **1**
      competition, contest, game, meet, tournament **3**

event|ful /ɪvɛntfəl/ ADJ 形容詞 If you describe an event or a period of time as **eventful**, you mean that a lot of interesting, exciting, or important things have happened in it. 多事の ❏ *This has been an eventful year for Tom, both professionally and personally.* 今年はトムにとって仕事の面でも個人的にも波乱に富んだ1年だった.

even|tual /ɪvɛntʃuəl/ ADJ 形容詞 You use **eventual** to indicate that something happens or is the case at the end of a process or period of time. 最終的な [ADJ n] ❏ *There are many who believe that civil war will be the eventual outcome of the racial tension in the country.* 内戦がその国の人種的な緊張関係の最終的な結末になるだろうと信じている人が多い.

even|tu|al|ity /ɪvɛntʃuælɪti/ (eventualities) N-COUNT 可算名詞 An **eventuality** is a possible future event or result, especially one that is unpleasant or surprising. 起こりうる事態 [FORMAL 形式ばった] ❏ *Every eventuality is covered, from running out of gas to needing water.* ガス欠から断水まであらゆる起こりうる事態が保証されている.

even|tu|al|ly /ɪvɛntʃuəli/ **1** ADV 副詞 **Eventually** means in the end, especially after a lot of delays, problems, or arguments. ついに ❏ *Eventually, the army caught up with him in Latvia.* ついに軍がラトビアで彼に追いつきました. **2** ADV 副詞 **Eventually** means at the end of a situation or process or as the final result of it. 最後には, 結局 ❏ *Eventually your child will leave home to lead her own life as a fully independent adult.* ゆくゆくは, あなたの子供は1人前の独立した成人として自分で人生を築くために家を出ることになりましょう.

Do not confuse **eventually** and **finally**. When something happens after a lot of delays or complications, you can say that it **eventually** happens. ❏ *Eventually they got to the hospital... I found Victoria Avenue eventually.* You can also use **eventually** to talk about what happens at the end of a series of events, often as a result of them. ❏ *Eventually, they were forced to return to Chicago.* You say that something **finally** happens after you have been waiting for it or expecting it for a long time. ❏ *Finally I went to bed...The heat of the sun finally became too much for me.* You can also use **finally** to show that something happens last in a series of events. ❏ *The sky turned red, then purple, and finally black.*

ever /ɛvər/

Ever is an adverb that you use to add emphasis in negative sentences, commands, questions, and conditional structures.

Ever は否定文, 命令, 質問, 条件構造で強調するために使う副詞である.

1 ADV 副詞 **Ever** means at any time. It is used in questions and negative statements. いつか, かつて ❏ *I'm not sure I'll ever trust people again.* 私は再び人を信用するようになる日がいつか来るか分からない. ❏ *Neither of us had ever skied.* 私たちは2人とも今までにスキーをしたことがなかった. **2** ADV 副詞 You use **ever** in expressions such as "did you ever" and "have you ever" to express surprise or shock at something you have just seen, heard, or experienced, especially when you expect people to agree with you. 疑問文で驚き・動揺などを表す ❏ *Have you ever seen anything like it?* あなたは今までにそのようなものを見たことがありますか. [EMPHASIS 強調] **3** ADV 副詞 You use **ever** after comparatives and superlatives to emphasize the degree to which something is true or when you are comparing a present situation with the past or the future. (最上級の文で) これまでで最高の (比較級の文で) これまでよりずっと [EMPHASIS 強調] ❏ *She's got a great voice and is singing better than ever.* 彼女の声は素晴らしく, これまでより上手に歌っている. ❏ *Japan is wealthier and more powerful than ever before.* 日本はかつてないほどの富と力を持っている.

Do not confuse **ever** and **always**. You use **ever**, for example in negative sentences, questions, and with superlatives, to talk about any time at all when referring to the past, present, or future. ❏ *No one ever came...Will I ever see France? ...the nicest thing anyone's ever said to me.* If something **always** happens, it happens regularly or on every occasion. ❏ *I would always ask for the radio to be turned down... He's always been an active person.* If something is **always** the case, it is true at all times. ❏ *No matter what she did, she would always be forgiven.*

4 ADV 副詞 You use **ever** to say that something happens more all the time. いつも [ADV adj/adv] ❏ *They grew ever further apart.* 彼らは終始ますます離れていった. **5** ADV 副詞 You can use **ever**

for emphasis after "never." never の後で強調して ❑ *I can never, ever, forgive myself*. 私は一生自分を許せない． [INFORMAL くだけた, EMPHASIS 強調] [ADV before V] **6** ADV 副詞 You use **ever** in questions beginning with words such as "why," "when," and "who" when you want to emphasize your surprise or shock. 疑問詞と共に用いて驚き・動揺の感情を表す ❑ *Why ever didn't you tell me?* 一体どうして私に話してくれなかったの． [EMPHASIS 強調] [quest ADV] **7** PHRASE 句 If something has been the case **ever since** a particular time, it has been the case all the time from then until now. 一以来ずっと ❑ *He's been there ever since you left!* あなたが去ってからずっと彼はそこにいる． ● ADV 副詞 Ever is also an adverb. 全面に用いられる ❑ *I simply gave in to him, and I've regretted it ever since*. 私はただ彼の言いなりになるのみだったが，その後ずっとそのこと後悔していた． **8** → see also **forever** **9** PHRASE 句 You use the expression **all** someone **ever does** when you want to emphasize that they do the same thing all the time, and this annoys you. いつもーするだけ [EMPHASIS 強調] ❑ *All she ever does is complain.* 彼女はいつだって文句を言うだけだ． **10** PHRASE 句 You use **as ever** in order to indicate that something or someone's behavior is not unusual because it is like that all the time or very often. 相変わらず ❑ *As ever, the meals are primarily fish-based.* 相変わらず，食事は主に魚が中心だ． **11** hardly ever → see **hardly**

Word Partnership ever は次の語句と用いられる:

V.	ever **forget**, ever **known**, ever **made**, ever **seen 1**
	have you ever **2**
ADV.	ever **again 1**
	better than ever, ever **more**, **more than** ever **3**
	never ever **5**
	hardly ever **11**
ADJ.	**best** ever **3**

ever- /ɛvər-/ COMB IN ADJ 形容詞の複合 You use **ever** in adjectives such as **ever-increasing** and **ever-present**, to show that something exists or continues all the time. 絶えず，ますます ❑ *...the ever-increasing traffic on our roads.* ますます増加する道路交通量

ever|green /ɛvərgrin/ (**evergreens**) N-COUNT 可算名詞 An **evergreen** is a tree or bush that has green leaves all year long. 常緑樹 ❑ *Holly, like ivy and mistletoe, is an evergreen.* ヒイラギは，ツタやヤドリギと同様に常緑樹です． ● ADJ 形容詞 Evergreen is also an adjective. 常緑の ❑ *Plant evergreen shrubs around the end of the month.* 月末頃に常緑低木を植えなさい．

every /ɛvri/ **1** DET 限定詞 You use **every** to indicate that you are referring to all the members of a group or all the parts of something and not only some of them. どのーも，すべての ❑ *Every room has a window facing the ocean.* 全室に海に面した窓がある． ❑ *Record every expenditure you make.* すべての出費を記録しなさい． ● ADJ 形容詞 Every is also an adjective. すべての [poss ADJ n] ❑ *His every utterance will be scrutinized.* 彼のすべての発言が詳細に調べられるでしょう． **2** DET 限定詞 You use **every** in order to say how often something happens or to indicate that something happens at regular intervals. 一ごとに，～ごとに ❑ *We were made to attend meetings every day.* 私たちは毎日会議へ出席させられた． ❑ *A burglary occurs every three minutes in London.* ロンドンでは3分ごとに押し込み強盗が発生する． **3** DET 限定詞 You use **every** in front of a number when you are saying what proportion of people or things something happens to or applies to. ～ごとに ❑ *Two out of every three people have a cell phone.* 3人に2人の割合で携帯電話を所有している． **4** DET 限定詞 You can use **every** before some nouns, for example "sign," "effort," "reason," and "intention" in order to emphasize what you are saying. 可能な限りの，十分な [EMPHASIS 強調] ❑ *The Congressional Budget Office says the federal deficit shows every sign of getting larger.* 連邦議会予算事務局によると，連邦政府の赤字が増大する十分な兆候がある． ❑ *I think that there is every chance that you will succeed.* あなたが成功する可能性が十分にあると思っている． **5** ADJ 形容詞 If you say that someone's **every** whim, wish, or desire will be satisfied, you are emphasizing that everything they want will happen or be provided. あらゆる [EMPHASIS 強調] [poss ADJ n] ❑ *Dozens of servants had catered to his every whim.* 何十人もの使用人が彼のあらゆる気まぐれに対応していた．

You use **every** to refer to all the members of a group that has more than two members. ❑ *He listened to every news bulletin.* *...an equal chance for every child.* You use **each** to refer to every person or thing in a group when you are thinking about them as individuals. Note that **each** can be used to refer to both members of a pair. ❑ *Each apartment has two bedrooms...We each carried a suitcase.* Note that **each** and **every** are only used with singular nouns.

6 PHRASE 句 You use **every** in the expressions **every now and then**, **every now and again**, **every once in a while**, and **every so often** in order to indicate that something happens occasionally. 時々 ❑ *Stir the batter every now and then to keep it from separating.* 分

離しないように，時々ころもをかき混ぜなさい． **7** PHRASE 句 If something happens **every other day** or **every second day**, for example, it happens one day, then does not happen the next day, then happens the day after that, and so on. You can also say that something happens **every third week**, **every fourth year**, and so on. 1日おきに，（起こる時間について）一おきに ❑ *I went home every other week.* 私は1週間おきに帰宅した． **8** **every bit as** good **as** → see **hit**

every|body /ɛvribɒdi, -bʌdi/ **Everybody** means the same as **everyone**. everyone と同義

every|day /ɛvrideɪ/ ADJ 形容詞 You use **everyday** to describe something that happens or is used every day, or forms a regular and basic part of your life, so it is not especially interesting or unusual. 毎日の，日常の ❑ *In the course of my everyday life, I had very little contact with teenagers.* 私の日常生活では10代の若者と接することはほとんどない．

every|one /ɛvriwʌn/

The form **everybody** is also used.

everybody 形も使われる.

1 PRON-INDEF 不定代名詞 You use **everyone** or **everybody** to refer to all the people in a particular group. みな ❑ *Everyone on the street was shocked when they heard the news.* その通りのだれもがそのニュースを聞いて動揺した． ❑ *Not everyone thinks that the government is being particularly generous.* 政府が特に気前よくやっていると全ての人が思っているわけではない． **2** PRON-INDEF 不定代名詞 You use **everyone** or **everybody** to refer to all people. だれでも ❑ *Everyone wrestles with self-doubt and feels like a failure at times.* だれでも自信喪失と戦い，時には落第者のように感じることがある． ❑ *Everyone needs some free time for rest and relaxation.* だれでも休息とくつろぎのためのいくらかの自由時間が必要だ．

Do not confuse **everyone** with **every one**. **Everyone** always refers to people. In the phrase **every one**, "one" is a pronoun that can refer to any person or thing, depending on the context. It is often followed by the word **of**. ❑ *We've saved seeds from every one of our plants... Every one of them phoned me.* In these examples, **every one** is a more emphatic way of saying **all**.

every|place /ɛvripleɪs/ → see **everywhere**

every|thing /ɛvriθɪŋ/ **1** PRON-INDEF 不定代名詞 You use **everything** to refer to all the objects, actions, activities, or facts in a particular situation. 何もかもすべて ❑ *He'd gone to Seattle long after everything else in his life had changed.* 彼がシアトルに行ったのは，彼の人生のほかのこと全てが変わってしまってからずっと後のことだ． **2** PRON-INDEF 不定代名詞 You use **everything** to refer to all possible or likely actions, activities, or situations. 起こりえるすべて ❑ *"This should have been decided long before now." — "We can't think of everything."* 「このことはずっと前に決めるべきだった」「何もかも考えるなんてできないよ」 ❑ *Najib and I do everything together.* ナジブと私は何でも一緒にする． **3** PRON-INDEF 不定代名詞 You use **everything** to refer to a whole situation or to life in general. 万事 ❑ *She says everything is going smoothly.* 彼女が言うには，万事順調だ． ❑ *Is everything all right?* 万事うまくいっていますか？ **4** PRON-INDEF 不定代名詞 If you say that someone or something is **everything**, you mean you consider them to be the most important thing in your life, or the most important thing that there is. 最も大切なもの ❑ *I love him. He is everything to me.* 彼を愛している．彼ほど大切な人はいない． **5** PRON-INDEF 不定代名詞 If you say that someone or something has **everything**, you mean they have all the things or qualities that most people consider to be desirable. 何もかも ❑ *This man had everything. He had the house, the sailboat and a full life with friends and family.* この男性はすべてを手に入れた．家，ヨット，それに友達や家族との充実した生活があった．

every|where /ɛvriwɛər/ also **everyplace** **1** ADV 副詞 You use **everywhere** to refer to a whole area or to all the places in a particular area. どこでも ❑ *Working people everywhere object to paying taxes.* 労働者がどこでも税金の支払いに反対する． ❑ *We went everywhere together.* 私たちはどこでも一緒に行った． **2** ADV 副詞 You use **everywhere** to refer to all the places that someone goes to. 至るところで ❑ *Mary Jo is still accustomed to traveling everywhere in style.* メアリー・ジョーは依然としてどこに行くときも豪勢に旅行する習慣がある． **3** ADV 副詞 You use **everywhere** to emphasize that you are talking about a large number of places, or all possible places. あらゆる場所，あちこちで [EMPHASIS 強調] ❑ *I saw her picture everywhere.* 私はあちこちで彼女の写真を見かけた． **4** ADV 副詞 If you say that someone or something is **everywhere**, you mean that they are present in a place in very large numbers. どこもーばかり ❑ *There were cartons of cigarettes everywhere.* どこもたばこの箱ばかりだった．

evict /ɪvɪkt/ (**evicts, evicting, evicted**) V-T 他動詞 If someone **is evicted from** the place where they are living, they are forced to leave it, usually because they have broken a law or contract. 立ち退かせる ❑ *They were evicted from their apartment after their mother*

became addicted to drugs. 母親が麻薬中毒になってから，彼らはアパートから強制退去になった． □ *In the first week, the city police evicted ten families.* 最初の週に市警察は10家族を立ち退かせた．

evic|tion /ɪvɪkʃ^ən/ (**evictions**) N-VAR 可変性名詞 **Eviction** is the act or process of officially forcing someone to leave a house or piece of land. 立ち退き □ *He was facing eviction, along with his wife and family.* 彼は妻と家族と共に立ち退きに直面していた．

evi|dence /ɛvɪdəns/ ■ N-UNCOUNT 不可算名詞 **Evidence** is anything that you see, experience, read, or are told that causes you to believe that something is true or has really happened. 証拠 □ *Ganley said he'd seen no evidence of widespread fraud.* ガンリーは広範囲にわたる詐欺行為の証拠は見たことがないと言った． ■ N-UNCOUNT 不可算名詞 **Evidence** is the information that is used in a court of law to try to prove something. **Evidence** is obtained from documents, objects, or witnesses. (物件) 証拠 証言 [LEGAL 法律的] □ *The evidence against him was purely circumstantial.* 彼に不利な証拠は全く状況証拠だけだった． ■ PHRASE 句 If you **give evidence** in a court of law or an official inquiry, you officially say what you know about people or events, or describe an occasion at which you were present. 証言する □ *The forensic scientists who carried out the original tests will be called to give evidence.* 最初の検査を行った科学捜査官たちは証言に呼び出されるでしょう． ■ PHRASE 句 If someone or something **is in evidence**, they are present and can be clearly seen. 目立つ，目につく □ *Few soldiers were in evidence.* 兵士はほとんど目につかなかった．

→ see **experiment, trial**

Word Partnership *evidence* は次の語句と使われる:
V.	**find** evidence, **gather** evidence, **present** evidence, **produce** evidence, evidence **to support** *something* ■ ■
ADJ.	**new** evidence, **physical** evidence, **scientific** evidence ■ ■
	circumstantial evidence ■

evi|dent /ɛvɪdənt/ ■ ADJ 形容詞 If something is **evident**, you notice it easily and clearly. はっきり分かる □ *His footprints were clearly evident in the heavy dust.* 彼の足跡は分厚いほこりの上にはっきりと残っていた． □ *The threat of inflation is already evident in bond prices.* インフレの兆しはすでに債券価格にはっきりと出ている． ■ ADJ 形容詞 You use **evident** to show that you are certain about a situation and your interpretation of it. 明白な [EMPHASIS 強調] □ *It was evident that she had once been a beauty.* 彼女がかつて美人だったということは明らかだった． ■ → see also **self-evident**

evi|dent|ly /ɛvɪdəntli, -dɛnt-/ ■ ADV 副詞 You use **evidently** to say that something is obviously true, for example, because you have seen evidence of it yourself. 明らかに，間違いなく □ *The man wore a bathrobe and had evidently just come from the bathroom.* その男はバスローブを着ていて，明らかに浴室から出てきたところだった． ■ ADV 副詞 You use **evidently** to show that you think something is true or have been told something is true, but that you are not sure, because you do not have enough information or proof. どうやら □ *From childhood, he was evidently at once rebellious and precocious.* 彼は子供時代からどうやら反抗的でしかも早熟だったようだ． ■ ADV 副詞 You can use **evidently** to introduce a statement or opinion and to emphasize that you feel that it is true or correct. 明白に [FORMAL 形式ばった, EMPHASIS 強調] [ADV with cl] □ *Evidently, it has nothing to do with social background.* 明らかにそれは社会的背景とは何の関係もない．

evil /iv^əl/ (**evils**) ■ N-UNCOUNT 不可算名詞 **Evil** is a powerful force that some people believe to exist, and that causes wicked and bad things to happen. 邪悪，悪 □ *There's always a conflict between good and evil in his plays.* 彼の劇には常に善と悪のかっとうがある． ■ N-UNCOUNT 不可算名詞 **Evil** is used to refer to all the wicked and bad things that happen in the world. 諸悪 □ *He could not, after all, stop all the evil in the world.* 結局のところ，彼は世界の諸悪をすべて止めることはできなかった． ■ N-COUNT 可算名詞 If you refer to an **evil**, you mean a very unpleasant or harmful situation or activity. 弊害 □ *Higher taxes may be a necessary evil.* 増税は必要悪かもしれない． ■ ADJ 形容詞 If you describe someone as **evil**, you mean that they are very wicked by nature and take pleasure in doing things that harm other people. 邪悪な，極悪な □ *...the country's most evil terrorists.* その国の最も邪悪なテロリストたち ■ ADJ 形容詞 If you describe something as **evil**, you mean that you think it causes a great deal of harm to people and is morally bad. 害悪の，非道な □ *A judge yesterday condemned heroin as evil.* 1人の判事が昨日ヘロインは害悪であるとの判決を下した． ■ ADJ 形容詞 If you describe something as **evil**, you mean that you think it is influenced by the devil. 悪魔の □ *I think this is an evil spirit at work.* これは悪霊が働いているのだと思う． ■ PHRASE 句 If you have two choices, but think that they are both bad, you can describe the less bad one as **the lesser of two evils**, or **the lesser evil**. 悪くてもまだましなほう □ *People voted for him as the lesser of two evils.* 人々は悪者のうちでもまだましな彼に投票した．

evoca|tive /ɪvɒkətɪv/ ADJ 形容詞 If you describe something as **evocative**, you mean that it is good or interesting because it produces pleasant memories, ideas, emotions, and responses in people. 喚情的な，呼び起こす [FORMAL 形式ばった] □ *Her story is sharply evocative of Italian provincial life.* 彼女の話を聞くとイタリアの田舎の生活がありありと思い浮かぶ．

evoke /ɪvoʊk/ (**evokes, evoking, evoked**) V-T 他動詞 To **evoke** a particular memory, idea, emotion, or response means to cause it to occur. 喚起する [FORMAL 形式ばった] □ *...the scene evoking memories of those old movies.* それらの古い映画を思い出させる光景

evo|lu|tion /ivəluʃ^ən, ɛv-/ (**evolutions**) ■ N-UNCOUNT 不可算名詞 **Evolution** is a process of gradual change that takes place over many generations, during which species of animals, plants, or insects slowly change some of their physical characteristics. 進化 □ *...the evolution of plants and animals.* 植物や動物の進化 ■ N-VAR 可変性名詞 **Evolution** is a process of gradual development in a particular situation or thing over a period of time. 発展 [FORMAL 形式ばった] □ *...a crucial period in the evolution of modern physics.* 現代物理学の発展における重要な時期

→ see **earth**

evo|lu|tion|ary /ivəluʃənɛri/ ADJ 形容詞 **Evolutionary** means relating to a process of gradual change and development. 進化の □ *...an evolutionary process.* 進化過程

evolve /ɪvɒlv/ (**evolves, evolving, evolved**) ■ V-I 自動詞 When animals or plants **evolve**, they gradually change and develop into different forms. 進化する □ *The bright plumage of many male birds was thought to have evolved to attract females.* 多くの雄鳥の鮮やかな羽毛は雌を引き付けるために進化したと考えられた． □ *Birds are widely believed to have evolved from dinosaurs.* 鳥は恐竜から進化したと広く信じられている． ■ V-T/V-I 他動詞/自動詞 If something **evolves** or you **evolve** it, it gradually develops over a period of time into something different and usually more advanced. 発展させる [他動詞] 発展する [自動詞] □ *...a tiny airline which eventually evolved into Pakistan International Airlines.* やがてはパキスタン国際航空に発展した小さな航空会社 □ *Popular music evolved from folk songs.* ポップミュージックはフォークソングから発展しました．

→ see **earth**

ewe /yu/ (**ewes**) N-COUNT 可算名詞 A **ewe** is an adult female sheep. 雌羊

ex|ac|er|bate /ɪgzæsərbeɪt/ (**exacerbates, exacerbating, exacerbated**) V-T 他動詞 If something **exacerbates** a problem or bad situation, it makes it worse. 悪化させる [FORMAL 形式ばった] □ *Longstanding poverty has been exacerbated by racial divisions.* 長年の貧困は人種対立により悪化した． ● **ex|ac|er|ba|tion** /ɪgzæsərbeɪʃ^ən/ N-UNCOUNT 不可算名詞 悪化 □ *...the exacerbation of global problems.* 地球規模の問題の深刻化

ex|act /ɪgzækt/ (**exacts, exacting, exacted**) ■ ADJ 形容詞 **Exact** means correct in every detail. For example, an **exact** copy is the same in every detail as the thing it is copied from. 正確な □ *I don't remember the exact words.* 私は正確な言葉は覚えていない． □ *The exact number of protest calls has not been revealed.* 抗議電話の正確な数は発表されていない． ● **ex|act|ly** ADV 副詞 □ *Try to locate exactly where the smells are entering the room.* どこからにおいが部屋に入っているのか正確に場所を突き止めてみなさい． □ *Both drugs will be exactly the same.* どちらの薬も全く同じものだろう． ■ ADJ 形容詞 [ADJ n] You use **exact** before a noun to emphasize that you are referring to that particular thing and no other, especially something that has a particular significance. ぴったりの [EMPHASIS 強調] □ *I hadn't really thought about it until this exact moment.* まさにこの瞬間までそのことを特に考えたことがなかった． ● **ex|act|ly** ADV [ADV n/wh] ぴったりと □ *These are exactly the people who do not vote.* 投票しないのはまさにこの人々だ． ■ V-T 他動詞 When someone **exacts** something, they demand and obtain it from another person, especially because they are in a superior or more powerful position. 強要する，取り立てる [FORMAL 形式ばった] □ *Already he has exacted a written apology from the chairman of the commission.* すでに彼はその委員会の委員長からわび状を強要して取っていた． ■ V-T 他動詞 If someone **exacts** revenge **on** a person, they have their revenge on them. (ふくしゅう) 果たす (復讐を) □ *She uses the media to help her exact a terrible revenge.* 彼女は恐ろしい復讐を果たす手助けにマスコミを使う． ■ V-T 他動詞 If something **exacts** a high price, it has a bad effect on a person or situation. (代償などを) 必要とする □ *The sheer physical effort had exacted a heavy price.* 純然たる肉体的努力が大きな犠牲をもたらした． ■ → see also **exactly** ■ PHRASE 句 You say **to be exact** to indicate that you are slightly correcting or giving more detailed information about what you have been saying. 正確に言えば，厳密には □ *A small number – five, to be exact – have been bad.* 少人数の者が，厳密には5人だが，いけなかったのだ．

Thesaurus *exact* また次を参照:
ADJ.	accurate, clear, precise, true; (*ant.*) inexact, wrong ■

Word Partnership *exact* は次の語句と使われる:

N. exact **change**, exact **duplicate**, exact **number**, exact
opposite, exact **replica**, exact **science**, exact **words** ■
exact **cause**, exact **location**, exact **moment** ■
exact **revenge** ■

ex|act|ing /ɪgzǽktɪŋ/ ADJ 形容詞 You use **exacting** to describe
something or someone that demands hard work and a great deal
of care. 骨の折れる □ *She didn't think that he was well enough to carry
out such an exacting task.* 彼女は、彼がそんなに骨の折れる仕事ができ
るほど元気だとは思わなかった.

ex|act|ly /ɪgzǽktli/ ■ ADV 副詞 You use **exactly** before an
amount, number, or position to emphasize that it is no more, no
less, or no different from what you are stating. 正確に、ちょうど
[EMPHASIS 強調] □ *Each corner had a guard tower, each of which was
exactly ten meters in height.* 角にはそれぞれ監視塔があり、どれも高
さがちょうど10メートルだった. ■ ADV 副詞 If you say "**Exactly**,"
you are agreeing with someone or emphasizing the truth of
what they say. If you say "**Not exactly**," you are telling them
politely that they are wrong in part of what they are saying. そ
の通り [ADV as reply] □ *Eve nodded, almost approvingly. "Exactly."* イ
ブは満足げにうなずいた. 「おっしゃるとおりですわ」 ■ ADV 副
詞 You use **not exactly** to indicate that a meaning or situation
is slightly different from what people think or expect. 少し違っ
て [VAGUENESS あいまいさ] □ *He's not exactly homeless, he just hangs
out in this park.* 彼はホームレスというわけではなくて、ただこの公園
でぶらぶらしているだけだ. ■ ADV 副詞 You can use **not exactly**
to show that you mean the opposite of what you are saying. 全
然一ではない [EMPHASIS 強調] □ *This was not exactly what I wanted
to hear.* これは全く私が聞きたいことではなかった. ■ ADV 副詞
You use **exactly** with a question to show that you disapprove of
what the person you are talking to is doing or saying. いったい
[DISAPPROVAL 不賛成] [ADV with quest] □ *What exactly do you mean?*
いったいどういう意味なんだ? ■ → see also **exact**

ex|ag|ger|ate /ɪgzǽdʒəreɪt/ (**exaggerates, exaggerating,
exaggerated**) ■ V-T/V-I 他動詞/自動詞 If you **exaggerate**,
you indicate that something is, for example, worse or more
important than it really is. 誇張する、大げさに言う □ *He
thinks I'm exaggerating.* 彼は私が誇張していると思っている.
●**ex|ag|ger|a|tion** /ɪgzǽdʒəreɪʃⁿn/ (**exaggerations**) N-VAR 可変性
名詞 誇張 □ *Like many stories about him, it smacks of exaggeration.* 彼
にまつわる多くのうわさ話のように、それは誇張気味だ. ■ V-T 他
動詞 If something **exaggerates** a situation, quality, or feature,
it makes the situation, quality, or feature appear greater, more
obvious, or more important than it really is. 強調しすぎる、際立た
せる □ *These figures exaggerate the loss of competitiveness.* これらの数
字は競争力の喪失を実際より際立たせている.

ex|ag|ger|at|ed /ɪgzǽdʒəreɪtɪd/ ADJ 形容詞 Something that is
exaggerated is or seems larger, better, worse, or more important
than it actually needs to be. 誇張された、大げさな □ *Western fears,
he insists, are greatly exaggerated.* 西欧諸国の懸念は、彼が主張すると
ころでは、大変誇張されて伝えられている.

Word Link *alt ≈ high : altar, altitude, exalted*

ex|alt|ed /ɪgzɔ́ltɪd/ ADJ 形容詞 Someone or something that is
at an **exalted** level is at a very high level, especially with regard
to rank or importance. 位の高い [FORMAL 形式ばった] □ *You must
decide how to make the best use of your exalted position.* あなたの高い地
位をどうすれば最大限に生かせるかを決断しなければなりません.

exam /ɪgzǽm/ (**exams**) ■ N-COUNT 可算名詞 An **exam** is a
formal test that you take to show your knowledge or ability
in a particular subject, or to obtain a qualification. 試験 □ *I
don't want to take any more exams.* 私はこれ以上試験を受けたくな
い. ■ N-COUNT 可算名詞 If you have a medical **exam**, a doctor
looks at your body, feels it, or does simple tests in order to check
how healthy you are. 健康診断、診察 [mainly AM 主に米国英語]
□ *These medical exams have shown I am in perfect physical condition.* こ
れらの健康診断の結果によると、私は完璧な健康状態にある.

ex|ami|na|tion /ɪgzǽmɪneɪʃⁿn/ (**examinations**) ■ N-COUNT
可算名詞 An **examination** is a formal test that you take to show
your knowledge or ability in a particular subject, or to obtain a
qualification. 試験 [FORMAL 形式ばった] □ *...college examination
results.* 大学の試験結果 ■ → see also **examine** ■ N-COUNT 可算
名詞 If you have a medical **examination**, a doctor looks at your
body, feels it, or does simple tests in order to check how healthy
you are. 健康診断、診察 □ *You must see your doctor for a thorough
examination.* あなたはかかりつけの医者に行って精密検査を受けなけ
ればいけません.
→ see **diagnosis**

ex|am|ine /ɪgzǽmɪn/ (**examines, examining, examined**)
■ V-T 他動詞 If you **examine** something, you look at it carefully.
検査する、調査する □ *He examined her passport and stamped it.* 彼

は彼女のパスポートを検査して、判を押した. ●**ex|ami|na|tion**
/ɪgzǽmɪneɪʃⁿn/ (**examinations**) N-VAR 可変性名詞 検査、調査
□ *The navy is to carry out an examination of the wreck tomorrow.* 海
軍が明日難破船の調査を行う予定です. ■ V-T 他動詞 If a doctor
examines you, he or she looks at your body, feels it, or does
simple tests in order to check how healthy you are. 診察する
□ *Another doctor examined her and could still find nothing wrong.* 別の
医者が彼女を診察したが、やはり何の異常もみとめられなかった.
●**ex|ami|na|tion** N-VAR 可変性名詞 診察 □ *He was later discharged
after an examination at the hospital.* 彼はその後、病院で診察を受け
たあと帰宅を許された. ■ V-T 他動詞 If an idea, proposal, or plan
is examined, it is considered very carefully. 考察する、検討す
る □ *The plans will be examined by officials.* それらの企画は役員によ
り検討されるであろう. ●**ex|ami|na|tion** N-VAR 可変性名詞 考
察 □ *The government said it was studying the implications, which
"required very careful examination and consideration."* 政府の発表によ
ると、政府はその影響について研究中だが、「非常に慎重な調査と熟
慮を必要とする」ということだった. ■ V-T 他動詞 [usu passive] If
you **are examined**, you are given a formal test in order to show
your knowledge of a subject. 試験する □ *...learning to cope with the
pressures of being judged and examined by our teachers.* 教師により評価
され、試験されるプレッシャーに対処することを学んで

Thesaurus *examine* また次を参照:

V. analyze, go over, inspect, investigate, research; (ant.)
scrutinize ■

ex|am|in|er /ɪgzǽmɪnər/ (**examiners**) ■ N-COUNT 可算名詞
An **examiner** is a person who conducts an examination. 試験官、
検査官 □ *...FBI senior fingerprint examiner Terry Green.* 連邦捜査局のテ
リー・グリーン上級指紋検査官 ■ → see also **medical examiner**

ex|am|ple /ɪgzǽmpⁿl/ (**examples**) ■ N-COUNT 可算名詞 An
example of something is a particular situation, object, or person
that shows that what is being claimed is true. 実例 □ *The doctors
gave numerous examples of patients being expelled from the hospital.*
医師側は同病院から強制退院になった患者の数々の実例を挙げま
した. ■ N-COUNT 可算名詞 An **example of** a particular class
of objects or styles is something that has many of the typical
features of such a class or style, and that you consider clearly
represents it. 見本 □ *Symphonies 103 and 104 stand as perfect examples
of early symphonic construction.* 交響曲103と104は初期の交響曲構成の
完璧な見本として存在する. ■ N-COUNT 可算名詞 If you refer to a
person or their behavior as an **example to** other people, you mean
that he or she behaves in a good or correct way that other people
should copy. 手本、模範 [APPROVAL 賛成] □ *He is a model professional
and an example to the younger boys.* 彼は模範的な職業人で、少年たち
にとっての手本だ. ■ PHRASE 句 You use **for example** to introduce
and emphasize something that shows that something is true. 例
えば □ *Take, for example, the simple sentence: "The man climbed up the
hill."* 例えば、The man climbed up the hill. (男はその丘を登った)
という簡単な文を取り上げましょう. ■ PHRASE 句 If you **follow**
someone's **example**, you behave in the same way as they did
in the past, or in a similar way, especially because you admire
them. 人の例を見習う □ *Following the example set by her father, she
has fulfilled her role and done her duty.* 彼女は父親を見習って、自分の
役割と義務を果たしてきた. ■ PHRASE 句 To **make an example of**
someone who has done something wrong means to punish them
severely as a warning to other people not to do the same thing. 人
を見せしめに罰する □ *Let us at least see our courts make an example of
these despicable criminals.* せめて裁判所がこれらの卑劣な犯罪者を見せ
しめに罰するのを見たい. ■ PHRASE 句 If you **set an example**, you
encourage or inspire people by your behavior to behave or act in a
similar way. 手本を示す □ *An officer's job was to set an example.* 将校
の仕事は手本を示すことだった.

Thesaurus *example* また次を参照:

N. model, representation, sample ■ ■
ideal, role model, standard ■

Word Partnership *example* は次の語句と使われる:

ADJ. **classic** example, **obvious** example, **perfect** example,
typical example ■ ■
good example ■ – ■
give an example ■ ■
follow an example ■

Word Link *sper ≈ hope : desperate, exasperate, prosperity*

ex|as|per|ate /ɪgzǽspəreɪt/ (**exasperates, exasperating,
exasperated**) V-T 他動詞 If someone or something **exasperates**
you, they annoy you and make you feel frustrated or upset. 怒
らせる、いらいらさせる □ *The sheer futility of it all exasperates
her.* それがすべて全く役に立たないのに彼女は腹を立てている.

ex|as|pera|tion /ɪgzæspəreɪʃᵊn/ N-UNCOUNT 不可算名詞 憤慨, 激怒 ❑*Mahoney clenched his fist in exasperation.* マホニーは激怒してこぶしを固く握った.

ex|as|per|at|ed /ɪgzæspəreɪtɪd/ ADJ 形容詞 If you describe a person as **exasperated**, you mean that they are frustrated or angry because of something that is happening or something that another person is doing. いらいらした, 怒った ❑*The president was clearly exasperated by the whole saga.* 大統領は明らかにその一連の事件に憤慨していた.

Word Link cav ≈ hollow : *cave, cavity, excavate*

ex|ca|vate /ɛkskəveɪt/ (excavates, excavating, excavated) **1** V-T 他動詞 When archaeologists or other people **excavate** a piece of land, they remove earth carefully from it and look for things such as pots, bones, or buildings that are buried there, in order to discover information about the past. 発掘する ❑*A new Danish expedition is again excavating the site in annual summer digs.* 新しいデンマークの探検隊が例年の夏季発掘調査で再びその場所を発掘している. ● **ex|ca|va|tion** /ɛkskəveɪʃᵊn/ (excavations) N-VAR 可変性名詞 発掘 ❑*She worked on the excavation of a Mayan archeological site.* 彼女はマヤ文明の考古学的跡地の発掘に関わっていた. **2** V-T 他動詞 To **excavate** means to dig a hole in the ground, for example, in order to build there. 掘る ❑*A contractor was hired to drain the reservoir and to excavate soil from one area for replacement with clay.* 貯水池を排水し, 1か所から土壌を掘り出して粘土に交換するために土建業者が雇われた. ● **ex|ca|va|tion** N-VAR 可変性名詞 掘削 ❑*...the excavation of canals.* 運河の掘削

Word Link ex ≈ away, from, out : *exceed, exit, explode*

ex|ceed /ɪksi:d/ (exceeds, exceeding, exceeded) **1** V-T 他動詞 If something **exceeds** a particular amount or number, it is greater or larger than that amount or number. 超過する [FORMAL 形式ばった] ❑*Its research budget exceeds $700 million a year.* それの研究予算は年間7億ドルを超過する. **2** V-T 他動詞 If you **exceed** a limit or rule, you go beyond it, even though you are not supposed to or it is against the law. 超える [FORMAL 形式ばった] ❑*He accepts that he was exceeding the speed limit.* 彼は制限速度を超えていたことを認めている.

ex|ceed|ing|ly /ɪksi:dɪŋli/ ADV 副詞 **Exceedingly** means very or very much. 非常に [OLD-FASHIONED 古風な] ❑*We had an exceedingly good lunch.* 私たちはとても素晴らしい昼食をとった.

ex|cel /ɪksɛl/ (excels, excelling, excelled) V-T/V-I 他動詞/自動詞 If someone **excels** in something or **excels at** it, they are very good at doing it. 抜きんでる, 秀でる ❑*Mary was a better rider than either of them and she excelled at outdoor sports.* メアリーはほかの2人よりも乗馬が上手で, 戸外のスポーツに秀でていた. ❑*Academically he began to excel.* 彼の学業成績がどんどん伸び始めた.

Word Link ence ≈ state, condition : *dependence, excellence, independence*

ex|cel|lence /ɛksələns/ N-UNCOUNT 不可算名詞 If someone or something has the quality of **excellence**, they are extremely good in some way. 優秀 ❑*...the top award for excellence in journalism and the arts.* ジャーナリズムと芸術における最優秀賞

ex|cel|lent /ɛksələnt/ **1** ADJ 形容詞 Something that is **excellent** is extremely good. 優れた, 素晴らしい ❑*The recording quality is excellent.* 録音の音質は素晴らしい. ● **ex|cel|lent|ly** ADV 副詞 素晴らしく ❑*They're both playing excellently.* 彼らは2人とも素晴らしい演奏をしている. **2** EXCLAM 感嘆詞 Some people say "**Excellent!**" to show that they approve of something. 最高だ, やった― [FEELINGS 感情] ❑*"Excellent!" he shouted, yelping happily at the rain. "Now we'll see how this boat really performs!"* 「やったー!」と彼は雨に向かってうれしそうにはしゃぎながら叫んだ.「やっとこのボートの性能を試せるよ!」

ex|cept /ɪksɛpt/ **1** PREP 前置詞 You use **except** to introduce the only thing or person that a statement does not apply to, or a fact that prevents a statement from being completely true. 一以外は ❑*I wouldn't have accepted anything except a job in New York.* 私はニューヨーク市内での仕事以外は引き受けなかったでしょう. ● CONJ 接続詞 **Except** is also a conjunction. 一を除いて ❑*Freddie would tell me nothing about what he was writing, except that it was to be a Christmas play.* フレディは何を書いているのかについて私に何も話そうとしなかったので, クリスマス劇になる予定だということ以外はね. **2** PHRASE 句 You use **except** or **except for** to introduce the only thing or person that prevents a statement from being completely true. 一以外は, 一を除いて ❑*He hadn't eaten a thing except for one forkful of salad.* 彼はサラダ1口を除いては何も食べていなかった.

Do not confuse **except**, **except for**, **besides**, and **unless**. You use **except** to introduce the only things, situations, people, or ideas that a statement does not apply to. ❑*All of his body relaxed except his right hand...Traveling was impossible, except in the cool of the morning.* You use **except for** before something that prevents a statement from being completely true. ❑*The classrooms were silent, except for the scratching of pens on paper...I had absolutely no friends except for Tom.* You use **besides** to introduce extra things in addition to the ones you are mentioning already. ❑*Fruit will give you, besides enjoyment, a source of vitamins.* However, note that if you talk about "the only thing" or "the only person" **besides** a particular person or thing, **besides** means the same as "apart from." ❑*He was the only person besides Gertrude who talked to Guy.* **Unless** is used to introduce the only situation in which something will take place or be true. ❑*In the 1940s, unless she wore gloves a woman was not properly dressed...You must not give compliments unless you mean them.*

ex|cept|ed /ɪksɛptɪd/ ADV 副詞 You use **excepted** after you have mentioned a person or thing to show that you do not include them in the statement you are making. 除外して [FORMAL 形式ばった] [N ADV] ❑*Jeremy excepted, the men seemed personable.* ジェレミーを除外して, その男性陣は魅力的だった.

ex|cept|ing /ɪksɛptɪŋ/ PREP 前置詞 You use **excepting** to introduce the only thing that prevents a statement from being completely true. ~を除外して [FORMAL 形式ばった] ❑*The source of meat for much of this region (excepting Japan) has traditionally been the pig.* この地域の大部分で食肉源は（日本を除き）伝統的に豚だった.

ex|cep|tion /ɪksɛpʃᵊn/ (exceptions) **1** N-COUNT 可算名詞 An **exception** is a particular thing, person, or situation that is not included in a general statement, judgment, or rule. 例外 ❑*Few guitarists can sing as well as they can play; Eddie, however, is an exception.* ギター演奏家で演奏と同じくらい上手に歌える者はほとんどいない. しかし, エディーは例外だ. ❑*The law makes no exceptions.* その法律は例外を認めません. **2** PHRASE 句 If you make a general statement, and then say that something or someone is **no exception**, you are emphasizing that they are included in that statement. 例外ではない [EMPHASIS 強調] ❑*Marketing is applied to everything these days, and books are no exception.* マーケティングは最近ではすべてに適用されており, 書籍も例外ではありません. **3** PHRASE 句 If you **take exception to** something, you feel offended or annoyed by it, usually with the result that you complain about it. 腹を立てる ❑*He also took exception to having been spied on.* 彼はひそかに探られていたことにも腹を立てた. **4** PHRASE 句 You use **with the exception of** to introduce a thing or person that is not included in a general statement that you are making. 一を除いて ❑*Yesterday was a day off for everybody, with the exception of Lorenzo.* 昨日はロレンゾを除いて, 全員が休みを取った. **5** PHRASE 句 You use **without exception** to emphasize that the statement you are making is true in all cases. 例外なく [EMPHASIS 強調] ❑*The vehicles are without exception old, rusty and dented.* 乗り物は例外なく古く, さびつや, へこみがあった.

ex|cep|tion|al /ɪksɛpʃənᵊl/ **1** ADJ 形容詞 You use **exceptional** to describe someone or something that has a particular quality, usually a good quality, in an unusually high degree. 並外れた, 抜群の [APPROVAL 賛成] ❑*...children with exceptional ability.* 抜群の能力を持つ子供たち ● **ex|cep|tion|al|ly** ADV 副詞 [ADV adj/adv] 並外れて ❑*He's an exceptionally talented dancer and needs to practice several hours every day.* 彼は並外れた才能のあるダンサーで, 毎日数時間の練習が必要だ. **2** ADJ 形容詞 **Exceptional** situations and incidents are unusual and only likely to happen infrequently. 例外的な, まれな [FORMAL 形式ばった] ❑*A review panel concluded that there were no exceptional circumstances that would warrant a lesser penalty for him.* 再調査団は, 彼への刑罰を軽減するような例外的な事情はないと結論を下した. ● **ex|cep|tion|al|ly** ADV 副詞 [ADV with cl] 例外的に ❑*Exceptionally, in times of emergency, we may send a team of experts.* 例外的に, 緊急の際は専門家のチームを派遣するかもしれない.

ex|cerpt /ɛksɜ:rpt/ (excerpts) N-COUNT 可算名詞 An **excerpt** is a short piece of writing or music taken from a larger piece. 抜粋, 引用 ❑*...an excerpt from Tchaikovsky's Nutcracker.* チャイコフスキーのくるみ割り人形からの引用

ex|cess (excesses)

The noun is pronounced /ɪksɛs/ or /ɛksɛs/. The adjective is pronounced /ɛksɛs/.

名詞は /ɪksɛs/ または /ɛksɛs/ と発音される. 形容詞は /ɛksɛs/ と発音される.

1 N-VAR 可変性名詞 An **excess of** something is a larger amount than is needed, allowed, or usual. 過剰, 超過 ❑*An excess of house plants in a small apartment can be oppressive.* 小さなアパートでの過剰な観葉植物は重苦しくなりかねない. **2** ADJ 形容詞 **Excess** is used to describe amounts that are greater than what is needed, allowed, or usual. 過剰な, 余分な [ADJ n] ❑*After cooking the fish, pour off any*

excess fat. 魚の調理後には，余分なあぶらを捨てなさい． **3** ADJ 形容詞 **Excess** is used to refer to additional amounts of money that need to be paid for services and activities that were not originally planned or taken into account. (料金が) 超過の [FORMAL 形式ばった] [ADJ n] □ *Make sure that you don't have to pay expensive excess charges.* 高額な超過料金を支払わないようにご確認しなさい． **4** PHRASE 句 **In excess of** means more than a particular amount. ～を超過して [FORMAL 形式ばった] □ *The value of the company is well in excess of $2 billion.* その会社の価値はゆうに20億ドルを超過している． **5** PHRASE 句 If you do something **to excess**, you do it too much. 過度に [DISAPPROVAL 不賛成] □ *I was reasonably fit, played a lot of tennis, and didn't smoke or drink to excess.* 私はまずまず健康で，よくテニスをし，たばこや酒は適度にたしなむ程度だった．

ex|ces|sive /ɪksɛsɪv/ ADJ 形容詞 If you describe the amount or level of something as **excessive**, you disapprove of it because it is more or higher than is necessary or reasonable. 過度の，法外な [DISAPPROVAL 不賛成] □ *Their spending on research is excessive and is slowing developments of new treatments.* 彼らの過剰な研究費のために，新しい治療法の開発が遅れている． ● **ex|ces|sive|ly** ADV 副詞 過度に □ *Managers are also accused of paying themselves excessively high salaries.* 経営者たちは法外に高い給料を取っていることでも非難されている．

ex|change /ɪkstʃeɪndʒ/ (exchanges, exchanging, exchanged) **1** V-RECIP 相互動詞 If two or more people **exchange** things of a particular kind, they give them to each other at the same time. 交換する □ *We exchanged addresses.* 私たちは住所を知らせ合った． □ *The two men exchanged glances.* その2人の男は視線を交わした． ● N-COUNT 可算名詞 **Exchange** is also a noun. 交換 □ *He ruled out any exchange of prisoners with the militants.* 彼は過激派と囚人のどんな交換も否定した． **2** V-T 他動詞 If you **exchange** something, you replace it with a different thing, especially something that is better or more satisfactory. (よい品に) 交換する □ *...the chance to sell back or exchange goods.* 商品を売り戻すか交換する機会 **3** N-COUNT 可算名詞 An **exchange** is a brief conversation, usually an angry one. 言葉のやり取り，口論 [FORMAL 形式ばった] □ *There've been some bitter exchanges between the two groups.* その2組の間で激しい口論がありました． **4** N-COUNT 可算名詞 An **exchange** of fire, for example, is an incident in which people use guns or missiles against each other. 交戦 □ *There was an exchange of fire during which the gunman was wounded.* 銃撃戦があり，銃を持った犯人が負傷した． **5** N-COUNT 可算名詞 An **exchange** is an arrangement in which people from two different countries visit each other's country, to strengthen links between them. 交流，交換 □ *...a series of sporting and cultural exchanges with Seoul.* ソウル市との一連のスポーツと文化の交流 **6** → see also **foreign exchange, stock exchange** **7** PHRASE 句 If you do or give something **in exchange for** something else, you do it or give it in order to get that thing. 引き換えに □ *It is illegal for public officials to solicit gifts or money in exchange for favors.* 公務員が便宜の提供と引き換えに金品をせがむのは違法だ．
→ see **stock market**

Word Partnership	exchange は次の語句と使われる：
N.	exchange **gifts**, exchange **greetings** **1**
	exchange **student** **5**
ADJ.	**brief** exchange **3**
	cultural exchange **5**

ex|change rate (exchange rates) N-COUNT 可算名詞 The **exchange rate** of a country's unit of currency is the amount of another country's currency that you get in exchange for it. 為替相場 □ *...a high exchange rate for the Canadian dollar.* カナダドルに対する高い為替相場

ex|cise /ɛksaɪz/ (excises) N-VAR 可変性名詞 **Excise** is a tax that the government of a country puts on particular goods, such as cigarettes and alcoholic drinks, which are produced for sale in its own country. 物品税 □ *...this year's rise in excise duties.* 本年度の物品税の上昇

ex|cit|able /ɪksaɪtəb³l/ ADJ 形容詞 If you describe someone as **excitable**, you mean that they behave in a nervous way and become excited very easily. 興奮しやすい □ *Mary sat beside Elaine, who today seemed excitable.* メアリーはイレインの横に座ったが，イレインは今日は興奮気味のようだった．

ex|cite /ɪksaɪt/ (excites, exciting, excited) **1** V-T 他動詞 If something **excites** you, it makes you feel very happy, eager, or enthusiastic. 興奮させる □ *I only take on work that excites me, even if it means turning down lots of money.* 私は，刺激のある仕事しか引き受けない．たとえそれが高給な仕事を断ることになったとしても． **2** V-T 他動詞 If something **excites** a particular feeling, emotion, or reaction in someone, it causes them to experience it. (感情を) かきたてる □ *Daniel's early exposure to motor racing did not excite his interest.* ダニエルは早い時期にカーレースを体験したが，彼の興味をそそらなかった．

ex|cit|ed /ɪksaɪtɪd/ **1** ADJ 形容詞 If you are **excited**, you are so happy that you cannot relax, especially because you are thinking about something pleasant that is going to happen to you. わくわくした □ *I was excited about the possibility of playing football again.* 私はまたサッカーができると思うとわくわくした． ● **ex|cit|ed|ly** ADV 副詞 [ADV with v] わくわくして □ *"You're coming?" he said excitedly. "That's fantastic! That's incredible!"* 「君も来るの?」と彼は興奮して言った．「そりゃすごい！信じられない！」 **2** ADJ 形容詞 If you are **excited**, you are worried or angry about something, and so you are very alert and cannot relax. 取り乱した，気が立った □ *I don't think there's any reason to get excited about inflation.* インフレに関して心配する理由は何もないと思います． ● **ex|cit|ed|ly** ADV 副詞 [ADV with v] 気が立って □ *Larry rose excitedly to the edge of his seat, shook a fist at us and spat.* ラリーは腹を立てて椅子の端まで前のめりになり，私たちに向かってこぶしを振り，つばを吐いた．

ex|cite|ment /ɪksaɪtmənt/ (excitements) N-VAR 可変性名詞 You use **excitement** to refer to the state of being excited, or to something that excites you. 興奮 □ *Everyone is in a state of great excitement.* だれもかれもひどい興奮状態である．

ex|cit|ing /ɪksaɪtɪŋ/ ADJ 形容詞 If something is **exciting**, it makes you feel very happy or enthusiastic. わくわくさせる，刺激的な □ *The race itself is very exciting.* レースそのものが非常にエキサイティングだ．

Word Link	claim, clam ≈ shouting : ac**claim**, **clam**or, ex**claim**

ex|claim /ɪkskleɪm/ (exclaims, exclaiming, exclaimed) V-T 動詞 Writers sometimes use **exclaim** to show that someone is speaking suddenly, loudly, or emphatically, often because they are excited, shocked, or angry. 叫ぶ □ *"He went back to the lab," Inez exclaimed impatiently.* 「彼は実験室に戻りました」とイネズはいらだったようにに叫んだ．

ex|cla|ma|tion /ɛkskləmeɪʃ³n/ (exclamations) N-COUNT 可算名詞 An **exclamation** is a sound, word, or sentence that is spoken suddenly, loudly, or emphatically and that expresses excitement, admiration, shock, or anger. 突然の叫び声 □ *Sue gave an exclamation as we got a clear sight of the house.* その家がはっきり見えたとき，スーは突然叫び声を上げた．

ex|cla|ma|tion point (exclamation points) also **exclamation mark** N-COUNT 可算名詞 An **exclamation point** is the sign ! which is used in writing to show that a word, phrase, or sentence is an exclamation. 感嘆符 (! の記号)

ex|clude /ɪksklud/ (excludes, excluding, excluded) **1** V-T 動詞 If you **exclude** someone **from** a place or activity, you prevent them from entering it or taking part in it. 締め出す，仲間はずれにする □ *Many of the youngsters feel excluded.* その若者たちの多くが孤独感を感じている． **2** V-T 他動詞 If you **exclude** something that has some connection with what you are doing, you deliberately do not use it or consider it. 除外する □ *In some schools, Christmas carols are being modified to exclude any reference to Christ.* 学校によっては，クリスマスキャロルがキリストへの言及を除くように修正されてきている． **3** V-T 他動詞 To **exclude** a possibility means to decide or prove that it is wrong and not worth considering. (可能性を) 排除する [usu with brd-neg] □ *I cannot entirely exclude the possibility that some form of pressure was applied to the neck.* 私は何らかの圧力が首にかけられたという可能性を完全に排除できない． **4** V-T 他動詞 To **exclude** something such as the sun's rays or harmful germs means to prevent them physically from reaching or entering a particular place. 防止する □ *This was intended to exclude the direct rays of the sun.* これは直射日光防止用だった．

ex|clud|ing /ɪkskludɪŋ/ PREP 前置詞 You use **excluding** before mentioning a person or thing to show that you are not including them in your statement. 除いて □ *Excluding water, half of the body's weight is protein.* 水分を除くと，体重の半分はたんぱく質だ．

ex|clu|sion /ɪksklʊʒ³n/ (exclusions) **1** N-VAR 可変性名詞 The **exclusion** of something is the act of deliberately not using, allowing, or considering it. 除外，排除 □ *It calls for the exclusion of all commercial lending institutions from the college loan program.* それは全ての民間貸出機関を大学ローン計画から除外することを求めています． **2** N-UNCOUNT 不可算名詞 **Exclusion** is the act of preventing someone from entering a place or taking part in an activity. 排斥 □ *...women's exclusion from political power.* 政治権力からの女性排斥 **3** PHRASE 句 If you do one thing **to the exclusion of** something else, you only do the first thing and do not do the second thing at all. ～を除外して □ *Diane had dedicated her life to caring for him to the exclusion of all else.* ダイアンはほかの全てを投げ出して，彼の介護に人生をささげた．

ex|clu|sive /ɪksklusɪv/ (exclusives) **1** ADJ 形容詞 If you describe something as **exclusive**, you mean that it is limited to people who have a lot of money or who are privileged, and is therefore not available to everyone. 上流向けの，高級な □ *It used to be a private, exclusive club, and now it's open to all New Yorkers.* かつては私営の高級クラブだったが，今では全てのニューヨーク市民に開放

されている。 **2** ADJ 形容詞 Something that is **exclusive** is used or owned by only one person or group, and not shared with anyone else. 独占的な。 ❑ *Our group will have exclusive use of a 60-foot boat.* 我々のグループは60フィートのボートを専用する予定だ。 **3** 形容詞 If a newspaper, magazine, or broadcasting organization describes one of its reports as **exclusive**, they mean it is a special report that does not appear in any other publication or on any other channel. (記事など) 独占の ❑ *He told the magazine in an exclusive interview: "All my problems stem from drinking."* 彼はその雑誌社の独占インタビューで「僕の問題の全ては飲酒のせいだ」と言った。 ● N-COUNT 可算名詞 An **exclusive** is an exclusive article or report. 独占記事、スクープ ❑ *Some papers thought they had an exclusive.* 自社が独占記事をものにしたと思った新聞社もあった。 **4** ADJ 形容詞 If a company states that its prices, goods, or services are **exclusive of** something, that thing is not included in the stated price, although it usually still has to be paid for. 除いて ❑ *...the average cost of a three-course dinner exclusive of tax, tip and beverage.* 税金、チップ、飲み物分を除いた3品料理のディナーの平均料金。 **5** PHRASE 句 If two things are **mutually exclusive**, they are separate and very different from each other, so that it is impossible for them to exist or happen together. 両立しない ❑ *They both have learned that ambition and successful fatherhood can be mutually exclusive.* 出世欲と立派な父親であることは相入れないものでありうることを彼ら両人は知った。

ex|clu|sive|ly /ɪksklúːsɪvli/ ADV 副詞 **Exclusively** is used to refer to situations or activities that involve only the thing or things mentioned, and nothing else. もっぱら、独占的に ❑ *...an exclusively male domain.* もっぱら男性の領分

ex|crete /ɪkskríːt/ (**excretes, excreting, excreted**) V-T 他動詞 When a person or animal **excretes** waste matter from their body, they get rid of it in feces, urine, or sweat. 排せつする [FORMAL 形式ばった] ❑ *Your open pores excrete sweat and dirt.* 開いた毛穴が汗とあかを排出する。

ex|cru|ci|at|ing /ɪkskrúːʃieɪtɪŋ/ ADJ 形容詞 If you describe something as **excruciating**, you are emphasizing that it is extremely painful, either physically or emotionally. 耐えがたい [EMPHASIS 強調] ❑ *I was in excruciating pain and one leg wouldn't move.* 私は耐えがたい痛みがあり、どうしても片足が動かなかった。

ex|cur|sion /ɪkskɜ́rʒən/ (**excursions**) **1** N-COUNT 可算名詞 You can refer to a short trip as an **excursion**, especially if it is taken for pleasure or enjoyment. 遠足、小旅行 ❑ *In Bermuda, Sam's father took him on an excursion to a coral barrier.* バミューダ島では父親がサムをサンゴ礁まで遠足に連れていった。 **2** N-COUNT 可算名詞 An **excursion** is a trip or visit to an interesting place, especially one that is arranged or recommended by a travel agency or tourist organization. 観光旅行 ❑ *Another pleasant excursion is Matamoros, 18 miles away.* もう1つの楽しい観光旅行は18マイル先のマタモーロス行きです。

ex|cuse (**excuses, excusing, excused**)

The noun is pronounced /ɪkskjúːs/. The verb is pronounced /ɪkskjúːz/.

名詞は /ɪkskjúːs/ と発音される。 動詞は /ɪkskjúːz/ と発音される。

1 N-COUNT 可算名詞 An **excuse** is a reason that you give in order to explain why something has been done or has not been done, or in order to avoid doing something. 言い訳、口実 ❑ *It is easy to find excuses for his indecisiveness.* 彼の優柔不断さの言い訳を見つけるのはたやすい。 ❑ *If you stop making excuses and do it you'll wonder what took you so long.* 言い訳ばかりしていそれをやってみれば、なぜもっと早くしなかったんだろうと思うよ。 PHRASE 句 ● If you say that there is **no excuse for** something, you are emphasizing that it should not happen, or expressing disapproval that it has happened. 弁解の余地はない [DISAPPROVAL 不賛成] ❑ *There's no excuse for behavior like that.* あんな振る舞いには弁解の余地はない。 **2** V-T 他動詞 To **excuse** someone or **excuse** their behavior means to provide reasons for their actions, especially when other people disapprove of these actions. 言い訳をする ❑ *He excused himself by saying he was "forced to rob to maintain my wife and cat."* 彼は「妻と猫を養うためには強盗せざるをえな」かったと弁解した。 **3** V-T 他動詞 If you **excuse** someone **for** something wrong that they have done, you forgive them for it. 許す ❑ *Many people might have excused them for shirking some of their responsibilities.* 多くの人は彼らが責任の1部を回避したのを許したかもしれないだろう。 **4** V-T 他動詞 If someone **is excused from** a duty or responsibility, they are told that they do not have to carry it out. 免除する [usu passive] ❑ *She is usually excused from her duties during summer vacation.* 通常彼女は夏休みの間は務めを免除される。 **5** V-T 他動詞 If you **excuse yourself**, you use a phrase such as "Excuse me" as a polite way of saying that you are about to leave. 退出を断る ❑ *He excused himself and went up to his room.* 彼は一言断って自分の部屋に行った。 **6** CONVENTION 慣習表現 You say "**Excuse me**" when you want to politely get someone's attention, especially when you are about to ask them a question. 失礼ですが [FORMULAE 決まり文句] ❑ *Excuse me, but are you Mr.*

Honig? 失礼ですが、ホーニッグさんですか。 **7** CONVENTION 慣習表現 You use **excuse me** to apologize to someone when you have disturbed or interrupted them. すみません [FORMULAE 決まり文句] ❑ *Excuse me interrupting, but there's something I need to say.* 話の腰を折るようで恐縮ですが、言わなきゃいけないことがあるんです。 **8** CONVENTION 慣習表現 You use **excuse me** or a phrase such as **if you'll excuse me** as a polite way of indicating that you are about to leave or that you are about to stop talking to someone. 失礼します [POLITENESS 丁寧さ] ❑ *"Excuse me," she said to José, and left the room.* します」と彼女はホセに言い、部屋を出た。 **9** CONVENTION 慣習表現 You use **excuse me, but** to indicate that you are about to disagree with someone. すみませんが ❑ *Excuse me, but I want to know what all this has to do with us.* すみませんが、これがみんな私たちとどんな関係があるのか知りたいものです。 **10** PHRASE 句 You say **excuse me** to apologize when you have bumped into someone, or when you need to move past someone in a crowd. 失礼 [FORMULAE 決まり文句] ❑ *Saying excuse me, Seaton pushed his way into the crowded living room.* 「失礼」と言いながら、シートンは込み合った居間に人を押し分けて入った。 **11** CONVENTION 慣習表現 You say **excuse me** to apologize when you have done something slightly embarrassing or impolite, such as burping, hiccuping, or sneezing. 失礼、すみません [FORMULAE 決まり文句] **12** CONVENTION 慣習表現 You say "**Excuse me?**" to show that you want someone to repeat what they have just said. もう1度言ってください、何ですって [AM 米国英語; FORMULAE 決まり文句] ❑ *"Excuse me?" Kate said, not sure she'd heard correctly.* 「何ですって」とケイトは自分がちゃんと聞いたのか確信が持てずに言った。

Thesaurus		*excuse* また次を参照:
N.	apology, explanation, reason	**1**
V.	forgive, pardon, spare; (ant.) accuse, blame, punish	**3**

ex-directory ADJ 形容詞 If a person or their telephone number is **ex-directory**, the number is not listed in the telephone directory, and the telephone company will not give it to people who ask for it. 電話帳に載っていない [BRIT 英国英語; AM **unlisted** 米国英語]

exec /ɪgzék/ (**execs**) N-COUNT 可算名詞 **Exec** is an abbreviation for executive. 管理職の [INFORMAL くだけた]

ex|ecute /éksɪkjuːt/ (**executes, executing, executed**) **1** V-T 他動詞 To **execute** someone means to kill them as a punishment for a serious crime. 死刑を執行する ❑ *He said nobody had been executed as a direct result of the events.* 彼はそれらの出来事の直接的な結果として誰も処刑されてないと述べた。 ❑ *One group claimed to have executed the hostage.* 1つのグループが人質を処刑したと公言した。 ● **ex|ecu|tion** /éksɪkjúːʃən/ (**executions**) N-VAR 可変性名詞 処刑 ❑ *Execution by lethal injection is scheduled for July 30th.* 薬物注射による処刑が7月30日に予定されています。 **2** V-T 他動詞 If you **execute** a plan, you carry it out. 実行する [FORMAL 形式ばった] ❑ *We are going to execute our campaign plan to the letter.* 我々はキャンペーン計画をそのまま厳密に実行するつもりだ。 ● **ex|ecu|tion** N-UNCOUNT 不可算名詞 遂行 ❑ *U.S. forces are fully prepared for the execution of any action once the order is given by the president.* 米軍は大統領から命令があり次第どのような行動でも遂行する準備が完全に整っている。 **3** V-T 他動詞 If you **execute** a difficult action or movement, you successfully perform it. 達成する ❑ *The landing was skilfully executed.* 着陸はうまくいった。

ex|ecu|tive /ɪgzékjətɪv/ (**executives**) **1** N-COUNT 可算名詞 An **executive** is someone who is employed by a business at a senior level. Executives decide what the business should do, and ensure that it is done. 管理職、重役 ❑ *...an advertising executive.* 宣伝担当重役 **2** ADJ 形容詞 The **executive** sections and tasks of an organization are concerned with the making of decisions and with ensuring that decisions are carried out. 管理職の [ADJ n] ❑ *A successful job search needs to be as well organised as any other executive task.* 職探しを成功させるためには、他の管理職の仕事と同じようにしっかり計画準備しておく必要がある。 **3** ADJ 形容詞 **Executive** goods are expensive products designed or intended for executives and other people at a similar social or economic level. 重役用の [ADJ n] ❑ *...an executive briefcase.* 重役用書類かばん。 **4** N-SING 単数名詞 The **executive** committee or board of an organization is a committee within that organization that has the authority to make decisions and ensures that these decisions are carried out. 執行部 ['the' N, n n] ❑ *They opted to put an executive committee in charge of the project rather than a single person.* 彼らは個人よりは執行委員会にその事業を担当させることを選んだ。 **5** N-SING 単数名詞 The **executive** is the part of the government of a country that is concerned with carrying out decisions or orders, as opposed to the part that makes laws or the part that deals with criminals. 行政府 ['the' N, n n] ❑ *The government, the executive and the judiciary are supposed to be separate.* 政府、行政、司法は分離しているべきものである。

ex|em|pla|ry /ɪgzémpləri/ ADJ 形容詞 If you describe someone or something as **exemplary**, you think they are extremely good.

模範的な ▢*Underpinning this success has been an exemplary record of innovation.* この成功は革新の模範的な経歴が土台になっている.

ex|em|pli|fy /ɪgzɛmplɪfaɪ/ (**exemplifies, exemplifying, exemplified**) V-T 他動詞 If a person or thing **exemplifies** something such as a situation, quality, or class of things, they are a typical example of it. 例示する [FORMAL 形式ばった] ▢*The room's style exemplifies their ideal of "beauty and practicality."* その部屋の様式は彼らの理想とする「美と実用性」を例示している.

ex|empt /ɪgzɛmpt/ (**exempts, exempting, exempted**) **1** ADJ 形容詞 If someone or something is **exempt from** a particular rule, duty, or obligation, they do not have to follow it or do it. 免除された ▢*Men in college were exempt from military service.* 大学在学中の男性は兵役を免除された. **2** V-T 他動詞 To **exempt** a person or thing **from** a particular rule, duty, or obligation means to state officially that they are not bound or affected by it. 免除する ▢*South Carolina claimed the government had the power to exempt its citizens from the obligation to obey federal law.* 南カロライナ州はその市民が連邦法に従う義務を免除する権限を主張した. ●**ex|emp|tion** /ɪgzɛmpʃⁿn/ (**exemptions**) N-VAR 可変性名詞 [oft n 'from' n] 免除 ▢*...the exemption of employer-provided health insurance from taxation.* 雇い主が提供する健康保険の課税免除.

ex|er|cise /ɛksərsaɪz/ (**exercises, exercising, exercised**) **1** V-T 他動詞 If you **exercise** something such as your authority, your rights, or a good quality, you use it or put it into effect. 行使する [FORMAL 形式ばった] ▢*They are merely exercising their right to free speech.* 彼らは単に言論の自由の権利を行使しているだけです. ●N-SING 単数名詞 **Exercise** is also a noun. 行使 ▢*Social structures are maintained through the exercise of political and economic power.* 社会構造は政治力や経済力を行使することにより維持されている. **2** V-I 自動詞 When you **exercise**, you move your body energetically in order to get in shape and to remain healthy. 運動する ▢*She exercises two or three times a week.* 彼女は週に2, 3回運動する. ●N-UNCOUNT 不可算名詞 **Exercise** is also a noun. 運動 ▢*Lack of exercise can lead to feelings of depression and exhaustion.* 運動不足はうつ感や疲労感を招くことがある. **3** V-T 他動詞 If a movement or activity **exercises** a part of your body, it keeps it strong, healthy, or in good condition. 働かせる ▢*They call rowing the perfect sport. It exercises every major muscle group.* 彼らはボート漕ぎは完璧なスポーツだと言っている. 全ての主要な筋肉群を使うのからだ. **4** N-COUNT 可算名詞 **Exercises** are a series of movements or actions that you do in order to get in shape, remain healthy, or practice for a particular physical activity. 体操 ▢*I do special neck and shoulder exercises.* わたしは首と肩の特別な体操をする. **5** N-COUNT 可算名詞 **Exercises** are military activities and operations that are not part of a real war, but that allow the armed forces to practice for a real war. 演習 [usu pl, also 'on' N] ▢*General Powell predicted that in the future it might even be possible to stage joint military exercises.* パウエル大将は, 将来は共同軍事演習を行うことも可能かもしれないと予言した. **6** N-COUNT 可算名詞 An **exercise** is a short activity or piece of work that you do, in school for example, which is designed to help you learn a particular skill. 課題 ▢*Try working through the opening exercises in this chapter.* この章の最初の課題をやってしまうようにしなさい.
→ see **muscle**

Thesaurus	exercise また次を参照:
V.	practice, use **1**
	work out **2**

ex|ert /ɪgzɜrt/ (**exerts, exerting, exerted**) **1** V-T 他動詞 If someone or something **exerts** influence, authority, or pressure, they use it in a strong or determined way, especially in order to produce a particular effect. (影響などを) 及ぼす, ふるう [FORMAL 形式ばった] ▢*He exerted considerable influence on the thinking of the scientific community on these issues.* 彼はこれらの問題に関する科学者たちの考え方にかなりの影響を及ぼした. **2** V-T 他動詞 If you **exert yourself**, you make a great physical or mental effort, or work hard to do something. 努力する ▢*Do not exert yourself unnecessarily.* 必要のない努力はするな. ●**ex|er|tion** /ɪgzɜrʃⁿn/ (**exertions**) N-UNCOUNT 不可算名詞 [also N in pl] 努力 ▢*He clearly found the physical exertion exhilarating.* 明らかに彼は体を使うのを爽快 (そうかい) だと感じたのだ.
→ see **motion**

ex|hale /ɛkshеɪl/ (**exhales, exhaling, exhaled**) V-T/V-I 他動詞/自動詞 When you **exhale**, you breathe out the air that is in your lungs. 息を吐き出す [FORMAL 形式ばった] ▢*Hold your breath for a moment and exhale.* しばらく息を止めてから息を吐き出しなさい.
→ see **respiratory**

ex|haust /ɪgzɔst/ (**exhausts, exhausting, exhausted**) **1** V-T 他動詞 If something **exhausts** you, it makes you so tired, either physically or mentally, that you have no energy left. 疲れ果てさせる ▢*Don't exhaust him.* 彼をへとへとにするな. ●**ex|haust|ed** ADJ 形容詞 疲れ果てた ▢*She was too exhausted and distressed to talk*

about the tragedy. その惨事について話すには彼女は疲れ過ぎ悲し み過ぎていた. ●**ex|haust|ing** ADJ 形容詞 とても疲れさせる ▢*It was an exhausting schedule she had set herself.* 彼女が自分で立てた計画はとても疲れるものであった. **2** V-T 他動詞 If you **exhaust** something such as money or food, you use or finish it all. 使い果たす ▢*We have exhausted all our material resources.* 私たちは物的資源を全て使い果たしました. **3** V-T 他動詞 If you **have exhausted** a subject or topic, you have talked about it so much that there is nothing more to say about it. 述べつくす ▢*She and Chantal must have exhausted the subject of clothes.* 彼女とシャンタルは洋服について述べつくしたに違いない. **4** N-UNCOUNT 不可算名詞 [also N in pl] **Exhaust** is the gas or steam that is produced when the engine of a vehicle is running. 排気ガス ▢*...the exhaust from a car engine.* 自動車のエンジンの排気ガス. ▢*The city's streets are filthy and choked with exhaust fumes.* 同市の街路は汚くて排気ガスでいっぱいだった. **5** N-COUNT 可算名詞 The **exhaust** is the same as the **exhaust pipe**. 排気管 [BRIT 英国英語]
→ see **engine, pollution**

ex|haus|tion /ɪgzɔstʃn/ N-UNCOUNT 不可算名詞 **Exhaustion** is the state of being so tired that you have no energy left. 極度の疲労 ▢*He is suffering from exhaustion.* 彼は疲労困憊 (こんぱい) している.

ex|haus|tive /ɪgzɔstɪv/ ADJ 形容詞 If you describe a study, search, or list as **exhaustive**, you mean that it is very thorough and complete. 余すところのない ▢*This is by no means an exhaustive list but it gives an indication of the many projects taking place.* これは全てを網羅した一覧表だとは言えないが, 数多くの事業が行われていることを示すものである. ●**ex|haus|tive|ly** ADV 副詞 徹底的に ▢*Martin said these costs were scrutinized exhaustively by independent accountants.* マーティンはこれらの経費は独立会計士によって徹底的に詳細調査されていると言った.

ex|hib|it /ɪgzɪbɪt/ (**exhibits, exhibiting, exhibited**) **1** V-T 他動詞 If someone or something shows a particular quality, feeling, or type of behavior, you can say that they **exhibit** it. 示す [FORMAL 形式ばった] ▢*He has exhibited symptoms of anxiety and overwhelming worry.* 彼は不安でどうしようもなく心配している兆候を示している. **2** V-T 他動詞 When a painting, sculpture, or object of interest **is exhibited**, it is put in a public place such as a museum or art gallery so that people can come to look at it. You can also say that animals **are exhibited** in a zoo. 展示する, 公開する [usu passive] ▢*His work was exhibited in the best galleries in America, Europe and Asia.* 彼の作品はアメリカ, ヨーロッパ, アジアの一流美術館に展示された. ●**ex|hi|bi|tion** N-UNCOUNT 不可算名詞 展示, 公開 ▢*Five large pieces of the wall are currently on exhibition.* 壁の大きな断片が5つ現在公開されています. **3** V-I 自動詞 When artists **exhibit**, they show their work in public. 出品する ▢*He has also exhibited at galleries and museums in New York and Washington.* 彼はニューヨークやワシントンの美術館や博物館にも出品した. **4** N-COUNT 可算名詞 An **exhibit** is a painting, sculpture, or object of interest that is displayed to the public in a museum or art gallery. 出品物 ▢*Shona showed me around the exhibits.* ショーナは私に出品物を案内してまわってくれた. **5** N-COUNT 可算名詞 An **exhibit** is a public display of paintings, sculpture, or objects of interest in a museum or art gallery. 展覧会 [AM 米国英語] ▢*...an exhibit at the Metropolitan Museum of Art.* メトロポリタン美術館の展覧会. **6** N-COUNT 可算名詞 An **exhibit** is an object that a lawyer shows in court as evidence in a legal case. 証拠物件 ▢*The jury has already asked to see more than 40 exhibits from the trial.* 陪審は裁判の証拠物件をすでに40件以上見るように言われていた.

ex|hi|bi|tion /ɛksɪbɪʃⁿn/ (**exhibitions**) **1** N-COUNT 可算名詞 An **exhibition** is a public event at which pictures, sculptures, or other objects of interest are displayed, for example at a museum or art gallery. 展覧会, 展示会 ▢*...an exhibition of expressionist art.* 表現派芸術の展覧会. **2** N-SING 単数名詞 An **exhibition of** a particular skillful activity is a display or example of it that people notice or admire. 披露 ▢*He responded in champion's style by treating the fans to an exhibition of power and speed.* 彼はファンに力と速度を披露して優勝者らしく応えた. **3** → see also **exhibit 2**

ex|hi|bi|tion game (**exhibition games**) N-COUNT 可算名詞 In sports, an **exhibition game** is a game that is not part of a competition, and is played for entertainment or practice, often without any serious effort to win. 模範試合 [AM 米国英語]

ex|hib|i|tor /ɪgzɪbɪtər/ (**exhibitors**) N-COUNT 可算名詞 An **exhibitor** is a person or company whose work or products are being shown in an exhibition. 出品者 ▢*Schedules will be sent out to all exhibitors.* 全ての出品者に予定表が送られる.

ex|hil|ar|at|ing /ɪgzɪləreɪtɪŋ/ ADJ 形容詞 If you describe an experience or feeling as **exhilarating**, you mean that it makes you feel very happy and excited. 陽気にさせる ▢*It was exhilarating to be on the road again and his spirits rose.* 再び旅に出るのを心を浮き立たせるもので, 彼は元気が出た.

ex|hila|ra|tion /ɪgzɪləreɪʃⁿn/ N-UNCOUNT 不可算名詞 **Exhilaration** is a strong feeling of excitement and happiness. 爽快 (そうかい) な気分 興奮 ▢*The exhilaration of winning such a famous*

event has stayed with him. そのように有名な競技で優勝したという興奮が彼に残っていた.

ex|ile /ɛksaɪl, ɛgz-/ (**exiles, exiling, exiled**) 1 N-UNCOUNT 不可算名詞 If someone is living **in exile**, they are living in a foreign country because they cannot live in their own country, usually for political reasons. 亡命 ❑ He is now living in exile in Egypt. 彼は今エジプトで亡命生活を送っています. ❑ He returned from exile earlier this year. 彼は今年の早い時期に亡命から帰還しました. 2 V-T 他動詞 If someone **is exiled**, they are living in a foreign country because they cannot live in their own country, usually for political reasons. 国外追放する ❑ His second wife, Hilary, had been widowed, then exiled from South Africa. 彼の2人目の妻であるヒラリーは前夫と死別し、その後南アフリカから追放されていた. ❑ They threatened to exile her in southern Spain. スペイン南部で彼女は国外に追放にすると脅された. 3 N-COUNT 可算名詞 An **exile** is someone who has been exiled. 亡命者 ❑ He is also an exile, a native of Palestine who has long given up the idea of going home. 彼もパレスチナ生まれで故郷に戻るのはとっくにあきらめている亡命者の1人である. 4 V-T 他動詞 If you say that someone **has been exiled from** a particular place or situation, you mean that they have been sent away from it or removed from it against their will. 追放する [usu passive] ❑ He served less than a year of a five-year prison sentence, but was permanently exiled from the sport. 彼は懲役5年の判決の刑期を1年足らずつとめたが、その競技からは永久追放された. ● N-UNCOUNT 不可算名詞 **Exile** is also a noun. 追放 ❑ ...the Left's long exile from power from 1958 to 1981. 1958年から1981年までの長期間左派が政権から追放されていたこと.

ex|ist /ɪgzɪst/ (**exists, existing, existed**) 1 V-I 自動詞 If something **exists**, it is present in the world as a real thing. ある、実在する [no cont] ❑ He thought that if he couldn't see something, it didn't exist. 彼は目に見えないものは実在しないと思っていた. ❑ Research opportunities exist in a wide range of areas. 研究する機会は広範な分野に存在する. 2 V-I 自動詞 To **exist** means to live, especially under difficult conditions or with very little food or money. やっと生きてゆく ❑ I was barely existing. 私は生きてゆくのがやっとだった. ❑ Some people exist on melons or coconuts for weeks at a time. 1度に数週間にわたりメロンやココナッツで生き延びている人たちもいる.

ex|ist|ence /ɪgzɪstəns/ (**existences**) 1 N-UNCOUNT 不可算名詞 The **existence** of something is the fact that it is present in the world as a real thing. 存在 ❑ ...the existence of other galaxies. 他の銀河の存在. ❑ Public worries about accidents are threatening the very existence of the nuclear power industry. 事故についての公衆の心配が原子力産業の存在そのものを脅かしている. 2 N-COUNT 可算名詞 You can refer to someone's way of life as an **existence**, especially when they live under difficult conditions. 生活、暮らし ❑ You may be stuck with a miserable existence for the rest of your life. あなたは今後一生惨めな暮らしを送り続けることになるかもしれない.

ex|ist|ing /ɪgzɪstɪŋ/ ADJ 形容詞 **Existing** is used to describe something that is now present, available, or in operation, especially when you are contrasting it with something that is planned for the future. 現存する [ADJ n] ❑ ...the need to improve existing products and develop new lines. 今ある製品を改良し新しい品目の開発をする必要性. ❑ Existing timbers are replaced or renewed. 使ってある材木は取り替えるか新しくする.

exit /ɛgzɪt, ɛksɪt/ (**exits, exiting, exited**) 1 N-COUNT 可算名詞 The **exit** is the door through which you can leave a public building. (公共の建物の) 出口 ❑ He picked up the case and walked toward the exit. 彼は箱を手に取り、出口に向かって歩いた. 2 N-COUNT 可算名詞 An **exit** on a highway is a place where traffic can leave it. (高速道路の) 出口 ❑ She continued to the next exit, got off the highway and pulled into a parking lot. 彼女は次の出口まで行き、高速道路を降りて駐車場に車を止めた. 3 N-COUNT 可算名詞 If you refer to someone's **exit**, you are referring to the way that they left a room or building, or the fact that they left it. 退出 [FORMAL 形式ばった] ❑ I made a hasty exit and managed to open the gate. 私はあわてて退出し、なんとか門を開けた. 4 N-COUNT 可算名詞 If you refer to someone's **exit**, you are referring to the way that

they left a situation or activity, or the fact that they left it. 退場、退去 [FORMAL 形式ばった] ❑ It's her earliest exit from Wimbledon since going out in the opening round in 1997. 1997年に開幕戦で負けて以来の彼女のウィンブルドンからの最も早い退場である. 5 V-T/V-I 他動詞/自動詞 If you **exit** from a room or building, you leave it. 出て行く、退去する [FORMAL 形式ばった] ❑ She exits into the tropical storm. 彼女は台風が吹き荒れる外に出た. ❑ As I exited the final display, I entered a hexagonal room. 最後の展示を出ると、私は六角形の部屋に入った. 6 V-T 他動詞 If you **exit** a computer program or system, you stop running it. 終了する [COMPUTING コンピューティング] ❑ I can open other applications without having to exit WordPerfect. 私はワードパーフェクトを終了しなくても、他のアプリケーションを開くことができる. ● N-SING 単数名詞 **Exit** is also a noun. 終了 ❑ Press Exit to return to your document. あなたの文書に戻るには「終了」を押してください.

exit visa (**exit visas**) N-COUNT 可算名詞 An **exit visa** is an official stamp in someone's passport, or an official document, which allows them to leave the country that they are visiting or living in. 出国査証

exo|dus /ɛksədəs/ N-SING 単数名詞 If there is an **exodus of** people **from** a place, a lot of people leave that place at the same time. 集団的出国 ❑ The medical system is facing collapse because of an exodus of doctors. 医師の大流出のため医療制度は崩壊に直面している.

ex|or|bi|tant /ɪgzɔrbɪtənt/ ADJ 形容詞 If you describe something such as a price or fee as **exorbitant**, you are emphasizing that it is much higher than it should be. 途方もない、法外な [EMPHASIS 強調] ❑ Exorbitant housing prices have created an acute shortage of affordable housing for the poor. 住宅価格が法外なために、貧民に手の届く住宅が深刻な不足状態になっている.

ex|ot|ic /ɪgzɒtɪk/ ADJ 形容詞 Something that is **exotic** is unusual and interesting, usually because it comes from or is related to a distant country. 異国情緒の、エキゾチックな ❑ ...brilliantly colored, exotic flowers. 色鮮やかでエキゾティックな花. ● **ex|oti|cal|ly** ADV 副詞 異国風に ❑ ...exotically beautiful scenery. 異国情緒にあふれていて美しい景色.

ex|pand /ɪkspænd/ (**expands, expanding, expanded**) 1 V-T/V-I 他動詞/自動詞 If something **expands** or **is expanded**, it becomes larger. 膨張させる、膨張する ❑ Engineers noticed that the pipes were not expanding as expected. 技師たちは管が予想したほど膨張していないことに気づいた. ❑ We have to expand the size of the image. 我々はその画像を拡大しなければならない. 2 V-T/V-I 他動詞/自動詞 If something such as a business, organization, or service **expands**, or if you **expand** it, it becomes bigger and includes more people, goods, or activities. 発達させる、拡張する [BUSINESS 実業] ❑ The popular ceramics industry expanded toward the middle of the 19th century. 大衆向けの窯業が19世紀の中ごろにかけて発達した.
▶ **expand on** or **expand upon** PHRASAL VERB 句動詞 If you **expand on** or **expand upon** something, you give more information or details about it when you write or talk about it. さらに詳しく述べる ❑ The president used today's speech to expand on remarks he made last month. 大統領は先月の発言についてさらに詳しく述べることに本日の演説を費やした.

ex|panse /ɪkspæns/ (**expanses**) N-COUNT 可算名詞 An **expanse** of something, usually sea, sky, or land, is a very large amount of it. 広がり ❑ ...a vast expanse of grassland. 果てしなく広がる草原.

ex|pan|sion /ɪkspænʃᵊn/ (**expansions**) N-VAR 可変性名詞 **Expansion** is the process of becoming greater in size, number, or amount. 拡大、膨張 ❑ ...the rapid expansion of private health insurance. 民間の健康保険の急速な増加.

ex|pan|sive /ɪkspænsɪv/ ADJ 形容詞 If you are **expansive**, you talk a lot, or are friendly or generous, because you are feeling happy and relaxed. 開放的な ❑ He was becoming more expansive as he relaxed. 彼は緊張が解けるといっそう開放的になりだした.

ex|pat|ri|ate /ɛkspeɪtriət, -pæt-/ (**expatriates**) N-COUNT 可算名詞 An **expatriate** is someone who is living in a country that is not their own. 国外在住者 ❑ ...British expatriates in Spain. スペインに住む英国人. ● ADJ 形容詞 **Expatriate** is also an adjective. 国外在住者の [ADJ n] ❑ The expatriate vote could help determine who wins in November. 11月の勝者を決定するのに国外在住者の票が1役買うかもしれない.

ex|pect /ɪkspɛkt/ (**expects, expecting, expected**) 1 V-T 他動詞 If you **expect** something to happen, you believe that it will happen. 予期する、思う ❑ ...a workman who expects to lose his job in the next few weeks. この数週間で失業すると思っている労働者. ❑ The talks are expected to continue until tomorrow. 話し合いは明日まで続くと思われます. 2 V-T 他動詞 If you **are expecting** something or someone, you believe that they will be delivered to you or come to you soon, often because this has been arranged earlier. 来るだろうと思う [usu cont] ❑ I wasn't expecting a visitor. 私は客が来るとは思っていなかった.

Do not confuse **expect**, **wait for**, and **look forward to**. When you are **expecting** someone or something, you think that the person or thing is going to arrive or that the thing is going to happen.❑ *I sent a postcard so they were expecting me…We are expecting rain.* When you **wait for** someone or something, you stay in the same place until the person arrives or the thing happens.❑ *Whisky was served while we waited for him …We got off the plane and waited for our luggage.* When you **look forward to** something that is going to happen, you feel happy because you think you will enjoy it.❑ *I'll bet you're looking forward to your holidays… I always looked forward to seeing her.*

❸ V-T 他動詞 If you **expect** something, or **expect** a person **to do** something, you believe that it is your right to have that thing, or the person's duty to do it for you. 当然期待する ❑ *He wasn't expecting our hospitality.* 彼は私たちの歓待を受けるとは期待していなかった. ❑ *I do expect to have some time to myself in the evenings.* 私は毎晩自分の時間が多少持てることを本当に期待している. ❹ V-T 他動詞 If you tell someone not to **expect** something, you mean that the thing is unlikely to happen as they have planned or imagined, and they should not hope that it will. あてにする [with brd-neg] ❑ *Don't expect an instant cure.* すぐに治るとは思わないように. ❑ *You cannot expect to like all the people you will work with.* 一緒に働く人たち全員を好きになるなんて無理だ. ❺ V-T/V-I 他動詞/自動詞 If you say that a woman **is expecting** a baby, or that she **is expecting**, you mean that she is pregnant. 妊娠している [only cont] ❑ *She was expecting another baby.* 彼女は次の子が生まれる予定だった. ❻ PHRASE 句 You say "**I expect**" to suggest that a statement is probably correct, or a natural consequence of the present situation, although you have no definite knowledge. 思う [SPOKEN 口語] ❑ *I expect you can guess what follows.* あなたは次に何か来るか分かるでしょう. ❑ *I expect you're tired.* あなたは疲れたでしょう.

ex|pec|tan|cy /ɪkspɛktənsi/ N-UNCOUNT 不可算名詞
Expectancy is the feeling or hope that something exciting, interesting, or good is about to happen. 期待 ❑ *The supporters had a tremendous air of expectancy.* 応援者たちはものすごく期待に満ちた様子だった.

ex|pec|tant /ɪkspɛktənt/ ❶ ADJ 形容詞 If someone is **expectant**, they are excited because they think something interesting is about to happen. 待ち設けている ❑ *An expectant crowd gathered.* 待ちかねている群集が集まった. ● **ex|pect|ant|ly** ADV 副詞 [ADV after v] ❑ *The others waited, looking at him expectantly.* 他の者たちは彼を期待に満ちた目で見つめながら待っていた. ❷ ADJ 形容詞 An **expectant** mother or father is someone whose baby is going to be born soon. 出産を待っている [ADJ n] ❑ *…a magazine for expectant mothers.* 妊婦のための雑誌.

ex|pec|ta|tion /ɛkspɛkteɪʃᵊn/ (expectations) ❶ N-UNCOUNT 不可算名詞 Your **expectations** are your strong hopes or beliefs that something will happen or that you will get something that you want. 期待 [also N in pl] ❑ *Their hope, and their expectation, was that she was going to be found safe and that she would be returned to her family.* 彼らが望みそして期待しているのは, 彼女が無事に見つかり家に戻ってくることだった. ❷ N-COUNT 可算名詞 A person's **expectations** are strong beliefs they have about the proper way someone should behave or something should happen. 期待 ❑ *Stephen Chase had determined to live up to the expectations of the company.* ステファン・チェースはあくまでも会社の期待にこたえるつもりだった.

Word Partnership *expectation* は次の語句と使われる:

N.	expectation **of privacy**, **sense of** expectation ❶
ADJ.	**reasonable** expectation, **realistic** expectation ❶ ❷

ex|pe|di|en|cy /ɪkspidiənsi/ N-UNCOUNT 不可算名詞
Expediency means doing what is convenient rather than what is morally right. 便宜 [FORMAL 形式ばった] ❑ *This was a matter less of morals than of expediency.* これは倫理よりも便宜の問題であった.

ex|pe|di|ent /ɪkspidiənt/ (expedients) ❶ N-COUNT 可算名詞 An **expedient** is an action that achieves a particular purpose, but may not be morally right. 手段 ❑ *The curfew regulation is a temporary expedient made necessary by a sudden emergency.* 夜間外出禁止令は突然の非常事態のため必要となった臨時処置である. ❷ ADJ 形容詞 If it is **expedient to** do something, it is useful or convenient to do it, even though it may not be morally right. 便宜の, 好都合の ❑ *Governments frequently ignore human rights abuses in other countries if it is politically expedient to do so.* 政府というものは, 他国での人権侵害を無視するのが政治的に得策であれば, しばしば無視する.

ex|pe|di|tion /ɛkspɪdɪʃᵊn/ (expeditions) ❶ N-COUNT 可算名詞 An **expedition** is an organized trip made for a particular purpose such as exploration. 探検 ❑ *…Byrd's 1928 expedition to Antarctica.* バードの1928年の南極探検. ❷ N-COUNT 可算名詞 You can refer to a group of people who are going on an expedition as an **expedition**.

探検隊 ❑ *Forty-three members of the expedition were killed.* 探検隊の43人が死亡した. ❸ N-COUNT 可算名詞 An **expedition** is a short trip that you make for pleasure. 小旅行, お出かけ ❑ *…Officer Goss was on a fishing expedition.* ゴス巡査は魚釣りに行っていた.

Word Link pel ≈ driving, forcing : compel, expel, propel

ex|pel /ɪkspɛl/ (expels, expelling, expelled) ❶ V-T 他動詞 If someone **is expelled from** a school or organization, they are officially told to leave because they have behaved badly. 退学させる, 除名する [usu passive] ❑ *More than five-thousand high school students have been expelled for cheating.* 不正行為で5千人以上の高校生が退学になりました. ❷ V-T 他動詞 If people **are expelled from** a place, they are made to leave it, often by force. 追放する, 追い払う ❑ *An American academic was expelled from the country yesterday.* 米国人の学者が昨日国外追放になった. ❑ *They were told that they should expel the refugees.* 彼らは難民を追放すべきだと言われた. ❸ V-T 他動詞 To **expel** something means to force it out from a container or from your body. 勢いよく排出する ❑ *As the lungs exhale this waste, gas is expelled into the atmosphere.* 肺がこの老廃物を吐き出すと, ガスが大気に勢いよく排出される.

ex|pend /ɪkspɛnd/ (expends, expending, expended) V-T 他動詞 To **expend** something, especially energy, time, or money, means to use it or spend it. 使う, 費やす [FORMAL 形式ばった] ❑ *Children expend a lot of energy and may need more high-energy food than adults.* 子供はエネルギーをたくさん使い, 大人より高エネルギー食品が必要かもしれない.

ex|pen|di|ture /ɪkspɛndɪtʃər/ (expenditures) N-VAR 可変性名詞 **Expenditure** is the spending of money on something, or the money that is spent on something. 支出, 経費 [FORMAL 形式ばった] ❑ *Policies of tax reduction must lead to reduced public expenditure.* 減税政策は公的支出の削減がなければならない.

ex|pense /ɪkspɛns/ (expenses) ❶ N-VAR 可変性名詞 **Expense** is the money that something costs you or that you need to spend in order to do something. 費用 ❑ *He's bought a big TV at vast expense so that everyone can see properly.* 彼はみんながちゃんと見られるように大きなテレビを大金を出して買った. ❷ N-PLURAL 複数名詞 **Expenses** are amounts of money that you spend while doing something in the course of your work, which will be paid back to you afterwards. 経費 [BUSINESS 実業] ❑ *Her airfare and hotel expenses were paid by the committee.* 彼女の航空運賃と宿泊料は委員会が支払った. ❸ PHRASE 句 If you do something **at** someone's **expense**, they provide the money for it. 人の費用で ❑ *Should architects continue to be trained for five years at public expense?* 公費で建築士を5年間養成するのを続けるべきか. ❹ PHRASE 句 If someone laughs or makes a joke **at** your **expense**, they do it to make you seem foolish. 人をからかって ❑ *I think he's having fun at our expense.* 私たちをだしに彼は楽しんでいるって思うわ. ❺ PHRASE 句 If you achieve something **at the expense of** someone, you do it in a way that might cause them some harm or disadvantage. 〜に迷惑をかけて ❑ *According to this study, women have made notable gains at the expense of men.* この研究によると, 男性を尻目に女性は著しい得をしてきた. ❻ PHRASE 句 If you say that someone does something **at the expense of** another thing, you are expressing concern that they are not doing the second thing, because the first thing uses all their resources. 犠牲にして [DISAPPROVAL 不賛成] ❑ *The orchestra has more discipline now, but at the expense of spirit.* オーケストラは今でより規律がとれているが, 意気を失った. ❼ PHRASE 句 If you **go to the expense of** doing something, you do something that costs a lot of money. If you **go to great expense to** do something, you spend a lot of money in order to achieve it. 金を使う ❑ *Why go to the expense of buying an electric saw when you can borrow one?* 電気のこぎりを借りられるのになぜ金を出して買うのですか.

Word Partnership *expense* は次の語句と使われる:

ADJ.	**additional** expense, **extra** expense, **medical** expense ❶
N.	**business** expense ❶ ❷

ex|pense ac|count (expense accounts) N-COUNT 可算名詞 An **expense account** is an arrangement between an employer and an employee that allows the employee to spend the company's money on things relating to their job, such as traveling or dealing with clients. 所要経費, 交際費 [BUSINESS 実業] ❑ *He put Elizabeth's motel bill and airfare on his expense account.* 彼はエリザベスのモーテル宿泊料と航空運賃を交際費で落とした.

ex|pen|sive /ɪkspɛnsɪv/ ADJ 形容詞 If something is **expensive**, it costs a lot of money. 高価な ❑ *Broadband is still more expensive than dial-up services.* ブロードバンドはダイアルアップのサービスよりまだ高い. ● **ex|pen|sive|ly** ADV 副詞 高価に, 費用をかけて ❑ *She was expensively dressed, with fine furs and jewels.* 彼女は素晴らしい毛皮と宝石を付けてぜいたくな身なりをしていた.

Thesaurus *expensive* また次を参照：

ADJ. costly, pricey, upscale; (ant.) cheap, economical, inexpensive

ex|pe|ri|ence /ɪkspɪəriəns/ (experiences, experiencing, experienced) ◾ N-UNCOUNT 不可算名詞 **Experience** is knowledge or skill in a particular job or activity that you have gained because you have done that job or activity for a long time. 経験 □ *He has also had managerial experience on every level.* 彼にはすべての段階での管理の経験もあった. ◾ N-UNCOUNT 不可算名詞 **Experience** is used to refer to the past events, knowledge, and feelings that make up someone's life or character. 体験 □ *I should not be in any danger here, but experience has taught me caution.* わたしはここでは何も危険もないはずだが, 体験から注意が必要だということがわかっている. ◾ N-COUNT 可算名詞 An **experience** is something that you do or that happens to you, especially something important that affects you. (具体的な) 体験 □ *His only experience of gardening so far proved immensely satisfying.* 彼の庭仕事の唯一の体験は今のところ素晴らしく満足感のあるものであった. ◾ V-T 他動詞 If you **experience** a particular situation, you are in that situation or it happens to you. 体験する □ *We had never experienced this kind of vacation before and had no idea what to expect.* 私たちはこの手の休暇はそれまで全く未経験だったので, 何を期待できるのか全く見当がつかなかった. ◾ V-T 他動詞 If you **experience** a feeling, you feel it or are affected by it. 味わう □ *Widows seem to experience more distress than widowers.* 夫を亡くした妻は妻を亡くした夫より大きな苦しみを味あうようだ. ● N-SING 単数名詞 **Experience** is also a noun. 味わうこと □ *...the experience of pain.* 痛みを感じること

Thesaurus *experience* また次を参照：

N. know-how, knowledge, wisdom; (ant.) inexperience ◾

Word Partnership *experience* は次の語句と使われる：

ADJ. **professional** experience ◾
valuable experience ◾ - ◾
past experience, **shared** experience ◾ ◾
learning experience, **religious** experience,
traumatic experience ◾
N. **work** experience ◾
life experience ◾
experience **a loss** ◾
experience **symptoms** ◾

ex|pe|ri|enced /ɪkspɪəriənst/ ADJ 形容詞 If you describe someone as **experienced**, you mean that they have been doing a particular job or activity for a long time, and therefore know a lot about it or are very skillful at it. 経験を積んだ □ *...lawyers who are experienced in these matters.* これらの問題に経験のある弁護士たち. □ *It's a team packed with experienced and mature professionals.* これは経験を積んだ円熟した専門家たちのたくさんいるチームである.

ex|peri|ment (experiments, experimenting, experimented)

The noun is pronounced /ɪkspɛrɪmənt/. The verb is pronounced /ɪkspɛrɪmɛnt/.

名詞は /ɪkspɛrɪmənt/ と発音される. 動詞は /ɪkspɛrɪmɛnt/ と発音される.

◾ N-VAR 可変性名詞 An **experiment** is a scientific test done in order to discover what happens to something in particular conditions. 実験 □ *The astronauts are conducting a series of experiments to learn more about how the body adapts to weightlessness.* 宇宙飛行士たちはいかに身体が無重力状態へ順応するかについてさらに知るために一連の実験を実施中である. ◾ V-I 自動詞 If you **experiment with** something or **experiment on** it, you do a scientific test on it in order to discover what happens to it in particular conditions. 実験する □ *In 1857 Mendel started experimenting with peas in his monastery garden.* メンデルは1857年に自分の修道院の庭で豆を使った実験を始めました. □ *The scientists have*

experimented on the tiny neck arteries of rats. 科学者たちはネズミの非常に小さな頚部 (けいぶ) 動脈で実験を行った. ● **ex|peri|men|ta|tion** /ɪkspɛrɪmɛnteɪʃⁿn/ N-UNCOUNT 不可算名詞 *...the ethical aspects of animal experimentation.* 動物実験の倫理的側面. ◾ N-VAR 可変性名詞 An **experiment** is the trying out of a new idea or method in order to see what it is like and what effects it has. 試み □ *As an experiment, we bought Ted a watch.* 試しに私たちはテッドに腕時計を買ってやった. ◾ V-I 自動詞 To **experiment** means to try out a new idea or method to see what it is like and what effects it has. 試みる □ *...if you like cooking and have the time to experiment.* もし料理が好きで試す時間があるなら ● **ex|peri|men|ta|tion** N-UNCOUNT 不可算名詞 試み, 実験 □ *Decentralization and experimentation must be encouraged.* 地方分権と実地での試みは奨励されなければならない.
→ see Word Web: **experiment**
→ see **laboratory, science**

Word Partnership *experiment* は次の語句と使われる：

V. **conduct an** experiment ◾
perform an experiment, **try an** experiment ◾ ◾
ADJ. **scientific** experiment ◾
simple experiment ◾ ◾

ex|peri|men|tal /ɪkspɛrɪmɛntⁿl/ ◾ ADJ 形容詞 Something that is **experimental** is new or uses new ideas or methods, and might be modified later if it is unsuccessful. 実験的な □ *...an experimental air-conditioning system.* 試験段階の空調システム. ◾ ADJ 形容詞 **Experimental** means using, used in, or resulting from scientific experiments. 実験用の □ *...the main techniques of experimental science.* 実験科学の主な技術. ● **ex|peri|men|tal|ly** ADV 副詞 [ADV with v] 実験的に □ *...an ecology laboratory, where communities of species can be studied experimentally under controlled conditions.* 種の群集が制御された条件下で実験的に研究できる生態実験室 ◾ ADJ 形容詞 An **experimental** action is done in order to see what it is like, or what effects it has. 試験的な □ *The senator is ready to argue for an experimental lifting of the ban.* その上院議員は禁止令の試験的な解除に賛成する論議をする用意ができている. ● **ex|peri|men|tal|ly** ADV 副詞 [ADV with v] 試験的に □ *This system is being tried out experimentally at many universities.* この制度は多くの大学で試験的に施行中である.

ex|pert /ɛkspɜrt/ (experts) ◾ N-COUNT 可算名詞 An **expert** is a person who is very skilled at doing something or who knows a lot about a particular subject. 専門家, 達人 □ *...a yoga expert.* ヨガの達人. ◾ ADJ 形容詞 Someone who is **expert at** doing something is very skilled at it. 上手な □ *The Japanese are expert at lowering manufacturing costs.* 日本人は製造コストを下げるのが上手だ. ● **ex|pert|ly** ADV 副詞 [ADV with v] 上手に □ *Shopkeepers expertly rolled spices up in bay leaves.* 商店主たちは香辛料を月桂樹の葉で上手にくるんだ. ◾ ADJ 形容詞 If you say that someone has **expert** hands or an **expert** eye, you mean that they are very skillful or experienced in using their hands or eyes for a particular purpose. 熟練した [ADJ n] □ *Harvey cured the pain with his own expert hands.* 熟練したハーヴィーは自分の手で痛みを治した. ◾ ADJ 形容詞 **Expert** advice or help is given by someone who has studied a subject thoroughly or who is very skilled at a particular job. 専門家の [ADJ n] □ *We'll need an expert opinion.* 私たちは専門家の意見が必要でしょう.

Word Partnership *expert* は次の語句と使われる：

ADJ. **leading** expert ◾
N. expert **advice**, expert **opinion**, expert **witness** ◾

ex|per|tise /ɛkspɜrtiz/ N-UNCOUNT 不可算名詞 **Expertise** is special skill or knowledge that is acquired by training, study, or practice. 専門的技術・知識 □ *She was not an accountant and didn't have the expertise to verify all of the financial details.* 彼女は会計士ではなく, 財務の詳細全てを確認する専門知識がなかった.

ex|pi|ra|tion date (expiration dates) N-COUNT 可算名詞 The **expiration date** on a food container is the date by which the food should be sold or eaten before it starts to decay. 賞味期限 [AM 米

Word Web experiment

Scientists learn much of what they know through **controlled experiments**. The scientific method provides a dependable way to understand natural **phenomena**. The first step in any experiment is **observation**. During this stage researchers examine the situation and ask a question about it. They may also read what others have discovered about it. Next, they state a **hypothesis**. Then they use the hypothesis to design an experiment and **predict** what will happen. Next comes the **testing** phase. Often researchers do several experiments using different **variables**. If all of the **evidence** supports the hypothesis, it becomes a new **theory**.

国英語] ❑ *But soda past its expiration date goes flat and loses much of its taste.* しかし賞味期限をすぎた炭酸飲料は気が抜けてすごく味が落ちる.

ex|pire /ɪkspaɪər/ (**expires, expiring, expired**) V-I 自動詞 When something such as a contract, deadline, or visa **expires**, it comes to an end or is no longer valid. 満了する, 失効する ❑ *He had lived illegally in the United States for five years after his visitor's visa expired.* 彼は米国に観光ビザが切れた後5年間不法滞在をしていた.

ex|plain /ɪkspleɪn/ (**explains, explaining, explained**) **1** V-T/V-I 他動詞/自動詞 If you **explain** something, you give details about it or describe it so that it can be understood. 説明する [他動詞・自動詞] ❑ *Not every judge, however, has the ability to explain the law in simple terms.* しかしながら全ての裁判官が法律を簡単な言葉で説明できる能力を持っているわけではない. ❑ *Don't sign anything until your lawyer has explained the contract to you.* あなたの弁護士が契約について説明するまでは何にも署名しないでください. ❑ *Professor Griffiths explained how the drug appears to work.* グリフィス教授はその薬がどのように効くと思われるかを説明しました. **2** V-T/V-I 他動詞/自動詞 If you **explain**, or **explain** something that has happened, you give people reasons for it, especially in an attempt to justify it. (理由を) 説明する 釈明する ❑ *"Let me explain, sir." — "Don't tell me about it. I don't want to know."* 「先生, わたしに説明させてください」「いや, それについては何も言うな. 知りたくもない」 ❑ *Before she ran away, she left a note explaining her actions.* 彼女は逃げる前に自分の行動を説明する手紙を書き残した. ❑ *Explain why you didn't telephone.* 電話をしなかった理由を説明しなさい.

▶ **explain away** PHRASAL VERB 句動詞 If someone **explains away** a mistake or a bad situation they are responsible for, they try to indicate that it is unimportant or that it is not really their fault. うまく言い逃れる ❑ *He evaded her questions about the war and tried to explain away the atrocities.* 彼は戦争に関する彼女の質問をはぐらかし, 残虐行為について言い逃れようとした.

ex|pla|na|tion /ɛkspləneɪʃ⁰n/ (**explanations**) **1** N-COUNT 可算名詞 If you give an **explanation** of something that has happened, you give people reasons for it, especially in an attempt to justify it. 説明 [also 'of/in' N] ❑ *She told the court she would give a full explanation of the prosecution's decision on Monday.* 彼女は検察側の判断については月曜に十分に説明すると法廷で述べた. **2** N-COUNT 可算名詞 If you say there is an **explanation** for something, you mean that there is a reason for it. 説明となる理由 ❑ *The deputy airport manager said there was no apparent explanation for the crash.* 墜落の理由ははっきりと説明がつかないと空港の副支配人は言った. **3** N-COUNT 可算名詞 If you give an **explanation** of something, you give details about it or describe it so that it can be understood. 釈明 ❑ *He has given a very clear explanation of his remarks and the context in which they were made.* 彼は自分の発言内容とその背景について非常に明確に釈明した.

ex|pla|na|tory /ɪksplænətɔri/ ADJ 形容詞 **Explanatory** statements or theories are intended to make people understand something by describing it or giving the reasons for it. 説明的な [FORMAL 形式ばった] ❑ *These statements are accompanied by a series of explanatory notes.* これらの陳述には一連の注釈がついている.

ex|plic|it /ɪksplɪsɪt/ **1** ADJ 形容詞 Something that is **explicit** is expressed or shown clearly and openly, without any attempt to hide anything. はっきりした, 露骨な ❑ *Sexually explicit scenes in movies and books were taboo under the old regime.* 映画や本の性的に露骨な場面は旧政権下では禁止されていた. ● **ex|plic|it|ly** ADV 副詞 はっきりと ❑ *The play was the first commercially successful work dealing explicitly with homosexuality.* その戯曲は同性愛をはっきりと扱った作品としては始めて営利的に成功したものであった. **2** ADJ 形容詞 [v-link ADJ, oft ADJ 'about' n] If you are **explicit about** something, you speak about it very openly and clearly. 明白に述べた ❑ *He was explicit about his intention to overhaul the party's internal voting system.* 彼は党内の投票制度を徹底的に見直す意図を明言していた. ● **ex|plic|it|ly** ADV 副詞 [ADV with v] はっきりと, 率直に ❑ *She has been talking very explicitly about AIDS to these groups.* 彼女はこれらのグループにはエイズについて非常に率直に話してきた.

ex|plode /ɪksploʊd/ (**explodes, exploding, exploded**) **1** V-T/V-I 他動詞/自動詞 If an object such as a bomb **explodes** or if someone or something **explodes** it, it bursts loudly and with great force, often causing damage or injury. 爆発する, 爆発させる ❑ *They were clearing up when the second bomb exploded.* 2つ目の爆弾が爆発したとき, 彼らは後片付けをしているところだった. **2** V-I 自動詞 If someone **explodes**, they express strong feelings suddenly and violently. 激発する ❑ *Do you fear that you'll burst into tears or explode with anger in front of her?* 彼女の目の前で突然泣き出すか怒りが爆発するのをあなたは恐れていますか. ❑ *"What happened!" I exploded.* 「何が起こったんだ」と私は叫んだ. **3** V-I 自動詞 If something **explodes**, it increases suddenly and rapidly in number or intensity. 爆発的に増える ❑ *The population explodes to 40,000 during the tourist season.* 観光シーズンには人口が4万人に激増する. **4** V-T 他動詞 If someone **explodes** a theory or myth, they prove that it is wrong or impossible. 打破する ❑ *Electricity privatization has exploded the myth of cheap nuclear power.* 電力の民営化が原子力発電は安いという神話を打破した.

→ see **firework**

ex|ploit (**exploits, exploiting, exploited**)

The verb is pronounced /ɪksplɔɪt/. The noun is pronounced /ɛksplɔɪt/.

動詞は /ɪksplɔɪt/ と発音される. 名詞は /ɛksplɔɪt/ と発音される.

1 V-T 他動詞 If you say that someone **is exploiting** you, you think that they are treating you unfairly by using your work or ideas and giving you very little in return. 搾取する ❑ *Critics claim he exploited black musicians for personal gain.* 批判者たちは, 彼は私益のために黒人音楽家たちを搾取したと主張する. ● **ex|ploi|ta|tion** /ɛksplɔɪteɪʃ⁰n/ N-UNCOUNT 不可算名詞 搾取 ❑ *Extra payments should be made to protect the interests of the staff and prevent exploitation.* 職員の利益を守り搾取を防ぐため割り増し手当てを支払うべきだ. **2** V-T 他動詞 If you say that someone **is exploiting** a situation, you disapprove of them because they are using it to gain an advantage for themselves, rather than trying to help other people or do what is right. 利用する, 乱用する [DISAPPROVAL 不賛成] ❑ *The government and its opponents compete to exploit the troubles to their advantage.* 政府と反政府派はこれらの問題を自分たちに有利に利用しようと競いあっている. ● **ex|ploi|ta|tion** N-SING 単数名詞 私利的利用 ❑ *...the exploitation of the famine by local politicians.* 地元の政治家による飢饉の私利的利用. **3** V-T 他動詞 If you **exploit** something, you use it well, and achieve something or gain an advantage from it. 活用する ❑ *You'll need a good antenna to exploit the radio's performance.* ラジオの性能を生かすには良いアンテナが必要でしょう. **4** V-T 他動詞 To **exploit** resources or raw materials means to develop them and use them for industry or commercial activities. 開発する, 活用する ❑ *I think we're being very short-sighted in not exploiting our own coal.* 私たちが自分たちの石炭を活用しないのはとても近視眼的だと私は思う. ● **ex|ploi|ta|tion** N-UNCOUNT 不可算名詞 ❑ *...the planned exploitation of its potential oil and natural gas reserves.* 潜在的な石油と天然ガスの開発予定. **5** N-COUNT 可算名詞 If you refer to someone's **exploits**, you mean the brave, interesting, or amusing things that they have done. 功績 ❑ *His wartime exploits were later made into a film and a television series.* 彼の戦時中の偉業はその後映画とテレビシリーズになった.

ex|plora|tory /ɪksplɔrətɔri/ ADJ 形容詞 **Exploratory** actions are done in order to discover something or to learn the truth about something. 探検の, 診査の ❑ *Exploratory surgery revealed her liver cancer.* 診査のための手術で彼女の肝臓ガンが見つかった.

ex|plore /ɪksplɔr/ (**explores, exploring, explored**) **1** V-T/V-I 他動詞/自動詞 If you **explore**, or **explore** a place, you travel around it to find out what it is like. 探検する, 探検に行く ❑ *I just wanted to explore on my own.* 私は1人で探検したかっただけだ. ❑ *After exploring the old part of town there is a guided tour of the cathedral.* 旧市街を見てまわった後で, 大聖堂のガイド付き見学がある. ● **ex|plo|ra|tion** /ɛksplɔreɪʃ⁰n/ (**explorations**) N-VAR 可変性名詞 探検 ❑ *We devote several days to the exploration of the magnificent Maya sites of Copan.* 我々はコパンの素晴らしいマヤ遺跡の踏査に数日を費やす. **2** V-T 他動詞 If you **explore** an idea or suggestion, you think about it or comment on it in detail, in order to assess it carefully. 探究する ❑ *The movie is eloquent as it explores the relationship between artist and instrument.* その映画は音楽家と楽器の関係を探っていて感銘深い映画です. ● **ex|plo|ra|tion** N-VAR 可変性名詞 探求 ❑ *I looked forward to*

the exploration of their theories. 私は彼らの理論を探究するのを楽しみにしていた. **3** V-I 自動詞 If people **explore for** a substance such as oil or minerals, they study an area and do tests on the land to see whether they can find it. 探査する □ *Central to the operation is a mile-deep well, dug originally to explore for oil.* この作業の中心となるのは、もともとは石油を探査するために掘られた1マイルの深さの井戸である. ●**ex|plo|ra|tion** N-UNCOUNT 不可算名詞 探査 □ *Oryx is a Dallas-based oil and gas exploration and production concern.* オリックスはダラスに本社を置く石油・天然ガス探査・生産の会社である. **4** V-T 他動詞 If you **explore** something with your hands or fingers, you touch it to find out what it feels like. 探る □ *He explored the wound with his finger, trying to establish its extent.* 彼は傷口の大きさを確認しようと傷口を指で探った.

ex|plor|er /ɪksplɔ́rər/ (explorers) N-COUNT 可算名詞 An **explorer** is someone who travels to places about which very little is known, in order to discover what is there. 探検家 □ *...the travels of Columbus, Magellan, and many other explorers.* コロンブス、マゼランをはじめとする多くの探検家の旅行記.

ex|plo|sion /ɪksplóuʒ³n/ (explosions) **1** N-COUNT 可算名詞 An **explosion** is a sudden, violent burst of energy, such as one caused by a bomb. 爆発 □ *After the second explosion, all of London's main train and subway stations were shut down.* 2つ目の爆発の後、ロンドンの鉄道と地下鉄の主要な駅は全て閉鎖された. **2** N-VAR 可変性名詞 **Explosion** is the act of deliberately causing a bomb or similar device to explode. 爆破 □ *Bomb disposal experts blew up the bag in a controlled explosion.* 爆発物処理の専門家たちはそのかばんを遠隔操作で爆破し処理した. **3** N-COUNT 可算名詞 An **explosion** is a large rapid increase in the number or amount of something. 急激な増加 □ *The study also forecast an explosion in the diet soft-drink market.* その調査はダイエット清涼飲料水の市場が急激に拡大することも予測した. **4** N-COUNT 可算名詞 An **explosion** is a sudden violent expression of someone's feelings, especially anger. 激発 □ *Every time they met, Myra anticipated an explosion.* 彼らが会うたびに、マイラは感情が爆発するのではないかと心配した. **5** N-COUNT 可算名詞 An **explosion** is a sudden and serious political protest or violence. 暴発 □ *...the explosion of protest and violence sparked off by the killing of seven workers.* 7人の労働者の殺害がきっかけとなった抗議と暴力行動の暴発.

ex|plo|sive /ɪksplóusɪv/ (explosives) **1** N-VAR 可変性名詞 An **explosive** is a substance or device that can cause an explosion. 爆発物、爆薬 □ *...one-hundred-and-fifty pounds of Semtex explosive.* 150ポンドのセムテックス爆薬. **2** ADJ 形容詞 Something that is **explosive** is capable of causing an explosion. 爆発性の □ *The explosive device was timed to go off at the rush hour.* 爆発装置はラッシュ時に爆発するように仕掛けられていた. **3** ADJ 形容詞 An **explosive** growth is a sudden, rapid increase in the size or quantity of something. 爆発的な □ *The explosive growth in casinos is one of the most conspicuous signs of Westernization.* カジノの爆発的な増加は欧米化の最も目立つ兆候の1つである. **4** ADJ 形容詞 An **explosive** situation is likely to have difficult, serious, or dangerous effects. 爆発寸前の □ *He appeared to be treating the potentially explosive situation with some sensitivity.* 彼は爆発する可能性のある情勢を相当に細心の注意で対処しているようだった. **5** ADJ 形容詞 If you describe someone as **explosive**, you mean that they tend to express sudden violent anger. 激情的な □ *He's inherited his father's explosive temper.* 彼は父親から激情的な気性を受け継いでいる.

→ see **tunnel**

expo /ékspou/ (expos) also **Expo** N-COUNT 可算名詞 An **expo** is a large event where goods, especially industrial goods, are displayed. 博覧会 □ *...the 1995 Queensland Computer Expo.* 1995年のクイーンズランド州コンピュータ博覧会.

ex|po|nent /ɪkspóunənt/ (exponents) **1** N-COUNT 可算名詞 An **exponent** of an idea, theory, or plan is a person who supports and explains it, and who tries to persuade other people that it is a good idea. 擁護者 [FORMAL 形式ばった] □ *...a leading exponent of test-tube baby techniques.* 試験管ベビーの技術の主な擁護者. **2** N-COUNT 可算名詞 An **exponent of** a particular skill or activity is a person who is good at it. 代表者 □ *The Alvin Ailey American Dance Theater was formed in the 1950s and quickly established itself as a leading exponent of progressive choreography and contemporary dance.* アルビン・エイリー・アメリカン・ダンス・シアターは1950年代に設立され、すぐに進歩的な振り付けと現代舞踏を先導する代表的グループとしての地位を確立した.

Word Link	*port ≈ carrying : export, import, portable*

ex|port (exports, exporting, exported)

The verb is pronounced /ɪkspɔ́rt/. The noun is pronounced /ékspɔrt/.
動詞は /ɪkspɔ́rt/ と発音される. 名詞は /ékspɔrt/ と発音される.

1 V-T/V-I 他動詞/自動詞 To **export** products or raw materials means to sell them to another country. 輸出する □ *The nation also exports beef.* その国は牛肉の輸出もしている. □ *They expect the*

antibiotic products to be exported to Southeast Asia and Africa. 彼らは抗生物質製品が東南アジアやアフリカへ輸出されることを期待している. □ *The company now exports to Japan.* その会社は現在日本へ輸出している. ●N-UNCOUNT 不可算名詞 **Export** is also a noun. 輸出 [also N in pl] □ *...the production and export of cheap casual wear.* 安いふだん着の製造と輸出. □ *A lot of our land is used to grow crops for export.* 我々の土地の多くが輸出向けの作物を栽培するのに使われている. **2** N-COUNT 可算名詞 **Exports** are goods sold to another country and sent there. 輸出品 □ *Ghana's main export is cocoa.* ガーナの主な輸出品はココアである. **3** V-T 他動詞 To **export** something means to introduce it into another country or make it happen there. 伝える □ *It has exported inflation at times.* それは時にはインフレも国外に広めた. **4** V-T 他動詞 In computing, if you **export** files or information from one type of software into another type, you change their format so that they can be used in the new software. エクスポートする □ *Files can be exported in ASCII or PCX formats.* ファイルはASCIIかPCXフォーマットでエクスポートできる.

ex|port|able /ɪkspɔ́rtəb³l/ ADJ 形容詞 **Exportable** products are suitable for being exported. 輸出できる、輸出向けの □ *They are reliant on a very limited number of exportable products.* 彼らは非常に限られた数の輸出向け製品に依存している.

ex|port|er /ékspɔrtər, ɪkspɔ́rtər/ (exporters) N-COUNT 可算名詞 An **exporter** is a country, company, or person that sells and sends goods to another country. 輸出元 □ *France is the world's second-biggest exporter of agricultural products.* フランスは世界で2番目に大きい農作物輸出国である.

ex|pose /ɪkspóuz/ (exposes, exposing, exposed) **1** V-T 他動詞 To **expose** something that is usually hidden means to uncover it so that it can be seen. 露出する □ *Lowered sea levels exposed the shallow continental shelf beneath the Bering Sea.* 海面が低下したためベーリング海の浅瀬の大陸棚が露出した. **2** V-T 他動詞 To **expose** a person or situation means to reveal that they are bad or immoral in some way. 暴露する □ *...the story of how the press helped expose the truth about the Nixon administration.* いかに報道機関が手を貸してニクソン政権についての真実を暴露したかという話 **3** V-T 他動詞 If someone **is exposed to** something dangerous or unpleasant, they are put in a situation in which it might affect them. さらす □ *They had not been exposed to most diseases common to urban populations.* 彼らは都市の住民に一般的な病気のほとんどにさらされたことがなかった. □ *A wise mother never exposes her children to the slightest possibility of danger.* 賢明な母親は子供たちをほんのわずかでも危ない可能性のあることに決してさらすことはない. **4** V-T 他動詞 If someone **is exposed to** an idea or feeling, usually a new one, they are given experience of it, or introduced to it. さらす □ *...local people who've not been exposed to glimpses of Western life before.* いままで欧米の生活に全くさらされたことのなかった地元の人たち

ex|po|sure /ɪkspóuʒər/ (exposures) **1** N-UNCOUNT 不可算名詞 **Exposure to** something dangerous means being in a situation where it might affect you. さらすこと □ *Exposure to lead is known to damage the brains of young children.* 幼児の脳が鉛にさらされると障害を受けることが知られている. **2** N-UNCOUNT 不可算名詞 **Exposure** is the harmful effect on your body caused by very cold weather. 低体温症 □ *He was suffering from exposure and shock but his condition was said to be stable.* 彼は低体温症とショックにかかっていたが、状態は安定しているということだった. **3** N-UNCOUNT 不可算名詞 The **exposure** of a well-known person is the revealing of the fact that they are bad or immoral in some way. 露見 □ *He undertook increasingly dangerous assignments until his exposure as a spy.* 彼がスパイであることが露見するまで彼はますます危険な任務を引き受けた. **4** N-UNCOUNT 不可算名詞 **Exposure** is publicity that a person, company, or product receives. 露出 □ *All the candidates have been getting an enormous amount of exposure on television and in the press.* 全ての候補者はテレビや報道陣にものすごく取り上げられてきた. **5** N-COUNT 可算名詞 In photography, an **exposure** is a single photograph. 一こま [TECHNICAL 技術的] □ *Larger drawings tend to require two or three exposures to cover them.* より大きなデッサンの全面を撮るには2,3こまが必要になりがちである.

ex|pound /ɪkspáund/ (expounds, expounding, expounded) V-T 他動詞 If you **expound** an idea or opinion, you give a clear and detailed explanation of it. 詳しく説明する [FORMAL 形式ばった] □ *Schmidt continued to expound his views on economics and politics.* シュミットは経済と政治に関する見解を詳しく説明し続けた. ●PHRASAL VERB 句動詞 **Expound on** means the same as **expound**. 詳しく説明する □ *Lawrence expounded on the military aspects of guerrilla warfare.* ロレンスはゲリラ戦の軍事面を詳述した.

ex|press /ɪksprés/ (expresses, expressing, expressed) **1** V-T 他動詞 When you **express** an idea or feeling, or **express yourself**, you show what you think or feel. 述べる、表わす □ *He expressed grave concern over American attitudes.* 彼は米国の姿勢について強い懸念を示した. **2** V-T 他動詞 If an idea or feeling **expresses itself** in some way, it can be clearly seen in someone's actions or in its effects on a situation. 外に出る □ *The anxiety of the separation often expresses*

itself as anger toward the child for getting lost. 離れ離れになったことの不安は迷子になった子供への怒りとして表に出ることが多い. ❸ ADJ 形容詞 An **express** command or order is one that is clearly and deliberately stated. 明示された [FORMAL 形式ばった] [ADJ n] ❏ This mighty electricity-generating power station was built on the express orders of the president. この巨大な発電所は大統領が特に命令したため建設された. ● **ex|press|ly** ADV 副詞 [ADV before v] 明白に ❏ He has expressly forbidden her to go out on her own. 彼は彼女が1人で外出するのをはっきりと禁じた. ❹ ADJ 形容詞 If you refer to an **express** intention or purpose, you are emphasizing that it is a deliberate and specific one that you have before you do something. 特殊の [EMPHASIS 強調] [ADJ n] ❏ The express purpose of the flights was to get Americans out of the danger zone. それらの飛行便は危険地帯から米国人を脱出させることを特別の目的としていた. ● **ex|press|ly** ADV 副詞 特に ❏ ...projects expressly designed to support cattle farmers. 牛を飼う牧畜業者たちを支援するために特に計画されたプロジェクト ❺ ADJ 形容詞 [ADJ n] **Express** is used to describe special services provided by companies or organizations such as the U.S. Postal Service, in which things are sent or done faster than usual for a higher price. 至急便の ❏ A special express service is available by fax. 特別至急便はファックスで可能です. ● ADV 副詞 **Express** is also an adverb. 至急便で ❏ Send it express. それは至急便で送れ. ❻ N-COUNT 可算名詞 An **express** or an **express** train is a fast train that stops at very few stations. 急行 ❏ Punctually at 7:45, the express to Kuala Lumpur left Singapore station. 時間通り7時45分にクアラルンプール行き急行がシンガポール駅を出た.

Word Partnership	express は次の語句と使われる:
N.	express **appreciation**, express **your emotions**, express **gratitude**, express **sympathy**, **words to** express **something** ❶ express **purpose** ❹ express **mail**, express **service** ❺

ex|pres|sion /ɪkspr**ɛ**ʃ⁰n/ (expressions) ❶ N-VAR 可変性名詞 The **expression** of ideas or feelings is the showing of them through words, actions, or artistic activities. 表現 ❏ Laughter is one of the most infectious expressions of emotion. 笑いは最もうつりやすい感情表現の1つである. ❏ ...the rights of the individual to freedom of expression. 表現の自由に対する個人の権利. ❷ N-VAR 可変性名詞 Your **expression** is the way that your face looks at a particular moment. It shows what you are thinking or feeling. 表情 ❏ Levin sat there, an expression of sadness on his face. レビンは悲しそうな表情を顔に浮かべてそこに座っていた. ❸ N-UNCOUNT 不可算名詞 **Expression** is the showing of feeling when you are acting, singing, or playing a musical instrument. 表現 ❏ I think I put more expression into my lyrics than a lot of other singers do. 私は他の多くの歌手たちより歌詞にもっと感情を入れていると思う. ❹ N-COUNT 可算名詞 An **expression** is a word or phrase. 言い回し ❏ She spoke in a quiet voice but used remarkably coarse expressions. 彼女は静かな声で話したが, 非常に下品な言い回しをした.

ex|pres|sive /ɪkspr**ɛ**sɪv/ ADJ 形容詞 If you describe a person or their behavior as **expressive**, you mean that their behavior clearly indicates their feelings or intentions. 表現的な, 表情豊かな ❏ You can train people to be more expressive. あなたは人がもっと表情豊かになるように訓練することができる. ❏ ...the present fashion for intuitive, expressive painting. 現今の直観的で表現的な絵画の流行. ● **ex|pres|sive|ly** ADV 副詞 [ADV with v] 表情豊かに ❏ He moved his hands expressively. 彼は手を感情豊かに動かした.

Word Link	puls ≈ driving, pushing : compulsion, expulsion, impulse

ex|pul|sion /ɪksp**ʌ**lʃⁿn/ (expulsions) ❶ N-VAR 可変性名詞 **Expulsion** is when someone is forced to leave a school, university, or organization. 除名, 放校 ❏ Her hatred of authority led to her expulsion from high school. 彼女は権威が大嫌いで, そのために高校を退学になった. ❷ N-VAR 可変性名詞 **Expulsion** is when someone is forced to leave a place. 追放 [FORMAL 形式ばった] ❏ ...the expulsion of Yemeni workers. イエメン人労働者の追放.

ex|qui|site /ɪkskw**ɪ**zɪt, ɛksk**w**ɪzɪt/ ADJ 形容詞 Something that is **exquisite** is extremely beautiful or pleasant, especially in a delicate way. 非常にすばらしい, 精妙な ❏ The Indians brought in exquisite beadwork to sell. インディアンたちが精妙なビーズ細工を売りに持ってきた. ● **ex|qui|site|ly** ADV 副詞 精妙に ❏ ...exquisitely crafted dollshouses. 見事な手作りの人形の家.

ext. N-VAR 可変性名詞 **Ext.** is the written abbreviation for **extension** when it is used to refer to a particular telephone number. 内線番号 [N num] ❏ For a full festival program call 206-555-7115, ext. 239. 祭のプログラムの詳細については206-555-7115, 内線239までお電話ください.

ex|tend /ɪkst**ɛ**nd/ (extends, extending, extended) ❶ V-I 自動詞 If you say that something, usually something large, **extends** **for** a particular distance or **extends from** one place **to** another,

you are indicating its size or position. 伸びる, 広がる ❏ The caves extend for some 12 miles. その洞窟群は約12マイルにもわたっている. ❏ The main stem will extend to around 12 ft, if left to develop naturally. 自然の成長に任せれば, その主茎は12フィート前後まで伸びるだろう. ❷ V-I 自動詞 If an object **extends from** a surface or place, it sticks out from it. 伸びる, 突き出る ❏ A table extended from the front of her desk to create a T-shaped seating arrangement. テーブルが1つ彼女の机の前部から突き出ていて, 座席がT字型に並べられるようになっていた. ❸ V-I 自動詞 If an event or activity **extends over** a period of time, it continues for that time. わたる ❏ The normal cyclone season extends from December to April. 通常のサイクロンの季節は12月から4月にわたっている. ❹ V-I 自動詞 If something **extends to** a group of people, things, or activities, it includes or affects them. 及ぶ ❏ The service also extends to wrapping and delivering gifts. サービスはまた贈答品の包装と配達にまで及ぶ. ❏ The talks will extend to the church, human rights groups, and other social organizations. その話し合いは教会, 人権団体, その他の社会団体にまで及ぶだろう. ❺ V-T 他動詞 If you **extend** something, you make it longer or bigger. 伸ばす ❏ This year they have introduced three new products to extend their range. 今年彼らは品揃えを拡張するために3種類の新製品を導入した. ❏ The building was extended in 1500. その建物は1500年に拡張された. ❻ V-I 自動詞 If a piece of equipment or furniture **extends**, its length can be increased. 伸びる ❏ ...a table that extends to accommodate extra guests. 伸びて臨時の客の席が設けられる食卓 ❼ V-T 他動詞 If you **extend** something, you make it last longer than before or end at a later date. 延長する ❏ They have extended the deadline by twenty-four hours. 彼らは締め切りを24時間遅らせた. ❽ V-T 他動詞 If you **extend** something to other people or things, you make it include or affect more people or things. 広げる ❏ It might be possible to extend the technique to other crop plants. ことによるとその技術を他の作物にまで広げることが可能かもしれない. ❾ V-T 他動詞 If someone **extends** their hand or things, they stretch out their arm and hand to shake hands with someone. (握手のため手を) 伸ばす ❏ The man extended his hand: "I'm Chuck." 男は手を差し出して「チャックです」と言った.

ex|ten|sion /ɪkst**ɛ**nʃⁿn/ (extensions) ❶ N-COUNT 可算名詞 An **extension** is a new room or building that is added to an existing building or group of buildings. 増築部 ❏ We are thinking of having an extension built, as we now require an extra bedroom. 今追加の寝室が必要なので, 私たちは増築を考えている. ❷ N-COUNT 可算名詞 An **extension** is a new section of a road or railroad that is added to an existing road or railroad. 延長部分 ❏ ...a proposed extension to the No. 7 subway line. 地下鉄7番線の延長提案部分 ❸ N-COUNT 可算名詞 An **extension** is an extra period of time for which something lasts or is valid, usually as a result of official permission. 延長期間 ❏ He first entered the country on a six-month visa, and was given a further extension of six months. 彼は最初6か月のビザで入国したが, さらに6か月の延長が許された. ❹ N-COUNT 可算名詞 Something that is an **extension of** something else is a development of it that includes or affects more people, things, or activities. 延長 ❏ Many Filipinos see the bases as an extension of American colonial rule. 多くのフィリピン人が基地を米国の植民地支配の延長と見なしている. ❺ N-COUNT 可算名詞 An **extension** is a telephone line that is connected to the switchboard of a company or institution, and that has its own number. The written abbreviation **ext.** is also used. 内線 [also N num] ❏ She can get me on extension 308. 彼女は内線308番で私をつかまえられる. ❻ N-COUNT 可算名詞 An **extension** is a part connected to a piece of equipment in order to make it reach something further away. 延長 ❏ ...a 30-foot extension cord. 30フィートの延長コード.

ex|ten|sive /ɪkst**ɛ**nsɪv/ ❶ ADJ 形容詞 Something that is **extensive** covers or includes a large physical area. 広範囲の ❏ ...an extensive tour of Latin America. ラテンアメリカの広範囲の旅行 ● **ex|ten|sive|ly** ADV 副詞 [ADV after v] 広範囲に ❏ Mark, however, needs to travel extensively with his varied business interests. しかしマークは多様な仕事上の利害関係で広範囲に旅行する必要がある. ❷ ADJ 形容詞 Something that is **extensive** covers a wide range of details, ideas, or items. 広範な ❏ She recently completed an extensive study of elected officials who began their political careers before the age of 35. 彼女は35歳以前に政治の仕事を始めた公選官吏についての広範な研究を最近完成した. ● **ex|ten|sive|ly** ADV 副詞 広範に ❏ All these issues have been extensively researched in recent years. これらの問題はすべて近年広範に研究されている. ❸ ADJ 形容詞 If something is **extensive**, it is very great. 大規模な ❏ The security forces have extensive powers of search and arrest. 保安部隊は捜索および逮捕の大規模な権限を持っている. ● **ex|ten|sive|ly** ADV 副詞 大規模に ❏ Hydrogen is used extensively in industry for the production of ammonia. 水素はアンモニア製造の産業で大量に利用されている.

ex|tent /ɪkst**ɛ**nt/ ❶ N-SING 単数名詞 If you are talking about how great, important, or serious a difficulty or situation is, you can refer to the **extent** of it. 程度 ❏ The government itself has little information on the extent of industrial pollution. 政府自体は産業公害の程度についてほとんど情報を持っていない. ❷ N-SING 単数名詞 The **extent of** something is its length, area, or size. 範囲 ❏ Industry representatives made it clear that their commitment was only to maintain

the extent of forests, not their biodiversity. 産業界の代表者は，彼らの責任は森林の範囲を維持することのみであり，その生命系の多様性には及ばないと明言した． **3** PHRASE 句 You use expressions such as **to a large extent, to some extent,** or **to a certain extent** in order to indicate that something is partly true, but not entirely true. 大部分は，ある程度は [VAGUENESS あいまいさ] ❑ *It was and, to a large extent, still is a good show.* かつてそれはいい番組だったし，大いに今でもそうだ． ❑ *To some extent this was the truth.* ある程度それは真実だった． **4** PHRASE 句 You use expressions such as **to what extent, to that extent,** or **to the extent that** when you are discussing how true a statement is, or in what ways it is true. どの程度まで [VAGUENESS あいまいさ] ❑ *It's still not clear to what extent this criticism is originating from within the ruling party.* この批判がどの程度まで与党内部から生まれているのかは，いまだに明らかでない． **5** PHRASE 句 You use expressions such as **to the extent of, to the extent that,** or **to such an extent that** in order to emphasize that a situation has reached a difficult, dangerous, or surprising stage. 一程度まで [EMPHASIS 強調] ❑ *Ford kept his suspicions to himself, even to the extent of going to jail for a murder he obviously didn't commit.* フォードは明らかに自分がやっていない殺人で投獄されることになってすら，自分の疑念を胸中に秘めていた．

Word Partnership   extent は次の語句と使われる:

N.	extent **of the damage** **1**
V.	**determine the** extent, **know the** extent **1**
ADJ.	**lesser** extent **1**
	full extent **1** **2**
	a certain extent **3**

ex|te|ri|or /ɪkstɪəriər/ (**exteriors**) **1** N-COUNT 可算名詞 The **exterior** of something is its outside surface. 外観 ❑ *The exterior of the building was a masterpiece of architecture, elegant and graceful.* その建物の外装は建築の傑作であり，上品で優雅だった． **2** N-COUNT 可算名詞 You can refer to someone's usual appearance or behavior as their **exterior**, especially when it is very different from their real character. 外観，うわべ ❑ *According to Mandy, Pat's tough exterior hides a shy and sensitive soul.* マンディーによると，パットはタフな外見の下に内気で繊細な魂を隠している． **3** ADJ 形容詞 You use **exterior** to refer to the outside parts of something or things that are outside something. 外側の ❑ *The exterior walls were made of preformed concrete.* 外壁は成型コンクリートでできていた．

Thesaurus   exterior また次を参照:

| N. | coating, cover, shell, skin **1** |
| ADJ. | external, outer, outermost, surface **3** |

ex|ter|mi|nate /ɪkstɜːrmɪneɪt/ (**exterminates, exterminating, exterminated**) V-T 他動詞 To **exterminate** a group of people or animals means to kill all of them. 絶滅させる ❑ *A huge effort was made to exterminate the rats.* ネズミを根絶するため甚大な努力がなされた． ● **ex|ter|mi|na|tion** /ɪkstɜːrmɪneɪʃ³n/ N-UNCOUNT 不可算名詞 根絶 ❑ *...the extermination of hundreds of thousands of their brethren.* 彼らの何十万もの同胞の殺戮 (さつりく)

ex|ter|nal /ɪkstɜːrn³l/ **1** ADJ 形容詞 **External** is used to indicate that something is on the outside of a surface or body, or that it exists, happens, or comes from outside. 外側の ❑ *...a much reduced heat loss through external walls.* 大幅に改善された外壁からの熱損失 ● **ex|ter|nal|ly** ADV 副詞 ❑ *Vitamins can be applied externally to the skin.* ビタミンは皮膚に外用できる． **2** ADJ 形容詞 [ADJ n] **External** means involving or intended for foreign countries. 対外的な ❑ *...the commissioner for external affairs.* 対外問題長官 ❑ *...Jamaica's external debt.* ジャマイカの対外債務 ● **ex|ter|nal|ly** ADV 副詞 対外的に ❑ *...protecting the value of the dollar both internally and externally.* 内外におけるドルの価値を防衛して **3** ADJ 形容詞 [ADJ n] **External** means happening or existing in the world in general and affecting you in some way. 外界の ❑ *Such events occur only when the external conditions are favorable.* そうした出来事は外的条件が好ましい場合のみ発生する．
→ see **ear**

ex|tinct /ɪkstɪŋkt/ **1** ADJ 形容詞 A species of animal or plant that is **extinct** is no longer has any living members, either in the world or in a particular place. 絶滅した ❑ *At the current rate of decline, many of the rain forest animals could become extinct in less than 10 years.* 現在の減少率では，熱帯雨林の多くの動物が10年以内に絶滅するかもしれない． **2** ADJ 形容詞 If a particular kind of worker, way of life, or type of activity is **extinct**, it no longer exists, because of changes in society. 廃れた ❑ *Herbalism had become an all but extinct skill in the Western world.* 西洋では薬草治療はほとんど廃れた技法になっていた． **3** ADJ 形容詞 An **extinct** volcano is one that does not erupt or is not expected to erupt anymore. 活動を停止した ❑ *Its tallest volcano, long extinct, is Olympus Mons.* その最高峰の火山は，遠い昔に死火山になっているが，オリンポス山だ．

ex|tinc|tion /ɪkstɪŋkʃ³n/ **1** N-UNCOUNT 不可算名詞 The **extinction** of a species of animal or plant is the death of all its

remaining living members. 絶滅 ❑ *An operation is beginning to try to save a species of crocodile from extinction.* ワニの1種類を絶滅から救おうとする作戦が始まろうとしている． **2** N-UNCOUNT 不可算名詞 If someone refers to the **extinction** of a way of life or type of activity, they mean that the way of life or activity stops existing. 消滅 ❑ *The loggers say their jobs are faced with extinction because of declining timber sales.* きこりたちは，木材の売り上げ落ち込みにより自分たちの仕事が廃業に直面していると言う．

ex|tin|guish /ɪkstɪŋgwɪʃ/ (**extinguishes, extinguishing, extinguished**) **1** V-T 他動詞 If you **extinguish** a fire or a light, you stop it from burning or shining. 消す [FORMAL 形式ばった] ❑ *It took about 50 minutes to extinguish the fire.* 消火には約50分かかった． **2** V-T 他動詞 If something **extinguishes** a feeling or idea, it destroys it. 絶やす ❑ *The message extinguished her hopes of Richard's return.* その伝言によりリチャードが戻ってくるという彼女の望みは消えた．

ex|tol /ɪkstoʊl/ (**extols, extolling, extolled**) also **extoll** V-T 他動詞 If you **extol** something or someone, you praise them enthusiastically. 激賞する ❑ *Now experts are extolling the virtues of the humble potato.* 現在専門家たちがその地味なジャガイモの良さを激賞している．

ex|tor|tion|ate /ɪkstɔːrʃ³nɪt/ ADJ 形容詞 If you describe something such as a price as **extortionate**, you are emphasizing that it is much greater than it should be. 法外な [EMPHASIS 強調] ❑ *...a specially prepared menu on which basic dishes are charged at extortionate prices.* 簡単な料理に法外な値段のついている特別に用意されたメニュー

ex|tra /ɛkstrə/ (**extras**) **1** ADJ 形容詞 You use **extra** to describe an amount, person, or thing that is added to others of the same kind, or that can be added to others of the same kind. 予備の [ADJ n] ❑ *Police warned motorists to allow extra time to get to work.* 警察は自動車通勤者に勤務先に着くのに余分な時間を見ておくように警告した． ❑ *There's an extra blanket in the bottom drawer of the cupboard.* 食器棚の一番下の引き出しに予備の毛布がある． **2** ADJ 形容詞 If something is **extra**, you have to pay more money for it in addition to what you are already paying for something. 追加の [v-link ADJ] ❑ *For foreign orders postage is extra.* 外国の注文には郵便料金が別に必要である． ● PRON 代名詞 **Extra** is also a pronoun. 追加のもの ❑ *She won't pay any extra.* 彼女はいかなる追加料金も払おうとしない． ● ADV 副詞 **Extra** is also an adverb. 追加で ❑ *You may be charged 10% extra for this service.* このサービスには10%の追加費用がかかるかもしれません． **3** N-COUNT 可算名詞 **Extras** are additional amounts of money that are added to the price that you have to pay for something. 追加料金 ❑ *There are no hidden extras.* 記載のない追加料金はありません． **4** N-COUNT 可算名詞 **Extras** are things that are not necessary in a situation, activity, or object, but that make it more comfortable, useful, or enjoyable. 特別なもの ❑ *Optional extras include cooking classes at a top restaurant.* 随意の特別サービスには最高のレストランでの料理教室も含まれます． **5** N-COUNT 可算名詞 The **extras** in a movie are the people who play unimportant parts, for example, as members of a crowd. エキストラ ❑ *In 1944, Kendall entered films as an extra.* 1944年にケンダルはエキストラとして映画界に入った． **6** ADV 副詞 You can use **extra** in front of adjectives and adverbs to emphasize the quality that they are describing. 特別に [INFORMAL くだけた, EMPHASIS 強調] [ADV adj/adv] ❑ *I said you'd have to be extra careful.* 特に注意するようにと言ったはずだ．

Word Link   extra ≈ outside of : extract, extradite, extraordinary

ex|tract (**extracts, extracting, extracted**)

> The verb is pronounced /ɪkstrækt/. The noun is pronounced /ɛkstrækt/.
>
> 動詞は /ɪkstrækt/ と発音される．名詞は /ɛkstrækt/ と発音される．

1 V-T 他動詞 To **extract** a substance means to obtain it from something else, for example, by using industrial or chemical processes. 抽出する ❑ *...the traditional method of pick and shovel to extract coal.* つるはしとシャベルを使って石炭を掘る伝統的方法 ❑ *Citric acid can be extracted from the juice of oranges, lemons, limes or grapefruit.* クエン酸はオレンジ，レモン，ライム，グレープフルーツの果汁から抽出できる． ● **ex|trac|tion** N-UNCOUNT 不可算名詞 抽出 ❑ *Petroleum engineers plan and manage the extraction of oil.* 石油技師たちは石油の抽出を計画し，処理する． **2** V-T 他動詞 If you **extract** something **from** a place, you take it out or pull it out. 引き出す ❑ *He extracted a small notebook from his hip pocket.* 彼は尻のポケットから小さな手帳を取り出した． **3** V-T 他動詞 When a dentist **extracts** a tooth, they remove it from the patient's mouth. 抜く ❑ *A dentist may decide to extract the tooth to prevent recurrent trouble.* 歯医者は痛みの再発を防ぐためにその歯を抜くことを決めるかもしれない． ● **ex|trac|tion** (**extractions**) N-VAR 可変性名詞 抜歯 ❑ *In those days, dentistry was basic. Extractions were carried out without anesthetic.* 当時は歯科医術は初歩的なものであった．抜歯は麻酔なしで行われた． **4** V-T 他動詞 If you say that someone **extracts** something,

you disapprove of them because they take it for themselves to gain an advantage. 引き出す，手に入れる [DISAPPROVAL 不賛成] ❑ *He sought to extract the maximum political advantage from the cut in interest rates.* 彼は利率引き下げから最大限の政治的に有利な立場を手に入れようとした. **5** V-T 他動詞 If you **extract** information or a response **from** someone, you get it from them with difficulty, because they are unwilling to say or do what you want. 引き出す ❑ *He made the mistake of trying to extract further information from our director.* 彼は我々の監督からさらに情報を引き出そうとするミスを犯した. **6** V-T 他動詞 If you **extract** a particular piece of information, you obtain it from a larger amount or source of information. 抜き出す ❑ *I've simply extracted a few figures.* 私は単にいくつかの数字を抜き出した. ❑ *Britain's trade figures can no longer be extracted from export-and-import documentation at ports.* 英国の貿易額は港での輸出入記録から引き出すことはもはやできない. **7** V-T PASSIVE 受動態他動詞 If part of a book or text **is extracted from** a particular book, it is printed or published. 抜粋する [JOURNALISM ジャーナリズム] ❑ *This material has been extracted from "Collins Good Wood Handbook."* この資料は『コリンズ木工手引き』から抜粋されたものだ. **8** N-COUNT 可算名詞 An **extract** from a book or piece of writing is a small part of it that is printed or published separately. 抜粋 ❑ *Read this extract from an information booklet about the work of an airline cabin crew.* この航空乗務員の仕事に関する情報冊子からの抜粋を読みなさい. **9** N-MASS 質量名詞 **Extract** is a very concentrated liquid that is used for flavoring food or for its smell. 濃縮液 ❑ *Blend in the vanilla extract, lemon peel, and walnuts.* バニラエキス，レモンの皮，クルミを混ぜなさい.
→ see **industry, mineral**

Word Link extra ≈ outside of : extract, extradite, extraordinary

extra|dite /ˈɛkstrədaɪt/ (extradites, extraditing, extradited) V-T 他動詞 If someone **is extradited**, they are officially sent back to their own or another country or state to be tried for a crime that they have been accused of. 引き渡す [FORMAL 形式ばった] ❑ *A judge agreed to extradite him to Texas.* 裁判官は彼をテキサス州に引き渡すことに同意した. ● **extra|di|tion** /ˌɛkstrədɪʃ³n/ (extraditions) N-VAR 可変性名詞 引き渡し ❑ *A New York court turned down the British government's request for his extradition.* ニューヨークの裁判所は英国政府からの彼の引き渡し要求を拒んだだ.

extraor|di|nary /ɪkstrɔrd³neri/ **1** ADJ 形容詞 If you describe something or someone as **extraordinary**, you mean that they have some extremely good or special quality. 並外れた [APPROVAL 賛成] ❑ *We've made extraordinary progress as a society in that regard.* その点では我々の社会は並外れた進歩を遂げた. ❑ *The task requires extraordinary patience and endurance.* その仕事は並外れた忍耐と持久力が必要だ. ● **extraor|di|nari|ly** /ɪkstrɔrdənerɪli/ ADV 副詞 [ADV adj] 並外れて ❑ *She's extraordinarily disciplined.* 彼女は極めてしつけがよい. **2** ADJ 形容詞 If you describe something as **extraordinary**, you mean that it is very unusual or surprising. 異常な [EMPHASIS 強調] ❑ *What an extraordinary thing to happen!* なんという途方もないことが起きたんだ. ● **extraor|di|nari|ly** ADV 副詞 異常な ❑ *Apart from the hair, he looked extraordinarily unchanged.* 髪型以外では，彼は驚くほど変わっていないように見えた. **3** ADJ 形容詞 [ADJ n] An **extraordinary** meeting is arranged to deal with a particular situation or problem, rather than happening regularly. 臨時の [FORMAL 形式ばった] ❑ *The U.S. has called for an extraordinary emergency meeting of the UN Human Rights Commission to examine the crisis.* 米国は国連人権委員会にその危機を検討するための臨時の緊急対策会議開催を要求した.

ex|trapo|late /ɪkstræp³leɪt/ (extrapolates, extrapolating, extrapolated) V-I 自動詞 If you **extrapolate from** known facts, you use them as a basis for general statements about a situation or about what is likely to happen in the future. 推定する [FORMAL 形式ばった] ❑ *Extrapolating from his latest findings, he reckons about 80% of these deaths might be attributed to smoking.* 彼の最新の研究結果から推測して，彼はこれらの死亡者数の80%は喫煙に起因する可能性があると考えている. ● **ex|trapo|la|tion** /ɪkstræpəleɪʃ³n/ (extrapolations) N-VAR 可変性名詞 推定 ❑ *His estimate of half a million HIV-positive cases was based on an extrapolation of the known incidence of the virus.* 50万人がHIV陽性であるという彼の概算は，このウィルスの既知の発生率からの推定に基づいていた.

ex|trava|gance /ɪkstrævəgəns/ (extravagances) **1** N-UNCOUNT 不可算名詞 **Extravagance** is the spending of more money than is reasonable or than you can afford. ぜいたく，浪費 ❑ *When the company went under, tales of his extravagance surged through the industry.* 会社が破産したとき，産業界で彼の浪費に関する噂話が噴出した. **2** N-COUNT 可算名詞 An **extravagance** is something that you spend money on but cannot really afford. ぜいたく品 ❑ *Why waste money on such extravagances?* なぜそんなぜいたく品で金を無駄にするのだ.

ex|trava|gant /ɪkstrævəgənt/ **1** ADJ 形容詞 Someone who is **extravagant** spends more money than they can afford or uses more of something than is reasonable. ぜいたくな ❑ *We are not extravagant; restaurant meals are a luxury and designer clothes are out.*

私たちはぜいたくではない．レストランの食事はぜいたくでできないし，デザイナーの服なんてない. ● **ex|trava|gant|ly** ADV 副詞 [ADV with v] ぜいたくに ❑ *The day before they left Jeff had shopped extravagantly for presents for the whole family.* 彼らが去る前の日，ジェフは家族全員への贈り物のためぜいたくな買い物をしていた. **2** ADJ 形容詞 Something that is **extravagant** costs more money than you can afford or uses more of something than is reasonable. ぜいたくな ❑ *Her aunt gave her an uncharacteristically extravagant gift.* 彼女の伯母は彼女に珍しくぜいたくな贈り物を与えた. ❑ *Baking a whole cheese in pastry may seem extravagant.* 練り粉にチーズを丸ごと入れて焼くのはぜいたくに思えるかもしれない. ● **ex|trava|gant|ly** ADV 副詞 [ADV adj/-ed] ぜいたくに ❑ *By supercar standards, though, it is not extravagantly priced for a beautifully engineered machine.* しかしスーパーカーの標準では，美しく設計された車に対してこの値段は法外ではない. **3** ADJ 形容詞 **Extravagant** behavior is extreme behavior that is often done for a particular effect. 仰々しい ❑ *He was extravagant in his admiration of Hellas.* 彼のヘラスへの賞賛は大げさだった. ● **ex|trava|gant|ly** ADV 副詞 仰々しく ❑ *She had on occasion praised him extravagantly.* 彼女は折にふれて彼を大げさにほめていた. **4** ADJ 形容詞 **Extravagant** claims or ideas are unrealistic or impractical. 非現実的な [DISAPPROVAL 不賛成] ❑ *Don't be afraid to consider apparently extravagant ideas.* 一見馬鹿げた着想をよく考えてみることを恐れるな.

ex|trava|gan|za /ɪkstrævəgænzə/ (extravaganzas) N-COUNT 可算名詞 An **extravaganza** is a very elaborate and expensive show or performance. 豪華な見世物 ❑ *...a magnificent fireworks extravaganza.* 豪華な花火大会

ex|treme /ɪkstrim/ (extremes) **1** ADJ 形容詞 **Extreme** means very great in degree or intensity. 極度の ❑ *The girls were afraid of snakes and picked their way along with extreme caution.* 少女たちはヘビを恐れて，極度に注意を払って進んで行った. ❑ *...people living in extreme poverty.* 極貧の生活をしている人々 **2** ADJ 形容詞 You use **extreme** to describe situations and behavior that are much more severe or unusual than you would expect, especially when you disapprove of them because of this. 極端な [DISAPPROVAL 不賛成] ❑ *The extreme case was Poland, where 29 parties won seats.* 極端な例はポーランドで，29の政党が議席を得た. ❑ *It is hard to imagine Jesse capable of anything so extreme.* ジェシーにそこまで極端なことができるとは想像し難い. **3** ADJ 形容詞 You use **extreme** to describe opinions, beliefs, or political movements that you disapprove of because they are very different from those that most people would accept as reasonable or normal. 極端な，過激な [DISAPPROVAL 不賛成] ❑ *This extreme view hasn't captured popular opinion.* この極端な見解は大衆の支持を得ていない. **4** N-COUNT 可算名詞 You can use **extremes** to refer to situations or types of behavior that have opposite qualities to each other, especially when each situation or type of behavior has such a quality to the greatest degree possible. 極端 ❑ *...a "middle way" between the extremes of success and failure, wealth and poverty.* 成功と失敗の両極端の間の「中道」 **5** ADJ 形容詞 The **extreme** end or edge of something is its farthest end or edge. 先端の ❑ *...the room at the extreme end of the corridor.* 廊下の一番端の部屋 **6** PHRASE 句 If a person **goes to extremes** or **takes** something **to extremes**, they do or say something in a way that people consider to be unacceptable, unreasonable, or foolish. 極端に走る ❑ *The police went to the extremes of installing the most advanced safety devices in the man's house.* 警察は最も進んだ安全装置をその男の家に設置するという極端な措置をした.

Word Partnership extreme は次の語句と使われる：

N.	extreme **caution**, extreme **difficulty** **1**
	extreme **case**, extreme **sports** **2**
	extreme **left**, extreme **right**, extreme **views** **3**
ADJ.	**the opposite** extreme **4**

ex|treme|ly /ɪkstrimli/ ADV 副詞 You use **extremely** in front of adjectives and adverbs to emphasize that the specified quality is present to a very great degree. 極端に [EMPHASIS 強調] [ADV adj/adv] ❑ *My cellphone is extremely useful.* 私の携帯電話はものすごく便利だ. ❑ *Three of them are working extremely well.* 彼ら3人はひどく熱心に働いている.

Thesaurus extremely また次を参照：

| ADV. | awfully, exceedingly, greatly, highly, terribly, very; (ant.) mildly, moderately |

ex|trem|ism /ɪkstrimɪzəm/ N-UNCOUNT 不可算名詞 **Extremism** is the behavior or beliefs of extremists. 過激主義 ❑ *Greater demands were being placed on the police by growing violence and left and right-wing extremism.* 暴力行為の増加と左翼および右翼の過激主義のために警察への要求が高まっていた.

ex|trem|ist /ɪkstrimɪst/ (extremists) **1** N-COUNT 可算名詞 If you describe someone as an **extremist**, you disapprove of them

because they try to bring about political change by using violent or extreme methods. 過激主義者, 過激派 [DISAPPROVAL 不賛成] ❑He said the country needed a strong intelligence service to counter espionage, terrorism, and foreign extremists. スパイ行為, テロ行為, 外国人過激派へ対抗するため国は強力な諜報機関を必要としていると彼は述べた. ❑A previously unknown extremist group has said it carried out Friday's bomb attack. あらかじめ把握されていなかった過激派集団が金曜の爆弾攻撃を実行したのは自分たちだと言っている. **2** ADJ 形容詞 If you say that someone has **extremist** views, you disapprove of them because they believe in bringing about change by using violent or extreme methods. 過激主義的な, 過激派の [DISAPPROVAL 不賛成] ❑his determination to purge the growth of extremist views. 党から過激主義的見解を一掃しようとする彼の決意

extro|vert /ˈɛkstrəvɜrt/ (**extroverts**) ADJ 形容詞 Someone who is **extrovert** is very active, lively, and friendly. 外向的な [mainly BRIT 主に英国英語] in AM usually **extroverted** 米国英語では通常 **extroverted**] ❑His footballing skills and extrovert personality won the hearts of the public. 彼のフットボールの技量と外向的な人柄が大衆の心をつかんだ. ● N-COUNT 可算名詞 An **extrovert** is someone who is extrovert. 外向的性格の人

extro|vert|ed /ˈɛkstrəvɜrtɪd/ ADJ 形容詞 Someone who is **extroverted** is very active, lively, and friendly. 外向的な [mainly AM 主に米国英語] ❑Some young people who were easy-going and extroverted as children become self-conscious in early adolescence. 子供の頃はのんびりとして外向的であった若者の中には, 青年期の初期に自意識過剰になる者もいる.

exu|ber|ance /ɪgˈzuːbərəns/ N-UNCOUNT 不可算名詞 **Exuberance** is behavior that is energetic, excited, and cheerful. あふれんばかりの活気 ❑Her burst of exuberance and her brightness overwhelmed me. 彼女のあふれんばかりの活気と明るさに私は圧倒された.

exu|ber|ant /ɪgˈzuːbərənt/ ADJ 形容詞 If you are **exuberant**, you are full of energy, excitement, and cheerfulness. 活気にあふれた ❑So the exuberant young girl with dark hair and blue eyes decided to become a screen actress. そこでその黒い髪と青い目の活気にあふれた少女は映画女優になろうと決心した. ● **exu|ber|ant|ly** ADV 副詞 活気にあふれて ❑They both laughed exuberantly. 彼らは2人とも元気いっぱいに笑った.

ex|ude /ɪgˈzuːd, ɪkˈsuːd/ (**exudes, exuding, exuded**) **1** V-T 他動詞 If someone **exudes** a quality or feeling, or if it **exudes**, they show that they have it to a great extent. 発散する [FORMAL 形式ばった] ❑The guerrillas exude confidence. Every town, they say, is under their control. そのゲリラたちは自信にあふれている. すべての町を支配下に置いていると彼らは言っている. ❑She exudes an air of relaxed calm. 彼女はくつろいだ穏やかな雰囲気を発散している. **2** V-T/V-I 他動詞/自動詞 If something **exudes** a liquid or smell or if a liquid or smell **exudes from** it, the liquid or smell comes out of it slowly and steadily. にじみ出す, にじみ出る [FORMAL 形式ばった] ❑Nearby was a factory which exuded a pungent smell. 近所に刺激臭を出す工場があった.

---

eye

❶ PART OF THE BODY, ABILITY TO SEE
❷ PART OF AN OBJECT

❶ eye /aɪ/ (**eyes, eyeing** or **eying, eyed**) **1** N-COUNT 可算名詞 Your **eyes** are the parts of your body with which you see. 目 ❑I opened my eyes and looked. 私は目を開いて見た. ❑...a tall, thin white-haired lady with piercing dark brown eyes. 鋭いこげ茶色の目を持ち, 背が高くてやせた白髪の女性

Eye contact is an important aspect of North American culture. If someone does not look at the person with whom he or she is speaking, the speaker is thought to be rude or even dishonest. An honest person is praised for **looking you straight in the eye**. Take care not to look for too long, or you'll be guilty of **staring**, which is considered bad manners.

2 V-T 他動詞 If you **eye** someone or something in a particular way, you look at them carefully in that way. じっと見る ❑Sally eyed Claire with interest. サリーは興味を持ってクレアを見つめた. ❑We eyed each other thoughtfully. 私たちは思いやり深くお互いを見つめ合った. **3** N-COUNT 可算名詞 You use **eye** when you are talking about a person's ability to judge things or about the way in which they are considering or dealing with things. 見る目 ❑William was a man of discernment, with an eye for quality. ウィリアムは質を見分ける目を持つ眼識のある男だった. ❑He first learned to fish under the watchful eye of his grandmother. 彼は最初祖母の油断のない監視の下で魚釣りを学んだ. **4** → see also **black eye** **5** PHRASE 句 If you say that something happens **before your eyes, in front of your eyes,** or **under your eyes,** you are emphasizing that it happens where you can see it clearly and often implying that it is surprising or unpleasant. 眼前で [EMPHASIS 強調] ❑A lot of them died in front of our eyes. 我々の目の前で彼らの多くが死んだ. **6** PHRASE 句 If you

cast your **eye** or **run** your **eye** over something, you look at it or read it quickly. 視線を走らせる ❑I would be grateful if he could cast an expert eye over it and tell me what he thought of it. 彼が専門家の目で内容を走り読みし, 彼の意見を聞かせてくれるとありがたい. **7** PHRASE 句 If something **catches** your **eye,** you suddenly notice it. 気づく ❑As she turned back, a movement across the lawn caught her eye. 彼女が振り返ったとき, 芝生の上を何かが横切るのに気づいた. **8** → see also **eye-catching** **9** PHRASE 句 If you **catch** someone's **eye,** you do something to attract their attention, so that you can speak to them. 注意を引く ❑He tried to catch Annie's eye as he walked by her seat. 彼女の座席のそばを通るとき, 彼はアニーの注意を引こうとした. **10** PHRASE 句 If you **close** your **eyes to** something bad or if you **shut** your **eyes to** it, you ignore it. 目をつむる ❑Most governments must simply be shutting their eyes to the problem. たいていの政府はきっとその問題に目をつむっているにちがいない. **11** PHRASE 句 If you **cry** your **eyes out,** you cry very hard. 目を泣きはらす [INFORMAL くだけた] ❑He didn't mean to be cruel but I cried my eyes out. 彼は邪険にするつもりではなかったが, 私はひどく泣いた. **12** PHRASE 句 If there is something **as far as the eye can see,** there is a lot of it and you cannot see anything else beyond it. 見渡す限り ❑There are pine trees as far as the eye can see. 見渡す限り松の木だ. **13** PHRASE 句 If you say that someone **has an eye for** something, you mean that they are good at noticing it or making judgments about it. 一を見る目がある ❑Susan has a keen eye for detail, so each dress is beautifully finished. スーザンは細部への鋭い目を持っているので, ひとつひとつの服が美しく仕上がっている. **14** PHRASE 句 You use expressions such as **in his eyes** or **to her eyes** to indicate that you are reporting someone's opinion and that other people might think differently. 一の目にとって ❑The other serious problem in the eyes of the new government is communalism. 新政府の目にとって他の深刻な問題は地方自治主義だ. **15** PHRASE 句 If you **keep** your **eyes open** or **keep an eye out for** someone or something, you watch for them carefully. 油断なく見張る [INFORMAL くだけた] ❑I ask the mounted patrol to keep their eyes open. 私は騎馬警備隊に油断なく見張るよう頼む. **16** PHRASE 句 If you **keep an eye on** something or someone, you watch them carefully, for example to make sure that they are satisfactory or safe, or not causing trouble. 一を監視する ❑I went for a run there, keeping an eye on the children the whole time. 私はそこまで走りに行き, その間中子供たちに目を配っていた. **17** PHRASE 句 If you say that **all eyes are on** something or that the **eyes of the world are on** something, you mean that everyone is paying careful attention to it and what will happen. 耳目が注がれている [JOURNALISM ジャーナリズム] ❑All eyes will be on tomorrow's vote. 明日の投票に世間の注目が集まるだろう. **18** PHRASE 句 If someone **has their eye on** you, they are watching you carefully to see what you do. 一を監視する ❑A spokesman for the store said: "He comes here quite a lot. We've had our eye on him before." その店の代表者は「彼は随分よくここに来る. 我々は前から彼に目をつけていた」と言った. **19** PHRASE 句 If you **have** your **eye on** something, you want to have it. 目をつける [INFORMAL くだけた] ❑If you're saving up for a new outfit you've had your eye on, cheap dinners for a month might let you buy it. あなたが目をつけている新しい衣装のために貯金をしているなら, 1か月間安い夕食ですませればそれを買えるかもしれない. **20** PHRASE 句 If you say that you did something **with** your **eyes open** or **with** your **eyes wide open,** you mean that you knew about the problems and difficulties that you were likely to have. よくわきまえて ❑We want all our members to undertake this trip responsibly, with their eyes open. 我々はメンバー全員がよくわきまえた上で, 責任を持ってこの旅行に出て欲しい. **21** PHRASE 句 If something **opens** your **eyes,** it makes you aware that something is different from the way that you thought it was. 目を開かせる ❑Watching your child explore the world about her can open your eyes to delights long forgotten. あなたの子供が自分の周りの世界を探検するのを観察すれば, 長い間忘れていた喜びに気づくことができる. **22** PHRASE 句 If you **see eye to eye with** someone, you agree with them and have the same opinions and views. 意見が一致する ❑Yuriko saw eye to eye with Yul on almost every aspect of the production. 百合子は演出のほとんどすべての面でユルと意見が一致した. **23** PHRASE 句 When you **take** your **eyes off** the thing you have been watching or looking at, you stop looking at it. 一から目を離す ❑She took her eyes off the road to glance at me. 彼女は私のほうに視線を向けるために道路から目を離した. **24** to **turn a blind eye** → see **blind** **25** to **feast** your **eyes** → see **feast** **26** in your **mind's eye** → see **mind**
→ see Word Web: **eye**
→ see **face, cry, hurricane**

❷ eye /aɪ/ (**eyes**) **1** N-COUNT 可算名詞 An **eye** is a small metal loop that a hook fits into, as a fastening on a piece of clothing. 留め穴 ❑There were lots of hooks and eyes in Victorian costumes! ビクトリア朝の衣装にはホックと留め穴がたくさんあったんだ. **2** N-COUNT 可算名詞 The **eye** of a needle is the small hole at one end that the thread passes through. 針穴 ❑The only difficult part was threading the cotton through the eye of the needle! 唯一の困難な点は針穴に綿糸を通すことだった. **3** N-SING 単数名詞 The **eye** of a storm, tornado, or hurricane is the center of it. (台風などの) 目 ❑The eye of the

E

Word Web   eye

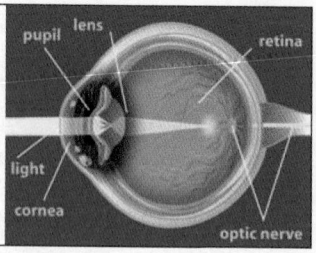

Light enters the **eye** through the cornea. The cornea bends the light and directs it through the **pupil**. The colored **iris** opens and closes the **lens**. This helps focus the **image** clearly on the **retina**. Nerve cells in the retina change the light into electrical signals. The **optic nerve** then carries these signals to the brain. In a **nearsighted** person the light rays focus in front of the lens. The image comes into focus in back of the lens in a **farsighted** person. An irregularity in the cornea can cause astigmatism. Glasses or **contact lenses** can correct all three problems.

hurricane hit Florida just south of Miami. ハリケーンの目がフロリダ州を マイアミのちょうど南の地点で襲った。

eye|ball /aɪbɔl/ (**eyeballs, eyeballing, eyeballed**) **1** N-COUNT 可算名詞 Your **eyeballs** are your whole eyes, rather than just the part which can be seen between your eyelids. 眼球 **2** V-T 他動詞 If you **eyeball** someone or something, you stare at them. じっと見る [INFORMAL くだけた] □*"Can you handle that?" Savage asked, eyeballing Cameron.* 「それを扱えるか」サヴィジは尋ね，キャメロンをじっと見た． **3** PHRASE 句 You use **up to the eyeballs** to emphasize that someone is in an undesirable state to a very great degree. ひどく困って [INFORMAL くだけた, EMPHASIS 強調] □*He is out of a job and up to his eyeballs in debt.* 彼は失業していて，借金で首が回らない．

eye|brow /aɪbraʊ/ (**eyebrows**) **1** N-COUNT 可算名詞 Your **eyebrows** are the lines of hair that grow above your eyes. 眉 **2** PHRASE 句 If something causes you to **raise an eyebrow** or to **raise** your **eyebrows**, it causes you to feel surprised or disapproving. 驚く，不満を感じる □*An intriguing item on the news pages caused me to raise an eyebrow over my morning coffee.* ニュースの頁の興味深い記事が朝のコーヒーを飲んでいた私を驚かせた． □*He raised his eyebrows over some of the suggestions.* 彼はその提案のいくつかに眉をつり上げた．

→ see **face**

eye-catching ADJ 形容詞 Something that is **eye-catching** is very noticeable. 目を引く □*...a series of eye-catching ads.* 一連の目を引く広告

eye|glasses /aɪglæsɪz/ N-PLURAL 複数名詞 **Eyeglasses** are two lenses in a frame that some people wear in front of their eyes in order to help them see better. 眼鏡 [AM 米国英語, FORMAL 形式ばった] □*...the 140 million Americans who wear eyeglasses or contact lenses.* 眼鏡かコンタクトレンズを使用している1億4千万人の米国人

eye|lash /aɪlæʃ/ (**eyelashes**) N-COUNT 可算名詞 Your **eyelashes**

are the hairs that grow on the edges of your eyelids. まつげ

→ see **face**

eye|lid /aɪlɪd/ (**eyelids**) N-COUNT 可算名詞 Your **eyelids** are the two pieces of skin that cover your eyes when they are closed. まぶた

→ see **face**

eye-opener (**eye-openers**) N-COUNT 可算名詞 If you describe something as an **eye-opener**, you mean that it surprises you and that you learn something new from it. 目を見張らせるもの [INFORMAL くだけた] □*Writing these scripts has been quite an eye-opener for me. It proves that you can do anything if the need is urgent.* これらの脚本の執筆は私にとってまったく驚くべきことだった．このことから，切羽詰っていればなんでもできるということが証明される．

eye|sight /aɪsaɪt/ N-UNCOUNT 不可算名詞 Your **eyesight** is your ability to see. 視力 □*He suffered from poor eyesight and could no longer read properly.* 彼は視力が弱くなり，もう満足に読むことができなかった．

eye|sore /aɪsɔr/ (**eyesores**) N-COUNT 可算名詞 You describe a building or place as an **eyesore** when it is extremely ugly and you dislike it or disapprove of it. 目障りなもの [DISAPPROVAL 不賛成] [usu sing] □*Poverty leads to slums, which are an eyesore and a health hazard.* 貧困が貧民街を生み，そうした場所は見苦しくて健康を脅かすものだ．

eye|witness /aɪwɪtnɪs/ (**eyewitnesses**) N-COUNT 可算名詞 An **eyewitness** is a person who was present at an event and can therefore describe it, for example in a law court. 目撃者 □*Eyewitnesses say the police then opened fire on the crowd.* 目撃者はそのとき警察が群集に発砲したと言っている．

e-zine /izin/ (**e-zines**) N-COUNT 可算名詞 An **e-zine** is a website which contains the kind of articles, pictures, and advertisements that you would find in a magazine. 電子雑誌

Ff

F also **f** /ɛf/ (**F's, f's**) N-VAR 可変性名詞 F is the sixth letter of the English alphabet. アルファベットの第6字

fa|ble /feɪbəl/ (**fables**) **1** N-VAR 可変性名詞 A **fable** is a story which teaches a moral lesson. Fables sometimes have animals as the main characters. 寓話（ぐうわ）❏ ...*the fable of the tortoise and the hare.* ウサギとカメの物語 **2** N-VAR 可変性名詞 You can describe a statement or explanation that is untrue but that many people believe as **fable**. 作り話 ❏ *Is reincarnation fact or fable?* 霊魂再来は事実か作り話か.

fab|ric /fæbrɪk/ (**fabrics**) **1** N-MASS 質量名詞 **Fabric** is cloth or other material produced by weaving together cotton, nylon, wool, silk, or other threads. Fabrics are used for making things such as clothes, curtains, and sheets. 布 ❏ ...*small squares of red cotton fabric.* 小さな正方形の赤い木綿の布 **2** N-SING 単数名詞 The **fabric** of a society or system is its basic structure, with all the customs and beliefs that make it work successfully. 組織 ❏ *The fabric of society has been deeply damaged by the previous regime.* 社会組織は前政権によりひどく壊された.
→ see **cotton, quilt**

fab|ri|cate /fæbrɪkeɪt/ (**fabricates, fabricating, fabricated**) V-T 他動詞 If someone **fabricates** information, they invent it in order to deceive people. でっち上げる ❏ *All four claim that officers fabricated evidence against them.* 警官が彼らに不利な証拠をでっち上げたと4人全員が主張している. ●**fab|ri|ca|tion** /fæbrɪkeɪʃən/ (**fabrications**) N-VAR 可変性名詞 でっち上げ ❏ *She described the interview as a "complete fabrication."* 彼女はインタビューが「まったくの作り事」だと言った.

| **Word Link** | *ous ≈ having the qualities of :* danger*ous*, fabul*ous*, glamor*ous* |
---

fabu|lous /fæbjələs/ ADJ 形容詞 If you describe something as **fabulous**, you are emphasizing that you like it a lot or think that it is very good. とても素晴らしい [INFORMAL くだけた, EMPHASIS 強調] ❏ *This is a fabulous album. It's fresh, varied, fun.* これはとてもステキなアルバムだ. 新鮮で変化に富んでいて楽しい.

fa|cade /fəsɑd/ (**facades**) also **façade 1** N-COUNT 名詞 The **facade** of a building, especially a large one, is its front wall or the wall that faces the street. 建物の正面 ❏ ...*the repairs to the building's facade.* 建物の正面の手入れ **2** N-SING 単数名詞 A **facade** is an outward appearance which is deliberately false and gives you a wrong impression about someone or something. 見せかけ ❏ *They hid the troubles plaguing their marriage behind a facade of family togetherness.* 彼らはうわべは仲が良さそうにつくろって彼らの結婚生活を蝕んでいる問題を隠した.

---
face
❶ NOUN USES
❷ VERB AND PHRASAL VERB USES
---

❶ **face** /feɪs/ (**faces**)
⇨ Please look at meaning **19** to see if the expression you are looking for is shown under another headword. **1** N-COUNT 可算名詞 Your **face** is the front part of your head from your chin to the top of your forehead, where your mouth, eyes, nose, and other features are. 顔 ❏ *He rolled down his window and stuck his face out.* 彼は窓を開け, 顔を突き出した. ❏ *He was going red in the face and breathing with difficulty.* 彼の顔が赤くなり呼吸困難に陥った. ❏ *She had a beautiful face.* 彼女は美しい顔をしていた. **2** N-COUNT 可算名詞 If your **face** is happy, sad, or serious, for example, the expression on your face shows that you are happy, sad, or serious. 顔つき ❏ *He was walking around with a sad face.* 彼は悲しそうな顔つきで歩き回っていた. **3** N-COUNT 可算名詞 The **face** of a cliff, mountain, or building is a vertical surface or side of it. 表面 ❏ *Harrer was one of the first to climb the north face of the Eiger.* ハラーはアイガー山の北壁を初めて登頂した者の1人だった. **4** N-COUNT 可算名詞 The **face** of a clock or watch is the surface with the numbers or hands on it, which shows the time. 文字板 ❏ *It was too dark to see the face of my watch.* 暗すぎて腕時計の文字板が見えなかった. **5** N-SING 単数名詞 If you say that **the face of** an area, institution, or field of activity is changing, you mean its appearance or nature is changing. 様

相 ❏ ...*the changing face of the countryside.* 田園地帯の変貌する様相 **6** N-SING 単数名詞 If you refer to something as **the particular face of** an activity, belief, or system, you mean that it is one particular aspect of it, in contrast to other aspects. 側面 ❏ *Brothels, she insists, are the acceptable face of prostitution.* 売春宿は売春の容認できる側面であると彼女は主張する. **7** N-UNCOUNT 不可算名詞 If you lose **face**, you do something which makes you appear weak and makes people respect or admire you less. If you do something in order to save **face**, you do it in order to avoid appearing weak and losing people's respect or admiration. メンツ ❏ *They don't want a war, but they don't want to lose face.* 彼らは戦争をしたくはないが, メンツを失いたくもない ❏ *To cancel the airport would mean a loss of face for the present governor.* 空港を取りやめれば, 現知事はメンツを失うことになるだろう. **8** → see also **face value 9** PHRASE 句 If someone or something is **face down**, their face or front points downward. If they are **face up**, their face or front points upward. うつぶせに; あおむけに ❏ *All the time Stephen was lying face down and unconscious in the bathtub.* スティーブンはその間ずっと浴槽でうつぶせに意識を失ったまま横たわっていた. **10** PHRASE 句 If you come **face to face** with someone, you meet them and can talk to them or look at them directly. 面と向かって ❏ *We were strolling into the town when we came face to face with Jacques Dubois.* 私たちはぶらぶら歩いて町に入って行ったときにジャック・デュボワと出くわした. **11** PHRASE 句 If you come **face to face with** a difficulty or reality, you cannot avoid it and have to deal with it. 直面する ❏ *Eventually, he came face to face with discrimination again.* 結局は, 彼は再び差別に直面した. **12** PHRASE 句 If an action or belief **flies in the face of** accepted ideas or rules, it seems to completely oppose or contradict them. ...に公然と反対する ❏ ...*scientific principles that seem to fly in the face of common sense.* 常識と正反対に見える科学的原理 **13** PHRASE 句 If you take a particular action or attitude **in the face of** a problem or difficulty, you respond to that problem or difficulty in that way. ...に直面して ❏ *The president has called for national unity in the face of the violent anti-government protests.* 大統領は激しい反政府抗議行動に直面して国民の団結を呼びかけた. **14** PHRASE 句 If you **make a face**, you show a feeling such as dislike or disgust by putting an exaggerated expression on your face, for example, by sticking out your tongue. しかめっ面をする ❏ *Opening the door, she made a face at the musty smell.* 彼女はドアを開け, かび臭い匂いに顔をしかめた. **15** PHRASE 句 You say **on the face of it** when you are describing how something seems when it is first considered, in order to suggest that people's opinion may change when they know or think more about the subject. 見たところでは ❏ *On the face of it that seems to make sense. But the figures don't add up.* 一見あれはもっともなように見える. しかし計算が合っていない. **16** PHRASE 句 If you **show your face** somewhere, you go there and see people, although you are not welcome, are somewhat unwilling to go, or have not been there for some time. 顔を出す ❏ *If she shows her face again back in Massachusetts she'll find a warrant for her arrest waiting.* 彼女が再びマサチューセッツ州に現われれば, 逮捕状が待っていることが分かるだろう. **17** PHRASE 句 If you manage to keep **a straight face**, you manage to look serious, although you want to laugh. 真顔 ❏ *What went through Tom's mind I can't imagine, but he did manage to keep a straight face.* 私にはトムが何を考えていたかは分からないが, どうにか笑わずにいられたことは確かだった. **18** PHRASE 句 If you say something **to someone's face**, you say it openly in their presence. 面と向かって ❏ *Her opponent called her a liar to her face.* 彼女の対抗者は面と向かって彼女をうそつきと呼んだ. **19** to **shut the door in** someone's **face** → see **door 20** to **have egg on** your **face** → see **egg**
→ see Picture Dictionary: **face**

❷ **face** /feɪs/ (**faces, facing, faced**)
⇨ Please look at meaning **8** to see if the expression you are looking for is shown under another headword. **1** V-T/V-I 他動詞/自動詞 If someone or something **faces** a particular thing, person, or direction, they are positioned opposite them or are looking in that direction. 面する ❏ *They stood facing each other.* 彼らは互いに向き合って立っていた. ❏ *Our house faces south.* 私たちの家は南向きだ. **2** V-T 他動詞 If you **face** someone or something, you turn so that you are looking at them. 向く ❏ *She stood up from the table and faced him.* 彼女はテーブルから立ち上がり, 彼の方を向いた. **3** V-T 他動詞 If you have to **face** a person or group, you have to stand or sit in front of them and talk to them, although it may be difficult

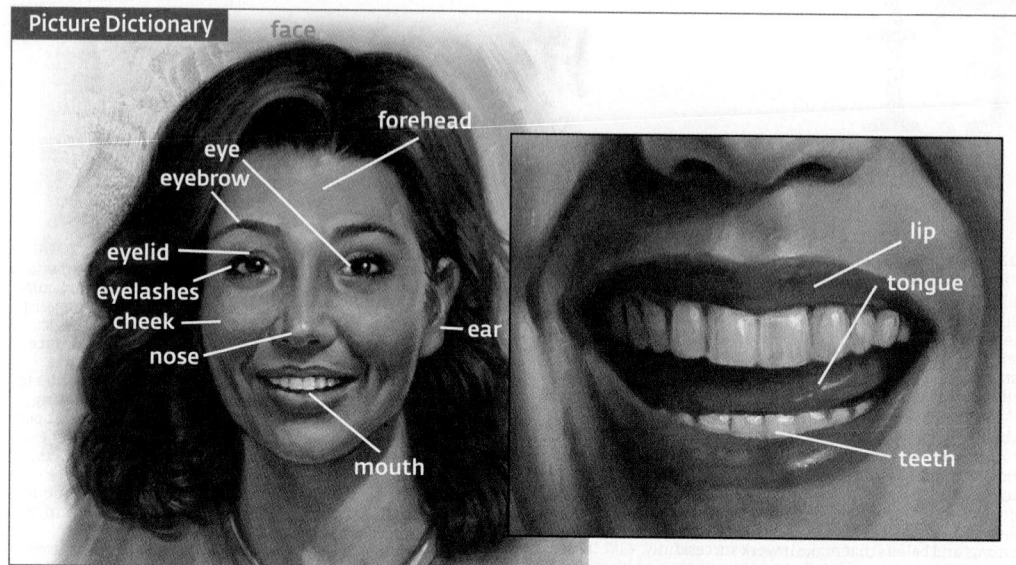

Picture Dictionary face

forehead
eye
eyebrow
eyelid
eyelashes
cheek
nose
ear
mouth

lip
tongue
teeth

and unpleasant. 立ち向かう ❏Christie looked relaxed and calm as he faced the press. クリスティは報道陣に立ち向かったとき，リラックスして落ち着いて見えた．**4** V-T 他動詞 If you **face** or **are faced** with something difficult or unpleasant, or if it **faces** you, it is going to affect you and you have to deal with it. 直面する ❏Williams faces life in prison if convicted of attempted murder. ウィリアムズは殺人未遂で有罪になれば終身刑に処せられる．❏The immense difficulties facing European businessmen in Russia were only too evident. ロシアで欧州の事業家が直面するとてつもない障害は残念なことに明白だった．**5** V-T 他動詞 If you **face** the truth or **face** the facts, you accept that something is true. If you **face** someone with the truth or with the facts, you try to make them accept that something is true. 直視する，認める ❏Although your heart is breaking, you must face the truth that a relationship has ended. あなたは胸が張り裂ける気持ちでしょうが，関係は終わったという真実を認めなければならない．❏He accused the Government of refusing to face facts about the economy. 彼は政府が経済の実態を直視しようとしないと非難した．● PHRASAL VERB 句動詞 **Face up to** means the same as **face**. 直視する ❏I have grown up now and I have to face up to my responsibilities. 私はもう大人なのだから，自分の責任を直視しなければならない．**6** V-T 他動詞 If you **cannot face** something, you do not feel able to do it because it seems so difficult or unpleasant. 立ち向かう [with neg] ❏I couldn't face the prospect of spending a Saturday night there, so I decided to press on. 私はそこで土曜日の夜を過ごす気にはとてもなれなかったので，がんばって先に進むことにした．❏My children want me with them for Christmas Day, but I can't face it. 子供たちはクリスマスを私と過ごしたがっているが，それは耐えられない．**7** PHRASE 句 You use the expression "**let's face it**" when you are stating a fact or making a comment about something which you think the person you are talking to may find unpleasant or be unwilling to admit. それを正直に受け入れよう，正直なところ ❏She was always attracted to younger men. But, let's face it, who is not? 彼女はいつも若い男に引かれた．でも，正直言ってそうでない人っている？**8** face the music → see music
▶ **face up to** → see **face ❷5**

face|less /feɪslɪs/ ADJ 形容詞 If you describe someone or something as **faceless**, you dislike them because they are uninteresting and have no character. 顔のない，誰ともわからない [DISAPPROVAL 不賛成] ❏Ordinary people are at the mercy of faceless bureaucrats. 普通の人々は顔の見えない官僚の意のままだ．

face|lift /feɪslɪft/ (**facelifts**) also **face-lift** **1** N-COUNT 可算名詞 If you give a place or thing a **facelift**, you do something to make it look better or more attractive. 模様替え ❏Nothing gives a room a faster facelift than a coat of paint. ペンキ塗り替えほど短時間に部屋の模様替えをするものはない．**2** N-COUNT 可算名詞 A **facelift** is an operation in which a surgeon tightens the skin on someone's face in order to make them look younger. 美容整形術 ❏I had a facelift in 1995, which went wrong. 私は1995年に美容整形術を受けたが，失敗した．

fac|et /fæsɪt/ (**facets**) **1** N-COUNT 可算名詞 A **facet** of something is a single part or aspect of it. 面 ❏The caste system shapes nearly every facet of Indian life. カースト制度がインドの生活のほとんどすべての面を形成している．**2** N-COUNT 可算名詞 The **facets** of a diamond or other precious stone are the flat surfaces that

have been cut on its outside. （宝石の）小面
→ see **diamond**

face value **1** N-SING 単数名詞 The **face value** of things such as coins, paper money, investment documents, or tickets is the amount of money that they are worth, and that is written on them. 額面価格 ❏Tickets were selling at twice their face value. チケットは額面価格の2倍で売れていた．**2** PHRASE 句 If you take something **at face value**, you accept it and believe it without thinking about it very much, even though it might untrue. 文字通りに ❏Public statements from the various groups involved should not necessarily be taken at face value. 関係した様々なグループの出す公の声明は，必ずしも文字通りに受け取るべきではない．

fa|cial /feɪ°l/ (**facials**) **1** ADJ 形容詞 **Facial** means appearing on or being part of your face. 顔の [ADJ n] ❏Cross didn't answer; his facial expression didn't change. クロスは返事をしなかった．彼の表情は変らなかった．**2** N-COUNT 可算名詞 A **facial** is a sort of beauty treatment in which someone's face is massaged, and creams and other substances are rubbed into it. 美顔術 ❏Where's the best place to get a facial in New York City? ニューヨーク市で美顔術を受ける一番いい店はどこにありますか．

fa|cili|tate /fəsɪlɪteɪt/ (**facilitates, facilitating, facilitated**) V-T 他動詞 To **facilitate** an action or process, especially one that you would like to happen, means to make it easier or more likely to happen. 容易にする，促進する ❏The new airport will facilitate the development of tourism. 新空港は観光業の発展を促進するだろう．

fa|cili|ta|tor /fəsɪlɪteɪtər/ (**facilitators**) N-COUNT 可算名詞 A **facilitator** is a person or organization that helps another person or organization to do or to achieve a particular thing. 進行役 [FORMAL 形式ばった] ❏The conference is chaired by a highly skilled facilitator who has been fully trained. その会議は完全に訓練された熟練した進行役が議長を務める．

fa|cil|ity /fəsɪlɪti/ (**facilities**) **1** N-COUNT 可算名詞 **Facilities** are buildings, pieces of equipment, or services that are provided for a particular purpose. 施設 ❏What recreational facilities are now available? どのようなリクリエーション施設が現在利用できるか．**2** N-COUNT 可算名詞 A **facility** is something such as an additional service provided by an organization or an extra feature on a machine which is useful but not essential. 便宜を図るもの，機能 ❏One of the new models has the facility to reproduce speech as well as text. 新型の1つには文章だけでなく会話を再生する機能がある．**3** N-COUNT 可算名詞 If you have a **facility** for something, for example learning a language, you find it easy to do. 才能 [usu sing, usu N 'for' n, N to-inf] ❏He and Marcia shared a facility for languages. 彼とマーシアには共に言語の才能があった．

fact /fækt/ (**facts**) **1** N-COUNT 可算名詞 **Facts** are pieces of information that can be discovered. 事実 ❏There is so much information you can almost effortlessly find the facts for yourself. こんなに多くの情報があるので，ほとんど努力せずに独力で事実を発見することができる．❏His opponent swamped him with facts and figures. 彼の対抗者は正確な情報で彼を圧倒した．**2** PHRASE 句 You use **the fact that** after some verbs or prepositions, especially in expressions such as **in view of the fact that**, **apart from the fact that**, and **despite the fact that**, to link the verb or preposition with a clause.

～という事実 ◻ *His chances do not seem good in view of the fact that the Chief Prosecutor has already voiced his public disapproval.* 検察長官が既に不賛成を公然と表明したという事実を考えると、彼が勝つ見込みはなさそうだ。◻ *Despite the fact that the disease is so prevalent, treatment is still far from satisfactory.* その病気があれほど流行しているという事実にもかかわらず、満足できる治療法はまだない。 **3** PHRASE 句 You use **the fact that** instead of a simple that-clause either for emphasis or because the clause is the subject of your sentence. ～という事実 ◻ *My family now accepts the fact that I don't eat sugar or bread.* 私の家族は私が砂糖もパンも避けているという事実を今では受け入れている。 **4** PHRASE 句 You use **in fact, in actual fact**, or **in point of fact** to indicate that you are giving more detailed information about what you have just said. 実は ◻ *We've had a pretty bad time while you were away. In fact, we very nearly split up this time.* 僕達はきみが留守をしている間、かなり不愉快な時を過ごした。実のところ、僕達は今度は別れる寸前だった。◻ *He apologized as soon as he realized what he had done. In actual fact he wrote a nice little note to me.* 彼は自分のしたことに気づくやいなや謝った。実際のところ彼は私に短い手紙を書いた。 **5** PHRASE 句 You use **in fact, in actual fact**, or **in point of fact** to introduce or draw attention to a comment that modifies, contradicts, or contrasts with a previous statement. 実際は、それどころか ◻ *That sounds rather simple, but in fact it's very difficult.* それはかなり簡単に聞こえるが、実際は大変難しい。◻ *They complained that they had been trapped inside the police station, but in fact most were seen escaping over the adjacent roofs to safety in nearby buildings.* 彼らは警察署に閉じ込められたと苦情を言ったが、実際は大半の人々は隣接した屋根越しに近くの建物の安全なところに逃げているのが見られた。 **6** PHRASE 句 You use **as a matter of fact** to introduce a statement that gives more details about what has just been said, or an explanation of it, or something that contrasts with it. 実を言うと ◻ *The local people saw the suffering to which these deportees were subjected. And, as a matter of fact, the local people helped the victims.* 地元の人々はこうした被追放者たちが受けた苦難を目撃した。そして実を言うと、地元の人々はその犠牲者たちを助けたのであった。 **7** PHRASE 句 If you say that you know something **for a fact**, you are emphasizing that you are completely certain that it is true. 事実として [EMPHASIS 強調] ◻ *I know for a fact that baby corn is very expensive in Europe.* 私はヨーロッパではベビーコーンが大変高価なことを事実として知っている。 **8** PHRASE 句 You use **the fact is** or **the fact of the matter is** to introduce and draw attention to a summary or statement of the most important point about what you have been saying. 実は～だ ◻ *The fact is blindness hadn't stopped the children from doing many of the things that sighted children enjoy.* 実は目の見えない子供たちでも目の見える子供たちが楽しむ活動の多くに参加することができたのだ。 **9** N-VAR 可変性名詞 When you refer to something as a **fact** or as **fact**, you mean that you think it is true or correct. 事実 ◻ *...a statement of verifiable historical fact.* 立証できる歴史的事実の陳述

→ see **history**

fac|tion /fǽkʃ^on/ (**factions**) N-COUNT 可算名詞 A **faction** is an organized group of people within a larger group, which opposes some of the ideas of the larger group and fights for its own ideas. 党派、派閥 ◻ *A peace agreement will be signed by the leaders of the country's warring factions.* 和平協定は同国の互いに交戦している党派の指導者たちが署名するであろう。

fac|tion|al /fǽkʃən^ol/ ADJ 形容詞 **Factional** arguments or disputes involve two or more small groups from within a larger group. 派閥の ◻ *...factional disputes between the various groups that make up the leadership.* 党の主流派を構成する様々な派閥間の派閥争い

fac|tor /fǽktər/ (**factors, factoring, factored**) **1** N-COUNT 可算名詞 A **factor** is one of the things that affects an event, decision, or situation. 要因 ◻ *Physical activity is an important factor in maintaining fitness.* 肉体の活動は健康を維持する上で重要な要因だ。 **2** N-COUNT 可算名詞 If an amount increases by **a factor of** two, for example, or by **a factor of** eight, then it becomes two times bigger or eight times bigger. 因数 ◻ *The cost of butter quadrupled and bread prices increased by a factor of five.* バターの原価は4倍になり、パンの値段は5倍に上昇した。 **3** N-SING 単数名詞 You can use **factor** to refer to a particular level on a scale of measurement. 指数、ファクター ◻ *A sunscreen with a protection factor of 30 allows you to stay in the sun without burning.* 防御指数30の日焼け止め剤を使えば、日焼けせずに日に当たることができる。

▸ **factor in** or **factor into** PHRASAL VERB 句動詞 If you **factor** a particular cost or element **into** a calculation you are making, or if you **factor** it **in**, you include it. 計算に入れる ◻ *You'd better consider this and factor this into your decision making.* あなたは意思決定を行う際にはこの点を考慮し計算に入れた方がいいだろう。

fac|to|ry /fǽktəri, -tri/ (**factories**) N-COUNT 可算名詞 A **factory** is a large building where machines are used to make large quantities of goods. 工場 ◻ *He owned furniture factories in New York State.* 彼はニューヨーク州に家具工場を持っていた。
→ see Word Web: **factory**
→ see **mass production**

fact sheet (**fact sheets**) N-COUNT 可算名詞 A **fact sheet** is a short, printed document with information about a particular subject, especially a summary of information that has been given on a radio or television program. 概況報告書 ◻ *...the institute's free fact sheet, Driving Abroad.* 協会の無料の概況報告書『海外での自動車運転』

fac|tual /fǽktʃuəl/ ADJ 形容詞 Something that is **factual** is concerned with facts or contains facts, rather than giving theories or personal interpretations. 事実の ◻ *The editorial contained several factual errors.* その社説には事実に関する間違いがいくつか含まれていた。

fac|ul|ty /fǽkəlti/ (**faculties**) **1** N-COUNT 可算名詞 Your **faculties** are your physical and mental abilities. （身体・精神の）機能 ◻ *He was drunk and not in control of his faculties.* 彼は酔っ払っていて自分の能力を働かせられなかった。 **2** N-VAR 可変性名詞 A **faculty** is all the teaching staff of a university or college, or of one department. （大学・学部の）教職員 [AM 米国英語] ◻ *The faculty agreed on a change in the requirements.* 教授陣は必要条件の変更に同意した。◻ *How can faculty improve their teaching so as to encourage creativity?* 創造性を促進するためには教員はどのように指導方法を改善できるか。

fad /fǽd/ (**fads**) N-COUNT 可算名詞 You use **fad** to refer to an activity or topic of interest that is very popular for a short time, but which people become bored with very quickly. 一時的流行 ◻ *Hamnett does not believe environmental concern is a passing fad.* ハムネットは環境への関心が一時的な流行だとは考えていない。
→ see **diet**

fade /féɪd/ (**fades, fading, faded**) **1** V-T/V-I 他動詞/自動詞 When a colored object **fades** or when the light **fades** it, it gradually becomes paler. 色をあせさせる、あせる ◻ *All color fades – especially under the impact of direct sunlight.* どんな色でもあせる、特に直射日光にさらされると。◻ *No matter how soft the light is, it still fades carpets and curtains in every room.* 日光はどんなに弱くても、すべての部屋のカーペットとカーテンの色をあせさせる。 ● **fad|ed** ADJ 形容

詞 色あせた □ *...a girl in a faded dress.* 色のあせたワンピースを着た少女 ② V-I 自動詞 When light **fades**, it slowly becomes less bright. When a sound **fades**, it slowly becomes less loud. 弱まる □ *Seaton lay on his bed and gazed at the ceiling as the light faded.* 日が暮れる中シートンはベッドに横たわり、天井をじっと見ていた。 ③ V-I 自動詞 If memories, feelings, or possibilities **fade**, they slowly become less intense or less strong. 薄らぐ □ *Sympathy for the rebels, the government claims, is beginning to fade.* 反乱軍への同情は薄らぎ始めていると政府は主張している。 □ *Prospects for peace had already started to fade.* 和平の見通しはすでに消え始めていた。

Word Partnership	*fade* は次の語句と使われる:
N.	**colors** fade, **images** fade ①
	memories fade ③
V.	**begin to** fade ① – ③
ADV.	fade **quickly** ① – ③

fae|ces /fiːsiz/ → see **feces**

Fahr|en|heit /færənhaɪt/ ADJ 形容詞 **Fahrenheit** is a scale for measuring temperature, in which water freezes at 32 degrees and boils at 212 degrees. It is represented by the symbol °F. カ氏の [n/num ADJ] □ *By mid-morning, the temperature was already above 100 degrees Fahrenheit.* 午前の中ごろ温度はすでにカ氏100度を超えていた。 ● N-UNCOUNT 不可算名詞 **Fahrenheit** is also a noun. カ氏温度, カ氏温度計 □ *He was asked for the boiling point of water in Fahrenheit.* 彼はカ氏温度の水の沸騰点を尋ねられた。

→ see **climate**

fail /feɪl/ (**fails, failing, failed**) ① V-T/V-I 他動詞/自動詞 If you **fail** to do something that you were trying to do, you are unable to do it or do not succeed in doing it. しそこなう, 失敗する □ *The party failed to win the election.* その政党は選挙に勝てなかった。 □ *He failed in his attempt to take control of the company.* 彼は会社の支配権を握る企てに失敗した。 ② V-T/V-I 他動詞/自動詞 If an activity, attempt, or plan **fails**, it is not successful. 失敗する □ *We tried to develop plans for them to get along, which all failed miserably.* 私たちは彼らがうまくやっていける計画を進めようとしたが、すべて惨めに失敗した。 □ *He was afraid the revolution that had started would fail.* 彼は彼らが始めた革命が失敗するのではないかと心配だった。 □ *...a failed military coup.* 失敗した軍のクーデター ③ V-T 他動詞 If someone or something **fails** to do a particular thing that they should have done, they do not do it. 怠る, しない [FORMAL 形式ばった] □ *Some schools fail to require any homework.* 一部の学校は宿題を何も出さない。 □ *He failed to file tax returns for 1982.* 彼は1982年の確定申告書を提出しなかった。 ④ V-I 自動詞 If something **fails**, it stops working properly, or does not do what it is supposed to do. 作動しなくなる □ *The lights mysteriously failed, and we stumbled around in complete darkness.* 照明が不思議なことに消えてしまい、私たちは真っ暗闇をよろめきながら歩き回った。 ⑤ V-I 自動詞 If a business, organization, or system **fails**, it becomes unable to continue in operation or in existence. 破綻 (はたん) する [BUSINESS 実業] □ *So far this year, 104 banks have failed.* 今年は現在までに104行の銀行が破綻した。 □ *...a failed hotel business.* 破綻したホテル事業 ⑥ V-I 自動詞 If something such as your health or a physical quality **is failing**, it is becoming gradually weaker or less effective. 衰える □ *He was 58, and his health was failing rapidly.* 彼は58歳であったが、健康状態は急速に衰えつつあった。 □ *Here in the hills, the light failed more quickly.* ここ高原地帯では他より急速に日が暮れる。 ⑦ V-T 他動詞 If someone **fails** you, they do not do what you had expected or trusted them to do. 失望させる □ *We waited twenty-one years, don't fail us now.* 我々は21年間待った。今になって我々を失望させるな。 ⑧ V-T 他動詞 If someone **fails** a test, examination, or course, they perform badly in it and do not reach the standard that is required. 落ちる □ *I lived in fear of failing my final exams.* 私は最終試験に落ちるのではないかとびくびくして過ごしていた。 ● N-COUNT 可算名詞 **Fail** is also a noun. 落第 □ *It's the difference between a pass and a fail.* それは合格と不合格の違いだ。 ⑨ V-T 他動詞 If someone **fails** you in a test, examination, or course, they judge that you have not reached a high enough standard in it. 落第する □ *...the two professors who had failed him during his first year of law school.* 法科大学院の1年目に彼に落第点をつけた2人の教授 ⑩ PHRASE 句 You say **if all else fails** to suggest what could be done in a certain situation if all the other things you have tried are unsuccessful. 他のすべてがだめな場合には □ *If all else fails, I could always drive a truck.* 他が全部だめな場合には、私はいつでもトラックの運転手になれる。 ⑪ PHRASE 句 You use **without fail** to emphasize that something always happens. 間違いなく [EMPHASIS 強調] □ *He attended every meeting without fail.* 彼はすべての会合に間違いなく出席した。 ⑫ PHRASE 句 You use **without fail** to emphasize an order or a promise. 確実に [EMPHASIS 強調] □ *On the 30th you must without fail hand in some money for Alex.* あなたは30日には確実にアレックスに金をいくらか渡す必要がある。

fail|ing /feɪlɪŋ/ (**failings**) ① N-COUNT 可算名詞 The **failings** of someone or something are their faults or unsatisfactory features. 欠点 □ *Like many in Russia, she blamed the country's failings on futile attempts to catch up with the West.* ロシアの多く人と同様に、彼女は

ロシアの弱点を西欧諸国に追いつこうとする無駄な試みのせいにした。 ② PHRASE 句 You say **failing that** to introduce an alternative, in case what you have just said is not possible. もしそれがだめな場合には □ *Find someone who will let you talk things through, or failing that, write down your thoughts.* 話をすっかり聞いてくれる人を見つけなさい。もしそれがだめな場合には思っていることを書き留めなさい。

fail|ure /feɪlyər/ (**failures**) ① N-UNCOUNT 不可算名詞 **Failure** is a lack of success in doing or achieving something, especially in relation to a particular activity. 失敗 □ *This policy is doomed to failure.* この政策は失敗する運命にある。 □ *Three attempts on the 200-meter record ended in failure.* 200メートルの新記録への3回の試みは失敗に終わった。 ② N-UNCOUNT 不可算名詞 Your **failure** to do a particular thing is the fact that you do not do it, even though you were expected to do it. 怠ること □ *They see their failure to produce an heir as a curse from God.* 彼らは跡継ぎができないことは神ののろいと考えている。 ③ N-COUNT 可算名詞 If something is **a failure**, it is not a success. 失敗 □ *The marriage was a failure and they both wanted to be free of it.* その結婚は失敗で、2人とも結婚を望んでいた。 ④ N-COUNT 可算名詞 If you say that someone is **a failure**, you mean that they have not succeeded in a particular activity, or that they are unsuccessful at everything they do. 失敗者 □ *Elgar received many honors and much acclaim and yet he often considered himself a failure.* エルガーは多くの勲章を受け、絶賛を多々浴びたが、それでもしばしば自分自身を失敗者と見なした。 ⑤ N-VAR 可変名詞 If there is a **failure** of something, for example, a machine or part of the body, it goes wrong and stops working or developing properly. 機能不全, 故障 □ *There were also several accidents mainly caused by engine failures on take-off.* 主に離陸時のエンジン故障が原因で起こった事故もいくつかあった。 ⑥ N-VAR 可変名詞 If there is a **failure** of a business or bank, it is no longer able to continue operating. 破綻 (はたん) [BUSINESS 実業] □ *Business failures rose 16% last month.* 倒産率は先月16%上昇した。

Word Partnership	*failure* は次の語句と使われる:
ADJ.	**afraid of** failure, **doomed to** failure ①
	complete failure ① ③ ④
	dismal failure ③ ④
N.	**feelings of** failure, **risk of** failure, **success or** failure ①
	engine failure, **heart** failure, **kidney** failure, **liver** failure ⑤
	business failure ⑥
V.	failure **to communicate** ① ②

faint /feɪnt/ (**fainter, faintest, faints, fainting, fainted**) ① ADJ 形容詞 A **faint** sound, color, mark, feeling, or quality has very little strength or intensity. かすかな □ *He became aware of the soft, faint sounds of water dripping.* 彼は水がたれる低いかすかな音に気づいた。 □ *There was still the faint hope deep within him that she might never need to know.* 彼女が知る必要がないかもしれないというかすかな希望がまだ彼の心の奥にあった。 ● **faint|ly** ADV 副詞 かすかに □ *He was already asleep in the bed, which smelled faintly of mildew.* 彼はベッドですでに眠っていたが、そのベッドにはかすかに白かびの匂いがした。 ② ADJ 形容詞 [ADJ n] A **faint** attempt at something is one that is made without proper effort and with little enthusiasm. 気のない □ *Caroline made a faint attempt at a laugh.* キャロラインは無理に笑おうとした。 □ *A faint smile crossed the Monsignor's face and faded quickly.* かすかなほほえみがモンシニョールの顔に浮かんだが、すぐに消えた。 ● **faint|ly** ADV 副詞 [ADV after v] かすかに □ *John smiled faintly and shook his head.* ジョンはかすかにほほえみ、首を振った。 ③ ADJ 形容詞 Someone who is **faint** feels weak and unsteady as if they are about to lose consciousness. めまいがして [v-link ADJ] □ *Other signs of angina are nausea, sweating, feeling faint and shortness of breath.* 狭心症の他の症状は吐き気、発汗、めまい、息切れだ。 ④ V-I 自動詞 If you **faint**, you lose consciousness for a short time, especially because you are hungry, or because of pain, heat, or shock. 気を失う □ *She suddenly fell forward on to the table and fainted.* 彼女は突然テーブルの上に倒れ、気絶した。 ● N-COUNT 可算名詞 **Faint** is also a noun. 気絶 □ *She slumped to the ground in a faint.* 彼女は気絶して地面にばったり倒れた。

faint|est /feɪntɪst/ ADJ 形容詞 You can use **faintest** for emphasis in negative statements. For example, if you say that someone hasn't the **faintest** idea what to do, you are emphasizing that they do not know what to do. まるで [EMPHASIS 強調] [ADJ n, with neg] □ *I haven't the faintest idea how to care for a snake.* ヘビの世話の仕方についてはまるで見当がつかない。

fair /fɛər/ (**fairer, fairest, fairs**) ① ADJ 形容詞 Something or someone that is **fair** is reasonable, right, and just. 公正な □ *It didn't seem fair to leave out her father.* 彼女の父を除外するのは公正ではないように思えた。 □ *Do you feel they're paying their fair share?* あなたは彼らがちゃんと当然の負担をしていると思うか。 □ *I wanted them to get a fair deal.* 私は彼らが公正な扱いを受けることを望んだ。 ● **fair|ly** ADV 副詞 公正に □ *...demonstrating concern for employees and solving their problems quickly and fairly.* 被雇用者に対する気遣いを示し、彼ら

の問題を素早く公正に解決して ② ADJ 形容詞 [ADJ n] A **fair** amount, degree, size, or distance is quite a large amount, degree, size, or distance. かなりの ❑ *My neighbors across the street travel a fair amount.* 通りを隔てて真向かいに住んでいる私の隣人たちはかなり頻繁に旅行する. ③ ADJ 形容詞 A **fair** guess or idea about something is one that is likely to be correct. まあまあの [ADJ n] ❑ *It's a fair guess to say that the damage will be extensive.* 被害は広範なものになろうと言うのは, 当たらずといえども遠からずの推測だ. ④ ADJ 形容詞 If you describe someone or something as **fair**, you mean that they are average in standard or quality, neither very good nor very bad. 並の ❑ *Reimar had a fair command of English.* レイマーはまあまあの英語力があった. ⑤ ADJ 形容詞 Someone who is **fair**, or who has **fair** hair, has light-colored hair. 金髪の ❑ *Both children were very like Robina, but were much fairer than she was.* 子供たちは2人ともロビナによく似ていたが, 彼女よりずっと金髪だった. ● COMB IN ADJ 形容詞の複合 **Fair** is also a combining form. 金髪の ❑ *...a tall, fair-haired man.* 長身で金髪の男性 ⑥ ADJ 形容詞 **Fair** skin is very pale and usually burns easily. 色白の ❑ *It's important to protect my fair skin from the sun.* 私の色白の肌を日差しから保護するのが重要だ. ● COMB IN ADJ 形容詞の複合 **Fair** is also a combining form. 色白の ❑ *Fair-skinned people who spend a great deal of time in the sun have the greatest risk of skin cancer.* 長時間日に当たる肌の白い人たちは, 皮膚がんにかかるリスクが最も大きい. ⑦ ADJ 形容詞 When the weather is **fair**, it is quite sunny and not raining. 晴れの [FORMAL 形式ばった] ❑ *Weather conditions were fair.* 天気は快晴だった. ⑧ N-COUNT 可算名詞 A county, state, or country **fair** is an event where there are, for example, displays of goods and animals, and amusements, games, and competitions. 品評会 ❑ *Every fall I go to the county fair.* 毎秋私は郡の品評会に行く. ⑨ N-COUNT 可算名詞 A **fair** is an event at which people display and sell goods, especially goods of a particular type. 展示会 ❑ *...an antiques fair.* 骨董(こっとう)市 ⑩ → see also **trade fair** ⑪ PHRASE 句 You use **fair enough** when you want to say that a statement, decision, or action seems reasonable to a certain extent, but that perhaps there is more to be said or done. まあいいだろう [mainly SPOKEN 主に口語] ❑ *If you don't like it, fair enough, but that's hardly a justification to attack the whole thing.* きみはそれが気に入らないとしても, まあいいだろう. だがとてもすべてのことを非難する根拠にはならない. ⑫ PHRASE 句 If you say that someone won a competition **fair and square**, you mean that they won honestly and without cheating. 公明正大に ❑ *There are no excuses. We were beaten fair and square.* 言い訳はない. 我々は正々堂々と戦って負けたんだ.

Word Partnership   **fair** は次の語句と使われる:

ADJ.	fair **and balanced** ①
N.	fair **chance**, fare **deal**, fair **fight**, fair **game**, fair **play**, fair **price**, fair **share**, fair **trade**, fair **treatment**, fair **trial** ①
	fair **amount** ⑤
	fair **hair** ⑤
	fair **skin** ⑥
	craft fair ⑨

fair|ground /fɛərgraʊnd/ (**fairgrounds**) N-COUNT 可算名詞 A **fairground** is an area of land where a fair is held. 品評会会場

fair|ly /fɛərli/ ① ADV 副詞 **Fairly** means to quite a large degree. For example, if you say that something is **fairly** old, you mean that it is old but not very old. まあまあ [ADV adj/adv] ❑ *We did fairly well but only fairly well.* 我々はまあうまくやったが, それだけだった. ② ADV 副詞 You use **fairly** instead of "very" to add emphasis to an adjective or adverb without making it sound too forceful. 相当に [VAGUENESS あいまいさ] [ADV adj/adv] ❑ *Were you always fairly bright at school?* きみは学校ではいつも相当できたのか. ❑ *You've got to be fairly single-minded about it.* きみはそれについてかなりひたむきにならなければいけない. ③ → see also **fair**

fair|ness /fɛərnɪs/ N-UNCOUNT 不可算名詞 **Fairness** is the quality of being reasonable, right, and just. 公正さ ❑ *...concern about the fairness of the election campaign.* 選挙運動の公正さについての懸念.

fair trade N-UNCOUNT 不可算名詞 **Fair trade** is the practice of buying goods directly from producers in developing countries at a fair price. 公正取引 ❑ *...fair trade coffee.* 公正取引によるコーヒー.

fairy /fɛəri/ (**fairies**) N-COUNT 可算名詞 A **fairy** is an imaginary creature with magical powers. Fairies are often represented as small people with wings. 妖精 → see **fantasy**

fairy tale (**fairy tales**) also **fairytale** N-COUNT 可算名詞 A **fairy tale** is a story for children involving magical events and imaginary creatures. おとぎ話 ❑ *She was like a princess in a fairy tale.* 彼女はおとぎ話の王女のようだった.

faith /feɪθ/ (**faiths**) ① N-UNCOUNT 不可算名詞 If you have **faith** in someone or something, you feel confident about their ability or goodness. 信用 ❑ *People have lost faith in the government.* 人々は

政府を信用しなくなった. ② N-UNCOUNT 不可算名詞 **Faith** is strong religious belief in a particular God. 信仰 ❑ *Umberto Eco's loss of his own religious faith is reflected in his novels.* ウンベルト・エーコが自分自身の信仰を失ったことは彼の小説に反映されている. ③ N-COUNT 可算名詞 A **faith** is a particular religion, for example, Christianity, Buddhism, or Islam. (特定の) 宗教 ❑ *England shifted officially from a Catholic to a Protestant faith in the 16th century.* イングランドは16世紀に正式にカトリック教から新教に転じた. ④ PHRASE 句 If you do something **in good faith**, you seriously believe that what you are doing is right, honest, or legal, even though this may not be the case. 誠実に ❑ *This report was published in good faith but we regret any confusion which may have been caused.* この報告は誠意を持って発表したものですが, その結果発生したかもしれないどんな混乱についても遺憾に思います.

Word Partnership   **faith** は次の語句と使われる:

ADJ.	**blind** faith, **little** faith ① ②
	religious faith ②
V.	**have** faith, **lose** faith ① ②
	practice *your* faith ②
N.	faith **in God** ②

faith|ful /feɪθfəl/ ① ADJ 形容詞 Someone who is **faithful to** a person, organization, idea, or activity remains firm in their belief in them or support for them. 忠実な ❑ *She had been faithful to her promise to guard this secret.* 彼女はこの秘密を守るという約束に忠実だった. ● N-PLURAL 複数名詞 The **faithful** are people who are faithful to someone or something. 忠実な人々 ❑ *He spends his time making speeches at factories or gatherings of the Party faithful.* 彼は工場や同党の忠実な支持者の集まりで演説をして時間を費やす. ● **faith|ful|ly** ADV 副詞 [ADV with v] 忠実に ❑ *He has since 1965 faithfully followed and supported every twist and turn of government policy.* 彼は1965年以来政府の政策のあらゆる紆余 (うよ) 曲折に忠実に従い支持してきた. ② ADJ 形容詞 Someone who is **faithful to** their husband, wife, or lover does not have a sexual relationship with anyone else. 貞節な ❑ *I'm very faithful when I love someone.* 私は愛する人がいる時にはとても貞淑だ. ③ ADJ 形容詞 A **faithful** account, translation, or copy of something represents or reproduces the original accurately. 正確な ❑ *Colin Welland's screenplay is faithful to the novel.* コリン・ウェランドの脚本はその小説に忠実だ. ● **faith|ful|ly** ADV 副詞 [ADV with v] 正確に ❑ *When I adapt something I translate from one meaning to another as faithfully as I can.* 私は脚色を行なう時にはできるだけ正確に内容を書き換える.

faith|ful|ly /feɪθfəli/ ① CONVENTION 慣習表現 When you start a formal or business letter with "Dear Sir" or "Dear Madam," you write **Yours faithfully** before your signature at the end. (手紙の結びとして *yours* とともに用いて) 敬具 ② → see also **faithful**

fake /feɪk/ (**fakes, faking, faked**) ① ADJ 形容詞 A **fake** fur or a **fake** painting, for example, is a fur or painting that has been made to look valuable or genuine, usually in order to deceive people. 偽の ❑ *The bank manager is said to have issued fake certificates.* その銀行支店長は偽の証明書を発行したと言われている. ● N-COUNT 可算名詞 A **fake** is something that is fake. 偽物 ❑ *The gallery is filled with famous works of art, and every one of them is a fake.* その画廊には有名な芸術品がいっぱいあるが, そのすべてが贋作 (がんさく) である. ② V-T 他動詞 If someone **fakes** something, they try to make it look valuable or genuine, although in fact it is not. 見せかける ❑ *It's safer to fake a tan with make-up rather than subject your complexion to the harsh rays of the sun.* 肌を強い太陽光線にさらすよりも, メークアップで日焼け色に見せかけたほうが安全だ. ❑ *...faked evidence.* でっち上げの証拠 ③ V-T 他動詞 If you **fake** a feeling, emotion, or reaction, you pretend that you are experiencing it when you are not. ふりをする ❑ *He tried to fake sincerity as he smiled at them.* 彼は彼らにほほえみながら誠実なふりをしようとした. ④ N-COUNT 可算名詞 Someone who is a **fake** is not what they claim to be, for example, because they do not have the qualifications that they claim to have. いかさま師 ❑ *I think Jack is a good man. He isn't a fake.* 私はジャックがよい男だと思う. 彼はいかさま師なんかではない.

Thesaurus   **fake** また次を参照:

ADJ.	artificial, counterfeit, imitation ①
V.	falsify, pretend ②

fall /fɔl/ (**falls, falling, fell, fallen**) ① V-I 自動詞 If someone or something **falls**, they move quickly downward onto or toward the ground, by accident or because of a natural force. 落ちる ❑ *He has again fallen from his horse.* 彼はまた落馬した. ❑ *Bombs fell in the town.* 爆弾はその町に落とされた. ● N-COUNT 可算名詞 **Fall** is also a noun. 落下 ❑ *The helmets are designed to withstand impacts equivalent to a fall from a bicycle.* ヘルメットは自転車から落ちた時の衝撃と同等の衝撃に耐えるように設計されている. ② V-I 自動詞 If a person or structure that is standing somewhere **falls**, they move from their upright position, so that they are then lying on the ground. 倒れる ❑ *The woman gripped the shoulders of her man to stop herself from*

F

falling. その女性は自分が転倒しないように夫の両肩をしっかりつかんだ. ❑ *He lost his balance and fell backwards.* 彼はバランスを失って、あおむけに倒れた. ● N-COUNT 可算名詞 **Fall** is also a noun. 転倒 ❑ *She broke her right leg in a bad fall.* 彼女はひどい転倒で右足を骨折した. ● PHRASAL VERB 句動詞 **Fall down** means the same as **fall**. 倒れる ❑ *I hit him so hard he fell down.* 私が彼をあまりひどく殴ったので、彼は転倒した. ● **fall|en** ADJ 形容詞 [ADJ n] 倒れた ❑ *A number of roads have been blocked by fallen trees.* いくつかの道路は倒木で通行止めになっている.

> Note that you can use **fall down** to talk about people and objects, but for things like prices you should use the verb **fall** by itself. ❑ *Suddenly she just fell down beside me... Share prices fell sharply during the day.* Do not confuse **fall** and **drop**. Although things can **drop** or **fall** by accident, note that **fall** is not followed by an object, so you cannot say that someone "falls" something. However, you can say that they **drop** something, or that something **drops**. ❑ *Leaves were falling to the ground... He dropped his cigar... Plate after plate dropped from his fingers.* You say that a person **drops** when they jump straight down from something, for example, when someone jumps from a plane using a parachute. If someone **falls** it is usually because of an accident. ❑ *He stumbled and fell.* **Drop** and **fall** are also nouns. A **drop** is the height of something when you imagine falling off it. ❑ *Sixteen hundred feet is a considerable drop.* A **fall** is what happens when someone has an accident. ❑ *I had been badly bruised by the fall.*

❸ V-I 自動詞 When rain or snow **falls**, it comes down from the sky. 降る ❑ *Winds reached up to 100 mph in some places with an inch of rain falling within 15 minutes.* 風速が時速100マイル、降雨量が15分間に1インチに達した地域もいくつかあった. ● N-COUNT 可算名詞 **Fall** is also a noun. 降下 ❑ *One night there was a heavy fall of snow.* ある夜大雪が降った. ❹ → see also **rainfall** ❺ V-I 自動詞 If you **fall** somewhere, you allow yourself to drop there in a hurried or disorganized way, often because you are very tired. 倒れる ❑ *Totally exhausted, he tore his clothes off and fell into bed.* 疲れ果てて、彼は服を脱ぎ捨てベッドに倒れこんだ. ❻ V-I 自動詞 If something **falls**, it decreases in amount, value, or strength. 減る ❑ *Output will fall by 6%.* 生産高は6%減少する見込みだ. ❑ *The rate of convictions has fallen.* 有罪判決の比率は低下した. ● N-COUNT 可算名詞 **Fall** is also a noun. 減少 ❑ *There was a sharp fall in the value of the dollar.* ドルの為替相場は急落した. ❼ V-I 自動詞 If a powerful or successful person **falls**, they suddenly lose their power or position. 失脚する ❑ *Regimes fall, revolutions come and go, but places never really change.* 政権は崩壊し、革命は次々と起こるが、場所は決して本当に変ることはない. 失脚 ● N-SING 単数名詞 **Fall** is also a noun. 失脚 ❑ *Following the fall of the military dictator in March, the country has had a civilian government.* 3月に軍の独裁者が失脚した後、その国は文民政権が続いていた. ❽ V-I 自動詞 If a place **falls** in a war or election, an enemy army or a different political party takes control of it. 陥落する ❑ *Croatian army troops retreated from northern Bosnia and the area fell to the Serbs.* クロアチアの軍隊はボスニア北部から撤退し、その地域はセルビア人の手に落ちた. ● N-SING 単数名詞 **Fall** is also a noun. 陥落 ❑ *...the fall of Rome.* ローマの滅亡 ❾ V-I 自動詞 If you say that something or someone **falls into** a particular group or category, you mean that they belong in that group or category. (ある範囲に) 入る ❑ *The problems generally fall into two categories.* それらの問題は通常2つのカテゴリーに分かれる. ❿ V-I 自動詞 If a celebration or other special event **falls on** a particular day or date, it happens to be on that day or date. 当たる ❑ *...the oddly named Quasimodo Sunday which falls on the first Sunday after Easter.* 復活祭の次の日曜日に当たる奇妙な名前のカジモド日曜日 ⓫ V-I 自動詞 When light or shadow **falls** on something, it covers it. かぶさる ❑ *Nancy, out of the corner of her eye, saw the shadow that suddenly fell across the doorway.* ナンシーは目の端に戸口に突然かぶさった影が見えた. ⓬ V-I 自動詞 If you say that someone's eyes **fell on** something, you mean they suddenly noticed it. (目が) 向けられる [WRITTEN 書き言葉] ❑ *As he laid the flowers on the table, his eye fell upon a note in Grace's handwriting.* 彼が花をテーブルの上に置いたとき、彼の目はグレースの手書きのメモに注がれた. ⓭ V-I 自動詞 When night or darkness **falls**, night begins and it becomes dark. 訪れる ❑ *As darkness fell outside, they sat down to eat at long tables.* 外が暗くなると、彼らは長いテーブルで食事をするために座った. ⓮ V-LINK 連結動詞 You can use **fall** to show that someone or something passes into another state. For example, if someone **falls ill**, they become ill, and if something **falls into disrepair**, it is then in a state of disrepair. なる (一の状態・関係に) ❑ *It is almost impossible to visit Florida without falling in love with the state.* フロリダを訪れてこの州が大好きにならないなんてほとんど不可能だ. ❑ *Almost without exception these women fall victim to exploitation.* ほとんど例外なしにこうした女たちは搾取の犠牲になる. ⓯ N-PLURAL; N-IN-NAMES 複数名詞、名称中の名詞 You can refer to a **waterfall** as **the falls**. 滝 ❑ *The falls have always been an insurmountable obstacle for salmon and sea trout.* その滝は常にサケや降海マスにとって越せない障害であった. ⓰ N-VAR 可変性名詞 **Fall** is the season between summer and winter when the weather becomes cooler. 秋 [AM 米国英語] ❑ *He was elected judge in*

the fall of 1991. 彼は1991年の秋に判事に選ばれた. ⓱ → see also **fallen** ⓲ PHRASE 句 To **fall to pieces** means the same as to **fall apart**. 壊れる ❑ *At that point the radio handset fell to pieces.* その時に無線ハンドセットは壊れた. ⓳ to **fall on your feet** → see **foot** ⓴ to **fall foul of** → see **foul** ㉑ to **fall flat** → see **flat** ㉒ to **fall into place** → see **place** ㉓ to **fall short** → see **short**

▶ **fall apart** ❶ PHRASAL VERB 句動詞 If something **falls apart**, it breaks into pieces because it is old or badly made. 崩壊する ❑ *The work was never finished and bit by bit the building fell apart.* 作業は決して終了せず、少しずつその建物は崩壊した. ❷ PHRASAL VERB 句動詞 If an organization or system **falls apart**, it becomes disorganized or unable to work effectively, or breaks up into its different parts. 分裂する ❑ *Europe's monetary system is falling apart.* ヨーロッパの通貨制度は崩壊しつつある. ❸ PHRASAL VERB 句動詞 If you say that someone is **falling apart**, you mean that they are becoming emotionally disturbed and are unable to think calmly or to deal with the difficult or unpleasant situation that they are in. 精神的に動揺する [INFORMAL くだけた] ❑ *I was falling apart. I wasn't getting any sleep.* 私は精神的に動揺していた. 全然眠れなかった.
▶ **fall back on** PHRASAL VERB 句動詞 If you **fall back on** something, you do it or use it after other things have failed. 一に頼る ❑ *When necessary, instinct is the most reliable resource you can fall back on.* 必要な時には直感が頼れる最も信頼できる手段だ.
▶ **fall behind** ❶ PHRASAL VERB 句動詞 If you **fall behind**, you do not make progress or move forward as fast as other people. 遅れる ❑ *Boris is falling behind all the top players.* ボリスはすべての一流選手に遅れを取っている. ❷ PHRASAL VERB 句動詞 If you **fall behind** with something or let it **fall behind**, you do not do it or produce it when you should, according to an agreement or schedule. 遅れる ❑ *He faces losing his home after falling behind with the payments.* 支払いを滞納した後、彼は家を失う事態に直面する. ❑ *Thousands of people could die because the relief effort has fallen so far behind.* 救済活動があれほど遅れたために、何千人もの人々が死亡することもありえる.
▶ **fall for** ❶ PHRASAL VERB 句動詞 If you **fall for** someone, you are strongly attracted to them and start loving them. ほれ込む ❑ *He was fantastically handsome – I just fell for him right away.* 彼はすごくハンサムだった. 私はたちまち彼に夢中になった. ❷ PHRASAL VERB 句動詞 If you **fall for** a lie or trick, you believe it or are deceived by it. だまされる ❑ *It was just a line to get you out here, and you fell for it!* それはお前をここに呼び出すためのほらに過ぎなかったのに、お前はそれにだまされたんだ.
▶ **fall off** ❶ PHRASAL VERB 句動詞 If something **falls off**, it separates from the thing to which it was attached and moves toward the ground. 取れて落ちる ❑ *When your exhaust pipe falls off, you have to replace it.* 排気管が取れたら、取り替える必要がある. ❷ PHRASAL VERB 句動詞 If the degree, amount, or size of something **falls off**, it decreases. 減少する ❑ *Unemployment is rising again and retail buying has fallen off.* 失業は再び増えつつあり、消費は減少した.
▶ **fall out** ❶ PHRASAL VERB 句動詞 If something such as a person's hair or a tooth **falls out**, it comes out. 抜ける ❑ *Her hair started falling out as a result of radiation treatment.* 彼女の髪は放射線治療により抜け始めた. ❷ PHRASAL VERB 句動詞 If you **fall out** with someone, you have an argument and stop being friendly with them. You can also say that two people **fall out**. けんかする ❑ *She fell out with her husband.* 彼女は夫と仲たがいした. ❸ → see also **fallout**
▶ **fall over** PHRASAL VERB 句動詞 If a person or object that is standing **falls over**, they accidentally move from their upright position so that they are then lying on the ground or on the surface supporting them. 転ぶ ❑ *If he drinks more than two glasses of wine he falls over.* 彼はワインをグラスに2杯以上飲むと立っていられなくなる.
▶ **fall through** PHRASAL VERB 句動詞 If an arrangement, plan, or deal **falls through**, it fails to happen. だめになる ❑ *They wanted to turn the estate into a private golf course and offered $20 million, but the deal fell through.* 彼らはその土地を一般人立入禁止のゴルフ場にしたくて2千万ドル提供したが、取引は失敗した.
▶ **fall to** PHRASAL VERB 句動詞 If a responsibility, duty, or opportunity **falls to** someone, it becomes their responsibility, duty, or opportunity. 一のものとなる ❑ *He's been very unlucky that no chances have fallen to him.* 彼は運悪く好機に恵まれることがなかった.

Thesaurus	*fall* また次を参照:
v.	fall down, plunge, topple over ❶ ❷ come down ❸ drop, plunge; (ant.) increase, rise ❺

fal|la|cy /fǽləsi/ (**fallacies**) N-VAR 可変性名詞 A **fallacy** is an idea which many people believe to be true, but which is in fact false because it is based on incorrect information or reasoning. 間違った考え ❑ *It's a fallacy that the affluent give relatively more to charity than the less prosperous.* 裕福であればあるほど慈善への寄付が増えるという考えは間違っている.

fall|en /fɔlən/ **Fallen** is the past participle of **fall**. fallの過去分詞

fall|out /fɔlaʊt/ **1** N-UNCOUNT 不可算名詞 **Fallout** is the radiation that affects a particular place or area after a nuclear explosion has taken place. 放射性降下物 ❏ They were exposed to radioactive fallout during nuclear weapons tests. 彼らは核兵器実験中に放射性降下物にさらされた. **2** N-UNCOUNT 不可算名詞 If you refer to the **fallout** from something that has happened, you mean the unpleasant consequences that follow it. 付随的結果 ❏ Grundy lost his job in the fallout from the incident. グランディはその事件の影響で職を失った.

false /fɔls/ **1** ADJ 形容詞 If something is **false**, it is incorrect, untrue, or mistaken. 間違った ❏ It was quite clear the president was being given false information by those around him. 大統領は側近から間違った情報を与えられていたことは全く明らかだった. ❏ You do not know whether what you're told is true or false. あなたは受けた説明が正しいのか正しくないのか分かっていない. ●**false|ly** ADV 副詞 [ADV with v] 間違って ❏ ...a man who is falsely accused of a crime. 間違って犯罪で告訴された男 **2** ADJ 形容詞 You use **false** to describe objects which are artificial but which are intended to look like the real thing or to be used instead of the real thing. 人工の ❏ ...a set of false teeth. 一そろいの入れ歯 **3** ADJ 形容詞 If you describe a person or their behavior as **false**, you are criticizing them for being insincere or for hiding their real feelings. 不誠実な [DISAPPROVAL 不賛成] ❏ "Thank you," she said with false enthusiasm. 「ありがとう」と彼女はしぶしぶ言った. ●**false|ly** ADV 副詞 不実に ❏ They smiled at one another, somewhat falsely. 彼らは何となくうわべだけお互いにほほ笑み合った.

false alarm (false alarms) N-COUNT 可算名詞 When you think something dangerous is about to happen, but then discover that you were mistaken, you can say that it was a **false alarm**. にせの警報 ❏ ...a bomb threat that turned out to be a false alarm. 根も葉もないことが分かった爆破の脅かし

false start (false starts) **1** N-COUNT 可算名詞 A **false start** is an attempt to start something, such as a speech, project, or plan, which fails because you were not properly prepared or ready to begin. 出だしの失敗 ❏ Any economic reform, he said, faced false starts and mistakes. どんな経済改革にも出だしの失敗と過ちが付き物だと彼は述べた. **2** N-COUNT 可算名詞 If there is a **false start** at the beginning of a race, one of the competitors moves before the person who starts the race has given the signal. フライング ❏ He powered away after two false starts to win comfortably. 2回のフライングの後に彼はものすごい勢いで走って楽勝した.

fal|si|fy /fɔlsɪfaɪ/ (falsifies, falsifying, falsified) V-T 他動詞 If someone **falsifies** something, they change it or add untrue details to it in order to deceive people. 改ざんする, 偽造する ❏ The charges against him include fraud, bribery, and falsifying business records. 彼に対する嫌疑は詐欺, わいろそして事業記録の改ざんである.

fal|ter /fɔltər/ (falters, faltering, faltered) **1** V-I 自動詞 If something **falters**, it loses power or strength in an uneven way, or no longer makes much progress. 弱まる ❏ Normal life is at a standstill, and the economy is faltering. 普通の暮らしは停滞し, 経済は低迷している. **2** V-I 自動詞 If you **falter**, you lose your confidence and stop doing something or start making mistakes. くじける ❏ I have not faltered in my quest for a new future. 私は新しい未来をひるまず探求し続けてきた.

fame /feɪm/ N-UNCOUNT 不可算名詞 If you achieve **fame**, you become very well-known. 名声 ❏ At the height of his fame, his every word was valued. 人気の絶頂期に彼の発言はすべて重んじられた. ❏ The film earned him international fame. その映画のおかげで彼は国際的な名声を得た.

	Word Partnership fameは次の語句と使われる:
V.	bring fame, gain fame, rise to fame
N.	claim to fame, fame and fortune, hall of fame
ADJ.	international fame

famed /feɪmd/ ADJ 形容詞 If people, places, or things are **famed** for a particular thing, they are very well known for it. 有名な ❏ The city is famed for its outdoor restaurants. その市は屋外レストランで有名だ.

fa|mil|iar /fəmɪlyər/ **1** ADJ 形容詞 If someone or something is **familiar** to you, you recognize them or know them well. よく知っている ❏ He talked of other cultures as if they were more familiar to him than his own. 彼は他の文化についてあたかも自分自身の文化よりも熟知しているかのように語った. ❏ They are already familiar faces on our TV screens. 彼らは既にテレビの画面で見慣れた顔だ. ●**fa|mil|iar|ity** /fəmɪliærɪti/ N-UNCOUNT 不可算名詞 よく知っていること ❏ Tony was unnerved by the uncanny familiarity of her face. トニーは彼女の顔がうす気味悪いほど見慣れたものであるのにびっくりした. **2** ADJ 形容詞 [v-link ADJ 'with' n] If you are **familiar with** something, you know or understand it well. 精通している ❏ Most people are familiar with this figure from Wagner's opera. 大半の人々はワーグナーの歌劇の

中のこの人物をよく知っている. ●**fa|mil|iar|ity** N-UNCOUNT 不可算名詞 精通 ❏ The enemy would always have the advantage of familiarity with the rugged terrain. 敵は岩だらけの地形に精通しているという点で常に有利な立場にあるだろう. **3** ADJ 形容詞 If someone you do not know well behaves in a **familiar** way toward you, they treat you very informally in a way that you might find offensive. なれなれしい [DISAPPROVAL 不賛成] ❏ It isn't appropriate for an officer to be overly familiar with an enlisted man. 将校が志願兵に対して過度になれなれしくするのは適切ではない. ●**fa|mil|iar|ity** N-UNCOUNT 不可算名詞 なれなれしさ ❏ She needed to control her surprise at the easy familiarity with which her host greeted the head waiter. 彼女は招待主がボーイ長に気軽になれなれしく挨拶したことへの驚きを抑えなければならなかった. ●**fa|mil|iar|ly** ADV 副詞 気安く ❏ "Gerald, isn't it?" I began familiarly. 「ジェラルドじゃない」と私は気安く話し始めた.

	Thesaurus familiarまた次を参照:
ADJ.	accustomed to **1**
	aware of, informed about **2**

	Word Partnership familiarは次の語句と使われる:
N.	familiar face, familiar to someone **1**
V.	look familiar, seem familiar, sound familiar **1**
	become familiar **2**
PREP.	familiar with someone/something **2**

fa|mil|iar|ize /fəmɪlyəraɪz/ (familiarizes, familiarizing, familiarized) V-T 他動詞 If you **familiarize** yourself with something, or if someone **familiarizes** you **with** it, you learn about it and start to understand it. 慣れ親しませる ❏ The goal of the experiment was to familiarize the people with the new laws. その試みの目標は国民を新しい法律に慣れ親しませることだった.

fam|i|ly /fæmɪli, fæmli/ (families) **1** N-COUNT-COLL 集合可算名詞 A **family** is a group of people who are related to each other, especially parents and their children. 家族 ❏ There's room in there for a family of five. そこには5人家族が住める広さがある. ❏ Does he have any family? 彼には家族がいるのか. **2** N-COUNT-COLL 集合可算名詞 When people talk about a **family**, they sometimes mean children. 子供たち ❏ They decided to start a family. 彼らは子をもうけることに決めた. **3** N-COUNT-COLL 集合可算名詞 When people talk about their **family**, they sometimes mean their ancestors. 先祖 ❏ Her family came to Los Angeles at the turn of the century. 彼女の先祖は世紀の変わり目にロサンジェルスにやって来た. **4** ADJ 形容詞 You can use **family** to describe things that belong to a particular family. 一家の [ADJ n] ❏ He returned to the family home. 彼は実家に戻った. **5** ADJ 形容詞 You can use **family** to describe things that are designed to be used or enjoyed by both parents and children. 家族用の [ADJ n] ❏ It had been designed as a family house. それは家族用の家として設計されていた. **6** N-COUNT 可算名詞 A **family** of animals or plants is a group of related species. 科 ❏ ...foods in the cabbage family, such as Brussels sprouts. 芽キャベツなどのキャベツ科の食物
→ see Picture Dictionary: family

fam|i|ly plan|ning N-UNCOUNT 不可算名詞 **Family planning** is the practice of using contraception to control the number of children you have. 家族計画 ❏ ...a family planning clinic. 家族計画クリニック

fam|ine /fæmɪn/ (famines) N-VAR 可変性名詞 **Famine** is a situation in which large numbers of people have little or no food, and many of them die. 飢饉(ききん) ❏ Thousands of refugees are trapped by war, drought and famine. 何千人もの避難民が戦争, 旱魃(かんばつ), 飢饉(ききん)から抜け出すことができない.

fa|mous /feɪməs/ ADJ 形容詞 Someone or something that is **famous** is very well-known. 有名な ❏ ...one of Kentucky's most famous landmarks. ケンタッキー州で最も有名な名所の1つ

A **famous** person or thing is known to more people than a **well-known** one. A **notorious** person or thing is famous because they are connected with something bad or undesirable. **Infamous** is not the opposite of **famous**. It has a similar meaning to **notorious**, but is a stronger word. Someone or something that is **notable** is important or interesting.

	Thesaurus famousまた次を参照:
ADJ.	acclaimed, celebrated, prominent, renowned; (ant.) anonymous, obscure, unknown

fa|mous|ly /feɪməsli/ ADV 副詞 You use **famously** to refer to a fact that is well known, usually because it is remarkable or extreme. 有名なことに ❏ Authors are famously ignorant about the realities of publishing. 作家は出版の実情について無知なことで定評がある.

fan /fæn/ (fans, fanning, fanned) **1** N-COUNT 可算名詞 If you are a **fan** of someone or something, especially a famous person or

f

Picture Dictionary family

grandfather grandmother

uncle aunt father mother father-in-law mother-in-law

brother-in-law sister sister-in-law brother husband

wife

a sport, you like them very much and are very interested in them. ファン ❏ If you're a Billy Crystal fan, you'll love this movie. もしあなたがビリー・クリスタルのファンなら、この映画が気に入ると思う。 ❏ I am a great fan of rave music. 私はレイブ音楽の大ファンだ。 **2** N-COUNT 可算名詞 A **fan** is a piece of electrical or mechanical equipment with blades that go around and around. It keeps a room or machine cool or gets rid of unpleasant smells. 扇風機 ❏ He cools himself in front of an electric fan. 彼は扇風機の前で涼んだ。 **3** N-COUNT 可算名詞 A **fan** is a flat object that you hold in your hand and wave in order to move the air and make yourself feel cooler. 扇 ❏ ...hundreds of dancing girls waving peacock fans. くじゃくの扇を振っている何百人もの踊り子 **4** V-T 他動詞 If you **fan** yourself or your face when you are hot, you wave a fan or other flat object in order to make yourself feel cooler. あおぐ ❏ She would have to wait in the truck, fanning herself with a piece of cardboard. 彼女はボール紙であおぎながらトラックの中で待たねばならないだろう。
→ see **concert**
▶ **fan out** PHRASAL VERB 句動詞 If a group of people or things **fan out**, they move forward away from a particular point in different directions. 扇形に広がる ❏ The main body of British, American, and French troops had fanned out to the west. 英国、米国そしてフランスの部隊の主力は西方に扇形に散開した。

fa|nat|ic /fənǽtɪk/ (**fanatics**) **1** N-COUNT 可算名詞 If you describe someone as a **fanatic**, you disapprove of them because you consider their behavior or opinions to be very extreme, for example, in the way they support particular religious or political ideas. 狂信者 [DISAPPROVAL 不賛成] ❏ I am not a religious fanatic but I am a Christian. 私は宗教的な狂信者ではないが、キリスト教徒だ。 **2** N-COUNT 可算名詞 If you say that someone is a **fanatic**, you mean that they are very enthusiastic about a particular activity, sport, or way of life. 熱狂的な愛好者 ❏ Both Rod and Phil are football fanatics. ロッドもフィルもフットボール狂だ。 **3** ADJ 形容詞 **Fanatic** means the same as **fanatical**. 熱狂的な

fa|nati|cal /fənǽtɪkᵊl/ ADJ 形容詞 If you describe someone as **fanatical**, you disapprove of them because you consider their behavior or opinions to be very extreme. 熱狂的な [DISAPPROVAL 不賛成] ❏ He is a fanatical fan of Mozart. 彼はモーツァルトの熱狂的なファンだ。

fan|ci|ful /fǽnsɪfᵊl/ ADJ 形容詞 If you describe an idea as **fanciful**, you disapprove of it because you think it comes from someone's imagination, and is therefore unrealistic or unlikely to be true. 空想的な [DISAPPROVAL 不賛成] ❏ ...fanciful ideas about Martian life. 火星人の生活についての空想的な考え

fancy

❶ ELABORATE OR EXPENSIVE
❷ WANTING, LIKING, OR THINKING

❶ **fan|cy** /fǽnsi/ (**fancier, fanciest**) **1** ADJ 形容詞 If you describe something as **fancy**, you mean that it is special, unusual, or elaborate, for example because it has a lot of decoration. 装飾的な ❏ The magazine was packaged in a fancy plastic case with attractive graphics. その雑誌は魅力的なグラフィックアート付きの意匠を凝らしたプラスチックのケースに入っていた。 **2** ADJ 形容詞 If you describe something as **fancy**, you mean that it is very expensive or of very high quality, and you often dislike it because of this. 極上の [INFORMAL くだけた] ❏ My parents sent me to a fancy private school. 両親は私をすごく金のかかる私立学校にやった。

Thesaurus *fancy* また次を参照：

ADJ. elegant, lavish, showy; (ant.) plain, simple ❶ **2**

❷ **fan|cy** /fǽnsi/ (**fancies, fancying, fancied**) **1** V-T 他動詞 If you **fancy yourself as** a particular kind of person or fancy **yourself** doing a particular thing, you like the idea of being that kind of person or doing that thing. 心に描く [mainly BRIT 主に英国英語] ❏ So you fancy yourself as the boss someday? それじゃきみはいつか社長になりたいと思うんだね。 **2** V-T 他動詞 If you say that someone **fancies themselves as** a particular kind of person, you mean that they think, often wrongly, that they have the good qualities which that kind of person has. うぬぼれる ❏ She fancies herself a bohemian. 彼女はいっぱしのボヘミアンのつもりでいる。 **3** V-T 他動詞 If you **fancy** something, you want to have it or to do it. ほしいと思う [mainly BRIT 主に英国英語, INFORMAL くだけた] ❏ I just fancied a drink. 私はただ1杯やりたかっただけだ。 **4** V-T 他動詞 If you **fancy** someone, you feel attracted to them, especially in a sexual way. (性的に) ひかれる [BRIT 英国英語, INFORMAL くだけた] **5** EXCLAM 感嘆詞 You say "**fancy**" or "**fancy that**" when you want to express surprise or disapproval. 想像してごらん [FEELINGS 感情] ❏ "Fancy that!" smiled Conti. 「そんなことがあるなんて」とコンティはほほえんだ。 **6** PHRASE 句 If you **take a fancy to** someone or something, you start liking them, usually for no understandable reason. 人・物が好きになる ❏ Sylvia took quite a fancy to him. シルビアは彼がすごく好きになった。 **7** PHRASE 句 If something **takes** your **fancy** or **tickles** your **fancy**, you like it a lot when you see it or think of it. 人の気に入る ❏ She makes most of her own clothes, copying any fashion which takes her fancy. 彼女は気に入ったファッションをまねて洋服の大部分を自分で作る。

fan|fare /fǽnfɛər/ (fanfares) **1** N-COUNT 可算名詞 A **fanfare** is a short, loud tune played on trumpets or other similar instruments to announce a special event. ファンファーレ ❑*The ceremony opened with a fanfare of trumpets.* その式典はトランペットのファンファーレで開幕した. **2** N-VAR 可変名詞 If something happens with a **fanfare**, it happens or is announced with a lot of publicity. If something happens without a **fanfare**, it happens without a lot of fuss or publicity. 派手な誇示, 派手な歓迎 [oft N 'of' N] ❑*...a fanfare of publicity.* 派手な宣伝活動

fang /fǽŋ/ (fangs) N-COUNT 可算名詞 **Fangs** are the two long, sharp, upper teeth that some animals have. きば, 犬歯 ❑*The cobra sank its venomous fangs into his hand.* コブラはその毒牙を彼の手に突き立てた.

fan|ta|size /fǽntəsaɪz/ (fantasizes, fantasizing, fantasized) V-T/V-I 他動詞/自動詞 If you **fantasize** about an event or situation that you would like to happen, you give yourself pleasure by imagining that it is happening, although it is untrue or unlikely to happen. 空想する ❑*I fantasized about writing music.* 私は作曲することを夢見た.

fan|tas|tic /fæntǽstɪk/ **1** ADJ 形容詞 If you say that something is **fantastic**, you are emphasizing that you think it is very good and that you like it a lot. 素晴らしい [INFORMAL くだけた, EMPHASIS 強調] ❑*I have a fantastic social life.* 私は素晴らしい社会生活を過ごしている. **2** ADJ 形容詞 A **fantastic** amount or quantity is an extremely large one. (額・量が) ばくだいな [ADJ n] ❑*...fantastic amounts of money.* 巨額の金 ● **fan|tas|ti|cal|ly** /fæntǽstɪkli/ ADV 副詞 [ADV adj/adv] 法外に ❑*...a fantastically expensive restaurant.* 法外に高いレストラン

fan|ta|sy /fǽntəsi/ (fantasies) **1** N-COUNT 可算名詞 A **fantasy** is a pleasant situation or event that you think about and that you want to happen, especially one that is unlikely to happen. 空想の出来事・状況 ❑*...fantasies of romance and true love.* 恋と真実の愛の絵空事 **2** N-VAR 可変名詞 You can refer to a story or situation that someone creates from their imagination and that is not based on reality as **fantasy**. 空想的作品, ファンタジー ❑*The film is more of an ironic fantasy than a horror story.* その映画はホラーストーリーというよりも風刺的な空想物語だ. **3** N-UNCOUNT 不可算名詞 **Fantasy** is the activity of imagining things. 空想 ❑*...a world of imagination, passion, fantasy, reflection.* 想像, 情熱, 空想, 熟考の世界 **4** ADJ 形容詞 **Fantasy** football, baseball, or another sport is a game in which players choose an imaginary team and score points based on the actual performances of the members of their team in real games. 空想的な [ADJ n] ❑*Haskins said he has been playing fantasy baseball for the past five years.* ハスキンズはファンタジーベースボールをもう5年もやっていると言った.
→ see Word Web: **fantasy**

FAO You use **FAO** when addressing a letter or parcel to a particular person. **FAO** is a written abbreviation for "for the attention of." (手紙・小包で) 一あて [BRIT 英国英語; AM **Attn.** 米国英語 **Attn.**]

FAQ /fǽk/ (FAQs) N-PLURAL 複数名詞 **FAQ** is used especially on websites to refer to questions about a particular topic. **FAQ** is an abbreviation for "frequently asked questions." よくある質問

---

far

❶ DISTANT IN SPACE OR TIME
❷ THE EXTENT TO WHICH SOMETHING HAPPENS
❸ EMPHATIC USES

---

❶ far /fɑ́r/ **1** ADV 副詞 If one place, thing, or person is **far** away from another, there is a great distance between them. 遠くに ❑*I know a nice little Italian restaurant not far from here.* 私はここからそう遠くない所にすてきで小さなイタリア料理店を知っている. ❑*Both of my sisters moved even farther away from home.* わたしの姉は2人とも家からさらに遠くへ引っ越した. **2** ADV 副詞 If you ask **how far** a place is, you are asking what distance it is from you or from another place. If you ask **how far** someone went, you are asking what distance they traveled, or what place they reached. (疑問形でhowと共に用いて) どのくらいの距離に ❑*How far is Pawtucket from Providence?* ポータケットはプロヴィダンスからどのくらい離れていますか. ❑*How far is it to Malcy?* マルシーまでのどのくらい距離がありますか. ❑*She followed the tracks as far as the road.* 彼女はその道路まで足跡をたどった.

> **Far** is used in negative sentences and questions about distance, but not usually in affirmative sentences. ❑*We stood by a stream not far from our house.* If you want to state the distance of a particular place from where you are, you can say that it is that distance **away**. ❑*...Omaha, which is over 300 miles away.* If a place is very distant, you can say that it is **a long way away**, or that it is **a long way from** another place. ❑*It is a long way from Atlanta...* *Anna was still a long way away.*

3 ADV 副詞 A time or event that is **far** away in the future or the past is a long time from the present or from a particular point in time. (時間的に) 遠くに ❑*...hidden conflicts whose roots lie far back in time.* 遠い昔に起因するひそかな対立 ❑*I can't see any farther than the next six months.* 先のことは半年以上先のことは分からないよ. **4** ADJ 形容詞 When there are two things of the same kind in a place, the **far** one is the one that is a greater distance from you. 遠いほうの [ADJ n] ❑*He had wandered to the far end of the room.* 彼は部屋の向こう側にぶらぶらと歩いて行っていた. **5** ADJ 形容詞 You can use **far** to refer to the part of an area or object that is the greatest distance from the center in a particular direction. For example, **the far north of** a country is the part of it that is the greatest distance to the north. 最も遠い地点の [ADJ n] ❑*A storm was brewing off Port Angeles in the far north of Washington State.* ワシントン州の最北端のポートアンジェルス沖で嵐が起こっていた. **6** ❐ **near and far** → see **near**

❷ far /fɑ́r/ **1** ADV 副詞 You can use **far** to talk about the extent or degree to which something happens or is true. (範囲・程度が) 一まで ❑*How far did the film tell the truth about Barnes Wallis?* その映画はバーンズ・ウォリスについてどれくらい真実を伝えていたか. **2** ADV 副詞 You can talk about how **far** someone or something gets to describe the progress that they make. (進展が) 一の地点まで ❑*Discussions never progressed very far.* 話し合いはたいして進まなかった. ❑*Think of how far we have come in a little time.* ほんの短い間に私たちがどれほど進んで来たかを考えよう. **3** ADV 副詞 You can talk about how **far** a person or action goes to describe the degree to which someone's behavior or actions are extreme. 極端に [ADV with v] ❑*It's still not clear how far the Russian parliament will go to implement its own plans.* ロシアの国会が (計画実行の) ためにためにどこまでやるかはまだよく分からない. ❑*Competition can be healthy, but if it is pushed too far it can result in bullying.* 競争は健全でありえるが, やり過ぎると弱い者いじめになる可能性がある. **4** ADV 副詞 You can use **far** in expressions like "**as far as I know**" and "**so far as I remember**" to indicate that you are not absolutely sure of the statement you are about to make or have just made, and you may be wrong. 一の限り [VAGUENESS あいまいさ] ['as/so' ADV 'as'] ❑*It only lasted a couple of years, as far as I know.* 私が知っていた限りでは, それは2年しか続かなかった. **5** PHRASE 句 If you say that someone **will go far**, you mean that they will be very successful in their career. 成功するだろう ❑*I was very impressed with the talent of Michael Ball. He will go far.* 私はマイケル・ボールの才能にとても感心した. 彼は大物になるだろう. **6** PHRASE 句 Someone or something

---

Word Web   fantasy

All **fictional** writing involves the use of **imaginary** situations and characters. However, **fantasy** goes a few steps further. This **genre** leaves **reality** behind and moves into the area of **imagination**. It involves creating new creatures, **myths**, and **legends**. A **novelist** usually incorporates **realistic** people and settings. But a fantasy writer is free to create a whole different world where earthly laws no longer apply. Contemporary movies have found a rich source of stories in the genre. Today you can see a wide variety of films about **fairies**, **wizards**, and **dragons**.

that is **far gone** is in such a bad state or condition that not much can be done to help or improve them. (病状が) ひどく進行して □ *In his last few days the pain seemed to have stopped, but by then he was so far gone that it was no longer any comfort.* 彼の最後の数日は痛みは止まったようだったが、すでに症状がかなり進行していて、それはもうなんの慰めにもならなかった. **7** PHRASE 句 You can use the expression "**as far as I can see**" when you are about to state your opinion of a situation, or have just stated it, to indicate that it is your personal opinion. 私に分かる限りでは □ *That's the problem as far as I can see.* 私に分かる限りでは、それが問題なのよ. **8** PHRASE 句 If you say that something only goes **so far** or can only go **so far**, you mean that its extent, effect, or influence is limited. そこまで □ *Their loyalty only went so far.* 彼らの忠誠心はそこまでが限界だった. **9** PHRASE 句 If you tell or ask someone what has happened **so far**, you are telling or asking them what has happened up until the present point in a situation or story, and often implying that something different might happen later. 今までのところ □ *It's been quiet so far.* 今のところは静かだ. □ *So far, they have met with no success.* 今のところ、彼らはまだ成功していない. **10** PHRASE 句 You can say **so far so good** to express satisfaction with the way that a situation or activity is progressing, developing, or happening. これまでは順調だ [FEELINGS 感情] □ *Of course, it's a case of so far, so good, but it's only one step.* もちろん、それは今のところうまく行っているケースだけれども、まだ第1段階にしか過ぎない.

❸ **far** /fɑr/ **1** ADV 副詞 You can use **far** to mean "very much" when you are comparing two things and emphasizing the difference between them. For example, you can say that something is **far better** or **far worse** than something else to indicate that it is very much better or worse. You can also say that something is, for example, **far too big** to indicate that it is very much too big. [EMPHASIS 強調] □ *Women who eat plenty of fresh vegetables are far less likely to suffer anxiety or depression.* 新鮮な野菜をたっぷり食べている女性は、不安やうつ病になる可能性が非常に低い. □ *The police say the response has been far better than expected.* 警察によると、その反応は予想よりはるかによかったらしい. **2** ADJ 形容詞 You can describe people with extreme left-wing or right-wing political views as the **far** left or the **far** right. 過激な、極端な [ADJ n] □ *The far right is now a greater threat than the extreme left.* 極右派はいまや極左派よりも大きな脅威となっている. **3** PHRASE 句 You use the expression **by far** when you are comparing something or someone with others of the same kind, in order to emphasize how great the difference is between them. For example, you can say that something is **by far the best** or **the best by far** to indicate that it is definitely the best. 圧倒的に、はるかに [EMPHASIS 強調] □ *By far the most important issue for them is unemployment.* 彼らにとってはるかに最重要の問題は失業だ. **4** PHRASE 句 If you say that something is **far from** a particular thing or **far from** being the case, you are emphasizing that it is not that particular thing or not at all the case, especially when people expect or assume that it is. 一にはほど遠い [EMPHASIS 強調] □ *It was obvious that much of what they recorded was far from the truth.* 彼らが記録したものの多くが真実からほど遠いということは明らかだった. □ *Far from being relaxed, we both felt so uncomfortable we hardly spoke.* くつろぐにはほど遠くとても居心地が悪かったので、私たちはほとんど口をきかなかった. **5** PHRASE 句 You can use the expression "**far from it**" to emphasize a negative statement that you have just made. とんでもない [EMPHASIS 強調] □ *Being dyslexic does not mean that one is unintelligent. Far from it.* 失読症であることと頭が悪いということはまったく別問題だ. 全然違う.

Far has two comparatives, **farther** and **further**, and two superlatives, **farthest** and **furthest**. **Farther** and **farthest** are used mainly in sense **1**, and are dealt with here. **Further** and **furthest** are dealt with in separate entries.

---

far|a|way /fɑrəweɪ/ ADJ 形容詞 A **faraway** place is a long distance from you or from a particular place. 遠く離れた [ADJ n] □ *They have just returned from faraway places with wonderful stories to tell.* 彼らは遠く離れた土地から素晴らしい土産話を持って帰って来たところだ.

farce /fɑrs/ (**farces**) **1** N-COUNT 可算名詞 A **farce** is a humorous play in which the characters become involved in complicated and unlikely situations. 笑劇 □ *...an off-Broadway farce called "Lucky Stiff."* 『幸福な死体』と呼ばれるオフ・ブロードウェイの道化芝居 **2** N-UNCOUNT 不可算名詞 **Farce** is the style of acting and writing that is typical of farces. 笑劇の様式 □ *The plot often borders on farce.* その筋はしばしば笑劇もどきになっている. **3** N-SING 単数名詞 If you describe a situation or event as a **farce**, you mean that it is so disorganized or ridiculous that you cannot take it seriously. ばかげていること、茶番 [DISAPPROVAL 不賛成] [also no det] □ *The elections have been reduced to a farce.* 選挙はばかげた様相を呈してきた.

far|ci|cal /fɑrsɪkəl/ ADJ 形容詞 If you describe a situation or event as **farcical**, you mean that it is so silly or extreme that you are unable to take it seriously. ばかげた [DISAPPROVAL 不賛成] □ *...a farcical nine months' jail sentence imposed yesterday on a killer.* 昨日殺人犯に言い渡された9か月のばかげた実刑判決

fare /fɛr/ (**fares, faring, fared**) **1** N-COUNT 可算名詞 A **fare** is the money that you pay for a trip that you make, for example, in a bus, train, or taxi. 運賃 □ *He could barely afford the fare.* 彼はかろうじて運賃が払えた. **2** V-I 自動詞 If you say that someone or something **fares** well or badly, you are referring to the degree of success they achieve in a particular situation or activity. やっていく、暮らす □ *It is unlikely that the marine industry will fare any better in September.* 水産業が9月にこれ以上うまくいく見込みはない.

Far East N-PROPER 固有名詞 The **Far East** is used to refer to all the countries of Eastern Asia, including China, Japan, North and South Korea, and Indonesia. 極東

fare|well /fɛrwɛl/ (**farewells**) CONVENTION 慣習表現 **Farewell** means the same as goodbye. さようなら [LITERARY, OLD-FASHIONED 文語的、古風な] ● N-COUNT 可算名詞 **Farewell** is also a noun. 別れの挨拶、別れ □ *They said their farewells there at the cafe.* 彼らはそこのカフェで別れの挨拶を交わした.

far-fetched ADJ 形容詞 If you describe a story or idea as **far-fetched**, you are criticizing it because you think it is unlikely to be true or practical. 信じ難い、無理な [DISAPPROVAL 不賛成] □ *The storyline was too far-fetched and none of the actors was particularly good.* 話の筋があまりにも強引な上、特に素晴らしい俳優は1人もいなかった.

farm /fɑrm/ (**farms, farming, farmed**) **1** N-COUNT 可算名詞 A **farm** is an area of land, together with the buildings on it, that is used for growing crops or raising animals, usually in order to sell them. 農場 □ *Farms in France are much smaller than those in the United States or even Britain.* フランスの農場は米国、さらに英国の農場よりもはるかに小さい. **2** N-COUNT 可算名詞 A mink **farm** or a fish **farm**, for example, is a place where a particular kind of animal or fish is bred and kept in large quantities in order to be sold. 飼育場 □ *...trout fresh from a local trout farm.* 地元のマスの養殖場から釣ったばかりのマス **3** V-T/V-I 他動詞/自動詞 If you **farm** an area of land, you grow crops or keep animals on it. 耕作する、飼育する [他動詞]、農業を営む [自動詞] □ *They farmed some of the best land in the country.* 彼らはその国で最良の農地のいくつかを耕作していた. □ *Bease has been farming for 30 years.* ビーズは30年間農業を営んでいる. ▶ **farm out** PHRASAL VERB 句動詞 If you **farm out** something that is your responsibility, you send it to other people for them to deal with or look after. 外注する、下請けに出す □ *Scores of U.S. companies farm out software development.* 多くの米国企業はソフトウェアの開発を外注している. □ *She may have farmed the child out in order to remarry.* 彼女は再婚するためにその子を里子に出したのかもしれない. → see Word Web: **farm** → see **dairy**

farm|er /fɑrmər/ (**farmers**) N-COUNT 可算名詞 A **farmer** is a person who owns or manages a farm. 農場主、農家の人 → see **farm**

farm|house /fɑrmhaʊs/ (**farmhouses**) N-COUNT 可算名詞 A **farmhouse** is the main house on a farm, usually where the farmer lives. 農場主の家

Word Web   farm

Gone are the days of simply planting a **crop** and **harvesting** it. Today's **farmer** relies on engineering and technology to make a living. Careful **irrigation** and **drainage** control the amount of water **plants** receive. **Insecticides** and fungicides protect plants from insect damage. **Fertilizers** guarantee maximum growth. Another high-tech **agricultural** approach promises to increase the world's **food** supply. Employing hydroponic methods, farmers use **chemical** solutions to **cultivate** plants. This has several advantages. **Soil** can contain **pests** and diseases not present in water alone. Growing plants hydroponically also requires less water and less labor than conventional growing methods.

farm|ing /fɑrmɪŋ/ N-UNCOUNT 不可算名詞 **Farming** is the activity of growing crops or keeping animals on a farm. 農業, 飼育 ❏ ...a career in farming. 農業歴

farm|land /fɑrmlænd/ (**farmlands**) N-UNCOUNT 不可算名詞 **Farmland** is land which is farmed, or which is suitable for farming. 農業用地 [also N in pl] ❏ It is surrounded by 62 acres of farmland. それは62エーカーの農地に囲まれている.

farm|yard /fɑrmyɑrd/ (**farmyards**) N-COUNT 可算名詞 On a farm, the **farmyard** is an area of land near the farmhouse which is enclosed by walls or buildings. 農場構内, 農家の庭 ❏ ...farmyard animals including chickens, geese and rabbits. 鶏やガチョウ, ウサギなどの農家構内の動物

far off (**further off, furthest off**) ■ ADJ 形容詞 If you describe a moment in time as **far off**, you mean that it is a long time from the present, either in the past or the future. (時間的に) 遠い ❏ In those far off days it never entered anyone's mind that a woman could be prime minister. その遠い昔には女性が首相になりえるなど誰も決して考え及ばなかった. ② ADJ 形容詞 If you describe something as **far off**, you mean that it is a long distance from you or from a particular place. (距離が) 遠い ❏ ...stars in far-off galaxies. 遠い銀河の星 ● ADV 副詞 **Far off** is also an adverb. 遠くで [ADV after v] ❏ The band was playing far off in their blue and yellow uniforms. そのバンドは青と黄色のそろいの服を着て遠くで演奏していた.

far-reaching ADJ 形容詞 If you describe actions, events, or changes as **far-reaching**, you mean that they have a very great influence and affect a great number of things. 広く影響する ❏ The economy is in danger of collapse unless far-reaching reforms are implemented. 大規模な改革が行われない限り, その経済は崩壊の危機に瀕している.

far|sighted /fɑrsaɪtɪd/ also **far-sighted** ■ ADJ 形容詞 If you describe someone as **farsighted**, you admire them because they understand what is likely to happen in the future, and therefore make wise decisions and plans. 先見の明がある [APPROVAL 賛成] ❏ Haven't farsighted economists been telling us that in the future we will work less, not more? 先見の明がある経済専門家たちが, 我々の労働時間は将来, 増加ではなく減少すると言わなかったか? ② ADJ 形容詞 **Farsighted** people cannot see things clearly that are close to them, and therefore need to wear glasses. 遠視の → see eye

far|ther /fɑrðər/ **Farther** is a comparative form of **far**. far の比較級

far|thest /fɑrðɪst/ **Farthest** is a superlative form of **far**. far の最上級

fas|ci|nate /fæsɪneɪt/ (**fascinates, fascinating, fascinated**) V-T 他動詞 If something **fascinates** you, it interests and delights you so much that your thoughts tend to concentrate on it. 魅惑する, 心をとらえる ❏ Politics fascinated Franklin's father. 政治がフランクリンの父の心を魅了した.

fas|ci|nat|ed /fæsɪneɪtɪd/ ADJ 形容詞 If you are **fascinated by** something, you find it very interesting and attractive, and your thoughts tend to concentrate on it. 魅了されて ❏ I sat on the stairs and watched, fascinated. 私は階段に座り, すっかり心を奪われ見つめた.

fas|ci|nat|ing /fæsɪneɪtɪŋ/ ADJ 形容詞 If you describe something as **fascinating**, you find it very interesting and attractive, and your thoughts tend to concentrate on it. 魅惑的な, 興味をかきたてる ❏ Madagascar is the most fascinating place I have ever been to. マダガスカルは私が今まで訪れた中で最も魅力的な所だ.

fas|ci|na|tion /fæsɪneɪʃən/ N-UNCOUNT 不可算名詞 **Fascination** is the state of being greatly interested in or delighted by something. 魅了された状態 ❏ I've had a lifelong fascination with the sea and with small boats. 私は一生, 海と小舟に魅せられてきた.

fas|cism /fæʃɪzəm/ N-UNCOUNT 不可算名詞 **Fascism** is a set of right-wing political beliefs that includes strong control of society and the economy by the state, a powerful role for the armed forces, and the stopping of political opposition. ファシズム ❏ ...the rise of fascism in the 1930s. 1930年代のファシズムの台頭

fas|cist /fæʃɪst/ (**fascists**) ■ ADJ 形容詞 You use **fascist** to describe organizations, ideas, or systems that follow the principles of fascism. ファシズムの ❏ ...an upsurge of support for extreme rightist, nationalist and fascist organizations. 極右団体, 国家主義的団体, そしてファシスト団体に対する支持の急増 ● N-COUNT 可算名詞 A **fascist** is someone who has fascist views. ファシスト ❏ ...a reluctant supporter of Mussolini's Fascists. ムッソリーニのファシスト党員をいやいや支持する人

fash|ion /fæʃən/ (**fashions**) ■ N-UNCOUNT 不可算名詞 **Fashion** is the area of activity that involves styles of clothing and appearance. ファッション ❏ There are 20 full-color pages of fashion for men. 男性ファッションがオールカラーで20ページにわたっている. ② N-COUNT 可算名詞 A **fashion** is a style of clothing or a way of behaving that is popular at a particular time. 流行 ❏ In the early seventies I wore false eyelashes, as was the fashion. 70年代の初めに私は

当時流行していた付けまつげをしていた. ❏ The demand for perfume resulted in a fashion for fancy scent bottles. 香水への需要がしゃれた香水瓶を流行させた. ③ N-SING 単数名詞 If you do something in a particular **fashion** or after a particular **fashion**, you do it in that way. やり方, 流儀 ❏ There is another drug called DHE that works in a similar fashion. 他にも同じような効き目を持つDHEという薬がある. ④ → see also old-fashioned ⑤ PHRASE 句 If something is **in fashion**, it is popular and approved of at a particular time. If it is **out of fashion**, it is not popular or approved of. 流行中の; 時代遅れの ❏ That sort of house is back in fashion. その手の家がまた流行している.

fash|ion|able /fæʃənəbəl/ ADJ 形容詞 Something or someone that is **fashionable** is popular or approved of at a particular time. 流行の ❏ It became fashionable to eat certain kinds of fish. ある種の魚を食べるのがはやりとなった. ● **fash|ion|ably** ADV 副詞 流行を追って ❏ ...women who are perfectly made up and fashionably dressed. 完璧なお化粧をし, 流行の服を着た女性たち

fast /fæst/ (**faster, fastest, fasts, fasting, fasted**) ■ ADJ 形容詞 **Fast** means happening, moving, or doing something at great speed. You also use **fast** in questions or statements about speed. (速度が) 速い ❏ ...fast cars with flashing lights and sirens. ライトを点滅させ, サイレンを鳴らして疾走する車 ❏ The only question is how fast the process will be. 唯一の問題はその進行がどれだけ早いだろうかということだ. ● ADV 副詞 **Fast** is also an adverb. 速く [ADV with v] ❏ They work terrifically fast. 彼らは素晴らしく仕事が速い. ❏ It would be nice to go faster and break the world record. もっと速く走り, 世界記録を破れるといいだろうな. ❏ How fast would the disease develop? その病気はどのくらい速く進行するのだろうか. ② ADJ 形容詞 If a watch or clock is **fast**, it is showing a time that is later than the real time. (時計が) 進んでいる [v-link ADJ] ❏ That clock's an hour fast. その時計は1時間進んでいる. ③ ADJ 形容詞 If colors or dyes are **fast**, they do not come out of the fabrics they are used on when they get wet. (色が) あせない ❏ The fabric was ironed to make the colors fast. その布は色落ちしないようアイロンがけてあせてあった. ④ ADV 副詞 You use **fast** to say that something happens without any delay. 直ちに [ADV after v] ❏ When you've got a crisis like this you need professional help – fast!. こんな危機に直面した時, 専門家の助けが必要だよ. 今すぐにだ. ● ADJ 形容詞 **Fast** is also an adjective. 迅速な [ADJ n] ❏ That would be an astonishingly fast action on the part of the Congress. それは議会側の驚くべき迅速な対応と言えるだろう. ⑤ ADV 副詞 If you hold something **fast**, you hold it tightly and firmly. If something is stuck **fast**, it is stuck very firmly and cannot move. しっかりと [ADV after v] ❏ She climbed the staircase cautiously, holding fast to the rail. 彼女は手すりをしっかりとつかみ, 階段を慎重に上った. ⑥ ADV 副詞 If you hold **fast** to a principle or idea, or if you stand **fast**, you do not change your mind about it, even though people are trying to persuade you to. かたくなに [ADV after v] ❏ We can only try to hold fast to the age-old values of honesty, decency and respect. 私たちは正直さ, 礼儀正しさや他人への思いやりといった昔からの価値観を固守するよう努力することができるのみだ. ⑦ V-I 自動詞 If you **fast**, you eat no food for a period of time, usually for either religious or medical reasons, or as a protest. 断食する ❏ I fasted for a day and half and asked God to help me. 私は1日半断食して神の助けを求めた. ● N-COUNT 可算名詞 **Fast** is also a noun. 断食 ❏ The fast is broken at sunset, traditionally with dates and water. 断食は日が沈むと中断され, 伝統的にナツメヤシと水を取る. ● **fast|ing** N-UNCOUNT 不可算名詞 断食 ❏ ...the Muslim holy month of fasting and prayer. イスラム教徒の断食と祈りの聖なる月 ⑧ PHRASE 句 Someone who is **fast asleep** is completely asleep. ぐっすり眠って ❏ When he went upstairs five minutes later, she was fast asleep. 彼が5分後に2階へ上がると, 彼女はぐっすり眠っていた. ⑨ to **make a fast buck** → see **buck**

Thesaurus		**fast** また次を参照:
ADJ.		hasty, quick, rapid, speedy, swift; (ant.) leisurely, slow ■
ADV.		quickly, rapidly, soon, swiftly; (ant.) leisurely, slowly ④ firmly, tightly; (ant.) loosely, unsteadily ⑤

fas|ten /fæsən/ (**fastens, fastening, fastened**) ■ V-T/V-I 他動詞/自動詞 When you **fasten** something, you close it by means of buttons or a strap, or some other device. If something **fastens** with buttons or straps, you can close it in this way. しっかり締める (ボタン・紐などで) 留める [他動詞], しっかり締まる [自動詞] ❏ She got quickly into her Mini and fastened the seat-belt. 彼女は素早く自分のミニに乗り込み, シートベルトを締めた. ❏ Her long fair hair was fastened at the nape of her neck by an elastic band. 彼女は首筋で長い金髪をゴムバンドで束ねていた. ② V-T 他動詞 If you **fasten** one thing **to** another, you attach the first thing to the second, for example, with a piece of string or tape. (ひも・テープで) つなぐ ❏ There were no instructions on how to fasten the carrying strap to the box. その持ち運び用の皮ひもを箱にどうやって付けるかの説明書がなかった. ③ → see also **fastening**

fas|ten|ing /fæsənɪŋ/ (**fastenings**) N-COUNT 可算名詞 A

fastening is something such as a clasp or zipper that you use to fasten something and keep it shut. 締め具, 留め具 □*The sundress has a neat back zipper fastening.* そのサンドレスの背中には小粋なファスナーが付いている.

fast food N-UNCOUNT 不可算名詞 **Fast food** is hot food, such as hamburgers and French fries, that you obtain from particular types of restaurants, and which is served quickly after you order it. ファーストフード □*James works at a fast food restaurant.* ジェイムズはファーストフードのレストランで働いている.
→ see **meal**

fast for|ward (**fast forwards, fast forwarding, fast forwarded**) also **fast-forward** V-T/V-I 他動詞/自動詞 When you **fast forward** the tape in a video or tape recorder or when you **fast forward,** you make the tape go forward. Compare **rewind.** 早送りする □*Just fast forward the video.* いいからそのビデオを早送りしてよ. □*He fast-forwarded the tape past the explosion.* 彼はそのテープの爆発の部分を早送りした.

fas|tid|ious /fæstɪdiəs, fə-/ ADJ 形容詞 If you say that someone is **fastidious,** you mean that they pay great attention to detail because they like everything to be very neat, accurate, and in good order. 細部までこだわった □*...her fastidious attention to historical detail.* 歴史的な詳細に対する彼女の細心の注意

fast lane (**fast lanes**) ■ N-COUNT 可算名詞 On a highway, the **fast lane** is the part of the road where the vehicles that are traveling fastest go. 追い越し車線 □*I cut across the expressway and took the fast lane back to Miami.* 私は高速道路に入り, 追い越し車線を通ってマイアミまで帰った. ② N-SING 単数名詞 If someone is living in the **fast lane,** they have a very busy, exciting life, although they sometimes seem to have a lot of risks. 忙しく緊張感のある人生 □*..a tale of life in the fast lane.* 多忙で緊張感のある人生の話

fast track (**fast tracks, fast tracking, fast tracked**) also **fast-track** ■ N-SING 単数名詞 The **fast track to** a particular goal, especially in politics or in your career, is the quickest route to achieving it. 出世コース, 成功への近道 □*Many Croats and Slovenes saw independence as the fast track to democracy.* 多くのクロアチア人とスロベニア人は独立が民主主義への近道だと思った. ② V-T 他動詞 To **fast track** something means to make it happen or progress faster or earlier than normal. (出来事を) 早めに起こす, 早める □*A Federal Court case had been fast tracked to Wednesday.* 連邦裁判所の訴訟が水曜日に繰り上げられていた.

fat /fæt/ (**fatter, fattest, fats**) ■ ADJ 形容詞 If you say that a person or animal is **fat,** you mean that they have a lot of flesh on their body and that they weigh too much. You usually use the word **fat** when you think that this is a bad thing. 太った (悪い意味で使うことが多い) [DISAPPROVAL 不賛成] □*I could eat what I liked without getting fat.* 私は食べたい物を食べても太らなかった.

If you describe someone as **fat,** you are speaking in a very direct way, and this may be considered rude. If you want to say more politely that someone is rather fat, it is better to describe them as **plump,** or more informally, as **chubby. Overweight** and **obese** are used to describe someone who may have health problems because of their size or weight. **Obese** is also a medical term used to describe someone who is extremely fat or overweight. In general you should avoid using any of these words in the presence of the person you are describing.

② N-MASS 質量名詞 **Fat** is a substance contained in foods such as meat, cheese, and butter which forms an energy store in your body. 脂肪 □*An easy way to cut the amount of fat in your diet is to avoid eating red meats.* 脂肪の摂取量を減らす簡単な方法は赤身の肉を食べないことだ. ③ N-MASS 質量名詞 **Fat** is a solid or liquid substance obtained from animals or vegetables, which is used in cooking. 油脂 □*When you use oil or fat for cooking, use as little as possible.* 料理用の油や油脂を使う時は, できるだけ量を少なくしなさい. ④ ADJ 形容詞 A **fat** object, especially a book, is very thick or wide. (本などが) 分厚い □*..."Europe in Figures," a fat book published on September 22nd.* 9月22日に出版された『数字で見るヨーロッパ』という分厚い本 ⑤ ADJ 形容詞 A **fat** profit or fee is a large one. (利益・手数料が) 多い [INFORMAL くだけた] [ADJ n] □*They are set to make a big fat profit.* 彼らは巨額の利益を上げる準備ができている. ⑥ N-UNCOUNT 不可算名詞 **Fat** is the extra flesh that animals and humans have under their skin, which is used to store energy and to help keep them warm. 脂肪 □*Because you're not burning calories, everything you eat turns to fat.* あなたはカロリーを消費してないから, 食べる物がすべて脂肪になるのよ. ⑦ PHRASE 句 If you say that there is **fat chance of** something happening, you mean that you do not believe that it will happen. 見込み薄 [INFORMAL, mainly SPOKEN くだけた, 主に口語, FEELINGS 感情] □*"Would your car be easy to steal?" — "Fat chance. I've got a device that shuts down the gas and ignition."* 「きみの車は簡単に盗まれるかい?」,「その可能性は低いさ. ぼくはガソリンと点火装置を切ってしまう機器を持っているんだ」.
→ see **calorie**

Thesaurus *fat* また次を参照:

ADJ. big, chunky, heavy, obese, overweight, stout, thick; (*ant.*) lean, skinny, slim, thin ■

Word Partnership *fat* は次の語句と使われる:

ADJ.	big and fat, short and fat ■
	high/low in fat, saturated fat ③
	excess fat ③ ⑥
V.	get fat ■
	burn fat, lose fat ⑥

fa|tal /feɪt³l/ ■ ADJ 形容詞 A **fatal** action has very undesirable effects. (行動が) 致命的な □*It would be fatal for the nation to overlook the urgency of the situation.* 事態の緊急性を見落とすことは国家にとって致命的となる. □*He made the fatal mistake of compromising early.* 彼は早々と妥協するという取り返しのつかない過ちを犯した. ●**fa|tal|ly** ADV 副詞 [ADV with v] 致命的に □*Failure now could fatally damage his chances in the future.* この時点での失敗は彼の将来の可能性を致命的につぶしかねないだろう. ② ADJ 形容詞 A **fatal** accident or illness causes someone's death. (事故・病気が) 致命的な, 命取りの □*...the fatal stabbing of a police sergeant.* 巡査部長の刺殺 ●**fa|tal|ly** ADV 副詞 致命的に □*The dead soldier is reported to have been fatally wounded in the chest.* その死亡した兵士は胸に致命傷を負っていたと報告されている.

fa|tal|ity /fətælɪti/ (**fatalities**) N-COUNT 可算名詞 A **fatality** is a death caused by an accident or by violence. (事故・暴力による) 死 [FORMAL 形式ばった] □*Drunk driving fatalities have declined more than 10 percent over the past 10 years.* 飲酒運転による死亡事故は過去10年間で10パーセント以上減少している.

fat cat (**fat cats**) N-COUNT 可算名詞 If you refer to a businessman or politician as a **fat cat,** you are indicating that you disapprove of the way they use their wealth and power. 金持ち, 権力者 [INFORMAL くだけた BUSINESS 実業, DISAPPROVAL 不賛成] □*...the fat cats who run the bank.* その銀行を経営している金持ち連中

fate /feɪt/ (**fates**) ■ N-UNCOUNT 不可算名詞 **Fate** is a power that some people believe controls and decides everything that happens, in a way that cannot be prevented or changed. You can also refer to **the fates.** 運命 [also N in pl] □*I see no use arguing with fate.* 私は運命に逆らっても無駄だと思う. □*...the fickleness of fate.* 運命の気まぐれ ② N-COUNT 可算名詞 A person's or thing's **fate** is what happens to them. 運命, (人や物に) 起こる事 □*The Russian Parliament will hold a special session later this month to decide his fate.* ロシア国会は彼の運命を決定するために今月後半に特別会議を開く. □*He seems for a moment to be again holding the fate of the country in his hands.* 彼はその国の運命を再び彼の手中にしばらく握っていそうだ.

fate|ful /feɪtfəl/ ADJ 形容詞 If an action or a time when something happened is described as **fateful,** it is considered to have an important, and often very bad, effect on future events. 運命を決する □*It was a fateful decision, one which was to break the Government.* それは政府を倒すという重大な決定だった.

fa|ther /fɑðər/ (**fathers, fathering, fathered**) ■ N-FAMILY 家族名詞 Your **father** is your male parent. You can also call someone your **father** if he brings you up as if he were this man. 父親 □*His father was a painter.* 彼の父は画家だった. □*He would be a good father to my children.* 彼は子供たちの良い父親になると思うの. ② V-T 他動詞 When a man **fathers** a child, he makes a woman pregnant and their child is born. (子供の) 父となる □*She claims Mark fathered her child.* 彼女はマークが子供の父親だと主張している. ③ N-COUNT 可算名詞 The man who invented or started something is sometimes referred to as the **father of** that thing. 創始者 □*Max Dupain, regarded as the father of modern photography.* 現代写真の父とされているマックス・デュペイン
→ see **family**

Father's Day is a special day on which children give cards and presents to their fathers as a sign of their love for them. Grown-up children often try to visit, and perhaps take their father out for the day or for a special meal. "Father's Day" is the third Sunday in June.

father|hood /fɑðərhʊd/ N-UNCOUNT 不可算名詞 **Fatherhood** is the state of being a father. 父親であること □*...the joys of fatherhood.* 父親であることの喜び

father-in-law (**fathers-in-law**) N-COUNT 可算名詞 Someone's **father-in-law** is the father of their husband or wife. 義父
→ see **family**

fath|om /fæðəm/ (**fathoms, fathoming, fathomed**) ■ N-COUNT 可算名詞 A **fathom** is a measurement of 6 feet or 1.8 meters, used when referring to the depth of water. (水深の単位) ひろ, ファゾム □*We sailed into the bay and dropped anchor in five fathoms of water.* 私たちはその湾内に船を進め, 水深5ひろのところにいかりを下ろした. ② V-T 他動詞 If you cannot **fathom** something,

you are unable to understand it, although you think carefully about it. 理解する [no cont, oft with brd-neg] ❏ *I really couldn't fathom what Steiner was talking about.* 私はシュタイナーが何の話をしているかまったく分からなかった. ● PHRASAL VERB 句動詞 **Fathom out** means the same as **fathom**. 理解する ❏ *We're trying to fathom out what's going on.* 我々は状況を把握しようとしている.

fa|tigue /fətiːɡ/ (**fatigues**) **1** N-UNCOUNT 不可算名詞 **Fatigue** is a feeling of extreme physical or mental tiredness. 疲労 ❏ *She continued to have severe stomach cramps, aches, fatigue, and depression.* 彼女のひどい胃けいれん, 痛み, 疲労感やうつ状態は続いた. **2** N-UNCOUNT 不可算名詞 You can say that people are suffering from a particular kind of **fatigue** when they have been doing something for a long time and feel they can no longer continue to do it. 倦(けん)怠感 ❏ *...compassion fatigue caused by endless TV and celebrity appeals.* 果てしないテレビや有名人の訴えによって引き起こされた共感疲労 **3** N-UNCOUNT 不可算名詞 **Fatigue** in metal or wood is a weakness in it that is caused by repeated stress. Fatigue can cause the metal or wood to break. (金属・木などの)疲労 ❏ *The problem turned out to be metal fatigue in the fuselage.* その問題は機体の金属疲労であることが判明した. **4** N-PLURAL 複数名詞 **Fatigues** are clothes that soldiers wear when they are fighting or when they are doing routine jobs. (兵士の)戦闘服, 作業服 ❏ *He never expected to return home wearing combat fatigues.* 彼は戦闘服を着て家に戻れるとは決して思わなかった.

fat|ten /fætᵊn/ (**fattens, fattening, fattened**) V-T 他動詞 If you say that someone is **fattening** something such as a business or its profits, you mean that they are increasing the value of the business or its profits, in a way that you disapprove of. (事業や利益を)太らせる [BUSINESS 実業, DISAPPROVAL 不賛成] ❏ *They have kept the price of sugar artificially high and so fattened the company's profits.* 彼らは砂糖の値段を人為的に高く保ち, 会社の利益を太らせた. ● PHRASAL VERB 句動詞 **Fatten up** means the same as **fatten**. 太らせる ❏ *The Government is making the taxpayer pay to fatten up a public sector business for private sale.* 政府は民営化のために公共部門の事業を太らせようと納税者に税金を支払わせている.

fat|ten|ing /fætᵊnɪŋ/ ADJ 形容詞 Food that is **fattening** is considered to make people fat easily. (人などを)太らせる ❏ *Some foods are more fattening than others.* 食べ物の一部は他の物よりずっと太るもとになる.

fat|ty /fæti/ (**fattier, fattiest**) **1** ADJ 形容詞 **Fatty** food contains a lot of fat. 脂肪の多い ❏ *Don't eat fatty food or chocolates.* 脂っこい食べ物やチョコレートを食べるな. **2** ADJ 形容詞 **Fatty** acids or **fatty** tissues, for example, contain or consist of fat. 脂肪の [ADJ n] ❏ *...fatty acids.* 脂肪酸

fau|cet /fɔːsɪt/ (**faucets**) N-COUNT 可算名詞 A **faucet** is a device that controls the flow of a liquid or gas from a pipe or container. Sinks and baths have faucets attached to them. (水道の)蛇口, (ガスの)コック [mainly AM 主に米国英語] ❏ *She turned off the faucet and dried her hands.* 彼女は蛇口を閉め, 手を乾かした.

fault /fɔːlt/ (**faults, faulting, faulted**) **1** N-SING 単数名詞 If a bad or undesirable situation is your **fault**, you caused it or are responsible for it. 責任 ❏ *There was no escaping the fact: it was all his fault.* その事実からは逃れようがなかった. それはすべて彼のせいだった. **2** N-COUNT 可算名詞 A **fault** is a mistake in what someone is doing or in what they have done. 誤り, 過失 ❏ *It is a big fault to think that you can learn how to manage people in business school.* 経営学大学院で人の管理方法を学べると思ったら大きな間違いだ. **3** N-COUNT 可算名詞 A **fault** in someone or something is a weakness in them or something that is not perfect. 欠点, 欠陥 ❏ *His manners had always made her blind to his faults.* 彼の物腰のせいで彼女はいつも彼の欠点に気づかなかった. **4** N-COUNT 可算名詞 A **fault** is a large crack in the surface of the earth. (地殻の)断層 ❏ *...the San Andreas Fault.* サンアンドレアス断層 **5** N-COUNT 可算名詞 A **fault** in tennis is a service that is wrong according to the rules. (テニスの)フォールト ❏ *He caught the ball on his first toss and then served a fault.* 彼は最初のトスでボールを引っかけ, サーブを失敗した. **6** V-T 他動詞 If you **cannot fault** someone, you cannot find any reason for criticizing them or the things that they are doing. あらを探す, 批判する [with brd-neg] ❏ *You can't fault them for lack of invention.* きみは彼らが創意に乏しいことを責めてはいけないよ. **7** PHRASE 句 If someone or something is **at fault**, they are to blame or are responsible for a particular situation that has gone wrong. 責任のある ❏ *He could never accept that he had been at fault.* 彼は自分に責任があったとは決して認めることはできなかった. **8** PHRASE 句 If you **find fault with** something or someone, you look for mistakes and complain about them. あら探しをする ❏ *I was disappointed whenever the cook found fault with my work.* 私はその料理人が私の作ったものにけちをつけるたびにがっかりした.

→ see **earthquake**

Thesaurus *fault* また次を参照:

N.	blunder, error, mistake, wrongdoing **1**
	defect, flaw, imperfection, weakness **2**

Word Partnership *fault* は次の語句と使われる:

ADJ.	generous to a fault **3**
PREP.	to a fault **3**
	at fault **7**
V.	find fault **8**

fault|less /fɔːltlɪs/ ADJ 形容詞 Something that is **faultless** is perfect and has no mistakes at all. 過失のない, 非の打ちどころのない ❏ *...Mary Thomson's faultless and impressive performance on the show.* そのショーでのメアリー・トムソンの非の打ちどころのない感動的な演技

faulty /fɔːlti/ **1** ADJ 形容詞 A **faulty** piece of equipment has something wrong with it and is not working properly. 欠陥のある ❏ *The money will be used to repair faulty equipment.* そのお金は機器の欠陥の修理に充てられるでしょう. **2** ADJ 形容詞 If you describe someone's argument or reasoning as **faulty**, you mean that it is wrong or contains mistakes, usually they have not been thinking in a logical way. 誤った ❏ *Their interpretation was faulty – they had misinterpreted things.* 彼らの説明は筋が通っていなかった. 彼らは事態を誤解していた.

fau|na /fɔːnə/ (**faunas**) N COUNT-COLL 集合可算名詞 Animals, especially the animals in a particular area, can be referred to as **fauna**. (特定の地域の)動物相 [TECHNICAL 技術的] ❏ *...the flora and fauna of the African jungle.* アフリカのジャングルの動植物相

fa|vor /feɪvər/ (**favors, favoring, favored**) **1** N-UNCOUNT 不可算名詞 If you regard something or someone with **favor**, you like or support them. 好意, 支持 ❏ *It remains to be seen if the show will find favor with an audience.* そのショーが観客の支持を得るかどうかは, まだ様子を見ないと分からない. ❏ *No one would look with favor on the continuing military rule.* 継続している軍事政権を支持する者は1人もないだろう. **2** N-COUNT 可算名詞 If you **do** someone **a favor**, you do something for them even though you do not have to. 親切な行為 ❏ *I've come to ask you to do me a favor.* 私はあなたにお願いがあって来たんです. **3** V-T 他動詞 If you **favor** something, you prefer it to the other choices available. 好む, 賛成する ❏ *The French say they favor a transition to democracy.* フランス人は彼らが民主主義への移行することを望んでいると言っている. **4** V-T 他動詞 If you **favor** someone, you treat them better or in a kinder way than you treat other people. (人を)ひいきする ❏ *The company has no rules about favoring U.S. citizens during layoffs.* その会社には一時解雇中に米国市民を特別扱いする規則が一切ない. **5** PHRASE 句 If you are **in favor of** something, you support it and think that it is a good thing. 賛成して, 支持して ❏ *I wouldn't be in favor of income tax cuts.* 私は所得税の減税には賛成しない. ❏ *Yet this is a Government which proclaims that it is all in favor of openness.* それにもかかわらず, この政府は公開を完全支持することを明言している政府なのだ. **6** PHRASE 句 If someone makes a judgment **in your favor**, they say that you are right about something. ~の正しさを認めて ❏ *The Supreme Court ruled in Fitzgerald's favor.* 最高裁判所はフィッツジェラルドに有利な判決を出した. **7** PHRASE 句 If something is **in your favor**, it helps you or gives you an advantage. ~の手助けになるように, ~の有利に ❏ *The protection that farmers have enjoyed amounts to a bias in favor of the countryside.* 農業主たちが受けている保護は地方に有利になるように偏向しているということだ. **8** PHRASE 句 If one thing is rejected **in favor of** another, the second thing is done or chosen instead of the first. ~の方を選んで ❏ *The policy was rejected in favor of a more cautious approach.* その政策は却下されて, もっと慎重な手段が採られた. **9** PHRASE 句 If someone or something is **in favor**, people like or support them. If they are **out of favor**, people no longer like or support them. 気に入って; 気に入られなくて ❏ *Governments and party leaders can only hope to remain in favor with the public for so long.* 政府と党の指導者は一般大衆が長年に渡り支持し続けてくれることを願うしかない.

Word Partnership *favor* は次の語句と使われる:

PREP.	with favor **1**
	out of favor **9**
	in *someone's* favor **6 7**
V.	ask for a favor, do *someone* a favor, need a favor, return a favor **2**
ADJ.	big favor **2**

fa|vor|able /feɪvərəbᵊl/ **1** ADJ 形容詞 If your opinion or your reaction is **favorable** to something, you agree with it and approve of it. 賛成の, 好意的な [ADJ n, v-link ADJ 'to' n] ❏ *The president's convention speech received favorable reviews.* 大統領の大会演説は好意的に評価された. **2** ADJ 形容詞 **Favorable** conditions make something more likely to succeed or seem more attractive. 有

望な，魅力的な ❑*It's believed the conditions in which the elections are being held are too favorable to the government.* その選挙が行われている状況は政府にとって有利すぎると思われている． ❸ ADJ 形容詞 If you make a **favorable** comparison between two things, you say that the first is better than or as good as the second. 優位な，遜（そん）色のない ❑*The film bears favorable technical comparison with Hollywood productions costing 10 times as much.* その映画はハリウッドの10倍も費用をかけた作品と比べても技術的に見劣りしない．

fa|vor|ite /ˈfeɪvərɪt, ˈfeɪvrɪt/ (**favorites**) ❶ ADJ 形容詞 Your **favorite** thing or person of a particular type is the one you like most. お気に入りの [ADJ n] ❑*He celebrated by opening a bottle of his favorite champagne.* 彼はお気に入りのシャンパンを1瓶開けて祝った． ● N-COUNT 可算名詞 **Favorite** is also a noun. お気に入り ❑*The Metropole is my favorite. I love those huge, anonymous hotels.* メトロポール・ホテルは私のお気に入りだ．私はそうした巨大で没個性的なホテルが大好きだ． ● PHRASE 句 If you refer to something as an **old favorite**, you mean that it has been in existence for a long time and everyone knows it or likes it. 昔から人気のあるもの ❑*This recipe is an adaptation of an old favorite.* このレシピは昔から人気の料理に手を加えたものだ． ❷ N-COUNT 可算名詞 The **favorite** in a race or contest is the competitor that is expected to win. In a team game, the team that is expected to win is referred to as the **favorites**. 優勝候補 ❑*The U.S. team is considered one of the favorites in next month's games.* その米国チームは来月の試合の優勝候補の1つとみなされている．

fa|vor|it|ism /ˈfeɪvərɪtɪzəm, ˈfeɪvrɪt-/ N-UNCOUNT 不可算名詞 If you accuse someone of **favoritism**, you disapprove of them because they unfairly help or favor one person or group much more than another. えこひいき [DISAPPROVAL 不賛成] ❑*Maria loved both the children. There was never a hint of favoritism.* マリアは両方の子供を愛していた．えこひいきはほんの少しもなかった．

fawn /fɔn/ (**fawns**) ❶ N-COUNT 可算名詞 A **fawn** is a very young deer. 子じか ❑*The fawn ran to the top of the ridge.* 子じかは尾根の頂上へ駆け上がった． ❷ COLOR 色彩語 **Fawn** is a pale yellowish-brown color. 淡黄褐色 ❑*Tania was standing there in her light fawn coat.* タニアは薄い淡黄褐色のコートを着てそこに立っていた．

fax /fæks/ (**faxes, faxing, faxed**) ❶ N-COUNT 可算名詞 A **fax** or a **fax machine** is a piece of equipment used to copy documents by sending information electronically along a telephone line, and to receive copies that are sent in this way. ファックス [also 'by' n] ❑*...a modern reception desk with telephone and fax.* 電話とファックスのある現代風の受付． ❷ N-COUNT 可算名詞 You can refer to a copy of a document that is transmitted by a fax machine as a **fax**. ファックスで送られる文書 ❑*I sent him a long fax, saying I didn't need a maid.* 私はお手伝いさんなど必要ないことを伝える長いファックスを彼に送った． ❸ V-T 他動詞 If you **fax** a document to someone, you send it from one fax machine to another. ファックスで送る ❑*I faxed a copy of the agreement to each of the investors.* 私は投資家1人1人に契約書のコピーをファックスした． ❑*Did you fax him a reply?* あなたは彼に返事をファックスしましたか．

fear /fɪr/ (**fears, fearing, feared**) ❶ N-VAR 可変性名詞 **Fear** is the unpleasant feeling you have when you think that you are in danger. 恐怖 ❑*I was sitting on the floor shivering with fear because a bullet had been fired through a window.* 銃弾が窓から打ち込まれたので，私は恐怖に震えながら床に座っていた． ❷ N-VAR 可変性名詞 A **fear** is a thought that something unpleasant might happen or might have happened. (いやなことが起こる) 恐れ，不安 ❑*These youngsters are motivated by fear of failure.* この若者たちは失敗するのが怖くてやっている． ❑*Then one day his worst fears were confirmed.* そしてある日彼の最も恐れていたことが現実になった． ❸ N-VAR 可変性名詞 If you say that there is a **fear that** something unpleasant or undesirable will happen, you mean that you think it is possible or likely. (いやなことが起こる) 可能性 ❑*There is a fear that the freeze on bank accounts could prove a lasting deterrent to investors.* 銀行口座の凍結は投資家に長期にわたって投資を思いとどまらせる可能性がある． ❹ N-VAR 可変性名詞 If you have **fears for** someone or something, you are very worried because you think that they might be in danger. 危機感 ❑*He also spoke of his fears for the future of his country's culture.* 彼は自国の文化の将来に危機感を抱いているとも話した． ❺ V-T 他動詞 If you **fear** someone or something, you are frightened because you think that they will harm you. 恐れる ❑*It seems to me that if people fear you they respect you.* もし人々があなたを恐れているとしたら，私には彼らがあなたを尊敬しているのだと思える． ❻ V-T 他動詞 If you **fear** something unpleasant or undesirable, you are worried that it might happen or might have happened. (いやなことが起こるのではないかと) 心配する ❑*She had feared she was coming down with pneumonia or bronchitis.* 彼女は自分が肺炎か気管支炎になりかけているのではないかと心配していた． ❼ V-I 自動詞 If you **fear for** someone or something, you are very worried because you think that they might be in danger. 危機感を抱く ❑*Carla fears for her son.* カーラは息子のことをとても心配している． ❽ PHRASE 句 If you are **in fear of** doing or experiencing something unpleasant, you are very worried that you might have to do it or experience it. ～を恐れて ❑*The elderly*

live in fear of assault and murder. 高齢者は暴行や殺人におびえながら生活している． ❾ PHRASE 句 If you take a particular course of action **for fear of** something, you take the action in order to prevent that thing happening. ～しないように，～を恐れて ❑*She was afraid to say anything to them for fear of hurting their feelings.* 彼女は彼らの心を傷つけるのを恐れて彼らに何も言えなかった．
→ see **emotion**

Thesaurus *fear* また次を参照：

N.	alarm, dread, panic, terror ❶
	concern, worry ❷

Word Partnership *fear* は次の語句と使われる：

ADJ.	constant fear ❶
	irrational fear ❶ ❷
	worst fear ❷
V.	face *your* fear, hide *your* fear, live in fear, overcome *your* fear ❶ ❷
N.	fear of failure, fear of rejection, fear of the unknown ❷
	nothing to fear, fear the worst ❺
	fear change ❻

fear|ful /ˈfɪrfəl/ ADJ 形容詞 If you are **fearful of** something, you are afraid of it. 恐れて [FORMAL 形式ばった] ❑*Bankers were fearful of a world banking crisis.* 銀行家たちは世界の金融危機を恐れていた． ❷ ADJ 形容詞 You use **fearful** to emphasize how serious or bad a situation is. ひどい [FORMAL 形式ばった，EMPHASIS 強調] [ADJ n] ❑*The region is in a fearful recession.* その地方はひどい不況に見舞われている．

fear|less /ˈfɪrlɪs/ ADJ 形容詞 If you say that someone is **fearless**, you mean that they are not afraid at all, and you admire them for this. 恐れを知らない，勇敢な [APPROVAL 賛成] ❑*...his fearless campaigning for racial justice.* 人種の公平を求める彼の勇敢な運動

Word Link *some ≈ causing : awe**some**, fear**some**, trouble**some***

fear|some /ˈfɪrsəm/ ADJ 形容詞 **Fearsome** is used to describe things that are frightening, for example, because of their large size or extreme nature. 恐るべき ❑*He had developed a fearsome reputation for intimidating people.* 彼は人を脅すという恐ろしい評判がたっていた．

fea|sible /ˈfizəbəl/ ADJ 形容詞 If something is **feasible**, it can be done, made, or achieved. (物事が) 実行可能な，実現可能な ❑*She questioned whether it was feasible to stimulate investment in these regions.* 彼女はこれらの地方への投資を活性化することは可能かどうか尋ねた． ● **fea|sibil|ity** /ˌfizəˈbɪlɪti/ N-UNCOUNT 不可算名詞 実行（実現）の可能性 ❑*The committee will study the feasibility of setting up a national computer network.* その委員会は全国的なコンピュータ・ネットワークを構築できるかどうかを検討していく予定だ．

feast /fist/ (**feasts, feasting, feasted**) ❶ N-COUNT 可算名詞 A **feast** is a large and special meal. ごちそう ❑*Lunch was a feast of meat and vegetables, cheese, yogurt and fruit, with unlimited wine.* 昼食は肉料理と野菜，チーズ，ヨーグルトと果物，そして飲み放題のワインというごちそうだった． ❷ N-COUNT 可算名詞 A **feast** is a day or time of the year when a special religious celebration takes place. (宗教的な) 祭り，(祝日) ❑*The Jewish feast of Passover began last night.* ユダヤ人の過ぎ越しの祝祭が昨夜始始まった． ❸ V-I 自動詞 If you **feast on** a particular food, you eat a large amount of it with great enjoyment. 大いに食べる ❑*They feasted well into the afternoon on mutton and corn stew.* 彼らは午後まで羊ととうもろこしのシチューを大いに愉しんだ． ❹ V-I 自動詞 If you **feast**, you take part in a feast. 宴会に列する ❑*Only a few feet away, their captors feasted in the castle's banqueting hall.* すぐ横では彼らを捕まえた連中が城の宴会場で宴会に加わっていた． ● **feast|ing** N-UNCOUNT 不可算名詞 宴会 ❑*The feasting, drinking, dancing and revelry continued for several days.* ごちそうに酒に踊りといったお祭り騒ぎが7日間続いた． ❺ PHRASE 句 If you **feast your eyes on** something, you look at it for a long time with great attention because you find it very attractive. ～を見て楽しむ ❑*She stood feasting her eyes on the view.* 彼女はその眺めに目を楽しませながら立っていた．

feat /fit/ (**feats**) N-COUNT 可算名詞 If you refer to an action, or the result of an action, as a **feat**, you admire it because it is an impressive and difficult achievement. 偉業 [APPROVAL 賛成] ❑*A racing car is an extraordinary feat of engineering.* レーシングカーは工学技術の驚くべき成果だ．

feath|er /ˈfɛðər/ (**feathers**) ❶ N-COUNT 可算名詞 A bird's **feathers** are the soft covering on its body. Each **feather** consists of a lot of smooth hairs on each side of a thin stiff center. (鳥の) 羽 ❑*...a hat that she had made herself from black ostrich feathers.* 彼女が黒いダチョウの羽を自分で作った帽子 ❷ → see also **feathered** ❸ to **ruffle** someone's **feathers** → see **ruffle**
→ see **bird**

feath|ered /fɛðərd/ ADJ 形容詞 If you describe something as **feathered**, you mean that it has feathers on it. 羽をつけた、羽毛の生えた □ *Her mother was the proud lady in the feathered hat.* 彼女の母は羽の付いた帽子をかぶったあの高慢な女性だった.

fea|ture /fiːtʃər/ (features, featuring, featured) **1** N-COUNT 可算名詞 A **feature of** something is an interesting or important part or characteristic of it. 特徴、重要な点 □ *Patriotic songs have long been a feature of Kuwaiti life.* 愛国的な歌は長い間クウェート人の生活の特徴の1つとなっている. □ *The spacious gardens are a special feature of this property.* 広大な庭がこの地所の特別な特徴となっている. **2** N-COUNT 可算名詞 A **feature** is a special article in a newspaper or magazine, or a special program on radio or television. (新聞・雑誌の) 特集記事、(ラジオ・テレビの) 特集番組 □ *We are delighted to see the Sunday Times running a long feature on breast cancer.* 私たちはサンデー・タイムズが乳がんについての長い特集記事を載せているのを見て喜んでいる. **3** N-COUNT 可算名詞 A **feature** or a **feature** film or movie is a full-length film about a fictional situation, as opposed to a short film or a documentary. 長編映画 □ *...the first feature-length cartoon, Snow White and the Seven Dwarfs.* 最初の長編アニメ映画である『白雪姫と7人のこびと』 **4** N-COUNT 可算名詞 A geographical **feature** is something noticeable in a particular area of a country, for example, a hill, river, or valley. 地形 □ *...one of the area's oddest geographical features - an eight-mile bank of pebbles shelving abruptly into the sea.* その地域の最も奇妙な地理的特徴の1つ—緩い勾配を斜面に突然海に入り込む8マイルの小石の洲 **5** N-PLURAL 複数名詞 Your **features** are your eyes, nose, mouth, and other parts of your face. 顔立ち □ *His features seemed to change.* 彼の顔立ちが変わるように見えた. **6** V-T 他動詞 When something such as a movie or exhibition **features** a particular person or thing, they are an important part of it. (展覧会の) 呼び物にする、(映画に人を) 主演させる、特集する □ *It's a great movie and it features a Spanish actor who is going to be a world star within a year.* それは素晴らしい映画で、1年以内に世界的スターになるだろうスペイン人の俳優が主演している. □ *The hour-long program will be updated each week and feature highlights from recent games.* その1時間番組は毎週更新され、最近の試合のハイライトを特集していく予定だ. **7** V-I 自動詞 If someone or something **features in** something such as a show, exhibition, or magazine, they are an important part of it. 呼び物になる、主演する □ *Jon featured in one of the show's most thrilling episodes.* ジョンはその連続番組の最もわくわくさせる回の1つに主演した.

Word Partnership	feature は次の語句と使われる:
ADJ.	**key** feature **1**
	special feature **1** **2**
	best feature, **striking** feature **1** **5**
	animated feature, **double** feature, **full-length** feature **3**
	facial feature **5**

Feb. **Feb.** is a written abbreviation for **February**. February (2月) の略語

Feb|ru|ary /fɛbyuɛri, fɛbru-/ (Februaries) N-VAR 可変性名詞 **February** is the second month of the year in the Western calendar. (西暦の) 2月 □ *He joined the Army in February 1943.* 彼は1943年2月に陸軍へ入隊した. □ *His exhibition opens on February 5.* 彼の展覧会は2月5日に開かれる.

fe|ces /fiːsiz/ N-UNCOUNT 不可算名詞 **Feces** is the solid waste substance that people and animals get rid of from their body by passing it through the anus. 大便 [FORMAL 形式ばった] □ *...grass contaminated by feces from infected dogs.* 感染した犬のふんによって汚染された草地

fed /fɛd/ **1** **Fed** is the past tense and past participle of **feed**. See also **fed up**. feed の過去・過去分詞 **2** N-SING 単数名詞 The **Fed** is the **Federal Reserve**. 連邦準備制度 [INFORMAL くだけた] ['the' N] □ *The Fed has already eased rates three times since late October.* 連邦準備制度は昨年10月からすでに3度も金利を緩和している.

fed|er|al /fɛdərəl/ **1** ADJ 形容詞 A **federal** country or system of government is one in which the different states or provinces of the country have important powers to make their own laws and decisions. 連邦制の [ADJ n] □ *Five of the six provinces are to become autonomous regions in a new federal system of government.* 政治体制の新しい連邦制度では、6つの州のうち5つが自治州となる予定だ. **2** ADJ 形容詞 **Federal** also means belonging or relating to the national government of a federal country rather than to one of the states within it. 連邦政府の [ADJ n] □ *The federal government controls just 6% of the education budget.* その連邦政府は教育予算の6%を管理しているに過ぎない. ● **fed|er|al|ly** ADV 副詞 [ADV -ed] 連邦制によって □ *...residents of public housing and federally subsidized apartments.* 公営住宅と連邦政府の補助金を受けたアパートの住人たち

fed|er|al|ist /fɛdərəlɪst/ (federalists) ADJ 形容詞 Someone or something that is **federalist** believes in, supports, or follows a

federal system of government. 連邦主義の □ *The new constitution includes federalist principles.* 新しい憲法には連邦主義の原理が盛り込まれている. ● N-COUNT 可算名詞 **Federalist** is also a noun. 連邦主義者 □ *Many Quebeckers are federalists.* ケベック州の住民には連邦主義者が多い.

fed|era|tion /fɛdəreɪʃ°n/ (federations) **1** N-COUNT 可算名詞 A **federation** is a federal country. 連邦 □ *...the Russian Federation.* ロシア連邦 **2** N-COUNT 可算名詞 A **federation** is a group of societies or other organizations which have joined together, usually because they share a common interest. 連合 □ *...the American Federation of Government Employees.* 米国公務員連合

fed up ADJ 形容詞 If you are **fed up**, you are unhappy, bored, or tired of something, especially something that you have been experiencing for a long time. うんざりした [INFORMAL くだけた] [v-link ADJ] □ *I am fed up with reading how women should dress to please men.* 私は女性が男性を喜ばせるための着こなし方について読み飽きていた. □ *He had become fed up with city life.* 彼は都市生活にうんざりしていた.

fee /fiː/ (fees) **1** N-COUNT 可算名詞 A **fee** is a sum of money that you pay to be allowed to do something. 料金 □ *He paid his license fee, and walked out with a brand-new driver's license.* 彼は免許料を支払い、真新しい運転免許証を持って外に出た. **2** N-COUNT 可算名詞 A **fee** is the amount of money that a person or organization is paid for a particular job or service that they provide. 手数料 □ *Lawyer's fees can be substantial.* 弁護料はかなりの金額になりうる.

fee|ble /fiːb°l/ (feebler, feeblest) **1** ADJ 形容詞 If you describe someone or something as **feeble**, you mean that they are weak. 弱い □ *He told them he was old and feeble and was not able to walk so far.* 彼は自分が年老いて弱く、そんなに遠くまで歩けないと彼らに伝えた. ● **fee|bly** ADV 副詞 [ADV with v] 弱弱しく □ *His left hand moved feebly at his side.* 彼の左手が体の脇でかすかに動いた. **2** ADJ 形容詞 If you describe something that someone says as **feeble**, you mean that it is not very good or convincing. 不十分な □ *This is a particularly feeble argument.* これは特に説得力のない主張だ. ● **fee|bly** ADV 副詞 [ADV with v] 不十分に、弱く □ *I said "Sorry," very feebly, feeling rather embarrassed.* 私はとても当惑して消え入りそうな声で「ごめん」と言った.

feed /fiːd/ (feeds, feeding, fed) **1** V-T 他動詞 If you **feed** a person or animal, you give them food to eat and sometimes actually put it in their mouths. 食べ物を与える □ *We brought along pieces of old bread and fed the birds.* 私たちは古いパンをなん切れか持って来て、それを鳥たちに与えること、授乳 □ *The feeding of dairy cows has undergone a revolution.* 乳牛の飼育は大変革を経てきた. **2** V-T 他動詞 To **feed** a family or a community means to supply food for them. (家族の) 養う □ *Feeding a hungry family can be expensive.* 食欲旺盛な家族を養うのは金がかかることもある. **3** V-I 自動詞 When an animal **feeds**, it eats or drinks something. (動物が) えさを取る □ *After a few days the caterpillars stopped feeding.* 数日後に毛虫はえさを食べなくなった. **4** V-T/V-I 他動詞/自動詞 When a baby **feeds**, or when you **feed** it, it drinks milk or milk from a bottle. (赤ちゃんに) 授乳する [他動詞]、(赤ちゃんが) 乳を飲む [自動詞] □ *When a baby is thirsty, it feeds more often.* 赤ちゃんはのどが渇いていると、より頻繁に乳を飲む. **5** V-T 他動詞 To **feed** something to a place, means to supply it to that place in a steady flow. 供給する □ *...blood vessels that feed blood to the brain.* 脳に血液を送り込む血管 **6** V-T 他動詞 If you **feed** something **into** a container or piece of equipment, you put it in it. (物を容器などに) 入れる □ *He took the compact disc from her, then fed it into the player.* 彼は彼女からCDを受け取り、それをプレーヤーに入れた. **7** V-T 他動詞 If you **feed** a plant, you add substances to it to make it grow well. (植物に) 肥料を与える □ *Feed plants to encourage steady growth.* 順調に成長するよう植物に肥料を与えなさい. **8** V-I 自動詞 If one thing **feeds on** another, it becomes stronger as a result of the other thing's existence. 助長される □ *The drinking and the guilt fed on each other.* 飲酒と罪悪感が相互に助長された. **9** V-T 他動詞 To **feed** information **into** a computer means to gradually put it into it. (コンピュータに情報を) 入力する □ *An automatic weather station feeds information on wind direction to the computer.* 自動気象観測所は風向き情報をコンピュータに入力する. **10** N-MASS 質量名詞 [usu N n] Animal **feed** is food given to animals, especially farm animals. 飼料 □ *The grain just rotted and all they could use it for was animal feed.* 穀物はほぼ腐っていて、動物の飼料にしか使えなかった. **11** to **bite the hand that feeds** you → see **bite** **12** **mouths to feed** → see **mouth**

Word Partnership	feed は次の語句と使われる:
N.	**feed the baby**, **feed the cat**, **feed the children**, **feed your family**, **feed the hungry** **1** **bird** feed **10**
V.	**feed and clothe** **2**

feed|back /fiːdbæk/ **1** N-UNCOUNT 不可算名詞 If you get **feedback on** your work or progress, someone tells you how well or

badly you are doing, and how you could improve. If you get good feedback you have worked or performed well. フィードバック, 意見 □ Continue to ask for feedback on your work. 自分の仕事に対するフィードバックを求め続けなさい. **2** N-UNCOUNT 不可算名詞 **Feedback** is the unpleasant high-pitched sound produced by a piece of electrical equipment when part of the signal that comes out goes back into it. (音響の) ハウリング □ The microphone screeched with feedback. マイクがハウリングでキーンといやな音を立てた.

feel /fíl/ (feels, feeling, felt) **1** V-LINK 連結動詞 If you **feel** a particular emotion or physical sensation, you experience it. 感じる □ I am feeling very depressed. 私はとても気が滅入っている. □ Suddenly I felt a sharp pain in my shoulder. 私は突然肩に鋭い痛みを感じた. □ I felt as if all my strength had gone. 私は力がみな抜けたかのように感じた. □ I felt like I was being kicked in the teeth every day. 私は毎日つらく当たられているような気分だった. **2** V-LINK 連結動詞 If you talk about how an experience or event **feels**, you talk about the emotions and sensations connected with it. (経験・出来事が—のように) 感じられる [no cont] □ It feels good to have finished a piece of work. 作品を1つ仕上げてそういかい気分だ. □ The speed at which everything moved felt strange. すべてのものが動く速さが変な感じがした. □ Within five minutes of arriving back from vacation, it feels as if I've never been away. 休暇から戻って5分もすると, どこにも行っていなかったような感じがする. **3** V-LINK 連結動詞 If you talk about how an object **feels**, you talk about the physical quality that you notice when you touch or hold it. For example, if something **feels** soft, you notice that it is soft when you touch it. [no cont] □ The metal felt smooth and cold. その金属はなめらかで冷たい感じがした. □ The ten-foot oars felt heavy and awkward. 10フィートのオールは重くて使いづらい感じだった. ● N-SING 単数名詞 **Feel** is also a noun. 感触 □ He remembered the feel of her skin. 彼は彼女の肌の感触を思い出した. **4** V-LINK 連結動詞 If you talk about how the weather **feels**, you describe the weather, especially the temperature or whether or not you think it is going to rain or snow. (温度が—に) 感じられる, (天気が—に) なりそうだ [no cont] □ It felt wintry cold that day. その日は冬らしい寒さの日だった. **5** V-T/V-I 他動詞/自動詞 If you **feel** an object, you touch it deliberately with your hand, so that you learn what it is like, for example, what shape it is or whether it is rough or smooth. 触ってみる □ The doctor felt his head. 医者は彼の頭に触った. □ Feel how soft the skin is in the small of the back. 腰のくびれの肌がどんなに柔らかいか触ってごらん. **6** V-T 他動詞 If you can **feel** something, you are aware of it because it is touching you. (感触で) 分かる [no cont] □ Through several layers of clothes I could feel his muscles. 服を何枚も重ね着していたにもかかわらず, 私には彼の筋肉が分かった. **7** V-T 他動詞 If you **feel** something happening, you become aware of it because of the effect it has on your body. (—するのを) 感じる, 知覚する □ She felt something being pressed into her hands. 彼女は何かが両手の中に押し込まれるのを感じた. □ He felt something move beside him. 彼は何かが彼のそばで動くのを感じた. **8** V-T 他動詞 If you **feel yourself** doing something or being in a particular state, you are aware that something is happening to you which you are unable to control. (自分が—となるのを) 意識する □ I felt myself blush. 私は顔が赤くなるのを意識した. □ At any point you feel yourself becoming tense, make a conscious effort to relax. どの時点でも自分が緊張するのを感じたら, 意識的にリラックスするようにしてください. **9** V-T 他動詞 If you **feel** the presence of someone or something, you become aware of them, even though you cannot see or hear them. (気配を) 感じる [no cont] □ He felt her eyes on him. 彼は彼女の視線を感じた. □ I could feel that a man was watching me very intensely. 男が私をじっと凝視しているのが感じられた. **10** V-T 他動詞 If you **feel** that something is the case, you have a strong idea in your mind that it is the case. 痛感する [no cont] □ I feel that not enough is being done to protect the local animal life. 私はその地域の動物の生態を守る十分な努力がなされていないと痛感する. □ I feel certain that it will all turn out well. 私は最後にはすべてがうまく行くと確信している. **11** V-T 他動詞 If you feel that you should do something, you think that you should do it. (—すべきだと) 思う [no cont] □ I feel I should resign. 私は自分が辞任すべきだと思う. □ You need not feel obliged to commit. 寄付しなければならないとは考えなくていいのです. **12** V-T/V-I 他動詞/自動詞 If you talk about how you **feel about** something, you talk about your opinion, attitude, or reaction to it. (—について—だと) 思う [no cont] □ We'd like to know what you feel about abortion. 私たちはあなたが妊娠中絶についてどう思うか知りたい. □ She feels guilty about spending less time lately with her two kids. 彼女は最近2人の子供と過ごす時間が少なくなったことに罪悪感を感じている. **13** V-I 自動詞 If you **feel like** doing something or having something, you want to do it or have it because you are in the right mood for it and think you would enjoy it. したい気分である □ Neither of them felt like going back to sleep. 彼らのどちらももう1度寝ようという気にならなかった. **14** → see also **feeling, felt 15** **feel free** → see **free**

▶ **feel for 1** PHRASAL VERB 句動詞 If you **feel for** something, for example, in the dark, you try to find it by moving your hand around until you touch it. —を手探りで探す □ I felt for my wallet and

papers in my inside pocket. 私は内ポケットの中を手探りで財布と書類を探した. **2** PHRASAL VERB 句動詞 If you **feel for** someone, you have sympathy for them. —に同情する □ She cried on the phone and I really felt for her. 彼女は電話で泣いた. そして私は彼女に心から同情した.

Thesaurus	feel また次を参照:
V-LINK.	experience, perceive, sense **1**

feelgood /fílgʊd/ also **feel-good 1** ADJ 形容詞 A **feelgood** movie is a movie which presents people and life in a way which makes the people who watch it feel happy and optimistic. 心が温まる [ADJ n] □ This could be the feelgood movie of the season. これは今シーズン一の心温まる映画となるかもしれないでしょう. **2** PHRASE 句 When journalists refer to **the feelgood factor**, they mean that people are feeling hopeful and optimistic about the future. 楽観的気分にさせる要因 [BRIT 英国英語]

feeling /fíliŋ/ (feelings) **1** N-COUNT 可算名詞 A **feeling** is an emotion, such as anger or happiness. 感情 □ It gave me a feeling of satisfaction. 満足感を受けた. □ He was unable to contain his own destructive feelings. 彼は自分の破壊的な感情を抑えることができなかった. **2** N-COUNT 可算名詞 If you have a **feeling** of hunger, tiredness, or other physical sensation, you experience it. 感覚 □ I also have a strange feeling in my neck. 私は首に変な感覚を感じた. □ Focus on the feeling of relaxation. ゆったりとした気分に精神を集中させなさい. **3** N-COUNT 可算名詞 If you have a **feeling that** something is the case or **that** something is going to happen, you think that is probably the case or that it is probably going to happen. 予感 □ I have a feeling that everything will be all right. 私には全部うまくいくような気がする. **4** N-PLURAL 複数名詞 Your **feelings** about something are the things that you think and feel about it, or your attitude toward it. 考え, 意見 □ She has strong feelings about the alleged growth in violence against female officers. 彼女は女性警官に対する暴力が増加していると言われていることについて強い意見を持っている. □ I think that sums up the feelings of most discerning and intelligent Indians. それは大部分の見識があり理知的なインド人の考えを集約していると私は思う. **5** N-PLURAL 複数名詞 When you refer to someone's **feelings**, you are talking about the things that might embarrass, offend, or upset them. For example, if you hurt someone's **feelings**, you upset them by something that you say or do. 気持ち, 感情 □ He was afraid of hurting my feelings. 彼は私の気持ちを傷つけるのを恐れていた. **6** N-UNCOUNT 不可算名詞 **Feeling** is a way of thinking and reacting to things which is emotional and not planned rather than logical and practical. 感情, 激情 □ He was prompted to a rare outburst of feeling. 彼は刺激されてめったにない感情の爆発を起こした. **7** N-UNCOUNT 不可算名詞 **Feeling** for someone is love, affection, sympathy, or concern for them. 愛情; 思いやり □ Thomas never lost his feeling for Harriet. トマスはハリエットに対する愛情を全然失わなかった. **8** N-UNCOUNT 不可算名詞 **Feeling** in part of your body is the ability to experience the sense of touch in that part of the body. 感覚 □ After the accident she had no feeling in his legs. 事故の後彼は足の感覚がなかった. **9** N-UNCOUNT 不可算名詞 **Feeling** is used to refer to a general opinion that a group of people has about something. (一般的な) 考え □ There is still some feeling in the art world that the market for such works may be declining. そのような作品の市場は衰退してきているのかもしれないとの美術界の考えがまだ多分ある. **10** N-SING 単数名詞 If you have a **feeling of** being in a particular situation, you feel that you are in that situation. 意識, 気分 □ I had the terrible feeling of being left behind to bring up the baby while he had fun. 私は彼が楽しんでいるのに, 自分は1人残されて赤ん坊を育てているといういやな気分だった. **11** N-SING 単数名詞 If something such as a place or book creates a particular kind of **feeling**, it creates a particular kind of atmosphere. 雰囲気 □ That's what we tried to portray in the book, this feeling of opulence and grandeur. それがこの本で描写しようとしたことなのだ. この華やかさと壮大さの雰囲気は. **12** → see also **feel 13** PHRASE 句 **Bad feeling** or **ill feeling** is bitterness or anger which exists between people, for example, after they have had an argument. 敵意, 反感 □ There's been some bad feeling between the two families. 両家の間には多少反感がある. **14** PHRASE 句 **Hard feelings** are feelings of anger or bitterness toward someone who you have had an argument with or who has upset you. If you say "**no hard feelings**," you are making an agreement with someone not to be angry or bitter about something. 悪感情 □ I don't want any hard feelings between our companies. 私は会社間で悪感情が何もないようにしたい.

Word Partnership feeling は次の語句と使われる:

ADJ. sinking feeling **1**
funny feeling **1 – 3 6 7**
strange feeling **1 – 3 6 7 8**
strong feeling **1 – 3 5 7**
good feeling **1 3**
bad feeling **1 3 9**

N. feeling of inadequacy, feeling of satisfaction **1**
depth of feeling **1 5 7**

V. get a feeling **1 – 3**
have a feeling **1 3 5**
express a feeling **1 5**

feet /fit/ **Feet** is the plural of **foot.** foot の複数形

feign /feɪn/ **(feigns, feigning, feigned)** v-т 他動詞 If someone **feigns** a particular feeling, attitude, or physical condition, they try to make other people think that they have it or are experiencing it, although this is not true. ふりをする [FORMAL 形式ばった] ❑ One morning, I didn't want to go to school, and decided to feign illness. ある朝、私は学校に行きたくなかったので仮病を装うことにした。

fell /fɛl/ **(fells, felling, felled)** **1** **Fell** is the past tense of **fall.** fall の過去形 **2** v-т 他動詞 If trees are **felled,** they are cut down. 伐採する [usu passive] ❑ Badly infected trees should be felled and burned. 感染のひどい木は伐採して焼却すべきだ。 **3** **in one fell swoop** → see **swoop**

fellow /fɛloʊ/ **(fellows)** **1** ADJ 形容詞 You use **fellow** to describe people who are in the same situation as you, or people you feel you have something in common with. 仲間 [ADJ n] ❑ She discovered to her pleasure, a talent for making her fellow guests laugh. うれしいことに、彼女は仲間の客を笑わせる才が自分にあることを発見した。 **2** N-COUNT 可算名詞 A **fellow** is a man or boy. 男、少年 [INFORMAL, OLD-FASHIONED くだけた、古風な] ❑ By all accounts, Rodger would appear to be a fine fellow. どこで聞いてみても、ロジャーはいいやつのようだ。 **3** N-COUNT 可算名詞 A **fellow of** an academic or professional association is someone who is a specially elected member of it, usually because of their work or achievements or as a mark of honor. 特別会員 ❑ ...the fellows of the Zoological Society. 動物学会の特別会員 **4** N-PLURAL Your **fellows** are the people who you work with, do things with, or who are like you in some way. 同僚 [FORMAL 形式ばった] [poss N] ❑ He stood out in terms of competence from all his fellows. 彼は能力に関して同僚の中で際立っていた。
→ see **hospital**

fellowship /fɛloʊʃɪp/ **(fellowships)** **1** N-COUNT 可算名詞 A **fellowship** is a group of people that join together for a common purpose or interest. 団体 ❑ ...the National Schizophrenia Fellowship. 全国統合失調症協会 **2** N-COUNT 可算名詞 A **fellowship** at a university is a post which involves research work. 奨学金給付研究員の地位 ❑ He was offered a research fellowship at Yale. エール大学での研究奨学生の採用通知があった。 **3** N-UNCOUNT 不可算名詞 **Fellowship** is a feeling of friendship that people have when they are talking or doing something together and sharing their experiences. 仲間意識 ❑ ...a sense of community and fellowship. 同じ共同体で仲間であるという意識

felony /fɛləni/ **(felonies)** N-COUNT 可算名詞 In countries where the legal system distinguishes between very serious crimes and less serious ones, a **felony** is a very serious crime such as armed robbery. 重罪 [LEGAL 法律的] ❑ He pleaded guilty to six felonies. 彼は重罪6件の有罪を認めた。

felt /fɛlt/ **1** **Felt** is the past tense and past participle of **feel.** feel の過去・過去分詞 **2** N-UNCOUNT 不可算名詞 **Felt** is a thick cloth made from wool or other fibers packed tightly together. フェルト [oft N n] ❑ She had on an old felt hat. 彼女はフェルトの古い帽子をかぶっていた。

felt-tip **(felt-tips)** N-COUNT 可算名詞 A **felt-tip** or a **felt-tip pen** is a pen which has a piece of fiber at the end that the ink comes through. フェルトペン

female /fimeɪl/ **(females)** **1** ADJ 形容詞 Someone who is **female** is a woman or a girl. 女性の、女の子の ❑ ...a sixteen-piece dance band with a female singer. 女性ボーカルのいる16人構成のダンスバンド **2** ADJ 形容詞 **Female** matters and things relate to, belong to, or affect women rather than men. 女性の [ADJ n] ❑ ...female infertility. 女性不妊症 **3** N-COUNT 可算名詞 Women and girls are sometimes referred to as **females** when they are being considered as a type. 女性 ❑ Hay fever affects males more than females. 花粉症は女性よりも男性の方が多くかかる。 **4** N-COUNT 可算名詞 You can refer to any creature that can lay eggs or produce babies from its body as a **female.** 雌 ❑ Each female will lay just one egg in April or May. 雌は4月から5月にそれぞれ卵をたった1つしか産まない。 ● 形容詞 **Female** is also an adjective. 雌の ❑ ...the scent given off by the female aphid to attract the male. 雌のアブラムシが雄を引きつけるため出すにおい

Word Link fem, femin ≈ woman : female, feminine, femininity

feminine /fɛmɪnɪn/ **1** ADJ 形容詞 **Feminine** qualities and things relate to or are considered typical of women, in contrast to men. 女性特有の ❑ ...male leaders worrying about their women abandoning traditional feminine roles. 女性が伝統的な女性の役割を放棄することを心配する男性指導者たち **2** ADJ 形容詞 Someone or something that is **feminine** has qualities that are considered typical of women, especially being pretty or gentle. 女らしい [APPROVAL 賛成] ❑ I've always been attracted to very feminine women who are not overpowering. 私は圧倒的でないとても女らしい女にいつも魅力を感じている。 **3** ADJ 形容詞 In some languages, a **feminine** noun, pronoun, or adjective has a different form from a masculine or neuter one, or behaves in a different way. 女性の

femininity /fɛmɪnɪniti/ **1** N-UNCOUNT 不可算名詞 A woman's **femininity** is the fact that she is a woman. 女であること ❑ ...the drudgery behind the ideology of motherhood and femininity. 母性と女性のイデオロギーの裏にある単調な骨の折れる労働 **2** N-UNCOUNT 不可算名詞 **Femininity** means the qualities that are considered to be typical of women. 女らしさ ❑ I wonder if there isn't a streak of femininity in him, a kind of sweetness. 彼には女性的な面、つまり優しさのようなものがないのかしらと私は思う。

feminism /fɛmɪnɪzəm/ N-UNCOUNT 不可算名詞 **Feminism** is the belief and aim that women should have the same rights, power, and opportunities as men. 男女同権主義 ❑ ...Barbara Johnson, that champion of radical feminism. 急進的な女性解放論のあの闘士バーバラ・ジョンソン
→ see **society**

feminist /fɛmɪnɪst/ **(feminists)** **1** N-COUNT 可算名詞 A **feminist** is a person who believes in and supports feminism. 男女同権主義者 ❑ Only 16 percent of young women in a 1990 survey considered themselves feminists. 1990年の調査では、男女同権主義者であると考えている若い女性は16%のみであった。 **2** ADJ 形容詞 **Feminist** groups, ideas, and activities are involved in feminism. 女性解放論（者）の [ADJ n]

fence /fɛns/ **(fences, fencing, fenced)** **1** N-COUNT 可算名詞 A **fence** is a barrier between two areas of land, made of wood or wire supported by posts. 柵（さく） ❑ Villagers say the fence would restrict public access to the hills. 村人たちは、柵があれば一般人の丘陵地帯への立ち入りが抑制されるだろうと言っている。 **2** N-COUNT 可算名詞 A **fence** in show jumping or horse racing is an obstacle or barrier that horses have to jump over. 障害物 ❑ The horse fell at the last fence. その馬は最後の障害物で転倒した。 **3** v-т 他動詞 If you **fence** an area of land, you surround it with a fence. 囲いをする ❑ The first task was to fence the wood to exclude sheep. まず最初の仕事は羊が入らないように木で柵を作ることであった。 **4** PHRASE 句 If you **sit on the fence,** you avoid supporting a particular side in a discussion or argument. 形勢を見る ❑ They are sitting on the fence and refusing to commit themselves. 彼らは日和見していて、態度をはっきりさせるのを拒んでいる。

fencing /fɛnsɪŋ/ **1** N-UNCOUNT 不可算名詞 **Fencing** is a sport in which two competitors fight each other using very thin swords. The ends of the swords are covered and the competitors wear protective clothes, so that they do not hurt each other. フェンシング ❑ ...the amateur fencing champion. アマチュアフェンシングのチャンピオン **2** N-UNCOUNT 不可算名詞 Materials such as wood or wire that are used to make fences are called **fencing.** 柵（さく）の材料 ❑ ...old wooden fencing. 古い木の柵材

fend /fɛnd/ **(fends, fending, fended)** v-I 自動詞 If you have to **fend for** yourself, you have to look after yourself without relying on help from anyone else. 独力で ❑ The woman and her young baby had been thrown out and left to fend for themselves. その女と幼い赤ん坊は追い出され、独力で何とかやっていかなければならなかった。

▶ **fend off** **1** PHRASAL VERB 句動詞 If you **fend off** unwanted questions, problems, or people, you stop them from affecting you or defend yourself from them, but often only for a short time and without dealing with them completely. かわす、しのぐ ❑ He looked relaxed and determined as he fended off questions from the world's Press. 世界の報道陣の質問を受け流しながら、彼はリラックスしていて、かつ決意は固いように見えた。 **2** PHRASAL VERB 句動詞 If you **fend off** someone who is attacking you, you use your arms or something such as a stick to defend yourself from their blows. かわす ❑ He raised his hand to fend off the blow. 彼は打撃をかわそうと片手を挙げた。

Word Link fend ≈ striking : defend, fender, offend

fender /fɛndər/ **(fenders)** N-COUNT 可算名詞 The **fenders** of a car are the parts of the body over the wheels. 泥よけ [AM 米国英語] ❑ Todd sat on the front fender, his legs dangling toward the ground. トッドは前のフェンダーの上に座り、足を地面のほうに垂らしてぶらぶらさせていた。

fer|ment (ferments, fermenting, fermented)

> The noun is pronounced /fɜrmɛnt/. The verb is pronounced /fərmɛnt/.
>
> 名詞は /fɜrmɛnt/ と発音される。動詞は /fərmɛnt/ と発音される。

1 N-UNCOUNT 不可算名詞 **Ferment** is excitement and trouble caused by change or uncertainty. 騒ぎ □ *The whole country was in a state of political ferment for some months.* 国全体がこの数か月間政治的動乱状態になっている。 **2** V-T/V-I 他動詞/自動詞 If a food, drink, or other natural substance **ferments**, or if it **is fermented**, a chemical change takes place in it so that alcohol is produced. This process forms part of the production of alcoholic drinks such as wine and beer. 発酵させる [他動詞]、発酵する [自動詞] □ *The dried grapes are allowed to ferment until there is no sugar left and the wine is dry.* 干しぶどうは糖分が無くなってワインが辛口になるまで発酵させる。 ●**fer|men|ta|tion** /fɜrmɛntɛɪʃⁿn/ N-UNCOUNT 不可算名詞 発酵 □ *Yeast is essential for the fermentation that produces alcohol.* 酵母菌はアルコールを生み出す発酵に必須なものである。
→ see **fungus**

fern /fɜrn/ (ferns) N-VAR 可変性名詞 A **fern** is a plant that has long stems with feathery leaves and no flowers. There are many types of fern. シダ

fe|ro|cious /fərouʃəs/ **1** ADJ 形容詞 A **ferocious** animal, person, or action is very fierce and violent. 凶暴な □ *By its very nature a lion is ferocious.* ライオンは生来どうもうである。 **2** ADJ 形容詞 A **ferocious** war, argument, or other form of conflict involves a great deal of anger, bitterness, and determination. ひどい □ *Fighting has been ferocious.* 戦いはひどかった。

fe|roc|ity /fərɒsɪti/ N-UNCOUNT 不可算名詞 The **ferocity** of something is its fierce or violent nature. どうもうさ □ *The armed forces seem to have been taken by surprise by the ferocity of the attack.* 武装勢力は猛烈な攻撃に不意をつかれたように見える。

fer|ry /fɛri/ (ferries, ferrying, ferried) **1** N-COUNT 可算名詞 A **ferry** is a boat that transports passengers and sometimes also vehicles, usually across rivers or short stretches of sea. 連絡船 [also 'by' N] □ *They had recrossed the River Gambia by ferry.* ガンビア川を渡し舟で再度渡った。 **2** V-T 他動詞 If a vehicle **ferries** people or goods, it transports them, usually by means of regular trips between the same two places. 運ぶ □ *Every day, a plane arrives to ferry guests to and from Bird Island Lodge.* 毎日飛行機がバードアイランドロッジまで往復し、客を運ぶ。
→ see **ship**

fer|tile /fɜrtⁿl/ **1** ADJ 形容詞 Land or soil that is **fertile** is able to support the growth of a large number of strong healthy plants. 肥えた □ *...fertile soil.* 肥沃（ひよく）な土壌 ●**fer|til|ity** /fɜrtɪlɪti/ N-UNCOUNT 不可算名詞 肥沃（ひよく）□ *He was able to bring large sterile acreages back to fertility.* 彼は大きな不毛地を肥えた土地に戻すことができた。 **2** ADJ 形容詞 A **fertile** mind or imagination is able to produce a lot of good, original ideas. 発想の豊かな □ *...a product of Flynn's fertile imagination.* フリンの豊かな想像力の成果 **3** ADJ 形容詞 [ADJ n] A situation or environment that is **fertile** in relation to a particular activity or feeling encourages the activity or feeling. よく結ぶ □ *...a fertile breeding ground for this kind of violent racism.* この種の暴力的人種差別を増長させる温床 **4** ADJ 形容詞 A person or animal that is **fertile** is able to reproduce and have babies or young. 繁殖力のある □ *The operation cannot be reversed to make her fertile again.* この手術は元に戻すことはできず、彼女は再び子を産めるようにならない。 ●**fer|til|ity** N-UNCOUNT 不可算名詞 生殖能力 □ *Doctors will tell you that pregnancy is the only sure test for fertility.* 医者は妊娠が唯一確実な受精能力のテストだと言うでしょう。

fer|ti|lize /fɜrtⁿlaɪz/ (fertilizes, fertilizing, fertilized) **1** V-T 他動詞 When an egg from the ovary of a woman or female animal **is fertilized**, a sperm from the male joins with the egg, causing a baby or young animal to begin forming. A female plant **is fertilized** when its reproductive parts come into contact with pollen from the male plant. 受精させる、受粉させる □ *Certain varieties cannot be fertilized with their own pollen.* ある種の品種は自己受粉できない。 □ *...the normal sperm levels needed to fertilize the egg.* 卵子を受精させるのに必要な精子の正常レベル ●**fer|ti|li|za|tion** /fɜrtⁿlɪzeɪʃⁿn/ N-UNCOUNT 不可算名詞 受精 □ *From fertilization until birth is about 266 days.* 受精から出産まで約266日である。 **2** V-T 他動詞 To **fertilize** land means to improve its quality in order to make plants grow well on it, by spreading solid animal waste or a chemical mixture on it. 肥やす □ *The feces contain nitrogen which fertilizes the soil.* ふん便は土壌を肥やす窒素が含まれている。
→ see **flower**

fer|ti|liz|er /fɜrtⁿlaɪzər/ (fertilizers) N-MASS 質量名詞 **Fertilizer** is a substance such as solid animal waste or a chemical mixture that you spread on the ground in order to make plants grow more successfully. 肥料 □ *...farming without any purchased chemical, fertilizer or pesticide.* 購入した薬品や肥料や殺虫剤を何も使わない農業
→ see **farm**, **pollution**

fer|vent /fɜrvⁿnt/ ADJ 形容詞 A **fervent** person has or shows strong feelings about something, and is very sincere and enthusiastic about it. 熱烈な □ *...a fervent admirer of Morisot's work.* モリゾーの作品の熱烈な称賛者 ●**fer|vent|ly** ADV 副詞 熱烈に □ *Their claims will be fervently denied.* 彼らの主張は激しく否定されるだろう。

fer|vor /fɜrvər/ N-UNCOUNT 不可算名詞 **Fervor** for something is a very strong feeling for or belief in it. 熱情 [FORMAL 形式ばった] □ *They were concerned only with their own religious fervor.* 彼らは自らの宗教的熱情のみに関心があった。

fes|ter /fɛstər/ (festers, festering, festered) **1** V-I 自動詞 If you say that a situation, problem, or feeling is **festering**, you disapprove of the fact that it is being allowed to grow more unpleasant or full of anger, because it is not being properly recognized or dealt with. つのる [DISAPPROVAL 不賛成] □ *Resentments are starting to fester.* 憤慨がつのり始めている。 **2** V-I 自動詞 If a wound **festers**, it becomes infected, making it worse. うむ □ *The wound is festering, and gangrene has set in.* 傷口がうんでいて、えそが起こっている。

fes|ti|val /fɛstɪvⁿl/ (festivals) **1** N-COUNT 可算名詞 A **festival** is an organized series of events such as musical concerts or drama productions. 祭り □ *Many towns hold their own summer festivals of music, theater, and dance.* 多くの町が音楽や劇やダンスの夏祭りを催す。 **2** N-COUNT 可算名詞 A **festival** is a day or time of the year when people do not go to work or school and celebrate some special event, often a religious event. 祭日 □ *Shavuot is a two-day festival for Orthodox Jews.* 五旬節は、ユダヤ教正統派の2日間にわたる祭礼である。

fes|tive /fɛstɪv/ **1** ADJ 形容詞 Something that is **festive** is special, colorful, or exciting, especially because of a holiday or celebration. お祝いの □ *The town has a festive holiday atmosphere.* 町には祝日のお祝い気分がある。 **2** ADJ 形容詞 **Festive** means relating to a holiday or celebration, especially Christmas. 祝祭（特にクリスマス）の [ADJ n] □ *With Christmas just around the corner, you should start your festive cooking now.* クリスマスがすぐそこまで来ているので、今からクリスマス料理を作り始めるべきです。

Thesaurus	*festive* また次を参照：
ADJ.	happy, joyous, merry; (ant.) gloomy, somber **1**

fes|tiv|ity /fɛstɪvɪti/ (festivities) **1** N-UNCOUNT 不可算名詞 **Festivity** is the celebration of something in a happy way. お祭り騒ぎ □ *There was a general air of festivity and abandon.* 祭り騒ぎや羽目をはずすような気分が全般的にあった。 **2** N-COUNT 可算名詞 **Festivities** are events that are organized in order to celebrate something. お祝い行事 □ *The festivities included a huge display of fireworks.* お祝い行事には大掛かりな花火の打ち上げも入っていた。

fetch /fɛtʃ/ (fetches, fetching, fetched) **1** V-T 他動詞 If you **fetch** something or someone, you go and get them from the place where they are. 行って取ってくる、行って連れてくる □ *Sylvia fetched a towel from the bathroom.* シルビアは浴室に行ってタオルを取ってきた。 □ *Fetch me a glass of water.* 水をコップに1杯持ってきてくれ。 **2** V-T 他動詞 If something **fetches** a particular sum of money, it is sold for that amount. （ある値で）売れる □ *The painting is expected to fetch between two and three million dollars.* その絵は2〜3百万ドルで売れるだろうと考えられている。 **3** → see also **far-fetched**

fete /feɪt, fɛt/ (fetes, feting, feted) also **fête** **1** N-COUNT 可算名詞 A **fete** is a fancy party or celebration. 祝宴 [AM 米国英語] □ *The pop star flew 100 friends in from London and Paris for a two-day fete.* そのポップ音楽のスターは、2日間の祝宴（きょうえん）のためにロンドンやパリから友達を100人飛行機で招いた。 **2** V-T 他動詞 If someone is **feted**, they are celebrated, welcomed, or admired by the public. 宴をはって祝う [usu passive] □ *Vera Wang was feted in New York this week at a spectacular dinner.* ベラ・ワングは今週ニューヨークで豪勢な晩餐（ばんさん）会でお祝いを受けた。

fe|tus /fitəs/ (fetuses) N-COUNT 可算名詞 A **fetus** is an animal or human being in its later stages of development before it is born. 胎児 □ *Pregnant women who are heavy drinkers risk damaging the unborn fetus.* 大酒飲みの妊娠中の女性は、体内の胎児に障害を与える恐れがある。

feud /fyud/ (feuds, feuding, feuded) **1** N-COUNT 可算名詞 A **feud** is a quarrel in which two people or groups remain angry with each other for a long time, although they are not always fighting or arguing. 確執、反目 □ *...a long and bitter feud between the state government and the villagers.* 州政府と村民との間の長期に渡る激しい反目 **2** V-RECIP 相互動詞 If one person or group **feuds** with another, they have a quarrel that lasts a long time. You can also say that two people or groups **feud**. 反目する □ *He feuded with his ex-wife.* 彼は別れた妻と不和である。

feu|dal /fyudⁿl/ ADJ 形容詞 **Feudal** means relating to the system or the time of feudalism. 封建制度の、封建時代の [ADJ n] □ *...the emperor and his feudal barons.* 皇帝とその封建領主たち

feu|dal|ism /fyudⁿlɪzəm/ N-UNCOUNT 不可算名詞 **Feudalism** was a system in which people were given land and protection by

people of higher rank, and worked and fought for them in return. 封建制度 ❏ *As feudalism decayed in the West it gave rise to a mercantile class.* 西洋では封建制度が衰退するにつれ、商人階級が台頭してきた.

fe|ver /fíːvər/ (fevers) **1** N-VAR 可変性名詞 If you have a **fever** when you are ill, your body temperature is higher than usual. 発熱 ❏ *My Uncle Jim had a high fever.* ジム叔父さんは熱が高かった. **2** → see also **hay fever**
→ see **illness**

fe|ver|ish /fíːvərɪʃ/ **1** ADJ 形容詞 **Feverish** activity is done extremely quickly, often in a state of nervousness or excitement because you want to finish it as soon as possible. 大あわての、猛烈な ❏ *Hours of feverish activity lay ahead. The tents had to be erected, the stalls set up.* 何時間も続く猛烈な活動が待っていた. テントを張ったり、屋台店を設けたりしなければならなかった. **2** ADJ 形容詞 If you are **feverish**, you are suffering from a fever. 熱のある ❏ *A feverish child refuses to eat and asks only for cold drinks.* 熱のある子供は食べたがらず、冷たい飲み物だけを欲しがる. ● **fe|ver|ish|ly** ADV 副詞 熱っぽくて ❏ *He slept feverishly all afternoon and into the night.* 彼は熱っぽく午後からずっと夜まで眠った.

few /fjuː/ (fewer, fewest) **1** DET 限定詞 You use **a few** to indicate that you are talking about a small number of people or things. You can also say **a very few**. いくらかの ❏ *I gave a dinner party for a few close friends.* 親友数人を夕食会に招いた. ❏ *Here are a few more ideas to consider.* ほら、考えてみるアイデアがまだいくつかあります. ● PRON 代名詞 **Few** is also a pronoun. 少数 ❏ *Doctors work an average of 90 hours a week, while a few are on call for up to 120 hours.* 医者は平均週に90時間働き、同時に最高120時間も待機する医者も少数いる. ● QUANT 数量詞 **Few** is also a quantifier. 少数 [QUANT 'of' def-pl-n] ❏ *There are many ways eggs can be prepared; here are a few of them.* 卵の料理法はたくさんありますが、これはその2, 3の例です. **2** DET 限定詞 You use **few** to indicate that you are talking about a small number of people or things. You can use "so," "too," and "very" in front of **few**. わずかしかない ❏ *She had few friends, and was generally not functioning up to her potential.* 彼女は友だちがほとんどなく、概して持てる能力を発揮できていなかった. ❏ *Few members planned to vote for him.* 彼に投票するつもりの会員はほとんどいなかった. ● PRON 代名詞 **Few** is also a pronoun. 少数しかない物（人）❏ *Few can survive more than a week without water.* 水なしで1週間以上生き残ることができる人はほとんどいない. ● QUANT 数量詞 **Few** is also a quantifier. 少数（しかない）[QUANT 'of' def-pl-n] ❏ *Few of the beach houses still had lights on.* まだ灯りのついている海辺の家はほんのわずかしかなかった. ● ADJ 形容詞 **Few** is also an adjective. わずかしかない ❏ *...spending her few waking hours in front of the TV.* 彼女のわずかしかない目覚めている時間をテレビの前で過ごして. **3** ADJ 形容詞 You use **few** after adjectives and determiners to indicate that you are talking about a small number of things or people. 少数の [adj/det ADJ n] ❏ *The past few weeks of her life had been the most pleasant she could remember.* ここ数週間は記憶にある彼女の人生の中でも最も楽しいものだった. ❏ *...in the last few chapters.* 最後のいくつかの章で. **4** N-SING 単数名詞 **The few** means a small set of people considered as separate from the majority, especially because they share a particular opportunity or quality that the others do not have. 少数の人たち、少数の選ばれた人たち ❏ *This should not be an experience for the few.* これは少数の人たちの経験であってはならない.

Few and **a few** are both used in front of the plural of count nouns, but they do not have the same meaning. For example, if you say **I have a few friends**, this is a positive statement and you are saying that you have some friends. However, if you say **I have few friends**, this is a negative statement and you are saying that you have almost no friends. You use **fewer** to talk about things that can be counted. ❏ *...fewer potatoes.* When you are talking about amounts that cannot be counted, you should use **less**. ❏ *...less meat.*

5 PHRASE 句 You use **as few as** before a number to suggest that it is surprisingly small. わずか [EMPHASIS 強調] ❏ *One study showed that even as few as ten cigarettes a day can damage fertility.* 1日わずか10本のタバコでも生殖能力に障害を与える場合があることを示した研究が1つあった. **6** PHRASE 句 Things that are **few and far between** are very rare or do not happen very often. きわめてまれ [EMPHASIS 強調] ❏ *Successful women politicians are few and far between.* 政治家で成功している女性はごくまれである. **7** PHRASE 句 You use **no fewer than** to emphasize that a number is surprisingly large. 〜ほどの [EMPHASIS 強調] ❏ *No fewer than thirteen foreign ministers attended the session.* その会合には13もの外務大臣が参加した.

fi|as|co /fiǽskoʊ/ (fiascos) N-COUNT 算名詞 If you describe an event or attempt to do something as a **fiasco**, you are emphasizing that it fails completely. 大失敗 [EMPHASIS 強調] ❏ *The blame for the Charleston fiasco did not lie with him.* チャールストンの大失敗の責任は彼にはなかった.

fi|ber /fáɪbər/ (fibers) **1** N-COUNT 可算名詞 A **fiber** is a thin thread of a natural or artificial substance, especially one that is used to make cloth or rope. 繊維 ❏ *If you look at the paper under*

a microscope you will see the fibers. その紙を顕微鏡で見てみると、繊維が見えるでしょう. **2** N-COUNT 可算名詞 A **fiber** is a thin piece of flesh like a thread which connects nerve cells in your body or which muscles are made of. 繊維組織 ❏ *...the nerve fibers.* 神経繊維組織 **3** N-VAR 可変性名詞 A particular **fiber** is a type of cloth or other material that is made from or consists of threads. （布など の）繊維製品 ❏ *The ball is made of rattan – a natural fiber.* ボールは天然繊維の籐（とう）から作られている. **4** N-UNCOUNT 不可算名詞 **Fiber** consists of the parts of plants or seeds that your body cannot digest. Fiber is useful because it makes food pass quickly through your body. 繊維質 ❏ *Most vegetables contain fiber.* ほとんどの野菜は繊維質を含んでいる.
→ see **laser, paper, rope, vegetable**

fi|ber op|tics

The form **fiber optic** is used as a modifier.

fiber optic 形は修飾語として使われる.

1 N-UNCOUNT 不可算名詞 **Fiber optics** is the use of long thin threads of glass to carry information in the form of light. 繊維光学、光ファイバー ❏ *Thanks to fiber optics, it is now possible to illuminate many of the body's remotest organs and darkest orifices.* 光ファイバーのお陰で現在は体内の最も奥深い臓器や最も暗い開口部を照らすことができる. **2** ADJ 形容詞 **Fiber optic** means relating to or involved in fiber optics. 繊維光学の、光ファイバーの [ADJ n] ❏ *...fiber optic cables.* 光ファイバーケーブル

fick|le /fíkəl/ **1** ADJ 形容詞 If you describe someone as **fickle**, you disapprove of them because they keep changing their mind about what they like or want. 気まぐれな [DISAPPROVAL 不賛成] ❏ *The group has been notoriously fickle in the past.* そのグループは以前から気まぐれで悪名が高い. **2** ADJ 形容詞 If you say that something is **fickle**, you mean that it often changes and is unreliable. 変わりやすい ❏ *New England's weather can be fickle.* ニューイングランドの天候は変わりやすいこともある.

fic|tion /fíkʃən/ (fictions) **1** N-UNCOUNT 不可算名詞 **Fiction** refers to books and stories about imaginary people and events, rather than books about real people or events. 小説 ❏ *Immigrant tales have always been popular themes in fiction.* 移民の話は小説でいつでも人気があるテーマだ. **2** → see also **science fiction** **3** N-UNCOUNT 不可算名詞 A statement or account that is **fiction** is not true. 作り話 ❏ *The truth or fiction of this story has never been truly determined.* この話しが真実か作り話かどうかはいまだに確定されていない. **4** N-COUNT 可算名詞 If something is a **fiction**, it is not true, although people sometimes pretend that it is true. 虚構 ❏ *Total recycling is a fiction.* 完全なる再利用は虚構だ.
→ see **genre, library**

fic|tion|al /fíkʃənəl/ ADJ 形容詞 **Fictional** characters or events occur only in stories, plays, or movies and never actually existed or happened. 架空の ❏ *It is drama featuring fictional characters.* それは架空の人物が登場する劇だ.
→ see **fantasy**

fic|ti|tious /fɪktíʃəs/ **1** ADJ 形容詞 **Fictitious** is used to describe something that is false or does not exist, although some people claim that it is true or exists. 虚偽の ❏ *We're interested in the source of these fictitious rumors.* 我々はこのようなうその噂の出所に関心があるのだ. **2** ADJ 形容詞 A **fictitious** character, thing, or event occurs in a story, play, or film but never really existed or happened. 架空の ❏ *The persons and events portrayed in this production are fictitious.* この作品で描写されている人物や出来事は架空のものである.

fid|dle /fídəl/ (fiddles, fiddling, fiddled) **1** V-I 自動詞 If you **fiddle with** an object, you keep moving it or touching it with your fingers. いじくる ❏ *Harriet fiddled with a pen on the desk.* ハリエットは机の上でペンをもてあそんだ. **2** V-I 自動詞 If you **fiddle with** something, you change it in minor ways. 手直しをする ❏ *She told Whistler that his portrait of her was finished and to stop fiddling with it.* ホィッスラーが描いた彼女の肖像画は仕上がっているので、それ以上手直しをしないようにと彼女はホィッスラーに言った. **3** V-I 自動詞 If you **fiddle with** a machine, you adjust it. 調整する ❏ *He turned on the radio and fiddled with the knob until he got a talk show.* 彼はラジオをつけて、インタビュー番組が見つかるまでつまみを調整していた. **4** N-VAR 可変性名詞 Some people call violins **fiddles**, especially when they are used to play folk music. バイオリン ❏ *Hardy played the fiddle at local dances.* ハーディは地元のダンスパーティーでバイオリンを弾いていた.

fi|del|ity /fɪdélɪti/ **1** N-UNCOUNT 不可算名詞 **Fidelity** is loyalty to a person, organization, or set of beliefs. 忠実、忠誠 [FORMAL 形式ばった] ❏ *People have failed to act in fidelity to their vows.* 人々は誓いに忠実に行動しなかった. **2** N-UNCOUNT 不可算名詞 **Fidelity** is being loyal to your husband, wife, or partner by not having a sexual relationship with anyone else. 貞節 ❏ *Women expect fidelity from their men.* 女は夫の貞節を期待する.

fidg|et /fídʒɪt/ (fidgets, fidgeting, fidgeted) **1** V-I 自動詞 If you **fidget**, you keep moving your hands or feet slightly or changing

your position slightly, for example, because you are nervous, bored, or excited. もじもじする、そわそわする ● *Brenda fidgeted in her seat.* ブレンダは席でもじもじした. ● PHRASAL VERB 句動詞 **Fidget around** and **fidget about** mean the same as **fidget**. もじもじする、そわそわする ● *There were two new arrivals, fidgeting around, waiting to ask questions.* 2人が新しく到着して、もじもじしながら質問する機会を持っていた. **2** V-I 自動詞 If you **fidget with** something, you keep moving it or touching it with your fingers with small movements, for example, because you are nervous or bored. いじくる ● *He fidgeted with his tie.* 彼はネクタイをいじくった.

field /fíld/ (**fields, fielding, fielded**) **1** N-COUNT 可算名詞 A **field** is an area of grass, for example, in a park or on a farm. A **field** is also an area of land on which a crop is grown. 芝地; 牧草地; 畑 ● *...a field of wheat.* 小麦畑 **2** N-COUNT 可算名詞 A sports **field** is an area of grass where sports are played. 競技場 ● *a football field.* フットボール場 ● *He was the fastest thing I ever saw on a baseball field.* 彼は今までに野球場で見たうちの1番早いやつだった. **3** N-COUNT 可算名詞 A **field** is an area of land or sea bed under which large amounts of a particular mineral have been found. 産地 ● *...an extensive natural gas field in Alaska.* アラスカにある大規模な天然ガス産地 **4** N-COUNT 可算名詞 A magnetic, gravitational, or electric **field** is the area in which that particular force is strong enough to have an effect. 界 ● *Some people are worried that electromagnetic fields from electric power lines could increase the risk of cancer.* 送電線の電磁界のためにがんの危険が増大するかもしれないと、一部の人は心配している. **5** N-COUNT 可算名詞 A particular **field** is a particular subject of study or type of activity. 分野 ● *Each of the authors of the tapes is an expert in his field.* テープの各著者はそれぞれの分野の専門家である. **6** N-COUNT 可算名詞 A **field** is an area of a computer's memory or a program where data can be entered, edited, or stored. 記録指定域, フィールド [COMPUTING コンピューティング] ● *Go to a site like Yahoo! Finance and enter "AOL" in the Get Quotes field.* ヤフーファイナンスのようなサイトに行って、「見積もり入手」の欄に 'AOL' と入力しなさい. **7** N-COUNT 可算名詞 Your **field** of vision or your visual **field** is the area that you can see without turning your head. 視野 ● *Our field of vision is surprisingly wide.* 視野は意外と広い. **8** N-COUNT-COLL 集合可算名詞 The **field** is a way of referring to all the competitors taking part in a particular race or sports contest. 全競技者; 全出走馬 ● *Going into the fourth lap, the two most broadly experienced riders led the field.* 4周目に入り、最も広く経験を積んだ騎手2人が全員をリードしていた. **9** ADJ 形容詞 You use **field** to describe work or study that is done in a real, natural environment rather than in a theoretical way or in controlled conditions. 現場の、実地の [ADJ n] ● *I also conducted a field study among the boys about their attitude to relationships.* 私は人間関係に対する少年たちの考えについて彼らの間で実地調査も行った. **10** V-I 自動詞 In a game of baseball or cricket, the team that **is fielding** is trying to catch the ball, while the other team is trying to hit it. 守備につく [usu cont] ● *When we are fielding, the umpires keep looking at the ball.* 守備についている間、審判員たちはずっとボールを見ている. **11** V-T 他動詞 If you say that someone **fields** a question, you mean that they answer it or deal with it, usually successfully. うまく答える [JOURNALISM ジャーナリズム] ● *He was later shown on television, fielding questions.* その後に質問をうまくさばいている彼の様子がテレビで放映された. **12** V-T 他動詞 If a sports team **fields** a particular number or type of players, the players are chosen to play for the team on a particular occasion. 出場させる ● *We are going to field an exciting and younger team.* 我々はわくわくするもっと若いチームを出場させるつもりだ. **13** V-T 他動詞 If a candidate in an election is representing a political party, you can say that the party **is fielding** that candidate. 出馬させる [JOURNALISM ジャーナリズム] ● *There are signs that the new party aims to field candidates in elections scheduled for February next year.* 新政党は来年の2月予定の選挙に候補者の擁立(ようりつ)を目指している気配がある. **14** → see also **minefield, playing field**
→ see **oil**

ADJ.	**open** field **1**
	magnetic field **4**
N.	**ball** field, field **hockey**, **track and** field **2**
	oil field **3**
	expert in a field, field **trip 5**
	field **of vision 7**
	field **of battle 8**
	field **questions 11**
V.	**work in a** field **5**

field|er /fíldər/ (**fielders**) N-COUNT 可算名詞 A **fielder** is a player in baseball or cricket who is fielding or one who has a particular skill at fielding. 野手 ● *He hit 10 home runs in the Coast League and he's also a good fielder.* 彼はコーストリーグで10本のホームランを出したし、よい野手でもある.

field hock|ey N-UNCOUNT 不可算名詞 **Field hockey** is an

outdoor game played on a grass field between two teams of 11 players who use long curved sticks to hit a small ball and try to score goals. ホッケー [AM 米国英語] [oft N n]

fierce /fíərs/ (**fiercer, fiercest**) **1** ADJ 形容詞 A **fierce** animal or person is very aggressive or angry. どう猛な ● *They look like the teeth of some fierce animal.* 何かどう猛な動物の歯のように見える. ● **fierce|ly** ADV 副詞 激しく ● *"I don't know," she said fiercely.* 「知らないわよ」と彼女は激しく言った. **2** ADJ 形容詞 **Fierce** feelings or actions are very intense or enthusiastic, or involve great activity. 猛烈な ● *Consumers have a wide array of choices and price competition is fierce.* 消費者には幅広い選択があり、価格競合は激烈である. ● *The town was captured after a fierce battle with rebels.* 反乱軍との猛烈な戦いの後にその町を占領した. ● **fierce|ly** ADV 副詞 猛烈に ● *He has always been ambitious and fiercely competitive.* 彼は常に野心に満ち、猛烈な競争心を持ってきた.

fiery /fáiəri/ (**fieriest**) **1** ADJ 形容詞 If you describe something as **fiery**, you mean that it is burning strongly or contains fire. 火の、猛火の [LITERARY 文語的] ● *A helicopter crashed in a fiery explosion in Vallejo.* バレーオでヘリコプターが墜落し、爆発して燃上した. **2** ADJ 形容詞 You can use **fiery** for emphasis when you are referring to bright colors such as red or orange. 火のような [LITERARY 文語的, EMPHASIS 強調] ● *The sky turned from fiery orange to lemon yellow.* 空は火のようなオレンジ色からレモン色の黄色に変化した.

fif|teen /fiftí:n/ (**fifteens**) NUM 数詞 **Fifteen** is the number 15. 15 ● *In India, there are fifteen official languages.* インドでは公式言語が15ある.

fif|teenth /fiftíːnθ/ ORD 序数詞 The **fifteenth** item in a series is the one that you count as number fifteen. 15番目の ● *...the invention of the printing press in the fifteenth century.* 15世紀の印刷機の発明

fifth /fífθ/ (**fifths**) **1** ORD 序数詞 The **fifth** item in a series is the one that you count as number five. 5番目の ● *Joe has recently returned from his fifth trip to Australia.* ジョーは5回目のオーストラリア旅行から最近帰ってきた. **2** FRACTION 端数詞 A **fifth** is one of five equal parts of something. 5分の1 ● *India spends over a fifth of its budget on defense.* インドは予算の5分の1以上を防衛に費やす. **3** N-SING 単数名詞 If you **take** or **plead the fifth**, you take the Fifth Amendment. (憲法修正第5条で保障された)黙秘権

fif|ti|eth /fíftiəθ/ ORD 序数詞 The **fiftieth** item in a series is the one that you count as number fifty. 50番目の ● *He retired in 1970, on his fiftieth birthday.* 彼は1970年に50歳の誕生日に引退した.

fif|ty /fífti/ (**fifties**) **1** NUM 数詞 **Fifty** is the number 50. 50 **2** N-PLURAL 複数名詞 When you talk about the **fifties**, you are referring to numbers between 50 and 59. For example, if you are in your **fifties**, you are aged between 50 and 59. If the temperature is **in the fifties**, the temperature is between 50 and 59 degrees. 50番台; 50歳代 ● *People probably look as if I'm in my fifties rather than my seventies.* 私はおそらく70歳代というよりも50歳代に見えるようだ. **3** N-PLURAL 複数名詞 The **fifties** is the decade between 1950 and 1959. 1950年代 ● *He began performing in the early fifties, singing and playing guitar.* 彼は50年代初めに舞台でギターを演奏して、歌を歌い始めた.

fifty-fifty ADV 副詞 If something such as money or property is divided or shared **fifty-fifty** between two people, each person gets half of it. 半々に [INFORMAL くだけた] [ADV after v] ● *The proceeds of the sale are split fifty-fifty.* セールの売上高は5分5分に分けられる. ● ADJ 形容詞 **Fifty-fifty** is also an adjective. 半々の ● *The new firm was owned on a fifty-fifty basis by the two parent companies.* 新会社は2つの親会社が半々のベースで所有していた.

fig /fíg/ (**figs**) **1** N-COUNT 可算名詞 A **fig** is a soft sweet fruit that grows in hot areas. It is full of tiny seeds and is often eaten dried. イチジク **2** N-COUNT 可算名詞 A **fig** or a **fig tree** is a tree on which figs grow. イチジクの木

fig. In books and magazines, **fig.** is used as an abbreviation for **figure** in order to tell the reader which picture or diagram is being referred to. 図 ● *Draw the basic outlines in black felt-tip pen (see fig. 4).* 黒のフェルトペンで基本的な輪郭を描きなさい. (図4参照)

fight /fáit/ (**fights, fighting, fought**) **1** V-T/V-I 他動詞/自動詞 If you **fight** something unpleasant, you try in a determined way to prevent it or stop it from happening. (阻止するために)戦う ● *More units to fight forest fires are planned.* 山火事と戦うためさらに多くの消防隊が計画されている. ● *I've spent a lifetime fighting against racism and prejudice.* 私は人種差別や偏見と戦うために人生をかけてきた. ● N-COUNT 可算名詞 **Fight** is also a noun. 戦い ● *...the fight against drug addiction.* 麻薬中毒に対する戦い **2** V-I 自動詞 If you **fight** for something, you try in a determined way to get it or achieve it. (獲得しようと)戦う ● *Lee had to fight hard for his place on the expedition.* リーは探検隊の1員になるために一生懸命努力しなければならなかった. ● *I told him how we had fought to hold on to the company.* 私は我々が会社を手放さないようにいかに奮闘してきたかを彼に話した. ● N-COUNT 可算名詞 **Fight** is also a noun. 奮闘 ● *I*

too am committing myself to continue the fight for justice. 私も本気で正義のための戦いを続けていくつもりだ. ■ V-T/V-I 他動詞/自動詞 If a person or army **fights** in a battle or a war, they take part in it. 戦闘する □ *He fought in the war and was taken prisoner by the Americans.* 彼はその戦争で戦い, 米軍の捕虜になった. □ *If I were a young man I would sooner go to prison than fight for this country.* 私が若者だったら, この国のために戦うよりも監獄に行った方がました. ●**fight|ing** N-UNCOUNT 不可算名詞 戦闘 □ *More than nine hundred people have died in the fighting.* その戦闘で900人以上の人が死んだ. ■ V-T 他動詞 If you **fight** your way to a place, you move toward it with great difficulty, for example, because there are a lot of people or obstacles in your way. もがきながら進む □ *I fought my way into a carriage just before the doors closed.* 私はドアが閉まる直前に客車にもがくようにして入った. ■ V-T/V-I 他動詞/自動詞 To **fight** means to take part in a boxing match. 拳闘する □ *In a few hours' time one of the world's most famous boxers will be fighting here for the first time.* 数時間したら世界で最も有名なボクサーの1人が初めてここで試合をしているだろう. □ *I'd like to fight him because he's undefeated and I want to be the first man to beat him.* 彼は負けたことがないので, 私は彼と戦いたい. そして彼を倒す最初の男になりたい. ■ V-T 他動詞 If you **fight** an election, you are a candidate in the election and try to win it. (選挙を) 戦う □ *He helped raise almost $40 million to fight the election campaign.* 彼はその選挙戦を戦うために4千万ドル近く集める手助けした. ■ V-T 他動詞 If you **fight** a case or a court action, you make a legal case against someone in a very determined way, or you put forward a defense when a legal case is made against you. (訴訟を) 起こす, 弁護する □ *Watkins sued the Army and fought his case in various courts for 10 years.* ワトキンズは陸軍を訴え, 10年間さまざまな法廷で自分の訴訟のために戦った. ■ V-T/V-I 他動詞/自動詞 If you **fight** an emotion or desire, you try very hard not to feel it, show it, or act on it, but do not always succeed. 克服しようとする □ *I desperately fought the urge to giggle.* 私はくすくすと笑いたい衝動を必死で抑えようとした. □ *He fought with the urge to smoke one of the cigars he'd given up a while ago.* 彼はしばらく前に止めた葉巻を1本吸いたい衝動を抑えようとした. ■ V-RECIP 相互動詞 If an army or group **fights** a battle with another army or group, they oppose each other with weapons. You can also say that two armies or groups **fight** a battle. 交戦する □ *Police fought a gun battle with a gang which used hand grenades against them.* 警察は彼らに対して手投げ弾を使う1団と銃撃戦をした. ■ V-RECIP 相互動詞 If one person **fights** with another, or **fights** them, the two people hit or kick each other because they want to hurt each other. You can also say that two people **fight**. 殴り合う □ *As a child she fought with her younger sister.* 彼女は子供のときに妹と取っ組み合いのけんかをした. □ *I did fight him, I punched him but it was like hitting a wall.* 私は実際彼とけんかして, げんこつで殴ったけれど, 壁を殴っているようだった. ●N-COUNT 可算名詞 [oft N 'with' n] **Fight** is also a noun. 殴り合いのけんか □ *He had a fight with Smith and bloodied his nose.* 彼はスミスと殴り合いをして, 鼻血を出させた. ■ V-RECIP 相互動詞 If one person **fights** with another, or **fights** them, they have an angry disagreement or quarrel. You can also say that two people **fight**. 言い争う [INFORMAL くだけた] □ *She was always arguing with him and fighting with him.* 彼女はいつも彼と口論し言い争っていた. □ *Gwendolen started fighting her teachers.* グエンドリンは先生たちと言い争い始めた. ●N-COUNT 可算名詞 **Fight** is also a noun. 言い争い □ *We think maybe he could have had a big fight with his dad the night before.* 彼は父親と前の晩に大げんかをして, 出ていったのではないかと思う. ■ N-COUNT 可算名詞 A **fight** is a boxing match. ボクシングの試合 □ *The referee stopped the fight.* 審判はその試合をとめた. ■ N-COUNT 可算名詞 You can use **fight** to refer to a contest such as an election or a sports competition. 競争 [JOURNALISM ジャーナリズム] □ *...the fight for power between the two parties.* 両政党間の権力争い. ■ N-UNCOUNT 不可算名詞 **Fight** is the desire or ability to keep fighting. 闘志 □ *I thought that we had a lot of fight in us.* 私は自分たちには闘志がたくさんあると思った. ■ PHRASE 句 Someone who **is fighting for** their **life** is making a great effort to stay alive, either when they are being physically attacked or when they are very ill. 生死をさまよう □ *He is still fighting for his life in the hospital.* 彼はまだ病院で危篤状態である.

▶ **fight back** ■ PHRASAL VERB 句動詞 If you **fight back** against someone or something that is attacking or harming you, you resist them actively or attack them. 反撃する □ *We should take some comfort from the ability of the judicial system to fight back against corruption.* 司法制度が汚職に反撃を加える能力があるのが少しは慰めとすべきだ. ■ PHRASAL VERB 句動詞 If you **fight back** an emotion or a desire, you try very hard not to feel it, show it, or act on it. 気持ちを抑える □ *She fought back the tears.* 彼女は泣くまいと涙をこらえた.

▶ **fight off** ■ PHRASAL VERB 句動詞 If you **fight off** something, for example, an illness or an unpleasant feeling, you succeed in getting rid of it and in not letting it overcome you. 寄せつけない □ *Unfortunately these drugs are quite toxic and hinder the body's ability to fight off infection.* 残念ながらこれらの薬はかなり毒性があり, 体が感染を撃退しようとする力を妨げる. ■ PHRASAL VERB 句動詞 If you **fight off** someone who has attacked you, you fight with them,

and succeed in making them go away or stop attacking you. 撃退する □ *She fought off three armed robbers.* 彼女は3人の武装した強盗を撃退した.

→ see **army**

fight|er /faɪtər/ (**fighters**) ■ N-COUNT 可算名詞 A **fighter** or a **fighter plane** is a fast military aircraft that is used for destroying other aircraft. 戦闘機 □ *...a fighter pilot.* 戦闘機のパイロット. ■ N-COUNT 可算名詞 If you describe someone as a **fighter**, you approve of them because they continue trying to achieve things in spite of great difficulties or opposition. 闘志のある人 [APPROVAL 賛成] □ *From the start it was clear this tiny girl was a real fighter.* この小さな女の子が本当にがんばり屋であることは最初から明白であった. ■ N-COUNT 可算名詞 A **fighter** is a person who physically fights another person, especially a professional boxer. けんか好きな人, 拳闘選手 □ *He was a real street fighter who'd do anything to win.* 彼は勝つためには何でもする本当の街のファイターだった. ■ → see also **firefighter**

fig|ura|tive /fɪgjərətɪv/ ■ ADJ 形容詞 If you use a word or expression in a **figurative** sense, you use it with a more abstract or imaginative meaning than its ordinary literal one. 比ゆの □ *...an event that will change your route – in both the literal and figurative sense.* 文字通りでも比ゆ的な意味でも進路を変えるような出来事. ●**fig|ura|tive|ly** ADV 副詞 比ゆ的に □ *I saw that she was, both literally and figuratively, up against a wall.* 私には彼女が文字通りにも比ゆ的にも壁にぶつかっているのがわかった. ■ ADJ 形容詞 **Figurative** art is a style of art in which people and things are shown in a realistic way. 造形の □ *His career spanned some 50 years and encompassed both abstract and figurative painting.* 彼のキャリアはおよそ50年間にわたり, 抽象および造形絵画の両方を包含していた.

fig|ure /fɪgjər/ (**figures, figuring, figured**) ■ N-COUNT 可算名詞 A **figure** is a particular amount expressed as a number, especially a statistic. 数値 □ *It would be very nice if we had a true figure of how many people in this country haven't got a job.* この国で仕事がない人がどれほどいるのか正確な数値があれば大変いいのだが. □ *It will not be long before the inflation figure starts to fall.* もう少しすればインフレーションの数値が下がり始めるだろう. ■ N-COUNT 可算名詞 A **figure** is any of the ten written symbols from 0 to 9 that are used to represent a number. 数字 □ *...the glowing red figures on the radio alarm clock which read 4:22 a.m.* 午前4時22分を示しているラジオ付き目覚まし時計の赤く輝いている数字. ■ N-COUNT 可算名詞 You refer to someone that you can see as a **figure** when you cannot see them clearly or when you are describing them. 人の姿 □ *Ernie saw the dim figure of Rose in the chair.* アーニーは椅子に座っているローズのぼやけた姿を見た. ■ N-COUNT 可算名詞 In art, a **figure** is a person in a drawing or a painting, or a statue of a person. 人物像 □ *...a life-size bronze figure of a brooding, hooded woman.* 考え込んでいる, ずきんをかぶった女の実物大の銅像. ■ N-COUNT 可算名詞 Your **figure** is the shape of your body. 体型 □ *Take pride in your health and your figure.* 自分の健康とスタイルに誇りを持ちなさい. ■ N-COUNT 可算名詞 Someone who is referred to as a **figure** of a particular kind is a person who is well-known and important in some way. 重要人物 □ *The movement is supported by key figures in the three main political parties.* その運動は3党の重要人物が支持している. ■ N-COUNT 可算名詞 If you say that someone is, for example, a mother **figure** or a hero **figure**, you mean that other people regard them as the type of person stated or suggested. 象徴 □ *Daniel Boone, the great hero figure of the frontier.* 辺境の偉大な英雄の象徴であるダニエル・ブーン. ■ N-COUNT 可算名詞 In books and magazines, the diagrams which help to show or explain information are referred to as **figures**. 図 [also N num] □ *If you look at a world map (see Figure 1) you can identify the major wine-producing regions.* 世界地図 (図1参照) を見れば, 主要なワイン生産地域を確認できる. ■ N-COUNT 可算名詞 In geometry, a **figure** is a shape, especially a regular shape. 図形 [TECHNICAL 技術的] □ *Draw a pentagon, a regular five-sided figure.* 5辺が等しい図形である5角形を描きなさい. ■ N-PLURAL 複数名詞 An amount or number that is in

single **figures** is between zero and nine. An amount or number that is in double **figures** is between ten and ninety-nine. You can also say, for example, that an amount or number is in three **figures** when it is between one hundred and nine hundred and ninety-nine. けた ❑ *Inflation, which has usually been in single figures, is running at more than 12%.* 普通は1けたであったインフレーションが、今は12%以上にも上っている。 **11** V-T 他動詞 If you **figure** that something is the case, you think or guess that it is the case. ～だと思う [INFORMAL くだけた] ❑ *She figured that both she and Ned had learned a lot from the experience.* 彼女も木ッドもその経験からたくさんのことを学んだと彼女は思った。 **12** V-I 自動詞 If you say "**That figures**" or "**It figures**," you mean that the fact referred to is not surprising. やっぱり思った通りだ。[INFORMAL くだけた] ❑ *When I finished, he said, "Yeah. That figures."* 私が話し終えたときに、彼は「うん、やっぱり思った通りだな」と言った。 **13** V-I 自動詞 If a person or thing **figures** in something, they appear in or are included in it. 現れる、目立つ [no passive] ❑ *Human rights violations figured prominently in the report.* 人権違反が報告書で目立った。

▶ **figure out** PHRASAL VERB 句動詞 If you **figure out** a solution to a problem or the reason for something, you succeed in solving it or understanding it. 解決する；理解する [INFORMAL くだけた] ❑ *It took them about one month to figure out how to start the equipment.* 彼らが装置をスタートさせる方法を理解するのに1か月くらいかかった。 ❑ *They're trying to figure out the politics of this whole situation.* 彼らはこの状況全体の利害関係を理解しようとしている。

figure|head /fɪɡjərhɛd/ (**figureheads**) **1** N-COUNT 可算名詞 If someone is the **figurehead** of an organization or movement, they are recognized as being its leader, although they have little real power. 名目上の最高責任者 ❑ *The president will be little more than a figurehead.* 大統領は名目上の最高責任者にしかすぎないだろう。 **2** N-COUNT 可算名詞 A **figurehead** is a large wooden model of a person that was put just under the pointed front of a sailing ship in former times. 船首像

file /faɪl/ (**files, filing, filed**) **1** N-COUNT 可算名詞 A **file** is a box or a folded piece of heavy paper or plastic in which letters or documents are kept. ファイル、書類整理箱 ❑ *...a file of insurance papers.* 保険書類のファイル **2** N-COUNT 可算名詞 A **file** is a collection of information about a particular person or thing. 記録、資料 ❑ *We already have files on people's tax details.* 人々の税金詳細に関する資料は既にある。 **3** N-COUNT 可算名詞 In computing, a **file** is a set of related data that has its own name. ファイル ❑ *Be sure to save the revised version of the file under a new filename.* 更新したファイルは必ず新しいファイル名で保存するようにしてください。 **4** N-COUNT 可算名詞 A **file** is a hand tool which is used for rubbing hard objects to make them smooth, shape them, or cut through them. やすり **5** V-T 他動詞 If you **file** a document, you put it in the correct place. とじ込んで整理する ❑ *They are all filed alphabetically under author.* それらはすべて著者名でアルファベット順に整理されている。 **6** V-T/V-I 他動詞/自動詞 If you **file** a formal or legal accusation, complaint, or request, you make it officially. 提起する ❑ *I filed for divorce on the grounds of adultery a few months later.* 私は数か月後に不貞を理由に離婚を申し立てた。 **7** V-T 他動詞 When someone **files** a report or a news story, they send or give it to their employer. (記事などを) 送る ❑ *He had to rush back to the office and file a housing story before the secretaries went home.* 彼は秘書たちが退社する前に急いで事務所に戻り、住宅記事を送らなければならなかった。 **8** V-T 他動詞 If you **file** an object, you smooth it, shape it, or cut it with a file. やすりをかける ❑ *Manicurists are skilled at shaping and filing nails.* マニキュア師は爪に形を整えたり、やすりをかけたりすることに熟練している。 **9** → see also **rank and file 10** PHRASE 句 A group of people who are walking or standing in **single file** or **single file** are in a line, one behind the other. 1列に ❑ *We were walking in single file to the lake.* 我々は湖に向かって1列に歩いていた。 → see **office, tool**

fil|ing cabi|net (**filing cabinets**) N-COUNT 可算名詞 A **filing cabinet** is a piece of office furniture, usually made of metal, which has drawers in which files are kept. 書類整理キャビネット → see **office**

fill /fɪl/ (**fills, filling, filled**) **1** V-T/V-I 他動詞/自動詞 If you **fill** a container or area, or if it **fills**, an amount of something enters it that is enough to make it full. いっぱいにする、満たす [他動詞]、いっぱいになる [自動詞] ❑ *She went to the bathroom, filled a glass with water, returned to the bed.* 彼女は浴室に行き、コップにいっぱい水を入れてベッドに戻った。 ● PHRASAL VERB 句動詞 **Fill up** means the same as **fill**. いっぱいにする、いっぱいになる ❑ *Warehouses at the frontier between the two countries fill up with sacks of rice and flour.* 両国間の国境にある倉庫は米や小麦粉の袋でいっぱいである。 **2** V-T 他動詞 If something **fills** a space, it is so big, or there are such large quantities of it, that there is very little room left. 占める ❑ *He cast his eyes at the rows of cabinets that filled the enormous work area.* 彼は広大な仕事場をふさいでいるキャビネットの並んだ列をざっと見た。 ● PHRASAL VERB 句動詞 **Fill up** means the same as **fill**. 占める ❑ *...the complicated machines that fill up today's laboratories.* 今日の

研究所をうずめる複雑な機械類 ● **filled** ADJ 形容詞 [v-link ADJ 'with' n] ～でいっぱいの ❑ *...four museum buildings filled with historical objects.* 歴史的な物体でいっぱいの博物館の4棟 **3** V-T 他動詞 If you **fill** a crack or hole, you put a substance into it in order to make the surface smooth again. ふさぐ ❑ *Fill small holes with wood filler in a matching color.* 一致する色の埋め木で小さい穴をふさぎなさい。 ● PHRASAL VERB 句動詞 **Fill in** means the same as **fill**. ふさぐ ❑ *Start by filling in any cracks and gaps between window and door frames and the wall.* 窓枠やドア枠と壁との間にあるひび割れや隙間を埋めることから始めなさい。 **4** V-T 他動詞 If a sound, smell, or light **fills** a space, or the air, it is very strong or noticeable. 充満する ❑ *In the parking lot of the school, the siren filled the air.* 学校の駐車場でサイレンが響き渡った。 **5** V-T 他動詞 If something **fills** you **with** an emotion, or if an emotion **fills** you, you experience this emotion strongly. 心をいっぱいにする ❑ *I admired my father, and work filled me with awe and curiosity.* 私は父を尊敬し、父の仕事に対する畏敬（いけい）の念と好奇心でいっぱいだった。 **6** V-T 他動詞 If you **fill** a period of time with a particular activity, you spend the time in this way. 時間を過ごす ❑ *If she wants a routine to fill her day, let her do community work.* 彼女が日を過ごす日課が欲しいのであれば、社会奉仕活動をさせよう。 ● PHRASAL VERB 句動詞 **Fill up** means the same as **fill**. 時間を過ごす ❑ *On Thursday night she went to her yoga class, glad to have something to fill up the evening.* 木曜日の夜は彼女はヨガ教室に通って、夕方の時間をうめることができるのがうれしかった。 **7** V-T 他動詞 If something **fills** a need or a gap, it puts an end to this need or gap by existing or being active. うめる ❑ *She brought him a sense of fun, of gaiety that filled a gap in his life.* 彼女はその愉快さや陽気さで彼の人生の隙間をうめた。 **8** V-T 他動詞 If something **fills** a role, position, or function, they have that role or position, or perform that function, often successfully. 果たす ❑ *Dena was filling the role of diplomat's wife with the skill she had learned over the years.* ディーナは長い年月の間に覚えた腕前で外交官の妻の役割をやりこなしていた。 **9** V-T 他動詞 If a company or organization **fills** a job vacancy, they choose someone to do the job. If someone **fills** a job vacancy, they accept a job that they have been offered. 補充する ❑ *A vacancy has arisen which I intend to fill.* 空席が1つ生じ、それに着こうと思っている。 **10** V-T 他動詞 When a dentist **fills** someone's tooth, he or she puts a filling in it. 詰める ❑ *Dentists fill teeth and repair broken ones.* 歯医者は歯を充填（じゅうてん）したり、破損した歯を直したりする。 **11** V-T 他動詞 If you **fill** an order or a prescription, you provide the things that are asked for. 応じる [mainly AM 主に米国英語] ❑ *A pharmacist can fill any prescription if, in his or her judgment, the prescription is valid.* 薬剤師は処方せんが有効であると判断すれば、どんな処方せんでも調剤することができる。 **12** to **fill the bill** → see **bill**

▶ **fill in 1** PHRASAL VERB 句動詞 If you **fill in** a form or other document requesting information, you write information in the spaces on it. 記入する ❑ *Fill in the coupon and send it first class to the address shown.* 申し込み票に記入して、表記の所在に第1種郵便で返送してください。 **2** PHRASAL VERB 句動詞 If you **fill in** a shape, you cover the area inside the lines with color or shapes so that none of the background is showing. ❑ *With a lip pencil, outline lips and fill them in.* 唇用の鉛筆で唇の輪郭を描いてから塗りなさい。 **3** PHRASAL VERB 句動詞 If you **fill** someone **in**, you give them more details about something that you know about. [INFORMAL くだけた] ❑ *He filled her in on Wilbur Kantor's visit.* 彼女はウイルバー・カントー来訪についての情報を彼女に教えた。 **4** PHRASAL VERB 句動詞 If you **fill in** for someone, you do the work or task that they normally do because they are unable to do it. 臨時に代わりをする ❑ *Vice-presidents' wives would fill in for first ladies.* 副大統領の妻が大統領夫人の代理をするでしょう。 **5** → see also **fill 3**

▶ **fill out 1** PHRASAL VERB 句動詞 If you **fill out** a form or other document requesting information, you write information in the spaces on it. 書き込む [mainly AM 主に米国英語] ❑ *Fill out the application carefully, and keep copies of it.* 申請書に注意して書き込み、控えを取っておきなさい。 **2** PHRASAL VERB 句動詞 If someone or something **fills out**, they become fuller, thicker, or rounder. 肉がつく ❑ *A girl may fill out before she reaches her full height.* 女子は身長が伸びきる前にふっくらしてくることがある。

▶ **fill up 1** PHRASAL VERB 句動詞 If you **fill up** or **fill** yourself **up** with food, you eat so much that you do not feel hungry. 満腹させる、満腹する ❑ *Fill up on potatoes, bread and pasta, which are high in carbohydrate and low in fat.* 炭水化物が多くて脂肪の少ない、ジャガイモやパンやパスタを腹いっぱい食べなさい。 **2** PHRASAL VERB 句動詞 A type of food that **fills** you **up** makes you feel that you have eaten a lot, even though you have only eaten a small amount. 満腹感を与える ❑ *Potatoes fill us up without overloading us with calories.* ジャガイモは満腹感があり、カロリーを取り過ぎることもない。 **3** → see also **fill 1, 2, 6**

Thesaurus	*fill* また次を参照:
v.	inflate, load, pour into, put into; (*ant.*) empty, pour out **1** crowd, take up **2** block, close, plug, seal **3**

fil|let /fɪleɪ/ (**fillets, filleting, filleted**) ◨ N-VAR 可変性名詞 **Fillet** is a strip of meat, especially beef, that has no bones in it. ヒレ肉 ◻ …*fillet of beef with shallots*. エシャロットをそえた牛ヒレ肉 ◻ …*chicken breast fillets*. 鶏の笹身 ◨ N-COUNT 可算名詞 A **fillet** of fish is the side of a fish with the bones removed. 切り身 ◻ …*anchovy fillets*. アンチョビーの切り身 ◨ V-T 他動詞 When you **fillet** fish or meat, you prepare it by taking the bones out. 切り身にする ◻ *Fillet the fish and roll the fillets in flour*. 魚をさばいて切り身にし、小麦粉の中で切り身を転がして粉をつけなさい。

fill|ing /fɪlɪŋ/ (**fillings**) ◨ N-COUNT 可算名詞 A **filling** is a small amount of metal or plastic that a dentist puts in a hole in a tooth to prevent further decay. 充填（てん）材 ◻ *The longer your child can go without needing a filling, the better*. 子供が歯に詰め物をする必要がない期間が長ければ長いほどよい。 ◨ N-MASS 質量名詞 The **filling** in something such as a cake, pie, or sandwich is a substance or mixture that is put inside it. 具 ◻ *Spread some of the filling over each cold pancake and then either roll or fold*. 冷えたパンケーキのそれぞれの上に具の一部を広げて、巻くか折り畳みなさい。 ◨ N-MASS 質量名詞 The **filling** in a piece of soft furniture or in a cushion is the soft substance inside it. 詰め物 ◻ …*second-hand sofas with old-style foam fillings*. 旧式の気泡ゴムが詰められた中古のソファ ◨ ADJ 形容詞 Food that is **filling** makes you feel full when you have eaten it. 食べ応えがある ◻ *Although it is tasty, crab is very filling*. カニはおいしいけれど、お腹がいっぱいになる。
→ see **teeth**

film /fɪlm/ (**films, filming, filmed**) ◨ N-COUNT 可算名詞 A **film** consists of moving pictures that have been recorded so that they can be shown in a theater or on television. A film tells a story, or shows a real situation. 映画 ◻ *Everything about the film was good. Good acting, good story, good fun*. その映画は何もかもよかった。よい演技とよい筋でとても楽しかった。 ◨ N-COUNT 可算名詞 A **film** of powder, liquid, or oil is a very thin layer of it. 薄い層 ◻ *The sea is coated with a film of raw sewage*. 海は生汚水の薄膜で覆われている。 ◨ V-T 他動詞 If you **film** something, you use a camera to take moving pictures which can be shown on a screen or on television. 撮影する ◻ *He had filmed her life story*. 彼は彼女の伝記を映画に撮影した。 ◨ N-UNCOUNT 不可算名詞 **Film** of something is moving pictures of a real event that are shown on television or on a screen. 記録映画 ◻ *He likes to look at film of old-time players*. 彼は昔の選手の記録映画を見るのが好きだ。 ◨ N-UNCOUNT 不可算名詞 The making of films, considered as a form of art or a business, can be referred to as **film** or **films**. 映画, 映画産業 [also N in pl] ◻ *Film is a business with limited opportunities for actresses*. 映画は女優には機会が限られた産業だ。 ◨ N-UNCOUNT 不可算名詞 Plastic **film** is a very thin sheet of plastic used to wrap and cover things. フィルム [BRIT 英国英語; AM **plastic wrap, Saran wrap** 米国英語 **plastic wrap, Saran wrap**] ◨ N-VAR 可変性名詞 A **film** is the narrow roll of plastic that is used in a camera to take photographs. フィルム ◻ *The photographers had already shot a dozen rolls of film*. 写真家たちはすでに何本ものフィルムを撮っていた。
→ see **photography**

film|ing /fɪlmɪŋ/ N-UNCOUNT 不可算名詞 **Filming** is the activity of making a film including the acting, directing, and camera shots. 映画撮影 ◻ *Filming was due to start next month*. 映画撮影は来月開始される予定だ。

fil|ter /fɪltər/ (**filters, filtering, filtered**) ◨ V-T 他動詞 To **filter** a substance means to pass it through a device which is designed to remove certain particles contained in it. ろ過する ◻ *The best prevention for cholera is to boil or filter water, and eat only well-cooked food*. コレラを防ぐ最善の方法は水を沸騰または煮沸し、十分火の通った食べ物のみを食べることだ。 ◨ V-I 自動詞 If light or sound **filters into** a place, it comes in weakly or slowly, either through a partly covered opening, or from a long distance away. 漏れる ◻ *Light filtered into my kitchen through the soft, green shade of the honey locust tree*. 光がアメリカサイカチの木の柔らかい緑の陰を通して私の台所に漏れてきた。 ◨ V-I 自動詞 When news or information **filters** through to people, it gradually reaches them. 徐々に知れわたる ◻ *It took months before the findings began to filter through to the politicians*. その調査結果が徐々に政治家に知られるようになるのに数か月を要した。 ◻ *News of the attack quickly filtered through the college*. 攻撃のニュースは即座に大学じゅうに知れわたった。 ◨ N-COUNT 可算名詞 A **filter** is a device through which a substance is passed when it is being filtered. ろ過器 ◻ …*a paper coffee filter*. 紙のコーヒーフィルター ◨ N-COUNT 可算名詞 A **filter** is a device through which sound or light is passed and which blocks or reduces particular sound or light frequencies. フィルター ◻ *You might use a yellow filter to improve the clarity of a hazy horizon*. かすんだ地平線をより明瞭にするには黄色のフィルターを使うとよいでしょう。
→ see **coffee**

▶ **filter out** PHRASAL VERB 句動詞 To **filter out** something from a substance or from light means to remove it by passing the substance or light through something acting as a filter. ろ過して取り除く ◻ *Children should have glasses which filter out UV rays*. 子供たちは紫外線をカットする眼鏡を持つべきだ。 ◻ *Plants and trees filter carbon dioxide out of the air and produce oxygen*. 植物や木は空気から二酸化炭素を取り除き、酸素を生み出す。

filth /fɪlθ/ ◨ N-UNCOUNT 不可算名詞 **Filth** is a disgusting amount of dirt. 汚物 ◻ *Thousands of tons of filth and sewage pour into the Ganges every day*. 毎日何千トンもの汚物と汚水がガンジス川に流れ込む。 ◨ N-UNCOUNT 不可算名詞 People refer to words or pictures, usually ones relating to sex, as **filth** when they think they are very disgusting and rude. わいせつなもの [DISAPPROVAL 不賛成] ◻ *The dialogue was all filth and innuendo*. 会話はひわいな言葉や中傷だらけだった。

filthy /fɪlθi/ (**filthier, filthiest**) ◨ ADJ 形容詞 Something that is **filthy** is very dirty. 不潔な ◻ *He never washed, and always wore a filthy old jacket*. 彼は決して洗濯をせず、いつも汚れた古い上着を着ていた。 ◨ ADJ 形容詞 If you describe something as **filthy**, you mean that you think it is morally very unpleasant and disgusting, sometimes in a sexual way. みだらな, 不道徳な [DISAPPROVAL 不賛成] ◻ *Apparently, well known actors were at these filthy parties*. 明らかに、これらのみだらなパーティーには有名な俳優たちが出席していた。

fin /fɪn/ (**fins**) ◨ N-COUNT 可算名詞 A fish's **fins** are the flat parts which stick out of its body and help it to swim and keep its balance. ひれ ◨ N-COUNT 可算名詞 A **fin** on something such as an airplane, rocket, or bomb is a flat part which sticks out and which is intended to help control its movement. ひれ状のもの

fi|nal /faɪnᵊl/ (**finals**) ◨ ADJ 形容詞 In a series of events, things, or people, the **final** one is the last one. 最後の [det ADJ] ◻ *Astronauts will make a final attempt today to rescue a communications satellite from its useless orbit*. 本日, 宇宙飛行士が通信衛星をむだな軌道から救う最後の試みをする。 ◻ *This is the fifth and probably final day of testimony before the Senate Judiciary Committee*. これは上院司法委員会での証言の5日目で, おそらく最終日になるだろう。 ◨ ADJ 形容詞 **Final** means happening at the end of an event or series of events. 最終の [ADJ n] ◻ *You must have been on stage until the final curtain*. きみは終演まで舞台にいたに違いない。 ◨ ADJ 形容詞 If a decision or someone's authority is **final**, it cannot be changed or questioned. 最終的な ◻ *The judges' decision is final*. その裁判官たちの判決は最終的だ。 ◨ N-COUNT 可算名詞 The **final** is the last game or contest in a series and decides who is the winner. 決勝 ◻ …*the Gold Cup final*. ゴールドカップの決勝戦 ◨ → see also **quarterfinal, semifinal** ◨ N-PLURAL 複数名詞 The **finals** of a sports tournament consist of a smaller tournament that includes only players or teams that have won earlier games. The finals decide the winner of the whole tournament. 決勝 ◻ *Poland knows it has a chance of qualifying for the World Cup Finals*. ポーランドはワールドカップファイナルに残るチャンスがあることを知っている。

fi|na|le /fɪnɑli, -næli/ (**finales**) N-COUNT 可算名詞 The **finale** of a show, piece of music, or series of shows is the last part of it or the last one of them, especially when this is exciting or impressive. フィナーレ ◻ …*the finale of Shostakovich's Fifth Symphony*. ショスタコビッチの交響曲第5番の終楽章

fi|nal|ist /faɪnᵊlɪst/ (**finalists**) N-COUNT 可算名詞 A **finalist** is someone who reaches the last stages of a competition or tournament by doing well or winning in its earlier stages. 決勝戦出場選手 ◻ *The twelve finalists will be listed in the Sunday Times*. 『サンデータイムズ』には12名の決勝戦出場選手がリストされる。

fi|nal|ize /faɪnᵊlaɪz/ (**finalizes, finalizing, finalized**) V-T 他動詞 If you **finalize** something such as a plan or an agreement, you complete the arrangements for it, especially by discussing it with other people. 決着をつける ◻ *Negotiators from the three countries finalized the agreement in August*. 3か国からの交渉担当者は8月にその協定を最終的に取りまとめた。 ◻ *We are saying nothing until all the details have been finalized*. 詳細がすべて決まるまで, 我々は何も言わない。

fi|nal|ly /faɪnᵊli/ **1** ADV 副詞 You use **finally** to suggest that something happens after a long period of time, usually later than you wanted or expected it to happen. ついに □ *The food finally arrived at the end of last week and distribution began.* その食糧は先週末にやっと到着し，配布が始まった． **2** ADV 副詞 You use **finally** to indicate that something is last in a series of actions or events. 最後に [ADV with cl/group] □ *The action slips from comedy to melodrama and finally to tragedy.* その話の展開はコメディーからメロドラマになり，最終的には悲劇で終わるものだ．

Do not confuse **finally** and **eventually**. You say that something **finally** happens after you have been waiting for it or expecting it for a long time. □ *Finally I went to bed…The heat of the sun finally became too much for me.* You can also use **finally** to show that something happens last in a series of events. □ *The sky turned red, then purple, and finally black.* When something happens after a lot of delays or complications, you can say that it **eventually** happens. □ *Eventually they got to the hospital… I found Victoria Avenue eventually.* You can also use **eventually** to talk about what happens at the end of a series of events, often as a result of them. □ *Eventually, they were forced to return to Chicago.*

---

fi|nance /faɪnæns, fɪnæns/ (**finances, financing, financed**) **1** V-T 他動詞 When someone **finances** something such as a project or a purchase, they provide the money that is needed to pay for them. 融資する □ *The fund has been used largely to finance the construction of federal prisons.* 基金のほとんどは連邦刑務所の建設に融資するために使用された． ● N-UNCOUNT 不可算名詞 **Finance** is also a noun. 融資 □ *A United States delegation is in Japan seeking finance for a major scientific project.* ある米国代表団が日本で主要な科学プロジェクトへの融資を求めている． **2** N-UNCOUNT 不可算名詞 **Finance** is the commercial or government activity of managing money, debt, credit, and investment. 財政，財務 [also N in pl] □ *…a major player in the world of high finance.* 大型金融取引界の大手 □ *The report recommends an overhaul of public finances.* 報告書は国家財政の見直しを勧告している． **3** N-UNCOUNT 不可算名詞 You can refer to the amount of money that you have and how well it is organized as your **finances**. 財政状態 [also N in pl] □ *Be prepared for unexpected news concerning your finances.* きみの財政状態に関して予想外のニュースがあるから覚悟しなさい．

fi|nance com|pa|ny (**finance companies**) N-COUNT 可算名詞 A **finance company** is a business which lends money to people and charges them interest while they pay it back. 金融会社 [BUSINESS 実業]

fi|nan|cial /faɪnænʃᵊl, fɪn-/ ADJ 形容詞 **Financial** means relating to or involving money. 財政上の □ *The company is in financial difficulties.* その会社は財政難だ． ● **fi|nan|cial|ly** ADV 副詞 財政的に □ *She would like to be more financially independent.* 彼女は経済的にもっと独立したい．

fi|nan|ci|er /fɪnænsiər, faɪn-/ (**financiers**) N-COUNT 可算名詞 A **financier** is a person, company, or government that provides money for projects or businesses. 融資者 [BUSINESS 実業] □ *The Connells were leading financiers of the Democratic Party in Congress.* コネルズ社は連邦議会の民主党の主要な融資業者だった．

find /faɪnd/ (**finds, finding, found**) **1** V-T 他動詞 If you **find** someone or something, you see them or learn where they are. 見つける □ *The police also found a pistol.* 警察は拳銃も発見した． □ *They have spent ages looking at the map and can't find a trace of anywhere called Darrowby.* 彼らは長いことその地図を見ているが，ダロウビーと呼ばれる場所は全然見つけられない． **2** V-T 他動詞 If you **find** something that you need or want, you succeed in achieving or obtaining it. 手に入れる，得る □ *Many people here cannot find work.* ここにいる多くの人は仕事を見つけることができない． □ *He has to apply for a permit and we have to find him a job.* 彼は許可証を申請し，私たちは彼の仕事を探してやらなければならない． **3** V-T 他動詞 If you **find** someone or something in a particular situation, they are in that situation when you see them or come into contact with them. 認める，見つける □ *They found him walking alone and depressed on the beach.* 彼らは彼女が1人で海辺を意気消沈して歩いているのを見つけた． □ *She returned to her home to find her back door forced open.* 彼女は帰宅し，勝手口のドアがこじ開けられていることに気づいた． **4** V-T 他動詞 If you **find yourself** doing something, you are doing it without deciding or intending to do it. 気づく □ *It's not the first time that you've found yourself in this situation.* きみがこの状態になっているのに気づいたのは初めてではない． □ *I found myself having more fun than I had had in years.* 私は何年もこんなに楽しんだことがないことに気づいた． **5** V-T 他動詞 If you **find** that something is the case, you become aware of it or realize that it is the case. わかる □ *The two biologists found, to their surprise, that both groups of birds survived equally well.* その2人の生物学者は，驚いたことに両方の鳥グループが同じようにうまく生き延びていることがわかった． □ *At my age I would find it hard to get another job.* 私の年齢では，別の仕事を得るのは難しいことがわかるだろう． **6** V-T 他動詞 When a court or jury decides that a person on trial is guilty or innocent, you say that the person **has been found** guilty or not guilty. 評決する □ *She was found guilty of manslaughter and put on probation for two years.* 彼女は過失致死罪で有罪と評決され，2年間の執行猶予が処分を受けた． **7** V-T 他動詞 You can use **find** to express your reaction to someone or something. 感ずる □ *I find most of the young men of my own age so boring.* 私は同年代の若い男性のほとんどに大変退屈だと思う． □ *I find it ludicrous that nothing has been done to protect passengers from fire.* 火災から乗客を保護するために何の策も取られていないのはばかげていると思う． **8** V-T 他動詞 If you **find** a feeling such as pleasure or comfort **in** a particular thing or activity, you experience the feeling mentioned as a result of this thing or activity. 経験する □ *How could anyone find pleasure in hunting and killing this beautiful creature?* この美しい生き物を狩って殺すことにどうして快楽を見出せるのか． **9** V-T 他動詞 If you **find** the time or money **to** do something, you succeed in making or obtaining enough time or money to do it. 見つける □ *I was just finding more time to write music.* 私は作曲するのにもっと時間を割いていただけだ． **10** V-T PASSIVE 受動態他動詞 If something **is found** in a particular place or thing, it exists in that place. 存在する □ *Two thousand of France's 4,200 species of flowering plants are found in the park.* その公園にはフランスの4200種の顕花植物の内2000種がある． **11** N-COUNT 可算名詞 If you describe someone or something that has been discovered as a **find**, you mean that they are valuable, interesting, good, or useful. 掘り出し物 □ *Another of his lucky finds was a pair of candleholders.* 彼の幸運な掘り出し物のもう1つはろうそく立て1対だった． **12** → see also **finding, found**

You can use **find, find out,** or **discover** to talk about learning that something is the case. □ *The young child finds that noise attracts attention… He discovered the whole school knew about it… We found out that she was wrong.* **Discover** is a slightly more formal word than **find,** and is often used to talk about scientific research or formal investigations. For example, you can **discover** a cure for a particular disease. You can also use **discover** when you find something by accident. □ *This well-known flower was discovered in 1903.* Note that if you cannot see something you are looking for, you say that you cannot **find** it. You do not use "discover" or "find out" in this way. □ *I'm lost – I can't find the bridge.* You can also say that someone **finds out** facts when this is easy to do, but you cannot use "discover" or "find" in this way. □ *I found out the train times.*

---

13 PHRASE 句 If you **find** your **way** somewhere, you successfully get there by choosing the right way to go. (人が) たどり着く □ *He was an expert at finding his way, even in strange surroundings.* 彼は見知らぬ環境でも目的地を見つけるのが得意だった． **14** PHRASE 句 If something **finds** its **way** somewhere, it comes to that place, especially by chance. (物が) たどり着く □ *It is one of the very few Michelangelos that have found their way out of Italy.* それはイタリアから首尾よく持ち出された数少ないミケランジェロの1つだ． **15** **to find fault with** → see **fault** **16** **to find one's feet** → see **foot**

▸ **find out 1** PHRASAL VERB 句動詞 If you **find** something **out,** you learn something that you did not already know, especially by making a deliberate effort to do so. 発見する □ *It makes you want to watch the next episode to find out what's going to happen.* それで，どんな展開になるのか知るために次回を見たくなる． □ *I was relieved to find out that my problems were due to a genuine disorder.* 私の問題は本物の病気のせいだとわかってほっとした． **2** PHRASAL VERB 句動詞 If you **find** someone **out,** you discover that they have been doing something dishonest. 見破る □ *Her face was so grave, I wondered for a moment if she'd found me out.* 彼女はとても深刻な表情をしていたので，彼女が私の正体を見破ったのかと一瞬心配した．

find|ing /faɪndɪŋ/ (**findings**) **1** N-COUNT 可算名詞 Someone's **findings** are the information they get or the conclusions they come to as the result of an investigation or some research. 研究の成果 □ *One of the main findings of the survey was the confusion about the facilities already in place.* その調査の主要結果の1つとして，すでに設置されている施設に関する混乱がある． **2** N-COUNT 可算名詞 The **findings** of a court are the decisions that it reaches after a trial or an investigation. 事実認定，評決 □ *The government hopes the court will announce its findings before the end of the month.* 政府は裁判所が月末前に事実認定を発表することを望んでいる．
→ see **laboratory, science**

---

fine

❶ ADJECTIVE USES
❷ PUNISHMENT

---

❶ fine /faɪn/ (**finer, finest**) **1** ADJ 形容詞 You use **fine** to describe something that you admire and think is very good. みごとな □ *There is a fine view of the countryside.* 田舎の壮大な眺めが見られる． □ *This is a fine book.* これは立派な本だ． ● **fine|ly** ADV 副詞 [ADV -ed] みごとに □ *They are finely engineered boats.* これらは精巧に設計された船だ． **2** ADJ 形容詞 If you say that you are **fine,** you mean that you are in good health or reasonably happy. 元気で [v-link ADJ] □ *Lina is fine and sends you her love and best wishes.* リナは元気で，きみ

によろしくと言っていた. ③ ADJ 形容詞 If you say that something is **fine**, you mean that it is satisfactory or acceptable. 申し分ない ❑ The skiing is fine. そのスキーは申し分ない. ❑ Everything was going to be just fine. すべてうまくいくはずだった. ● ADV 副詞 **Fine** is also an adverb. みごとに ❑ All the instruments are working fine. 機器はすべてうまく機能している. ④ ADJ 形容詞 Something that is **fine** is very delicate, narrow, or small. 繊細な ❑ The heat scorched the fine hairs on her arms. 熱が彼女の腕の繊細な毛を焦がした. ●**fine**|**ly** ADV 副詞 [ADV with v] 細かく ❑ Chop the ingredients finely and mix them together. 材料を細かく刻んで, 混ぜなさい. ⑤ ADJ 形容詞 **Fine** objects or clothing are of good quality, delicate, and expensive. 上等な, 立派な ❑ We waited in our fine clothes. 私たちは上等の服を着て待した. ⑥ ADJ 形容詞 A **fine** detail or distinction is very delicate, small, or exact. 細かい ❑ Johnson likes the broad outline but is reserving judgment on the fine detail. ジョンソンは大綱は気に入ったが, 細部については判断を差し控えている. ●**fine**|**ly** ADV 副詞 細かく ❑ They had to take the finely balanced decision to let the visit proceed. 訪問を続行させるため, 彼らは微妙に均衡のとれた決断を下さなくてはならなかった. ⑦ ADJ 形容詞 A **fine** person is someone you consider good, moral, and worth admiring. 立派な [APPROVAL 賛成] ❑ He was an excellent journalist and a very fine man. 彼は卓越したジャーナリストであり, 大変立派な人であった. ⑧ ADJ 形容詞 When the weather is **fine**, the sun is shining and it is not raining. 晴れた ❑ He might be doing some gardening if the weather is fine. 天気が晴れなら, 彼は園芸をしているかもしれないでしょう. ⑨ CONVENTION 慣習表現 You say "**fine**" or "**that's fine**" to show that you do not object to an arrangement, action, or situation that has been suggested. 結構 [FORMULAE 決まり文句] ❑ If competition is the best way to achieve it, then, fine. 競争がそれを達成する最良の方法なら, それも結構だ.
→ see **coffee**

❷ **fine** /faɪn/ (**fines, fining, fined**) ① N-COUNT 可算名詞 A **fine** is a punishment in which a person is ordered to pay a sum of money because they have done something illegal or broken a rule. 罰金 ② V-T 他動詞 If someone **is fined**, they are punished by being ordered to pay a sum of money because they have done something illegal or broken a rule. 罰金を科する ❑ She was fined $300 and banned from driving for one month. 彼女は300ドルの罰金を科され, 1か月間運転を禁止された.

fine art (**fine arts**) ① N-UNCOUNT 不可算名詞 Painting and sculpture, in which objects are produced that are beautiful rather than useful, can be referred to as **fine art** or as the **fine arts**. 美術 [also N in pl] ❑ He deals in antiques and fine art. 彼は骨董品と美術品を取り扱っている. ② PHRASE 句 If you **have** something **down to a fine art**, you are able to do it in a very skillful or efficient way because you have had a lot of experience of doing it. 熟達している ❑ They've got fruit retailing down to a fine art. You can be sure that your pears will ripen in day. 彼らは果物の小売に熟達している. きみの買った梨は1日で熟れると信じてよい.

fine print N-UNCOUNT 不可算名詞 In a contract or agreement, the **fine print** is the same as the **small print**. 細字部分

fi|**nesse** /fɪnɛs/ N-UNCOUNT 不可算名詞 If you do something with **finesse**, you do it with great skill and style. 技巧, 腕のさえ ❑ ...handling momentous diplomatic challenges with tact and finesse. 重大な外交問題を機転と手腕で処理して

fine-tune (**fine-tunes, fine-tuning, fine-tuned**) V-T 他動詞 If you **fine-tune** something, you make very small and precise changes to it in order to make it as successful or effective as it possibly can be. 微調整する ❑ We do not try to fine-tune the economy on the basis of short-term predictions. 我々は短期予測を基に経済の微調整をしようとしない.

fin|**ger** /fɪŋɡər/ (**fingers, fingering, fingered**) ① N-COUNT 可算名詞 Your **fingers** are the long thin parts at the end of each hand, sometimes also including the thumb. 手の指 ❑ She suddenly held up a small, bony finger and pointed across the room. 彼女は突然小さな骨ばった指をかざして, 部屋の向こう側を指差した. ❑ She ran her fingers through her hair. 彼女は指で髪を整えた. ② N-COUNT 可算名詞 The **fingers** of a glove are the parts that a person's fingers fit into. 手袋の指 ❑ He bit the fingers of his right glove and pulled it off. 彼は右の手袋の指をかんで外した. ③ N-COUNT 可算名詞 A **finger of** something such as smoke or land is an amount of it that is shaped rather like a finger. 指状のもの ❑ ...a thin finger of land that

separates Pakistan from the former Soviet Union. パキスタンを旧ソ連から隔てる細い指状の土地 ④ V-T 他動詞 If you **finger** something, you touch or feel it with your fingers. 指を触れる ❑ He fingered the few coins in his pocket. 彼はポケットの中にある数枚の硬貨を指でいじった. ⑤ PHRASE 句 If you **cross** your **fingers**, you put one finger on top of another and hope for good luck. If you say that someone **is keeping their fingers crossed**, you mean they are hoping for good luck. 幸運を祈る ❑ He crossed his fingers, asking for luck for the first time in his life. 彼は人生で初めて幸運を祈った. ⑥ PHRASE 句 If you say that someone did not **lay a finger on** a particular person or thing, you are emphasizing that they did not touch or harm them at all. 手を出す [EMPHASIS 強調] ❑ I must make it clear I never laid a finger on her. 私は彼女に決して手を出していないことをはっきりさせる必要がある. ⑦ PHRASE 句 If you say that a person does not **lift a finger** or **raise a finger** to do something, especially to help someone, you are critical of them because they do nothing. 手助けなどをする [DISAPPROVAL 不賛成] ❑ She never lifted a finger around the house. 彼女は人差し指に中指を当てて, 家事の手伝いを決してしなかった. ⑧ PHRASE 句 If you **point the finger at** someone or **point an accusing finger at** someone, you blame them or accuse them of doing wrong. 責める ❑ He said he wasn't pointing an accusing finger at anyone in the government or the army. 彼は政府や陸軍の誰かを非難しているわけではないと言った. ⑨ PHRASE 句 If you **put your finger on** something, for example, a reason or problem, you see and identify exactly what it is. 的確に指摘する ❑ Midge couldn't quite put her finger on the reason. ミッジは理由をはっきり突き止めることができなかった.

finger|**nail** /fɪŋɡərneɪl/ (**fingernails**) N-COUNT 可算名詞 Your **fingernails** are the thin hard areas at the end of each of your fingers. 指の爪
→ see **hand**

finger|**print** /fɪŋɡərprɪnt/ (**fingerprints, fingerprinting, fingerprinted**) ① N-COUNT 可算名詞 **Fingerprints** are marks made by a person's fingers which show the lines on the skin. Everyone's fingerprints are different, so they can be used to identify criminals. 指紋 ❑ The detective discovered no fewer than 35 fingerprints. その刑事は35以上もの指紋を発見した. ❑ ...his fingerprint on the murder weapon. 凶器に付いた彼の指紋 ● PHRASE 句 If the police **take** someone's **fingerprints**, they make that person press their fingers onto a pad covered with ink, and then onto paper, so that they know what that person's fingerprints look like. 人の指紋をとる ② V-T 他動詞 If someone **is fingerprinted**, the police take their fingerprints. 指紋をとる [usu passive] ❑ He took her to jail, where she was fingerprinted and booked. 彼は彼女を拘置所に送り, そこで彼女は指紋をとられ調書をとられた

finger|**tip** /fɪŋɡərtɪp/ (**fingertips**) also **finger-tip** ① N-COUNT 可算名詞 Your **fingertips** are the ends of your fingers. 指先 ❑ The butter and flour are rubbed together with the fingertips. バターと小麦粉を指先でこすり合わせる. ② PHRASE 句 If you say that something is **at** your **fingertips**, you approve of the fact that you can reach it easily or that it is easily available to you. すぐに手に入る, じきに利用できる [APPROVAL 賛成] ❑ I had the information at my fingertips and hadn't used it. 私はその情報をすぐ使えることができたのに利用しなかった.

fin|**ish** /fɪnɪʃ/ (**finishes, finishing, finished**) ① V-T 他動詞 When you **finish** doing or dealing with something, you do or deal with the last part of it, so that there is no more for you to do or deal with. 終える, 済ます ❑ As soon as he'd finished eating, he excused himself. 彼は食べ終えるとすぐに中座した. ❑ Mr. Gould was given a standing ovation and loud cheers when he finished his speech. グールド氏が演説を終えると, 総立ちの拍手と大きな歓声が沸き起こった. PHRASAL VERB 句動詞 **Finish up** means the same as **finish**. 終える [AM 米国英語] ❑ We waited a few minutes outside his office while he finished up his meeting. 私たちは彼が会議を終える間, オフィスの外で数分待った. ② V-T 他動詞 When you **finish** something that you are making or producing, you reach the end of making or producing it, so that it is complete. 完成する, 仕上げる ❑ The consultants had been working to finish a report this week. 顧問団は今週中に報告書を完成するために働いていた. ● PHRASAL VERB 句動詞 **Finish off** and **finish up** mean the same as **finish**. 仕上げる ❑ Now she is busy finishing off a biography of Queen Caroline. 今彼女はキャロライン王妃の伝記を仕上げるのに忙しい. ③ V-T/V-I 他動詞/自動詞 When something such as a course, show, or sale **finishes**, especially at a planned time, it ends. 終了する ❑ The teaching day finishes at around 4 p.m. 授業日はだいたい午後4時に終わる. ④ V-T/V-I 他動詞/自動詞 You say that someone or something

F

finishes a period of time or an event in a particular way to indicate what the final situation was like. You can also say that a period of time or an event **finishes** in a particular way. (〜して) 終える [他動詞] (〜して) 終わる [自動詞] □ *The two of them finished by kissing each other goodbye.* その2人は最後にはお互いキスをして別れた。□ *The evening finished with the welcoming of three new members.* 夜会は3人の新しいメンバーを歓迎して終わった。 **5** V-I 自動詞 If someone **finishes** second, for example, in a race or competition, they are in second place at the end of the race or competition. 決勝戦に入る □ *He finished second in the championship four years in a row.* 彼はその選手権で4年続けて2位でゴールした。 **6** V-I 自動詞 To **finish** means to reach the end of saying something. 締めくくりをつける □ *Her eyes flashed, but he held up a hand. "Let me finish."* 彼女の眼が光ったが、彼は手を挙げて「最後まで言わせてくれ」と言った。 **7** N-SING 単数名詞 The **finish** of something is the end of it or the last part of it. 終わり ['the' N, with poss] □ *I intend to continue it and see the job through to the finish.* 私はそれを継続し、その仕事を最後まで見届けるつもりだ。 **8** N-COUNT 可算名詞 The **finish** of a race is the end of it. フィニッシュ □ *Win a trip to see the finish of the Tour de France!* ツール・ド・フランスのフィニッシュを見に行く旅を当てよう！ **9** N-COUNT 可算名詞 If the surface of something that has been made has a particular kind of **finish**, it has the appearance or texture mentioned. 仕上げ □ *The finish and workmanship of the woodwork were excellent.* その木工細工の仕上げと出来栄えはすばらしかった。 **10** → see also **finished** **11** PHRASE 句 If you add **the finishing touches** to something, you add or do the last things that are necessary to complete it. 最後の仕上げ □ *Right up until the last minute, workers were still putting the finishing touches on the pavilions.* 時間ぎりぎりまで、作業員たちはまだ展示館に最後の仕上げを施していた。

▶ **finish off** **1** PHRASAL VERB 句動詞 If you **finish off** something that you have been eating or drinking, you eat or drink the last part of it with the result that there is none left. 平らげる □ *Kelly finished off his coffee.* ケリーはコーヒーを飲みほえた。 **2** PHRASAL VERB 句動詞 If someone **finishes off** a person or thing that is already badly injured or damaged, they kill or destroy them. 破壊しつくす，殺す □ *They meant to finish her off, swiftly and without mercy.* 彼らは素早く，情け容赦なく彼女を殺してしまうつもりだった。 **3** → see also **finish 2**

▶ **finish up** **1** PHRASAL VERB 句動詞 If you **finish up** something that you have been eating or drinking, you eat or drink the last part of it. 平らげる □ *Finish up your drinks now, please.* さあ、飲み干してください。 **2** → see also **finish 1, 2**

▶ **finish with** PHRASAL VERB 句動詞 If you **finish with** someone or something, you stop dealing with them or being involved with them. 関係を絶つ，手を切る □ *My boyfriend was threatening to finish with me.* 私の恋人は別れると私を脅していた。

Thesaurus *finish* また次を参照：

V.	conclude, end, wrap up; (ant.) begin, start **1** **2**

Word Partnership *finish* は次の語句と使われる：

N.	finish **a conversation**, finish **school**, finish **work** **1** finish **a job**, **time to** finish **1** **2** finish **line** **3**
ADV.	finish **first**, finish **last** **5**

---

fin|ished /fínɪʃt/ **1** ADJ 形容詞 Someone who is **finished with** something is no longer doing it or dealing with it or is no longer interested in it. 終わった，やめた [v-link ADJ 'with'n] □ *One suspects he will be finished with boxing.* 彼はボクシングをやめてしまうのではと疑われている。 **2** ADJ 形容詞 Something that is **finished** no longer exists or is no longer happening. 滅びた，終えてしまった [v-link ADJ] □ *After each game is finished, a message flashes on the screen.* 試合が終わる毎に，メッセージがスクリーンにパッと表示される。 **3** ADJ 形容詞 Someone or something that is **finished** is no longer important, powerful, or effective. だめになった [v-link ADJ] □ *Her power over me is finished.* 彼女はもはや私に対して力を持たない。

---

fi|nite /fáɪnaɪt/ ADJ 形容詞 Something that is **finite** has a definite fixed size or extent. 限りのある [FORMAL 形式ばった] □ *...a finite set of elements.* 有限の1組の要素 □ *Only a finite number of situations can arise.* 起こりうる状況には限りがある。

fir /fɜːr/ (firs) N-VAR 可変性名詞 A **fir** or a **fir tree** is a tall evergreen tree that has thin needle-like leaves. モミ

---

fire

❶ BURNING, HEAT, OR ENTHUSIASM
❷ SHOOTING OR ATTACKING
❸ DISMISSAL

---

❶ fire /fáɪər/ (fires, firing, fired)

⇨ Please look at meaning **11** to see if the expression you are looking for is shown under another headword. **1** N-UNCOUNT 不可算名詞 **Fire** is the hot, bright flames produced by things that are burning. 火 □ *They saw a big flash and a huge ball of fire reaching hundreds of feet into the sky.* 彼らは大きな閃（せん）光と巨大な火の玉が数百フィート上空に達するのを見た。 **2** N-VAR 可変性名詞 **Fire** or a **fire** is an occurrence of uncontrolled burning which destroys buildings, forests, or other things. 火事 □ *87 people died in a fire at the Happy Land Social Club.* ハッピーランド社交クラブの火事で87人が死亡した。 □ *A forest fire is sweeping across portions of north Maine this evening.* 山火事が今夜メイン州北部の一部を焼き尽くしている。 **3** N-COUNT 可算名詞 A **fire** is a burning pile of wood, coal, or other fuel that you make, for example, to use for heat, light, or cooking. 火 □ *There was a fire in the grate.* 暖炉には火があった。 **4** N-COUNT 可算名詞 A **fire** is a device that uses electricity or gas to give out heat and warm a room. 暖房 [BRIT 英国英語; AM **heater** 米国英語 **heater**] **5** V-T 他動詞 When a pot or clay object is **fired**, it is heated at a high temperature in a special oven, as part of the process of making it. 焼成する □ *After the pot is dipped in this mixture, it is fired.* つぼはこの混合物にさっと浸したあと焼成します。 **6** V-I 自動詞 When the engine of a motor vehicle **fires**, an electrical spark is produced which causes the fuel to burn and the engine to work. 発火する □ *The engine fired and we moved off.* エンジンが発火し，我々は出発した。 **7** V-T 他動詞 If you **fire** someone with enthusiasm, you make them feel very enthusiastic. If you **fire** someone's imagination, you make them feel interested and excited. 刺激する □ *...the potential to fire the imagination of an entire generation.* 世代全体の想像力をかきたてる可能性 □ *It was Allen who fired this rivalry with real passion.* 本物の情熱でこのライバル心を燃え立たせたのはアレンだった。 **8** PHRASE 句 If an object or substance **catches fire**, it starts burning. 火がつく □ *The blast caused several buildings to catch fire.* その爆発により建物がいくつか燃え出した。 **9** PHRASE 句 If something is **on fire**, it is burning and being damaged or destroyed by an uncontrolled fire. 炎上中で □ *The captain radioed that the ship was on fire.* 船長は船が火事だと無線で連絡した。 **10** PHRASE 句 If you **set fire** to something or if you **set** something **on fire**, you start it burning in order to damage or destroy it. 〜に火をつける □ *They set fire to vehicles outside that building.* 彼らはその建物の外にある車に火をつけた。 **11** have irons in the fire → see **iron** **12** like a house on fire → see **house** **13** there's no smoke without fire → see **smoke**

▶ **fire up** **1** PHRASAL VERB 句動詞 If you **fire up** a machine, you switch it on. 始動させる □ *Fire up your engine and head out.* エンジンを作動させて出発しなさい。 **2** PHRASAL VERB 句動詞 If you **fire** someone **up**, you make them feel very enthusiastic or motivated. 刺激する □ *The president knows his task is to fire up the delegates.* 大統領は自分の役目は代表団を発奮させることであることを知っている。
→ see Word Web: **fire**
→ see **pottery**

❷ fire /fáɪər/ (fires, firing, fired) **1** V-T/V-I 他動詞/自動詞 If someone **fires** a gun or a bullet, or if they **fire**, a bullet is sent from a gun that they are using. 発砲する □ *Seven people were wounded when soldiers fired rubber bullets to disperse crowds.* 群集を追い散らすために兵隊がゴム弾を発砲した際に7人が負傷した。 ● **fir|ing** N-UNCOUNT 不可算名詞 発砲 □ *The firing continued even while the protestors were fleeing.* 抗議者たちが逃げているときでも、発砲は止

Word Web *fire*

A single **match**, a campfire, or even a bolt of lightning can **spark** a **wildfire**. Wildfires race across grasslands and **burn down** forests. Huge firestorms can **burn** out of control for days. They cause death and destruction. However, some ecosystems depend on fire. Once the fire passes, the **smoke** clears, the **smoldering embers** cool, and the **ash** settles. Then the cycle of life begins again. Humans have learned to use fire. The **heat** cooks our food. People build fires in **fireplaces** and **wood** stoves. The **flames** warm our hands. And before electricity, the **glow** of candlelight lit our homes.

Word Web　　fireworks

Fireworks originated in China over a thousand years ago. Historians believe that the discovery was made by alchemists who were looking for the elixir of life. They heated **sulfur**, potassium **nitrate**, **charcoal**, and arsenic together and the mixture **exploded**. It produced an extremely hot, bright fire. Later they mixed these **chemicals** in a hollow bamboo tube and threw it in the fire. Thus the firecracker was born. Marco Polo brought firecrackers to Europe from the Orient in 1292. Soon the Italians began experimenting with ways of producing elaborate, colorful fireworks displays. This launched the era of modern pyrotechnics.

まなかった. **2** V-T 他動詞 If you **fire** an arrow, you send it from a bow. 射る ❑ *He fired an arrow into a clearing in the forest.* 彼は森の中の空き地に矢を射た. **3** V-T 他動詞 If you **fire** questions at someone, you ask them a lot of questions very quickly, one after another. (質問などを) 集中的に浴びせる ❑ *They were bombarded by more than 100 representatives firing questions on pollution.* 彼らは100人以上の代表者からの公害についての質問で攻め立てられた. **4** N-UNCOUNT 不可算名詞 You can use **fire** to refer to the shots fired from a gun or guns. 銃火, 発砲 ❑ *His car was raked with fire from automatic weapons.* 彼の車は自動銃からの銃撃で掃射された. **5** PHRASE 句 If someone **holds** their **fire** or **holds fire**, they stop shooting or they wait before they start shooting. 射撃を中断する, 発砲を待つ ❑ *Devereux ordered his men to hold their fire until the ships got closer.* デヴェリューは船がもっと近づくまで発砲を待つよう部下に命令した. **6** PHRASE 句 If you are in the **line of fire**, you are in a position where someone is aiming their gun at you. If you move into their **line of fire**, you move into a position between them and the thing they were aiming at. 弾道 ❑ *He cheerfully blows away any bad guy stupid enough to get in his line of fire.* 彼は弾道に入ってくるばかな悪者すべてを楽しげに射殺する. **7** PHRASE 句 If you **open fire on** someone, you start shooting at them. 火ぶたを切る ❑ *Then without warning, the troops opened fire on the crowd.* そして警告なしで軍隊は群集に向かって火ぶたを切った. **8** PHRASE 句 If you **return fire** or you **return** someone's **fire**, you shoot back at someone who has shot at you. 応射する ❑ *The soldiers returned fire after being attacked.* 兵士たちは攻撃されてから反撃した. **9** PHRASE 句 If you come **under fire** or are **under fire**, someone starts shooting at you. 砲火を浴びて ❑ *The Belgians fell back as the infantry came under fire.* ベルギー軍は歩兵が砲火を浴びたので後退した. **10** PHRASE 句 If you come **under fire from** someone or are **under fire**, they criticize you strongly. 非難を浴びて ❑ *The president's plan first came under fire from critics who said he hadn't included enough spending cuts.* 大統領の計画は最初は, 十分な支出削減が含まれていないと批判者たちに非難された.

❾ **fire** /ˈfaɪər/ (**fires, firing, fired**) V-T 他動詞 If an employer **fires** you, they dismiss you from your job. If he hadn't been so good at the rest of his job, I probably would have fired him. もし彼が仕事のそれ以外の面でそんなによくなかったら, おそらく私は彼を解雇していただろう. ● **firing** N-UNCOUNT 不可算名詞 ❑ *There was yet another round of firings.* さらにもう1回の解雇があった.

fire alarm (**fire alarms**) N-COUNT 可算名詞 A **fire alarm** is a device that makes a noise, for example, with a bell, to warn people when there is a fire. 火災報知機 ❑ *The smoke sets off the fire alarm.* 煙によって火災報知機が作動する.

fire|arm /ˈfaɪərɑːrm/ (**firearms**) N-COUNT 可算名詞 **Firearms** are guns. 火器 [FORMAL 形式ばった] ❑ *He was also charged with illegal possession of firearms.* 彼は違法な火器の所持でも告発された.
→ see **war**

fire de|part|ment (**fire departments**) N-COUNT-COLL 集合可算名詞 The **fire department** is an organization which has the job of putting out fires. 消防署 [AM 米国英語] [usu 'the' N]

fire en|gine (**fire engines**) N-COUNT 可算名詞 A **fire engine** is a large vehicle which carries firefighters and equipment for putting out fires. 消防自動車

fire es|cape (**fire escapes**) also **fire-escape** N-COUNT 可算名詞 A **fire escape** is a metal staircase on the outside of a building, which can be used to escape from the building if there is a fire. 火災避難装置

fire ex|tin|guish|er (**fire extinguishers**) also **fire-extinguisher** N-COUNT 可算名詞 A **fire extinguisher** is a metal cylinder which contains water or chemicals at high pressure which can put out fires. 消火器

fire|fight|er /ˈfaɪərfaɪtər/ (**firefighters**) N-COUNT 可算名詞 **Firefighters** are people whose job is to put out fires. 消防士 [usu pl]

fire|man /ˈfaɪərmən/ (**firemen**) N-COUNT 可算名詞 A **fireman** is a person, usually a man, whose job is to put out fires. 消防士

fire|place /ˈfaɪərpleɪs/ (**fireplaces**) N-COUNT 可算名詞 In a room, the **fireplace** is the place where a fire can be lit and the area on the wall and floor surrounding this place. 暖炉 ❑ *In the evenings, we gathered around the fireplace and talked in hushed whispers.* 夜になると, 私たちは暖炉の周りに集まって, 静かに小声で話した.
→ see **fire**

fire|power /ˈfaɪərpaʊər/ N-UNCOUNT 不可算名詞 The **firepower** of an army, ship, tank, or aircraft is the amount of ammunition it can fire. 火力 ❑ *The U.S. also had superior firepower.* 米国も優勢な火力を持っていた.

fire truck (**fire trucks**) N-COUNT 可算名詞 A **fire truck** is a large vehicle which carries firefighters and equipment for putting out fires. 消防自動車 [mainly AM, AUSTRALIAN 主に米国英語, オーストラリア英語]

fire|wall /ˈfaɪərwɔːl/ (**firewalls**) N-COUNT 可算名詞 A **firewall** is a computer system or program that automatically prevents an unauthorized person from gaining access to a computer when it is connected to a network such as the Internet. ファイアウォール [COMPUTING コンピューティング] ❑ *New technology should provide a secure firewall against hackers.* 新しい技術はハッカー予防の安全なファイアウォールを提供すべきだ.
→ see **Internet**

fire|wood /ˈfaɪərwʊd/ N-UNCOUNT 不可算名詞 **Firewood** is wood that has been cut into pieces so that it can be burned on a fire. まき ❑ *Young Geoffrey made money by chopping and selling firewood.* 若いジェフリーはまきを切って売ることで金を稼いだ.

fire|work /ˈfaɪərwɜːrk/ (**fireworks**) N-COUNT 可算名詞 **Fireworks** are small objects that are lit to entertain people on special occasions. They contain chemicals and burn brightly or attractively, often with a loud noise, when you light them. 花火 ❑ *They drank champagne, set off fireworks and tooted their car horns.* 彼らはシャンペンを飲み, 花火を上げ, 車の警笛を鳴らした.
→ see Word Web: **fireworks**

firm /fɜːrm/ (**firms, firmer, firmest**) **1** N-COUNT 可算名詞 A **firm** is an organization which sells or produces something or which provides a service which people pay for. 会社 ❑ *The firm's employees were expecting large bonuses.* その会社の従業員は多額のボーナスを期待していた. ❑ *...a legal assistant at a Chicago law firm.* シカゴの法律事務所の弁護士助手 **2** ADJ 形容詞 If something is **firm**, it does not change much in shape when it is pressed but is not completely hard. 堅い ❑ *Fruit should be firm and in excellent condition.* 果物は堅く, 良好な状態でなければならない. **3** ADJ 形容詞 If someone's grip is **firm** or if they perform a physical action in a **firm** way, they do it with quite a lot of force or pressure but also in a controlled way. しっかりした ❑ *The quick handshake was firm and cool.* 素早い握手は堅く, 冷たいものだった. ● **firm|ly** ADV 副詞 [ADV after v] しっかりと ❑ *She held me firmly by the elbow and led me to my aisle seat.* 彼女は私のひじをしっかりとって, 通路側の席に案内した. **4** ADJ 形容詞 If you describe someone as **firm**, you mean they behave in a way that shows that they are not going to change their mind, or that they are the person who is in control. 断固たる ❑ *She had to be firm with him. "I don't want to see you again."* 彼女は彼に「もう会いたくない」ときっぱり言わなければならなかった. ● **firm|ly** ADV 副詞 [ADV with v] 断固として ❑ *"A good night's sleep is what you want,"* he said firmly. 「きみはよく眠ることが必要だよ」と彼は断言した. **5** ADJ 形容詞 A **firm** decision or opinion is definite and unlikely to change. 確固不抜の ❑ *He made a firm decision to leave Fort Multry by boat.* 彼は船でマルトリー砦 (とりで) を去ることを堅く決意した. ● **firm|ly** ADV 副詞 堅固に ❑ *Political values and opinions are firmly held, and can be slow to change.* 政治的価値観と意見は固守され, 変わるのには時間がかかる. **6** ADJ 形容詞 [ADJ n] **Firm** evidence or information is based on facts and so is likely to be true. 確固たる ❑ *This man may have killed others but unfortunately we have no firm evidence.* この男は他にも人を殺したかもしれないが, 残念ながら我々には確固たる証拠がない. **7** ADJ 形容詞 You use **firm** to describe control or a basis or position when it is strong and unlikely to be ended or

F

removed. しっかりした □*Although the Yakutians are a minority, they have firm control of the territory.* ヤクート人は少数民族だが、領土をしっかり支配している. ● **firm|ly** ADV 副詞 しっかりと □*This tradition is also firmly rooted in the past.* この伝統も過去にしっかり根付いている. **8** ADJ 形容詞 If something is **firm**, it does not shake or move when you put weight or pressure on it, because it is strongly made or securely fastened. 固定した □*If you have to climb up, use a firm platform or a sturdy ladder.* 登らなければならないなら、安定した踏み台か頑丈なはしごを使いなさい. ● **firm|ly** ADV 副詞 堅く □*The front door is locked and all the windows are firmly shut.* 玄関のドアは鍵がかかっており、すべての窓は堅く閉じられている. **9** PHRASE 句 If someone **stands firm**, they refuse to change their mind about something. 断固として譲らない □*The council is standing firm against the protest.* 議会は抗議に対して断固とした姿勢をとっている.

▸ **firm up** **1** PHRASAL VERB 句動詞 If you **firm up** something or if it **firms up**, it becomes firmer and more solid. 堅くする □*This treatment helps tone the body, firm up muscles and tighten the skin.* この手当ては体の調子を整え、筋肉を堅くし、肌を引き締めるのに役立つ. **2** PHRASAL VERB 句動詞 If you **firm** something **up** or if it **firms up**, it becomes clearer, stronger, or more definite. 固める、固まる □*We can give you more detail as our plans firm up.* 我々の計画が固まったら、詳細をお知らせできます.

Thesaurus	*firm* また次を参照:
N.	business, company, enterprise, organization **1**
ADJ.	dense, hard, sturdy, unyielding; (*ant.*) yielding **2**

first /fɜːrst/ ORD 序数詞 The **first** thing, person, event, or period of time is the one that happens or comes before all the others of the same kind. 1番目の □*She lost 16 pounds in the first month of her diet.* 彼女はダイエットを始めて最初の月に16ポンド体重を落とした. □*...the first few flakes of snow.* 雪の最初の数片 ● PRON 代名詞 **First** is also a pronoun. 第1番目 □*The second paragraph startled me even more than the first.* 第2段落は第1段落以上に私をびっくりさせた. **2** ORD 序数詞 When something happens or is done for the **first** time, it has never happened or been done before. 最初の □*This is the first time she has experienced disappointment.* これは彼女が失望を味わった最初だ. ● ADV 副詞 **First** is also an adverb. 最初に [ADV with v] □*Anne and Steve got engaged two years after they had first started going out.* アンとスティーブは最初にデートしてから2年後に婚約した. **3** ORD 序数詞 The **first** thing, person, or place in a line is the one that is nearest to you or nearest to the front. 先頭の □*Before him, in the first row, sat the president.* 大統領は彼の前、最前列に座った. **4** ORD 序数詞 You use **first** to refer to the best or most important thing or person of a particular kind. 最も重要な □*The first duty of any government must be to protect the interests of the taxpayers.* いかなる政府においても最も重要な責務は納税者の利益を守ることであるにちがいない. **5** ADV 副詞 If you do something **first**, you do it before anyone else does, or before you do anything else. 最初に □*I do not remember who spoke first, but we all expressed the same opinion.* 誰が最初に言ったのか覚えていないが、私たちは皆同じ意見を述べた. □*First, tell me what you think of my products.* まず、私の作品についての意見を聞かせてください. **6** ADV 副詞 You use **first** when you are talking about what happens in the early part of an event or experience, in contrast to what happens later. 最初のころ [ADV before v] □*When he first came home he wouldn't say anything about what he'd been doing.* 帰宅当初、彼は何をしていたのかについて何も言おうとしなかった. ● ORD 序数詞 **First** is also an ordinal. 第1の □*She told him that her first reaction was disgust.* 彼女は最初の反応は嫌悪感だったと彼に言った. **7** ADV 副詞 In order to emphasize your determination not to do a particular thing, you can say that rather than do it, you would do something else **first**. いっそのこと [EMPHASIS 強調] [ADV after v] □*I'd die first, before I let you have all my money!* 金を全部きみに取られるくらいなら、私はいっそ死んでしまいたい. **8** N-SING 単数名詞 An event that is described as **a first** has never happened before and is important or exciting. 最初の物 □*It is a first for New York. An outdoor exhibition of Fernando Botero's sculpture on Park Avenue.* それはニューヨークにとって最初だ。パークアベニューで開催のフェルナンド・ボテロの彫刻の野外展覧会だ. **9** PRON 代名詞 The **first** you hear of something or the **first** you know about it is the time when you first become aware of it. 最初 ['the' PRON that] □*We heard it on the TV last night – that was the first we heard of it.* 私たちはそれを昨夜テレビで聞いたが、それを聞いたのはそれが初めてだった. **10** PHRASE 句 You use **first of all** to introduce the first of a number of things that you want to say. まず第1に □*The cut in the interest rates has not had very much impact in California for two reasons. First of all, banks are still afraid to loan.* カリフォルニア州では2つの理由で利率の引き下げの影響はあまり出ていない。まず第1に、銀行はいまだに貸付けを恐れている. **11** PHRASE 句 You use **at first** when you are talking about what happens in the early stages of an event or experience, or just after something else has happened, in contrast to what happens later. 最初は □*At first, he seemed surprised by my questions.* 最初は彼は私の質問に驚いたようだった. **12** PHRASE 句 If you say that someone or something **comes first** for a particular person, you mean they treat or consider that person or thing as more important than anything else. 優先させる □*There's no time for boyfriends, my career comes first.* ボーイフレンドなんか作っている暇はない。私には仕事が何よりも大切である. **13** PHRASE 句 If you learn or experience something **at first hand**, you experience it yourself or learn it directly rather than being told about it by other people. 直接に □*He arrived in Natal to see at first hand the effects of the recent heavy fighting.* 彼は最近起こった猛烈な戦闘の影響を自分でじかに見るためにナタールに到着した. **14** PHRASE 句 If you say that you **do not know the first thing about** something, you are emphasizing that you know absolutely nothing about it. 基本的なことも何も知らない [EMPHASIS 強調] □*You don't know the first thing about farming.* きみは農業について基本的なことも知らない. **15** PHRASE 句 If you **put** someone or something **first**, you treat or consider them as more important than anything else. 最重要する □*Somebody has to think for the child and put him first.* 誰かがその子のことを考え、最優先してやらねばならない. **16** **first and foremost** → see **foremost**

first aid N-UNCOUNT 不可算名詞 **First aid** is simple medical treatment given as soon as possible to a person who is injured or who suddenly becomes ill. 応急手当 □*There are many emergencies which need prompt first aid treatment.* 迅速な応急手当を必要とする非常事態が多くある.

first-class also **first class** **1** ADJ 形容詞 If you describe something or someone as **first-class**, you mean that they are extremely good and of the highest quality. 最高級の □*The food was first-class.* その食事は一流だった. **2** ADJ 形容詞 You use **first-class** to describe something that is in the group that is considered to be of the highest standard. 第1級の [ADJ n] □*They always stayed in first-class hotels.* 彼らは常に一流ホテルに泊まった. **3** ADJ 形容詞 **First-class** accommodations on a train, airplane, or ship are the best and most expensive type of accommodations. 1等の [ADJ n] □*He won himself two first-class tickets to fly to Dublin.* 彼はダブリンへのファーストクラス航空券が2枚当たった. ● ADV 副詞 **First-class** is also an adverb. 1等で [ADV v] □*She had never flown first class before.* 彼女はそれまで飛行機のファーストクラスに乗ったことが全然なかった. ● N-UNCOUNT 不可算名詞 **First-class** is the first-class accommodations on a train, airplane, or ship. 1等 □*He paid for and was assigned a cabin in first class.* 彼は料金を払って、ファーストクラスの船室を与えられた. **4** ADJ 形容詞 In the United States, **first-class** postage is the type of postage that is used for sending letters and postcards. 第1種の [ADJ n] □*Two first-class stamps, please.* 第1種の切手を2枚ください.

first floor (**first floors**) **1** N-COUNT 可算名詞 The **first floor** of a building is the one at ground level. 1階 [AM 米国英語] **2** N-COUNT 可算名詞 The **first floor** of a building is the floor immediately above the one at ground level. 2階 [BRIT 英国英語; AM **second floor** 米国英語 **second floor**] → see **house**

first hand also **first-hand** or **firsthand** **1** ADJ 形容詞 **First hand** information or experience is gained or learned directly, rather than from other people or from books. じかに得た [ADJ n] □*School trips give children firsthand experience not available in the classroom.* 学校の遠足では、子供たちは教室では得られない直接体験をする. ● ADV 副詞 **First-hand** is also an adverb. じかに [ADV after v] □*We've been through Germany and seen first-hand what's happening there.* 私たちはドイツをあちこち回り、そこで何が起こっているかをじかに見てきた. **2** **at first hand** → see **first**

first|ly /fɜːrstli/ ADV 副詞 You use **firstly** in speech or writing when you want to give a reason, make a point, or mention an item that will be followed by others connected with it. 第1に [ADV with cl/group] □*The program is now seven years behind schedule as a result, firstly of increased costs, then of technical problems.* その計画は現在予定よりも7年遅れています。それは第1に費用の増加、次に技術的な問題の結果です.

first name (**first names**) N-COUNT 可算名詞 Your **first name** is the first of the names that were given to you when you were born. 名 □*Her first name was Mary. I don't know what her surname was.* 彼女の名はマリーだ。彼女の姓は知らない.

first-rate also **first rate** ADJ 形容詞 If you say that something or someone is **first-rate**, you mean that they are extremely good and of the highest quality. 一流の [APPROVAL 賛成] □*People who used his service knew they were dealing with a first-rate professional.* 彼のサービスを利用した人たちは、一流の専門家を相手にしていることがわかった.

fis|cal /fɪskəl/ ADJ 形容詞 **Fiscal** is used to describe something that relates to government money or public money, especially taxes. 国庫収入の、財政の [ADJ n] □*...in 1987, when the government tightened fiscal policy.* 政府が財政政策を引き締めた1987年

fis|cal year (**fiscal years**) N-COUNT 可算名詞 A **fiscal year** is a period of twelve months, used by government, business, and other organizations in order to calculate their budgets, profits, and losses. 会計年度 [BUSINESS 実業] □*...the budget for the coming fiscal year.* 次の会計年度の予算

Word Web fish

Commercial **fishing** has become very efficient. Fishing **trawlers** pull huge **nets** behind them and harvest thousands of fish at once. Some boats **trawl** with hundreds of meters of **fishing line** and **hooks**. Overfishing is a major problem for many countries. Some popular species of fish are disappearing from **fishing grounds**. Each year there is a smaller supply of **cod** and **sole**. So companies are changing the names of some fish to make them sound more appetizing. For example, "slimehead" is now "orange roughy." Hawaiian "dolphin fish" is now "mahi mahi." No one wants to eat a dolphin.

cod

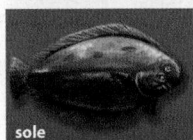

sole

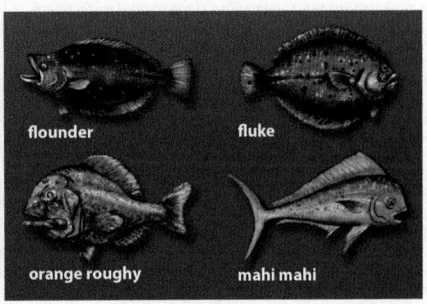

flounder   fluke

orange roughy   mahi mahi

---

fish /fɪʃ/ (fish or fishes, fishes, fishing, fished)

> The form **fish** is usually used for the plural, but **fishes** can also be used.

> fish 形は通常複数に使われるが、 **fishes** も使える.

1 N-COUNT 可算名詞 A **fish** is a creature that lives in water and has a tail and fins. There are many different kinds of fish. 魚類 □ *An expert angler was casting his line and catching a fish every time.* ベテランの釣り師が釣り糸を投げる度に魚を釣っていた. **2** N-UNCOUNT 不可算名詞 **Fish** is the flesh of a fish eaten as food. 魚肉 □ *Does dry white wine go best with fish?* 魚と最もよく合うのは辛口の白ワインですか. **3** V-I 自動詞 If you **fish**, you try to catch fish, either for food or as a form of sport or recreation. 魚を捕る, 釣りをする □ *Brian remembers learning to fish in the Colorado River.* ブライアンはコロラド川で釣りを習ったことを思い出した. **4** V-I 自動詞 If you say that someone is **fishing for** information or praise, you disapprove of the fact that they are trying to get it from someone in an indirect way. 得ようとする [DISAPPROVAL 不賛成] □ *He didn't want to create the impression that he was fishing for information.* 彼は情報を探っているような印象を与えたくなかった. **5** → see also **fishing**
→ see Word Web: **fish**
→ see **pet, shark**

fisher|man /fɪʃərmən/ (fishermen) N-COUNT 可算名詞 A **fisherman** is a person who catches fish as a job or for sport. 漁師 □ *The Algarve is a paradise for fishermen whether river anglers or deep-sea fishermen.* アルガルベ地域は, 川釣り師であろうが深海の漁師であろうが, 漁師にとって楽園だ.

Word Link ery ≈ place where something happens : bak**ery**, fish**ery**, refin**ery**

fish|ery /fɪʃəri/ (fisheries) **1** N-COUNT 可算名詞 **Fisheries** are areas of the sea where fish are caught in large quantities for commercial purposes. 漁場 □ *...the fisheries off Newfoundland.* ニューファンドランド州沖の漁場 **2** N-COUNT 可算名詞 A **fishery** is a place where fish are bred and reared. 養魚場

fish|ing /fɪʃɪŋ/ N-UNCOUNT 不可算名詞 **Fishing** is the sport, hobby, or business of catching fish. 魚釣り, 漁業 □ *Despite the poor weather the fishing has been pretty good.* 悪天候にもかかわらず, 魚釣りの成果はずいぶんよかった.

fist /fɪst/ (fists) N-COUNT 可算名詞 Your hand is referred to as your **fist** when you have bent your fingers in toward the palm in order to hit someone, to make an angry gesture, or to hold something. 握りこぶし □ *Angry protesters with clenched fists shouted their defiance.* 憤慨した抗議者たちはこぶしを握りしめて挑戦的な言葉を叫んだ.

fit

❶ BEING RIGHT OR GOING IN THE RIGHT PLACE
❷ HEALTHY
❸ UNCONTROLLABLE MOVEMENTS OR EMOTIONS

❶ fit /fɪt/ (fits, fitting, fitted or fit)
↪ Please look at meaning **13** to see if the expression you are looking for is shown under another headword. **1** V-T/V-I 他動詞/自動詞 If something **fits**, it is the right size to go onto a person's body or onto a particular object. ぴったりする [他動詞・自動詞] □ *The sash, kimono, and other garments were made to fit a child.* 帯, 着物, その他の衣類は子供に合うように作られた. □ *She has to go to the men's department to find trousers that fit at the waist.* ウェストが

ぴったりするズボンを見つけるためには, 彼女は紳士服売り場に行かなければならなかい.

> You do not use the verb **fit** to say that something looks attractive on a person or in a place. The verb you need is **suit**. □ *It is really feminine and pretty and it certainly suits you.* You use the verb **fit** to say that clothes are the right size for you. □ *The size 12 gown is gorgeous and fits perfectly... The gloves didn't fit.* You cannot usually say that one color, pattern, or object **suits** another. The verb you need is **match**. □ *She wears a straw hat with a yellow ribbon to match her yellow cotton dress... His clothes don't quite match.*

2 V-T 他動詞 If you **are fitted for** a particular piece of clothing, you try it on so that the person who is making it can see where it needs to be altered. 合い具合を見る [usu passive] □ *She was being fitted for her wedding dress.* 彼女はウェディングドレスの仮縫いをしてもらっていた. **3** V-I 自動詞 If something **fits** somewhere, it can be put there or is designed to be put there. 合う, はまる □ *...a pocket computer which is small enough to fit into your pocket.* ポケットに入るほど小さいポケコン □ *He folded his long legs to fit under the table.* 彼は長い脚を折り曲げてテーブルの下に入れた. **4** V-T 他動詞 If you **fit** something into a particular space or place, you put it there. はめ込む □ *...she fitted her key in the lock.* 彼女は鍵を錠前に差し込んだ. □ *Who could cut the millions of stone blocks and fit them together?* 何百万もの石の固まりを切って組み合わせられる人なんているのか. **5** V-T 他動詞 If you **fit** something somewhere, you attach it there, or put it there carefully and securely. 取り付ける □ *Fit hinge bolts to give extra support to the door lock.* ドアの錠を補強するためにヒンジボルトを取り付けなさい. □ *Peter had built the overhead ladders, and the next day he fitted them to the wall.* ピーターは雲梯を作り, 次の日壁に取り付けた. **6** V-T/V-I 他動詞/自動詞 If something **fits** something else or **fits** into it, it goes together well with that thing or is able to be part of it. 適合する □ *Her daughter doesn't fit the current feminine ideal.* 彼女の娘は現在の女性理想像には適合しない. □ *Fostering is a full-time job and you should carefully consider how it will fit into your career.* 里子育ては片手間の仕事ではないから, それがあなたの仕事にどう組み入れられるかを慎重に考えるべきです. **7** V-T 他動詞 You can say that something **fits** a particular person or thing when it is appropriate or suitable for them or it. 相応する □ *The punishment must always fit the crime.* 罰は常に罪に見合うものでなくてはならない. **8** V-T 他動詞 If something **fits** someone for a particular task or role, it makes them good enough or suitable for it. 資格をつける [FORMAL 形式ばった] □ *...a man whose past experience fits him for the top job in education.* 過去の経験で教育の最も重要な職につく資格がある男性 **9** N-SING 単数名詞 If something is a good **fit**, it fits well. ぴったり合うもの □ *Eventually he was happy that the sills and doors were a reasonably good fit.* 最終的に, 敷居と扉が適度に合ったので彼は満足した. **10** ADJ 形容詞 If something is **fit** for a particular purpose, it is suitable for that purpose. うってつけの □ *Of the seven bicycles we had, only two were fit for the road.* 私たちの所有した7台の自転車の内, 道路を走れるのは2台だけだった. **11** ADJ 形容詞 If someone is **fit** to do something, they have the appropriate qualities or skills that will allow them to do it. 適任の □ *You're not fit to be a mother!* きみは母親になるには不適任だ. □ *In a word, this government isn't fit to rule.* 要するに, この政府は統治する力がない. ● **fit|ness** N-UNCOUNT 不可算名詞 適合性 □ *There is a debate about his fitness for the highest office.* その最高の地位に彼が適任かをめぐって議論がめぐらされている. **12** PHRASE 句 If you say that someone **sees fit to** do something, you mean that they are entitled to do it, but that you disapprove of their decision to do it. ーするのを適当と思う [FORMAL 形式ばった, DISAPPROVAL 不賛成] □ *He's not a friend, you say, yet you saw fit to lend him money.* 彼は友達ではないといいながら, きみはお金を貸してもよいと思った. **13** → see also **fitted, fitting** **14 fit the bill** → see **bill 15 fit like a glove** → see **glove 16 not in a fit state** → see **state**

▶ **fit in** ■ PHRASAL VERB 句動詞 If you manage to **fit** a person or task **in**, you manage to find time to deal with them. (予定に)組み込む, 都合をつける ❑ *We work long hours both outside and inside the home and we rush around trying to fit everything in.* 私たちは家の内外の両方で長時間働き, すべてをやり遂げようと走り回っている. ■ PHRASAL VERB 句動詞 If you **fit in** as part of a group, you seem to belong there because you are similar to the other people in it. 一に溶け込む ❑ *She was great with the children and fit in beautifully.* 彼女はその子供たちの扱いがうまく, 見事に溶け込んだ. ■ PHRASAL VERB 句動詞 If you say that someone or something **fits in**, you understand how they form part of a particular situation or system. ぴったり合う, 調和する ❑ *He knew where I fitted in and what he had to do to get the best out of me.* 彼は私が何に適任か, 私を最大限に利用するにはどうすべきかを知っていた.

▶ **fit out** PHRASAL VERB 句動詞 If you **fit** someone or something **out**, or you **fit** them **up**, you provide them with equipment and other things that they need. 支度をしてやる ❑ *We helped to fit him out for a trip to the Baltic.* 私たちは彼がバルト海への旅行の支度をするのを手伝った. ❑ *I suggest we fit you up with an office suite.* あなたにオフィススイートを用意したらどうかと思う.

❷ **fit** /fɪt/ (fitter, fittest) ADJ 形容詞 Someone who is **fit** is healthy and physically strong. よい健康状態で ❑ *An averagely fit person can master easy ski runs within a few days.* 平均的に健康な人なら簡単なスキーコースを数日の内にマスターできる. ● **fit|ness** N-UNCOUNT 不可算名詞 ❑ *Squash was once thought to offer all-round fitness.* スカッシュをすると総合的に健康になれるとかつて考えられていた.

❸ **fit** /fɪt/ (fits) ■ N-COUNT 可算名詞 If you have a **fit** of coughing or laughter, you suddenly start coughing or laughing in an uncontrollable way. 発作 ❑ *Halfway down the cigarette she had a fit of coughing.* 彼女はたばこを半分吸ったところで, 咳き込んだ. ■ N-COUNT 可算名詞 If you do something in a **fit of** anger or panic, you are very angry or afraid when you do it. 激発 ❑ *Pattie shot Tom in a fit of jealous rage.* パティーは激しいしっとで発作的にトムを撃った. ■ N-COUNT 可算名詞 If someone has a **fit** they suddenly lose consciousness and their body makes uncontrollable movements. ひきつけ ❑ *About two in every five epileptic fits occur during sleep.* てんかんの発作の約5件の内は2件は睡眠中に起こる. ■ N-COUNT 可算名詞 If someone **has a fit** or **throws a fit**, they suddenly become very agitated because they are angry or worried about something. ひどく興奮する [INFORMAL くだけた] ❑ *When my landlady said she wanted to keep $380 of my deposit to paint the walls, I threw a fit.* 女家主が私の敷金の内380ドルを壁塗装のために取っておくと言ったとき, 私はカッとなった. ❑ *"Cathy will have a fit when she finds out you bought all that fishing gear," Harrington said.* 「きみがそんなに釣具を買ったのを見つけたらキャシーはカンカンに怒るぜ」とハリントンは言った.

fit|ted /fɪtɪd/ ■ ADJ 形容詞 A **fitted** piece of clothing is designed so that it is the same size and shape as your body rather than being loose. 合うように作られた ❑ *...baggy trousers with fitted jackets.* だぶだぶのズボンとそれに合った上着 ■ ADJ 形容詞 A **fitted** sheet has the corners sewn so that they fit over the corners of the mattress and do not have to be folded. ボックス型の [ADJ n] → see bed

fit|ting /fɪtɪŋ/ (fittings) ■ N-COUNT 可算名詞 A **fitting** is one of the smaller parts on the outside of a piece of equipment or furniture, for example, a handle or a faucet. 取付け部品 ❑ *...brass light fittings.* 真ちゅうの照明器具 ❑ *...industrial fittings for kitchen and bathroom.* 台所と浴室用の工業製の備品 ■ N-COUNT 可算名詞 If someone has a **fitting**, they try on a piece of clothing that is being made for them to see if it fits. 仮縫い ❑ *She lunched and shopped and went for fittings for clothes she didn't need.* 彼女は昼食を食べ, 買い物をして, いりもしない衣服の仮縫いに行った. ■ N-PLURAL 複数名詞 **Fittings** are things such as ovens or heaters, that are fitted inside a building, but can be removed if necessary. 備品 ❑ *...a detailed list of what fixtures and fittings are included in the purchase price.* 購入価格に含まれている据付品や備品の詳細なリスト ■ ADJ 形容詞 Something that is **fitting** is right or suitable. ぴったりの ❑ *A solitary man, it was perhaps fitting that he should have died alone.* 孤独な男性だったから, 彼が独りで死んだのは恐らくふさわしかっただろう. ● **fit|ting|ly** ADV 副詞 ぴったりと ❑ *He closed out his career, fittingly, by hitting a home run.* 彼は彼にふさわしく, ホームランを放って, そのキャリアを終えた.

five /faɪv/ (fives) NUM 数詞 **Five** is the number 5. 5 ❑ *I spent five years there and had a really good time.* 私はそこで5年を過ごし, とても楽しかった.

fiv|er /faɪvər/ (fivers) N-COUNT 可算名詞 A **fiver** is a five dollar bill. 5ドル札 [INFORMAL くだけた]

fix /fɪks/ (fixes, fixing, fixed) ■ V-T 動詞 If you **fix** something which is damaged or which does not work properly, you repair it. 修理する ❑ *He cannot fix the electricity.* 彼は電気を直せない. ■ V-T 他動詞 If you **fix** a problem or a bad situation, you deal with it and make it satisfactory. 解決する ❑ *It's not too late to fix the problem,*

although time is clearly getting short. その問題の解決にはまだ間に合います. 明らかに時間が限られてきていますが. ■ V-T 他動詞 If you **fix** some food or a drink for someone, you make it or prepare it for them. 作る, 用意する ❑ *Sarah fixed some food for us.* サラは私たちに食事を作ってくれた. ❑ *Let me fix you a drink.* 飲み物を出すわ. ■ V-T 他動詞 If you **fix** your hair, clothes, or makeup, you arrange or adjust them so you look neat and tidy, showing you have taken care with your appearance. 整える, 直す [INFORMAL くだけた] [no passive] ❑ *"I've got to fix my hair," I said and retreated to my bedroom.* 「髪を直さなくっちゃ」と私は言って, 寝室に戻った. ■ V-T 他動詞 If you **fix** something, for example, a date, price, or policy, you decide and say exactly what it will be. 決定する ❑ *He's going to fix a time when I can see him.* 彼が私と会える面会時間を決めるところだ. ❑ *The date of the election was fixed.* 選挙日が決定した. ■ V-T 他動詞 If you **fix** something for someone, you arrange for it to happen or you organize it for them. 手配する ❑ *I've fixed it for you to see Bonnie Lachlan.* 私はあなたがボニー・ラックランに会えるよう手配した. ❑ *It's fixed. He's going to meet us at the airport.* 段取りはついた. 彼が私たちを空港で出迎えてくれる予定だ. ❑ *He vanished after you fixed him with a job.* きみが彼に仕事の手配をしてやったあと彼はいなくなった. ■ V-T 他動詞 If something **is fixed** somewhere, it is attached there firmly or securely. 固定する, 取り付ける ❑ *It is fixed on the wall.* それは壁に固定されている. ❑ *Most blinds can be fixed directly to the top of the window-frame.* ほとんどのブラインドは窓枠の上部に直接取り付けられる. ■ V-T/V-I 他動詞/自動詞 If you **fix** your eyes **on** someone or something or if your eyes **fix on** them, you look at them with complete attention. (視線・注意を)注ぐ ❑ *She fixes her steel-blue eyes on an unsuspecting local official.* 彼女は怪しんでいない地方官吏にはがね色の目をじっと向ける. ❑ *Her soft brown eyes fixed on Kelly.* 彼女の優しい茶色の目がケリーに注がれた. ■ V-T 他動詞 If someone or something **is fixed in** your mind, you remember them well, for example, because they are very important, interesting, or unusual. (心に)留める ❑ *Leonard was now fixed in his mind.* レオナルドのことが今や彼の心に留められた. ■ V-T 他動詞 If someone **fixes** a gun, camera, or radar **on** something, they point it at that thing. 向ける ❑ *The U.S. crew fixed its radar on the Turkish ship.* 米軍乗務員はレーダーをそのトルコ船に向けた. ■ V-T 他動詞 If someone **fixes** a race, election, contest, or other event, they make unfair or illegal arrangements or use deception to affect the result. 八百長する, 不正工作をする [DISAPPROVAL 不賛成] ❑ *They offered opposing players bribes to fix a decisive game.* 彼らは決定的な試合を八百長するように相手の選手たちにわいろの申し出をした. ● N-COUNT 可算名詞 **Fix** is also a noun. 不正行為, 八百長試合 ❑ *It's all a fix, a deal they've made.* それは全部前もって取引をした八百長だ. ■ V-T 他動詞 If you accuse someone of **fixing** prices, you accuse them of making unfair arrangements to charge a particular price for something, rather than allowing market forces to decide it. 不正に操作する, 談合する [BUSINESS 実業, DISAPPROVAL 不賛成] ❑ *...a suspected cartel that had fixed the price of steel for the construction market.* 建築市場での鋼鉄の価格を談合したという容疑がかかっているカルテル ■ N-COUNT 可算名詞 You can refer to a solution to a problem as a **fix**. 解決策 [INFORMAL くだけた] ❑ *Many of those changes could just be a temporary fix.* これらの変更の多くは一時しのぎに過ぎない可能性がある. ■ → see also quick fix ■ N-SING 単数名詞 If you get a **fix on** someone or something, you have a clear idea or understanding of them. 理解 [INFORMAL くだけた] ❑ *It's been hard to get a steady fix on what's going on.* 起こっている状況をはっきりとつかむのは難しい状態だ. ■ → see also **fixed**

▶ **fix up** ■ PHRASAL VERB 句動詞 If you **fix** something **up**, you do work that is necessary in order to make it more suitable or attractive. 修理する, 整える ❑ *I've fixed up Matthew's old room.* マシューの古い部屋を修理した. ■ PHRASAL VERB 句動詞 If you **fix** someone **up with** something they need, you provide it for them. 用意する ❑ *We'll fix him up with a tie.* 私たちが彼にネクタイを用意しましょう. ■ PHRASAL VERB 句動詞 If you **fix** something **up**, you arrange it. 手配する [BRIT 英国英語]

Thesaurus		*fix* また次を参照:
v.	adjust, correct, repair, restore ■	
	agree on, decide, establish, work out ■ ■	
	arrange, plan ■	
	fasten, nail, secure ■	

fixed /fɪkst/ ■ ADJ 形容詞 You use **fixed** to describe something which stays the same and does not or cannot vary. 固定した ❑ *They issue a fixed number of shares that trade publicly.* それらは一般に取引される一定数の株を発行する. ❑ *Many restaurants offer fixed-price menus.* 定額の料理を出すレストランが多い. ■ ADJ 形容詞 If you say that someone has **fixed** ideas or opinions, you mean that they do not often change their ideas and opinions, although perhaps they should. 固執的な ❑ *...people who have fixed ideas about things.* 物事について固定観念を持つ人々 ■ ADJ 形容詞 If someone has a **fixed** smile on their face, they are smiling even though they do not feel happy or pleased. こわばった ❑ *I had to go through the rest of*

the evening with a fixed smile on my face. 私はこわばった笑顔でその夜の残りを過ごさねばならなかった. **4** PHRASE 句 Someone who is of **no fixed address** does not have a permanent place to live. 住所不定 [FORMAL 形式ばった] ❑ They are not able to get a job interview because they have no fixed address. 彼らは住所不定なので就職試験の面接は受けられない. **5** → see also **fix**

fix|ture /fɪkstʃər/ (**fixtures**) N-COUNT 可算名詞 **Fixtures** are fittings or furniture which belong to a building and are legally part of it, for example, a bathtub or a toilet. 据え付け品 ❑ ...a detailed list of what fixtures and fittings are included in the purchase price. 購入価格に含まれている家具什器（じゅうき）の詳細リスト

fizz /fɪz/ (**fizzes, fizzing, fizzed**) V-I 自動詞 If a drink **fizzes**, it produces a lot of little bubbles of gas and makes a sound like a long "s." シューと泡立つ ❑ After a while their mother was back, holding a tray of glasses that fizzed. しばらくすると彼らの母親が炭酸飲料の入ったグラスを盆に載せて戻ってきた. ● N-UNCOUNT 不可算名詞 **Fizz** is also a noun. 炭酸飲料の気泡, シューという音 ❑ I wonder if there's any fizz left in the lemonade. そのレモネードに炭酸が少しでも残っているのかしら.

fizzy /fɪzi/ (**fizzier, fizziest**) ADJ 形容詞 **Fizzy** liquids contain small bubbles of carbon dioxide. They make a sound like a long "s" when you pour them. 発泡性の, 炭酸入りの ❑ ...fizzy water. 炭酸水

flag /flæɡ/ (**flags, flagging, flagged**) **1** N-COUNT 可算名詞 A **flag** is a piece of cloth which can be attached to a pole and which is used as a sign, signal, or symbol of something, especially of a particular country. 旗 ❑ The Marines climbed to the roof of the embassy building to raise the American flag. 海兵隊員が星条旗を揚げるために大使館の屋根に上った. **2** N-COUNT 可算名詞 Journalists sometimes refer to the **flag** of a particular country or organization as a way of referring to the country or organization itself and its values or power. 旗が示す国・組織 ❑ Every person who serves under the American flag will answer to his or her own superiors and to military law. 星条旗の下に仕える者は皆, それぞれの上官と軍法に従うことになります. **3** V-I 自動詞 If you **flag** or if your spirits **flag**, you begin to lose enthusiasm or energy. （熱意・気力が）衰える ❑ His enthusiasm was in no way flagging. 彼の熱意は決して衰えてきていなかった.
→ see Word Web: **flag**

fla|grant /fleɪɡrənt/ ADJ 形容詞 You can use **flagrant** to describe an action, situation, or someone's behavior that you find extremely bad or shocking in a very obvious way. 目に余る [DISAPPROVAL 不賛成] [ADJ n] ❑ The judge called the decision "a flagrant violation of international law." 判事はその決定を「国際法の甚だしい違反行為」と呼んだ.

flag|ship /flæɡʃɪp/ (**flagships**) **1** N-COUNT 可算名詞 The **flagship** of a group of things that are owned or produced by a particular organization is the most important one. 最も重要なもの ❑ The company plans to open a flagship store in New York this month. その会社は今月ニューヨーク市に本店をオープンする予定だ. **2** N-COUNT 可算名詞 A **flagship** is the most important ship in a fleet of ships, especially the one on which the commander of the fleet is sailing. 旗艦 [mainly BRIT 主に英国英語]

flail /fleɪl/ (**flails, flailing, flailed**) V-T/V-I 他動詞/自動詞 If your arms or legs **flail** or if you **flail** them about, they wave about in an energetic but uncontrolled way. 振り回す, 振り回る ❑ His arms were flailing in all directions. 彼の両腕は四方八方に振り回されていた. ● PHRASAL VERB 句動詞 **Flail around** means the same as **flail**. 振り回す ❑ He started flailing around and hitting Vincent in the chest. 彼は腕を振り回してヴィンセントの胸を打ちだした.

flair /flɛər/ **1** N-SING 単数名詞 If you have **a flair for** a particular thing, you have a natural ability to do it well. 才能 ❑ ...a friend who has a flair for languages. 語学の才のある友人 **2** N-UNCOUNT 不可算名詞 If you have **flair**, you do things in an original, interesting, and stylish way. センスの良さ [APPROVAL 賛成] ❑ Their work has all the usual punch, panache and flair you'd expect. 彼らの作品には期待通りふだんの迫力, 華やかさ, そしてセンスの良さがある.

flak /flæk/ N-UNCOUNT 不可算名詞 If you get a lot of **flak** from someone, they criticize you severely. If you take **flak**, you get the

blame for something. 激しい非難 [INFORMAL くだけた] ❑ The president is getting a lot of flak for that. そのことで大統領はひどく非難攻撃されています.

flake /fleɪk/ (**flakes, flaking, flaked**) **1** N-COUNT 可算名詞 A **flake** is a small thin piece of something, especially one that has broken off a larger piece. 破片, かけら ❑ Large flakes of snow began swiftly to fall. ぼたん雪が勢いよく降り始めた. **2** V-I 自動詞 If something such as paint **flakes**, small thin pieces of it come off. はげ落ちる ❑ They can see how its colors have faded and where paint has flaked. その色のあせ方やペンキのはがれ落ちた場所が見られる. ● PHRASAL VERB 句動詞 **Flake off** means the same as **flake**. はげ落ちる ❑ The surface corrosion was worst where the paint had flaked off. 表面腐食はペンキがはげ落ちた場所が最もひどかった. **3** N-COUNT 可算名詞 If you refer to someone as a **flake**, you mean that you think they are very unreliable. 当てにならない人 [INFORMAL くだけた] ❑ Sophie turned out to be such a flake. She said she'd meet me here and instead I'm just lying around this hotel room and I'm totally bored. 結局ソフィーは全く当てにならない人だと分かった. ここで私に会うと言ったのに, 結局私はこのホテルで暇をつぶしているだけで, すっかり飽き飽きしている.

flam|boy|ant /flæmbɔɪənt/ ADJ 形容詞 If you say that someone or something is **flamboyant**, you mean that they are very noticeable, stylish, and exciting. 華やかな ❑ Freddie Mercury was a flamboyant star of the hard rock scene. フレディー・マーキュリーはハードロックの舞台ウやかなスターだった. ● **flam|boy|ance** N-UNCOUNT 不可算名詞 華やかさ ❑ Campese was his usual mixture of flamboyance and flair キャンピーズはいつもの華やかさとセンスを持ち合わせていた.

Word Link   **flam ≈ burning : flame, flammable, inflame**

---

flame /fleɪm/ (**flames, flaming, flamed**) **1** N-VAR 可変性名詞 A **flame** is a hot bright stream of burning gas that comes from something that is burning. 炎 ❑ The heat from the flames was so intense that roads melted. 炎から出る熱があまりにも強くて道路が溶けた. **2** N-COUNT 可算名詞 A **flame** is an e-mail message which severely criticizes or attacks someone. 怒りのメール, フレーム [INFORMAL くだけた COMPUTING コンピューティング] ❑ The best way to respond to a flame is to ignore it. 怒りのメールへの最善の対応策は無視することだ. ● V-T 他動詞 **Flame** is also a verb. 怒りのメールを送る ❑ Ever been flamed? 怒りのメールが送られて来たことがあるか. **3** → see also **flaming** **4** PHRASE 句 If something **bursts into flames** or **bursts into flame**, it suddenly starts burning strongly. 一気に燃え上がる ❑ She managed to scramble out of the vehicle as it burst into flames. 車が一気に炎上したときに, 彼女はどうにか車からはい出た. **5** PHRASE 句 Something that is **in flames** is on fire. 炎上して ❑ I woke to a city in flames. 私が目覚めると市が炎上していた.
→ see **fire**

flam|ing /fleɪmɪŋ/ ADJ 形容詞 **Flaming** is used to describe something that is burning and producing a lot of flames. 炎上している ❑ The plane, which was full of fuel, scattered flaming fragments over a large area. その飛行機は燃料が満タンで, 燃え上がった火の粉が広い範囲にわたって散乱しました.

flam|mable /flæməbəl/ ADJ 形容詞 **Flammable** chemicals, gases, cloth, or other things catch fire and burn easily. 可燃性の ❑ ...flammable liquids such as gasoline or kerosene. ガソリンや灯油などの可燃性液体

flank /flæŋk/ (**flanks, flanking, flanked**) **1** N-COUNT 可算名詞 An animal's **flank** is its side, between the ribs and the hip. 脇腹 ❑ He put his hand on the dog's flank. 彼は犬の脇腹に手を当てた. **2** N-COUNT 可算名詞 A **flank** of an army or navy force is one side of it when it is organized for battle. （戦闘部隊の）側面 ❑ The assault element, led by Captain Ramirez, opened up from their right flank. ラミレス大尉によって率いられた急襲分隊は部隊の右側から攻撃を開始した. **3** N-COUNT 可算名詞 The side of anything large can be referred to as its **flank**. （大きなものの）側面 ❑ They continued along the flank of the mountain. 彼らは山の中腹を進み続けた. **4** V-T 他動詞 If something **is flanked by** things, it has them on both sides of it, or sometimes on one side of it. 側面に立つ ❑ The altar was flanked by two Christmas trees. 祭壇の両側にはそれぞれクリスマスツリーがあった.

Word Web   flag

Flags are **symbols**. Some flags **symbolize** countries. At the Olympics, each group of athletes proudly carries their country's standard. The Olympics even has its own flag. It **flies** at all Olympic games. Flags can also send messages. Most people understand that a white flag means "we **surrender**." Before radios, people used semaphore to communicate between ships. They used different colored flags. They hoisted them in special positions to spell out words. Flags can also signal danger. When people carry long pieces of wood on their cars, they use a red flag to warn other drivers.

flan|nel /ˈflænᵊl/ (flannels) **1** N-UNCOUNT 不可算名詞 **Flannel** is a soft cloth, usually made of cotton or wool, that is used for making clothes. フランネル，ネル [oft N n] ❑ He wore a faded red flannel shirt. 彼は色あせた赤色のネルのシャツを着ていた． **2** N-COUNT 可算名詞 A **flannel** is a small cloth that you use for washing yourself. フランネルのタオル [BRIT 英国英語; AM 米国英語 **washcloth** ⇨ **washcloth**]

flap /flæp/ (flaps, flapping, flapped) **1** V-T/V-I 他動詞/自動詞 If something such as a piece of cloth or paper **flaps** or if you **flap** it, it moves quickly up and down or from side to side. パタパタと動く [他動詞]，パタパタと動く [自動詞] ❑ Gray sheets flapped on the clothes line. 灰色のシーツが物干しロープでパタパタしていた． **2** V-T/V-I 他動詞/自動詞 If a bird or insect **flaps** its wings or if its wings **flap**, the wings move quickly up and down. 羽ばたかせる [他動詞]，羽ばたく [自動詞] ❑ The bird flapped its wings furiously. その鳥は猛烈に翼を羽ばたかせた． **3** V-T 他動詞 If you **flap** your arms, you move them quickly up and down as if they were the wings of a bird. (腕を) パタパタと動かす ❑ ...a kid running and flapping her arms. 走りながら腕をパタパタ動かしている子供 **4** N-COUNT 可算名詞 A **flap** of cloth or skin, for example, is a flat piece of it that can move freely up and down or from side to side because it is held or attached by only one edge. (布・皮などの) パタパタするもの ❑ He drew back the tent flap and strode out into the blizzard. 彼はテントのフラップを開けて猛吹雪の中に大股に歩いていった． **5** N-COUNT 可算名詞 A **flap** on the wing of an aircraft is an area along the edge of the wing that can be raised or lowered to control the movement of the aircraft. (飛行機の翼の) フラップ ❑ ...the sudden slowing as the flaps were lowered. フラップが下げられ急に速度が低下

flare /flɛər/ (flares, flaring, flared) **1** N-COUNT 可算名詞 A **flare** is a small device that produces a bright flame. Flares are used as signals, for example, on ships. 発火信号，照明弾 ❑ ...a ship which had fired a distress flare. 遭難発火信号を打ち上げた船 **2** V-I 自動詞 If a fire **flares**, the flames suddenly become larger. 燃え上がる [自動詞] ❑ Camp fires flared like beacons in the dark. キャンプファイヤーが暗闇の中でのろしのように燃え上がった． ● PHRASAL VERB 句動詞 **Flare up** means the same as **flare**. 燃え上がる ❑ Don't spill too much fat on the barbecue as it could flare up. バーベキューの炭火にあまり脂をこぼさないように，火が燃え上がる可能性がある． **3** V-I 自動詞 If something such as trouble, violence, or conflict **flares**, it starts or becomes more violent. 勃発 (ぼっぱつ) する，激化する ❑ Even as the president appealed for calm, trouble flared in several American cities. 大統領が事態の沈静化を訴えたにも関わらず，紛争はアメリカの数都市で激化した． ● PHRASAL VERB 句動詞 **Flare up** means the same as **flare**. 激化する ❑ Dozens of people were injured as fighting flared up. 戦いが激化するにつれて何十人もの人々が負傷した． **4** V-I 自動詞 If people's tempers **flare**, they get angry. カッと怒り出す ❑ Tempers flared and harsh words were exchanged. 感情が爆発し，辛らつな言葉が交わされた．

flare-up (flare-ups) N-COUNT 可算名詞 If there is a **flare-up** of violence or of an illness, it suddenly starts or gets worse. (暴動などの) 突発，(病気の) 急な再発 ❑ There's been a flare-up of violence in South Africa. 南アフリカで暴動が勃発 (ぼっぱつ) した．

flash /flæʃ/ (flashes, flashing, flashed) **1** N-COUNT 可算名詞 A **flash** is a sudden burst of light or of something shiny or bright. 閃光 (せんこう) ❑ A sudden flash of lightning lit everything up for a second. 突然の稲妻で一瞬すべてが明るく出された． ❑ The wire snapped at the wall plug with a blue flash. コードが壁のコンセントで青い閃光 (せんこう) を放ちぶつんと切れた． **2** V-T/V-I 他動詞/自動詞 If a light **flashes** or if you **flash** a light, it shines with a sudden bright light, especially as quick, regular flashes of light. ぱっとつける [他動詞]，ぴかっと光る [自動詞] ❑ Lightning flashed among the distant dark clouds. 遠くの暗黒雲の中で稲妻がぴかっと光った． ❑ He lost his temper after a driver flashed her headlights as he overtook. 彼が追い越しをする際に女性ドライバーにヘッドライトをぱっと照らされて，彼は腹を立てた． **3** V-I 自動詞 If something **flashes** past or by, it moves past you so fast that you cannot see it properly. さっと通り過ぎる ❑ It was a busy road, cars flashed by every few minutes. そこは交通量が多く，車が数分ごとに通りすぎた． **4** V-I 自動詞 If something **flashes through** or **into** your mind, you suddenly think about it. 頭をよぎる ❑ A ludicrous thought flashed through Harry's mind. ばかばかしい考えがハリーの頭をよぎった． **5** V-T 他動詞 If you **flash** something such as an identification card, you show it to people quickly and then put it away again. ちらっと見せる [INFORMAL くだけた] ❑ Halim flashed his official card, and managed to get hold of a soldier to guard the Land Rover. ハリムは警察証をちらりと見せ，なんとかランドローバーの見張りをさせる兵士を見つけた． **6** V-T/V-I 他動詞/自動詞 If a picture or message **flashes up** on a screen, or if you **flash** it **onto** a screen, it is displayed there briefly or suddenly, and often repeatedly. ぱっと表示する [他動詞]，ぱっと表示される [自動詞] ❑ The figures flashed up on the scoreboard. 得点掲示板に数字が点灯する． ❑ The words "Good Luck" were flashing on the screen. 「幸運を祈る」という言葉が画面に点滅していた． **7** V-T 他動詞 If you **flash** a look or a smile at someone, you suddenly look at them or smile at them. (視線・ほほえを) ちらりと向ける [WRITTEN 書

き言葉] ❑ I flashed a look at Sue. 私はスーにちらりと視線を向けた． **8** N-UNCOUNT 不可算名詞 **Flash** is the use of special bulbs to give more light when taking a photograph. フラッシュ ❑ He was one of the first people to use high speed flash in bird photography. 彼は鳥の撮影で高スピードのフラッシュを使用した最初の1人だった． **9** N-COUNT 可算名詞 A **flash** is the same as a **flashlight**. 懐中電灯 [AM 米国英語, INFORMAL くだけた] ❑ Stopping to rest, Pete shut off the flash. ピートは休憩のために立ち止まり，懐中電灯を切った． **10** PHRASE 句 If you say that something happens **in a flash**, you mean that it happens suddenly and lasts only a short time. あっという間に ❑ The answer had come to him in a flash. 即座にその答えが彼の頭に浮かんだ． **11** PHRASE 句 If you say that someone reacts to something **quick as a flash**, you mean that they react to it extremely quickly. 即座に ❑ Quick as a flash, the man said, "I have to, don't I?" 即座にその男は「僕がしなくちゃ，ね」と言った．

flash|back /ˈflæʃbæk/ (flashbacks) **1** N-COUNT 可算名詞 In a movie, novel, or play, a **flashback** is a scene that returns to events in the past. 回想シーン ❑ There is even a flashback to the murder itself. その殺人そのものの回想シーンすらある． **2** N-COUNT 可算名詞 If you have a **flashback** to a past experience, you have a sudden and very clear memory of it. 突然思い出すこと ❑ He has recurring flashbacks to the night his friends died. 彼は友人たちが死んだ夜が繰り返し思い出される．

flash|light /ˈflæʃlaɪt/ (flashlights) N-COUNT 可算名詞 A **flashlight** is a small electric light which gets its power from batteries and which you can carry in your hand. 懐中電灯 [mainly AM 主に米国英語] [also 'by' N] ❑ Len studied it a moment in the beam of his flashlight. レンは懐中電灯の光で少しの間それを調べた．

flashy /ˈflæʃi/ (flashier, flashiest) ADJ 形容詞 If you describe a person or thing as **flashy**, you mean they are fashionable and noticeable, but in a somewhat vulgar way. 派手な [INFORMAL くだけた, DISAPPROVAL 不賛成] ❑ He was much less flashy than his brother. 彼は弟ほど派手ではなかった．

flask /flæsk/ (flasks) **1** N-COUNT 可算名詞 A **flask** is a bottle which you use for carrying drinks around with you. 水筒，魔法瓶 ❑ He took out a metal flask from a canvas bag. 彼はキャンバスバッグから金属性の魔法瓶を取り出した． ● N-COUNT 可算名詞 A **flask** of liquid is the flask and the liquid which it contains. 魔法瓶に入った飲み物 ❑ There are some sandwiches here and a flask of coffee. ここにサンドイッチと魔法瓶に入ったコーヒーがある． **2** N-COUNT 可算名詞 A **flask** is a bottle or other container which is used in science laboratories and industry for holding liquids. フラスコ ❑ Flasks for the transport of spent fuel are extremely strong containers made of steel or steel and lead. 使用済み燃料の輸送用フラスコは鋼鉄製，あるいは鋼鉄と鉛の合成の非常に丈夫な容器だ．

---

flat

❶ SURFACES, SHAPES, AND POSITIONS

❷ OTHER USES

❸ AN APARTMENT

---

❶ flat /flæt/ (flats, flatter, flattest) **1** ADJ 形容詞 Something that is **flat** is level, smooth, or even, rather than sloping, curved, or uneven. 平らな ❑ Tiles can be fixed to any surface as long as it's flat, firm and dry. タイルは平らで堅く乾燥しているかぎり，どんな表面にでも貼ることができる． ❑ ...windows which a thief can reach from a drainpipe or flat roof. 配水管あるいは平屋根から泥棒がたどり着ける窓． **2** ADJ 形容詞 **Flat** means horizontal and not upright. 横の，水平の ❑ Two men near him threw themselves flat. 彼の近くにいた2人の男がばたんと横になった． **3** PHRASE 句 If you **fall flat** on your face, you fall over. うつぶせに倒れる ❑ A man walked in off the street and fell flat on his face, unconscious. 男が通りから中に歩いてきて，バタンとうつぶせに倒れ，意識不明だった． **4** ADJ 形容詞 A **flat** object is not very tall or deep in relation to its length and width. 薄い，平べったい ❑ Ellen is walking down the drive with a square flat box balanced on one hand. エレンは四角くて平べったい箱を片手に乗せて玄関先を歩いている． **5** ADJ 形容詞 **Flat** land is level, with no high hills or other raised parts. 平坦 (ひよく) な ❑ To the north lie the flat and fertile farmlands of Nebraska. 北方にはネブラスカ州の平坦 (へいたん) で肥沃 (へいたん) な農地が広がっている． **6** ADJ 形容詞 **Flat** shoes have no heels or very low heels. かかとの低い，ローヒールの ❑ People wear slacks, sweaters, flat shoes, and all manner of casual attire for travel. 人々はズボン，セーター，かかとの低い靴，そして様々な旅行用のカジュアルな服装を身につけていた． N-PLURAL 複数名詞 ● **Flats** are flat shoes. ローヒール [AM 米国英語] ❑ His mother looked ten years younger in jeans and flats. 彼の母親はジーンズとローヒールを履いていて10歳若く見えた． **7** ADJ 形容詞 A **flat** tire, ball, or balloon does not have enough air in it. 空気が抜けた ❑ One vehicle with a flat tire can bring the highway to a standstill. 車が1台パンクするだけで，その高速道路は交通まひが起きる可能性がある． **8** N-COUNT 可算名詞 You can refer to one of the broad flat surfaces of an object as **the flat of** that object. 平らな面 ❑ He slammed the counter

with the flat of his hand. 彼は手のひらでカウンターをバンとたたいた。 **9** N-COUNT 可算名詞 A **flat** is a tire that does not have enough air in it. パンクしたタイヤ □ Then, after I finally got back on the highway, I developed a flat. そして、私がやっと高速道路に戻ったあとで、タイヤがパンクした。 **10** N-COUNT 可算名詞 A low flat area of uncultivated land, especially an area where the ground is soft and wet, can be referred to as **flats** or a **flat**. 湿地 □ The salt marshes and mud flats attract large numbers of waterfowl. 塩水の沼地や泥の湿地を水鳥をたくさん引き寄せる。 **11** ADJ 形容詞 If you have **flat** feet, the arches of your feet are too low. 偏平足の □ The condition of flat feet runs in families. 偏平足の状態は遺伝する。

Thesaurus　　flat また次を参照:

ADJ.　even, horizontal, level, smooth **❶ 1 2**

---

❷ flat /flæt/ (**flatter, flattest**) **1** ADJ 形容詞 A drink that is **flat** has lost its fizz. 気が抜けた □ Could this really stop the champagne from going flat? これで本当にシャンパンの気が抜けるのを止められるのだろうか。 **2** ADJ 形容詞 A **flat** battery has lost some or all of its electrical charge. 切れた [BRIT 英国英語; AM dead 米国英語 dead] **3** ADJ 形容詞 If you say that something happened, for example, in ten seconds **flat** or ten minutes **flat**, you are emphasizing that it happened surprisingly quickly and only took ten seconds or ten minutes. きっかり [EMPHASIS 強調] [num n ADJ] □ You're sitting behind an engine that'll move you from 0 to 60mph in six seconds flat. あなたは時速60マイルまでをほんの6秒で加速できるエンジンの後ろに座っている。 **4** ADJ 形容詞 A **flat** rate, price, or percentage is one that is fixed and which applies in every situation. 定額の [ADJ n] □ Fees are charged at a flat rate, rather than on a percentage basis. 手数料は歩合制ではなく定額料金で請求される。 **5** ADJ 形容詞 If trade or business is **flat**, it is slow and inactive, rather than busy and improving or increasing. 低迷した □ During the first eight months of this year, sales of big pickups were up 14% while car sales stayed flat. 今年1-8月期では自動車の売り上げが低迷する一方で、大型集配トラックの売り上げは14%伸びた。 **6** ADJ 形容詞 **Flat** is used after a letter representing a musical note to show that the note should be played or sung half a tone lower than the note which otherwise matches that letter. **Flat** is often represented by the symbol Ð after the letter. フラットの、半音下がった [n ADJ] □ ...Schubert's B flat Piano Trio (Opus 99). シューベルトのピアノ三重奏曲変ロ長調 (作品99) **7** ADV 副詞 If someone sings **flat** or if a musical instrument is **flat**, their singing or the instrument is slightly lower in pitch than it should be. 低く外れて [ADV after v] □ She had a tendency to sing flat. 彼女は低く外れて歌う傾向にある。 ● ADJ 形容詞 **Flat** is also an adjective. 低く外れた □ He had been fired because his singing was flat. 彼は歌声が低く外れるために解雇されていた。 **8** ADJ 形容詞 A **flat** denial or refusal is definite and firm, and is unlikely to be changed. はっきりとした、断固とした [ADJ n] □ The Foreign Ministry has issued a flat denial of any involvement. 外務大臣はいかなる関与も断固として否定した。 ● **flatly** ADV 副詞 きっぱりと、断固として □ He flatly refused to discuss it. 彼はそれについての論議を断固として拒否した。 **9** ADJ 形容詞 If you describe something as **flat**, you mean that it is dull and not exciting or interesting. つまらない □ The past few days have seemed comparatively flat and empty. 過去数日は比較的単調で何事もなく過ぎたようだ。 **10** PHRASE 句 If an event or attempt **falls flat** or **falls flat** on **its face**, it is unsuccessful. 不成功に終わる □ Liz meant it as a joke but it fell flat. リズは冗談のつもりで言ったが、受けなかった。 **11** PHRASE 句 If you do something **flat out**, you do it as fast or as hard as you can. 全力で □ Everyone is working flat out to try to trap those responsible. 全員が責任者を捕えようと全力を尽くしている。 □ ...a flat-out sprint. 全力疾走(しっそう)! **12** PHRASE 句 You use **flat out** to emphasize that something is completely the case. 全くの [mainly AM 主に米国英語, INFORMAL くだけた, EMPHASIS 強調] □ That allegation is a flat-out lie. その申し立ては真っ赤なうそだ。

❸ flat /flæt/ (**flats**) N-COUNT 可算名詞 A **flat** is a set of rooms for living in, usually on one floor and part of a larger building. A flat usually includes a kitchen and bathroom. アパート [BRIT 英国英語; AM apartment 米国英語 apartment]

flat|mate /flætmeɪt/ (**flatmates**) also **flat-mate** N-COUNT 可算名詞 Someone's **flatmate** is a person who shares a flat with them. 同居人、ルームメート [BRIT 英国英語; AM roommate 米国英語 roommate]

flat|ten /flætᵊn/ (**flattens, flattening, flattened**) **1** V-T/V-I 他動詞/自動詞 If you **flatten** something or if it **flattens**, it becomes flat or flatter. 平らにする、ぺちゃんこにする [他動詞]、平らになる、ぺちゃんこになる [自動詞] □ He carefully flattened the wrappers and put them between the leaves of his book. 彼は本のカバーを注意深く折り、ページの間に挟んだ。 □ The dog's ears flattened slightly as Cook spoke his name. クックが名前を呼ぶと、その犬の耳がかすかに垂れた。 ● PHRASAL VERB 句動詞 **Flatten out** means the same as **flatten**. 平らにする、平らになる □ The hills flattened out just south of the mountain. それらの丘はその山のすぐ南で平らになっていた。 **2** V-T 他動詞 To **flatten** something such as a building, town, or plant

means to destroy it by knocking it down or crushing it. 取り壊す □ ...explosives capable of flattening a five-story building. 5階建ての建物を取り壊せる爆発物 □ ...bombing raids flattened much of the area. 爆撃がその地域の大部分を破壊した。 **3** V-T 他動詞 If you **flatten yourself against** something, you press yourself flat against it, for example, to avoid getting in the way or being seen. (再帰動詞を伴い) へばりつく □ He flattened himself against a brick wall as I passed. 私が通り過ぎるとき、彼はれんがの塀にぴったり体を寄せた。 **4** V-T 他動詞 If you **flatten** someone, you make them fall over by hitting them violently. 殴り倒す □ "I've never seen a woman flatten someone like that," said a crew member. "She knocked him out cold." 「女があんなふうに誰かを殴り倒すのは見たことがない」と乗務員が言った。 「彼女は彼を殴って意識を失わせたよ」

flat|ter /flætər/ (**flatters, flattering, flattered**) **1** V-T 他動詞 If someone **flatters** you, they praise you in an exaggerated way that is not sincere, because they want to please you or to persuade you to do something. おだてる、おせじを言う [DISAPPROVAL 不賛成] □ I knew she was just flattering me. 彼女が私をおだてているだけだと知っていた。 **2** V-T 他動詞 If you **flatter yourself that** something good is the case, you believe that it is true, although others may disagree. If someone says to you "**you're flattering yourself**" or "**don't flatter yourself**," they mean that they disagree with your good opinion of yourself. うぬぼれる □ I flatter myself that this campaign will put an end to the war. 私はこの運動によって戦争を終結できると自負している。 **3** → see also **flat, flattered, flattering**

flat|tered /flætərd/ ADJ 形容詞 If you are **flattered** by something that has happened, you are pleased about it because it makes you feel important or special. 喜んで [v-link ADJ] □ She was flattered by Roberto's long letter. 彼女はロベルトから長い手紙をもらって喜んだ。

flat|ter|ing /flætərɪŋ/ **1** ADJ 形容詞 If something is **flattering**, it makes you appear more attractive. 実物以上に見える □ It wasn't a very flattering photograph. あまり写りのいい写真ではなかった。 **2** ADJ 形容詞 If someone's remarks are **flattering**, they praise you and say nice things about you. おせじの、褒め言葉の □ Most of his colleagues had positive, even flattering things to say. 彼の同僚のほとんどは肯定的な意見で、褒め言葉さえ出た。

flat|ware /flætweər/ N-UNCOUNT 不可算名詞 You can refer to the knives, forks, and spoons that you eat your food with as **flatware**. 食卓用金物類 [AM 米国英語] □ An assortment of pots, pans, plates, cups, and flatware is provided. 鍋、フライパン、皿、カップ、ナイフ・フォークなどの食器一式が用意されている。

flaunt /flɔnt/ (**flaunts, flaunting, flaunted**) V-T 他動詞 If you say that someone **flaunts** their possessions, abilities, or qualities, you mean that they display them in a very obvious way, especially in order to try to obtain other people's admiration. ひけらかす [DISAPPROVAL 不賛成] □ They drove around in Rolls-Royces, openly flaunting their wealth. 彼らは裕福さをおおっぴらにひけらかしてロールスロイスを乗り回した。

fla|vor /fleɪvər/ (**flavors, flavoring, flavored**) **1** N-VAR 可変性名詞 The **flavor** of a food or drink is its taste. 味 □ I always add some paprika for extra flavor. 私は特別な味を出すためにいつもパプリカを少し足す。 **2** N-COUNT 可算名詞 If something is orange **flavor** or beef **flavor**, it is made to taste of orange or beef. 風味 □ It has an orange flavor and smooth texture. それはオレンジの風味がして滑らかな舌触りだ。 **3** V-T 他動詞 If you **flavor** food or drink, you add something to it to give it a particular taste. 味付けする、風味を加える □ Lime preserved in salt is a North African specialty which is used to flavor chicken dishes. ライムの塩漬けは北アフリカの特産品で、チキン料理の味付けに使用される。

-flavored /-fleɪvərd/ COMB IN ADJ 形容詞の複合 **-flavored** is used after nouns such as strawberry and chocolate to indicate that a food or drink is flavored with strawberry or chocolate. 一風味の、一味の □ ...strawberry-flavored candies. イチゴ味のキャンディー

fla|vor|ing /fleɪvərɪŋ/ (**flavorings**) N-VAR 可変性名詞 **Flavorings** are substances that are added to food or drink to give it a particular taste. 調味料、香味料 □ ...lemon flavoring. レモン調味料

flaw /flɔ/ (**flaws**) **1** N-COUNT 可算名詞 A **flaw** in something such as a theory or argument is a mistake in it, which causes it to be less effective or valid. 欠陥、不備 □ There were, however, a number of crucial flaws in his monetary theory. しかしながら、彼の金融論には数々の重大な欠陥があった。 **2** N-COUNT 可算名詞 A **flaw** in someone's character is an undesirable quality that they have. 欠点、短所 □ The only flaw in his character seems to be a short temper. 彼は短気なことが唯一の欠点のようだ。 **3** N-COUNT 可算名詞 A **flaw** in something such as a pattern or material is a fault in it that should not be there. (模様・生地などの) 欠陥 □ It's like having a flaw in a piece of material - the longer you leave it, the weaker it gets. それは生地に欠陥があるようなものだ。 放っておけば置くほど、ますます弱くなる。

flawed /flɔd/ ADJ 形容詞 Something that is **flawed** has a mark, fault, or mistake in it. 欠陥のある □ These tests were so seriously

flawed as to render the results meaningless. これらのテストは欠陥がひ
どすぎたのでその結果は無効となった.

flaw|less /flɔ́ːlɪs/ ADJ 形容詞 If you say that something or
someone is **flawless**, you mean that they are extremely good and
that there are no faults or problems with them. 完璧(かんぺき)な
□ *Discovery's takeoff this morning from Cape Canaveral was flawless.* ケ
ープ・カナベラル宇宙基地からの今朝のディスカバリー号の離陸は完
璧なものだった. ●**flaw|less|ly** ADV 副詞 完璧に □ *Each stage of the
battle was carried off flawlessly.* 戦闘の各段階が滞りなく遂行された.

flea /flíː/ (**fleas**) N-COUNT 可算名詞 A **flea** is a very small
jumping insect that has no wings and feeds on the blood of
humans or animals. ノミ

fleck /flék/ (**flecks**) N-COUNT 可算名詞 **Flecks** are small marks
on a surface, or objects that look like small marks. 斑点(はんてん)
しみ □ *He went to the men's room to wash flecks of blood from his shirt.*
彼は男子用トイレに行ってシャツに付いた血のしみを洗った.

fled /fléd/ **Fled** is the past tense and past participle of **flee**.

fledg|ling /fléʤlɪŋ/ (**fledglings**) ① N-COUNT 可算名詞 A
fledgling is a young bird that has its feathers and is learning to
fly. ひな鳥 □ *...when fledglings are almost ready to leave the nests.* ひな
鳥がほぼ巣立つ準備ができたとき ② ADJ 形容詞 You use **fledgling** to
describe a person, organization, or system that is new or without
experience. 未熟な [ADJ n] □ *...Russia's fledgling
democracy.* ロシアの未熟な民主主義

flee /flíː/ (**flees, fleeing, fled**) V-T/V-I 他動詞/自動詞 If you **flee**
from something or someone, or **flee** a person or thing, you escape
from them. 逃亡する, 逃げる [WRITTEN 書き言葉]
□ *He slammed the bedroom door behind him and fled.* 彼は後ろ手で寝
室のドアをバタンと閉めて逃げた. □ *...refugees fleeing persecution or
torture.* 迫害や拷問から逃れてきた避難民

fleece /flíːs/ (**fleeces, fleecing, fleeced**) ① N-COUNT 可算名詞
A sheep's **fleece** is the coat of wool that covers it. (ヒツジの) 毛
□ *...a special protein which triggers the animal to shed its fleece.* その
動物の脱毛を引き起こす特別なたんぱく質 ② N-COUNT 可算名詞 A
fleece is the wool that is cut off one sheep in a single piece. (1匹
分の) 羊毛 □ *Wool can be spun from fleeces.* ウールは羊毛から紡ぐこ
とができる ③ V-T 他動詞 If you **fleece** someone, you get a lot of
money from them by tricking them or charging them too much.
巻き上げる, ふんだくる [INFORMAL くだけた] □ *She claims she fleeced
her out of thousands of dollars.* 彼に数千ドルを巻き上げられたと彼女は
主張している. ④ N-VAR 可変性名詞 **Fleece** is a soft warm artificial
fabric. A **fleece** is also a jacket or other garment made from this
fabric. フリース, フリース衣料 □ *...white leather slippers with fleece
lining.* フリースの裏地が付いた白い皮のスリッパ

fleet /flíːt/ (**fleets**) ① N-COUNT 可算名詞 A **fleet** is a group of
ships organized to do something together, for example, to fight
battles or to catch fish. 艦隊, 船団 □ *A fleet sailed for New South
Wales to establish the first European settlement in Australia.* 1つの船団
がオーストラリアに最初のヨーロッパ人の植民地を設立するためにニュ
ーサウスウェールズに向けて航海した. ② N-COUNT 可算名詞 A **fleet**
of vehicles is a group of them, especially when they all belong to
a particular organization or business, or when they are all going
somewhere together. 保有車両, 車隊 □ *With its own fleet of trucks,
the company delivers most orders overnight.* その会社は自社のトラック
群を使って, ほとんどの注文を一晩で配達する.

fleet|ing /flíːtɪŋ/ ADJ 形容詞 **Fleeting** is used to describe
something which lasts only for a very short time. つかの間の
□ *The girls caught only a fleeting glimpse of the driver.* 少女たちはその
運転者をちらっと見ただけだった. ●**fleet|ing|ly** ADV 副詞 すばや
く □ *A smile passed fleetingly across his face.* 彼の顔に一瞬だけ笑顔が
見えた.

flesh /fléʃ/ (**fleshes, fleshing, fleshed**) ① N-UNCOUNT 不可算名
詞 **Flesh** is the soft part of a person's or animal's body between
the bones and the skin. 肉, 身 □ *...the pale pink flesh of trout and
salmon.* マスやサケの薄いピンク色の身 ② N-UNCOUNT 不可算名詞
You can use **flesh** to refer to human skin and the human body,
especially when you are considering it in a sexual way. 肌, 肉体
□ *...the warmth of her flesh.* 彼女の肉体の温かさ ③ N-UNCOUNT 不
可算名詞 The **flesh** of a fruit or vegetable is the soft inside part of
it. 果肉, 実 □ *Cut the flesh from the olives and discard the stones.* オ
リーブの実の果肉を切り取って, 種を捨てなさい. ④ PHRASE 句
You use **flesh and blood** to emphasize that someone has human
feelings or weaknesses, often when contrasting them with
machines. 血の通った人間 [EMPHASIS 強調] □ *I'm only flesh and
blood, like anyone else.* 私もほかの人たちと同様に血の通った人間にす
ぎない. ⑤ PHRASE 句 If you say that someone is your **own flesh
and blood**, you are emphasizing that they are a member of your
family. 肉親 [EMPHASIS 強調] □ *The kid, after all, was his own flesh
and blood. He deserved a second chance.* その子は, 結局は彼の肉親だ
った. 彼はやり直しの機会が与えられて当然だった. ⑥ PHRASE 句 If
something **makes** your **flesh creep** or **makes** your **flesh crawl**, it
makes you feel disgusted, shocked or frightened. 人をぞっとさせ
る □ *It makes my flesh creep to think of it.* 私はそのことを考えるとぞっ

とする. ⑦ PHRASE 句 If you meet or see someone **in the flesh**, you
actually meet or see them, rather than, for example, seeing them
in a movie or on television. 実物に (会う・見る) □ *The first thing
viewers usually say when they see me in the flesh is "You're smaller than
you look on TV."* 視聴者が通常私に実際に会って真っ先に言うことは「テ
レビで見るより小柄なんですね」だ.

▶ **flesh out** PHRASAL VERB 句動詞 If you **flesh out** something such
as a story or plan, you add details and more information to it. 肉
付けする □ *Permission for a warehouse development has already been
granted and the developers are merely fleshing out the details.* 倉庫開発
の許可はすでに下りており, 開発者は単に細部を具体化しているわ
けだ.

→ see **fruit**

flew /flúː/ **Flew** is the past tense of **fly**.

| **Word Link** | flex ≈ bending : *flex, flexible, reflex* |

flex /fléks/ (**flexes, flexing, flexed**) ① V-T 他動詞 If you **flex** your
muscles or parts of your body, you bend, move, or stretch them for
a short time in order to exercise them. (筋肉・体の一部を) 動かす
□ *He slowly flexed his muscles and tried to stand.* 彼はゆっくりと筋肉を
動かし立とうとした. ② N-VAR 可変性名詞 A **flex** is an electric cable
containing two or more wires that is connected to an electrical
appliance. 電気コード [mainly BRIT 主に英国英語; AM cord 米国英
語 cord] ③ to **flex** your **muscles** → see **muscle**

| **Word Link** | ible ≈ able to be : *audible, flexible, possible* |

flex|ible /fléksɪbəl/ ① ADJ 形容詞 A **flexible** object or material
can be bent easily without breaking. 柔軟な □ *...brushes with long,
flexible bristles.* 毛が長くて柔軟なブラシ ●**flexi|bil|ity** /fléksɪbɪliti/
N-UNCOUNT 不可算名詞 柔軟性 □ *The flexibility of the lens decreases
with age; it is therefore common for our sight to worsen as we get older.* 水
晶体の柔軟性は年齢に伴って低下する. したがって, 加齢すると視力が
落ちるのが普通なことだ. ② ADJ 形容詞 Something or someone
that is **flexible** is able to change easily and adapt to different
conditions and circumstances as they occur. 臨機応変な, 融通
の利く [APPROVAL 賛成] □ *...flexible working hours.* 自由勤務時間制
●**flexi|bil|ity** N-UNCOUNT 不可算名詞 順応性 □ *The flexibility
of distance learning would be particularly suited to busy managers.* 通
信教育は融通が利くので, 特に多忙な管理職の人々に適しているでし
ょう.

flex|time /flékstaɪm/ also **flexitime** N-UNCOUNT 不可算名詞
Flextime is a system that allows employees to vary the time that
they start or finish work, provided that an agreed total number of
hours are spent at work. 自由勤務時間制 [BUSINESS 実業] □ *I have
recently introduced flextime for all my staff.* 私は最近全職員に自由勤務
時間制を導入した.

flick /flík/ (**flicks, flicking, flicked**) ① V-T/V-I 他動詞/自動詞 If
something **flicks** in a particular direction, or if someone **flicks** it,
it moves with a short, sudden movement. ピシッとはじく [他動詞],
さっと動く [自動詞] □ *His tongue flicked across his lips.* 彼は舌で唇をす
っとなめた. □ *He flicked his cigarette out of the window.* 彼はたばこを
窓からさっと投げ出した. ● N-COUNT 可算名詞 さっと動かすこと □ *...a flick of a paintbrush.* 絵筆の一振り ② V-T 他動詞
If you **flick** something away, or off something else, you remove it
with a quick movement of your hand or finger. さっと払いのける
□ *Shirley flicked a piece of lint from the sleeve of her black suit.* シャーリ
ーは黒いスーツの袖から糸くずをさっと払いのけた. ③ V-T 他動詞 If
you **flick** something such as a whip or a towel, or **flick** something
with it, you hold one end of it and move your hand quickly up and
then forward, so that the other end moves. (むち・タオルなどを)
バシッと振る □ *She sighed and flicked a dishcloth at the counter.* 彼女は
ため息をつき, カウンターをタオルでさっと拭いた. ● N-COUNT 可算
名詞 **Flick** is also a noun. 軽い一振り □ *...a flick of the whip.* むちの
軽い一振り ④ V-T 他動詞 If you **flick** a switch, or **flick** an electrical
appliance on or off, you press the switch sharply so that it moves
into a different position and works the equipment. (スイッチ・
電源ボタンを) パチンと押す □ *Sam was flicking a flashlight on and off.*
サムは懐中電灯をパチパチとつけたり消したりしていた. ⑤ V-I 自
動詞 If you **flick through** a book or magazine, you turn its pages
quickly, for example, to get a general idea of its contents or to look
for a particular item. If you **flick through** television channels,
you continually change channels very quickly, usually using a
remote control. さっと目を通す, (チャンネルを) パチパチ変える
□ *She was flicking through some magazines on a table.* 彼女はテーブルの
上の数冊の雑誌にさっと目を通していた. ● N-SING 単数名詞 **Flick** is
also a noun. さっと目を通すこと, チャンネルをパチパチ変えること
□ *I thought I'd have a quick flick through some recent issues.* 私は最近の
いくつかの問題についてさっと目を通そうと思った.

flick|er /flíkər/ (**flickers, flickering, flickered**) V-I 自動詞 If
a light or flame **flickers**, it shines unsteadily. ちらちらする
□ *Fluorescent lights flickered, and then the room was blindingly bright.*
蛍光灯がちかちかし, そして部屋が目がくらむほど明るくなった.
● N-COUNT 可算名詞 **Flicker** is also a noun. ちらつき □ *Looking*

through the window I saw the flicker of flames. 窓から眺めると，炎がちらついているのが見えた.

flight /flaɪt/ (**flights**) **1** N-COUNT 可算名詞 A **flight** is a trip made by flying, usually in an airplane. 飛行機の旅 □*The flight will take four hours.* 飛行機で4時間かかるだろう. **2** N-COUNT 可算名詞 You can refer to an airplane carrying passengers on a particular trip as a particular **flight**. 飛行便, フライト [also N num] □*BA flight 286 was two hours late.* 英国航空286便に2時間の遅れが出た. **3** N-COUNT 可算名詞 A **flight** of steps or stairs is a set of steps or stairs that lead from one level to another without changing direction. (階段) ひと続き □*We walked in silence up a flight of stairs and down a long corridor.* 私たちは黙って上の階まで階段を上り，長い廊下を歩いた. **4** N-UNCOUNT 不可算名詞 **Flight** is the action of flying, or the ability to fly. 飛行, 飛行能力 □*Supersonic flight could become a routine form of travel in the 21st century.* 超音速飛行が21世紀には日常的な旅行手段になる可能性があります. **5** N-UNCOUNT 不可算名詞 **Flight** is the act of running away from a dangerous or unpleasant situation or place. 逃亡 □*The family was often in flight, hiding out in friends' houses.* その家族はよく逃げ出して，友人たちの家に隠れていた.
→ see Word Web: **flight**
→ see **fly**

flight at|tend|ant (**flight attendants**) N-COUNT 可算名詞 On an airplane, the **flight attendants** are the people whose job is to take care of the passengers and serve their meals. 客室乗務員

flim|sy /flɪmzi/ (**flimsier, flimsiest**) **1** ADJ 形容詞 A **flimsy** object is weak because it is made of a weak material, or is badly made. もろい □*...a flimsy wooden door.* もろい木製の戸 **2** ADJ 形容詞 **Flimsy** cloth or clothing is thin and does not give much protection. 薄っぺらな □*...a very flimsy pink chiffon nightgown.* 非常に薄くてピンク色のシフォンの寝巻き **3** ADJ 形容詞 If you describe something such as evidence or an excuse as **flimsy**, you mean that it is not very good or convincing. 説得力がない, 薄弱な □*The charges were based on very flimsy evidence.* 告訴は非常にいいかげんな証拠に基づいていた.

flinch /flɪntʃ/ (**flinches, flinching, flinched**) **1** V-I 自動詞 If you **flinch**, you make a small sudden movement, especially when something surprises you or hurts you. ひるむ [usu neg] □*Leo stared back at him without flinching.* リオはひるみもせずに彼をにらみ返した. **2** V-I 自動詞 If you **flinch from** something unpleasant, you are unwilling to do it or think about it, or you avoid doing it. しり込みする，たじろぐ □*The world community should not flinch in the face of this challenge.* 国際社会はこのような難題に直面してたじろぐべきではない.

fling /flɪŋ/ (**flings, flinging, flung**) **1** V-T 他動詞 If you **fling** something somewhere, you throw it there using a lot of force. 投げつける □*The woman flung the cup at him.* その女は彼にカップを投げつけた. **2** V-T 他動詞 If you **fling yourself** somewhere, you move or jump there suddenly and with a lot of force. (身を) おどらせる □*He flung himself to the floor.* 彼は床に身を投げつけた. **3** V-T 他動詞 If you **fling** a part of your body in a particular direction, especially your arms or head, you move it there suddenly. さっと動かす □*She flung her arms around my neck and kissed me.* 彼女はいきなり両腕を僕の首に回して，キスをした. **4** V-T 他動詞 If you **fling** someone to the ground, you push them very roughly so that they fall over. 投げ倒す □*The youth got him by the front of his shirt and flung him to the ground.* その若者は彼のシャツを前からつかみ，地面に投げ倒した. **5** V-T 他動詞 If you **fling** something into a particular place or position, you put it there in a quick or angry way. 投げつける □*Peter flung his shoes into the corner.* ピーターは靴を隅に投げつけた. **6** V-T 他動詞 If you **fling yourself into** a particular activity, you do it with a lot of enthusiasm and energy. 精を出す，打ち込む □*She flung herself into her career.* 彼女は仕事に打ち込んだ. **7** **Fling** can be used instead of "throw" in many expressions that usually contain "throw." 投げる **8** N-COUNT 可算名詞 If two people have a **fling**, they have a brief sexual relationship. 浮気 [INFORMAL くだけた] □*She claims she had a brief fling with him 30 years ago.* 彼女は30年前に彼とちょっと浮気したと言っている.

flip /flɪp/ (**flips, flipping, flipped**) **1** V-T 他動詞 If you **flip** a device on or off, or if you **flip** a switch, you turn it on or off by pressing the switch quickly. (スイッチを) パチッと入れる・切

る □*He didn't flip on the headlights until he was two blocks away.* 彼は2街区先に行くまでヘッドライトをつけなかった. □*Then he walked out, flipping the lights off.* そして彼は電灯をパチッと消して，外に出た. **2** V-I 自動詞 If you **flip** through the pages of a book, for example, you quickly turn over the pages in order to find a particular one or to get an idea of the contents. パラパラめくる □*He was flipping through a magazine in the living room.* 彼は居間で雑誌をパラパラとめくっていた. **3** V-T/V-I 他動詞/自動詞 If something **flips** over, or if you **flip** it over or into a different position, it moves or is moved into a different position. ひっくり返す [他動詞]，ひっくり返る [自動詞] □*The plane then flipped over and burst into flames.* その飛行機はそのとき転覆し，炎上しました. **4** V-T 他動詞 If you **flip** something, especially a coin, you use your thumb to make it turn over and over, as it goes through the air. はじき飛ばす □*I pulled a coin from my pocket and flipped it.* 私はポケットからコインを出して，はじき飛ばした.

flip|chart /flɪptʃɑrt/ (**flipcharts**) N-COUNT 可算名詞 A **flipchart** is a stand with large sheets of paper which is used when presenting information at a meeting. フリップチャート □*There are three conference rooms each of which is equipped with a screen, flipchart and audio visual equipment.* 会議室は3室あり，それぞれにスクリーン，フリップチャート，視聴覚設備が備えられている.

flirt /flɜrt/ (**flirts, flirting, flirted**) **1** V-RECIP 相互動詞 If you **flirt with** someone, you behave as if you are sexually attracted to them, in a playful or not very serious way. いちゃつく □*Dad's flirting with all the ladies, or they're all flirting with him, as usual.* いつものように親父は女の性たちみんなといちゃついている. あるいは女性たちがみんな親父といちゃついていると言うべきか. ● **flir|ta|tion** /flɜrteɪᵊn/ (**flirtations**) N-VAR 可変性名詞 [oft N 'with' n] いちゃつき，もてあそぶこと □*She was aware of his attempts at flirtation.* 彼女は彼がもてあそぼうとしていることに気づいていた. **2** N-COUNT 可算名詞 Someone who is a **flirt** likes to flirt a lot. 浮気者 □*I've always been a real flirt, I had a different boyfriend every week.* 私はいつも全くの浮気者であって，週ごとに別の彼氏がいた. **3** V-I 自動詞 If you **flirt with** something, you consider it but do not do anything about it. 考えをもてあそぶ，ぼうっと考える □*My mother used to flirt with Anarchism.* 私の母は以前無政府主義に少しかぶれた. ● **flir|ta|tion** N-VAR 可変性名詞 一時的な関心 □*...the party's brief flirtation with economic liberalism.* その党が経済的自由主義と一時的に関わったこと

flit /flɪt/ (**flits, flitting, flitted**) **1** V-I 自動詞 If you **flit around** or **flit** between one place and another, you go to lots of places without staying for very long in any of them. あちこち渡り歩く □*Laura flits about New York hailing taxis at every opportunity.* ローラは機会があるごとにタクシーを呼んでニューヨーク市内をあちこち行く. **2** V-I 自動詞 If someone **flits from** one thing or situation to another, they move or turn their attention from one to the other very quickly. 気が変わる □*He's prone to flit between subjects with amazing ease.* 彼はいとも簡単に話題を変える傾向がある. **3** V-I 自動詞 If something such as a bird or a bat **flits** quickly from one place to another. すいすい飛び回る □*...the parrot that flits from tree to tree.* 木から木へと飛び回るオウム

float /floʊt/ (**floats, floating, floated**) **1** V-T/V-I 他動詞/自動詞 If something or someone is **floating** in a liquid, they are in the liquid, on or just below the surface, and are being supported by it. You can also **float** something on a liquid. 浮かべる [他動詞]，浮かぶ [自動詞] □*They noticed fifty and twenty dollar bills floating in the water.* 彼らは50ドル札と20ドル札が水に浮かんでいるのに気づいた. □*It's below freezing and small icebergs are floating by.* 気温は氷点下で，そばに小さな氷山が浮かんでいる. **2** V-I 自動詞 Something that **floats** lies on or just below the surface of a liquid when it is put in it and does not sink. (液体中で) 浮く □*They will also float if you drop them in the water.* これらも水に落とすと浮くでしょう. **3** V-I 自動詞 Something that **floats** in or through the air hangs in it or moves slowly and gently through it. 空に浮かぶ □*The white cloud of smoke floated away.* 白い煙の雲が漂い去った. **4** V-T 他動詞 If you **float** a project, plan, or idea, you suggest it for others to think about. 提案する □*The French had floated the idea of placing the diplomatic work in the hands of the UN.* フランス国民は外交業務を国連に移行させるという案を持ち出していた. **5** V-T 他動詞 If a company director **floats** their company, they start to sell shares in it to the

Word Web   **flight**

In order for an airplane to **fly**, it must overcome the force of **gravity** and also move forward through the air. The **propellers** or **jet engines** provide the **thrust** that helps the plane move ahead. This force is opposed by the **drag** on the wings as they encounter **air resistance**. The upper part of the wing is **curved**, which reduces the **air pressure** over it. This airflow over the wing provides the **lift** that allows the plane to rise from the ground.

public. 株式を公開する [BUSINESS 実業] ❑*He floated his firm on the stock market.* 彼は自分の会社の株式を証券市場に公開した. ⑥ V-T/V-I 他動詞/自動詞 If a government **floats** its country's currency or allows it to **float**, it allows the currency's value to change freely in relation to other currencies. 変動相場制にする [他動詞], 変動する [自動詞] [BUSINESS 実業] ❑*On January 15th Brazil was forced to float its currency.* 1月15日にブラジルはその通貨を変動相場制に移行せざるを得なかった. ⑦ N-COUNT 可算名詞 A **float** is a light object that is used to help someone or something float. 浮き輪, ビート板 ❑*Floats will provide confidence in the water.* 浮き輪を使用することによって水中での自信がつくでしょう. ⑧ N-COUNT 可算名詞 A **float** is a small object attached to a fishing line which floats on the water and moves when a fish has been caught. 浮き ⑨ N-COUNT 可算名詞 A **float** is a truck on which displays and people in special costumes are carried in a parade. 山車, パレードカー ❑*...a procession of makeshift floats bearing loudspeakers and banners.* スピーカーを設置し横断幕を張った間に合わせのパレードカーの行列

flock /flɒk/ (**flocks, flocking, flocked**) ① N-COUNT-COLL 集合可算名詞 A **flock** of birds, sheep, or goats is a group of them. (鳥・ヒツジ・ヤギなどの) 群れ ❑*They kept a small flock of sheep.* 彼らは小規模に牧羊していました. ② N-COUNT-COLL 集合可算名詞 You can refer to a group of people or things as a **flock** of them to emphasize that there are a lot of them. (人の) 群れ (物が) たくさん [EMPHASIS 強調] ❑*These cases all attracted flocks of famous writers.* これらの事件はすべて多くの有名な作家を引きつけた. ③ V-I 自動詞 If people **flock to** a particular place or event, a very large number of them go there, usually because it is pleasant or interesting. 押し寄せる ❑*The public has flocked to the show.* 一般の人々がそのショーを見に押し寄せた. ❑*The criticisms will not stop people flocking to see the film.* それらの批評のせいで人々がその映画を見に詰めかけるのを止めたりはしないだろう.

flog /flɒg/ (**flogs, flogging, flogged**) V-T 他動詞 If someone **is flogged**, they are hit very hard with a whip or stick as a punishment. (むち・棒で) 強く打つ ❑*In these places people starved, were flogged, were clubbed to death.* これらの地域では人々は餓え死にし, むちやこん棒で打ち殺された. ●**flog|ging** (**floggings**) N-VAR 可変性名詞 むち打ち ❑*He gets dragged off to court and sentenced to a flogging and life imprisonment.* 彼は裁判所に引きずり出され, むち打ちの刑と終身刑を言い渡される.

flood /flʌd/ (**floods, flooding, flooded**) ① N-VAR 可変性名詞 If there is a **flood**, a large amount of water covers an area which is usually dry, for example, when a river flows over its banks or a pipe bursts. 洪水 ❑*More than 70 people were killed in the floods, caused when a dam burst.* ダムの決壊による洪水で70名以上が死亡しました. ❑*This is the type of flood dreaded by cavers.* これは洞くつ探険家が恐れていたたぐいの洪水だ. ② V-T/V-I 他動詞/自動詞 If something such as a river or a burst pipe **floods** an area that is usually dry or if the area **floods**, it becomes covered with water. 水浸しにする [他動詞], 水浸しになる [自動詞] ❑*The kitchen flooded.* 台所が水浸しになった. ③ V-I 自動詞 If a river **floods**, it overflows, especially after very heavy rain. 氾濫 (はんらん) する ❑*...the relentless rain that caused twenty rivers to flood.* 20の川の氾濫を引き起こした容赦ない雨 ④ V-I 自動詞 If you say that people or things **flood** into a place, you are emphasizing that they arrive there in large numbers. 殺到する [EMPHASIS 強調] ❑*Large numbers of immigrants flooded into the area.* 大勢の移民がその地域に押し寄せた. ❑*Inquiries flooded in from all over the world.* 世界中から問い合わせが殺到した. ⑤ V-T 他動詞 If you **flood** a place **with** a particular type of thing, or if a particular type of thing **floods** a place, the place becomes full of so many of them that it cannot hold or deal with any more. 氾濫させる, いっぱいにする ❑*Manufacturers are destroying American jobs by flooding the market with cheap imports.* 製造業者は米国市場を安価な輸入品であふれさせて米国内の雇用を破壊している. ⑥ N-COUNT 可算名詞 If you say that a **flood** of people or things arrive somewhere, you are emphasizing that a very large number of them arrive there. 殺到 [EMPHASIS 強調] ❑*The administration is trying to stem the flood of refugees out of Haiti and into Florida.* 政府はハイチからフロリダ州への避難民の殺到を食い止めようとしている.
→ see **disaster**

flood|ing /flʌdɪŋ/ N-UNCOUNT 不可算名詞 If **flooding** occurs, an area of land that is usually dry is covered with water after heavy rain or after a river or lake flows over its banks. 洪水 ❑*The flooding, caused by three days of torrential rain, is the worst in sixty-five years.* 3日間に及ぶ豪雨によりもたらされた洪水は, 過去65年間で最悪である.
→ see **dam, storm**

flood|light /flʌdlaɪt/ (**floodlights, floodlighting, floodlit**) ① N-COUNT 可算名詞 **Floodlights** are very powerful lamps that are used outside to light public buildings, sports grounds, and other places at night. フラッドライト, 投光照明灯 ❑*A group of men were playing soccer under the glare of floodlights.* フラッドライトのまぶしい光の下で一群の男たちがサッカーをしていた. ② V-T 他動詞 If a building or place **is floodlit**, it is lit by floodlights. 投光照明で照らす ❑*In the evening the facade is floodlit.* 日が暮れると正面は投光照明で照らされる.

floor /flɔr/ (**floors, flooring, floored**) ① N-COUNT 可算名詞 The **floor** of a room is the part of it that you walk on. 床 ❑*Jack's sitting on the floor watching TV.* ジャックは床に座ってテレビを見ている. ② N-COUNT 可算名詞 A **floor** of a building is all the rooms that are on a particular level. 階 ❑*The café was on the top floor of the hospital.* その喫茶店は病院の最上階にあった.

> In North America, the **floor** at street level is the first floor and the next floor up is the second floor. In Britain, the floor at street level is the ground floor and the first floor is one floor up.

③ N-COUNT 可算名詞 The ocean **floor** is the ground at the bottom of an ocean. The valley **floor** is the ground at the bottom of a valley. 底 ❑*They spend hours feeding on the ocean floor.* それらは海底で何時間もえさを取り続ける. ④ N-COUNT 可算名詞 The place where official debates and discussions are held, especially between members of a legislature, is referred to as **the floor**. 議場 ❑*The issues were debated on the floor of the House.* それらの問題は下院の議場で議論された. ⑤ N-SING-COLL 集合的単数名詞 In a debate or discussion, **the floor** is the people who are listening to the arguments being put forward but who are not among the main speakers. 聴衆 ❑*The president is taking questions from the floor.* 大統領は聴衆からの質問に応じているところだ. ⑥ V-T 他動詞 If you **are floored by** something, you are unable to respond to it because you are so surprised by it. あぜんとさせる [usu passive] ❑*He was floored by the announcement.* 彼はその発表にあぜんとした. ⑦ → see also **floored, flooring, dance floor, first floor, ground floor, shop floor** ⑧ PHRASE 句 If someone **has the floor**, they are the person who is speaking in a debate or discussion. 発言権を持つ ❑*Since I have the floor for the moment, I want to go back to a previous point.* 差し当たり私に発言権があるので, 先ほどの話題に戻らせていただきます. ⑨ PHRASE 句 If you **take to the floor**, you start dancing at a dance or disco. 踊り始める ❑*The happy couple and their respective parents took to the floor.* 幸せそうな新郎新婦と両家の親がダンスを始めた. ⑩ PHRASE 句 If you **wipe the floor with** someone, you defeat them completely in a competition or discussion. こてんぱんにやっつける [INFORMAL くだけた] ❑*He could wipe the floor with the opposition.* 彼は相手をこてんぱんにやっつけることだってできるだろう.

Word Partnership   floor は次の語句と使われる:

V.	**fall on the** floor; **sit on the** floor; **sweep the** floor ①
N.	floor **to ceiling**, floor **space** ① floor **plan** ② **forest** floor, **ocean** floor ③

floor|board /flɔrbɔrd/ (**floorboards**) N-COUNT 可算名詞 **Floorboards** are the long pieces of wood that a wooden floor is made up of. 床板

floor|ing /flɔrɪŋ/ (**floorings**) N-MASS 質量名詞 **Flooring** is a material that is used to make the floor of a room. 床材 ❑*Quarry tiles are a popular kitchen flooring.* クォーリータイルは台所用の床材として人気がある.

flop /flɒp/ (**flops, flopping, flopped**) ① V-I 自動詞 If you **flop** into a chair, for example, you sit down suddenly and heavily because you are so tired. どさっと座る ❑*Bunbury flopped down upon the bed and rested his tired feet.* バンベリーはベッドにどさっと座り, 疲れた足を休めた. ② V-I 自動詞 If something **flops** onto something else, it falls there heavily or untidily. どさっと落ちる ❑*The briefcase flopped onto the desk.* 書類かばんがどさっと机に落ちた. ③ V-I 自動詞 If something **flops**, it is completely unsuccessful. 失敗する [INFORMAL くだけた] ❑*The film flopped badly at the box office.* その映画の興行成績はひどく悪かった. ④ N-COUNT 可算名詞 If something is a **flop**, it is completely unsuccessful. 失敗作 [INFORMAL くだけた] ❑*The film is the public who decide whether a film is a hit or a flop.* 映画がヒット作か失敗作かを決めるのは一般大衆だ.

flop|py /flɒpi/ ADJ 形容詞 Something that is **floppy** is loose rather than stiff, and tends to hang downward. くったりした ❑*...the girl with the floppy hat and glasses.* くったりした帽子をかぶって眼鏡を掛けた少女

flop|py disk (**floppy disks**) N-COUNT 可算名詞 A **floppy disk** is a small magnetic disk that is used for storing computer data and programs. Floppy disks are used especially with personal computers. フロッピーディスク

Word Link   flor ≈ flower : flora, floral, florist

flo|ra /flɔrə/ N-UNCOUNT-COLL 集合的不可算名詞 You can refer to plants as **flora**, especially the plants growing in a particular area. 植物, 植物相 [FORMAL 形式ばった] ❑*...the variety of food crops and flora which now exists in Dominica.* ドミニカに現在生存する多種の食用作物と植物相

flo|ral /flɔrəl/ ① ADJ 形容詞 A **floral** fabric or design has flowers

Word Web flower

People love **flowers** because they are **colorful** and they smell good. But the **color** and **scent** of flowers are also important in **reproduction**. Sometimes the wind helps pollinate a plant. However, most plants must attract **insects**, hummingbirds, or **bats** to guarantee **fertilization**. If this doesn't happen, no **seeds** form. As one of these creatures lands on a flower, **grains** of pollen stick to its body. It carries these to another flower. Different colors attract different insects and animals. Yellow and blue flowers seem to draw **bees** and **butterflies**. Red flowers attract hummingbirds. At night, **bats** seek out white flowers.

on it. 花柄の □…a bright yellow floral fabric. 鮮やかな黄色の花柄の布 ② ADJ 形容詞 You can use **floral** to describe something that contains flowers or is made of flowers. 花の [ADJ n] □…eye-catching floral arrangements. 人目を引く生け花

flo|rist /flɔ́rɪst/ (**florists**) ① N-COUNT 可算名詞 A **florist** is a storekeeper who arranges and sells flowers and sells houseplants. 花屋の店主 ② N-COUNT 可算名詞 A **florist** or a **florist's** is a store where flowers and houseplants are sold. 花屋 □ He bought her some roses at the florist's in the mall. モールの花屋で彼女にバラの花を買った.

flo|ta|tion /floʊtéɪʃ⁰n/ (**flotations**) N-VAR 可変性名詞 The **flotation** of a company is the selling of shares in it to the public. 株式の売り出し [BUSINESS 実業] □ Prudential's flotation is the third largest this year, behind Kraft Foods and Agere Systems. プルデンシャル社の株式の売出しはクラフト・フーズ社, アギア・システムズ社に次いで今年3番目の規模となるである.

floun|der /floʊ́ndər/ (**flounders, floundering, floundered**) ① V-I 自動詞 If something **is floundering**, it has many problems and may soon fail completely. □ What a pity that his career was left to flounder. 彼の仕事がうまく行かない状態に残されたのは何と残念なことだ. ② V-I 自動詞 If you say that someone **is floundering**, you are criticizing them for not making decisions or for not knowing what to say or do. まごつく [DISAPPROVAL 不賛成] □ Right now, you've got a president who's floundering, trying to find some way to get his campaign jump-started. 今, 選挙運動に活を入れる方法をなんとか見つけようとしてまごついている大統領がいるわけだ. ③ V-I 自動詞 If you **flounder** in water or mud, you move in an uncontrolled way, trying not to sink. もがく □ Three men were floundering about in the water. 3人の男が水の中でもがきまわっていた.

flour /flaʊ́ər/ (**flours**) N-MASS 質量名詞 **Flour** is a white or brown powder that is made by grinding grain. It is used to make bread, cakes, and pastry. 小麦粉
→ see **grain**

flour|ish /flə́rɪʃ/ (**flourishes, flourishing, flourished**) ① V-I 自動詞 If something **flourishes**, it is successful, active, or common, and developing quickly and strongly. 栄える □ Business flourished and within six months they were earning 18,000 roubles a day. 事業は栄え6か月以内に1日当たり1万8千ルーブルの収益を上げていた. ●**flour|ish|ing** ADJ 形容詞 栄えている □ Boston quickly became a flourishing port. ボストンはすぐに栄えた港になった. ② V-I 自動詞 If a plant or animal **flourishes**, it grows well or is healthy because the conditions are right for it. 繁茂する, 繁殖する □ The plant flourishes particularly well in slightly harsher climes. その植物は少しより厳しい気候下で特に良く繁茂する. ●**flour|ish|ing** ADJ 形容詞 繁茂している, 繁殖している □…a flourishing fox population. 繁殖しているキツネの集団. ③ V-T 他動詞 If you **flourish** an object, you wave it about in a way that makes people notice it. 振り回す □ He flourished the glass to emphasize the point. 彼はそれを強調するためにグラスを振り回した. ●**Flourish** is also a noun. 派手な身ぶり □ He took his cap from under his arm with a flourish and pulled it low over his eyes. 彼は小脇に抱えていた帽子を派手な身ぶりで手にとり, 目を深くかぶった.

flout /flaʊ́t/ (**flouts, flouting, flouted**) V-T 他動詞 If you **flout** something such as a law, an order, or an accepted way of behaving, you deliberately do not obey it or follow it. ばかにする, 無視する □…illegal campers who persist in flouting the law. 法律を無視し続ける違法キャンプ生活者.

flow /floʊ́/ (**flows, flowing, flowed**) ① V-I 自動詞 If a liquid, gas, or electrical current **flows** somewhere, it moves there steadily and continuously. 流れる □ A stream flowed gently down into the valley. 小川はゆっくり谷へと流れた. □ The current flows into electric motors that drive the wheels. 電流が車輪を駆動する電動機に流れ込む. ●N-VAR 可変性名詞 **Flow** is also a noun. 流れ □ It works only in the veins, where the blood flow is slower. これは静脈でのみ正しく機能する. そこでは血流がより遅いからだ. ② V-I 自動詞 If a number of people or things **flow** from one place to another, they move there steadily in large groups, usually without stopping. 流出する □ Large numbers of refugees continue to flow from the troubled region

into the no-man's land. 紛争地域から多数の難民が無人地帯に流出し続けている. ●N-VAR 可変性名詞 **Flow** is also a noun. 流れ □ She watched the frantic flow of cars and buses along the street. 彼女は通りの車やバスのあわただしい流れを見つめた. ③ V-I 自動詞 If information or money **flows** somewhere, it moves freely between people or organizations. 流れ出る □ A lot of this information flowed through other police departments. この情報の大部分が他の警察署から流出しました. ●N-VAR 可変性名詞 **Flow** is also a noun. 流れ □…the opportunity to control the flow of information. 情報の流れを管理する好機. ④ → see also **cash flow** ⑤ PHRASE 句 If you say that an activity, or the person who is performing the activity, is in **full flow**, you mean that the activity has started and is being carried out with a great deal of energy and enthusiasm. 真っ盛り □ Lunch at Harry's Bar was in full flow when Irene made a splendid entrance. アイリーンが華麗に登場した時には, ハリーズ・バーは昼食の真っ盛りであった.
→ see **ocean, traffic**

flow chart (**flow charts**) N-COUNT 可算名詞 A **flow chart** or a **flow diagram** is a diagram which represents the sequence of actions in a particular process or activity. 流れ図 □ This flow chart, shown below, summarizes the overall costing process. 下記の流れ図に全部の見積もりの概要を示す.

flow|er /flaʊ́ər/ (**flowers, flowering, flowered**) ① N-COUNT 可算名詞 A **flower** is the part of a plant which is often brightly colored, grows at the end of a stem, and only survives for a short time. 花 □ Each individual flower is tiny. 個々の花はとても小さい. ② N-COUNT 可算名詞 A **flower** is a stem of a plant that has one or more flowers on it and has been picked, usually with others, for example, to give as a present or to put in a vase. 切り花 □…a bunch of flowers sent by a new admirer. 新しいファンから贈られた花束. ③ N-COUNT 可算名詞 **Flowers** are small plants that are grown for their flowers as opposed to trees, shrubs, and vegetables. 草花 □…a lawned area surrounded by screening plants and flowers. 仕切りになっている草木や草花で囲まれた芝地. ④ V-I 自動詞 When a plant or tree **flowers**, its flowers appear and open. 咲く □ Several of these rhododendrons will flower this year for the first time. これらのシャクナゲのいくつかが今年初めて咲くだろう. ⑤ V-I 自動詞 When something **flowers**, for example, a political movement or a relationship, it gets stronger and more successful. 栄える □ Their relationship flowered. 彼らの関係は栄えた.
→ see Word Web: **flower**

<table>
<tr><td colspan="2">Word Partnership flower は次の語句と使われる:</td></tr>
<tr><td>V.</td><td>**pick a** flower ②</td></tr>
<tr><td>N.</td><td>flower **arrangement**, flower **garden**, flower **shop**, flower **show** ② ③</td></tr>
<tr><td>ADJ.</td><td>**dried** flower, **fresh** flower ② ③</td></tr>
</table>

flow|er|ing /flaʊ́ərɪŋ/ ① N-UNCOUNT 不可算名詞 The **flowering** of something such as an idea or artistic style is the development of its popularity and success. 開花 □ He may be happy with the flowering of new thinking, but he has yet to contribute much to it himself. 彼は新しい思想の開花に満足しているかもしれないが, 彼自身はまだそれに大いに貢献しなくてはならない. 開花 ② ADJ 形容詞 **Flowering** shrubs, trees, or plants are those which produce noticeable flowers. 花の咲く [ADJ n] □…a late summer flowering plant like an aster. アスターのような夏の終わりに花の咲く植物

flown /floʊ́n/ **Flown** is the past participle of **fly**. fly の過去分詞

flu /flúː/ N-UNCOUNT 不可算名詞 **Flu** is an illness which is similar to a bad cold but more serious. It often makes you feel very weak and makes your muscles hurt. インフルエンザ [also 'the' N] □ I got the flu. 私はインフルエンザにかかった.

fluc|tu|ate /flʌ́ktʃueɪt/ (**fluctuates, fluctuating, fluctuated**) V-I 自動詞 If something **fluctuates**, it changes a lot in an irregular way. 変動する □ Body temperature can fluctuate if you are ill. 病気のときは体温が上下することがある. ●**fluc|tua|tion** /flʌ̀ktʃueɪʃ⁰n/ (**fluctuations**) N-VAR 可変性名詞 変動 □ Don't worry about tiny fluctuations in your weight. 体重のわずかな変動は気にするな.

flu|ent /flˈuːənt/ 🔢 ADJ 形容詞 Someone who is **fluent in** a particular language can speak the language easily and correctly. You can also say that someone speaks **fluent** French, Chinese, or some other language. 流暢(りゅうちょう)な □ *She studied eight foreign languages but is fluent in only six of them.* 彼女は外国語を8か国語習ったが, 流暢なのはそのうち6か国語だけである. ● **flu|en|cy** N-UNCOUNT 不可算名詞 流暢 □ *To work as a translator, you need fluency in at least one foreign language.* 翻訳家として仕事をするには, たんのうな外国語が最低1つは必要であある. ● **flu|ent|ly** ADV 副詞 流暢に □ *He spoke three languages fluently.* 彼は3か国語を流暢に話した. 🔢 ADJ 形容詞 If your speech, reading, or writing is **fluent**, you speak, read, or write easily, smoothly, and clearly with no mistakes. 雄弁な, よどみのない □ *He had emerged from being a hesitant and unsure candidate into a fluent debater.* 彼はためらいがちで自信のない候補だったのが, 雄弁な討論者となっていた. ● **flu|en|cy** N-UNCOUNT 不可算名詞 雄弁 □ *His son was praised for speeches of remarkable fluency.* 彼の息子は並外れて雄弁な演説を褒められた. ● **flu|ent|ly** ADV 副詞 [ADV with v] 雄弁に, すらすらと □ *Alex didn't read fluently till he was nearly seven.* アレックスは7歳近くになるまですらすらと読めなかった.

fluff /flˈʌf/ (**fluffs, fluffing, fluffed**) 🔢 N-UNCOUNT 不可算名詞 **Fluff** consists of soft threads or fibers in the form of small, light balls or lumps. For example, you can refer to the fur of a small animal as **fluff**. ふわふわしたもの □ *The nest contained two chicks: just small gray balls of fluff.* 巣にはひなが2羽いた. ちょうど小さな灰色の綿毛の玉のようだった. 🔢 V-T 他動詞 If you **fluff** something that you are trying to do, you are unsuccessful or you do it badly. しくじる [INFORMAL くだけた] □ *She fluffed her interview at Harvard.* 彼女はハーバード大の面接でしくじった.

fluffy /flˈʌfi/ (**fluffier, fluffiest**) 🔢 ADJ 形容詞 If you describe something such as a towel or a toy animal as **fluffy**, you mean that it is very soft. ふわふわの □ *...fluffy white towels.* ふわふわの白いタオル 🔢 ADJ 形容詞 A cake or other food that is **fluffy** is very light because it has a lot of air in it. ふわふわした □ *Cream together the margarine and sugar with a wooden spoon until light and fluffy.* 軽くふわふわしたクリーム状になるまで, マーガリンと砂糖を木のスプーンで混ぜ合わせなさい.

flu|id /flˈuːɪd/ (**fluids**) 🔢 N-MASS 質量名詞 A **fluid** is a liquid. 液体 [FORMAL 形式ばった] □ *The blood vessels may leak fluid, which distorts vision.* 血管から液体が漏れ出すことがあり, それが視野をゆがめる. □ *Make sure that you drink plenty of fluids.* 必ずたくさん飲み物を摂取するようにしなさい. 🔢 ADJ 形容詞 **Fluid** movements or lines or designs are smooth and graceful. 流れるような □ *His painting became less illustrational and more fluid.* 彼の油絵はイラスト調ではなくなり, もっと流れるようになった.

fluke /flˈuːk/ (**flukes**) N-COUNT 可算名詞 If you say that something good is a **fluke**, you mean that it happened accidentally rather than by being planned or arranged. まぐれ当たり [INFORMAL くだけた] [usu sing, also 'by' n] □ *The discovery was something of a fluke.* その発見はまぐれ当たりみたいなものであった.

flung /flˈʌŋ/ **Flung** is the past tense and past participle of **fling**. flingの過去・過去分詞

flunk /flˈʌŋk/ (**flunks, flunking, flunked**) V-T 他動詞 If you **flunk** an exam or a course, you fail to reach the required standard. 落第する [mainly AM 主に米国英語, INFORMAL くだけた] □ *Your son is upset because he flunked a history exam.* あなたの息子は歴史の試験に落ちて動転している.

▶ **flunk out** PHRASAL VERB 句動詞 If you **flunk out**, you are dismissed from a school or college because your grades are not satisfactory. 成績不良で退学になる [mainly AM 主に米国英語, INFORMAL くだけた] □ *He flunked out, a school official told CNN.* 彼は退学になったと学校側はCNNに伝えた. □ *If he doesn't find a solution to his problem soon, he'll surely flunk out of college.* 彼は早く自分の問題の解決策を見つけないと, 大学退学は確実だろう.

fluo|res|cent /flʊərˈesᵊnt/ 🔢 ADJ 形容詞 A **fluorescent** surface, substance, or color has a very bright appearance when light is directed onto it, as if it is actually shining itself. 蛍光性の □ *...a piece of fluorescent tape.* 1片の蛍光テープ 🔢 ADJ 形容詞 A **fluorescent** light shines with a very hard, bright light and is usually in the form of a long strip. 蛍光の □ *Fluorescent lights flickered, and then the room was brilliantly, blindingly bright.* 蛍光灯がちらついたあと, 部屋はあかあかと目がくらむほどに明るくなった.
→ see **light**

fluo|ride /flˈʊəraɪd/ N-UNCOUNT 不可算名詞 **Fluoride** is a mixture of chemicals that is sometimes added to drinking water and toothpaste because it is considered to be good for people's teeth. フッ化物
→ see **teeth**

flur|ry /flˈɜːri/ (**flurries**) 🔢 N-COUNT 可算名詞 A **flurry** of something such as activity or excitement is a short intense period of it. 慌ただしさ, ろうばい □ *...a flurry of diplomatic activity aimed at ending the war.* 戦争を終わらせるための慌ただしい外交活動 🔢 N-COUNT 可算名詞 A **flurry** of something such as snow is a

small amount of it that suddenly appears for a short time and moves in a quick, swirling way. にわか雪 □ *The Alps expect heavy cloud over the weekend with light snow flurries and strong winds.* この週末のアルプスは厚い雲に覆われ, 軽いにわか雪と強風が予測されている.

flush /flˈʌʃ/ (**flushes, flushing, flushed**) 🔢 V-I 自動詞 If you **flush**, your face gets red because you are hot or ill, or because you are feeling a strong emotion such as embarrassment or anger. ほてる, 顔を赤くする □ *Do you sweat a lot or flush a lot?* 汗をたくさんかいたり, 顔赤にほてったりしますか. ● N-COUNT 可算名詞 **Flush** is also a noun. ほてり, 紅潮 □ *There was a slight flush on his cheeks.* 彼はわずかにほおを赤らめた. ● **flushed** ADJ 形容詞 紅潮した □ *Her face was flushed with anger.* 彼女は怒りで顔を真っ赤にしていた. 🔢 V-T/V-I 他動詞/自動詞 When someone **flushes** a toilet after using it, they fill the toilet bowl with water in order to clean it, usually by pressing a handle or pulling a chain. You can also say that a toilet **flushes**. 流す, 流れる □ *She flushed the toilet and went back in the bedroom.* 彼女はトイレを流して寝室に戻った. ● N-COUNT 可算名詞 **Flush** is also a noun. 流すこと □ *He heard the flush of a toilet.* 彼にはトイレを流す音が聞こえた. 🔢 V-T 他動詞 If you **flush** something **down** the toilet, you get rid of it by putting it into the toilet bowl and flushing the toilet. 流して捨てる □ *He was found trying to flush the pills down the toilet.* 彼はトイレに錠剤を流して捨てようとしているところを見つかった. 🔢 V-T 他動詞 If you **flush** a part of your body, you clean it or make it healthier by using a large amount of liquid to get rid of dirt or harmful substances. 洗い流す □ *Flush the eye with clean cold water for at least 15 minutes.* きれいな冷水で目を最低15分間洗い流しなさい. ● PHRASAL VERB 句動詞 **Flush out** means the same as **flush**. 洗い流す □ *...an "alternative" therapy that gently flushes out the colon to remove toxins.* 大腸をゆっくり洗い流して毒素を取り除く, いわゆる代替療法 🔢 V-T 他動詞 If you **flush** dirt or a harmful substance **out** of a place, you get rid of it by using a large amount of liquid. 洗い流す □ *That won't flush out all the sewage, but it should unclog some stinking drains.* あれではすべての下水は洗い流せないが, 悪臭を放っている下水管の流れはある程度良くなるだろう. 🔢 V-T 他動詞 If you **flush** people or animals **out** of a place where they are hiding, you find or capture them by forcing them to come out of that place. 追い出す □ *They flushed them out of their hiding places.* 彼らは隠場から彼らを追い出しました.
→ see **plumbing**

Word Partnership	*flush* は次の語句と使われる:
ADJ.	**slight** flush 🔢
N.	**someone's** face flushes, flush **of** embarrassment 🔢 flush **a toilet** 🔢

flushed /flˈʌʃt/ ADJ 形容詞 If you say that someone is **flushed with** success or pride you mean that they are very excited by their success or pride. 意気揚々として [v-link ADJ 'with' n] □ *Grace was flushed with the success of the venture.* グレースは投機的事業の成功に意気揚々としていた.

flus|ter /flˈʌstər/ (**flusters, flustering, flustered**) V-T 他動詞 If you **fluster** someone, you make them feel nervous and confused by rushing them and preventing them from concentrating on what they are doing. 慌てさせる □ *The General refused to be flustered.* 将軍は断固として動じなかった. ● **flus|tered** ADJ 形容詞 慌てて □ *She was so flustered that she forgot her reply.* 彼女はとても慌てていて返事をするのを忘れた.

flute /flˈuːt/ (**flutes**) N-VAR 可変性名詞 A **flute** is a musical instrument of the woodwind family. You play it by blowing over a hole near one end while holding it sideways to your mouth. フルート
→ see **orchestra**

flut|ter /flˈʌtər/ (**flutters, fluttering, fluttered**) 🔢 V-T/V-I 他動詞/自動詞 If something thin or light **flutters**, or if you **flutter** it, it moves up and down or from side to side with a lot of quick, light movements. はためく, ひらひらと翻す □ *Her chiffon skirt was fluttering in the night breeze.* 彼女のシフォンのスカートが夜風に翻っていた. □ *...a butterfly fluttering its wings.* 羽ばたきをしている蝶. ● N-COUNT 可算名詞 **Flutter** is also a noun. 羽ばたき, ひらひらさせること □ *...a flutter of white cloth.* ひらひらと翻る白い布. 🔢 V-I 自動詞 If something light such as a small bird or a piece of paper **flutters** somewhere, it moves through the air with small quick movements. ひらひらと飛ぶ □ *The paper fluttered to the floor.* 紙が床にひらひらと落ちた.

flux /flˈʌks/ N-UNCOUNT 不可算名詞 If something is in **a** state of **flux**, it is constantly changing. 不安定 □ *Education remains in a state of flux which will take some time to settle down.* 教育は不安定な状態にあり, 落ち着くのには多少の時間がかかるでしょう.

fly /flˈaɪ/ (**flies, flying, flew, flown**) 🔢 N-COUNT 可算名詞 A **fly** is a small insect with two wings. There are many kinds of flies, and the most common are black in color. ハエ □ *Flies buzzed at the animals' swishing tails.* その動物たちの振っているしっぽにハエ

Word Web　fly

About 500 years ago, Leonardo da Vinci* designed some simple flying machines. His sketches look a lot like modern **parachutes** and **helicopters**. About 300 years later, the Montgolfier Brothers amazed the king of France with **hot-air balloon** flights. Soon inventors in many countries began experimenting with blimps, hang gliders, and human-powered **aircraft**. Most inventors tried to imitate the **flight** of birds. Then in 1903, the Wright brothers invented the first true **airplane**. Their gasoline-powered **craft** carried one **passenger**. The trip lasted 59 seconds. And amazingly, 70 years later **jumbo jets** carrying 400 passengers became an everyday occurrence.

Leonardo da Vinci (1452-1519): an Italian artist.

が飛び交った. **2** N-COUNT 可算名詞 The front opening on a pair of pants is referred to as the **fly**. It usually consists of a zipper or row of buttons behind a band of cloth. ズボンの前開き ❏ *I'm the kind of person who checks to see if my fly is undone.* 私はズボンの前が開いていないかちゃんと確認するような男です. **3** V-I 自動詞 When something such as a bird, insect, or aircraft **flies**, it moves through the air. 飛ぶ ❏ *The planes flew through the clouds.* 飛行機は雲の中を飛んだ. **4** V-I 自動詞 If you **fly** somewhere, you travel there in an aircraft. 飛行機で飛ぶ ❏ *He flew to Los Angeles.* 彼はロサンジェルスに飛んだ. ❏ *He flew back to London.* 彼はロンドンに飛行機で帰った. **5** V-T/V-I 他動詞/自動詞 When someone **flies** an aircraft, they control its movement in the air. 飛ばす, 操縦する [他動詞], 飛行機を操縦する [自動詞] ❏ *Parker had successfully flown both aircraft.* パーカーは両方の航空機の操縦に成功していた. ❏ *He flew a small plane to Cuba.* 彼は小型飛行機をキューバまで操縦した. ❏ *I learned to fly in Vietnam.* 私はベトナムで飛行機の操縦を習った. ●**flying** N-UNCOUNT 不可算名詞 飛行 ❏ *...a flying instructor.* 飛行教官. **6** V-T 他動詞 To **fly** someone or something somewhere means to take or send them there in an aircraft. 飛行機で運ぶ ❏ *It may be possible to fly the women and children out on Thursday.* 木曜に女性と子供たちを飛行機で送り出すことが可能かもしれません. **7** V-I 自動詞 If something such as your hair **is flying** about, it is moving about freely and loosely in the air. 風になびく ❏ *His long, uncovered hair flew back in the wind.* 彼の帽子をかぶっていない長髪が風で後にたなびいた. **8** V-T/V-I 他動詞/自動詞 If you **fly** a flag or if it **is flying**, you display it at the top of a pole. 掲揚する [他動詞], 揚がる [自動詞] ❏ *They flew the flag of the African National Congress.* 彼らはアフリカ民族会議の旗を掲揚した. **9** V-I 自動詞 If you say that someone or something **flies** in a particular direction, you are emphasizing that they move there with a lot of speed or force. 飛んで行く [EMPHASIS 強調] ❏ *She flew to their bedsides when they were ill.* 彼らが病気のときには, 彼女は枕元に飛んで行った. **10** → see also **flying** **11** PHRASE 句 If you say that someone wouldn't **hurt a fly** or wouldn't **harm a fly**, you are emphasizing that they are very kind and gentle. 虫も殺さない; とても優しい [EMPHASIS 強調] ❏ *Ray wouldn't hurt a fly.* レイはとても優しい男だ. **12** PHRASE 句 If you **let fly**, you attack someone, either physically by hitting them, or with words by insulting them. 食ってかかる ❏ *A simmering dispute ended with her letting fly with a stream of obscenities.* くすぶり続けた口論は彼女が口汚い言葉で続けざまにののしって終了した. **13** PHRASE 句 If you **send** someone or something **flying** or if they **go flying**, they move through the air and fall down with a lot of force. 投げ飛ばす ❏ *The blow sent the young man flying.* その強打で若者は吹き飛ばされた. **14** PHRASE 句 [V PHR] If you do something **on the fly**, you do it quickly or automatically, without planning it in advance. 大急ぎで [mainly AM 主に米国英語] ❏ *You've got to be able to make decisions on the fly as deadlines loom.* 期限が迫ったとき, あなたは大急ぎで決断を下せるようでなくてはならない. **15** **to fly in the face of** → see **face** **16** **to fly off the handle** → see **handle** **17** **a fly in the ointment** → see **ointment** **18** **when pigs fly** → see **pig** **19** **sparks fly** → see **spark** **20** **time flies** → see **time**

▶ **fly into** PHRASAL VERB 句動詞 If you **fly into** a bad temper or a panic, you suddenly become very angry or anxious and show this in your behavior. 突然〜の状態になる ❏ *Losing a game would cause him to fly into a rage.* ゲームに負けると, 彼はかっとなって怒るだろう.

→ see Word Web: **fly**
→ see **flag**, **flight**

fly|er /flaɪr/ (**flyers**) also **flier** **1** N-COUNT 可算名詞 A **flyer** is a pilot of an aircraft. 飛行士 ❏ *The American flyers sprinted for their planes and got into the cockpit.* 米国の飛行士たちは飛行機まで全速力で走って行き操縦室に入った. **2** N-COUNT 可算名詞 You can refer to someone who travels by airplane as a **flyer**. 飛行機で旅する人 ❏ *...regular business flyers.* 仕事でいつも飛行機を使う人たち **3** N-COUNT 可算名詞 A **flyer** is a small printed notice which is used to advertise a particular company, service, or event. ちらし ❏ *Thousands of flyers advertising the tour were handed out during the festival.* そのツアーを宣伝するちらしが何千枚も祭りの間に配られた.

→ see **advertising**

fly|ing /flaɪɪŋ/ **1** ADJ 形容詞 A **flying** animal has wings and is able to fly. 空を飛ぶ [ADJ n] ❏ *...species of flying insects.* 空を飛ぶ昆虫の種類 **2** PHRASE 句 If someone or something **gets off to a flying start**, or **makes a flying start**, they start very well, for example, in a race or a new job. 好調な滑り出しをする ❏ *Advertising revenue in the new financial year has got off to a flying start.* 新しい営業年度の広告収入は好調な滑り出しを見せた.

fly|over /flaɪoʊvər/ (**flyovers**) N-COUNT 可算名詞 A **flyover** is a structure which carries one road over the top of another road. 高架道路 [BRIT 英国英語; AM **overpass** 米国英語 **overpass**]

FM /ɛf ɛm/ **FM** is a method of transmitting radio waves that can be used to broadcast high quality sound. **FM** is an abbreviation for "frequency modulation." 周波数変調

foal /foʊl/ (**foals, foaling, foaled**) **1** N-COUNT 可算名詞 A **foal** is a very young horse. 子馬 **2** V-I 自動詞 When a female horse **foals**, it gives birth. 子馬を生む ❏ *The mare is due to foal today.* その雌馬は今日子馬を生む予定だ.

foam /foʊm/ (**foams**) **1** N-UNCOUNT 不可算名詞 **Foam** consists of a mass of small bubbles that are formed when air and a liquid are mixed together. 泡 ❏ *The water curved round the rocks in great bursts of foam.* その川水はものすごく泡を吹き出しながら岩の周りを曲がって流れていた. **2** N-MASS 質量名詞 **Foam** is used to refer to various kinds of manufactured products which have a soft, light texture like a thick liquid. フォーム ❏ *...shaving foam.* ひげそり用フォーム. **3** N-MASS 質量名詞 **Foam** or **foam rubber** is soft rubber full of small holes which is used, for example, to make mattresses and cushions. 気泡ゴム ❏ *...modern three-piece suites filled with foam rubber.* 気泡ゴムの詰めてある現今の3点セットの家具.

fo|cal point /foʊkəl pɔɪnt/ (**focal points**) N-COUNT 可算名詞 The **focal point** of something is the thing that people concentrate on or pay most attention to. 関心の的, 中心 ❏ *The focal point for the town's many visitors is the museum.* 同町へ来る多くの観光客の関心の的は美術館です.

fo|cus /foʊkəs/ (**focuses, focusing** or **focussing, focused** or **focussed**)

> The plural of the noun can be either **focuses** or **foci** /foʊsaɪ/.

> 名詞の複数は **focuses** と **foci** /foʊsaɪ/ のいずれかである.

1 V-T/V-I 他動詞/自動詞 If you **focus on** a particular topic or if your attention **is focused** on it, you concentrate on it and think about it, discuss it, or deal with it, rather than dealing with other topics. (特定の話題に) 焦点を合わせる, 集中する ❏ *The research effort has focused on tracing the effects of growing levels of five compounds.* 5つの化合物の増大する濃度の影響を追跡することに研究の努力が向けられている. ❏ *Today he was able to focus his message exclusively on the economy.* 今日彼はそのメッセージをもっぱら経済だけに焦点を合わせることができた. **2** V-T/V-I 他動詞/自動詞 If you **focus** your eyes or if your eyes **focus**, your eyes adjust so that you can clearly see the thing that you want to look at. If you **focus** a camera, telescope, or other instrument, you adjust it so that you can see clearly through it. (目・カメラなどの) 焦点を合わせる, 焦点が合う ❏ *Kelly couldn't focus his eyes well enough to tell if the figure was male or female.* ケリーは人影の性別を区別できるほど十分に目の焦点を合わせられなかった. ❏ *His eyes slowly began to focus on what looked like a small dark ball.* 小さな黒っぽいボールのように見えるものに彼の目の焦点が徐々に合い始めた. **3** V-T 他動詞 If you **focus** rays of light on a particular point, you pass them through a lens or reflect them from a mirror so that they meet at that point. 集める ❏ *Magnetic coils focus the electron beams into fine spots.* 磁気コイルは電子ビームを小さな点に集める. **4** N-COUNT 可算名詞 The **focus** of something is the main topic or main thing that it is concerned with. 焦点, 中心, 的 ❏ *The UN's role in promoting peace is increasingly the focus of international attention.* 平和を促進する国連の役割がますます国際的な関心の的となっている. ❏ *The new system is the focus of controversy.* その新しい制度が物議の中心です. **5** N-COUNT 可算名詞 Your **focus** on something is the special attention that you pay it. 焦点 ❏ *He said his sudden focus on foreign policy was not motivated by presidential politics.* 彼が急に外交政策に焦点を当てたのは大統領の

F

政見に刺激を受けたからではないと彼は言った. **6** N-UNCOUNT 不可算名詞 If you say that something has a **focus**, you mean you can see a purpose in it. 意図, 重点 □ *Somehow, though, their latest CD has a focus that the others have lacked.* しかしどうしたわけか、彼らの最新のCDには他のものに欠けている意図が見られる. **7** N-UNCOUNT 不可算名詞 You use **focus** to refer to the fact of adjusting your eyes or a camera, telescope, or other instrument, and to the degree to which you can see clearly. 焦点, ピント □ *His focus switched to the little white ball.* 彼は焦点をその小さな白い球に移した. **8** PHRASE 句 If an image or a camera, telescope, or other instrument is in **focus**, the edges of what you see are clear and sharp. 焦点が合って □ *Pictures should be in focus, with realistic colors and well composed groups.* 写真は焦点が合っていて、写実的な色で、群がく構成されているべきです. **9** PHRASE 句 If something is in **focus**, it is being discussed or its purpose and nature are clear. 焦点が当って □ *We want to keep the real issues in focus.* 私たちは実際の問題に焦点を当てて行きたいです. **10** PHRASE 句 If an image or a camera, telescope, or other instrument is out of **focus**, the edges of what you see are unclear. 焦点がはずれて、ぼやけて □ *In some of the pictures the subjects are out of focus while the background is sharp.* その写真の中には被写体がぼやけているのに背景がはっきりしているものがある.

→ see **photography, telescope**

Word Partnership *focus は次の語句と使われる:*

N.	focus **attention** **1**
	focus *your* **eyes**, focus **a camera** **2**
V.	shift *your* focus **4** **5**
	come into focus **7**

fo|cus group (**focus groups**) N-COUNT 可算名詞 A **focus group** is a specially selected group of people who are intended to represent the general public. Focus groups have discussions in which their opinions are recorded as a form of market research. フォーカスグループ □ *The market research company BMRB conducted 12 focus groups for the project.* 市場調査会社BMRBはその計画のために12のフォーカスグループ調査を実施した.

fod|der /fɒdər/ **1** N-UNCOUNT 不可算名詞 **Fodder** is food that is given to cows, horses, and other animals. 家畜の飼料、かいば □ *...fodder for horses.* 馬の飼料. **2** N-UNCOUNT 不可算名詞 If you say that something is **fodder** for a particular purpose, you mean that it is useful for that purpose and perhaps nothing else. 材料 [DISAPPROVAL 不賛成] □ *The press conference simply provided more fodder for another attack on his character.* 記者会見は彼の人格をもう1度攻撃する材料をさらに提供しただけだった.

foe /foʊ/ (**foes**) N-COUNT 可算名詞 Someone's **foe** is their enemy. 敵 [WRITTEN 書き言葉] □ *But he soon discovers that his old foe may be leading him into a trap.* しかし昔からの敵が彼を計略にかけようとしているのかもしれないと彼はじきに気づく.

foe|tus /fiːtəs/ → see **fetus**

fog /fɒg/ (**fogs**) **1** N-VAR 可変性名詞 When there is **fog**, there are tiny drops of water in the air which form a thick cloud and make it difficult to see things. 霧 □ *The crash happened in thick fog.* その衝突は濃い霧の中で起こりました. **2** N-SING 単数名詞 A **fog** is an unpleasant cloud of something such as smoke inside a building or room. (タバコなどの)こもった煙 □ *...a fog of stale cigarette smoke.* むっとするタバコのこもった煙

fog|gy /fɒgi/ (**foggier, foggiest**) **1** ADJ 形容詞 When it is **foggy**, there is fog. 霧のかかった □ *It's quite foggy now.* 今かなり霧が濃い. **2** PHRASE 句 If you say that you **haven't the foggiest** or you **haven't the foggiest idea**, you are emphasizing that you do not know something. さっぱり分からない [INFORMAL くだけた, EMPHASIS 強調] □ *I did not have the foggiest idea what he meant.* 彼が何を言いたかったのか私にはさっぱり分からなかった.

foil /fɔɪl/ (**foils, foiling, foiled**) **1** N-UNCOUNT 不可算名詞 **Foil** consists of sheets of metal as thin as paper. It is used to wrap food in. ホイル □ *Pour cider around the meat and cover with foil.* 肉のあちこちにりんご酒を注ぎ、ホイルで覆いなさい. **2** V-T 他動詞 If you **foil** someone's plan or attempt to do something, for example, to commit a crime, you succeed in stopping them from doing what they want. 食い止める [JOURNALISM ジャーナリズム] □ *A brave police chief foiled an armed robbery by grabbing the raider's shotgun.* 勇敢な警察署長が侵入者の散弾銃をつかんで武装強盗を食い止めた.

fold /foʊld/ (**folds, folding, folded**) **1** V-T 他動詞 If you **fold** something such as a piece of paper or cloth, you bend it so that one part covers another part, often pressing the edge so that it stays in place. 折りたたむ □ *He folded the paper carefully.* 彼は丁寧に紙を折りたたんだ. □ *Fold the omelette in half.* オムレツを半分に折りたたみなさい. **2** V-T/V-I 他動詞/自動詞 If a piece of furniture or equipment **folds** or if you can **fold** it, you can make it smaller by bending or closing parts of it. たたむ、たためる □ *The back of the bench folds forward to make a table.* ベンチの背もたれを前方に折り返すとテーブルになる. □ *This portable seat folds flat for easy storage.* この携帯用椅子は収納しやすいように平たくたためる. ● PHRASAL VERB

句動詞 **Fold up** means the same as **fold**. たたむ、たためる □ *When not in use it folds up out of the way.* 不用なときは邪魔にならないようにたためる. **3** V-T 他動詞 If you **fold** your arms or hands, you bring them together and cross or link them, for example, over your chest. 組む □ *Meer folded his arms over his chest and turned his head away.* ミーアは腕組みをして顔を背けた. **4** N-COUNT 可算名詞 A **fold** in a piece of paper or cloth is a bend that you make in it when you put one part of it over another part and press the edge. 折り目 □ *Make another fold and turn the ends together.* もう1回折り目を入れて、両端を折り返して合わせなさい. **5** N-COUNT 可算名詞 The **folds** in a piece of cloth are the curved shapes which are formed when it is not hanging or lying flat. ひだ □ *The priest fumbled in the folds of his gown.* 司祭はガウンのひだの中を手探りした.

▶ **fold up** PHRASAL VERB 句動詞 If you **fold** something **up**, you make it into a smaller, neater shape by folding it, usually several times. たたむ □ *She folded it up, and tucked it into her purse.* 彼女はそれをたたんで財布にしまった. → see also **fold 2**

Word Partnership *fold は次の語句と使われる:*

ADV.	fold **carefully**, fold **gently**, fold **neatly** **1**
N.	fold **clothes**, fold **paper** **1**
	fold *your* **arms/hands** **3**

fold|er /foʊldər/ (**folders**) **1** N-COUNT 可算名詞 A **folder** is a thin piece of cardboard in which you can keep loose papers. 紙ばさみ **2** N-COUNT 可算名詞 A **folder** is a group of files that are stored together on a computer. フォルダ

fo|li|age /foʊliɪdʒ/ N-UNCOUNT 不可算名詞 The leaves of a plant are referred to as its **foliage**. 葉 □ *...shrubs with gray or silver foliage.* 葉が灰色か銀色の低木.

folk /foʊk/ (**folks**)

Folk can also be used as the plural form for meaning **1**.

Folk は **1** を意味する複数形としても使える.

1 N-PLURAL 複数名詞 You can refer to people as **folk** or **folks**. 人たち □ *Country folk can tell you that there are certain places which animals avoid.* 田舎の人たちは動物が避ける特定の場所があることを知っている. □ *These are the folks from the local TV station.* この人たちは地元のテレビ局の人たちです. **2** N-PLURAL 複数名詞 You can refer to your close family, especially your mother and father, as your **folks**. 家族、両親 [INFORMAL くだけた] □ *I've been avoiding my folks lately.* 最近わたしは両親を避けている. **3** N-VOC 呼格名詞 You can use **folks** as a term of address when you are talking to several people. 皆さん [INFORMAL くだけた] □ *"It's a question of money, folks," I said.* 「これは金の問題なんですよ、皆さん」と私は言った. **4** ADJ 形容詞 **Folk** art and customs are traditional or typical of a particular community or nation. 民間の、民俗の [ADJ n] □ *...South American folk art.* 南米の民芸 **5** ADJ 形容詞 **Folk** music is music which is traditional or typical of a particular community or nation. 民俗の [ADJ n] ● N-UNCOUNT 不可算名詞 **Folk** is also a noun. 民俗音楽、フォーク □ *...a variety of music including classical and folk.* クラシックやフォークなど各種の音楽.

folk|lore /foʊklɔːr/ N-UNCOUNT 不可算名詞 **Folklore** is the traditional stories, customs, and habits of a particular community or nation. 民間伝承 □ *In Chinese folklore the bat is a symbol of good fortune.* 中国の民間伝承ではコウモリは幸運の象徴だ.

follow

1 GO OR COME AFTER

2 ACT ACCORDING TO SOMETHING, OBSERVE SOMETHING

3 UNDERSTAND

4 PHRASAL VERBS

1 **fol|low** /fɒloʊ/ (**follows, following, followed**) **1** V-T/V-I 他動詞/自動詞 If you **follow** someone who is going somewhere, you move along behind them because you want to go to the same place. ついて行く、ついて来る □ *We followed him up the steps into a large hall.* 私たちは彼について階段を上り大広間に出た. □ *Please follow me, madam.* 奥様、私について来てください. □ *They took him into a small room and I followed.* 彼らが彼を小さな部屋に連れて行ったので、私は後について行った. **2** V-T 他動詞 If you **follow** someone who is going somewhere, you move along behind them without their knowledge, in order to catch them or find out where they are going. 後をつける □ *She realized that the Mercedes was following her.* メルセデスベンツが彼女の後をつけてるのに彼女は気づいた. **3** V-T 他動詞 If you **follow** someone to a place where they have recently gone and where they are now, you go to join them there. 追う □ *He followed Janice to New York, where she was preparing an exhibition.* 彼はニューヨークまでジャニスを追って行ったが、そこで彼女が展覧会の準備をしていたからだ. **4** V-T/V-I 他動詞/自動

詞 An event, activity, or period of time that **follows** a particular thing happens or comes after that thing, at a later time. 次に来る、次に起こる、続く □...*the rioting and looting that followed the verdict.* その評決の後に起こった暴動と略奪。□*Other problems may follow.* 別の問題がこの後に起こるかもしれない。 **5** V-T 他動詞 If you **follow** one thing **with** another, you do or say the second thing after you have done or said the first thing. 続ける □*Her first major role was in Martin Scorsese's "Goodfellas" and she followed this with a part in Spike Lee's "Jungle Fever."* 彼女はマーティン・スコッセジの『いいやつら』で初めて主要な役を演じ、それに続いてスパイク・リーの『蜜林熱』に出演した。 ●PHRASAL VERB 句動詞 **Follow up** means the same as **follow**. 続ける □*The book proved such a success that the authors followed it up with "The Messianic Legacy."* その本がすごい成功だったので、その著者たちは続編として『救世主の遺産』を出版した。 **6** V-T/V-I 他動詞/自動詞 If it **follows** that a particular thing is the case, that thing is a logical result of something else being true or being the case. 結果として起こる、当然...になる □*Just because a bird does not breed one year, it does not follow that it will fail the next.* 鳥がある年ひなをかえさないからといって、その翌年も失敗するとは限らない。 □*If the explanation is right, two things follow.* その説明が正しいとすれば、当然2つのことが言えるはずだ。 **7** V-T/V-I 他動詞/自動詞 If you refer to the words that **follow** or **followed**, you are referring to the words that come next or came next in a piece of writing or speech. 次に来る、次に続く □*What follows is an eye-witness account.* 次に来るのは目撃者の話だ。 □*There followed a list of places where Hans intended to visit.* 次にハンスが訪れるつもりの場所のリストだった。 **8** V-T 他動詞 If you **follow** a path, route, or set of signs, you go somewhere using the path, route, or signs to direct you. たどる □*If they followed the road, they would be certain to reach a village.* もし彼らがその道をたどったのなら、村に着くはずだ。 □*All we had to do was follow the map.* 地図をたどればいいだけだった。 **9** V-T 他動詞 If something such as a path or river **follows** a particular route or line, it goes along that route or line. 沿って行く、沿って流れる □*Our route follows the Pacific coast through densely populated neighborhoods.* 私たちは太平洋沿岸に沿って行き、人口密度の高い地域を経由する。 **10** V-T 他動詞 If you **follow** something with your eyes, or if your eyes **follow** it, you watch it as it moves or you look along its route or course. 目で追う □*Ann's eyes followed a police car as it drove slowly past.* アンはパトカーがゆっくり過ぎ去るのを目で追った。 **11** V-T 他動詞 Something that **follows** a particular course of development happens or develops in that way. ならう、従う □*His release turned out to follow the pattern set by that of the other six hostages.* 結局彼は他の6人の人質が解放された手順に従い解放された。 **12** V-T 他動詞 If you **follow** someone in what you do, you do the same thing or job as they did previously. 後を継ぐ □*He followed his father and became a surgeon.* 彼は彼の父親の後を継いで外科医になった。 **13** PHRASE 句 You use **as follows** in writing or speech to introduce something such as a list, description, or an explanation. 下記の通り、次の通り □*The winners are as follows: E. Walker; R. Foster; R. Gates; A. Mackintosh.* 勝者は次の通りです：E. ウォーカーさん、R. フォスターさん、R. ゲーツさん、A. マッキントッシュさん。 **14** PHRASE 句 You use **followed by** to say what comes after something else in a list or ordered set of things. その後に □*Potatoes are still the most popular food, followed by white bread.* ジャガイモは今も最も人気のある食品で、そのあとに白パンが来ます。 **15** → see also **following** **16** to **follow** in someone's **footsteps** → see **footstep** **17** to **follow** your **nose** → see **nose** **18** to **follow suit** → see **suit**

Thesaurus

follow また次を参照：

V.	pursue, shadow, trail **1** **2**
	succeed **1** **12**

2 fol|low /fɒloʊ/ (follows, following, followed) **1** V-T 他動詞 If you **follow** advice, an instruction, or a recipe, you act or do something in the way that it indicates. 従う □*Take care to follow the instructions carefully.* 指示に慎重に従うように気をつけなさい。 **2** V-T 他動詞 If you **follow** what someone else has done, you do it too because you think it is a good thing or because you want to copy them. まねる、手本とする □*His admiration for the athlete did not extend to the point where he would follow his example in taking drugs.* 彼はその運動選手を崇拝したが、その選手をまねて薬物を乱用するまでには至らなかった。 **3** V-T 他動詞 If you **follow** something, you take an interest in it and keep informed about what happens. 興味を持ってたどる、関心を示す □*...the millions of people who follow football because they genuinely love it.* フットボールが本当に大好きなのでその動向に関心を示す何百万の人びと。 **4** V-T 他動詞 If you **follow** a particular religion or political belief, you have that religion or belief. 信じる □*"Do you follow any particular religion?" — "Yes, we're all Hindus."* 「何か特定の宗教を信じていますか」「はい、私たちはみんなヒンドゥー教徒です」

3 fol|low /fɒloʊ/ (follows, following, followed) **1** V-T/V-I 他動詞/自動詞 If you are able to **follow** something such as an explanation or the story of a movie, you understand it as it

continues and develops. 話についてゆく、理解する □*Can you follow the plot so far?* ここまでの話の筋を理解できましたか。 □*I'm sorry, I don't follow.* すみませんが、おっしゃることが分かりません。 **2** → see also **following**

4 fol|low /fɒloʊ/ (follows, following, followed) ▶ **follow through** PHRASAL VERB 句動詞 If you **follow through** an action, plan, or idea or **follow through** with it, you continue doing or thinking about it until you have done everything possible. 最後までやり通す、最後まで考え抜く □*The leadership has been unwilling to follow through the implications of these ideas.* 指導者たちにはこれらの案の影響について徹底的に考える気はなかった。 □*I was trained to be an actress but I didn't follow it through.* 私は女優となるように養成されたが、最後までやり通さなかった。 ▶ **follow up** PHRASAL VERB 句動詞 If you **follow up** something that has been said, suggested, or discovered, you try to find out more about it or take action about it. どこまでも追求する、追跡する □*State police are following up several leads.* 州警察はいくつかの手がかりを追跡している。 → see also **follow** **5** → see also **follow-up**

fol|low|er /fɒloʊər/ (followers) N-COUNT 可算名詞 A **follower** of a particular person, group, or belief is someone who supports or admires this person, group, or belief. 信奉者 □*...followers of the Zulu Inkatha movement.* ズールー族のインカタ運動の信奉者たち。

fol|low|ing /fɒloʊɪŋ/ (followings) **1** PREP 前置詞 **Following** a particular event means after that event. 一の後で □*In the centuries following Christ's death, Christians genuinely believed the world was about to end.* キリストの死後数世紀の中で、キリスト教信者たちは世界が今にも終わろうとしていると本気で信じていた。 **2** ADJ 形容詞 The **following** day, week, or year is the day, week, or year after the one you have just mentioned. 次の [det ADJ] □*The following day the picture appeared on the front pages of every newspaper in the world.* 翌日その写真が世界中のすべての新聞の第1面に載った。 □*We went to dinner the following Monday evening.* その次の月曜の晩にわたしたちは食事に出かけた。 **3** ADJ 形容詞 You use **following** to refer to something that you are about to mention. 次の [det ADJ] □*Write down the following information: name of product, type, date purchased and price.* 次の情報を記録すること：製品名、型、購買日、値段。 ● PRON 代名詞 The **following** refers to the thing or things that you are about to mention. 次に述べること、下記のもの ['the' PRON] □*The following is a paraphrase of what was said.* 発言内容を言い換えると以下の通りになる。 **4** N-COUNT 可算名詞 A person or organization that has a **following** has a group of people who support or admire their beliefs or actions. 支持者、愛好者 □*Australian rugby league enjoys a huge following in New Zealand.* オーストラリアのラグビーリーグはニュージーランドのファンがすごく多い。

follow-up (follow-ups) N-VAR 可変性名詞 A **follow-up** is something that is done to continue or add to something done previously. 続き □*They are recording a follow-up to their successful 1989 album.* 彼らは今1989年のヒットアルバムに続く新盤を録音している。

fol|ly /fɒli/ (follies) N-VAR 可変性名詞 If you say that a particular action or way of behaving is **folly** or a **folly**, you mean that it is foolish. 愚かさ □*It's sheer folly to build nuclear power stations in a country that has dozens of earthquakes every year.* 毎年何十もの地震がある国に原子力発電所を建てるのは全く愚かなことだ。

fond /fɒnd/ (fonder, fondest) **1** ADJ 形容詞 If you are **fond of** someone, you feel affection for them. 好んで [v-link ADJ 'of' n] □*I am very fond of Michael.* 私はマイケルがとても好きです。 ● **fond|ness** N-UNCOUNT 不可算名詞 好き □*...a great fondness for children.* 子供が大好き **2** ADJ 形容詞 [ADJ n] You use **fond** to describe people or their behavior when they show affection. 優しい □*...a fond father.* 甘い父 ● **fond|ly** ADV 副詞 [ADV after v] 優しく □*Liz saw their eyes meet fondly across the table.* リズは彼らがテーブル越しに優しい視線を交わしているのを見た。 **3** ADJ 形容詞 If you are **fond of** something, you like it or you like doing it very much. 大好きで [v-link ADJ 'of' n/-ing] □*He was fond of marmalade.* 彼はマーマレードが大好きだった。 ● **fond|ness** N-UNCOUNT 不可算名詞 大好き □*I've always had a fondness for chocolate cake.* わたしは昔からチョコレートケーキが大好きだ。 **4** ADJ 形容詞 [ADJ n] If you have **fond** memories of someone or something, you remember them with pleasure. 楽しい □*I have very fond memories of living in our village.* 私は村に住んでいたときのとても楽しい思い出がある。 ● **fond|ly** ADV 副詞 [ADV with v] 楽しく □*My dad took us there when I was about four and I remembered it fondly.* 私のお父さんは私が4歳くらいのときに私たちをそこに連れて行ってく

Word Web food

The food chain begins with sunlight. Green **plants** absorb and store **energy** from the sun through photosynthesis. This energy is passed on to an herbivore (such as a mouse) that **eats** these plants. The mouse is then eaten by a carnivore (such as a snake). The snake may be eaten by a **top predator** (such as a hawk). When the hawk dies, its body is broken down by bacteria. Soon its **nutrients** become food for plants and the cycle begins again.

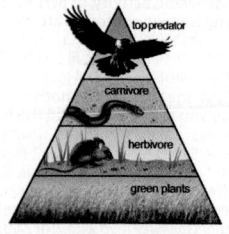

Food chain

れたが, 私はそのことをとても楽しく思い出した. 5 ADJ 形容詞 You use **fond** to describe hopes, wishes, or beliefs which you think are foolish because they seem unlikely to be fulfilled. たわいない [ADJ n] □*My fond hope is that we will be ready by Christmastime.* 私のたわいもない望みは準備がクリスマス季節までに整うことです. ●**fond|ly** ADV 副詞 [ADV with v] 愚かにも □*I fondly imagined that surgery meant a few stitches and an overnight stay in the hospital.* 私は愚かにも手術といっても少し縫い合わせるだけで, 1晩入院すればすむのだろうと思った.

font /fɒnt/ (**fonts**) N-COUNT 可算名詞 In printing, a **font** is a set of characters of the same style and size. フォント □*...the immense variety of fonts available in Microsoft Word and Publisher.* マイクロソフト・ワードとパブリッシャーにある膨大な種類のフォント.

food /fuːd/ (**foods**) 1 N-MASS 質量名詞 **Food** is what people and animals eat. 食物, 食品 □*Enjoy your food.* どうぞ召し上がれ. □*...frozen foods.* 冷凍食品. 2 → see also **fast food, junk food** 3 PHRASE 句 If you give someone **food for thought**, you make them think carefully about something. 考えるべき材料 □*Her speech offers much food for thought.* 彼女のスピーチには考えさせられる点が多くあった.
→ see Word Web: **food**
→ see **can, farm, rice, sugar, vegetarian**

food|stuff /fuːdstʌf/ (**foodstuffs**) N-VAR 可変化名詞 **Foodstuffs** are substances which people eat. 食料, 食材 □*...basic foodstuffs such as sugar, cooking oil and cheese.* 砂糖, 食用油, チーズなどの基本的な食材

fool /fuːl/ (**fools, fooling, fooled**) 1 N-COUNT 可算名詞 If you call someone a **fool**, you are indicating that you think they are not at all sensible and show a lack of good judgment. 愚か者, ばか [DISAPPROVAL 不賛成] □*"You fool!" she shouted.* 「ばか者だ」と彼女は叫んだ. 2 ADJ 形容詞 **Fool** is used to describe an action or person that is not at all sensible and shows a lack of good judgment. ばかな [mainly AM 主に米国英語, INFORMAL くだけた, DISAPPROVAL 不賛成] [ADJ n] □*What a damn fool thing to do!* 何というばかなことをするのだ！ 3 V-T 他動詞 If someone **fools** you, they deceive or trick you. だます □*Art dealers fool a lot of people.* 画商は多くの人をだます. □*Don't be fooled by his appearance.* 彼の見かけにだまされるな. 4 V-I 自動詞 If you say that a person **is fooling with** something or someone, you mean that the way they are behaving is likely to cause problems. もてあそぶ □*What are you doing fooling with such a staggering sum of money?* あんなに大金をもてあそんで, 一体あなたは何しているのだ？ 5 PHRASE 句 If you **make a fool of** someone, you make them seem silly by telling people about something stupid that they have done, or by tricking them. ばかにする □*Your brother is making a fool of you.* きみの兄貴はきみのことをばかにしているのだ. 6 PHRASE 句 If you **make a fool of** yourself, you behave in a way that makes other people think that you are silly or lacking in good judgment. ばかなまねをして物笑いになる □*He was drinking and making a fool of himself.* 彼は酒を飲んでいて, ばかなまねをして物笑いになっていた. 7 PHRASE 句 If you **play the fool** or **act the fool**, you behave in a playful, childish, and foolish way, usually in order to make other people laugh. ふざける □*They used to play the fool together, calling each other silly names and giggling.* 彼女たちはたわいもない悪口を言い合ったり, くすくす笑ったりして, よく一緒にふざけていた.
▶**fool around** PHRASAL VERB 句動詞 If you **fool around**, you behave in a silly, dangerous, or irresponsible way. ふざける, ぶらぶらする □*They were fooling around on an Army firing range.* 彼らは陸軍の射撃練習場でふざけまわっていた.

fool|ish /fuːlɪʃ/ 1 ADJ 形容詞 If someone's behavior or action is **foolish**, it is not sensible and shows a lack of good judgment. 愚かな, ばかげた □*It would be foolish to raise hopes unnecessarily.* むだに期待を持たせるのはばかげているでしょう. ●**fool|ish|ly** ADV 副詞 愚かにも □*He admitted that he had acted foolishly.* 彼は自分がばかなことをしたことを認めた. ●**fool|ish|ness** N-UNCOUNT 不可算名詞 □*They don't accept any foolishness when it comes to spending money.* 金を使うこととなると, 彼らは真剣だった. 2 ADJ 形容詞 If you look or feel **foolish**, you look or feel so silly or ridiculous that people are likely to laugh at you. きまりの悪い □*I just stood there feeling foolish and watching him.* 私はきまりの悪い思いをしながら, 彼

をじっと見てそこにたたずむだけだった. ●**fool|ish|ly** ADV 副詞 [ADV after v] きまり悪そうに □*He saw me standing there, grinning foolishly at him.* 彼は私がそこに立ってきまり悪そうに彼にニヤッと笑いかけていた.

fool|proof /fuːlpruːf/ ADJ 形容詞 Something such as a plan or a machine that is **foolproof** is so well designed, easy to understand, or easy to use that it cannot go wrong or be used wrongly. ばかにでも扱える □*The system is not 100 per cent foolproof.* これは完全に誰にでも簡単に扱えるシステムではない.

---

foot

❶ PART OF BODY
❷ UNIT OF MEASUREMENT
❸ LOWER END OF SOMETHING

---

❶ **foot** /fʊt/ (**feet**) 1 N-COUNT 可算名詞 Your **feet** are the parts of your body that are at the ends of your legs, and that you stand on. 足 (足首から下の部分) □*She stamped her feet again.* 彼女はまた片足を踏み鳴らした. □*...a foot injury.* 足の負傷. 2 ADJ 形容詞 A **foot** brake or **foot** pump is operated by your foot rather than by your hand. 足踏み式の [ADJ n] □*I tried to reach the foot brakes but I couldn't.* 私は足踏みブレーキに足を伸ばしたけれど届かなかった. 3 ADJ 形容詞 A **foot** patrol or **foot** soldiers walk rather than traveling in vehicles or on horseback. 徒歩の [ADJ n] □*Paratroopers and foot-soldiers entered the building on the government's behalf.* 落下傘兵と歩兵が政府に代わってその建物に入った. 4 → see also **footing** 5 PHRASE 句 If you get **cold feet** about something, you become nervous or frightened about it because you think it will fail. おじけ, 逃げ腰 □*The Government is getting cold feet about the reforms.* 政府は改革に逃げ腰になっている. 6 PHRASE 句 If you say that someone **is finding** their **feet** in a new situation, you mean that they are starting to feel confident and to deal with things successfully. 慣れる, 自信がつく □*I don't know anyone here but I am sure I will manage when I find my feet.* ここは私の知らない人ばかりだけれども, 慣れたらきっとうまくやって行ける. 7 PHRASE 句 If you say that someone has their **feet on the ground**, you approve of the fact that they have a sensible and practical attitude toward life, and do not have unrealistic ideas. 足を地に着けている [APPROVAL 賛成] □*In that respect he needs to keep his feet on the ground and not get carried away.* その点で彼はしっかり足を地に着けて, 我を忘れないようにする必要がある. 8 PHRASE 句 If you go somewhere **on foot**, you walk, rather than using any form of transport. 徒歩で □*We rowed ashore, then explored the island on foot for the rest of the day.* 彼は岸まで漕いで行き, その日はその後徒歩で島を探索して過ごした. 9 PHRASE 句 If you are **on your feet**, you are standing up. 立ち上がって □*Everyone was on their feet applauding wildly.* みんな立ち上がり熱狂的に拍手した. 10 PHRASE 句 If you say that someone or something is **on their feet** again after an illness or difficult period, you mean that they have recovered and are back to normal. 元気になって, 立ち直って □*You need someone to take the pressure off and help you get back on your feet.* あなたの元気を回復させてくれる人があなたには必要だ. 11 PHRASE 句 If you say that someone always **lands on** their **feet**, you mean that they are always successful or lucky, although they do not seem to achieve this by their own efforts. 首尾よく難を免れる, 運が良い □*He has good looks and charm, and always lands on his feet.* 彼はハンサムで魅力的でいつも運が良い. 12 PHRASE 句 If someone **puts** their **foot down**, they use their authority in order to stop something from happening. 断固とした態度をとる, 反対する □*He had planned to go skiing on his own in March but his wife had decided to put her foot down.* 彼は3月に独りでスキーに行く計画をしていたが, 妻が断固として反対していた. 13 PHRASE 句 If someone **puts** their **foot down** when they are driving, they drive as fast as they can. スピードをできる限り上げる [BRIT 英国英語] 14 PHRASE 句 If someone **puts** their **foot in it** or **puts** their **foot in** their **mouth**, they accidentally do or say something which embarrasses or offends people. どじを踏む, へまなことを言う [INFORMAL くだけた] □*Our chairman has really put his foot in it, poor man, though he doesn't know it.* 私たちの会長はかわいそうに, 本当にへまなことを言った. でもまだ自分では気がついていないが. 15 PHRASE 句 If you **put** your **feet up**, you relax or have a

Picture Dictionary　foot

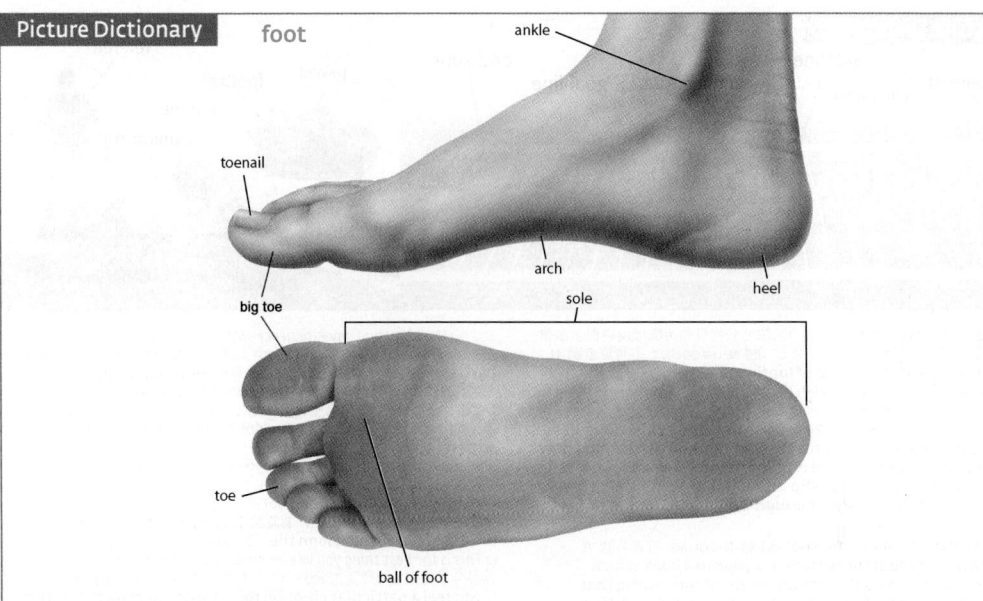

ankle

toenail

arch

heel

big toe

sole

toe

ball of foot

rest, especially by sitting or lying with your feet supported off the ground. くつろぐ，一休みする □ *After supper he'd put his feet up and read.* 彼は夕飯のあとにはくつろいで読書したものだ. **16** PHRASE 句 If you never **put a foot wrong**, you never make any mistakes. しくじらない [mainly BRIT 主に英国英語] □ *When he's around, we never put a foot wrong.* 彼がいる時には私たちは絶対にしくじらない. **17** PHRASE 句 If you say that someone **sets foot** in a place, you mean that they enter it or reach it, and you are emphasizing the significance of their action. If you say that someone **never sets foot** in a place, you are emphasizing that they never go there. 入る，着く [EMPHASIS 強調] □ *...the day the first man set foot on the moon.* 人類が始めて月に着いた日 **18** PHRASE 句 If someone has to **stand on their own two feet**, they have to be independent and manage their lives without help from other people. 自立する □ *My father didn't mind whom I married, so long as I could stand on my own two feet and wasn't dependent on my husband.* 私が自立できて夫婦りでない限り，私の父は私が誰と結婚しようと気にしなかった. **19** PHRASE 句 If you get or rise **to your feet**, you stand up. 立つように □ *Malone got to his feet and followed his superior out of the suite.* マローンは立ち上がり，上役の後を追って部屋を出た. □ *The delegates cheered and rose to their feet.* 代議員たちはかっさいして立ち上がった. **20** PHRASE 句 If someone **gets off on the wrong foot** in a new situation, they make a bad start by doing something in completely the wrong way. 出だしでしくじる □ *Even though they called the election and had been preparing for it for some time, they got off on the wrong foot.* 選挙を求めその準備もしばらくしていたのに，彼らは出だしでしくじった. **21 foot in the door** → see **door** **22 to drag** your **feet** → see **drag** **23 to vote with** your **feet** → see **vote**
→ see Picture Dictionary: **foot**
→ see **body**

❷ foot /fʊt/ (feet) N-COUNT 可算名詞 A **foot** is a unit for measuring length, height, or depth, and is equal to 12 inches or 30.48 centimeters. When you are giving measurements, the form "foot" is often used as the plural instead of the plural form "feet." フィート □ *This beautiful and curiously shaped lake lies at around fifteen thousand feet.* この美しくて珍しい形をした湖は標高約1万5千フィートにある. □ *He occupies a cell 10 foot long, 6 foot wide and 10 foot high.* 彼は長さ10フィート，幅6フィート，高さ10フィートの独房に入っている.

❸ foot /fʊt/ (feet) **1** N-SING 単数名詞 The **foot of** something is the part that is farthest from its top. 最下部，ふもと □ *David called to the children from the foot of the stairs.* デービットは階段の下から子供たちを呼んだ. □ *...the foot of the hill.* 丘のふもと. **2** N-SING 単数名詞 The **foot of** a bed is the end nearest to the feet of the person lying in it. 足部，すそ □ *Friends stood at the foot of the bed, looking at her with serious faces.* 友人たちは真剣な顔で彼女を見つめながらベッドのすそに立っていた.

foot|age /fʊtɪdʒ/ N-UNCOUNT 不可算名詞 **Footage** of a particular event is a film of it or the part of a film which shows this event. 映画，映画の1場面 □ *They are planning to show exclusive footage from this summer's festivals.* 彼らは今年の夏祭りの独占録画を放映する計画だ.

foot-and-mouth dis|ease N-UNCOUNT 不可算名詞 **Foot-and-mouth disease** or **foot-and-mouth** is a serious and highly infectious disease that affects cattle, sheep, pigs, and goats. 口てい疫

foot|ball /fʊtbɔl/ (footballs) **1** N-UNCOUNT 不可算名詞 **Football** is a game played by two teams of eleven players using an oval ball. Players carry the ball in their hands or throw it to each other as they try to score goals that are called touchdowns. フットボール，アメリカンフットボール [AM 米国英語] □ *Two blocks beyond our school was a field where boys played football.* 私たちの学校から2街区ほど向こうに男の子たちがフットボールをする球場があった. **2** N-COUNT 可算名詞 A **football** is a ball that is used for playing football. フットボール用ボール □ *...a heavy leather football.* 重い皮製のフットボールのボール. **3** N-UNCOUNT 不可算名詞 **Football** is a game played by two teams of eleven players using a round ball. Players kick the ball to each other and try to score goals by kicking the ball into a large net. フットボール，サッカー [BRIT 英国英語; AM **soccer** 米国英語 **soccer**]
→ see Picture Dictionary: **football**

foot|ball|er /fʊtbɔlər/ (footballers) N-COUNT 可算名詞 A **footballer** is a person who plays football (soccer), especially as a profession. サッカー選手，フットボール選手 [BRIT 英国英語; AM **soccer player** 米国英語 **soccer player**]

foot|er /fʊtər/ (footers) **1** N-COUNT 可算名詞 A **footer** is text such as a name or page number that can be automatically displayed at the bottom of each page of a printed document. Compare **header**. フッター [COMPUTING コンピューティング] □ *Page Mode shows headers, footers, footnotes and page numbers.* ページモードではヘッダー，フッター，脚注，ページ番号が表示される. **2** → see also **header**

foot|hills /fʊthɪlz/ N-PLURAL 複数名詞 The **foothills** of a mountain or a range of mountains are the lower hills or mountains around its base. 山麓（さんろく）の丘陵地帯 □ *Pasadena lies in the foothills of the San Gabriel mountains.* パサディナはサンガブリエル山脈の丘陵地帯にある.

foot|hold /fʊthoʊld/ (footholds) **1** N-COUNT 可算名詞 A **foothold** is a strong or favorable position from which further advances or progress may be made. 足掛かり □ *Businesses are investing millions of dollars to gain a foothold in this new market.* この新しい市場で足掛かりを得るために諸企業が何百万ドルもの投資をしている. **2** N-COUNT 可算名詞 A **foothold** is a place such as a small hole or area of rock where you can safely put your foot when climbing. 足掛かり，足場 □ *He lowered his legs until he felt he had a solid foothold on the rockface beneath him.* 彼の真下の岩面にしっかりした足場があると感じるまで足を下げた.

foot|ing /fʊtɪŋ/ **1** N-UNCOUNT 不可算名詞 If something is put on a particular **footing**, it is defined, established, or changed in a particular way, often so that it is able to develop or exist successfully. 立場 □ *The new law will put official corruption on the*

Picture Dictionary — football

goalpost · sideline · yard line · fifty-yard line · goal line · end zone

player · football · referee · helmet · uniform · face mask

same legal footing as treason. その新法で公務員の汚職は反逆罪と法律的に同じ立場に置かれるようになる. **2** N-UNCOUNT 不可算名詞 If you are **on** a particular kind of **footing** with someone, you have that kind of relationship with them. 立場, 関係 ❑ They decided to put their relationship on a more formal footing. 彼らは関係をより正式なものとすることに決めた. **3** N-UNCOUNT 不可算名詞 You refer to your **footing** when you are referring to your position and how securely your feet are placed on the ground. For example, if you lose your **footing**, your feet slip and you fall. 足元, 足場 ❑ He was cautious of his footing, wary of the edge. 彼は縁に油断せず足元に用心した.

foot|note /fʊtnoʊt/ (**footnotes**) **1** N-COUNT 可算名詞 A **footnote** is a note at the bottom of a page in a book which provides more detailed information about something that is mentioned on that page. 脚注 **2** N-COUNT 可算名詞 If you refer to what you are saying as a **footnote**, you mean that you are adding some information that is related to what has just been mentioned. 補足情報 ❑ As a footnote, I should add that there was one point on which his bravado was more than justified. 彼が正当化しきれないほど虚勢を張った点もあったことを補足として加えたい. **3** N-COUNT 可算名詞 If you describe an event as a **footnote**, you mean that it is fairly unimportant although it will probably be remembered. 付随的なこと ❑ I'm afraid that his name will now become a footnote in history. 残念ながら, 今では彼の名前は歴史には付随的なものとしてしか残らないだろう.

foot|path /fʊtpæθ/ (**footpaths**) N-COUNT 可算名詞 A **footpath** is a path for people to walk on, especially in the countryside. 歩行者用の小道

foot|print /fʊtprɪnt/ (**footprints**) N-COUNT 可算名詞 A **footprint** is a mark in the shape of a foot that a person or animal makes in or on a surface. 足跡 ❑ His footprints were clearly evident in the heavy dust. 分厚く積もったほこりの中で彼の足跡ははっきりと見えた.
→ see **fossil**

foot|step /fʊtstɛp/ (**footsteps**) **1** N-COUNT 可算名詞 A **footstep** is the sound or mark that is made by someone walking each time their foot touches the ground. 足音, 足跡 ❑ I heard footsteps outside. 外で足音がした. **2** PHRASE 句 If you **follow in** someone's **footsteps**, you do the same things as they did earlier. 見習う ❑ My father is extremely proud that I followed in his footsteps and became a doctor. 父は私が父を見習って医者になったことを大変誇りに思っている.

foot|wear /fʊtwɛər/ N-UNCOUNT 不可算名詞 **Footwear** refers to things that people wear on their feet, for example, shoes and boots. 履物 ❑ Some football players get paid millions for endorsing footwear. フットボール選手の中には履物を推奨することで何百万もの収入を得ている人もいる.

for
1 SAYING WHO OR WHAT SOMETHING RELATES TO, OR WHO BENEFITS
2 MENTIONING A PURPOSE, REASON, OR DESTINATION
3 BEFORE NUMBERS, AMOUNTS, AND TIMES
4 WANTING OR SUPPORTING

1 for /fər, STRONG fɔr/ **1** PREP 前置詞 If something is **for** someone, they are intended to have it or benefit from it. 一のために, 一のための ❑ Isn't that enough for you? あれだけではあなたには足りませんか? ❑ ...a table for two. 2人の席. ❑ He wanted all the running of the business for himself. 彼は自分でその事業をすべて経営したかった. **2** PREP 前置詞 If you work or do a job **for** someone, you are employed by them. 一で, 一のために ❑ I knew he worked for a security firm. 私は彼が警備会社で働いていることを知ってい

た. ❑ Have you had any experience writing for radio? ラジオの原稿を書いた経験がありますか. **3** PREP 前置詞 If you speak or act **for** a particular group or organization, you represent them. 一を代表して ❑ She appears nightly on the television news, speaking for the State Department. 彼女は国務省を代弁してテレビのニュースに毎晩出ている. **4** PREP 前置詞 If someone does something **for** you, they do it so that you do not have to do it. 一の代わりに, 一のために ❑ If your pharmacy doesn't stock the product you want, have them order it for you. もし薬局にあなたの欲しい薬が置いてない場合は, 薬局に注文してもらいなさい. ❑ I hold a door open for an old person. 私は年寄りのためにはドアを開けて持つ. **5** PREP 前置詞 If you feel a particular emotion **for** someone, you feel it on their behalf. 一のために [adj/n PREP] ❑ This is the best thing you've ever done – I am so happy for you! これはきみが今までにしたことで最高のことだね. よかった. **6** PREP 前置詞 If you feel a particular emotion **for** someone or something, they are the object of that emotion, and you feel it when you think about them. 一に対して [adj/n PREP] ❑ John, I'm sorry for Steve, but I think you've made the right decisions. ジョン, スティーブには気の毒だが, きみは正しい判断を下したと私は思う. **7** PREP 前置詞 You use **for** after words such as "time," "space," "money," or "energy" when you say how much there is or whether there is enough of it in order to be able to do or use a particular thing. 一のための ❑ Many new trains have space for wheelchair users. 新しい列車の多くに車椅子使用者の乗るスペースがある. ❑ ...a huge room with plenty of room for books. 本を置くための場所が十分にある巨大な大部屋. **8** PREP 前置詞 You use **for** when you make a statement about something in order to say how it affects or relates to someone, or what their attitude to it is. 一にとって ❑ What matters for most scientists is money and facilities. 大部分の科学者にとって重要なのは金と施設だ. ❑ For her, books were as necessary to life as bread. 彼女にとって本はパンと同様に生活に欠かせないものであった. **9** PREP 前置詞 After some adjective, noun, and verb phrases, you use **for** to introduce the subject of the action indicated by the following infinitive verb. 一が (一することは) [PREP n to-inf] ❑ It might be possible for a single woman to be accepted as a foster parent. 独身女性が里親として認められることもあり得るだろう. ❑ I had made arrangements for my affairs to be dealt with by one of my children. 私は後のことは自分の子供の1人に任せるように手はずを整えておいた. **10** PREP 前置詞 If you say that something is **not for** you, you mean that you do not enjoy it or that it is not suitable for you. 一に向いて, 一に適して [INFORMAL くだけた] [with neg] ❑ Wendy decided the sport was not for her. ウェンディーはそのスポーツは自分には向いていないと思った. **11** PREP 前置詞 If it is **for** you to do something, it is your responsibility or right to do it. 一が (一するべき) [PREP n to-inf] ❑ I wish you would come back to Washington with us, but that's for you to decide. きみに私たちと一緒にワシントンに戻って欲しいと私は思うけれど, それはきみ次第だ. **12** PREP 前置詞 **For** is the preposition that is used after some nouns, adjectives, or verbs in order to introduce more information or to indicate what a quality, thing, or action relates to. 一のため, 一に関して ❑ Reduced-calorie cheese is a great substitute for cream cheese. 低カロリーのチーズはクリームチーズの素晴らしい代用品だ. ❑ Parking lot owners should be legally responsible for protecting vehicles. 駐車場の持ち主が車を保護する法的責任を負うべきである. **13** PREP 前置詞 If a word or expression has the same meaning as another word or expression, you can say that the first one is another word or expression **for** the second one. 一を表わす ❑ The technical term for sunburn is erythema. 日焼けの専門用語は紅斑 (こうはん) である. **14** PREP 前置詞 To be named **for** someone means to be given the same name as them. 一にちなんで [AM 米国英語] ❑ The Brady Bill is named for former White House Press Secretary James Brady. ブレイディー法はホワイトハウスの前報道官ジェームズ・ブレイディーにちなんで命名されている. **15** PREP 前置詞 You use **for** in a piece of writing when you mention information which will be found somewhere else. 一については ❑ For further information on the life of William James Sidis, see Amy Wallace, "The Prodigy." ウィリアム・ジェーム・サイディズの生涯の詳細についてはエイミー・ウォレス著『神童』を参照せよ. **16** PREP 前置詞 **For** is used in conditional sentences, in expressions such as "**if not for**" and "**were it not for**,"

to introduce the only thing which prevents the main part of the sentence from being true. 一のおかげが（なかったら）❑ *If not for John, Brian wouldn't have learned the truth.* ジョンのおかげがなかったら、ブライアンは真実を知らなかったであろう。❑ *The earth would be a frozen ball if it were not for the radiant heat of the sun.* 太陽の放射熱がなかったら、地球は凍った球体だろう。**17** **as for** → see **as** **18** **but** **for** → see **but** **19** **for all** → see **all**

❷ for /fər, STRONG fɔːr/ **1** PREP 前置詞 You use **for** when you state or explain the purpose of an object, action, or activity. （目的・行為など）のために、一のための [PREP n/-ing] ❑ *...drug users who use unsterile equipment for injections of drugs.* 薬物注射のため未殺菌の器具を使用する薬物使用者 ❑ *The knife for cutting sausage was sitting in the sink.* ソーセージを切るための包丁は流しに放置されていた。**2** PREP 前置詞 You use **for** after nouns expressing reason or cause. 一のための [n PREP n/-ing] ❑ *He's soon to make a speech explaining his reasons for going.* 彼は去る理由を説明する演説をまもなくするはずだ。❑ *The county hospital could find no physical cause for Sumner's problems.* その郡立病院はサムナーの健康問題の身体的原因は何も発見できなかった。**3** PREP 前置詞 If something is **for** sale, hire, or use, it is available to be sold, hired, or used. 一のために、一のための ❑ *Freshwater fish for sale.* 販売用の淡水魚 ❑ *...a room for rent.* 貸し部屋。**4** PREP 前置詞 If you do something **for** a particular occasion, you do it on that occasion or to celebrate that occasion. 一のために、一のための ❑ *He asked his daughter what she would like for her birthday.* 彼は娘に誕生日に何が欲しいか尋ねた。**5** PREP 前置詞 If you leave **for** a particular place or if you take a bus, train, plane, or boat **for** a place, you are going there. 一に向かって ❑ *They would be leaving for Rio early the next morning.* 彼らは翌朝早くリオに向かっていたのだろう。

❸ for /fər, STRONG fɔːr/ **1** PREP 前置詞 You use **for** to say how long something lasts or continues. 一の間 [PREP amount] ❑ *The toaster was on for more than an hour.* トースターは1時間以上つけっぱなしだった。❑ *They talked for a bit.* 彼らはしばらく話をした。**2** PREP 前置詞 You use **for** to say how far something extends. 一の間 [PREP amount] ❑ *We drove on for a few miles.* 我々は数マイルほどドライブを続けた。**3** PREP 前置詞 If something is bought, sold, or done **for** a particular amount of money, that amount of money is its price. （ある金額）で [PREP amount] ❑ *We got the bus back to Tange for 30 cents.* 我々は30セントでタンゲに戻るバスに乗った。❑ *The Martins sold their house for about 1.4 million dollars.* マーティン家は約140万ドルで自宅を売った。**4** PREP 前置詞 If something is planned **for** a particular time, it is planned to happen then. （ある日時）に ❑ *...the Baltimore Boat Show, planned for January 21 – 29.* 1月21日から29日までに予定されているバルティモア・ボートショー。❑ *The designer will be unveiling her latest fashions for fall and winter.* そのデザイナーは秋と冬に彼女の最新ファッションを披露しているだろう。**5** PHRASE 句 You use expressions such as **for the first time** and **for the last time** when you are talking about how often something has happened before. 初めて、最後に ❑ *He was married for the second time.* 彼は2度目の結婚をした。**6** PREP 前置詞 You use **for** when you say that one aspect of something or someone is surprising in relation to other aspects of them. 一のわりには ❑ *He was tall for an eight-year-old.* 彼は8歳にしては背が高かった。**7** PREP 前置詞 You use **for** with "every" when you are stating a ratio, to introduce one of the things in the ratio. 一に対して ❑ *For every farm job that is lost, two or three other jobs in the area are put at risk.* 農場での失業1件に対して、その地域の他の仕事2件ないし3件が危険にさらされる。**8** PREP 前置詞 You can use **for** in expressions such as **dollar for dollar** or **mile for mile** when you are making comparisons between the values or qualities of different things. （ある単位で）比較すると [n PREP n] ❑ *...the Antarctic, mile for mile one of the planet's most lifeless areas.* マイル当たりでは地球上で最も生物が少ない地域の1つである南極圏

❹ for /fər, STRONG fɔːr/ **1** PREP 前置詞 If you say that you are **for** a particular activity, you mean that this is what you want or intend to do. 一を求めて ❑ *Right, who's for a toasted sandwich then?* よし。では誰がトーストのサンドイッチを欲しいの？ **2** PREP 前置詞 If you are **for** something, you agree with it or support it. 一に賛成して ❑ *Are you for or against public transportation?* あなたは公共交通手段に賛成ですか、それとも反対ですか。**3** PREP 前置詞 You use **for** after words such as "argue," "case," "evidence," or "vote" in order to introduce the thing that is being supported or proved. 一を支持して [n/v PREP n] ❑ *Another union has voted for industrial action in support of a pay claim.* もう1つの組合では賃上げ要求支持の労働争議に賛成の投票結果が出た。❑ *The case for nuclear power is impressive.* その原子力擁護論は印象深い。● ADV 副詞 **For** is also an adverb. ❑ *833 delegates voted for, and only 432 against.* 833名の代表が賛成に投じ、反対は432名のみだった。**4** PHRASE 句 If you say that you are **all for** doing something, you agree or strongly believe that it should be done, but you are also often suggesting that other people disagree with you or that there are practical difficulties. 全面的に支持して ❑ *He is all for players earning what they can while they are in the game.* 彼は選手が試合に出ている間に可能な稼ぎをするのを全面的に支持している。

In addition to the uses shown below, **for** is used after some verbs, nouns, and adjectives in order to introduce extra information, and in phrasal verbs such as "account for" and "make up for." It is also used with some verbs that have two objects in order to introduce the second object.

for|age /fɔːrɪdʒ/ (forages, foraging, foraged) **1** V-I 自動詞 If someone **forages for** something, they search for it in a busy way. 捜し回る ❑ *They were forced to forage for clothing and fuel.* 彼らは衣類と燃料を捜し回らざるを得なかった。**2** V-I 自動詞 When animals **forage**, they search for food. えさをあさる ❑ *We disturbed a wild boar that had been foraging by the roadside.* 我々は道端でえさをあさっていたイノシシのじゃまをした。

for|ay /fɔːreɪ/ (forays) **1** N-COUNT 可算名詞 If you make a **foray into** a new or unfamiliar type of activity, you start to become involved in it. 進出 ❑ *Emporio Armani, the Italian fashion house, has made a discreet foray into furnishings.* イタリアの高級服飾メーカーのエンポリオ・アルマーニは慎重に家具類への進出を始めた。**2** N-COUNT 可算名詞 You can refer to a short trip that you make as a **foray** if it seems to involve excitement or risk, for example, because it is to an unfamiliar place or because you are looking for a particular thing. 小旅行 ❑ *Most guests make at least one foray into the town.* たいていの訪問客が少なくとも1度はその町に足を伸ばす。**3** N-COUNT 可算名詞 If a group of soldiers make a **foray into** enemy territory, they make a quick attack there, and then return to their own territory. 急襲 ❑ *These base camps were used by the PKK guerrillas to make forays into Turkey.* これらの前線基地はクルド労働者党ゲリラのトルコ急襲に使われた。

for|bid /fərbɪd, fɔːr-/ (forbids, forbidding, forbade, forbidden) **1** V-T 他動詞 If you **forbid** someone **to** do something, or if you **forbid** an activity, you order that it must not be done. 禁じる ❑ *They'll forbid you to marry.* 彼らはあなたが結婚するのを禁じるだろう。❑ *She was shut away and forbidden to read.* 彼女は閉じ込められ、読書を禁じられた。**2** V-T 他動詞 If something **forbids** a particular course of action or state of affairs, it makes it impossible for the course of action or state of affairs to happen. 妨げる ❑ *His own pride forbids him to ask Arthur's help.* 彼自身の自尊心がアーサーに助けを求めることを許さない。

for|bid|den /fərbɪdⁿ, fɔːr-/ **1** ADJ 形容詞 If something is **forbidden**, you are not allowed to do it or have it. 禁じられた ❑ *Smoking was forbidden everywhere.* すべての場所が禁煙だった。**2** ADJ 形容詞 A **forbidden** place is one that you are not allowed to visit or enter. 禁制の ❑ *This was a forbidden area for foreigners.* ここは外国人禁制区域だった。**3** ADJ 形容詞 **Forbidden** is used to describe things that people strongly disapprove of or feel guilty about, and that are not often mentioned or talked about. 禁断の ❑ *The war was a forbidden subject.* その戦争についての話題は禁制だった。❑ *Men fantasize as a substitute for acting out forbidden desires.* 男性は禁断の欲望を実行するための代役を務めることを夢想する。

---

force

❶ VERB USES
❷ NOUN USES: POWER OR STRENGTH
❸ THE ARMY, POLICE, ETC.

---

❶ force /fɔːrs/ (forces, forcing, forced) **1** V-T 他動詞 If someone **forces** you **to** do something, they make you do it even though you do not want to, for example, by threatening you. 強制する ❑ *He took two women hostage and forced them to drive away from the area.* 彼は2人の女性を人質に取り、彼女らにその地域から運転して逃げることを強制した。❑ *They were grabbed by three men who appeared to force them into a car.* 彼らは3人の男につかまれ、男たちは彼らを車に押し込もうとしているようだった。**2** V-T 他動詞 If a situation or event **forces** you to do something, it makes it necessary for you to do something that you would not otherwise have done. 強制する ❑ *A back injury forced her to withdraw from Wimbledon.* 背中のけがのせいで彼女はウィンブルドン出場を取り消さざるを得なかった。**3** V-T 他動詞 He turned right, down a dirt road that forced him into four-wheel drive. 彼は右折し、四輪駆動で運転せざるを得ない未舗装の道路を下った。**3** V-T 他動詞 If someone **forces** something **on** or **upon** you, they make you accept or use it when you would prefer not to. 押しつける ❑ *To force this agreement on the nation is wrong.* この合意を国民に押しつけるのは間違っている。**4** V-T 他動詞 If you **force** something into a particular position, you use a lot of strength to make it move there. 無理に押しやる ❑ *They were forcing her head under the icy waters, drowning her.* 彼らは彼女の頭を氷のように冷たい水面下に無理やり押し込み、彼女をおぼれさせた。**5** V-T 他動詞 If someone **forces** a lock, a door, or a window, they break the lock or fastening in order to get into a building without using a key. こじあける ❑ *That evening police forced the door of the apartment and arrested Mr. Roberts.* その晩警察はアパートの扉をこじあけ、ロバーツ

氏を逮捕した. ⑥ PHRASE 句 If you **force** your **way through** or **into** somewhere, you have to push or break things that are in your way in order to get there. 無理やり通る ❑ *The miners forced their way through a police cordon.* 鉱夫たちは警察の非常線を無理やり通った.

❷ **force** /fɔrs/ (forces) ❶ N-UNCOUNT 不可算名詞 If someone uses **force** to do something, or if it is done by **force**, strong and violent physical action is taken in order to achieve it. 武力, 暴力 ❑ *The government decided against using force to break up the demonstrations.* 政府はデモ隊を解散させるのに実力行使をしないことに決めた. ❷ N-UNCOUNT 不可算名詞 **Force** is the power or strength which something has. 力, 威力 ❑ *The force of the explosion shattered the windows of several buildings.* 爆発の力でいくつかの建物の窓が破壊された. ❸ N-UNCOUNT 不可算名詞 The **force** of something is the powerful effect or quality that it has. 影響力 ❑ *He changed our world through the force of his ideas.* 彼はその思想の影響力で我々の世界を変えた. ❹ N-UNCOUNT 不可算名詞 **Force** is used before a number to indicate a wind of a particular speed or strength, especially a very strong wind. ❑ *The airlift was conducted in force ten winds.* その空輸は風力10の風の中で行われた. ❺ N-COUNT 可算名詞 If you refer to someone or something as a **force** in a particular type of activity, you mean that they have a strong influence on it. 影響力を持つ人・物 ❑ *For years the army was the most powerful political force in the country.* 何年もの間, その国では軍が最強の政治勢力だった. ❑ *The band is still an innovative force in music.* そのバンドはいまだに音楽における革新的影響力を持っている. ❻ N-COUNT 可算名詞 You can use **forces** to refer to processes and events that do not appear to be caused by human beings, and are therefore difficult to understand or control. (自然などの) 力 ❑ *...the protection of mankind against the forces of nature: epidemics, predators, floods, hurricanes.* 疫病, 猛獣, 洪水, ハリケーンなど, 自然の猛威からの人類の保護 ❑ *The principle of market forces was applied to some of the country's most revered institutions.* 市場の力の原理はその国で最も重んじられている機関の一部でも用いられていた. ❼ N-VAR 可変性名詞 In physics, a **force** is the pulling or pushing effect that something has on something else. 力 ❑ *...the Earth's gravitational force.* 地球の重力 ❽ PHRASE 句 If you do something **from force of habit**, you do it because you have always done it in the past, rather than because you have thought carefully about it. 習慣の力 ❑ *He looked around from force of habit, but nobody paid any attention to him.* 彼は習慣的にあたりを見回したが, 誰も彼に注意を払わなかった. ❾ PHRASE 句 A law, rule, or system that is **in force** exists or is being used. 有効な ❑ *Although the new tax is already in force, you have until November to lodge an appeal.* 新税がすでに実施されているのに, 訴えの提出は11月まで待たねばならない. ❿ PHRASE 句 When people do something **in force**, they do it in large numbers. 大挙して ❑ *Voters turned out in force for their first taste of multiparty elections.* 初めての経験となる複数政党選挙に投票者は大挙して押し寄せた. ⓫ PHRASE 句 If you **join forces** with someone, you work together in order to achieve a common aim or purpose. 力を合わせる ❑ *Both groups joined forces to persuade voters to approve a tax break for the industry.* 両陣営は協力してその産業に対する減税に賛成するように投票者の説得にあたった.
→ see **motion**

Thesaurus	force また次を参照:
V.	coerce, make ❶ ❶ ❷
	push, thrust ❶ ❹
	break in, break open ❶ ❻
N.	energy, pressure, strength ❷ ❷

❸ **force** /fɔrs/ (forces) ❶ N-COUNT 可算名詞 **Forces** are groups of soldiers or military vehicles that are organized for a particular purpose. 部隊 ❑ *...the deployment of American forces in the region.* その地域への米軍の展開 ❷ N-PLURAL 複数名詞 The **forces** means the army, the navy, or the air force, or all three. 軍隊, 陸海空軍 ❑ *The more senior you become in the forces, the more likely you are to end up in a desk job.* 軍隊で年配になるにつれ, 事務的な仕事につく羽目になる可能性が高まる. ❸ N-SING 単数名詞 The **force** is sometimes used to mean the police force. 警察, 警官隊 ❑ *It was hard for a police officer to make friends outside the force.* 警官が警察の外で友だちを作ることは難しかった. ❹ → see also **air force, armed forces, labor force, workforce**

Word Partnership	force は次の語句と使われる:
V.	force to resign ❶ ❶ ❷
N.	force a smile ❶ ❷
	use of force ❷ ❶ ❷
	force of gravity ❷ ❼
ADJ.	excessive force, necessary force ❷ ❶
	driving force, powerful force ❷ ❸
	full force ❷ ❿
	enemy forces, military forces ❸ ❶ ❷

forced /fɔrst/ ❶ ADJ 形容詞 A **forced** action is something that you do because someone else makes you do it. 強制された [ADJ n] ❑ *A system of forced labor was used on the cocoa plantations.* ココアの栽培農場で強制労働が使われていた. ❷ ADJ 形容詞 A **forced** action is something that you do because circumstances make it necessary. やむを得ない [ADJ n] ❑ *He made a forced landing on a highway.* 彼は幹線道路に不時着した. ❸ ADJ 形容詞 If you describe something as **forced**, you mean it does not happen naturally and easily. 不自然な ❑ *...a forced smile.* 不自然な笑み

force|ful /fɔrsfəl/ ❶ ADJ 形容詞 If you describe someone as **forceful**, you approve of them because they express their opinions and wishes in a strong, emphatic, and confident way. 力強い [APPROVAL 賛成] ❑ *He was a man of forceful character, with considerable insight and diplomatic skills.* 彼は力強い性格の人物で, かなりの洞察力と外交手腕を持っていた. ● **force|ful|ly** ADV 副詞 [ADV with v] 力強く ❑ *Mrs. Dambar was talking very rapidly and somewhat forcefully.* ダンバー夫人はとても早口でやや力強く話していた. ❷ ADJ 形容詞 Something that is **forceful** has a very powerful effect and causes you to think or feel something very strongly. 力強い ❑ *It made a very forceful impression on me.* それはとても力強い印象を私に与えた. ● **force|ful|ly** ADV 副詞 [ADV with v] 力強く ❑ *Daytime television tended to remind her too forcefully of her own situation.* 昼間のテレビを見ると彼女は自分の現状についてあまりにも強く自覚させられることが多かった. ❸ ADJ 形容詞 A **forceful** point or argument in a discussion is one that is good, valid, and convincing. 説得力のある ❑ *You may need to be armed with some forceful arguments to persuade a partner into seeing things your way.* 相手を説得し物事をあなたのやり方で考えさせるためには, あなたは何か力強い論拠で武装する必要があるかもしれない.

for|cible /fɔrsɪbᵊl/ ADJ 形容詞 **Forcible** action involves physical force or violence. 強制的な ❑ *Reports are coming in of the forcible resettlement of villagers from the countryside into towns.* 農村部から都市部への住民の強制再移住に関する報告が入ってきている.

fore /fɔr/ ❶ PHRASE 句 If someone or something comes **to the fore** in a particular situation or group, they become important or popular. 目立って ❑ *A number of low-budget independent films brought new directors and actors to the fore.* 数多くの低予算独立系映画のおかげで新しい監督と役者が目立ってきた. ❷ ADJ 形容詞 **Fore** is used to refer to parts at the front of an animal, ship, or aircraft. 前部の [ADJ n] ❑ *There had been no direct damage in the fore part of the ship.* その船の前部には直接の損傷はなかった.

fore|arm /fɔrɑrm/ (forearms) N-COUNT 可算名詞 Your **forearm** is the part of your arm between your elbow and your wrist. 前腕 ❑ *...the tattoo on his forearm.* 彼の前腕部の刺青

Word Link	fore ≈ before : **forecast, foresight, foreword**

fore|cast /fɔrkæst/ (forecasts, forecasting, forecasted)

The forms **forecast** and **forecasted** can both be used for the past tense and past participle.

forecast 形と forecasted 形は両者ともに過去時制と過去分詞として使える

❶ N-COUNT 可算名詞 A **forecast** is a statement of what is expected to happen in the future, especially in relation to a particular event or situation. 予測 ❑ *...a forecast of a 2.25 percent growth in the economy.* 経済成長率2.25パーセントの予測 ❑ *He delivered his election forecast.* 彼は選挙予測を出した. ❷ V-T 他動詞 If you **forecast** future events, you say what you think is going to happen in the future. 予測する ❑ *They forecast a humiliating defeat for the president.* 彼らは大統領の屈辱的敗北を予測した. ❸ → see also **weather forecast**
→ see Word Web: **forecast**

fore|close /fɔrkloʊz/ (forecloses, foreclosing, foreclosed) V-I 自動詞 If the person or organization that lent someone money **forecloses**, they take possession of a property that was bought with the borrowed money, for example, because regular repayments have not been made. 抵当権を行使する, 差し押さえる [BUSINESS 実業] ❑ *The bank foreclosed on the mortgage for his previous home.* 銀行は彼の以前の家の抵当権を行使した.

fore|clo|sure /fɔrkloʊʒər/ (foreclosures) N-VAR 可変性名詞 **Foreclosure** is when someone who has lent money to a person or organization so that they can buy property takes possession of the property because the money has not been repaid. 抵当権の行使, 差し押さえ [BUSINESS 実業] ❑ *If homeowners can't keep up the payments, they face foreclosure.* 家の所有者が支払いを続けられなければ, 差し押さえに直面する.

fore|court /fɔrkɔrt/ (forecourts) ❶ N-COUNT 可算名詞 In sports such tennis and badminton, the **forecourt** is the section of each side of the court that is nearest to the net. フォアコート ❷ N-COUNT 可算名詞 The **forecourt** of a large building or gas station is the open area at the front of it. 前庭 [usu 'the']
→ see **tennis**

fore|finger /fɔrfɪŋgər/ (forefingers) N-COUNT 可算名詞 Your

Word Web   forecast

Meteorologists depend on good information. They make **observations**. They gather **data** about **barometric pressure**, **temperature**, and **humidity**. They track **storms** with **radar** and **satellites**. They track cold **fronts** and warm fronts. They put all of this information into their computers and **model** possible weather patterns. Today scientists are trying to make better **weather forecasts**. They are installing thousands of small, inexpensive **radar** units on rooftops and cell phone towers. They will gather information near the Earth's surface and high in the sky. This will give meteorologists more information to help them **predict** tomorrow's weather.

forefinger is the finger that is next to your thumb. 人差し指 ❏*He took the pen between his thumb and forefinger.* 彼はそのペンを親指と人差し指の間に持った.

fore|front / fɔːrfrʌnt / ◼ N-SING 単数名詞 If you are at the **forefront** of a campaign or other activity, you have a leading and influential position in it. 最前線 ❏*They have been at the forefront of the campaign for political change.* 彼らは政治改革運動の最前線に立ってきた. ◼ N-SING 単数名詞 If something is **at the forefront of** people's minds or attention, they think about it a lot because it is particularly important to them. 中心 ❏*The pension issue was not at the forefront of his mind in the spring of 1985.* 1985年の春には年金問題は彼の心の中心にはなかった.

fore|go /fɔːrgoʊ / (foregoes, foregoing, forewent, foregone) also **forgo** V-T 他動詞 If you **forego** something, you decide to do without it, although you would like it. なしで済ませる [FORMAL 形式ばった] ❏*Many skiers are happy to forego a summer vacation to go skiing.* 多くのスキーヤーはスキーに行くため夏休みをあきらめることをよしとする.

fore|gone /fɔːrgɒn / ◼ **Foregone** is the past participle of **forego**. foregoの過去分詞 ◼ PHRASE 句 If you say that a particular result is **a foregone conclusion**, you mean you are certain that it will happen. 既定の結末 ❏*Most voters believe the result is a foregone conclusion.* 多くの有権者が結果ははじめから分かりきっていると信じている.

fore|ground /fɔːrgraʊnd / (foregrounds) ◼ N-VAR 可変性名詞 The **foreground** of a picture or scene you are looking at is the part or area of it that appears nearest to you. 前景 ❏*He is the bowler-hatted figure in the foreground of Orpen's famous painting.* 彼はオーペンの有名な絵画の前景で山高帽をかぶっている人物だ. ◼ N-SING 単数名詞 If something or someone is **in the foreground**, or comes **to the foreground**, they receive a lot of attention. 最も目立つ位置 ❏*This is another worry that has come to the foreground in recent years.* これが近年になって非常に注目されてきたもう1つの心配だ.

fore|head /fɔːrhɛd, fɔːrɪd / (foreheads) N-COUNT 可算名詞 Your **forehead** is the area at the front of your head between your eyebrows and your hair. 額 ❏*...the lines on her forehead.* 彼女の額のしわ
→ see **face**

for|eign /fɔːrɪn / ◼ ADJ 形容詞 Something or someone that is **foreign** comes from or relates to a country that is not your own. 外国の ❏*She was on her first foreign vacation without her parents.* 彼女は初めての両親なしでの海外旅行だった. ❏*...a foreign language.* 外国語 ◼ ADJ 形容詞 In politics and journalism, **foreign** is used to describe people, jobs, and activities relating to countries that are not the country of the person or government concerned. 対外の [ADJ n] ❏*...the German foreign minister.* ドイツの外務大臣 ❏*I am the foreign correspondent in Washington of La Tribuna newspaper of Honduras.* 私はホンジュラスのラ・トリブーナ紙のワシントン駐在海外特派員です. ◼ ADJ 形容詞 A **foreign** object is something that has got into something else, usually by accident, and should not be there. 異質の [FORMAL 形式ばった] ❏*The patient's immune system would reject the transplanted organ as a foreign object.* その患者の免疫系は移植臓器を異物として拒絶反応を起こすだろう.

Thesaurus   foreign また次を参照:

ADJ.   alien, exotic, strange; (ant.) domestic, native ◼

for|eign|er /fɔːrɪnər / (foreigners) N-COUNT 可算名詞 A **foreigner** is someone who belongs to a country that is not your own. 外国人 ❏*They are discouraged from becoming close friends with foreigners.* 彼らは外国人と親しい友達となることを反対されている.

for|eign ex|change (foreign exchanges) ◼ N-PLURAL 複数名詞 **Foreign exchanges** are the institutions or systems involved with changing one currency into another. 外国為替 ❏*On the foreign exchanges, the U.S. dollar is up point forty-five.* 外国為替に関しては、米ドルが0.45値上がりした. ◼ N-UNCOUNT 不可算名詞 **Foreign exchange** is used to refer to foreign currency that is obtained through the foreign exchange system. 外貨 ❏*...an important source of foreign exchange.* 外貨の重要な源泉 ◼ N-COUNT 可算名詞 A **foreign exchange** is an arrangement in which people from two different countries visit each other's country, to strengthen links between them. 外国との交流 [oft N n] ❏*He recently hosted a foreign exchange student from Argentina.* 彼は最近アルゼンチンの交換留学生を接待した.

Word Link   man ≈ human being : fore**man**, hu**man**e, wo**man**

fore|man /fɔːrmən / (foremen) ◼ N-COUNT 可算名詞 A **foreman** is a person, especially a man, in charge of a group of workers. 職長主任, 親方 ❏*He still visited the dairy daily, but left most of the business details to his manager and foreman.* 彼はまだ毎日その乳製品製造所を見に行ったが, 細かい仕事の大半を支配人と職場主任に任せていた. ◼ N-COUNT 可算名詞 The **foreman** of a jury is the person who is chosen as their leader. 陪審長 ❏*There was applause as the foreman of the jury announced the verdict.* 陪審長が評決を発表したとき拍手が起こった.

fore|most /fɔːrmoʊst / ◼ ADJ 形容詞 The **foremost** thing or person in a group is the most important or best. 最重要の ❏*He was one of the world's foremost scholars of ancient Indian culture.* 彼は古代インド文化に関する世界で最高の学者の1人だった. ◼ PHRASE 句 You use **first and foremost** to emphasize the most important quality of something or someone. 真っ先に [EMPHASIS 強調] ❏*It is first and foremost a trade agreement.* それは真っ先に貿易協定だ.

fore|name /fɔːrneɪm / (forenames) N-COUNT 可算名詞 Your **forename** is your first name. Your **forenames** are your names other than your surname. 名 [FORMAL 形式ばった] ❏*...the unusual spelling of his forename.* 彼の名の珍しいつづり

fo|ren|sic /fərɛnsɪk / ◼ ADJ 形容詞 **Forensic** is used to describe the work of scientists who examine evidence in order to help the police solve crimes. 犯罪科学の, 法医学の [ADJ n] ❏*They were convicted on forensic evidence alone.* 彼らは法医学的証拠のみで有罪となった. ❏*Forensic experts searched the area for clues.* 科学捜査の専門家が手掛かりを求めてその地域を捜索した. ◼ N-UNCOUNT 不可算名詞 **Forensics** is the use of scientific techniques to solve crimes. 犯罪科学, 法医学 ❏*...the newest advances in forensics.* 犯罪科学の最新の進展

fore|run|ner /fɔːrʌnər / (forerunners) N-COUNT 可算名詞 If you describe a person or thing as the **forerunner of** someone or something similar, you mean they existed before them and either influenced their development or were a sign of what was going to happen. 先駆者, 先触れ ❏*...a machine which, in some respects, was the forerunner of the modern helicopter.* いくつかの点で現代のヘリコプターの先駆となった機械

fore|see /fɔːrsiː / (foresees, foreseeing, foresaw, foreseen) V-T 他動詞 If you **foresee** something, you expect and believe that it will happen. 予知する, 予測する ❏*He did not foresee any problems.* 彼はなんの問題も予測しなかった.

fore|see|able /fɔːrsiːəbəl / ◼ ADJ 形容詞 If a future event is **foreseeable**, you know that it will happen or that it can happen, because it is a natural or obvious consequence of something else that you know. 予知できる ❏*It seems to me that this crime was foreseeable and this death preventable.* この犯罪は予知できるものだったし, この死は避けられるものだったと私には思える. ◼ PHRASE 句 If you say that something will happen **for the foreseeable future**, you think that it will continue to happen for a long time. 当分の間 ❏*Profit and dividend growth looks above average for the foreseeable future.* 利益と配当の伸びが, ここしばらくは平均以上と思われる.

Word Link   fore ≈ before : **fore**cast, **fore**sight, **fore**word

fore|sight /fɔːrsaɪt / N-UNCOUNT 不可算名詞 Someone's **foresight** is their ability to see what is likely to happen in the future and to take appropriate action. 先見の明 [APPROVAL 賛成] ❏*They had the foresight to invest in new technology.* 彼らは新技術に投資する先見性を持っていた.

Word Web   forest

Four hundred years ago, newly arrived colonists in North America encountered endless **forests**. This abundant supply of **wood** helped them get started. They used **timber** to build homes and make furniture. They burned wood for cooking and heating. They cut down the **woods** to create farmland. By the late 1800s, most of the old growth forests on the East Coast had disappeared. The **lumber** industry has also destroyed millions of trees. Reforestation has replaced some of them. However, logging companies usually plant single species forests. Some people say these are not really forests at all—just **tree** farms.

for|est /fɔ́rɪst/ (forests) N-VAR 可変性名詞 A **forest** is a large area where trees grow close together. 森 ❑ *Parts of the forest are still dense and inaccessible.* 森のところどころはまだ木々が密集しており足を踏み入れることができない.
→ see Word Web: **forest**

fore|stall /fɔrstɔ́l/ (forestalls, forestalling, forestalled) V-T 他動詞 If you **forestall** someone, you realize what they are likely to do and prevent them from doing it. 機先を制する ❑ *Large numbers of police were in the square to forestall any demonstrations.* いかなるデモでも機先を制しようと広場には大勢の警官がいた.

for|est|ry /fɔ́rɪstri/ N-UNCOUNT 不可算名詞 **Forestry** is the science or skill of growing and taking care of trees in forests, especially in order to obtain wood. 林学, 林業 ❑ *...his great interest in forestry.* 彼の林学への大きな関心
→ see **industry**

for|ever /fərévər, fɔr-/ **1** ADV 副詞 If you say that something will happen or continue **forever**, you mean that it will always happen or continue. 永久に [ADV with v] ❑ *I think that we will live together forever.* 私は私たちが永久に一緒に暮らすと思う. **2** ADV 副詞 If something has gone or changed **forever**, it has gone or changed completely and permanently. 永遠に [ADV after v] ❑ *The old social order was gone forever.* 古い社会秩序は永遠に失われた. **3** ADV 副詞 If you say that something takes **forever** or lasts **forever**, you are emphasizing that it takes a very long time, or that it seems to. 非常に長い間 [INFORMAL くだけた, EMPHASIS 強調] [ADV after v] ❑ *The drive seemed to take forever.* ドライブは永久に続くように思われた.

Thesaurus   forever また次を参照:

ADV.   always, endlessly, eternally **1**
permanently **2**
permanently **2**

fore|went /fɔrwént/ **Forewent** is the past tense of **forego**. foregoの過去形

Word Link   fore ≈ before : forecast, foresight, foreword

fore|word /fɔ́rwɜrd/ (forewords) N-COUNT 可算名詞 The **foreword** to a book is an introduction by the author or by someone else. 序文 ❑ *She has written the foreword to a book of recipes.* 彼女は料理法の本に序文を書いた.

forex /fɔ́rɛks/ N-UNCOUNT 不可算名詞 **Forex** is an abbreviation for **foreign exchange**. 外為 ❑ *...the forex market.* 外為市場

for|feit /fɔ́rfɪt/ (forfeits, forfeiting, forfeited) **1** V-T 他動詞 If you **forfeit** something, you lose it or are forced to give it up because you have broken a rule or done something wrong. 失う, 没収される ❑ *He was ordered to forfeit more than $1.5m.* 彼は150万ドル以上没収の命令を受けた. **2** V-T 他動詞 If you **forfeit** something, you give it up willingly, especially so that you can achieve something else. 犠牲にする ❑ *Do you think that they would forfeit profit in the name of safety?* 彼らが安全の名の下に利益を犠牲にすると思いますか. **3** N-COUNT 可算名詞 A **forfeit** is something that you have to give up because you have done something wrong. 没収物 ❑ *That is the forfeit he must pay.* それが彼の払うべき罰金だ.

for|gave /fərgéɪv/ **Forgave** is the past tense of **forgive**. forgiveの過去形

forge /fɔrdʒ/ (forges, forging, forged) **1** V-RECIP 相互動詞 If one person or institution **forges** an agreement or relationship with another, they create it with a lot of hard work, hoping that it will be strong or lasting. 作りあげる ❑ *The prime minister is determined to forge a good relationship with the country's new leader.* 首相はその国の新しい指導者との良い関係を築き上げることを決意している. ❑ *They agreed to forge closer economic ties.* 彼らはより緊密な経済的関係を作りあげることで合意した. **2** V-T 他動詞 If someone **forges** something such as paper money, a document, or a painting, they copy it or make it so that it looks genuine, in order to deceive people. 偽造する ❑ *He admitted seven charges including forging passports.* 彼は旅券偽造を含む7件の罪を認めた. ❑ *They used forged documents to leave the country.* 彼らはその国を出るために偽造書類を使った. ● **forg|er**

(forgers) N-COUNT 可算名詞 偽造者 ❑ *...the most prolific art forger in the country.* その国で最も多作な美術品贋（がん）作者
▶ **forge ahead** PHRASAL VERB 句動詞 If you **forge ahead** with something, you continue with it and make a lot of progress with it. 躍進する ❑ *He again pledged to forge ahead with his plans for reform.* 彼は再び彼の改革計画を躍進させることを誓った.

Word Partnership   forge は次の語句と使われる:

N.   forge **a bond**, forge **a friendship**, forge **links**, forge **a relationship**, forge **ties 1**
forge **documents**, forge **an identity**, forge **a signature 2**

for|gery /fɔ́rdʒəri/ (forgeries) **1** N-UNCOUNT 不可算名詞 **Forgery** is the crime of forging money, documents, or paintings. 偽造 ❑ *He was found guilty of forgery.* 彼は偽造で有罪となった. **2** N-COUNT 可算名詞 You can refer to a forged document, bill, or painting as a **forgery**. 偽造品, 贋（がん）作 ❑ *The letter was a forgery.* その手紙は偽造だった.

for|get /fərgét/ (forgets, forgetting, forgot, forgotten) **1** V-T 他動詞 If you **forget** something or **forget** how to do something, you cannot think of it or think how to do it, although you knew it or knew how to do it in the past. 忘れる ❑ *She forgot where she left the car and it took us two days to find it.* 彼女は車を置いた場所を忘れ, 私たちがそれを見つけるのに2日かかった. **2** V-T/V-I 他動詞/自動詞 If you **forget** something or **forget** to do it, you fail to think about it or fail to remember to do it, for example, because you are thinking about other things. 忘れる ❑ *She never forgets her daddy's birthday.* 彼女は決して父親の誕生日を忘れない. ❑ *She forgot to lock her door one day and two men got in.* ある日彼女は扉の鍵をかけ忘れ, 2人の男が侵入した. ❑ *When I close my eyes, I forget about everything.* 目を閉じると, 私はすべてを忘れる. **3** V-T 他動詞 If you **forget** something that you had intended to bring with you, you do not bring it because you did not think about it at the right time. 置き忘れる ❑ *Once when we were going to Paris, I forgot my passport.* かつて我々がパリに行こうとしたとき, 私は旅券を忘れた.

Note that you cannot use the verb **forget** to say that you have put something somewhere and left it there. Instead you use the verb **leave**. ❑ *I left my bag on the bus.*

4 V-T/V-I 他動詞/自動詞 If you **forget** something or someone, you deliberately put them out of your mind and do not think about them any more. 忘れる ❑ *I hope you will forget the bad experience you had today.* 私は今日の嫌な経験をあなたが忘れてくれることを望む. ❑ *I found it very easy to forget about Sumner.* サムナーのことを忘れるのはとても易しいことだとわかった. **5** CONVENTION 慣習表現 You say "**Forget it**" in reply to someone as a way of telling them not to worry or bother about something, or as an emphatic way of saying no to a suggestion. 気にするな, だめです [SPOKEN 口語, FORMULAE 決まり文句] ❑ *"Sorry, Liz. I think I was a bit rude to you."—"Forget it, but don't do it again!"* 「ごめん, リズ. どうもきみに対してちょっと失礼だったようだ」「いいわよ. でも2度としないで」 **6** PHRASE 句 You say **not forgetting** a particular thing or person when you want to include them in something that you have already talked about. 忘れずに ❑ *Leave a message, not forgetting your name and address.* 名前と住所を添え伝言を頼みなさい.

Thesaurus   forget また次を参照:

V.   disregard, ignore, neglect, overlook **2**

Word Partnership   forget は次の語句と使われる:

ADV.   **never** forget, **quickly** forget, **soon** forget **1**
almost forget **1** – **3**
ADJ.   **easy/hard to** forget **1** – **4**

for|get|ful /fərgétfəl/ ADJ 形容詞 Someone who is **forgetful** often forgets things. 忘れっぽい ❑ *My mother has become very forgetful and confused.* 私の母はとても忘れっぽく, まごつくようになった.

for|give /fərgɪv/ (forgives, forgiving, forgave, forgiven) **1** V-T 他動詞 If you **forgive** someone who has done something bad or wrong, you stop being angry with them and no longer want to punish them. 許す ❑ *Hopefully Jane will understand and forgive you, if she really loves you.* ジェーンが本当にあなたを愛しているなら、あなたを理解し許してくれることでしょう。❑ *Irene forgave Terry for stealing her money.* アイリーンは彼女の金を盗んだテリーを許した。❑ *He could forgive Petal anything if the children were safe.* 子供たちが無事なら、彼はペタルのどんなことでも許せるでしょう。**2** V-T 他動詞 **Forgive** is used in polite expressions and apologies like "**forgive me**" and "**forgive my ignorance**" when you are saying or doing something that might seem rude, silly, or complicated. 許す [POLITENESS 丁寧さ] ❑ *Forgive me, I don't mean to insult you.* 申し訳ありませんが、あなたを侮辱するつもりはないのです。❑ *I do hope you'll forgive me but I've got to leave.* まことに申し訳ないのですが、おいとませねばなりません。**3** V-T PASSIVE 受動態他動詞 If you say that someone could **be forgiven for** doing something, you mean that they were wrong or mistaken, but not seriously, because many people would have done the same thing in those circumstances. 大目に見る ❑ *Looking at the figures, you could be forgiven for thinking the recession is already over.* その数字を見れば、不況はすでに終わったと考えたとしても無理はないかもしれない。

for|give|ness /fərgɪvnɪs/ N-UNCOUNT 不可算名詞 If you ask for **forgiveness**, you ask to be forgiven for something wrong that you have done. 寛大の精神と国民の和解 ❑ *a spirit of forgiveness and national reconciliation.* 寛大の精神と国民の和解。

for|giv|ing /fərgɪvɪŋ/ ADJ 形容詞 Someone who is **forgiving** is willing to forgive. 寛大な ❑ *Voters can be remarkably forgiving of presidents who fail to keep their campaign promises.* 有権者は選挙期間中の公約を守れない大統領に極めて寛大になりえる。

for|go /fɔrgoʊ/ → see **forego**

for|got /fərgɒt/ **Forgot** is the past tense of **forget**. forgetの過去形

for|got|ten /fərgɒtⁿn/ **Forgotten** is the past participle of **forget**. forgetの過去分詞
→ see **memory**

fork /fɔrk/ (forks, forking, forked) **1** N-COUNT 可算名詞 A **fork** is a tool used for eating food which has a row of three or four long metal points at the end. フォーク ❑ *...knives and forks.* ナイフとフォーク **2** N-COUNT 可算名詞 A **fork** in a road, path, or river is a point at which it divides into two parts and forms a "Y" shape. 分岐点 ❑ *We arrived at a fork in the road.* 我々はその道路の分岐点に到着した。❑ *The road divides; you should take the right fork.* 道が分かれる。右のほうに行くべきだ。**3** V-T 他動詞 If you **fork** food **into** your mouth or **onto** a plate, you put it there using a fork. フォークで運ぶ ❑ *He forked an egg onto a piece of bread and folded it into a sandwich.* 彼はフォークで卵を1枚のパンの上に運び、折り曲げてサンドイッチにした。**4** V-I 自動詞 If a road, path, or river **forks**, it divides into a fork. 分岐する [no cont] ❑ *Beyond the village the road forked.* その村を越えると道路は分岐した。**5** N-COUNT 可算名詞 A garden **fork** is a tool used for breaking up soil which has a row of three or four long metal points at the end. またぐわ [mainly BRIT 主に英国英語; AM usually **pitchfork** 米国英語では通常 **pitchfork**]
→ see **lightning, silverware**
▶ **fork out** PHRASAL VERB 句動詞 If you **fork out for** something, you spend a lot of money on it. 支払う [INFORMAL くだけた] ❑ *Visitors to the castle had to fork out for a guidebook.* その城の観光客は案内書に高い金を払わねばならなかった。
▶ **fork over** PHRASAL VERB 句動詞 If you **fork** something **over** to someone, for example money, you give it to them. 支払う [INFORMAL くだけた] ❑ *Nonresidents who work in Philadelphia fork over 3.88 percent of their pay to the city.* フィラデルフィア市で働く非居住者は給与の3.88パーセントを市に払わねばならない。

for|lorn /fərlɔrn/ **1** ADJ 形容詞 If someone is **forlorn**, they feel alone and unhappy. わびしい [LITERARY 文語的] ❑ *One of the demonstrators, a young woman, sat forlorn on the sidewalk.* デモ参加者の1人の若い女性が歩道にひとりぼっちと座りこんでいた。**2** ADJ 形容詞 A **forlorn** hope or attempt is one that you think has no chance of success. 見込みのない ❑ *Peasants have left the land in the forlorn hope of finding a better life in cities.* 小作農たちは都市でよりよい生活を見つけるというはかない望みでその土地を離れた。

form /fɔrm/ (forms, forming, formed) **1** N-COUNT 可算名詞 A **form** of something is a type or kind of it. 種類 ❑ *He contracted a rare form of cancer.* 彼は珍しい型のがんを患った。❑ *I am against hunting in any form.* 私はどんな種類の狩猟にも反対だ。**2** N-COUNT 可算名詞 When something can exist or happen in several possible ways, you can use **form** to refer to one particular way in which it exists or happens. 形式 ❑ *They received a benefit in the form of a tax reduction.* 彼らは給与の3.88という形式で恩恵を受けた。**3** N-COUNT 可算名詞 The **form** of something is its shape. 形 ❑ *...the form of the body.* 体形 **4** N-COUNT 可算名詞 You can refer to something that you can see as a **form** if you cannot see it clearly, or if its outline is the clearest or most striking aspect of it. 形、物影 ❑ *His form lay still*

under the blankets. 彼の形がまだ毛布の下にあった。**5** N-COUNT 可算名詞 A **form** is a paper with questions on it and spaces marked where you should write the answers. Forms usually ask you to give details about yourself, for example, when you are applying for a job or joining an organization. 書式 ❑ *You will be asked to fill in a form with details of your birth and occupation.* 生年月日、職業などの詳細を用紙に記入することを求められるでしょう。**6** V-T/V-I 他動詞/自動詞 When a particular shape **forms** or is **formed**, people or things move or are arranged so that this shape is made. 形作る [他動詞]、(形が)できる [自動詞] ❑ *A line formed to use the bathroom.* トイレを使うために行列ができた。❑ *They formed a circle and sang "Auld Lang Syne."* 彼らは輪になって『蛍の光』を歌った。**7** V-T 他動詞 If something is arranged or changed so that it becomes similar to a thing with a particular structure or function, you can say that it **forms** that thing. 形作る ❑ *These panels folded up to form a screen some five feet tall.* これらの板が高さ5フィートほどのついたてになるよう折りたたまれた。**8** V-T 他動詞 If something consists of particular things, people, or features, you can say that they **form** that thing. 形成する ❑ *...the articles that formed the basis of Randolph's book.* ランドルフの著書の基礎を形成した論文 **9** V-T 他動詞 If you **form** an organization, group, or company, you start it. 組織する ❑ *They tried to form a study group on human rights.* 彼らは人権に関する研究団体を組織しようとした。**10** V-T/V-I 他動詞/自動詞 When something natural **forms** or is **formed**, it begins to exist and develop. 形成する [他動詞]、生ずる [自動詞] ❑ *The stars must have formed 10 to 15 billion years ago.* それらの星は100億年から150億年前にできたに違いない。**11** V-T/V-I 他動詞/自動詞 If you **form** a relationship, a habit, or an idea, or if it **forms**, it begins to exist and develop. 形成する ❑ *She had formed the habit of giving herself freely to men.* 彼女には簡単に男に自分を与える習慣がついていた。❑ *An idea formed in his mind.* ある考えが彼の頭に浮かんだ。**12** V-T 他動詞 If you say that something **forms** a person's character or personality, you mean that it has a strong influence on them and causes them to develop in a particular way. (性格・人格を) 作り上げる ❑ *Anger at injustice formed his character.* 不正への怒りが彼の性格を形成していた。**13** N-UNCOUNT 不可算名詞 In sports, **form** refers to the ability or success of a person or animal over a period of time. 調子 ❑ *His form this season has been brilliant.* 今期の彼の調子は素晴らしかった。

Thesaurus	form また次を参照:
N.	class, description, kind **1**
	body, figure, frame, shape **3**
	application, document, sheet **5**
V.	construct, create, develop, establish **7** – **11**

for|mal /fɔrmⁿl/ (formals) **1** ADJ 形容詞 **Formal** speech or behavior is very correct and serious rather than relaxed and friendly, and is used especially in official situations. 形式ばった、改まった ❑ *He wrote a very formal letter of apology to Douglas.* 彼はダグラスにとても改まった謝罪の手紙を書いた。● **for|mal|ly** ADV 副詞 [ADV with v] 礼儀正しく ❑ *He took her back to Vincent Square in a taxi, saying goodnight formally on the doorstep.* 彼はタクシーでヴィンセント広場まで彼女を連れ帰り、戸口の階段で礼儀正しくお休みを言った。● **for|mal|ity** N-UNCOUNT 不可算名詞 形式ばった ❑ *Lillith's formality and seriousness amused him.* リリスの形式ばった態度と生まじめさが彼にはおかしかった。**2** ADJ 形容詞 [ADJ n] A **formal** action, statement, or request is an official one. 正式な ❑ *UN officials said a formal request was passed to American authorities.* 国連の職員がアメリカ当局に正式な要請を送ったと述べた。❑ *No formal announcement had been made.* 正式の発表はなされていなかった。● **for|mal|ly** ADV 副詞 [ADV with v] 正式に ❑ *Diplomats haven't formally agreed to Anderson's plan.* 外交官たちはアンダーソンの計画には正式には同意していない。**3** ADJ 形容詞 **Formal** occasions are special occasions at which people wear elegant clothes and behave according to a set of accepted rules. 格式ばった ❑ *One evening the company arranged a formal dinner after the play.* ある晩その会社は芝居の後に格式ばった晩さん会を用意した。● N-COUNT 可算名詞 **Formal** is also a noun. 格式ばった行事 ❑ *...a wide array of events, including school formals and speech nights, weddings, and balls.* 学校の公式行事、演説の夕べ、結婚式、舞踏会など幅広い行事 **4** ADJ 形容詞 **Formal** clothes are very elegant clothes that are suitable for formal occasions. 儀礼用の [ADJ n] ❑ *They wore ordinary ties instead of the more formal high collar and cravat.* 彼らはいっそう儀礼的な高襟とクラバットの代わりに普通のネクタイを着用していた。● **for|mal|ly** ADV 副詞 儀礼的に ❑ *It was really too warm for her to dress so formally.* 彼女にとってそこまで正式に装うには本当に暑すぎた。**5** ADJ 形容詞 [ADJ n] **Formal** education or training is given officially, usually in a school, college, or university. 正式の ❑ *Wendy didn't have any formal dance training.* ウェンディは正式の舞踏の訓練をまったく受けていなかった。● **for|mal|ly** ADV 副詞 [ADV -ed] 正規に ❑ *Usually only formally-trained artists from established schools are chosen.* 通常は有名校で正規の教育を受けた芸術家のみが選ばれる。**6** → see also **formality**

for|mal|ity /fɔrmælɪti/ (formalities) **1** N-COUNT 可算名詞 If

you say that an action or procedure is just a **formality**, you mean that it is done only because it is normally done, and that it will not have any real effect on the situation. 形式的行為 □ *Some contracts are a mere formality.* 契約には単なる形式でしかないものがある. **2** N-COUNT 可算名詞 **Formalities** are formal actions or procedures that are carried out as part of a particular activity or event. 正式手続き □ *They are whisked through the immigration and customs formalities in a matter of minutes.* 彼らは数分間ほどで入国および通関の手続きをさっさとすませてもらう. **3** → see also **formal**

for|mal|ize /fɔ̱rməlaɪz/ (**formalizes, formalizing, formalized**) V-T 他動詞 If you **formalize** a plan, idea, arrangement, or system, you make it formal and official. 正式な形にする □ *A recent treaty signed by Russia, Canada and Japan formalized an agreement to work together to stop the pirates.* ロシア, カナダ, 日本により調印された最近の条約により海賊防止のための協力合意が正式な形をとった.

for|mat /fɔ̱rmæt/ (**formats, formatting, formatted**) **1** N-COUNT 可算名詞 The **format** of something is the way or order in which it is arranged and presented. 構成 □ *I had met with him to explain the format of the program and what we had in mind.* 私はその計画の構成と我々の考えていることを説明するため彼に会ったことがあった. **2** N-COUNT 可算名詞 The **format** of a piece of computer software, a movie or a musical recording is the type of equipment on which it is designed to be used or played. For example, possible formats for a movie are DVD and video cassette. 形式 □ *His latest album is available on all formats.* 彼の最新アルバムはあらゆる形式で入手できる. **3** V-T 他動詞 To **format** a computer disk means to run a program so that the disk can be written on. 初期化する [COMPUTING コンピューティング] □ *...a menu that includes the choice to format a disk.* ディスク初期化の選択を含むメニュー **4** V-T 他動詞 To **format** a piece of computer text or graphics means to arrange the way in which it appears when it is printed or is displayed on a screen. 体裁を整える [COMPUTING コンピューティング] □ *When text is saved from a Web page, it is often very badly formatted with many short lines.* ウェブページからセーブしたテキストは, しばしば短い行がたくさん入っていてひどくまずい体裁になっている.

for|ma|tion /fɔrme̱ɪʃ³n/ (**formations**) **1** N-UNCOUNT 不可算名詞 The **formation of** something is the starting or creation of it. 編成, 成立 □ *Time is running out for the formation of a new government.* 新政府の樹立のための時間がなくなりつつある. **2** N-UNCOUNT 不可算名詞 The **formation of** an idea, habit, relationship, or character is the process of developing and establishing it. 形成 □ *My profession had an important influence in the formation of my character and temperament.* 私の職業が私の性格および気性の形成に重要な影響を与えた. **3** N-COUNT 可算名詞 If people or things are **in formation**, they are arranged in a particular pattern as they move. 陣形, 編隊 □ *He was flying in formation with seven other jets.* 彼は他の7機のジェット機と編隊を組んで飛んでいた. **4** N-COUNT 可算名詞 A rock or cloud **formation** is rock or cloud of a particular shape or structure. 形成物 □ *...a vast rock formation shaped like a pillar.* 柱のような形の巨大な岩の組成物

forma|tive /fɔ̱rmətɪv/ ADJ 形容詞 A **formative** period of time or experience is one that has an important and lasting influence on a person's character and attitudes. 人格形成の □ *She was born in Barbados but spent her formative years growing up in Miami.* 彼女はバルバドスで生まれたが, 人格形成期をマイアミで過ごした.

for|mer /fɔ̱rmər/ **1** ADJ 形容詞 **Former** is used to describe someone who used to have a particular job, position, or role, but no longer has it. 前の [ADJ n] □ *The unemployed executives include former sales managers, directors and accountants.* その失業した役員には前の販売部長, 重役, 会計士が含まれる. □ *...former president Richard Nixon.* 前大統領リチャード・ニクソン **2** ADJ 形容詞 **Former** is used to refer to countries which no longer exist or whose boundaries have changed. 旧 [ADJ n] □ *...the former Soviet Union.* 旧ソビエト連邦 **3** ADJ 形容詞 **Former** is used to describe something which used to belong to someone or which used to be a particular thing. 以前の [ADJ n] □ *...the former home of Robert E. Lee.* ロバート・E・リーのかつての家 **4** PRON 代名詞 When two people, things, or groups have just been mentioned, you can refer to the first of them as **the former**. 前者 ['the' PRON] □ *They grappled with the problem of connecting the electricity and water supplies. The former proved simple compared with the latter.* 彼らは電力供給と水道の問題に取り組んだ. 前者は後者と比べると簡単であることが分かった.

The latter should only be used to refer to the second of two items which have already been mentioned: □ *Given the choice between working for someone else and being on call day and night for the family business, she'd prefer the latter.* The last of three or more items can be referred to as **the last-named**. Compare this with **the former** which is used to talk about the first of two things already mentioned.

Thesaurus *former* また次を参照:

ADJ. prior **1**
past, previous **1 3**

for|mer|ly /fɔ̱rmərli/ ADV 副詞 If something happened or was true **formerly**, it happened or was true in the past. 以前に □ *He had formerly been in the navy.* 彼はかつて海軍にいた.

for|mi|dable /fɔ̱rmɪdəb³l, fərmɪ̱d-/ ADJ 形容詞 If you describe something or someone as **formidable**, you mean that you feel slightly frightened by them because they are very great or impressive. 恐るべき □ *We have a formidable task ahead of us.* 我々の前には恐るべき仕事が待っていた.

for|mu|la /fɔ̱rmyələ/ (**formulae** /fɔ̱rmyəli/ or **formulas**) **1** N-COUNT 可算名詞 A **formula** is a plan that is invented in order to deal with a particular problem. 解決策, 方法 □ *...a peace formula.* 和平策 **2** N-COUNT 可算名詞 A **formula** is a group of letters, numbers, or other symbols which represents a scientific or mathematical rule. 公式 □ *He developed a mathematical formula describing the distances of the planets from the Sun.* 彼は惑星の太陽からの距離を記述する数式を展開した. **3** N-COUNT 可算名詞 In science, the **formula** for a substance is a list of the amounts of various substances which make up that substance, or an indication of the atoms that it is composed of. 化学式 □ *Glucose and fructose have the same chemical formula but have very different properties.* ブドウ糖と果糖の化学式は同じだが, 性質は大きく異なる. **4** N-SING 単数名詞 A **formula for** a particular situation, usually a good one, is a course of action or a combination of actions that is certain or likely to result in that situation. 決まったやり方 □ *After he was officially pronounced the world's oldest man, he offered this simple formula for a long and happy life.* 自分が世界最高齢の男性であると公式に宣言された後で, 彼は長く幸せに生きるためのこの単純な秘訣を示した.

for|mu|late /fɔ̱rmyəleɪt/ (**formulates, formulating, formulated**) **1** V-T 他動詞 If you **formulate** something such as a plan or proposal, you invent it, thinking about the details carefully. 系統立てて計画する □ *Little by little, he formulated his plan for escape.* 少しずつ彼は自分の脱出計画を練った. **2** V-T 他動詞 If you **formulate** a thought, opinion, or idea, you express it or describe it using particular words. 系統立てて述べる □ *I was impressed by the way he could formulate his ideas.* 私は彼が自分の考えを明確に述べることができるのに感心した.

for|mu|la|tion /fɔ̱rmyəle̱ɪʃ³n/ (**formulations**) **1** N-VAR 可変性名詞 A **formulation** is the way in which you express your thoughts and ideas. 定式化, 明確な表現 □ *This is a far weaker formulation than is in the draft resolution which is being proposed.* 提案中の決議案の草案にあるものと比べると, これははるかに弱い立案だ. **2** N-UNCOUNT 不可算名詞 The **formulation** of something such as a policy or plan is the process of creating or inventing it. 策定 □ *...the process of policy formulation and implementation.* 政策の策定および施行の過程 **3** N-VAR 可変性名詞 The **formulation** of something such as a medicine or a beauty product is the way in which different ingredients are combined to make it. You can also say that the finished product is a **formulation**. 調合, 調合物 [mainly BRIT 主に英国英語]

for|sake /fərse̱ɪk/ (**forsakes, forsaking, forsook** /fərsʊ̱k/, **forsaken**) **1** V-T 他動詞 If you **forsake** someone, you leave them when you should have stayed, or you stop helping them or looking after them. 見捨てる [LITERARY 文語的, DISAPPROVAL 不賛成] □ *I still love him and I would never forsake him.* 私はまだ彼を愛しているし, 私は決して彼を見捨てないでしょう. **2** V-T 他動詞 If you **forsake** something, you stop doing it, using it, or having it. やめる [LITERARY 文語的] □ *He developed their claim to have forsaken military solutions to the civil war.* 彼は内戦の武力解決は放棄したという彼らの主張を疑っていた.

fort /fɔ̱rt/ (**forts**) **1** N-COUNT 可算名詞, N-IN-NAMES 名称中の名詞 A **fort** is a strong building or a place with a wall or fence around it where soldiers can stay and be safe from the enemy. とりで **2** PHRASE 句 If you **hold the fort** for someone or if you **hold down the fort**, you take care of things for them while they are somewhere else or are busy doing something else. 留守を預かる □ *His business partner is holding the fort while he is away.* 彼が出かけているまに, 彼の事業の共同経営者が留守を預かっている. □ *"I'll hold down the fort until he's back," Clark said.* 「彼が戻るまで留守を預かるつもりだ」クラークは言った.

forth /fɔ̱rθ/

In addition to the uses shown below, **forth** is also used in the phrasal verbs "put forth" and "set forth."

下記の用法に加えて, **forth** は put forth や set forth 句動詞にも使われる.

1 ADV 副詞 When someone goes **forth** from a place, they leave it. 前方へ [LITERARY 文語的] [ADV after v] □ *Go forth into the desert.* 前進して砂漠の中に入れ. **2** ADV 副詞 If one thing brings **forth**

another, the first thing produces the second. 外へ [LITERARY 文語的] [ADV after v] ❑ *My reflections brought forth no conclusion.* 私はよく考えたが、結論には至らなかった。 **3** ADV 副詞 When someone or something is brought **forth**, they are brought to a place or moved into a position where people can see them. 外へ [LITERARY 文語的] [ADV after v] ❑ *Pilate ordered Jesus to be brought forth.* ピラトがキリストを引き出すように命じた。 **4** **back and forth** → see **back** **5** **to hold forth** → see **hold**

forth|com|ing /fɔrθkʌmɪŋ/ **1** ADJ 形容詞 A **forthcoming** event is planned to happen soon. これから来る [ADJ n] ❑ *...his opponents in the forthcoming elections.* 来たる選挙戦での彼の対抗相手 **2** ADJ 形容詞 If something that you want, need, or expect is **forthcoming**, it is given to you or it happens. 手に入る [FORMAL 形式ばった] [v-link ADJ] ❑ *They promised that the money would be forthcoming.* 彼らはその金は手に入ると約束した。 ❑ *One source predicts no major shift in policy will be forthcoming at the committee hearings.* ある情報筋は委員会の聴聞会で大きな政策変更は得られないだろうと予測している。 **3** ADJ 形容詞 If you say that someone is **forthcoming**, you mean that they willingly give information when you ask them. 協力的な ❑ *William, sadly, was not very forthcoming about any other names he might have, where he lived or what his phone number was.* 残念ながら、ウィリアムは彼が知っているかもしれない他の人物の名前、彼の居所、彼の電話番号についてはあまり協力的ではなかった。

forth|right /fɔrθraɪt/ ADJ 形容詞 If you describe someone as **forthright**, you admire them because they show clearly and strongly what they think and feel. 率直な [APPROVAL 賛成] ❑ *...a deeply religious man with forthright opinions.* 率直な意見を持つとても信心深い男

for|ti|eth /fɔrtiəθ/ ORD 序数詞 The **fortieth** item in a series is the one that you count as number forty. 40番目の ❑ *It was the fortieth anniversary of the death of the composer.* それはその作曲家の没後40周年記念日だった。

for|ti|fy /fɔrtɪfaɪ/ (fortifies, fortifying, fortified) **1** V-T 他動詞 To **fortify** a place means to make it stronger and more difficult to attack, often by building a wall or ditch round it. 防備を固める ❑ *...soldiers working to fortify an airbase in Bahrain.* バーレーンの空軍基地の防備を強化するために作業する兵士たち **2** V-T 他動詞 If food or drink is **fortified**, another substance is added to it to make it healthier or stronger. アルコールを添加する、栄養強化する [usu passive] ❑ *Choose margarine or butter fortified with vitamin D.* マーガリンかビタミンD強化バターを選びなさい。 ❑ *All sherry is made from wine fortified with brandy.* すべてのシェリー酒はブランデーで強化したワインからできている。

fort|night /fɔrtnaɪt/ (fortnights) N-COUNT 可算名詞 A **fortnight** is a period of two weeks. 2週間 [mainly BRIT 主に英国英語] ❑ *I hope to be back in a fortnight.* 私は2週間で戻って来られればと思う。

fort|night|ly /fɔrtnaɪtli/ ADJ 形容詞 A **fortnightly** event or publication happens or appears once every two weeks. 2週間に1度の [BRIT 英国英語; AM biweekly 米国英語 biweekly] ● ADV 副詞 **Fortnightly** is also an adverb. 2週間に1度

for|tress /fɔrtrɪs/ (fortresses) N-COUNT 可算名詞 A **fortress** is a castle or other large strong building, or a well-protected place, which is intended to be difficult for enemies to enter. 要塞(ようさい)、城塞 ❑ *...a 13th-century fortress.* 13世紀の城塞

for|tu|nate /fɔrtʃənɪt/ ADJ 形容詞 If you say that someone or something is **fortunate**, you mean that they are lucky. 幸運な ❑ *He was extremely fortunate to survive.* 彼はきわめて運良く生き延びた。 ❑ *She is in the fortunate position of having plenty of choice.* 彼女は選択の余地の多い幸運な立場にいる。

for|tu|nate|ly /fɔrtʃənɪtli/ ADV 副詞 **Fortunately** is used to introduce or indicate a statement about an event or situation that is good. 運良く ❑ *Fortunately, the weather this winter was reasonably mild.* 幸運にもこの冬の気候はほどよく穏やかだった。

for|tune /fɔrtʃən/ (fortunes) **1** N-COUNT 可算名詞 You can refer to a large sum of money as a **fortune** or a small **fortune** to emphasize how large it is. 大金 [EMPHASIS 強調] ❑ *He made a small fortune in the property boom.* 彼は不動産景気で大もうけをした。 **2** N-COUNT 可算名詞 Someone who has a **fortune** has a very large amount of money. 資産 ❑ *He made his fortune in car sales.* 彼は自動車販売で資産形成した。 **3** N-UNCOUNT 不可算名詞 **Fortune** or good **fortune** is good luck. Ill **fortune** is bad luck. 運 ❑ *Investors are starting to wonder how long their good fortune can last.* 投資家たちはどのくらい自分たちの幸運が続くのか考え始めている。 **4** N-PLURAL 複数名詞 If you talk about someone's **fortunes** or the **fortunes** of something, you are talking about the extent to which they are doing well or being successful. 運勢、盛衰 ❑ *The company had to do something to reverse its sliding fortunes.* 会社は社運衰退の動きを逆転するため何かをせねばならなかった。 **5** PHRASE 句 When someone **tells** your **fortune**, they tell you what they think will happen to you in the future, which they say is shown, for example, by the lines on your hand. 運勢を占う ❑ *I was just going to have my fortune*

told by a gypsy. 私はちょうどジプシーに自分の運勢を占ってもらいに行こうとしていた。

for|ty /fɔrti/ (forties) **1** NUM 数詞 **Forty** is the number 40. 40 **2** N-PLURAL 複数名詞 When you talk about the **forties**, you are referring to numbers between 40 and 49. For example, if you are in your **forties**, you are aged between 40 and 49. If the temperature is **in the forties**, the temperature is between 40 and 49 degrees. 40代 ❑ *He was a big man in his forties, smartly dressed in a suit and tie.* 彼は40代の大男で背広にネクタイのきちんとした身なりをしていた。 **3** N-PLURAL 複数名詞 The **forties** is the decade from 1940 and 1949. 1940年代 ❑ *Steel cans were introduced sometime during the forties.* 鋼製の缶が40年代のある時期に導入された。

fo|rum /fɔrəm/ (forums) N-COUNT 可算名詞 A **forum** is a place, situation, or group in which people exchange ideas and discuss issues, especially important public issues. 公開討論の場 ❑ *Members of the council agreed that was an important forum for discussion.* 評議会の面々は、あれは議論のための重要なフォーラムであるという見解で一致した。

for|ward /fɔrwərd/ (forwards, forwarding, forwarded) **1** ADV 副詞 If you move or look **forward**, you move or look in a direction that is in front of you. 前方に ❑ *He came forward with his hand out. "Mr. and Mrs. Selby?" he said.* 彼は片手を突き出しながら前に来た。「セルビーさん御夫妻ですね」彼は言った。 ❑ *She fell forward on to her face.* 彼女はうつぶせに倒れた。 **2** ADV 副詞 **Forward** means in a position near the front of something such as a building or a vehicle. 前方に ❑ *The best seats are in the aisle and as far forward as possible.* 最も良い座席は通路側のできるだけ前のほうだ。 ● ADJ 形容詞 **Forward** is also an adjective. 前方の [ADJ n] ❑ *Reinforcements were needed to allow more troops to move to forward positions.* より多くの部隊が前方に移動できるように増援部隊が必要だった。 **3** ADV 副詞 If you say that someone looks **forward**, you approve of them because they think about what will happen in the future and plan for it. 将来に向けて、今後 [APPROVAL 賛成] ❑ *Now the leadership wants to look forward, and to outline a strategy for the rest of the century.* 今、指導者層は将来を見すます今世紀の今後のための戦略の輪郭を描こうとしている。 ❑ *People should forget and look forward.* 人々は忘れて将来のことを考えるべきだ。 ● ADJ 形容詞 **Forward** is also an adjective. 将来に向けての [ADJ n] ❑ *The university system requires more forward planning.* 大学の制度はもっと将来に向けての計画が必要である。 **4** ADV 副詞 If you move a clock or watch **forward**, you change the time shown on it so that it shows a later time, for example, when the time changes to daylight saving time. 前に [ADV after v] ❑ *When we put the clocks forward in March we go into daylight saving time.* 3月に時計を進めると夏時間に入る。 **5** ADV 副詞 When you are referring to a particular time, if you say that something was true **from** that time **forward**, you mean that it became true at that time, and continued to be true afterward. 以後 ['from' n ADV] ❑ *Velzquez's work from that time forward was confined largely to portraits of the royal family.* ラスケスの作品は、それ以降、主として王室の肖像画に限定された。 **6** ADV 副詞 You use **forward** to indicate that something progresses or improves. 先に ❑ *And by boosting economic prosperity in Mexico, Canada and the United States, it will help us move forward on issues that concern all of us.* そしてメキシコ、カナダ、米国における経済的繁栄を増進することで、それは我々すべてに関わる諸問題を前に進めることを助けるだろう。 ❑ *They just couldn't see any way forward.* 彼らにはまったく先が見えなかった。 **7** ADV 副詞 If something or someone is put **forward**, or comes **forward**, they are suggested or offered as suitable for a particular purpose. 前に [ADV after v] ❑ *Over the years several similar theories have been put forward.* ここ数年間でいくつかの類似の理論が提唱されてきた。 ❑ *Investigations have ground to a standstill because no witnesses have come forward.* 目撃者が1人も出てこないので、調査は難航して行き詰まってしまった。 **8** V-T 他動詞 If a letter or message is **forwarded to** someone, it is sent to the place where they are, after having been sent to a different place earlier. 転送する ❑ *When he's out on the road, office calls are forwarded to the cellular phone in his truck.* 彼が仕事で地方に出ているときは、事務所の電話は彼のトラックの携帯電話に転送される。 **9** N-COUNT 可算名詞 In basketball, soccer, or hockey, a **forward** is a player whose usual position is in the opponents' half of the field, and whose usual job is to attack or score goals. 前衛 ❑ *Junior forward Sam McCracken added 14 points for the home team.* 3年生の前衛サム・マクラケンが地元チームに14点を追加した。 **10** **backward and forward** → see **backward**

fos|sil /fɒsəl/ (fossils) N-COUNT 可算名詞 A **fossil** is the hard remains of a prehistoric animal or plant that are found inside a rock. 化石 → see Word Web: fossil

fos|sil fuel (fossil fuels) also fossil-fuel N-MASS 質量名詞 **Fossil fuel** is fuel such as coal or oil that is formed from the decayed remains of plants or animals. 化石燃料 ❑ *Burning fossil fuels uses oxygen and produces carbon dioxide.* 化石燃料の燃焼には酸素を消費

Word Web   fossil

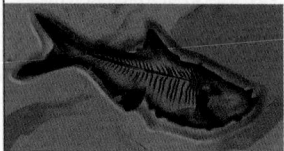

There are two types of animal **fossils**—body fossils and **trace** fossils. Body fossils help us understand how the animal looked when it was alive. Trace fossils, such as **tracks** and **footprints**, show us how the animal moved. Since we don't find tracks of dinosaurs' tails, we know they lifted them up as they walked. Footprints tell us about the weight of the dinosaur and how fast it moved. Scientists use two methods to calculate the date of a fossil. They sometimes count the number of **rock** layers covering it. They also use carbon dating.

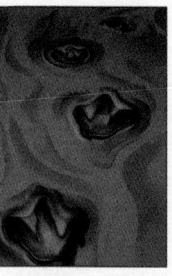

し，二酸化炭素を発生する.
→ see **greenhouse, solar system**

fos|ter /fɔ̱stər/ (fosters, fostering, fostered) **1** ADJ 形容詞 **Foster** parents are people who officially take a child into their family for a period of time, without becoming the child's legal parents. The child is referred to as their **foster** child. 里親の，里子の [ADJ n] ❑ Little Jack was placed with foster parents. 小さなジャックは里親に預けられた. **2** V-T 他動詞 If you **foster** a child, you take it into your family for a period of time, without becoming its legal parent. 里子として養育する ❑ She has since gone on to find happiness by fostering more than 100 children. 彼女はそれ以来100人以上の子供を養育することで幸福を見つけ続けている. **3** V-T 他動詞 To **foster** something such as an activity or idea means to help it to develop. はぐくむ ❑ He said that developed countries had a responsibility to foster global economic growth to help new democracies. 彼は先進国には新興民主主義国の援助のため世界的な経済成長をはぐくむ責任があると言った.

fought /fɔ̱t/ **Fought** is the past tense and past participle of **fight**. fightの過去・過去分詞

foul /fa̱ʊl/ (fouler, foulest, fouls, fouling, fouled) **1** ADJ 形容詞 If you describe something as **foul**, you mean it is dirty and smells or tastes unpleasant. 汚い，臭い ❑ …foul polluted water. 汚染された臭い水 **2** ADJ 形容詞 **Foul** language is offensive and contains swear words or rude words. 口汚い ❑ The teachers had to deal with her foul language, disruptive behavior, and low academic performance. 教師たちは彼女の汚い言葉づかい，破壊的な行動，芳しくない学業成績などに対処しなければならなかった. **3** ADJ 形容詞 If someone has a **foul** temper or is in a **foul** mood, they become angry or violent very suddenly and easily. 不快な ❑ Collins was in a foul mood even before the interviews began. コリンズは取材が始まる前ですら機嫌が悪かった. **4** ADJ 形容詞 **Foul** weather is unpleasant, windy, and stormy. ひどい ❑ No amount of foul weather, whether hail, wind, rain or snow, seems to deter them. ひょう，風，雨，あるいは雪であろうが，どんなにひどい悪天候でも彼らを思いとどまらせるようには思えない. **5** V-T 他動詞 If an animal **fouls** a place, it drops feces onto the ground. ふんで汚す ❑ It is an offense to let your dog foul a footpath. 犬にふんで小道を汚さすのは犯罪だ. **6** V-T 他動詞 In a game or sport, if a player **fouls** another player, they touch them or block them in a way which is not allowed according to the rules. 反則する ❑ Nowitzki fouled Mitchell early in the third quarter. 第3クォーターの始めのほうでノウィツキーがミッチェルに反則行為をした. **7** N-COUNT 可算名詞 A **foul** is an act in a game or sport that is not allowed according to the rules. 反則 ❑ Harridge was charged with a flagrant foul and ejected from the game. ハリッジは目に余る反則行為に問われ，退場となった. ● ADJ 形容詞 **Foul** is also an adjective. 反則の [ADJ n] ❑ …a foul tackle. 反則のタックル **8** PHRASE 句 If you **run foul of** someone or **fall foul of** them, you do something which gets you into trouble with them. —と問題を起こす ❑ He had fallen foul of the FBI. 彼は連邦捜査局と問題を起こしていた.

▶ **foul up** PHRASAL VERB 句動詞 If someone or something **fouls up**, or if they **foul** something **up**, they make a serious mistake that causes things to go badly wrong. 台無しにする，台無しになる ❑ A computer software glitch fouled up their presentation. コンピュータのソフトウェアの突然の不調で彼らの発表は台無しになった.

found /fa̱ʊnd/ (founds, founding, founded) **1 Found** is the past tense and past participle of **find**. findの過去・過去分詞 **2** V-T 他動詞 When an institution, company, or organization **is founded** by someone or by a group of people, they get it started, often by providing the necessary money. 設立する ❑ The New York Free-Loan Society was founded in 1892. ニューヨーク無利子融資協会は1892年に設立された. ❑ His father founded the American Socialist Party. 彼の父は米国社会党を創設した. ● **foun|da|tion** /fa̱ʊndeɪʃ°n/ N-SING 単数名詞 [with poss] 設立 ❑ …the foundation of the National Association of Evangelicals in 1942. 1942年の全国福音主義協会の創設 ● **found|ing** N-SING 単数名詞 設立 ❑ The firm has never had an unprofitable year since its founding 65 years ago. その会社は65年前の設立以来，赤字に転落した年は1度もない. **3** V-T 他動詞 [usu passive] When a town, important building, or other place **is founded** by someone or by a group of people, they cause it to be built. 創建する ❑ The town was

founded in 1610. その町は1610年に創建された. **4** → see also **founded, founding**

Word Link   found ≈ base : foundation, founded, founder

foun|da|tion /fa̱ʊndeɪʃ°n/ (foundations) **1** N-COUNT 可算名詞 The **foundation of** something such as a belief or way of life is the things on which it is based. 基盤 ❑ The issue strikes at the very foundation of our community. その問題は我々の地域社会の基盤そのものを揺るがしかねない. **2** N-COUNT 可算名詞 A **foundation** is an organization which provides money for a special purpose such as research or charity. 財団 ❑ …the National Foundation for Educational Research. 全国教育研究財団 **3** N-PLURAL 複数名詞 The **foundations** of a building or other structure are the layer of bricks or concrete below the ground that it is built on. 土台 **4** N-UNCOUNT 不可算名詞 If a story, idea, or argument has **no foundation**, there are no facts to prove that it is true. 根拠 ❑ The allegations were without foundation. それらの申し立てには根拠がなかった. **5** N-MASS 質量名詞 **Foundation** is a skin-colored cream that you put on your face before putting on the rest of your makeup. ファンデーション ❑ Use foundation and/or face powder afterwards for an even skin tone. 後でファンデーションと／またはフェースパウダーをつけると，むらのない肌の色が得られる. **6** → see also **found**
→ see **makeup**

Word Partnership   foundation は次の語句と使われる：

V.	**establish a** foundation **1 2**
	build a foundation, **lay a** foundation **3**
	apply foundation **5**
ADJ.	**firm** foundation, **solid** foundation **1 3**
	charitable foundation **2**

found|ed /fa̱ʊndɪd/ **1** ADJ 形容詞 If something is **founded on** a particular thing, it is based on it. 基づいた [v-link ADJ 'on' n] ❑ The criticisms are founded on facts as well as on convictions. それらの批判は確信だけでなく事実に基づいたものだ. **2** → see also **found**

found|er /fa̱ʊndər/ (founders, foundering, foundered) **1** N-COUNT 可算名詞 The **founder** of an institution, organization, or building is the person who got it started or caused it to be built, often by providing the necessary money. 創設者 ❑ He was one of the founders of the university's medical faculty. 彼はその大学の医学部の創設者の1人だった. **2** V-I 自動詞 If something such as a plan or project **founders**, it fails because of a particular point, difficulty, or problem. 失敗する ❑ The talks have foundered, largely because of the reluctance of some members of the government to do a deal with criminals. その話し合いは犯罪者と取引することに反対する者が政府内にいたことが主な原因で物別れとなった.

found|ing /fa̱ʊndɪŋ/ **1** ADJ 形容詞 **Founding** means relating to the starting of a particular institution or organization. 創設の [ADJ n] ❑ The committee held its founding congress in the capital, Riga. その委員会は首都のリガで創設会議を開催した. **2** → see also **found**

foun|tain /fa̱ʊntɪn/ (fountains) **1** N-COUNT 可算名詞 A **fountain** is an ornamental feature in a pool or lake which consists of a long narrow stream of water that is forced up into the air by a pump. 噴水 ❑ …the fountains on the 16th Street Mall. 16番街の遊歩道の噴水 **2** N-COUNT 可算名詞 A **fountain of** a liquid is an amount of it which is sent up into the air and falls back. 噴流 [LITERARY 文語的] ❑ The volcano spewed a fountain of molten rock 650 feet in the air. その火山は溶岩の噴流を空中に650フィート吹き出した.

four /fɔ̱r/ (fours) **1** NUM 数詞 **Four** is the number 4. (基数の) 4 ❑ Judith is married with four children. ジュディスは既婚で4人の子供がいる. **2** PHRASE 句 If you are **on all fours**, your knees, feet, and hands are on the ground. 四つんばいで ❑ She crawled on all fours over to the window. 彼女は四つんばいで窓の方に這って行った.

four|some /fɔ̱rsəm/ (foursomes) N-COUNT-COLL 集合可算名詞 A **foursome** is a group of four people or things. 4人組 ❑ The foursome released their second CD this month. 4人組は今月2枚目のCDを売り出した.

four|teen /fɔ́rtín/ (fourteens) NUM 数詞 Fourteen is the number 14. (基数の) ❑ I'm fourteen years old. 私は14歳です.

four|teenth /fɔ́rtínθ/ ORD 序数詞 The fourteenth item in a series is the one that you count as number fourteen. 14番目の ❑ The Festival, now in its fourteenth year, has become a major international jazz event. そのフェスティバルは現在14年目だが, 主要な国際的ジャズ行事となった.

fourth /fɔ́rθ/ (fourths) ➊ ORD 序数詞 The fourth item in a series is the one that you count as number four. 4番目の ❑ Last year's winner Greg Lemond of the United States is in fourth place. 昨年の優勝者である米国のグレッグ・ルモンドは第4位だ. ➋ FRACTION 端数 A fourth is one of four equal parts of something. 4分の1 [AM 米国英語] ❑ Three-fourths of the public say they favor a national referendum on the issue. 国民の4分の3はその問題について国民投票をすべきだと言っている.

four-wheel drive (four-wheel drives) N-COUNT 可算名詞 A four-wheel drive is a vehicle in which all four wheels receive power from the engine to help with steering. This makes the vehicle easier to drive on rough roads or surfaces such as sand or snow. 四輪駆動車

fowl /fául/ (fowls)

Fowl can also be used as the plural form.

Fowl は複数形としても使える.

N-COUNT 可算名詞 A fowl is a bird, especially one that can be eaten as food, such as a duck or a chicken. 家禽 (かきん) ❑ Carve the fowl into 8 pieces. とり肉を8つに切り分けよ.

fox /fɑ́ks/ (foxes) N-COUNT 可算名詞 A fox is a wild animal which looks like a dog and has reddish-brown fur, a pointed face and ears, and a thick tail. Foxes eat smaller animals. キツネ → see Arctic

foy|er /fɔ́iər, fɔ́iei, fwɑyéi/ (foyers) N-COUNT 可算名詞 The foyer is the large area where people meet or wait just inside the main doors of a building such as a theater or hotel. ロビー, ホワイエ ❑ I went and waited in the foyer. 私は行ってロビーで待った.

<u>**Word Link**</u>   fract, frag ≈ breaking : fraction, fracture, fragile

frac|tion /frǽkʃn/ (fractions) ➊ N-COUNT 可算名詞 A fraction of something is a tiny amount or proportion of it. ほんの少し ❑ She hesitated for a fraction of a second before responding. 彼女は返事をする前にほんの一瞬ためらった. ❑ Here's how to eat like the stars, at a fraction of the cost. さあこれがわずかの費用でスターのように食事をする方法だ. ➋ N-COUNT 可算名詞 A fraction is a number that can be expressed as a proportion of two whole numbers. For example, F(1/2) and F(1/3) are both fractions. 分数 ❑ The students had a grasp of decimals, percentages and fractions. 学生たちは小数, 百分率, 分数を理解していた.

frac|ture /frǽktʃər/ (fractures, fracturing, fractured) ➊ N-COUNT 可算名詞 A fracture is a crack or break in something, especially a bone. 破損 ❑ At least one-third of all women over ninety have sustained a hip fracture. 90歳以上の女性の少なくとも3分の1は腰の骨折を抱えている. ➋ V-T/V-I 他動詞/自動詞 If something such as a bone is fractured or fractures, it gets a crack or break in it. 折る [他動詞], 折れる [自動詞] ❑ You've fractured a rib, maybe more than one. あなたはろっ骨をおそらく1本以上骨折している. ❑ One strut had fractured and been crudely repaired in several places. 1本の支柱が破損し, 数箇所でぞんざいに修理されていた. ➌ V-T/V-I 他動詞/自動詞 If something such as an organization or society is fractured or fractures, it splits into several parts or stops existing. 分裂させる [他動詞], 分裂する [自動詞] ❑ His policy risks fracturing the coalition. 彼の政策は連立を分裂させる危険がある. [FORMAL 形式ばった]

frag|ile /frǽdʒəl/ ➊ ADJ 形容詞 If you describe a situation as fragile, you mean that it is weak or uncertain, and unlikely to be able to resist strong pressure or attack. もろい [JOURNALISM ジャーナリズム] ❑ The fragile economies of several southern African nations could be irreparably damaged. 南部アフリカ諸国の脆弱 (ぜいじゃく) な経済は回復できないほどに損害を受ける可能性がある. ● **fra|gil|ity** /frədʒíliti/ N-UNCOUNT 不可算名詞 もろさ ❑ By mid-1988 there were clear indications of the extreme fragility of the Right-wing coalition. 1988年の半ばまでには右翼の連立が非常にもろいことが明確となった. ➋ ADJ 形容詞 Something that is fragile is easily broken or damaged. 壊れやすい ❑ He leaned back in his fragile chair. 彼は壊れやすい椅子にもたれた. ● **fra|gil|ity** N-UNCOUNT 不可算名詞 壊れやすさ ❑ Older drivers are more likely to be seriously injured because of the fragility of their bones. 年配の運転者のほうが, 骨がもろいために事故で重傷を負いやすい.

<u>**Thesaurus**</u>   fragile また次を参照:

ADJ.   unstable, weak ➊
       breakable, delicate; (ant.) sturdy ➋

frag|ment (fragments, fragmenting, fragmented)

The noun is pronounced /frǽgmənt/. The verb is pronounced /frægmɛ́nt/.

名詞は /frǽgmənt/ と発音される. 動詞は /frægmɛ́nt/ と発音される.

➊ N-COUNT 可算名詞 A fragment of something is a small piece or part of it. 破片 ❑ The only reminder of the shooting is a few fragments of metal in my shoulder. その銃撃事件を思い出させる唯一のものは, 私の肩に入っている数片の金属破片である. ❑ She read everything, digesting every fragment of news. 彼女はニュースのあらゆる断片をよく考えながらすべて読んだ. ➋ V-T/V-I 他動詞/自動詞 If something fragments or is fragmented, it breaks or separates into small pieces or parts. ばらばらにする [他動詞], ばらばらになる [自動詞] ❑ The clouds fragmented and out came the sun. 雲が割れて太陽が出てきた. ● **frag|men|ta|tion** /frægmɛntéiʃn/ N-UNCOUNT 不可算名詞 分裂 ❑ ...the extraordinary fragmentation of styles on the music scene. 音楽界における様式の異常な分裂

fra|grance /fréigrəns/ (fragrances) ➊ N-VAR 可変性名詞 A fragrance is a pleasant or sweet smell. 芳香 ❑ ...a shrubby plant with a strong characteristic fragrance. 独特の強い芳香を放つ低木 ➋ N-MASS 質量名詞 Fragrance is a pleasant-smelling liquid which people put on their bodies to make themselves smell nice. 香水 ❑ The advertisement is for a men's fragrance. その広告は男性用香水のものだ.

fra|grant /fréigrənt/ ADJ 形容詞 Something that is fragrant has a pleasant, sweet smell. よいにおいの ❑ ...fragrant oils and perfumes. よいにおいのオイルと香水

frail /fréil/ (frailer, frailest) ➊ ADJ 形容詞 Someone who is frail is not very strong or healthy. ひ弱な ❑ She lay in bed looking frail. 彼女はか弱そうにベッドに横たわっていた. ➋ ADJ 形容詞 Something that is frail is easily broken or damaged. 壊れやすい ❑ The frail boat rocked as he clambered in. もろいボートは彼がはい登って入ると揺れた.

frail|ty /fréilti, frɛ́əl-/ (frailties) ➊ N-VAR 可変性名詞 If you refer to the frailties or frailty of people, you are referring to their weaknesses. 弱さ ❑ ...the frailties of human nature. 人間性の弱み ➋ N-UNCOUNT 不可算名詞 Frailty is the condition of having poor health. 衰弱 ❑ She died after a long period of increasing frailty. ますます衰弱して行く状態が長い間続いた後に死亡した.

frame /fréim/ (frames, framing, framed) ➊ N-COUNT 可算名詞 The frame of a picture or mirror is the wood, metal, or plastic that is fitted around it, especially when it is displayed or hung on a wall. 額縁 ❑ Estelle kept a photograph of her mother in a silver frame on the kitchen mantelpiece. エステルは母親の写真を銀の額縁に入れて台所の戸棚の上に飾っていた. ➋ N-COUNT 可算名詞 The frame of an object such as a building, chair, or window is the arrangement of wooden, metal, or plastic bars between which other material is fitted, and which give the object its strength and shape. 骨組み ❑ He supplied housebuilders with modern timber frames. 彼は家屋建築業者に近代的な木製の骨組みを供給した. ❑ With difficulty he released the mattress from the metal frame, and groped beneath it. 彼はやっとのことで金属の骨組みからマットレスをはずし, その下を手探りした. ➌ N-COUNT 可算名詞 The frames of a pair of glasses are all the metal or plastic parts of it, but not the lenses. フレーム ❑ He was wearing new glasses with gold wire frames. 彼は金の針金状のフレームの新しい眼鏡をかけていた. ➍ N-COUNT 可算名詞 A frame of movie film is one of the many separate photographs that it consists of. こま ❑ Standard 8mm projects at 16 frames per second. 標準的8ミリは毎秒16のこまを映写する. ➎ V-T 他動詞 When a picture or photograph is framed, it is put in a frame. 額縁に入れる [usu passive] ❑ The picture is now ready to be mounted and framed. その絵はもう表装して額縁に入れられる準備ができている. ➏ V-T 他動詞 If an object is framed by a particular thing, it is surrounded by that thing in a way that makes the object more striking or attractive to look at. 囲まれる [usu passive] ❑ The swimming pool is framed by tropical gardens. 水泳プールは熱帯庭園で囲まれている. ➐ V-T 他動詞 If someone frames an innocent person, they make other people think that that person is guilty of a crime, by lying or inventing evidence. ぬれ衣を着せる [INFORMAL くだけた] ❑ I need to find out who tried to frame me. 誰が私をはめようとしたのか見つけ出す必要がある. ➑ N-COUNT 可算名詞 You can refer to someone's body as their frame, especially when you are describing the general shape of their body. 体格 ❑ Their belts are pulled tight against their bony frames. ベルトは彼らの骨ばった体にきつく締められた. → see animation, bed, painting

frame of mind (frames of mind) N-COUNT 可算名詞 Your frame of mind is the mood that you are in, which causes you to have a particular attitude to something. 心の状態 ❑ Lewis was not in the right frame of mind to continue. ルイスは続けるのにふさわしい気分ではなかった.

frame|work /fréimwɜrk/ (frameworks) ➊ N-COUNT 可算名詞 A framework is a particular set of rules, ideas, or beliefs which you use in order to deal with problems or to decide what to do. 枠

組み ❑ ...within the framework of federal regulations. 連邦規定の枠組み内で ❷ N-COUNT 可算名詞 A **framework** is a structure that forms a support or frame for something. 骨組み ❑ ...wooden shelves on a steel framework. 鋼製の骨組みにつけられた木製の棚

fran|chise /fræntʃaɪz/ (**franchises, franchising, franchised**) ❶ N-COUNT 可算名詞 A **franchise** is an authority that is given by an organization to someone, allowing them to sell its goods or services or to take part in an activity which the organization controls. 一手販売権, 特権 [BUSINESS 実業] ❑ ...fast-food franchises. ファーストフードの一手販売権 ❑ ...the franchise to build and operate the tunnel. トンネルを建設・営業する特権 ❷ V-T 他動詞 If a company **franchises** its business, it sells franchises to other companies, allowing them to sell its goods or services. 一手販売権を売る [BUSINESS 実業] ❑ She has recently franchised her business. 彼女は最近自分の事業の一手販売権を売った。 ❸ N-UNCOUNT 不可算名詞 **Franchise** is the right to vote in an election. 選挙権 [also 'the' N] ❑ ...the introduction of universal franchise. 普通選挙権の導入

fran|chi|see /fræntʃaɪziː/ (**franchisees**) N-COUNT 可算名詞 A **franchisee** is a person or group of people who buy a particular franchise. 一手販売業者 [BUSINESS 実業] ❑ ...National Restaurants, a New York franchisee for Pizza Hut. ピザハットのニューヨークの一手販売業者であるナショナル・レストラン

fran|chi|ser /fræntʃaɪzər/ (**franchisers**) N-COUNT 可算名詞 A **franchiser** is an organization which sells franchises. 一手販売権を売る企業 [BUSINESS 実業] ❑ Coca-Cola, Pepsi and Cadbury use franchisers to manufacture, bottle and distribute their products within geographical areas. コカ・コーラ，ペプシおよびキャドベリーは地域内での商品の生産・瓶詰め・流通にフランチャイザーを利用した。

frank /fræŋk/ (**franker, frankest**) ADJ 形容詞 If someone is **frank**, they state or express things in an open and honest way. 率直な ❑ "It is clear that my client has been less than frank with me," said his lawyer. 「私の依頼人が私に率直ではなかったことは明らかだ」と彼の弁護士は言った。 ● **frank|ly** ADV 副詞 [ADV with v] 率直に ❑ You can talk frankly to me. 私には率直に話したほうがいい。 ● **frank|ness** N-UNCOUNT 不可算名詞 率直さ ❑ The reaction to his frankness was hostile. 彼の率直さに対する反応は敵意あるものだった。

frank|ly /fræŋkli/ ADV 副詞 You use **frankly** when you are expressing an opinion or feeling to emphasize that you mean what you are saying, especially when the person you are speaking to may not like it. 率直に [EMPHASIS 強調] ❑ "You don't give a damn about my feelings, do you." —"Quite frankly, I don't." 「きみは私の気持ちなんてどうでもいいんだろう」「全く率直に言うと，その通りだ」 ❑ Frankly, Thomas, this question of your loan is beginning to worry me. 率直に言って，トマス，このきみのローンの問題は僕の心配の種になりつつある。 ❷ → see also **frank**

fran|tic /fræntɪk/ ❶ ADJ 形容詞 If you are **frantic**, you are behaving in a wild and uncontrolled way because you are frightened or worried. 狂乱した ❑ A bird had been locked in and was by now quite frantic. 鳥が1羽閉じ込められ，今では半狂乱になっていた。 ● **fran|ti|cal|ly** /fræntɪkli/ ADV 副詞 [ADV with v] 狂乱して ❑ She clutched frantically at Emily's arm. 彼女は半狂乱でエミリーの腕をつかんだ。 ❷ ADJ 形容詞 If an activity is **frantic**, things are done quickly and in an energetic but disorganized way, because there is very little time. 大急ぎの，大あわての ❑ A busy night in the restaurant can be frantic in the kitchen. レストランが忙しい夜は厨（ちゅう）房がてんてこ舞いになることがある。 ● **fran|ti|cal|ly** ADV 副詞 [ADV with v] 大急ぎで ❑ We have been frantically trying to save her life. 我々は大あわてで彼女の命を救おうとしていた。

fra|ter|nity /frətɜːrnɪti/ (**fraternities**) ❶ N-COUNT 可算名詞 You can refer to people who have the same profession or the same interests as a particular **fraternity**. 同業者仲間 ❑ ...the spread of stolen guns among the criminal fraternity. 犯罪者仲間での盗んだ銃器の蔓延（まんえん） ❷ N-UNCOUNT 不可算名詞 **Fraternity** refers to friendship and support between people who feel they are closely linked to each other. 友愛 [FORMAL 形式ばった] ❑ Bob needs the fraternity of others who share his mission. ボブは彼の使命を共有する他の人たちの友愛を必要としている。 ❸ N-COUNT 可算名詞 In the United States, a **fraternity** is a society of male university or college students. 友愛会 ❑ He must have been the most popular guy at the most popular fraternity in college. 彼は大学で最も人気のある友愛会で最も人気のある男だったにちがいない。

fraud /frɔːd/ (**frauds**) ❶ N-VAR 可変性名詞 **Fraud** is the crime of gaining money or financial benefits by a trick or by lying. 詐欺 ❑ He was jailed for two years for fraud and deception. 彼は詐欺罪で2年間投獄された。 ❷ N-COUNT 可算名詞 A **fraud** is something or someone that deceives people in a way that is illegal or dishonest. 偽物，詐欺師 ❑ He's a fraud and a cheat. 彼はずるいペテン師だ。

Word Link   ***ulent ≈ full of*: frau**dulent**, op**ulent**, vir**ulent**

fraudu|lent /frɔːdʒələnt/ ADJ 形容詞 A **fraudulent** activity is deliberately deceitful, dishonest, or untrue. 詐欺的な ❑ ...fraudulent claims about being a nurse. 看護婦であるという不正直な主張 ● **fraudu|lent|ly** ADV 副詞 [ADV with v] 詐欺的に ❑ All 5,000

of the homes were fraudulently obtained. その家屋の5千軒はすべて不正に取得された。

fraught /frɔːt/ ❶ ADJ 形容詞 If a situation or action is **fraught with** problems or risks, it is filled with them. (問題・危険などに)満ちた [v-link ADJ 'with' n] ❑ The earliest operations employing this technique were fraught with dangers. この技術を使った最も初期の手術は危険を伴っていた。 ❷ ADJ 形容詞 If you say that a situation or action is **fraught**, you mean that it is worrisome or difficult. 気にかかる ❑ It has been a somewhat fraught day. ちょっと心配の多い1日だった。

fray /freɪ/ (**frays, fraying, frayed**) ❶ V-T/V-I 他動詞/自動詞 If something such as cloth or rope **frays**, or if something **frays** it, its threads or fibers start to come apart from each other and spoil its appearance. すり切らす [他動詞]，すり切れる [自動詞] ❑ The fabric is very fine or frays easily. その生地は非常に繊細で簡単にすり切れる。 ❑ The stitching had begun to fray at the edges. 縫い目は端ですり切れ始めていた。 ❷ V-T/V-I 他動詞/自動詞 If your nerves or your temper **fray**, or if something **frays** them, you become nervous or easily annoyed because of mental strain and anxiety. 平静さを失う [他動詞]，平静さが失われる [自動詞] ❑ Tempers began to fray as the two teams failed to score. 両チームが得点し損なうにつれて，神経がささくれ立ち始めた。

freak /friːk/ (**freaks**) ❶ ADJ 形容詞 A **freak** event or action is one that is a very unusual or extreme example of its type. 風変わりな [ADJ n] ❑ Weir broke his leg in a freak accident playing golf. ウィアーはゴルフをしている最中の珍しい事故で足の骨を折った。 ❷ N-COUNT 可算名詞 If you describe someone as a particular kind of **freak**, you are emphasizing that they are very enthusiastic about a thing or activity, and often seem to think about nothing else. 凝る人 [INFORMAL くだけた] ❑ Diaz is a fitness freak who's trained in martial arts. ディアズは武術の訓練を受けたフィットネス狂だ。 ❸ N-COUNT 可算名詞 People are sometimes referred to as **freaks** when their behavior or attitude is very different from that of the majority of people. 変人 [DISAPPROVAL 不賛成] ❑ Not so long ago, transsexuals were regarded as freaks. ごく最近まで性倒錯者は変人と見なされていた。

freck|le /frekəl/ (**freckles**) N-COUNT 可算名詞 **Freckles** are small light brown spots on someone's skin, especially on their face. そばかす ❑ He had short ginger-colored hair and freckles. 彼は短い赤毛でそばかすがあった。

free /friː/ (**freer, freest, frees, freeing, freed**) ❶ ADJ 形容詞 If something is **free**, you can have it or use it without paying for it. 無料の ❑ The seminars are free, with lunch provided. そのセミナーは無料でランチ付きだ。 ❷ **free of charge** → see **charge** ❸ ADJ 形容詞 Someone or something that is **free** is not restricted, controlled, or limited, for example, by rules, customs, or other people. 自由な ❑ The government will be free to pursue its economic policies. 政府は経済政策を自由に推し進められるだろう。 ❑ The elections were free and fair. 選挙は自由で公正だった。 ● **free|ly** ADV 副詞 [ADV with v] 自由に ❑ They cast their votes freely and without coercion on election day. 選挙日に強制されることなく自由に投票した。 ❹ ADJ 形容詞 Someone who is **free** is no longer a prisoner or a slave. 自由な身の ❑ He walked from the court house a free man. 彼は自由の身となって裁判所を出た。 ❺ ADJ 形容詞 If someone or something is **free of** or **free from** an unpleasant thing, they do not have it or they are not affected by it. 免れている [v-link ADJ 'of/from' n] ❑ ...a future far more free of fear. はるかにずっと不安のない将来 ❑ She retains her slim figure and is free of wrinkles. 彼女はスリムな体型を保っていて，しわがない。 ❻ ADJ 形容詞 A sum of money or type of goods that is **free** of tax or duty is one that you do not have to pay tax on. 免除されている [v-link ADJ 'of' n] ❑ This benefit is free of tax under current legislation. この手当は現在の法律では無税だ。 ❼ → see also **duty-free, interest-free, tax-free** ❽ ADJ 形容詞 If you have a **free** period of time or are **free** at a particular time, you are not working or occupied then. 暇な ❑ She spent her free time shopping. 彼女は余暇をショッピングで費やした。 ❑ I used to write during my free periods at school. 私は学校の自由時間を作文して過ごしたものです。 ❾ ADJ 形容詞 If something such as a table or seat is **free**, it is not being used or occupied by anyone, or is not reserved for anyone to use. 空いて ❑ There was only one seat free on the train. 列車には空席が1つしかなかった。 ❿ ADJ 形容詞 If you get something **free** or if it gets **free**, it is no longer trapped by anything or attached to anything. 縛られていない ❑ He pulled his arm free, and strode for the door. 彼は腕を振りほどき，ドアに向かって大またに歩いた。 ⓫ ADJ 形容詞 When someone is using one hand or arm to hold or move something, their other hand or arm is referred to as their **free** one. 自由に動かせる [ADJ n] ❑ He snatched up the receiver and his free hand groped for the switch on the bedside lamp. 彼は受話器を取り上げ，空いているほうの手でベッド脇の電気スタンドのスイッチを探した。 ⓬ V-T 他動詞 If you **free** someone of something that is unpleasant or restricting, you remove it from them. 取り除く ❑ It will free us of a whole lot of debt. それにより私たちの多額の借金はなくなるだろう。 ⓭ V-T 他動詞 To **free** a prisoner or a slave means to let them go or release them from prison. 解放する ❑ Israel is set to free more Lebanese prisoners. イスラエルはもっ

と多くのレバノン人の囚人を解放する予定だ. **14** V-T 他動詞 To **free** someone or something means to make them available for a task or function that they were previously not available for. 自由にする ❑ *Toolbelts free both hands and lessen the risk of dropping hammers.* 道具ベルトは両手を解放し, 金づちを落とすリスクを減らす. ❑ *His deal with Disney will run out shortly, freeing him to pursue his own project.* ディズニーとの彼の取引契約はまもなく切れるので, 彼は自由に独自の企画を推し進めることができる. ● PHRASAL VERB 句動詞 **Free up** means the same as **free**. 自由にする ❑ *It can handle even the most complex graphic jobs, freeing up your computer for other tasks.* それは最も複雑な図表作業ですら処理できるので, コンピュータを他の作業に自由に使える. **15** V-T 他動詞 If you **free** someone or something, you remove them from the place in which they have been trapped or become fixed. 救出する ❑ *Rescue workers tried to free him by cutting away part of the car.* 救助隊は車の一部を切断することで彼を救出しようとした. **16** PHRASE 句 You say "**feel free**" when you want to give someone permission to do something, in a very willing way. 遠慮なく~する [INFORMAL くだけた, FORMULAE 決まり文句] ❑ *If you have any questions at all, please feel free to ask me.* 何か質問があったら, 遠慮なく私に聞いてください. **17** PHRASE 句 If you do something or get something **for free**, you do it without being paid or get it without having to pay for it. ただで [INFORMAL くだけた] ❑ *I wasn't expecting you to do it for free.* 私はきみがそれをただでやってくれるとは思っていなかった. **18** to give someone **a free hand** → see **hand 19** to give someone **free rein** → see **rein**

▶ **free up 1** → see **free 12 2** PHRASAL VERB 句動詞 To **free up** a market, economy, or system means to make it operate with fewer restrictions and controls. 解放する [BUSINESS 実業] ❑ *...policies for freeing up markets and extending competition.* 市場を開放し, 競争を広げるための政策

Thesaurus	*free* また次を参照:
ADJ.	complimentary **1**
	independent, unattached, unrestricted **2**
	available, unoccupied, vacant **7**
V.	emancipate, let go, liberate **10 11**
	disentangle, unshackle **13**

Word Link	*dom ≈ state of being : bore*dom, *free*dom, *wis*dom

free|dom /frídəm/ (**freedoms**) **1** N-UNCOUNT 不可算名詞 **Freedom** is the state of being allowed to do what you want to do. **Freedoms** are instances of this. 自由 [also N in pl] ❑ *...freedom of speech.* 言論の自由 ❑ *The United Nations Secretary-General has spoken of the need for individual freedoms and human rights.* 国連事務総長は個人の自由の必要性と人権について話した. **2** N-UNCOUNT 不可算名詞 When prisoners or slaves are set free or escape, they gain their **freedom**. 自由, 自由の身 ❑ *...the agreement worked out by the UN, under which all hostages and detainees would gain their freedom.* すべての人質と抑留者が自由の身になるであろう国連の作成した協定 **3** N-UNCOUNT 不可算名詞 **Freedom from** something you do not want means not being affected by it. ～からの解放 ❑ *...all the freedom from pain that medicine could provide.* 薬のおかげで得られた痛みからの全面的な解放

Word Partnership	*freedom* は次の語句と使われる:
ADJ.	**artistic** freedom, **political** freedom, **religious** freedom **1**
N.	freedom **of choice, feeling/sense of** freedom, freedom **of the press,** freedom **of speech 1** **struggle for** freedom **1 2**

free en|ter|prise N-UNCOUNT 不可算名詞 **Free enterprise** is an economic system in which businesses compete for profit without much government control. 自由企業 [BUSINESS 実業] ❑ *...a believer in democracy and free enterprise.* 民主主義と自由企業の信奉者

free|lance /frílæns/ ADJ 形容詞 Someone who does **freelance** work or who is, for example, a **freelance** journalist or photographer is not employed by one organization, but is paid for each piece of work they do by the organization they do it for. フリーランスの [BUSINESS 実業] ❑ *Michael Cross is a freelance journalist.* マイケル・クロスはフリーランスのジャーナリストだ. ● ADV 副詞 **Freelance** is also an adverb. フリーランサーとして [ADV after v] ❑ *He is now working freelance from his home in New Hampshire.* 彼は現在ニューハンプシャーの自宅でフリーランサーの仕事をしている.

free|ly /fríli/ **1** ADV 副詞 **Freely** means many times or in large quantities. 十分に ❑ *We have referred freely to his ideas.* 我々は彼の考えに何度も言及してきた. ❑ *George was spending very freely.* ジョージはひどく浪費していた. **2** ADV 副詞 If you can talk **freely**, you can talk without needing to be careful about what you say. 打ち解けて [ADV after v] ❑ *She wondered whether he had someone to whom he could talk freely.* 彼女は彼に打ち解けて話せる人物がいたかどうか考えた. **3** ADV 副詞 If someone gives or does something **freely**, they give or do it willingly, without being ordered or forced to do

it. 快く [ADV with v] ❑ *Danny shared his knowledge freely with anyone interested.* ダニーは自分の知識を関心のある人物なら誰とでも進んで分かち合った. **4** ADV 副詞 If something or someone moves **freely**, they move easily and smoothly, without any obstacles or resistance. 支障なく [ADV after v] ❑ *The clay court was slippery and he was unable to move freely.* クレーコートは滑りやすく, 彼はスムーズに動くことができなかった. **5** → see also **free**

free mar|ket (**free markets**) N-COUNT 可算名詞 A **free market** is an economic system in which business organizations decide things such as prices and wages, and are not controlled by the government. 自由市場 [BUSINESS 実業] ❑ *...the creation of a free market.* 自由市場の創造

free-range ADJ 形容詞 **Free-range** means relating to a system of keeping animals in which they can move and feed freely on an area of open ground. 放し飼いの ❑ *...free-range eggs.* 放し飼いの鶏の卵

free|ware /fríweər/ N-UNCOUNT 不可算名詞 **Freeware** is computer software that you can use without payment. フリーウェア [COMPUTING コンピューティング] ❑ *Is there a freeware program that I can use to produce my own clip art?* 私独自のクリップアートを制作できるフリーウェアのプログラムがありますか.

free|way /fríweɪ/ (**freeways**) N-COUNT 可算名詞 A **freeway** is a major road that has been specially built for fast travel over long distances. Freeways have several lanes and special places where traffic gets on and leaves. 高速道路 [AM 米国英語] ❑ *The speed limit on the freeway is 55mph.* 高速道路の制限速度は時速55マイルだ.

free will 1 N-UNCOUNT 不可算名詞 If you believe in **free will**, you believe that people have a choice in what they do and that their actions have not been decided in advance by God or by any other power. 自由意志 ❑ *...the free will of the individual.* 個人の自由意志 **2** PHRASE 句 If you do something **of** your **own free will**, you do it by choice and not because you are forced to do it. 自分の自由意志で ❑ *Would Bethany return of her own free will, as she had promised?* ベサニーは約束通りに彼女の自由意志で戻ってくるだろうか.

freeze /fríz/ (**freezes, freezing, froze, frozen**) **1** V-T/V-I 他動詞/自動詞 If a liquid or a substance containing a liquid **freezes**, or if something **freezes** it, it becomes solid because of low temperatures. 凍らせる [他動詞], 凍る [自動詞] ❑ *If the temperature drops below 0°C, water freezes.* 温度が氷点下に達すれば, 水は凍る. ❑ *The ground froze solid.* 地面は凍結して固くなった. **2** V-T/V-I 他動詞/自動詞 If you **freeze** something such as food, you preserve it by storing it at a temperature below freezing point. You can also talk about how well food **freezes**. 冷凍する [他動詞], 冷凍できる [自動詞] ❑ *You can freeze the soup at this stage.* スープはこの段階で冷凍することができます. **3** V-I 自動詞 When it **freezes** outside, the temperature falls below freezing point. 氷点下まで冷え込む ❑ *What if it rained and then froze all through those months?* もし雨が降り, それからその何か月かの間じゅう氷点下まで冷え込んだらどうなるのか. ● N-COUNT 可算名詞 **Freeze** is also a noun. 凍結状態 ❑ *The trees were damaged by a freeze in December.* 12月の寒波で樹木に被害が出た. **4** V-I 自動詞 If you **freeze**, you feel extremely cold. 凍える ❑ *The windows didn't fit at the bottom so for a while we froze even in the middle of summer.* 窓は下の方がぴったり合わなかったので, しばらくの間我々は夏の盛りですらひどく寒い思いをした. **5** V-I 自動詞 If someone who is moving **freezes**, they suddenly stop and become completely still and quiet. 動けなくなる [WRITTEN 書き言葉] ❑ *She froze when the beam of the flashlight struck her.* 彼女は懐中電灯の光が当たったときに体がすくんだ. **6** V-T 他動詞 If the government or a company **freeze** things such as prices or wages, they state officially that they will not allow them to increase for a fixed period of time. (物価・賃金を) 凍結する [BUSINESS 実業] ❑ *They want the government to freeze prices.* 彼らは政府が物価を凍結することを望んでいる. ● N-COUNT 可算名詞 **Freeze** is also a noun. 凍結 ❑ *A wage freeze was imposed on all staff earlier this month.* 今月初めに職員全員に賃金凍結が課された. **7** V-T 他動詞 If someone in authority **freezes** something such as a bank account, fund, or property, they obtain a legal order which states that it cannot be used or sold for a particular period of time. (銀行口座・資産を) 凍結する [BUSINESS 実業] ❑ *The governor's action freezes 300,000 accounts.* 知事の措置により30万の口座が凍結される. ● N-COUNT 可算名詞 **Freeze** is also a noun. 凍結 [with supp] ❑ *...a freeze on private savings.* 個人預金の凍結 **8** → see also **freezing, frozen** → see **refrigerator, water**

freez|er /frízər/ (**freezers**) N-COUNT 可算名詞 A **freezer** is a large container like a refrigerator in which the temperature is kept below freezing point so that you can store food inside it for long periods. 冷凍庫 → see **refrigerator**

freez|ing /frízɪŋ/ **1** ADJ 形容詞 If you say that something is **freezing** or **freezing cold**, you are emphasizing that it is very cold. 非常に寒い [EMPHASIS 強調] ❑ *The movie theater was freezing.* 映画館はひどく寒かった.

If you want to emphasize how cold the weather is, you can say that it is **freezing**, especially in winter when there is ice or frost. In summer, if the temperature is below average, you can say that it is **cool**. In general, **cold** suggests a lower temperature than **cool**, and **cool** things may be pleasant or refreshing. □ *A cool breeze swept off the ocean; it was pleasant out there.* If it is very **cool** or too **cool**, you can also say that it is **chilly**.

2 ADJ 形容詞 If you say that you are freezing or freezing cold, you emphasizing that you feel very cold. 凍えるほど寒い [EMPHASIS 強調] [v-link ADJ] □ *"You must be freezing," she said.* 「あなたはとても寒いにちがいない」と彼女は言った。 **Freezing** means the same as **freezing point**. 氷点 □ *It's 15 degrees below freezing.* 氷点下15度だ。 **4** → see also **freeze**

freez|ing point (freezing points) also **freezing-point** **1** N-UNCOUNT 不可算名詞 **Freezing point** is 32°Fahrenheit or 0°Celsius, the temperature at which water freezes. Freezing point is often used when talking about the weather. (水の) 氷点 □ *The temperature remained below freezing point throughout the day.* 気温は1日中氷点下のままだった。 **2** N-COUNT 可算名詞 The **freezing point** of a particular substance is the temperature at which it freezes. (物質の) 凝固点 □ *It was the seventeenth century before Newton determined the freezing point of water.* それはニュートンが水の凝固点を決定する前の17世紀だった。

freight /freɪt/ **1** N-UNCOUNT 不可算名詞 **Freight** is the movement of goods by trucks, trains, ships, or airplanes. 貨物運送 □ *France derives 16% of revenue from air freight.* フランスは歳入の16%を航空貨物運送から得ている。 **2** N-UNCOUNT 不可算名詞 **Freight** is goods that are transported by trucks, trains, ships, or airplanes. 運送貨物 □ *...26 tons of freight.* 26トンの運送貨物
→ see **train**

freight car (freight cars) N-COUNT 可算名詞 On a train, a **freight car** is a large container in which goods are transported. 貨車 [mainly AM 主に米国英語]

freight|er /freɪtər/ (freighters) N-COUNT 可算名詞 A **freighter** is a large ship or airplane that is designed for carrying freight. 貨物船, 貨物輸送機

French fries N-PLURAL 複数名詞 **French fries** are long, thin pieces of potato fried in oil or fat. フライドポテト

fre|net|ic /frɪnɛtɪk/ ADJ 形容詞 If you describe an activity as **frenetic**, you mean that it is fast and energetic, but rather uncontrolled. 熱狂的な □ *...the frenetic pace of life in New York.* ニューヨーク生活の気が狂ったようなペース

fren|zied /frɛnzid/ ADJ 形容詞 **Frenzied** activities or actions are wild, excited, and uncontrolled. 熱狂した □ *...the frenzied activity of the election.* 熱狂的な選挙活動

fren|zy /frɛnzi/ (frenzies) N-VAR 可変性名詞 **Frenzy** or a **frenzy** is great excitement or wild behavior that often results from losing control of your feelings. 逆上 □ *"Get out!" she ordered in a frenzy.* 「出て行って」と彼女は逆上して指図した。

fre|quen|cy /frɪkwənsi/ (frequencies) **1** N-UNCOUNT 不可算名詞 The **frequency** of an event is the number of times it happens during a particular period. 頻度 □ *The frequency of Kara's phone calls increased rapidly.* カーラの電話の回数が急に増えた。 **2** N-VAR 可変性名詞 In physics, the **frequency** of a sound wave or a radio wave is the number of times it vibrates within a specified period of time. 周波数 □ *You can't hear waves of such a high frequency.* そのような高周波数を聞くことはできない。 □ *...a frequency of 24 kilohertz.* 24kHzの周波数
→ see **sound, wave**

fre|quent ADJ 形容詞 If something is **frequent**, it happens often. 頻繁な □ *Bordeaux is on the main Paris-Madrid line so there are frequent trains.* ボルドーはパリとマドリッドを結ぶ本線上にあるため、列車の本数が多い。 ● **fre|quent|ly** ADV 副詞 頻繁に □ *Iron and folic acid supplements are frequently given to pregnant women.* 鉄と葉酸の補助剤は妊娠した女性に頻繁に与えられる。

Thesaurus	frequent また次を参照:
ADJ.	common, everyday, habitual; (ant.) occasional, rare

fresh /frɛʃ/ (fresher, freshest) **1** ADJ 形容詞 A **fresh** thing or amount replaces or is added to a previous thing or amount. 新たな [ADJ n] □ *He asked the police, who carried out the original investigation, to make fresh inquiries.* 彼は最初の捜査を行なった警察に新たな調査を行なうよう依頼した。 **2** ADJ 形容詞 Something that is **fresh** has been done, made, or experienced recently. 真新しい □ *There were no fresh car tracks or footprints in the snow.* 雪には真新しい車の跡や足跡は何もなかった。 □ *A puppy stepped in the fresh cement.* 子犬が塗りたてのセメントに足を踏み入れた。 **3** ADJ 形容詞 **Fresh** food has been picked or produced recently, and has not been preserved, for example, by being frozen or put in a can. 新鮮な □ *...locally caught fresh fish.* 地元で捕れた鮮魚 **4** ADJ 形容詞 If you describe something as **fresh**, you like it because it is new and

exciting. 新奇な □ *These designers are full of fresh ideas.* こうしたデザイナーたちは新しい考えでいっぱいだ。 **5** ADJ 形容詞 If you describe something as **fresh**, you mean that it is pleasant, bright, and clean in appearance. 鮮やかな □ *Gingham fabrics always look fresh and pretty.* ギンガムの生地はいつも鮮やかできれいに見える。 **6** ADJ 形容詞 If something smells, tastes, or feels **fresh**, it is clean or cool. さわやかな □ *The air was fresh and for a moment she felt revived.* 空気はさわやかで, 少しの間彼女は生き返ったように感じた。 **7** ADJ 形容詞 If you feel **fresh**, you feel full of energy and enthusiasm. 生き生きした □ *It's vital we are as fresh as possible for those games.* そうした試合のためにできるだけ元気でいることがきわめて重要だ。 **8** ADJ 形容詞 **Fresh** paint is not yet dry. 塗りたての [AM 米国英語] □ *There was fresh paint on the walls.* 壁はペンキ塗りたてだった。 **9** ADJ 形容詞 If you are **fresh from** a particular place or experience, you have just come from that place or you have just had that experience. You can also say that someone is **fresh out of** a place. 来たばかりの [v-link ADJ 'from/out of' n] □ *I returned to the office, fresh from the airport.* 私は空港から出てまっすぐ事務所に帰った。
→ see **vegetable**

fresh air N-UNCOUNT 不可算名詞 You can describe the air outside as **fresh air**, especially when you mean that it is good for you because it does not contain dirt or dangerous substances. さわやかな空気 [also 'the' N] □ *"Let's take the baby outside," I suggested. "We all need some fresh air."* 「赤ちゃんを外に連れ出しましょう。私たち全員にさわやかな空気がちょっと必要よ」と私は提案した。

fresh|ly /frɛʃli/ ADV 副詞 If something is **freshly** made or done, it has been recently made or done. 新しく [ADV -ed] □ *...freshly baked bread.* 焼きたてのパン

fresh|water /frɛʃwɔtər/ ADJ 形容詞 A **freshwater** lake contains water that is not salty, usually in contrast to the sea. **Freshwater** creatures live in water that is not salty. 淡水の [ADJ n] □ *...Lake Balaton, the largest freshwater lake in Europe.* ヨーロッパ最大の淡水湖であるバラトン湖
→ see **wetland**

fret /frɛt/ (frets, fretting, fretted) **1** V-T/V-I 他動詞/自動詞 If you **fret** about something, you worry about it. じらす [他動詞], じれる [自動詞] □ *I was working all hours and constantly fretting about everyone else's problems.* 私は四六時中働き, 常に他の人たち全員の問題にやきもきしていた。 □ *But congressional staffers fret that the project will eventually cost billions more.* しかし議会職員はその計画の最終的費用が数十億増えるのではないかと心配している。 **2** N-COUNT 可算名詞 The **frets** on a musical instrument such as a guitar are the raised lines across its neck. フレット

Fri. **Fri.** is a written abbreviation for **Friday**. Fridayの略

fric|tion /frɪkʃən/ (frictions) **1** N-UNCOUNT 不可算名詞 If there is **friction** between people, there is disagreement and argument between them. もめごと [also N in pl] □ *Sara sensed that there had been friction between her children.* セアラは自分の子供たちの間でもめごとがあったことに気づいた。 **2** N-UNCOUNT 不可算名詞 **Friction** is the force that makes it difficult for things to move freely when they are touching each other. 摩擦 □ *The pistons are graphite-coated to reduce friction.* ピストンは摩擦を減らすために黒鉛が塗ってある。

Fri|day /fraɪdeɪ, -di/ (Fridays) N-VAR 可変性名詞 **Friday** is the day after Thursday and before Saturday. 金曜日 □ *Mr. Cook is intending to go to the Middle East on Friday.* クック氏は金曜日に中東に行くつもりだ。 □ *...Friday November 6.* 11月6日金曜日

fridge /frɪdʒ/ (fridges) N-COUNT 可算名詞 A **fridge** is the same as a **refrigerator**. 冷蔵庫 [INFORMAL くだけた]

friend /frɛnd/ (friends) **1** N-COUNT 可算名詞 A **friend** is someone who you know well and like, but who is not related to you. 友人 □ *I had a long talk about this with my best friend.* 私は親友とこのことについてじっくり話し合った。 □ *She never was a close friend of mine.* 彼女が私の親しい友人であったことは決してない。 **2** N-COUNT 可算名詞 If one country refers to another as a **friend**, they mean that the other country is not an enemy of theirs. 友好国 □ *The president said that Japan is now a friend and international partner.* 大統領は日本は今や友好国で国際的パートナーだと言った。 **3** N-PLURAL 複数名詞 If you are **friends** with someone, you are their friend and they are yours. 友だち □ *I still wanted to be friends with Alison.* 私はやはりアリソンと友だちになりたかった。 □ *We remained good friends.* 私たちは良い友達のままだった。 **4** N-PLURAL; N-IN-NAMES 複数名詞, 名称中の名詞 The **friends** of a country, cause, organization, or a famous politician are the people and organizations who help and support them. 支援者 □ *...the friends of Israel.* イスラエルの支援者 **5** PHRASE 句 If you **make friends** with someone, you begin a friendship with them. You can also say that two people **make friends**. 友だちになる □ *He has made friends with the kids on the street.* 彼は街の子供たちと友だちになった。 □ *Dennis made friends easily.* デニスはたやすく友だちができた。

Word Partnership *friend* は次の語句と使われる:

ADJ.	**best** friend, **close** friend, **dear** friend, **faithful** friend, **former** friend, **good** friend, **loyal** friend, **mutual** friend, **old** friend, **personal** friend, **trusted** friend **1**
N.	**childhood** friend, friend **of the family**, friend **or relative** **1** friend **or foe** **1** **2**
V.	**tell** a friend **1** **make** a friend **1** **5**

friend|ly /frɛndli/ (friendlier, friendliest, friendlies) **1** ADJ 形容詞 If someone is **friendly**, they behave in a pleasant, kind way, and like to be with other people. 友好的な, 親切な □ *Godfrey had been friendly to me.* ゴッドフリーは私に親切だった. □ *...a man with a pleasant, friendly face.* 愉快で親しみのある顔をした男 ● **friend|li|ness** N-UNCOUNT 不可算名詞 友好的なこと □ *She also loves the friendliness of the people.* 彼女はそこの人々の人なつっこさも好きだ. **2** ADJ 形容詞 [v-link ADJ] If you are **friendly with** someone, you like each other and enjoy spending time together. 親しい □ *I'm friendly with his mother.* 私は彼のお母さんとも親しい. **3** ADJ 形容詞 You can describe another country or their government as **friendly** when they have good relations with your own country rather than being an enemy. 友好的な □ *...a worsening in relations between the two previously friendly countries.* 以前友好的だった2か国間の関係の悪化

Do not confuse **friendly** and **sympathetic**. A person who is **friendly** or has a **friendly** attitude is kind and pleasant and behaves the way a friend would. □ *...a friendly woman who offered me a coffee. ...a pleasant, friendly smile.* If you have a problem and someone is **sympathetic** or shows a **sympathetic** attitude, they show that they care and would like to help you. □ *My boyfriend was very sympathetic.* Note that people sometimes refer to characters in a play or novel who are easy to like as **sympathetic**. □ *There were no sympathetic characters in my book.* You usually say that real people are "nice" or "likable."

4 N-COUNT 可算名詞 In sports, a **friendly** is a game which is not part of a competition, and is played for entertainment or practice, often without any serious effort to win. 親善試合 [BRIT 英国英語] [ADJ n] [AM **exhibition game** 米国英語 **exhibition game**] ● ADJ 形容詞 **Friendly** is also an adjective. 親善のための → see **dump**

Word Partnership *friendly* は次の語句と使われる:

N.	friendly **atmosphere**, friendly **face**, friendly **neighbors**, friendly **service**, friendly **voice** **1** friendly **relationship** **2** friendly **game**, friendly **match** **4**
V.	**become** friendly **2**

-friendly /-frɛndli/ **1** COMB IN ADJ 形容詞の複合 **-friendly** combines with nouns to form adjectives which describe things that are not harmful to the specified part of the natural world. ～に害を及ぼさない □ *Palm oil is environment-friendly.* パーム油は環境に優しい. **2** COMB IN ADJ 形容詞の複合 **-friendly** combines with nouns to form adjectives which describe things which are intended for or suitable for the specified person, especially things that are easy for them to understand, appreciate, or use. ～に適した, ～に使いやすい □ *...customer-friendly banking facilities.* 顧客に親切な銀行設備 **3** → see also **user-friendly**

Word Link *ship ≈ condition or state :* censor**ship**, citizen**ship**, friend**ship**

friend|ship /frɛndʃip/ (friendships) **1** N-VAR 可変性名詞 A **friendship** is a relationship between two or more friends. 交友関係 □ *Giving advice when it's not called for is the quickest way to end a good friendship.* 求められないのに忠告をすることは, 親しい交友関係を終わらせる最も速い方法だ. □ *She struck up a close friendship with Desiree during the week of rehearsals.* 彼女はリハーサルの週の間にデジレーと親しくなった. **2** N-VAR 可変性名詞 **Friendship** is a relationship between two countries in which they help and support each other. 友好 □ *The president set the targets for the future to promote friendship with East Europe.* 大統領は東欧との友好関係を推進するために将来の目標を設定した. **3** N-UNCOUNT 不可算名詞 You use **friendship** to refer in a general way to the state of being friends, or the feelings that friends have for each other. 友情 □ *...a hobby which led to a whole new world of friendship and adventure.* 友情と冒険の全く新しい世界につながった趣味

frig|ate /frɪgət/ (frigates) N-COUNT 可算名詞 A **frigate** is a fairly small ship owned by the navy that can move at fast speeds. Frigates are often used to protect other ships. フリゲート

fright /fraɪt/ (frights) **1** N-UNCOUNT 不可算名詞 **Fright** is a

sudden feeling of fear, especially the fear that you feel when something unpleasant surprises you. 恐怖 □ *The steam pipes rattled suddenly, and Franklin jumped with fright.* 蒸気管が突然音を立てたので, フランクリンはぎょっとして飛び上がった. □ *The birds smashed into the top of their cages in fright.* 鳥は怖がってかごの上部に激突した. **2** N-COUNT 可算名詞 A **fright** is an experience which makes you suddenly afraid. 恐怖感 □ *The snake picked up its head and stuck out its tongue which gave everyone a fright.* ヘビは頭を持ち上げて舌を出したため, 全員恐怖に襲われた.

fright|en /fraɪt³n/ (frightens, frightening, frightened) **1** V-T 他動詞 If something or someone **frightens** you, they cause you to suddenly feel afraid, anxious, or nervous. 怖がらせる □ *He knew that Soli was trying to frighten him, so he smiled to hide his fear.* 彼はソーリが彼を怖がらせようとしていることを知っていたので, 恐怖感を隠すためにほほえんだ. **2** PHRASE 句 If something **frightens the life out of** you, **frightens the wits out of** you, or **frightens you out of your wits**, it causes you to feel suddenly afraid or gives you a very unpleasant shock. 人を震え上がらせる [EMPHASIS 強調] □ *Fairground rides are intended to frighten the life out of you.* 遊園地の乗り物は人を震え上がらせるためのものだ.
▶ **frighten away** or **frighten off** **1** PHRASAL VERB 句動詞 If you **frighten** a person or animal or **frighten** them **off**, you make them afraid so that they run away or stay some distance away from you. おどかして追い払う □ *The fishermen said the company's seismic survey was frightening away fish.* 漁師たちは会社の地震調査のせいで魚がよりつかなくなったと言った. **2** PHRASAL VERB 句動詞 To **frighten** someone **away** or **frighten** them **off** means to make them nervous so that they decide not to become involved with a particular person or activity. おどかしてやめさせる □ *Repossessions have frightened buyers off.* 住宅を回収されることが心配で買い手は購入に消極的だ.
▶ **frighten off** → see **frighten away**

fright|ened /fraɪt³nd/ ADJ 形容詞 If you are **frightened**, you are anxious or afraid, often because of something that has just happened or that you think may happen. 怖がって □ *She was frightened of making a mistake.* 彼女は誤りを犯すことを恐れていた.

fright|en|ing /fraɪt³nɪŋ/ ADJ 形容詞 If something is **frightening**, it makes you feel afraid, anxious, or nervous. 恐ろしい □ *It was a very frightening experience and they were very courageous.* それは非常に恐ろしい体験で, 彼らは非常に勇敢だった. ● **fright|en|ing|ly** ADV 副詞 恐ろしく □ *The country is frighteningly close to possessing nuclear weapons.* その国は核兵器の所有に恐ろしいほど近づいている.

fright|ful /fraɪtfəl/ **1** ADJ 形容詞 **Frightful** means very bad or unpleasant. いやな [OLD-FASHIONED 古風な] □ *My father was unable to talk about the war, it was so frightful.* 私の父は戦争について話すことができなかったが, それほどいやなものだったのだ. **2** ADJ 形容詞 **Frightful** is used to emphasize the extent or degree of something, usually something bad. 大変な [INFORMAL, OLD-FASHIONED くだけた, 古風な] [ADJ n] 強調] □ *He got himself into a frightful muddle.* 彼はひどい混乱状態に陥った.

frill /frɪl/ (frills) **1** N-COUNT 可算名詞 A **frill** is a long narrow strip of cloth or paper with many folds in it, which is attached to something as a decoration. フリル □ *...curtains with frills.* フリルのついたカーテン **2** N-COUNT 可算名詞 If you describe something as having **no frills**, you mean that it has no extra features, but is acceptable or good if you want something simple. 余分なもの [APPROVAL 賛成]

fringe /frɪndʒ/ (fringes) **1** N-COUNT 可算名詞 A **fringe** is a decoration attached to clothes, or other objects such as curtains, consisting of a row of hanging strips or threads. ふさ飾り, 縁取り □ *The jacket had leather fringes.* その上着には皮製のふさ飾りがついていた. **2** N-COUNT 可算名詞 To be **on the fringe** or **the fringes** of a place means to be on the outside edge of it, or to be in one of the parts that are farthest from its center. 外れ □ *...black townships located on the fringes of the city.* 市のはずれにある黒人居住区 **3** N-COUNT 可算名詞 The **fringe** or the **fringes of** an activity or organization are its less important, least typical, or most extreme parts, rather than its main and central part. 非主流 □ *The party remained on the fringe of the political scene until last year.* その政党は昨年まで政界の非主流派だった. **4** N-COUNT 可算名詞 A **fringe** is hair which is cut so that it hangs over your forehead. 切り下げ前髪 [BRIT 英国英語; AM **bangs** 米国英語 **bangs**] **5** ADJ 形容詞 **Fringe** groups or events are less important or popular than other related groups or events. 非主流の [ADJ n] □ *The monarchists are a small fringe group who quarrel fiercely among themselves.* きみ主制主義者は内部で激しく抗争している小規模な非主流派である.

fringe ben|efit (fringe benefits) N-COUNT 可算名詞 **Fringe benefits** are extra things that some people get from their job in addition to their salary, for example, a car. 付加給付 [BUSINESS 実業] □ *...insecure, badly paid jobs without any of the fringe benefits such as healthcare.* 健康保険などの付加給付の何もない不安定で低賃金の仕事

fringed /frɪndʒd/ ◨ ADJ 形容詞 Fringed clothes, curtains, or lampshades are decorated with fringes. ふさ飾りのついた [ADJ n] ◻Emma wore a fringed scarf round her neck. エマはふさ飾りのあるスカーフを首に巻いていた. ◨ ADJ 形容詞 If a place or object **is fringed with** something, that thing forms a border around it or is situated along its edges. 縁取られた [v-link ADJ 'with' n] ◻Her eyes were large and brown and fringed with incredibly long lashes. 彼女の目は大きく茶色で, 大変長いまつげで縁取られていた.

frivolous /frɪvələs/ ◨ ADJ 形容詞 If you describe someone as **frivolous**, you mean they behave in a silly or light-hearted way, rather than being serious and sensible. 軽薄な, 不真面目な ◻I just decided I was a bit too frivolous to be a doctor. 私は医者になるにはちょっと不真面目すぎるとの結論に達したところだ. ◨ ADJ 形容詞 If you describe an activity as **frivolous**, you disapprove of it because it is not useful and wastes time or money. くだらない [DISAPPROVAL 不賛成] ◻The group says it wants politicians to stop wasting public money on what it believes are frivolous projects. その集団は政治家たちがそれがくだらない計画だと信じているものに公金を費やすのをやめて欲しいと言っている.

fro /froʊ/ **to and fro** → see **to**

frog /frɒg/ (**frogs**) N-COUNT 可算名詞 A **frog** is a small creature with smooth skin, big eyes, and long back legs which it uses for jumping. Frogs usually live near water. カエル

frolic /frɒlɪk/ (**frolics, frolicking, frolicked**) V-I 自動詞 When people or animals **frolic**, they play or move in a lively, happy way. 遊び戯れる ◻Tourists sunbathe and frolic in the ocean. 観光客は日光浴をし, 海で遊び戯れる.

from
❶ MENTIONING THE SOURCE, ORIGIN, OR STARTING POINT
❷ MENTIONING A RANGE OF TIMES, AMOUNTS, OR THINGS
❸ MENTIONING SOMETHING YOU WANT TO PREVENT OR AVOID

❶ **from** /frəm, STRONG frʌm/ ◨ PREP 前置詞 If something comes **from** a particular person or thing, or if you get something **from** them, they give it to you or they are the source of it. (出所) ～からの ◻He appealed for information from anyone who saw the attackers. 彼は襲撃者たちを目撃した人物からの情報提供を呼びかけた. ◻...an anniversary present from his wife. 彼の妻からの記念日のプレゼント

> When you are talking about the person who has written you a letter or sent a message to you, you say that the letter or message is **from** that person. ◻He received a message from Vito Corleone. When you are talking about an author, a composer, or a painter, you say the work is **by** that person or is written or painted **by** him or her. ◻...three books by Michael Moorcock. ...a collection of piano pieces by Mozart.

◨ PREP 前置詞 Someone who comes **from** a particular place lives in that place or originally lived there. Something that comes **from** a particular place was made in that place. (出身地) ～出身の ◻...an art dealer from Zurich. チューリッヒ出の美術商 ◻Katy Jones is nineteen and comes from Biloxi. ケイティ・ジョーンズは19歳で, ビロクシの出身である. ◨ PREP 前置詞 A person **from** a particular organization works for that organization. (組織) ～からの ◻...a representative from the Israeli embassy. イスラエル大使館からの代表者 ◨ PREP 前置詞 If someone or something moves or is moved **from** a place, they leave it or are removed, so that they are no longer there. (場所の起点) ～から ◻The guests watched as she fled from the room. 客たちは彼女が部屋から逃げ出すのをじっと見ていた. ◨ PREP 前置詞 If you take one thing or person **from** another, you move that thing or person so that they are no longer with the other or attached to the other. (場所の起点) ～から ◻In many bone transplants, bone can be taken from other parts of the patient's body. 骨の移植手術では患者の体の他の部分から取った骨を利用することが多い. ◨ PREP 前置詞 If you take something **from** an amount, you reduce the amount by that much. (数量の起点) ～から ◻The $103 is deducted from Mrs. Adams' salary. 103ドルはアダムス夫人の給料から差し引かれる. ◨ PREP 前置詞 **From** is used in expressions such as **away from** or **absent from** to say that someone or something is not present in a place where they are usually found. (不在を表して) ～から離れて ◻Her husband worked away from home a lot. 彼女の夫は出張で不在なことが多かった. ◨ PREP 前置詞 If you return **from** a place or an activity, you return after being in that place or doing that activity. (場所・活動などの起点) ～から ◻My son has just returned from Amsterdam. 私の息子はアムステルダムから戻ってきたばかりだ. ◨ PREP 前置詞 If you are back **from** a place or activity, you have left it and have returned to your former place. (場所・活動などの起点) ～から ◻Elaine was just back from work when he called. 彼が電話をしたとき, エレーンはちょうど勤め先から戻ってきたところだった. ◨ PREP 前置詞 If you see or hear something

from a particular place, you are in that place when you see it or hear it. (視点を表して) ～から ◻Visitors see the painting from behind a plate glass window. 参観者は板ガラスの窓の後ろから絵画を見る. ◨ PREP 前置詞 If something hangs or sticks out **from** an object, it is attached to it or held by it. (物を起点として) ～から [v PREP n] ◻Hanging from his right wrist is a heavy gold bracelet. 彼の右の手首から下がっているのは重い金の腕輪だ. ◻...large fans hanging from ceilings. 天井から下がっている大きな扇風機 ◨ PREP 前置詞 You can use **from** when giving distances. For example, if a place is fifty miles **from** another place, the distance between the two places is fifty miles. (距離を表して) ～から離れて [amount PREP n] ◻...a small park only a few hundred yards from Zurich's main shopping center. チューリッヒの主なショッピングセンターからほんの数百ヤード離れたところにある小さな公園 ◻How far is it from here? それはここからどの位離れているのか. ◨ PREP 前置詞 If a road or railroad line goes **from** one place to another, you can travel along it between the two places. (移動の出発点を表して) ～から ◻...the road from St. Petersburg to Tallinn. サンクトペテルブルグからタリンへの道路 ◨ PREP 前置詞 **From** is used, especially in the expression **made from**, to say what substance has been used to make something. (原料・材料を表して) ～で, ～から [v PREP n] ◻bread made from white flour. 白色小麦粉でできたパン ◨ PREP 前置詞 If something changes **from** one thing **to** another, it stops being the first thing and becomes the second thing. (変化を表して) ～から ◻The expression on his face changed from sympathy to surprise. 彼の表情は同情から驚きに変わった. ◻Unemployment has fallen from 7.5 to 7.2%. 失業率は7.5%から7.2%に低下した. ◨ PREP 前置詞 You use **from** after some verbs and nouns when mentioning the cause of something. (原因を表して) ～から [PREP n/-ing] ◻The problem simply resulted from a difference of opinion. その問題は単に意見の相違から発生した. ◻They really do get pleasure from spending money on other people. 彼らは本当に他人のために金を使うことが好きだ. ◨ PREP 前置詞 You use **from** when you are giving the reason for an opinion. (根拠を表して) ～から ◻She knew from experience that Dave was about to tell her the truth. 彼女は経験からデイブが彼女に真実を告げようとしていることが分かった. ◻He sensed from the expression on her face that she had something to say. 彼は表情から彼女には何か言いたいことがあるに気づいた.

❷ **from** /frəm, STRONG frʌm/ ◨ PREP 前置詞 You can use **from** when you are talking about the beginning of a period of time. (時間の起点を表して) ～から ◻She studied painting from 1926 and also worked as a commercial artist. 彼女は1926年から絵画を学び, 商業アーティストとしても働いた. ◻Breakfast is available to fishermen from 6 a.m. 漁師向けの朝食は午前6時から出ます. ◨ PREP 前置詞 You say **from** one thing **to** another when you are stating the range of things that are possible, or when saying that the range of things includes everything in a certain category. (範囲の起点を表して) ～から [PREP n/-ing] ◻There are 94 countries represented in Barcelona, from Algeria to Zimbabwe. バルセロナにはアルジェリアからジンバブエまで94ヶ国の代表が送られている.

❸ **from** /frəm, STRONG frʌm/ PREP 前置詞 **From** is used after verbs with meanings such as "protect," "free," "keep," and "prevent" to introduce the action that does not happen, or that someone does not want to happen. (抑制・防止を表して) ～から ◻Such laws could protect the consumer from harmful or dangerous remedies. そうした法律は消費者を有害または危険な療法から守ることができるであろう.

> In addition to the uses shown here, **from** is used in phrasal verbs such as "date from" and "grow away from."

front /frʌnt/ (**fronts**) ◨ N-COUNT 可算名詞 The **front** of something is the part of it that faces you, or that faces forward, or that you normally see or use. 前面 ◻One man sat in an armchair, and the other sat on the front of the desk. 1人の男が肘掛けいすに座り, もう1人は机の前に座っていた. ◻Stand at the front of the line. 列の最前部に立ちなさい. ◨ N-COUNT 可算名詞 The **front** of a building is the side or part of it that faces the street. 正面 ◻Attached to the front of the house, there was a large veranda. 家の正面には大きなベランダが取り付けられていた. ◨ N-COUNT 可算名詞 In a war, the **front** is a line where two opposing armies are facing each other. 最前線 ◻Sonja's husband is fighting at the front. ソニャの夫は最前線で戦っている. ◨ → see also **front line** ◨ N-COUNT 可算名詞 If you say that something is happening on a particular **front**, you mean that it is happening with regard to a particular situation or field of activity. 活動分野 ◻...research across a wide academic front. 広範な学問分野にまたがる研究 ◨ N-COUNT 可算名詞 If someone puts on a particular kind of **front**, they pretend to have a particular quality. 見せかけ ◻Michael kept up a brave front both to the world and in his home. マイケルは世間に対しても家庭でも勇敢なふりをし続けた. ◨ N-COUNT 可算名詞 An organization or activity that is **a front for** one that is illegal or secret is used to hide it. 隠れみの ◻...a firm later identified by the police as a front for crime syndicates. 後に警察の調べで犯罪組織の隠れみのであることが判明した会社 ◨ N-COUNT 可算名詞 In relation to the weather, a **front** is a line where a mass of cold air meets a mass of warm air. 前線 ◻The snow signaled the

arrival of a front, and a high-pressure area seemed to be settling in. 雪は前線の到来を伝え，高気圧の地域は居座っているようだ． **9** N-SING 単数名詞 A person's or animal's **front** is the part of their body between their head and their legs that is on the opposite side to their back. 前部 □ *When baby is lying on his front, hold something so that he has to raise his head to look at it.* 赤ちゃんがうつぶせで寝ているときに，何かを持って赤ちゃんがそれを見るためには頭を上げなければならないようにしなさい． **10** ADJ 形容詞 **Front** is used to refer to the side or part of something that is toward the front or nearest to the front. 表側の [ADJ n] □ *I went out there on the front porch.* 私はその表側のポーチに出た． □ *She was only six and still missing her front teeth.* 彼女はたった6歳で，まだ前歯が抜けていなかった． **11** ADJ 形容詞 The **front** page of a newspaper is the outside of the first page, where the main news stories are printed. 第1面の [ADJ n] □ *The front page carries a photograph of the two foreign ministers.* 第1面には2人の外務大臣の写真が載っている． **12** → see also **front-page** **13** PHRASE 句 If a person or thing is **in front**, they are ahead of others in a moving group, or further forward than someone or something else. 前に □ *Officers will crack down on lunatic motorists who speed or drive too close to the car in front.* 警官はスピード違反を犯したり，前の車の直後にぴったりつけて走る狂気じみたドライバーを厳重に取り締まる予定だ． **14** PHRASE 句 Someone who is **in front** in a competition or contest at a particular point is winning at that point. 先頭に立って □ *Richard Dunwoody is in front in the jockeys' title race.* リチャード・ダンウッディは騎手の選手権で先頭に立っている． **15** PHRASE 句 If someone or something is **in front of** a particular thing, they are facing it, ahead of it, or close to the front part of it. ～の前に □ *She sat down in front of her dressing-table mirror to look at herself.* 彼女は自分の姿を見るために化粧台の鏡の前に座った． □ *Something darted out in front of my car, and my car hit it.* 何かが私の車の前に飛び出してきて，私の車にぶつかった． **16** PHRASE 句 If you do or say something **in front of** someone else, you do or say it when they are present. ～の前で □ *They never argued in front of their children.* 彼らは子供たちの前では決して言い争いをしなかった．
→ see **forecast**

Word Partnership	*front* は次の語句と使われる:

N.   front **of the line** **1**
     front **door**, front **end**, front **porch**, front **room**, front
     tire, front **wheel**, front **window** **1** **9**
     front **paws**, front **teeth** **8**

front|al /frʌntᵊl/ ADJ 形容詞 **Frontal** means relating to or involving the front of something, for example, the front of an army, a vehicle, or the brain. 前面の [FORMAL 形式ばった] □ *Military leaders are not expecting a frontal assault by the rebels.* 軍首脳陣は反乱軍による正面攻撃は想定していないようです．

front desk N-SING 単数名詞 The **front desk** in a hotel is the desk or office that books rooms for people and answers their questions. フロント [mainly AM 主に米国英語] □ *Call the hotel's front desk and cancel your early morning wake-up call.* フロントに電話をかけて早朝のモーニングコールをキャンセルしてください．
→ see **hotel**

fron|tier /frʌntɪər, frɒn-/ (**frontiers**) **1** N-COUNT 可算名詞 When you are talking about the western part of America before the twentieth century, you use **frontier** to refer to the area beyond the part settled by Europeans. 開拓時代のアメリカ西部地方 □ *...a far-flung outpost on the frontier.* アメリカ西部辺境の開拓集落． **2** N-COUNT 可算名詞 The **frontiers** of something, especially knowledge, are the limits to which it extends. 限界，最先端 □ *...pushing back the frontiers of science.* 科学に新境地を開く． **3** N-COUNT 可算名詞 A **frontier** is a border between two countries. 国境 □ *It wasn't difficult then to cross the frontier.* 当時は国境を越えるのは難しいことではなかった．

front line (**front lines**) also **front-line** **1** N-COUNT 可算名詞 The **front line** is the place where two opposing armies are facing each other and where fighting is going on. 前線 □ *...a massive concentration of soldiers on the front line.* 前線へ集結した兵士の大部隊． **2** PHRASE 句 Someone who is **in the front line** has to play a very important part in defending or achieving something. 第一線で □ *Information officers are in the front line of putting across government policies.* 広報幹部は政府の方針を伝える最も重要な役割を担っている．

front-page ADJ 形容詞 A **front-page** article or picture appears on the front page of a newspaper because it is very important or interesting. 第1面の [ADJ n] □ *...a front-page article in last week's paper.* 先週の新聞の第1面記事．

front-runner (**front-runners**) N-COUNT 可算名詞 In a competition or contest, the **front-runner** is the person who seems most likely to win it. 有力候補 □ *Neither of the front-runners in the presidential election is a mainstream politician.* 大統領選挙の有力候補はどちらも主流派ではありません．

frost /frɒst/ (**frosts, frosting, frosted**) **1** N-VAR 可変性名詞 When there is **frost** or a **frost**, the temperature outside falls below freezing point and the ground becomes covered in ice crystals. 霜 □ *There is frost in the ground and snow is forecast.* 霜が降り雪になるでしょう． **2** V-T 他動詞 If you **frost** a cake, you cover and decorate it with frosting. 粉砂糖をまぶす [AM 米国英語] □ *She was frosting the cupcakes while we talked.* 私たちが歓談している間に彼女はカップケーキに粉砂糖をまぶしていた．

frost|ing /frɒstɪŋ/ N-UNCOUNT 不可算名詞 **Frosting** is a sweet substance made from powdered sugar that is used to cover and decorate cakes. 砂糖衣，アイシング [AM 米国英語] □ *...a huge pastry with green frosting on it.* 緑色でアイシングされた大きなケーキ．

frosty /frɒsti/ (**frostier, frostiest**) **1** ADJ 形容詞 If the weather is **frosty**, the temperature is below freezing. 凍るように寒い □ *...sharp, frosty nights.* 厳しい寒さ続きの夜． **2** ADJ 形容詞 You describe the ground or an object as **frosty** when it is covered with frost. 霜の降りた □ *The street was deserted except for a cat lifting its paws off the frosty stones.* 通りには人気がなく，1匹の猫だけが霜のついた石畳を冷たそうに歩いていた．

froth /frɒθ/ (**froths, frothing, frothed**) **1** N-UNCOUNT 不可算名詞 **Froth** is a mass of small bubbles on the surface of a liquid. 泡 □ *...the froth of bubbles on the top of a glass of beer.* グラスに浮かぶビールの泡． **2** V-I 自動詞 If a liquid **froths**, small bubbles appear on its surface. 泡立つ □ *The sea froths over my feet.* 波が足にかかって泡立った．

frown /fraʊn/ (**frowns, frowning, frowned**) V-I 自動詞 When someone **frowns**, their eyebrows become drawn together, because they are annoyed, worried, or puzzled, or because they are concentrating. まゆをひそめる □ *Nancy shook her head, frowning.* ナンシーはまゆをひそめて首を横に振った． □ *He frowned at her anxiously.* 彼は心配そうにまゆをひそめて彼女を見た． ● N-COUNT 可算名詞 **Frown** is also a noun. しかめ面 □ *There was a deep frown on the boy's face.* 少年は苦々しい表情を浮かべていた．
▶ **frown upon** or **frown on** PHRASAL VERB 句動詞 If something is **frowned upon** or is **frowned on**, people disapprove of it. 認められていない □ *This practice is frowned upon as being wasteful.* 人々はこれを無駄な慣習だと冷ややかに見ています．

froze /froʊz/ **Froze** is the past tense of **freeze**. freezeの過去形

fro|zen /froʊzᵊn/ **1** **Frozen** is the past participle of **freeze**. freezeの過去分詞 **2** ADJ 形容詞 If the ground is **frozen** it has become very hard because the weather is very cold. 凍った □ *It was bitterly cold now and the ground was frozen hard.* そのときは非常に寒く，道はかちかちに凍った． **3** ADJ 形容詞 **Frozen** food has been preserved by being kept at a very low temperature. 冷凍の □ *Frozen fish is a very healthy convenience food.* 冷凍魚は，健康的で便利な食品です． **4** ADJ 形容詞 If you say that you are **frozen**, or a part of your body is **frozen**, you are emphasizing that you feel very cold. 凍えるように寒い [EMPHASIS 強調] □ *He put one hand up to his frozen face.* 彼は凍えた顔に片手を当てた． □ *I'm frozen out here.* ここは寒くて凍えそうだよ． ● PHRASE 句 **Frozen stiff** means the same as **frozen**. 凍えそうに寒い
→ see **glacier**

fru|gal /fruːgᵊl/ **1** ADJ 形容詞 People who are **frugal** or who live **frugal** lives do not spend much money on themselves. 質素な □ *She lives a frugal life.* 彼女は質素な生活をしている． ● **fru|gal|ity** /fruːɡælɪti/ N-UNCOUNT 不可算名詞 □ *We must practice the strictest frugality and economy.* 極めて質素で倹約的な実施が求められる． **2** ADJ 形容詞 A **frugal** meal is small and not expensive. 簡素な □ *The diet was frugal: cheese and water, rice and beans.* 食事は，チーズと水，お米と豆といった簡素なものでした．

fruit /fruːt/ (**fruit, fruits, fruiting, fruited**)

The plural form is usually **fruit**, but can also be **fruits**.
複数は通常 **fruit** であるが，**fruits** も使われる．

1 N-VAR 可変性名詞 **Fruit** or a **fruit** is something which grows on a tree or bush and which contains seeds or a pit covered by a substance that you can eat. 果物 □ *Fresh fruit and vegetables provide fiber and vitamins.* 生の果物や野菜からは食物繊維とビタミンが取れます． □ *...bananas and other tropical fruits.* バナナやトロピカルフルーツ類． **2** V-I 自動詞 If a plant **fruits**, it produces fruit. 果実をつける □ *The scientists will study the variety of trees and observe which are fruiting.* 科学者は木を広く調査し，どの種類が果実をつけるかを観察する予定だ． **3** N-COUNT 可算名詞 The **fruits** or the **fruit** of someone's work or activity are the good things that result from it. 成果 □ *The team has really worked hard and Mansell is enjoying the fruits of that labor.* チームはこれまで懸命な努力を続け，マンセルはレースでその成果を享受している． **4** → see also **kiwi fruit** **5** PHRASE 句 If the effort that you put into something or a particular way of doing something **bears fruit**, it is successful and produces good results. 実を結ぶ □ *Eleanor's work among the women will, I trust, bear fruit.* エレノアの女性のための活動は実を結ぶと確信しています．
→ see Word Web: **fruit**
→ see **dessert, grain**

Word Web fruit

Fruits only appear on **flowering plants**. They are fleshy and **sweet** and contain **seeds** or a **stone** or **pit**. The fruit serves the plant in two ways. First, it protects seeds from damage. Secondly, it helps make sure seeds are carried to new places. After an animal eats a seed, it passes through its body unharmed. When the animal leaves droppings in a new location, the seed may start a new plant there. Fruits contain a **sugar** called fructose—an important source of energy for animals and humans. But not all fruits are sweet. **Lemons**, for example, are **sour**.

fruit|ful /frútfəl/ ADJ 形容詞 Something that is **fruitful** produces good and useful results. 実りの多い ❑ *We had a long, happy, fruitful relationship.* 私たちの関係は、長く、幸福で、実りの多いものでした.

frui|tion /fruíʃᵊn/ N-UNCOUNT 不可算名詞 If something comes **to fruition**, it starts to succeed and produce the results that were intended or hoped for. 結実 [FORMAL 形式ばった] ❑ *These plans take time to come to fruition.* これらの計画は結実するまで時間がかかる.

fruit|less /frútlɪs/ ADJ 形容詞 **Fruitless** actions, events, or efforts do not achieve anything at all. 実りのない ❑ *It was a fruitless search.* それは実りのない捜査だった.

fruity /frúti/ (**fruitier, fruitiest**) **1** ADJ 形容詞 Something that is **fruity** smells or tastes of fruit. フルーティーな ❑ *This shampoo smells fruity and leaves the hair beautifully silky.* このシャンプーはフルーティーな香りで、髪を美しくつやややかに保ちます. **2** ADJ 形容詞 A **fruity** voice or laugh is pleasantly rich and deep. よく響く ❑ *Jerrold laughed again, a solid, fruity laugh.* ジェロルドは再び大きくよく響く声で笑った.

frus|trate /frʌ́streɪt/ (**frustrates, frustrating, frustrated**) **1** V-T 他動詞 If something **frustrates** you, it upsets or angers you because you are unable to do anything about the problems it creates. いらだたせる ❑ *These questions frustrated me.* 私はそれらの質問にいらいらした. ● **frus|trat|ed** ADJ 形容詞 いらいらした ❑ *Roberta felt frustrated and angry.* ロベルタはいらだちと怒りを覚えた. ● **frus|tra|tion** /frʌstreɪʃᵊn/ (**frustrations**) N-VAR 可変性名詞 欲求不満 ❑ *The results show the level of frustration among hospital doctors.* その調査結果は、勤務医がどの程度欲求不満を抱えているのかを示している. **2** V-T 他動詞 If someone or something **frustrates** a plan or attempt to do something, they prevent it from succeeding. くじく ❑ *The government has deliberately frustrated his efforts to gain work permits for his foreign staff.* 行政は意図的に、彼が外国人労働者の就労許可を取得しようとするのを阻止してきました.

frus|trat|ing /frʌ́streɪtɪŋ/ ADJ 形容詞 Something that is **frustrating** annoys you or makes you angry because you cannot do anything about the problems it causes. いらだたしい ❑ *The current situation is very frustrating for us.* 我々にとって非常にいらだたしい状況だ.

→ see **anger**

fry /fraɪ/ (**fries, frying, fried**) **1** V-T 他動詞 When you **fry** food, you cook it in a pan that contains hot fat or oil. 油で揚げる、油でいためる ❑ *Fry the breadcrumbs until golden brown.* パン粉をこんがり色づくまでいためてください. **2** N-PLURAL 複数名詞 **Fries** are the same as **French fries**. フライドポテト

→ see **cook, egg**

fry|ing pan (**frying pans**) N-COUNT 可算名詞 A **frying pan** is a flat metal pan with a long handle, in which you fry food. フライパン

→ see **pan**

ft. ft. is a written abbreviation for **feet** or **foot**. フィートの略号 ❑ *Flying at 1,000 ft., he heard a peculiar noise from the rotors.* 高度1,000フィートを飛行中、彼は回転翼が奇妙な音をたてているのに気づいた.

fuck /fʌk/ (**fucks, fucking, fucked**)

Fuck is a vulgar and offensive word which you should avoid using.

Fuck は野卑で無礼な語で使うのを避けるべき語である.

1 EXCLAM 感嘆詞 **Fuck** is used to express anger or annoyance. ちくしょう、くそっ [OFFENSIVE, VULGAR 無礼な、下品な、FEELINGS 感情] **2** V-RECIP 相互動詞 To **fuck** someone means to have sex with them. 性交する [OFFENSIVE, VULGAR 無礼な、下品な] ▶ **fuck off** PHRASAL VERB 句動詞 Telling someone to **fuck off** is an insulting way of telling them to go away. 消えうせろ [OFFENSIVE, VULGAR 無礼な、下品な] [usu imper]

fuck|ing /fʌ́kɪŋ/ ADJ 形容詞 **Fucking** is used by some people to emphasize a word or phrase, especially when they are feeling angry or annoyed. 形容詞的な強調語で、特にいらだちなどの感情を表す際に使用する. ● ADV 副詞 **Fucking** is also an adverb. 副詞的な強調語としても用いられる.

fudge /fʌdʒ/ (**fudges, fudging, fudged**) **1** N-UNCOUNT 不可算名詞 **Fudge** is a soft brown candy that is made from butter, cream, and sugar. ファッジ (バター、クリーム、砂糖などでできた柔らかいキャンディー) **2** V-T 他動詞 If you **fudge** something, you avoid making a clear and definite decision, distinction, or statement about it. ごまかす [他動詞] ❑ *Both have fudged their calculations and avoided specifics.* 両者とも計算をごまかし、詳細には触れることはなかった.

fuel /fyúəl/ (**fuels, fueling** or **fuelling, fueled** or **fuelled**) **1** N-MASS 質量名詞 **Fuel** is a substance such as coal, oil, or gasoline that is burned to provide heat or power. 燃料 ❑ *They ran out of fuel.* 彼らは燃料を使い果たした. **2** V-T 他動詞 To **fuel** a situation means to make it become worse or more intense. あおる ❑ *The result will inevitably fuel speculation about the prime minister's future.* この結果、必然的に大統領の進退について憶測があおられることになるでしょう.

→ see **car, energy, engine, oil**

Word Partnership fuel は次の語句と使われる:

N.	**cost of** fuel, fuel **oil**, fuel **pump**, fuel **shortage**, fuel **supply**, fuel **tank** **1**
ADJ.	**unleaded** fuel **1**

fu|gi|tive /fyúdʒɪtɪv/ (**fugitives**) N-COUNT 可算名詞 A **fugitive** is someone who is running away or hiding, usually in order to avoid being caught by the police. 逃亡者 ❑ *The rebel leader was a fugitive from justice.* 反体制派の指導者は逃亡犯だったのです.

ful|fill /fʊlfɪ́l/ (**fulfills, fulfilling, fulfilled**) **1** V-T 他動詞 If you **fulfill** something such as a promise, dream, or hope, you do what you said or hoped you would do. 実現させる ❑ *President Kaunda fulfilled his promise of announcing a date for the referendum.* カウンダ大統領は国民投票の日程を発表するという公約を果たしました. **2** V-T 他動詞 To **fulfill** a task, role, or requirement means to do or be what is required, necessary, or expected. 終える ❑ *Without them you will not be able to fulfill the tasks you have before you.* 彼らがいなければきみは課された仕事を完遂できない. **3** V-T 他動詞 If something **fulfills** you, or if you **fulfill yourself**, you feel happy and satisfied with what you are doing or with what you have achieved. 満足させる ❑ *The war was the biggest thing in her life and nothing after that quite fulfilled her.* 彼女にとってはその戦争が人生最大の出来事で、その後何かに満足感を覚えることはなかった. ● **ful|filled** ADJ 形容詞 満足した ❑ *She has courageously continued to lead a fulfilled life.* 彼女は気丈にも充実した人生を送ってきた. ● **ful|fill|ing** ADJ 形容詞 充実した ❑ *...a fulfilling career.* 充実した経歴.

Word Partnership fulfill は次の語句と使われる:

N.	fulfill *your* **destiny**, fulfill a **dream**, fulfill a **promise** **1** fulfill a **role**, fulfill **obligations** **2**

ful|fill|ment /fʊlfɪ́lmənt/ **1** N-UNCOUNT 不可算名詞 **Fulfillment** is a feeling of satisfaction that you get from doing or achieving something, especially something useful. 達成感 ❑ *...professional fulfillment.* 仕事のやりがい. **2** N-UNCOUNT 不可算名詞 The **fulfillment of** a promise, threat, request, hope, or duty is the event or act of it happening or being made to happen. 実現 ❑ *Visiting Angkor was the fulfillment of a childhood dream.* アンコールを訪れたいという子供のころからの夢がかなった.

full

❶ CONTAINING AS MANY PEOPLE/THINGS AS POSSIBLE
❷ COMPLETE, INCLUDING THE MAXIMUM POSSIBLE
❸ OTHER USES

❶ full /fʊl/ (**fuller, fullest**) **1** ADJ 形容詞 If something is **full**, it contains as much of a substance or as many objects as it can. いっぱいの ❑ *Once the container is full, it stays shut until you turn it*

clockwise. いったん容器の中がいっぱいになると，それを時計回りに回すまでは閉じたままになります. **2** ADJ 形容詞 If a place or thing **is full of** things or people, it contains a large number of them. 〜でいっぱいの [v-link ADJ 'of' n] □ *The case was full of clothes.* ケースには衣服が詰まっていた. □ *The streets are still full of debris from two nights of rioting.* 二晩続いた暴動で通りにはがれきあ散乱あれています. **3** ADJ 形容詞 You say that a place or vehicle is **full** when there is no space left in it for any more people or things. 満車，満員 □ *The parking lot was full when I left about 10:45.* 10:45ごろに駐車場を出たけど，そのときは満車だったよ. □ *They stay here a few hours before being sent to refugee camps, which are now almost full.* 難民キャンプはほぼ収容限界に達しており，彼らはキャンプに送られる前に数時間ここで待機する. **4** ADJ 形容詞 If your hands or arms are **full**, you are carrying or holding as much as you can carry. 両手いっぱいの [v-link ADJ] □ *Sylvia entered, her arms full of packages.* シルビアは両手いっぱいに荷物を抱えて入ってきた. **5** ADJ 形容詞 If you feel **full**, you have eaten or drunk so much that you do not want anything else. 満腹の [v-link ADJ] □ *It's healthy to eat when I'm hungry and to stop when I'm full.* 空腹を感じたときに食事をし，満腹になればやめるのは健康です. ●**full**|**ness** N-UNCOUNT 不可算名詞 満腹感 □ *High fiber diets give the feeling of fullness.* 食物繊維が豊富な食べ物は満腹感を与えてくれる.

Thesaurus
full また次を参照：

ADJ. brimming; *(ant.)* ;, empty ❶ **1**
bursting ❶ **1**
sated, stuffed ❶ **5**

❷ full /fʊl/ (**fuller, fullest**) **1** ADJ 形容詞 If someone or something **is full of** a particular feeling or quality, they have a lot of it. 〜にあふれる [v-link ADJ 'of' n] □ *I feel full of confidence and so open to possibilities.* 私は自信に満ち，常に新たな可能性を求めています. □ *Mom's face was full of pain.* 母の表情は苦痛に満ちていた. **2** ADJ 形容詞 You use **full** before a noun to indicate that you are referring to all the details, things, or people that it can possibly include. すべての [ADJ n] □ *Full details will be sent to you once your application has been accepted.* お申し込みの受け付けを完了次第，全詳細をお送りします. □ *May I have your full name?* フルネームを教えていただけますか. **3** ADJ 形容詞 **Full** is used to describe a sound, light, or physical force which is being produced with the greatest possible power or intensity. 最高限度の [ADJ n] □ *From his study came the sound of Mahler, playing at full volume.* 彼の書斎からマーラーの曲が大音量で流れてきた. □ *Officials say the operation will be carried out in full daylight.* 当局によると，その作戦は白昼に実行されるとのことです. **4** ADJ 形容詞 You use **full** to emphasize the completeness, intensity, or extent of something. 完全な [EMPHASIS 強調] [ADJ n] □ *We should conserve oil and gas by making full use of other energy sources.* 石油とガス資源の保存のために，その他のエネルギー源を最大限活用しなければならない. □ *The lane leading to the farm was in full view of the house windows.* 家の窓からは農場に続く小道がよく見えた. **5** ADJ 形容詞 A **full** statement or report contains a lot of information and detail. 詳細な [ADJ n] □ *Mr. Primakov gave a full account of his meeting with the president.* プリマコフ氏は大統領との会談の内容を詳細に語りました. **6** ADJ 形容詞 If you say that someone has or leads a **full** life, you approve of the fact that they are always busy and do a lot of different things. 充実した [APPROVAL 賛成] □ *You will be successful in whatever you do and you will have a very full and interesting life.* あなたは何をやっても成功し，面白く充実した人生を送るでしょう. **7** ADJ 形容詞 You use **full** to refer to something which gives you all the rights, status, or importance for a particular position or activity, rather than just some of them. すべての権利を有する，正規の [ADJ n] □ *How did the meeting go, did you get your full membership?* 面談はどうだった？正会員になれたの？ **8** ADV 副詞 You use **full** to emphasize the force or directness with which someone or something is hit or looked at. 十分に [EMPHASIS 強調] [ADV prep] □ *She kissed him full on the mouth.* 彼女は彼にたっぷりとロづけした. **9** PHRASE 句 You say that something has been done or described **in full** when everything that was necessary has been done or described. すっかり □ *The medical experts have yet to report in full.* 医療関係者はまだ詳細を語っていない. **10** PHRASE 句 If you say that a person **knows full well** that something is true, especially something unpleasant, you are emphasizing that they are definitely aware of it, although they may behave as if they are not. 十分承知している [EMPHASIS 強調] □ *He knew full well he'd be ashamed of himself later.* 彼は後から自分を恥じるようになると十分承知していた. **11** PHRASE 句 Something that is done or experienced **to the full** is done to as great an extent as is possible. 最大限に □ *She probably has a good mind, which should be used to the full.* 彼女はすぐれた知性の持ち主なのだろうから，それを最大限生かすべきだ. **12** full blast → see blast **13** to have your hands full → see hand **14** in full swing → see swing

❸ full /fʊl/ (**fuller, fullest**) **1** ADJ 形容詞 A **full** flavor is strong and rich. 豊かな [ADJ n] □ *Italian plum tomatoes have a full flavor, and are best for cooking.* イタリア産プラムトマトは香りが豊かで，料理に最適です. **2** ADJ 形容詞 If you describe a part of someone's body as **full**, you mean that it is rounded and quite large. まるまるとした □ *The Juno Collection specializes in large sizes for ladies with a fuller figure.* ジュノーは，ふくよかな女性向けのサイズを専門に扱うコレクションです. **3** ADJ 形容詞 A **full** skirt or sleeve is wide and has been made from a lot of fabric. ゆったりした □ *My wedding dress has a very full skirt so I need to wear a good quality slip.* ウェディングドレスのスカートはとてもゆったりしているから，上質のランジェリーをつけないといけないわ. ●**full**|**ness** N-UNCOUNT 不可算名詞 ゆったりしていること □ *The coat has raglan sleeves, and is cut to give fullness at the back.* コートはラグラン袖で，背中がゆったりしたデザインになっている. **4** ADJ 形容詞 When there is a **full** moon, the moon appears as a bright, complete circle. 満月の □ *...those nights when the moon is full.* 月が満ちる夜に.

full-blown ADJ 形容詞 **Full-blown** means having all the characteristics of a particular type of thing or person. 本格的，成熟した [ADJ n] □ *Before becoming a full-blown director, he worked as the film editor on Citizen Kane.* 彼は，監督として花開くまでは『市民ケーン』のフィルム編集者だった.

full-fledged ADJ 形容詞 **Full-fledged** means complete or fully developed. 成熟した □ *Hungary is to have a full-fledged Stock Exchange from today.* 今日，ハンガリーに本格的な株式市場が開かれる予定です.

full-length **1** ADJ 形容詞 A **full-length** book, record, or movie is the normal length, rather than being shorter than normal. ノーカットの [ADJ n] □ *...his first full-length recording in well over a decade.* 10年以上経て初めて出た彼のノーカット版. **2** ADJ 形容詞 A **full-length** coat or skirt is long enough to reach the lower part of a person's leg, almost to the ankles. A full-length sleeve reaches a person's wrist. フルレングスの [ADJ n] **3** ADJ 形容詞 **Full-length** curtains or other furnishings reach to the floor. 床まで届く長さの [ADJ n] **4** ADJ 形容詞 A **full-length** mirror or painting shows the whole of a person. 全体が映る，全体を描いた [ADJ n] **5** ADV 副詞 Someone who is lying **full-length**, is lying down flat and stretched out. 体をまっすぐに伸ばして [ADV after v] □ *She stretched herself out full-length.* 彼女は体をうんと伸ばしてストレッチをした.

full-scale **1** ADJ 形容詞 **Full-scale** means as complete, intense, or great in extent as possible. 完全な，全面的な [ADJ n] □ *...the possibility of a full-scale nuclear war.* 全面的な核戦争の可能性. **2** ADJ 形容詞 A **full-scale** drawing or model is the same size as the thing that it represents. 実物大の [ADJ n] □ *...working, full-scale prototypes.* 実物大の試作品を使って.

full-size also **full-sized** ADJ 形容詞 A **full-size** or **full-sized** model or picture is the same size as the thing or person that it represents. 等身大の [ADJ n] □ *I made a full-size cardboard model.* 私はボール紙で等身大の型を作った.

full stop (**full stops**) N-COUNT 可算名詞 A **full stop** is the punctuation mark . which you use at the end of a sentence when it is not a question or exclamation. 終止符 [BRIT 英国英語; AM period 米国英語 period]

full-time also **full time** ADJ 形容詞 **Full-time** work or study involves working or studying for the whole of each normal working week rather than for part of it. フルタイムの □ *...a full-time job.* フルタイムの仕事. ●ADV 副詞 **Full-time** is also an adverb. フルタイムで [ADV after v] □ *Deirdre works full-time.* ディアドラはフルタイムで働いている.

full up also **full-up** **1** ADJ 形容詞 Something that is **full up** has no space left for any more people or things. いっぱいの [v-link ADJ] □ *The prisons are all full up.* それらの刑務所はすべて満員だ. **2** ADJ 形容詞 If you are **full up** you have eaten or drunk so much that you do not want to eat or drink anything else. 満腹の [INFORMAL くだけた] [v-link ADJ] □ *He found that he was so full-up from all the liquid in his diet that he hardly had room for his evening meal.* 彼は，食べた物の水分でお腹がぱんぱんで，これでは晩ごはんがほとんど食べられない，と思った.

ful|**ly** /fʊli/ **1** ADV 副詞 **Fully** means to the greatest degree or extent possible. 完全に □ *She was fully aware of my thoughts.* 彼女は私の考えを完全に見抜いていた. **2** ADV 副詞 You use **fully** to say that a process is completely finished. すっかり [ADV with v] □ *He had still not fully recovered.* 彼はまだ完全には回復していなかった. **3** ADV 副詞 If you describe, answer, or deal with something **fully**, you leave out nothing that should be mentioned or dealt with. 余さず [ADV with v] □ *Fiers promised to testify fully and truthfully.* フィアーズは余すことなく正直に証言すると約束した.

Word Partnership   *fully* は次の語句と使われる:

ADJ.	fully **adjustable**, fully **aware**, fully **clothed**, fully **formed**, fully **functional**, fully **operational**, fully **prepared** **1**
V.	fully **agree**, fully **expect**, fully **extend**, fully **understand** **1** fully **decide**, fully **develop**, fully **heal**, fully **realize**, fully **recover** **2** fully **explain** **3**

fully-fledged ADJ 形容詞 **Fully-fledged** means the same as **full-fledged**. 成熟した [BRIT 英国英語]

fum|ble /fˈʌmbəl/ (fumbles, fumbling, fumbled) **1** V-I 自動詞 If you **fumble for** something or **fumble with** something, you try to reach for it or hold it in a clumsy way. ぎこちなく探る □*She crept from the bed and fumbled for her dressing gown.* 彼女はベッドからはい出て部屋着をまさぐった. **2** V-T/V-I 他動詞/自動詞 When you are trying to say something, if you **fumble** for the right words, you speak in a clumsy and unclear way. 口ごもる □*I fumbled for something to say.* 私は何か言おうとして口ごもった.

fume /fjuːm/ (fumes, fuming, fumed) **1** N-PLURAL 複数名詞 **Fumes** are the unpleasant and often unhealthy smoke and gases that are produced by fires or by things such as chemicals, fuel, or cooking. ガス, 煙 □*...car exhaust fumes.* 車の排気ガス. **2** V-T 他動詞 If you **fume** over something, you express annoyance and anger about it. 怒りを表す □*"It's monstrous!" Jackie fumed.* 「なんてひどいの」とジャッキーは怒りをあらわにした.

fun /fʌn/ **1** N-UNCOUNT 不可算名詞 You refer to an activity or situation as **fun** if you think it is pleasant and enjoyable and it causes you to feel happy. 楽しみ □*It's been a learning adventure and it's also been great fun.* それは知的な冒険であり, 大きな楽しみでもあった. □*It could be fun to watch them.* それらを見るのは面白そうだ. **2** N-UNCOUNT 不可算名詞 If you say that someone is **fun**, you mean that you enjoy being with them because they say and do interesting or amusing things. 面白い人 [APPROVAL 賛成] □*Liz was fun to be with.* リズは一緒にいて面白い人だった. **3** ADJ 形容詞 If you describe something as a **fun** thing, you mean that you think it is enjoyable. If you describe someone as a **fun** person, you mean that you enjoy being with them. 楽しい [INFORMAL くだけた] [ADJ n] □*It was a fun evening.* 楽しい夜だった. **4** PHRASE 句 If you do something **for fun** or **for the fun of it**, you do it in order to enjoy yourself rather than because it is important or necessary. 面白半分で □*We used to drive too fast, just for fun.* 我々は面白半分に猛スピードで運転していたものです. **5** PHRASE 句 If you do something **in fun**, you say or do it as a joke or for amusement, without intending to cause any harm. ふざけて □*Don't say such things, even in fun.* 戯れだとしても, そんなことは言ってはいけないよ. **6** PHRASE 句 If you **make fun of** someone or something or **poke fun at** them, you laugh at them, tease them, or make jokes about them in a way that causes them to seem ridiculous. からかう □*Don't make fun of me.* からかわないでよ.

Thesaurus   *fun* また次を参照:

N.	amusement, enjoyment, play; (ant.) misery **1**
ADJ.	amusing, enjoyable, entertaining, happy, pleasant; (ant.) boring **3**

Word Partnership   *fun* は次の語句と使われる:

N.	**your** idea of fun, fun **part**, **sense of** fun, fun **stuff**, fun **time 1**
V.	**have** fun, **join the** fun, **ought to/should be** fun, fun **to watch 1 3**

func|tion /fˈʌŋkʃən/ (functions, functioning, functioned) **1** N-COUNT 可算名詞 The **function** of something or someone is the useful thing that they do or are intended to do. 機能 □*The main function of the investment banks is to raise capital for industry.* 投資銀行の主な機能は, 産業向けに資金を調達することだ. **2** N-COUNT 可算名詞 A **function** is a large formal dinner or party. (公式な) 会合 □*...a private function hosted by one of his students.* 彼の生徒の1人が主催した内々の会合. **3** V-I 自動詞 If a machine or system **is functioning**, it is working or operating. 機能する □*The authorities say the prison is now functioning normally.* 当局によれば, その刑務所は, 今は通常に機能しているとのことです. **4** V-I 自動詞 If someone or something **functions as** a particular thing, they do the work or fulfill the purpose of that thing. 役割を果たす □*On weekdays, one third of the room functions as workspace.* 平日は, 部屋の3分の1が作業場になります.

Thesaurus   *function* また次を参照:

N.	action, duty, job, responsibility **1** celebration, gathering, occasion **2**
V.	operate, perform, work **3**

func|tion|al /fˈʌŋkʃənəl/ **1** ADJ 形容詞 **Functional** things are useful rather than decorative. 実用的な □*...modern, functional furniture.* モダンで実用的な家具. **2** ADJ 形容詞 **Functional** equipment works or operates in the way that it is supposed to. 機能を果たせる □*We have fully functional smoke alarms on all staircases.* すべての階段に高性能な煙探知機を設置しています.

func|tion key (function keys) N-COUNT 可算名詞 **Function keys** are the keys along the top of a computer keyboard, usually numbered from F1 to F12. Each key is designed to make a particular thing happen when you press it. ファンクションキー [COMPUTING コンピューティング] □*Just hit the F5 function key to send and receive your e-mails.* Eメールを送受信するにはファンクションキーのF5を押せばよい.

fund /fʌnd/ (funds, funding, funded) **1** N-PLURAL 複数名詞 **Funds** are amounts of money that are available to be spent, especially money that is given to an organization or person for a particular purpose. 基金 □*The concert will raise funds for research into AIDS.* そのコンサートではエイズの研究基金が集められるでしょう. **2** → see also **fund-raising** **3** N-COUNT 可算名詞 A **fund** is an amount of money that is collected or saved for a particular purpose. 資金 □*...a scholarship fund for undergraduate engineering students.* 工学専攻大学院生向けの奨学資金. **4** → see also **trust fund** **5** V-T 他動詞 When a person or organization **funds** something, they provide money for it. 資金を供給する □*The Bush Foundation has funded a variety of faculty development programs.* ブッシュ基金はさまざまな能力開発プログラムを支援している. □*The airport is being privately funded by a construction group.* 空港は, ある建築会社グループの私費により建設される予定です.

fun|da|men|tal /fˌʌndəmˈentəl/ **1** ADJ 形容詞 You use **fundamental** to describe things, activities, and principles that are very important or essential. They affect the basic nature of other things or are the most important element upon which other things depend. 根本的な □*Our constitution embodies all the fundamental principles of democracy.* わが国の憲法は民主主義の根本原則のすべてを具現化したものです. □*A fundamental human right is being withheld from these people.* 基本的人権はこれらの人々には認められないだろう. **2** ADJ 形容詞 You use **fundamental** to describe something which exists at a deep and basic level, and is therefore likely to continue. 根本的な □*But on this question, the two leaders have very fundamental differences.* しかし, この点では両リーダーに非常に根本的な相違が認められます. **3** ADJ 形容詞 If one thing **is fundamental to** another, it is absolutely necessary to it, and the second thing cannot exist, succeed, or be imagined without it. 欠かせない [v-link ADJ 'to' n] □*He believes better relations with China are fundamental to the well-being of the area.* 彼は, その地域の安泰のためには中国とよりよい関係を築くことが不可欠だと考えています. **4** ADJ 形容詞 You can use **fundamental** to show that you are referring to what you consider to be the most important aspect of a situation, and that you are not concerned with less important details. 主要な [ADJ n] □*The fundamental problem lies in their inability to distinguish between reality and invention.* 主な問題は, 彼らが事実と作り事を区別できないことだ.

Thesaurus   *fundamental* また次を参照:

ADJ.	basic, essential, necessary, original, primary **1** **2**

fun|da|men|tal|ism /fˌʌndəmˈentəlɪzəm/ N-UNCOUNT 不可算名詞 **Fundamentalism** is the belief in the original form of a religion or theory, without accepting any later ideas. 原理主義 □*Religious fundamentalism was spreading in the region.* 宗教的原理主義がその地区に広がりつつありました. ●**fun|da|men|tal|ist** (fundamentalists) N-COUNT 可算名詞 原理主義者 □*...fundamentalist Christians.* キリスト教原理主義者.

fun|da|men|tal|ly /fˌʌndəmˈentəli/ **1** ADV 副詞 You use **fundamentally** for emphasis when you are stating an opinion, or when you are making an important or general statement about something. 基本的に [EMPHASIS 強調] [ADV with cl/group] □*Fundamentally, women like him for his sensitivity and charming vulnerability.* 基本的に, 女性は, 彼の繊細さと愛すべき弱さを好むのだ. **2** ADV 副詞 You use **fundamentally** to indicate that something affects or relates to the deep, basic nature of something. 根本的に [ADV with v] □*He disagreed fundamentally with the president's judgment.* 彼は根本的には大統領の判断に反対だった. □*Environmentalists say the treaty is fundamentally flawed.* 環境保護主義者は, その条約には根本的な欠陥があると述べています.

fun|da|men|tals /fˌʌndəmˈentəlz/ N-PLURAL 複数名詞 The **fundamentals** of something are its simplest, most important elements, ideas, or principles, in contrast to more complicated

Word Web funeral

Many modern **funeral** practices may have their roots in ancient beliefs. Today's **wake** resembles the early custom of providing plentiful food for the departed. In some cultures the food was meant to pacify the spirits. In others, it was for the **deceased** to eat in the afterlife. In some societies **mourners** waited by the **dead** in hopes that the person would return to life. People brought flowers to please the spirit of the dead person. **Ceremonial** candles resemble the fires lit to protect the living from dangerous spirits. Wearing special clothing was also supposed to confuse the spirits.

or detailed ones. 基本 ❑ *They agree on fundamentals, like the need for further political reform.* 彼らは、政治改革推進の必要性などの基本事項では合意しています。

fund|ing /fʌndɪŋ/ N-UNCOUNT 不可算名詞 **Funding** is money which a government or organization provides for a particular purpose. 財政支援 ❑ *They hope for government funding for the program.* 彼らは政府にその計画への財政支援を望んでいます。

fund|rais|er /fʌndreɪzər/ (**fundraisers**) also **fund-raiser** ◼ N-COUNT 可算名詞 A **fundraiser** is an event which is intended to raise money for a particular purpose, for example, a charity. 資金調達のための催し ❑ *Organize a fundraiser for your church.* 教会には資金調達イベントの開催が必要ですよ。 ◼ N-COUNT 可算名詞 A **fundraiser** is someone who works to raise money for a particular purpose, for example, a charity. 資金を調達する人 ❑ *...a fundraiser for the Democrats.* 民主党の資金調達者。

fund-raising also **fundraising** N-UNCOUNT 不可算名詞 **Fund-raising** is the activity of collecting money to support a charity or political campaign or organization. 資金調達 ❑ *Encourage her to get involved in fund-raising for charity.* チャリティの資金調達活動に加わるよう、彼女に勧めてください。

fu|ner|al /fyunərəl/ (**funerals**) N-COUNT 可算名詞 A **funeral** is the ceremony that is held when the body of someone who has died is buried or cremated. 葬儀 ❑ *The funeral will be held in Joplin, Missouri.* 葬儀はミズーリ州、ジョプリンで行われます。
→ see Word Web: **funeral**

fun|gus /fʌŋgəs/ (**fungi**) N-MASS 質量名詞 A **fungus** is a plant that has no flowers, leaves, or green coloring, such as a mushroom or a toadstool. Other types of fungus such as mold are extremely small and look like a fine powder. 菌類
→ see Word Web: **fungus**

funky /fʌŋki/ (**funkier, funkiest**) ◼ ADJ 形容詞 **Funky** jazz, blues, or pop music has a very strong, repeated bass part. ファンク（強いベース音が繰り返される音楽のスタイル）の ❑ *It's a funky sort of rhythm.* それはファンクスタイルのリズムだ。 ◼ ADJ 形容詞 If you describe something or someone as **funky**, you mean that they are stylish and modern in an unconventional way. いかした [APPROVAL 賛成] ❑ *She would love to buy her daughter funky little leopard-print skirts.* 彼女なら、かっこいい、ミニヒョウ柄プリントのスカートを娘さんに買ってあげたいと思うでしょう。 ❑ *The place is quirky, funky and dazzlingly imaginative in design.* そこのデザインは独特で、素敵なうえにとても創造的です。 ◼ ADJ 形容詞 Something that is **funky** has a strong, offensive odor. 強い悪臭のする ❑ *There were dirty clothes everywhere, and they all had that funky overripe smell.* 不潔な服が散乱していて、それら全部がすえたにおいを放っていた。

fun|nel /fʌnºl/ (**funnels, funneling** or **funnelling, funneled** or **funnelled**) ◼ N-COUNT 可算名詞 A **funnel** is an object with a wide, circular top and a narrow short tube at the bottom. Funnels are used to pour liquids into containers which have a small opening, for example, bottles. じょうご ❑ *Rain falls through the funnel into the jar below.* 雨水はじょうごを介して下に置かれたつぼに集められる。 ◼ N-COUNT 可算名詞 A **funnel** is a metal chimney on a ship or railroad engine powered by steam. (汽船や蒸気機関車の) 煙突 ❑ *...a ship with three masts and two funnels.* 3本のマストと2本の煙突を備えた船。 ◼ N-COUNT 可算名詞 You can describe as a **funnel** something that is narrow, or narrow at one end, through which

a substance flows and is directed. じょうご形の物 ❑ *Along the road, funnels of dark gray smoke rose from bombed villages.* 爆撃を受けた村では、通りに沿って暗い灰色の煙が幾筋も立ち上っていた。 ◼ V-T/V-I 他動詞/自動詞 If something **funnels** somewhere or **is funneled** there, it is directed through a narrow space. 狭い所を通す [他動詞]、狭い所を通る [自動詞] ❑ *The winds came from the north, across the plains, funneling down the valley.* 風は北から平原を渡り、谷間に吹き下りた。 ◼ V-T 他動詞 If you **funnel** money, goods, or information from one place or group to another, you cause it to be sent there as it becomes available. (資金や情報を) 流す ❑ *He secretly funneled credit-card information to counterfeiters.* 彼はクレジットカード情報を裏で偽造組織に流していた。

fun|ni|ly /fʌnɪli/ PHRASE 句 You use **funnily enough** to indicate that, although something is surprising, it is true or really happened. 不思議なことに ❑ *Funnily enough I can remember what I had for lunch on July 5th, 1956, but I've forgotten what I had for breakfast today.* 不思議なことに、1956年の7月5日の昼食に何を食べたかは言えるのですが、今朝、朝食に何を食べたか思い出せないのです。

fun|ny /fʌni/ (**funnier, funniest**) ◼ ADJ 形容詞 Someone or something that is **funny** is amusing and likely to make you smile or laugh. おかしな ❑ *I'll tell you a funny story.* おかしな話をしてあげるよ。 ◼ ADJ 形容詞 If you describe something as **funny**, you think it is strange, surprising, or puzzling. 奇妙な ❑ *Children get some very funny ideas sometimes!.* 子供というのは時にとても奇妙な発想をするものだな。 ❑ *There's something funny about him.* 彼にはどこか変なところがある。 ◼ ADJ 形容詞 If you feel **funny**, you feel slightly ill. 気分が少しすぐれない [INFORMAL くだけた] ❑ *My head had begun to ache and my stomach felt funny.* 頭痛がし始めて、胃の調子が少しおかしくなりました。

Thesaurus   *funny* また次を参照:

ADJ. amusing, comical, entertaining; (*ant.*) serious ◼
bizarre, odd, peculiar ◼

fur /fɜr/ (**furs**) ◼ N-MASS 質量名詞 **Fur** is the thick and usually soft hair that grows on the bodies of many mammals. 毛皮 ❑ *This creature's fur is short, dense and silky.* この動物は短毛ですが、毛皮は密でなめらかです。 ◼ N-MASS 質量名詞 **Fur** is an artificial fabric that looks like fur and is used, for example, to make clothing, soft toys, and seat covers. フェイクファー、人工毛皮 ◼ N-VAR 可変性名詞 **Fur** is the fur-covered skin of an animal that is used to make clothing or small carpets. 毛皮 ❑ *She had on a black coat with a fur collar.* 彼女は毛皮の襟がついた黒いコートを着ていた。 ❑ *...the trading of furs from Canada.* カナダからの毛皮の輸入。 ◼ N-COUNT 可算名詞 A **fur** is a coat made from real or artificial fur, or a piece of fur worn around your neck. 毛皮のコート ❑ *There were women in furs and men in comfortable overcoats.* そこでは女性は毛皮、男性は着心地のよさそうなコートを身に着けていた。

fu|ri|ous /fyuəriəs/ ◼ ADJ 形容詞 Someone who is **furious** is extremely angry. 憤慨する ❑ *He is furious at the way his wife has been treated.* 彼は妻が受けてきた待遇に憤慨している。 ● **fu|ri|ous|ly** ADV 副詞 憤慨して ❑ *He stormed out of the apartment, slamming the door furiously behind him.* 彼は、腹立たしげにバタンとドアを閉め、アパートを飛び出した。

Word Web fungus

Some **fungi** are destructive. For example, **mold** and mildew destroy crops, ruin clothing, cause diseases, and can even lead to death. But many fungi are useful. For instance, a single-cell fungus called **yeast** makes bread rise. Another form of yeast helps wine **ferment**. It turns the sugar in grape juice into alcohol. And **mushrooms** are a part of the diet of people all over the world. Cheese makers use a specific fungus to produce the creamy white skin on brie. A different **microorganism** gives blue cheese its characteristic color. Truffles, the most expensive fungi, cost more than $100 an ounce.

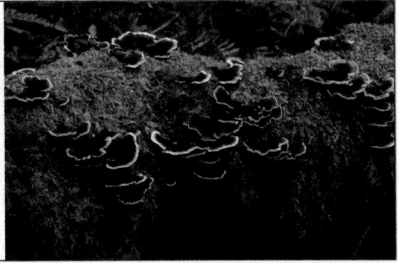

Angry is normally used to talk about someone's mood or feelings on a particular occasion. If someone is often angry, you can describe them as **bad-tempered**. ❑ *She's a bad-tempered young lady.* If someone is very angry, you can describe them as **furious**. ❑ *Senior police officers are furious at the blunder.* If they are less angry, you can describe them as **annoyed** or **irritated**. ❑ *The premier looked annoyed but calm. …a man irritated by the barking of his neighbor's dog.* Typically, someone is **irritated** by something because it happens constantly or continually. If someone is often irritated, you can describe them as **irritable**.

2 ADJ 形容詞 **Furious** is also used to describe something that is done with great energy, effort, speed, or violence. 激しい ❑ *A furious gunbattle ensued.* 続いて激しい銃撃戦が起こった. ● **fu|ri|ous|ly** ADV 副詞 激しく ❑ *Officials worked furiously to repair the center court.* 係員はセンターコートの修復に向け懸命に働きました.

→ see **anger**

fur|long /fɜ̃rlɒŋ/ (furlongs) N-COUNT 可算名詞 A **furlong** is a unit of length that is equal to 220 yards or 201.2 meters. ファーロング（長さの単位）, ハロン（競馬で用いる距離の単位） ❑ *"Although he was beaten in his first race at seven furlongs, I was thrilled with his performance," the trainer said.* 「7ハロンのデビュー戦には負けたが, その走りにはワクワクさせられたよ」とトレーナーはコメントしました.

fur|lough /fɜ̃rloʊ/ (furloughs, furloughing, furloughed) **1** N-VAR 可変化名詞 If workers are given **furlough**, they are told to stay away from work for a certain period because there is not enough for them to do. 一時帰休 [AM 米国英語] ❑ *This could mean a massive furlough of government workers.* これは公務員の大量一時帰休をも意味しかねません. **2** V-T 他動詞 If people who work for a particular organization **are furloughed**, they are given a furlough. 一時帰休させる [AM 米国英語] ❑ *We regret to inform you that you are being furloughed indefinitely.* 残念ですが, あなたは無期限の一時帰休となります.

fur|nace /fɜ̃rnɪs/ (furnaces) N-COUNT 可算名詞 A **furnace** is a container or enclosed space in which a very hot fire is made, for example, to melt metal, burn trash, or produce heat for a building or house. かまど

fur|nish /fɜ̃rnɪʃ/ (furnishes, furnishing, furnished) **1** V-T 他動詞 If you **furnish** a room or building, you put furniture and furnishings into it. （家具などを）備え付ける ❑ *Many proprietors try to furnish their hotels with antiques.* ホテル経営者の多くは, 客室にアンティーク家具を設置したいのだ. **2** V-T 他動詞 If you **furnish** someone **with** something, you provide or supply it. 供給する [FORMAL 形式ばった] ❑ *They'll be able to furnish you with the rest of the details.* 彼らが残りの詳細を明らかにしてくれるでしょう.

fur|nish|ings /fɜ̃rnɪʃɪŋz/ N-PLURAL 複数名詞 The **furnishings** of a room or house are the furniture, curtains, carpets, and decorations such as pictures. 調度品 ❑ *To enable rental increases, you have to have luxurious furnishings.* 高い賃貸料を得るには, 部屋の調度品を豪華にする必要がある.

fur|ni|ture /fɜ̃rnɪtʃər/ N-UNCOUNT 不可算名詞 **Furniture** consists of large objects such as tables, chairs, or beds that are used in a room for sitting or lying on or for putting things on or in. 家具 ❑ *Each piece of furniture in their home suited the style of the house.* 一つ一つの家具が彼らの家のスタイルにぴったり合っていた.

Note that **furniture** is only ever used as an uncount noun. You cannot say "a furniture" or "furnitures." If you want to refer in general terms to something such as a table, a chair, or a bed, you can say **a piece of furniture** or **an item of furniture**.

fu|ror /fyʊərɔr, -ər/ N-SING 単数名詞 A **furor** is a very angry or excited reaction by people to something. 激高, 騒動 ❑ *…an international furor over the plan.* その計画をめぐる国際的な騒動.

fur|row /fɜ̃roʊ/ (furrows) **1** N-COUNT 可算名詞 A **furrow** is a long, thin line in the earth which a farmer makes in order to plant seeds or to allow water to flow along. 畝間, 農業用の溝 ❑ *…furrows of roses and corn.* バラととうもろこしを植えつける溝. **2** N-COUNT 可算名詞 A **furrow** is a deep, fairly wide line in the surface of something. 溝 ❑ *I saw a dark brown fertile field in which a plow was cutting large furrows.* 私は, 濃い茶色をした肥沃（よく）な土地にすきで大きな溝が作られていくのを目にした. **3** N-COUNT 可算名詞 A **furrow** is a deep fold or line in the skin of someone's face. 深いしわ ❑ *He was his old self again, except for the deep furrows that marked the corners of his mouth.* 口元に刻まれた深いしわを除けば, 彼は以前の自分を取り戻したのだった.

fur|ry /fɜ̃ri/ (furrier, furriest) **1** ADJ 形容詞 A **furry** animal is covered with thick, soft hair. 毛皮を持つ ❑ *People like having small furry animals to stroke, but pets can be expensive to feed.* 手触りのよい毛皮を持つ小動物はペットとして好まれるが, えさ代は高くつく. **2** ADJ 形容詞 If you describe something as **furry**, you mean that it has a soft rough texture like fur. ふわふわした ❑ *The leaves are soft, round and rather furry.* その葉っぱは丸くて柔らかく, 思ったよりふわふわしている.

fur|ther /fɜ̃rðər/ (furthers, furthering, furthered)

Further is a comparative form of **far**. It is also a verb.

Further は **far** の比較形であり, 動詞でもある

1 ADV 副詞 **Further** means to a greater extent or degree. さらに [ADV with v] ❑ *Inflation is below 5% and set to fall further.* インフレ率は5パーセントを下回っているけど, きっともっと下がるさ. ❑ *The rebellion is expected to further damage the country's image.* その反乱は国のイメージをさらに傷つけることがねらいでしょう. **2** ADV 副詞 If you go or get **further with** something, or take something **further**, you make more progress. さらに進む [ADV with v] ❑ *They lacked the scientific personnel to develop the technical apparatus much further.* 彼らが欲しいのは, 工学機械の改良をさらに推進できる科学要員だった. **3** ADV 副詞 If someone goes **further** in a discussion, they make a more extreme statement or deal with a point more thoroughly. さらに深く [ADV after v] ❑ *To have a better comparison, we need to go further and address such issues as repairs and insurance.* よりよい比較を行うためには, 修理費や保険などの問題についてさらに深く検証しなければなりません. **4** ADV 副詞 **Further** means a greater distance than before or than something else. より離れて [ADV adv/prep] ❑ *People are living further away from their jobs.* 居住地は仕事場からより遠い所になりつつある. **5** ADV 副詞 **Further** is used in expressions such as "further back" and "further ahead" to refer to a point in time that is earlier or later than the time you are talking about. さらに [ADV adv/prep] ❑ *Looking still further ahead, by the end of the next century world population is expected to be about ten billion.* さらに先の予測をすれば, 次の世紀末までに世界人口は約100億になるだろう. **6** ADJ 形容詞 A **further** thing, number of things, or amount of something is an additional thing, number of things, or amount. さらなる [ADJ n, pron-indef ADJ] ❑ *Further evidence of slowing economic growth is likely to emerge this week.* 今週, 経済成長がさらに鈍化する兆候が見られるでしょう. **7** V-T 他動詞 If you **further** something, you help it to progress, to be successful, or to be achieved. 促進する ❑ *Education needn't only be about furthering your career.* 教育の目的は, あなたのキャリアを高めることだけではない.

fur|ther edu|ca|tion N-UNCOUNT 不可算名詞 **Further education** is the education of people who have left school but who are not at a university or a college of education. 継続教育, 成人教育 [BRIT 英国英語; AM continuing education, adult education 米国英語 continuing education, adult education]

further|more /fɜ̃rðərmɔr/ ADV 副詞 **Furthermore** is used to introduce a piece of information or opinion that adds to or supports the previous one. そのうえ [FORMAL 形式ばった] [ADV with cl] ❑ *Furthermore, they claim that any such interference is completely ineffective.* さらに, 彼らはそういった妨害は何であれまったく無効だと主張している.

fur|thest /fɜ̃rðɪst/

Furthest is a superlative form of **far**.

Furthest は **far** の最上級形である.

1 ADV 副詞 **Furthest** means to a greater extent or degree than ever before or than anything or anyone else. 最も~な [ADV with v] ❑ *The south, where prices have fallen furthest, will remain the weakest market.* 南部は, ここのところ物価の下落が一番激しく, 最も弱い市況が続くだろう. **2** ADV 副詞 **Furthest** means at a greater distance from a particular point than anyone or anything else, or for a greater distance than anyone or anything else. 最も遠くに ❑ *The risk of thunder is greatest in those areas furthest from the coast.* 海岸から最も遠いそれらの地区は, 落雷のリスクが最大である. ● ADJ 形容詞 **Furthest** is also an adjective. 最も遠い [ADJ n] ❑ *…the furthest point from earth that any controlled spacecraft has ever been.* 制御下にある宇宙船がかつて到達した地球から最も遠い地点.

fur|tive /fɜ̃rtɪv/ ADJ 形容詞 If you describe someone's behavior as **furtive**, you disapprove of them behaving as if they want to keep something secret or hidden. うさんくさい [DISAPPROVAL 不賛成] ❑ *With a furtive glance over her shoulder, she unlocked the door and entered the house.* 肩越しに人目を気にしながら, 彼女はかぎを開け家に入った.

fury /fyʊəri/ N-UNCOUNT 不可算名詞 **Fury** is violent or very strong anger. 激怒 ❑ *She screamed, her face distorted with fury and pain.* 彼女は悲鳴を上げ, 激しい怒りと苦痛に顔をゆがめた.

fuse /fyuz/ (fuses, fusing, fused)

The spelling **fuze** is also used for meaning **2**.

つづりの **fuze** は **2** の意味にも使われる.

1 N-COUNT 可算名詞 A **fuse** is a safety device in an electric plug or circuit. It contains a piece of wire which melts when there is a fault so that the flow of electricity stops. ヒューズ ❑ *The fuse blew as he pressed the button to start the motor.* 彼がモーターの作動

ボタンを押すとヒューズが飛んだ. **2** N-COUNT 可算名詞 A **fuse** is a device on a bomb or firework which delays the explosion so that people can move a safe distance away. 導火線 ❑A bomb was deactivated at the last moment, after the fuse had been lit. 導火線に火がつけられましたが, 爆発は寸前で阻止されました. **3** V-RECIP 相互動詞 When things **fuse** or **are fused**, they join together physically or chemically, usually to become one thing. You can also say that one thing **fuses** with another. 融合させる, 融合する ❑The skull bones fuse between the ages of fifteen and twenty-five. 頭がい骨は15から25歳で縫合が完成する. ❑Manufactured glass is made by fusing various types of sand. 工業ガラスは異種類の原料石を溶解し製造する.

fu｜selage /fyuˑsɪlɑʒ, -lɪdʒ, -zɪ-/ (fuselages) N-COUNT 可算名詞 The **fuselage** is the main body of an airplane, missile, or rocket. It is usually cylindrical in shape. 機体 ❑The force of the impact ripped apart the plane's fuselage. 衝撃力で機体がバラバラになった.

fu｜sion /fyuˑʒ^ən/ (fusions) **1** N-COUNT 可算名詞 A **fusion** of different qualities, ideas, or things is something new that is created by joining them together. 融合 ❑His previous fusions of jazz, pop and African melodies have proved highly successful. 彼のジャズ, ポップス, アフリカンメロディを融合させるこれまでの試みは大きな成功を収めてきた. **2** N-VAR 可変性名詞 The **fusion** of two or more things involves joining them together to form one thing. 統合 ❑His final reform was the fusion of regular and reserve forces. 彼が行った最後の改革は正規軍と予備軍の統合だった. **3** N-UNCOUNT 不可算名詞 In physics, **fusion** is the process in which atomic particles combine and produce a large amount of nuclear energy. 核融合 ❑...research into nuclear fusion. 核融合の研究.
→ see **sun**

fuss /fʌs/ (fusses, fussing, fussed) **1** N-SING 単数名詞 **Fuss** is anxious or excited behavior which serves no useful purpose. 空騒ぎ [also no det] ❑I don't know what all the fuss is about. いったいこの騒ぎは何なのか. **2** V-I 自動詞 If you **fuss**, you worry or behave in a nervous, anxious way about unimportant matters or rush around doing unnecessary things. やきもきする, せかせかする ❑Carol fussed about getting me a drink. キャロルは私に飲み物を出そうとやきもきした. ❑My wife was fussing over the food and clothing we were going to take. 妻はいつも自分達の服装や食べ物にあれこれ口うるさい. ❑"Stop fussing," he snapped. 彼は「やきもきするな」とぴしゃりと言った. **3** V-I 自動詞 If you **fuss over** someone, you pay them a lot of attention and do things to make them happy or comfortable. あれこれ世話を焼く ❑Auntie Hilda and Uncle Jack couldn't fuss over them enough. ヒルダおばさんとジャックおじさんは彼らにあまり手をかけられなかった. **4** PHRASE 句 If you **make a fuss** or **kick up a fuss** about something, you become angry or excited about it and complain. 大騒ぎする [INFORMAL くだけた] ❑I don't know why everybody makes such a fuss about a few mosquitoes. なぜみんな数匹の蚊ごときでそんなに大騒ぎをするんだろう.

fussy /fʌsi/ (fussier, fussiest) ADJ 形容詞 Someone who is **fussy** is very concerned with unimportant details and is difficult to please. うるさい [DISAPPROVAL 不賛成] ❑She is not fussy about her food. 彼女は自分が食べる物にはうるさくない.

fu｜tile /fyuˑt^əl/ ADJ 形容詞 If you say that something is **futile**, you mean there is no point in doing it, usually because it has no chance of succeeding. 無益な ❑He brought his arm up in a futile attempt to ward off the blow. 彼は攻撃をかわそうと腕を上げたが, それは無益な試みだった.

fu｜til｜ity /fyuˑtɪlɪti/ N-UNCOUNT 不可算名詞 **Futility** is a total lack of purpose or usefulness. 無益性 ❑Brown's article tells of the tragedy and futility of war. ブラウンの記事には戦争の悲劇性と無益さが表現されています.

fu｜ture /fyuˑtʃər/ (futures) **1** N-SING 単数名詞 The **future** is the period of time that will come after the present, or the things that will happen then. 未来 ❑The spokesman said no decision on the proposal was likely in the immediate future. スポークスマンは, その提案に関する決定が近々行われることはないと述べました. ❑He was making plans for the future. 彼は今後の計画を立てようとしていた. **2** ADJ 形容詞 **Future** things will happen or exist after the present time. 未来の [ADJ n] ❑She said if the world did not act conclusively now, it would only bequeath the problem to future generations. 世界が断固とした行動を起こさない限り, 後世に問題を引き継ぐだけだ, と彼女は言った. ❑...the future king and queen. 未来の王と王妃. **3** N-COUNT 可算名詞 Someone's **future**, or the **future** of something, is what will happen to them or what they will do after the present time. 将来 ❑His future depends on the outcome of the elections. 彼の将来は選挙の結果にかかっている. ❑...a proposed national conference on the country's political future. 国の政治的将来に関する全国会議の開催案. **4** N-PLURAL 複数名詞 When people trade in **futures**, they buy stocks and shares, commodities such as coffee or oil, or foreign currency at a price that is agreed at the time of purchase for items which are delivered some time in the future. 先物取引 [BUSINESS 実業] ❑This report could spur some buying in corn futures when the market opens today. 市場が開けたら, このレポートによって, とうもろこしの先物取引に買いが集まるでしょう. **5** PHRASE 句 You use **in the future** when saying what will happen from now on, which will be different from what has previously happened. これからは ❑I asked her to be more careful in the future. これからはもっと気をつけてね, と彼女に頼んだ.

fu｜tur｜is｜tic /fyuˑtʃərɪstɪk/ **1** ADJ 形容詞 Something that is **futuristic** looks or seems very modern and unusual, like something from the future. 超現代的な ❑The theater is a futuristic steel and glass structure. その劇場は鉄とガラスでできた超現代的な建造物です. **2** ADJ 形容詞 A **futuristic** movie or book tells a story that is set in the future, when things are different. 未来を描いた [ADJ n] ❑...the futuristic hit film, "Terminator 2." 未来を描いたヒット映画『ターミネーター2』.

fuzzy /fʌzi/ (fuzzier, fuzziest) **1** ADJ 形容詞 **Fuzzy** hair sticks up in a soft, curly mass. 柔らかくて縮れた ❑He had fuzzy black hair and bright black eyes. 彼の髪は黒いソフトな縮れ毛で, 瞳は黒く輝いていた. **2** ADJ 形容詞 If something is **fuzzy**, it has a covering that feels soft and like fur. 綿毛の ❑...fuzzy material. 綿毛状の生地. **3** ADJ 形容詞 A **fuzzy** picture, image, or sound is unclear and hard to see or hear. ぼやけた ❑A couple of fuzzy pictures have been published. 不鮮明な写真数枚が公開された. **4** ADJ 形容詞 If you or your thoughts are **fuzzy**, you are confused and cannot think clearly. はっきりとしない ❑He had little patience for fuzzy ideas. 彼は, 釈然としない考えにはほとんど容赦がない.

Gg

G also **g** /dʒiː/ (**G's, g's**) N-VAR 可変性名詞 **G** is the seventh letter of the English alphabet. 英語アルファベットの第7字

gadget /gædʒɪt/ (**gadgets**) N-COUNT 可算名詞 A **gadget** is a small machine or device which does something useful. You sometimes refer to something as a **gadget** when you are suggesting that it is complicated and unnecessary. 小さい機械装置 ❏ …sales of kitchen gadgets including toasters, kettles, and percolators. トースター、やかん、パーコレータなどの台所用品のセールス

→ see **technology**

Gaelic /ˈɡeɪlɪk, ˈɡælɪk/ **1** N-UNCOUNT 不可算名詞 **Gaelic** is a language spoken by people in parts of Scotland and Ireland. ゲール語 ❏ We weren't allowed to speak Gaelic at school. 私たちは学校ではゲール語を話すことは許されていなかった。 ● ADJ 形容詞 **Gaelic** is also an adjective. ゲール人の ❏ …the Gaelic language. ゲール語 **2** ADJ 形容詞 **Gaelic** means coming from or relating to Scotland and Ireland, especially the parts where Gaelic is spoken. ゲールの ❏ …an evening of Gaelic music and drama. ゲールの音楽と演劇の夕べ

gag /ɡæɡ/ (**gags, gagging, gagged**) **1** N-COUNT 可算名詞 A **gag** is something such as a piece of cloth that is tied around or put inside someone's mouth in order to stop them from speaking. さるぐつわ ❏ His captors had put a gag of thick leather in his mouth. 彼を捕らえた者たちは彼に厚い革のさるぐつわをかませた。 **2** V-T 他動詞 If someone **gags** you, they tie a piece of cloth around your mouth in order to stop you from speaking or shouting. さるぐつわをかませる [他動詞] ❏ I gagged him with a towel. 私はタオルで彼にさるぐつわをした。 **3** V-T 他動詞 If a person **is gagged** by someone in authority, they are prevented from expressing their opinion or from publishing certain information. 言論の自由を抑圧する [DISAPPROVAL 不賛成] [他動詞] ❏ Judges must not be gagged. 裁判官の発言の自由を奪ってはならない。 **4** V-I 自動詞 If you **gag**, you cannot swallow and nearly vomit. 吐きそうになる [自動詞] ❏ I knelt by the toilet and gagged. 私はトイレの側にひざまずいて吐こうとした。 **5** N-COUNT 可算名詞 A **gag** is a joke. ギャグ [INFORMAL くだけた] ❏ The running gag is that the band never gets to play. そのバンドがいつも演奏の機会を逃すことはよくジョークのネタにされる。 **6** N-COUNT 可算名詞 A **gag** is a humorous trick that you play on someone. 悪ふざけ [AM 米国英語, INFORMAL くだけた] ❏ Richard must have thought colleagues were playing a gag on him. リチャードは同僚が彼をからかっていると思ったに違いない。

gain /ɡeɪn/ (**gains, gaining, gained**) **1** V-T/V-I 他動詞/自動詞 If a person or place **gains** something such as an ability or quality, they gradually get more of it. 得る [他動詞] 増大する [自動詞] ❏ Students can gain valuable experience by working on the campus radio or magazine. 学生は学内ラジオや雑誌の仕事をすれば貴重な経験を得ることができる。 ❏ His reputation abroad has gained in stature. 国外での彼の名声は上がった。 **2** V-T/V-I 他動詞/自動詞 If you **gain from** something such as an event or situation, you get some advantage or benefit from it. 稼ぐ [他動詞・自動詞] 利益を収める [自動詞] ❏ The company didn't disclose how much it expects to gain from the two deals. その会社は2つの取引からの予測利益額を公開しなかった。 ❏ There is absolutely nothing to be gained by feeling bitter. 憤慨したって得るものは全くない。 **3** V-T 他動詞 To **gain** something such as weight or speed means to have an increase in that particular thing. 増す [他動詞] ❏ The BMW started coming forward, passing the other cars and gaining speed as it approached. BMWは前進し始め、他の車を追い越し、速度を上げて近づいた。 ● N-VAR 可変性名詞 **Gain** is also a noun. 増加 [usu with supp] ❏ News on new home sales is brighter, showing a gain of nearly 8% in June. 新築住宅販売のニュースはさらに明るいものとなり、6月には8%近い増加を示している。 **4** V-T 他動詞 If you **gain** something, you obtain it, especially after a lot of hard work or effort. 獲得する [他動詞] ❏ To gain a promotion, you might have to work overtime. 昇進するには、残業しなくてはならないかもしれない。 **5** PHRASE 句 If something such as an idea or an ideal **gains ground**, it gradually becomes more widely known or more popular. 広まる ❏ There are strong signs that his views are gaining ground. 彼の見解が優勢になっているというはっきりした兆候がある。

gait /ɡeɪt/ (**gaits**) N-COUNT 可算名詞 A particular kind of **gait** is a particular way of walking. 歩きぶり [WRITTEN 書き言葉] ❏ …a tubby little man in his fifties, with sparse hair and a rolling gait. 千鳥足の髪の薄い50台のずんぐりした小男

gala /ˈɡeɪlə/ (**galas**) N-COUNT 可算名詞 A **gala** is a special public celebration, entertainment, performance, or festival. 祝祭 ❏ …a gala evening at the Metropolitan Opera House. メトロポリタンオペラハウスでの特別公演の夕べ

galaxy /ˈɡæləksi/ (**galaxies**) also **Galaxy** **1** N-COUNT 可算名詞 A **galaxy** is an extremely large group of stars and planets that extends over many billions of light years. 星雲 ❏ Astronomers have discovered a distant galaxy. 天文学者は遠くの星雲を発見した。 **2** N-PROPER 固有名詞 **The Galaxy** is the extremely large group of stars and planets to which the Earth and the solar system belong. 銀河系 ❏ The Galaxy consists of 100 billion stars. 銀河系には1000億の星がある。

→ see Word Web: **galaxy**
→ see **star**

gale /ɡeɪl/ (**gales**) **1** N-COUNT 可算名詞 A **gale** is a very strong wind. 疾風 ❏ …forecasts of fierce gales over the next few days. これから数日間疾風が吹き荒れるという予報 **2** N-COUNT 可算名詞 You can refer to the loud noise made by a lot of people all laughing at the same time as a **gale of** laughter or **gales of** laughter. 激発 [WRITTEN 書き言葉] ❏ This was greeted with gales of laughter from the audience. これは観客の爆笑で迎えられた。

→ see **wind**

gall /ɡɔːl/ (**galls, galling, galled**) **1** N-UNCOUNT 不可算名詞 If you say that someone has **the gall to** do something, you are criticizing them for behaving in a rude or disrespectful way. ずうずうしさ [DISAPPROVAL 不賛成] ❏ He has the gall to accuse reporters of exploiting a tragedy for their own ends. 彼は報道陣が自分たちの目的のため悲劇につけこんだとあつかましくも非難した。 **2** V-T 他動詞 If someone's action **galls** you, it makes you feel very angry or annoyed, often because it is unfair to you and you cannot do anything about it. 怒らせる [他動詞] ❏ It must have galled him that Nick thwarted each of these measures. ニックに措置をすべて阻止されて彼はいらだったに違いない。

Word Web galaxy

The word **galaxy** with a small "g" refers to an extremely large group of **stars** and **planets**. It measures billions of **light years** across. There are about 100 billion galaxies in the **universe**. **Astronomers** classify galaxies into four different types. Irregular galaxies have no particular shape. Elliptical galaxies look like flattened spheres. Spiral galaxies have long curving arms. A barred spiral galaxy has straight lines of stars extending from its nucleus. Galaxy with a capital "G" refers to our own **solar system**. The name of this galaxy is the Milky Way. It is about 100,000 light years wide.

Word Web   gallery

The Uffizi **Gallery** in Florence, Italy, is a world-famous art **museum**. It contains many magnificent **paintings** and **sculptures**. These include **works of art** by da Vinci, Botticelli, and Michelangelo. The building was constructed in the 1550s to house government offices. The Medici family, who ruled the area at that time, were great art **collectors**. Gradually they began to convert parts of the building into art galleries. In 1737, the Medici family gave their art collection to the people of Italy.

gal|lant /gǽlənt/

Pronounced /gəlǽnt/ or /gǽlənt/ for meaning **2**.

2 の意味では /gǽlənt/ か/gəlǽnt/ と発音される。

1 ADJ 形容詞 If someone is **gallant**, they behave bravely and honorably in a dangerous or difficult situation. 勇敢な [OLD-FASHIONED 古風な] ❏ *The gallant soldiers lost their lives so that peace might reign again.* 再度平和の世の中になるように、勇敢な兵士たちが命を落とした。● **gal|lant|ly** ADV 副詞 [ADV with v] 勇敢に ❏ *The town responded gallantly to the war.* その町は戦争に堂々と立ち向かった。**2** ADJ 形容詞 If a man is **gallant**, he is kind, polite, and considerate toward women. 騎士的な [OLD-FASHIONED 古風な] ❏ *Douglas was a complex man, thoughtful, gallant, and generous.* ダグラスは複雑な男で、思いやりがあり騎士的で寛大だった。● **gal|lant|ly** ADV 副詞 [ADV with v] 女性に優しく ❏ *He gallantly kissed Marie's hand as we prepared to leave.* 私たちが去ろうとすると、彼はマリーの手に優しくキスした。

gall blad|der (gall bladders) N-COUNT 可算名詞 Your **gall bladder** is the organ in your body which contains bile and is next to your liver. 胆嚢(たんのう)

gal|lery /gǽləri/ (galleries) **1** N-COUNT; N-IN-NAMES 可算名詞、名称中の名詞 A **gallery** is a place that has permanent exhibitions of works of art in it. 美術展示室 ❏ *...an art gallery.* アートギャラリー **2** N-COUNT 可算名詞 A **gallery** is a privately owned building or room where people can look at and buy works of art. 画廊 ❏ *The painting is in the gallery upstairs.* その絵は上の階の画廊にあります。**3** N-COUNT 可算名詞 A **gallery** is an area high above the ground at the back or at the sides of a large room or hall. 回廊 ❏ *A crowd eagerly filled the gallery.* 回廊はすぐに観衆でいっぱいだった。**4** N-COUNT 可算名詞 The **gallery** in a theater or concert hall is an area high above the ground that usually contains the cheapest seats. 天井桟敷 ❏ *They had been forced to find cheap tickets in the gallery.* 彼らは天井桟敷の安い切符を探さざるをえなかった。● PHRASE 句 If you **play to the gallery**, you do something in public in a way which you hope will impress people. 俗うけをねらう ❏ *...but I must tell you that in my opinion you're both now playing to the gallery.* だが私が思うに、きみたちは今2人とも俗うけをねらっていると言わねばならない。

→ see Word Web: **gallery**

gal|ley /gǽli/ (galleys) **1** N-COUNT 可算名詞 On a ship or aircraft, the **galley** is the kitchen. 調理室 ❏ *I awoke to the smell of sizzling bacon in the galley.* 私が起きると調理室からジュージューというベーコンの匂いがしていた。**2** N-COUNT 可算名詞 In former times, a **galley** was a ship with sails and a lot of oars, which was often rowed by slaves or prisoners. ガレー船 ❏ *...his months pulling the oar on the galleys.* 彼がガレー船のオールをこいだ数か月

gal|lon /gǽlən/ (gallons) N-COUNT 可算名詞 A **gallon** is a unit of measurement for liquids that is equal to eight pints or 3.785 liters. ガロン ❏ *...80 million gallons of water a day.* 1日あたり水800万ガロン

gal|lop /gǽləp/ (gallops, galloping, galloped) **1** V-T/V-I 他動詞/自動詞 When a horse **gallops**, it runs very fast so that all four legs are off the ground at the same time. If you **gallop** a horse, you make it gallop. ギャロップさせる [他動詞] ギャロップする [自動詞] ❏ *The horses galloped away.* 馬たちはギャロップして去っていった。**2** V-I 自動詞 If you **gallop**, you ride a horse that is galloping. 馬をギャロップで走らせる ❏ *Major Winston galloped into the distance.* ウィンストン少佐は馬をギャロップで遠くへ走らせた。**3** N-SING 単数名詞 A **gallop** is a ride on a horse that is galloping. ギャロップ ❏ *I was forced to attempt a gallop.* 私はギャロップをやってみるよう強要された。**4** V-I 自動詞 If something such as a process **gallops**, it develops very quickly and is often difficult to control. 急速に進行する [自動詞] ❏ *China's economy galloped ahead.* 中国の経済は急速に成長した。**5** PHRASE 句 If you do something **at a gallop**, you do it very quickly. 全速力で ❏ *I read the book at a gallop.* 私はその本を全速力で読んだ。

ga|lore /gəlɔ́ːr/ ADJ 形容詞 You use **galore** to emphasize that something you like exists in very large quantities. 豊富に [INFORMAL, WRITTEN くだけた、書き言葉, EMPHASIS 強調] [n ADJ] ❏ *You'll be able to win prizes galore.* きみは景品をどっさり獲得できるでしょう。

gal|va|nize /gǽlvənaɪz/ (galvanizes, galvanizing, galvanized) V-T 他動詞 To **galvanize** someone means to cause them to take action, for example by making them feel very excited, afraid, or angry. 駆り立てる [他動詞] ❏ *The aid appeal has galvanized the country's business community.* 援助要請は国の経済界を活気づけた。

gam|ble /gǽmbəl/ (gambles, gambling, gambled) **1** N-COUNT 可算名詞 A **gamble** is a risky action or decision that you take in the hope of gaining money, success, or an advantage over other people. かけ事 ❏ *Yesterday, he named his cabinet and took a big gamble in the process.* 昨日、彼は内閣を指名し、その過程でいちばちかのかけをした。**2** V-T 他動詞/自動詞 If you **gamble on** something, you take a risky action or decision in the hope of gaining money, success, or an advantage over other people. かける [他動詞・自動詞] ❏ *Few firms will be willing to gamble on new products.* 新製品にかけるのを厭わない会社は少ないだろう。❏ *They are not prepared to gamble their careers on this matter.* 彼らはこの事態に自らのキャリアをかけるつもりはない。**3** V-T/V-I 他動詞/自動詞 If you **gamble** an amount of money, you bet it in a game such as cards or on the result of a race or competition. People who **gamble** usually do it frequently. かけ事をする [他動詞・自動詞] ❏ *Most people visit Las Vegas to gamble their hard-earned money.* ほとんどの人は苦労してやっと得たお金でかけ事をするためにラスベガスを訪問する。❏ *John gambled heavily on the horses.* ジョンは競馬にのめりこんでいた。

→ see **lottery**

gam|bler /gǽmblər/ (gamblers) **1** N-COUNT 可算名詞 A **gambler** is someone who gambles regularly, for example in card games or horse racing. ばくち打ち ❏ *There was a fellow in that casino tonight who's a very heavy gambler.* そのカジノには今夜度を過ぎたばくち打ちがいた。**2** N-COUNT 可算名詞 If you describe someone as a **gambler**, you mean that they are ready to take risks in order to gain advantages or success. ギャンブラー ❏ *He had never been afraid of failure: he was a gambler, ready to go off somewhere else and start all over again.* 彼は失敗を恐れたことはない。彼はギャンブラーで、いつでもどこかに逃げて最初からやり直す心構えができている。

gam|bling /gǽmblɪŋ/ N-UNCOUNT 不可算名詞 **Gambling** is the act or activity of betting money, for example in card games or on horse racing. 賭博 ❏ *Gambling is a form of entertainment.* 賭博は一種の娯楽だ。

game /geɪm/ (games) **1** N-COUNT 可算名詞 A **game** is an activity or sport usually involving skill, knowledge, or chance, in which you follow fixed rules and try to win against an opponent or to solve a puzzle. ゲーム ❏ *...the wonderful game of football.* すばらしいサッカー競技 ❏ *...a playful game of hide-and-seek.* おもしろい遊び、かくれんぼ **2** N-COUNT 可算名詞 A **game** is one particular occasion on which a game is played. 試合 ❏ *It was the first game of the season.* それがシーズン最初の試合だった。❏ *He regularly watched our games from the stands.* 彼はスタンドから我々の試合を定期的に観戦した。**3** N-COUNT 可算名詞 A **game** is a part of a match, for example in tennis or bridge, consisting of a fixed number of points. ゲーム ❏ *She won six games to love in the second set.* 彼女は第2セットを6-0で取った。**4** N-PLURAL 複数名詞 **Games** are an organized event in which competitions in several sports take place. 競技会 ❏ *...the 1996 Olympic Games at Atlanta.* 1996年のアトランタオリンピック大会 **5** N-COUNT 可算名詞 You can use **game** to describe a way of behaving in which a person uses a particular plan, usually in order to gain an advantage for himself or herself. やり方 ❏ *Until now, the Americans have been playing a very delicate political game.* 今まで、アメリカは非常に微妙な政治ゲームをしてきた。**6** N-UNCOUNT 不可算名詞 Wild animals or birds that are hunted for sport and sometimes cooked and eaten are referred to as **game**. 猟鳥獣 ❏ *As men who shot game for food, they were natural marksmen.* 食料にする鳥獣を撃っていたため、男たちは当然のように弓がうまかった。**7** ADJ 形容詞 If you are **game for** something, you are willing to do something new, unusual, or risky. する気がある [v-link ADJ] ❏ *He said he's game for a similar challenge next year.* 彼は来年も同じような挑戦をする気が十分あると言った。**8** PHRASE 句 If someone or something **gives the game away**, they reveal a secret or reveal their feelings, and this puts them at a disadvantage. 手の内を見せる ❏ *The faces of the two conspirators gave the game away!* 2人の共謀者の顔で計画が漏れてしまった。**9** PHRASE 句 If you are **new to** a particular **game**, you have not done a particular activity

or been in a particular situation before. 初めてである □ *Don't forget that she's new to this game and will take a while to complete the task.* 彼女は新顔で仕事を完了するには時間がかかることを忘れてはならない。 **10 PHRASE** 句 If you beat someone **at** their **own game**, you use the same methods that they have used, but more successfully, so that you gain an advantage over them. 相手の得意の手で逆にやっつける □ *He must anticipate the maneuvers of the other lawyers and beat them at their own game.* 彼は他の弁護士の計略を予想し、逆にそれを利用して勝たねばならない。 **11 PHRASE** 句 If you say that someone is **playing games** or **playing silly games**, you mean that they are not treating a situation seriously and you are annoyed with them. いいかげんにやる [DISAPPROVAL 不賛成] □ *This seemed to annoy Professor Steiner.* "*Don't play games with me,*" *he thundered.* これはシュタイナー教授をいらだたせたようだった。「私にお遊びは通用せんぞ」と彼は雷を落とした。

→ see **chess, mammal**

game show (game shows) N-COUNT 可算名詞 **Game shows** are television programs on which people play games in order to win prizes. ゲームショー □ *Being a good game-show host means getting to know your contestants.* ゲームショーでいい司会者とは出場者のことをよく知ることだ。

gam|ing /ɡeɪmɪŋ/ N-UNCOUNT 不可算名詞 **Gaming** means the same as **gambling**. 賭博 □ *...offenses connected with vice, gaming, and drugs.* 悪徳、賭博および麻薬に関連した犯罪

gang /ɡæŋ/ (gangs, ganging, ganged) **1** N-COUNT 可算名詞 A **gang** is a group of people, especially young people, who go around together and often deliberately cause trouble. ギャング □ *During the fight with a rival gang he lashed out with his flick knife.* 対立するギャングとのけんかの際、彼は飛び出しナイフを持って襲いかかった。 □ *Gang members were behind a lot of the violence.* 多くの暴力の裏には暴力団員がいた。 **2** N-COUNT 可算名詞 A **gang** is a group of criminals who work together to commit crimes. 暴力団 □ *Police were hunting for a gang that had allegedly stolen fifty-five cars.* 警察は車を55台盗んだとされている一味を捜している。 □ *...an underworld gang.* やくざ **3** N-SING 単数名詞 **The gang** is a group of friends who frequently meet. 遊び仲間 [INFORMAL くだけた] □ *Come on over, we've got lots of the old gang here.* ここへいよ、昔の連中がたくさんいるぞ。 **4** N-COUNT 可算名詞 A **gang** is a group of workers who do physical work together. (労働者の) 一群 □ *...a gang of laborers.* 一団の労働者

▶ **gang up** PHRASAL VERB 句動詞 If people **gang up on** someone, they unite against them for a particular reason, for example in a fight or argument. 徒党を組む [INFORMAL くだけた] □ *Harrison complained that his colleagues ganged up on him.* ハリソンは同僚たちが自分に対して結託したと文句を言った。 □ *All the other parties ganged up to keep them out of power.* その他の党すべてが徒党を組んで彼らに政権を取らせないようにした。

Thesaurus   *gang* また次を参照:

N.	crowd, group, pack **1**
	mob, ring **2**

gan|grene /ɡæŋɡrin/ N-UNCOUNT 不可算名詞 **Gangrene** is the decay that can occur in a part of a person's body if the blood stops flowing to it, for example as a result of illness or injury. 壊疽 (え そ) □ *Once gangrene has developed, the tissue is dead, and the only hope is to contain the damage.* 壊疽になると組織が死ぬので、損傷を抑えることにしか希望はない。

Word Link   *ster ≈ one who does : barrister, gangster, youngster*

gang|ster /ɡæŋstər/ (gangsters) N-COUNT 可算名詞 A **gangster** is a member of an organized group of violent criminals. 暴力団の一員 □ *...a gangster movie.* ギャング映画

gap /ɡæp/ (gaps) **1** N-COUNT 可算名詞 A **gap** is a space between two things or a hole in the middle of something solid. 割れ目 □ *He pulled the thick curtains together, leaving just a narrow gap.* 彼は少しだけ隙間を残して、厚いカーテンを引き寄せた。 **2** N-COUNT 可算名詞 A **gap** is a period of time when you are not busy or when you stop doing something that you normally do. とぎれ □ *There followed a gap of four years, during which William joined the Army.* その後4年間の空白があり、その間ウィリアムは陸軍に入隊した。 **3** N-COUNT 可算名詞 If there is something missing from a situation that prevents it from being complete or satisfactory, you can say that there is a **gap**. 欠陥 □ *The manifesto calls for a greater effort to recruit young scientists to fill the gap left by a wave of retirements expected over the next decade.* 声明書は、次の10年間に予想される退職者の急増による欠員を補うため若い科学者を雇用する一層の努力を行うよう要求している。 **4** N-COUNT 可算名詞 A **gap between** two groups of people, things, or sets of ideas is a big difference between them. ずれ □ *...the gap between rich and poor.* 富裕層と貧困層の格差 □ *America's trade gap widened.* アメリカの貿易不均衡が広がった。

Word Partnership   *gap* は次の語句と使われる:

ADJ.	**narrow** gap **1 2**
V.	**bridge a** gap **1**
	fill a gap, **leave a** gap, **widen a** gap **1** – **4**
PREP.	gap **between** *something* **1 4**

gape /ɡeɪp/ (gapes, gaping, gaped) **1** V-I 自動詞 If you **gape**, you look at someone or something in surprise, usually with an open mouth. 驚いた顔でみる [自動詞] □ *His secretary stopped taking notes to gape at me.* 彼の秘書はメモを取るのをやめ、ぽかんと口を開けて私のことを見た。 □ *He was not the type to wander around gaping at everything like a tourist.* 彼は観光客のように何もかもに見とれてウロウロするようなタイプではなかった。 **2** V-I 自動詞 If you say that something such as a hole or a wound **gapes**, you are emphasizing that it is big or wide. [EMPHASIS 強調] □ *The front door was missing. A hole gaped in the roof.* 玄関のドアがなくなり、屋根に大きな穴が開いた。 ● **gap|ing** ADJ 形容詞 大きく割れた □ *The aircraft took off with a gaping hole in its fuselage.* 飛行機は機体に大穴があいたままで離陸した。

gar|age /ɡɑrɑʒ/ (garages) **1** N-COUNT 可算名詞 A **garage** is a building in which you keep a car. A garage is often built next to or as part of a house. ガレージ □ *They have turned the garage into a study.* 彼らはガレージを書斎に変えた。 **2** N-COUNT; N-IN-NAMES 可算名詞, 名称中の名詞 A **garage** is a place where you can get your car repaired. 自動車修理場 □ *Nancy took her car to a local garage for a check-up.* ナンシーは点検のため、車を近くの自動車修理場に持っていった。

gar|bage /ɡɑrbɪdʒ/ **1** N-UNCOUNT 不可算名詞 **Garbage** is waste material, especially waste from a kitchen. 台所ごみ [mainly AM 主に米国英語] □ *This morning a bomb in a garbage bag exploded and injured 15 people.* 今朝、ごみ袋内の爆弾が破裂して15人が負傷した。 **2** N-UNCOUNT 不可算名詞 If someone says that an idea or opinion is **garbage**, they are emphasizing that they believe it is untrue or unimportant. くだらないもの [INFORMAL くだけた, DISAPPROVAL 不賛成] □ *I personally think this is complete garbage.* 個人的にはこれは完全なくずだと思う。

→ see **pollution**

In American English, the words **garbage** and **trash** are most commonly used to refer to waste material that is thrown away. □ *...the smell of rotting garbage... She threw the bottle into the trash.* In British English, **rubbish** is the usual word. **Garbage** and **trash** are sometimes used in British English, but only informally and metaphorically. □ *I don't have to listen to this garbage... The book was trash.*

Thesaurus   *garbage* また次を参照:

N.	junk, litter, rubbish, trash **1**
	foolishness, nonsense **2**

gar|bage can (garbage cans) N-COUNT 可算名詞 A **garbage can** is a container that you put waste material into. ごみ入れ [AM 米国英語] □ *A bomb planted in a garbage can exploded early today.* 本日早朝にごみバケツに仕掛けられた爆弾が破裂した。

gar|bage dump (garbage dumps) N-COUNT 可算名詞 A **garbage dump** is a place where waste material is left. 廃棄物集積場 [AM 米国英語]

gar|bage truck (garbage trucks) N-COUNT 可算名詞 A **garbage truck** is a large truck which collects the garbage from outside people's houses. ごみ回収車 [AM 米国英語]

gar|bled /ɡɑrbᵊld/ ADJ 形容詞 A **garbled** message or report contains confused or wrong details, often because it is spoken by someone who is nervous or in a hurry. 混乱した □ *The Coast Guard needs to decipher garbled messages in a few minutes.* 沿岸警備隊員は混乱したメッセージを数分の内に解読しなければならない。

gar|den /ɡɑrdᵊn/ (gardens, gardening, gardened) **1** N-COUNT 可算名詞 A **garden** is the part of a yard which is used for growing flowers and vegetables. 庭 □ *...the most beautiful garden on Earth.* 地球で最も美しい庭園 **2** V-I 自動詞 If you **garden**, you do work in your garden such as weeding or planting. 園芸をする [自動詞] □ *Jim gardened at the homes of friends on weekends.* ジムは週末友人の家で庭いじりをした。 ● **gar|den|ing** N-UNCOUNT 不可算名詞 園芸 □ *I have taken up gardening again.* 私は園芸を再開した。 **3** N-PLURAL 複数名詞 **Gardens** are places like a park that have areas of plants, trees, and grass, and that people can visit and walk around. 庭園 □ *The Gardens are open from 10:30 a.m. until 5:00 p.m.* 庭園は午前10:30から午後5:00まで開園している。 **4** N-IN-NAMES 名称中の名詞 **Gardens** is sometimes used as part of the name of a street. ガーデン □ *He lives at 9 Acacia Gardens.* 彼はアカシアガーデンズ9番地に住んでいる。

→ see **park**

gar|den|er /ɡɑrdᵊnər/ (gardeners) **1** N-COUNT 可算名詞 A

gardener is a person who is paid to work in someone else's garden. 庭師 ❏ *She employed a gardener.* 彼女は庭師を雇った. ❷ N-COUNT 可算名詞 A **gardener** is someone who enjoys working in their own garden growing flowers or vegetables. 園芸愛好家 ❏ *The majority of sweet peas are still bred by enthusiastic amateur gardeners.* スイートピーの新種の大部分はいまだに熱心なアマチュア園芸愛好家によって品種改良されている.

gar|gle /gɑrg°l/ (**gargles, gargling, gargled**) V-I 自動詞 If you **gargle**, you wash your mouth and throat by filling your mouth with a liquid, tipping your head back and using your throat to blow bubbles through the liquid, and finally spitting it out. うがいをする [自動詞] ❏ *Try gargling with salt water as soon as a cough begins.* 咳が始まったらすぐに塩水でうがいをしてみなさい.

gar|ish /gɛərɪʃ/ ADJ 形容詞 You describe something as **garish** when you dislike it because it is very bright in an unattractive, showy way. けばけばしい [DISAPPROVAL 不賛成] ❏ *They climbed the garish, purple-carpeted stairs.* 彼らはけばけばしい紫のカーペットが敷かれた階段を上った.

gar|land /gɑrlənd/ (**garlands**) N-COUNT 可算名詞 A **garland** is a circular decoration made from flowers and leaves. People sometimes wear garlands of flowers on their heads or around their necks. 花輪 ❏ *They wore blue silk dresses with cream sashes and garlands of summer flowers in their hair.* 彼女らは青色の絹のドレスにクリーム色の帯を締め, 髪に夏の花の冠をかぶっていた.

gar|lic /gɑrlɪk/ N-UNCOUNT 不可算名詞 **Garlic** is the small, white, round bulb of a plant that is related to the onion plant. Garlic has a very strong smell and taste and is used in cooking. ニンニク ❏ *a clove of garlic.* ニンニクの一片
→ see **spice**

gar|ment /gɑrmənt/ (**garments**) N-COUNT 可算名詞 A **garment** is a piece of clothing; used especially in contexts where you are talking about the manufacture or sale of clothes. 衣類 ❏ *Many of the garments have the customers' name tags sewn into the linings.* 多くの衣類の裏地には顧客の名札が縫いこまれている.

gar|ner /gɑrnər/ (**garners, garnering, garnered**) V-T 他動詞 If someone **has garnered** something useful or valuable, they have gained it or collected it. 獲得する [FORMAL 形式ばった] [他動詞] ❏ *Durham had garnered three times as many votes as Carey.* ダーハムはキャリーの3倍の票を集めた. ❏ *He has garnered extensive support for his proposals.* 彼は提案で広範な支持を得た.

gar|nish /gɑrnɪʃ/ (**garnishes, garnishing, garnished**) ❶ N-VAR 可変性名詞 A **garnish** is a small amount of salad, herbs, or other food that is used to decorate cooked or prepared food. つま ❏ *a garnish of chopped raw onion, tomato, and fresh coriander.* みじん切りの生ねぎ, トマト, 新鮮なコリアンダーのつけあわせ ❷ V-T 他動詞 If you **garnish** cooked or prepared food, you decorate it with a garnish. つまを添える [他動詞] ❏ *She had finished the vegetables and was garnishing the roast.* 彼女は野菜の料理を終え, ロースト肉につけあわせを添えていた.

gar|ri|son /gærɪs°n/ (**garrisons, garrisoning, garrisoned**) ❶ N-COUNT-COLL 集合可算名詞 A **garrison** is a group of soldiers whose task is to guard the town or building where they live. 守備隊 ❏ *a five-hundred-man French army garrison.* 500人のフランス軍守備隊 ❷ N-COUNT 可算名詞 A **garrison** is the buildings which the soldiers live in. 要塞 ❏ *The approaches to the garrison have been heavily mined.* 要塞への進路には多数の地雷が敷設されていた. ❸ V-T 他動詞 To **garrison** a place means to put soldiers there in order to protect it. You can also say that soldiers **are garrisoned** in a place. 兵を駐留させる ❏ *American troops still garrisoned the country.* 米軍はいまだにその国に駐留していた. ❏ *No other soldiers were garrisoned there.* その他の兵士はそこに駐留していなかった.

gas /gæs/ (**gases, gasses, gassing, gassed**)

The form **gases** is the plural of the noun. The form **gasses** is the third person singular of the verb.

gases 形は名詞の複数である. gasses 形は動詞の3人称単数である.

❶ N-UNCOUNT 不可算名詞 **Gas** is a substance like air that is neither liquid nor solid and burns easily. It is used as a fuel for cooking and heating. ガス ❏ *Coal is actually cheaper than gas.* 石炭は実際には天然ガスよりも安価だ. ❷ N-VAR 可変性名詞 A **gas** is any substance that is neither liquid nor solid, for example oxygen or hydrogen. 気体 ❏ *Helium is a very light gas.* ヘリウムは大変軽い気体だ. ❸ N-MASS 質量名詞 **Gas** is a poisonous gas that can be used as a weapon. 毒ガス ❏ *The problem was that the exhaust gases contain many toxins.* 問題は排ガスに毒素が多く含まれていることだった. ❹ N-UNCOUNT 不可算名詞 **Gas** is the fuel which is used to drive motor vehicles. ガソリン [AM 米国英語] ❏ *a tank of gas.* ひとタンク分のガソリン ❺ V-T 他動詞 To **gas** a person or animal means to kill them by making them breathe poisonous gas. 毒ガスで殺す [他動詞] ❏ *Her husband ran a pipe from her car exhaust to the bedroom in an attempt to gas her.* 夫は, 彼女を中毒死させるために, 彼女の車の排気ガス管から寝室に管を走らせた. ❻ → see also **gas mask,**

greenhouse gas, tear gas
→ see **air, greenhouse, matter, solar**

gash /gæʃ/ (**gashes, gashing, gashed**) ❶ N-COUNT 可算名詞 A **gash** is a long, deep cut in your skin or in the surface of something. 深く長い裂け目 ❏ *There was an inch-long gash just above his right eye.* 彼の右目のすぐ上には1インチの深傷があった. ❷ V-T 他動詞 If you **gash** something, you accidentally make a long and deep cut in it. 裂傷をつくる [他動詞] ❏ *He gashed his leg while felling trees.* 木から落ちる途中, 彼は脚に裂傷を負った.

gas mask (**gas masks**) N-COUNT 可算名詞 A **gas mask** is a device that you wear over your face in order to protect yourself from poisonous gases. ガスマスク

gaso|line /gæsəlin/ N-UNCOUNT 不可算名詞 **Gasoline** is the fuel which is used to drive motor vehicles. ガソリン [AM 米国英語]
→ see **dry-cleaning, oil**

gasp /gæsp/ (**gasps, gasping, gasped**) ❶ N-COUNT 可算名詞 A **gasp** is a short, quick breath of air that you take in through your mouth, especially when you are surprised, shocked, or in pain. あえぎ ❏ *An audible gasp went around the court as the jury announced the verdict.* 陪審員が判決を発表すると, 聞き取れるほどのあえぎが法廷内で起こった. ❷ V-I 自動詞 When you **gasp**, you take a short, quick breath through your mouth, especially when you are surprised, shocked, or in pain. あえぐ [自動詞] ❏ *She gasped for air and drew in a lungful of water.* 彼女は苦しそうにあえいで肺いっぱい水を飲んでしまった. ❸ PHRASE 句 You describe something as the **last gasp** to emphasize that it is the final part of something or happens at the last possible moment. 最後のあがき [EMPHASIS 強調] ❏ *the last gasp of a dying system of censorship.* 消滅しつつある検閲システムの最後のあがき

gas sta|tion (**gas stations**) N-COUNT 可算名詞 A **gas station** is a place where you can buy fuel for your car. ガソリンスタンド [AM 米国英語]

gas|tric /gæstrɪk/ ADJ 形容詞 You use **gastric** to describe processes, pain, or illnesses that occur in someone's stomach. 胃の [MEDICAL 医学の] [ADJ n] ❏ *He suffered from diabetes and gastric ulcers.* 彼は糖尿病と胃かいようをわずらっていた.

gate /geɪt/ (**gates**) ❶ N-COUNT 可算名詞 A **gate** is a structure like a door which is used at the entrance to a field, a garden, or the grounds of a building. 門 ❏ *He opened the gate and started walking up to the house.* 彼は門を開けて家の方に歩き始めた. ❷ N-COUNT 可算名詞 In an airport, a **gate** is a place where passengers leave the airport and get on their airplane. 搭乗口 ❏ *Passengers with hand luggage can go straight to the departure gate to check in there.* 持ち込み手荷物の乗客はそのまま出発搭乗口に行ってチェックインできる. ❸ N-UNCOUNT 不可算名詞 The **gate** is the total amount of money that is paid by the people who go to a sports match or other event. 入場料の総額

gate|way /geɪtweɪ/ (**gateways**) ❶ N-COUNT 可算名詞 A **gateway** is an entrance where there is a gate. 門口 ❏ *He walked across the park and through a gateway.* 彼は公園を横切り門口を通り過ぎた. ❷ N-COUNT 可算名詞 A **gateway to** somewhere is a place which you go through because it leads you to a much larger place. 入り口 ❏ *Denver is the gateway to some of the best skiing in the world.* デンバーは世界で最高のスキー場への入り口だ. ❸ N-COUNT 可算名詞 If something is a **gateway to** a job, career, or other activity, it gives you the opportunity to make progress or get further success in that activity. (成功などに至る) 道 ❏ *The prestigious title offered a gateway to success in the highly competitive world of modeling.* 一流の肩書きは, 非常に競争の激しいモデル界で成功をつかむ手段となった. ❹ N-COUNT 可算名詞 In computing, a **gateway** connects different computer networks so that information can be passed between them. ゲートウェイ [COMPUTING コンピューティング] ❏ *The network has a gateway into the hospital mainframe.* その病院のメインフレームへのゲートウェイがある.
→ see **Internet**

gath|er /gæðər/ (**gathers, gathering, gathered**) ❶ V-T/V-I 他動詞/自動詞 If people **gather** somewhere, or if someone **gathers** people somewhere, they come together in a group. 集める [他動詞] 集まる [自動詞] ❏ *In the evenings, we gathered around the fireplace and talked.* 夜になると, 私たちは暖炉の周りに集まって話した. ❷ V-T 他動詞 If you **gather** things, you collect them together so that you can use them. 集める [他動詞] ❏ *I suggest we gather enough firewood to last the night.* 夜の分を絶やさないのに十分な薪を集めたらどうだろう. ● PHRASAL VERB 句動詞 **Gather up** means the same as **gather**. 拾い集める ❏ *When Steinberg had gathered up his papers, he went out.* スタインバーグは論文をかき集めると出て行った. ❸ V-T 他動詞 If you **gather** information or evidence, you collect it, especially over a period of time and after a lot of hard work. 収集する [他動詞] ❏ *a private detective using a hidden tape recorder to gather information.* 隠れたテープレコーダで情報を収集する私立探偵 ❹ V-T 他動詞 If something **gathers** speed, momentum, or force, it gradually becomes faster or more powerful. (速度, 勢い, 力などが) 次第に増す [他動詞] ❏ *Demands for his dismissal have gathered momentum in*

recent weeks. ここ数週間、彼を免職する要求は勢いが増した. **5** V-T 他動詞 When you **gather** something such as your strength, courage, or thoughts, you make an effort to prepare yourself to do something. (力、勇気などを) 奮い起こす [他動詞] □ *You must gather your strength for the journey.* 旅行に備えて力を蓄えなくてはなりませんよ. ● PHRASAL VERB 句動詞 **Gather up** means the same as **gather**. 寄せ集める □ *She was gathering up her courage to approach him when he called to her.* 彼が呼んだとき、彼女は彼にアプローチする勇気を奮い起こそうとしていたところだった. **6** V-T 他動詞 You use **gather** in expressions such as "**I gather**" and "**as far as I can gather**" to introduce information that you have found out, especially when you have found it out in an indirect way. 推測する [他動詞] □ *I gather his report is highly critical of the trial judge.* 彼の報告書は予審判事に対して非常に批判的なものだと推測する. □ *"He speaks English," she said to Graham. "I gathered that."* 「彼は英語を話すのよ」と彼女はグレアムに言った.「私の推測ではね.」 **7** to **gather dust** → see **dust**

▶ **gather up** → see **gather 2, 5**

gath|er|ing /gǽðərɪŋ/ (**gatherings**) **1** N-COUNT 可算名詞 A **gathering** is a group of people meeting together for a particular purpose. 集まり □ *The twenty-second annual gathering of the South Pacific Forum.* 南太平洋フォーラムの第22回年次集会 **2** ADJ 形容詞 If there is **gathering** darkness, the light is gradually decreasing, usually because it is nearly night. 深まる [ADJ n] □ *The lighthouse beam was quite distinct in the gathering dusk.* 灯台が発する光線は深まる暮色の中で非常にはっきり見えた. **3** → see also **gather**

gaudy /gɔ́di/ (**gaudier, gaudiest**) ADJ 形容詞 If something is **gaudy**, it is very brightly colored and showy. はなやかな [DISAPPROVAL 不賛成] □ *...her gaudy orange-and-purple floral hat.* 彼女のはなやかなオレンジと紫の花模様の帽子

gauge /geɪdʒ/ (**gauges, gauging, gauged**) **1** V-T 他動詞 If you **gauge** the speed or strength of something, or if you **gauge** an amount, you measure or calculate it, often by using a device of some kind. 測定する [他動詞] □ *He gauged the wind at over thirty knots.* 風は30ノット以上と彼は測定した. **2** N-COUNT 可算名詞 A **gauge** is a device that measures the amount or quantity of something and shows the amount when measured. 計量器 [oft n n] □ *...temperature gauges.* 温度計 **3** V-T 他動詞 If you **gauge** people's actions, feelings, or intentions in a particular situation, you carefully consider and judge them. 評価する [他動詞] □ *His mood can be gauged by his reaction to the most trivial of incidents.* 彼の機嫌はいたってくだらない出来事に対する反応で分かる. **4** N-SING 単数名詞 A **gauge of** someone's feelings or a situation is a fact or event that can be used to judge them. (判断の) 尺度 □ *The index is the government's chief gauge of future economic activity.* 指標は政府が将来の経済活動を評価するための主要な標準だ.

→ see **scuba diving**

gaunt /gɔnt/ **1** ADJ 形容詞 If someone looks **gaunt**, they look very thin, usually because they have been very ill or worried. やせ衰えた □ *Looking gaunt and tired, he denied there was anything to worry about.* やせ衰え、疲れて見えたが、彼は心配することはないと打ち消した. **2** ADJ 形容詞 If you describe a building as **gaunt**, you mean it is very plain and unattractive. 荒涼とした [LITERARY 文語の] [ADJ n] □ *Above on the hillside was a large, gaunt, gray house.* 丘の中腹には荒涼とした大きな灰色の家が建っていた.

gaunt|let /gɔ́ntlɪt/ (**gauntlets**) **1** N-COUNT 可算名詞 **Gauntlets** are long, thick, protective gloves. 長手袋 □ *The smart biker also wears boots, gauntlets, and protective clothing.* 賢いライダーは、ブーツ、長手袋、保護服も着用する. **2** PHRASE 句 If you **pick up the gauntlet** or **take up the gauntlet**, you accept the challenge that someone has made. 挑戦に応ずる □ *She picked up the gauntlet in her incisive keynote address to the conference.* 彼女は会議での鋭い基調演説で挑戦に応じた. **3** PHRASE 句 If you **run the gauntlet**, you go through an unpleasant experience in which a lot of people criticize or attack you. 方々から批判される □ *The trucks tried to drive to the American base, running the gauntlet of marauding bands of gunmen.* トラックは、武装集団から襲撃を受けながらも、米軍基地へ走ろうとした. **4** PHRASE 句 If you **throw down the gauntlet** to someone, you say or do something that challenges them to argue or compete with you. 挑戦する □ *Luxury car firm Jaguar has thrown down the gauntlet to competitors by giving the best guarantee on the market.* 高級車会社ジャガーは、市場で最高の保証をつけ競合会社に戦いを挑んだ.

gave /geɪv/ **Gave** is the past tense of **give**. give の過去形

gay /geɪ/ (**gays**) ADJ 形容詞 A **gay** person is homosexual. 同性愛の □ *The quality of life for gay men has improved over the last two decades.* 過去20年間で同性愛男性の生活の質は向上した. ● N-PLURAL 複数名詞 **Gays** are homosexual people, especially homosexual men. 同性愛者 □ *More importantly, gays have proved themselves to be style leaders.* さらに重要なことに、ゲイはスタイルリーダーであることを証明した. ● **gay|ness** N-UNCOUNT 不可算名詞 ゲイであること

□ *...Mike's admission of his gayness.* ゲイであるとのマイクの告白

gaze /geɪz/ (**gazes, gazing, gazed**) **1** V-I 自動詞 If you **gaze at** someone or something, you look steadily at them for a long time, for example because you find them attractive or interesting, or because you are thinking about something else. 見つめる [自動詞] □ *...gazing at herself in the mirror.* 鏡に映った自分自身を熟視する □ *Sitting in his wicker chair, he gazed reflectively at the fire.* 彼は籐いすに座り、考え込むように火を見つめた.

The verbs **gaze** and **stare** are both used to talk about looking at something for a long time. If you **gaze at** something, it is often because you think it is marvelous or impressive. □ *A fresh-faced little girl gazes in wonder at the bright fairground lights.* If you **stare at** something or someone, it is often because you think they are strange or shocking. □ *Various families came out and stared at us.*

---

2 N-COUNT 可算名詞 You can talk about someone's **gaze** as a way of describing how they are looking at something, especially when they are looking steadily at it. 凝視 [WRITTEN 書き言葉] □ *The Monsignor turned his gaze from the flames to meet the Colonel's.* モンシニョールは視線を炎から大佐の眼に移した. □ *She felt increasingly uncomfortable under the woman's steady gaze.* 彼女は女性に凝視されてますます不愉快に感じた. **3** PHRASE 句 If someone or something is **in the public gaze**, they are receiving a lot of attention from the general public. 人目にさらされて □ *You won't find a couple more in the public gaze than Michael and Lizzie.* マイケルとリジーほど世間の注目を集めているカップルはいない.

ga|zette /gəzɛ́t/ (**gazettes**) N-IN-NAMES 名称中の名詞 **Gazette** is often used in the names of newspapers. 新聞 [n n] □ *...the Arkansas Gazette.* アーカンソー・ガゼット紙

G.B. /dʒi bi/ N-PROPER 固有名詞 **G.B.** is an abbreviation for **Great Britain**. Great Britain の略

GDP /dʒi di pi/ (**GDPs**) N-VAR 可変性名詞 In economics, a country's **GDP** is the total value of goods and services produced within a country in a year, not including its income from investments in other countries. **GDP** is an abbreviation for **gross domestic product**. Compare **GNP**. 国内総生産. gross domestic product の略.

gear /gɪər/ (**gears, gearing, geared**) **1** N-COUNT 可算名詞 The **gears** on a machine or vehicle are a device for changing the rate at which energy is changed into motion. ギア □ *On hills, he must use low gears.* 彼は丘では低速ギアを使わねばならない. □ *The car was in fourth gear.* 車は4速ギアに入っていた. **2** N-UNCOUNT 不可算名詞 The **gear** involved in a particular activity is the equipment or special clothing that you use. 用具 □ *About 100 officers in riot gear were needed to break up the fight.* 戦いをやめさせるには暴動鎮圧用装備をした警官が約100人必要だった. □ *...fishing gear.* 釣具 **3** N-UNCOUNT 不可算名詞 **Gear** means clothing. 衣服 [INFORMAL くだけた] □ *I used to wear trendy gear but it just looked ridiculous.* 私はかつて流行の服を着ていたが、ばかげてみえただけだった. **4** V-T PASSIVE 受動態他動詞 If someone or something is **geared to** or **toward** a particular purpose, they are organized or designed in order to achieve that purpose. 合わせる □ *Colleges are not always geared to the needs of mature students.* 大学はいつも社会人学生のニーズを満足させるようにはできていない. □ *My training was geared toward winning gold.* 私のトレーニングは金メダル獲得を目指すものだった.

▶ **gear up** PHRASAL VERB 句動詞 If someone is **gearing up for** a particular activity, they are preparing to do it. If they are **geared up to** do a particular activity, they are prepared to do it. 態勢をとる □ *...another indication that the country is gearing up for an election.* その国が選挙態勢に入っているもうひとつの兆候

Word Partnership gear は次の語句と使われる:

v.	put *something* in gear, shift gear **1**
	change gear **1** **2**
ADJ.	protective gear **2**

---

gear lev|er → see **gearshift**

gear|shift /gɪ́ərʃɪft/ (**gearshifts**) N-COUNT 可算名詞 In a vehicle, the **gearshift** is the lever that you use to change gear in a car or other vehicle. 変速レバー

gee /dʒi/ EXCLAM 感嘆詞 People sometimes say **gee** to emphasize a reaction or remark. おや [AM 米国英語, INFORMAL くだけた, EMPHASIS 強調] □ *Gee, it's hot.* わあ、暑い.

geese /gis/ **Geese** is the plural of **goose**. goose の複数形

gel /dʒɛl/ (**gels, gelling, gelled**)

The spelling **jell** is usually used for meanings **1** and **2**.

つづりの **jell** は通常 **1** と **2** を意味するのに使われる.

---

1 V-RECIP 相互動詞 If people **gel with** each other, or if two groups of people **gel**, they work well together because their skills and personalities fit together well. うまくやる □ *They have gelled very*

well with the rest of the side. 彼らは他のチームメンバーととても仲良くやっていた。 □ *Their partnership gelled, and scriptwriting for television followed.* 彼らのパートナーシップはうまくいき、テレビ用の脚本の台本も書かれた。 **2** V-I 自動詞 *If a vague shape, thought, or creation* **gels**, *it becomes clearer or more definite.* 具現化する [自動詞] □ *Even if her musicianship has not yet gelled into a satisfying whole, she displays real musicianship.* 解釈がまだ満足のいく統一一体として具現化したものでなかったとしても、彼女は本当の楽才を発揮している。 **3** N-MASS 質量名詞 **Gel** *is a thick, jelly-like substance, especially one used to keep your hair in a particular style.* ゲル

gem /dʒεm/ (**gems**) **1** N-COUNT 可算名詞 A **gem** *is a jewel or stone that is used in jewelry.* 宝石 □ *The mask is formed of a gold-platinum alloy inset with emeralds and other gems.* 仮面はエメラルドなどの宝石をはめ込んだ金と白金の合金で形づくられている。 **2** N-COUNT 可算名詞 *If you describe something or someone as a* **gem**, *you mean that they are especially pleasing, good, or helpful.* 逸品 [INFORMAL くだけた] □ *...a gem of a hotel, Castel Clara.* 珠玉のホテル、カステル・クララ

gen|der /dʒεndər/ (**genders**) **1** N-VAR 可変性名詞 *A person's* **gender** *is the fact that they are male or female.* 性 □ *Women are sometimes denied opportunities solely because of their gender.* 女性は性別だけで機会を奪われることがある。 **2** N-COUNT 可算名詞 *You can refer to all male people or all female people as a particular* **gender**. 性 □ *While her observations may be true about some men, they could really apply to the entire gender.* 彼女の観察は一部の男性については当てはまるかも知れないが、男性全体についてはほとんど当てはまらない。 **3** N-VAR 可変性名詞 *In grammar, the* **gender** *of a noun, pronoun, or adjective is whether it is masculine, feminine, or neuter. A word's gender can affect its form and behavior. In English, only personal pronouns such as "she," reflexive pronouns such as "itself," and possessive determiners such as "his" have gender.* 性 □ *In both Welsh and Irish the word for "moon" is of feminine gender.* ウェールズ語とアイルランド語の両方で「月」は女性名詞だ。

gene /dʒin/ (**genes**) N-COUNT 可算名詞 *A* **gene** *is the part of a cell in a living thing which controls its physical characteristics, growth, and development.* 遺伝子 □ *The gene for asthma has been identified.* ぜんそくの遺伝子が特定された。
→ see Word Web: **gene**

ge|neal|ogy /dʒiniǽlədʒi/ N-UNCOUNT 不可算名詞 **Genealogy** *is the study of the history of families, especially through studying historical documents to discover the relationships between particular people and their families.* 家系学
● **ge|nea|logi|cal** /dʒiniəlɒdʒikəl/ ADJ 形容詞 [ADJ n] 系図の □ *He had engaged in genealogical research on his family shortly before the War.* 彼は戦争直前に自分の家族に関する系図研究に従事した。

gen|era /dʒεnərə/ **Genera** *is the plural of* **genus**. genusの複数形

gen|er|al /dʒεnrəl/ (**generals**) **1** N-COUNT; N-TITLE; N-VOC 可算名詞, 称号名詞, 呼格名詞 *A* **general** *is a high-ranking officer in the armed forces, usually in the army.* 将官 □ *The General's visit to Sarajevo is part of preparations for the deployment of extra troops.* 将軍のサラエボ訪問は、部隊追加配備の準備の一環である。 **2** ADJ 形容詞 *If you talk about the* **general** *situation somewhere or talk about something in* **general** *terms, you are describing the situation as a whole rather than considering its details or exceptions.* 全般的な [ADJ n] □ *The figures present a general decline in employment.* 数値は雇用の全体的な減少を示している。 □ *...a general deterioration in the quality of life.* 生活の質の全般的な低下 ● PHRASE 句 *If you describe something in* **general** *terms, you describe it without giving details.* 概括的に言って **3** ADJ 形容詞 *You use* **general** *to describe several items or activities when there are too many of them or when they are not important enough to mention separately.* 一般的な [ADJ n] □ *$2,500 for software is soon swallowed up in general costs.* ソフトウェアの2500ドルはすぐに一般費用に飲み込まれる。 **4** ADJ 形容詞 *You use* **general** *to describe something that involves or affects most people, or most people in a particular group.* 全般に共通な [ADJ n] □ *The project should raise general awareness about bullying.* プロジェクトはいじめについての一般の意識を高めるはずだ。 **5** ADJ 形容詞 *If you describe something as* **general**, *you mean*

that it is not restricted to any one thing or area. ひとつの場所や物に特定されない [ADJ n] □ *...a general ache radiating from the back of the neck.* 首の後ろから広がる痛み **6** ADJ 形容詞 **General** *is used to describe a person's job, usually as part of their title, to indicate that they have complete responsibility for the administration of an organization or business.* 長官の [BUSINESS 実業] [ADJ n] □ *He joined Sanders Roe, moving on later to become general manager.* 彼はサンダース・ロウに入社し、後に総支配人に昇格した。 **7** → see also **generally** **8** PHRASE 句 *You use* **in general** *to indicate that you are talking about something as a whole, rather than about part of it.* 概して □ *I think we need to improve our educational system in general.* 我々は教育制度全般を改善する必要があると思う。 **9** PHRASE 句 *You say* **in general** *to indicate that you are referring to most people or things in a particular group.* 一般に □ *People in general will support us.* 一般大衆は我々を支持してくれるだろう。

gen|er|al elec|tion (**general elections**) N-COUNT 可算名詞 *In the United States, a* **general election** *is a local, state, or national election where the candidates have been selected by a primary election. Compare* **primary**. 最終選挙 □ *Street raised $10 million during his primary and general election.* ストリートは予備選挙と最終選挙で1000万ドルの資金を集めた。

gen|er|ali|za|tion /dʒεnrəlaizeiʃən/ (**generalizations**) N-VAR 可変性名詞 *A* **generalization** *is a statement that seems to be true in most situations or for most people, but that may not be completely true in all cases.* 一般化 □ *He is making sweeping generalizations to get his point across.* 彼は言いたいことをわかってもらうために大胆な一般化をしている。

gen|er|al|ize /dʒεnrəlaiz/ (**generalizes, generalizing, generalized**) **1** V-I 自動詞 *If you* **generalize**, *you say something that seems to be true in most situations or for most people, but that may not be completely true in all cases.* 一般的に論ずる [自動詞] □ *Critics love to generalize, to formulate trends into which all new work must be fitted, however contradictory.* 批評家は、それがどんなに矛盾していようとも、新作品すべてが当てはまる傾向を一般化し定式化することを好む。 **2** V-T 他動詞 *If you* **generalize** *something such as an idea, you apply it more widely than its original context, as if it was true in many other situations.* 広げて適用する、普遍化する [他動詞] □ *A child first labels the household pet cat as a "cat" and then generalizes this label to other animals that look like it.* 子供はまず家のペットを「猫」と分類し、それからそれと似た他の動物にもこの分類を広げて適用する。

gen|er|al|ized /dʒεnrəlaizd/ **1** ADJ 形容詞 **Generalized** *means involving many different things, rather than one or two specific things.* 全般的な □ *...a generalized discussion about admirable singers.* 立派な歌手についての全般的な論議 **2** ADJ 形容詞 *You use* **generalized** *to describe medical conditions or problems which affect the whole of someone's body, or the whole of a part of their body.* 全身の [MEDICAL 医学の] □ *She experienced an increase in generalized aches and pains.* 彼女は全身的なうずきと痛みの悪化を経験した。

gen|er|al knowl|edge N-UNCOUNT 不可算名詞 **General knowledge** *is knowledge about many different things, as opposed to detailed knowledge about one particular subject.* 一般的な知識 □ *...a general-knowledge quiz show.* 雑学クイズショー

gen|er|al|ly /dʒεnrəli/ **1** ADV 副詞 *You use* **generally** *to give a summary of a situation, activity, or idea without referring to the particular details of it.* 概して □ *University teachers generally have admitted a lack of enthusiasm about their subjects.* 大学の教員は概して専門教科について熱意が足りないことを認めた。 **2** ADV 副詞 *You use* **generally** *to say that something happens or is used on most occasions but not on every occasion.* ふつう □ *As women we generally say and feel too much about these things.* 女性である我々はだいたいこれらについて言い過ぎるし、感じすぎる。 □ *In the diet, it is generally true that the darker the fruit the higher its iron content.* 食べ物においては、果物は色が濃ければ濃いほど鉄分の含有量が高いというのはたいがい正しい。

Word Web — gene

Gregor Mendel* studied the **inheritance** of **traits** in plants. He discovered how plants pass on their physical **characteristics** from **generation** to generation. He **bred** and **cross-bred** seven varieties of pea plants. He showed that each new plant was not just a general blend of its parents. Each characteristic (for example, flower color) is inherited separately. Some characteristics are **dominant** and some are recessive. When dominant and recessive **genes** combine, there is predictable pattern of inheritance. Today we know that genes form long strings called **DNA**.

first generation
second generation
third generation

Gregor Mendel (1822-1884): a scientist.

G

Thesaurus   *generally* また次を参照:

ADV. commonly, mainly, usually **1** **2**

---

gen|er|al prac|ti|tion|er (general practitioners) N-COUNT 可算名詞 A **general practitioner** is the same as a **GP**. GP, 一般開業医 [FORMAL 形式ばった]

gen|er|al pub|lic N-SING-COLL 集合的単数名詞 You can refer to the people in a society as **the general public**, especially when you are contrasting people in general with a small group. 公衆 ❑ *These charities depend on the compassionate feelings and generosity of the general public.* これらの慈善事業は公衆の同情心と寛大さに依存している.

gen|er|al strike (general strikes) N-COUNT 可算名詞 A **general strike** is a situation where most or all of the workers in a country are on strike and are refusing to work. ゼネスト

gen|er|ate /dʒɛnəreɪt/ (generates, generating, generated) **1** V-T 他動詞 To **generate** something means to cause it to begin and develop. 生ずる [他動詞] ❑ *The labor secretary said the reforms would generate new jobs.* 労働長官は, 改革により雇用が創出されるだろうと言った. **2** V-T 他動詞 To **generate** a form of energy or power means to produce it. 発電する [他動詞] ❑ *The company, New England Electric, burns coal to generate power.* その会社, ニューイングランドエレクトリックは石炭を燃やして発電している.
→ see **energy**

gen|era|tion /dʒɛnəreɪʃ°n/ (generations) **1** N-COUNT 可算名詞 A **generation** is all the people in a group or country who are of a similar age, especially when they are considered as having the same experiences or attitudes. 世代 ❑ *...the younger generation of party members.* 若い世代の党員 **2** N-COUNT 可算名詞 A **generation** is the period of time, usually considered to be about thirty years, that it takes for children to grow up and become adults and have children of their own. 一世代 ❑ *Within a generation, flight has become the method used by many travelers.* 一世代の間に, 空の旅は多くの旅行者に利用される方法になった. **3** N-COUNT 可算名詞 You can use **generation** to refer to a stage of development in the design and manufacture of machines or equipment. 世代 [N 'of' n] ❑ *...a new generation of Apple computers.* 新世代のアップルコンピュータ **4** ADJ 形容詞 **Generation** is used to indicate how long members of your family have had a particular nationality. For example, second generation means that you were born in the country you live in, but your parents were not. 世 [ord ADJ n] ❑ *...second-generation Jamaicans in New York.* ニューヨークのジャマイカ系二世
→ see **gene**

gen|era|tor /dʒɛnəreɪtər/ (generators) **1** N-COUNT 可算名詞 A **generator** is a machine which produces electricity. 発電機 ❑ *The house is far from water mains and electricity and relies on its own generators.* その家は水道や電気から遠く, 独自の発電機に頼っている. **2** N-COUNT 可算名詞 A **generator** of something is a person, organization, product, or situation which produces it or causes it to happen. 生む人, 生むもの ❑ *The company has been a very good cash generator.* その会社はずいぶんともうけてきた.
→ see **electricity**

gen|er|ic /dʒɪnɛrɪk/ (generics) **1** ADJ 形容詞 You use **generic** to describe something that relates or refers to a whole class of similar things. 属に特有の ❑ *Parmesan is a generic term used to describe a family of hard Italian cheeses.* パルメザンはイタリアの硬いチーズ各種の総称である. **2** ADJ 形容詞 A **generic** drug or other product is one that does not have a trademark and that is known by a general name, rather than the manufacturer's name. 商標登録されていない ❑ *Doctors sometimes prescribe cheaper generic drugs instead of more expensive brand names.* 医師は高価なブランドの代わりに安価な商標登録されていない薬を処方することもある. ● N-COUNT 可算名詞 **Generic** is also a noun. 一般名 ❑ *The program saved $11 million in 1988 by substituting generics for brand-name drugs.* そのプログラムは, 1988年, ブランド薬品の代わりに一般品を使用することで1100万ドルを節約した.

gen|er|os|ity /dʒɛnərɒsɪti/ N-UNCOUNT 不可算名詞 If you refer to someone's **generosity**, you mean that they are generous, especially in doing or giving more than is usual or expected. 気前のよさ ❑ *There are stories about his generosity, the massive amounts of money he gave to charities.* 彼の気前のよさ, 慈善事業に寄付したばくだいなお金については逸話がある.

gen|er|ous /dʒɛnərəs/ **1** ADJ 形容詞 A **generous** person gives more of something, especially money, than is usual or expected. 気前のよい ❑ *Dietler is generous with his time and money.* ディエトラーは自分の時間とお金を物惜しみなく与える. ● **gen|er|ous|ly** ADV 副詞 [ADV with v] 気前よく ❑ *We would like to thank all the judges who gave so generously of their time.* 惜しみなく時間を割いてくださった裁判官の皆様に感謝の意を表します. **2** ADJ 形容詞 A **generous** person is friendly, helpful, and willing to see the good qualities in someone or something. 寛大な ❑ *He was always generous in sharing*

his enormous knowledge. 彼はいつも膨大な知識を人と分かち合う雅量を持っていた. ● **gen|er|ous|ly** ADV 副詞 [ADV with v] 寛大にも ❑ *The students generously gave them instruction in social responsibility.* 学生たちは彼らに社会責任をたっぷり教授した. **3** ADJ 形容詞 A **generous** amount of something is much larger than is usual or necessary. たくさんな ❑ *He should be able to keep his room tidy with the generous amount of storage space.* 収納スペースはたっぷりあるのだから, 彼は部屋を片付けておけるはずだ. ● **gen|er|ous|ly** ADV 副詞 たっぷりと ❑ *Season the steaks generously with salt and pepper.* ステーキにたっぷりの塩とこしょうで味付けする.

Thesaurus   *generous* また次を参照:

ADJ. charitable, kind, unselfish; (ant.) mean, selfish, stingy **1** **2**
abundant, overflowing; (ant.) meager **3**

---

ge|net|ic /dʒɪnɛtɪk/ ADJ 形容詞 You use **genetic** to describe something that is concerned with genetics or with genes. 遺伝子の ❑ *Cystic fibrosis is the most common fatal genetic disease in the United States.* 嚢 (のう) 胞性線維症は米国で最もよくみられる致命的な遺伝的疾患である. ● **ge|net|ical|ly** /dʒɪnɛtɪkli/ ADV 副詞 遺伝的に ❑ *Some people are genetically predisposed to diabetes.* 遺伝的に糖尿病にかかりやすい人もいる.

ge|net|ical|ly modi|fied ADJ 形容詞 **Genetically modified** plants and animals have had one or more genes changed, for example so that they resist pests and diseases better. **Genetically modified** food contains ingredients made from genetically modified plants or animals. The abbreviation **GM** is often used. 遺伝子組み換えが行われた ❑ *Top supermarkets are to ban many genetically modified foods.* 一流スーパーマーケットは遺伝子操作された食品の多くを売らない方針だ.

ge|net|ic en|gi|neer|ing N-UNCOUNT 不可算名詞 **Genetic engineering** is the science or activity of changing the genetic structure of an animal, plant, or other organism in order to make it stronger or more suitable for a particular purpose. 遺伝子工学 ❑ *Scientists have used genetic engineering to protect tomatoes against the effects of freezing.* 科学者たちは遺伝子組み換え技術を使用して氷結の影響からトマトを保護した.
→ see **clone**

ge|net|ics /dʒɪnɛtɪks/ N-UNCOUNT 不可算名詞 **Genetics** is the study of heredity and how qualities and characteristics are passed on from one generation to another by means of genes. 遺伝学 ❑ *Genetics is also bringing about dramatic changes in our understanding of cancer.* 遺伝学はがんの理解に劇的な変化ももたらしている.

gen|ial /dʒiːnjəl/ ADJ 形容詞 Someone who is **genial** is kind and friendly. 親切な [APPROVAL 賛成] ❑ *Bob was always genial and welcoming.* ボブはいつも親切で友好的だった. ● **geni|al|ly** ADV 副詞 親切に ❑ *"If you don't mind," Mrs. Dambar said genially.* 「よろしかったら」とダンバー夫人はにこやかに言った. ● **geni|al|ity** /dʒiːniælɪti/ N-UNCOUNT 不可算名詞 親切 ❑ *He soon recovered his habitual geniality.* 彼はすぐにいつものにこやかさを取り戻した.

geni|tal /dʒɛnɪt°l/ (genitals) **1** N-PLURAL 複数名詞 Someone's **genitals** are their external sexual organs. 生殖器 ❑ *Without thinking, Neil cupped his hands over his genitals.* ニールは無意識に性器に手をかぶせた. **2** ADJ 形容詞 **Genital** means relating to a person's external sexual organs. 生殖の [ADJ n] ❑ *Wear loose clothing in the genital area.* 性器あたりがゆったりした衣服を着用する.

ge|ni|us /dʒiːnjəs/ (geniuses) **1** N-UNCOUNT 不可算名詞 **Genius** is very great ability or skill in a particular subject or activity. 特殊な才能 ❑ *This is the mark of her real genius as a designer.* これは彼女のデザイナーとしての真に非凡な才能を示すものである. **2** N-COUNT 可算名詞 A **genius** is a highly talented, creative, or intelligent person. 天才 ❑ *Chaplin was not just a genius, he was among the most influential figures in film history.* チャップリンは単に天才であっただけではなく, 映画史で最も影響力のある人物の1人だった.

Word Link   *cide* ≈ *killing : geno**cide**, homi**cide**, pesti**cide***

geno|cide /dʒɛnəsaɪd/ N-UNCOUNT 不可算名詞 **Genocide** is the deliberate murder of a whole community or race. 大虐殺 ❑ *They have alleged that acts of genocide and torture were carried out.* 彼らは大虐殺と拷問行為が行われたと主張した.

gen|re /ʒɒnrə/ (genres) N-COUNT 可算名詞 A **genre** is a particular type of literature, painting, music, film, or other art form which people consider as a class because it has special characteristics. ジャンル [FORMAL 形式ばった] ❑ *...his love of films and novels in the horror genre.* ホラージャンルの映画と小説に対する彼の情熱
→ see Word Web: **genre**
→ see **fantasy**

Word Web   genre

Each of the arts includes a variety of types called **genre**. The four basic types of **literature** are **fiction**, nonfiction, **poetry**, and **drama**. In painting, some of the special areas are **realism**, expressionism, and Cubism. In music, they include **classical**, **jazz**, and **popular** forms. Each genre contains several subdivisions. For example, popular music takes in country and western, **rap music**, and **rock**. Modern movie-making has produced a wide variety of genres. These include **horror films**, **comedies**, **action movies**, film noir, and **westerns**. Some artists don't like working within just one genre.

gent /dʒɛnt/ (**gents**) ■ N-COUNT 可算名詞 **Gent** is an informal and old-fashioned word for **gentleman**. 紳士 ❑ *Mr. Blake was a gent. He knew how to behave.* ブレーク氏は紳士だった. ふるまい方を知っていた. ■ N-VOC 呼格名詞 **Gents** is used when addressing men in an informal, humorous way, especially in the expression "ladies and gents." 皆さん [HUMOROUS, INFORMAL ユーモアのある, くだけた] ❑ *Don't be left standing, ladies and gents, while a bargain slips past your eyes.* 皆さん, 突っ立ったままだと, お買い得品はあっという間になくなってしまいますよ.

gen|teel /dʒɛntiːl/ ■ ADJ 形容詞 A **genteel** person is respectable and well-mannered, and comes or seems to come from a high social class. 上品な ❑ *It was a place to which genteel families came in search of health and quiet.* それは上流社会の家族が健康と静寂を求めて来る場所だった. ■ ADJ 形容詞 A **genteel** place or area is quiet and traditional, but may also be old-fashioned and dull. 上品ぶった ❑ *...the genteel towns of Winchester and Chichester.* ウィンチェスターとチチェスターの上品ぶった町

gen|tle /dʒɛntəl/ (**gentler**, **gentlest**) ■ ADJ 形容詞 Someone who is **gentle** is kind, mild, and calm. 温和な ❑ *My son was a quiet and gentle man who liked sports and enjoyed life.* 私の息子は, スポーツを好む無口で温和な子で, 人生を楽しみました. ● **gen|tly** ADV 副詞 [ADV with v] 優しく ❑ *She smiled gently at him.* 彼女は彼に優しくほほえみかけた. ● **gen|tle|ness** N-UNCOUNT 不可算名詞 ❑ *...the gentleness with which she treated her pregnant mother.* 彼女が妊娠した母親に対して見せた優しさ ■ ADJ 形容詞 **Gentle** actions or movements are performed in a calm and controlled manner, with little force. もの静かな ❑ *...a gentle game of tennis.* 穏やかなテニスの試合 ● **gen|tly** ADV 副詞 穏やかに ❑ *Patrick took her gently by the arm and led her to a chair.* パトリックは優しく彼女の腕をとって椅子まで導いた. ■ ADJ 形容詞 A **gentle** slope or curve is not steep or severe. ゆるやかな ❑ *...gentle, rolling meadows.* ゆるやかに起伏する牧草地 ● **gen|tly** ADV 副詞 ゆるやかに ❑ *With its gently rolling hills it looks like Tuscany.* ゆるやかに起伏する丘はトスカーナのようだ. ■ ADJ 形容詞 A **gentle** heat is a fairly low heat. 強くない ❑ *Cook for 30 minutes over a gentle heat.* とろ火で30分間煮ます. ● **gen|tly** ADV 副詞 [ADV with v] とろ火で ❑ *Add the onion and cook gently for about 5 minutes.* 玉ねぎを加えて約5分とろ火で料理する.

gentle|man /dʒɛntəlmən/ (**gentlemen**) ■ N-COUNT 可算名詞 If you say that a man is a **gentleman**, you mean he is polite and educated, and can be trusted. 紳士 ❑ *He was always such a gentleman.* 彼はいつもとても紳士だった. ■ N-COUNT 可算名詞 A **gentleman** is a man from a family of high social standing. 家柄のよい人 ❑ *...this wonderful portrait of English gentleman Joseph Greenway.* 英国紳士ジョーゼフ・グリーンウェイのこのすばらしい肖像 ■ N-COUNT 可算名詞; N-VOC 呼格名詞 You can address men as **gentlemen**, or refer politely to them as **gentlemen**. 皆さん [POLITENESS 丁寧さ] ❑ *This way, please, ladies and gentlemen.* 皆さん, どうぞ, こちらです. ❑ *It seems this gentleman was waiting for the doctor.* この紳士は医者を待っていたようだ.

genu|ine /dʒɛnyuɪn/ ■ ADJ 形容詞 **Genuine** is used to describe people and things that are exactly what they appear to be, and are not false or an imitation. 本物の ❑ *There was a risk of genuine refugees being returned to Vietnam.* 正真正銘の難民がベトナムに帰される危険があった. ❑ *...genuine leather.* 本革 ■ ADJ 形容詞 **Genuine** refers to things such as emotions that are real and not pretended. 心からの ❑ *If this offer is genuine, I will gladly accept it.* この申し出が本当なら, よろこんで引き受けます. ● **genu|ine|ly** ADV 副詞 心から ❑ *He was genuinely surprised.* 彼は心底おどろいた. ■ ADJ 形容詞 If you describe a person as **genuine**, you approve of them because they are honest, truthful, and sincere in the way they live and in their relationships with other people. 誠実な [APPROVAL 賛成] ❑ *She is very caring and very genuine.* 彼女はとても思いやりがあり, 大変誠実だ.

Thesaurus   *genuine* また次を参照:

ADJ.   actual, original, real, true; (*ant.*) bogus, fake ■ ■
honest, open, sincere, true, valid; (*ant.*) dishonest,
insincere ■

ge|nus /dʒiːnəs/ (**genera** /dʒɛnərə/) N-COUNT 可算名詞 A **genus** is a class of similar things, especially a group of animals or plants that includes several closely related species. (生物分類上の) 属 [TECHNICAL 技術的] ❑ *...a genus of plants called Sinningia.* シンニンギアと呼ばれる植物属

geo|graphi|cal /dʒiːəgræfɪkəl/

The form **geographic** /dʒiːəgræfɪk/ is also used.

geographic /dʒiːəgræfɪk/ 形も使われる.

ADJ 形容詞 **Geographical** or **geographic** means concerned with or relating to geography. 地理的な ❑ *Its geographical location stimulated overseas mercantile enterprise.* 地理的な位置が海外貿易企業を活性化させた. ● **geo|graphi|cal|ly** /dʒiːəgræfɪkli/ ADV 副詞 地理的に ❑ *It is geographically more diverse than any other continent.* それは他のどの大陸よりも地理的な特徴に富んでいる.

ge|og|ra|phy /dʒiɒgrəfi/ ■ N-UNCOUNT 不可算名詞 **Geography** is the study of the countries of the world and of such things as the land, seas, climate, towns, and population. 地理学 ■ N-UNCOUNT 不可算名詞 The **geography** of a place is the way that features such as rivers, mountains, towns, or streets are arranged within it. 地形 ❑ *...policemen who knew the local geography.* 地元の様子に詳しかった警官

geo|logi|cal /dʒiːəlɒdʒɪkəl/ ADJ 形容詞 **Geological** means relating to geology. 地質学の ❑ *With geological maps, books, and atlases you can find out all the proven sites of precious minerals.* 地質学の地図や本, 地図帳などから, 重要鉱物の調査済みの場所をすべて見つけ出せる.

Word Link   logy, ology ≈ study of : anthropology, biology, geology

ge|ol|ogy /dʒiɒlədʒi/ ■ N-UNCOUNT 不可算名詞 **Geology** is the study of the Earth's structure, surface, and origins. 地質学 ❑ *He was visiting professor of geology at the University of Georgia.* 彼はジョージア大学の地質学教授を訪ねるところだった. ● **ge|ol|ogist** (**geologists**) N-COUNT 可算名詞 地質学者 ❑ *Geologists have studied the way that heat flows from the earth.* 地質学者たちはどのように地球から熱が放出されるかを調べている. ■ N-UNCOUNT 不可算名詞 The **geology** of an area is the structure of its land, together with the types of rocks and minerals that exist within it. 地質 ❑ *...the geology of Asia.* アジアの地質

geo|met|ric /dʒiːəmɛtrɪk/

The form **geometrical** /dʒiːəmɛtrɪkəl/ is also used.

geometrical /dʒiːəmɛtrɪkəl/形も使われる.

■ ADJ 形容詞 **Geometric** or **geometrical** patterns or shapes consist of regular shapes or lines. 幾何学的な ❑ *Geometric designs were popular wall decorations in the 14th century.* 14世紀に幾何学模様の壁の装飾がはやった. ■ ADJ 形容詞 **Geometric** or **geometrical** means relating to or involving the principles of geometry. 幾何学の ❑ *Euclid was trying to convey his idea of a geometrical point.* ユークリッドは幾何学上の点についての自分の考えを伝えようとしていた.

ge|om|etry /dʒiɒmɪtri/ ■ N-UNCOUNT 不可算名詞 **Geometry** is the branch of mathematics concerned with the properties and relationships of lines, angles, curves, and shapes. 幾何学 ❑ *...the very ordered way in which mathematics and geometry describe nature.* 数学と幾何学が自然を表現する極めて秩序だった方式 ■ N-UNCOUNT 不可算名詞 The **geometry** of an object is its shape or the relationship of its parts to each other. 形状, 配置 ❑ *...the geometry of the curved roof.* カーブした屋根の形状
→ see **mathematics**

Geor|gian /dʒɔːrdʒən/ ADJ 形容詞 **Georgian** means belonging to or connected with Britain in the eighteenth and early nineteenth centuries, during the reigns of King George I to King George IV. (英国の) ジョージ王朝時代の (18世紀から19世紀の始め頃) の ❑ *...the restoration of his Georgian house.* ジョージ王朝様式の家の修復

Word Link   iatr ≈ healing : geriatric, pediatrics, psychiatrist

geri|at|ric /dʒɛriætrɪk/ (**geriatrics**) ■ ADJ 形容詞 **Geriatric**

is used to describe things relating to the illnesses and medical care of old people. 老人病の [MEDICAL 医学の] [ADJ n] ❏ *There is a question mark over the future of geriatric care.* 高齢者看護の将来は不透明だ. ② N-COUNT 可算名詞 If you describe someone as a **geriatric**, you are implying that they are old and that their mental or physical condition is poor. This use could cause offense. 老いぼれ [DISAPPROVAL 不賛成] ❏ *He will complain about having to spend time with such a boring bunch of geriatrics.* 彼は退屈な老いぼれたちと過ごさねばならなかったことについて文句を言うだろう.

germ /dʒɜːrm/ (**germs**) ❶ N-COUNT 可算名詞 A **germ** is a very small organism that causes disease. 細菌, 病原菌 ❏ *Chlorine is widely used to kill germs.* 塩素は殺菌のため広く使用されている. ② N-SING 単数形 The **germ** of something such as an idea is something which developed or might develop into that thing. (考えなどの) 芽, 初期段階 ❏ *This was the germ of a book.* これが本の初期段階だった.
→ see **medicine**, **spice**

ger|mi|nate /ˈdʒɜːrmɪneɪt/ (**germinates, germinating, germinated**) ❶ V-T/V-I 他動詞/自動詞 If a seed **germinates** or if it **is germinated**, it starts to grow. 発芽させる [他動詞], (種が) 芽を出す [自動詞] ❏ *Some seed varieties germinate fast, so check every day or so.* 種の品種によっては早く発芽するものがあるので, 日に一度くらいチェックしてください. ● **ger|mi|na|tion** /ˌdʒɜːrmɪˈneɪʃ°n/ N-UNCOUNT 不可算名詞 [usu with supp] 発芽 ❏ *The poor germination of your seed could be because the soil was too cold.* あなたの種があまり発芽しなかったのは土が冷たすぎたせいかもしれない. ② V-I 自動詞 If an idea, plan, or feeling **germinates**, it comes into existence and begins to develop. (考えや感情が) 生まれる ❏ *...a big book that was germinating in his mind.* 彼の頭に浮かびつつある大きな本.
→ see **tree**

ger|und /ˈdʒɛrənd/ (**gerunds**) N-COUNT 可算名詞 A **gerund** is a noun formed from a verb which refers to an action, process, or state. In English, gerunds end in "-ing," for example "running" and "thinking." 動名詞

ges|ture /ˈdʒɛstʃər/ (**gestures, gesturing, gestured**) ❶ N-COUNT 可算名詞 A **gesture** is a movement that you make with a part of your body, especially your hands, to express emotion or information. 身ぶり ❏ *Sarah made a menacing gesture with her fist.* サラは握りこぶしで威嚇する身ぶりをした. ② N-COUNT 可算名詞 A **gesture** is something that you say or do in order to express your attitude or intentions, often something that you know will not have much effect. 意思表示, みせかけ ❏ *He questioned the government's commitment to peace and called on it to make a gesture of good will.* 彼は政府の平和への公約を疑問視し, 政府に誠意を見せよう求めた. ③ V-I 自動詞 If you **gesture**, you use movements of your hands or head in order to tell someone something or draw their attention to something. 手ぶりで示す, 頭の動きで示す ❏ *I gestured toward the boathouse, and he looked inside.* わたしが舟小屋の方を指し示すと, 彼は中をのぞいた.

---

get

❶ CHANGING, CAUSING, MOVING, OR REACHING
❷ OBTAINING, RECEIVING, OR CATCHING
❸ PHRASES AND PHRASAL VERBS

---

❶ **get** /ɡɛt/ (**gets, getting, got, gotten** or **got**)

In most of its uses **get** is a fairly informal word.

get はその用法のほとんどでかなりくだけた語である.

❶ V-LINK 連結動詞 You use **get** with adjectives to mean "become." For example, if someone **gets cold**, they become cold, and if they **get angry**, they become angry. なる ❏ *The boys were getting bored.* その男の子たちは退屈し始めていた. ❏ *From here on, it can only get better.* ここからはよくなって行くだけだよ. ② V-LINK 連結動詞 **Get** is used with expressions referring to states or situations. For example, to **get into trouble** means to start being in trouble. (一の状態に) なる ❏ *Half the pleasure of an evening out is getting ready.* 夜出かけるときの楽しみの半分は準備をするところにある. ❏ *Perhaps I shouldn't say that – I might get into trouble.* 多分こんな事を言うべきじゃないんだろうけど. 面倒に巻き込まれるかもしれない. ③ V-T 他動詞 To **get** someone or something into a particular state or situation means to cause them to be in it. (一の状態に) する ❏ *I don't know if I can get it clean.* 汚れが落とせるかなあ. ❏ *Brian will get them out of trouble.* ブライアンが彼らを助けてくれるよ. ④ V-T 他動詞 If you **get** someone **to** do something, you cause them to do it by asking, persuading, or telling them to do it. (依頼や説得, 命令で人に) させる ❏ *...a long campaign to get U.S. politicians to take the AIDS epidemic more seriously.* 米国の政治家にもっとエイズ禍を真剣に受け止めさせようとする長期運動 ⑤ V-T 他動詞 If you **get** something done, you cause it to be done. (人が一を一) してもらう, させる ❏ *I might benefit from getting my teeth fixed.* 歯の治療をすれ

ば楽になるかもしれない. ⑥ V-I 自動詞 To **get** somewhere means to move there. 動く ❏ *I got off the bed and opened the door.* わたしはベッドから起き上がり, ドアを開けた. ❏ *How can I get past her without her seeing me?* どうやって彼女に見られずにわたしがそばを通れるというの? ⑦ V-I 自動詞 When you **get** to a place, you arrive there. 着く ❏ *Generally I get to work at 9:30 a.m.* 普通, わたしは午前9時半に職場に着く. ⑧ V-T 他動詞 To **get** something or someone into a place or position means to cause them to move there. 動かす, 持って行く ❏ *Mack got his wallet out.* マックは財布を取り出した. ❏ *Go and get your coat on.* コートを着てきなさい. ⑨ AUX 助動詞 **Get** is often used in place of "be" as an auxiliary verb to form passives. be の代わりに用いて受身形を作る ❏ *A pane of glass got broken.* 窓ガラスが割れた. ⑩ V-T 他動詞 If you **get to** do something, you eventually or gradually reach a stage at which you do it. (最終的にまたは次第に一の状態に) たどり着く ❏ *No one could figure out how he got to be so wealthy.* 彼がどうやってあんなに裕福になったか誰も分からない. ⑪ V-T 他動詞 If you **get to** do something, you manage to do it or have the opportunity to do it. できるようになる, する機会を得る ❏ *How do these people get to be the bosses of major companies?* この人々がどうやって大企業の経営者になれるのか? ❏ *Do you get to see him often?* 最近, 彼に会う機会がよくある? ⑫ V-T 他動詞 You can use **get** in expressions like **get moving, get going**, and **get working** when you want to tell people to begin moving, going, or working quickly. (行動を) 始める ❏ *I aim to be at the lake before dawn, so let's get moving.* 夜明け前には湖に到着する目標だから, そろそろ行こう. ⑬ V-I 自動詞 If you **get to** a particular stage in your life or in something you are doing, you reach that stage. (状態や地点に) 達する ❏ *We haven't gotten to the stage of a full-scale military conflict.* わたしたちはまだ全面的な軍事衝突の段階には至っていない. ❏ *It got to the point where I was so ill I was waiting to die.* わたしの病気はとてもひどく, 死を待つだけの状態になった. ⑭ V-T/V-I 他動詞/自動詞 You can use **get** to talk about the progress that you are making. For example, if you say that you **are getting somewhere**, you mean that you are making progress, and if you say that something **won't get** you **anywhere**, you mean it will not help you to progress at all. 進展させる [他動詞], 進展する [自動詞] ❏ *Radical factions say the talks are getting nowhere and they want to withdraw.* 急進派は交渉にまったく進展がなく手を引きたいと言っている. ❏ *This bout of self-pity was getting me nowhere.* こんな具合に自己れんびんにとらわれて私はどうしようもなかった. ⑮ V-LINK 連結動詞 When it **gets to be** a particular time, it is that time. If **it is getting toward** a particular time, it is approaching that time. (時間に) なる, 近づく ❏ *It got to be after 1 a.m. and I was exhausted.* 時間は午前1時を過ぎており, わたしは疲れ切っていた. ❏ *It was getting toward evening when we got back.* わたしたちが戻ったのは夕方近くだった. ⑯ V-I 自動詞 If something that has continued for some time **gets to** you, it starts causing you to suffer. 苦痛になる ❏ *That's the first time I lost my cool in 20 years in this job. This whole thing's getting to me.* この仕事に従事している20年でわたしが平静を失ったのはあれが初めてだ. この件全体がだんだん苦痛になってきている.

❷ **get** /ɡɛt/ (**gets, getting, got, gotten** or **got**) ❶ V-T 他動詞 If you **get** something that you want or need, you obtain it. 手に入れる ❏ *I got a job at the sawmill.* 製材工場での仕事が決まった. ② V-T 他動詞 If you **get** something, you receive it or are given it. 受け取る ❏ *I'm getting a bike for my birthday.* ぼく, 誕生日に自転車をもらうんだ. ❏ *He gets a lot of letters from women.* 彼はたくさんの女性から手紙を受け取る. ③ V-T 他動詞 If you **get** someone or something, you go and bring them to a particular place. 連れてくる, 取ってくる ❏ *I came down this morning to get the newspaper.* 今朝, わたしは新聞を取りに下りてきた. ❏ *Go and get me a large brandy.* ブランデー, 大きいの買ってきて. ④ V-T 他動詞 If you **get** a particular result, you obtain it from some action that you take, or from a calculation or experiment. (結果を) 得る ❏ *What do you get if you multiply six by nine?* 6掛ける9は何になる? ⑤ V-T 他動詞 If you **get** a particular price for something that you sell, you obtain that amount of money by selling it. (一の値段で) 売る ❏ *He can't get a good price for his crops.* 彼の作物はよい値では売れないだろう. ⑥ V-T 他動詞 If you **get** the time or opportunity to do something, you have the time or opportunity to do it. (時間や機会を) 持つ ❏ *You get time to think in prison.* 刑務所では考える時間ができる. ⑦ V-T 他動詞 If you **get** an idea, impression, or feeling, you begin to have that idea, impression, or feeling as you learn or understand more about something. (アイデアを) 思いつく, (印象を) 受ける ❏ *I get the feeling that you're not the man.* わたしはあなたが正直な人のような気がするの. ⑧ V-T 他動詞 If you **get** a feeling or benefit from an activity or experience, the activity or experience gives you that feeling or benefit. (活動や経験から感情や利益を) 受ける ❏ *Charles got a shock when he saw him.* チャールズは彼を見てショックを受けた. ❏ *She gets enormous pleasure out of working freelance.* 彼女はフリーランスの仕事をとても楽しんでいる. ⑨ V-T 他動詞 If you **get** a look, view, or glimpse of something, you manage to see it. (視野などを) 確保する ❏ *Young men climbed on buses and fences to get a better view.* 若者たちはよく見えるようにバスやフェンスに登った. ⑩ V-T 他動詞 If you **get** a joke or **get** the point of something that is said,

you understand it. (冗談や要点を) 理解する □ *Did you get that joke, Ann? I'll explain later.* アン、あの冗談分かった？後で説明してあげるよ。 **11** V-T 他動詞 If you **get** an illness or disease, you become ill with it. (病気に) なる □ *When I was five I got measles.* わたしは5歳の時にはしかにかかった。 **12** V-T 他動詞 When you **get** a train, bus, plane, or boat, you leave a place on a particular train, bus, plane, or boat. (乗り物に) 乗る □ *We had to get a dollar to get the bus.* バスの料金は1ドルだろう。 **13** → see also **got**

Thesaurus		*get* また次を参照:
V-LINK.	become ❶ **1**	
V.	bring, collect, pick up ❷ **3**	
	know, sense ❷ **7**	

❸ **get** /gɛt/ (gets, getting, got, gotten or got) **1** PHRASE 句 You can say that something is, for example, **as good as you can get** to mean that it is as good as it is possible for that thing to be. この上なく素晴らしい/小さい □ *Consort has a population of 714 and is about as rural and isolated as you can get.* コンソートの人口は714人。そしてこれ以上ないほどの田舎で孤立している。 □ *...the diet that is as near to perfect as you can get it.* 食べ物の中で最も完璧に近いもの **2** PHRASE 句 If you say **you can't get away from** something or **there is no getting away from** something, you are emphasizing that it is true, even though people might prefer it not to be true. 逃れようのない (事実) [INFORMAL くだけた, EMPHASIS 強調] □ *There is no getting away from the fact that he is on the left of the party.* 彼が党の中でも左寄りであるのは逃れようのない事実だ。 **3** PHRASE 句 If you **get away from it all**, you have a holiday in a place that is very different from where you normally live and work. 日常のすべてから開放される □ *...the ravishing island of Ischia, where rich Italians get away from it all.* 裕福なイタリア人が日常のわずらわしさから逃れる魅惑の島、イスキア島 **4** PHRASE 句 You can use **you get** instead of "there is" or "there are" to say that something exists, happens, or can be experienced. (事態や状況が) 存在する、起きる [SPOKEN 口語] □ *That's where you get some differences of opinion.* それは意見がさまざまに分かれるところだ。

▶ **get across** PHRASAL VERB 句動詞 When an idea **gets across** or when you **get** it **across**, you succeed in making other people understand it. (考えを) 理解させる □ *Officers felt their point of view was not getting across to the generals.* 将校たちは自分たちの考え方が軍司令官たちに理解されていないのを感じとった。

▶ **get along** PHRASAL VERB 句動詞 If you **get along with** someone, you have a friendly relationship with them. You can also say that two people **get along**. 仲良くする □ *It's impossible to get along with him.* 彼とうまくやっていくのは無理だよ。

▶ **get around** **1** PHRASAL VERB 句動詞 To **get around** a problem or difficulty means to overcome it. (問題や困難を) 克服する □ *None of these countries has found a way yet to get around the problem of the polarization of wealth.* これらのどの国も、富の偏りという問題の解決策をまだ見出していない。 **2** PHRASAL VERB 句動詞 If you **get around** a rule or law, you find a way of doing something that the rule or law is intended to prevent, without actually breaking it. (法律や規則を) くぐり抜ける □ *Although tobacco ads are prohibited, companies get around the ban by sponsoring music shows.* たばこの広告は禁止されているが、企業は音楽ショーのスポンサーになることで禁止令をかいくぐっている。 **3** PHRASAL VERB 句動詞 If news **gets around**, it becomes well known as a result of being told to lots of people. (ニュースが口伝えで) 広まる □ *They threw him out because word got around that he was taking drugs.* 彼が麻薬をやっているといううわさが広がり、彼らは彼を追い出した。 **4** PHRASAL VERB 句動詞 If you **get around** someone, you persuade them to allow you to do or have something by pleasing them or flattering them. うまくはやして) うまく説き伏せる □ *Max could always get around her.* マックスはいつも彼女をうまく説き伏せられた。 **5** PHRASAL VERB 句動詞 If you **get around**, you visit a lot of different places as part of your way of life. あちこち訪れる □ *He claimed to be a journalist, and he got around.* 彼はジャーナリストと自称し、あちこちを訪れた。 **6** PHRASAL VERB 句動詞 The way that someone **gets around** is the way they walk or go from one place to another. 歩き回る □ *It is difficult for Gail to get around since she broke her leg.* ゲイルは足を骨折したので歩き回るのが難しい。

▶ **get around to** PHRASAL VERB 句動詞 When you **get around to** doing something that you have delayed doing or have been too busy to do, you finally do it. やっとーに取りかかる □ *I said I would write to you, but as usual I never got around to it.* ぼくはきみに手紙を書くって言ったけど、例のごとくとてもそこまで手が回らなかったんだ。

▶ **get at** **1** PHRASAL VERB 句動詞 To **get at** something means to succeed in reaching it. ーに届く □ *A goat was standing up against a tree on its hind legs, trying to get at the leaves.* ヤギが葉っぱに届くよう木に向かって後足で立ち上がっていた。 **2** PHRASAL VERB 句動詞 If you **get at** the truth about something, you succeed in discovering it. (真実を) 見いだす □ *We want to get at the truth. Who killed him? And why?* わたしたちは真実を見つけ出したいのだ。誰が彼を殺したか。そしてなぜ。 **3** PHRASAL VERB 句動詞 If you ask someone what

they **are getting at**, you are asking them to explain what they mean, usually because you think that they are being unpleasant or are suggesting something that is untrue. ーを言おうとする、ほのめかす □ *"What are you getting at now?" demanded Rick.* 「今度は何が言いたいの？」とリックが詰問した。

▶ **get away** **1** PHRASAL VERB 句動詞 If you **get away**, you succeed in leaving a place or a person's company. (場所や仕事を) 離れる □ *She'd gladly have gone anywhere to get away from the city.* 彼女はその都市を離れるためならどこへでも喜んで行っただろう。 **2** PHRASAL VERB 句動詞 If you **get away**, you go away for a period of time in order to have a vacation. 休暇を取る □ *He is too busy to get away.* 彼は忙し過ぎて休暇が取れない。 **3** PHRASAL VERB 句動詞 When someone or something **gets away**, or when you **get** them **away**, they escape. 逃れる □ *Dr. Dunn was apparently trying to get away when he was shot.* ダン博士はどうやら撃たれた時に逃げようとしていたらしい。

▶ **get away with** PHRASAL VERB 句動詞 If you **get away with** doing something wrong or risky, you do not suffer any punishment or other bad consequences because of it. (悪い事をしたにもかかわらず) 罰を受けずに済む □ *The criminals know how to play the system and get away with it.* 犯罪者は誰にも見つからずシステムに細工をする方法を知っている。

▶ **get back** **1** PHRASAL VERB 句動詞 If someone or something **gets back** to a state they were in before, they are then in that state again. (ーの状態に) 戻る □ *Then life started to get back to normal.* そして生活はいつもの状態に戻り始めた。 **2** PHRASAL VERB 句動詞 If you **get back** to a subject that you were talking about before, you start talking about it again. (話を) 戻す □ *It wasn't until we sat down to eat that we got back to the subject of Tom Halliday.* わたしたちが再びトム・ハリデーの話を始めたのは食事の席についてからだった。 **3** PHRASAL VERB 句動詞 If you **get** something **back** after you have lost it or after it has been taken from you, you then have it again. 取り戻す □ *You have 14 days in which you can cancel the contract and get your money back.* 14日以内なら契約を解除し、払い戻しを受けることができます。

▶ **get back to** **1** PHRASAL VERB 句動詞 If you **get back to** an activity, you start doing it again after you have stopped doing it. 再開する □ *I think I ought to get back to work.* わたしは仕事を再開すべきだろう。 **2** PHRASAL VERB 句動詞 If you **get back to** someone, you contact them again after a short period of time, often by telephone. 再度連絡する □ *We'll get back to you as soon as possible.* できるだけ早く連絡します。

▶ **get by** PHRASAL VERB 句動詞 If you can **get by** with what you have, you can manage to live or do things in a satisfactory way. なんとかやっていく □ *I'm a survivor. I'll get by.* わたしは逆境に強いの。なんとかやっていくわ。

▶ **get down** **1** PHRASAL VERB 句動詞 If something **gets** you **down**, it makes you unhappy. がっかりさせる □ *At times when my work gets me down, I like to fantasize about being a farmer.* わたしは仕事で落ち込んだとき、農場主の自分を空想するのが好きだ。 **2** PHRASAL VERB 句動詞 If you **get down**, you lower your body until you are sitting, kneeling, or lying on the ground. かがむ、体を伏せる □ *"Get down!" she yelled. "Somebody's shooting!"* 「伏せて！」と彼女が叫んだ。「誰かが銃を撃っているわ！」

▶ **get down to** PHRASAL VERB 句動詞 If you **get down to** something, especially something that requires a lot of attention, you begin doing it. 本腰を入れて取り組む □ *With the election out of the way, the government can get down to business.* 選挙も終わったので、政府は仕事に本格的に取り組むことができる。

▶ **get in** **1** PHRASAL VERB 句動詞 If a political party or a politician **gets in**, they are elected. 当選する □ *If the Republicans got in they might decide to change it.* もし共和党が当選したら、彼らはそれを変更するよう決めるかもしれない。 **2** PHRASAL VERB 句動詞 If you **get** something **in**, you manage to do it at a time when you are very busy doing other things. (忙しい中一の) 時間を見つける □ *I plan to get a few lessons in.* わたしはいくつか授業の時間を見つけるつもり。 **3** PHRASAL VERB 句動詞 When a train, bus, or plane **gets in**, it arrives. (乗り物が) 到着する □ *We would have come straight here, except our flight got in too late.* わたしたちの飛行機があれほど遅れて到着していなければ、ここへまっすぐに来るつもりだった。

▶ **get into** **1** PHRASAL VERB 句動詞 If you **get into** a particular kind of work or activity, you manage to become involved in it. (仕事や活動に) 参加する □ *He was eager to get into politics.* 彼は政界に入りたがっていた。 **2** PHRASAL VERB 句動詞 If you **get into** a school, college, or university, you are accepted there as a student. (学校や大学に) 入る □ *I was working hard to get into Yale.* わたしはエール大学に入るため一生懸命勉強していた。

▶ **get off** **1** PHRASAL VERB 句動詞 If someone who has broken a law or rule **gets off**, they are not punished, or are given only a very small punishment. (罰を) 逃れる □ *He is likely to get off with a small fine.* 彼は罰金を少し払うだけで済みそうだ。 **2** PHRASAL VERB 句動詞 If you tell someone to **get off** a piece of land or a property, you are telling them to leave, because they have no right to be there and you do not want them there. (場所を) 去る □ *I told you. Get off the farm.* おまえに言ったはずだ。農場から出て行け。 **3** PHRASAL VERB 句

動詞 You can tell someone to **get off** when they are touching something and you do not want them to. (物に) 手を触れない □*I kept telling him to get off.* わたしは彼に手をどけるよう言い続けた.

▶ **get on** PHRASAL VERB 句動詞 If you **get on with** something, you continue doing it or start doing it. (物事に) 取りかかる □*Jane got on with her work.* ジェーンは彼女の仕事に取りかかった.

▶ **get on to** PHRASAL VERB 句動詞 If you **get on to** a topic when you are speaking, you start talking about it. (話題に) 入る □*We got on to the subject of relationships.* わたしたちは恋愛関係の話題に入った.

▶ **get out** ◼ PHRASAL VERB 句動詞 If you **get out**, you leave a place because you want to escape from it, or because you are made to leave it. 出て行く, 逃げ出す □*They probably wanted to get out of the country.* 彼らはおそらくその国から逃げ出したかったのだろう. ◾ PHRASAL VERB 句動詞 If you **get out**, you go to places and meet people, usually in order to have a more enjoyable life. 外出する □*Get out and enjoy yourself, make new friends.* 外に出かけて楽しみなさい. 新しい友達を作るのよ. ◾ PHRASAL VERB 句動詞 If you **get out of** an organization or a commitment, you withdraw from it. (組織から) 去る □*I wanted to get out of the group, but they wouldn't let me.* ぼくはそのグループから抜けたかったけど, 彼らは抜けさせてくれなかったんだ. ◾ PHRASAL VERB 句動詞 If news or information **gets out**, it becomes known. (ニュースや情報が) 漏れる □*If word got out now, a scandal could be disastrous.* その事が今漏れたら, 破滅的な醜聞になるぞ.

▶ **get out of** PHRASAL VERB 句動詞 If you **get out of** doing something that you do not want to do, you succeed in avoiding doing it. (やりたくない事を) 逃れる □*It's amazing what people will do to get out of paying taxes.* 人々が税金を逃れるためにやることには驚かされる.

▶ **get over** ◼ PHRASAL VERB 句動詞 If you **get over** an unpleasant or unhappy experience or an illness, you recover from it. (いやな経験などを) 乗り越える □*It took me a very long time to get over the shock of her death.* わたしが彼女の死の打撃から立ち直るにはとても長い時間がかかった. ◾ PHRASAL VERB 句動詞 If you **get over** a problem or difficulty, you overcome it. (問題や困難を) 克服する □*"How would they get over that problem?" he wondered.* 「彼らはどうやってその問題を解決するだろう?」と彼はいぶかった.

▶ **get round** → see **get around**

▶ **get round to** → see **get around to**

▶ **get through** ◼ PHRASAL VERB 句動詞 If you **get through** a task or an amount of work, especially when it is difficult, you complete it. (難しい任務や仕事を) やり遂げる (BRIT 英国英語; BRIT 英国英語) □*I think you can get through the first two chapters.* わたしはきみなら最初の2章はやれると思うよ. ◾ PHRASAL VERB 句動詞 If you **get through** a difficult or unpleasant period of time, you manage to live through it. (難しい時期を) 切り抜ける □*It is hard to see how people will get through the winter.* 人々がどうやってその冬を切り抜けるか見通しを立てにくい. ◾ PHRASAL VERB 句動詞 If you **get through to** someone, you succeed in making them understand something that you are trying to tell them. (人に自分の言いたい事を) 理解させる □*An old friend might well be able to get through to her and help her.* 昔からの友達なら彼女に理解させ, 彼女を教えるかもしれない. ◾ PHRASAL VERB 句動詞 If you **get through to** someone, you succeed in contacting them on the telephone. (電話で) ─に連絡がつく □*Look, I can't get through to this number.* ちょっと, この電話番号はつながらないわよ. ◾ PHRASAL VERB 句動詞 If a law or proposal **gets through**, it is officially approved by something such as a parliament or committee. (法案などが) 通過する □*Such a radical proposal would never get through Congress.* そんな過激な提案が議会を通過するわけがない.

▶ **get together** ◼ PHRASAL VERB 句動詞 When people **get together**, they meet in order to discuss something or to spend time together. (人が) 集まる ◾ → see also **get-together** □*A whole range of people from all backgrounds can get together and enjoy themselves.* あらゆる背景を持ったすべての人々が集まり楽しめる. ◾ PHRASAL VERB 句動詞 If you **get** something **together**, you organize it. 組織する □*Paul and I were getting a band together, and we needed a new record deal.* ポールと僕はバンドを結成しようとしており, 新しいレコード契約が必要だった. ◾ PHRASAL VERB 句動詞 If you **get** an amount of money **together**, you succeed in getting all the money that you need in order to pay for something. (お金を) かき集める □*Now you've finally got enough money together to put a down payment on your dream home.* さて, きみはやっと夢のマイホームに十分な頭金を集めたんだね.

▶ **get up** ◼ PHRASAL VERB 句動詞 When someone who is sitting or lying down **gets up**, they rise to a standing position. 起き上がる □*I got up and walked over to where he was.* わたしは起き上がり, 彼がいる所へ歩いて行った. ◾ PHRASAL VERB 句動詞 When you **get up**, you get out of bed. 起床する □*They have to get up early in the morning.* 彼らは朝早く起きなければならない.

get|away /gɛtəweɪ/ (**getaways**) ◼ N-COUNT 可算名詞 If someone makes a **getaway**, they leave a place quickly, especially after committing a crime or when trying to avoid someone. 逃走 □*They made their getaway on a stolen motorcycle.* 彼らは盗んだオート

バイで逃げた. ◾ N-COUNT 可算名詞 A **getaway** is a short vacation somewhere. 短い休暇 [INFORMAL くだけた] □*Weekend tours are ideal for families who want a short getaway.* 週末旅行は短い休暇を取りたい家族には理想的だ.

get|ting /gɛtɪŋ/ **Getting** is the present participle of **get**. getの現在分詞

get-together (**get-togethers**) N-COUNT 可算名詞 A **get-together** is an informal meeting or party, usually arranged for a particular purpose. (非公式の) 集まり □*...a get-together I had at my home.* わたしの家で開いた集まり

ghast|ly /gæstli/ ADJ 形容詞 If you describe someone or something as **ghastly**, you mean that you find them very unpleasant or shocking. ぞっとする [INFORMAL くだけた] □*...a mother accompanied by her ghastly, unruly child.* ぞっとするような手に負えない子供を連れた母親 □*It was the worst week of my life. It was ghastly.* それはわたしの人生で最悪の一週間だった. まったくひどかった.

ghet|to /gɛtoʊ/ (**ghettos** or **ghettoes**) N-COUNT 可算名詞 A **ghetto** is a part of a city in which many poor people or many people of a particular race, religion, or nationality live separately from everyone else. スラム街 □*...the black ghettos of New York and Los Angeles.* ニューヨークとロサンゼルスの黒人スラム街

ghost /goʊst/ (**ghosts**) ◼ N-COUNT 可算名詞 A **ghost** is the spirit of a dead person that someone believes they can see or feel. 幽霊 □*...the ghost of Marie Antoinette.* マリー・アントワネットの幽霊 ◾ N-COUNT 可算名詞 The **ghost** of something, especially of something bad that has happened, is the memory of it. 過去の記憶 (しばしば忌まわしい記憶を意味する) □*...the ghost of anti-Americanism.* 反米主義の忌まわしい記憶

ghost|ly /goʊstli/ ◼ ADJ 形容詞 Something that is **ghostly** seems unreal or unnatural and may be frightening because of this. 非現実的な, 不自然な □*...Sonia's ghostly laughter.* ソニアの不自然な笑い ◾ ADJ 形容詞 A **ghostly** presence is the ghost or spirit of a dead person. 幽霊の [ADJ n] □*...the ghostly presences which haunt these islands.* これらの島に出現する幽霊

GI /dʒi aɪ/ (**GIs**) N-COUNT 可算名詞 A **GI** is a soldier in the United States armed forces, especially the army. (米陸軍) 兵士 □*...the GIs who came to Europe to fight the Nazis.* ナチスと戦うためにヨーロッパへ来た米軍兵士

gi|ant /dʒaɪənt/ (**giants**) ◼ ADJ 形容詞 Something that is described as **giant** is much larger or more important than most others of its kind. 巨大な [ADJ n] □*...America's giant car maker, General Motors.* アメリカの巨大自動車メーカー, ゼネラル・モーターズ □*...a giant oak table.* 巨大なオークのテーブル ◾ N-COUNT 可算名詞 **Giant** is often used to refer to any large, successful business organization or country. 大企業, 強国 [JOURNALISM ジャーナリズム] □*...Japanese electronics giant, Sony.* 日本のエレクトロニクス大手企業, ソニー ◾ N-COUNT 可算名詞 A **giant** is an imaginary person who is very big and strong, especially one mentioned in old stories. 巨人 □*...a Nordic saga of giants.* 北欧の巨人の英雄伝説

Thesaurus	*giant* また次を参照:
ADJ.	colossal, enormous, gigantic, huge, immense, mammoth; (ant.) miniature ◼

gibe /dʒaɪb/ → see **jibe**

gid|dy /gɪdi/ (**giddier, giddiest**) ◼ ADJ 形容詞 If you feel **giddy**, you feel unsteady and think that you are about to fall over, usually because you are not well. 目まいがする □*He felt giddy and light-headed.* 彼は目まいがし頭がぼおっとした. ◾ ADJ 形容詞 If you feel **giddy with** delight or excitement, you feel so happy or excited that you find it hard to think or act normally. 有頂天の □*Anthony was giddy with self-satisfaction.* アンソニーは自己満足で有頂天だった.

gift /gɪft/ (**gifts**) ◼ N-COUNT 可算名詞 A **gift** is something that you give someone as a present. 贈り物 □*...a gift of $50.00.* 50ドルの贈り物 □*They believed the unborn child was a gift from God.* 彼らはやがて生まれてくる子が神からの授かり物であると信じていた. ◾ N-COUNT 可算名詞 If someone has a **gift for** doing something, they have a natural ability for doing it. 天賦の才能 □*As a youth he discovered a gift for teaching.* 若い頃, 彼は教えることに天賦の才能があることを発見した.

Thesaurus	*gift* また次を参照:
N.	present ◼
	ability, talent ◾

gift|ed /gɪftɪd/ ◼ ADJ 形容詞 Someone who is **gifted** has a natural ability to do something well. 天賦の才能に恵まれた □*...one of the most gifted players in the world.* 世界で最も才能のある演奏者の一人 ◾ ADJ 形容詞 A **gifted** child is much more intelligent or talented than average. 知能や才能の優れた □*...a state program for gifted children.* 英才児に対する国のカリキュラム

gig /gɪg/ (**gigs**) N-COUNT 可算名詞 A **gig** is a live performance by someone such as a musician or a comedian. （ミュージシャンやコメディアンの）生演奏，ライブ [INFORMAL くだけた] ❑ *The two bands join forces for a gig at Madison Square Garden on November 28.* その2つのバンドは11月28日にマジソン・スクエア・ガーデンで開かれるライブで共演する.

gi|ga|byte /gɪgəbaɪt/ (**gigabytes**) N-COUNT 可算名詞 In computing, a **gigabyte** is one thousand and twenty-four megabytes. ギガバイト（1ギガバイトは1,024メガバイト）

gi|gan|tic /dʒaɪgæntɪk/ ADJ 形容詞 If you describe something as **gigantic**, you are emphasizing that it is extremely large in size, amount, or degree. 巨大な，膨大な [EMPHASIS 強調] ❑ *In Red Rock Valley the road is bordered by gigantic rocks.* レッド・ロック・バレーでは道路に沿って巨大な岩が立ち並んでいる.

gig|gle /gɪgʲl/ (**giggles, giggling, giggled**) ■ V-T/V-I 他動詞/自動詞 If someone **giggles**, they laugh in a childlike way, because they are amused, nervous, or embarrassed. クスクス笑いながらーと言う [他動詞]，クスクス笑う [自動詞] ❑ *Both girls began to giggle.* どちらの少女もクスクス笑い始めた. ❑ *"I beg your pardon?" she giggled.* 「なんでおっしゃったの？」と言って彼女はクスクス笑った. ● N-COUNT 可算名詞 **Giggle** is also a noun. クスクス笑い，忍び笑い ❑ *She gave a little giggle.* 彼女は小さく忍び笑いをした. ② N-PLURAL 複数名詞 If you say that someone has **the giggles**, you mean they cannot stop giggling. 止まらない忍び笑い ❑ *I was so nervous I got the giggles.* わたしはとても緊張していたので，忍び笑いが止まらなかった.
→ see **laugh**

gilt /gɪlt/ ADJ 形容詞 A **gilt** object is covered with a thin layer of gold or gold paint. 金ぱくの，金めっきの ❑ *...marble columns and gilt spires.* 大理石の柱と金ぱくに覆われた尖頂（せんちょう）

gim|mick /gɪmɪk/ (**gimmicks**) N-COUNT 可算名詞 A **gimmick** is an unusual and unnecessary feature or action whose purpose is to attract attention or publicity. （注意を引く為や広告の為の）策略 [DISAPPROVAL 不賛成] ❑ *It is just a public relations gimmick.* それは宣伝活動のためのただのやらせだ.

gin /dʒɪn/ (**gins**) N-MASS 質量名詞 **Gin** is a strong, colorless, alcoholic drink made from grain and juniper berries. ジン（無色透明の蒸留酒）● N-COUNT 可算名詞 A **gin** is a glass of gin. グラス一杯のジン ❑ *...another gin and tonic.* ジン・トニックのお代わり

gin|ger /dʒɪndʒər/ ■ N-UNCOUNT 不可算名詞 **Ginger** is the root of a plant that is used to flavor food. It has a sweet, spicy flavor and is often sold in powdered form. しょうが ② COLOR 色彩語 **Ginger** is used to describe things that are orangey brown in color. 赤褐色，（髪の）赤毛色 ❑ *She was a mature lady with dyed ginger hair.* 彼女は髪を赤毛に染めた落ち着いた女性だった.

gin|ger|ly /dʒɪndʒərli/ ADV 副詞 If you do something **gingerly**, you do it in a careful manner, usually because you expect it to be dangerous, unpleasant, or painful. とても用心深く [WRITTEN 書き言葉] [ADV with v] ❑ *She was touching the dressing gingerly with both hands.* 彼女は慎重に両手で包帯に触っていた.

gip|sy /dʒɪpsi/ → see **gypsy**

gi|raffe /dʒɪræf/ (**giraffes**) N-COUNT 可算名詞 A **giraffe** is a large African animal with a very long neck, long legs, and dark patches on its body. キリン

girl /gɜrl/ (**girls**) ■ N-COUNT 可算名詞 A **girl** is a female child. 女の子 ❑ *...an eleven-year-old girl.* 11歳の少女 ② N-COUNT 可算名詞 You can refer to someone's daughter as a **girl**. 娘，女の子 ❑ *We had a little girl.* わたしたちには小さな娘がいたのよ. ③ N-COUNT 可算名詞 Young women are often referred to as **girls**. This use could cause offense. 女性（しばしば大人の女性に使われるが，失礼になる場合がある）❑ *...a pretty twenty-year-old girl.* かわいい20歳の女性 ④ N-COUNT 可算名詞 Some people refer to a man's girlfriend as his **girl**. （女性の）恋人，ガールフレンド [INFORMAL くだけた] ❑ *I've been with my girl for nine years.* ぼくは彼女とつきあって9年になる.

girl|friend /gɜrlfrɛnd/ (**girlfriends**) ■ N-COUNT 可算名詞 Someone's **girlfriend** is a girl or woman with whom they are having a romantic or sexual relationship. （女性の）恋人，ガールフレンド ❑ *He had been going out with his girlfriend for seven months.* 彼は恋人と7か月つきあっていた. ② N-COUNT 可算名詞 A **girlfriend** is a female friend. 女友達 ❑ *I met a girlfriend for lunch.* わたしは女友達と昼食に落ち合った.

A **girlfriend** is the female person in a romantic relationship. Women can also describe their female friends as their **girlfriends**, but men do not usually use this word to talk about anyone except the woman they are in a romantic relationship with.

girth /gɜrθ/ (**girths**) N-VAR 可変性名詞 The **girth** of an object, for example a person's or an animal's body, is its width or thickness, considered as the measurement around its circumference. 周囲の長さ，（人や動物の）胴回り [FORMAL 形式ばった] ❑ *A girl he knew had upset him by commenting on his increasing*

girth. 彼の知りあいの女性は，彼の胴回りが増えたことに触れて彼の気分を害していた.

gist /dʒɪst/ N-SING 単数名詞 The **gist** of a speech, conversation, or piece of writing is its general meaning. （演説や文章の）要点 ❑ *He related the gist of his conversation to Sam.* 彼は会話の要点をサムに話した.

---

give

❶ USED WITH NOUNS DESCRIBING ACTIONS
❷ TRANSFERRING
❸ OTHER USES, PHRASES, AND PHRASAL VERBS

---

❶ give /gɪv/ (**gives, giving, gave, given**) ■ V-T 他動詞 You can use **give** with nouns that refer to physical actions. The whole expression refers to the performing of the action. For example, **She gave a smile** means almost the same as "She smiled." 後ろに動作の名詞を伴い，その動作を行うことを示す. ❑ *She stretched her arms out and gave a great yawn.* 彼女は両腕を伸ばして大きなあくびをした. [no cont] ❑ *He gave her a fond smile.* 彼は彼女に優しくほほえんだ. ② V-T 他動詞 You use **give** to say that a person does something for another person. For example, if you **give** someone a lift, you take them somewhere in your car. （人に行為を）してあげる ❑ *I gave her a lift back to her house.* わたしは彼女を車で家に送って行った. ❑ *He was given mouth-to-mouth resuscitation.* 彼は口移しの人工呼吸を施された. ③ V-T 他動詞 You use **give** with nouns that refer to information, opinions, or greetings to indicate that something is communicated. For example, if you **give** someone some news, you tell it to them. （情報や意見を）伝える ❑ *He gave no details.* 彼は詳細をまったく語らなかった. ❑ *Would you like to give me your name?* あなたの名前をお聞かせ願えますか? ④ V-T 他動詞 You use **give** to say how long you think something will last or how much you think something will be. （期間や数値が―に）なる ❑ *A recent poll gave Campbell a 68 percent support rating.* 最近の世論調査によると，キャンベルに対する支持率は68パーセントだった. ⑤ V-T 他動詞 People use **give** in expressions such as **I don't give a damn** to show that they do not care about something. （関心を）払う [INFORMAL くだけた, FEELINGS 感情] [no cont, no passive, with brd-neg] ❑ *They don't give a damn about the country.* やつらはその国のことなんて気にもかけていない. ⑥ V-T 他動詞 If someone or something **gives** you a particular idea or impression, it causes you to have that idea or impression. （考えを）ひらめかせる，（印象を）与える ❑ *They gave me the impression that they were doing exactly what they wanted in life.* わたしは彼らが人生の中でやりたいこととそのものをやっているという印象を受けた. ⑦ V-T 他動詞 If someone or something **gives** you a particular physical or emotional feeling, it makes you experience it. （肉体的または心理的な感覚を）経験させる ❑ *He gave me a shock.* 彼はぼくをびっくりさせた. ⑧ V-T 他動詞 If you **give** a performance or speech, you perform or speak in public. （公演やスピーチを）する ❑ *Kotto gives a stupendous performance.* コットーは並外れて素晴らしい演技だ. ⑨ V-T 他動詞 If you **give** something thought or attention, you think about it, concentrate on it, or deal with it. 考える，（注意を）払う ❑ *I've been giving it some thought.* わたしはそれについて考えている. ⑩ V-T 他動詞 If you **give** a party or other social event, you organize it. （パーティーや催しを）開く ❑ *That evening, I gave a dinner party for a few close friends.* その夜わたしは数人の親しい友達を招いて食事会を開いた.

❷ give /gɪv/ (**gives, giving, gave, given**) ■ V-T/V-I 他動詞/自動詞 If you **give** someone something that you own or have bought, you provide them with it, so that they have it or can use it. 提供する ❑ *They gave us T-shirts and stickers.* 彼らはわたしたちにTシャツとシールをくれた. ❑ *He gave money to the World Health Organization to help defeat smallpox.* 彼は世界保健機関に天然痘撲滅のための資金を提供した. ❑ *Americans are still giving to charity despite hard times.* アメリカ人は厳しい時代でもなおチャリティーに寄付している. ② V-T 他動詞 If you **give** someone something that you are holding or that is near you, you pass it to them, so that they are then holding it. （物を）渡す ❑ *Give me that pencil.* その鉛筆を取ってちょうだい. ③ V-T 他動詞 To **give** someone or something a particular power or right means to allow them to have it. （権力や権利を）与える ❑ *The new law would give the president the power to appoint the central bank's chairman.* その新しい法律は大統領に中央銀行の総裁を指名する権限を与える.

❸ give /gɪv/ (**gives, giving, gave, given**)
⇨ Please look at meaning ⑧ to see if the expression you are looking for is shown under another headword. ■ V-I 自動詞 If something **gives**, it collapses or breaks under pressure. （圧力で）崩れ落ちる ❑ *My knees gave under me.* わたしはひざの力が抜けた. ② V-T PASSIVE 受動態他動詞 You say that you **are given to** understand or believe that something is the case when you do not want to say how you found out about it, or who told you. （～であると）聞いている（～であると）聞いている（情報源を明らかにしたくない時の表現）[FORMAL 形式ばった, VAGUENESS あいま

いさ] □*We were given to understand that he was ill.* わたしたちは彼が病気だと聞いた. ❸ → see also **given** ❹ PHRASE 句 You use **give me** to say that you would rather have one thing than another, especially when you have just mentioned the thing that you do not want. 〜の方がよい □*"I hate Sundays," he said. "They're endless. Give me a Saturday night any day."* 「わたしは日曜日が嫌いだ」と彼は言った.「日曜日は際限がない. どの日も土曜日の夜にしてくれ.」 ❺ PHRASE 句 If you say that something requires **give-and-take**, you mean that people must compromise or cooperate for it to be successful. 持ちつ持たれつ □*...a happy relationship where there's a lot of give-and-take.* 持ちつ持たれつの精神に満ちた円満な関係 ❻ PHRASE 句 **Give or take** is used to indicate that an amount is approximate. For example, if you say that something is fifty years old, **give or take** a few years, you mean that it is approximately fifty years old. 〜の増減を伴って □*They grow to a height of 12 in. – give or take a couple of inches.* それらは12インチの高さに成長するが, 数インチの違いはあるかもしれないが. ❼ PHRASE 句 If an audience is asked to **give it up** for a performer, they are being asked to applaud. 〜に拍手かっさいする [INFORMAL くだけた] □*Ladies and gentlemen, give it up for Fred Durst.* 皆様, フレッド・ダーストに拍手をお願いします. ❽ to **give the game away** → see **game** ❾ to **give notice** → see **notice** ❿ to **give rise to** → see **rise** ⓫ to **give way** → see **way**

▸ **give away** ❶ PHRASAL VERB 句動詞 If you **give away** something that you own, you give it to someone, rather than selling it, often because you no longer want it. 無料で譲る □*He was giving his collection away for free.* 彼は所蔵品をただであげていた. ❷ PHRASAL VERB 句動詞 If someone **gives away** an advantage, they accidentally cause their opponent or enemy to have that advantage. (競争相手にチャンスを) 与える □*Military advantages should not be given away.* 軍事的利点をふいにしてはならない. ❸ PHRASAL VERB 句動詞 If you **give away** information that should be kept secret, you reveal it to other people. (秘密を) 漏らす □*She would give nothing away.* 彼女は何も漏らしたりしない. ❹ PHRASAL VERB 句動詞 To **give** someone or something **away** means to show their true nature or identity, which is not obvious. 正体を現す □*Although they are pretending hard to be young, gray hair and cellulite give them away.* 彼らは懸命に若作りをしているが, 白髪や皮下脂肪に年齢が現れている.

▸ **give back** PHRASAL VERB 句動詞 If you **give** something **back**, you return it to the person who gave it to you. 〜を返す □*I gave the textbook back to him.* わたしは彼に教科書を返した. □*You gave me back the projector.* きみは映写機をわたしに返してくれた.

▸ **give in** ❶ PHRASAL VERB 句動詞 If you **give in**, you admit that you are defeated or that you cannot do something. 降参する □*"I wasn't going to give in. I was going to fight like hell."* 「おれは降伏なんかする気はなかった. 打ち負かされるつもりじゃなかった. おれは鬼のように戦うつもりだったんだ.」 ❷ PHRASAL VERB 句動詞 If you **give in**, you agree to do something that you do not want to do. 折れる □*I pressed my parents until they finally gave in and registered me for skating classes.* わたしは, 両親が折れてスケート教室に登録してくれるまでせがんだ.

▸ **give off** or **give out** PHRASAL VERB 句動詞 If something **gives off** or **gives out** a gas, heat, or a smell, it produces it and sends it out into the air. (気体や熱, 臭いなどを) 発する □*...natural gas, which gives off less carbon dioxide than coal.* 石炭よりも二酸化炭素の放出が少ない天然ガス

▸ **give out** ❶ PHRASAL VERB 句動詞 If you **give out** a number of things, you distribute them among a group of people. 配布する □*There were people at the entrance giving out leaflets.* 出口でチラシを配っている人たちがいた. ❷ PHRASAL VERB 句動詞 If you **give out** information, you make it known to people. (情報を) 提供する □*He wouldn't give out any information.* 彼はどんな情報も漏らしたりしないよ. ❸ → see also **give off**

▸ **give over to** or **give up to** PHRASAL VERB 句動詞 If something **is given over** or **given up to** a particular use, it is used entirely for that purpose. 〜のためだけに使われる □*Much of the garden was given over to vegetables.* その庭の大部分は野菜の栽培に使われていた.

▸ **give up** ❶ PHRASAL VERB 句動詞 If you **give up** something,

you stop doing it or having it. 中止する, 手離す □*The Coast Guard had given up all hope of finding the two divers alive.* 沿岸警備隊は2人のダイバー救出の望みを捨て去っていた. ❷ PHRASAL VERB 句動詞 If you **give up**, you decide that you cannot do something and stop trying to do it. あきらめる □*After a fruitless morning sitting at his desk he had given up.* 彼は机に座って午前中を無駄にした後, 努力をやめた. ❸ PHRASAL VERB 句動詞 If you **give up** your job, you resign from it. (仕事を) 辞める □*She gave up her job to join her husband's campaign.* 彼女は夫の選挙運動に加わるため仕事を辞めた. ❹ PHRASAL VERB 句動詞 If you **give up** something that you have or that you are entitled to, you allow someone else to have it. (所有物や資格を) 譲る □*One of the men with him gave up his place on the bench.* 彼と一緒にいた男性陣の一人が長いすの自分の場所を譲った. ❺ PHRASAL VERB 句動詞 If you **give yourself up**, you let the police or other people know where you are, after you have been hiding from them. (警察に) 自首する, 出頭する □*A 28-year-old man later gave himself up and will appear in court today.* その後28歳の男性は自首し, 今日裁判所に出廷する予定だ.

▸ **give up on** PHRASAL VERB 句動詞 If you **give up on** something or someone, you decide that you will never succeed in doing what you want to with them, and you stop trying. 〜に見切りをつける, 見捨てる □*He urged them not to give up on peace efforts.* 彼は和平実現への努力をあきらめないよう強く促した.

▸ **give up to** → see **give over to**

give|away /gívəweɪ/ (**giveaways**) also **give-away**
N-COUNT 可算名詞 A **giveaway** is something that a company or organization gives to someone, usually in order to encourage people to buy a particular product. 無料サンプル, 景品 □*Free book giveaway for all who attend.* 参加者にはもれなく本の景品があります.

giv|en /gívən/ ❶ Given is the past participle of **give**. giveの過去分詞 ❷ ADJ 形容詞 If you talk about, for example, any **given** position or a **given** time, you mean the particular position or time that you are discussing. 与えられた [det ADJ] □*In chess there are typically about 36 legal moves from any given board position.* チェスには通常, どの局面からでも約36種の合法手がある. ❸ PREP 前置詞 **Given** is used when indicating a possible situation in which someone has the opportunity or ability to do something. For example, **given the chance** means "if I had the chance." (仮定で) 〜があれば □*Write down the sort of thing you would like to do, given the opportunity.* 機会があればしてみたいということを書いてください. ❹ PHRASE 句 If you say **given that** something is the case, you mean taking that fact into account. (that以下であることを) 考えると □*Usually, I am sensible with money, as I have to be, given that I don't earn that much.* 普通わたしは分別のあるお金の使い方をしているわ. 自分にそんなに収入がないことを考えると, そうせざるを得ないもの. ❺ PREP 前置詞 If you say **given** something, you mean taking that thing into account. (物事を) 考慮に入れると □*Given the uncertainty over Leigh's future I was left with little other choice.* リーの将来の不確かさを思うと, わたしに残された選択の余地はほとんどなかった.

gla|cial /gléɪʃəl/ ❶ ADJ 形容詞 **Glacial** means relating to or produced by glaciers or ice. 氷河の, 氷の [TECHNICAL 技術的] □*...a true glacial landscape with U-shaped valleys.* U字型のくぼみがある本物の氷河の景観 ❷ ADJ 形容詞 If you say that something moves or changes at a **glacial** pace, you are emphasizing that it moves or changes very slowly. 進行の遅い [EMPHASIS 強調] [usu ADJ n] □*Change occurs at a glacial pace.* 変化はゆっくりと起きる.
→ see **lake**

gla|cier /gléɪʃər/ (**glaciers**) N-COUNT 可算名詞 A **glacier** is an extremely large mass of ice which moves very slowly, often down a mountain valley. 氷河
→ see Word Web: **glacier**
→ see **climate, glacier, mountain**

glad /glǽd/ ❶ ADJ 形容詞 If you are **glad** about something, you are happy and pleased about it. うれしい [v-link ADJ] □*The people seem genuinely glad to see you.* 人々は彼らに会えて本当にうれしそうだ. □*I'd be glad if the boys slept a little longer so I could do some ironing.*

Word Web glacier

Two-thirds of all **fresh water** is **frozen**. The largest **glaciers** in the world are the **polar ice caps** of Antarctica and Greenland. They cover more than six million square miles. Their average depth is almost one mile. If all the glaciers **melted**, the average **sea level** would rise by over 250 feet. Glaciologists have noted that the Antarctic is about 1º C* warmer than it was 50 years ago. Some of them are worried. Continued warming might cause floating **ice** shelves there to begin to disintegrate. This, in turn, could cause disastrous coastal flooding in low-lying areas around the world.

1º Celsius = 33.8º Fahrenheit.

Word Web   glass

The basic recipe for **glass** includes silica (found in **sand**) and **ash** (left over from burning wood). The earliest glass objects are glass **beads** made in Egypt around 3500 BC. By 14 AD, the Syrians had learned how to **blow** glass to form hollow containers. These included primitive **bottles** and **vases**. By 100 AD, the Romans were making clear glass windowpanes. Modern factories now produce **safety glass** which doesn't **shatter** when it breaks. It includes a layer of cellulose between two **sheets** of glass. **Bulletproof** glass consists of several layers of glass with a tough, **transparent** plastic between the layers.

アイロンがけができるよう息子たちがもう少し長く寝てくれたらうれしいのに. ●**glad|ly** ADV 副詞 [ADV with v] 喜んで ❑*Malcolm gladly accepted the invitation.* マルコムは喜んでその招待を受けた. ❷ ADJ 形容詞 If you say that you will be **glad to** do something, usually for someone else, you mean that you are willing and eager to do it. (〜することに) 前向きな [FEELINGS 感情] [v-link ADJ to-inf] ❑*I'll be glad to show you everything.* わたしは喜んであなたにすべてをお見せしますよ. ●**glad|ly** ADV 副詞 [ADV with v] 喜んで ❑*The counselors will gladly baby-sit during their free time.* 相談員たちは空き時間に喜んで子守をしてくれるだろう.

glam|or /ɡlǽmər/ N-UNCOUNT 不可算名詞 → see **glamour**

Word Link   ous ≈ having the qualities of : danger*ous*, fabul*ous*, glamor*ous*

glam|or|ous /ɡlǽmərəs/ ADJ 形容詞 If you describe someone or something as **glamorous**, you mean that they are more attractive, exciting, or interesting than ordinary people or things. 魅力的な, 魅惑的な ❑*...some of the world's most beautiful and glamorous women.* 世界で最も美しく魅力的な女性たち

glance /ɡlǽns/ (**glances, glancing, glanced**) ❶ V-I 自動詞 If you **glance at** something or someone, you look at them very quickly and then look away again immediately. ちらっと見る ❑*He glanced at his watch.* 彼は腕時計をちらっと見た. ❷ V-I 自動詞 If you **glance through** or **at** a newspaper, report, or book, you spend a short time looking at it without reading it very carefully. (新聞や報告書などに) ざっと目を通す ❑*I picked up the phone book and glanced through it.* わたしは電話帳を手に取り, ざっと目を通した. ❸ N-COUNT 可算名詞 A **glance** is a quick look at someone or something. いちべつ, ちらりと見ること ❑*Trevor and I exchanged a glance.* トレバーとわたしはちらりと視線を交わした. ❹ PHRASE 句 If you see something **at a glance**, you see or recognize it immediately, and without having to look or look carefully. 一目で ❑*One could tell at a glance that she was a compassionate person.* 彼女が心の優しい人だということは一目でわかった. ❺ PHRASE 句 If you say that something is true or seems to be true **at first glance**, you mean that it seems to be true when you first see it or think about it, but that your first impression may be wrong. 一見したところでは ❑*At first glance, organic farming looks much more expensive for the farmer.* 一見したところ, 有機農業は農家の人にとってずっと高くつくように思える.

Word Partnership   glance は次の語句と使われる:

PREP.	glance **at** *someone*, glance **over** *someone's* shoulder ❶ glance **at** *something*, glance **over** ❶ ❷ glance **through** ❷
V.	**exchange a** glance, **steal a** glance ❸
ADJ.	**quick** glance ❸

gland /ɡlǽnd/ (**glands**) N-COUNT 可算名詞 A **gland** is an organ in the body which produces chemical substances for the body to use or get rid of. 腺 [usu supp N] ❑*...the hormones secreted by our endocrine glands.* わたしたちの内分泌腺から分泌されるホルモン → see **sweat**

glare /ɡlέər/ (**glares, glaring, glared**) ❶ V-I 自動詞 If you **glare at** someone, you look at them with an angry expression on your face. にらみつける ❑*The old woman glared at him.* その老婦人は彼をにらみつけた. ❑*Jacob glared and muttered something.* ジェイコブはにらみつけて, 何かをブツブツつぶやいた. ❷ N-COUNT 可算名詞 A **glare** is an angry, hard, and unfriendly look. にらみつけること ❑*His glasses magnified his irritable glare.* 眼鏡で彼の怒った視線が強調されて見えた. ❸ V-I 自動詞 If the sun or a light **glares**, it shines with a very bright light which is difficult to look at. (太陽や光が) ぎらぎら光る ❑*The sunlight glared.* 太陽の光がまぶしく輝いた. ❹ N-UNCOUNT 不可算名詞 **Glare** is very bright light that is difficult to look at. まぶしい光 ❑*...the glare of a car's headlights.* 車のヘッドライトのまぶしい光 ❺ N-SING 単数名詞 If someone is **in the glare of** publicity or public attention, they are constantly being watched and talked about by a lot of people. 注目の的

❑*Norma is said to dislike the glare of publicity.* ノーマはメディアに注目されるのが嫌らしい.

Word Partnership   glare は次の語句と使われる:

PREP.	glare **at** *someone* ❶
ADJ.	**irritable** glare ❷ **full** glare ❸ ❹
N.	glare **of light** ❸ ❹ glare **of publicity** ❺

glar|ing /ɡlέərɪŋ/ ❶ ADJ 形容詞 If you describe something bad as **glaring**, you are emphasizing that it is very obvious and easily seen or noticed. 明白な, 目立つ [EMPHASIS 強調] ❑*I never saw such a glaring example of misrepresentation.* わたしはあそこまで虚偽の陳述をした例を見たことがない. ●**glar|ing|ly** ADV 副詞 紛れもなく ❑*It was glaringly obvious.* それは火を見るよりも明らかだった. ❷ → see also **glare**

glass /ɡlάs, ɡlǽs/ (**glasses**) ❶ N-UNCOUNT 不可算名詞 **Glass** is a hard, transparent substance that is used to make things such as windows and bottles. ガラス ❑*...a pane of glass.* 窓ガラス ❷ N-COUNT 可算名詞 A **glass** is a container made from glass, which you can drink from and which does not have a handle. グラス, コップ ❑*Grossman raised the glass to his lips.* グロスマンはそのグラスを口元に持っていった. ●N-COUNT 可算名詞 The contents of a glass can be referred to as a **glass** of something. グラスに一杯 ❑*...a glass of milk.* コップ1杯の牛乳 ❸ N-UNCOUNT 不可算名詞 **Glass** is used to mean objects made of glass, for example drinking containers and bowls. ガラス製品 ❑*There's a glittering array of glass to choose from at markets.* 市場にはよりどりのきらきら輝くガラス製品がずらりと並んでいる. ❹ N-PLURAL 複数名詞 **Glasses** are two lenses in a frame that some people wear in front of their eyes in order to help them see better. 眼鏡 ❑*He took off his glasses.* 彼は眼鏡を外した.
→ see Word Web: **glass**
→ see **light**

glass ceil|ing (**glass ceilings**) N-COUNT 可算名詞 When people refer to a **glass ceiling**, they are talking about the attitudes and traditions in a society that prevent women from rising to the top jobs. ガラスの天井 (女性の昇進を妨げる目に見えない壁) [JOURNALISM ジャーナリズム] ❑*In her current role she broke through the glass ceiling as the first woman to reach senior management level in the company.* 彼女は現在の職務で, 障害を克服し会社初の女性上級管理職になった.

glaze /ɡlέɪz/ (**glazes, glazing, glazed**) ❶ N-COUNT 可算名詞 A **glaze** is a thin layer of liquid which is put on a piece of pottery and becomes hard and shiny when the pottery is heated in a very hot oven. (陶芸の) 上薬, 釉 (ゆう) 薬 ❑*...hand-painted French tiles with decorative glazes.* 装飾的な上薬がついた手描きのフレンチタイル ❷ N-COUNT 可算名詞 A **glaze** is a thin layer of beaten egg, milk, or other liquid that you spread onto food in order to make the surface shine and look attractive. 料理でつや出しのため表面に塗る卵やシロップなどの液体 ❑*Brush the glaze over the top and sides of the hot cake.* 熱いケーキの上と横にはけでつや出しを塗る. ❸ V-T 他動詞 When you **glaze** food such as bread or pastry, you spread a layer of beaten egg, milk, or other liquid onto it before you cook it in order to make its surface shine and look attractive. (卵やシロップなどの) つや出しを塗る ❑*Glaze the pie with beaten egg.* パイにつや出しの溶き卵を塗る.
▶ **glaze over** PHRASAL VERB 句動詞 If your eyes **glaze over**, they become dull and lose all expression, usually because you are bored or are thinking about something else. (目の) 輝きが曇る ❑*...movie actors whose eyes glaze over as soon as the subject wavers from themselves.* 話題が自分の事からそれるや否や目の輝きを失う映画俳優たち
→ see **pottery**

glazed /ɡlέɪzd/ ❶ ADJ 形容詞 If you describe someone's eyes as **glazed**, you mean that their expression is dull or dreamy, usually because they are tired or are having difficulty concentrating on something. (目が) うつろな ❑*Doctors with glazed eyes sat chain-*

smoking in front of a television set. どんよりとした目の医師たちがテレビの前に座り，立て続けにたばこを吸っていた．**2** ADJ 形容詞 **Glazed** pottery is covered with a thin layer of a hard, shiny substance. 上薬を塗った □...*a large glazed pot.* 上薬を塗った大きな鉢 **3** ADJ 形容詞 A **glazed** window or door has glass in it. ガラスをはめた □...*the new office, with glazed windows to the corridor.* 廊下に向かってガラス張りの窓がついた新しい事務所

gleam /gliːm/ (gleams, gleaming, gleamed) **1** V-I 自動詞 If an object or a surface **gleams**, it reflects light because it is shiny and clean. (物の表面などが光を受けて) 輝く □*His black hair gleamed in the sun.* 彼の黒髪が太陽の光に輝いた．**2** N-COUNT 可算名詞 A **gleam of** something is a faint sign of it. かすかな兆候 □*There was a gleam of hope for a peaceful settlement.* 平和的解決へのかすかな望みがあった．

glean /gliːn/ (gleans, gleaning, gleaned) V-T 他動詞 If you **glean** something such as information or knowledge, you learn or collect it slowly and patiently, and perhaps indirectly. (情報や知識を) 少しずつ収集する □*At present we're gleaning information from all sources.* 現在，わたしたちはあらゆる筋から情報を集めている．

glee /gliː/ N-UNCOUNT 不可算名詞 **Glee** is a feeling of happiness and excitement, often caused by someone else's misfortune. 歓喜，(他人の不幸を) 喜ぶこと □*His victory was greeted with glee by his fellow American golfers.* 彼の勝利はアメリカ人のゴルフ仲間から大喜びで迎えられた．

glee|ful /gliːfʊl/ ADJ 形容詞 Someone who is **gleeful** is happy and excited, often because of someone else's bad luck. (しばしば他人の不幸に) 大喜びの [WRITTEN 書き言葉] □*He took an almost gleeful delight in showing how wrong they can be.* 彼は彼らがどれだけ間違っているかを示すことにほとんど喜びを感じていた．●**glee|ful|ly** ADV 副詞 [ADV with v] 大喜びで □*I spent the rest of their visit gleefully boring them with tedious details.* 彼らの訪問の残りの時間を，私はこれでもかというほど細かい話で退屈させて愉快に過ごした．

glib /glɪb/ ADJ 形容詞 If you describe what someone says as **glib**, you disapprove of it because it implies that something is simple or easy, or that there are no problems involved, when this is not the case. 軽薄な，誠意のない [DISAPPROVAL 不賛成] □...*the glib talk of "past misery."* 「過去の苦難」に対する誠意のない話し合い ●**glib|ly** ADV 副詞 [ADV with v] □*We talk glibly of equality of opportunity.* わたしたちは機会の均等に関して口先だけで語っている．

glide /glaɪd/ (glides, gliding, glided) **1** V-I 自動詞 If you **glide** somewhere, you move silently and in a smooth and effortless way. なめらかに動く □*Waiters glide between tightly packed tables bearing trays of pasta.* ウェイターたちはパスタの乗った盆を手に，人でいっぱいのテーブルの間をすべるように動く．**2** V-I 自動詞 When birds or airplanes **glide**, they float on air currents. (鳥や飛行機が) 滑空する □*Our only companion is the wandering albatross, which glides effortlessly and gracefully behind the yacht.* 我々の唯一の連れはヨットの後ろをすいすいと優雅に飛ぶワタリアホウドリだ．

glid|er /glaɪdər/ (gliders) N-COUNT 可算名詞 A **glider** is an aircraft without an engine, which flies by floating on air currents. グライダー

glim|mer /glɪmər/ (glimmers, glimmering, glimmered) **1** V-I 自動詞 If something **glimmers**, it produces or reflects a faint, gentle, often unsteady light. ちらちら光る □*The moon glimmered faintly through the mists.* 霧を通して月の光がかすかに輝いた．**2** N-COUNT 可算名詞 A **glimmer** is a faint, gentle, often unsteady light. ちらちらする光 □*In the east there is the slightest glimmer of light.* 東の方にきわめてかすかな光が見える．**3** N-COUNT 可算名詞 A **glimmer of** something is a faint sign of it. わずかな兆候 □*Despite an occasional glimmer of hope, this campaign has not produced any results.* 時折わずかな希望の兆しが見えたが，この運動はまだ何の成果も生み出していない．

glimpse /glɪmps/ (glimpses, glimpsing, glimpsed) **1** N-COUNT 可算名詞 If you get a **glimpse** of someone or something, you see them very briefly and not very well. ちらりと見ること □*Some of the fans had waited 24 hours outside the hotel to catch a glimpse of their heroine.* ファンの中には憧れの女性を一目見ようと，ホテルの外で24時間待っていた者もいた．**2** V-T 他動詞 If you **glimpse** someone or something, you see them very briefly and not very well. ちらりと見る □*She glimpsed a group of people standing on the bank of a river.* 彼女は川岸に立っている人々の群れをちらべつした．**3** N-COUNT 可算名詞 A **glimpse of** something is a brief experience of it or an idea about it that helps you understand or appreciate it better. (物事を) 垣間見させる経験，または考え □*As university campuses become increasingly multiethnic, they offer a glimpse of the conflicts society will face tomorrow.* 大学キャンパスの多民族化が進み，社会が将来直面するだろうかっとうを垣間見ることができる．

glint /glɪnt/ (glints, glinting, glinted) **1** V-I 自動詞 If something **glints**, it produces or reflects a quick flash of light. きらめく，きらきらと光る [WRITTEN 書き言葉] □*The sea glinted in the sun.* 海が日光にきらめいた．□*Sunlight glinted on his glasses.* 日の光が彼の眼鏡に反射しきらきらと光った．**2** N-COUNT 可算名詞 A **glint** is a quick flash of light. きらめき [WRITTEN 書き言葉] [usu N

'of' n] □...*glints of sunlight.* 日光のきらめき．

glis|ten /glɪsən/ (glistens, glistening, glistened) V-I 自動詞 If something **glistens**, it shines, usually because it is wet or oily. きらきら輝く □*The calm sea glistened in the sunlight.* 穏やかな海が日光を受けてきらきらと輝いた．□*Deborah's face was white and glistening with sweat.* デボラの顔は青ざめ，汗で光っていた．

glit|ter /glɪtər/ (glitters, glittering, glittered) **1** V-I 自動詞 If something **glitters**, light comes from or is reflected off different parts of it. きらきら輝く □*The bay glittered in the sunshine.* 日光が降り注いで入り江がきらきら輝いていた．**2** N-UNCOUNT 不可算名詞 **Glitter** consists of tiny, shining pieces of metal. It is glued to things for decoration. グリッター，ラメ □*Cut out a piece of sandpaper and sprinkle it with glitter.* 紙やすりを切り抜き，グリッターを降りかけること．**3** N-UNCOUNT 不可算名詞 You can use **glitter** to refer to superficial attractiveness or to the excitement connected with something. きらびやかさ □*She was blinded by the glitter and the glamour of her own life.* 彼女は自分の生活のきらびやかさと魅力に目がくらんでいた．

gloat /gloʊt/ (gloats, gloating, gloated) V-I 自動詞 If someone is **gloating**, they are showing pleasure at their own success or at other people's failure in an arrogant and unpleasant way. ほくそえむ [DISAPPROVAL 不賛成] □*Anti-abortionists are gloating over the court's decision.* 人工中絶反対者たちは法廷の決定にほくそえんでいる．

glob|al /gloʊbəl/ **1** ADJ 形容詞 You can use **global** to describe something that happens in all parts of the world or affects all parts of the world. 全世界の，全面的な □...*a global ban on nuclear testing.* 核実験の全面禁止．●**glob|al|ly** ADV 副詞 世界中に □...*a globally familiar trade name.* 世界中に知られている商品名．**2** ADJ 形容詞 A **global** view or vision of a situation is one in which all the different aspects of it are considered. 全体的な □...*a global vision of contemporary societies.* 現代社会の全体的展望．

→ see **greenhouse**

glob|al|ize /gloʊbəlaɪz/ (globalizes, globalizing, globalized) V-T/V-I 他動詞/自動詞 When industry **globalizes** or **is globalized**, companies from one country link with companies from another country in order to do business with them. 世界的規模になる，世界的にする，世界化する [BUSINESS 実業] □*One way to lower costs will be to forge alliances with foreign companies or to expand internationally through appropriate takeovers – in short, to "globalize."* コストを下げる方法としては外国の企業と提携するか，適切な企業買収を行って国際的に拡大するかだ．要するにグローバル化だ．●**glob|al|i|za|tion** /gloʊbəlɪzeɪʃən/ N-UNCOUNT 不可算名詞 世界化 □*Trends toward the globalization of industry have dramatically affected food production in California.* 業界の世界化の流れはカリフォルニア州の食品生産に劇的な影響を及ぼした．

glob|al vil|lage N-SING 単数名詞 People sometimes refer to the world as a **global village** when they want to emphasize that all the different parts of the world form one community linked together by electronic communications, especially the Internet. 世界村 □*Now that we are all part of the global village, everyone becomes a neighbor.* 現在われわれはみんな世界村の一員で，だれもが同胞だ．

glob|al warm|ing N-UNCOUNT 不可算名詞 **Global warming** is the gradual rise in the Earth's temperature caused by high levels of carbon dioxide and other gases in the atmosphere. 地球の温暖化 □*The threat of global warming will eventually force the U.S. to slow down its energy consumption.* 地球の温暖化の脅威によりやがて米国はエネルギー消費量を低減せざるを得なくなるでしょう．

→ see **air**

globe /gloʊb/ (globes) **1** N-SING 単数名詞 You can refer to the world as **the globe** when you are emphasizing how big it is or that something happens in many different parts of it. 地球 □...*bottles of beer from every corner of the globe.* 地球のすみずみからのびんビール □*70% of our globe's surface is water.* 地球の表面の70%が水に覆われている．**2** N-COUNT 可算名詞 A **globe** is a ball-shaped object with a map of the world on it. It is usually fixed on a stand. 地球儀 □*Three large globes stand on the floor.* 大きな地球儀が三つ床の上に置いてある．**3** N-COUNT 可算名詞 Any ball-shaped object can be referred to as a **globe**. 球状のも □*The overhead light was covered now with a white globe.* 今は天井の照明には白い球状のかさがかぶせてあった．

→ see Picture Dictionary: **globe**

gloom /gluːm/ **1** N-SING 単数名詞 The **gloom** is a state of near darkness. うす暗さ □...*the gloom of a foggy November morning.* 霧に包まれた11月の朝のうす暗さ．**2** N-UNCOUNT 不可算名詞 **Gloom** is a feeling of sadness and lack of hope. 陰気，悲観 □...*the deepening gloom over the economy.* いっそう増す景気の暗さ．

gloomy /gluːmi/ (gloomier, gloomiest) **1** ADJ 形容詞 If a place is **gloomy**, it is almost dark so that you cannot see very well. 薄暗い □*Inside it's gloomy after all that sunshine.* あんなに日光が降り注いでいただけに室内は暗い．**2** ADJ 形容詞 If people are **gloomy**, they are unhappy and have no hope. 陰気な，悲観的な，憂鬱な，暗い □*Miller is gloomy about the fate of the serious playwright in America.* ミ

Picture Dictionary

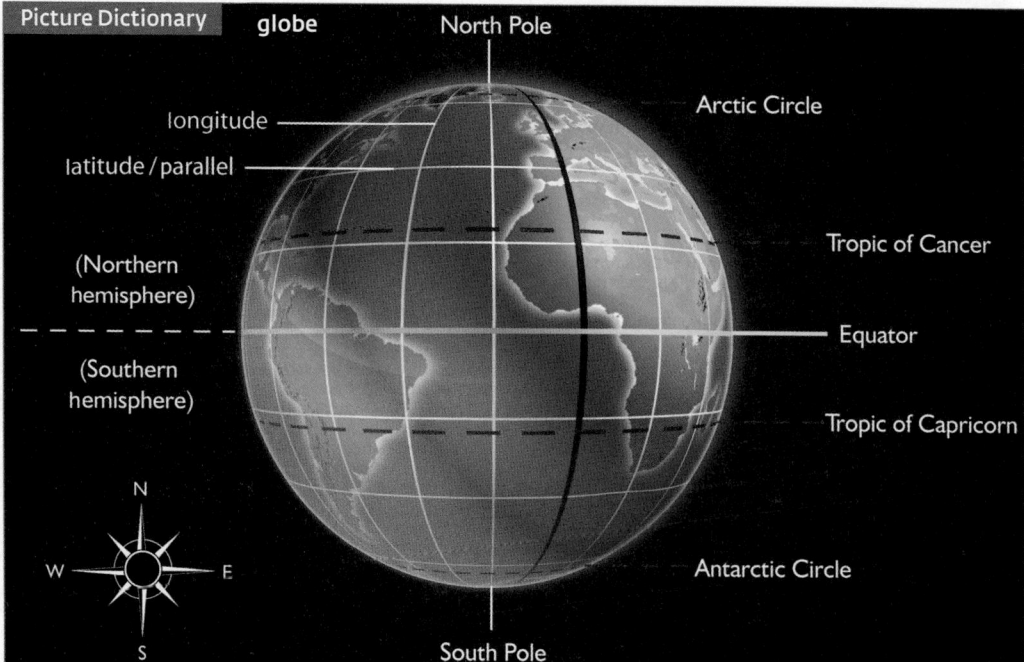

globe

- North Pole
- longitude
- latitude / parallel
- Arctic Circle
- (Northern hemisphere)
- Tropic of Cancer
- Equator
- (Southern hemisphere)
- Tropic of Capricorn
- Antarctic Circle
- South Pole

N W E S

g

ラーは米国でその本格的な劇作家がどういう運命を迎えるかについて悲観的だ. ● **gloomi|ly** ADV 副詞 [ADV with v] 陰気に □ *He tells me gloomily that he has been called up for army service.* 軍隊から徴集命令が来たと彼は陰気な声で言う. **3** ADJ 形容詞 If a situation is **gloomy**, it does not give you much hope of success or happiness. 暗さ, 悲観的な □ ...*a gloomy picture of an economy sliding into recession.* 景気が滑るように後退してゆく悲観的情勢. □ *Officials say the outlook for next year is gloomy.* 当局は来年の見通しは暗いと言っています.

→ see weather

glo|ri|fied /glɔrɪfaɪd/ ADJ 形容詞 You use **glorified** to indicate that something is less important or impressive than its name suggests. 美化した [ADJ n] □ *Sometimes they tell me I'm just a glorified waitress.* 私はウェイトレスに毛のはえたようなものだろうって言われることがある.

glo|ri|fy /glɔrɪfaɪ/ (**glorifies, glorifying, glorified**) V-T 他動詞 To **glorify** something means to praise it or make it seem good or special, usually when it is not. 美化する □ *This magazine in no way glorifies gangs.* この雑誌は決してギャングを美化していない. ● **glo|ri|fi|ca|tion** /glɔrɪfɪkeɪʃ°n/ N-UNCOUNT 不可算名詞 美化 □ ...*the glorification of violence.* 暴力の美化.

glo|ri|ous /glɔriəs/ **1** ADJ 形容詞 Something that is **glorious** is very beautiful and impressive. 素晴らしい, 美しい □ ...*a glorious rainbow in the air.* 空に広がる素晴らしい虹. □ *She had missed the glorious blooms of the desert spring.* 彼女は砂漠の春の素晴らしい花盛りを逃した. ● **glo|ri|ous|ly** ADV 副詞 美しく □ *A tree, gloriously lit by autumn, pressed against the windowpane.* 美しく紅葉した木が窓ガラスを押していた. **2** ADJ 形容詞 If you describe something as **glorious**, you are emphasizing that it is wonderful and it makes you feel very happy. 輝かしい [EMPHASIS 強調] □ *The win revived glorious memories of his championship-winning days.* この勝利によって彼が選手権で優勝していたころの輝かしい記憶がよみがえった. ● **glo|ri|ous|ly** ADV 副詞 輝かしく □ ...*her gloriously happy love life.* 彼女の素晴らしく幸せな異性関係. **3** ADJ 形容詞 A **glorious** career, victory, or occasion involves great fame or success. 素晴らしい □ *Harrison had a glorious career spanning more than six decades.* ハリソンには六十年にわたる素晴らしい経歴があった. ● **glo|ri|ous|ly** ADV 副詞 素晴らしく □ *But the mission was successful, gloriously successful.* しかし, 任務は成功, 見事に成功したのだった.

glo|ry /glɔri/ (**glories**) **1** N-UNCOUNT 不可算名詞 **Glory** is the fame and admiration that you gain by doing something impressive. 光栄 □ *Walsham had his moment of glory when he won a 20km race.* 20キロレース優勝はウォルシャムの栄光の瞬間だった. **2** N-PLURAL 複数名詞 A person's **glories** are the occasions when they have done something people greatly admire which makes them famous. 全盛期 □ *The album sees them re-living past glories but not really breaking any new ground.* アルバムで彼らは過ぎ去りし全盛期を復活させているようだが新地を開くには至っていない.

gloss /glɔs/ (**glosses, glossing, glossed**) **1** N-SING 単数名詞 A **gloss** is a bright shine on the surface of something. 光沢 □ *Sheets of rain were falling and produced a black gloss on the asphalt.* 豪雨が降っていてアスファルトの表面が黒く光っていた. **2** N-UNCOUNT 不可算名詞 **Gloss** is an appearance of attractiveness or good quality which sometimes hides less attractive features or poor quality. 見せかけ □ *Television commercials might seem more professional, but beware of mistaking the gloss for the content.* テレビ宣伝は本格的に見えるかもしれないが, 見せかけを中身だと思い違いしないよう用心することだ. **3** N-SING 単数名詞 If you put **a gloss on** a bad situation, you try to make it seem more attractive or acceptable by giving people a false explanation or interpretation of it. うわべを飾る □ *He used his diary to put a fine gloss on the horrors the regime perpetrated.* 彼は政権の犯した惨事をごまかすのに自分の日記を使った. **4** N-MASS 質量名詞 **Gloss** is the same as **gloss paint**. 光沢仕上げ用ペンキ **5** V-T 他動詞 If you **gloss** a difficult word or idea, you provide an explanation of it. 解釈する □ *"Aventure" is often glossed as simply good or bad "fortune" or "chance."* 「Aventure」という言葉はしばしば単に良いあるいは悪い「運」あるいは「偶然」と解釈される.

▶ **gloss over** PHRASAL VERB 句動詞 If you **gloss over** a problem, a mistake, or an embarrassing moment, you try to make it seem unimportant by ignoring it or by dealing with it very quickly. うまくうわべを飾る, うまくごまかす □ *Some foreign governments gloss over human rights abuses.* 人権侵害を言いつくろう外国政府もある.

glos|sa|ry /glɔsəri/ (**glossaries**) N-COUNT 可算名詞 A **glossary** of special, unusual, or technical words or expressions is an alphabetical list of them giving their meanings, for example at the end of a book on a particular subject. 用語集 □ *A glossary of terms is included for the reader's convenience.* 読者に便利なように用語集が入っている.

gloss paint N-UNCOUNT 不可算名詞 **Gloss paint** is paint that forms a shiny surface when it dries. 光沢仕上げ用ペンキ □ ...*a fresh coat of white gloss paint.* 白い光沢塗料の新しい塗装.

glossy /glɔsi/ (**glossier, glossiest**) **1** ADJ 形容詞 **Glossy** means smooth and shiny. 光沢のある □ ...*glossy black hair.* 光沢のある黒髪. **2** ADJ 形容詞 You can describe something as **glossy** if you think that it has been designed to look attractive but has little practical value or may have hidden faults. 見掛けのいい □ ...*a glossy new office.* 見掛けのいい新しい事務所. **3** ADJ 形容詞 **Glossy** magazines, leaflets, books, and photographs are produced on

expensive, shiny paper. 光沢紙の [ADJ n] □...a glossy magazine. グラビア誌

glove /glʌv/ (gloves) **1** N-COUNT 可算名詞 **Gloves** are pieces of clothing which cover your hands and wrists and have individual sections for each finger. You wear gloves to keep your hands warm or dry or to protect them. 手袋 □He stuck his gloves in his pocket. 彼は手袋をポケットに突っ込んだ. **2** PHRASE 句 If you say that something **fits like a glove**, you are emphasizing that it fits exactly. ぴったり合う [EMPHASIS 強調] □I gave one of the bikinis to my sister Sara and it fit like a glove. 妹のサラにそのビキニを一つあげたら、ぴったりだった.
→ see **baseball**

glow /gloʊ/ (glows, glowing, glowed) **1** N-COUNT 可算名詞 A **glow** is a dull, steady light, for example the light produced by a fire when there are no flames. 輝き, 光 □The cigarette's red glow danced about in the darkness. タバコが赤く燃える光が暗闇の中で揺れり動いた. **2** N-SING 単数名詞 A **glow** is a pink color on a person's face, usually because they are healthy or have been exercising. 色つや □The moisturizer gave my face a healthy glow that lasted all day. 保湿剤のおかげで一日中わたしの顔は健康な色つやをしていた. **3** N-SING 単数名詞 If you feel a **glow** of satisfaction or achievement, you have a strong feeling of pleasure because of something that you have done or that has happened. 喜び □Exercise will give you a glow of satisfaction at having achieved something. 運動は何かを達成した満悦感をもたらす. **4** V-I 自動詞 If something **glows**, it produces a dull, steady light. 炎を上げずに光る □The night lantern glowed softly in the darkness. 常夜灯が暗闇の中で柔らかな光を放った. **5** V-I 自動詞 If someone's skin **glows**, it looks pink because they are healthy or excited, or have been doing physical exercise. 紅潮する □Her freckled skin glowed with health again. 彼女のそばかすのある皮膚は健康そうな色つやを取り戻した. **6** V-I 自動詞 If someone **glows with** an emotion such as pride or pleasure, the expression on their face shows how they feel. 光り輝く □The expectant mothers that Amy had encountered positively glowed with pride. エーミーが出会ったことのある妊婦たちは誇りを持って断然光り輝いていた. **7** → see also **glowing**
→ see **fire, light**

Thesaurus	glow また次を参照:
N.	beam, glimmer, light **1**
	blush, flush, radiance **2**
V.	gleam, radiate, shine **4 6**

glow|er /glaʊr/ (glowers, glowering, glowered) V-I 自動詞 If you **glower at** someone or something, you look at them angrily. 渋い顔をする □He glowered at me but said nothing. 彼はわたしをにらみつけたが何も言わなかった.

glow|ing /gloʊɪŋ/ **1** ADJ 形容詞 A **glowing** description or opinion about someone or something praises them highly or supports them strongly. 絶賛の □The media has been speaking in glowing terms of the relationship between the two countries. メディアは両国関係を称賛する論調だった. **2** → see also **glow**

glu|cose /gluːkoʊs/ N-UNCOUNT 不可算名詞 **Glucose** is a type of sugar that gives you energy. ぶどう糖

glue /gluː/ (glues, glueing or gluing, glued) **1** N-MASS 質量名詞 **Glue** is a sticky substance used for joining things together, often for repairing broken things. 接着剤, のり □...a tube of glue. 1本のチューブ入り接着剤 **2** V-T 他動詞 If you **glue** one object to another, you stick them together using glue. のり付けする, 張る □Glue the fabric around the window. 窓のまわりにその布を張る. □The material is cut and glued in place. 素材を切り、所定位置にのり付けした. **3** V-T PASSIVE 受動態他動詞 If you say that someone **is glued to** something, you mean that they are giving it all their attention. くぎ付けになる □They are all glued to the Olympic Games. 彼らはみんなオリンピックにくぎ付けだ.

glum /glʌm/ (glummer, glummest) ADJ 形容詞 Someone who is **glum** is sad and quiet because they are disappointed or unhappy about something. ふさぎ込んだ □She was very glum and was obviously missing her children. 彼女はとてもふさぎ込んでいて、明らかに子供と離れているのが寂しいのだった. ● **glum|ly** ADV 副詞 [ADV with v] むっつりして □When Eleanor returned, I was still sitting glumly on the couch. エリナーが帰ってきたとき私はまだ浮かぬ顔をしてソファーに座っていた.

glut /glʌt/ (gluts, glutting, glutted) **1** N-COUNT 可算名詞 If there is a **glut of** something, there is so much of it that it cannot all be sold or used. だぶつき, 供給過剰 [usu sing, usu with supp] □Exports have become increasingly important to wineries as they battle a global wine glut. 世界的なワインの供給過剰と戦う上で、ぶどう酒醸造所にとって輸出はますます重要になってきた. **2** V-T 他動詞 If a market **is glutted with** something, there is a glut of that thing. 供給過剰にする [BUSINESS 実業] □The region is glutted with hospitals. この地域には病院が有り余るほどあります.

gm. (gm.)

The plural can be **gm.** or **gms.**

複数は **gm.** か **gms.** である.

gm. is a written abbreviation for **gram**. グラム □...450 gm. (1 lb) mixed soft summer fruits. 柔らかい夏の果物の取り合わせ450グラム (1ポンド).

GM /dʒiː ɛm/ ADJ 形容詞 **GM** crops have had one or more genes changed, for example in order to make them resist pests better. **GM** food contains ingredients made from GM crops. **GM** is an abbreviation for **genetically modified**. 遺伝子組み換えをされた □Many of us may be eating food containing GM ingredients without realizing it. 多くの人は知らないうちに遺伝子組み換え原料を含む食品を食べている可能性がある.

GMO /dʒiː ɛm oʊ/ (GMOs) N-COUNT 可算名詞 A **GMO** is an animal, plant, or other organism whose genetic structure has been changed by genetic engineering. **GMO** is an abbreviation for "genetically modified organism." 苦しめる, 悩ませる [WRITTEN 書き言葉] □...the presence of GMOs in many processed foods. 遺伝子組み換え生物が多くの加工食品中に存在すること.

GMT /dʒiː ɛm tiː/ **GMT** is the standard time in Great Britain which is used to calculate the time in the rest of the world. **GMT** is an abbreviation for **Greenwich Mean Time**. グリニッジ標準時 □New Mexico is seven hours behind GMT. ニューメキシコ州の時間はグリニッジ標準時より7時間遅い.

gnaw /nɔː/ (gnaws, gnawing, gnawed) **1** V-T/V-I 他動詞/自動詞 If people or animals **gnaw** something or **gnaw at** it, they bite it repeatedly. かじる, 齧食する □Woodlice attack living plants and gnaw at the stems. シロアリは生きている植物を攻撃し、幹を食い荒らす. **2** V-I 自動詞 If a feeling or thought **gnaws at** you, it causes you to keep worrying. 苦しめる, 悩ませる [WRITTEN 書き言葉] □...the nagging disquiet that had gnawed at him for days. 彼を何日にもわたり悩ませたしつこい心配事.

GNP /dʒiː ɛn piː/ (GNPs) N-VAR 可変性名詞 In economics, a country's **GNP** is the total value of all the goods produced and services provided by that country in one year. **GNP** is an abbreviation for **gross national product**. Compare **GDP**. 国民総生産

go
❶ MOVING OR LEAVING
❷ LINK VERB USES
❸ OTHER VERB USES, NOUN USES, AND PHRASES
❹ PHRASAL VERBS

❶ go /goʊ/ (goes, going, went, gone)

In most cases the past participle of **go** is **gone**, but occasionally you use 'been': see **been**.

たいていは **go** の過去分詞は **gone** であるが, 時々 **been** が使われる. **been** 参照.

1 V-T 他動詞/自動詞 When you **go** somewhere, you move or travel there. 行く, 進む [自動詞], 出て行く [他動詞] □We went to Rome. わたしたちはローマに行った. □I went home for the weekend. わたしたちは週末, 帰郷した. □It took us an hour to go three miles. 3マイル進むのに一時間かかった. **2** V-I 自動詞 When you **go**, you leave the place where you are. 行く □Let's go. さあ行こう. **3** V-T/V-I 他動詞/自動詞 You use **go** to say that someone leaves the place where they are and does an activity, often a leisure activity. 出かける, しに行く □We went swimming very early. わたしたちは朝とても早くに泳ぎに行った. □Maybe they've just gone shopping. 彼らは単に買い物に出かけてるのかもしれない. **4** V-T/V-I 他動詞/自動詞 When you **go do** something, you move to a place in order to do it and you do it. You can also **go and do** something, but you always say that someone **went and** did something. 行く, しに行く □I have to go see the doctor. わたしは医者に行かなければならない. □I finished my beer, then went and got another. わたしはビールを飲み干してから次のビールを取りに行った. **5** V-I 自動詞 If you **go to** school, work, or church, you attend it regularly as part of your normal life. 行く, 通う □She will have to go to school. 彼女は学校に行かなければいけないでしょう. **6** V-I 自動詞 When you say where a road or path **goes**, you are saying where it begins or ends, or what places it is in. 行く, 向かう □There's a mountain road that goes from Blairstown to Millbrook Village. ブレアーズタウンからミルブルック村に向かう山道があります. **7** V-I 自動詞 You can use **go** with words like "further" and "beyond" to show the degree or extent of something. ～まですると □The governor went further by agreeing that all policy announcements should be made first in the House. さらに政府はすべての政策を下院で最初に発表することに合意しました. **8** V-I 自動詞 If you say that a period of time **goes** quickly or slowly, you mean that it seems to

pass quickly or slowly. 経過する □ *The weeks go so quickly!* その数週間はあっという間に過ぎちゃうね. **9** V-I 自動詞 If you say where money **goes**, you are saying what it is spent on. 使われる □ *Most of my money goes toward bills.* わたしは請求書の支払いにほとんどお金を使い果たしてしまう. **10** V-I 自動詞 If you say that something **goes to** someone, you mean that it is given to them. 与えられる □ *A lot of credit must go to the chairman and his father.* これはほとんど会長と会長の父親の功績と言わざるを得ない. **11** V-I 自動詞 If someone **goes on** television or radio, they take part in a television or radio program. 出る □ *The president has gone on television to defend stringent new security measures.* 大統領は厳しい新たな公安措置を擁護するためテレビに出演した. **12** V-I 自動詞 If something **goes**, someone gets rid of it. なくなる □ *Exactly how many jobs will go remains unclear.* どのぐらい失業者が出るかはいまだ不明だ. **13** V-I 自動詞 If someone **goes**, they leave their job, usually because they are forced to. 職を去る □ *He had made a humiliating tactical error and he had to go.* 彼はかけひきで不面目な誤りを犯し、辞職せざるをえなくなった. **14** V-I 自動詞 If something **goes into** something else, it is put in it as one of the parts or elements that form it. 入る □ *...the really interesting ingredients that go into the dishes that we all love to eat.* わたしたちみんなが とても好きな料理に入っている大変興味深い素材. **15** V-I 自動詞 If something **goes** in a particular place, it belongs there or should be put there, because that is where you normally keep it. 置かれる □ *The shoes go on the shoe shelf.* 靴は靴棚に置きます. **16** V-I 自動詞 If you say that one number **goes into** another number a particular number of times, you are dividing the second number by the first. 割る □ *Six goes into thirty five times.* 6で30を割ると5だ. **17** V-I 自動詞 If one of a person's senses, such as their sight or hearing, **is going**, it is getting weak and they may soon lose it completely. 悪くなる [INFORMAL くだけた] □ *His eyes are going; he says he has glaucoma.* 彼は目が悪くなってきている. 彼の話では緑内障なんだそうだ. **18** V-I 自動詞 If something such as a light bulb or a part of an engine **is going**, it is no longer working properly and will soon need to be replaced. だめになる、なくなる □ *I thought it looked as though the battery was going.* 電池がなくなってきてるみたいだとわたしは思った.

❷ go /goʊ/ (goes, going, went, gone) V-LINK 連結動詞 You can use **go** to say that a person or thing changes to another state or condition. For example, if someone **goes crazy**, they become crazy, and if something **goes bad**, it deteriorates. □ *I'm going bald.* わたしは頭がはげだした. □ *Sometimes food goes bad, but people don't know it, so they eat it anyway and then they get sick.* たべものが悪くなっていても気づかずにとにかく食べて、あとで具合が悪くなることがある.

❸ go /goʊ/ (goes, going, went, gone) **1** V-I 自動詞 You use **go** to talk about the way something happens. For example, if an event or situation **goes well**, it is successful. 行く、進行する □ *She says everything is going smoothly.* 彼女はすべてうまく行っていると言う. **2** V-I 自動詞 If a machine or device **is going**, it is working. 動く、機能する □ *What about my copier? Can you get it going again?* わたしのコピー機は？直せる？ **3** V-RECIP 相互動詞 If something **goes with** something else, or if two things **go together**, they look or taste good together. 調和する、似合う □ *I was searching for a pair of gray gloves to go with my new gown.* わたしは新しいドレスに合う灰色の手袋を探していた. □ *I can see that some colors go together and some don't.* 色によって合う色と合わない色があるのは分かる. **4** V-T/V-I 他動詞/自動詞 You use **go** to introduce something you are quoting. For example, you say **the story goes** or **the argument goes** just before you quote all or part of it. なっている、書いてある、展開する □ *The story goes that she went home with him that night.* その夜彼女は彼と家に帰ったらしい. □ *The story goes like this.* それはこんな話だ. **5** V-T 他動詞 You use **go** when indicating that something makes or produces a sound. For example, if you say that something **goes "bang,"** you mean it produces the sound "bang." 鳴る、鳴く □ *She stopped in front of a painting of a dog and she started going "woof woof."* 彼女は犬の絵の前で立ち止まり、「ワンワン」と吠え出した. **6** V-T 他動詞 You can use **go** instead of "say" when you are quoting what someone has said or what you think they will say. 言う [INFORMAL くだけた] □ *He goes to me: "Oh, what do you want?"* 彼は「あれ、何か用？」と私に聞く. **7** N-COUNT 可算名詞 A **go** is an attempt at doing something. やってみること、試み □ *I always wanted to have a go at football.* わたしはずっとフットボールをやってみたかったのだ. □ *She won on her first go.* 一回目で彼女は勝った. **8** N-COUNT 可算名詞 If it is your **go** in a game, it is your turn to do something, for example to play a card or move a piece. 番 [poss N] □ *Now whose go is it?* 今だれの番かな？ **9** → see also **going, gone** **10** PHRASE 句 If you do something **as you go along**, you do it while you are doing another thing, without preparing it beforehand. 実際にやりながら □ *Learning how to become a parent takes time. It's a skill you learn as you go along.* ちゃんとした親になる方法を学ぶには時間がかかる. 実際にやって行くうちに身につくものだ. **11** CONVENTION 慣習表現 If someone says **"Where do we go from here?"** they are asking what should be done next, usually because a problem has not been solved in a satisfactory way. この

後どうしようか. **12** PHRASE 句 If you say that someone is **making a go of** something such as a business or relationship, you mean that they are having some success with it. うまくやってゆく □ *I knew we could make a go of it and be happy.* わたしたちはうまくやっていけて幸せになれるとわたしは思った. **13** PHRASE 句 If you say that someone is always **on the go**, you mean that they are always busy and active. 絶えず行動して、働きづめで [INFORMAL くだけた] □ *I got a new job this year where I am on the go all the time.* わたしは今年新しい職について、そこではずっと働きづめで. **14** PHRASE 句 If you say that there are a particular number of things **to go**, you mean that they still remain to be dealt with. 残りが □ *I still had another five operations to go.* まだあと手術が5件残っていました. **15** PHRASE 句 If you say that there is a certain amount of time **to go**, you mean that there is that amount of time left before something happens or ends. 残されている □ *There is a week to go until the elections.* 選挙まであと1週間あります. **16** PHRASE 句 If you are in a café or restaurant and ask for an item of food **to go**, you mean that you want to take it with you and not eat it there. 持ち帰りの [mainly AM 主に米国英語] □ *...large fries to go.* 持ち帰り用のフライドポテト大で.

❹ go /goʊ/ (goes, going, went, gone)

▶ **go about** **1** PHRASAL VERB 句動詞 The way you **go about** a task or problem is the way you approach it and deal with it. 取り組む □ *I want him back, but I just don't know how to go about it.* わたしは彼に戻ってきて欲しいが、どうしたらいいのか分からない. **2** PHRASAL VERB 句動詞 When you **are going about** your normal activities, you are doing them. せっせとする □ *We were simply going about our business when we were pounced upon by these police officers.* わたしたちが警察官たちに突然捕らえられたとき、わたしたちは自分たちのことをしていただけだ.

▶ **go after** PHRASAL VERB 句動詞 If you **go after** something, you try to get it, catch it, or hit it. 追いかける □ *We're not going after civilian targets.* わたしたちは非軍事的な標的に矛先は向けていない.

▶ **go against** **1** PHRASAL VERB 句動詞 If a person or their behavior **goes against** your wishes, beliefs, or expectations, their behavior is the opposite of what you want, believe in, or expect. 反する □ *Changes are being made here which go against my principles and I cannot agree with them.* わたしの主義に反してここで手が加えられ、納得できなかった. **2** PHRASAL VERB 句動詞 If a decision, vote, or result **goes against** you, you do not get the decision, vote, or result that you wanted. 不利になる □ *The mayor will resign if the vote goes against him.* もしも採決の結果が不利ならば市長は辞任するでしょう.

▶ **go ahead** **1** PHRASAL VERB 句動詞 If someone **goes ahead with** something, they begin to do it or make it, especially after planning, promising, or asking permission to do it. 着手する □ *The district board will vote today on whether to go ahead with the plan.* 計画に着手するかどうかについて今日、地区委員会で投票がある予定だ. **2** PHRASAL VERB 句動詞 If a process or an organized event **goes ahead**, it takes place or is carried out. 行う □ *The event will go ahead as planned in Chicago next summer.* イベントは計画通りに来年の夏シカゴで行われるでしょう.

▶ **go along with** **1** PHRASAL VERB 句動詞 If you **go along with** a rule, decision, or policy, you accept it and obey it. 従う □ *Whatever the majority decided I was prepared to go along with.* わたしは多数決による決定はどんなことであろうと従うつもりだった. **2** PHRASAL VERB 句動詞 If you **go along with** a person or an idea, you agree with them. 賛成する □ *"I don't think a government has properly done it for about the past twenty-five years."—"I'd go along with that."* 「この25年間ぐらい政府はそれをおざなりにしてきたと思う。」「わたしもそう思います。」

▶ **go around** **1** PHRASAL VERB 句動詞 If you **go around to** someone's house, you go to visit them at their house. 訪ねる □ *I asked them to go around to the house to see if they were there.* わたしは彼らがいるか家に見に来るように言った. **2** PHRASAL VERB 句動詞 If you **go around** in a particular way, you behave or dress in that way, often as part of your normal life. いる □ *I got in the habit of going around with bare feet.* わたしは裸足でいる習慣がついた. **3** PHRASAL VERB 句動詞 If a piece of news or a joke **is going around**, it is being told by many people in the same period of time. 広まる □ *There's a nasty sort of rumor going around about it.* それに関してたちの悪い噂が広まっている. **4** PHRASAL VERB 句動詞 If there is enough of something **to go around**, there is enough of it to be shared among a group of people, or to do all the things for which it is needed. 行き渡る □ *Eventually we will not have enough water to go around.* ゆくゆくはみんなに行き渡るだけの水がなくなるだろう.

▶ **go away** **1** PHRASAL VERB 句動詞 If you **go away**, you leave a place or a person's company. 立ち去る □ *I think we need to go away and think about this.* これについては場を変えて考えてみる必要があると思う. **2** PHRASAL VERB 句動詞 If you **go away**, you leave a place and spend a period of time somewhere else, especially as a vacation. 出かける □ *Why don't you and I go away this weekend?* 今週末にわたしと二人で出かけませんか.

▶ **go back on** PHRASAL VERB 句動詞 If you **go back on** a promise or agreement, you do not do what you promised or agreed to do. 撤回する ❏ *The budget crisis has forced the president to go back on his word.* 予算上の問題から大統領は発言を撤回せざるを得なかった.

▶ **go back to** 1 PHRASAL VERB 句動詞 If you **go back to** a task or activity, you start doing it again after you have stopped doing it for a period of time. 戻る ❏ *I now look forward to going back to work as soon as possible.* 今はできるだけ早く仕事に戻りたいと思っている. 2 PHRASAL VERB 句動詞 If you **go back to** a particular point in a lecture, discussion, or book, you start to discuss it. 戻る ❏ *Let me just go back to the point I was making.* 前の論点にちょっと戻ってみましょう.

▶ **go before** 1 PHRASAL VERB 句動詞 Something that **has gone before** has happened or been discussed at an earlier time. 先行するもの ❏ *This is a rejection of most of what has gone before.* これは今まで話し合ってきたことをほとんどすべて却下するものだ. 2 PHRASAL VERB 句動詞 To **go before** a judge, tribunal, or court of law means to be present there as part of an official or legal process. 法廷にもちこまれる ❏ *The case went before Justice Henry on December 23 and was adjourned.* この件は12月23日にヘンリー判事に審理され, 休廷となった.

▶ **go by** 1 PHRASAL VERB 句動詞 If you say that time **goes by**, you mean that it passes. 経つ ❏ *My grandmother was becoming more and more sad and frail as the years went by.* 祖母は年をおうごとにみじめでか弱くなっていった. 2 PHRASAL VERB 句動詞 If you **go by** something, you use it as a basis for a judgment or action. したがって行動する ❏ *If they prove that I was wrong, then I'll go by what they say.* もしもわたしが間違っていると彼らに証明できるのなら, 言い分に従いましょう.

▶ **go down** 1 PHRASAL VERB 句動詞 If a price, level, or amount **goes down**, it becomes lower or less than it was. 低下する ❏ *Income from sales tax went down.* 消費税からの収入が低下した. ❏ *Crime has gone down 70 percent.* 犯罪は7割低下した. 2 PHRASAL VERB 句動詞 If you **go down on** your knees or **on** all fours, you lower your body until it is supported by your knees, or by your hands and knees. 体を低くする ❏ *I went down on my knees and prayed for guidance.* わたしはひざまづいてお導きを祈った. 3 PHRASAL VERB 句動詞 If you say that a remark, idea, or type of behavior **goes down** in a particular way, you mean that it gets a particular kind of reaction from a person or group of people. 受け入れられる ❏ *Lawyers advised their clients that a neat appearance went down well with the judges.* 弁護士たちは依頼人にきちんとした身だしなみは裁判官に受けがいいと助言した. 4 PHRASAL VERB 句動詞 When the sun **goes down**, it goes below the horizon. 沈む ❏ *...the glow left in the sky after the sun has gone down.* 太陽が沈んだあとの空に残った輝き. 5 PHRASAL VERB 句動詞 If a ship **goes down**, it sinks. If a plane **goes down**, it crashes out of the sky. 沈む, 落ちる ❏ *Their aircraft went down during a training exercise.* 彼らの飛行機は訓練中に墜落した. 6 PHRASAL VERB 句動詞 If a computer **goes down**, it stops functioning temporarily. 停止する ❏ *The main computers went down for 30 minutes.* メインコンピューターが30分間停止した. 7 PHRASAL VERB 句動詞 Something that **is going down** is happening. 起こる [INFORMAL くだけた] [usu cont] ❏ *The patrol can detect if something is going down or is about to go down.* 見回りの人は何か起こっているか, 何か起こりそうかどうかを察知できる.

▶ **go for** 1 PHRASAL VERB 句動詞 If you **go for** a particular thing or way of doing something, you choose it. 選ぶ ❏ *People tried to persuade him to go for a more gradual reform program.* 人びとはさらに暫時的な改革計画を採用するように彼を説得しようとした. 2 PHRASAL VERB 句動詞 If you **go for** someone, you attack them. 襲う ❏ *Pantieri went for him, gripping him by the throat.* パンティエリは彼ののど元を握って襲いかかった. 3 PHRASAL VERB 句動詞 If you say that a statement you have made about one person or thing also **goes for** another person or thing, you mean that the statement is also true of this other person or thing. 当てはまる ❏ *It is illegal to dishonor reservations; that goes for restaurants as well as customers.* 予約をしたのに守らないのは違法だ. これはレストランにも客にも当てはまる. 4 PHRASAL VERB 句動詞 If something **goes for** a particular price, it is sold for that amount. 値で売れる ❏ *Some old machines go for as much as 35,000 dollars.* 古い機械のなかには3万5千ドルもの値で売れるものもある.

▶ **go in** PHRASAL VERB 句動詞 If the sun **goes in**, a cloud comes in front of it and it can no longer be seen. 雲に隠れる ❏ *The sun went in, and the breeze became cold.* 太陽が雲に隠れ, そよ風が冷たくなった.

▶ **go in for** PHRASAL VERB 句動詞 If you **go in for** a particular activity, you decide to do it as a hobby or interest. 趣味である, 好む, 凝っている ❏ *They go in for tennis and bowling.* 彼らはテニスとボーリングに凝っている.

▶ **go into** 1 PHRASAL VERB 句動詞 If you **go into** something, you describe or examine it fully or in detail. 説明する, 検討する ❏ *It was a private conversation and I don't want to go into details about what was said.* それは個人的な会話でどんな話をしたかは詳しく説明したくない. 2 PHRASAL VERB 句動詞 If you **go into** something, you decide to do it as your job or career. 就く ❏ *Mr. Pok has now gone into*

the tourism business. ポク氏はいまや観光業に従事している. 3 PHRASAL VERB 句動詞 If an amount of time, effort, or money **goes into** something, it is spent or used to do it, get it, or make it. 費やす ❏ *Is there a lot of effort and money going into this sort of research?* この種の研究にたくさんの労力と資金が費やされているのですか.

▶ **go off** 1 PHRASAL VERB 句動詞 If an explosive device or a gun **goes off**, it explodes or fires. 爆発する, 発射する ❏ *A few minutes later the bomb went off, destroying the vehicle.* 数分後に爆弾が爆発し車両を破壊した. 2 PHRASAL VERB 句動詞 If an alarm bell **goes off**, it makes a sudden loud noise. 鳴る ❏ *Then the fire alarm went off. I just grabbed my clothes and ran out.* そのとき火災警報が鳴りだした. わたしは自分の服をつかんで外に走って出るのがやっとだった. 3 PHRASAL VERB 句動詞 If an electrical device **goes off**, it stops operating. 止まる, 消える ❏ *As the water came in the windows, all the lights went off.* 水が窓から入ってくると明かりがすべて消えた.

▶ **go off with** 1 PHRASAL VERB 句動詞 If someone **goes off with** another person, they leave their husband, wife, or lover and have a relationship with that person. 夫や妻などを捨て一のもとに走る ❏ *I suppose Carolyn went off with some man she'd fallen in love with.* キャロラインはほれた男のところに走ったんだろうと思う. 2 PHRASAL VERB 句動詞 If someone **goes off with** something that belongs to another person, they leave and take it with them. 持ち逃げする, 持ち去る ❏ *He's gone off with my passport.* 彼はわたしのパスポートを持ち去った.

▶ **go on** 1 PHRASAL VERB 句動詞 If you **go on** doing something, or **go on with** an activity, you continue to do it. 続ける ❏ *Unemployment is likely to go on rising this year.* 今年失業率は上昇し続けるであろう. ❏ *I'm all right here. Go on with your work.* 私はここで大丈夫です. あなたは自分の仕事を続けてください. 2 PHRASAL VERB 句動詞 If something **is going on**, it is happening. 進行中である ❏ *While this conversation was going on, I was listening with earnest attention.* この会話が続いている間, わたしはとても大きな関心を寄せて聞いていた. 3 PHRASAL VERB 句動詞 If a process or institution **goes on**, it continues to happen or exist. 続ける ❏ *The population failed to understand the necessity for the war to go on.* 住民たちには戦争を続ける必要性を理解できなかった. 4 PHRASAL VERB 句動詞 If you say that a period of time **goes on**, you mean that it passes. 過ぎる ❏ *Renewable energy will become progressively more important as time goes on.* 再生可能エネルギーは漸次的にますます重要になってゆくであろう. 5 PHRASAL VERB 句動詞 If you **go on to** do something, you do it after you have done something else. 続けてする ❏ *Alliss retired from golf in 1969 and went on to become a successful broadcaster.* アリスはゴルフから1969年に現役引退し, その後放送人として成功した. 6 PHRASAL VERB 句動詞 If you **go on to** a place, you go to it from the place that you have reached. さらに一まで進む ❏ *He goes on to New Orleans tomorrow.* 彼は明日ニューオリンズへと旅を続けます. 7 PHRASAL VERB 句動詞 If you **go on**, you continue saying something or talking about something. 話を続ける ❏ *Meer cleared his throat several times before he went on.* ミーアは数回咳払いをしてから話を続けた. 8 PHRASAL VERB 句動詞 If you **go on about** something, you continue talking about the same thing, often in an annoying way. しゃべり続ける [INFORMAL くだけた] ❏ *He's always going on about his son and daughter.* 彼はいつも自分の息子と娘の話ばかりする. 9 PHRASAL VERB 句動詞 You say "**Go on**" to someone to persuade or encourage them to do something. どうぞ [INFORMAL くだけた] [only imper] ❏ *Go on, it's fun.* さあどうぞ, 面白いですよ. 10 PHRASAL VERB 句動詞 If you talk about the information you have **to go on**, you mean the information you have available to base an opinion or judgment on. 基づく ❏ *But you have to go on the facts.* しかし事実に基づいて話さねばならないよ. 11 PHRASAL VERB 句動詞 If an electrical device **goes on**, it begins operating. つく ❏ *A light went on at seven every evening.* 毎晩7時に明かりがついた.

▶ **go out** 1 PHRASAL VERB 句動詞 If you **go out**, you leave your home in order to do something enjoyable, for example to go to a party, a bar, or the movies. 外出する ❏ *I'm going out tonight.* わたし今夜外出するの. 2 PHRASAL VERB 句動詞 If you **go out with** someone, the two of you spend time together socially, and have a romantic or sexual relationship. つきあう ❏ *I once went out with a French man.* 一時わたしはフランス人の男性とつきあっていた. 3 PHRASAL VERB 句動詞 If you **go out to** do something, you make a deliberate effort to do it. そのつもりでする ❏ *You do not go out to injure opponents.* 相手にけがをさせるつもりでは臨まないものだ. 4 PHRASAL VERB 句動詞 If a light **goes out**, it stops shining. 消える ❏ *The bedroom light went out after a moment.* しばらくすると寝室の明かりが消えた. 5 PHRASAL VERB 句動詞 If something that is burning **goes out**, it stops burning. 消える ❏ *The fire seemed to be going out.* 火は消えそうだった. 6 PHRASAL VERB 句動詞 If a message **goes out**, it is announced, published, or sent out to people. 伝えられる ❏ *Word went out that a column of tanks was on its way.* 戦車隊がこちらに向かっているという話が伝えられた. 7 PHRASAL VERB 句動詞 When the tide **goes out**, the water in the sea gradually moves back to a lower level. 引く ❏ *The tide was going out.* 潮が引いていた. 8 PHRASE 句 You can say "**My heart**

goes out to him" or "**My sympathy goes out to her**" to express the strong sympathy you have for someone in a difficult or unpleasant situation. 深く同情する [FEELINGS 感情] ❑*My heart goes out to Mrs. Adams and her fatherless children.* アダムス夫人と父親を失った子供たちに心から哀悼の意を表します.

▶ **go over** PHRASAL VERB 句動詞 If you **go over** a document, incident, or problem, you examine, discuss, or think about it very carefully. 詳しく調べる, 点検する ❑*I won't know how successful it is until an accountant has gone over the books.* これがどれぐらい成功しているのかは経理担当者が帳簿を詳しく調べるまで分からない.

▶ **go round** → see **go around**

▶ **go through** ❶ PHRASAL VERB 句動詞 If you **go through** an experience or a period of time, especially an unpleasant or difficult one, you experience it. 体験する [BRIT 英国英語] ❑*He was going through a very difficult time.* 彼はとてもつらい目にあっていた. ❷ PHRASAL VERB 句動詞 If you **go through** a lot of things such as papers or clothes, you look at them, usually in order to sort them into groups or to search for a particular item. くまなく調べる, 探す ❑*It was evident that someone had gone through my possessions.* 誰かがわたしの持ち物をくまなく調べたのは明らかだった. ❸ PHRASAL VERB 句動詞 If you **go through** a list, story, or plan, you read or check it from beginning to end. 通して読む, 1つずつ調べる ❑*Going through his list of customers is a massive job.* 彼の顧客名簿を通して調べるのは大仕事だ. ❹ PHRASAL VERB 句動詞 If a law, agreement, or official decision **goes through**, it is approved by a legislature or committee. 通過する ❑*The bill might have gone through if the economy was growing.* この法案は景気が上向きだったら承認されたかもしれない.

▶ **go through with** PHRASAL VERB 句動詞 If you **go through with** an action you have decided on, you do it, even though it may be very unpleasant or difficult for you. 最後までやり通す ❑*Richard pleaded for Belinda to reconsider and not to go through with the divorce.* リチャードはベリンダに考え直して離婚はやめてくれと嘆願した.

▶ **go under** PHRASAL VERB 句動詞 If a business or project **goes under**, it becomes unable to continue in operation or in existence. つぶれる [BUSINESS 実業] ❑*If one firm goes under it could provoke a cascade of bankruptcies.* 1つの会社がつぶれると連鎖倒産が起きることがある.

▶ **go up** ❶ PHRASAL VERB 句動詞 If a price, amount, or level **goes up**, it becomes higher or greater than it was. 上がる ❑*Interest rates went up.* 金利が上がった. ❑*The cost has gone up to $1.95 a minute.* コストが毎分1.95ドルにまで上がった. ❷ PHRASAL VERB 句動詞 When a building, wall, or other structure **goes up**, it is built or fixed in place. 建てられる ❑*He noticed a new building going up near Whitaker Park.* 彼はウィテカー公園の近くに新しいビルが建築中なのに気づいた. ❸ PHRASAL VERB 句動詞 If something **goes up**, it explodes or starts to burn, usually suddenly and with great intensity. 炎上する ❑*The hotel went up in flames.* ホテルは突然炎上した. ❹ PHRASAL VERB 句動詞 If a shout or cheer **goes up**, it is made by a lot of people together. 沸き起こる ❑*A cheer went up from the other passengers.* 他の乗客から声援が沸き起こった.

▶ **go with** ❶ PHRASAL VERB 句動詞 If one thing **goes with** another thing, the two things officially belong together, so that if you get one, you also get the other. 付いて来る ❑*...the lucrative $250,000 salary that goes with the job.* その仕事の25万ドルという高い給与. ❷ PHRASAL VERB 句動詞 If one thing **goes with** another thing, it is usually found or experienced together with the other thing. 伴う ❑*For many women, the status which goes with being a wife is important.* 多くの女性にとって, 妻であるという地位が重要だ.

▶ **go without** PHRASAL VERB 句動詞 If you **go without** something that you need or usually have or do, you do not get it or do it. なしで済ませる ❑*I have known what it is like to go without food for days.* 何も食べずに何日も過ごすのがどんな事だかわたしは承知していた.

goad /goʊd/ (**goads, goading, goaded**) V-T 他動詞 If you **goad** someone, you deliberately make them feel angry or irritated, often causing them to react by doing something. わざといらだたせる, 刺激する ❑*Charles was always goading me.* チャールズにはいつもいらいらさせられた. ● N-COUNT 可算名詞 **Goad** is also a noun. 刺激, 突き棒 ❑*Her presence was just one more goad to Joanna's unraveling nerves.* 彼女の存在はぼろぼろになっているジョアナの神経を刺激するもう1つの材料だった.

go-ahead ❶ N-SING 単数名詞 If you give someone or something **the go-ahead**, you give them permission to start doing something. 許可 ❑*Chuck gave Pellman the go-ahead to speak publicly about the injury he sustained.* チャックは自分の負った傷についてペルマンが公言することを許した. ❷ ADJ 形容詞 A **go-ahead** person or organization tries hard to succeed, often by using new methods. 積極的な [ADJ n] ❑*Fairview Estate is one of the oldest and the most go-ahead wine producers in South Africa.* フェアビューぶどう園は南アフリカ最古で, 最も積極的なワイン生産地の1つである.

goal /goʊl/ (**goals**) ❶ N-COUNT 可算名詞 In games such as soccer or hockey, the **goal** is the space into which the players try to get the ball in order to score a point for their team. ゴール ❑*The Dragons had only one shot on goal.* ドラゴンズはシュートを1本しかゴ

ールしなかった. ❷ N-COUNT 可算名詞 In games such as soccer or hockey, a **goal** is when a player gets the ball into the goal, or the point that is scored by doing this. 得点 ❑*They scored five goals in the first half of the match.* 彼らは試合の前半に5点入れた. ❸ N-COUNT 可算名詞 Something that is your **goal** is something that you hope to achieve, especially when much time and effort will be needed. 目標, 目的 ❑*It's a matter of setting your own goals and following them.* 自分で目標を立ててそれに向かって進めばすむことだ.
→ see **football, soccer**

Word Partnership	*goal* は次の語句と使われる:
V.	**shoot at a** goal ❶ **score a** goal ❷ **accomplish a** goal, **share a** goal ❸
ADJ.	**winning** goal ❷ **attainable** goal, **main** goal ❸

goalie /goʊli/ (**goalies**) N-COUNT 可算名詞 A **goalie** is the same as a **goalkeeper**. ゴールキーパー [INFORMAL くだけた]

goal|keeper /goʊlkipər/ (**goalkeepers**) N-COUNT 可算名詞 A **goalkeeper** is the player on a sports team whose job is to guard the goal. ゴールキーパー

goal|less /goʊllɪs/ ADJ 形容詞 In soccer, a **goalless** draw is a game which ends without any goals having been scored. 無得点の ❑*The fixture ended in a goalless draw.* その試合の結果は無得点引き分けでした.

goal|post /goʊlpoʊst/ (**goalposts**) also **goal post** N-COUNT 可算名詞 A **goalpost** is one of the two upright wooden posts that are connected by a crossbar and form the goal in games such as soccer and hockey. ゴールポスト
→ see **football**

goat /goʊt/ (**goats**) N-COUNT 可算名詞 A **goat** is a farm animal or a wild animal that is about the size of a sheep. Goats have horns, and hairs on their chin which resemble a beard. ヤギ

gob|ble /gɒbəl/ (**gobbles, gobbling, gobbled**) V-T 他動詞 If you **gobble** food, you eat it quickly and greedily. むさぼり食う, ぺろりと平らげる ❑*Pete gobbled all the beef stew.* ピートはビーフシチューを全部平らげた. ● PHRASAL VERB 句動詞 **Gobble down** and **gobble up** mean the same as **gobble**. がつがつ食う, 丸のみにする ❑*There were dangerous beasts in the river that might gobble you up.* あなたを丸のみにできるような危険な動物たちが川にいた.

go-between (**go-betweens**) N-COUNT 可算名詞 A **go-between** is a person who takes messages between people who are unable or unwilling to meet each other. 仲介者, 仲立ち人 ❑*He will act as a go-between to try and work out an agenda.* 彼は仲介役となり議事日程を組もうとするでしょう.

god /gɒd/ (**gods**) ❶ N-PROPER 固有名詞 The name **God** is given to the spirit or being who is worshipped as the creator and ruler of the world, especially by Jews, Christians, and Muslims. 神 ❑*He believes in God.* 彼は神を信じている. ❷ CONVENTION 慣習表現 People sometimes use **God** in exclamations to emphasize something that they are saying, or to express surprise, fear, or excitement. This use could cause offense. うわあ！, あらっ！, やばい！ [EMPHASIS 強調] ❑*Oh my God, he's shot somebody.* 何てこった！だれかが彼に撃たれた. ❑*Good God, it's Mr. Harper!* ひえ~やばい, ハーパー先生だ！ ❸ N-COUNT 可算名詞 In many religions, a **god** is one of the spirits or beings that are believed to have power over a particular part of the world or nature. 神 ❑*...Zeus, king of the gods.* 神々の王, ゼウス. ❹ N-COUNT 可算名詞 Someone who is admired very much by a person or group of people, and who influences them a lot, can be referred to as a **god**. 神様 ❑*To his followers he was a god.* 彼は信奉者にとって神様であった. ❺ PHRASE 句 You can say **God knows**, **God only knows**, or **God alone knows** to emphasize that you do not know something. 神のみぞ知る, だれも知らない [EMPHASIS 強調] ❑*God alone knows what she thinks.* 彼女がどう思っているかはだれも知らない. ❻ PHRASE 句 If someone says **God knows** in reply to a question, they mean that they do not know the answer. 知らない [EMPHASIS 強調] ❑*"Where is he now?" —"God knows."* 「彼は今どこにいるの？」「知らない！」 ❼ PHRASE 句 If someone uses expressions such as **what in God's name**, **why in God's name**, or **how in God's name**, they are emphasizing how angry, annoyed, or surprised they are. 一体全体 [INFORMAL くだけた, EMPHASIS 強調] ❑*What in God's name do you expect me to do?* 一体全体わたしに何をしろって言うの？ ❽ PHRASE 句 If a person thinks they are **God's gift to** someone or something, they think they are perfect or extremely good. 神の恵み [INFORMAL くだけた] ❑*Are men God's gift to women? Some of them think they are.* 男性は女性にとって神の恵みか？ 中にはそう思う人もいる. ❾ PHRASE 句 If someone **plays God**, they act as if they have unlimited power and can do anything they want. 神のようにふるまう [DISAPPROVAL 不賛成] ❑*You have no right to play God in my life!* あなたには私の人生で神のようにふるまう権利なんてないわ！ ❿ PHRASE 句 You can use **God** in expressions such as **I hope to God**, or **I wish to God**,

or I **swear to God**, in order to emphasize what you are saying. ぜ ひとも [EMPHASIS 強調] ❑ I hope to God they are paying you well. せ めてきみがいい給料をもらっているのならいいけど. **11** PHRASE 句 If you say **God willing**, you are saying that something will happen if all goes well. 神のおぼしめしがあれば ❑ God willing, there will be a breakthrough. 神のおぼしめしがあれば、進展があるだろ う. **12** honest to God → see honest **13** for God's sake → see sake **14** thank God → see thank
→ see religion

god|dess /gɒdɪs/ (goddesses) N-COUNT 可算名詞 In many religions, a **goddess** is a female spirit or being that is believed to have power over a particular part of the world or nature. 女神 ❑...Diana, the goddess of war. 戦争の女神、ディアナ.
→ see religion

going /gəʊɪŋ/ **1** PHRASE 句 If you say that something **is going to** happen, you mean that it will happen in the future, usually quite soon. するだろう ❑ I think it's going to be successful. わたしは これは成功すると思う. ❑ You're going to enjoy this. あなたはこれを 楽しむでしょう. **2** PHRASE 句 You say that you **are going to** do something to express your intention or determination to do it. す るつもりである、しようと思っている ❑ I'm going to go to bed. わたしは 寝ようと思っている. ❑ He announced that he's going to resign. 彼は辞 任するつもりだと発表した. **3** N-UNCOUNT 不可算名詞 You use **the going** to talk about how easy or difficult it is to do something. You can also say that something is, for example, **hard going** or **tough going**. 進み具合、状況 ❑ He has her support to fall back on when the going gets tough. 状況が悪くなったら彼は彼女を頼りにできる. **4** ADJ 形容詞 The **going** rate or the **going** salary is the usual amount of money that you expect to pay or receive for something. 相場の [ADJ n] ❑ That's about half the going price on world oil markets. それは 世界の石油市場の相場の約半値です. **5** → see also **go 6** PHRASE 句 If someone or something **has a lot going for** them, they have a lot of advantages. 有利な点がある ❑ This area has a lot going for it. この 地域は有利な点がたくさんあります. **7** PHRASE 句 When you **get going**, you start doing something or start a journey, especially after a delay. 始める ❑ Now what about that shopping list? I've got to get going. ところであの買い物リストはどうしたの？わたしはそろそ ろ行かなきゃならないわ. **8** PHRASE 句 If you say that someone should do something **while the going is good**, you are advising them to do it while things are going well and they still have the opportunity, because you think it will become much more difficult to do. 状況がいいうちに ❑ People are leaving in the thousands while the going is good. 状況が悪化する前にと何千人もが去ろうとして いる. **9** PHRASE 句 If you **keep going**, you continue doing things or doing a particular thing. 続ける ❑ I like to keep going. I hate to sit still. わたしはこのまま続けたい. じっとしてるのは嫌い. **10** **going concern** → see concern

goings-on N-PLURAL 複数名詞 If you describe events or activities as **goings-on**, you mean that they are strange, interesting, amusing, or dishonest. 出来事 ❑ The Mexican girl had found out about the goings-on in the factory. メキシコ人の女の子は工場 での出来事に気づいていた.

gold /gəʊld/ (golds) **1** N-UNCOUNT 不可算名詞 **Gold** is a valuable, yellow-colored metal that is used for making jewelry and ornaments, and as an international currency. 金 ❑...a sapphire set in gold. 金にはめ込んであるサファイア. ❑ The price of gold was going up. 金の価格は上昇していた. **2** N-UNCOUNT 不可算 名詞 **Gold** is jewelry and other things that are made of gold. 金 製品 ❑ We handed over all our gold and money. わたしたちは金製品や お金をすべて手渡した. **3** COLOR 色彩語 Something that is **gold** is a bright yellow color, and is often shiny. 金色 ❑ I'd been wearing Michel's black and gold shirt. わたしはミシェルの黒と金色のシャツを 着ていた. **4** N-VAR 可変性名詞 A **gold** is the same as a **gold medal**. 金メダル [INFORMAL くだけた] ❑ His ambition was to win gold at the Atlanta Games in 1996. 1996年のアトランタ大会で金メダルを獲得する ことが彼の夢だった. **5** PHRASE 句 If you say that a child is being **as good as gold**, you are emphasizing that they are behaving very well and are not causing you any problems. 行儀がよい [EMPHASIS 強調] ❑ The boys were as good as gold on our walk. 男の子たちは歩い ている最中、とても行儀がよかった. **6** PHRASE 句 If you say that someone has **a heart of gold**, you are emphasizing that they are very good and kind to other people. 親切な心 [EMPHASIS 強調] ❑ They are all good boys with hearts of gold. They would never steal. 彼ら はみんな親切なよい子たちだ. 絶対に盗みはしないだろうに.
→ see metal, mineral, money

gold card (gold cards) N-COUNT 可算名詞 A **gold card** is a special type of credit card that gives you extra benefits such as a higher spending limit. ゴールドカード

gold|en /gəʊldən/ **1** ADJ 形容詞 Something that is **golden** is bright yellow in color. 金色の ❑ She combed and arranged her golden hair. 彼女は黄金色の髪をとかして整えた. **2** ADJ 形容詞 **Golden** things are made of gold. 金製の ❑...a golden chain with a golden locket. 金のロケットのついた金の鎖. **3** ADJ 形容詞 If you describe

something as **golden**, you mean it is wonderful because it is likely to be successful and rewarding, or because it is the best of its kind. すばらしい、絶好の ❑ He says there's a golden opportunity for peace which must be seized. 絶対につかまなければ いけない、平和へのまたとないチャンスがあると彼は言っていま す. **4** PHRASE 句 If you refer to a man as a **golden boy** or a woman as a **golden girl**, you mean that they are especially popular and successful. 人気者、売れっ子 ❑ When the movie came out the critics went wild, hailing Tarantino as the golden boy of the 1990s. 映画が公開 された時、評論家は狂喜し、タランティーノを1990年代の寵児 (ちょう じ) と呼んだ.

gold|en hand|shake (golden handshakes) N-COUNT 可算名詞 A **golden handshake** is a large sum of money that a company gives to an employee when he or she leaves, as a reward for long service or good work. 多額の退職金 [BUSINESS 実業] ❑ And if Mr. Pell, 49, is axed following a takeover, he would be in line to collect a golden handshake of $1 million. さらに、もし会社買収に伴って首になれば、49 歳のペルさんは100万ドルの退職金をもらえる立場にあるだろう.

gold|en para|chute (golden parachutes) N-COUNT 可算名 詞 A **golden parachute** is an agreement to pay a large amount of money to a senior executive of a company if they are forced to leave. 多額の退職金 [BUSINESS 実業] ❑ Golden parachutes entitle them to a full year's salary if they get booted out of the company. もしも会社を 首になったら、一年分の給料をそっくり退職金としてもらえる権利が 彼らにはある.

gold|en rule (golden rules) N-COUNT 可算名詞 A **golden rule** is a principle you should remember because it will help you to be successful. 黄金律 ❑ Hanson's golden rule is to add value to whatever business he buys. ハンソンの黄金律は買収したたとえどんな事業でも価 値を付加することにある.

gold|fish /gəʊldfɪʃ/ (goldfish)

> Goldfish is both the singular and the plural form.

> Goldfish は単数形でも複数形でもある.

N-COUNT 可算名詞 **Goldfish** are small gold or orange fish which are often kept as pets. 金魚

gold med|al (gold medals) N-COUNT 可算名詞 A **gold medal** is a medal made of gold which is awarded as first prize in a contest or competition. 金メダル ❑...her ambition to win a gold medal at the Winter Olympics. 冬季オリンピックで金メダルを獲得するという彼女 の野心.

gold|mine /gəʊldmaɪn/ N-SING 単数名詞 If you describe something such as a business or idea as a **goldmine**, you mean that it produces large profits. 宝の山 ❑ The book is a goldmine. その 本は宝の山だ.

golf /gɒlf/ N-UNCOUNT 不可算名詞 **Golf** is a game in which you use long sticks called clubs to hit a small, hard ball into holes that are spread out over a large area of grassy land. ゴルフ ❑ "Do you play golf?" he asked me suddenly. 「ゴルフするの？」と彼は突然聞 いた.
→ see Picture Dictionary: golf

golf club (golf clubs) **1** N-COUNT 可算名詞 A **golf club** is a long, thin, metal stick with a piece of wood or metal at one end that you use to hit the ball in golf. ゴルフのクラブ **2** N-COUNT 可算名 詞 A **golf club** is a social organization which provides a golf course and a building to meet in for its members. ゴルフクラブ

golf course (golf courses) N-COUNT 可算名詞 A **golf course** is a large area of grass which is specially designed for people to play golf on. ゴルフ場

golf|er /gɒlfər/ (golfers) N-COUNT 可算名詞 A **golfer** is a person who plays golf for pleasure or as a profession. ゴルファー ❑...one of the world's top golfers. 世界一流のゴルファーの一人.
→ see golf

golf|ing /gɒlfɪŋ/ **1** ADJ 形容詞 **Golfing** is used to describe things that involve the playing of golf or that are used while playing golf. ゴルフの、ゴルフ用の [ADJ n] ❑ He was wearing a cream silk shirt and a tartan golfing cap. 彼はクリーム色の絹のシャツを着て タータンチェックのゴルフの帽子をかぶっていた. **2** N-UNCOUNT 不 可算名詞 **Golfing** is the activity of playing golf. ゴルフをすること ❑ You can play tennis or go golfing. あなたはテニスかゴルフをすること ができます.

gone /gɒn/ **1** **Gone** is the past participle of **go**. goの過去分詞 **2** ADJ 形容詞 When someone is **gone**, they have left the place where you are and are no longer there. When something is **gone**, it is no longer present or no longer exists. 留守をする [v-link ADJ] ❑ He knows how hard it was for her while he was gone. 彼には自分の留 守中、彼女がどんなに苦労するかが分かっていた. ❑ He's already been gone four hours! 彼が出掛けてからもう4時間経っている！

gong /gɒn/ (gongs) N-COUNT 可算名詞 A **gong** is a large, flat, circular piece of metal that you hit with a hammer to make a sound like a loud bell. Gongs are sometimes used as musical

G

Picture Dictionary

golf

club house · cart path · sand trap · green · golfer · sand trap · golf cart · golf club · golf ball · hole · green

instruments, or to give a signal that it is time to do something. ど
ら □ *On the stroke of seven, a gong summons guests into the diningroom.*
7時きっかりにどらの音で客は食堂に呼ばれる。

gon|na /ɡɔnə/ **Gonna** is used in written English to represent
the words "going to" when they are pronounced informally. する
つもり □ *Then what am I gonna do?* じゃあ、わたしはどうしようか？

---

good

❶ DESCRIBING QUALITY,
   EXPRESSING APPROVAL
❷ BENEFICIAL
❸ MORALLY RIGHT
❹ OTHER USES

---

❶ **good** /ɡʊd/ (**better, best**) **1** ADJ 形容詞 **Good** means pleasant
or enjoyable. 楽しい、愉快な、快適な □ *We had a really good time
together.* わたしたちはとても楽しい時を共にした。 □ *I know they
would have a better life here.* あの子達はここのほうが良い生活が送れ
るだろうとは思う。 **2** ADJ 形容詞 **Good** means of a high quality,
standard, or level. 上質な、質の良い、水準の高い □ *Exercise is just
as important to health as good food.* 運動は良い食べ物と同じように健
康に大切です。 □ *His parents wanted Raymond to have the best possible
education.* 両親はレイモンドに最良の教育を受けさせたいと思っ
た。 **3** ADJ 形容詞 If you are **good at** something, you are skillful
and successful at doing it. 上手で、有能で □ *He was very good at his
work.* 彼はとても仕事ができる男だった。 □ *I'm not very good at singing.*
わたしは歌があまりうまくない。 **4** ADJ 形容詞 If you describe a
piece of news, an action, or an effect as **good**, you mean that it is
likely to result in benefit or success. 都合の良い □ *On balance,
biotechnology should be good news for developing countries.* あらゆる
ことを考慮すると、バイオ技術は発展途上国にとって朗報であろう。
□ *I think the response was good.* よい反応が得られたと思う。 **5** ADJ
形容詞 A **good** idea, reason, method, or decision is a sensible or
valid one. 良い、適切な、もっともな □ *They thought it was a good
idea to make some offenders do community service.* 彼らは一部の犯罪者
たちに社会奉仕をさせるのは名案だと思った。 □ *There is good reason
to doubt this.* これを疑うのにはそれ相応の理由がある。 **6** ADJ 形容
詞 If you say that **it is good that** something should happen or
good to do something, you mean it is desirable, acceptable, or
right. けっこうな、望ましい □ *I think it's good that some people are
going.* わたしは一部の人たちがいなくなるのはけっこうなことだと
思う。 **7** N-UNCOUNT 不可算名詞 If someone or something is **no
good** or is **not any good**, they are not satisfactory or are of a low
standard. 良いこと [with brd-neg] □ *If the weather's no good then I
won't take any pictures.* 天気がよくなければ写真は撮らない。 **8** ADJ
形容詞 A **good** estimate or indication of something is an accurate
one. 正確な、確実な □ *We have a fairly good idea of what's going on.* わ
たしたちは状況がかなり正確にわかっている。 □ *This is a much better
indication of what a school is really like.* こちらの方が学校の実態を正確
に示している。 **9** ADJ 形容詞 If you get a **good** deal or a **good**
price when you buy or sell something, you receive a lot in exchange
for what you give. もうかる、てごろな □ *Whether such properties
are a good deal will depend on individual situations.* このような不動産
がいい買いものになるかどうかはその人の状況次第だ。 **10** ADJ 形容
詞 Someone who is in a **good** mood is cheerful and pleasant to be
with. 機嫌の良い □ *People were in a pretty good mood.* 人びとはかな
りいい機嫌だった。 □ *He exudes natural charm and good humor.* かれ
は持ち前の魅力と陽気さにあふれている。 **11** ADJ 形容詞 If people are
good friends, they get along well together and are very close. 親
しい、仲の良い [ADJ n] □ *She and Gavin are good friends.* 彼女とギャビ

ンは親友です。 **12** ADJ 形容詞 You use **good** to emphasize the great
extent or degree of something. たっぷりの、かなりの [EMPHASIS
強調] ['a' ADJ n] □ *We waited a good fifteen minutes.* わたしたちはた
っぷり15分は待った。 **13** CONVENTION 慣用表現 You say "**Good**" or
"**Very good**" to express pleasure, satisfaction, or agreement with
something that has been said or done, especially when you are
in a position of authority. よかった！、よし！ □ *"Are you all right?"*
— *"I'm fine."* — *"Good. So am I."* 「大丈夫かい？」「はい」「よかった、
僕も大丈夫だ」 □ *Oh good, Tom's just come in.* あーよかった、ちょう
どトムがやって来た。 **14** PHRASE 句 If you say **it's a good thing that**
something is the case, you mean that it is fortunate. よかった、幸
運だ □ *It's a good thing you aren't married.* あなたが結婚しなくて
よかった。 **15** PHRASE 句 If you say that something or someone is
as good as new, you mean that they are in a very good condition
or state, especially after they have been damaged or ill. 新品同様
で □ *I only use that on special occasions, so it's as good as new.* あれは
特別な場合にしか使わないから、新品同様だ。 **16** PHRASE 句 You
use **good old** before the name of a person, place, or thing when
you are referring to them in an affectionate way. いとしい、親愛
な [FEELINGS 感情] □ *Good old Harry. Reliable to the end.* 親愛なるハ
リー。最後まで頼りにできた。 **17** → see also **best, better 18** good
deal → see **deal 19** in good faith → see **faith 20** so far so good → see
far 21 good job → see **job 22** the good old days → see **old 23** in good
shape → see **shape 24** to stand someone in good stead → see **stead
25** in good time → see **time 26** too good to be true → see **true**

Thesaurus   good また次を参照：

ADJ.	agreeable, enjoyable, nice, pleasant; (ant.) disagreeable, unpleasant ❶ **1**
	able, capable, skilled; (ant.) unqualified, unskilled ❶ **3**

---

❷ **good** /ɡʊd/ (**better, best**) **1** ADJ 形容詞 If something is
good for a person or organization, it benefits them. 役に立つ、
体によい [v-link ADJ 'for' n] □ *Rain water was once considered to be
good for the complexion.* 雨水はかつて顔のつやによいと考えられて
いた。 **2** N-SING 単数名詞 If something is done **for the good** of
a person or organization, it is done in order to benefit them. 利
益、改善 [with poss] □ *The president urged him to resign for the good
of the country.* 大統領は国家のために彼が辞任することを強く勧告し
た。 □ *Victims want to see justice done not just for themselves, but for the
greater good of society.* 被害者は自分たちのためだけでなく社会全体の
利益のために法の裁きが下されることを望んでいる。 **3** N-UNCOUNT
不可算名詞 If you say that doing something is **no good** or does
not do any good, you mean that doing it is not of any use or will
not bring any success. (否定形で) 役に立たない □ *It's no good
worrying about it now.* そのことを今更心配しても何にもならない。
□ *We gave them water and kept them warm, but it didn't do any good.* 私
たちはそれらに水をやり暖かいところに置いたが、何の効果もなか
った。 **4** PHRASE 句 If you say that something will **do** someone
good, you mean that it will benefit them or improve them. ため
になる □ *The outing will do me good.* 出かけることは私のためになるだ
ろう。 □ *It's probably done you good to get away for a few hours.* 数時間
休むことはきっときみのためになったよ。 **5** → see also **best, better**

---

❸ **good** /ɡʊd/ (**better, best**) **1** N-UNCOUNT 不可算名詞 **Good**
is what is considered to be right according to moral standards
or religious beliefs. 善 □ *Good and evil may co-exist within one
family.* 善悪はひとつの家族の中で共存することがある。 **2** ADJ 形容
詞 Someone who is **good** is morally correct in their attitudes and
behavior. 善良な □ *The president is a good man.* 大統領は善良な人間
だ。 **3** ADJ 形容詞 Someone, especially a child, who is **good** obeys
rules and instructions and behaves in a socially correct way. 行

儀のよい，おりこうな □ *The children were very good.* 子供たちはとても行儀がよかった. □ *I'm going to be a good boy now.* 僕はこれからおりこうさんになるよ. **4** ADJ 形容詞 Someone who is **good** is kind and thoughtful. 優しい □ *You are good to me.* あなたは私に優しいね. □ *Her good intentions were thwarted almost immediately.* 彼女の親切な気持ちはほぼ瞬間的に無駄になった. **5** → see also **best, better** **6** **good as gold** → see **gold**

❹ good /gʊd/ **1** PHRASE 句 **As good as** can be used to mean "almost". ほとんど □ *His career is as good as over.* 彼のキャリアは終わったも同然だ. **2** PHRASE 句 If something changes or disappears **for good**, it never changes back or comes back as it was before. 永遠に □ *Some of the nation's manufacturing jobs may be gone for good.* 国内の製造業の仕事の一部が永久的に失われたのかもしれない. **3** PHRASE 句 If someone **makes good** a threat or promise or **makes good on** it, they do what they have threatened or promised to do. (脅迫に) 応じる，(約束を) 守る [mainly AM 主に米国英語] □ *He was confident the allies would make good on their pledges.* 彼は，同盟国が誓約を守ることに自信を持っていました. **4** → see also **goods** **5** **good gracious** → see **gracious** **6** **good grief** → see **grief** **7** **good heavens** → see **heaven** **8** **good lord** → see **lord**

good after|noon CONVENTION 慣習表現 You say "**Good afternoon**" when you are greeting someone in the afternoon. こんにちは [FORMAL 形式ばった，FORMULAE 決まり文句]

good|bye /gʊdbaɪ/ (**goodbyes**) also **good-bye** **1** CONVENTION 慣習表現 You say "**Goodbye**" to someone when you or they are leaving, or at the end of a telephone conversation. さようなら，失礼します [FORMULAE 決まり文句] **2** N-COUNT 可算名詞 When you say your **goodbyes**, you say something such as "Goodbye" when you leave. 別れの言葉 □ *He said his goodbyes knowing that a long time would pass before he would see his child again.* 彼は子供に再開できる日が遠い先であることを知りつつ別れを告げた. □ *Perry and I exchanged goodbyes.* ペリーと私は別れの言葉を交わした. **3** PHRASE 句 If you **say goodbye** or **wave goodbye** to something that you want or usually have, you accept that you are not going to have it. 見切りをつける □ *He has probably said goodbye to his last chance of Olympic gold.* おそらく彼はオリンピック金への最後のチャンスをあきらめたのだろう. **4** **to kiss** something **goodbye** → see **kiss**

good eve|ning CONVENTION 慣習表現 You say "**Good evening**" when you are greeting someone in the evening. こんばんは [FORMAL 形式ばった，FORMULAE 決まり文句]

good-looking (**better-looking, best-looking**) ADJ 形容詞 Someone who is **good-looking** has an attractive face. (男性に対して) ハンサムな，(女性に対して) きれいな □ *Cassandra noticed him because he was good-looking.* カッサンドラが彼のことに気づいたのはハンサムだったからだ.

When you are describing someone's appearance, you generally use **pretty** and **beautiful** to describe women, girls, and babies. **Beautiful** is a much stronger word than **pretty**. The equivalent word for a man is **handsome**. **Good-looking** and **attractive** can be used to describe people of either sex. **Pretty** can also be used to modify adjectives and adverbs but is less strong than **very**. In this sense, **pretty** is informal.

good morn|ing CONVENTION 慣習表現 You say "**Good morning**" when you are greeting someone in the morning. おはようございます [FORMAL 形式ばった，FORMULAE 決まり文句]

good-natured ADJ 形容詞 A **good-natured** person or animal is naturally friendly and does not get angry easily. 穏やかな □ *Bates looks like a good-natured fellow.* ベーツは穏やかな男のようだ.

good|ness /gʊdnəs/ **1** EXCLAM 感嘆詞 People sometimes say "**goodness**" or "**my goodness**" to express surprise. 「あら！」，「ええっ！」など驚きを表す □ *Goodness, I wonder if he knows.* あらまあ，彼は知っているのかしら. [FEELINGS 感情] **2** **for goodness sake** → see **sake** **3** **thank goodness** → see **thank** **4** N-UNCOUNT 不可算名詞 **Goodness** is the quality of being kind, helpful, and honest. 善良さ，善 □ *He retains a faith in human goodness.* 彼は性善説を信じている.

good night also **goodnight** **1** CONVENTION 慣習表現 You say "**Good night**" to someone late in the evening before one of you goes home or goes to sleep. おやすみなさい（夜の別れの言葉としても用いられる）[FORMULAE 決まり文句] **2** PHRASE 句 If you **say good night** to someone or **kiss** them **good night**, you say something such as "Good night" to them or kiss them before one of you goes home or goes to sleep. おやすみの言葉をかける/キスをする □ *Eleanor went upstairs to say good night to the children.* エレノアは子供たちにおやすみの言葉をかけるために2階に行った. □ *Both men rose to their feet and kissed her goodnight.* 両方の男が立ち上がって彼女におやすみのキスをした.

goods /gʊdz/ **1** N-PLURAL 複数名詞 **Goods** are things that are made to be sold. 商品，製品 □ *Money can be exchanged for goods or services.* お金は商品やサービスと交換できる. **2** N-PLURAL 複数名詞 Your **goods** are the things that you own and that can be moved. 所有物 □ *You can give your unwanted goods to charity.* 不要なものはチ

ャリティーに寄付してよい.
→ see **economics**

good|will /gʊdwɪl/ **1** N-UNCOUNT 不可算名詞 **Goodwill** is a friendly or helpful attitude toward other people, countries, or organizations. 善意 □ *I invited them to dinner, a gesture of goodwill.* 私は好意のしるしとして彼らを夕食に誘った. **2** N-UNCOUNT 不可算名詞 The **goodwill** of a business is something such as its good reputation, which increases the value of the business. 信頼，信頼関係 [BUSINESS 実業] □ *We do not want to lose the goodwill built up over 175 years.* 我々が175年にわたって築いた信頼関係を失いたくない.

goose /gus/ (**geese**) **1** N-COUNT 可算名詞 A **goose** is a large bird that has a long neck and webbed feet. Geese are often farmed for their meat. ガチョウ **2** N-UNCOUNT 不可算名詞 **Goose** is the meat from a goose that has been cooked. ガチョウの肉 □ *...roast goose.* ローストしたガチョウの肉

gore /gɔr/ (**gores, goring, gored**) **1** V-T 他動詞 If someone **is gored** by an animal, they are badly wounded by its horns or tusks. 傷つける [usu passive] □ *Carruthers had been gored by a rhinoceros.* キャラザーズはサイに襲われ負傷した. **2** N-UNCOUNT 不可算名詞 **Gore** is blood from a wound that has become thick. 血のり □ *There were pools of blood and gore on the pavement.* 歩道は血や血のりがたまっていた.

gorge /gɔrdʒ/ (**gorges, gorging, gorged**) **1** N-COUNT 可算名詞 A **gorge** is a deep, narrow valley with very steep sides, usually where a river passes through mountains or an area of hard rock. 峡谷 □ *...the deep gorge between these hills.* 山と山の間のの深い峡谷 **2** V-T/V-I 他動詞/自動詞 If you **gorge on** something or **gorge yourself on** it, you eat lots of it in a very greedy way. がつがつ食べる □ *I could spend each day gorging on chocolate.* 私は毎日チョコレートをむしゃむしゃ食べながら過ごすことができる.
→ see **river**

gor|geous /gɔrdʒəs/ **1** ADJ 形容詞 If you say that something is **gorgeous**, you mean that it gives you a lot of pleasure or is very attractive. 素晴らしい [INFORMAL くだけた] □ *...gorgeous mountain scenery.* 素晴らしい山の風景 □ *It's a gorgeous day.* とてもいい天気だ. **2** ADJ 形容詞 If you describe someone as **gorgeous**, you mean that you find them very sexually attractive. 色っぽい，セクシーな [INFORMAL くだけた] □ *The cosmetics industry uses gorgeous women to sell its skincare products.* 化粧品業界はスキンケア製品の販売に魅力的な女性を利用する.

go|ril|la /gərɪlə/ (**gorillas**) N-COUNT 可算名詞 A **gorilla** is a very large ape. It has long arms, black fur, and a black face. ゴリラ
→ see **primate**

gory /gɔri/ (**gorier, goriest**) ADJ 形容詞 **Gory** situations involve people being injured or dying in a horrible way. せいさんな，むごたらしい □ *...the gory details of Mayan human sacrifices.* マヤ文明における人身御供のむごたらしい詳細

gosh /gɒʃ/ EXCLAM 感嘆詞 Some people say "**Gosh**" when they are surprised. 「おや」，「まあ」などの驚きを表す □ *Gosh, there's a lot of noise.* あら，とても騒がしいわね. [OLD-FASHIONED 古風な]

go-slow (**go-slows**) N-COUNT 可算名詞 A **go-slow** is a protest by workers in which they deliberately work slowly in order to cause problems for their employers. サボタージュ，怠業 [BRIT 英国英語; AM slowdown 米国英語 **slowdown**]

gos|pel /gɒspəl/ (**gospels**) **1** N-COUNT; N-IN-NAMES 可算名詞，名称中の名詞 In the New Testament of the Bible, the **Gospels** are the four books which describe the life and teachings of Jesus Christ. 福音書 □ *...the parable in St. Matthew's Gospel.* マタイによる福音書の中の例え話 **2** N-SING 単数名詞 In the Christian religion, the **gospel** refers to the message and teachings of Jesus Christ, as explained in the New Testament. 福音 □ *I didn't shirk my duties. I visited the sick and I preached the gospel.* 私は責務逃れをしたのではない。病人を見舞って福音を説いたのだ. **3** N-UNCOUNT 不可算名詞 **Gospel** or **gospel music** is a style of religious music that uses strong rhythms and vocal harmony. It is especially popular among black Christians in the southern United States. ゴスペル □ *I had to go to church, so I grew up singing gospel.* 私は教会に行かされたものでした。それで，ゴスペルを歌って育ったんです. **4** N-UNCOUNT 不可算名詞 If you take something **as gospel**, or it is **the gospel truth**, you believe that it is completely true. 絶対的真理 □ *He wouldn't say this if it weren't the gospel truth.* 絶対に本当じゃなければ彼はこのことを言わない.

gos|sip /gɒsɪp/ (**gossips, gossiping, gossiped**) **1** N-UNCOUNT 不可算名詞 **Gossip** is informal conversation, often about other people's private affairs. うわさ話 [also 'a' N] □ *He spent the first*

hour talking gossip. 彼は最初の1時間はうわさ話をして過ごしました. ❑ There has been much gossip about the possible reasons for his absence. 彼の不在理由についてかなりのうわさが流れています. **2** V-RECIP 相互動詞 If you **gossip with** someone, you talk informally, especially about other people or local events. You can also say that two people **gossip**. うわさ話をする ❑ We spoke, debated, gossiped into the night. 私たちは夜遅くまで会話し、議論し、うわさ話をした. ❑ Eva gossiped with Sarah. イーバはサラとうわさ話をした. **3** N-COUNT 可算名詞 If you describe someone as a **gossip**, you mean that they enjoy talking informally to people about the private affairs of others. うわさ好き、おしゃべり [DISAPPROVAL 不賛成] ❑ He was a vicious gossip. 彼はかなりのうわさ好きだ.

got /gɒt/ **1** **Got** is the past tense and sometimes the past participle of **get**. getの過去・過去分詞 **2** PHRASE 句 You use **have got** to say that someone has a particular thing, or to mention a quality or characteristic that someone or something has. In informal American English, people sometimes just use "got." 持っている（アメリカ口語では単にgotもいう.）[SPOKEN 口語] ❑ I've got a coat just like this. 私はこれとそっくりなコートを持っている. ❑ After a pause he asked, "You got any identification?" しばらくして彼は「身分証明書を持っていますか. 」と尋ねた. **3** PHRASE 句 You use **have got to** when you are saying that something is necessary or must happen in the way stated. In informal American English, the "have" is sometimes omitted. 〜する必要がある（アメリカ口語ではhaveを省略することがある.）[SPOKEN 口語] ❑ I'm not happy with the situation, but I've just got to accept it. 状況に不満はあるけど、ただ受け入れるしかない. ❑ You got to come clean about things. 本当のことを白状しろよ. **4** PHRASE 句 People sometimes use **have got to** in order to emphasize that they are certain that something is true, because of the facts or circumstances involved. In informal American English, the "have" is sometimes omitted. 〜にちがいない [SPOKEN 口語, EMPHASIS 強調] ❑ "You've got to be joking!" he wisely replied. 「冗談だろう！」と彼は抜け目なく答えた.

Goth|ic /ɡɒθɪk/ **1** ADJ 形容詞 **Gothic** architecture and religious art was produced in the Middle Ages. Its features include tall pillars, high curved ceilings, and pointed arches. ゴシック建築の ❑ ...a vast, lofty Gothic cathedral. 巨大で堂々としたゴシック建築の大聖堂 ❑ ...Gothic stained glass windows. ゴシック建築のステンドグラスの窓 **2** ADJ 形容詞 In **Gothic** stories, strange, mysterious adventures happen in dark and lonely places such as graveyards and old castles. ゴシック文学の ❑ This novel is not science fiction, nor is it Gothic horror. この小説はSFでもゴシックホラーでもない.

got|ta /ɡɒtə/ **Gotta** is used in written English to represent the words "got to" when they are pronounced informally, with the meaning "have to" or "must." 〜しなきゃ（got toのくだけた表現）❑ Prices are high and our kids gotta eat. 料金は高いし、子供たちは食べなきゃならない.

got|ten /ɡɒtⁿn/ **Gotten** is the past participle of **get** in American English. getの過去分詞

gouge /ɡaʊdʒ/ (**gouges**, **gouging**, **gouged**) V-T 他動詞 If you **gouge** something, you make a hole or a long cut in it, usually with a pointed object. くりぬく ❑ He gouged her cheek with a screwdriver. 彼はねじ回しで彼女のほおをえぐった.

▶ **gouge out** PHRASAL VERB 句動詞 To **gouge out** a piece or part of something means to cut, dig, or force it from the surrounding surface. You can also **gouge out** a hole in the ground. えぐり出す, ほじくり出す ❑ He has accused her of threatening to gouge his eyes out. 彼は、彼女に目をほじくり出すと脅迫されたと告発した.

gour|met /ɡʊrmeɪ/ (**gourmets**) **1** ADJ 形容詞 **Gourmet** food is nicer or more unusual or sophisticated than ordinary food, and is often more expensive. グルメの [ADJ n] ❑ Flavored coffee is sold at gourmet food stores and coffee shops. フレーバーコーヒーはグルメ食品店やコーヒー専門店で販売されている. ❑ The couple share a love of gourmet cooking. その夫婦は共にグルメ料理に凝っている. **2** N-COUNT 可算名詞 A **gourmet** is someone who enjoys good food, and who knows a lot about food and wine. グルメ, 食通 ❑ The seafood here is a gourmet's delight. ここのシーフード料理にはグルメも大満足をする.

gov|ern /ɡʌvərn/ (**governs**, **governing**, **governed**) **1** V-T 他動詞 To **govern** a place such as a country, or its people, means to be officially in charge of the place, and to have responsibility for making laws, managing the economy, and controlling public services. 治める, 統治する ❑ They go to the polls on Friday to choose the people they want to govern their country. 国民は国政を任せる人を選ぶため金曜日に投票する. **2** V-T 他動詞 If a situation or activity **is governed by** a particular factor, rule, or force, it is controlled by that factor, rule, or force. 管理する, 統制する ❑ Marine insurance is governed by a strict series of rules and regulations. 海上保険は厳しい規則や規定に管理されている.

Thesaurus *govern* また次を参照：

v. administer, command, control, direct, guide, head up; (ant.) lead, manage, reign, rule **1**

gov|ern|ment /ɡʌvərnmənt/ (**governments**) **1** N-COUNT-COLL 集合可算名詞 The **government** of a country is the group of people who are responsible for governing it. 政府 ❑ The Government has insisted that confidence is needed before the economy can improve. 政府は景気回復には信頼感が前提条件であると主張した. ❑ ...democratic governments in countries like Britain and the U.S. 英国や米国のような国々における民主政府 **2** N-UNCOUNT 不可算名詞 **Government** consists of the activities, methods, and principles involved in governing a country or other political unit. 行政, 政治 ❑ The first four years of government were completely disastrous. 最初の4年間の統治は完全に大失敗だった.
→ see **country**

In the United States, the head of the government is the **President**, who appoints the members of his **administration**. Policies are debated and approved by **Congress**, which consists of the **House of Representatives** and the **Senate**. Members of the House of Representatives are known as **congressmen** and **congresswomen**, and members of the **Senate** are called **senators**. In Britain, the head of the government is the **Prime Minister**. The Prime Minister appoints the other **ministers**, who are responsible for particular areas of policy. The Prime Minister and other senior ministers together form the **Cabinet**. The policies of the government are debated and approved by **Parliament**, which consists of the **House of Commons** and the **House of Lords**. There are around 650 elected **Members of Parliament** (or **MPs**) in the House of Commons.

gov|ern|men|tal /ɡʌvərnmentⁿl/ ADJ 形容詞 **Governmental** means relating to a particular government, or to the practice of governing a country. 政府の, 政治の [ADJ n] ❑ ...a governmental agency for providing financial aid to developing countries. 発展途上国に経済援助を提供するための政府機関

gov|er|nor /ɡʌvərnər/ (**governors**) **1** N-COUNT; N-TITLE 可算名詞, 称号名詞 In some systems of government, a **governor** is a person who is in charge of the political administration of a state, colony, or region. 知事, 総督 ❑ He was governor of Iowa in the late 1970s. 彼は1970年代後半にアイオワ州の知事だった. **2** N-COUNT 可算名詞 A **governor** is a member of a committee which controls an organization such as a university or a hospital. 理事, 運営委員会 ❑ Wayne Hansen was added to the board of governors at City University, Bellevue. ウェイン・ハンセンはシティ大学ベルビュー校の理事会に加わった.

gown /ɡaʊn/ (**gowns**) **1** N-COUNT 可算名詞 A **gown** is a dress, usually a long dress, which women wear on formal occasions. 正装ドレス ❑ The new ball gown was a great success. 新しい夜会服は大成功だった. **2** N-COUNT 可算名詞 A **gown** is a loose black garment worn on formal occasions by people such as lawyers and academics. 正服, 法服 ❑ ...an old headmaster in a flowing black gown. ゆったりとした黒の正服を着た年配の校長

GP /dʒi pi/ (**GPs**) also **G.P.** N-COUNT 可算名詞 A **GP** is a doctor who does not specialize in any particular area of medicine, but who has a medical practice in which he or she treats all types of illness. **GP** is an abbreviation for "general practitioner." 一般医 (general practitionerの略) ❑ Her husband called their local GP. 彼女の夫は地域の医者に電話した.

grab /ɡræb/ (**grabs**, **grabbing**, **grabbed**) **1** V-T 他動詞 If you **grab** something, you take it or pick it up suddenly and roughly. さっとつかむ ❑ I managed to grab her hand. 僕は何とか彼女の手を捕まえた. **2** V-I 自動詞 If you **grab at** something, you try to grab it. つかもうとする ❑ He was clumsily trying to grab at Alfred's arms. 彼はぎこちなくアルフレッドの腕をつかもうとしていた. ● N-COUNT 可算名詞 **Grab** is also a noun. さっとつかむこと [usu sing, N 'for/at' n] ❑ I made a grab for the knife. 私はナイフにさっと手を伸ばした. **3** V-T 他動詞 If you **grab** someone who is walking past, you succeed in getting their attention. 注意を引く [INFORMAL くだけた] ❑ Grab that waiter, Mary Ann. あのウェイターを呼んで, メアリー・アン. **4** V-T 他動詞 If you **grab** someone's attention, you do something in order to make them notice you. （気を）引く ❑ I jumped on the wall to grab the attention of the crowd. 私は群衆の気を引くために壁に跳びかかったんだ. **5** V-T 他動詞 If you **grab** something such as food, drink, or sleep, you manage to get some quickly. （飲食物を）素早くとる, ちょっと眠る [INFORMAL くだけた] ❑ Grab a beer. ビールでも飲め. **6** to **grab hold of** → see **hold** **7** PHRASE 句 If something is **up for grabs**, it is available to anyone who is interested. だれにでも手に入れられる [INFORMAL くだけた] ❑ The famous Ritz hotel is up for grabs for $100 million. 有名なリッツホテルが1億ドルで売り出されている.

g

Thesaurus

grab また次を参照：

v.　capture, catch, seize, snap up; (ant.) release **1**

Word Link

*grac ≈ pleasing : dis*grace*,* grace*,* grace*ful*

grace /greɪs/ (**graces, gracing, graced**) **1** N-UNCOUNT 不算名詞 If someone moves with **grace**, they move in a smooth, controlled, and attractive way. 優雅さ □*He moved with the grace of a trained boxer.* 彼は鍛えられたボクサーらしく滑らかに動いた. **2** N-PLURAL 複数名詞 The **graces** are the ways of behaving and doing things which are considered polite and well-mannered. 礼儀作法 □*She didn't fit in and she had few social graces.* 彼女は場に不釣合いで社交上の作法をほとんど知らなかった. **3** V-T 他動詞 If you say that something **graces** a place or a person, you mean that it makes them more attractive. 引き立てる [FORMAL 形式ばった] □*He went to the beautiful old Shaker dresser that graced this homely room.* 彼は、この素朴な部屋を引き立てている立派な年代物のシェーカーのたんすのところまで行った. **4** N-UNCOUNT 不可算名詞 In Christianity and some other religions, **grace** is the kindness that God shows to people because he loves them. 恩寵 (おんちょう) □*It was only by the grace of God that no one died.* 死者が出なかったのは神のお恵みのおかげだ. **5** N-VAR 可変性名詞 When someone says **grace** before or after a meal, they say a prayer in which they thank God for the food and ask Him to bless it. 感謝の祈り □*Leo, will you say grace?* レオ、祈りを唱えてくださる？

Word Partnership

grace は次の語句と使われる：

N.	**grace of a dancer 1** **grace of God 4**
ADJ.	**good** graces, **social** graces **2**
V.	**fall from** grace **4**

grace|ful /greɪsfəl/ **1** ADJ 形容詞 Someone or something that is **graceful** moves in a smooth and controlled way that is attractive to watch. 優雅な □*His movements were so graceful they seemed effortless.* 彼の動きはとても優雅で無理がないようだ. ● **grace|ful|ly** ADV 副詞 [ADV with v] □*She stepped gracefully onto the stage.* 彼女は優雅にステージに上った. **2** ADJ 形容詞 Something that is **graceful** is attractive because it has a pleasing shape or style. 優美な □*His handwriting, from earliest young manhood, was flowing and graceful.* 彼の筆跡は若い頃から流麗だった. ● **grace|ful|ly** ADV 副詞 [ADV adj/-ed] 優美に □*She loved the gracefully high ceiling, with its white-painted cornice.* 彼女は、白塗りのコーニスがある優美で高い天井がとても気に入った.

gra|cious /greɪʃəs/ **1** ADJ 形容詞 If you describe someone as **gracious**, you mean that they are very well-mannered and pleasant. 丁重な、上品な [FORMAL 形式ばった] □*She is a lovely and gracious woman.* 彼女は美しく丁重な女性だ. **2** ADJ 形容詞 If you describe the behavior of someone in a position of authority or high social standing as **gracious**, you mean that they behave in a polite and considerate way. いんぎんな [FORMAL 形式ばった] □*She closed with a gracious speech of thanks.* 彼女はいんぎんな感謝のスピーチで締めくくった. ● **gra|cious|ly** ADV 副詞 [ADV with v] いんぎんに □*Hospitality at the presidential guest house was graciously declined.* 大統領貴賓館での接待は丁重に断られた. **3** ADJ 形容詞 You use **gracious** to describe the comfortable way of life of wealthy people. 贅沢な □*He drove through the gracious suburbs with the swimming pools and tennis courts.* 彼はプールやテニスコートのある郊外の高級住宅地を車で通り抜けた. **4** EXCLAM 感嘆詞 Some people say **good gracious** or **goodness gracious** in order to express surprise or annoyance. 「おや」、「まあ」など驚きやいらだちを表す [FEELINGS 感情] □*Good gracious, look at that specimen, will you?* おやまあ、あの標本を見てくれませんか.

grade /greɪd/ (**grades, grading, graded**) **1** V-T 他動詞 If something **is graded**, its quality is judged, and it is often given a number or a name that indicates how good or bad it is. 格付けする、等級分けする □*Dust masks are graded according to the protection they offer.* 防じんマスクは保護レベルによって格付けされている. □*Hampshire College does not grade the students' work.* ハンプシャー・カレッジは学生の成績を段階付けしません. **2** N-COUNT 可算名詞 The **grade** of a product is its quality, especially when this has been officially judged. 等級 □*...a good grade of plywood.* 高い等級のベニア板 ● COMB IN ADJ 形容詞の複合 **Grade** is also a combining form. 一等級の □*...weapons-grade plutonium.* 兵器級プルトニウム **3** N-COUNT 可算名詞 Your **grade** in an examination or piece of written work is the mark you get, usually in the form of a letter or number, that indicates your level of achievement. 成績、評価 □*What grade are you hoping to get?* どのぐらいの成績を期待していますか？ **4** N-COUNT 可算名詞 Your **grade** in a company or organization is your level of importance or your rank. 地位 □*Staff turnover is particularly high among junior grades.* 離職率は下級社員で特に高い. **5** N-COUNT 可算名詞 In the United States, a **grade** is a group of classes in which all the children are of a similar age.

When you are six years old you go into the first grade and you leave school after the twelfth grade. 学年 □*Mr. White teaches first grade in south Georgia.* ホワイト先生はジョージア州南部で小学1年生を教えています. **6** N-COUNT 可算名詞 A **grade** is a slope. 坂 [AM 米国英語] □*She drove up a steep grade and then began the long descent into the desert.* 彼女は車で急な坂を上り、そして砂漠に向かう長い坂を下り始めた. **7** N-COUNT 可算名詞 Someone's **grade** is their military rank. 階級 [AM 米国英語] □*I was a naval officer, lieutenant junior grade.* 私は海軍少尉だった. **8** PHRASE 句 If someone **makes the grade**, they succeed, especially by reaching a particular standard. 合格する □*She had a strong desire to be a dancer but failed to make the grade.* 彼女はダンサーになりたいという強い願望があったが、試験に落ちた.

grade cross|ing (**grade crossings**) N-COUNT 可算名詞 A **grade crossing** is a place where a railroad track crosses a road at the same level. 踏切 [AM 米国英語]

grade school (**grade schools**) N-VAR 可変性名詞 In the United States, a **grade school** is the same as an **elementary school**. 小学校 □*I was just in grade school at the time, but I remember it perfectly.* 私はその頃まだ小学生だったが、そのことをはっきりと覚えている.

gra|di|ent /greɪdiənt/ (**gradients**) N-COUNT 可算名詞 A **gradient** is a slope, or the degree to which the ground slopes. 勾配 (こうばい)、傾斜度 [mainly BRIT 主に英国英語; AM usually **grade** 米国英語では通常 **grade**]

gradu|al /grædʒuəl/ ADJ 形容詞 A **gradual** change or process occurs in small stages over a long period of time, rather than suddenly. 除々の □*Losing weight is a slow, gradual process.* 体重はゆっくりと徐々に減る.

gradu|al|ly /grædʒuəli/ ADV 副詞 If something changes or is done **gradually**, it changes or is done in small stages over a long period of time, rather than suddenly. 徐々に [ADV with v] □*Electricity lines to 30,000 homes were gradually being restored yesterday.* 3万件の民家への電線が昨日徐々に復旧した.

gradu|ate (**graduates, graduating, graduated**)

The noun is pronounced /grædʒuɪt/. The verb is pronounced /grædʒueɪt/.

名詞は /grædʒuɪt/ と発音される. 動詞は /grædʒueɪt/ と発音される.

1 N-COUNT 可算名詞 A **graduate** is a student who has successfully completed a course at a high school, college, or university. 卒業生 □*The top one-third of all high school graduates are entitled to an education at California State University.* 高校卒業生の上位3分の1は、カリフォルニア州立大学への入学資格がある. **2** V-I 自動詞 When a student **graduates**, they complete their studies successfully and leave their school or university. 卒業する □*When the boys graduated from high school, Ann moved to a small town in Vermont.* 息子たちが高校を卒業したとき、アンはバーモント州の小さな町に引っ越した. **3** V-I 自動詞 If you **graduate** from one thing to another, you go from a less important job or position to a more important one. 段階が上がる □*Bruce graduated to chef at the Bear Hotel.* ブルースはベアーホテルのシェフという要職を得た. → see **graduation**

gradu|ate school (**graduate schools**) N-VAR 可変性名詞 In the United States, a **graduate school** is a division of a university or college where graduate students are taught. 大学院 □*She was in graduate school, studying for a master's degree in social work.* 彼女は大学院生で、ソーシャルワークの修士号を目指して勉強していた.

gradu|ate stu|dent (**graduate students**) N-COUNT 可算名詞 In the United States, a **graduate student** is a student with a bachelor's degree from a university who is studying or doing research at a more advanced level. 大学院生 [AM 米国英語]

gradua|tion /grædʒueɪʃən/ (**graduations**) **1** N-UNCOUNT 不可算名詞 **Graduation** is the successful completion of a course of study at a university, college, or school, for which you receive a degree or diploma. 卒業 □*They asked what his plans were after graduation.* 彼らは卒業後の彼の計画は何かと尋ねた. **2** N-COUNT 可算名詞 A **graduation** is a special ceremony at a university, college, or school, at which degrees and diplomas are given to students who have successfully completed their studies. 卒業式 □*...the graduation ceremony at Yale.* エール大学の卒業式 → see Word Web: **graduation**

graf|fi|ti /grəfiti/ N-UNCOUNT-COLL 集合的不可算名詞 **Graffiti** is words or pictures that are written or drawn in public places, for example on walls or posters. 落書き □*Buildings old and new are thickly covered with graffiti.* 古い建物も新しい建物も一面が落書きで覆われていた.

graft /græft/ (**grafts, grafting, grafted**) **1** N-COUNT 可算名詞 A **graft** is a piece of healthy skin or bone, or a healthy organ, which is attached to a damaged part of your body by a medical operation in order to replace it. 移植片、移植臓器 □*I am having a skin graft on my arm soon.* 私はもうすぐ腕の皮膚移植を受ける. **2** V-T 他動詞 If a

Word Web graduation

High school and college **graduations** are important **rites of passage**. This **ceremony** tells the world that the **student** is an accomplished scholar. In college, **graduates** receive different types of **diplomas** depending on their subject and level of study. After four years of study, students earn a Bachelor of Arts or Bachelor of Science degree. A Master of Arts or Master of Science usually takes one or two more years. The **PhD**, or doctor of philosophy degree, may require several additional years. In addition, a PhD student must write a **thesis** and defend it in front of a group of **professors**.

piece of healthy skin or bone or a healthy organ **is grafted onto** a damaged part of your body, it is attached to that part of your body by a medical operation. 移植する [usu passive] ❑ *The top layer of skin has to be grafted onto the burns.* 皮膚の最上層をやけど跡に移植しなければなりません. ❸ V-T 他動詞 If a part of one plant or tree **is grafted** onto another plant or tree, they are joined together so that they will become one plant or tree, often in order to produce a new variety. 接ぎ木する ❑ *Pear trees are grafted on quince rootstocks.* ナシの木がマルメロの台木に接ぎ木される.

grain /greɪn/ (**grains**) ❶ N-COUNT 可算名詞 A **grain** of wheat, rice, or other cereal crop is a seed from it. 種子 ❑ *...a grain of wheat.* 小麦1粒 ❷ N-MASS 質量名詞 **Grain** is a cereal crop, especially wheat or corn, that has been harvested and is used for food or in trade. 穀物 ❑ *...a bag of grain.* 穀物1袋 ❸ N-COUNT 可算名詞 A **grain** of something such as sand or salt is a tiny, hard piece of it. 1粒 ❑ *...a grain of sand.* 砂の粒 ❹ N-SING 単数名詞 A **grain** of a quality is a very small amount of it. ごくわずかな [N 'of' n] ❑ *There's more than a grain of truth in that.* それには真実のかけら以上のものがある. ❺ N-SING 単数名詞 The **grain** of a piece of wood is the direction of its fibers. You can also refer to the pattern of lines on the surface of the wood as **the grain**. 布目, 木目 ❑ *Brush the paint generously over the wood in the direction of the grain.* 木目に沿ってその木材にたっぷりとペンキを塗りなさい. ❻ PHRASE 句 If you say that an idea or action **goes against the grain**, you mean that it is very difficult for you to accept it or do it, because it conflicts with your previous ideas, beliefs, or principles. 性に合わない ❑ *Privatization goes against the grain of their principle of opposition to private ownership of industry.* 民営化は産業の私有反対という原則と矛盾します.

→ see Word Web: **grain**

→ see **flower, rice**

gram /græm/ (**grams**) N-COUNT 可算名詞 A **gram** is a unit of weight. One thousand grams are equal to one kilogram. グラム ❑ *A soccer ball weighs about 400 grams.* サッカーボールは重さ約400グラムだ.

gram|mar /græmər/ (**grammars**) ❶ N-UNCOUNT 不可算名詞 **Grammar** is the ways that words can be put together in order to make sentences. 文法 ❑ *He doesn't have mastery of the basic rules of grammar.* 彼は基本的な文法規則に精通していない. ❷ N-UNCOUNT 不可算名詞 Someone's **grammar** is the way in which they obey or do not obey the rules of grammar when they write or speak. 語法, 言葉使い ❑ *His vocabulary was sound and his grammar excellent.* 彼は語彙(ごい)力があり, 言葉使いが見事だ.

→ see **English**

gram|mar school (**grammar schools**) N-VAR; N-IN-NAMES 可変性名詞, 名称中の名詞 A **grammar school** is the same as an **elementary school**. 小学校 [AM 米国英語] ❑ *Jennifer hadn't been home to watch television in the afternoon since grammar school.* ジェニファーは小学校以来午後テレビを見るために家にいたことがない.

gram|mati|cal /grəmætɪkˀl/ ❶ ADJ 形容詞 **Grammatical** is used to indicate that something relates to grammar. 文法上の [ADJ n] ❑ *Should the teacher present grammatical rules to students?* 教師は文法上の規則を生徒に示すべきだろうか. ❷ ADJ 形容詞 If someone's language is **grammatical**, it is considered correct because it obeys the rules of grammar. 文法的に正しい ❑ *...a new test to determine whether students can write grammatical English.* 学生が文法的に正しい

英文を書けるかを判断する新テスト

gramme /græm/ (**grammes**) → see **gram**

grand /grænd/ (**grander, grandest, grand**)

The form **grand** is used as the plural for meaning ❻.

grand 形は❻を意味する複数として使われる.

❶ ADJ 形容詞 If you describe a building or a piece of scenery as **grand**, you mean that its size or appearance is very impressive. 壮大な ❑ *This grand building in the center of town used to be the hub of the capital's social life.* 町の真ん中にあるこの壮大な建物はかつて首都における社交生活の中心となっていた. ❷ ADJ 形容詞 **Grand** plans or actions are intended to achieve important results. 重大な ❑ *Hamilton revealed his grand design for the economic future of the United States.* ハミルトンは, 将来の合衆国経済に関する大計画を明らかにした. ❸ ADJ 形容詞 People who are **grand** think they are important or socially superior. 尊大な, 偉そうな [DISAPPROVAL 不賛成] ❑ *He is grander and even richer than the Prince of Wales.* 彼は英国皇太子よりも尊大で裕福でさえある. ❹ ADJ 形容詞 A **grand** total is one that is the final amount or the final result of a calculation. 最終的な [ADJ n] ❑ *It came to a grand total of $220,329.* 総計22万329ドルに達した. ❺ ADJ 形容詞 **Grand** is often used in the names of buildings such as hotels, especially when they are very large. ホテルなどの建物が非常に大きい場合に名前の一部として使われる ❑ *They stayed at The Grand Hotel, Budapest.* 彼らはブダペスト市のグランド・ホテルに滞在した. [ADJ n] ❻ N-COUNT 可算名詞 A **grand** is a thousand dollars or a thousand pounds. 1000ドルあるいは1000ポンド ❑ *They're paying you ten grand now for those adaptations of old plays.* 現代ではそうした古い劇の翻案に1万ドル支払っている. [INFORMAL くだけた]

gran|dad /grændæd/ (**grandads**) → see **granddad**

grand|child /græntʃaɪld/ (**grandchildren**) N-COUNT 可算名詞 Someone's **grandchild** is the child of their son or daughter. 孫 ❑ *Mary loves her grandchildren.* メアリーは孫を愛している.

grand|dad /grændæd/ (**granddads**) also **grandad** N-FAMILY 家族名詞 Your **granddad** is your grandfather. おじいちゃん [INFORMAL くだけた] ❑ *My granddad is 85.* 私のおじいちゃんは85歳だ.

grand|daugh|ter /grændɔːtər/ (**granddaughters**) N-COUNT 可算名詞 Someone's **granddaughter** is the daughter of their son or daughter. 孫娘 ❑ *...a drawing of my granddaughter Amelia.* 孫娘のアメリアが描いた絵

gran|deur /grændʒər/ ❶ N-UNCOUNT 不可算名詞 If something such as a building or a piece of scenery has **grandeur**, it is impressive because of its size, its beauty, or its power. 雄大さ, 壮大さ ❑ *Venezuela is the ideal starting point to explore the grandeur and natural beauty of South America.* ベネズエラは, 南アメリカの雄大さと自然の美しさを探検するには理想的なスタート地点だ. ❷ N-UNCOUNT 不可算名詞 Someone's **grandeur** is the great importance and social status that they have, or think they have. 偉大さ ❑ *He is wholly concerned with his own grandeur.* 彼は自分自身の威光のことばかり気にしている.

grand|father /grænfɑːðər/ (**grandfathers**) N-FAMILY 家族名詞 Your **grandfather** is the father of your father or mother. 祖父 ❑ *His grandfather was a professor.* 彼の祖父は教授だった.

→ see **family**

Word Web grain

People first began **cultivating grain** about 10,000 years ago in Asia. Working in groups made growing and **harvesting** the **crop** easier. This probably led Stone Age people to form the first communities. Today grain is still the principal food source for humans and domestic animals. Half of all the farmland in the world is used to produce grain. The most popular are **wheat, rice, corn**, and **oats**. An individual kernel of grain is actually a dry, one-seeded **fruit**. It combines the walls of the seed and the flesh of the fruit. Grain is often **ground** into **flour** or meal.

gran|di|ose /grændioʊs/ ADJ 形容詞 If you describe something as **grandiose**, you mean it is bigger or more elaborate than necessary. 大きな [DISAPPROVAL 不賛成] ❑ *The sad truth is that not one of Tim's grandiose plans has even begun.* 悲しい現実はティムの大げさな計画はどれも始まりさえしなかったことだ.

grand jury (**grand juries**) N-COUNT 可算名詞 A **grand jury** is a jury, usually in the United States, which considers a criminal case in order to decide if someone should be tried in a court of law. 大陪審 ❑ *They have already given evidence before a grand jury in Washington.* 彼らはすでにワシントンの大陪審の前で証言した.

grand|ma /grænma/ (**grandmas**) N-FAMILY 家族名詞 Your **grandma** is your grandmother. おばあちゃん [INFORMAL くだけた] ❑ *Grandma was from Scotland.* おばあちゃんはスコットランド出身だった.

grand|mother /grænmʌðər/ (**grandmothers**) N-FAMILY 家族名詞 Your **grandmother** is the mother of your father or mother. 祖母 ❑ *My grandmothers are both widows.* 私の祖母は2人とも夫を亡くしている.
→ see **family**

grand|pa /grænpa/ (**grandpas**) N-FAMILY 家族名詞 Your **grandpa** is your grandfather. おじいちゃん [INFORMAL くだけた] ❑ *Grandpa was not yet back from the war.* おじいちゃんは戦争からまだ帰っていなかった.

grand|parent /grænpɛrənt, -pær-/ (**grandparents**) N-COUNT 可算名詞 Your **grandparents** are the parents of your father or mother. 祖父母 ❑ *Tammy was raised by her grandparents.* タミーは祖父母に育てられた.

grand|son /grænsʌn/ (**grandsons**) N-COUNT 可算名詞 Someone's **grandson** is the son of their son or daughter. 孫息子 ❑ *My grandson's birthday was on Tuesday.* 私の孫息子の誕生日は火曜日だった.

grand|stand /grændstænd/ (**grandstands**) N-COUNT 可算名詞 A **grandstand** is a covered stand with rows of seats for people to sit on at sporting events. 特別観覧席, グランドスタンド

Word Link ite ≈ mineral, rock : granite, graphite, meteorite

gran|ite /grænɪt/ (**granites**) N-MASS 質量名詞 **Granite** is a very hard rock used in building. かこう岩

gran|ny /græni/ (**grannies**) also **grannie** N-FAMILY 家族名詞 Some people refer to their grandmother as **granny**. おばあちゃん [INFORMAL くだけた] ❑ *...my old granny.* 私の年老いたおばあちゃん

grant /grænt/ (**grants, granting, granted**) ❶ N-COUNT 可算名詞 A **grant** is an amount of money that a government or other institution gives to an individual or to an organization for a particular purpose such as education or home improvements. 補助金, 助成金 ❑ *They'd got a special grant to encourage research.* 彼らは研究奨励のための特別交付金をもらった. ❷ V-T 他動詞 If someone in authority **grants** you something, or if something **is granted** to you, you are allowed to have it. 与える [FORMAL 形式ばった] ❑ *France has agreed to grant him political asylum.* フランス政府は彼に政治亡命を認めることに承諾した. ❑ *Single parents tend to grant more independence to their children than other parents do.* 片親はほかの親よりも自分の子供に自立性を認める傾向がある. ❸ V-T 他動詞 If you **grant that** something is true, you accept that it is true, even though your opinion about it does not change. 認める ❑ *The magistrates granted that the charity was justified in bringing the action.* 判事はその慈善事業が訴訟を起こすということにおいて正当化されたことを認めた. ❹ PHRASE 句 If you say that someone **takes** you **for granted**, you are complaining that they benefit from your help,

efforts, or presence without showing that they are grateful. 当然のことだと思う ❑ *What right has the family to take me for granted, Martin?* どんな権利があって家族は私のことを当たり前に思っているのかしら, マーティン? ❺ PHRASE 句 If you **take** something **for granted**, you believe that it is true or accept it as normal without thinking about it. 当然のことだと思う ❑ *I was amazed that virtually all the things I took for granted up north just didn't happen in Savannah.* 事実上私が北部で当然だと思っていたすべてのことがサバナでは起こらなかったことに私は驚いた. ❻ PHRASE 句 If you **take it for granted that** something is the case, you believe that it is true or you accept it as normal without thinking about it. ...ということが当然だと思う ❑ *He seemed to take it for granted that he should speak as a representative.* 彼は自分が代表者として話すべきだということを当たり前に思っているようだった.

Word Partnership grant は次の語句と使われる:

| N. | grant **amnesty**, grant **equal rights**, grant **independence**, grant **membership**, grant **money**, grant **permission**, grant **a wish** ❷ |
| V. | **refuse to** grant ❷ |

grape /greɪp/ (**grapes**) ❶ N-COUNT 可算名詞 **Grapes** are small green or purple fruit which grow in bunches. Grapes can be eaten raw, used for making wine, or dried. ブドウ ❑ *...a bunch of grapes.* ブドウ1房 ❷ PHRASE 句 If you describe someone's attitude as **sour grapes**, you mean that they say something is worthless or undesirable because they want it themselves but cannot have it. 負け惜しみ ❑ *These accusations have been going on for some time now, but it is just sour grapes.* これらの非難はすでにかなりの長い間続いているが, 単なる負け惜しみに過ぎない.

grape|fruit /greɪpfrut/ (**grapefruit**)

The plural can also be **grapefruits**.

複数は **grapefruits** もある.

N-VAR 可変性名詞 A **grapefruit** is a large, round, yellow fruit, similar to an orange, that has a sharp, slightly bitter taste. グレープフルーツ

grape|vine /greɪpvaɪn/ N-SING 単数名詞 If you hear or learn something **on** or **through the grapevine**, you hear it or learn it in casual conversation with other people. 口コミ, うわさで ❑ *I had heard through the grapevine that he was quite critical of what we were doing.* うわさで聞いたところによると, 彼は私たちがやっていることにかなり批判的だということだった.

Word Link graph ≈ writing : autograph, biography, graph

graph /græf/ (**graphs**) N-COUNT 可算名詞 A **graph** is a mathematical diagram which shows the relationship between two or more sets of numbers or measurements. グラフ, 図表 ❑ *...a graph showing that breast cancer deaths rose about 20 percent from 1960 to 1985.* 乳がんによる死亡率が1960年から1985年の間で20%上昇したのを示すグラフ
→ see Word Web: **graph**

graph|ic /græfɪk/ (**graphics**) ❶ ADJ 形容詞 If you say that a description or account of something unpleasant is **graphic**, you are emphasizing that it is clear and detailed. 生々しい [EMPHASIS 強調] ❑ *The descriptions of sexual abuse are graphic.* 性的虐待の描写が生々しい. ● **graphi|cal|ly** /græfɪkli/ ADV 副詞 [ADV with v] 生々しく ❑ *Here, graphically displayed, was confirmation of the entire story.* ここに生々しく展示されているのはその事件全体の証拠だ. ❷ ADJ 形容詞 **Graphic** means concerned with drawing or pictures, especially

---

Word Web graph

There are three main elements in a **line** or **bar graph**:
- a **vertical axis** (the y-axis)
- a **horizontal axis** (the x-axis)
- at least one line or set of bars.

To understand a **graph**, do the following:
1. Read the **title** of the graph.
2. Read the **labels** and the **range** of numbers along the side (the **scale** or vertical axis).
3. Read the information along the bottom (horizontal axis) of the graph.
4. Determine what **units** the graph uses. This information can be found on the axis or in the **key**.
5. Look for patterns, groups, and differences.

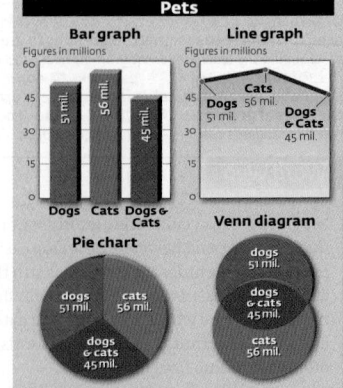

Pets

Bar graph — Figures in millions

Dogs 51 mil. Cats 56 mil. Dogs & Cats 45 mil.

Line graph — Figures in millions

Cats 56 mil. Dogs 51 mil. Dogs & Cats 45 mil.

Venn diagram

dogs 51 mil. dogs & cats 45 mil. cats 56 mil.

Pie chart

dogs 51 mil. cats 56 mil. dogs & cats 45 mil.

in publishing, industry, or computing. グラフィックの [ADJ n] □...fine and graphic arts. 美術とグラフィックアート ❸ N-UNCOUNT 不可算名詞 **Graphics** is the activity of drawing or making pictures, especially in publishing, industry, or computing. グラフィック製作、画像製作 □...a computer manufacturer that specializes in graphics. 画像を専門としているコンピュータ・メーカー ❹ N-UNCOUNT 可算名詞 **Graphics** are drawings and pictures that are composed using simple lines and sometimes strong colors. グラフィック，絵 □The Agriculture Department today released a new graphic to replace the old symbol. 農務省は本日古いシンボルマークに取って代わる新しいデザインを発表した。

graph|ic de|sign N-UNCOUNT 不可算名詞 **Graphic design** is the art of designing advertisements, magazines, and books by combining pictures and words. グラフィックデザイン □...the graphic design department. グラフィックデザイン課

> **Word Link** ite ≈ mineral, rock : granite, graphite, meteorite

graph|ite /ɡræfaɪt/ N-UNCOUNT 不可算名詞 **Graphite** is a soft black substance that is a form of carbon. It is used in pencils and electrical equipment. 黒鉛，グラファイト
→ see **drawing**

graph pa|per N-UNCOUNT 不可算名詞 **Graph paper** is paper that has small squares printed on it so that you can use it for drawing graphs. 方眼紙，グラフ用紙

grap|ple /ɡræpªl/ (grapples, grappling, grappled) ❶ V-I 自動詞 If you **grapple with** a problem or difficulty, you try hard to solve it. 取り組む □The economy is just one of several critical problems the country is grappling with. 経済は国が取り組んでいる重要な問題の1つに過ぎない。 ❷ V-RECIP 相互動詞 If you **grapple with** someone, you take hold of them and struggle with them, as part of a fight. You can also say that two people **grapple**. 取っ組み合う □He was grappling with an alligator in a lagoon. 彼は沼でワニと取っ組み合いをしていた。

grasp /ɡræsp/ (grasps, grasping, grasped) ❶ V-T 他動詞 If you **grasp** something, you take it in your hand and hold it firmly. しっかりつかむ □He grasped both my hands. 彼は私の両手をぎゅっとつかんだ。 ❷ N-SING 単数名詞 A **grasp** is a very firm hold or grip. 握ること □His hand was taken in a warm, firm grasp. 彼の手は温かい手でしっかりと握られた。 ❸ N-SING 単数名詞 If you say that something is in someone's **grasp**, you disapprove of the fact that they possess or control it. If something slips **from** your **grasp**, you lose it or lose control of it. 支配 □The people in your grasp are not guests, they are hostages. 支配下にある人々は客ではなくて人質である。 □She allowed victory to slip from her grasp. 彼女は勝利を逃してしまった。 ❹ V-T 他動詞 If you **grasp** something that is complicated or difficult to understand, you understand it. 把握する □The government has not yet grasped the seriousness of the crisis. 政府は危機の深刻さをまだ把握していない。 ❺ N-SING 単数名詞 A **grasp** of something is an understanding of it. 把握 □They have a good grasp of foreign languages. 彼らは外国語をよく理解している。 ❻ PHRASE 句 If you say that something is **within** someone's **grasp**, you mean that it is very likely that they will achieve it. 達成可能な □Peace is now within our grasp. 今や平和を実現できそうだ。

grass /ɡræs/ (grasses) ❶ N-MASS 質量名詞 **Grass** is a very common plant consisting of large numbers of thin, spiky, green leaves that cover the surface of the ground. 芝 □Small things stirred in the grass around the tent. テントの周りの芝生で小さなものがもぞもぞと動いた。 ❷ PHRASE 句 If you say **the grass is greener** somewhere else, you mean that other people's situations always seem better or more attractive than your own, but may not really be so. 隣の芝は青い □He was very happy with us but wanted to see if the grass was greener elsewhere. 彼は私たちに何の不満もなかったが、ほかにもっといい場所がないかを確かめたかった。

grass|hopper /ɡræshɒpər/ (grasshoppers) N-COUNT 可算名詞 A **grasshopper** is an insect with long back legs that jumps high into the air and makes a high, vibrating sound. キリギリス・バッタ・イナゴなどのバッタ科の昆虫

grass|roots /ɡræsru:ts/ N-PLURAL 複数名詞 The **grassroots** of an organization or movement are the ordinary people who form the main part of it, rather than its leaders. 草の根、一般構成員 □You have to join the party at grassroots level from what I understand. 私が理解するところでは、一般大衆レベルで党に入会しなければならない。

grassy /ɡræsi/ (grassier, grassiest) ADJ 形容詞 A **grassy** area of land is covered in grass. 草で覆われた □The buildings are hidden behind grassy banks. 建物は草の岸の向こうに隠れている。

grate /ɡreɪt/ (grates, grating, grated) ❶ N-COUNT 可算名詞 A **grate** is a framework of metal bars in a fireplace, which holds the wood or coal. 火床 □A wood fire burned in the grate. 暖炉で まきが燃えた。 ❷ V-T 他動詞 If you **grate** food such as cheese or carrots, you rub it over a metal tool called a grater so that the food is cut into very small pieces. おろす □Grate the cheese into a mixing bowl. チーズをボールにおろしなさい。 ❸ V-I 自動詞 When something **grates**,

it rubs against something else, making a harsh, unpleasant sound. きしむ，ギーギーという音がする □His chair grated as he got to his feet. 彼が立ったとき、いすがきしんだ。 ❹ V-I 自動詞 If something such as someone's behavior **grates on** you or **grates**, it makes you feel annoyed. いらいらさせる □His manner always grated on me. 彼の態度にはいつも不快を感じた。
→ see **cut**

grate|ful /ɡreɪtfəl/ ADJ 形容詞 If you are **grateful for** something that someone has given you or done for you, you have warm, friendly feelings towards them and wish to thank them. ありがたく思う，感謝している □She was grateful to him for being so good to her. 彼女は、彼がとても親切にしてくれたことに感謝した。 ●**grate|ful|ly** ADV 副詞 [ADV with v] 感謝して □"That's kind of you, Sally," Claire said gratefully. 「どうもありがとう、サリー.」とクレアは感謝して言った。

> **Thesaurus** grateful また次を参照：
> ADJ. appreciative, thankful; (ant.) ungrateful

grat|er /ɡreɪtər/ (graters) N-COUNT 可算名詞 A **grater** is a kitchen tool which has a rough surface that you use for cutting food into very small pieces. おろし金、おろし器

> **Word Link** grat ≈ pleasing : congratulate, gratify, gratitude

grati|fy /ɡrætɪfaɪ/ (gratifies, gratifying, gratified) ❶ V-T 他動詞 If you **are gratified by** something, it gives you pleasure or satisfaction. 喜ばせる，満足させる [FORMAL 形式ばった] □Mr. Dambar was gratified by his response. ダンバー氏は彼の回答に満足した。 ●**grati|fy|ing** ADJ 形容詞 満足を与える □We took a chance and we've won. It's very gratifying. 我々は一か八かにかけてうまくいった。非常にうれしい。 ●**grati|fi|ca|tion** /ɡrætɪfɪkeɪʃən/ N-UNCOUNT 不可算名詞 喜び、満足 □He is waiting for them to recognize him and eventually they do, much to his gratification. 彼は、彼らが自分に気付くのを待っていて、やっと気付いたときは満足感で一杯になる。 ❷ V-T 他動詞 If you **gratify** your own or another person's desire, you do what is necessary to please yourself or them. 満足させる [FORMAL 形式ばった] □We gratified our friend's curiosity. 我々は友人の好奇心を満たした。 ●**grati|fi|ca|tion** N-UNCOUNT 不可算名詞 満たすこと、満足 □...sexual gratification. 性的満足

gra|tis /ɡrætɪs, ɡrɑ-/ ADV 副詞 If something is done or provided **gratis**, it does not have to be paid for. 無料で [ADV after v] □David gives the first consultation gratis. ディビッドは初回の相談は無料で行う。 ●ADJ 形容詞 **Gratis** is also an adjective. 無料の □What I did for you was free, gratis, you understand? 私が今日あなたにしたことはただ、無料です、お分かりですか？

grati|tude /ɡrætɪtud/ N-UNCOUNT 不可算名詞 **Gratitude** is the state of feeling grateful. 感謝 □I wish to express my gratitude to Kathy Davis for her immense practical help. 私は、ケイティ・ディビスが多大な実践面での支援をしてくれたことに感謝を表します。

gra|tui|tous /ɡrətu:ɪtəs/ ADJ 形容詞 If you describe something as **gratuitous**, you mean that it is unnecessary, and often harmful or upsetting. 余計な，不当な □There's too much crime and gratuitous violence on TV. テレビには犯罪や意味のない暴力が多すぎる。 ●**gra|tui|tous|ly** ADV 副詞 無意味に □They wanted me to change the title to something less gratuitously offensive. 彼らは私に題名をそれほど無意味に侮辱的でないものに変更するよう希望した。

gra|tu|ity /ɡrətu:ɪti/ (gratuities) N-COUNT 可算名詞 A **gratuity** is a gift of money to someone who has done something for you. チップ，心付け [FORMAL 形式ばった] □The porter expects a gratuity. ポーターはチップを受け取ることを当然だと思っている。

> **Word Link** grav ≈ heavy : grave, gravitate, gravity

grave (graves, graver, gravest)

Pronounced /ɡreɪv/, except for meaning ❹, when it is pronounced /ɡrɑv/.

/ɡreɪv/と発音される❹の意味の場合以外では、/ɡrɑv/と発音される。

❶ N-COUNT 可算名詞 A **grave** is a place where a dead person is buried. 墓 □They used to visit her grave twice a year. 彼らはかつて彼女の墓参りを年に2回行ったものだった。 ❷ ADJ 形容詞 A **grave** event or situation is very serious, important, and worrying. 重大な □He said that the situation in his country is very grave. 彼は国内の事態がかなり深刻だと言いました。 ●**grave|ly** ADV 副詞 深刻に □They had gravely impaired the credibility of the government. それによって、政府の信頼性が著しく損なわれた。 ❸ ADJ 形容詞 A **grave** person is quiet and serious in their appearance or behavior. 重々しい、深刻な □Anxiously, she examined his unusually grave face. 彼女は心配そうに彼のいつにない深刻な表情をじろじろと見た。 ●**grave|ly** ADV 副詞 深刻に □"I think I've covered that business more than adequately," he said gravely. 「その件に関しては十分すぎるほど取り扱ったと思います。」と彼は深刻そうに言った。 ❹ ADJ 形容詞 [ADJ n] In some languages,

such as French, a **grave** accent is a symbol that is placed over a vowel in a word to show how the vowel is pronounced. For example, the word "mère" has a grave accent over the first "e." アクセント **5** PHRASE 句 If you say that someone who is dead would **turn** or **turn over in** their **grave at** something that is happening now, you mean that they would be very shocked or upset by it, if they were alive. 草葉の陰で嘆く ❑ *Darwin must be turning in his grave at the thought of what is being perpetrated in his name.* ダーウィンは自分の名前で人が何をしているかと思うと草葉の陰で嘆いていることだろう.

grav|el /grǽvˀl/ N-UNCOUNT 不可算名詞 **Gravel** consists of very small stones. It is often used to make paths. 砂利 ❑ *...a gravel path leading to the front door.* 玄関へ続く砂利道

grave|yard /gréɪvyɑrd/ (**graveyards**) N-COUNT 可算名詞 A **graveyard** is an area of land, sometimes near a church, where dead people are buried. 墓地 ❑ *They made their way to a graveyard to pay their traditional respects to the dead.* 彼らは亡くなった人に習わし通りのお参りをするため墓地に行った.

Word Link grav ≈ heavy : grave, gravitate, gravity

---

gravi|tate /grǽvɪteɪt/ (**gravitates, gravitating, gravitated**) V-I 自動詞 If you **gravitate toward** a particular place, thing, person, or activity, you are attracted by it and go to it or get involved in it. 引き付けられる ❑ *You naturally gravitate toward people with shared values.* 共通の価値観を持つ人に自然に引き寄せられる.

gravi|ta|tion|al /grævɪteɪʃənˀl/ ADJ 形容詞 **Gravitational** means relating to or resulting from the force of gravity. 重力の [TECHNICAL 技術的] ❑ *If a spacecraft travels faster than 11 km a second, it escapes the Earth's gravitational pull.* もし宇宙船が秒速11km以上で移動すれば、地球の引力から逃れる.

→ see **tide**

grav|ity /grǽviti/ **1** N-UNCOUNT 不可算名詞 **Gravity** is the force that causes things to drop to the ground. 重力 ❑ *Arrows would continue to fly forward forever in a straight line were it not for gravity, which brings them down to earth.* 矢はもし地上に落とす重力がなければ、永遠に直線に飛び続けるだろう. **2** N-UNCOUNT 不可算名詞 The **gravity of** a situation or event is its extreme importance or seriousness. 重大さ ❑ *The president said those who grab power through violence deserve punishment which matches the gravity of their crime.* 大統領は、暴力により権力を得る者はその犯罪の深刻さにふさわしい罰が与えられるべきだと述べた. **3** N-UNCOUNT 不可算名詞 The **gravity** of someone's behavior or speech is the extremely serious way in which they behave or speak. 厳粛さ ❑ *There was an appealing gravity to everything she said.* 彼女の言ったすべての言葉には、訴えかけるような真剣さがあった.

→ see **flight, moon**

gra|vy /gréɪvi/ (**gravies**) N-MASS 質量名詞 **Gravy** is a sauce made from the juices that come from meat when it cooks. グレービーソース

gray /gréɪ/ (**grayer, grayest, grays**) **1** COLOR 色彩語 **Gray** is the color of ashes or of clouds on a rainy day. 灰色の、グレーの ❑ *...a gray suit.* グレーのスーツ **2** ADJ 形容詞 If the weather is **gray**, there are many clouds in the sky and the light is dull. どんよりした、曇った ❑ *It was a gray, wet, April Sunday.* どんより雨模様の4月の日曜日だった. **3** ADJ 形容詞 If you describe a situation as **gray**, you mean that it is dull, unpleasant, or difficult. つまらない ❑ *Brazilians look gloomily forward to a New Year that even the president admits will be gray and cheerless.* ブラジル人はゆううつ気に新年を迎えるが、大統領も暗く活気がないだろうと認めている. **4** ADJ 形容詞 If you describe someone or something as **gray**, you think that they are boring and unattractive, and very similar to other things or other people. 平凡な [DISAPPROVAL 不賛成] ❑ *Miles is one of those little gray men you find in every company.* マイルズはどこの会社にでもいるような平凡な男だ.

Word Partnership gray は次の語句と使われる:

N.	gray **eyes**, gray **hair**, **shades of** gray, gray **sky**, gray **suit** **1**
V.	**go** gray, **turn** gray **1**

---

gray area (**gray areas**) N-COUNT 可算名詞 If you refer to something as a **gray area**, you mean that it is unclear, for example because nobody is sure how to deal with it or who is responsible for it, or it falls between two separate categories of things. あいまいな部分、グレーゾーン ❑ *At the moment, the law on compensation is very much a gray area.* 現在の段階では、賠償金に関する法律は非常にあいまいだ.

gray mar|ket (**gray markets**) **1** N-SING 単数名詞 **Gray-market** goods are bought unofficially and then sold to customers at lower prices than usual. グレーマーケット [BUSINESS 実業] ❑ *Gray-market perfumes and toiletries are now commonly sold by mail.* グレーマーケットの香水や化粧品類は現在は一般的に通信販売されている. **2** N-SING 単数名詞 **Gray-market** shares are sold to investors

before they have been officially issued. 公開取引前の新株取引 [BUSINESS 実業] ❑ *An unofficial gray market in the shares has been operating for about two weeks.* 非公式の新株取引が約2週間ほど行われている.

graze /gréɪz/ (**grazes, grazing, grazed**) **1** V-T/V-I 他動詞/自動詞 When animals **graze** or **are grazed**, they eat the grass or other plants that are growing in a particular place. You can also say that a field **is grazed** by animals. 牧草を食べさせる [他動詞]、牧草を食べる [自動詞] ❑ *Five cows graze serenely around a massive oak.* 5頭の牛が大きなオークの木の周りで穏やかに草を食べている. ❑ *Several horses grazed the meadowland.* 数頭の馬が牧草地で草を食べた. **2** V-T 他動詞 If you **graze** a part of your body, you injure your skin by scraping against something. 擦りむく ❑ *I had grazed my knees a little.* 私はひざを少し擦りむいた. **3** N-COUNT 可算名詞 A **graze** is a small wound caused by scraping against something. 擦り傷 ❑ *Although cuts and grazes are not usually very serious, they can be quite painful.* 切り傷や擦り傷はふつうそんなにあまり深刻なものではないが、かなり痛むことがある. **4** V-T 他動詞 If something **grazes** another thing, it touches that thing lightly as it passes by. かする ❑ *A bullet had grazed his arm.* 弾丸が彼の腕をかすった.

GRE /dʒi ɑr i/ N-PROPER 固有名詞 The **GRE** is the examination which you have to take to be admitted to graduate schools. **GRE** is an abbreviation for "Graduate Record Examination." 大学院進学適性試験 (Graduate Record Examinationの略)

grease /grís/ (**greases, greasing, greased**) **1** N-UNCOUNT 不可算名詞 **Grease** is a thick, oily substance which is put on the moving parts of cars and other machines in order to make them work smoothly. グリース、潤滑油 ❑ *...grease-stained hands.* グリースで汚れた手 **2** V-T 他動詞 If you **grease** a part of a car, machine, or device, you put grease on it in order to make it work smoothly. グリースを塗る ❑ *I greased front and rear hubs and adjusted the brakes.* 私は前輪と後輪のハブにグリースを塗り、ブレーキを調整した. **3** N-UNCOUNT 不可算名詞 **Grease** is an oily substance that is produced by your skin. 皮脂 ❑ *His hair is thick with grease.* 彼の髪は油でべったりした. **4** N-UNCOUNT 不可算名詞 **Grease** is animal fat that is produced by cooking meat. You can use **grease** for cooking. 油脂、脂肪 ❑ *He could smell the bacon grease.* ベーコンの脂のにおいがした. **5** V-T 他動詞 If you **grease** a dish, you put a small amount of fat or oil around the inside of it in order to prevent food from sticking to it during cooking. 油を塗る ❑ *Grease two sturdy baking sheets and heat the oven to 400 degrees.* 丈夫な天パン2枚に油を塗って、オーブンを400度に加熱しなさい.

greasy /grísi, -zi/ (**greasier, greasiest**) ADJ 形容詞 Something that is **greasy** has grease on it or in it. 油でべたべたした、油っこい ❑ *He propped his elbows upon a greasy counter.* 彼は油でべとついたカウンターにひじをついた.

great /gréɪt/ (**greater, greatest, greats**) **1** ADJ 容詞 You use **great** to describe something that is very large. **Great** is more formal than **big**. 大きい [ADJ n] ❑ *The room had a great bay window.* その部屋は大きな出窓があった. **2** ADJ 形容詞 **Great** means large in amount or degree. 多い、高い ❑ *Benjamin Britten did not live to a great age.* ベンジャミン・ブリテンは長生きしなかった. **3** ADJ 形容詞 You use **great** to describe something that is important, famous, or exciting. 素晴らしい ❑ *...the great cultural achievements of the past.* 過去の素晴らしい文化面での業績 ● **great|ness** N-UNCOUNT 不可算名詞 素晴らしさ ❑ *A nation must take certain risks to achieve greatness.* 偉大な国になるためにはある程度のリスクを冒さなければならない. **4** ADJ 形容詞 You can describe someone who is successful and famous for their actions, knowledge, or skill as **great**. 偉大な ❑ *He has the potential to be a great player.* 彼は名選手になる可能性がある. ● **great|ness** N-UNCOUNT 不可算名詞 偉大さ ❑ *Abraham Lincoln achieved greatness.* エイブラハム・リンカーンは偉業を成し遂げた. **5** N-PLURAL 複数名詞 The **greats** in a particular subject or field of activity are the people who have been most successful or famous in it. 大物、名士 [JOURNALISM ジャーナリズム] ❑ *...all the greats of Hollywood.* ハリウッドの大物全員 **6** ADJ 形容詞 If you describe someone or something as **great**, you approve of them or admire them. いい、素敵な [INFORMAL くだけた、APPROVAL 賛成] ❑ *Arturo has this great place in Cozumel.* アーチュロはコズメルにこの素敵な家を持っている. ❑ *They're a great bunch of guys.* いいやつらだ. **7** ADJ 形容詞 ['feel' ADJ] If you **feel great**, you feel very healthy, energetic, and enthusiastic. 健康な、元気はつらつな ❑ *I feel just great.* 私はとても体調がいい. **8** ADJ 形容詞 You use **great** in order to emphasize the size or degree of a characteristic or quality. とても [EMPHASIS 強調] ❑ *...a great big Italian wedding.* 盛大なイタリア風の結婚式 **9** EXCLAM 感嘆詞 You say **great** in order to emphasize that you are pleased or enthusiastic about something. すごい、そりゃあいい [FEELINGS 感情] ❑ *Oh great! That'll be good for Fred.* すごい！それはフレッドのためになるよ.

Great, big, and large are all used to talk about size. In general, great is more formal than large, and large is more formal than big. You normally use great to emphasize the importance of someone or something. □ *...the great English architect, Inigo Jones.* However, you can also use great to suggest that something is impressive because of its size. □ *The great bird of prey was a dark smudge against the sun.* Big and large are normally used to describe objects, but you can also use big to suggest that something is important or impressive. □ *...his influence over the big advertisers.* You can use large or great, but not big, to describe amounts. □ *...a large amount of blood on the floor. ...the coming of tourists in great numbers.* Both great and big can be used to emphasize the intensity of something, although great is more formal. □ *It gives me great pleasure to welcome you... Most of them act like big fools.*

Thesaurus
great また次を参照:

| ADJ. | enormous, immense, vast; (*ant.*) small **1** **2** |
| | distinguished, famous, important; (*ant.*) remarkable, successful **3** **4** |

great|ly /ɡreɪtli/ ADV 副詞 You use **greatly** to emphasize the degree or extent of something. 非常に [FORMAL 形式ばった, EMPHASIS 強調] □ *People would benefit greatly from a pollution-free vehicle.* 無公害車は人類に多大な恩恵をもたらすことであろう.

greed /ɡriːd/ N-UNCOUNT 不可算名詞 **Greed** is the desire to have more of something, such as food or money, than is necessary or fair. 欲, 貪欲 □ *...an insatiable greed for personal power.* 個人的な権力に対する飽くなき貪欲さ

greedy /ɡriːdi/ (**greedier, greediest**) ADJ 形容詞 If you describe someone as **greedy**, you mean that they want to have more of something such as food or money than is necessary or fair. 欲深い, 貪欲な □ *He attacked greedy bosses for awarding themselves big raises.* 彼は, 欲深い経営陣が多額の昇給を得たことを非難した. ● **greed|ily** ADV 副詞 [ADV with v] □ *Laurie ate the pastries greedily and with huge enjoyment.* ローリーはペイストリーを大喜びでむさぼるように食べた.

green /ɡriːn/ (**greener, greenest, greens**) **1** COLOR 色彩語 **Green** is the color of grass or leaves. 緑色, 青 □ *Yellow and green together make a pale green.* 黄色と緑色を混ぜると黄緑色になる. **2** ADJ 形容詞 A place that is **green** is covered with grass, plants, and trees and not with houses or factories. 緑が多い □ *Every street ends at a park or bit of green space.* それぞれの通りの終わりには公園か小さな緑地がある. ● **green|ness** N-UNCOUNT 不可算名詞 緑が多いこと □ *...the lush greenness of the river valleys.* 緑に溢れる川の流域 **3** ADJ 形容詞 [ADJ n] **Green** issues and political movements relate to or are concerned with the protection of the environment. 環境保護に関した □ *The power of the Green movement in Germany has made that country a leader in the drive to recycle more waste materials.* 緑の党の力で, ドイツは廃棄物リサイクル運動でのリーダー的存在となった. **4** ADJ 形容詞 If you say that someone or something is **green**, you mean they harm the environment as little as possible. 環境に優しい □ *...trying to persuade governments to adopt greener policies.* 環境に優しい政策を取り入れるよう各国政府を説得しようとして ● **green|ness** N-UNCOUNT 不可算名詞 環境への優しさ □ *If you'd like to recognize the greenness of an individual or organization, why not nominate them for an Environmental Achievement Award.* 個人や組織の環境への配慮を評価するのなら, 環境功績賞に彼らを指名してはどうだろうか. **5** N-COUNT 可算名詞 **Greens** are members of green political movements. 緑の党の党員 □ *The Greens see themselves as a radical alternative to the two major political parties.* 緑の党は根本的に主要2党に取って代わる存在だと自認している. **6** N-COUNT 可算名

詞 A **green** is a smooth, flat area of grass around a hole on a golf course. グリーン □ *...the 18th green.* 18番グリーン **7** N-COUNT 可算名詞 A **green** is an area of land covered with grass, especially in a town or in the middle of a village. 緑地, 草地 □ *...the village green.* 村の緑地 **8** ADJ 形容詞 If you say that someone is **green**, you mean that they have had very little experience of life or a particular job. 未熟な, 青一 □ *He was a young fellow, very green, very immature.* 彼は若くて未熟な青二才だった. **9** PHRASE 句 If someone has **a green thumb**, they are very good at gardening and their plants grow well. 園芸の才がある [AM 米国英語] □ *She has an unbelievably green thumb, she can grow anything.* 彼女は信じられないほど園芸が上手で何でも育てられる. **10** to **give** someone **the green light** → see **light** → see **color, golf, rainbow**

green belt (**green belts**) also **greenbelt** N-VAR 可変性名詞 A **green belt** is an area of land with fields or parks around a town or city, where people are not allowed to build houses or factories by law. 緑地帯 □ *The room features a 20 feet wall of glass that overlooks a greenbelt.* その部屋には緑地帯を見下ろす20フィートのガラスの窓がある.

green card (**green cards**) N-COUNT 可算名詞 A **green card** is a document showing that someone who is not a citizen of the United States has permission to live and work there. グリーンカード □ *Nicollette married Harry so she could get a green card.* ニコレットはグリーンカード取得のためにハリーと結婚した.

An alien resident may apply to stay in the U.S. through the help of his employer or family. The **green card** identifies a legal resident and permits the cardholder to apply for citizenship after 5 years (in the case of singles) or 3 years (if they are married to an American).

green|ery /ɡriːnəri/ N-UNCOUNT 不可算名詞 Plants that make a place look green are referred to as **greenery**. 緑の草木 □ *Adriana misses the trees and greenery of her native mountains.* エイドリアナは故郷の山の木々や緑が恋しい.

green|house /ɡriːnhaʊs/ (**greenhouses**) **1** N-COUNT 可算名詞 A **greenhouse** is a glass building in which you grow plants that need to be protected from bad weather. 温室 **2** ADJ 形容詞 **Greenhouse** means relating to or causing the greenhouse effect. 温室の, 温室効果の [ADJ n] □ *...controls on greenhouse emissions.* 温室効果ガスの排出規制 → see **barn**

green|house ef|fect N-SING 単数名詞 The **greenhouse effect** is the problem caused by increased quantities of gases such as carbon dioxide in the air. These gases trap the heat from the sun, and cause a gradual rise in the temperature of the Earth's atmosphere. 温室効果 □ *...gases that contribute to the greenhouse effect.* 温室効果の一因となるガス → see Word Web: **greenhouse effect** → see **greenhouse**

green|house gas (**greenhouse gases**) N-VAR 可変性名詞 **Greenhouse gases** are the gases which are responsible for causing the greenhouse effect. The main greenhouse gas is carbon dioxide. 温室効果ガス

green|mail /ɡriːnmeɪl/ N-UNCOUNT 不可算名詞 **Greenmail** is when a company buys enough shares in another company to threaten a takeover and makes a profit if the other company buys back its shares at a higher price. グリーンメール [mainly AM 主に米国英語 BUSINESS 実業] □ *Family control would prevent any hostile takeover or greenmail attempt.* 同族支配により敵対的買収やグリーンメールは防止されるだろう

greet /ɡriːt/ (**greets, greeting, greeted**) **1** V-T 他動詞 When you **greet** someone, you say "Hello" or shake hands with them. あいさつする, 迎える □ *She liked to be home to greet Steve when he came in*

Word Web greenhouse effect

Over the past 100 years, the global average **temperature** has risen dramatically. Researchers believe that this **global warming** comes from added **carbon dioxide** and other **gases** in the **atmosphere**. With **water vapor**, they form a shield that holds in heat. It acts a little like the glass in a greenhouse. Scientists call this the **greenhouse effect**. Some natural causes of this warming may include increased **solar radiation** and tiny changes in the earth's orbit. However, human activities, such as **deforestation**, and the use of **fossil fuels** seem to play a much more important role.

Sun
Some heat gets out.
Solar radiation comes in.
Some heat can't get out.
Heat is absorbed by greenhouse gases.

g

from school. スティーブが学校から帰ったときに迎えられるよう彼女は家にいることを好んだ． **2** V-T 他動詞 If something **is greeted** in a particular way, people react to it in that way. 迎える，反応する [usu passive] ❏ *His research was greeted with skepticism by advocates for children, who thought it was based on faulty data.* 子供の立場を支援する活動家たちは，彼の研究が欠陥のあるデータに基づいたものだと考え，懐疑心で迎えた．

greet|ing /grítɪŋ/ (**greetings**) N-VAR 可変性名詞 A **greeting** is something friendly that you say or do when you meet someone. あいさつ ❏ *His greeting was familiar and friendly.* 彼のあいさつは聞き覚えがあり親しみのあるものだった． ❏ *They exchanged greetings.* 彼らはあいさつを交わした．

gre|nade /grɪnéɪd/ (**grenades**) N-COUNT 可算名詞 A **grenade** or a **hand grenade** is a small bomb that can be thrown by hand. 手榴弾 ❏ *A hand grenade was thrown at an army patrol.* 手投げ弾が陸軍巡察に投げかけられました．

grew /grú/ **Grew** is the past tense of **grow**. *grow*の過去形

grey /greɪ/ → see **gray**

grey|hound /gréɪhaʊnd/ (**greyhounds**) **1** N-COUNT 可算名詞 A **greyhound** is a dog with a thin body and long thin legs, which can run very fast. Greyhounds sometimes run in races and people bet on them. グレーハウンド ❏ *...his love of greyhound racing.* ドッグレースへの愛情 **2** N-COUNT 可算名詞 In the United States, a **Greyhound** or a **Greyhound bus** is a bus that travels between towns or cities rather than within a particular town or city. グレイハウンドバス [AM 米国英語, TRADEMARK] ❏ *I didn't fly. I took the Greyhound.* 私は飛行機ではなくグレイハウンドバスに乗った．

grid /grɪd/ (**grids**) **1** N-COUNT 可算名詞 A **grid** is something which is in a pattern of straight lines that cross over each other, forming squares. On maps, the grid is used to help you find a particular thing or place. 格子，碁盤目 ❏ *...a grid of ironwork.* 碁盤目状の鉄格子 ❏ *...a grid of narrow streets.* 碁盤目状の細い通り **2** N-COUNT 可算名詞 A **grid** is a network of wires and cables by which sources of power, such as electricity, are distributed throughout a country or area. 配電網 ❏ *...breakdowns in communications and electric-power grids.* 通信網と配電網の断絶 **3** N-COUNT 可算名詞 **The grid** or **the starting grid** is the starting line on a car-racing track. スターティンググリッド ❏ *The Ferrari driver was starting second on the grid.* フェラーリのドライバーがスターティンググリッドの2列目でスタートするところだった．

grid|lock /grɪdlɒk/ **1** N-UNCOUNT 不可算名詞 **Gridlock** is the situation that exists when all the roads in a particular place are so full of vehicles that none of them can move. 交通渋滞 ❏ *The streets are wedged solid with the chaos of poorly regulated parking and near-constant traffic gridlock.* 街は十分な駐車規制とほぼ絶え間なく続く交通渋滞による混乱状態で停滞している． **2** N-UNCOUNT 不可算名詞 You can use **gridlock** to refer to a situation in an argument or dispute when neither side is prepared to give in, so no agreement can be reached. 膠着(こうちゃく)状態，行き詰まり ❏ *He agreed that these policies will lead to gridlock in the future.* これらの政策が原因で将来的には行き詰っていくことに彼は同意した．

→ see **traffic**

grief /gríf/ (**griefs**) **1** N-VAR 可変性名詞 **Grief** is a feeling of extreme sadness. 深い悲しみ，悲嘆 ❏ *...a huge outpouring of national grief for the victims of the shootings.* その襲撃の被害者に対する国民の悲しみがほとばしること **2** PHRASE 句 If something **comes to grief**, it fails. If someone **comes to grief**, they fail in something they are doing, and may be hurt. 失敗に終わる ❏ *So many marriages have come to grief over lack of money.* あまりにも多くの結婚がお金が足りないために失敗に終わった． **3** EXCLAM 感嘆詞 Some people say "**Good grief**" when they are surprised or shocked. 「やれやれ」「なんてこった」など驚いたりショックを受けたときに使う表現 [FEELINGS 感情] ❏ *"He's been arrested for theft and burglary." — "Good grief!"* 「彼は窃盗罪で逮捕されたのよ．」「なんてこった！」

Word Link *griev ≈ heavy, serious:* **aggrieved, grievance, grieve**

griev|ance /grívˀns/ (**grievances**) N-VAR 可変性名詞 If you have a **grievance** about something that has happened or been done, you believe that it was unfair. 不平，不満 ❏ *They had a legitimate grievance.* 彼らには正当な不満がありました． ❏ *The main grievance of the drivers is the imposition of higher fees for driver's licenses.* ドライバーからの主な苦情は運転免許証発行の手数料の値上げについてです．

grieve /grív/ (**grieves, grieving, grieved**) V-I 自動詞 If you **grieve over** something, especially someone's death, you feel very sad about it. 深く悲しむ，悲嘆にくれる ❏ *He's grieving over his dead wife and son.* 彼は妻と息子の死を嘆き悲しんでいる． ❏ *I didn't have any time to grieve.* 私には嘆き悲しむ暇がなかった．

griev|ous /grívəs/ **1** ADJ 形容詞 If you describe something such as a loss as **grievous**, you mean that it is extremely serious or worrying in its effects. 深刻な ❏ *Mr. Morris said the victims had*

suffered from a very grievous mistake. モリス氏によると，被害者は非常に深刻な過ちのために苦しんだとのことです． ● **griev|ous|ly** ADV 副詞 [ADV with v] 深刻に ❏ *Birds, sea life and the coastline all suffered grievously.* 鳥類，海洋生物，そして海岸線すべてが深刻な被害を被った． **2** ADJ 形容詞 A **grievous** injury to your body is one that causes you great pain and suffering. けがなどの程度がひどい ❏ *He survived in spite of suffering grievous injuries.* 彼は重傷を負ったにもかかわらず生き延びた． ● **griev|ous|ly** ADV 副詞 けがなどの程度がひどく ❏ *Nelson Piquet, three times world champion, was grievously injured.* 3度目の世界チャンピオンの座についたネルソン・ピケットは重傷を負った．

grill /grɪl/ (**grills, grilling, grilled**) **1** N-COUNT 可算名詞 A **grill** is a flat frame of metal bars on which food can be cooked over a fire. 焼き網 ❏ *Jerry forced scrap wood through the vents in the grill to stoke the fire.* ジェリーは火をかき立てるのに焼き網の隙間から無理やり廃材を押し込んだ． **2** N-COUNT 可算名詞 A **grill** is a part of a stove which produces strong direct heat to cook food that has been placed underneath it. グリル [BRIT 英国英語; AM **broiler** 米国英語 **broiler**] **3** V-T 他動詞 When you **grill** food, or when it **grills**, you cook it on metal bars above a fire or barbecue. 焼き網で焼く，直火で焼く ❏ *Grill the steaks over a wood or charcoal fire that is quite hot.* 強火のかなり火か炭火でステーキを焼きなさい． **4** V-T/V-I 他動詞/自動詞 When you **grill** food, or when it **grills**, you cook it in a stove using very strong heat directly above it. グリルで焼く [他動詞]，グリルで焼ける [自動詞] [AM **broil** 米国英語 **broil**] ❏ *Grill the meat for 20 minutes on each side.* 肉を片側20分ずつグリルしなさい． [BRIT 英国英語] ❏ *Apart from peppers and eggplant, many other vegetables grill well.* ピーマンとナスを除き，ほかの野菜の多くはグリルでうまく焼ける． ● **grill|ing** N-UNCOUNT 不可算名詞 グリルで焼くこと ❏ *The breast can be cut into portions for grilling.* 胸肉をグリル焼きするためいくつかに切りなさい． **5** V-T 他動詞 If you **grill** someone **about** something, you ask them a lot of questions for a long period of time. 質問攻めにする [INFORMAL くだけた] ❏ *Grill your travel agent about the facilities for families with children.* 旅行会社に子供のいる家族向けの施設についていろいろと質問しなさい． ● **grill|ing** (**grillings**) N-COUNT 可算名詞 質問攻め，厳しい尋問 ❏ *He faced a hostile grilling from the committee's Republicans.* 彼は委員会の共和党員からとげとげしい尋問にあいました． **6** N-COUNT 可算名詞 A **grill** is a restaurant that serves grilled food. 焼肉専門のレストラン ❏ *...patrons of the Savoy Grill.* サボイ・グリルの常連客

grille /grɪl/ (**grilles**) also **grill** N-COUNT 可算名詞 A **grille** is a framework of metal bars or wire which is placed in front of a window or a piece of machinery, in order to protect it or to protect people. 鉄格子 ❏ *The single window was protected by a rusted iron grille.* その1重窓はさび付いた鉄格子で保護されていた．

grim /grɪm/ (**grimmer, grimmest**) **1** ADJ 形容詞 A situation or piece of information that is **grim** is unpleasant, depressing, and difficult to accept. 不快な，厳しい ❏ *They painted a grim picture of growing crime.* 彼らは犯罪増加についての不快な絵を描いた． ❏ *There was further grim economic news yesterday.* 昨日，さらに暗い経済ニュースが流れた． **2** ADJ 形容詞 A place that is **grim** is unattractive and depressing in appearance. うっとうしい ❏ *The city might be grim at first, but there is a vibrancy and excitement.* その街は初めはうっとうしく感じるかもしれないが，活気と刺激がある．

gri|mace /grɪmɪs, grɪméɪs/ (**grimaces, grimacing, grimaced**) V-I 自動詞 If you **grimace**, you twist your face in an ugly way because you are annoyed, disgusted, or in pain. しかめ面をする，顔をゆがめる [WRITTEN 書き言葉] ❏ *She started to sit up, grimaced, and sank back weakly against the pillow.* 彼女は起き上がろうとしたが，顔をゆがめ，弱々しく再び横になった． ● N-COUNT 可算名詞 **Grimace** is also a noun. しかめ面 ❏ *He took another drink of his coffee. "Awful," he said with a grimace.* 彼はもう1口コーヒーを飲み，「まずい」としかめ面をして言った．

grime /graɪm/ N-UNCOUNT 不可算名詞 **Grime** is dirt that has collected on the surface of something. すす，あか ❏ *Kelly got the grime off his hands before rejoining her in the kitchen.* ケリーはキッチンに戻る前に彼の手の汚れを取った．

grimy /graɪmi/ (**grimier, grimiest**) ADJ 形容詞 Something that is **grimy** is very dirty. とても汚い ❏ *...a grimy industrial city.* かなり汚れた産業都市

grin /grɪn/ (**grins, grinning, grinned**) **1** V-I 自動詞 When you **grin**, you smile broadly. にっこり笑う ❏ *He grins, delighted at the memory.* 彼はにっこりと思い出し笑いをした． ❏ *Sarah tried several times to catch Philip's eye, but he just grinned at her.* サラは何度かフィリップと目を合わそうとしたが，彼は彼女ににっこりほほえんだだけだった． **2** N-COUNT 可算名詞 A **grin** is a broad smile. にこやかな笑い ❏ *...a big grin on her face.* 満面の笑み **3** PHRASE 句 If you **grin and bear it**, you accept a difficult or unpleasant situation because you know there is nothing you can do to make things better. 笑ってこらえる ❏ *They cannot stand the sight of each other, but they will just have to grin and bear it.* 彼らはお互いの存在に耐えられないが，笑ってこらえるしかない．

grind /graɪnd/ (**grinds, grinding, ground**) **1** V-T 他動詞 If you

grind a substance such as corn, you crush it between two hard surfaces or with a machine until it becomes a fine powder. ひく、すりつぶす □ *Store the peppercorns in an airtight container and grind the pepper as you need it.* コショウの実を密閉容器に入れて保管し、必要に応じてコショウをひきなさい. ● PHRASAL VERB 句動詞 **Grind up** means the same as **grind**. ひく、すりつぶす □ *He makes his own paint, grinding up the pigment with a little oil.* 彼は少量の油を混ぜて色素をひき、自分専用の絵の具を作る. **2** V-T 他動詞 If you **grind** something **into** a surface, you press and rub it hard into the surface using small circular or sideways movements. こすりつける □ *"Well," I said, grinding my cigarette nervously into the granite step.* 「えーっと」と私はタバコを緊張して玄関の階段にこすりつけながら言った. ● PHRASE 句 If you **grind** your **teeth**, you rub your upper and lower teeth together as though you are chewing something. 歯ぎしりをする **3** V-T 他動詞 If you **grind** something, you make it smooth or sharp by rubbing it against a hard surface. 磨ぐ、研ぐ □ *It was beyond my ability to grind a blade this broad.* これほど幅広の刃物を研ぐのは私にはとても無理だった. **4** V-I 自動詞 If a vehicle **grinds** somewhere, it moves there very slowly and noisily. ギーギーッと音を立てる □ *Tanks had crossed the border at five fifteen and were grinding south.* 戦車が5時15分に国境を越え、南に向かってゆっくり走った. **5** N-SING 単数名詞 The **grind of** a machine is the harsh, scraping noise that it makes, usually because it is old or is working too hard. きしむ音 □ *The grind of heavy machines could get on their nerves.* 大型機械のきしむ音は神経に障ることがある. **6** N-SING 単数名詞 If you refer to routine tasks or activities as the **grind**, you mean they are boring and take up a lot of time and effort. 単調で骨が折れること [INFORMAL くだけた, DISAPPROVAL 不賛成] □ *Life continues to be a terrible grind for the ordinary person.* 一般の人にとっては人生はひどく単調で骨が折れることの繰り返しだ. **7** PHRASE 句 If a country's economy or something such as a process **grinds to a halt**, it gradually becomes slower or less active until it stops. 徐々に停滞する □ *The peace process has ground to a halt while Israel struggles to form a new government.* イスラエルが新政府の発足に苦闘している間、和平へのプロセスは徐々に停滞した. **8** PHRASE 句 If a vehicle **grinds to a halt**, it stops slowly and noisily. きしみながらゆっくり停車する □ *The tanks ground to a halt after a hundred yards because the fuel had been siphoned out.* 燃料が流出したため、その戦車は100ヤード進んだ後できしみながら停車した.

▶ **grind down** PHRASAL VERB 句動詞 If you say that someone **grinds** you **down**, you mean that they treat you very harshly and cruelly, reducing your confidence or your will to resist them. 苦しめる、虐げる □ *"You see," said Hughes, "there's people who want to humiliate you and grind you down."* 「ほらね。」とヒューズは言った. 「きみを侮辱して虐げようとする人がいるんだよ。」

▶ **grind up** → see **grind 1**

grind|er /gráɪndər/ (**grinders**) **1** N-COUNT 可算名詞 In a kitchen, a **grinder** is a device for crushing food such as coffee or meat into small pieces or into a powder. 粉ひき器、肉ひき器 □ *...an electric coffee grinder.* 電気コーヒーひき器 **2** N-COUNT 可算名詞 A **grinder** is a machine or tool for sharpening, smoothing, or polishing the surface of something. 研磨機、研削盤 □ *The grinder is used for making precision tooling.* その研磨機は精密工作機械を作るために使用される.

grip /grɪp/ (**grips, gripping, gripped**) **1** V-T 他動詞 If you **grip** something, you take hold of it with your hand and continue to hold it firmly. しっかりつかむ □ *She gripped the rope.* 彼女はロープをしっかりとつかんだ. **2** N-COUNT 可算名詞 A **grip** is a firm, strong hold on something. しっかりつかむこと □ *His strong hand eased the bag from her grip.* 彼は力強い手で彼女が握っていたバッグをもぎ取った. **3** N-SING 単数名詞 Someone's **grip on** something is the power and control they have over it. 支配 □ *The president maintains an iron grip on his country.* 大統領は自国における確固たる支配力を維持しています. **4** V-T 他動詞 If something **grips** you, it affects you very strongly. 引き付ける □ *The entire community has been gripped by fear.* 住民全員が恐怖心にとらわれている. **5** V-T 他動詞 If you **are gripped by** something such as a story or a series of events, your attention is concentrated on it and held by it. （人の）心をつかむ [usu passive] □ *The nation is gripped by the dramatic story.* 国中がその劇的な話に心をつかまれた. ● **grip|ping** ADJ 形容詞 興奮させる □ *The film turned out to be a gripping thriller.* その映画は手に汗を握るスリラーだということが分かった. **6** N-UNCOUNT 不可算名詞 If things such as shoes or car tires have **grip**, they do not slip. 握り、グリップ □ *...a new way of reinforcing rubber which gives car tires a better grip.* 車のタイヤのグリップを良くする新しいゴム補強方法 **7** PHRASE 句 If you **come to grips with** a problem, you consider it seriously, and start taking action to deal with it. 取り組む □ *The administration's first task is to come to grips with the economy.* 政府の最初の任務は経済問題に取り組むことです. **8** PHRASE 句 If you **get a grip** on yourself, you make an effort to control or improve your behavior or work. 自制する、しっかりする □ *Part of me was very frightened and I consciously had to get a grip on myself.* 私の一部はとても怖がっていたので意識的に落ち着きを取り戻さなければならなかった. **9** PHRASE 句 If a person, group, or place is **in the grip of**

something, they are being severely affected by it. 〜に捕らえられて、〜に陥って **10** PHRASE 句 If you **lose** your **grip**, you become less efficient and less confident, and less able to deal with things. 能力がなくなる □ *He wondered if perhaps he was getting old and losing his grip.* 彼は高齢のために能力が衰えたのかなと思った. **11** PHRASE 句 If you say that someone has a **grip on reality**, you mean they recognize the true situation and do not have mistaken ideas about it. 現実に対する理解 □ *Shakur loses his fragile grip on reality and starts blasting away at friends and foes alike.* シャカールは現実がますます理解できなくなり、友人、敵を問わず射撃し始める.

gripe /graɪp/ (**gripes, griping, griped**) **1** V-I 自動詞 If you say that someone **is griping**, you mean they are annoying you because they keep on complaining about something. ぼやく、愚痴る [INFORMAL くだけた, DISAPPROVAL 不賛成] □ *Why are football players griping when the average salary is half a million dollars?* 平均給料が50万ドルだというのにどうしてサッカー選手はぼやいているんだ? ● **grip|ing** N-UNCOUNT 不可算名詞 愚痴 □ *Still, the griping went on.* いまだに愚痴は続いた. **2** N-COUNT 可算名詞 A **gripe** is a complaint about something. 不平、ぼやき [INFORMAL くだけた] □ *My only gripe is that one main course and one dessert were unavailable.* 気に入らなかったことといえば、あるメインコースとデザートがなかったことくらいだ.

gris|ly /grízli/ (**grislier, grisliest**) ADJ 形容詞 Something that is **grisly** is extremely unpleasant, and usually involves death and violence. ぞっとするような □ *He was insane when he carried out the grisly murders.* 彼が陰惨な殺人を犯したとき正気ではなかった.

grit /grɪt/ (**grits, gritting, gritted**) **1** N-UNCOUNT 不可算名詞 **Grit** is very small pieces of stone. 砂、砂利 □ *He felt tiny pieces of grit and sand peppering his knees.* 彼はひざに小さな砂粒がかかるのを感じた. **2** N-UNCOUNT 不可算名詞 If someone has **grit**, they have the determination and courage to continue doing something even though it is very difficult. 根性 □ *If they gave gold medals for grit, Karen would be right up there on the winners' podium.* もし根性で金メダルが取れるなら、カレンは表彰台に乗っているだろうに. **3** N-PLURAL 複数名詞 **Grits** are coarsely ground grains of corn which are cooked and eaten for breakfast or as part of a meal in the southern United States. ひき割りトウモロコシ [AM 米国英語] □ *I want grits with my eggs instead of hash browns.* ハッシュ・ブラウンズの代わりに卵添えのひき割りトウモロコシが欲しい. **4** V-T 他動詞 If you **grit** your **teeth**, you press your upper and lower teeth tightly together, usually because you are angry about something. 歯を食いしばってこらえる □ *Gritting my teeth, I did my best to stifle one or two remarks.* 歯を食いしばって、一言か二言発言するのを精一杯我慢した. **5** PHRASE 句 If you **grit** your **teeth**, you make up your mind to carry on even if the situation is very difficult. 歯を食いしばって頑張る □ *There is going to be hardship, but we have to grit our teeth and get on with it.* つらいことはあるだろうが、我々は歯を食いしばって続けなければなりません.

grit|ty /gríti/ (**grittier, grittiest**) **1** ADJ 形容詞 Something that is **gritty** contains grit, is covered with grit, or has a texture like that of grit. 砂の入った、砂だらけの □ *The sheets fell on the gritty floor, and she just let them lie.* シーツを砂だらけの床に敷いて、彼女はただ彼らを寝かせた. **2** ADJ 形容詞 Someone who is **gritty** is brave and determined. 根性がある □ *We have to prove how gritty we are.* 私たちは根性があるのを示さなければならない. **3** ADJ 形容詞 A **gritty** description of a tough or unpleasant situation shows it in a very realistic way. 生々しい □ *...gritty social comment.* 生々しい社会の批評

groan /groʊn/ (**groans, groaning, groaned**) **1** V-I 自動詞 If you **groan**, you make a long, low sound because you are in pain, or because you are upset or unhappy about something. うなる、うめく □ *Slowly, he opened his eyes. As he did so, he began to groan with pain.* ゆっくりと彼は目を開けた。目を開けながら、彼は苦痛のためうめき始めた. □ *They glanced at the man on the floor, who began to groan.* 彼らは床でうめき始めた男をちらりと見た. ● N-COUNT 可算名詞 **Groan** is also a noun. うめき声 □ *She heard him let out a pitiful, muffled groan.* 彼女は彼が哀れでくぐもったうめき声をあげるのを聞いた. **2** V-T 他動詞 If you **groan** something, you say it in a low, unhappy voice. ぼそぼそ言う □ *"My leg - I think it's broken," Eric groaned.* 「足が。骨折していると思う。」とエリックは言った. **3** V-I 自動詞 If you **groan about** something, you complain about it. 不平を言う □ *His parents were beginning to groan about the price of college tuition.* 彼の両親は大学の授業料について不平を言い始めていた. ● N-COUNT 可算名詞 **Groan** is also a noun. 不平 □ *Listen sympathetically to your child's moans and groans about what she can't do.* 子供が出来ないことについて不平不満を言うのに対し好意的に耳を傾けなさい. **4** V-I 自動詞 If wood or something made of wood **groans**, it makes a loud sound when it moves. ギーギーいう □ *The timbers groan and creak and the floorboards shift.* 板がきしんで床板が少し動いた. **5** V-I 自動詞 If you say that something such as a table **groans under** the weight of food, you are emphasizing that there is a lot of food on it. （食べ物など）でいっぱいだ [EMPHASIS 強調] □ *The bar counter groans under the weight of huge plates of the freshest fish.* バーのカウンターはとても新鮮な魚を載せた大きなお皿の重みできしむほどだ. **6** V-I 自動詞 If

you say that someone or something **is groaning under** the weight of something, you think there is too much of that thing. 苦しむ [DISAPPROVAL 不賛成] [usu cont] ❑ *Consumers were groaning under the weight of high interest rates.* 消費者は高金利に苦しんでいた.

gro|cer /ˈɡroʊsər/ (**grocers**) ◼ N-COUNT 可算名詞 A **grocer** is a storekeeper who sells foods such as flour, sugar, and canned foods. 食料雑貨店主 ◪ N-COUNT 可算名詞 A **grocer** or a **grocer's** is the same as a **grocery**. 食料雑貨店 [mainly BRIT 主に英国英語]

gro|cery /ˈɡroʊsəri, ˈɡroʊsri/ (**groceries**) ◼ N-COUNT 可算名詞 A **grocery** or a **grocery store** is a small store that sells foods such as flour, sugar, and canned goods. 食料雑貨店 [mainly AM 主に米国英語] ❑ *They run a small grocery store.* 彼らは小さな食料雑貨店を経営しています. ◪ → see also **supermarket** ◾ N-PLURAL 複数名詞 **Groceries** are foods you buy at a grocery or at a supermarket. 食料品 ❑ *...a small bag of groceries.* 小さな買い物袋に入った食料品

groin /ɡrɔɪn/ (**groins**) N-COUNT 可算名詞 Your **groin** is the front part of your body between your legs. 股間 (こかん) ❑ *I underwent an operation on my groin once.* 私はかつて股間 (こかん) の手術を受けた.

groom /ɡruːm/ (**grooms, grooming, groomed**) ◼ N-COUNT 可算名詞 A **groom** is the same as a **bridegroom**. 新郎, 花婿 ❑ *...the bride and groom.* 新郎新婦 ◪ N-COUNT 可算名詞 A **groom** is someone whose job is to look after the horses in a stable and to keep them clean. 馬丁 ◾ V-T 他動詞 If you **groom** an animal, you clean its fur, usually by brushing it. 手入れする, ブラシをかける ❑ *The horses were exercised and groomed with special care.* その馬は運動し, 特別の手入れを受けた. ◼ V-T 他動詞 If you **are groomed for** a special job, someone prepares you for it by teaching you the skills you will need. 教育する [usu passive] ❑ *George was already being groomed for the top job.* ジョージはすでに最高位職に就くための教育を受けていた.

groomed /ɡruːmd/ ADJ 形容詞 You use **groomed** in expressions such as **well groomed** and **badly groomed** to say how neat and clean a person is. 身だしなみのよさ・悪さを表現するときに用いる ❑ *...a very well groomed man.* とても身だしなみのよい男性

groom|ing /ˈɡruːmɪŋ/ N-UNCOUNT 不可算名詞 **Grooming** refers to the things that people do to keep themselves clean and make their face, hair, and skin look nice. 身だしなみ ❑ *...a growing concern for personal grooming.* ルックスへの関心の高まり

groove /ɡruːv/ (**grooves**) N-COUNT 可算名詞 A **groove** is a deep line cut into a surface. 溝 ❑ *Prior to assembly, grooves were made in the shelf, base, and sides to accommodate the back panel.* 組み立てる前に, 棚, 底板, 横板に裏板をはめるための溝を入れた.

grope /ɡroʊp/ (**gropes, groping, groped**) ◼ V-I 自動詞 If you **grope for** something that you cannot see, you try to find it by moving your hands around in order to feel it. 手探りする ❑ *With his left hand he groped for the knob, turned it, and pulled the door open.* 彼は左手でドアノブを手探りで見付けて回し, ドアを開けた. ◪ V-T 他動詞 If you **grope** your **way** to a place, you move there, holding your hands in front of you and feeling the way because you cannot see anything. 手探りで進む ❑ *I didn't turn on the light, but groped my way across the room.* 私は電灯をつけずに, 部屋に手探りで入っていった. ◾ V-I 自動詞 If you **grope for** something, for example the solution to a problem, you try to think of it, when you have no real idea what it could be. (解決策などを) 模索する ❑ *He groped for solutions to his problems.* 彼は自分の問題への解決法を模索した.

gross /ɡroʊs/ (**grosser, grossest, grosses, grossing, grossed**)

The plural of the number is **gross**.

その数の複数は **gross** である.

◼ ADJ 形容詞 You use **gross** to describe something unacceptable or unpleasant to a very great amount, degree, or intensity. 甚だしい [ADJ n] ❑ *The company was guilty of gross negligence.* その会社は甚だしい過失を犯した. ● **gross|ly** ADV 副詞 [ADV -ed/adj] 大いに ❑ *Funding of education has been grossly inadequate for years.* 教育への財政的支援は長年にわたり非常に不十分でした. ◪ ADJ 形容詞 If you say that someone's speech or behavior is **gross**, you think it is very coarse, vulgar, or unacceptable. 下品な [DISAPPROVAL 不賛成] ❑ *He abused the Admiral in the grossest terms.* 彼は提督を非常に下品な言葉でののしった. ◾ ADJ 形容詞 If you describe something as **gross**, you think it is very unpleasant. 気持ち悪い, むかつく [INFORMAL くだけた, DISAPPROVAL 不賛成] ❑ *They had a commercial on the other night for Drug Free America that was so gross I thought Dad was going to faint.* 先日Drug Free America (アメリカの薬物追放運動) のコマーシャルが流れたが, あまりにも気持ち悪くて父が気を失うのではないかと思った. ◼ ADJ 形容詞 If you describe someone as **gross**, you mean that they are extremely fat and unattractive. デブの, ブタ (のように太った) [DISAPPROVAL 不賛成] [v-link ADJ] ❑ *I only resist things like chocolate if I feel really gross.* 私は本当にブタのように太ったと思ったらチョコレートのようなものを控えるだけだ. ◼ ADJ 形容詞 **Gross** means the total amount of something, especially money, before any has been taken away. 総一 (税などの差し引き前

の額) [ADJ n] ❑ *...a fixed rate account guaranteeing 10.4% gross interest or 7.8% net until October.* 10月まで粗利子10.4%あるいは純利子7.8%を保証する固定金利型の口座 ● ADV 副詞 **Gross** is also an adverb. 税込みで [ADV after v] ❑ *Interest is paid gross, rather than having tax deducted.* 利子は税引きではなくて, 税込みで支払われる. ◼ ADJ 形容詞 **Gross** means the total amount of something, after all the relevant amounts have been added together. 総一, 総計一 [ADJ n] ❑ *Gross sales reached nearly $2 million a year.* 売り上げ総計額が1年でほぼ2百万ドルに達した. ◼ V-T 他動詞 If a person or a business **grosses** a particular amount of money, they earn that amount of money before tax has been taken away. [BUSINESS 実業] ❑ *The company grossed $16.8 million last year.* その会社は昨年1680万ドルの総収益を上げた. ◼ NUM 数詞 A **gross** is a group of 144 things. グロス (12ダース, 144個) ❑ *In all honesty he could not have justified ordering more than twelve gross of the disks.* 正直言って, 彼は12グロス以上のディスクを注文したことを正当化できるはずがなかった.

Word Partnership	*gross* は次の語句と使われる:
N.	act of gross **injustice**, gross **mismanagement**, gross **negligence** ◼
	gross **income**, gross **margin** ◼
V.	**feel** gross ◾

gross do|mes|tic prod|uct (**gross domestic products**) N-VAR 可変性名詞 A country's **gross domestic product** is the total value of all the goods it has produced and the services it has provided in a particular year, not including its income from investments in other countries. 国内総生産 [BUSINESS 実業]

gross na|tion|al prod|uct (**gross national products**) N-VAR 可変性名詞 A country's **gross national product** is the total value of all the goods it has produced and the services it has provided in a particular year, including its income from investments in other countries. 国民総生産 [BUSINESS 実業]

gro|tesque /ɡroʊˈtɛsk/ (**grotesques**) ◼ ADJ 形容詞 You say that something is **grotesque** when it is so unnatural, unpleasant, and exaggerated that it upsets or shocks you. グロテスクな, 奇怪な ❑ *...the grotesque disparities between the wealthy few and nearly everyone else.* 限られた裕福層とそれ以外の一般層との奇怪な格差 ● **gro|tesque|ly** ADV 副詞 グロテスクに ❑ *He called it the most grotesquely tragic experience he's ever had.* 彼は, それがこれまでで最もグロテスクに悲劇的な経験だと言いました. ◪ ADJ 形容詞 If someone or something is **grotesque**, they are very ugly. 醜い ❑ *They tried to avoid looking at his grotesque face and his crippled body.* 彼らは, 彼の醜い顔と不自由な体を見るのを避けようとした. ● **gro|tesque|ly** ADV 副詞 [ADV adj/-ed] 恐ろしいほどに ❑ *...grotesquely deformed beggars.* 恐ろしいほどに奇形のこじき ◾ N-COUNT 可算名詞 A **grotesque** is a person who is very ugly in a strange or unnatural way, especially one in a novel or painting. グロテスクな人 ❑ *Grass's novels are peopled with outlandish characters: grotesques, clowns, scarecrows, dwarfs.* グラスの小説には風変わりな登場人物が多い. 例えば, グロテスクな人, 道化師, かかし, 小人など.

ground

❶ NOUN USES
❷ VERB AND ADJECTIVE USES
❸ PHRASES

❶ **ground** /ɡraʊnd/ (**grounds**) ◼ N-SING 単数名詞 The **ground** is the surface of the earth. 地面 ['the' N] ❑ *Forty or fifty women were sitting cross-legged on the ground.* 40から50人の女性が地べたに足を組んで座っていた. ❑ *We slid down the roof and dropped to the ground.* 私たちは屋根から滑って地面に落ちた. ● PHRASE 句 Something that is **below ground** is under the Earth's surface or under a building. Something that is **above ground** is on top of the earth's surface. 地上で/地下で ◪ N-SING 単数名詞 If you say that something takes place **on the ground**, you mean it takes place on the surface of the earth and not in the air. 地上で ❑ *Coordinating airline traffic on the ground is as complicated as managing the traffic in the air.* 地上の航空便の交通を調整するのは飛行中の航空便の管理するのと同じくらい複雑です. ◾ N-SING 単数名詞 The **ground** is the soil and rock on the earth's surface. 土, 土壌 ❑ *The ground had eroded.* 土壌が侵食していた. ◼ N-UNCOUNT 不可算名詞 You can refer to land as **ground**, especially when it has very few buildings or when it is considered to be special in some way. 土地, 平地 ❑ *...a stretch of waste ground.* 一面に広がる荒地 ◼ N-COUNT 可算名詞 You can use **ground** to refer to an area of land, sea, or air which is used for a particular activity. 一場 ❑ *The best fishing grounds are around the islands.* 最高の釣り場は島の周辺にある. ◼ N-PLURAL 複数名詞 The **grounds** of a large or important building are the garden or area of land which surrounds it. 庭園, 敷地 ❑ *...the palace grounds.* 宮殿の敷地 ◼ N-VAR 可変性名詞 You can use **ground** to refer to a place or situation in which particular methods or ideas can develop and be successful. 状況, 立場 ❑ *The company has maintained its reputation as the developing ground for new techniques.* その会社は新し

い技術を開発する立場にあるとの評判を維持してきた. **8** N-UNCOUNT 不可算名詞 You can use **ground** in expressions such as **on shaky ground** and **the same ground** to refer to a particular subject, area of experience, or basis for an argument. 意見, 立場 □ *Sensing she was on shaky ground, Marie changed the subject.* 彼女があやふやな発言をしていることに気付いて, マリーは話題を変えた. □ *This is the most solid ground for optimism.* これが楽観している最もはっきりとした根拠だ. **9** N-UNCOUNT 不可算名詞 **Ground** is used in expressions such as **gain ground**, **lose ground**, and **give ground** in order to indicate that someone gains or loses an advantage. 勢力 [JOURNALISM ジャーナリズム] □ *There are signs that the party is gaining ground in the latest polls.* 最近の世論調査においてその党が前進している兆しがある. **10** N-VAR 可変性名詞 If something is **grounds for** a feeling or action, it is a reason for it. If you do something **on the grounds** of a particular thing, that thing is the reason for your action. 理由 □ *In the interview he gave some grounds for optimism.* インタビューで彼は楽観の理由をいくつか述べた. □ *The court overturned that decision on the grounds that the prosecution had withheld crucial evidence.* 検察側が重要な証拠を提供しなかったという理由で法廷は判決を覆した. **11** N-COUNT 可算名詞 The **ground** in an electric plug or piece of electrical equipment is the wire through which electricity passes into the ground and which makes the equipment safe. アース [AM 米国英語] [usu sing] □ *...an insulated ground.* 絶縁アース → see **coffee**, **fish**, **grain**

❷ ground /graʊnd/ (grounds, grounding, grounded) **1** V-T 他動詞 If an argument, belief, or opinion **is grounded in** something, that thing is used to justify it. 基づく □ *Her argument was grounded in fact.* 彼女の反論は事実に基づいていた. **2** V-T 他動詞 If an aircraft or its passengers **are grounded**, they are made to stay on the ground and are not allowed to take off. 地上待機にする, 飛行禁止にする □ *The civil aviation minister ordered all the planes to be grounded.* 民間航空大臣は民間機の全面的な飛行禁止を命じした. **3** V-T 他動詞 When parents **ground** a child, they forbid them to go out and enjoy themselves for a period of time, as a punishment. 外出を禁止する □ *They grounded him for a month, and banned television.* 彼らは, 彼に1か月間外出を禁止し, テレビも禁止した. **4** V-T/V-I 他動詞/自動詞 If a ship or boat **is grounded** or if it **grounds**, it touches the bottom of the sea, lake, or river it is on, and is unable to move off. 座礁させる [他動詞], 座礁する [自動詞] □ *Residents have been told to stay away from the region where the ship was grounded.* 住民は, その船が座礁した地域から離れるように言い渡された. □ *The boat finally grounded on a soft, underwater bank.* そのボートはついに柔らかい浅瀬に座礁した. **5** V-T 他動詞 If something **grounds** you, it causes you to have a sensible and practical attitude toward life and not to have unrealistic ideas. まともにさせる □ *These things have grounded me and made me who I am.* こういうことのおかげで私はまともになり, 現在の私がある. ● **ground|ed** ADJ 形容詞 しっかりした □ *She seems very grounded and down-to-earth.* **6** ADJ 形容詞 **Ground** meat has been cut into very small pieces in a machine. ひいた [mainly AM 主に米国英語] □ *...The sausages are made of coarsely ground pork.* そのソーセージは粗びきポークで作られている. **7** **Ground** is the past tense and past participle of **grind**. grindの過去形・過去分詞形 **8** → see also **grounding**

❸ ground /graʊnd/ **1** PHRASE 句 If you **break new ground**, you do something completely different or you do something in a completely different way. 新しい分野に踏み出す, 新天地を切り開く [APPROVAL 賛成] □ *Gellhorn may have broken new ground when she filed her first report on the Spanish Civil War.* ゲリホーンは初めてスペイン内戦についてのレポートをしたとき新天地を切り開いたかもしれない. **2** PHRASE 句 If you say that a town or building **is burned to the ground** or **is razed to the ground**, you are emphasizing that it has been completely destroyed by fire. 全焼する [EMPHASIS 強調] □ *The town was razed to the ground after the French Revolution.* フランス革命のあと, 町は全焼した. **3** PHRASE 句 If two people or groups find **common ground**, they agree about something, especially when they do not agree about other things. 共通の意見 □ *The participants seem unable to find common ground on the issue of agriculture.* 参加者は農業問題について共通の見地に達することが不可能なようだ. **4** PHRASE 句 The **middle ground** between two groups, ideas, or plans involves things which do not belong to either of these groups, ideas, or plans but have elements of each, often in a less extreme form. 中立の立場, 妥協点 □ *The sooner we find a middle ground between freedom of speech and protection of the young, the better for everyone.* 我々が言論の自由と若者の保護の間での妥協点を見出すのが早ければ早いほど, 皆のためになる. **5** PHRASE 句 If something such as a project gets **off the ground**, it begins or starts functioning. 軌道に乗る □ *We help small companies to get off the ground.* 当社は零細企業を軌道に乗せるお手伝いをします. **6** PHRASE 句 If you **prepare the ground** for a future event, course of action, or development, you make it easier for it to happen. 基礎を築く, 下準備する □ *...a political initiative which would prepare the ground for war.* 戦争のための地盤を築く政治主導 **7** PHRASE 句 If you **shift** your **ground** or **change** your **ground**, you

change the basis on which you are arguing. 意見を変える □ *Robert considered this, then shifted his ground slightly in line with a new thought.* ロバートはこれを考慮したが, そのあとで新しい考えの方に少し意見を変えた. **8** PHRASE 句 If you **stand** your **ground** or **hold** your **ground**, you do not run away from a situation, but face it bravely. 一歩も引かない □ *This is the most solid ground for optimism.* She had to force herself to stand her ground when she heard someone approaching. 彼女はだれかが近づいてくるのが聞こえたとき勇気を出して立ち向かわなければならなかった.

ground floor (ground floors) **1** N-COUNT 可算名詞 The **ground floor** of a building is the floor that is level or almost level with the ground outside. 1階 [AM also **first floor** 米国英語, また **first floor**] □ *She showed him around the ground floor of the empty house.* 彼女は彼にその空き家の1階を案内した. **2** If you **get in on the ground floor**, you become involved in a business or plan in the early stages, in order to gain an advantage. 最初から参加する □ *A supplier wants to get in on the ground floor and grow with the business.* 供給業者が最初からかかわってそのビジネスと共に成長することを願っている.

Word Link ground ≈ bottom : back**ground**, **ground**ing, **ground**work

ground|ing /graʊndɪŋ/ N-SING 単数名詞 If you have a **grounding in** a subject, you know the basic facts or principles of that subject, especially as a result of a particular course of training or instruction. 基礎知識 □ *The degree provides a thorough grounding in both mathematics and statistics.* その学位課程では数学と統計学の両方の徹底的な基礎知識を身につけることができる.

ground|less /graʊndlɪs/ ADJ 形容詞 If you say that a fear, accusation, or story is **groundless**, you mean that it is not based on evidence and is unlikely to be true or valid. 根拠のない □ *Fears that the world was about to run out of fuel proved groundless.* 世界がまもなく燃料切れになるという恐れは根拠がないと分かった.

Word Partnership groundless は次の語句と使われる:

N.	**charges are** groundless
V.	**call** *something* groundless, **dismiss** *something* **as** groundless, **prove** groundless

ground rule (ground rules) N-COUNT 可算名詞 The **ground rules for** something are the basic principles on which future action will be based. 基本原則 □ *The panel says the ground rules for the current talks should be maintained.* 委員会の発表によると, 現在の話し合いのための基本原則は維持されるべきだとのことです.

ground|work /graʊndwɜrk/ N-SING 単数名詞 The **groundwork for** something is the early work on it which forms the basis for further work. 基礎, 土台作り □ *Yesterday's meeting was to lay the groundwork for the task ahead.* 昨日の会議はこれからの任務への土台作りであった.

group /grup/ (groups, grouping, grouped) **1** N-COUNT-COLL 集合可算名詞 A **group** of people or things is a number of people or things that are together in one place at one time. グループ, 群れ □ *The trouble involved a small group of football fans.* その騒動はサッカーファンの少人数のグループを巻き込みました. **2** N-COUNT 可算名詞 A **group** is a set of people who have the same interests or aims, and who organize themselves to work or act together. 団体 □ *Members of an environmental group are staging a protest inside a chemical plant.* 環境団体のメンバーが化学プラントの中で抗議行動を行っている. **3** N-COUNT 可算名詞 A **group** is a set of people, organizations, or things which are considered together because they have something in common. 群, 層 □ *She is among the most promising players in her age group.* 彼女は同じ年齢層の中では最も将来性が高いプレーヤーの1人だ. **4** N-COUNT 可算名詞 A **group** is a number of separate commercial or industrial firms that all have the same owner. 企業グループ [BUSINESS 実業] □ *The group made a pretax profit of $1.05 million.* その企業グループは105万ドルの経常利益を出した. **5** N-COUNT 可算名詞 A **group** is a number of musicians who perform together, especially ones who play popular music. グループ, バンド □ *At school he played bass in a pop group called The Urge.* 学校時代に彼は「ザ・アージ」という名のポップ・バンドでベースギターを演奏していた. **6** V-T/V-I 他動詞/自動詞 If a number of things or people **are grouped together** or **group together**, they are together in one place or within one organization or system. 分類する □ *Plants are grouped into botanical "families" that have certain characteristics in common.* 植物は共通の特徴を持つ植物学上の「科」に分類される. □ *The Species Survival Network groups together 80 international environmental organizations.* 80の国際環境機関がSpecies Survival Networkに属しています. **7** → see also **grouping**, **pressure group**

Thesaurus group また次を参照:

N.	collection **1**
	crowd, gang, organization, society **1** **2**
V.	arrange, categorize, class, order, rank, sort **6**

group|ing /grúpɪŋ/ (groupings) N-COUNT 可算名詞 A **grouping** is a set of people or things that have something in common. 集団，グループ □ *There were two main political groupings pressing for independence.* 独立を強く要求している政治団体が2団体あった.

grov|el /grɒvᵊl/ (grovels, groveling, groveled) **1** V-I 自動詞 If you say that someone **grovels**, you think they are behaving too respectfully towards another person, for example because they are frightened or because they want something. ぺこぺこする [DISAPPROVAL 不賛成] □ *I don't grovel to anybody.* 私はだれにもへつらわない. □ *Speakers have been shouted down, classes disrupted, teachers made to grovel.* 演説者は黙らされ，授業は妨害され，教師は屈服させられた. **2** V-I 自動詞 If you **grovel**, you crawl on the ground, for example in order to find something. 横ばいになる □ *We groveled around the room on our knees.* 私たちは四つんばいになって部屋をはった.

grow /gróʊ/ (grows, growing, grew, grown) **1** V-I 自動詞 When people, animals, and plants **grow**, they increase in size and change physically over a period of time. 育つ，成長する □ *We stop growing at maturity.* 成人すると成長が止まる. **2** V-I 自動詞 If a plant or tree **grows** in a particular place, it is alive there. 生えている □ *The station had roses growing at each end of the platform.* その駅ではプラットホームの両端にバラが生えていた. **3** V-T 他動詞 If you **grow** a particular type of plant, you put seeds or young plants in the ground and take care of them as they develop. 育てる，栽培する □ *Lettuce was grown by the ancient Romans.* レタスは古代ローマ人によって栽培された. **4** V-I 自動詞 When someone's hair **grows**, it gradually becomes longer. Your nails also **grow**. (髪・つめが) 伸びる [自動詞] □ *Then the hair began to grow again and I felt terrific.* そのあと髪がまた伸び始め，すごく嬉しかった. **5** V-T 他動詞 If someone **grows** their hair, or **grows** a beard or mustache, they stop cutting their hair or shaving so that their hair becomes longer. You can also **grow** your nails. (髪・ひげ・つめを) 伸ばす[他動詞] □ *I'd better start growing my hair.* 髪を伸ばし始めなくっちゃ. **6** V-I 自動詞 If someone **grows** mentally, they change and develop in character or attitude. 成長する，向上する □ *They began to grow as individuals.* 彼らは個人として成長し始めました. **7** V-LINK 連結動詞 You use **grow** to say that someone or something gradually changes until they have a new quality, feeling, or attitude. 〜になる □ *I grew a little afraid of the guy next door.* 私は隣の住人を少し恐れるようになった. **8** V-I 自動詞 If an amount, feeling, or problem **grows**, it becomes greater or more intense. 増える □ *From 2000 to 2002, the number of uninsured grew by almost 4 million.* 2000年から2002年にかけて，無保険の数がほぼ400万件増えた. **9** V-I 自動詞 If one thing **grows into** another, it develops or changes until it becomes that thing. 成長して〜になる □ *The boys grew into men.* その少年たちは成人男性となった. **10** V-I 自動詞 If something such as an idea or a plan **grows out of** something else, it develops from it. 〜から発展する □ *The idea for this book grew out of conversations with Philippa Brewster.* この本のアイデアはフィリッパ・ブルースターとの会話から発展した. **11** V-I 自動詞 If the economy or a business **grows**, it increases in wealth, size, or importance. 成長する [BUSINESS 実業] [自動詞] □ *The economy continues to grow.* 経済が成長し続けます. **12** V-T 他動詞 If someone **grows** a business, they take actions that will cause it to increase in wealth, size, or importance. 成長させる，拡大させる [BUSINESS 実業] □ *To grow the business, he needs to develop management expertise and innovation across his team.* 事業を拡大するには，彼は経営の手腕とチーム改革を育成しなければならない. **13** → see also **grown** → see **plant**

▶ **grow apart** PHRASAL VERB 句動詞 If people who have a close relationship **grow apart**, they gradually start to have different interests and opinions from each other, and their relationship starts to fail. 疎遠になる，気持ちが離れる □ *He and his wife grew apart.* 彼と彼の妻の気持ちが離れていった.

▶ **grow into** PHRASAL VERB 句動詞 When a child **grows into** an item of clothing, they become taller or bigger so that it fits them properly. (服が) 着られるようになる □ *It's a little big, but she'll soon grow into it.* 少し大きめだけど，彼女はすぐに大きくなって着られるようになるわ.

▶ **grow on** PHRASAL VERB 句動詞 If someone or something **grows on** you, you start to like them more and more. だんだん好きになる (onの後にくる語を訳文の主語にする) □ *Slowly and strangely, the place began to grow on me.* 徐々にそして不思議なことに，私はその場所がだんだん好きになった.

▶ **grow out of** **1** PHRASAL VERB 句動詞 If you **grow out of** a type of behavior or an interest, you stop behaving in that way or having that interest, as you develop or change. 〜しなくなる □ *Most children who stammer grow out of it.* どもる子供のほとんどは成長につれてそれが治る. **2** PHRASAL VERB 句動詞 When a child **grows out of** an item of clothing, they become so tall or big that it no longer fits them properly. 成長して着られなくなる □ *You've grown out of your shoes again.* 足が大きくなって，また靴がはけなくなった.

▶ **grow up** **1** PHRASAL VERB 句動詞 When someone **grows up**, they gradually change from being a child into being an adult. 成長する，育つ □ *She grew up in Tokyo.* 彼女は東京で育った. **2** → see also **grown-up** **3** PHRASAL VERB 句動詞 If you tell someone to **grow up**, you are telling them to stop behaving in a silly or childish way. 大人になる，ちゃんとする [INFORMAL くだけた，DISAPPROVAL 不賛成] □ *It's time you grew up.* もう少しちゃんとしなさい. **4** PHRASAL VERB 句動詞 If something **grows up**, it starts to exist and then becomes larger or more important. 発展する □ *A variety of heavy industries grew up alongside the port.* 様々な重工業が港に沿って発展した.

<table>
<tr><td colspan="2">**Thesaurus**   *grow* また次を参照：</td></tr>
<tr><td>v.</td><td>develop, mature **1** **6**
germinate, spring up, thrive **2**
cultivate, plant, produce **3**
heighten, intensify **7** **8**</td></tr>
</table>

<table>
<tr><td colspan="2">**Word Partnership**   *grow* は次の語句と使われる：</td></tr>
<tr><td>v.</td><td>**continue to** grow **1** **4** **5** – **8** **11**
try to grow **3** **5** **12**</td></tr>
<tr><td>ADJ.</td><td>grow **older** **1** **7**
grow **bored**, grow **closer**, grow **louder**, grow **silent** **8**</td></tr>
<tr><td>N.</td><td>grow **food** **3**</td></tr>
</table>

grow|er /gróʊər/ (growers) N-COUNT 可算名詞 A **grower** is a person who grows large quantities of a particular plant or crop in order to sell them. 栽培者 □ *The state's apple growers are fighting an uphill battle against foreign competition.* 国内のリンゴ栽培者は対外競合に対して苦戦を強いられている.

growl /gráʊl/ (growls, growling, growled) **1** V-I 自動詞 When a dog or other animal **growls**, it makes a low noise in its throat, usually because it is angry. うなる □ *The dog was biting, growling, and wagging its tail.* そのイヌはかみつき，うなり，しっぽを振っていた. ● N-COUNT 可算名詞 **Growl** is also a noun. うなり声 □ *Their noise modulated to a concerted menacing growl punctuated by sharp yaps.* その鳴き声はだんだん声をそろえて脅かすようなうなり声に変わり，たびたびかん高いキャンキャン声で中断された. **2** V-T 他動詞 If someone **growls** something, they say something in a low, rough, and angry voice. うなるように言う [WRITTEN 書き言葉] □ *His fury was so great he could hardly speak. He growled some unintelligible words at Pete.* 彼は怒りのあまりほとんど話せなかった. ピートにわけの分からない言葉をうなるように言った. ● N-COUNT 可算名詞 **Growl** is also a noun. どなり声，うなり声 □ *…with an angry growl of contempt for her own weakness.* 自分自身の弱さに対して軽蔑し怒りのうなり声を出して

grown /gróʊn/ ADJ 形容詞 A **grown** man or woman is one who is fully developed and mature, both physically and mentally. 成人の，大人の [ADJ n] □ *Few women can understand a grown man's love of sports.* 大人の男性のスポーツに対する情熱を理解できる女性はほとんどいない.

grown-up (grown-ups)

The spelling **grownup** is also used. The syllable **up** is not stressed when it is a noun.

つづりの **grownup** も使われる. 音節の **up** は名詞のときは強勢がない.

1 N-COUNT 可算名詞 A **grown-up** is an adult; used by or to children. 大人 □ *Jan was almost a grown-up.* ジャンはほぼ大人だった. **2** ADJ 形容詞 Someone who is **grown-up** is physically and mentally mature and no longer depends on their parents or another adult. 成人した □ *I seem to have everything anyone could want – a good husband, a lovely home, grown-up children who're doing well.* 私はだれもが欲しがっているようなものはすべて持っているようだ. −よい夫，素敵な家，一人前に成長した子供たちなど. **3** ADJ 形容詞 If you say that someone is **grown-up**, you mean that they behave in an adult way, often when they are in fact still a child. 大人びた，大人っぽい □ *She's very grown-up.* 彼女はとても大人びている. **4** ADJ 形容詞 **Grown-up** things seem suitable for or typical of adults. 大人向きの [INFORMAL くだけた] □ *Her songs tackle grown-up subjects.* 彼女の歌は大人向けのテーマを扱っている.

growth /gróʊθ/ (growths) **1** N-UNCOUNT 不可算名詞 The **growth of** something such as an industry, organization, or idea is its development in size, wealth, or importance. 発展，成長 □ *…the growth of nationalism.* 国家主義の発展 □ *…Japan's enormous economic growth.* 日本の巨大な経済の発展 **2** N-UNCOUNT 不可算名詞 The **growth** in something is the increase in it. 増加 [also 'a' n] □ *A steady growth in the popularity of two smaller parties may upset the polls.* 野党2党の人気が恒常的に上昇しているため，投票結果を覆す可能性があります. □ *The area has seen a rapid population growth.* この地域では人口が急増しました. **3** ADJ 形容詞 A **growth** industry, area, or market is one that is increasing in size or activity. 成長

している [BUSINESS 実業] [ADJ n] ❑ *Computers and electronics are growth industries and need skilled technicians.* コンピュータと電子工学は成長産業で熟練した専門家を必要としている. **4** N-UNCOUNT 不可算名詞 Someone's **growth** is the development and progress of their character. 発達, 成長 ❑ *...the child's emotional and intellectual growth.* その子の情緒的および知的発達 **5** N-UNCOUNT 不可算名詞 **Growth** in a person, animal, or plant is the process of increasing in physical size and development. 成長, 発育 ❑ *...hormones which control fertility and body growth.* 受胎能力と身体発育をコントロールするホルモン **6** N-VAR 可変性名詞 You can use **growth** to refer to plants that have recently developed or that developed at the same time. 生えてきたもの ❑ *This helps to ripen new growth and makes it flower profusely.* これによって新しい芽の成長が促され, たくさんの花が咲くようになる. **7** N-COUNT 可算名詞 A **growth** is a lump that grows inside or on a person, animal, or plant, and that is caused by a disease. 腫瘍 (しゅよう) ❑ *This type of surgery could even be used to extract cancerous growths.* このような手術によってがん腫 (しゅ) を取り除くことさえできる.

grub /grʌb/ (grubs, grubbing, grubbed) **1** N-COUNT 可算名詞 A **grub** is a young insect which has just come out of an egg and looks like a short, fat worm. 幼虫 **2** N-UNCOUNT 不可算名詞 **Grub** is food. 食いもん [INFORMAL くだけた] ❑ *Get yourself some grub and come and sit down.* 何か食いもんを取ってきて座れよ. **3** V-I 自動詞 If you **grub** around, you search for something. 探し回る ❑ *I simply cannot face grubbing through all this paper.* 私は単にこの書類全部から探すなんてできない.

grub|by /grʌbi/ (grubbier, grubbiest) **1** ADJ 形容詞 A **grubby** person or object is rather dirty. 汚い, 汚れた ❑ *His white coat was grubby and stained.* 彼の白いコートは汚れていた. **2** ADJ 形容詞 If you call an activity or someone's behavior **grubby**, you mean that it is not completely honest or respectable. 汚い, 下劣な [DISAPPROVAL 不賛成] ❑ *...the grubby business of politics.* 汚い政治取引

grudge /grʌdʒ/ (grudges) N-COUNT 可算名詞 If you have or bear a **grudge against** someone, you have unfriendly feelings toward them because of something they did in the past. 恨み ❑ *He appears to have a grudge against certain players.* 彼はある選手に対して恨みを持っているようだ.

grudg|ing /grʌdʒɪŋ/ ADJ 形容詞 A **grudging** feeling or action is felt or done very unwillingly. いやいやながらの, しぶしぶの ❑ *He even earned his opponents' grudging respect.* 彼は対戦相手からいやいやながらも敬意を受けた. **● grudg|ing|ly** ADV 副詞 [ADV with v] しぶしぶ ❑ *The film studio grudgingly agreed to allow him to continue working.* その映画撮影所は彼が勤務を続けることにしぶしぶ承諾した.

gru|el|ing /gruəlɪŋ/ ADJ 形容詞 A **grueling** activity is extremely difficult and tiring to do. 激しい, つらい ❑ *He had complained of exhaustion after his grueling schedule over the past week.* 彼は, 過去1週間のハードスケジュールのために疲労こんぱいしていると文句を言った.

grue|some /grusəm/ ADJ 形容詞 Something that is **gruesome** is extremely unpleasant and shocking. ぞっとする ❑ *There has been a series of gruesome murders in the capital.* 首都で一連の残虐な殺人事件がありました.

grum|ble /grʌmbəl/ (grumbles, grumbling, grumbled) **1** V-T/V-I 他動詞/自動詞 If someone **grumbles**, they complain about something in a bad-tempered way. ぶつぶつ文句を言う ❑ *They grumble about how hard they have to work.* 彼らは, どんなに仕事がきついかぶつぶつ文句を言う. ❑ *Taft grumbled that the law so favored the criminal that trials seemed like a game of chance.* 法律はあまりにも犯罪者びいきなため裁判は運次第のゲームのようだとタフトはぼやいた. **● ** N-COUNT 可算名詞 **Grumble** is also a noun. ぼやき ❑ *My only grumble is that there isn't a non-smoking section.* 私の不満は喫煙コーナーがないことだけだ. **2** V-I 自動詞 If something **grumbles**, it makes a low continuous sound. ゴロゴロ鳴る, うなる [LITERARY 文語的] ❑ *It was quiet now, the thunder had grumbled away to the west.* 雷がゴロゴロと鳴りながら西に行ってしまったので, 静かになった. **● ** N-SING 単数名詞 **Grumble** is also a noun. ゴロゴロ鳴る音 [usu N 'of' n] ❑ *One could often hear, far to the east, the grumble of guns.* 遠く東の方で銃声がたびたび聞こえた.

grumpy /grʌmpi/ (grumpier, grumpiest) ADJ 形容詞 If you say that someone is **grumpy**, you mean that they are bad tempered and miserable. 不機嫌な ❑ *Some folks think I'm a grumpy old man.* わしを気難しい老人だと思っているやつがいる. **● grump|i|ly** ADV 副詞 [ADV with v] 不機嫌そうに ❑ *"I know, I know," said Ken, grumpily, without looking up.* 「わかった, わかった」とケンは下を向いたまま不機嫌そうに言った.

grunt /grʌnt/ (grunts, grunting, grunted) **1** V-T/V-I 他動詞/自動詞 If you **grunt**, you make a low sound, especially because you are annoyed or not interested in something. うなるように言う [他動詞], フンと言う, うなるような声を出す [自動詞] ❑ *The driver grunted, convinced that Michael was crazy.* 運転手は, マイケルは頭がおかしいと確信してフンと言った. ❑ *Harvey grunted disgustedly as he*

tossed in his cards. ハービーはトランプを投げ出し, うんざりとした様子でうなり声を出した. **● ** N-COUNT 可算名詞 **Grunt** is also a noun. うめくような声 [oft N 'of' n] ❑ *Their replies were no more than grunts of acknowledgement.* 彼らの反応はただ承認を示すうなり声だけだった. **2** V-I 自動詞 When an animal **grunts**, it makes a low, rough noise. ブーブー言う ❑ *...the sound of a pig grunting.* ブタのブーブーという鳴き声 **3** N-COUNT 可算名詞 A **grunt** is a soldier of low rank in the infantry or the marines. 歩兵 [AM 米国英語, INFORMAL くだけた] ❑ *I'm just a grunt. I have to follow everybody's orders.* 俺はただの歩兵だ. 全員の命令に従わなきゃならないんだ.

GSM /dʒiː ɛs ɛm/ N-UNCOUNT 不可算名詞 **GSM** is a digital mobile telephone system. **GSM** is an abbreviation for "global system for mobile communication." GSM (デジタル携帯電話に使われている無線通信方式の一つ) ❑ *Their latest financial performance was a direct result of consistent growth in GSM cell phone subscribers.* 最近の財務実績はGSM携帯電話の契約者が着実に増えたことの直接的な結果だ.

guar|an|tee /gærənti/ (guarantees, guaranteeing, guaranteed) **1** V-T 他動詞 If one thing **guarantees** another, the first is certain to cause the second thing to happen. 確実にする, 確保する ❑ *Surplus resources alone do not guarantee growth.* 余剰資産だけでは確実に成長できるわけではない. **2** N-COUNT 可算名詞 Something that is a **guarantee** of something else makes it certain that it will happen or that it is true. 保証 ❑ *A famous old name on a firm is not necessarily a guarantee of quality.* 昔ながらの有名な会社名だからといって質の保証にはなるとは限らない. **3** V-T 他動詞 If you **guarantee** something, you promise that it will definitely happen, or that you will do or provide it for someone. 保証する, 約束する ❑ *Most states guarantee the right to free and adequate education.* ほとんどの州が無料で適切な教育を受ける権利を保障している. ❑ *We guarantee that you will find a community with which to socialize.* あなたが付き合いのできる人々を見つけられることを保証する. **● ** N-COUNT 可算名詞 **Guarantee** is also a noun. 保証, 約束 ❑ *The editors can give no guarantee that they will fulfil their obligations.* 編集者は彼らが義務を果たすという保証をできない. **4** N-COUNT 可算名詞 A **guarantee** is a written promise by a company to replace or repair a product free of charge if it has any faults within a particular time. 保証書 [also 'under' n] ❑ *Whatever a guarantee says, when something goes wrong, you can still claim your rights from the store.* 保証書の記載事項に関わらず, 故障の場合は販売店を通して権利を主張できる. **5** V-T 他動詞 If a company **guarantees** its product or work, they provide a guarantee for it. 保証をつける ❑ *Some builders guarantee their work.* 保証付きの仕事をする建築業者もある. ❑ *All Dreamland's electric blankets are guaranteed for three years.* ドリームランドの電気毛布は全商品3年間の保証付きです. **6** N-COUNT 可算名詞 A **guarantee** is money or something valuable that you give to someone to show that you will do what you have promised. 保証金, 保証 ❑ *Males between 18 and 20 had to leave a deposit as a guarantee of returning to do their military service.* 18歳から20歳の男性は兵役のため戻ることの保証として支払いをしなければならなかった.

guar|an|tor /gærəntɔr/ (guarantors) N-COUNT 可算名詞 A **guarantor** is a person who gives a guarantee or who is bound by one. 保証人 [LEGAL 法律的] ❑ *Someone thinking about acting as a guarantor should be clear about their obligations will be.* 保証人を引き受けようと考えている人はその責任の内容をはっきりとするべきだ.

guard /gɑrd/ (guards, guarding, guarded) **1** V-T 他動詞 If you **guard** a place, person, or object, you stand near them in order to watch and protect them. 守る, 警護する ❑ *Gunmen guarded homes near the cemetery with shotguns.* 武装集団が散弾銃を持って墓地の近くの住宅を警護した. **2** V-T 他動詞 If you **guard** someone, you watch them and keep them in a particular place to stop them from escaping. 監視する ❑ *Marines with rifles guarded them.* ライフル銃を持った海兵隊員が彼らを監視した. **3** N-COUNT 可算名詞 A **guard** is someone such as a soldier, police officer, or prison officer who is guarding a particular place or person. 警備員 ❑ *The prisoners overpowered their guards and locked them in a cell.* 囚人が看守を取り押さえ監房に閉じ込めた. **4** N-SING-COLL 集合的単数名詞 A **guard** is a specially organized group of people, such as soldiers or police officers, who protect or watch someone or something. 警備隊 ❑ *We have a security guard around the whole area.* この地域全体に警備隊がいます. **5** V-T 他動詞 If you **guard** some information or advantage that you have, you try to protect it or keep it for yourself. 守る ❑ *He closely guarded her identity.* 彼はしっかりと彼女の身元を守った. **6** N-COUNT 可算名詞 A **guard** is a protective device which covers a part of someone's body or a dangerous part of a piece of equipment. ―ガード, ―当て [usu with supp] ❑ *...the chin guard of my helmet.* ヘルメットのあご当て **7** N-COUNT 可算名詞 On a train, a **guard** is a person whose job is to travel on the train in order to help passengers, check tickets, and make sure that the train travels safely and on time. 車掌 [BRIT 英国英語; AM 米国英語 **conductor** 米国英語 **conductor**] **8** → see also **guarded, bodyguard, coast guard, lifeguard** **9** PHRASE 句 If someone **catches** you **off guard**, they surprise you by doing something you do not expect. If something **catches** you **off guard**, it surprises you by happening when you are not expecting it. 不

意をつく □*Charm the audience and catch them off guard.* 聴衆を魅了して不意をつきなさい. **10** PHRASE 句 If you **lower** your **guard, let** your **guard down** or **drop** your **guard,** you relax when you should be careful and alert, often with unpleasant consequences. 油断する □*The ANC could not afford to lower its guard until everything had been carried out.* アフリカ民族会議はすべてが実行されるまで油断することができなかった. □*You can't let your guard down.* 油断してはいけません. **11** PHRASE 句 If you are **on** your **guard** or **on guard,** you are being very careful because you think a situation might become difficult or dangerous. 警戒して, 注意して □*The police have questioned him thoroughly, and he'll be on his guard.* 警察は彼に徹底的に尋問をしたので, 彼は気をつけるだろう. **12** PHRASE 句 If someone is **on guard,** they are on duty and responsible for guarding a particular place or person. 見張って, 警戒して □*Police were on guard at Barnet town hall.* 警察がバーネット・タウンホールで警備に当たっていた. **13** PHRASE 句 If you **stand guard,** you stand near a particular person or place because you are responsible for watching or protecting them. 見張りをする, 監視する □*One young policeman stood guard outside the locked embassy gates.* 若い警官が施錠された大使館門の外で警備をしていた. **14** PHRASE 句 If someone is **under guard,** they are being guarded. 監視されている □*Three men were arrested and one was under guard in a hospital.* 3人の男性が逮捕され, 1人は病院で監視下に置かれた.

→ see **soccer**

▶ **guard against** PHRASAL VERB 句動詞 If you **guard against** something, you are careful to prevent it from happening, or to avoid being affected by it. 〜から守る □*The armed forces were on high alert to guard against any retaliation.* 軍隊はいかなる報復行為も防ぐために厳戒態勢にあった.

Word Partnership   guard は次の語句と使われる:

N.	guard **a door/house/prisoner 1 2**
	prison guard, **security** guard **3 4**
V.	catch *someone* **off** guard **9**
	let your guard **down, be on** guard,
	stand guard **10 – 13**

---

guard|ed /gɑːrdɪd/ ADJ 形容詞 If you describe someone as **guarded,** you mean that they are careful not to show their feelings or give away information. 用心深い □*The boy gave him a guarded look.* 少年は彼に対して慎重な態度を見せた.

guard|ian /gɑːrdiən/ (**guardians**) **1** N-COUNT 可算名詞 A **guardian** is someone who has been legally appointed to take charge of the affairs of another person, for example a child or someone who is mentally ill. 後見人 □*Destiny's legal guardian was her grandmother.* デスティニーの法的後見人は彼女の祖母だった. **2** N-COUNT 可算名詞 The **guardian of** something is someone who defends and protects it. 保護者 □*...an institution acting as the guardian of democracy in Europe.* ヨーロッパでの民主主義保護のため活動している組織

guer|ril|la /gərɪlə/ (**guerrillas**) also **guerilla** N-COUNT 可算名詞 A **guerrilla** is someone who fights as part of an unofficial army, usually against an official army or police force. 遊撃隊員 □*The guerrillas threatened to kill their hostages.* ゲリラは人質を殺すと言って脅迫した.

guess /ges/ (**guesses, guessing, guessed**) **1** V-T/V-I 他動詞/自動詞 If you **guess** something, you give an answer or provide an opinion which may not be true because you do not have definite knowledge about the matter concerned. 推測する □*Yvonne guessed that he was a very successful publisher or a banker.* イボンヌは彼のことを出版で大成功した人物か銀行家だと推測した. □*You can only guess at what mental suffering they endure.* あなたには彼らがどんな精神的苦痛に耐えてきたかを推測することしかできない. □*Guess what I did for the whole of the first week.* 最初の一週間の全体で私がしたことを推測してください. **2** V-T 他動詞 If you **guess that** something is the case, you correctly form the opinion that it is the case, although you do not have definite knowledge about it. 推測する □*By now you will have guessed that I'm back in Ohio.* 今ごろあなたは私がオハイオ州に戻ったと推測しているだろう. □*He should have guessed what would happen.* 彼は何が起こるかを推測するべきだった. **3** N-COUNT 可算名詞 A **guess** is an attempt to give an answer or provide an opinion which may not be true because you do not have definite knowledge about the matter concerned. 推測 □*My guess is that the chance that these vaccines will work is zero.* 私の推測では三つのワクチンが効力を発揮する機会はない. □*He'd taken her pulse and made a guess at her blood pressure.* 彼は彼女の脈を取り, 彼女の血圧を推測した. **4** PHRASE 句 If you say that something is **anyone's guess** or **anybody's guess,** you mean that no one can be certain about what is really true. 誰にもわからないこと [INFORMAL くだけた] □*Just when this will happen is anyone's guess.* いつがいい起こるかは誰にもわからない. **5** PHRASE 句 You say **at a guess** to indicate that what you are saying is only an estimate or what you believe to be true, rather than being a definite fact. 推測では [mainly BRIT 主に英国英語, VAGUENESS あいまいさ] □*At a guess he's been dead*

for two days. 推測では彼は二日前に死んだ. **6** PHRASE 句 You say **I guess** to show that you are slightly uncertain or reluctant about what you are saying. 思う [mainly AM 主に米国英語, INFORMAL くだけた, VAGUENESS あいまいさ] □*I guess he's right.* おそらく彼は正しい. □*"I think you're being paranoid." — "Yeah. I guess so."* 「きみはこだわりすぎなんじゃないかな」 – 「うん, たぶんね」 **7** PHRASE 句 If someone **keeps** you **guessing,** they do not tell you what you want to know. 気をもませておく □*The author's intention is to keep everyone guessing until the bitter end.* 著者の意図は辛らつな結末に至るまで読者をはらはらさせておくことだ. **8** CONVENTION 慣習表現 You say **guess what** to draw attention to something exciting, surprising, or interesting that you are about to say. 想像できるかい [INFORMAL くだけた] □*Guess what, I just got my first part in a movie.* 何だと思う. 初めて映画の役が回ってきたよ.

Thesaurus   guess また次を参照:

V.	estimate, predict, suspect **1**
N.	assumption, prediction, theory **3**

Word Partnership   guess は次の語句と使われる:

N.	guess **a secret 1 2**
V.	**make a** guess **3**
ADJ.	**educated** guess, **good** guess, **wild** guess **3**

---

guess|ti|mate /gestɪmət/ (**guesstimates**) N-COUNT 可算名詞 A **guesstimate** is an approximate calculation which is based mainly or entirely on guessing. 当て推量 [INFORMAL くだけた] □*The 30 percent figure may be no more than a guesstimate.* その30パーセントという数字は当て推量に過ぎないのかもしれない.

guest /gest/ (**guests**) **1** N-COUNT 可算名詞 A **guest** is someone who is visiting you or is at an event because you have invited them. 客 □*She was a guest at the wedding.* 彼女は結婚式の客だった. **2** N-COUNT 可算名詞 A **guest** is someone who visits a place or organization or appears on a radio or television show because they have been invited to do so. 特別出演者 □*...a frequent talk show guest.* トーク番組によく特別出演する人物 □*Dr. Gerald Jeffers is the guest speaker.* ジェラルド・ジェファーズ博士の特別出演です. **3** N-COUNT 可算名詞 A **guest** is someone who is staying in a hotel. 宿泊客 □*I was the only hotel guest.* 私が唯一の宿泊客だった. **4** CONVENTION 慣習表現 If you say **be my guest** to someone, you are giving them permission to do something. ご遠慮なく □*If anybody wants to work on this, be my guest.* これに取り組みたい人がいれば誰でも, 遠慮しないでください.

→ see **hotel**

Word Partnership   guest は次の語句と使われる:

ADJ.	**unwelcome** guest **1 2**
V.	**be** *someone's* guest, **entertain a** guest **1 2**
	accommodate a guest **1 – 3**
N.	guest **appearance,** guest **list,** guest **speaker 1 2**
	hotel guest **3**

---

guest house (**guest houses**) also **guesthouse 1** N-COUNT 可算名詞 A **guest house** is a small hotel. 小旅館 **2** N-COUNT 可算名詞 A **guest house** is a small house in the grounds of a large house, where visitors can stay. 客用の離れ

guid|ance /gaɪdəns/ N-UNCOUNT 不可算名詞 **Guidance** is help and advice. 指導 □*...an opportunity for young people to improve their performance under the guidance of professional coaches.* 専門指導員の手ほどきのもとで若者が自分たちの演技を向上させる機会

guide /gaɪd/ (**guides, guiding, guided**) **1** N-COUNT; N-IN-NAMES 可算名詞, 名称中の名詞 A **guide** is a book that gives you information or instructions to help you do or understand something. 手引書 □*Our 10-page guide will help you to change your life for the better.* 我々の10ページの手引書が, よりよい生活への変化をお手伝いします. **2** N-COUNT; N-IN-NAMES 可算名詞, 名称中の名詞 A **guide** is a book that gives tourists information about a town, area, or country. 旅行案内書 □*The Rough Guide to Paris lists accommodations for as little as $35 a night.* その大まかなパリの案内書にわずか35ドルで泊まれる宿泊施設の一覧がある. **3** N-COUNT 可算名詞 A **guide** is someone who shows tourists around places such as museums or cities. 案内人 □*We've arranged a walking tour of the city with your guide.* 徒歩での市内見学と案内人を手配した. **4** V-T 他動詞 If you **guide** someone around a city, museum, or building, you show it to them and explain points of interest. 案内する □*...a young Egyptologist who guided us through tombs and temples with enthusiasm.* 霊廟(れいびょう)と寺院で我々を熱心に案内した若いエジプト学者 **5** N-COUNT 可算名詞 A **guide** is someone who shows people the way to a place in a difficult or dangerous region. 案内人 □*The mountain people say that, with guides, the journey can be done in fourteen days.* 山の住民は, 案内人がいれば14日間でその旅をこなせると言う. **6** N-COUNT 可算名詞 A **guide** is

something that can be used to help you plan your actions or to form an opinion about something. 指針 ❑ *As a rough guide, a horse needs 2.5 percent of its body weight in food every day.* おおよその指針として、馬は毎日、体重の2.5パーセントに相当する食物を必要とする. **7** V-T 他動詞 If you **guide** someone somewhere, you go there with them in order to show them the way. 案内する ❑ *He took the bewildered Elliott by the arm and guided him out.* 彼は当惑するエリオットの腕を取って連れ出し、彼を案内した. **8** V-T 他動詞 If you **guide** a vehicle somewhere, you control it carefully to make sure that it goes in the right direction. 導く ❑ *Captain Shelton guided his plane down the runway and took off.* シェルトン機長は飛行機を滑走路に導き離陸した. **9** V-T 他動詞 If something **guides** you somewhere, it gives you the information you need in order to go in the right direction. 導く ❑ *They sailed across the Caribbean with only a compass to guide them.* 彼らは羅針盤の案内のみでカリブ海を横断した. **10** V-T 他動詞 If something or someone **guides** you, they influence your actions or decisions. 指導する ❑ *He should have let his instinct guide him.* 彼は本能に従うべきだった. ❑ *Development has been guided by a concern for the ecology of the area.* 発展はその地域の環境への考慮から導かれてきた. **11** V-T 他動詞 If you **guide** someone through something that is difficult to understand or to achieve, you help them to understand it or to achieve success in it. 指導する ❑ *Gym owner David Barton will guide them through a workout.* ジムの所有者デビッド・バートンが彼らの準備運動を指導するだろう.

Thesaurus
guide また次を参照:

N. directory, handbook, information **1** **2**
V. accompany, direct, instruct, lead, navigate; (*ant.*) follow **4** **7**

guide|book /ɡaɪdbʊk/ (**guidebooks**) also **guide book** N-COUNT 可算名詞 A **guidebook** is a book that gives tourists information about a town, area, or country. 旅行案内書

guide|line /ɡaɪdlaɪn/ (**guidelines**) **1** N-COUNT 可算名詞 If an organization issues **guidelines on** something, it issues official advice about how to do it. 指針 ❑ *The government should issue clear guidelines on the content of religious education.* 政府は宗教教育の内容について明確な指針を示すべきだ. **2** N-COUNT 可算名詞 A **guideline** is something that can be used to help you plan your actions or to form an opinion about something. 基準 ❑ *A written IQ test is merely a guideline.* 記述式の知能試験はたんにひとつの基準に過ぎない.

guild /ɡɪld/ (**guilds**) N-COUNT 可算名詞 A **guild** is an organization of people who do the same job. 同業者組合 ❑ *...the Writers' Guild of America.* アメリカの文筆業者組合

guilt /ɡɪlt/ **1** N-UNCOUNT 不可算名詞 **Guilt** is an unhappy feeling that you have because you have done something wrong or think that you have done something wrong. 罪悪感 ❑ *Her emotions had ranged from anger to guilt in the space of a few seconds.* 彼女の感情は、数秒のうちに怒りから罪悪感にまで及んでいた. **2** N-UNCOUNT 不可算名詞 **Guilt** is the fact that you have done something wrong or illegal. 罪 ❑ *The trial is concerned only with the determination of guilt according to criminal law.* 裁判は刑法にのっとって罪の判定にのみ関わる.

Word Partnership
guilt は次の語句と使われる:

N. burden of guilt, feelings of guilt, sense of guilt, guilt trip **1**
V. admit guilt **2**

guilty /ɡɪlti/ (**guiltier, guiltiest**) **1** ADJ 形容詞 If you feel **guilty**, you feel unhappy because you think that you have done something wrong or have failed to do something which you should have done. 後ろめたい ❑ *I feel so guilty, leaving all this to you.* これを全部きみに任せてしまって、本当に悪いと思う. ● **guilti|ly** ADV 副詞 [ADV with v] やましい気持ちで ❑ *He glanced guiltily over his shoulder.* 彼は後ろめたそうに肩越しに視線を投げた. **2** ADJ 形容詞 **Guilty** is used of an action or fact that you feel guilty about. 後ろめたい ❑ *Many may be keeping in a guilty secret.* 多くの人がそれを後ろめたい秘密のままにしておくかもしれない. **3** **guilty conscience** → see **conscience** **4** ADJ 形容詞 If someone is **guilty of** a crime or offense, they have committed that crime or offense. 有罪の ❑ *They were found guilty of murder.* 彼らは殺人で有罪となった. **5** ADJ 形容詞 If someone is **guilty of** doing something wrong, they have done that thing. (過失などを) 犯した ❑ *He claimed Mr. Brooke had been guilty of a "gross error of judgment."* 彼はブルック氏が「とんでもない誤判」を犯してきたと主張した.
→ see **trial**

Word Partnership
guilty は次の語句と使われる:

V. feel guilty, look guilty **1**
find someone guilty, plead (not) guilty, prove someone guilty **3** **4**
N. guilty conscience, guilty secret **2**
guilty party, guilty plea, guilty verdict **3** **4**
PREP. guilty of something **3** **4**

guinea pig (**guinea pigs**) **1** N-COUNT 可算名詞 If someone is used as a **guinea pig** in an experiment, something is tested on them that has not been tested on people before. モルモット ❑ *Dr. Roger Altounyan used himself as a human guinea pig.* ロジャー・アルトニアン博士は自らを人間モルモットとして使った. **2** N-COUNT 可算名詞 A **guinea pig** is a small, furry animal without a tail. Guinea pigs are often kept as pets. モルモット

guise /ɡaɪz/ (**guises**) N-COUNT 可算名詞 You use **guise** to refer to the outward appearance or form of someone or something, which is often temporary or different from their real nature. 外観 ❑ *He turned up at an Easter party in the guise of a white rabbit.* 彼は復活祭のパーティーに白ウサギの扮装で登場した.

gui|tar /ɡɪtɑr/ (**guitars**) N-VAR 可変性名詞 A **guitar** is a musical instrument with six strings and a long neck. You play the guitar by plucking or strumming the strings. ギター

gui|tar|ist /ɡɪtɑrɪst/ (**guitarists**) N-COUNT 可算名詞 A **guitarist** is someone who plays the guitar. ギター奏者

gulf /ɡʌlf/ (**gulfs**) **1** N-COUNT 可算名詞 A **gulf** is an important or significant difference between two people, things, or groups. 隔たり ❑ *Within society, there is a growing gulf between rich and poor.* 社会内の貧富の格差が広がりつつある. **2** N-COUNT 可算名詞 A **gulf** is a large area of sea which extends a long way into the surrounding land. 湾 ❑ *Hurricane Andrew was last night heading into the Gulf of Mexico.* 昨晩、ハリケーン・アンドリューはメキシコ湾に向かっていた.

gul|lible /ɡʌlɪbəl/ ADJ 形容詞 If you describe someone as **gullible**, you mean they are easily tricked because they are too trusting. だまされやすい ❑ *What point is there in admitting that the stories fed to the gullible public were false?* だまされやすい大衆向きの話を間違いだと認めることにどんな利点があるんだ. ● **gul|li|bil|ity** /ɡʌləbɪlɪti/ N-UNCOUNT 不可算名詞 だまされやすさ ❑ *Was she taking part of the blame for her own gullibility?* 彼女は自分自身のだまされやすさへの非難に加担していたのか.

gul|ly /ɡʌli/ (**gullies**) also **gulley** N-COUNT 可算名詞 A **gully** is a long, narrow valley with steep sides. 峡谷 ❑ *The bodies of the three climbers were located at the bottom of a steep gully.* 3人の登山者の死体は狭い峡谷の底にあった.
→ see **erosion**

gulp /ɡʌlp/ (**gulps, gulping, gulped**) **1** V-T 他動詞 If you **gulp** something, you eat or drink it very quickly by swallowing large quantities of it at once. 勢いよく飲む ❑ *She quickly gulped her soda.* 彼女は炭酸水をすばやくあおった. ● PHRASAL VERB 句動詞 **Gulp down** means the same as **gulp**. 勢いよく飲む ❑ *Paige gulped down more coffee and a candy bar from the machine.* ペイジは機械からさらなるコーヒーと板チョコをとってのどに詰め込んだ. **2** V-T/V-I 他動詞/自動詞 If you **gulp**, you swallow air, often making a noise in your throat as you do so, because you are nervous or excited. 息を飲む [WRITTEN 書き言葉] ❑ *I gulped, and then proceeded to tell her the whole story.* 私は息を飲み、それからその一部始終を彼女に話し続けた. **3** V-T 他動詞 If you **gulp** air, you breathe in a large amount of air quickly through your mouth. 飲み込む ❑ *She gulped air into her lungs.* 彼女は肺の中に空気を吸い込んだ. **4** N-COUNT 可算名詞 A **gulp** of air, food, or drink, is a large amount of it that you swallow at once. 一気に飲む量 ❑ *I took in a large gulp of air.* 私は大きな空気の塊を飲み込んだ.

gum /ɡʌm/ (**gums**) **1** N-MASS 質量名詞 **Gum** is a substance, usually tasting of mint, which you chew for a long time but do not swallow. ガム ❑ *I do not chew gum in public.* 私は人前でガムをかまない. **2** N-COUNT 可算名詞 Your **gums** are the areas of firm, pink flesh inside your mouth, which your teeth grow out of. 歯茎 ❑ *The toothbrush gently removes plaque without damaging the gums or causing bleeding.* その歯ブラシは、歯茎を傷つけたり出血を引き起こしたりすることなく、やさしく歯垢（こう）を取り除く.
→ see **teeth**

gun /ɡʌn/ (**guns, gunning, gunned**) **1** N-COUNT 可算名詞 A **gun** is a weapon from which bullets or other things are fired. 銃 ❑ *He fled, pointing the gun at officers as they chased him.* 追跡されたとき、彼は警官たちに銃を向けながら逃げた. ❑ *He just seemed like a normal military guy who liked guns.* 彼は単に銃の好きな普通の軍人に見えた. **2** N-COUNT 可算名詞 A **gun** or a **starting gun** is an object like a gun that is used to make a noise to signal the start of a race. 出発合図用のピストル ❑ *The starting gun blasted and they were off.* 合図の拳銃が火を噴き、彼らはスタートした. **3** V-T 他動詞 To **gun** an

engine or a vehicle means to make it start or go faster by pressing on the accelerator pedal. ふかす, 加速する [mainly AM 主に米国英語] ❑ *He gunned his engine and drove off.* 彼はエンジンをかけ出発した. ◧ → see also **shotgun** ◩ PHRASE 句 If you come out with **guns blazing** or with **all guns blazing**, you put all your effort and energy into trying to achieve something. 全力を注いで ❑ *The company came out with guns blazing.* その会社は猛烈な勢いで世に出てきた. ◪ PHRASE 句 If you **jump the gun**, you do something before everyone else or before the proper or right time. 先走る [INFORMAL くだけた] ❑ *It wasn't due to be released until September 10, but some booksellers have jumped the gun and decided to sell it early.* その本は9月10日までは売り出してはいけないはずだったが，書店の中には先走って早めの発売を決めたところもある. ◫ PHRASE 句 If you **stick to** your **guns**, you continue to have your own opinion about something even though other people are trying to tell you that you are wrong. 持論を譲らない [INFORMAL くだけた] ❑ *He should have stuck to his guns and refused to meet her.* 彼は自分の主張を貫き，彼女と会うことを拒むべきだった.

▸ **gun down** PHRASAL VERB 句動詞 If someone **is gunned down**, they are shot and severely injured or killed. 銃で撃つ [JOURNALISM ジャーナリズム] ❑ *He had been gunned down and killed at point-blank range.* 彼は至近距離から撃たれて死亡していた.

Word Partnership	*gun* は次の語句と使われる:
v.	**aim** a gun, **carry** a gun, **fire** a gun, **load** a gun, **own** a gun, **shoot** a gun, **use** a gun ◨
N.	**hand** gun, **toy** gun ◨ **starting** gun ◩ gun **an engine** ◪

gun|fire /gʌnfaɪr/ N-UNCOUNT 不可算名詞 **Gunfire** is the repeated shooting of guns. 砲火 ❑ *The sound of gunfire and explosions grew closer.* 銃撃と爆撃の音が近づいてきた.

gun|man /gʌnmən/ (**gunmen**) N-COUNT 可算名詞 A **gunman** is a man who uses a gun to commit a crime such as murder or robbery. 銃撃犯 [JOURNALISM ジャーナリズム] ❑ *Two policemen were killed when gunmen opened fire on their patrol vehicle.* 銃撃犯がパトカーで発砲し，2名の警官が死亡した.

gun|point /gʌnpɔɪnt/ PHRASE 句 If you are held **at gunpoint**, someone is threatening to shoot and kill you if you do not obey them. 銃を突きつけられて ❑ *She and her two daughters were held at gunpoint by a gang who burst into their home.* 彼女とふたりの娘は家に押し入った悪党に銃を突きつけられた.

gun|shot /gʌnʃɒt/ (**gunshots**) ◧ N-UNCOUNT 不可算名詞 **Gunshot** is used to refer to bullets that are fired from a gun. 発砲された銃弾 ❑ *They had died of gunshot wounds.* 彼らは銃弾を受けた傷で死んでいた. ◨ N-COUNT 可算名詞 A **gunshot** is the firing of a gun or the sound of a gun being fired. 発砲 ❑ *They heard thousands of gunshots.* 彼らは何千もの銃声を聞いた.

gur|gle /gɜrgºl/ (**gurgles, gurgling, gurgled**) ◧ V-I 自動詞 If water **is gurgling**, it is making the sound that it makes when it flows quickly and unevenly through a narrow space. ゴボゴボと音を立てる ❑ *...a narrow stone-edged channel along which water gurgles unseen.* 見えないところで水が音を立てる狭く険しい海峡. ● N-COUNT 可算名詞 **Gurgle** is also a noun. ゴボゴボいう音 ❑ *We could hear the swish and gurgle of water against the hull.* 水が殻にぶつかるゴボゴボとした音が聞こえた. ◨ V-I 自動詞 If someone, especially a baby, **is gurgling**, they are making a sound in their throat similar to the gurgling of water. のどを鳴らす ❑ *Henry gurgles happily in his baby chair.* ヘンリーは赤ん坊用の椅子に座り幸せそうにのどを鳴らす. ● N-COUNT 可算名詞 **Gurgle** is also a noun. のどを鳴らす音 ❑ *There was a gurgle of laughter on the other end of the line.* 列の反対側の端では，のどを鳴らして笑う声が聞こえた.

gur|ney /gɜrni/ (**gurneys**) N-COUNT 可算名詞 A **gurney** is a bed on wheels that is used in hospitals for moving sick or injured people. 台車付き担架 [AM 米国英語] ❑ *A man on a gurney was being handled by an orderly.* 台車付き担架に乗った男が看護兵に世話をされていた.

guru /guru/ (**gurus**) ◧ N-COUNT 可算名詞 A **guru** is a person who some people regard as an expert or leader. 指導者 ❑ *Fashion gurus dictate crazy ideas such as squeezing oversized bodies into tight trousers.* ファッションリーダーたちは大きすぎる体を細いズボンに無理やり押し込むなど，おかしな考えを押し付ける. ◨ N-COUNT; N-TITLE 可算名詞, 称号名詞 A **guru** is a religious and spiritual leader and teacher, especially in Hinduism. 導師

gush /gʌʃ/ (**gushes, gushing, gushed**) ◧ V-T/V-I 他動詞/自動詞 When liquid **gushes** out of something, or when something **gushes** a liquid, the liquid flows out very quickly and in large quantities. ほとばしる ❑ *Piping-hot water gushed out.* 鋭い音を立てる熱湯がほとばしった. ◨ N-SING 単数名詞 A **gush of** liquid is a sudden, rapid flow of liquid, or a quantity of it that suddenly flows out. ほとばしり [usu N 'of' n] ❑ *I heard a gush of water.* 水がほとばしる音が聞こえた. ◪ V-T/V-I 他動詞/自動詞 If someone

gushes, they express their admiration or pleasure in an exaggerated way. 大げさに言う ❑ *"Oh, it was brilliant,"* he *gushes.* 「ああ，それは素晴らしかった」彼は大げさに言う. ● **gush|ing** ADJ 形容詞 大げさに表した ❑ *He delivered a gushing speech.* 彼は大げさに感情を込めて演説した.

gust /gʌst/ (**gusts, gusting, gusted**) ◧ N-COUNT 可算名詞 A **gust** is a short, strong, sudden rush of wind. 突風 ❑ *A gust of wind drove down the valley.* 一陣の風が谷を走り抜けた. ◨ V-I 自動詞 When the wind **gusts**, it blows with short, strong, sudden rushes. 急に強く吹く ❑ *The wind gusted again.* 再び突風が吹いた. ◪ N-COUNT 可算名詞 If you feel a **gust** of emotion, you feel the emotion suddenly and intensely. 激発 [N 'of' n] ❑ *...a small gust of pleasure.* 小さな喜びのほとばしり

gut /gʌt/ (**guts, gutting, gutted**) ◧ N-PLURAL 複数名詞 A person's or animal's **guts** are all the organs inside them. 臓物 ❑ *By the time they finish, the crewmen are standing ankle-deep in fish guts.* 終わったときには乗組員たちはくるぶしまで魚の内臓にまみれて立っている. ◨ V-T 他動詞 When you **guts** a dead animal or fish, they prepare it for cooking by removing all the organs from inside it. 内臓を取る ❑ *It is not always necessary to gut the fish prior to freezing.* 冷凍する前に魚の内臓を取ることが必要だとは限らない. ◪ N-SING 単数名詞 The **gut** is the tube inside the body of a person or animal through which food passes while it is being digested. 消化器官 ['the'/poss N] ❑ *Toxins can leak from the gut into the bloodstream.* 毒素が消化器官から血管に入り込むかもしれない. ◫ N-UNCOUNT 不可算名詞 **Guts** is the will and courage to do something that is difficult or unpleasant, or which might have unpleasant results. 根性 [INFORMAL くだけた] ❑ *The new governor has the guts to push through unpopular tax increases.* 新政府は不評の増税を推し進める根性を持っている. ◬ ADJ 形容詞 A **gut** feeling is based on instinct or emotion rather than reason. 直感的な ❑ *Let's have your gut reaction to the facts as we know them.* 事実を知っているのだから，それに対して直感的に反応しよう. ◭ N-COUNT 可算名詞 You can refer to someone's stomach as their **gut**, especially when it is very large and sticks out. 腹 [INFORMAL くだけた] ❑ *His gut sagged out over his belt.* 彼の腹はベルトの上にたわんでせりだしていた. ◮ V-T 他動詞 To **gut** a building means to destroy the inside of it so that only its outside walls remain. 内部を破壊する ❑ *Over the weekend, a firebomb gutted a building where 60 people lived.* 週末，60名の住人がいた建物の内部を焼い弾が焼き尽くした. ◰ N-UNCOUNT 不可算名詞 **Gut** is string made from part of the stomach of an animal. Traditionally, it is used to make the strings of sports rackets or musical instruments such as violins. 腸線 ❑ *Gerald's violin strings are made of gut rather than steel.* ジェラルドのバイオリンの弦は金属ではなく腸線でできている. ◱ PHRASE 句 If you **hate** someone's **guts**, you dislike them very much. 心底嫌う [INFORMAL くだけた, EMPHASIS 強調] ❑ *We hate each other's guts.* 我々は互いを徹底的に嫌っている. ◲ PHRASE 句 If you say that you **are working** your **guts out**, you are emphasizing that you are working as hard as you can. 身を粉にして働く [INFORMAL くだけた, EMPHASIS 強調] ❑ *Most have worked their guts out and made sacrifices.* たいていの者が身を粉にして働き，犠牲を払った.

gut|ter /gʌtər/ (**gutters**) ◧ N-COUNT 可算名詞 The **gutter** is the edge of a road next to the pavement, where rainwater collects and flows away. 溝 ❑ *It is supposed to be washed down the gutter and into the city's vast sewerage system.* それは溝を洗い流して下り，町の巨大な下水網に流れ込むはずだ. ◨ N-COUNT 可算名詞 A **gutter** is a plastic or metal channel attached to the lower edge of the roof of a building, which rainwater drains into. 雨どい ❑ *Did you fix the gutter?* 雨どいを修理したか. ◪ N-SING 単数名詞 If someone is **in the gutter**, they are very poor and live in a very bad way. どん底で ❑ *Instead of ending up in jail or in the gutter he was remarkably successful.* 刑務所や社会の底辺で終わるどころか彼は目覚しい成功をした.

guy /gaɪ/ (**guys**) ◧ N-COUNT 可算名詞 A **guy** is a man. 男 [INFORMAL くだけた] ❑ *I was working with a guy from Milwaukee.* 私はミルウォーキー出身の男と働いていた. ◨ N-VOC; N-PLURAL 呼格名詞, 複数名詞 Americans sometimes address a group of people, whether they are male or female, as **guys** or **you guys**. みんな [INFORMAL くだけた] ['you' N] ❑ *Hi, guys. How are you doing?* やあ，みんな. 元気かい.

gym /dʒɪm/ (**gyms**) ◧ N-COUNT 可算名詞 A **gym** is a club, building, or large room, usually containing special equipment, where people go to do physical exercise and get fit. 体育施設 ❑ *While the boys are golfing, I work out in the gym.* 男の子たちがゴルフをしている間，私はジムで準備運動をする. ◨ N-UNCOUNT 不可算名詞 **Gym** is the activity of doing physical exercises in a gym, especially at school. 体操 ❑ *...gym classes.* 体操の授業

gym|na|sium /dʒɪmneɪziəm/ (**gymnasiums** or **gymnasia** /dʒɪmneɪziə/) N-COUNT 可算名詞 A **gymnasium** is the same as a **gym**. 体育施設 [FORMAL 形式ばった]

gym|nast /dʒɪmnæst/ (**gymnasts**) N-COUNT 可算名詞 A **gymnast** is someone who is trained in gymnastics. 体操選手 → see **gymnastics**

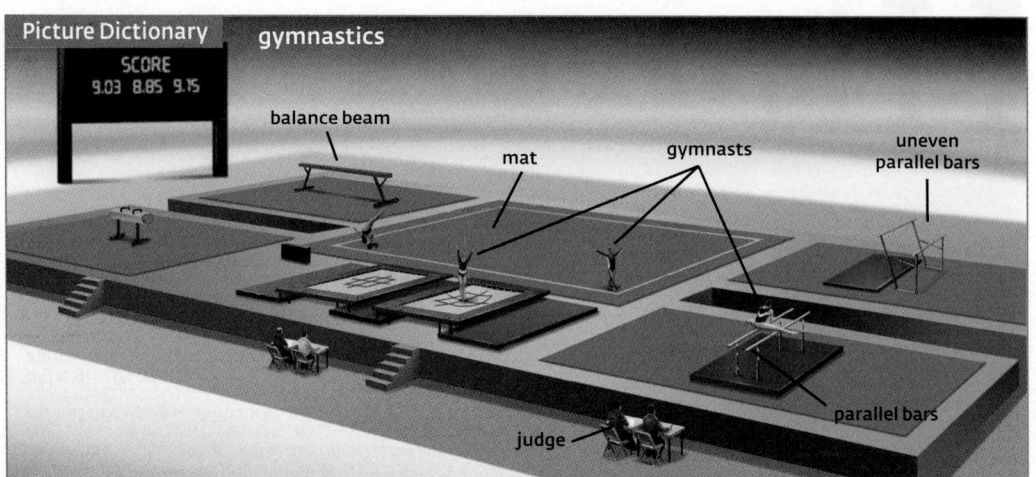

Picture Dictionary

gymnastics

SCORE
9.03 8.85 9.15

balance beam

mat

gymnasts

uneven parallel bars

parallel bars

judge

g

gym|nas|tics /dʒɪmnæstɪks/

The form **gymnastic** is used as a modifier.

gymnastic 形は修飾語として使われる.

N-UNCOUNT 不可算名詞 **Gymnastics** consists of physical exercises that develop your strength, coordination, and ease of movement. 体操 ❑ *She competes in gymnastics, with hopes of making it to the Olympics.* 彼女は体操競技に出場し，オリンピックへの期待も持っている.
→ see Picture Dictionary: **gymnastics**

gy|ne|col|ogy /gaɪnɪkɒlədʒi/ N-UNCOUNT 不可算名詞 **Gynecology** is the branch of medical science that deals with women's diseases and medical conditions. 婦人科

● **gy|ne|colo|gist** (**gynecologists**) N-COUNT 可算名詞 婦人科医 ❑ *Gynecologists at the hospital have successfully used the drug on 60 women.* その病院の婦人科医は60人の女性にその薬を投与し成功を収めている. ● **gy|ne|co|logi|cal** /gaɪnɪkəlɒdʒɪkᵊl/ ADJ 形容詞 [ADJ n] 婦人科の ❑ *Breast examination is a part of a routine gynecological examination.* 胸部診断は婦人科の通常検査の一部だ.

gyp|sy /dʒɪpsi/ (**gypsies**) N-COUNT 可算名詞 A **gypsy** is a member of a race of people who travel from place to place, usually in caravans, rather than living in one place. Some people find this word offensive. ジプシー ❑ *I'm proud of being brought up by gypsies.* 私はジプシーに育てられたことを誇りに思っている. ● ADJ 形容詞 **Gypsy** is also an adjective. ジプシーの ❑ *...the largest gypsy community of any country.* すべての国の最大のジプシー共同体

Hh

H also **h** /ˈeɪtʃ/ (**H's, h's** /ˈeɪtʃɪz/) H is the eighth letter of the English alphabet. アルファベットの第8字

hab|it /ˈhæbɪt/ (**habits**) **1** N-VAR 可変性名詞 A habit is something that you do often or regularly. 習慣 □ *He has an endearing habit of licking his lips when he's nervous.* 彼にはそわそわしている時に唇をなめる愛らしい癖がある。 □ *Many people add salt to their food out of habit, without even tasting it first.* 味見もせずに習慣で食べ物に塩をふりかける人が多い。 **2** N-COUNT 可算名詞 A habit is an action considered bad that someone does repeatedly and finds it difficult to stop doing. 癖 □ *A good way to break the habit of eating too quickly is to put your knife and fork down after each mouthful.* 早食いの癖を直す良い方法は一口毎にナイフとフォークを休ませることだ。 **3** N-COUNT 可算名詞 A drug habit is an addiction to a drug such as heroin or cocaine. 常用癖 □ *She became a prostitute in order to pay for her cocaine habit.* 彼女はコカインの常用癖を維持するために売春婦になった。 **4** PHRASE 句 If you say that someone is **a creature of habit**, you mean that they usually do the same thing at the same time each day, rather than doing new and different things. 習慣に縛られた人 □ *Jesse is a creature of habit and always eats breakfast.* ジェスは習慣で毎日朝食を食べる。 **5** PHRASE 句 If you are **in the habit of** doing something, you do it regularly or often. If you **get into the habit of** doing something, you begin to do it regularly or often. 習慣で □ *They were in the habit of giving two or three dinner parties a month.* 彼らは月に2~3回ディナーパーティを開くのが習慣になっていた。 **6** PHRASE 句 If you **make a habit of** doing something, you do it regularly or often. 習慣にする □ *You can phone me at work as long as you don't make a habit of it.* それを習慣にしないのなら私の勤務先に電話してもよい。

Word Partnership	*habit* は次の語句と使われる:
N.	**force of** habit **1**
	cocaine habit, **drug** habit **3**
V.	**develop/form a** habit, **a** habit **of doing** *something*, **do** *something* **out of** habit **1 6**
	break a habit, **kick a** habit, **give up a** habit, **smoking** habit **2**
ADJ.	**bad/nasty** habit **2**

habi|tat /ˈhæbɪtæt/ (**habitats**) N-VAR 可変性名詞 The **habitat** of an animal or plant is the natural environment in which it normally lives or grows. 生息環境 □ *In its natural habitat, the hibiscus will grow up to 25 ft.* ハイビスカスは自然の生息環境で25フィートまで育つ。

ha|bitu|al /həˈbɪtʃuəl/ **1** ADJ 形容詞 A **habitual** action, state, or way of behaving is one that someone usually does or has, especially one that is considered to be typical or characteristic of them. 悪い姿勢が習慣になると長期的な影響を受ける可能性がある。 □ *If bad posture becomes habitual, you risk long-term effects.* 悪い姿勢が習慣になると長期的な影響を受ける可能性がある。 ● **ha|bitu|al|ly** ADV 副詞 いつも □ *His mother had a patient who habitually flew into rages.* 彼の母にはいつもかっと怒り出す患者がいた。 **2** ADJ 形容詞 [ADJ n] You use **habitual** to describe someone who usually or often does a particular thing. 常習的な □ *Three out of four of them would become habitual criminals if actually sent to jail.* 実際に投獄された場合には、彼ら4人のうち3人は常習的な犯罪者になるだろう。

hack /hæk/ (**hacks, hacking, hacked**) **1** V-T/V-I 他動詞/自動詞 If you **hack** something or **hack** at it, you cut it with strong, rough strokes using a sharp tool such as an ax or a knife. たたき切る □ *An armed gang barged onto the train and began hacking and shooting anyone in sight.* 武装したギャングが列車に乗り込み、手当たり次第にめった切りと発砲を始めた。 □ *Matthew desperately hacked through the leather.* マシューは必死で革をたたき切った。 **2** V-I 自動詞 If someone **hacks into** a computer system, they break into the system, especially in order to get secret information. システムの中に侵入する □ *The saboteurs had demanded money in return for revealing how they hacked into the systems.* ハッカーたちはどのように システムの中に侵入したかを明らかにする代償として金を要求した。 ● **hack|ing** N-UNCOUNT 不可算名詞 ハッキング □ *...the common and often illegal art of computer hacking.* 広く行き渡り、違法なことの多いコンピュータ・ハッキングの技術 **3** N-COUNT 可算名詞 If you refer to a politician as a **hack**, you disapprove of them because they are too

loyal to their party and perhaps do not deserve the position they have. 党に従順すぎる政治家 [DISAPPROVAL 不賛成] □ *Far too many party hacks from the old days still hold influential jobs.* 昔からの党のいいなりになって要職にとどまっている政治家が余りに多い。 **4** N-COUNT 可算名詞 If you refer to a professional writer, such as a journalist, as a **hack**, you disapprove of them because they write for money without worrying very much about the quality of their writing. 売文家 [DISAPPROVAL 不賛成] □ *...tabloid hacks, always eager to find victims in order to sell newspapers.* 販売数を増やすために熱心にカモを探すタブロイド紙の二流記者 **5** N-COUNT 可算名詞 A **hack** is the same as a **taxi**. タクシー [AM 米国英語] □ *I will pay for a hack. There is no need for you to return home on foot.* タクシー代は私が払う。歩いて家に変える必要はない。 **6** PHRASE 句 If you say that someone **can't hack it** or **couldn't hack it**, you mean that they do not or did not have the qualities needed to do a task or cope with a situation. うまくやり遂げられない [INFORMAL くだけた] □ *You have to be strong and confident, and never give the slightest impression that you can't hack it.* 君は頑強で自信に満ちていなければならない。やり遂げられないという印象は少しも与えてはならない。

hack|er /ˈhækər/ (**hackers**) **1** N-COUNT 可算名詞 A computer **hacker** is someone who tries to break into computer systems, especially in order to get secret information. ハッカー □ *...a hacker who steals credit card numbers.* クレジットカード番号を盗むハッカー **2** N-COUNT 可算名詞 A computer **hacker** is someone who uses a computer a lot, especially so much that they have no time to do anything else. コンピュータばかり使う人
→ see **Internet**

had

The auxiliary verb is pronounced /həd/, STRONG hæd/. For the main verb, and for meanings **2** to **5**, the pronunciation is /hæd/.

助動詞は /həd, STRONG hæd/ と発音される。本動詞と **2** から **5** の意味では発音は /hæd/ である。

1 Had is the past tense and past participle of **have**. have の過去・過去分詞形 **2** AUX 助動詞 **Had** is sometimes used instead of "if" to begin a clause which refers to a situation that might have happened but did not. For example, the clause "had he been elected" means the same as "if he had been elected." 仮定法過去 □ *Had he succeeded, he would have acquired a monopoly.* もし彼が成功していれば独占権を獲得していただろう。 **3** PHRASE 句 If you **have been had**, someone has tricked you, for example by selling you something at too high a price. だまされる [INFORMAL くだけた] □ *If your customer thinks he's been had, you have to make him happy.* 顧客がだまされたと感じた場合には、彼を喜ばす必要がある。 **4** PHRASE 句 If you say that someone **has had it**, you mean they are in very serious trouble or have no hope of succeeding. 駄目になる [INFORMAL くだけた] □ *Unless she loses some weight, she's had it.* 彼女は減量しないともう駄目だ。 **5** PHRASE 句 If you say that you **have had it**, you mean that you are very tired of something or very annoyed about it, and do not want to continue doing it or it to continue happening. うんざりする [INFORMAL くだけた] □ *I've had it. Let's call it a day.* もううんざりだ。今日はこの位にしておこう。

had|dock /ˈhædək/ (**haddock**) N-VAR 可変性名詞 **Haddock** is a type of edible saltwater fish found in the North Atlantic. コダラ □ *...fishing boats which normally catch a mix of cod, haddock, and whiting.* 通常はタラ、コダラ、ホワイティングを捕える漁船

hadn't /ˈhædⁿt/ **Hadn't** is the usual spoken form of "had not." had not の縮約形

haemo|philia /ˌhiməˈfɪliə/ → see **hemophilia**

haemo|phili|ac /ˌhiməˈfɪliæk/ → see **hemophiliac**

haem|or|rhage /ˈhɛmərɪdʒ/ → see **hemorrhage**

hag|gle /ˈhægⁿl/ (**haggles, haggling, haggled**) V-RECIP 相互動詞 If you **haggle**, you argue about something before reaching an agreement, especially about the cost of something that you are buying. 値切る交渉をする □ *Ella showed her the best places to go for a good buy, and taught her how to haggle with used furniture dealers.* エラはいい買い物ができる場所と、中古家具業者との値切り交渉のやり方を彼女に教えた。 □ *Of course he'll still haggle over the price.* もちろん彼はまだ値段について交渉を続けるだろう。 ● **hag|gling** N-UNCOUNT

不可算名詞 値切り交渉をすること ❑*After months of haggling, they recovered only three-quarters of what they had lent.* 数か月間に及ぶ交渉の後、彼らは融資の4分の3しか回収できなかった.

hail /heɪl/ (**hails, hailing, hailed**) ① V-T 他動詞 If a person, event, or achievement **is hailed as** important or successful, they are praised publicly. 称賛する [usu passive] ❑*Faulkner has been hailed as the greatest American novelist of his generation.* フォークナーは彼の世代で最も偉大なアメリカの小説家として称賛されてきた. ② N-UNCOUNT 不可算名詞 **Hail** consists of small balls of ice that fall like rain from the sky. あられ ❑*...a sharp short-lived storm with heavy hail.* 大降りのあられを伴うつかの間の嵐 ③ V-I 自動詞 When **it hails**, hail falls like rain from the sky. あられが降る ❑*It started to hail, huge great stones.* 大きな石のようなあられが降り始めた. ④ N-SING 単数名詞 A **hail of** things, usually small objects, is a large number of them that hit you at the same time and with great force. の雨 ❑*The victim was hit by a hail of bullets.* 犠牲者は雨あられと飛ぶ弾丸に当たった. ⑤ V-I 自動詞 Someone who **hails from** a particular place was born there or lives there. の出身だ [FORMAL 形式ばった] ❑*He hails from Memphis.* 彼はメンフィスの出身である. ⑥ V-T 他動詞 If you **hail** a taxi, you wave at it in order to stop it because you want the driver to take you somewhere. 呼び止める ❑*I hurried away to hail a taxi.* 私はタクシーを呼び止めるために急いだ. → see **storm**

hair /heər/ (**hairs**) ① N-VAR 可変性名詞 Your **hair** is the fine threads that grow in a mass on your head. 髪 ❑*I wash my hair every night.* 私は毎晩髪を洗う. ❑*I get some gray hairs but I pull them out.* 私には白髪があるが、抜いている. ② N-VAR 可変性名詞 **Hair** is the short, fine threads that grow on different parts of your body. 体毛 ❑*The majority of men have hair on their chest.* 男性の大半は胸毛がある. ③ N-VAR 可変性名詞 **Hair** is the threads that cover the body of an animal such as a dog, or make up a horse's mane and tail. 毛 ❑*I am allergic to cat hair.* 私は猫の毛アレルギーだ. ④ PHRASE 句 If you **let** your **hair down**, you relax completely and enjoy yourself. くつろぐ ❑*...the world-famous Oktoberfest, a time when everyone in Munich really lets their hair down.* 世界的に有名な十月祭は誰もが気楽に振舞う時 ⑤ PHRASE 句 Something that **makes** your **hair stand on end** shocks or frightens you very much. ぞっとさせる ❑*This was the kind of smile that made your hair stand on end.* これは身の毛がよだつような微笑みだった. ⑥ PHRASE 句 If you say that someone has **not a hair out of place**, you are emphasizing that they are extremely neat and well dressed. 一分の隙(すき)もなく [EMPHASIS 強調] ❑*She had a lot of makeup on and not a hair out of place.* 彼女は厚化粧で完璧な身だしなみだった. ⑦ PHRASE 句 If you say that someone **is splitting hairs**, you mean that they are making unnecessary distinctions between things when the differences between them are so small they are not important. 必要以上に細かい区別立てをする ❑*Don't split hairs. You know what I'm getting at.* 重箱の隅をつつくな. 何のことか分かるだろう. → see **Word Web: hair**

Word Partnership *hairは次の語句と使われる:*

ADJ.	**black/blonde/brown/gray** hair, **curly/straight/wavy** hair ①
V.	**bleach your** hair, **brush/comb your** hair, **color your** hair, **cut your** hair, **do your** hair, **dry your** hair, **fix your** hair, **lose your** hair, **pull someone's** hair, **wash your** hair ①
N.	**lock of** hair ①

hair|cut /heərkʌt/ (**haircuts**) ① N-COUNT 可算名詞 If you get a **haircut**, someone cuts your hair for you. 散髪 ❑*Your hair is all right; it's just that you need a haircut.* あなたの髪は悪くない. 散髪が必要なだけだ. ② N-COUNT 可算名詞 A **haircut** is the style in which your hair has been cut. ヘアスタイル ❑*Who's that guy with the funny haircut?* 変なヘアスタイルをしたあの男は誰だ.

hair|dresser /heərdresər/ (**hairdressers**) ① N-COUNT 可算名詞 A **hairdresser** is a person who cuts, colors, and arranges people's hair. 美容師 ② N-COUNT 可算名詞 A **hairdresser** or a **hairdresser's** is a place where a hairdresser works. 美容院 ❑*I work in this new*

hairdresser's. 私はこの新しい美容院で働いている.

hair|dressing /heərdresɪŋ/ N-UNCOUNT 不可算名詞 **Hairdressing** is the job or activity of cutting, coloring, and arranging people's hair. 調髪業 ❑*...personal services such as hairdressing and dry cleaning.* 調髪業やドライクリーニングなどのパーソナルなサービス

hair|style /heərstaɪl/ (**hairstyles**) N-COUNT 可算名詞 Your **hairstyle** is the style in which your hair has been cut or arranged. 髪型 ❑*I think her new short hairstyle looks simply great.* 彼女の新しい短い髪型はとても素敵だと思う.

hairy /heəri/ (**hairier, hairiest**) ① ADJ 形容詞 Someone or something that is **hairy** is covered with hairs. 毛深い ❑*He was wearing shorts which showed his long, muscular, hairy legs.* 彼はショートパンツをはいており、長い筋肉質の毛深い足が見えた. ② ADJ 形容詞 If you describe a situation as **hairy**, you mean that it is exciting, worrying, and somewhat frightening. 冷や冷やする [INFORMAL くだけた] ❑*His driving was a bit hairy.* 彼の運転にはやや冷や冷やさせられた.

half /hæf/ (**halves** /hævz/) ① FRACTION 端数 **Half of** a number, an amount, or an object is one of two equal parts that together make up the whole number, amount, or object. 半分 ❑*She wore a diamond ring worth half a million dollars.* 彼女は50万ドルの値打ちがあるダイアの指輪をはめていた. ❑*More than half of all U.S. households are heated with natural gas.* アメリカの家庭の半分以上は天然ガスによる暖房を使っている. ● PREDET 前限定詞 **Half** is also a predeterminer. 半分の数量 ❑*We just sat and talked for half an hour or so.* 私達は30分ほど座って話をした. ❑*They had only received half the money promised.* 彼らは約束の金額の半分だけ受け取った. ● ADJ 形容詞 **Half** is also an adjective. 半分の [ADJ n] ❑*...a half measure of fresh lemon juice.* コップ半分の作りたてのレモンジュース ● ADV 副詞 You use **half** to say that something is only partly the case or happens to only a limited extent. 不完全に [ADJ n] ❑*His eyes were half closed.* 彼は半分目を閉じていた. ❑*His refrigerator frequently looked half empty.* 彼の冷蔵庫はしばしば半分空のようだった. ③ N-COUNT 可算名詞 In games such as football, soccer, rugby, and basketball, games are divided into two equal periods of time which are called **halves**. ハーフ ❑*The only goal was scored by Jakobsen early in the second half.* 唯一のゴールは後半の初めにヤコブセンが入れた. ④ ADV 副詞 You use **half** to say that someone has parents of different nationalities. For example, if you are **half** German, one of your parents is German but the other is not. 混血で ❑*She was half Italian and half English.* 彼女はイタリア人とイギリス人の混血だった. ⑤ PHRASE 句 You use **half past** to refer to a time that is thirty minutes after a particular hour. (正時から) 30分過ぎで ❑*"What time were you planning lunch?" — "Half past twelve, if that's convenient."* 「昼食は何時に食べる予定か.」「都合がよければ12時半に.」 ⑥ ADV 副詞 You can use **half** before an adjective describing an extreme quality, as a way of emphasizing and exaggerating something. ほどで [INFORMAL くだけた, EMPHASIS 強調] [ADV adj] ❑*He felt half dead with tiredness.* 彼は疲れて死にそうだった. ● PREDET 前限定詞 **Half** can also be used in this way with a noun referring to a long period of time or a large quantity. ほとんど ❑*I thought about you half the night.* 私はほとんど一晩中あなたのことを考えていた. ⑦ ADV 副詞 You use **not half** to emphasize a negative quality that someone has. 少しも—でない [EMPHASIS 強調] ❑*You're not half the man you think you are.* あなたは自分で思っているほどの男ではない. ⑧ PHRASE 句 If two people **go halves**, they divide the cost of something equally between them. 費用を均等に負担する ❑*She went halves on gas.* 彼女はガソリン代を半額支払った.

half brother (**half brothers**) N-COUNT 可算名詞 Someone's **half brother** is a boy or man who has either the same mother or the same father as they have. 片親の違う兄弟

half-day (**half-days**) also **half day** N-COUNT 可算名詞 A **half-day** is a day when you work only in the morning or in the afternoon, but not all day. 半日勤務 ❑*"If I could have just what I wanted," Sharon mused, "I'd work half days."* 「願いがかなうのなら半日ずつ働くわ.」とシャロンは思慮深く言った.

half|heart|ed /hæfhɑrtɪd/ ADJ 形容詞 If someone does something in a **halfhearted** way, they do it without any real

---

Word Web hair

At any given moment, only about 90 percent of the **hair** on your **scalp** is alive. The other 10 percent is dead and getting ready to **fall out**. Each hair grows about a centimeter a month for two to six years. Then it falls out and the cycle starts all over again. It's normal to lose about 100 hairs a day from your scalp. To keep hair healthy, eat a healthy diet and use a good **shampoo** and conditioner. Gently **brush** and **comb** your hair. Avoid strong **dyes**. Using the "cool" setting on your hairdryer also helps.

effort, interest, or enthusiasm. 気乗りのしない ❑…*a halfhearted apology.* いやいやながらの謝罪 ● **half|heart|ed|ly** ADV 副詞 [ADV with v] 生半可で ❑ *I can't do anything halfheartedly. I have to do everything 100 percent.* 私は生半可で物ができない性質だ. 何でも本腰をいれないと気がすまない.

half-price ◼ ADJ 形容詞 If something is **half-price**, it costs only half what it usually costs. 半額の ❑ *Main courses are half price from 12:30 p.m. to 2 p.m.* 午後12時半から2時まではメーンコースが半額になります. ❑ *A half-price suit still cost $400.* 半額のスーツでも400ドルする. ◼ N-UNCOUNT 不可算名詞 If something is sold **at** or **for half-price**, it is sold for only half of what it usually costs. 半額で ❑ *By yesterday she was selling off stock at half-price.* 昨日までには彼女は在庫品を半額で売り払っていた.

half sister (**half sisters**) N-COUNT 可算名詞 Someone's **half sister** is a girl or woman who has either the same mother or the same father as they have. 片親の違う姉妹

half|time /hǽftaɪm/ N-UNCOUNT 不可算名詞 **Halftime** is the short period of time between the two parts of a sports event such as a football, rugby, or basketball game, when the players take a short rest. ハーフタイム ❑ *The game started in brilliant sunshine but during halftime fog closed in.* その試合は素晴らしい晴天で始まったがハーフタイム中に霧が立ち込めてきた.

half|way /hǽfwéɪ/ ◼ ADV 副詞 **Halfway** means in the middle of a place or between two points, at an equal distance from each of them. 中途まで ❑ *He was halfway up the ladder.* 彼ははしごを上る途中だった. ◼ ADV 副詞 **Halfway** means in the middle of a period of time or of an event. 中間点 [ADV prep/adv] ❑ *By then, it was October and we were more than halfway through our tour.* そのころはもう10月で私たちのツアーは半分以上が終わっていた. ● ADJ 形容詞 **Halfway** is also an adjective. 中間の [ADJ n] ❑ *Cleveland held a 12-point advantage at the halfway point.* クリーブランドは中間点で12点リードしていた. ◼ PHRASE 句 If you meet someone **halfway**, you accept some of the points they are making so that you can come to an agreement with them. 妥協する ❑ *The Democrats are willing to meet the president halfway.* 民主党は妥協して大統領の要求をある程度認める心構えだ. ◼ ADV 副詞 **Halfway** means fairly or reasonably. 多少なりとも [INFORMAL くだけた] [ADV adj] ❑ *You need hard currency to get anything halfway decent.* 多少なりともまともなものを手に入れるためには交換可能通貨が必要だ.

half-yearly ◼ ADJ 形容詞 **Half-yearly** means happening in the middle of a calendar year or a financial year. 半年ごとの [BRIT 英国英語] [ADJ n] [AM **semiannual** 米国英語 **semiannual**] ◼ ADJ 形容詞 A company's **half-yearly** profits are the profits that it makes in six months. 企業の半期利益とは6か月間に生み出す半期の利益のことだ. [BRIT 英国英語] [ADJ n] [AM **semiannual** 米国英語 **semiannual**]

hall /hɔ́l/ (**halls**) ◼ N-COUNT 可算名詞 The **hall** in a house or an apartment is the area just inside the front door, into which some of the other rooms open. 入り口の広間 ❑ *The lights were on in the hall and in the bedroom.* 玄関広間と寝室の明かりがついていた. ◼ N-COUNT 可算名詞 A **hall** in a building is a long passage with doors into rooms on both sides of it. 廊下 [mainly AM 主に米国英語] ❑ *There are 10 rooms along each hall.* 各通路には10室ある. ◼ N-COUNT 可算名詞 A **hall** is a large room or building which is used for public events such as concerts, exhibitions, and meetings. 集会場 ❑ *We picked up our conference materials and filed into the lecture hall.* 私達は会議の資料を集め, 列を作って講堂に繰り込んだ. ◼ → see also **town hall** → see **house**

PREP. **across the** hall, **down the** hall, **in the** hall ◼ ◼
N. **concert** hall, **lecture** hall, **meeting** hall, **pool** hall ◼

hall|mark /hɔ́lmɑrk/ (**hallmarks**) ◼ N-COUNT 可算名詞 The **hallmark** of something or someone is their most typical quality or feature. 特徴 ❑ *It's a technique that has become the hallmark of Amber Films.* それはアンバー・フィルムズ社の特徴となった技術だ. ◼ N-COUNT 可算名詞 A **hallmark** is an official mark put on things made of gold, silver, or platinum that indicates the quality of the metal, where the object was made, and who made it. ホールマーク ❑ *Early pieces of Scottish silver carry the hallmarks of individual silversmiths.* スコットランド製の初期の銀の作品には銀細工師のホールマークがついている.

hal|lo /hæloʊ/ → see **hello**

hall of resi|dence (**halls of residence**) N-COUNT 可算名詞 **Halls of residence** are buildings with rooms or apartments, usually built by universities or colleges, in which students live during the term. 学生寮 [mainly BRIT 主に英国英語; AM **dormitory**, **residence hall** 米国英語 **dormitory**, **residence hall**]

hal|lowed /hǽloʊd/ ◼ ADJ 形容詞 **Hallowed** is used to describe something that is respected and admired, usually because it is old, important, or has a good reputation. 尊い [ADJ n] ❑ *They protested that there was no place for a school of commerce*

in their hallowed halls of learning. 彼らは尊い学習の場には商学部のための場所はないと抗議した. ◼ ADJ 形容詞 **Hallowed** is used to describe something that is considered to be holy. 神聖な [ADJ n] ❑ …*hallowed ground.* 神聖な場所

hal|lu|ci|nate /həlúsɪneɪt/ (**hallucinates, hallucinating, hallucinated**) V-I 自動詞 If you **hallucinate**, you see things that are not really there, either because you are ill or because you have taken a drug. 幻覚を感じる ❑ *Hunger made him hallucinate.* 彼は空腹のあまり幻覚を感じた.

hal|lu|ci|na|tion /həlùsɪnéɪʃən/ (**hallucinations**) N-VAR 可変性名詞 A **hallucination** is the experience of seeing something that is not really there because you are ill or have taken a drug. 幻覚 ❑ *The drug induces hallucinations at high doses.* その薬物は大量に服用すると幻覚が起こる.

hall|way /hɔ́lweɪ/ (**hallways**) ◼ N-COUNT 可算名詞 A **hallway** in a building is a long passage with doors into rooms on both sides of it. 廊下 ❑ *They took the elevator up to the third floor and walked along the quiet hallway.* 彼らはエレベーターで3階に上り, 静かな廊下を歩いた. ◼ N-COUNT 可算名詞 A **hallway** in a house or an apartment is the area just inside the front door, into which some of the other rooms open. 玄関 ❑ …*the coats hanging in the hallway.* 玄関にかかっているコート

halo /héɪloʊ/ (**haloes** or **halos**) N-COUNT 可算名詞 A **halo** is a circle of light that is shown in pictures around the head of a holy figure such as a saint or angel. 後光

halt /hɔ́lt/ (**halts, halting, halted**) ◼ V-T/V-I 他動詞/自動詞 When a person or a vehicle **halts** or when something **halts** them, they stop moving in the direction they were going and stand still. 停止する, 停止させる ❑ *They halted at a short distance from the house.* 彼らは家から近い所で停止した. ◼ V-T/V-I 他動詞/自動詞 When something, such as growth, development, or activity **halts** or when you **halt** it, it stops completely. 停止する ❑ *Striking workers halted production at the auto plant yesterday.* スト中の労働者は昨日, 自動車工場の製造を停止した. ◼ PHRASE 句 If someone **calls a halt to** something such as an activity, they decide not to continue with it or to end it immediately. 中止を決定する ❑ *The Russian government had called a halt to the construction of a new project in the Rostov region.* ロシア政府はロストフ地域の新しいプロジェクトの建設中止を決定した. ◼ PHRASE 句 If someone or something comes **to a halt**, they stop moving. 止まる ❑ *The elevator creaked to a halt at the ground floor.* エレベーターは1階できしむ音をあげて止まった. ◼ PHRASE 句 If something such as growth, development, or activity **comes** or **grinds to a halt** or **is brought to a halt**, it stops completely. 終わる ❑ *Her political career came to a halt in December 1988.* 彼女の政治生活は1988年12月に終わった.

V. **call** a halt **to** *something* ◼
bring *something* **to** a halt, **come/grind/screech to** a halt ◼

halve /hǽv/ (**halves, halving, halved**) ◼ V-T/V-I 他動詞/自動詞 When you **halve** something or when it **halves**, it is reduced to half its previous size or amount. 半分に減らす, 半分に減る ❑ *Dr. Lee believes that men who exercise can halve their risk of colon cancer.* リー博士は運動によって大腸がんのリスクは半減すると考えている. ◼ V-T 他動詞 If you **halve** something, you divide it into two equal parts. 半分にする ❑ *Halve the pineapple and scoop out the inside.* パイナップルを半分にし, 中味を削り取りなさい. ◼ **Halves** is the plural of **half**. *half*の複数形

ham /hǽm/ (**hams**) N-VAR 可変性名詞 **Ham** is meat from the top of the back leg of a pig, specially treated so that it can be kept for a long period of time. ハム ❑ …*ham sandwiches.* ハムのサンドイッチ

ham|burg|er /hǽmbɜrgər/ (**hamburgers**) N-COUNT 可算名詞 A **hamburger** is ground meat which has been shaped into a flat circle. Hamburgers are fried or grilled and then eaten, often on a bun. ハンバーガー

ham|mer /hǽmər/ (**hammers, hammering, hammered**) ◼ N-COUNT 可算名詞 A **hammer** is a tool that consists of a heavy piece of metal at the end of a handle. It is used, for example, to hit nails into a piece of wood or a wall, or to break things into pieces. 金づち ❑ *He used a hammer and chisel to chip away at the wall.* 彼は金づちとのみを使って壁をこつこつ削った. ◼ V-T 他動詞 If you **hammer** an object such as a nail, you hit it with a hammer. 金づちで打つ ❑ *To avoid damaging the tree, hammer a wooden peg into the hole.* 木を傷つけないように穴に木製の釘（くぎ）を金づちで打ち込みなさい. ◼ V-I 自動詞 If you **hammer on** a surface, you hit it several times in order to make a noise, or to emphasize something you are saying when you are angry. 強打する ❑ *We had to hammer and shout*

before they would open up. 我々がどんどんたたき，大声で叫んでからようやく彼らは戸を開けた． ❏ *A crowd of reporters was hammering on the door.* 記者の集団がドアをどんどんたたいていた． ◳ V-T/V-I 他動詞/自動詞 If you **hammer** something such as an idea **into** people or you **hammer at** it, you keep repeating it forcefully so that it will have an effect on people. たたき込む ❏ *He hammered it into me that I had not suddenly become a rotten goalkeeper.* 彼は私が突然ひどいゴールキーパーになったのではないという考えを私の頭にたたきこんだ． ◵ V-T 他動詞 If you say that someone **hammers** another person, you mean that they attack, criticize, or punish the other person severely. 厳しく攻撃する ❏ *Democrats insisted they will continue to hammer Bush on his tax plan.* 民主党は税制計画についてブッシュ大統領を厳しく批判し続けると主張した． ◶ V-T 他動詞 In sports, if you say that one player or team **hammers** another, you mean that the first player or team defeated the second completely and easily. 圧勝する ❏ *He hammered the young left-hander in three straight sets.* 彼は若い左利きの選手に3セット連続で快勝した． ◷ N-COUNT 可算名詞 In track and field, a **hammer** is a heavy weight on a piece of wire, which the athlete throws as far as possible. ハンマー ● N-SING 単数名詞 The **hammer** also refers to the sport of throwing the hammer. ハンマー投げ ❏ *Events like the hammer and the discus are not traditional crowd-pleasers in the West.* ハンマー投げや円盤投げは欧米で昔から人気のある種目ではない． ◸ PHRASE 句 If you say that someone **was going at** something **hammer and tongs**, you mean that they were doing it with great enthusiasm or energy. 猛烈な勢いで ❏ *He loved gardening. He went at it hammer and tongs as soon as he got back from work.* 彼は園芸が趣味だった．仕事から戻るやいなや彼は猛烈に取り掛かった．

→ see **tool**

▸ **hammer out** PHRASAL VERB 句動詞 If people **hammer out** an agreement or treaty, they succeed in producing it after a long or difficult discussion. 苦心して作り上げる ❏ *I think we can hammer out a solution.* 私達は解決策を考案できると思う．

ham|per /hǽmpər/ (**hampers, hampering, hampered**) ◳ V-T 他動詞 If someone or something **hampers** you, they make it difficult for you to do what you are trying to do. 阻止する ❏ *The bad weather hampered rescue operations.* 悪天候は救助活動を妨げた． ◵ N-COUNT 可算名詞 A **hamper** is a basket containing food of various kinds that is given to someone as a present. 食べ物入りの詰めかご ❏ ...*a luxury food hamper.* 高級食品の詰め合わせ ◶ N-COUNT 可算名詞 A **hamper** is a large basket with a lid, used especially for carrying food. 大型バスケット ❏ ...*a picnic hamper.* ピクニック用バスケット ◷ N-COUNT 可算名詞 A **hamper** is a storage container for soiled laundry. 洗濯かご ❏ *He tossed his damp towel into the laundry hamper.* 彼は湿ったタオルを洗濯かごに入れた．

ham|ster /hǽmstər/ (**hamsters**) N-COUNT 可算名詞 A **hamster** is a small furry animal which is similar to a mouse, and which is often kept as a pet. ハムスター

ham|string /hǽmstrɪŋ/ (**hamstrings, hamstringing, hamstrung**) ◳ N-COUNT 可算名詞 A **hamstring** is a length of tissue or tendon behind your knee which joins the muscles of your thigh to the bones of your lower leg. 膝腱（しつけん） ❏ *Webster has not played since suffering a hamstring injury in the opening game.* ウェブスターは初日の試合で膝腱（しつけん）を負傷して以来，試合に出ていない． ◵ V-T 他動詞 If you are **hamstrung** by a person, problem, or difficulty, they make it very difficult for you to take any action. 無力にする [usu v-link ADJ 'by' n] ❏ *Rural schools were hamstrung by their inability to attract and keep experienced staff.* 農村部の学校は経験豊かな職員を引き寄せ，引き留めることができないため，行き詰まった．

hand
❶ NOUN USES AND PHRASES
❷ VERB USES

❶ **hand** /hǽnd/ (**hands**)
⇨ Please look at meaning ◷◷ to see if the expression you are looking for is shown under another headword. ◳ N-COUNT 可算名詞 Your **hands** are the parts of your body at the end of your arms. Each hand has four fingers and a thumb. 手 ❏ *I put my hand into my pocket and pulled out the letter.* 私は手をポケットに入れ，手紙を引っ張り出した． ◵ N-SING 単数名詞 The **hand** of someone or something is their influence in an event or situation. 影響力 ❏ *The hand of the military authorities can be seen in the entire electoral process.* 軍当局の影響力が全選挙過程に見られる． ◶ N-PLURAL 複数名詞 If you say that something is **in** a particular person's **hands**, you mean that they are taking care of it, own it, or are responsible for it. 管理 ❏ *I feel that possibly the majority of these dogs are in the wrong hands.* 私はこれらの犬の大多数が不適切な人に保護されているのではないかと思う． ❏ *We're in safe hands.* 我々は安全に保護されている． ◷ N-SING 単数名詞 If you ask someone for a **hand** with something, you are asking them to help you in what you are doing. 手伝い ❏ *Come and give me a hand in the garden.* 私の庭仕事を手伝って． ◸ N-SING 単数名詞 If someone asks an audience to give someone a **hand**, they

are asking the audience to clap loudly, usually before or after that person performs. 拍手かっさいをする ❏ *Let's give 'em a big hand.* 彼らに盛大な拍手を送りましょう． ◺ N-COUNT 可算名詞 In a game of cards, your **hand** is the set of cards that you are holding in your hand at a particular time or the cards that are dealt to you at the beginning of the game. 持ち札 ❏ *He carefully inspected his hand.* 彼は注意深く持ち札を調べた． ◿ N-COUNT 可算名詞 The **hands** of a clock or watch are the thin pieces of metal or plastic that indicate what time it is. （時計の）針 ❏ *The hands of the clock on the wall moved with a slight click. Half past ten.* 壁にかかった時計の針はカチッとかすかな音をたてて動いた．10時半． ⓼ PHRASE 句 If something is **at hand**, **near at hand**, or **close at hand**, it is very near in place or time. すぐ手の届く所に ❏ *Having the right equipment at hand will be enormously helpful.* 適切な道具が手近にあれば非常に便利だ． ⓽ PHRASE 句 If someone experiences a particular kind of treatment, especially unpleasant treatment, **at the hands of** a person or organization, they receive it from them. 手にかかって ❏ *The civilian population was suffering greatly at the hands of the security forces.* 民間人は治安部隊の手にかかって辛酸をなめていた． ⓾ PHRASE 句 If you do something **by hand**, you do it using your hands rather than a machine. 手で ❏ *Each pleat was stitched in place by hand.* プリーツの一本一本が手で縫い合わされた． ⓫ PHRASE 句 When something **changes hands**, its ownership changes, usually because it is sold to someone else. 持ち主が変る ❏ *The firm has changed hands many times over the years.* その会社は長年にわたり何度も持ち主が変った． ⓬ PHRASE 句 If you **have** your **hands full with** something, you are very busy because of it. 手がふさがっている ❏ *She had her hands full with new arrivals.* 彼女は新しくきた人たちの対応で手が一杯だった． ⓭ PHRASE 句 If someone gives you a **free hand**, they give you the freedom to use your own judgment and to do exactly as you wish. 自由裁量を与える ❏ *He gave Stephanie a free hand in the decoration.* 彼はステファニーが自由に装飾をすることを許した． ⓮ PHRASE 句 If you **get** your **hands on** something or **lay** your **hands on** something, you manage to find it or obtain it, usually after some difficulty. みつけだす [INFORMAL くだけた] ❏ *Patty began reading everything she could get her hands on.* パティは手に入れたものを片っ端から読み始めた． ⓯ PHRASE 句 If two people are **hand in hand**, they are holding each other's nearest hand, usually while they are walking or sitting together. People often do this to show their affection for each other. 手に手を取って ❏ *I saw them making their way, hand in hand, down the path.* 私は彼らが手をつないで小道を歩いていくのを見た． ⓰ PHRASE 句 If two things **go hand in hand**, they are closely connected and cannot be considered separately from each other. 深く結びついて ❏ *For us, research and teaching go hand in hand.* 我々にとって研究と指導は深く結びついている． ⓱ PHRASE 句 If you **have a hand in** something such as an event or activity, you are involved in it. に関与する ❏ *He thanked all who had a hand in his release.* 彼は自分の釈放に関与した人々全員にお礼を述べた． ⓲ PHRASE 句 If two people are **holding hands**, they are holding each other's nearest hand, usually while they are walking or sitting together. People often do this to show their affection for each other. 手を握る ❏ *She approached a young couple holding hands on a bench.* 彼女はベンチに座って手を握り合っている若いカップルに近づいた． ⓳ PHRASE 句 The job or problem **in hand** is the job or problem that you are dealing with at the moment. 関与している ❏ *The business in hand was approaching some kind of climax.* かかわっている事業はある種の最高潮に近づいていた． ⓴ PHRASE 句 If a situation is **in hand**, it is under control. 制御されて ❏ *The Olympic organizers say that matters are well in hand.* オリンピックの主催者は事態はうまく管理されていると言っている． ㉑ PHRASE 句 If you **lend** someone a **hand**, you help them. 手を貸す ❏ *I'd be glad to lend a hand.* 喜んで手伝うよ． ㉒ PHRASE 句 If someone **lives hand to mouth** or **lives from hand to mouth**, they have hardly enough food or money to live on. その日暮らしをする ❏ *I have a wife and two children and we live from hand to mouth on what I earn.* 私には妻と子供が2人いるが，私たちは私の給料でその日暮らしをしている． ㉓ → see also **hand-to-mouth** ㉔ PHRASE 句 If you tell someone to **keep** their **hands off** something or to **take** their **hands off** it, you are telling them in a slightly aggressive way not to touch it or interfere with it. 手を出さない ❏ *Keep your hands off my milk.* 私の牛乳にさわらないで． ㉕ PHRASE 句 If you do not know something **off hand**, you do not know it without having to ask someone else or look it up in a book. 深く考えずに [SPOKEN 口語] ❏ *I can't think of any off hand.* すぐには思いつかない． ㉖ PHRASE 句 If you have a problem or responsibility **on** your **hands**, you have to deal with it. If it is **off** your **hands**, you no longer have to deal with it. 自分の責任となって，自分の役目が済んで ❏ *They now have yet another drug problem on their hands.* 彼らは今度は別の麻薬問題の責任を負っている． ㉗ PHRASE 句 If someone or something is **on hand**, they are near and able to be used if they are needed. 身近に ❏ *There are experts on hand to give you all the help and advice you need.* 必要な支援と忠告を与えてくれる専門家が身近にいる． ㉘ PHRASE 句 You use **on the one hand** to introduce the first of two contrasting points, facts, or ways of looking at something. It is always followed later by "on the other hand" or "on the other." 一方では ❏ *On the one hand, if the*

h

body doesn't have enough cholesterol, we would not be able to survive. On the other hand, if the body has too much cholesterol, the excess begins to line the arteries. 一方で体内のコレステロールが不十分だと生きていくことができないが、他方では体内のコレステロールが多すぎると過剰分が動脈の内側を覆い始める。 ㉙ PHRASE 句 You use **on the other hand** to introduce the second of two contrasting points, facts, or ways of looking at something. 他方 ❑ *The movie lost money; reviews, on the other hand, were by and large favorable.* その映画は赤字だったが、他方では批評が概して好意的だった。

> Do not confuse **on the other hand** with **on the contrary**. **On the other hand** is used to state a different, often contrasting aspect of the situation you are considering. **On the contrary** is used to contradict someone, to say that they are wrong. ❑ *He had no wish to hurt her. On the contrary, he thought of her with warmth and affection.*

㉚ PHRASE 句 If a person or a situation gets **out of hand**, you are no longer able to control them. 抑えきれないで ❑ *His drinking got out of hand.* 彼の飲酒は手に負えなくなった。 ㉛ PHRASE 句 If you dismiss or reject something **out of hand**, you do so immediately and do not consider believing or accepting it. すぐに ❑ *I initially dismissed the idea out of hand.* 私は最初その意見を考えもせずに退けた。 ㉜ PHRASE 句 If you **take** something or someone **in hand**, you take control or responsibility over them, especially in order to improve them. の世話を引き受ける ❑ *She took the twins in hand, encouraging them to turn their thoughts to the future.* 彼女は双子の世話を引き受け、彼らが将来のことを考えるよう奨励した。 ㉝ PHRASE 句 If you say that your **hands are tied**, you mean that something is preventing you from acting in the way that you want to. 自分の好きに行動できない ❑ *Politicians are always saying that they want to help us but their hands are tied.* 我々を援助したいが自分の思う通りには行動できないというのが政治家の口癖だ。 ㉞ PHRASE 句 If you **try** your **hand at** an activity, you attempt to do it, usually for the first time. 一度やってみる ❑ *He tried his hand at fishing, but he wasn't really very good at it.* 彼は魚釣りを一度やってみたが大した成果が得られなかった。 ㉟ PHRASE 句 If you **turn** your **hand to** something such as a practical activity, you learn about it and do it for the first time. 手がける ❑ *...a person who can turn his hand to anything.* 何でも手がけられる人 ㊱ PHRASE 句 If you **wash** your **hands of** someone or something, you refuse to be involved with them any more or to take responsibility for them. 関係を絶つ ❑ *He seems to have washed his hands of the job.* 彼はその仕事から手を引いたようだ。 ㊲ PHRASE 句 If you **win hands down**, you win very easily. 楽に勝つ ❑ *We have been beaten in some games which we should have won hands down.* 我々は楽勝すべきだった試合に負けた。 ㊳ **with** one's **bare hands** → see **bare** ㊴ to **shake** someone's **hand** → see **shake** ㊵ to **shake hands** → see **shake**
→ see Picture Dictionary: hand
→ see **body**

❷ **hand** /hǽnd/ (hands, handing, handed) V-T 他動詞 If you **hand** something **to** someone, you pass it to them. 手渡す ❑ *He*

handed me a little rectangle of white paper. 彼は私に小さな長方形の白い紙を手渡した。

▸ **hand back** PHRASAL VERB 句動詞 If you **hand back** something that you have borrowed or taken from someone, you return it to them. 返す ❑ *He handed the book back.* 彼はその本を返した。

▸ **hand down** PHRASAL VERB 句動詞 If you **hand down** something such as knowledge, a possession, or a skill, you give or leave it to people who belong to a younger generation. 伝える ❑ *The idea of handing down his knowledge from generation to generation is important to McLean.* 後世に彼の知識を伝えるという概念はマクリーンにとって重要だ。

▸ **hand in** ➊ PHRASAL VERB 句動詞 If you **hand in** something such as homework or something that you have found, you give it to a teacher, police officer, or other person in authority. 提出する ❑ *I'm supposed to have handed in a first draft of my dissertation.* 私は卒論の最初の草稿を提出していなければいけないはずだ。 ➋ PHRASAL VERB 句動詞 If you **hand in** your notice or resignation, you tell your employer, in speech or in writing, that you no longer wish to work there. 提出する ❑ *I handed my notice in on Saturday.* 私は土曜日に辞表を提出した。

▸ **hand on** PHRASAL VERB 句動詞 If you **hand** something **on**, you give it or transfer it to another person, often someone who replaces you. 残す ❑ *Natural resources should be handed on to the next generation intact.* 天然資源はそっくりそのまま次の世代に残されるべきだ。

▸ **hand out** ➊ PHRASAL VERB 句動詞 If you **hand** things **out** to people, you give one or more to each person in a group. 配る ❑ *One of my jobs was to hand out the prizes.* 私の仕事の1つは賞品を配ることだった。 ➋ PHRASAL VERB 句動詞 When people in authority **hand out** something such as advice or permission to do something, they give it. 与える ❑ *I listened to a lot of people handing out a lot of advice.* 私は多くの人が多くのアドバイスを与えるのを聞いた。 ➌ → see also **handout**

▸ **hand over** ➊ PHRASAL VERB 句動詞 If you **hand** something **over** to someone, you give them the responsibility for dealing with a particular situation or problem. 引き渡す ❑ *I wouldn't dare hand this project over to anyone else.* 私にはこのプロジェクトをあえて他人に引き渡すつもりはない。 ➋ PHRASAL VERB 句動詞 If you **hand over** to someone or **hand** something **over** to them, you give them the responsibility for dealing with a particular situation or problem. 責任などを委譲する ❑ *The present leaders have to decide whether to hand over to a younger generation.* 現在の指導者達は若い世代に引き継がせるかどうかを決める必要がある。

hand|bag /hǽndbæg/ (handbags) N-COUNT 可算名詞 A **handbag** is a small bag which a woman uses to carry things such as her money and keys when she goes out. ハンドバッグ

hand|book /hǽndbʊk/ (handbooks) N-COUNT 可算名詞 A **handbook** is a book that gives you advice and instructions about a particular subject, tool, or machine. 案内書 ❑ *...a handbook on pool maintenance.* プール管理の手引き

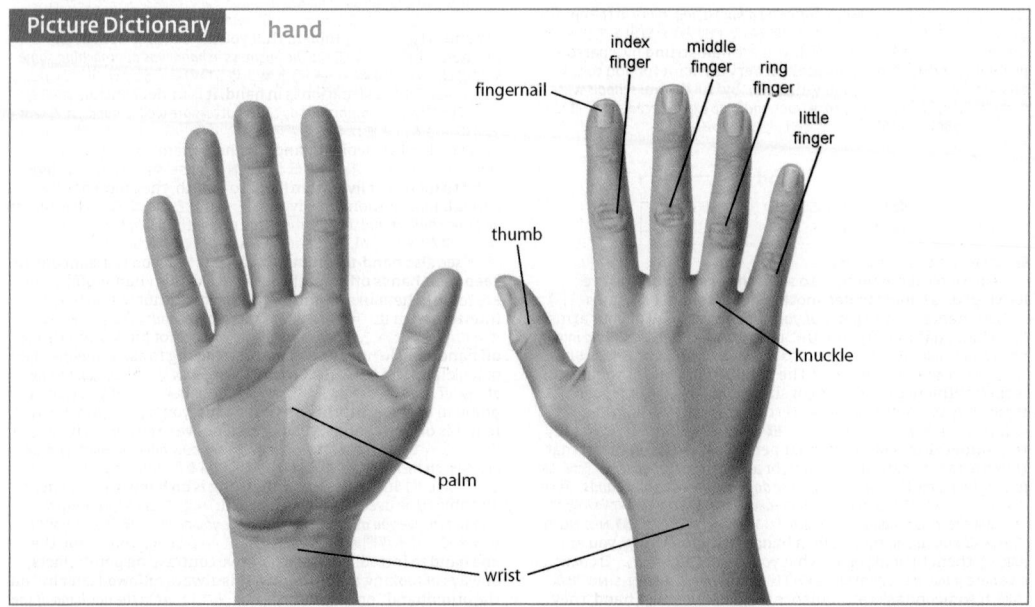

Picture Dictionary   hand

index finger
middle finger
ring finger
fingernail
little finger
thumb
knuckle
palm
wrist

hand|cuff /hǽndkʌf/ (handcuffs, handcuffing, handcuffed) ▪ N-PLURAL 複数名詞 **Handcuffs** are two metal rings which are joined together and can be locked around someone's wrists, usually by the police during an arrest. 手錠 [also 'a pair of' N] ▫ *He was led away to jail in handcuffs.* 彼は手錠をかけられ、刑務所に連行された. ▪ V-T 他動詞 If you **handcuff** someone, you put handcuffs around their wrists. 手錠をかける ▫ *They tried to handcuff him but, despite his injuries, he fought his way free.* 彼らは彼に手錠をかけようとしたが、けがにもかかわらず彼はもがいて振りほどいた.

hand|ful /hǽndfʊl/ (handfuls) ▪ N-SING 単数名詞 **A handful of** people or things is a small number of them. 少数の ▫ *He surveyed the handful of customers at the bar.* 彼はカウンターに座っている少数の客を見回した. ▪ N-COUNT 可算名詞 **A handful of** something is the amount of it that you can hold in your hand. 一握りの ▫ *She scooped up a handful of sand and let it trickle through her fingers.* 彼女は一握りの砂をすくい上げ、さらさらと指の間から落とした. ▪ N-SING 単数名詞 If you say that someone, especially a child, is **a handful**, you mean that they are difficult to control. 手に余ること [INFORMAL くだけた] ▫ *Zara can be a handful sometimes.* ザーラは手に余ることがある.

hand|held /hǽndhɛld/ (handhelds) ADJ 形容詞 A **handheld** device such as a camera or a computer is small and light enough to be used while you are holding it. 手に持てるほど小型の ▫ *a handheld electric mixer.* 手持ち型電気ミキサー ● N-COUNT 可算名詞 **Handheld** is also a noun. 小型機器 ▫ *Users will be able to use their handhelds to look up timetables on the net, search for a local hotel, and check their bank accounts.* ユーザーは携帯機器を使ってインターネットで時刻表のチェック、地元のホテル検索、銀行口座の照会ができるようになる.

handi|cap /hǽndikæp/ (handicaps, handicapping, handicapped) ▪ N-COUNT 可算名詞 A **handicap** is a physical or mental disability. （身体的・精神的な） 障害 ▫ *He lost his leg when he was ten, but learned to overcome his handicap.* 彼は10歳の時に足を失ったが、身体障害を克服できるようになった. ▪ N-COUNT 可算名詞 A **handicap** is an event or situation that places you at a disadvantage and makes it harder for you to do something. 不利な条件 ▫ *Being a foreigner was not a handicap.* 外国人であることは不利な条件ではなかった. ▪ V-T 他動詞 If an event or a situation **handicaps** someone or something, it places them at a disadvantage. 不利な立場に立たせる ▫ *Greater levels of stress may seriously handicap some students.* ストレスレベルがあがると一部の学生はかなり不利になるかもしれない. ▪ N-COUNT 可算名詞 In golf, a **handicap** is an advantage given to someone who is not a good player, in order to make the players more equal. As you improve, your handicap gets lower. ゴルフのハンディキャップ ▫ *I see your handicap is down from 16 to 12.* 君のハンディは16から12に下がったんだね. ▪ N-COUNT 可算名詞 In horse racing, a **handicap** is a race in which some competitors are given a disadvantage of extra weight in an attempt to give everyone an equal chance of winning. ハンディキャップ付きの試合 ▫ *...the Melbourne Cup, a two-mile handicap.* 2マイルのハンディキャップ付き試合、メルボルン杯.

handi|capped /hǽndikæpt/ ADJ 形容詞 Someone who is **handicapped** has a physical or mental disability that prevents them from living a totally normal life. 障害のある ▫ *I'm going to work two days a week teaching handicapped kids to fish.* 私は週に2日、障害のある子供たちに魚釣りを教える予定だ. ● N-PLURAL 複数名詞 You can refer to people who are handicapped as **the handicapped**. 障害者 ▫ *...measures to prevent discrimination against the handicapped.* 障害者差別を防止する措置

hand|ker|chief /hǽŋkərtʃɪf/ (handkerchiefs) N-COUNT 可算名詞 A **handkerchief** is a small square piece of fabric which you use for blowing your nose. ハンカチ

han|dle /hǽndəl/ (handles, handling, handled) ▪ N-COUNT 可算名詞 A **handle** is a small round object or a lever that is attached to a door and is used for opening and closing it. 取っ手 ▫ *I turned the handle and found the door was open.* 私は取っ手を回し、ドアが空いていることに気づいた. ▪ N-COUNT 可算名詞 A **handle** is the part of an object such as a tool, bag, or cup that you hold in order to be able to pick up and use the object. 取っ手 ▫ *...a broom handle.* ほうきの取っ手 ▪ V-T 他動詞 If you say that someone can **handle** a problem or situation, you mean that they have the ability to deal with it successfully. うまく処理する ▫ *To tell the truth, I don't know if I can handle the job.* 実を言うと、その仕事をうまく処理できるかどうか分からない. ▪ V-T 他動詞 If you talk about the way that someone **handles** a problem or situation, you mention whether or not they are successful in achieving the result they want. 扱う ▫ *I think I would handle a meeting with Mr. Siegel very badly.* 私はシーゲル氏との会合に非常におそまつに応対するのではないかと思う. ● **han|dling** N-UNCOUNT 不可算名詞 扱い方 ▪ V-T 他動詞 If you **handle** a particular area of work, you have responsibility for it. 担当する ▫ *She handled travel arrangements for the press corps during the presidential campaign.* 彼女は大統領選のキャンペーン中に記者団の旅行手配を担当した. ▪ V-T 他動詞 When you **handle** something,

you hold it or move it with your hands. 手で扱う ▫ *Wear rubber gloves when handling cat litter.* 猫の砂を処理する時にはゴムの手袋をはめなさい. ▪ PHRASE 句 If you **fly off the handle**, you suddenly and completely lose your temper. かっとなる [INFORMAL くだけた] ▫ *He flew off the handle at the slightest thing.* 彼はちょっとしたことでかっとなった.
→ see **silverware**

Word Partnership	*handle* は次の語句と使われる:
N.	**handle** a **job/problem/situation**, handle **pressure/responsibility** ▪ ▪ **ability to** handle *something* ▪ – ▪
ADJ.	**difficult/easy/hard to** handle ▪ ▪

han|dler /hǽndlər/ (handlers) ▪ N-COUNT 可算名詞 A **handler** is someone whose job is to be in charge of and control an animal. 調教師 ▫ *Fifty officers, including dog handlers, are searching for her.* 警察犬係を含む50名の警官が彼女を探している. ▪ N-COUNT 可算名詞 A **handler** is someone whose job is to deal with a particular type of object. 取り扱う人 ▫ *...baggage handlers at the airport.* 空港の手荷物取扱い係

hand lug|gage N-UNCOUNT 不可算名詞 When you travel by air, your **hand luggage** is the luggage you have with you in the plane, rather than the luggage that is carried in the hold. 手荷物 ▫ *a ban on all knives in hand luggage.* 手荷物内のナイフ全面禁止

hand|made /hǽndméɪd/ also **hand-made** ADJ 形容詞 **Handmade** objects have been made by someone using their hands or using tools rather than by machines. 手作りの ▫ *Because they're handmade, each one varies slightly.* それらは手製のため一つ一つ微妙に違う.

hand|out /hǽndaʊt/ (handouts) ▪ N-COUNT 可算名詞 A **handout** is a gift of money, clothing, or food, which is given free to poor people. 施し物 ▫ *Each family is being given a cash handout of six thousand rupees.* 各家族には6000ルピーの現金の施しを受けている. ▪ N-COUNT 可算名詞 If you call money that is given to someone a **handout**, you disapprove of it because you believe that the person who receives it has done nothing to earn or deserve it. 援助金 [DISAPPROVAL 不賛成] ▫ *...the tendency of politicians to use money on vote-buying handouts rather than on investment in the future.* 政治家が将来のための投資ではなく票を獲得するための財政援助に金を使う傾向 ▪ N-COUNT 可算名詞 A **handout** is a document which contains news or information about something and which is given, for example, to journalists or members of the public. 印刷物 ▫ *Official handouts describe the Emperor as "particularly noted as a scholar."* 公式な印刷物には「学者として注目される」皇帝と書いてある. ▪ N-COUNT 可算名詞 A **handout** is a paper given out to students by a teacher, that contains a summary of the information or topics that will be dealt with in a lesson. 配布物 ▫ *Many teachers are opting for group discussions instead of handouts.* 多くの教師はプリントを配布するかわりにグループ討論を選択している.

hand|set /hǽndset/ (handsets) ▪ N-COUNT 可算名詞 The **handset** of a telephone is the part that you hold next to your face in order to speak and listen. 受話器 ▫ *...the cord that connects the telephone handset to the phone itself.* 受話器を電話本体に接続するコード ▪ N-COUNT 可算名詞 You can refer to a device such as the remote control of a television or stereo as a **handset**. ハンドセット ▫ *Most VCRs can be programmed using a remote control handset.* 大半のVCRはリモートコントロールのハンドセットを使ってセットできる.

hands-free ADJ 形容詞 A **hands-free** telephone or other device can be used without being held in your hand. 手を用いなくてもよい [ADJ n] ▫ *...legislation to ban both handheld and hands-free cellphones in moving vehicles.* 走行中の自動車内で端末を使っても使わせても携帯電話の使用を禁じる規制

hand|shake /hǽndʃeɪk/ (handshakes) ▪ N-COUNT 可算名詞 If you give someone a **handshake**, you take their right hand with your own right hand and hold it firmly or move it up and down, as a sign of greeting or to show that you have agreed about something such as a business deal. 握手 ▫ *He has a strong handshake.* 彼は力強い握手をする. ▪ → see also **golden handshake**

hand|some /hǽnsəm/ ▪ ADJ 形容詞 A **handsome** man has an attractive face with regular features. ハンサムな ▫ *a tall, dark, handsome sheep farmer.* 背が高く浅黒いハンサムな牧羊業者

When you are describing someone's appearance, you generally use **pretty** and **beautiful** to describe women, girls, and babies. **Beautiful** is a much stronger word than **pretty**. The equivalent word for a man is **handsome**. **Good-looking** and **attractive** can be used to describe people of either sex. **Pretty** can also be used to modify adjectives and adverbs but is less strong than **very**. In this sense, **pretty** is informal.

▪ ADJ 形容詞 A **handsome** sum of money is a large or generous amount. 相当の [FORMAL 形式ばった] [ADJ n] ▫ *They will make a handsome profit on the property.* 彼らは不動産から相当な利益を得るだろう.

hands-on ADJ 形容詞 **Hands-on** experience or work involves actually doing a particular thing, rather than just talking about it or getting someone else to do it. 実際に参加する ❑ *This hands-on management approach often stretches his workday from 6 a.m. to 11 p.m.* 経営陣の直接参加型アプローチにより彼は朝6時から夜11時までの長時間勤務になることがたびたびある.

hand-to-mouth also **hand to mouth** ADJ 形容詞 A **hand-to-mouth** existence is a way of life in which you have hardly enough food or money to live on. その日暮らしの ❑ *Unloved and uncared-for, they live a meaningless hand to mouth existence.* 愛されることもなく, ほったらかしで彼らは意味のないその日暮らしの生活をしている. ● ADV 副詞 **Hand to mouth** is also an adverb. その日暮らしで [ADV after v] ❑ *I just can't live hand to mouth, it's too frightening.* 私にはその日暮らしの生活はできない. 恐ろしすぎる.

hand|writing /hǽndraɪtɪŋ/ N-UNCOUNT 不可算名詞 Your **handwriting** is your style of writing with a pen or pencil. 手書き ❑ *The address was in Anna's handwriting.* 住所はアンナの手書きだった.

hand|writ|ten /hǽndrɪtᵊn/ ADJ 形容詞 A piece of writing that is **handwritten** is one that someone has written using a pen or pencil rather than by typing it. 手書きの ❑ *...a handwritten note.* 手書きのメモ.

handy /hǽndi/ (**handier, handiest**) ◼ ADJ 形容詞 Something that is **handy** is useful. 便利な ❑ *The book gives handy hints on looking after indoor plants.* その本からは室内植物の世話についての便利な助言が得られる. ◻ PHRASE 句 If something **comes in handy**, it is useful in a particular situation. 役立つ ❑ *The $20 check came in very handy.* 20ドルの小切手は非常に役立った. ◻ ADJ 形容詞 A thing or place that is **handy** is nearby and therefore easy to get or reach. 身近にある ❑ *It would be good to have a pencil and paper handy.* 紙と鉛筆を手近に用意しておくと良いだろう.

hang /hǽŋ/ (**hangs, hanging, hung** or **hanged**)

> The form **hanged** is used as the past tense and past participle for meaning ◻.
>
> **hanged** 形は◻を意味する過去時制と過去分詞として使われる.

◼ V-T/V-I 他動詞/自動詞 If something **hangs** in a high place or position, or if you **hang** it there, it is attached there so it does not touch the ground. 掛ける, 掛かる ❑ *Notices painted on sheets hang at every entrance.* 板にペンキ書きの通知がどの入り口にも掛かっている. ❑ *...small hanging lanterns.* 釣り下がった小さなちょうちん. ● PHRASAL VERB 句動詞 **Hang up** means the same as **hang**. 掛かる ❑ *I found his jacket, which was hanging up in the hallway.* 私は玄関に掛かっている彼のジャケットを見つけた. ◻ V-I 自動詞 If a piece of clothing or fabric **hangs** in a particular way or position, that is how it is worn or arranged. すらりと垂れる ❑ *...a ragged fur coat that hung down to her calves.* 彼女のふくらはぎまであるぼろぼろの毛皮のコート ◻ V-I 自動詞 If something **hangs** loose or **hangs** open, it is partly fixed in position, but is not firmly held, supported, or controlled, often in a way that it moves freely. 垂れ下がる ❑ *...her long golden hair which hung loose about her shoulders.* 肩のあたりに垂れ下がる彼女の長い金髪 ◻ V-T 他動詞 If something such as a wall **is hung with** pictures or other objects, they are attached to it. 壁に掛ける [usu passive] ❑ *The walls were hung with huge modern paintings.* 壁には巨大な近代絵画が掛かっていた. ◻ V-T/V-I 他動詞/自動詞 If someone **is hanged** or if they **hang**, they are killed, usually as a punishment, by having a rope tied around their neck and the support taken away from under their feet. 絞首刑にする ❑ *The five were expected to be hanged at 7 a.m. on Tuesday.* 5人は火曜日の午前7時に絞首刑にされる予定だった. ❑ *He hanged himself two hours after arriving at a mental hospital.* 彼は精神病院に着いてから2時間後に首をつって死んだ. ◻ V-I 自動詞 If something such as someone's breath or smoke **hangs** in the air, it remains there without appearing to move or change position. 漂う ❑ *His breath was hanging in the air before him.* 彼の息は空中に漂っていた. ◻ V-I 自動詞 If a possibility **hangs over** you, it worries you and makes your life unpleasant or difficult because you think it might happen. のしかかっている ❑ *A constant threat of unemployment hangs over thousands of university researchers.* 失業の脅威が常に何千人もの大学の研究者にのしかかっている. ◻ → see also **hung** ◻ PHRASE 句 If you **get the hang of** something such as a skill or activity, you begin to understand or realize how to do it. 取扱いのこつが分かる [INFORMAL くだけた] ❑ *It's a bit tricky at first till you get the hang of it.* 扱い方が分かるまで最初はちょっとやりにくい. ◻ PHRASE 句 If you tell someone to **hang in there** or to **hang on in there**, you are encouraging them to keep trying to do something and not to give up even though it might be difficult. 踏みとどまる [INFORMAL くだけた] ❑ *Hang in there and you never know what is achievable.* がんばれば何でも達成できるかもしれない.

▸ **hang back** ◼ PHRASAL VERB 句動詞 If you **hang back**, you move or stay slightly behind a person or group, usually because you are shy or nervous about something. しりごみをする ❑ *I saw him step forward momentarily but then hang back, nervously massaging his hands.* 私は彼が一瞬前に出て, それから両手を神経質そうにすり合わせ

ながらしりごみしたのを見た. ◻ PHRASAL VERB 句動詞 If a person or organization **hangs back**, they do not do something immediately. 渋る ❑ *They will then hang back on closing the deal.* 彼らはそれから取引をまとめるのを渋るだろう.

▸ **hang on** ◼ PHRASAL VERB 句動詞 If you ask someone to **hang on**, you ask them to wait or stop what they are doing or saying for a moment. 待つ [INFORMAL くだけた] ❑ *Can you hang on for a minute?* ちょっと待ってくれるか. ◻ PHRASAL VERB 句動詞 If you **hang on**, you manage to survive, achieve success, or avoid failure in spite of great difficulties or opposition. 努力を続ける ❑ *He hung on to finish second.* 彼は頑張って2位に食い込んだ. ◻ PHRASAL VERB 句動詞 If you **hang on to** or **hang onto** something that gives you an advantage, you succeed in keeping it for yourself, and prevent it from being taken away or given to someone else. すがりつく ❑ *The driver was unable to hang on to his lead.* ドライバーはリードを維持することができなかった. ◻ PHRASAL VERB 句動詞 If you **hang on to** or **hang onto** something, you hold it very tightly, for example to stop it from falling or to support yourself. しがみつく ❑ *She was conscious of a second man hanging on to the rail.* 彼女は2人目の男が手すりにしがみついているのに気づいていた. ❑ *...a flight attendant who helped save the life of a pilot by hanging onto his legs.* パイロットの足にしがみついて彼の命を救ったスチュワーデス ◻ PHRASAL VERB 句動詞 If you **hang on to** or **hang onto** something, you keep it for a longer time than you would normally expect. 手放さない [INFORMAL くだけた] ❑ *You could, alternatively, hang onto it in the hope that it will be worth millions in 10 years time.* またはあなたは10年後には数百万ポンドもの価値になることを期待してそれを保持することもできる. ◻ PHRASAL VERB 句動詞 If one thing **hangs on** another, it depends on it in order to be successful. 次第である ❑ *Much hangs on the success of the collaboration between the Group of Seven governments and Brazil.* 多くはG7諸国とブラジル間の協力の成否にかかっている.

▸ **hang out** ◼ PHRASAL VERB 句動詞 If you **hang out** clothes that you have washed, you hang them on a clothes line to dry. 外に干す ❑ *I was worried I wouldn't be able to hang my laundry out.* 私は洗濯物を外に干せないのではないかと心配だった. ◻ PHRASAL VERB 句動詞 If you **hang out** in a particular place or area, you go and stay there for no particular reason, or spend a lot of time there. うろつく [INFORMAL くだけた] ❑ *I often used to hang out in supermarkets.* 私はよくスーパーをうろついた.

▸ **hang up** ◼ → see **hang 1** ◻ PHRASAL VERB 句動詞 If you **hang up** or you **hang up** the phone, you end a phone call. If you **hang up on** someone you are speaking to on the phone, you end the phone call suddenly and unexpectedly, usually because you are angry or upset with the person you are speaking to. 電話を切る ❑ *Mom hung up the phone.* 母は電話を切った. ❑ *Don't hang up!* 電話を切らないで.

Word Partnership	**hang** は次の語句と使われる:
N.	hang *up* clothes ◼
ADV.	hang *something* upside down ◼

hang|ar /hǽŋər/ (**hangars**) N-COUNT 可算名詞 A **hangar** is a large building in which aircraft are kept. ＜格納庫（航空機の）

hang|er /hǽŋər/ (**hangers**) N-COUNT 可算名詞 A **hanger** is the same as a **coat hanger**. 洋服掛け

hang|over /hǽŋoʊvər/ (**hangovers**) ◼ N-COUNT 可算名詞 If someone wakes up with a **hangover**, they feel sick and have a headache because they drank a lot of alcohol the night before. 二日酔い ❑ *It was a great night and I had a massive hangover.* 楽しい夜で私はひどい二日酔いになった. ◻ N-COUNT 可算名詞 Something that is a **hangover from** the past is an idea or way of behaving which people used to have in the past but which people no longer generally have. 遺物 ❑ *As a hangover from rationing, they mixed butter and margarine.* 配給を受けていた頃の名残で彼らはバターとマーガリンを混ぜ合わせた.

hap|haz|ard /hǽphæzərd/ ADJ 形容詞 If you describe something as **haphazard**, you are critical of it because it is not at all organized or is not arranged according to a plan. 計画性のない [DISAPPROVAL 不賛成] ❑ *The investigation does seem haphazard.* その調査は全く計画性がないように思われる. ● **hap|haz|ard|ly** ADV 副詞 無計画に ❑ *She looked at the books jammed haphazardly in the shelves.* 彼女は本が本棚にめちゃめちゃに詰め込まれているのを見た.

hap|less /hǽplɪs/ ADJ 形容詞 A **hapless** person is unlucky. 不運な [FORMAL 形式ばった] [ADJ n] ❑ *...his hapless victim.* 彼の犠牲になった不運な人

hap|pen /hǽpən/ (**happens, happening, happened**) ◼ V-I 自動詞 Something that **happens** occurs or is done without being planned. 起こる ❑ *We cannot say for sure what will happen.* 何が起こるかは分からない. ◻ V-I 自動詞 If something **happens**, it occurs as a result of a situation or course of action. 起こる ❑ *She wondered what would happen if her parents found her.* 彼女は両親に見つかったらどうなるだろうと思った. ◻ V-I 自動詞 When something, especially something unpleasant, **happens to** you, it takes place and affects you. 起こる ❑ *If we had been spotted at that point, I don't*

know what would have happened to us. あの時点で発見されていたら私達はどうなっていたか分からない。 **4** V-T 他動詞 If you **happen to** do something, you do it by chance. 偶然にする **If it happens that** something is the case, it occurs by chance. 偶然にする **We happened to discover we had a friend in common.** 私達は共通の友人がいたことに偶然気づいた。 **5** PHRASE 句 You use **as it happens** in order to introduce a statement, especially one that is rather surprising. たまたま □He called Amy to see if she knew where his son was. As it happened, Amy did know. 彼は彼の息子の居場所を聞くためにエイミーに電話した。折りよくエイミーは知っていた。

hap|pen|ing /hǽpənɪŋ/ (**happenings**) N-COUNT 可算名詞 **Happenings** are things that happen, often in a way that is unexpected or hard to explain. 出来事 □The Budapest office plans to hire freelance reporters to cover the latest happenings. ブダペスト事務所は最近の出来事を取材するフリーランス記者を雇う予定だ.

hap|pi|ly /hǽpɪli/ **1** ADV 副詞 You can add **happily** to a statement to indicate that you are glad that something happened. 幸いにも [ADV with cl] □Happily, his neck injuries were not serious. 運良く彼の首のけがは大したことなかった。 **2** → see also **happy**

hap|py /hǽpi/ (**happier**, **happiest**) **1** ADJ 形容詞 Someone who is **happy** has feelings of pleasure, usually because something nice has happened or because they feel satisfied with their life. 幸福な □Marina was a confident, happy child. マリーナは自信に満ちた幸福な子供だった。 ●**hap|pi|ly** ADV 副詞 幸せそうに □Albert leaned back happily and lit a cigarette. アルバートは満足そうに上体を後ろに反らし、タバコに火をつけた。 ●**hap|pi|ness** N-UNCOUNT 不可算名詞 幸福 □I think mostly she was looking for happiness. 彼女はおおかた幸せを探していたのだと思う。 **2** ADJ 形容詞 A **happy** time, place, or relationship is full of happy feelings and pleasant experiences, or has an atmosphere in which people feel happy. 幸せな □Except for her illnesses, she had a particularly happy childhood. 病気になったこと以外では彼女はとても幸せな子供時代を過ごした。 □It had always been a happy place. それはいつも楽しい場所だった。 **3** ADJ 形容詞 [v-link ADJ] If you are **happy about** a situation or arrangement, you are satisfied with it, for example, because you think that something is being done in the right way. 満足する □If you are not happy about a repair, go back and complain. 修理に満足していなければ戻って苦情を言いなさい。 □He's happy that I deal with it myself. 彼は私が独力でそれに取り組んでいることに満足している。 **4** ADJ 形容詞 If you say you are **happy** to do something, you mean that you are very willing to do it. 喜んでーする [v-link ADJ] □I'll be happy to answer questions if there are any. 質問があれば喜んでお答えします。 ●**hap|pi|ly** ADV 副詞 [ADV with v] 喜んで □If I've caused any offense over something I have written, I will happily apologize. 私の書いたものが人の感情を害するようなことがあったら、私は喜んでお詫びします。 **5** ADJ 形容詞 **Happy** is used in greetings and other conventional expressions to say that you hope someone will enjoy a special occasion. おめでとう [ADJ n] □Happy Birthday! 誕生日おめでとう
→ see **emotion**

ha|rangue /hərǽŋ/ (**harangues**, **haranguing**, **harangued**) V-T 他動詞 If someone **harangues** you, they try to persuade you to accept their opinions or ideas in a forceful way. 長いお説教をする □An argument ensued, with various band members joining in and haranguing Simpson and his girlfriend for over two hours. 言い争いが起こり、それに複数のバンドメンバーが加わり、シンプソンと彼のガールフレンドを2時間以上も長々とお説教した.

har|ass /hərǽs, hǽrəs/ (**harasses**, **harassing**, **harassed**) V-T 他動詞 If someone **harasses** you, they trouble or annoy you, for example by attacking you repeatedly or by causing you as many problems as they can. しつこく悩ます □A woman reporter complained one of them sexually harassed her in the locker room. ある女性記者は彼らの1人からロッカールームでセクハラを受けたと訴えた.

har|assed /hərǽst, hǽrəst/ ADJ 形容詞 If you are **harassed**, you are anxious and tense because you have too much to do or too many problems to cope with. 疲れきった □This morning, looking harassed and drawn, Lewis tendered his resignation. 今朝ルイスは疲れきってやつれた顔つきで辞表を提出した.

har|ass|ment /hərǽsmənt, hǽrəs-/ N-UNCOUNT 不可算名詞 **Harassment** is behavior which is intended to trouble or annoy someone, for example repeated attacks on them or attempts to cause them problems. ハラスメント □Another survey found that

51 percent of women had experienced some form of sexual harassment in their working lives. 別のアンケート調査によると、女性の51%が勤務中に何らかのセクハラを体験したことがある.

har|bor /hɑ́rbər/ (**harbors**, **harboring**, **harbored**) **1** N-COUNT; N-IN-NAMES 可算名詞, 名称中の名詞 A **harbor** is an area of the sea at the coast which is partly enclosed by land or strong walls, so that boats can be left there safely. 港 □She led us to a room with a balcony overlooking the harbor. 彼女は私達を港を見下ろすバルコニー付きの部屋に案内した。 **2** V-T 他動詞 If you **harbor** an emotion, thought, or secret, you have it in your mind over a long period of time. 心に持つ □He might have been murdered by a former client or someone harboring a grudge. 彼は昔の依頼人あるいは恨みを持っている人物に殺された可能性がある。 **3** V-T 他動詞 If a person or country **harbors** someone who is wanted by the police, they let them stay in their house or country and offer them protection. かくまう □Accusations of harboring suspects were raised against the former Hungarian leadership. ハンガリーのもと指導者は容疑者をかくまっていると訴えられた.

hard /hɑ́rd/ (**harder**, **hardest**) **1** ADJ 形容詞 Something that is **hard** is very firm and stiff to touch and is not easily bent, cut, or broken. 堅い □He shuffled his feet on the hard wooden floor. 彼は木でできた固い床の上で足をもぞもぞ動かした。 ●**hard|ness** N-UNCOUNT 不可算名詞 堅さ □He felt the hardness of the iron railing press against his spine. 彼は背骨が堅い鉄の手すりに押し付けられるのを感じた。 **2** ADJ 形容詞 Something that is **hard** is very difficult to do or deal with. 困難な □It's hard to tell what effect this latest move will have. この最近の動きがどんな効果をもたらすかを知るのは難しい。 □That's a very hard question. それは非常に難しい質問だ。 **3** ADV 副詞 [ADV after v] If you work **hard** doing something, you are very active or work intensely, with a lot of effort. 懸命に □I'll work hard. I don't want to let him down. 一生懸命に働くつもりだ。彼を失望させるわけにはいかない。 ●ADJ 形容詞 **Hard** is also an adjective. 勤勉な [ADJ n] □I admired him as a true scientist and hard worker. 私は真の科学者そして仕事熱心な人物として彼を尊敬している。 **4** ADJ 形容詞 **Hard** work involves a lot of activity and effort. □Coping with three babies is very hard work. 3人の赤ちゃんの世話をするのは重労働だ。 □...a hard day's work. 骨の折れる1日の仕事 **5** ADV 副詞 If you look, listen, or think **hard**, you do it carefully and with a great deal of attention. じっと [ADV after v] □He looked at me hard. 彼は私をじっと見つめた。 ●ADJ 形容詞 **Hard** is also an adjective. 鋭い □It might be worth taking a long hard look at your frustrations and resentments. 君の失望と怒りをじっくり考慮してみる価値があるかもしれない。 **6** ADV 副詞 If you strike or take hold of something **hard**, you strike or take hold of it with a lot of force. 強く [ADV after v] □I kicked a trash can very hard and broke my toe. 私はゴミ入れを非常に強く蹴り、足の指の骨を折った。 ●ADJ 形容詞 **Hard** is also an adjective. 強い [ADJ n] □He gave her a hard push which toppled her backwards into an armchair. 彼は彼女を強く押したので、彼女はひじ掛け椅子に後ろ向きに倒れた。 **7** ADV 副詞 You can use **hard** to indicate that something happens intensely and for a long time. 激しく [ADV after v] □I've never seen Terry laugh so hard. 私はテリーがあんなに大笑いするのを初めて見た。 **8** ADJ 形容詞 If a person or their expression is **hard**, they show no kindness or sympathy. 無情な □His father was a hard man. 彼の父親は無情な男だった。 **9** ADJ 形容詞 If you are **hard on** someone, you treat them severely or unkindly. つらく当たって [v-link ADJ 'on' n] □Don't be so hard on yourself. そんなに自分につらく当たるな。 ●ADV 副詞 **Hard** is also an adverb. 厳しく [ADV after v] □He said the security forces would continue to crack down hard on the protestors. 防衛隊は抗議者を厳重に取り締まり続けるだろうと彼は言った。 **10** ADJ 形容詞 If you say that something is **hard on** a person or thing, you mean it affects them in a way that is likely to cause them damage or suffering. 不快な [v-link ADJ 'on' n] □The gray light was hard on the eyes. 灰色の照明は目にきつかった。 **11** ADJ 形容詞 If you have a **hard** life or a **hard** period of time, your life or that period is difficult and unpleasant for you. つらい □It had been a hard life for her. 彼女にとってはつらい人生だった。 ●**hard|ness** N-UNCOUNT 不可算名詞 つらさ □In America, people don't normally admit to the hardness of life. アメリカでは普通人々は人生が苛酷であることを認めない。 **12** ADJ 形容詞 [ADJ n] **Hard** evidence or facts are definitely true and do not need to be questioned. 厳然たる □He wanted more hard evidence. かれは厳然たる証拠をより多く求めた。 **13** ADJ 形容詞 **Hard** drugs are very strong illegal drugs such as heroin or cocaine. 中毒性の [ADJ n] □He then graduated from soft drugs to hard ones. 彼はその後、習慣性が少ない麻薬から中毒性の麻薬に移った。 **14** PHRASE 句 If you say that something is **hard going**, you mean it is difficult and requires a lot of effort. 進みにくい □The talks had been hard going at the start. 話合いは最初から難航していた。 **15** PHRASE 句 To be **hard hit by** something means to be affected very severely by it. 非常に打撃を受ける □California's been particularly hard hit by the recession. カリフォルニアは特に景気後退の打撃を受けた。 **16** PHRASE 句 If someone **plays hard to get**, they pretend not to be interested in another person or in what someone is trying to persuade them to do. その気がない振りをする □I wanted her and she was playing hard to get. 僕は彼女に会いたかったが彼女はその気がないふりをしていた。

h

Thesaurus   *hard* また次を参照：

ADJ firm, solid, tough; (*ant.*) gentle, soft **1**
complicated, difficult, tough; (*ant.*) easy **2**

hard|back /hɑrdbæk/ (**hardbacks**) N-COUNT 可算名詞 A **hardback** is a book which has a stiff hard cover. Compare **paperback**. ハードカバーの本 [also'in' n] ❑ *The book was published in hardback last October.* その本のハードカバーは昨年10月に出版された。

hard cash N-UNCOUNT 不可算名詞 **Hard cash** is money in the form of bills and coins as opposed to a check or a credit card. 現金 ❑ *There is no confusion about what the real dividend is since the payment comes in hard cash.* 支払いは現金で行なわれるため、本当の配当が何かについての混乱はない。

hard copy (**hard copies**) N-VAR 可変性名詞 A **hard copy** of a document is a printed version of it, rather than a version that is stored on a computer. ハードコピー ❑ *...eight pages of hard copy.* 8ページのハードコピー

hard cur|ren|cy (**hard currencies**) N-VAR 可変性名詞 A **hard currency** is one which is unlikely to lose its value and so is considered to be a good one to have or to invest in. 交換可能通貨 ❑ *The country is running short of hard currency to pay for imports.* その国は輸入の代金となる交換可能通貨が不足している。

hard disk (**hard disks**) N-COUNT 可算名詞 A computer's **hard disk** is a stiff magnetic disk on which data and programs can be stored. ハードディスク

hard|en /hɑrd°n/ (**hardens, hardening, hardened**) **1** V-T/V-I 他動詞/自動詞 When something **hardens** or when you **harden** it, it becomes stiff or firm. 堅くする、堅くなる ❑ *Mold the mixture into shape while hot, before it hardens.* 混合物が熱いうちに、それが固まる前に成型しなさい。 **2** V-T/V-I 他動詞/自動詞 When an attitude or opinion **hardens** or is **hardened**, it becomes harsher, stronger, or fixed. 強固になる ❑ *Their action can only serve to harden the attitude of landowners.* 彼らの行動は地主の態度を益々確固たるものにするだけだ。 ● **hard|en|ing** N-SING 単数名詞 強固になること ❑ *...a hardening of the government's attitude toward rebellious parts of the army.* 軍の反抗的な要素に対する政府の態度の強化 **3** V-T/V-I 他動詞/自動詞 When events **harden** people or when people **harden**, they become less easily affected emotionally and less sympathetic and gentle than they were before. 無情にする、無情になる ❑ *Her years of drunken bickering hardened my heart.* 長年に及ぶ彼女の酔った口争いは私の心を無感覚にした。 **4** V-I 自動詞 If you say that someone's face or eyes **harden**, you mean that they suddenly look serious or angry. 厳しくなる ❑ *His smile died and the look in his face hardened.* 微笑みが消え、彼の顔はこわばった。

hard-line also **hardline** ADJ 形容詞 If you describe someone's policy or attitude as **hard-line**, you mean that it is strict or extreme, and they refuse to change it. 強硬路線 ❑ *The United States has taken a lot of criticism for its hard-line stance.* 米国はその強硬路線の姿勢に対して多くの批判を受けた。

hard|ly /hɑrdli/ **1** ADV 副詞 You use **hardly** to modify a statement when you want to emphasize that it is only a small amount or detail which makes it true, and that therefore it is best to consider the opposite statement as being true. ほとんど～ない [EMPHASIS 強調] ❑ *I hardly know you.* 私はあなたをほとんど知らない。 ❑ *I've hardly slept in three days.* 私は3日間ほとんど眠っていない。 **2** ADV 副詞 You use **hardly** in expressions such as **hardly ever, hardly any,** and **hardly anyone** to mean almost never, almost none, or almost no one. ほとんど～ない [ADV 'ever/any'] ❑ *We hardly ever eat fish.* 私達は魚はほとんど食べない。 ❑ *Most of the others were so young they had hardly any experience.* その他の人々の大半は若すぎて経験がほとんどなかった。 **3** ADV 副詞 You use **hardly** before a negative statement in order to emphasize that something is usually true or usually happens. 少しも～ない [EMPHASIS 強調] [ADV n] ❑ *Hardly a day goes by without a visit from someone.* 誰かが訪ねてこない日はない。 **4** ADV 副詞 When you say that you can **hardly** do something, you are emphasizing that it is very difficult for you to do it. ほとんど～ない [EMPHASIS 強調] ['can/could' ADV inf] ❑ *My garden was covered with so many butterflies that I could hardly see the flowers.* 庭は蝶が沢山飛びまわり花々はほとんど見えなかった。 **5** ADV 副詞 You use **hardly** to mean "not" when you want to suggest that you are expecting your listener or reader to agree with your comment. とても～できる ❑ *We have not seen the letter, so we can hardly comment on it.* 我々はその手紙を見ていないのでとても意見を述べることはできない。 **6** CONVENTION 慣習表現 You use "**hardly**" to mean "no," especially when you want to express surprise or annoyance at a statement that you disagree with. 全く～ない [SPOKEN 口語] ❑ *"They all thought you were marvelous!" —"Well, hardly."* 「いや、そんなことはないでしょう」

hard-pressed also **hard pressed** **1** ADJ 形容詞 If someone is **hard-pressed**, they are under a great deal of strain and worry, usually because they do not have enough money. 追い詰められた [JOURNALISM ジャーナリズム] ❑ *The region's hard-pressed consumers are spending less on luxuries.* その地域の追い詰められた消費者はぜいたく品の出費を抑えている。 **2** ADJ 形容詞 If you will be **hard-pressed** to do something, you will have great difficulty doing it. 困難な [v-link ADJ to-inf] ❑ *This year the airline will be hard-pressed to make a profit.* 今年その航空会社は黒字になるのが難しいだろう。

hard sell N-SING 単数名詞 A **hard sell** is a method of selling in which the salesperson puts a lot of pressure on someone to make them buy something. 強引な販売法 ❑ *...a company whose hard sell techniques were exposed by a consumer program.* 強引な販売法が消費者の手で暴露された会社

hard|ship /hɑrdʃɪp/ (**hardships**) N-VAR 可変性名詞 **Hardship** is a situation in which your life is difficult or unpleasant, often because you do not have enough money. 苦労 ❑ *Many people are suffering economic hardship.* 経済的な苦労をしている人は多い。

Word Link   *ware* ≈ *merchandise :* **hard**ware, **silver**ware, **soft**ware

hard|ware /hɑrdwɛr/ **1** N-UNCOUNT 不可算名詞 In computer systems, **hardware** refers to the machines themselves as opposed to the programs which tell the machines what to do. Compare **software**. ハードウェア ❑ *To be totally secure, you need a piece of hardware that costs about $200.* 安全性を確実にするためには約200ドルのハードウェアが必要だ。 **2** N-UNCOUNT 不可算名詞 Military **hardware** is the machinery and equipment that is used by the armed forces, such as tanks, aircraft, and missiles. 戦闘用器材 ❑ *...the billions which are spent on military hardware.* 戦闘用器材に費やされた数十億 **3** N-UNCOUNT 不可算名詞 **Hardware** refers to tools and equipment that are used in the home and garden, for example nuts and bolts, screwdrivers, and hinges. 金物類 ❑ *...a shop from which an uncle had sold hardware and timber.* 叔父が金物と木材を販売していた店

har|dy /hɑrdi/ (**hardier, hardiest**) ADJ 形容詞 Plants that are **hardy** are able to survive cold weather. 耐寒性の ❑ *The silver-leaved varieties of cyclamen are not quite as hardy.* 銀葉のシクラメンはそれ程寒さに強くない。

hare /hɛər/ (**hares**) N-VAR 可変性名詞 A **hare** is an animal like a rabbit but larger with long ears, long legs, and a small tail. 野ウサギ

hark /hɑrk/ (**harks, harking, harked**)
▸ **hark back to** PHRASAL VERB 句動詞 If you say that one thing **harks back to** another thing in the past, you mean it is similar to it or takes it as a model. 戻る ❑ *...pitched roofs, which hark back to the Victorian era.* 傾斜した屋根はビクトリア時代にさかのぼる。

harm /hɑrm/ (**harms, harming, harmed**) **1** V-T 他動詞 To **harm** a person or animal means to cause them physical injury, usually on purpose. 危害を加える ❑ *The hijackers seemed anxious not to harm anyone.* ハイジャック犯人は乗客には危害を加えたくないようだった。 **2** N-UNCOUNT 不可算名詞 **Harm** is physical injury to a person or an animal which is usually caused on purpose. 危害 ❑ *All dogs are capable of doing harm to human beings.* どんな犬にも人間に危害を加える能力がある。 **3** V-T 他動詞 To **harm** a thing, or sometimes a person, means to damage them or make them less effective or successful than they were. 害する ❑ *...a warning that the product may harm the environment.* その商品は環境に害を及ぼすかもしれないという警告 **4** N-UNCOUNT 不可算名詞 **Harm** is the damage to something which is caused by a particular course of action. 悪影響 ❑ *The abuse of your powers does harm to all other officers who do their job properly.* 職権の悪用は正しく任務を遂行する他の公務員全員に悪影響を与える。 **5** PHRASE 句 If you say **it does no harm to** do something or **there is no harm in** doing something, you mean that it might be worth doing, and you will not be blamed for doing it. 差し支えない ❑ *They are not always willing to take on untrained workers, but there's no harm in asking.* 彼らは訓練を受けていない作業員をいつも喜んで引き受けるとは限らないが、聞いてみる分には差し支えない。 **6** PHRASE 句 If someone or something is **out of harm's way**, they are in a safe place away from danger or from the possibility of being damaged. 害を受けないように ❑ *For parents, it is an easy way of keeping their children entertained, or simply out of harm's way.* 親にとってそれは子供たちを楽しませる、あるいは安全にしておく簡単な方法だ。 **7** PHRASE 句 If you say that there is **no harm done**, you are telling someone not to worry about something that has happened because it has not caused any serious injury or damage. 被害なし ❑ *There, now, you're all right. No harm done.* ほらあなた達は全員無事だ。被害はない。 **8** PHRASE 句 If you say that someone or something **will come to no harm** or that **no harm will come to** them, you mean that they will not be hurt or damaged in any way. 危害を受けない ❑ *There is always a lifeguard to ensure that no one comes to any harm.* 人々の安全を確認するために救護員が常に監視している。

Thesaurus

harm また次を参照：

v.	abuse, damage, hurt, injure, ruin, wreck; (ant.) benefit **1** **3**
N.	abuse, damage, hurt, injury, ruin, violence **2** **4**

Word Partnership

harm は次の語句と使われる：

v.	cause harm **2** **4** not mean any harm **4**
N.	harm the environment **3**
ADJ.	bodily harm **4**
ADV.	more harm than good **1**

harm|ful /hɑrmfəl/ ADJ 形容詞 Something that is **harmful** has a bad effect on something else, especially on a person's health. 有害な □ ...the harmful effects of smoking. 喫煙の悪影響

Word Link

less ≈ without : aimless, harmless, worthless

harm|less /hɑrmlɪs/ **1** ADJ 形容詞 Something that is **harmless** does not have any bad effects, especially on people's health. 無害な □ This experiment was harmless to the animals. この実験は動物に無害だ. **2** ADJ 形容詞 If you describe someone or something as **harmless**, you mean that they are not important and therefore unlikely to annoy other people or cause trouble. 無害の □ He seemed harmless enough. 彼は十分無害に見えた.

har|mon|ic /hɑrmɒnɪk/ ADJ 形容詞 **Harmonic** means composed, played, or sung using two or more notes which sound right and pleasing together. 和声の □ I had been looking for ways to combine harmonic and rhythmic structures. 私は和声的な構造とリズミカルな構造を組み合わせる方法を探していた.

har|mo|ni|ous /hɑrmoʊniəs/ ADJ 形容詞 A **harmonious** relationship, agreement, or discussion is friendly and peaceful. 仲のよい □ Their harmonious relationship resulted in part from their similar goals. 彼らの仲のよさは目標が似ていることにある程度起因した. ● **har|mo|ni|ous|ly** ADV 副詞 [ADV after v] 仲良く □ To live together harmoniously as men and women is an achievement. 男と女が仲むつまじく生活を共にすることは偉業だ.

har|mo|nize /hɑrmənaɪz/ (**harmonizes, harmonizing, harmonized**) **1** V-RECIP 相互動詞 If two or more things **harmonize with** each other, they fit in well with each other. 調和する □ How well all her garments harmonized with each other. 彼女の洋服は全て何てよく調和しているんだろう. **2** V-T 他動詞 When governments or organizations **harmonize** laws, systems, or regulations, they agree in a friendly way to make them the same or similar. 一致させる □ The leaders have agreed to harmonize their national policies on immigration and asylum. 指導者達は移民と亡命に関する国家政策を一致させることに合意した. **3** V-I 自動詞 When people **harmonize**, they sing or play notes which are different from the main tune but which sound nice with it. 調和音を加える □ ...a perfectly pitched gospel group that harmonized perfectly. 完璧に和声を加えた音の高さが完璧なゴスペル合唱隊

Word Link

mony ≈ resulting state : ceremony, harmony, testimony

har|mo|ny /hɑrməni/ (**harmonies**) **1** N-UNCOUNT 不可算名詞 If people are living **in harmony with** each other, they are living together peacefully rather than fighting or arguing. 仲よく □ ...the notion that man should dominate nature rather than live in harmony with it. 自然に合わせて生活するのではなく自然を支配すべきだという考え. **2** N-VAR 可変性名詞 **Harmony** is the pleasant combination of different notes of music played at the same time. 和声 □ ...singing in harmony. 和声合唱 **3** N-UNCOUNT 不可算名詞 The **harmony** of something is the way in which its parts are combined into a pleasant arrangement. 調和 □ ...the ordered harmony of the universe. 宇宙の調和

har|ness /hɑrnɪs/ (**harnesses, harnessing, harnessed**) **1** V-T 他動詞 If you **harness** something such as an emotion or natural source of energy, you bring it under your control and use it. 利用する □ Turkey plans to harness the waters of the Tigris and Euphrates rivers for big hydro-electric power projects. トルコはチグリスおよびユーフラテス川を流れる水を大規模な水力発電プロジェクトに利用する予定だ. **2** N-COUNT 可算名詞 A **harness** is a set of straps which fit under a person's arms and fasten around their body in order to keep a piece of equipment in place or to prevent the person moving from a place. 安全ベルト **3** N-COUNT 可算名詞 A **harness** is a set of leather straps and metal links fastened around a horse's head or body so that the horse can have a carriage, cart, or plow fastened to it. 引き具 **4** V-T 他動詞 If a horse or other animal is **harnessed**, a harness is put on it, especially so that it can pull a carriage, cart, or plow. 引き具でつながれる [usu passive] □ On Sunday the horses were harnessed to a heavy wagon for a day-long ride over the border. 日曜日に馬は1日かけて国境を横断するために大きな荷物車に引き具でつながれた.

harp /hɑrp/ (**harps, harping, harped**) N-VAR 可変性名詞 A **harp** is a large musical instrument consisting of a row of strings stretched from the top to the bottom of a frame. You play the harp by plucking the strings with your fingers. ハープ
→ see string
▶ **harp on** PHRASAL VERB 句動詞 If you say that someone **harps on** a subject, or **harps on about** it, you mean that they keep on talking about it in a way that other people find annoying. 繰り返し話す □ Jones harps on this theme more than on any other. ジョーンズは他のどんな話題よりもこの話題について繰り返して話す.

har|row|ing /hæroʊɪŋ/ ADJ 形容詞 A **harrowing** experience is extremely upsetting or disturbing. 悲惨な □ You've had a harrowing time this past month. 君はこの1か月間、ひどい経験をした.

harsh /hɑrʃ/ (**harsher, harshest**) **1** ADJ 形容詞 **Harsh** climates or conditions are very difficult for people, animals, and plants to live in. 厳しい □ ...the harsh desert environment. 破滅の厳しい環境 ● **harsh|ness** N-UNCOUNT 不可算名詞 厳しさ □ ...the harshness of their living conditions. 彼らの生活状態の厳しさ **2** ADJ 形容詞 **Harsh** actions or speech are unkind and show no understanding or sympathy. 苛酷な □ He said many harsh and unkind things about his opponents. 彼は敵対者について苛酷で不親切なことを沢山述べた. ● **harsh|ly** ADV 副詞 [ADV with v] 厳しく □ She's been told that her husband is being harshly treated in prison. 彼女は夫が刑務所で厳しい待遇を受けていると聞いた. ● **harsh|ness** N-UNCOUNT 不可算名詞 厳しさ □ ...treating him with great harshness. 彼をひどく厳しく扱うこと **3** ADJ 形容詞 Something that is **harsh** is so hard, bright, or rough that it seems unpleasant or harmful. どぎつい □ Tropical colors may look rather harsh in our dull northern light. 熱帯的な色彩はわが国のどんよりした北部の光線ではややどぎつく見える. ● **harsh|ness** N-UNCOUNT 不可算名詞 不快さ □ As the wine ages, it loses its bitter harshness. 熟成するにつれ、ワインは苦味を失う. **4** ADJ 形容詞 **Harsh** voices and sounds are ones that are rough and unpleasant to listen to. 耳ざわりな □ It's a pity she has such a loud harsh voice. 彼女はひどく耳ざわりな大声で話すのが惜しいことだ. ● **harsh|ly** ADV 副詞 [ADV with v] 耳ざわりになるほど □ Chris laughed harshly. クリスは耳ざわりになるほど大声で笑った. ● **harsh|ness** N-UNCOUNT 不可算名詞 とげとげしさ □ Then in a tone of abrupt harshness, he added, "Open these trunks!" それから突然とげとげしい口調で彼は「これらの大かばんを開けろ」と付け加えた. **5** ADJ 形容詞 If you talk about **harsh** realities or facts, or the **harsh** truth, you are emphasizing that they are true or real, although they are unpleasant and people try to avoid thinking about them. 厳しい [EMPHASIS 強調] □ The harsh truth is that luck plays a big part in who will live or die. 人々の生死には運が大きな役割を務めているというのが厳然たる事実だ.

har|vest /hɑrvɪst/ (**harvests, harvesting, harvested**) **1** N-SING 単数名詞 The **harvest** is the gathering of a crop. 収穫 □ There was about 300 million tons of grain in the fields at the start of the harvest. 収穫期の初めには約3億トンの穀物が畑にあった. **2** N-COUNT 可算名詞 A **harvest** is the crop that is gathered in. 収穫物 □ Millions of people are threatened with starvation as a result of drought and poor harvests. 干ばつと乏しい収穫で、何百万もの人々が飢餓の危険にさらされている. **3** V-T 他動詞 When you **harvest** a crop, you gather it in. 収穫する □ Rice farmers here still plant and harvest their crops by hand. この米農業従事者はまだ穀物を手で植え、収穫する.
→ see farm, grain

has

The auxiliary verb is pronounced /həz/, STRONG hæz/. The main verb is usually pronounced /hæz/.
助動詞は /həz, STRONG hæz/ と発音される. 本動詞は通常 /hæz/ と発音される.

Has is the third person singular of the present tense of **have**. have の三人称単数現在形

has-been (**has-beens**) N-COUNT 可算名詞 If you describe someone as a **has-been**, you are indicating in an unkind way that they were important or respected in the past, but they are not now. 盛りを過ぎた人 [DISAPPROVAL 不賛成] □ ...the so-called experts and various has-beens who foist opinions on us. 我々に意見を押し付けるいわゆる専門家と様々な盛りを過ぎた人たち

hash /hæʃ/ (**hashes, hashing, hashed**) **1** N-UNCOUNT 不可算名詞 **Hash** is a dish made from meat cut into small lumps and fried with other ingredients such as onions or potato. ハヤシ肉料理 □ ...corned beef hash. コンビーフハッシュ **2** N-COUNT 可算名詞 A **hash** is the sign Ð, found on telephone keypads and computer keyboards. らの記号 [mainly BRIT 主に英国英語, SPOKEN 口語] [usu sing] [AM usually pound sign 米国英語では通常 pound sign] **3** PHRASE 句 If you **make a hash of** a job or task, you do it very badly. めちゃくちゃにする [INFORMAL くだけた] □ The government made a total hash of things and squandered a small fortune. 政府は何もかもめちゃくちゃにし、大金を浪費した.
▶ **hash out 1** PHRASAL VERB 句動詞 If people **hash out** something such as a plan or an agreement, they decide on it after a lot of discussion. 徹底的に討議する [AM 米国英語] [also V n P]

h

❑*The House and Senate are to begin soon hashing out an agreement for sanctions legislation.* 上院と下院はまもなく経済制裁規制のための協定を徹底的に討議し始める予定だ. ❷ PHRASAL VERB 句動詞 If people **hash out** a problem or a dispute, they discuss it thoroughly until they reach an agreement. とことん話し合う [AM 米国英語] ❑*…while the parties try to hash out their differences in court.* 当事者たちが裁判所で意見の相違についてとことん話し合う間に

hasn't /hˈæzⁿt/ **Hasn't** is the usual spoken form of "has not." has notの短縮形

has|sle /hˈæsⁿl/ (**hassles, hassling, hassled**) ❶ N-VAR 可変性名詞 A **hassle** is a situation that is difficult and involves problems, effort, or arguments with people. いざこざ [INFORMAL くだけた] ❑*I don't think it's worth the money or the hassle.* それは金を出す価値も手間をかける価値もないと思う. ❷ V-T 他動詞 If someone **hassles** you, they cause problems for you, often by repeatedly telling you or asking you to do something, in an annoying way. 悩ます [INFORMAL くだけた] ❑*Then my husband started hassling me.* それから夫は私を悩まし始めた.

haste /hˈeɪst/ ❶ N-UNCOUNT 不可算名詞 **Haste** is the quality of doing something quickly, sometimes too quickly so that you are careless and make mistakes. 慌てること ❑*In their haste to escape the rising water, they dropped some expensive equipment.* 増水から慌てて逃れる途中で彼らは高価な機器を落とした. ❷ PHRASE 句 If you do something **in haste**, you do it quickly and hurriedly, and sometimes carelessly. 慌てて行動したり、せっかちにはなってはいけない. ❑*Don't act in haste or be hot-headed.* 慌てて行動したり、せっかちにはなってはいけない.

has|ten /hˈeɪsⁿn/ (**hastens, hastening, hastened**) ❶ V-T 他動詞 If you **hasten** an event or process, often an unpleasant one, you make it happen faster or sooner. 早める ❑*But if he does this, he may hasten the collapse of his own country.* しかし彼がこれを行なえば自国の崩壊を早めるかもしれない. ❷ V-T 他動詞 If you **hasten to** do something, you are quick to do it. 急いで〜する ❑*She more than anyone had hastened to sign the contract.* 彼女は他の誰よりも急いで契約に署名した.

has|ty /hˈeɪsti/ (**hastier, hastiest**) ❶ ADJ 形容詞 A **hasty** movement, action, or statement is sudden, and often done in reaction to something that has just happened. 慌ただしい ❑*Donald had overturned a chair in his hasty departure.* ドナルドは慌だしく出発しようとして椅子をひっくり返した. ●**hastily** /hˈeɪstɪli/ ADV 副詞 [ADV with v] 慌ただしく ❑*The council was hastily convened after his father said he was resigning.* 審議会は彼の父が辞任を表明した後、慌ただしく開催された. ❷ ADJ 形容詞 If you describe a person or their behavior as **hasty**, you mean that they are acting too quickly, without thinking carefully, for example because they are angry. 早まった [DISAPPROVAL 不賛成] ❑*A number of the United States' allies had urged him not to make a hasty decision.* 米国の同盟国数か国は早まった決断をしないよう強く勧めた. ●**hastily** ADV 副詞 [ADV with v] 早まって ❑*I decided that nothing should be done hastily, that things had to be sorted out carefully.* 私はどんなことでは急いでやってはならない、物事は注意深く処理するべきだという結論に達した.

hat /hˈæt/ (**hats**) ❶ N-COUNT 可算名詞 A **hat** is a head covering, often with a brim around it, which is usually worn outdoors to give protection from the weather. 帽子 ❑*…a plump woman in a red hat.* 赤い帽子を被ったふくよかな女性 ❷ N-COUNT 可算名詞 If you say that someone is wearing a particular **hat**, you mean that they are performing a particular role at that time. If you say that they wear several **hats**, you mean that they have several roles or jobs. 役割 ❑*Now I'll take off my "friend hat" and put on my "therapist hat."* さて私はこれから「友人」から「セラピスト」の役目に変ります. ❸ PHRASE 句 If you say that you are ready to do something **at the drop of a hat**, you mean that you are willing to do it immediately, without hesitating. 待っていたばかりに ❑*India is one part of the world I would go to at the drop of a hat.* 私はためらわずに行きたい国の1つだ. ❹ PHRASE 句 If you tell someone to **keep a piece of information under their hat**, you are asking them not to tell anyone else about it. 内証にしておく ❑*If I tell you something, will you promise to keep it under your hat?* これから君に言うことを内証にすると約束してくれるか. ❺ PHRASE 句 If you say that you **take** your **hat off** to someone, you mean that you admire them for something that they have done. 敬意を表する [APPROVAL 賛成] ❑*I take my hat off to Mr. Clarke for taking this action.* この行動を取ったことに対してクラーク氏に敬意を表する. ❻ PHRASE 句 To **pull** something **out of the hat** means to do something unexpected which helps you to succeed, often when you are failing. やすやすと生み出す ❑*There are expectations that he'll pull a cease-fire out of a hat.* 彼が停戦を可能にするという期待がある. ❼ PHRASE 句 In competitions, if you say that the winners will be drawn or picked **out of the hat**, you mean that they will be chosen randomly, so everyone has an equal chance of winning. 任意に選択する ❑*The first 10 correct entries drawn out of the hat will win a pair of tickets, worth $30 each.* 任意に選択された正解者10名に各々30ドルの価値のあるチケット2枚が贈られます.

hatch /hˈætʃ/ (**hatches, hatching, hatched**) ❶ V-T/V-I 他動詞/自

動詞 When a baby bird, insect, or other animal **hatches**, or when it **is hatched**, it comes out of its egg by breaking the shell. 孵る(かえる), 卵から孵す ❑*The young disappeared soon after they were hatched.* ふ化した後まもなくして子はいなくなった. ❷ V-T/V-I 他動詞/自動詞 When an egg **hatches** or when a bird, insect, or other animal **hatches** an egg, the egg breaks open and a baby comes out. 卵から孵る ❑*The eggs hatch after a week or ten days.* 1週間から10日間後に卵は孵った. ❸ V-T 他動詞 If you **hatch** a plot or a scheme, you think of it and work it out. 企てる ❑*He has accused opposition parties of hatching a plot to assassinate the pope.* 彼は野党がローマ法王を暗殺する陰謀を企てていると主張した. ❹ N-COUNT 可算名詞 A **hatch** is an opening in the deck of a ship, through which people or cargo can go. You can also refer to the door of this opening as a **hatch**. ハッチ ❑*He stuck his head up through the hatch.* 彼はハッチから頭を突き出した.

hatch|et /hˈætʃɪt/ (**hatchets**) ❶ N-COUNT 可算名詞 A **hatchet** is a small ax that you can hold in one hand. 手おの ❷ PHRASE 句 If two people **bury the hatchet**, they become friendly again after a quarrel or disagreement. 仲直りする ❑*It is time to bury the hatchet and forget about what has happened in the past.* 仲直りし、過去に起きたことを忘れる時が来た.

hate /hˈeɪt/ (**hates, hating, hated**) ❶ V-T 他動詞 If you **hate** someone or something, you have an extremely strong feeling of dislike for them. 憎む ❑*Most people hate him, but they don't dare to say so, because he still rules the country.* 大半の人は彼を憎んでいるがそう言う勇気はない, 何故なら彼はまだ国を牛耳っているから. ●N-UNCOUNT 不可算名詞 **Hate** is also a noun. 憎しみ ❑*I was 17 and filled with a lot of hate.* 私は17歳で, 憎しみの感情で一杯だった. ❷ V-T 他動詞 If you say that you **hate** something such as a particular activity, you mean that you find it very unpleasant. 嫌う [no cont] ❑*Ted hated parties, even gatherings of people he liked individually.* テッドは個人的には好きな人が集まっていても, パーティは嫌いだった. ❑*He hates to be interrupted during training.* 彼は訓練中に中断されるのが嫌いだ. ❑*He hated coming home to the empty house.* 彼は誰もいない家に帰って来るのが嫌いだった. ❸ V-T 他動詞 You can use **hate** in expressions such as "**I hate to trouble you**" or "**I hate to bother you**" when you are apologizing to someone for interrupting them or asking them to do something. 残念に思う [POLITENESS 丁寧さ] [no cont] ❑*I hate to rush you but I have another appointment later on.* 急かせてすみませんが, 私には後で別の約束があります. ❹ V-T 他動詞 You can use **hate** in expressions such as "**I hate to say it**" or "**I hate to tell you**" when you want to express regret about what you are about to say, because you think it is unpleasant or should not be the case. いやである [FEELINGS 感情] [no cont] ❑*I hate to tell you this, but tomorrow's your last day.* これを君に言いたくないのだが, 明日が君の最後の日だ. ❺ to **hate** someone's **guts** → see **gut** ❻ V-T 他動詞 You can use **hate** in expressions such as "**I hate to see**" or "**I hate to think**" when you are emphasizing that you find a situation or an idea unpleasant. 嫌う [EMPHASIS 強調] [no cont] ❑*I just hate to see you doing this to yourself.* 私はあなたが自分自身にそうするのをとても見ていられない. ❼ V-T 他動詞 You can use **hate** in expressions such as "**I'd hate to think**" when you hope that something is not true or that something will not happen. 嫌う [no cont] ❑*I'd hate to think my job would not be secure if I left it temporarily.* もし休職したら私の職は保証されなくなるとはとても考えたくない.

→ see **emotion**

Word Partnership		hate は次の語句と使われる:
N.	hate **the thought of** *something* ❷	
V.	hate **to admit** *something* ❹	
	hate **to see** *something* ❻	
	hate **to think** *something* ❼	

ha|tred /hˈeɪtrɪd/ (**hatreds**) N-UNCOUNT 不可算名詞 **Hatred** is an extremely strong feeling of dislike for someone or something. 憎しみ ❑*Her hatred of them would never lead her to murder.* 彼らをどんなに憎んでいても彼女が殺人を犯すことは決してないだろう.

hat trick (**hat tricks**) also **hat-trick** N-COUNT 可算名詞 A **hat trick** is a series of three achievements, especially in a sports event, for example three goals scored by the same person in a soccer game. ハットトリック ❑*I scored a hat-trick in my first game.* 僕は最初の試合で3得点挙げた.

haul /hˈɔl/ (**hauls, hauling, hauled**) ❶ V-T 他動詞 If you **haul** something which is heavy or difficult to move, you move it using a lot of effort. 引きずる ❑*A crane had to be used to haul the car out of the stream.* 車を小川から引き上げるにはクレーンを使う必要があった. ❷ V-T 他動詞 If someone **is hauled before** a court or someone in authority, they are made to appear before them because they are accused of having done something wrong. 召喚される [usu passive] ❑*He was hauled before the managing director and fired.* 彼は社長の前に呼び出され, 首になった. ●PHRASAL VERB 句動詞 **Haul up** means the same as **haul**. 呼び出す ❑*He was hauled up before the board of trustees.* 彼は評議員会の前に呼び出された. ❸ N-COUNT 可

算名詞 A **haul** is a quantity of things that are stolen, or a quantity of stolen or illegal goods found by police or customs. 押収した密輸品 ☐ *The size of the drug haul shows that the international trade in heroin is still flourishing.* 麻薬の密輸品の規模はヘロインの国際取引は今でも盛んなことを示している。 **4** PHRASE 句 If you say that a task or a journey is a **long haul**, you mean that it takes a long time and a lot of effort. 長くてつらい道のり ☐ *Revitalizing the Romanian economy will be a long haul.* ルーマニア経済の民営化は長くてつらい道のりとなるだろう。 **5** → see also **long-haul**

haul|er /hɔ́lər/ (**haulers**) N-COUNT 可算名詞 A **hauler** is a company or a person that transports goods by road. 運送業者 [AM 米国英語]

haunt /hɔ́nt/ (**haunts, haunting, haunted**) **1** V-T 他動詞 If something unpleasant **haunts** you, you keep thinking or worrying about it over a long period of time. 付きまとう ☐ *He would always be haunted by that scene in Well Park.* 彼はウェル公園のあの光景を決して忘れられないだろう。 **2** V-T 他動詞 Something that **haunts** a person or organization regularly causes them problems over a long period of time. 付きまとう ☐ *The stigma of being a bankrupt is likely to haunt him for the rest of his life.* 破産者の汚名は彼を一生付きまとうだろう。 **3** N-COUNT 可算名詞 A place that is the **haunt** of a particular person is one which they often visit because they enjoy going there. よく行く場所 ☐ *The islands are a favorite summer haunt for yachtsmen.* その島はヨット愛好家が好んでよく行く所だ。 **4** V-T 他動詞 A ghost or spirit that **haunts** a place or a person regularly appears in the place, or is seen by the person and frightens them. 出没する ☐ *His ghost is said to haunt some of the rooms, banging a toy drum.* 彼の幽霊はおもちゃのドラムをたたきながら部屋に出没すると言われている。

haunt|ed /hɔ́ntɪd/ ADJ 形容詞 A **haunted** building or other place is one where a ghost regularly appears. 幽霊が出没する ☐ *Tracy said the cabin was haunted.* トレイシーはそのキャビンには幽霊が出ると言った。 **2** ADJ 形容詞 Someone who has a **haunted** expression looks very worried or troubled. 取り付かれたような ☐ *She looked so haunted, I almost didn't recognize her.* 彼女はひどく取り付かれたように見え、もう少しで別人かと思った。

haunt|ing /hɔ́ntɪŋ/ ADJ 形容詞 **Haunting** sounds, images, or words remain in your thoughts because they are very beautiful or sad. 容易に忘れられない ☐ *...the haunting calls of wild birds in the mahogany trees.* マホガニーの木に止まった野鳥の心に残るさえずり。 ●**haunt|ing|ly** ADV 副詞 忘れられない ☐ *Each one of these ancient towns is hauntingly beautiful.* 古びた町のどれも忘れられないほど美しい。

---

have

❶ AUXILIARY VERB USES
❷ USED WITH NOUNS DESCRIBING ACTIONS
❸ OTHER VERB USES AND PHRASES
❹ MODAL PHRASES

---

❶ have /həv, STRONG hǽv/ (**has, having, had**)

In spoken English, forms of **have** are often shortened, for example **I have** is shortened to **I've** and **has not** is shortened to **hasn't**.

口語英語では **have** の諸形はしばしば短縮される。例えば、**I have** は **I've** に短縮できるし、**has not** は **hasn't** に短縮できる。

1 AUX 助動詞 You use the forms **have** and **has** with a past participle to form the present perfect tense of verbs. してしまった ☐ *Alex has already gone.* アレックスは既に行ってしまった。 ☐ *What have you found so far?* 今までに何を発見したか。 ☐ *Frankie hasn't been feeling well for a long time.* フランキーは長い間体調がすぐれない。 **2** AUX 助動詞 You use the form **had** with a past participle to form the past perfect tense of verbs. していた ☐ *When I met her, she had just returned from a job interview.* 私が彼女にあった時、彼女はちょうど面接から戻ってきたばかりだった。 **3** AUX 助動詞 **Have** is used in question tags. したか ☐ *You haven't sent her away, have you?* あなたは彼女を追いやっていないだろうね。 **4** AUX 助動詞 You use **have** when you are confirming or contradicting a statement containing "have," "has," or "had," or answering a question. したことがある ☐ *"You'd never seen the Marilyn Monroe film?" —"No I hadn't."* 「君はマリリンモンローの映画は一度も観たことなかったね。」「はい、観たことありません。」 **5** AUX 助動詞 The form **having** with a past participle can be used to introduce a clause in which you mention an action which had already happened before another action began. してから ☐ *He arrived in San Francisco, having left New Jersey on January 19th.* 彼は1月19日にニュージャージーを出発してからサンフランシスコに到着した。

Thesaurus   *have* また次を参照：
v.   own, possess **❸ 1**
      suffer **❸ 10**

❷ have /hǽv/ (**has, having, had**)

Have is used in combination with a wide range of nouns, where the meaning of the combination is mostly given by the noun.

Have は広範囲の名詞と結合して用いられ、その場合結合表現の意味は大部分その名詞によって与えられる。

1 V-T 他動詞 You can use **have** followed by a noun to talk about an action or event, when it would be possible to use the same word as a verb. For example, you can say "**I had a look at the photos**" instead of "I looked at the photos." する [no passive] ☐ *I went out and had a walk around.* 私は散歩に出かけた。 ☐ *We had a laugh over that one.* 私はそのことについて笑った。 **2** V-T 他動詞 In normal spoken or written English, people use **have** with a wide range of nouns to talk about actions and events, often instead of a more specific verb. For example people are more likely to say "**we had ice cream**" or "**he's had a shock**" than "we ate ice cream," or "he's suffered a shock." 食べる、行なう [no passive] ☐ *Come and have a meal with us tonight.* 今夜私達の家に食事に来ませんか。 ☐ *We will be having a meeting to decide what to do.* 私達は対策を練るために打ち合わせを行なう予定だ。

❸ have /hǽv/ (**has, having, had**)

For meanings **1** – **4**, people often use **have gotten** in spoken American English, and **have got** in spoken British English, instead of **have**. In this case, **have** is pronounced as an auxiliary verb. For more information and examples of the use of "have got" and "have gotten," see **got**.

1 – **4** の意味には、**have gotten** の代わりに口語米語では **have got** が、口語英国英語では **have** がしばしば使われる。この場合、**have** は助動詞として発音される。より詳細な情報と **have got** と **have gotten** の用法の例文は、got を参照。

⊳ **Please look at meaning 17 to see if the expression you are looking for is shown under another headword. 1** V-T 他動詞 You use **have** to say that someone or something owns a particular thing, or when you are mentioning one of their qualities or characteristics. 所有する [no passive] ☐ *Oscar had a new bicycle.* オスカーは新しい自転車を買ってもらった。 ☐ *I want to have my own business.* 私は自分の事業を持ちたい。 ☐ *She had no job and no money.* 彼女には仕事もお金もなかった。 ☐ *You have beautiful eyes.* あなたはきれいな目をしている。 ☐ *Do you have any brothers and sisters?* あなたには兄弟・姉妹がいますか。 **2** V-T 他動詞 If you **have** something **to do**, you are responsible for doing it or must do it. 抱える [no passive] ☐ *He had plenty of work to do.* 彼は大量の作業を抱えていた。 **3** V-T 他動詞 You can use **have** instead of "there is" to say that something exists or happens. For example, you can say "**you have no alternative**" instead of "there is no alternative," or "**he had a good view from his window**" instead of "there was a good view from his window." ある [no passive] ☐ *He had two tenants living with him.* 彼は2人のテナントと同居していた。 **4** V-T 他動詞 If you **have** something such as a part of your body in a particular position or state, it is in that position or state. (―の状態に) 保つ [no passive] ☐ *Mary had her eyes closed.* メアリーは目を閉じていた。 ☐ *They had the curtains open.* 彼らはカーテンを開けていた。 **5** V-T 他動詞 If you **have** something **done**, someone does it for you or you arrange for it to be done. してもらう、させる [no passive] ☐ *I had your rooms cleaned and aired.* あなた達の部屋の掃除と空気の入れ換えをしてもらった。 ☐ *They had him killed.* 彼らは彼を殺させた。 **6** V-T 他動詞 If someone **has** something unpleasant happen to them, it happens to them. 経験する [no passive] ☐ *We had our money stolen.* 我々は金を盗まれた。 **7** V-T 他動詞 If you **have** someone do something, you persuade, cause, or order them to do it. させる [no passive] ☐ *The bridge is not as impressive as some guides would have you believe.* その橋はツアーガイドが言うほど印象的ではない。 **8** V-T 他動詞 If someone **has** you **by** a part of your body, they are holding you there and they are trying to hurt you or force you to go somewhere. つかむ [no passive] ☐ *He had her by the arm and he was screaming at her.* 彼は彼女の腕をつかみ、彼女に大声で叫んでいた。 **9** V-T 他動詞 If you **have** something from someone, they give it to you. 得る [no passive] ☐ *You can have my ticket.* 私のチケットは君にあげるよ。 ☐ *Can I have your name please?* 名前を教えてください。 **10** V-T 他動詞 If you **have** an illness or disability, you suffer from it. わずらう [no passive] ☐ *I had a headache.* 私は頭痛がした。 **11** V-T 他動詞 If a woman **has** a baby, she gives birth to it. If she is **having** a baby, she is pregnant. 産む [no passive] ☐ *My wife has just had a baby boy.* 私の妻は男の赤ちゃんを出産したばかりだ。 **12** V-T 他動詞 You can use **have** in expressions such as "**I won't have it**" or "**I'm not having that,**" to mean that you will not allow or put up with something. 受け入れる [with neg] ☐ *I'm not having any of that*

nonsense. そんなばかな話は1つも信じない. **13** PHRASE 句 You can use **has it** in expressions such as "**rumor has it that**" or "**as legend has it**" when you are quoting something that you have heard, but you do not necessarily think it is true. 言う [VAGUENESS あいまいさ] □ *Rumor has it that tickets were being sold for $300.* うわさではチケットは300ドルで販売されているそうだ. **14** PHRASE 句 If someone **has it in for** you, they do not like you and they want to make life difficult for you. 恨みを抱いている [INFORMAL くだけた] □ *He's always had it in for the Dawkins family.* 彼は常にドーキンズ一家に恨みを抱いてきた. **15** PHRASE 句 If you **have it in** you, you have abilities and skills which you do not usually use and which only show themselves in a difficult situation. 能力がある □ *"You were brilliant!" he said. "I didn't know you had it in you."* 「君は素晴らしかった. 君にそんな能力があるとは知らなかった. 」と彼は言った. **16** PHRASE 句 If you **have it out** or **have things out with** someone, you discuss a problem or disagreement very openly with them, even if it means having an argument, because you think this is the best way to solve the problem. 決着をつける □ *Why not have it out with your critic, discuss the whole thing face to face?* 面と向かって全てを討論し, 批評家と決着をつけたらどうか. **17** to **be had** → see **had** **18** to **have had it** → see **had**

❹ have /hæv, hæf/ (**has, having, had**) **1** PHRASE 句 You use **have to** when you are saying that something is necessary or required, or must happen. If you do not **have to** do something, it is not necessary or required. しなければならない □ *He had to go to Germany.* 彼はドイツに行かなければならなかった. □ *You have to be careful what you say on TV.* テレビ出演した時の発言には注意する必要がある. **2** PHRASE 句 You can use **have to** in order to say that you feel certain that something is true or will happen. するにちがいない □ *There has to be some kind of way out.* 何か解決法はあるはずだ.

ha|ven /heɪvᵊn/ (**havens**) **1** N-COUNT 可算名詞 A **haven** is a place where people or animals feel safe, secure, and happy. 避難所 □ *...Lake Baringo, a freshwater haven for a mixed variety of birds.* 多種類の鳥類のための淡水の避難所, バリンゴ湖. **2** → see also **safe haven**

haven't /hævᵊnt/ **Haven't** is the usual spoken form of "have not."

hav|oc /hævək/ **1** N-UNCOUNT 不可算名詞 **Havoc** is great disorder and confusion. 大混乱 □ *Rioters caused havoc in the center of the town.* 暴動者たちは町の中心部を破壊した. **2** PHRASE 句 If one thing **plays havoc with** another or **wreaks havoc on** it, it prevents it from continuing or functioning as normal, or damages it. 混乱させる □ *The weather played havoc with airline schedules.* 天候は航空便の時刻表をめちゃくちゃにした.

hawk /hɔk/ (**hawks**) **1** N-COUNT 可算名詞 A **hawk** is a large bird with a short, hooked beak, sharp claws, and very good eyesight. Hawks catch and eat small birds and animals. タカ **2** N-COUNT 可算名詞 In politics, if you refer to someone as a **hawk**, you mean that they believe in using force and violence to achieve something, rather than using more peaceful or diplomatic methods. Compare **dove**. タカ派 □ *Both hawks and doves have expanded their conditions for ending the war.* タカ派とハト派は双方とも, 戦争終結の条件を広げた. **3** PHRASE 句 If you **watch** someone **like a hawk**, you observe them very carefully, usually to make sure that they do not make a mistake or do something you do not want them to do. 厳重に見張る □ *If we hadn't watched him like a hawk, he would have escaped.* もし彼を厳重に監視していなければ彼は脱走していただろう.

hay /heɪ/ **1** N-UNCOUNT 不可算名詞 **Hay** is grass which has been cut and dried so that it can be used to feed animals. 干し草 □ *...bales of hay.* 干し草1俵. **2** PHRASE 句 If you say that someone **is making hay** or **is making hay while the sun shines**, you mean that they are taking advantage of a situation that is favorable to them while they have the chance to. 好機を逃さない □ *We knew war was coming, and were determined to make hay while we could.* 我々は戦争が起こることは知っており, 好機を逃さないことを固く決心していた. → see **barn**

hay fe|ver N-UNCOUNT 不可算名詞 If someone is suffering from **hay fever**, they sneeze and their eyes itch, because they are allergic to grass or flowers. 花粉症

haz|ard /hæzərd/ (**hazards, hazarding, hazarded**) **1** N-COUNT 可算名詞 A **hazard** is something which could be dangerous to you, your health or safety, or your plans or reputation. 危険 □ *A new report suggests that chewing gum may be a health hazard.* 新しいリポートによると, ガムをかむことは健康によくない可能性がある. **2** V-T 他動詞 If you **hazard** or if you **hazard a guess**, you make a suggestion about something which is only a guess and which you know might be wrong. 思い切って発言する □ *I would hazard a guess that they'll do fairly well in the next election.* 彼らは次の選挙でかなり成功するだろうと思い切って言いたい.

haz|ard|ous /hæzərdəs/ ADJ 形容詞 Something that is **hazardous** is dangerous, especially to people's health or safety. 危ない □ *They have no way to dispose of the hazardous waste they produce.* 彼らには生みだす有害廃棄物を処分する方法がない.

haze /heɪz/ (**hazes**) **1** N-VAR 可変性名詞 **Haze** is light mist, caused by particles of water or dust in the air, which prevents you from seeing distant objects clearly. Haze often forms in hot weather. もや □ *They vanished into the haze near the horizon.* 彼らは水平線近くのもやの中に消えた. **2** N-SING 単数名詞 If there is a **haze** of something such as smoke or steam, you cannot see clearly through it. もうろう [LITERARY 文語的] □ *Dan smiled at him through a haze of smoke and steaming coffee.* ダンはもうろうとしたタバコの煙とコーヒーの蒸気越しに微笑んだ.

ha|zel /heɪzᵊl/ (**hazels**) **1** N-VAR 可変性名詞 A **hazel** is a small tree which produces nuts that you can eat. ハシバミ **2** COLOR 色彩語 **Hazel** eyes are greenish brown in color. ハシバミ色の目は緑がかった茶色のことだ.

hazy /heɪzi/ (**hazier, haziest**) **1** ADJ 形容詞 **Hazy** weather conditions are those in which things are difficult to see, because of light mist, hot air, or dust. かすんだ □ *The air was thin and crisp, filled with hazy sunshine and frost.* 弱々しい太陽と霜で, 空気は希薄でひんやりしていた. **2** ADJ 形容詞 If you are **hazy about** ideas or details, or if they are **hazy**, you are uncertain or confused about them. はっきりしない □ *I'm a bit hazy about that.* 私はそれについてはよく分からない. **3** ADJ 形容詞 If things seem **hazy**, you cannot see things clearly, for example because you are feeling ill. ぼんやりした □ *My vision has grown so hazy.* 私の視力はひどく衰えた.

he /hi, STRONG hi/

He is a third person singular pronoun. **He** is used as the subject of a verb.

He は3人称単数の代名詞である. **He** は動詞の主語として用いられる.

1 PRON-SING 単数代名詞 You use **he** to refer to a man, boy, or male animal. 彼は □ *He could never quite remember all our names.* 彼は私達全員の名前をどうしても覚えられなかった. **2** PRON-SING 単数代名詞 In written English, **he** is sometimes used to refer to a person without saying whether that person is a man or a woman. Some people dislike this use and prefer to use "he or she" or "they." その人 □ *The teacher should encourage the child to proceed as far as he can, and when he is stuck, ask for help.* 教師は子供ができる所まで学習を進め, 行き詰った時に援助を求めることを奨励するべきだ.

---

head
❶ NOUN AND ADVERB USES
❷ VERB USES
❸ PHRASES

❶ head /hɛd/ (**heads**) **1** N-COUNT 可算名詞 Your **head** is the top part of your body, which has your eyes, mouth, and brain in it. 頭 □ *She turned her head away from him.* 彼女は彼と反対方向に頭を向けた. **2** N-COUNT 可算名詞 You can use **head** to refer to your mind and your mental abilities. 頭脳 □ *...an exceptional analyst who could do complex math in his head.* 暗算で複雑な計算ができる抜群のアナリスト **3** N-SING 単数名詞 The **head** of a line of people or vehicles is the front of it, or the first person or vehicle in the line. 先頭 □ *He made his way to the head of the line.* 彼は最前列に進んだ. **4** N-COUNT 可算名詞 The **head** of a company or organization is the person in charge of it and in charge of the people in it. 長 □ *Heads of government from more than 100 countries gather in Geneva tomorrow.* 100か国以上の国のリーダーが明日ジュネーブに集まる. **5** N-COUNT 可算名詞 The **head** of something long and thin is the end which is wider than or a different shape from the rest, and which is often considered to be the most important part. 上部 □ *There should be no exposed screw heads.* ねじ頭がむき出しになってはならない. **6** ADV 副詞 If you flip a coin and it comes down **heads**, you can see the side of the coin which has a picture of a head on it. 表 □ *"We might flip a coin for it," suggested Ted. "If it's heads, then we'll talk."* 「硬貨を投げて表が上だったら話そう」とテッドは提案した. → see **body, engine**

❷ head /hɛd/ (**heads, heading, headed**) **1** V-T 他動詞 If someone or something **heads** a line or procession, they are at the front of it. 先頭に立つ □ *The parson, heading the procession, had just turned right toward the churchyard.* 行列の先頭に立つ牧師はちょうど教会の構内の方向に右折したところだった. **2** V-T 他動詞 If something **heads** a list or group, it is at the top of it. 最高位を占める □ *Running a business heads the list of ambitions among the 1,000 people interviewed by Good Housekeeping magazine.* グッドハウスキーピング誌が野望について1000名の読者にアンケート調査を実施したところ, 事業経営がトップを占めた. **3** V-T 他動詞 If you **head** a department, company, or organization, you are the person in charge of it. 率いる □ *...Michael Williams, who heads the department's Office of Civil Rights.* 市民権局の局長を務めるマイケル・ウィリアムズ **4** V-T/V-I 他動詞/自動詞 If you **are heading** or **are headed** for a particular place, you are going toward that place. 向かう □ *He was headed for the bus stop.* 彼はバス停に向かっていた. □ *It is not clear how many of them will be heading back to Saudi Arabia tomorrow.* 彼らのうち何人がサウ

ジアラビアに戻るのかは明らかでない。 **5** V-T/V-I 他動詞/自動詞 If something or someone **is heading for** or **is headed for** a particular result, the situation they are in is developing in a way that makes that result very likely. 進んでいる ❑ *The latest talks aimed at ending the civil war appear to be heading for deadlock.* 内戦を終結させるための最近の話合いは行き詰まりそうだ。 **6** V-T 他動詞 If a piece of writing **is headed** a particular title, it has that title written at the beginning of it. 見出しのある [usu passive] ❑ *One chapter is headed, "Beating the Test."* 1つの章は「試験を打ち負かすこと」という見出しだ。 **7** V-T 他動詞 If you **head** a ball in soccer, you hit it with your head in order to make it go in a particular direction. ヘディングする ❑ *He headed the ball across the face of the goal.* 彼はゴール正面を横切ってボールにヘディングした。 **8** → see also **heading**

Thesaurus head また次を参照:

N.	brain, mind ❶ **2**
	beginning, front ❶ **3**
	director, leader ❶ **4**
V.	lead ❷ **1**
	command, control, govern, manage ❷ **3**

❸ **head** /hɛd/ (**heads**) **1** PHRASE 句 You use **a head** or **per head** after stating a cost or amount in order to indicate that that cost or amount is for each person in a particular group. 1人前 ❑ *This simple chicken dish costs less than $3 a head.* このシンプルなチキン料理は1人前3ドル以下だ。 **2** PHRASE 句 If you a have **a head for** something, you can deal with it easily. For example, if you have **a head for** figures, you can do arithmetic easily, and if you have **a head for** heights, you can climb to a great height without feeling afraid. 才能 ❑ *I don't have a head for business.* 私には事業の才はない。 **3** PHRASE 句 If you **get** a fact or idea **into your head**, you suddenly realize or think that it is true and you usually do not change your opinion about it. 思い込む ❑ *Once they get an idea into their heads, they never give up.* 彼らは一旦思い込むと絶対にあきらめない。 **4** PHRASE 句 If you say that someone has **got** or **gotten** something **into** their **head**, you mean that they have finally understood or accepted it, and you are usually criticizing them because it has taken them a long time to do this. 理解する ❑ *Managers have at last got it into their heads that they can no longer rest content with inefficient operations.* マネジャーたちは非効率的な操業に満足していられないことをようやく理解した。 **5** PHRASE 句 If alcoholic drink **goes to** your **head**, it makes you feel drunk. 酔わせる ❑ *That wine was strong, it went to your head.* あのワインは強くて酔っ払った。 **6** PHRASE 句 If you say that something such as praise or success **goes to** someone's **head**, you are criticizing them because you think that it makes them too proud or confident. のぼせ上がる [DISAPPROVAL 不賛成] ❑ *Ford is definitely not a man to let a little success go to his head.* フォードはちょっとした成功でのぼせ上がるような男では絶対にない。 **7** PHRASE 句 If you are **head over heels** or **head over heels in love**, you are very much in love. すっかり ❑ *I was very attracted to men and fell head over heels many times.* 私は男性に大変魅力を感じ、何度も夢中になったことがある。 **8** PHRASE 句 If you **keep** your **head**, you remain calm in a difficult situation. If you **lose** your **head**, you panic or do not remain calm in a difficult situation. 冷静さを失わない、気が動転する ❑ *She was able to keep her head and not panic.* 彼女は冷静さを失わずにいられた。 **9** PHRASE 句 Phrases such as **laugh** your **head off** and **scream** your **head off** can be used to emphasize that someone is laughing or screaming a lot or very loudly. [EMPHASIS 強調] ❑ *He carried on telling a joke, laughing his head off.* 彼は大笑いしながら冗談を言い続けた。 **10** PHRASE 句 If something such as an idea, joke, or comment goes **over** someone's **head**, it is too difficult for them to understand. 理解力を超えた ❑ *I admit that a lot of the ideas went way over my head.* 多くの発想を私は全く理解できなかったことを認める。 **11** PHRASE 句 If someone does something **over** another person's **head**, they do it without asking them or discussing it with them, especially when they should do so because the other person is in a position of authority. さしおいて ❑ *He was reprimanded for trying to go over the heads of senior officers.* 彼は上級役人を通り越そうとしたことで懲戒処分を受けた。 **12** PHRASE 句 If you say that something unpleasant or embarrassing **rears its ugly head** or **raises its ugly head**, you mean that it occurs, often after not occurring for some time. 頭をもたげる ❑ *There was a problem which reared its ugly head about a week after she moved back in.* 戻ってきてから約1週間後に問題が持ち上がった。 **13** PHRASE 句 If you **stand on** your **head**, you balance upside down with the top of your head and your hands on the ground. 逆立ちする ❑ *He was photographed standing on his head doing yoga.* 彼は逆さ姿でヨガをするところを写真に撮られた。 **14** PHRASE 句 If you say that you cannot **make head nor tail of** something or you cannot **make heads or tails of** it, you are emphasizing that you cannot understand it at all. 理解する [INFORMAL くだけた] ❑ *I couldn't make head nor tail of the damn film.* わたしにはその映画が理解できなかった。 **15** PHRASE 句 If somebody **takes it into** their **head to** do something, especially

something strange or foolish, they suddenly decide to do it. 思いつく ❑ *He suddenly took it into his head to go out to Australia to stay with his son.* 彼は突然息子に会いにオーストラリアに行くことを思いついた。 **16** PHRASE 句 If a problem or disagreement **comes to a head** or **is brought to a head**, it becomes so bad that something must be done about it. 危機に陥る ❑ *These problems came to a head in September when five of the station's journalists were fired.* こうした問題は9月に放送局のジャーナリスト5名が解雇された時、危機に陥った。 **17** PHRASE 句 If two or more people **put** their **heads together**, they talk about a problem they have and try to solve it. 互いの知恵を出し合う ❑ *So everyone put their heads together and eventually an amicable arrangement was reached.* それで全員が知恵を出し合い、最後に友好的な解決策に達した。 **18** PHRASE 句 If you **keep** your **head above water**, you just avoid getting into difficulties; used especially to talk about business. 破産せずにいる ❑ *We are keeping our head above water, but our cash flow position is not too good.* 我々は破産せずにいるが、キャッシュフローは好ましくない。 **19** PHRASE 句 If you say that **heads will roll** as a result of something bad that has happened, you mean that people will be punished for it, especially by losing their jobs. 首切りが行なわれる ❑ *The group's problems have led to speculation that heads will roll.* そのグループの問題は首切りが行なわれるという推測につながった。

> **Head** is used in a large number of expressions which are explained under other words in the dictionary. For example, the expression "off the top of your head" is explained at "top."

head|ache /hɛdeɪk/ (**headaches**) **1** N-COUNT 可算名詞 If you have **a headache**, you have a pain in your head. 頭痛 ❑ *I have had a terrible headache for the last two days.* わたしはこの2日間ひどい頭痛に悩まされた。 **2** N-COUNT 可算名詞 If you say that something is a **headache**, you mean that it causes you difficulty or worry. 頭痛の種 ❑ *The airline's biggest headache is the increase in the price of aviation fuel.* 航空会社が抱える最大の問題は航空燃料価格の上昇である。

head count (**head counts**) N-COUNT 可算名詞 If you do a **head count**, you count the number of people present. You can also use **head count** to talk about the number of people that are present at an event, or that an organization employs. 人数調べ ❑ *The troops rushed back onto the chopper and took off - but a head count showed one man was missing.* 軍隊はヘリコプターに急いで戻り離陸したが、人数調べによると1人足りなかった。

head|er /hɛdər/ (**headers**) N-COUNT 可算名詞 A **header** is text such as a name or a page number that can be automatically displayed at the top of each page of a printed document. Compare **footer**. ヘッダー [COMPUTING コンピューティング] ❑ *page formatting like headers, footers, and page numbers.* ヘッダー、フッター、ページ番号などのページフォーマット

head|hunt /hɛdhʌnt/ (**headhunts, headhunting, headhunted**) V-T 他動詞 If someone who works for a particular company **is headhunted**, they leave that company because another company has approached them and offered them another job with better pay and higher status. 引き抜く ❑ *He was headhunted by Barkers last October to build an advertising team.* 彼は広告チーム構築のために昨年10月、バーカーズに引き抜かれた。

head|hunter /hɛdhʌntər/ (**headhunters**) N-COUNT 可算名詞 A **headhunter** is a person who tries to persuade someone to leave their job and take another job which has better pay and more status. ヘッドハンター ❑ *...a headhunter for a bank.* 銀行のヘッドハンター

head|ing /hɛdɪŋ/ (**headings**) **1** N-COUNT 可算名詞 A **heading** is the title of a piece of writing, which is written or printed at the top of the page. 見出し ❑ *...helpful chapter headings.* 役に立つ章の見出し **2** → see also **head**

head|light /hɛdlaɪt/ (**headlights**) N-COUNT 可算名詞 A vehicle's **headlights** are the large powerful lights at the front. ヘッドライト ❑ *Motorists were forced to turn on their headlights at midday.* 自家用車の運転手は真昼にヘッドライトをつけることを余儀なくされた。

head|line /hɛdlaɪn/ (**headlines, headlining, headlined**) **1** N-COUNT 可算名詞 A **headline** is the title of a newspaper story, printed in large letters at the top of the story, especially on the front page. 大見出し ❑ *The Sydney Morning Herald carried the headline: "Sorry Ma'am, Most Australians Want a Republic."* シドニー・モーニング・ヘラルド誌には「オーストラリア人の大半は共和国を望む」という大見出しが載った。 **2** N-PLURAL 複数名詞 The **headlines** are the main points of the news which are read on radio or television. 主な項目 ❑ *I'm Claudia Polley with the news headlines.* ニュースの主な項目を担当するクローディア・ポリーです。 **3** V-T 他動詞 If a newspaper or magazine article **is headlined** a particular thing, that is the headline that introduces it. 見出しをつける [usu passive] ❑ *The article was headlined "Tell us the truth."* その記事には「我々は真実を求めている」との見出しがついていた。 **4** PHRASE 句 Someone or something that **hits the headlines** or **grabs the headlines** gets a lot of publicity from the media. 重大ニュースに

なる ❑ *El Salvador first hit the world headlines at the beginning of the 1980s.* エルサルバドルはまず1980年代初期に世界中の重大ニュースになった.

head|long /hɛdlɒŋ/ **1** ADV 副詞 If you move **headlong** in a particular direction, you move there very quickly. 迅速に [ADV after v] ❑ *He ran headlong for the open door.* 彼は開いたドアの方向に一目散で走った. **2** ADV 副詞 If you fall or move **headlong**, you fall or move with your head furthest forward. 真っ逆さまに [ADV after v] ❑ *She missed her footing and fell headlong down the stairs.* 彼女は足場を失い, 階段をまっさかさまに落ちた. **3** ADV 副詞 If you rush **headlong into** something, you do it quickly without thinking carefully about it. 向こう見ずに [ADV after v] ❑ *Do not leap headlong into decisions.* 性急に物事を決定してはいけない. ● ADJ 形容詞 **Headlong** is also an adjective. 大急ぎの [ADJ n] ❑ *...the headlong rush to independence.* 独立への慌しい活動

head of state (**heads of state**) N-COUNT 可算名詞 A **head of state** is the leader of a country, for example a president, king, or queen. 国家元首 ❑ *The Algerian authorities have still not named a new head of state.* アルジェリア当局はまだ新しい国家元首を指名していない.

head-on **1** ADV 副詞 If two vehicles hit each other **head-on**, they hit each other with their fronts pointing toward each other. 正面から [ADV after v] ❑ *The car collided head-on with a van.* その車は大型バンと正面衝突した. ● ADJ 形容詞 **Head-on** is also an adjective. 正面衝突の [ADJ n] ❑ *Their car was in a head-on collision with a truck.* 彼らの車はトラックと正面衝突した. **2** ADJ 形容詞 A **head-on** conflict or approach is direct, without any attempt to compromise or avoid the issue. 真っ向からの [ADJ n] ❑ *The only victors in a head-on clash between the president and the assembly would be the hardliners on both sides.* 大統領と議会間の真っ向からの対決で勝つのは双方の強硬派だけだろう. ● ADV 副詞 **Head-on** is also an adverb. 真っ向から [ADV after v] ❑ *Once again, I chose to confront the issue head-on.* 今回も私はその問題に真っ向から立ち向かうことに決めた.

head|phones /hɛdfoʊnz/ N-PLURAL 複数名詞 **Headphones** are a pair of padded speakers which you wear over your ears in order to listen to a radio, CD player, or tape recorder without other people hearing it. ヘッドフォン [also 'a pair of' N] ❑ *...while out cycling one evening and listening to your program on headphones.* ある夜, 君のプログラムをヘッドフォンで聞きながら自転車を乗り回していたとき

head|quarters /hɛdkwɔrtərz/ N-SING-COLL 集合的単数名詞 The **headquarters** of an organization are its main offices. 本部 ❑ *...fraud squad officers from Chicago's police headquarters.* シカゴ警察本部からの偽特捜班警官

head|rest /hɛdrɛst/ (**headrests**) N-COUNT 可算名詞 A **headrest** is the part of the back of a seat on which you can lean your head, especially one on the front seat of a car. ヘッドレスト

head|set /hɛdsɛt/ (**headsets**) **1** N-COUNT 可算名詞 A **headset** is a small pair of headphones that you can use for listening to a radio or recorded music, or for using a telephone. ヘッドセット ❑ *During the race Mr. Taylor talks to the driver using a headset.* レースの間, タイラー氏はヘッドセットでドライバーと会話する. **2** N-COUNT 可算名詞 A **headset** is a piece of equipment that you wear on your head so you can see computer images or images from a camera in front of your eyes. ヘッドセット ❑ *Soon the wearer of a virtual reality headset will be able to be "present" at sporting or theatrical events staged thousands of miles away.* もうすぐ, バーチャルリアリティヘッドセットを着用すると, 何千マイルも離れた場所で行われるスポーツや演劇イベントに居合せることができるようになるだろう.

head start (**head starts**) N-COUNT 可算名詞 If you have a **head start** on other people, you have an advantage over them in something such as a competition or race. 先手 ❑ *A good education gives your child a head start in life.* 子供は優れた教育を受けることにより人生を幸先よくスタートできる.

head|strong /hɛdstrɒŋ/ ADJ 形容詞 If you refer to someone as **headstrong**, you are slightly critical of the fact that they are determined to do what they want. 頑固な ❑ *He's young, very headstrong, but he's a good man underneath.* 彼は若く, 非常に強情だが, 根はよい男だ.

head|way /hɛdweɪ/ PHRASE 句 If you **make headway**, you progress toward achieving something. 進捗する ❑ *There was concern in the city that police were making little headway in the investigation.* 町では, 警察の捜査がほとんど進んでいないことが懸念されていた.

heady /hɛdi/ (**headier, headiest**) ADJ 形容詞 A **heady** drink, atmosphere, or experience strongly affects your senses, for example, by making you feel drunk or excited. 陶酔させる ❑ *...in the heady days just after their marriage.* 結婚直後の陶酔の日々

heal /hil/ (**heals, healing, healed**) **1** V-T/V-I 他動詞/自動詞 When a broken bone or other injury **heals**, or if someone or something **heals** it, it becomes healthy and normal again. いやす [他動詞] いえる [自動詞] ❑ *Within six weeks the bruising had gone,*

but it was six months before it all healed. 6週間の間に傷はなくなったが, すべてがいえるのには6ヶ月かかった. **2** V-T/V-I 他動詞/自動詞 If you **heal** something such as a rift or a wound, or if it **heals**, the situation is put right so that people are friendly or happy again. 和解させる [他動詞] 回復する [自動詞] ❑ *We have begun to heal the wounds of war in our society.* 我々は社会が受けた戦争の傷の回復にとりかかった.

heal|er /hilər/ (**healers**) N-COUNT 可算名詞 A **healer** is a person who heals people, especially a person who heals through prayer and religious faith. 治療者

health /hɛlθ/ **1** N-UNCOUNT 不可算名詞 A person's **health** is the condition of their body and the extent to which it is free from illness or is able to resist illness. 健康状態 ❑ *Tea contains caffeine. It's bad for your health.* お茶にはカフェインが含まれている. これは健康に悪い. **2** N-UNCOUNT 不可算名詞 **Health** is a state in which a person is not suffering from any illness and is feeling well. 健康 ❑ *In the hospital they nursed me back to health.* 病院で彼らは私を看病し, 元の健全な体に戻してくれた. **3** N-UNCOUNT 不可算名詞 The **health** of something such as an organization or a system is its success and the fact that it is working well. 健全 ❑ *There's no way to predict the future health of the banking industry.* 銀行業界の将来的な安寧を予測することはできない.

healthy /hɛlθi/ (**healthier, healthiest**) **1** ADJ 形容詞 Someone who is **healthy** is well and is not suffering from any illness. 健康な ❑ *Most of us need to lead more balanced lives to be healthy and happy.* 私たちのほとんどはよりバランスのとれた生活をして, 健康を増進し, 幸せになる必要がある. ● **health|ily** /hɛlθɪli/ ADV 副詞 健康で ❑ *What I really want is to live healthily for as long as possible.* 私が真に欲することは, できるだけ長く健康に生きることだ. **2** ADJ 形容詞 Something that is **healthy** is good for your health. 健康によい ❑ *...a healthy diet.* 健康食 **3** ADJ 形容詞 A **healthy** organization or system is successful. 健全な ❑ *...an economically healthy socialist state.* 経済的に健全な社会主義国 **4** ADJ 形容詞 A **healthy** amount of something is a large amount that shows success. 大量の ❑ *He predicts a continuation of healthy profits in the current financial year.* 彼は現会計年度にはかなりの収益が継続すると予想している. **5** ADJ 形容詞 If you have a **healthy** attitude about something, you show good sense. 健全な ❑ *She has a refreshingly healthy attitude to work.* 彼女は仕事に対し, 爽快なまでに健全な姿勢を保持している.

Thesaurus	*healthy* また次を参照:
ADJ.	fit, lively **1**
	beneficial, nourishing **2**

Word Partnership	*healthy* は次の語句と使われる:
N.	healthy **baby**, healthy **glow**, healthy **skin** **1**
	healthy **appetite**, healthy **diet/food**, healthy **lifestyle** **2**
	healthy **attitude about** *something* **5**

heap /hip/ (**heaps, heaping, heaped**) **1** N-COUNT 可算名詞 A **heap** of things is a pile of them, especially a pile arranged in a rather messy way. 積み重なったもの ❑ *...a heap of bricks.* れんがの山

A **heap** of things is usually untidy, and often has the shape of a hill or mound. ❑ *Now, the house is a heap of rubble.* A **stack** is usually tidy, and often consists of flat objects placed directly on top of each other. ❑ *...a neat stack of dishes.* A **pile** of things can be tidy or untidy. ❑ *...a neat pile of clothes.*

2 V-T 他動詞 If you **heap** things in a pile, you arrange them in a large pile. 積み上げる ❑ *Mrs. Madrigal heaped more carrots onto Michael's plate.* マドリガル夫人がマイケルの皿にさらなる人参を山盛りにした. ● PHRASAL VERB 句動詞 **Heap up** means the same as **heap**. 積み上げる ❑ *Off to one side, the militia was heaping up wood for a bonfire.* 向こうでは, 市民軍がたき木用の木材を積み上げていた. **3** V-T 他動詞 If you **heap** praise or criticism **on** someone or something, you give them a lot of praise or criticism. ふんだんに与える [他動詞] ❑ *The head of the navy heaped scorn on both the methods and motives of the conspirators.* 海軍の長は方法と動機の両方を大いにあざ笑った. **4** QUANT 数量詞 **Heaps of** something or a **heap of** something is a large quantity of it. たくさん [INFORMAL くだけた] ❑ *You have heaps of time.* 時間はたっぷりある.

hear /hɪər/ (**hears, hearing, heard** /hɜrd/) **1** V-T/V-I 他動詞/自動詞 When you **hear** a sound, you become aware of it through your ears. 聞く [他動詞・自動詞] ❑ *She heard no further sounds.* 彼女はそれ以上何も聞かなかった. ❑ *They heard the protesters shout: "No more fascism!"* 彼らは「ファシズム撲滅」と抗議者が叫ぶのを聞いた. ❑ *He doesn't hear very well.* 彼は聴力が弱い. **2** V-T 他動詞 If you **hear** something such as a lecture or a piece of music, you listen to it. 耳を傾ける [他動詞] ❑ *You can hear commentary on the game at halftime.* ハーフタイムに試合の解説を聴くことができる. ❑ *I don't think you've ever heard Doris talking about her emotional life before.* ドリスが恋愛面について話しているのをあなたがかつて聴いたことはない

と思う。 ③ V-T 他動詞 When a judge or a court of law **hears** a case, or evidence in a case, they listen to it officially in order to make a decision about it. 審理する [FORMAL 形式ばった] [他動詞] ❑The jury has heard evidence from defense witnesses. 陪審は弁護側証人による証言を審理した。 ④ V-I 自動詞 If you **hear from** someone, you receive a letter or telephone call from them. 便りをもらう [自動詞] ❑Drop us a line, it's always great to hear from you. 一筆お便りください。あなたからのお便りをいつも楽しみにしています。 ⑤ V-T/V-I 他動詞/自動詞 If you **hear** some news or information about something, you find out about it by someone telling you, or from the radio or television. 聞き知る [他動詞] 伝え聞く [他動詞] ❑My mother heard of this school through Leslie. 母はこの学校のことをレスリーから聞いた. ❑He had heard that the trophy had been sold. 彼はそのトロフィーが売却されたことを聞いた。 ⑥ V-I 自動詞 If you **have heard of** something or someone, you know about them, but not in great detail. 耳にする [no cont] [自動詞] ❑Many people haven't heard of reflexology. 多くの人はリフレクソロジーの名にしたことがない。

Do not confuse **hear** and **listen**. You use **hear** to talk about sounds that you are aware of because they reach your ears. You often use **can** with **hear**. ❑I can hear him yelling and swearing. If you want to say that someone is paying attention to something they can hear, you say that they **are listening to** it. ❑He turned on the radio and listened to the news. Note that **listen** is not followed directly by an object. You must always say that you listen **to** something. However, **listen** can also be used on its own without an object. ❑I was laughing too much to listen.

---

⑦ PHRASE 句 If you say that you **have heard** something **before**, you mean that you are not interested in it, or do not believe it, or are not surprised about it, because you already know about it or have experienced it. 聞き飽きている、そうだろう ❑Frank shrugs wearily. He has heard it all before. フランクはうんざりして肩をすくめた。すべて聞き飽きたことだったのだ. ⑧ PHRASE 句 If you say that you **can't hear yourself think**, you are complaining and emphasizing that there is a lot of noise, and that it is disturbing you or preventing you from doing something. じっくり考えられない [INFORMAL くだけた, EMPHASIS 強調] ❑...those noisy late-night clubs where you can't even hear yourself think. 物を考えることさえできないうるさい深夜クラブ ⑨ PHRASE 句 If you say that you **won't hear** of someone doing something, you mean that you refuse to let them do it. 容認しない ❑I've always wanted to be an actor but Dad wouldn't hear of it. 私は常に役者になりたいと思っていたが、父が聞き入れてくれなかった.

Thesaurus hear また次を参照：

v.	listen ⑤
	detect, pick up ⑤

hear|ing /hɪərɪŋ/ (hearings) ① N-UNCOUNT 不可算名詞 A person's or animal's **hearing** is the sense which makes it possible for them to be aware of sounds. 聴力 ❑His mind still seemed clear and his hearing was excellent. 彼の知力はまだ明晰のようで、聴力も優れていた。 ② N-COUNT 可算名詞 A **hearing** is an official meeting which is held in order to collect facts about an incident or problem. 聴聞会 ❑After more than two hours of pandemonium, the judge adjourned the hearing until next Tuesday. 2時間以上もの大混乱のあと、裁判官は来週の火曜日まで尋問を延期した。 ③ PHRASE 句 If someone gives you a **fair hearing** or a **hearing**, they listen to you when you give your opinion about something. 話を公平に聞いてやる ❑Weber gave a fair hearing to anyone who held a different opinion. ウェーバーは、意見の異なるすべての人の話を公平に聞いた。 ④ PHRASE 句 If someone says something in your **hearing** or within your **hearing**, you can hear what they say because they are with you or near you. 聞こえるところで ❑No one spoke disparagingly of her father in her hearing. 彼女に聞こえる所では誰も彼女の父を軽蔑するような話はしなかった。
→ see **disability**

Word Partnership hearing は次の語句と使われる：

N.	hearing **impairment/loss** ①
	court hearing ②
V.	**hold a** hearing, **testify at/before a** hearing ②

---

heart
❶ NOUN USES
❷ PHRASES

❶ **heart** /hɑrt/ (hearts) ① N-COUNT 可算名詞 Your **heart** is the organ in your chest that pumps the blood around your body. People also use **heart** to refer to the area of their chest that is closest to their heart. 心臓、胸 ❑The bullet had passed less than an inch from Andrea's heart. 銃弾はアンドレアの心臓から1インチ未満のところを貫通した。 ② N-COUNT 可算名詞 You can refer to

someone's **heart** when you are talking about their deep feelings and beliefs. 感情、心 [LITERARY 文語的] ❑Alik's words filled her heart with pride. アリクの言葉は彼女の心を自尊心で満たした。 ③ N-VAR 可変性名詞 You use **heart** when you are talking about someone's character and attitude toward other people, especially when they are kind and generous. 心情 [APPROVAL 賛成] ❑She loved his brilliance and his generous heart. 彼女は彼の優れた才気とおおらかな心を愛した。 ④ N-SING 単数名詞 The **heart of** something is the most central and important part of it. 核心 ❑The heart of the problem is supply and demand. 問題の核心は供給と需要だ。 ⑤ N-SING 単数名詞 The **heart of** a place is its center. 中心 ❑...a busy dentists' practice in the heart of the city. 都心における多忙な歯科医の業務 ⑥ N-COUNT 可算名詞 A **heart** is a shape that is used as a symbol of love: ♡. ハート ❑...heart-shaped chocolates. ハート形のチョコレート ⑦ N-UNCOUNT-COLL 集合的不可算名詞 **Hearts** is one of the four suits in a deck of playing cards. Each card in the suit is marked with one or more symbols in the shape of a heart. ハート ● N-COUNT 可算名詞 A **heart** is a playing card of this suit. ハートの札 ❑West had to decide whether to play a heart. ウェストはハートを出すかどうかを決めなければならなかった。
→ see **donor**

❷ **heart** /hɑrt/ (hearts) ① PHRASE 句 If you feel or believe something **with all** your **heart**, you feel or believe it very strongly. 真心こめて [EMPHASIS 強調] ❑My own family I loved with all my heart. 私は家族を心から愛していた。 ② PHRASE 句 If you say that someone is a particular kind of person **at heart**, you mean that that is what they are really like, even though they may seem very different. 心底は ❑He was a very gentle boy at heart. 彼は心根はとても優しい少年だった。 ③ PHRASE 句 If you say that someone has your interests or your welfare **at heart**, you mean that they are concerned about you and that is why they are doing something. 気にかけて ❑She told him she only had his interests at heart. 彼女は、彼の利益しか気にかけていなかったと彼に言った。 ④ PHRASE 句 If someone **breaks** your **heart**, they make you very sad and unhappy, usually because they end a love affair or close relationship with you. 悲嘆にくれさせる [LITERARY 文語的] ❑I fell in love on vacation but the girl broke my heart. 僕は休暇中に恋に落ちたが、その少女は私に胸の張り裂ける思いをさせた。 ⑤ PHRASE 句 If something **breaks** your **heart**, it makes you feel very sad and depressed, especially because people are suffering but you can do nothing to help them. 悲嘆にくれさせる ❑It really breaks my heart to see them this way. 彼らにこのような状態で会うのは本当につらい. ⑥ PHRASE 句 If you know something such as a poem **by heart**, you have learned it so well that you can remember it without having to read it. 暗記して ❑Mack knew this passage by heart. マックはこの一節をそらで覚えていた。 ⑦ PHRASE 句 If someone has a **change of heart**, their attitude toward something changes. 心変わり ❑Several brokers have had a change of heart about prospects for the company. ブローカーには、その企業の見通しについて翻意を示したものもある。 ⑧ PHRASE 句 If something such as a subject or project is **close to** your **heart** or **near to** your **heart**, it is very important to you and you are very interested in it and concerned about it. 大事な ❑This is a subject very close to my heart. これは私にとって最も大事なテーマだ. ⑨ PHRASE 句 If you can do something **to** your **heart's content**, you can do it as much as you want. 存分に ❑I was delighted to be able to eat my favorite dishes to my heart's content. 心ゆくまで好物を食べられて大変うれしかった。 ⑩ CONVENTION 慣習表現 You can say **"cross my heart"** when you want someone to believe that you are telling the truth. You can also ask **"cross your heart?"** when you are asking someone if they are really telling the truth. 誓って言う [SPOKEN 口語] ❑And I won't tell any of the other girls anything you tell me about it. I promise, cross my heart. それに関して君が私に話すことは他の女の子たちの誰にも言わないよ。誓って約束するよ。 ⑪ PHRASE 句 If you say something **from the heart** or **from the bottom of** your **heart**, you sincerely mean what you say. 心の底から ❑He spoke with confidence, from the heart. 彼は、心の底から、自信を持って話した。 ⑫ PHRASE 句 If you want to do something but do **not have the heart to** do it, you do not do it because you know it will make someone unhappy or disappointed. するに忍びない ❑We knew all along but didn't have the heart to tell her. 私たちは最初から知っていたが、彼女に伝える勇気を持ち合わせていなかった。 ⑬ PHRASE 句 If you believe or know something **in** your **heart of hearts**, that is what you really believe or think, even though it may sometimes seem that you do not. 心の奥底で ❑I know in my heart of hearts that I am the right man for that mission. 私はその任務に適任なのは私であるとひそかに思っていた。 ⑭ PHRASE 句 If your **heart isn't in** the thing you are doing, you have very little enthusiasm for it, usually because you are depressed or are thinking about something else. 熱中できない ❑I tried to learn some lines but my heart wasn't really in it. 何行かを覚えようとしたが、とても集中できなかった。 ⑮ PHRASE 句 If you **lose heart**, you become sad and depressed and are no longer interested in something, especially because it is not progressing as you would like. 意気消沈する ❑He appealed to his countrymen not to lose heart. 彼は同胞に弱気になってはだめだと訴えた。 ⑯ PHRASE 句 If your **heart is in** your **mouth**, you feel very excited, worried,

or frightened. びっくりしている ❑My heart was in my mouth when I walked into her office. 私は彼のオフィスに入っていきょうてんした.

17 PHRASE 句 If you **open** your **heart** or **pour out** your **heart** to someone, you tell them your most private thoughts and feelings. 本心を明かす，心を開く ❑She opened her heart to millions yesterday and told how she came close to suicide. 昨日彼女は何百万もの人に本心を明かし，どうして自殺しそうになったかを説明した. **18** PHRASE 句 If you say that someone's **heart is in the right place**, you mean that they are kind, considerate, and generous, although you may disapprove of other aspects of their character. 人が根が親切だ ❑He's rich, handsome, funny, and his heart is in the right place. 彼はお金持ちで，ハンサムで，ユーモアがあり，根が優しい. **19** PHRASE 句 If you have **set** your **heart on** something, you want it very much or want to do it very much. 欲しがる ❑He had always set his heart on a career in the fine arts. 彼は常に芸術関連の仕事に就きたがっていた. **20** PHRASE 句 If you **take heart from** something, you are encouraged and made to feel optimistic by it. 勇気づけられる ❑Investors and dealers also took heart from the better than expected industrial production figures. 投資家とディーラーも期待より高い工業産業値に勇気づけられた. **21** PHRASE 句 If you **take** something **to heart**, for example someone's behavior, you are deeply affected and upset by it. 心に留める ❑If someone says something critical I take it to heart. 誰かに批判的なことを言われると，私はそれを深刻に受け止めてしまう.

heart|ache /hɑrteɪk/ (**heartaches**) N-VAR 可変性名詞 **Heartache** is very great sadness and emotional suffering. 心痛 ❑...after suffering the heartache of her divorce from her first husband. 最初の夫との離婚で悲嘆にくれたあと

heart at|tack (**heart attacks**) N-COUNT 可算名詞 If someone has a **heart attack**, their heart begins to beat very irregularly or stops completely. 心臓発作 ❑He died of a heart attack brought on by overwork. 彼は過労による心臓発作で死んだ.

heart|beat /hɑrtbit/ (**heartbeats**) N-SING 単数名詞 Your **heartbeat** is the regular movement of your heart as it pumps blood around your body. 鼓動 ❑Your baby's heartbeat will be monitored continuously. あなたの赤ちゃんの鼓動は継続的にモニターされます.

heart|break /hɑrtbreɪk/ (**heartbreaks**) N-VAR 可変性名詞 **Heartbreak** is very great sadness and emotional suffering, especially after the end of a love affair or close relationship. 悲嘆 ❑...suffering and heartbreak for those close to the victims. 被害者と親しい人の苦痛と悲嘆

heart|breaking /hɑrtbreɪkɪŋ/ ADJ 形容詞 Something that is **heartbreaking** makes you feel extremely sad and upset. 断腸の思いをさせる ❑This year we won't even be able to buy presents for our grandchildren. It's heartbreaking. 今年，私たちは孫にプレゼントを買うことさえできない，なんてつらいことだろう.

heart|broken /hɑrtbroʊkən/ ADJ 形容詞 Someone who is **heartbroken** is very sad and emotionally upset. 悲嘆にくれた ❑Was your daddy heartbroken when they got a divorce? 君のお父さんは離婚したとき悲嘆にくれていたかい.

heart|en /hɑrtən/ (**heartens, heartening, heartened**) V-T 他動詞 If someone **is heartened by** something, it encourages them and makes them cheerful. 元気づける [他動詞] ❑The news heartened everybody. そのニュースは誰をも勇気づけた. ●**heart|ened** ADJ 形容詞 [v-link ADJ] 励まされた ❑I feel heartened by her progress. 私は彼女の進歩に励まされた気がする. ●**heart|en|ing** ADJ 形容詞 励みになる ❑This is heartening news. これは励みになるニュースだ.

heart fail|ure N-UNCOUNT 不可算名詞 **Heart failure** is a serious medical condition in which someone's heart does not work as well as it should, sometimes stopping completely so that they die. 心臓病 ❑He remained in a critical condition after suffering heart failure. 彼は心臓麻痺を患ったあとも危篤状態が続いた.

heart|felt /hɑrtfelt/ ADJ 形容詞 **Heartfelt** is used to describe a deep or sincere feeling or wish. 心からの ❑My heartfelt sympathy goes out to all the relatives. 親族の方々に心よりお悔み申し上げます.

hearth /hɑrθ/ (**hearths**) N-COUNT 可算名詞 The **hearth** is the floor of a fireplace, which sometimes extends into the room. 火床 ❑It was winter and there was a huge fire roaring in the hearth. それは冬のことで，暖炉には大きな火が燃え盛っていた.

heart|land /hɑrtlænd/ (**heartlands**) **1** N-COUNT 可算名詞 Journalists use **heartland** or **heartlands** to refer to the area or region where a particular set of activities or beliefs is most significant. 中心地 ❑...his six-day bus tour around the industrial heartland of America. 彼がアメリカの工業中心地をめぐる6日間のバス旅行. **2** N-COUNT 可算名詞 The most central area of a country or continent can be referred to as its **heartland** or **heartlands**. 中核地域 [WRITTEN 書き言葉] ❑For many, the essence of French living is to be found in the rural heartlands. 多くの人にとって，フランスの生活の真髄は田舎のハートランドである.

hearty /hɑrti/ (**heartier, heartiest**) **1** ADJ 形容詞 **Hearty** people or actions are loud, cheerful, and energetic. 元気な ❑Wade

was a hearty, athletic sort of guy. ウェードは，元気な筋骨型の男だった. ●**heartily** ADV 副詞 [ADV after v] 元気よく ❑He laughed heartily. 彼は腹の底から笑った. **2** ADJ 形容詞 **Hearty** feelings or opinions are strongly felt or strongly held. 心からの ❑With the last sentiment, Arnold was in hearty agreement. 最後に意見に，アーノルドは心から同意した. ●**heartily** ADV 副詞 本気で ❑Most Afghans are heartily sick of war. ほとんどのアフガニスタン人は戦争に心底うんざりしている. **3** ADJ 形容詞 A **hearty** meal is large and very satisfying. 腹いっぱいの ❑The men ate a hearty breakfast. 男たちは朝食をたらふく食べた. ●**heartily** ADV 副詞 [ADV after v] 腹いっぱい ❑He ate heartily but would drink only beer. 彼は腹いっぱい食べたが，ビールしか飲もうとしなかった.

heat /hit/ (**heats, heating, heated**) **1** V-T 他動詞 When you **heat** something, you raise its temperature, for example, by using a flame or a special piece of equipment. 熱する [他動詞] ❑Meanwhile, heat the tomatoes and oil in a pan. その間に，トマトと油をフライパンで熱します. **2** N-UNCOUNT 不可算名詞 **Heat** is warmth or the quality of being hot. 熱さ ❑The seas store heat and release it gradually during cold periods. 寒冷期間には，海は熱を保存し，徐々に放出する. **3** N-UNCOUNT 不可算名詞 The **heat** is very hot weather. 暑気 [also 'the' N] ❑As an asthmatic, he cannot cope with the heat and humidity. 彼はぜんそく患者なので，暑さと湿気に耐えられない. **4** N-UNCOUNT 不可算名詞 The **heat of** something is the temperature of something that is warm or that is being heated. 温度 ❑Adjust the heat of the barbecue by opening and closing the air vents. 換気口を開閉して，バーベキューの温度を調節する. **5** N-SING 単数名詞 You use **heat** to refer to a source of heat, for example a burner on a stove or the heating system of a house. 熱 ❑Immediately remove the pan from the heat. フライパンをすぐに火から下ろします. **6** N-UNCOUNT 不可算名詞 You use **heat** to refer to a state of strong emotion, especially of anger or excitement. 熱烈さ ❑It was all done in the heat of the moment and I have certainly learned by my mistake. それはすべて一時的な憤激でやってしまったことで，もちろん私は自分の間違いから学んだ. **7** N-SING 単数名詞 The **heat of** a particular activity is the point when there is the greatest activity or excitement. 最高潮 ❑People say all kinds of things in the heat of an argument. 論議の最中には人々はあらゆることを言う. **8** N-COUNT 可算名詞 A **heat** is one of a series of races or competitions. The winners of a heat take part in another race or competition, against the winners of other heats. (予選などの) 一回 ❑...the heats of the men's 100 meter breaststroke. 男子100メートル平泳ぎの予選

▶ **heat up** **1** PHRASAL VERB 句動詞 When you **heat** something **up**, especially food which has already been cooked and allowed to go cold, you make it hot. 暖める ❑Freda heated up a pie for me but I couldn't eat it. フレダは私のためにパイを暖めてくれたが，私は食べられなかった. **2** PHRASAL VERB 句動詞 When a situation **heats up**, things start to happen much more quickly and with increased interest and excitement among the people involved. 一段と熱気をおびる ❑Then in the last couple of years, the movement for democracy began to heat up. そして過去数年の間，民主主義運動は加熱し始めた. **3** PHRASAL VERB 句動詞 When something **heats up**, it gradually becomes hotter. 加熱する ❑In the summer her mobile home heats up like an oven. 夏季には，彼女のトレーラーハウスはオーブンのように暑くなる.

→ see **cooking, fire, pan, weather**

heat|ed /hitɪd/ **1** ADJ 形容詞 A **heated** discussion or quarrel is one where the people involved are angry and excited. 激した ❑It was a very heated argument and they were shouting at each other. それは非常な激論で，彼らはお互いに叫びあっていた. **2** ADJ 形容詞 If someone gets **heated about** something, they get angry and excited about it. 興奮した [v-link ADJ 'about/over' n] ❑You will understand that people get a bit heated about issues such as these. 人々がこういった問題に多少興奮するのは理解できるだろう. ●**heat|ed|ly** ADV 副詞 [ADV with v] 興奮して ❑The crowd continued to argue heatedly about the best way to tackle the problem. 問題の対処の仕方について民衆は熱っぽく論議し続けた.

heat|er /hitər/ (**heaters**) N-COUNT 可算名詞 A **heater** is a piece of equipment or a machine which is used to raise the temperature of something, especially of the air inside a room or a car. 暖房装置 ❑There's an electric heater in the bedroom. 寝室には電気ストーブがある.

heath|er /hɛðər/ N-UNCOUNT 不可算名詞 **Heather** is a low, spreading plant with small purple, pink, or white flowers that grows wild on high land with poor soil. ヒース

heat|ing /hitɪŋ/ **1** N-UNCOUNT 不可算名詞 **Heating** is the process of heating a building or room, considered especially from the point of view of how much this costs. 暖房 ❑We wanted to reduce the cost of heating and air-conditioning. 我々は暖房と空調の費用を削減したかった. **2** N-UNCOUNT 不可算名詞 **Heating** is the system and equipment that is used to heat a building. 暖房装置 ❑I wish I knew how to turn on the heating. 暖房装置の入れ方を知っていたらなあ. **3** → see also **central heating**

heave /hiːv/ (**heaves, heaving, heaved**) **1** V-T 他動詞 If you **heave** something heavy or difficult to move somewhere, you push, pull, or lift it using a lot of effort. 持ち上げる [他動詞] ❏ *It took five strong men to heave it up a ramp and lower it into place.* それを斜面から持ち上げて所定場所まで下ろすのには力持ちが5人必要だった. ●N-COUNT 可算名詞 **Heave** is also a noun. 持ち上げること ❏ *It took only one heave to hurl him into the river.* 彼は一回だけで川に投げ込むことができた. **2** V-I 自動詞 If something **heaves**, it moves up and down with large regular movements. 上下する [自動詞] ❏ *His chest heaved, and he took a deep breath.* 彼は胸を上下させて、深く息を吸った. **3** V-I 自動詞 If you **heave**, or if your stomach **heaves**, you vomit or feel as if you are about to vomit. 吐く、胸がむかつく [自動詞] ❏ *He gasped and heaved again.* 彼はあえいで、もう一度吐いた. **4** V-T 他動詞 If you **heave a sigh**, you give a big sigh. ため息をつく [他動詞] ❏ *Mr. Collier heaved a sigh and got to his feet.* コリヤ氏はため息をついて立ち上がった. **5** V-I 自動詞 If a place **is heaving** or if it **is heaving with** people, it is full of people. 膨れ上がる [mainly BRIT 主に英国英語, INFORMAL くだけた] [usu cont] [自動詞] ❏ *The Happy Bunny club was heaving.* ハッピーバニークラブは人で溢れていた. ❏ *Father Auberon's Academy Club positively heaved with dashing young men.* オベロン神父のアカデミークラブは確かに元気のよい若者でいっぱいだった. **6** to heave **a sigh of relief →** see **sigh**

heav|en /hɛvən/ (**heavens**) **1** N-PROPER 固有名詞 In some religions, **heaven** is said to be the place where God lives, where good people go when they die, and where everyone is always happy. It is usually imagined as being high up in the sky. 天国 ❏ *I believed that when I died I would go to heaven and see God.* 私は死んだら天国に行って神様に会えると信じていた. **2** N-UNCOUNT 不可算名詞 You can use **heaven** to refer to a place or situation that you like very much. 極楽 [INFORMAL くだけた] ❏ *I would go to movies in the afternoon and to ball games in the evening. It was heaven.* 私は午後には映画館に行き、夜には球技を見る. これは極楽だった. **3** EXCLAM 感嘆詞 You say "**Good heavens!**" or "**Heavens!**" to express surprise or to emphasize that you agree or disagree with someone. おやまあ！[SPOKEN 口語, FEELINGS 感情] ❏ *Good Heavens! That explains a lot!* おやまあ！なるほどそういうことか. **4** PHRASE 句 You say "**Heaven help someone**" when you are worried that something bad is going to happen to them, often because you disapprove of what they are doing or the way they are behaving. 神よ助けたまえ [SPOKEN 口語, DISAPPROVAL 不賛成] ❏ *If this makes sense to our leaders, then heaven help us all.* 我々のリーダーがこれを当然と思うのなら、神よ我々を助けたまえ. **5** PHRASE 句 You can say "**Heaven knows**" to emphasize that you do not know something, or that you find something very surprising. 神のみぞ知る [SPOKEN 口語, EMPHASIS 強調] ❏ *Heaven knows what they put in it.* 彼らがそれに何を入れたかは誰にもわからない. **6** PHRASE 句 You can say "**Heaven knows**" to emphasize something that you feel or believe very strongly. 確かに [SPOKEN 口語, EMPHASIS 強調] ❏ *Heaven knows they have enough money.* 彼らがお金を十分持っていることは確かだ. **7** PHRASE 句 If **the heavens open**, it suddenly starts raining very heavily. 土砂降りになる ❏ *The match had just begun when the heavens opened and play was suspended.* 試合が始まったとたんに土砂降りになり、試合は中断された. **8** for heaven's sake **→** see **sake 9** thank heavens **→** see **thank**

heav|en|ly /hɛvənli/ **1** ADJ 形容詞 **Heavenly** things are things that are connected with the religious idea of heaven. 天国の ❏ *...heavenly beings whose function it is to serve God.* 神に仕えることを職務とする聖なる者. **2** ADJ 形容詞 Something that is **heavenly** is very pleasant and enjoyable. すばらしい [INFORMAL くだけた] ❏ *The idea of spending two weeks with him may seem heavenly.* 彼と2週間を過ごすというのは素敵なアイデアに思えるかもしれない.

heavy /hɛvi/ (**heavier, heaviest, heavies**) **1** ADJ 形容詞 Something that is **heavy** weighs a lot. 重い ❏ *These scissors are awfully heavy.* このはさみはとても重い. ●**heavi|ness** N-UNCOUNT 不可算名詞 重さ ❏ *...a sensation of warmth and heaviness in the muscles.* 筋肉における暖かさと重さの感覚. **2** ADJ 形容詞 You use **heavy** to ask or talk about how much someone or something weighs. 重い ❏ *How heavy are you?* 体重はいくらですか. **3** ADJ 形容詞 **Heavy** means great in amount, degree, or intensity. 大量の、激しい ❏ *Heavy fighting has been going on.* 激しい戦いが繰り広げられていた. ●**heavi|ly** ADV 副詞 [ADV after v] ひどく ❏ *It has been raining heavily all day.* 一日中雨が激しく降っていた. ●**heavi|ness** N-UNCOUNT 不可算名詞 激しさ ❏ *...the heaviness of the blood loss.* 失血のひどさ. **4** ADJ 形容詞 A **heavy** meal is large in amount and often difficult to digest. 胃にもたれる ❏ *He had been feeling drowsy, the effect of an unusually heavy meal.* いつになくたっぷりの食事をしたために、彼はうとうとしていた. **5** ADJ 形容詞 [v-link ADJ 'with' n] Something that is **heavy with** things is full of them or loaded with them. いっぱいに含んだ [LITERARY 文語的] ❏ *The air is heavy with moisture.* 空気は湿っぽい. **6** ADJ 形容詞 If a person's breathing is **heavy**, it is very loud and deep. 重苦しい ❏ *Her breathing became slow and heavy.* 彼女の息づかいは遅く、荒くなった. ●**heavi|ly** ADV 副詞 [ADV after v] 重苦しく ❏ *She sank back on the pillow and closed her eyes, breathing heavily as if asleep.* 彼女は枕に頭を沈めて眼を閉じ、眠っているかのように荒く

呼吸した. **7** ADJ 形容詞 A **heavy** movement or action is done with a lot of force or pressure. 激しい [ADJ n] ❏ *...a heavy blow on the back of the skull.* 頭蓋骨の後ろへの大打撃 ●**heavi|ly** ADV 副詞 [ADV after v] 激しく ❏ *I sat down heavily on the ground beside the road.* 私は道の脇の地面にドカッと腰をおろした. **8** ADJ 形容詞 A **heavy** machine or piece of military equipment is very large and very powerful. 重装備の [ADJ n] ❏ *...government militia backed by tanks and heavy artillery.* タンクと重砲で支援された政府の国民軍 **9** ADJ 形容詞 If you describe a period of time or a schedule as **heavy**, you mean it involves a lot of work. 密な ❏ *It's been a heavy day and I'm tired.* 忙しい日だったので疲れた. **10** ADJ 形容詞 **Heavy** work requires a lot of strength or energy. 骨の折れる ❏ *The business is thriving and Philippa employs two full-timers for the heavy work.* 事業は盛況で、フィリッパは重作業要員として常勤者を2名雇う. **11** ADJ 形容詞 If you say that something is **heavy** on another thing, you mean that it uses a lot of that thing or too much of that thing. 大量に消費する [v-link ADJ 'on' n] ❏ *Tanks are heavy on fuel, destructive to roads and difficult to park.* タンク車は燃料を大量に消費し、道を破壊する上に駐車が困難である. **12** ADJ 形容詞 Air or weather that is **heavy** is unpleasantly still, hot, and damp. どんよりした ❏ *The outside air was heavy and moist and sultry.* 外気は、どんよりじっとりして、蒸し暑かった. **13** ADJ 形容詞 A situation that is **heavy** is serious and difficult to cope with. 重大な [INFORMAL くだけた] ❏ *I don't want any more of that heavy stuff.* そういった困難なことはもうたくさんだ. **14** N-COUNT 可算名詞 A **heavy** is a large strong man who is employed to protect a person or place, often by using violence. You can also use **heavy** to refer to a male character who represents such a man in a movie or play. 用心棒 [INFORMAL くだけた] ❏ *They had employed heavies to evict squatters from neighboring sites.* 近隣地区から無断移住者を強制退去させるため、彼らはチンピラを雇った. ❏ *In 1943, he received his first role as a heavy in "Double Indemnity."* 1943年、彼は『深夜の告白』で荒くれ者として最初の役をもらった.

Thesaurus	heavy また次を参照:
N.	complex, difficult, tough **13**

Word Partnership	heavy は次の語句と使われる:
N.	heavy **competition**, heavy **drinking**, heavy **fighting 3**

heavy-duty ADJ 形容詞 A **heavy-duty** piece of equipment is very strong and can be used a lot. 激務に耐えうる ❏ *...a heavy-duty plastic bag.* 特別に丈夫なポリ袋

heavy-handed ADJ 形容詞 If you say that someone's behavior is **heavy-handed**, you mean that they are too forceful or too rough. 重圧的な [DISAPPROVAL 不賛成] ❏ *...heavy-handed police tactics.* 圧制的な警察の方策

heavy in|dus|try (**heavy industries**) N-VAR 可変性名詞 **Heavy industry** is industry in which large machines are used to produce raw materials or to make large objects. 重工業 ❏ *...the policy of redirecting investment to heavy industries like steel and energy.* 鋼鉄やエネルギーといった、重工業に投資を向けなおす政策 **→** see **industry**

heavy|weight /hɛviweɪt/ (**heavyweights**) **1** N-COUNT 可算名詞 A **heavyweight** is a boxer weighing more than 175 pounds and therefore in the heaviest class. ヘビー級のボクサー **2** N-COUNT 可算名詞 If you refer to a person or organization as a **heavyweight**, you mean that they have a lot of influence, experience, and importance in a particular field, subject, or activity. 有力者、大企業 ❏ *He was a political heavyweight.* 彼は政治的経験の豊富な人材だった.

He|brew /hiːbruː/ **1** N-UNCOUNT 不可算名詞 **Hebrew** is a language that was spoken by Jews in former times. A modern form of Hebrew is spoken now in Israel. ヘブライ語 ❏ *He is a fluent speaker of Hebrew.* 彼はヘブライ語を流暢に話す. **2** ADJ 形容詞 **Hebrew** means belonging to or relating to the Hebrew language or people. ヘブライ人の、ヘブライ語の ❏ *...the respected Hebrew newspaper Haarez.* 高い評価を受けているヘブライ語の新聞『Haarez』紙

heck|le /hɛkl/ (**heckles, heckling, heckled**) V-T/V-I 他動詞/自動詞 If people in an audience **heckle** public speakers or performers, they interrupt them, for example by making rude remarks. 妨害する [他動詞・自動詞] ❏ *They heckled him and interrupted his address with angry questions.* 彼らは怒って彼を質問攻めにし、演説を中断させた. ●N-COUNT 可算名詞 **Heckle** is also a noun. やじ ❏ *The offending comment was in fact a heckle from an audience member.* 不愉快なコメントは、実は観客からのやじだった. ●**heck|ling** N-UNCOUNT 不可算名詞 やじを飛ばすこと ❏ *The ceremony was disrupted by unprecedented heckling and slogan-chanting.* 儀式は前代未聞のやじとスローガンのシュプレヒコールにより中断された. ●**heck|ler** /hɛklər/ (**hecklers**) N-COUNT 可算名詞 やじを飛ばす人 ❏ *As he began his speech, a heckler called out asking for his opinion on gun control.* 彼が演説を始めると、妨

害者が叫び出し，銃砲取り締まりについての意見を求めた.

hec|tare /hɛkteər/ (hectares) N-COUNT 可算名詞 A **hectare** is a measurement of an area of land which is equal to 10,000 square meters, or 2.471 acres. ヘクタール

hec|tic /hɛktɪk/ ADJ 形容詞 A **hectic** situation is one that is very busy and involves a lot of rushed activity. てんやわんやの □ Despite his hectic work schedule, Benny has rarely suffered poor health. 多忙な勤務スケジュールにもかかわらず，ベニーが健康を害することはめったになかった.

he'd /hid, STRONG hɪd/ **1** **He'd** is the usual spoken form of "he had," especially when "had" is an auxiliary verb. he hadの短縮形 □ He'd never learned to read. 彼は読み方を習ったことがない. **2** **He'd** is a spoken form of "he would." he wouldの短縮形 □ He'd come into the clubhouse every day. 彼は毎日クラブハウスに来るだろう.

hedge /hɛdʒ/ (hedges, hedging, hedged) **1** N-COUNT 可算名詞 A **hedge** is a row of bushes or small trees, usually along the edge of a lawn, garden, field, or road. 生垣 **2** V-I 自動詞 If you **hedge against** something unpleasant or unwanted that might affect you, especially losing money, you do something which will protect you from it. 保護する [自動詞] □ You can hedge against illness with insurance. 保険で疾病に対する防御策を講じることができる. **3** N-COUNT 可算名詞 Something that is a **hedge against** something unpleasant will protect you from its effects. 防衛手段 □ Gold is traditionally a hedge against inflation. 金は伝統的なインフレ防衛策である. **4** PHRASE 句 If you **hedge your bets**, you reduce the risk of losing a lot by supporting more than one person or thing in a situation where they are opposed to each other. 危険を分散する □ The company tried to hedge its bets by diversifying into other fields. その会社はその他の分野に多角化することにより危険を回避しようとした.

hedge fund (hedge funds) N-COUNT 可算名詞 A **hedge fund** is an investment fund that invests large amounts of money using methods that involve a lot of risk. ヘッジファンド [BUSINESS 実業]

hedge|hog /hɛdʒhɔg/ (hedgehogs) N-COUNT 可算名詞 A **hedgehog** is a small brown animal with sharp spikes covering its back. ハリネズミ

he|don|ism /hidᵊnɪzəm/ N-UNCOUNT 不可算名詞 **Hedonism** is the belief that gaining pleasure is the most important thing in life. 快楽主義 [FORMAL 形式ばった] □ ...the life of hedonism that she embraced in her youth. 彼女が若いときに信奉した快楽的生活

he|don|is|tic /hidᵊnɪstɪk/ ADJ 形容詞 **Hedonistic** means relating to hedonism. 快楽主義の [FORMAL 形式ばった] □ ...an eccentric and flamboyant nobleman with a hedonistic lifestyle. 快楽的生き方をする，風変わりで派手な貴族

heed /hid/ (heeds, heeding, heeded) **1** V-T 他動詞 If you **heed** someone's advice or warning, you pay attention to it and do what they suggest. 心に留める [FORMAL 形式ばった] [他動詞] □ But few at the conference in London last week heeded his warning. しかし，先週ロンドンで開催された会議で彼の警告に気を留めた人はわずかだった. **2** PHRASE 句 If you **take heed** of what someone says or if you **pay heed to** them, you pay attention to them and consider carefully what they say. 気をつける [FORMAL 形式ばった] □ But what if the government takes no heed? でも，もし政府が無視したらどうするのだ.

heel /hil/ (heels) **1** N-COUNT 可算名詞 Your **heel** is the back part of your foot, just below your ankle. かかと □ He had an operation on his heel last week. 先週彼はかかとに手術を受けた. **2** N-COUNT 可算名詞 The **heel** of a shoe is the raised part on the bottom at the back. 靴のかかと □ ...the shoes with the high heels. ハイヒールの靴 **3** N-PLURAL 複数名詞 **Heels** are women's shoes that are raised very high at the back. ヒール □ She was dressed in heels and a clingy dress. 彼女はハイヒールと体にぴったりしたドレスを身に着けていた. **4** PHRASE 句 If you **dig your heels in** or **dig in** your **heels**, you refuse to do something such as change your opinions or plans, especially when someone is trying very hard to make you do so. 頑として譲らない □ It was really the British who, by digging their heels in, prevented any last-minute deal. 自分の意見を固守して，土壇場での合意すべてを阻止したのは実際にはイギリス人だった. **5** PHRASE 句 If you say that one event follows **hard on the heels of** another or **hot on the heels of** another, you mean that one happens very quickly or immediately after another. 直後に □ Unfortunately, bad news has come hard on the heels of good. 残念なことに，朗報の直後に悪い知らせが届いた. **6** PHRASE 句 If you say that someone is **hot on** your **heels**, you are emphasizing that they are chasing you and are not very far behind you. 後ろにぴったりとついている [EMPHASIS 強調] □ They sped through the southwest with the law hot on their heels. 彼らは警察に追われて南西中を疾走した. **7** **head over heels** → see **head** **8** to **drag** your **heels** → see **drag** → see **foot**

hefty /hɛfti/ (heftier, heftiest) **1** ADJ 形容詞 **Hefty** means large in size, weight, or amount. 大きな [INFORMAL くだけた] □ She was quite a hefty woman. 彼女はかなりの大女だった. **2** ADJ 形容詞 A **hefty** movement is done with a lot of force. 大きな [INFORMAL く

だけた] □ Max grabbed Sascha's hair and she retaliated by giving him a hefty push. マックスはサッシャの髪をひっつかみ，彼女は彼を激しく押して仕返しした.

height /haɪt/ (heights) **1** N-VAR 可変性名詞 The **height** of a person or thing is their size or length from the bottom to the top. 高さ □ Her weight is about normal for her height. 彼女の体重は身長を考えると標準だ. □ I am 5'6" in height. 私の身長は5フィート6インチだ. **2** N-UNCOUNT 不可算名詞 **Height** is the quality of being tall. 高いこと □ She admits that her height is intimidating for some men. 彼女は，その身長のために男性に近寄り難い思われることがあることを認めている. **3** N-VAR 可変性名詞 A particular **height** is the distance that something is above the ground or above something else mentioned. 高度 □ At the speed and height at which he was moving, he was never more than half a second from disaster. 彼の動く速度と高度では，惨事を避ける時間は0.5秒しかなかった. **4** N-COUNT 可算名詞 A **height** is a high position or place above the ground. 高所 □ I'm not afraid of heights. 私は高所恐怖症ではない. **5** N-SING 単数名詞 When an activity, situation, or organization is at its most successful, powerful, or intense. 絶頂 □ At its height, the antiwar movement drew supporters from nearly every political camp. 反戦運動は絶頂期にはほとんどすべての政治陣営から支持者を取り付けた. **6** N-SING 単数名詞 If you say that something is **the height of** a particular quality, you are emphasizing that it has that quality to the greatest degree possible. 卓越 [EMPHASIS 強調] □ The hip-hugging black and white polka-dot dress was the height of fashion. ヒップを包み込む黒と白のポルカドットのドレスは流行の最先端だった. **7** N-PLURAL 複数名詞 If something reaches great **heights**, it becomes very extreme or intense. 極致 □ ...the mid-1980s, when prices rose to absurd heights. 物価がとんでもなく急騰した1980年代半ば → see **area**

Thesaurus　　　height また次を参照：

N.　　altitude, elevation **3**
　　　peak **5**

Word Partnership　　height は次の語句と使われる：

ADJ.　**average** height, **medium** height, **the right** height **1**
N.　　height **and weight**, height **and width** **1**
　　　the height of someone's **career** **5**
　　　the height of **fashion/popularity/style** **6**
V.　　**reach a** height **1** **5**

height|en /haɪtᵊn/ (heightens, heightening, heightened) V-T/V-I 他動詞/自動詞 If something **heightens** a feeling or if the feeling **heightens**, the feeling increases in degree or intensity. 高める [他動詞] 高まる [自動詞] □ The move has heightened tension in the state. その運動は国内の対立を高めた. □ Cross's interest heightened. クロスの興味は増した.

heir /eər/ (heirs) N-COUNT 可算名詞 An **heir** is someone who has the right to inherit a person's money, property, or title when that person dies. 相続人 □ ...the heir to the throne. 王位継承者

Word Link　　ess ≈ female : actress, heiress, princess

heir|ess /eərɪs/ (heiresses) N-COUNT 可算名詞 An **heiress** is a woman or girl who has the right to inherit property or a title, or who has inherited it, especially when this involves great wealth. 女性の遺産相続人 □ ...the heiress to a jewelry empire. 宝石帝国の女相続人

held /hɛld/ **Held** is the past tense and past participle of **hold**. holdの過去形

heli|cop|ter /hɛlikɑptər/ (helicopters) N-COUNT 可算名詞 A **helicopter** is an aircraft with long blades on top that go around very fast. It is able to stay still in the air and to move straight upward or downward. ヘリコプター → see **fly**

heli|pad /hɛlipæd/ (helipads) N-COUNT 可算名詞 A **helipad** is a place where helicopters can land and take off. ヘリポート □ Each house had a helipad for a fast evacuation. 各家にはすぐに避難できるようヘリパッドがあった.

hell

❶ NOUN USES
❷ PHRASES

❶ hell /hɛl/ (hells) **1** N-PROPER; N-COUNT 固有名詞，可算名詞 In some religions, **hell** is the place where the Devil lives, and where wicked people are sent to be punished when they die. Hell is usually imagined as being under the ground and full of flames. 地獄 □ I've never believed. Not in heaven or hell or God or Satan until now. 私は，天国も地獄も，神も悪魔も今まで信じたことはなかった. **2** N-VAR 可変性名詞 If you say that a particular situation or place is **hell**, you are emphasizing that it is extremely unpleasant. 地獄のような状態 [EMPHASIS 強調] □ ...the hell of the Siberian labor camps.

シベリア強制労働集容所の地獄のような状況 ③ EXCLAM 感嘆詞 **Hell** is used by some people when they are angry or excited, or when they want to emphasize what they are saying. This use could cause offense. ちくしょう [EMPHASIS 強調] □ "Hell, no!" the doctor snapped. 「冗談じゃない」と医師は吐き捨てるように言った.

❷ **hell** /hel/ ① PHRASE 句 You can use **as hell** after adjectives or some adverbs to emphasize the adjective or adverb. ものすごく [INFORMAL くだけた, EMPHASIS 強調] □ The men might be armed, but they sure as hell weren't trained. 男どもは武装しているかもしれないが, 訓練されていないことは疑いがない. ② PHRASE 句 If someone does something **for the hell of it**, or **just for the hell of it**, they do it for fun or for no particular reason. 意味もなく [INFORMAL くだけた] □ I started shouting in German, just for the hell of it. 私は面白半分にドイツ語で叫び始めた. ③ PHRASE 句 You can use **from hell** after a noun when you are emphasizing that something or someone is extremely unpleasant or evil. ひどく不快な [INFORMAL くだけた, EMPHASIS 強調] □ He's a child from hell. 彼は非常に不愉快な子供だ. ④ PHRASE 句 If you tell someone to **go to hell**, you are angrily telling them to go away and leave you alone. ほっといてくれ [INFORMAL, VULGAR くだけた, 下品な, FEELINGS 感情] □ "Well, you can go to hell!" He swept out of the room. 「ああ, ほっといてくれ」と言って彼はさっさと部屋を出て行った. ⑤ PHRASE 句 If you say that someone can **go to hell**, you are emphasizing angrily that you do not care about them and that they will not stop you doing what you want. くたばってしまえ [INFORMAL, VULGAR くだけた, 下品な, EMPHASIS 強調] □ Peter can go to hell. It's my money and I'll leave it to who I want. ピーターなんかくたばってしまえ. これは僕の金で, 僕の望む者に残す. ⑥ PHRASE 句 If you say that someone is **going hell for leather**, you are emphasizing that they are doing something or are moving very quickly and perhaps carelessly. 全速力で [INFORMAL くだけた, EMPHASIS 強調] □ The first horse often goes hell for leather, hits a few fences but gets away with it. 最初の馬は往々にして猛烈に飛ばし, 柵に多少ぶつかってもうまくやり過ごす. ⑦ PHRASE 句 Some people say **like hell** to emphasize that they strongly disagree with you or are strongly opposed to what you say. とんでもない [INFORMAL くだけた, EMPHASIS 強調] □ "I'll go myself." — "Like hell you will!" 「自分で行くわ」「とんでもない」 ⑧ PHRASE 句 Some people use **like hell** to emphasize how strong an action or quality is. 猛烈に [INFORMAL くだけた, EMPHASIS 強調] □ It hurts like hell. 猛烈に痛む. ⑨ PHRASE 句 If you say that **all hell breaks loose**, you are emphasizing that a lot of arguing or fighting suddenly starts. 大混乱が起きる [INFORMAL くだけた, EMPHASIS 強調] □ He had an affair, I found out and then all hell broke loose. 彼は不倫をし, それを私が見つけて大変なことになった. ⑩ PHRASE 句 If you talk about **a hell of a lot of** something, or **one hell of a lot of** something, you mean that there is a large amount of it. ものすごくたくさんの [INFORMAL くだけた, EMPHASIS 強調] □ The manager took a hell of a lot of money out of the club. 管理人はクラブからお金をしこたま持ち出した. ⑪ PHRASE 句 Some people use **a hell of a** or **one hell of a** to emphasize that something is very good, very bad, or very big. ものすごく [INFORMAL くだけた, EMPHASIS 強調] □ Whatever the outcome, it's going to be one hell of a fight. 結果がどうであろうとも, ものすごい戦いになるだろう. ⑫ PHRASE 句 Some people use **the hell out of** for emphasis after verbs such as "scare," "irritate," and "beat." 徹底的に [INFORMAL くだけた, EMPHASIS 強調] □ I patted the top of her head in the condescending way I knew irritated the hell out of her. 私が恩着せがましく彼女の頭を軽くたたいたことが彼女をものすごくいらつかせた. ⑬ PHRASE 句 If you say **there'll be hell to pay**, you are emphasizing that there will be serious trouble. 一大事になる [INFORMAL くだけた, EMPHASIS 強調] □ There would be hell to pay when Ferguson and Tony found out about it. ファーガソンとトニーがそれを知ったら一大事になる. ⑭ PHRASE 句 To **play hell with** something means to have a bad effect on it or cause great confusion. ひどくかき乱す [INFORMAL くだけた] □ The rain had played hell with business. 商売は雨でだいなしになった. ⑮ PHRASE 句 People sometimes use **the hell** for emphasis in questions, after words such as "what," "where," and "why," often in order to express anger. 一体 [INFORMAL, VULGAR くだけた, 下品な, EMPHASIS 強調] □ Where the hell have you been? 一体どこに行っていたの. ⑯ PHRASE 句 If you **go through hell**, or if someone **puts you through hell**, you have a very difficult or unpleasant time. 大変に難儀をする [INFORMAL くだけた] □ All of you seem to have gone through hell making this record. 君たち全員このレコードをつくるために大変な苦労をしたみたいだ. ⑰ PHRASE 句 If you **hope to hell** or **wish to hell that** something is true, you are emphasizing that you strongly hope or wish it is true. ぜひともそうであってほしい [INFORMAL, EMPHASIS くだけた, 強調] □ I hope to hell you're right. 是非とも君が正しいことを祈る. ⑱ PHRASE 句 You can say "**what the hell**" when you decide to do something in spite of the doubts that you have about it. かまうものか [INFORMAL, FEELINGS くだけた, 感情] □ What the hell, I thought, at least it will give the lazy old man some exercise. かまうものか, 少なくとも怠け者の老人に多少運動させてやることになるんだと僕は思った. ⑲ PHRASE 句 If you say "**to hell with**" something, you are emphasizing that you do not care about

something and that it will not stop you from doing what you want to do. くそ食らえ [INFORMAL くだけた, EMPHASIS 強調] □ To hell with this, I'm getting out of here. これが何だ, 僕は行くぞ.

he'll /hɪl, hil/ **He'll** is the usual spoken form of "he will." he will の省略形 □ By the time he's twenty he'll know everyone worth knowing in Washington. 20歳になるまでには, 彼はワシントンで知る価値のある者すべてを知るだろう.

hel|lo /heloʊ/ (**hellos**) also **hallo** or **hullo** ① CONVENTION 慣習表現 You say "**Hello**" to someone when you meet them. やあ [FORMULAE 決まり文句] □ Hello, Trish. I won't shake hands, because I'm filthy. やあ, トリッシュ. 僕は汚れているから握手はしないよ. ● N-COUNT 可算名詞 Hello is also a noun. Helloというあいさつ □ The salesperson greeted me with a warm hello. 店員は暖かくこんにちわと私にあいさつした. ② CONVENTION 慣習表現 You say "**Hello**" to someone at the beginning of a telephone conversation, either when you answer the phone or before you give your name or say why you are phoning. もしもし [FORMULAE 決まり文句] □ A moment later, Cohen picked up the phone. "Hello?" そのすぐあと, コーエンは電話を取った. 「もしもし」 ③ CONVENTION 慣習表現 You can call "**hello**" to attract someone's attention. ちょっと □ Very softly, she called out: "Hello? Who's there?" 彼女は非常に優しく「ちょっと, 誰なの」と声をかけた.

hel|met /helmɪt/ (**helmets**) N-COUNT 可算名詞 A **helmet** is a hat made of a strong material which you wear to protect your head. ヘルメット
→ see **army, football, skateboarding**

help /help/ (**helps, helping, helped**) ① V-T/V-I 他動詞/自動詞 If you **help** someone, you make it easier for them to do something, for example by doing part of the work for them or by giving them advice or money. 助ける [他動詞・自動詞] □ He has helped to raise a lot of money. 彼は大金を工面するのを手伝った. □ You can of course help by giving them a donation directly. もちろん, 彼らに直接寄付することで援助できます. ● N-UNCOUNT 不可算名詞 Help is also a noun. 助け □ Thanks very much for your help. ご援助感謝いたします. ② V-T/V-I 他動詞/自動詞 If you say that something **helps**, you mean that it makes something easier to do or get, or that it improves a situation to some extent. 役に立つ [他動詞・自動詞] □ The right style of swimsuit can help to hide, minimize, or emphasize what you want it to. 正しいスタイルの水着なら, 思いどおりに隠したり, 最小限にしたり, 強調したりが簡単だ. □ Building more bypasses will help the environment by reducing pollution and traffic jams in towns and cities. さらなるバイパスを作ることにより, 町や市の公害や渋滞を軽減でき, 環境が保護される. □ If it would help, I'd be happy to take photographs. お役に立つのなら喜んで写真を撮ります. ③ V-T 他動詞 If you **help** someone go somewhere or move in some way, you give them support so that they can move more easily. 手伝う [他動詞] □ Martin helped Tanya over the rail. マーチンはタニヤがレールを越すのを助けた. ④ N-SING 単数名詞 If you say that someone or something has been **a help** or has been some **help**, you mean that they have helped you to solve a problem. 助け ['a' N, also no det] □ Thank you. You've been a great help already. ありがとう. もう十分助かりました. ⑤ N-UNCOUNT 不可算名詞 Help is action taken to rescue a person who is in danger. You shout "**help!**" when you are in danger in order to attract someone's attention so that they can come and rescue you. 救助, 助けて □ He was screaming for help. 彼は大声で救いを求めた. ⑥ N-UNCOUNT 不可算名詞 In computing, **help**, or the **help** menu, is a file that gives you information and advice, for example about how to use a particular program. ヘルプ [COMPUTING コンピューティング] □ If you get stuck, click on Help. 困ったらヘルプをクリックする. ⑦ V-T 他動詞 If you **help yourself to** something, you serve yourself or you take it for yourself. If someone tells you to **help yourself**, they are telling you politely to serve yourself anything you want or to take anything you want. 自分で取って食べる [他動詞] □ There's bread on the table. Help yourself. テーブルにパンがあります. 自由にお取りください. ⑧ V-T 他動詞 If someone **helps themselves to** something, they steal it. 勝手に取る [INFORMAL くだけた] [他動詞] □ Two men forced the clerks to flee before helping themselves to the cash register. 2人の男はレジからお金を盗む前に, 店員を無理やり逃げさせた. ⑨ PHRASE 句 If you **can't help** the way you feel or behave, you cannot control it or stop it from happening. You can also say that you **can't help yourself**. することを避けられない □ I can't help feeling sorry for the poor man. そのかわいそうな男に同情しないではいられない. ⑩ PHRASE 句 If you say you **can't help** thinking something, you are expressing your opinion in an indirect way, often because you think it seems rude. しないではいられない [VAGUENESS あいまいさ] □ I can't help feeling that this may just be another of her schemes. これも彼女の陰謀にすぎないという気がしてならない. ⑪ PHRASE 句 If someone or something **is of help**, they make a situation easier or better. 役に立つ □ Can I be of help to you? 何かお役に立てることはありますか.

▶ **help out** PHRASAL VERB 句動詞 If you **help** someone **out**, you help them by doing some work for them or by lending them some money. 援助する □ I help out with the secretarial work. 私は秘書の仕事を援助した. □ All these presents came to more money than I had, and my

mother had to help me out. これらプレゼントの総額は私の全財産よりも多く，母が援助しなければならなかった．
→ see donor

Thesaurus　　help また次を参照：

V.	aid, assist, support; (ant.) hinder 1
N.	aid, assistance, guidance, support 1

Word Partnership　　help は次の語句と使われる：

ADJ.	**financial** help, **professional** help 1
V.	**ask for** help, **get** help, **need** help, **want to** help 1
	try to help 1 3
	cry/scream/shout for help 5
	can't help thinking/feeling something 9 10

help|er /hɛlpər/ (helpers) N-COUNT 可算名詞 A **helper** is a person who helps another person or group with a job they are doing. 助手 □*Phyllis and her helpers provided us with refreshment.* フィリスと助手は私たちに軽食を用意した．

help|ful /hɛlpfʊl/ 1 ADJ 形容詞 If you describe someone as **helpful**, you mean that they help you in some way, such as doing part of your job for you or by giving you advice or information. 助けになる □*The staff in the branch office are helpful but only have limited information.* 支店の職員は助けにはなるが，限られた情報しか持っていない． ● **help|ful|ly** ADV 副詞 [ADV with v] 有用に □*They had helpfully provided us with instructions on how to find the house.* 彼らはその家への行きかたをわかり易く教えてくれた． 2 ADJ 形容詞 If you describe information or advice as **helpful**, you mean that it is useful for you. 重宝な □*The catalog includes helpful information on the different bike models available.* カタログには，入手可能な様々なバイクのモデルに関する有用な情報が含まれていた． 3 ADJ 形容詞 Something that is **helpful** makes a situation more pleasant or more easy to tolerate. 役に立つ □*It is often helpful to have your spouse in the room when major news is expected.* 重大な知らせが予想される場合には，配偶者に同席してもらうと助けになることが多い．

help|less /hɛlpləs/ ADJ 形容詞 If you are **helpless**, you do not have the strength or power to do anything useful or to control or protect yourself. 無力な □*Parents often feel helpless, knowing that all the hugs in the world won't stop the tears.* 親は，往々にして，いくら抱きしめても涙を止めることはできないことがわかると，ふがいなく感じる． ● **help|less|ly** ADV 副詞 力なく □*Their son watched helplessly as they vanished beneath the waves.* 息子は波にさらわれていくのを，その息子は力なく見つめた． ● **help|less|ness** N-UNCOUNT 不可算名詞 無力 □*I remember my feelings of helplessness.* 私は無力感を覚えている．

help|line /hɛlplaɪn/ (helplines) N-COUNT 可算名詞 A **helpline** is a special telephone service that people can call to get advice about a particular subject. 悩み事相談電話 □*...Greece's first helpline for gamblers who need counseling.* カウンセリングを必要とするギャンブラーのための，ギリシャ初のヘルプライン

hem /hɛm/ (hems, hemming, hemmed) N-COUNT 可算名詞 A **hem** on something such as a piece of clothing is an edge that is folded over and stitched down to prevent threads coming loose. The **hem** of a skirt or dress is the bottom edge. へり □*She lifted the hem of her dress and brushed her knees.* 彼女はドレスのすそをあげて，ひざを払った．
▶ **hem in** 1 PHRASAL VERB 句動詞 If a place **is hemmed in by** mountains or **by** other places, it is surrounded by them. 囲む □*The canyon is hemmed in by towering walls of rock.* 峡谷はそびえ立つ岩壁に囲まれている． 2 PHRASAL VERB 句動詞 If someone **is hemmed in** or if someone **hems** them **in**, they are prevented from moving or changing, for example because they are surrounded by people or obstacles. 束縛する □*The company's competitors complain that they are hemmed in by rigid legal contracts.* その会社の競合会社は，融通の利かない適法契約で束縛されていると文句をいった．

Word Link　　sphere ≈ ball : atmosphere, hemisphere, sphere

hemi|sphere /hɛmɪsfɪər/ (hemispheres) N-COUNT 可算名詞 A **hemisphere** is one half of the earth. 半球 □*...the depletion of the ozone layer in the northern hemisphere.* 北半球のオゾン層の枯渇
→ see globe, solid

hemo|philia /himəfɪliə/ N-UNCOUNT 不可算名詞 **Hemophilia** is a medical condition in which a person's blood does not thicken or clot properly when they are injured, so they continue bleeding. 血友病

hemo|phili|ac /himəfɪliæk/ (hemophiliacs) N-COUNT 可算名詞 A **hemophiliac** is a person who suffers from haemophilia. 血友病患者 □*...a hemophiliac who contracted the AIDS virus through a blood transfusion.* 輸血によりAIDウィルスに感染した血友病患者

hem|or|rhage /hɛmərɪdʒ/ (hemorrhages, hemorrhaging, hemorrhaged) 1 N-VAR 可変性名詞 A **hemorrhage** is serious bleeding inside a person's body. 出血 □*Shortly after his admission into the hospital he had a massive brain hemorrhage and died.* 入院

直後，彼は多量な脳内出血を起こして死亡した． 2 V-I 自動詞 If someone **is hemorrhaging**, there is serious bleeding inside their body. 出血する [自動詞] □*I hemorrhaged badly after the birth of all three of my sons.* 3人の息子すべてを生んだあと，私は多量に出血した． ● **hem|or|rhag|ing** N-UNCOUNT 不可算名詞 大出血 □*A post mortem showed he died from shock and hemorrhaging.* 死体解剖により，彼はショックと大出血で死んだことがわかった．

hen /hɛn/ (hens) N-COUNT 可算名詞 A **hen** is a female chicken. People often keep hens in order to eat or sell their eggs. めんどり

hence /hɛns/ 1 ADV 副詞 You use **hence** to indicate that the statement you are about to make is a consequence of what you have just said. この故に [FORMAL 形式ばった] [ADV cl/group] □*The trade imbalance is likely to rise again in 2007. Hence a new set of policy actions will be required soon.* 貿易不均衡は2007年に再度高まる見込みである．したがって，一連の新しい政策的措置がもうじき必要になるだろう． 2 ADV 副詞 You use **hence** in expressions such as "**several years hence**" or "**six months hence**" to refer to a time in the future, especially a long time in the future. 今後 [FORMAL 形式ばった] [amount ADV] □*The gases that may be warming the planet will have their main effect many years hence.* 惑星の温度を上昇させている恐れのあるガスの主要効果は今から何年もあとに現れる．

hence|forth /hɛnsfɔrθ/ ADV 副詞 **Henceforth** means from this or that time onward. 今後 [FORMAL 形式ばった] [ADV with cl] □*Henceforth all branches of the naval officer corps were equal to one another.* それからは，海軍士官軍団の支部はすべて平等だった．

Word Link　　itis ≈ inflammation : arthritis, hepatitis, meningitis

hepa|ti|tis /hɛpətaɪtɪs/ N-UNCOUNT 不可算名詞 **Hepatitis** is a serious disease which affects the liver. 肝炎

her /hər, STRONG hɜr/

Her is a third person singular pronoun. **Her** is used as the object of a verb or a preposition. **Her** is also a possessive determiner.

Her は3人称単数代名詞である．**Her** は動詞または前置詞の目的語に使われる．**Her** はまた所有限定詞でもある．

1 PRON-SING 単数代名詞 You use **her** to refer to a woman, girl, or female animal. 彼女 [V PRON, prep PRON] □*I went in the room and told her I had something to say to her.* 私は部屋に行って，彼女に言いたいことがあると言った． ● DET 限定詞 **Her** is also a possessive determiner. 彼女の □*Liz traveled around the world for a year with her boyfriend James.* リズは，恋人のジェームスと一年間世界旅行をした． 2 PRON-SING 単数代名詞 In written English, **her** is sometimes used to refer to a person without saying whether that person is a man or a woman. Some people dislike this use and prefer to use "him or her" or "them." 彼の代わり [V PRON, prep PRON] □*Talk to your baby, play games, and show her how much you enjoy her company.* 赤ちゃんに話しかけ，ゲームをし，一緒にいるのを楽しんでいることを示しなさい． ● DET 限定詞 **Her** is also a possessive determiner. 彼女の □*The non-drinking, non-smoking model should do nothing to risk her reputation.* その飲酒も喫煙もしないモデルは名声を危険に晒すようなことをすべきではない． 3 PRON-SING 単数代名詞 **Her** is sometimes used to refer to a country or nation. 国や国家を指す [FORMAL OR WRITTEN 形式ばった，または書き言葉] [V PRON, prep PRON] ● DET 限定詞 **Her** is also a possessive determiner. 国の □*America and her partners are helping to rebuild roads and bridges and buildings.* アメリカとそのパートナーは道路，橋，建物の再建を援助している． 4 PRON-SING 単数代名詞 People sometimes use **her** to refer to a car, machine, or ship. 車，機械，船を指す [V PRON, prep PRON] □*Kemp got out of his truck. "Just fill her up, thanks."* ケンプはトラックから降りた．「満タンお願いします．」 ● DET 限定詞 **Her** is also a possessive determiner. 号の □*This dramatic photograph was taken from Carpathia's deck by one of her passengers.* この劇的な写真はカルパチア号のデッキから乗客により撮影された．

her|ald /hɛrəld/ (heralds, heralding, heralded) 1 V-T 他動詞 Something that **heralds** a future event or situation is a sign that it is going to happen or appear. 到来を告げる [FORMAL 形式ばった] □*...the sultry evening that heralded the end of the baking hot summer.* 焼けつくような夏の終わりを告げた蒸し暑い夜 2 N-COUNT 可算名詞 Something that is a **herald** of a future event or situation is a sign that it is going to happen or appear. 先触れ [FORMAL 形式ばった] □*I welcome the report as a herald of more freedom.* より多くの自由の先触れとして私はそのリポートを歓迎する． 3 V-T 他動詞 If an important event or action **is heralded by** people, announcements are made about it so that it is publicly known and expected. 予告する [FORMAL 形式ばった] [usu passive] □*Janet Jackson's new album has been heralded by a massive media campaign.* ジャネット・ジャクソンの新作アルバムを予告する大規模な広告キャンペーンが行なわれた．

Word Link　　herb ≈ grass : herb, herbal, herbivorous

herb /ɜrb/ (herbs) N-COUNT 可算名詞 A **herb** is a plant whose leaves are used in cooking to add flavor to food, or as a medicine. ハーブ □*...beautiful, fragrant herbs such as basil and coriander.* バジルやコリアンダーなどの美しくよいにおいのハーブ

Word Link
herb ≈ grass : herb, herbal, herbivorous

herb|al /ɜrbᵊl/ ADJ 形容詞 **Herbal** means made from or using herbs. 薬草の [ADJ n] □ *...herbal remedies for colds.* 風邪用の漢方薬

Word Link
vor ≈ eating : herbivorous, savory, voracious

herbivorous /hɜrbɪvərəs, 3r-/ ADJ 形容詞 **Herbivorous** animals only eat plants. 草食の

herd /hɜrd/ (herds, herding, herded) **1** N-COUNT 可算名詞 A **herd** is a large group of animals of one kind that live together. 群れ □ *Chobe is also renowned for its large herds of elephant and buffalo.* チョベ川は象とバッファローの大きな群れでも有名だ. **2** N-SING 単数名詞 If you say that someone has joined **the herd** or follows **the herd**, you are criticizing them because you think that they behave just like everyone else and do not think for themselves. 大衆 [DISAPPROVAL 不賛成] □ *They are individuals; they will not follow the herd.* 彼らは個別の人間だ. 大衆に従うことはない. **3** V-T 他動詞 If you **herd** people somewhere, you make them move there in a group. 人の集団を目的地まで導く □ *He began to herd the prisoners out.* 彼は囚人たちを外に連れ出し始めた. **4** V-T 他動詞 If you **herd** animals, you make them move along as a group. 家畜の群れを移動させる □ *Stefano used a motorcycle to herd the sheep.* ステファーノはオートバイで羊の群れを移動させた.

here /hɪər/ **1** ADV 副詞 You use **here** when you are referring to the place where you are. ここに □ *I'm here all by myself and I know I'm going to get lost.* 私はたった一人でここにいるので道に迷うことは確かだ. **2** ADV 副詞 You use **here** when you are pointing toward a place that is near you, in order to draw someone else's attention to it. ここに □ *...if you will just sign here.* ここにちょっと署名してくれれば **3** ADV 副詞 You use **here** in order to indicate that the person or thing that you are talking about is near you or is being held by you. ここにいる □ *My friend here writes for radio.* ここにいる私の友人はラジオ番組の原稿を書いている. **4** ADV 副詞 If you say that you are **here to** do something, that is your role or function. ここに ['be' ADV to-inf] □ *I'm here to help you.* 私の仕事はあなたを助けることだ. **5** ADV 副詞 You use **here** in order to draw attention to something or someone who has just arrived in the place where you are, or to draw attention to the place you have just arrived at. ほらここに □ *"Here's the taxi," she said politely.* 「さあタクシーが着きました」と彼女は礼儀正しく言った. **6** ADV 副詞 You use **here** to refer to a particular point or stage of a situation or subject that you have come to or that you are dealing with. この点 □ *It's here that we come up against the difference of approach.* アプローチについて意見が異なるのはこの点だ. **7** ADV 副詞 You use **here** to refer to a period of time, a situation, or an event that is present or happening now. ここにある □ *Economic recovery is here.* 経済回復は既に始まっている. **8** ADV 副詞 You use **here** at the beginning of a sentence in order to draw attention to something or to introduce something. ほらここに [ADV be n/wh] □ *Now here's what I want you to do.* さてこれが君にやってもらいたいことだ. **9** ADV 副詞 You use **here** when you are offering or giving something to someone. さあどうぞ [ADV 'be' n] □ *Here's your coffee, just the way you like it.* さあコーヒーをどうぞ. あなたの好みに入れました. □ *Here are some letters I want you to sign.* はい, こちらがあなたに署名してほしい手紙です. **10** CONVENTION 慣習表現 You say **"here we are"** when you have just found something that you have been looking for. ほらここにありますよ □ *I rummaged through the drawers and came up with Amanda's folder. "Here we are."* 私は引き出しの中をかき回して探し, アマンダのフォルダーを見つけた. 「ほらここにあった.」 **11** CONVENTION 慣習表現 You say **"here goes"** when you are about to do or say something difficult or unpleasant. さあ始めるぞ □ *Dr. Culver nervously muttered "Here goes," and gave the little girl an injection.* ドクター・カルバーは神経質に「よし行くぞ」とつぶやき, 少女に注射した. **12** PHRASE 句 You use expressions such as **"here we go"** and **"here we go again"** in order to indicate that something is happening again in the way that you expected, especially something unpleasant. ああ, またか [INFORMAL くだけた] □ *"Police! Open up!" —"Oh well," I thought, "here we go."* 「警察だ. 開けろ」 「ああ, またか」と私は思った. **13** PHRASE 句 You use **here and now** to emphasize that something is happening at the present time, rather than in the future or past, or that you would like it to happen at the present time. 今この場で [EMPHASIS 強調] □ *I'm a practicing physician trying to help people here and now.* 私は人々を今この場で助けようとしている医者だ. **14** PHRASE 句 If something happens **here and there**, it happens in several different places. あちこちで □ *I do a bit of teaching here and there.* 私はあちこちで少しばかり教えている. **15** CONVENTION 慣習表現 You use expressions such as **"here's to us"** and **"here's to your new job"** before drinking a toast in order to wish someone success or happiness. 乾杯 [FORMULAE 決まり文句] □ *He raised his glass. "Here's to neighbors."* 彼はグラスを持ち上げて「隣人たちに乾杯」と言った.

he|redi|tary /hɪrɛdɪteri/ **1** ADJ 形容詞 A **hereditary** characteristic or illness is passed on to a child from its parents before it is born. 遺伝の □ *Cystic fibrosis is the commonest fatal hereditary disease.* 嚢胞(のうほう)性線維症は最もありふれた命にかかわる遺伝性の病気だ. **2** ADJ 形容詞 A title or position in society that is **hereditary** is one that is passed on as a right from parent to child. 世襲の □ *The position of the head of state is hereditary.* 元首の地位は世襲である.

her|esy /hɛrɪsi/ (heresies) **1** N-VAR 可変性名詞 **Heresy** is a belief or action that most people think is wrong, because it disagrees with beliefs that are generally accepted. 異論 □ *It might be considered heresy to suggest such a notion.* そうした想念の提唱は通説に反すると見なされる可能性がある. **2** N-VAR 可変性名詞 **Heresy** is a belief or action which seriously disagrees with the principles of a particular religion. 異説 □ *He said it was a heresy to suggest that women should not conduct services.* 彼は女性が礼拝を行なうことに反対するのは異説だと言った.

her|it|age /hɛrɪtɪdʒ/ (heritages) N-VAR 可変性名詞 A country's **heritage** is all the qualities, traditions, or features of life there that have continued over many years and have been passed on from one generation to another. 継承物 □ *The historic building is as much part of our heritage as the paintings.* 歴史的建造物は絵画と同様に我が国の文化遺産の一部である.

her|mit /hɜrmɪt/ (hermits) N-COUNT 可算名詞 A **hermit** is a person who lives alone, away from people and society. 隠者 □ *I've spent the past ten years living like a hermit.* 私は過去10年間, 隠者のような生活をしてきた.

her|nia /hɜrniə/ (hernias) N-VAR 可変性名詞 A **hernia** is a medical condition which is often caused by strain or injury. It results in one of your internal organs sticking through a weak point in the surrounding tissue. ヘルニア

hero /hɪəroʊ/ (heroes) **1** N-COUNT 可算名詞 The **hero** of a book, play, movie, or story is the main male character, who usually has good qualities. 主人公 □ *The hero of Doctor Zhivago dies in 1929.* ドクトル・ジバゴの主人公は1929年に死ぬ. **2** N-COUNT 可算名詞 A **hero** is someone, especially a man, who has done something brave, new, or good, and who is therefore greatly admired by a lot of people. 英雄的人物 □ *He called Mr. Mandela a hero who had inspired millions.* 彼はマンデラ氏を何百人もの人々に希望を与えた英雄と呼んだ. **3** N-COUNT 可算名詞 If you describe someone as your **hero**, you mean that you admire them a great deal, usually because of a particular quality or skill that they have. 理想的人物 □ *My boyhood hero was Kit Carson.* 私の少年時代のあこがれはキット・カーソンだった.

→ see Word Web: **hero**
→ see **hero, myth**

Word Web   hero

Odysseus is a **hero** from Greek **mythology**. He is a warrior. He shows great courage in battle. He faces many **dangers** and temptations. However he knows he must return home after the Trojan War*. During his **epic** journey home, Odysseus faces many trials. He must survive wild storms at sea and fight a monster. He must also resist the temptations of the Sirens and outwit the goddess Circe*. At home Penelope, Odysseus' wife, **defends** their home and **protects** their son. She remains **loyal** and **brave** through many trials. She is the **heroine** of the story.

Trojan War: a legendary war between Greece and Troy.
Circe: a Greek goddess.

Odysseus saves his men from the Cyclops.

he|ro|ic /hɪroʊɪk/ (**heroics**) **1** ADJ 形容詞 If you describe a person or their actions as **heroic**, you admire them because they show extreme bravery. 勇敢な ❑ *His heroic deeds were celebrated in every corner of India.* 彼の勇敢な行為はインドで全国的に有名だ。● **he|roi|cal|ly** /hɪroʊɪkli/ ADV 副詞 [ADV with v] 勇敢に ❑ *He had acted heroically during the liner's evacuation.* 彼は定期船の避難中に勇敢に行動した。**2** ADJ 形容詞 If you describe an action or event as **heroic**, you admire it because it involves great effort or determination to succeed. 思い切った [APPROVAL 賛成] ❑ *The company has made heroic efforts at cost reduction.* その会社は経費削減のために思い切った努力をした。● **he|roi|cal|ly** ADV 副詞 堂々と ❑ *Single parents cope heroically in doing the job of two people.* 1人で子供を育てる親は2人分の仕事を堂々とこなしている。**3** ADJ 形容詞 **Heroic** means being or relating to the hero or heroine of a story. 主人公の ❑ *...the book's central, heroic figure.* その本の主人公 **4** N-PLURAL 複数名詞 **Heroics** are actions involving bravery, courage, or determination. 英雄的行為 ❑ *...the man whose aerial heroics helped save the helicopter pilot.* ヘリコプターのパイロットを救援した英雄的行為の男 **5** N-PLURAL 複数名詞 If you describe someone's actions or plans as **heroics**, you think that they are foolish or dangerous because they are too difficult or brave for the situation in which they occur. 誇張した言動 [SPOKEN 口語, DISAPPROVAL 不賛成] ❑ *He said his advice was: "No heroics, stay within the law."* 彼は「大げさな言動はしないこと、法律違反は犯すな。」が彼の忠告だと言った。

hero|in /hɛroʊɪn/ N-UNCOUNT 不可算名詞 **Heroin** is a powerful drug which some people take for pleasure, but which they can become addicted to. ヘロイン

hero|ine /hɛroʊɪn/ (**heroines**) **1** N-COUNT 可算名詞 The **heroine** of a book, play, movie, or story is the main female character, who usually has good qualities. ヒロイン ❑ *The heroine is a senior TV executive.* ヒロインはテレビ局の重役である。**2** N-COUNT 可算名詞 A **heroine** is a woman who has done something brave, new, or good, and who is therefore greatly admired by a lot of people. 女英雄 ❑ *The national heroine of the day was Xing Fen, winner of the first gold medal of the Games.* その日の国民的英雄は競技大会の最初の金メダル受賞者、シアン・フェンだった。**3** N-COUNT 可算名詞 If you describe a woman as your **heroine**, you mean that you admire her greatly, usually because of a particular quality or skill that she has. 敬服の的の女性 ❑ *My heroine was Elizabeth Taylor.* 私が敬服する女性はエリザベス・テイラーだった。
→ see **hero**

hero|ism /hɛroʊɪzəm/ N-UNCOUNT 不可算名詞 **Heroism** is great courage and bravery. 英雄的行為 ❑ *...individual acts of heroism.* 個人的な英雄的行為

her|ring /hɛrɪŋ/ (**herring, herrings**) N-VAR 可変性名詞 A **herring** is a long silver-colored fish. Herring live in large groups in the ocean. ニシン ❑ *...a shoal of herring.* ニシンの群れ ● N-UNCOUNT 不可算名詞 **Herring** is a piece of this fish eaten as food. ニシン ❑ *a can of herring.* ニシンの缶詰

hers /hɜrz/

Hers is a third person possessive pronoun.

Hersは3人称所有代名詞である。

1 PRON-POSS 所有代名詞 You use **hers** to indicate that something belongs or relates to a woman, girl, or female animal. 彼女のもの ❑ *His hand as it shook hers was warm and firm.* 彼女と握手した彼の手は温かくてしっかりとしていた。❑ *Professor Camm was a great friend of hers.* カム教授は彼女の良い友人だった。**2** PRON-POSS 所有代名詞 In written English, **hers** is sometimes used to refer to a person without saying whether that person is a man or a woman. Some people dislike this use and prefer to use "his or hers" or "theirs." 人のもの ❑ *The author can report other people's results which more or less agree with hers.* 筆者は自分のものとおおよそ一致する他の人々の決果を報告することができる。

her|self /hərsɛlf/

Herself is a third person singular reflexive pronoun. **Herself** is used when the object of a verb or preposition refers to the same person as the subject of the verb, except in meaning **3**.

Herselfは3人称単数の再帰代名詞である。 **Herself** は、 **3** を意味する場合以外は、動詞または前置詞の目的語が動詞の主語と同じ人物を指すときに用いられる。

1 PRON-REFL 再帰代名詞 You use **herself** to refer to a woman, girl, or female animal. 彼女自身 [v PRON, prep PRON] ❑ *She let herself out of the room.* 彼女は自分で部屋から出た。❑ *Jennifer believes she will move out on her own when she is financially able to support herself.* ジェニファーは経済的に自立できるようになったら、人で引っ越すつもりだと考えている。**2** PRON-REFL 再帰代名詞 In written English, **herself** is sometimes used to refer to a person without saying whether that person is a man or a woman. Some people dislike this use and prefer to use "himself or herself" or "themselves." その人は

身 ❑ *How can anyone believe stories for which she feels herself to be in no way responsible?* 自分に全く責任はないと彼女が感じている話を一体誰が信じることができるのか。**3** PRON-REFL-EMPH 強調的再帰代名詞 You use **herself** to emphasize the person or thing that you are referring to. **Herself** is sometimes used instead of "her" as the object of a verb or preposition. 彼女自身 [EMPHASIS 強調] ❑ *She herself was not a keen gardener.* 彼女自身はガーデニングには熱心でなかった。

he's /hiz, STRONG hiz/ **He's** is the usual spoken form of "he is" or "he has," especially when "has" is an auxiliary verb. he is または he has の縮約形 ❑ *He's working maybe twenty-five hours a week.* 彼は多分週に25時間働いている。

hesi|tant /hɛzɪtənt/ ADJ 形容詞 If you are **hesitant about** doing something, you do not do it quickly or immediately, usually because you are uncertain, embarrassed, or worried. ためらう ❑ *She was hesitant about coming forward with her story.* 彼女は彼女の説明を提供するのをためらった。● **hesi|tan|cy** /hɛzɪtənsi/ N-UNCOUNT 不可算名詞 ためらい ❑ *A trace of hesitancy showed in Dr. Stockton's eyes.* ドクター・ストックマンの目にはかすかなためらいがあった。● **hesi|tant|ly** ADV 副詞 [ADV with v] ためらって ❑ *"Would you do me a favor?" she asked hesitantly.* 「お願いがあるのですが」と彼女はためらいがちに聞いた。

hesi|tate /hɛzɪteɪt/ (**hesitates, hesitating, hesitated**) **1** V-I 自動詞 If you **hesitate**, you do not speak or act for a short time, usually because you are uncertain, embarrassed, or worried about what you are going to say or do. ためらう ❑ *The telephone rang. Catherine hesitated, debating whether to answer it.* 電話が鳴った。キャサリンは応えるかどうか迷った。● **hesi|ta|tion** /hɛzɪteɪʃən/ (**hesitations**) N-VAR 可変性名詞 口ごもること ❑ *Asked if he would go back, Mr. Searle said after some hesitation, "I'll have to think about that."* 戻るかどうか聞かれ、シール氏はしばらく間をおいて「まだ決まっていない」と答えた。**2** V-T 他動詞 If you **hesitate to** do something, you delay doing it or are unwilling to do it, usually because you are not certain it would be right. If you do not **hesitate to** do something, you do it immediately. 嫌がる ❑ *Some parents hesitate to take these steps because they suspect that their child is exaggerating.* 子供が誇張していることを疑っているため、こうした手段を取るのを嫌がる親もいる。**3** V-T 他動詞 [only imper, with neg] You can use **hesitate** in expressions such as "**don't hesitate to call me**" or "**don't hesitate to contact us**" when you are telling someone that they should do something as soon as it needs to be done and should not worry about disturbing other people. 遠慮する ❑ *In the event of difficulties, please do not hesitate to contact our Customer Service Department.* 問題が発生した場合には当社の顧客サービス部門に遠慮なくご連絡ください。

Thesaurus	*hesitate* また次を参照:
V.	falter, pause, wait **1** **2**

hesi|ta|tion /hɛzɪteɪʃən/ (**hesitations**) **1** N-VAR 可変性名詞 **Hesitation** is an unwillingness to do something, or a delay in doing it, because you are uncertain, worried, or embarrassed about it. 優柔決断 ❑ *He promised there would be no more hesitations in pursuing reforms.* 彼は迷わずに改革を続けると約束した。**2** → see also **hesitate** **3** PHRASE 句 If you say that you **have no hesitation in** doing something, you are emphasizing that you will do it immediately or willingly because you are certain that it is the right thing to do. なんのためらいもなく [EMPHASIS 強調] ❑ *The board said it had no hesitation in unanimously rejecting the offer.* 理事会は満場一致ですぐその申出を拒否すると述べた。**4** PHRASE 句 If you say that someone does something **without hesitation**, you are emphasizing that they do it immediately and willingly. すぐさま [EMPHASIS 強調] ❑ *The great majority of players would, of course, sign the contract without hesitation.* 選手の大半は勿論すぐさま契約に署名するだろう。

hetero|sexual /hɛtəroʊsɛkʃuəl/ (**heterosexuals**) **1** ADJ 形容詞 A **heterosexual** relationship is a sexual relationship between a man and a woman. 異性間の ❑ *An increasing number of people are becoming infected with HIV through heterosexual sex.* 異性間の性交を通じてHIVに感染する人々の数が増えつつある。**2** ADJ 形容詞 Someone who is **heterosexual** is sexually attracted to people of the opposite sex. 異性愛の ❑ *It doesn't matter whether people are heterosexual or homosexual.* 人々が異性愛者か同性愛者かは重要ではない。● N-COUNT 可算名詞 **Heterosexual** is also a noun. 異性愛の人 ❑ *In Denmark the age of consent is fifteen for both heterosexuals and homosexuals.* デンマークの丁年は異性愛者も同性愛者も15歳である。● **hetero|sexu|al|ity** /hɛtəroʊsɛkʃuæliti/ N-UNCOUNT 不可算名詞 異性愛 ❑ *...a challenge to the assumption that heterosexuality was "normal."* 異性愛が「正常」だという前提への反論

hexa|gon /hɛksəgɒn/ (**hexagons**) N-COUNT 可算名詞 A **hexagon** is a shape that has six straight sides. 六角形
→ see **shape**

hex|ago|nal /hɛksægənəl/ ADJ 形容詞 A **hexagonal** object or

shape has six straight sides. 六角形の

hey /heɪ/ **1** CONVENTION 慣習表現 In informal situations, you say or shout "**hey**" to attract someone's attention, or to show surprise, interest, or annoyance. ちょっと [FEELINGS 感情] ❑ "Hey! Look out!" shouted Patty. 「ちょっと見て」とパティは叫んだ. **2** CONVENTION 慣習表現 In informal situations, you can say "**hey**" to greet someone. やあ ❑ She watched as he smiled, opened his mouth, and said, "Hey, Kate." 彼女は彼が微笑みながら口を開き「やあケイト」と言うのを見た.

hey|day /heɪdeɪ/ N-SING 単数名詞 Someone's **heyday** is the time when they are most powerful, successful, or popular. 盛り ❑ In its heyday, the studio's boast was that it had more stars than there are in heaven. 全盛期には非常に多数のスターがいたというのがスタジオの自慢だった.

hi /haɪ/ CONVENTION 慣習表現 In informal situations, you say "**hi**" to greet someone. やあ, こんにちわ [FORMULAE 決まり文句] ❑ "Hi, Liz," she said shyly. 「こんにちわ、リズ」と彼女は恥ずかしそうに言った.

hic|cup /hɪkʌp/ (**hiccups, hiccuping** or **hiccupping, hiccuped** or **hiccupped**) also **hiccough** **1** N-COUNT 可算名詞 You can refer to a small problem or difficulty as a **hiccup**, especially if it does not last very long or is easily corrected. 一時的な問題 ❑ A recent sales hiccup is nothing to panic about. 最近の販売高の一時的落ち込みはうろたえることはない. **2** N-UNCOUNT 不可算名詞 When you have **hiccups**, you make repeated sharp sounds in your throat, often because you have been eating or drinking too quickly. しゃっくり [also 'the' N] ❑ A baby may frequently get a bout of hiccups during or soon after a feeding. 赤ん坊は授乳中または授乳直後にしばしばしゃっくりをする. **3** V-I 自動詞 When you **hiccup**, you make repeated sharp sounds in your throat. しゃっくりをする ❑ She was still hiccuping from the egg she had swallowed whole. 彼女は丸のまま飲み込んだ卵のせいでしゃっくりが止まらなかった.

hid /hɪd/ **Hid** is the past tense of **hide**. hideの過去形

hid|den /hɪdⁿn/ **1** **Hidden** is the past participle of **hide**. hideの過去分詞形 **2** ADJ 形容詞 **Hidden** facts, feelings, activities, or problems are not easy to notice or discover. 隠された ❑ Under all the innocent fun, there are hidden dangers, especially for children. 無邪気な楽しみには、特に子供たちにとって危険が潜んでいる. **3** ADJ 形容詞 A **hidden** place is difficult to find. 隠れた ❑ As you descend, suddenly you see at last the hidden waterfall. 下降するにつれ、突然やっと隠れた滝が見える.

hid|den agen|da (**hidden agendas**) N-COUNT 可算名詞 If you say that someone has a **hidden agenda**, you are criticizing them because you think they are secretly trying to achieve or cause a particular thing, while they appear to be doing something else. 隠された意図 [DISAPPROVAL 不賛成] ❑ He accused foreign nations of having a hidden agenda to harm French influence. 彼は諸外国が密かにフランスの影響力を弱めようとしていると非難した.

hide /haɪd/ (**hides, hiding, hid, hidden**) **1** V-T 他動詞 If you **hide** something or someone, you put them in a place where they cannot easily be seen or found. 隠す ❑ He hid the bicycle in the hawthorn hedge. 彼はサンザシの垣根に自転車を隠した. **2** V-T/V-I 他動詞/自動詞 If you **hide** or if you **hide yourself**, you go somewhere where you cannot easily be seen or found. 身を隠す ❑ At their approach the little boy scurried and hid. 彼らが近づいてきた時、その少年は急いで身を隠した. **3** V-T 他動詞 If you **hide** your face, you press your face against something or cover your face with something, so that people cannot see it. 覆い隠す ❑ She hid her face under the collar of his jacket and started to cry. 彼女は彼のジャケットの襟の下に顔を隠し、泣き始めた. **4** V-T 他動詞 If you **hide** what you feel or know, you keep it a secret, so that no one knows about it. 秘密にする ❑ Lee tried to hide his excitement. リーは興奮を包み隠そうとした. **5** V-T 他動詞 If something **hides** an object, it covers it and prevents it from being seen. 覆い隠す ❑ The man's heavy mustache hid his upper lip completely. その男の濃い口ひげは上唇を完全に覆い隠した. **6** N-VAR 可変性名詞 A **hide** is the skin of a large animal such as a cow, horse, or elephant, which can be used for making leather. 皮革 ❑ ...the process of tanning animal hides. 獣皮の製革プロセス **7** → see also **hidden, hiding**

Thesaurus hide また次を参照:

| V. | camouflage, conceal, cover, lock up **1** **5** |

Word Partnership hide は次の語句と使われる:

ADV.	nowhere to hide **1** **2**
V.	attempt/try to hide **1** **2** **4** **5**
	run and hide **2**
N.	hide your face **3**
	hide a fact/secret, hide your fear/feelings/tears/ disappointment **4**

hid|eous /hɪdiəs/ **1** ADJ 形容詞 If you say that someone or

something is **hideous**, you mean that they are very ugly or unattractive. ひどく醜い ❑ She saw a hideous face at the window and screamed. 彼女は窓のところでひどく醜い顔を見て叫び声をあげた. **2** ADJ 形容詞 You can describe an event, experience, or action as **hideous** when you mean that it is very unpleasant, painful, or difficult to bear. 恐ろしい ❑ His family was subjected to a hideous attack by the gang. 彼の家族はギャングの恐ろしい攻撃を受けた.

hid|eous|ly /hɪdiəsli/ **1** ADV 副詞 You use **hideously** to emphasize that something is very ugly or unattractive. ひどく [EMPHASIS 強調] ❑ Everything is hideously ugly. 全てのものはひどく醜い. **2** ADV 副詞 You can use **hideously** to emphasize that something is very unpleasant or unacceptable. ひどく [EMPHASIS 強調] [ADV adj/-ed] ❑ ...a hideously complex program. ひどく複雑なプログラム

hid|ing /haɪdɪŋ/ N-UNCOUNT 不可算名詞 If someone is in **hiding**, they have secretly gone somewhere where they cannot be seen or found. 隠れている ❑ Gray is thought to be in hiding near the France/Italy border. グレーはフランスとイタリアの国境付近に潜伏中だと考えられている.

hi|er|ar|chi|cal /haɪərɑrkɪkⁿl/ ADJ 形容詞 A **hierarchical** system or organization is one in which people have different ranks or positions, depending on how important they are. 階層性の ❑ ...the traditional hierarchical system of military organization. 軍隊組織の伝統的な階層制度

Word Link arch ≈ rule : an**arch**y, hier**arch**y, mon**arch**

hi|er|ar|chy /haɪərɑrki/ (**hierarchies**) **1** N-VAR 可変性名詞 A **hierarchy** is a system of organizing people into different ranks or levels of importance, for example in society or in a company. 階層性 ❑ Like most other American companies with a rigid hierarchy, workers and managers had strictly defined duties. 厳格な階層性を持つその他米国企業の大半同様に、平社員と管理職には厳格に定められた職務があった. **2** N-COUNT-COLL 集合可算名詞 The **hierarchy** of an organization is the group of people who manage and control it. 権力者集団 ❑ The church hierarchy today feels the church should reflect the social and political realities of the country. 教会の権力者集団は現在、教会がその国の社会的・政治的現実を反映すべきだと感じている.

hi-fi /haɪ faɪ/ (**hi-fis**) N-VAR 可変性名詞 A **hi-fi** is a set of equipment on which you play CDs and tapes, and which produces stereo sound of very good quality. ハイファイ装置 [OLD-FASHIONED 古風な]

Word Link er ≈ more : cold**er**, high**er**, larg**er**

Word Link est ≈ most : cold**est**, high**est**, larg**est**

high /haɪ/ (**higher, highest, highs**) **1** ADJ 形容詞 Something that is **high** extends a long way from the bottom to the top when it is upright. You do not use **high** to describe people, animals, or plants. 高い ❑ ...a house with a high wall all around it. 周りを高い壁で囲まれた家 ❑ Mount Marcy is the highest mountain in the Adirondacks. マーシー山はアディロンダック山脈で最高峰の山だ. ● ADV 副詞 **High** is also an adverb. 高く [ADV after v] ❑ ...wagons packed high with bureaus, bedding, and cooking pots. 机、寝具、調理鍋がいっぱい詰まった荷馬車

The word you should use to describe people, animals, or plants is **tall**, not "high". ❑ She was rather tall for a woman. **Tall** is also used to describe buildings such as skyscrapers, and other things whose height is much greater than their width. ❑ ...tall pine trees. ...a tall glass vase.

2 ADJ 形容詞 You use **high** to talk or ask about how much something upright measures from the bottom to the top. 高さが ❑ ...an elegant bronze horse only nine inches high. 高さがたったの9インチのエレガントなブロンズの馬 ❑ The grass in the yard was a foot high. 庭の芝生はフートの高さだった. **3** ADJ 形容詞 If something is **high**, it is a long way above the ground, above sea level, or above a person or thing. 高い ❑ I looked down from the high window. 私は高い窓から見下ろした. ❑ The sun was high in the sky, blazing down on us. 太陽は空高く私達に照りつけた. ● ADV 副詞 **High** is also an adverb. 高く [ADV after v] ❑ ...being able to run faster or jump higher than other people. 他の人々よりも早く走り、高く飛べること ● PHRASE 句 If something is **high up**, it is a long way above the ground, above sea level, or above a person or thing. 高所の ❑ His farm was high up in the hills. 彼の農場は丘の高い場所にあった. **4** ADJ 形容詞 You can use **high** to indicate that something is great in amount, degree, or intensity. 高い, 大きい ❑ The European country with the highest birth rate is Ireland. ヨーロッパで出生率が最も高い国はアイルランドである. ❑ Official reports said casualties were high. 公報によると多数の死傷者が出た. ● ADV 副詞 **High** is also an adverb. 高く [ADV after v] ❑ He expects the unemployment figures to rise even higher in coming months. 彼は失業率が今後数ヶ月間に一段と上昇すると見込んでいる. ● PHRASE 句 You can use phrases such as "**in the high 80s**" to indicate that a number or level is, for example,

H

more than 85 but not as much as 90. 後半の **5** ADJ 形容詞 If a food or other substance is **high** in a particular ingredient, it contains a large amount of that ingredient. 大量に含んだ [v-link ADJ 'in' n] ❑ *Don't indulge in rich sauces, fried food, and thick pastry as these are high in fat.* こってりしたソース、揚げ物、厚みのあるペーストリー一脂肪を大量に含んでいるため食べない方がよい. **6** N-COUNT 可算名詞 If something reaches a **high of** a particular amount or degree, that is the greatest it has ever been. 最高水準 [oft N 'of' amount] ❑ *Traffic from Jordan to Iraq is down to a dozen loaded trucks a day, compared with a high of 200 a day.* ヨルダンからイラクへの交通量はピークの1日当たり荷を積んだトラック200車から12車に減っている. **7** ADJ 形容詞 If you say that something is a **high** priority or is **high on** your list, you mean that you consider it to be one of the most important things you have to do or deal with. 重要な ❑ *The party has not made the issue a high priority.* その党はその問題を最優先事項にしなかった. **8** ADJ 形容詞 Someone who is **high in** a particular profession or society, or has a **high** position, has a very important position and has great authority and influence. 高い [v-link ADJ 'in' n, ADJ n] ❑ *Was there anyone particularly high in the administration who was an advocate of a different policy?* 異なる政策を提唱する政府高官がいたか. ❑ *...corruption in high places.* 有力者の中の不正行為 ● PHRASE 句 Someone who is **high up in** a profession or society has a very important position. 地位の高い ❑ *His cousin is somebody quite high up in the navy.* 彼のいとこはかなり高い地位についている. **9** ADV 副詞 If you aim **high**, you try to obtain or to achieve the best that you can. 高位に [ADV after v] ❑ *You should not be afraid to aim high in the quest for an improvement in your income.* 所得の向上を追求する際には高い目標を持つことを恐れてはならない. **10** ADJ 形容詞 If someone has a **high** reputation, or people have a **high** opinion of them, people think they are very good in some way, for example at their work. 大きい ❑ *People have such high expectations of you.* 人々はあなたに大いに期待している. **11** ADJ 形容詞 If the quality or standard of something is **high**, it is extremely good. 高級な ❑ *This is high quality stuff.* これは高級な食べ物である. **12** ADJ 形容詞 A **high** sound or voice is close to the top of a particular range of notes. 高い ❑ *Her high voice really irritated Maria.* 彼女のかん高い声はマリアを本当にいらいらさせた. **13** ADJ 形容詞 If your spirits are **high**, you feel happy and excited. 意気が高まった ❑ *Her spirits were high with the hope of seeing Nick in minutes rather than hours.* 彼女は数時間後ではなく数分後にニックに会えるという期待で上機嫌だった. **14** ADJ 形容詞 If someone is **high on** alcohol or drugs, they are affected by the alcoholic drink or drugs they have taken. 酔った状態で [INFORMAL くだけた] [v-link ADJ] ❑ *He was too high on drugs and alcohol to remember them.* 彼は麻薬と酒にひどく酔っていたため彼らのことを思い出せなかった. **15** N-COUNT 可算名詞 A **high** is a feeling or mood of great excitement or happiness. 大いに興奮した [INFORMAL くだけた] ❑ *"I'm still on a high," she said after the show.* 「私はまだ興奮からさめないわ」と彼女はショーの後で言った. **16** PHRASE 句 If you say that something came from **on high**, you mean that it came from a person or place of great authority. 高い地位の ❑ *Orders had come from on high that extra care was to be taken during this week.* 今週中は特別の注意が必要だとの命令が高位の有力者から与えられた. **17** PHRASE 句 If you say that you were left **high and dry**, you are emphasizing that you were left in a difficult situation and were unable to do anything about it. 見捨てられて [EMPHASIS 強調] ❑ *Schools with better reputations will be flooded with applications while poorer schools will be left high and dry.* 評価の高い学校には志願者が殺到する一方で、劣った学校は見捨てられるだろう. **18** PHRASE 句 If you refer to the **highs and lows of** someone's life or career, you are referring to both the successful or happy times, and the unsuccessful or bad times. 浮き沈み ❑ *Here, she talks about the highs and lows of her life.* ここで彼女は彼女の人生の浮き沈みについて語る. **19** PHRASE 句 If you say that you looked **high and low** for something, you are emphasizing that you looked for it in every place that you could think of. あらゆる所を [EMPHASIS 強調] ❑ *...and I rambled around the apartment looking high and low for an aspirin or painkiller.* そして私はアスピリンか鎮痛剤を求めてアパートをくまなく探し回った.
→ see **tide**

high また次を参照:
ADJ. | tall **1 2**
elevated, lofty, tall; (*ant.*) low **3**

high|boy /ˈhɑːɪˌbɔɪ/ (**highboys**) N-COUNT 可算名詞 A **highboy** is a high chest of drawers consisting of two sections which are placed one on top of the other. 脚付きの高いタンス [AM 米国英語] ❑ *She saw him methodically searching the drawers of a highboy.* 彼女は彼がタンスの引き出しを丹念に探すのを見た.

high-class ADJ 形容詞 If you describe something as **high-class**, you mean that it is of very good quality or of superior social status. 高級の ❑ *...a high-class jeweler.* 高級宝石店

high-end ADJ 形容詞 **High-end** products, especially electronic products, are the most expensive of their kind. 最高級の ❑ *...high-*

end personal computers and computer workstations. 最高級のパソコンとコンピュータ端末

high|er edu|ca|tion N-UNCOUNT 不可算名詞 **Higher education** is education at universities and colleges. 高等教育 ❑ *...students in higher education.* 高等教育を受ける学生

high-flying ADJ 形容詞 A **high-flying** person is successful or is likely to be successful in their career. 野心的な ❑ *...her high-flying newspaper-editor husband.* 野心的な新聞の論説委員である彼女の夫

high|lands /ˈhɑɪləndz/ N-PLURAL 複数名詞 **Highlands** are mountainous areas of land. 山岳地方

high|light /ˈhɑɪlaɪt/ (**highlights, highlighting, highlighted**) **1** V-T 他動詞 If someone or something **highlights** a point or problem, they emphasize it or make you think about it. 浮き彫りにする ❑ *Last year Collins wrote a moving ballad which highlighted the plight of the homeless.* 昨年コリンズはホームレスの人々の状態を浮き彫りにした心を動かすバラードを書いた. **2** V-T 他動詞 To **highlight** a piece of text means to mark it in a different color, either with a special type of pen or on a computer screen. マーカーで印をつける ❑ *Highlight the chosen area by clicking and holding down the left mouse button.* 左側のマウスボタンをクリックし、押さえることによって望む場所にマーカーで印をつけなさい. **3** N-COUNT 可算名詞 The **highlights** of an event, activity, or period of time are the most interesting or exciting parts of it. 重要な部分 ❑ *...a match that is likely to prove one of the highlights of the tournament.* トーナメントの見ものの1つとなりそうな試合

highlight は次の語句と使われる:
N. | highlight **concerns/problems**, highlight **differences 1**
highlight of *someone's* career **3**

high|ly /ˈhɑɪli/ **1** ADV 副詞 **Highly** is used before some adjectives to mean "very." 非常に [ADV adj] ❑ *Mr. Singh was a highly successful salesman.* シング氏は高い業績を持つ営業社員だ. ❑ *It seems highly unlikely that she ever existed.* 彼女が実際に存在したことは非常に疑わしい. **2** ADV 副詞 You use **highly** to indicate that someone has an important position in an organization or set of people. 高い地位に [ADV -ed] ❑ *...a highly placed government advisor.* 高位の政府顧問 **3** ADV 副詞 If someone is **highly** paid, they receive a large salary. 高く [ADV -ed] ❑ *...the 30 most highly paid athletes in the world.* 世界で最も高給取りのアスリート30名 **4** ADV 副詞 If you think **highly** of something or someone, you think they are extremely good. 高く評価して ❑ *Daphne and Michael thought highly of the school.* ダフネとマイケルはその学校を高く評価した.

highly は次の語句と使われる:
V. | highly **recommended**, highly **respected 1**
ADJ. | highly **addictive**, highly **competitive**, highly **contagious**, highly **controversial**, highly **critical**, highly **educated**, highly **intelligent**, highly **qualified**, highly **skilled**, highly **successful**, highly **technical**, highly **trained**, highly **unlikely**, highly **visible 1**
highly **paid 3**

High|ness /ˈhɑɪnɪs/ (**Highnesses**) N-VOC 呼格名詞 Expressions such as "**Your Highness**" or "**His Highness**" are used to address or refer to a member of a royal family other than a king or queen. 殿下 [POLITENESS 丁寧さ] ❑ *That would be best, Your Highness.* 殿下、それが最善だと思われます.

high-pitched ADJ 形容詞 A **high-pitched** sound is shrill and high in pitch. 甲高い ❑ *A woman squealed in a high-pitched voice.* 1人の女は甲高い声で悲鳴を上げた.

high-powered **1** ADJ 形容詞 A **high-powered** machine or piece of equipment is very powerful and efficient. 高性能の ❑ *...high-powered lasers.* 高性能のレーザー **2** ADJ 形容詞 Someone who is **high-powered** or has a **high-powered** job has a very important and responsible job which requires a lot of ability. 非常に有能な ❑ *...a high-powered lawyer.* 有力な弁護士

high-profile ADJ 形容詞 A **high-profile** person or a **high-profile** event attracts a lot of attention or publicity. 人の注意を引く ❑ *...high-profile criminal defense lawyer, Gerald Shargel.* 著名な被告人のための刑事専門弁護士、ジェラルド・シャーゲル

high-rise (**high-rises**) **1** ADJ 形容詞 **High-rise** buildings are modern buildings which are very tall and have many levels or floors. 高層の [ADJ n] ❑ *...high-rise office buildings.* 高層のオフィスビル ● N-COUNT 可算名詞 A **high-rise** is a high-rise building. 高層の建物 ❑ *That big high-rise above us is where Brian lives.* 上に見える大きな高層アパートにはブリアンが住んでいる.

high school (**high schools**) N-VAR; N-IN-NAMES 可変性名詞、名称中の名詞 A **high school** is a school for children usually aged between fourteen and eighteen. ハイスクール ❑ *...an 18-year-old*

inner-city kid who dropped out of high school. ハイスクールを中退したスラム地区の18歳の子供
→ see **graduation**

high street /high streets/ N-COUNT; N-IN-NAMES 可算名詞, 名称中の名詞 The **high street** of a town is the main street where most of the stores and banks are. 大通り [mainly BRIT 主に英国英語; AM **main street** 米国英語 **main street**]

high-tech /haɪ tɛk/ also **high tech** or **hi tech** ADJ 形容詞 **High-tech** activities or equipment involve or result from the use of high technology. ハイテク □ *...such high-tech industries as computers or telecommunications.* コンピュータや通信などのハイテク産業

high tech|nol|ogy N-UNCOUNT 不可算名詞 **High technology** is the practical use of advanced scientific research and knowledge, especially in relation to electronics and computers, and the development of new advanced machines and equipment. 先端技術 □ *...a limited war using high technology.* 先端技術を使った限定戦争

high|way /haɪweɪ/ (highways) N-COUNT 可算名詞 A **highway** is a main road, especially one that connects towns or cities. 主要道路 [mainly AM 主に米国英語] □ *I crossed the highway, dodging the traffic.* 私は交通をさっと避け、主要道路を渡った.
→ see **traffic**

hi|jack /haɪdʒæk/ (hijacks, hijacking, hijacked) **1** V-T 他動詞 If someone **hijacks** a plane or other vehicle, they illegally take control of it by force while it is traveling from one place to another. ハイジャックする □ *Two men tried to hijack a plane on a flight from Riga to Murmansk.* 2人の男がリガ発ムルマンスク行きの便をハイジャックしようとした. ● N-COUNT 可算名詞 **Hijack** is also a noun. ハイジャック □ *Every minute during the hijack seemed like a week.* ハイジャックされている間は1分が1週間のように感じた. ● **hi|jack|ing** (hijackings) N-COUNT 可算名詞 ハイジャックすること □ *Car hijackings are running at a rate of nearly 50 a day.* 車のハイジャックは1日当り50件近くのペースで推移している. **2** V-T 他動詞 If you say that someone **has hijacked** something, you disapprove of the way in which they have taken control of it when they had no right to do so. 乗っ取る [DISAPPROVAL 不賛成] □ *A peaceful demonstration had been hijacked by anarchists intent on causing trouble.* 平和なデモは問題を起こそうとするアナキストに乗っ取られた.

hi|jack|er /haɪdʒækər/ (hijackers) N-COUNT 可算名詞 A **hijacker** is a person who hijacks a plane or other vehicle. ハイジャック犯人

hike /haɪk/ (hikes, hiking, hiked) **1** N-COUNT 可算名詞 A **hike** is a long walk in the country, especially one that you go on for pleasure. ハイキング □ *The site is reached by a 30-minute hike through dense forest.* その場所は密林を30分歩いて到達できます. **2** V-I 自動詞 If you **hike**, you go for a long walk in the country. ハイキングする □ *You could hike through the Fish River Canyon – it's entirely up to you.* フィッシュ川峡谷を通ってハイキングできる. 全く君次第だ. ● **hik|ing** N-UNCOUNT 不可算名詞 □ *...some harder, more strenuous hiking on cliff pathways.* 崖の小道のやや難しくより大変なハイキング **3** N-COUNT 可算名詞 A **hike** is a sudden or large increase in prices, rates, taxes, or quantities. 引き上げ [INFORMAL くだけた] □ *...a sudden 1.75 percent hike in interest rates.* 1.75%の突然の利上げ **4** V-T 他動詞 To **hike** prices, rates, taxes, or quantities means to increase them suddenly or by a large amount. 引き上げる [INFORMAL くだけた] □ *It has now been forced to hike its rates by 5.25 percent.* 今や比率を5.25%引き上げることを余儀なくされた. ● PHRASAL VERB 句動詞 **Hike up** means the same as **hike**. 引き上げる □ *The insurers have started hiking up premiums by huge amounts.* 保険会社は保険料を大幅に引き上げ始めた.

hik|er /haɪkər/ (hikers) N-COUNT 可算名詞 A **hiker** is a person who is going for a long walk in the countryside for pleasure. ハイカー

hi|lari|ous /hɪlɛəriəs/ ADJ 形容詞 If something is **hilarious**, it is extremely funny and makes you laugh a lot. とてもおかしい □ *We thought it was hilarious when we first heard about it.* 私達は始めてそれを知った時とてもおかしいと思った. ● **hi|lari|ous|ly** 副詞 ひどく □ *She found it hilariously funny.* 彼女はそれがひどくおかしいと思った.

hill /hɪl/ (hills) **1** N-COUNT; N-IN-NAMES 可算名詞, 名称中の名詞 A **hill** is an area of land that is higher than the land that surrounds it. 丘 □ *...the shady street that led up the hill to the office building.* 坂の上のオフィスビルに通じる木陰の道 **2** PHRASE 句 If you say that someone is **over the hill**, you are saying rudely that they are old and no longer fit, attractive, or capable of doing useful work. もう年の [INFORMAL くだけた, DISAPPROVAL 不賛成] □ *He doesn't take kindly to suggestions that he is over the hill.* 彼はもう年だという提案にはすんなりと耳を貸さない.

hilly /hɪli/ (hillier, hilliest) ADJ 形容詞 A **hilly** area has many hills. 丘陵の多い □ *The areas where the fighting is taking place are hilly and densely wooded.* 戦闘が行なわれている地域は丘陵が多く、密林だ.

him /hɪm/

Him is a third person singular pronoun. **Him** is used as the object of a verb or a preposition.

Him は3人称単数の代名詞である. **Him** は動詞または前置詞の目的語として用いられる.

1 PRON-SING 単数代名詞 You use **him** to refer to a man, boy, or male animal. 彼を [V PRON, prep PRON] □ *John's aunt died suddenly and left him a surprisingly large sum.* ジョンの叔母は急死し、驚くほどの大金を彼に残した. □ *Is Sam there? Let me talk to him.* サムはそこにいるか. 彼に話させてくれ. **2** PRON-SING 単数代名詞 In written English, **him** is sometimes used to refer to a person without saying whether that person is a man or a woman. Some people dislike this use and prefer to use "him or her" or "them." あの人 [V PRON, prep PRON] □ *If the child encounters "hear," we should show him that this is the base word in "hearing" and "hears."* 子供が「聞く」という言葉に出くわした場合、これは「聞くこと」と「聞く」の基本語だとその子供に教えるべきだ.

him|self /hɪmsɛlf/

Himself is a third person singular reflexive pronoun. **Himself** is used when the object of a verb or preposition refers to the same person as the subject of the verb, except in meaning **3**.

Himself は3人称単数の再帰代名詞である. **Himself** は, **3** を意味する場合以外は, 動詞または前置詞の目的語が動詞の主語と同じ人物を指すときに用いられる.

1 PRON-REFL 再帰代名詞 You use **himself** to refer to a man, boy, or male animal. 彼自身に [V PRON, prep PRON] □ *He poured himself a whiskey and sat down in the chair.* 彼はウィスキーを注ぎ、椅子に座った. □ *William went away muttering to himself.* ウィリアムは独り言を言いながら立ち去った. **2** PRON-REFL 再帰代名詞 In written English, **himself** is sometimes used to refer to a person without saying whether that person is a man or a woman. Some people dislike this use and prefer to use "himself or herself" or "themselves." 自分自身を [V PRON, prep PRON] □ *There is nothing more dangerous than someone who thinks of himself as a victim.* 自分自身を被害者だと思う人ほど危険な人物はいない. **3** PRON-REFL-EMPH 強調的再帰代名詞 You use **himself** to emphasize the person or thing that you are referring to. **Himself** is sometimes used instead of "him" as the object of a verb or preposition. 彼自身 [EMPHASIS 強調] □ *The president himself is on a visit to Beijing.* 大統領ご自身は北京訪問中である.

hind /haɪnd/ ADJ 形容詞 An animal's **hind** legs are at the back of its body. 後ろの [ADJ n] □ *Suddenly the cow kicked up its hind legs.* 牛は突然後ろ足をけった.

hin|der /hɪndər/ (hinders, hindering, hindered) **1** V-T 他動詞 If something **hinders** you, it makes it more difficult for you to do something or make progress. 妨害する □ *Further investigation was hindered by the loss of all documentation on the case.* 更なる調査はその事件に関する全ての書類が失われたため遅れた. **2** V-T 他動詞 If something **hinders** your movement, it makes it difficult for you to move forward or move around. 邪魔する □ *A thigh injury increasingly hindered her mobility.* 大腿（たい）部の負傷により彼女の活動は一層の制約を受けるようになった.

hin|drance /hɪndrəns/ (hindrances) N-COUNT 可算名詞 A **hindrance** is a person or thing that makes it more difficult for you to do something. 妨害 □ *The higher rates have been a hindrance to economic recovery.* 金利の引き上げは経済回復を妨げてきた.

hind|sight /haɪndsaɪt/ N-UNCOUNT 不可算名詞 **Hindsight** is the ability to understand and realize something about an event after it has happened, although you did not understand or realize it at the time. あと知恵 □ *With hindsight, we'd all do things differently.* あとから考えてみると、我々は皆異なる行動を取るだろう.

Hin|du /hɪndu/ (Hindus) **1** N-COUNT 可算名詞 A **Hindu** is a person who believes in Hinduism and follows its teachings. ヒンドゥー教信者 **2** N-UNCOUNT 不可算名詞 **Hindu** is used to describe things that belong or relate to Hinduism. ヒンドゥー教の □ *...a Hindu temple.* ヒンドゥー教寺院
→ see **religion**

Hin|du|ism /hɪnduɪzəm/ N-UNCOUNT 不可算名詞 **Hinduism** is an Indian religion. It has many gods and teaches that people have another life on earth after they die. ヒンドゥー教

hinge /hɪndʒ/ (hinges, hinging, hinged) N-COUNT 可算名詞 A **hinge** is a piece of metal, wood, or plastic that is used to join a door to its frame or to join two things together so that one of them can swing freely. ちょうつがい □ *The top swung open on well-oiled hinges.* 上部はよく油を差したちょうつがいでさっと開いた.
▶ **hinge on** PHRASAL VERB 句動詞 Something that **hinges on** one thing or event depends entirely on it. 次第である □ *The plan hinges on a deal being struck with a new company.* 計画は新しい会社と結んだ取引次第だ.

hint /hɪnt/ (hints, hinting, hinted) **1** N-COUNT 可算名詞 A **hint** is a suggestion about something that is made in an indirect way. 暗示 □ *I'd dropped a hint about having an exhibition of his work up here.* 私は彼の作品の展示をここで開くことについてほのめかした. ● PHRASE 句 If you **take a hint**, you understand something that is suggested

to you indirectly. その意を悟る ❑*"I think I hear the telephone ringing."* —*"Okay, I can take a hint."* 「電話が鳴っているのが聞こえる。」「分かったよ。」 **2** V-I 自動詞 If you **hint at** something, you suggest it in an indirect way. 言外にほのめかす ❑*She hinted at the possibility of a treat of some sort.* 彼女は何らかのもてなしの可能性をほのめかした。 **3** N-COUNT 可算名詞 A **hint** is a helpful piece of advice, usually about how to do something. 助言 ❑*Here are some helpful hints to make your journey easier.* これはあなたの旅を楽にするための助言です。 **4** N-SING 単数名詞 A **hint** of something is a very small amount of it. 微量 ❑*She added only a hint of vermouth to the gin.* 彼女はジンにほんのわずかのベルモットを加えた。

hip /hɪp/ (**hips**) **1** N-COUNT 可算名詞 Your **hips** are the two areas at the sides of your body between the tops of your legs and your waist. 腰 ❑*Tracey put her hands on her hips and sighed.* トレーシーは腰に手を当ててため息をついた。 **2** N-COUNT 可算名詞 You refer to the bones between the tops of your legs and your waist as your **hips**. 股（こ）関節 ❑*Eventually, surgeons replaced both hips and both shoulders.* 結局外科医は両方の股関節と肩関節の置換えを行なった。 **3** ADJ 形容詞 If you say that someone is **hip**, you mean that they are very modern and follow all the latest fashions, for example in clothes and ideas. 最近のことに明るい [INFORMAL くだけた] ❑*...a hip young character with tight-cropped blond hair and stylish glasses.* 丸刈りの金髪とスタイリッシュなメガネをかけたナウい若者 **4** EXCLAM 感嘆詞 If a large group of people want to show their appreciation or approval of someone, one of them says "**Hip hip**" and they all shout "**hooray**." ヒップ **5** PHRASE 句 If you say that someone **shoots from the hip**, you mean that they react to situations or give their opinion very quickly, without stopping to think. 考えなしに行動する ❑*Judges don't have to shoot from the hip. They have the leisure to think, to decide.* 判事は急いで行動する必要はない。彼らにはよく考えて決める余裕がある。

hip|pie /hɪpi/ (**hippies**) also **hippy** N-COUNT 可算名詞 **Hippies** were young people in the 1960s and 1970s who rejected conventional ways of living, dressing, and behaving, and tried to live a life based on peace and love. Hippies often had long hair and many took drugs. ヒッピー

hire /haɪər/ (**hires, hiring, hired**) **1** V-T/V-I 他動詞/自動詞 If you **hire** someone, you employ them or pay them to do a particular job for you. 雇う ❑*Sixteen of the contestants have hired lawyers and are suing the organizers.* 16名の競技者が弁護士を雇い、主催者を起訴している。 ❑*He will be in charge of all hiring and firing at PHA.* 彼はPHAの人事の全てを管理することになっている。 **2** V-T 他動詞 If you **hire** something, you pay money to the owner so that you can use it for a period of time. 借りる [mainly BRIT 主に英国英語; AM usually **rent** 米国英語では通常 **rent**] **3** N-UNCOUNT 不可算名詞 You use **hire** to refer to the activity or business of hiring something. 賃貸し [mainly BRIT 主に英国英語; AM usually **rental** 米国英語では通常 **rental**] **4** PHRASE 句 If something is **for hire**, it is available for you to hire. 賃貸し [mainly BRIT 主に英国英語; AM usually **for rent** 米国英語では通常 **for rent**]

▸ **hire out** PHRASAL VERB 句動詞 If you **hire out** a person's services, you allow them to be used in return for payment. 貸し出す ❑*...employment agencies which hire out personnel to foreign companies.* 外国企業に従業員を貸し出す人材会社

hire pur|chase N-UNCOUNT 不可算名詞 **Hire purchase** is a way of buying goods gradually. You make regular payments until you have paid the full price and the goods belong to you. The abbreviation **HP** is often used. 分割払い購入制度 [BRIT 英国英語] [oft N n] [AM **installment plan** 米国英語 **installment plan**]

his

The determiner is pronounced /hɪz/. The pronoun is pronounced /hɪz/.

限定詞は /hɪz/ と発音される. 代名詞は /hɪz/ と発音される.

His is a third person singular possessive determiner. **His** is also a possessive pronoun.

His は3人称単数所有限定詞である. **His** はまた所有代名詞である.

DET 限定詞 You use **his** to indicate that something belongs or relates to a man, boy, or male animal. 彼の ❑*Brian splashed water on his face, then brushed his teeth.* ブライアンは顔を洗い、歯を磨いた。 ❑*He spent a large part of his career in Hollywood.* 彼は経歴の大部分をハリウッドで積んだ。 ● PRON-POSS 所有代名詞 **His** is also a possessive pronoun. 彼のもの ❑*Staff say the decision was his.* スタッフはその決定は彼が行なったと言っている。

His|pan|ic /hɪspænɪk/ (**Hispanics**) ADJ 形容詞 A **Hispanic** person is a citizen of the United States of America who originally came from Latin America, or whose family originally came from Latin America. ラテンアメリカ系の ❑*...a group of Hispanic doctors in Washington.* ワシントンのラテンアメリカ系医者の集団 ● N-COUNT 可算名詞 A **Hispanic** is someone who is Hispanic. ラテンアメリカ系の人 ❑*About 80 percent of Hispanics here are U.S. citizens.* ここにいるラテンアメリカ系の人の約8割は米国市民だ。

hiss /hɪs/ (**hisses, hissing, hissed**) **1** V-I 自動詞 To **hiss** means to make a sound like a long "s." シューという音を出す ❑*The tires of Lenny's bike hissed over the wet pavement as he slowed down.* レニーの自転車のタイヤはスピードを落とすにつれて濡れた歩道でシューシューと音を立てた。 ❑*My cat hissed when I stepped on its tail.* 私の猫は私に尻尾を踏まれてシューという音を立てた。 ● N-COUNT 可算名詞 **Hiss** is also a noun. シューという声音 ❑*...the hiss of water running into the burned pan.* こげた鍋にジュッと水が流れる音 ● **hiss|ing** N-UNCOUNT 不可算名詞 シューという音 ❑*...a silence broken only by a steady hissing from above my head.* 頭上から絶え間なくシューという音にのみ壊されている沈黙 **2** V-I 自動詞 If people **hiss at** someone such as a performer or a person making a speech, they express their disapproval or dislike of that person by making long loud "s" sounds. シーと言う ❑*One had to listen hard to catch the words of the president's speech as the delegates booed and hissed.* 代議員のブーイングと野次のため、大統領の演説を聞き取るためには集中して聞く必要があった。 ● N-COUNT 可算名詞 **Hiss** is also a noun. シーという音 ❑*She was greeted with boos and hisses.* 彼女はブーイングに迎えられた。

his|to|rian /hɪstɔriən/ (**historians**) N-COUNT 可算名詞 A **historian** is a person who specializes in the study of history, and who writes books and articles about it. 歴史家 → see **history**

his|tor|ic /hɪstɔrɪk/ ADJ 形容詞 Something that is **historic** is important in history, or likely to be considered important at some time in the future. 歴史上重要な ❑*...the historic changes in Eastern Europe.* 歴史上重要な東欧の変化

his|tori|cal /hɪstɔrɪkᵊl/ **1** ADJ 形容詞 **Historical** people, situations, or things existed in the past and are considered to be a part of history. 歴史的な [ADJ n] ❑*...an important historical figure.* 重要な歴史的人物 ❑*...the historical impact of Western capitalism on the world.* 西欧の資本主義が世界に与えた歴史的影響 ● **his|tori|cal|ly** ADV 副詞 歴史的に ❑*Historically, royal marriages have been cold, calculating affairs.* 皇室の結婚は歴史的に冷淡で計算ずくの出来事だった。 **2** ADJ 形容詞 [ADJ n] **Historical** books, movies, or pictures describe or represent people, situations, or things that existed in the past. 歴史に基づく ❑*He is writing a historical novel about nineteenth-century France.* 彼は19世紀のフランスについて歴史小説を執筆中だ。 **3** ADJ 形容詞 **Historical** information, research, and discussion is related to the study of history. 歴史に関する [ADJ n] ❑*...historical records.* 史的記録文書

his|to|ry /hɪstəri, -tri/ (**histories**) **1** N-UNCOUNT 不可算名詞 You can refer to the events of the past as **history**. You can also refer to the past events which concern a particular topic or place as its **history**. 歴史 ❑*The Catholic Church has played a prominent role throughout Polish history.* カソリック教会はポーランドの歴史を通じて重要な役割を演じた。 ❑*...the most evil mass killer in history.* 歴史上最も邪悪な大量殺人者 ● PHRASE 句 Someone who **makes history** does something that is considered to be important and significant in the development of the world or of a particular society. 歴史に残るようなことをする ❑*Willy Brandt made history by visiting East Germany in 1970.* ウィリー・ブラントは1970年に東独を訪問することによって画期的なことをした。 ● PHRASE 句 If someone or something **goes down in history**, people in the future remember them because of particular actions that they have done or because of particular

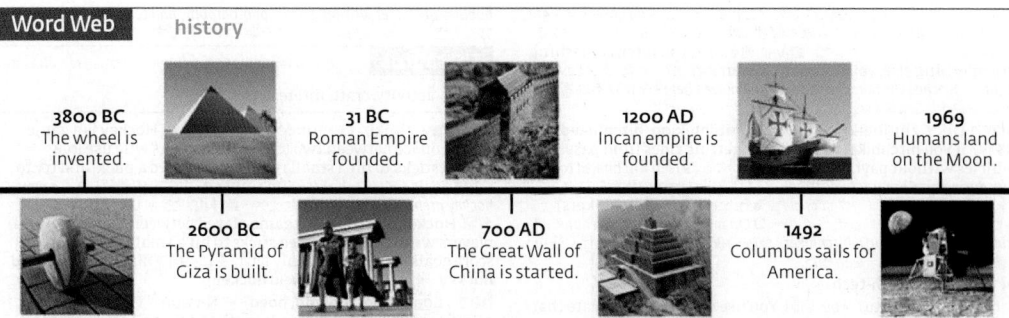

Word Web   history

3800 BC
The wheel is invented.

31 BC
Roman Empire founded.

1200 AD
Incan empire is founded.

1969
Humans land on the Moon.

2600 BC
The Pyramid of Giza is built.

700 AD
The Great Wall of China is started.

1492
Columbus sails for America.

Open any history textbook and you will find **timelines**. They show important dates for **ancient civilizations**—when **empires** appeared and disappeared, and when **wars** were fought. But, how much of what we read in **history** books is **fact**? **Accounts** of the **past** are often based on how archeologists interpret the **artifacts** they find. **Scholars** often rely on the **records** of the people who were in power. These **historians** included certain facts and left out others. Historians today look beyond official records. They research **primary source documents** such as **diaries**. They describe **events** from different **points of view**.

h

events that have happened. 歴史に残る ❏ *Bradley will go down in history as Los Angeles' longest serving mayor*. ブラッドリーは最も長期間ロサンジェルスの知事を務めた人物として歴史に名をとどめるだろう. **2** N-UNCOUNT 不可算名詞 **History** is a subject studied in schools, colleges, and universities that deals with events that have happened in the past. 歴史学 ❏ *...a lecturer in history at Birmingham University*. バーミンガム大学の歴史学の講師 **3** N-COUNT 可算名詞 A **history** is an account of events that have happened in the past. 経歴 ❏ *...his magnificent history of broadcasting in Canada*. カナダの彼の素晴らしい放送の経歴 **4** N-COUNT 可算名詞 If a person or a place has **a history of** something, it has been very common or has happened frequently in their past. の前歴がある ❏ *He had a history of drinking problems*. 彼には酒乱の気がある. **5** N-COUNT 可算名詞 Someone's **history** is the set of facts that are known about their past. 履歴 ❏ *He couldn't get a new job because of his medical history*. 彼は病歴のために新しい職を得ることができなかった. **6** PHRASE 句 If you are telling someone about an event and say **the rest is history**, you mean that you do not need to tell them what happened next because everyone knows about it already. 後は知ってのとおりだ ❏ *We met in college, the rest is history*. 我々は大学で出会った. 後はご存知の通りだ.

→ see Word Web: **history**

Word Partnership   history は次の語句と使われる:

N.	the course of history, world history **1**
	family history **1** **5**
	life history **5**
V.	go down in history, make history **1**
	teach history **2**

hit /hɪt/ (hits, hitting)

The form **hit** is used in the present tense and is the past and present participle.

hit 形は現在時制に使われ, 過去と現在分詞でもある.

1 V-T 他動詞 If you **hit** someone or something, you deliberately touch them with a lot of force, with your hand or an object held in your hand. 打つ ❏ *Find the exact grip that allows you to hit the ball hard*. ボールを強く打てる正確な握り方を見つけなさい. **2** V-T 他動詞 When one thing **hits** another, it touches it with a lot of force. 衝突する ❏ *The car had apparently hit a traffic sign before skidding out of control*. 車はスキッドして制御できなくなる前に信号に衝突したらしい. **3** V-T 他動詞 If a bomb or missile **hits** its target, it reaches it. 命中する ❏ *...multiple-warhead missiles that could hit many targets at a time*. 一度に多くの標的に命中させられる多弾頭ミサイル ● N-COUNT 可算名詞 **Hit** is also a noun. 打撃 ❏ *First a house took a direct hit and then the rocket exploded*. まず家屋は直撃弾を受け, それからロケットは爆発した. **4** V-T 他動詞 If something **hits** a person, place, or thing, it affects them very badly. 打撃を与える [JOURNALISM ジャーナリズム] ❏ *The plan to charge motorists to use the freeway is going to hit me hard*. 高速道路を有料にする計画は私に大きな打撃となるだろう. ❏ *About two hundred people died in the earthquake which hit northern Peru*. ペルー北部を襲った地震で約200人が死亡した. **5** V-T 他動詞 When a feeling or an idea **hits** you, it suddenly affects you or comes into your mind. 思い浮かぶ ❏ *It hit me that I had a choice*. 私には選択肢があることを思い出した. **6** V-T 他動詞 If you **hit** a particular high or low point on a scale of something such

as success or health, you reach it. 達する [JOURNALISM ジャーナリズム] ❏ *He admits to having hit the lowest point in his life*. 彼は人生のどん底に達したことを認めている. **7** N-COUNT 可算名詞 If a CD, movie, or play is a **hit**, it is very popular and successful. ヒット ❏ *The song became a massive hit in 1945*. その歌は1945年に大ヒットした. **8** N-COUNT 可算名詞 A **hit** is a single visit to a website. ヒット [COMPUTING コンピューティング] ❏ *Our small company has had 78,000 hits on its Internet pages*. わが社は小企業だがインターネットで78000のヒットがあった. **9** N-COUNT 可算名詞 If someone who is searching for information on the Internet gets a **hit**, they find a website where there is that information. データのある場所をうまく突き止めること **10** PHRASE 句 If two people **hit it off**, they like each other and become friendly as soon as they meet. うまくやっていく [INFORMAL くだけた] ❏ *Dad and Walter hit it off straight away*. お父さんとウォルターはすぐに仲良くなった. **11** to **hit the headlines** → see **headline** **12** to **hit home** → see **home** **13** to **hit the nail on the head** → see **nail** **14** to **hit the roof** → see **roof**

▶ **hit on** or **hit upon** PHRASAL VERB 句動詞 **1** If you **hit on** an idea or a solution to a problem, or **hit upon** it, you think of it. ふと思いつく ❏ *After running through the numbers in every possible combination, we finally hit on a solution*. ありとあらゆる数字の組み合わせを考慮した後, 我々はやっと解決策を思いついた. **2** PHRASAL VERB 句動詞 If someone **hits on** you, they speak or behave in a way that shows they want to have a sexual relationship with you. 言い寄る [INFORMAL くだけた] ❏ *She was hitting on me and I was surprised and flattered*. 彼女は私にしつこく言い寄ってきたので, 私は驚くと共にうれしくなった.

▶ **hit up** PHRASAL VERB 句動詞 If you **hit** somebody **up** for something, especially for money, you ask them for it. (借金など を) 求める [AM 米国英語, INFORMAL くだけた] ❏ *They hit up Hector for the last $250*. 彼はヘクターに最後の250ドルを求めた.

Thesaurus   hit また次を参照:

V.	bang, beat, knock, pound, slap, smack, strike **1**
N.	smash, success, triumph; (*ant.*) failure **7**

Word Partnership   hit は次の語句と使われる:

N.	hit a ball, hit a button, hit the brakes **1**
	earthquakes/famine/storms hit *someplace* **4**
	a hit movie/show/song

hit-and-run **1** ADJ 形容詞 A **hit-and-run** accident is an accident in which the driver of a vehicle hits someone and then drives away without stopping. ひき逃げの [ADJ n] ❏ *...the victim of a hit-and-run accident*. ひき逃げ事故の被害者 **2** ADJ 形容詞 A **hit-and-run** attack on an enemy position relies on surprise and speed for its success. ヒットアンドランによる [ADJ n] ❏ *The rebels appear to be making hit-and-run guerrilla style attacks on military targets*. 反逆者は軍の標的にヒットアンドラン戦法によるゲリラ式の攻撃をしているようである.

hitch /hɪtʃ/ (hitches, hitching, hitched) **1** N-COUNT 可算名詞 A **hitch** is a slight problem or difficulty which causes a short delay. 思いがけない障害 ❏ *After some technical hitches the show finally got under way*. 技術的問題の後, ショーはやっと始まった. **2** V-T/V-I 他動詞/自動詞 If you **hitch**, **hitch** a lift, or **hitch** a ride, you hitchhike.

ヒッチハイクする [INFORMAL くだけた] ❏*There was no garage in sight, so I hitched a lift into town.* 自動車修理工場は全く見かけなかったので私は町までヒッチハイクした. **2** V-T 他動詞 If you **hitch** something **to** something else, you hook it or fasten it there. つなぐ ❏*Last night we hitched the horse to the cart and moved here.* 昨夜我々は馬を荷車につないでここに移動した.

hitch|hike /ˈhɪtʃhaɪk/ (**hitchhikes, hitchhiking, hitchhiked**) V-I 自動詞 If you **hitchhike**, you travel by getting rides from passing vehicles without paying. ヒッチハイクする ❏*Neff hitchhiked to New York during his Christmas vacation.* ネフはクリスマスの休暇中にヒッチハイクしてニューヨークに行った. ● **hitch|hiker** (**hitchhikers**) N-COUNT 可算名詞 ヒッチハイカー ❏*On my way to Vancouver one Friday night I picked up a hitchhiker.* 金曜の夜, バンクーバーに行く途中で私はヒッチハイカーを拾った.

hi tech → see **high-tech**

hither|to /ˌhɪðərˈtuː/ ADV 副詞 You use **hitherto** to indicate that something was true up until the time you are talking about, although it may no longer be the case. 今まで [FORMAL 形式ばった] ❏*The ruling party is likely to be opened up to let in people hitherto excluded.* 与党は今まで除外されていた人々に解放されそうだ.

hit list (**hit lists**) **1** N-COUNT 可算名詞 If someone has a **hit list of** people or things, they are intending to take action concerning those people or things. 対象者リスト ❏*Some banks also have a hit list of people whom they threaten to sue for damages.* 一部の銀行は損害賠償のために提訴を脅かしている人々のリストも持っている. **2** N-COUNT 可算名詞 A **hit list** is a list that someone makes of people they intend to have killed. 暗殺者リスト ❏*...a group of killers instructed by the deputy minister to attack people on his hit list.* 大臣代理から彼の暗殺者リスト上の人々を攻撃するよう指示された殺人者の集団

HIV /ˌeɪtʃaɪ ˈviː/ **1** N-UNCOUNT 不可算名詞 **HIV** is a virus which reduces people's resistance to illness and can cause AIDS. **HIV** is an abbreviation for "human immunodeficiency virus." ヒト免疫不全ウィルス **2** PHRASE 句 If someone is **HIV positive**, they are infected with the HIV virus, and may develop AIDS. If someone is **HIV negative**, they are not infected with the virus. HIV陽性, HIV陰性

hive /haɪv/ (**hives**) **1** N-COUNT 可算名詞 A **hive** is a structure in which bees are kept, which is designed so that the beekeeper can collect the honey that they produce. ミツバチの巣箱 **2** N-COUNT 可算名詞 If you describe a place as a **hive of** activity, you approve of the fact that there is a lot of activity there or that people are busy working there. 活動の中心地 [APPROVAL 賛成] ❏*In the morning the house was a hive of activity.* 朝, その家は活気に満ちていた.

hoard /hɔːrd/ (**hoards, hoarding, hoarded**) **1** V-T 他動詞 If you **hoard** things such as food or money, you save or store them, often in secret, because they are valuable or important to you. ため込む ❏*They've begun to hoard food and gasoline and save their money.* 彼らは食料とガソリンをため込み, 貯金し始めた. **2** N-COUNT 可算名詞 A **hoard** is a store of things that you have saved and that are valuable or important to you or you do not want other people to have. 秘蔵物 ❏*The case involves a hoard of silver and jewels valued at up to $40m.* その事件は最高4千万ドルの価値のある銀などの宝石の秘蔵物が関与している.

hoard|ing /ˈhɔːrdɪŋ/ (**hoardings**) N-COUNT 可算名詞 A **hoarding** is a very large board at the side of a road or on the side of a building, which is used for displaying advertisements and posters. 広告掲示板 [BRIT 英国英語; AM **billboard** 米国英語 **billboard**]

hoarse /hɔːrs/ (**hoarser, hoarsest**) ADJ 形容詞 If your voice is **hoarse** or if you are **hoarse**, your voice sounds rough and unclear, for example because your throat is sore. しわがれた ❏*"So what do you think?" she said in a hoarse whisper.* 「じゃああなたはどう思う?」と彼女はかすれた声でささやいた. ● **hoarse|ly** ADV 副詞 かすれた声で ❏*"Thank you," Maria said hoarsely.* 「ありがとう」とマリアはハスキーな声で言った.

hoax /hoʊks/ (**hoaxes**) N-COUNT 可算名詞 A **hoax** is a trick in which someone tells people a lie, for example that there is a bomb somewhere when there is not, or that a picture is genuine when it is not. でっち上げ ❏*He denied making the hoax call but was convicted after a short trial.* 彼はいたずら電話をしたことを否定したが, 短期間の裁判の後で有罪の判決を受けた.

hob /hɒb/ (**hobs**) N-COUNT 可算名詞 A **hob** is a surface on top of a stove or set into a work surface, which can be heated in order to cook things on it. 調理用レンジの最上部 [BRIT 英国英語; AM **cooktop** 米国英語 **cooktop**]

hob|ble /ˈhɒbəl/ (**hobbles, hobbling, hobbled**) V-I 自動詞 If you **hobble**, you walk in an awkward way with small steps, for example because your foot is injured. 足を引きずって歩く ❏*He got up slowly and hobbled over to the coffee table.* 彼はのっそりと起き上がり, コーヒーテーブルまでよろよろと歩いていった.

hob|by /ˈhɒbi/ (**hobbies**) N-COUNT 可算名詞 A **hobby** is an activity that you enjoy doing in your spare time. 趣味 ❏*My*

hobbies are letter writing, music, photography, and tennis. 趣味は手紙を書くこと, 音楽, 写真, テニスを楽しむことです.

hock|ey /ˈhɒki/ **1** N-UNCOUNT 不可算名詞 **Hockey** is a game played on ice between two teams of 11 players who use long curved sticks to hit a small rubber disk, called a puck, and try to score goals. アイスホッケー [mainly AM 主に米国英語] ❏*...a new hockey arena.* 新しいアイスホッケー 競技場. **2** N-UNCOUNT 不可算名詞 **Hockey** is an outdoor game played between two teams of 11 players who use long curved sticks to hit a small ball and try to score goals. ホッケー [mainly BRIT 主に英国英語; AM usually **field hockey** 米国英語では通常 **field hockey**]

hoe /hoʊ/ (**hoes, hoeing, hoed**) **1** N-COUNT 可算名詞 A **hoe** is a gardening tool with a long handle and a small square blade, which you use to remove small weeds and break up the surface of the soil. くわ **2** V-T 他動詞 If you **hoe** a field or crop, you use a hoe on the weeds or soil there. くわで耕す, くわを使って掘る ❏*I have to feed the chickens and hoe the potatoes.* トリに餌をやって, イモを掘らないといけない.

hog /hɒɡ/ (**hogs, hogging, hogged**) **1** N-COUNT 可算名詞 A **hog** is a pig. 豚 ❏*We picked the corn by hand and we fed it to the hogs and the cows.* 私たちはコーンを手で摘み, 豚と牛に与えた. **2** V-T 他動詞 If you **hog** something, you take all of it in a greedy or impolite way. 独り占めする [INFORMAL くだけた] ❏*Are you done hogging the bathroom?* 風呂場の独り占めはもう済んだかい? **3** PHRASE 句 If you **go whole hog** or **go the whole hog**, you do something bold or extravagant in the most complete way possible. 徹底的に行う [INFORMAL くだけた] ❏*Well, I thought, I've already lost half my job, I might as well go the whole hog and lose it completely.* もう仕事を半分失ったんだから, やるだけやって全部失ったっていいのさ.

hoist /hɔɪst/ (**hoists, hoisting, hoisted**) **1** V-T 他動詞 If you **hoist** something heavy somewhere, you lift it or pull it up there. 持ち上げる, 引き上げる ❏*Hoisting my suitcase on to my shoulder, I turned and headed toward my hotel.* 私はスーツケースを肩に乗せて, 体の向きを変え, ホテルに向かった. **2** V-T 他動詞 If something heavy **is hoisted** somewhere, it is lifted there using a machine such as a crane. つり上げる ❏*A twenty-foot steel pyramid is to be hoisted into position on top of the tower.* 20フィートの鉄製ピラミッドがつり上げられ, 塔の上に設置されることになっています. **3** N-COUNT 可算名詞 A **hoist** is a machine for lifting heavy things. 巻き上げ機, ホイスト ❏*He uses a hydraulic hoist to unload two empty barrels.* 彼は油圧ホイストを使って2本の空のたるを降ろす. **4** V-T 他動詞 If you **hoist** a flag or a sail, you pull it up to its correct position by using ropes. 揚げる ❏*A group forced their way through police cordons and hoisted their flag on top of the disputed monument.* ある集団が警察の非常線を突破し, 問題となっているモニュメントの上に団旗を揚げました.

hold

❶ PHYSICALLY TOUCHING, SUPPORTING, OR CONTAINING
❷ HAVING OR DOING
❸ CONTROLLING OR REMAINING
❹ PHRASES
❺ PHRASAL VERBS

❶ hold /hoʊld/ (**holds, holding, held**) **1** V-T 他動詞 When you **hold** something, you carry or support it, using your hands or your arms. 持つ ❏*Hold the knife at an angle.* ナイフを斜めに持ってください. ● N-COUNT 可算名詞 **Hold** is also a noun. 握ること ❏*He released his hold on the camera.* 彼はカメラを手から放した. **2** N-UNCOUNT 不可算名詞 **Hold** is used in expressions such as **grab hold of, catch hold of,** and **get hold of,** to indicate that you close your hand tightly around something, for example to stop something moving or falling. しっかりつかむ ❏*I was woken up by someone grabbing hold of my sleeping bag.* 誰かが私の寝袋をぎゅっとつかんだため, 目が覚めた. ❏*A doctor and a nurse caught hold of his arms.* 医師と看護師が彼の両腕をしっかりとつかんだ. **3** V-T 他動詞 When you **hold** someone, you put your arms around them, usually because you want to show them how much you like them or because you want to comfort them. 抱きしめる ❏*If only he would hold her close to him.* 彼が彼女を抱きよせてくれたらいいのに. **4** V-T 他動詞 If you **hold** someone in a particular position, you use force to keep them in that position and stop them from moving. 一な状態にしておく ❏*He then held the man in an armlock until police arrived.* そうして彼は警察が来るまでその男の腕を固めていた. **5** N-COUNT 可算名詞 A **hold** is a particular way of keeping someone in a position using your own hands, arms, or legs. 拘束すること ❏*The man wrestled the Indian to the ground, locked in a hold he couldn't escape.* 男はそのインド人を地面に組み伏せ, 逃げられないように押さえ込んだ. **6** V-T 他動詞 When you **hold** a part of your body, you put your

hand on or against it, often because it hurts. (痛い所などに) 手を当てる □ *Soon she was crying bitterly about the pain and was holding her throat.* 程なくすると、彼女は痛みのあまり激しく叫び、のどを押さえていた. **7** V-T 他動詞 When you **hold** a part of your body in a particular position, you put it into that position and keep it there. 保つ □ *Hold your hands in front of your face.* 両手を顔の前に掲げてください. **8** V-T 他動詞 If one thing **holds** another in a particular position, it keeps it in that position. 保持する □ *...the wooden wedge which held the heavy door open.* その重厚な扉を開放しておくための木製ドアストッパー. **9** V-T 他動詞 If one thing is used to **hold** another, it is used to store it. 収納する □ *Two knife racks hold her favorite knives.* 彼女のお気に入り包丁が納められた2つのナイフラック. **10** N-COUNT 可算名詞 In a ship or airplane, a **hold** is a place where cargo or luggage is stored. 貨物室 □ *A fire had been reported in the cargo hold.* 貨物室で火災が発生したとの報告がありました. **11** V-T 他動詞 If a place **holds** something, it keeps it available for reference or for future use. 取っておく □ *The Better Business Bureau holds an enormous amount of information on any business problem.* ベター・ビジネス・ビューローは、いかなる経営問題にも対処しうる膨大な情報をご用意いたしております. **12** V-T 他動詞 If something **holds** a particular amount of something, it can contain that amount. 収容する [no cont] □ *One CD-ROM disk can hold over 100,000 pages of text.* 1枚のCD-ROMには10万ページ余りの文書が保存できます.

Thesaurus	hold また次を参照:
v.	carry, support **❶ 1**
	cradle, embrace, hug **❶ 3**
	hang on to, pin down, restrain **❶ 4**

❷ hold /hoʊld/ (holds, holding, held)

Hold is often used to indicate that someone or something has the particular thing, characteristic, or attitude that is mentioned. Therefore it takes most of its meaning from the word that follows it.

Hold はしばしばある人かある物が言及された特定のもの、特徴あるいは態度を持っていることを示すのに用いられる。それゆえに、それは後に来る語からその意味の大部分を受け取る.

1 V-T 他動詞 **Hold** is used with words and expressions indicating an opinion or belief, to show that someone has a particular opinion or believes that something is true. (考えなどを) 抱く [no cont] □ *He held firm opinions which usually conflicted with my own.* 彼が抱いた断固とした考えは、たいてい私の意見と相容れなかった. □ *Current thinking holds that obesity is more a medical than a psychological problem.* 今主流なのは、肥満の原因は心理的ではなく医学的な問題だ、という考え方だ. **2** V-T 他動詞 **Hold** is used with words such as "fear" or "mystery" to indicate someone's feelings toward something, as if those feelings were a characteristic of the thing itself. 抱く [no passive] □ *Death doesn't hold any fear for me.* 死ぬことなんて怖くも何ともないさ. **3** V-T 他動詞 **Hold** is used with nouns such as "office," "power," and "responsibility" to indicate that someone has a particular position of power or authority. (地位、役職に) 就く (責任を) 持つ □ *She has never held an elected office.* 彼女はこれまで選出公職に就いたことはありません. **4** V-T 他動詞 **Hold** is used with nouns such as "permit," "degree," or "ticket" to indicate that someone has a particular document that allows them to do something. 所有する □ *Applicants should normally hold a good degree.* 応募者は相応の学歴を有すること. □ *He did not hold a firearms licence.* 彼は銃器使用許可証を持っていなかった. **5** V-T 他動詞 **Hold** is used with nouns such as "party," "meeting," "talks," "election," and "trial" to indicate that people are organizing a particular activity. 開催する □ *The country will hold democratic elections within a year.* その国では民主的選挙が1年以内に行われるでしょう. ● **holding** N-UNCOUNT 不可算名詞 □ *They also called for the holding of multi-party general elections.* 彼らは複数政党による総選挙の開催も要求しました. **6** V-RECIP 相互動詞 **Hold** is used with nouns such as "conversation," "interview," and "talks" to indicate that two or more people meet and discuss something. (話し合いなどを) 持つ □ *The prime minister is holding consultations with his colleagues to finalize the deal.* 政策を固めるため、首相は閣僚と協議を行う予定です. □ *The engineer and his son held frequent meetings concerning technical problems.* その技師は技術上の問題について息子と何度も話し合った. **7** V-T 他動詞 **Hold** is used with nouns such as "shares" and "stock" to indicate that someone owns a particular proportion of a business. 持つ □ *The group said it continues to hold 1,774,687 shares in the company.* そのグループは、その会社の177万4,687株をまだ所有していると述べました. **8** → see also **holding** **9** V-T 他動詞 **Hold** is used with nouns such as "attention" or "interest" to indicate that what you do or say keeps someone interested or listening to you. 引く □ *If you want to hold someone's attention, look them directly in the eye but don't stare.* 注意を引きたければ、相手の目をまっすぐに見ることです. でも、凝視してはいけません. **10** V-T 他動詞 If you **hold** someone responsible, liable, or accountable for something, you will blame them if anything

goes wrong. 〜のせいだと思う □ *It's impossible to hold any individual responsible.* 個々人に責任を問うのは不可能です.

❸ hold /hoʊld/ (holds, holding, held) **1** V-T 他動詞 If someone **holds** you in a place, they keep you there as a prisoner and do not allow you to leave. 留置する □ *The inside of a van was as good a place as any to hold a kidnap victim.* ライトバンの車内は誘拐した人を留置するのに絶好の場所だった. □ *Somebody is holding your wife hostage.* 何者かがあなたの奥さんを人質にとっています. **2** V-T 他動詞 If people such as an army or a violent crowd **hold** a place, they control it by using force. 占領する □ *Demonstrators have been holding the square since Sunday.* デモ隊が日曜以来広場を占拠している. **3** N-SING 単数名詞 If you have a **hold** over someone, you have power or control over them, for example because you know something about them you can use to threaten them or because you are in a position of authority. 支配力 □ *He had ordered his officers to keep an exceptionally firm hold over their men.* 彼は将校に、引き続き下士官を厳重に統制するよう命じた. **4** V-T/V-I 他動詞/自動詞 If you ask someone to **hold**, or to **hold the line**, when you are answering a telephone call, you are asking them to wait for a short time, for example so that you can find the person they want to speak to. 電話を切らずに待つ [no passive] □ *Could you hold the line and I'll just get my pen.* 書くものを用意しますのでしばらくお待ちください. **5** V-T 他動詞 If you **hold** telephone calls for someone, you do not allow people who phone to speak to that person, but take messages instead. (電話を) 取り次がない □ *He tells his secretary to hold his calls.* 彼は電話を取り次がないよう秘書に指示している. **6** V-T/V-I 他動詞/自動詞 If something **holds** at a particular value or level, or is **held** there, it is kept at that value or level. (水準などを) 保つ □ *OPEC production is holding at around 21.5 million barrels a day.* OPECの原油産出量は、1日2,150万バレルを維持している. **7** V-T 他動詞 If you **hold** a sound or musical note, you continue making it. (音などを) 持続させる □ *...a voice which hit and held every note with perfect ease and clarity.* どんな音程にも易々と持続できた全く無理のない、明るい声. **8** V-T 他動詞 If you **hold** something such as a train or an elevator, you delay it. (運行を) 止める □ *A spokesman defended the decision to hold the train until police arrived.* 広報官は、警察が到着するまで列車を止めるという決定を擁護した. **9** V-I 自動詞 If an offer or invitation still **holds**, it is still available for you to accept. 有効のままである □ *Does your offer still hold?* 先のオファーはまだ生きていますか. **10** V-I 自動詞 If a good situation **holds**, it continues and does not get worse or fail. 〜のままである □ *Our luck couldn't hold forever.* この幸運はずっと続くわけじゃないさ. **11** V-I 自動詞 If an argument or theory **holds**, it is true or valid, even after close examination. 妥当性を有する □ *Today, most people think that argument no longer holds.* 今では、その議論が妥当だと考える人はほとんどいない. ● PHRASAL VERB 句動詞 **Hold up** means the same as **hold**. □ *Democrats say arguments against the bill won't hold up.* 民主党員は、法案に反対するのは妥当ではないだろう、と述べています. **12** V-I 自動詞 If part of a structure **holds**, it does not fall or break although there is a lot of force or pressure on it. 持ちこたえる □ *How long would the roof hold?* 屋根の耐用期間はどのくらいですか. **13** V-I 自動詞 If laws or rules **hold**, they exist and remain in force. 効力を有する □ *These laws also hold for universities.* これらの法律は大学にも適用される. **14** V-I 自動詞 If you **hold** to a promise or to high standards of behavior, you keep that promise or continue to behave according to those standards. 守る [FORMAL 形式ばった] □ *Will the president be able to hold to this commitment?* 大統領はこの公約を守れるのでしょうか. **15** V-T 他動詞 If someone or something **holds** you to a promise or to high standards of behavior, they make you keep that promise or those standards. 守らせる □ *"I won't make you marry him."—"I'll hold you to that."* 「彼との結婚は許さない」「絶対に認めないからな」

❹ hold /hoʊld/ (holds, holding, held) ▷ Please look at meaning **12** to see if the expression you are looking for is shown under another headword. **1** PHRASE 句 If you **hold forth on** a subject, you speak confidently and for a long time about it, especially to a group of people. 〜について長々と話す □ *Barry was holding forth on something.* バリーは何かを長々と語っていた. **2** PHRASE 句 If you **get hold of** an object or information, you obtain it, usually after some difficulty. 手に入れる □ *It is hard to get hold of guns in this country.* この国では銃を入手するのは困難だ. **3** PHRASE 句 If you **get hold of** someone, you manage to contact them. 連絡をつける □ *The only electrician we could get hold of was miles away.* 唯一連絡可能だった電気技師は数マイル離れたところにいた. **4** CONVENTION 慣習表現 If you say "**Hold it**," you are telling someone to stop what they are doing and to wait. 止まれ □ *Hold it! Don't move!* 止まれ！動くな！ **5** PHRASE 句 If you put something **on hold**, you decide not to do it, deal with it, or change it now, but to leave it until later. 保留にする □ *He put his retirement on hold to work 16 hours a day, seven days a week to find a solution.* 彼は退職を保留にし、解決策を求めて毎日16時間無休で働いた. **6** PHRASE 句 If you **hold** your **own**, you are able to resist someone who is attacking or opposing you. 屈しない □ *The Frenchman held his own against the challenger.* そのフランス人は挑戦者に屈しなかった. **7** PHRASE 句 If you can do something well enough to **hold**

your **own**, you do not appear foolish when you are compared with someone who is generally thought to be very good at it. 引けを取らない □*She can hold her own against almost any player.* 彼女は他のどの選手にも引けを取らないでしょう。 **8** PHRASE 句 If you **hold still**, you do not move. じっとしている □*Can't you hold still for a second?* 少しはじっとできないの。 **9** PHRASE 句 If something **takes hold**, it gains complete control or influence over a person or thing. 支配する □*She felt a strange excitement taking hold of her.* 彼女は奇妙な興奮に捕らわれる感じがした。 **10** PHRASE 句 If you **hold tight**, you put your hand around or against something in order to prevent yourself from falling over. A bus driver might say "Hold tight!" to you if you are standing on a bus when it is about to move. 一にしっかりとつかまる □*He held tight to the rope.* 彼はロープをしっかりとつかんだ。 **11** PHRASE 句 If you **hold tight**, you do not immediately start a course of action that you have been planning or thinking about. 見合わせる □*The advice for individual investors is to hold tight.* 個人投資家は、今は動かないほうがよいでしょう。 **12** to **hold** something **at bay** → see **bay** **13** to **hold** something **in check** → see **check** **14** to **hold fast** → see **fast** **15** to **hold the fort** → see **fort** **16** to **hold your ground** → see **ground** **17** to **hold** someone **ransom** → see **ransom** **18** to **hold sway** → see **sway**

❻ hold /hoʊld/ (**holds, holding, held**)

▶ **hold against** PHRASAL VERB 句動詞 If you **hold** something **against** someone, you let their actions in the past influence your present attitude toward them and cause you to deal severely or unfairly with them. 過去のことを持ち出して一を責める、過去のことを一を不当に扱う □*Bernstein lost the case, but never held it against Grundy.* バーンスタインは敗訴したが、それでグランディを責めることはなかった。

▶ **hold back** **1** PHRASAL VERB 句動詞 If you **hold back** or if something **holds** you **back**, you hesitate before you do something because you are not sure whether it is the right thing to do. しり込みする □*The Bush administration had several reasons for holding back.* ブッシュ政権が思いとどまった裏にはいくつかの理由があったのです。 **2** PHRASAL VERB 句動詞 To **hold** someone or something **back** means to prevent someone from doing something, or to prevent something from happening. 抑える □*Stagnation in home sales is holding back economic recovery.* 国内販売の低迷が景気回復の妨げとなっています。 **3** PHRASAL VERB 句動詞 If you **hold** something **back**, you keep it in reserve to use later. 取っておく □*Farmers apparently hold back produce in the hope that prices will rise.* 農家は、明らかに値上がりを見越して作物を出し惜しみしています。 **4** PHRASAL VERB 句動詞 If you **hold** something **back**, you do not include it in the information you are giving about something. （情報などを）出さないでおく □*You seem to be holding something back.* あなたは何かを隠していますね。 **5** PHRASAL VERB 句動詞 If you **hold back** something such as tears or laughter, or if you **hold back**, you make an effort to stop yourself from showing how you feel. 抑える □*She kept trying to hold back her tears.* 彼女はずっと涙をこらえていた。 **6** PHRASAL VERB 句動詞 If a teacher **holds** a student **back**, they keep them in the same grade instead of promoting them to a higher grade, because their work is not good enough. 留年させる □*16 percent of eighth-graders were held back for poor performance.* 8年生の16パーセントが成績不良で留年になった。

▶ **hold down** **1** PHRASAL VERB 句動詞 If you **hold down** a job or a place on a team, you manage to keep it. （職業や地位に）とどまる □*He never could hold down a job.* かれが一つの仕事に落ち着くことはないだろう。 **2** PHRASAL VERB 句動詞 If you **hold** someone **down**, you keep them under control and do not allow them to have much freedom or power or many rights. 押さえつける □*Everyone thinks there is some vast conspiracy wanting to hold down the younger generation.* 若い世代を掌握しようとする大きな陰謀がある、と誰もが考えている。

▶ **hold off** **1** PHRASAL VERB 句動詞 If you **hold off** doing something, you delay doing it or delay making a decision about it. 遅らせる □*The hospital staff held off taking Rosenbaum in for an X-ray.* 病院スタッフはローゼンバームのX線検査を先送りにした。 **2** PHRASAL VERB 句動詞 If you **hold off** a challenge in a race or competition, you do not allow someone to pass you. 寄せつけない □*Between 1987 and 1990, Steffi Graf largely held off Navratilova's challenge for the crown.* 1987年から1990年まで、シュテフィ・グラフはほとんどの大会でナブラチロワを決勝で退け女王の座を守っていた。

▶ **hold on** or **hold onto** **1** PHRASAL VERB 句動詞 If you **hold on**, or **hold onto** something, you keep your hand on it or around it, for example to prevent the thing from falling or to support yourself. しっかりつかまえる □*His right arm was extended up beside his head, still holding on to a coffee cup.* コーヒーカップを握ったまま彼は右腕を頭の横まで上げた。 □*He was struggling to hold onto a rock on the face of the cliff.* 彼は切り立った崖で岩をつかもうと必死だった。 **2** PHRASAL VERB 句動詞 If you **hold on**, you manage to achieve success or avoid failure in spite of great difficulties or opposition. からくも一する □*The Rams held on to defeat the Nevada Wolf Pack in Reno, 32-28.* ラムズは、ネバダ州立大学リノ校・ウルフパック戦を38対32でからくも制した。 **3** PHRASAL VERB 句動詞 If you ask someone to **hold on**, you are asking them to wait for a short time. お待ち

ください [SPOKEN 口語] □*The manager asked him to hold on while he investigated.* マネージャーは彼に調べる間待っているようにと言った。

▶ **hold out** **1** PHRASAL VERB 句動詞 If you **hold out** your hand or something you have in your hand, you move your hand away from your body, for example to shake hands with someone. 差し出す □*"I'm Nancy Drew," she said, holding out her hand.* 彼女は手を差し出し、「ナンシー・ドルーです」と言った。 **2** PHRASAL VERB 句動詞 If you **hold out** for something, you refuse to accept something which you do not think is good enough or large enough, and you continue to demand more. （望むものを）あくまで要求する □*I should have held out for a better deal.* もっと良い条件をあくまで要求するべきだった。 **3** PHRASAL VERB 句動詞 If you say that someone **is holding out on** you, you think that they are refusing to give you information that you want. 一に隠し事をする [INFORMAL くだけた] □*He had always believed that kids could sense it when you held out on them.* 彼は、隠し事をしても子供たちにはかぎつけることができるだろう、と考えていた。 **4** PHRASAL VERB 句動詞 If you **hold out**, you manage to resist an enemy or opponent in difficult circumstances and refuse to give in. 持ちこたえる □*One prisoner was still holding out on the roof of the jail.* 囚人の1人は、刑務所の屋上でまだ抵抗を続けていました。 **5** PHRASAL VERB 句動詞 If you **hold out** hope of something happening, you hope that in the future something will happen as you want it to. 期待を抱く □*He still holds out hope that they could be a family again.* 彼はまだ、彼らが家族としてやり直せるかもしれないという希望を抱いている。

▶ **hold up** **1** PHRASAL VERB 句動詞 If you **hold up** your hand or something you have in your hand, you move it upward into a particular position and keep it there. 持ち上げる □*She held up her hand stiffly.* 彼女はぎこちなく手を上げた。 **2** PHRASAL VERB 句動詞 If one thing **holds up** another, it is placed under the other thing in order to support it and prevent it from falling. 支える □*Mills have iron pillars all over the place holding up the roof.* 工場の屋根は、各所にある鉄柱が支えている。 **3** PHRASAL VERB 句動詞 To **hold up** a person or process means to make them late or delay them. 遅らせる □*Why were you holding everyone up?* なぜ君は皆の進行を妨げていたんだ？

If you **cancel** or **call off** an arrangement or an appointment, you stop it from happening. □*His failing health forced him to cancel the meeting… The European Community has threatened to call off peace talks.* If you **postpone** or **put off** an arrangement or an appointment, you make another arrangement for it to happen at a later time. □*Elections have been postponed until next year… The senate put off a vote on the nomination for one week.* If you **delay** something that has been arranged, you make it happen later than planned. □*Space agency managers decided to delay the launch of the space shuttle.* If something **delays** you or **holds** you **up**, you start or finish what you are doing later than you planned. □*He was delayed in traffic… Delivery of equipment had been held up by delays and disputes.*

4 PHRASAL VERB 句動詞 If someone **holds up** a place such as a bank or a store, they point a weapon at someone there to make them give you money or valuable goods. 強盗を働く □*When his money was gone he held up a gas station with a toy gun.* 彼は一文無しになり、おもちゃの銃を使いガソリンスタンドで強盗を働いた。 **5** PHRASAL VERB 句動詞 If you **hold up** something such as someone's behavior, you make it known to other people, so that they can criticize or praise it. 示す □*He had always been held up as an example to the younger ones.* 彼はいつも若い人たちに手本として示されていた。 **6** PHRASAL VERB 句動詞 If something such as a type of business **holds up** in difficult conditions, it stays in a reasonably good state. よく持ちこたえる □*Children's wear is one area that is holding up well in the recession.* 子供服は不況に強い事業の一つだ。 **7** PHRASAL VERB 句動詞 If an argument or theory **holds up**, it is true or valid, even after close examination. 真実だとわかる、妥当性がある □*I'm not sure if the argument holds up, but it's stimulating.* その議論が妥当か否かは不確かだが、よい刺激剤にはなっている。 **8** → see also **holdup**

hold|er /hoʊldər/ (**holders**) **1** N-COUNT 可算名詞 A **holder** is someone who owns or has something. 所有者 □*This season the club has had 73,500 season-ticket holders.* 今期は7万3,500人がそのチームのシーズン観戦券を購入した。 **2** N-COUNT 可算名詞 A **holder** is a container in which you put an object, usually in order to protect it or to keep it in place. 容器 □*…a toothbrush holder.* 歯ブラシホルダー。

Word Partnership holder は次の語句と使われる：

N.	**cup** holder, **pot** holder **2**

hold|ing /hoʊldɪŋ/ (**holdings**) N-COUNT 可算名詞 If you have a **holding** in a company, you own shares in it. 持ち株 [BUSINESS 実業] □*That would increase Olympia & York's holding to 35%.* それによりオリンピア・アンド・ヨークの持ち株比率は35パーセントに増えるでしょう。

hold|ing com|pa|ny (**holding companies**) N-COUNT 可算名詞 A **holding company** is a company that has enough shares in one or more other companies to be able to control the other companies. 持ち株会社 [BUSINESS 実業] ❑ ...*a Montreal-based holding company with interests in telecommunications, gas, and natural resources.* 電気通信、ガス、天然資源事業に関心を寄せるモントリオールに本拠を置く持ち株会社.

holdup /hoʊldʌp/ (**holdups**) also **hold-up** **1** N-COUNT 可算名詞 A **holdup** is a situation in which someone is threatened with a weapon in order to make them hand over money or valuables. 追いはぎ ❑ *What could have happened? A hold-up? There'd been no gunshot or scream.* いったい何が起こったのだ？追いはぎか？銃声や悲鳴は聞こえなかったぞ. **2** N-COUNT 可算名詞 A **holdup** is a delay. 停滞 ❑ ...*bureaucratic holdups and legal wrangles over the contract.* 契約をめぐる官僚主義的な遅滞と法廷論争. **3** N-COUNT 可算名詞 A **holdup** is the stopping or very slow movement of traffic, sometimes causes by an accident which happened earlier. 交通渋滞 ❑ *They arrived late due to a freeway holdup.* ハイウェイの渋滞で彼らの到着が遅れた.

hole /hoʊl/ (**holes**) **1** N-COUNT 可算名詞 A **hole** is a hollow space in something solid, with an opening on one side. 穴 ❑ *He took a shovel, dug a hole, and buried his once-prized possessions.* 彼はシャベルを手にして穴を掘り、かつては価値のあった所持品を埋めた. **2** N-COUNT 可算名詞 A **hole** is an opening in something that goes right through it. 穴 ❑ ...*kids with holes in the knees of their jeans.* ひざに穴があいたジーンズをはいた子供たち. **3** N-COUNT 可算名詞 A **hole** is the home or hiding place of a mouse, rabbit, or other small animal. 巣穴 ❑ ...*a rabbit hole.* うさぎの巣穴. **4** N-COUNT 可算名詞 A **hole** in a law, theory, or argument is a fault or weakness that it has. 欠陥、穴 ❑ *There were some holes in that theory, some unanswered questions.* その理論にはいくつか穴があった。うやむやな問題が残っていたんだ. **5** N-COUNT 可算名詞 A **hole** is also one of the nine or eighteen sections of a golf course. ホール ❑ *I played nine holes with Gary Carter today.* 今日はグレイ・カーターと9ホール回った. **6** PHRASE 句 If you say that you are **in a hole**, you mean that you are in a difficult or embarrassing situation. 窮地に陥って [INFORMAL くだけた] ❑ *We were in a hole, but I was proud with the way we came back.* 我々は苦境にあったが、そこから復活した過程を誇りに思っていた. **7** PHRASE 句 If a person or organization is **in the hole**, they owe money to someone else. 借金をして [AM 米国英語、INFORMAL くだけた] ❑ *Some estimates show next year's budget could be $2.5 billion in the hole.* 来年度は25億ドルの赤字が計上されるだろう、との予測もあります. **8** PHRASE 句 If you get a **hole in one** in golf, you get the golf ball into the hole with a single stroke. ホール・イン・ワン ❑ *All they ever dream about is getting a hole in one.* 彼らがいつも夢見ているのはホール・イン・ワンの達成です. **9** PHRASE 句 If you **pick holes in** an argument or theory, you find weak points in it so that it is no longer valid. あら探しをする [INFORMAL くだけた] ❑ *He then goes on to pick holes in the article before reaching his conclusion.* 彼は結論を出す前に記事のあら探しをしようとします.
→ see **golf**

ADJ.	**deep** hole **1**
	big/huge/small hole, **gaping** hole **1 2**
V.	**dig** a hole, **fill/plug** a hole **1**
	cut/punch a hole in *something*, **drill/bore** a hole in *something* **1 2**

holi|day /hɒlɪdeɪ/ (**holidays, holidaying, holidayed**) **1** N-COUNT 可算名詞 A **holiday** is a day when people do not go to work or school because of a religious or national celebration. 休日 ❑ *New Year's Day is a public holiday.* 元旦は祝日です. **2** → see **bank holiday** **3** N-COUNT 可算名詞 A **holiday** is a period of time during which you relax and enjoy yourself away from home. People sometimes refer to their holiday as **holidays**. 休暇 [BRIT 英国英語; AM **vacation** 米国英語 **vacation**] **4** N-PLURAL 複数名詞 The **holidays** are the time when children do not have to go to school. (学校の) 休み [BRIT 英国英語; AM **vacation** 米国英語 **vacation**] **5** N-UNCOUNT 不可算名詞 If you have a particular number of days' or weeks' **holiday**, you do not have to go to work for that number of days or weeks. 休暇 [BRIT 英国英語; AM **vacation** 米国英語 **vacation**] **6** V-I 自動詞 If you are **holidaying** in a place away from home, you are on holiday there. 休暇を過ごす [BRIT 英国英語; AM **vacation** 米国英語 **vacation**]

holi|day|maker /hɒlɪdeɪmeɪkər/ (**holidaymakers**) N-COUNT 可算名詞 A **holidaymaker** is a person who is away from their home on holiday. 行楽客 [BRIT 英国英語; AM **vacationer** 米国英語 **vacationer**]

ho|lism /hoʊlɪzəm/ N-UNCOUNT 不可算名詞 **Holism** is the belief that everything in nature is connected in some way. 全体論 [FORMAL 形式ばった] ❑ *Nature by itself, he writes, runs on "principles of balance and holism."* 自然はそれ自体「調和と全体論の法則」に従ってい

る、と彼は記している.

ho|lis|tic /hoʊlɪstɪk/ ADJ 形容詞 **Holistic** means based on the principles of holism. 全体的な、ホリスティックな [FORMAL 形式ばった] ❑ ...*practitioners of holistic medicine.* ホリスティック医学を実践する医師.

hol|ler /hɒlər/ (**hollers, hollering, hollered**) V-T/V-I 他動詞/自動詞 If you **holler**, you shout loudly. 大声を上げる [mainly AM 主に米国英語、INFORMAL くだけた] ❑ *The audience whooped and hollered.* 観衆は歓喜と興奮の声を上げました. ❑ *"Watch out!" he hollered.* 「危ない」と彼は叫んだ. ● N-COUNT 可算名詞 **Holler** is also a noun. 叫び声 ❑ *She spun round as the man, with a holler, burst through the door.* 男が叫びながらドアから飛び込んできたので、彼女は振り返った. ● PHRASAL VERB 句動詞 **Holler out** means the same as **holler**. 大声で叫ぶ ❑ *I hollered out the names.* 私は大声で彼らの名前を叫んだ.

hol|low /hɒloʊ/ (**hollows, hollowing, hollowed**) **1** ADJ 形容詞 Something that is **hollow** has a space inside it, as opposed to being solid all the way through. 空洞の ❑ ...*a hollow tree.* 中が空洞化した木. **2** ADJ 形容詞 A surface that is **hollow** curves inward. くぼんだ ❑ *He looked young, dark and sharp-featured, with hollow cheeks.* 彼は、ほほがくぼみ、浅黒くシャープな顔立ちで、若く見えた. **3** N-COUNT 可算名詞 A **hollow** is an area that is lower than the surrounding surface. くぼ地 ❑ *Below him the town lay warm in the hollow of the hill.* 彼が見下ろす谷合いの盆地には、暖かな雰囲気の町が広がっていた. **4** ADJ 形容詞 If you describe a statement, situation, or person as **hollow**, you mean they have no real value, worth, or effectiveness. 空疎な ❑ *Any threat to bring in the police is a hollow one.* 警察に対するいかなる脅しも無意味だ. ● **hol|low|ness** N-UNCOUNT 不可算名詞 空疎なこと ❑ *One month before the deadline we see the hollowness of these promises.* 期日の1月前に約束が口先だけのものだとわかる. **5** ADJ 形容詞 [ADJ n] If someone gives a **hollow** laugh, they laugh in a way that shows that they do not really find something amusing. うわべだけの ❑ *Murray Pick's hollow laugh had no mirth in it.* マレー・ピックはうつろに笑ったが、そこには楽しさのかけらもなかった. **6** ADJ 形容詞 A **hollow** sound is dull and echoing. 鈍く響く [ADJ n] ❑ ...*the hollow sound of a gunshot.* 鈍く響いた銃声. **7** V-T 他動詞 If something **is hollowed**, its surface is made to curve inward or downward. へこませる [usu passive] ❑ *The mule's back was hollowed by the weight of its burden.* ラバの背中は荷物の重みで曲がった.

ADJ.	empty **1**
	empty, meaningless **4 5**

hol|ly /hɒli/ (**hollies**) N-VAR 可変性名詞 **Holly** is an evergreen tree or shrub which has hard, shiny leaves with sharp points, and red berries in winter. ヒイラギ

holo|caust /hɒləkɔst, hoʊlə-/ (**holocausts**) **1** N-VAR 可変性名詞 A **holocaust** is an event in which there is a lot of destruction and many people are killed, especially one caused by war. 大虐殺 ❑ *A nuclear holocaust seemed a very real possibility in the '50s.* 1950年代は核兵器による大惨事がまさに起こるかのようだったのです. **2** N-SING 単数名詞 The **Holocaust** is used to refer to the killing by the Nazis of millions of Jews during the Second World War. ホロコースト ❑ ...*an Israeli-based fund for survivors of the Holocaust and their families.* ホロコーストの生存者と家族に向けたイスラエルからの基金.

holy /hoʊli/ (**holier, holiest**) ADJ 形容詞 If you describe something as **holy**, you mean that it is considered to be special because it is connected with God or a particular religion. 神聖な ❑ *To them, as to all Poles, this is a holy place.* 彼らにとっては、全てのポーランド人にとって同じく、ここは神聖な場所です.

hom|age /hɒmɪdʒ, ɒm-/ N-UNCOUNT 不可算名詞 **Homage** is respect shown toward someone or something you admire, or to a person in authority. 敬意 [usu N 'to' n] ❑ *Palace has released two marvelous films that pay homage to our literary heritage.* パレス社は、我々の文学的遺産を称える2本のすばらしい映画を公開した.

---

home

❶ NOUN, ADJECTIVE, AND ADVERB USES
❷ PHRASAL VERB USES

---

❶ home /hoʊm/ (**homes**) **1** N-COUNT 可算名詞 Someone's **home** is the house or apartment where they live. 自宅 [oft poss N, also 'at' N] ❑ *Last night they stayed at home and watched TV.* 昨夜、彼らは家でテレビを見ていた. ❑ *The general divided his time between his shabby offices and his home in Hampstead.* 司令官は、簡素な執務室で仕事をすることもあれば、ハムステッドにある自宅にいることもあった.

When people move to a new **home,** they often hold a **housewarming** party. Friends and neighbors usually bring gifts for the house such as plants, soap, kitchen towels, and other non-personal items to welcome the new people to the neighborhood and make them feel welcome.

2 N-UNCOUNT 不可算名詞 You can use **home** to refer in a general way to the house, town, or country where someone lives now or where they were born, often to emphasize that they feel they belong in that place. 故郷, 母国 □ *She gives frequent performances of her work, both at home and abroad.* 彼女はしばしば自作曲の演奏会を海外と母国の両方で開く. □ *His father worked away from home for much of Jim's first five years.* ジムの誕生後の5年間は, 父親はほとんど故郷を離れて仕事をしていた. **3** ADV 副詞 **Home** means to or at the place where you live. 家 □ *His wife wasn't feeling too well and she wanted to go home.* 彼の奥さんは気分が優れず, 家に帰りたがった. □ *I'll call you as soon as I get home.* 帰宅次第電話をします. **4** ADJ 形容詞 **Home** means made or done in the place where you live. 家庭の [ADJ n] □ *...cheap but healthy home cooking.* お金がかからず健康的な家庭料理. **5** ADJ 形容詞 **Home** means relating to your own country as opposed to foreign countries. 自国の [ADJ n] □ *Europe's software companies still have a growing home market.* ヨーロッパのソフトメーカーは自国市場で以前と成長を誇っている. **6** N-COUNT 可算名詞 A **home** is a large house or institution where a number of people live and are cared for, instead of living in their own houses or apartments. They usually live there because they are too old or ill to take care of themselves or for their families to care for them. ホーム □ *It's going to be a home for handicapped children.* そこは体の不自由な子供たちのホームになる予定です. **7** N-COUNT 可算名詞 You can refer to a family unit as a **home.** 家庭 □ *She had, at any rate, provided a peaceful and loving home for Harriet.* 彼女は, ともかく, ハリエットに穏やかで愛情あふれる家庭を提供してきた. **8** N-SING 単数名詞 If you refer to the **home of** something, you mean the place where it began or where it is most typically found. 本場 □ *This southwest region of France is the home of claret.* フランス南西部の当地は, クラレットの発祥地です. **9** N-COUNT 可算名詞 If you find a **home for** something, you find a place where it can be kept. 収納場所 □ *The equipment itself is getting smaller, neater and easier to find a home for.* 装置自体がより小さくすっきりとしたデザインになっていますので, 以前ほど置き場所に困ることはありません. **10** ADV 副詞 If you press, drive, or hammer something **home,** you explain it to people as forcefully as possible. 十分に [ADV after v] □ *It is now up to all of us to debate this issue and press home the argument.* 今我々全員が成すべきは, この問題を熟考し徹底的に議論することだ. **11** N-UNCOUNT 不可算名詞 When a sports team plays **at home,** they play a game on their own field, rather than on the opposing team's field. 本拠地, ホーム □ *I scored in both games; we tied at home and beat them away.* 試合結果を集計したら, ホームでは五分五分, アウェイでは勝ち越していた. ●ADJ 形容詞 **Home** is also an adjective. 本拠地の [ADJ n] □ *All three are fans, and attend all home games together.* 3人ともチームのファンで, 全てのホームゲームを一緒に観戦します. **12** PHRASE 句 If you feel at **home,** you feel comfortable in the place or situation that you are in. くつろいで □ *He spoke very good English and appeared pleased to see us, and we soon felt quite at home.* 彼はとても上手な英語で私たちを歓迎してくれたので, すぐにとてもくつろいだ気分になった. **13** PHRASE 句 To **bring** something **home to** someone means to make them understand how important or serious it is. はっきりと認識させる □ *Their sobering conversation brought home to everyone present the serious and worthwhile work the Red Cross does.* 彼らの真剣な話を聞き, 出席者全員が赤十字の活動が重要で価値のあるものだと認識した. **14** PHRASE 句 If you say that someone is **home free** you mean that they have been successful or that they are certain to be successful. うまくいく □ *Just when she thought she was home free, her father spoke from behind her.* 彼女がうまくいったと思ったとたん, 背後からお父さんが話しかけてきた. **15** PHRASE 句 If a situation or what someone says **hits home** or **strikes home,** people accept that it is real or true, even though it may be painful for them to realize. 胸にささる □ *Did the reality of war finally hit home?* 人々は戦争の実態に心を痛めたのでしょうか. **16** PHRASE 句 You can say a **home away from home** to refer to a place in which you are as comfortable as in your own home. わが家のような場所 [APPROVAL 賛成] □ *The café seems to be her home away from home these days.* ところで, 彼女はその カフェを自宅さながらに感じているようだ. **17** CONVENTION 慣習表現 If you say to a guest "**Make yourself at home,**" you are making them feel welcome and inviting them to behave in an informal, relaxed way. くつろいでください [POLITENESS 丁寧な] □ *Take off your jacket and make yourself at home.* 上着を脱いで, ゆっくりおくつろぎください. **18** PHRASE 句 If you say that something is **nothing to write home about,** you mean that it is not very interesting or exciting. 大したことではない [INFORMAL くだけた] □ *I see growth slightly up, but nothing to write home about.* 若干の成長は見られるものの特筆すべきことは何もありません. **19** PHRASE 句 If something that is thrown or fired **strikes home,** it reaches its target. 命中す

る [WRITTEN 書き言葉] □ *Only two torpedoes struck home.* 魚雷は2発だけ命中した.

Thesaurus   *home* また次を参照:

N.   dwelling, house, residence **1** **1**
        birthplace, home town **1** **2**

Word Partnership   *home* は次の語句と使われる:

ADJ.   new home **1** **1** **2**
        close to home **1** **1** **2** **15**
V.   bring/take *someone/something* home, **build** a home,
        buy a home, call/phone home, come home, drive
        home, feel at home, fly home, get home, go home,
        head for home, leave home, return home, ride home,
        sit *at* home, stay *at* home, walk home, work at home
        1 **1** – **3**

❷ home /hoʊm/ (homes, homing, homed)

▶ **home in 1** PHRASAL VERB 句動詞 If you **home in on** one particular aspect of something, you give all your attention to it. 的を絞る □ *The critics immediately homed in on the group's essential members.* 批評家は直ちにグループの主要メンバーにねらいを定めた. **2** PHRASAL VERB 句動詞 If something such as a missile **homes in on** something else, it is aimed at that thing and moves toward it. 目標に向かう □ *Two rockets homed in on it from behind without a sound.* 2発のロケット弾が背後から音もなくそこに飛んでいった.

home|coming /hoʊmkʌmɪŋ/ (homecomings) **1** N-VAR 可変性名詞 Your **homecoming** is your return to your home or your country after being away for a long time. 帰郷 □ *Her homecoming was tinged with sadness.* 彼女の帰郷には哀愁が漂っていた. **2** N-UNCOUNT 不可算名詞 **Homecoming** is a day or weekend each year when former students of a particular school, college, or university go back to it to meet each other again and go to parties and sports events. ホームカミング (同窓生を迎えて開催される学園祭) [AM 米国英語] □ *...a recent Penn State graduate who was back for Homecoming weekend.* ホームカミングのために帰郷したペンシルバニア州立大の近年の卒業生.

home|grown /hoʊmgroʊn/ ADJ 形容詞 **Homegrown** fruit and vegetables have been grown in your garden, rather than on a farm, or in your country rather than abroad. 自家栽培の, 国内産の □ *Martinelli reminds visitors often that he uses 100 percent homegrown fruit from California's Bajaro Valley.* 自分が使うのはカリフォルニア, バハロ・バレーの純国産フルーツだけだ, とマルティネリは来客によく言うのだ.

home|land /hoʊmlænd/ (homelands) **1** N-COUNT 可算名詞 Your **homeland** is your native country. 祖国 [mainly WRITTEN 主に書き言葉] □ *Many are planning to return to their homeland.* 多くの人が祖国に帰ろうとしています. **2** N-COUNT 可算名詞 The **homelands** were regions within South Africa in which black South Africans had a limited form of self-government. ホームランド (南アフリカ共和国内の黒人住民のための自治区)

home|less /hoʊmlɪs/ ADJ 形容詞 **Homeless** people have nowhere to live. 住む家がない. 家がない人たちの □ *the growing number of homeless families.* 増加傾向にある家がない家庭. ●N-PLURAL 複数名詞 The **homeless** are people who are homeless. ホームレス □ *...shelters for the homeless.* ホームレスのための保護施設. ●**home|less|ness** N-UNCOUNT 不可算名詞 住む家のないこと □ *The only way to solve homelessness is to provide more homes.* ホームレス問題を解決するには住宅供給を増やすしかありません.

home|ly /hoʊmli/ **1** ADJ 形容詞 If you say that someone is **homely,** you mean that they are not very attractive to look at. やぼったい [AM 米国英語] □ *The man was homely, overweight, and probably only two or three years younger than Lou.* その男はやぼったくて, 太っている. たぶん, ルーより2つ3つ若いだけだろう. **2** ADJ 形容詞 If you describe a room or house as **homely,** you like it because you feel comfortable and relaxed there. 暖かい雰囲気の [BRIT 英国英語, APPROVAL 賛成] [AM **homey** 米国英語 **homey**]

home|made /hoʊmmeɪd/ ADJ 形容詞 Something that is **homemade** has been made in someone's home, rather than in a store or factory. 自家製の □ *The bread, pastry and mayonnaise are homemade.* パン, 焼き菓子, マヨネーズは自家製です.

homeo|path /hoʊmioʊpæθ/ (homeopaths) N-COUNT 可算名詞 A **homeopath** is someone who treats illness by homeopathy. ホメオパシー医 □ *The homeopath will test various strengths of remedies on the patient.* ホメオパシー医はその患者に様々な強さの薬を試すつもりだ.

homeo|path|ic /hoʊmioʊpæθɪk/ ADJ 形容詞 **Homeopathic** means relating to or used in homeopathy. ホメオパシーの □ *...homeopathic remedies.* ホメオパシーの療法.

homeo|pa|thy /hoʊmiɒpəθi/ N-UNCOUNT 不可算名詞 **Homeopathy** is a way of treating an illness in which the patient

is given very small amounts of a drug that produces signs of the illness in healthy people. ホメオパシー

home page (**home pages**) N-COUNT 可算名詞 On the Internet, a person's or organization's **home page** is the main page of information about them, which often contains links to other pages about them. ホームページ ❏ ...*the home page of a new sex education website.* 新しい性教育関連ウェブサイトのホームページ.

home shop|ping N-UNCOUNT 不可算名詞 **Home shopping** is shopping that people do by ordering goods they see in catalogs or on television channels, using the telephone or computers. ホームショッピング [oft N n] ❏ ...*America's most successful home-shopping channel.* アメリカで最も利用されているホームショッピング・チャンネル.

home|sick /hoʊmsɪk/ ADJ 形容詞 If you are **homesick**, you feel unhappy because you are away from home and are missing your family, friends, and home very much. ホームシックの ❏ *She's feeling a little homesick.* 彼女はちょっとホームシックにかかっています. ● **home|sick|ness** N-UNCOUNT 不可算名詞 ホームシック ❏ *There were inevitable bouts of homesickness.* 逃れようのないホームシックに何度もかかりました.

Word Link stead ≈ place, stand : home**stead**, in**stead**, **stead**y

home|stead /hoʊmstɛd/ (**homesteads**) ■ N-COUNT 可算名詞 A **homestead** is a farmhouse, together with the land around it. (付属の建物も含む) 農場 ◢ N-COUNT 可算名詞 In United States history, a **homestead** was a piece of government land in the west, which was given to someone so they could settle there and develop a farm. (移民へ移譲される) 自作農場 [AM 米国英語]

home|work /hoʊmwɜrk/ ■ N-UNCOUNT 不可算名詞 **Homework** is schoolwork that teachers give to students to do at home in the evening or on the weekend. 宿題 ❏ *Have you done your homework, Gemma?* ジェマ, 宿題は済んだの? ◢ N-UNCOUNT 不可算名詞 If you **do** your **homework**, you find out what you need to know in preparation for something. 下調べ ❏ *Before you go near a stockbroker, do your homework.* 株の売買に手を出すなら, その前にちゃんと勉強することだね.

homey /hoʊmi/ ADJ 形容詞 If you describe a room or house as **homey**, you like it because you feel comfortable and relaxed there. 居心地がいい 主に米国英語, INFORMAL くだけた, APPROVAL 賛成 ❏ ...*a large, homey dining room.* 広くて居心地のいいダイニング.

homi|ci|dal /hɒmɪsaɪdəl, hoʊmɪ-/ ADJ 形容詞 **Homicidal** is used to describe someone who is dangerous because they are likely to kill someone. 殺人を犯す傾向のある ❏ *That man is a homicidal maniac.* あの男は殺人狂だ.

Word Link cide ≈ killing : geno**cide**, homi**cide**, pesti**cide**

homi|cide /hɒmɪsaɪd, hoʊmɪ-/ (**homicides**) N-VAR 可変性名詞 **Homicide** is the illegal killing of a person. 殺人 [mainly AM 主に米国英語] ❏ *The police arrived at the scene of the homicide.* 警察が殺人現場に到着した.

homeo|path|ic /hoʊmiəpæθɪk/ → see **homeopathic**

homeopa|thy /hoʊmiɒpəθi/ → see **homeopathy**

Word Link homo ≈ same : homo**genous**, homo**phobia**, homo**sexual**

homo|geneous /hɒmədʒiniəs, hoʊ-/ also **homogenous** ADJ 形容詞 **Homogeneous** is used to describe a group or thing which has members or parts that are all the same. 同種の [FORMAL 形式ばった] ❏ *The unemployed are not a homogeneous group.* 失業者全体に共通する特性があるわけではない.

homo|pho|bia /hɒməfoʊbiə/ N-UNCOUNT 不可算名詞 **Homophobia** is a strong and unreasonable dislike of gay people, especially gay men. 同性愛嫌悪

Word Link phob ≈ fear : homo**phobic**, **phob**ia, xeno**phob**ia

ho|mo|pho|bic /hɒmǝfoʊbɪk/ ADJ 形容詞 **Homophobic** means involving or related to a strong and unreasonable dislike of gay people, especially gay men. 同性愛嫌悪の ❏ *I'm not homophobic in any way and certainly don't condemn gay relationships.* 私は何ら同性愛を嫌悪しているわけではないし, 彼らを非難したりもしない.

homo|sex|ual /hoʊmoʊsɛkʃuəl/ (**homosexuals**) ■ ADJ 形容詞 A **homosexual** relationship is a sexual relationship between people of the same sex. 同性愛の ❏ ...*partners in a homosexual relationship.* 同性愛カップル. ◢ ADJ 形容詞 Someone who is **homosexual** is sexually attracted to people of the same sex. 同性愛志向の ❏ ...*a fraud trial involving two homosexual lawyers.* 同性愛者である弁護士2人が関係した偽りの裁判. ● N-COUNT 可算名詞 **Homosexual** is also a noun. 同性愛者 ❏ *The judge said that discrimination against homosexuals is deplorable.* 裁判官は, 同性愛者差別は受け入れられざる行為である, と述べた. ● **homo|sex|ual|ity** /hoʊmoʊsɛkʃuæliti/ N-UNCOUNT 不可算名詞 同性愛 ❏ ...*a place*

where gays could openly discuss homosexuality. ゲイの人たちが公然と同性愛について話し合える場所.

hone /hoʊn/ (**hones, honing, honed**) V-T 他動詞 If you **hone** something, for example a skill, technique, idea, or product, you carefully develop it over a long period of time so that it is exactly right for your purpose. 磨く ❏ *Leading companies spend time and money on honing the skills of senior managers.* 大手企業は上級管理職のスキル向上には時間と費用を惜しまない.

hon|est /ɒnɪst/ ■ ADJ 形容詞 If you describe someone as **honest**, you mean that they always tell the truth, and do not try to deceive people or break the law. 誠実な ❏ *I know she's honest and reliable.* 彼女は誠実で信頼できますよ. ● **hon|est|ly** ADV 副詞 [ADV after v] 誠実に ❏ *She fought honestly for a just cause and for freedom.* 彼女は正当な理由と自由を求めて実直に戦った. ◢ ADJ 形容詞 If you are **honest** in a particular situation, you tell the complete truth or give your sincere opinion, even if this is not very pleasant. 偽りのない ❏ *I was honest about what I was doing.* 私は自分がしていたことを偽りなく話した. ❏ *He had been honest with her and she had tricked him!* 彼は隠し事はしていなかったのに, 彼女は彼をだましてたんだ! ● **hon|est|ly** ADV 副詞 [ADV with v] あからさまに ❏ *It came as a shock to hear an old friend speak so honestly about Ted.* テッドのことを旧友があのようにあからさまに話すのはショックだった. ◣ ADV 副詞 You say "**honest**" before or after a statement to emphasize that you are telling the truth and that you want people to believe you. 本当に [INFORMAL くだけた, EMPHASIS 強調] [ADV with cl] ❏ *I'm not sure, honest.* わからないよ. 本当に. ◤ PHRASE 句 Some people say "**honest to God**" to emphasize their feelings or to emphasize that something is really true. 誓って [INFORMAL くだけた, EMPHASIS 強調] ❏ *I wish we weren't doing this, Lillian, honest to God, I really do.* リリアン, 僕たちはこんなことをしていてはだめなんだ. 本当にそう思うよ. ◥ PHRASE 句 You can say "**to be honest**" before or after a statement to indicate that you are telling the truth about your own opinions or feelings, especially if you think these will disappoint the person you are talking to. 率直に言えば [FEELINGS 感情] ❏ *To be honest the house is not quite our style.* 率直に言いますが, その家は我々の好みではありません.

Thesaurus honest また次を参照:

ADJ.	fair, genuine, sincere, true, truthful, upright ■ candid, frank, straight, truthful ◢

hon|est|ly /ɒnɪstli/ ■ ADV 副詞 You use **honestly** to emphasize that you are referring to your, or someone else's, true beliefs or feelings. 本当に [EMPHASIS 強調] [ADV before v] ❏ *But did you honestly think we wouldn't notice?* しかし, 本当に君は我々が気づかないとでも思ってたのかい? ◢ ADV 副詞 You use **honestly** to emphasize that you are telling the truth and that you want people to believe you. 本当のところ [SPOKEN 口語, EMPHASIS 強調] [ADV with cl] ❏ *Honestly, I don't know anything about it.* 正直言って, 何も知らないんです. ◣ ADV 副詞 You use **honestly** to indicate that you are annoyed or impatient. まったく [SPOKEN 口語, FEELINGS 感情] [ADV with cl] ❏ *Honestly, Nev! Must you be so crude!.* まったく, ネブっ. なんでそんなにがさつなのよ!. ◤ → see also **honest**

hon|es|ty /ɒnɪsti/ N-UNCOUNT 不可算名詞 **Honesty** is the quality of being honest. 誠実さ ❏ *They said the greatest virtues in a politician were integrity, correctness, and honesty.* 政治家の最大の美徳といえば, 高潔で礼儀正しく誠実なことだとされていた. PHRASE 句 ● You say **in all honesty** when you are saying something that might be disappointing or upsetting, and you want to soften its effect by emphasizing your sincerity. 実を言うと [EMPHASIS 強調]

hon|ey /hʌni/ (**honeys**) ■ N-VAR 可変性名詞 **Honey** is a sweet, sticky, yellowish substance that is made by bees. はちみつ ◢ N-VOC 呼格名詞 You call someone **honey** as a sign of affection. 親密な人に対するよびかけ ❏ *Honey, I don't really think that's a good idea.* ねえ, あなた. それはあんまりいい考えではないと思うわ. [mainly AM 主に米国英語]

> **Honey** is a term commonly used to express affection between two people. Other words used in a similar way include: **dear**, **darling**, **sweetheart**, or **angel**. Sometimes these words are used by adults when speaking to a child.

honey|moon /hʌnimun/ (**honeymoons, honeymooning, honeymooned**) ■ N-COUNT 可算名詞 A **honeymoon** is a vacation taken by a man and a woman who have just gotten married. ハネムーン ❏ *The next time I went abroad was on my honeymoon.* 次に海外に出たのは新婚旅行だったわ. ◢ V-I 自動詞 When a recently married couple **honeymoon** somewhere, they go there on their honeymoon. ハネムーンでーに行く ❏ *They honeymooned in Venice.* 彼らのハネムーン先はベニスだった. ◣ N-COUNT 可算名詞 You can use **honeymoon** to refer to a period of time after the start of a new job or when a newly elected official takes office when everyone is pleased with the person or people concerned and is nice to them. 蜜月期間 (最初のうまくいっている期間) ❏ *Brett is enjoying a honeymoon period with both press and public.* ブレットはマスコミと大

衆の両方との蜜月期間を謳歌(おうか)している.
→ see **wedding**

honk /hɒŋk/ (honks, honking, honked) V-T/V-I 他動詞/自動詞
If you **honk** the horn of a vehicle or if the horn **honks**, you make
the horn produce a short loud sound. (警笛を) 鳴らす（警笛が）鳴
る ❏ *Drivers honked their horns in solidarity with the peace marchers.* 平
和行進に合わせてドライバーたちがクラクションを鳴らしました.
❏ *Horns honk. An angry motorist shouts.* クラクションが鳴り響き，怒
り心頭のドライバーが叫んでいます. ● N-COUNT 可算名詞 **Honk** is
also a noun. 警笛 ❏ *She pulled to the right with a honk.* 彼女はクラクシ
ョンを鳴らして右側に車を止めた.

hon|or /ɒnər/ (honors, honoring, honored) **1** N-UNCOUNT 不可
算名詞 **Honor** means doing what you believe to be right and being
confident that you have done what is right. 道徳規範 ❏ *The officers
died faithful to the honor of a soldier.* 将校たちは兵士たるべき死に方を
しました. **2** N-COUNT 可算名詞 An **honor** is a special award that
is given to someone, usually because they have done something
good or because they are greatly respected. 賞 ❏ *He was showered
with honors – among them an Oscar.* 彼は多くの賞を獲得しましたが，
その一つはアカデミー賞です. **3** V-T 他動詞 If someone is **honored**,
they are given public praise or an award for something they have
done. 表彰する [usu passive] ❏ *Diego Maradona was honored with
an award presented by Argentina's soccer association.* ディエゴ・マラ
ドーナはアルゼンチンサッカー協会賞を贈られた. **4** N-SING 単数名
詞 If you describe doing or experiencing something as an **honor**,
you mean you think it is something special and desirable. 名
誉 ❏ *Five other cities had been competing for the honor of staging the
Games.* 他にも5都市が大会開催の栄誉を勝ち取るためしのぎを削って
きました. **5** V-T PASSIVE 受動態他動詞 If you say that you **would
be honored** to do something, you are saying very politely and
formally that you would be pleased to do it. If you say that you
are honored by something, you are saying that you are grateful
for it and pleased about it. 光栄に思う [POLITENESS 丁寧さ] ❏ *Ms.
Payne said she was honored to accept the appointment and looked
forward to its challenges.* ペイン女史は，任命を受諾できて光栄で
あり，任務の遂行を楽しみにしている，と述べました. **6** V-T 他動
詞 To **honor** someone means to treat them or regard them with
special attention and respect. 敬意を払う ❏ *They honored me with
a seat at the head of the table.* 彼らは私に上席を用意し礼遇してくれ
た. **7** V-T 他動詞 If you **honor** an arrangement or promise, you
do what you said you would do. 履行する ❏ *The two sides agreed to
honor a new ceasefire.* 両陣営は新たに停戦を履行することを確認しま
した. **8** N-VOC 呼格名詞 Judges and mayors are sometimes called
your honor or referred to as **his honor** or **her honor**. 裁判官，市長
などへの呼びかけ言葉 ❏ *I bring this up, your honor, because I think it is
important to understand the background of the defendant.* 裁判官，提示
したいものがあります. これは被告人の背景を理解するために重要な
ものです. [POSS N; PRON: POSS PRON] **9** PHRASE 句 If something is
arranged **in honor of** a particular event, it is arranged in order to
celebrate that event. 〜を祝して ❏ *The Foundation is holding a dinner
at the Museum of American Art in honor of the opening of its new show.*
アメリカンアート美術館の新展示のオープニングを祝し，協会が晩餐
会を開催した. **10** PHRASE 句 If something is arranged or happens
in someone's **honor**, it is done specially to show appreciation
of them. 〜の栄誉をたたえて ❏ *Mr. Mandela will attend an outdoor
concert in his honor.* マンデラ氏は彼のために開催される野外コンサー
トに出席する予定です.

Thesaurus　　　　*honor* また次を参照:

N.	award, distinction, recognition **2**
V.	commend, praise, recognize **3**

Word Partnership　　　*honor* は次の語句と使われる:

N.	**code of** honor, **sense of** honor **1**
	honor **a ceasefire 7**
	honor **the memory of** *someone/something* **9 10**
ADJ.	**great/highest** honor **2 4**

hon|or|able /ɒnrəbəl/ ADJ 形容詞 If you describe people or
actions as **honorable**, you mean that they are good and deserve
to be respected and admired. 尊敬すべき ❏ *He argued that the only
honorable course of action was death.* 彼は，取るべき道は死だけだ，と
論じた. ● **hon|or|ably** /ɒnrəbli/ ADV 副詞 立派に ❏ *He also felt she
had not behaved honorably in the leadership election.* 彼もまた，指導者
選挙での彼女のふるまいはほめられたものではないと思った.

hon|or|ary /ɒnərɛri/ **1** ADJ 形容詞 An **honorary** title or
membership of a group is given to someone without their
needing to have the necessary qualifications, usually because
of their public achievements. 名誉上の [ADJ N] ❏ *Harvard awarded
him an honorary degree.* ハーバード大学は彼に名誉学位を授与し
た. **2** ADJ 形容詞 **Honorary** is used to describe an official job that
is done without payment. (無給の) 名誉職 [ADJ N] ❏ *...the honorary
secretary of the Beekeepers' Association.* 養蜂業協会の名誉幹事.

hon|our /ɒnər/ → see **honor**
hon|our|able /ɒnrəbəl/ → see **honorable**

hood /hʊd/ (hoods) **1** N-COUNT 可算名詞 A **hood** is a part of a
coat which you can pull up to cover your head. It is in the shape
of a triangular bag attached to the neck of the coat at the back. フー
ド ❏ *She threw back the hood of her cloak.* 彼女は外とうのフードを後
ろに払った. **2** N-COUNT 可算名詞 The **hood** of a car is the metal
cover over the engine at the front. ボンネット [AM 米国英語] ❏ *He
raised the hood of McKee's truck.* 彼はマッキーのトラックのボンネット
を開けた.

hood|ed /hʊdɪd/ **1** ADJ 形容詞 A **hooded** piece of clothing or
furniture has a hood. フード付きの ❏ *...a blue hooded sweatshirt.*
青いフード付きトレーナー. **2** ADJ 形容詞 A **hooded** person is
wearing a hood or a piece of clothing pulled down over their face,
so they are difficult to recognize. 覆面をかぶった [ADJ N] ❏ *The class
was held hostage by a hooded gunman.* そのクラスは覆面の武装犯に人
質に取られた.

hoof /huf, hʊf/ (hoofs or hooves) N-COUNT 可算名詞 The
hooves of an animal such as a horse are the hard lower parts of its
feet. ひづめ ❏ *The horses' hooves often could not get a proper grip.* 馬の
ひづめは接地が不安定になることもある.

hook /hʊk/ (hooks, hooking, hooked) **1** N-COUNT 可算名詞 A
hook is a bent piece of metal or plastic that is used for catching
or holding things, or for hanging things up. フック ❏ *One of his
jackets hung from a hook.* 彼のジャケットが1枚フックにぶら下がってい
た. **2** V-T/V-I 他動詞/自動詞 If you **hook** one thing to another, you
attach it there using a hook. If something **hooks** somewhere, it
can be hooked there. フックで留める ❏ *Paul hooked his tractor to the
car and pulled it to safety.* ポールはトラクターに車をつなぎ安全な場所
まで牽引(けんいん)した. **3** V-T 他動詞 If you **hook** your arm, leg,
or foot round an object, you place it like a hook round the object
in order to move it or hold it. 曲げてつかむ ❏ *She latched on to his
arm, hooking her other arm around a tree.* 彼女は片手を木に巻きつけ，
彼の腕にしがみついた. **4** V-T 他動詞 If you **hook** a fish, you catch
it with a hook on the end of a line. 釣り針で引っかける ❏ *At the first
cast I hooked a huge fish, probably a tench.* 最初の一投で大きな魚がか
かったんだ. たぶんテンチだな. **5** N-COUNT 可算名詞 A **hook** is a
short sharp blow with your fist that you make with your elbow
bent, usually in a boxing match. フック ❏ *Lewis desperately needs
to keep clear of Ruddock's big left hook.* ルイスは是が非でもラドックの
強烈な左フックをかわし続けなければならない. **6** V-T/V-I 他動詞/自
動詞 If you **are hooked into** something, or **hook into** something,
you get involved with it. 引き込む，関わる [mainly AM 主に米国
英語] ❏ *I'm guessing again now because I'm not hooked into the political
circles.* 私は政界関係者ではないのですから，やはり推測でお話をする
ことになります. **7** PHRASE 句 If someone gets **off the hook** or
is let **off the hook**, they manage to get out of the awkward or
unpleasant situation that they are in. 窮地を脱して [INFORMAL
くだけた] ❏ *Officials accused of bribery and corruption get off the hook
with monotonous regularity.* 収賄で告訴された官僚はお決まりの責任
逃れをする. **8** PHRASE 句 If you take a phone **off the hook**, you
take the receiver off the part that it normally rests on, so that the
phone will not ring. 受話器が外れて ❏ *I'd taken my phone off the hook
in order to get some sleep.* 少し眠りたかったので受話器を外しておきま
した. **9** PHRASE 句 If your phone **is ringing off the hook**, so many
people are trying to telephone you that it is ringing constantly.
電話が立て続けに鳴る ❏ *Since war broke out, the phones at donation
centers have been ringing off the hook.* 戦争が勃発(ぼっぱつ)して以来，
寄付金センターの電話は鳴り続けています.
→ see **fish**

▶ **hook up 1** PHRASAL VERB 句動詞 If someone **hooks up with**
another person, they begin a sexual or romantic relationship
with that person. You can also say that two people **hook up**. 親
密な関係になる [INFORMAL くだけた] ❏ *I could be about to hook up
with this incredibly intelligent, beautiful girl.* とびきりの知性派美人
ともう少しで関係が持てるところだったんだ. ❏ *We haven't exactly
hooked up yet.* 私たちはまだきちんとおつきあいしているわけではない
の. **2** PHRASAL VERB 句動詞 If you **hook up with** someone, you
meet them and spend time with them. You can also say that two
people **hook up**. つきあうようになる [mainly AM 主に米国英語，
INFORMAL くだけた] ❏ *He hooked up with fellow cycling enthusiasts
and joined several clubs.* 彼はサイクリング同好者たちと親しくなり，複
数のクラブに入会した. ❏ *This afternoon Iz and Jude and Chris hooked
up.* イズ，ジュード，クリスは今日の午後はつるんでいた. **3** PHRASAL
VERB 句動詞 When someone **hooks up** a computer or other
electronic machine, they connect it to other similar machines
or to a central power supply. 接続する ❏ *...technicians who hook up
computer systems and networks.* コンピュータシステムとネットワー
ク接続の技術者. ❏ *He brought it down, hooked it up, and we got the
generator going.* 彼がそれをいったん止めてから接続し直すと，発電機
は動き出した.

v.	**bait** a **hook**, **hang** *something* **from a hook** 🔳
ADJ.	**sharp hook** 🔳

hooked /hʊkt/ 🔳 ADJ 形容詞 If you describe something as **hooked**, you mean that it is shaped like a hook. かぎ状の 🔲 *He was thin and tall, with a hooked nose.* かれはやせていて背が高く、鼻はかぎ鼻だった. 🔳 ADJ 形容詞 If you are **hooked on** something, you enjoy it so much that it takes up a lot of your interest and attention. 夢中になって [INFORMAL くだけた] [v-link ADJ] 🔲 *Many of the leaders have become hooked on power and money.* これまでの指導者の多くが金と権力のとりこになった. 🔳 ADJ 形容詞 If you are **hooked on** a drug, you are addicted to it. 中毒になって [INFORMAL くだけた] [v-link ADJ] 🔲 *He spent a number of years hooked on cocaine, heroin, and alcohol.* 彼は永年、コカイン、ヘロイン、アルコールの中毒だった.

hook|er /hʊkər/ (hookers) N-COUNT 可算名詞 A **hooker** is a prostitute. 売春婦 [mainly AM 主に米国英語, INFORMAL くだけた]

hoo|li|gan /huːlɪɡən/ (hooligans) N-COUNT 可算名詞 If you describe people, especially young people, as **hooligans**, you are critical of them because they behave in a noisy and violent way in a public place. フーリガン [DISAPPROVAL 不賛成] 🔲 *...the problem of soccer hooligans.* サッカーのフーリガンが起こす問題.

hoo|li|gan|ism /huːlɪɡənɪzəm/ N-UNCOUNT 不可算名詞 **Hooliganism** is the behavior and actions of hooligans. フーリガン行為 🔲 *Officials dismiss these incidents as simple hooliganism.* 当局が一連の事件を単なるフーリガン行為だとして片付ける.

hoop /huːp/ (hoops) 🔳 N-COUNT 可算名詞 A **hoop** is a ring made of wood, metal, or plastic. 輪 🔲 *A boy came towards them, rolling an iron hoop.* 男の子が鉄の輪を転がしながら彼らに近づいてきた. 🔳 N-COUNT 可算名詞 A basketball **hoop** is the ring that players try to throw the ball into in order to score points for their team. (バスケットボールの) リング 🔳 PHRASE 句 If someone makes you **jump through hoops**, they make you do lots of difficult or boring things in order to please them or achieve something. どんな指示にも従う 🔲 *He had the receptionist almost jumping through hoops for him. But to no avail.* 彼は受付係を服従させようとしたが、無駄だった.

hoot /huːt/ (hoots, hooting, hooted) 🔳 V-I 自動詞 If you **hoot**, you make a loud high-pitched noise when you are laughing or showing disapproval. 大声で笑う、大声でやじる 🔲 *The protesters chanted, blew whistles and hooted at the name of Governor Pete Wilson.* デモ参加者はシュプレヒコールを上げ、口笛を吹き鳴らし、ピート・ウィルソン知事の名でやじりました. ● N-COUNT 可算名詞 **Hoot** is also a noun. 大声のやじ、大きな笑い声 🔲 *His confession was greeted with derisive hoots.* 彼の告白は大声であざけられた. 🔳 PHRASE 句 If you say that you **don't give a hoot** or **don't care two hoots** about something, you are emphasizing that you do not care at all about it. 全く関心がない [INFORMAL くだけた, EMPHASIS 強調] 🔲 *Alan doesn't care two hoots about politics.* アランは政治問題にてんで関心がない. 🔳 V-T/V-I 他動詞/自動詞 If you **hoot** the horn on a vehicle or if it **hoots**, it makes a loud noise on one note. (クラクションを) 鳴らす [mainly BRIT 主に英国英語; AM usually honk, toot 米国英語では通常 honk, toot]

hooves /huːvz/ **Hooves** is a plural of **hoof**.

hop /hɒp/ (hops, hopping, hopped) 🔳 V-I 自動詞 If you **hop**, you move along by jumping on one foot. 片足で跳ぶ 🔲 *I hopped down three steps.* 私は階段をぴょんぴょんぴょんと降りた. ● N-COUNT 可算名詞 **Hop** is also a noun. 片足で跳ぶこと 🔲 *"This really is a catching rhythm, huh?" he added, with a few little hops.* 彼は数回軽くホップして「このリズムはほんとに乗りやすいだろ?」と言った. 🔳 V-I 自動詞 When birds and some small animals **hop**, they move along by jumping on both or all four feet. ぴょんとはねる 🔲 *A small brown fawn hopped across the trail in front of them.* 彼らの目の前を小さな茶色い小鹿がぴょんぴょんと道を渡っていった. ● N-COUNT 可算名詞 **Hop** is also a noun. ぴょんとはねること 🔲 *The rabbit got up, took four hops and turned around.* うさぎが立ち上がり、4歩はねて振り返りました. 🔳 V-I 自動詞 If you **hop** somewhere, you move there quickly or suddenly. さっと動く [INFORMAL くだけた] 🔲 *My wife and I were the first to arrive and hopped on board.* 私と妻はゲートに一番乗りだったので、すばやく搭乗できました. 🔳 N-COUNT 可算名詞 A **hop** is a short, quick trip, usually by plane. 飛行機で短距離を飛ぶ [INFORMAL くだけた] 🔲 *It is a three-hour drive but can be reached by a 20-minute hop in a private helicopter.* 車で3時間かかるけど、ヘリコプターだと20分で飛べるよ. 🔳 N-COUNT 可算名詞 **Hops** are flowers that are dried and used for making beer. ホップ

hope /hoʊp/ (hopes, hoping, hoped) 🔳 V-T/V-I 他動詞/自動詞 If you **hope** that something is true, or you **hope** for something, you want it to be true or to happen, and you usually believe that it is possible or likely. 望む 🔲 *She had decided she must go on as usual, follow her normal routine, and hope and pray.* 彼女はいつも通り暮らし、通常の日課に従い、希望を持ち祈ることを決意した. 🔲 *He hesitates*

before leaving, almost as though he had been hoping for conversation. まるで彼はずっと会話を望んでいたかのようにその場を去るのをためらう. 🔳 V-T/V-I 他動詞/自動詞 If you say that you cannot **hope for** something, or if you talk about the only thing that you can **hope to** get, you mean that you are in a bad situation, and there is very little chance of improving it. 望む [with brd-neg] 🔲 *Things aren't ideal, but that's the best you can hope for.* 事態は理想的ではないが、それはあなたが望みうる最上のものだ. ● N-VAR 可変性名詞 **Hope** is also a noun. 希望 🔲 *The only hope for underdeveloped countries is to become, as far as possible, self-reliant.* 開発の遅れた国の唯一の望みは可能な限りの自立である. 🔳 N-UNCOUNT 不可算名詞 **Hope** is a feeling of desire and expectation that things will go well in the future. 期待 🔲 *Now that he has become president, many people once again have hope for genuine changes in the system.* 今や彼は大統領となったのだから、多くの人が本当に変わることを期待している. 🔲 *But Kevin hasn't given up hope of getting in shape.* しかしケビンは体調を整える望みを捨てていない. 🔳 N-COUNT 可算名詞 If someone wants something to happen, and considers it likely or possible, you can refer to their **hopes of** that thing, or to their **hope that** it will happen. 見込み 🔲 *They have hopes of increasing trade between the two regions.* 彼らは二つの地域での取引が増えると見込んでいる. 🔲 *My hope is that, in the future, I will go over there and marry her.* 私の希望としては、いずれ向こうに行き彼女と結婚したい. 🔳 N-COUNT 可算名詞 If you think that the help or success of a particular person or thing will cause you to be successful or to get what you want, you can refer to them as your **hope**. 希望 🔲 *Roemer represented the best hope for a businesslike climate in Louisiana.* ローマーはルイジアナ州の商業風土の最良の希望を体現している. 🔳 PHRASE 句 If you are in a difficult situation and do something and **hope for the best**, you hope that everything will happen in the way you want, although you know that it may not. うまくいくことを望む 🔲 *Some companies are cutting costs and hoping for the best.* 費用を削減しうまくいくことを望んでいる会社もある. 🔳 PHRASE 句 If you **tell** someone not to **get** their **hopes up**, or not to **build** their **hopes up**, you are warning them that they should not become too confident of progress or success. 望みを抱く 🔲 *There is no reason for people to get their hopes up over this mission.* 人々がこの仕事に対して期待する理由がない. 🔳 PHRASE 句 If you say that someone has **not got a hope in hell** of doing something, you are emphasizing that they will not be able to do it. 見込みがまったくない [INFORMAL くだけた, EMPHASIS 強調] 🔲 *Everybody knows they haven't got a hope in hell of forming a government anyway.* 誰もがともかく政府を作る見込みがまったくないことを知っている. 🔳 PHRASE 句 If you have **high hopes** or **great hopes that** something will happen, you are confident that it will happen. 大きな望み 🔲 *I had high hopes that Derek Randall might play an important part.* 私はデレク・ランドールが重要な役割を果たすことを大いに期待していた. 🔳 PHRASE 句 If you **hope against hope** that something will happen, you hope that it will happen, although it seems impossible. 淡い期待を抱く 🔲 *She glanced about the hall, hoping against hope that Richard would be waiting for her.* リチャードが広間にいるのではないかという淡い期待を抱き、彼女は広間をちらりと見た. 🔳 PHRASE 句 You use "**I hope**" in expressions such as "**I hope you don't mind**" and "**I hope I'm not disturbing you**," when you are being polite and want to make sure that you have not offended someone or disturbed them. 願う [POLITENESS 丁寧さ] 🔲 *I hope you don't mind me coming to see you.* お目にかかりに伺ったことがご迷惑でなければいいのですが. 🔳 PHRASE 句 You say "**I hope**" when you want to warn someone not to do something foolish or dangerous. だといいのですが 🔲 *You're not trying to see him, I hope?* していませんよね. 🔳 PHRASE 句 If you do one thing **in the hope of** another thing happening, you do it because you think it might cause or help the other thing to happen, which is what you want. 期待し 🔲 *He was studying in the hope of being admitted to an engineering college.* 彼は工科大学へ入学することを望み勉強していた. 🔳 PHRASE 句 If you **live in hope** that something will happen, you continue to hope that it will happen, although it seems unlikely, and you realize that you are being foolish. あてのない希望を持ち続ける 🔲 *I just live in hope that one day she'll talk to me.* 私はいつか彼女が話しかけてくれるのではないかといううあてのない希望を持ち続けている.

V.	aspire, desire, dream, wish 🔳
N.	ambition, aspiration, desire, dream, wish 🔳

N.	**glimmer of hope** 🔳
ADJ.	**faint hope, false hope, little hope** 🔳 🔳
V.	**give** *someone* **hope, give up** *all* **hope, hold out hope, lose** *all* **hope** 🔳 🔳

hope|ful /hoʊpfəl/ (hopefuls) 🔳 ADJ 形容詞 If you are **hopeful**, you are fairly confident that something that you want to happen will happen. 見込みがあると思う 🔲 *I am hopeful this*

misunderstanding will be rectified very quickly. 私はこの誤解が非常に早く修正されうると見込んでいる。 ●**hope|ful|ly** ADV 副詞 [ADV with v] 期待して ❑ *"Am I welcome?" He smiled hopefully, leaning on the door.* 「私もよろしいですか」彼は期待の笑みを浮かべ、扉にもたれた。 ❷ ADJ 形容詞 If something such as a sign or event is **hopeful**, it makes you feel that what you want to happen will happen. 見込みがある ❑ *The result of the election is yet another hopeful sign that peace could come to the Middle East.* しかし選挙の結果は中東に平和がもたらされうるというさらなる希望の兆候である。 ❸ ADJ 形容詞 A **hopeful** action is one that you do in the hope that you will get what you want to get. 期待に満ちた [ADJ n] ❑ *We've chartered the aircraft in the hopeful anticipation that the government will allow them to leave.* 政府が彼らの出発を許可するという希望的予測の下、われわれはその飛行機を借り上げた。 ❹ N-COUNT 可算名詞 If you refer to someone as a **hopeful**, you mean that they are hoping and trying to achieve success in a particular career, election, or competition. 有望な人 ❑ *His skills continue to be put to good use in his job as coach to young hopefuls.* 彼の技術は若手有望株の指導の仕事のため引き続き有効活用されている。

hope|ful|ly /hoʊpfəli/ ADV 副詞 You say **hopefully** when mentioning something that you hope will happen. Some careful speakers of English think that this use of **hopefully** is not correct, but it is very frequently used. うまくいけば [ADV with cl/group] ❑ *Hopefully, you won't have any problems after reading this.* うまくいけばこれを読んだあとは問題がなくなるでしょう。

hope|less /hoʊplɪs/ ❶ ADJ 形容詞 If you feel **hopeless**, you feel very unhappy because there seems to be no possibility of a better situation or success. 望みのない ❑ *I looked around hopelessly.* 私は失望して辺りを見回した。 ●**hope|less|ness** N-UNCOUNT 不可算名詞 失望 ❑ *She had a feeling of hopelessness about the future.* 彼女は未来に対する失望感を持っていた。 ❷ ADJ 形容詞 Someone or something that is **hopeless** is certain to fail or be unsuccessful. 希望のない ❑ *I don't believe your situation is as hopeless as you think. If you love each other, you'll work it out.* 私はあなたの状況があなたの考えるほど希望のないものだとは思わない。 ❸ ADJ 形容詞 If someone is **hopeless at** something, they are very bad at it. 無能な [INFORMAL くだけた] ❑ *I'd be hopeless at working for somebody else.* 私は誰かに雇われるのがひどく苦手だ。 ❹ ADJ 形容詞 You use **hopeless** to emphasize how bad or inadequate something or someone is. どうしようもない [EMPHASIS 強調] ❑ *Argentina's economic policies were a hopeless mess.* アルゼンチンの経済政策はとんでもないめちゃくちゃな状態だった。 ●**hope|less|ly** ADV 副詞 どうしようもなく ❑ *Harry was hopelessly lost.* ハリーはどうしようもなく道に迷っていた。

horde /hɔrd/ (**hordes**) N-COUNT 可算名詞 If you describe a crowd of people as a **horde**, you mean that the crowd is very large and excited and, often, rather frightening or unpleasant. 大群 ❑ *This attracts hordes of tourists to Las Vegas.* これが非常に多くの旅行客をラスベガスに引きつける。

ho|ri|zon /həraɪzᵊn/ (**horizons**) ❶ N-SING 単数名詞 The **horizon** is the line in the far distance where the sky seems to meet the land or the sea. 地平線，水平線 ❑ *In the distance, the dot of a boat appeared on the horizon.* 彼方では水平線に小船が点在していた。 ❷ N-COUNT 可算名詞 Your **horizons** are the limits of what you want to do or of what you are interested or involved in. 視野 ❑ *As your horizons expand, these new ideas can give a whole new meaning to life.* 視野を広げればこうした新しい考えから人生の新しい意味のすべてを得ることができる。 ❸ PHRASE 句 If something is **on the horizon**, it is almost certainly going to happen or be done quite soon. 兆しが見える ❑ *With breast cancer, as with many common diseases, there is no obvious breakthrough on the horizon.* 乳がんに関しては、多くの一般的な病気と同じに、はっきりとした解決の意図口は見えない。

hori|zon|tal /hɔrɪzɒntᵊl/ ADJ 形容詞 Something that is **horizontal** is flat and level with the ground, rather than at an angle to it. 水平の ❑ *The board consists of vertical and horizontal lines.* 垂直線と水平線で構成された板 ❑ N-SING 単数名詞 **Horizontal** is also a noun. 水平なもの ❑ *Do not raise your left arm above the horizontal.* 水平棒よりも上に左腕を上げてはいけない。 ●**hori|zon|tal|ly** ADV 副詞 水平に ❑ *The wind was cold and drove the snow at him almost horizontally.* 風は冷たく、彼に対してほとんど垂直に雪を吹きつけた。 → see **graph**

hor|mo|nal /hɔrmoʊnᵊl/ ADJ 形容詞 **Hormonal** means relating to or involving hormones. ホルモンの ❑ *...our individual hormonal balance.* 自分のホルモンバランス

hor|mone /hɔrmoʊn/ (**hormones**) N-COUNT 可算名詞 A **hormone** is a chemical, usually occurring naturally in your body, that makes an organ of your body do something. ホルモン ❑ *...the male sex hormone testosterone.* 男性ホルモン，テストステロン → see **emotion**

horn /hɔrn/ (**horns**) ❶ N-COUNT 可算名詞 On a vehicle such as a car, the **horn** is the device that makes a loud noise as a signal or warning. 警笛 ❑ *He sounded the car horn.* 彼は車の警笛を鳴らした。 ❷ N-COUNT 可算名詞 The **horns** of an animal such as a cow or deer are the hard pointed things that grow from its head. 角 ❑ *A mature cow has horns.* 大人のウシは角を持っている。 ❸ N-COUNT 可算名詞 A **horn** is a musical instrument of the brass family. It is a long circular metal tube, wide at one end, which you play by blowing. ホルン ❑ *He started playing the horn when he was eight.* 彼は8歳のときにホルンの演奏を始めた。 ❹ N-COUNT 可算名詞 A **horn** is a simple musical instrument consisting of a metal tube that is wide at one end and narrow at the other. You play it by blowing into it. 角笛 ❑ *...a hunting horn.* 狩猟用角笛 ❺ PHRASE 句 If two people **lock horns**, they argue about something. 論争する ❑ *During his six years in office, Seidman has often locked horns with lawmakers.* 6年間の在職中、ザイドマンはしばしば議員と議論を戦わせた。

Word Link *scope ≈ looking : horoscope, microscope, telescope*

horo|scope /hɔrəskoʊp/ (**horoscopes**) N-COUNT 可算名詞 Your **horoscope** is a prediction of events which some people believe will happen to you in the future. Horoscopes are based on the position of the stars when you were born. 星占い ❑ *I always read my horoscope and follow the advice.* 私はいつも自分の星占いを読み、忠告に従う。

hor|ren|dous /hɔrendəs, hɒ-, hə-/ ❶ ADJ 形容詞 Something that is **horrendous** is very unpleasant or shocking. すさまじい ❑ *He described it as the most horrendous experience of his life.* 彼はそれを自分の人生で最もすさまじい経験だと述べる。 ❷ ADJ 形容詞 Some people use **horrendous** to describe something that is so big or great that they find it extremely unpleasant. ものすごい [INFORMAL くだけた] ❑ *...the usually horrendous traffic jams.* いつもながらのすさまじい交通渋滞 ●**hor|ren|dous|ly** ADV 副詞 ものすごく ❑ *The man in the photo was horrendously fat.* 写真の男は恐ろしく太っていた。

hor|ri|ble /hɔrɪbᵊl, hɒr-/ ❶ ADJ 形容詞 If you describe something or someone as **horrible**, you do not like them at all. 身の毛のよだつ [INFORMAL くだけた] ❑ *Her voice sounds horrible.* 彼女の声を聞くと身の毛がよだつ。 ●**hor|ri|bly** /hɔrɪbli, hɒr-/ ADV 副詞 [ADV with v] ひどく ❑ *When trouble comes they behave selfishly and horribly.* 問題が起こると彼らは自分勝手にひどい振る舞いをとる。 ❷ ADJ 形容詞 You can call something **horrible** when it causes you to feel great shock, fear, and disgust. 恐ろしい ❑ *Still the horrible shrieking came out of his mouth.* まだ彼の口からは恐ろしい悲鳴があがっていた。 ●**hor|ri|bly** ADV 副詞 [ADV with v] 恐ろしく ❑ *A two-year-old boy was horribly murdered.* 2歳の男の子がひどい殺され方をした。 ❸ ADJ 形容詞 **Horrible** is used to emphasize how bad something is. ひどい [EMPHASIS 強調] [ADJ n] ❑ *That seems like a horrible mess that will drag on for years.* それは数年にわたる影響を残しかねないとんでもない混乱に思える。 ●**hor|ri|bly** ADV 副詞 ひどく ❑ *Our plans have gone horribly wrong.* 我々の計画はひどくまずい状態になった。

hor|rid /hɔrɪd, hɒr-/ ❶ ADJ 形容詞 If you describe something as **horrid**, you mean that it is extremely unpleasant. 忌まわしい [INFORMAL くだけた] ❑ *What a horrid smell!* なんというひどい臭いだ。 ❷ ADJ 形容詞 If you describe someone as **horrid**, you mean that they behave in a very unpleasant way toward other people. ひどい [INFORMAL くだけた] ❑ *I must have been a horrid little girl.* 私はひどく嫌な幼い少女だったに違いない。

hor|rif|ic /hɔrɪfɪk, hɒ-, hə-/ ❶ ADJ 形容詞 If you describe a physical attack, accident, or injury as **horrific**, you mean that it is very bad, so that people are shocked when they see it or think about it. すさまじい ❑ *I have never seen such horrific injuries.* こんなにすさまじい損傷は見たことがない。 ●**hor|rif|ical|ly** ADV 副詞 すさまじく ❑ *He had been horrifically assaulted before he died.* 彼は死ぬ前にひどい暴行を受けていた。 ❷ ADJ 形容詞 If you describe something as **horrific**, you mean that it is so big that it is extremely unpleasant. ものすごい ❑ *...piling up horrific extra amounts of money on top of your original debt.* あなたの元の負債の上に途方もない追加金額を積み上げること ●**hor|rif|ical|ly** ADV 副詞 [ADV adj] ものすごく ❑ *Opera productions are horrifically expensive.* オペラの制作には途方もなく金がかかる。

hor|ri|fy /hɔrɪfaɪ, hɒr-/ (**horrifies, horrifying, horrified**) V-T 他動詞 If someone **is horrified**, they feel shocked or disgusted, usually because of something that they have seen or heard. ぞっとさせる ❑ *His family was horrified by the change.* 彼の家族はその変化におびえた。

hor|ri|fy|ing /hɔrɪfaɪɪŋ, hɒr-/ ADJ 形容詞 If you describe something as **horrifying**, you mean that it is shocking or disgusting. ぞっとする ❑ *These were horrifying experiences.* それはぞっとする体験だった。

hor|ror /hɔrər, hɒr-/ ❶ N-UNCOUNT 不可算名詞 **Horror** is a feeling of great shock, fear, and worry caused by something extremely unpleasant. 恐怖 ❑ *I felt numb with horror.* 私は恐怖でぼう然となった。 ❷ N-SING 単数名詞 If you have a **horror of** something, you are afraid of it or dislike it very much. 恐怖

Word Web   horse

The earliest use of **horses** was as a source of meat for prehistoric man. Then, around 4000 BC, groups began to carry goods on **horseback**. These people also probably milked the mares. Later on, early farmers used a primitive form of **bridle** to help guide their horses. In the Middle Ages, knights used horses in battle. Special **saddles** and stirrups helped them stay on the horse during combat. In the 1800s, **cowboys** had to move large herds of cattle thousands of miles. Some spent weeks at a time with only a horse for company.

❏ ...*his horror of death.* 彼の死に対する恐れ ❸ N-SING 単数名詞 The **horror** of something, especially something that hurts people, is its very great unpleasantness. 恐怖 ❏ ...*the horror of this most bloody of civil wars.* この最も血なまぐさい内戦の恐怖 ❹ N-COUNT 可算名詞 You can refer to extremely unpleasant or frightening experiences as **horrors**. 惨事 ❏ *Can you possibly imagine all the horrors we have undergone since I last wrote you?* 私があなたに最後に手紙を書いてから我々が経験したすべての惨事を想像することがあなたにはできるだろうか. ❺ ADJ 形容詞 A **horror** film or story is intended to be very frightening. 恐怖の [ADJ n] ❏ ...*a psychological horror film.* 心理的恐怖映画. ❻ ADJ 形容詞 You can refer to an account of a very unpleasant experience or event as a **horror** story. 恐ろしい [ADJ n] ❏ ...*a horror story about lost luggage while flying.* 飛行機に乗っている間に荷物が紛失したとんでもない話
→ see **genre**

horse /hɔrs/ (**horses, horsing, horsed**) ❶ N-COUNT 可算名詞 A **horse** is a large animal which people can ride. Some horses are used for pulling plows and carts. ウマ ❏ *A small man on a gray horse had appeared.* 灰色のウマに乗った小さな男が現れた. ❷ PHRASE 句 If you hear something **from the horse's mouth**, you hear it from someone who knows that it is definitely true. 確かな筋から ❏ *He has got to hear it from the horse's mouth. Then he can make a judgment as to whether his policy is correct or not.* 彼は確かな筋から情報を得ねばならない. そうすれば彼は自分の政策が正しいかどうかの判断を下すことができるだろう.
→ see Word Web: **horse**
→ see **train, transportation**

▶ **horse around** PHRASAL VERB 句動詞 If you **horse around**, you play roughly and carelessly, and could hurt someone or damage something. 暴れる [INFORMAL くだけた] ❏ *My friends and I would horse around and try to push each other.* 友人たちと私は暴れてお互いに押し合うだろう.

horse|back /hɔrsbæk/ ❶ N-UNCOUNT 不可算名詞 If you do something **on horseback**, you do it while riding a horse. ウマの背 ❏ *In remote mountain areas, voters arrived on horseback.* 遠く離れた山間部で有権者はウマに乗って投票に訪れた. ❷ ADJ 形容詞 A **horseback** ride is a ride on a horse. ウマの背の [ADJ n] ❏ ...*a horseback ride into the mountains.* 山間部へのウマ乗り ● ADV 副詞 **Horseback** is also an adverb. ウマに乗って ❏ *Many people in this area ride horseback.* この地域にはウマに乗る人が多い.
→ see **horse**

horse|man /hɔrsmən/ (**horsemen**) N-COUNT 可算名詞 A **horseman** is a man who is riding a horse, or who rides horses well. 騎手 ❏ *Gerald was a fine horseman.* ジェラルドはよい騎手だった.

horse|power /hɔrspaʊər/ N-UNCOUNT 不可算名詞 **Horsepower** is a unit of power used for measuring how powerful an engine is. 馬力 ❏ ...*a 300-horsepower engine.* 300馬力のエンジン

horse|shoe /hɔrsʃu/ (**horseshoes**) ❶ N-COUNT 可算名詞 A **horseshoe** is a piece of metal shaped like a U, which is fixed with nails to the bottom of a horse's foot in order to protect it. 蹄鉄 (ていてつ) ❷ N-COUNT 可算名詞 A **horseshoe** is an object in the shape of a horseshoe which is used as a symbol of good luck. 蹄鉄 (ていてつ)

horse-trading also **horsetrading** N-UNCOUNT 不可算名詞 When negotiation or bargaining is forceful and shows clever and careful judgment, you can describe it as **horse-trading**. 抜け目のない取引 [AM 米国英語] ❏ ...*an adroit piece of political horse-trading by Senator Orrin Hatch.* オリン・ハッチ上院議員による抜け目ない取引のひとつ

hor|ti|cul|tur|al /hɔrtɪkʌltʃərəl/ ADJ 形容詞 **Horticultural** means concerned with horticulture. 園芸の ❏ ...*the John A. Sibley Horticultural Center.* ジョン・A・シブリー園芸場

hor|ti|cul|ture /hɔrtɪkʌltʃər/ N-UNCOUNT 不可算名詞 **Horticulture** is the study and practice of growing plants. 園芸

hose /hoʊz/ (**hoses, hosing, hosed**) ❶ N-COUNT 可算名詞 A **hose** is a long, flexible pipe made of rubber or plastic. Water is directed through a hose in order to do things such as put out fires, clean cars, or water gardens. ホース ❏ *You've left the garden*

hose on. あなたは庭のホースを出しっぱなしにしている. ❷ N-COUNT 可算名詞 A **hose** is a pipe made of rubber or plastic, along which a liquid or gas flows, for example from one part of an engine to another. 管 ❏ *Water in the engine compartment is sucked away by a hose.* エンジン区画の水を管で吸い出す. ❸ V-T 他動詞 If you **hose** something, you wash or water it using a hose. ホースで散水する ❏ *We wash our cars and hose our gardens without even thinking of the water that uses.* 我々は使用する水のことを考えもせず, 車を洗い, 庭に水をやる.
→ see **scuba diving**

hos|pice /hɒspɪs/ (**hospices**) ❶ N-COUNT; N-IN-NAMES 可算名詞, 名称中の名詞 A **hospice** is a special hospital for people who are dying, where their practical and emotional needs are dealt with as well as their medical needs. ホスピス ❏ ...*a hospice for cancer patients.* がん患者のためのホスピス ❷ ADJ 形容詞 **Hospice** care is medical care that is provided for people, either in a hospice or in their own home, when they are dying. ホスピスの [ADJ n] ❏ *Berle was diagnosed with colon cancer last year and had been under hospice care for the past few weeks.* 昨年, バールは結腸がんの診断を受け, 数週間にわたりホスピス治療を受けていた. ❏ ...*a hospice nurse.* ホスピスの看護師

hos|pi|table /hɒspɪtəbəl, hɒspɪt-/ ❶ ADJ 形容詞 A **hospitable** person is friendly, generous, and welcoming to guests or people they have just met. 親切にもてなす ❏ *The locals are hospitable and welcoming.* 地元の人たちは親切にもてなし歓迎してくれる. ❷ ADJ 形容詞 A **hospitable** climate or environment is one that encourages the existence or development of particular people or things. 快適な ❏ *Even in summer this place did not look exactly hospitable: in winter, conditions must have been exceedingly harsh.* 夏でさえこの場所はそれほど快適には見えなかった. 冬には極めて厳しい状態だったに違いない.

Word Link   hosp, host ≈ guest : hospital, hospitality, hostage

hos|pi|tal /hɒspɪtəl/ (**hospitals**) N-VAR 可変性名詞 A **hospital** is a place where people who are ill are cared for by nurses and doctors. 病院 ❏ ...*a children's hospital with 120 beds.* 120床の小児科病院
→ see Word Web: **hospital**

Word Partnership   hospital は次の語句と使われる:

v.	**admit** *someone* **to a** hospital, **bring/rush/take** *someone* **to a** hospital, **end up in a** hospital, **go to a** hospital, **visit** *someone* **in a** hospital

hos|pi|tal|ity /hɒspɪtælɪti/ N-UNCOUNT 不可算名詞 **Hospitality** is friendly, welcoming behavior toward guests or people you have just met. もてなし ❏ *Every visitor to Georgia is overwhelmed by the kindness, charm, and hospitality of the people.* ジョージア州へのすべての訪問客が人々の親切, 魅力, 歓待に圧倒される. ❷ N-UNCOUNT 不可算名詞 **Hospitality** is the food, drink, and other privileges which some companies provide for their visitors or clients at major sports events or other public events. もてなし ❏ ...*corporate hospitality tents.* 会社の接待用テント

hos|pi|tal|ize /hɒspɪtəlaɪz/ (**hospitalizes, hospitalizing, hospitalized**) V-T 他動詞 If someone **is hospitalized**, they are sent or admitted to a hospital. 入院させる [usu passive] ❏ *Most people do not have to be hospitalized for asthma or pneumonia.* たいていの人はぜんそくや肺炎で入院の必要はない. ● **hos|pi|tali|za|tion** /hɒspɪtəlaɪzeɪʃən/ N-UNCOUNT 不可算名詞 入院 ❏ *Occasionally hospitalization is required to combat dehydration.* ときおり戦闘による脱水症状で入院が必要となる.

host /hoʊst/ (**hosts, hosting, hosted**) ❶ N-COUNT 可算名詞 The **host** at a party is the person who has invited the guests and provides the food, drink, or entertainment. 主催者 ❏ *Apart from my host, I didn't know a single person there.* 主催者をのぞけば, その場で私は誰一人知らなかった. ❷ V-T 他動詞 If someone **hosts** a party, dinner, or other function, they have invited the guests and provide the food, drink, or entertainment. 主催する ❏ *Tonight she hosts a ball for 300 guests.* 今晩, 彼女は300名を招き舞踏会を主催する. ❸ N-COUNT 可算名詞 A country, city, or organization

Word Web · hospital

Children's **Hospital** in Boston has one of the best **pediatric wards** in the country. Its Advanced Fetal Care Center can even treat babies before they are born. The hospital records about 18,000 inpatient **admissions** every year. It also has over 150 **outpatient** programs and handles more than 300,000 **emergency cases**. The staff includes 700 **residents** and **fellows**. Many of its **physicians** teach at nearby Harvard University. The hospital also employs excellent **researchers**. Their work led to the discovery of **vaccines** for **polio** and **measles**. The hospital has also led the way in liver, heart, and lung **transplants** in children.

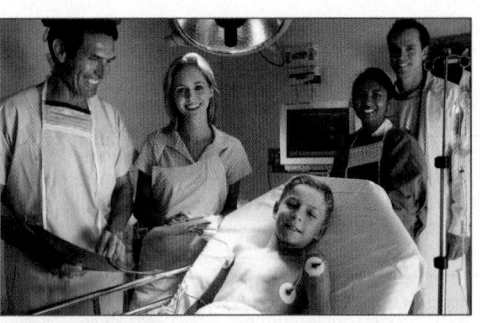

that is the **host** of an event provides the facilities for that event to take place. 主催地 ❑ *Atlanta was chosen to be host of the 1996 Olympic games.* アトランタは1996年のオリンピック開催地として選ばれた. ◢ V-T 他動詞 If a country, city, or organization **hosts** an event, they provide the facilities for the event to take place. 主催する ❑ *New Bedford hosts a number of lively festivals throughout the summer months.* 夏の数ヶ月を通じ、ニューベッドフォードは数々の活気ある祭典を主催する. ◣ PHRASE 句 If a person or country **plays host to** an event or an important visitor, they host the event or the visit. 主催者となる ❑ *Bush played host to Russian President Vladimir Putin.* ブッシュはロシア大統領ウラジミール・プーチンをもてなした. ◢ N-COUNT 可算名詞 The **host** of a radio or television show is the person who introduces it and talks to the people who appear in it. 司会者 ❑ *I am host of a live radio program.* 私は生放送のラジオ番組の司会者です. ◢ V-T 他動詞 The person who **hosts** a radio or television show introduces it and talks to the people who appear in it. 司会する ❑ *She also hosts a show on St. Petersburg Radio.* 彼女はセント・ペテルスブルグ・ラジオの番組でも司会をしている. ◢ QUANT 数量詞 A **host of** things is a lot of them. 大量、多数 ❑ *A host of problems may delay the opening of the new bridge.* 多くの問題が新しい橋の開通を遅らせるかもしれない. ◢ N-COUNT 可算名詞 A **host** or a **host computer** is the main computer in a network of computers, which controls the most important files and programs. ホスト ❑ *Subscribers dial directly from their computers into the BBS host computer.* 加入者は自分のコンピューターからBBSのホストコンピューターに直接ダイヤルできる.

Word Link · *hosp, host ≈ guest : hospital, hospitality, hostage*

hos|tage /hɒstɪdʒ/ (**hostages**) ◢ N-COUNT 可算名詞 A **hostage** is someone who has been captured by a person or organization and who may be killed or injured if people do not do what that person or organization demands. 人質 ❑ *It is hopeful that two hostages will be freed in the next few days.* 人質ふたりの数日後の解放は期待できる. ◢ PHRASE 句 If someone **is taken hostage** or **is held hostage**, they are captured and kept as a hostage. 人質にとる ❑ *He was taken hostage while on his first foreign assignment as a television journalist.* テレビの記者としての最初の外国勤務で彼は人質となった. ◢ N-VAR 可変性名詞 If you say you are **hostage to** something, you mean that your freedom to take action is restricted by things that you cannot control. 人質の状態 ❑ *Wine growers say they've been held hostage to the interests of cereal farmers.* ワイン生産者は自分たちが穀物農家の利益に縛られているという.

host|ess /hoʊstɪs/ (**hostesses**) N-COUNT 可算名詞 The **hostess** at a party is the woman who has invited the guests and provides the food, drink, or entertainment. 女性主催者 ❑ *The hostess introduced them.* 女性の主催者が彼らを紹介した.

hos|tile /hɒstl/ ◢ ADJ 形容詞 If you are **hostile to** another person or an idea, you disagree with them or disapprove of them, often showing this in your behavior. 反感のある ❑ *Many people felt he would be hostile to the idea of foreign intervention.* 多くの人が彼は外国からの干渉という考えに反感を持つだろうと感じていた. ❑ *The West has gradually relaxed its hostile attitude to this influential state.* 西側諸国は次第にこの有力な国家に対する敵対的態度を緩和してきた. ◢ ADJ 形容詞 Someone who is **hostile** is unfriendly and aggressive. 敵意のある ❑ *Drinking may make a person feel relaxed and happy, or it may make her hostile, violent, or depressed.* 飲酒により、くつろいで幸福感を感じるかもしれないし、敵対的で暴力的な状態やうつ状態に陥るかもしれない. ◢ ADJ 形容詞 **Hostile** situations and conditions make it difficult for you to achieve something. 適さない ❑ *...some of the most hostile climatic conditions in the world.* 世界で最も厳しい気候条件のいくつか ◢ ADJ 形容詞 A **hostile** takeover bid is one that is opposed by the company that is being bid for. 敵対的 [BUSINESS 実業] ❑ *Soon after he arrived, Kingfisher launched a hostile bid for Dixons.* 彼が到着してまもなくキングフィッシャー社はディクソン社の敵対的買収を開始した. ◢ ADJ 形容詞 In a war, you use **hostile** to describe your enemy's forces, organizations, weapons, land, and activities. 敵側の [ADJ n] ❑ *The city is encircled by a hostile army.* その

都市は敵軍に包囲されている.

Word Partnership · *hostile* は次の語句と使われる:

N.	hostile **attitude/feelings/intentions** ◢
	hostile **act/action**, hostile **environment** ◢
	hostile **takeover** ◢
ADV.	**increasingly** hostile ◢ - ◢

hos|til|ities /hɒstɪlɪtiz/ N-PLURAL 複数名詞 You can refer to fighting between two countries or groups who are at war as **hostilities**. 戦争状態 [FORMAL 形式ばった] ❑ *The authorities have urged people to stock up on fuel in case hostilities break out.* 戦争状態の勃発に備え、当局は人々に燃料の備蓄を促してきた.

hos|til|ity /hɒstɪliti/ ◢ N-UNCOUNT 不可算名詞 **Hostility** is unfriendly or aggressive behavior toward people or ideas. 敵対的態度 ❑ *The last decade has witnessed a serious rise in the levels of racism and hostility to black and ethnic groups.* 過去10年、人種差別の度合いと黒人やその他の人種集団に対する敵対的態度が深刻化した. ◢ N-UNCOUNT 不可算名詞 Your **hostility to** something you do not approve of is your opposition to it. 反感 ❑ *There is hostility among traditionalists to this method of teaching history.* 伝統主義者の間にこの歴史教育の方法への反感がある.

hot /hɒt/ (**hotter, hottest**) ◢ ADJ 形容詞 Something that is **hot** has a high temperature. 熱い ❑ *When the oil is hot, add the sliced onion.* 油が熱くなったら薄く切ったたまねぎを加える. ❑ *What he needed was a hot bath and a good sleep.* 彼が必要としていたのは熱い風呂に入りよく眠ることだった. ◢ ADJ 形容詞 **Hot** is used to describe the weather or the air in a room or building when the temperature is high. 暑い ❑ *It was too hot even for a gentle stroll.* ゆったりとした散歩に出るのにすら暑すぎた.

In informal English, if you want to emphasize how hot the weather is, you can say that it is **boiling** or **scorching**. In winter, if the temperature is above average, you can say that it is **mild**. In general, **hot** suggests a higher temperature than **warm**, and **warm** things are usually pleasant. ❑ *...a warm evening.*

◢ ADJ 形容詞 If you are **hot**, you feel as if your body is at an unpleasantly high temperature. 熱のある ❑ *I was too hot and tired to eat more than a few mouthfuls.* 私はとても熱っぽくて体がだるく、ほんの一口か二口しか食べられなかった. ◢ ADJ 形容詞 You can say that food is **hot** when it has a strong, burning taste caused by chilies, pepper, or other spices. 辛い ❑ *...hot curries.* 辛いカレー ◢ ADJ 形容詞 A **hot** issue or topic is one that is very important at the present time and is receiving a lot of publicity. 話題となっている [JOURNALISM ジャーナリズム] ❑ *The role of women in war has been a hot topic of debate since the Gulf conflict.* 戦争における女性の役割は、湾岸紛争以来、話題となってきた. ◢ ADJ 形容詞 **Hot** news is new, recent, and fresh. 最新の [INFORMAL くだけた] ❑ *...eight pages of the latest movies, video releases, and the hot news from Tinseltown.* 新作映画、新発売のビデオ、ティンゼルタウンからの最新ニュースの8ページ ◢ ADJ 形容詞 You can use **hot** to describe something that is very exciting and that many people want to see, use, obtain, or become involved with. 注目の [INFORMAL くだけた] ❑ *When I was in Chicago in 1990 a friend got me a ticket for the hottest show in town: the Monet Exhibition at the Art Institute.* 私が1990年にシカゴにいたとき、町で一番の話題となっていた展示の入場券を友達からもらった. 芸術学校でのモネの展覧会だった. ◢ ADJ 形容詞 A **hot** contest is one that is intense and involves a great deal of activity and determination. 苛烈(かれつ)な [INFORMAL くだけた] ❑ *It took hot competition from abroad, however, to show us just how good our product really is.* 海外からの激しい競争相手があったが、ただ我々の商品がどれほど本当に優れているかを示すのみだった. ◢ ADJ 形容詞 If a person or team is the **hot** favorite, people think that they are the one most likely to win a race or competition. 人気のある [ADJ n] ❑ *Atlantic City is the hot favorite to stage the fight.* アトランタ市がその試合の開催地の本命である. ◢ ADJ 形容詞 Someone who has a **hot** temper gets angry very quickly and easily. 短気な ❑ *His hot temper was making it increasingly*

difficult for others to work with him. 彼の短気のせいで周りの者が彼と働くことが次第に困難となっていた。 ⑪ ADJ 形容詞 If you describe someone as **hot**, you mean that they are sexually attractive or sexually desirable. 性的魅力のある [INFORMAL くだけた] □"He's great," Caroline said, "hot." 「彼、すごい」キャロラインは言った。「熱くなるわ」 □If a hot chick comes on to you, smile and walk away. 魅力的な若い女が近づいてきたら、微笑んで立ち去れ。 ⑫ PHRASE 句 If someone **blows hot and cold**, they keep changing their attitude toward something, sometimes being very enthusiastic and at other times expressing no interest at all. 態度をくるくる変える □The media, meanwhile, has blown hot and cold over the affair. 一方、報道機関はその件に関して態度を頻繁に変えてきた。 ⑬ PHRASE 句 If you are **hot and bothered**, you are so worried and anxious that you cannot think clearly or behave sensibly. 気をもんで熱くなる □Ray was getting very hot and bothered about the argument. レイはその考えにひどく気をもみ熱くなってきた。 ⑭ PHRASE 句 If you say that one person **has the hots for** another, you mean that they feel a strong sexual attraction to that person. 熱を上げる [INFORMAL くだけた] □I've had the hots for him ever since he arrived. 私は彼がやってきたときから彼に熱を上げてきた。
→ see **weather**

hot but|ton (**hot buttons**) N-COUNT 可算名詞 A **hot button** is a subject or problem that people have very strong feelings about. 関心を集める話題 [mainly AM 主に米国英語 JOURNALISM ジャーナリズム] [oft N n] □Abortion is still one of the hot button issues of U.S. life. 中絶はいまだにアメリカの生活における熱い問題のひとつだ。

hot dog (**hot dogs**) N-COUNT 可算名詞 A **hot dog** is a long bun with a hot sausage inside it. You can also use **hot dog** to refer to the sausage inside the bun. ホットドッグ

ho|tel /hoʊtέl/ (**hotels**) N-COUNT 可算名詞 A **hotel** is a building where people stay, for example on vacation, paying for their rooms and meals. ホテル、旅館
→ see Word Web: **hotel**

In addition to **hotels**, there are several other types of accommodation for travelers and tourists. A **bed and breakfast** or **B & B** is a private home that rents out rooms and serves only breakfast. A **motel** is similar in size to a hotel but particularly is designed for those traveling by car, so the parking lot is very convenient. **Youth hostels** provide dormitories for young people who want low-priced lodgings.

ho|tel|ier /oʊtέlyeɪ/ (**hoteliers**) N-COUNT 可算名詞 A **hotelier** is a person who owns or manages a hotel. ホテル経営者

hot key (**hot keys**) N-COUNT 可算名詞 A **hot key** is a key, or a combination of keys, on a computer keyboard that you can press in order to make something happen, without having to type the full instructions. ホットキー □All macros can be set to run when a hot key is pressed. すべてのマクロはホットキーを押すと作動するよう設定できる。 [COMPUTING コンピューティング]

hot|line /hɒtlaɪn/ (**hotlines**) also **hot line** ① N-COUNT 可算名詞 A **hotline** is a telephone line that the public can use to contact an organization about a particular subject. Hotlines allow people to obtain information from an organization or to give the organization information. 直通電話 □...a telephone hotline for gardeners seeking advice. 助言の必要な園芸愛好家のための直通電話 ② N-COUNT 可算名詞 A **hotline** is a special, direct telephone line between the heads of government in different countries. 緊急直通電話 □They have discussed setting up a military hotline between Hanoi

and Bangkok. 彼らはハノイとバンコクを結ぶ軍事用ホットラインの設置について話し合った。

hot link (**hot links**) N-COUNT 可算名詞 A **hot link** is a word or phrase in a hypertext document that can be selected in order to access additional information. ホットリンク □Each of these pages has hot links to other documents throughout the network. こうしたページのそれぞれにネットワークの他の文書へのホットリンクがある。 [COMPUTING コンピューティング]

hot|ly /hɒtli/ ① ADV 副詞 If people discuss, argue, or say something **hotly**, they speak in a lively or angry way, because they feel strongly. 熱く [ADV with v] □The bank hotly denies any wrongdoing. その銀行はいかなる悪行も強く否定する。 ② ADV 副詞 If you are being **hotly** pursued, someone is trying hard to catch you and is close behind you. 熱心に [ADV with v] □He'd snuck out of the U.S. hotly pursued by the CIA. 彼は米中央情報局の厳しい追跡を受け、こっそりとアメリカを出た。

hound /haʊnd/ (**hounds, hounding, hounded**) ① N-COUNT 可算名詞 A **hound** is a type of dog that is often used for hunting or racing. 猟犬 □Rainey's chief interest in life is hunting with hounds. レイニーにとって人生における主要な関心事は猟犬を使った狩猟である。 ② V-T 他動詞 If someone **hounds** you, they constantly disturb or speak to you in an annoying or upsetting way. 追い回す □Newcomers are constantly hounding them for advice. 新参者たちが助言を求め絶え間なく彼らを追い回す。 ③ V-T 他動詞 If someone **is hounded out of** a job or place, they are forced to leave it, often because other people are constantly criticizing them. 追い出す [usu passive] □There is a general view around that he has been hounded out of office by the press. 彼は報道機関によって辞職に追い込まれたという一般的見解がある。

hour /aʊər/ (**hours**) ① N-COUNT 可算名詞 An **hour** is a period of sixty minutes. 一時間 □They waited for about two hours. 彼らは約二時間待った。 □I only slept about half an hour that night. その晩、私は30分だけ眠った。 ② N-PLURAL 複数名詞 People say that something takes or lasts **hours** to emphasize that it takes or lasts a very long time, or what seems like a very long time. 長い時間 [EMPHASIS 強調] □Getting there would take hours. そこに着くのに何時間もかかるだろう。 ③ N-SING 単数名詞 A clock that strikes **the hour** strikes when it is exactly one o'clock, two o'clock, and so on. 正時 □She'd heard a clock somewhere strike the hour as she'd slipped from her room. 彼女がこっそりと部屋から出たとき、正時を告げる時計の音がどこかから聞こえた。 ④ N-SING 単数名詞 You can refer to a particular time or moment as a particular **hour**. 時刻 [LITERARY 文語的] □...the hour of his execution. 彼の死刑執行の時刻 ⑤ N-COUNT 可算名詞 If you refer, for example, to someone's **hour** of need or **hour** of happiness, you are referring to the time in their life when they are or were experiencing that condition or feeling. 時 [LITERARY 文語的] □He recalled her devotion to her husband during his hour of need. 必要とされる間、彼女が夫に対して献身的であったことを彼は思い出した。 ⑥ N-PLURAL 複数名詞 You can refer to the period of time during which something happens or operates each day as the **hours** during which it happens or operates. 時間 □...the hours of darkness. 暗闇の時間 □Phone us on this number during office hours. 営業時間中にこの電話番号におかけください。 ⑦ N-PLURAL 複数名詞 If you refer to the **hours** involved in a job, you are talking about how long you spend each week doing it and when you do it. 時間 □I worked quite irregular hours. 私の勤務時間はまったく不規則だった。 ⑧ → see also **rush hour** ⑨ PHRASE 句 If you do something **after hours**, you do it outside normal business hours or the time when you are usually at work. 勤務時間後 □...a local restaurant where steel workers unwind after hours. 鉄鋼労働者が仕事のあとにくつろぐ地元の食堂 ⑩ PHRASE 句 If you say that something happens **at all hours** of the day or night, you disapprove of it happening at the time that it does or as often as it does. 迷惑な時間に [DISAPPROVAL 不賛成] □She didn't want her fourteen-year-old daughter coming home at all hours of the morning. 彼女は14歳の娘が朝のとんでもない時間に帰宅することを望んでいなかった。 ⑪ PHRASE 句 If something happens **in the early hours**, **in the small hours**, or **in the wee hours**, it happens in the early morning after midnight. 未明に □Gibbs was arrested in the early hours of yesterday morning. ギブズは昨日の未明に逮捕された。 ⑫ PHRASE 句 If something happens

Word Web   hotel

When making **reservations** at a hotel, most people request a **single** or a **double** room. Sometimes the **clerk** invites the person to **upgrade** to a **suite**. When arriving at the hotel, the first person to greet the **guest** is the bellhop. He will put the person's suitcases on a **luggage cart**. The guest then goes to the **front desk** and **checks in**. The clerk often describes **amenities** such as a **gym** or **spa**. Most hotels provide **room service** for late night snacks. There is often a concierge to help arrange dinners and other entertainment outside of the hotel.

on the hour, it happens every hour at, for example, nine o'clock, ten o'clock, and so on, and not at any number of minutes past an hour. 毎時正時に □ *During this war in the Persian Gulf, NPR will have newscasts every hour on the hour.* このペルシャ湾での戦争中、NPRは毎時正時にニュースを放送するだろう。

hour|ly /aʊərli/ ■ ADJ 形容詞 An **hourly** event happens once every hour. 一時間毎の [ADJ n] □ *He flipped on the radio to get the hourly news broadcast.* 彼は一時間毎のニュース放送を聴くためラジオのスイッチを入れた。 ● ADV 副詞 **Hourly** is also an adverb. 一時間毎に [ADV after v] □ *The hospital issued press releases hourly.* その病院は一時間毎に報道陣への発表を行った。 ② ADJ 形容詞 Your **hourly** earnings are the money that you earn in one hour. 一時間の [ADJ n] □ *They have little prospect of finding new jobs with the same hourly pay.* 彼らが同じ時給で新しい仕事を見つけられる見込みは薄い。

house (houses, housing, housed)

> The noun and adjective are pronounced /haʊs/. The verb is pronounced /haʊz/. The form **houses** is pronounced /haʊzɪz/.
>
> 名詞と形容詞は /haʊs/ と発音される。動詞は /haʊz/ と発音される。**houses** 形は /haʊzɪz/ と発音される。

■ N-COUNT 可算名詞 A **house** is a building in which people live, usually the people belonging to one family. 家 □ *She has moved to a small house and is living off her meager savings.* 彼女は小さな家に移り、乏しい貯金で暮らしている。 ② N-SING 単数名詞 You can refer to all the people who live together in a house as **the house**. 家族 □ *If he set his alarm clock for midnight, it would wake the whole house.* 彼が目覚まし時計を真夜中に設定するなら、家族全員が目を覚ますだろう。 ③ N-COUNT 可算名詞 **House** is used in the names of types of places where people go to eat and drink. 食堂 □ *...a steak house.* ステーキハウス。 ④ N-COUNT 可算名詞 **House** is used in the names of types of companies, especially ones which publish books, lend money, or design clothes. 会社 □ *Many of the clothes come from the world's top fashion houses.* 世界最高級の洋品店から多くの洋服がもたらされる。 ⑤ N-COUNT 可算名詞 You can refer to one of the two bodies of the U.S. Congress as a **House**. The House of Representatives is sometimes referred to as **the House**. 議会 □ *Some members of the House and Senate worked all day yesterday.* 下院と上院では昨日一日中働いていた議員もいた。 ⑥ ADJ 形容詞 A restaurant's **house** wine is the cheapest wine it sells, which is not listed by name on the wine list. その店の [ADJ n] □ *Tweed ordered a carafe of the house wine.* トウィードはハウスワインをガラス瓶で頼んだ。 ⑦ V-T 他動詞 To **house** someone means to provide a house or apartment for them to live in. 住む場所を与える □ *...homes that house up to nine people.* 9人まで収容可能な家屋。 ⑧ V-T 他動詞 A building or container that **houses** something is the place where it is located or from where it operates. 中に持つ [no cont] □ *The building is open to the public and houses a museum of motorcycles and cars.* その建物は一般に開放されており、オートバイと自動車の博物館がある。 ⑨ V-T 他動詞 If you say that a building **houses** a number of people, you mean that is the place where they live or where they are staying. 収容する [no cont] □ *The building will house twelve boys and eight girls.* その建物は12人の男の子と8人の女の子を収容するだろう。 ⑩ → see also **clearinghouse,**

White House ⑪ PHRASE 句 If a person or their performance or speech **brings the house down**, the audience claps, laughs, or shouts loudly because the performance or speech is very impressive or amusing. 大かっさいを浴びる [INFORMAL くだけた] □ *It's really an amazing dance. It just always brings the house down.* それは本当に楽しい踊りだ。常に大かっさいを受ける。 ⑫ PHRASE 句 If two people **get on like a house on fire**, they quickly become close friends, for example because they have many interests in common. 意気投合する [INFORMAL くだけた] □ *I went over and struck up a conversation, and we got on like a house on fire.* 私は訪問し会話を始め、われわれはすぐに意気投合した。 ⑬ PHRASE 句 If you are given something in a restaurant or bar **on the house**, you do not have to pay for it. 店のおごりで □ *The owner knew about the engagement and brought them glasses of champagne on the house.* 店主はその契約のことを知っており、グラスのシャンパンを店のおごりで彼らに出した。 ⑭ PHRASE 句 If someone **gets** their **house in order**, **puts** their **house in order**, or **sets** their **house in order**, they arrange their affairs and solve their problems. 自分の問題を片付ける □ *He's got his house in order and made some tremendous decisions.* 彼は自分の問題を片付け、いくつかの大きな決心をした。
→ see Picture Dictionary: **house**

Thesaurus	*house* また次を参照:
N.	dwelling, home, place, residence ■

Word Partnership	*house* は次の語句と使われる:
V.	**break into** a house, **build** a house, **buy** a house, **find** a house, **live in** a house, **own** a house, **rent** a house, **sell** a house ■
ADJ.	**empty** house, **expensive** house, **little** house, **new/old** house ■
N.	house **prices**, a **room in** a house ■

house ar|rest N-UNCOUNT 不可算名詞 If someone is **under house arrest**, they are officially ordered not to leave their home, because they are suspected of being involved in an illegal activity. 自宅軟禁 □ *The main opposition leaders had been arrested or placed under house arrest.* 主な野党指導者は逮捕あるいは自宅軟禁の状態に置かれていた。

house|hold /haʊshoʊld/ (households) ■ N-COUNT 可算名詞 A **household** is all the people in a family or group who live together in a house. 家族 □ *...growing up in a male-only household.* 男だけの家族で育って。 ② N-SING 単数名詞 The **household** is your home and everything that is connected with taking care of it. 家庭 □ *...household chores.* 家庭の雑用。 ③ ADJ 形容詞 Someone or something that is a **household** name or word is very well known. よく知られた [ADJ n] □ *Today, fashion designers are household names.* 今日、ファッション・デザイナーの名前はよく知られている。

house|holder /haʊshoʊldər/ (householders) N-COUNT 可算名詞 The **householder** is the person who owns or rents a particular house. 家主 □ *Officials appealed to householders to open their homes to the thousands of persons made homeless by the storm.* 役人は家屋の所有

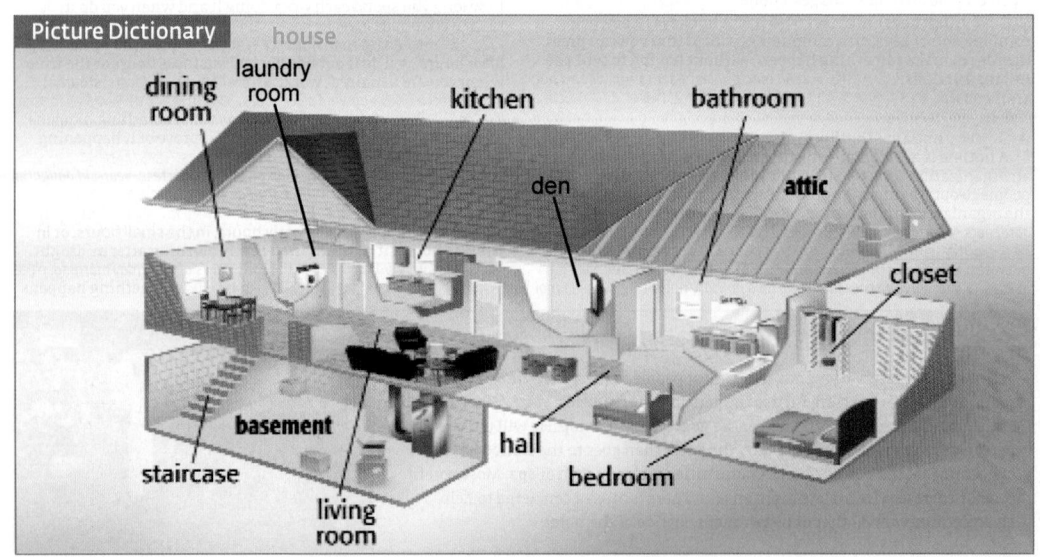

Picture Dictionary house

dining room
laundry room
kitchen
bathroom
den
attic
closet
basement
hall
bedroom
staircase
living room

者に嵐で家をなくした数千人の人々に自分の家を開放するよう訴えた.

house|keep|er /ha͜ʊskipər/ (**housekeepers**) N-COUNT 可算名詞 A **housekeeper** is a person whose job is to cook, clean, and take care of a house for its owner. 家政婦

house|keep|ing /ha͜ʊskipɪŋ/ N-UNCOUNT 不可算名詞 **Housekeeping** is the work and organization involved in running a home, including the shopping and cleaning. 家事 □ *I thought that cooking and housekeeping were unimportant, easy tasks.* 私は料理や家事は取るに足りない易しい仕事だと思った.

House of Rep|re|senta|tives N-PROPER 固有名詞 The **House of Representatives** is the larger of the two parts of Congress in the United States, or the equivalent part of the system of government in some other countries. 下院 □ *The House of Representatives approved a new budget.* 下院が新予算を承認した.

house|wife /ha͜ʊswa͟ɪf/ (**housewives**) N-COUNT 可算名詞 A **housewife** is a married woman who does not have a paid job, but instead takes care of her home and children. 主婦 □ *Married at nineteen, she was a traditional housewife and mother of four children.* 19歳で結婚し、彼女は伝統的な主婦かつ4人の子の母親となった.

Homemaker is the preferred term in the U.S. for a woman who takes care of her home and children full time. Housewife is not the modern term in the U.S., although it is still quite common in the UK.

house|work /ha͜ʊsw3rk/ N-UNCOUNT 不可算名詞 **Housework** is the work such as cleaning, washing, and ironing that you do in your home. 家事 □ *Men are doing more housework nowadays.* 今日、男性はより多くの家事をこなしている.

hous|ing /ha͜ʊzɪŋ/ N-UNCOUNT 不可算名詞 You refer to the buildings in which people live as **housing** when you are talking about their standard, price, or availability. 住宅 □ *...a shortage of affordable housing.* 手の届く住宅の不足

hov|er /hʌ͟vər/ (**hovers, hovering, hovered**) **1** V-I 自動詞 To **hover** means to stay in the same position in the air without moving forward or backward. Many birds and insects can hover by moving their wings very quickly. 空中で静止する □ *Beautiful butterflies hovered above the wild flowers.* 美しい蝶が野生の花々の上を舞っていた. **2** V-I 自動詞 If you **hover**, you stay in one place and move slightly in a nervous way, for example because you cannot decide what to do. うろつく □ *Judith was hovering in the doorway.* ジュディスは戸口でためらっていた. **3** V-I 自動詞 If you **hover**, you are in an uncertain situation or state of mind. さまよう □ *She hovered on the brink of death for three months as doctors battled to save her.* 医者たちが彼女を救うため戦っていた間、彼女は3ヶ月間、死の淵をさまよっていた. **4** V-I 自動詞 If a something such as a price, value, or score **hovers** around a particular level, it stays at more or less that level and does not change much. 前後する □ *In September 1989 the exchange rate hovered around 140 yen to the dollar.* 1989年9月、為替レートは1ドル140円前後で推移していた.

hover|craft /hʌ͟vərkræft/ (**hovercraft**) N-COUNT 可算名詞 A **hovercraft** is a vehicle that can travel across land and water. It floats above the land or water on a cushion of air. ホバークラフト □ *Traveling at speeds of up to thirty five knots, these hovercraft can easily outpace most boats.* 最高時速35ノットで進み、これらのホバークラフトは簡単にたいていのボートを追い抜くことができる. [also 'by' N]

how /ha͜ʊ/

The conjunction is pronounced /ha͜ʊ/.

接続詞は /ha͜ʊ/ と発音される.

1 QUEST 疑問詞 You use **how** to ask about the way in which something happens or is done. どのように □ *How do I make payments into my account?* どうすれば自分の口座に支払いこむことができるのですか. □ *How do you manage to keep the place so neat?* どうやってその場所をそれほど整頓しているのですか. ● CONJ 接続詞 **How** is also a conjunction. どのように □ *I don't want to know how he died.* 彼がどんな風に死んだのかを知りたくはない. **2** CONJ 接続詞 You use **how** after certain adjectives and verbs to introduce a statement or fact, often something that you remember or expect other people to know about. どのように □ *It's amazing how people collect so much stuff over the years.* 人々が何年にもわたりこれだけ多くのものを集めてきたやり方には驚く. □ *It's funny how I never seem to get a thing done on my day off.* 休みの日には物事をうまくやれたためしがないように思えるのはおかしなことだ. **3** QUEST 疑問詞 You use **how** to ask questions about the quantity or degree of something. どのくらい □ *How much money are we talking about?* どのくらいの金額について話しているのですか. □ *How many full-time staff have we got?* 常勤の人員は何人いますか. □ *How long will you be staying?* どのくらい滞在しているつもりですか. □ *How old is your son now?* 今、息子さんはおいくつですか. **4** QUEST 疑問詞 You use **how** when you are asking whether something was successful or enjoyable. どのような □ *How was your trip down to Orlando?* オーランドへ下る旅はいかがでしたか. □ *How did your date go?* 君のお相手はどんな様子だったの. **5** QUEST 疑問詞 You use **how** to ask about someone's

health or to find out someone's news. どのような □ *Hi! How are you doing?* やあ、元気かい. □ *How's Rosie?* ロージーは元気か.

You do not use **how** to ask questions about the appearance or character of someone or something. You use an expression with **what** and **like**. For example, if you ask "**How is Susan?**," you are asking about her health. If you want to know about her appearance, you ask "**What does Susan look like?**" If you want to know about her personality, you ask "**What is Susan like?**"

6 ADV 副詞 You use **how** to emphasize the degree to which something is true. どのくらい [EMPHASIS 強調] [ADV adj/adv] □ *I didn't realize how heavy that bag was going to be.* あのかばんがどれほどの重さになるかわかっていなかった. **7** ADV 副詞 You use **how** in exclamations to emphasize an adjective, adverb, or statement. なんという [EMPHASIS 強調] [ADV adj/adv/cl] □ *How strange that something so simple as a walk on the beach could suddenly mean so much.* 浜辺の散歩のようにとても単純なものが突然大きな意味を持つことができるのはなんと不思議なことだろう. **8** QUEST 疑問詞 You use **how** in expressions such as "**How can you...**" and "**How could you...**" to indicate that you disapprove of what someone has done or that you find it hard to believe. どうして [DISAPPROVAL 不賛成] [QUEST 'can/could'] □ *How can you drink so much beer, Luke?* ルーク、なぜそんなにも大量のビールを飲むんだい. **9** QUEST 疑問詞 You use **how** in expressions such as "**How about...**" or "**How would you like...**" when you are making an offer or a suggestion. いかが □ *How about a cup of coffee?* コーヒーを一杯、いかがですか. **10** CONVENTION 慣習表現 If you ask someone "**How about you?**" you are asking them what they think or want. あなたはどうですか. □ *Well, I enjoyed that. How about you two?* ええと、私は楽しかった. 君たちふたりはどうかな. **11** PHRASE 句 You use **how about** to introduce a new subject which you think is relevant to the conversation you have been having. いかが □ *Are your products and services competitive? How about marketing?* あなた方の製品とサービスには競争力がありますか. 市場戦略はいかがですか. **12** PHRASE 句 You ask "**How come?**" or "**How so?**" when you are surprised by something and are asking why it happened or was said. なぜ [INFORMAL くだけた] □ *"They don't say a single word to each other."—"How come?"* 「彼らはお互い一言も口をきかなかった」 – 「どうして」

how|ev|er /ha͜ʊe͟vər/ **1** ADV 副詞 You use **however** when you are adding a comment which is surprising or which contrasts with what has just been said. けれども [ADV with cl] □ *This was not an easy decision. It is, however, a decision that we feel is dictated by our duty.* これは簡単な決定ではなかった. しかしそれは我々の義務から導かれると感じられる決定だ. **2** ADV 副詞 You use **however** before an adjective or adverb to emphasize that the degree or extent of something cannot change a situation. どれほど [EMPHASIS 強調] □ *You should always strive to achieve more, however well you have done before.* あなたがかつてどれほどのことをやってきたにせよ、さらなる達成のために努力すべきだ. □ *However hard she tried, nothing seemed to work.* 彼女がどれほど懸命に試みようと、なにもうまくいかないようだった. **3** CONJ 接続詞 You use **however** when you want to say that it makes no difference how something is done. たとえ □ *However we adopt healthcare reform, it isn't going to save major amounts of money.* たとえ医療制度改革を行ったとしても、大きな金額の節約にはならない. **4** ADV 副詞 You use **however** in expressions such as **or however long it takes** and **or however many there were** to indicate that the figure you have just mentioned may not be accurate. どれほど [VAGUENESS あいまいさ] □ *Wait 30 to 60 minutes or however long it takes.* 30分でも60分でも、どれほど長い時間でも待つように. **5** QUEST 疑問詞 You can use **however** to ask in an emphatic way how something has happened which you are very surprised about. Some speakers of English think that this form is incorrect and prefer to use "how ever." どうやって [EMPHASIS 強調] □ *However did you find this place in such weather?* こんな天気でどうやってこの場所を見つけたんだい.

howl /ha͜ʊl/ (**howls, howling, howled**) **1** V-I 自動詞 If an animal such as a wolf or a dog **howls**, it makes a long, loud, crying sound. 遠ぼえする □ *Somewhere a dog suddenly howled, baying at the moon.* どこかで犬が突然声を上げ、月に向かってほえた. ● N-COUNT 可算名詞 **Howl** is also a noun. 遠ぼえ □ *The dog let out a savage howl and, wheeling round, flew at him.* その犬はどうもうなうなり声を出し、突然向きを変え、彼に飛びかかった. **2** V-I 自動詞 If a person **howls**, they make a long, loud cry expressing pain, anger, or unhappiness. うめく □ *He howled like a wounded animal as blood spurted from the gash.* 傷口から血があふれ、彼は傷ついた動物のようにうめいた. ● N-COUNT 可算名詞 **Howl** is also a noun. うめき □ *With a howl of rage, he grabbed the neck of a broken bottle and advanced.* 怒りにうめき、彼は割れた瓶の首をつかみ前進した. **3** V-I 自動詞 When the wind **howls**, it blows hard and makes a loud noise. うなる □ *The wind howled all night, but I slept a little.* 一晩中、風がうなったが、私は少し眠った. **4** V-T 他動詞 If you **howl** something, you say it in a very loud voice. わめく [INFORMAL くだけた] □ *"Get away, get away, get away," he howled.* 「出て行け、出て行け、出て行け」彼はわめいた. **5** V-I 自動詞 If you **howl with** laughter, you laugh very

loudly. 大笑いする ❑*Joe, Pink, and Booker howled with delight.* ジョーとピンクとブッカーは嬉しそうに大笑いした. ● N-COUNT 可算名詞 **Howl** is also a noun. 大笑い ❑*His stories caused howls of laughter.* 彼の話が大笑いを引き起こした.
→ see **laugh**

HQ /ˌeɪtʃ ˈkjuː/ (**HQs**) N-VAR 可変性名詞 **HQ** is an abbreviation for **headquarters.** 本部 ❑*The regimental HQ is a tiny office manned by two retired officers.* 連隊の本部はふたりの退役仕官の配置された小さな事務所である.

hr (**hrs**) **hr** is a written abbreviation for **hour.** 時間 ❑*Let this cook on low for another 1 hr 15 mins.* これをさらに1時間15分間, 弱火で料理する.

HR /ˌeɪtʃ ˈɑr/ In a company or other organization, the **HR** department is the department with responsibility for the recruiting, training, and welfare of the staff. **HR** is an abbreviation for **human resources.** 人事 [BUSINESS 実業]

HTML /ˌeɪtʃ tiː ɛm ˈɛl/ N-UNCOUNT 不可算名詞 **HTML** is a system of codes for producing documents for the Internet. **HTML** is an abbreviation for "hypertext markup language." ❑*...HTML documents.* HTML文書 [COMPUTING コンピューティング]

HTTP /ˌeɪtʃ tiː tiː ˈpiː/ N-UNCOUNT 不可算名詞 **HTTP** is a way of formatting and transmitting messages on the Internet. **HTTP** is an abbreviation for "hypertext transfer protocol." HTTP

hub /ˈhʌb/ (**hubs**) ◼ N-COUNT 可算名詞 You can describe a place as a **hub of** an activity when it is a very important center for that activity. 中枢 ❑*The island's social hub is the Cafe Sport.* その島の社交の中心地はカフェ・スポーツである. ◼ N-COUNT 可算名詞 The **hub** of a wheel is the part at the center. 中軸 ◼ N-COUNT 可算名詞 A **hub** or a **hub** airport is a large airport from which you can travel to many other airports. 基幹空港 ❑*...a campaign to secure Heathrow's place as Europe's main international hub.* ヒースローのヨーロッパにおける国際主要基幹空港としての地位を守るための運動

hud|dle /ˈhʌdəl/ (**huddles, huddling, huddled**) ◼ V-I 自動詞 If you **huddle** somewhere, you sit, stand, or lie there holding your arms and legs close to your body, usually because you are cold or frightened. 身を縮める ❑*Mr. Pell huddled in a corner with his notebook on his knees.* ペル氏は隅でノートをひざに縮こまった. ◼ V-I 自動詞 If people **huddle together** or **huddle around** something, they stand, sit, or lie close to each other, usually because they all feel cold or frightened. 身を寄せ合う ❑*Tired and lost, we huddled together.* 疲れて途方にくれ我々は身を寄せ合った. ◼ V-RECIP 相互動詞 If people **huddle** in a group, they gather together to discuss something quietly or secretly. 集まって密談する ❑*Off to one side, Sticht, Macomber, Jordan, and Kreps huddled to discuss something.* 片側に寄り, スティヒト, マコンバー, ジョーダン, クレプスはこっそりと何かを相談するために集まった. ❑*The president has been huddling with his most senior aides.* 大統領は最古参の側近と集まって密談してきた. ◼ N-COUNT 可算名詞 A **huddle** is a small group of people or things that are standing very close together or lying on top of each other, usually in a disorganized way. 群がり ❑*We lay there: a huddle of bodies, gasping for air.* 我々はそこに横たわっていた. 体を寄せ集め, 空気を求めあえいでいた.

huff /ˈhʌf/ (**huffs, huffing, huffed**) ◼ V-T 他動詞 If you **huff,** you indicate that you are annoyed or offended about something, usually by the way that you say something. 憤慨する ❑*"This," huffed Mr. Buthelezi, "was discrimination."* 「これは差別であった」ブゼレジ氏は憤慨して言った. ◼ PHRASE 句 If someone is **in a huff,** they are behaving in a bad-tempered way because they are annoyed and offended. 憤慨して [INFORMAL くだけた] ❑*He was so disappointed that he drove off in a huff.* 彼は失望のあまり憤慨し車で去り去った.

hug /ˈhʌg/ (**hugs, hugging, hugged**) ◼ V-RECIP 相互動詞 When you **hug** someone, you put your arms around them and hold them tightly, for example because you like them or are pleased to see them. You can also say that two people **hug** each other or that they **hug.** 抱きかかえる ❑*She had hugged him exuberantly and invited him to dinner the next day.* 彼女は嬉々として彼を抱擁し, 翌日, 彼を夕食に招待した. ● N-COUNT 可算名詞 **Hug** is also a noun. 抱擁 ❑*She leapt out of the back seat, and gave him a hug.* シャールは後部座席から飛び出し, 彼に抱きついた. ◼ V-T 他動詞 If you **hug** something, you hold it close to your body with your arms tightly around it. 抱え込む ❑*Shaerl trudged toward them, hugging a large box.* シャールは大きな箱を抱えながら, 足を引きずって彼らのほうに近寄ってきた. ◼ V-T 他動詞 Something that **hugs** the ground or a stretch of land or water stays very close to it. 沿って進む [WRITTEN 書き言葉] ❑*The road hugs the coast for hundreds of miles.* その道は何百マイルにも渡り海岸線に沿って走っている.

Thesaurus hug また次を参照:

v. cling, embrace, hold ◼

huge /ˈhjuːdʒ/ (**huger, hugest**) ◼ ADJ 形容詞 Something or someone that is **huge** is extremely large in size. 巨大な ❑*...a*

---

tiny little woman with huge black glasses. とても大きな黒い眼鏡をかけた小さなかわいい女性 ◼ ADJ 形容詞 Something that is **huge** is extremely large in amount or degree. 莫大な ❑*I have a huge number of ties because I never throw them away.* 私はネクタイを捨てたことがないので, 莫大な数のネクタイを持っている. ● **huge|ly** ADV 副詞 途方もなく ❑*In summer this hotel is a hugely popular venue for wedding receptions.* 夏にはこのホテルは結婚式場として途方もない人気を呼ぶ. ◼ ADJ 形容詞 Something that is **huge** exists or happens on a very large scale, or involves a lot of different people or things. 巨大な ❑*Another team is looking at the huge problem of debts between companies.* 別のチームは企業間負債の巨大な問題に目をつけている.

hull /ˈhʌl/ (**hulls**) N-COUNT 可算名詞 The **hull** of a boat or tank is the main body of it. 船体, 車体 ❑*The hull had suffered extensive damage to the starboard side.* 船体は右側に甚だしい損傷を受けていた.

hul|lo /hʌˈloʊ/ → see **hello**

hum /ˈhʌm/ (**hums, humming, hummed**) ◼ V-I 自動詞 If something **hums,** it makes a low continuous noise. 低くうなる ❑*The birds sang, the bees hummed.* 鳥はさえずり, ミツバチは低くうなった. ● N-SING 単数名詞 **Hum** is also a noun. 低いうなり ❑*...the hum of traffic.* 交通の騒音 ◼ V-T/V-I 他動詞/自動詞 When you **hum,** or **hum** a tune, you sing a tune with your lips closed. 鼻歌を歌う ❑*She was humming a merry little tune.* 彼女は陽気なかわいい曲を鼻歌で歌った. ◼ V-I 自動詞 If you say that a place **hums,** you mean that it is full of activity. 活気づく ❑*The place is really beginning to hum.* その場所は本当に活気づき始めている.

hu|man /ˈhjuːmən/ (**humans**) ◼ ADJ 形容詞 **Human** means relating to or concerning people. 人間の [ADJ n] ❑*...the human body.* 人体 ◼ N-COUNT 可算名詞 You can refer to people as **humans,** especially when you are comparing them with animals or machines. 人間 ❑*Like humans, cats and dogs are omnivores.* ヒトと同様, ネコやイヌは雑食である. ◼ ADJ 形容詞 **Human** feelings, weaknesses, or errors are ones that are typical of humans rather than machines. 人間的な ❑*...an ever-growing risk of human error.* 常に高まる人的過誤の危険
→ see **primate**

Word Partnership human は次の語句と使われる:

N.	human **behavior,** human **body,** human **brain,** human **dignity,** human **life** ◼ human **error,** human **weakness** ◼

hu|man be|ing (**human beings**) N-COUNT 可算名詞 A **human being** is a man, woman, or child. 人類 ❑*The treatment will be tried out on human beings only after it has been shown to be safe and foolproof in animals.* その治療は動物に対して安全で絶対確実であることが示されたのちにのみ, 人間に対して試行される.

Word Link man ≈ human being : fore**man,** hu**man,** wo**man**

hu|mane /hjuːˈmeɪn/ ◼ ADJ 形容詞 **Humane** people act in a kind, sympathetic way toward other people and animals, and try to do them as little harm as possible. 人道的な ❑*In the mid-nineteenth century, Dorothea Dix began to campaign for humane treatment of the mentally ill.* 19世紀の半ば, ドロシア・ディックスは精神疾患の人道的治療のための運動を開始した. ● **hu|mane|ly** ADV 副詞 [ADV with v] 人間的に ❑*Suffering animals should be humanely euthanized on the farm.* 罹患 (りかん) した動物は農場において人道的やり方で安楽死の処置をとられるべきだ. ◼ ADJ 形容詞 **Humane** values and societies encourage people to act in a kind and sympathetic way toward others, even toward people they do not agree with or like. 人道的な ❑*...the humane values of socialism.* 社会主義における人道的価値観

hu|man|ism /ˈhjuːmənɪzəm/ N-UNCOUNT 不可算名詞 **Humanism** is the belief that people can achieve happiness and live well without religion. 人道主義 ● **hu|man|ist** (**humanists**) N-COUNT 可算名詞 人道主義者 ❑*He is a practical humanist, who believes in the dignity of mankind.* 彼は現実的な人道主義者で, 人類の尊厳を信じている.

Word Link arian ≈ believing in, having : authorit**arian,** humanit**arian,** veget**arian**

hu|mani|tar|ian /hjuːˌmænɪˈtɛəriən/ ADJ 形容詞 If a person or society has **humanitarian** ideas or behavior, they try to avoid making people suffer or they help people who are suffering. 人道主義 ❑*Air bombardment raised criticism on the humanitarian grounds that innocent civilians might suffer.* 空爆は人道主義団体に対して無垢な市民が被害を被ったのではないかという避難を引き起こした.

hu|man|ity /hjuːˈmænɪti/ ◼ N-UNCOUNT 不可算名詞 All the people in the world can be referred to as **humanity.** 人類 ❑*They face charges of committing crimes against humanity.* 彼らは人道に対する罪を犯したという嫌疑を受けている. ◼ N-UNCOUNT 不可算名詞 A person's **humanity** is their state of being a human being,

rather than an animal or an object. 人間性 [FORMAL 形式ばった] ❑ *He was under discussion and it made him feel deprived of his humanity.* 彼は審議中で，そのため自分の人間性を剥奪（はくだつ）されたように感じていた． ■ N-UNCOUNT 不可算名詞 **Humanity** is the quality of being kind, thoughtful, and sympathetic toward others. 人間性 ❑ *Her speech showed great maturity and humanity.* 彼女の話し方には素晴らしい成熟と人間性が現れていた． ■ N-PLURAL 複数名詞 **The humanities** are the subjects such as history, philosophy, and literature which are concerned with human ideas and behavior. 人文学 ❑ *The number of students majoring in the humanities has declined by about half.* 人文系を選考する学生の数が半分にまで減ってきた．

hu|man na|ture N-UNCOUNT 不可算名詞 **Human nature** is the natural qualities and ways of behavior that most people have. 人間性 ❑ *It seems to be human nature to worry.* 心配するのは人間の特性のようである．

hu|man race N-SING 単数名詞 **The human race** is the same as **mankind**. 人類 ❑ *Can the human race carry on expanding and growing the same way that it is now?* 人類は，現在と同様にこれからも拡大成長を続けることができるか．

hu|man re|sources N-UNCOUNT 不可算名詞 In a company or other organization, the department of **human resources** is the department with responsibility for the recruiting, training, and welfare of the staff. The abbreviation **HR** is often used. 人事部門 [BUSINESS 実業] ❑ *...Geoff May, the firm's head of human resources.* 会社の人材部長であるジェフ・メイ

hu|man rights N-PLURAL 複数名詞 **Human rights** are basic rights which many societies believe that all people should have. 人権 ❑ *In the treaty both sides pledge to respect human rights.* その条約では両者とも人権を尊重すると誓約している．

hum|ble /hʌmbᵊl/ (humbler, humblest, humbles, humbling, humbled) ■ ADJ 形容詞 A **humble** person is not proud and does not believe that they are better than other people. 謙虚な ❑ *He gave a great performance, but he was very humble.* 彼はすばらしい演技をしたが，非常に謙虚であった． ● **hum|bly** ADV 副詞 [ADV with v] 謙虚に ❑ *"I'm a lucky man, undeservedly lucky," he said humbly.* 「私は幸運な男だ，身に余るほど幸運だ」と彼は謙虚に言った． ■ ADJ 形容詞 People with low social status are sometimes described as **humble**. (身分や地位が) 低い ❑ *Spyros Latsis started his career as a humble fisherman in the Aegean.* スピロス・ラーツイスの経歴はエーゲ海のつつましい漁師としてはじまった． ■ ADJ 形容詞 A **humble** place or thing is ordinary and not special in any way. 質素な ❑ *There are restaurants, both humble and expensive, that specialize in noodles.* めん類専門のレストランには質素なものも高級なものもある． ■ ADJ 形容詞 People use **humble** in a phrase such as **in my humble opinion** as a polite way of emphasizing what they think, even though they do not feel humble about it. つまらない [POLITENESS 丁寧さ] ❑ *It is, in my humble opinion, perhaps the best steak restaurant in the city.* 卑見を述べれば，たぶん街の中では一番のステーキレストランです． ● **hum|bly** ADV 副詞 [ADV before v] 謙そんして ❑ *So may I humbly suggest we all do something next time.* では，次は全員が何かすることを提案してもよろしいでしょうか． ■ PHRASE 句 If you **eat humble pie**, you speak or behave in a way which tells people that you admit you were wrong about something. 屈辱に甘んじる ❑ *Anson was forced to eat humble pie and publicly apologize to her.* アンソンは屈辱に甘んじて，公衆の面前で彼女に謝罪させられた． ■ V-T 他動詞 If you **humble** someone who is more important or powerful than you, you defeat them easily. 敗北させる ❑ *Honda won fame in the 1980s as the little car company that humbled the industry giants.* ホンダは，1980年代に自動車業界大手の威信を傷つけた小企業として有名になった． ■ V-T 他動詞 If something or someone **humbles** you, they make you realize that you are not as important or good as you thought you were. 謙虚にする ❑ *Ted's words humbled me.* テッドの言葉でわたしは謙虚になった． ● **hum|bling** ADJ 形容詞 プライドを傷つける ❑ *Giving up an addiction is a humbling experience.* 依存症から脱するのはみじめな体験だ．

hu|mid /hyuːmɪd/ ADJ 形容詞 You use **humid** to describe an atmosphere or climate that is very damp, and usually very hot. 多湿の ❑ *Visitors can expect hot and humid conditions.* 訪れると蒸し暑いかもしれない．
→ see **weather**

hu|mid|ity /hyuːmɪdɪti/ ■ N-UNCOUNT 不可算名詞 You say there is **humidity** when the air feels very heavy and damp. 湿気 ❑ *The heat and humidity were insufferable.* 暑さと湿気は我慢できないほどであった． ■ N-UNCOUNT 不可算名詞 **Humidity** is the amount of water in the air. 湿度 ❑ *The humidity is relatively low.* 湿度は比較的低い．
→ see **forecast**

Word Link   ate ≈ causing to be : complicate, humiliate, motivate

hu|mili|ate /hyuːmɪlieɪt/ (humiliates, humiliating, humiliated) V-T 他動詞 To **humiliate** someone means to say or do something which makes them feel ashamed or stupid. 恥をかか

せる ❑ *She had been beaten and humiliated by her husband.* 夫に殴られ辱めを受けたことがあった． ● **hu|mili|at|ed** ADJ 形容詞 屈辱を受けた ❑ *I have never felt so humiliated in my life.* 生まれてこのかたこれほど屈辱を感じたことはなかった．

hu|mili|at|ing /hyuːmɪlieɪtɪŋ/ ADJ 形容詞 If something is **humiliating**, it embarrasses you and makes you feel ashamed and stupid. 不面目な ❑ *The Democrats have suffered a humiliating defeat.* 民主党は屈辱的な敗北を受けた．

hu|milia|tion /hyuːmɪlieɪʃᵊn/ (humiliations) ■ N-UNCOUNT 不可算名詞 **Humiliation** is the embarrassment and shame you feel when someone makes you appear stupid, or when you make a mistake in public. 恥 ❑ *She faced the humiliation of discussing her husband's affair.* 自分の夫の情事について話す恥ずかしい思いをした． ■ N-COUNT 可算名詞 A **humiliation** is an occasion or a situation in which you feel embarrassed and ashamed. 恥をかく状況 ❑ *The result is a humiliation for the president.* 大統領にとって不面目な結果である．

hu|mil|ity /hyuːmɪlɪti/ N-UNCOUNT 不可算名詞 Someone who has **humility** is not proud and does not believe they are better than other people. 謙遜 ❑ *...a deep sense of humility.* 深い謙遜心

hu|mor /hyuːmər/ (humors, humoring, humored) ■ N-UNCOUNT 不可算名詞 You can refer to the amusing things that people say as their **humor**. ユーモア ❑ *Her humor and determination were a source of inspiration to others.* 彼女のユーモアと決意は他の人にとって激励の源となった． ■ → see also **sense of humor** ■ N-UNCOUNT 不可算名詞 **Humor** is a quality in something that makes you laugh, for example in a situation, in someone's words or actions, or in a book or movie. おかしみ ❑ *She felt sorry for the man but couldn't ignore the humor of the situation.* その男をかわいそうに思ったが，こっけいな状況を見ないふりはできなかった． ■ N-VAR 可変性名詞 If you are **in a good humor**, you feel cheerful and happy, and are pleasant to people. If you are **in a bad humor**, you feel bad tempered and unhappy, and are unpleasant to people. 気分 ❑ *Christina was still not clear why he had been in such ill humor.* クリスティーナには，なぜ彼がそんなに機嫌が悪かったのかまだはっきりわからなかった． ■ N-UNCOUNT 不可算名詞 If you do something with **good humor**, you do it cheerfully and pleasantly. 気性 ❑ *Hugo bore his illness with great courage and good humor.* ヒューゴは非常な勇気と快活さで病気に耐えた． ■ V-T 他動詞 If you **humor** someone who is behaving strangely, you try to please them or pretend to agree with them, so that they will not become upset. 機嫌をとる ❑ *She disliked Dido but was prepared to tolerate her for a weekend in order to humor her husband.* 彼女はディドは嫌いであったが，夫の機嫌をとるためにその週末は我慢をすることにした．
→ see **laugh**

Word Partnership	humorは次の語句と使われる:
N.	**brand of** humor, **sense of** humor ■
ADJ.	**good** humor ■ ■

hu|mor|ous /hyuːmərəs/ ADJ 形容詞 If someone or something is **humorous**, they are amusing, especially in a clever or witty way. ユーモアのある ❑ *He was quite humorous, and I liked that about him.* 彼はとてもユーモアがあり，わたしはそういうところが気に入っていた． ● **hu|mor|ous|ly** ADV 副詞 こっけいに ❑ *He looked at me humorously as he wrestled with the door.* 彼はドアと取っ組み合いながらこっけいに私の顔を見た．

hu|mour /hyuːmər/ → see **humor**

hump /hʌmp/ (humps) ■ N-COUNT 可算名詞 A **hump** is a small hill or raised area. 低い円丘; 盛り上がり ❑ *The path goes over a large hump by a tree before running near a road.* その小道は，木の横にある大きく盛り上がった場所を越えた後，道路の近くを走っている． ■ N-COUNT 可算名詞 A camel's **hump** is the large lump on its back. こぶ ❑ *Camels rebuild fat stores in their hump.* ラクダはこぶに脂肪の蓄えを再蓄積する． ■ PHRASE 句 If you are **over the hump** in an unpleasant or difficult situation, you are past the worst part of it. 難関を脱して [v-link PHR] ❑ *It has been a traumatic week, but they are over the hump.* 精神的な衝撃の続いた1週間であったが，彼らは危機を脱した．

hunch /hʌntʃ/ (hunches, hunching, hunched) ■ N-COUNT 可算名詞 If you have a **hunch** about something, you are sure that it is correct or true, even though you do not have any proof. 予感 [INFORMAL くだけた] ❑ *I had a hunch that Susan and I would work well together.* わたしはスーザンとうまく一緒に仕事ができるだろうという予感があった． ■ V-I 自動詞 If you **hunch forward**, you raise your shoulders, put your head down, and lean forward, often because you are cold, ill, or unhappy. 体を丸くする ❑ *He got out his map and hunched over it to read the small print.* 地図を取り出して，小さな字を読むためにその上に身をかがめた． ■ V-T 他動詞 If you **hunch** your shoulders, you raise them and lean forward slightly. 背を丸める ❑ *Wes hunched his shoulders and leaned forward on the edge of the counter.* ウェスは背を丸くすぼめて，カウンターの端で身を前に乗り出した．

h

hun|dred /hʌndrɪd/ (hundreds)

> The plural form is **hundred** after a number, or after a word or expression referring to a number, such as "several" or "a few."
>
> 複数形は数の後、あるいは **several** や **a few** のような数を指す単語や表現の後では **hundred** である。

1 NUM 数詞 **A hundred** or **one hundred** is the number 100. 100 □ According to one official more than a hundred people have been arrested. 関係者によれば100人以上が逮捕されたということである。 **2** QUANT 数量詞 If you refer to **hundreds of** things or people, you are emphasizing that there are very many of them. 多数の [EMPHASIS 強調] [QUANT 'of' pl-n] □ Hundreds of tree species face extinction. 何百という木の種類が絶滅に面している。 ● PRON 代名詞 You can also use **hundreds** as a pronoun. 多数の物（人）□ Hundreds have been killed in the fighting and thousands made homeless. その戦いで何百人もが殺され、何千人もが家を失った。 **3** PHRASE 句 You can use **a hundred percent** or **one hundred percent** to emphasize that you agree completely with something or that it is completely right or wrong. 100％完全に [INFORMAL くだけた, EMPHASIS 強調] □ Are you a hundred percent sure it's your neighbor? 近所の人であることは100％確実ですか？

hun|dredth /hʌndrɪdθ/ (hundredths) **1** ORD 序数詞 The **hundredth** item in a series is the one that you count as number one hundred. 100番目の □ The bank celebrates its hundredth anniversary in December. その銀行は12月に100周年記念の祝典を開く。 **2** FRACTION 端数 **A hundredth** of something is one of a hundred equal parts of it. 100分の □ Mitchell beat Lewis by three-hundredths of a second. ミッチェルは100分の3秒の差でルイスに勝った。

hung /hʌŋ/ **1** Hung is the past tense and past participle of most of the senses of **hang**. **2** ADJ 形容詞 A **hung** jury is the situation that occurs when a jury is unable to reach a decision because there is not a clear majority of its members in favor of any one decision. 全員一致の評決がない □ His first trial ended in a hung jury. 最初の裁判は陪審評決が不一致で終わった。

hun|ger /hʌŋgər/ (hungers, hungering, hungered) **1** N-UNCOUNT 不可算名詞 **Hunger** is the feeling of weakness or discomfort that you get when you need something to eat. 空腹 □ Hunger is the body's signal that levels of blood sugar are too low. 空腹は血糖レベルが低すぎるという体の徴候である。 **2** N-UNCOUNT 不可算名詞 **Hunger** is a severe lack of food which causes suffering or death. 飢餓 □ Three hundred people in this town are dying of hunger every day. この町では毎日300人が飢餓のため死んでいる。 **3** N-SING 単数名詞 If you have a **hunger for** something, you want or need it very much. 切望 [WRITTEN 書き言葉] [also no det] □ Geffen has a hunger for success that seems bottomless. ゲフェンの出世欲は底知らずのようだ。 **4** V-I 自動詞 If you say that someone **hungers for** something or **hungers after** it, you are emphasizing that they want it very much. 切望する [FORMAL 形式ばった, EMPHASIS 強調] □ But Jules was not eager for classroom learning, but he hungered for adventure. しかしジュールズは教室での学習には熱心でなく、冒険を熱望した。

hun|ger strike (hunger strikes) N-VAR 可変性名詞 If someone goes **on hunger strike** or goes **on a hunger strike**, they refuse to eat as a way of protesting about something. ハンスト □ The protesters have been on hunger strike for 17 days. 抗議者たちは17日間ハンストをしている。

hun|gry /hʌŋgri/ (hungrier, hungriest) **1** ADJ 形容詞 When you are **hungry**, you want some food because you have not eaten for some time and have an uncomfortable or painful feeling in your stomach. 空腹の □ My friend was hungry, so we drove to a shopping mall to get some food. わたしの友達は空腹だったので、何か食べるために一緒にショッピングセンターまで車で行った。 ● **hun|gri|ly** /hʌŋgrɪli/ ADV 副詞 [ADV with v] ひもじそうに □ James ate hungrily. ジェームズはがつがつと食べた。 **2** PHRASE 句 If people **go hungry**, they do not have enough food to eat. 飢える □ They brought her meat so that she never went hungry. 彼女が空腹にならないように肉を持ってきた。 **3** ADJ 形容詞 If you say that someone is **hungry for** something, you are emphasizing that they want it very much. 切望する [LITERARY 文語的, EMPHASIS 強調] □ I was hungry to be heard by my contemporaries. 同輩の人たちにぜひとも理解してもらいたかった。 ● COMB IN ADJ 形容詞の複合 **Hungry** is also a combining form. 切望している（他の語との連結形で）□ ...power-hungry politicians. 権力欲の強い政治家たち ● **hun|gri|ly** ADV 副詞 [ADV with v] 熱望して □ He looked at her hungrily. What eyes! What skin! 彼は飢えたように彼女を見た。なんという目！なんという肌！

hunk /hʌŋk/ (hunks) **1** N-COUNT 可算名詞 A **hunk of** something is a large piece of it. 切り取った大きな塊 □ ...a thick hunk of bread. パンの厚切り **2** N-COUNT 可算名詞 If you refer to a man as a **hunk**, you mean that he is big, strong, and sexually attractive. たくましくて魅力的な男 [INFORMAL くだけた, APPROVAL 賛成] □ ...a blond, blue-eyed hunk. ブロンドで青い目のたくましくていかす男

hunt /hʌnt/ (hunts, hunting, hunted) **1** V-I 自動詞 If you **hunt** for something or someone, you try to find them by searching carefully or thoroughly. くまなく探す（捜す）□ A forensic team was hunting for clues. 犯罪科学チームは手がかりを求めてくまなく捜していた。 ● N-COUNT 可算名詞 **Hunt** is also a noun. □ The couple had helped in the hunt for the toddlers. その夫婦はよちよち歩きの子供たちの捜索を手伝った。 **2** V-T 他動詞 If you **hunt** a criminal or an enemy, you search for them in order to catch or harm them. 追跡する □ Detectives have been hunting him for seven months. 刑事は7か月間彼を追跡している。 ● N-COUNT 可算名詞 **Hunt** is also a noun. 追跡 □ Despite a nationwide hunt for the kidnap gang, not a trace of them was found. 誘拐者一味の全国的な追跡にもかかわらず、まったく何の形跡も見つからなかった。 **3** V-T/V-I 他動詞/自動詞 When people or animals **hunt**, or **hunt** something, they chase and kill wild animals for food or as a sport. 狩る □ As a child I learned to hunt and fish. 子供の頃に狩りと魚釣りを覚えた。 ● N-COUNT 可算名詞 **Hunt** is also a noun. 狩り □ He set off for a nineteen-day moose hunt in Nova Scotia. ノバスコシアで19日間のヘラジカ狩りに出かけた。 **4** PHRASE 句 If a team or competitor is **in the hunt for** something, they still have a chance of winning it. 求めて □ Six teams were still in the hunt for the team title. 6組がまだ優勝を争っている。

▶ **hunt down** PHRASAL VERB 句動詞 If you **hunt down** a criminal or an enemy, you find them after searching for them. 追跡して捕らえる □ Last December they hunted down and killed one of the gangsters. 去年の12月にギャングを追い詰め、1人を殺した。

hunt|er /hʌntər/ (hunters) **1** N-COUNT 可算名詞 A **hunter** is a person who hunts wild animals for food or as a sport. 狩りをする人 □ The hunters stalked their prey. 狩りをする人たちは獲物に忍び寄った。 **2** N-COUNT 可算名詞 People who are searching for things of a particular kind are often referred to as **hunters**. 探求者 □ ...job-hunters. 求職者たち **3** → see also **headhunter**

hunt|ing /hʌntɪŋ/ **1** N-UNCOUNT 不可算名詞 **Hunting** is the chasing and killing of wild animals by people or other animals, for food or as a sport. 狩猟 □ He'd gone deer hunting with his cousins. 彼はいとこたちとシカ狩りに出かけて行った。 **2** N-UNCOUNT 不可算名詞 **Hunting** is the activity of searching for a particular thing. 捜し求めること □ Job hunting should be approached as a job in itself. 求職は仕事そのものとして取り組むべきである。 ● COMB IN N-UNCOUNT 不可算名詞の複合 **Hunting** is also a combining form. 探求すること（他の語と連結形で）□ Make job-hunting a full-time job until you find one. 仕事が見つかるまで求職を本職としなさい。

hur|dle /hɜrdəl/ (hurdles, hurdling, hurdled) **1** N-COUNT 可算名詞 A **hurdle** is a problem, difficulty, or part of a process that may prevent you from achieving something. 障害 □ Two-thirds of candidates fail at this first hurdle and are sent home. 3分の2の候補者はこの最初の障害で失敗し家に帰される。 **2** N-COUNT-COLL 集合可算名詞 **Hurdles** is a race in which people have to jump over a number of obstacles that are also called hurdles. You can use **hurdle** to refer to one or more races. ハードル競走 □ Davis won the 400 meter hurdles in a new Olympic time of 49.3 sec. デイビスは新オリンピック記録49.3秒を出して400mハードルを優勝した。 **3** V-T/V-I 他動詞/自動詞 If you **hurdle**, you jump over something while you are running. 乗り越える □ He crossed the lawn and hurdled the short fence. 芝を横切り、低い柵を走って飛び越えた。

hurl /hɜrl/ (hurls, hurling, hurled) **1** V-T 他動詞 If you **hurl** something, you throw it violently and with a lot of force. 強く投げつける □ Groups of angry youths hurled stones at police. 怒った若者たちの群れが警察に向かって石を投げつけた。 □ Simon caught the grenade and hurled it back. サイモンは手りゅう弾を捕まえて投げ戻した。 **2** V-T 他動詞 If you **hurl** abuse or insults **at** someone, you shout insults at them aggressively. 浴びせる □ How would you handle being locked in the back of a cab while the driver hurled abuse at you? タクシー運転手から悪口を浴びながら後部座席で動けない状況に、あなたならどのように対処するか？

hur|ri|cane /hɜrɪkən, hʌr-/ (hurricanes) N-COUNT 可算名詞 A **hurricane** is an extremely violent storm that begins over ocean water. 大暴風
→ see Word Web: **hurricane**
→ see **disaster**

hur|ried /hɜrid, hʌr-/ **1** ADJ 形容詞 A **hurried** action is done quickly, because you do not have much time to do it in. あわただしい □ ...a hurried breakfast. あわただしい朝食 ● **hur|ried|ly** ADV 副詞 [ADV with v] あわただしく □ ...students hurriedly taking notes. 大急ぎでメモを取っている学生たち **2** ADJ 形容詞 A **hurried** action is done suddenly, in reaction to something that has just happened. あわてた □ There had been a hurried overnight redrafting of the text. 文章は一夜であわてて書き直された。 ● **hur|ried|ly** ADV 副詞 [ADV with v] あわてて □ The moment she saw it, she blushed and hurriedly

H

Word Web   hurricane

A **hurricane** is a tropical **cyclone** that develops in the Atlantic or Caribbean. When a hurricane develops in the Pacific it is known as a **typhoon**. A hurricane is a violent storm. It begins as a **tropical depression**. It becomes a **tropical storm** when its winds reach 39 miles per hour (mph). When wind speeds reach 74 mph, a distinct **eye** forms in the center. Then the storm is officially a hurricane. It has heavy rains and very high winds. When a hurricane makes **landfall** or moves over cool water, it loses some of its power.

left the room. それを見た瞬間彼女は顔を赤らめて，あわてて部屋を出て行った. ❸ ADJ 形容詞 Someone who is **hurried** does things more quickly than they should because they do not have much time to do them. せきたてられた ❑ *Parisians on the street often looked worried, hurried, and unfriendly*. 街のパリ市民の多くは心配顔でせかせかしていて冷淡な感じだった.

hur|ry /hɜri, har-/ (**hurries, hurrying, hurried**) ❶ V-I 自動詞 If you **hurry** somewhere, you go there as quickly as you can. 急ぐ ❑ *Claire hurried along the road*. クレアは道を急いだ. ❷ V-T 他動詞 If you **hurry to** do something, you start doing it as soon as you can, or try to do it quickly. あわててする ❑ *Mrs. Hardie hurried to make up for her tactlessness by asking her guest about his holiday*. ハーディ夫人は要領の悪さをなんとかしようと，あわてて客の休暇について質問した. ❸ N-SING 単数名詞 If you are **in a hurry to** do something, you need or want to do something quickly. If you do something **in a hurry**, you do it quickly or suddenly. あせって ❑ *Kate was In a hurry to grow up, eager for knowledge and experience*. ケイトは知識や経験が欲しくて，あせって大人になりたがっていた. ❹ V-T 他動詞 To **hurry** something means the same as to **hurry up** something. 急がせる ❑ *...the president's attempt to hurry the process of independence*. 独立プロセスを急がせようとする大統領の試み. ❺ V-T 他動詞 If you **hurry** someone to a place or into a situation, you try to make them go to that place or get into that situation quickly. せきたてる ❑ *They say they are not going to be hurried into any decision*. 性急に判断を迫られることはないと彼らは言っている. ❻ PHRASE 句 If you say to someone "**There's no hurry**" or "**I'm in no hurry**" you are telling them that there is no need for them to do something immediately. 急ぐ必要はない ❑ *I'll need to talk with you, but there's no hurry*. 君に話をする必要があるが，急がなくていい. ❼ PHRASE 句 If you are **in no hurry** to do something, you are very unwilling to do it. する気がない ❑ *I love it here so I'm in no hurry to go anywhere*. ここがとても気に入っているのでどこにも行く気はない.

▶ **hurry along** → see **hurry up 2**
▶ **hurry up** ❶ PHRASAL VERB 句動詞 If you tell someone to **hurry up**, you are telling them to do something more quickly than they were doing. 急がせる ❑ *Franklin told Howe to hurry up and take his bath; otherwise, they'd miss their train*. フランクリンは急いで風呂に入るようハウに言った. 列車に乗り遅れそうだったからだ. ❷ PHRASAL VERB 句動詞 If you **hurry** something **up** or **hurry** it **along**, you make it happen faster or sooner than it would otherwise have done. 急いでする ❑ *...if you're not a traditionalist and you want to hurry up the process*. もし伝統主義者でなく，その過程を急いでしたければ

Thesaurus   hurry また次を参照:

v.	run, rush; (ant.) slow down, relax ❶

hurt /hɜrt/ (**hurts, hurting, hurt**) ❶ V-T 他動詞 If you **hurt** yourself or **hurt** a part of your body, you feel pain because you have injured yourself. けがをする ❑ *Yasin had seriously hurt himself while trying to escape from the police*. ヤシンは警察から逃れようとしてひどくけがをした. ❷ V-I 自動詞 If a part of your body **hurts**, you feel pain there. 痛む ❑ *His collar bone only hurt when he lifted his arm*. 腕を上げたときだけ鎖骨が痛んだ. ❸ ADJ 形容詞 If you are **hurt**, you have been injured. 傷ついた ❑ *His comrades asked him if he was hurt*. けがをしたのかと仲間は彼に尋ねた. ❹ V-T/V-I 他動詞/自動詞 If you **hurt** someone, you cause them to feel pain. 痛みを与える ❑ *I didn't mean to hurt her, only to keep her still*. 彼女に痛みを与えるつもりはなくて，じっとさせたかっただけだ. ❑ *That hurts!* 痛い! ❺ V-T/V-I 他動詞/自動詞 If someone **hurts** you, they say or do something that makes you unhappy. 感情を害する ❑ *He is afraid of hurting Bessy's feelings*. ベシーの感情を傷つけるのを恐れている. ❑ *What hurts most is the betrayal*. もっとも痛いのは裏切りだ. ❻ ADJ 形容詞 If you are **hurt**, you are upset because of something that someone has said or done. 感情を害した ❑ *She was deeply hurt and shocked by what Smith had said*. 彼女はスミスが言ったことに深く傷つきショックを受けた. ❼ V-I 自動詞 If you say that you **are hurting**, you mean that you are experiencing emotional pain. 心が痛む [only cont] ❑ *I am lonely and I am hurting*. 寂しくて苦痛だ. ❽ V-T 他

動詞 To **hurt** someone or something means to have a bad effect on them or prevent them from succeeding. 悪い影響をおよぼす; 妨げる ❑ *The combination of hot weather and decreased water supplies is hurting many industries*. 猛暑と水不足が重なり，多数の企業が損害をこうむっている. ❾ N-VAR 可変性名詞 A feeling of **hurt** is a feeling that you have when you think that you have been treated badly or judged unfairly. 精神的苦痛 ❑ *I was full of jealousy and hurt*. 嫉妬と苦痛でいっぱいだった. ❿ PHRASE 句 If you say "**It won't hurt to** do something" or "**It never hurts to** do something," you are recommending an action which you think is helpful or useful. してもいいでしょう [INFORMAL くだけた] ❑ *It never hurts to ask*. 質問しても全然かまわないでしょう.

Thesaurus   hurt また次を参照:

v.	harm, injure, wound ❶
	ache, smart, sting ❷
ADJ.	injured, wounded ❸
	saddened, upset ❻

Word Partnership   hurt は次の語句と使われる:

ADV.	**badly/seriously** hurt ❶ ❸
v.	**get** hurt ❸
	feel hurt ❻
N.	hurt *someone's* **chances**, hurt the **economy**, hurt *someone's* **feelings**, hurt **sales** ❽

hurt|ful /hɜrtfəl/ ADJ 形容詞 If you say that someone's comments or actions are **hurtful**, you mean that they are unkind and upsetting. 感情を害する ❑ *Her comments can only be very hurtful to Mrs. Green's family*. 彼女のコメントはグリーン夫人の家族にとって不快に他ならない.

hur|tle /hɜrt°l/ (**hurtles, hurtling, hurtled**) V-I 自動詞 If someone or something **hurtles** somewhere, they move there very quickly, often in a rough or violent way. 突進する ❑ *A pretty young girl came hurtling down the stairs*. かわいい小さな少女が階段をまっしぐらに駆け下りてきた.

hus|band /hʌzbənd/ (**husbands**) N-COUNT 可算名詞 A woman's **husband** is the man she is married to. 夫 ❑ *Eva married her husband Jack in 1957*. エバは1957年に夫のジャックと結婚した.
→ see **family, love**

hush /hʌʃ/ (**hushes, hushing, hushed**) ❶ CONVENTION 慣習表現 You say "**Hush!**" to someone when you are asking or telling them to be quiet. しっ! ❑ *Hush, my love, it's all right*. 静かにしなさい，いい子ね，大丈夫よ. ❷ V-T/V-I 他動詞/自動詞 If you **hush** someone or if they **hush**, they stop speaking or making a noise. 黙らせる [他動詞], 黙る [自動詞] ❑ *She tried to hush her noisy father*. うるさい父親を黙らせようとした. ❸ N-SING 単数名詞 You say there is a **hush** in a place when everything is quiet and peaceful, or suddenly becomes quiet. 沈黙 [also no det] ❑ *A hush fell over the crowd and I knew something terrible had happened*. 群衆は静まり返り，わたしは何か恐ろしいことが起こったのだと直感した.
▶ **hush up** PHRASAL VERB 句動詞 If someone **hushes** something **up**, they prevent other people from knowing about it. もみ消す ❑ *I thought it would reflect badly on me so I tried to hush the whole thing up*. 私の不名誉になるだろうと思い，その件すべてをもみ消そうとした.

hushed /hʌʃt/ ❶ ADJ 形容詞 A **hushed** place is peaceful and much quieter and calmer than usual. 普段より静かな ❑ *The house seemed muted, hushed as if it had been deserted*. 家はまるで見捨てられたように音もなく静かなように思えた. ❷ ADJ 形容詞 A **hushed** voice or **hushed** conversation is very quiet. ひそひそ声の ❑ *At first we spoke in hushed voices and crept about in order not to alarm them*. 彼らをびっくりさせないように，私たちは最初はひそひそ声で話し，忍び足で歩いた.

hus|tle /hʌs°l/ (**hustles, hustling, hustled**) ❶ V-T 他動詞 If you **hustle** someone, you try to make them go somewhere or do something quickly, for example by pulling or pushing them

h

along. せかす ❑*The guards hustled Harry out of the car.* 守衛はせかしてハリーを車から乱暴に降ろした. **2** v-I 自動詞 If you **hustle**, you go somewhere or do something as quickly as you can. 急ぐ ❑*You'll have to hustle if you're to get home for supper.* 夕食までに家に帰る予定なら急ぐ必要がある. **3** v-I 自動詞 If someone **hustles**, they try hard to earn money or to gain an advantage from a situation. はりきる [mainly AM 主に米国英語] ❑*I like it here. It forces you to hustle and you can earn money.* ここが好きだ. とにかく張り切らなきゃいけないし, 金も稼げる. ❑*Hustling for social contacts isn't something that just happens. You have to make it happen.* やたら人と知り合いになろうとしても無理だ. そうなるよう持っていかなければ. **4** v-T 他動詞 If someone **hustles** you, or if they **hustle** something, they try hard to get something, often by using dishonest or illegal means. だまし取る [mainly AM 主に米国英語] ❑*Two teenage boys asked us for money, saying they were forming a baseball team. Anna said they were hustling us.* 十代の少年2人が野球チームを作るからと金をくれと言ってきた. アンナはだまし取ろうとしているんだと言った. ❑*He hustled several daytime jobs and finished his education at night.* 昼の仕事をかけもちして, 夜学を終えた. **5** N-UNCOUNT 不可算名詞 **Hustle** is busy, noisy activity. 押し合いへし合い ❑*...the hustle and bustle of New York.* ニューヨークの雑踏

hut /hʌt/ (**huts**) **1** N-COUNT 可算名詞 A **hut** is a small house with only one or two rooms, especially one which is made of wood, mud, grass, or stones. 小屋 **2** N-COUNT 可算名詞 A **hut** is a small wooden building in someone's garden, or a temporary building used by builders or repair workers. 物置; 仮屋 [BRIT 英国英語; AM **shed** 米国英語 **shed**]

hy|brid /ˈhaɪbrɪd/ (**hybrids**) **1** N-COUNT 可算名詞 A **hybrid** is an animal or plant that has been bred from two different species of animal or plant. 交配種 [TECHNICAL 技術的] ❑*All these brightly colored hybrids are so lovely in the garden.* 庭では鮮やかな色の交配種がどれも大変きれいです. ● ADJ 形容詞 **Hybrid** is also an adjective. 交配種の [ADJ n] ❑*...the hybrid corn seed.* 交配種のとうもろこしの種 **2** N-COUNT 可算名詞 A **hybrid** or a **hybrid car** is a car that can be powered by either gasoline or electricity. ハイブリッド車 ❑*Hybrids, unlike pure electric cars, never need to be plugged in.* 純粋な電気自動車と違ってハイブリッド車に充電の必要はない. ❑*Hybrid cars can go almost 600 miles between refueling.* ハイブリッド車は一回燃料を入れれば600マイル近く走ることができる. **3** N-COUNT 可算名詞 You can use **hybrid** to refer to anything that is a mixture of other things, especially two other things. 混成物 ❑*...a hybrid of solid and liquid fuel.* 固体および液体燃料の混合 ● ADJ 形容詞 **Hybrid** is also an adjective. 混成物の [ADJ n] ❑*...a hybrid system.* 混成体制
→ see **car**

hy|drau|lic /haɪˈdrɔlɪk, -ˈdrɒl-/ ADJ 形容詞 **Hydraulic** equipment or machinery involves or is operated by a fluid that is under pressure, such as water or oil. 水圧の, 油圧の [ADJ n] ❑*The boat has no fewer than five hydraulic pumps.* 船には5基以上の水圧ポンプがある.

hydro|gen /ˈhaɪdrədʒən/ N-UNCOUNT 不可算名詞 **Hydrogen** is a colorless gas that is the lightest and commonest element in the universe. 水素
→ see **sun**

hydro|log|ic cy|cle /ˌhaɪdrəlɒdʒɪk ˈsaɪkəl/ N-SING 単数名詞 The **hydrologic cycle** is the process by which the Earth's water is circulated from the surface to the atmosphere and back to the surface through rainfall. 水の循環 [TECHNICAL 技術的] [ˈthe' N]
→ see **water**

hy|giene /ˈhaɪdʒin/ N-UNCOUNT 不可算名詞 **Hygiene** is the practice of keeping yourself and your surroundings clean, especially in order to prevent illness or the spread of diseases. 衛生 ❑*Be extra careful about personal hygiene.* 身の回りの衛生については特に注意しなさい.

hy|gien|ic /ˈhaɪdʒɛnɪk/ ADJ 形容詞 Something that is **hygienic** is clean and unlikely to cause illness. 衛生的な ❑*...a white, clinical-looking kitchen that was easy to keep clean and hygienic.* 衛生的で清潔

維持しやすかった白い飾り気のないキッチン

hymn /hɪm/ (**hymns**) **1** N-COUNT 可算名詞 A **hymn** is a religious song that Christians sing in church. 賛美歌 ❑*I like singing hymns.* 賛美歌を歌うのが好きだ. **2** N-COUNT 可算名詞 If you describe a movie, book, or speech as a **hymn to** something, you mean that it praises or celebrates that thing. 賛歌 [MAINLY JOURNALISM 主にジャーナリズム] ❑*...a hymn to freedom and rebellion.* 自由と反逆の賛歌

hype /haɪp/ (**hypes, hyping, hyped**) **1** N-UNCOUNT 不可算名詞 **Hype** is the use of a lot of publicity and advertising to make people interested in something such as a product. 誇大宣伝 [DISAPPROVAL 不賛成] ❑*We are certainly seeing a lot of hype by some companies.* 確かに一部の会社による誇大宣伝が多数見受けられる. **2** v-T 他動詞 To **hype** a product means to advertise or praise it a lot. 誇大宣伝する [DISAPPROVAL 不賛成] ❑*We had to hype the film to attract the financiers.* 投資家を引きつけるために映画の誇大宣伝をしなければならなかった. ● PHRASAL VERB 句動詞 **Hype up** means the same as **hype**. 誇大宣伝をする ❑*The media seems obsessed with hyping up individuals or groups.* メディアはとりつかれたように個人やグループのことを大げさに報道している.

hyper|ac|tive /ˌhaɪpərˈæktɪv/ ADJ 形容詞 Someone who is **hyperactive** is unable to relax and is always moving around or doing things. 異常なほどに活動的な ❑*His research was used in planning treatments for hyperactive children.* 彼の研究は過度に落ち着きのない子供たちの治療計画に使用された.

hyper|in|fla|tion /ˌhaɪpərɪnˈfleɪʃən/ N-UNCOUNT 不可算名詞 **Hyperinflation** is very severe inflation. 超インフレーション ❑*In the hyperinflation of 1922-23 a dollar could be bought for 4.2 billion marks.* 1922年から23年の超インフレーションでは1ドルは42億マルクで買うことができた.

hyper|link /ˈhaɪpərlɪŋk/ (**hyperlinks, hyperlinking, hyperlinked**) **1** N-COUNT 可算名詞 In an HTML document, a **hyperlink** is a link to another part of the document or to another document. Hyperlinks are shown as words with a line under them. ハイパーリンク [COMPUTING コンピューティング] ❑*...Web pages full of hyperlinks.* ハイパーリンクでいっぱいのウェブのページ **2** v-T 他動詞 If a document or file **is hyperlinked**, it contains hyperlinks. ハイパーリンクのある [COMPUTING コンピューティング] [usu passive] ❑*The database is fully hyperlinked both within the database and to thousands of external links.* データベースは, データベース内と数千の外部リンクの両方にしっかりハイパーリンクをはっている.

hyper|text /ˈhaɪpərtɛkst/ N-UNCOUNT 不可算名詞 In computing, **hypertext** is a way of connecting pieces of text so that you can go quickly and directly from one to another. ハイパーテキスト [COMPUTING コンピューティング] ❑*...information embroidered with colorful graphics and tied together by hypertext links.* 華麗なグラフィックスで飾られ, ハイパーテキストのリンクでまとめられた情報

hy|phen /ˈhaɪfən/ (**hyphens**) N-COUNT 可算名詞 A **hyphen** is the punctuation sign used to join words together to make a compound, as in "left-handed." People also use a hyphen to show that the rest of a word is on the next line. ハイフン

hyp|no|sis /hɪpˈnoʊsɪs/ **1** N-UNCOUNT 不可算名詞 **Hypnosis** is a state in which a person seems to be asleep but can still see, hear, or respond to things said to them. 催眠状態 ❑*Bevin is now an adult and has re-lived her birth experience under hypnosis.* ベビンはもう大人なのだが, 催眠状態で生まれたときのことを再体験した. **2** N-UNCOUNT 不可算名詞 **Hypnosis** is the art or practice of hypnotizing people. 催眠術
→ see Word Web: **hypnosis**

hyp|not|ic /hɪpˈnɒtɪk/ **1** ADJ 形容詞 If someone is in a **hypnotic** state, they have been hypnotized. 催眠の ❑*The hypnotic state actually lies somewhere between being awake and being asleep.* 実際に催眠とは覚醒と睡眠の中間の状態だ. **2** ADJ 形容詞 Something that

Hypnosis is a **mental** state somewhere between wakefulness and sleep. When hypnotized, a person's mind is **alert** and **calm** at the same time. Scientists believe this kind of **trance** helps the **conscious** mind relax. This gives the **hypnotist** access to the **subconscious** mind. Some hypnotists are entertainers. They do things like getting **subjects** on stage to bark like dogs. Hypnotherapists, on the other hand, use the trance state to help people. For example, the therapist may suggest that smoking will make the person feel nauseous. This idea stays in the subconscious mind and helps the subject give up cigarettes.

is **hypnotic** holds your attention or makes you feel sleepy, often because it involves repeated sounds, pictures, or movements. 催眠作用のある ❑ *His songs are often both hypnotic and reassuringly pleasant.* 彼の歌はしばしば催眠効果があり，安心するほど心地よい.

hyp|no|tism /hɪpnətɪzəm/ N-UNCOUNT 不可算名詞 **Hypnotism** is the practice of hypnotizing people. 催眠術 ❑ *Dulcy also saw a psychiatrist who used hypnotism to help her deal with her fear.* ダルシーは，恐怖心に対処できるように催眠術を使う精神科医にも見てもらった. ●**hyp|no|tist** (**hypnotists**) N-COUNT 可算名詞 催眠術師 ❑ *He was put into a trance by a police hypnotist.* 彼は警察の催眠術師に催眠術をかけられた.
→ see hypnosis

hyp|no|tize /hɪpnətaɪz/ (**hypnotizes, hypnotizing, hypnotized**) ◼ V-T 他動詞 If someone **hypnotizes** you, they put you into a state in which you seem to be asleep but can still see, hear, or respond to things said to you. 催眠術をかける ❑ *A hypnotherapist will hypnotize you and will stop you from smoking.* 催眠療法師が催眠術をかけて，禁煙させます. ◻ V-T 他動詞 If you **are hypnotized by** someone or something, you are so fascinated by them that you cannot think of anything else. 魅了する [usu passive] ❑ *He's hypnotized by that black hair and that white face.* その黒髪，その白い肌の顔に魅惑されている.

hy|poc|ri|sy /hɪpɒkrɪsi/ (**hypocrisies**) N-VAR 可変性名詞 If you accuse someone of **hypocrisy**, you mean that they pretend to have qualities, beliefs, or feelings that they do not really have. みせかけ [DISAPPROVAL 不賛成] ❑ *He accused newspapers of hypocrisy in their treatment of the story.* その話の取り扱い方について，ないものをあるという新聞社を非難した.

hypo|crite /hɪpəkrɪt/ (**hypocrites**) N-COUNT 可算名詞 If you accuse someone of being a **hypocrite**, you mean that they pretend to have qualities, beliefs, or feelings that they do not really have. 偽善者 [DISAPPROVAL 不賛成] ❑ *The magazine wrongly suggested he was a liar and a hypocrite.* その雑誌は誤って彼をうそつきで偽善者だと示唆した.

hypo|criti|cal /hɪpəkrɪtɪkəl/ ADJ 形容詞 If you accuse someone of being **hypocritical**, you mean that they pretend to have qualities, beliefs, or feelings that they do not really have. 偽善的な [DISAPPROVAL 不賛成] ❑ *It would be hypocritical to say I travel at 70 mph simply because that is the law.* 法律だから時速70マイルで運転すると言うのは偽善になるだろう.

Word Link hypo ≈ below, under : hypodermic, hypothesis, hypothetical

---

hypo|der|mic /haɪpədɜrmɪk/ (**hypodermics**) ADJ 形容詞 A **hypodermic** needle or syringe is a medical instrument with a hollow needle, which is used to give injections. 皮下用の [ADJ n] ●N-COUNT 可算名詞 **Hypodermic** is also a noun. 皮下注射器 ❑ *He held up a hypodermic to check the dosage.* 薬量を確認するために皮下注射器を目の前にすえた.

hy|poth|esis /haɪpɒθɪsɪs/ (**hypotheses**) N-VAR 可変性名詞 A **hypothesis** is an idea which is suggested as a possible explanation for a particular situation or condition, but which has not yet been proved to be correct. 仮説 [FORMAL 形式ばった]

❑ *Work will now begin to test the hypothesis in rats.* 仮説をネズミでテストする作業が今から始まる.
→ see experiment, science

hypo|theti|cal /haɪpəθɛtɪkəl/ ADJ 形容詞 If something is **hypothetical**, it is based on possible ideas or situations rather than actual ones. 仮説の ❑ *Let's look at a hypothetical situation in which Carol, a recovering alcoholic, gets invited to a party.* 仮に，アル中から立ち直ろうとしているキャロルがパーティに招待されるという想定状況を検討してみよう. ●**hypo|theti|cal|ly** /haɪpəθɛtɪkli/ ADV 副詞 仮定的に ❑ *He was invariably willing to discuss the possibilities hypothetically.* 彼はいつも仮定の可能性を進んで検討した.

hys|ter|ec|to|my /hɪstərɛktəmi/ (**hysterectomies**) N-COUNT 可算名詞 A **hysterectomy** is a surgical operation to remove a woman's uterus. 子宮摘出手術 ❑ *I had to have a hysterectomy.* 子宮摘出の手術を受けなければならなかった.

hys|te|ria /hɪstɪəriə/ N-UNCOUNT 不可算名詞 **Hysteria** among a group of people is a state of uncontrolled excitement, anger, or panic. 病的な異常興奮 ❑ *No one could help getting carried away by the hysteria.* 誰も異常な興奮で夢中にならないわけにはいかなかった.

hys|teri|cal /hɪstɛrɪkəl/ ◼ ADJ 形容詞 Someone who is **hysterical** is in a state of uncontrolled excitement, anger, or panic. 狂乱の ❑ *Police and bodyguards had to form a human shield around him as the almost hysterical crowds struggled to approach him.* ほとんど半狂乱の群集がなにがなんでも彼に近づこうとする，警察と警備の人が体を張って盾となった. ●**hys|teri|cal|ly** /hɪstɛrɪkli/ ADV 副詞 異常に興奮して ❑ *I don't think we can go around screaming hysterically: "Ban these dogs. Muzzle all dogs."* 「この種の犬を禁止せよ．犬は全部口輪をかけよ」と，理性をなくしたかのように叫び歩くことはできないと思う. ◻ ADJ 形容詞 **Hysterical** laughter is loud and uncontrolled. 笑いが止まらないくらいおかしい [INFORMAL くだけた] ❑ *The young woman burst into hysterical laughter.* 若い女はおかしくてたまらないように急にげらげらと笑い出した. ●**hys|teri|cal|ly** ADV 副詞 [ADV with v] 腹の皮がよじれるほどに ❑ *She says she hasn't laughed as hysterically since she was 13.* 13歳のときからこれほど腹の皮がよじれるくらい笑ったことはないと言う. ▨ ADJ 形容詞 If you describe something or someone as **hysterical**, you think that they are very funny and they make you laugh a lot. ひどくおかしい [INFORMAL くだけた] ❑ *Paul Mazursky was Master of Ceremonies, and he was pretty hysterical.* ポール・マザースキィは司会者で，とてもおもしろい人だった. ●**hys|teri|cal|ly** ADV 副詞 [ADV adj] ひどくおかしく ❑ *It wasn't supposed to be a comedy but I found it hysterically funny.* 喜劇になるはずじゃなかったのに，私には笑い転げるくらいおかしかった.

hys|ter|ics /hɪstɛrɪks/ ◼ N-PLURAL 複数名詞 If someone is **in hysterics** or is having **hysterics**, they are in a state of uncontrolled excitement, anger, or panic. ヒステリーの発作 [INFORMAL くだけた] ❑ *I'm sick of your having hysterics, okay?* いいかい，君がヒステリーを起こすのにはもううんざりだ. ◻ N-PLURAL 複数名詞 You can say that someone is **in hysterics** or is having **hysterics** when they are laughing loudly in an uncontrolled way. 抱腹絶倒の状態 [INFORMAL くだけた] ❑ *He'd often have us all in absolute hysterics.* 彼はよく私たちみんなを抱腹絶倒させたものだった.

h

I i

I /aɪ/ PRON-SING 単数代名詞 A speaker or writer uses **I** to refer to himself or herself. **I** is a first person singular pronoun. **I** is used as the subject of a verb. わたしは [PRON v] ❑ *Jim and I are getting married.* ジムとわたしは結婚するの.

I also **i** /aɪ/ (**I's, i's**) N-VAR 可変性名詞 **I** is the ninth letter of the English alphabet. 英語アルファベットの第9字

ibid. CONVENTION 慣習表現 **Ibid.** is used in books and journals to indicate that a piece of text taken from somewhere else is from the same source as the previous piece of text. 同じ箇所(同じ本, 同じ章, 同じページなど)に

ice /aɪs/ (**ices, icing, iced**) **1** N-UNCOUNT 不可算名詞 **Ice** is frozen water. 氷 ❑ *Glaciers are moving rivers of ice.* 氷河は動く氷の川だ. **2** V-T 他動詞 If you **ice** a cake, you cover it with icing. (ケーキを)糖衣で覆う ❑ *I've made the cake. I've iced and decorated it.* わたしがケーキを作ったのよ. アイシングを乗せて, 飾り付けをしたの. **3** → see also **iced, icing 4** PHRASE 句 If you **break the ice** at a party or meeting, or in a new situation, you say or do something to make people feel relaxed and comfortable. (パーティーや会議で)堅苦しい雰囲気を和ませる ❑ *That sort of approach should go a long way toward breaking the ice.* ああいうやり方は場を和ませるのにとても役立つ. **5** PHRASE 句 If you say that something **cuts no ice with** you, you mean that you are not impressed or influenced by it. 影響を与えない ❑ *That sort of romantic attitude cuts no ice with moneymen.* あの手の空想的な態度では財政家に影響を与えられない. **6** PHRASE 句 If someone puts a plan or project **on ice**, they delay doing it. (計画などを)保留にする ❑ *There would be a three-month delay while the deal would be put on ice.* 取引が保留されると, その間3か月の遅れが出るだろう. **7** PHRASE 句 If you say that someone is **on thin ice** or is **skating on thin ice**, you mean that they are doing something risky that may have serious or unpleasant consequences. 危険な状態で, 薄氷を踏むような ❑ *I had skated on thin ice on many assignments and somehow had gotten away with it.* わたしは任務の中で何度も危ない思いをしたが, どうにか難を逃れていた.

→ see **Arctic, crystal, glacier**

ice|berg /aɪsbɜrg/ (**icebergs**) **1** N-COUNT 可算名詞 An **iceberg** is a large tall mass of ice floating in the sea. 氷山 **2 the tip of the iceberg** → see **tip**

→ see **Arctic**

ice cream (**ice creams**) **1** N-MASS 質量名詞 **Ice cream** is a very cold sweet food made from frozen cream or a substance like cream and has a flavor such as vanilla, chocolate, or strawberry. アイスクリーム ❑ *I'll get you some ice cream.* きみにアイスクリームを買ってあげる. **2** N-COUNT 可算名詞 An **ice cream** is an amount of ice cream sold in a small container or a cone made of a thin cookie. (カップやコーンに入った)アイスクリーム ❑ *Do you want an ice cream?* アイスクリームいる?

→ see **dessert**

iced /aɪst/ **1** ADJ 形容詞 An **iced** drink has been made very cold, often by putting ice in it. 氷で冷やした [ADJ n] ❑ *…iced tea.* アイスティー **2** ADJ 形容詞 An **iced** cake is covered with a layer of icing. アイシングで覆った

ice hock|ey N-UNCOUNT 不可算名詞 **Ice hockey** is a game played on ice between two teams of 11 players who use long curved sticks to hit a small rubber disk, called a puck, and try to score goals. アイスホッケー [AM usually **hockey** 米国英語では通常 **hockey**]

ice skate (**ice skates, ice skating, ice skated**) **1** N-COUNT 可算名詞 **Ice skates** are boots with a thin metal blade underneath that people wear to move quickly on ice. スケート靴 **2** V-I 自動詞 If you **ice skate**, you move around on ice wearing ice skates. アイススケートをする ❑ *We never learned to ice skate or ski.* わたしたちはアイススケートもスキーもしなかった. ● **ice skat|ing** N-UNCOUNT 不可算名詞 アイススケート ❑ *I love watching ice skating on television.* わたしはテレビでアイススケートを見るのが大好きだ. ❑ *We went ice skating on a frozen lake.* わたしたちは凍った湖にスケートをしに行った.

ici|cle /aɪsɪkᵊl/ (**icicles**) N-COUNT 可算名詞 An **icicle** is a long pointed piece of ice hanging down from a surface. It forms when water comes slowly off the surface, and freezes as it falls. つらら

ic|ing /aɪsɪŋ/ **1** N-UNCOUNT 不可算名詞 **Icing** is a sweet substance made from powdered sugar that is used to cover and decorate cakes. アイシング, 糖衣(ケーキの表面に塗ったり飾り付けに使う) ❑ *Paul made five-year-old Michelle a birthday cake with yellow icing.* ポールは5歳になるミシェルのために黄色いアイシングをかけたケーキを作った. **2** PHRASE 句 If you describe something as **icing on the cake** or **the icing on the cake**, you mean that it makes a good thing even better, but it is not essential. 花を添えるもの, 絶対必要ではないがあれば喜ばれるもの ❑ *Qualifying was my only goal, so winning is icing on the cake.* 予選通過だけが目標だったので, 優勝は思いがけない喜びだ.

icon /aɪkɒn/ (**icons**) also **ikon 1** N-COUNT 可算名詞 If you describe something or someone as an **icon**, you mean that they are important as a symbol of a particular thing. あこがれの対象 ❑ *…only Marilyn has proved as enduring a fashion icon.* マリリンだけが永遠のファッションアイドルであることを示している. **2** N-COUNT 可算名詞 An **icon** is a picture of Christ, his mother, or a saint painted on a wooden panel. (キリストや聖母, 聖人の)聖像 ❑ *…a painter of religious icons.* 宗教画家 **3** N-COUNT 可算名詞 An **icon** is a picture on a computer screen representing a particular computer function. If you want to use it, you move the cursor onto the icon using a mouse. アイコン(コンピュータの機能内容を図形化したもの)[COMPUTING コンピューティング] ❑ *Kate clicked on the mail icon on her computer screen.* ケイトはコンピュータ画面のメールのアイコンをクリックした.

icy /aɪsi/ (**icier, iciest**) **1** ADJ 形容詞 If you describe something as **icy** or **icy cold**, you mean that it is extremely cold. とても冷たい ❑ *An icy wind blew hard across the open spaces.* 空き地に氷のように冷たい風が吹き渡った. **2** ADJ 形容詞 An **icy** road has ice on it. 氷で覆われた ❑ *The roads were icy.* それらの道路は凍結していた. **3** ADJ 形容詞 If you describe a person or their behavior as **icy**, you mean that they are not affectionate or friendly, and they show their dislike or anger in a quiet, controlled way. (態度が)冷淡な [DISAPPROVAL 不賛成] ❑ *His response was icy.* 彼の返事はよそよそしかった.

ID /aɪ di/ (**IDs**) N-VAR 可変性名詞 If you have **ID** or an **ID**, you are carrying a document such as an identity card or driver's license that tells who you are. 身分証明書 ❑ *I had no ID on me so the police couldn't establish that I was the owner of the car.* わたしは身分証明書も持っていなかったので, 警察はわたしがその車の持ち主であることを確認できなかった.

I'd /aɪd/ **1** **I'd** is the usual spoken form of "I had," especially when "had" is an auxiliary verb. I had の口語体. had が助動詞の時によく使われる. ❑ *I felt absolutely certain that I'd seen her before.* わたしは絶対彼女を前にも見た確信があった. **2** **I'd** is the usual spoken form of "I would." I would の口語体 ❑ *There are some questions I'd like to ask.* 私の聞きたいことがいくつかあるの.

idea /aɪdiə/ (**ideas**) **1** N-COUNT 可算名詞 An **idea** is a plan, suggestion, or possible course of action. 考え, 提案 ❑ *It's a good idea to have your blood pressure checked regularly.* あなたの血圧を定期的に測ってもらうのはいいことだわ. ❑ *I really like the idea of helping people.* わたしは人を助けるというのはとてもいい考えだと思う. **2** N-COUNT 可算名詞 An **idea** is an opinion or belief about what something is like or should be like. 意見, 信念 ❑ *Some of his ideas about democracy are entirely his own.* 民主主義に関する彼の意見の中にはまったく彼独自のものもある. **3** N-SING 単数名詞 If someone gives you an **idea of** something, they give you information about it without being very exact or giving a lot of detail. 見当 ❑ *This table will give you some idea of how levels of ability in a foreign language can be measured.* この表を見れば, 外国語の能力レベルをどうやって測るかが大まかに分かるだろう. **4** N-SING 単数名詞 If you have an **idea of** something, you know about it to some extent. 見当 ❑ *No one has any real idea how much the company will make next year.* その会社が来年どれほど利益を上げるかは当分かつかない. ❑ *We had no idea what was happening.* わたしたちは何が起こっているのかまったく分からなかった. **5** N-SING 単数名詞 If you have an **idea that** something is the case, you think that it may be the case, although you are not certain. 想像 [VAGUENESS あいまいさ] ❑ *I had an idea that he joined the army later, after college, but I may be wrong.* 彼は大学を卒業してから軍隊に入るだろうとわたしは思っていたのだが, 違っているかもしれない. **6** N-SING 単数名詞 **The idea** of an action or activity is its aim or purpose. 目的 ❑ *The idea is to get industry to be more efficient in the way it uses energy.* 会社側により効果的なエネルギーの使い方をさせることがその狙いだ. **7** N-COUNT 可算名詞 If

you have the **idea of** doing something, you intend to do it. （〜する）つもり ❑ *He sent for a number of books he admired with the idea of rereading them.* 彼はお気に入りの本をまた読むつもりで大量に取り寄せた.

| N. | plan, suggestion **1** |
| | belief, concept, opinion, thought, viewpoint **2** |

Word Partnership　*idea* は次の語句と使われる:

ADJ.	**bad** idea, **bright** idea, **brilliant** idea, **great** idea **1**
	crazy idea, **different** idea, **dumb** idea, **interesting** idea, **new** idea, **original** idea **1 2**
	the main idea, **the whole** idea **1 2 6**
V.	**get an** idea, **have an** idea **1 3 4 5**

Word Link　*ide, ideo* ≈ *idea* : *ideal, idealize, ideology*

ideal /aɪdiəl/ (**ideals**) **1** N-COUNT 可算名詞 An **ideal** is a principle, idea, or standard that seems very good and worth trying to achieve. 理念, 理想 ❑ *Walt Disney stayed true to his ideals.* ウォルト・ディズニーは自分の理念に忠実であり続けた. **2** N-SING 単数名詞 Your **ideal of** something is the person or thing that seems to you to be the best possible example of it. 理想的な人 (物) ❑ *Her features were almost the opposite of the Japanese ideal of beauty in those days.* 彼女の顔立ちは当時の日本の理想美とはほとんど逆だった. **3** ADJ 形容詞 The **ideal** person or thing for a particular task or purpose is the best possible person or thing for it. 理想的な ❑ *She decided that I was the ideal person to take over the job.* 彼女はわたしがその仕事を引き継ぐのに最適だと判断した. **4** ADJ 形容詞 An **ideal** society or world is the best possible one that you can imagine. 究極の [ADJ n] ❑ *We do not live in an ideal world.* わたしたち理想郷に住んでいるわけではない.

ideal|**ise** /aɪdiəlaɪz/ → see **idealize**

ideal|**ism** /aɪdiəlɪzəm/ N-UNCOUNT 不可算名詞 **Idealism** is the beliefs and behavior of someone who has ideals and who tries to base their behavior on these ideals. 理想主義 ❑ *She never lost her respect for the idealism of the 1960s.* 彼女は1960年代の理想主義に敬意を抱き続けた. ● **ideal**|**ist** (**idealists**) N-COUNT 可算名詞 理想主義者 ❑ *He is not such an idealist that he cannot see the problems.* 彼はそれほどの理想主義者ではないので, その問題に気づかない.

ideal|**is**|**tic** /aɪdiəlɪstɪk, aɪdiə-/ ADJ 形容詞 If you describe someone as **idealistic**, you mean that they have ideals, and base their behavior on these ideals, even though this may be impractical. 理想主義の ❑ *Idealistic young people died for the cause.* 理想主義の若者たちが大義のために死んでいった.

ideal|**ize** /aɪdiəlaɪz/ (**idealizes, idealizing, idealized**) V-T 他動詞 If you **idealize** something or someone, you think of them, or represent them to other people, as being perfect or much better than they really are. 理想化する ❑ *People idealize the past.* 人々は過去を美化する.

ideal|**ly** /aɪdiəli/ **1** ADV 副詞 If you say that **ideally** a particular thing should happen or be done, you mean that this is what you would like to happen or be done, but you know that this may not be possible or practical. 理想を言えば [ADV with cl/group] ❑ *People should, ideally, be persuaded to eat a diet with much less fat or oil.* 理想を言えば, みんなもっと脂肪分や油分の少ない食事を取るという真心に耳を傾けるべきだ. **2** ADV 副詞 If you say that someone or something is **ideally** suited, **ideally** located, or **ideally** qualified, you mean that they are as well suited, located, or qualified as they could possibly be. 申し分なく ❑ *They were an extremely happy couple, ideally suited.* 彼らは理想的な相性のとても幸せな夫婦だった.

Word Link　*ident* ≈ *same* : *identical, identification, unidentified*

iden|**ti**|**cal** /aɪdɛntɪkəl/ ADJ 形容詞 Things that are **identical** are exactly the same. まったく同じの ❑ *The three bombs were virtually identical.* その3発の爆弾はほとんど同じものだった. ● **iden**|**ti**|**cal**|**ly** /aɪdɛntɪkli/ ADV 副詞 同一に ❑ *...nine identically dressed female dancers.* 同じ衣装を着た9人の女性ダンサー → see **clone**

iden|**ti**|**fi**|**able** /aɪdɛntɪfaɪəbəl/ ADJ 形容詞 Something or someone that is **identifiable** can be recognized. 確認できる ❑ *In the corridor were four dirty, ragged bundles, just identifiable as human beings.* 廊下には, やっと人間と分かる4つの汚れたぼろぼろの塊があった.

iden|**ti**|**fi**|**ca**|**tion** /aɪdɛntɪfɪkeɪʃən/ (**identifications**) **1** N-VAR 可変性名詞 The **identification** of something is the recognition that it exists, is important, or is true. （存在や事実の）確認, 認識 ❑ *Early identification of a disease can prevent death and illness.* 病気の早期発見で死亡や疾病を防止できる. **2** N-VAR 可変性名詞 The **identification** of a particular person or thing is the ability to name them because you know them or recognize them.

（人や物が）同一であることの確認 ❑ *Officials are awaiting positive identification before charging the men with war crimes.* 当局はそれらの男を戦争犯罪で起訴する前に, 彼らが本人であるという身元確認を待っている. **3** N-UNCOUNT 不可算名詞 If someone asks you for some **identification**, they want to see something such as a driver's license, that proves who you are. 身分証明書 ❑ *He did not have any identification when he arrived at the hospital.* 彼は病院に着いた時に身元を証明できるものを何も持っていなかった. **4** N-VAR 可変性名詞 The **identification of** one person or thing with another is the close association of one with the other. 一体化, 強いつながり ❑ *...the identification of Spain with Catholicism.* スペインとカトリック教との強いつながり **5** N-UNCOUNT 不可算名詞 **Identification with** someone or something is the feeling of sympathy and support for them. 共感, 支持 ❑ *Marilyn had an intense identification with animals.* マリリンは動物に強い共感を抱いていた.

iden|**ti**|**fy** /aɪdɛntɪfaɪ/ (**identifies, identifying, identified**) **1** V-T 他動詞 If you can **identify** someone or something, you are able to recognize them or distinguish them from others. 認める, 識別する ❑ *There are a number of distinguishing characteristics by which you can identify a Hollywood epic.* ハリウッドの大作を見分ける目立った特徴はたくさんある. **2** V-T 他動詞 If you **identify** someone or something, you name them or say who or what they are. （人の身元や物を）確認する ❑ *Police have already identified 10 murder suspects.* 警察はすでに10人の殺人容疑者の身元をつきとめている. **3** V-T 他動詞 If you **identify** something, you discover or notice its existence. 発見する ❑ *Scientists claim to have identified chemicals produced by certain plants which have powerful cancer-fighting properties.* 科学者は, 強力な抗がん作用を持つ特定の植物によって作り出される化学物質を発見した. **4** V-T 他動詞 If a particular thing **identifies** someone or something, it makes them easy to recognize, by making them different in some way. （〜であると）分かるようにする ❑ *She wore a little nurse's hat on her head to identify her.* 彼女は小さなナース帽をかぶって彼女であることが分かるようにした. **5** V-I 自動詞 If you **identify with** someone or something, you feel that you understand them or their feelings and ideas. （感情や考えを）共有する ❑ *She would only play a role if she could identify with the character.* 彼女はその人物像に共鳴できる役だけを演じていた. **6** V-T 他動詞 If you **identify** one person or thing **with** another, you think that they are closely associated or involved in some way. 密接に結びつける ❑ *Moore really hates to play the sweet, passive women that audiences have identified her with.* ムーアは, 観客が彼女に重ね合わせるかわいい受身の女性を演じることが大嫌いだ.

iden|**ti**|**ty** /aɪdɛntɪti/ (**identities**) **1** N-COUNT 可算名詞 Your **identity** is who you are. 身元 ❑ *Abu is not his real name, but it's one he uses to disguise his identity.* アブーというのは彼の本名ではなくて, 彼が身元を隠す時に使う名前だ. **2** N-VAR 可変性名詞 The **identity** of a person or place is the characteristics that distinguish them from others. （人や場所の）特徴 ❑ *I wanted a sense of my own identity.* わたしは私独自の個性感を持ちたかった.

Word Partnership　*identity* は次の語句と使われる:

N.	**identity theft 1**
	identity **crisis, sense of** identity **2**
ADJ.	**ethnic** identity, **national** identity, **personal** identity **2**

iden|**ti**|**ty card** (**identity cards**) N-COUNT 可算名詞 An **identity card** is a card with a person's name, photograph, date of birth, and other information on it. In some countries, people are required to carry identity cards in order to prove who they are. The abbreviation **ID card** is also used. 身分証明書

ideo|**logi**|**cal** /aɪdiəlɒdʒɪkəl, ɪdi-/ ADJ 形容詞 **Ideological** means relating to principles or beliefs. 理念的な, 信念の ❑ *Others left the party for ideological reasons.* 他の者は政治的理念を理由にその党を離脱した. ● **ideo**|**logi**|**cal**|**ly** /aɪdiəlɒdʒɪkli, ɪdi-/ ADV 副詞 信念的に ❑ *...an ideologically sound organization.* しっかりした理念を持つ組織

ideol|**ogy** /aɪdiɒlədʒi, ɪdi-/ (**ideologies**) N-VAR 可変性名詞 An **ideology** is a set of beliefs, especially the political beliefs on which people, parties, or countries base their actions. 観念, 考え方 ❑ *...capitalist ideology.* 資本主義思想

idi|**om** /ɪdiəm/ (**idioms**) N-COUNT 可算名詞 An **idiom** is a group of words that have a different meaning when used together from the one they would have if you took the meaning of each word separately. 熟語, 慣用句 [TECHNICAL 技術的] ❑ *...familiar idioms and metaphors, such as "turning over a new leaf."* 「心機一転」のような慣れ親しんだ慣用句やたとえ

id|**iot** /ɪdiət/ (**idiots**) N-COUNT 可算名詞 If you call someone an **idiot**, you are showing that you think they are very stupid or have done something very stupid. ばか者, まぬけ [DISAPPROVAL 不賛成] ❑ *I knew I'd been an idiot to stay there.* わたしは, そこに留まるなんて自分がばかだったことを知っていた.

idle /aɪdəl/ (**idles, idling, idled**) **1** ADJ 形容詞 If people who were working are **idle**, they have no jobs or work. 働いていない, 仕事

のない [v-link ADJ] ❑4,000 workers have been idle for 12 of the first 27 weeks of this year. 今年は最初の27週間のうち12週間，4千人の人が失業している． ❷ ADJ 形容詞 If machines or factories are **idle**, they are not working or being used. (機械や工場が) 稼動していない，使用されていない [v-link ADJ] ❑Now the machine is lying idle. その機械はもう使われていない． ❸ ADJ 形容詞 If you say that someone is **idle**, you disapprove of them because they are not doing anything and you think they should be. 怠けた [DISAPPROVAL 不賛成] ❑…idle bureaucrats who spent the day reading newspapers. 新聞を読んでその日を過ごした怠惰な役人たち ● **idly** ADV 副詞 [ADV with v] 怠けて ❑We were not idly sitting around. ぼくたちは何もしないで座っていたわけじゃない． ❹ ADJ 形容詞 **Idle** is used to describe something that you do for no particular reason, often because you have nothing better to do. これといった目的もなく [ADJ n] ❑Brian kept up the idle chatter for another five minutes. ブライアンはたわいのないおしゃべりをもう5分間続けた． ● **idly** ADV 副詞 意味もなく，無駄に ❑We talked idly about magazines and baseball. わたしたちは暇つぶしに雑誌や野球の話をした． ❺ ADJ 形容詞 [ADJ n] You refer to an **idle** threat or boast when you do not think the person making it will or can do what they say. 実質を伴わない ❑It was more of an idle threat than anything. それはただの脅し以外の何ものでもなかった． ❻ V-I 自動詞 If an engine or vehicle is **idling**, the engine is running slowly and quietly because it is not in gear, and the vehicle is not moving. (エンジンや車が) アイドリングする ❑Beyond a stand of trees a small plane idled. 並木の向こうで小型飛行機がアイドリングした．

Thesaurus

idle また次を参照:

ADJ. inactive, jobless, unemployed ❶
lazy, passive, shiftless, wasteful; *(ant.)* busy, productive ❸

idol /ˈaɪdəl/ (**idols**) ❶ N-COUNT 可算名詞 If you refer to someone such as a movie, pop, or sports star as an **idol**, you mean that they are greatly admired or loved by their fans. (映画やポップスターなどの) アイドル，あこがれのスター ❑A great cheer went up from the crowd as they caught sight of their idol. あこがれのスターの姿が見えると，群衆から大歓声が上がった． ❷ N-COUNT 可算名詞 An **idol** is a statue or other object that is worshipped by people who believe that it is a god. (宗教的な) 偶像

idol|ize /ˈaɪdəlaɪz/ (**idolizes, idolizing, idolized**) V-T 他動詞 If you **idolize** someone, you admire them very much. 崇拝する ❑Naomi idolized her father as she was growing up. ネイオミは大きくなるにつれ，父親を崇拝した．

idyl|lic /ɪˈdɪlɪk/ ADJ 形容詞 If you describe something as **idyllic**, you mean that it is extremely pleasant, simple, and peaceful without any difficulties or dangers. のどかな，牧歌的な ❑…an idyllic setting for a summer romance. ひと夏の恋のための素材な環境

i.e. /ˌaɪ ˈiː/ **i.e.** is used to introduce a word or sentence that makes what you have just said clearer or gives details. すなわち (ラテン語の id est の略) ❑…an artificial intelligence system, i.e. a computer program. 人工知能システム，すなわちコンピュータ・プログラム

if /ɪf/

Often pronounced /ɪf/ at the beginning of the sentence.

文頭ではしばしば /ɪf/ と発音される．

❶ CONJ 接続詞 You use **if** in conditional sentences to introduce the circumstances in which an event or situation might happen, might be happening, or might have happened. もし〜ならば ❑She gets very upset if I exclude her from anything. 彼女はわたしが彼女抜きで何かしようとするととても怒る． ❑You can go if you want. もしあなたが行きたいなら，そうしていいよ． ❷ CONJ 接続詞 You use **if** in indirect questions where the answer is either "yes" or "no." 〜かどうか ❑He asked if I had left with you, and I said no. 彼はわたしがあなたと一緒に退出したか尋ねたので，わたしはいいえと答えた． ❸ CONJ 接続詞 You use **if** to suggest that something might be slightly different from what you are stating in the main part of the sentence, for example, that there might be slightly more or less of a particular quality. (挿入句として) 〜ではないにしても ❑Sometimes that standard is quite difficult, if not impossible, to achieve. 時おり，その基準を達成するのは，不可能でなくても，とても難しい． ❹ CONJ 接続詞 You use **if**, usually with "can," "could," "may," or "might," in a conversation when you are politely trying to make a point, change the subject, or interrupt another speaker. can, could, may, might と共に，失礼にならないよう要点を述べる時や，話題を変える時，人の話に割り込む時の言い方 ❑If I could just make another small point about the weightlifters in the Olympics. もしよければ，小さなことがオリンピックの重量挙げ選手たちについてもう1点述べたいと思います． ❺ CONJ 接続詞 You use **if** at or near the beginning of a clause when politely asking someone to do something. 〜していただけませんか (相手に丁寧にものを頼む時の言い方) [POLITENESS 丁寧さ] ❑I wonder if you'd be kind enough to give us some information, please? わたしたちに情報を提供してくださらないでしょうか？ ❻ PHRASE 句 You use **if not** in front of a word

or phrase to indicate that your statement does not apply to that word or phrase, but to something closely related to it that you also mention. 〜ではないにしても ❑She understood his meaning, if not his words, and took his advice. 彼女は彼の言葉は理解しなかったにしても，言わんとすることを理解し，そのアドバイスを受け入れた． ❼ CONJ 接続詞 You use **if** to introduce a subordinate clause in which you admit a fact that you regard as less important than the statement in the main clause. もし〜であるとしても ❑If there was any disappointment it was probably temporary. もし失望したことがあったとしても，それは恐らく一時的なものだった． ❽ PHRASE 句 You use **if ever** with past tenses when you are introducing a description of a person or thing, to emphasize how appropriate it is. 間違いなく [EMPHASIS 強調] ❑I became a distraught, worried mother, a useless role if ever there was one. わたしは取り乱して心配する母親になっていた．間違いなく役立たずの役割だった． ❾ PHRASE 句 You use **if only** with past tenses to introduce what you think is a fairly good reason for doing something, although you realize it may not be a very good one. ただ〜のためだけに ❑She always writes me once a month, if only to scold me because I haven't answered her last letter yet. 彼女は，その前の手紙に返事を出していないからただ叱るためにいつも月1回手紙を書いてくる． ❿ PHRASE 句 You use **if only** to express a wish or desire, especially one that cannot be fulfilled. ただ〜すればいいのに，ただ〜であればいいのに [FEELINGS 感情] ❑If only you had told me that some time ago. ただあなたがこれをこの前わたしに話してくれればよかったのに． ⓫ PHRASE 句 You use **as if** when you are making a judgment about something that you see or notice. Your belief or impression might be correct, or it might be wrong. まるで〜であるかのように ❑It looked as if she had forgotten how to breathe. 彼女は呼吸の仕方を忘れてしまっているかのようだった． ⓬ PHRASE 句 You use **as if** to describe something or someone by comparing them with another thing or person. (2つの人／ものを比較して) 〜はあたかも〜のようで ❑He points two fingers at his head, as if he were holding a gun. 彼はあたかも銃を持っているかのように，2本の指を彼の頭に向ける． ⓭ PHRASE 句 You use **as if** to emphasize that something is not true. 〜というわけではあるまいし [SPOKEN 口語，EMPHASIS 強調] ❑Getting my work done! My God! As if it mattered. 私の仕事を片付けている！まあまあ！そんなのどうでもよかったのに．

ig|nite /ɪɡˈnaɪt/ (**ignites, igniting, ignited**) ❶ V-T/V-I 他動詞 自動詞 When you **ignite** something or when it **ignites**, it starts burning or explodes. 他動詞 点火する 自動詞 発火する ❑The bombs ignited a fire which destroyed some 60 houses. その爆弾で火災が起き，約60家屋が破壊された． ❷ V-T 他動詞 If something or someone **ignites** your feelings, they cause you to have very strong feelings about something. (感情を) 燃え上がらせる [LITERARY 文語的] [他動詞]，(感情が) 燃え立つ [自動詞] ❑There was one teacher who really ignited my interest in words. 1人の教師が，言葉に対するわたしの興味を非常にかきたてた．

ig|ni|tion /ɪɡˈnɪʃən/ (**ignitions**) ❶ N-VAR 可変性名詞 In a car engine, the **ignition** is the part where the fuel is ignited. (車の) イグニッション，点火装置 ❑The device automatically disconnects the ignition. その装置はイグニッションを自動的に切る． ❷ N-SING 単数名詞 Inside a car, the **ignition** is the part where you turn the key so that the engine starts. (車の) キーの差し込み口 ❑Abruptly he turned the ignition key and started the engine. 彼は急にイグニッションキーを回し，エンジンをかけた． ❸ N-UNCOUNT 不可算名詞 **Ignition** is the process of something starting to burn. 発火，着火 ❑The ignition of methane gas killed eight men. メタンガスの発火で8人の男性が死亡した．

ig|no|rance /ˈɪɡnərəns/ N-UNCOUNT 不可算名詞 **Ignorance of** something is lack of knowledge about it. 無知 ❑I am beginning to feel embarrassed by my complete ignorance of world history. わたしは世界史をまったく知らないことを恥ずかしく思い始めている．

ig|no|rant /ˈɪɡnərənt/ ❶ ADJ 形容詞 If you describe someone as **ignorant**, you mean that they do not know things they should know. If someone is **ignorant of** a fact, they do not know it. 無知な ❑People don't like to ask questions for fear of appearing ignorant. 人々は無教養だと思われるのを恐れて質問したがらない． ❷ ADJ 形容詞 People are sometimes described as **ignorant** when they do something that is not polite or kind. 無礼な ❑I met some ignorant people who called me all kinds of names. わたしをいろんな呼び名で呼ぶ何人かの失礼な人たちに会った．

ig|nore /ɪɡˈnɔːr/ (**ignores, ignoring, ignored**) ❶ V-T 他動詞 If you **ignore** someone or something, you pay no attention to them. 無視する ❑She said her husband ignored her. 彼女は夫が彼女を無視すると言った． ❷ V-T 他動詞 If you say that an argument or theory **ignores** an important aspect of a situation, you are criticizing it because it fails to consider that aspect or to take it into account. (議論や学説の大事な要素を) 見落とす ❑Such arguments ignore the question of where ultimate responsibility lay. そのような議論は最終責任がどこにあるかという問題点を見落としている．

Word Web illness

Most **infectious diseases** pass from person to person. However, some people have **contracted viruses** from animals. During the 2002 SARS **epidemic**, doctors discovered that the disease came from birds. SARS caused over 800 deaths in 32 countries.The disease had to be stopped quickly. Hospitals **quarantined** SARS patients. Medical workers used **symptoms** such as **fever**, **chills**, and a **cough** to help **diagnose** the disease. **Treatment** was not simple. By the time the symptoms appeared, the disease had already caused a lot of damage. **Patients** received oxygen and **physical therapy** to help clear the lungs.

Word Partnership　ignore は次の語句と使われる：

N.	ignore **advice**, ignore **a warning** 1
V.	**choose to** ignore *someone/something*, **try to** ignore *someone/something* 1
ADJ.	**hard to** ignore, **impossible to** ignore 1

ill /ɪl/ (**ills**) **1** ADJ 形容詞 Someone who is **ill** is suffering from a disease or a health problem. 病気の □ *In November 1941 Payne was seriously ill with pneumonia.* 1941年11月，ペインは重症の肺炎を患っていた。● N-PLURAL 複数名詞 People who are **ill** in some way can be referred to as, for example, **the** mentally **ill**. 病人 □ *The hospice provides care for the terminally ill.* そのホスピスは末期患者の看護をする。

The words **ill** and **sick** are very similar in meaning, but are used in slightly different ways. **Ill** is generally not used before a noun, and can be used in verbal expressions such as **fall ill** and **be taken ill.** □ *He fell ill shortly before Christmas… One of the jury members was taken ill.* **Sick** is often used before a noun. □ *…sick children.* In British English, **ill** is a slightly more polite, less direct word than **sick**. **Sick** often suggests the actual physical feeling of being ill, for example nausea or vomiting. □ *I spent the next 24 hours in bed, groaning and being sick.* In American English, **sick** is often used where British people would say **ill**. □ *Some people get hurt in accidents or get sick.*

2 N-COUNT 可算名詞 Difficulties and problems are sometimes referred to as **ills**. 困難，災難 [FORMAL 形式ばった] □ *His critics maintain that he's responsible for many of Algeria's ills.* 彼を非難する人たちは，アルジェリアの多くの問題は彼の責任だと主張している。**3** ADJ 形容詞 You can use **ill** in front of some nouns to indicate that you are referring to something harmful or unpleasant. 有害な，不快な [FORMAL 形式ばった] [ADJ n] □ *She had brought ill luck into her family.* 彼女は自分の家族に不運をもたらしていた。**4** N-UNCOUNT 不可算名詞 **Ill** is evil or harm. 邪悪，害 [LITERARY 文語的] □ *They say they mean you no ill.* 彼らはあなたに害を与えるつもりはないそうだ。**5** ADV 副詞 **Ill** means the same as "badly." 悪く [FORMAL 形式ばった] [ADV with v] □ *The company's conservative instincts sit ill with competition.* その会社の保守的な体質は競争で不利になる。**6** PHRASE 句 If you say that someone **can ill afford to** do something, or **can ill afford** something, you mean that they must prevent it from happening because it would be harmful or embarrassing to them. 〜すると困る [FORMAL 形式ばった] □ *It's possible he won't play but I can ill afford to lose him.* 彼が出演しない可能性はあるが，わたしは彼がいなくなると困るんだ。**7** PHRASE 句 If you **fall ill** or **are taken ill**, you suddenly become ill. 突然病気になる □ *Shortly before Christmas, he was mysteriously taken ill.* 彼は不可解にも病気になった。**8** to **speak ill of** someone → see **speak**

Word Partnership　ill は次の語句と使われる：

V.	**become** ill, **feel** ill, **look** ill 1
ADV.	**critically** ill, **mentally** ill, **physically** ill, **seriously** ill, **terminally** ill, **very** ill 1

I'll /aɪl/ **I'll** is the usual spoken form of "I will" or "I shall." I will または I shall の口語体 □ *I'll be leaving town in a few weeks.* わたしは数週間後には町を離れるつもりだ。

Word Link　il ≈ not : illegal, illiterate, illogical

il|legal /ɪliːgəl/ (**illegals**) **1** ADJ 形容詞 If something is **illegal**, the law says that it is not allowed. 不法な □ *It is illegal to intercept radio messages.* 無線電信を妨害するのは違法だ。□ *…illegal drugs.* 違法薬物 ● **il|legal|ly** ADV 副詞 [ADV with v] 不法に □ *He was convicted of illegally using a handgun.* 彼は拳銃の不法使用により有罪判決を受けた。**2** ADJ 形容詞 **Illegal** immigrants or workers have traveled into a country or are working without official permission. 正規の許可なく [ADJ n] ● N-COUNT 可算名詞 Illegal immigrants or workers are sometimes referred to as **illegals**. 不法入国者，不法労働者 □ *…a clothing factory where many other illegals also worked.* 他の多くの不法労働者も働いていた縫製工場

il|legi|ti|mate /ɪlɪdʒɪtɪmɪt/ **1** ADJ 形容詞 A person who is **illegitimate** was born of parents who were not married to each other. 非嫡出の □ *They discovered he had an illegitimate child.* 彼らは彼に私生児がいることを発見した。**2** ADJ 形容詞 **Illegitimate** is used to describe activities and institutions that are not in accordance with the law or with accepted standards of what is right. 非合法の，基準違反の □ *He realized that, otherwise, the election would have been dismissed as illegitimate by the international community.* そうでもしないと，彼はその選挙が国際社会で違法とみなされ却下されていただろうことに気づいた。

ill-fated ADJ 形容詞 If you describe something as **ill-fated**, you mean that it ended or will end in an unsuccessful or unfortunate way. 不運な □ *…the ill-fated merger between AOL and Time Warner.* AOLとタイム・ワーナー間の不幸な合併

ill health N-UNCOUNT 不可算名詞 Someone who suffers from **ill health** has an illness or keeps being ill. 不健康 □ *He was forced to retire because of ill health.* 彼は健康上の理由から退職せざるを得なかった。

il|lic|it /ɪlɪsɪt/ ADJ 形容詞 An **illicit** activity or substance is not allowed by law or by the social customs of a country. 不法な，社会的に許されない □ *Dante clearly condemns illicit love.* ダンテは不倫をはっきりと非難した。

Word Link　liter ≈ letter : illiterate, literal, literature

il|lit|er|ate /ɪlɪtərɪt/ (**illiterates**) ADJ 形容詞 Someone who is **illiterate** does not know how to read or write. 読み書きのできない □ *A large percentage of the population is illiterate.* 人口に対する文盲率は高い。● N-COUNT 可算名詞 An **illiterate** is someone who is illiterate. 文盲者 □ *…a subclass of illiterates.* 文盲者の下位分類

ill|ness /ɪlnɪs/ (**illnesses**) **1** N-UNCOUNT 不可算名詞 **Illness** is the fact or experience of being ill. 病気であること □ *If your child shows any signs of illness, take her to the doctor.* あなたの子供が何かの病気の兆候を見せた時は，医者に連れて行きなさい。**2** N-COUNT 可算名詞 An **illness** is a particular disease such as measles or pneumonia. （はしかや肺炎などの）特定疾患 □ *She returned to her family home to recover from an illness.* 彼女は病気の療養のため実家に戻った。
→ see Word Web: **illness**

Thesaurus　illness また次を参照：

N.	ailment, disease, sickness; (ant.) health, wellness 1 2

Word Partnership　illness は次の語句と使われる：

N.	**signs/symptoms of an** illness 1 2
ADJ.	**mental** illness, **serious** illness, **terminal** illness 1 2 **long/short** illness, **mysterious** illness, **sudden** illness 2
V.	**suffer from an** illness, **treat an** illness 1 2 **diagnose an** illness, **have an** illness 2

il|logi|cal /ɪlɒdʒɪkəl/ ADJ 形容詞 If you describe an action, feeling, or belief as **illogical**, you are critical of it because you think that it does not result from a logical and ordered way of thinking. 非論理的な，筋の通らない [DISAPPROVAL 不賛成] □ *It was absurd and illogical to go out into such a storm.* そんな嵐の中へ出て行くなんて，まったくばかげていた。

il|lu|mi|nate /ɪluːmɪneɪt/ (**illuminates, illuminating, illuminated**) **1** V-T 他動詞 To **illuminate** something means to shine light on it and to make it brighter and more visible. （光を）照らす 明るくする [FORMAL 形式ばった] □ *No streetlights illuminated the street.* その通りには街灯が1つもなかった。**2** V-T 他動詞 If you **illuminate** something that is unclear or difficult to understand, you make it clearer by explaining it carefully or giving information about it. （問題点を）解明する [FORMAL 形式ばった] □ *Instead of formulas and charts, the two instructors use games and drawings to illuminate their subject.* その2人の講師はそれぞれの教科を分かりやすく説明するため，従来の方法や表の代わりにゲームや絵を使っている。● **il|lu|mi|nat|ing** ADJ 形容詞 （問題を）解明する □ *It*

would be illuminating to hear the views of the club vice-chairman. そのクラブの副会長の意見を聞くとはっきりするだろう.

il|lu|mi|na|tion /ɪluːmɪneɪʃ³n/ N-UNCOUNT 不可算名詞 **Illumination** is the lighting that a place has. 照明 [FORMAL 形式ばった] □*The only illumination came from a small window high in the opposite wall.* 唯一の明かりは反対側の壁の高い所にある小窓から差し込んでいた.

il|lu|sion /ɪluːʒ³n/ (**illusions**) ■ N-VAR 可変性名詞 An **illusion** is a false idea or belief. 誤った考え, 誤った信念 □*No one really has any illusions about winning the war.* その戦争に勝つなどと信じている者はほとんどいなかった. ② N-COUNT 可算名詞 An **illusion** is something that appears to exist or be a particular thing but does not actually exist or is in reality something else. 錯覚 □*Floor-to-ceiling windows can look stunning, giving the illusion of extra height.* 床から天井に届く窓は, 実際よりも天井を高く見せ, 素晴らしいものになりうる.

Word Partnership　illusion は次の語句と使われる:

V.　**be under an** illusion ■
　　create an illusion, **give an** illusion **about/of/that something** ■ ②

il|lus|trate /ɪləstreɪt/ (**illustrates, illustrating, illustrated**) ■ V-T 他動詞 If you say that something **illustrates** a situation that you are drawing attention to, you mean that it shows that the situation exists. 実証する □*The example of the United States illustrates this point.* 米国の例はこの点を実証している. □*The situation illustrates how vulnerable the president is.* その事態は大統領がいかに危ういかを証明している. ② V-T 他動詞 If you use an example, story, or diagram to **illustrate** a point, you use its show that what you are saying is true or to make your meaning clearer. 例証する □*Let me give another example to illustrate this difficult point.* この難しい点を分かりやすくするためにもう1つ例を挙げましょう. ●**il|lus|tra|tion** N-UNCOUNT 不可算名詞 例証, 実例 □*Here, by way of illustration, are some extracts from our new catalog.* 我々の新しいカタログから, 実例として, いくつかの抜粋がある. ③ V-T 他動詞 If you **illustrate** a book, you put pictures, photographs or diagrams into it. 挿絵 (写真, 図表) を入れる □*She went on to art school and is now illustrating a book.* 彼女は美術学校に進み, 今は本の挿絵をかいている. ●**il|lus|tra|tion** N-UNCOUNT 不可算名詞 挿絵 □*...the world of children's book illustration.* 児童図書の挿絵の世界
→ see **animation**

il|lus|tra|tion /ɪləstreɪʃ³n/ (**illustrations**) ■ N-COUNT 可算名詞 An **illustration** is an example or a story that is used to make a point clear. (要点を明確にするための) 実例 □*An illustration of China's dynamism is that a new company is formed in Shanghai every 11 seconds.* 中国の力強さの一例は, 上海で11秒間に1社新しい会社が設立されていることだ. ② N-COUNT 可算名詞 An **illustration** in a book is a picture, design, or diagram. (本の) 挿絵 デザイン, 図表 □*She looked like a princess in a nineteenth-century illustration.* 彼女は19世紀の挿絵にある王女様のようだった. ③ → see also **illustrate**

il|lus|tri|ous /ɪlʌstriəs/ ADJ 形容詞 If you describe someone as an **illustrious** person, you mean that they are extremely well known because they have a high position in society or they have done something impressive. 著名な, 傑出した □*...the most illustrious scientists of the century.* その世紀でもっとも著名な科学者

I'm /aɪm/ **I'm** is the usual spoken form of "I am." I am の口語体 □*I'm sorry.* ごめんなさい.

im|age /ɪmɪdʒ/ (**images**) ■ N-COUNT 可算名詞 If you have an **image** of something or someone, you have a picture or idea of them in your mind. (心の中の) イメージ, 心象 □*The image of art theft as a gentleman's crime is outdated.* 美術品盗難が紳士の犯罪というイメージは時代遅れだ. ② N-COUNT 可算名詞 The **image** of a person, group, or organization is the way that they appear to other people. (人や組織の) イメージ 印象 □*...the government's negative public image.* 国民の政府に対する悪いイメージ ③ N-COUNT 可算名詞 An **image** is a picture of someone or something. 像 [FORMAL 形式ばった] □*...photographic images of young children.* 幼い子供たちの写真像 ④ N-COUNT 可算名詞 An **image** is a poetic description of something. 詩的描写 [FORMAL 形式ばった] □*The natural images in the poem are meant to be suggestive of realities beyond themselves.* その詩の中の自然描写は, 描写だけに留まらず現実を暗示するよう意図されている. ⑤ PHRASE 句 If you **are the image of** someone else, you look very much like them. 一によく似ている □*Marianne's son was the image of his father.* マリアンヌの息子は, 彼の父親にそっくりだった. ⑥ **spitting image** → see **spit**
→ see **copy, eye, photography, telescope, television**

Word Partnership　image は次の語句と使われる:

N.　**body** image, **self-image** ■ ②
　　image **on a screen** ③
ADJ.　**corporate** image, **negative/positive** image, **public** image ②
V.　**project an** image ② ③
　　display an image ③

im|age|ry /ɪmɪdʒri/ ■ N-UNCOUNT 不可算名詞 You can refer to the descriptions in something such as a poem or song, and the pictures they create in your mind, as its **imagery**. ひゆの描写 [FORMAL 形式ばった] □*...the nature imagery of the ballad.* そのバラードの自然描写 ② N-UNCOUNT 不可算名詞 You can refer to pictures and representations of things as **imagery**, especially when they act as symbols. (象徴としての) 画像, 描写 [FORMAL 形式ばった] □*This is an ambitious and intriguing movie, full of striking imagery.* これは印象的な映像に満ちた意欲的で面白い映画だ.

im|agi|nable /ɪmædʒɪnəb³l/ ■ ADJ 形容詞 You use **imaginable** after a superlative such as "best" or "worst" to emphasize that something is extreme in some way. 極度の [EMPHASIS 強調] □*...their imprisonment under some of the most horrible circumstances imaginable.* 想像しうる数値の最悪の状況下で起きた彼らの投獄 ② ADJ 形容詞 You use **imaginable** after a word like "every" or "all" to emphasize that you are talking about all the possible examples of something. You use **imaginable** after "no" to emphasize that something does not have the quality mentioned. 考えられる限りの [EMPHASIS 強調] [ADJ n, n ADJ] □*Parents encourage every activity imaginable.* 親は考えられる限りすべての活動を勧める. □*...a place of no imaginable strategic value.* 戦略的価値がまったく考えられない場所

im|agi|nary /ɪmædʒɪneri/ ADJ 形容詞 An **imaginary** person, place, or thing exists only in your mind or in a story, and not in real life. 想像上の, 架空の □*Lots of children have imaginary friends.* 子供たちの多くは想像上の友達を持っている.
→ see **fantasy**

im|agi|na|tion /ɪmædʒɪneɪʃ³n/ (**imaginations**) ■ N-VAR 可変性名詞 Your **imagination** is the ability that you have to form pictures or ideas in your mind of things that are new and exciting, or things that you have not experienced. 想像力 □*Latanya is a woman with a vivid imagination.* ラターニャは生き生きとした想像力を持つ女性だ. ② N-COUNT 可算名詞 Your **imagination** is the part of your mind that allows you to form pictures or ideas of things that do not necessarily exist in real life. 想像 □*Long before I ever went there, Africa was alive in my imagination.* わたしがそこに行くよりだいぶ前から, アフリカは私の想像をかき立てた. ③ PHRASE 句 If you say that someone or something **captured** your **imagination**, you mean that you thought they were interesting or exciting when you saw them or heard them for the first time. 心をとらえる □*Their music continues to capture the imagination of the American public.* 彼らの音楽は米国民の心をとらえ続けている. ④ **not by any stretch of the imagination** → see **stretch**
→ see **fantasy**

Word Partnership　imagination は次の語句と使われる:

ADJ.　**active** imagination, **lively** imagination, **vivid** imagination ■
PREP.　**beyond (someone's)** imagination ■
N.　**lack of** imagination ■

im|agi|na|tive /ɪmædʒɪnətɪv/ ADJ 形容詞 If you describe someone or their ideas as **imaginative**, you are praising them because they are easily able to think of or create new or exciting things. 想像力に富んだ [APPROVAL 賛成] □*...an imaginative writer.* 想像力豊かな作家 ●**im|agi|na|tive|ly** ADV 副詞 [ADV with v] □*The hotel is decorated imaginatively and attractively.* そのホテルの装飾は独創的で素敵だ.

im|ag|ine /ɪmædʒɪn/ (**imagines, imagining, imagined**) ■ V-T 他動詞 If you **imagine** something, you think about it and your mind forms a picture or idea of it. 想像する □*He could not imagine a more peaceful scene.* 彼はそれ以上穏やかな光景を思いつかなかった. ② V-T 他動詞 If you **imagine** that something is the case, you think that it is the case. 思う □*I imagine you're referring to Jean-Paul Sartre.* わたしはあなたがジャンポール・サルトルのことを言っているんだと思う. ③ V-T 他動詞 If you **imagine** something, you think that you have seen, heard, or experienced that thing, although actually you have not. 思い違いをする □*Looking back on it now, I realized that I must have imagined the whole thing.* 今振り返ると, すべてが気のせいだったに違いないとわたしは思った.

Thesaurus　imagine また次を参照:

V.　picture, see, visualize ■
　　believe, guess, think ②

Word Link *im ≈ not : imbalance, immature, impossible*

im|bal|ance /ɪmbæləns/ (imbalances) N-VAR 可変он性名詞 If there is an **imbalance** in a situation, the things involved are not the same size, or are not the right size in proportion to each other. 不均衡 □ ...the imbalance between the two sides in this war. この戦争における2者間の不均衡

im|bue /ɪmbyu/ (imbues, imbuing, imbued) V-T 他動詞 If someone or something **is imbued** with an idea, feeling, or quality, they become filled with it. （考えや特質を）吹き込む，満たす [FORMAL 形式ばった] □ The film is imbued with the star's rebellious spirit. その映画はスターの反抗精神に満ちていた.

IMF /aɪ em ef/ N-PROPER 固有名詞 The **IMF** is an international agency that tries to promote trade and improve economic conditions in poorer countries, sometimes by lending them money. **IMF** is an abbreviation for "International Monetary Fund." 国際通貨基金 (International Monetary Fundの略)

imi|tate /ɪmɪteɪt/ (imitates, imitating, imitated) 1 V-T 他動詞 If you **imitate** someone, you copy what they do or produce. まねる □ ...a genuine German musical that does not try to imitate the American model. アメリカの原型をまねようとしない本物のドイツ・ミュージカル 2 V-T 他動詞 If you **imitate** a person or animal, you copy the way they speak or behave, usually because you are trying to be funny. （ふざけて人や動物を）まねる □ Clarence screws up his face and imitates the Colonel again. クラレンスは顔をしかめて，また大佐の真似をする.

imi|ta|tion /ɪmɪteɪʃ³n/ (imitations) 1 N-COUNT 可算名詞 An **imitation** of something is a copy of it. 複製 □ ...the most accurate imitation of Chinese architecture in Europe. ヨーロッパで最も正確な中国建築の複製 2 N-UNCOUNT 不可算名詞 **Imitation** means copying someone else's actions. 模倣 □ They discussed important issues in imitation of their elders. 彼らは年長者に倣い，重要な問題について話し合った. 3 ADJ 形容詞 **Imitation** things are not genuine but are made to look as if they are. 偽の [ADJ n] □ ...a complete set of Dickens bound in imitation leather. 合成皮革で製本されたディケンズの完全なセット 4 N-COUNT 可算名詞 If someone does an **imitation** of another person, they copy the way they speak or behave, sometimes in order to be funny. 物まね □ One boy did an imitation of a soldier with a loudspeaker. 男の子が1人，拡声器を持った兵士の物まねをした.

im|macu|late /ɪmækyʊlɪt/ 1 ADJ 形容詞 If you describe something as **immaculate**, you mean that it is extremely clean, tidy, or neat. 汚れ一つない □ Her kitchen was kept immaculate. 彼女の台所はまったくきれいにしてあった. ●**im|macu|late|ly** ADV 副詞 汚れ一つなく □ As always he was immaculately dressed. いつものことだが，彼の服にはしみ一つなかった. 2 ADJ 形容詞 If you say that something is **immaculate**, you are emphasizing that it is perfect, without any mistakes or bad parts at all. （失敗や欠陥がなく）かんぺきな [EMPHASIS 強調] □ The goalie's performance was immaculate. そのゴールキーパーの試合はかんぺきだった. ●**im|macu|late|ly** ADV 副詞 [ADV with v] かんぺきに □ The orchestra plays immaculately. そのオーケストラの演奏はかんぺきだ.

im|ma|teri|al /ɪmətɪəriəl/ ADJ 形容詞 If you say that something is **immaterial**, you mean that it is not important or not relevant. 重要でない，関係ない [v-link ADJ] □ Whether we like him or not is immaterial. 我々が彼を好きかどうかは関係ない.

im|ma|ture /ɪmətʃʊər, -tʊər/ 1 ADJ 形容詞 Something or someone that is **immature** is not yet completely grown or fully developed. 未成熟な □ She is emotionally immature. 彼女は情緒的に未熟だ. 2 ADJ 形容詞 If you describe someone as **immature**, you are being critical of them because they do not behave in a sensible or responsible way. 大人気ない [DISAPPROVAL 不賛成] □ She's just being childish and immature. 彼女はただ子供じみた大人気ないまねをしているだけよ.

im|medi|ate /ɪmidiɪt/ 1 ADJ 形容詞 An **immediate** result, action, or reaction happens or is done without any delay. 即時の □ These tragic incidents have had an immediate effect. これらの悲劇的な事件は即座に影響をもたらしている. 2 ADJ 形容詞 **Immediate** needs and concerns exist at the present time and must be dealt with quickly. 差し迫った □ Relief agencies say the immediate problem is not a lack of food, but transportation. 救援組織によると，差し迫った問題は食糧不足ではなく，輸送手段の不足だということだ. 3 ADJ

形容詞 The **immediate** person or thing comes just before or just after another person or thing in a sequence. （時間的に）近い [ADJ n] □ In the immediate aftermath of the riots, a mood of hope and reconciliation sprang up. 暴動の直後に，希望と和解の空気が生じた. 4 ADJ 形容詞 You use **immediate** to describe an area or position that is next to or very near a particular place or person. （場所的に）すぐ近くの [ADJ n] □ Only a handful had returned to work in the immediate vicinity. ほんの一握りの人が近くの仕事場に戻っていた. 5 ADJ 形容詞 Your **immediate** family are the members of your family who are most closely related to you, such as your parents, children, brothers, and sisters. （血縁が）最も近い [ADJ n] □ The presence of his immediate family is obviously having a calming effect on him. 彼の肉親の存在が，明らかに彼を落ち着かせている.

im|medi|ate|ly /ɪmidiɪtli/ 1 ADV 副詞 If something happens **immediately**, it happens without any delay. 即座に [ADV with v] □ He immediately flung himself to the floor. 彼は間髪を入れずに床へ身を投げ出した. 2 ADV 副詞 If something is **immediately** obvious, it can be seen or understood without any delay. 一見して [ADV adj] □ The cause of the accident was not immediately apparent. その事故の原因は一見しただけでは分からなかった. 3 ADV 副詞 **Immediately** is used to indicate that someone or something is closely and directly involved in a situation. 直接に [ADV adj/-ed] □ The man responsible for this misery is the province's governor. この苦境の直接責任は州知事にある. 4 ADV 副詞 **Immediately** is used to emphasize that something comes next, or is next to something else. 一の後に，すぐ近くに [ADV prep/adj] □ They wish to begin immediately after dinner. 彼らは夕食後すぐに始めたがっている.

im|mense /ɪmɛns/ ADJ 形容詞 If you describe something as **immense**, you mean that it is extremely large or great. 巨大な，素晴らしい □ ...an immense cloud of smoke. もうもうたる煙

im|mense|ly /ɪmɛnsli/ ADV 副詞 You use **immensely** to emphasize the degree or extent of a quality, feeling, or process. 非常に [EMPHASIS 強調] □ I enjoyed this movie immensely. この映画は非常に面白かった.

im|merse /ɪmɜrs/ (immerses, immersing, immersed) 1 V-T 他動詞 If you **immerse** yourself in something that you are doing, you become completely involved in it. 没頭する 2 □ Their commitments do not permit them to immerse themselves in current affairs as fully as they might wish. 彼らは契約のせいで，これらの件に思うほど完全には専念できない. ●**im|mersed** ADJ 形容詞 [v-link ADJ 'in' n] 没頭して □ He's really becoming immersed in his work. 彼は仕事に熱中し始めているところだ. 2 V-T 他動詞 If something **is immersed** in a liquid, someone puts it into the liquid so that it is completely covered. （液体に）浸す，沈める [usu passive] □ The electrodes are immersed in liquid. それらの電極が液体に浸されている.

Word Link *migr ≈ moving, changing : emigrant, immigrant, migrant*

im|mi|grant /ɪmɪgrənt/ (immigrants) N-COUNT 可算名詞 An **immigrant** is a person who has come to live in a country from some other country. Compare **emigrant**. （外国からの）移民 □ ...illegal immigrants. 密入国者たち → see **culture**

im|mi|gra|tion /ɪmɪgreɪʃ³n/ 1 N-UNCOUNT 不可算名詞 **Immigration** is the coming of people into a country in order to live and work there. （外国からの）移住 □ The government has decided to tighten its immigration policy. 政府は移民政策を厳しくすることを決定した. 2 N-UNCOUNT 不可算名詞 **Immigration** or **immigration control** is the place at a port, airport, or international border where officials check the passports of people who wish to come into the country. 出入国管理 □ First, you have to go through immigration and customs. 最初にあなたは入国管理と税関を通らないといけません.

im|mi|nent /ɪmɪnənt/ ADJ 形容詞 If you say that something is **imminent**, especially something unpleasant, you mean it is almost certain to happen very soon. （嫌な事が）目前に迫った □ There appeared no imminent danger. 差し迫った危険はなさそうだった.

im|mo|bi|liz|er /ɪmoʊbɪlaɪzər/ (immobilizers) N-COUNT 可算名詞 An **immobilizer** is a device on a car that prevents it from

starting unless a special key is used, so that no one can steal the car. エンジン始動ロック

im|mor|al /ɪmɒrəl/ ADJ 形容詞 If you describe someone or their behavior as **immoral**, you believe that their behavior is morally wrong. 不道徳な [DISAPPROVAL 不賛成] ❏...*those who think that birth control and abortion are immoral.* 産児制限や妊娠中絶が道徳に反すると考える人たち

Word Link   mort ≈ death : im**mortal**, **mortify**, **mortuary**

im|mor|tal /ɪmɔrtəl/ (**immortals**) ❶ ADJ 形容詞 Someone or something that is **immortal** is famous and likely to be remembered for a long time. (人や作品が) 不朽の ❏...*Wuthering Heights, Emily Bronte's immortal love story.* エミリー・ブロンテの不朽の恋愛小説である『嵐が丘』● N-COUNT 可算名詞 An **immortal** is someone who will be remembered for a long time. 名声不朽の人 ❏...*the players considered to be the immortals of the game.* そのゲームで不朽の名声を残すであろう選手たち ● **im|mor|tal|ity** /ɪmɔrtælɪti/ N-UNCOUNT 不可算名詞 不朽の名声 ❏*Some people want to achieve immortality through their works.* ある人たちは彼らの作品を通して永遠の名声を残したいと願う. ❷ ADJ 形容詞 Someone or something that is **immortal** will live or last forever and never die or be destroyed. 不死身の ❏*The pharaohs, after all, were considered gods and therefore immortal.* ファラオたちはつまるところ, 神とみなされ, それゆえに不死身であると考えられていた. ● N-COUNT 可算名詞 An **immortal** is an immortal being. 不死身の存在 ❏...*porcelain figurines of the Chinese immortals.* 中国の不死身の存在である陶器の人形 ● **im|mor|tal|ity** N-UNCOUNT 不可算名詞 不死 ❏*The Greeks accepted belief in the immortality of the soul.* ギリシャ人たちは, 魂は死なないという考えを受け入れていた. ❸ ADJ 形容詞 [ADJ n] If you refer to someone's **immortal** words, you mean that what they said is well-known, and you are usually about to quote it. (言葉などが) 有名な ❏*Everyone knows Teddy Roosevelt's immortal words, "Speak softly and carry a big stick."* 誰もがテディー・ルーズベルトの「こん棒を手に, 穏やかに話せ」という, 不朽の言葉を知っている.

im|mor|tal|ize /ɪmɔrtəlaɪz/ (**immortalizes, immortalizing, immortalized**) V-T 他動詞 If someone or something is **immortalized** in a story, movie, or work of art, they appear in it, and will be remembered for a long time. (名声などを) 不朽のものにする [WRITTEN 書き言葉] ❏*His original interior design is immortalized in at least seven movies and television shows.* 彼独自のインテリア・デザインは少なくとも7つの映画やテレビ番組に使われ, 不朽の名作となっている.

im|mune /ɪmyun/ ❶ ADJ 形容詞 If you are **immune** to a particular disease, you cannot be affected by it. (病気に) 免疫のある [v-link ADJ] ❏*About 93 percent of U.S. residents are immune to measles either because they were vaccinated or they had the disease as a child.* 米国在住者の約93パーセントが, はしかに対し予防接種を受けたか, 子供の時にかかったかで免疫を持っている. ● **im|mun|ity** /ɪmyunɪti/ N-UNCOUNT 不可算名詞 免疫 ❏*Birds in outside cages develop immunity to airborne bacteria.* かごの外の鳥たちは空中のバクテリアに対し免疫を持つようになる. ❷ ADJ 形容詞 [v-link ADJ] If you are **immune to** something that happens or is done, you are not affected by it. 影響されていない ❏*Higher education is no longer immune to state budget cuts.* 高等教育は, もはや国家予算の削減に影響されない. ❸ ADJ 形容詞 Someone or something that is **immune from** a particular process or situation is able to escape it. 免れて [v-link ADJ] ❏*People with diplomatic passports are immune from criminal prosecution.* 外交旅券を持つ者は刑事訴追を免除される. ● **im|mun|ity** N-UNCOUNT 不可算名詞 免除 ❏*The police are offering immunity to witnesses who help identify the murderers.* 警察は殺人犯人の特定に協力した証人に訴追免除を提示している.

Word Partnership   immune は次の語句と使われる :

N.   immune **disorder**, immune **response** ❶
     immune **from attack**, immune **from prosecution** ❸

im|mune sys|tem (**immune systems**) N-COUNT 可算名詞 Your **immune system** consists of all the organs and processes in your body that protect you from illness and infection. 免疫システム ❏*His immune system completely broke down and he became very ill.* 免疫システムが完全に崩壊し, 彼はひどい病気になった.

im|mun|ize /ɪmyənaɪz/ (**immunizes, immunizing, immunized**) V-T 他動詞 If people or animals **are immunized**, they are made immune to a particular disease, often by being given an injection. 免疫性を与える [usu passive] ❏*We should require that every student is immunized against hepatitis B.* 全学生はB型肝炎の予防接種を受けるよう求めるべきだ. ❏*The monkeys used in these experiments had previously been immunized with a vaccine made from killed infected cells.* その研究に使われた猿たちは事前に, 不活性化された感染細胞から作られたワクチンの予防接種を受けていた. ● **im|mun|iza|tion** /ɪmyənaɪzeɪʃən/ (**immunizations**) N-VAR 可変性名詞 予防接種 ❏...*universal immunization against childhood diseases.* 小児疾患に対する世界共通の予防接種

im|pact (**impacts, impacting, impacted**)

The noun is pronounced /ɪmpækt/. The verb is pronounced /ɪmpækt/ or /ɪmpækt/.

名詞は /ɪmpækt/ と発音される. 動詞は /ɪmpækt/ または /ɪmpækt/ と発音される.

❶ N-COUNT 可算名詞 The **impact** that something has **on** a situation, process, or person is a sudden and powerful effect that it has on them. 影響 ❏*They say they expect the meeting to have a marked impact on the future of the country.* 彼らはその会議が国の将来に大きな影響を持つことを予期しているとのことだ. ❷ N-VAR 可変性名詞 An **impact** is the action of one object hitting another, or the force with which one object hits another. 衝突, 衝撃 ❏*The plane is destroyed, a complete wreck: the pilot must have died on impact.* その飛行機は破壊され, まったくの残骸となっている. パイロットは衝突で死亡したに違いない. ❸ V-T/V-I 他動詞/自動詞 To **impact** a situation, process, or person means to affect them. 影響を及ぼす ❏*Such schemes mean little unless they impact people.* そんな計画は人々に影響を与えない限り, ほとんど意味がない. ❹ V-T/V-I 他動詞/自動詞 If one object **impacts** on another, it hits it with great force. 激突する [FORMAL 形式ばった] ❏...*the sharp tinkle of metal impacting on stone.* 金属が石にぶつかる鋭いベルのような音
→ see **crash**

Word Partnership   impact は次の語句と使われる :

ADJ.   **historical** impact, **important** impact ❶
V.   **have an** impact, **make an** impact ❶
     die on impact ❷
PREP.   **on** impact ❷

im|pair /ɪmpɛər/ (**impairs, impairing, impaired**) V-T 他動詞 If something **impairs** something such as an ability or the way something works, it damages it or makes it worse. 悪化させる [FORMAL 形式ばった] ❏*Consumption of alcohol impairs your ability to drive a car or operate machinery.* 飲酒はあなたが車を運転したり機械を操作する能力を低下させる. ● **im|paired** ADJ 形容詞 損なわれた, 悪化した ❏*The blast left him with permanently impaired hearing.* その爆発によって彼は永久に聴力を失った.

im|pair|ment /ɪmpɛərmənt/ (**impairments**) N-VAR 可変性名詞 If someone has an **impairment**, they have a condition that prevents their eyes, ears, limbs or brain from working properly. (身体の) 機能障害 ❏*He has a visual impairment in the right eye.* 彼は右目に視力障害がある.
→ see **disability**

im|part /ɪmpɑrt/ (**imparts, imparting, imparted**) ❶ V-T 他動詞 If you **impart** information to people, you tell it to them. (情報などを) 伝える [FORMAL 形式ばった] ❏*The ability to impart knowledge and command respect is the essential qualification for teachers.* 知識を授け, 尊敬を勝ち取る能力は教師にとって欠かせない資質だ. ❷ V-T 他動詞 To **impart** a particular quality to something means to give it that quality. 添える [FORMAL 形式ばった] ❏*She managed to impart great elegance to the unpretentious dress she was wearing.* 彼女は自分の着ている控えめなドレスに, 素晴らしい優雅さを加えていた.

im|par|tial /ɪmpɑrʃəl/ ADJ 形容詞 Someone who is **impartial** is not directly involved in a particular situation, and is therefore able to give a fair opinion or decision about it. 公平な, 偏らない ❏*Career counselors offer impartial advice, guidance and information to all pupils.* 職業相談員たちはすべての学生に公平なアドバイスや指導, また情報提供を行っている. ● **im|par|ti|al|ity** /ɪmpɑrʃiælɪti/ N-UNCOUNT 不可算名詞 公平さ ❏...*a justice system lacking impartiality by democratic standards.* 民主主義の基準からすると公平さに欠ける司法制度 ● **im|par|tial|ly** ADV 副詞 [ADV with v] 公平に ❏*He has vowed to oversee the elections impartially.* 彼は選挙を公平に監督することを誓っている.

im|passe /ɪmpæs/ N-SING 単数名詞 If people are in a difficult position in which it is impossible to make any progress, you can refer to the situation as an **impasse**. 行き詰まり ❏*The company says it has reached an impasse in negotiations with the union.* 会社側は労働組合との交渉が行き詰まったと伝えている.

im|pas|sioned /ɪmpæʃənd/ ADJ 形容詞 An **impassioned** speech or piece of writing is one in which someone expresses their strong feelings about an issue in a forceful way. 熱烈な [WRITTEN 書き言葉] ❏*He made an impassioned appeal for peace.* 彼は熱烈に平和を訴えた.

im|pas|sive /ɪmpæsɪv/ ADJ 形容詞 If someone is **impassive** or their face is **impassive**, they are not showing any emotion. 感情を表に表さない, 無表情な [WRITTEN 書き言葉] ❏*He searched Hill's impassive face for some indication that he understood.* 彼はヒルの無表情な顔の中に, 彼が理解したことを示す何かを探そうとした. ● **im|pas|sive|ly** ADV 副詞 [ADV with v] 無表情に, 冷静に ❏*The lawyer looked impassively at him and said nothing.* 弁護士は無表情に彼を見つめ, 何も言わなかった.

im|pa|tient /ɪmpeɪʃ³nt/ ADJ 形容詞 If you are **impatient**, you are annoyed because you have to wait too long for something. しびれを切らした [v-link ADJ] ❏ Investors are growing impatient with promises of improved earnings. 投資家たちは配当増額の約束にだんだんしびれを切らし始めている. ● **im|pa|tient|ly** ADV 副詞 [ADV with v] 我慢できずに ❏ People have been waiting impatiently for a chance to improve the situation. 人々は状況改善の機会をしびれを切らしながら待っている. ● **im|pa|tience** /ɪmpeɪʃ³ns/ N-UNCOUNT 不可算名詞 せっかち, 焦燥 ❏ There is considerable impatience with the slow pace of political change. ゆっくりとした政変のペースにかなり焦燥がつのっている. ❷ ADJ 形容詞 If you are **impatient**, you are easily irritated by things. いらいらした ❏ Beware of being too impatient with others. 他の人に対していらいらしすぎないように気を付けて. ● **im|pa|tient|ly** ADV 副詞 [ADV with v] いらいらして ❏ "Come on, David," Harry said impatiently. 「急いで, デイビッド」とハリーがいらいらして言った. ● **im|pa|tience** N-UNCOUNT 不可算名詞 いらだち ❏ There was a hint of impatience in his voice. 彼の口調が少しいらだっていた. ❸ ADJ 形容詞 [v-link ADJ] If you are **impatient** to do something or **impatient for** something to happen, you are eager to do it or for it to happen and do not want to wait. しきりにーしたがって ❏ He didn't want to tell Mr. Morrisson why he was impatient to get home. 彼はモリソン氏に自分が家へ帰りたがっている理由を言いたくなかった. ● **im|pa|tience** N-UNCOUNT 不可算名詞 切望 ❏ She showed impatience to continue the climb. 彼女は登山を続けたい気持ちを示した.

im|pec|cable /ɪmpɛkəb³l/ ADJ 形容詞 If you describe something such as someone's behavior or appearance as **impeccable**, you are emphasizing that it is perfect and has no faults. 非の打ちどころがない, 申し分のない [EMPHASIS 強調] ❏ She had impeccable taste in clothes. 彼女の服のセンスは非の打ちどころがなかった. ● **im|pec|cably** /ɪmpɛkəbli/ ADV 副詞 申し分なく, かんぺきに ❏ He was charming, considerate and impeccably mannered. 彼は魅力的で, 思いやり深く, 礼儀作法はかんぺきだった.

im|pede /ɪmpid/ (**impedes, impeding, impeded**) V-T 他動詞 If you **impede** someone or something, you make their movement, development, or progress difficult. (動きや発達などを) 妨げる [FORMAL 形式ばった] ❏ Debris and fallen rock are impeding the progress of the rescue workers. がれきや落下した岩が救助隊の進行を遅らせている.

im|pedi|ment /ɪmpɛdɪmənt/ (**impediments**) ❶ N-COUNT 可算名詞 Something that is an **impediment** to a person or thing makes their movement, development, or progress difficult. 妨害 [FORMAL 形式ばった] ❏ He was satisfied that there was no legal impediment to the marriage. 彼はその結婚への法的な障害がまったくないことに満足した. ❷ N-COUNT 可算名詞 Someone who has a speech **impediment** has a disability that makes speaking difficult. (言語の) 障害 ❏ John's slight speech impediment made it difficult for his mother to understand him. ジョンの軽い言語障害のため彼女の母親は彼を理解するのが難しかった.

im|pend|ing /ɪmpɛndɪŋ/ ADJ 形容詞 An **impending** event is one that is going to happen very soon. 差し迫った [FORMAL 形式ばった] [ADJ n] ❏ On the morning of the expedition I awoke with a feeling of impending disaster. 遠征の朝, わたしは今にも大惨事が起こりそうな予感で目が覚めた.

im|pen|etrable /ɪmpɛnɪtrəb³l/ ❶ ADJ 形容詞 If you describe something such as a barrier or a forest as **impenetrable**, you mean that it is impossible or very difficult to get through. 通り抜けられない ❏ ...the Caucasus range, an almost impenetrable barrier between Europe and Asia. ヨーロッパとアジアの間のほとんど人が足を踏み込めない境界, コーカサス山脈. ❷ ADJ 形容詞 If you describe something such as a book or a theory as **impenetrable**, you are emphasizing that it is impossible or very difficult to understand. 不可解な, 難解な [EMPHASIS 強調] ❏ His philosophical work is notoriously impenetrable. 彼の哲学作品は, 難しいことで有名だ.

im|pera|tive /ɪmpɛrətɪv/ (**imperatives**) ❶ ADJ 形容詞 If it is **imperative** that something be done, that thing is extremely important and must be done. 欠かせない, 必須の [FORMAL 形式ばった] ❏ It was imperative that he act as naturally as possible. 彼ができるだけ自然にふるまうことがとても重要だった. ❷ N-COUNT 可算名詞 An **imperative** is something that is extremely important and must be done. 重要なすべきこと, 義務 [FORMAL 形式ばった] ❏ The most important political imperative is to limit the number of U.S. casualties. 国家の最重要課題は, 米国民の犠牲者数を抑えることだ. ❸ N-SING 単数名詞 In grammar, a clause that is in **the imperative**, or in **the imperative** mood, contains the base form of a verb and usually has no subject. Examples are "Go away" and "Please be careful." Clauses of this kind are typically used to tell someone to do something. 命令法 ❹ N-COUNT 可算名詞 An **imperative** is a verb in the base form that is used, usually without a subject, in an imperative clause. 動詞の命令形

Word Partnership _imperative_ は次の語句と使われる:

ADV.	**absolutely** imperative ❶
N.	imperative **need** ❶
ADJ.	**economic/political** imperative, **moral** imperative ❷

im|per|fect /ɪmpɜrfɪkt/ ADJ 形容詞 Something that is **imperfect** has faults and is not exactly as you would like it to be. 不完全な [FORMAL 形式ばった] ❏ We live in an imperfect world. 私たちは不完全な世界に住んでいる.

im|per|fec|tion /ɪmpərfɛkʃ³n/ (**imperfections**) ❶ N-VAR 可変性名詞 An **imperfection in** someone or something is a fault, weakness, or undesirable feature that they have. 不完全, 欠点 ❏ He concedes that there are imperfections in the socialist system. 彼は社会主義体制に欠点があることを認めている. ❷ N-COUNT 可算名詞 An **imperfection in** something is a small mark or damaged area that may spoil its appearance. 欠陥, 傷 ❏ Optical scanners ensure that imperfections in the cloth are located and removed. オプティカルスキャナによって, 布地の傷が見つけられ取り除かれていることを確実にする.

im|perial /ɪmpɪəriəl/ ❶ ADJ 形容詞 **Imperial** is used to refer to things or people that are or were connected with an empire. 帝国の, 皇帝の [ADJ n] ❏ ...the Imperial Palace in Tokyo. 東京の皇居. ❷ ADJ 形容詞 The **imperial** system of measurement uses inches, feet, yards and miles to measure length, ounces and pounds to measure weight, and pints, quarts and gallons to measure volume. ヤード・ポンド法では長さの測定にインチ, フィート, ヤード, マイルを使用し, 重さの測定にオンス, ポンドを用い, 容積の測定にパイント, クオート, ガロンを使用する. [ADJ n]

im|peri|al|ism /ɪmpɪəriəlɪzəm/ N-UNCOUNT 不可算名詞 **Imperialism** is a system in which a rich and powerful country controls other countries, or a desire for control over other countries. 帝国主義 ❏ ...nations or groups which have been victims of imperialism. 帝国主義の犠牲になった国家と集団

im|peri|al|ist /ɪmpɪəriəlɪst/ (**imperialists**) ADJ 形容詞 **Imperialist** means relating to or based on imperialism. 帝国主義の ❏ The developed nations have all benefited from their imperialist exploitation. 先進国は全て帝国主義による搾取の恩恵を受けてきた. ● N-COUNT 可算名詞 An **imperialist** is someone who has imperialist views. 帝国主義者 ❏ He claims that imperialists are trying to re-establish colonial rule in the country. 帝国主義者はその国で植民地主義の支配を復旧させようとしていると, 彼は主張する.

im|per|son|al /ɪmpɜrsən³l/ ❶ ADJ 形容詞 If you describe a place, organization, or activity as **impersonal**, you mean that it is not very friendly and makes you feel unimportant because it involves or is used by a large number of people. 人間的な感情に欠けた [DISAPPROVAL 不賛成] ❏ Before then many children were cared for in large impersonal orphanages. それ以前は多くの子供達が人間的な温かさに欠けた大きな孤児院で育てられた. ❷ ADJ 形容詞 If you describe someone's behavior as **impersonal**, you mean that they do not show any emotion about the person they are dealing with. 個人の感情を交えない ❏ We must be as impersonal as a surgeon with his knife. 我々はメスを持つ外科医と同じくらい客観的になる必要がある. ❸ ADJ 形容詞 An **impersonal** room or statistic does not give any information about the character of the person to whom it belongs or relates. 個性のない ❏ The rest of the room was neat and impersonal. 残りの部屋はきちんと整頓され, 個性に欠けていた.

im|per|son|ate /ɪmpɜrsəneɪt/ (**impersonates, impersonating, impersonated**) V-T 他動詞 If someone **impersonates** a person, they pretend to be that person, either to deceive people or to make people laugh. なりすます ❏ He was returned to prison in 1977 for impersonating a police officer. 彼は警官になりすましたかどで1977年に刑務所に連れ戻された. ● **im|per|sona|tion** /ɪmpɜrsəneɪʃ³n/ (**impersonations**) N-COUNT 可算名詞 物まねをすること ❏ She excelled at impersonations of his teachers, which provided great amusement for him. 彼女は彼の教師の物まねがとても上手で, 彼はそれをとてもおもしろがった.

im|per|ti|nent /ɪmpɜrt³nənt/ ADJ 形容詞 If someone talks or behaves in a rather impolite and disrespectful way, you can say that they are being **impertinent**. でしゃばりの ❏ Would it be impertinent to ask where exactly you were? あなたの正確な居場所を聞くのは失礼でしょうか.

im|petus /ɪmpɪtəs/ N-UNCOUNT 不可算名詞 Something that gives a process **impetus** or an **impetus** makes it happen or progress more quickly. 衝動 [also 'a' N, oft N 'for' n] ❏ The impetus for change came from lawyers. 変化を推進したのは弁護士だった.

im|plac|able /ɪmplækəb³l/ ADJ 形容詞 If you say that someone is **implacable**, you mean that they have very strong feelings of hostility or disapproval that nobody can change. 冷酷無情な ❏ ...the threat of invasion by a ruthless and implacable enemy. 残酷で無慈悲な敵が侵略する恐れ ● **im|plac|ably** ADV 副詞 執念深く ❏ ...two implacably hostile groups. 執念深く敵対的な2つのグループ

im|plant (implants, implanting, implanted)

> The verb is pronounced /ɪmplǽnt/. The noun is pronounced /ɪ́mplænt/.
>
> 動詞は /ɪmplǽnt/ と発音される。名詞は /ɪ́mplænt/ と発音される。

1 V-T 他動詞 To **implant** something into a person's body means to put it there, usually by means of a medical operation. 移植する □ Two days later, they implanted the fertilized eggs back inside me. 彼らは2日後に受精卵を私の子宮壁に着床させた。**2** N-COUNT 可算名詞 An **implant** is something that is implanted into a person's body. インプラント □ They felt a woman had a right to choose to have a breast implant. 彼らは女性には豊胸手術を受ける権利があると考えた。**3** V-I 自動詞 When an egg or embryo **implants** in the womb, it becomes established there and can then develop. 着床する □ Non-identical twins are the result of two fertilized eggs implanting in the uterus at the same time. 非一卵性双生児は2つの受精卵が子宮壁に着床した決果生まれる。**4** V-T 他動詞 If you **implant** an idea or attitude **in** people, you make it become accepted or believed. 吹き込む □ The diagram implanted a dangerous prejudice firmly in the minds of countless economics students. その図式は無数の経済学部の学生の心に危険な偏見をしっかりと吹き込んだ。

im|ple|ment (implements, implementing, implemented)

> The verb is pronounced /ɪ́mplɪmɛnt/ or /ɪ́mplɪmənt/. The noun is pronounced /ɪ́mplɪmənt/.
>
> 動詞は /ɪ́mplɪmɛnt/ または /ɪ́mplɪmənt/ と発音される。名詞は /ɪ́mplɪmənt/ と発音される。

1 V-T 他動詞 If you **implement** something such as a plan, you ensure that what has been planned is done. 実施させる □ The government promised to implement a new system to control financial loan institutions. 政府は金融機関を管理するための新制度を導入すると約束した。● **im|ple|men|ta|tion** /ɪ̀mplɪmɛntéɪʃᵊn, -mən-/ N-UNCOUNT 不可算名詞 実施すること □ Very little has been achieved in the implementation of the peace agreement signed last January. 昨年1月に署名された和平条約はほとんど実施されていない。**2** N-COUNT 可算名詞 An **implement** is a tool or other piece of equipment. 道具 [FORMAL 形式ばった] □ ...writing implements. 筆記用具

Thesaurus implement また次を参照：

V. bring about, carry out, execute, fulfill **1**

im|pli|cate /ɪ́mplɪkeɪt/ (implicates, implicating, implicated) V-T 他動詞 To **implicate** someone means to show or claim that they were involved in something wrong or criminal. 巻き込む □ He was obliged to resign when one of his own aides was implicated in a financial scandal. 彼は助手が金融スキャンダルに巻き込まれた際に辞任を余儀なくされた。● **im|pli|ca|tion** N-UNCOUNT 不可算名詞 掛かりあい □ Implication in a murder finally brought him to the gallows. 殺人に荷担したことで彼はついに絞首刑に処せられた。

im|pli|ca|tion /ɪ̀mplɪkéɪʃᵊn/ (implications) **1** N-COUNT 可算名詞 The **implications** of something are the things that are likely to happen as a result. 含み □ The Attorney General was aware of the political implications of his decision to prosecute. 法務長官は起訴の決断が政治的に何を意味するのかを知っていた。**2** N-COUNT 可算名詞 The **implication** of a statement, event, or situation is what it implies or suggests is the case. 言外の意味 □ The implication was obvious: vote for us or it will be very embarrassing for you. 我々に投票しなさい、さもないと非常に厄介なことになる。● PHRASE 句 If you say that something is the case **by implication**, you mean that a statement, event, or situation implies that it is the case. 暗に □ Now his authority and, by implication, that of the whole management team are under threat as never before. 今や彼の権限と、含蓄的には経営陣全体の権限がかつてないほど脅かされている。**3** → see also **implicate**

Word Partnership implication は次の語句と使われる：

ADJ. **clear** implication, **important** implication, **obvious** implication **2**

im|plic|it /ɪmplɪ́sɪt/ **1** ADJ 形容詞 Something that is **implicit** is expressed in an indirect way. 暗黙の □ ...an implicit warning to the Moroccans not to continue or repeat the military actions they began a week ago. モロッコが1週間前に開始した軍隊活動を継続しないよう暗黙のうちに警告すること ● **im|plic|it|ly** ADV 副詞 [ADV with v] 暗黙のうちに □ The jury implicitly criticized the government by their verdict. 陪審員はその判決で政府を暗黙のうちに批判した。**2** ADJ 形容詞 If a quality or element is **implicit in** something, it is involved in it or is shown by it. 事実上含まれた [FORMAL 形式ばった] [v-link ADJ 'in' n] □ Trust is implicit in the system. 信頼はその制度に内在する。**3** ADJ 形容詞 If you say that someone has an **implicit** belief or faith in something, you mean that they have complete faith in it and no doubts at all. 絶対の □ He had implicit faith in the noble intentions

of the Emperor. 彼は皇帝の崇高な心構えに絶対の信頼を寄せていた。● **im|plic|it|ly** ADV 副詞 [ADV after v] 絶対的に □ I trust him implicitly. 私は彼を絶対的に信頼する。

im|plore /ɪmplɔ́r/ (implores, imploring, implored) V-T 他動詞 If you **implore** someone to do something, you ask them to do it in a forceful, emotional way. 懇願する □ We will implore both parties to stay at the negotiating table. 我々は交渉の場にとどまるよう両当事者に懇願するつもりだ。

im|ply /ɪmplάɪ/ (implies, implying, implied) **1** V-T 他動詞 If you **imply that** something is the case, you say something that indicates that it is the case in an indirect way. ほのめかす □ "Are you implying that I have something to do with those attacks?" she asked coldly. 「あなたは私がそうした攻撃に関与しているとでも言いたいの」と彼女は冷ややかに聞いた。**2** V-T 他動詞 If an event or situation **implies** that something is the case, it makes you think that it is the case. 意味する □ Exports in June rose 1.5%, implying that the economy was stronger than many investors had realized. 6月の輸出は1.5%増加したが、これは経済は多くの投資家が考えるよりも堅実なことを意味していた。

> Do not confuse **imply** and **infer**. If you **imply** that something is the case, you suggest that it is the case without actually saying so. □ Rose's lawyer implied that he had married her for her money. If you **infer** that something is the case, you decide that it must be the case because of what you know, but without actually being told. □ From this simple statement I could infer a lot about his wife. Note that some English speakers use **infer** with the same meaning as **imply**, but this is considered incorrect by careful speakers.

Thesaurus imply また次を参照：

v. hint, insinuate, point to, suggest **1 2**

Word Partnership imply は次の語句と使われる：

V. **not mean to** imply **1**
seem to imply **2**
ADV. **not necessarily** imply **1 2**

im|po|lite /ɪ̀mpəláɪt/ ADJ 形容詞 If you say that someone is **impolite**, you mean that they are rather rude and do not have good manners. 無礼な □ The count acknowledged the two newcomers as briefly as was possible without being impolite. 伯爵は無礼にならない程度にできるだけ手短に2人の新来者にあいさつした。

Thesaurus impolite また次を参照：

ADJ. ill-mannered, rude, ungracious; (ant.) courteous, polite

Word Link port ≈ carrying : ex**port**, im**port**, **port**able

im|port (imports, importing, imported)

> The verb is pronounced /ɪmpɔ́rt/ or /ɪ́mpɔrt/. The noun is pronounced /ɪ́mpɔrt/.
>
> 動詞は /ɪmpɔ́rt/ または /ɪ́mpɔrt/ と発音される。名詞は /ɪ́mpɔrt/ と発音される。

1 V-T/V-I 他動詞/自動詞 To **import** products or raw materials means to buy them from another country for use in your own country. 輸入する □ Rich countries benefited from importing Indonesia's timber. 先進国はインドネシア産の木材輸入の恩恵を受けた。□ To import from Russia, a Ukrainian firm needs Russian roubles. ロシアから輸入するためにはウクライナ企業にはルーブルが必要だ。● N-UNCOUNT 不可算名詞 **Import** is also a noun. 輸入 [also N in pl] □ Germany, however, insists on restrictions on the import of Polish coal. だがドイツはポーランド産の石炭の輸入を制限することを主張している。● **im|por|ta|tion** /ɪ̀mpɔrtéɪʃᵊn/ N-UNCOUNT 不可算名詞 □ ...restrictions concerning the importation of birds. 鳥類の輸入に関する制限 **2** N-COUNT 可算名詞 **Imports** are products or raw materials bought from another country for use in your own country. 輸入品 □ ...cheap imports from other countries. 他の諸国からの安い輸入品 **3** N-UNCOUNT 不可算名詞 The **import** of something is its importance. 重要性 [FORMAL 形式ばった] □ Such arguments are of little import. そうした論議はほとんど重要ではない。**4** V-T 他動詞 If you **import** files or information into one type of software from another type, you open them in a format that can be used in the new software. インポート [COMPUTING コンピューティング] □ Users can import files made in other packages. 利用者は他のソフトで作成したファイルをインポートできる。

im|por|tance /ɪmpɔ́rtᵊns/ **1** N-UNCOUNT 不可算名詞 The **importance** of something is its quality of being significant, valued, or necessary in a particular situation. 重要性 □ China has been stressing the importance of its ties with third world countries. 中国は第三世界諸国とのつながりの重要性を強調していた。**2** N-UNCOUNT

不可算名詞 **Importance** means having influence, power, or status. 重要な地位 ❑*Obviously a man of his importance is going to be missed.* 明らかに彼のような重要人物はいないのを残念がられるだろう.

Word Partnership
importance は次の語句と使われる:

ADJ.	**critical** importance, **enormous** importance, **growing/increasing** importance, **utmost** importance ■
V.	**place less/more** importance on *something*, **recognize** the importance, **understand** the importance ■
N.	**self**-importance, **sense of** importance ②

im|por|tant /ɪmpɔːrtʰnt/ ■ ADJ 形容詞 Something that is **important** is very significant, is highly valued, or is necessary. 重要な ❑*The most important thing in my life was my career.* 私の人生で最も重要なのは仕事だった. ❑*It's important to answer her questions as honestly as you can.* 彼女の質問にできるだけ正直に答えることが重要だ. ● **im|por|tant|ly** ADV 副詞 重要なことに ❑*I was hungry, and, more importantly, my children were hungry.* 私は空腹だったが, もっと重要なことに子供達は腹をすかせていた. ② ADJ 形容詞 Someone who is **important** has influence or power within a society or a particular group. 大きな影響力のある ❑*...an important figure in the media world.* メディア界の重要人物

You do not use **important** to say that an amount or quantity is very large. Instead, you use words such as **large**, **considerable**, or **substantial**. ❑*...a large sum of money.* ❑*...a man with considerable influence...* ❑*The armed forces face substantial cuts.*

Thesaurus
important また次を参照:

| ADJ. | critical, essential, principal, significant; (ant.) unimportant ■ distinguished, high-ranking ② |

im|port|er /ɪmpɔːrtər/ (**importers**) N-COUNT 可算名詞 An **importer** is a country, company, or person that buys goods from another country for use in their own country. 輸入国 ❑*Japan is the biggest importer of US beef.* 日本は米国産牛肉の最大の輸入国である.

im|pose /ɪmpouz/ (**imposes, imposing, imposed**) ■ V-T 他動詞 If you **impose** something **on** people, you use your authority to force them to accept it. 課する ❑*Fines are imposed on retailers who sell tobacco to minors.* 年少者にタバコを売る小売業者には罰金が課される. ❑*A third of companies reviewing pay since last August have imposed a pay freeze of up to a year.* 昨年の8月以降, 賃金の再考を行なう企業の3分の1が最高1年間の賃金凍結を強いた. ● **im|po|si|tion** /ɪmpəzɪʃ°n/ N-UNCOUNT 不可算名詞 賦課 ❑*...the imposition of sanctions against Pakistan.* パキスタンに対する経済制裁の賦課 ② V-T 他動詞 If you **impose** your opinions or beliefs **on** other people, you try and make people accept them as a rule or as a model to copy. 押し付ける ❑*Parents should beware of imposing their own tastes on their children.* 親は自分の好みを子供に押し付けないように気をつける必要がある. ③ V-T 他動詞 If something **imposes** strain, pressure, or suffering **on** someone, it causes them to experience it. 負わせる ❑*The filming imposed an additional strain on her.* 撮影は彼女に追加の重圧を与えた. ④ V-I 自動詞 If someone **imposes on** you, they unreasonably expect you to do something for them which you do not want to do. 無理強いする ❑*I was afraid you'd feel we were imposing on you.* 私は私達があなたに無理強いしていると思われたくなかった. ● **im|po|si|tion** N-COUNT 可算名詞 厚かましい言動 ❑*I know this is an imposition. But please hear me out.* これは随分厚かましいお願いだとは思いますが, 最後まで聞いてください. ⑤ V-T 他動詞 If someone **imposes themselves on** you, they force you to accept their company although you may not want to. 押しかける ❑*I didn't want to impose myself on my married friends.* 私は結婚した友人の所に押しかけたくはなかった.

Word Partnership
impose は次の語句と使われる:

| N. | impose **a fine**, impose **limits**, impose **order**, impose **a penalty**, impose **restrictions**, impose **sanctions**, impose **a tax** |

im|pos|ing /ɪmpouzɪŋ/ ADJ 形容詞 If you describe someone or something as **imposing**, you mean that they have an impressive appearance or manner. たいへん印象的な ❑*He was an imposing man.* 彼は人目をひく男だった.

Word Link
im ≈ not : imbalance, immature, impossible

im|pos|sible /ɪmpɒsɪb°l/ ■ ADJ 形容詞 Something that is **impossible** cannot be done or cannot happen. 不可能な ❑*It was impossible for anyone to get in because no one knew the password.* パスワードを知らなかったので誰も入ることはできなかった. ❑*He thinks the tax is impossible to administer.* 彼は税金を管理するのは不可能だと考えている. ● N-SING 単数名詞 The **impossible** is something that is

impossible. 不可能なこと ❑*They were expected to do the impossible.* 彼らは不可能なことをすることを求められていた. ● **im|pos|sibly** ADV 副詞 [ADV adj] 信じがたいほど ❑*Mathematical physics is an almost impossibly difficult subject.* 数理物理学はほとんど信じがたいほど難しい科目である. ● **im|pos|sibil|ity** /ɪmpɒsɪbɪliti/ (**impossibilities**) N-VAR 可変性名詞 不可能なこと ❑*...the impossibility of knowing absolute truth.* 完全な真実を知ることの不可能性 ② ADJ 形容詞 [ADJ n] An **impossible** situation or an **impossible** position is one that is very difficult to deal with. 耐えられない ❑*I think he was in an impossible position.* 彼は我慢のならない立場だったと, 私は思う. ③ ADJ 形容詞 If you describe someone as **impossible**, you are annoyed that their bad behavior or strong views make them difficult to deal with. どうしようもない [DISAPPROVAL 不賛成] ❑*The woman is impossible, thought Francesca.* あの女は手に負えないと, フランチェスカは思った.

Word Partnership
impossible は次の語句と使われる:

V.	impossible **to describe**, impossible **to find**, impossible **to ignore**, impossible **to prove**, impossible **to say/tell, seem** impossible ■
ADV.	**absolutely** impossible, **almost** impossible, **nearly** impossible ■ ②
N.	**an** impossible **task** ■ ②

im|po|tence /ɪmpətəns/ ■ N-UNCOUNT 不可算名詞 **Impotence** is a lack of power to influence people or events. 無力 ❑*...a sense of impotence in the face of deplorable events.* 嘆かわしい出来事の前での無力感 ② N-UNCOUNT 不可算名詞 **Impotence** is a man's sexual problem in which his penis fails to get hard or stay hard. インポテンツ ❑*Impotence affects 10 million men in the U.S. alone.* アメリカだけでも1000万人の男性が性交不能になっている.

Word Link
potent ≈ ability, power : impotent, potent, potential

im|po|tent /ɪmpətənt/ ■ ADJ 形容詞 If someone feels **impotent**, they feel that they have no power to influence people or events. 無力な ❑*The aggression of a bully leaves people feeling hurt, angry and impotent.* いじめにあう人々は傷つき, 立腹し, 無力に感じる. ② ADJ 形容詞 If a man is **impotent**, he is unable to have sex normally, because his penis fails to get hard or stay hard. 性交不能 ❑*At the age of 40, 1.9 percent of men are impotent.* 40歳までに男性の1.9%が性交不能である.

im|pound /ɪmpaund/ (**impounds, impounding, impounded**) V-T 他動詞 If something **is impounded** by police officers, customs officers, or other officials, they officially take possession of it because a law or rule has been broken. 押収される ❑*The ship was impounded under the terms of the UN trade embargo.* その船は国連の通商禁止の約定の下で押収された.

im|pov|er|ish /ɪmpɒvərɪʃ/ (**impoverishes, impoverishing, impoverished**) ■ V-T 他動詞 Something that **impoverishes** a person or a country makes them poor. 貧しくする ❑*We need to reduce the burden of taxes that impoverish the economy.* 我々は経済を衰退させる税金の負担を減らす必要がある. ● **im|pov|er|ished** ADJ 形容詞 貧窮化した ❑*The goal is to lure businesses into impoverished areas by offering them tax breaks.* 目標は税制優遇措置を提供することによって貧窮化した地域に企業を誘致することだ. ② V-T 他動詞 A person or thing that **impoverishes** something makes it worse in quality. 不毛にする ❑*A top dressing of fertilizer should be added to improve growth as mint impoverishes the soil quickly.* ミントは土をすばやく不毛にするため, 肥料を加えて成長を促進する必要がある.

im|prac|ti|cal /ɪmpræktɪk°l/ ■ ADJ 形容詞 If you describe an object, idea, or course of action as **impractical**, you mean that it is not sensible or realistic, and does not work well in practice. 実用的でない ❑*There were regularly scheduled airlines, but it became impractical to make a business trip by ocean liner.* 航空会社の定期便が就航してからは大洋航路船による出張は実用的ではなくなった. ② ADJ 形容詞 If you describe someone as **impractical**, you mean that they do not have the abilities or skills to do practical work such as making, repairing, or organizing things. 実際にうとい ❑*Geniuses are supposed to be difficult, eccentric and hopelessly impractical.* 天才は気難しく, エキセントリックでどうしようもなく実際にうといことになっている.

im|press /ɪmpres/ (**impresses, impressing, impressed**) ■ V-T/V-I 他動詞/自動詞 If something **impresses** you, you feel great admiration for it. 感動させる ❑*What impressed him most was their speed.* 彼が最も感動したのは彼らの速度だった. ● **im|pressed** ADJ 形容詞 [v-link ADJ] 印象を受けた ❑*I was very impressed by one young man at my lectures.* 私は講義に出席した1人の若い男に非常に好印象を受けた. ② V-T 他動詞 If you **impress** something **on** someone, they must understand its importance or degree. 熱心に説く ❑*I had always impressed upon the children that if they worked hard they would succeed in life.* 私はいつも子供達に努力すれば人生に成功すると熱心に言い聞かせた. ❑*I've impressed upon them the need for more professionalism.* 私はより優れたプロ意識の必要性を彼ら

に痛感させた. **3** V-T 他動詞 If something **impresses itself on** your mind, you notice and remember it. 刻み付ける ❏ *But this change has not yet impressed itself on the minds of the public.* しかしこの変化はまだ国民の心に刻み付けられていない. **4** V-T 他動詞 If someone or something **impresses** you **as** a particular thing, usually a good one, they gives you the impression of being that thing. 印象を与える ❏ *It didn't impress me as a good place to live.* 私はそこが住むのに適した場所という印象を受けなかった.

im|pres|sion /ɪmprɛʃ³n/ (**impressions**) **1** N-COUNT 可算名詞 Your **impression** of a person or thing is what you think they are like, usually after having seen or heard them. Your **impression** of a situation is what you think is going on. 印象 ❏ *What were your first impressions of college?* 大学の第一印象はどうでしたか. ❏ *My impression is that they are totally out of control.* 私は彼らは全く手に負えないという印象を受けた. **2** N-SING 単数名詞 If someone gives you a particular **impression**, they cause you to believe that something is the case, often when it is not. 印象 ❏ *I don't want to give the impression that I'm running away from the charges.* 私は負債から逃げているという印象を与えたくない. **3** N-COUNT 可算名詞 An **impression** is an amusing imitation of someone's behavior or way of talking, usually someone well-known. 物まね ❏ *I did an impression of daddy saying "do as I say, not as I do."* 私は「俺のする通りではなく言う通りにしろ」というお父さんの物まねをした. **4** N-COUNT 可算名詞 An **impression** of an object is a mark or outline that it has left after being pressed hard onto a surface. 跡 ❏ *...the world's oldest fossil impressions of plant life.* 世界最古の植物の化石の跡 **5** PHRASE 句 If someone or something **makes an impression**, they have a strong effect on people or a situation. 影響を与える ❏ *The type of aid coming in makes no immediate impression on the horrific death rates.* 入ってくるタイプの援助はものすごい死亡率にすぐには影響を与えない. **6** PHRASE 句 If you are **under the impression that** something is the case, you believe that it is the case, usually when it is not actually the case. 考えている ❏ *He had apparently been under the impression that a military coup was in progress.* 彼はどうやら軍のクーデターが進行中だと思っていたらしい.

im|pres|sive /ɪmprɛsɪv/ ADJ 形容詞 Something that is **impressive** impresses you, for example, because it is great in size or degree, or is done with a lot of skill. 印象的な ❏ *It is an impressive achievement.* それは立派な功績である. ●**im|pres|sive|ly** ADV 副詞 すばらしく ❏ *...an impressively bright and energetic woman called Cathie Gould.* 非常に頭が良くエネルギッシュなキャシー・グールドという名前の女性

im|print (**imprints, imprinting, imprinted**)

The noun is pronounced /ɪmprɪnt/. The verb is pronounced /ɪmprɪnt/.

名詞は /ɪmprɪnt/ と発音される. 動詞は /ɪmprɪnt/ と発音される.

1 N-COUNT 可算名詞 If something leaves an **imprint** on a place or on your mind, it has a strong and lasting effect on it. 印象 ❏ *World War I left an indelible imprint on the twentieth-century world.* 第一次世界大戦は20世紀の世界にぬぐい去れない跡を残した. **2** V-T 他動詞 When something is **imprinted** on your memory, it is firmly fixed in your memory so that you will not forget it. 刻み付けられる ❏ *As I arrived, the shimmering skyline of domes and minarets was imprinted on my memory.* 私が到着したとたんに丸屋根とミナレットのかすかに光る地平線が私の記憶に刻み込まれた. **3** N-COUNT 可算名詞 An **imprint** is a mark or outline made by the pressure of one object on another. 跡 ❏ *She could see the imprint of his fingers on his pale face.* 彼女は彼の青白い顔に彼の指の跡を見ることができた. **4** V-T 他動詞 If a surface is **imprinted with** a mark or design, that mark or design is printed on the surface or pressed into it. 刻印される [usu passive] ❏ *The company carries a variety of binders that can be imprinted with your message or logo.* その企業はあなたのメッセージやロゴの刻印入りの各種バインダーを扱っている.

im|pris|on /ɪmprɪz³n/ (**imprisons, imprisoning, imprisoned**) V-T 他動詞 If someone **is imprisoned**, they are locked up or kept somewhere, usually in prison, as a punishment for a crime or for political opposition. 刑務所に入れられる ❏ *He was imprisoned for 18 months on charges of theft.* 彼は窃盗罪で18ヶ月間投獄された.

im|pris|on|ment /ɪmprɪz³nmənt/ N-UNCOUNT 不可算名詞 **Imprisonment** is the state of being imprisoned. 投獄 ❏ *She was sentenced to seven years' imprisonment.* 彼女は7年の禁固刑を受けた.

im|prob|able /ɪmprɒbəb³l/ **1** ADJ 形容詞 Something that is **improbable** is unlikely to be true or to happen. 起こりそうにもない ❏ *Ordered arrangements of large groups of atoms and molecules*

are highly improbable. 原子と微粒子の大集団が規律正しく配列されることはとうていあり得ない. ●**im|prob|abil|ity** /ɪmprɒbəbɪlɪti/ (**improbabilities**) N-VAR 可変性名詞 起こりそうにないこと **2** ❏ *...the improbability of such an outcome.* そのような結果が起こりそうにないこと **2** ADJ 形容詞 If you describe something as **improbable**, you mean it is strange, unusual, or ridiculous. 奇抜な ❏ *On the face of it, their marriage seems an improbable alliance.* 一見したところでは, 彼らの結婚は変てこな婚姻のようだ. ●**im|prob|ably** ADV 副詞 信じられないほど ❏ *The sea is an improbably pale turquoise.* 海は信じられないほど淡い碧青色だ.

im|promp|tu /ɪmprɒmptu/ ADJ 形容詞 An **impromptu** action is one that you do without planning or organizing it in advance. 即席の ❏ *This afternoon the Palestinians held an impromptu press conference.* 今日の午後, パレスチナ人は即席の記者会見を行なった.

im|prop|er /ɪmprɒpər/ **1** ADJ 形容詞 **Improper** activities are illegal or dishonest. 不適切な [FORMAL 形式ばった] ❏ *25 officers were investigated following allegations of improper conduct.* 不適切行為の申し立ての後, 25名の警察官が調査された. ●**im|prop|er|ly** ADV 副詞 [ADV with v] 不適切に ❏ *I acted neither fraudulently nor improperly.* 私は詐欺行為も不適切行為もしていない. **2** ADJ 形容詞 **Improper** conditions or methods of treatment are not suitable or good enough for a particular purpose. 不適切な [FORMAL 形式ばった] [ADJ n] ❏ *The improper use of medicine could lead to severe adverse reactions.* 薬の不適切な使用は深刻な悪反応を引き起こすことがある. ●**im|prop|er|ly** ADV 副詞 [ADV with v] 不適切に ❏ *The study confirmed many reports that doctors were improperly trained.* その研究は医者が間違った教育を受けているという多くのリポートを裏付けた. **3** ADJ 形容詞 If you describe someone's behavior as **improper**, you mean it is rude or shocking or in some way socially unacceptable. 無作法な ❏ *Such improper behavior and language from a young lady left me momentarily incapable of speech.* 若い女性の余りにも下品な行動と言葉遣いに私はちょっとの間口もきけなかった. ●**im|prop|er|ly** ADV 副詞 [ADV with v] 不適切に ❏ *The company turns down people who show up at job interviews improperly dressed.* その企業は不適切な服装で面接に来る人々を不採用にしている.

im|prove /ɪmpruv/ (**improves, improving, improved**) **1** V-T/V-I 他動詞/自動詞 If something **improves** or if you **improve** it, it gets better. 改善する ❏ *Within a month, both the texture and condition of your hair should improve.* あなたの髪は1ヶ月以内にしっとりしてつやのある髪になるはずだ. **2** V-T/V-I 他動詞/自動詞 If a skill you have **improves** or you **improve** a skill, you get better at it. 改善する, 向上する ❏ *Their French has improved enormously.* 彼らのフランス語はかなり上達した. **3** V-I 自動詞 If you **improve** after an illness or an injury, your health gets better or you get stronger. 回復する ❏ *He had improved so much the doctor had cut his dosage.* 彼はかなり回復したので医者は薬の服用量を減らした. **4** V-I 自動詞 If you **improve on** a previous achievement of your own or of someone else, you achieve a better standard or result. より良いものにする ❏ *We need to improve on our performance against Nabisco.* 我々はナビスコに対する業績をより良いものにする必要がある.

im|prove|ment /ɪmpruvmənt/ (**improvements**) **1** N-VAR 可変性名詞 If there is an **improvement** in something, it becomes better. If you make **improvements to** something, you make it better. 改善 ❏ *...the dramatic improvements in organ transplantation in recent years.* 臓器の移植における最近の劇的な改善 **2** N-COUNT 可算名詞 If you say that something is an **improvement** on a previous thing or situation, you mean that it is better than that thing. より優れたもの ❏ *The new governor is an improvement on his predecessor.* 新しい知事は前任者より優れている.

im|pro|vise /ɪmprəvaɪz/ (**improvises, improvising, improvised**) **1** V-T/V-I 他動詞/自動詞 If you **improvise**, you make or do something using whatever you have or without having planned it in advance. 間に合わせで急場をしのぐ ❏ *You need a wok with a steaming rack for this; if you don't have one, improvise.* これには

蒸しラックつきの中華なべが必要です. ない場合には間に合わせの鍋を使ってください. ❑ *The vet had improvised a harness.* 獣医は間に合わせの首輪を作った. ❷ V-T/V-I 他動詞/自動詞 When performers **improvise**, they invent music or words as they play, sing, or speak. 即席で作る ❑ *I asked her what the piece was and she said, "Oh, I'm just improvising."* 私が彼女に曲名を聞くと彼女は「即席で演奏しているだけよ」と言った. ❑ *Uncle Richard read a chapter from the Bible and improvised a prayer.* リチャードおじさんは聖書抜節を読み, 即席で祈祷(きとう)した.

im|pu|dent /ˈɪmpyədənt/ ADJ 形容詞 If you describe someone as **impudent**, you mean they are rude or disrespectful, or do something they have no right to do. 厚かましい [FORMAL 形式ばった, DISAPPROVAL 不賛成] ❑ *Some of them spoke pleasantly and were well behaved, while others were impudent and insulting.* 彼らの中には愛想がよく行儀良い人もいたが, 横柄で失敬な人もいた.

im|pulse /ˈɪmpʌls/ (**impulses**) ❶ N-VAR 可変性名詞 An **impulse** is a sudden desire to do something. 衝動 ❑ *Unable to resist the impulse, he glanced at the sea again.* 衝動を抑えきれずに彼は海を再び眺めた. ❷ N-COUNT 可算名詞 An **impulse** is a short electrical signal that is sent along a wire or nerve or through the air, usually as one of a series. インパルス ❑ *It works by sending a series of electrical impulses which are picked up by hi-tech sensors.* それは高度技術センサーの捕える一連の電気インパルスを送ることによって機能する. ❸ ADJ 形容詞 An **impulse** buy or **impulse** purchase is something that you decide to buy when you see it, although you had not planned to buy it. 衝動的な [ADJ n] ❑ *The curtains were an impulse buy.* カーテンは衝動買いだった. ❹ PHRASE 句 If you do something on **impulse**, you suddenly decide to do it, without planning it. 衝動的に ❑ *Sean's a fast thinker, and he acts on impulse.* ショーンは頭の回転が早く, 衝動的に行動する.

im|pul|sive /ˈɪmpʌlsɪv/ ADJ 形容詞 If you describe someone as **impulsive**, you mean that they do things suddenly without thinking about them carefully first. 衝動的な ❑ *He is too impulsive to be a responsible mayor.* 彼は信頼できる市長になるには衝動的すぎる. ● **im|pul|sive|ly** ADV 副詞 [ADV with v] 衝動的に ❑ *He studied her face for a moment, then said impulsively: "Let's get married."* 彼はちょっとの間彼女の顔をしげしげと眺めてから衝動的に「結婚しよう」と言った.

im|pure /ˈɪmpyʊər/ ADJ 形容詞 A substance that is **impure** is not of good quality because it has other substances mixed with it. 不純な ❑ *...diarrhea, dysentery and other diseases borne by impure water.* 不潔な水によって運ばれた下痢, 赤痢などの病気

im|pu|rity /ˈɪmpyʊərɪti/ (**impurities**) N-COUNT 可算名詞 **Impurities** are substances that are present in small quantities in another substance and make it dirty or of an unacceptable quality. 不純物 ❑ *The air in the factory is filtered to remove impurities.* 工場の空気は濾過(ろか)して不純物が取り除かれる.

---

in

❶	POSITION OR MOVEMENT
❷	INCLUSION OR INVOLVEMENT
❸	TIME AND NUMBERS
❹	STATES AND QUALITIES
❺	OTHER USES AND PHRASES

---

❶ **in**

The preposition is pronounced /ɪn/. The adverb is pronounced /ˈɪn/.

前置詞は /ɪn/ と発音される. 副詞は /ˈɪn/ と発音される.

In addition to the uses shown below, **in** is used after some verbs, nouns, and adjectives in order to introduce extra information. **In** is also used with verbs of movement such as "walk" and "push," and in phrasal verbs such as "give in" and "dig in."

下記の用法に加えて, **in** は余分な情報を伝えるために1部の動詞, 名詞, 形容詞の後に使われる. **In** はまた **walk** や **push** のような移動の動詞と共に使われるし, また **give in** や **dig in** のような句動詞にも使われる.

❶ PREP 前置詞 Someone or something that is **in** something else is enclosed by it or surrounded by it. If you put something **in** a container, you move it so that it is enclosed by the container. の中に ❑ *He was in his car.* 彼は車の中にいた. ❷ PREP 前置詞 If something happens **in** a place, it happens there. に ❑ *...spending a few days in a hotel.* ホテルに数日宿泊すること ❸ ADV 副詞 If you are **in**, you are present at your home or place of work. 在宅して ['be' ADV] ❑ *My roommate was in at the time.* 私のルームメートはその時家にいた. ❹ ADV 副詞 When someone comes **in**, they enter a room or building. 中へ [ADV after v] ❑ *She looked up anxiously as he came in.* 彼女は彼が入ってきたとたん不安そうに見上げた. ❺ ADV 副詞 If a train, boat, or plane has come **in** or is **in**, it has arrived at a station, port, or airport. 到着する ❑ *...every plane coming in from Melbourne.* メルボルンから到着する全ての飛行機 ❻ ADV 副詞 When the sea or tide comes **in**, the sea moves toward the shore rather than away from it. 満ち潮になる ❑ *She thought of the tide rushing in, covering the wet sand.* 彼女は勢いよく潮が満ち, 濡れた砂浜を覆うことを考えた. ❼ PREP 前置詞 Something that is **in** a window, especially a store window, is just behind the window so that you can see it from outside. に ❑ *There was a camera for sale in the window.* ショーウィンドーに売りに出されているカメラがあった. ❽ PREP 前置詞 When you see something in a mirror, the mirror shows an image of it. の中の ❑ *I couldn't bear to see my reflection in the mirror.* 私は鏡に映った自分の姿を見るのが耐えられなかった. ❾ PREP 前置詞 If you are dressed in a piece of clothing, you are wearing it. を着て ❑ *He was a big man, dressed in a suit and tie.* 彼はスーツとネクタイ姿の大男だった. ❿ PREP 前置詞 Something that is covered or wrapped in something else has that thing over or around its surface. で包んで ❑ *His legs were covered in mud.* 彼の両足は泥だらけだった. ⓫ PREP 前置詞 If there is something such as a crack or hole **in** something, there is a crack or hole on its surface. に ❑ *There was a deep crack in the ceiling above him.* 彼の頭上の天井には深い割れ目があった.

❷ **in** /ɪn/ ❶ PREP 前置詞 If something is in a book, movie, play, or picture, you can read it or see it there. の中に ❑ *Don't stick too precisely to what it says in the book.* 本の内容に忠実すぎてはならない. ❷ PREP 前置詞 If you are **in** something such as a play or a race, you are one of the people taking part. の中の ❑ *Alfredo offered her a part in the play he was directing.* アルフレッドは彼が監督する演劇の役を彼女に提供した. ❸ PREP 前置詞 Something that is **in** a group or collection is a member of it or part of it. の中で ❑ *The New England team is the worst in the league.* ニューイングランドのチームはメジャーリーグの選手の中で最も劣っている. ❹ PREP 前置詞 You use **in** to specify a general subject or field of activity. で ❑ *...those working in the defense industry.* 防衛産業で働く人々

❸ **in** /ɪn/ ❶ PREP 前置詞 If something happens **in** a particular year, month, or other period of time, it happens during that time. の時に ❑ *...that early spring day in April 1949.* 1949年4月の初春の日 ❑ *Export orders improved in the last month.* 輸出の注文は先月, 改善した. ❷ PREP 前置詞 If something happens **in** a particular situation, it happens while that situation is going on. の中 ❑ *His father had been badly wounded in the last war.* 彼の父親はこの前の戦争中にひどく負傷した. ❸ PREP 前置詞 If you do something **in** a particular period of time, that is how long it takes you to do it. の間 [PREP amount] ❑ *He walked two hundred and sixty miles in eight days.* 彼は8日間で260マイル歩いた. ❹ PREP 前置詞 If something will happen **in** a particular length of time, it will happen after that length of time. の後に [PREP amount] ❑ *I'll have some breakfast ready in a few minutes.* 後数分で朝食の準備が整います. ❺ PREP 前置詞 You use **in** to indicate roughly how old someone is. For example, if someone is **in** their fifties, they are between 50 and 59 years old. の間 [PREP poss pl-num] ❑ *...young people in their twenties.* 20代の若者 ❻ PREP 前置詞 You use **in** to indicate roughly how many people or things do something. をなして ❑ *...men who came there in droves.* 大挙してそこに押し寄せた男達 ❼ PREP 前置詞 You use **in** to express a ratio, proportion, or probability. のうちで [num PREP num] ❑ *One in three fourth-graders couldn't find their state on a map of the U.S.* 4年生の3人に1人はアメリカの地図上に住んでいる州を見つけることができなかった.

❹ **in** /ɪn/ ❶ PREP 前置詞 If something or someone is **in** a particular state or situation, that is their present state or situation. の状態で [v-link PREP n] ❑ *The economy was in trouble.* 経済は問題を抱えてた. ❑ *Dave was in a hurry to get back to work.* デイブは急いで仕事に戻りたがった. ❷ PREP 前置詞 You use **in** to indicate the feeling or desire that someone has when they do something, or which causes them to do it. の状態で ❑ *Simpson looked at them in surprise.* シンプソンは驚いて彼らを見た. ❸ PREP 前置詞 If a particular quality or ability is **in** you, you naturally have it. には ❑ *Violence is not in his nature.* 彼は生まれつき暴力を振るうような男ではない. ❹ PREP 前置詞 You use **in** when saying that someone or something has a particular quality. の中に ❑ *He had all the qualities I was looking for in a partner.* 彼は私が伴侶に求める全ての性質が備わっていた. ❺ PREP 前置詞 You use **in** to indicate how someone is expressing something. で ❑ *Information is given to the patient verbally and in writing.* 情報は口頭および書面で患者に与えられる. ❻ PREP 前置詞 You use **in** in expressions such as **in a row** or **in**

a ball to describe the arrangement or shape of something. `をなして ❏ *The cards need to be laid out in two rows.* カードは2列に並べる必要がある. ▪ PREP 前置詞 If something is **in** a particular color, it has that color. の色の ❏ *...white flowers edged in pink.* ピンク色で縁取られた白い花 ▪ PREP 前置詞 You use **in** to specify which feature or aspect of something you are talking about. `に関して ❏ *The movie is nearly two hours in length.* その映画の上映時間は約2時間だ. ❏ *There is a big difference in the amounts that banks charge.* 銀行の手数料には大きな格差がある.

❾ in (ins)

Pronounced /ɪn/ for meanings ▪ and ▪ to ▪, and /ɪn/ for meaning ▪.
/ɪn/ および ▪ から ▪ の意味では ▪ と発音される. /ɪn/の意味では ▪ と発音される.

▪ ADJ 形容詞 If you say that something is **in**, or is the **in** thing, you mean it is fashionable or popular. 人気のある [INFORMAL くだけた] ❏ *A few years ago jogging was the thing.* 数年前ジョギングは人気があった. ▪ PREP 前置詞 You use **in** with a present participle to indicate that when you do something, something else happens as a result. `する際に [PREP -ing] ❏ *He shifted uncomfortably on his feet. In doing so he knocked over Steven's briefcase.* 彼は居心地悪そうに位置を変えた. その際に彼はスティーブンのブリーフケースをひっくり返した. ▪ PHRASE 句 If you say that someone **is in for** a shock or a surprise, you mean that they are going to experience it. 直面しそうで ❏ *You might be in for a shock at the sheer hard work involved.* 君はまったくの厳しい作業にショックを受けるかもしれない. ▪ PHRASE 句 If someone **has it in for** you, they dislike you and try to cause problems for you. 悪意を抱いている [INFORMAL くだけた] ❏ *The other kids had it in for me.* 他の子供達は私に悪意を抱いていた. ▪ PHRASE 句 If you are **in on** something, you are involved in it or know about it. 関係して ❏ *I don't know. I wasn't in on that particular argument.* 私は知らない. その議論には関与していなかったので. ▪ PHRASE 句 If you **are in with** a person or group, they like you and accept you, and are likely to help you. と親しくしている [INFORMAL くだけた] ▪ PHRASE 句 You use **in that** to introduce an explanation of a statement you have just made. という点で ❏ *I'm lucky in that I've got four sisters.* 私は4人の姉妹がいるので幸運だ. ▪ PHRASE 句 The **ins and outs** of a situation are all the detailed points and facts about it. 詳細 ❏ *...the ins and outs of high finance.* 大型金融取引の一部始終

in|abil|ity /ɪnəbɪlɪti/ N-UNCOUNT 不可算名詞 If you refer to someone's **inability to** do something, you are referring to the fact that they are unable to do it. 不能 ❏ *Her inability to concentrate could cause an accident.* 彼女は集中力不足で事故を引き起こすかもしれない.

in|ac|ces|sible /ɪnəksɛsɪbəl/ ▪ ADJ 形容詞 An **inaccessible** place is very difficult or impossible to reach. 到達しがたい ❏ *...people living in remote and inaccessible parts of China.* 中国の遠く到達しがたい地域に住む人々 ▪ ADJ 形容詞 If something is **inaccessible**, you are unable to see, use, or buy it. 手に入らない ❏ *Ninety-five percent of its magnificent collection will remain inaccessible to the public.* その素晴らしいコレクションの95%は国民の手に入らないままであろう. ▪ ADJ 形容詞 Someone or something that is **inaccessible** is difficult or impossible to understand or appreciate. 理解できない [DISAPPROVAL 不賛成] ❏ *...language that is inaccessible to working people.* 労働者には理解できない言語

in|ac|cu|ra|cy /ɪnækyərəsi/ (inaccuracies) N-VAR 可変性名詞 The **inaccuracy** of a statement or measurement is the fact that it is not accurate or correct. 不正確な点 ❏ *He was disturbed by the inaccuracy of the answers.* 彼は回答の不正確さにどぎまぎした.

in|ac|cu|rate /ɪnækyərɪt/ ADJ 形容詞 If a statement or measurement is **inaccurate**, it is not accurate or correct. 不正確な ❏ *The book is both inaccurate and exaggerated.* その本は不正確な上に誇張されている.

in|ac|tion /ɪnækʃən/ N-UNCOUNT 不可算名詞 If you refer to someone's **inaction**, you disapprove of the fact that they are doing nothing. 不活動 [DISAPPROVAL 不賛成] ❏ *He is bitter about the inaction of the other political parties.* 彼は他の政党の不活動について苦々しく感じている.

in|ac|tive /ɪnæktɪv/ ADJ 形容詞 Someone or something that is **inactive** is not doing anything or is not working. 活動しない ❏ *He certainly was not politically inactive.* 彼は確かに政治的に不活発ではなかった. ● **in|ac|tiv|ity** /ɪnæktɪvɪti/ N-UNCOUNT 不可算名詞 活動しないこと ❏ *The players have comparatively long periods of inactivity.* 選手達は比較的長期間活動を止める.

in|ad|equa|cy /ɪnædɪkwəsi/ (inadequacies) ▪ N-VAR 可変性名詞 The **inadequacy** of something is the fact that there is not enough of it, or that it is not good enough. 不足 ❏ *...the inadequacy of the water supply.* 不十分な水の供給量 ▪ N-UNCOUNT 不可算名詞 If someone has feelings of **inadequacy**, they feel that they do not have the qualities and abilities necessary to do something

or to cope with life in general. 欠陥 ❏ *...his deep-seated sense of inadequacy.* 彼の心にしっかりと植えつけられた不適格者であるという気持ち

in|ad|equate /ɪnædɪkwɪt/ ▪ ADJ 形容詞 If something is **inadequate**, there is not enough of it or it is not good enough. 不十分な ❏ *Supplies of food and medicines are inadequate.* 食料と薬の供給は不十分である. ● **in|ad|equate|ly** ADV 副詞 [ADV with v] 不十分に ❏ *The projects were inadequately funded.* そのプロジェクトの資金調達は不十分だった. ▪ ADJ 形容詞 If someone feels **inadequate**, they feel that they do not have the qualities and abilities necessary to do something or to cope with life in general. 不適格な ❏ *I still feel inadequate, useless and mixed up.* 私はまだ不適格で, 役に立たず, 不安定だと感じている.

Word Partnership	*inadequate* は次の語句と使われる:
N.	inadequate **funding**, inadequate **supply**, inadequate **training** ▪
ADV.	**woefully** inadequate ▪ ▪
V.	**feel** inadequate ▪

in|ad|vert|ent /ɪnædvɜrtᵊnt/ ADJ 形容詞 An **inadvertent** action is one that you do without realizing what you are doing. 故意でない ❏ *The government has said it was an inadvertent error.* 政府はそれが不注意による間違いだったと述べた. ● **in|ad|vert|ent|ly** ADV 副詞 [ADV with v] うっかりして ❏ *You may have inadvertently pressed the wrong button.* 君はうっかりして間違ったボタンを押したのかもしれない.

in|ap|pro|pri|ate /ɪnəproʊpriɪt/ ▪ ADJ 形容詞 Something that is **inappropriate** is not useful or suitable for a particular situation or purpose. 不適当な ❏ *There is no suggestion that clients have been sold inappropriate policies.* 顧客が不適切な保険を売りつけられたという示唆は全くない. ▪ ADJ 形容詞 If you say that someone's speech or behavior in a particular situation is **inappropriate**, you are criticizing it because you think it is not suitable for that situation. 不適当な [DISAPPROVAL 不賛成] ❏ *I feel the remark was inappropriate for such a serious issue.* そのコメントはそのように深刻な問題には不適切だと私は思う.

in|as|much as /ɪnəzmʌtʃæz/ PHRASE 句 You use **inasmuch as** to introduce a statement that explains something you have just said, and adds to it. だから [FORMAL 形式ばった] ❏ *We were doubly lucky inasmuch as my friend was living on the island and spoke Greek fluently.* 我々は友人がその島に住み, ギリシャ語を流暢にしゃべるので二重に恵まれていた.

in|augu|ral /ɪnɔgyərəl/ ADJ 形容詞 An **inaugural** meeting or speech is the first meeting of a new organization or the first speech by the new leader of an organization or a country. 就任の [ADJ n] ❏ *In his inaugural address, the president appealed for national unity.* 大統領は就任演説で国家の統一を呼びかけた.

in|augu|rate /ɪnɔgyəreɪt/ (inaugurates, inaugurating, inaugurated) ▪ V-T 他動詞 When a new leader **is inaugurated**, they are formally given their new position at an official ceremony. 就任する [usu passive] ❏ *The new president will be inaugurated on January 20th.* 新大統領は1月20日に就任する予定だ. ● **in|augu|ra|tion** /ɪnɔgyəreɪʃən/ (inaugurations) N-VAR 可変性名詞 就任式 ❏ *...the inauguration of the new Governor.* 新知事の就任式 ▪ V-T 他動詞 [usu passive] When a new building or institution **is inaugurated**, it is declared open in a formal ceremony. 開通式を行なう ❏ *A Mafia Museum was inaugurated in Corleone.* コルレオーネでマフィア博物館の除幕式が行なわれた. ● **in|augu|ra|tion** N-COUNT 可算名詞 開会式 ❏ *They later attended the inauguration of the University.* 彼らは後に大学の開校式に参加した. ▪ V-T 他動詞 If you **inaugurate** a new system or service, you start it. 開始する [FORMAL 形式ばった] ❏ *Pan Am inaugurated the first scheduled international flight.* パンナムは最初の国際定期便を就航させた.

in|box /ɪnbɒks/ (inboxes) also in-box ▪ N-COUNT 可算名詞 An **inbox** is a shallow container used in offices to put letters and documents in before they are dealt with. 未処理書類入れ [AM 米国英語] ▪ N-COUNT 可算名詞 On a computer, your **inbox** is the part of your mailbox which stores e-mails that have arrived for you. 受信箱 ❏ *I returned home and checked my inbox.* 私は家に戻りメールの受信箱をチェックした.

inc. In written advertisements, **inc.** is an abbreviation for **including**. including の縮約形 ❏ *The hotel offers a two-night stay for $210 per person, inc. breakfast and dinner.* そのホテルは朝食および夕食込みの2泊の宿泊料金を1名210ドルで提供している.

Inc. Inc. is an abbreviation for **Incorporated** when it is used after a company's name. Incorporated の縮約形 [AM 米国英語 BUSINESS 実業] ❏ *...Sun Microsystems Inc.* サン・マイクロシステムズ有限会社

in|ca|pable /ɪnkeɪpəbᵊl/ ▪ ADJ 形容詞 Someone who is **incapable of** doing something is unable to do it. できない [V-link ADJ 'of' -ing/n] ❏ *She seemed incapable of making the decision.* 彼女は決断を下せないようだった. ▪ ADJ 形容詞 An **incapable** person is weak or stupid. 無能な ❏ *He lost his job for allegedly being incapable.*

彼はうわさによると無能なために職を失ったらしい.

in|car|cer|ate /ɪnkɑ́rsəreɪt/ (**incarcerates, incarcerating, incarcerated**) V-T 他動詞 If people **are incarcerated**, they are kept in a prison or other place. 監禁される [FORMAL 形式ばった] ❑ *They were incarcerated for the duration of the war.* 彼らは戦争が終わるまで監禁されていた. ● **in|car|cera|tion** N-UNCOUNT 不可算名詞 監禁 ❑ *...her mother's incarceration in a psychiatric hospital.* 彼女の母親の精神病院監禁

Word Link carn ≈ flesh : carnage, incarnation, reincarnation

in|car|na|tion /ɪnkɑ́rneɪʃ⁰n/ (**incarnations**) **1** N-COUNT 可算名詞 If you say that someone is the **incarnation of** a particular quality, you mean that they represent that quality or are typical of it in an extreme form. 具体化した姿 ❑ *The regime was the very incarnation of evil.* その政権は悪の権化だった. **2** N-COUNT 可算名詞 An **incarnation** is an instance of being alive on earth in a particular form. Some religions believe that people have several incarnations in different forms. 化身 ❑ *She began recalling a series of previous incarnations.* 彼女は一連の過去の化身を思い出し始めた.

in|cen|di|ary /ɪnséndieri/ (**incendiaries**) **1** ADJ 形容詞 **Incendiary** weapons or attacks are ones that cause large fires. 発焼用の [ADJ n] ❑ *Five incendiary devices were found in her house.* 5つの発火装置が彼女の家で見つかった. **2** N-COUNT 可算名詞 An **incendiary** is an incendiary bomb. 焼い弾 ❑ *A shower of incendiaries struck the Opera House.* 焼い弾の雨がオペラハウスに衝突した. **3** ADJ 形容詞 If you accuse someone of saying or doing **incendiary** things, you mean that what they say or do is likely to make people react very angrily. 扇動的な [DISAPPROVAL 不賛成] ❑ *...incendiary slogans such as "Hospital closures kill more than car bombs."* 「病院の閉鎖は自動車爆弾よりも多くの死者を出す」といった扇動的なスローガン

in|cense (**incenses, incensing, incensed**)

The noun is pronounced /ɪ́nsɛns/. The verb is pronounced /ɪnsɛ́ns/.

名詞は /ɪ́nsɛns/ と発音される. 動詞は /ɪnsɛ́ns/ と発音される.

1 N-UNCOUNT 不可算名詞 **Incense** is a substance that is burned for its sweet smell, often as part of a religious ceremony. 香 **2** V-T 他動詞 If you say that something **incenses** you, you mean that it makes you extremely angry. ひどく怒らせる ❑ *This proposal will incense conservation campaigners.* この提案は保守党のキャンペーン活動者をひどく怒らせるだろう. ● **in|censed** ADJ 形容詞 激怒した ❑ *Mom was incensed at his lack of compassion.* お母さんは彼の思いやりのなさに激怒した.

in|cen|tive /ɪnséntɪv/ (**incentives**) N-VAR 可変性名詞 If something is an **incentive** to do something, it encourages you to do it. 誘因 ❑ *There is little or no incentive to adopt such measures.* そうした措置の採用させようとする動機は全くあるいはほとんどない.

in|ces|sant /ɪnsés⁰nt/ ADJ 形容詞 An **incessant** process or activity is one that continues without stopping. 絶え間のない ❑ *Incessant rain made conditions almost intolerable.* 絶え間なく降る雨によりほとんど耐えられないといっていい状況になった. ● **in|ces|sant|ly** ADV 副詞 絶え間なく ❑ *Dee talked incessantly about herself.* ディーは自分のことを絶え間なく話した.

in|cest /ɪ́nsɛst/ N-UNCOUNT 不可算名詞 **Incest** is the crime of two members of the same family having sexual intercourse, such as a father and daughter, or a brother and sister. 近親相姦(そうかん) ❑ *Oedipus, according to ancient Greek legend, killed his father and committed incest with his mother.* 古代ギリシャの伝説によると, オイディプスは父親を殺し, 母親と近親相姦を犯した.

inch /ɪ́ntʃ/ (**inches, inching, inched**) **1** N-COUNT 可算名詞 An **inch** is an imperial unit of length, approximately equal to 2.54 centimeters. There are twelve inches in a foot. インチ ❑ *...18 inches below the surface.* 表面から18インチ下に **2** V-T/V-I 他動詞/自動詞 To **inch** somewhere means to move there very slowly and carefully, or to make something do this. 徐々に動く, 徐々に動かす ❑ *...a climber inching up a vertical wall of rock.* 垂直の岸壁を少しずつよじ登る登山者 ❑ *He inched the van forward.* 彼は小型トラックを前方にゆっくり動かした. **3** PHRASE 句 If you say that someone looks **every inch** a certain type of person, you are emphasizing that they look exactly like that kind of person. あらゆる点で [EMPHASIS 強調] ❑ *He looks every inch the businessman, with his grey suit, dark blue shirt and blue tie.* グレーの背広, 暗青色のシャツ, ブルーのネクタイ姿の彼は典型的な実業家に見える.

in|ci|dence /ɪ́nsɪdəns/ (**incidences**) N-VAR 可変性名詞 The **incidence** of something, especially something bad such as a disease, is the frequency with which it occurs, or the occasions when it occurs. 発生率 ❑ *The incidence of breast cancer increases with age.* 乳がんの発生率は年と共に増える.

in|ci|dent /ɪ́nsɪdənt/ (**incidents**) N-COUNT 可算名詞 An **incident** is something that happens, often something that is unpleasant. 出来事 [FORMAL 形式ばった] [also 'without' N] ❑ *These*

incidents were the latest in a series of disputes between the two nations. こうした出来事は2か国間の一連の紛争の最近のものだった.

Thesaurus incident また次を参照:

N. episode, event, fact, happening, occasion, occurrence

in|ci|den|tal /ɪnsɪdént⁰l/ ADJ 形容詞 If one thing is **incidental** to another, it is less important than the other thing or is not a major part of it. 偶発の ❑ *The playing of music proved to be incidental to the main business of the evening.* 音楽演奏はその晩の主な商取引に付随的なものであることが分かった.

in|ci|den|tal|ly /ɪnsɪdéntli/ **1** ADV 副詞 You use **incidentally** to introduce a point that is not directly relevant to what you are saying, often a question or extra information that you have just thought of. ところで [ADV with cl] ❑ *"I didn't ask you to come. Incidentally, why have you come?"* 「私は君に来てくれとは頼まなかった. ところで, 君は何故来たのか」 **2** ADV 副詞 If something occurs only **incidentally**, it is less important than another thing or is not a major part of it. 付随的に [ADV with v] ❑ *The letter mentioned my great aunt and uncle only incidentally.* その手紙は私の一代離れたおばとおじについて付随的にしか言及してなかった.

in|cin|er|ate /ɪnsɪ́nəreɪt/ (**incinerates, incinerating, incinerated**) V-T 他動詞 When authorities **incinerate** garbage or waste material, they burn it completely in a special container. 焼く ❑ *They were incinerating hazardous waste without a license.* 彼らは免許なしに有害な廃棄物を焼却していた. ● **in|cin|era|tion** /ɪnsɪnəreɪ́ʃ⁰n/ N-UNCOUNT 不可算名詞 焼却 ❑ *South Pacific nations have protested against the incineration of the weapons.* 南太平洋の国家は武器の焼却に対して抗議した.

→ see **dump**

in|cin|era|tor /ɪnsɪ́nəreɪtər/ (**incinerators**) N-COUNT 可算名詞 An **incinerator** is a special large container for burning garbage at a very high temperature. 焼却装置

in|ci|sive /ɪnsáɪsɪv/ ADJ 形容詞 You use **incisive** to describe a person, their thoughts, or their speech when you approve of their ability to think and express their ideas clearly, briefly, and forcefully. 鋭い [APPROVAL 賛成] ❑ *He is a very shrewd operator with an incisive mind.* 彼は明敏な頭脳を持つ非常に抜け目のない人物だ.

in|cite /ɪnsáɪt/ (**incites, inciting, incited**) V-T 他動詞 If someone **incites** people to behave in a violent or illegal way, they encourage people to behave in that way, usually by making them excited or angry. 扇動する ❑ *He incited his fellow citizens to take their revenge.* 彼は復讐をするよう市民を扇動した. ❑ *The party agreed not to incite its supporters to violence.* その政党は支持者を扇動して暴力をふるわせないことに合意した.

in|cite|ment /ɪnsáɪtmənt/ (**incitements**) N-VAR 可変性名詞 If someone is accused of **incitement to** violent or illegal behavior, they are accused of encouraging people to behave in that way. 扇動 ❑ *Insults can lead to the incitement of violence.* 侮辱は暴力の扇動につながることがある.

incl. **1** In written advertisements, **incl.** is an abbreviation for **including** or **included**. includedの縮約形 ❑ *...blood pressure monitor with batteries, case and 1 year warranty incl.* 電池, ケースそして1年間の保証書付きの血圧測定器 **2** In written advertisements, **incl.** is an abbreviation for **inclusive**. inclusiveの縮約形 ❑ *Open July 19th - September 6th, Sun. to Thurs. incl.* 7月19日ー9月6日の日曜から木曜まで開館

in|cli|na|tion /ɪnklɪneɪ́ʃ⁰n/ (**inclinations**) N-VAR 可変性名詞 An **inclination** is a feeling that makes you want to act in a particular way. 好み ❑ *He had neither the time nor the inclination to think of other things.* 彼には他のことを考える時間も気持ちもなかった. ❑ *She showed no inclination to go.* 彼女は行くそぶりも見せなかった.

Word Link clin ≈ leaning : decline, incline, recline

in|cline (**inclines, inclining, inclined**)

The noun is pronounced /ɪ́nklaɪn/. The verb is pronounced /ɪnklaɪ́n/.

名詞は /ɪ́nklaɪn/ と発音される. 動詞は /ɪnklaɪ́n/ と発音される.

1 N-COUNT 可算名詞 An **incline** is land that slopes at an angle. 傾斜面 [FORMAL 形式ばった] ❑ *He came to a halt at the edge of a steep incline.* 彼は急な斜面の端で止まった. **2** V-T 他動詞 If you **incline** your head, you bend your neck so that your head is leaning forward. 下げる [WRITTEN 書き言葉] ❑ *Jack inclined his head very slightly.* ジャックは頭をゆっくり下げた. **3** V-T 他動詞 If you **incline to** think or act in a particular way, or if something **inclines** you **to** it, you are likely to think or act in that way. 心を向けさせる [FORMAL 形式ばった] ❑ *...the factors that incline us toward particular beliefs.* 私達に特定の信念を持ちたいと思わせる要因 ❑ *Those who fail incline to blame the world for their failure.* 失敗する者は失敗を世間のせいにしたがる.

in|clined /ɪnklaɪnd/ ■ ADJ 形容詞 If you are **inclined to** behave in a particular way, you often behave in that way, or you want to do so. ～したいと思う [v-link ADJ] □Nobody felt inclined to argue with Smith. スミスと議論しようと思う人はいなかった。□He was inclined to self-pity. 彼は自己憐憫（れんびん）に陥りがちだった。 ■ ADJ 形容詞 If you say that you are **inclined to** have a particular opinion, you mean that you hold this opinion but you are not expressing it strongly. ～しがちの [VAGUENESS あいまいさ] [v-link ADJ to-inf] □I am inclined to agree with Alan. 私はアランと議論しがちだ。 ■ ADJ 形容詞 Someone who is mathematically **inclined** or artistically **inclined**, for example, has a natural talent for mathematics or art. 性向を示して [adv ADJ] □...the needs of academically inclined pupils. 学問の好きな生徒のニーズ ■ → see also **incline**

Word Partnership   *inclined* は次の語句と使われる:

V.	inclined **to agree**, inclined **to believe** *someone/ something*, inclined **to think** ■

in|clude /ɪnklud/ (includes, including, included) ■ V-T 他動詞 If one thing **includes** another thing, it has the other thing as one of its parts. 含む □The trip has been extended to include a few other events. その旅行は他の行事を含むために延長された。 ■ V-T 他動詞 If someone or something **is included in** a large group, system, or area, they become a part of it or are considered a part of it. 入れる □I had worked hard to be included in a project like this. 私はこうしたプロジェクトに入れてもらうために努力した。

in|clud|ed /ɪnkludɪd/ ADJ 形容詞 You use **included** to emphasize that a person or thing is part of the group of people or things that you are talking about. 含まれた [EMPHASIS 強調] [n ADJ, v-link ADJ] □Many runners, myself included, are loners. 私自身を含む多くのランナーは一匹狼だ。

in|clud|ing /ɪnkludɪŋ/ PREP 前置詞 You use **including** to introduce examples of people or things that are part of the group of people or things that you are talking about. ～を含む [PREP n /-ing] □Thousands were killed, including many women and children. 多くの女性と子供を含む何千人もの人々が殺された。

in|clu|sion /ɪnkluʒᵊn/ (inclusions) N-VAR 可変性名詞 **Inclusion** is the act of making a person or thing part of a group or collection. 包含すること □...a confident performance that justified his inclusion in the team. 彼がチームの一員となることを正当化した自信たっぷりのパフォーマンス

in|clu|sive /ɪnklusɪv/ ■ ADJ 形容詞 If you describe a group or organization as **inclusive**, you mean that it allows all kinds of people to belong to it, rather than just one kind of person. 開放的な □The academy is far more inclusive now than it used to be. 学会は現在、以前よりずっと開放的である。 ■ ADJ 形容詞 After stating the first and last item in a set of things, you can add **inclusive** to make it clear that the items stated are included in the set. 含めた [n ADJ] □You are also invited to join us on our prayer days (this year, June 6 to June 14 inclusive). 礼拝日（今年は6月6日－14日）にもお出でください。 ■ ADJ 形容詞 If a price is **inclusive**, it includes all the charges connected with the goods or services offered. If a price is **inclusive of** shipping and handling, it includes the charge for this. 算入した □...all prices are inclusive of delivery. すべての価格は配達料金込みである。 ● ADV 副詞 **Inclusive** is also an adverb. ～を含めて [amount ADV] □The outpatient program costs $105 per day, all inclusive. 外来患者プログラムは1日105ドルかかります。

in|co|her|ent /ɪnkoʊhɪərənt/ ■ ADJ 形容詞 If someone is **incoherent**, they are talking in a confused and unclear way. 支離滅裂の □The man was almost incoherent with fear. その男は恐怖でほとんどしどろもどろに近かった。 ■ ADJ 形容詞 If you say that something such as a policy is **incoherent**, you are criticizing it because the different parts of it do not fit together properly. 論理的一貫性のない [DISAPPROVAL 不賛成] □...an incoherent set of objectives. 一貫性のない一連の目標

in|come /ɪnkʌm/ (incomes) N-VAR 可変性名詞 A person's or organization's **income** is the money that they earn or receive, as opposed to the money that they have to spend or pay out. 収入 [BUSINESS 実業] □Many families on low incomes will be unable to afford to buy their own home. 低収入の家庭の多くはマイホームを購入できないだろう。

Word Partnership   *income* は次の語句と使われる:

ADJ.	**average** income, **fixed** income, **large/small** income, **a second** income, **steady** income, **taxable** income
V.	**earn an** income, **supplement your** income
N.	**loss of** income, **source of** income

in|come tax (income taxes) N-VAR 可変性名詞 **Income tax** is a part of your income that you have to pay regularly to the government. 所得税 [BUSINESS 実業] □You pay income tax on all your earnings, not just your salary. 給料だけでなく全ての収入に所得税を支払う。

in|com|ing /ɪnkʌmɪŋ/ ■ ADJ 形容詞 An **incoming** message or phone call is one that you receive. 入ってくる [ADJ n] □We keep a tape of incoming calls. 我々は外からかかってきた電話のテープを保存する。 ■ ADJ 形容詞 An **incoming** plane or passenger is one that is arriving at a place. 着陸しようとする [ADJ n] □The airport was closed for incoming flights. 空港は着陸しようとする飛行機に対して閉鎖された。 ■ ADJ 形容詞 An **incoming** official or government is one that has just been appointed or elected. 後継の [ADJ n] □the problems confronting the incoming government. 後継の政府の直面する問題

in|com|pa|rable /ɪnkɒmpərəbᵊl/ ■ ADJ 形容詞 If you describe someone or something as **incomparable**, you mean that they are extremely good or impressive. 比類のない □...the incomparable Tony Bennet singing "It had to be you." 「It had to be you」を歌う比類のないほどすばらしいトニー・ベネット ■ ADJ 形容詞 You use **incomparable** to emphasize that someone or something has a good quality to a great degree. 無比の [FORMAL 形式ばった、EMPHASIS 強調] [ADJ n] □...an area of incomparable beauty. ずば抜けて美しい地域

in|com|pat|ible /ɪnkəmpætɪbᵊl/ ■ ADJ 形容詞 If one thing or person is **incompatible with** another, they are very different in important ways, and do not suit each other or agree with each other. 両立しない □They feel strongly that their religion is incompatible with the political system. 彼らは彼らの宗教が政治システムと両立しないと強く感じている。 ● **in|com|pat|ibil|ity** /ɪnkəmpætɪbɪlɪti/ N-UNCOUNT 不可算名詞 □Incompatibility between the mother's and the baby's blood groups may cause jaundice. 母親と赤ん坊の血液型が不適合な場合には黄だんが起こる可能性がある。 ■ ADJ 形容詞 If one type of computer or computer system is **incompatible with** another, they cannot use the same programs or be linked up. 互換性のない □This made its mini-computers incompatible with its mainframes. この決果ミニコンピュータは本体と互換性がなくなった。

in|com|pe|tence /ɪnkɒmpɪtəns/ N-UNCOUNT 不可算名詞 If you refer to someone's **incompetence**, you are criticizing them because they are unable to do their job or a task properly. 無能 [DISAPPROVAL 不賛成] □The incompetence of government officials is appalling. 政府高官の無能さにはあきれる。

in|com|pe|tent /ɪnkɒmpɪtənt/ (incompetents) ADJ 形容詞 If you describe someone as **incompetent**, you are criticizing them because they are unable to do their job or a task properly. 無能な、役に立たない [DISAPPROVAL 不賛成] □He wants the power to fire incompetent employees. 彼は無能な従業員を首にする権限が欲しいのだ。 ● N-COUNT 可算名詞 An **incompetent** is someone who is incompetent. 無能な人 □The president turned furiously on his staff. "I'm surrounded by incompetents!" 「どこを見ても無能なやつらばかりだ！」と大統領は怒り狂ってスタッフに食ってかかった。

Word Partnership   *incompetent* は次の語句と使われる:

ADJ.	**corrupt and** incompetent, **lazy and** incompetent
N.	incompetent **leadership**, incompetent **management**

in|com|plete /ɪnkəmplit/ ADJ 形容詞 Something that is **incomplete** is not yet finished, or does not have all the parts or details that it needs. 不完全な □The clearing of garbage and drains is still incomplete. 台所ごみと配水管の処理はまだ完了していません。

in|com|pre|hen|sible /ɪnkɒmprɪhɛnsɪbᵊl/ ADJ 形容詞 Something that is **incomprehensible** is impossible to understand. 理解できない □He spent his time devising incomprehensible mathematics puzzles. 彼は理解不能な数学パズルを考案するのに明け暮れた。

in|con|ceiv|able /ɪnkənsivəbᵊl/ ADJ 形容詞 If you describe something as **inconceivable**, you think it is very unlikely to happen or be true. 想像もつかない □It was inconceivable to me that Toby could have been my attacker. 私を襲ったのがトービーだったかもしれないなんて思いもよらなかった。

in|con|clu|sive /ɪnkənklusɪv/ ■ ADJ 形容詞 If research or evidence is **inconclusive**, it has not proved anything. 結論に達しない、決定的でない □Research has so far proved inconclusive. 今のところ研究の確定的な結果は得られていない。 ■ ADJ 形容詞 If a contest or conflict is **inconclusive**, it is not clear who has won or who is winning. 決定的でない □The past two elections were inconclusive. 過去2回の選挙では、決定的な結果が得られませんでした。

in|con|gru|ous /ɪnkɒŋgruəs/ ADJ 形容詞 Someone or something that is **incongruous** seems strange when considered together with other aspects of a situation. 不釣合いな [FORMAL 形式ばった] □She was small and fragile and looked incongruous in an army uniform. 彼女は小柄でか弱く、軍服を着ているのが不釣合いに見えた。 ● **in|con|gru|ous|ly** ADV 副詞 不釣合いに、調和しないで □...a town of Western-style buildings perched incongruously in a high green valley. 青々とした谷の高みに場違いの感じで存在している洋風建物の並ぶ町。

in|con|sid|er|ate /ɪnkənsɪdərɪt/ ADJ 形容詞 If you accuse someone of being **inconsiderate**, you mean that they do not take enough care over how their words or actions will affect other people. 思いやりのない[DISAPPROVAL 不賛成] □ *It's a bit inconsiderate of her not to let you know when she expects to arrive.* いつ到着する予定かあなたに知らせないとは, 彼女はちょっと思いやりに欠けてますね.

in|con|sist|en|cy /ɪnkənsɪstənsi/ (**inconsistencies**) **1** N-UNCOUNT 不可算名詞 If you refer to someone's **inconsistency**, you are criticizing them for not behaving in the same way every time a similar situation occurs. 一貫性の欠如[DISAPPROVAL 不賛成] □ *His worst fault was his inconsistency.* 彼の最悪の欠点は一貫性に欠けることだった. **2** N-VAR 可変性名詞 If there are **inconsistencies** between two statements, one cannot be true if the other is true. 矛盾 □ *We were asked to investigate the alleged inconsistencies in his evidence.* 彼の証言で矛盾していると言われている点について調査するように依頼された.

in|con|sist|ent /ɪnkənsɪstənt/ **1** ADJ 形容詞 If you describe someone as **inconsistent**, you are criticizing them for not behaving in the same way every time a similar situation occurs. 一貫性がない[DISAPPROVAL 不賛成] □ *You are inconsistent and unpredictable.* あなたは一貫性がなくて気まぐれだ. **2** ADJ 形容詞 Someone or something that is **inconsistent** does not stay the same, being sometimes good and sometimes bad. むらがある, 当たり外れが多い □ *We had a terrific start to the season, but recently we've been inconsistent.* 我々はシーズンの始まりは素晴らしかったけれども, 最近はむらがある. **3** ADJ 形容詞 If two statements are **inconsistent**, one cannot possibly be true if the other is true. 矛盾する, つじつまが合わない □ *The evidence given in court was inconsistent with what he had previously told them.* 法廷での証言は以前彼が言っていたことと食い違っていた. **4** ADJ 形容詞 If something is **inconsistent with** a set of ideas or values, it does not fit in well with them or match them. 一致しない, 相反する [v-link ADJ 'with' n] □ *This legislation is inconsistent with what they call Free Trade.* この法律はいわゆる自由貿易に反する.

in|con|ti|nence /ɪnkɒntɪnəns/ N-UNCOUNT 不可算名詞 **Incontinence** is the inability to control urine or feces from coming out of your body. 失禁 □ *Incontinence is not just a condition of old age.* 失禁は老齢の体調の1つであるだけではない.

in|con|ti|nent /ɪnkɒntɪnənt/ ADJ 形容詞 Someone who is **incontinent** is unable to control urine or feces from coming out of their body. 失禁の □ *His diseased bladder left him incontinent.* 彼は膀胱疾患のため失禁症状が残った.

in|con|ven|ience /ɪnkənvinyəns/ (**inconveniences, inconveniencing, inconvenienced**) **1** N-VAR 可変性名詞 If someone or something causes **inconvenience**, they cause problems or difficulties. 迷惑, 不便 □ *We apologize for any inconvenience caused during the repairs.* 修理中に何かご迷惑をおかけしましたらお詫びいたします. **2** V-T 他動詞 If someone **inconveniences** you, they cause problems or difficulties for you. 迷惑をかける □ *He promised to be quick so as not to inconvenience them any further.* 彼らにこれ以上迷惑をかけないように早くすると彼は約束した.

in|con|ven|ient /ɪnkənvinyənt/ ADJ 形容詞 Something that is **inconvenient** causes problems or difficulties for someone. 都合が悪い □ *Can you come at 10:30? I know it's inconvenient, but I have to see you.* 10時半に来れますか. 都合が悪いことは分かっているけど, 会わなきゃいけないのです.

Word Link   *corp ≈ body : corporal, corpse, in corporate*

in|cor|po|rate /ɪnkɔrpəreɪt/ (**incorporates, incorporating, incorporated**) **1** V-T 他動詞 If one thing **incorporates** another thing, it includes the other thing. 含む, 取り入れる [FORMAL 形式ばった] □ *The new cars will incorporate a number of major improvements.* 新車には数々の大きな改良を加える予定です. **2** V-T 他動詞 If someone or something **is incorporated into** a large group, system, or area, they become a part of it. 組み入れる, 編入する [FORMAL 形式ばった] □ *The agreement would allow the rebels to be incorporated into a new national police force.* その合意によって反乱軍が新しい国家警察隊に編入されることになりましょう.

In|cor|po|rated /ɪnkɔrpəreɪtɪd/ ADJ 形容詞 **Incorporated** is used after a company's name to show that it is a legally established company. 法人組織の, 有限責任の [AM 米国英語 BUSINESS 実業] [n ADJ] □ *...MCA Incorporated.* MCA社

in|cor|rect /ɪnkərɛkt/ **1** ADJ 形容詞 Something that is **incorrect** is wrong and untrue. 間違った, 正しくない □ *He denied that his evidence about the telephone call was incorrect.* 彼はその通話に関する彼の証言が間違っていることはないと言った. ● **in|cor|rect|ly** ADV 副詞 [ADV with v] 間違って □ *The magazine suggested, incorrectly, that he was planning to announce his retirement.* 彼は引退準備をしようとしているのではないかとその雑誌は間違って報じた. **2** ADJ 形容詞 Something that is **incorrect** is not the thing that is required or is most suitable in a particular situation. 不適当な, 妥当でない

□ *...injuries caused by incorrect posture.* 悪い姿勢によって起こった負傷 ● **in|cor|rect|ly** ADV 副詞 [ADV with v] 不適当に, 正しくなく □ *He was told that the doors had been installed incorrectly.* ドアが正しく取り付けられていなかったのだと彼は知らされた.

Word Link   *cresc, creas ≈ growing : crescent, decrease, in crease*

in|crease (**increases, increasing, increased**)

> The verb is pronounced /ɪnkris/. The noun is pronounced /ɪnkris/.
>
> 動詞は /ɪnkris/ と発音される. 名詞は /ɪnkris/ と発音される.

1 V-T/V-I 他動詞/自動詞 If something **increases** or you **increase** it, it becomes greater in number, level, or amount. 増やす, 増える □ *The population continues to increase.* 人口は増加し続ける. □ *Japan's industrial output increased by 2%.* 日本の工業生産高は2%増加した. **2** N-COUNT 可算名詞 If there is an **increase** in the number, level, or amount of something, it becomes greater. 増加, 増大, 増進 □ *...a sharp increase in productivity.* 生産性の急激な増進 **3** PHRASE 句 If something is **on the increase**, it is happening more often or becoming greater in number or intensity. 増加して □ *Crime is on the increase.* 犯罪が増加している.

Thesaurus   *increase* また次を参照:

V.	expand, extend, raise; (ant.) decrease, reduce **1**
N.	gain, hike, raise, rise; (ant.) decrease, reduction **2**

Word Partnership   *increase* は次の語句と使われる:

ADV.	increase **dramatically**, increase **rapidly** **1**
ADJ.	**big** increase, **marked** increase, **sharp** increase **1 2**
N.	increase **in size**, increase **in temperature**, increase **in value** **1 2** increase in crime, increase **in demand**, increase **in spending**, **population** increase, **price** increase, **salary** increase **2**

in|creas|ing|ly /ɪnkrisɪŋli/ ADV 副詞 You can use **increasingly** to indicate that a situation or quality is becoming greater in intensity or more common. ますます, だんだん □ *He was finding it increasingly difficult to make decisions.* 彼はますます決断しにくくなったと感じていた. □ *The U.S. has increasingly relied on Japanese capital.* 米国はますます日本の資本に依存している.

Word Partnership   *increasingly* は次の語句と使われる:

ADJ.	increasingly **clear**, increasingly **common**, increasingly **complex**, increasingly **difficult**, increasingly **important**, increasingly **popular**

Word Link   *cred ≈ to believe : credentials, credibility, in credible*

in|cred|ible /ɪnkrɛdɪbəl/ **1** ADJ 形容詞 If you describe something or someone as **incredible**, you like them very much or are impressed by them, because they are extremely or unusually good. すばらしい, すごくいい[APPROVAL 賛成] □ *The wildflowers will be incredible after this rain.* この雨の後は野生の花がすごくいいでしょう. ● **in|cred|ibly** /ɪnkrɛdɪbli/ ADV 副詞 [ADV adj/adv] すばらしく, すごく □ *Their father was incredibly good-looking.* 彼らの父親はすごくハンサムだった. **2** ADJ 形容詞 If you say that something is **incredible**, you mean that it is very unusual or surprising, and you cannot believe it is really true, although it may be. 信じられない, 驚くべき □ *It seemed incredible that people would still want to play football during a war.* 戦争中でもみんながフットボールをしたがるのは驚くべきことだと思いました. ● **in|cred|ibly** ADV 副詞 信じられないほど □ *Incredibly, some people don't like the name.* 信じられないことに, その名前が嫌いな人もいます. **3** ADJ 形容詞 You use **incredible** to emphasize the degree, amount, or intensity of something. 途方もない, 非常な[EMPHASIS 強調] □ *I work an incredible amount of hours.* 私は途方もなく長い時間働く. ● **in|cred|ibly** ADV 副詞 [ADV adj/adv] 途方もなく, 非常に □ *It was incredibly hard work.* それは非常にきつい仕事だった.

Word Partnership   *incredible* は次の語句と使われる:

N.	incredible **discovery**, incredible **prices** **1** incredible **experience** **1 – 3**
ADV.	**absolutely** incredible **1 – 3**

in|credu|lous /ɪnkrɛdʒələs/ ADJ 形容詞 If someone is **incredulous**, they are unable to believe something because it is very surprising or shocking. 疑い深い, 疑うような □ *"He made you do it?" Her voice was incredulous.* 「彼にやらされたって?」彼女は怪しむように言った. ● **in|credu|lous|ly** ADV 副詞 [ADV with v] 疑い深く, 疑うように □ *"You told Pete?" Rachel said incredulously. "I can't believe it!"* 「ピーターに言ったって?信じられないわ!」とレイチェルは疑い深く言った.

in|cre|ment /ɪnkrɪmənt/ (**increments**) **1** N-COUNT 可算名詞 An **increment** in something or **in** the value of something is an amount by which it increases. 増加量 [FORMAL 形式ばった] □ The average yearly increment in productivity was 4.5 per cent. 生産性の年平均増加率は4.5%であった. **2** N-COUNT 可算名詞 An **increment** is an amount by which your salary automatically increases after a fixed period of time. 定期昇給額 [BRIT 英国英語, FORMAL 形式ばった] [AM raise 米国英語 raise]

in|crimi|nate /ɪnkrɪmɪneɪt/ (**incriminates, incriminating, incriminated**) V-T 他動詞 If something **incriminates** you, it suggests that you are responsible for something bad, especially a crime. 有罪にする, 罪を負わせる □ He claimed that the drugs had been planted to incriminate him. その麻薬は彼に罪を着せるために、こっそり置かれたのだと彼は主張した. ●**in|crimi|nat|ing** ADJ 形容詞 罪に陥れるような, 罪があることを示す □ Police had reportedly searched his house and found incriminating evidence. 報道によると, 警察は彼の家を捜査し彼が有罪であることを示す証拠を発見した.

in|cu|bate /ɪnkyəbeɪt, ɪŋ/ (**incubates, incubating, incubated**) V-T/V-I 他動詞/自動詞 When birds **incubate** their eggs, or when they **incubate**, they keep the eggs warm until the baby birds come out. (卵を) 抱く [他動詞], 卵を抱く, (卵が) かえる [自動詞] □ The birds returned to their nests and continued to incubate the eggs. その鳥たちはそれぞれの巣に戻り, 卵を抱き続けた. □ They lay eggs that incubate through the winter. それらは卵を産んで冬の間にかえる. ●**in|cu|ba|tion** /ɪnkyəbeɪʃⁿn, ɪŋ/ N-UNCOUNT 不可算名詞 抱卵 □ Male albatrosses share in the incubation of eggs. アホウドリの雄は抱卵を分担する.

in|cum|bent /ɪnkʌmbənt/ (**incumbents**) **1** N-COUNT 可算名詞 An **incumbent** is someone who holds an official post at a particular time. 現職者 [FORMAL 形式ばった] □ In general, incumbents have a 94 percent chance of being re-elected. 一般的に現職者が再選される確率は94%です. ●ADJ 形容詞 **Incumbent** is also an adjective. 現職の [ADJ n] □ ...the only candidate who defeated an incumbent senator. 現職の上院議員を破った唯一の候補者. **2** ADJ 形容詞 If it is **incumbent on** or **upon** you to do something, it is your duty or responsibility to do it. 義務の [FORMAL 形式ばった] □ She felt it was incumbent on herself to act immediately. 彼女はすぐ対処するのが自分の義務だと感じた.

in|cur /ɪnkɜr/ (**incurs, incurring, incurred**) V-T 他動詞 If you **incur** something unpleasant, it happens to you because of something you have done. 招く, 負う [WRITTEN 書き言葉] □ The government had also incurred huge debts. 政府は巨大な負債も負っていました.

Word Link　　　able ≈ able to be : incurable, portable, unavoi

in|cur|able /ɪnkyʊərəbⁿl/ **1** ADJ 形容詞 If someone has an **incurable** disease, they cannot be cured of it. 治らない, 不治の □ He is suffering from an incurable skin disease. 彼は不治の皮膚疾患にかかっている. ●**in|cur|ably** /ɪnkyʊərəbli/ ADV 副詞 [ADV adj] 治しようもないほど □ ...youngsters who are disabled, or incurably ill. 身体障害があるか, 不治の病にかかった若者たち. **2** ADJ 形容詞 You can use **incurable** to indicate that someone has a particular quality or attitude and will not change. 救いがたい [ADJ n] □ Poor old Willy is an incurable romantic. かわいそうに, ウィリーのやつは度しがたいロマンチストだ. ●**in|cur|ably** ADV 副詞 [ADV adj] 救いがたいほど □ I know you think I'm incurably nosy, but the truth is I'm concerned about you. あなたが私のことをどうしようもないおせっかいだと思っているのは分かっているけれども, 本当のところ, あなたのことを心配しているのよ.

in|debt|ed /ɪndɛtɪd/ **1** ADJ 形容詞 If you say that you are **indebted to** someone for something, you mean that you are very grateful to them for something. 恩を受けて [v-link ADJ 'to' n] □ I am deeply indebted to him for his help. 私は彼の援助を深く恩に着ています. **2** ADJ 形容詞 **Indebted** countries, organizations, or people are ones that owe money to other countries, organizations, or people. 負債のある □ The treasury secretary identified the most heavily indebted countries. 財務長官は最も負債の大きい国々を確認した.

in|de|cen|cy /ɪndisⁿnsi/ (**indecencies**) **1** N-UNCOUNT 不可算名詞 If you talk about the **indecency** of something or someone, you are indicating that you find them morally or sexually offensive. 下品 □ ...the indecency of their language. 彼らの言葉遣いの下品さ. **2** N-COUNT 可算名詞 In law, an **indecency** is an illegal sexual act. わいせつ行為 □ ...sexual indecencies. 性的わいせつ行為

in|de|cent /ɪndisⁿnt/ **1** ADJ 形容詞 If you describe something as **indecent**, you mean that it is shocking and offensive, usually because it relates to sex or nakedness. みだらな □ He accused Mrs. Moore of making an indecent suggestion. 彼はみだらなことをほのめかしたとムーア夫人を責めた. ●**in|de|cent|ly** ADV 副詞 みだらなほどに □ ...an indecently short skirt. みだらなほどに短いスカート **2** ADJ 形容詞 If you describe the speed or amount of something as **indecent**, you are indicating, often in a humorous way, that it is much quicker or larger than is usual or desirable. 不適当な □ She finished her first glass of wine with indecent haste. 彼女は大あわてで1杯目のワ

インを飲み干した. ●**in|de|cent|ly** ADV 副詞 不適当なほどに □ ...an indecently large office. 不当なほど大きい事務所

in|de|ci|sion /ɪndɪsɪʒⁿn/ N-UNCOUNT 不可算名詞 If you say that someone suffers from **indecision**, you mean that they find it very difficult to make decisions. 優柔不断, ためらい □ After months of indecision, the government gave the plan the go-ahead on Monday. 何か月間も迷った末, 政府は月曜にその計画に許可を出した.

in|de|ci|sive /ɪndɪsaɪsɪv/ **1** ADJ 形容詞 If you say that someone is **indecisive**, you mean that they find it very difficult to make decisions. 優柔不断な □ He was criticized as a weak and indecisive leader. 彼は気弱で優柔不断な指導者だと批判されていた. **2** ADJ 形容詞 An **indecisive** result in a contest or election is one that is not clear or definite. 決定的でない, 不明確な □ The outcome of the battle was indecisive. その戦いの結果ははっきりしていなかった.

in|deed /ɪndid/ **1** ADV 副詞 You use **indeed** to confirm or agree with something that has just been said. 本当に [EMPHASIS 強調] □ Later, he admitted that the payments had indeed been made. その後彼は本当に支払いがあったと認めた. □ "Did you know him?"—"I did indeed." 「彼のこと知っていたの?」「本当に知っていました」 **2** ADV 副詞 You use **indeed** to introduce a further comment or statement that strengthens the point you have already made. いやそれどころか [EMPHASIS 強調] [ADV with cl] □ We have nothing against diversity; indeed, we want more of it. 私たちは多様性には何ら反対していません. いやそれどころか, もっと多様性があったほうがいいぐらいです. **3** ADV 副詞 You use **indeed** at the end of a clause to give extra force to the word "very," or to emphasize a particular word. 実に, 全く [EMPHASIS 強調] [adj ADV] □ The results are often strange indeed. 実に変な結果が出ることが多いです.

in|defi|nite /ɪndɛfɪnɪt/ **1** ADJ 形容詞 If you describe a situation or period as **indefinite**, you mean that people have not decided when it will end. 不定の □ The trial was adjourned for an indefinite period. 裁判は無期延期された. **2** ADJ 形容詞 Something that is **indefinite** is not exact or clear. 明確でない □ ...at some indefinite time in the future. 将来いつしか

in|defi|nite ar|ti|cle (**indefinite articles**) N-COUNT 可算名詞 The words "a" and "an" are sometimes called **the indefinite article**. 不定冠詞

in|defi|nite|ly /ɪndɛfɪnɪtli/ ADV 副詞 If a situation will continue **indefinitely**, it will continue forever or until someone decides to change it or end it. 無期限に [ADV with v] □ The visit has now been postponed indefinitely. その訪問は現在のところ無期限延期となっている.

Word Link　　　damn, demn ≈ harm, loss : condemn, damning, indemnify

in|dem|ni|fy /ɪndɛmnɪfaɪ/ (**indemnifies, indemnifying, indemnified**) V-T 他動詞 To **indemnify** someone against something bad happening means to promise to protect them, especially financially, if it happens. 保障する [FORMAL 形式ばった] □ They agreed to indemnify the taxpayers against any loss. 彼らは納税者がどんな損失も受けないように保障することを合意した.

in|dem|ni|ty /ɪndɛmnɪti/ N-UNCOUNT 不可算名詞 If something provides **indemnity**, it provides insurance or protection against damage or loss. 損害補償, 免責保護 [FORMAL 形式ばった] □ Political exiles had not been given indemnity from prosecution. 政治亡命者は起訴を免れるような保護を受けていなかった.

Word Link　　　ence ≈ state, condition : dependence, excellence, independence

in|de|pend|ence /ɪndɪpɛndəns/ **1** N-UNCOUNT 不可算名詞 If a country has or gains **independence**, it has its own government and is not ruled by any other country. 独立 □ In 1816, Argentina declared its independence from Spain. 1816年にアルゼンチンはスペインからの独立を宣言した. **2** N-UNCOUNT 不可算名詞 Someone's **independence** is the fact that they do not rely on other people. 自立, 非依存 □ He was afraid of losing his independence. 彼は自立できなくなることを恐れていた.

Word Partnership　　　independence は次の語句と使われる:

N.	a struggle for independence **1**
V.	fight for independence, gain independence **1**
ADJ.	economic/financial independence **1** **2**

in|de|pend|ent /ɪndɪpɛndənt/ (**independents**) **1** ADJ 形容詞 If one thing or person is **independent of** another, they are separate and not connected, so the first one is not affected or influenced by the second. 独立した □ Your questions should be independent of each other. あなたの質問はそれぞれ独立したものであるべきです. □ We're going independent from the university and setting up our own group. 私たちは大学から独立して, 自分たちのグループを設立するつもりだ. ●**in|de|pen|dent|ly** ADV 副詞 独立して, 単独で □ ...several people working independently in different areas of the

world. 世界の異なる地域で単独で仕事をしている何人かの人たち **2** ADJ 形容詞 If someone is **independent**, they do not need help or money from anyone else. 独立した，頼らない ◻ *Phil was now much more independent of his parents.* フィルは今では前ほど両親に頼ってなかった． ● **in|de|pen|dent|ly** ADV 副詞 独立して ◻ *...helping disabled students to live and study as independently as possible.* 身体障害のある学生ができるだけ独立して生活し勉強できるように援助して **3** ADJ 形容詞 **Independent** countries and states are not ruled by other countries but have their own government. 独立した ◻ *Papua New Guinea became independent from Australia in 1975.* パプアニューギニアは1975年にオーストラリアから独立した． **4** ADJ 形容詞 [ADJ n] An **independent** organization or other body is one that controls its own finances and operations, rather than being controlled by someone else. 独立した ◻ *...an independent television station.* 独立テレビ局 **5** ADJ 形容詞 An **independent** inquiry or opinion is one that involves people who are not connected with a particular situation, and should therefore be fair. 独自の [ADJ n] ◻ *There were calls in Congress for an independent inquiry.* 議会内には独自の調査を求める声があった． **6** ADJ 形容詞 An **independent** politician is one who does not represent any political party. 無所属の ◻ *There's been a late surge of support for an independent candidate.* 無所属の候補者に対する支持が最近急上昇している． ● N-COUNT 可算名詞 An **independent** is an independent politician. 無所属の政治家 ◻ *Mr. Vassiliou, standing as an independent, succeeded in convincing a significant number of voters of his argument.* 無所属で立候補しているヴァシリウ氏は，その主張をかなり多くの有権者に納得させることに成功した．

Thesaurus independent また次を参照：

ADJ. self-reliant, self-supporting; (ant.) dependent **1** **2** liberated, self-governing **3**

in|dex /ɪ́ndɛks/ (**indices**, **indexes**, **indexing**, **indexed**)

The usual plural is **indexes**, but the form **indices** can be used for meaning **1**.

普通の複数は **indexes** であるが，**indices** 形が**1**を意味するのに使える．

1 N-COUNT 可算名詞 An **index** is a system by which changes in the value of something and the rate at which it changes can be recorded, measured, or interpreted. 指標，指数 ◻ *...the consumer price index.* 消費者物価指数 **2** N-COUNT 可算名詞 An **index** is an alphabetical list that is printed at the back of a book and tells you on which pages important topics are referred to. 索引 ◻ *There's even a special subject index.* 特殊事項の索引さえもあります． **3** V-T 他動詞 If you **index** a book or a collection of information, you make an alphabetical list of the items in it. 索引をつける，索引に載せる ◻ *A quarter of this vast archive has been indexed and made accessible to researchers.* この膨大な公文書の4分の1は索引が作成されており，研究者が利用できるようになっている． **4** V-T 他動詞 If a quantity or value **is indexed to** another, a system is arranged so that it increases or decreases whenever the other one increases or decreases. (変動に応じて) 調整する [usu passive] ◻ *Minimum benefits and wages are to be indexed to inflation.* 最低手当てと賃金はインフレに応じて調整されるべきだ． **5** → see also **card index** → see **hand**

in|di|cate /ɪ́ndɪkeɪt/ (**indicates**, **indicating**, **indicated**) **1** V-T 他動詞 If one thing **indicates** another, the first thing shows that the second is true or exists. 示す ◻ *A survey of retired people has indicated that most are independent and enjoying life.* 退職者たちについてのある調査は，大部分の人たちが自立して楽しく暮らしていることを示した． ◻ *Our vote today indicates a change in United States policy.* 本日の投票結果は米国の政策の変化を示している． **2** V-T 他動詞 If you **indicate** an opinion, an intention, or a fact, you mention it in an indirect way. 暗に示す，それとなく知らせる ◻ *Mr. Rivers has indicated that he may resign.* リバーズ氏は辞任するかもしれないことをほのめかした． **3** V-T 他動詞 If you **indicate** something to someone, you show them where it is, especially by pointing to it. 指し示す [FORMAL 形式ばった] ◻ *He indicated a chair. "Sit down."* 彼は椅子を指して「お座りなさい」と言った． **4** V-T 他動詞 If one thing **indicates** something else, it is a sign of that thing. 兆しである，表わす ◻ *Dreams can help indicate your true feelings.* 夢はあなたの本当の気持ちの兆しになっていることがある． **5** V-T 他動詞 If a technical instrument **indicates** something, it shows a measurement or reading. 表示する，指示する ◻ *...an instrument used to indicate wind direction.* 風向を表示するのに用いられる器具 **6** V-T/V-I 他動詞/自動詞 When drivers **indicate**, they make lights flash on one side of their vehicle to show that they are going to turn in that direction. 指示を出す，示す [mainly BRIT 主に英国英語; AM **signal** 米国英語 **signal**]

Thesaurus indicate また次を参照：

V. demonstrate, hint, mean, reveal, show **1** **2**

Word Partnership indicate は次の語句と使われる：

N. **polls** indicate, **records** indicate, **reports** indicate, **results** indicate, **statistics** indicate, **studies** indicate, **surveys** indicate **1** indicate **a change in** *something* **1** **2**

in|di|ca|tion /ɪ̀ndɪkéɪʃ⁰n/ (**indications**) N-VAR 可変性名詞 An **indication** is a sign that suggests, for example, what people are thinking or feeling. 表示，兆候 ◻ *He gave no indication that he was ready to compromise.* 彼は妥協する用意がある様子はまったく見せなかった．

Word Partnership indication は次の語句と使われる：

ADJ. **a clear** indication, **a strong** indication
V. **give an** indication

in|dica|tive /ɪndɪ́kətɪv/ ADJ 形容詞 If one thing is **indicative** of another, it suggests what the other thing is likely to be. 示して [FORMAL 形式ばった] ◻ *His action is indicative of growing concern about the shortage of skilled labor.* 彼の行動は熟練労働者の不足に関する懸念が高まっていることを示している．

in|dica|tor /ɪ́ndɪkeɪtər/ (**indicators**) **1** N-COUNT 可算名詞 An **indicator** is a measurement or value that gives you an idea of what something is like. 指標 ◻ *...vital economic indicators, such as inflation, growth and the trade gap.* インフレ，成長，貿易赤字などの極めて重要な経済指標 **2** N-COUNT 可算名詞 A car's **indicators** are the flashing lights that tell you when it is going to turn left or right. 方向指示器 [mainly BRIT 主に英国英語; AM **turn signals** 米国英語 **turn signals**]

Word Partnership indicator は次の語句と使われる：

ADJ. **economic** indicator, **good** indicator, **important** indicator, **reliable** indicator **1**

in|di|ces /ɪ́ndɪsiz/ **Indices** is a plural form of **index**. index の複数形

in|dict /ɪndáɪt/ (**indicts**, **indicting**, **indicted**) V-T 他動詞 If someone **is indicted for** a crime, they are officially charged with it. 起訴する [mainly AM 主に米国英語 LEGAL 法律的] [usu passive] ◻ *He was later indicted on corruption charges.* 彼はその後汚職罪で起訴された．

in|dict|ment /ɪndáɪtmənt/ (**indictments**) **1** N-COUNT 可算名詞 If you say that one thing is **an indictment of** another thing, you mean that it shows how bad the other thing is. 非難，告発 ◻ *The movie is an indictment of Hollywood.* その映画はハリウッドを非難したものである． **2** N-VAR 可変性名詞 An **indictment** is a formal accusation that someone has committed a crime. 起訴 [mainly AM 主に米国英語 LEGAL 法律的] ◻ *Prosecutors may soon seek an indictment on racketeering and fraud charges.* 検察当局はまもなく恐喝罪と詐欺罪での起訴をしようとするかもしれない．

in|die /ɪ́ndi/ (**indies**) **1** ADJ 形容詞 **Indie** music refers to rock or pop music produced by new bands working with small, independent record companies. (音楽の) 独立プロの，インディーの [ADJ n] ◻ *...a multi-racial indie band.* 多民族インディーバンド ● N-COUNT 可算名詞 An **indie** is an indie band or record company. 独立プロ，インディー ◻ *The fact is that the indies are selling a lot more CDs than the major record labels.* 独立プロは大手レーベルよりCDの売り上げ枚数がずっと多いというのが真相だ． **2** ADJ 形容詞 **Indie** films are produced by small independent companies rather than by major studios. (映画の) 独立プロの，インディーの [ADJ n] ◻ *With a role in the indie movie "Happiness," her career is now swimming along.* インディー映画『幸福』に出演したことにより，彼女のキャリアは順調に前進している． ● N-COUNT 可算名詞 An **indie** is an indie film or film company. 独立プロ ◻ *The indies convert their digital movies to film.* 独立プロはそのデジタル映画をフィルム化している．

in|dif|fer|ence /ɪndɪ́fərəns/ N-UNCOUNT 不可算名詞 If you accuse someone of **indifference** to something, you mean that they have a complete lack of interest in it. 無関心さ ◻ *...his callous indifference to the plight of his son.* 息子の苦境に対する彼の冷淡な無関心さ

in|dif|fer|ent /ɪndɪ́fərənt/ **1** ADJ 形容詞 If you accuse someone of being **indifferent to** something, you mean that they have a complete lack of interest in it. 無関心な ◻ *People have become indifferent to the suffering of others.* 人々は他人の苦しみに無関心になりました． ● **in|dif|fer|ent|ly** ADV 副詞 無関心で ◻ *"Not that it matters," said Trujillo indifferently.* 「別にどうでもいいけどね」とトルヒーヨは無関心さそうに言った． **2** ADJ 形容詞 If you describe something or someone as **indifferent**, you mean that their standard or quality is not very good, and often quite bad. 平凡な，まずい ◻ *She had starred in several very indifferent movies.* 彼女はいくつかの全くぱっとしない映画で主役を演じた． ● **in|dif|fer|ent|ly** ADV

副詞 [ADV with v] 平凡に，まずく ❑...*a shoddy piece of work, poorly written, indifferently performed.* 脚本はお粗末で，演技は平凡な，見かけ倒しの作品.

in|dig|enous /ɪndɪdʒɪnəs/ ADJ 形容詞 **Indigenous** people or things belong to the country in which they are found, rather than coming there or being brought there from another country. 土着の，原産の [FORMAL 形式ばった] ❑...*the country's indigenous population.* その国の先住民族

in|di|ges|tion /ɪndɪdʒestʃ°n, -daɪ-/ N-UNCOUNT 不可算名詞 If you have **indigestion**, you have pains in your stomach and chest that are caused by difficulties in digesting food. 消化不良

Word Link dign ≈ proper, worthy : dignified, dignitary, indignant

in|dig|nant /ɪndɪgnənt/ ADJ 形容詞 If you are **indignant**, you are shocked and angry, because you think that something is unjust or unfair. 憤慨した，怒った ❑*He is indignant at suggestions that they were secret agents.* 彼らがスパイだったとの示唆に彼は憤慨しています. ❑*He was indignant that his rival was offered the job.* 彼の競争相手にその仕事が行ったので彼は腹を立てた. ●**in|dig|nant|ly** 副詞 [ADV with v] 怒って ❑*"That is not true,"* Erica said *indignantly.* 「それは事実と違うわ」とエリカは怒って言った.

in|dig|na|tion /ɪndɪgneɪʃ°n/ N-UNCOUNT 不可算名詞 **Indignation** is a feeling of shock and anger when you think that something is unjust or unfair. 憤慨，憤り ❑*She was filled with indignation at the conditions under which miners were forced to work.* 鉱夫たちが働かされているひどい状態に彼女は激しい憤りを感じた.

in|dig|nity /ɪndɪgnɪti/ (**indignities**) N-VAR 可変性名詞 If you talk about **the indignity of** doing something, you mean that it makes you feel embarrassed or unimportant. 侮辱 [FORMAL 形式ばった] ❑*Later, he suffered the indignity of having to flee angry protesters.* その後，彼は怒って抗議する人たちから逃げなければならないという辱めを受けた.

in|di|rect /ɪndaɪrekt, -dɪr-/ ■ ADJ 形容詞 An **indirect** result or effect is not caused immediately and obviously by a thing or person, but happens because of something else that they have done. 間接的な ❑*Businesses are feeling the indirect effects from the recession that's going on elsewhere.* 企業はよそで景気が後退していることの間接的な影響を感じています. ●**in|di|rect|ly** ADV 副詞 間接的に ❑*Drugs are indirectly responsible for the violence.* 麻薬は間接的に暴力の原因となっている. ■ ADJ 形容詞 An **indirect** route or journey does not use the shortest or easiest way between two places. 遠回りの ❑*He took an indirect route back home.* 彼は回り道をして家に帰った. ■ ADJ 形容詞 **Indirect** remarks and information suggest something or refer to it, without actually mentioning it or stating it clearly. 遠回しの ❑*His remarks amounted to an indirect appeal for economic aid.* 彼の発言は結局のところ遠回しに経済援助を求めているものでした. ●**in|di|rect|ly** ADV 副詞 [ADV with v] 遠回しに ❑*He referred indirectly to the territorial dispute.* 彼は遠回しに領土問題に触れた.

in|di|rect dis|course N-UNCOUNT 不可算名詞 **Indirect discourse** is speech that tells you what someone said, but does not use the person's actual words; for example, "They said you didn't like it." , "I asked him what his plans were." , and "Citizens complained about the smoke." 間接話法

in|di|rect ob|ject (**indirect objects**) N-COUNT 可算名詞 An **indirect object** is an object that is used with a transitive verb to indicate who benefits from an action or gets something as a result. For example, in "She gave him her address." , "him" is the indirect object. Compare **direct object**. 間接目的語

in|di|rect speech N-UNCOUNT 不可算名詞 **Indirect speech** is the same as **indirect discourse**. 間接話法

in|dis|crimi|nate /ɪndɪskrɪmɪnət/ ADJ 形容詞 If you describe an action as **indiscriminate**, you are critical of it because it does not involve any careful thought or choice. 無差別の [DISAPPROVAL 不賛成] ❑*The indiscriminate use of fertilizers is damaging to the environment.* 化学肥料を無差別に使用することは環境に有害です. ●**in|dis|crimi|nate|ly** ADV 副詞 無差別に ❑*The men opened fire indiscriminately.* 彼らは無差別に発砲した.

in|dis|pen|sable /ɪndɪspensəb°l/ ADJ 形容詞 If you say that someone or something is **indispensable**, you mean that they are absolutely essential and other people or things cannot function without them. 不可欠な，絶対必要な ❑*She was becoming indispensable to him.* 彼は彼女なしではやっていけなくなっていた.

Word Link put ≈ thinking : computer, dispute, indisputable

in|dis|put|able /ɪndɪspyutəb°l/ ADJ 形容詞 If you say that something is **indisputable**, you are emphasizing that it is true and cannot be shown to be untrue. 議論の余地のない，明白な [EMPHASIS 強調] ❑*It is indisputable that birds are harboring this illness.* 鳥がこの病気を持っているのは明白だ.

in|dis|tin|guish|able /ɪndɪstɪŋgwɪʃəb°l/ ADJ 形容詞 If one thing is **indistinguishable from** another, the two things are so

similar that it is difficult to know which is which. 区別できない ❑*Replica weapons are indistinguishable from the real thing.* 複製の武器は本物と見分けがつかない.

in|di|vid|ual /ɪndɪvɪdʒuəl/ (**individuals**) ■ ADJ 形容詞 **Individual** means relating to one person or thing, rather than to a large group. 個人の，個々の [ADJ n] ❑...*waiting for the group to decide rather than making individual decisions.* 個人的な決定をするよりはグループが決定を下すのを待って. ●**in|di|vid|ual|ly** ADV 副詞 個人で，個々で ❑...*individually crafted tiles.* 個別に手作りしたタイル. ■ N-COUNT 可算名詞 An **individual** is a person. 個人，人 ❑...*anonymous individuals who are doing good things within our community.* 私たちの地域社会内でよい活動をしている無名の人たち. ■ ADJ 形容詞 If you **describe** someone or something as **individual**, you mean that you admire them because they are very unusual and do not try to imitate other people or things. 個性的な [APPROVAL 賛成] ❑*It was really all part of her very individual personality.* まさにそれはすべて彼女のとても個性的な性格の一部だった.

Thesaurus *individual* また次を参照:

N. human being, person, somebody, someone ■
ADJ. distinctive, original, unique ■

in|di|vidu|al|ity /ɪndɪvɪdʒuælɪti/ N-UNCOUNT 不可算名詞 The **individuality** of a person or thing consists of the qualities that make them different from other people or things. 個性 ❑*People should be free to express their individuality.* 人々は自分の個性を自由に表わすのは当然だ.

in|di|vidu|al|ize /ɪndɪvɪdʒuəlaɪz/ (**individualizes, individualizing, individualized**) V-T 他動詞 To **individualize** a thing or person means to make them different from other things or people and to give them a recognizable identity. 個性を与える，個別化する [FORMAL 形式ばった] ❑*You can individualize a document by adding comments in the margins.* 余白にコメントを入れて個人に合った文書にすることが可能だ. ●**in|di|vidu|al|ized** ADJ 個人に合わせた，個別化した ❑*Doctors feel that a more individualized approach to patients should now be adopted.* 今では医師たちはもっと患者個人に合った接し方をすべきだと感じている.

in|door /ɪndɔr/ ADJ 形容詞 **Indoor** activities or things are ones that happen or are used inside a building and not outside. 屋内の [ADJ n] ❑*No smoking in any indoor facilities.* 屋内の施設は全て禁煙.

in|doors /ɪndɔrz/ ADV 副詞 If something happens **indoors**, it happens inside a building. 屋内で ❑*I think perhaps we should go indoors.* 恐らくみんな屋内に入ったほうがいいと思う.

in|duce /ɪndus/ (**induces, inducing, induced**) ■ V-T 他動詞 To **induce** a state or condition means to cause it. 引き起こす，誘発する ❑*Doctors said surgery could induce a heart attack.* 手術が心臓麻痺を誘発することもあると医師たちは言った. ■ V-T 他動詞 If you **induce** someone to do something, you persuade or influence them to do it. 勧めて～させる ❑*More than 4,000 teachers were induced to take early retirement.* 4千人以上の教師が早期退職するように説得された.

in|duce|ment /ɪndusmənt/ (**inducements**) N-COUNT 可算名詞 If someone is offered an **inducement to** do something, they are given or promised gifts or benefits in order to persuade them to do it. 勧誘 ❑*They offer every inducement to foreign businesses to invest in their states.* 彼らは外国の企業が自分の州に投資するようにあらゆる手を使って勧誘する.

in|duc|tion /ɪndʌkʃ°n/ (**inductions**) N-VAR 可変性名詞 **Induction** is a procedure or ceremony for introducing someone to a new job, organization, or way of life. 就任式，導入 ❑...*his induction as president.* 彼の社長就任式

in|dulge /ɪndʌldʒ/ (**indulges, indulging, indulged**) ■ V-T/V-I 他動詞/自動詞 If you **indulge in** something or if you **indulge** yourself, you allow yourself to have or do something that you know you will enjoy. 楽しむ，ふける ❑*Only rarely will she indulge in a glass of wine.* 彼女がぶどう酒を1杯楽しむのは極めて稀なことでしょう. ❑*He returned to Ohio so that he could indulge his passion for football.* 彼は満足行くまで大好きなフットボールができるようにオハイオ州に戻った. ■ V-T 他動詞 If you **indulge** someone, you let them have or do what they want, even if this is not good for them. 甘やかす ❑*He did not agree with indulging children.* 子供を甘やかすことは良くないと彼は思っていた.

Word Partnership *indulge* は次の語句と使われる:

ADV. freely indulge ■
PREP. indulge in *something* ■
N. indulge children ■

in|dul|gence /ɪndʌldʒ°ns/ (**indulgences**) N-VAR 可変性名詞 **Indulgence** means treating someone with special kindness, often when it is not a good thing. 甘やかし ❑*The king's indulgence toward his sons angered the business community.* 国王は息子たちを甘やかし，

実業界の怒りを買った.

in|dul|gent /ɪndʌldʒⁿnt/ ADJ 形容詞 If you are **indulgent**, you treat a person with special kindness, often in a way that is not good for them. 甘い ❑ *His indulgent mother was willing to let him do anything he wanted.* 彼に甘い母は彼がやりたいことは何でも喜んでさせていた. ● **in|dul|gent|ly** ADV 副詞 甘く，優しく ❑ *Najib smiled at him indulgently and said, "Come on over when you feel like it."* ナジブは彼に優しく微笑みかけ，「いつでも気が向いたとき来なさい」と言った.

in|dus|trial /ɪndʌstriəl/ ◼ ADJ 形容詞 You use **industrial** to describe things that relate to or are used in industry. 産業の，工業の ❑ *...industrial machinery and equipment.* 工業用機械と設備 ◻ ADJ 形容詞 An **industrial** city or country is one in which industry is important or highly developed. 産業の発達した ❑ *...leading western industrial countries.* 西側の先進工業諸国

Word Partnership	*industrial* は次の語句と使われる:
N.	industrial **machinery**, industrial **production**, industrial **products** ◼ industrial **area**, industrial **city**, industrial **country** ◻

in|dus|trial es|tate (**industrial estates**) N-COUNT 可算名詞 An **industrial estate** is the same as an **industrial park**. 工業団地 [BRIT 英国英語]

in|dus|trial|ist /ɪndʌstriəlɪst/ (**industrialists**) N-COUNT 可算名詞 An **industrialist** is a powerful businessperson who owns or controls large industrial companies or factories. 大実業家 ❑ *...prominent Japanese industrialists.* 日本の著名な大実業家たち

in|dus|trial|ize /ɪndʌstriəlaɪz/ (**industrializes**, **industrializing**, **Industrialized**) V-T/V-I 他動詞/自動詞 When a country **industrializes** or is **industrialized**, it develops a lot of industries. 産業化する，工業化する ❑ *Energy consumption rises as countries industrialize.* 諸国が工業化するにつれエネルギー消費量が増加する. ● **in|dus|tri|ali|za|tion** /ɪndʌstriəlɪzeɪʃⁿn/ N-UNCOUNT 不可算名詞 産業化 ❑ *Industrialization began early in Spain.* スペインの産業化の始まりは早かった.

in|dus|trial park (**industrial parks**) N-COUNT 可算名詞 An **industrial park** is an area that has been specially planned for a lot of factories. 工業団地 [AM 米国英語]

in|dus|trial re|la|tions N-PLURAL 複数名詞 **Industrial relations** refers to the relationship between employers and employees in industry, and the political decisions and laws that affect it. 労使関係 [BUSINESS 実業] ❑ *The offer is seen as an attempt to improve industrial relations.* その提案は労使関係の改善を図ったものだと見られている.

in|dus|try /ɪndəstri/ (**industries**) ◼ N-UNCOUNT 不可算名詞 **Industry** is the work and processes involved in collecting raw materials, and making them into products in factories. 産業，工業 ❑ *Our industry suffers through insufficient investment in research.* 研究に対する不十分な投資のため，我が国の産業は痛手を受けている. ◻ N-COUNT 可算名詞 A particular **industry** consists of all the people and activities involved in making a particular product or providing a particular service. (特定の) 産業界 ❑ *...the motor vehicle and textile industries.* 自動車産業と繊維産業 ▨ N-COUNT 可算名詞 If you refer to a social or political activity as an **industry**, you are criticizing it because you think it involves a lot of people in unnecessary or useless work. 産業 [DISAPPROVAL 不賛成] ❑ *...the industry of western capitalism.* 西側資本主義という産業 ▧ N-UNCOUNT 不可算名詞 **Industry** is the fact of working very hard. 勤勉 [FORMAL 形式ばった] ❑ *No one doubted his ability, his industry or his integrity.* 誰も彼の能力，勤勉さ，誠実さを疑わなかった. ▩ → see also **cottage industry, service industry**
→ see Word Web: **industry**
→ see **cotton**

in|ed|ible /ɪnɛdɪbⁿl/ ADJ 形容詞 If you say that something is **inedible**, you mean you cannot eat it, for example, because it tastes bad or is poisonous. 食用に適さない ❑ *Detainees complained of being given inedible food.* 抑留者たちは支給される食べ物がとても食べられるものではないと文句を言った.
→ see **cooking**

in|ef|fec|tive /ɪnɪfɛktɪv/ ADJ 形容詞 If you say that something is **ineffective**, you mean that it has no effect on a process or situation. 効果のない ❑ *Economic reform will continue to be painful and ineffective.* 経済改革は引き続き苦痛を招くだけで効果はないでしょう.

in|ef|fec|tual /ɪnɪfɛktʃuəl/ ADJ 形容詞 If someone or something is **ineffectual**, they fail to do what they are expected to do or are trying to do. 役に立たない ❑ *The mayor had become ineffectual in the struggle to clamp down on drugs.* 市長は麻薬を厳重に取り締まる戦いで効果を挙げられなくなっていた. ● **in|ef|fec|tu|al|ly** ADV 副詞 効果なく ❑ *Her voice trailed off ineffectually.* 彼女の声は効果なく次第に消えていった.

in|ef|fi|cient /ɪnɪfɪʃⁿnt/ ADJ 形容詞 **Inefficient** people, organizations, systems, or machines do not use time, energy, or other resources in the best way. 非能率的な ❑ *Their communication systems are inefficient in the extreme.* 彼らの通信体制ははなはだしく非能率的である. ● **in|ef|fi|cien|cy** (**inefficiencies**) N-VAR 可変性名詞 非能率 ❑ *The inefficiency of the distribution system has led to the loss of millions of tons of food.* 流通機構の効率が悪いために何百万トンもの食品が無駄になってしまった. ● **in|ef|fi|cient|ly** ADV 副詞 [ADV with v] 効率悪く ❑ *Energy prices have been kept low, so energy is used inefficiently.* エネルギーの価格が低く抑えられてきた．したがってエネルギーの使用効率が悪い.

in|ept /ɪnɛpt/ ADJ 形容詞 If you say that someone is **inept**, you are criticizing them because they do something with a complete lack of skill. 不適切な，無能な [DISAPPROVAL 不賛成] ❑ *He was inept and lacked the intelligence to govern.* 彼は無能で，統治する知性に欠けていた.

in|equal|ity /ɪnɪkwɒlɪti/ (**inequalities**) N-VAR 可変性名詞 **Inequality** is the difference in social status, wealth, or opportunity between people or groups. 不平等 ❑ *People are concerned about corruption and social inequality.* 人々は腐敗と社会的不平等に関心を持っている.

Word Partnership	*inequality* は次の語句と使われる:
ADJ.	**economic** inequality, **growing/increasing** inequality, **racial** inequality, **social** inequality
N.	**gender** inequality, **income** inequality

in|ert /ɪnɜrt/ ◼ ADJ 形容詞 Someone or something that is **inert** does not move at all. 全く動かない ❑ *He covered the inert body with a blanket.* 彼はその動きのない体を毛布で覆った. ◻ ADJ 形容詞 If you describe something as **inert**, you are criticizing it because it is not very lively or interesting. 緩慢な，活気のない [DISAPPROVAL 不賛成] ❑ *The novel itself remains oddly inert.* その小説そのものは妙に緩慢なままだ. ▨ ADJ 形容詞 An **inert** substance is one that does not react with other substances. 不活性の [TECHNICAL 技術的] ❑ *...inert gases like neon and argon.* ネオンやアルゴンなどの不活性ガス

in|er|tia /ɪnɜrʃə/ ◼ N-UNCOUNT 不可算名詞 If you have a feeling of **inertia**, you feel very lazy and unwilling to move or be active. 不活発，ものぐさ ❑ *He resented her inertia, her lack of energy and self-direction.* 彼女がものぐさで活動力や自主性がないところが彼には腹立たしかった. ◻ N-UNCOUNT 不可算名詞 **Inertia** is the tendency of a physical object to remain still or to continue moving, unless a force is applied to it. 慣性 [TECHNICAL 技術的]

in|es|cap|able /ɪnɪskeɪpəbⁿl/ ADJ 形容詞 If you describe a fact, situation, or activity as **inescapable**, you mean that it is difficult

Word Web	industry

There are three general categories of **industry**. Primary industry involves **extracting raw materials** from the environment. Examples include **agriculture**, **forestry**, and **mining**. Secondary industry involves **refining** raw materials to make new **products**. It also includes **assembling** parts created by other **manufacturers**. There are two types of secondary industry—**light industry** (such as **textile weaving**) and **heavy industry** (such as shipbuilding).Tertiary industry deals with **services** which don't involve a concrete product. Some examples are **banking**, **tourism**, and education. Recently, computers have created millions of jobs in the **information technology** field. Some researchers describe this as a fourth type of industry.

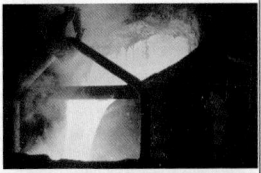

not to notice it or be affected by it. 避けられない，必然的な ❑*The inescapable conclusion is that he was trying to avenge the death of his friend.* これは死んだ友達の敵を討とうとしていたというのが必然的な結論である。 ●**in|es|cap|ably** /ˌɪnɪskeɪpəbli/ ADV 副詞 避けられなく ❑*...the inescapably dreary hopelessness of the universe.* 宇宙のどうしようもないほど荒涼とした絶望状態

in|evi|tabil|ity /ɪnˌevɪtəˈbɪlɪti/ (**inevitabilities**) N-VAR 可変性名詞 The **inevitability** of something is the fact that it is certain to happen and cannot be prevented or avoided. 避けられないこと ❑*We are all bound by the inevitability of death.* 我々はだれも死を避けることはできない。

in|evi|table /ɪnˈevɪtəbəl/ ADJ 形容詞 If something is **inevitable**, it is certain to happen and cannot be prevented or avoided. 避けられない，必然的な ❑*If the case succeeds, it is inevitable that other trials will follow.* もしこの訴訟が成功すれば，他の裁判がこれに続くことは避けられないでしょう。 ●N-SING 単数名詞 The **inevitable** is something that is inevitable. 避けられない事物 ❑*"It's just delaying the inevitable," he said.* 「それは避けられないことを遅らせているだけだよ」と彼は言った。

in|evi|tably /ɪnˈevɪtəbli/ ADV 副詞 If something will **inevitably** happen, it is certain to happen and cannot be prevented or avoided. 必然的に ❑*Technological changes will inevitably lead to unemployment.* 技術の変化は必然的に失業につながるものだ。

in|exo|rable /ɪnˈeksərəbəl/ ADJ 形容詞 You use **inexorable** to describe a process that cannot be prevented from continuing or progressing. 容赦のない，動かしえない [FORMAL 形式ばった] ❑*...the seemingly inexorable rise in unemployment.* 容赦なく増え続けるように見える失業率●**in|exo|rably** /ɪnˈeksərəbli/ ADV 副詞 [ADV with v] 容赦なく，頑として ❑*Spending on health is growing inexorably.* 医療費は容赦なく増大している。

in|ex|pen|sive /ˌɪnɪkspensɪv/ ADJ 形容詞 Something that is **inexpensive** does not cost very much. 高価でない ❑*There is a large variety of good, inexpensive restaurants.* いろいろな種類の手ごろないいレストランがある。

in|ex|pe|ri|ence /ˌɪnɪkspɪəriəns/ N-UNCOUNT 不可算名詞 If you refer to someone's **inexperience**, you mean that they have little knowledge or experience of a particular situation or activity. 無経験 ❑*Critics attacked the youth and inexperience of his staff.* 彼のスタッフが若くて経験がないことを批判者たちは非難した。

in|ex|pe|ri|enced /ˌɪnɪkspɪəriənst/ ADJ 形容詞 If you are **inexperienced**, you have little knowledge or experience of a particular situation or activity. 無経験の ❑*Routine tasks are often delegated to inexperienced young doctors.* 日常的な仕事は経験のない若い医師たちに任せられることがよくある。

in|ex|pli|cable /ˌɪnɪkspˈlɪkəbəl, ɪnɪksplɪk-/ ADJ 形容詞 If something is **inexplicable**, you cannot explain why it happens or why it is true. 説明がつかない ❑*His behavior was extraordinary and inexplicable.* 彼の行動は異常で不可解だった。 ●**in|ex|pli|cably** /ˌɪnɪksplˈɪkəbli, ɪnɪksplɪk-/ ADV 副詞 どういうわけか ❑*She suddenly and inexplicably announced her retirement.* 彼女は突然どういうわけか退職すると発表した。

in|ex|tri|cably /ˌɪnɪkstrˈɪkəbli, ɪnɪkstrɪk-/ ADV 副詞 If two or more things are **inextricably** linked, they cannot be considered separately. ほどけないほど [FORMAL 形式ばった] [ADV with v] ❑*Our survival is inextricably linked to the survival of the rainforest.* 私たちが生き残れるかどうかは，熱帯雨林が生き残れるかどうかと切っても切れないほど結びついている。

in|fa|mous /ˈɪnfəməs/ ADJ 形容詞 **Infamous** people or things are well-known because of something bad. 悪名の高い [FORMAL 形式ばった] ❑*He was infamous for his anti-feminist attitudes.* 彼は反女権拡張主義的な姿勢で悪名高い。

A **famous** person or thing is known to more people than a **well-known** one. A **notorious** person or thing is famous because they are connected with something bad or undesirable. **Infamous** is not the opposite of **famous**. It has a similar meaning to **notorious**, but is a stronger word. Someone or something that is **notable** is important or interesting.

in|fan|cy /ˈɪnfənsi/ ❶ N-UNCOUNT 不可算名詞 **Infancy** is the period of your life when you are a very young child. 幼年期 ❑*...the development of the mind from infancy onwards.* 幼年期以降の精神の発達 ❷ N-UNCOUNT 不可算名詞 If something is **in its infancy**, it is new and has not developed very much. 初期，未発達時代 ❑*Computing science was still in its infancy.* コンピュータ科学はまだあまり発達していなかった。

in|fant /ˈɪnfənt/ (**infants**) ❶ N-COUNT 可算名詞 An **infant** is a baby or very young child. 幼児 [FORMAL 形式ばった] ❑*...holding the infant in his arms.* 幼児を腕に抱きながら ❑*They are saying that he is tiring of playing daddy to their infant son.* 彼は彼らのまだ幼い息子の父親ぶるのにあきてきたのだ，と彼らは言っている。 ❷ ADJ 形容詞 **Infant** means designed especially for very young children. 幼児用の [BRIT 英国英語，AM 米国英語 **baby**] [ADJ n] ❸ ADJ 形容詞 An **infant** organization or system is new and has not developed very

much. 初期の，できたばかりの [ADJ n] ❑*The infant company was based in Nebraska.* その創立したばかりの会社はネブラスカにあった。 → see **age, child**

in|fan|try /ˈɪnfəntri/ N-UNCOUNT-COLL 集合的不可算名詞 **Infantry** are soldiers who fight on foot rather than in tanks or on horses. 歩兵 ❑*...an infantry division.* 歩兵師団

in|fect /ɪnˈfekt/ (**infects, infecting, infected**) ❶ V-T 他動詞 To **infect** people, animals, or plants means to cause them to have a disease or illness. 感染させる，病気をうつす ❑*A single mosquito can infect a large number of people.* たった1匹の蚊が多くの人たちに病気をうつすことができる。 ❑*...objects used by an infected person.* 病気に感染した人の使った物●**in|fec|tion** /ɪnˈfekʃən/ N-UNCOUNT 不可算名詞 伝染，感染 ❑*...plants that are resistant to infection.* 伝染に抵抗性のある植物 ❷ V-T 他動詞 To **infect** a substance or area means to cause it to contain harmful germs or bacteria. 汚染する ❑*The birds infect the milk.* 鳥類は牛乳を汚染する。 ❸ V-T 他動詞 When people, places, or things are **infected** by a feeling or influence, it spreads to them. 影響を与える ❑*For an instant I was infected by her fear.* 一瞬私は彼女につられておびえた。 ❑*He thought they might infect others with their bourgeois ideas.* 彼らのブルジョア思想が他の人たちに影響を与えるかもしれないと彼は思った。 ❹ V-T 他動詞 If a virus **infects** a computer, it damages or destroys files or programs. 感染する [COMPUTING コンピューティング] ❑*This virus infected thousands of computers across the U.S. and Europe within days.* このウイルスは数日間で米国と欧州の何千ものコンピューターに感染した。

Word Partnership	*infect* は次の語句と使われる:
PRON.	infect **others** ❶ ❷
N.	**bacteria** infect, infect **cells**, infect **people** ❶ ❷
	viruses infect, infect **with a virus** ❶ ❹

in|fec|tion /ɪnˈfekʃən/ (**infections**) ❶ N-COUNT 可算名詞 An **infection** is a disease caused by germs or bacteria. 感染症 ❑*Ear infections are common in preschool children.* 耳感染症は就学前の児童によく見られる。 ❷ → see also **infect** → see **diagnosis**

Word Partnership	*infection* は次の語句と使われる:
N.	**cases of** infection, **rates of** infection, **risk of** infection, **symptoms of** infection
V.	**cause an** infection, **have an** infection, **prevent** infection, **spread an** infection

in|fec|tious /ɪnˈfekʃəs/ ❶ ADJ 形容詞 A disease that is **infectious** can be caught by being near a person who has it. Compare **contagious**. 感染性の，伝染性の ❑*...infectious diseases such as measles.* はしかなどの伝染病 ❷ ADJ 形容詞 If a feeling is **infectious**, it spreads to other people. 伝わりやすい ❑*She radiates an infectious enthusiasm for everything she does.* 何をするにしても，彼女の熱意はすぐあたり一面に広まる。 → see **illness**

in|fer /ɪnˈfɜr/ (**infers, inferring, inferred**) ❶ V-T 他動詞 If you **infer** that something is the case, you decide that it is true on the basis of information that you already have. 推定する ❑*I inferred from what she said that you have not been well.* 私はあなたが言ったことからあなたの健康が優れないのだと推定した。 ❷ V-T 他動詞 Some people use **infer** to mean "imply," but this use is incorrect. ほのめかす ❑*The police inferred, though they didn't exactly say it, that they found her behavior rather suspicious.* 警察ははっきりとは言わなかったが，彼女の態度をかなり疑わしく思っていることをほのめかした。

Do not confuse **infer** and **imply**. If you **infer** that something is the case, you decide that it must be the case because of what you know, but without actually being told. ❑*From this simple statement I could infer a lot about his wife.* If you **imply** that something is the case, you suggest that it is the case without actually saying so. ❑*Rose's lawyer implied that he had married her for her money.*

in|fer|ence /ˈɪnfərəns/ (**inferences**) ❶ N-COUNT 可算名詞 An **inference** is a conclusion that you draw about something by using information that you already have about it. 推定 ❑*There were two inferences to be drawn from her letter.* 彼女の手紙からは2つのことが推定できた。 ❷ N-UNCOUNT 不可算名詞 **Inference** is the act of drawing conclusions about something on the basis of information that you already have. 推論 ❑*It had an extremely tiny head and, by inference, a tiny brain.* その頭部は非常に小さく，推論によれば脳も極めて小さかった。

in|fe|ri|or /ɪnˈfɪəriər/ (**inferiors**) ❶ ADJ 形容詞 Something that is **inferior** is not as good as something else. 質の悪い，粗悪な ❑*The cassettes were of inferior quality.* カセットは品質の劣るものだった。 ❑*This resulted in overpriced and often inferior products.* これは価格の高すぎる，ともすれば粗悪な製品を生む結果となりました。 ❷ ADJ 形容詞 If one person is regarded as **inferior to** another,

they are regarded as less important because they have less status or ability. 劣る，低い □*He preferred the company of those who were intellectually inferior to himself.* 彼は自分より知的に劣った人たちと付き合うのを好んだ. ●N-COUNT 可算名詞 **Inferior** is also a noun. 劣った人，目下の者 □*It was a gentleman's duty always to be civil, even to his inferiors.* 常に礼儀正しくするのは紳士の務めであり，たとえ目下の者に対してでもそうであった. ●**in|fe|ri|or|ity** /ɪnfɪriɒrɪti/ N-UNCOUNT 不可算名詞 劣等 □*I found it difficult to shake off a sense of social inferiority.* 私には社会的劣等感を振り払うことは難しかった.

Thesaurus   *inferior* また次を参照:

ADJ.   mediocre, second-rate, substandard ❶

in|fer|tile /ɪnfɜrtəl/ ❶ ADJ 形容詞 A person or animal that is **infertile** is unable to produce babies. 繁殖力のない，不妊症の □*According to one survey, one woman in eight is infertile.* 1つの調査によると，8人に1人の女性が不妊症である. ●**in|fer|til|ity** /ɪnfɜrtɪlɪti/ N-UNCOUNT 不可算名詞 不妊，不妊症 □*Male infertility is becoming commonplace.* 男性の不妊症は一般的になっている. ❷ ADJ 形容詞 **Infertile** soil is of poor quality because it lacks substances that plants need. やせた □*The land was barren and infertile.* その土地は不毛でやせていた.

in|fest /ɪnfɛst/ (**infests, infesting, infested**) ❶ V-T 他動詞 When creatures such as insects or rats **infest** plants or a place, they are present in large numbers and cause damage. 寄生する，たかる □*...pests like aphids which infest cereal crops.* 穀物にたかるアブラムシなどの害虫 ●**in|fest|ed** ADJ 形容詞 はびこった □*The prison is infested with rats.* 刑務所にはネズミがはびこっている. ❷ V-T 他動詞 If you say that people or things you disapprove of or regard as dangerous **are infesting** a place, you mean that there are large numbers of them in that place. 横行する [DISAPPROVAL 不賛成] □*Crime and drugs are infesting the inner cities.* 犯罪や麻薬が都市の中心部に横行している. ●**in|fest|ed** ADJ 形容詞 横行して □*The road further south was infested with bandits.* その道路のさらに南には山賊が横行していた.

in|fi|del|ity /ɪnfɪdɛlɪti/ (**infidelities**) N-VAR 可変性名詞 **Infidelity** occurs when a person who is married or in a steady relationship has sex with another person. 不貞 □*George turned a blind eye to his partner's infidelities.* ジョージは配偶者の不貞に気づかぬふりをした.

in|fil|trate /ɪnfɪltreɪt/ (**infiltrates, infiltrating, infiltrated**) ❶ V-T/V-I 他動詞/自動詞 If people **infiltrate** a place or organization, or **infiltrate into** it, they enter it secretly in order to spy on it or influence it. 潜入する，入り込む □*Activists had infiltrated the student movement.* その学生運動には活動家たちが入り込んでいた. ●**in|fil|tra|tion** /ɪnfɪltreɪʃən/ (**infiltrations**) N-VAR 可変性名詞 潜入 □*...an inquiry into alleged infiltration by the far left group.* 極左グループの潜入の疑いの調査 ❷ V-T 他動詞 To **infiltrate** people **into** a place or organization means to get them into it secretly in order to spy on it or influence it. 潜入させる □*He claimed that some countries have been trying to infiltrate their agents into the republic.* いくつかの国がその共和国に諜報員を潜入させようとしていると彼は主張した.

in|fi|nite /ɪnfɪnɪt/ ❶ ADJ 形容詞 If you describe something as **infinite**, you are emphasizing that it is extremely great in amount or degree. 莫大な，無数の [EMPHASIS 強調] □*...an infinite variety of landscapes.* 無数の多種多様な景観 □*With infinite care, John shifted position.* 膨大な注意を払ってジョンは位置を変えた. ●**in|fi|nite|ly** ADV 副詞 [ADV adj/adv] 無限に □*His design was infinitely better than anything I could have done.* 彼のデザインのほうが私ができるどんなものよりずっと比べ物にならないぐらいよかった. ❷ ADJ 形容詞 Something that is **infinite** has no limit, end, or edge. 無限な □*...an infinite number of atoms.* 無限の数の原子 ●**in|fi|nite|ly** ADV 副詞 [ADV with v] 無限に □*A centimeter can be infinitely divided into smaller units.* 1センチはより小さい単位に無限に割ってゆくことが可能である.

in|fini|tive /ɪnfɪnɪtɪv/ (**infinitives**) N-COUNT 可算名詞 The **infinitive** of a verb is the basic form, for example, "do," "be," "take," and "eat." The infinitive is often used with "to" in front of it. 不定詞

in|fin|ity /ɪnfɪnɪti/ ❶ N-UNCOUNT 不可算名詞 **Infinity** is a number that is larger than any other number and can never be given an exact value. 無限大 [also 'a' N 'of' n] □*These permutations multiply toward infinity.* これらの順列は無限大に増加する ❷ N-UNCOUNT 不可算名詞 **Infinity** is a point that is further away than any other point and can never be reached. 無限 □*...the darkness of a starless night stretching to infinity.* 無限に広がる，星明かりのない夜の暗さ.

Word Link   *firm ≈ making strong : affirm, confirm, infirm*

in|firm /ɪnfɜrm/ ADJ 形容詞 A person who is **infirm** is weak or ill, and usually old. 弱い，衰弱した [FORMAL 形式ばった] □*...her aging, infirm husband.* 彼女の年老いて衰弱した夫 ●N-PLURAL 複数名詞

The **infirm** are people who are infirm. 衰弱した人々 □*We are here to protect and assist the weak and infirm.* 私たちは弱く衰えた人たちを保護し，援助するためにここにいます.

in|fir|ma|ry /ɪnfɜrməri/ (**infirmaries**) N-COUNT 可算名詞 An **infirmary** is a place in a school or other institution that is used to take care of people who are sick or injured. 医務室，診療所

Word Link   *flam ≈ burning : flame, flammable, inflame*

in|flame /ɪnfleɪm/ (**inflames, inflaming, inflamed**) V-T 他動詞 If something **inflames** a situation or **inflames** people's feelings, it makes people feel even more strongly about something. たきつける，あおる [JOURNALISM ジャーナリズム] □*They are responsible for inflaming the situation.* 彼らは状況をあおった責任がある.

in|flamed /ɪnfleɪmd/ ADJ 形容詞 If part of your body is **inflamed**, it is red or swollen, usually as a result of an infection, injury, or illness. 赤くはれた，炎症を起こした □*Symptoms include red, itchy and inflamed skin.* 皮膚が赤くなり，かゆくなり，炎症を起こすなどの症状がある.

in|flam|mable /ɪnflæməbəl/ ADJ 形容詞 An **inflammable** material or chemical catches fire and burns easily. 引火しやすい，燃えやすい □*A highly inflammable liquid escaped from the drilling equipment.* 極めて引火しやすい液体が漏れて穴あけ装置に入った.

in|flam|ma|tion /ɪnfləmeɪʃən/ (**inflammations**) N-VAR 可変性名詞 An **inflammation** is a painful redness or swelling of a part of your body that results from an infection, injury, or illness. 炎症 □*The drug can cause inflammation of the liver.* その薬は肝臓の炎症をおこすことがある.

in|flam|ma|tory /ɪnflæmətɔri/ ❶ ADJ 形容詞 If you accuse someone of saying or doing **inflammatory** things, you mean that what they say or do is likely to make people react very angrily. 扇動的な [DISAPPROVAL 不賛成] □*...nationalist policies that are too drastic and inflammatory.* あまりにも思い切った扇動的な国家主義的政策 ❷ ADJ 形容詞 An **inflammatory** condition or disease is one in which the patient suffers from inflammation. 炎症性の [FORMAL 形式ばった] [ADJ n] □*...the inflammatory reactions that occur in asthma.* ぜんそくに起こる炎症性反応

in|flat|able /ɪnfleɪtəbəl/ (**inflatables**) ❶ ADJ 形容詞 An **inflatable** object is one that you fill with air when you want to use it. ふくらませる □*The children were playing on the inflatable castle.* 子供たちは空気注入式のお城で遊んでいた. ❷ N-COUNT 可算名詞 An **inflatable** is an inflatable object, especially a small boat. 膨張式の物（特にゴムボート）□*...floats, tubes and other inflatables.* 浮き袋，チューブ，その他の膨張式の器具

in|flate /ɪnfleɪt/ (**inflates, inflating, inflated**) ❶ V-T/V-I 他動詞/自動詞 If you **inflate** something such as a balloon or tire, or if it **inflates**, it becomes bigger as it is filled with air or a gas. ふくらませる，ふくれる □*Stuart jumped into the sea and inflated the liferaft.* スチュアートは海に飛び込んで，救命いかだを膨らませた. ❷ V-T/V-I 他動詞/自動詞 If you say that someone **inflates** the price of something, or that the price **inflates**, you mean that the price increases. つり上げる，つり上がる □*The promotion of a big release can inflate a film's final cost.* 大々的な封切りの宣伝は映画の最終的な制作費用をつり上げることがある. ●**in|flat|ed** ADJ 形容詞 つり上がった，高くしてある □*They had to buy everything at inflated prices at the ranch store.* 彼らはその農園の店ですべてのものを高い値段で買わなければならなかった. ❸ V-T 他動詞 If someone **inflates** the amount or effect of something, they say it is bigger, better, or more important than it really is, usually so that they can profit from it. 誇張する，水増しする □*They inflated their clients' medical injuries and treatment to defraud insurance companies.* 保険会社から金をだまし取るために，依頼人の怪我と治療の医療費を水増しした.

in|fla|tion /ɪnfleɪʃən/ N-UNCOUNT 不可算名詞 **Inflation** is a general increase in the prices of goods and services in a country. インフレ [BUSINESS 実業] □*...rising unemployment and high inflation.* 上昇する失業率と高度インフレ

Word Partnership   *inflation* は次の語句と使われる:

ADJ.	**high/low** inflation
N.	inflation **fears**, **increase in** inflation, inflation **rate**
V.	**control** inflation, **reduce** inflation

in|fla|tion|ary /ɪnfleɪʃənɛri/ ADJ 形容詞 **Inflationary** means connected with inflation or causing inflation. インフレの，インフレを誘発する [BUSINESS 実業] □*The bank is worried about mounting inflationary pressures.* 銀行はインフレの圧力が高まっていることを懸念している.

in|flec|tion /ɪnflɛkʃən/ (**inflections**) N-VAR 可変性名詞 An **inflection** in someone's voice is a change in its tone or pitch as they are speaking. 音調の変化 [WRITTEN 書き言葉] □*...the upward inflection of her voice.* 彼女の声の上昇調

in|flex|ible /ɪnflɛksɪbəl/ ❶ ADJ 形容詞 Something that is **inflexible** cannot be altered in any way, even if the situation

changes. 柔軟性がない，曲げられない □*Workers insisted the new system was too inflexible.* 労働者たちは新しい制度には柔軟性がなさ過ぎると主張した． ●**in|flex|ibil|ity** /ɪnfleksɪbɪlɪti/ N-UNCOUNT 不可算名詞 柔軟性のなさ □*The system's inflexibility was highlighted by several recent failures.* その制度の柔軟性のなさは最近の数々の失敗例にはっきり示されている． □*Marvin's father was exceptional for the inflexibility of his rules.* マービンの父親は自分のやり方を曲げないことでは他に類をみなかった． **2** ADJ 形容詞 If you say that someone is **inflexible**, you are criticizing them because they refuse to change their mind or alter their way of doing things. 頑固な，融通が利かない [DISAPPROVAL 不賛成] □*His opponents viewed him as stubborn, dogmatic, and inflexible.* 彼に反対する者たちは彼を頑固で独断的で融通が利かないとみなした． ●**in|flex|ibil|ity** N-UNCOUNT 不可算名詞 頑固さ □*Joyce was irritated by the inflexibility of her colleagues.* ジョイスは彼女の同僚たちの融通の利かなさにいらだっていた．

Word Link flict ≈ striking : affliction, conflict, inflict

in|flict /ɪnflɪkt/ (**inflicts, inflicting, inflicted**) V-T 他動詞 To **inflict** harm or damage on someone or something means to make them suffer it. （危害・損害を）与える □*...the damage being inflicted on industries by the recession.* 不況が産業界に与えている損害

in|flu|ence /ɪnfluəns/ (**influences, influencing, influenced**) **1** N-UNCOUNT 不可算名詞 **Influence** is the power to make other people agree with your opinions or do what you want. 影響力 □*He used his influence to get his son into medical school.* 彼はコネを使って息子を医学部に入れた． □*He denies exerting any political influence over them.* 彼は彼らに政治的影響力を使ったことを否定している． **2** V-T 他動詞 If you **influence** someone, you use your power to make them agree with you or do what you want. 影響を及ぼす，（同意するように）しむける □*He is trying to improperly influence a witness.* 彼は証人に不当な影響を与えようとしている． **3** N-COUNT 可算名詞 To have an **influence on** people or situations means to affect what they do or what happens. 影響 □*Van Gogh had a major influence on the development of modern painting.* ヴァン・ゴッホは近代絵画の発展に大きな影響を与えた． **4** V-T 他動詞 If someone or something **influences** a person or situation, they have an effect on that person's behavior or that situation. 影響を与える □*We became the best of friends and he influenced me deeply.* 僕たちは親友になり，彼は僕に深い影響を与えた． **5** N-COUNT 可算名詞 Someone or something that is a good or bad **influence on** people has a good or bad effect on them. 感化 □*I thought Sonny would be a good influence on you.* 私はソニーがあなたに良い感化を与えると思っていた． **6** PHRASE 句 If you are **under the influence** of someone or something, you are being affected or controlled by them. ～の影響を受けて □*He was arrested on suspicion of driving under the influence of alcohol.* 彼は酒気帯び運転の容疑で逮捕された．

Word Partnership influence は次の語句と使われる：

ADJ. **political** influence **1**
considerable influence, **important** influence, **major** influence, **powerful** influence, **strong** influence **1** **3**
good/bad influence **5**
N. influence **behavior**, influence **opinion**, influence **people** **2** **4**

in|flu|en|tial /ɪnfluenʃəl/ ADJ 形容詞 Someone or something that is **influential** has a lot of influence over people or events. 影響力の大きい □*It helps to have influential friends.* 影響力の大きい友人を持つと助かる． □*He had been influential in shaping economic policy.* 彼は経済政策をまとめるのに大きな影響を与えた．

in|flux /ɪnflʌks/ (**influxes**) N-COUNT 可算名詞 An **influx** of people or things into a place is their arrival there in large numbers. 流入，殺到 □*...problems caused by the influx of refugees.* 難民の流入によって引き起こされた問題

info /ɪnfoʊ/ N-UNCOUNT 不可算名詞 **Info** is information. 情報 [INFORMAL くだけた] □*For more info call 414-3935.* 詳細は414-3935までお電話下さい．

in|form /ɪnfɔrm/ (**informs, informing, informed**) **1** V-T 他動詞 If you **inform** someone **of** something, you tell them about it. 知らせる □*They would inform him of any progress they had made.* 彼らはどんな進展でもあれば彼に報告するだろう． □*My daughter informed me that she was pregnant.* 娘が私に妊娠したことを告げた． **2** V-I 自動詞 If someone **informs on** a person, they give information about the person to the police or another authority, which causes the person to be suspected or proved guilty of doing something bad. 通報する □*Thousands of American citizens have informed on these organized crime syndicates.* 何千人もの米国市民がこれらの組織暴力団連合のことを通報した． **3** V-T 他動詞 If a situation or activity **is informed** by an idea or a quality, that idea or quality is very noticeable in it. （観念・特質に）満たす [FORMAL 形式ばった] □*All great songs are informed by a certain sadness and tension.* 素晴らしい歌はみな，ある種の悲しみや緊張感に満ちている．

Word Partnership inform は次の語句と使われる：

N. inform **parents**, inform **people**, inform **the police**, inform **readers**, inform *someone* **in writing** **1**

in|for|mal /ɪnfɔrməl/ **1** ADJ 形容詞 **Informal** speech or behavior is relaxed and friendly rather than serious, very correct, or official. 打ち解けた □*She is refreshingly informal.* 彼女は感じよく気さくだ． ●**in|for|mal|ly** ADV 副詞 [ADV after v] 打ち解けて □*She was always there at half past eight, chatting informally to the children.* 彼女はいつも8時半にはそこにいて，子供たちに気さくに話しかけていた． ●**in|for|mal|ity** /ɪnfɔrmælɪti/ N-UNCOUNT 不可算名詞 気さくさ □*He was overwhelmed by their friendly informality.* 彼は彼らの親しげな気さくさに胸がいっぱいになった． **2** ADJ 形容詞 An **informal** situation is one that is relaxed and friendly and not very serious or official. 形式ばらない □*The house has an informal atmosphere.* その家にはくつろいだ雰囲気がある． ●**in|for|mal|ity** N-UNCOUNT 不可算名詞 形式ばらないこと □*She enjoyed the relative informality of island life.* 彼女は島の生活の比較的ざっくばらんなところが気に入った． **3** ADJ 形容詞 **Informal** clothes are casual and suitable for wearing when you are relaxing, but not on formal occasions. 普段着の □*For lunch, dress is informal.* 昼食時の服装はカジュアルでよい． ●**in|for|mal|ly** ADV 副詞 普段着で，カジュアルに □*Everyone dressed informally in shorts or faded jeans, and baggy sweatshirts.* みんなショートパンツやあせたジーンズ，だぶだぶのトレーナーといったカジュアルな服装をしていた． **4** ADJ 形容詞 You use **informal** to describe something that is done unofficially or casually without planning. 非公式の □*The two leaders will retire to Camp David for informal discussions.* 両指導者たちは非公式会談のためにキャンプ・デービッドに引きこもる予定だ． ●**in|for|mal|ly** ADV 副詞 非公式に □*He began informally to handle Ted's tax affairs for him.* 彼は非公式にテッドの税金問題を処理し始めた．

Thesaurus informal また次を参照：

ADJ. natural, relaxed; (ant.) formal **1**
unofficial; (ant.) formal **2**
casual; (ant.) formal **3**

in|form|ant /ɪnfɔrmənt/ (**informants**) **1** N-COUNT 可算名詞 An **informant** is someone who gives another person a piece of information. 資料提供者，インフォーマント [FORMAL 形式ばった] □*On the basis of data furnished by her informants, Mead concluded that adolescents in Samoa had complete sexual freedom.* 彼女のインフォーマントたちが提供した資料に基づき，ミードはサモア諸島の若者が性的にまったく自由であるとの結論を下した． **2** N-COUNT 可算名詞 An **informant** is the same as an **informer**. 情報提供者，密告者

in|for|ma|tion /ɪnfərmeɪʃ⁰n/ **1** N-UNCOUNT 不可算名詞 **Information** about someone or something consists of facts about them. 情報 □*Pat refused to give her any information about Sarah.* パットは彼女にセイラについてどんな情報も与えることを断った． □*Each center would provide information on technology and training.* 各センターは技術に関する情報提供と訓練を行うだろう． **2** N-UNCOUNT 不可算名詞 **Information** consists of the facts and figures that are stored and used by a computer program. 情報，データ [COMPUTING コンピューティング] □*Pictures are scanned into a form of digital information that computers can recognize.* 写真はコンピュータが認識できるデジタル情報の形式に読み取られる． **3** N-UNCOUNT 不可算名詞 **Information** is a service that you can telephone to find out someone's telephone number. 電話番号案内 [AM 米国英語] □*He called information, and they gave him the number.* 彼は電話番号案内に電話して，電話番号を教えてもらった．

Note that **information** is only ever used as an uncount noun. You cannot say "an information" or "informations." However, you can say a **piece of information** or an **item of information** when you are referring to a particular fact that someone has informed you of.

Word Partnership information は次の語句と使われる：

ADJ. **additional** information, **background** information, **classified** information, **important** information, **new** information, **personal** information **1**
V. **find** information, **get** information, **have** information, **need** information, **provide** information, **want** information **1**
retrieve information, **store** information **2**

in|for|ma|tion tech|nol|ogy N-UNCOUNT 不可算名詞 **Information technology** is the theory and practice of using computers to store and analyze information. The abbreviation **IT** is often used. 情報技術（略はIT） □*...the information technology industry.* IT産業
→ see **industry**

in|forma|tive /ɪnfɔrmətɪv/ ADJ 形容詞 Something that is

informative gives you useful information. （情報が）参考になる □ *Both men termed the meeting friendly and informative.* 彼らは2人ともその会議が友好的で有益だったと言った.

Thesaurus *informative* また次を参照：

ADJ. educational, informational, instructional

in|formed /ɪnfɔ́rmd/ ■ ADJ 形容詞 Someone who is **informed** knows about a subject or what is happening in the world. 情報に通じた, 見聞の広い □ *Informed people know the company is shaky.* 情報に通じた人々はその会社が危ないことを知っている. ② → see also **well-informed** ③ ADJ 形容詞 When journalists talk about **informed** sources, they mean people who are likely to give correct information because of their private or special knowledge. 消息通の [ADJ n] □ *According to informed sources, those taken into custody include at least one major-general.* 消息筋によると, 拘留された人々の中には少なくとも少将が1名いる. ④ ADJ 形容詞 An **informed** guess or decision is one that likely to be good, because it is based on definite knowledge or information. 情報に基づく [ADJ n] □ *Science is now enabling us to make more informed choices about how we use common drugs.* 現在, 科学のおかげで我々が一般的な薬の使い方についてより情報に基づいた選択ができるようになってきている. ⑤ → see also **inform**

in|form|er /ɪnfɔ́rmər/ (informers) N-COUNT 可算名詞 An **informer** is a person who tells the police that someone has done something illegal. 通報者, 密告者 □ *...two men suspected of being police informers.* 警察の密告者として疑われている2人の男

info|tain|ment /ɪ́nfoʊteɪnmənt/ N-UNCOUNT 不可算名詞 **Infotainment** is used to refer to radio or television programs that are intended both to entertain people and to give information. The word is formed from "information" and "entertainment." インフォテインメント（楽しみながら情報を得られるラジオやテレビの番組）□ *Cable TV's Food Network offers a buffet of food-related infotainment.* ケーブルテレビの『フード・ネットワーク』はビュッフェ形式の食べ物に関するインフォテインメントを提供している.

infra|struc|ture /ɪ́nfrəstrʌktʃər/ (infrastructures) N-VAR 可変性名詞 The **infrastructure** of a country, society, or organization consists of the basic facilities such as transportation, communications, power supplies, and buildings, which enable it to function. （交通・通信・電力など）基盤施設 □ *...improvements in the country's infrastructure.* 国の基盤施設の向上

in|fringe /ɪnfrɪ́ndʒ/ (infringes, infringing, infringed) ■ V-T 他動詞 If someone **infringes** a law or a rule, they break it or do something that disobeys it. （法律・規則を）破る □ *The film exploited his image and infringed his copyright.* その映画は彼の映像を不正に使用し, 著作権を侵害した. ② V-T/V-I 他動詞/自動詞 If something **infringes** people's rights, or **infringes on** them, it interferes with these rights and does not allow people the freedom they are entitled to. （権利などを）侵害する □ *They rob us, they infringe our rights, they kill us.* 彼らは私たちから略奪し, 私たちの権利を侵害し, 私たちを殺害する.

in|fringe|ment /ɪnfrɪ́ndʒmənt/ (infringements) ■ N-VAR 可変性名詞 An **infringement** is an action or situation that interferes with your rights and the freedom you are entitled to. （権利・自由などの）侵害 □ *...infringement of privacy.* プライバシーの侵害 ② N-VAR 可変性名詞 An **infringement of** a law or rule is the act of breaking it or disobeying it. 違反 □ *There might have been an infringement of the rules.* 規則違反があったかもしれないだろう.

in|furi|ate /ɪnfyʊ́ərieɪt/ (infuriates, infuriating, infuriated) V-T 他動詞 If something or someone **infuriates** you, they make you extremely angry. 激怒させる □ *His manner infuriated him.* 彼の態度に彼は激怒した.

in|furi|at|ing /ɪnfyʊ́ərieɪtɪŋ/ ADJ 形容詞 Something that is **infuriating** annoys you very much. ひどく腹立たしい □ *A man of indecision is infuriating to watch.* 優柔不断な男を見ているとひどく腹が立つ.

in|fuse /ɪnfyúz/ (infuses, infusing, infused) V-T 他動詞 To **infuse** a quality **into** someone or something, or to **infuse** them **with** a quality, means to fill them with it. 吹き込む, 満たす [FORMAL 形式ばった] □ *Many of the girls seemed to be infused with excitement on seeing the snow.* 女の子たちの多くは, 雪を見てすっかり興奮しているようだった.

in|gen|ious /ɪndʒíːnyəs/ ADJ 形容詞 Something that is **ingenious** is very clever and involves new ideas, methods, or equipment. 独創的な □ *...a truly ingenious invention.* まったく独創的な発明

in|genu|ity /ɪ̀ndʒənúːɪti/ N-UNCOUNT 算名詞 **Ingenuity** is skill at working out how to achieve things or skill at inventing new things. 創意, 発明の才能 □ *Inspecting the nest can be difficult and may require some ingenuity.* その巣を調べるのは難しい場合もあるし, なんらかの工夫が必要かもしれない.

in|grained /ɪngréɪnd/ ADJ 形容詞 **Ingrained** habits and beliefs

are difficult to change or remove. （習慣・考えが）深くしみついた変え難い □ *Morals tend to be deeply ingrained.* 道徳というものは深く根づいていがちだ.

in|gre|di|ent /ɪngríːdiənt/ (ingredients) ■ N-COUNT 可算名詞 **Ingredients** are the things that are used to make something, especially all the different foods you use when you are cooking a particular dish. （料理などの）材料 □ *Mix in the remaining ingredients.* 残りの材料を入れて混ぜなさい. ② N-COUNT 可算名詞 An **ingredient** of a situation is one of the essential parts of it. 要素 □ *The meeting had all the ingredients of high political drama.* その会議は高度な政治劇のすべての要素を含んでいた.

Word Partnership *ingredient* は次の語句と使われる：

ADJ. **active** ingredient, **a common** ingredient, **secret** ingredient ■
important ingredient, **key** ingredient, **main** ingredient ■ ②

in|hab|it /ɪnhǽbɪt/ (inhabits, inhabiting, inhabited) V-T 他動詞 If a place or region **is inhabited** by a group of people or a species of animal, those people or animals live there. 住む □ *The valley is inhabited by the Dani tribe.* その谷にはダニ族が住んでいる. □ *...the people who inhabit these islands.* これらの島々に住む人々

in|hab|it|ant /ɪnhǽbɪtənt/ (inhabitants) N-COUNT 可算名詞 The **inhabitants** of a place are the people who live there. 居住者, 住民 □ *...the inhabitants of Boise.* ボイシ市の住民

in|hale /ɪnhéɪl/ (inhales, inhaling, inhaled) V-T/V-I 他動詞/自動詞 When you **inhale**, you breathe in. When you **inhale** something such as smoke, you take it into your lungs when you breathe in. （肺まで）吸い込む □ *He took a long slow breath, inhaling deeply.* 彼は時間をかけてゆっくりと呼吸し, 息を深く吸い込んだ

in|her|ent /ɪnhɛ́rənt, -hɪ́ər-/ ADJ 形容詞 The **inherent** qualities of something are the necessary and natural parts of it. 本来の, 内在して □ *Stress is an inherent part of dieting.* ダイエットにストレスは付きものだ. ● **in|her|ent|ly** ADV 副詞 本来的に □ *Man is not inherently violent.* 人間は本来凶暴ではない.

in|her|it /ɪnhɛ́rɪt/ (inherits, inheriting, inherited) ■ V-T 他動詞 If you **inherit** money or property, you receive it from someone who has died. （遺産を）相続する □ *He has no son to inherit his land.* 彼には自分の土地を相続する息子が1人もいない. ② V-T 他動詞 If you **inherit** something such as a task, problem, or attitude, you get it from the people who used to have it, for example, because you have taken over their job or been influenced by them. （仕事・問題などを）引き継ぐ □ *The Endara government inherited an impossibly difficult situation from its predecessors.* エンダラ政権は前政権から途方もなく困難な状況を引き継いだ. ③ V-T 他動詞 If you **inherit** a characteristic or quality, you are born with it, because your parents or ancestors also had it. （親・先祖から性質などを）受け継ぐ □ *We inherit from our parents many of our physical characteristics.* 我々は親から身体的特徴の多くを受け継ぐ. □ *Her children have inherited her love of sports.* 彼女の子供たちは彼女のスポーツ好きを引き継いでいる.

in|her|it|ance /ɪnhɛ́rɪtəns/ (inheritances) ■ N-VAR 可変性名詞 An **inheritance** is money or property that you receive from someone who has died. 遺産, 相続財産 □ *She feared losing her inheritance to her stepmother.* 彼女は継母に遺産を取られることを恐れた. ② N-COUNT 可算名詞 If you get something such as job, problem, or attitude from someone who used to have it, you can refer to this as an **inheritance**. （仕事・問題などの）継承 □ *...starvation and disease over much of Europe and Asia, which was Truman's inheritance as president.* トルーマンが大統領として継承した, ヨーロッパとアジアの多くに広がる飢餓や病気 ③ N-SING 単数名詞 Your **inheritance** is the particular characteristics or qualities that your parents or ancestors had and that you are born with. 遺伝的体質 □ *Eye color shows more than your genetic inheritance.* 目の色は人の遺伝的体質以上のものを示す.
→ see gene

in|her|it|ance tax (inheritance taxes) N-COUNT 可算名詞 An **inheritance tax** is a tax paid on the money and property of someone who has died. 相続税

in|hib|it /ɪnhɪ́bɪt/ (inhibits, inhibiting, inhibited) ■ V-T 他動詞 If something **inhibits** an event or process, it prevents it or slows it down. （出来事・過程を）抑制する □ *The high cost of borrowing is inhibiting investment by industry in new equipment.* 借り入れ金の高金利のため, 産業界は新しい設備投資を控えている. ② V-T 他動詞 To **inhibit** someone **from** doing something means to prevent them from doing it, although they want to do it or should be able to do it. （人が~するのを）妨げる □ *Officers will be inhibited from doing their duty.* 警官たちは自分たちの職務の遂行を妨げられるだろう.

in|hib|it|ed /ɪnhɪ́bɪtɪd/ ADJ 形容詞 If you say that someone is **inhibited**, you mean that they find it difficult to behave naturally and show their feelings, and that you think this is a bad thing.

(行動・感情が) 抑制された [DISAPPROVAL 不賛成] ❑*Men are more inhibited about touching each other than women are.* 男性は女性ほど気軽にお互いに触れ合わない.

in|hi|bi|tion /ɪnɪbɪʃ⁰n/ (**inhibitions**) N-VAR 可変性名詞 **Inhibitions** are feelings of fear or embarrassment that make it difficult for you to behave naturally. 抑制, 引っ込み思案 ❑*The whole point about dancing is to stop thinking and lose all your inhibitions.* ダンスで一番大事な点は, 考えることをやめて自分をまったく自由に解き放つことだ.

in-house ADJ 形容詞 **In-house** work or activities are done by employees of an organization or company, rather than by workers outside the organization or company. 社内の ❑*A lot of companies do in-house training.* たくさんの会社が社内教育を行っている. ●ADV 副詞 **In-house** is also an adverb. 社内で, 組織内で ❑*The magazine is still produced in-house.* その雑誌は今も社内で制作されている.

in|hu|man /ɪnhyumən/ ■ ADJ 形容詞 If you describe treatment or an action as **inhuman**, you mean that it is extremely cruel. 冷酷な, 非人間的な ❑*The detainees are often held in cruel and inhuman conditions.* 抑留者はしばしば残酷かつ非人間的な状況で拘束されている. ■ ADJ 形容詞 If you describe someone or something as **inhuman**, you mean that they are strange or bad because they do not seem human in some way. 非人間的な ❑*...inhuman screams and moans.* 人間のものとは思えぬ叫び声とうなり声

in|hu|mane /ɪnhyumeɪn/ ADJ 形容詞 If you describe something as **inhumane**, you mean that it is extremely cruel. 残酷な ❑*He was kept under inhumane conditions.* 彼は過酷な状況下に拘留された.

ini|tial /ɪnɪʃ⁰l/ (**initials, initialing, initialed**) ■ ADJ 形容詞 You use **initial** to describe something that happens at the beginning of a process. 初期の, 最初の [ADJ n] ❑*The initial reaction has been excellent.* 最初の反応は非常に素晴らしかった. ■ N-COUNT 可算名詞 **Initials** are the capital letters that begin each word of a name. For example, if your full name is Michael Dennis Stocks, your initials are M.D.S. 頭文字, イニシャル ❑*...a silver Porsche with her initials JB on the side.* 側面に彼女の頭文字JBが入った銀色のポルシェ ■ V-T 他動詞 If someone **initials** an official document, they write their initials on it, to show that they have seen it or that they accept or agree with it. 頭文字を書く ❑*Would you mind initialing this voucher?* この商品券に頭文字で署名をしていただけませんか.

ini|tial|ly /ɪnɪʃəli/ ADV 副詞 **Initially** means soon after the beginning of a process or situation, rather than in the middle or at the end of it. 最初に ❑*Forecasters say the storms may not be as bad as they initially predicted.* 気象予報士は嵐は当初予報したほどひどくないかもしれないと言っている.

ini|ti|ate /ɪnɪʃieɪt/ (**initiates, initiating, initiated**) ■ V-T 他動詞 If you **initiate** something, you start it or cause it to happen. 始める ❑*They wanted to initiate a discussion on economics.* 彼らは経済問題に関する議論を始めたかった. ■ V-T 他動詞 If you **initiate** someone **into** something, you introduce them to a particular skill or type of knowledge and teach them about it. (技術・知識などの) 手ほどきをする ❑*He initiated her into the study of other cultures.* 彼は彼女に他文化の研究の手ほどきをした. ■ V-T 他動詞 If someone **is initiated into** something such as a religion, secret society, or social group, they become a member of it by taking part in special ceremonies. 入門させる, 入会させる ❑*In many societies, young people are formally initiated into their adult roles.* 多くの社会で若者たちは正式に大人の役割を担うようになる.

ini|tia|tion /ɪnɪʃieɪʃ⁰n/ (**initiations**) ■ N-UNCOUNT 不可算名詞 The **initiation** of something is the starting of it. 開始 ❑*...the initiation of a rural development program.* 農村部開発計画の始動 ■ N-VAR 可変性名詞 Someone's **initiation** into a particular group is the act or process by which they officially become a member, often involving special ceremonies. 入会 (式), 入社 (式) ❑*This was my initiation into the peace movement.* これが私の平和運動への参加だった.

ini|tia|tive /ɪnɪʃiətɪv, -ʃətɪv/ (**initiatives**) ■ N-COUNT 可算名詞 An **initiative** is an important act or statement that is intended to solve a problem. (問題解決のための) 施策 構想 ❑*Local initiatives to help young people have been inadequate.* 若者を援助するための地元の施策は不十分なままだ. ■ N-SING 単数名詞 In a fight or contest, if you have **the initiative**, you are in a better position than your opponents to decide what to do next. 主導権, 先制 ❑*We have the initiative; we intend to keep it.* 我々が先制している. これを維持するつもりだ. ■ N-UNCOUNT 不可算名詞 If you have **initiative**, you have the ability to decide what to do next and to do it, without needing other people to tell you what to do. 自ら行動する力, 自発性 ❑*She was disappointed by his lack of initiative.* 彼女は彼の自発

性のなさにがっかりした. ■ N-COUNT 可算名詞 An **initiative** is a political procedure in which a group of citizens propose a new law or a change to the law, which all voters can then vote on. 発議 [mainly AM 主に米国英語] ❑*If they reject or ignore the initiative, the public will vote on it in November.* もし彼らがこの発案を拒否するか無視するなら, 国民は11月にそれに対する投票を行う予定だ. ■ PHRASE 句 If you **take the initiative** in a situation, you are the first person to act, and are therefore able to control the situation. 率先する, 主導権を持つ ❑*We are the only power willing to take the initiative in the long struggle to end the war.* 我々は戦争を終わらせるための長期闘争に率先している唯一の勢力だ.

in|ject /ɪndʒɛkt/ (**injects, injecting, injected**) ■ V-T 他動詞 To **inject** a substance such as a medicine into someone means to put it into their body using a device with a needle called a syringe. 注射する ❑*His son was injected with strong drugs.* 彼の息子は強い薬を注射された. ❑*The technique consists of injecting healthy cells into the weakened muscles.* その技術は弱った筋肉に健康な細胞を注入することから成り立つ. ■ V-T 他動詞 If you **inject** a new, exciting, or interesting quality **into** a situation, you add it. (新しい特質を) 加える ❑*She kept trying to inject a little fun into their relationship.* 彼女はいつも2人の関係にちょっとした楽しみを取り入れようした. ■ V-T 他動詞 If you **inject** money or resources **into** a business or organization, you provide more money or resources for it. (資金・資産を) 投入する [BUSINESS 実業] ❑*The insurance fund would inject $750 into the banks.* 保険基金は銀行に750ドルを投入するだろう.

in|jec|tion /ɪndʒɛkʃ⁰n/ (**injections**) ■ N-COUNT 可算名詞 If you have an **injection**, a doctor or nurse puts a medicine into your body using a device with a needle called a syringe. 注射 [also 'by' N] ❑*They gave me an injection to help me sleep.* 彼らは私が眠れるように注射をした. ■ N-COUNT 可算名詞 An **injection of** money or resources into an organization is the act of providing it with more money or resources, to help it become more efficient or profitable. (資金・資源の) 投入 [BUSINESS 実業] ❑*An injection of cash is needed to fund some of these projects.* これらの計画のいくつかに資金を供給するために, 現金の投入が必要だ.

in|junc|tion /ɪndʒʌŋkʃ⁰n/ (**injunctions**) ■ N-COUNT 可算名詞 An **injunction** is a court order, usually one telling someone not to do something. (裁判所の) 禁止命令 [LEGAL 法律的] ❑*He took out a court injunction against the newspaper demanding the return of the document.* 彼はその新聞社からの書類返還要求に対する裁判所の差し止め命令を取得した. ■ N-COUNT 可算名詞 An **injunction to** do something is an order or strong request to do it. 命令, 強い要請 [FORMAL 形式ばった] ❑*We hear endless injunctions to managers to build commitment and a sense of community among their staff.* 私たちは支配人たちに対して自分のスタッフ間に献身的精神と共同体意識を築くことを求める絶え間ない要望を耳にしている.

in|jure /ɪndʒər/ (**injures, injuring, injured**) V-T 他動詞 If you **injure** a person or animal, you damage some part of their body. 傷つける ❑*A number of bombs have exploded, seriously injuring at least five people.* 爆弾がいくつか爆発して, 少なくとも5人が重傷を負った. → see **war**

in|jured /ɪndʒərd/ ■ ADJ 形容詞 An **injured** person or animal has physical damage to part of their body, usually as a result of an accident or fighting. けがをして ❑*The other injured man had a superficial stomach wound.* もう1人の負傷した男性は腹部に軽い傷を負った. ● N-PLURAL 複数名詞 **The injured** are people who are injured. 負傷者たち ❑*Army helicopters tried to evacuate the injured.* 陸軍のヘリコプターが負傷者たちを避難させようとした. ■ ADJ 形容詞 If you have **injured** feelings, you feel upset because you believe someone has been unfair or unkind to you. (感情が) 傷ついた ❑*...a look of injured pride.* プライドを傷つけられた様子

in|ju|ry /ɪndʒəri/ (**injuries**) ◫ N-VAR 可変性名詞 An **injury** is damage done to a person's or an animal's body. 負傷 ◻ *Four police officers sustained serious injuries in the explosion.* 4人の警官がその爆発で重傷を負った.

> Note that when someone is hurt accidentally, for example, in a car crash or when they are playing sports, you do not use the word **wound**. You use **injury** instead.◻ *A man and his baby were injured in the explosion… Many of the deaths that occur in cycling are due to head injuries.* In more formal English, **injury** can also be an uncount noun. ◻ *Two teenagers escaped serious injury when their car rolled down an embankment.* **Wound** is normally restricted to soldiers who are injured in battle, or to deliberate acts of violence against a particular person.◻ *…stab wounds.*

◫ N-VAR 可変性名詞 If someone suffers **injury** to their feelings, they are badly upset by something. If they suffer **injury** to their reputation, their reputation is seriously harmed. (感情・評判を) 傷つけること [LEGAL 法律的] ◻ *She was awarded $3,500 for injury to her feelings.* 彼女は感情を傷つけられたことに対して3千5百ドルの損害賠償を与えられた. ◫ **to add insult to injury** → see **insult**

in|jus|tice /ɪndʒʌstɪs/ (**injustices**) ◫ N-VAR 可変性名詞 **Injustice** is a lack of fairness in a situation. 不公平, 不正 ◻ *They'll continue to fight injustice.* 彼らは不公平に対し戦い続けるであろう. ◫ N-COUNT 可算名詞 An **injustice** is an action or statement in which someone judges you or treats you unfairly. 不当な評価, 不当な処置 ◻ *Calling them a bunch of capricious kids with half-formed ideas does them an injustice.* 彼らのことを考え方が未熟で気まぐれな子供たちと呼ぶのは不当な評価だ.

ink /ɪŋk/ (**inks**) N-MASS 質量名詞 **Ink** is the colored liquid used for writing or printing. インク ◻ *The letter was handwritten in black ink.* その手紙は黒いインクで手書きされていた.

in|laid /ɪnleɪd/ ADJ 形容詞 An object that is **inlaid** has a design on it that is made by putting materials such as wood, gold, or silver into the surface of the object. (木や金・銀などが) はめ込まれた ちりばめた ◻ *…a box inlaid with little triangles.* 小さな三角形をちりばめた箱

in|land

> The adverb is pronounced /ɪnlænd/ or /ɪnlənd/. The adjective is pronounced /ɪnlənd/.
>
> 副詞は /ɪnlænd/ または /ɪnlənd/ と発音される. 形容詞は /ɪnlənd/ と発音される.

◫ ADV 副詞 If something is situated **inland**, it is away from the coast, toward or near the middle of a country. If you go **inland**, you go away from the coast, toward the middle of a country. 内陸に ◻ *The vast majority live further inland.* 大部分の人々はさらに内陸に住んでいる. ◻ *It's about 15 minutes' drive inland from Pensacola.* そこはペンサコラから車で15分ほど内陸へ入ったところだ. ◫ ADJ 形容詞 **Inland** areas, lakes, and places are not on the coast, but in or near the middle of a country. 内陸の [ADJ n] ◻ *…a rather quiet inland town.* かなり静かな内陸の町

in-laws N-PLURAL 複数名詞 Your **in-laws** are the parents and close relatives of your husband or wife. 自分の伴侶の両親や近親者 ◻ *…meals with the in-laws.* 夫 (妻) の近親者との食事

in|let /ɪnlet, -lɪt/ (**inlets**) N-COUNT 可算名詞 An **inlet** is a narrow strip of water that goes from a sea or lake into the land. 入り江 ◻ *A tiny fishing village by a rocky inlet.* 岩の多い入り江近くの小さな漁村

in|mate /ɪnmeɪt/ (**inmates**) N-COUNT 可算名詞 The **inmates** of a prison or mental hospital are the prisoners or patients who are living there. 囚人, (精神病院の) 入院患者 ◻ *…education for prison inmates.* 囚人への教育

inn /ɪn/ (**inns**) N-COUNT; N-IN-NAMES 可算名詞, 名称中の名詞 An **inn** is a hotel, bar, or restaurant, often one in the country. (田舎の) 宿屋 ◻ *…the Waterside Inn.* ウォーターサイド旅館

in|nate /ɪneɪt/ ADJ 形容詞 An **innate** quality or ability is one that a person is born with. 生まれつきの, 天性の ◻ *Americans have an innate sense of fairness.* 米国人は生まれつきの公正感を備えている.

in|nate|ly ADV 副詞 [ADV adj] 生まれつき, 生来 ◻ *I believe everyone is innately psychic.* 私は誰でも生まれつき霊能力を持っていると信じている.

in|ner /ɪnər/ ◫ ADJ 形容詞 The **inner** parts of something are the parts contained or enclosed inside the other parts, closest to the center. 内部の [ADJ n] ◻ *She got up and went into an inner office.* 彼女は立ち上がり, 奥の事務所に入って行った. ◫ ADJ 形容詞 Your **inner** feelings are feelings that you have but do not show to other people. (心の) 奥の 内面的な [ADJ n] ◻ *Loving relationships a child makes will give him an inner sense of security.* 子供が作る愛情関係はその子に内面的な安心感を与えるだろう.

→ see **core**, **ear**

in|ner cir|cle (**inner circles**) N-COUNT 可算名詞 An **inner circle** is a small group of people within a larger group who have a lot of power, influence, or special information. (組織の) 中枢 ◻ *…the inner circle of company executives.* 会社重役の中枢グループ

in|ner city (**inner cities**) N-COUNT 可算名詞 You use **inner city** to refer to the areas in or near the center of a large city where people live and where there are often social and economic problems. (スラム化した) 都市の中心部 ◻ *No one could deny that problems of crime in the inner city exist.* 市の中心部が犯罪問題を抱えているのは誰も否定できないでしょう.

→ see **city**

in|no|cence /ɪnəsəns/ ◫ N-UNCOUNT 不可算名詞 **Innocence** is the quality of having no experience or knowledge of the more complex or unpleasant aspects of life. 無邪気, 純真 ◻ *…the sweet innocence of youth.* 青年時代の快い純真さ ◫ N-UNCOUNT 不可算名詞 If someone proves their **innocence**, they prove that they are not guilty of a crime. 無罪 ◻ *He claims he has evidence which could prove his innocence.* 彼は身の潔白を証明できる証拠があると主張している.

in|no|cent /ɪnəsənt/ (**innocents**) ◫ ADJ 形容詞 If someone is **innocent**, they did not commit a crime that they have been accused of. 無罪の ◻ *He was sure that the man was innocent of any crime.* 彼はその男がなんの罪も犯していないことを確信していた. ◫ ADJ 形容詞 If someone is **innocent**, they have no experience or knowledge of the more complex or unpleasant aspects of life. 無邪気な, 純真な ◻ *They seemed so young and innocent.* 彼らはとても若く, 無邪気に見えた. ● N-COUNT 可算名詞 An **innocent** is someone who is innocent. 無邪気な人 ◻ *She had always regarded Greg as a hopeless innocent where women were concerned.* 彼女はグレッグのことをいつも, 女性に関してはどうしようもないほうぶな人だと考えていた. ● **in|no|cent|ly** ADV 副詞 無邪気に ◻ *The baby gurgled innocently on the bed.* 赤ちゃんが無邪気にベッドでのどを鳴らした. ◫ ADJ 形容詞 **Innocent** people are those who are not involved in a crime or conflict, but are injured or killed as a result of it. (犯罪・戦争などとは) 無関係の ◻ *All those wounded were innocent victims.* その負傷者はみな罪のない犠牲者だった. ◫ ADJ 形容詞 An **innocent** question, remark, or comment is not intended to offend or upset people, even if it does so. 悪意のない ◻ *It was probably an innocent question, but Michael got flustered anyway.* それは恐らく他意のない質問だったのだろうが, とにかくマイケルは狼狽した.

in|no|cent|ly /ɪnəsəntli/ ◫ ADV 副詞 If you say that someone does or says something **innocently**, you mean that they are pretending not to know something about a situation. 何食わぬ顔で [ADV with v] ◻ *"What do you mean?" Annie asked innocently.* 「どういう意味」とアニーが何食わぬ顔で聞いた. ◫ → see also **innocent**

in|nocu|ous /ɪnɒkyuəs/ ADJ 形容詞 Something that is **innocuous** is not at all harmful or offensive. 害のない [FORMAL 形式ばった] ◻ *Both mushrooms look innocuous but are in fact deadly.* どちらのキノコも無毒に見えるが, 実際は極めて毒性が強い.

in|no|vate /ɪnəveɪt/ (**innovates**, **innovating**, **innovated**) V-I 自動詞 To **innovate** means to introduce changes and new ideas in the way something is done or made. (変化・新しい考えを) 導入する ◻ *What sets Rice apart from most engineers is his constant desire to innovate and experiment.* ライスがたいていの技術者と違うところは, 彼はいつも新しいことを取り入れたがり実験したがっていることだ.

in|no|va|tion /ɪnəveɪʃ°n/ (**innovations**) N-COUNT 可算名詞 An **innovation** is a new thing or a new method of doing something. 革新的なもの, 新手法 ◻ *They produced the first vegetarian beanburger – an innovation which was rapidly exported.* 彼らが最初に菜食主義のビーンバーガーを作った. それは急速に輸出さ

れた新製品だった. **2 N-UNCOUNT** 不可算名詞 **Innovation** is the introduction of new ideas, methods, or things. (新しい考え・方法などの) 導入 革新 ❏*We must promote originality, inspire creativity and encourage innovation.* わたしたちは独創性を発展させ, 創造性を刺激し, 革新を奨励しなくてはならない.
→ see **inventor**

in|no|va|tive /ɪnəveɪtɪv/ **1 ADJ** 形容詞 Something that is **innovative** is new and original. 革新的な ❏…*products which are cheaper, more innovative and more reliable than those of their competitors.* ライバル社の製品よりもより廉価で, より革新的で, より信頼性のある製品 **2 ADJ** 形容詞 An **innovative** person introduces changes and new ideas. 独創的な ❏*He was one of the most creative and innovative engineers of his generation.* 彼は同世代の中でも最も独創的で革新的な技術者の1人だった.
→ see **technology**

Word Link *ator ≈ one who does : creator, innovator, spectator*

in|no|va|tor /ɪnəveɪtər/ (**innovators**) **N-COUNT** 可算名詞 An **innovator** is someone who introduces changes and new ideas. 革新者 ❏*He is an innovator in this field.* 彼はこの分野の革新者だ.

in|nu|en|do /ɪnjuɛndoʊ/ (**innuendoes or innuendos**) **N-VAR** 可変名詞 **Innuendo** is indirect reference to something rude or unpleasant. 当てこすり, ほのめかし ❏*The report was based on rumors, speculation, and innuendo.* その記事はうわさと推測と当てこすりに基づいていた.

Word Link *numer ≈ number : innumerable, numerical, numerous*

in|nu|mer|able /ɪnuːmərəbəl/ **ADJ** 形容詞 **Innumerable** means very many, or too many to be counted. 数え切れない [FORMAL 形式ばった] ❏*He has invented innumerable excuses, told endless lies.* 彼は数え切れないほどの言い訳を考え出し, 際限なく嘘をついてきた.

in|or|di|nate /ɪnɔrdᵊnɪt/ **ADJ** 形容詞 If you describe something as **inordinate**, you are emphasizing that it is unusually or excessively great in amount or degree. 法外な, 過度の [FORMAL 形式ばった, EMPHASIS 強調] ❏*They spend an inordinate amount of time talking.* 彼らはおしゃべりに途方もない時間を費やす.
●**in|or|di|nate|ly** **ADV** 副詞 過度に, 法外に ❏*He is inordinately proud of his wife's achievements.* 彼は妻の業績を異常なほど誇りにしている.

in|or|gan|ic /ɪnɔrgænɪk/ **ADJ** 形容詞 **Inorganic** substances are substances such as stone and metal that do not come from living things. 無機の ❏…*roofing made from organic and inorganic fibers.* 有機繊維と無機繊維から作られた屋根ふき材

in|put /ɪnpʊt/ (**inputs, inputting**)

The form **input** is used in the present tense and is the past and past participle.

input 形は現在時制に使われ, 過去時制と過去分詞でもある.

1 N-VAR 可変名詞 **Input** consists of information or resources that a group or project receives. 情報 ❏*It's up to the teacher to provide a variety of types of input in the classroom.* 教室でさまざまな種類の情報を提供するのは先生の責任だ. **2 N-UNCOUNT** 不可算名詞 **Input** is information that is put into a computer. (コンピュータに入力する) データ [COMPUTING コンピューティング] ❏*The x-ray detectors feed the input into computer programs.* X線探知機はコンピュータプログラムにそのデータを入力する. **3 V-T** 他動詞 If you **input** information into a computer, you feed it in, for example, by typing it on a keyboard. (データをコンピュータに) 入力する [COMPUTING コンピューティング] ❏*The computer acts as a word processor where the text of a speech can be input at any time.* そのコンピュータは演説の本文をいつでも入力できるワードプロセッサーの働きをする.

in|put de|vice (**input devices**) **N-COUNT** 可算名詞 An **input device** is a piece of computer equipment such as a keyboard that enables you to put information into a computer. (コンピュータのキーボードのような) 入力機器 [COMPUTING コンピューティング] ❏*The officers use stylus pen-based input devices to write their reports onto touch-sensitive screens.* 警官たちはスタイラスペン式の入力機器を使って, タッチスクリーン上に報告書を書く.

input/output **1 N-UNCOUNT** 不可算名詞 **Input/output** refers to the information that is passed into or out of a computer. (コンピュータへ/からの) 入力/出力 [COMPUTING コンピューティング] ❏…*input/output delays.* 入力・出力遅延 **2 N-UNCOUNT** 不可算名詞 **Input/output** refers to the hardware or software that controls the passing of information into or out of a computer. 入力/出力を管理するハードウェアまたはソフトウェア ❏…*an input/output system.* 入力/出力システム [COMPUTING コンピューティング]

in|quest /ɪnkwɛst/ (**inquests**) **1 N-COUNT** 可算名詞 When an **inquest** is held, a public official hears evidence about someone's death in order to find out the cause. 死因審問 ❏*The inquest into their deaths opened yesterday in Little Rock.* 彼らの死因に関する審問が昨日リトルロックで開かれた. **2 N-COUNT** 可算名詞 You can refer to

an investigation by the people involved in a defeat or failure as an **inquest**. (失敗・故障などの) 調査 ❏*His plea came last night as party chiefs held an inquest into the election disaster.* 党のリーダーたちが選挙惨敗に対する調査を行っているとき, 昨夜彼から弁解があった.

in|quire /ɪnkwaɪər/ (**inquires, inquiring, inquired**) also **enquire** **1 V-T/V-I** 他動詞/自動詞 If you **inquire** about something, you ask for information about it. 尋ねる, 問い合わせる [FORMAL 形式ばった] ❏*"What are you doing there?" she inquired.* 「あなたはそこで何をしているの」と彼女は尋ねた. ❏*He called them several times to inquire about job possibilities.* 彼は就職口の可能性について問い合わせるために彼らに何度も電話した. **2 V-I** 自動詞 If you **inquire** something, you investigate it carefully. 調査する ❏*Inspectors were appointed to inquire into the affairs of the company.* その会社の事件を調査するために調査官たちが任命された.

Thesaurus inquire また次を参照:

v.	ask, question, quiz **1**

in|quir|ing /ɪnkwaɪərɪŋ/ also **enquiring** **1 ADJ** 形容詞 If you have an **inquiring** mind, you have a great interest in learning new things. 探究心旺盛な, 好奇心の強い [ADJ n] ❏*All this helps children to develop an inquiring attitude to learning.* このすべては, 子供たちが学問に対する向学心を培うのに役立つ. **2 ADJ** 形容詞 If someone has an **inquiring** expression on their face, they are showing that they want to know something. 不審そうな, 問いかけるような [WRITTEN 書き言葉] [ADJ n] ❏*"That's right," she said in reply to his inquiring glance.* 彼の問いかけるようないちべつに, 彼女は「そうよ」と答えた. ●**in|quir|ing|ly** **ADV** 副詞 不審そうに, 問いかけるように ❏*She looked at me inquiringly. "Well?"* 彼女は問いかけるようにわたしを見た.「それで」.

in|quiry /ɪnkwaɪəri, ɪŋkwɪri/ (**inquiries**) also **enquiry** **1 N-COUNT** 可算名詞 An **inquiry** is a question you ask in order to get some information. 問い合わせ ❏*He made some inquiries and discovered she had gone to Connecticut.* 彼女がコネチカット州に行ってしまったことを発見した. **2 N-COUNT** 可算名詞 An **inquiry** is an official investigation. (公の) 調査, 取調べ ❏…*a shocking murder inquiry.* 衝撃的な殺人事件の取調べ **3 N-UNCOUNT** 不可算名詞 **Inquiry** is the process of asking about or investigating something in order to find out more about it. 調査すること ❏*The investigation has suddenly switched to a new line of inquiry.* その調査は急に新しい方向の調査に切り替わった.

Word Partnership inquiry は次の語句と使われる:

N.	**board of** inquiry, **the outcome of an** inquiry **2**
V.	**conduct an** inquiry, **hold an** inquiry **2**
ADJ.	**scientific** inquiry **3**

in|quisi|tive /ɪnkwɪzɪtɪv/ **ADJ** 形容詞 An **inquisitive** person likes finding out about things, especially secret things. 好奇心の旺盛な, 詮索好きな ❏*Barrow had an inquisitive nature.* バローは好奇心旺盛な性格だった.

in|roads /ɪnroʊdz/ **PHRASE** 句 If one thing **makes inroads into** another, the first thing starts affecting or destroying the second. 侵入する ❏*In Italy, as elsewhere, television has made deep inroads into movies.* 他の国と同様にイタリアでは, テレビが映画に深刻な影響を与えている.

Word Link *san ≈ health : insane, sane, sanitation*

in|sane /ɪnseɪn/ **1 ADJ** 形容詞 Someone who is **insane** is severely mentally ill. 狂気の ❏*Some people simply can't take it and they just go insane.* ある人々はとてもそれに耐えられず, 正気を失う. **2 ADJ** 形容詞 If you describe a decision or action as **insane**, you think it is very foolish or excessive. 大変ばかげた, 非常識な [DISAPPROVAL 不賛成] ❏*He asked me what I thought and I said, "Listen, this is completely insane."* 彼が私にどう思うか尋ねたので, 私は「いいかい, これは全くばかげている」と言った. ●**in|sane|ly** **ADV** 副詞 非常識に, 狂ったように ❏*I would be insanely jealous if Bill left me for another woman.* もしビルが私を捨てて他の女のところへ行ったら, 私は狂ったように嫉妬すると思う.

in|san|ity /ɪnsænɪti/ **1 N-UNCOUNT** 不可算名詞 **Insanity** is the state of being insane. 狂気 ❏…*a psychiatrist who specialized in diagnosing insanity.* 精神異常の診断を専門にしていた精神科医 **2 N-UNCOUNT** 不可算名詞 If you describe a decision or an action as **insanity**, you think it is very foolish. ひどくばかげたこと [DISAPPROVAL 不賛成] ❏…*the final financial insanity of the 1980s.* 1980年代の最後の財政上の愚行

Word Link *sat, satis ≈ enough : dissatisfaction, insatiable, satisfy*

in|sa|tiable /ɪnseɪʃəbᵊl, -ʃiə-/ **ADJ** 形容詞 If someone has an **insatiable** desire for something, they want as much of it as they can possibly get. 貪欲な ❏*A section of the reading public has an*

insatiable appetite for dirty stories about the famous. 一般読者層の1部は有名人の醜聞話を貪欲に欲しがる.

Word Link scrib ≈ writing : inscribe, scribble, transcribe

in|scribe /ɪnskráɪb/ (inscribes, inscribing, inscribed) **1** V-T 他動詞 If you **inscribe** words **on** an object, you write or carve the words on the object. (言葉を物に) 書く, 刻む □*Some galleries commemorate donors by inscribing their names on the walls.* 美術館の中には寄贈者の名前を壁に刻んで記念にしているところがある. **2** V-T 他動詞 If you **inscribe** something in the front of a book or on a photograph, you write it there, often before giving it to someone. (本・写真に) 献呈の辞を書く □*On the back I had inscribed the words: "Here's to Great Ideas! John."* 本の後ろに私は次の言葉を書いていた. 「偉大なる思想に乾杯! ジョン」

in|scrip|tion /ɪnskrɪ́pʃ⁰n/ (inscriptions) **1** N-COUNT 可算名詞 An **inscription** is writing carved into something made of stone or metal, such as a gravestone or medal. 銘, 碑文 □*The medal bears the inscription "For distinguished service."* そのメダルには「殊勲に対して」と刻まれている. **2** N-COUNT 可算名詞 An **inscription** is something written by hand in the front of a book or on a photograph. (本・写真の手書き) 献呈の辞 □*The inscription reads: "To Emma, with love from Harry."* 献呈の辞は「エマへ. 愛を込めてハリーより」と書かれている.

in|sect /ɪ́nsɛkt/ (insects) N-COUNT 可算名詞 An **insect** is a small animal that has six legs. Most insects have wings. Ants, flies, butterflies, and beetles are all insects. 昆虫
→ see **flower**

in|sec|ti|cide /ɪnsɛ́ktɪsaɪd/ (insecticides) N-MASS 質量名詞 **Insecticide** is a chemical substance that is used to kill insects. 殺虫剤 □*Spray the plants with insecticide.* 草木に殺虫剤を吹きかけよ.
→ see **farm**

in|secure /ɪ̀nsɪkjʊ́ər/ **1** ADJ 形容詞 If you are **insecure**, you lack confidence because you think that you are not good enough or are not loved. 自信のない, 不安な □*Most mothers are insecure about their performance as mothers.* ほとんどの母親は, 自分の母親ぶりに自信がない. ●**in|se|cur|ity** /ɪ̀nsɪkjʊ́ərɪti/ (insecurities) N-VAR 可変性名詞 自信のなさ, 不安 □*She is always assailed by self-doubt and emotional insecurity.* 彼女はいつも自信喪失と情緒不安に悩まされている. **2** ADJ 形容詞 Something that is **insecure** is not safe or protected. 不安定な, 不確かな □*...low-paid, insecure jobs.* 給料が安く不安定な仕事 ●**in|se|cu|rity** N-UNCOUNT 不可算名詞 不安感 □*...the increase in crime, which has created feelings of insecurity in the population.* 住民の中に不安感を生み出している犯罪の増加

in|sen|si|tive /ɪnsɛ́nsɪtɪv/ **1** ADJ 形容詞 If you describe someone as **insensitive**, you are criticizing them for being unaware of or unsympathetic to other people's feelings. (人の気持ちに) 鈍感な 思いやりのない[DISAPPROVAL 不賛成] □*I feel my husband is very insensitive about my problem.* 私の夫が私の問題にとても鈍感だと思う. ●**in|sen|si|tiv|ity** /ɪnsɛ̀nsɪtɪ́vɪti/ N-UNCOUNT 不可算名詞 鈍感さ, 思いやりのなさ □*I was ashamed and appalled at my clumsiness and insensitivity toward her.* 私は彼女に対する自分の気の利かなさと思いやりのなさに恥じ入るとともにがく然とした. **2** ADJ 形容詞 Someone who is **insensitive to** a situation or to a need does not think or care about it. (状況などに) 配慮のない □*...women's and Latino organizations that say he is insensitive to civil rights.* 彼は公民権への配慮に欠けると言っている女性とラテンアメリカ人の組織 ●**in|sen|si|tiv|ity** N-UNCOUNT 不可算名詞 無神経さ □*...insensitivity to the environmental consequences.* 環境への影響に対する配慮のなさ **3** ADJ 形容詞 Someone who is **insensitive to** a physical sensation is unable to feel it. (体などが) 無感覚な □*He had become insensitive to cold.* 彼は寒さを感じなくなっていた.

in|sepa|rable /ɪnsɛ́pərəb⁰l/ **1** ADJ 形容詞 If one thing is **inseparable from** another, the things are so closely connected that they cannot be considered separately. 切り離せない □*He firmly believes liberty is inseparable from social justice.* 彼は自由は社会正義と切り離すことができないと固く信じている. ●**in|sepa|rably** ADV 副詞 密接に, 不可分に □*In his mind, religion and politics were inseparably intertwined.* 彼の中では宗教と政治は密接に結びついていた. **2** ADJ 形容詞 If you say that two people are **inseparable**, you are emphasizing that they are very good friends and spend a lot of time together. 親友の[EMPHASIS 強調] □*She and Kristin were inseparable.* 彼女とクリスティンは親友だった.

in|sert (inserts, inserting, inserted)

The verb is pronounced /ɪnsɜ́rt/. The noun is pronounced /ɪ́nsɜrt/.

動詞は /ɪnsɜ́rt/ と発音される. 名詞は /ɪ́nsɜrt/ と発音される.

1 V-T 他動詞 If you **insert** an object **into** something, you put the object inside it. 挿入する □*He took a small key from his pocket and slowly inserted it into the lock.* 彼はポケットから小さな鍵を取り出し, ゆっくりと錠に差し込んだ. ●**in|ser|tion** /ɪnsɜ́rʃ⁰n/ (insertions) N-VAR 可変性名詞 挿入 □*...the first experiment involving the insertion*

of a new gene into a human being. 人間に対する新しい遺伝子の組み込みを含む最初の実験 **2** V-T 他動詞 If you **insert** a comment into a piece of writing or a speech, you add it. (コメントを文章・演説に) 書き込む 加える □*They joined with the monarchists to insert a clause calling for a popular vote on the issue.* 彼らはその問題に対し国民投票を求める条項を盛り込むために君主制主義者と手を結んだ. ●**in|ser|tion** N-VAR 可変性名詞 書き込み □*...an item for insertion in the program.* プログラムに加える項目 **3** N-COUNT 可算名詞 An **insert** is something that is inserted somewhere, especially an advertisement on a piece of paper that is placed between the pages of a book or magazine. 挿入物 □*Sunday is the preferred day for advertising inserts in newspapers.* 新聞に折り込み広告を入れるのは日曜日が好まれる.

in-service ADJ 形容詞 If people working in a particular profession are given **in-service** training, they attend special courses to improve their skills or to learn about new developments in their field. 現職の[ADJ n] □*...in-service courses for people such as doctors, teachers, and civil servants.* 医師, 教師, 公務員といった人々の現職研修コース

in|side /ɪnsáɪd/ (insides)

The preposition is usually pronounced /ɪnsáɪd/.

前置詞は通常 /ɪnsáɪd/ と発音される.

The form **inside of** can also be used as a preposition in American English.

inside of 形は米国英語では前置詞としても使える

1 PREP 前置詞 Something or someone that is **inside** a place, container, or object is in it or is surrounded by it. ...の中に □*Inside the passport was a folded slip of paper.* 旅券の中にたたんだ紙片が1枚入っていた. ●ADV 副詞 **Inside** is also an adverb. 中に □*The couple chatted briefly on the doorstep before going inside.* そのカップルは中へ入る前に戸口の階段で短いおしゃべりをした. ●ADJ 形容詞 **Inside** is also an adjective. 中の[ADJ n] □*...an inside wall.* 内部の壁 **2** N-COUNT 可算名詞 The **inside** of something is the part or area that its sides surround or contain. 内側 □*The doors were locked from the inside.* それらの扉は内側から鍵がかかっていた. ●ADJ 形容詞 **Inside** is also an adjective. 内側の[ADJ n] □*The popular papers all have photo features on their inside pages.* すべての大衆紙は中面に写真の特集記事を載せている. ●ADV 副詞 **Inside** is also an adverb. 内側に[adj ADV] □*The potato cakes can be shallow or deep-fried until crisp outside and meltingly soft inside.* ポテトケーキは外側がカリカリで内側がとろけるように柔らかくなるまで, 軽くまたはしっかり揚げてよい. **3** ADJ 形容詞 **Inside** information is obtained from someone who is involved in a situation and therefore knows a lot about it. 秘密の, 内幕の[ADJ n] □*Sloane used inside diplomatic information to make himself rich.* スローンは金持ちになるために外交上の秘密情報を利用した. □*I cannot claim any inside knowledge of government policies.* 私は政府の政策の内幕を何か知っていると主張できない. **4** PREP 前置詞 If you are **inside** an organization, you belong to it. ...の内部で □*75 percent of chief executives come from inside the company.* 最高経営責任者の75パーセントは社内から出ている. ●ADJ 形容詞 **Inside** is also an adjective. 内部の[ADJ n] □*...a recent book about the inside world of pro football.* プロフットボールの内側の世界に関する最近の本 ●N-SING 単数名詞 **Inside** is also a noun. 内部 □*McAvoy was convinced he could control things from the inside but he lost control.* マッカヴォイは事態を内部から統制できると確信していたが, 彼は統制力を失った. **5** ADV 副詞 You can say that someone is **inside** when they are in prison. 刑務所に入って[INFORMAL くだけた] □*They've both done prison time – he's been inside three times.* 彼らは2人とも服役した. 彼は3度刑務所に入ったことがある. **6** N-PLURAL 複数名詞 Your **insides** are your internal organs, especially your stomach. 内臓, 腹[INFORMAL くだけた] □*Every pill made my insides turn upside down.* どの錠剤も私のおなかの調子を壊してしまった. **7** ADV 副詞 If you say that someone has a feeling **inside**, you mean that they have it but have not expressed it. 心の中に □*There is nothing left inside – no words, no anger, no tears.* 心の中に何も残っていない. 言葉も怒りも涙も. ●PREP 前置詞 **Inside** is also a preposition. ...の心の中に □*He felt a great weight of sorrow inside him.* 彼は悲しみで心の中がとても重かった. ●N-SING 単数名詞 **Inside** is also a noun. 心の中 □*What is needed is a change from the inside, a real change in outlook and attitude.* 必要なのは心の内側からの変化, つまり考え方や態度を本当に変えることだ. **8** PREP 前置詞 If you do something **inside** a particular time, you do it before the end of that time. (特定の時間) 以内に[PREP amount] □*They should have everything working inside an hour.* 彼らはすべてを1時間以内に稼動させるべきだ. **9** PHRASE 句 If something such as a piece of clothing is **inside out**, the part that is normally inside now faces outward. (服などが) 裏返しに □*Her umbrella blew inside out.* 彼女の傘は風で裏返ってしまった. **10** PHRASE 句 If you say that you know something or someone **inside out**, you are emphasizing that you know them extremely well. 隅から隅まで, 完全に[EMPHASIS 強調] □*He knew the game inside out.* 彼はそのゲームを熟知していた.

in|sid|er /ɪnsaɪdər/ (**insiders**) N-COUNT 可算名詞 An **insider** is someone who is involved in a situation and who knows more about it than other people. 内部関係者，内情に明るい人 □ *An insider said, "Katharine has told friends it is time to end her career."* ある内部関係者は，「キャサリンは仕事を辞めしおどきだと友人たちに話している」と語った.

in|sid|er trad|ing N-UNCOUNT 不可算名詞 **Insider trading** is the illegal buying or selling of a company's stock by someone who has secret or private information about the company. インサイダー取引 [BUSINESS 実業] □ *...a friend of Ms. Stewart's who is accused of insider trading in shares of his own company.* スチュアートさんの友人で，自社株のインサイダー取引で告訴されている男性

in|sid|i|ous /ɪnsɪdiəs/ ADJ 形容詞 Something that is **insidious** is unpleasant or dangerous and develops gradually without being noticed. 陰湿な，(病気などが) 潜行性の □ *The changes are insidious, and will not produce a noticeable effect for 15 to 20 years.* 変化は潜行性で，15年から20年は目立った影響が現れない.

in|sight /ɪnsaɪt/ (**insights**) ■ N-VAR 可変性名詞 If you gain **insight** or an **insight into** a complex situation or problem, you gain an accurate and deep understanding of it. 識見 □ *The project would give scientists new insights into what is happening to the Earth's atmosphere.* その計画を通じて，科学者たちは地球の大気圏に何が起こっているかについての新たな識見を得るであろう. ■ N-UNCOUNT 不可算名詞 If someone has **insight**, they are able to understand complex situations. 洞察力 □ *He was a man of forceful character, with considerable insight and diplomatic skills.* 彼は少なからぬ洞察力と外交的手腕を備えた力強い性格の男だった.

in|sig|nifi|cance /ɪnsɪgnɪfɪkəns/ N-UNCOUNT 不可算名詞 **Insignificance** is the quality of being insignificant. 重要でないこと，無意味 □ *These prices pale into insignificance when compared with what was paid for two major works by the late Alfred Stieglitz.* 故アルフレッド・スティーグリッツの2つの主要作品に支払われた金額に比べたとき，これらの価格は取るに足りないものになる.

in|sig|nifi|cant /ɪnsɪgnɪfɪkənt/ ADJ 形容詞 Something that is **insignificant** is unimportant, especially because it is very small. 重要でない，取るに足りない □ *In 1949 Bonn was a small, insignificant city.* 1949年にボンは小さな取るに足りない市だった.

in|sin|cere /ɪnsɪnsɪər/ ADJ 形容詞 If you say that someone is **insincere**, you are being critical of them because they say things they do not really mean, usually pleasant, admiring, or encouraging things. 誠意のない，偽善的な [DISAPPROVAL 不賛成] □ *Some people are so terribly insincere you can never tell if they are telling the truth.* ある人たちはあまりにもひどく不誠実だから，彼らが本当のことを言っているかどうかは決して分からない.

in|sist /ɪnsɪst/ (**insists, insisting, insisted**) ■ V-T/V-I 他動詞/自動詞 If you **insist that** something should be done, you say so very firmly and refuse to give in about it. If you **insist on** something, you say firmly that it must be done or provided. 強く要求する □ *My family insisted that I should not give in, but stay and fight.* 私の家族は私が屈服せずに，とどまり戦うことを強く求めた. □ *She insisted on being present at all the interviews.* 彼女はすべてのインタビューに出席すると言ってきかなかった. ■ V-T/V-I 他動詞/自動詞 If you **insist** that something is the case, you say so very firmly and refuse to say otherwise, even though other people do not believe it. 主張する □ *The president insisted that he was acting out of compassion, not political opportunism.* 大統領は，彼は同情の念から行動しているのであって，政治的なご都合主義からではないと主張した. □ *"It's not that difficult," she insists.* 「それはそんなに難しくないわよ」と彼女は言い張る. □ *He insisted on his innocence.* 彼は自分の無罪を主張した.

in|sist|ence /ɪnsɪstəns/ N-UNCOUNT 不可算名詞 Someone's **insistence** on something is the fact that they insist that it should be done or insist that it is the case. 強い主張，強要 □ *...her insistence on personal privacy.* 彼女の個人のプライバシーに対する要求

in|sist|ent /ɪnsɪstənt/ ■ ADJ 形容詞 Someone who is **insistent** keeps insisting that a particular thing should be done or is the case. 主張して，強く要求して □ *Stalin was insistent that the war would be won and lost in the machine shops.* その戦争に勝つか負けるかは，武器の製造工場にかかっているとスターリンは主張した. ● **in|sist|ent|ly** ADV 副詞 [ADV with v] 強情に，しつこく □ *"What is it?" his wife asked again, gently but insistently.* 「それは何？」と彼の妻

が再び優しいがしつこい調子で聞いた. ■ ADJ 形容詞 An **insistent** noise or rhythm keeps going on for a long time and holds your attention. 長々と耳につく □ *...the insistent rhythms of the Caribbean and Latin America.* カリブ海とラテンアメリカの耳につくリズム

in|so|far as /ɪnsəfɑr æz, ɪnsoʊ-/ PHRASE 句 You use **insofar as** to introduce a statement that explains and adds to something you have just said. 〜する限りでは [FORMAL 形式ばった] □ *Looking back helps insofar as it helps you learn from your mistakes.* あなたが自分の失敗から学ぶ助けになる限り，後ろを振り返ることも役に立つ.

in|so|lent /ɪnsələnt/ ADJ 形容詞 If you say that someone is being **insolent**, you mean they are being rude to someone they ought to be respectful to. 無礼な，横柄な □ *...her insolent stare.* 彼女のじろじろと生意気な視線

in|sol|uble /ɪnsɒljəbəl/ ■ ADJ 形容詞 An **insoluble** problem is so difficult that it is impossible to solve. (問題が) 解決できない □ *I pushed the problem aside; at present it was insoluble.* 私はその問題を脇へ押しやった. 今のところこれは解決できなかった. ■ ADJ 形容詞 If a substance is **insoluble**, it does not dissolve in a liquid. (液体に) 溶けない □ *Carotenes are insoluble in water and soluble in oils and fats.* カロチンは水には溶けないが，油や脂肪に溶ける.

in|sol|ven|cy /ɪnsɒlvənsi/ (**insolvencies**) N-VAR 可変性名詞 **Insolvency** is the state of not having enough money to pay your debts. 支払不能 [FORMAL 形式ばった BUSINESS 実業] □ *...eight mortgage companies, seven of which are on the brink of insolvency.* 住宅金融専門会社8社，そのうちの7社が破産寸前状態

in|sol|vent /ɪnsɒlvənt/ ADJ 形容詞 A person or organization that is **insolvent** does not have enough money to pay their debts. 支払不能の [FORMAL 形式ばった BUSINESS 実業] □ *Two years later, the bank was declared insolvent.* 2年後，その銀行は破産宣告を受けた.

in|som|nia /ɪnsɒmniə/ N-UNCOUNT 不可算名詞 Someone who suffers from **insomnia** finds it difficult to sleep. 不眠症
→ see **sleep**

in|spect /ɪnspɛkt/ (**inspects, inspecting, inspected**) ■ V-T 他動詞 If you **inspect** something, you look at every part of it carefully in order to find out about it or check that it is all right. 点検する □ *Elaine went outside to inspect the playing field.* イレインは運動場を点検するため外に出た. ● **in|spec|tion** /ɪnspɛkʃən/ (**inspections**) N-VAR 可変性名詞 点検 □ *"Excellent work," he said when he had completed his inspection of the painted doors.* 彼はペンキを塗ったドアを点検し終えると，「素晴らしいできだ」と言った. ■ V-T 他動詞 When an official **inspects** a place or a group of people, they visit it and check it carefully, for example, in order to find out whether regulations are being obeyed. 視察する，検分する □ *The Public Utilities Commission inspects us once a year.* 私たちは年に1度，公共事業委員会の検分を受ける. ● **in|spec|tion** N-VAR 可変性名詞 視察，検分 □ *Officers making a routine inspection of the vessel found fifty kilograms of cocaine.* その船の定期立ち入り検査を行っていた警官は50キログラムのコカインを発見した.

in|spec|tor /ɪnspɛktər/ (**inspectors**) ■ N-COUNT 可算名詞 An **inspector** is a person, usually employed by a government agency, whose job is to find out whether people are obeying official regulations. 検査官 □ *The mill was finally shut down by state safety inspectors.* その工場は州の安全検査官によってついに閉鎖された. ■ N-COUNT; N-TITLE; N-VOC 可算名詞，称号名詞，呼格名詞 An **inspector** is an officer in the police who is next in rank to a superintendent or police chief. 警視正 □ *...San Francisco police inspector Tony Camileri.* サンフランシスコ警察のトニー・カミレリ警視正

in|spi|ra|tion /ɪnspəreɪʃən/ (**inspirations**) ■ N-UNCOUNT 不可算名詞 **Inspiration** is a feeling of enthusiasm you get from someone or something, that gives you new and creative ideas. 霊感，インスピレーション □ *My inspiration comes from poets like Baudelaire and Jacques Prévert.* ボードレールやジャック・プレヴェールのような詩人からインスピレーションを得ている. ■ N-SING 単数名詞 If you describe someone or something good as **an inspiration**, you mean that they make you or other people want to do or achieve something. 刺激する人/もの [APPROVAL 賛成] □ *Powell's unusual journey to high office is an inspiration to millions.* パウエルの高い地位への異例の出世は何百万もの人々を鼓舞するものである. ■ N-SING 単数名詞 If something or someone is **the inspiration for** a particular book, work of art, or action, they are the source of the ideas in it or act as a model for it. 着想の基になる人/もの，(本や作品などの) モデル □ *India's myths and songs are the inspiration for her books.* 彼女の本はインドの神話や歌が基になっている. ■ N-COUNT 可算名詞 If you suddenly have an **inspiration**, you suddenly think of an idea of what to do or say. ひらめき □ *She had an inspiration, "Could we take Janice?"* 彼女はひらめいた. 「ジャニスを連れて行ったらどうかしら？」.

Word Partnership

inspiration は次の語句と使われる:

N. **source of** inspiration 1 – 3
V. **provide an** inspiration 1 – 3
  draw inspiration **from** *someone/something*, **find**
  inspiration 1 3
  have an inspiration 4

Word Link

*spir ≈ breath : a*spire, in*spire, re*spiratory

in|spire /ɪnspaɪər/ (**inspires, inspiring, inspired**) 1 V-T 他動詞 If someone or something **inspires** you **to** do something new or unusual, they make you want to do it. ～する気にさせる □ *Our challenge is to motivate those voters and inspire them to join our cause.* 我々の課題はあの有権者たちを刺激して、我々の運動に加わらせることだ. 2 V-T 他動詞 If someone or something **inspires** you, they give you new ideas and a strong feeling of enthusiasm. (考えや感情を) 吹き込む, 感激させる □ *In the 1960s, the electric guitar virtuosity of Jimi Hendrix inspired a generation.* 1960年代にジミ・ヘンドリックスの高度なエレキギターの妙技は同世代の人々を感激させた. 3 V-T 他動詞 If a book, work of art, or action **is inspired by** something, that thing is the source of the idea for it. (本・芸術品の) 基となる [usu passive] □ *The book was inspired by a real person, namely Tamara de Treaux.* この本は実在の人物、すなわちタマラ・ド・トローから着想を得た. ● **-inspired** COMB IN ADJ 形容詞の複合 ～の影響を受けた □ *...Mediterranean-inspired ceramics in bright yellow and blue.* 鮮やかな黄と青の地中海風の陶磁器 4 V-T 他動詞 Someone or something that **inspires** a particular emotion or reaction in people makes them feel that emotion or reaction. (感情・反応を) 引き起こす □ *The car's performance is effortless and its handling is precise and quickly inspires confidence.* その車の性能は余裕があり、操縦は正確であっという間に安心感を与える.

Word Partnership

inspire は次の語句と使われる:

N. inspire **people** 1 2
  ability to inspire 1 2 4
  inspire **affection**, inspire **confidence**, inspire **fear** 4

in|spir|ing /ɪnspaɪərɪŋ/ ADJ 形容詞 Something or someone that is **inspiring** is exciting and makes you feel strongly interested and enthusiastic. 刺激的な、奮い立たせる □ *She was a very strong, impressive character and one of the most inspiring people I've ever met.* 彼女は非常に強くて印象深い人物であって、私がいままで会った人の中で最も刺激的な人々の1人だった.

Word Link

*stab ≈ steady : de*stabilize, e*stablish, in*stability

in|sta|bil|ity /ɪnstəbɪlɪti/ (**instabilities**) N-UNCOUNT 不可算名詞 **Instability** is the quality of being unstable. 不安定さ □ *...unpopular policies, which resulted in social discontent and political instability.* 社会的不満や政治不安を招いた不評の政策

in|stall /ɪnstɔl/ (**installs, installing, installed**) 1 V-T 他動詞 If you **install** a piece of equipment, you put it somewhere so that it is ready to be used. (機器を) 設置する □ *They had installed a new phone line in the apartment.* 彼らはアパートに新しい電話線を引いていた. ● **in|stal|la|tion** N-UNCOUNT 不可算名詞 設置 □ *Hundreds of lives could be saved if the installation of alarms was more widespread.* 警報機の設置がもっと広く普及すれば、何百人もの命が救われるのに. 2 V-T 他動詞 If someone **is installed** in a new job or important position, they are officially given the job or position, often in a special ceremony. 就任させる、任命する □ *A temporary government was installed.* 暫定政府が任命された. □ *Professor Sawyer was formally installed as president last Thursday.* 先週の木曜日にソーヤー教授は正式に学長に就任した. ● **in|stal|la|tion** N-UNCOUNT 不可算名詞 就任、任命 □ *He sent a letter inviting Naomi to attend his installation as chief of his tribe.* 彼は自分の部族長就任式に出席するようネイオーミに招待状を送った. 3 V-T 他動詞 If you **install yourself** in a particular place, you settle there and make yourself comfortable. (場所に) 落ち着かせる [FORMAL 形式ばった] □ *Before her husband's death she had installed herself in a modern villa.* 彼女は夫が亡くなる前にモダンな大邸宅に落ち着いていた.

Word Partnership

install は次の語句と使われる:

ADJ. **easy to** install 1
N. install **equipment**, install **machines**, install **software** 1

in|stal|la|tion /ɪnstəleɪʃᵊn/ (**installations**) 1 N-COUNT 可算名詞 An **installation** is a place that contains equipment and machinery that are being used for a particular purpose. 施設 □ *The building was turned into a secret military installation.* その建物は秘密軍事施設に変えられた. 2 → see also **install**

in|stall|ment /ɪnstɔlmənt/ (**installments**) 1 N-COUNT 可算名詞 If you pay for something in **installments**, you pay small

sums of money at regular intervals over a period of time, rather than paying the whole amount at once. 分割払い □ *Upper-bracket taxpayers who elected to pay their tax increase in installments must pay the third installment by April 15.* 増税分を分割払いするよう選んだ高額納税者は、第3回目の支払いを4月15日までに行わなければならない. 2 N-COUNT 可算名詞 An **installment** of a story or plan is one of its parts that are published or carried out separately one after the other. (連載の話・一連の計画の) 1回分 □ *The next installment of this four-part series deals with the impact of the war on the continent of Africa.* 4回シリーズの次回はその戦争のアフリカ大陸への影響について扱う.

in|stall|ment plan (**installment plans**) N-COUNT 可算名詞 An **installment plan** is a way of buying products gradually. You make regular payments to the seller until, after some time, you have paid the full price. 分割払い購入 [AM 米国英語]

in|stance /ɪnstəns/ (**instances**) 1 PHRASE 句 You use **for instance** to introduce a particular event, situation, or person that is an example of what you are talking about. 例えば □ *In sub-Saharan Africa today, for instance, gross investment accounts for roughly 15% of national income.* 例えば、今日のサハラ砂漠以南のアフリカでは、総投資額は国民所得の約15パーセントを占める. 2 N-COUNT 可算名詞 An **instance** is a particular example or occurrence of something. 事例 □ *...an investigation into a serious instance of corruption.* 汚職の深刻な事例に対する捜査 3 PHRASE 句 You say **in the first instance** to mention something that is the first step in a series of actions. まず、第1に [INFORMAL くだけた] □ *In the first instance your child will be seen by an ear, nose and throat specialist.* まず最初に、お子さんは耳鼻咽喉専門の先生の診察をうけてもらいます.

in|stant /ɪnstənt/ (**instants**) 1 N-COUNT 可算名詞 An **instant** is an extremely short period of time. 瞬時 □ *For an instant, Barney was tempted to flee.* バーニーは一瞬逃げたくなった. 2 N-SING 単数名詞 If you say that something happens **at** a particular **instant**, you mean that it happens at exactly the time you have been referring to, and you are usually suggesting that it happens quickly or immediately. 瞬間 □ *At that instant the museum was plunged into total darkness.* その瞬間、博物館は真っ暗になった. 3 PHRASE 句 To do something **the instant** something else happens means to do it immediately. ～するとすぐに [EMPHASIS 強調] □ *I bolted the door the instant I saw the bat.* 私はそのコウモリを見るや否やドアにかんぬきをかけた. 4 ADJ 形容詞 You use **instant** to describe something that happens immediately. 即時の □ *Mr. Porter's book was an instant hit.* ポーター氏の本はあっという間にヒットした. ● **in|stant|ly** ADV 副詞 即時に □ *The man was killed instantly.* その男は即死だった. 5 ADJ 形容詞 [ADJ n] **Instant** food is food that you can prepare very quickly, for example, by just adding water. インスタントの □ *He stirred instant coffee into a mug of hot water.* 彼は湯の入ったマグカップにインスタントコーヒーを入れてかき混ぜた.

Thesaurus

instant また次を参照:

N. minute, second, split second 1

Word Partnership

instant は次の語句と使われる:

PREP. **for an** instant, **in an** instant 1
ADJ. **the next** instant 1 2
N. instant **access**, instant **messaging**, instant **success** 4

in|stan|ta|neous /ɪnstənteɪniəs/ ADJ 形容詞 Something that is **instantaneous** happens immediately and very quickly. 即時の □ *Death was not instantaneous because none of the bullets hit the heart.* どの弾丸も心臓に当たらなかったので、即死ではなかった. ● **in|stan|ta|neous|ly** ADV 副詞 [ADV with v] 即座に □ *Airbags inflate instantaneously on impact to form a cushion between the driver and the steering column.* エアバッグは衝撃により瞬時に膨らみ、運転者とステアリングコラム間にクッションを形成する.

Word Link

*stead ≈ place, stand : home*stead, in*stead, *steady

in|stead /ɪnsted/ 1 PHRASE 句 If you do one thing **instead of** another, you do the first thing and not the second thing, as the result of a choice or a change of behavior. ～の代わりに □ *They raised prices and cut production, instead of cutting costs.* 彼らはコストを削減する代わりに価格を上げて生産を縮小した. 2 ADV 副詞 If you do not do something, but do something else **instead**, you do the second thing and not the first thing, as the result of a choice or a change of behavior. その代わりに [ADV with cl] □ *My husband asked why I couldn't just forget about dieting and eat normally instead.* 夫は、なぜ私がダイエットのことを忘れてしまい、その代わりに普通に食べることができないのかと聞いた.

in|sti|gate /ɪnstɪgeɪt/ (**instigates, instigating, instigated**) V-T 他動詞 Someone who **instigates** an event causes it to happen. 扇動する □ *He did not instigate the coup or even know of it beforehand.* 彼はクーデターを扇動しなかったし、そのことを事前に知ってさえいな

かった. ●in|sti|ga|tion /ɪnstɪɡeɪʃⁿn/ N-UNCOUNT 不可算名詞 扇動 ❑ *The talks are taking place at the instigation of Germany.* その会談はドイツの扇動で行われている.

in|sti|ga|tor /ɪnstɪɡeɪtər/ (**instigators**) N-COUNT 可算名詞 The **instigator** of an event is the person who causes it to happen. 扇動者 ❑ *He was accused of being the main instigator of the coup.* 彼はクーデターの主要扇動者として告訴された.

in|still /ɪnstɪl/ (**instills, instilling, instilled**) V-T 他動詞 If you **instill** an idea or feeling in someone, especially over a period of time, you make them think it or feel it. (思想などを) しみこませる ❑ *The tough thing is trying to instill a winning attitude in the kids.* 困難なのは, 勝つ姿勢を子供たちに教え込もうとすることである.

in|stinct /ɪnstɪŋkt/ (**instincts**) ◼ N-VAR 可変性名詞 **Instinct** is the natural tendency that a person or animal has to behave or react in a particular way. 本能 ❑ *I didn't have as strong a maternal instinct as some other mothers.* 私は一部の母親のように母性本能が強くなかった. ◼ N-COUNT 可算名詞 If you have an **instinct for** something, you are naturally good at it or able to do it. 天性 ❑ *He seems to have an instinct for smart advertising and marketing.* 彼は目先が利く広告とマーケティングの才があるようだ. ◼ N-VAR 可変性名詞 If it is your **instinct to** do something, you feel that it is right to do it. 勘 ❑ *I should've gone with my first instinct, which was not to do the interview.* インタビューをしないという最初の勘に頼るべきではなかった. ◼ N-VAR 可変性名詞 **Instinct** is a feeling, rather than an opinion or idea based on facts, that something is the case. 直感 ❑ *There is scientific evidence to support our instinct that being surrounded by plants is good for health.* 植物に囲まれていることは健康に良いという私たちの直感には, それを裏付ける科学的証拠がある.

Word Partnership *instinct は次の語句と使われる:*

ADJ.	**basic** instinct, **maternal** instinct, **natural** instinct ◼
N.	**survival** instinct ◼

in|stinc|tive /ɪnstɪŋktɪv/ ADJ 形容詞 An **instinctive** feeling, idea, or action is one that you have or do without thinking or reasoning. 本能的な ❑ *It's an instinctive reaction – if a child falls you pick it up.* 子供が転ぶと起こしてやるのは本能的な反応だ. ●in|stinc|tive|ly ADV 副詞 [ADV with v] 本能的に ❑ *Jane instinctively knew all was not well with her 10-month old son.* ジェーンは10か月の息子に何か問題があることを本能的に悟った.

in|sti|tute /ɪnstɪtut/ (**institutes, instituting, instituted**) ◼ N-COUNT; N-IN-NAMES 可算名詞, 名称中の名詞 An **institute** is an organization set up to do a particular type of work, especially research or teaching. You can also use **institute** to refer to the building the organization occupies. 学会, 会館 ❑ *...the National Cancer Institute.* 国立がん研究所 ◼ V-T 他動詞 If you **institute** a system, rule, or course of action, you start it. 設ける [FORMAL 形式ばった] ❑ *We will institute a number of measures to better safeguard the public.* 我々は一般市民をよりよく保護するための施策をいくつか制定するつもりだ.

in|sti|tu|tion /ɪnstɪtuʃⁿn/ (**institutions**) ◼ N-COUNT; N-IN-NAMES 可算名詞, 名称中の名詞 An **institution** is a large important organization such as a university, church, or bank. (大学・教会・銀行などの) 機関 ❑ *...financial institutions.* 金融機関 ◼ N-COUNT; N-IN-NAMES 可算名詞, 名称中の名詞 An **institution** is a building where certain people are cared for, such as people who are mentally ill or children who have no parents. (精神病院・孤児院などの) 施設 ❑ *Larry has been in an institution since he was four.* ラリーは4歳のときから施設で育った. ◼ N-COUNT 可算名詞 An **institution** is a custom or system that is considered an important or typical feature of a particular society or group, usually because it has existed for a long time. 慣行 ❑ *I believe in the institution of marriage.* 私は結婚制度はよいことだと思っている. ◼ N-UNCOUNT 不可算名詞 The **institution** of a new system is the act of starting it or bringing it in. 設立, 制定 ❑ *There was never an official institution of censorship in Albania.* アルバニアに検閲制度が正式に制定されたことはない.

in|sti|tu|tion|al /ɪnstɪtuʃⁿnⁿl/ ◼ ADJ 形容詞 **Institutional** means relating to a large organization, such as a university, bank, or church. 機関の [ADJ n] ❑ *NATO remains the United States' chief institutional anchor in Europe.* NATOは依然として欧州における米国の主要な頼りになる機関である. ◼ ADJ 形容詞 **Institutional** means relating to a building where people are cared for or held. 施設の [ADJ n] ❑ *Outside the protected environment of institutional care he could not survive.* 彼は施設の世話になるという保護された環境外では生きられなかった. ◼ ADJ 形容詞 An **institutional** value or quality is considered an important and typical feature of a particular society or group, usually because it has existed for a long time. 慣習の [ADJ n] ❑ *...social and institutional values.* 社会的および慣習的価値 ◼ ADJ 形容詞 If someone accuses an organization of **institutional** racism or sexism, they mean that the organization is deeply racist or sexist and has been so for a long time. 制度上の [usu ADJ n] ❑ *The report accused the police department of*

institutional racism. その報道は警察の制度的な人種差別を告発した. ●in|sti|tu|tion|al|ly /ɪnstɪtuʃⁿnəli/ ADV 副詞 [ADV adj] 制度的に ❑ *The government's policy still appeared to be institutionally racist.* 政府の政策はいまだに制度的に人種差別をしているように見えた.

in|sti|tu|tion|al|ize /ɪnstɪtuʃⁿnəlaɪz/ (**institutionalizes, institutionalizing, institutionalized**) ◼ V-T 他動詞 If someone such as a sick, mentally ill, or old person **is institutionalized**, they are sent to stay in a special hospital or home, usually for a long period. (病人・精神病患者・老人などを) 施設に入れる [usu passive] ❑ *She became seriously ill and had to be institutionalized for a lengthy period.* 彼女は重態となり, 長期間入院していなければならなかった. ◼ V-T 他動詞 To **institutionalize** something means to establish it as part of a culture, social system, or organization. 制度化する ❑ *The goal is to institutionalize family planning into community life.* 目標は家族計画を地域社会生活に組み入れるように制度化することである.

Word Link *struct ≈ building : construct, destructive, instruct*

in|struct /ɪnstrʌkt/ (**instructs, instructing, instructed**) ◼ V-T 他動詞 If you **instruct** someone to do something, you formally tell them to do it. 指令する [FORMAL 形式ばった] ❑ *A doctor will often instruct patients to exercise.* 医師は往々にして患者に運動するよう指示するものだ. ❑ *"Go and have a word with her, Ken," Wojtowicz instructed.* 「行って彼女と話せよ」とヴォイトヴィッツは指図した. ◼ V-T 他動詞 Someone who **instructs** people **in** a subject or skill teaches it to them. 教える ❑ *He instructed family members in nursing techniques.* 彼は家族の人たちに看護技術を教えた.

in|struc|tion /ɪnstrʌkʃⁿn/ (**instructions**) ◼ N-COUNT 可算名詞 An **instruction** is something that someone tells you to do. 指図 ❑ *Two lawyers were told not to leave the building but no reason for this instruction was given.* 2人の弁護士はその建物を出てはならないと言われたが, この指示に対する理由は教えてもらえなかった. ◼ N-UNCOUNT 不可算名詞 If someone gives you **instruction** in a subject or skill, they teach it to you. 教授 [FORMAL 形式ばった] ❑ *Each candidate is given instruction in safety.* 各候補者は安全に関する教育を受ける. ◼ N-PLURAL 複数名詞 **Instructions** are clear and detailed information on how to do something. 取り扱い指示 ❑ *This book gives instructions for making a wide range of skin and hand creams.* 本書は様々な種類のスキンクリームおよびハンドクリームの作り方を説明している.

Thesaurus *instruction また次を参照:*

N.	direction, order ◼
	education, learning ◼

Word Partnership *instruction は次の語句と使われる:*

ADJ.	**explicit** instruction ◼ ◼
N.	**classroom** instruction, instruction **manual** ◼
V.	**give** instruction, **provide** instruction, **receive** instruction ◼

in|struc|tive /ɪnstrʌktɪv/ ADJ 形容詞 Something that is **instructive** gives useful information. 有益な ❑ *...an entertaining and instructive documentary.* 楽しくてためになる記録映画

in|struc|tor /ɪnstrʌktər/ (**instructors**) N-COUNT 可算名詞 An **instructor** is someone who teaches a skill such as driving or skiing. An **instructor** can also be used to refer to a schoolteacher or to a university teacher of low rank. 指導者, 専任講師 ❑ *...a fitness instructor.* フィットネス教室の先生

Thesaurus *instructor また次を参照:*

N.	educator, leader, professor, teacher

in|stru|ment /ɪnstrəmənt/ (**instruments**) ◼ N-COUNT 可算名詞 An **instrument** is a tool or device that is used to do a particular task, especially a scientific task. 器具 ❑ *...instruments for cleaning and polishing teeth.* 歯を洗浄し, 磨くための器具 ◼ N-COUNT 可算名詞 A musical **instrument** is an object such as a piano, guitar, or flute, which you play in order to produce music. 楽器 ❑ *Learning a musical instrument introduces a child to an understanding of music.* 楽器を習うことで, 子供は音楽を理解するようになる. ◼ N-COUNT 可算名詞 An **instrument** is a device that is used for making measurements of something such as speed, height, or sound, for example, on a ship or plane or in a car. 計器 ❑ *The design of crucial instruments on the control panel will have to be improved.* 制御盤の極めて重要な計器の設計を改善する必要があるだろう. ◼ N-COUNT 可算名詞 Something that is an **instrument** for achieving a particular aim is used by people to achieve that aim. 手段 ❑ *The veto has been a traditional instrument of diplomacy for centuries.* 拒否権の行使は何世紀にもわたり, 伝統的な外交手段であった.

→ see **concert, drum, orchestra**

in|stru|men|tal /ɪnstrəmɛntⁿl/ (**instrumentals**) ◼ ADJ 形容詞 Someone or something that is **instrumental in** a process or event

helps to make it happen. 役に立つ, 助けになる ❑ *In his first years as chairman he was instrumental in raising the company's wider profile.* 会長としての最初の何年かに彼は会社の知名度を上げる力になった. ❷ ADJ 形容詞 **Instrumental** music is performed by instruments and not by voices. 楽器の [ADJ n] ❑ *...a CD of vocal and instrumental music.* 声楽と器楽のCD ● N-COUNT 可算名詞 **Instrumentals** are pieces of instrumental music. 器楽曲 ❑ *After a couple of brief instrumentals, he puts his guitar down.* 2, 3の短い器楽曲を演奏したあと, 彼はギターを置いた.

in|suf|fi|cient /ɪnsəfɪʃᵊnt/ ADJ 形容詞 Something that is **insufficient** is not large enough in amount or degree for a particular purpose. 不十分な [FORMAL 形式ばった] ❑ *He decided there was insufficient evidence to justify criminal proceedings.* 彼は刑事訴訟を正当とするには証拠が不十分だと結論した. ● **in|suf|fi|cient|ly** ADV 副詞 [ADV adj/-ed] 不十分に ❑ *Food that is insufficiently cooked can lead to food poisoning.* 十分に調理されていない食べ物は食中毒を起こすことがある.

in|su|lar /ɪnsələr/ ADJ 形容詞 If you say that someone is **insular**, you are being critical of them because they are unwilling to meet new people or to consider new ideas. 偏狭な, 島国根性の [DISAPPROVAL 不賛成] ❑ *They were an insular family.* 彼らは偏狭な一家だった. ● **in|su|lar|ity** /ɪnsəlærɪti/ N-UNCOUNT 不可算名詞 偏狭さ, 島国根性 ❑ *But at least they have started to break out of their old insularity.* しかし少なくとも彼らは古い島国根性から脱却し始めている.

in|su|late /ɪnsəleɪt/ (insulates, insulating, insulated) ❶ V-T 他動詞 To **insulate** something such as a building means to protect it from cold, heat, or noise by placing a layer of other material around it or inside it. (寒気・熱・騒音などを) 遮断する 絶縁する ❑ *People should insulate their homes to conserve energy.* 人々は住居を断熱してエネルギーを節約すべきだ. ❑ *Is there any way we can insulate our home from the noise?* その騒音に対して私たちの家を防音する方法は何かありますか. ❷ V-T 他動詞 If a piece of equipment **is insulated**, it is covered with rubber or plastic to prevent electricity from passing through it and giving the person using it an electric shock. 絶縁する ❑ *In order to make it safe, the element is electrically insulated.* 素子は安全のために電気的に絶縁されている. ❸ V-T 他動詞 If a person or group **is insulated from** the rest of society or from outside influences, they are protected from them. 隔離する, 防護する ❑ *They wonder if their community is no longer insulated from big city problems.* 彼らの住む地域は大都市問題からもはや護られていないのではと彼らは思っている. ● **in|su|la|tion** N-UNCOUNT 不可算名詞 隔離 ❑ *They lived in happy insulation from brutal facts.* 彼らはきびしい事実から隔離されて幸せに生活した.

in|su|la|tion /ɪnsəleɪʃᵊn/ ❶ N-UNCOUNT 不可算名詞 **Insulation** is a thick layer of a substance that keeps something warm, especially a building. 絶縁体 ❑ *High electricity bills point to a poor heating system or bad insulation.* 電気料金が高いということは, 暖房装置の不良か絶縁の悪さを意味する. ❷ → see also **insulate**

in|su|lin /ɪnsəlɪn/ N-UNCOUNT 不可算名詞 **Insulin** is a substance that most people produce naturally in their body and that controls the level of sugar in their blood. インシュリン ❑ *Sufferers from the more severe form of diabetes have faulty insulin-producing cells.* より重症の種類の糖尿病の患者はインシュリン産生細胞に欠陥がある.

in|sult (insults, insulting, insulted)

The verb is pronounced /ɪnsʌlt/. The noun is pronounced /ɪnsʌlt/.

動詞は /ɪnsʌlt/ と発音される. 名詞は /ɪnsʌlt/ と発音される.

❶ V-T 他動詞 If someone **insults** you, they say or do something that is rude or offensive. 侮辱する ❑ *I did not mean to insult you.* 僕は君を侮辱するつもりじゃなかったんだ. ● **in|sult|ed** ADJ 形容詞 侮辱されて, むっとして ❑ *I mean, I was a bit insulted that they thought I needed bribing to shut up.* つまり, 私を黙らすのに賄賂が必要だと彼らが思ったことにちょっとむっとしたのだ. ❷ N-COUNT 可算名詞 An **insult** is a rude remark, or something a person says or does which insults you. 侮辱 ❑ *Their behavior was an insult to the people they represent.* 彼らの振る舞いは彼らが代表している人々に対する侮辱だった. ❸ PHRASE 句 You say **to add insult to injury** when mentioning an action or fact that makes an unfair or unacceptable situation even worse. ひどい目にあわせた上になお侮辱を加える ❑ *It is the victim who is often put on trial and, to add insult to injury, she is presumed guilty until proven innocent of provoking the rape.* 裁判にかけられるのは往々にして被害者であり, さらにひどいことには, レイプ挑発の罪を犯していないと証明されるまで有罪と推定される.

in|sult|ing /ɪnsʌltɪŋ/ ADJ 形容詞 Something that is **insulting** is rude or offensive. 侮辱的な ❑ *...insulting language.* 失礼な言葉遣い

in|sur|ance /ɪnʃʊərəns/ (insurances) ❶ N-VAR 可変性名詞 **Insurance** is an arrangement in which you pay money to a

company, and they pay you if something unpleasant happens to you, for example, if your property is stolen or damaged, or if you get a serious illness. 保険 ❑ *The house was a total loss and the insurance company promptly paid us the policy limit.* その家屋は全損で, 保険会社はすぐさま保険限度額を我々に支払った. ❷ N-VAR 可変性名詞 If you do something as **insurance against** something unpleasant happening, you do it to protect yourself in case the unpleasant thing happens. 備え ❑ *Attentive proofreading is the only insurance against the kind of omissions described in this section.* 注意深い校正が本節で説明されている種類の脱落に対する唯一の安全策だ.

in|sur|ance ad|just|er (insurance adjusters) N-COUNT 可算名詞 An **insurance adjuster** is the same as a **claims adjuster**. 保険の支払額査定人 [AM 米国英語 BUSINESS 実業]

in|sure /ɪnʃʊər/ (insures, insuring, insured) ❶ V-T/V-I 他動詞/自動詞 If you **insure** yourself or your property, you pay money to an insurance company so that, if you become ill or if your property is damaged or stolen, the company will pay you a sum of money. 保険をかける [他動詞] 保険契約を結ぶ [自動詞] ❑ *For protection against unforeseen emergencies, you insure your house, your furnishings and your car.* 予期せぬ非常事態に備えて, あなたは家, 家具および車に保険をかける. ❑ *While many people insure against death, far fewer take precautions against long-term loss of income because of sickness.* 多くの人々が死亡保険をかける一方, 疾病による長期所得喪失に対して予防措置を取る者は非常に少ない. ❷ V-T 他動詞 If you **insure yourself against** something unpleasant that might happen in the future, you do something to protect yourself in case it happens, or to prevent it from happening. 身を守る ❑ *All the electronics in the world cannot insure people against accidents, though.* しかし世界中の電子機器すべてが事故から人々を守ることができるわけではない.

in|sur|er /ɪnʃʊərər/ (insurers) N-COUNT 可算名詞 An **insurer** is a company that sells insurance. 保険業者 [BUSINESS 実業]

in|sur|gen|cy /ɪnsɜːrdʒᵊnsi/ (insurgencies) N-VAR 可変性名詞 An **insurgency** is a violent attempt to oppose a country's government carried out by citizens of that country. 暴動, 反乱 [FORMAL 形式ばった] ❑ *Both countries were threatened with communist insurgencies in the 1960s.* それら両国は1960年代に共産主義者の暴動に脅かされた.

in|sur|rec|tion /ɪnsərekʃᵊn/ (insurrections) N-VAR 可変性名詞 An **insurrection** is violent action that is taken by a large group of people against the rulers of their country, usually in order to remove them from office. 暴動, 反乱 [FORMAL 形式ばった] ❑ *They were plotting to stage an armed insurrection if negotiations with the government should fail.* 政府との交渉が万一失敗に終わった場合は, 彼らは武装蜂起をすることをたくらんでいた.

in|tact /ɪntækt/ ADJ 形容詞 Something that is **intact** is complete and has not been damaged or changed. 無傷で ❑ *Customs men put dynamite in the water to destroy the cargo, but most of it was left intact.* 税関職員はその貨物を破壊するためにダイナマイトを海中に入れたが, 貨物はほとんど無傷のままだった.

in|take /ɪnteɪk/ (intakes) ❶ N-SING 単数名詞 Your **intake** of a particular kind of food, drink, or air is the amount that you eat, drink, or breathe in. 摂取量 ❑ *Your intake of alcohol should not exceed two units per day.* あなたのアルコール摂取量は1日に2単位を超えてはならない. ❷ N-COUNT 可算名詞 The people who are accepted into an organization or place at a particular time are referred to as a particular **intake**. 受け入れ人員 [BRIT 英国英語] ❑ *...one of this year's intake of students.* 今年受け入れた学生の1人

in|tan|gible /ɪntændʒɪbᵊl/ (intangibles) ADJ 形容詞 Something that is **intangible** is abstract or is hard to define or measure. つかみ難い ❑ *...the intangible and non-material dimensions*

of our human and social existence. 私たちの人間的および社会的存在の不可解かつ非物質的な特質 ● N-PLURAL 複数名詞 You can refer to intangible things as **intangibles**. 手に触れられないもの □ *That approach fails to take into consideration intangibles such as pride of workmanship, loyalty and good work habits.* その方法は技量に対する誇り，忠誠心，優れた作業慣行といった無形の財産を考慮していない.

in|te|gral /ɪntɪɡrəl/ ADJ 形容詞 Something that is an **integral** part of something is an essential part of that thing. 絶対必要な □ *Rituals, celebrations, and festivals form an integral part of every human society.* 儀式，祝典，祭りはあらゆる人間社会に欠かせないものである.

in|te|grate /ɪntɪɡreɪt/ (integrates, integrating, integrated) ■ V-T/V-I 他動詞/自動詞 If someone **integrates** into a social group, or **is integrated** into it, they behave in such a way that they become part of the group or are accepted into it. (社会に) 溶け込ませる [他動詞] 同化する [自動詞] □ *He didn't integrate successfully into the Italian way of life.* 彼はイタリアの生活様式にうまく同化しなかった. □ *Integrating the kids with the community is essential.* 子供を地域社会に溶け込ませることは必須だ. ● **in|grat|ed** ADJ 形容詞 融和した □ *He thinks we are living in a fully integrated, supportive society.* 我々は完全に融和した協力的な社会に住んでいると彼は考えている. ● **in|te|gra|tion** /ɪntɪɡreɪʃ⁰n/ N-UNCOUNT 不可算名詞 融和 □ *Americans overwhelmingly support the integration of disabled people into mainstream society.* アメリカ人は身体障害者を社会の主流へ溶け込ませることに圧倒的賛意を見せる. ② V-T/V-I 他動詞/自動詞 When races **integrate** or when schools and organizations **are integrated**, people who belong to ethnic minorities can join others in their schools and organizations. 人種差別を撤廃する [AM 米国英語] [他動詞] 人種差別がなくなる [自動詞] □ *The Marine Corps was the last service to integrate.* アメリカ海兵隊は最後まで人種差別撤廃が行われえない軍隊だった. ● **in|te|grat|ed** ADJ 形容詞 [ADJ n] 人種差別廃止の □ *...a black honor student in Chicago's integrated Lincoln Park High School.* シカゴにある人種差別撤廃のリンカーンパーク高校の黒人の優等生 ● **in|te|gra|tion** N-UNCOUNT 不可算名詞 人種差別廃止 □ *Lots of people in Chicago don't see that racial border. They see progress toward integration.* シカゴの住民の多くにはあの人種的な境界線が見えない. 人種差別廃止への進展が見えているのだ. ③ V-RECIP 相互動詞 If you **integrate** one thing **with** another, or one thing **integrates with** another, the two things become closely linked or form part of a whole idea or system. You can also say that two things **integrate**. 統合する □ *Writing about a topic helps you integrate new knowledge with what you already know.* ある主題について書くことは，新しい知識をすでに持っている知識と統合させるのに役立つ. □ *...historic landmarks that integrate with the community.* 地域社会と調和する歴史的建造物 ● **in|te|grat|ed** ADJ 形容詞 統合した □ *There is, he said, a lack of an integrated national transportation policy.* 統合された全国的な運輸政策が欠落していると彼は言った. ● **in|te|gra|tion** N-UNCOUNT 不可算名詞 統合 □ *With Germany, France has been the prime mover behind closer European integration.* ドイツと共に，フランスはより密接な欧州統合の原動力だった.

V.　　assimilate, combine, consolidate, incorporate, synthesize, unite; (*ant.*) separate ③

N.　　integrate **schools** ②
　　　　integrate **efforts**, integrate **information/knowledge** ③

in|te|grat|ed /ɪntɪɡreɪtɪd/ ■ ADJ 形容詞 An **integrated** institution is intended for use by all races or religious groups. (人種・宗教上の) 差別をしない □ *We believe that students of integrated schools will have more tolerant attitudes.* 人種差別撤廃の学校の学生はより寛容な態度を持つと信じている. ② → see also **integrate**

in|teg|rity /ɪntɛɡrɪti/ ■ N-UNCOUNT 不可算名詞 If you have **integrity**, you are honest and firm in your moral principles. 誠実，高潔 □ *I have always regarded him as a man of integrity.* 私は常に彼を高潔な人だと評価していた. ② N-UNCOUNT 不可算名詞 The **integrity** of something such as a group of people or a text is its state of being a united whole. 完全な状態 [FORMAL 形式ばった] □ *Separatist movements are a threat to the integrity of the nation.* 分離主義的運動は国の統一に対する脅威である.

N.　　**honesty and** integrity, **a man of** integrity, **sense of** integrity ■
ADJ.　　**moral** integrity, **personal** integrity ■
　　　　structural integrity, **territorial** integrity ②

in|tel|lect /ɪntɪlɛkt/ (intellects) ■ N-VAR 可変性名詞 **Intellect** is the ability to understand or deal with ideas and information.

知力 □ *Do the emotions develop in parallel with the intellect?* 情緒は知力と並行して発達しますか. ② N-VAR 可変性名詞 **Intellect** is the quality of being intelligent. 知性 □ *She is famed for her intellect.* 彼女はその知性で有名である.

in|tel|lec|tual /ɪntɪlɛktʃuəl/ (intellectuals) ■ ADJ 形容詞 **Intellectual** means involving a person's ability to think and to understand ideas and information. 知力の [ADJ n] □ *High levels of lead could damage the intellectual development of children.* 高レベルの鉛は子供の知力発達を損なう可能性があるだろう. ● **in|tel|lec|tual|ly** ADV 副詞 知的に □ *...intellectually satisfying work.* 知的満足を与える仕事 ② N-COUNT 可算名詞 An **intellectual** is someone who spends a lot of time studying and thinking about complicated ideas. 知識人 □ *Teachers, artists and other intellectuals urged political parties to launch a united movement against the government.* 教師，芸術家，その他の知識人たちは，政府に反対する統一行動を開始するよう諸政党に働きかけた. ● ADJ 形容詞 **Intellectual** is also an adjective. 聡明な □ *They were very intellectual and witty.* 彼らは非常に聡明で機知に富んでいた.

N.　　intellectual **ability**, intellectual **activity**, intellectual **freedom**, intellectual **interests** ■

in|tel|li|gence /ɪntɛlɪdʒəns/ ■ N-UNCOUNT 不可算名詞 **Intelligence** is the quality of being intelligent or clever. 知性，聡明 □ *She's a woman of exceptional intelligence.* 彼女は卓抜した知性の持ち主だ. ② N-UNCOUNT 不可算名詞 **Intelligence** is the ability to think, reason, and understand instead of doing things automatically or by instinct. 知能 □ *Nerve cells, after all, do not have intelligence of their own.* 結局のところ，神経細胞そのものに知能はない. ③ N-UNCOUNT 不可算名詞 **Intelligence** is information that is gathered by the government or the army about their country's enemies and their activities. 諜報 (ちょうほう) □ *Why was military intelligence so lacking?* どうして軍情報がそんなに欠けていたのか.

N.　　**human** intelligence ②
　　　　intelligence **agent**, intelligence **expert**, **military** intelligence, **secret** intelligence ③

in|tel|li|gent /ɪntɛlɪdʒənt/ ■ ADJ 形容詞 A person or animal that is **intelligent** has the ability to think, understand, and learn things quickly and well. 知能のある □ *Susan's a very bright and intelligent woman who knows her own mind.* スーザンは自分自身の意見を持っている，非常に頭脳明晰で聡明な女性だ. ● **in|tel|li|gent|ly** ADV 副詞 聡明に □ *They are incapable of thinking intelligently about politics.* 彼らは政治を理知的に考えることができない. ② ADJ 形容詞 Something that is **intelligent** can think and understand instead of doing things automatically or by instinct. □ *Intelligent computers will soon be an indispensable diagnostic tool for every doctor.* インテリジェントコンピュータはもうじき，すべての医師になくてはならない診断器具になるだろう.

ADJ.　　bright, clever, sharp, smart; (*ant.*) dumb, stupid ■ ②

in|tel|li|gi|ble /ɪntɛlɪdʒɪbəl/ ADJ 形容詞 Something that is **intelligible** can be understood. 理解できる □ *The language of Darwin was intelligible to experts and non-experts alike.* ダーウィンの言葉は専門家，非専門家の別なく理解できた.

in|tend /ɪntɛnd/ (intends, intending, intended) ■ V-T 他動詞 If you **intend** to do something, you have decided or planned to do it. つもりである □ *Maybe he intends to leave her.* おそらく彼は彼女から去るつもりだ. □ *What do you intend doing when you get to this place?* この場所に着いたら何をするつもりかね. ② V-T 他動詞 If something **is intended** for a particular purpose, it has been planned to fulfill that purpose. If something **is intended** for a particular person, it has been planned to be used by that person or to affect them in some way. ～を対象/目的としている [usu passive] □ *This money is intended for the development of the tourist industry.* この金は観光産業の発展のためのものだ. □ *Columns are usually intended in architecture to add grandeur and status.* 円柱は通常建築で威厳と格式を加えるためのものである. ③ V-T 他動詞 If you **intend** a particular idea or feeling in something that you say or do, you want to express it or want it to be understood. 意図する □ *He didn't intend any sarcasm.* 彼は皮肉をいうつもりは全くなかった. □ *Barzun's response seemed a little patronizing, though he undoubtedly hadn't intended it that way.* わざとしたのでなかったのは明らかだったが，バーザンの返事は少し横柄に思えた.

V.　intend **to be**, intend **to continue**, intend **to do**, intend **to go**, intend **to leave**, intend **to make**, intend **to return**, intend **to say**, intend **to stay** 1

in|tense /ɪntɛns/ 1 ADJ 形容詞 **Intense** is used to describe something that is very great or extreme in strength or degree. 激しい □*He was sweating from the intense heat.* 彼は酷暑で汗をかいていた。□*Stevens's murder was the result of a deep-seated and intense hatred.* スティーブンズの殺人は，根深くて激しい憎悪の結果であった。●**in|tense|ly** ADV 副詞 激しく □*The fast-food business is intensely competitive.* ファストフード業界は競争が非常に激しい。●**in|ten|sity** /ɪntɛnsɪti/ (**intensities**) N-VAR 可変性名詞 激烈 □*The attack was anticipated but its intensity came as a shock.* 攻撃は予想されていたが，その猛烈さはショックだった。 2 ADJ 形容詞 If you describe an activity as **intense**, you mean that it is very serious and concentrated, and often involves doing a lot in a short time. 一心不乱の □*The battle for third place was intense.* 3位争いは熱がこもっていた。 3 ADJ 形容詞 If you describe the way someone looks at you as **intense**, you mean that they look at you very directly and seem to know what you are thinking or feeling. 集中した □*I felt so self-conscious under Luke's mother's intense gaze.* ルークの母親にじっと凝視されて，私は非常に気まずく感じた。●**in|tense|ly** ADV 副詞 集中して □*He sipped his drink, staring intensely at me.* 彼は私をじっと見つめながら飲み物を飲んだ。 4 ADJ 形容詞 If you describe a person as **intense**, you mean that they appear to concentrate very hard on everything that they do, and they feel their emotions very strongly. 熱心な □*I know he's an intense player, but he does enjoy what he's doing* 彼は努力型の選手だが，やっていることを楽しんでいるのを私は知っている。●**in|ten|sity** N-UNCOUNT 不可算名詞 熱心さ □*His intensity and the ferocity of his feelings alarmed me.* 彼の熱心さと感情の凶暴性に私は恐れを抱いた。

N.　intense **concentration**, intense **feelings**, intense **pain**, intense **pressure** 1
　　intense **activity**, intense **competition**, intense **debate**, intense **fighting**, intense **relationship** 2
　　intense **scrutiny** 2 3

in|ten|si|fy /ɪntɛnsɪfaɪ/ (**intensifies, intensifying, intensified**) V-T/V-I 他動詞/自動詞 If you **intensify** something or if it **intensifies**, it becomes greater in strength, amount, or degree. 強める [他動詞] 強まる [自動詞] □*I jump, intensifying the pain in all my muscles.* 私はジャンプすると，全筋肉の痛みがより激しくなる。

in|ten|sive /ɪntɛnsɪv/ 1 ADJ 形容詞 **Intensive** activity involves concentrating a lot of effort or people on one particular task in order to try to achieve a lot in a short time. 集中的な □*...after several days and nights of intensive negotiations.* 昼夜数日間にわたる徹底的な交渉の後に。●**in|ten|sive|ly** ADV 副詞 [ADV with v] 集中して □*Caitlin's parents opted to educate her intensively at home.* ケイトリンの両親は家庭で彼女を集中的に教育することを選んだ。 2 ADJ 形容詞 **Intensive** farming involves producing as many crops or animals as possible from your land, usually with the aid of chemicals. 集約的な □*...intensive methods of rearing poultry.* 集約的養鶏法 ●**in|ten|sive|ly** ADV 副詞 [ADV with v] 集約して □*Will they farm the rest of their land less intensively?* 彼らは残りの土地では集約度のもっと低い農業をするつもりだろうか。

N.　intensive **efforts**, intensive **negotiations**, intensive **program**, intensive **study**, intensive **training**, intensive **treatment** 1

in|ten|sive care N-UNCOUNT 不可算名詞 If someone is **in intensive care**, they are being given extremely thorough care in a hospital because they are very ill or very badly injured. 集中治療 □*She spent the night in intensive care after the operation.* 手術後，彼女は集中治療室で夜を明かした。

in|tent /ɪntɛnt/ 1 ADJ 形容詞 If you are **intent on** doing something, you are eager and determined to do it. 没頭して [v-link ADJ 'on/upon' -ing/n] □*The rebels are obviously intent on keeping up the pressure.* 反乱軍は圧力をかけ続けることに余念がないことは明らかだ。 2 ADJ 形容詞 If someone does something in an **intent** way, they pay great attention to what they are doing. 専心の [WRITTEN 書き言葉] □*She looked from one intent face to another.* 彼女は熱心な顔を次々に見た。●**in|tent|ly** ADV 副詞 [ADV after v] 一心に □*He listened intently, then slammed down the phone.* 彼は熱心に聞いてから，電話をガチャンと切った。 3 N-VAR 可変性名詞 A person's **intent** is their intention to do something. 意図 [FORMAL 形式ば

った] □*The timing of this strong statement of intent on arms control is crucial.* 軍縮に関するこの力強い主旨書のタイミングは極めて重大である。 4 PHRASE 句 You say **to all intents and purposes** to suggest that a situation is not exactly as you describe it but the effect is the same as if it were. 事実上 □*To all intents and purposes he was my father.* どの点からみても彼は私の父だった。

in|ten|tion /ɪntɛnʃᵊn/ (**intentions**) 1 N-VAR 可変性名詞 An **intention** is an idea or plan of what you are going to do. 意向 □*The company has every intention of keeping the share price high.* その会社は株価を高く維持することを固く決意している。□*It is my intention to remain in my position until a successor is elected.* 私は後継者が選ばれるまで自分の職にとどまるつもりだ。 2 PHRASE 句 If you say that you **have no intention** of doing something, you are emphasizing that you are not going to do it. If you say that you **have every intention of** doing something, you are emphasizing that you intend to do it. 〜するつもりは少しもない，固く決心している [EMPHASIS 強調] □*I have no intention of allowing you to continue living here alone.* ここで君が1人暮らしを続けるのを許す気は毛頭ない。

ADJ.　**clear** intention, **original** intention 1
V.　express **your** intention, state **your** intention 1
　　have every intention of, have no intention of 2

in|ten|tion|al /ɪntɛnʃənᵊl/ ADJ 形容詞 Something that is **intentional** is deliberate. 故意の □*Women who are the victims of intentional discrimination will be able to get compensation.* 意図的差別の被害を受けた女性は賠償金を受け取ることができるようになる。●**in|ten|tion|al|ly** ADV 副詞 故意に □*I've never intentionally hurt anyone.* 私はわざと誰かを傷つけたことは決してない。

in|ter|act /ɪntərækt/ (**interacts, interacting, interacted**) 1 V-RECIP 相互動詞 When people **interact** with each other or **interact**, they communicate as they work or spend time together. 交流する □*While the other children interacted and played together, Ted ignored them.* 他の子供たちは交流して一緒に遊んでいたのに，テッドは彼らを無視した。●**in|ter|ac|tion** /ɪntərækʃᵊn/ (**interactions**) N-VAR 可変性名詞 交流 □*...superficial interactions with other people.* 他人との表面的な交流 2 V-I 自動詞 When people **interact with** computers, or when computers **interact with** other machines, information or instructions are exchanged. 対話する □*...new, simplified ways of interacting with a computer.* コンピュータと対話するための，新しくて簡単な方法 ●**in|ter|ac|tion** N-VAR 可変性名詞 (**interactions**) 対話 □*...experts on human-computer interaction.* 人間とコンピュータの対話の専門家 3 V-RECIP 相互動詞 When one thing **interacts with** another or two things **interact**, the two things affect each other's behavior or condition. 影響し合う □*You have to understand how cells interact.* 君は細胞がどう影響し合っているかを理解しなければならない。●**in|ter|ac|tion** N-VAR 可変性名詞 相互作用 □*...the interaction between physical and emotional illness.* 身体的疾患と情緒障害間の相互作用

in|ter|ac|tive /ɪntəræktɪv/ 1 ADJ 形容詞 An **interactive** computer program or electronic device is one that allows direct communication between the user and the machine. 対話式の，双方向の □*This will make computer games more interactive than ever.* これにより，コンピュータゲームの双方向性は今までになく高まる。●**in|ter|ac|tiv|ity** /ɪntəræktɪvɪti/ N-UNCOUNT 不可算名詞 対話性，双方向性 □*...digital television, with more channels and interactivity.* チャンネル数が増え，双方向性が向上したデジタルテレビ 2 ADJ 形容詞 If you describe a group of people or their activities as **interactive**, you mean that the people communicate with each other. 交流的な □*There is little evidence that this encouraged flexible, interactive teaching in the classroom.* これにより教室における柔軟な対話式授業が促進されたという証拠はほとんどない。

in|ter|cept /ɪntərsɛpt/ (**intercepts, intercepting, intercepted**) V-T 他動詞 If you **intercept** someone or something that is traveling from one place to another, you stop them before they get to their destination. (人・物を) 途中で止める □*Gunmen intercepted him on his way to the airport.* 武装強盗たちが彼を空港へ向かう途中で捕らえた。●**in|ter|cep|tion** /ɪntərsɛpʃᵊn/ (**interceptions**) N-VAR 可変性名詞 途中で捕らえること，妨害 □*...the interception of a ship off the coast of Oregon.* オレゴン海岸沖での船舶妨害

in|ter|change (**interchanges, interchanging, interchanged**)

The noun is pronounced /ɪntərtʃeɪndʒ/. The verb is pronounced /ɪntərtʃeɪndʒ/.

名詞は /ɪntərtʃeɪndʒ/ と発音される．動詞は /ɪntərtʃeɪndʒ/ と発音される．

1 N-VAR 可変性名詞 If there is an **interchange** of ideas or information among a group of people, each person talks about his or her ideas or gives information to the others. 交換する

❏*What made the meeting exciting was the interchange of ideas from different disciplines.* 会議を面白くしたのは様々な研究分野からの意見交換であった. **2** V-RECIP 相互動詞 If you **interchange** one thing **with** another, or you **interchange** two things, each thing takes the place of the other or is exchanged for the other. You can also say that two things **interchange**. 置き換える ❏*You cannot interchange a "male" with a "female" electric plug.* 「雄」電気用プラグを「雌」プラグで置き替えることはできない. ❏*Your task is to interchange words so that the sentence makes sense.* 君の仕事はその文の意味が通るように言葉を置き換えることだ. ●N-VAR 可変性名詞 **Interchange** is also a noun. 相互交換 ❏*...the interchange of matter and energy at atomic or sub-atomic levels.* 原子または亜原子レベルにおける物質とエネルギーの相互交換 **3** N-COUNT 可算名詞 An **interchange** on a highway, freeway, or road is a place where it joins a main road or another highway or freeway. インターチェンジ ❏*...Sudley Road in Manassas, near the interchange with Interstate 66.* 州間高速道路66とのインターチェンジの近くにある, マナッサスのサドリー道路

inter|change|able /ɪntərtʃeɪndʒəbᵊl/ ADJ 形容詞 Things that are **interchangeable** can be exchanged with each other without it making any difference. 交換できる ❏*His greatest innovation was the use of interchangeable parts.* 彼の最も偉大な新機軸は交換可能部品の利用であった. ●**inter|change|ably** ADV 副詞 [ADV after v] 交換できるように ❏*These expressions are often used interchangeably, but they do have different meanings.* これらの表現は往々にして交互に使用されるが, 意味は異なる.

inter|com /ɪntərkɒm/ (**intercoms**) N-COUNT 可算名詞 An **intercom** is a small box with a microphone that is connected to a loudspeaker in another room. You use it to talk to the people in the other room. インターホン ❏*I pushed a button on my intercom and told Viktor Ilyushin that I needed to see him.* 私はインターホンのボタンを押して, ビクター・イリューシンに, 会う必要があると告げた.

Word Link inter ≈ between : interchange, interconnect, internal

inter|con|nect /ɪntərkənɛkt/ (**interconnects, interconnecting, interconnected**) V-RECIP 相互動詞 Things that **interconnect** or **are interconnected** are connected to or with each other. You can also say that one thing **interconnects with** another. 相互に連結させる, 相互に連結している ❏*The causes are many and may interconnect.* 原因は多数あり, それらが相互に関連している可能性がある.

inter|con|nec|tion /ɪntərkənɛkʃᵊn/ (**interconnections**) N-VAR 可変性名詞 If you say that there is an **interconnection** between two or more things, you mean that they are very closely connected. 相互連結 [FORMAL 形式ばった] ❏*...the alarming interconnection of drug abuse and AIDS infection.* 薬物乱用とAIDS感染の憂慮すべき相互関係性

inter|con|ti|nen|tal /ɪntərkɒntɪnɛntᵊl/ ADJ 形容詞 **Intercontinental** is used to describe something that exists or happens between continents. 大陸間の [ADJ n] ❏*...intercontinental flights.* 大陸間の飛行便

inter|course /ɪntərkɔrs/ **1** N-UNCOUNT 不可算名詞 **Intercourse** is the act of having sex. 性交 [FORMAL 形式ばった] ❏*...sexual intercourse.* 性交 **2** N-UNCOUNT 不可算名詞 Social **intercourse** is communication between people as they spend time together. 交際 [OLD-FASHIONED 古風な] ❏*There was social intercourse between the old and the young.* 老人たちと若者たちの間に社交があった.

inter|de|pend|ence /ɪntərdɪpɛndəns/ N-UNCOUNT 不可算名詞 **Interdependence** is the condition of a group of people or things that all depend on each other. 相互依存 ❏*...the interdependence of nations.* 国家間の相互依存

inter|de|pend|ent /ɪntərdɪpɛndənt/ ADJ 形容詞 People or things that are **interdependent** all depend on each other. 互いに依存する ❏*We live in an increasingly interdependent world.* 我々はますます相互依存が高まる世界に住んでいる.

inter|dict /ɪntərdɪkt/ (**interdicts, interdicting, interdicted**) V-T 他動詞 If an armed force **interdicts** something or someone, they stop them and prevent them from moving. If they **interdict** a route, they block it or cut it off. 阻止する, 遮断 (しゃだん) する [AM 米国英語, FORMAL 形式ばった] ❏*Troops could be ferried in to interdict drug shipments.* 麻薬の出荷を阻止するために部隊を船で送り込むことができた.

in|ter|est /ɪntrɪst, -tərɪst/ (**interests, interesting, interested**) **1** N-UNCOUNT 不可算名詞 If you have an **interest** in something, you want to learn or hear more about it. 関心, 興味 [also 'a' n] ❏*There has been a lively interest in the elections in the last two weeks.* 過去2週間, 選挙に対する関心が高まった. ❏*She'd liked him at first, but soon lost interest.* 彼女は最初彼が気に入っていたが, すぐに興味をなくした. **2** N-COUNT 可算名詞 Your **interests** are the things that you enjoy doing. 関心事 ❏*Encourage your child in her interests and hobbies.* 子供が関心のあることや趣味に取り組むよう励ましなさい. **3** V-T 他動詞 If something **interests** you, it attracts your attention so that you want to learn or hear more about it or

continue doing it. 興味を起こさせる ❏*Your financial problems do not interest me.* 私は君の金銭問題には興味がない. **4** V-T 他動詞 If you are trying to persuade someone to buy or do something, you can say that you are trying to **interest** them in it. 関心を持たせる ❏*Can I interest you in a new car?* 新車に興味ありませんか. **5** N-COUNT 可算名詞 If something is in the **interests** of a particular person or group, it will benefit them in some way. 利益 ❏*Did those directors act in the best interests of their club?* あの重役たちはクラブの最善の利益になるように行動しましたか. **6** N-COUNT 可算名詞 You can use **interests** to refer to groups of people who you think use their power or money to benefit themselves. 関係者たち ❏*The government accused unnamed "foreign interests" of inciting the trouble.* 政府は「外国の事業グループ」を, 名指しせずに, その事態を扇動したと非難した. **7** N-COUNT 可算名詞 A person or organization that has an **interest** in an area, a company, a property or in a particular type of business owns stock in it. 利権 [BUSINESS 実業] ❏*My father had many business interests in Vietnam.* 父はベトナムに多くの事業利権を持っていた. **8** N-COUNT 可算名詞 If a person, country, or organization has an **interest** in a possible event or situation, they want that event or situation to happen because they are likely to benefit from it. 利害関係 ❏*The West has an interest in promoting democratic forces in Eastern Europe.* 西側諸国は東欧における民主主義勢力の助長に利害関係がある. **9** N-UNCOUNT 不可算名詞 **Interest** is extra money that you receive if you have invested a sum of money. **Interest** is also the extra money that you pay if you have borrowed money or are buying something on credit. 利息 ❏*Does your checking account pay interest?* 君の当座預金には利息が付きますか. **10** → see also **interested, interesting, compound interest, self-interest, vested interest** **11** PHRASE 句 If you do something **in the interests of** a particular result or situation, you do it in order to achieve that result or maintain that situation. ～のために ❏*...a call for all businessmen to work together in the interests of national stability.* 国家の安定のために一致協力せよという, 全実業家への要請 **12** to have someone's **interests at heart** → see **heart** → see **bank, interest rate**

Word Partnership *interest*は次の語句と使われる:

N.	**level of** interest, **places of** interest, **self**-interest **1** **conflict of** interest **7 8** interest **charges**, interest **expenses**, interest **payments 9**
V.	**attract** interest, **express** interest, **lose** interest **1** **earn** interest, **pay** interest **9**
ADJ.	**great** interest, **little** interest, **strong** interest **1 8**

in|ter|est|ed /ɪntərɛstɪd, -trɪstɪd/ **1** ADJ 形容詞 If you are **interested in** something, you think it is important and want to learn more about it or you spend time doing it. 興味をもった ❏*I thought she might be interested in Paula's proposal.* 私は彼女がポーラの提案に興味があるかもしれないと思った. **2** ADJ 形容詞 An **interested** party or group of people is affected by or involved in a particular event or situation. 利害関係をもつ [ADJ n] ❏*The success was only possible because all the interested parties eventually agreed to the idea.* 最後には当事者全員がその考えに賛成したので, 成功はやっと可能だった. **3** ADJ 形容詞 If you say that one person is **interested in** another person, you mean that the first person would like to have a romantic or sexual relationship with the other person. 気のある [usu v-link ADJ 'in' n] ❏*I heard there are a lot of guys interested in her.* 私は彼女に気のある男がたくさんいると聞いた.

Word Partnership *interested*は次の語句と使われる:

V.	**become** interested, interested **in buying**, **get** interested, interested **in getting**, interested **in helping**, interested **in learning**, interested **in making**, **seem** interested **1**
ADV.	**really** interested, **very** interested **1**

interest-free ADJ 形容詞 An **interest-free** loan has no interest charged on it. 無利子の ❏*He was offered a $10,000 interest-free loan.* 彼は1万ドルの無利子のローンを提供された. ●ADV 副詞 **Interest-free** is also an adverb. 無利子で [ADV after v] ❏*Customers allowed the banks to use their money interest-free.* 顧客は彼らの金を無利子で使うことを銀行に許可した.

in|ter|est|ing /ɪntərɛstɪŋ, -trɪstɪŋ/ ADJ 形容詞 If you find something **interesting**, it attracts your attention, for example, because you think it is exciting or unusual. 興味を起こさせる ❏*It was interesting to be in a different environment.* 違った環境にいるのはおもしろかった.

Thesaurus *interesting*また次を参照:

ADJ.	absorbing, compelling, engrossing, unusual; (*ant.*) boring

Word Web interest rate

Borrowers have several options when choosing a **mortgage** to purchase a new home. The most common home **loan** is the **fixed rate** mortgage. With this loan the interest rate does not change, so the borrower pays the same amount of principal and interest each month. The interest on an **adjustable rate** mortgage does change. With an **interest only** mortgage, the borrower pays only the interest every month and owes the **lender** the entire **principal** amount at the end of the period.

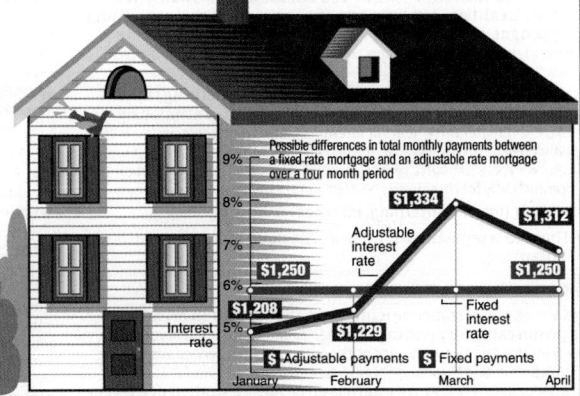

→ see Word Web: **interest rate**

Word Partnership interesting は次の語句と使われる:

ADV. **especially** interesting, **really** interesting, **very** interesting
N. interesting **idea**, interesting **people**, interesting **point**, interesting **question**, interesting **story**, interesting **things**

in|ter|est|ing|ly /ɪntərestɪŋli, -trɪstɪŋli/ ADV 副詞 You use **interestingly** to introduce a piece of information that you think is interesting or unexpected. おもしろく [ADV with cl] ❑ *Interestingly enough, a few weeks later, Benjamin remarried.* 大変興味深いことに、ベンジャミンは数週間後再婚した.

in|ter|est rate (**interest rates**) N-COUNT 可算名詞 The **interest rate** is the amount of interest that must be paid. It is expressed as a percentage of the amount that is borrowed or gained as profit. 金利 [BUSINESS 実業] ❑ *The Federal Reserve lowered interest rates by half a point.* 連邦準備金は金利を0.5%下げた.
→ see Word Web: **interest rate**

inter|face /ɪntərfeɪs/ (**interfaces, interfacing, interfaced**) ◼ N-COUNT 可算名詞 The **interface** between two subjects or systems is the area in which they affect each other or have links with each other. 境界領域 ❑ *...a witty exploration of that interface between bureaucracy and the working world.* 官僚社会と労働階級の接点に関する機知に富んだ調査 ◼ N-COUNT 可算名詞 The user **interface** of a particular piece of computer software is its presentation on the screen and how easy it is to operate. インターフェース [COMPUTING コンピューティング] ❑ *...the development of better user interfaces.* よりよいユーザーインターフェースの開発 ◼ V-RECIP 相互動詞 If one thing **interfaces with** another, or if two things **interface**, they have connections with each other. If you **interface** one thing with another, you connect the two things. 連結する [FORMAL 形式ばった] ❑ *...the way we interface with the environment.* 我々が環境と調和する方法 ❑ *He had interfaced all this machinery with a master computer.* 彼はこれらの機械すべてをインターフェースでマスターコンピュータにつないだ.

inter|fere /ɪntərfɪər/ (**interferes, interfering, interfered**) ◼ V-I 自動詞 If you say that someone **interferes in** a situation, you mean they get involved in it although it does not concern them and their involvement is not wanted. 干渉する [DISAPPROVAL 不賛成] ❑ *I wish everyone would stop interfering and just leave me alone.* みんな口出しを止めて、私をただほっておいてくれたらいいのに. ◼ V-I 自動詞 Something that **interferes with** a situation, activity, or process has a damaging effect on it. 妨げる ❑ *Smoking and drinking interfere with your body's ability to process oxygen.* 喫煙と飲酒は酸素を処理する身体の能力を妨害する.

Word Partnership interfere は次の語句と使われる:

N. **ability to** interfere, **right to** interfere ◼
V. **try to** interfere, **not want to** interfere ◼

inter|fer|ence /ɪntərfɪərəns/ ◼ N-UNCOUNT 不可算名詞 **Interference** by a person or group is their unwanted or unnecessary involvement in something. 干渉 [DISAPPROVAL 不賛成] ❑ *Airlines will be able to set cheap fares without further interference from the government.* 航空会社は、政府からのさらなる干渉なしに、安い料金を設定することができるようになるだろう. ◼ N-UNCOUNT 不可算名詞 When there is **interference**, a radio signal is affected by other radio waves or electrical activity so that it cannot be received properly. 干渉 ❑ *...electrical interference.* 電気的干渉

in|ter|im /ɪntərɪm/ ◼ ADJ 形容詞 **Interim** is used to describe something that is intended to be used until something permanent is done or established. 当座の、臨時の [ADJ n] ❑ *She was sworn in as head of an interim government in March.* 彼女は3月に暫定政府の首相に宣誓就任した. ◼ PHRASE 句 **In the interim** means until a particular thing happens or until a particular thing happened. 当座の間 [FORMAL 形式ばった] ❑ *But, in the interim, we obviously have a duty to maintain law and order.* しかし、その間我々には法と秩序を維持する任務があることは明らかだ.

in|te|ri|or /ɪntɪəriər/ (**interiors**) ◼ N-COUNT 可算名詞 The **interior** of something is the inside part of it. 内部 ❑ *The interior of the house was furnished with heavy, old-fashioned pieces.* 家の内部には重い旧式の家具が置かれていた. ◼ ADJ 形容詞 You use **interior** to describe something that is inside a building or vehicle. 内部の [ADJ n] ❑ *The interior walls were painted green.* 内壁は緑に塗られていた. ◼ N-SING 単数名詞 The **interior** of a country or continent is the central area of it. 内陸 ❑ *The Yangtze River would give access to much of China's interior.* 揚子江を利用すれば、中国内陸部の多くの地域への行くことが可能であろう. ◼ ADJ 形容詞 An **interior** minister, ministry, or department in some countries deals with affairs within that country, such as law and order. 内政の [ADJ n] ❑ *The French Interior Minister has intervened in a scandal over the role of a secret police force.* フランスの内務大臣は秘密警察部隊の役割に関するスキャンダルに干渉した.

Thesaurus interior また次を参照:

N. inside; (ant.) exterior, outside ◼

inter|lude /ɪntərlud/ (**interludes**) N-COUNT 可算名詞 An **interlude** is a short period of time when an activity or situation stops and something else happens. 合間

Word Link med ≈ middle : intermediary, media, mediate

inter|medi|ary /ɪntərmidieri/ (**intermediaries**) N-COUNT 可算名詞 An **intermediary** is a person who passes messages or proposals between two people or groups. 仲介者 ❑ *She wanted him to act as an intermediary in the dispute with Moscow.* 彼女は彼がモスクワとの紛争の仲介者になってくれることを望んでいた.

inter|medi|ate /ɪntərmidiɪt/ ◼ ADJ 形容詞 An **intermediate** stage, level, or position is one that occurs between two other stages, levels, or positions. 中間の ❑ *Do you make any intermediate stops between your home and work?* 家と職場を往復する途中で寄り道をしますか. ◼ ADJ 形容詞 **Intermediate** learners of something have some knowledge or skill but are not yet advanced. 中級の ❑ *Students are categorized as novice, intermediate, or advanced.* 学生は初級、中級、上級に分けられる. ● N-COUNT 可算名詞 An **intermediate** is an intermediate learner. 中級学習者 ❑ *The ski school coaches beginners, intermediates, and advanced skiers.* そのスキー学校は初心者、中級者、上級のスキーヤーを指導する.

in|ter|mi|nable /ɪntɜrmɪnəbəl/ ADJ 形容詞 If you describe something as **interminable**, you are emphasizing that it continues for a very long time and indicating that you wish it was shorter or would stop. 果てしない [EMPHASIS 強調] ❑ *...an interminable meeting.* だらだらと続く会議 ● **in|ter|mi|nably** ADV 副詞 果てしなく ❑ *He talked to me interminably about his first wife.* 彼は私に最初の妻についてとめどなく話した.

inter|mis|sion /ɪntərmɪʃən/ (**intermissions**) ◼ N-COUNT 可算名詞 An **intermission** is a short break between two parts of a concert, show, or movie. 休憩時間 ❑ *...during the intermission of the musical "Steppin' Out."* ミュージカル『ステッピング・アウト』の幕あ

いの間に **2** N-COUNT 可算名詞 You can use **intermission** to refer to a short break between two parts of a game, or say that something happens **at**, **after**, or **during intermission**. 中休み □ *Fraser did not perform until after intermission.* フレイザーは幕あい後まで出演しなかった.

inter|mit|tent /ɪntərmɪtᵊnt/ ADJ 形容詞 Something that is **intermittent** happens occasionally rather than continuously. 断続的 □ *After three hours of intermittent rain, the game was abandoned.* 雨が3時間降ったりやんだりしたあと，試合は中止された. ● **inter|mit|tent|ly** ADV 副詞 断続的に □ *The talks went on intermittently for three years.* その話し合いは断続的に3年間続いた.

in|tern (**interns**, **interning**, **interned**)

The verb is pronounced /ɪntɜrn/. The noun is pronounced /ɪntɜrn/.

動詞は /ɪntɜrn/ と発音される. 名詞は /ɪntɜrn/ と発音される.

1 V-T 他動詞 If someone **is interned**, they are put in prison or in a prison camp for political reasons. 抑留する [usu passive] □ *He was interned as an enemy alien at the outbreak of the Second World War.* 第2次世界大戦勃発（ぼっぱつ）時に彼は敵国人として抑留された. **2** N-COUNT 可算名詞 An **intern** is an advanced student or a recent graduate, especially in medicine, who is being given practical training under supervision. インターン [AM 米国英語] □ *…a medical intern.* 研修医

Word Link inter ≈ between : interchange, interconnect, internal

in|ter|nal /ɪntɜrnᵊl/ **1** ADJ 形容詞 **Internal** is used to describe things that exist or happen inside a country or organization. 内部の [ADJ n] □ *The country stepped up internal security.* その国は国内の保安対策を強化した. ● **in|ter|nal|ly** ADV 副詞 内部に □ *The state is not a unified and internally coherent entity.* その国は統合された，内的に統一のとれた国ではない. **2** ADJ 形容詞 [ADJ n] **Internal** is used to describe things that exist or happen inside a particular person, object, or place. 内部の □ *The doctor said the internal bleeding had been massive.* 医師は内出血がひどかったと言った. ● **in|ter|nal|ly** ADV 副詞 内部に □ *Evening primrose oil is used on the skin as well as taken internally.* 月見草油は内服されるのみでなく外用もされる.

inter|na|tion|al /ɪntərnæʃənᵊl/ ADJ 形容詞 **International** means between or involving different countries. 国際の，国家間の □ *…an international agreement against exporting arms to that country.* その国に対する武器輸出を禁止する国際協定 ● **inter|na|tion|al|ly** ADV 副詞 国際的に □ *…internationally agreed-upon rules.* 国際的に合意された規則

In|ter|net /ɪntərnɛt/ also **internet** N-PROPER 固有名詞 The **Internet** is the network that allows computer users to connect with computers all over the world, and that carries e-mail. インターネット

→ see Word Web: **Internet**
→ see **Internet**

in|tern|ship /ɪntɜrnʃɪp/ (**internships**) N-COUNT 算名詞 An **internship** is the position held by an intern, or the period of time when someone is an intern. インターンの地位・期間 [AM 米国英語] □ *…an internship in surgery in New York.* ニューヨークでの外科の実務研修

inter|per|son|al /ɪntərpɜrsənᵊl/ ADJ 形容詞 **Interpersonal** means relating to relationships between people. 対人関係の [ADJ n] □ *Training in interpersonal skills is essential.* 対人技術の訓練は必須である.

in|ter|pret /ɪntɜrprɪt/ (**interprets**, **interpreting**, **interpreted**) **1** V-T 他動詞 If you **interpret** something in a particular way, you decide that this is its meaning or significance. 解釈する □ *The fact that they had decided to come was interpreted as a positive sign.* 彼らが来ることに決めたという事実は，肯定的な兆候と解釈された. □ *The judge quite rightly says that he has to interpret the law as it's been passed.* その裁判官は，法は可決されたとおりに解釈しなければならないとしごく当然に言う. **2** V-T/V-I 他動詞/自動詞 If you **interpret** what someone is saying, you translate it immediately into another language. 通訳する □ *The chambermaid spoke little English, so her husband came with her to interpret.* その客室係のメードはほとんど英語を話さなかったので，彼女の夫が通訳するために一緒に来た.
→ see **dream**

Word Partnership interpret は次の語句と使われる:

| N. | interpret **data**, interpret **the meaning of** *something*, interpret **results**, **ways to** interpret **1** |
| ADJ. | **difficult to** interpret **1 2** |

in|ter|pre|ta|tion /ɪntɜrprɪteɪʃᵊn/ (**interpretations**) **1** N-VAR 可変性名詞 An **interpretation** of something is an opinion about what it means. 解釈 □ *Professor Wolfgang gives the data a very different interpretation.* ヴォルフガング教授はそのデータに非常に異なる解釈を与えている. **2** N-COUNT 可算名詞 A performer's **interpretation** of something such as a piece of music or a role in a play is the particular way in which they choose to perform it. 演出，演奏 □ *…a pianist celebrated for his interpretation of Chopin.* ショパンの演奏で名高いピアニスト
→ see **art**

Word Partnership interpretation は次の語句と使われる:

| ADJ. | **correct** interpretation, **literal** interpretation, **open to** interpretation, **strict** interpretation **1** |
| N. | **data** interpretation, interpretation **of results 1** |

in|ter|pret|er /ɪntɜrprɪtər/ (**interpreters**) N-COUNT 可算名詞 An **interpreter** is a person whose job is to translate what someone is saying into another language. 通訳者 □ *Speaking through an interpreter, Aristide said that Haitians had hoped coups were behind them.* アリスティドは通訳者を通して，ハイチ人はクーデターが終わることを願っていたと語った.

in|ter|ro|gate /ɪntɛrəgeɪt/ (**interrogates**, **interrogating**, **interrogated**) V-T 他動詞 If someone, especially a police officer, **interrogates** someone, they question them thoroughly for a long time in order to get some information from them. 尋問する □ *I interrogated everyone even slightly involved.* 私は少しでも係わり合いのある者すべてを尋問した.

in|ter|ro|ga|tion /ɪntɛrəgeɪʃᵊn/ (**interrogations**) N-VAR 可変性名詞 An **interrogation** is the act of interrogating someone. 尋問 □ *…the right to silence in police interrogations.* 警察の尋問における黙秘権

Word Link rupt ≈ breaking : disrupt, erupt, interrupt

in|ter|rupt /ɪntərʌpt/ (**interrupts**, **interrupting**, **interrupted**) **1** V-T/V-I 他動詞/自動詞 If you **interrupt** someone who is speaking, you say or do something that causes them to stop. さえぎる [他動詞・自動詞] □ *Turkin tapped him on the shoulder. "Sorry to interrupt, Colonel."* ターキンは彼の肩を軽くたたいて，「大佐，お話の邪魔をして申し訳ありませんが」と言った. ● **in|ter|rup|tion** /ɪntərʌpʃᵊn/ (**interruptions**) N-VAR 可変性名詞 妨害 □ *The sudden interruption stopped Justin in mid-sentence.* 突然じゃまが入り，文の途中でジャスティンの話の腰を折った. **2** V-T 他動詞 If someone or something **interrupts** a process or activity, they stop it for a period of time. 中断する □ *People kept nosing around the place, interrupting my work.* 人々はその場所をかぎまわり，私の仕事は中断された. ● **in|ter|rup|tion** N-VAR 可変性名詞 中断 □ *…interruptions in the supply of food and fuel.* 食物と燃料の供給の中断 **3** V-T 他動詞 If something **interrupts** a line, surface, or view, it stops it from being continuous or makes it look irregular. さえぎる □ *Taller plants interrupt the views from the house.* いっそう高い植物が家からの眺めをさえぎっている.

Word Link sect ≈ cutting : dissect, intersect, section

inter|sect /ɪntərsɛkt/ (**intersects**, **intersecting**, **intersected**) **1** V-RECIP 相互動詞 If two or more lines or roads **intersect**, they

The Internet

meet or cross each other. You can also say that one line or road **intersects** another. 交差する ❑ *The orbit of this comet intersects the orbit of the Earth.* このすい星の軌道は地球の軌道と交差する. ❷ V-RECIP 相互動詞 If one thing **intersects with** another or if two things **intersect**, the two things connect at a particular point. 相交わる ❑ *...the ways in which historical events intersect with individual lives.* 歴史的出来事が個々の人生と関わる仕方

inter|sec|tion /ɪntərsɛkʃən/ (intersections) N-COUNT 可算名詞 An **intersection** is a place where roads or other lines meet or cross. 交差点 ❑ *We crossed at a busy intersection.* 私たちは交通量の多い交差点を渡った.

inter|spersed /ɪntərspɜrst/ ADJ 形容詞 If one group of things are **interspersed with** another or **interspersed among** another, the second things occur between or among the first things. 散在して [v-link ADJ prep] ❑ *...a series of bursts of gunfire, interspersed with single shots.* 単発射撃の混じった連続射撃

inter|state /ɪntərsteɪt/ (interstates) ❶ ADJ 形容詞 **Interstate** means between states, especially the states of the United States. 各州間の [ADJ n] ❑ *...interstate commerce.* 州際通商 ❷ N-COUNT 可算名詞 An **interstate** or **interstate highway** is a major road linking states. 州間高速自動車道 ❑ *...the southbound lane of Interstate 75.* 州間高速自動車道75号線の南行き車線

inter|val /ɪntərvəl/ (intervals) ❶ N-COUNT 可算名詞 An **interval** between two events or dates is the period of time between them. 間隔 ❑ *The process is repeated after a short interval of time.* その過程は短い間隔を置いて繰り返される. ❷ N-COUNT 可算名詞 An **interval** during a concert, show, movie, or game is a short break between two of the parts. 合間 [mainly BRIT 主に英国英語; AM usually **intermission** 米国英語では通常 **intermission**] ❸ PHRASE 句 If something happens **at intervals**, it happens several times with gaps or pauses in between. 時々 ❑ *She woke him for his medicines at intervals throughout the night.* 彼女は, その夜じゅう折々彼を起こして薬を与えた. ❹ PHRASE 句 If things are placed **at particular intervals**, there are spaces of a particular size between them. (特定の) 間隔で ❑ *Several red and white barriers marked the road at intervals of about a mile.* 数個の赤と白のバリアで約1マイルごとに道路に目印がつけられていた.

inter|vene /ɪntərvin/ (intervenes, intervening, intervened) ❶ V-I 自動詞 If you **intervene in** a situation, you become involved in it and try to change it. 介入する ❑ *The situation calmed down when police intervened.* 警察の介入により, 状況は沈静した. ❷ V-I 自動詞 If you **intervene**, you interrupt a conversation in order to add something to it. さえぎる ❑ *Hernandez intervened and told me to stop it.* エルナンデスはさえぎって, 私にやめるように言った. ❸ V-I 自動詞 If an event **intervenes**, it happens suddenly in a way that stops, delays, or prevents something from happening. じゃまをする ❑ *The mailboat arrived on Friday mornings unless bad weather intervened.* 悪天候で遅れない限り, 郵便船は金曜日の朝に到着する.

inter|ven|ing /ɪntərvinɪŋ/ ❶ ADJ 形容詞 An **intervening** period of time is one that separates two events or points in time. 中間の [ADJ n] ❑ *During those intervening years Bridget had married her husband Robert.* その間の数年間はブリジットは夫のロバートと結婚していた. ❷ ADJ 形容詞 An **intervening** object or area comes between two other objects or areas. 介在する [ADJ n] ❑ *They had scoured the intervening miles of desert.* 彼らは間にある数マイルにわたる砂漠を探し回った.

inter|ven|tion /ɪntərvɛnʃən/ (interventions) N-VAR 可変性名詞 **Intervention** is the act of intervening in a situation. 介入 ❑ *...the role of the United States and its intervention in the internal affairs of many countries.* 米国の役割と, 多くの国の内政問題への米国の介入

inter|view /ɪntərvyu/ (interviews, interviewing, interviewed) ❶ N-VAR 可変性名詞 An **interview** is a formal meeting at which someone is asked questions in order to find out if they are suitable for a job or school. 面接 ❑ *The interview went well.* 面接はうまく行った. ❷ V-T 他動詞 If you **are interviewed** for a particular job or school, someone asks you questions about yourself to find out if you suitable for it. 面接する [usu passive] ❑ *When Wardell was interviewed, he was impressive, and on that basis, he was hired.* ワーデルは面接を受けた際に強い印象を与え, そのために採用された. ❸ N-COUNT 可算名詞 An **interview** is a conversation in which a journalist puts questions to someone such as a famous person or politician. インタビュー ❑ *The trouble began when Allan gave an interview to the Chicago Tribune last month.* 問題は, アランが先月『シカゴ・トリビューン』のインタビューに応じたことから起こった. ❹ V-T 他動詞 When a journalist **interviews** someone such as a famous person, they ask them a series of questions. インタビューする ❑ *I'd interviewed him often in the past.* 私はかつてよく彼にインタビューした. ❺ V-T 他動詞 When the police **interview** someone, they ask them questions about a crime that has been committed. 事情聴取する ❑ *The police interviewed the driver, but had no evidence to go on.* 警察は運転者から事情聴取したが, 継続するために必要な証拠は何もなかった.

Word Partnership *interview* は次の語句と使われる:

N.	**job** interview ❶
	(tele)phone interview ❶ ❸
	magazine/newspaper/radio/television interview ❸
V.	**conduct an** interview, **give an** interview, **request an** interview ❶ ❸

inter|view|ee /ɪntərvyui/ (interviewees) N-COUNT 可算名詞 An **interviewee** is a person who is being interviewed. 被面接者 ❑ *Is there any interviewee who stands out as memorable?* 面接を受けた者で特に印象に残る誰かいますか.

inter|view|er /ɪntərvyuər/ (interviewers) N-COUNT 可算名詞 An **interviewer** is a person who is asking someone questions at an interview. 面接者 ❑ *Being a good interviewer, however, requires much preparation and skill.* しかし, 良い面接者になるには, 十分な準備と技術が必要である.

in|tes|tine /ɪntɛstɪn/ (intestines) N-COUNT 可算名詞 Your **intestines** are the tubes in your body through which food passes when it has left your stomach. 腸 ❑ *This area is always tender to the touch if the intestines are not functioning properly.* 腸が適切に機能していない場合, この部位を触ると常に痛い.

in|ti|ma|cy /ɪntɪməsi/ ❶ N-UNCOUNT 不可算名詞 **Intimacy** between two people is a very close personal relationship between them. 親密 ❑ *...a means of achieving intimacy with another person.* 別の人と親密になる方法 ❷ N-UNCOUNT 不可算名詞 You sometimes use **intimacy** to refer to sex or a sexual relationship. 情交 ❑ *He did not feel like intimacy with any woman.* 彼はどんな女性とも肉体関係を持つ気にならなかった.

in|ti|mate (intimates, intimating, intimated)

The adjective is pronounced /ɪntɪmɪt/. The verb is pronounced /ɪntɪmeɪt/.

形容詞は /ɪntɪmɪt/ と発音される. 動詞は /ɪntɪmeɪt/ と発音される.

❶ ADJ 形容詞 If you have an **intimate** friendship with someone, you know them very well and like them a lot. 親密な ❑ *I discussed with my intimate friends whether I would immediately have a baby.* 私が赤ちゃんをすぐに作るべきか親しい友人たちと話し合った. ●**in|ti|mate|ly** ADV 副詞 親密に ❑ *He did not feel like he had gotten to know them intimately.* 彼は彼らを親しく知るようになったとは感じなかった. ❷ ADJ 形容詞 If two people are in an **intimate** relationship, they are involved with each other in a loving or sexual way. 肉体関係にある, 親密な ❑ *...their intimate moments with their boyfriends.* 彼女たちが恋人と親密に過ごす時間 ●**in|ti|mate|ly** ADV 副詞 [ADV after v] 親しく ❑ *You have to be willing to get to know yourself and your partner intimately.* あなたは喜んで自分自身と恋人を親しく知るようにならなければならない. ❸ ADJ 形容詞 An **intimate** conversation or detail, for example, is very personal and private. 個人的な ❑ *He wrote about the intimate details of his family life.* 彼は彼の個人的な家庭生活について詳しく書いた. ●**in|ti|mate|ly** ADV 副詞 [ADV after v] 個人的に ❑ *It was the first time they had attempted to talk intimately.* その時, 彼らは初めて個人的な会話を試みた. ❹ ADJ 形容詞 If you use **intimate** to describe an occasion or the atmosphere of a place, you like it because it is quiet and pleasant, and seems suitable for close conversations between friends. 居心地のよい [APPROVAL 賛成] ❑ *...an intimate candlelit dinner for two.* くつろいだ, ろうそくを灯した2人用の夕食 ❺ ADJ 形容詞 An **intimate** connection between ideas or organizations, for example, is a very strong link between them. 密接な ❑ *...an intimate connection between madness and wisdom.* 狂気と賢明さの密接な繋がり ●**in|ti|mate|ly** ADV 副詞 [ADV after v] 密接に ❑ *Scientific research and conservation are intimately connected.* 科学的研究と自然保護は密接な関係がある. ❻ ADJ 形容詞 An **intimate** knowledge of something is a deep and detailed knowledge of it. 詳細な ❑ *He surprised me with his intimate knowledge of Kierkegaard and Schopenhauer.* 彼はキルケゴールとショーペンハウアーを熟知しており, 私は驚いた. ●**in|ti|mate|ly** ADV 副詞 詳しく ❑ *...a golden age of musicians whose work she knew intimately.* 彼女が作品を熟知している音楽家たちの黄金時代 ❼ V-T 他動詞 If you **intimate** something, you say it in an indirect way. 暗示する [FORMAL 形式ばった] ❑ *He went on to intimate that he was indeed contemplating a shake-up of the company.* さらに彼は, 自分が確かに会社の大改革を考えていることをほのめかした.

Word Partnership *intimate* は次の語句と使われる:

N.	intimate **friend** ❶
	intimate **relationship** ❷
	intimate **details** ❸
	intimate **atmosphere** ❹

in|timi|date /ɪntɪmɪdeɪt/ (intimidates, intimidating, intimidated) V-T 他動詞 If you **intimidate** someone, you

deliberately make them frightened enough to do what you want them to do. 脅す □ *Jones had set out to intimidate and dominate Paul.* ジョーンズはポールを威圧し、支配しようとしていた. ● **in|timi|da|tion** /ɪntɪmɪdeɪʃᵊn/ N-UNCOUNT 不可算名詞 脅迫 □ *...an inquiry into allegations of intimidation during last week's vote.* 先週の投票中に脅迫が行われたという申し立てについての調査

in|timi|dat|ed /ɪntɪmɪdeɪtɪd/ ADJ 形容詞 Someone who feels **intimidated** feels frightened and lacks confidence because of the people they are with or the situation they are in. おじけづいて □ *Women can come in here and not feel intimidated.* 女性は安心してここに来ることができる.

in|timi|dat|ing /ɪntɪmɪdeɪtɪŋ/ ADJ 形容詞 If you describe someone or something as **intimidating**, you mean that they are frightening and make people lose confidence. 怖い □ *He was a huge, intimidating figure.* 彼は人をおびえさせるような大男だった.

into /ɪntu/

Pronounced /ɪntu/ or /ɪntu/, particularly before pronouns and for meaning 14.

特に代名詞の前と /ɪntu/の意味には /ɪntu/または 14 と発音される.

In addition to the uses shown below, **into** is used after some verbs and nouns in order to introduce extra information. **Into** is also used with verbs of movement, such as "walk" and "push," and in phrasal verbs such as "enter into" and "talk into."

下記の用法に加えて, **into** は余分な情報を伝えるために1部の動詞や名詞の後に使われる. **Into** はまた walk や push のような移動の動詞と共に使われるし, また **enter into** や **talk into** のような句動詞にも使われる.

1 PREP 前置詞 If you put one thing **into** another, you put the first thing inside the second. ～の中に □ *Combine the remaining ingredients and put them into a dish.* 残りの材料を混ぜ合わせてお皿に入れなさい. 2 PREP 前置詞 If you go into a place or vehicle, you move from being outside it to being inside it. ～の中に □ *I have no idea how he got into Iraq.* 私は彼がどのような方法でイラクに入国したのか分からない. 3 PREP 前置詞 If one thing goes **into** another, the first thing moves from the outside to the inside of the second thing, by breaking or damaging the surface of it. ～の中に □ *The blade missed his kidney, but went into his bowel.* ナイフは彼の腎臓をはずれ, 腸に刺さった. 4 PREP 前置詞 If one thing gets **into** another, the first thing enters the second and becomes part of it. ～の中に □ *Poisonous chemicals got into the water supply.* 有毒性の化学物質が水道に入り込んだ. 5 PREP 前置詞 If you are walking or driving a vehicle and you bump **into** something or crash **into** something, you hit it accidentally. ～に □ *A train from New Jersey plowed into the barrier at the end of the track.* ニュージャージー発の電車は線路の端の柵 (さく) に激しくぶつかった. 6 PREP 前置詞 When you get **into** a piece of clothing, you put it on. ～に □ *She could change into a different outfit in two minutes.* 彼女は2分で着替えることができた. 7 PREP 前置詞 If someone or something gets **into** a particular state, they start being in that state. (ある状態への推移) ～に [v PREP n, n PREP n] □ *I slid into a depression.* 私はうつ状態に陥った. 8 PREP 前置詞 If you talk someone **into** doing something, you persuade them to do it. (受諾) ～に [v n PREP n/-ing] □ *They sweet-talked him into selling the farm.* 彼らは彼をおだてて農場を売らせた. 9 PREP 前置詞 If something changes **into** something else, it then has a new form, shape, or nature. (ある状態への変化) ～に □ *...to turn a nasty episode into a joke.* 嫌な出来事を冗談に変えること 10 PREP 前置詞 If something is cut or split **into** a number of pieces or sections, it is divided so that it becomes several smaller pieces or sections. (分割) ～に □ *Sixteen teams are taking part, divided into four groups.* 16のチームが4つのグループに分かれて参加する. 11 PREP 前置詞 An investigation **into** a subject or event is concerned with that subject or event. ～に関する [n PREP n] □ *It would provide hundreds of millions of dollars for research into alternative energy sources.* それは代替エネルギー源の研究に数億ドルの資金を提供するだろう. 12 PREP 前置詞 If you move or go **into** a particular career or business, you start working in it. (職業・商売) ～に □ *In the early 1980s, it was easy to get into the rental business.* 1980年代の初期は簡単にレンタルビジネスを始められた. 13 PREP 前置詞 If something continues **into** a period of time, it continues until after that period of time has begun. (時間の継続) ～まで □ *He had three children, and lived on into his sixties.* 彼は3人の子供をもうけ, 60代まで生きた. 14 PREP 前置詞 If you are very interested in something and like it very much, you can say that you are **into** it. ～に熱中して [INFORMAL くだけた] [v-link PREP n] □ *I'm into electronics myself.* 私自身も電子工学にのめり込んでいる.

in|tol|er|able /ɪntɒlərəbᵊl/ ADJ 形容詞 If you describe something as **intolerable**, you mean that it is so bad or extreme that no one can bear it or tolerate it. 耐えられない □ *They felt this would put intolerable pressure on them.* 彼らはこれが耐えがたい重圧となると感じた. ● **in|tol|er|ably** /ɪntɒlərəbli/ ADV 副詞 耐えられない

ほどに □ *...intolerably cramped conditions.* ひどく狭苦しい状態

in|tol|er|ance /ɪntɒlərəns/ N-UNCOUNT 不可算名詞 **Intolerance** is unwillingness to let other people act in a different way or hold different opinions from you. 狭量 [DISAPPROVAL 不賛成] □ *...his intolerance of any opinion other than his own.* 自分の意見と違う意見を全く受け入れられない彼の狭量

in|tol|er|ant /ɪntɒlərənt/ ADJ 形容詞 If you describe someone as **intolerant**, you mean that they do not accept behavior and opinions that are different from their own. 狭量な [DISAPPROVAL 不賛成] □ *...intolerant attitudes toward non-Catholics.* 非カトリック教徒への偏狭な態度

in|toxi|cat|ed /ɪntɒksɪkeɪtɪd/ 1 ADJ 形容詞 Someone who is **intoxicated** is drunk. 酔った [FORMAL 形式ばった] □ *He appeared intoxicated, police said.* 彼は酔っていたようだと警察は言った. 2 ADJ 形容詞 If you are **intoxicated by** or **with** something such as a feeling or an event, you are so excited by it that you find it hard to think clearly and sensibly. 興奮した [LITERARY 文語的] [v-link ADJ 'by/with' n] □ *My cousins seem to have become intoxicated by their success.* 私の従兄弟たちはその成功に有頂天になっていたようだ.

in|trac|table /ɪntræktəbᵊl/ 1 ADJ 形容詞 **Intractable** people are very difficult to control or influence. 頑固な [FORMAL 形式ばった] □ *What may be done to reduce the influence of intractable opponents?* 頑固な反対者たちの影響力を減らすためには何ができるか. 2 ADJ 形容詞 **Intractable** problems or situations are very difficult to deal with. 扱いにくい [FORMAL 形式ばった] □ *The economy still faces intractable problems.* 経済にはまだ扱いにくい問題が残っている.

in|tra|net /ɪntrənet/ (**intranets**) N-COUNT 可算名詞 An **intranet** is a network of computers, similar to the Internet, within a particular company or organization. イントラネット → see **Internet**

in|tran|si|gence /ɪntrænsɪdʒᵊns/ N-UNCOUNT 不可算名詞 If you talk about someone's **intransigence**, you mean that they refuse to behave differently or to change their attitude to something. 妥協しないこと, 頑固さ [FORMAL 形式ばった, DISAPPROVAL 不賛成] □ *He often appeared angry and frustrated by the intransigence of both sides.* 彼はしばしば双方の非妥協的な態度に腹を立て, いらだっているようだった.

in|tran|si|gent /ɪntrænsɪdʒᵊnt/ ADJ 形容詞 If you describe someone as **intransigent**, you mean that they refuse to behave differently or to change their attitude to something. 妥協しない [FORMAL 形式ばった, DISAPPROVAL 不賛成] □ *...Sami's opinionated and intransigent father.* サミーの独断的で頑固な父親

in|tran|si|tive /ɪntrænsɪtɪv/ ADJ 形容詞 An **intransitive** verb does not have an object. 自動詞の

intra|venous /ɪntrəvinəs/ ADJ 形容詞 **Intravenous** foods or drugs are put into people's bodies through their veins, rather than their mouths. 静脈内の [MEDICAL 医学の] [ADJ n] □ *...an intravenous drip.* 静脈内点滴 ● **intra|venous|ly** ADV 副詞 [ADV after v] 静脈内に □ *Premature babies have to be fed intravenously.* 未熟児は静脈内点滴で栄養を与えなければならない.

in tray (**in trays**) also **in-tray** N-COUNT 可算名詞 An **in tray** is a shallow container used in offices to put letters and documents in before they are dealt with. Compare **out tray**. 未決書類入れ [mainly BRIT 主に英国英語; AM usually **inbox**] 米国英語では通常 **inbox**]

in|trep|id /ɪntrepɪd/ ADJ 形容詞 An **intrepid** person acts in a brave way. 勇敢な □ *...an intrepid space traveler.* 勇敢な宇宙旅行者

in|tri|ca|cy /ɪntrɪkəsi/ N-UNCOUNT 不可算名詞 **Intricacy** is the state of being made up of many small parts or details. 複雑さ □ *The price depends on the intricacy of the work.* 価格は作業の複雑さによって決まる.

in|tri|cate /ɪntrɪkət/ ADJ 形容詞 You use **intricate** to describe something that has many small parts or details. 複雑な □ *...the production of carpets with highly intricate patterns.* 非常に複雑な模様のカーペットの製造 ● **in|tri|cate|ly** ADV 副詞 複雑に □ *...intricately carved sculptures.* 複雑に彫られた彫刻

in|trigue (**intrigues, intriguing, intrigued**)

The noun is pronounced /ɪntrig/. The verb is pronounced /ɪntrig/.

名詞は /ɪntrig/と発音される. 動詞は /ɪntrig/と発音される.

1 N-VAR 可変性名詞 **Intrigue** is the making of secret plans to harm or deceive people. 陰謀 □ *...political intrigue.* 政治的陰謀 2 V-T 他動詞 If something, especially something strange, **intrigues** you, it interests you and you want to know more about it. 興味を抱かせる □ *The novelty of the situation intrigued him.* 状況の目新しさに彼は興味をそそられた.

in|trigued /ɪntrigd/ ADJ 形容詞 If you are **intrigued by** something, especially something strange, it interests you and you want to know more about it. 興味をそそられた □ *I would be intrigued to hear others' views.* 私は他の人々の考えを聞きたい.

in|tri|guing /ɪntriːgɪŋ/ ADJ 形容詞 If you describe something as **intriguing**, you mean that it is interesting or strange. 興味をそそる ❑ *This intriguing book is both thoughtful and informative.* この面白い本は思慮に富み、参考になる. ●**in|tri|guing|ly** ADV 副詞 興味をそそるように ❑ *...the intriguingly-named newspaper Le Canard Enchain (The Chained Duck).* 興味深い名前の新聞『鎖でつながれたカモ』

in|trin|sic /ɪntrɪnsɪk/ ADJ 形容詞 If something has **intrinsic** value or **intrinsic** interest, it is valuable or interesting because of its basic nature or character, and not because of its connection with other things. 本質的な [FORMAL 形式ばった] [ADJ n] ❑ *Diamonds have little intrinsic value and their price depends almost entirely on their scarcity.* ダイアモンドには本質的な価値はほとんどなく、その価格はほとんど全部珍しさに左右される. ●**in|trin|si|cal|ly** /ɪntrɪnsɪkli/ ADV 副詞 本質的に ❑ *Sometimes I wonder if people are intrinsically evil.* 私は時々人間は本質的に邪悪なのではないかと思うことがある.

in|tro|duce /ɪntrədjuːs/ (introduces, introducing, introduced) **1** V-T 他動詞 To **introduce** something means to cause it to enter a place or exist in a system for the first time. 導入する ❑ *MGM introduced a new system for hiring writers.* MGMは作家を雇用するための新しい制度を導入した. ●**in|tro|duc|tion** N-UNCOUNT 不可算名詞 導入 ❑ *What he is better remembered for is the introduction of the moving assembly-line in Detroit in 1913.* 彼についていっそう記憶されることは、1913年にデトロイトで動く組立ラインを導入したことだ. **2** V-T 他動詞 If you **introduce** one person **to** another, or you **introduce** two people, you tell them each other's names, so that they can get to know each other. If you **introduce yourself** to someone, you tell them your name. 紹介する ❑ *Tim, may I introduce you to my uncle's secretary, Mary Waller?* ティム、こちらは私の叔父の秘書のメアリー・ウォーカーさんだ. ❑ *We haven't been introduced. My name is Nero Wolfe.* まだ紹介されていませんが、私はネロ・ウォルフといいます. ●**in|tro|duc|tion** N-VAR 可変性名詞 紹介 ❑ *With considerable shyness, Elaine performed the introductions.* エレーンはかなり恥ずかしそうに紹介をした. **3** V-T 他動詞 If you **introduce** someone **to** something, you cause them to learn about it or experience it for the first time. 初めて体験させる ❑ *He introduced us to the delights of natural food.* 彼は私たちに自然食の楽しみを教えてくれた. ●**in|tro|duc|tion** N-SING 単数名詞 手ほどきすること, 入門 ❑ *His introduction to fieldwork was a series of expeditions.* 彼は実地調査の入門として一連の探検旅行を行なった. **4** V-T 他動詞 The person who **introduces** a television or radio program speaks at the beginning of it, and often between the different items in it, in order to explain what the program or the items are about. 前置きをつけて始める ❑ *...talk shows introduced by women.* 女性が前置きを務めるトークショー

Word Partnership	introduce は次の語句と使われる:
N.	introduce **a bill**, introduce **changes**, introduce **legislation**, introduce **reform** **1**
V.	**allow me to** introduce, **let me** introduce, **want to** introduce **3** **4**

in|tro|duc|tion /ɪntrədʌkʃən/ (introductions) **1** N-COUNT 可算名詞 The **introduction** to a book or talk is the part that comes at the beginning and tells you what the rest of the book or talk is about. 序文 ❑ *Ellen Malos, in her introduction to "The Politics of Housework," provides a summary of the debates.* エレン・マロス著『家事の策略』の序文には討議の要約がある. **2** N-COUNT 可算名詞 If you refer to a book as an **introduction to** a particular subject, you mean that it explains the basic facts about that subject. 入門書 ❑ *The book is a friendly, down-to-earth introduction to physics.* その本は物理学の親しみやすく実際的な入門書である. **3** N-COUNT 可算名詞 You can refer to a new product as an **introduction** when it becomes available in a place for the first time. 新製品 ❑ *There are two among their recent introductions that have greatly impressed me.* 最近の新製品の中には私に大きな印象を与えたものが2つある. **4** → see also **introduce**

in|tro|duc|tory /ɪntrədʌktəri/ **1** ADJ 形容詞 An **introductory** remark, talk, or part of a book gives a small amount of general information about a particular subject, often before a more detailed explanation. 入門的な, 序文の [ADJ n] ❑ *...an introductory course in religion and theology.* 宗教と神学の入門講座 **2** ADJ 形容詞 An **introductory** offer or price on a new product is something such as a free gift or a low price that is meant to attract new customers. 紹介の [BUSINESS 実業] [ADJ n] ❑ *...a special introductory offer.* 新商品の特価提供

in|trude /ɪntruːd/ (intrudes, intruding, intruded) **1** V-I 自動詞 If you say that someone **is intruding into** a particular place or situation, you mean that they are not wanted or welcome there. 押しかける ❑ *The press has been blamed for intruding into people's personal lives in an unacceptable way.* 報道機関は容認できない方法で人々の私生活を侵害していると非難されてきた. **2** V-I 自動詞 If something **intrudes on** your mood or your life, it disturbs it or

has an unwanted effect on it. じゃまする ❑ *Do you feel anxious when unforeseen incidents intrude on your day?* あなたは予期できない出来事が日常をじゃますると不安に感じるか. **3** V-I 自動詞 If someone **intrudes into** a place, they go there even though they are not allowed to be there. 侵入する ❑ *An American officer on the scene said no one had intruded into the space he was defending.* 現場にいた米軍将校は彼が防衛している区域には誰も侵入していないと言った.

in|trud|er /ɪntruːdər/ (intruders) N-COUNT 可算名詞 An **intruder** is a person who goes into a place where they are not supposed to be. 侵入者 ❑ *He owned a gun for scaring off intruders.* 彼は侵入者を追い払うために銃を持っていた.

in|tru|sion /ɪntruːʒən/ (intrusions) **1** N-VAR 可変性名詞 If someone disturbs you when you are in a private place or having a private conversation, you can call this event an **intrusion**. じゃま ❑ *I hope you don't mind this intrusion, Jon.* ジョン、じゃましてごめんなさい. **2** N-VAR 可変性名詞 An **intrusion** is something that disturbs your mood or your life in a way you do not like. 侵害行為 ❑ *I felt it was a grotesque intrusion into our lives.* 私はそれが私たちの生活へのひどい侵害行為だと感じた.

in|tru|sive /ɪntruːsɪv/ ADJ 形容詞 Something that is **intrusive** disturbs your mood or your life in a way you do not like. じゃまになる ❑ *The cameras were not an intrusive presence.* カメラはじゃまな存在ではなかった.

in|tui|tion /ɪntuɪʃən/ (intuitions) N-VAR 可変性名詞 Your **intuition** or your **intuitions** are unexplained feelings that something is true even when you have no evidence or proof of it. 直感, 直観 ❑ *Her intuition was telling her that something was wrong.* 彼女は何か変だと直感的に感じていた.

in|tui|tive /ɪntuɪtɪv/ ADJ 形容詞 If you have an **intuitive** idea or feeling about something, you feel that it is true although you have no evidence or proof of it. 直感により認識する ❑ *A positive pregnancy test soon confirmed her intuitive feelings.* 陽性の妊娠テストはじきに彼女の直感が正しいことを確認した. ●**in|tui|tive|ly** ADV 副詞 直感的に ❑ *He seemed to know intuitively that I must be missing my mother.* 彼は私が母に会いたがっているのを直感的に知っているようだった.

in|un|date /ɪnʌndeɪt/ (inundates, inundating, inundated) **1** V-T 他動詞 If you say that you **are inundated with** things such as letters, demands, or requests, you are emphasizing that you receive so many of them that you cannot deal with them all. 殺到する [EMPHASIS 強調] ❑ *Her office was inundated with requests for tickets.* 彼女の事務所にはチケットの注文が殺到した. **2** V-T 他動詞 If an area of land **is inundated**, it becomes covered with water. 水浸しにする [usu passive] ❑ *Their neighborhood is being inundated by the rising waters of the Colorado River.* 彼らの近所はコロラド川の増水で水浸しになりつつある.

in|vade /ɪnveɪd/ (invades, invading, invaded) **1** V-T/V-I 他動詞/自動詞 To **invade** a country means to enter it by force with an army. 侵略する ❑ *In autumn 1944 the Allies invaded the Italian mainland at Anzio and Salerno.* 1944年秋に連合軍はイタリア本土にアンツィオとサレルノの地点で侵入した. **2** V-T 他動詞 If you say that people or animals **invade** a place, you mean that they enter it in large numbers, often in a way that is unpleasant or difficult to deal with. 押し寄せる ❑ *People invaded the streets in victory processions almost throughout the day.* ほぼ1日中人々は戦勝行進で街路に押し寄せた.

in|vad|er /ɪnveɪdər/ (invaders) **1** N-COUNT 可算名詞 **Invaders** are soldiers who are invading a country. 侵略部隊 ❑ *The city was destroyed by foreign invaders.* その市は外国の侵略軍に破壊された. **2** N-COUNT 可算名詞 You can refer to a country or army that has invaded or is about to invade another country as an **invader**. 侵略者 ❑ *...action against a foreign invader.* 外国の侵略者に対する行動

in|va|lid (invalids)

The noun is pronounced /ɪnvəlɪd/. The adjective is pronounced /ɪnvælɪd/ and is hyphenated in|val|id.

名詞は /ɪnvəlɪd/ と発音される. 形容詞は /ɪnvælɪd/ と発音され, in|val|id とハイフンで結ぶ.

1 N-COUNT 可算名詞 An **invalid** is someone who needs to be cared for because they have an illness or disability. 病人 ❑ *I hate being treated as an invalid.* 病人扱いされるのは大嫌いだ. **2** ADJ 形容詞 If an action, procedure, or document is **invalid**, it cannot be accepted, because it breaks the law or some official rule. 無効な ❑ *The trial was stopped and the results declared invalid.* 裁判は中止となり, 結果は無効だと宣言された. **3** ADJ 形容詞 An **invalid** argument or conclusion is wrong because it is based on a mistake. 根拠のない ❑ *We think that those arguments are rendered invalid by the facts.* 我々はそうした議論は事実により根拠が失われたと考えている.

in|vali|date /ɪnvælɪdeɪt/ (invalidates, invalidating, invalidated) V-T 他動詞 If something **invalidates** something such as a law, contract, or election, it causes it to be considered illegal. 無効にする ❑ *An official decree invalidated the vote in the capital.* 公式の

法令により首都で行われた投票は無効となった.

in|valu|able /ɪnvǽlyuəbᵊl/ ADJ 形容詞 If you describe something as **invaluable**, you mean that it is extremely useful. 非常に貴重な ❑ *I was able to gain invaluable experience over that year.* 私はその年じゅうに非常に貴重な経験をすることができた.

in|vari|ably /ɪnvέəriəbli/ ADV 副詞 If something **invariably** happens or is **invariably** true, it always happens or is always true. 常に ❑ *They almost invariably get it wrong.* 彼らはほとんど常に誤解する.

in|va|sion /ɪnvéɪʒᵊn/ (**invasions**) ◼ N-VAR 可変性名詞 If there is an **invasion** of a country, a foreign army enters it by force. 侵略 ❑ *…seven years after the Roman invasion of Britain.* ローマがブリテン島を侵略してから7年後 ◼ N-VAR 可変性名詞 If you refer to the arrival of a large number of people or things as an **invasion**, you are emphasizing that they are unpleasant or difficult to deal with. 襲来 ❑ *…this year's annual invasion of flies, wasps and ants.* 今年のハエ, ハチ, アリの例年の襲来 ◼ N-VAR 可変性名詞 If you describe an action as an **invasion**, you disapprove of it because it affects someone or something in a way that is not wanted. 侵害 [DISAPPROVAL 不賛成] ❑ *Is reading a child's diary always a gross invasion of privacy?* 子供の日記を読むことはいつもプライバシーの大侵害となるか.

in|va|sive /ɪnvéɪsɪv/ ◼ ADJ 形容詞 You use **invasive** to describe something undesirable that spreads very quickly and that is very difficult to stop from spreading. 浸潤性の ❑ *They found invasive cancer during a routine examination.* 彼らは定期検査中に浸潤ガンを発見した. ◼ ADJ 形容詞 An **invasive** medical procedure involves operating on a patient or examining the inside of their body. 切開する ❑ *Many people find the idea of any kind of invasive surgery unbearable.* 多くの人々はどんな手術でも体を切開するのは耐えられないと考えている.

in|vent /ɪnvént/ (**invents, inventing, invented**) ◼ V-T 他動詞 If you **invent** something such as a machine or process, you are the first person to think of it or make it. 発明する ❑ *He invented the first electric clock.* 彼は最初の電気時計を発明した. ◼ V-T 他動詞 If you **invent** a story or excuse, you try to make other people believe that it is true when in fact it is not. でっち上げる ❑ *I stood still, trying to invent a plausible excuse.* 私はじっと立って, もっともらしい言い訳をこしらえようとしていた.

in|ven|tion /ɪnvénʃᵊn/ (**inventions**) ◼ N-COUNT 可算名詞 An **invention** is a machine, device, or system that has been invented by someone. 発明品 ❑ *The spinning wheel was a Chinese invention.* 紡ぎ車は中国の発明品だ. ◼ N-UNCOUNT 不可算名詞 **Invention** is the act of inventing something that has never been made or used before. 発明 ❑ *…the invention of the telephone.* 電話の発明 ◼ N-VAR 可変性名詞 If you refer to someone's account of something as an **invention**, you think that it is untrue and that they have made it up. でっち上げ ❑ *The story was certainly a favorite one, but it was undoubtedly pure invention.* その話は確かにお気に入りだったが, ただの作り話だったことは疑いない. ◼ N-UNCOUNT 不可算名詞 **Invention** is the ability to invent things or to have clever and original ideas. 発明の才 ❑ *Perhaps, with such powers of invention and mathematical ability, he will be offered a job in computers.* あのような発明の才と数学的な能力を持っているので, 彼は多分コンピュータ関連の仕事に就くだろう.

in|ven|tive /ɪnvéntɪv/ ADJ 形容詞 An **inventive** person is good at inventing things or has clever and original ideas. 発明の才のある, 創意に富んだ ❑ *It inspired me to be more inventive with my own cooking.* そのおかげで私自身が料理する時にもっと工夫する気になった. ●**in|ven|tive|ness** N-UNCOUNT 不可算名詞 独創性 ❑ *He has surprised us before with his inventiveness.* 彼は以前私たちを独創性で驚かしたことがある.

in|ven|tor /ɪnvéntər/ (**inventors**) N-COUNT 可算名詞 An **inventor** is a person who has invented something, or whose job is to invent things. 発明家 ❑ *…Alexander Graham Bell, the inventor of the telephone.* 電話の発明家のアレキサンダー・グレアム・ベル → see Word Web: **inventor**

in|ven|tory /ɪnvᵊntɔri/ (**inventories**) ◼ N-VAR 可変性名詞 An **inventory** is a supply or stock of something. 在庫品目 [AM 米国英語] ❑ *…one inventory of twelve sails for each yacht.* 各ヨットにつき12の帆の在庫品 ◼ N-COUNT 可算名詞 An **inventory** is a written list of all the objects in a particular place such as all the merchandise in a store. 商品目録 ❑ *Before starting, he made an inventory of everything that was to stay.* 始める前に彼はそのまま残るべき全ての品目の目録を作成した.

in|vert /ɪnvɜ́rt/ (**inverts, inverting, inverted**) V-T 他動詞 If you **invert** something, you turn it upside down or inside out. ひっくり返す [FORMAL 形式ばった] ❑ *Invert the cake onto a serving plate.* ケーキをひっくり返してお皿に移しなさい.

in|vert|ed com|mas N-PLURAL 複数名詞 **Inverted commas** are punctuation marks that are used in writing to show where speech or a quotation begins and ends. They are usually written or printed as " " or ' '. **Inverted commas** are also sometimes used around the titles of books, plays, or songs, or around a word or phrase that is being discussed. 逆コンマ [BRIT 英国英語; AM **quotation marks** 米国英語 **quotation marks**]

in|vest /ɪnvést/ (**invests, investing, invested**) ◼ V-T/V-I 他動詞/自動詞 If you **invest** in something, or if you **invest** a sum of money, you use your money in a way that you hope will increase its value, for example, by putting it in a bank, or buying securities or property. 投資する ❑ *Many people don't like to invest in stocks.* 株式へ投資するのを好まない人々は多い. ❑ *I'm tired of watching you invest our money in insane projects.* 私はあなたがばかげた企画に私たちのお金を投資するのを見ているのがいやになった. ◼ V-T/V-I 他動詞/自動詞 If you **invest in** something useful, you buy it, because it will help you to do something more efficiently or more cheaply. 投資する ❑ *The company has invested a six-figure sum in an electronic order-control system which is used to keep stores stocked.* その会社は在庫を確保するための電子注文管理システムに6桁の金額を投資した. ◼ V-T/V-I 他動詞/自動詞 When a government or organization **invests in** something, it gives or lends money for a purpose that it considers useful or profitable. 投資する ❑ *…the need to invest in new technology.* 新しいテクノロジーに投資する必要性 ❑ *Government agencies must invest more funds in training and development programs.* 政府機関は研修と開発プログラムにより多くの資金を投資する必要がある. ◼ V-T 他動詞 If you **invest** time or energy in something, you spend a lot of time or energy on it because you think it will be useful or successful. 使う ❑ *I would rather invest time in Rebecca than in the kitchen.* 私はどちらかと言うと台所仕事よりもレベッカに時間を費やしたい. ◼ V-T 他動詞 To **invest** someone **with** rights or responsibilities means to give them those rights or responsibilities legally or officially. 授ける [FORMAL 形式ばった] ❑ *The constitution invested him with certain powers.* 憲法は彼に一定の権限を与えた. → see **stock market**

in|ves|ti|gate /ɪnvéstɪgeɪt/ (**investigates, investigating, investigated**) V-T/V-I 他動詞/自動詞 If someone, especially an official, **investigates** an event, situation, or claim, they try to find out what happened or what is the truth. 調査する, 捜査する ❑ *They're still investigating the accident.* 彼らはまだその事故を捜査中

だ. ● in|ves|ti|ga|tion /ɪnvɛstɪɡeɪʃ°n/ (investigations) N-VAR 可変性名詞 調査, 捜査 □He ordered an investigation into the affair. 彼はその事件の捜査を命じた.

Word Partnership investigate は次の語句と使われる:

N.	investigate **complaints**, investigate **a crime**, **police** investigate, investigate **the possibility of** something
ADV.	**fully** investigate, investigate **further**

in|ves|ti|ga|tive /ɪnvɛstɪɡeɪtɪv/ ADJ 形容詞 **Investigative** work, especially journalism, involves investigating things. 調査の □…an investigative reporter. 調査記者

in|ves|ti|ga|tor /ɪnvɛstɪɡeɪtər/ (investigators) N-COUNT 可算名詞 An **investigator** is someone who carries out investigations, especially as part of their job. 調査者, 捜査官 □…an undercover investigator. 秘密捜査官

in|vest|ment /ɪnvɛstmənt/ (investments) **1** N-UNCOUNT 不可算名詞 **Investment** is the activity of investing money. 投資 □He said the government must introduce tax incentives to encourage investment. 政府は投資を推進するために税制上の優遇措置を導入しなければならないと彼は言った. **2** N-VAR 可変性名詞 An **investment** is an amount of money that you invest, or the thing that you invest in it. 投資額 □…an investment of twenty-eight million dollars. 2800万ドルの投資額 **3** N-COUNT 可算名詞 If you describe something you buy as an **investment**, you mean that it will be useful, especially because it will help you to do a task more cheaply or efficiently. 投資の対象 □When selecting boots, fine, quality leather will be a wise investment. ブーツを選ぶ時には上等で品質の優れた革が賢明な投資の対象となるだろう. **4** N-UNCOUNT 不可算名詞 **Investment** of time or effort is the spending of time or effort on something in order to make it a success. 投入 □I worry about this big investment of time not working. この多大な時間の投入が効果をもたらしていないのではないかと心配だ.

Word Partnership investment は次の語句と使われる:

V.	**encourage** investment, **stimulate** investment **1** **make an** investment **2** – **4**
N.	**capital** investment **1** **2** investment **advisor**, investment **banker**, investment **company**, investment **fund**, investment **opportunity**, investment **plan** **2**
ADJ.	**long-term/short-term** investment **2**

in|ves|tor /ɪnvɛstər/ (investors) N-COUNT 可算名詞 An **investor** is a person or organization that buys securities or property in order to receive a profit. 投資者 □The main investor in the project is the French bank Credit National. その計画の主な投資者はフランスの銀行, クレディナショナルだ.

Word Link vig ≈ awake, strong : in**vig**orating, **vig**il, **vig**ilant

in|vig|or|at|ing /ɪnvɪɡəreɪtɪŋ/ ADJ 形容詞 If you describe something as **invigorating**, you mean that it makes you feel more energetic. 爽快(そうかい)な気分にさせる □…the invigorating northern air. 爽快な気分になる北の空気

Word Link vict, vinc ≈ conquering : con**vict**, con**vinc**e, in**vinc**ible

in|vin|ci|ble /ɪnvɪnsɪb°l/ **1** ADJ 形容詞 If you describe an army or sports team as **invincible**, you believe that they cannot be defeated. 打ち負かせない □You couldn't help feeling the military's fire power was invincible. 軍の火力は無敵だと感ぜずにはいられなかった. **2** ADJ 形容詞 If someone has an **invincible** belief or attitude, it cannot be changed. ゆるぎない □He also had an invincible faith in the medicinal virtues of garlic. また彼はにんにくの薬効をかたくなに信じていた.

in|vis|ible /ɪnvɪzɪb°l/ **1** ADJ 形容詞 If you describe something as **invisible**, you mean that it cannot be seen, for example, because it is transparent, hidden, or very small. 見えない □The lines were so finely etched as to be invisible from a distance. そのエッチングの線は遠くからは見えないほど細く描かれていた. ● in|vis|ibly /ɪnvɪzɪbli/ 副詞 [ADV with v] 目に見えないほど □A thin coil of smoke rose almost invisibly into the sharp, bright sky. 薄い煙の輪が晴れ渡った空に上っていくのがほのかすかに見えた. **2** ADJ 形容詞 You can use **invisible** when you are talking about something that cannot be seen but has a definite effect. In this sense, **invisible** is often used before a noun that refers to something visible. 隠れた [ADJ n] □All the time you are in doubt about the cause of your illness, you are fighting against an invisible enemy. 病気の原因が不明な時はずっと, 隠れた敵と戦っている. ● in|vis|ibly ADV 副詞 [ADV with v] 気づかれずに □…the tradition that invisibly shapes things in the present. 現在の事柄をそれとなく形づくる伝統 **3** ADJ 形容詞 If you say that you feel **invisible**, you are complaining that you are being ignored by other people. If you say that a particular problem or situation is **invisible**, you are complaining that it is

not being considered or dealt with. 無視されて □It was strange, how invisible a clerk could feel. 事務員がいかに無視されていると感じることがあるかは不思議だった. ● in|vis|ibil|ity /ɪnvɪzɪbɪlɪti/ N-UNCOUNT 不可算名詞 目に見えないこと, 軽視 □She takes up the issue of the invisibility of women and women's concerns in society. 彼女は社会での女性に対する軽視や女性の社会への関心の問題を取り上げる. **4** ADJ 形容詞 In stories, **invisible** people or things have a magic quality that makes people unable to see them. 透明な □…The Invisible Man. 透明人間 **5** ADJ 形容詞 [ADJ n] In economics, **invisible** earnings are the money that a country makes as a result of services such as banking and tourism, rather than by producing goods. 財務諸表に表れない, 貿易外の [BUSINESS 実業] □The revenue from tourism is the biggest single item in the country's invisible earnings. 観光業による収入はその国の貿易外所得の最大の単一の項目である. → see **sun**

in|vi|ta|tion /ɪnvɪteɪʃ°n/ (invitations) **1** N-COUNT 可算名詞 An **invitation** is a written or spoken request to come to an event such as a party, a meal, or a meeting. 招待 □…an invitation to lunch. 昼食への招待 □The Syrians have not yet accepted an invitation to attend. シリア人たちはまだ参加への招待に応じていない. **2** N-COUNT 可算名詞 An **invitation** is the card or paper on which an invitation is written or printed. 招待状 □Hundreds of invitations are being sent out this week. 今週は何百枚もの招待状が発送されている. **3** N-SING 単数名詞 If you believe that someone's action is likely to have a particular result, especially a bad one, you can refer to the action as an **invitation to** that result. 誘惑 □Don't leave your shopping on the back seat of your car – it's an open invitation to a thief. 車の後部席に買った品物を置きっぱなしにしてはならない. 泥棒への公然たる誘惑だ.

Word Partnership invitation は次の語句と使われる:

V.	**accept an** invitation, **decline an** invitation, **extend an** invitation **1** **get/receive an** invitation **1** **2**

in|vite (invites, inviting, invited)

The verb is pronounced /ɪnvaɪt/. The noun is pronounced /ɪnvaɪt/.

動詞は /ɪnvaɪt/ と発音される. 名詞は /ɪnvaɪt/ と発音される.

1 V-T 他動詞 If you **invite** someone to something such as a party or a meal, you ask them to come to it. 招く □She invited him to her 26th birthday party in New Jersey. 彼女はニュージャージー州での26歳の誕生パーティーに彼を招待した. □Barron invited her to accompany him to the races. バロンは彼女を競馬に同行するように招待した. **2** V-T 他動詞 If you **are invited to** do something, you are formally asked or given permission to do it. 要請する, 勧める □At a future date, managers will be invited to apply for a management buy-out. 後日経営陣は自社株取得を申し込むことを要請されるでしょう. □He invited me to go into partnership with him. 彼は私に彼と提携するように頼んだ. **3** V-T 他動詞 If something you say or do **invites** trouble or criticism, it makes trouble or criticism more likely. もたらす, 招く □Their refusal to compromise will inevitably invite more criticism from the UN. 彼らが歩み寄りを拒否すれば, 国連からより多くの批判を受けるのは避けられないだろう. **4** N-COUNT 可算名詞 An **invite** is an invitation to something such as a party or a meal. 招待 [INFORMAL くだけた] □She tried to wangle an invite to the party. 彼女はうまくそのパーティーへの招待にあずかろうとした.

Word Partnership invite は次の語句と使われる:

N.	invite someone **to dinner**, invite **friends**, invite **people** **1** invite **criticism**, invite **questions** **3**

in|vit|ing /ɪnvaɪtɪŋ/ **1** ADJ 形容詞 If you say that something is **inviting**, you mean that it has good qualities that attract you or make you want to experience it. 気をそそる □The February air was soft, cool, and inviting. 2月の空気は柔らかく, すずしく, 爽快(そうかい)だった. ● in|vit|ing|ly ADV 副詞 心を奪うように □The waters of the tropics are invitingly clear. 熱帯地方の海水は吸い込まれそうなほど澄んでいる. **2** → see also **invite**

in|voice /ɪnvɔɪs/ (invoices, invoicing, invoiced) **1** N-COUNT 可算名詞 An **invoice** is a document that lists goods that have been supplied or services that have been done, and says how much money you owe for them. 送り状, 明細記入請求書 □We will then send you an invoice for the total course fees. 当方はそれから受講料全額の請求書をあなたに送ります. **2** V-T 他動詞 If you **invoice** someone, you send them a bill for goods or services you have provided them with. 送り状を送る, 請求書を送る □The agency invoices the client who then pays the full amount to the agency. 代理店は顧客に送り状を送り, 顧客はそれから代理店に全額を支払う.

in|voke /ɪnvoʊk/ (invokes, invoking, invoked) **1** V-T 他動詞 If you **invoke** a law, you state that you are taking a particular action

because that law allows or tells you to. 発動する ❑ *The judge invoked an international law that protects refugees.* 判事は避難民を保護する国際法を発動した. ❷ V-T 他動詞 If you **invoke** something such as a principle, a saying, or a famous person, you refer to them in order to support your argument. 引き合いに出す ❑ *...economists who invoke the principle of "consumer sovereignty" to support their arguments.* 自分の主張を裏付けるために「消費者主権」の原則を引き合いに出す経済専門家 ❸ V-T 他動詞 If something such as a piece of music **invokes** a feeling or an image, it causes someone to have the feeling or to see the image. Many people consider this use to be incorrect because **evoke** is the correct word for this. 呼びさます ❑ *"Appalachian Spring" by Aaron Copland invoked the atmosphere of the wide open spaces of the prairies.* アーロン・コプランド作曲の「アパラチア山脈の春」は草原地帯の広い空間の雰囲気を呼び起こした.

Word Link vol ≈ will : bene**vol**ent, in**vol**untary, **vol**unteer

in|vol|un|tary /ɪnvɒləntəri/ ❶ ADJ 形容詞 If you make an **involuntary** movement or exclamation, you make it suddenly and without intending to because you are unable to control yourself. 無意識の ❑ *Another surge of pain in my ankle caused me to give an involuntary shudder.* 足首の痛みがまた急に始まり, 私は思わず身震いした. ● in|vol|un|tari|ly /ɪnvɒləntɛərɪli/ ADV 副詞 [ADV with v] 無意識に ❑ *His left eyelid twitched involuntarily.* 彼の左まぶたは不随意にびくびく動いた. ❷ ADJ 形容詞 You use **involuntary** to describe an action or situation that is forced on someone. 不本意の ❑ *...insurance policies that cover death, accident, sickness and involuntary unemployment.* 死亡, 事故, 疾病, 故意でない失業をカバーする保険契約

→ see **muscle**

in|volve /ɪnvɒlv/ (**involves, involving, involved**) ❶ V-T 他動詞 If a situation or activity **involves** something, that thing is a necessary part or consequence of it. 伴う, 必要とする ❑ *Running a kitchen involves lots of discipline and speed.* 厨房を切り盛りするには多大な訓練とスピードが必要だ. ❷ V-T 他動詞 If a situation or activity **involves** someone, they are taking part in it. 巻き込む, 参加させる ❑ *If there was a cover-up, it involved people at the very highest levels of government.* もしもみ消し工作があったとしたら, 政府高官が関与していたのだ. ❸ V-T 他動詞 If you say that someone **involves** themselves **in** something, you mean that they take part in it, often in a way that is unnecessary or unwanted. (oneselfを伴って) かかわる ❑ *I seem to have involved myself in something I don't understand.* 私は自分が理解できないことにかかわったようだ. ❹ V-T 他動詞 If you **involve** someone **in** something, you get them to take part in it. 参加させる ❑ *Nasser and I do everything together, he involves me in everything.* ナサーと私は何でも一緒にする. 彼は私を何にでも参加させる. ❺ V-T 他動詞 If one thing **involves** you **in** another thing, especially something unpleasant or inconvenient, the first thing causes you to do or deal with the second. 携わらせる ❑ *I don't want to do anything that will involve me in a long-term commitment.* 私は長期的な係わり合いが伴うようなことは何もしたくない.

in|volved /ɪnvɒlvd/ ❶ ADJ 形容詞 If you are **involved in** a situation or activity, you are taking part in it or have a strong connection with it. 巻き込まれた [v-link ADJ] ❑ *If she were involved in business, she would make a strong chief executive.* 彼女が事業を手がけていれば, 有能な経営責任者になるだろう. ❷ ADJ 形容詞 If you are **involved in** something, you give a lot of time, effort, or attention to it. 打ち込んだ [v-link ADJ] ❑ *The family was deeply involved in Jewish culture.* その家族はユダヤ文化にのめり込んでいた. ❸ ADJ 形容詞 The things **involved in** something such as a job or system are the necessary parts or consequences of it. 必要な [v-link ADJ] ❑ *We believe the time and hard work involved in completing such an assignment are worthwhile.* 我々はそうした任務を遂行するために必要な時間と労力は価値があると信じている. ❹ ADJ 形容詞 If a situation or activity is **involved**, it has a lot of different parts or aspects, often making it difficult to understand, explain, or do. 入り組んだ ❑ *The operations can be quite involved, requiring many procedures in order to restructure the anatomy.* その手術は, 解剖学的構造を作り直すために多くの処置を必要とするので, 全く複雑なものになる可能性がある. ❺ ADJ 形容詞 If one person is **involved with** another, especially someone they are not married to, they are having a sexual or romantic relationship. 深い仲になって ❑ *During a visit to Kenya in 1928 he became romantically involved with a married woman.* 1928年のケニア訪問中に彼は既婚女性と深い仲になった.

Word Partnership **involved** は次の語句と使われる:

N.	**involved in an accident, involved in planning, involved in politics** ❶ ❷
	people involved, involved **in a process** ❶ ❷
	risks involved, **work** involved ❸
ADJ.	**actively** involved, **directly** involved, **heavily** involved, **personally** involved ❶ ❷
	deeply involved, **emotionally** involved ❶ ❷ ❺
	romantically involved ❺

in|volve|ment /ɪnvɒlvmənt/ (**involvements**) ❶ N-UNCOUNT 不可算名詞 Your **involvement in** or **with** something is the fact that you are taking part in it. 掛かり合い ❑ *She disliked his involvement with the group and disliked his friends.* 彼女が彼がそのグループと掛かり合っていることを好まず, 彼の友人たちを嫌っていた. ❷ N-UNCOUNT 不可算名詞 **Involvement** is the enthusiasm that you feel when you care deeply about something. 熱中 ❑ *Ben has always felt a deep involvement with animals.* ベンはいつも動物に対して深い結びつきを感じてきた. ❸ N-VAR 可変性名詞 An **involvement** is a close relationship between two people, especially if they are not married to each other. 親密な関係, 不倫関係 ❑ *They were very good friends but there was no romantic involvement.* 彼らは仲の良い友達だったが, 恋愛関係はなかった.

Word Partnership **involvement** は次の語句と使われる:

N.	**community** involvement ❶
ADJ.	**active** involvement, **direct** involvement, **parental** involvement ❶
	romantic involvement ❸

Word Link ward ≈ in the direction of : back**ward**, for**ward**, in**ward**

in|ward /ɪnwərd/ ❶ ADJ 形容詞 Your **inward** thoughts or feelings are the ones that you do not express or show to other people. 内心の [ADJ n] ❑ *I sighed with inward relief.* 私は内心ほっとしてため息をついた. ● in|ward|ly ADV 副詞 心の中で ❑ *Sara was inwardly furious.* サラは内心ひどく腹を立てていた. ❷ ADJ 形容詞 [ADJ n] An **inward** movement is one toward the inside or center of something. 内部への ❑ *...a sharp, inward breath like a gasp.* あえぎのような鋭い体内へ吸い込む呼吸 ❸ ADV 副詞 If something moves or faces **inward**, it moves or faces toward the inside or center of something. 内側に [ADV after v] ❑ *He pushed open the front door, which swung inward with a groan.* 彼が正面玄関のドアを押し開けると, ギーギーという音を立てて内側に開いた.

iodine /aɪədaɪn/ N-UNCOUNT 不可算名詞 **Iodine** is a dark-colored substance used in medicine and photography. ヨウ素

IOU /aɪ oʊ yu/ (**IOUs**) N-COUNT 可算名詞 An **IOU** is a written promise that you will pay back some money that you have borrowed. **IOU** is an abbreviation for "I owe you." 借用証書

iPod /aɪpɒd/ (**iPods**) N-COUNT 可算名詞 An **iPod** is a portable MP3 player that can play music downloaded from the Internet. iポッド [COMPUTING, TRADEMARK]

IQ /aɪ kyu/ (**IQs**) N-VAR 可変性名詞 Your **IQ** is your level of intelligence, as indicated by a special test that you do. **IQ** is an abbreviation for "intelligence quotient." intelligence quotientの略, 知能指数 ❑ *His IQ is above average.* 彼の知能指数は平均以上だ.

irate /aɪreɪt/ ADJ 形容詞 If someone is **irate**, they are very angry about something. 立腹した ❑ *The owner was so irate he almost threw me out of the place.* 持ち主は立腹の余り, もう少しで私をその場所から追い出すところだった.

IRC /aɪ ɑr si/ N-UNCOUNT 不可算名詞 **IRC** is a way of having conversations with people who are using the Internet, especially people you do not know. **IRC** is an abbreviation for "Internet Relay Chat." Internet Relay Chatの略, インターネット上の会話 ❑ *Not long ago, just being in IRC was enough to forge bonds between chatters.* 最近までチャットラインに参加しているだけで, 他の参加者と友情のきずなを結ぶことができた.

iris /aɪrɪs/ (**irises**) N-COUNT 可算名詞 The **iris** is the round colored part of a person's eye. (眼球の) 虹彩 (こうさい)
→ see **eye, muscle**

iron /aɪərn/ (**irons, ironing, ironed**) ❶ N-UNCOUNT 不可算名詞 **Iron** is an element that is usually takes the form of a hard, dark gray metal. It is used to make steel, and also forms part of many tools, buildings, and vehicles. Very small amounts of iron occur in your blood and in food. 鉄 ❑ *The huge, iron gate was locked.* 巨大な鉄の門は錠が下ろされていた. ❑ *...the highest grade iron ore deposits in the world.* 世界で最高級の鉄鉱石の鉱床 ❷ N-COUNT 可算名詞 An **iron** is an electrical device with a flat metal base. You heat it until the base is hot, then rub it over clothes to remove creases. アイロン ❸ V-T 他動詞 If you **iron** clothes, you remove the creases from them using an iron. アイロンをかける ❑ *She used*

to iron his shirts. 彼女は以前は彼のシャツにアイロンをかけていた. ● **iron|ing** N-UNCOUNT 不可算名詞 アイロンかけ ❑ *I managed to get all the ironing done this morning.* 私は今朝なんとか全てのアイロンかけを終わらせた. ❹ ADJ 形容詞 You can use **iron** to describe the character or behavior of someone who is very firm in their decisions and actions, or who can control their feelings well. 強固な ❑ *...a man of icy nerve and iron will.* 物事に動じず，強固な意志を持つ男 ❺ ADJ 形容詞 **Iron** is used in expressions such as **an iron hand** and **iron discipline** to describe strong, harsh, or unfair methods of control that do not allow people much freedom. 圧制的な [ADJ n] ❑ *He died in 1985 after ruling Albania with an iron fist for 40 years.* 彼はアルバニアを40年間過酷に支配した後，1985年に死亡した. ❻ PHRASE 句 If someone has a lot of **irons in the fire**, they are involved in several different activities or have several different plans. 手がけている仕事 ❑ *Too many irons in the fire can sap your energy and prevent you from seeing which path to take.* 1度にいろんなことに手を出しすぎると精力を使い果たし，どちらに進むべきか判断力が失われることがある.

▶ **iron out** PHRASAL VERB 句動詞 If you **iron out** difficulties, you resolve them and bring them to an end. 解決する ❑ *"It was in the beginning, when we were still ironing out problems," a company spokesman said.* 「それは問題がまだ解決されていない初期のことだった」と会社のスポークスマンは言った.

Word Partnership   iron は次の語句と使われる:

ADJ.	cast iron, wrought iron ❶
	a hot iron ❶
N.	iron bar, iron gate ❶
	iron a shirt ❸
	an iron fist/hand ❺

---

iron|ic /aɪrɒnɪk/ also **ironical** /aɪrɒnɪkᵊl/ ❶ ADJ 形容詞 When you make an **ironic** remark, you say the opposite of what you really mean, as a joke. ❑ *At the most solemn moments he will flash a mocking smile or make an ironic remark.* 最も厳粛な瞬間に彼は決まってあざ笑を投げかけたり，皮肉たっぷりなことを言う. ❷ ADJ 形容詞 If you say that it is **ironic** that something happens, you mean that it is odd or amusing because it involves a contrast. 皮肉な ❑ *It is ironic that so many women are anti-feminist.* あれほど多くの女性が反フェミニズム主義者なのは皮肉なことだ.

ironi|cal|ly /aɪrɒnɪkli/ ❶ ADV 副詞 You use **ironically** to draw attention to a situation that is odd or amusing because it involves a contrast. 皮肉なことに [ADV with cl] ❑ *Ironically, for a man who hated war, he would have made a superb war cameraman.* 戦争を憎んでいた男にとっては皮肉なことだが，彼は素晴らしい戦争カメラマンになっていただろう. ❷ ADV 副詞 If you say something **ironically**, you say the opposite of what you really mean, as a joke. 皮肉で [ADV with v] ❑ *Classmates at West Point had ironically dubbed him Beauty.* ウエストポイントの同級生たちは彼を皮肉っぽく美男子と呼んだ.

iro|ny /aɪrəni, aɪər-/ (**ironies**) ❶ N-UNCOUNT 不可算名詞 **Irony** is a subtle form of humor that involves saying things that are the opposite of what you really mean. 皮肉 ❑ *His tone was tinged with irony.* 彼の口調は皮肉めいていた. ❷ N-VAR 可変性名詞 If you talk about the **irony** of a situation, you mean that it is odd or amusing because it involves a contrast. 皮肉な成り行き ❑ *The irony is that many officials in Washington agree in private that their policy is inconsistent.* 皮肉なのはワシントンの多くの当局者は彼らの政策は一貫性に欠けると密かに認めていることだ.

Word Partnership   irony は次の語句と使われる:

ADJ.	bitter irony ❶
	ultimate irony ❶ ❷
N.	hint of irony, sense of irony, trace of irony ❶
	irony of a situation ❷

Word Link   ir ≈ not : irrational, irregular, irresponsible

Word Link   ratio ≈ reasoning : irrational, rational, rationale

---

ir|ra|tion|al /ɪræʃənᵊl/ ADJ 形容詞 If you describe someone's feelings and behavior as **irrational**, you mean they are not based on logical reasons or clear thinking. 不合理な ❑ *...an irrational fear of science.* 科学に対するばかげた恐怖心 ● **ir|ra|tion|al|ly** ADV 副詞 不合理に ❑ *My husband is irrationally jealous over my past loves.* 私の夫はばかげたことに私の過去の恋愛にやきもちを焼いている. ● **ir|ra|tion|al|ity** /ɪræʃᵊnælɪti/ N-UNCOUNT 不可算名詞 不合理な行動な ❑ *...the irrationality of his behavior.* 彼の態度の不合理さ

ir|rec|on|cil|able /ɪrɛkənsaɪləbᵊl/ ❶ ADJ 形容詞 If two things such as opinions or proposals are **irreconcilable**, they are so different from each other that it is not possible to believe or have both of them. 相容れない [FORMAL 形式ばった] ❑ *These old concepts are irreconcilable with modern life.* こうした古い考えは現代生活と両立しない. ❷ ADJ 形容詞 An **irreconcilable** disagreement or conflict is so serious that it cannot be settled. 妥協できない [FORMAL 形式ばった] ❑ *...an irreconcilable clash of personalities.* 個性の和解できない衝突

ir|regu|lar /ɪrɛgyələr/ (**irregulars**) ❶ ADJ 形容詞 If events or actions occur at **irregular** intervals, the periods of time between them are of different lengths. 不規則な ❑ *Cars passed at irregular intervals.* 車が不規則な間隔で通った. ❑ *She was taken to a hospital suffering from an irregular heartbeat.* 彼女は不整脈のために病院に連れて行かれた. ● **ir|regu|lar|ly** ADV 副詞 [ADV with v] 不規則に ❑ *He was eating irregularly, steadily losing weight.* 彼は不規則な食生活をしていたので，段々やせてきた. ● **ir|regu|lar|ity** /ɪrɛgyələrɪti/ (**irregularities**) N-VAR 可変性名詞 不規則さ ❑ *...a dangerous irregularity in her heartbeat.* 彼女の危険な不整脈 ❷ ADJ 形容詞 Something that is **irregular** is not smooth or straight, or does not form a regular pattern. 不ぞろいの ❑ *He had bad teeth, irregular and discolored.* 彼の歯は悪くて，不ぞろいで，変色していた. ● **ir|regu|lar|ly** ADV 副詞 不ぞろいに ❑ *Located off-center in the irregularly shaped lake was a fountain.* 不均整な形をした湖の中心からはずれたところに噴水があった. ● **ir|regu|lar|ity** N-VAR 可変性名詞 不ぞろいさ ❑ *...treatment of abnormalities or irregularities of the teeth.* 歯の異常または歯並びの悪さの治療 ❸ ADJ 形容詞 **Irregular** behavior is dishonest or not in accordance with the normal rules. 不正な ❑ *...irregular business practices.* 不法な取引慣行 ● **ir|regu|lar|ity** N-VAR 可変性名詞 不法行為 ❑ *He faced charges arising from alleged financial irregularities.* 彼は財務上の不正行為の嫌疑から来る告発に直面した. ❹ ADJ 形容詞 An **irregular** verb, noun, or adjective has different forms from most other verbs, nouns, or adjectives in the language. For example, "break" is an irregular verb because its past form is "broke," not "breaked." (文法上の) 不規則変化の

ir|rel|evance /ɪrɛlɪvᵊns/ (**irrelevances**) ❶ N-UNCOUNT 不可算名詞 If you talk about the **irrelevance** of something, you mean that it is irrelevant. 無関係，見当違い ❑ *...the utter irrelevance of the debate.* 討論が全く見当違いであること ❷ N-COUNT 可算名詞 If you describe something as an **irrelevance**, you have a low opinion of it because it is not important in a situation. 今日的な意義のなさ ❑ *The Patriotic Front has been a political irrelevance since it was abandoned by its foreign backers.* 愛国戦線は外国の支援者から見捨てられてから政治的意義を失っている.

ir|rel|evant /ɪrɛlɪvᵊnt/ ❶ ADJ 形容詞 If you describe something such as a fact or remark as **irrelevant**, you mean that it is not connected with what you are discussing or dealing with. 無関係の，見当はずれの ❑ *...irrelevant details.* 無関係の詳細 ❷ ADJ 形容詞 If you say that something is **irrelevant**, you mean that it is not important in a situation. 重要でない ❑ *The choice of subject matter is irrelevant.* 主題の選択は重要でない.

ir|re|sist|ible /ɪrɪzɪstɪbᵊl/ ❶ ADJ 形容詞 If you describe something such as a desire or force as **irresistible**, you mean that it is so powerful that it makes you act in a certain way, and there is nothing you can do to prevent this. 抑えがたい ❑ *It proved an irresistible temptation to Bob to go back.* 戻ることはボブにとって抑えがたい誘惑であることが分かった. ● **ir|re|sist|ibly** ADV 副詞 [ADV with v] いやおうなく ❑ *I found myself irresistibly drawn to Steve's world.* 私はいやおうなくスティーヴの世界に引き寄せられるのを感じた. ❷ ADJ 形容詞 If you describe something or someone as **irresistible**, you mean that they are so good or attractive that you cannot stop yourself from liking them or wanting them. たまらなく魅力的な [INFORMAL くだけた] ❑ *The music is irresistible.* その音楽はほんとに素晴らしい. ● **ir|re|sist|ibly** ADV 副詞 [ADV adj] たまらないほど ❑ *She had a charm that men found irresistibly attractive.* 彼女には男性がたまらないほど愛らしいと感じる魅力があった.

ir|re|spec|tive /ɪrɪspɛktɪv/ PHRASE 句 If you say that something happens or should happen **irrespective of** a particular thing, you mean that it is not affected or should not be affected by that thing. 〜にかかわりなく [FORMAL 形式ばった] ❑ *...their commitment to a society based on equality for all citizens irrespective of ethnic origin.* 出身民族にかかわりなく全ての市民のための平等に基づく社会に対する彼らの傾向

ir|re|spon|sible /ɪrɪspɒnsɪbᵊl/ ADJ 形容詞 If you describe someone as **irresponsible**, you are criticizing them because they do things without properly considering their possible consequences. 無責任な [DISAPPROVAL 不賛成] ❑ *I felt that it was irresponsible to advocate the legalization of drugs.* 私は麻薬の合法化を提唱することは無責任だと感じた. ● **ir|re|spon|sibly** ADV 副詞 無責任に ❑ *They resent the implication that they have behaved irresponsibly.* 彼らは無責任にふるまったとのほのめかしに憤慨している. ● **ir|re|spon|sibil|ity** /ɪrɪspɒnsɪbɪlɪti/ N-UNCOUNT 不可算名詞 無責任さ ❑ *I can only wonder at the irresponsibility of people who advocate such destruction to our environment.* 私はそうした環境破壊を提唱する人々の無責任さにただ驚くばかりだ.

Word Link   vere ≈ fear, awe : irreverent, revere, reverence

---

ir|rev|er|ent /ɪrɛvərənt/ ADJ 形容詞 If you describe someone as **irreverent**, you mean that they do not show respect for people

or things that are generally respected. 不敬な，不遜な [APPROVAL 賛成] ❑ Taylor combined great knowledge with an irreverent attitude to history. テイラーは偉大な知識を歴史へのふそんな態度と結び付けていた。● ir|rev|er|ence N-UNCOUNT 不可算名詞 不敬 ❑ His irreverence for authority marks him out as a troublemaker. 彼は権威に対する不遜な態度により厄介な男として目立っている。

ir|re|vers|ible /ɪrɪvɜ́rsɪbəl/ ADJ 形容詞 If a change is **irreversible**, things cannot be changed back to the way they were before. 元に戻せない ❑ She could suffer irreversible brain damage if she is not treated within seven days. 彼女は7日間以内に治療を受けないと，取り返しのつかない脳損傷を受けるだろう。

ir|revo|cable /ɪrévəkəbəl/ ADJ 形容詞 If a decision, action, or change is **irrevocable**, it cannot be changed or reversed. 取り消せない [FORMAL 形式ばった] ❑ He said the decision was irrevocable. 彼はその決定は変更できないと言った。● ir|revo|cably /ɪrévəkəbli/ ADV 副詞 変更できないほど ❑ My relationships with friends have been irrevocably altered by their reactions to my illness. 友人たちとの関係は，私の病気への彼らの対応により取り消せないほど変化した。

ir|ri|gate /ɪ́rɪgeɪt/ (irrigates, irrigating, irrigated) V-T 他動詞 To **irrigate** land means to supply it with water in order to help crops grow. 灌漑(かんがい)する ❑ None of the water from Lake Powell is used to irrigate the area. パウエル湖の水はその地域を灌漑するのに全く使われていない。● ir|ri|ga|tion /ɪrɪgéɪʃən/ N-UNCOUNT 不可算名詞 灌漑 ❑ The agricultural land is hilly and the irrigation poor. 農地は丘陵が多く，灌漑が不十分である。
→ see **dam, farm**

ir|ri|table /ɪ́rɪtəbəl/ ADJ 形容詞 If you are **irritable**, you are easily annoyed. 怒りっぽい ❑ He had been waiting for over an hour and was beginning to feel irritable. 彼は1時間以上待たされたので，いらいらし始めていた。● ir|ri|tably /ɪ́rɪtəbli/ ADV 副詞 [ADV with v] いらいらして ❑ "Why are you whispering?" he asked irritably. 「なぜささやいているのか」と彼はいらいらして言った。● ir|ri|tabil|ity /ɪ̀rɪtəbɪ́lɪti/ N-UNCOUNT 不可算名詞 怒りやすいこと ❑ Patients usually suffer from memory loss, personality changes, and increased irritability. 患者は通常記憶喪失，性格の変化，怒りやすさの増大をこうむる。

ir|ri|tant /ɪ́rɪtənt/ (irritants) ❶ N-COUNT 可算名詞 If you describe something as an **irritant**, you mean that it keeps annoying you. いらだたせるもの [FORMAL 形式ばった] ❑ He said the issue was not a major irritant. 彼はその問題は大して怒るほどのものではないと言った。❷ N-COUNT 可算名詞 An **irritant** is a substance that causes a part of your body to itch or become sore. 刺激物 [FORMAL 形式ばった] ❑ Many pesticides are irritants. 殺虫剤は刺激物であることが多い。

ir|ri|tate /ɪ́rɪteɪt/ (irritates, irritating, irritated) ❶ V-T 他動詞 If something **irritates** you, it keeps annoying you. いらいらさせる ❑ Their attitude irritates me. 彼らの態度にはいらいらさせられる。● ir|ri|tat|ed ADJ 形容詞 いらいらした ❑ Not surprisingly, her teacher is getting irritated with her. 予想通り，彼女の教師は彼女にいらだちを感じている。❷ V-T 他動詞 If something **irritates** a part of your body, it causes it to itch or become sore. 刺激する ❑ Wear rubber gloves while chopping chilies as they can irritate the skin. とうがらしを刻む時には，肌がひりひりすることがあるのでゴムの手袋をしなさい。

ir|ri|tat|ing /ɪ́rɪteɪtɪŋ/ ❶ ADJ 形容詞 Something that is **irritating** keeps annoying you. いらいらさせる ❑ They also have the irritating habit of interrupting. また彼らには話の腰を折るという腹立たしい癖がある。● ir|ri|tat|ing|ly ADV 副詞 腹立たしいほど ❑ They can be irritatingly indecisive at times. 彼らは時々腹立たしいほど優柔不断なことがある。

> **Angry** is normally used to talk about someone's mood or feelings on a particular occasion. If someone is often angry, you can describe them as **bad-tempered**. ❑ She's a bad-tempered young lady. If someone is very angry, you can describe them as **furious**. ❑ Senior police officers are furious at the blunder. If they are less angry, you can describe them as **annoyed** or **irritated**. ❑ The premier looked annoyed but calm. …a man irritated by the barking of his neighbor's dog. Typically, someone is **irritated** by something because it happens constantly or continually. If someone is often irritated, you can describe them as **irritable**.

❷ ADJ 形容詞 An **irritating** substance can cause your body to itch or become sore. ひりひりさせる，炎症を起こさせる ❑ In heavy concentrations, ozone is irritating to the eyes, nose and throat. オゾンは濃度が高まった場合に目，鼻，のどをひりひりさせる。

ir|ri|ta|tion /ɪrɪtéɪʃən/ (irritations) ❶ N-UNCOUNT 不可算名詞 **Irritation** is a feeling of annoyance, especially when something is happening that you cannot easily stop or control. いらだち ❑ He tried not to let his irritation show as he blinked in the glare of the television lights. 彼はテレビの照明のまぶしさでまばたきしながら，いらだちを見せないようにした。❷ N-COUNT 可算名詞 An **irritation** is something that keeps annoying you. いらいらさせるもの ❑ Don't allow a minor irritation in the workplace to mar your ambitions. 職場でささいな問題が起こったからといって大望を台無しにしてはならない。❸ N-VAR 可変性名詞 **Irritation** in a part of your body is a feeling

of slight pain and discomfort there. 炎症，かぶれ ❑ These oils may cause irritation to sensitive skins. こうした油は敏感な皮膚に炎症を起こすことがある。

IRS /áɪ ɑr ɛ́s/ N-PROPER 固有名詞 The **IRS** is the federal government authority that collects taxes. **IRS** is an abbreviation for **Internal Revenue Service**. Internal Revenue Serviceの略，米国の国税局

is /ɪz/ **Is** is the third person singular of the present tense of **be**. **Is** is often added to other words and shortened to **-'s**. beの三人称単数現在形。しばしば **-'** sと略して使われる。

ISDN /áɪ ɛ́s di ɛ́n/ N-UNCOUNT 不可算名詞 **ISDN** is a telephone network that can send voice and computer messages. **ISDN** is an abbreviation for "Integrated Services Digital Network." Integrated Service Digital Network (総合ディジタル通信網サービス) の略 ❑ …an ISDN phone line. ISDN電話線

Is|lam /ɪslɑ́m/ ❶ N-UNCOUNT 不可算名詞 **Islam** is the religion of the Muslims, which was started by Mohammed. イスラム教 ❑ He converted to Islam at the age of 16. 彼は16歳の時にイスラム教に改宗した。❷ N-UNCOUNT 不可算名詞 Some people use **Islam** to refer to all the countries where Islam is the main religion. イスラム世界 ❑ …relations between Islam and the West. イスラム世界と欧米諸国間の関係
→ see **religion**

Is|lam|ic /ɪslǽmɪk, -lɑ́-/ ADJ 形容詞 **Islamic** means belonging or relating to Islam. イスラム教の [ADJ n] ❑ …Islamic law. イスラム教の戒律
→ see **religion**

is|land /áɪlənd/ (islands) N-COUNT; N-IN-NAMES 可算名詞，名称中の名詞 An **island** is a piece of land that is completely surrounded by water. 島 ❑ …the Canary Islands. カナリア諸島

is|land|er /áɪləndər/ (islanders) N-COUNT 可算名詞 **Islanders** are people who live on an island. 島の住民 ❑ The islanders endured centuries of exploitation. 島民は何世紀もの搾取に耐えた。

isle /áɪl/ (isles) N-COUNT; N-IN-NAMES 可算名詞，名称中の名詞 An **isle** is an island; often used as part of an island's name, or in literary English. 島 ❑ …the Isle of Pines. パインズ島

isn't /ɪ́zənt/ **Isn't** is the usual spoken form of "is not." 口語で用いられるis notの短縮形

iso|late /áɪsəleɪt/ (isolates, isolating, isolated) ❶ V-T 他動詞 To **isolate** a person or organization means to cause them to lose their friends or supporters. 孤立させる ❑ This policy could isolate the country from the other permanent members of the United Nations Security Council. この政策は同国を国連安全保障理事会の他の常任国から孤立させる可能性がある。● iso|lat|ed ADJ 形容詞 孤立した ❑ They are finding themselves increasingly isolated within the teaching profession. 彼らは教職の世界で一段と孤立しているのに気づいている。● iso|la|tion /áɪsəléɪʃən/ N-UNCOUNT 不可算名詞 孤立 ❑ Diplomatic isolation could lead to economic disaster. 外交的孤立は経済の大失敗につながる可能性がある。❷ V-T 他動詞 If you **isolate yourself**, or if something **isolates** you, you become physically or socially separated from other people. (oneselfを伴って) 交際を絶つ ● iso|la|tion N-UNCOUNT 不可算名詞 [oft N n] 他人と接触のない状態，孤立 ❑ She seemed determined to isolate herself from everyone, even him. 彼女は他人との接触を，彼との接触さえも絶つ決心を固めたようだった。❑ His radicalism and refusal to compromise isolated him. 彼はその急進キ義と妥協を拒むことにより孤立した。❸ V-T 他動詞 If you **isolate** something such as an idea or a problem, you separate it from others that it is connected with, so that you can concentrate on it or consider it on its own. 分離する，隔離する ❑ Our anxieties can also be controlled by isolating thoughts, feelings and memories. 我々の心配は思考，感情，記憶を分離することによって抑制することもできる。❹ V-T 他動詞 To **isolate** a substance means to obtain it by separating it from other substances using scientific processes. 分離する [TECHNICAL 技術的] ❑ We can use genetic engineering techniques to isolate the gene that is responsible. 遺伝子工学の技術を使って原因となる遺伝子を分離することができる。❺ V-T 他動詞 To **isolate** a sick person or animal means to keep them apart from other people or animals, so that their illness does not spread. (病人を) 隔離する ❑ Patients will be isolated from other people for between three days and one month after treatment. 患者は治療後3日から1か月の間他人から隔離されるでしょう。● iso|la|tion N-UNCOUNT 不可算名詞 [oft N n] 隔離 ❑ Hayley contracted tuberculosis and had to be put in an isolation ward. ヘイリーは結核に感染し，隔離病棟に移されなければならなかった。

iso|lat|ed /áɪsəleɪtɪd/ ❶ ADJ 形容詞 An **isolated** place is a long way away from large towns and is difficult to reach. 孤立した ❑ Many of the refugee villages are in isolated areas. 難民の村の多くは孤立した地域にある。❷ ADJ 形容詞 If you feel **isolated**, you feel lonely and without friends or help. 孤独な ❑ Some patients may become very isolated and depressed. 一部の患者は孤独感を強く抱き，うつ状態になることがある。❸ ADJ 形容詞 An **isolated** example is an example of something that is not very common. 例外的な [ADJ n]

❏ *They said the allegations related to an isolated case of cheating.* 彼らはその申し立てがカンニングの例外的な事例に関するものだと言った。

iso|la|tion /ˌaɪsəˈleɪʃ⁰n/ **1** N-UNCOUNT 不可算名詞 **Isolation** is the state of feeling alone and without friends or help. 孤独 ❏ *Many deaf people have feelings of isolation and loneliness.* 耳の聞こえない人々の多くは孤独感を味わっている。 **2** → see also **isolate** **3** PHRASE 句 If something is considered **in isolation from** other things that it is connected with, it is considered separately, and those other things are not considered. 離して ❏ *Punishment cannot, therefore, be discussed in isolation from social and political theory.* それゆえ刑罰は社会的・政治的理論と離して論ずることはできない。 **4** PHRASE 句 If someone does something **in isolation**, they do it without other people present or without their help. 独りで ❏ *Malcolm, for instance, works in isolation but I have no doubts about his abilities.* 例えばマルカムは独りで仕事をしているが、私は彼の能力を全面的に信頼している。

ISP /ˌaɪ ɛs ˈpi/ (**ISPs**) N-COUNT 可算名詞 An **ISP** is a company that provides Internet and e-mail services. **ISP** is an abbreviation for "Internet service provider." Internet service providerの略、インターネット接続業者

is|sue /ˈɪʃu/ (**issues, issuing, issued**) **1** N-COUNT 可算名詞 An **issue** is an important subject that people are arguing about or discussing. 問題 ❏ *Agents will raise the issue of prize-money for next year's world championships.* 代理人たちは来年の世界選手権の賞金問題を取り上げる予定だ。 ❏ *A key issue for higher education in the 1990s is the need for greater diversity of courses.* 1990年代の高等教育の主な問題の1つは、よりいっそう多様なコースを設ける必要性だ。 **2** N-SING 単数名詞 If something is **the issue**, it is the thing you consider to be the most important part of a situation or discussion. 核心 ❏ *I was earning a lot of money, but that was not the issue.* 私は多額の金を稼いでいたが、それは重要な点ではなかった。 ❏ *Do not draw it on the chart, however, as this will confuse the issue.* しかし、これは核心点を分かりにくくするので、表に描いてはならない。 **3** N-COUNT 可算名詞 An **issue** of something such as a magazine or newspaper is the version of it that is published, for example, in a particular month or on a particular day. 刊行物 ❏ *The growing problem is underlined in the latest issue of the Scientific American.* その増大する問題はScientific American誌の最新号で強調されている。 **4** V-T 他動詞 If you **issue** a statement or a warning, you make it known formally or publicly. 発布する、出す ❏ *Last night he issued a statement denying the allegations.* 昨夜彼は申し立てを否定する声明を発表した。 ❏ *The government issued a warning that the strikers should end their action or face dismissal.* 政府はストライキを行なっている者はその行為を止めないと解雇されるという警告を出した。 **5** V-T 他動詞 If you **are issued with** something, it is officially given to you. 交付する、支給する [usu passive] ❏ *On your appointment you will be issued with a written statement of particulars of employment.* 任命後にあなたは雇用の詳細な文書が交付されます。 ● N-UNCOUNT 不可算名詞 **Issue** is also a noun. 交付、支給 ❏ *...a standard army issue rifle.* 軍支給の標準的ライフル。 **6** PHRASE 句 The question or point **at issue** is the question or point that is being argued about or discussed. 係争中の ❏ *The problems of immigration were not the question at issue.* 移民問題は係争中の問題ではなかった。 **7** PHRASE 句 If you **make an issue of** something, you try to make other people think about it or discuss it, because you are concerned or annoyed about it. ～を問題にする ❏ *It seemed the Colonel had no desire to make an issue of the affair.* 大佐はその事件を問題にする気が全くないように見えた。 **8** PHRASE 句 If you **take issue with** someone or something they said, you disagree with them, and start arguing about it. ～に異議を唱える ❏ *I will not take issue with the fact that we have a recession.* 私は我が国が景気後退の局面にあるという事実に反対しない。 **9** PHRASE 句 If someone **has issues with** a particular aspect of their life, they have problems connected with it. ～について問題を持つ [oft PHR 'with/about' n] ❏ *Once you have issues with food, you're going to have them for the rest of your life.* 1度食べ物に問題が起こると、それは一生ついてまわるだろう。

→ see **philosophy**

is|sue price (**issue prices**) N-COUNT 可算名詞 The **issue price** of shares is the price at which they are offered for sale when they first become available to the public. 発行価格 [BUSINESS 実業] ❏ *Shares in the company slipped below their issue price on their first day of trading.* 同社の株価は取引の初日に発行価格を下回った。

it /ɪt/

It is a third person singular pronoun. **It** is used as the subject or object of a verb, or as the object of a preposition.

It は3人称単数の代名詞である。**It** は動詞の主語または目的語として、または前置詞の目的語として用いられる。

1 PRON-SING 単数代名詞 You use **it** to refer to an object, animal, or other thing that has already been mentioned. それは ❏ *It's a wonderful city, really. I'll show it to you if you want.* それは実に素晴らしい町です。よければご案内します。 ❏ *My wife has become crippled by arthritis. She is embarrassed to see the doctor about it.* 私の妻は関節炎で体が不自由になった。彼女はそれについて医者に相談するのを恥ずかしがっている。 **2** PRON-SING 単数代名詞 You use **it** to refer to a child or baby whose sex you do not know or whose sex is not relevant to what you are saying. その子供 ❏ *She could compel him to support the child after it was born.* 彼女は出産後、子供の扶養を彼に強いることができた。 **3** PRON-SING 単数代名詞 You use **it** to refer in a general way to a situation that you have just described. 既出の状況を指して ❏ *He was through with sports, not because he had to be but because he wanted it that way.* 彼は強制的にではなく自発的にスポーツを止めた。 **4** PRON-SING 単数代名詞 You use **it** before certain nouns, adjectives, and verbs to introduce your feelings or point of view about a situation. 状況への見解を指して ❏ *It was nice to see Steve again.* スティーブとまた会えてよかった。 ❏ *It's a pity you never got married, Sarah.* サラ、あなたが一度も結婚しなかったのは残念だ。 **5** PRON-SING 単数代名詞 You use **it** in passive clauses that report a situation or event. 状況を漠然と指して ❏ *It has been said that stress causes cancer.* ストレスがガンの原因になると言われてきた。 **6** PRON-SING 単数代名詞 You use **it** with some verbs that need a subject or object, although there is no noun that "it" refers to. 状況を漠然と指して ❏ *Of course, as it turned out, three-fourths of the people in the group were psychiatrists.* もちろん、結局グループの4分の3は心理学者だった。 **7** PRON-SING 単数代名詞 You use **it** as the subject of "be" to say what the time, day, or date is. be動詞の主語として ❏ *It's three o'clock in the morning.* 朝の3時だ。 ❏ *It was a Monday, so she was at home.* 月曜日だったので彼女は家にいた。 **8** PRON-SING 単数代名詞 You use **it** as the subject of a linking verb to describe the weather, the light, or the temperature. 天候・明暗・気温などを表して ❏ *It was very wet and windy the day I drove over the hill to Del Norte.* 私が丘を登ってデル・ノーテに車で行った日は雨で風が強かった。 **9** PRON-SING 単数代名詞 You use **it** when you are telling someone who you are, or asking them who they are, especially at the beginning of a phone call. You also use **it** in statements and questions about the identity of other people. 特に電話での会話で自分を名乗る場合や相手の名を尋ねる場合に使われる。また他の人を特定する場合にも使われる。 ❏ *"Who is it?" he called. — "It's your neighbor."* 「誰だ」と彼は呼びかけた。「近所の者です」 **10** PRON 代名詞 When you are emphasizing or drawing attention to something, you can put that thing immediately after **it** and a form of the verb "be." 強調構文 [EMPHASIS 強調] ❏ *It's really the poor countries that don't have an economic base that have the worst environmental records.* 環境の実績が最悪なのは経済基盤を持たない貧しい国々だ。 **11** PHRASE 句 You use **it** in expressions such as **it's not that** or **it's not just that** when you are giving a reason for something and are suggesting that there are several other reasons. ということではない ❏ *It's not that I didn't want to be with my family.* 私は家族と一緒にいたくなかったということではない。 **12** **if it wasn't for** → see **be**

IT /ˌaɪ ˈti/ **IT** is an abbreviation for **information technology**. 情報工学 ❏ *...people with IT skills.* ITの技能を持つ人々

ital|ic /ɪˈtælɪk/ (**italics**) **1** N-PLURAL 複数名詞 **Italics** are letters that slope to the right. Italics are often used to emphasize a particular word or sentence. The examples in this dictionary are printed in italics. イタリック体 ❏ *The title is printed in italics.* 題名はイタリック体で印刷されている。 **2** ADJ 形容詞 **Italic** letters slope to the right. イタリック体の [ADJ n] ❏ *She addressed them by hand in her beautiful italic script.* 彼女は美しいイタリック体の文字で手書きで宛名を書いた。

itch /ɪtʃ/ (**itches, itching, itched**) **1** V-I 自動詞 When a part of your body **itches**, you have an unpleasant feeling on your skin that makes you want to scratch. かゆい ❏ *When someone has hay fever, the eyes and nose will stream and itch.* 花粉症になると涙と鼻水が流れ、鼻がかゆくなる。 ● N-COUNT 可算名詞 **Itch** is also a noun. かゆみ ❏ *Scratch my back – I've got an itch.* 背中がかいてよ。かゆいんだ。 ● **itch|ing** N-UNCOUNT 不可算名詞 かゆみ ❏ *It may be that the itching is caused by contact with irritant material.* かゆみは刺激物に触れたことが原因の可能性がある。 **2** V-T/V-I 他動詞/自動詞 [usu cont] If you **are itching** to do something, you are very eager or impatient to do it. したくてたまらない [INFORMAL くだけた] ❏ *I was itching to get involved.* 私は係わりあいになりたくてたまらなかった。 ● N-SING 単数名詞 **Itch** is also a noun. したくてたまらないこと ❏ *...cable TV viewers with an insatiable itch to switch from channel to channel.* チャン

ネルを変えたくてたまらないケーブルテレビの視聴者

itchy /ɪtʃi/ ■ ADJ 形容詞 If a part of your body or something you are wearing is **itchy**, you have an unpleasant feeling on your skin that makes you want to scratch. かゆい [INFORMAL くだけた] ❑ ...itchy, sore eyes. かゆくて痛い目 ② PHRASE 句 If you have **itchy feet**, you have a strong desire to leave a place and to travel. どこかに出かけたくてたまらない [INFORMAL くだけた] ❑ The thought gave me really itchy feet so within a couple of months I decided to leave. その考えで私は出かけたくてたまらなくなり, 2か月以内に私は出発することに決めた.

it'd /ɪtəd/ ■ **It'd** is a spoken form of "it would." it wouldの短縮形 ❑ It'd be better for a place like this to remain closed. このような場所は閉鎖したままの方がいいだろう. ② **It'd** is a spoken form of "it had," especially when "had" is an auxiliary verb. it hadの短縮形 ❑ Marcie was watching the news. It'd just started. マーシーはニュースを見ていた. それは始まったばかりだった.

item /aɪtəm/ (items) ■ N-COUNT 可算名詞 An **item** is one of a collection or list of objects. 品目 ❑ The most valuable item on show will be a Picasso drawing. 陳列された品目で最も高価なものはピカソの素描となるだろう. ② N-COUNT 可算名詞 An **item** is one of a list of things for someone to do, deal with, or talk about. 項目 ❑ The other item on the agenda is the tour. 議題のもう1つの項目はツアーである. ③ N-COUNT 可算名詞 An **item** is a report or article in a newspaper or magazine, or on television or radio. 記事 ❑ There was an item in the paper about him. 新聞に彼に関する記事があった. ④ N-SING 単数名詞 If you say that two people are an **item**, you mean that they are having a romantic or sexual relationship. 恋人同士 [INFORMAL くだけた] ❑ She and Gino were an item. 彼女とジーノはできていた.

Thesaurus *item* また次を参照:

N. issue, subject, task ②
article, story ③; (ant.) couple ④

Word Partnership *item* は次の語句と使われる:

N. item **of clothing** ■
agenda item (or item **on an agenda**) ②
newspaper item ③

---

item|ize /aɪtəmaɪz/ (itemizes, itemizing, itemized) V-T 他動詞 If you **itemize** a number of things, you make a list of them. 列挙する ❑ The report will itemize the cost of various improvements. その報告書には様々な改善の費用明細が記載される.

itin|er|ary /aɪtɪnərɛri/ (itineraries) N-COUNT 可算名詞 An **itinerary** is a plan of a trip, including the route and the places that you will visit. 旅行計画 ❑ The next place on our itinerary was Sedona. 旅程で次の訪問地はセドナだった.

it'll /ɪtᵊl/ **It'll** is a spoken form of "it will." it willの短縮形 ❑ It's been a while since I've seen her so it'll be nice to meet her in town on Thursday. 彼女とはごぶさたなので木曜日に町で会えればいいな.

its /ɪts/

Its is a third person singular possessive determiner.

Its は3人称単数所有限定詞である.

DET 限定詞 You use **its** to indicate that something belongs or relates to a thing, place, or animal that has just been mentioned or whose identity is known. You can use **its** to indicate that something belongs or relates to a child or baby. itの所有格 ❑ He held the knife by its blade. 彼はナイフを刃のところで握った.

Do not confuse **its** and **it's**. Its means "belonging to it." It's is short for "it is" or "it has." ❑ The horse raised its head... It's hot in here... It's stopped raining.

it's /ɪts/ ■ **It's** is the usual spoken form of "it is." it isの短縮形 ❑ It's the best news I've heard in a long time. それほど素晴らしい知らせは聞いたのはしばらくぶりだ. ② **It's** is the usual spoken form of "it has," especially when "has" is an auxiliary verb. it hasの短縮形 ❑ It's been such a long time since I played. しばらくプレーをしていない.

it|self /ɪtsɛlf/ ■ PRON-REFL 再帰代名詞 **Itself** is used as the object of a verb or preposition when it refers to something that is the same thing as the subject of the verb. それ自身 [v PRON, prep PRON] ❑ Scientists have discovered remarkable new evidence showing how the body rebuilds itself while we sleep. 科学者は睡眠中に人体がどのように再生するかを示す驚くべき新証拠を発見した. ② PRON-REFL-EMPH 強調的再帰代名詞 You use **itself** to emphasize the thing you are referring to. それ自体 [EMPHASIS 強調] ❑ I think life itself is a learning process. 私は生きること自体が学ぶことだと思う. ③ PRON-REFL-EMPH 強調的再帰代名詞 If you say that someone is, for example, politeness **itself** or kindness **itself**, you are emphasizing that they are extremely polite or extremely kind. そのもの [EMPHASIS 強調] [N PRON] ❑ He is rarely satisfied with anything less than perfection itself. 彼は完璧以外のものに満足することはほとんどない.

I've /aɪv/ **I've** is the usual spoken form of "I have," especially when "have" is an auxiliary verb. I haveの短縮形 ❑ I've been invited to meet with the ambassador. 私は大使との会談に招待された.

IVF /aɪ vi ɛf/ N-UNCOUNT 不可算名詞 **IVF** is a method of helping a woman to have a baby in which an egg is removed from one of her ovaries, fertilized outside her body, and then replaced in her womb. IVF is an abbreviation for "in vitro fertilization." 体外受精 ❑ When she first underwent IVF it was still a relatively new procedure. 彼女が初めて体外受精を受けたときそれはまだ比較的新しい治療だった.

ivo|ry /aɪvəri/ ■ N-UNCOUNT 不可算名詞 **Ivory** is a hard cream-colored substance that forms the tusks of elephants and some other animals. It is valuable and can be used for making carved ornaments. 象牙(ぞうげ) ❑ ...the international ban on the sale of ivory. 象牙販売の国際的な禁止 ② COLOR 色彩語 **Ivory** is a creamy-white color. アイボリー ❑ ...small ivory flowers. アイボリー色の小さな花

ivy /aɪvi/ (ivies) N-VAR 可変性名詞 **Ivy** is an evergreen plant that grows up walls or along the ground. セイヨウキヅタ

Jj

J also **j** /dʒeɪ/ (**J's, j's**) N-VAR 可変性名詞 **J** is the tenth letter of the English alphabet. 英語アルファベットの第10字

jab /dʒæb/ (**jabs, jabbing, jabbed**) **1** V-T/V-I 他動詞/自動詞 If you **jab** one thing into another, you push it there with a quick, sudden movement and with a lot of force. ぐいと突っ込む、ぐいと突く □ *He saw her jab her thumb on a red button – a panic button.* 彼は、彼女が親指で赤い非常ボタンをぐいと押すのを見た。 □ *Stern jabbed at me with his glasses.* スターンは眼鏡で私を突いた。 **2** N-COUNT 可算名詞 A **jab** is a sudden, sharp punch. 鋭い突き、突き □ *He was simply too powerful for his opponent, rocking him with a steady supply of left jabs.* 彼は単に対戦相手にとって強すぎた。しっかりとした左ジャブを出して彼を揺り動かした。

jack /dʒæk/ (**jacks**) **1** N-COUNT 可算名詞 A **jack** is a device for lifting a heavy object, such as a car, off the ground. ジャッキ **2** N-COUNT 可算名詞 A **jack** is a playing card whose value is between a ten and a queen. A jack is usually represented by a picture of a young man. (トランプの) ジャック □ *...the jack of spades.* スペードのジャック

jack|et /dʒækɪt/ (**jackets**) **1** N-COUNT 可算名詞 A **jacket** is a short coat with long sleeves. 上着、ジャケット □ *...a black leather jacket.* 黒の皮ジャン **2** N-COUNT 可算名詞 The **jacket** of a book is the paper cover that protects the book. (本の) カバー [mainly AM 主に米国英語] □ *A beautiful girl gazes from the jacket of this book.* きれいな女の子のカバーから見つめている。 **3** → see also **dinner jacket, straitjacket**
→ see **clothing**

jack|pot /dʒækpɒt/ (**jackpots**) **1** N-COUNT 可算名詞 A **jackpot** is the most valuable prize in a game or lottery, especially when the game involves increasing the value of the prize until someone wins it. 特賞 □ *A nurse who gambled $5 in a slot machine walked away with the biggest ever jackpot of more than $5 million.* スロットマシンで5ドルかけた看護婦が過去最高の500万ドルの賞金を獲得した。 **2** PHRASE 句 If you **hit the jackpot**, you have a great success, for example by winning a lot of money or having a piece of good luck. 大当たりする、一山当てる [INFORMAL くだけた] □ *Tennis player Michael Stich hit the jackpot yesterday when he won $2 million.* テニスプレーヤーのマイケル・スティッチは昨日200万ドルを当て、一獲千金を実現した。
→ see **lottery**

Ja|cuz|zi /dʒəkuːzi/ (**Jacuzzis**) N-COUNT 可算名詞 商標 A **Jacuzzi** is a large circular bath fitted with a device that makes the water move around. ジャグジー風呂 [TRADEMARK]

jade /dʒeɪd/ **1** N-UNCOUNT 不可算名詞 **Jade** is a hard stone, usually green in color, that is used for making jewelry and ornaments. ひすい □ *The Burmese jade choker in the catalog was very beautiful.* カタログに載っているビルマ製ひすいのチョーカーはとても美しい。 **2** COLOR 色彩語 Something that is **jade** or **jade green** is bright green in color. ひすい色、明るい緑 □ *Amy had bought a soft, jade green cashmere jacket for Helen.* エイミーは柔らかくてひすい色のカシミアの上着をヘレンに買った。

jad|ed /dʒeɪdɪd/ ADJ 形容詞 If you are **jaded**, you feel bored, tired, and not enthusiastic, because you have had too much of the same thing. 飽き飽きした □ *We had both become jaded, disinterested, and disillusioned.* 私たちは2人とも飽き飽きして、関心がなくなり、失望してしまった。

jag|ged /dʒægɪd/ ADJ 形容詞 Something that is **jagged** has a rough, uneven shape or edge with lots of sharp points. ぎざぎざの、ごつごつした □ *...jagged black cliffs.* ごつごつした黒いがけ

jail /dʒeɪl/ (**jails, jailing, jailed**) **1** N-VAR 可変性名詞 A **jail** is a place where criminals are kept in order to punish them, or where people waiting to be tried are kept. 刑務所、拘置所 □ *Three prisoners escaped from a jail.* 3人の囚人が脱獄した。 **2** V-T 他動詞 If someone **is jailed**, they are put into jail. 投獄する、拘置する [usu passive] □ *He was jailed for twenty years.* 彼は20年間投獄された。

jam /dʒæm/ (**jams, jamming, jammed**) **1** V-T 他動詞 If you **jam** something somewhere, you push or put it there roughly. 押し込む □ *Pete jammed his hands into his pockets.* ピートは手をポケットに押し込んだ。 **2** V-T/V-I 他動詞/自動詞 If something such as a part of a machine **jams**, or if something **jams** it, the part becomes fixed in position and is unable to move freely or work properly. 動かな

くなる、故障する [自動詞]、動かなくする [他動詞] □ *The second time he fired his gun jammed.* 彼が2度目に発砲したとき、銃が故障した。 □ *A rope jammed the boat's propeller.* ロープがボートのプロペラに詰まった。 **3** V-T 他動詞 If vehicles **jam** a road, there are so many of them that they cannot move. ふさぐ □ *Hundreds of departing motorists jammed roads that had been closed during the height of the storm.* 何百台もの自動車が出発し、嵐のまっただ中に閉鎖されていた道路がふさがれた。 ● N-COUNT 可算名詞 **Jam** is also a noun. 渋滞 □ *400 trucks may sit in a jam for ten hours waiting to cross the limited number of bridges.* 限られた数の橋を渡るために400台のトラックが渋滞に10時間に巻き込まれる。 ● **jammed** ADJ 形容詞 渋滞した □ *Nearby roads and the dirt track to the beach were jammed with cars.* 周辺道路やビーチへの砂利道は車で渋滞していた。 **4** V-T/V-I 他動詞/自動詞 If a lot of people **jam** a place, or **jam into** a place, they are pressed tightly together so that they can hardly move. 詰めかける □ *Hundreds of people jammed the boardwalk to watch.* 何百人もの人々が見るためにボードウォークに詰めかけた。 ● **jammed** ADJ 形容詞 混雑した □ *The stadium was jammed and they had to turn away hundreds of disappointed fans.* スタジアムは満員で何百人ものファンが入場を断られ落胆していた。 **5** V-T 他動詞 To **jam** a radio or electronic signal means to interfere with it and prevent it from being received or heard clearly. 妨害する □ *They will try to jam the transmissions electronically.* 電子的に通信を妨害しようとするでしょう。 ● **jam|ming** N-UNCOUNT 不可算名詞 妨害 □ *The plane is used for electronic jamming and radar detection.* その飛行機は電子的妨害とレーダー探知のために使われている。 **6** V-T 他動詞 If callers **are jamming** telephone lines, there are so many callers that the people answering the telephones find it difficult to deal with them all. 回線をパンクさせる □ *Hundreds of callers jammed the switchboard for more than an hour.* 大量の電話コールのために回線が1時間以上パンクしていた。 **7** N-MASS 質量名詞 **Jam** is a sweet food consisting of pieces of fruit cooked with a large amount of sugar until it is thickened. It is usually spread on bread. ジャム [mainly BRIT 主に英国英語; AM **jelly** 米国英語 **jelly**]
→ see **traffic**

<table>
<tr><td colspan="2">Word Partnership jam は次の語句と使われる:</td></tr>
<tr><td>N.</td><td>traffic jam **3**
jam jar, strawberry jam **7**</td></tr>
</table>

Jan. Jan. is a written abbreviation for **January**. Januaryの略

jan|gle /dʒæŋgəl/ (**jangles, jangling, jangled**) V-T/V-I 他動詞/自動詞 When objects strike against each other and make a ringing noise, you can say that they **jangle** or **are jangled**. ジャラジャラと鳴る [自動詞]、ジャラジャラと鳴らす [他動詞] □ *Her bead necklaces and bracelets jangled as she walked.* 彼女が歩くとビーズのネックレスとブレスレットがジャラジャラと音を立てた。

jani|tor /dʒænɪtər/ (**janitors**) N-COUNT 可算名詞 A **janitor** is a person whose job is to take care of a building. 管理人、用務員 [mainly AM 主に米国英語] □ *Ed Roberts had been a school janitor for a long time.* エド・ロバーツは長い間学校の用務員をした。

Janu|ary /dʒænyueri/ (**Januaries**) N-VAR 可変性名詞 **January** is the first month of the year in the Western calendar. 1月 □ *We always have snow in January.* 1月にはいつも雪が降る。

jar /dʒɑr/ (**jars, jarring, jarred**) **1** N-COUNT 可算名詞 A **jar** is a glass container with a lid that is used for storing food. 瓶 □ *...cucumbers in glass jars.* ガラス瓶に入ったキュウリ **2** N-COUNT 可算名詞 You can use **jar** to refer to a jar and its contents, or to the contents only. 瓶に入ったもの □ *She opened up a jar of plums.* 彼女はスモモの瓶を開けた。 **3** V-T/V-I 他動詞/自動詞 If something **jars** you, you find it unpleasant, disturbing, or shocking. 不快感を与える、神経に障る、ショックを与える □ *...televised congressional hearings that jarred the nation's faith in the presidency.* 国民の大統領への信頼感を揺らいだ連邦議会公聴会のテレビ放送 ● **jar|ring** ADJ 形容詞 神経に障るような □ *In the context of this chapter, Dore's comments strike a jarring note.* この章の文脈ではドレのコメントは不快感を表している。 **4** V-T/V-I 他動詞/自動詞 If an object **jars**, or if something **jars** it, the object moves with a fairly hard shaking movement. ガタガタする、振動する [自動詞]、ガタガタさせる [他動詞] □ *The ship jarred a little.* 船が少し揺れた。 □ *The sudden movement jarred the box and it fell off the table.* 突然の動きで箱がガタガタし、テーブルから落ちた。
→ see **can**

jar|gon /dʒɑːrgən/ N-UNCOUNT 不可算名詞 You use **jargon** to refer to words and expressions that are used in special or technical ways by particular groups of people, often making the language difficult to understand. 業界用語, 特殊用語, 仲間ことば □ *The manual is full of the jargon and slang of self-improvement courses.* 説明書は自己啓発コースの特殊用語と俗語だらけだ.

jaun|ty /dʒɔːnti/ (**jauntier, jauntiest**) ADJ 形容詞 If you describe someone or something as **jaunty**, you mean that they are full of confidence and energy. さっそうとした, 意気揚々とした □ *...a jaunty little man.* さっそうとした小柄な男性 ●**jaun|ti|ly** /dʒɔːntɪli/ ADV 副詞 さっそうと □ *He walked jauntily into the café.* さっそうと喫茶店に入った.

Java /dʒɑːvə/ N-UNCOUNT 不可算名詞 商標 **Java** is a computer programming language. It is used especially in creating websites. ジャバ [TRADEMARK] □ *...applications written in Java.* ジャバで書かれたアプリケーション

jave|lin /dʒævlɪn/ (**javelins**) ◼ N-COUNT 可算名詞 A **javelin** is a long spear that is used in sports competitions. Competitors try to throw the javelin as far as possible. やり ◼ N-SING 単数名詞 You can refer to the competition in which the javelin is thrown as **the javelin**. やり投げ □ *...Steve Backley who won the javelin.* スティーブ・バックリーがやり投げで優勝した.

jaw /dʒɔː/ (**jaws**) ◼ N-COUNT 可算名詞 Your **jaw** is the lower part of your face below your mouth. The movement of your jaw is sometimes considered to express a particular emotion. For example, if your **jaw drops**, you are very surprised. あご □ *He thought for a moment, stroking his well-defined jaw.* 彼は角張ったあごを触りながらしばらく考えた. ◼ N-COUNT 可算名詞 A person's or animal's **jaws** are the two bones in their head that their teeth are attached to. あごの骨 □ *...a forest rodent with powerful jaws.* 力強いあごを持った森ネズミ ◼ N-PLURAL 複数名詞 If you talk about the **jaws of** something unpleasant such as death or hell, you are referring to a dangerous or unpleasant situation. 窮地 □ *A family dog rescued a newborn boy from the jaws of death.* 飼いイヌが新生児を窮地から救った.

jaw-dropping ADJ 形容詞 Something that is **jaw-dropping** is extremely surprising, impressive, or shocking. びっくり仰天の, 開いた口がふさがらないほどの [INFORMAL くだけた JOURNALISM ジャーナリズム] □ *One insider who has seen the report said it was pretty jaw-dropping stuff.* その報告書を見た部内者は開いた口がふさがらないような驚くべき内容だったと言った.

jazz /dʒæz/ N-UNCOUNT 不可算名詞 **Jazz** is a style of music that was invented by African American musicians in the early part of the twentieth century. Jazz music has very strong rhythms and often involves improvisation. ジャズ □ *The club has live jazz on Sundays.* そのクラブでは毎週土曜日にライブのジャズ演奏がある.
→ see **genre**

jeal|ous /dʒeləs/ ◼ ADJ 形容詞 If someone is **jealous**, they feel angry or bitter because they think that another person is trying to take a lover or friend, or a possession, away from them. 嫉妬 (しっと) した, やきもちをやいた □ *She got insanely jealous and there was a terrible fight.* 彼女は気が狂ったように嫉妬 (しっと) し, ひどいけんかになった. ●**jeal|ous|ly** ADV 副詞 [ADV with v] 嫉妬 (しっと) して やきもちをやいて □ *The formula is jealously guarded.* その調法は固く守られている. ◼ ADJ 形容詞 If you are **jealous of** another person's possessions or qualities, you feel angry or bitter because you do not have them. 嫉妬 (しっと) した ねたんだ □ *She was jealous of his wealth.* 彼女は彼の富をねたんでいた. ●**jeal|ous|ly** ADV 副詞 [ADV after v] 嫉妬 (しっと) して ねたんで □ *Gloria eyed them jealously.* グロリアはうらやましげに彼らを見た.

jeal|ousy /dʒeləsi/ ◼ N-UNCOUNT 不可算名詞 **Jealousy** is the feeling of anger or bitterness that someone has when they think that another person is trying to take a lover or friend, or a possession, away from them. 嫉妬, やきもち □ *At first his jealousy only showed in small ways – he didn't mind me talking to other guys.* 初めの頃, 彼はほとんどやきもちをやかなくて, 私がほかの男性と話しても気にしなかった. ◼ N-UNCOUNT 不可算名詞 **Jealousy** is the feeling of anger or bitterness that someone has when they wish that they could have the qualities or possessions that another person has. ねたみ, 羨望 (せんぼう) □ *Her beauty causes envy and jealousy.* 彼女の美ぼうは羨望 (せんぼう) の的だ.

jeans /dʒiːnz/ N-PLURAL 複数名詞 **Jeans** are casual pants that are usually made of strong cotton cloth called denim. ジーンズ, ジーパン [also 'a pair of' N] □ *...a young man in jeans and a worn T-shirt.* ジーンズでボロTシャツを身に着けた若い男性
→ see **clothing**

Jeep /dʒiːp/ (**Jeeps**) N-COUNT 可算名詞 商標 A **Jeep** is a type of car that can travel over rough ground. ジープ [TRADEMARK] □ *...a U.S. Army Jeep.* 米軍ジープ

jeer /dʒɪər/ (**jeers, jeering, jeered**) ◼ V-T/V-I 他動詞/自動詞 To **jeer at** someone means to say or shout rude and insulting things to them to show that you do not like or respect them. やじる, あ

ざける □ *Marchers jeered at white passers-by, but there was no violence, nor any arrests.* デモ行進者は通りがかりの白人にやじったが, 暴力行為はなく逮捕者も出なかった. □ *Demonstrators jeered the mayor as he arrived for a week-long visit.* 一週間の視察で到着した市民に向かってデモの参加者は罵声 (ばせい) を浴びせた. ●**jeer|ing** N-UNCOUNT 不可算名詞 やじ, あざけり □ *There was constant jeering and interruption from the floor.* 議場からは, 絶えずやじが飛ばされ妨害が続きました. ◼ N-COUNT 可算名詞 **Jeers** are rude and insulting things that people shout to show they do not like or respect someone. やじ, ひやかし □ *...the heckling and jeers of his audience.* 観客からのやじやひやかし

Jell-O N-UNCOUNT 不可算名詞 商標 **Jell-O** is a transparent, usually colored food that is eaten as a dessert. It is made from gelatin, fruit juice, and sugar. ジェロー, ジェリー [AM 米国英語, TRADEMARK] □ *...a bowl of Jell-O.* ボール一杯のゼリー
→ see **dessert**

jel|ly /dʒeli/ (**jellies**) ◼ N-MASS 質量名詞 **Jelly** is a sweet food that is made by cooking fruit or fruit juice with a large amount of sugar until it is thickened. It is usually spread on bread. ジャム, ジェリー状ジャム □ *I had two peanut butter and jelly sandwiches.* ピーナツバターとジャムのサンドイッチを2切れ食べました. ◼ N-VAR 可変性名詞 **Jelly** is the same as **Jell-o.** ゼリー [BRIT 英国英語]

jeop|ard|ize /dʒepərdaɪz/ (**jeopardizes, jeopardizing, jeopardized**) V-T 他動詞 To **jeopardize** a situation or activity means to do something that may destroy it or cause it to fail. 危険にさらす [他動詞] □ *He has jeopardized his future career.* 彼は将来の仕事を台無しにした.

jeop|ard|y /dʒepərdi/ PHRASE 句 If someone or something is **in jeopardy**, they are in a dangerous situation where they might fail, be lost, or be destroyed. 危険にさらされて, 危うくなって □ *A series of setbacks have put the whole project in jeopardy.* 失敗が連続したのでプロジェクト全体が危機に陥りました.

jerk /dʒɜːrk/ (**jerks, jerking, jerked**) ◼ V-T/V-I 他動詞/自動詞 If you **jerk** something or someone in a particular direction, or they **jerk** in a particular direction, they move a short distance very suddenly and quickly. 急に動かす [他動詞], 急に動く [自動詞] □ *Mr. Griffin jerked forward in his chair.* グリフィン氏は, 椅子にかけたままガタンと前に動いた. □ *"This is Brady Coyne," said Sam, jerking his head in my direction.* 「こちらがブラディ・コインさんです」とサムは言いながら, 私のほうに頭をちょっと傾けた. ●N-COUNT 可算名詞 **Jerk** is also a noun. 急な動き □ *He indicated the bedroom with a jerk of his head.* 彼は, 頭をちょっと傾げて寝室を指した. ◼ N-COUNT 可算名詞 If you call someone a **jerk**, you are insulting them because you think they are stupid or you do not like them. ばか, まぬけ [INFORMAL, OFFENSIVE くだけた, DISAPPROVAL 不賛成] □ *The guy is such a jerk! He only cares about himself.* あの男, サイテー！ 自分のことしか気にかけないんだから.

jerky /dʒɜːrki/ (**jerkier, jerkiest**) ADJ 形容詞 **Jerky** movements are very sudden and quick, and do not flow smoothly. ぎくしゃくした □ *Mr. Griffin made a jerky gesture.* グリフィン氏はぎくしゃくしたしぐさをした. ●**jerk|i|ly** /dʒɜːrkɪli/ ADV 副詞 [ADV with v] ぎこちなさそうに □ *Using his cane heavily, he moved jerkily toward the car.* 彼は杖を重そうに使いながら, ぎこちなさそうに車の方へ歩いた.

jer|sey /dʒɜːrzi/ (**jerseys**) ◼ N-COUNT 可算名詞 A **jersey** is a knitted piece of clothing that covers the upper part of your body and your arms and does not open at the front. Jerseys are usually worn over a shirt or blouse. ジャージ [OLD-FASHIONED 古風な] □ *...a sports jersey.* スポーツジャージ ◼ N-VAR 可変性名詞 **Jersey** is a knitted, slightly stretchy fabric used especially to make women's clothing. ジャージー □ *Sheila had come to dinner in a black jersey top.* シーラはジャージーの服を来てディナーにやって来た. ◼ N-VAR 可変性名詞 A **jersey** is a shirt that you wear when playing football, soccer, or some other sports. ジャージ, メリヤスのシャツ

Jesus /dʒiːzəs/ ◼ N-PROPER 固有名詞 **Jesus** or **Jesus Christ** is the name of the man who Christians believe was the son of God, and whose teachings are the basis of Christianity. イエス (キリスト) □ ◼ EXCLAM 感嘆詞 **Jesus** is used by some people to express surprise, shock, or annoyance. This use could cause offense. (驚き・いらだちなどを表す) ちきしょう, くそ [FEELINGS 感情]

jet /dʒet/ (**jets, jetting, jetted**) ◼ N-COUNT 可算名詞 A **jet** is an aircraft that is powered by jet engines. ジェット機 [also 'by' N] □ *Her private jet landed in the republic on the way to Japan.* 彼女の自家用ジェット機が日本に行く途中その共和国に着陸した. □ *He had arrived from Key West by jet.* 彼女はキー・ウェストからジェット機でやって来た. ◼ V-I 自動詞 If you **jet** somewhere, you travel there in a fast plane. ジェット機で旅行する □ *The president will be jetting off to Germany today.* 大統領は今日ドイツに飛行機で行く. ◼ N-COUNT 可算名詞 A **jet** of liquid or gas is a strong, fast, thin stream of it. 噴出する □ *A jet of water poured through the windows.* 窓から水が噴出した.
→ see **fly**

jet en|gine (**jet engines**) N-COUNT 可算名詞 A **jet engine** is an engine in which hot air and gases are forced out at the back. Jet

Picture Dictionary
jewelry

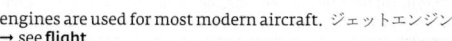

engagement ring

wedding ring

class ring

identification bracelet

charm bracelet

watch

necklace

bracelet

tie pin

pendant

earrings

tie bar

brooch

engines are used for most modern aircraft. ジェットエンジン
→ see flight

jet lag N-UNCOUNT 不可算名詞 If you are suffering from **jet lag**, you feel tired and slightly confused after a long trip by airplane, especially after traveling between places that have a time difference of several hours. 時差ぼけ □ ...the best way to avoid jet lag. 時差ぼけを防ぐ最善法

Jet Ski (Jet Skis) also **jet ski** or **jet-ski** N-COUNT 可算名詞 商標 A **Jet Ski** is a small machine like a motorcycle that is powered by a jet engine and can travel on the surface of water. ジェットスキー [TRADEMARK] □ I watched as they got on the jet ski. 私は、彼らがジェットスキーに乗るのを見ていた。 ● **jet skiing** N-UNCOUNT 不可算名詞 ジェットスキーをすること □ I like jet skiing, being out on boats, doing stuff like that. 私はジェットスキーをしたり、ボートで出かけたりというようなことが好きだ。

jet|ti|son /dʒɛtɪsən, -zən/ (jettisons, jettisoning, jettisoned) **1** V-T 他動詞 If you **jettison** something, such as an idea or a plan, you deliberately reject it or decide not to use it. 放棄する □ The governor seems to have jettisoned the plan. 知事はその計画を放棄したようだ。 **2** V-T 他動詞 To **jettison** something that is not needed or wanted means to throw it away or get rid of it. 投げ捨てる □ The crew jettisoned excess fuel and made an emergency landing. 乗務員は余分な燃料を投下し、緊急着陸をしました。

jet|ty /dʒɛti/ (jetties) **1** N-COUNT 可算名詞 A **jetty** is a wide stone wall or wooden platform where boats stop to let people get on or off, or to load or unload goods. 桟橋、波止場 **2** N-COUNT 可算名詞 A **jetty** is a structure that is built at the edge of a shore in order to protect a harbor or to reduce the force of currents and waves. 防波堤

Jew /dʒu/ (Jews) N-COUNT 可算名詞 A **Jew** is a person who believes in and practices the religion of Judaism. ユダヤ教徒、ユダヤ人

jew|el /dʒuəl/ (jewels) **1** N-COUNT 可算名詞 A **jewel** is a precious stone used to decorate valuable things that you wear, such as rings or necklaces. 宝石 □ ...a golden box containing precious jewels. 貴重な宝石が入った金の箱 **2** N-COUNT 可算名詞 If you describe something or someone as a **jewel**, you mean that they are better, more beautiful, or more special than other similar things or than other people. 大切な人、大切なもの □ ...a small jewel of a theater. 大切な劇場 **3** PHRASE 句 If you refer to an achievement or thing as the **jewel in** someone's **crown**, you mean that it is considered to be their greatest achievement or the thing they can be most proud of. 輝かしいもの □ His achievement is astonishing and this book is the jewel in his crown. 彼の功績は素晴らしく、この本は彼の最高傑作だ。

jew|el|er /dʒuələr/ (jewelers) **1** N-COUNT 可算名詞 A **jeweler** is a person who makes, sells, and repairs jewelry and watches. 宝石商、宝石職人 **2** N-COUNT 可算名詞 A **jeweler** is a store where jewelry and watches are made, sold, and repaired. 宝石店 □ ...a jeweler on Fifth Avenue that sells Rolex. ロレックスを販売している五番街の宝石店
→ see diamond

jew|el|ry /dʒuəlri/ N-UNCOUNT 不可算名詞 **Jewelry** is ornaments that people wear, such as rings, bracelets, and necklaces. It is often made of a valuable metal such as gold, and sometimes decorated with precious stones. 宝石類、アクセサリー □ Discover a full selection of fine watches and jewelry at these two Upper

Manhattan stores. アッパーマンハッタンにあるこの2軒の宝石店で素敵な時計や宝石類のセレクションを見つけよう。
→ see Picture Dictionary: jewelry

Jew|ish /dʒuɪʃ/ ADJ 形容詞 **Jewish** means belonging or relating to the religion of Judaism, or to Jews as an ethnic group. ユダヤ教徒の、ユダヤ人の □ ...the Jewish festival of Passover. ユダヤ教の過ぎ越しの祭り
→ see religion

jibe /dʒaɪb/ (jibes, jibing, jibed)

The spelling **gibe** is also used for meanings **1** and **2**.

1と**2**の意味には**gibe**のつづりも使われる。

1 N-COUNT 可算名詞 A **jibe** is a rude or insulting remark about someone that is intended to make them look foolish. あざけり □ ...a cheap jibe about his loss of hair. 彼の髪が薄くなったことについての意地悪なあざけり **2** V-T 他動詞 To **jibe** means to say something rude or insulting that is intended to make another person look foolish. あざける、からかう [WRITTEN 書き言葉] □ "No doubt he'll give me the chance to fight him again," he jibed. 「間違いなく彼はまた闘うチャンスをくれるだろうよ。」と彼は愚ろうした。 **3** V-RECIP 相互動詞 If numbers, statements, or events **jibe**, they are exactly the same as each other or they are consistent with each other. 一致する [mainly AM 主に米国英語] □ The numbers don't jibe. 数字が一致しない。

jig /dʒɪg/ (jigs, jigging, jigged) **1** N-COUNT 可算名詞 A **jig** is a lively dance. ジグ □ She danced an Irish jig. 彼女はアイリッシュ・ジグを踊った。 **2** V-I 自動詞 To **jig** means to dance or move energetically, especially bouncing up and down. 激しく踊る □ His son, Louis, laughed and jigged around to the music. 彼の息子のルイは笑い、音楽に合わせて激しくダンスした。

jig|saw /dʒɪgsɔ/ (jigsaws) **1** N-COUNT 可算名詞 A **jigsaw** or **jigsaw puzzle** is a picture on cardboard or wood that has been cut up into odd shapes. You have to make the picture again by putting the pieces together correctly. ジグソーパズル □ Both her children did jigsaw puzzles easily. 彼女の子供は2人ともジクソーパズルをたやすく終えた。 **2** N-COUNT 可算名詞 You can describe a complicated situation as a **jigsaw**. 複雑な状況 □ ...the jigsaw of high-level diplomacy. 高レベルの外交の複雑な状況

jin|gle /dʒɪŋgəl/ (jingles, jingling, jingled) **1** V-T/V-I 他/自動詞 When something **jingles** or when you **jingle** it, it makes a gentle ringing noise, like small bells. チリンチリンと鳴る [自動詞]、チリンチリンと鳴らす [他動詞] □ Brian put his hands in his pockets and jingled some change. ブライアンはポケットに手を入れて小銭をチャラチャラと鳴らした。 ● N-SING 単数名詞 **jingle** is also a noun. チャラチャラという音 □ ...the jingle of money in a man's pocket. 男のポケットのチャラチャラという小銭の音 **2** N-COUNT 可算名詞 A **jingle** is a short, simple tune, often with words, that is used to advertise a product or program on radio or television. 短いコマーシャルソング □ ...advertising jingles. 広告用のCMソング

jit|ters /dʒɪtərz/ N-PLURAL 複数名詞 If you have the **jitters**, you feel extremely nervous, for example because you have to do something important or because you are expecting important news. 緊張感 [INFORMAL くだけた] □ This only increased market jitters. これによって市場が不安定化した。

jit|tery /dʒɪtəri/ ADJ 形容詞 If someone is **jittery**, they feel nervous or are behaving nervously. 緊張した [INFORMAL くだけた] □ International investors have become jittery about the country's

economy. 国際投資家はその国の経済に対して神経過敏になった.

job /dʒɒb/ (**jobs**) **1** N-COUNT 可算名詞 A **job** is the work that someone does to earn money. 仕事, 職 □ *Once I'm in Miami I can get a job.* マイアミに行けば仕事のあてはあるよ. □ *Thousands have lost their jobs.* 数千人が失業した. **2** N-COUNT 可算名詞 A **job** is a particular task. 仕事, 作業 □ *He said he hoped that the job of putting together a coalition wouldn't take too much time.* 速やかな連立政権の樹立を期待すると彼は述べた. **3** N-COUNT 可算名詞 The **job** of a particular person or thing is their duty or function. 任務 □ *Their main job is to preserve health rather than treat illness.* 主な任務は, 病気の治療というより健康の維持だ. □ *His first job will be to try and get talks going between the two sides.* 彼の最初の任務は, 双方間の話し合いを進めるよう努めることだ. **4** N-SING 単数名詞 If you say that someone is doing a good **job**, you mean that they are doing something well. do a good job で「うまくやる」 □ *We could do a far better job of managing it than they have.* それの管理においては, 私共が担当したほうがよほどよくやれる. **5** N-SING 単数名詞 If you say that you have a **job** doing something, you are emphasizing how difficult it is. 大変なこと [EMPHASIS 強調] □ *He may have a hard job selling that argument to investors.* 彼はたやすくその根拠を投資家に納得させられないであろう. **6** PHRASE 句 If someone is **on the job**, they are actually doing a particular job or task. 仕事中で, 作業中で □ *The top pay scale after five years on the job would reach $5.00 an hour.* その仕事を5年勤続すると, 最高賃金が時給5ドルまで上がります. **7** **the job in hand** → see **hand**

	Thesaurus	*job* また次を参照:
N.	employment, occupation, profession, vocation; (ant.) work **1**	
	assignment, duty, obligation, task **2** **3**	

job de|scrip|tion (**job descriptions**) N-COUNT 可算名詞 A **job description** is a written account of all the duties and responsibilities involved in a particular job or position. 職務内容説明書 □ *...the job description for the position of division general manager.* 本部長職の職務内容説明書

job|less /dʒɒblɪs/ ADJ 形容詞 Someone who is **jobless** does not have a job, although they would like one. 失業中の □ *He has turned his back on millions of jobless Americans.* 彼は何百万人もの失業中のアメリカ人を見放した. ● N-PLURAL 複数名詞 The **jobless** are people who are jobless. 失業者 □ *They joined the ranks of the jobless.* 彼らは失業者の仲間入りをした.

job share (**job shares, job sharing, job shared**) V-I 自動詞 If two people **job share**, they share the same job by working part-time, for example, one person working in the mornings and the other in the afternoons. ジョブシェアリングをする □ *They both want to job share.* 二人ともジョブシェアリングを希望しています.

jock|ey /dʒɒki/ (**jockeys, jockeying, jockeyed**) **1** N-COUNT 可算名詞 A **jockey** is someone who rides a horse in a race. 騎手 **2** PHRASE 句 If you say that someone **is jockeying for** something, you mean that they are using whatever methods they can in order to get it or do it before their competitors can get it or do it. 〜のために画策する □ *The rival political parties are already jockeying for power.* 対抗する政治家どうしがすでに権力闘争をしている. ● PHRASE 句 If someone **is jockeying for position**, they are using whatever methods they can in order to get into a better position than their rivals. 有利な位置をとろうと画策する

jog /dʒɒg/ (**jogs, jogging, jogged**) **1** V-I 自動詞 If you **jog**, you run slowly, often as a form of exercise. ジョギングする □ *I got up early the next morning to jog.* 私は翌朝ジョギングをするために早起きした. ● N-COUNT 可算名詞 **Jog** is also a noun. □ *He went for another early morning jog.* 彼はまた早朝のジョギングに出かけた. ● **jog|ging** N-UNCOUNT 不可算名詞 ジョギング □ *It isn't the walking and jogging that got his weight down.* 彼の減量はウォーキングではなくてジョギングのおかげだ. **2** V-T 他動詞 If you **jog** something, you push or bump it slightly so that it moves. ちょっと突く □ *Avoid jogging the camera.* カメラを動かさないように. **3** PHRASE 句 If something or someone **jogs** your **memory**, they cause you to suddenly remember something that you had forgotten. 記憶を呼び覚ます □ *Police have planned a reconstruction of the crime tomorrow in the hope that this will jog the memory of passersby.* 通行人の記憶を呼び覚ますことを期待して, 警察は明日事件の再現を予定している.

jog|ger /dʒɒgər/ (**joggers**) N-COUNT 可算名詞 A **jogger** is a person who jogs as a form of exercise. ジョギングをする人

join /dʒɔɪn/ (**joins, joining, joined**) **1** V-T 他動詞 If one person **joins** another, they move or go to the same place, for example, so that both of them can do something together. 合流する, 加わる □ *His wife and children moved to join him in their new home.* 新しい家に妻と子供が引っ越して彼と一緒に住み始めた. **2** V-T 他動詞 If you **join** an organization, you become a member of it or start work as an employee of it. 入会する, 入社する □ *He joined the Army five years ago.* 彼は5年前, 陸軍に入隊した. **3** V-T/V-I 他動詞/自動詞 If you **join** an activity that other people are doing, you take part in it or

become involved with it. 参加する □ *The United States joined the war in April 1917.* 合衆国は1917年4月に参戦した. □ *The pastor requested the women present to join him in prayer.* その牧師は参列中の女性に一緒に祈りをするよう求めた. □ *Nine Republicans joined in supporting the measure.* 9名の共和党員がその法案の賛成派に加わった. **4** V-T 他動詞 If you **join** a line, you stand at the end of it so that you are part of it. 列に並ぶ □ *It is advised that fans seeking autographs join the line before practice starts.* サインを求めているファンは, 練習が始まる前に列に並ぶように忠告された. **5** V-T 他動詞 To **join** two things means to attach or fasten them together. 連結する □ *The opened link is used to join the two ends of the chain.* オープンリンクは2つの鎖をつなぐ環として使われる. □ *...the conjunctiva, the skin which joins the eye to the lid.* まぶたと眼球を覆う膜である結膜 **6** V-T 他動詞 If something such as a line or path **joins** two things, it connects them. つなげる □ *...a global highway of cables joining all the continents together.* 全ての大陸を結びつける世界規模の高速回線 **7** V-RECIP 相互動詞 If two roads or rivers **join**, they meet or come together at a particular point. 合流する □ *Do you know the highway to Tulsa? The airport road joins it.* タルサへの幹線道路を知っていますか？空港行きがその道に合流します. **8** **join forces** → see **force**

▶ **join in** PHRASAL VERB 句動詞 If you **join in** an activity, you take part in it or become involved in it. 参加する □ *I hope everyone will join in the fun.* 皆が参加して楽しむといいですね.

▶ **join up** **1** PHRASAL VERB 句動詞 If someone **joins up**, they become a member of the army, the navy, or the air force. 入隊する □ *When hostilities broke out he joined up.* 戦争が開始したとき, 彼は入隊した. **2** PHRASAL VERB 句動詞 If one person or organization **joins up with** another, they start doing something together. 提携する □ *Dwight decided to withdraw from the committee and join up with the opposition.* ドワイトは委員会から身を引いて, 野党側に加わることを決心した.

joint /dʒɔɪnt/ (**joints**) **1** ADJ 形容詞 **Joint** means shared by or belonging to two or more people. 共有の, 共同の [ADJ n] □ *She and Frank had never gotten around to opening a joint account.* 彼女とフランクは結局共同預金口座を開設できなかった. ● **joint|ly** ADV 副詞 [ADV with v] 共同で □ *The Port Authority is an agency jointly run by New York and New Jersey.* 湾岸管理委員会はニューヨーク州とニュージャージー州が共同で運営している機関です. **2** N-COUNT 可算名詞 A **joint** is a part of your body such as your elbow or knee where two bones meet and are able to move together. 関節 □ *Her joints ache if she exercises.* 彼女が運動をすると関節が痛む. **3** N-COUNT 可算名詞 A **joint** is the place where two things are fastened or joined together. 接合箇所, つなぎ目 □ *...the joint between the inner and outer panels.* 内外パネルの接合箇所 **4** N-COUNT 可算名詞 You can refer to a cheap place where people go for some form of entertainment as a **joint**. 安酒場, たまり場 [INFORMAL くだけた] □ *They had come to the world's most famous pick-up joint.* 彼らは世界でもっとも有名なナンパバーに来た. **5** N-COUNT 可算名詞 A **joint** is a cigarette that contains cannabis or marijuana. マリファナ [INFORMAL くだけた] □ *He's smoking a joint.* 彼はマリファナを吸っている. **6** PHRASE 句 If something puts someone's **nose out of joint**, it upsets or offends them because it makes them feel less important or less valued. 鼻をあかす, 出し抜く [INFORMAL くだけた] □ *Barry had his nose put out of joint by Lucy's aloof sophistication.* バリーはルーシーのお高くとまった態度に頭にきた.

	Word Partnership	*joint* は次の語句と使われる:
N.	joint **account**, joint **agreement**, joint **effort**, joint **resolution**, joint **statement** **1**	

joint-stock com|pany (**joint-stock companies**) N-COUNT 可算名詞 A **joint-stock company** is a company that is owned by the people who have bought shares in that company and who are responsible for its debts. 共同出資会社 [BUSINESS 実業]

joke /dʒoʊk/ (**jokes, joking, joked**) **1** N-COUNT 可算名詞 A **joke** is something that is said or done to make you laugh, such as a funny story. 冗談, ジョーク □ *No one told worse jokes than Claus.* クローズほどひどいジョークを言った者はいない. **2** V-I 自動詞 If you **joke**, you tell funny stories or say amusing things. 冗談を言う □ *She would joke about her appearance.* 彼女は自分の外見について冗談だって言うだろう. □ *Luanne was laughing and joking with Tritt.* ルアンはトリットと笑って冗談を言っていた. **3** N-COUNT 可算名詞 A **joke** is something untrue that you tell another person in order to amuse yourself. いたずら, 悪ふざけ, からかい □ *It was probably just a joke to them, but it wasn't funny to me.* 彼らにとっては単なる悪ふざけだろうが, 私にとってはおもしろくなかった. **4** V-I 自動詞 If you **joke**, you tell someone something that is not true in order to amuse yourself. からかう □ *Don't get defensive, Charlie. I was only joking.* チャーリー, むきになるなよ. ただの冗談だよ. **5** N-SING 単数名詞 If you say that something or someone is a **joke**, you think they are ridiculous and do not deserve respect. 話にならない [INFORMAL くだけた, DISAPPROVAL 不賛成] □ *It's ridiculous, it's pathetic, it's a joke.* ばかげている, 情けない, 話にならないよ. **6** PHRASE 句 If you **make a joke of** something, you laugh at

it even though it is in fact serious or sad. 冗談ですませる ❑ *I wish I had your courage, Michael, to make a joke of it like that.* マイケル，あなたみたいにそんな風に冗談ですませられるような強さがあったらなあ． **7** PHRASE 句 If you describe a situation as **no joke**, you are emphasizing that it is very difficult or unpleasant. 笑い事ではない，大変だ [INFORMAL くだけた，EMPHASIS 強調] ❑ *Eight hours on a bus is no joke, is it.* バスに8時間も乗っているなんて笑い事じゃないだろう． **8** PHRASE 句 If you say that **the joke is on** a particular person, you mean that they have been made to look very foolish by something. 笑いものになる ❑ *"For once," he said, "the joke's on me. And it's not very funny."* 「今回だけは」と彼は言った． 「僕が笑いものだ．あまりおもしろくないね． 」 **9** CONVENTION 慣習表現 You say **you're joking** or **you must be joking** to someone when they have just told you something that is so surprising or unreasonable that you find it difficult to believe. 冗談でしょう，まさか [SPOKEN 口語, FEELINGS 感情] ❑ *You're joking. Are you serious?* 冗談でしょう．本気なの？

Word Partnership   joke は次の語句と使われる：

ADJ.	**dirty** joke, **old** joke, **practical** joke **bad** joke, **cruel** joke, **funny** joke, **good** joke **1**
V.	**crack** a joke, **laugh at** a joke, **make** a joke, **play** a joke, **tell** a joke **1**
	make a joke of *something* **6**

---

jok|er /dʒoʊkər/ (jokers) **1** N-COUNT 可算名詞 Someone who is a **joker** likes making jokes or doing amusing things. 冗談好きの人 ❑ *He is, by nature, a joker, a witty man with a sense of fun.* 彼は生まれつき笑いのセンスがあって冗談好きで機知に富む人だ． **2** N-COUNT 可算名詞 The **joker** in a deck of playing cards is the card that does not belong to any of the four suits. ジョーカー **3** N-COUNT 可算名詞 You can call someone a **joker** if you think they are behaving in a stupid or dangerous way. ばか，あほ [INFORMAL くだけた, DISAPPROVAL 不賛成] ❑ *Keep your eye on these jokers, you never know what they will come up with.* こいつらに気をつけるんだ．何をしでかすか分からないからな．

jol|ly /dʒɒli/ (jollier, jolliest) **1** ADJ 形容詞 Someone who is **jolly** is happy and cheerful in their appearance or behavior. 陽気な ❑ *She was a jolly, kindhearted woman.* 彼女は陽気で優しい女性だった． **2** ADJ 形容詞 A **jolly** event is lively and enjoyable. 楽しい ❑ *She had a very jolly time in Korea.* 彼女は韓国でとても楽しいひとときを過ごした．

jolt /dʒoʊlt/ (jolts, jolting, jolted) **1** V-T/V-I 他動詞/自動詞 If something **jolts** or if something **jolts** it, it moves suddenly and quite violently. ガタガタと揺れる [自動詞]，ガタガタと揺らす [他動詞] ❑ *The wagon jolted again.* 荷馬車が再びガタガタと揺れた． ❑ *The train jolted into motion.* 電車がガタガタと動きだした． ● N-COUNT 可算名詞 **Jolt** is also a noun. 揺れ ❑ *We were worried that one tiny jolt could worsen her injuries.* 少しでも揺れると彼女の傷が悪化すると私たちは心配した． **2** V-T 他動詞 If something **jolts** someone, it gives them an unpleasant surprise or shock. 衝撃を与える ❑ *A stinging slap across the face jolted her.* 顔をパシッと平手打ちされて彼女はショックを受けた． ● N-COUNT 可算名詞 **Jolt** is also a noun. 衝撃 ❑ *Then my husband left me. It gave me the jolt I needed.* そして夫に捨てられた．私にはそんな衝撃が必要だった．

jos|tle /dʒɒsəl/ (jostles, jostling, jostled) **1** V-T/V-I 他動詞/自動詞 If people **jostle** you, they bump against you or push you in a way that annoys you, usually because you are in a crowd and they are trying to get past you. 押しのける ❑ *You get 2,000 people jostling each other and bumping into furniture.* 2000人もの人々が家具に向って押しのけ合うんだ． ❑ *We spent an hour jostling with the crowds as we did our shopping.* 私たちは買い物をする間大勢の客と押しのけ合いながら1時間過ごした． **2** V-I 自動詞 If people or things **are jostling for** something such as attention or a reward, they are competing with other people or things in order to get it. 一のために競り合う ❑ *...the contenders who have been jostling for the top job.* 最高位職に就くために競り合っていた候補者たち

jot /dʒɒt/ (jots, jotting, jotted) V-T 他動詞 If you **jot** something short such as an address somewhere, you write it down so that you will remember it. メモを取る ❑ *Could you just jot his name on there?* 彼の名前をあそこに書き留めてくれませんか． ● PHRASAL VERB 句動詞 **Jot down** means the same as **jot**. メモを取る ❑ *Christine uses her journal to jot down ideas and lists of things to do.* クリスティンは思いついたことやするべきことのリストを書くのに日記帳を使う．

jour|nal /dʒɜrnəl/ (journals) **1** N-COUNT 可算名詞 A **journal** is a magazine, especially one that deals with a specialized subject. 雑誌 ❑ *All our results are published in scientific journals.* 我々の研究結果は全て科学雑誌に記載されている． **2** N-COUNT 可算名詞 A **journal** is a daily or weekly newspaper. The word journal is often used in the name of the paper. 一新聞，一紙 ❑ *...ads in The New York Times, the Wall Street Journal and other publications.* ニューヨークタイムズ紙，ウォールストリートジャーナル紙，またほかの出版物での広告 **3** N-COUNT 可算名詞 A **journal** is an account that you write of

your daily activities. 日記 ❑ *Sara confided to her journal.* 彼女は日記に秘密ごとを書いた．

jour|nal|ism /dʒɜrnəlɪzəm/ N-UNCOUNT 算名詞 **Journalism** is the job of collecting news and writing about it for newspapers, magazines, television, or radio. ジャーナリズム，報道業界 ❑ *He began a career in journalism, working for the Rocky Mountain News.* 彼は報道業界で，ロッキー・マウンテン・ニュース社で仕事を始めた．

jour|nal|ist /dʒɜrnəlɪst/ (journalists) N-COUNT 可算名詞 A **journalist** is a person whose job is to collect news and write about it for newspapers, magazines, television, or radio. ジャーナリスト，記者

→ see newspaper

jour|ney /dʒɜrni/ (journeys, journeying, journeyed) **1** N-COUNT 可算名詞 When you make a **journey**, you travel from one place to another. 旅行，旅 [FORMAL 形式ばった] ❑ *There is an express service from Paris that completes the journey to Bordeaux in under 4 hours.* パリからボルドーまで4時間未満で行ける急行列車がある．

The noun **travel** is used to talk about the general activity of traveling. It is either uncount or plural. You cannot say "a travel," you would use the word **trip** or **journey** instead. ❑ *First-class rail travel to Paris or Brussels is included...We were going to go on a trip to Florida together.*

2 N-COUNT 可算名詞 You can refer to a person's experience of changing or developing from one state of mind to another as a **journey**. 道のり ❑ *My films try to describe a journey of discovery, both for myself and the viewer.* 私の映画は私自身と観客の両方のために発見への道のりを描こうとしている． **3** V-I 自動詞 If you **journey** somewhere, you travel there. 旅する [FORMAL 形式ばった] ❑ *In February 1935, Naomi journeyed to the United States for the first time.* 1935年2月に，ナオミは初めてアメリカへ旅をした．

Thesaurus   journey また次を参照：

N.	adventure, trip, visit, voyage **1**
V.	cruise, fly, go, travel **3**

Word Partnership   journey は次の語句と使われる：

V.	**begin** a journey, **complete** a journey, **make** a journey **1 2**
N.	**end of** a journey, **first/last leg of** a journey **1 2**
	journey **of discovery 2**

---

joy /dʒɔɪ/ (joys) **1** N-UNCOUNT 不可算名詞 **Joy** is a feeling of great happiness. 喜び ❑ *Salter shouted with joy.* ソルターは歓声を上げた． **2** N-COUNT 可算名詞 A **joy** is something or someone that makes you feel happy or gives you great pleasure. 喜びの種 ❑ *Spending evenings outside is one of the joys of summer.* 夕方野外で過ごすのは夏の楽しみの1つだ． **3** PHRASE 句 If you say that someone **is jumping for joy**, you mean that they are very pleased or happy about something. 大喜びをする ❑ *He jumped for joy on being told the news.* 彼はそのニュースを聞いて大喜びした．

→ see emotion

Word Partnership   joy は次の語句と使われる：

V.	**bring** *someone* joy, **cry/weep for** joy, **feel** joy **1**
ADJ.	**filled with** joy, **great** joy, **pure** joy, **sheer** joy **1**
N.	**tears of** joy **1**

Word Link   joy ≈ being glad : *enjoy, joyful, joyous*

joy|ful /dʒɔɪfəl/ **1** ADJ 形容詞 Something that is **joyful** causes happiness and pleasure. 喜ばしい [FORMAL 形式ばった] ❑ *A wedding is a joyful celebration of love.* 結婚式は喜ばしい愛の祝福だ． **2** ADJ 形容詞 Someone who is **joyful** is extremely happy. うれしい [FORMAL 形式ばった] ❑ *We're a very joyful people; we're very musical people and we love music.* 私たちはとても楽しいんだ．音楽の才能があって，音楽が大好きなんだ． ● **joy|ful|ly** ADV 副詞 うれしそうに ❑ *They greeted him joyfully.* 彼らはうれしそうに彼にあいさつした．

joy|ous /dʒɔɪəs/ ADJ 形容詞 **Joyous** means extremely happy. 歓喜した [LITERARY 文語的] ❑ *She had made their childhood so joyous and carefree.* 彼女のおかげで彼らは楽しくのんびりとした子供時代を送った． ● **joy|ous|ly** ADV 副詞 歓喜して ❑ *Sarah accepted joyously.* サラは喜んで承諾した．

joy|rider /dʒɔɪraɪdər/ (joyriders) N-COUNT 可算名詞 A **joyrider** is someone who steals cars in order to drive around in them at high speed. 無謀運転をする人 ❑ *...a car crash caused by joyriders.* 無謀運転が原因の交通事故

joy|stick /dʒɔɪstɪk/ (joysticks) N-COUNT 可算名詞 In some computer games, the **joystick** is the lever that the player uses in order to control the direction of the things on the screen. 操作レバー

JPEG /dʒeɪpɛg/ (**JPEGs**) also **Jpeg** N-UNCOUNT 不可算名詞 **JPEG** is a standard file format for compressing pictures so they can be stored or sent by e-mail more easily. **JPEG** is an abbreviation for "Joint Photographic Experts Group." JPEG [COMPUTING コンピューティング] ❑ *...JPEG images.* JPEGの画像 ● N-COUNT 可算名詞 A **JPEG** is a JPEG file or picture. JPEGのファイル，JPEGの画像 ❑ *You can add edge enhancement or smoothness to a Jpeg, or vary the color depth.* JPEG の画像でエッジの鋭角化あるいはスムーズ化ができ，また色調調整も出来る.

ju|bi|lant /dʒuːbɪlənt/ ADJ 形容詞 If you are **jubilant**, you feel extremely happy because of a success. 歓喜に満ちた ❑ *The team were greeted by thousands of jubilant supporters.* チームは数千人の歓喜に満ちた支持者に迎えられた.

ju|bi|lee /dʒuːbɪliː/ (**jubilees**) N-COUNT 可算名詞 A **jubilee** is a special anniversary of an event, especially the 25th or 50th anniversary. 記念祭，祝典 ❑ *...Queen Victoria's jubilee.* ビクトリア女王の祝典

Ju|da|ism /dʒuːdeɪɪzəm, -deɪ-/ N-UNCOUNT 不可算名詞 **Judaism** is the religion of the Jewish people. It is based on the Old Testament of the Bible and the Talmud. ユダヤ教

judge /dʒʌdʒ/ (**judges**, **judging**, **judged**) ■ N-COUNT; N-TITLE 可算名詞，称号名詞 A **judge** is the person in a court of law who decides how the law should be applied, for example how criminals should be punished. 裁判官，判事 ❑ *The judge adjourned the hearing until next Tuesday.* 裁判官は来週の火曜日まで公聴会を休会とした. ② N-COUNT 可算名詞 A **judge** is a person who decides who will be the winner of a competition. 審査員 ❑ *A panel of judges is now selecting the finalists.* 審査員一団が決勝戦出場者を選んでいる最中です. ③ V-T 他動詞 If you **judge** something such as a competition, you decide who or what is the winner. 審査する ❑ *He was asked to judge a literary competition.* 彼は文芸コンテストの審査をするように頼まれた. ④ V-T 他動詞 If you **judge** something or someone, you form an opinion about them after you have examined the evidence or thought carefully about them. 判断する，評価する ❑ *It will take a few more years to judge the impact of these ideas.* これらの案の影響を評価するにはあと数年かかるだろう. ❑ *I am ready to judge any book on its merits.* わたしは喜んでどんな本の是非に関してでも評価する. ❑ *It's for other people to judge how much I have improved.* 私がどのくらい上達したかはほかの人の判断すること だ. ⑤ V-T 他動詞 If you **judge** something, you guess its amount, size, or value or you guess what it is. 推測する ❑ *It is important to judge the weight of your washing load correctly.* 洗濯物の重さを正確に推量することが大切だ. ❑ *I judged him to be about forty.* 彼は40歳くらいだと思う. ⑥ N-COUNT 可算名詞 If someone is a good **judge** of something, they understand it and can make sensible decisions about it. If someone is a bad **judge** of something, they cannot do this. 見る目 ❑ *I'm a pretty good judge of character.* 私はかなり人を見る目がある. ⑦ PHRASE 句 You use **judging by**, **judging from**, or **to judge from** to introduce the reasons why you believe or think something. 〜から判断すると ❑ *Judging by the opinion polls, he seems to be succeeding.* 世論調査によると，彼は成功しているようだ. ❑ *Judging from the way he laughed as he told it, it was meant to be humorous.* 彼がそれを言ったときの笑い方から判断して，ユーモアのつもりだったのだ.
→ see **gymnastics**, **trial**

Word Partnership *judge* は次の語句と使われる:

V.	judge **approves** *something*, judge **asks** *something*, judge **decides** *something*, judge **denies a motion/request**, judge **grants** *something*, judge **orders** *something*, judge **rules** *something*, judge **says** *something*, judge **sentences** *someone* ■
N.	**decision by/of** a judge, **trial** judge ■

judg|ment /dʒʌdʒmənt/ (**judgments**) ■ N-VAR 可変性名詞 A **judgment** is an opinion that you have or express after thinking carefully about something. 判断，評価 ❑ *In your judgment, what has changed over the past few years?* あなたの考えでは，過去数年で変わったことは何ですか. ② N-UNCOUNT 不可算名詞 **Judgment** is the ability to make sensible guesses about a situation or sensible decisions about what to do. 判断力 ❑ *I respect his judgment and I'll follow any advice he gives me.* 彼の判断力を尊敬し，彼からのアドバイスに従います. ③ N-VAR 可変性名詞 A **judgment** is a decision made by a judge or by a court of law. 判決 ❑ *We are awaiting a judgment from the Supreme Court.* 私たちは最高裁の判決を待っている. ④ PHRASE 句 If something is **against** your **better judgment**, you believe that it would be more sensible or better not to do it. 心ならずも，不本意ながら ❑ *Against our better judgment, we buy the products of manufacturers whose claims seem too good to be true.* 不本意ながら，私たちは宣伝文句がまゆつばものの製造会社の商品を購入する. ⑤ PHRASE 句 If you **pass judgment** on someone or something, you give your opinion about it, especially if you are making a criticism. 批判する ❑ *They won't pass judgment on their*

friends or family. 彼らは友人や家族の批判はしない. ⑥ PHRASE 句 If you **reserve judgment on** something, you refuse to give an opinion about it until you know more about it. 判断を差し控える ❑ *I think I'd have to reserve judgment on whether it'll make any difference until I see some of those key details.* 重要な詳細事項を見るまではそれの影響があるかどうかについての判断は差し控えるべきだと思います.

Word Partnership *judgment* は次の語句と使われる:

V.	**make** a judgment, **rush to** judgment ■ **exercise** judgment, **trust** *someone's* judgment, **use** judgment ②
ADJ.	**bad** judgment, **good** judgment, **poor** judgment ②

judg|men|tal /dʒʌdʒmɛntəl/ ADJ 形容詞 If you say that someone is **judgmental**, you are critical of them because they form opinions of people and situations very quickly, when it would be better for them to wait until they know more about the person or situation. 批判的な [DISAPPROVAL 不賛成] ❑ *We tried not to seem critical or judgmental while giving advice that would protect him from ridicule.* 私たちは，彼がからかわれないようにアドバイスを与えるとき，批判的に思われないように努めた.

ju|di|cial /dʒuːdɪʃəl/ ADJ 形容詞 **Judicial** means relating to the legal system and to judgments made in a court of law. 司法の，裁判の [ADJ n] ❑ *...an independent judicial system.* 独立司法制度 ❑ *...efforts to manipulate the judicial process.* 司法過程を操作しようとする努力 ● **ju|di|cial|ly** ADV 副詞 [ADV with v] 裁判で ❑ *Even if the amendment is passed it can be defeated judicially.* 仮に修正案が通ったとしても裁判で否決される可能性がある.

ju|di|ci|ary /dʒuːdɪʃieri/ N-SING 単数名詞 The **judiciary** is the branch of authority in a country that is concerned with law and the legal system. 裁判官 [FORMAL 形式ばった] ❑ *The judiciary must think very hard before jailing nonviolent offenders.* 裁判官は，知能犯罪者に実刑判決を出す前にじっくり考えなければならない.

ju|di|cious /dʒuːdɪʃəs/ ADJ 形容詞 If you describe an action or decision as **judicious**, you approve of it because you think that it shows good judgment and sense. 賢明な [FORMAL 形式ばった，APPROVAL 賛成] ❑ *The president authorizes the judicious use of military force to protect our citizens.* 大統領は国民を守るために軍事力の賢明な使用を許可する. ● **ju|di|cious|ly** ADV 副詞 [ADV with v] 賢明に ❑ *Modern fertilizers should be used judiciously.* 現代の化学肥料は賢明に使用されるべきだ.

judo /dʒuːdoʊ/ N-UNCOUNT 不可算名詞 **Judo** is a sport in which two people fight without weapons and try to throw each other to the ground. 柔道 ❑ *He was also a black belt in judo.* 彼はまた柔道でも黒帯だ.

jug /dʒʌg/ (**jugs**) ■ N-COUNT 可算名詞 A **jug** is a cylindrical container with a handle and is used for holding and pouring liquids. ジャグ ② N-COUNT 可算名詞 You can use **jug** to refer to the jug and its contents, or to the contents only. ジャグに入ったもの ❑ *...a jug of water.* 水差し1杯の水
→ see **dish**

jug|gle /dʒʌgəl/ (**juggles**, **juggling**, **juggled**) ■ V-T 他動詞 If you **juggle** lots of different things, such as your work and your family, you try to give enough time or attention to all of them. やりくりする ❑ *The management team meets several times a week to juggle budgets and resources.* 予算と資金をやりくりするために経営陣は週に数回ミーティングをする. ② V-T/V-I 他動詞/自動詞 If you **juggle**, you entertain people by throwing things into the air, catching each one, and throwing it up again so that there are several of them in the air at the same time. ジャグリングする ❑ *Soon she was juggling five eggs.* まもなく彼女は5つの卵をジャグリングしていた. ● **jug|gling** N-UNCOUNT 不可算名詞 ジャグリング ❑ *He can perform an astonishing variety of acts, including mime and juggling.* 彼は，パントマイムやジャグリングを含めて驚くほど様々な芸が出来る.

jug|gler /dʒʌglər/ (**jugglers**) N-COUNT 可算名詞 A **juggler** is someone who juggles in order to entertain people. 曲芸師

juice /dʒuːs/ (**juices**, **juicing**, **juiced**) ■ N-MASS 質量名詞 **Juice** is the liquid that can be obtained from a fruit or vegetable. ジュース，果汁 ❑ *...fresh orange juice.* 新鮮なオレンジジュース ② N-PLURAL 複数名詞 The **juices** of a piece of meat are the liquid that comes out of it when you cook it. 肉汁 ❑ *When cooked, drain off the juices and put the meat in a processor.* 調理をしたら肉汁を捨て，肉をフードプロセッサーに入れなさい.
▶ **juice up** PHRASAL VERB 句動詞 If you **juice up** a place or event, you do something to make it more lively or exciting. 活気づける [AM 米国英語，INFORMAL くだけた] ❑ *Look at the ads for Chamber of Secrets, and you'll see that the filmmakers are doing all they can to juice up the formula.* 『秘密の部屋』の広告をご覧下さい. 映画制作者がお決まりの宣伝を活気づけようと全力を尽くしているのが分るでしょう.

Word Partnership   *juice* は次の語句と使われる:

N.   **bottle of** juice, **fruit** juice, **glass of** juice **1**

ADJ.   **fresh-squeezed** juice **1**

juicy /dʒúsi/ (**juicier, juiciest**) **1** ADJ 形容詞 If food is **juicy**, it has a lot of juice in it and is very enjoyable to eat. 汁がたっぷりの，ジューシーな □ *...a thick, juicy steak.* 分厚くてジューシーなステーキ **2** ADJ 形容詞 **Juicy** gossip or stories contain details about people's lives, especially details that are normally kept private. 興味をそそる [INFORMAL くだけた] □ *It provided some juicy gossip for a few days.* それのせいで興味をそそるうわさ話が数日間続いた.

Jul. **Jul.** is a written abbreviation for **July**. Julyの略

July /dʒʊláɪ/ (**Julys**) N-VAR 可変性名詞 **July** is the seventh month of the year in the Western calendar. 7月 □ *In July 1969, Neil Armstrong walked on the moon.* 1969年7月にニール・アームストロングは月面を歩いた.

jum|ble /dʒʌ́mbªl/ (**jumbles, jumbling, jumbled**) **1** N-COUNT 可算名詞 A **jumble** of things is a lot of different things that are all mixed together in a disorganized or confused way. ごちゃ混ぜ □ *The shoreline was made up of a jumble of huge boulders.* 海岸線は巨石の集まりで出来ていた. **2** V-T/V-I 他動詞/自動詞 If you **jumble** things, they become mixed together so that they are untidy or are not in the correct order. ごちゃ混ぜにする □ *He's making a new film by jumbling together bits of his other movies.* 彼は過去の映画の場面をごちゃ混ぜにして新しい映画を製作している. ● PHRASAL VERB 句動詞 To **jumble up** means the same as to **jumble**. ごちゃ混ぜにする □ *They had jumbled it all up into a heap.* 彼らはそれを全部ごちゃ混ぜにして山のように積み上げた. □ *The bank scrambles all that money together, jumbles it all up and lends it out to hundreds and thousands of borrowers.* 銀行はお金を全部寄せ集め，ごちゃ混ぜにし，そして何万人もの客に貸し出す.

jum|bo /dʒʌ́mboʊ/ (**jumbos**) **1** ADJ 形容詞 **Jumbo** means very large; used mainly in advertising and in the names of products. 特大の [ADJ n] □ *...a jumbo box of tissues.* 特大のティッシュ箱 **2** N-COUNT 可算名詞 A **jumbo** or a **jumbo jet** is a very large jet aircraft that can carry several hundred passengers. ジャンボジェット機

jump /dʒʌmp/ (**jumps, jumping, jumped**) **1** V-T/V-I 他動詞/自動詞 If you **jump**, you bend your knees, push against the ground with your feet, and move quickly upward into the air. 跳ぶ，ジャンプする [自動詞]，跳び越える [他動詞] □ *I jumped over the fence.* 僕は塀を飛び越えた. □ *I'd jumped seventeen feet six in the long jump, which was a school record.* 走り幅跳びで17フィート6インチジャンプしたんだ. それって学校の新記録だよ. ● N-COUNT 可算名詞 **Jump** is also a noun. ジャンプ □ *The longest jumps by a man and a woman were witnessed in Sestriere, Italy, yesterday.* 男性および女性による走り幅跳びの最高新記録が昨日イタリア，セストリエレで更新された. **2** V-T/V-I 他動詞/自動詞 If you **jump** from something above the ground, you deliberately push yourself into the air so that you drop toward the ground. 跳び降りる □ *I jumped the last six feet down to the deck.* デッキまでの最後の6フィートを跳び降りた. □ *He jumped out of a third-floor window.* 彼は，3階の窓から跳び降りた. **3** V-T 他動詞 If you **jump** something such as a fence, you move quickly up and through the air over or across it. 飛び越える □ *He jumped the first fence beautifully.* 彼は最初の障害物を見事に跳び越えた. **4** V-I 自動詞 If you **jump** somewhere, you move there quickly and suddenly. 飛び起きる，飛びのく □ *Adam jumped from his seat at the girl's cry.* アダムは，女の子の泣き声を聞いて椅子から飛び上がった. **5** V-I 自動詞 If something **makes** you **jump**, it makes you make a sudden movement because you are frightened or surprised. どきっとする □ *The phone shrilled, making her jump.* 電話がけたたましく鳴ったので，彼女はどきっとした. **6** V-T/V-I 他動詞/自動詞 If an amount or level **jumps**, it suddenly increases or rises by a large amount in a short time. 急増する □ *Sales jumped from $94 million to over $101 million.* 売上高が9400万ドルから1億100万ドル以上に急増した. □ *The number of crimes jumped by ten percent last year.* 昨年の犯罪数は10%急増した. □ *Squibb shares jumped $2.50.* スクィブの株価が2.5ドル急騰した. ● N-COUNT 可算名詞 **Jump** is also a noun. 急増 □ *A big jump in energy conservation could be achieved without much disruption of anyone's standard of living.* 生活水準にほとんど影響を及ぼさずにエネルギーの使用量を急減することが可能だ. **7** V-I 自動詞 If you **jump at** an offer or opportunity, you accept it quickly and eagerly. 飛びつく [no cont] □ *Members of the public would jump at the chance to become part owners of the corporation.* 一般の人々は，その会社の共同所有者になれるチャンスに飛びつくであろう. **8** V-I 自動詞 If someone **jumps on** you, they quickly criticize you for doing something that they do not approve of. しかる □ *A lot of people jumped on me about that, you know.* 多くの人々がそのことについて私をとがめたんですよ. **9** V-T 他動詞 If someone **jumps** you, they attack you suddenly or unexpectedly. 突然襲いかかる [mainly AM 主に米国英語, INFORMAL くだけた] □ *Half a dozen sailors jumped him.* 半ダースもの水兵が彼に突然襲いかかった. **10** PHRASE 句 If you **get a jump**

on something or someone or **get the jump on** them, you gain an advantage over them. 先手を取る [AM 米国英語] □ *Helicopters helped fire crews get a jump on the blaze.* ヘリコプターのおかげで消防隊は火事の先手を取ることができました. **11** to **jump on the bandwagon** → see **bandwagon** **12** to **jump bail** → see **bail** **13** to **jump the gun** → see **gun** **14** to **jump for joy** → see **joy**

Thesaurus   *jump* また次を参照:

V.   bound, hop, leap, lunge **1**
     dive, leap, parachute **2**
     hurdle **3**
     startle **5**
     increase, rise, shoot up **6**

Word Partnership   *jump* は次の語句と使われる:

ADJ.   **big** jump **1** **6**

N.   jump **to** *your* **feet** **4**
     jump **in prices**, jump **in sales** **6**

jump|er /dʒʌ́mpər/ (**jumpers**) **1** N-COUNT 可算名詞 If you refer to a person or a horse as a particular kind of **jumper**, you are describing how good they are at jumping or the way that they jump. 跳ぶ人・動物 □ *He is a terrific athlete and a brilliant jumper.* 彼は素晴らしい運動選手でジャンプが得意だ. **2** N-COUNT 可算名詞 A **jumper** is a sleeveless dress that is worn over a blouse or sweater. ジャンパースカート [AM 米国英語] □ *She wore a checkered jumper and had ribbons in her hair.* 彼女はチェックのジャンパースカートをはいて髪にリボンを付けていた. **3** N-COUNT 可算名詞 A **jumper** is a warm knitted piece of clothing that covers the upper part of your body and your arms. セーター [BRIT 英国英語; AM **sweater** 米国英語 **sweater**]

jump|start /dʒʌ́mpstɑrt/ (**jumpstarts, jumpstarting, jumpstarted**) **1** V-T 他動詞 To **jumpstart** a vehicle that has a dead battery means to make the engine start by getting power from the battery of another vehicle, using special cables called jumper cables. ジャンプスタート □ *He was huddled with John trying to jumpstart his car.* 彼は車をジャンプスタートさせようとしてジョンと身を寄せ合っていた. ● N-COUNT 可算名詞 **Jumpstart** is also a noun. ジャンプスタート □ *I drove out to give him a jumpstart because his battery was dead.* 私は彼の車のバッテリーが切れていたのでジャンプさせようとして車を動かした. **2** V-T 他動詞 To **jumpstart** a system or process that has stopped working or progressing means to do something that will make it start working quickly or effectively. 活性化する □ *The EU is trying to jumpstart the peace process.* 欧州連合は和平プロセスを推進させようとしている. ● N-COUNT 可算名詞 **Jumpstart** is also a noun. 活性化 □ *...attempts to give the industry a jumpstart.* 産業活性化の試み

Jun. **Jun.** is a written abbreviation for **June**. Juneの略

junc|tion /dʒʌ́ŋkʃən/ (**junctions**) N-COUNT; N-IN-NAMES 可算名詞，名称中の名詞 A **junction** is a place where roads or railroad lines join. 交差点，連結駅 [BRIT 英国英語; AM usually **intersection** 米国英語では通常 **intersection**]

June /dʒun/ (**Junes**) N-VAR 可変性名詞 **June** is the sixth month of the year in the Western calendar. 6月 □ *He spent two and a half weeks with us in June 1986.* 彼は1986年6月に2週間半私たちと過ごした. □ *I am moving out on June 5th.* 私は6月5日に引っ越す.

jun|gle /dʒʌ́ŋgªl/ (**jungles**) **1** N-VAR 可変性名詞 A **jungle** is a forest in a tropical country where large numbers of tall trees and plants grow very close together. ジャングル □ *...the mountains and jungles of Papua New Guinea.* パプアニューギニアの山々と密林 **2** N-SING 単数名詞 If you describe a place as a **jungle**, you are emphasizing that it is full of lots of things and very messy. ジャングルのように雑然としたところ □ *...a jungle of stuffed sofas, stuffed birds, knick-knacks, potted plants.* ソファー，剝製（はくせい）の鳥，小物，観葉植物などが散らかった場所 [EMPHASIS 強調] **3** N-SING 単数名詞 If you describe a situation as a **jungle**, you dislike it because it is complicated and difficult to get what you want from it. 迷宮 [DISAPPROVAL 不賛成] □ *Social Security law and procedure remain a jungle of complex rules.* 社会保障の法律と訴訟手続きは複雑な規則の迷宮のままである.

jun|ior /dʒúniər/ (**juniors**) **1** ADJ 形容詞 A **junior** official or employee holds a low-ranking position in an organization or profession. 下位の □ *A handful of junior officers were made to bear responsibility for the incident.* 少数の下級将校がその事件の責任を負わされた. ● N-COUNT 可算名詞 **Junior** is also a noun. 下位 □ *He has said legal aid work is for juniors when they start out in the law.* 法律相談は若手の弁護士の取りかかりの仕事だと彼は言った. **2** N-SING 単数名詞 If you are someone's **junior**, you are younger than they are. 年下 □ *She now lives with actor Denis Lawson, 10 years her junior.* 彼女は現在，10歳年下の俳優デニス・ローソンと暮らしている. **3** N-COUNT 可算名詞 In the United States, a student in the third year of high school or college is called a **junior**. 3年生 □ *Their youngest daughter*

Amy's a junior at the University of Evansville in Indiana. 末娘のエイミーはインディアナ州エバンズビル大学の3年生だ。 **4** N-IN-NAMES 名称中の名詞 **Junior** is sometimes used after the name of the younger of two men in a family who have the same name, sometimes in order to prevent confusion. The abbreviation **Jr.** is also used. ―ジュニア，―2世 [AM 米国英語] □*His son, Arthur Ochs Junior, is expected to succeed him as publisher.* 彼の息子のアーサー・オクス・ジュニアは発行者として彼の跡を継ぐとみられる。

Word Partnership *junior* は次の語句と使われる：

N. junior **executive**, junior **officer**, junior **partner**, junior **senator** **1**

jun|ior high school (junior high schools) also **junior high**
N-VAR; N-IN-NAMES 可変性名詞，名称中の名詞 A **junior high school** or a **junior high** is a school for students from 7th through 9th or 10th grade. 中学校 [AM 米国英語] □*He dropped out of junior high school.* 中学校を中退した。 □*...Benjamin Franklin Junior High.* ベンジャミン・フランクリン中学校

junk /dʒʌŋk/ (junks, junking, junked) **1** N-UNCOUNT 不可算名詞 **Junk** is old and used things that have little value and that you do not want any more. がらくた □*Rose finds her furniture in junk shops.* ローズは中古品店で家具を買う。 **2** V-T 他動詞 If you **junk** something, you get rid of it or stop using it. 捨てる [INFORMAL くだけた] □*Consumers will not have to junk their old cassettes to use the new format.* 消費者は，新形式を使うために古いカセットを捨てる必要はない。

junk bond (junk bonds) N-COUNT 可算名詞 If a company issues **junk bonds**, it borrows money from investors, usually at a high rate of interest, in order to finance a particular deal that is risky. くず物債権 [BUSINESS 実業]

junk food (junk foods) N-MASS 質量名詞 If you refer to food as **junk food**, you mean that it is quick and easy to prepare but is not good for your health. 低栄養価の即製食品 □*Sharon fears that her love of junk food may have contributed to her cancer.* シャーロンは，即製食品が大好きなためにガンになったのではないかと不安に思っている。

junkie /dʒʌŋki/ (junkies) **1** N-COUNT 可算名詞 A **junkie** is a drug addict. 麻薬中毒者 [INFORMAL くだけた] □*...those desperate junkies who have tried every known drug.* 全ての麻薬を試してやけそになった麻薬中毒者 **2** N-COUNT 可算名詞 You can use **junkie** to refer to someone who is very interested in a particular activity, especially when they spend a lot of time on it. 中毒者 [INFORMAL くだけた] □*...a computer junkie.* コンピューター気違い

junk mail N-UNCOUNT 不可算名詞 **Junk mail** is advertisements and publicity materials in your mail that you have not asked for and that you do not want. くず郵便物 □*We still get junk mail from the previous occupants.* 前の住人宛のくず郵便物がまだある。

ju|ris|dic|tion /dʒʊərɪsdɪkʃən/ (jurisdictions) **1** N-UNCOUNT 不可算名詞 **Jurisdiction** is the power that a court of law or an official has to carry out legal judgments or to enforce laws. 裁判権；管轄権 [FORMAL 形式ばった] □*The British police have no jurisdiction over foreign bank accounts.* 英国警察は外国銀行口座に対しては管轄権がない。 **2** N-COUNT 可算名詞 A **jurisdiction** is a state or other area in which a particular court and system of laws has authority. 管轄区 [LEGAL 法律的] □*In the U.K., unlike in most other European jurisdictions, there is no right to strike.* 英国では欧州の他司法管轄区の大部分と違ってストをする権利はない。

ju|ror /dʒʊərər/ (jurors) N-COUNT 可算名詞 A **juror** is a member of a jury. 陪審員 □*The foreman was asked by the clerk whether the jurors had reached verdicts on which they all agreed.* 書記は陪審長に全員一致の評決が決まったかどうか尋ねた。

jury /dʒʊəri/ (juries) **1** N-COUNT-COLL 集合可算名詞 In a court of law, the **jury** is the group of people who have been chosen from the general public to listen to the facts about a crime and to decide whether the person accused is guilty or not. 陪審団 [also 'by' N] □*The jury convicted Mr. Hampson of all offenses.* 陪審団はすべての罪に対してハンプソン氏を有罪とした。 **2** N-COUNT-COLL 集合可算名詞 A **jury** is a group of people who choose the winner of a competition. 審査委員会 □*I am not surprised that the jury chose to award this novel the prize.* 審査委員会が授賞にこの小説を選んだのは当然だと思う。 **3** PHRASE 句 If you say that **the jury is out** or that **the jury is still out** on a particular subject, you mean that people in general have still not made a decision or formed an opinion about that subject. 決定が下されていない □*The jury is out on whether or not this is true.* これが本当かどうかはまだ決定が下されていない。
→ see **trial**

Word Partnership *jury* は次の語句と使われる：

N.	jury **duty**, **trial by** jury **1**
V.	jury **convicts 1**
	jury **announces 1 2**
ADJ.	**hung** jury **1**
	unbiased jury **1 2**

just

❶ ADVERB USES
❷ ADJECTIVE USE

❶ just /dʒʌst/
↪ Please look at meaning **17** to see if the expression you are looking for is shown under another headword. **1** ADV 副詞 You use **just** to say that something happened a very short time ago, or is starting to happen at the present time. For example, if you say that someone **just arrived** or **has just arrived**, you mean that they arrived a very short time ago. たった今；すぐに [ADV before v] □*I've just bought a new house.* 新しい家を買ったばかりだ。 □*I just had the most awful dream.* 最悪の夢をつい今しがた見た。 **2** ADV 副詞 If you say that you are **just** doing something, you mean that you are doing it now and will finish it very soon. If you say that you are **just about to** do something, or **just going to** do it, you mean that you will do it very soon. 今ちょっと，今まさにしようとしている □*I'm just making the sauce for the cauliflower.* 今ちょっとカリフラワー用のソースを作っているのよ。 □*I'm just going to go mail a letter.* ちょうど今から手紙を出しに行くところだ。 **3** ADV 副詞 You can use **just** to emphasize that something is happening at exactly the moment of speaking or at exactly the moment that you are talking about. ちょうど今 [EMPHASIS 強調] □*Randall would just now be getting the Sunday paper.* ランドルは今ちょうど日曜版新聞を取ってきているところだろうよ。 □*Just then the phone rang.* まさにそのときに電話が鳴った。 **4** ADV 副詞 You use **just** to indicate that something is no more important, interesting, or difficult, than you say it is, especially when you want to correct a wrong idea that someone may get or has already gotten. 単なる [EMPHASIS 強調] [ADV group/cl] □*It's just a suggestion.* ただの提案だ。 □*It's not just a financial matter.* 単なる財政の問題だけではない。 **5** ADV 副詞 You use **just** to emphasize that you are talking about a small part, not the whole of an amount. ほんの [EMPHASIS 強調] [ADV n] □*Just one example of the kind of experiments you can do.* きみたちがやってみることできる実験のほんの一例だ。 **6** ADV 副詞 You use **just** to emphasize how small an amount is or how short a length of time is. たった [EMPHASIS 強調] [ADV amount] □*Stephanie and David redecorated a room in just three days.* ステファニーとデイビットはたった3日で部屋の内装をやりかえた。 **7** ADV 副詞 You can use **just** in front of a verb to indicate that the result of something is unfortunate or undesirable and is likely to make the situation worse rather than better. とても [ADV before v] □*By doing what they did, they just hurt the people in their community.* 彼らがそういうことをしたので，地域社会の人たちにたいそう迷惑がかかった。 **8** ADV 副詞 You use **just** to indicate that what you are saying is the case, but only by a very small degree or amount. やっとのことで □*Her hand was just visible in the dimly lit room.* 薄暗いあかりの部屋の中で彼女の手がかろうじて見えた。 □*I arrived just in time for my flight to London.* ロンドン行きの飛行機にやっとのことで間に合うように到着した。 **9** ADV 副詞 You use **just** with "might," "may," and "could," when you mean that there is a small chance of something happening, even though it is not very likely. ほんの少しは [ADV with modal] □*It's an old trick but it just might work.* 使い古しの手だが少しは役に立つかもしれない。 **10** ADV 副詞 You use **just** to emphasize the following word or phrase, in order to express feelings such as annoyance, admiration, or certainty. いったい；まったく [EMPHASIS 強調] □*She just won't relax.* 彼女ったら全然リラックスしないのよ。 **11** ADV 副詞 You use **just** in expressions such as **just a minute** and **just a moment** to ask someone to wait for a short time. ちょっと [SPOKEN 口語] [ADV n] □*"Let me in, Di." — "Okay. Just a minute."* 「入れてくれよ，ダイ」―「うん，ちょっと待って」 **12** ADV 副詞 You can use **just** in expressions such as **just a second** and **just a moment** to interrupt someone, for example, in order to disagree with them, explain something, or calm them down. ともかくちょっと [SPOKEN 口語] [ADV n] □*Well, now just a second, I don't altogether agree.* ええ，まあちょっと待ってください。まったく賛成というわけじゃないんです。 **13** ADV 副詞 You say that you can **just** see or hear something, you mean that it is easy for you to imagine seeing or hearing it. 容易に（―しているのが）想像できる [ADV before v] □*I can just hear her telling her friends, "Well, I blame his mother!"* 彼女の友達に「それでね，悪いのは彼のお母さんなのよ」と言いふらしている姿が目に浮かぶよ。 **14** ADV 副詞 You use **just** in expressions such as **just like**, **just as...as**, and **just the same** when you are emphasizing the similarity between two things or two people. まるで―のように

[EMPHASIS 強調] ❑ *Behind the facade they are just like the rest of us.* 仮面の裏は彼らもまったくわれわれと同じだ。❑ *He worked just as hard as anyone.* 皆と全く同じように一生懸命働いた。 **15** PHRASE 句 You use **just about** to indicate that what you are talking about is so close to being the case that it can be regarded as being the case. ほぼ同然 ❑ *There are those who believe that Nick Price is just about the best golfer in the world.* ニック・プライスは世界一と言えるゴルフ選手と考えている人もいる。 **16** PHRASE 句 You use **just about** to indicate that what you are talking about is in fact the case, but only by a very small degree or amount. ようやく ❑ *I can just about tolerate it at the moment.* 今はなんとか我慢できる。 **17 just my luck →** see **luck 18 not just →** see **not 19 just now →** see **now 20** it **just goes to show →** see **show**

<table>
<tr><td colspan="2">**Thesaurus**   *just* また次を参照:</td></tr>
<tr><td>ADV.</td><td>now, presently ❶ ② ③
only, merely ❶ ④ – ⑥
barely ❶ ⑥ ⑧</td></tr>
</table>

❷ just /dʒʌst/ ADJ 形容詞 If you describe a situation, action, or idea as **just**, you mean that it is right or acceptable according to particular moral principles, such as respect for all human beings. 正義の；正当な [FORMAL 形式ばった] ❑ *They believe that they are fighting a just war.* 彼らは正義の戦争のために戦っていると信じている。 ●**just|ly** ADV 副詞 [ADV with v] 正しく；公正に ❑ *They were not treated justly in the past.* 過去彼らは公正には取り扱われていなかった。

jus|tice /dʒʌstɪs/ (justices) **1** N-UNCOUNT 不可算名詞 **Justice** is fairness in the way that people are treated. 正義；公平 ❑ *He has a good overall sense of justice and fairness.* 彼は全般的に公平公正な感覚を持っている。 ❑ *He only wants freedom, justice and equality.* 自由，正義，平等を望んでいるだけだ。 **2** N-UNCOUNT 不可算名詞 The **justice** of a cause, claim, or argument is its quality of being reasonable, fair, or right. 妥当性；公正；正義 ❑ *We are a minority and must convince people of the justice of our cause.* 我々は少数派であり，大義の正当性を人々に説得しなければならない。 **3** N-UNCOUNT 不可算名詞 **Justice** is the legal system that a country uses in order to deal with people who break the law. 司法 ❑ *Many in Toronto's black community feel that the justice system does not treat them fairly.* トロントの黒人社会の大部分は，司法制度から公平な扱いを受けていないと思っている。 **4** N-COUNT 可算名詞 A **justice** is a judge. 裁判官，判事 [AM 米国英語] ❑ *Thomas will be sworn in today as a justice on the Supreme Court.* トマスは最高裁判所の裁判官として今日宣誓就任する。 **5** N-TITLE 称号名詞 **Justice** is used before the names of judges. 一裁判官，一判事 ❑ *A preliminary hearing was due to start today before Justice Hutchison, but was adjourned.* 今日ハッチソン裁判官のもとで事前審理が開始される予定だったが延期となった。 **6** PHRASE 句 If a criminal is **brought to justice**, he or she is punished for a crime by being arrested and tried in a court of law. 裁判にかける ❑ *They demanded that those responsible be brought to justice.* 責任者たちを裁判にかけるように要求した。 **7** PHRASE 句 To **do justice** to a person or thing means to reproduce them accurately and show how good they are. 真価を示す ❑ *The photograph I had seen didn't do her justice.* 私が見た写真は彼女のよさが写っていなかった。 **8** PHRASE 句 If you **do justice to** someone or something, you deal with them properly and completely. 公平に扱う ❑ *No one article can ever do justice to the topic of fraud.* 詐欺の話題についてはどのような記事でも公平に評価することはできない。 **9** PHRASE 句 If you **do yourself justice**, you do something as well as you are capable of doing it. 発揮する ❑ *I don't think he did himself justice in the game today.* 今日の試合では彼は実力を発揮していなかったと思う。

<table>
<tr><td colspan="2">**Word Partnership**   *justice* は次の語句と使われる:</td></tr>
<tr><td>V.</td><td>**seek** justice ❶</td></tr>
<tr><td>ADJ.</td><td>**racial** justice, **social** justice ❶
criminal justice, **equal** justice ❸</td></tr>
<tr><td>N.</td><td>**obstruction of** justice, justice **system** ❸</td></tr>
</table>

jus|ti|fi|able /dʒʌstɪfaɪəbᵊl/ ADJ 形容詞 An action, situation, emotion, or idea that is **justifiable** is acceptable or correct because

there is a good reason for it. 筋の通った ❑ *The violence of the revolutionary years was justifiable on the grounds of political necessity.* 革命時代の暴力は政治的必要性を根拠として正当と認められた。 ●**jus|ti|fi|ably** /dʒʌstɪfaɪəbli/ ADV 副詞 当然のこととして ❑ *He was justifiably proud of his achievements.* 自分の業績を当然誇りにしていた

jus|ti|fi|ca|tion /dʒʌstɪfɪkeɪʃᵊn/ (justifications) N-VAR 可変性名詞 A **justification for** something is an acceptable reason or explanation for it. 弁明 ❑ *To me the only justification for a zoo is educational.* 動物園があってもいいというのは私にすれば教育的な理由だけだ。

jus|ti|fied /dʒʌstɪfaɪd/ **1** ADJ 形容詞 If you describe a decision, action, or idea as **justified**, you think it is reasonable and acceptable. 正しいとする ❑ *In my opinion, the decision was wholly justified.* 私の意見ではその判断はまったく正しかった。 **2** ADJ 形容詞 If you think that someone is **justified** in doing something, you think that their reasons for doing it are good and valid. 正当化する [v-link ADJ 'in' -ing] ❑ *He's absolutely justified in resigning. He was treated shamefully.* 彼が辞職するのもまったくだ。けしからぬ扱いを受けたから。

jus|ti|fy /dʒʌstɪfaɪ/ (justifies, justifying, justified) **1** V-T 他動詞 To **justify** a decision, action, or idea means to show or prove that it is reasonable or necessary. 正当化する ❑ *No argument can justify a war.* どのような議論も戦争を正当化することはできない。 **2** V-T 他動詞 To **justify** printed text means to adjust the spaces between the words so that each line of type is exactly the same length. 行末をそろえる ❑ *Click on this icon to align or justify text at both the left and right margins.* 左端と右端で行をそろえるためにはこのアイコンをクリックする。 **3 →** see also **left-justify**

just|ly /dʒʌstli/ **1** ADV 副詞 You use **justly** to show that you approve of someone's attitude toward something, because it seems to be based on truth or reality. 正当に [APPROVAL 賛成] ❑ *Australians are justly proud of their native wildlife.* オーストラリア人は当然ながら土地の野生動物を誇りにしている。 **2 →** see also **just**

jut /dʒʌt/ (juts, jutting, jutted) **1** V-I 自動詞 If something **juts out**, it sticks out above or beyond a surface. 突き出る ❑ *The northern end of the island juts out like a long, thin finger into the sea.* その島の北端は細長い指のように海に突き出ている。 **2** V-T/V-I 他動詞/自動詞 If you **jut** a part of your body, especially your chin, or if it **juts**, you push it forward in an aggressive or determined way. 張り出す ❑ *His jaw jutted stubbornly forward; he would not be denied.* 彼はあごを前に頑固に突き出した。拒否されてたまるか。❑ *Gwen jutted her chin forward, her nose in the air, and did not bother to answer the teacher.* グエンはあごの先を突き出し，鼻をツンと上に向けて，先生に答えようとはしなかった。

ju|ve|nile /dʒuvənᵊl, -naɪl/ (juveniles) **1** N-COUNT 可算名詞 A **juvenile** is a child or young person who is not yet old enough to be regarded as an adult. 未成年者 [FORMAL 形式ばった] ❑ *The number of juveniles in the general population has fallen by a fifth in the past 10 years.* 一般人口の未成年者数は過去10年間で5分の1減少している。 **2** ADJ 形容詞 **Juvenile** activity or behavior involves young people who are not yet adults. 未成年の [ADJ n] ❑ *Juvenile crime is increasing at a terrifying rate.* 未成年者の犯罪は恐ろしいほどの割合で増加している。

jux|ta|pose /dʒʌkstəpoʊz/ (juxtaposes, juxtaposing, juxtaposed) V-T 他動詞 If you **juxtapose** two contrasting objects, images, or ideas, you place them together or describe them together, so that the differences between them are emphasized. 並列する [FORMAL 形式ばった] ❑ *The technique Mr. Wilson uses most often is to juxtapose things for dramatic effect.* ウイルソン氏が最もよく使う技法は，劇的な効果のために物事を並列することだ。 ❑ *Contemporary photographs are juxtaposed with a sixteenth century, copper Portuguese mirror.* 近代写真は，16世紀のポルトガル銅鏡と並置されている。

jux|ta|po|si|tion /dʒʌkstəpəzɪʃᵊn/ (juxtapositions) N-VAR 可変性名詞 The **juxtaposition of** two contrasting objects, images, or ideas is the fact that they are placed together or described together, so that the differences between them are emphasized. 並列 [FORMAL 形式ばった] ❑ *This juxtaposition of brutal reality and lyrical beauty runs through Park's stories.* パークの小説は，残酷な現実と叙情的な美の並列でつらぬかれている。

Kk

K also k /keɪ/ **(K's, k's)** N-VAR 可変性名詞 K is the eleventh letter of the English alphabet. 英字5番目のアルファベット

kan|ga|roo /kæŋgərˈuː/ **(kangaroos)** N-COUNT 可算名詞 A **kangaroo** is a large Australian animal which moves by jumping on its back legs. Female kangaroos carry their babies in a pouch on their stomach. カンガルー

ka|ra|te /kərˈɑːti/ N-UNCOUNT 不可算名詞 **Karate** is a Japanese sport or way of fighting in which people fight using their hands, elbows, feet, and legs. 空手

keel /kiːl/ **(keels, keeling, keeled)** ■ N-COUNT 可算名詞 The **keel** of a boat is the long, specially shaped piece of wood or steel along the bottom of it. 竜骨 ❑ *The keel hit the rock first.* まず竜骨が岩にぶつかった. ② PHRASE 句 If you say that someone or something is **on an even keel**, you mean that they are working or progressing smoothly and steadily, without any sudden changes. 安定して ❑ *Jason had helped him out with a series of loans, until he could get back on an even keel.* ジェーソンは彼が安定を取り戻すまで一連のローンの支払いを援助した.
▶ **keel over** PHRASAL VERB 句動詞 If someone **keels over**, they collapse because they are tired or ill. 気絶する, 倒れる [INFORMAL くだけた] ❑ *He then keeled over and fell flat on his back.* そして彼は気絶したりとおあむけに倒れた.

keen /kiːn/ **(keener, keenest)** ■ ADJ 形容詞 If you say that someone has a **keen** mind, you mean that they are very clever and aware of what is happening around them. 鋭い, 鋭敏な [ADJ n] ❑ *They described him as a man of keen intellect.* 彼らは彼のことを鋭敏な知性の持ち主だと言った. ● **keen|ly** ADV 副詞 鋭く, 痛烈に ❑ *They're keenly aware that whatever they decide will set a precedent.* 彼らはどのような決定を下してもそれが前例になることを強く意識していた. ② ADJ 形容詞 If you have a **keen** eye or ear, you are able to notice things that are difficult to detect. 鋭敏な ❑ *...an amateur artist with a keen eye for detail.* 細かいところにまで目の届くアマチュア芸術家. ● **keen|ly** ADV 副詞 [ADV with v] 鋭敏に ❑ *Charles listened keenly.* チャールズは熱心に聞き入った. ③ ADJ 形容詞 A **keen** interest or emotion is one that is very intense. 強い [mainly BRIT 主に英国英語] ❑ *He had retained a keen interest in the progress of the work.* 彼はその作業の進行に強い関心を持ち続けた. ● **keen|ly** 副詞 強い ❑ *She remained keenly interested in international affairs.* 相変わらず彼女は国際情勢に強い関心を持っていた. ④ ADJ 形容詞 [v-link ADJ] If you are **keen on** doing something, you very much want to do it. とてもしたい, 熱心で ❑ *You're not keen on going, are you?* あんまり行く気がしないんでしょう? ● **keen|ness** N-UNCOUNT 不可算名詞 熱心さ ❑ *...Doyle's keenness to please.* ドイルの人を楽しませることへの情熱. ⑤ ADJ 形容詞 [v-link ADJ 'on' n] If you are **keen on** something, you like it a lot and are very enthusiastic about it. 大好き ❑ *I wasn't too keen on physics and chemistry.* 物理と科学はあまり好きではなかった. ⑥ ADJ 形容詞 You use **keen** to indicate that someone has a lot of enthusiasm for a particular activity and spends a lot of time doing it. 熱心な ❑ *She was a keen amateur photographer.* 彼女は熱心なアマチュア写真家だった. ⑦ ADJ 形容詞 A **keen** fight or competition is one in which the competitors are all trying very hard to win, and it is not easy to predict who will win. 激しい [mainly BRIT 主に英国英語] ● **keen|ly** ADV 副詞 激しく ❑ *The contest should be very keenly fought.* その競争はとても激しい戦いとなるであろう.

---

keep

❶ REMAIN, STAY, OR CONTINUE TO HAVE/DO
❷ STOP OR PREVENT
❸ SUPPORT, PROVIDE FOR
❹ NOUN USE
❺ PHRASAL VERBS

---

❶ **keep** /kiːp/ **(keeps, keeping, kept)** ■ V-LINK 連結動詞 If someone **keeps** or **is kept** in a particular state, they remain in it. 保つ ❑ *The noise kept him awake.* 騒音のせいで彼は眠れなかった. ❑ *People had to burn these trees to keep warm during harsh winters.* 過酷な冬の間, 人々は暖を取るためにこれらの木を燃やさなければならなかった. ② V-T/V-I 他動詞/自動詞 If you **keep** or you **are kept** in a particular position or place, you remain in it. 保つ ❑ *Keep away*

from the doors while the train is moving. 電車が動いている間はドアから離れてください. ❑ *He kept his head down, hiding his features.* 彼は目立たないように隠れていた. ③ V-I 自動詞 If you **keep off** something or **keep away from** it, you avoid it. If you **keep out of** something, you avoid getting involved in it. 避ける ❑ *I managed to stick to the diet and keep off sweet foods.* わたしはその食事療法を守って甘い物を避けることができた. ④ V-T 他動詞 If you **keep** doing something, you do it repeatedly or continue to do it. 続ける ❑ *I keep forgetting it's December.* 今は12月だということを忘れてばかりいる. ● PHRASAL VERB 句動詞 **Keep on** means the same as **keep**. 続ける ❑ *Did he give up or keep on trying?* 彼はあきらめたか, それとも頑張り続けたか? ⑤ V-T 他動詞 **Keep** is used with some nouns to indicate that someone does something for a period of time or continues to do it. For example, if you **keep a grip on** something, you continue to hold or control it. ～し続ける ❑ *Until last year, the regime kept a tight grip on the country.* 昨年までは政権は国をしっかり支配していた. ⑥ V-T 他動詞 If you **keep** something, you continue to have it in your possession and do not throw it away, give it away, or sell it. 持ち続ける, 取っておく ❑ *We must decide what to keep and what to give away.* 何を取っておいて, 何を寄付するのか決めなければならない. ⑦ V-T 他動詞 If you **keep** something in a particular place, you always have it or store it in that place so that you can use it whenever you need it. しまっておく ❑ *She kept her money under the mattress.* 彼女はお金をマットレスの下にしまっていた. ⑧ V-T 他動詞 When you **keep** something such as a promise or an appointment, you do what you said you would do. 守る ❑ *I'm hoping you'll keep your promise to come for a long visit.* あなたがお約束を守ってうちにゆっくり滞在しに来てくれるといいと思っている. ⑨ V-T 他動詞 If you **keep** a record of a series of events, you write down details of it so that they can be referred to later. つける ❑ *Eleanor began to keep a diary.* エレナーは日記をつけ始めた. ⑩ V-I 自動詞 If food **keeps** for a certain length of time, it stays fresh and suitable to eat for that time. もつ ❑ *Whatever is left over may be put into the refrigerator, where it will keep for 2-3 weeks.* 残ったものは全て冷蔵庫に入れておけば2-3週間もつでしょう. ⑪ V-I 自動詞 You can say or ask how someone **is keeping** as a way of saying or asking whether they are well. ～している [only cont] ❑ *She hasn't been keeping too well lately.* 彼女は最近あまり調子が良くなかった. ⑫ PHRASE 句 If you **keep at it**, you continue doing something that you have started, even if you are tired and would prefer to stop. 根気良く続ける ❑ *It may take a number of attempts, but it is worth keeping at it.* 何度か試さなければだめかもしれないけど, 根気良く続ける価値はある. ⑬ PHRASE 句 If you **keep going**, you continue moving or doing something that you have started, even if you are tired and would prefer to stop. 頑張る ❑ *She forced herself to keep going.* 彼女は無理してまで頑張った. ⑭ PHRASE 句 If one thing is **in keeping with** another, it is suitable in relation to that thing. If one thing is **out of keeping with** another, you mean that it is not suitable in relation to that thing. 調和して, 調和しないで ❑ *This is not in keeping with our objective of representing the community.* これは地域を代表するという我々の目標から外れている. ⑮ PHRASE 句 If you **keep it up**, you continue working or trying as hard as you have been in the past. 頑張り続ける ❑ *There are fears that he will not be able to keep it up when he gets to the particularly demanding third year.* 特に過酷な3年目になると彼はついて行けなくなる恐れがあった. ⑯ PHRASE 句 If you **keep** something **to yourself**, you do not tell anyone else about it. 秘密にする ❑ *I have to tell someone. I can't keep it to myself.* 誰かに言わなくてはならなかった. 人に言わないわけにはいかなかった. ⑰ PHRASE 句 If you **keep to yourself**, you stay on your own most of the time and do not mix socially with other people. つきあいを避ける ❑ *He was a quiet man who always kept to himself.* 彼は物静かな男で, いつも人づきあいを避けていた. ⑱ **to keep** someone **company** → see **company** ⑲ **to keep a straight face** → see **face** ⑳ **to keep** your **head** → see **head** ㉑ **to keep pace** → see **pace** ㉒ **to keep the peace** → see **peace** ㉓ **to keep quiet** → see **quiet** ㉔ **to keep a secret** → see **secret** ㉕ **keep time** → see **time** ㉖ **to keep track** → see **track**

❷ **keep** /kiːp/ **(keeps, keeping, kept)** ■ V-T 他動詞 If someone or something **keeps** you **from** a particular action, they prevent you from doing it. ～させない ❑ *Embarrassment has kept me from doing all sorts of things.* わたしはきまりが悪くてできないことが多かった. ② V-T 他動詞 If someone or something **keeps** you, they delay you and make you late. 引き留める ❑ *Sorry to keep you, Jack.* 待たせ

てごめんなさいね、ジャック. ❸ V-T 他動詞 If you **keep** something from someone, you do not tell them about it. 隠す *She knew that Gabriel was keeping something from her.* ガブリエルが何か隠し事をしていることに彼女は気づいていた.

❸ **keep** /kiːp/ (keeps, keeping, kept) ■ N-SING 単数名詞 Someone's **keep** is the cost of food and other things that they need in their daily life. 糧 *Ray will earn his keep on local farms while studying.* レイは勉強している間、地元の農場で働いて糧を得るつもりです. ❷ V-T 他動詞 If you **keep** animals, you own them and take care of them. 飼う *I've brought you some eggs. We keep chickens.* 卵を持ってきたよ. わたしたちは鶏を飼っているんだ. ❸ V-T 他動詞 If you **keep** yourself or **keep** someone else, you support yourself or the other person by earning enough money to provide food, clothing, money, and other necessary things. 養う [mainly BRIT 主に英国英語] *She could just about afford to keep her five kids.* 彼女は5人の子供を養うのがやっとだった. *I just cannot afford to keep myself.* わたしはとても自活できない.

❹ **keep** /kiːp/ (keeps) N-COUNT 可算名詞 A **keep** is the main tower of a medieval castle, in which people lived. 本丸 *...the first stone-built castle keep in Britain.* 英国で最初の石造りの本丸.

❺ **keep** /kiːp/ (keeps, keeping, kept)
▶ **keep down** ■ PHRASAL VERB 句動詞 If you **keep** the number, size, or amount of something **down**, you do not let it get bigger or go higher. 保つ *The prime aim is to keep inflation down.* 最も重要なのはインフレを低く保つことだ. ❷ PHRASAL VERB 句動詞 If someone **keeps** a group of people **down**, they prevent them from getting power and status and being completely free. 抑圧する *No matter what a woman tries to do to improve her situation, there is some barrier or attitude to keep her down.* 女性が状況改善を目指してどんなことをしようとも、女性を抑圧しようとする障壁や態度にぶち当たる. ❸ PHRASAL VERB 句動詞 If you **keep** food or drink **down**, you manage to swallow it properly and not vomit, even though you feel sick. 吐き戻さないようにする *I tried to give her something to drink but she couldn't keep it down.* 彼女に飲み物をあげようとしたが、吐いてしまった.
▶ **keep on** ■ → see keep ❸ ❹ ❷ PHRASAL VERB 句動詞 If you **keep** someone **on**, you continue to employ them, for example after other employees have lost their jobs. 雇い続ける *They concluded that firing him would be more damaging than keeping him on.* 彼を雇い続けるより首にしたほうが弊害が大きいとの結論を出した.
▶ **keep to** ■ PHRASAL VERB 句動詞 If you **keep to** a rule, plan, or agreement, you do exactly what you are expected or supposed to do. 守る *You've got to keep to the speed limit.* 速度制限は守らなければいけない. ❷ PHRASAL VERB 句動詞 If you **keep to** something such as a path or river, you do not move away from it as you go somewhere. それない *Please keep to the paths.* 歩道からそれないでください. ❸ PHRASAL VERB 句動詞 If you **keep to** a particular subject, you talk only about that subject, and do not talk about anything else. それない *Let's keep to the subject, or you'll get me too confused.* 本題からそれないようにしましょう. そうでなければ私は混乱します. ❹ PHRASAL VERB 句動詞 If you **keep** something **to** a particular number or quantity, you limit it to that number or quantity. 抑える *Keep costs to a minimum.* 費用を最低限に抑えること.
▶ **keep up** ■ PHRASAL VERB 句動詞 If you **keep up with** someone or something that is moving near you, you move at the same speed. 遅れない *He lengthened his stride to keep up with his father.* 父親に遅れないようにするため、彼は歩幅を広げた. ❷ PHRASAL VERB 句動詞 To **keep up with** something that is changing means to be able to cope with the change, usually by changing at the same rate. 同じ速度で進む *The union called the strike to press for wage increases which keep up with inflation.* インフレ率に合わせた賃上要求で、組合はストライキを呼びかけた. ❸ PHRASAL VERB 句動詞 If you **keep up with** your work or **with** other people, you manage to do or understand all your work, or to do or understand it as well as other people. 遅れないようにする *Penny tended to work through her lunch hour in an effort to keep up with her work.* ペニーは仕事をこなすため、お昼休みも働き続けることがままあった. ❹ PHRASAL VERB 句動詞 If you **keep up with** what is happening, you make sure that you know about it. 遅れない *She did not bother to keep up with the news.* 彼女はわざわざニュースを追おうとはしなかった. ❺ PHRASAL VERB 句動詞 If you **keep** something **up**, you continue to do it or provide it. 維持する *I was so hungry all the time that I could not keep the diet up for longer than a month.* 常におなかがすいていたので1ヵ月以上ダイエットを続けることは不可能だった. ❻ PHRASAL VERB 句動詞 If you **keep** something **up**, you prevent it from growing less in amount, level, or degree. 維持する *The riders had to keep their pace up.* 乗り手は速度を保たねばならなかった. ❼ → see also keep ❸ 15

keep|er /kiːpər/ (keepers) ■ N-COUNT 可算名詞 In football, a **keeper** is a play in which the quarterback keeps the ball. キープ [AM 米国英語] ❷ N-COUNT 可算名詞 A **keeper** at a zoo is a person who takes care of the animals. 飼育係 ❸ N-COUNT 可算名詞 A **keeper** is something or someone that you value and that you feel is worth keeping. 保つのに値するもの [AM 米国英語, INFORMAL くだけた] *The show's a keeper – daring, imaginative and provocative.* そのショーは続ける価値があった. 大胆で、創意に富んでいて、挑発的だったのだ. *His sweet nature and kindness made him a keeper, she said.* 思いやりのある性格とやさしさが彼にはあるから気に入っているのよ、と彼女は言った.

ken|nel /kenᵊl/ (kennels) ■ N-COUNT 可算名詞 A **kennel** is a place where dogs are bred and trained, or cared for when their owners are away. 犬舎、犬を預る所 *Once you have chosen a kennel, make a booking for your pet.* ペットを預ってくれる場所を選んだら、予約をするように. ❷ N-COUNT 可算名詞 A **kennel** is a small building made especially for a dog to sleep in. 犬小屋 [mainly BRIT 主に英国英語; AM usually **doghouse** 米国英語では通常 **doghouse**]

kept /kept/ **Kept** is the past tense and past participle of **keep**. keepの過去・過去分詞

kerb /kɜːrb/ → see **curb** 3

kero|sene /kerəsiːn/ N-UNCOUNT 不可算名詞 **Kerosene** is a clear, strong-smelling liquid which is used as a fuel, for example in heaters and lamps. 灯油 [mainly AM 主に米国英語] *...a kerosene lamp.* 灯油ランプ.
→ see **dry-cleaning**

ket|tle /ketᵊl/ (kettles) ■ N-COUNT 可算名詞 A **kettle** is a covered container that you use for boiling water. It has a handle, and a spout for the water to come out of. やかん *I'll put the kettle on and make us some tea.* お湯を沸かしてお茶を入れましょうね. ❷ N-COUNT 可算名詞 A **kettle of** water is the amount of water contained in a kettle. やかんいっぱい [AM also **teakettle** 米国英語、また **teakettle**] *Pour a kettle of boiling water over the onions.* 玉ねぎにやかんいっぱいの熱湯をかけること. ❸ PHRASE 句 If you say that something is a **different kettle of fish**, you mean that it is very different from another related thing that you are talking about. 別のもの [INFORMAL くだけた] *Banking today is a very different kettle of fish from the industry of the past.* 現在の銀行業は過去のものとはまったく別のものだ.

key /kiː/ (keys, keying, keyed) ■ N-COUNT 可算名詞 A **key** is a specially shaped piece of metal that you place in a lock and turn in order to open or lock a door, or to start or stop the engine of a vehicle. 鍵 *They put the key in the door and entered.* 彼らは鍵をドアに差し込んで中に入った. ❷ N-COUNT 可算名詞 The **keys** on a computer keyboard or typewriter are the buttons that you press in order to operate it. キー *Finally, press the Delete key.* 最後に削除キーを押すこと. ❸ N-COUNT 可算名詞 The **keys** of a piano or organ are the long narrow pieces of wood or plastic that you press in order to play it. 鍵 *...the black and white keys on a piano keyboard.* ピアノ鍵盤の黒鍵と白鍵. ❹ N-VAR 可変性名詞 In music, a **key** is a scale of musical notes that starts on one specific note. 主音 *...the key of A minor.* イ短調. ❺ N-COUNT 可算名詞 The **key** on a map or diagram or in a technical book is a list of the symbols or abbreviations used and their meanings. 略語・記号一覧 *You will find a key at the front of the book.* 略語および記号一覧は本の最初にあります. ❻ ADJ 形容詞 The **key** person or thing in a group is the most important one. 重要な [ADJ n] *He is expected to be the key witness at the trial.* 彼はその裁判の重要な証人になるでしょう. ❼ N-COUNT 可算名詞 The **key** to a desirable situation or result is the way in which it can be achieved. 秘訣 *The key to success is to be ready from the start.* 成功の秘訣は始めから準備を整えていることです. ❽ N-COUNT 可算名詞 A **key** is a small low island or reef, especially one in the Gulf of Mexico. キー *...the Florida Keys.* フロリダ・キーズ.
▶ **key in** PHRASAL VERB 句動詞 If you **key** something **in**, you put information into a computer or you give the computer a particular instruction by typing the information or instruction on the keyboard. キーを打って入力する *Brian keyed in his personal code.* ブライアンは個人暗号を打ち込んだ.
→ see **graph**

Thesaurus		*key* また次を参照:
N.	code, explanation, guide	❺
ADJ.	critical, important, major, vital	❻

Word Partnership		*key* は次の語句と使われる:
V.	turn a key	■
N.	key component, key decision, key factor, key figure, key ingredient, key issue, key official, key player, key point, key question, key role, key word	❻
	key to success	❼

key|board /kiːbɔːrd/ (keyboards) ■ N-COUNT 可算名詞 The **keyboard** of a typewriter or computer is the set of keys that you press in order to operate it. キーボード *He was in his office, battering the keyboard of his computer as if it were an old manual typewriter.* 彼は事務所でコンピューターのキーボードを古い手動のタイプライターであるかのように乱打していた. ❷ N-COUNT 可算名詞 The **keyboard** of a piano or organ is the set of black and

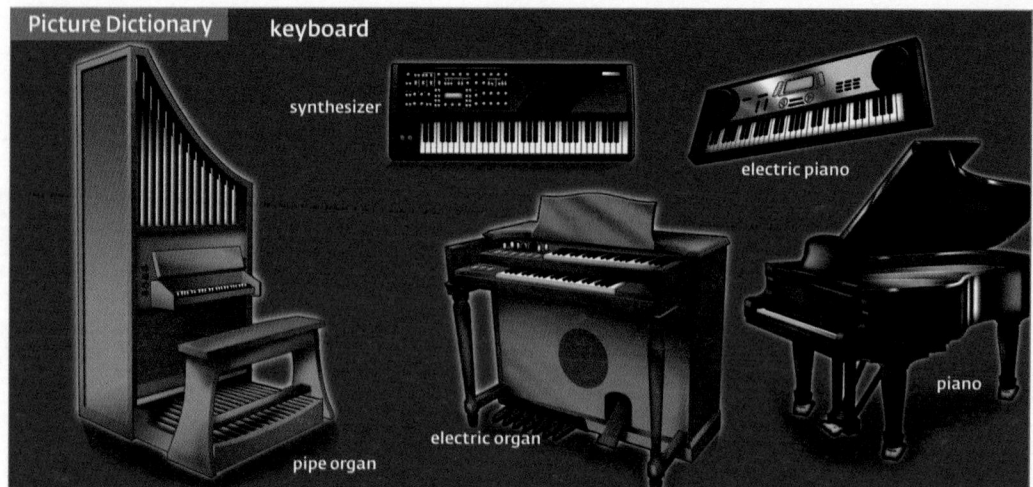

Picture Dictionary   **keyboard**

synthesizer

electric piano

electric organ

pipe organ

piano

white keys that you press in order to play it. けん盤 □ *Tanya's hands rippled over the keyboard.* タニアの手はけん盤の上でさざ波のように動いた. **3** N-COUNT 可算名詞 People sometimes refer to musical instruments that have a keyboard as **keyboards**. キーボード □ *...Sean O'Hagan on keyboards.* キーボード担当、ショーン・オ・ヘイガン.
→ see Picture Dictionary: **keyboard**
→ see **computer**

key card (key cards) N-COUNT 可算名詞 A **key card** is a small plastic card which you can use instead of a key to open a door or barrier, for example in some hotels and parking lots. カード式かぎ □ *The electronic key card to Julie's room would not work.* ジューリーの部屋のカード式かぎは作動しなかった.

key|note /kíːnoʊt/ (keynotes) N-COUNT 可算名詞 The **keynote** of a policy, speech, or idea is the main theme of it or the part of it that is emphasized the most. 基調 □ *He would be setting out his plans for the party in a keynote speech.* 彼は基調演説で自らの党のための計画をはっきりと述べるであろう.

key|pad /kíːpæd/ (keypads) N-COUNT 可算名詞 The **keypad** on a telephone is the set of buttons that you press in order to operate it. Some other machines, such as ATMs, also have a keypad. キーパッド □ *...an elevator's push-button keypad.* エレベーターの押しボタンのキーパッド.

key|stone /kíːstoʊn/ (keystones) **1** N-COUNT 可算名詞 A **keystone** of a policy, system, or process is an important part of it, which is the basis for later developments. 基本原理 □ *The government's determination to beat inflation has so far been the keystone of its economic policy.* インフレを克服すると言う政府が決意したことが現在のところ経済政策の基本原理をなしている. **2** N-COUNT 可算名詞 A **keystone** is a stone at the top of an arch, which keeps the other stones in place by its weight and position. かなめ石 [TECHNICAL 技術的]
→ see **architecture**

key|stroke /kíːstroʊk/ (keystrokes) N-COUNT 可算名詞 A **keystroke** is one touch of one of the keys on a computer or typewriter keyboard. キーのひと打ち □ *With a few keystrokes, Rebecca was connected to her computer at Liberty Air Service.* レベッカは少しキーを打っただけで、リバティーエアサービス社の自分のコンピュータに接続した.

kg kg is a written abbreviation for **kilogram** or **kilograms**. kilogramの略

kha|ki /kǽki/ **1** N-UNCOUNT 不可算名詞 **Khaki** is a strong material of a beige color, used especially to make uniforms for some soldiers. カーキ色布の □ *On each side of me was a figure in khaki.* カーキ色の服を着た人がわたしの両側に一人ずついた. **2** COLOR 色彩語 Something that is **khaki** is beige in color. カーキ色 □ *He was dressed in khaki trousers.* 彼はカーキ色のズボンをはいていた.

kick /kík/ (kicks, kicking, kicked) **1** V-T/V-I 他動詞/自動詞 If you **kick** someone or something, you hit them forcefully with your foot. ける □ *He kicked the door hard.* 彼はドアを激しくけった. □ *He threw me to the ground and started to kick.* 彼はわたしを地べたに投げ飛ばしてけり始めた. ●N-COUNT 可算名詞 **Kick** is also a noun. けること、けり □ *He suffered a kick to the knee.* 彼は膝をけられた. **2** V-T 他動詞 When you **kick** a ball or other object, you hit it with your foot so that it moves through the air. ける、け飛ばす □ *I went to kick the ball and I completely missed it.* わたしはボールをけ

ろうとしたが完全に逃した. □ *He kicked the ball away.* 彼はボールをけ飛ばした. ●N-COUNT 可算名詞 **Kick** is also a noun. キック □ *He missed an easy kick.* 彼は簡単なキックを逃した. **3** V-T/V-I 他動詞/自動詞 If you **kick** or if you **kick** your legs, you move your legs with very quick, small, and forceful movements, once or repeatedly. けり上げる、ける □ *They were dragged away struggling and kicking.* 彼らはもがきながら引きずられて行った. □ *First he kicked the left leg, then he kicked the right.* まず彼は左足をけり上げ、そして右足をけり上げた. ●PHRASAL VERB 句動詞 **Kick out** means the same as **kick**. ける □ *As its rider tried to free it, the horse kicked out and rolled over, crushing her.* 騎手がそれを手放そうとすると馬は脚をけり上げ彼女を押しつぶして横倒しになった. **4** V-T 他動詞 If you **kick** your legs, you lift your legs up very high one after the other, for example when you are dancing. けり上げる □ *...kicking his legs like a cancan dancer.* カンカンの踊り子のように脚をけり上げながら. **5** V-T 他動詞 If you **kick** a habit, you stop doing something that is bad for you and that you find difficult to stop doing. やめる [INFORMAL くだけた] □ *She's kicked her drug habit and learned that her life has value.* 彼女は麻薬をやめて、自分が生きてゆく価値があることに気づいた. **6** N-SING 単数名詞 If something gives you **a kick**, it makes you feel very excited or very happy for a short period of time. 興奮 [INFORMAL くだけた] □ *I got a kick out of seeing my name in print.* 自分の名前が印刷されているのを見てわたしは興奮した. **7** PHRASE 句 If you say that someone **kicks** you **when you are down**, you think they are behaving unfairly because they are attacking you when you are in a weak position. □ *In the end I just couldn't kick Jimmy when he was down.* 結局のところ落ち込んでいるジミーの弱みにつけこむことは出来なかった. **8** PHRASE 句 If you say that someone does something **for kicks**, you mean that they do it because they think it will be exciting. 刺激を求めて [INFORMAL くだけた] □ *They made a few small bets for kicks.* 彼らは刺激を求めて数回だけ小さい賭けをした. **9** PHRASE 句 If you say that someone is dragged **kicking and screaming into** a particular course of action, you are emphasizing that they are very unwilling to do what they are being made to do. 泣きわめくほどいやいやながら [EMPHASIS 強調] □ *He had to be dragged kicking and screaming into action.* ジタバタする彼に無理やりやらせなければならなかった. **10** PHRASE 句 If you describe an event as **a kick in the teeth**, you are emphasizing that it is very disappointing and upsetting. ひどい仕打ち、失望 [INFORMAL くだけた, EMPHASIS 強調] □ *We've been struggling for years and it's a real kick in the teeth to see a new band make it ahead of us.* 長年苦労しているので新しいバンドが自分たちより先に成功してひどい挫折感を味わっている. **11** to **kick up a fuss** → see **fuss**

▶ **kick around** PHRASAL VERB 句動詞 If you **kick around** ideas or suggestions, you discuss them informally. あれこれ考える、検討する □ *We kicked a few ideas around.* わたしたちはいくつかのアイディアを検討した. □ *They started to kick around the idea of going to Brazil next month.* 来月ブラジルに行くという案について彼らは検討し始めた.

▶ **kick off 1** PHRASAL VERB 句動詞 In soccer or football, when the players **kick off**, they start a game by kicking the ball. 試合を開始する □ *They kicked off an hour ago.* 試合は1時間前に始まりました. **2** PHRASAL VERB 句動詞 In football, when the players **kick off**, they resume a game by kicking the ball. 再開する **3** PHRASAL VERB 句動詞 If an event, game, series, or discussion **kicks off**, or is **kicked off**, it begins. 始める □ *The shows kick off on October 24th.* ショーは10月24日に始まる. □ *The mayor kicked off the party.* 市長がパーティーを開始した. **4** PHRASAL VERB 句動詞 If you **kick off** your

shoes, you shake your feet so that your shoes come off. けって脱ぐ ❑ *She stretched out on the sofa and kicked off her shoes.* 彼女はソファーの上で足を伸ばし靴をけって脱いだ. **5** PHRASAL VERB 句動詞 To **kick** someone **off** an area of land means to force them to leave it. 追い払う [INFORMAL くだけた] ❑ *We can't kick them off the island.* 彼らを島から追い払うわけには行かない. ▶ **kick out** PHRASAL VERB 句動詞 To **kick** someone **out of** a place or an organization means to force them to leave it. 追い出す [INFORMAL くだけた] ❑ *The country's leaders kicked five foreign journalists out of the country.* その国の指導者たちは5人の外国人ジャーナリストを国外に追放した. → see also **kick 3**

kick|off /kɪkɔf/ (**kickoffs**) **1** N-VAR 可変性名詞 In football or soccer, the **kickoff** is the time at which a particular game starts. キックオフ ❑ *Hakan Sukur netted the goal just 10.8 seconds after the kickoff.* ハカン・シュクールはキックオフからわずか10.8秒後にゴールを決めた. **2** N-COUNT 可算名詞 In football, a **kickoff** is the kick that begins a play, for example at the beginning of a half or after a touchdown or goal has been scored. キックオフ [AM 米国英語] ❑ *Gunn fumbled away the opening kickoff for the second straight week.* ガンは2週間続けて試合開始のキックオフでファンブルしてボールを失った. **3** N-SING 単数名詞 The **kickoff** of an event or activity is its beginning. 開始 [INFORMAL くだけた] ❑ *Memorial Day weekend marks the kickoff of the summer vacation season.* 戦没兵士記念日の週末から夏の休暇のシーズンが始まる.

kick-start (**kick-starts, kick-starting, kick-started**) also **kickstart 1** V-T 他動詞 To **kick-start** a process that has stopped working or progressing is to take a course of action that will quickly start it going again. 弾みをつける ❑ *The president has chosen to kick-start the economy by slashing interest rates.* 大統領は金利を大幅に下げて経済に弾みをつける道を選んだ. ● N-COUNT 可算名詞 **Kick-start** is also a noun. 弾みをつけること ❑ *The housing market needs a kick-start.* 住宅市場は弾みをつける必要がある. **2** V-T 他動詞 If you **kick-start** a motorcycle, you press the lever that starts it with your foot. キックスターターをふんでエンジンを始動させる ❑ *He lifted the bike off its stand and kick-started it.* 彼はバイクをスタンドから外しスターターをふんで始動させた.

kid /kɪd/ (**kids, kidding, kidded**) **1** N-COUNT 可算名詞 You can refer to a child as a **kid**. 子供 [INFORMAL くだけた] ❑ *They've got three kids.* 彼らには子供が3人いる. **2** V-I 自動詞 If you **are kidding**, you are saying something that is not really true, as a joke. 冗談を言う [INFORMAL くだけた] [usu cont] ❑ *I'm not kidding, Frank. There's a cow out there, just standing around.* フランク、本当だよ. 外に牛が突っ立っているんだ. ❑ *I'm just kidding.* 単なる冗談ですよ. **3** V-T 他動詞 If you **kid** someone, you tease them. からかう ❑ *He liked to kid Ingrid a lot.* 彼はイングリッドを目一杯からかうのが好きだった. **4** V-T 他動詞 If people **kid themselves**, they allow themselves to believe something that is not true because they wish that it was true. 現実を無視する ❑ *We're kidding ourselves, Bill. We're not winning, we're not even doing well.* 僕たちは現実を無視しているよ、ビル、勝ってないし、良くやってるとすらいえない. **5** N-COUNT 可算名詞 A **kid** is a young goat. 子ヤギ **6** PHRASE 句 You can say **"you've got to be kidding"** or **"you must be kidding"** to someone if they have said something that you think is ridiculous or completely untrue. ご冗談でしょう [INFORMAL くだけた, FEELINGS 感情] ❑ *You've got to be kidding! I can't live here!* ご冗談でしょう！ここには住めないわ！

kid|nap /kɪdnæp/ (**kidnaps, kidnaping** or **kidnapping, kidnaped** or **kidnapped**) **1** V-T/V-I 他動詞/自動詞 To **kidnap** someone is to take them away illegally and by force, and usually to hold them prisoner in order to demand something from their family, employer, or government. 誘拐する ❑ *Police in Brazil uncovered a plot to kidnap him.* ブラジルの警察は彼を誘拐する計画を暴いた. ❑ *They were middle-class university students, intelligent and educated, yet they chose to kidnap and kill.* 彼らは中流階級出の大学生で知能も高く、教育も受けていたが、人を誘拐して殺害する道を選んだ. ● **kid|nap|per**

N-COUNT 可算名詞 (**kidnappers**) 誘拐者 ❑ *His kidnappers have threatened that they will kill him unless three militants are released from prison.* 彼を誘拐した者たちは3人の過激派を刑務所から解放しない限り彼を殺すと脅している. ● **kid|nap|ping** (**kidnappings**) N-VAR 可変性名詞 誘拐 ❑ *Two youngsters have been arrested and charged with kidnapping.* 2人の未成年者が誘拐の疑いで逮捕、告発された. **2** N-VAR 可変性名詞 **Kidnap** or a **kidnap** is the crime of taking someone away by force. 誘拐 ❑ *Stewart denies attempted murder and kidnap.* スチュアートは殺人未遂と誘拐罪を否定している.

kid|ney /kɪdni/ (**kidneys**) **1** N-COUNT 可算名詞 Your **kidneys** are the organs in your body that take waste matter from your blood and send it out of your body as urine. 腎臓 ❑ *...a kidney transplant.* 腎移植. **2** N-VAR 可変性名詞 **Kidneys** are the kidneys of an animal, for example a lamb, calf, or pig, that are eaten as meat. 食べ物としての腎臓 ❑ *...lambs' kidneys.* 子羊の腎臓.
→ see **donor**

kill /kɪl/ (**kills, killing, killed**) **1** V-T/V-I 他動詞/自動詞 If a person, animal, or other living thing **is killed**, something or someone causes them to die. 殺す，死なせる，人を殺す ❑ *More than 1,000 people have been killed by the armed forces.* 軍隊により千人以上が殺された. ❑ *He had attempted to kill himself on several occasions.* 彼は幾度も自殺を企てた. ❑ *Drugs can kill.* 麻薬で死ぬことがある. ● **killing** N-UNCOUNT 不可算名詞 殺すこと，殺害 ❑ *There is tension in the region following the killing of seven civilians.* 市民が7人殺害されて以来その地域は緊張状態にある. **2** N-COUNT 可算名詞 The act of killing an animal after hunting it is referred to as **the kill**. 仕留めること ❑ *After the kill the men and old women collect in an open space and eat a meal of whale meat.* 獲物を仕留めたあと、男たちと老女たちは空き地に集まってクジラ肉で食事をする. **3** V-T 他動詞 If someone or something **kills** a project, activity, or idea, they completely destroy or end it. 没にする、つぶす ❑ *His objective was to kill the space station project altogether.* 彼の目標は宇宙ステーションの計画を完全につぶす事だった. ● PHRASAL VERB 句動詞 **Kill off** means the same as **kill**. つぶす ❑ *He would soon launch a second offensive, killing off the peace process.* 彼はすぐに2回目の攻撃に出て和平プロセスを台無しにするであろう. **4** V-T 他動詞 If something **kills** pain, it weakens it so that it is no longer as strong as it was. 鎮める ❑ *He was forced to take opium to kill the pain.* 彼は痛みを鎮めるためアヘンを使わなければならなくなった. **5** V-T 他動詞 [only cont] If you say that something **is killing** you, you mean that it is causing you physical or emotional pain. ひどい苦痛を与える [INFORMAL くだけた] ❑ *My feet are killing me.* 足が痛くてしょうがない. **6** V-T 他動詞 If you say that you **kill yourself to** do something, you are emphasizing that you make a great effort to do it, even though it causes you a lot of trouble or suffering. 無理をしてへとへとになる [INFORMAL くだけた, EMPHASIS 強調] ❑ *I'm killing myself to get my work done.* わたしは自分の仕事を片付けるのにへとへとだ. **7** V-T 他動詞 If you say that you will **kill** someone for something they have done, you are emphasizing that you are extremely angry with them. 殺してやる [EMPHASIS 強調] ❑ *Tell Richard I'm going to kill him when I get hold of him.* とっ捕まえてひどい目にあわせてやると言っていたとリチャードに伝えてくれ. **8** V-T 他動詞 If you say that something will not **kill** you, you mean that it is not really as difficult or unpleasant as it might seem. 我慢できない [INFORMAL くだけた] ❑ *Three or four more weeks won't kill me!* もうあと3～4週間は何てことないわ！ **9** V-T 他動詞 If you **are killing** time, you are doing something because you have some time available, not because you really want to do it. つぶす ❑ *I'm just killing time until I can talk to the other witnesses.* わたしは他の目撃者の話が聞けるようになるまで暇をつぶしているだけだ.

10 PHRASE 句 If you say that you will do something **if it kills you**, you are emphasizing that you are determined to do it even though it is extremely difficult or painful. 何が何でも [EMPHASIS 強調] ❑ *I'll make this marriage work if it kills me.* 何が何でもこの結婚がうまく行くようにするわ. **11** PHRASE 句 If you say that you **killed yourself laughing**, you are emphasizing that you laughed a lot because you thought something was extremely funny. 笑い転げる [INFORMAL くだけた, EMPHASIS 強調] ❑ *I eventually got to the top about an hour after everyone else, and they were all killing themselves laughing.* やがてほかの人たちより1時間ぐらい遅れて頂上に到着したら、みんな笑い転げていた. **12** PHRASE 句 If you **move in for the kill** or if you **close in for the kill**, you take advantage of a changed situation in order to do something that you have been preparing to do. 仕留めにかかる ❑ *Seeing his chance, Dennis moved in for the kill.* チャンスがあるのを見て、デニスは仕留めにかかった. **13** **dressed to kill** → see **dressed** **14** **to be killed outright** → see **outright**

▶ **kill off** ■ → see **kill 3** ■ PHRASAL VERB 句動詞 If you say that a group or an amount of something **has been killed off**, you mean that all of them or all of it have been killed or destroyed. 絶滅させる、皆殺しにする □ *Their natural predators have been killed off.* 彼らの天敵は絶滅した. □ *It is an effective treatment for the bacteria and does kill it off.* これは効果的な治療法でその細菌を全滅させる.
→ see **war**

Thesaurus	kill また次を参照:
v.	execute, murder, put down, slay, wipe out ■

kill|er /kɪlər/ (**killers**) ■ N-COUNT 可算名詞 A **killer** is a person who has killed someone, or who intends to kill someone. 殺人者 □ *The police are searching for his killers.* 警察は彼を殺害した犯人を捜している. ■ N-COUNT 可算名詞 You can refer to something that causes death or is likely to cause death as a **killer**. 死因 □ *Heart disease is the biggest killer of men in developed countries.* 先進国では心臓病が男性の一番大きな死因だ.

kill|ing /kɪlɪŋ/ (**killings**) ■ N-COUNT 可算名詞 A **killing** is an act of deliberately killing a person. 殺人行為 □ *This is a brutal killing.* これは残忍な殺人行為だ. ■ PHRASE 句 If you **make a killing**, you make a large profit very quickly and easily. 大もうけ [INFORMAL くだけた] □ *They have made a killing on the deal.* 彼らはその取引で大もうけした.

kilo /kiːloʊ/ (**kilos**) N-COUNT 可算名詞 A **kilo** is the same as a **kilogram**. キロ □ *He'd lost ten kilos in weight.* 彼は10キロ減量した.

kilo|byte /kɪləbaɪt/ (**kilobytes**) N-COUNT 可算名詞 In computing, a **kilobyte** is one thousand bytes of data. キロバイト

kilo|gram /kɪləgræm/ (**kilograms**) N-COUNT 可算名詞 A **kilogram** is a metric unit of weight. One kilogram is a thousand grams, or a thousandth of a metric ton, and is equal to 2.2 pounds. キログラム □ *...a parcel weighing around 4.5 kilograms.* 約4.5キログラムの小包.

kilo|hertz /kɪləhɜrts/ (**kilohertz**)

Kilohertz is both the singular and the plural form.

Kilohertz は単数形でも複数形でもある.

N-COUNT 可算名詞 A **kilohertz** is a unit of measurement of radio waves. One kilohertz is a thousand hertz. キロヘルツ □ *Their instruments detected very faint radio waves at a frequency of 3 kilohertz.* 彼らの計器は周波数3キロヘルツの大変弱い電波を感知した.

Word Link	meter ≈ measuring : kilometer, meter, perimeter

kilo|meter /kɪləmitər, kɪləmitər/ (**kilometers**) N-COUNT 可算名詞 A **kilometer** is a metric unit of distance or length. One kilometer is a thousand meters and is equal to 0.62 miles. キロメートル □ *...only one kilometer from the border.* 国境から1キロメートルだけ.

kilo|watt /kɪləwɒt/ (**kilowatts**) N-COUNT 可算名詞 A **kilowatt** is a unit of power. One kilowatt is a thousand watts. キロワット □ *...a prototype system which produces 25 kilowatts of power.* 25キロワットの出力のある試作システム.

kin /kɪn/ ■ N-PLURAL 複数名詞 Your **kin** are your relatives. 血族 [DIALECT OR OLD-FASHIONED 方言、または古風な] ■ → see also **next of kin**

kind

❶ NOUN USES AND PHRASES
❷ ADJECTIVE USES

❶ **kind** /kaɪnd/ (**kinds**) ■ N-COUNT 可算名詞 If you talk about a particular **kind of** thing, you are talking about one of the types or sorts of that thing. 種類 □ *The party needs a different kind of leadership.* その党は異なった種類の統率力が必要だ. □ *Had Jamie ever been in any kind of trouble?* ジェーミーは今までに苦境に陥ったことは一切ないのか. ■ N-COUNT 可算名詞 If you refer to someone's **kind**, you are referring to all the other people that are like them or that belong to the same class or set. ような [DISAPPROVAL 不賛成] □ *I can take care of your kind.* あなたのような人の世話はできる. ■ PHRASE 句 You can use **all kinds of** to emphasize that there are a great number and variety of particular things or people. いろいろな [EMPHASIS 強調] □ *Adoption can fail for all kinds of reasons.* いろいろな理由から養子縁組はうまく行かないことがある. ■ PHRASE 句 You use **kind of** when you want to say that something or someone can be roughly described in a particular way. まあ [SPOKEN 口語, VAGUENESS あいまいさ] □ *It was kind of sad, really.* 実際まあ悲しかった. ■ PHRASE 句 If you refer to someone or something as **one of a kind**, you mean that there is nobody or nothing else like them. 独特な [APPROVAL 賛成] □ *She's a very unusual woman, one of a kind.* 彼女はとても変わった女性で独特

だ. ■ PHRASE 句 If you refer, for example, to **two, three**, or **four of a kind**, you mean two, three, or four similar people or things that seem to go well or belong together. 似たもの同士 □ *They were two of a kind, from the same sort of background.* 2人とも似たような生い立ちで似たもの同士だった. ■ PHRASE 句 If you respond **in kind**, you react to something that someone has done to you by doing the same thing to them. 同じやり方で □ *They hurled defiant taunts at the riot police, who responded in kind.* 彼らは機動隊に挑戦的な野次を飛ばし、機動隊は同様に応対した. ■ PHRASE 句 If you pay a debt **in kind**, you pay it in the form of goods or services and not money. 現物で □ *...benefits in kind.* 現物手当て. ■ PHRASE 句 You can use **of a kind** to indicate that something is not as good as it might be expected to be, but that it seems to be the best that is possible or available. 名ばかりの [mainly BRIT 主に英国英語] □ *She finds solace of a kind in alcohol.* 彼女はアルコールに名ばかりのなぐさめを見出した.

❷ **kind** /kaɪnd/ (**kinder, kindest**) ■ ADJ 形容詞 Someone who is **kind** behaves in a gentle, caring, and helpful way toward other people. 優しい、思いやりがある □ *I must thank you for being so kind to me.* とてもご親切にしていただいて、感謝しております. ● **kind|ly** ADV 副詞 [ADV after v] 優しく □ *"You seem tired this morning, Jenny,"* she said kindly. 「ジェニー、今朝は疲れてるみたいね」と彼女はやさしく言った. ■ ADJ 形容詞 You can use **kind** in expressions such as **please be so kind as to** and **would you be kind enough to** in order to ask someone to do something in a firm but polite way. どうか [POLITENESS 丁寧さ] [v-link ADJ] □ *Please be so kind as to see to it that all the alterations are made at once!* どうか責任を持って全ての変更をすぐ加えるようにしてください! ■ → see also **kindly, kindness**

Thesaurus	kind また次を参照:
N.	sort, type ❶ ■
ADJ.	affectionate, considerate, gentle ❷ ■

kin|der|gar|ten /kɪndərgɑrtᵊn/ (**kindergartens**) N-COUNT 可算名詞 A **kindergarten** is a school or class for children aged 4 to 6 years old. It prepares them to go into the first grade. 幼稚園 [also 'in/to/at' N] □ *She's in kindergarten now.* 彼女は今は幼稚園に通っています.

kind|ly /kaɪndli/ ■ ADJ 形容詞 A **kindly** person is kind, caring, and sympathetic. 思いやりがある □ *He was a stern critic but an extremely kindly man.* 彼は厳しい評論家だがとても思いやりがある男だった. ■ ADV 副詞 If someone **kindly** does something for you, they act in a thoughtful and helpful way. 快く [ADV before v] □ *She kindly offered to go and fetch him some beer.* 彼女は快く彼にビールを持ってきてあげると申し出た. ■ ADV 副詞 If someone asks you to **kindly** do something, they are asking you in a way which shows that they have authority over you, or that they are angry with you. どうか [FORMAL 形式ばった] [ADV before v] □ *Will you kindly obey the instructions I am about to give?* わたしがいま出す指示にどうか従ってください. ■ → see also **kind**

Word Link	ness ≈ state, condition : cleanliness, consciousness, kindness

kind|ness /kaɪndnɪs/ N-UNCOUNT 不可算名詞 **Kindness** is the quality of being gentle, caring, and helpful. 思いやり、優しさ □ *We have been treated with such kindness by everybody.* わたしたちはみんなからとても思いやりのあるもてなしを受けた.

king /kɪŋ/ (**kings**) ■ N-TITLE; N-COUNT 称号名詞, 可算名詞 A **king** is a man who is the most important member of the royal family of his country, and who is considered to be the head of state of that country. 王 □ *...the king and queen of Spain.* スペインの王と王妃. ■ N-COUNT 可算名詞 If you describe a man as **the king** of something, you mean that he is the most important person doing that thing or he is the best at doing it. 王者 □ *He was the king of the cowboys.* 彼はカウボーイの王者だった. ■ N-COUNT 可算名詞 A **king** is a playing card with a picture of a king on it. トランプのキング札 □ *...the king of diamonds.* ダイヤのキング. ■ N-COUNT 可算名詞 In chess, the **king** is the most important piece. When you are in a position to capture your opponent's king, you win the game. 王将
→ see **chess**

king|dom /kɪŋdəm/ (**kingdoms**) ■ N-COUNT 可算名詞 A **kingdom** is a country or region that is ruled by a king or queen. 王国 □ *The kingdom's power declined.* 王国の力は弱まった. ■ N-SING 単数名詞 All the animals, birds, and insects in the world can be referred to together as the animal **kingdom**. All the plants can be referred to as the plant **kingdom**. 界 □ *The animal kingdom is full of fine and glorious creatures.* 動物界はすばらしい見事な生き物に満ちている.

ki|osk /kiɒsk/ (**kiosks**) N-COUNT 可算名詞 A **kiosk** is a small structure with an open window at which people can buy things like newspapers, pay an attendant at a parking lot, or get information about something. キオスク、売店 □ *I was getting*

Word Web   kiss

Some anthropologists believe mothers invented the **kiss**. They chewed a bit of food and then used their lips to place it in their child's mouth. Others believe that primates started the practice. There are many types of kisses. Kisses express affection or accompany a greeting or a goodbye. Friends and family members exchange **social kisses** on the **lips** or sometimes on the **cheek**. When people are about to kiss they pucker their lips. In European countries, friends kiss each other lightly on both cheeks. And in the Middle East, a kiss between two political figures indicates a pledge of mutual support.

cigarettes at the kiosk. 売店でタバコを買っているところだった. ❏ *...an information kiosk.* 案内所.

kiss /kɪs/ (**kisses, kissing, kissed**) **1** V-RECIP 相互動詞 If you **kiss** someone, you touch them with your lips to show affection or sexual desire, or to greet them or say goodbye. キスする ❏ *She leaned up and kissed him on the cheek.* 彼女は反り返って彼の頬にキスした. ❏ *Her parents kissed her goodbye as she set off from their home.* 彼女が家から出発するとき両親が別れのキスをした. ● N-COUNT 可算名詞 **Kiss** is also a noun. キス ❏ *I put my arms around her and gave her a kiss.* わたしは彼女に抱きついてキスをした. **2** V-T 他動詞 If you say that something **kisses** another thing, you mean that it touches that thing very gently. 軽く触れる ❏ *The wheels of the aircraft kissed the runway.* 飛行機の車輪が滑走路に軽く触れた. **3** PHRASE 句 If you **blow** someone **a kiss** or **blow a kiss**, you touch the palm of your hand lightly with your lips, and then blow across your hand toward the person, in order to show them your affection. 投げキスをする ❏ *Maria blew him a kiss.* マリアは彼に投げキスを送った. **4** PHRASE 句 If you say that you **kiss** something **goodbye** or **kiss goodbye to** something, you accept the fact that you are going to lose it, although you do not want to. あきらめる [INFORMAL くだけた] ❏ *I felt sure I'd have to kiss my dancing career goodbye.* わたしはダンスの仕事を断念しなければならないと本当に思った. → see Word Web: **kiss**

Word Partnership   *kiss* は次の語句と使われる:

ADJ.	**big kiss, first kiss, quick kiss 1**
N.	**kiss** *someone* **on the cheek/lips/mouth, kiss** *(someone)* **goodbye/goodnight, hug and kiss 1**
V.	**give** *someone* **a kiss, plant a kiss on** *someone*, **want to kiss** *someone* **1**

kit /kɪt/ (**kits, kitting, kitted**) **1** N-COUNT 可算名詞 A **kit** is a group of items that are kept together, often in the same container, because they are all used for similar purposes. 道具一式 ❏ *Make sure you keep a well-stocked first aid kit ready to deal with any emergency.* あらゆる非常時に備えて, 中身の揃った救急箱を必ず保管するように. **2** N-COUNT 可算名詞 A **kit** is a set of parts that can be put together in order to make something. キット ❏ *Her popular potholder is also available in do-it-yourself kits.* 好評な彼女のなべ敷は手作り用キットとしても市販されています. **3** N-UNCOUNT 不可算名詞 **Kit** is special clothing and equipment that you use when you take part in a particular activity, especially a sport. 服装 [mainly BRIT 主に英国英語] 米国英語では通常 **gear**]

kitch|en /kɪtʃ°n/ (**kitchens**) N-COUNT 可算名詞 A **kitchen** is a room that is used for cooking and for household jobs such as washing dishes. 台所 → see **house**

kite /kaɪt/ (**kites**) **1** N-COUNT 可算名詞 A **kite** is an object, usually used as a toy, which is flown in the air. It consists of a light frame covered with paper or cloth and has a long string attached which you hold while the kite is flying. たこ ❏ *Willy asks if I've ever flown a kite before.* ウィリーはたこを揚げたことがあるかと私に聞く. **2** PHRASE 句 If you say that someone is **as high as a kite**, you mean that they are very excited or that they are greatly affected by alcohol or drugs. ひどく興奮状態の ❏ *The steroids made me feel so strange. I was as high as a kite some of the time.* ステロイドを使うととても妙な感じがした. 大変な興奮状態になったこともあった.

kitsch /kɪtʃ/ N-UNCOUNT 不可算名詞 You can refer to a work of art or an object as **kitsch** if it is showy and thought by some people to be in bad taste. 人目を引く安っぽい物, キッチュ ❏ *...a hideous ballgown verging on the kitsch.* キッチュに近い不細工な夜会服. ● ADJ 形容詞 **Kitsch** is also an adjective. 人目を引いて安っぽい, キッチュな ❏ *Blue and green eyeshadow has long been considered kitsch.* 青と緑のアイシャドーは以前から俗悪だと思われていた.

kit|ten /kɪt°n/ (**kittens**) N-COUNT 可算名詞 A **kitten** is a very young cat. 子猫

kit|ty /kɪti/ (**kitties**) **1** N-COUNT 可算名詞 A **kitty** is an amount of money gathered from several people, which is meant to be spent on things that these people will share or use together. 共同出資金 ❏ *You haven't put any money in the kitty for three weeks.* 君は3週間前から共同資金に一銭も入れてないね. **2** N-COUNT 可算名詞 A **kitty** is the total amount of money which is bet in a gambling game, and which is taken by the winner or winners. 総かけ金 ❏ *Each month the total prize kitty is $13.5 million.* 毎月の賞金総額は1350万ドルだ. **3** N-COUNT 可算名詞 A **kitty** is a cat, especially a young cat. 猫 [INFORMAL くだけた] ❏ *...a cute little kitty.* かわいい子猫. ❏ *...kitty litter made of wood shavings.* 木の削りくずでできた猫用トイレ. **4** N-COUNT 可算名詞 **Kitty** is sometimes used as an affectionate way of referring to a cat or a kitten. 猫ちゃん [INFORMAL くだけた] ❏ *"Gertie!" the kids were calling into the yard. "Here kitty, kitty, kitty!"* 「ガーティー!」と子供たちは庭にむかって叫んでいた. 「猫ちゃん, おいで!」

kiwi /kiwi/ (**kiwis**) A **kiwi** is the same as a **kiwi fruit**. キーウィ **kiwi fruit** (**kiwi fruits**)

Kiwi fruit can also be used as the plural form.

Kiwi fruit は複数形としても使える.

N-VAR 可変性名詞 A **kiwi fruit** is a fruit with a brown hairy skin and green flesh. キーウィフルーツ

km (**kms**) **km** is a written abbreviation for **kilometer**. キロメートル

knack /næk/ (**knacks**) N-COUNT 可算名詞 A **knack** is a particularly clever or skillful way of doing something successfully, especially something which most people find difficult. こつ ❏ *He's got the knack of getting people to listen.* 彼は人に話を聞かせるこつを心得ている.

knap|sack /næpsæk/ (**knapsacks**) also **backpack** N-COUNT 可算名詞 A **knapsack** is a cloth or leather bag that you carry on your back or over your shoulder, for example when you are walking in the countryside. ナップサック

knead /niːd/ (**kneads, kneading, kneaded**) **1** V-T 他動詞 When you **knead** dough or other food, you press and squeeze it with your hands so that it becomes smooth and ready to bake. こねる ❏ *Lightly knead the mixture on a floured surface.* 打ち粉をした上で混ぜ合わせた物を軽くこねます. **2** V-T 他動詞 If you **knead** a part of someone's body, you press or squeeze it with your fingers. こねるようにもむ ❏ *She felt him knead the aching muscles.* 彼女は彼がうずく筋肉をこねるようにもんでいるのを感じた.

knee /niː/ (**knees, kneeing, kneed**) **1** N-COUNT 可算名詞 Your **knee** is the place where your leg bends. ひざ ❏ *He will receive physical therapy on his damaged left knee.* 彼は損傷した左ひざの理学療法を受けるでしょう. **2** N-COUNT 可算名詞 If something or someone is **on your knee** or **on your knees**, they are resting or sitting on the upper part of your legs when you are sitting down. ひざ ❏ *He sat with the package on his knees.* 彼はその包みをひざに置いて座った. **3** N-PLURAL 複数名詞 If you are **on your knees**, your legs are bent and your knees are on the ground. ひざ ❏ *She fell to the ground on her knees and prayed.* 彼女は地べたにひざまずいて祈った. **4** V-T 他動詞 If you **knee** someone, you hit them using your knee. ひざげりを食わす ❏ *Ian kneed him in the groin.* イアンは彼の急所にひざげりを食わした. **5** PHRASE 句 If a country or organization **is brought to its knees**, it is almost completely destroyed by someone or something. 屈服させる ❏ *The country was being brought to its knees by the loss of 2.4 million manufacturing jobs.* 製造業で240万の失業者が出てその国はぼろぼろになった. **6** on **bended knee** → see **bended** → see **body**

Word Partnership   *knee* は次の語句と使われる:

N.	knee **injury** ◼️1
ADJ.	**left/right** knee, **weak-**kneed ◼️1
V.	**bend your** knees, knees **buckle** ◼️1
	fall on your knees ◼️3

kneel /niːl/ (**kneels, kneeling, kneeled** or **knelt**) V-I 自動詞 When you **kneel**, you bend your legs so that your knees are touching the ground. ひざまずく ❑ *She knelt by the bed and prayed.* 彼女はベッドの横にひざまずいて祈った. ❑ *Other people were kneeling, but she just sat.* ほかの人たちはひざまずいていたが彼女はただ座っていた. ● PHRASAL VERB 句動詞 **Kneel down** means the same as **kneel**. ひざまずく ❑ *He kneeled down beside him.* 彼女は彼のわきにひざまずいた.

knew /njuː/ **Knew** is the past tense of **know**. know の過去形

knick|ers /ˈnɪkərz/

The form **knicker** is used as a modifier.

knicker 形は修飾語として使われる.

N-PLURAL 複数名詞 **Knickers** are the same as **panties**. パンティー [BRIT 英国英語] [also 'a pair of' N]

knife /naɪf/ (**knives, knifes, knifing, knifed**)

Knives is the plural form of the noun and **knifes** is the third person singular of the present tense of the verb.

Knives は名詞の複数形であり, **knifes** は動詞の3人称単数現在形.

◼️1 N-COUNT 可算名詞 A **knife** is a tool for cutting or a weapon and consists of a flat piece of metal with a sharp edge on the end of a handle. ナイフ, 小刀 ❑ *...a knife and fork.* ナイフとフォーク. ◼️2 V-T 他動詞 To **knife** someone means to attack and injure them with a knife. ナイフで刺す ❑ *Dawson takes revenge on the man by knifing him to death.* ドーソンはその男を刺し殺して仕返しをした. ◼️3 PHRASE 句 If you **twist the knife in someone's wound**, you do or say something to make an unpleasant situation they are in even more unpleasant. 追い討ちをかける ❑ *Hearing his own plans was like having a knife twisted in his wound.* 彼が作った計画について聞くことは追い討ちをかけられたようなものだった.
→ see **tool**

knight /naɪt/ (**knights, knighting, knighted**) ◼️1 N-COUNT 可算名詞 In medieval times, a **knight** was a man of noble birth, who served his king or lord in battle. 騎士 ❑ *...King Arthur's faithful knight, Gawain.* アーサー王の忠実な騎士, ガウェイン. ◼️2 V-T 他動詞 If someone **is knighted**, they are given a knighthood. ナイト爵に叙する [usu passive] ❑ *He was knighted in 1988.* 彼は1988年の6月にナイト爵に叙せられた. ◼️3 N-COUNT 可算名詞 In chess, a **knight** is a piece which is shaped like a horse's head. チェスのナイト ◼️4 PHRASE 句 If you refer to someone as a **knight in shining armor**, you mean that they are kind and brave, and likely to rescue you from a difficult situation. 輝くよろいに身を包んだ騎士（おとぎ話に出てくるような勇敢で優しい男性）❑ *The love songs tricked us all into believing in happy endings and knights in shining armor.* ラブソングは私んなをたぶらかして, 輝くよろいに身を包んだ騎士が救いに来てくれてハッピーエンドが迎えられるって信じさせた.

knight|hood /ˈnaɪthʊd/ (**knighthoods**) N-COUNT 可算名詞 A **knighthood** is a title that is given to a man by a British king or queen for his achievements or his service to his country. A man who has been given a knighthood can put "Sir" in front of his name instead of "Mr." ナイト爵位 ❑ *When he finally received his knighthood in 1975 Chaplin was 85.* 1975年にやっとナイト爵位を受けたときにはチャップリンは85歳だった.

knit /nɪt/ (**knits, knitting, knitted**) ◼️1 V-T/V-I 他動詞/自動詞 If you **knit** something, especially an article of clothing, you make it from wool or a similar thread by using two knitting needles or a machine. 編む, 編み物をする ❑ *I had endless hours to knit and sew.* 編み物や縫い物をする時間が限りなくあった. ❑ *I have already started knitting baby clothes.* もう赤ちゃんの服を編み始めている. ● COMB IN ADJ 形容詞の複合 **Knit** is also a combining form. ニット [ADJ n] ❑ *Ferris wore a heavy knit sweater.* フェリスは厚手のニットのセーターを着た. ◼️2 V-T 他動詞 If someone or something **knits** things or people **together**, they make them fit or work together closely and successfully. 団結させる ❑ *The best thing about sports is that they knit the whole family close together.* スポーツの最もいい点は家族みんなの団結を強めることだ. ● COMB IN ADJ 形容詞の複合 **Knit** is also a combining form. 強く結ぶ ❑ *...a closer-knit family.* もっと結びつきの強い家族. ◼️3 V-I 自動詞 When broken bones **knit**, the broken pieces grow together again. 接合する ❑ *The bone hasn't knitted together properly.* 骨はまだちゃんと接合していない.

Word Partnership   *knit* は次の語句と使われる:

N.	knit **a sweater** ◼️1
ADV.	**closely/tightly** knit, knit **together** ◼️2

knit|ting /ˈnɪtɪŋ/ ◼️1 N-UNCOUNT 不可算名詞 **Knitting** is something, such as an article of clothing, that is being knitted. 編み物 ❑ *She had been sitting with her knitting at her fourth-floor window.* 彼女は5階の自分の部屋の窓辺に編み物を手にして腰掛けていた. ◼️2 N-UNCOUNT 不可算名詞 **Knitting** is the action or process of knitting. 編み物をすること ❑ *Take up a relaxing hobby, such as knitting.* 編み物などのくつろげる趣味を始めなさい.

knives /naɪvz/ **Knives** is the plural of **knife**. knife の複数形

knob /nɒb/ (**knobs**) ◼️1 N-COUNT 可算名詞 A **knob** is a round handle on a door or drawer which you use in order to open or close it. 取っ手 ❑ *He turned the knob and pushed against the door.* 彼は取っ手を回してドアを押した. ◼️2 N-COUNT 可算名詞 A **knob** is a round switch on a piece of machinery or equipment. つまみ ❑ *...the volume knob.* ボリュームのつまみ.

knock /nɒk/ (**knocks, knocking, knocked**) ◼️1 V-I 自動詞 If you **knock on** something such as a door or window, you hit it, usually several times, to attract someone's attention. たたく, ノックする ❑ *She went directly to Simon's apartment and knocked on the door.* 彼女はサイモンのアパートに直行しドアをたたいた. ● N-COUNT 可算名詞 **Knock** is also a noun. 扉をたたく音 ❑ *They heard a knock at the front door.* 表玄関の扉をたたく音 ● N-SING 単数名詞 [also no det] 扉をたたく音 ❑ *They were wakened by a loud knocking at the door.* 彼らはドアをたたく大きな音で目が覚めた. ◼️2 V-T 他動詞 If you **knock** something, you touch or hit it roughly, especially so that it falls or moves. たたく ❑ *She accidentally knocked the glass off the shelf.* 彼女はうっかりコップをたたいて棚から落としてしまった. ● N-COUNT 可算名詞 **Knock** is also a noun. ❑ *The bags have tough exterior materials to protect against knocks, rain, and dust.* その袋は衝撃や雨やホコリに対して保護するため外側に丈夫な素材が使ってある. ◼️3 V-T 他動詞 To **knock** them into a particular position or condition means to hit them very hard so that they fall over or become unconscious. 打ち倒す ❑ *The third wave was so strong it knocked me backwards.* 3つ目の波はとても強くてわたしを仰向けに打ち倒した. ◼️4 V-T 他動詞 To **knock** a particular quality or characteristic **out of** someone means to make them lose it. たたき出す [no cont] ❑ *The school system is designed to knock passion out of people.* 学校制度は人々の情熱を失わせるように設定されている. ◼️5 V-T 他動詞 If you **knock** something or someone, you criticize them and say unpleasant things about them. 非難する [INFORMAL くだけた] ❑ *I'm not knocking them: if they want to do it, it's up to them.* わたしは彼らを非難しているわけではない. もしそうしたいのなら彼ら次第だ. ◼️6 N-COUNT 可算名詞 If someone receives a **knock**, they have an unpleasant experience which prevents them from achieving something or which causes them to change their attitudes or plans. ひどい仕打ち ◼️7 to **knock** someone or something **into shape** → see **shape**
▸ **knock about** → see **knock around**
▸ **knock around** ◼️1 PHRASAL VERB 句動詞 If someone **knocks around** somewhere, they spend time there, experiencing different situations or just passing time. 歩き回る [BRIT 英国英語] ❑ *...reporters who knock around in troubled parts of the world.* 世界の紛争地域を歩き回る記者たち. ❑ *They knock around on weekends in grubby sweaters and pants.* 彼らは週末は汚いセーターとズボンを着てぶらつく. ◼️2 PHRASAL VERB 句動詞 If someone **knocks** you **around**, they hit or kick you several times. こづき回す, 虐待する [INFORMAL くだけた] ❑ *He lied to me constantly and started knocking me around.* 彼はわたしに絶え間なく嘘をつき虐待し始めた.
▸ **knock down** ◼️1 PHRASAL VERB 句動詞 If someone **is knocked down** or **is knocked over** by a vehicle or its driver, they are hit by a car and fall to the ground, and are often injured or killed. はねる ❑ *He died after being knocked down by a car.* 彼は車にはねられたあと死亡した. ❑ *A drunk driver knocked down and killed two girls.* 飲酒運転をしていた人が少女2人をはね殺した. ❑ *A car knocked him over.* 自動車が彼を引き倒した. ◼️2 PHRASAL VERB 句動詞 To **knock down** a building or part of a building means to demolish it. 取り壊す ❑ *Why doesn't he just knock the wall down?* 単に壁を取り壊したらすむのに. ◼️3 PHRASAL VERB 句動詞 To **knock down** a price or amount means to decrease it. 下げる [mainly AM 主に米国英語] ❑ *The market might abandon the stock, and knock down its price.* 市場はその株を放棄し, 安値を引き起こすかもしれない. ◼️4 PHRASAL VERB 句動詞 If someone **is knocked down** or **is knocked over** by a vehicle or its driver, they are hit by a car and fall to the ground, and are often injured or killed. はねる [mainly BRIT 主に英国英語; AM usually **hit** 米国英語では通常 **hit**]
▸ **knock off** ◼️1 PHRASAL VERB 句動詞 To **knock off** an amount from a price, time, or level means to reduce it by that amount. 値下げする ❑ *We have knocked 10% off admission prices.* 入場料を10%の値下げした. ◼️2 PHRASAL VERB 句動詞 When you **knock off**, you finish work at the end of the day or before a break. 済ませる [INFORMAL

くだけた] *If I get this report finished I'll knock off early.* この報告書を終わらせられたらわたしは早退する.

▶ **knock out** ◨ PHRASAL VERB 句動詞 To **knock** someone **out** means to cause them to become unconscious or to go to sleep. 意識を失わせる ◻ *The three drinks knocked him out.* 酒3杯で彼は意識を失った. ◪ PHRASAL VERB 句動詞 If a person or team **is knocked out** of a competition, they are defeated in a game, so that they take no more part in the competition. ノックアウトする ◻ *He got knocked out in the first inning.* 第1イニングで彼はノックアウトになった. ◫ → see also **knockout** PHRASAL VERB 句動詞 If something **is knocked out** by enemy action or bad weather, it is destroyed or stops functioning because of it. 破壊する, 使えなくする ◻ *Our bombers have knocked out the mobile launchers.* 我々の爆撃機が移動式発射装置を破壊した.

▶ **knock over** → see **knock down** 1, 4

▶ **knock up** ◨ PHRASAL VERB 句動詞 If you **knock** something **up**, you make it or build it very quickly, using whatever materials are available. 大急ぎで作る [BRIT 英国英語, INFORMAL くだけた] ◪ PHRASAL VERB 句動詞 If a woman **is knocked up** by a man, she is made pregnant by him. 妊娠させる [INFORMAL, VULGAR くだけた, 下品な] [usu passive] ◻ *When I got knocked up, the whole town knew it.* わたしが妊娠した時, 町中に発覚した.

Thesaurus   *knock* また次を参照:

V.	rap, tap ◨
	bash, hit, strike ◪
	belittle, criticize, denounce; (ant.) praise ◳

Word Partnership   *knock* は次の語句と使われる:

V.	answer a knock, hear a knock ◨
N.	knock on/at a door ◨
ADJ.	loud knock ◨
	knock *someone* out cold, knock *someone* unconscious ◳

---

knock|out /nɒkaʊt/ (**knockouts**) also **knock-out** ◨ N-COUNT 可算名詞 In boxing, a **knockout** is a situation in which a boxer wins the fight by making his opponent fall to the ground and be unable to stand up before the referee has counted to ten. ノックアウト [also 'by' N] ◻ *Lennox Lewis ended the scheduled 12-round fight with a knockout in the eighth round.* レノックス・ルイスは予定されていた12ラウンド戦の8ラウンド目で相手をノックアウトして試合を終えた. ◪ ADJ 形容詞 A **knockout** blow is an action or event that completely defeats an opponent. 痛烈な [ADJ n] ◻ *He delivered a knockout blow to all of his rivals.* 彼はライバル全員に痛烈な一撃を与えた. ◳ ADJ 形容詞 A **knockout** competition is one in which the players or teams that win continue playing until there is only one winner left. 勝ち抜きの [mainly BRIT 主に英国英語] [ADJ n] [AM elimination 米国英語 **elimination**] ◴ N-SING 単数名詞 If you describe someone as a **knockout**, you think that they are extremely attractive or impressive. すごくかっこいい人 [INFORMAL くだけた, APPROVAL 賛成] ◻ *Jill was a knockout with her biker leathers and t-shirt.* ジルはバイク用のレザーとTシャツを着て, ものすごくかっこよかった.

knot /nɒt/ (**knots, knotting, knotted**) ◨ N-COUNT 可算名詞 If you tie a **knot** in a piece of string, rope, cloth, or other material, you pass one end or part of it through a loop and pull it tight. 結び目 ◻ *One lace had broken and been tied in a knot.* 一本のひもは切れており結んでつないであった. ◪ V-T 他動詞 If you **knot** a piece of string, rope, cloth, or other material, you pass one end or part of it through a loop and pull it tight. 結ぶ ◻ *He knotted the laces securely together.* 彼はひもをしっかりと結び合わせた. ◻ *He knotted the bandanna around his neck.* 彼は首にバンダナを巻いた. ◳ N-COUNT 可算名詞 If you feel a **knot** in your stomach, you get an uncomfortable tight feeling in your stomach, usually because you are afraid or excited. 緊張で胃が締めつけられた感じ ◻ *There was a knot of tension in his stomach.* 緊張で胃が締めつけられた. ◴ V-T/V-I 他動詞/自動詞 If your stomach **knots** or if something **knots** it, it feels tight because you are afraid or excited. 締めつける, 締めつく ◻ *I felt my stomach knot with apprehension.* 心配で胃が締めつけられるのを感じた. ◵ V-I 自動詞 If part of your face or your muscles **knot**, they become tense, usually because you are worried or angry. しわを寄せる ◻ *His forehead knotted in a frown.* 彼はおでこにしわを寄せてしかめ面をしていた. ◶ N-COUNT 可算名詞 A **knot** in a piece of wood is a small hard area where a branch grew. 節 ◻ *A carpenter often rejects half his wood because of knots or cracks.* 大工は節やワレのある木材を半分使わないことがしばしばある. ◷ N-COUNT 可算名詞 A **knot** is a unit of speed. The speed of ships, aircraft, and wind is measured in knots. ノット ◻ *They travel at speeds of up to 30 knots.* 最大30ノットの速度が出る.

→ see **rope**

---

know

❶ VERB USES
❷ PHRASES

---

❶ **know** /noʊ/ (**knows, knowing, knew, known**) ◨ V-T/V-I 他動詞/自動詞 If you **know** a fact, a piece of information, or an answer, you have it correctly in your mind. 知っている, 承知している, 分かっている [no cont] ◻ *I don't know the name of the place.* わたしはその場所の地名を知らない. ◻ *"People like doing things for nothing."—"I know they do."* 「人はわけもなくしたがるものだよ. 」「それは分かっている」 ◻ *I don't know what happened to her husband.* 彼女の夫がどうなったのかは分からない. ◻ *"How did he meet your mother?"—"I don't know."* 「どのようにして彼はきみのお母さんと出会ったの?」「知らない」 ◪ V-T 他動詞 If you **know** someone, you are familiar with them because you have met them and talked to them before. 知り合いである [no cont] ◻ *Gifford was a friend. I'd known him for nine years.* ギフォードは友達だった. 9年前から知っていた. ◳ V-I 自動詞 If you say that you **know of** something, you mean that you have heard about it but you do not necessarily have a lot of information about it. 聞いている [no cont] ◻ *We know of the incident but have no further details.* その出来事のことは聞いているけれども詳しいことは知らない. ◻ *The president admitted that he did not know of any rebels having surrendered so far.* 大統領はこれまでに反政府分子の投降例は聞いていないと認めた. ◴ V-I 自動詞 If you **know about** a subject, you have studied it or taken an interest in it, and understand part or all of it. 知識がある [no cont] ◻ *Hire someone with experience, someone who knows about real estate.* 経験があり, 不動産について知識のある人を雇いなさい. ◻ *She didn't know anything about music.* 彼女は音楽に関する知識は全くなかった. ◵ V-T 他動詞 If you **know** a language, you have learned it and can understand it. 分かる [no cont] ◻ *It helps to know French and Creole if you want to understand some of the lyrics.* 歌詞を理解したいのならフランス語とクレオール語の知識が助けになる. ◶ V-T 他動詞 If you **know** something such as a place, a work of art, or an idea, you have visited it, seen it, read it, or heard about it, and so you are familiar with it. 知っている [no cont] ◻ *No matter how well you know this city, it is easy to get lost.* どれほど詳しくこの都市を知っていようと, すぐに道に迷ってしまう. ◷ V-T 他動詞 If you **know how to** do something, you have the necessary skills and knowledge to do it. 心得ている [no cont] ◻ *The health authorities now know how to deal with the disease.* 保健当局は今ではその病気への対処のしかたを心得ている. ◸ V-T 他動詞 You can say that someone **knows that** something is happening when they become aware of it. 気づく [no cont] ◻ *Then I saw a gun under the hall table so I knew that something was wrong.* それから玄関の下のテーブルの下に拳銃が落ちているのを見て何かおかしいと気づいた. ◹ V-T 他動詞 If you **know** something or someone, you recognize them when you see them or hear them. わかる, 区別ができる [no cont] ◻ *Would she know you if she saw you on the street?* もし通りで彼女があなたを見たかけたら, あなただってわかるかしら. ◺ V-T 他動詞 If someone or something **is known as** a particular name, they are called by that name. 呼び習わす [no cont] ◻ *The disease is more commonly known as Mad Cow Disease.* もっと一般的にその病気は狂牛病と呼ばれています. ◻ *...Peter and his wife Antonella (also known as Tony).* ピーターと彼の妻アントネラ (別名トニー). ◻ V-T 他動詞 If you **know** someone or something **as** a person or thing that has particular qualities, you consider that they have those qualities. 知られている ◻ *Lots of people know her as a very kind woman.* 彼女はとても優しい女性として多くの人に知られている. ◻ → see also **knowing, known**

Thesaurus   *know* また次を参照:

V.	comprehend, recognize, understand ❶ ◨
	be acquainted, be familiar with ❶ ◪

❷ **know** /noʊ/ (**knows, knowing, knew, known**) ◨ PHRASE 句 If you talk about a thing or system **as we know it**, you are referring to the form in which it exists now and which is familiar to most people. 今ある形の ◻ *He planned to end the welfare system as we know it.* 彼は現行福祉制度の廃止を計画した. ◪ PHRASE 句 If you **get to know** someone, you find out what they are like by spending time with them. 知り合う ◻ *The new neighbors were getting to know each other.* 新しい隣人たちは知り合いになり始めていた. ◳ PHRASE 句 People use expressions such as **goodness knows, Heaven knows,** and **God knows** when they do not know something and want to suggest that nobody could possibly know it. 知らない [INFORMAL くだけた] ◻ *"Who's he?"—"God knows."* 「あれだれ」「誰も知らないよ」 ◴ CONVENTION 慣習表現 You say "**I know**" to show that you agree with what has just been said. そうだ ◻ *"This country is so awful."—"I know, I know."* 「この国はとてもひどい」「そうなの, そうなの」 ◵ PHRASE 句 You can use **I don't know** to indicate that you do not completely agree with something or do not really think that it is true. さあそれはどうか ◻ *"He should quite simply resign."—"I don't know about that."* 「はっ

きり言って彼は辞めればいいんだよ」「さあそれはどんなもんかね」 **⑥** PHRASE 句 You can say "**I don't know about you**" to indicate that you are going to give your own opinion about something and you want to find out if someone else feels the same. あなたはどうだか知らないけど ❑ *I don't know about the rest of you, but I'm hungry.* ほかの人たちはどうだか知らないけど、わたしはお腹がすいた. **⑦** PHRASE 句 You use **I don't know** in expressions which indicate criticism of someone's behavior. For example, if you say that you **do not know how** someone can do something, you mean that you cannot understand or accept them doing it. どうしてか理解しかねる [DISAPPROVAL 不賛成] ❑ *I don't know how he could do this to his own daughter.* どうして彼は自分の娘にそんなことができるのか理解しかねる. **⑧** PHRASE 句 If you are **in the know** about something, especially something that is not known about or understood by many people, you have information about it. よく知っている, 内情に通じている ❑ *It was gratifying to be in the know about important people.* 重要な人たちの内情に通じているのは心地よいものだった. **⑨** CONVENTION 慣習表現 You can use expressions such as **you know what I mean** and **if you know what I mean** to suggest that the person listening to you understands what you are trying to say, and so you do not have to explain any more. 言わなくても分かるでしょう [SPOKEN 口語] ❑ *None of us stayed long. I mean, the atmosphere wasn't – well, you know what I mean.* だれも長居はしなかった. つまり雰囲気が今ひとつ、なんて言うか、ほら、分かるだろう、おれが言いたいこと. **⑩** CONVENTION 慣習表現 You say "**You never know**" or "**One never knows**" to indicate that it is not definite or certain what will happen in the future, and to suggest that there is some hope that things will turn out well. 先のことは分からない [VAGUENESS あいまいさ] ❑ *You never know, I might get lucky.* 先のことは分からないわよ、幸運が回って来るかも知れないし. **⑪** CONVENTION 慣習表現 You say "**Not that I know of**" when someone has asked you whether or not something is true and you think the answer is "no" but you cannot be sure because you do not know all the facts. わたしの知る限りではそうではない [VAGUENESS あいまいさ] ❑ *"Is he married?" — "Not that I know of."* 「彼、結婚してるの?」「わたしの知る限りでは結婚してないわ」 **⑫** CONVENTION 慣習表現 You use **you know** to emphasize or to draw attention to what you are saying. ですからね、でしょう [SPOKEN 口語, EMPHASIS 強調] ❑ *The conditions in there are awful, you know.* 何せあそこはひどい状況ですからね. **⑬** PHRASE 句 You can say "**You don't know**" in order to emphasize how strongly you feel about the remark you are going to make. とてもひとには分かるまい [SPOKEN 口語, EMPHASIS 強調] ❑ *You don't know how good it is to speak to somebody from home.* 同郷の人と話ができるのがどんなに楽しいかはとてもひとにはわかってもらえないでしょう. **⑭** to **know best** → see **best** **⑮** to **know better** → see **better** **⑯** to **know** something **for a fact** → see **fact** **⑰** as far as I know → see **far** **⑱** not to **know the first thing about** something → see **first** **⑲** to **know full well** → see **full** **⑳** to **let** someone **know** → see **let** **㉑** to **know** your **own mind** → see **mind** **㉒** to **know the ropes** → see **rope**

know-how N-UNCOUNT 不可算名詞 **Know-how** is knowledge of the methods or techniques of doing something, especially something technical or practical. こつ [INFORMAL くだけた] ❑ *He hasn't got the know-how to run a farm.* 彼は農場を経営するこつを知らない.

know|ing /nʊɪŋ/ ADJ 形容詞 A **knowing** gesture or remark is one that shows that you understand something, for example the way that someone is feeling or what they really mean, even though it has not been mentioned directly. 了解していることを示す ❑ *Ron gave her a knowing smile.* ロンは何のことか分かっているというような笑顔を彼女に向けた. ● **know|ing|ly** ADV 副詞 了解していることを示すように ❑ *He smiled knowingly.* 彼は心得顔で微笑んだ.

know|ing|ly /nʊɪŋli/ ADV 副詞 If you **knowingly** do something wrong, you do it even though you know it is wrong. 故意に [ADV before v] ❑ *He repeated that he had never knowingly taken illegal drugs.* 彼は故意に禁止薬物を使用したことはない、と言い続けた.

know-it-all (**know-it-alls**) N-COUNT 可算名詞 If you say that someone is a **know-it-all**, you are critical of them because they think that they know a lot more than other people. 利口ぶる人 [AM 米国英語, INFORMAL くだけた, DISAPPROVAL 不賛成] ❑ *Don't act like a know-it-all. You listen to your mother.* 利口ぶったふりをするな. お母さんの言うことを聞け.

knowl|edge /nɒlɪdʒ/ **①** N-UNCOUNT 不可算名詞 **Knowledge** is information and understanding about a subject which a person has, or which all people have. 知識 ❑ *She disclaims any knowledge of her husband's business concerns.* 彼女は夫の仕事関係については全く関知していないと主張している. **②** PHRASE 句 If you say that something is true **to your knowledge** or **to the best of your knowledge**, you mean that you believe it to be true but it is possible that you do not know all the facts. 自分が知る限りでは ❑ *Alec never carried a gun to my knowledge.* わたしが知る限りではアレックが拳銃を持ち歩くことはなかった.

Thesaurus	knowledge また次を参照:
N.	comprehension, consciousness, education, intelligence, wisdom; (ant.) ignorance **①**

Word Partnership	knowledge は次の語句と使われる:
V.	acquire knowledge, gain knowledge, have knowledge, lack knowledge, require knowledge, test your knowledge, use your knowledge **①**
ADJ.	background knowledge, common knowledge, general knowledge, prior knowledge, scientific knowledge, useful knowledge, vast knowledge **①**
N.	knowledge base **①**

knowl|edge|able /nɒlɪdʒəbᵊl/ also **knowledgable** ADJ 形容詞 Someone who is **knowledgeable** has or shows a clear understanding of many different facts about the world or about a particular subject. 知識のある ❑ *Do you think you are more knowledgeable about life than your parents were at your age?* あなたの両親が今のあなたの年齢だったころより今のあなたの方が人生について良く知っていると思いますか.

known /noʊn/ **①** Known is the past participle of **know**. know の過去分詞 **②** ADJ 形容詞 You use **known** to describe someone or something that is clearly recognized by or familiar to all people or to a particular group of people. 既知の ❑ *...He was a known drug dealer.* 彼は名の通った麻薬の密売人だった. **③** ADJ 形容詞 If someone or something is **known for** a particular achievement or feature, they are familiar to many people because of that achievement or feature. 知られている, 有名である [v-link 'for' n/-ing] ❑ *He is better known for his film and TV work.* 彼は映画とテレビの仕事の方が有名である. **④** PHRASE 句 If you **let it be known** that something is the case, or you **let** something **be known**, you make sure that people know it or can find out about it. 吹聴する ❑ *The president has let it be known that he is against it.* 大統領は自分がそれに反対であることを吹聴した.

knuck|le /nʌkᵊl/ (**knuckles**) **①** N-COUNT 可算名詞 Your **knuckles** are the rounded pieces of bone that form lumps on your hands where your fingers join your hands, and where your fingers bend. こぶし ❑ *Brenda's knuckles were white as she gripped the arms of the chair.* 椅子のひじかけを強く握ったのでブレンダのこぶしは真っ白だった. **②** a **rap on the knuckles** → see **rap** → see **hand**

Ko|ran /kɔrɑn/ N-PROPER 固有名詞 The **Koran** is the sacred book on which the religion of Islam is based. コーラン

kph /keɪ pi eɪtʃ/ **kph** is written after a number to indicate the speed of something such as a vehicle. **kph** is an abbreviation for "kilometers per hour." 時速〜キロ

kW also **KW** **kW** is a written abbreviation for **kilowatt**. キロワット

Ll

L also l /ɛl/ (**L's, l's**) N-VAR 可変性名詞 **L** is the twelfth letter of the English alphabet. アルファベットの第12字

lab /læb/ (**labs**) N-COUNT 可算名詞 A **lab** is the same as a **laboratory**. laboratoryの短縮形

la|bel /leɪbəl/ (**labels, labeling** or **labelling, labeled** or **labelled**) ■ N-COUNT 可算名詞 A **label** is a piece of paper or plastic that is attached to an object in order to give information about it. ラベル □ *He peered at the label on the bottle.* 彼は瓶のラベルをじっと見た. ■ V-T 他動詞 If something **is labeled**, a label is attached to it giving information about it. ラベルを貼る [usu passive] □ *It requires foreign frozen-food imports to be clearly labeled.* 輸入品の冷凍食品は分かりやすいラベルを貼る必要がある. □ *The produce was labeled "Made in China."* その産物には「中国産」のラベルが貼ってあった. ■ V-T 他動詞 If you say that someone or something **is labeled as** a particular thing, you mean that people generally describe them that way and you think that this is unfair. 呼ぶ, 名付りる [DISAPPROVAL 不賛成] [usu passive] □ *It won't be labeled in any way as a military expedition.* それが軍事的遠征と呼ばれることは決してないだろう. □ *It does not matter whether these duties are labeled "duties" or "tasks."* こうした任務を任務と呼ぶか作業と呼ぶかはどうでもよいことだ.
→ see **graph**

la|bor /leɪbər/ (**labors, laboring, labored**) ■ N-UNCOUNT 不可算名詞 **Labor** is very hard work, usually physical work. 労働 [also N in pl] □ *...the labor of hauling the rocks away.* 岩を引っ張って運び去る労働. ■ V-I 自動詞 Someone who **labors** works hard using their hands. 労働する □ *...he will be laboring 14 hundred meters below ground.* 彼は地下1400メートルのところで働いている予定だ. ■ V-T/V-I 他動詞/自動詞 If you **labor to** do something, you do it with difficulty. 努力する □ *Scientists labored for months to unravel the mysteries of Neptune and still remain baffled.* 科学者たちが何か月間も海王星の神秘の解明に努めたが、まだ解明できていない. □ *We're laboring under an unfair disadvantage.* 我々は不公平な不利な立場で悪戦苦闘している. ■ N-UNCOUNT 不可算名詞 **Labor** is used to refer to the workers of a country or industry, considered as a group. 労働者, 労働階級 □ *We have a problem of skilled labor.* 我々は熟練労働力の問題を抱えている. □ *Employers want cheap labor and consumers want cheap houses.* 雇用主は低賃金の労働者を求め、消費者は低価格の住宅を求める. ■ N-UNCOUNT 不可算名詞 The work done by a group of workers or by a particular worker is referred to as their **labor**. 仕事 □ *He exhibits a profound humility in the low rates he pays himself for his labor.* 自らの仕事に低賃金を支払っていることから彼が非常に謙虚な人物であることが分かる. ■ N-UNCOUNT 不可算名詞 **Labor** is the last stage of pregnancy, in which the baby is gradually pushed out of the womb by the mother. 出産 □ *Her labor had lasted ten hours before the doctor arranged a Cesarean section.* 彼女の陣痛は医者が帝王切開を手配するまで10時間続いた.

la|bora|tory /læbrətɔri/ (**laboratories**) ■ N-COUNT 可算名詞 A **laboratory** is a building or a room where scientific experiments, analyses, and research are carried out. 研究室 □ *...a brain research laboratory at Columbia University.* コロンビア大学の脳研究室 ■ N-COUNT 可算名詞 A **laboratory** in a school, college, or university is a room containing scientific equipment where students are taught science subjects such as chemistry. 実験室 □ *...my old school chemistry laboratory.* 私の母校の化学実験室
→ see Word Web: **laboratory**

la|bor|er /leɪbərər/ (**laborers**) N-COUNT 可算名詞 A **laborer** is a person who does a job which involves a lot of hard physical work. 肉体労働者 □ *He still lives on the farm where he worked as a laborer.* 彼女は彼が人夫として働いた農場にまだ住んでいる.
→ see **union**

la|bor force (**labor forces**) N-COUNT 可算名詞 The **labor force** consists of all the people who are able to work in a country or area, or all the people who work for a particular company. 労働力 [BUSINESS 実業] □ *He says the reduction of the labor force could be significant.* 彼は労働力の削減はかなりなものになる可能性があると言っている.

labor-intensive ADJ 形容詞 **Labor-intensive** industries or methods of making things involve a lot of workers. Compare **capital-intensive**. 労働集約的な [BUSINESS 実業] □ *For labor-intensive businesses like garments, factory labor is cheap.* 衣類などの労働集約的な企業にとって、工場労働は安上がりだ.

la|bo|ri|ous /ləbɔriəs/ ADJ 形容詞 If you describe a task or job as **laborious**, you mean that it takes a lot of time and effort. 労力を要する □ *Keeping the yard tidy all year round can be a laborious task.* 1年中庭をきちんとしておくことは骨の折れる仕事である. ● **la|bo|ri|ous|ly** ADV 副詞 [ADV with v] 苦労して □ *...the embroidery she'd worked on so laboriously during the long winter nights.* 長い冬の夜に彼女があれほど骨を折って取り組んだ刺繍(ししゅう)

la|bor mar|ket (**labor markets**) N-COUNT 可算名詞 When you talk about **the labor market**, you are referring to all the people who are able to work and want jobs in a country or area, in relation to the number of jobs there are available in that country or area. 労働市場 [BUSINESS 実業] □ *In a tight labor market, demand by employers exceeds the available supply of workers.* 逼迫(ひっぱく)した労働市場では、雇用主の需要は利用できる労働者の供給より大きい.

Word Web — laboratory

The discovery of the life-saving drug penicillin was a fortunate accident. While cleaning up his **laboratory**, a **researcher** named Alexander Fleming* noticed that the bacteria in one petri dish had been killed by some kind of **mold**. He took a **sample** and found that it was a form of penicillin. Fleming and others did further **research** and **published** their **findings** in 1928, but few people took notice. However, ten years later a team at Oxford University read Fleming's **study** and began animal and human **experiments**. Within a decade, companies were manufacturing 650 billion units of penicillin a month!

Alexander Fleming (1881-1955): a Scottish biologist and pharmacologist.

la|bor re|la|tions N-PLURAL 複数名詞 **Labor relations** refers to the relationship between employers and employees in industry, and the political decisions and laws that affect it. 労使関係 ❑ *We have to balance good labor relations against the need to cut costs.* 我々は良好な労使関係を経費削減の必要性とバランスを取らなければならない.

la|bor un|ion (**labor unions**) N-COUNT 可算名詞 A **labor union** is an organization that represents the rights and interests of workers to their employers, for example in order to improve working conditions or wages. 労働組合 [AM 米国英語] ❑ *...NYSUT, the state's largest labor union.* 州最大の労働組合であるNYSUT

la|bour /leɪbər/ → see **labor**

la|boured /leɪbərd/ → see **labored**

la|bour|er /leɪbərər/ → see **laborer**

lab|y|rinth /læbɪrɪnθ/ (**labyrinths**) ◼ N-COUNT 可算名詞 If you describe a place as a **labyrinth**, you mean that it is made up of a complicated series of paths or passages, through which it is difficult to find your way. 入り組んだ迷路 [LITERARY 文語的] ❑ *...the labyrinth of corridors.* 迷路のような廊下 ◼ N-COUNT 可算名詞 If you describe a situation, process, or area of knowledge as a **labyrinth**, you mean that it is very complicated. 複雑な状況 [FORMAL 形式ばった] ❑ *...a labyrinth of conflicting political and sociological interpretations.* 矛盾する政治的・社会学的解釈の複雑な関係

lace /leɪs/ (**laces, lacing, laced**) ◼ N-UNCOUNT 不可算名詞 **Lace** is a very delicate cloth which is made with a lot of holes in it. It is made by twisting together very fine threads of cotton to form decorative patterns. レース ❑ *She finally found the perfect gown, a beautiful creation trimmed with lace.* 彼女は完璧なドレス, レースの縁取りのある美しいドレスをやっと見つけた. ◼ N-COUNT 可算名詞 **Laces** are thin pieces of material that are put through special holes in some types of clothing, especially shoes. The laces are tied together in order to tighten the clothing. 締めひも ❑ *Barry was sitting on the bed, tying the laces of an old pair of running shoes.* バリーはベッドに腰掛けて, 使い古したランニングシューズのひもを結んでいた. ◼ V-T 他動詞 If you **lace** something such as a pair of shoes, you tighten the shoes by pulling the laces through the holes, and usually tying them together. 締めひもで締める ❑ *I have a good pair of skates, but no matter how tightly I lace them, my ankles wobble.* 私は立派なスケート靴を持っているが, どんなに強くひもで締めても足首がぐらぐらする. ● PHRASAL VERB 句動詞 **Lace up** means the same as **lace**. ひもを結ぶ ❑ *He sat on the steps, and laced up his boots.* 彼は階段に腰掛けてブーツのひもを結んだ. ◼ V-T 他動詞 To **lace** food or drink with a substance such as alcohol or a drug means to put a small amount of the substance into the food or drink. 少量加える ❑ *She laced his food with sleeping pills.* 彼女は彼の食べ物に睡眠薬を少し入れた.

lack /læk/ (**lacks, lacking, lacked**) ◼ N-UNCOUNT 不可算名詞 If there is a **lack** of something, there is not enough of it or it does not exist at all. 不足 [also 'a' N, usu N 'of' n] ❑ *Despite his lack of experience, he got the job.* 彼は経験不足だったにもかかわらず採用された. ❑ *The charges were dropped for lack of evidence.* 告訴は証拠不足のため撤回された. ◼ V-T/V-I 他動詞/自動詞 If you say that someone or something **lacks** a particular quality or that a particular quality is **lacking** in them, you mean that they do not have any or enough of it. 欠けている ❑ *It lacked the power of the Italian cars.* それにはイタリア製の車の力がなかった. ❑ *He lacked the judgment and political acumen for the post of chairman.* 彼には会長の地位に必要な判断力と政治的な洞察力が欠けていた. ◼ PHRASE 句 If you say there is **no lack of** something, you are emphasizing that there is a great deal of it. 一が十分 [EMPHASIS 強調] ❑ *He said there was no lack of things for them to talk about.* 彼は話すことがいっぱいあると言った.

Thesaurus   lack また次を参照：

N.   absence, shortage; (*ant.*) abundance ◼

V.   be without, miss, need, require, want; (*ant.*) have, own ◼

Word Partnership   lack は次の語句と使われる：

N.   lack *of* confidence, lack *of* control, lack *of* enthusiasm, lack *of* evidence, lack *of* exercise, lack *of* experience, lack *of* food, lack *of* information, lack *of* knowledge, lack *of* money, lack *of* progress, lack *of* resources, lack *of* skills, lack *of* sleep, lack *of* support, lack *of* trust, lack *of* understanding ◼ ◼

---

lack|ing /lækɪŋ/ ADJ 形容詞 If something or someone is **lacking** in a particular quality, they do not have any of it or enough of it. 足りない [v-link ADJ] ❑ *...if your hair is lacking in luster and feeling dry.* 髪につやがなく乾燥している場合には ❑ *She felt nervous, increasingly lacking in confidence about herself.* 彼女は自信をますます失い, 胸がどきどきした.

lack|luster /læklʌstər/ ADJ 形容詞 If you describe something or someone as **lackluster**, you mean that they are not exciting or energetic. 活気のない ❑ *He has already been blamed for his party's lackluster performance during the election campaign.* 彼は選挙運動中に彼の政党の活動がぱっとしなかった責任を既に負わされていた.

lac|quer /lækər/ (**lacquers**) N-MASS 質量名詞 **Lacquer** is a special liquid which is painted on wood or metal in order to protect it and to make it shiny. ラッカー ❑ *We put on the second coating of lacquer.* 我々はラッカーの2度目の上塗りをした.

lacy /leɪsi/ (**lacier, laciest**) ADJ 形容詞 **Lacy** things are made from lace or have pieces of lace attached to them. レースの ❑ *...lacy nightgowns.* レースのナイトガウン

lad /læd/ (**lads**) N-COUNT; N-VOC 可算名詞, 呼格名詞 A **lad** is a young man or boy. 若者 [OLD-FASHIONED 古風な] ❑ *When I was a lad his age I would laugh at the strangest things.* 私が彼くらいの年齢の若者だったときには, 非常に見慣れない物はあざ笑っていたものだ.

lad|der /lædər/ (**ladders**) ◼ N-COUNT 可算名詞 A **ladder** is a piece of equipment used for climbing up something or down from something. It consists of two long pieces of wood, metal, or rope with steps fixed between them. はしご ❑ *He climbed the ladder to the next deck.* 彼ははしごを上って次の甲板に出た. ◼ N-SING 単数名詞 You can use **the ladder** to refer to something such as a society, organization, or system which has different levels that people can progress up or drop down. 階段 ❑ *If they want to climb the ladder of success they should be given that opportunity.* 彼らが成功の階段を上りたいのなら, その機会を与えられるべきだ. ◼ N-COUNT 可算名詞 A **ladder** is a hole or torn part in a woman's stocking or pantyhose, where some of the vertical threads have broken, leaving only the horizontal threads. 伝線 [BRIT 英国英語; AM 米国英語 **run**]

lad|en /leɪdⁿn/ ◼ ADJ 形容詞 If someone or something is **laden with** a lot of heavy things, they are holding or carrying them. 積んだ [LITERARY 文語的] ❑ *I came home laden with cardboard boxes.* 私はボール箱をたくさん抱えて帰宅した. ❑ *The following summer the peach tree was laden with fruit.* 次の夏, 桃の木は鈴なりに実っていた. ◼ ADJ 形容詞 If you describe a person or thing as **laden with** something, particularly something bad, you mean that they have a lot of it. 苦しんで [v-link ADJ 'with' n] ❑ *We're so laden with guilt.* 我々は罪悪感で大変悩んでいる.

lady /leɪdi/ (**ladies**) ◼ N-COUNT 可算名詞 You can use **lady** when you are referring to a woman, especially when you are showing politeness or respect. 女性 ❑ *She's a very sweet old lady.* 彼女はとても感じのよい老婦人だ. ❑ *...a cream-colored lady's shoe.* クリーム色の女性用の靴 ◼ N-VOC 呼格名詞 "**Lady**" is sometimes used by men as a form of address when they are talking to a woman that they do not know, especially in stores and on the street. (呼びかけに) 奥様 [AM 米国英語, INFORMAL くだけた, POLITENESS 丁寧さ] ❑ *What seems to be the trouble, lady?* 奥さん, どうしましたか. ◼ N-TITLE 称号名詞 In Britain, **Lady** is a title used in front of the names of some female members of the nobility, or the wives of knights. レディー

lag /læg/ (**lags, lagging, lagged**) ◼ V-I 自動詞 If one thing or person **lags behind** another thing or person, their progress is slower than that of the other thing or person. 遅れる ❑ *Western banks still lag behind financial institutions in most other regions of the country.* 西欧の銀行はその国のほとんどの他の地域で金融機関にまだ遅れを取っている. ❑ *The restructuring of the pattern of consumption also lagged behind.* 消費型の建て直しも遅れた. ◼ N-COUNT 可算名詞 A time **lag** or a **lag** of a particular length of time is a period of time between one event and another related event. 時間のずれ ❑ *There's a time lag between infection with HIV and developing AIDS.* HIVに感染してからAIDSの発症まで時間のずれがある.

la|goon /ləgun/ (**lagoons**) N-COUNT 可算名詞 A **lagoon** is an area of calm sea water that is separated from the ocean by a line of rock or sand. 潟 (かた)

laid /leɪd/ **Laid** is the past tense and past participle of **lay**. layの過去・過去分詞

laid-back ADJ 形容詞 If you describe someone as **laid-back**, you mean that they behave in a calm relaxed way as if nothing will ever worry them. のんびりした [INFORMAL くだけた] ❑ *Everyone here has a really laid-back attitude.* ここではだれでも本当にゆったり構えている.

lain /leɪn/ **Lain** is the past participle of **lie**. lieの過去分詞

laissez-faire /leɪseɪ fɛər, lɛs-/ N-UNCOUNT 不可算名詞 **Laissez-faire** is the policy which is based on the idea that governments and the law should not interfere with business, finance, or the conditions of people's working lives. 自由放任主義, レッセフェール [BUSINESS 実業] ❑ *...the doctrine of laissez-faire and unbridled individualism.* レッセフェールと無制限な個人主義の理論

lake /leɪk/ (**lakes**) N-COUNT 可算名詞 A **lake** is a large area of fresh water, surrounded by land. 湖 ❑ *They can go fishing in the lake.*

Several forces create **lakes**. The movement of a glacier can carve out a deep **basin** in the soil. The Great Lakes between the U.S. and Canada are **glacial** lakes. Very deep lakes appear when large pieces of the earth's crust suddenly shift. Lake Baikal in Russia is over a mile deep. When a volcano erupts, it creates a **crater**. Crater Lake in Oregon is the perfectly round remains of a volcanic cone. It contains **water** from melted snow and rain. Erosion also creates lakes. When the wind blows away sand, the hole left behind forms a natural lake **bed**.

彼らは湖で魚釣りができる.
→ see Word Web: **lake**
→ see **river**

lamb /læm/ (lambs) N-COUNT 可算名詞 A lamb is a young sheep. 子羊● N-UNCOUNT 不可算名詞 **Lamb** is the flesh of a lamb eaten as food. 子羊の肉 ❏ Laura was basting the leg of lamb. ローラは子羊の脚肉をあぶりながらたれをつけていた.

lame /leɪm/ (lamer, lamest) ① ADJ 形容詞 If someone is **lame**, they are unable to walk properly because of damage to one or both of their legs. 足の不自由な ❏ He was aware that she was lame in one leg. 彼は片足が不自由なことを知っていた. ● N-PLURAL 複数名詞 **The lame** are people who are lame. 足の不自由な人たち ❏ ...the wounded and the lame of the last war. この前の戦争で負傷した人たちや足が不自由になった人たち ② ADJ 形容詞 If you describe an excuse, argument, or remark as **lame**, you mean that it is poor or weak. 不十分な, へたな ❏ He mumbled some lame excuse about having gone to sleep. 彼は眠ってしまったことについて苦しい言い訳をぶつぶつつぶやいた. ● **lame|ly** ADV 副詞 [ADV with v] ぎこちなく "Lovely house," I said lamely. 「ステキな家ね」と私はぎこちなく言った.

la|ment /ləmɛnt/ (laments, lamenting, lamented) ① V-T/V-I 自動詞 If you **lament** something, you express your sadness, regret, or disappointment about it. 嘆き悲しむ, 残念に思う [mainly FORMAL OR WRITTEN 主に形式ばった, または書き言葉] ❏ Ken began to lament the death of his only son. ケンは彼の1人息子の死を嘆き始めた. ❏ He laments that people in Villa El Salvador are suspicious of the police. 彼はヴィラ・エルサルバドルの人々が警察を信用していないことを残念がっている. ② N-UNCOUNT 不可算名詞 Someone's **lament** is an expression of their sadness, regret, or disappointment about something. 悲嘆, 嘆き [mainly FORMAL OR WRITTEN 主に形式ばった, または書き言葉] ❏ She spoke of the professional woman's lament that a woman's judgment is questioned more than a man's. 彼女は男性の判断力よりも女性の判断力のほうが疑われることを専門職の女性が残念に思っていることについて話した. ③ N-COUNT 可算名詞 A **lament** is a poem, song, or piece of music which expresses sorrow that someone has died. 哀歌 ❏ ...Shelley's lament for the death of Keats. キーツの死に対するシェリーの哀歌

lamp /læmp/ (lamps) N-COUNT 可算名詞 A **lamp** is a light that works by using electricity or by burning oil or gas. ランプ ❏ She switched on the bedside lamp. 彼女はベッド脇のランプをつけた.

LAN /læn/ (LANs) N-COUNT 可算名詞 A **LAN** is a group of personal computers and associated equipment that are linked by cable, for example in an office building, and that share a communications line. **LAN** is an abbreviation for **local area network**. local area networkの略, ラン [COMPUTING コンピューティング] ❏ You can take part in multiplayer games either on a LAN network or via the Internet. マルチプレイヤー・ゲームではランまたはインターネット経由で参加できる.

land /lænd/ (lands, landing, landed) ① N-UNCOUNT 不可算名詞 **Land** is an area of ground, especially one that is used for a particular purpose such as farming or building. 土地 ❏ Good agricultural land is in short supply. 優れた農地は不足している. ❏ ...160 acres of land. 160エーカーの土地 ② N-COUNT 可算名詞 You can refer to an area of land which someone owns as their **land** or their **lands**. 所有地, 地所 ❏ Their home is on his father's land. 彼らの家は彼の父親の所有地にある. ③ N-SING 単数名詞 If you talk about **the land**, you mean farming and the way of life in farming areas, in contrast to life in the cities. 農地, 田園 ❏ Living off the land was hard enough at the best of times. 農地で生計を立てることは最良の時代にあっても大変だった. ④ N-UNCOUNT 不可算名詞 **Land** is the part of the world that consists of ground, rather than sea or air. 陸 [also 'the' N] ❏ It isn't clear whether the plane went down over land or sea. 飛行機が墜落したのが陸だったのか海だったのかはっきりしない. ⑤ N-COUNT 可算名詞 You can use **land** to refer to a country in a poetic or emotional way. 国 [LITERARY 文語的] ❏ ...America, land of opportunity. 機会の国, アメリカ

Country is the most usual word to use when you are talking about the major political units that the world is divided into. **State** is used when you are talking about politics or government institutions. ❏ ...the new German state created by the unification process. ...Italy's state-controlled telecommunications company. **State** can also refer to a political unit within a particular country. ❏ ...the state of California. **Nation** is often used when you are talking about a country's inhabitants, and their cultural or ethnic background. ❏ Wales is a proud nation with its own traditions...A senior government spokesman will address the nation. **Land** is a less precise and more literary word, which you can use, for example, to talk about the feelings you have for a particular country. ❏ She was fascinated to learn about this strange land at the edge of Europe.

⑥ V-I 自動詞 When someone or something **lands**, they come down to the ground after moving through the air or falling. 着地する ❏ He was sent flying into the air and landed 20 feet away. 彼は空中に飛ばされ, 20フィート離れたところに着地した. ⑦ V-T/V-I 他動詞/自動詞 When someone **lands** a plane, ship, or spacecraft, or when it **lands**, it arrives somewhere after a journey. 着陸させる, 着陸する ❏ The jet landed after a flight of just under three hours. ジェット機は3時間弱飛行した後に着陸した. ❏ He landed his troops on the western shore. 彼は西岸に軍隊を上陸させた. ⑧ V-T/V-I 他動詞/自動詞 If you **land** in an unpleasant situation or place or if something **lands** you in it, something causes you to be in it. 陥らせる, 陥る [INFORMAL くだけた] ❏ He landed in a psychiatric ward. 彼は精神科の病棟に入った. ⑨ V-I 自動詞 If something **lands** somewhere, it arrives there unexpectedly, often causing problems. 到着する [INFORMAL くだけた] ❏ Two days later the book had already landed on his desk. 2日後にその本はすでに彼の机の上に届いていた. ⑩ to **land on** your **feet** → see **foot**
→ see **continent**, **earth**, **skyscraper**

Thesaurus land また次を参照:

N.	acreage, area, country, real estate ①
V.	arrive, touch down; (ant.) take off ⑥ ⑦

Word Partnership land は次の語句と使われる:

N.	**acres of** land, **area of** land, **desert** land, land **development**, land **management**, land **ownership**, **parcel of** land, **piece of** land, **plot of** land, **strip of** land, **tract of** land, land **use** ① ②
ADJ.	**agricultural** land, **fertile** land, **flat** land, **grazing** land, **private** land, **public** land, **undeveloped** land, **vacant** land, **vast** land ① ②
V.	**buy** land, **own** land, **sell** land ① ②

land|fill /lændfɪl/ (landfills) ① N-UNCOUNT 不可算名詞 **Landfill** is a method of getting rid of very large amounts of garbage by burying it in a large deep hole. ゴミ埋め立て ❏ ...the environmental costs of landfill. ゴミ埋め立ての環境保全経費 ② N-COUNT 可算名詞 A **landfill** is a large deep hole in which very large amounts of garbage are buried. ゴミ処理場 ❏ The rubbish in modern landfills does not rot. 近代的なゴミ処理場のゴミは腐らない.
→ see **dump**

land|ing /lændɪŋ/ (landings) ① N-COUNT 可算名詞 In a house or other building, the **landing** is the area at the top of the staircase which has rooms leading off it. 踊り場 ❏ I ran out onto the landing. 私は走り出て踊り場の上に出た. ② N-VAR 可変性名詞 A **landing** is an act of bringing an aircraft or spacecraft down to the ground. 着陸 ❏ I had to make a controlled landing into the sea. 私は海に制御着水をしなければならなかった. ③ N-COUNT 可算名詞 When a **landing** takes place, troops are unloaded from boats or aircraft at the beginning of a military invasion or other operation. 上陸 ❏ American forces have begun a big landing. 米軍は大規模な上陸を始めた.

land|lady /lændleɪdi/ (landladies) N-COUNT 可算名詞 Someone's **landlady** is the woman who allows them to live or

work in a building which she owns, in return for rent. 女家主 ❑ *There was a note under the door from my landlady.* 私の女家主からのメモがドアの下にあった。

land|lord /lǽndlɔːrd/ (**landlords**) N-COUNT 可算名詞 Someone's **landlord** is the man who allows them to live or work in a building which he owns, in return for rent. 家主 ❑ *His landlord doubled the rent.* 彼の家主は家賃を2倍に上げた。

land|mark /lǽndmɑːrk/ (**landmarks**) **1** N-COUNT 可算名詞 A **landmark** is a building or feature which is easily noticed and can be used to judge your position or the position of other buildings or features. 目印となるもの, 陸標 ❑ *The Menger Hotel is a San Antonio landmark.* メンジャー・ホテルはサンアントニオ市の目印になる建物だ。 **2** N-COUNT 可算名詞 You can refer to an important stage in the development of something as a **landmark**. 際立った出来事 ❑ *...a landmark arms control treaty.* 画期的な軍備縮小協定

land|scape /lǽndskeɪp/ (**landscapes, landscaping, landscaped**) **1** N-VAR 可変性名詞 The **landscape** is everything you can see when you look across an area of land, including hills, rivers, buildings, trees, and plants. 風景 ❑ *...Arizona's desert landscape.* アリゾナ州の砂漠の風景

Do not confuse **landscape**, **scenery**, **countryside**, and **nature**. With **landscape**, the emphasis is on the physical features of the land, while **scenery** includes everything you can see when you look out over an area of land. ❑ *...the landscape of steep woods and distant mountains. ...unattractive urban scenery.* **Countryside** is land which is away from towns and cities. ❑ *3,500 acres of mostly flat countryside.* **Nature** includes the landscape, the weather, animals, and plants. ❑ *These creatures roamed the Earth as the finest and rarest wonders of nature.*

2 N-COUNT 可算名詞 A **landscape** is all the features that are important in a particular situation. 状況 ❑ *June's events completely altered the political landscape.* 6月の出来事は政治的状況を完全に変えた。 **3** N-COUNT 可算名詞 A **landscape** is a painting which shows a scene in the countryside. 風景画 ❑ *Kenna's latest series of landscapes is on show at the Zelda Cheatle Gallery.* ケナの風景写真の最近の連作はゼルダ・チートル画廊で展示されている。 **4** V-T 他動詞 If an area of land **is landscaped**, it is changed to make it more attractive, for example, by adding streams or ponds and planting trees and bushes. 美化する ❑ *The gravel pits have been landscaped and planted to make them attractive to wildfowl.* 砂利採取場は野鳥を引き寄せるために庭園化され, 植物が植えられた。 ❑ *They had landscaped their property with trees, shrubs, and lawns.* 彼らは自分たちの地所を樹木, 低木, 芝生を植えて整備した。 ● **land|scap|ing** N-UNCOUNT 不可算名詞 景観設計 ❑ *The landowner insisted on a high standard of landscaping.* その地主は高水準の造園設計を強く求めた。 **5** N-UNCOUNT 不可算名詞 [oft N N] If a sheet of paper is in **landscape** format or mode, the longer edge of the paper is horizontal and the shorter edge is vertical. 横長 ❑ *Most powerpoint presentations are prepared for screens in landscape format.* パワーポイント・プレゼンテーションの大半はスクリーン用に横長のフォーマットで作成される。
→ see **art, painting**

land|slide /lǽndslaɪd/ (**landslides**) **1** N-COUNT 可算名詞 A **landslide** is a victory in an election in which a person or political party gets far more votes or seats than their opponents. 大勝利 ❑ *He won last month's presidential election by a landslide.* 彼は先月の大統領選挙に圧勝した。 **2** N-COUNT 可算名詞 A **landslide** is a large amount of earth and rocks falling down a cliff or the side of a mountain. 地滑り ❑ *The storm caused landslides and flooding in Savona.* その嵐はサヴォナ市で地滑りと洪水を引き起こした。
→ see **disaster**

lane /leɪn/ (**lanes**) **1** N-COUNT 可算名詞 A **lane** is a narrow road, especially in the country. 小道 ❑ *...a quiet country lane.* 静かな田舎の小道 **2** N-IN-NAMES 名称中の名詞 **Lane** is also used in the names of roads, either in cities or in the country. 通り ❑ *They had a house on Spring Park Lane in East Hampton.* 彼らはイーストハンプトン町のスプリング・パーク通りに家を持っていた。 **3** N-COUNT 可算名詞 A **lane** is a part of a main road which is marked by the edge of the road and a painted line, or by two painted lines. 車線 ❑ *The truck was traveling at 20 mph in the slow lane.* トラックはスピードの遅い車線で時速20マイルで走っていた。 **4** N-COUNT 可算名詞 At a swimming pool, athletics track, or bowling alley, a **lane** is a long narrow section which is separated from other sections, for example by lines or ropes. コース ❑ *...after being disqualified for running out of his lane in the 200 meters.* 200メートル競技でコースからはずれたために失格してから **5** N-COUNT 可算名詞 A **lane** is a route that is frequently used by aircraft or ships. 航路 ❑ *The collision took place in one of the busiest shipping lanes in the world.* その衝突は世界で最も混雑した航路の1つで起こった。
→ see **traffic**

lan|guage /lǽŋgwɪdʒ/ (**languages**) **1** N-COUNT 可算名詞 A **language** is a system of communication which consists of a set of sounds and written symbols which are used by the people of a particular country or region for talking or writing. 言語 ❑ *...the*

English language. 英語 ❑ *Students are expected to master a second language.* 学生は第2言語を習得することになっている。 **2** N-UNCOUNT 不可算名詞 **Language** is the use of a system of communication which consists of a set of sounds or written symbols. 言葉 ❑ *Students examined how children acquire language.* 学生は子供が言葉を覚える方法を調べた。 **3** N-UNCOUNT 不可算名詞 You can refer to the words used in connection with a particular subject as **the language of** that subject. 専門用語 ❑ *...the language of business.* ビジネス用語 **4** N-UNCOUNT 不可算名詞 You can refer to someone's use of rude words or swearing as **bad language** when you find it offensive. 下品な言葉 ❑ *Television companies tend to censor bad language in feature films.* テレビ局は長編映画の下品な言葉を削除することがよくある。 **5** N-UNCOUNT 不可算名詞 The **language** of a piece of writing or speech is the style in which it is written or spoken. 言葉づかい ❑ *The tone of his language was diplomatic and polite.* 彼の口調はそつのない丁寧なものだった。 **6** N-VAR 可変性名詞 You can use **language** to refer to various means of communication involving recognizable symbols, nonverbal sounds, or actions. 伝達記号体系 ❑ *Some sign languages are very sophisticated means of communication.* 一部の手話は非常に高度な意思疎通の手段である。 ❑ *...the digital language of computers.* コンピュータのディジタル言語
→ see **culture**

Thesaurus	language また次を参照:
N.	communication, dialect, lexicon **1** **2** **6** jargon, slang, terminology **3** **5** swear **4**

Word Partnership	language は次の語句と使われる:
V.	**know** a language, **learn** a language, **speak** a language, **study** a language, **teach** a language, **understand** a language, **use** a language **1**
ADJ.	**a different** language, **foreign** language, **native** language, **official** language, **second** language, **universal** language **1** **bad** language, **foul** language, **vulgar** language **4** **plain** language, **simple** language, **technical** language **5**
N.	language **acquisition**, language **barrier**, **child** language, language **of children**, language **classes**, language **comprehension**, language **development**, **proficiency in** a language, language **skills** **1** **2** **body** language, **computer** language, **programming** language, **sign** language **6**

lan|guid /lǽŋgwɪd/ ADJ 形容詞 If you describe someone as **languid**, you mean that they show little energy or interest and are very slow and casual in their movements. 元気のない, もの憂い [LITERARY 文語的] ❑ *He's a large, languid man with a round and impassive face.* 彼は無表情の丸顔をしただらっとした大男だ。 ● **lan|guid|ly** ADV 副詞 元気なく ❑ *We sat about languidly after dinner.* 我々は食後もの憂くあたりに座っていた。

lan|guish /lǽŋgwɪʃ/ (**languishes, languishing, languished**) **1** V-I 自動詞 If someone **languishes** somewhere, they are forced to remain and suffer in an unpleasant situation. つらい生活をする ❑ *Pollard continues to languish in prison.* ポラードは刑務所で苦しい生活をし続けている。 **2** V-I 自動詞 If something **languishes**, it is not successful, often because of a lack of effort or because of a lot of difficulties. 活気がなくなる ❑ *Without the founder's drive and direction, the company gradually languished.* 創業者の気迫と指揮を失って, その会社は次第に活気がなくなった。

lan|tern /lǽntərn/ (**lanterns**) N-COUNT 可算名詞 A **lantern** is a lamp in a metal frame with glass sides and with a handle on top so you can carry it. 手提げランプ

lap /lǽp/ (**laps, lapping, lapped**) **1** N-COUNT 可算名詞 If you have something on your **lap** when you are sitting down, it is on top of your legs and near to your body. ひざ ❑ *She waited quietly with her hands in her lap.* 彼女は手をひざに置いて静かに待った。 **2** N-COUNT 可算名詞 In a race, a competitor completes a **lap** when they have gone around a course once. 1周 ❑ *...that last lap of the race.* 競争のあの最後の1周 **3** V-T 他動詞 In a race, if you **lap** another competitor, you go past them while they are still on the previous lap. 1周以上リードする ❑ *He then built a 10-bike lead before lapping his first rider on lap 14.* 彼はそれから14周目で最初の選手を1周以上リードする前に自転車10台を追い抜いた。 **4** N-COUNT 可算名詞 A **lap** of a long journey is one part of it, between two points where you stop. 1行程 ❑ *I had thought we might travel as far as Oak Valley, but we only managed the first lap of the journey.* 私はオーク渓谷まで行けるかもしれないと思っていたが, 我々は旅の最初の行程をやっとこなしただけだった。 **5** V-I 自動詞 When water **laps** against something such as the shore or the side of a boat, it touches it gently and

makes a soft sound. 打ち寄せる [WRITTEN 書き言葉] ❑ ...the water that lapped against the pillars of the boathouse. ボート小屋の柱にぴたぴたと打ち寄せた水. ❑ With a rising tide the water was lapping at his chin before rescuers arrived. 高潮のため, 救助隊が到着する前に水は彼のあごにひたひたと打ち寄せていた. ●**lapping** N-UNCOUNT 不可算名詞 小波の打ち寄せること ❑ The only sound was the lapping of the waves. 聞えるのは波の打ち寄せる音だけだった. ⑥ V-T 他動詞 When an animal **laps** a drink, it uses short quick movements of its tongue to take liquid up into its mouth. ぴちゃぴちゃ飲む ❑ It lapped milk from a dish. それは皿のミルクをぴちゃぴちゃ飲んだ. ●PHRASAL VERB 句動詞 **Lap up** means the same as **lap**. ぴちゃぴちゃ飲む ❑ She poured some water into a plastic bowl. Faust, her Great Dane, lapped it up with relish. 彼女はプラスチックのボウルに水を注いだ. 彼女のグレートデーン犬のファウストは喜んでそれを飲んだ.

▶ **lap up** ① PHRASAL VERB 句動詞 If you say that someone **laps up** something such as information or attention, you mean that they accept it eagerly, usually when you think they are being foolish for believing that it is sincere. 真に受ける ❑ Their audience will lap up whatever they throw at them. 彼らの聴衆は彼らの言うことなら何でも信じるだろう. ② → see lap 6

la|pel /ləpɛ́l/ (lapels) N-COUNT 可算名詞 The **lapels** of a jacket or coat are the two top parts at the front that are folded back on each side and join on to the collar. 下襟 ❑ He sports a small red flower in his lapel. 彼は下襟のところに小さな赤い花をつけて見せびらかしている.

Word Link
lapse ≈ falling : col**lapse**, e**lapse**, **lapse**

lapse /lǽps/ (lapses, lapsing, lapsed) ① N-COUNT 可算名詞 A **lapse** is a moment or instance of bad behavior by someone who usually behaves well. ささいな間違い ❑ On Friday he showed neither decency nor dignity. It was an uncommon lapse. 金曜日に彼には礼儀正しさも威厳も見られなかった. これは珍しい過ちだった. ② N-COUNT 可算名詞 A **lapse of** something such as concentration or judgment is a temporary lack of that thing, which can often cause you to make a mistake. 一時的な喪失 ❑ I had a little lapse of concentration in the middle of the race. 私は競技の最中に集中力をちょっと失ってしまった. ❑ He was a genius and because of it you could accept lapses of taste. 彼は天才だった. それゆえに彼が審美眼を時々失うのを許容できた. ③ V-I 自動詞 If you **lapse into** a quiet or inactive state, you stop talking or being active. (ある状態に) なる ❑ She muttered something unintelligible and lapsed into silence. 彼女は何か理解できないことをつぶやき, 黙りこんだ. ④ V-I 自動詞 If someone **lapses into** a particular way of speaking, or behaving, they start speaking or behaving in that way, usually for a short period. (ある話し方・振る舞い方に) なる ❑ She lapsed into a little girl voice to deliver a nursery rhyme. 彼女は童謡を伝えるために少女の声になった. ●N-COUNT 可算名詞 **Lapse** is also a noun. 陥ること ❑ Her lapse into German didn't seem peculiar. After all, it was her native tongue. 彼女がドイツ語になるのは別に不思議ではなかった. 何と言ってもそれは彼女の母語だった. ⑤ N-SING 単数名詞 A **lapse of** time is a period that is long enough for a situation to change or for people to have a different opinion about it. 経過 ❑ ...the restoration of diplomatic relations after a lapse of 24 years. 24年ぶりの外交関係の復活 ⑥ V-I 自動詞 If a period of time **lapses**, it passes. 経過する ❑ New products and production processes are transferred to the developing countries only after a substantial amount of time has lapsed. 新製品と製造プロセスは相当長い時間が経過してから初めて発展途上国に移転される. ⑦ V-I 自動詞 If a situation or legal contract **lapses**, it is allowed to end rather than being continued, renewed, or extended. 失効する ❑ The terms of the treaty lapsed in 1987. その条約の条項は1987年に失効した. ⑧ V-I 自動詞 If a member of a particular religion **lapses**, they stop believing in it or stop following its rules and practices. 離脱する ❑ I lapsed in my 20s, returned to it, then lapsed again, while writing the life of historical Jesus. 私は20代の時に信仰を捨て, それを取り戻し, 歴史的イエスの生涯について著述中に再び信仰を捨てた.

lap|top /lǽptɒp/ (laptops) N-COUNT 可算名詞 A **laptop** or a **laptop computer** is a small portable computer. ラップトップコンピュータ ❑ She used to work at her laptop until four in the morning. 彼女は朝の4時までラップトップコンピュータを使って作業したものだった.

Word Link
er ≈ more : cold**er**, high**er**, larg**er**

Word Link
est ≈ most : cold**est**, high**est**, larg**est**

large /lɑ́rdʒ/ (larger, largest) ① ADJ 形容詞 A **large** thing or person is greater in size than usual or average. 大きい ❑ The pike lives mainly in large rivers and lakes. カワマスは主に大きな川や湖に生息している. ❑ In the largest room about a dozen children and seven adults are sitting on the carpet. 最も広い部屋では12人ほどの子供と7人の大人がカーペットの上に座っている. ② ADJ 形容詞 A **large** amount or number of people or things is more than the average amount or number. 多い ❑ The gang finally fled with a large amount of cash and jewelry. 一味はとうとう多額の現金と多数の宝石を持って逃亡した. ❑ There are a large number of centers where you can take full-time courses. フルタイムのコースを受けられるセンターはたくさ

んある. ③ ADJ 形容詞 **Large** is used to indicate that a problem or issue which is being discussed is very important or serious. 重要な ❑ ...the already large problem of under-age drinking. 既に深刻な未成年の飲酒問題

Large, **big**, and **great** are all used to talk about size. In general, **large** is more formal than **big**, and **great** is more formal than **large**. **Large** and **big** are normally used to describe objects, but you can also use **big** to suggest that something is important or impressive. ❑ ...his influence over the big advertisers. You normally use **great** to emphasize the importance of someone or something. ❑ ...the great English architect, Inigo Jones. However, you can also use **great** to suggest that something is impressive because of its size. ❑ The great bird of prey was a dark smudge against the sun. You can use **large** or **great**, but not **big**, to describe amounts. ❑ ...a large amount of blood on the floor. ...the coming of tourists in great numbers. Both **big** and **great** can be used to emphasize the intensity of something, although **great** is more formal. ❑ It gives me great pleasure to welcome you... Most of them act like big fools.

④ PHRASE 句 You use **at large** to indicate that you are talking in a general way about most of the people mentioned. 全体として ❑ I think the chances of getting reforms accepted by the community at large remain extremely remote. 私は地域社会全般に改革を受け入れてもらう見込みはありそうにないと思う. ⑤ PHRASE 句 If you say that a dangerous person, thing, or animal is **at large**, you mean that they have not been captured or made safe. 捕らわれないで ❑ The man who tried to have her killed is still at large. 彼女の殺人をたくらんだ男はまだ逃走中である. ⑥ **to a large extent** → see **extent**

Thesaurus
large また次を参照 :
ADJ.   big, sizable, spacious, substantial; (ant.) small ①

large|ly /lɑ́rdʒli/ ① ADV 副詞 You use **largely** to say that a statement is not completely true but is mostly true. おおむね ❑ The fund is largely financed through government borrowing. 資金は主に政府借入を通じて調達される. ❑ I largely work with people who already are motivated. 私は主として既にやる気のある人々と働く. ② ADV 副詞 **Largely** is used to introduce the main reason for a particular event or situation. 主に [ADV prep] ❑ Retail sales dipped 6/10ths of a percent last month, largely because Americans were buying fewer cars. 小売販売高は先月, 主に米国人の自動車購買高が落ち込んだため, 0.6%減少した.

large-scale also **large scale** ① ADJ 形容詞 A **large-scale** action or event happens over a very wide area or involves a lot of people or things. 大規模な [ADJ n] ❑ ...a large scale military operation. 大規模な軍事作戦 ② ADJ 形容詞 A **large-scale** map or diagram represents a small area of land or a building or machine on a scale that is large enough for small details to be shown. 大縮尺の [ADJ n] ❑ ...a large-scale map of the county. その国の大縮尺地図

lar|va /lɑ́rvə/ (larvae /lɑ́rvi/) N-COUNT 可算名詞 A **larva** is an insect at the stage of its life after it has developed from an egg and before it changes into its adult form. 幼虫 ❑ The eggs quickly hatch into larvae. 卵はすぐに幼虫にかえる.

la|ser /léɪzər/ (lasers) N-COUNT 可算名詞 A **laser** is a narrow beam of concentrated light produced by a special machine. It is used for cutting very hard materials, and in many technical fields such as surgery and telecommunications. レーザー ❑ ...new laser technology. 新しいレーザー技術
→ see Word Web: laser

la|ser print|er (laser printers) N-COUNT 可算名詞 A **laser printer** is a computer printer that produces clear words and pictures by using laser beams. レーザープリンター

lash /lǽʃ/ (lashes, lashing, lashed) ① N-COUNT 可算名詞 Your **lashes** are the hairs that grow on the edge of your upper and lower eyelids. まつげ ❑ ...somber gray eyes, with unusually long lashes. 異常に長いまつげを持ったくすんだ灰色の目 ② V-T 他動詞 If you **lash** two or more things together, you tie one of them firmly to the other. 結ぶ ❑ Secure the anchor by lashing it to the rail. 錨 (いかり) を柵に結び付けて固定しなさい. ❑ The shelter is built by lashing poles together to form a small dome. 避難所は支柱を結び合わせて小さなドームを形成して造られた. ③ V-T/V-I 他動詞/自動詞 If wind, rain, or water **lashes** someone or something, it hits them violently. 激しく打ち当たる [WRITTEN 書き言葉] ❑ The worst winter storms of the century lashed the east coast of North America. 今世紀最悪の冬の嵐は北米の東海岸を激しく打った. ④ V-T/V-I 他動詞/自動詞 If someone **lashes** you or **lashes into** you, they speak very angrily to you, criticizing you or saying you have done something wrong. 激しく責める ❑ She went quiet for a moment while she summoned up the words to lash him. 彼女は彼を非難する言葉を呼び起こしている間, しばらく黙っていた. ⑤ N-COUNT 可算名詞 A **lash** is a blow with a whip, especially a blow on someone's back as a punishment. むち打ち ❑ The villagers sentenced one man to five lashes for stealing a ham from

Word Web   laser

Lasers are an amazing form of technology. Laser **beams** read **CDs** and **DVDs**. They can create three-dimensional holograms. Laser **light shows** add excitement at concerts. **Fiber optic cables** carry intense flashes of laser light. This allows a single cable to transmit thousands of email and phone messages at the same time. Laser **scanners** read prices from **bar codes**. Lasers are also used as scalpels in **surgery**, and to remove hair, birthmarks, and tattoos. Dentists use them to remove cavities. Laser eye surgery has become very popular. In manufacturing, lasers make precise cuts in everything from fabric to steel.

his neighbor. 村人たちは隣人からハムを盗んだ男をむち打ち5回の刑に処した.

▶ **lash out** 1 PHRASAL VERB 句動詞 If you **lash out**, you attempt to hit someone quickly and violently with a weapon or with your hands or feet. 激しく打つ ❑ Riot police fired in the air and lashed out with clubs to disperse hundreds of demonstrators. 機動隊は空中に発砲し, こん棒を振り回して, 何百人ものデモ参加者を追い散らした. 2 PHRASAL VERB 句動詞 If you **lash out at** someone or something, you speak to them or about them very angrily or critically. 非難をあびせる ❑ As a politician Jefferson frequently lashed out at the press. ジェファーソンは政治家として頻繁に報道記者団をしかりとばした.

lass /læs/ (**lasses**) N-COUNT; N-VOC 可算名詞, 呼格名詞 A **lass** is a young woman or girl. 若い女 [OLD-FASHIONED 古風な] ❑ Anne is a Lancashire lass from Longton, near Preston. アンはプレストン市に近接するロングトン出身のランカシャー娘だ.

last /læst/ (**lasts, lasting, lasted**) 1 DET 限定詞 You use **last** in expressions such as **last Friday, last night**, and **last year** to refer, for example, to the most recent Friday, night, or year. この前の ❑ I got married last July. 私は昨年の7月に結婚した. ❑ He never made it home at all last night. 彼は昨夜は全然帰宅できなかった. 2 ADJ 形容詞 The **last** event, person, thing, or period of time is the most recent one. この前の [det ADJ] ❑ Much has changed since my last visit. 私が先回訪問してから随分変った. ❑ I split up with my last boyfriend three years ago. 私は3年前に前の男友だちと別れた. ● PRON 代名詞 **Last** is also a pronoun. この前のもの ❑ The next tide, it was announced, would be even higher than the last. 次の潮はこの前よりもずっと高くなると発表された. 3 ADV 副詞 If something **last** happened on a particular occasion, that is the most recent occasion on which it happened. この前 [ADV with v] ❑ When were you there last? あなたがこの前そこにいたのはいつですか. ❑ The house is a little more dilapidated than when I last saw it. その家は私がこの前見た時よりも少し荒廃している. 4 ORD 序数詞 The **last** thing, person, event, or period of time is the one that happens or comes after all the others of the same kind. 最後の ❑ ...the last three pages of the chapter. その章の最後の3ページ ● PRON 代名詞 **Last** is also a pronoun. 最後 ❑ It wasn't the first time that this particular difference had divided them and it wouldn't be the last. 特にこの相違で彼らが対立したのは, 今回が彼らの最後ではなく, 最後になることもないだろう. 5 ADV 副詞 If you do something **last**, you do it after everyone else does, or after you do everything else. 最後に [ADV after v] ❑ I testified last. 私は最後に証言した. ❑ I was always picked last for the football team at school. 私は学生時代フットボールチームを組む時にいつも最後に選ばれた. 6 PRON 代名詞 If you are **the last to** do or know something, everyone else does or knows it before you. 最後の人 [PRON to-inf] ❑ She was the last to go to bed. 彼女は最後に寝た. 7 ADJ 形容詞 **Last** is used to refer to the only thing, person, or part of something that remains. 最後に残った [det ADJ] ❑ Jed nodded, finishing off the last piece of pizza. ジェッドはうなずいて, 最後に残ったピザを食べた. ● N-SING 単数名詞 **Last** is also a noun. 最後に残ったもの ❑ He finished off the last of the wine. 彼は残ったワインを飲み干した. 8 ADJ 形容詞 You can use **last** to indicate that something is extremely undesirable or unlikely. 最も望ましくない [EMPHASIS 強調] [det ADJ] ❑ The last thing I wanted to do was teach. 教えることは私がいちばんしたくないことだった. ● PRON 代名詞 **Last** is also a pronoun. 最もしそうにないもの [PRON to-inf] ❑ I would be the last to say that science has explained everything. 科学がすべてを説明したと私が言うはずはない. 9 PRON 代名詞 **The last** you see of someone or **the last** you hear of them is the final time that you see them or talk to them. 最後の姿 ['the' PRON that] ❑ She disappeared shouting, "To the river, to the river!" And that was the last we saw of her. 彼女は「川へ, 川へ」と叫びながら姿を消した. そしてあれが私たちが見た彼女の最後の姿だった. 10 V-T/V-I 他動詞/自動詞 If an event, situation, or problem **lasts** for a particular length of time, it continues to exist or happen for that length of time. 続く ❑ The marriage had lasted for less than two years. その結婚は2年も続かなかった. ❑ The games lasted only half the normal time. 試合は通常の時間の半分しか続かなかった. 11 V-T/V-I 他動詞/自動詞 If something **lasts** for a particular length of time, it continues to be able to be used for that time, for example, because there is some of it left or because it is in good

enough condition. もつ ❑ You only need a very small blob of glue, so one tube lasts for ages. ほんの少量の接着剤だけを使えばよいので, 1本のチューブは長い間もつ. ❑ The repaired sail lasted less than 24 hours. 修理された帆は24時間ももたなかった. 12 → see also **lasting** 13 PHRASE 句 If you say that something has happened **at last** or **at long last** you mean it has happened after you have been hoping for it for a long time. ようやく ❑ I'm so glad that we've found you at last! やっとあなたを見つけて本当に嬉しい. ❑ Here, at long last, was the moment he had waited for. やっとのことで彼が待っていた瞬間が来た. 14 PHRASE 句 You use expressions such as **the night before last, the election before last** and **the leader before last** to refer to the period of time, event, or person that came immediately before the most recent one in a series. 一昨ー, 先々ー ❑ It was the dog he'd heard the night before last. 一昨夜彼が聞いたのは犬の鳴き声だった. 15 PHRASE 句 You can use expressions such as **the last I heard** and **the last she heard** to introduce a piece of information that is the most recent that you have on a particular subject. この前聞いたところによると ❑ The last I heard, Joe and Irene were still happily married. この前聞いたところによると, ジョーとアイリーンはまだ幸せな結婚生活を送っていた. 16 PHRASE 句 If you **leave** something or someone **until last**, you delay using, choosing, or dealing with them until you have used, chosen, or dealt with all the others. 最後までーを残しておく ❑ I have left my best wine until last. 私はとっておきのワインを最後まで残しておいた. 17 **the last straw** → see **straw** 18 **last thing** → see **thing**

last-ditch ADJ 形容詞 A **last-ditch** action is done only because there are no other ways left to achieve something or to prevent something from happening. It is often done without much hope that it will succeed. 死力を尽くした [ADJ n] ❑ ...a last-ditch attempt to prevent civil war. 内戦を防ぐための懸命な試み

last|ing /læstɪŋ/ 1 ADJ 形容詞 You can use **lasting** to describe a situation, result, or agreement that continues to exist or have an effect for a very long time. 長続きする ❑ We are well on our way to a lasting peace. 我々は恒久平和に向けてうまく進んでいる. 2 → see also **last**

last|ly /læstli/ 1 ADV 副詞 You use **lastly** when you want to make a final point, ask a final question, or mention a final item that is connected with the other ones you have already asked or mentioned. 終わりに [ADV with cl/group] ❑ Lastly, I would like to ask about your future plans. 最後にあなたの将来の計画についてお尋ねしたい. 2 ADV 副詞 You use **lastly** when you are saying what happens after everything else in a series of actions or events. 最後に [ADV cl] ❑ They wash their hands, arms and faces, and lastly, they wash their feet. 彼らは手, 腕, 顔を洗い, 最後に足を洗う.

last-minute → see **minute**

latch /lætʃ/ (**latches, latching, latched**) 1 N-COUNT 可算名詞 A **latch** is a fastening on a door or gate. It consists of a metal bar which you lift in order to open the door. 掛け金 ❑ You left the latch off the gate and the dog escaped. あなたが門の掛け金をはずしていたので, 犬が逃げ出した. 2 N-COUNT 可算名詞 A **latch** is a lock on a door which locks automatically when you shut the door, so that you need a key in order to open it from the outside. 錠 ❑ ...a key clicked in the latch of the front door. 鍵は正面玄関のドアの錠にカチッとはまった.

▶ **latch onto** or **latch on** 1 PHRASAL VERB 句動詞 If someone **latches onto** a person or idea or **latches on**, they become very interested in the person or idea, often finding them so useful that they do not want to leave them. ーをしっかりつかむ, ーにくっついて離れない [INFORMAL くだけた] ❑ Rob had latched onto me. He followed me around and sat beside me at lunch. ロップは私にくっついて離れなかった. 彼は私につきまとい, 昼食時も私の隣に座った. 2 PHRASAL VERB 句動詞 If one thing **latches onto** another, or if it **latches on**, it attaches itself to it and becomes part of it. ーにくっつく ❑ These are substances which specifically latch onto the protein on the cell membrane. これらは特に細胞膜のたんぱく質にくっつく物質だ.

late /leɪt/ (**later, latest**) 1 ADV 副詞 **Late** means near the end of a day, week, year, or other period of time. 遅く ❑ It was late in the afternoon. 午後の遅い時刻だった. ❑ His autobiography was written late in life. 彼の自伝は晩年に書かれた. ● ADJ 形容詞 **Late** is also an

adjective. 遅い [ADJ n] ❑ *The talks eventually broke down in late spring.* 話合いはついに晩春に物別れに終わった. ❑ *He was in his late 20s.* 彼は20代後半だった. ❷ ADJ 形容詞 If it is **late**, it is near the end of the day or it is past the time that you feel something should have been done. 夜遅くの [v-link ADJ] ❑ *It was very late and the streets were deserted.* 夜ふけで街路には人がいなかった. ● **late|ness** N-UNCOUNT 不可算名詞 遅いこと ❑ *A large crowd had gathered despite the lateness of the hour.* 遅い時間にもかかわらず大きな人込みができていた. ❸ ADV 副詞 **Late** means after the time that was arranged or expected. 遅れて ❑ *Steve arrived late.* スティーヴは遅れて到着した. ❑ *The talks began some fifteen minutes late.* 会談は約15分遅れて始まった. ● ADJ 形容詞 **Late** is also an adjective. 遅れた ❑ *His campaign got off to a late start.* 彼の運動は遅れて始まった. ❑ *The train was 40 minutes late.* 電車は40分遅れた. ● **late|ness** N-UNCOUNT 不可算名詞 遅れること ❑ *He apologized for his lateness.* 彼は遅れたことを謝った. ❹ ADV 副詞 [ADV after v] **Late** means after the usual time that a particular event or activity happens. いつもより遅く ❑ *We went to bed very late.* 私達はいつもよりかなり遅い時間に寝た. ● ADJ 形容詞 **Late** is also an adjective. いつもより遅い [ADJ n] ❑ *They had a late lunch in a café.* 彼らはカフェでいつもより遅い昼食を取った. ❺ ADJ 形容詞 You use **late** when you are talking about someone who is dead, especially someone who has died recently. 最近死んだ [det ADJ] ❑ *...my late husband.* 私の亡夫 ❻ → see also **later**, **latest** ❼ PHRASE 句 If an action or event is **too late**, it is useless or ineffective because it occurs after the best time for it. 遅すぎる ❑ *It was too late to turn back.* 戻るには遅すぎた. ❽ **a late night** → see **night**

late|ly /ˈleɪtli/ ADV 副詞 You use **lately** to describe events in the recent past, or situations that started a short time ago. 最近 ❑ *Dad's health hasn't been too good lately.* 最近お父さんの健康状態はあまりよくない. ❑ *"Have you talked to her lately?" — "Not lately, really."* 「最近彼女と話をしたか」「実は最近はしていない」

la|tent /ˈleɪtˀnt/ ADJ 形容詞 **Latent** is used to describe something which is hidden and not obvious at the moment, but which may develop further in the future. 潜在性の ❑ *Advertisements attempt to project a latent meaning behind an overt message.* 広告は表立ったメッセージの裏にある隠れた意味を伝えようとする.

lat|er /ˈleɪtər/ ❶ **Later** is the comparative of **late**. late の比較級 ❷ ADV 副詞 You use **later** to refer to a time or situation that is after the one that you have been talking about or after the present one. その後 ❑ *He resigned ten years later.* 彼は10年後に辞職した. ● PHRASE 句 You use **later on** to refer to a time or situation that is after the one that you have been talking about or after the present one. 後で ❑ *Later on I'll be speaking to Patty Davis.* 後で私はパティ・デービスと話すことになっている. ❸ ADJ 形容詞 You use **later** to refer to an event, period of time, or other thing which comes after the one that you have been talking about or after the present one. もっと遅い [ADJ n, 'the' ADJ, 'the' ADJ 'of' n] ❑ *At a later news conference, he said differences should not be dramatized.* その後の記者会見で彼は相違点をオーバーに伝えるべきではないと言った. ❑ *The competition should have been re-scheduled for a later date.* その試合は後日に変更されるべきだった. ❹ ADJ 形容詞 You use **later** to refer to the last part of someone's life or career or the last part of a period of history. 後期の [ADJ n] ❑ *He found happiness in later life.* 彼は晩年に幸福をつかんだ. ❑ *...the later part of the 20th century.* 20世紀の後期

You use **after**, **afterward**, and **later** to talk about things that happen following the time when you are speaking, or following a particular event. Expressions such as "not long" and "shortly" can also be used with **after**. ❑ *After dinner she spoke to him... I returned to England after visiting India... Shortly after, she called me.* **Afterward** can be used when you do not need to mention the particular time or event. ❑ *Afterward we went to a night club.* You can also use words such as "soon" and "shortly" with **afterward**. ❑ *Soon afterward, he came to the clinic.* You can use **later** to refer to a time or situation that follows the time when you are speaking. ❑ *I'll go and see her later.* "A little," "much," and "not much" can also be used with **later**. ❑ *A little later, the lights went out... I learned all this much later.* You can use **after**, **afterward**, or **later** following a phrase that mentions a period of time, in order to say when something happens. ❑ *...five years after his death... She wrote about it six years afterward... Ten minutes later he left the house.*

❺ → see also **late**

lat|er|al /ˈlætərəl/ ADJ 形容詞 **Lateral** means relating to the sides of something, or moving in a sideways direction. 横の ❑ *McKinnon estimated that the lateral movement of the bridge to be between*

four and six inches. マッキノンはその橋の横ずれは4-6インチと推定した.

lat|est /ˈleɪtɪst/ ❶ **Latest** is the superlative of **late**. late の最上級 ❷ ADJ 形容詞 You use **latest** to describe something that is the most recent thing of its kind. 最新の ❑ *...her latest book.* 彼女の最新作 ❸ ADJ 形容詞 You can use **latest** to describe something that is very new and modern and is better than older things of a similar kind. 最新式の ❑ *Crooks are using the latest laser photocopiers to produce millions of fake banknotes.* 詐欺師は最新式のレーザー写真複写機を使って何百万もの偽造紙幣を製造している. ❑ *I got to drive the latest model.* 私は最新式のモデルを運転することができた. ❹ → see also **late** ❺ PHRASE 句 You use **at the latest** in order to indicate that something must happen at or before a particular time and not after that time. いくら遅くとも [EMPHASIS 強調] ❑ *She should be back by ten o'clock at the latest.* 彼女はいくら遅くとも10時までにはきっと戻ってくるでしょう.

lathe /ˈleɪð/ (**lathes**) N-COUNT 可算名詞 A **lathe** is a machine which is used for shaping wood or metal. 旋盤

Lat|in /ˈlætɪn, -tˀn/ ❶ N-UNCOUNT 不可算名詞 **Latin** is the language which the ancient Romans used to speak. ラテン語 ❷ ADJ 形容詞 **Latin** countries are countries where Spanish, or perhaps Portuguese, Italian, or French, is spoken. You can also use **Latin** to refer to things and people that come from these countries. ラテン系の、ラテン民族の ❑ *Cuba was one of the least Catholic of the Latin countries.* キューバはラテン系諸国の中でカソリック教徒が最も少ない国だった.

→ see **English**

Lat|in Ameri|can /ˈlætɪn əˈmɛrɪkən/ ADJ 形容詞 **Latin American** means belonging or relating to the countries of South America, Central America, and Mexico. **Latin American** also means belonging or relating to the people or culture of these countries. ラテンアメリカの ❑ *Leaders of eight Latin American countries are meeting in Caracas, Venezuela, today.* ラテンアメリカ8か国の指導者たちは今日ベネズエラのカラカス市で会談を行なう.

lati|tude /ˈlætɪtud/ (**latitudes**) ❶ N-VAR 可変性名詞 The **latitude** of a place is its distance from the equator. Compare **longitude**. 緯度 ❑ *In the middle to high latitudes rainfall has risen steadily over the last 20-30 years.* 中-高緯度の降雨量は過去20-30年間に徐々に増加した. ● ADJ 形容詞 **Latitude** is also an adjective. 緯度の ❑ *The army must cease military operations above 36° latitude north.* 陸軍は北緯36度超えた地点で軍事行動を停止しなければならない. ❷ N-UNCOUNT 不可算名詞 **Latitude** is freedom to choose the way in which you do something. 自由範囲 [FORMAL 形式ばった] ❑ *He would be given every latitude in forming a new government.* 彼は全く自由に新政府を樹立できるだろう.

→ see **globe**

lat|ter /ˈlætər/ ❶ PRON 代名詞 When two people, things, or groups have just been mentioned, you can refer to the second of them as **the latter**. 後者 'the' PRON ❑ *He tracked down his cousin and uncle. The latter was sick.* 彼はいとこと叔父の居場所を突き止めた. 後者は病気だった. ● ADJ 形容詞 **Latter** is also an adjective. 後者の [ADJ n] ❑ *There are the people who speak after they think and the people who think while they're speaking. Mike definitely belongs in the latter category.* 考えた後で話す人もいれば、話している間に考える人もいる. マイクは確実に後者の部類に属している. ❷ ADJ 形容詞 You use **latter** to describe the later part of a period of time or event. 後半の [ADJ n] ❑ *He is getting into the latter years of his career.* 彼のキャリアは後半にさしかかろうとしている.

The latter should only be used to refer to the second of two items which have already been mentioned: ❑ *Given the choice between working for someone else and being on call day and night for the family business, she'd prefer the latter.* The last of three or more items can be referred to as **the last-named**. Compare this with **the former** which is used to talk about the first of two things already mentioned.

lat|tice /ˈlætɪs/ (**lattices**) N-COUNT 可算名詞 A **lattice** is a pattern or structure made of strips of wood or another material which cross over each other diagonally leaving holes in between. 格子 ❑ *We were crawling along the narrow steel lattice of the bridge.* 我々は橋の鋼鉄の狭い格子細工沿いにのろのろ徐行していた.

laugh /ˈlæf/ (**laughs**, **laughing**, **laughed**) ❶ V-T/V-I 他動詞/自動詞 When you **laugh**, you make a sound with your throat while smiling and show that you are happy or amused. People also sometimes laugh when they feel nervous or are being unfriendly. 笑う ❑ *He was about to offer an explanation, but she was beginning to laugh.* 彼は説明しようとするところだったが、彼女は笑い始めていた. ❑ *I just couldn't laugh at his jokes the way I used to.* 私は昔のようには彼の冗談にちっとも笑えなかった. ❑ *"We could do with some help from our friends," he laughed.* 「友だちがちょっと手伝ってくれるといいのだが」と彼は笑った. ● N-COUNT 可算名詞 **Laugh** is also a noun. 笑い ❑ *Lysenko gave a deep rumbling laugh at his own joke.* ライセンコは自分の冗談に低く重々しい声で笑った. ❷ V-I 自動詞 If people **laugh**

Word Web   laugh

There is an old saying, "**Laughter** is the best medicine." New scientific research supports the idea that **humor** really is good for your health. For example, laughing 100 times provides the same exercise benefits as a 15-minute bike ride. When a person **bursts out laughing**, levels of stress hormones in the bloodstream immediately drop. And laughter is more than just a sound. **Howling with laughter** gives face, stomach, leg, and back muscles a good workout. From polite **giggles** to noisy guffaws, laughter allows the release of anger, sadness, and fear. And that has to be good for you.

at someone or something, they mock them or make jokes about them. あざ笑う □ *I thought they were laughing at me because I was ugly.* 彼らは私が醜いので私のことをあざ笑っているのだと私は思った. **3** PHRASE 句 If you do something **for a laugh** or **for laughs**, you do it as a joke or for fun. 気晴らしに □ *They were persuaded onstage for a laugh.* 彼らは説得されて面白半分に舞台に上がった. **4** PHRASE 句 If you describe a situation as **a laugh** or **a good laugh**, you think that it is fun and do not take it too seriously. 笑わせるもの [INFORMAL くだけた] □ *Working there's great. It's a good laugh.* そこで働くのはすてきだ. とても楽しい. **5** to **laugh** your **head off** → see **head** → see Word Web: **laugh**

▶ **laugh off** PHRASAL VERB 句動詞 If you **laugh off** a difficult or serious situation, you try to suggest that it is amusing and unimportant, for example, by making a joke about it. 笑い飛ばす □ *Frank tried to laugh off his aunt's worry.* フランクは伯母の心配を一笑に付そうとした.

Thesaurus   laugh また次を参照:

V.   chuckle, crack up, giggle, howl, snicker; (*ant.*) cry **1**

Word Partnership   laugh は次の語句と使われる:

V.   begin/start to laugh, hear *someone* laugh, make *someone* laugh, try to laugh **1**

ADJ.   big laugh, good laugh, hearty laugh, little laugh **1**

laugh|ter /lǽftər/ N-UNCOUNT 不可算名詞 **Laughter** is the sound of people laughing, for example, because they are amused or happy. 笑い声 □ *Their laughter filled the corridor.* 廊下は彼らの笑い声で一杯になった. □ *He delivered the line perfectly, and everybody roared with laughter.* 彼はそのせりふを完璧に言い, 誰もが大笑いした. → see **laugh**

Word Partnership   laughter は次の語句と使われる:

V.   burst into laughter, hear laughter, roar with laughter

N.   burst of laughter, sound of laughter

ADJ.   hysterical laughter, loud laughter, nervous laughter

launch /lɔntʃ/ (launches, launching, launched) **1** V-T 他動詞 To **launch** a rocket, missile, or satellite means to send it into the air or into space. 打ち上げる □ *NASA plans to launch a satellite to study cosmic rays.* NASAは宇宙線を研究するために衛星を打ち上げる予定だ. ● N-VAR 可変性名詞 **Launch** is also a noun. 打ち上げ □ *This morning's launch of the space shuttle Columbia has been delayed.* 今朝のスペース・シャトルのコロンビア号の打ち上げは延期された. **2** V-T 他動詞 To **launch** a ship or a boat means to put it into water, often for the first time after it has been built. 進水させる □ *There was no time to launch the lifeboats because the ferry capsized with such alarming speed.* フェリー船が驚くほどのスピードで転覆したため, 救命ボートを水面に下ろす時間がなかった. ● N-COUNT 可変性名詞 **Launch** is also a noun. 進水 □ *The launch of a ship was a big occasion.* 船の進水は大きな行事だった. **3** V-T 他動詞 To **launch** a large and important activity, for example, a military attack, means to start it. 開始する □ *A group of 80 attackers launched an all-out assault just before dawn.* 80人の攻撃部隊が夜明け直前に総力を挙げて突撃を開始した. □ *The police have launched an investigation into the incident.* 警察はその事件の調査に着手した. ● N-COUNT 可変性名詞 **Launch** is also a noun. 開始 □ *...the launch of a campaign to restore law and order.* 法と秩序を回復させるための運動の開始. **4** V-T 他動詞 If a company **launches** a new product, it makes it available to the public. 売り出す □ *...powerful allies to help the company launch a low-cost "network computer."* その会社が低コストの「ネットワーク・コンピュータ」を売り出すのを支援する強力な提携企業. ● N-COUNT 可変性名詞 **Launch** is also a noun. 売り出し □ *The company's spending has also risen following the launch of a new Sunday magazine.* その会社の経費も日曜雑誌が新発売された後に増加した. → see **satellite**

▶ **launch into** PHRASAL VERB 句動詞 If you **launch into** something such as a speech, task, or fight, you enthusiastically start it. 一に勢いよく乗り出す □ *Horrigan launched into a speech about the importance of new projects.* ホリガンは新計画の重要性についての演説を勢いよく始めた.

laun|der /lɔ́ndər/ (launders, laundering, laundered) **1** V-T To **launder** money that has been obtained illegally means to process it through a legitimate business or to send it abroad to a foreign bank, so that when it comes back nobody knows that it was illegally obtained. (不正の金を) 洗浄する, ロンダリングする □ *The House voted today to crack down on banks that launder drug money.* 下院は今日, 麻薬の利益をロンダリングする銀行の取り締まりに票決した. ● **laun|der|er** N-COUNT 可算名詞 ロンダリングをする人 □ *...a businessman and self-described money launderer.* 実業家で自称ロンダリングをする人 **2** V-T 他動詞 When you **launder** clothes, sheets, and towels, you wash and iron them. 洗濯してアイロンをかける [FORMAL 形式ばった] □ *How many guests who expect clean towels every day in an hotel launder their own every day at home?* 毎日清潔なタオルを期待するホテルの泊り客のうち, 自分の家でもタオルを毎日洗濯している人は何人いるだろうか.

laun|dry /lɔ́ndri/ (laundries) **1** N-UNCOUNT 不可算名詞 **Laundry** is used to refer to clothes, sheets, and towels that are about to be washed, are being washed, or have just been washed. 洗濯物 □ *I'll do your laundry.* 洗濯は私に任せてください. □ *...the room where I hang the laundry.* 私が洗濯物を干す部屋. **2** N-COUNT 可算名詞 A **laundry** is a business that washes and irons clothes, sheets, and towels for people. クリーニング屋 □ *We had to have the washing done at the laundry.* 私達はクリーニング屋で洗濯をしてもらわなければならなかった.

> A business where people go to wash their clothes for themselves is called a **Laundromat**. The machines are operated by inserting coins so another name for these is **coin laundry**. In the UK, the usual word is **launderette**.

3 N-COUNT 可算名詞 A **laundry** or a **laundry room** is a room in a house, hotel, or institution where clothes, sheets, and towels are washed. 洗濯室 □ *He worked in the laundry at Oxford prison.* 彼はオックスフォード刑務所の洗濯室で働いた. → see **house, soap**

lau|rel /lɔ́rəl/ (laurels) **1** N-VAR 可変性名詞 A **laurel** or a **laurel tree** is a small evergreen tree with shiny leaves. The leaves are sometimes used to make decorations such as wreaths. ゲッケイジュ **2** PHRASE 句 If someone is **resting on** their **laurels**, they appear to be satisfied with the things they have achieved and have stopped putting effort into what they are doing. すでに得た栄誉に満足する [DISAPPROVAL 不賛成] □ *The committee's chairman accused NASA of resting on its laurels after making it to the moon.* その委員会の委員長はNASAが月着陸後に得た成功に安んじてそれ以上やらないと非難した.

lava /lávə, lǽvə/ (lavas) N-MASS 質量名詞 **Lava** is the very hot liquid rock that comes out of a volcano. 溶岩 □ *Mexico's Mount Colima began spewing lava and ash last night.* メキシコのコリマ山は昨夜溶岩と灰を噴出し始めた. → see **rock, volcano**

lava|tory /lǽvətɔri/ (lavatories) N-COUNT 可算名詞 A **lavatory** is a toilet or a room with a toilet in it. 洗面所 [mainly BRIT 主に英国英語] □ *...the ladies' lavatory.* 女性用洗面所

lav|en|der /lǽvɪndər/ N-UNCOUNT 不可算名詞 **Lavender** is a garden plant with sweet-smelling, bluish-purple flowers. ラベンダー

lav|ish /lǽvɪʃ/ (lavishes, lavishing, lavished) **1** ADJ 形容詞 If you describe something as **lavish**, you mean that it is very elaborate and impressive and a lot of money has been spent on it. ぜいたくな □ *...a lavish party to celebrate Bryan's fiftieth birthday.* ブライアンの50歳の誕生日を祝うための豪華なパーティー □ *He staged the most lavish productions of Mozart.* 彼はモーツアルトの最も豪華な上演を演出した. ● **lav|ish|ly** ADV 副詞 [ADV with v] 豪華に □ *The apartment building was lavishly decorated.* そのアパートの建物は豪華な飾りつけがあった. **2** ADJ 形容詞 If you say that spending, praise, or the use of something is **lavish**, you mean that someone spends a lot or that something is praised or used a lot. たっぷりの □ *Critics attack his lavish spending and flamboyant style.* 批判者た

ちは彼のぜいたくな金遣いと派手なやり方を非難する. **3** ADJ 形容詞 If you say that someone is **lavish** in the way they behave, you mean that they give, spend, or use a lot of something. 気前よく使う □*Reviewers are lavish in their praise of this book.* 書評者たちはこの本を褒めちぎる. ●**lav|ish|ly** ADV 副詞 [ADV with v] 気前よく □*Entertaining in style needn't mean spending lavishly.* 上等なもてなしは気前よく金を使うことを意味するとは限らない. **4** V-T 他動詞 If you **lavish** money, affection, or praise **on** someone or something, you spend a lot of money on them or give them a lot of affection or praise. 惜しみなく使う □*He lavished praise on his opponents.* 彼は対抗者たちを褒めちぎった.

law /lɔː/ (laws) **1** N-SING 単数名詞 **The law** is a system of rules that a society or government develops in order to deal with crime, business agreements, and social relationships. You can also use **the law** to refer to the people who work in this system. 法律, 法; 法の執行者 □*Obscene and threatening phone calls are against the law.* わいせつ電話や脅迫電話は法律違反だ. □*They are beginning criminal proceedings against him for breaking the law on financing political parties.* 彼らは政党献金に関する法律違反で彼に対する刑事訴訟手続きを始めている. □*The book analyses why women kill and how the law treats them.* その本はなぜ女性が殺人を犯すか, そして法律が彼女たちをどう扱うかを分析している. **2** N-UNCOUNT 不可算名詞 **Law** is used to refer to a particular branch of the law, such as **criminal law** or **business law**. (特定分野の個々の) 法律 □*He was a professor of criminal law at Harvard University law school.* 彼はハーバード大学法学大学院で刑法の教授をしていた. □*Under international law, diplomats living in foreign countries are exempt from criminal prosecution.* 国際法に基づき外国に住む外交官は刑事訴追を免除されている. **3** N-COUNT 可算名詞 A **law** is one of the rules in a system of law which deals with a particular type of agreement, relationship, or crime. (特定の分野の法体系の中の) 法規 □*...the country's liberal political asylum law.* その国の寛大な政治亡命者保護法. **4** N-PLURAL 複数名詞 The **laws** of an organization or activity are its rules, which are used to organize and control it. (団体・活動の) 規則 □*...the laws of the Catholic Church.* カトリック教会の律法. **5** N-COUNT 可算名詞 A **law** is a rule or set of rules for good behavior which is considered right and important by the majority of people for moral, religious, or emotional reasons. 慣習, 模範的行動基準 □*...inflexible moral laws.* 不変の道徳律. **6** N-COUNT 可算名詞 A **law** is a natural process in which a particular event or thing always leads to a particular result. (自然の) 法則 □*The laws of nature are absolute.* 自然の法則は絶対的だ. **7** N-COUNT 可算名詞 A **law** is a scientific rule that someone has invented to explain a particular natural process. (科学的な) 法則, 原理 □*...the law of gravity.* 重力の法則. **8** N-UNCOUNT 不可算名詞 **Law** or **the law** is all the professions which deal with advising people about the law, representing people in court, or giving decisions and punishments. 法律を扱う職業, 法曹界 □*A career in law is becoming increasingly attractive to young people.* 法律家としての職はますます若い人たちを引き付けている. **9** N-UNCOUNT 不可算名詞 **Law** is the study of systems of law and how laws work. 法学 □*He studied law.* 彼は法律を勉強した. **10** PHRASE 句 If you accuse someone of thinking they are **above the law**, you criticize them for thinking that they are so clever or important that they do not need to obey the law. (巧妙さ・権力があって) 法の適用を受けない [DISAPPROVAL 不賛成] □*He accuses the government of wanting to be above the law.* 彼は政府が超法規的であろうとしていると非難している. **11** PHRASE 句 If you have to do something **by law** or if you are not allowed to do something **by law**, the law states that you have to do it or that you are not allowed to do it. 法律によって □*By law all restaurants must display their prices outside.* 法律により, すべてのレストランは外に値段を掲示しなければならない.

law-abiding ADJ 形容詞 A **law-abiding** person always obeys the law and is considered to be good and honest because of this. 法律を守る □*We believe that the law should protect decent law-abiding citizens and their property.* 法は法を守るまともな市民とその財産を守るべきだと私たちは信じている.

law and or|der N-UNCOUNT 不可算名詞 When there is **law and order** in a country, the laws are generally accepted and obeyed, so that society there functions normally. 法と秩序, 治安 □*If there was a breakdown of law and order, the army might be tempted to intervene.* もし法と秩序が崩壊したら, 軍隊が介入しようとするかもしれない.

law|ful /lɔːfəl/ ADJ 形容詞 If an activity, organization, or product is **lawful**, it is allowed by law. 合法的な [FORMAL 形式ばった] □*The detention of the fugitive was lawful.* その逃亡者の勾留 (そうはく) は合法だった. ●**law|ful|ly** ADV 副詞 [ADV with v] 合法的に, 法律に従い □*Amnesty International is trying to establish whether the police acted lawfully in shooting him.* 国際アムネスティは警察が合法的に行動して彼を撃ったかどうかを立証しようとしている.

law|less /lɔːlɪs/ **1** ADJ 形容詞 **Lawless** actions break the law, especially in a wild and violent way. 無法な, 法に従わない □*The government recognized there were problems in urban areas but these could never be an excuse for lawless behavior.* 政府は都市圏に問題があることを認めたが, それが無法行為の口実には決してなり得なかっ

た. ●**law|less|ness** N-UNCOUNT 不可算名詞 無法 □*Lawlessness is a major problem.* 無法は深刻な問題だ. **2** ADJ 形容詞 A **lawless** place or time is one where or when people do not respect the law. 無法状態の □*...lawless inner-city streets plagued by muggings, thefts, assaults and even murder.* 路上強盗, 窃盗, 暴行, そして殺人すらに悩まされる無法状態の都心の街路

lawn /lɔːn/ (lawns) N-VAR 可変性名詞 A **lawn** is an area of grass that is kept cut short and is usually part of someone's yard, or part of a park. 芝生 □*They were sitting on the lawn under a large beech tree.* 彼らは大きなブナの木の下の芝生に座っていた.

lawn|mow|er /lɔːnmoʊər/ (lawnmowers) N-COUNT 可算名詞 A **lawnmower** is a machine for cutting grass on lawns. 芝刈り機

law|suit /lɔːsuːt/ (lawsuits) N-COUNT 可算名詞 A **lawsuit** is a case in a court of law which concerns a dispute between two people or organizations. 訴訟 [FORMAL 形式ばった] □*The dispute culminated last week in a lawsuit against the government.* その論争は先週ついに政府に対する訴訟となった.

law|yer /lɔːɪər, lɔːyər/ (lawyers) N-COUNT 可算名詞 A **lawyer** is a person who is qualified to advise people about the law and represent them in court. 弁護士 □*Prosecution and defense lawyers are expected to deliver closing arguments next week.* 検察官と被告側弁護士は来週, 最終弁論を行うはずだ.
→ see **trial**

In both British and American English, **lawyer** is a general term for someone who is qualified in law and represents people in legal matters. American **lawyers** can prepare cases and can also represent their clients in court. Another American word commonly used for **lawyer** is **attorney**. In Britain, a **solicitor** prepares legal documents such as wills and contracts, and also prepares cases that are heard in court. **Solicitors** can also represent their clients, especially in lower courts. In higher courts, the argument for each side is usually presented by a **barrister**. In Scotland, a **barrister** is usually called an **advocate**.

Word Link lax ≈ allowing, loosening : lax, laxative, relax

lax /læks/ (laxer, laxest) ADJ 形容詞 If you say that a person's behavior or a system is **lax**, you mean they are not careful or strict about maintaining high standards. (人の行動が) たるんだ, (制度などが) 手ぬるい □*One of the problem areas is lax security for airport personnel.* 空港の職員に対する警備の甘さが問題領域の1つとなっている. □*There have been allegations from survivors that safety standards had been lax.* 生存者から安全基準が緩かったという主張が出ている. ●**lax|ity** N-UNCOUNT 不可算名詞 怠慢, 手ぬるさ □*The laxity of export control authorities has made a significant contribution to the problem.* 輸出管理当局の怠慢がその問題を大きく助長してきた.

laxa|tive /læksətɪv/ (laxatives) N-MASS 質量名詞 A **laxative** is something you eat or drink that makes you go to the toilet. 下剤, 便秘薬 □*Foods that ferment quickly in the stomach are excellent natural laxatives.* 胃の中ですぐに発酵する食べ物は, 素晴らしい自然の便秘薬だ.

lay
❶ VERB AND NOUN USES
❷ ADJECTIVE USES

❶ **lay** /leɪ/ (lays, laying, laid)

In standard English, the form **lay** is also the past tense of the verb **lie** in some meanings. In informal English, people sometimes use the word **lay** instead of **lie** in those meanings.

標準英語では **lay** 形はいくつかの意味で動詞**lie**の過去時制でもある. くだけた英語ではこれらの意味で **lay** の代わりに単語 **lie** が時々使われる.

↻ Please look at meaning **7** to see if the expression you are looking for is shown under another headword.

Do not confuse the verb **lay** with the verb **lie**. Because **lay** is used to talk about putting something in a particular place or position, it is related to the verb **lie**. If someone **lays** something somewhere, it **lies** there. The past tense and past participle of **lay** are both **laid** and it is usually a transitive verb. □*They laid him on the floor.* However, **lie** is an intransitive verb with the past tense **lay** and the past participle **lain**. □*I lay on the floor with my legs in the air.*

1 V-T 他動詞 If you **lay** something somewhere, you put it there in a careful, gentle, or neat way. (物を慎重にきちんと) 置く □*Lay a sheet of newspaper on the floor.* 新聞紙を1枚床に置きなさい. □*Mothers routinely lay babies on their backs to sleep.* 母親たちは普段赤ちゃんを仰向けに寝かせて眠らせる. **2** V-T 他動詞 If you **lay** something such as carpets, cables, or foundations, you put them into their permanent position. (じゅうたん・ケーブルなど

を）敷く □*A man came to lay the carpet.* 男がじゅうたんを敷きに来た． ❸ V-T/V-I 他動詞/自動詞 When a female bird **lays**, or **lays an egg**, it produces an egg by pushing it out of its body.（卵を）産む □*My canary has laid an egg.* 私のカナリアが卵を1個産んだ． ❹ V-T 他動詞 **Lay** is used with some nouns to talk about making official preparations for something. For example, if you **lay the basis** for something or **lay plans** for it, you prepare it carefully.（基礎・計画を）築く □*Diplomats meeting in Chile have laid the groundwork for far-reaching environmental regulations.* チリに集まった外交官たちが，大規模な環境規制の基盤を築いた． ❺ V-T 他動詞 **Lay** is used with some nouns in expressions about accusing or blaming someone. For example, if you **lay the blame** for a mistake on someone, you say it is their fault, or if the police **lay charges** against someone, they officially accuse that person of a crime.（責任・罪などを）帰する □*She refused to lay the blame on any one party.* 彼女はどれか一方の側に責任をかぶせることを拒否した． ❻ V-T 他動詞 If you **lay the table** or **lay** the places at a table, you arrange the knives, forks, and other things that people need on the table before a meal.（食卓の）準備をする [OLD-FASHIONED 古風な] □*The butler always laid the table.* その執事がいつも食卓の準備をした． ❼ to **lay** something **at** someone's **door** → see **door** to **lay a finger on** someone → see **finger** ❽ to **lay** your **hands on** something → see **hand** ❿ to **lay siege** to something → see **siege**

▸ **lay aside** ❶ PHRASAL VERB 句動詞 If you **lay aside** a feeling or belief, you reject it or give it up in order to progress with something.（感情・信条を）捨てる，やめる □*Perhaps the opposed parties will lay aside their sectional interests and rise to this challenge.* 恐らく対抗し合っている政党も，各自の利害関係を捨てて，この難問に立ち上がるだろう． ❷ PHRASAL VERB 句動詞 If you **lay** something **aside**, you put it down, usually because you have finished using it or want to save it to use later. かたわらに置く，しまって置く [BRIT 英国英語] □*He finished the tea and laid the cup aside.* 彼は茶を飲み終え，カップをかたわらに置いた．

▸ **lay down** ❶ PHRASAL VERB 句動詞 If you **lay** something **down**, you put it down, usually because you have finished using it. 下に置く □*Daniel finished the article and laid the newspaper down on his desk.* ダニエルはその記事を読み終え，新聞を机に置いた． ❷ PHRASAL VERB 句動詞 If rules or people in authority **lay down** what people should do or must do, they officially state what they should or must do.（規則などを）定める □*Not all companies lay down written guidelines and rules.* 全ての会社が文書で指針や規則を決めてはいない ❸ PHRASAL VERB 句動詞 If someone **lays down** their weapons, they stop fighting a battle or war and make peace.（武器を）捨てる □*The drug-traffickers have offered to lay down their arms.* 麻薬の密売人たちは武器を捨てることを申し出ている．

▸ **lay off** ❶ PHRASAL VERB 句動詞 If workers **are laid off**, they are told by their employers to leave their job, usually because there is no more work for them to do. 解雇する [BUSINESS 実業] □*100,000 federal workers will be laid off to reduce the deficit.* 赤字削減のため連邦政府の10万人の職員が解雇される予定だ． ❷ → see also **layoff**

▸ **lay on** PHRASAL VERB 句動詞 If you **lay on** something such as food, entertainment, or a service, you provide or supply it, especially in a generous or grand way.（食事・娯楽などを）気前よく提供する 用意する [mainly BRIT 主に英国英語] □*They laid on a superb evening.* 彼らは豪華な夜会を開いた．

▸ **lay out** ❶ PHRASAL VERB 句動詞 If you **lay out** a group of things, you spread them out and arrange them neatly, for example, so that they can all be seen clearly. きちんと配置する □*Grace laid out the knives and forks on the table.* グレースは食卓の上にナイフとフォークを並べた． ❷ PHRASAL VERB 句動詞 To **lay out** ideas, principles, or plans means to explain or present them clearly, for example, in a document or a meeting.（考え・計画などを）説明する，提示する □*Maxwell listened closely as Johnson laid out his plan.* マックスウェルはジョンソンが彼の計画を説明するのを注意して聞いた． ❸ → see also **layout**

▸ **lay up** PHRASAL VERB 句動詞 If someone **is laid up with** an illness, the illness makes it necessary for them to stay in bed.（病気が人を）寝たきりにさせる [INFORMAL くだけた] [usu passive] □*She was in the hospital for a week and laid up for a month after that.* 彼女は1週間入院し，その後1か月間，床についていた． □*Powell ruptured a disc in his back and was laid up for a year.* パウエルは椎間板ヘルニアを起こし，1年間寝たきりになっていた．

❷ **lay** /leɪ/ ❶ ADJ 形容詞 You use **lay** to describe people who are involved with a Christian church but are not members of the clergy or are not monks or nuns. 平信徒の [ADJ n] □*Edwards is a Methodist lay preacher and social worker.* エドワーズはメソジスト教会の平信徒説教師でありソーシャル・ワーカーだ． ❷ ADJ 形容詞 You use **lay** to describe people who are not experts or professionals in a particular subject or activity. 素人の [ADJ n] □*It is difficult for a lay person to gain access to medical libraries.* 一般人が医学図書館に出入りするのは難しい．

lay|er /leɪər/ (layers, layering, layered) ❶ N-COUNT 可算名詞 A **layer** of a material or substance is a quantity or piece of it that covers a surface or that is between two other things. 層 □*...the*

depletion of the ozone layer. オゾン層の消耗 ❷ N-COUNT 可算名詞 If something such as a system or an idea has many **layers**, it has many different levels or parts. 段階，階層 □*Critics and the public puzzle out the layers of meaning in his photos.* 評論家と一般の人々は彼の写真の何層にもなっている意味を解く． ❸ V-T 他動詞 If you **layer** something, you arrange it in layers.（重ねて）層にする □*Layer half the onion slices on top of the potatoes.* ジャガイモの上にスライスした玉ねぎの半分を重ねなさい．

lay|man /leɪmən/ (laymen) N-COUNT 可算名詞 A **layman** is a person who is not trained, qualified, or experienced in a particular subject or activity. 素人 □*The mere mention of the words "heart failure" can conjure up, to the layman, the prospect of imminent death.* 「心臓麻痺」という言葉を口にするだけで，素人は今にも死ぬように思いかねない．

lay|off /leɪɒf/ (layoffs) N-COUNT 可算名詞 When there are **layoffs** in a company, people become unemployed because there is no more work for them in the company. 解雇 [BUSINESS 実業] □*It will close more than 200 stores nationwide resulting in the layoffs of an estimated 2,000 employees.* それによって全国の200店舗以上が閉店に追い込まれ，結果的に推定2千人の従業員が職を失うだろう．

lay|out /leɪaʊt/ (layouts) N-COUNT 可算名詞 The **layout** of a park, building, or piece of writing is the way in which the parts of it are arranged. 配置，レイアウト □*He tried to recall the layout of the farmhouse.* 彼はその農家の間取りを思い出そうとした．

lazy /leɪzi/ (lazier, laziest) ❶ ADJ 形容詞 If someone is **lazy**, they do not want to work or make any effort to do anything. 怠惰な □*Lazy and incompetent police officers are letting the public down.* 怠惰で無能な警察官たちが一般人を失望させている． ● **la|zi|ness** N-UNCOUNT 不可算名詞 怠惰 □*Current employment laws will be changed to reward effort and punish laziness.* 現行の雇用法は，努力に報いに怠惰を罰するよう変更されるであろう． ❷ ADJ 形容詞 [ADJ n] You can use **lazy** to describe an activity or event in which you are very relaxed and which you do or take part in without making much effort. くつろいだ □*Her latest novel is perfect for a lazy summer's afternoon reading.* 彼女の最新作の小説は，夏の午後ののんびりした読書に最適だ． ● **la|zily** /leɪzili/ ADV 副詞 [ADV with v] のんびりと □*Liz went back into the kitchen, stretching lazily.* リズはゆっくりと伸びをしながら台所へ戻って行った．

lb (lbs) **lb** is a written abbreviation for **pound**, when it refers to weight. ポンド（重さの単位）の略語 □*The baby was born three months early at 3 lbs 5 oz.* 赤ちゃんは予定より3か月早く，体重3ポンド5オンスで生まれた．

LCD /ɛl si di/ (LCDs) N-COUNT 可算名詞 An **LCD** is a display of information on a screen, which uses liquid crystals that become visible when electricity is passed through them. **LCD** is an abbreviation for **liquid crystal display**. 液晶ディスプレイ □*...a color LCD screen.* カラー液晶ディスプレー画面

lead

❶ BEING AHEAD OR TAKING SOMEONE SOMEWHERE
❷ SUBSTANCES

❶ **lead** /liːd/ (leads, leading, led)
⊃ Please look at meaning ❿ to see if the expression you are looking for is shown under another headword. ❶ V-T 他動詞 If you **lead** a group of people, you walk or ride in front of them. 率いる，先導する □*The president and vice president led the mourners.* 大統領と副大統領が会葬者たちの先頭に立った． □*He walks with a stick but still leads his soldiers into battle.* 彼は杖をついて歩くが，それでもなお彼の兵士たちを率いて戦う． ❷ V-T 他動詞 If you **lead** someone to a particular place or thing, you take them there.（場所へ）連れて行く □*He took Dickon by the hand to lead him into the house.* 彼はディコンを家の中へ招き入れるため，その手を取った． □*She confessed to the killing and led police to his remains.* 彼女は殺害を自白し，彼の遺体のところへ警察を連れて行った． ❸ V-I 自動詞 If a road, gate, or door **leads** somewhere, you can get there by following the road or going through the gate or door.（場所に）至る，通じる □*...the door that led to the yard.* 庭に通じていた出入り口 □*...a hallway leading to the living room.* 居間に通じる廊下 ❹ V-I 自動詞 If you **are leading** at a particular point in a race or competition, you are winning at that point.（競争・競技で）リードする，優位に立つ □*He's leading in the presidential race.* 彼は大統領選挙戦でリードしている． □*So far Fischer leads by five wins to two.* 今のところフィッシャーが5勝対2勝でリードしている． ❺ N-SING 単数名詞 If you have **the lead** or are

in the lead in a race or competition, you are winning. (競争・競技中の) 優勢 ❑ *Harvard took the lead and remained unperturbed by the repeated challenges.* ハーバード大がリードし、度重なる巻き返しにも動じなかった。 **6** V-T 他動詞 If one company or country **leads** others in a particular activity such as scientific research or business, it is more successful or advanced than they are in that activity. (研究・事業などで他よりも) 優れる ❑ *In 1920, the United States led the world in iron and steel manufacturing.* 1920年に米国は鉄鋼製造で世界の頂点に立った。 **7** V-T 他動詞 If you **lead** a group of people, an organization, or an activity, you are in control or in charge of the people or the activity. (人々・組織などを) 統率する ❑ *He led the country between 1949 and 1984.* 彼は1949年から1984年までその国を統治した。 **8** N-COUNT 可算名詞 If you take **the lead**, you do something new or develop new ideas or methods that other people consider to be a good example or model to follow. 先駆、先導 ❑ *The American and Japanese navies took the lead in the development of naval aviation.* 米国と日本の海軍は、海軍の軍用機開発で先駆者となった。 **9** V-T 他動詞 You can use **lead** when you are saying what kind of life someone has. For example, if you **lead** a busy life, your life is busy. (生活を) 送る ❑ *She led a normal, happy life with her sister and brother.* 彼女は妹や弟と共に普通の幸せな生活を送った。 **10** V-I 自動詞 If something **leads to** a situation or event, usually an unpleasant one, it begins a process which causes that situation or event to happen. (ある状態に) 至る ❑ *Ethnic tensions among the republics could lead to civil war.* 共和国間の民族どうしの緊張は内戦に至る可能性がある。 **11** V-T 他動詞 If something **leads you to do** something, it influences or affects you in such a way that you do it. (〜するよう) 影響を与える、仕向ける ❑ *His abhorrence of racism led him to write The Algiers Motel Incident.* 人種差別に対する嫌悪感から彼は『アルジェー・モーテル事件』を書くに至った。 **12** V-T 他動詞 You can say that one point or topic in a discussion or piece of writing **leads you to** another in order to introduce a new point or topic that is linked with the previous one. (関連する話題などに) 導く ❑ *Well, I think that leads me to the real point.* さて、そこから本題に入ります。 **13** N-COUNT 可算名詞 A **lead** is a piece of information or an idea which may help people to discover the facts in a situation where many facts are not known, for example, in the investigation of a crime or in a scientific experiment. 手がかり、きっかけ ❑ *The inquiry team is also following up possible leads after receiving 400 calls from the public.* 捜査班は一般市民から400本の電話を受け、可能性のある手がかりを追ってもいる。 **14** N-COUNT 可算名詞 A dog's **lead** is a long, thin chain or piece of leather which you attach to the dog's collar so that you can control the dog. (犬をつなぐ) ひも [BRIT 英国英語; AM leash 米国英語 **leash**] **15** N-COUNT 可算名詞 A **lead** in a piece of equipment is a piece of wire covered in plastic which supplies electricity to the equipment or carries it from one part of the equipment to another. リード線 (電気の引き込み線) ❑ *...a lead that plugs into a socket on the camcorder.* ビデオカメラのソケットに接続するリード線 **16** N-COUNT 可算名詞 The **lead** in a play, film, or show is the most important part in it. The person who plays this part can also be called the **lead**. (劇・映画の) 主役 ❑ *Nina Ananiashvili and Alexei Fadeyechev from the Bolshoi Ballet dance the leads.* ボリショイ・バレエのニーナ・アナニアシュヴィリとアレクセイ・ファジェーチェフが主役を踊る。 ❑ *Neve Campbell is the lead, playing one of the dancers.* ニーヴ・キャンベルが主役でダンサーの1人を演じる。 **17** → see also **leading** **18** to **lead** someone **astray** → see **astray** **19** to **lead the way** → see **way**

▶ **lead up to** **1** PHRASAL VERB 句動詞 The events that **led up to** a particular event happened one after the other until that event occurred. 〜に至る ❑ *Alan Tomlinson has reconstructed the events that led up to the deaths.* アラン・トムリンソンはその死亡事件に至るまでの出来事を再現している。 **2** PHRASAL VERB 句動詞 If someone **leads up to** a particular subject, they gradually guide a conversation to a point where they can introduce it. 〜に話を持っていく ❑ *I'm leading up to something quite important.* 私はとても重要な話を持っていこうとしているのだ。

❷ **lead** /lɛd/ (leads) **1** N-UNCOUNT 不可算名詞 **Lead** is a soft, gray, heavy metal. 鉛 ❑ *...drinking water supplied by old-fashioned lead pipes.* 旧式の鉛のパイプで供給される飲料水 **2** N-COUNT 可算名詞 The **lead** in a pencil is the center part of it which makes a mark on paper. (鉛筆の) しん ❑ *He grabbed a pen, and the lead immediately broke.* 彼がペンを握りつかもうとすると、すぐにしんが折れた。
→ see **mineral**, **plumbing**

lead|er /líːdər/ (leaders) **1** N-COUNT 可算名詞 The **leader** of a group of people or an organization is the person who is in control of it or in charge of it. (グループ・組織の) 指導者 ❑ *We now need a new leader of the party and a new style of leadership.* 今や私たちには党の新しい指導者と新しい統率のスタイルが必要だ。 **2** N-COUNT 可算名詞 The **leader** at a particular point in a race or competition is the

person who is winning at that point. (競争・競技で) リードしている人 ❑ *The leaders came in two minutes clear of the field.* 先頭の走者たちはその他の走者を2分も離してゴールした。

lead|er|board /líːdərbɔːrd/ N-SING 単数名詞 The **leaderboard** is a board that shows the names and positions of the leading competitors in a competition, especially a golf tournament. リーダーボード (上位選手の名前やスコアを掲示) ❑ *I'm delighted to be on top of the leaderboard in a tournament that has so many star names playing.* 私はこんなにたくさんの有名選手が出場しているトーナメントのリーダーボードに最上位で載るなんて嬉しい。

lead|er|ship /líːdərʃɪp/ (leaderships) **1** N-COUNT 可算名詞 You refer to people who are in control of a group or organization as the **leadership**. (グループ・組織の) 指導者たち、指導部 ❑ *He is expected to hold talks with both the Croatian and Slovenian leaderships.* 彼はクロアチアとスロベニアの両方の指導者たちと会談することが見込まれている。 **2** N-UNCOUNT 不可算名詞 Someone's **leadership** is their position or state of being in control of a group of people. 指導者の地位、指導力 ❑ *He praised her leadership during the crisis.* 彼は危機の最中の彼女の指導力を称賛した。

lead|ing /líːdɪŋ/ **1** ADJ 形容詞 The **leading** person or thing in a particular area is the one which is most important or successful. 主要な、一流の [ADJ n] ❑ *...a leading member of the city's Sikh community.* その都市のシーク教徒社会の主要な1員 **2** ADJ 形容詞 The **leading** role in a play or movie is the main role. A **leading** lady or man is an actor who plays this role. (芝居や映画の) 主役の [ADJ n] ❑ *...an offer to play the leading role in an Arthur Miller play.* アーサー・ミラーのある劇の主役を演じないかという申し出 **3** ADJ 形容詞 The **leading** group, vehicle, or person in a race or procession is the one that is at the front. (競争の) 最上位の [ADJ n] ❑ *The leading car came to a halt.* 先頭を走る車が止まった。

lead|ing edge N-SING 単数名詞 The **leading edge of** a particular area of research or development is the area of it that seems most advanced or sophisticated. (研究・開発の) 最前線 ❑ *I think Israel tends to be at the leading edge of technological development.* 私はイスラエルが技術開発の最前線にいることが多いように思う。 ● **leading-edge** ADJ 形容詞 最前線の ❑ *...leading-edge technology.* 最先端技術

lead time (lead times) **1** N-COUNT 可算名詞 **Lead time** is the time between the original design or idea for a particular product and its actual production. リードタイム (製品の企画から生産までの時間)、準備期間 [BUSINESS 実業] ❑ *They aim to cut production lead times to under 18 months.* 彼らは製品化のリードタイムを18ヵ月以内にすることを目指している。 **2** N-COUNT 可算名詞 **Lead time** is the period of time that it takes for goods to be delivered after someone has ordered them. 発注から配達までの期間 [BUSINESS 実業] ❑ *Lead times on new equipment orders can run as long as three years.* 新設備の調達期間は3年もかかることもある。

leaf /liːf/ (leaves, leafs, leafing, leafed) **1** N-COUNT 可算名詞 The **leaves** of a tree or plant are the parts that are flat, thin, and usually green. Many trees and plants lose their leaves in the winter and grow new leaves in the spring. 葉 [usu pl, also 'in/into' N] ❑ *In the garden, the leaves of the horse chestnut had already fallen.* 庭ではトチノキの葉がすでに落ちていた。 **2** N-COUNT 可算名詞 A **leaf** is one of the pieces of paper of which a book is made. (本の紙) 1枚 ❑ *He flattened the wrappers and put them between the leaves of his book.* 彼は包装紙を平たくし、本のページの間に挟んだ。 **3** PHRASE 句 If you say that you are going to **turn over a new leaf**, you mean that you are going to start to behave in a better or more acceptable way. 心を入れ替える ❑ *He realized he was in the wrong and promised to turn over a new leaf.* 彼は自分が間違っていたことに気づき、心を入れ替えると約束した。

▶ **leaf through** PHRASAL VERB 句動詞 If you **leaf through** something such as a book or magazine, you turn the pages without reading or looking at them very carefully. (本・雑誌を) ぱらぱらめくる、ざっと目を通す ❑ *Most patients derive enjoyment from leafing through old picture albums.* ほとんどの患者は古い写真アルバムをぱらぱらめくって楽しむ。

leaf|let /líːflɪt/ (leaflets) N-COUNT 可算名詞 A **leaflet** is a little book or a piece of paper containing information about a particular subject. 小冊子、ちらし ❑ *Campaigners handed out leaflets on passive smoking.* 運動の参加者たちは受動喫煙に関するちらしを配った。

leafy /líːfi/ **1** ADJ 形容詞 **Leafy** trees and plants have lots of leaves on them. 葉の茂った ❑ *His two-story brick home was surrounded by tall, leafy trees.* 彼の2階建てのれんが造りの家は、葉の茂った高い木々に囲まれていた。 **2** ADJ 形容詞 You say that a place is

leafy when there are lots of trees and plants there. 緑の多い ❏...a gate leading to the narrow leafy streets at the top of the hill. 丘の上にある緑の生い茂った狭い通りに通じる門
→ see **vegetable**

league /liːɡ/ (leagues) **1** N-COUNT 可算名詞 A **league** is a group of people, clubs, or countries that have joined together for a particular purpose, or because they share a common interest. 同盟, 連盟 ❏...the League of Nations. 国際連盟 **2** N-COUNT 可算名詞 A **league** is a group of teams that play the same sport or activity against each other. 競技連盟, リーグ ❏...the American League series between the Boston Red Sox and World Champion Oakland Athletics. ボストン・レッドソックスとワールドチャンピオンの覇者, オークランド・アスレチックスとのアメリカンリーグ・シリーズ戦 **3** N-COUNT 可算名詞 You use **league** to make comparisons between different people or things, especially in terms of their quality. 同類 ❏ Her success has taken her out of my league. 彼女は成功して私の仲間から離れた. **4** PHRASE 句 If you say that someone is **in league with** another person to do something bad, you mean that they are working together to do that thing. 結束して, ぐるになって ❏ There is no evidence that the broker was in league with the fraudulent vendor. その仲買人が不正な売人と結託していたという証拠はなにもない.

Word Partnership   league は次の語句と使われる:
N.	league **leader**, league **record**, league **schedule** 2
V.	**lead** the league 2
PREP.	**out of** someone's league 3
	in league **with** someone 4

leak /liːk/ (leaks, leaking, leaked) **1** V-T/V-I 他動詞/自動詞 If a container **leaks**, there is a hole or crack in it which lets a substance such as liquid or gas escape. You can also say that a container **leaks** a substance such as liquid or gas. (液体・気体を) 漏らす [他動詞], (液体・気体が) 漏れる [自動詞] ❏ The roof leaked. 屋根は雨漏りしていた. ❏ The pool's fiberglass sides had cracked and the water had leaked out. プールの繊維グラスの面にひびが入っており, 水が漏れていた. ● N-COUNT 可算名詞 **Leak** is also a noun. (液体・気体が) 漏れること, 漏れ ❏ It's thought a gas leak may have caused the blast. ガス漏れがその爆発を起こした可能性があると思われる. **2** N-COUNT 可算名詞 A **leak** is a crack, hole, or other gap that a substance such as a liquid or gas can pass through. (液体・気体が漏れる) ひび, 漏れ口 ❏...a leak in the radiator. 冷却器のひび **3** V-T/V-I 他動詞/自動詞 If a secret document or piece of information **leaks** or **is leaked**, someone lets the public know about it. (秘密などを) 漏らす [他動詞], (秘密などが) 漏れる [自動詞] ❏ Mr. Ashton accused police of leaking information to the press. アシュトン氏は警察が報道機関に情報を漏らしたと非難した. ❏ We don't know how the transcript leaked. その写しがどうやって漏れたか, 我々には分からない. ● N-COUNT 可算名詞 **Leak** is also a noun. (秘密などの) 漏えい ❏ More serious leaks, possibly involving national security, are likely to be investigated by the police. 国家の安全に影響を与えるかもしれない, より深刻な機密の漏えいは警察によって調査される可能性が高い. ● PHRASAL VERB 句動詞 **Leak out** means the same as **leak**. 漏らす, 漏れる ❏ More details are now beginning to leak out. 現在, さらに詳しい情報が漏れ始めている.

Thesaurus   leak また次を参照:
V.	discharge, drip, ooze, seep, trickle 1
	come out, divulge, pass on 3
N.	crack, hole, opening 2

Word Partnership   leak は次の語句と使われる:
V.	**cause** a leak, **spring** a leak 1
N.	**fuel** leak, **gas** leak, **oil** leak, leak **in the roof**, **water** leak 1
	leak **information**, leak **news**, leak a **story** 3

leak|age /liːkɪdʒ/ (leakages) N-VAR 可変性名詞 A **leakage** is an amount of liquid or gas that is escaping from a pipe or container by means of a crack, hole, or other fault. (液体・気体の) 漏れた量 ❏ A leakage of kerosene has polluted water supplies. 漏れた灯油が水道水を汚染している.

lean /liːn/ (leans, leaning, leaned, leaner, leanest) **1** V-I 自動詞 When you **lean** in a particular direction, you bend your body in that direction. 体を曲げる ❏ Eileen leaned across and opened the passenger door. アイリーンは身を乗り出して, 客席のドアを開けた. **2** V-T/V-I 他動詞/自動詞 If you **lean on** or **against** someone or something, you rest against them so that they partly support your weight. If you **lean** an object **on** or **against** something, you place the object so that it is partly supported by that thing. (物に) 寄りかからせる [他動詞], (人・物に) 寄りかかる [自動詞] ❏ She was feeling tired and was glad to lean against him. 彼女は疲れていたので, 喜んで彼に寄りかかった. ❏ Lean the plants against a wall and cover the roots with peat. 苗木を壁にもたせかけ, ピートで根を覆い

なさい. **3** ADJ 形容詞 If you describe someone as **lean**, you mean that they are thin but look strong and healthy. (体が締まった) 細身の [APPROVAL 賛成] ❏ Like most athletes, she was lean and muscular. 多くの運動選手と同様に, 彼女は細身で筋肉質だった. **4** ADJ 形容詞 If meat is **lean**, it does not have very much fat. 脂身の少ない ❏ It is a beautiful meat, very lean and tender. それは脂身が少なくて柔らかい素晴らしい肉だ. **5** ADJ 形容詞 If you describe an organization as **lean**, you mean that it has become more efficient and less wasteful by getting rid of staff, or by dropping projects which were unprofitable. (組織の) 無駄を省いた ❏...reforms which turned us into a lean and competitive nation. 我々を無駄のない競争力のある国家に変えた改革 **6** ADJ 形容詞 If you describe periods of time as **lean**, you mean that people have less of something such as money or are less successful than they used to be. 収入の少ない ❏ My parents lived through the lean years of the 1930s. 私の両親は1930年代の不況の時期を生き延びた.

▶ **lean on** or **lean upon** PHRASAL VERB 句動詞 If you **lean on** someone or **lean upon** them, you depend on them for support and encouragement. 一に頼る ❏ She leaned on him to help her to solve her problems. 彼女は彼に頼って自分の問題の解決を手伝ってもらった.

Thesaurus   lean また次を参照:
V.	bend, incline, prop, tilt 1
	recline, rest 2
ADJ.	angular, lanky, slender, slim, wiry 3

Word Partnership   lean は次の語句と使われる:
ADV.	lean **heavily** 2
ADJ.	**long and** lean, **tall and** lean 3
N.	lean **body** 3
	lean **beef**, lean **meat** 4

leap /liːp/ (leaps, leaping, leaped or leapt) **1** V-T/V-I 他動詞/自動詞 If you **leap**, you jump high in the air or jump a long distance. 跳び上がる ❏ He leaped in the air and waved his fists to the fans as he ran out of the stadium. 彼は中へ跳び上がり, スタジアムを走り出ながらファンに両手のこぶしを振った. ❏ Frederick leaped 22 feet, 7-1/4 inches on his second attempt. フレデリックは2回目の跳躍で22フィート7インチ1/4を跳んだ. ● N-COUNT 可算名詞 **Leap** is also a noun. 跳ぶこと, 跳躍 ❏ The suspect took a leap out of a third-story window. 容疑者は3階の窓から跳び出した. **2** V-I 自動詞 If you **leap** somewhere, you move there suddenly and quickly. (人が) 急に動く ❏ The two men leaped into the jeep and roared off. その2人の男はジープに飛び乗って, ごう音を立てて走り去った. **3** V-I 自動詞 If a vehicle **leaps** somewhere, it moves there in a short sudden movement. (車が) 急に動く ❏ The car leaped forward. その車は前へ急発進した. **4** N-COUNT 可算名詞 A **leap** is a large and important change, increase, or advance. 大変化, 大増加 [JOURNALISM ジャーナリズム] ❏ The result has been a giant leap in productivity. その結果, 生産性が大躍進した. ❏...the leap in the unemployed from 35,000 to 75,000. 失業者数3万5千人から7万5千人への大幅な増加 **5** V-I 自動詞 If you **leap** to a particular place or position, you make a large and important change, increase, or advance. 大変化する, 急上昇する ❏ Bush's approval rating leaped to an astounding 88 percent. ブッシュの支持率が驚異的な88パーセントに急上昇した.

Word Partnership   leap は次の語句と使われる:
V.	**make a** leap, **take a** leap 1
ADJ.	**big** leap, **giant** leap, **sudden** leap 1 4
N.	leap **to your feet** 1

leap|frog /liːpfrɔɡ/ (leapfrogs, leapfrogging, leapfrogged) **1** N-UNCOUNT 不可算名詞 **Leapfrog** is a game which children play, in which a child bends over, while others jump over their back. 馬跳び ❏ The kids were playing leapfrog and doing somersaults in the backyard. 子供たちは裏庭で馬跳びや宙返りをしていた. **2** V-T/V-I 他動詞/自動詞 If one group of people **leapfrogs** into a particular position or **leapfrogs** someone else, they use the achievements of another person or group in order to make advances of their own. (他人の業績を利用して) 前進する ❏ It is already obvious that all four American systems have leapfrogged over the European versions. アメリカの4つの制度のすべてがヨーロッパのものを追い抜いて進んでいることはすでに明らかだ.

leap year (leap years) N-COUNT 可算名詞 A **leap year** is a year which has 366 days. The extra day is February 29th. There is a leap year every four years. うるう年
→ see **year**

learn /lɜːrn/ (learns, learning, learned) **1** V-T/V-I 他動詞/自動詞 If you **learn** something, you obtain knowledge or a skill through studying or training. (知識・技術を) 学ぶ, 習う ❏ Their children were going to learn English. 彼らの子供たちは英語を学ぶ予定だった. ❏ He is learning to play the piano. 彼はピアノを習っている. ❏ It's going to be tough, but these guys learn quickly. それは難しいだろうが, この

連中ならすぐに覚えるよ. ●**learn|ing** N-UNCOUNT 不可算名詞 学習 ❑...a bilingual approach to the learning of English. 2か国語を使って英語を学ぶ方法 ❷ V-T/V-I 他動詞/自動詞 If you **learn** of something, you find out about it. 知る ❑It was only after his death that she learned of his affair with Betty. 彼がベティと浮気をしていたことを彼女が知ったのは, 彼の死後だった. ❑It didn't come as a shock to learn that the fuel and cooling systems are the most common causes of breakdown. 燃料システムと冷却システムが故障の最も一般的な原因だと知っても驚かなかった. ❸ V-T 他動詞 If people **learn** to behave or react in a particular way, they gradually start to behave in that way as a result of a change in attitudes. できるようになる, (言動を) 身につける ❑You have to learn to face your problem. あなたは問題を直視できるようにならないといけません. ❹ V-T/V-I 他動詞/自動詞 If you **learn from** an unpleasant experience, you change the way you behave so that it does not happen again or so that, if it happens again, you can deal with it better. (不快な経験から) 学ぶ ❑I am convinced that he has learned from his mistakes. 私は彼が自分の失敗から学んだと確信している. ❑I just hope we all learn some lessons from this. ただ, 私たちみんながこのことから何か教訓を学ぶよう願うだけです. ❺ V-T 他動詞 If you **learn** something such as a poem or a role in a play, you study or repeat the words so that you can remember them. 暗記する ❑He learned this song as an inmate at a Texas prison. 彼はこの歌をテキサス州の刑務所で囚人だった時に覚えた. ❻ → see also **learned, learning** ❼ to **learn** something **the hard way** → see **hard** ❽ to **learn the ropes** → see **rope**

Thesaurus		learn また次を参照:
v.	master, pick up, study ❶	
	discover, find out, understand ❷	

Word Partnership		learn は次の語句と使われる:
v.	learn **to drive**, learn **to read**, learn **to speak**, learn **to swim**, learn **to use** something, learn **to write** ❶	
	have to learn, **must** learn, **need to** learn, **try to** learn, **want to** learn ❶ - ❺	
	learn **to cope with** someone/something ❸	
N.	learn **a language**, learn **a secret**, learn **a skill**, learn **things**, learn **the truth** ❶	
	children learn, learn **from experience**, learn **a lesson**, learn **from mistakes**, **opportunity to** learn, **people** learn, learn **in school**, **students** learn ❶ ❸ ❹	
ADJ.	**eager to** learn ❶ - ❸	
	shocked to learn ❷ ❹	

learn|ed /lɜrnɪd/ ADJ 形容詞 A **learned** person has gained a lot of knowledge by studying. 博学な, 教養のある ❑He is a scholar, a genuinely learned man. 彼は学者で, 本当に学識のある人だ.

learn|er /lɜrnər/ (learners) N-COUNT 可算名詞 A **learner** is someone who is learning about a particular subject or how to do something. 学習者 ❑Clinton proved to be a quick learner and soon settled into serious struggles over cutting the budget. クリントンは飲み込みが早く, 間もなく予算の削減に真剣に格闘し始めた.

learn|ing /lɜrnɪŋ/ ❶ N-UNCOUNT 不可算名詞 **Learning** is the process of gaining knowledge through studying. 学習 ❑The brochure described the library as the focal point of learning on the campus. パンフレットには図書館が学内で勉強する際の中心であると述べられていた. ❷ → see also **learn** → see **brain**

learn|ing curve (learning curves) N-COUNT 可算名詞 A **learning curve** is a process where people develop a skill by learning from their mistakes. A steep learning curve involves learning very quickly. 学習曲線, 学習の過程 [usu sing] ❑They are on a steep learning curve. 彼らは学習が急速に進んでいる.

lease /lis/ (leases, leasing, leased) ❶ N-COUNT 可算名詞 A **lease** is a legal agreement by which the owner of a building, a piece of land, or something such as a car allows someone else to use it for a period of time in return for money. 賃貸 ❑He took up a 10-year lease on the house. 彼は10年の賃貸契約でその家を借りた. ❷ V-T 他動詞 If you **lease** property or something such as a car from someone or if they **lease** it to you, they allow you to use it in return for regular payments of money. 賃借する, 賃貸する ❑He went to Toronto, where he leased an apartment. 彼はトロントへ行き, そこでアパートを借りた. ❑She hopes to lease the building to students. 彼女は学生たちにその建物を賃貸したいと思っている.

lease|hold /lishoʊld/ ADJ 形容詞 If a building or land is described as **leasehold**, it is allowed to be used in return for payment according to the terms of a lease. 賃借の ❑I went into a leasehold property at four hundred and fifty dollars rent per year. 私はある賃貸物件に年間450ドルの家賃で入った.

leash /liʃ/ (leashes) N-COUNT 可算名詞 A dog's **leash** is a long thin piece of leather or a chain, which you attach to the dog's collar so that you can keep the dog under control. (犬をつなぐ) 革

ひも, 鎖 ❑All dogs in public places should be on a leash. 公共の場では犬はすべて鎖につないでおかないといけない.

least /list/

Least is often considered to be the superlative form of **little**.

Least はしばしば **little** の最上級形であると考えられている.

❶ PHRASE 句 You use **at least** to say that a number or amount is the smallest that is possible or likely and that the actual number or amount may be greater. The forms **at the least** and **at the very least** are also used. (数・量が) 最低でも ❶Aim to have at least half a pint of milk each day. 少なくとも毎日, 半パイントの牛乳を飲むことを目指しなさい. ❑About two-thirds of adults consult their doctor at least once a year. 成人の約3分の2が少なくとも1年に1回医師の診察を受けている. ❷ PHRASE 句 You use **at least** to say that something is the minimum that is true or possible. The forms **at the least** and **at the very least** are also used. とにかく, いずれにせよ ❑She could take a nice vacation at least. 彼女はとにかく楽しい休暇が取れた. ❑His possession of classified documents in his home was, at the very least, a violation of navy security regulations. 彼が機密文書を自宅に持っていたことは, 控えめに言っても, 海軍の機密保持規則に違反していた. ❸ PHRASE 句 You use **at least** to indicate an advantage that exists in spite of the disadvantage or bad situation that has just been mentioned. (悪い状況の中) 少なくとも ❑We've no idea what his state of health is but at least we know he is still alive. 我々は彼の健康状態がどうなのかまったく分からないが, 少なくとも彼がまだ生きていることは分かっている. ❹ PHRASE 句 You use **at least** to indicate that you are correcting or changing something that you have just said. (前言を訂正・言い換えして) 正確に言うと, 少なくとも ❑It's not difficult to get money for research or at least it's not always difficult. 研究費を得るのは難しくない. いや少なくとも, いつも難しいわけではない. ❺ ADJ 形容詞 You use **the least** to mean a smaller amount than anyone or anything else, or the smallest amount possible. (量が) 最小限の ['the' ADJ n] ❑I try to offend the least amount of people possible. 私はできるだけ人に不快な思いをさせないように心がけている. ● PRON 代名詞 **Least** is also a pronoun. 最小のもの ['the' PRON] ❑On education funding, Japan performs best but spends the least per student. 教育資金供給に関しては, 日本が最もよい成績を上げているが, 学生1人当たりの金額は最も少ない. ● ADV 副詞 **Least** is also an adverb. 最小限で ['the' ADV after v] ❑Damming the river may end up benefiting those who need it the least. 川にダムを造ることは, 最もそれを必要としない人たちに恩恵をもたらすことになりかねない. ❻ ADV 副詞 You use **least** to indicate that someone or something has less of a particular quality than most other things of its kind. (性質の) 最も少なく [ADV adj/adv] ❑He was one of the least warm human beings I had ever met. 彼は私がそれまで会った人の中でも, 1番温かみのない人間の1人だった. ❼ ADJ 形容詞 You use **the least** to emphasize the smallness of something, especially when it hardly exists at all. 最小の [EMPHASIS 強調] ['the' ADJ n] ❑I don't have the least idea of what you're talking about. 私は君が何の話をしているのか全く分からないよ. ❽ ADV 副詞 You use **least** to indicate that something is true or happens to a smaller degree or extent than anything else or at any other time. 最も少なく [ADV with v] ❑He had a way of throwing Helen off guard with his charm when she least expected it. 彼は彼女が最も予期していない時に, その魅力で彼女の警戒心を解く方法を心得ていた. ❾ ADJ 形容詞 You use **least** in structures where you are emphasizing that a particular situation or event is much less important or serious than other possible or actual ones. 取るに足らない [EMPHASIS 強調] [ADJ 'of' def-n] ❑Having to get up at three o'clock every morning was the least of her worries. 彼女にとって毎朝3時に起きなければならないことは, 何の問題でもなかった. ❿ PRON 代名詞 You use **the least** in structures where you are suggesting the minimum that should be done in a situation, and suggesting that more should really be done. 最小限のもの, 最低限のこと ['the' PRON cl] ❑Well, the least you can do, if you won't help me yourself, is to tell me where to go instead. いいわ, もしあなたが私を助けてくれないなら, せめてどこに行けばいいかを代わりに教えてください.

Thesaurus	least また次を参照:
ADJ.	fewest, lowest, minimum, smallest ❺

leath|er /lɛðər/ (leathers) N-MASS 質量名詞 **Leather** is treated animal skin, usually from cows, which is used for making shoes, clothes, bags, and furniture. なめし革 ❑He wore a leather jacket and dark trousers. 彼は革のジャケットを着て, 黒ずんだズボンをはいていた.

leave
❶ VERB USES
❷ NOUN USE
❸ PHRASES AND PHRASAL VERBS

❶ **leave** /liv/ (leaves, leaving, left) ❶ V-T/V-I 他動詞/自動詞 If you **leave** a place or person, you go away from that place or

person. 去る、離れる ❏ *He would not be allowed to leave the country.* 彼はその国を離れることを許されないだろう。 ❏ *My flight leaves in less than an hour.* 私の飛行便は1時間以内に出発する。 **2** V-T/V-I 他動詞/自動詞 If you **leave** an institution, group, or job, you permanently stop attending that institution, being a member of that group, or doing that job. (機関・仕事を) 辞める ❏ *He left school with no qualifications.* 彼は何の資格も取らずに学校を退学した。 ❏ *I am leaving to concentrate on writing fiction.* 私は小説を書くことに専心するため退職するつもりだ。 **3** V-T/V-I 他動詞/自動詞 If you **leave** your husband, wife, or some other person with whom you have had a close relationship, you stop living with them or you end the relationship. (配偶者などと) 別居する 別れる ❏ *He'll never leave you. You needn't worry.* 彼は絶対あなたと別れないわ。心配する必要などない。 **4** V-T 他動詞 If you **leave** something or someone in a particular place, you let them remain there when you go away. If you **leave** something or someone with a person, you let them remain with that person so they are safe while you are away. 置いて行く、渡して行く ❏ *I left my bags in the car.* 私は鞄を車に置いてきた。 ❏ *From the moment that Philippe had left her in the bedroom at the hotel, she had heard nothing of him.* フィリップが彼女をホテルの寝室に置き去りにして以来、彼女は彼から何の連絡もなかった。 **5** V-T 他動詞 If you **leave** a message or an answer, you write it, record it, or give it to someone so that it can be found or passed on. (伝言・メモなどを) 残す ❏ *You can leave a message on our answering machine.* 私たちの留守電にメッセージを残してくれてもいいよ。 ❏ *I left my phone number with several people.* 私は自分の電話番号を数人に渡した。 **6** V-T 他動詞 If you **leave** someone doing something, they are doing that thing when you go away from them. (人がーしているのを) させておく ❏ *Salter drove off, leaving Callendar surveying the scene.* カレンダーが景色を見渡しているのをそのままにして、ソルターは車で走り去った。 **7** V-T 他動詞 If you **leave** someone **to** do something, you go away from them so that they do it on their own. If you **leave** someone **to** himself or herself, you go away from them and allow them to be alone. (人に物事を) させておく そっとしておく ❏ *I'll leave you to get to know each other.* 私は行くけど、お互いにお知り合いになってね。 ❏ *Diana took the hint and left them to it.* ダイアナは気配を察し、彼らをそっとしておいた。 **8** V-T 他動詞 To **leave** an amount of something means to keep it available after the rest has been used or taken away. (残りを) 取っておく ❏ *He always left a little food for the next day.* 彼はいつも次の日のために少し食べ物をとって置いた。 **9** V-T 他動詞 To **leave** someone **with** something, especially when that thing is unpleasant or difficult to deal with, means to make them have it or make them deal with it. (不快・難儀なことを) もたらす ❏ *...a crash which left him with a broken collar-bone.* 彼が鎖骨を骨折した衝突事故 **10** V-T 他動詞 If an event **leaves** people or things in a particular state, they are in that state when the event has finished. (人・物をーの状態に) しておく ❏ *...violent disturbances which have left at least ten people dead.* 少なくとも10人を死亡させた暴動 **11** V-T 他動詞 If you **leave** food or drink, you do not eat or drink it, often because you do not like it. (食べ物・飲み物を) 手をつけずに残す ❏ *If you don't like the cocktail you ordered, just leave it and try a different one.* 君の注文したカクテルが好みじゃなければ、そのまま残して違うものを頼めばいいよ。 **12** V-T 他動詞 If something **leaves** a mark, effect, or sign, it causes that mark, effect, or sign to remain as a result. (傷跡・影響などを) 後に残す ❏ *A muscle tear will leave a scar after healing.* 筋肉の裂傷は治った後、傷跡になって残るでしょう。 **13** V-T 他動詞 If you **leave** something in a particular state, position, or condition, you let it remain in that state, position, or condition. (物をーの状態・立場に) しておく ❏ *He left the album open on the table.* 彼はアルバムをテーブルの上に開いたままにしていた。 ❏ *I've left the car lights on.* 私は車のライトをつけっぱなしにして来た。 **14** V-T 他動詞 If you **leave** a space or gap in something, you deliberately make that space or gap. (隙間などを) 空けておく ❏ *Leave a gap at the top and bottom so air can circulate.* 空気が循環するように上部と底にすき間を空けておきなさい。 **15** V-T 他動詞 If you **leave** a job, decision, or choice to someone, you give them the responsibility for dealing with it or making it. (仕事・選択などを人に) 任せる ❏ *Affix the blue airmail label and leave the rest to us.* 航空郵便の青いシールを貼って、後は私たちに任せておいて。 ❏ *The judge should not have left it to the jury to decide.* 裁判官は陪審に評決を任せるべきではなかった。 **16** V-T 他動詞 To **leave** someone **with** a particular course of action or the opportunity to do something means to let it be available to them, while restricting them in other ways. (人にーの選択肢のみを) 残す、与える ❏ *He was left with no option but to resign.* 彼は辞任する以外に選択の余地はなかった。 **17** V-T 他動詞 If you **leave** something **until** a particular time, you delay doing it or dealing with it until then. (すべきことを) 放置しておく ❏ *Don't leave it all until the last minute.* ぎりぎりになるまでそれ全部を放っておくな。 ● PHRASE 句 If you **leave** something **too late**, you delay doing it so that when you eventually do it, it is useless or ineffective. 長い間放置しすぎる ❏ *We eventually ... (the* 彼が完治するまで待ちすぎた) **18** V-T 他動詞 If you **leave** a particular subject, you stop talking about it and start discussing something else. (特定の話題から) 離れる おしまいにする ❏ *I think we'd better leave the subject of nationalism.* 国家主義の話題はおしまいにした方がいいと私は思うよ。 **19** V-T 他動詞

詞 If you **leave** property or money **to** someone, you arrange for it to be given to them after you have died. (遺産などを) 残す ❏ *He died two and a half years later, leaving everything to his wife.* 彼は2年半後にすべてを妻に残して亡くなった。 **20** V-T 他動詞 If you **leave** something somewhere, you forget to bring it with you. 置き忘れる ❏ *I left my purse back there on the gas pump.* 私は財布をガソリン・ポンプの上に置き忘れてきた。 **21** → see also **left**

❷ **leave** /liːv/ N-UNCOUNT 不可算名詞 **Leave** is a period of time when you are not working at your job, because you are on vacation, or for some other reason. If you are **on leave**, you are not working at your job. 休暇 ❏ *Why don't you take a few days' leave?* きみ、2、3日休みを取ったらどう？ ❏ *...maternity leave.* 育児休暇

❸ **leave** /liːv/ (**leaves, leaving, left**) **1** 句 If you **leave** someone or something **alone**, or if you **leave** them **be**, you do not pay them any attention or bother them. 1人にしておく、放っておく ❏ *Some people need to confront a traumatic past; others find it better to leave it alone.* 深い心の傷となっている過去を直視する必要がある人もいるし、それをそのままにしておく方がよいと思う人もいる。 **2** PHRASE 句 If something continues **from where** it **left off**, it starts happening again at the point where it had previously stopped. 中断していたところ ❏ *As soon as the police disappear the violence will take up from where it left off.* 警察官が見えなくなるや、暴力はまた中断していたところからまた始まるだろう。 **3** **take it or leave it** → see **take**

▶ **leave behind 1** PHRASAL VERB 句動詞 If you **leave** someone or something **behind**, you go away permanently from them. (人・物を) 置き去りにする、ーを後にする ❏ *"I'd go and live there and leave Kentucky behind," says Brown.* 「私ならそこに行って住み、ケンタッキーとはお別れだ」とブラウンは言った。 **2** PHRASAL VERB 句動詞 If you **leave behind** an object or a situation, it remains after you have left a place. (物・事態を) 後に残す ❏ *I don't want to leave anything behind.* ぼくは何も残して行きたくない。 **3** PHRASAL VERB 句動詞 If a person, country, or organization **is left behind**, they remain at a lower level than others because they are not as quick at understanding things or developing. (人・組織を) 追い越す ❏ *We're going to be left behind by the rest of the world.* 我々は世界の他の国々に取り残されてしまうは。

▶ **leave off** PHRASAL VERB 句動詞 If someone or something **is left off** a list, they are not included on that list. (リストに) 入れない ❏ *She has been deliberately left off the guest list.* 彼女は故意に来客リストから外されていた。

▶ **leave out** PHRASAL VERB 句動詞 If you **leave** someone or something **out** of an activity, collection, discussion, or group, you do not include them in it. (活動・グループなどから) 除外する、締め出す ❏ *Some would question the wisdom of leaving her out of the team.* 1部の人たちは彼女をチームから排除することが賢明であるか疑問に思うだろう。 ❏ *If you prefer mild flavors reduce or leave out the chili.* もしろやかな味の方がよければ、チリ唐辛子を減らすか取り除きなさい。

leaves /liːvz/ **Leaves** is the plural form of **leaf**, and the third person singular form of **leave**. leafの複数形。またleaveの三人称単数現在形。

→ see **tea**

lec|tern /lɛktərn/ (**lecterns**) N-COUNT 可算名詞 A **lectern** is a high sloping desk on which someone puts their notes when they are standing up and giving a lecture. 講義台

lec|ture /lɛktʃər/ (**lectures, lecturing, lectured**) **1** N-COUNT 可算名詞 A **lecture** is a talk someone gives in order to teach people about a particular subject, usually at a university or college. 講義 ❏ *...a series of lectures by Professor Eric Robinson.* エリック・ロビンソン教授による一連の講義 **2** V-I 自動詞 If you **lecture on** a particular subject, you give a lecture or a series of lectures about it. 講義をする ❏ *She then invited him to Atlanta to lecture on the history of art.* それから彼女は、美術史の講義をしてくれるよう彼をアトランタへ招いた。 **3** V-T 他動詞 If someone **lectures** you about something, they criticize you or tell you how they think you should behave. 説教する、叱責する ❏ *He used to lecture me about getting too much sun.* 彼は私が日光に当たりすぎないようによくお説教をした。 ❏ *Chuck would lecture me, telling me to get a haircut.* チャックはぼくに散髪してくるよう言いつけがらよく小言を言っていた。 ● N-COUNT 可算名詞 **Lecture** is also a noun. 説教 ❏ *Our captain gave us a stern lecture on safety.* 我々の船長は安全について厳しい説教をした。

lec|tur|er /lɛktʃərər/ (**lecturers**) **1** N-COUNT 可算名詞 A **lecturer** is a teacher at a university or college. (大学の) 講師 ❏ *...a lecturer in law.* 法学の講師 **2** N-COUNT 可算名詞 A **lecturer** is a person who gives lectures. 講演者

led /lɛd/ **Led** is the past tense and past participle of **lead**. leadの過去・過去分詞

ledge /lɛdʒ/ (**ledges**) ■ N-COUNT 可算名詞 A **ledge** is a piece of rock on the side of a cliff or mountain, which is in the shape of a narrow shelf. (がけや山の壁面の) 岩棚 □...like a wounded bird seeking refuge on a mountain ledge. 山の岩陰で隠れる場所を探す傷ついた鳥のように ② N-COUNT 可算名詞 A **ledge** is a narrow shelf along the bottom edge of a window. (窓の下部の) 出っ張り □ Dorothy had climbed onto the ledge outside his window. ドロシーは窓の外側の出っ張りによじ登っていた.

ledg|er /lɛdʒər/ (**ledgers**) N-COUNT 可算名詞 A **ledger** is a book in which a company or organization writes down the amounts of money it spends and receives. 出納簿 [BUSINESS 実業]

leek /lik/ (**leeks**) N-VAR 可変性名詞 **Leeks** are long thin vegetables which smell like onions. They are white at one end, have long light green leaves, and are eaten cooked. リーキ, 西洋ネギ

leer /lɪər/ (**leers, leering, leered**) V-I 自動詞 If someone **leers** at you, they smile in an unpleasant way, usually because they are sexually interested in you. いやらしい目つきで見る [DISAPPROVAL 不賛成] □...men standing around, swilling beer and occasionally leering at passing females. あたりに突っ立ったままビールをがぶ飲みし, 時折, 通り過ぎる女性をいやらしい目つきで眺めている男たち

---

left
❶ REMAINING
❷ DIRECTION AND POLITICAL GROUPINGS

---

❶ left /lɛft/ ■ **Left** is the past tense and past participle of **leave**. leaveの過去・過去分詞 ② ADJ 形容詞 If there is a certain amount of something **left**, or if you have a certain amount of it **left**, it remains when the rest has gone or been used. 残された [v-link ADJ, v n ADJ] □ Is there any gin left? ジンはまだ残っている？ □ They still have six games left to play. 彼らにはまだ6試合残っている. ● PHRASE 句 If there is a certain amount of something **left over**, or if you have it **left over**, it remains when the rest has gone or been used. 使い残しの, 残り物の □ So much income is devoted to monthly mortgage payments that nothing is left over. 収入のあまりにも多くを月々の住宅ローンの支払いに充てるので, 後には何も残らない.

Thesaurus   left また次を参照:

ADJ.   extra, leftover, remaining ❶ ②

❷ left /lɛft/

The spelling **Left** is also used for meanings ③ and ④.

つづりの **Left** は ③ と ④ の意味にも使われる.

■ N-SING 単数名詞 The **left** is one of two opposite directions, sides, or positions. If you are facing north and you turn to the left, you will be facing west. In the word "to," the "t" is to the left of the "o." 左 □ Go back to the last fork in the road and take a left. 今来た別れ道まで戻り, 左に曲がれ. □...the brick wall to the left of the conservatory. 温室の左手にあるれんがの壁 ● ADV 副詞 **Left** is also an adverb. 左へ [ADV after v] □ Turn left at the crossroads into Clay Lane. 十字路を左へ曲がりクレイ・レーンに入れ. ② ADJ 形容詞 Your **left** arm, leg, or ear, for example, is the one which is on the left side of your body. Your **left** shoe or glove is the one which is intended to be worn on your left foot or hand. 左の [ADJ n] □ Ferdinand landed awkwardly on top of Delgado's right boot and twisted his left leg. ファーディナンドはデルガドの右のブーツの上にぶざまに落ちて, 左足をねんざした. ③ N-SING-COLL 集合的単数名詞 In the U.S., the **left** refers to people who want to use legislation and the tax system to improve social conditions. In most other countries, the **left** refers to people who support the ideas of socialism. 左派, 革新派 □...the traditional parties of the Left. 左派の伝統的な政党 ④ N-SING 単数名詞 If you say that a person or political party has moved **to the left**, you mean that their political beliefs have become more left-wing. 左翼 □ After 1979, the party moved sharply to the left. 1979年以降その党は急に左翼的になった.

left-click (**left-clicks, left-clicking, left-clicked**) V-I 自動詞 To **left-click** or to **left-click on** something means to press the left-hand button on a computer mouse. (コンピュータのマウスを) 左クリックする [COMPUTING コンピューティング] □ When the menu has popped up you should left-click on one of the choices to make it operate. メニューが出たら, 選択肢の1つを起動させるために左クリックすべきだ.

left-hand ADJ 形容詞 If something is on the **left-hand** side of something, it is positioned on the left of it. 左手の, 左側の [ADJ n] □ The Japanese drive on the left-hand side of the road. 日本人は道路の左側を運転する.

left-handed ADJ 形容詞 Someone who is **left-handed** uses their left hand rather than their right hand for activities such as writing and sports and for picking things up. 左利きの □ There is a

store in town that supplies practically everything for left-handed people. 町には左利き用のものをほとんど何でもそろえている店がある.

left|ist /lɛftɪst/ (**leftists**) N-COUNT 可算名詞 A **leftist** is someone who supports the ideas of the political left. 左派の人, 急進派の人 □ Two of the men were leftists and two were centrists. その男性たちの2人は左派で, 2人は中道派だった.

left-justify (**left-justifies, left-justifying, left-justified**) V-T 他動詞 If printed text is **left-justified**, each line begins at the same distance from the left-hand edge of the page or column. 左寄せする, 左揃えにする □ The data in the cells should be left-justified. セルの中の情報は左揃えにすべきだ.

left|over /lɛftoʊvər/ (**leftovers**) ■ N-PLURAL 複数名詞 You can refer to food that has not been eaten after a meal as **leftovers**. (食べ物の) 残り物 □ Refrigerate any leftovers. どんな残り物も冷蔵庫で保存しなさい. ② ADJ 形容詞 You use **leftover** to describe an amount of something that remains after the rest of it has been used or eaten. 残り物の, 使い残しの [ADJ n] □...leftover pieces of wallpaper. 使い残りの壁紙

left-wing also **left wing** ■ ADJ 形容詞 **Left-wing** people support the ideas of the political left. 左翼の □ They said they would not be voting for him because he was too left-wing. 彼らは彼が左翼的すぎるので彼には投票しないと言っていた. ② N-SING 単数名詞 The **left wing** of a group of people, especially a political party, consists of the members of it whose beliefs are closer to those of the political left than are those of its other members. 左翼 □ She belongs on the left wing of the Democratic Party. 彼女は民主党の中でも左翼だ.

leg /lɛg/ (**legs**) ■ N-COUNT 可算名詞 A person or animal's **legs** are the long parts of their body that they use to stand on. 脚, 足 □ He was tapping his walking stick against his leg. 彼は杖で自分の脚をコツコツとたたいていた. ② N-COUNT 可算名詞 The **legs** of a pair of pants are the parts that cover your legs. ズボンの足の部分 □ He moved on through wet grass that soaked the legs of his pants. 彼はズボンの足をずぶぬれにする湿った草の間をどんどん進んだ. ③ N-COUNT 可算名詞 A **leg** of lamb, pork, chicken, or other meat is a piece of meat that consists of the animal's or bird's leg, especially the thigh. (動物の) 足の肉, もも肉 □...a chicken leg. 鶏のもも肉 ④ N-COUNT 可算名詞 The **legs** of a table, chair, or other piece of furniture are the parts that rest on the floor and support the furniture's weight. (テーブル・いすなどの) 脚 □ His ankles were tied to the legs of the chair. 彼の両足は椅子の脚に縛りつけられていた. ⑤ N-COUNT 可算名詞 A **leg** of a long journey is one part of it, usually between two points where you stop. (長旅の) 1区間 □ The first leg of the journey was by boat to Lake Naivasha in Kenya. 旅の最初の行程は船でケニアのナイバシャ湖まで行くことだった. ⑥ N-COUNT 可算名詞 A **leg** of a sports competition is one of a series of games that are played to find an overall winner. (連戦の) 1試合 [mainly BRIT 主に英国英語] ⑦ PHRASE 句 If you **are pulling** someone's **leg**, you are teasing them by telling them something shocking or worrying as a joke. (人を) からかう [INFORMAL くだけた] □ Of course I won't tell them; I was only pulling your leg. もちろん, 彼らに言ったりしないよ. ぼくはただ君をからかっていただけだよ.
→ see **body**

Word Partnership   leg は次の語句と使われる：

V.	amputate a/your leg, break a/your leg, lose a/your leg ■
ADJ.	front leg, hind leg, left/right leg, lower leg ■ broken leg ■ ④
N.	leg bones, leg injury, leg muscles, leg pain ■ final/first/last/second leg of a journey/trip/tour ⑤

lega|cy /lɛgəsi/ (**legacies**) ■ N-COUNT 可算名詞 A **legacy** is money or property which someone leaves to you when they die. 遺産 □ You could make a real difference to someone's life by leaving them a generous legacy. あなたは人に多額の遺産を残すことで, その人の人生を大きく変えることができるでしょう. ② N-COUNT 可算名詞 A **legacy** of an event or period of history is something which is a direct result of it and which continues to exist after it is over. (出来事・時代の) 遺物 □...a program to overcome the legacy of inequality and injustice created by Apartheid. アパルトヘイトによって生み出された不平等と不公平という遺物を克服するための計画

le|gal /ligᵊl/ ■ ADJ 形容詞 **Legal** is used to describe things that relate to the law. 法律の, 法律に関する [ADJ n] □ He vowed to take legal action. 彼は法的措置を取ると断言した. □...the legal system. 法体制 ● **le|gal|ly** ADV 副詞 法律的に □ It could be a bit problematic, legally speaking. 法的に言うと, それには少し問題があるかもしれない. ② ADJ 形容詞 An action or situation that is **legal** is allowed or required by law. 合法的な, 適法の □ What I did was perfectly legal. 私がしたことは完全に合法的だった.

Word Partnership legal は次の語句と使われる:

N. legal **action**, legal **advice**, legal **battle**, legal **bills**, legal **costs/expenses**, legal **defense**, legal **department**, legal **documents**, legal **expert**, legal **fees**, legal **guardian**, legal **issue**, legal **liability**, legal **matters**, legal **obligation**, legal **opinion**, legal **problems/troubles**, legal **procedures/proceedings**, legal **profession**, legal **responsibility**, legal **rights**, legal **services**, legal **status**, legal **system** 1

ADV. **perfectly** legal 2

le|gal|ity /ligǽliti/ N-UNCOUNT 不可算名詞 If you talk about **the legality of** an action or situation, you are talking about whether it is legal or not. 合法性, 適法性 ❑ *The auditor has questioned the legality of the contracts.* 監査役はそれらの契約の合法性を問題にしている.

le|gal|ize /lígəlaɪz/ (**legalizes, legalizing, legalized**) V-T 他動詞 If something **is legalized**, a law is passed that makes it legal. 合法化する ❑ *Divorce was legalized in 1981.* 離婚は1981年に合法化された.

le|gal ten|der N-UNCOUNT 不可算名詞 **Legal tender** is money, especially a particular coin or banknote, which is officially part of a country's currency at a particular time. 法定貨幣 ❑ *The French franc was no longer legal tender after midnight last night.* フランス・フランは昨夜の真夜中以降にはもはや法定貨幣ではなくなった.

leg|end /lɛ́dʒənd/ (**legends**) 1 N-VAR 可変性名詞 A **legend** is a very old and popular story that may be true. 伝説, 言い伝え ❑ *...the legends of ancient Greece.* 古代ギリシャの伝説 2 N-COUNT 可算名詞 If you refer to someone as a **legend**, you mean that they are very famous and admired by a lot of people. 伝説的人物 [APPROVAL 賛成] ❑ *...blues legends John Lee Hooker and B.B. King.* ブルースの伝説的人物であるジョン・リー・フッカーとB・B・キング
→ see **fantasy**

leg|end|ary /lɛ́dʒənderi/ 1 ADJ 形容詞 If you describe someone or something as **legendary**, you mean that they are very famous and that many stories are told about them. 伝説的な ❑ *...the legendary jazz singer Adelaide Hall.* 伝説的なジャズ歌手, アデレード・ホール 2 ADJ 形容詞 A **legendary** person, place, or event is mentioned or described in an old legend. 伝説上の ❑ *The hill is supposed to be the resting place of the legendary King Lud.* その丘は伝説のルッド王の墓だと考えられている.

leg|gings /lɛ́gɪŋz/ N-PLURAL 複数名詞 **Leggings** are close-fitting pants, usually made out of a stretchy fabric, that are worn by women and girls. レギンス（女性や子供用のパンツ）[also 'a pair of' N] ❑ *She is wearing tight black leggings and a baggy green jersey.* 彼女は黒のぴったりしたレギンスをはき, だぼだぼの緑のジャージーを着ている.

le|gion /lídʒən/ (**legions**) N-COUNT 可算名詞 A **legion** is a large group of soldiers who form one section of an army. 軍団 ❑ *...the Sudan-based troops of the Libyan Islamic Legion.* リビアのイスラム教軍団のスーダンを拠点にした部隊

leg|is|late /lɛ́dʒɪsleɪt/ (**legislates, legislating, legislated**) V-T/V-I 他動詞/自動詞 When a government or state **legislates**, it passes a new law. 法制化する [他動詞], 法律を制定する [自動詞] ❑ *Most member countries have already legislated against excessive overtime.* ほとんどの加盟国はすでに過度の残業を禁止する法律を制定している. [FORMAL 形式ばった] ❑ *You cannot legislate to change attitudes.* 考え方を変えるために法律を制定することはできない.

leg|is|la|tion /lɛ́dʒɪsleɪʃən/ N-UNCOUNT 不可算名詞 **Legislation** consists of a law or laws passed by a government. （制定された）法律 [FORMAL 形式ばった] ❑ *...a letter calling for legislation to protect women's rights.* 女性の権利を守る法律制定を求める手紙

Word Partnership legislation は次の語句と使われる:

V. **draft** legislation, **enact** legislation, **introduce** legislation, **oppose** legislation, **pass** legislation, **support** legislation, **veto** legislation
ADJ. **federal** legislation, **new** legislation, **proposed** legislation

leg|is|la|tive /lɛ́dʒɪsleɪtɪv/ ADJ 形容詞 **Legislative** means involving or relating to the process of making and passing laws. 立法上の [FORMAL 形式ばった] [ADJ n] ❑ *Today's hearing was just the first step in the legislative process.* 今日の公聴会は立法過程の第1歩に過ぎなかった.

leg|is|la|tor /lɛ́dʒɪsleɪtər/ (**legislators**) N-COUNT 可算名詞 A **legislator** is a person who is involved in making or passing laws. 立法者, 国会議員 [FORMAL 形式ばった] ❑ *...an attempt to get U.S. legislators to change the system.* 米国の議会議員にその制度を変えさせようとする試み

leg|is|la|ture /lɛ́dʒɪsleɪtʃər/ (**legislatures**) N-COUNT 可算名詞 The **legislature** of a particular state or country is the group of

people in it who have the power to make and pass laws. 立法機関, 議会 [FORMAL 形式ばった] ❑ *The proposals before the legislature include the creation of two special courts to deal exclusively with violent crimes.* 議会に出された提案には, 暴力犯罪を専門に取り扱う特殊な裁判所を2か所設立することが含まれている.

le|giti|mate /lɪdʒítɪmɪt/ 1 ADJ 形容詞 Something that is **legitimate** is acceptable according to the law. 合法の ❑ *The French government has condemned the coup in Haiti and has demanded the restoration of the legitimate government.* フランス政府はハイチでのクーデターを非難し, 合法的な政府の復活を要求している. ●**le|giti|ma|cy** /lɪdʒítəmisi/ N-UNCOUNT 不可算名詞 合法性 ❑ *The opposition parties do not recognize the political legitimacy of his government.* 野党は彼の政府の政治的な正当性を認めていない. ●**le|giti|mate|ly** ADV 副詞 [ADV with v] 合法的に ❑ *The government has been legitimately elected by the people.* その政府は合法的に国民の選挙で選ばれた. 2 ADJ 形容詞 If you say that something such as a feeling or claim is **legitimate**, you think that it is reasonable and justified. 合理的な, 筋が通った ❑ *That's a perfectly legitimate fear.* それはまったく当然の不安だ. ●**le|giti|ma|cy** N-UNCOUNT 不可算名詞 妥当性 ❑ *Sampras beat Carl-Uwe Steeb by 6-1, 6-2, 6-1 to underline the legitimacy of his challenge for the title.* サンプラスはカール・ウベ・スティーブを6対1, 6対2, 6対1で破り, 選手権に挑戦する妥当性を明白に示した. ●**le|giti|mate|ly** ADV 副詞 [ADV with v] 合理的に ❑ *They could quarrel quite legitimately with some of my choices.* 彼らは私が選んだ者の何人かと全く筋の通った口論ができた.

lei|sure /lídʒər, lɛ́ʒ-/ 1 N-UNCOUNT 不可算名詞 **Leisure** is the time when you are not working and you can relax and do things that you enjoy. 暇, 余暇 ❑ *...a relaxing way to fill my leisure time.* 余暇をゆったりして過ごす方法. 2 PHRASE 句 If someone does something **at leisure** or **at their leisure**, they enjoy themselves by doing it when they want to, without hurrying. のんびりと ❑ *You will be able to stroll at leisure through the gardens.* 庭園をのんびり散策されるのもよろしいかと思います.

Word Partnership leisure は次の語句と使われる:

N. leisure **activity**, leisure **class**, leisure **goods**, leisure **hours**, leisure **time** 1

lei|sure|ly /lídʒərli, lɛ́ʒ-/ ADJ 形容詞 A **leisurely** action is done in a relaxed and unhurried way. のんびりした ❑ *Lunch was a leisurely affair.* 昼食はゆっくりするものだった. ●ADV 副詞 **Leisurely** is also an adverb. のんびりと [ADV with v] ❑ *We walked leisurely into the hotel.* 私たちはゆっくりと歩いてホテルに入った.

lem|on /lɛ́mən/ (**lemons**) N-VAR 可変性名詞 A **lemon** is a bright yellow fruit with very sour juice. Lemons grow on trees in warm countries. レモン ❑ *...a slice of lemon.* 1切れのレモン ❑ *...oranges, lemons and other citrus fruits.* オレンジ, レモンおよびその他のかんきつ類
→ see **fruit**

lem|on|ade /lɛ́mənéɪd/ N-UNCOUNT 不可算名詞 **Lemonade** is a drink that is made from lemons, sugar, and water. レモネード ❑ *He was pouring ice and lemonade into tall glasses.* 彼は細長いグラスに氷とレモネードを注いでいた.

lend /lɛ́nd/ (**lends, lending, lent**) 1 V-T/V-I 他動詞/自動詞 When people or organizations such as banks **lend** you money, they give it to you and you agree to pay it back at a future date, often with an extra amount as interest. 貸し付ける ❑ *The bank is reassessing its criteria for lending money.* その銀行は融資基準を見直している. ❑ *The government will lend you money at incredible rates, between zero percent and 3 percent.* ゼロから3パーセントというとても信じられないような金利で政府から融資を受けられる. ●**lend|ing** N-UNCOUNT 不可算名詞 融資 ❑ *...a financial institution that specializes in the lending of money.* 融資に特化した金融機関. 2 V-T 他動詞 If you **lend** something that you own, you allow someone to have it or use it for a period of time. 貸す ❑ *Will you lend me your jacket for a little while?* しばらく君の上着を貸してくれないかい?

Do not confuse **lend** and **borrow**. You say that you **borrow** something **from** another person. However, if you allow someone to **borrow** something that belongs to you, you say that you **lend** it to them. **Lend** is often followed by two objects. ❑ *Betty lent him some blankets... He lent Tim the money.* Both **borrow** and **lend** can be used without objects. ❑ *The poor had to borrow from the rich... Banks will not lend to them.* The noun related to **lend** is **loan**. ❑ *...a government loan of $3m.* **Loan** can also be used as a verb in the same way as **lend**, especially in American English. ❑ *I'll loan you fifty dollars.*

3 V-T 他動詞 If you **lend** your support **to** someone or something, you help them with what they are doing or with a problem that they have. （援助を）与える ❑ *He was approached by the organizers to lend support to a benefit concert.* チャリティコンサートに力を貸してくれないか, と彼は主催者側から打診された. 4 V-T 他動詞 If something **lends itself to** a particular activity or result, it is easy

for it to be used for that activity or to achieve that result. 役立つ, 適している □ *The room lends itself well to summer eating with its light, airy atmosphere.* その部屋は明るくて風通しがよく, 夏の食事に最適です. **5** → see also **lent** **6** to **lend a hand** → see **hand** → see **bank**

Word Partnership lend は次の語句と使われる:

N.	lend **money** **1**
	lend **support** **3**

lend|er /lɛndər/ (**lenders**) N-COUNT 可算名詞 A **lender** is a person or an institution that lends money to people. 貸し手 [BUSINESS 実業] □...*the six leading mortgage lenders.* 住宅ローンの大手6社.
→ see **interest rate**

lend|ing rate (**lending rates**) N-COUNT 可算名詞 The **lending rate** is the rate of interest that you have to pay when you are repaying a loan. 貸付金利 [BUSINESS 実業] □ *The bank left its lending rates unchanged.* その銀行は貸付金利を据え置いた.

length /lɛŋθ/ (**lengths**) **1** N-VAR 可変性名詞 The **length** of something is the amount that it measures from one end to the other along the longest side. 長さ □ *It is about a meter in length.* その長さは約1メートルです. □...*the length of the fish.* その魚の体長. **2** N-VAR 可変性名詞 The **length** of something such as a piece of writing is the amount of writing that is contained in it. 長さ □...*a book of at least 100 pages in length.* 少なくとも100ページの長さの本. **3** N-VAR 可変性名詞 The **length** of an event, activity, or situation is the period of time from beginning to end for which something lasts or during which something happens. 期間 □ *The exact length of each period may vary.* 各期間の正確な長さは変わる場合がある. **4** N-COUNT 可算名詞 A **length of** rope, cloth, wood, or other material is a piece of it that is intended to be used for a particular purpose or that exists in a particular situation. 全長 □...*a 30 feet length of rope.* 全長30フィートのロープ. **5** N-UNCOUNT 不可算名詞 The **length of** something is the quality of being long. 長さ □ *Many have been surprised at the length of time it has taken him to make up his mind.* 多くの人が, 彼が決心するまでに要した時間の長さに驚きました. **6** → see also **full-length** **7** at **arm's length** → see **arm** → see **ratio**

Word Partnership length は次の語句と使われる:

ADJ.	**average** length, **entire** length **1** – **4**
N.	length **and width** **1** **4**
	length **of your stay**, length **of time**, length **of treatment** **3**

length|en /lɛŋθən/ (**lengthens, lengthening, lengthened**) **1** V-T/V-I 他動詞/自動詞 When something **lengthens** or when you **lengthen** it, it increases in length. 長くする, 長くなる □ *The evening shadows were lengthening.* 夕方にできる影が長くなってきていた. **2** V-T/V-I 他動詞/自動詞 When something **lengthens** or when you **lengthen** it, it lasts for a longer time than it did previously. のばす, のびる □ *Vacations have lengthened and the work week has shortened.* 休暇が長くなり, 1週当たりの労働時間が短くなった.

length|wise /lɛŋθwaɪz/ also **lengthways** /lɛŋθweɪz/ ADV 副詞 **Lengthwise** or **lengthways** means in a direction or position along the length of something. 縦に, 長く [ADV after v] □ *She tore off two sections of paper towel and folded them lengthwise.* 彼女は紙タオルを2枚はぎ取って長く折り畳んだ.

lengthy /lɛŋθi/ (**lengthier, lengthiest**) **1** ADJ 形容詞 You use **lengthy** to describe an event or process which lasts for a long time. 長期の □ *The board members held a lengthy meeting to decide future policy.* 重役たちは今後の方針決定のために長時間にわたる会議を開いた. **2** ADJ 形容詞 A **lengthy** report, article, book, or document contains a lot of speech, writing, or other material. 長い □ *Friedman's lengthy report quoted an unnamed source.* フリードマンの長い報告書には出所不明の情報が引用されていた.

Word Partnership lengthy は次の語句と使われる:

N.	lengthy **period** **1**
	lengthy **description**, lengthy **discourse**, lengthy **discussion**, lengthy **report** **2**

le|ni|ent /liniənt, linyənt/ ADJ 形容詞 When someone in authority is **lenient**, they are not as strict or severe as expected. 寛大な □ *He believes the government already is lenient with drug traffickers.* 彼は政府がかねてから麻薬密売者に寛大だと考えている. ● **le|ni|ent|ly** ADV 副詞 [ADV after v] 寛大に □ *Many people believe reckless drivers are treated too leniently.* 多くの人は危険運転に対する処分が甘すぎると考えている.

lens /lɛnz/ (**lenses**) **1** N-COUNT 可算名詞 A **lens** is a thin

curved piece of glass or plastic used in things such as cameras, telescopes, and pairs of glasses. You look through a lens in order to make things look larger, smaller, or clearer. レンズ □...*a camera lens.* カメラのレンズ. **2** N-COUNT 可算名詞 In your eye, the **lens** is the part behind the pupil that focuses light and helps you to see clearly. 水晶体 □...*degenerative changes in the lens of the eye.* 目の水晶体の変質的な変化. **3** → see also **contact lens** → see **eye**

lent /lɛnt/ **Lent** is the past tense and past participle of **lend**. lendの過去・過去分詞

leop|ard /lɛpərd/ (**leopards**) N-COUNT 可算名詞 A **leopard** is a type of large, wild cat. Leopards have yellow fur and black spots, and live in Africa and Asia. ヒョウ

les|bian /lɛzbiən/ (**lesbians**) ADJ 形容詞 **Lesbian** is used to describe homosexual women. 同性愛の女性の, レスビアンの □...*a woman who had contacts in the homosexual and lesbian community.* ゲイとレスビアン社会に接触のあった女性 ● N-COUNT 可算名詞 A **lesbian** is a woman who is lesbian. レスビアン, レズ □...*a youth group for lesbians, gays and bisexuals.* レズ, ゲイ, 両性愛の若者グループ

less /lɛs/

Less is often considered to be the comparative form of little.

Less はしばしば little の比較級形であると考えられている.

1 DET 限定詞 You use **less** to indicate that there is a smaller amount of something than before or than average. You can use "a little," "a lot," "a bit," "far," and "much" in front of **less**. より少ない □ *People should eat less fat to reduce the risk of heart disease.* 心臓疾患の危険を減らしたければ, 脂肪の摂取量を減らすべきだ. □...*a dishwasher that uses less water and electricity than older machines.* 旧型より節水と節電ができる食器洗い機. ● PRON 代名詞 **Less** is also a pronoun. より少ない物 □ *Borrowers are striving to ease their financial position by spending less and saving more.* 借り手は消費を抑え貯蓄を増やし, 財政状態を軽減しようと努力している. ● QUANT 数量詞 **Less** is also a quantifier. より少ない量 □ *Last year less of the money went into high-technology companies.* 昨年のハイテク企業への投資額は減少した. **2** PHRASE 句 You use **less than** before a number or amount to say that the actual number or amount is smaller than this. ーより少ない □...*a country whose entire population is less than 12 million.* 全人口が1,200万人を下回る国. **3** DET 限定詞 You use **less** to indicate that something or someone has a smaller amount of a quality than they used to or than is average or usual. より少なく □ *I often think about those less fortunate than me.* 私は自分より不幸な人たちのことをよく考える. □ *Other amenities, less commonly available, include a library and exercise room.* より利用可能性が低い公共設備には図書館やトレーニングルームなどが該当する. **4** ADV 副詞 If you say that something is **less** one thing **than** another, you mean that it is like the second thing rather than the first. ーよりも (むしろー) □ *At first sight it looked less like a capital city than a mining camp.* 一見すると, その都市は首都というよりも鉱山町のようだった. **5** ADV 副詞 If you do something **less** than before or **less** than someone else, you do it to a smaller extent or not as often. より少なく [ADV with v] □ *We are eating more and exercising less.* 食事量が増加し運動量が減少している. **6** PREP 前置詞 When you are referring to amounts, you use **less** in front of a number or quantity to indicate that it is to be subtracted from another number or quantity already mentioned. ーを差し引いて □ *You will pay between ten and twenty five percent, less tax.* 10から25パーセントを税引きで支払ってください.

You use **less** to talk about amounts that cannot be counted. □...*less meat.* When you are talking about things that can be counted, you should use **fewer**. □...*fewer potatoes.*

7 PHRASE 句 You use **less than** to say that something does not have a particular quality. For example, if you describe something as **less than** perfect, you mean that it is not perfect at all. 決してーでない [EMPHASIS 強調] □ *Her greeting was less than enthusiastic.* 彼女の挨拶には全く心がこもっていなかった. **8** **couldn't care less** → see **care** **9** **more or less** → see **more**

less|en /lɛsⁿn/ (**lessens, lessening, lessened**) V-T/V-I 他動詞/自動詞 If something **lessens** or you **lessen** it, it becomes smaller in size, amount, degree, or importance. 少なくする, 少なくなる □ *He is used to a lot of attention from his wife, which will inevitably lessen when the baby is born.* 彼は妻にさんざん可愛がられているが, 赤ちゃんが生まれたら当然そんなにはかまってもらえなくなるでしょう. ● **less|en|ing** N-UNCOUNT 不可算名詞 低下 □...*increased trade and a lessening of tension on the border.* 国境での貿易の増加と緊張の緩和

less|er /lɛsər/ **1** ADJ 形容詞 You use **lesser** in order to indicate that something is smaller in extent, degree, or amount than another thing that has been mentioned. より少ない [ADJ n, 'the' ADJ 'of' n] □ *No medication works in isolation but is affected to a greater or lesser extent by many other factors.* 薬物療法は独立して機能するのではなく, 程度の多少はあれ他に多くの要因の影響を受ける. ● ADV 副詞 **Lesser** is also an adverb. より少なく [ADV -ed] □...*lesser known works by famous artists.* 有名芸術家のあまり知られていない

作品. **2** ADJ 形容詞 You can use **lesser** to refer to something or someone that is less important than other things or people of the same type. より重要でない [ADJ n, 'the' ADJ 'of' n] ❑ *They pleaded guilty to lesser charges of criminal damage.* 彼らはより軽い器物損壊容疑に対して罪を認めた. **3** **the lesser of two evils** → see **evil**

les|son /lɛsᵊn/ (**lessons**) **1** N-COUNT 可算名詞 A **lesson** is a fixed period of time when people are taught about a particular subject or taught how to do something. 授業 ❑ *It would be his last French lesson for months.* それが彼の数か月に及ぶフランス語の授業の最終回になるだろう. **2** N-COUNT 可算名詞 You use **lesson** to refer to an experience which acts as a warning to you or an example from which you should learn. 教訓 ❑ *There's still one lesson to be learned from the crisis – we all need to better understand the thinking of the other side.* その危機から学ぶべき教訓がもう1つあります. 我々全員が相手側の考えをもっと理解しなければならないということです. ● PHRASE 句 If you say that you are going to **teach** someone **a lesson**, you mean that you are going to punish them for something that they have done so that they do not do it again. 人を懲らしめる

let /lɛt/ (**lets, letting**)

The form **let** is used in the present tense and is the past tense and past participle.

let 形は現在時制に使われ, 過去時制と過去分詞でもある.

1 V-T 他動詞 If you **let** something happen, you allow it to happen without doing anything to stop or prevent it. ～するに任せる ❑ *People said we were interfering with nature, and that we should just let the animals die.* 人々は我々は自然に対して干渉しており, 我々はただそれらの動物が死ぬのに任せるべきだと言った. ❑ *I can't let myself be distracted by those things.* 私はそういうことに頭を痛めたくない. **2** V-T 他動詞 If you **let** someone do something, you give them your permission to do it. 許可する ❑ *I love candy but Mom doesn't let me have it very often.* 私はキャンディが大好きだけど, ママがあんまり食べさせてくれない. **3** V-T 他動詞 If you **let** someone into, out of, or through a place, you allow them to enter, leave, or go through it, for example, by opening a door or making room for them. (入室・退室などを) させる ❑ *I had to let them into the building because they had lost their keys.* 彼らはかぎを失くしたので, 私が中に入れてやらねばならなかった. **4** V-T 他動詞 You use **let me** when you are introducing something you want to say. ～させてもらう [only imper] ❑ *Let me tell you what I saw last night.* 私が昨夜見たことについて話させてもらいます. ❑ *Let me explain why.* わけを話させてください. **5** V-T 他動詞 You use **let me** when you are offering politely to do something. 私が～します [POLITENESS 丁寧さ] [only imper] ❑ *Let me take your coat.* コートをお預かりします. **6** V-T 他動詞 You say **let's** or, in more formal English, **let us**, to direct the attention of the people you are talking to toward the subject that you want to consider next. ～しましょう [only imper] ❑ *Let us look at these views in more detail.* これらの意見をもっと詳しく検討しましょう. **7** V-T 他動詞 You say **let's** or, in more formal English, **let us**, when you are making a suggestion that involves both you and the person you are talking to, or when you are agreeing to a suggestion of this kind. (一緒に) ～しよう [only imper] ❑ *I'm bored. Let's go home.* 退屈だ. もう帰ろうよ. **8** V-T 他動詞 Someone in authority, such as a teacher, can use **let's** or, in more formal English, **let us**, in order to make a polite instruction to another person or group of people. ～してください [POLITENESS 丁寧さ] [only imper] ❑ *Let's have some quiet, please.* もう少し静かにしましょう. **9** V-T 他動詞 You can use **let** when you are saying what you think someone should do, usually when they are behaving in a way that you think is unreasonable or wrong. ～してもらう [only imper] ❑ *Let him get his own cup of tea.* 彼には自分でお茶をいれてもらいましょう. **10** V-T 他動詞 If you **let** your house or land **to** someone, you allow them to use it in exchange for money that they pay you regularly. 貸す [mainly BRIT 主に英国英語; AM rent 米国英語 **rent**] ● PHRASAL VERB 句動詞 **Let out** means the same as **let**. 貸す ❑ *I couldn't sell the apartment, so I let it out.* アパートが売れなかったから, 賃貸にしたのだ.

Do not confuse **let**, **rent**, and **hire**. You can say that you **rent** a house or room to someone when they pay you money to live there. ❑ *We rented our house to a college professor.* You can also say that you **let** a house or room to someone. ❑ *They were letting a room to a school teacher.* In British English, if you pay a sum of money to use something for a short time, you say that you **hire** it. In American English, it is more common to say that you **rent** it. ❑ *He was unable to hire another car... He rented a car for the weekend.* If you make a series of payments to use something for a long time, you say that you **rent** it. ❑ *...the apartment he had rented... He rented a TV.*

11 PHRASE 句 **Let alone** is used after a statement, usually a negative one, to indicate that the statement is even more true of the person, thing, or situation that you are going to mention next. ～は言うまでもなく [EMPHASIS 強調] ❑ *It is incredible that the 12-year-old managed to even reach the pedals, let alone drive the car.* 12歳の子がその車を運転したことはもちろん, ペダルに足が届いたことは信じ難いことだ. **12** PHRASE 句 If you **let go of** someone or something, you stop holding them. ～を手放す ❑ *She let go of Mona's hand and took a sip of her drink.* 彼女はモナの手を離し, 自分の飲み物をすすった. **13** PHRASE 句 If you **let** someone or something **go**, you allow them to leave or escape. 行かせる ❑ *They held him for three hours and they let him go.* 彼らは彼を3時間拘束し, 釈放した. **14** PHRASE 句 When someone leaves a job, either because they are told to or because they want to, the employer sometimes says that they are **letting** that person **go**. 解雇する, 退職させる [BUSINESS 実業] ❑ *I've assured him I have no plans to let him go.* 辞めさせるつもりはないことを伝えて彼を安心させた. **15** PHRASE 句 If you say that you did not know what you were **letting yourself in for** when you decided to do something, you mean you did not realize how difficult, unpleasant, or expensive it was going to be. 自分を困難に陥らせる ❑ *He got the impression that Miss Hawes had no idea of what she was letting herself in for.* 彼が感じたのは, ホーズさんがどんな困難に身を投じようとしているのかを自覚していないのではないか, ということだった. **16** PHRASE 句 If you **let** someone **know** something, you tell them about it or make sure that they know about it. 知らせる ❑ *They want to let them know that they are safe.* 彼らは彼らに安全だと伝えたいのです. **17** to **let fly** → see **fly** **18** to **let your hair down** → see **hair** **19** to **let** someone **off the hook** → see **hook** **20** to **let it be known** → see **known** **21** PHRASAL VERB 句動詞 If you **let** someone **down**, you disappoint them, by not doing something that you have said you will do or that they expected you to do. がっかりさせる, 失望させる ❑ *Don't worry, Xiao, I won't let you down.* 心配するな, シャオ. 君をがっかりさせしないよ. ● **let down** ADJ 形容詞 [v-link ADJ] がっかりした ❑ *The company now has a large number of workers who feel badly let down.* 今やこの会社では多くの従業員がひどい失望感を味わっている. **22** PHRASAL VERB 句動詞 If something **lets** you **down**, it is the reason you are not as successful as you could have been. 失敗させる ❑ *Many believe it was his shyness and insecurity which let him down.* 彼の内気で不安定な性格が災いして成功しないのだ, と多くの人が思っている.

▶ **let in** PHRASAL VERB 句動詞 If an object **lets in** something such as air, light, or water, it allows air, light, or water to get into it, for example, because the object has a hole in it. 通す ❑ *...balconies shaded with lattice-work which lets in air but not light.* 空気を通すが, 光を遮る格子造りで陰になっているバルコニー

▶ **let off** **1** PHRASAL VERB 句動詞 If someone in authority **lets** you **off** a task or duty, they give you permission not to do it. 放免する ❑ *I realized that having a new baby lets you off going to boring dinner parties.* 私はあなたが新しい赤ちゃんを産んだら退屈なディナーパーティーに行かなくてすむと気づいた. **2** PHRASAL VERB 句動詞 If you **let** someone **off**, you give them a lighter punishment than they expect or no punishment at all. 軽い罰だけで許す, 放免する ❑ *Because he was a Christian, the judge let him off.* 裁判官は彼がクリスチャンだったので放免した. **3** PHRASAL VERB 句動詞 If you **let off** an explosive or a gun, you explode or fire it. 撃つ, 放つ ❑ *A resident of his neighborhood had let off fireworks to celebrate the revolution.* 彼の近所の住人が革命を祝して花火を打ち上げた.

▶ **let out** **1** PHRASAL VERB 句動詞 If something or someone **lets** water, air, or breath **out**, they allow it to flow out or escape. 出す, 逃す ❑ *It lets sunlight in but doesn't let heat out.* そこから太陽光は入りますが, 熱は逃げません. **2** PHRASAL VERB 句動詞 If you **let out** a particular sound, you make that sound. (音を) 出す [WRITTEN 書き言葉] ❑ *When she saw him, she let out a cry of horror.* 彼女は彼を見て恐怖のあまり悲鳴を上げた. **3** PHRASAL VERB 句動詞 If you **let out** a dress or pair of pants, you make it larger by undoing the seams and sewing closer to the edge of the material. (衣服を) 広げる ❑ *I'll have to let this dress out a bit before the wedding next week.* 来週の結婚式前にこのドレスを少し広げなければならない. **4** → see also **let** 10

▶ **let up** PHRASAL VERB 句動詞 If an unpleasant, continuous process **lets up**, it stops or becomes less intense. 止まる, 弱まる ❑ *The traffic in this city never lets up, even at night.* この市の往来は夜も決して絶えることはない.

Thesaurus *let* また次を参照：

v. allow, approve, permit; (ant.) prevent, stop 🔢 🔢

le|thal /liːθ°l/ ADJ 形容詞 A substance that is **lethal** can kill people or animals. 死をもたらす ❏...a lethal dose of sleeping pills. 睡眠薬の致死量. 🔢 ADJ 形容詞 If you describe something as **lethal**, you mean that it is capable of causing a lot of damage. 破壊的な ❏ Amorality and intelligence is probably the most lethal combination to be found within one personality. 道徳観念がなく、しかも頭が切れるという結びつきは、おそらく1人格内に見られる最も危険な結びつきであろう.

le|thar|gic /lɪθɑːrdʒɪk/ ADJ 形容詞 If you are **lethargic**, you do not have much energy or enthusiasm. 無気力な ❏ He felt too miserable and lethargic to get dressed. 彼はあまりにもゆううつで服を着るのもおっくうだった.

leth|ar|gy /lɛθərdʒi/ N-UNCOUNT 不可算名詞 **Lethargy** is the condition or state of being lethargic. 無気力 ❏ Symptoms include tiredness, paleness, and lethargy. 症状には疲労感、顔面蒼白（そうはく）、無気力などがある.

let's /lɛts/ **Let's** is the usual spoken form of "let us." let usの会話での形式

let|ter /lɛtər/ (letters) 🔢 N-COUNT 可算名詞 If you write a **letter** to someone, you write a message on paper and send it to them, usually through the mail. 手紙、書状 [also 'by' N] ❏ I had received a letter from a very close friend. 私はとても親しい友人から手紙を受け取っていた. ❏...a letter of resignation. 辞表. 🔢 N-COUNT 可算名詞 **Letters** are written symbols which represent one of the sounds in a language. 文字 ❏...the letters of the alphabet. アルファベット文字. 🔢 V-I 自動詞 If a student **letters** in sports or athletics by being part of the university or college team, they are entitled to wear on their jacket the initial letter of the name of their university or college. (優秀選手として) 大学の略字マークを受ける [AM 米国英語] ❏ Burkoth lettered in soccer. バーコスはサッカーで大学の略字マーク表彰を受けた. 🔢 → see also **covering letter, newsletter**

let|ter|box /lɛtərbɒks/ also **letter box** 🔢 N-COUNT 可算名詞 A **letterbox** is a rectangular hole in a door or a small box at the entrance to a building into which letters and small packages are delivered. 郵便受け [mainly BRIT 主に英国英語; AM usually **mailbox** 米国英語では通常 **mailbox**] 🔢 ADJ 形容詞 If something is displayed on a television or computer screen in **letterbox** format, it is displayed across the middle of the screen with dark bands at the top and bottom of the screen. レターボックス形式（テレビ放映で画面の上下が黒く切れる状態）

let|ter|ing /lɛtərɪŋ/ N-UNCOUNT 不可算名詞 **Lettering** is writing, especially when you are describing the type of letters used. 字体、レタリング ❏...a small blue sign with white lettering. 白いレタリングが施された小さな青い看板.

let|tuce /lɛtɪs/ (lettuces) N-VAR 可変性名詞 A **lettuce** is a plant with large green leaves that is the basic ingredient of many salads. レタス

leu|ke|mia /luːkiːmiə/ N-UNCOUNT 不可算名詞 **Leukemia** is a disease of the blood in which the body produces too many white blood cells. 白血病

lev|el /lɛv°l/ (levels, leveling or levelling, leveled or levelled) 🔢 N-COUNT 可算名詞 A **level** is a point on a scale, for example, a scale of amount, quality, or difficulty. 水準 ❏ If you don't know your cholesterol level, it's a good idea to have it checked. 自分のコレステロール値を知らないのなら、測ってもらうといい. ❏ We do have the lowest level of inflation for some years. ここ数年のインフレ率は確かに最低水準になっています. 🔢 N-SING 単数名詞 The **level** of a river, lake, or ocean or the **level** of liquid in a container is the height of its surface. 水位 ❏ The water level of the Mississippi River is already 6.5 feet below normal. ミシシッピー川の水位はすでに正常水位より6.5フィート低くなっている. 🔢 → see also **sea level** 🔢 N-SING 単数名詞 If something is at a particular **level**, it is at that height. 高さ ❏ Liz sank down until the water came up to her chin and the bubbles were at eye level. リズは湯があごにまで来て、泡が目の位置にくるまで身を沈めた. 🔢 N-COUNT 可算名詞 A **level** of a building is one of its different stories, which is situated above or below other stories. 階 ❏ Thurlow and Brown's rooms were on the second level, to the rear of the building. サーロウとブラウンの部屋は、その建物の2階の奥にあった. 🔢 N-COUNT 可算名詞 A **level** is a device for testing to see if a surface is level. It consists of a plastic, wood, or metal frame containing a glass tube of liquid with an air bubble in it. 水準儀 [AM 米国英語] 🔢 ADJ 形容詞 If one thing is **level** with another thing, it is at the same height as it. 同じ高さの [v-link ADJ] ❏ He leaned over the counter so his face was almost level with the boy's. 彼は少年と顔の位置がほぼ同じになるようにカウンターから身をのり出した. 🔢 ADJ 形容詞 When something is **level**, it is completely flat with no part higher than any other. 平らな ❏ The floor was level, but the ceiling sloped toward his head. 床は水平だったが、天井は彼の頭のほうに傾いていた. 🔢 ADV 副詞 If you draw **level** with someone

or something, you get closer to them until you are by their side. 近くに [ADV after v] ❏ Just before we drew level with the gates, he slipped out of the jeep and disappeared. まさに我々が門にさしかかろうとしていたとき、彼がジープから滑り出て姿をくらました. ADJ 形容詞 ● **Level** is also an adjective. 近くの [v-link ADJ] ❏ He waited until they were level with the door before he pivoted around sharply and punched Graham hard. 彼は彼らがドアの近くにくるまで待ち、急にくるりと向きを変えてグレアムに激しいパンチを浴びせた. 🔢 V-T 他動詞 If someone or something such as a violent storm **levels** a building or area of land, they destroy it completely or make it completely flat. 倒す ❏ The storm was the most powerful to hit Hawaii this century. It leveled sugar plantations and destroyed homes. それはハワイを襲った今世紀最大の嵐でした. サトウキビ畑がなぎ倒され、家屋が倒壊しました. 🔢 V-T 他動詞 If an accusation or criticism **is leveled at** someone, they are accused of doing wrong or they are criticized for something they have done. (非難などを) 向ける、あびせる ❏ Allegations of corruption were leveled at him and his family. 彼と家族に汚職疑惑が向けられた. 🔢 a **level playing field** → see **playing field** ▶ **level off** or **level out** 🔢 PHRASAL VERB 句動詞 If a changing number or amount **levels off** or **levels out**, it stops increasing or decreasing at such a fast speed. 横ばいになる ❏ The figures show evidence that murders in the nation's capital are beginning to level off. データから首都での殺人件数が横ばい状態になり始めていることがうかがえる. 🔢 PHRASAL VERB 句動詞 If an aircraft **levels off** or **levels out**, it travels horizontally after having been traveling in an upward or downward direction. 水平飛行に移る ❏ The aircraft leveled out at about 30,000 feet. 飛行機は高度3万フィートで水平飛行に移った.

Thesaurus *level* また次を参照：

ADJ. even, flat, horizontal, smooth 🔢

Word Partnership *level* は次の語句と使われる：

ADJ.	**basic** level, **increased** level, **intermediate** level, **top** level, **upper** level 🔢 **high/low** level 🔢 – 🔢
N.	level **of activity**, level **of awareness**, **cholesterol** level, **college** level, **comfort** level, level **of difficulty**, **energy** level, **noise** level, **reading** level, **skill** level, **stress** level, level **of violence** 🔢 **eye** level, **ground** level, **street** level 🔢

lev|el cross|ing (level crossings) N-COUNT 可算名詞 A **level crossing** is a place where a railroad track crosses a road at the same level. 踏切 [BRIT 英国英語; AM **grade crossing, railroad crossing** 米国英語 **grade crossing, railroad crossing**]

lev|er /lɪvər, lɛv-/ (levers, levering, levered) 🔢 N-COUNT 可算名詞 A **lever** is a handle or bar that is attached to a piece of machinery and which you push or pull in order to operate the machinery. レバー ❏ Push the tiny lever on the lock and let the door lock itself. 錠前についた小さなレバーを押すと、ドアは自然に施錠される. 🔢 → see also **gear lever** 🔢 N-COUNT 可算名詞 A **lever** is a long bar, one end of which is placed under a heavy object so that when you press down on the other end you can move the object. てこ ❏ He examined the machine, worked a lever that lifted the lid. 彼は機械を点検し、ふたを持ち上げるてこを動かした. 🔢 V-T 他動詞 If you **lever** something in a particular direction, you move it there, especially by using a lot of effort. 力を入れて動かす ❏ Neighbors eventually levered open the door with a crowbar. 近所の住人がついにかなてこでドアをこじ開けた.

lev|er|age /lɛvərɪdʒ/ (leverages, leveraging, leveraged) 🔢 N-UNCOUNT 不可算名詞 **Leverage** is the ability to influence situations or people so that you can control what happens. 影響力 ❏ His position as mayor gives him leverage to get things done. 彼は市長として物事を推進させる影響力を持っている. 🔢 V-T 他動詞 To **leverage** a company or investment means to use borrowed money in order to buy it or pay for it. 借入金で買収する [BUSINESS 実業] ❏ He might feel that leveraging the company at a time when he sees tremendous growth opportunities would be a mistake. 驚異的な成長の機会がうかがえるのに借入金でその会社を買収するのは誤りだろう、と彼は思うかもしれないでしょう.

levy /lɛvi/ (levies, levying, levied) 🔢 N-COUNT 可算名詞 A **levy** is a sum of money that you have to pay, for example, as a tax to the government. 賦課金 ❏...an annual levy on all drivers. 全運転者に課せられる通行税の年額. 🔢 V-T 他動詞 If a government or organization **levies** a tax or other sum of money, it demands it from people or organizations. 課す ❏ They levied religious taxes on Christian commercial transactions. キリスト教の商行為に対し宗教税が課されました.

lia|bil|ity /laɪəbɪlɪti/ (liabilities) 🔢 N-COUNT 可算名詞 If you say that someone or something is **a liability**, you mean that they cause a lot of problems or embarrassment. 不利になるもの ❏ As the president's prestige continues to fall, they're clearly beginning to

consider him a liability. 大統領の威信は低下の一途をたどっており，彼らは明らかに大統領をお荷物だと考え始めている. **2** N-COUNT 可算名詞 A company's or organization's **liabilities** are the sums of money which it owes. 負債 [BUSINESS OR LEGAL 実業，または法律的] □ *The company had assets of $138 million and liabilities of $120.5 million.* その会社の資産は1億3，800万ドル，負債は1億2，050万ドルでした. **3** → see also **liable**

lia|ble /láɪəbʰl/ **1** PHRASE 句 When something **is liable to** happen, it is very likely to happen. 〜しがちである □ *Only a small minority of the mentally ill are liable to harm themselves or others.* 精神障害者のごく少数のものしか自分や他人を傷つけるようなことはない. **2** ADJ 形容詞 If people or things are **liable to** something unpleasant, they are likely to experience it or do it. 陥りやすい [v-link ADJ 'to' n] □ *She will grow into a woman particularly liable to depression.* 彼女は大人になると特に落ち込みやすい性格になりそうだ. **3** ADJ 形容詞 If you are **liable for** something such as a debt, you are legally responsible for it. 責任があって [v-link ADJ] □ *The airline's insurer is liable for damages to the victims' families.* 航空保険会社は犠牲者の遺族への損害賠償責任を負う. ●**lia|bil|ity** N-UNCOUNT 不可算名詞 責任，義務 □ *The company does not accept liability for fragile, valuable or perishable articles.* 当社はこわれもの，貴重品，生ものなどには損害賠償を負いません.

li|aise /liéɪz/ (**liaises, liaising, liaised**) V-RECIP 相互動詞 When organizations or people **liaise**, or when one organization **liaises with** another, they work together and keep each other informed about what is happening. 連携する [mainly BRIT 主に英国英語] □ *Detectives are liaising with police following the bomb explosion early today.* 刑事たちは警察と連携し，今朝早くに起きた爆発事件を追跡している.

liai|son /liéɪzɒn/ **1** N-UNCOUNT 不可算名詞 **Liaison** is cooperation and the exchange of information between different organizations or between different sections of an organization. 連絡 □ *Liaison between police forces and the art world is vital to combat art crime.* 美術品の犯罪と戦うためには警察と美術界の連携が欠かせない. **2** N-UNCOUNT 不可算名詞 If someone acts as **liaison** with a particular group, or **between** two or more groups, their job is to encourage co-operation and the exchange of information. 連絡係 [also 'a' N, oft N 'with' n] □ *He is acting as liaison with the film crew.* 彼は撮影スタッフとの連絡係を務めている. □ *She acts as a liaison between patients and staff.* 彼女は患者と病院スタッフの連絡係になっている.

Word Link	ar, er ≈ one who acts as : buyer, liar, seller

liar /láɪər/ (**liars**) N-COUNT 可算名詞 If you say that someone is a **liar**, you mean that they tell lies. うそつき □ *He was a liar and a cheat.* 彼はうそつきでペテン師だった.

li|bel /láɪbʰl/ (**libels, libeling** or **libelling, libeled** or **libelled**) **1** N-VAR 可変性名詞 **Libel** is a written statement which wrongly accuses someone of something, and which is therefore against the law. Compare **slander**. 名誉棄損 [LEGAL 法律的] □ *Warren sued him for libel over the remarks.* ウォーレンは彼をその発言に関して名誉棄損として訴えた. **2** V-T 他動詞 To **libel** someone means to write or print something in a book, newspaper, or magazine which wrongly damages that person's reputation and is therefore against the law. 中傷する [LEGAL 法律的] □ *The newspaper which libeled him had already offered compensation.* 彼を誹謗（ひぼう）した新聞社はすでに補償を申し出ていた.

Word Link	liber ≈ free : liberal, liberate, liberty

lib|er|al /líbərəl, líbrəl/ (**liberals**) **1** ADJ 形容詞 Someone who has **liberal** views believes people should have a lot of freedom in deciding how to behave and think. 自由な □ *She is known to have liberal views on divorce and contraception.* 彼女は離婚や避妊について偏見のない見解を持っていることで知られています. ●N-COUNT 可算名詞 **Liberal** is also a noun. 自由な考え方をする人 □ *...a nation of free-thinking liberals.* 自由思想を持った自由な人たちの国家 **2** ADJ 形容詞 A **liberal** system allows people or organizations a lot of political or economic freedom. 自由主義の □ *...a liberal democracy with a multiparty political system.* 複数政制の自由民主主義. ●N-COUNT 可算名詞 **Liberal** is also a noun. 自由主義者 □ *These kinds of price controls go against all the financial principles of the free market liberals.* こういった種類の物価統制は，自由市場主義者の全ての財政原則に反することになる. **3** ADJ 形容詞 A **Liberal** politician or voter is a member of a Liberal Party or votes for a Liberal Party. 自由党員の，自由党支持者の [ADJ n] □ *She withdrew because she did not wish to split the liberal vote.* 彼女は自由党票を分割させたくないからと身を引いた. ●N-COUNT 可算名詞 **Liberal** is also a noun. 自由党員，自由党支持者 □ *The Liberals hold twenty-three seats.* 自由党は23議席を維持している. **4** ADJ 形容詞 **Liberal** means giving, using, or taking a lot of something, or existing in large quantities. たっぷりの □ *As always he is liberal with his jokes.* いつものように，彼はたくさんのジョークを飛ばしている. ●**lib|er|al|ly** ADV 副詞 [ADV with v] ふんだんに □ *Chemical products were used liberally over agricultural land.* 農地に

大量の化学製品が使われた.

lib|er|al|ize /líbərəlaɪz, líbrəl-/ (**liberalizes, liberalizing, liberalized**) V-T/V-I 他動詞/自動詞 When a country or government **liberalizes**, or **liberalizes** its laws or its attitudes, it becomes less strict and allows people more freedom in their actions. （規制を）緩和する，自由化する □ *...authoritarian states that have only now begun to liberalize.* 自由化が最近始まったばかりの独裁主義国家. ●**lib|er|ali|za|tion** /líbərəlɪzéɪʃʰn, líbrəl-/ N-UNCOUNT 不可算名詞 自由化 □ *...the liberalization of divorce laws in the late 1960s.* 1960年代後半の離婚法の緩和.

lib|er|ate /líbəreɪt/ (**liberates, liberating, liberated**) **1** V-T 他動詞 To **liberate** a place or the people in it means to free them from the political or military control of another country, area, or group of people. 解放する □ *They planned to march on and liberate the city.* 彼らはその市に進攻し解放しようと計画した. ●**lib|er|a|tion** /líbəréɪʃʰn/ N-UNCOUNT 不可算名詞 解放 □ *...a mass liberation movement.* 大規模な解放運動. **2** V-T 他動詞 To **liberate** someone **from** something means to help them escape from it or overcome it, and lead a better way of life. 解放する，自由にする □ *He asked how committed the leadership was to liberating its people from poverty.* 彼は指導者たちが民衆を貧困から解放するのにどれほど尽力しているのかと尋ねた. ●**lib|er|at|ing** ADJ 形容詞 解放するような □ *If you have the chance to spill your problems out to a therapist it can be a very liberating experience.* 機会があってセラピストに悩みを打ち明ければ，心が非常に解放される様な気持ちになる場合があります よ. ●**lib|era|tion** N-UNCOUNT 不可算名詞 解放 □ *...the women's liberation movement.* 女性解放運動.

Thesaurus		**liberate** また次を参照:
V.		emancipate, free, let out, release; (ant.) confine, enslave **1**

lib|er|ty /líbərti/ (**liberties**) **1** N-VAR 可変性名詞 **Liberty** is the freedom to live your life in the way that you want, without interference from other people or the authorities. 自由 □ *...the ideal of equality and the appreciation of liberty.* 平等の理想と自由の理解. **2** N-UNCOUNT 不可算名詞 **Liberty** is the freedom to go wherever you want, which you lose when you are a prisoner. 自由 □ *Why not say that three convictions before court for stealing cars means three months' loss of liberty.* 車の窃盗で3回有罪になると禁固3か月になる，となぜ言わないのかな. **3** PHRASE 句 If someone **is at liberty to** do something, they have been given permission to do it. 〜してもよい □ *The island's in the Pacific Ocean; I'm not at liberty to say exactly where, because we're still negotiating for its purchase.* その島は太平洋上にありますが，正確な場所はまだお伝えできません. というのも，その購入についてはまだ交渉中だからです.

Thesaurus		**liberty** また次を参照:
N.		freedom, independence, privilege **1** **2**

Word Partnership		**liberty** は次の語句と使われる:
ADJ.		**human** liberty, **individual** liberty, **personal** liberty, **religious** liberty **1**

li|brar|ian /laɪbréəriən/ (**librarians**) N-COUNT 可算名詞 A **librarian** is a person who is in charge of a library or who has been specially trained to work in a library. 図書館長，図書館員 □ *The new librarian is a friend of mine.* その新しい司書は私の友人です. → see **library**

li|brary /láɪbreri/ (**libraries**) **1** N-COUNT 可算名詞 A public **library** is a building where things such as books, newspapers, videos, and music are kept for people to read, use, or borrow. （公の）図書館 □ *...the local library.* 地元の図書館. **2** N-COUNT 可算名詞 A private **library** is a collection of things such as books or music, that is normally only used with the permission of the owner. 蔵書，コレクション □ *The company owns a very diverse library of Arabic music.* その会社はアラビア音楽の非常に多様なコレクションを所有している. **3** N-COUNT 可算名詞 A **library** is a public building or a room, for example in a school or hospital, where things such as books, newspapers, videos, and music are kept for people to read, use, or borrow. （学校・病院などの）付属図書館，図書室 **4** N-COUNT 可算名詞 In some large houses the **library** is the room where most of the books are kept. 書庫，書斎 □ *Guests were rarely entertained in the library.* 来客は書斎へ通されることはめったになかった. → see Word Web: library

lice /láɪs/ **Lice** is the plural of **louse**. louseの複数形

li|cence /láɪsʰns/ → see **license**

li|cense /láɪsʰns/ (**licenses, licensing, licensed**) **1** N-COUNT 可算名詞 A **license** is an official document which gives you permission to do, use, or own something. 免許 □ *The judge fined the man and suspended his license.* 裁判官はその男に罰金を課し免許を停止した. □ *The company has applied to the FDA for a license to sell the drug.*

Word Web   library

Public libraries are changing. You can still **borrow** and **return books**, **magazines**, DVDs, CDs, and other **media** free of charge. However, many new **services** are now available. Websites often allow you to search the library's **catalog** of books and **periodicals**. Many libraries have computers with Internet access for the public. Some offer literacy classes, tutoring, and homework assistance. You can still wander through the **fiction** section to find a good **novel**. You can also search the nonfiction bookshelves for an interesting **biography**. And if you need help, the **librarian** is still there to answer your questions.

その会社は食品医薬局へその薬の販売許可を申請した. **2** N-UNCOUNT 不可算名詞 If you say that something gives someone **license** or **a license to** act in a particular way, you mean that it gives them an excuse to behave in an irresponsible or excessive way. 放縦 [DISAPPROVAL 不賛成] [also 'a' N, N to-inf] ❑ *Partition would give license to other aggressors in other conflicts.* 分割によって他の紛争地域での他の侵略者たちの勝手な行動がはびこるだろう. **3** V-T 他動詞 To **license** a person or activity means to give official permission for the person to do something or for the activity to take place. 認可する ❑ *...a proposal that would require the state to license guns the way it does cars.* 車と同様に銃も州が認可することが必要になる議案.

Thesaurus   *license* また次を参照.

N.	authorization, certificate, permission, permit; (*ant.*) warrant **1**

Word Partnership   *license* は次の語句と使われる:

N.	**driver's** license, license **fees**, **hunting** license, **liquor** license, **marriage** license, **pilot's** license, **software** license **1**
V.	**get/obtain** a license, **renew** a license, **revoke** a license **1**
ADJ.	**suspended** license, **valid** license **1**

li|censed /laɪsənst/ **1** ADJ 形容詞 If you are **licensed to** do something, you have official permission from the government or from the authorities to do it. 許可された ❑ *There were about 250 people on board, about 100 more than the ferry was licensed to carry.* 約250人がそのフェリーに乗船していたが，100名ほど定員オーバーだった. **2** ADJ 形容詞 If something that you own or use is **licensed**, you have official permission to own it or use it. 認可された ❑ *While searching the house they discovered an unlicensed shotgun and a licensed rifle.* その家を捜査中に彼らは未認可の散弾銃と認可を受けたライフルを各1丁発見した.

li|cense num|ber (license numbers) N-COUNT 可算名詞 The **license number** of a car or other road vehicle is the series of letters and numbers shown on the back, and in many places also on the front, of a vehicle. 登録番号 [AM 米国英語] ❑ *...a maroon 1992 Ford Taurus, license number 2YMT 804.* えび茶色の1992年式フォード・トーラスで，ナンバーは2YMT 804

li|cense plate (license plates) N-COUNT 可算名詞 A **license plate** is a sign on the back, and in some places also on the front, of a vehicle that shows its license number. ナンバープレート [AM 米国英語] ❑ *...a car with Austrian license plates.* オーストリアのナンバープレートを付けた車.

lick /lɪk/ (licks, licking, licked) **1** V-T 他動詞 When people or animals **lick** something, they move their tongue across its surface. なめる ❑ *She folded up her letter, licking the envelope flap with relish.* 彼女は手紙を折りたたみ，封筒の折り返しをおいしそうになめた. ● N-COUNT 可算名詞 **Lick** is also a noun. なめること ❑ *It's incredible how long a cat can go without more than a lick of milk or water.* 猫がミルクや水を1なめほどでそんなに長く過ごせるのは驚きだ. **2** N-COUNT 可算名詞 A **lick** of something is a small amount of it. 少量 [INFORMAL くだけた] [usu N 'of' n] ❑ *It could do with a lick of paint to brighten up its premises.* ちょっとのペンキ塗りで店内が明るくなりますよ. **3** to **lick into shape** → see **shape**

Word Partnership   *lick* は次の語句と使われる:

N.	lick *someone's* **hand**, lick *your* **lips** **1**
PREP.	lick *something* **off** *something* **1**

lid /lɪd/ (lids) N-COUNT 可算名詞 A **lid** is the top of a box or other container which can be removed or raised when you want to open the container. ふた ❑ *She lifted the lid of the box and displayed the contents.* 彼女は箱のふたをあげ，中の物を陳列した.

→ see **can**

---

lie

❶ POSITION OR SITUATION
❷ THINGS THAT ARE NOT TRUE

❶ **lie** /laɪ/ (lies, lying, lay, lain) ⇨ Please look at meaning **8** to see if the expression you are looking for is shown under another headword. **1** V-I 自動詞 If you **are lying** somewhere, you are in a horizontal position and are not standing or sitting. 横たわる ❑ *There was a child lying on the ground.* 地面に寝そべっている子供がいた. **2** V-I 自動詞 If an object **lies** in a particular place, it is in a flat position in that place. 横になっている ❑ *...a newspaper lying on a nearby couch.* 近くの寝椅子に置かれている新聞. **3** V-I 自動詞 If you say that a place **lies** in a particular position or direction, you mean that it is situated there. 位置する ❑ *The islands lie at the southern end of the Kurile chain.* それらの島は千島列島の南端に位置しています. **4** V-LINK 連結動詞 You can use **lie** to say that something is or remains in a particular state or condition. For example, if something **lies forgotten**, it has been and remains forgotten. —のままである ❑ *The picture lay hidden in the archives for over 40 years.* その写真は40年以上も公文書館に秘蔵されたままだった. **5** V-I 自動詞 You can talk about where something such as a problem, solution, or fault **lies** to say what you think it consists of, involves, or is caused by. (問題などが—に)存在する ❑ *The problem lay with the family and the school system rather than with television.* 問題は家族と学校制度にあって，テレビではなかった. **6** V-I 自動詞 You use **lie** in expressions such as **lie ahead**, **lie in store**, and **lie in wait** when you are talking about what someone is going to experience in the future, especially when it is something unpleasant or difficult. (困難などが)待ち受ける ❑ *She'd need all her strength and bravery to cope with what lay in store.* これから起こることに立ち向かうには，彼女はあらゆる力と勇気を振り絞らなければならないだろう. **7** V-T/V-I 他動詞/自動詞 You can use **lie** to say what position a competitor or team is in during a competition. (競技である位置に)いる [BRIT 英国英語] ❑ *I was going well and was lying fourth.* 私は調子よく，4位につけていた. **8** to **lie in state** → see **state** **9** to **take** something **lying down** → see **take**

> Do not confuse the verb **lie** with the verb **lay**. Because **lay** is used to talk about putting something in a particular place or position, it is related to the verb **lie**. If someone **lays** something somewhere, it **lies** there. The past tense of **lie** is **lay** and the past participle is **lain**. It is an intransitive verb. ❑ *I lay on the floor with my legs in the air.* However, **lay**, whose past tense and past participle are both **laid**, is usually a transitive verb. ❑ *They laid him on the floor.*

▶ **lie around** PHRASAL VERB 句動詞 If things are left **lying around** or **lying about**, they are not put away but left casually somewhere where they can be seen. そこらに置いてある ❑ *People should be careful about their possessions and not leave them lying around.* 所持品には気をつけて，そこらに放って置くべきではない

▶ **lie behind** PHRASAL VERB 句動詞 If you refer to what **lies behind** a situation or event, you are referring to the reason the situation exists or the event happened. —の背後にある ❑ *It seems that what lay behind the clashes was disagreement over the list of candidates.* その衝突の背後には候補者選びに関するいざこざがあったようです.

▶ **lie down** PHRASAL VERB 句動詞 When you **lie down**, you move into a horizontal position, usually in order to rest or sleep. 横になる ❑ *Why don't you go upstairs and lie down for a bit?* 2階に上がってちょっと横になったら?

❷ **lie** /laɪ/ (lies, lying, lied) **1** N-COUNT 可算名詞 A **lie** is something that someone says or writes which they know is untrue. うそ ❑ *"Who else do you work for?" — "No one." — "That's a lie."* 「他にも親玉がいるんだろ?」「いませんよ」「うそをつけ」 ❑ *I've had enough of your lies.* おまえのうそは聞き飽きた. **2** V-I 自動詞 If someone **is lying**, they are saying something which they know is not true. うそをつく ❑ *I know he's lying.* 彼がうそをついているのは分かっている. ● **lying** N-UNCOUNT 不可算名詞 うそをつくこと

❏ *Lying is something that I will not tolerate.* うそをつくのは私が許せないものだ。 **3** → see also **lying**

lieu /lu/ **1** PHRASE 句 If you do, get, or give one thing **in lieu of** another, you do, get, or give it instead of the other thing, because the two things are considered to have the same value or importance. 一の代わりに [FORMAL 形式ばった] ❏ *He left what little furniture he owned to his landlord in lieu of rent.* 彼は家賃の代わりに家主になけなしの家具を置いていった。 **2** PHRASE 句 If you do, get, or give something **in lieu**, you do, get, or give it instead of something else, because the two things are considered to have the same value or importance. 代わりに [FORMAL 形式ばった] ❏ *...an increased salary or time off in lieu.* 給与を上げるか、代わりに休暇を増やすか

lieu|ten|ant /lutɛnənt/ (**lieutenants**) N-COUNT; N-TITLE 可算名詞，称号名詞 A **lieutenant** is a person who holds a junior officer's rank in the army, navy, marines, or air force, or in the U.S. police force. (陸軍の) 中尉，少尉，(海軍の) 大尉，警部補 ❏ *Lieutenant Campbell ordered the man at the wheel to steer for the gunboat.* キャンベル大尉はかじを取る下士官に砲艦に向かうよう命じた。

life /laɪf/ (**lives** /laɪvz/) **1** N-UNCOUNT 不可算名詞 **Life** is the quality which people, animals, and plants have when they are not dead, and which objects and substances do not have. 生命 ❏ *...a baby's first minutes of life.* 赤ちゃんが生を受けて間もないとき。 **2** N-UNCOUNT 不可算名詞 You can use **life** to refer to things or groups of things which are alive. 生物 ❏ *Is there life on Mars?* 火星に生物はいるのか。 **3** N-COUNT 可算名詞 If you refer to someone's **life**, you mean their state of being alive, especially when there is a risk or danger of them dying. 命 ❏ *Your life is in danger.* あなたの命は危険にさらされている。 ❏ *A nurse began to try to save his life.* 看護師は彼の命を救おうと乗り出した。 **4** N-COUNT 可算名詞 Someone's **life** is the period of time during which they are alive. 人生，生涯 ❏ *He spent the last fourteen years of his life in retirement.* 彼は人生最後の14年は隠居生活を送っていた。 **5** N-COUNT 可算名詞 You can use **life** to refer to a period of someone's life when they are in a particular situation or job. 一生活 ❏ *Interior designers spend their working lives keeping up to date with the latest trends.* インテリアデザイナーは最新の流行を追いかける職業生活を送る。 **6** N-COUNT 可算名詞 You can use **life** to refer to particular activities which people regularly do during their lives. 一生活 ❏ *My personal life has had to take second place to my career.* 私生活は常に仕事の二の次だった。 **7** N-UNCOUNT 不可算名詞 You can use **life** to refer to the things that people do and experience that are characteristic of a particular place, group, or activity. 一生活 ❏ *How did you adjust to college life?* どうやって大学生活に慣れましたか？ ❏ *He abhors the wheeling-and-dealing associated with conventional political life.* 伝統的な政治生活では決まって策略がめぐらされるが、彼はそれが大嫌いだ。 **8** N-UNCOUNT 不可算名詞 A person, place, book, or movie that is full of **life** gives an impression of excitement, energy, or cheerfulness. 活気 [APPROVAL 賛成] ❏ *The town itself was full of life and character.* その町自体は活気と特色にあふれていた。 **9** N-UNCOUNT 不可算名詞 If someone is sentenced to **life**, they are sentenced to stay in prison for the rest of their life or for a very long time. 終身刑 [INFORMAL くだけた] ❏ *He could get life in prison, if convicted.* 有罪になったら、彼は終身刑でしょう。 **10** N-COUNT 可算名詞 The **life** of something such as a machine, organization, or project is the period of time that it lasts for. 寿命 ❏ *The repairs did not increase the value or the life of the equipment.* その装置を修理しても有用性は上がらなかったし、寿命も延びなかった。 **11** PHRASE 句 If you **bring** something **to life** or if it **comes to life**, it becomes interesting or exciting. 一を活気づける，活気づく ❏ *The cold, hard cruelty of two young men is vividly brought to life in this true story.* 2人の若者の冷酷で無骨な残酷さがこの実話を生気あふれるものにしている。 **12** PHRASE 句 If you say that someone **is fighting for** their **life**, you mean that they are in a very serious condition and may die as a result of an accident or illness. 瀕死 (ひんし) の状態である [JOURNALISM ジャーナリズム] ❏ *...a horrifying*

robbery that left a man fighting for his life. 男性1人が瀕死 (ひんし) の重傷を負った凶悪な強盗事件。 **13** PHRASE 句 **For life** means for the rest of a person's life. 死ぬまでずっと ❏ *He was jailed for life in 1966 for the murder of three policemen.* 彼は警官3名を殺害したかどで1966年に終身刑になった。 ❏ *She may have been scarred for life.* 彼女は生涯傷あとが残ったかもしれない。 **14** PHRASE 句 If someone takes another person's **life**, they kill them. If someone **takes** their own **life**, they kill themselves. 命を奪う [FORMAL 形式ばった] ❏ *Before execution, he admitted to taking the lives of at least 35 more women.* 彼は処刑される前に少なくとも35名以上の女性を殺害したことを告白した。 **15** PHRASE 句 You can use expressions such as **to come to life**, **to spring to life**, and **to roar into life** to indicate that a machine or vehicle suddenly starts working or moving. 再び動き始める [LITERARY 文語的] ❏ *To his great relief the engine came to life.* エンジンが復活し、彼は本当に安心した。 **16** a matter of **life and death** → see **death**
→ see **earth**

life|boat /laɪfboʊt/ (**lifeboats**) **1** N-COUNT 可算名詞 A **lifeboat** is a medium-sized boat that is sent out from a port or harbor in order to rescue people who are in danger at sea. 救助艇 **2** N-COUNT 可算名詞 A **lifeboat** is a small boat that is carried on a ship, which people on the ship use to escape when the ship is in danger of sinking. 救命ボート ❏ *The captain ordered all passengers and crew into lifeboats.* 船長は全乗客と乗員に救命ボートに移るよう命じました。

life cy|cle (**life cycles**) **1** N-COUNT 可算名詞 The **life cycle** of an animal or plant is the series of changes and developments that it passes through from the beginning of its life until its death. 生活環 ❏ *...a plant that completes its life cycle in a single season.* たった1季節でライフサイクルが終わる植物。 **2** N-COUNT 可算名詞 The **life cycle** of something such as an idea, product, or organization is the series of developments that take place in it from its beginning until the end of its usefulness. 寿命 ❏ *Each new product would have a relatively long life cycle.* 個々の新製品の寿命は比較的長いものになるだろう。
→ see **plant**

life|guard /laɪfgɑrd/ (**lifeguards**) N-COUNT 可算名詞 A **lifeguard** is a person who works at a beach or swimming pool and rescues people when they are in danger of drowning. 救助員

life in|sur|ance N-UNCOUNT 不可算名詞 **Life insurance** is a form of insurance in which a person makes regular payments to an insurance company, in return for a sum of money to be paid to them after a period of time, or to their family if they die. 生命保険 ❏ *I have also taken out a life insurance policy on him just in case.* 念のため私も彼に生命保険をかけました。

life|less /laɪflɪs/ **1** ADJ 形容詞 If a person or animal is **lifeless**, they are dead, or are so still that they appear to be dead. 死んでいる，死んだ ❏ *Their cold-blooded killers had then dragged their lifeless bodies upstairs to the bathroom.* 血も涙もない殺人犯たちは、彼らの遺体を2階の浴室に引きずり上げた。 **2** ADJ 形容詞 If you describe an object or a machine as **lifeless**, you mean that they are not living things, even though they may resemble living things. 生物ではない ❏ *It was made of plaster, hard and white and lifeless, bearing no resemblance to human flesh.* それは硬くて白い無生物の石こうでできており、人間の肌とは似ても似つかぬものだった。 **3** ADJ 形容詞 A **lifeless** place or area does not have anything living or growing there at all. 生物の住まない ❏ *Dry stone walls may appear stark and lifeless, but they provide a valuable habitat for plants and animals.* モルタルを用いない石壁は殺風景で生物が住めないように思えるが、動植物の貴重な生息場所になる。

life|line /laɪflaɪn/ (**lifelines**) N-COUNT 可算名詞 A **lifeline** is something that enables an organization or group to survive or to continue with an activity. 生命線 ❏ *Information about the job market can be a lifeline for those who are out of work.* 雇用状況に関する情報は失業者にとっての生命線になりうる。

life|long /laɪflɔŋ/ ADJ 形容詞 **Lifelong** means existing or happening for the whole of a person's life. 一生の [ADJ n] ❏ *...her lifelong friendship with Naomi.* 彼女とナオミの生涯変わることのない友情。

life|span /laɪfspæn/ (**lifespans**) also **life span** **1** N-VAR 可変性名詞 The **lifespan** of a person, animal, or plant is the period of time for which they live or are normally expected to live. 寿命 ❏ *A 15-year lifespan is not uncommon for a dog.* 犬が15年生きるのは珍しいことではない。 **2** N-COUNT 可算名詞 The **lifespan** of a product, organization, or idea is the period of time for which it is expected to work properly or to last. 寿命 ❏ *Most boilers have a lifespan of 15 to 20 years.* ボイラーの寿命は大半が15年から20年です。

life|style /laɪfstaɪl/ (**lifestyles**) also **life-style** or **life style** **1** N-VAR 可変性名詞 The **lifestyle** of a particular person or group of people is the living conditions, behavior, and habits that are typical of them or are chosen by them. 生き方，ライフスタイル ❏ *They enjoyed an income and lifestyle that many people would envy.* 彼らは多くの人がうらやむような収入とライフスタイルを謳歌 (おうか) していた。 **2** ADJ 形容詞 **Lifestyle** magazines, television programs,

and products are aimed at people who wish to be associated with glamorous and successful lifestyles. 生活様式の，ライフスタイルの [ADJ n] □ *This year people are going for luxury and buying lifestyle products.* 今年はぜいたく志向で，ライフスタイル関連製品が売れている． ❸ ADJ 形容詞 **Lifestyle** drugs are drugs that are intended to improve people's quality of life rather than to treat particular medical disorders. (薬品が) ライフスタイル用の [ADJ n] □ *"I see anti-depressants as a lifestyle drug," says Dr. Charlton.* 「抗うつ剤はライフスタイル用薬品だと思う」とチャールトン博士が言っている．

life|time /ˈlaɪftaɪm/ (**lifetimes**) N-COUNT 可算名詞 A **lifetime** is the length of time that someone is alive. 生涯 □ *During my lifetime I haven't got around to much traveling.* これまでの人生で私はあまり旅行する機会がなかった． □ *...a trust fund to be administered throughout his wife's lifetime.* 彼の妻が生きている間じゅう運営される信託資金

lift /lɪft/ (**lifts, lifting, lifted**) ❶ V-T 他動詞 If you **lift** something, you move it to another position, especially upward. 持ち上げる □ *The colonel lifted the phone and dialed his superior.* 大佐は受話器を取り上げ，上官に電話した． ● PHRASAL VERB 句動詞 **Lift up** means the same as **lift**. 持ち上げる □ *She put her arms around him and lifted him up.* 彼女は彼を抱え込んで持ち上げた．

> Do not confuse **lift** and **carry**. When you **carry** something, you move it from one place to another without letting it touch the ground. When you **lift** something, you move it upwards using your hands or a machine. After you have lifted it, you may **carry** it to a different place.

❷ V-T 他動詞 If you **lift** your eyes or your head, you look up, for example, when you have been reading and someone comes into the room. 上げる □ *When he finished he lifted his eyes and looked out the window.* 終わると，彼は目を上げて窓の外を眺めた． ❸ V-T 他動詞 If people in authority **lift** a law or rule that prevents people from doing something, they end it. (禁止令などを) 解除する □ *The European Commission has urged France to lift its ban on imports of British beef.* 欧州委員会はフランスに対し英国産牛肉の輸入禁止を解除するよう促した． ❹ V-T/V-I 他動詞/自動詞 If something **lifts** your spirits or your mood, or if they **lift**, you start feeling more cheerful. 高揚させる，高揚する □ *He used his incredible sense of humor to lift my spirits.* 彼は持ち前の卓越したユーモアで私の心を晴らしてくれた． ❺ N-COUNT 可算名詞 If you give someone a **lift** somewhere, you take them there in your car as a favor to them. 車に乗せてやること □ *He had a car and often gave me a lift home.* 彼は車をもっていて，よく私を家まで送ってくれた． ❻ N-UNCOUNT 不可算名詞 **Lift** is the force that makes an aircraft leave the ground and stay in the air. 揚力 □ *An airplane has to reach a certain speed before there is enough lift to get it off the ground.* 飛行機が離陸に必要な揚力を得るには，ある速度に到達しなければならない． ❼ V-T 他動詞 If a government or organization **lifts** people or goods in or out of an area, it transports them there by aircraft, especially when there is a war. 空輸する □ *The army lifted people off rooftops where they had climbed to escape the flooding.* 洪水から逃れて屋根に非難した人たちが軍用ヘリで救出されました． ❽ V-T 他動詞 To **lift** something means to increase its amount or to increase the level or the rate at which it happens. 引き上げる [BRIT 英国英語] ❾ N-COUNT 可算名詞 A **lift** is a device that carries people or goods up and down inside tall buildings. エレベーター [BRIT 英国英語; AM **elevator** 米国英語] ❿ **to lift a finger** → see **finger**

Thesaurus   *lift* また次を参照：

V.	boost, hoist, pick up; (ant.) drop, lower, put down ❶ cancel, repeal, rescind, terminate ❸ boost, enhance, raise ❹

Word Partnership   *lift* は次の語句と使われる：

N.	lift **your** arm, lift **your** hand, lift **weights** ❶ lift a ban, lift a blockade, lift an embargo, lift restrictions, lift sanctions, lift a siege ❸

liga|ment /ˈlɪɡəmənt/ (**ligaments**) N-COUNT 可算名詞 A **ligament** is a band of strong tissue in a person's body which connects bones. 靱帯 (じんたい) □ *He suffered torn ligaments in his knee.* 彼はひざの靱帯を損傷しました．

light

❶ BRIGHTNESS OR ILLUMINATION
❷ NOT GREAT IN WEIGHT, AMOUNT, OR INTENSITY
❸ UNIMPORTANT OR NOT SERIOUS

❶ **light** /laɪt/ (**lights, lighting, lit** or **lighted, lighter, lightest**) ⇨ Please look at meaning ❶❺ to see if the expression you are looking for is shown under another headword. ❶ N-UNCOUNT 不可算名詞 **Light** is the brightness that lets you see things. Light

---

comes from sources such as the sun, moon, lamps, and fire. 光 [also 'the' N] □ *Cracks of light filtered through the shutters.* シャッターから光がきれぎれに漏れていた． □ *...ultraviolet light.* 紫外線． ❷ N-COUNT 可算名詞 A **light** is something such as an electric lamp which produces light. 明かり □ *The janitor comes around to turn the lights out.* 用務員は回って来て消灯する． ❸ N-PLURAL 複数名詞 You can use **lights** to refer to a set of traffic lights. 信号 □ *...the heavy city traffic with its endless delays at lights and crosswalks.* 信号や交差点で停止しない渋滞が起こる都市部のひどい交通 ❹ V-T 他動詞 If a place or object **is lit by** something, it has light shining on it. 照らす □ *It was dark and a giant moon lit the road so brightly you could see the landscape clearly.* 暗かったし，とても大きな月が大変明るく道路を照らしていたから景色がはっきり見えた． □ *The room was lit by only the one light.* 部屋には明かりがたった1つだけ灯っていた． ❺ ADJ 形容詞 If it is **light**, the sun is providing light at the beginning or end of the day. 明るい □ *It was still light when we arrived at Lalong Creek.* ラロング・クリークに到着したときはまだ明るかった． ❻ ADJ 形容詞 If a room or building is **light**, it has a lot of natural light in it, for example, because it has large windows. 明るい □ *It is a light room with tall windows.* 背の高い窓があって明るい部屋です． ● **light|ness** N-UNCOUNT 不可算名詞 明るさ □ *The dark green spare bedroom is in total contrast to the lightness of the large main bedroom.* 暗緑色の予備寝室は，大きな主寝室の明るさと全く対照的です． ❼ V-T/V-I 他動詞/自動詞 If you **light** something such as a cigarette or fire, or if it **lights**, it starts burning. 火をつける，火がつく □ *Stephen hunched down to light a cigarette.* ステファンは背中を丸めてたばこに火をつけた． □ *If the charcoal does fail to light, use a special liquid spray and light it with a long taper.* もしどうしても炭が着火しなかったら，専用の液体スプレーを使い，長細いろうそくで点火してください． ❽ N-COUNT 可算名詞 If something is presented in a particular **light**, it is presented so that you think about it in a particular way or so that it appears to be of a particular nature. 見方 □ *He has worked hard in recent months to portray New York in a better light.* 彼はニューヨークをより良いイメージで描こうと，ここ数か月懸命に取り組んでいる． ❾ → see also **lighter, lighting** ❿ PHRASE 句 If something **comes to light** or is **brought to light**, it becomes obvious or is made known to a lot of people. 明らかになる，明らかにする □ *Nothing about this sum has come to light.* この金額については何も明らかにされていない． ⓫ PHRASE 句 If someone in authority gives you a **green light**, they give you permission to do something. 許可する □ *The food industry was given a green light to extend the use of these chemicals.* 食品業界はこれらの化学薬品の使用範囲を広げる許可を受けた． ⓬ PHRASE 句 If something is **possible in the light of** particular information, it is only possible because you have this information. 一に照らして，一にかんがみて □ *In the light of this information it is now possible to identify a number of key issues.* この情報に照らして，いくつかの主要問題を特定することが今や可能だ． ⓭ PHRASE 句 To **shed light on, throw light on**, or **cast light on** something means to make it easier to understand, because more information is known about it. 一の解明に役立つ □ *A new approach offers an answer, and may shed light on an even bigger question.* 新しいやり方によって解決策が見えるし，もっと大きな問題を解決する手掛かりになるかもしれません． ⓮ PHRASE 句 If you **set light to** something, you make it start burning. 一に火をつける [mainly BRIT 主に英国英語; AM usually **set fire to** 米国英語では通常 **set fire to**] ⓯ **all sweetness and light** → see **sweetness**

▶ **light up** ❶ PHRASAL VERB 句動詞 If you **light** something **up** or if it **lights up**, it becomes bright, usually when you shine light on it. 照らす，明るくなる □ *...a keypad that lights up when you pick up the handset.* 受話器を取ると明かりがつく押しボタン． ❷ PHRASAL VERB 句動詞 If your face or your eyes **light up** you suddenly look very surprised or happy. (表情が) ぱっと変わる □ *Sue's face lit up with surprise.* びっくりしてスーの表情がぱっと変わった．

→ see **color, laser, light, telescope, wave**

Thesaurus   *light* また次を参照：

N.	brightness, gleam, glow, radiance, shine ❶ ❶
ADJ.	bright, sunny ❶ ❺ ❻ weightless; (ant.) heavy, solid ❷ ❶

❷ **light** /laɪt/ (**lighter, lightest**) ❶ ADJ 形容詞 Something that is **light** does not weigh very much, or weighs less than you would expect it to. 軽い □ *Modern tennis rackets are now apparently 20 per cent lighter.* 最新のテニスラケットは明らかに20パーセント軽量化されている． □ *...weight training with light weights.* 軽い負荷でのウェートトレーニング． ● **light|ness** N-UNCOUNT 不可算名詞 [usu with supp] 軽さ □ *The toughness, lightness, strength, and elasticity of whalebone gave it a wide variety of uses.* 丈夫で，軽く，強靱 (きょうじん) で，柔軟な鯨の骨は幅広く利用された． ❷ ADJ 形容詞 Something that is **light** is not very great in amount, degree, or intensity. 少ない，小さい □ *It's a Sunday like any other with the usual light traffic in the city.* いつもと変わらず都市部では交通量の少ない日曜日です． □ *Trading was very light ahead of yesterday's auction.* 取引は昨日のオークション以上にとても少なかった． ● **light|ly** ADV 副

Word Web light bulb

The incandescent **light bulb** has changed little since the 1870s. It consists of a **glass** globe containing an inert gas, such as argon, some wires, and a filament. **Electricity** flows through the wires and the tungsten filament. The filament heats up and **glows**. Light bulbs aren't very efficient. They give off more heat than **light**. **Fluorescent** lights are much more efficient. They contain liquid mercury and argon gas. A layer of phosphorus covers the inside of the tube. When electricity begins to flow, the mercury becomes a gas and **emits** ultraviolet light. This causes the phosphorus coating to **shine**.

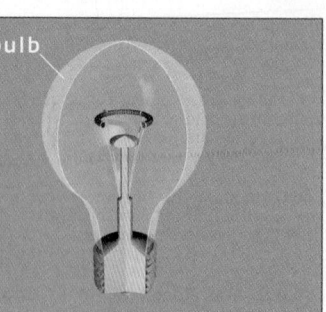

bulb

詞] 少し ❑ *Put the onions in the pan and cook until lightly browned.* たまねぎをフライパンに入れ，少し色づくまでいためてください． ❸ ADJ 形容詞 Something that is **light** is very pale in color. 淡い ❑ *He is light haired with gray eyes.* 彼は髪の色が淡く，灰色の目をしている． ●COMB IN COLOR 色彩語の複合 **Light** is also a combining form. 薄～色の ❑ *We know he has a light green van.* 彼が薄緑色の小型トラックを持っているのは我々には周知のことだ． ❹ ADJ 形容詞 [ADJ n] A **light** sleep is one that is easily disturbed and in which you are often aware of the things around you. If you are a **light** sleeper, you are easily woken when you are asleep. （眠りが）浅い ❑ *She had drifted into a light sleep.* 彼女はいつの間にかうとうとしていた． ●**light|ly** ADV 副詞 [ADV after v] 浅く ❑ *He was dozing lightly in his chair.* 彼はいすで少しまどろんでいた． ❺ ADJ 形容詞 A **light** meal consists of food that is easy to digest. 軽い ❑ *...a light, healthy lunch.* 軽くて健康的な昼食． ●**light|ly** ADV 副詞 [ADV after v] 軽く ❑ *She found it impossible to eat lightly.* 彼女は軽く食事をするのは不可能だと気づいた． ❻ ADJ 形容詞 **Light** work does not involve much physical effort. 軽い ❑ *He was on the training field for some light work yesterday.* 彼は昨日軽いメニューをこなすため練習場にいた． ❼ ADJ 形容詞 If you describe the result of an action or a punishment as **light**, you mean that it is less serious or severe than you expected. 軽い ❑ *She confessed her astonishment at her light sentence when her father visited her at the jail.* 彼女の父親が面会に来たとき，彼女は自分の判決が軽くて驚いたと告白した． ●**light|ly** ADV 副詞 [ADV after v] 軽く ❑ *One of the accused got off lightly in exchange for pleading guilty to withholding information from Congress.* 被告の１人は，議会に情報を渡さなかった罪を認めるのと引き換えに，刑が軽く済んだ． ❽ ADJ 形容詞 Movements and actions that are **light** are graceful or gentle and are done with very little force or effort. 軽い ❑ *Use a light touch when applying cream or makeup.* クリームや化粧をするときはそっと延ばしましょう． ●**light|ly** ADV 副詞 [ADV with v] 軽く ❑ *He kissed her lightly on the mouth.* 彼は彼女に軽く口づけた． ●**light|ness** N-UNCOUNT 不可算名詞 軽さ ❑ *She danced with a grace and lightness that were breathtaking.* 彼女の踊りは息をのむほど優雅で軽快だった． ❾ ADJ 形容詞 **Light** is used to describe foods or drinks that contain few calories or low amounts of sugar, fat, or alcohol. 低カロリーの ❑ *There's been a flood of low-fat and light ice creams on the market.* 市場には低脂肪，低カロリーのアイスクリームが山のように出回っている． ❑ *They refreshed themselves with cans of light beer.* 彼らは缶入りのライト・ビールで一息ついた．

❸ **light** /laɪt/ (lighter, lightest) ❶ ADJ 形容詞 If you describe things such as books, music, and movies as **light**, you mean that they entertain you without making you think very deeply. 軽い，肩の凝らない ❑ *He doesn't like me reading light novels.* 彼は私が娯楽小説を読むのを嫌がる． ❑ *...light classical music.* 軽快なクラシック音楽． ❷ ADJ 形容詞 If you say something in a **light** way, you sound as if you think that something is not important or serious. 軽い，気軽な ❑ *Talk to him in a friendly, light way about the relationship.* 親しげで気軽な調子で彼と交際について話し合いなさい． ●**light|ly** ADV 副詞 [ADV] 軽く ❑ *"Once a detective, always a detective," he said lightly.* 「１度探偵になると，いつだって探偵さ」と彼は軽い調子で言った． ●**light|ness** N-UNCOUNT 不可算名詞 軽さ ❑ *"I'm not an authority on them," Jessica said with forced lightness.* 「私はそれらのことの権威者じゃないの」とジェシカはわざと気軽そうに言った． ❸ PHRASE 句 If you **make light of** something, you treat it as though it is not serious or important, when in fact it is. 軽く受け止める，軽んじる ❑ *Roberts attempted to make light of his discomfort.* ロバートは不快感を軽く受け止めようとした．

light bulb (light bulbs) N-COUNT 可算名詞 A **light bulb** or **bulb** is the round glass part of an electric light or lamp which light shines from. 電球
→ see Word Web: light bulb

Word Link light = not heavy : lighten, lighthearted, lightweight

light|en /laɪt³n/ (lightens, lightening, lightened) ❶ V-T/V-I 他動詞/自動詞 When something **lightens** or when you **lighten** it, it becomes less dark in color. 明るくする [他動詞]，明るくなる [自動詞] ❑ *The sky began to lighten.* 空が明るくなり始めた． ❷ V-T 他動詞 If someone **lightens** a situation, they make it less serious or less boring. 和らげる ❑ *Anthony felt the need to lighten the atmosphere.* アントニーはその場の雰囲気を和らげる必要性を感じた． ❸ V-T/V-I 他動詞/自動詞 If your attitude or mood **lightens**, or if someone or something **lightens** it, they make you feel more cheerful, happy, and relaxed. 明るくする，楽しませる [他動詞]，晴れやかになる [自動詞] ❑ *As they approached the outskirts of the city, Ella's mood visibly lightened.* その市の郊外に近づくにつれて，エラの機嫌が明らかによくなった．

light|er /laɪtər/ (lighters) N-COUNT 可算名詞 A **lighter** is a small device that produces a flame which you can use to light cigarettes, cigars, and pipes. ライター

light|heart|ed /laɪthɑrtɪd/ ❶ ADJ 形容詞 Someone who is **lighthearted** is cheerful and happy. 陽気な，愉快な ❑ *I was amazingly lighthearted and peaceful.* 私は驚くほど陽気で穏やかな気持ちだった． ❷ ADJ 形容詞 Something that is **lighthearted** is intended to be entertaining or amusing, and not at all serious. 気楽な，軽快な ❑ *There have been many attempts, both lighthearted and serious, to locate the Loch Ness Monster.* ネッシーの居場所を突き止めるために気軽な捜査から深刻なものまで多くの試みがなされた．

light|house /laɪthaʊs/ (lighthouses) N-COUNT 可算名詞 A **lighthouse** is a tower containing a powerful flashing lamp that is built on the coast or on a small island. Lighthouses are used to guide ships or to warn them of danger. 灯台

light in|dus|try (light industries) N-VAR 可変性名詞 **Light industry** is industry in which only small items are made, for example, household goods and clothes. 軽工業 ❑ *State and local officials are hoping to bring some light industry to the site.* 州と地元の役人はその敷地に軽工業を誘致できるよう期待している．
→ see industry

light|ing /laɪtɪŋ/ N-UNCOUNT 不可算名詞 The **lighting** in a place is the way that it is lit, for example, by electric lights, by candles, or by windows, or the quality of the light in it. 照明 ❑ *...the bright fluorescent lighting of the laboratory.* 実験室のまぶしい蛍光灯の照明 ❑ *The whole room is bathed in soft lighting.* 部屋全体が柔らかな照明を浴びていた．
→ see concert, photography

light|ning /laɪtnɪŋ/ ❶ N-UNCOUNT 不可算名詞 **Lightning** is the very bright flashes of light in the sky that happen during thunderstorms. 稲光，稲妻 ❑ *One man died when he was struck by lightning.* 稲妻に打たれて男性が１人死亡した． ❑ *Another flash of lightning lit up the cave.* 再び稲光がひらめいて洞くつを照らした． ❷ ADJ 形容詞 **Lightning** describes things that happen very quickly or last for only a short time. 電光石火の，素早い [ADJ n] ❑ *Driving today demands lightning reflexes.* 今日の車の運転は素早い反射神経を要する．
→ see Word Web: lightning
→ see storm

light|weight /laɪtweɪt/ (lightweights) also **light-weight** ❶ ADJ 形容詞 Something that is **lightweight** weighs less than most other things of the same type. 軽い，薄手の ❑ *...lightweight denim.* 薄手のデニム ❷ N-UNCOUNT 不可算名詞 **Lightweight** is a category in some sports, such as boxing, judo, or rowing, based on the weight of the athlete. ライト級，軽量級 ❑ *By the age of sixteen he was the junior lightweight champion of Poland.* 16歳までに彼はポーランドでジュニアライト級のチャンピオンになった． ❸ N-COUNT 可算名詞 If you describe someone as a **lightweight**, you are critical of them because you think that they are not very important or skillful in a particular area of activity. 取るに足らない人物 [DISAPPROVAL 不賛成] ❑ *Brian considered Sam a lightweight, a real amateur.* ブライアンはサムのことをど素人でつまらない人物だと思った． ●ADJ 形容詞 **Lightweight** is also an adjective. 軽薄な ❑ *Some of the discussion in the book is lightweight and unconvincing.* その本の論述には内容が浅く説得力に欠けるものがある．

light year (light years) ❶ N-COUNT 可算名詞 A **light year** is the

Word Web — lightning

Lightning originates in storm clouds. Strong winds cause tiny **particles** within the clouds to rub together violently. This creates **positive charges** on some particles and **negative charges** on others. The negatively charged particles sink to the bottom of the cloud. There they are attracted by the positively charged surface of the earth. Gradually a large negative charge accumulates in a cloud. When it is large enough, a **bolt** of lightning strikes the earth. When a bolt branches out, the result is called **forked lightning**. Sheet lightning occurs when the bolt **discharges** within a cloud, instead of on the earth.

distance that light travels in a year. 光年 ❑ *...a star system millions of light years away.* 何百万光年も離れたところにある星雲 ❷ N-COUNT 可算名詞 You can say that two things are **light years** apart to emphasize a very great difference or a very long distance or period of time between them. 非常に長い距離・時間 [INFORMAL くだけた, EMPHASIS 強調] ❑ *She says the French education system is light years ahead of the English one.* フランスの教育制度はイギリスよりはるかに進歩していると彼女は言う.

→ see **galaxy**

lik|able /láɪkəbəl/ also **likeable** ADJ 形容詞 Someone or something that is **likable** is pleasant and easy to like. 好感の持てる, 感じのよい ❑ *He was a bright guy, a likable guy.* 彼は頭がよくて感じのよい男だった.

like

❶ PREPOSITION AND CONJUNCTION USES
❷ VERB USES
❸ NOUN USES AND PHRASES

❶ **like** /láɪk, láɪk/ (**likes**) ❶ PREP 前置詞 If you say that one person or thing is **like** another, you mean that they share some of the same qualities or features. 〜のような, 〜に似ている ❑ *He looks like Father Christmas.* 彼はサンタクロースに似ている. ❑ *It's a bit like going to the dentist; it's never as bad as you fear.* それは歯医者に行くのとちょっと似ているよ. 実際に行ってみると想像よりマシなんだ. ❑ *It's nothing like what happened in the mid-Seventies.* それは70年代の半ばに起きたこととは全く異なっている. ❷ PREP 前置詞 If you talk about what something or someone is **like**, you are talking about their qualities or features. 〜らしい（特徴などを表して） ❑ *What was Bulgaria like?* ブルガリアはどんな感じでしたか. ❑ *What did she look like?* 彼女の見た目はどんな感じだった？ ❸ PREP 前置詞 You can use **like** to introduce an example of the set of things or people that you have just mentioned. 〜のような [n PREP n/-ing] ❑ *The neglect that large cities like New York have received over the past 12 years is tremendous.* ニューヨークのような大都市が過去12年間どれほどおろそかにされたかは恐ろしいほどだ. ❹ PREP 前置詞 You can use **like** to say that someone or something is in the same situation as another person or thing. 〜と同様に ❑ *It also moved those who, like me, are too young to have lived through the war.* それはまた私のように若すぎてその戦争を経験していなかった人々も感動させた. ❺ PREP 前置詞 If you say that someone is behaving **like** something or someone else, you mean that they are behaving in a way that is typical of that kind of thing or person. **Like** is used in this way in many fixed expressions, for example, **to cry like a baby** and **to watch someone like a hawk**. 〜のように [v PREP n] ❑ *I was shaking all over, trembling like a leaf.* 私は木の葉がふるえるように全身がふるえていた. ❻ CONJ 接続詞 **Like** is sometimes used as a conjunction in order to say that something appears to be the case when it is not. Some people consider this use to be incorrect. まるで〜のように ❑ *His arms look like they might snap under the weight of his gloves.* 彼の両腕はグラブの重さで折れそうに見える. ❼ CONJ 接続詞 **Like** is sometimes used as a conjunction in order to indicate that something happens or is done in the same way as something else. Some people consider this use to be incorrect. 〜と同じように ❑ *People are strolling, buying ice cream for their children, just like they do every Sunday.* 人々は毎週日曜日にするように, 散歩をしたり子供たちにアイスクリームを買ってやったりしている. ❑ *He spoke exactly like I did.* 彼は私と全く同じ話し方をした. ❽ PREP 前置詞 You can use **like** in negative expressions such as **nothing like it** and **no place like it** to emphasize that there is nothing as good as the situation, thing, or person mentioned. 否定文で肯定の意味を強調する ❑ *There's nothing like candlelight for creating a romantic mood.* ロマンチックなムードを出すにはろうそくの光が1番だ. [EMPHASIS 強調] [with neg] ❾ PREP 前置詞 You can use **like** in expressions such as **nothing like** to make an emphatic negative statement. nothing likeで否定の意味を強調する ❑ *Three hundred million dollars*

will be nothing like enough. 3百万ドルでは決して十分ではない. [EMPHASIS 強調] [with neg]

Thesaurus — *like* また次を参照：

PREP.	alike, comparable, similar ❶ ❶
V.	admire, appreciate, enjoy; *(ant.)* dislike ❷ ❶

❷ **like** /láɪk/ (**likes, liking, liked**) ❶ V-T 他動詞 If you **like** something or someone, you think they are interesting, enjoyable, or attractive. 好きである [no cont] ❑ *He likes baseball.* 彼は野球が好きだ. ❑ *I just didn't like being in crowds.* 私はただ人混みにいるのが好きじゃなかった. ❑ *Do you like to go swimming?* 水泳に行くのは好きですか？ ❷ V-T 他動詞 If you ask someone how they **like** something, you are asking them for their opinion of it and whether they enjoy it or find it pleasant. 〜はいかがですか（howと共に用いて意見を尋ねるときに用いる） [no cont, no passive] ❑ *How do you like America?* アメリカをどう思いますか？ ❸ V-T 他動詞 If you say that you **like to** do something or that you **like** something to be done, you mean that you prefer to do it or prefer it to be done as part of your normal life or routine. （不定詞と共に用いて）〜するのが好きだ [no cont, no passive] ❑ *I like to get to airports in good time.* 私は空港には余裕を持って到着するのが好きだ. ❹ V-T 他動詞 If you say that you **would like** something or **would like** to do something, you are indicating a wish or desire that you have. （wouldと共に用いて）欲しい, したい [no cont, no passive] ❑ *I'd like a bath.* 私は風呂に入りたい. ❺ V-T 他動詞 If you ask someone if they **would like** something or **would like** to do something, you are making a polite offer or invitation. （wouldと共に用いて）〜はいかがですか [POLITENESS 丁寧さ] [no cont, no passive] ❑ *Here's your change. Would you like a bag?* お釣りをどうぞ. 袋はいかがですか？ ❑ *Perhaps while you wait you would like a drink at the bar.* 待っている間にバーで飲み物はいかがですか. ❻ V-T 他動詞 If you say to someone that you **would like** something or you **would like** them to do something, or ask them if they **would like** to do it, you are politely telling them what you want or what you want them to do. （wouldと共に用いて）〜していただきたい [POLITENESS 丁寧さ] [no cont, no passive] ❑ *I'd like an explanation.* ご説明をお願いしたい. ❑ *We'd like you to look around and tell us if anything is missing.* 見回って何か見当たらないものがないかを知らせてもらいたい.

❸ **like** /láɪk/ (**likes**) ❶ N-UNCOUNT 不可算名詞 You can use **like** in expressions such as **like attracts like**, when you are referring to two or more people or things that have the same or similar characteristics. 似たもの, 同類 ❑ *You have to make sure you're comparing like with like.* 必ず同種のものを比較しているようにしなければならない. ❷ N-PLURAL 複数名詞 Someone's **likes** are the things that they enjoy or find pleasant. 好み, 趣味 ❑ *I thought that I knew everything about Jemma: her likes and dislikes, her political viewpoints.* 私はジェマの好き嫌いや政治観まですべてを知っていると思っていた ❸ → see also **liking** ❹ PHRASE 句 You say **if you like** when you are making or agreeing to an offer or suggestion in a casual way. もしよろしかったら ❑ *You can stay here if you like.* よかったらここに泊まっていいですよ. ❺ PHRASE 句 You say **like this, like that**, or **like so** when you are showing someone how something is done. こういうふうに ❑ *It opens and closes, like this.* それはこのように開いたり閉じたりする. ❻ PHRASE 句 You use **like this** or **like that** when you are drawing attention to something that you are doing or that someone else is doing. こんなふうに ❑ *I'm sorry to intrude on you like this.* このようにおじゃまをして申し訳ございません. ❼ PHRASE 句 You use the expression **something like** with an amount, number, or description to indicate that it is approximately accurate. およそ ❑ *They can get something like $3,000 a year.* 彼らは年間約3000ドル稼げる.

-like /-láɪk/ COMB IN ADJ 形容詞の複合 **-like** combines with nouns to form adjectives which describe something as being similar to the thing referred to by the noun. 「〜のような」という意の形容詞を作る ❑ *...beautiful purple-red petunia-like flowers.* 美しい赤紫のペチュニアのような花 ❑ *...a tiny worm-like creature.* とても小さなミミズのような生物

like|able /laɪkəbᵊl/ → see **likable**

like|li|hood /laɪklihʊd/ **1** N-UNCOUNT 不可算名詞 The **likelihood of** something happening is how likely it is to happen. 可能性，見込み □ The likelihood of infection is minimal. 感染の可能性は極めて低い． **2** N-SING 単数名詞 If something is a **likelihood**, it is likely to happen. 有望さ，ありそうなこと □ But the likelihood is that people would be willing to pay if they were certain that their money was going to a good cause. しかし人々の払う金が大義のために使われることが確かであれば喜んで支払いをする可能性が高い．

like|ly /laɪkli/ (**likelier, likeliest**) **1** ADJ 形容詞 You use **likely** to indicate that something is probably the case or will probably happen in a particular situation. ありそうな □ Experts say a "yes" vote is still the likely outcome. 専門家によると，まだ賛成派の勝利の可能性が高い． □ If this is your first baby, it's far more likely that you'll get to the hospital too early. 初めての出産の場合，病院に行くのが早すぎる可能性がずっと高い． ● ADV 副詞 **Likely** is also an adverb. 恐らく [ADV with cl/group] □ Profit will most likely have risen by about $25 million. 利益は恐らく約2500万ドル増加しているだろう． **2** ADJ 形容詞 If someone or something is **likely to** do a particular thing, they will very probably do it. (不定詞と共に用いて) ～しそうだ [v-link ADJ to-inf] □ In the meantime the war of nerves seems likely to continue. それまでは神経戦が続きそうに見える．

like-minded ADJ 形容詞 **Like-minded** people have similar opinions, ideas, attitudes, or interests. 同じ考えの，同好の □ ...the opportunity to mix with hundreds of like-minded people. 何百人もの同好の士と交わる機会

lik|en /laɪkən/ (**likens, likening, likened**) V-T 他動詞 If you **liken** one thing or person **to** another thing or person, you say that they are similar. たとえる □ She likens marriage to slavery. 彼女は結婚を奴隷制になぞらえている．

Word Link　　like ≈ similar : alike, childlike, likeness

like|ness /laɪknɪs/ (**likenesses**) **1** N-SING 単数名詞 If two things or people have a **likeness** to each other, they are similar to each other. 類似 □ These myths have a startling likeness to one another. これらの神話は互いに驚くほど共通点が多い． **2** N-COUNT 可算名詞 A **likeness** of someone is a picture or sculpture of them. 肖像 □ The museum displays wax likenesses of every U.S. president. その美術館には歴代米国大統領全員のろう人形が展示されている． **3** N-COUNT 可算名詞 If you say that a picture of someone is a good **likeness**, you mean that it looks just like them. 外見が似たもの □ She says the artist's impression is an excellent likeness of her abductor. 彼女によると，その絵描きの描いたものが彼女の誘拐犯にそっくりだと言う．

Word Link　　wise ≈ in the direction or manner of : clockwise, likewise, otherwise

like|wise /laɪkwaɪz/ **1** ADV 副詞 You use **likewise** when you are comparing two methods, states, or situations and saying that they are similar. 同様に □ What is fair for homeowners likewise should be fair to businesses. 自宅所有者にとって公平なことは企業にとっても同様に公平であるべきだ． **2** ADV 副詞 If you do something and someone else does **likewise**, they do the same or a similar thing. 同じように [ADV after v] □ He lent money, made donations and encouraged others to do likewise. 彼は金を貸し，寄付をし，そしてほかの人にも同じことをするよう勧めた．

lik|ing /laɪkɪŋ/ **1** N-SING 単数名詞 If you have a **liking for** something or someone, you like them. 好き □ She had a liking for good clothes. 彼女はいい服がすきだった． □ He bought me CDs to encourage my liking for music. 彼は音楽に対する興味を伸ばすように私にCDを買ってくれた． **2** PHRASE 句 If something is, for example, too fast **for** your **liking**, you would prefer it to be slower. If it is not fast enough **for** your **liking**, you would prefer it to be faster. ～の好みには早すぎる；～の好みには遅すぎる □ He had become too powerful for their liking. 彼は強力になりすぎて彼らの好みに合わなくなった． **3** PHRASE 句 If something is **to** your **liking**, it suits your interests, tastes, or wishes. 好みに合って □ London was more to his liking than Rome. ロンドンはローマよりも彼の好みに合っていた．

li|lac /laɪlək, -læk, -lək/ (**lilacs**)

Lilac can also be used as the plural form.

Lilac は複数形としても使える．

1 N-VAR 可変性名詞 A **lilac** or a **lilac tree** is a small tree which has sweet-smelling purple, pink, or white flowers in large, cone-shaped groups. ライラック □ Lilacs grew against the side wall. ライラックが側壁に寄りかかって咲いていた． **2** COLOR 色彩語 Something that is **lilac** is pale pinkish-purple in color. 薄紫色の □ All shades of mauve, lilac, lavender and purple were fashionable. ふじ色，ライラック色，ラベンダー色，紫色のすべての色が流行していた．

lily /lɪli/ (**lilies**) N-VAR 可変性名詞 A **lily** is a plant with large flowers that are often white. ユリ

limb /lɪm/ (**limbs**) **1** N-COUNT 可算名詞 Your **limbs** are your arms and legs. 手足 □ She would be able to stretch her cramped limbs and rest for a few hours. 彼女は引きつった手足を伸ばして，数時間休憩することができるだろう． **2** PHRASE 句 If someone goes **out on a limb**, they do something they strongly believe in even though it is risky or extreme, and is likely to fail or be criticized by other people. 危険を冒す □ They can see themselves going out on a limb, voting for a very controversial energy bill. 彼らは危険を冒すのを承知で，激しい論争になっているエネルギー法案に賛成投票をする．

→ see **mammal**

lim|bo /lɪmboʊ/ N-UNCOUNT 不可算名詞 If you say that someone or something is **in limbo**, you mean that they are in a situation where they seem to be caught between two stages and it is unclear what will happen next. 宙ぶらりんの状態 □ The negotiations have been in limbo since mid-December. 交渉は12月中旬以来どちらつかずの状態が続いている．

lime /laɪm/ (**limes**) **1** N-VAR 可変性名詞 A **lime** is a green fruit that tastes like a lemon. Limes grow on trees in tropical countries. ライム □ ...peeled slices of lime. 皮をむいてスライスしたライム **2** N-UNCOUNT 不可算名詞 **Lime** is a substance containing calcium. It is found in soil and water. 石灰 □ If your soil is very acidic, add lime. 土の酸度が強ければ石灰を加えなさい．

lime|light /laɪmlaɪt/ N-UNCOUNT 不可算名詞 If someone is in the **limelight**, a lot of attention is being paid to them, because they are famous or because they have done something very unusual or exciting. 脚光，注目 □ Tony has now been thrust into the limelight, with a high-profile job. トニーは話題の仕事に就き今や脚光を浴びることになった．

lime|stone /laɪmstoʊn/ (**limestones**) N-MASS 質量名詞 **Limestone** is a whitish-colored rock which is used for building and for making cement. 石灰岩 □ ...high limestone cliffs. 石灰岩の高い崖

lim|it /lɪmɪt/ (**limits, limiting, limited**) **1** N-COUNT 可算名詞 A **limit** is the greatest amount, extent, or degree of something that is possible. 限界，極限 □ Her love for him was being tested to its limits. 彼女の彼への愛は究極の試練を受けていた． □ There is no limit to how much fresh fruit you can eat in a day. 1日に新鮮な果物をどれだけ摂取してもかまわない． **2** N-COUNT 可算名詞 A **limit** of a particular kind is the largest or smallest amount of something such as time or money that is allowed because of a rule, law, or decision. 限度 □ The three month time limit will be up in mid-June. 3か月の期限が6月の中旬に切れる． **3** N-COUNT 可算名詞 The **limit** of an area is its boundary or edge. 境界，区域 □ ...the city limits of Baghdad. バグダッド市の市域 **4** N-PLURAL 複数名詞 The **limits** of a situation are the facts involved in it which make only some actions or results possible. 制限 □ She has to work within the limits of a fairly tight budget. 彼女はかなり厳しい予算の範囲内で働かなければならない． **5** V-T 他動詞 If you **limit** something, you prevent it from becoming greater than a particular amount or degree. 制限する，限定する □ He limited payments on the country's foreign debt. 彼は国家の対外債務支払いを制限した． **6** V-T 他動詞 If you **limit yourself** to something, or if someone or something **limits** you, the number of things that you have or do is reduced. 削減する □ Please limit letters to 125 words or less. 文字数を125語かそれ以下に制限してください． ● **lim|it|ing** ADJ 形容詞 制約的な □ The conditions laid down to me were not too limiting. 私に与えられた条件はそれほど制約的ではなかった． **7** V-T 他動詞 [usu passive] If something **is limited to** a particular place or group of people, it exists only in that place, or is had or done only by that group. 限る □ The protests were not limited to New York. 抗議活動があったのはニューヨークだけではなかった． **8** → see also **limited** **9** PHRASE 句 If an area or a place is **off limits**, you are not allowed to go there. 立ち入り禁止の □ A one-mile area around the wreck is still off limits. 難破船の周囲1マイル区域は依然として立ち入り禁止です．

Thesaurus　　**limit** また次を参照：

N.	ceiling, maximum **1**
	border, edge, extremity, perimeter **3**
V.	cap, check, confine, reduce, restrict **5**

Word Partnership　　**limit** は次の語句と使われる：

ADJ.	lower limit, upper limit **1** **2**
	legal limit **2**
PREP.	beyond the limit, over the limit **2**
N.	credit limit, term limit, time limit **2**
	limit the amount of something, limit benefits,
	limit damage, limit growth, limit the number of
	something, limit spending **5**

---

limi|ta|tion /lɪmɪteɪʃᵊn/ (**limitations**) **1** N-UNCOUNT 不可算名詞 The **limitation** of something is the act or process of controlling or reducing it. 制限，規制 □ All the talk had been about the limitation of nuclear weapons. 話題すべて核兵器制限に関するものだった． **2** N-VAR 可変性名詞 A **limitation on** something is

a rule or decision which prevents that thing from growing or extending beyond certain limits. 限度，制約 ❑ *...a limitation on the tax deductions for people who make more than $100,000 a year.* 年収が10万ドル以上の者に対する税控除の制限 **3** N-PLURAL 複数名詞 If you talk about the **limitations** of someone or something, you mean that they can only do some things and not others, or cannot do something very well. 限界，弱点 ❑ *I realized how possible it was to overcome your limitations, to achieve well beyond what you believe yourself capable of.* 弱点を乗り越えて，自分ができると思っている以上のことを達成するのがいかに可能であるか，ということに私は気づいた。**4** N-VAR 可変性名詞 A **limitation** is a fact or situation that allows only some actions and makes others impossible. 限界 ❑ *This drug has one important limitation. Its effects only last six hours.* この薬に重要な限界がある。効果があるのは6時間だけだ。

lim|it|ed /límɪtɪd/ **1** ADJ 形容詞 Something that is **limited** is not very great in amount, range, or degree. わずかな，限られた ❑ *They may only have a limited amount of time to get their points across.* 自分たちの論点を伝えるのに限られた時間しかない可能性がある。**2** ADJ 形容詞 A **limited** company is one whose owners are legally responsible for only a part of any money that it may owe if it goes bankrupt. 有限責任の [BRIT, CANADIAN 英国英語，カナダ英語 BUSINESS 実業] [AM incorporated 米国英語で incorporated]

lim|it|ed edi|tion (**limited editions**) N-COUNT 可算名詞 A **limited edition** is a work of art, such as a book which is only produced in very small numbers, so that each one will be valuable in the future. 限定版 ❑ *The limited edition of 300 copies was edited by Rebekah Scott.* 300冊の限定版はレベーカー・スコットによって編集された。

lim|it|less /límɪtlɪs/ ADJ 形容詞 If you describe something as **limitless**, you mean that there is or appears to be so much of it that it will never be exhausted. 無限の ❑ *...a cheap and potentially limitless supply of energy.* 低価格で無限の可能性があるエネルギーの供給

lim|ou|sine /líməzin/ (**limousines**) N-COUNT 可算名詞 A **limousine** is a large and very comfortable car. Limousines are usually driven by a chauffeur and often hired for important occasions. リムジン

limp /límp/ (**limps, limping, limped, limper, limpest**) **1** V-I 自動詞 If a person or animal **limps**, they walk with difficulty or in an uneven way because one of their legs or feet is hurt. 片足を引きずって歩く ❑ *I wasn't badly hurt, but I injured my thigh and had to limp.* 私は傷はひどくなかったが，太ももをけがして片足を引きずらなければならなかった。● N-COUNT 可算名詞 **Limp** is also a noun. 足を引きずること ❑ *A stiff knee following surgery forced her to walk with a limp.* 彼女は手術後にひざが痛み，足を引きずって歩かざるをえなかった。**2** V-I 自動詞 If you say that something such as an organization, process, or vehicle **limps along**, you mean that it continues slowly or with difficulty, for example because it has been weakened or damaged. もたつく，のろのろ進む ❑ *In recent years the newspaper had been limping along on limited resources.* 過去数年，その新聞社は限られた資力で苦闘してきた。**3** ADJ 形容詞 If you describe something as **limp**, you mean that it is soft or weak when it should be firm or strong. 柔和な，柔弱な ❑ *She was told to reject applicants with limp handshakes.* 彼女は，弱い握手で申込者を断るように言われました。● **limp|ly** ADV 副詞 [ADV with v] だらりと ❑ *Flags and bunting hung limply in the still, warm air.* 旗や吹き流しが静かな暖かい空中にだらりとぶら下がっていた。**4** ADJ 形容詞 If someone is **limp**, their body has no strength and is not moving, for example, because they are asleep or unconscious. ぐにゃっとした ❑ *He carried her limp body into the room and laid her on the bed.* 彼は彼女のぐにゃっとした体を部屋まで運び，ベッドに寝かせた。

---

line

❶ NOUN USES
❷ PHRASES
❸ VERB USES
❹ PHRASAL VERB

---

❶ line /láɪn/ (**lines**) **1** N-COUNT 可算名詞 A **line** is a long thin mark which is drawn or painted on a surface. 線 ❑ *Draw a line down that page's center.* あのページの中央から下に線を引きなさい。❑ *...a dotted line.* 点線 **2** N-COUNT 可算名詞 The **lines** on someone's skin, especially on their face, are long thin marks that appear there as they grow older. しわ ❑ *He has a large, generous face with deep lines.* 彼は深いしわのある大きくふくよかな顔をしている。**3** N-COUNT 可算名詞 A **line** of people or things is a number of them arranged one behind the other or side by side. 並び，列 ❑ *The sparse line of spectators noticed nothing unusual.* まばらな列に並んだ観客は異常には何も気付かなかった。**4** N-COUNT 可算名詞 A **line** of people or vehicles is a number of them that are waiting one behind another, for example, in order to buy something or to go in a particular direction. 行列，列 ❑ *Children clutching empty bowls form a line.* 空のわんを持った子供たちが1列に並ぶ。**5** N-COUNT

可算名詞 A **line** of a piece of writing is one of the rows of words, numbers, or other symbols in it. 行 ❑ *The next line should read: Five days, 23.5 hours.* 次の行は「5日間，23.5時間」と書いてあるはずだ。**6** N-COUNT 可算名詞 A **line** of a poem, song, or play is a group of words that are spoken or sung together. If an actor **learns** his or her **lines** for a play or film, they learn what they have to say. 行，せりふ ❑ *...a line from Shakespeare's Othello: "one that loved not wisely but too well."* シェークスピアの『オセロ』からのせりふ「賢明にではなかったが，あまりにも深く愛してしまった男」 ❑ *Every time I sing that line, I have to compete with that darn trombone!* あの行を歌うたびに，私はあのにっくきトロンボーンと競わなければならない。**7** N-VAR 可変性名詞 You can refer to a long piece of wire, string, or cable as a **line** when it is used for a particular purpose. ひも，コード ❑ *She put her washing on the line.* 彼女は洗濯物をロープに干した。❑ *...a piece of fishing-line.* 1本の釣り糸 **8** N-COUNT 可算名詞 A **line** is a connection which makes it possible for two people to speak to each other on the telephone. 電話線 ❑ *The telephone lines went dead.* 電話が不通になった。❑ *It's not a very good line. Shall we call you back Susan?* 電話が遠いようです。スーザン，こちらからかけ直しましょうか。**9** N-COUNT 可算名詞 You can use **line** to refer to a telephone number which you can call in order to get information or advice. テレフォンサービス ❑ *...the 24-hours information line.* 24時間対応の電話案内サービス **10** N-COUNT 可算名詞 A **line** is a route, especially a dangerous or secret one, along which people move or send messages or supplies. ルート ❑ *The North American continent's geography severely limited the lines of attack.* 北アメリカ大陸の地形により攻撃ルートが大幅に制限された。❑ *Negotiators say they're keeping communication lines open.* 交渉者たちは，連絡ルートは閉ざしてはいないと言っている。**11** N-COUNT 可算名詞 The **line** in which something or someone moves is the particular route that they take, especially when they keep moving straight ahead. 進行方向 ❑ *Walk in a straight line.* まっすぐに歩きなさい。**12** N-COUNT 可算名詞 A **line** is a particular route, involving the same stations, roads, or stops along which a train or bus service regularly operates. 路線 ❑ *They've got to ride all the way to the end of the line.* 彼らはこの路線の終点までずっと乗らなければならない。**13** N-COUNT 可算名詞 A railroad **line** consists of the pieces of metal and wood which form the track that the trains travel along. 線路 ❑ *Floods washed out much of the railroad line.* 洪水で線路の大部分が押し流された。**14** N-COUNT 可算名詞 A shipping, air, or bus **line** is a company which provides services for transporting people or goods by sea, air, or bus. 運輸会社 [BUSINESS 実業] ❑ *The Cunard shipping line came up with a clever slogan: "Getting there is half the fun..."* キュナード海運会社が「目的地への到着は喜びの半分」という思いつきのいいスローガンを考え出した。**15** N-COUNT 可算名詞 A state or county **line** is a boundary between two states or counties. 境界線 [AM 米国英語] ❑ *...the California state line.* カリフォルニア州の境界線 **16** N-COUNT 可算名詞 You can use **lines** to refer to the set of physical defenses or the soldiers that have been established along the boundary of an area occupied by an army. 戦線，前線 ❑ *Their unit was shelling the German lines only seven miles away.* その部隊はわずか7マイル先のドイツ軍の前線を砲撃していた。**17** N-COUNT 可算名詞 The particular **line** that a person has toward a problem is the attitude that they have toward it. For example, if someone takes a **hard line** on something, they have a firm strict policy which they refuse to change. 方針，姿勢 ❑ *Forty members of the governing Conservative party rebelled, voting against the government line.* 与党の保守党員40名が造反して政府方針に反対投票した。**18** N-COUNT 可算名詞 You can use **line** to refer to the way in which someone's thoughts or activities develop, particularly if it is logical. 考え方，方法 ❑ *Our discussion in the previous chapter continues this line of thinking.* 前章の論議はこの考え方を引き継いでいる。**19** N-PLURAL 複数名詞 If you say that something happens **along** particular **lines**, or **on** particular **lines**, you are giving a general summary or approximate account of what happens, which may not be correct in every detail. 概略，たぐい ❑ *There followed an assortment of praise for the coffee along the lines of "Hey, this coffee is fantastic!"* そのコーヒーに対して「このコーヒーはとってもおいしい！」というたぐいのさまざまな称賛が続いた。❑ *He'd said something on those lines already.* 彼は何かそのようなことをすでに言っていた。**20** N-PLURAL 複数名詞 If something is organized **on** particular **lines**, or **along** particular **lines**, it is organized according to that method or principle. 方針，主義 ❑ *...so-called autonomous republics based on ethnic lines.* 民族的方針に基づいたいわゆる自治共和国 **21** N-COUNT 可算名詞 Your **line** of business or work is the kind of work that you do. 職業，職種 [BUSINESS 実業] ❑ *So what was your father's line of business?* それでお父さんの職業は何でしたか。**22** N-COUNT 可算名詞 In a factory, a **line** is an arrangement of workers or machines where a product passes from one worker to another until it is finished. 流れ作業，生産ライン ❑ *...a production line capable of producing three different products.* 3種類の製品を製造できる生産ライン **23** N-COUNT 可算名詞 You can use **line** when you are referring to a number of people who are ranked according to status. 序列 ❑ *Nicholas Paul Patrick was seventh in the line of succession to the throne.* ニコラス・ポール・パトリックは王位継承順位第7位だった。**24** N-COUNT 可算名詞 A

particular **line of** people or things is a series of them that has existed over a period of time, when they have all been similar in some way, or done similar things. 系統 □ *We were part of a long line of artists.* 我々は代々芸術家の家系だ. ☑ → see also **bottom line, front line, picket line**
→ see fish, football, graph, mass production, mathematics, soccer, tennis, train

❷ **line** /laɪn/ (lines) **1** PHRASE 句 If you say that someone has **crossed the line** or has **stepped over the line**, you mean that they have behaved in a way that is considered unacceptable. 一線を越える □ *He has crossed the line, and it must stop.* 彼は一線を越えてしまったので、終わりにしなければならない. □ *Sometimes, I think the administration steps over the line when they make these kinds of accusations.* 時折、私は政府がこのような非難をするとき一線を越えると思う. **2** PHRASE 句 If you **draw the line at** a particular activity, you refuse to do it, because you disapprove of it or because it is more extreme than what you normally do. 断る □ *Letters have come from prisoners, declaring that they would draw the line at hitting an old lady.* 囚人たちから「自分たちは老婦人を殴るようなことはしない」と断言する手紙が届いた. **3** PHRASE 句 If you do something or if it happens to you **in the line of duty**, you do it or it happens as part of your regular work or as a result of it. 職務中に □ *More than 3,000 police officers were wounded in the line of duty last year.* 昨年3千人以上の警官が勤務中に負傷した. **4** PHRASE 句 If you refer to a method as **the first line of**, for example, defense or treatment, you mean that it is the first or most important method to be used in dealing with a problem. 最前線 □ *Residents have the responsibility of being the first line of defense against wildfires.* 住民は森林火災に対して防御の最前線たる責任がある. **5** PHRASE 句 If one object is **in line with** others, or moves **into line with** others, they are arranged in a line. You can also say that a number of objects are **in line** or move **into line**. 列を成して □ *The device itself was right under the vehicle, almost in line with the gear lever.* 装置自体は変速レバーとほぼ並んで車両の真下にあった. **6** PHRASE 句 If one thing is **in line with** another, or is brought **into line with** it, the first thing is, or becomes, similar to the second, especially in a way that has been planned or expected. 一致して □ *The structure of our schools is now broadly in line with the major countries of the world.* 我々の学校組織は今では世界の主要国と概して一致している. □ *This brings the law into line with most medical opinion.* これによりその法律がたいていの医学界の意見と一致するようになる. **7** PHRASE 句 If you **keep** someone **in line** or **bring** them **into line**, you make them obey you, or you make them behave in the way you want them to. 従順に □ *All this was just designed to frighten me and keep me in line.* これはすべて私を怖がらせ従順にさせるように仕組まれただけだ. **8** PHRASE 句 If a machine or piece of equipment comes **on line**, it starts operating. If it is **off line**, it is not operating. 作動中の □ *The new machine will go on line in June 2006.* 新しい機械は2006年6月に稼働する. **9** PHRASE 句 If you do something **on line**, you do it using a computer or a computer network. オンラインの、ネットワーク上の □ *They can order their requirements on line.* オンラインで必要品を注文できる. **10** → see also **online** **11** **to sign on the dotted line** → see **dotted**

❸ **line** /laɪn/ (lines, lining, lined) **1** V-T 他動詞 If people or things **line** a road, room, or other place, they are present in large numbers along its edges or sides. 並ぶ □ *Thousands of local people lined the streets and clapped as the procession went by.* 何千人もの地元の住人が通りに沿って並び、行列が通り過ぎるときに拍手した. **2** V-T 他動詞 If you **line** a wall, container, or other object, you put a layer of something such as leaves or paper on the inside surface of it in order to make it stronger, warmer, or cleaner. 裏をつける、内側を覆う □ *Line the basket with a bright checkered napkin just before adding the cookies.* バスケットの内側に明るいチェックのナプキンを敷いてからクッキーを入れなさい. **3** → see also **lining**

❹ **line** /laɪn/ (lines, lining, lined)
▸ **line up** **1** PHRASAL VERB 句動詞 If people **line up** or if you **line** them **up**, they move so that they are standing in a line. 並ぶ、並ばせる □ *The senior leaders lined up behind him in orderly rows.* 年配の首脳陣がきちんと列を組んで彼の後ろに並んだ. □ *The gym teachers lined us up against the cement walls.* 体操教師がコンクリートの壁の前で私たちを1列に並ばせた. **2** PHRASAL VERB 句動詞 If you **line** things **up**, you move them into a straight row. 並べる □ *I would line up my toys on this windowsill and play.* 私はおもちゃをこの窓枠に並べて遊んだものでした. **3** PHRASAL VERB 句動詞 If you **line** one thing **up with** another, or one thing **lines up with** another, the first thing is moved into its correct position in relation to the second. You can also say that two things **line up**, or **are lined up**. 配置を調整する □ *You have to line the car up with the ones beside you.* 横にある車に位置を合わせて駐車しなければなりません. □ *The plane circled twice, trying in vain to line up with the runway.* 飛行機は滑走路に合わせようと2回旋回したが失敗した. **4** PHRASAL VERB 句動詞 If you **line up** an event

or activity, you arrange for it to happen. If you **line** someone **up** for an event or activity, you arrange for them to be available for that event or activity. 手配する □ *She lined up executives, politicians and educators to serve on the board of directors.* 彼女は経営者、政治家、教育者が理事会に参加するよう手配した. **5** → see also **lineup**

lin|ear /lɪniər/ **1** ADJ 形容詞 A **linear** process or development is one in which something changes or progresses straight from one stage to another, and has a starting point and an ending point. 連続的な □ *...decisions that lead the story in various directions, rather than follow traditional linear storytelling.* 従来どおりの連続的な物語の運び方に従うよりも、むしろさまざまな方向にその物語を展開するという決定 **2** ADJ 形容詞 A **linear** shape or form consists of straight lines. 直線の □ *...the sharp, linear designs of the Seventies and Eighties.* 70年代と80年代の鋭い直線型のデザイン **3** ADJ 形容詞 **Linear** movement or force occurs in a straight line rather than in a curve. 直線的な □ *...linear movement toward a goal.* ゴールに向かう直線的な動き

line man|ag|er (**line managers**) N-COUNT 可算名詞 Your **line manager** is the person at work who is in charge of your department, group, or project. 部門の責任者、直属の上司 [mainly BRIT 主に英国英語 BUSINESS 実業] □ *I believe that my wife is having an affair with her line manager.* 私は妻が彼女の上司と浮気をしていると思う.

lin|en /lɪnɪn/ (**linens**) **1** N-MASS 質量名詞 **Linen** is a kind of cloth that is made from a plant called flax. It is used for making clothes and things such as tablecloths and sheets. リネン、亜麻布 □ *...a white linen suit.* 白いリネンのスーツ **2** N-UNCOUNT 不可算名詞 **Linen** is tablecloths, sheets, pillowcases, and similar things made of cloth that are used in the home. リネン製品 □ *...embroidered bed linen.* 刺しゅう入りのベッドリネン [also N in pl]

lin|er /laɪnər/ (**liners**) N-COUNT 可算名詞 A **liner** is a large ship in which people travel long distances, especially on vacation. 大型船 □ *...luxury ocean liners.* 大洋横断豪華客船
→ see **ship**

lines|man /laɪnzmən/ (**linesmen**) N-COUNT 可算名詞 A **linesman** is an official who assists the referee or umpire in games such as football and tennis by indicating when the ball goes over the lines around the edge of the field or court. 線審、ラインズマン

line|up /laɪnʌp/ (**lineups**) **1** N-COUNT 可算名詞 A **lineup** is a group of people or a series of things that have been gathered together to be part of a particular event. 陣容、ラインアップ □ *One player sure to be in the lineup is star midfielder Landon Donovan.* 出場が確実な選手はミッドフィールダーのスター選手、ランドン・ドノバンだ. **2** N-COUNT 可算名詞 At a **lineup**, a witness to a crime tries to identify the criminal from among a line of people. （面通しのための）容疑者の列 □ *He failed to identify Graham from photographs, but later picked him out of a police lineup.* 彼は写真からはグレアムを確認できなかったが、後ほど警察の面通しで彼を識別した.

lin|ger /lɪŋgər/ (**lingers, lingering, lingered**) **1** V-I 自動詞 When something such as a smell, feeling, or illness **lingers**, it continues to exist for a long time, often much longer than expected. いつまでも残る □ *The scent of her perfume lingered on in the room.* 彼女の香水の香りがいつまでも部屋に残っていた. □ *He was ashamed. That feeling lingered, and he was never comfortable in church after that.* 彼は恥ずかしいと思った. その感情はいつまでも残り、以来彼はいつでも気まずい思いをした. **2** V-I 自動詞 If you **linger** somewhere, you stay there for a longer time than is necessary, for example, because you are enjoying yourself. 長居する □ *Customers are welcome to linger over coffee until around midnight.* 客は真夜中ごろまでコーヒーを飲みながらゆっくりして構わない.

lin|ge|rie /lɑnʒərei, læn-/ N-UNCOUNT 不可算名詞 **Lingerie** is women's underwear and nightclothes. ランジェリー、婦人用下着類 □ *...a new range of lingerie.* ランジェリー新商品

lin|guist /lɪŋgwɪst/ (**linguists**) **1** N-COUNT 可算名詞 A **linguist** is someone who is good at speaking or learning foreign languages. 諸外国語に通じた人 □ *He had a scholarly air and was an accomplished linguist.* 彼は学者的な雰囲気があり博学だった. **2** N-COUNT 可算名詞 A **linguist** is someone who studies or teaches linguistics. 言語学者 □ *Many linguists have looked at language in this way.* このように言語を見る言語学者が多い.

lin|guis|tic /lɪŋgwɪstɪks/ (**linguistics**) **1** ADJ 形容詞 **Linguistic** abilities or ideas relate to language or linguistics. 言語の □ *...linguistic skills.* 言語技能 **2** N-UNCOUNT 不可算名詞 **Linguistics** is the study of the way in which language works. 言語学 □ *Modern linguistics emerged as a distinct field in the nineteenth century.* 現代の言語学は19世紀に新しい分野として台頭した.

lin|ing /laɪnɪŋ/ (**linings**) **1** N-VAR 可変名詞 The **lining** of something such as a piece of clothing or a curtain is a layer of cloth attached to the inside of it in order to make it thicker or warmer, or in order to make it hang better. 裏地、裏張り □ *...a padded satin jacket with quilted lining.* キルトの裏地がついた肩パッ

ド入りのしゅすの上着 ② N-COUNT 可算名詞 The **lining** of your stomach or other organ is a layer of tissue on the inside of it. 内壁 ❏...*a bacterium that attacks the lining of the stomach.* 胃の内壁を冒すバクテリア ③ → see also **line**

link /lɪŋk/ (**links, linking, linked**) ❶ N-COUNT 可算名詞 If there is a **link between** two things or situations, there is a relationship between them, for example, because one thing causes or affects the other. 関連, つながり ❏...*the link between smoking and lung cancer.* 喫煙と肺がんの関連性 ② V-T 他動詞 If someone or something **links** two things or situations, there is a relationship between them, for example, because one thing causes or affects the other. 関連させる ❏ *The U.N. Security Council has linked any lifting of sanctions to compliance with the ceasefire terms.* 国連安全保障理事会はいかなる制裁解除も停戦条件の遵守と関連付けている. ❏ *The study further strengthens the evidence linking smoking with early death.* その研究は喫煙を早期死亡と関連づける証拠をさらに裏付ける. ③ N-COUNT 可算名詞 A **link between** two things or places is a physical connection between them. 連結 ❏...*the railroad link between Boston and New York.* ボストンとニューヨークを結ぶ鉄道 ❏ *Drivers ran into a field of weeds at the state border, where no link with the neighboring state had yet been planned.* 運転者たちが州境の草むらに入れ込んでしまったが, そこはまだ隣の州との連結道路の建設が予定されていなかったのだ. ❹ V-T 他動詞 If two places or objects **are linked** or something **links** them, there is a physical connection between them. 連絡する, 連結する ❏...*the Rama Road, which links the capital, Managua, with the Caribbean coast.* 首都マナグア市をカリブ海岸と結ぶラーマ道路 ❏ *Seven miles of track were installed to link the hotel to the golf course.* ゴルフコースにホテルを連結するために7マイルの通路が付けられた. ❺ N-COUNT 可算名詞 A **link** between two people, organizations, or places is a friendly or business connection between them. 結びつき, 絆 ❏ *Kiev hopes to cement close links with Bonn.* キエフはボンとの連携を強化させたいと願っている. ❏ *In 1984 the long link between AC Cars and the Hurlock family was severed.* AC社とハーロック家の長年の連携が1984年に断絶した. ❻ N-COUNT 可算名詞 A **link** to another person or organization is something that allows you to communicate with them or have contact with them. 連絡手段 ❏ *She was my only link with the past.* 彼女は私を過去と結びつける唯一の人だった. ❏ *The Red Cross was created to provide a link between soldiers in battle and their families at home.* 赤十字は戦場の兵士と母国の家族との連絡手段の提供するために創設されました. ❼ V-T 他動詞 If you **link** one person or thing to another, you claim that there is a relationship or connection between them. つなぐ, 連結する ❏ *Criminologist Dr. Ann Jones has linked the crime to social circumstances.* 犯罪学者のアン・ジョーンズ博士はその犯罪と社会環境を関連付けた. ❏ *They've linked her with various men, including magnate Donald Trump.* 彼らは彼女を大事業家ドナルド・トランプを含むさまざまな男性と結びつけた. ❽ N-COUNT 可算名詞 In computing, a **link** is a connection between different documents, or between different parts of the same document, using hypertext. リンク ❏ *Available in English, French, German and Italian, it has links to other relevant tourism sites.* それは英語, フランス語, ドイツ語, イタリア版版の利用可能で, 他の関連した観光サイトへのリンクがある. ●V-T 他動詞 **Link** is also a verb. リンクする ❏ *Certainly, Andreessen didn't think up using hypertext to link Internet documents.* もちろん, アンドリーセンはハイパーテキストを使ってインターネットのページへリンクさせることを思いつかなかった. ❾ N-COUNT 可算名詞 A **link** is one of the rings in a chain. 環 ❏...*a chain of heavy gold links.* 重い金の鎖 ❿ V-T 他動詞 If you **link** one thing with another, you join them by putting one thing through the other. 結ぶ, つなぐ ❏ *She linked her arm through his.* 彼女は彼と腕を組んだ. ● PHRASE 句 If two or more people **link arms**, or if one person **links arms** with another, they stand next to each other, and each person puts their arm around the arm of the person next to them. 腕を組む ❏ *Use so slippery that some of the walkers linked arms and proceeded very carefully.* とても滑りやすかったので, 腕を組んで非常に慎重に進む歩行者たちもいた. ⓫ → see also **linkup**

▶ **link up** PHRASAL VERB 句動詞 ❶ If you **link up** with someone, you join them for a particular purpose. 同盟を結ぶ ❏ *They linked up with a series of local anti-nuclear and anti-apartheid groups.* 彼らはいくつかの地元の反核団体・反アパルトヘート団体と同盟を結んだ. ❷ PHRASAL VERB 句動詞 If one thing **is linked up to** another, the two things are connected to each other. つなげる, 接続する ❏ *The television screens of the next century will be linked up to an emerging world telecommunications grid.* 次世紀のテレビ画面は新興の世界遠距離通信網と接続されるだろう.

Word Partnership		*link* は次の語句と使われる:
ADJ.	**direct** link, **possible** link, **vital** link	❶ ③ ⑤ ❻
	strong/weak link	❶ ⑤ ❻
V.	**establish** a link, **find** a link	❶ ② ⑤ ❻
	attempt to link	② ❹ ❼ ❿
	click on a link	❽

link|up /lɪŋkʌp/ (**linkups**) ❶ N-COUNT 可算名詞 A **linkup** is a

connection between two machines or communication systems. 接続, 交信 ❏...*a live satellite linkup with Bonn.* ボンと衛星生中継 ❷ N-COUNT 可算名詞 A **linkup** is a relationship or partnership between two organizations. 提携 ❏...*new linkups between school and commerce.* 学校と商業との新しい提携

lion /laɪən/ (**lions**) N-COUNT 可算名詞 A **lion** is a large wild member of the cat family that is found in Africa. Lions have yellowish fur, and male lions have long hair on their head and neck. ライオン

lion's share N-SING 単数名詞 If a person, group, or project gets **the lion's share of** something, they get the largest part of it, leaving very little for other people. 大部分 ❏ *Military and nuclear research have received the lion's share of public funding.* 軍事研究および核研究が公的資金の大部分を受け取った.

lip /lɪp/ (**lips**) N-COUNT 可算名詞 Your **lips** are the two outer parts of the edge of your mouth. 唇 ❏ *Wade stuck the cigarette between his lips.* ウェイドはたばこを口にくわえた.
→ see **face**, **kiss**

lip|stick /lɪpstɪk/ (**lipsticks**) N-MASS 質量名詞 **Lipstick** is a colored substance in the form of a stick which women put on their lips. 口紅, リップスティック ❏ *She was wearing red lipstick.* 彼女は赤い口紅をしていた.
→ see **makeup**

li|queur /lɪkɜr, -kyʊər/ (**liqueurs**) N-MASS 質量名詞 A **liqueur** is a strong alcoholic drink with a sweet taste. You drink it after a meal. リキュール ❏...*liqueurs such as Grand Marnier and Kirsch.* グランマルニエやキルシュなどのリキュール

liq|uid /lɪkwɪd/ (**liquids**) ❶ N-MASS 質量名詞 A **liquid** is a substance which is not solid but which flows and can be poured, for example, water. 液体 ❏ *Drink plenty of liquid.* 十分に水分を取りなさい. ❏ *Boil for 20 minutes until the liquid has reduced by half.* 水分が半減するまで20分間煮込みなさい. ❷ ADJ 形容詞 A **liquid** substance is in the form of a liquid rather than being solid or a gas. 液体の, 液状の ❏ *Wash in warm water with liquid detergent.* 液体洗剤を入れたお湯で洗いなさい. ❏ *The tanker was carrying liquid nitrogen.* そのタンカーは液体窒素を輸送していた. ❸ ADJ 形容詞 **Liquid** assets are the things that a person or company owns which can be quickly turned into cash if necessary. 流動性の [BUSINESS 実業] ❏ *The bank had sufficient liquid assets to continue operations.* その銀行には営業活動を続けるのに十分な流動資産があった.
→ see **matter**

liq|ui|date /lɪkwɪdeɪt/ (**liquidates, liquidating, liquidated**) ❶ V-T 他動詞 To **liquidate** a company is to close it down and sell all its assets, usually because it is in debt. 清算する, 解散する [BUSINESS 実業] ❏ *A unanimous vote was taken to liquidate the company.* 全会一致で会社を解散することが決定した. ● **liq|ui|da|tion** /lɪkwɪdeɪʃⁿn/ (**liquidations**) N-VAR 可変性名詞 清算, 整理 ❏ *The company went into liquidation.* その会社は倒産した. ❷ V-T 他動詞 If a company **liquidates** its assets, its property such as buildings or machinery is sold in order to get money. (会社が資産を) 整理する [BUSINESS 実業] ❏ *The company closed down operations and began liquidating its assets in January.* その会社は運営を停止し, 1月に資産の整理を開始した.

liq|ui|da|tor /lɪkwɪdeɪtər/ (**liquidators**) N-COUNT 可算名詞 A **liquidator** is a person who is responsible for settling the affairs of a company that is being liquidated. 精算人 [BUSINESS 実業] ❏...*the failed company's liquidators.* 破たんした会社の精算人

li|quid|ity /lɪkwɪdɪti/ N-UNCOUNT 不可算名詞 In finance, a company's **liquidity** is the amount of cash or liquid assets it has easily available. 換金性, 流動性 [BUSINESS 実業] ❏ *The company maintains a high degree of liquidity.* その会社は高い流動性を維持している.

liq|uid|iz|er /lɪkwɪdaɪzər/ (**liquidizers**) N-COUNT 可算名詞 A **liquidizer** is the same as a **blender**. ミキサー [BRIT 英国英語]

liq|uor /lɪkər/ (**liquors**) N-MASS 質量名詞 Strong alcoholic drinks such as whiskey, vodka, and gin can be referred to as **liquor**. 蒸留酒 [AM 米国英語] ❏ *The room was filled with cases of liquor.* 部屋は蒸留酒の箱でいっぱいだった.

liquor store (**liquor stores**) N-COUNT 可算名詞 A **liquor store** is a store which sells beer, wine, and other alcoholic drinks. 酒屋 [AM 米国英語]

list /lɪst/ (**lists, listing, listed**) ❶ N-COUNT 可算名詞 A **list** of things such as names or addresses is a set of them which all belong to a particular category, written down one below the other. リスト, 一覧 ❏ *We are making a list of the top ten men we would not want to be married to.* 結婚したくない男性トップ10のリストを作成しています. ❏ *There were six names on the list.* リストには6名の名前があった. ❷ → see also **hit list, mailing list, waiting list** ❸ N-COUNT 可算名詞 A **list** of things is a group of them that you think of as being in a particular order. リスト ❏ *High on the list of public demands is to end military control of broadcasting.* 国民の要求のリストの上位には放送の軍による支配の終結がある. ❏ *The criminal judicial system always*

comes up at the top of the list of voters' concerns in focus groups. 刑事司法制度は、常にフォーカスグループでの有権者の関心事のリストの冒頭に来る. **4** V-T 他動詞 To **list** several things such as reasons or names means to write or say them one after another, usually in a particular order. 一覧表にする，リストアップする □*The pupils were asked to list the sports they loved most and hated most.* 生徒は最も好きなスポーツと嫌いなスポーツをリストアップするように言われた. **5** V-T 他動詞 To **list** something in a particular way means to include it in that way in a list or report. 記載する □*A medical examiner has listed the deaths as homicides.* 検視官はそれらの死亡を殺人だと記載している. **6** V-T/V-I 他動詞/自動詞 If a company **is listed**, or if it **lists**, on a stock exchange, it obtains an official quotation for its shares so that people can buy and sell them. 上場する，株式公開をする [BUSINESS 実業] □*...a basket of blue chip stocks listed on the American Exchange.* 米国株式取引所に上場されている優良株のバスケット **7** → see also **listed company**

Word Partnership　list は次の語句と使われる:

ADJ.	**disabled** list, **injured** list **1**
	complete list, **long** list, **short** list **1 2**
V.	**add** *someone/something* **to a** list, list **includes**, **make a** list **1 2**
N.	list **of candidates**, list **of demands**, **guest** list, list **of ingredients**, list **of items**, list **of names**, **price** list, list **of questions**, **reading** list, list **of things**, **wine** list, **wish** list, list **of words** **1 2**

list|ed com|pa|ny (**listed companies**) N-COUNT 可算名詞 A **listed company** is a company whose shares are quoted on a stock exchange. 上場会社 [BUSINESS 実業] □*Some of Australia's largest listed companies are expected to announce huge interim earnings this week.* オーストラリアの大手上場会社の一部が今週莫大な利益の中間報告をする見込みだ.

lis|ten /lɪsˈn/ (**listens, listening, listened**) **1** V-I 自動詞 If you **listen** to someone who is talking or to a sound, you give your attention to them or it. 聞く □*He spent his time listening to the radio.* 彼はラジオを聴きながら時間を過ごした. ●**lis|ten|er** (**listeners**) N-COUNT 可算名詞 □*One or two listeners had fallen asleep while the president was speaking.* 大統領の演説中に聴衆の1人か2人が居眠りした. **2** V-I 自動詞 If you **listen for** a sound, you keep alert and are ready to hear it if it occurs. 耳を澄ます □*We listen for footsteps approaching.* 私たちは近づいてくる足音に耳を澄ます. **3** V-I 自動詞 If you **listen to** someone, you do what they advise you to do, or you believe them. 耳を貸す，聞き入れる □*Anne, you need to listen to me this time.* アン，今回は私の言うことを聞かないとだめよ. **4** CONVENTION 慣習表現 You say **listen** when you want someone to pay attention to you because you are going to say something important. ねえ，ちょっと □*Listen, I finish at one.* ねえ，私は1時に終わるよ.

Do not confuse **listen** and **hear**. If you want to say that someone is paying attention to something they can hear, you say that they **are listening to** it. □*He turned on the radio and listened to the news.* Note that **listen** is not followed directly by an object. You must always say that you listen **to** something. However, **listen** can also be used on its own without an object. □*I was laughing too much to listen.* You use **hear** to talk about sounds that you are aware of because they reach your ears. You often use **can** with **hear**. □*I can hear him yelling and swearing.*

▶ **listen in** PHRASAL VERB 句動詞 If you **listen in** to a private conversation, you secretly listen to it. 盗み聞きをする □*He assigned federal agents to listen in on Martin Luther King's phone calls.* 彼はマーティン・ルーサー・キングの電話を盗聴するために連邦捜査官を任命した.

Thesaurus　listen また次を参照:

V.	catch, pick up, tune in; (*ant.*) ignore **1**
	heed, mind **3**

Word Partnership　listen は次の語句と使われる:

V.	listen **to** *someone's* **voice 1**
	sit up and listen, **willing to** listen **1** – **3**
ADV.	listen **carefully**, listen **closely 1 2**

lis|ten|er /lɪsˈnər, lɪsnər/ (**listeners**) **1** N-COUNT 可算名詞 A **listener** is a person who listens to the radio or to a particular radio program. 聴取者，リスナー □*I'm a regular listener to her show.* 私はいつも彼女の番組を聴いています. **2** N-COUNT 可算名詞 If you describe someone as a good **listener**, you mean that they listen carefully and sympathetically to you when you talk, for example, about your problems. 聞き手，聞き役 □*Dr. Brian was a good listener.* ブライアン博士は聞き上手だった. **3** → see also **listen** → see **radio**

list|less /lɪstlɪs/ ADJ 形容詞 Someone who is **listless** has no energy or enthusiasm. やる気のない，無気力な □*He was listless and pale and wouldn't eat much.* 彼は青白くほとんど食べようとしなかった. ●**list|less|ly** ADV 副詞 [ADV with v] 無気力に □*Usually, you would just lie listlessly, too hot to do anything else.* ふだんは暑くて他に何もできないから，無気力に座っているだけだった.

list price (**list prices**) N-COUNT 可算名詞 The **list price** of an item is the price which the manufacturer suggests that a store should charge for it. 定価 □*...a small car with a list price of $18,000.* 定価1万8000ドルの小型車

lit /lɪt/ **Lit** is a past tense and past participle of **light**. light の過去・過去分詞

li|ter /liːtər/ (**liters**) N-COUNT 可算名詞 A **liter** is a metric unit of volume that is a thousand cubic centimeters. It is equal to 2.11 pints. リットル □*...a 13-thousand liter water tank.* 1万3000リットルの貯水槽 □*It is sold to the public at eight cents a liter.* 1リットル8セントで一般に販売されています.

lit|era|cy /lɪtərəsi/ N-UNCOUNT 不可算名詞 **Literacy** is the ability to read and write. 読み書き能力，識字 □*Many adults have problems with literacy and numeracy.* 読み書きや基礎的計算力で問題を抱えている成人が多い.

Word Link　liter ≈ letter : il**liter**ate, **liter**al, **liter**ature

lit|er|al /lɪtərəl/ **1** ADJ 形容詞 The **literal** sense of a word or phrase is its most basic sense. 文字どおりの □*In many cases, the people there are fighting, in a literal sense, for their homes.* 多くの場合，そこにいる人々は文字どおり家のために戦っている. **2** ADJ 形容詞 A **literal** translation is one in which you translate each word of the original work rather than giving the meaning of each expression or sentence using words that sound natural. 直訳の，逐語的な □*A literal translation of the name Tapies is "walls."* タピエスという名前の直訳は「壁」だ.

lit|er|al|ly /lɪtərəli/ **1** ADV 副詞 You can use **literally** to emphasize an exaggeration. Some careful speakers of English think that this use is incorrect. 全く，まさに [EMPHASIS 強調] □*We've got to get the economy under control or it will literally eat us up.* 我々は経済を何とか制御しないと，全く大変なことになるよ. **2** ADV 副詞 You use **literally** to emphasize that what you are saying is true, even though it seems exaggerated or surprising. 文字どおり [EMPHASIS 強調] □*Putting on an opera is a tremendous enterprise involving literally hundreds of people.* オペラを上演するのは文字どおり何百人もの人々を必要とする非常に大規模な企画だ. **3** ADV 副詞 If a word or expression is translated **literally**, its most simple or basic meaning is translated. 文字どおりに，逐語的に □*The word "volk" translates literally as "folk."* volk という語は直訳すると folk だ.

lit|er|ary /lɪtəreri/ **1** ADJ 形容詞 **Literary** means concerned with or connected with the writing, study, or appreciation of literature. 文学の，文学的な □*Her literary criticism focuses on the way great literature suggests ideas.* 彼女の文学批評は偉大な文学が着想を提示する仕方に集中している. □*She's the literary editor of the "Sunday Review."* 彼女は『サンデー・レビュー』の文芸編集者だ. **2** ADJ 形容詞 **Literary** words and expressions are often unusual in some way and are used to create a special effect in a piece of writing such as a poem, speech, or novel. 文語の □*...archaic, literary words from the Tang dynasty.* 唐王朝で使われた古くて文語的な単語 → see **book**

lit|er|ate /lɪtərɪt/ **1** ADJ 形容詞 Someone who is **literate** is able to read and write. 読み書きができる □*Over one-quarter of the adult population are not fully literate.* 成人人口の4分の1以上が十分に読み書きができない. **2** → see also **computer-literate**

lit|era|ture /lɪtərətʃər, -tʃʊr/ (**literatures**) **1** N-VAR 可変性名詞 Novels, plays, and poetry are referred to as **literature**, especially when they are considered to be good or important. 文学，文学作品 □*...classic works of literature.* 古典文学作品 □*I have spent my life getting to know diverse literatures of different epochs.* 私は生涯をかけて異なった時代の様々な文学作品を理解するようになった. **2** N-UNCOUNT 不可算名詞 The **literature** on a particular subject of study is all the books and articles that have been published about it. 文献 □*...the literature on immigration policy.* 移民政策に関する文献 **3** N-UNCOUNT 不可算名詞 **Literature** is written information produced by people who want to sell you something or give you advice. 印刷物，チラシ □*I am sending you literature from two other companies that provide a similar service.* よく似たサービスを提供する別の会社2社のパンフレットを郵送します. → see **genre**

liti|ga|tion /lɪtɪgeɪʃˈn/ N-UNCOUNT 不可算名詞 **Litigation** is the process of fighting or defending a case in a civil court of law. 訴訟 □*The settlement ends more than four years of litigation on behalf of the residents.* その和解により4年以上にわたり住民を代行して行われた訴訟が終結する.

li|tre /liːtər/ → see **liter**

lit|ter /lɪtər/ (**litters, littering, littered**) **1** N-UNCOUNT 不可算

名詞 **Litter** is garbage or trash that is left lying around outside. ごみ ❑ *If you see litter in the corridor, pick it up.* 廊下でごみを見かけたら，拾いなさい． **2** V-T 他動詞 If a number of things **litter** a place, they are scattered around it or over it. 散らかす ❑ *Glass from broken bottles litters the sidewalk.* 割れた瓶のガラスが歩道に散らばっていた． ●**lit|tered** ADJ 形容詞 [v-link ADJ prep] 散らかった ❑ *The entrance hall is littered with toys.* 玄関の広間はおもちゃで散らかっている． **3** ADJ 形容詞 If something is **littered with** things, it contains many examples of it. いっぱいである [v-link ADJ 'with' n] ❑ *History is littered with men and women spurred into achievement by a father's disregard.* 歴史は父親に無視されて偉業に駆り立てられた男性や女性が数多く登場する． **4** N-COUNT 可算名詞 A **litter** is a group of animals born to the same mother at the same time. ひと腹の子 ❑ *…a litter of pups.* ひと腹の子犬

Thesaurus	*litter* また次を参照:
N.	clutter, debris, garbage, trash **1**
V.	clutter, scatter, strew **2**

little

❶ DETERMINER, QUANTIFIER, AND ADVERB USES
❷ ADJECTIVE USES

❶ **lit|tle** /lɪtªl/ **1** DET 限定詞 You use **little** to indicate that there is only a very small amount of something. You can use "so," "too," and "very" in front of **little**. ほとんど〜ない ❑ *I had little money and little free time.* 私には金も暇もほとんどなかった． ❑ *I find that I need very little sleep these days.* このごろほとんど睡眠が必要でないことが分かった． ●QUANT 数量詞 **Little** is also a quantifier. ほとんど〜ない [QUANT 'of' def-n] ❑ *Little of the existing housing is of good enough quality.* 現存する住宅のほとんどが十分満足できる質ではない． ●PRON 代名詞 **Little** is also a pronoun. ほとんど〜ない ❑ *He ate little, and drank less.* 彼はほとんど食べず，さらに少ししか飲まなかった． ❑ *In general, employers do little to help the single working mother.* 一般的に，雇用主は働くシングルマザーの援助をほとんどしない． **2** ADV 副詞 **Little** means not very often or to only a small extent. ほとんど〜ない [ADV with v] ❑ *On their way back to Marseille they spoke very little.* マルセイユに戻る途中，彼らはほとんど口を利かなかった． **3** DET 限定詞 A **little** of something is a small amount of it, but not very much. You can also say **a very little**. 少しの ❑ *Mrs. Caan needs a little help getting her groceries home.* カーン夫人は食料品の買い物を家に運ぶのに少し手伝いが必要だ． ❑ *A little food would do us all some good.* 少し食事を取ればみんな多少体によいだろう． ●PRON 代名詞 **Little** is also a pronoun. 少し ❑ *They get paid for it. Not much.* 彼らはそれで手当てをもらっているんだ． たいした額じゃない．ほんの少しだ． ●QUANT 数量詞 **Little** is also a quantifier. 少し ❑ *Pour a little of the sauce over the chicken.* 鶏肉に少しソースをかけなさい． **4** ADV 副詞 If you do something **a little**, you do it for a short time. 少し ❑ *He walked a little by himself in the garden.* 彼は独りで庭を少し散歩した． **5** ADV 副詞 A **little** or **a little bit** means to a small extent or degree. 少し ❑ *He complained a little of a nagging pain between his shoulder blades.* 彼は肩甲骨の間のしつこい痛みを少し訴えた． ❑ *He was a little bit afraid of his father's reaction.* 彼は父親の反応を少し恐れていた．

> You can use the adjective **little** to talk about things that are small. ❑ *…a little house.* ❑ *…little children.* However, **little** is not normally used to emphasize or draw attention to the fact that something is small. For instance, you do not usually say "The town is little" or "I have a very little car," but you can say "**The town is small**" or "**I have a very small car.**" **Little** is a less precise word than **small**, and may be used to suggest the speaker's feelings or attitude toward the person or thing being described. For that reason, **little** is often used after another adjective. ❑ *What a nice little house you've got here!… Shut up, you horrible little boy!* **Little** and **a little** are both used as determiners in front of uncount nouns, but they do not have the same meaning. For example, if you say "**I have a little money**," this is a positive statement and you are saying that you have some money. However, if you say "**I have little money**," this is a negative statement and you are saying that you have almost no money.

❷ **lit|tle** /lɪtªl/ (littler, littlest)

> The comparative **littler** and the superlative **littlest** are sometimes used in spoken English for meanings **1**, **3**, and **4**, but otherwise the comparative and superlative forms of the adjective **little** are not used.

比較級の **littler** と最上級の **littlest** は時々口語英語で **1**，**3**，**4** の意味で使われるが，その他の点で形容詞 **little** の比較級形と最上級形は使われない．

1 ADJ 形容詞 **Little** things are small in size. **Little** is slightly more informal than **small**. 小さい ❑ *We sat around a little table, eating and drinking wine.* 私たちは小さいテーブルの周りに座って，食事をしてワインを飲んだ． **2** ADJ 形容詞 You use **little** to indicate that someone or something is small, in a pleasant and attractive way. 小さな，かわいい [ADJ n] ❑ *She's got the nicest little house not far from the library.* 彼女は図書館から遠くないところにとても素敵でかわいい家を持っている． ❑ *…a little old lady.* 小柄の老婦人 **3** ADJ 形容詞 Your **little** sister or brother is younger than you are.（自分の兄弟・姉妹で）年下の [ADJ n] ❑ *Whenever Daniel's little sister was asked to do something she always had a naughty reply.* ダニエルの妹は何かをするように言われるたびに，決まって反抗的な返事をした． **4** ADJ 形容詞 A **little** distance, period of time, or event is short in length. 短い，ちょっとの [ADJ n] ❑ *Why don't we just go down the road a little way, turn left, and cross the bridge.* その道をもう少しまっすぐ行って，左に曲がり橋を渡りなさい． ❑ *Why don't we just wait a little while and see what happens.* もう少しだけ待って様子を見たらどうでしょうか． **5** ADJ 形容詞 A **little** sound or gesture is quick. わずかな，素早い [ADJ n] ❑ *I had a little laugh to myself.* 私はふふっと1人笑いをした． **6** ADJ 形容詞 You use **little** to indicate that something is not serious or important. ささいな [ADJ n] ❑ *…irritating little habits.* 不愉快なちょっとした癖

Thesaurus	*little* また次を参照:
DET.	bit, dab, hint, touch, trace ❶ **1** **3**
ADJ.	miniature, petite, slight, small, young; (ant.) big ❷ **1** casual, insignificant, minor, small, unimportant; (ant.) important ❷ **6**

live

❶ VERB USES
❷ ADJECTIVE USES

❶ **live** /lɪv/ (lives, living, lived) ⇨ Please look at meaning **8** to see if the expression you are looking for is shown under another headword. **1** V-I 自動詞 If someone **lives** in a particular place or with a particular person, their home is in that place or with that person. 住む ❑ *She has lived here for 10 years.* 彼女はここに10年住んでいる． ❑ *Where do you live?* どちらにお住まいですか？ **2** V-T/V-I 他動詞／自動詞 If you say that someone **lives** in particular circumstances or that they **live** a particular kind of life, you mean that they are in those circumstances or that they have that kind of life. 生活する，暮らす ❑ *We lived quite grandly.* 私たちはけっこう派手な生活を送っていた． ❑ *Compared to people living only a few generations ago, we have greater opportunities to have a good time.* わずか数世代前の人たちの生活と比較して，私たちのほうが楽しく過ごす機会に恵まれている． **3** V-I 自動詞 If you say that someone **lives for** a particular thing, you mean that it is the most important thing in their life. 生きがいとする ❑ *He lived for his work.* 彼は自分の仕事が生きがいだった． **4** V-T/V-I 他動詞／自動詞 To **live** means to be alive. If someone **lives to** a particular age, they stay alive until they are that age. 生き延びる，生きる ❑ *He's got a terrible disease and will not live long.* 彼はひどい病気にかかってるから先は長くないだろう． ❑ *He lived to be 103.* 彼は103歳まで生きた． **5** V-I 自動詞 If people **live by** doing a particular activity, they get the money, food, or clothing they need by doing that activity. 生計を立てる，暮らす [no cont] ❑ *…the last indigenous people to live by hunting.* 狩猟生活をしている最後の原住民族． **6** → see also **living** **7** PHRASE 句 If you **live it up**, you have a very enjoyable and exciting time, for example by going to lots of parties or going out drinking with friends. 派手にやる，大いに楽しむ [INFORMAL くだけた] ❑ *There is no reason why you couldn't live it up once in a while.* たまには派手にやるのも悪くない． **8** to **live hand to mouth** → see **hand**

> When you are talking about someone's home, the verb **live** has a different meaning in the continuous tenses than it does in the simple tenses. For example, if you say "**I'm living in Boston**," this suggests that the situation is temporary and you may soon move to a different place. If you say "**I live in Boston**," this suggests that Boston is your permanent home.

▶ **live down** PHRASAL VERB 句動詞 If you are unable to **live down** a mistake, failure, or bad reputation, you are unable to make people forget about it. 〜をぬぐい去る，〜を償う ❑ *It was unable to live down its reputation as the party of high taxes.* 税金が高い政党という評判をぬぐい去ることはできなかった．

▶ **live off** PHRASAL VERB 句動詞 If you **live off** another person, you rely on them to provide you with money. 〜の厄介になる，〜を食い物にする ❑ *…a man who all his life had lived off his father.* 一生父親のすねをかじっていた男

▶ **live on** or **live off** **1** PHRASAL VERB 句動詞 If you **live on** or **live**

off a particular amount of money, you have that amount of money to buy things. 〜で生きてゆく，〜で生活してゆく □...*people trying to live on $100 a week.* 週100ドルで暮らそうとしている人たち． ◼ PHRASAL VERB 句動詞 If you **live on** or **live off** a particular source of income, that is where you get the money that you need. 〜で暮らす，〜で暮らす □*The proportion of Americans living on welfare rose.* 福祉に頼って暮らす米国人の割合が増えた． ◼ PHRASAL VERB 句動詞 If an animal **lives on** or **lives off** a particular food, this is the kind of food that it eats. 〜を常食とする □*The fish live on the plankton.* その魚はプランクトンを常食とする．

▶ **live on** PHRASAL VERB 句動詞 If someone **lives on**, they continue to be alive for a long time after a particular point in time or after a particular event. 生き永らえる，生き延びる □*I know my life has been cut short by this terrible virus but Daniel will live on after me.* このひどいウイルスのせいで私の人生は中途で終わるのがわかっているが，私が死んだ後もダニエルは生き続けるだろう．

▶ **live up to** PHRASAL VERB 句動詞 If someone or something **lives up to** what they were expected to be, they are as good as they were expected to be. 〜にこたえる □*Sales have not lived up to expectations this year.* 今年は期待したほど売り上げが良くない．

❷ **live** /laɪv/ ◼ ADJ 形容詞 **Live** animals or plants are alive, rather than being dead or artificial. 生きている，生きた [ADJ n] □...*a protest against the company's tests on live animals.* その会社の生きた動物を用いる実験に対する抗議． ◼ ADJ 形容詞 A **live** television or radio program is one in which an event or performance is broadcast at exactly the same time as it happens, rather than being recorded. 生中継の □*Murray was a guest on a live radio show.* マレーはラジオの生番組にゲストとして出た． □*They watch all the live matches.* 彼らは生中継の全試合を見る． ● ADV 副詞 **Live** is also an adverb. 生中継で [ADV after v] □*It was broadcast live in 50 countries.* それは50か国に生放送された． ◼ ADJ 形容詞 A **live** performance is given in front of an audience, rather than being recorded and then broadcast or shown in a movie. ライブの □*The Rainbow has not hosted live music since the end of 1981.* 1981年以来レインボーはライブの音楽イベントを主催していない． □*A live audience will pose the questions.* スタジオの観客がその質問をするでしょう． ● ADV 副詞 **Live** is also an adverb. ライブで [ADV after v] □*Kat Bjelland has been playing live with her new band.* キャット・ビーエランドは新しいバンドでライブ活動をしている． ◼ ADJ 形容詞 A **live** wire or piece of electrical equipment is directly connected to a source of electricity. 電気の流れている □*The plug broke, exposing live wires.* ソケットが壊れ，電線がむき出しになった． ◼ ADJ 形容詞 **Live** bullets are made of metal, rather than rubber or plastic, and are intended to kill people rather than injure them. 有効な，実の □*They trained in the jungle using live ammunition.* 彼らは実弾を使ってジャングルの中で訓練をした．

live-in /lɪv ɪn/ ◼ ADJ 形容詞 A **live-in** partner is someone who lives in the same house as the person they are having a sexual relationship with, but is not married to them. 同棲（どうせい）中の [ADJ n] □*She shared the apartment with her live-in partner.* 彼女は同棲（どうせい）中の相手とアパートを共用していた． ◼ ADJ 形容詞 A **live-in** servant or other domestic worker sleeps and eats in the house where they work. 住み込みの [ADJ n] □*I have a live-in nanny for my youngest daughter.* うちには1番下の娘の面倒を見る住み込みの乳母がいる．

live|li|hood /laɪvlihʊd/ (livelihoods) N-VAR 可変性名詞 Your **livelihood** is the job or other source of income that gives you the money to buy the things you need. 生計，暮らし □...*fishermen who depend on the seas for their livelihood.* 海で生計を立てる漁師たち．

live|ly /laɪvli/ (livelier, liveliest) ◼ ADJ 形容詞 You can describe someone as **lively** when they behave in an enthusiastic and cheerful way. 活発な □*She had a sweet, lively personality.* 彼女ははつらつとして陽気な気性の持ち主だった． ● **live|li|ness** N-UNCOUNT 不可算名詞 陽気さ □*Amy could sense his liveliness even from where she stood.* エイミーが立っているところからでさえ彼の陽気さは感じられた． ◼ ADJ 形容詞 A **lively** event or a **lively** discussion, for example, has lots of interesting and exciting things happening or being said in it. 活発な □*It turned out to be a very interesting session with a lively debate.* 活発な討論が交わされて，結局とても面白い会議となった． ● **live|li|ness** N-UNCOUNT 不可算名詞 活発さ，活気 □*Some may enjoy the liveliness of such a restaurant for a few hours a day or week.* 1日あるいは1週間に数時間ならこんなレストランのにぎやかさを楽しめる人もいるかもしれない． ◼ ADJ 形容詞 Someone who has a **lively** mind is intelligent and interested in a lot of different things. 鋭い □*She was a very well educated girl with a lively mind, a girl with*

ambition. 彼女は知性が鋭くとても教養のある，覇気に満ちた女の子だった．

liv|en /laɪvᵊn/ (livens, livening, livened)
▶ **liven up** ◼ PHRASAL VERB 句動詞 If a place or event **livens up**, or if something **livens it up**, it becomes more interesting and exciting. もっと陽気にする，もっと陽気になる □*How could we decorate the room to liven it up?* 部屋をもっと陽気な感じにするにはどんな室内装飾をしたらいいか． ◼ PHRASAL VERB 句動詞 If people **liven up**, or if something **livens them up**, they become more cheerful and energetic. もっと陽気にする，元気になる □*Talking about her daughters livens her up.* 彼女の娘のことを話していると彼女は元気になった．

liv|er /lɪvər/ (livers) ◼ N-COUNT 可算名詞 Your **liver** is a large organ in your body which processes your blood and helps to clean unwanted substances out of it. 肝臓 □*Three weeks ago, it was discovered the cancer had spread to his liver.* 3週間前に彼の肝臓にガンが移転しているのが見つかった． ◼ N-VAR 可変性名詞 **Liver** is the liver of some animals, especially lambs, pigs, and cows, which is cooked and eaten. 肝臓 □...*grilled calves' liver.* 子牛の肝臓の網焼き．
→ see **donor**

lives

Pronounced /laɪvz/ for meaning ◼, and /lɪvz/ for meaning ◼.

◼ の意味では /laɪvz/ と，◼ の意味では /lɪvz/ と発音される．

◼ **Lives** is the plural of **life**. lifeの複数形 ◼ **Lives** is the third person singular form of **live**. liveの三人称単数現在形

live|stock /laɪvstɒk/ N-UNCOUNT-COLL 集合的不可算名詞 Animals such as cattle and sheep which are kept on a farm are referred to as **livestock**. 家畜 □*The heavy rains and flooding killed scores of livestock.* 豪雨と洪水のため何十頭もの家畜が死んだ．

liv|id /lɪvɪd/ ADJ 形容詞 Someone who is **livid** is extremely angry. 激怒した [INFORMAL くだけた] □*I am absolutely livid about it.* 私はそれについてはまったく腹を立てている．

liv|ing /lɪvɪŋ/ (livings) ◼ N-COUNT 可算名詞 The work that you do for a **living** is the work that you do in order to earn the money that you need. 生計，生活の資 □*Father never talked about what he did for a living.* 父はどうやって生計を立てていたのかについては全く話題にしなかった． ◼ N-UNCOUNT 不可算名詞 You use **living** when you are talking about the quality of people's daily lives. 暮らし □*Olivia has always been a model of healthy living.* オリビアはいつも健康な暮らし方をしている見本のような人だ． ◼ ADJ 形容詞 You use **living** to talk about the places where people relax when they are not working. 生活の [ADJ n] □*The spacious living quarters were on the second floor.* 2階には広々とした住まいがあった．

living room (living rooms) also **living-room** N-COUNT 可算名詞 The **living room** in a house is the room where people sit and relax. 居間 □*We were sitting on the couch in the living room watching TV.* 私たちは居間のソファーに座ってテレビを見ていた．
→ see **house**

liz|ard /lɪzərd/ (lizards) N-COUNT 可算名詞 A **lizard** is a reptile with short legs and a long tail. トカゲ
→ see **desert**

load /loʊd/ (loads, loading, loaded) ◼ V-T 他動詞 If you **load** a vehicle or a container, you put a large quantity of things into it. 荷物を積む，どっさり載せる □*The three men seemed to have finished loading the truck.* その3人の男はトラックに荷物を積み終えたようだった． □*Mr. Dambar had loaded his plate with lasagne.* ダンバーさんは自分の皿にラザーニャを山盛りにした． ◼ N-COUNT 可算名詞 A **load** is something, usually a large quantity or heavy object, which is being carried. 積荷 □*He drove by with a big load of hay.* 彼は干し草をいっぱい車に積んで通り過ぎた． ◼ QUANT 数量詞 If you refer to a **load** of people or things or **loads of** them, you are emphasizing that there are a lot of them. どっさり，多数 [INFORMAL くだけた, EMPHASIS 強調] □*I've got loads of money.* 私は金がたっぷりある． □...*a load of kids.* たくさんの子供たち． ◼ V-T 他動詞 When someone **loads** a weapon such as a gun, they put a bullet or missile in it so that it is ready to use. 装填（そうてん）する □*I knew how to load and handle a gun.* 私は拳銃の装填（そうてん）のしかたと取り扱いを心得ていた． □*He carried a loaded gun.* 彼は弾を込めた拳銃を携行していた． ◼ V-T 他動詞 To **load** a camera or other piece of equipment means to put film, tape, or data into it so that it is ready to use. 入れる □*A photographer from the newspaper was loading his camera with film.* その新聞社のカメラマンはフイルムをカメラに入れているところだった． ◼ N-COUNT 可算名詞 You

can refer to the amount of work you have to do as a **load**. 負担 ☐ *She's taking some of the load off the secretaries.* 彼女は秘書たちの負担を減らしている. **7** N-COUNT 可算名詞 The **load** of a system or piece of equipment, especially a system supplying electricity or a computer, is the extent to which it is being used at a particular time. 負荷 ☐ *An efficient bulb may lighten the load of power stations.* 省エネの電球が発電所の負荷を減らすかもしれない. **8** N-SING 単数名詞 The **load on** something is the amount of weight that is pressing down on it or the amount of strain that it is under. 負荷 ☐ *Some of these chairs have flattened feet which spread the load on the ground.* これらの椅子の一部は地面にかかる重さを分散させるため脚を平たくしてある. **9** → see also **loaded** **10** **a load off** your mind → see **mind** → see **photography**

▶ **load down** PHRASAL VERB 句動詞 If you **load** someone **down** with things, especially heavy things, you give them a large number of them or put a large number of them on them. たくさん負わせる, たくさんあげる ☐ *She loaded me down with around a dozen cassettes.* 彼女は約1ダースのカセットをくれた. ☐ *They had come up from London loaded down with six suitcases.* 彼らはスーツケースを6つも持ってロンドンから北上してきた.

▶ **load up** PHRASAL VERB 句動詞 **Load up** means the same as **load**. 荷を積む ☐ *I've just loaded my truck up.* 私はちょうどトラックに荷物を積んだところだ. ☐ *The giggling couple loaded up their red sports car and drove off.* くすくす笑っている男女が赤いスポーツカーに荷物を積みこんで走り去った.

Thesaurus   *load* また次を参照:

V.	arrange, fill, pack, pile up, stack **1**
N.	bundle, cargo, freight, haul, shipment **2**

Word Partnership   *load* は次の語句と使われる:

N.	load **a truck 1**
ADJ.	**big** load, **full** load, **heavy** load **2 6**
V.	**carry** a load, **handle** a load, **lighten** a load, **take on** a load **2 6**

load|ed /loʊdɪd/ **1** ADJ 形容詞 A **loaded** question or word has more meaning or purpose than it appears to have, because the person who uses it hopes it will cause people to respond in a particular way. 含みのある ☐ *That's a loaded question.* それは含みのある質問ですね. **2** ADJ 形容詞 If something is **loaded with** a particular characteristic, it has that characteristic to a very great degree. たっぷり含んだ ☐ *The president's visit is loaded with symbolic significance.* 大統領の訪問は象徴的意義がたっぷり含まれている. **3** ADJ 形容詞 If a place or object is **loaded with** things, it has very many of them in it or it is full of them. たくさんある ☐ *...a tray loaded with cups.* カップがたくさん載っているお盆. ☐ *The second store you enter is loaded with jewelry.* 君たちが行く2番目の店には宝石が山のようにある. **4** ADJ 形容詞 If you say that something is **loaded in favor of** someone, you mean it works unfairly to their advantage. If you say it is **loaded against** them, you mean it works unfairly to their disadvantage. 偏った [DISAPPROVAL 不賛成] ☐ *The press is loaded in favor of this present government.* その新聞社は現政府に味方して偏向している. **5** ADJ 形容詞 If someone is **loaded**, they are intoxicated as a result of drinking alcohol or taking drugs. 酔っ払って [INFORMAL くだけた] ☐ *We gather as a group once or twice a year, for old times' sake, and get loaded.* 私たちは昔よしみで年に1回2回グループで集まって酔っ払う.

loaf /loʊf/ (**loaves, loafs, loafing, loafed**) **1** N-COUNT 可算名詞 A **loaf** of bread is bread which has been shaped and baked in one piece. It is usually large enough for more than one person and can be cut into slices. 斤, 塊 ☐ *...a loaf of crusty bread.* 皮の堅いパン1つ. **2** V-I 自動詞 If you **loaf**, you spend time in a lazy way, doing nothing in particular, especially when you should be working. ぶらつく, だらだらする ☐ *There were always a lot of men loafing in the shop.* その店にはいつもぶらついている男たちがたくさんいた.

loan /loʊn/ (**loans, loaning, loaned**) **1** N-COUNT 可算名詞 A **loan** is a sum of money that you borrow. 融資 ☐ *The country has no access to foreign loans or financial aid.* その国には海外からの融資や経済援助はありません. ☐ *The president wants to make it easier for small businesses to get bank loans.* 大統領は零細企業が銀行融資をもっと受けやすいようにしたいと思っている. **2** → see also **bridge loan, soft loan** **3** N-SING 単数名詞 If someone gives you a **loan of** something, you borrow it from them. 貸し出し, 借りること ☐ *I am in need of a loan of a bike for a few weeks.* 私は自転車を数週間借りる必要がある. **4** V-T 他動詞 If you **loan** something to someone, you lend it to them. 貸す ☐ *He had kindly offered to loan us all the plants required for the exhibit.* 親切にも彼は展示会に必要な植物をすべて私たちに貸してもいいと申し出てくれた. ● PHRASAL VERB 句動詞 **Loan out** means the same as **loan**. 貸し出す ☐ *It is common practice for clubs to loan out players to sides in the lower divisions.* クラブが選手を下位のリーグのチームに貸し出すのはよくあることだ. **5** PHRASE 句 If something is **on loan**, it has been borrowed. 貸し出し中の

☐ *...impressionist paintings on loan from the National Gallery.* 国立美術館から貸し出し中の印象派の絵画. → see **bank, interest rate**

Word Partnership   *loan* は次の語句と使われる:

N.	loan **agreement**, loan **application**, **bank** loan, **home** loan, **interest on a** loan, **mortgage** loan, loan **payment/repayment**, **savings and** loan, **student** loan **1**
V.	**apply for a** loan, **get/receive a** loan, **make a** loan, **pay off** a loan, **repay a** loan **1**

loath /loʊθ/ also **loth** ADJ 形容詞 If you are **loath to** do something, you do not want to do it. いやがって, 嫌って [V-LINK ADJ to-inf] ☐ *Sensing he held the advantage, Mr. Danbar was loath to change the subject.* 自分が優位に立っていると感じて, ダンバー氏は話題を変えるのをいやがった.

loathe /loʊð/ (**loathes, loathing, loathed**) V-T 他動詞 If you **loathe** something or someone, you dislike them very much. ひどく嫌う ☐ *The two men loathe each other.* その2人の男たちはお互いにひどく嫌っている.

loath|ing /loʊðɪŋ/ N-UNCOUNT 不可算名詞 **Loathing** is a feeling of great dislike and disgust. 大嫌い ☐ *She looked at him with loathing.* 彼女はとてもいやそうに彼を見た.

loaves /loʊvz/ **Loaves** is the plural of **loaf**. loafの複数形

lob|by /lɒbi/ (**lobbies, lobbying, lobbied**) **1** V-T/V-I 他動詞/自動詞 If you **lobby** someone such as a member of a government or council, you try to persuade them that a particular law should be changed or that a particular thing should be done. 働きかける, 圧力をかける ☐ *The Wilderness Society lobbied Congress to authorize the Endangered Species Act.* 原野協会は絶滅危惧種法を認可するように議会に働きかけた. **2** N-COUNT 可算名詞 A **lobby** is a group of people who represent a particular organization or campaign, and try to persuade a government or council to help or support them. 圧力団体 ☐ *Agricultural interests are some of the most powerful lobbies in Washington.* 農業関係業者たちはワシントンで最も力のある圧力団体の中に含まれている. **3** N-COUNT 可算名詞 In a hotel or other large building, the **lobby** is the area near the entrance that usually has corridors and staircases leading off it. ロビー ☐ *I met her in the lobby of the museum.* 私は彼女と美術館のロビーで会った.

lob|ster /lɒbstər/ (**lobsters**) N-VAR 可変性名詞 A **lobster** is a sea creature that has a hard shell, two large claws, and eight legs. ロブスター, ウミザリガニ ☐ *She sold me a couple of live lobsters.* 彼女は私に生きているロブスターを2匹売ってくれた. ● N-UNCOUNT 不可算名詞 **Lobster** is the flesh of a lobster eaten as food. ロブスターの身 ☐ *...lobster on a bed of fresh vegetables.* 生野菜の上に載っているロブスター

lo|cal /loʊkəl/ (**locals**) **1** ADJ 形容詞 **Local** means existing in or belonging to the area where you live, or to the area that you are talking about. 地元の [ADJ n] ☐ *We'd better check on the game in the local paper.* 地元の新聞でその試合について調べたほうがいいだろう. ☐ *Some local residents joined the students' protest.* 地元の住民の中には学生の抗議集会に参加した人もいる. ● N-COUNT 可算名詞 The **locals** are local people. 地元の人々 ☐ *Camping is a great way to meet the locals as the Portuguese themselves are enthusiastic campers.* ポルトガル人はキャンプするのがとても好きなので, キャンプ生活は地元の人たちと知り合うのもいい方法だ. ● **lo|cal|ly** ADV 副詞 地元で ☐ *We've got cards which are drawn and printed and designed by someone locally.* 地元の人が描いた絵を印刷・デザインしたカードがあります. **2** ADJ 形容詞 **Local** government is elected by people in one area of a country and controls aspects such as education, housing, and transportation within that area. 地方の ☐ *Education comprises two-thirds of all local government spending.* 教育は地方自治体の総支出の3分の2を占める. **3** ADJ 形容詞 A **local** anesthetic or condition affects only a small part of your body. 局所の [MEDICAL 医学の] ☐ *The procedure was done under local anesthetic in the physician's office.* その処置はその医師の医院で局所麻酔で行われた.

Thesaurus   *local* また次を参照:

ADJ.	neighboring, regional **1**

Word Partnership   *local* は次の語句と使われる:

N.	local **area**, local **artist**, local **business**, local **community**, local **customs**, local **group**, local **hospital**, local **library**, local **news**, local **newspaper**, local **office**, local **people**, local **phone call**, local **residents**, local **restaurant**, local **store 1** local **government**, local **officials**, local **police**, local **politicians**, local **politics 2**

lo|cal area net|work (**local area networks**) N-COUNT 可算名詞 A **local area network** is a group of computers and

associated equipment that are linked by cable, for example, in an office building, and that share a communications line. The abbreviation **LAN** is also used. ローカル・エリア・ネットワーク、ラン [COMPUTING コンピューティング] ❏ *Users can easily move files between PCs connected by local area networks or the Internet.* ユーザーはローカル・エリア・ネットワークかインターネットに接続しているPC間でファイルを簡単に移動することができる。

lo|cal author|ity (local authorities) N-COUNT 可算名詞 A **local authority** is the same as a **local government**. 地方自治体

lo|cal gov|ern|ment (local governments) **1** N-UNCOUNT 不可算名詞 **Local government** is the system of electing representatives to be responsible for the administration of public services and facilities in a particular area. 地方政治 ❏ *...careers in local government.* 地方政治での経歴 **2** N-COUNT 可算名詞 A **local government** is an organization that is officially responsible for all the public services and facilities in a particular area. 地方自治体 [AM 米国英語]

lo|cal|ity /loʊkælɪti/ (localities) N-COUNT 可算名詞 A **locality** is a small area of a country or city. 地方 [FORMAL 形式ばった] ❏ *Following the discovery of the explosives the president canceled his visit to the locality.* 爆発物が発見された後で大統領はその地方の訪問を中止した。

lo|cate /loʊkeɪt/ (locates, locating, located) **1** V-T 他動詞 If you **locate** something or someone, you find out where they are. 位置を突き止める [FORMAL 形式ばった] ❏ *The scientists want to locate the position of the gene on a chromosome.* 科学者たちはその遺伝子の染色体上に占める位置を確認したいと思っている。 **2** V-T 他動詞 If you **locate** something in a particular place, you put it there or build it there. 設置する、配置する [FORMAL 形式ばった] ❏ *Atlanta was voted the best city in which to locate a business by more than 400 chief executives.* 400人以上の最高経営責任者たちがアトランタ市を会社を設置するのに最も適した都市だと認めた。 **3** V-I 自動詞 If you **locate** in a particular place, you move there or open a business there. 構える、位置する [mainly AM 主に米国英語 BUSINESS 実業] ❏ *...tax breaks for businesses that locate in run-down neighborhoods.* 荒廃した地域に位置する企業の税政優遇措置。

lo|cat|ed /loʊkeɪtɪd/ ADJ 形容詞 If something is **located** in a particular place, it is present or has been built there. 位置して [FORMAL 形式ばった] [v-link ADJ prep, adv ADJ] ❏ *A boutique and beauty salon are conveniently located within the grounds.* ブティックと美容院が好都合にも敷地の中にある。

lo|ca|tion /loʊkeɪʃᵊn/ (locations) **1** N-COUNT 可算名詞 A **location** is the place where something happens or is situated. 位置、場所 ❏ *The first thing he looked at was his office's location.* まず最初に彼が確かめたのは自分の事務所の場所だった。 **2** N-COUNT 可算名詞 The **location** of someone or something is their exact position. 位置、場所 ❏ *She knew the exact location of The Eagle's headquarters.* 彼女はイーグルの本部のある正確な場所を知っていた。 **3** N-VAR 可変性名詞 A **location** is a place away from a studio where a movie or part of a movie is made. ロケ地 ❏ *...an art movie with dozens of exotic locations.* 異国風のロケ地がたくさんある芸術映画。

Word Partnership   *location* は次の語句と使われる:

| ADJ. | **central** location, **convenient** location, **secret** location **1** **exact** location, **geographic** location, **present** location, **specific** location **2** |
| V. | **pinpoint** a location **1 2** |

---

loch /lɒx, lɒk/ (lochs) N-COUNT 可算名詞 A **loch** is a large area of water in Scotland that is completely or almost completely surrounded by land. 湖 ❏ *...twenty miles north of Loch Ness.* ネス湖から20マイル北。

lock /lɒk/ (locks, locking, locked) **1** V-T 他動詞 When you **lock** something such as a door, drawer, or case, you fasten it, usually with a key, so that other people cannot open it. 錠を下ろす ❏ *Are you sure you locked the front door?* 玄関の錠は確かにかけたの? **2** N-COUNT 可算名詞 The **lock** on something such as a door or a drawer is the device which is used to keep it shut and prevent other people from opening it. Locks are opened with a key. 錠 ❏ *At that moment he heard Gill's key turning in the lock of the door.* その時彼はジルがドアの錠で鍵を回している音を聞いた。 **3** V-T 他動詞 If you **lock** something or someone in a place, room, or container, you put them there and fasten the lock. しまいこむ ❏ *Her maid locked the case in the safe.* 彼女の家政婦はそのケースを金庫にしまった。 **4** V-T/V-I 他動詞/自動詞 If you **lock** something in a particular position, or if it locks there, it is held or fitted firmly in that position. しっかり組み合わせる ❏ *He leaned back in the swivel chair and locked his fingers behind his head.* 彼は回転椅子の背にもたれて指を頭の後ろで組んだ。 **5** N-COUNT 可算名詞 On a canal or river, a **lock** is a place where walls have been built with gates at each end so that boats can move to a higher or lower section of the canal or river, by gradually changing the water level inside the gates. 閘

門(こうもん)❏ *As the lock filled, the ducklings rejoined their mother to wait for another vessel to go through.* 閘門(こうもん)がいっぱいになると、アヒルの子供たちは母親と再び一緒になって次の船が通り過ぎるのを待った。 **6** N-COUNT 可算名詞 A **lock** of hair is a small bunch of hairs on your head that grow together and curl or curve in the same direction. 房 ❏ *She brushed a lock of hair off his forehead.* 彼女は彼の額からひと房の髪を払いのけた。

▶ **lock away** **1** PHRASAL VERB 句動詞 If you **lock** something **away** in a place or container, you put or hide it there and fasten the lock. しまい込む ❏ *She meticulously cleaned the gun and locked it away in its case.* 彼女は細心の注意を払って拳銃の手入れをし、ケースに鍵をかけてしまった。 **2** PHRASAL VERB 句動詞 To **lock** someone **away** means to put them in prison or a secure psychiatric hospital. 閉じ込める、監禁する ❏ *Locking them away is not sufficient, you have to give them treatment.* 彼らは閉じ込めておくだけでは不十分で、治療する必要がある。

▶ **lock out** **1** PHRASAL VERB 句動詞 If someone **locks** you **out** of a place, they prevent you entering it by locking the doors. 閉め出す ❏ *His wife locked him out of their bedroom after the argument.* 口論のあとで彼の妻は彼を寝室から閉め出した。 **2** PHRASAL VERB 句動詞 In an industrial dispute, if a company **locks** its workers **out**, it closes the factory or office in order to prevent the employees coming to work. 締め出す [BUSINESS 実業] ❏ *The company locked out the workers, and then the rest of the work force went on strike.* 会社はその労働者たちを締め出し、その後、他の労働者たちはストに入った。

▶ **lock up** **1** PHRASAL VERB 句動詞 If you **lock** something **up** in a place or container, you put or hide it there and fasten the lock. しまい込む ❏ *Give away any food you have on hand, or lock it up and give the key to the neighbors.* 手元にある食料品は全部譲ってしまうか、しまい込んで鍵を近所の人に渡しなさい。 **2** PHRASAL VERB 句動詞 To **lock** someone **up** means to put them in prison or a secure psychiatric hospital. 監禁する、閉じ込める ❏ *Mr. Milner persuaded the federal prosecutors not to lock up his client.* ミルナーさんは彼の依頼人を監禁しないように連邦検察官を説得した。 **3** PHRASAL VERB 句動詞 When you **lock up** a building or car or **lock up**, you make sure that all the doors and windows are locked so that nobody can get in. 戸締りをする、ロックする ❏ *Don't forget to lock up.* 戸締りを忘れないように。

Word Partnership   *lock* は次の語句と使われる:

| N. | **lock** a **car**, **lock** a **door**, **lock** a **room** **1** **combination** lock, **door** lock, **lock and key**, **key** in a lock **2** |
| V. | **change** a lock, **open** a lock, **pick** a lock **2** |

---

lock|er /lɒkər/ (lockers) N-COUNT 可算名詞 A **locker** is a small metal or wooden cabinet with a lock, where you can put your personal possessions, for example in a school, place of work, or sports club. ロッカー

lock|out (lockouts) N-COUNT 可算名詞 A **lockout** is a situation in which employers close a place of work and prevent workers from entering it until the workers accept the employer's new proposals on pay or conditions of work. 工場締め出し、工場閉鎖 [BUSINESS 実業] ❏ *The lockout could resume if no new contract agreement is signed.* 新しい契約合意に調印がされないと再び労働者締め出しとなる可能性がある。

lo|cust /loʊkəst/ (locusts) N-COUNT 可算名詞 **Locusts** are large insects, similar to grasshoppers, that live mainly in hot areas and often cause serious damage to crops. バッタ、イナゴ ❏ *...a swarm of locusts.* イナゴの群れ。

lodge /lɒdʒ/ (lodges, lodging, lodged) **1** N-COUNT 可算名詞 A **lodge** is a house or hotel in the country or in the mountains where people stay on vacation, especially when they want to hunt or fish. 山荘、小屋 ❏ *...a Victorian hunting lodge.* ビクトリア朝時代の狩猟小屋。 **2** N-COUNT 可算名詞 A **lodge** is a small house at the entrance to the grounds of a large house. 小屋 ❏ *I drove out of the gates, past the keeper's lodge.* 私は自動車で管理人の小屋の前を通り過ぎて門を出た。 **3** V-T 他動詞 If you **lodge** a complaint, protest, accusation, or claim, you officially make it. 提出する、申し出る ❏ *He has four weeks in which to lodge an appeal.* 彼には4週間の上訴提起期間がある。 **4** V-T/V-I 他動詞/自動詞 If you **lodge** somewhere, such as in someone else's house or if you **are lodged** there, you live there, usually paying rent. 下宿する ❏ *...the story of the farming family she lodged with as a young teacher.* 彼女が若い教師の時に下宿した農家の話。 **5** V-I 自動詞 If an object **lodges** somewhere, it becomes stuck there. とどまる、突き刺さる ❏ *The bullet lodged in the sergeant's leg, shattering his thigh bone.* 弾丸は巡査部長の太い骨を粉砕して足の中にとどまっていた。 **6** → see also **lodging**

Word Partnership   *lodge* は次の語句と使われる:

| N. | **country** lodge, **hunting** lodge, **ski** lodge **1** |

---

lodg|er /lɒdʒər/ (lodgers) N-COUNT 可算名詞 A **lodger** is a

person who pays money to live in someone else's house. 下宿人 ❑Jennie took in a lodger to help with the mortgage. ジェニーは住宅ローン返済の助けになるように下宿人を置いた.

lodg|ing /lɒdʒɪŋ/ (**lodgings**) N-UNCOUNT 不可算名詞 If you are provided with **lodging** or **lodgings**, you are provided with a place to stay for a period of time. You can use **lodgings** to refer to one or more of these places. 宿, 宿泊場所 [also N in pl] ❑He was given free lodging. 彼は無料の宿を与えられた.

loft /lɒft/ (**lofts**) **1** N-COUNT 可算名詞 A **loft** is the space inside the sloping roof of a house or other building, where things are sometimes stored. 屋根裏 ❑A loft conversion can add considerably to the value of a house. 屋根裏を改造することにより家の価値をかなり上げることができる. **2** N-COUNT 可算名詞 A **loft** is an apartment in the upper part of a building, especially a building such as a warehouse or factory that has been converted for people to live in. Lofts are usually large and not divided into separate rooms. 上階, ロフト ❑...Andy Warhol's New York loft. アンディー・ウォーフォールのニューヨークのロフト.

lofty /lɒfti/ (**loftier, loftiest**) **1** ADJ 形容詞 A **lofty** ideal or ambition is noble, important, and admirable. 高尚な ❑It was a bank that started out with grand ideas and lofty ideals. それは立派な理念や崇高な理想を持って始まった銀行でした. **2** ADJ 形容詞 A **lofty** building or room is very high. 非常に高い [FORMAL 形式ばった] ❑...a light, lofty apartment in the suburbs of Salzburg. ザルツブルグの郊外にある明るくて非常に天井の高いアパート. **3** ADJ 形容詞 If you say that someone behaves in a **lofty** way, you are critical of them for behaving in a proud and somewhat overbearing way, as if they think they are very important. 高慢な [DISAPPROVAL 不賛成] ❑...the lofty disdain he often expresses for his profession. 彼が自らの職業に対してしばしば示すごうまんな侮蔑 (ぶべつ)

log /lɒg/ (**logs, logging, logged**) **1** N-COUNT 可算名詞 A **log** is a piece of a thick branch or of the trunk of a tree that has been cut so that it can be used for fuel or for making things. まき, 丸太 ❑He dumped the logs on the big stone hearth. 彼はまきを大きな石の暖炉にどさっと置いた. **2** N-COUNT 可算名詞 A **log** is an official written account of what happens each day, for example, on board a ship. 日誌 ❑The family made an official complaint to a ship's officer, which was recorded in the log. その一家は高級船員に苦情を正式に申し立て, それは日誌に記録された. **3** V-T 他動詞 If you **log** an event or fact, you record it officially in writing or on a computer. 記録する ❑They log everyone and everything that comes in and out of here. 彼らはここに出入りする人や物をすべて記録している.

→ see **blog**

▶ **log in** or **log on** PHRASAL VERB 句動詞 When someone **logs in** or **logs on**, or **logs into** a computer system, they start using the system, usually by typing their name or identity code and a password. ログインする, ログオンする ❑Customers pay to log on and gossip with other users. 客は料金を払ってログオンして他のユーザーと雑談をする.

▶ **log out** or **log off** PHRASAL VERB 句動詞 When someone who is using a computer system **logs out** or **logs off**, they finish using the system by typing a particular command. ログアウトする, ログオフする ❑If a computer user fails to log off, the system is accessible to all. もしコンピューターのユーザーがログオフしそこなうと, 誰でもシステムにアクセスできてしまう.

logic /lɒdʒɪk/ **1** N-UNCOUNT 不可算名詞 **Logic** is a method of reasoning that involves a series of statements, each of which must be true if the statement before it is true. 論理学 ❑Apart from criminal investigation techniques, students learn forensic medicine, philosophy and logic. 犯罪調査技術以外に学生は法医学と哲学と論理学を学ぶ. **2** N-UNCOUNT 不可算名詞 The **logic** of a conclusion or an argument is its quality of being correct and reasonable. 論理, 筋道 ❑I don't follow the logic of your argument. あなたの議論の筋道が私にはつかめない. **3** N-UNCOUNT 不可算名詞 A particular kind of **logic** is the way of thinking and reasoning about things that is characteristic of a particular type of person or particular field of activity. 理論 ❑The plan was based on sound commercial logic. その計画はしっかりした商業理論に基づいたものであった.

→ see **philosophy**

logi|cal /lɒdʒɪkᵊl/ **1** ADJ 形容詞 In a **logical** argument or method of reasoning, each step must be true if the step before it is true. 論理的な ❑Only when each logical step has been checked by other mathematicians will the proof be accepted. 他の数学者たちが論理的段階を全て照合した場合のみ, その証明は受け入れられるであろう. ● **logi|cally** /lɒdʒɪkli/ ADV 副詞 論理的に ❑My professional training has taught me to look at things logically. 私は職業訓練の中で物事を論理的に見るように教えられた. **2** ADJ 形容詞 The **logical** conclusion or result of a series of facts or events is the only one which can come from it, according to the rules of logic. 必然の, 当然の ❑If the climate gets drier, then the logical conclusion is that even more drought will occur. 気候がますます乾燥すると, 当然の結果として

干ばつはより一層頻繁になるでしょう. ● **logi|cal|ly** ADV 副詞 [ADV with v] 必然的に ❑From that it followed logically that he would not be meeting Hildegarde. このことから, 彼はヒルデガードとは当然面談しないことになった. **3** ADJ 形容詞 Something that is **logical** seems reasonable or sensible in the circumstances. 必然的な, 筋の通った ❑Connie suddenly struck her as a logical candidate. 彼女はコニーが必然的な候補である, と突然ひらめいた. ❑There was a logical explanation. 論理的に説明がついた. ● **logi|cal|ly** ADV 副詞 必然的に ❑This was the one possibility I hadn't taken into consideration, though logically I should have. これは1つの可能性として当然考えに入れるべきことではあったが, 私はこれだけは考えに入れていなかった.

logic bomb (**logic bombs**) N-COUNT 可算名詞 A **logic bomb** is an unauthorized program that is inserted into a computer system so that when it is started it affects the operation of the computer. ロジックボム [COMPUTING コンピューティング] ❑Viruses and logic bombs can doubtless do great damage under some circumstances. ウイルスとロジックボムは状況によりひどい被害を及ぼす可能性があることは確かだ.

lo|gis|tics /loʊdʒɪstɪks/ N-UNCOUNT-COLL 集合的不可算名詞 If you refer to the **logistics** of doing something complicated that involves a lot of people or equipment, you are referring to the skillful organization of it so that it can be done successfully and efficiently. 後方業務 ❑The skills and logistics of getting such a big show on the road pose enormous practical problems. このように大きなショーで地方巡業すると技術と後方業務の面で膨大な実際の問題を引き起こす.

logo /loʊgoʊ/ (**logos**) N-COUNT 可算名詞 The **logo** of a company or organization is the special design or way of writing its name that it puts on all its products, stationery, or advertisements. ロゴ, 商標 ❑...the famous MGM logo of the roaring lion. MGM社の有名な, ほえているライオンの商標.

→ see **advertising**

loi|ter /lɔɪtər/ (**loiters, loitering, loitered**) V-I 自動詞 If you **loiter** somewhere, you remain there or walk up and down without any real purpose. ぶらつく ❑Unemployed young men loiter at the entrance of the factory. 失業した若者たちが工場の入り口をぶらついている.

lone /loʊn/ ADJ 形容詞 If you talk about a **lone** person or thing, you mean that they are alone. 1人の ❑A lone woman motorist waited for six hours for help yesterday because of a name mix-up. 昨日, 名前に取り違えがあったため, たった1人で車を運転していた女性は6時間救助を待たなければならなかった.

lone|li|ness /loʊnlinɪs/ N-UNCOUNT 不可算名詞 **Loneliness** is the unhappiness that is felt by someone because they do not have any friends or do not have anyone to talk to. 孤独 ❑I have so many friends, but deep down, underneath, I have a fear of loneliness. 私には友人がたくさんいるが, 心の奥底深くで孤独を恐れている.

lone|ly /loʊnli/ (**lonelier, loneliest**) **1** ADJ 形容詞 Someone who is **lonely** is unhappy because they are alone or do not have anyone they can talk to. 孤独な ❑...lonely people who just want to talk. 単に話しをしたいだけの孤独な人々 **2** ADJ 形容詞 A **lonely** situation or period of time is one in which you feel unhappy because you are alone or do not have anyone to talk to. 孤独な ❑I desperately needed something to occupy me during those long, lonely nights. その長い孤独な夜の間じゅう何かに時間を費やすことが私にはどうしても必要だった. **3** ADJ 形容詞 A **lonely** place is one where very few people come. さびしい ❑It felt like the loneliest place in the world. そこは世界中で最もさびしい所に思えた.

lon|er /loʊnər/ (**loners**) N-COUNT 可算名詞 If you describe someone as a **loner**, you mean they prefer to be alone rather than with a group of people. 1人で行動する人 ❑I'm very much a loner – I never go out. 私は1人でいるのがとても好きだ. 全く外出もしない.

long
❶ TIME
❷ DISTANCE AND SIZE
❸ PHRASES
❹ VERB USES

❶ long /lɒŋ/ (**longer** /lɒŋgər/, **longest** /lɒŋgɪst/) **1** ADV 副詞 **Long** means a great amount of time or for a great amount of time. 長く ❑Repairs to the cable did not take too long. 電線の修理にはあまり時間がかからなかった. ❑Have you known her parents long? 彼女の両親をかなり前から知っていたの? ❑I learned long ago to avoid these invitations. これらの招待は避けたほうがいいって私はかなり前に教訓を得たのだよ. ● PHRASE 句 The expression **for long** is used to mean "for a great amount of time." 長い間 ❑"Did you live there?" — "Not for long." 「あそこに住んでいたの?」「さほど長くはなかったけどね」 **2** ADJ 形容詞 A **long** event or period of time lasts for a great amount of time or takes a great amount of time. 長時間の ❑We had a long meeting with the attorney general. 我々は司法長官と長時間の話し合いをした. ❑She is planning a long vacation in Europe. 彼女はヨ

ーロッパでの長い休暇を計画している． **③** ADV 副詞 You use **long** to ask or talk about amounts of time. 長く □ *How long have you lived around here?* どのぐらい前からこのあたりにお住まいですか？ □ *He has been on a diet for as long as any of his friends can remember.* 彼の友人たちが覚えている限り，彼はいつもダイエットをしていた． ● ADJ 形容詞 **Long** is also an adjective. 長い □ *So how long is your commute?* 通勤にどのぐらいかかりますか？ **④** ADJ 形容詞 A **long** speech, book, movie, or list contains a lot of information or a lot of items and takes a lot of time to listen to, read, watch, or deal with. 長たらしい，盛りだくさんの □ *He was making quite a long speech.* 彼は長々とスピーチをしていた． **⑤** ADJ 形容詞 If you describe a period of time or work as **long**, you mean it lasts for more hours or days than is usual, or seems to last for more time than it actually does. 長く感じられる □ *Go to sleep. I've got a long day tomorrow.* 寝なさい．明日は1日長いんだから． □ *She was a TV reporter and worked long hours.* 彼女はテレビのレポーターで長時間働いた． **⑥** ADJ 形容詞 If someone has a **long** memory, they are able to remember things that happened far back in the past. 前のことまで覚えている □ *Mr. Assad, who has a long memory, will not have forgotten that meeting.* アサッドさんは物事をよく覚えている人で，あの出会いのことを忘れていないだろう． **⑦** ADV 副詞 **Long** is used in expressions such as **all year long**, **the whole day long**, and **your whole life long** to say and emphasize that something happens for the whole of a particular period of time. 一中ずっと [EMPHASIS 強調] [N ADV] □ *We played that CD all night long.* 私たちは1晩中ずっとあのCDをかけていた．

② long /lɒŋ/ (longer /lɒŋɡər/, longest /lɒŋɡɪst/) **①** ADJ 形容詞 Something that is **long** measures a great distance from one end to the other. 長い □ *...a long table.* 細長いテーブル． □ *Lucy was 27, with long dark hair.* ルーシーは27歳で黒っぽくて長い髪をしていた． **②** ADJ 形容詞 A **long** distance is a great distance. A **long** journey or route covers a great distance. 遠い □ *These people were a long way from home.* この人々は遠くから来ていた． □ *The long journey tired him.* 彼は長旅に疲れた． **③** ADJ 形容詞 A **long** piece of clothing covers the whole of someone's legs or more of their legs than usual. Clothes with long sleeves cover the whole of someone's arms. 長い [ADJ n] □ *She is wearing a long black dress.* 彼女は黒いロングドレスを着ている． **④** ADJ 形容詞 You use **long** to talk or ask about the distance something measures from one end to the other. 長さで □ *An eight-week-old embryo is only an inch long.* 8週目の胎児の長さはたった1インチである． □ *How long is the tunnel?* そのトンネルの長さはどのぐらいか？ ● COMB IN ADJ 形容詞の複合 **Long** is also a combining form. 一の長さの □ *...a three-foot-long gash in the tanker's side.* タンカーの側面にある長さ3フィートの深い裂け目．
→ see **ratio**

③ long /lɒŋ/ (longer /lɒŋɡər/)
⇨ Please look at meaning **⑥** to see if the expression you are looking for is shown under another headword. **①** PHRASE 句 If you say that something is the case **as long as** or **so long as** something else is the case, you mean that it is only the case if the second thing is the case. 一する限りは，一さえすれば □ *He said he would still support them, as long as they didn't break the rules.* 彼は彼らが規則を破らない限り，彼らを依然として支援すると言った． **②** PHRASE 句 If you say that someone **won't be long**, you mean that they will arrive or be back soon. If you say that **it won't be long** before something happens, you mean that you think it will happen soon. もうすぐだろう □ *"What's happened to her?"—"I'm sure she won't be long."* 「彼女はどうしたのかしら？」「きっともうすぐ来るよ」 **③** PHRASE 句 If you say that something will happen or happened **before long**, you mean that it will happen or it happened soon. そのうちに □ *German interest rates will come down before long.* 近いうちにドイツの金利は下がるでしょう． **④** PHRASE 句 Something that is **no longer** the case used to be the case but is not the case now. You can also say that something is not the case **any longer**. もうーでない □ *Food shortages are no longer a problem.* 食糧不足はもう問題ではない． □ *She could no longer afford to keep him at school.* 彼女は彼を学校にやる余裕はなかった． **⑤** PHRASE 句 You can say **so long** as an informal way of saying goodbye. ではさようなら □ *Well, so long, pal, see you around.* さて，じゃあ，さようなら，また今度ね． **⑥ at long last** → see **last** **⑦ in the long run** → see **run** **⑧ a long shot** → see **shot** **⑨ in the long term** → see **term** **⑩ to go a long way** → see **way**

④ long /lɒŋ/ (longs, longing, longed) **①** V-T/V-I 他動詞/自動詞 If you **long for** something, you want it very much. あこがれる，切望する □ *Steve longed for the good old days.* スティーブは古き良き時代にあこがれていた． □ *I'm longing to meet her.* 私は彼女に会いたくてしかたがない． **②** → see also **longing**

long-distance **①** ADJ 形容詞 **Long-distance** is used to describe travel between places that are far apart. 長距離の [ADJ n] □ *Trains are reliable, cheap and best for long-distance travel.* 列車は信頼でき，安く，長距離の旅行には最適である． **②** ADJ 形容詞 **Long-distance** is used to describe communication that takes place between people who are far apart. 長距離の □ *He received a long-distance phone call from his girlfriend in Colorado.* 彼はコロラド州のガールフレンドから長

距離電話をもらった．

long-haul **①** ADJ 形容詞 **Long-haul** is used to describe things that involve transporting passengers or goods over long distances. Compare **short-haul**. 長距離の，長時間の [ADJ n] □ *...learning how to avoid the unpleasant side-effects of long-haul flights.* 長距離輸送飛行の不快な副作用をどうやって避けるかを習うこと **②** → see also **haul**

longing /lɒŋɪŋ/ (longings) N-VAR 可変性名詞 If you feel **longing** or a **longing** for something, you have a rather sad feeling because you want it very much. 恋しさ，切望 □ *He felt a longing for the familiar.* 彼は親友が恋しかった．

longitude /lɒndʒɪtuːd/ (longitudes) N-VAR 可変性名詞 The **longitude** of a place is its distance to the west or east of a line passing through Greenwich, England. Compare **latitude**. 経度 □ *He noted the latitude and longitude, then made a mark on the admiralty chart.* 彼は経度と緯度を書きとめてから海図に印をつけた． ● ADJ 形容詞 **Longitude** is also an adjective. 経度の □ *A similar feature is found at 13 degrees north between 230 degrees and 250 degrees longitude.* 似たような地形は北緯13度，経度230度と250度の間に見られる．
→ see **globe**

long-lost ADJ 形容詞 You use **long-lost** to describe someone or something that you have not seen for a long time. 長い間行方不明の [ADJ n] □ *For me it was like meeting a long-lost sister. We talked, and talked, and talked.* 私にとってはそれはずっと行方の分からなかった妹と再会したみたいだった．私たちは話して，話して，話まくった．

long-range **①** ADJ 形容詞 A **long-range** piece of military equipment or vehicle is able to hit or detect a target a long way away or to travel a long way in order to do something. 長距離に達する □ *He is eager to reach agreement with the U.S. on reducing long-range nuclear missiles.* 彼は米国と長距離核ミサイルを縮減する合意にぜひ達したいと思っている． **②** ADJ 形容詞 A **long-range** plan or prediction relates to a period extending a long time into the future. 長期の □ *Eisenhower was intensely aware of the need for long-range planning.* アイゼンハワーは長期計画の必要性にはっきり気づいていた．

long-running (longest-running) ADJ 形容詞 Something that is **long-running** has been in existence, or has been performed, for a long time. 長期の [ADJ n] □ *...a long-running trade dispute.* 長期にわたる貿易摩擦．

long-standing ADJ 形容詞 A **long-standing** situation has existed for a long time. 長年の □ *They are on the brink of resolving their long-standing dispute over money.* 彼らは金をめぐる長年の争いを今にも解決しそうだ．

long-suffering ADJ 形容詞 Someone who is **long-suffering** patiently puts up with a lot of trouble or unhappiness, especially when it is caused by someone else. 辛抱強い □ *He went back to his loyal, long-suffering wife.* 彼は彼の忠実で辛抱強い妻のもとへ戻った．

long-term (longer-term) **①** ADJ 形容詞 Something that is **long-term** has continued for a long time or will continue for a long time in the future. 長期の □ *They want their parents to have access to affordable long-term care.* 彼らは両親が手ごろな価格の長期医療を利用できるようにしたかった． **②** N-SING 単数名詞 When you talk about what happens in **the long term**, you are talking about what happens over a long period of time, either in the future or after a particular event. 長期 □ *In the long term the company hopes to open in Moscow and other major cities.* 長期的にはその会社はモスクワや他の主要都市で開店したいと思っている．
→ see **memory**

long-time ADJ 形容詞 You use **long-time** to describe something that has existed or been a particular thing for a long time. 長期の [ADJ n] □ *Newcomers had to pay far more in taxes than long-time land owners.* 新参者たちは昔からの地主たちよりずっと高い税金を払わなければならなかった．

---

look

❶ USING YOUR EYES OR YOUR MIND
❷ APPEARANCE

---

❶ look /lʊk/ (looks, looking, looked)
⇨ Please look at meaning **⑫** to see if the expression you are looking for is shown under another headword. **①** V-I 自動詞 If you **look** in a particular direction, you direct your eyes in that direction, especially so that you can see what is there or see what something is like. 見る □ *I looked down the hallway to room number nine.* 私は通路の先を見ると9号室があった． □ *If you look, you'll see what was a lake.* 見れば，以前湖だったものがわかるでしょう． ● N-SING 単数名詞 **Look** is also a noun. 見ること □ *Lucille took a last look in the mirror.* ルシールは最後にもう1回鏡を見た． **②** V-I 自動詞 If you **look at** a book, newspaper, or magazine, you read it fairly quickly or read part of it. 見る，目を通す □ *You've just got to look at the last bit of Act Three.* 第3幕の最後の部分には絶対目を通してね．

● N-SING 単数名詞 **Look** is also a noun. 目を通すこと ❑ A quick look at Monday's newspapers shows that there's plenty of interest in foreign news. 月曜の各新聞にさっと目を通したところ、外国のニュースにかなり関心が向いています。 **3** V-I 自動詞 If you **look at** someone in a particular way, you look at them with your expression showing what you are feeling or thinking. 見る、見つめる ❑ She looked at him earnestly. "You don't mind?" 彼女は真剣に彼を見つめた。「いいの?」 ● N-COUNT 可算名詞 **Look** is also a noun. 顔つき ❑ He gave her a blank look, as if he had no idea who she was. 彼は彼女が誰だか全く分かっていないかのように、うつろな顔つきで彼女を見た。 **4** V-I 自動詞 If you **look for** something, for example, something that you have lost, you try to find it. 探す ❑ I'm looking for a child. I believe your husband can help me find her. 私は子供を捜しています。あなたのご主人に彼女を見つける手助けをしていただけるかと思いまして。 ❑ I looked everywhere for ideas. 私はありとあらゆるところでアイディアを得ようとした。 ● N-SING 単数名詞 **Look** is also a noun. 探すこと ❑ Go and have another look. もう1回そこに行って探しなさい。 **5** V-I 自動詞 If you are **looking for** something such as the solution to a problem or a new method, you want and are trying to obtain it or think of it. 探す、探索する ❑ The working group will be looking for practical solutions to the problems faced by doctors. 作業部会は医師の直面している問題の現実的な解決策を探索しているであろう。 **6** V-I 自動詞 If you **look at** a subject, problem, or situation, you think about it or study it, so that you know all about it and can perhaps consider what should be done in relation to it. 考察する ❑ Next term we'll be looking at the Second World War period. 次学期には第2世界大戦期について見ることになるでしょう。 ❑ Anne Holker looks at the pros and cons of making changes to your property. アン・ホルカーがあなたの家屋敷を改造するプラス面とマイナス面について考えます。 ● N-SING 単数名詞 **Look** is also a noun. 見てみること、調査 ❑ A close look at the statistics reveals a troubling picture. その統計をよく調べると問題があることが明らかになる。 **7** V-I 自動詞 If you **look at** a person, situation, or subject from a particular point of view, you judge them or consider them from that point of view. 見る ❑ Brian had learned to look at her with new respect. ブライアンは新たな関心で彼女を見るようになっていた。 **8** CONVENTION 慣習表現 You say **look** when you want someone to pay attention to you because you are going to say something important. ほら! ❑ Look, I'm sorry. I didn't mean it. あら、ごめんなさい。本気じゃなかったのよ。 **9** V-T/V-I 他動詞/自動詞 You can use **look** to draw attention to a particular situation, person, or thing, for example because you find it very surprising, significant, or annoying. 現状を見る [only imper] ❑ Hey, look at the time! We'll talk about it tonight. All right? おっと、もうこんな時間だ!これについては今夜話そう。いいね。 ❑ I mean, look at how many people watch television and how few read books. つまり、みんなテレビばかり見て、本を読む人はほとんどいないのが現状でしょう。 ❑ Look what you've done! 何てことをしたのだ! **10** V-I 自動詞 If something such as a building or window **looks** somewhere, it has a view of a particular place. 向いている、面している ❑ The castle looks over private parkland. 城からは私有の緑地が見渡せる。 ● PHRASAL VERB 句動詞 **Look out** means the same as **look**. 面している ❑ Nine windows looked out over the sculpture gardens. 9つの窓は彫刻の庭に面していた。 **11** EXCLAM 感嘆詞 If you say or shout "**look out!**" to someone, you are warning them that they are in danger. 注意する ❑ "Look out!" somebody shouted, as the truck started to roll toward the sea. トラックが海に向かって動き出すと「気をつけろ!」と誰かが叫んだ。 **12** to **look down** your **nose at** someone → see nose

If you want to say that someone is paying attention to something they can see, you say that they **are looking at** it or **watching** it. In general, you **look at** something that is not moving, while you **watch** something that is moving or changing. ❑ I asked him to look at the picture above his bed... He watched Blake run down the stairs. **Look** is never followed directly by an object. You must always use **at** or some other preposition. ❑ I looked toward the plane. You use **see** to talk about things that you are aware of because a visual impression reaches your eyes. You often use **can** in this case. ❑ I can see the fax here on the desk.

▶ **look after** **1** PHRASAL VERB 句動詞 If you **look after** someone or something, you do what is necessary to keep them healthy, safe, or in good condition. ～の面倒を見る ❑ I love looking after the children. 私は子供たちの世話をするのが大好きだ。 **2** PHRASAL VERB 句動詞 If you **look after** something, you are responsible for it and deal with it or make sure it is all right, especially because it is your job to do so. 監督する ❑ ...the farm manager who looks after the day-to-day organization. 日々の管理を監督する農場支配人

▶ **look around** PHRASAL VERB 句動詞 If you **look around** or **look round** a building or place, you walk round it and look at the different parts of it. ～を見回す ❑ She left Annie and Cooper looking around the store and headed back onto the street. 彼女は店内を見回しているアニーとクーパーを残して、通りに戻って行った。

▶ **look back** PHRASAL VERB 句動詞 If you **look back**, you think about things that happened in the past. 振り返ってみる ❑ Looking back, I am staggered how easily it was all arranged. 振り返ってみると、

それを全部配列するのがどんなに簡単だったかに驚いている。

▶ **look down on** PHRASAL VERB 句動詞 To **look down on** someone means to consider that person to be inferior or unimportant, usually when this is not true. ～を見下す ❑ I wasn't successful, so they looked down on me. 私は出世しなかったので、彼らは私を見下した。

▶ **look forward to** **1** PHRASAL VERB 句動詞 If you **look forward to** something that is going to happen, you want it to happen because you think you will enjoy it. ～を楽しみにする ❑ He was looking forward to working with the new manager. 彼は新しい支配人と一緒に働くのを心待ちにしていた。 **2** PHRASAL VERB 句動詞 If you say that someone **is looking forward** to something useful or positive, you mean they expect it to happen. ～を期待する ❑ He now says that he's looking forward to increased trade after the war. 彼は戦後に貿易が伸びることを期待していると今では言っている。

Do not confuse **look forward to**, **expect**, and **wait for**. When you **look forward to** something that is going to happen, you feel happy because you think you will enjoy it. ❑ I'll bet you're looking forward to your holidays... I always looked forward to seeing her. When you are **expecting** someone or something, you think that the person or thing is going to arrive or that the thing is going to happen. ❑ I sent a postcard so they were expecting me...We are expecting rain. When you **wait for** someone or something, you stay in the same place until the person arrives or the thing happens. ❑ Soft drinks were served while we waited for him...We got off the plane and waited for our luggage.

▶ **look in** PHRASAL VERB 句動詞 If you **look in on** a person, you visit that person for a short time to check on their health or safety. ちょっと訪ねる、様子を見に立ち寄る ❑ Could I look in on Sam? サムを訪ねに行っていいですか? ❑ I think I'll look in on my parents on the way home from work. 私は両親の様子を見に会社の帰りに寄ろうと思う。

▶ **look into** PHRASAL VERB 句動詞 If a person or organization **is looking into** a possible course of action, a problem, or a situation, they are finding out about it and examining the facts relating to it. ～を調べる、～を検討する ❑ He had once looked into buying his own island off Nova Scotia. 彼はノバスコシア州の沖にある自分の島をかつて買うかどうかを検討したものだ。

▶ **look on** PHRASAL VERB 句動詞 If you **look on** while something happens, you watch it happening without taking part yourself. 傍観する、見守る ❑ About 150 local people looked on in silence as the two coffins were taken into the church. 2つのひつぎが教会の中に運ばれるのを約150人の地元の人たちが黙って見守った。

▶ **look on** or **look upon** PHRASAL VERB 句動詞 If you **look on** or **look upon** someone or something in a particular way, you think of them in that way. ～と見なす、～と思う ❑ A lot of people looked on him as a healer. 多くの人が彼を治療者だと見なしていた。 ❑ A lot of people look on it like that. 多くの人がそれをそんなふうに思っている。

▶ **look out** → see look **①** 10

▶ **look out for** PHRASAL VERB 句動詞 If you **look out for** something, you pay attention to things so that you notice it if or when it occurs. ～に注意する ❑ Look out for special deals. 特別販売を見逃さないように。

▶ **look over** PHRASAL VERB 句動詞 If you **look** something **over**, you examine it in order to get an idea of what it is like. ～を調べる、～にざっと目を通す ❑ They presented their draft to the president, who looked it over, nodded and signed it. 彼らは草案を大統領に提出し、大統領はそれにざっと目を通し、うなずいて、署名した。

▶ **look round** → see look around

▶ **look through** **1** PHRASAL VERB 句動詞 If you **look through** a group of things, you examine each one so that you can find or choose the one that you want. 1つ1つ調べる ❑ Peter starts looking through the mail as soon as the door shuts. ピーターはドアが閉まるや否やメールを1つ1つ調べ始める。 **2** PHRASAL VERB 句動詞 If you **look through** something that has been written or printed, you read it. ～を読む ❑ He happened to be looking through the medical book "Gray's Anatomy" at the time. その時彼はたまたま医学書『グレイの解剖学』を読んでいた。

▶ **look to** **1** PHRASAL VERB 句動詞 If you **look to** someone or something for a particular thing that you want, you expect or hope that they will provide it. ～に頼る ❑ He runs the team because he commands their respect. The kids really look to him. 彼はこのチームを運営しているから尊敬されるからだ。チームの子供たちは本当に彼を頼りにしている。 **2** PHRASAL VERB 句動詞 If you **look to** something that will happen in the future, you think about it. ～に気をつける ❑ Looking to the future, though, we asked him what the prospects are for a vaccine to prevent infection in the first place. しかし将来的に見てですが、ワクチンがそもそも感染を予防する見通しはどんなものであるかを彼に聞いてみました。

▶ **look up** **1** PHRASAL VERB 句動詞 If you **look up** a fact or a piece of information, you find it out by looking in something such as a reference book or a list. ～を調べる ❑ I looked your address up in the personnel file. 私はあなたの住所を人事ファイルで調べた。 **2** PHRASAL VERB 句動詞 If you **look** someone **up**, you visit them after not having seen them for a long time. ～を訪問する ❑ I'll try to look

him up, ask him a few questions. 彼を訪ねてみて，すこし質問しよう
と思う．

▶ **look up to** PHRASAL VERB 句動詞 If you **look up to** someone, especially someone older than you, you respect and admire them. ーを尊敬する □*You're a popular girl, Grace, and a lot of the younger ones look up to you.* あなたは人気のある女の子なのよ，グレース，そしてた くさんの年下の子供たちがあなたを尊敬しているのよ．

❷ **look** /lʊk/ (**looks, looking, looked**) **1** V-LINK 連結動詞 You use **look** when describing the appearance of a person or thing or the impression that they give. 見える □*Sheila was looking miserable.* シー ラはさえない顔をしていた．□*They look like stars to the naked eye.* それらは肉眼では星のように見える．□*He looked as if he was going to smile.* 彼は微笑を浮かべようとしているように見えた．**2** N-SING 単 数名詞 If someone or something has a particular **look**, they have a particular appearance or expression. 様子，見かけ □*She had the look of someone deserted and betrayed.* 彼女はいかにも見捨てられて裏 切られた者のように見えた．□*When he came to decorate the kitchen, Kenneth opted for a freshly rustic look.* ケニスは台所の内装について は田舎風で気さくな感じにすることを決めた．**3** N-PLURAL 複数名 詞 When you refer to someone's **looks**, you are referring to how beautiful or ugly they are, especially how beautiful they are. 容 貌，外観 □*I never chose people just because of their looks.* 私は外観だけ で人を選ぶようなことは絶対しなかった．**4** V-LINK 連結動詞 You use **look** when indicating what you think will happen in the future or how a situation seems to you. 見える，思われる □*He had lots of time to think about the future, and it didn't look good.* 彼は将来について 考える時間があった．そして見通しは良くなかった．□*So far it looks like Warner Brothers' gamble is paying off.* 今のところ，ワーナー ブラザーズ社のかけはうまく行っているようだ．□*The Europeans had hoped to win, and, indeed, had looked like they would win.* ヨーロッパ勢 は勝利を望んでいた．そして実際勝ちそうに見えていた．**5** PHRASE 句 You use expressions such as **by the look of him** and **by the looks of it** when you want to indicate that you are giving an opinion based on the appearance of someone or something. 様子から見る と，外見から判断すると □*He was not a well man by the look of him.* 彼 の様子から判断すると彼は健康な男ではない．**6** PHRASE 句 If you **don't like the look of** something or someone, you feel that they may be dangerous or cause problems. ーを怪しいと思う，ーの様 子が気に入らない □*I don't like the look of those clouds.* 雲行きが怪し いと思う．**7** PHRASE 句 If you ask **what** someone or something **looks like**, you are asking for a description of them. どんな人か， どんな物か

> ### Thesaurus
> *look* また次を参照：
>
> | | |
> |---|---|
> | N. | gaze, glance, glimpse, stare ❶ **1** |
> | V. | gaze, glance, observe, stare, view, watch ❶ **1**
examine, inspect, investigate, observe, study; (ant.)
survey ❶ **6** |
> | V-LINK | appear, seem ❷ **1** |

look|out /lʊkaʊt/ (**lookouts**) **1** N-COUNT 可算名詞 A **lookout** is a place from which you can see clearly in all directions. 見晴台， 監視所 □*Troops tried to set up a lookout post inside a refugee camp.* 難民 キャンプの中に軍隊は監視台を設置しようとした．**2** N-COUNT 可算 名詞 A **lookout** is someone who is watching for danger in order to warn other people about it. 見張り □*One of them, Bayer's girlfriend, helped plan the botched burglary and acted as a lookout.* その中の一人， ベイヤーのガールフレンドはその失敗に終わった押し込みの計画 を手伝い，さらに見張り役も務めた．**3** PHRASE 句 If someone **keeps a lookout**, especially on a boat, they look around all the time in order to make sure there is no danger. 見張る □*He denied that he'd failed to keep a proper lookout that night.* 彼はその夜しっかり見張りを するのを怠ったことを否定した．

loom /luːm/ (**looms, looming, loomed**) **1** V-I 自動詞 If something **looms over** you, it appears as a large or unclear shape, often in a frightening way. ぼんやりと現れる，立ちはだか る □*Vincent loomed over me, as pale and gray as a tombstone.* 墓石の ように顔色が青白いビンセントが私に立ちはだかってきた．**2** V-I 自 動詞 If a worrying or threatening situation or event **is looming**, it seems likely to happen soon. 迫る [JOURNALISM ジャーナリ ズム] □*Another government spending crisis is looming in the United States.* 米国ではまたもや財政支出の危機が迫っている．□*The threat of renewed civil war looms ahead.* 新たな内戦の恐れが前途に待ち受け ている．**3** N-COUNT 可算名詞 A **loom** is a machine that is used for weaving thread into cloth. 織機

loony /luːni/ (**loonies**) **1** N-COUNT 可算名詞 If you refer to someone as a **loony**, you mean that they behave in a way that seems crazy, strange, or eccentric. Some people consider this use offensive. きちがい [INFORMAL くだけた, DISAPPROVAL 不賛 成] □*At first they all thought I was a loony.* 最初彼らはみんな私のこ とをきちがいだと思った．**2** ADJ 形容詞 If you describe someone's behavior or ideas as **loony**, you mean that they seem mad, strange, or eccentric. Some people consider this use offensive. 気 の狂った [INFORMAL くだけた] □*What's she up to? She's as loony as*

her brother! 彼女は何をしているの？彼女はお兄さんと同じぐらい狂っ ているわ！

loop /luːp/ (**loops, looping, looped**) **1** N-COUNT 可算名詞 A **loop** is a curved or circular shape in something long, for example, in a piece of string. 輪，ループ □*Mrs. Morrell reached for a loop of garden hose.* モレルさんは庭のホースの輪に手を伸ばした．**2** V-T 他動詞 If you **loop** something such as a piece of rope around an object, you tie a length of it in a loop around the object, for example, in order to fasten it to the object. 輪にして巻きつける □*He looped the rope over the wood.* 彼はその木材に縄を巻きつけた．**3** V-I 自動詞 If something **loops** somewhere, it goes there in a circular direction that makes the shape of a loop. 孤を描く □*The enemy was looping around the south side.* 敵は南側で孤を描いていた．

loop|hole /luːphoʊl/ (**loopholes**) N-COUNT 可算名詞 A **loophole** in the law is a small mistake which allows people to do something that would otherwise be illegal. 抜け穴 □*It is estimated that 60,000 businesses are exploiting a loophole in the law to avoid prosecution.* 6万社が告発を避けるために法の抜け穴を使っていると推 定されている．

loose /luːs/ (**looser, loosest, looses, loosing, loosed**) **1** ADJ 形 容詞 Something that is **loose** is not firmly held or fixed in place. ゆるい，がたがたの □*If a tooth feels very loose, your dentist may recommend that it's taken out.* もしも歯がとてもぐらぐらしているよ うなら，歯医者は抜歯を薦めるかもしれません．□*Two wooden beams had come loose from the ceiling.* 2本の木の梁が天井から離れ落ちて きていた．● **loose|ly** ADV 副詞 ゆるく □*Tim clasped his hands together and held them loosely in front of his belly.* ティム は手を組んで腹の前に だらりと置いた．**2** ADJ 形容詞 Something that is **loose** is not attached to anything, or held or contained in anything. ばらの □*Frank emptied a handful of loose change on the table.* フランクは一握りの小銭を机の上に空けた．**3** ADJ 形容 詞 If people or animals break **loose** or are set **loose**, they are no longer held, tied, or kept somewhere and can move around freely. 放たれた，自由な □*She broke loose from his embrace and crossed to the window.* 彼女は彼の抱擁から逃れ，窓辺に行った．**4** ADJ 形 容詞 Clothes that are **loose** are somewhat large and do not fit closely. ゆったりとした，だぶだぶの □*A pistol wasn't that hard to hide under a loose shirt.* 拳銃をゆったりとしたシャツの下に隠すのは さほど難しくなかった．● **loose|ly** ADV 副詞 ゆったりと □*His shirt hung loosely over his shoulders.* 彼の肩はやせ細っていてシャツ がだぶだぶしていた．**5** ADJ 形容詞 If your hair is **loose**, it hangs freely around your shoulders and is not tied back. 結んでいな い □*She was still in her nightgown, with her hair hanging loose over her shoulders.* 彼女はまだ寝巻きを着ていて，結んでない髪の毛が肩にゆっ たりかかっていた．**6** ADJ 形容詞 A **loose** grouping, arrangement, or organization is flexible rather than strictly controlled or organized. あいまいな，厳密でない □*Murray and Alison came to some sort of loose arrangement before he went home.* マレーが帰る前 に彼とアリソンがある種のあいまいな取り決めを結んだ．● **loose|ly** ADV 副詞 [ADV with v] あいまいに □*The investigation had aimed at a loosely organized group of criminals.* 捜査はしっかり組織されていない 犯罪者の集団を対象に行われていた．**7** PHRASE 句 If a person or an animal is **on the loose**, they are free because they have escaped from a person or place. 束縛されないで，囚われの身でない □*Up to a thousand prisoners may be on the loose inside the jail.* 千人にも及 ぶ囚人が刑務所内で自由に振舞っているかもしれない．**8** a **loose cannon** → see **cannon 9** all hell breaks loose → see hell

> Do not confuse **loose** and **lose**. **Loose** is usually an adjective. If something is **loose**, it is not properly fixed or held in place. □*…the loose floorboards on the landing. …a loose tooth.* If you let an animal **loose**, you release it from where it was kept. □*He brought a pair of white rats into church, and let them loose on the floor.* **Lose** is a verb. If you **lose** something, you no longer have it and cannot find it. □*I've lost my wallet.* The past participle and past tense of **lose** are both **lost**.

> ### Thesaurus
> *loose* また次を参照：
>
> | | |
> |---|---|
> | ADJ. | slack, wobbly **1**
free **3**
loose-fitting, baggy **4** |

> ### Word Partnership
> *loose* は次の語句と使われる：
>
> | | |
> |---|---|
> | V. | **break** loose, **cut** *someone/something* loose, **set** *someone/*
something loose, **turn** *someone/something* loose **1** – **3**
hang loose **1 2 4 5**
come loose **1 2 5** |
> | N. | loose **coalition**, loose **confederation 6** |

loose end (**loose ends**) **1** N-COUNT 可算名詞 A **loose end** is part of a story, situation, or crime that has not yet been explained. 未 決事項 □*There are some annoying loose ends in the plot.* その話の筋には 気に触る未決事項がいくつかある．**2** PHRASE 句 If you are **at loose**

ends, you are bored because you do not have anything to do and cannot think of anything that you want to do. 暇な, 手持ちぶさたな [INFORMAL くだけた] □ *She had woken feeling at loose ends.* 彼女は手持ちぶさたな気分で目が覚めた.

loos|en /luːsən/ (**loosens, loosening, loosened**) 1 V-T 他動詞 If someone **loosens** restrictions or laws, for example, they make them less strict or severe. 緩和する □ *Many business groups have been pressing the Federal Reserve to loosen interest rates.* 多くの企業団体が連邦準備銀行に金利を緩和するよう強要してきた. ● **loos|en|ing** N-SING 単数名詞 緩和 □ *Domestic conditions did not justify a loosening of monetary policy.* 国内情勢は金融緩和政策を正当化しなかった. 2 V-T/V-I 他動詞/自動詞 If someone or something **loosens** the ties between people or groups of people, or if the ties **loosen**, they become weaker. 緩める, 弱める [他動詞], 緩む, 弱まる [自動詞] □ *The Federal Republic must loosen its ties with the United States.* 連邦共和国は合衆国との関係を緩めなければならない. □ *The deputy leader is cautious about loosening the links with the unions.* 副党首は労働組合との関係を緩和することに慎重だ. 3 V-T 他動詞 If you **loosen** your clothing or something that is tied or fastened, you undo it slightly so that it is less tight or less firmly held in place. 緩める, ほどく [他動詞] □ *He reached up to loosen the scarf around his neck.* 彼は首の周りのスカーフを緩めようと手を上に動かした. □ *Loosen the bolt so the bars can be turned.* バーを回せるようにボルトを緩めなさい. 4 V-T/V-I 他動詞/自動詞 If you **loosen** your grip on something, or if your grip **loosens**, you hold it less tightly. (握った手を) 緩める [他動詞], (握った手が) 緩む [自動詞] □ *Harry loosened his grip momentarily and Anna wriggled free.* ハリーは一瞬握った手を緩め, アナは体をくねって逃げた. 5 V-T/V-I 他動詞/自動詞 If a government or organization **loosens** its grip on a group of people or an activity, or if its grip **loosens**, it begins to have less control over it. (規制を) 緩和する [他動詞], (規制が) 緩まる [自動詞] □ *There is no sign that the party will loosen its grip on the country.* 党が国に対する規制を緩和する兆しはない.

▶ **loosen up** 1 PHRASAL VERB 句動詞 If a person or situation **loosens up**, they become more relaxed and less tense. 気が楽になる, リラックスする □ *Relax, smile; loosen up in mind and body.* 気を楽にして, にっこり笑いなさい. 心と体をリラックスさせなさい. □ *Things loosened up, in politics and the economy.* 政治や経済における状況は改善した. 2 PHRASAL VERB 句動詞 If you **loosen up** your body, or if it **loosens up**, you do simple exercises to get your muscles ready for a difficult physical activity, such as running or playing sports. 体をほぐす □ *Squeeze the foot with both hands to loosen up tight muscles.* 両手で足をぎゅっと握り緊張した筋肉をほぐしなさい.

loot /luːt/ (**loots, looting, looted**) 1 V-T/V-I 他動詞/自動詞 If people **loot**, or **loot** stores or houses, they steal things from them, for example, during a war or riot. (店・家などから) 略奪する □ *The trouble began when gangs began breaking windows and looting shops.* 問題の起こりは不良グループが窓を割って店から略奪を始めたときだった. ● **loot|ing** N-UNCOUNT 不可算名詞 略奪 □ *In the country's largest cities there has been rioting and looting.* その国の大都市では暴動や略奪事件が発生している. 2 V-T 他動詞 If someone **loots** things, they steal them, for example, during a war or riot. (商品を) 略奪する □ *The town has been plagued by armed thugs who have looted food supplies and terrorized the population.* 町は, 食料品を略奪し住民を恐怖に陥れた武装集団に悩まされてきた.

lop|sided /lɒpsaɪdɪd/ ADJ 形容詞 Something that is **lopsided** is uneven because one side is lower or heavier than the other. 一方に傾いた, 不均衡な □ *His suit had shoulders that made him look lopsided.* スーツの肩のせいで体が斜めに見えた.

lord /lɔːrd/ (**lords**) 1 N-COUNT; N-TITLE 可算名詞, 称号名詞 A **lord** is a man who has a high rank in the nobility, for example, an earl, a viscount, or a marquis. 貴族 □ *She married a lord and lives in this huge house in the Cotswolds.* 彼女は貴族と結婚しコッツウォールズのこの大邸宅に住んでいる. 2 N-PROPER 固有名詞 In the Christian church, people refer to God and to Jesus Christ as the **Lord**. 神, 主, イエス・キリスト [usu 'the' N; N-VOC] □ *I know the Lord will look after him.* 彼に神のご加護があることが分かっている. □ *She prayed now, "Lord, help me to find courage."* 彼女はさっとお祈りをした. 「神様, 私に勇気をお与えください」. 3 EXCLAM 感嘆詞 **Lord** is used in exclamations such as "**good Lord!**" and "**oh Lord!**" to express surprise, shock, frustration, or annoyance about something. おやまあ, おお [FEELINGS 感情] □ *"Good Lord, that's what he is: he's a policeman."* 「おやまあ, それが彼の仕事なのね. 警察官なんだ」

lor|ry /lɒri/ (**lorries**) N-COUNT 可算名詞 A **lorry** is the same as a **truck**. トラック [BRIT 英国英語]

lose /luːz/ (**loses, losing, lost**) 1 V-T/V-I 他動詞/自動詞 If you **lose** a contest, a fight, or an argument, you do not succeed because someone does better than you and defeats you. 負ける □ *The Golden Bears have lost three games this season.* ゴールデン・ベアーズは今シーズン中3試合で負けた. □ *The government lost the argument over the pace of reform.* 政府は改革の速度に関する議論で負けた. □ *No one likes to lose.* 負けるのが好きな人はいない. 2 V-T 他動詞 If you **lose** something, you do not know where it is, for example,

because you have forgotten where you put it. なくす, 紛失する □ *I lost my keys.* かぎをなくした. 3 V-T 他動詞 You say that you **lose** something when you no longer have it because it has been taken away from you or destroyed. なくす, 失う □ *I lost my job when the company moved to another state.* 会社が別の州に移転したときに仕事を失った. □ *He lost his license for six months.* 彼は6か月間免停になった. 4 V-T 他動詞 If someone **loses** a quality, characteristic, attitude, or belief, they no longer have it. なくす, 失う □ *He lost all sense of reason.* 彼は判断力をすべて失った. □ *The government had lost all credibility.* 政府は信頼をすべて失った. 5 V-T 他動詞 If you **lose** an ability, you stop having that ability because of something such as an accident. 失う (一できなくなる) □ *They lost their ability to hear.* 彼らは耳が聞こえなくなった. 6 V-T 他動詞 If someone or something **loses** heat, their temperature becomes lower. (体温が) 下がる □ *Babies lose heat much faster than adults.* 赤ん坊は大人よりもずっと体温が下がりやすい. 7 V-T 他動詞 If you **lose** blood or fluid from your body, it leaves your body so that you have less of it. (体内から) 失う □ *The victim suffered a dreadful injury and lost a lot of blood.* 被害者は出血多量の重傷を負った. 8 V-T 他動詞 If you **lose** weight, you become less heavy, and usually look thinner. (体重を) 減らす, やせる □ *I have lost a lot of weight.* かなりやせた. 9 V-T 他動詞 If someone **loses** their life, they die. 命を落とす, 死ぬ (一死亡する) □ *...the ferry disaster in 1987, in which 192 people lost their lives.* 192名が死亡した1987年のフェリー大惨事. 10 V-T 他動詞 If you **lose** a close relative or friend, they die. 死別する, 失う □ *My Grandma lost her brother in the war.* 祖母は戦争で兄を亡くした. 11 V-T 他動詞 If things **are lost**, they are destroyed in a disaster. 破れる [usu passive] □ *...the famous Nankin pottery that was lost in a shipwreck off the coast of China.* 中国の海岸沖での難破で壊れた有名な南京の陶器. 12 V-T 他動詞 If you **lose** time, something slows you down so that you do not make as much progress as you hoped. (時間を) 無駄にする □ *They claim that police lost valuable time in the early part of the investigation.* 彼らは, 捜査の初期に警察が貴重な時間を無駄にしたと主張している. 13 V-T 他動詞 If you **lose** an opportunity, you do not take advantage of it. (チャンスを) 逃す □ *If you don't do it soon you're going to lose the opportunity.* すぐに実行しないとチャンスを逃すことになるよ. □ *They did not lose the opportunity to say what they thought of events.* イベントについての感想を述べるチャンスを逃さなかった. 14 V-T 他動詞 If you **lose yourself** in something or if you **are lost** in it, you give a lot of attention to it and do not think about anything else. 引き込まれる, 没頭する □ *Michael held on to her arm, losing himself in the music.* マイケルは音楽に引き込まれながら, 彼女の腕をしっかりと握った. 15 V-T 他動詞 If a business **loses** money, it earns less money than it spends, and is therefore in debt. 損失する [BUSINESS 実業] □ *His stores stand to lose millions of dollars.* 彼の店は何百万ドルもの損失を出しそうな状況にある. 16 V-T 他動詞 If something **loses** you a contest or **loses** you something that you had, it causes you to fail or to no longer have what you had. 失わせる [他動詞] □ *My own stupidity lost me the match.* 自分の愚かさのせいで試合に負けた. 17 → see also **lost** 18 PHRASE 句 If you **lose your way**, you become lost when you are trying to get somewhere. 道に迷う □ *The men lost their way in a sandstorm.* 砂嵐で10人が道に迷った. 19 to **lose** your **balance** → see **balance** 20 to **lose** contact → see contact 21 to **lose face** → see **face** 22 to **lose** your **grip** → see **grip** 23 to **lose** your **head** → see **head** 24 to **lose heart** → see **heart** 25 to **lose** your **mind** → see **mind** 26 to **lose** your **nerve** → see **nerve** 27 to **lose sight of** → see **sight** 28 to **lose** your **temper** → see **temper** 29 to **lose touch** → see **touch** 30 to **lose track of** → see **track**

> Do not confuse **lose** and **loose**. **Lose** is a verb. If you lose something, you no longer have it and cannot find it. □ *I've lost my wallet.* The past participle and past tense of **lose** are both **lost**. **Loose** is usually an adjective. If something is **loose**, it is not properly fixed or held in place. □ *...the loose floorboards on the landing. ...a loose tooth.* If you let an animal **loose**, you release it from where it was kept. □ *He brought a pair of white rats into church, and let them loose on the floor.*

▶ **lose out** PHRASAL VERB 句動詞 If you **lose out**, you suffer a loss or disadvantage because you have not succeeded in what you were doing. 負ける, 損をする □ *We both lost out.* 我々は両方負けだ. □ *Laura lost out to Tom.* ローラはトムに負けた.

los|er /luːzər/ (**losers**) 1 N-COUNT 可算名詞 The **losers** of a game, contest, or struggle are the people who are defeated or beaten. 敗者 □ *...the Dallas Cowboys and Buffalo Bills, the winners and losers of this year's Super Bowl.* 今年のスーパーボールでの勝者チームと敗者チームのスーパーボールダラス・カウボーイズとバッファロー・ビルズ. ● PHRASE 句 If someone is a **good loser**, they accept that they have lost a game or contest without complaining. If someone is a **bad loser**, they hate losing and complain about it. good loser は「潔く負けを認める人」, bad loser は「負け惜しみなどをぐずぐず言う人」 □ *I'm a great winner and I try to be a good loser.* 私は勝つときは控えめに, 負けたときは負け惜しみを言わないようにしている. 2 N-COUNT 可算名詞 If you refer to someone as a **loser**, you have a low opinion of them because you think they are always

unsuccessful. 負け犬 [INFORMAL くだけた, DISAPPROVAL 不賛成] □ *They've only been trained to compete with other men, so a successful woman can make them feel like a real loser.* 最近の男性と張り合うように研修を受けたばかりなので，やり手の女性のせいで負け犬のように感じることがある． **2** N-COUNT 可算名詞 People who are **losers** as the result of an action or event, are in a worse situation because of it or do not benefit from it. 損を被る人 □ *Some of the top business successes of the 1980s became the country's greatest losers in the recession.* 1980年代に最も成功を収めた事業家の1部は景気後退中に損失額が国内で上位に入った.

loss /lɒs/ (**losses**) **1** N-VAR 可変性名詞 **Loss** is the fact of no longer having something or having less of it than before. 紛失，喪失 □ *...loss of sight.* 視力低下 □ *...hair loss.* 抜け毛 **2** N-VAR 可変性名詞 **Loss** of life occurs when people die. (命の) 喪失 □ *...a terrible loss of human life.* 恐ろしい人命の喪失 **3** N-UNCOUNT 不可算名詞 The **loss** of a relative or friend is their death. 死別 □ *They took the time to talk about the loss of Thomas and how their grief was affecting them.* 彼らは，トーマスの死といかに悲しみが与える影響について話し合う時間をとった. **4** N-UNCOUNT 不可算名詞 **Loss** is the feeling of sadness you experience when someone or something you like is taken away from you. 喪失感 □ *Talk to others about your feelings of loss and grief.* 喪失感と悲しみについてほかの人と話しなさい. **5** N-COUNT 可算名詞 A **loss** is the disadvantage you suffer when a valuable and useful person or thing leaves or is taken away. 痛手，損害 □ *She said his death was a great loss to herself.* 彼女は，彼の死はとてもつらかったと言った. **6** N-UNCOUNT 不可算名詞 The **loss** of something such as heat, blood, or fluid is the gradual reduction of it or of its level in a system or in someone's body. 失うこと □ *...blood loss.* 失血 □ *...a rapid loss of heat from the body.* 体温の急低下 **7** N-VAR 可変性名詞 If a business makes a **loss**, it earns less than it spends. 損失，損害 [BRIT 英国英語] □ *In 1986 Rover made a loss of nine hundred million dollars.* 1986年にローバー社は900万ドルの損失を出した. □ *The company said it will stop producing fertilizer in 1990 because of continued losses.* その会社は，損失が続いたため1990年に化学肥料の生産を打ち切ることを発表した. **8** PHRASE 句 If a business produces something **at a loss**, they sell it at a price which is less than it cost them to produce it or buy it. 損失を出して [BUSINESS 実業] □ *Timber owners have often produced lumber at a loss and survived these down cycles in demand.* 木材業者はよく損失を出して製材し，需要がある間この赤字のサイクルを切り抜けた. **9** PHRASE 句 If you say that you are **at a loss**, you mean that you do not know what to do in a particular situation. 途方に暮れて □ *I was at a loss for what to do next.* 私は次に何をしたらいいか途方に暮れていた.

→ see **disaster**

Word Partnership
loss は次の語句と使われる:

N.	loss **of appetite**, loss **of control**, loss **of income**, loss **of a job** **1**
	blood loss, **hair** loss, **hearing** loss, **memory** loss, **weight** loss **1** **6**
ADJ.	**great/huge/substantial** loss **1** – **7**
	tragic loss **2** **3**
	net loss **7**

loss ad·just·er (**loss adjusters**) also **loss adjustor 1** N-COUNT 可算名詞 A **loss adjuster** is someone who is employed by an insurance company to decide how much money should be paid to a person making a claim. 損害査定人 [BRIT 英国英語 BUSINESS 実業] **2** → see also **claims adjuster**, **insurance adjuster**

loss lead·er (**loss leaders**) also **loss-leader** N-COUNT 可算名詞 A **loss leader** is an item that is sold at such a low price that it makes a loss in the hope that customers will be attracted by it and buy other products at the same store. 客寄せ商品，おとり商品 [BUSINESS 実業] □ *Hoskins does not expect a huge profit from the cookies, viewing them more as a loss leader.* ホスキンズはクッキーをむしろ客寄せ商品とみなしていて巨額の利益を期待していない.

lost /lɒst/ **1 Lost** is the past tense and past participle of **lose**. lose の過去形・過去分詞形 **2** ADJ 形容詞 If you are **lost** or if you get **lost**, you do not know where you are or are unable to find your way. 道に迷った □ *Barely had I set foot in the street when I realized I was lost.* 町に出るとすぐに道に迷っていたことに気付いた. **3** ADJ 形容詞 If something is **lost**, or gets **lost**, you cannot find it, for example, because you have forgotten where you put it. 紛失した，なくした □ *...a lost book.* 紛失した本 □ *He was scrabbling for his pen, which had got lost somewhere under the sheets of paper.* 彼は手探りでペンを探していたが，そのペンは書類の下のどこかに紛失したのだった. **4** ADJ 形容詞 If you feel **lost**, you feel very uncomfortable because you are in an unfamiliar situation. 戸惑って □ *Of the funeral he remembered only the cold, the waiting, and feeling very lost.* 葬式で彼が覚えているのは，寒かったこと，待たされたこと，そしてどうしたらいいのか分からなくて困ったことだ. **5** ADJ 形容詞 If you describe something as **lost**, you mean that you no longer have it or it no longer exists. 失われた □ *...their lost homeland.* 彼らの失われ

れた母国 □ *The sense of community is lost.* コミュニティ感覚が失われた. **6** ADJ 形容詞 You use **lost** to refer to a period or state of affairs that existed in the past and no longer exists. 消滅した [ADJ n] □ *He seemed to pine for his lost youth.* 彼は失われた青春時代を恋しがっているようだった. □ *They are links to a lost age.* 失われた時代へつながっている. **7** ADJ 形容詞 If something is **lost**, it is not used properly and is considered wasted. 無駄にされた，逃した □ *Smith is not bitter about the lost opportunity to compete in the games.* スミスはその試合に出場する機会を逃したことを苦に思っていない.

Thesaurus
lost また次を参照:

| ADJ. | adrift, off-track **2** |
| | missing **3** |

lost and found 1 N-SING 単数名詞 **Lost and found** is the place where lost property is kept. 遺失物取扱所 [AM 米国英語] □ *Excuse me, can you tell me where the lost and found is?* すみません，遺失物取扱所の場所を教えてください. **2** ADJ 形容詞 **Lost-and-found** things are things which someone has lost and which someone else has found. 見つかった落とし物の □ *...the shelf where they stored lost-and-found articles.* 届けられた落し物を保管している棚

lot /lɒt/ (**lots**) **1** QUANT 数量詞 **A lot of** something or **lots of** it is a large amount of it. **A lot of** people or things, or **lots of** them, is a large number of them. たくさんの [QUANT 'of' n] □ *A lot of our land is used to grow crops for export.* 土地の大部分は輸出用の穀物栽培に使用されている. □ *He drank lots of milk.* 彼は牛乳をたくさん飲む. ● PRON 代名詞 **Lot** is also a pronoun. たくさん □ *I personally prefer to be in a town where there's lots going on.* 個人的にはいろんなことが次々と起こる街中にいるほうが好きだ. □ *I learned a lot from him about how to run a band.* バンドの運営方法について彼から多くを学んだ. **2** ADV 副詞 **A lot** means to a great extent or degree. かなり □ *Matthew's out quite a lot doing his research.* マシューはリサーチのために出かけることが非常に多い. □ *I like you, a lot.* 君のこと好きだよ，すごく. **3** ADV 副詞 If you do something **a lot**, you do it often or for a long time. しょっちゅう [ADV after v] □ *They went out a lot, to restaurants and bars.* 彼らはレストランやバーによく出かけた. **4** N-COUNT 可算名詞 You can use **lot** to refer to a set or group of things or people. 組，セット □ *He bought two lots of 1,000 shares in the company during August and September.* 彼は，8・9月期にその会社の1000株を2口購入した. **5** N-SING 単数名詞 You can refer to a specific group of people as a particular **lot**. 一な連中 [INFORMAL くだけた] □ *Future generations are going to think that we were a pretty boring lot.* 次世代の人々は我々を全くつまらない連中だと思うだろう. **6** N-SING 単数名詞 You can use **the lot** to refer to the whole of an amount that you have just mentioned. すべて，全部 [INFORMAL くだけた] □ *This may turn out to be the best football game of the lot.* これが今までで最高のフットボールの試合になるかもしれない. **7** N-SING 単数名詞 Your **lot** is the kind of life you have or the things that you have or experience. 運命，宿命 □ *She tried to accept her marriage as her lot in life but could not.* 彼女は結婚を人生における運命だと認めようとしたが，できなかった. **8** N-COUNT 可算名詞 A **lot** is a small area of land that belongs to a person or company. 土地，敷地 [AM 米国英語] □ *If oil or gold are discovered under your lot, you can sell the mineral rights.* 自分の所有地で原油や金が発見されれば，採掘権を売ることができる. **9** → see also **parking lot** **10** N-COUNT 可算名詞 A **lot** in an auction is one of the objects or groups of objects that are being sold. 一組 □ *The receivers are keen to sell the stores as one lot.* 管財人はその店をまとめて1組として販売することを強く望んでいる. **11** PHRASE 句 If people **draw lots** to decide who will do something, they each take a piece of paper from a container. One or more pieces of paper is marked, and the people who take marked pieces are chosen. くじを引く □ *For the first time in a World Cup finals, lots had to be drawn to decide who would finish second and third.* ワールドカップ決勝戦で初めて，どのチームが2位3位になるかを決定するのにくじが引かれた.

loth /loʊθ/ → see **loath**

lo·tion /loʊʃ°n/ (**lotions**) N-MASS 質量名詞 A **lotion** is a liquid that you use to clean, improve, or protect your skin or hair. ローション □ *...suntan lotion.* 日焼け止めローション

lot·tery /lɒtəri/ (**lotteries**) **1** N-COUNT 可算名詞 A **lottery** is a type of gambling game in which people buy numbered tickets. Several numbers are then chosen, and the people who have those numbers on their tickets win a prize. 宝くじ □ *...the national lottery.* 公営宝くじ **2** N-SING 単数名詞 If you describe something as a **lottery**, you mean that what happens depends entirely on luck or chance. 運任せ，巡り合わせ □ *The stockmarket is a lottery.* 株式市場は運任せのようなものだ.

→ see Word Web: **lottery**

loud /laʊd/ (**louder, loudest**) **1** ADJ 形容詞 If a noise is **loud**, the level of sound is very high and it can be easily heard. Someone or something that is **loud** produces a lot of noise. (音が) 大きい □ *Suddenly there was a loud bang.* 突然，ドカンという大きい音がした. □ *His voice became harsh and loud.* 彼の声がとげとげしく大きく

Word Web　lottery

People **gamble** for many different reasons. Some want to become rich. Some find it entertaining or exciting. Others need more **money** to live. **Lotteries** have become a popular form of **betting**. Most places have a lottery. **Winners** can choose between a **lump sum** payment and annual **payouts**. Either way, they usually have to pay the government about half their **winnings** in taxes. The **odds** of **winning** a lottery are very tiny. There is often only about one chance in 20 million of winning the **jackpot**. Studies have shown that poor people are the most likely to **play** the lottery.

なった. ●ADV 副詞 **Loud** is also an adverb. 大声で，大音量で [ADV after v] ❑ *She wonders whether Paul's hearing is OK because he turns the television up very loud.* 彼女は，ポールがテレビの音量をかなり上げたので耳が遠いのかと思った. ❷ **loud|ly** ADV 副詞 [ADV with v] 大声で，騒々しく ❑ *His footsteps echoed loudly in the tiled hall.* タイル張りのホールで彼の足音が大きくこだました. ❷ ADJ 形容詞 If you describe something, especially a piece of clothing, as **loud**, you dislike it because it has very bright colors or very large, bold patterns which look unpleasant. 派手な，けばけばしい [DISAPPROVAL 不賛成] ❑ *He liked to shock with his gold chains and loud clothes.* 彼は金の鎖や派手な服で人をぎょっとさせるのが好きだった. ❸ PHRASE 句 If you say or read something **out loud**, you say it or read it so that it can be heard, rather than just thinking it. 声に出して ❑ *Even Ford, who seldom smiled, laughed out loud a few times.* フォードでさえ，ふだんはめったに笑わないのに，何度か声に出して笑った. ❹ **for crying out loud** → see **cry**

Thesaurus　loud また次を参照:

ADJ.	deafening, noisy, piercing; (ant.) quiet, soft ❶
	flashy, gaudy, tasteless ❷

Word Partnership　loud は次の語句と使われる:

N.	loud **bang**, loud **crash**, loud **explosion**, loud **music**, loud **noise**, loud **voice** ❶
ADJ.	loud **and clear** ❶
V.	laugh out loud, read out loud, **say** *something* out loud, **think** out loud ❸

loud|speaker /laʊdspiːkər/ (**loudspeakers**) also **loud speaker** ❶ N-COUNT 可算名詞 A **loudspeaker** is a piece of electronic equipment that forms part of a public address system and transmits sound. 拡声器，スピーカー ❑ *The loudspeaker announced the arrival of the train.* スピーカーから電車の到着のアナウンスがあった. ❷ N-COUNT 可算名詞 A **loudspeaker** is a piece of equipment, for example, part of a radio or hi-fi system, through which sound comes out. スピーカー [BRIT 英国英語]

lounge /laʊndʒ/ (**lounges, lounging, lounged**) ❶ N-COUNT 可算名詞 In a hotel, club, or other public place, a **lounge** is a room where people can sit and relax. ラウンジ，休憩室 ❑ *I spoke to her in the lounge of a big Johannesburg hotel where she was attending a union meeting.* 彼女が出席する組合の会議が行われているヨハネスブルグの大きなホテルのラウンジで，彼女と話した. ❷ N-COUNT 可算名詞 In an airport, a **lounge** is a very large room where people can sit and wait for aircraft to arrive or leave. 待合室，ロビー ❑ *Instead of taking me to the departure lounge they took me right to my seat on the plane.* 出発ロビーに行く代わりに，まっすぐ飛行機の座席まで連れて行ってくれた. ❸ N-COUNT 可算名詞 In a house, a **lounge** is a room where people sit and relax. 居間，リビングルーム [BRIT 英国英語; AM family room 米国英語 **family room**] ❹ V-I 自動詞 If you **lounge** somewhere, you sit or lie there in a relaxed or lazy way. ゆったり座る，のんびり横になる ❑ *They ate and drank and lounged in the shade.* 彼らは飲み食いして，日陰でのんびりした.

louse /laʊs/ (**lice**) N-COUNT 可算名詞 **Lice** are small insects that live on the bodies of people or animals and bite them in order to feed off their blood. シラミ

lousy /laʊzi/ (**lousier, lousiest**) ❶ ADJ 形容詞 If you describe something as **lousy**, you mean that it is of very bad quality or that you do not like it. ひどい，お粗末な [INFORMAL くだけた] ❑ *He blamed Fiona for a lousy weekend.* 彼はひどい週末をフィオナのせいにした. ❑ *At Billy's Café, the menu is limited and the food is lousy.* ビリーズカフェーではメニューは限られていて食べ物はお粗末でした. ❷ ADJ 形容詞 If you describe someone as **lousy**, you mean that they are very bad at something they do. 下手な，ひどい [INFORMAL くだけた] ❑ *I was a lousy secretary.* 私はひどい秘書だった. ❸ ADJ 形容詞 If you describe the number or amount of something as **lousy**, you mean it is smaller than you think it should be. けちな [INFORMAL

くだけた] ❑ *The pay is lousy.* 給料は安い. ❹ ADJ 形容詞 If you feel **lousy**, you feel very ill. 気分が悪い [INFORMAL くだけた] ['feel/look' ADJ] ❑ *I wasn't actually sick but I felt lousy.* 実は吐き気はなかったけど，気分が悪かったの.

lout /laʊt/ (**louts**) N-COUNT 可算名詞 If you describe a man or boy as a **lout**, you are critical of them because they behave in an impolite or aggressive way. 不良 [DISAPPROVAL 不賛成] ❑ *...a drunken lout.* 酔っ払いの不良

lov|able /lʌvəbəl/ ADJ 形容詞 If you describe someone as **lovable**, you mean that they have attractive qualities, and are easy to like. 愛らしい ❑ *His vulnerability makes him even more lovable.* 彼のもろさがよけい愛らしく感じさせる.

love /lʌv/ (**loves, loving, loved**) ❶ V-T 他動詞 If you **love** someone, you feel romantically or sexually attracted to them, and they are very important to you. 愛する，恋をする ❑ *Oh, Amy, I love you.* ああ，エイミー，愛しているよ. ❷ N-UNCOUNT 不可算名詞 **Love** is a very strong feeling of affection toward someone who you are romantically or sexually attracted to. 愛，恋愛感情 ❑ *Our love for each other has been increased by what we've been through together.* 一緒に経験してきたことを通してお互いへの愛が増した. ❑ *...a old fashioned love story.* 古臭いラブストーリー ❸ V-T 他動詞 You say that you **love** someone when their happiness is very important to you, so that you behave in a kind and caring way toward them. 愛する，かわいがる ❑ *You'll never love anyone the way you love your baby.* 自分の赤ちゃんを愛するようにほかの人を愛することはないだろう. ❹ N-UNCOUNT 不可算名詞 **Love** is the feeling that a person's happiness is very important to you, and the way you show this feeling in your behavior toward them. 愛，愛情 ❑ *My love for all my children is unconditional.* 自分の子供全員に対する愛は絶対的だ. ❺ V-T 他動詞 If you **love** something, you like it very much. 大好きだ ❑ *We loved the food so much, especially the fish dishes.* 私たちは食べ物，特に魚料理が大好きだ. ❑ *...one of these people that loves to be in the outdoors.* アウトドア派の1人 ❻ V-T 他動詞 You can say that you **love** something when you consider that it is important and want to protect or support it. 愛する（大切に思い誇りを持つ）❑ *I love my country as you love yours.* だれもが母国を愛するように，私は母国を愛している. ❼ N-UNCOUNT 不可算名詞 **Love** is a strong liking for something, or a belief that it is important. 情熱，愛好 ❑ *This is no way to encourage a love of literature.* これは決して文学に対する情熱を促す方法ではない. ❽ N-COUNT 可算名詞 Your **love** is someone or something that you love. 愛する人，愛するもの ❑ *"She is the love of my life," he said.* 「彼女が生涯を通じての最愛の人だ」と彼は言った. ❾ V-T 他動詞 If you **would love to** have or do something, you very much want to have or do it. —したい ❑ *I would love to play for England again.* ぜひまたイングランドの代表選手になりたい. ❑ *I would love a hot bath and clean clothes.* 熱いお風呂と清潔な服が欲しい. ❿ NUM 数詞 In tennis, **love** is a score of zero. ラブ ❑ *He beat Thomas Muster of Austria three sets to love.* 彼はオーストリアのトーマス・マスターに3セットをラブで勝った. ⓫ CONVENTION 慣習表現 You can use expressions such as **love**, **love from**, and **all my love**, followed by your name, as an informal way of ending a letter to a friend or relative. 愛を込めて ❑ *...with love from Grandma and Grandpa.* おじいちゃんとおばあちゃんより愛を込めて ⓬ N-UNCOUNT 不可算名詞 If you send someone your **love**, you ask another person, who will soon be speaking or writing to them, to tell them that you are thinking about them with affection. 「よろしく伝えて」というときに用いる ❑ *Please give her my love.* 彼女によろしくお伝えください. ⓭ → see also **loving** ⓮ PHRASE 句 If you **fall in love with** someone, you start to be in love with them. 恋に落ちる ❑ *I fell in love with him because of his kind nature.* 彼の優しい性格にほれ込んだ. ⓯ PHRASE 句 If you **fall in love with** something, you start to like it very much. 好きになる ❑ *I fell in love with the movies.* それらの映画が好きになった. ⓰ PHRASE 句 If you **are in love with** someone, you feel romantically or sexually attracted to them, and they are very important to you. 恋している ❑ *Laura had never before been in love.* ローラはそれまでに恋をしたことがなかった. ⓱ PHRASE 句 If you **are in love with** something, you like it

Word Web   love

Until the Middle Ages, **romance** was not an important part of **marriage**. Parents decided who their children would marry. Often social class and political connections were the deciding factor. No one expected a couple to **fall in love**. However, during the Middle Ages, poets and musicians began to write about love in a new way. These **romantic** poems and songs describe a new type of courtship. In them, the man **woos** a woman for her **affection**. This is the basis for the modern idea of a romantic **bond** between **husband** and **wife**.

very much. 大好きだ ❑*He had always been in love with the enchanted landscape of the West.* 彼はいつも西洋のうっとりするような景色が大好きだった. **16** PHRASE 句 When two people **make love**, they have sex. セックスする, 寝る ❑*Have you ever made love to a girl before?* 今までに女の子と寝たことある?
→ see Word Web: **love**
→ see **emotion**

Thesaurus   *love* また次を参照:

v.	adore, cherish, treasure; (ant.) dislike, hate **1 3 5**
N.	adoration, devotion, tenderness; (ant.) hate **2 4 7**

Word Partnership   *love* は次の語句と使われる:

N.	love **a girl/guy**, love-**hate relationship**, love **your husband/wife**, love **a man/woman**, love **and marriage 1 3** love **of books**, love **of life**, love **music**, love **of nature 7**
ADJ.	**passionate** love, **romantic** love, **sexual** love **2** **great** love, **true** love **2 4 7 8**

love af|fair (love affairs) **1** N-COUNT 可算名詞 A **love affair** is a romantic and usually sexual relationship between two people who love each other but who are not married or living together. 情事, 浮気 ❑*...a stressful love affair with a married man.* ストレスが多い既婚男性との不倫 **2** N-SING 単数名詞 If you refer to someone's **love affair with** something, you mean that they like it a lot and are very enthusiastic about it. 熱狂, 夢中になること ❑*...the American love affair with firearms.* 銃器に対するアメリカ人の熱狂ぶり

love life (love lives) N-COUNT 可算名詞 Someone's **love life** is the part of their life that consists of their romantic and sexual relationships. 恋愛生活 ❑*His love life was complicated, and involved intense relationships.* 彼の恋愛生活は複雑で緊迫した関係がかかわっていた.

love|ly /lʌvli/ (lovelier, loveliest) **1** ADJ 形容詞 If you describe someone or something as **lovely**, you mean that they are very beautiful and therefore pleasing to look at or listen to. かわいい, すてきな ❑*You look lovely, Marcia.* マーシャ, すてきよ. ❑*He had a lovely voice.* 彼はすてきな声をしていた. ●**love|li|ness** N-UNCOUNT 不可算名詞 ❑*You are a vision of loveliness.* 君は夢かと思うほどの美人だ. **2** ADJ 形容詞 If you describe something as **lovely**, you mean that it gives you pleasure. うれしい, 素晴らしい [mainly SPOKEN 主に口語] ❑*Mary! How lovely to see you!.* メアリー! 会えて嬉しいよ! ❑*It's a lovely day.* とてもいい天気だ.

lov|er /lʌvər/ (lovers) **1** N-COUNT 可算名詞 Someone's **lover** is someone who they are having a sexual relationship with but are not married to. 愛人 ❑*Every Thursday she would meet her lover Leon.* 毎週木曜日に彼女は愛人のレオンに会っていた. **2** N-COUNT 可算名詞 If you are a **lover** of something such as animals or the arts, you enjoy them very much and take great pleasure in them. 愛好者 ❑*She is a great lover of horses and horse racing.* 彼女は馬と乗馬が大好きだ.

Word Partnership   *lover* は次の語句と使われる:

ADJ.	**former** lover, **great** lover, **jealous** lover, **married** lover **1**
N.	**animal** lover, **music** lover, **nature** lover **2**

lov|ing /lʌvɪŋ/ **1** ADJ 形容詞 Someone who is **loving** feels or shows love to other people. 愛情深い ❑*Jim was a most loving husband and father.* ジムはとても愛情深い夫であり父親だった. ●**lov|ing|ly** ADV 副詞 愛情を込めて ❑*Brian gazed lovingly at Mary Ann.* ブライアンは愛情を込めてメアリー・アンをじっと見た. **2** ADJ 形容詞 **Loving** actions are done with great enjoyment and care. 愛情に満ちた ❑*The house has been restored with loving care.* その家は大切に手入れされて修復した. ●**lov|ing|ly** ADV 副詞 愛情に満ちて ❑*I lifted the box and ran my fingers lovingly over the top.* 私は箱を持ち上げてさっと愛情を込めて上部に指を走らせた.

low /loʊ/ (lower, lowest, lows) **1** ADJ 形容詞 Something that is **low** measures only a short distance from the bottom to the top, or

from the ground to the top. (高さが) 低い ❑*...the low garden wall that separated the front garden from next door.* 隣の前庭を隔てている低い庭塀 ❑*The country, with its low, rolling hills was beautiful.* その国には低く起伏する丘陵があり, 美しかった. **2** ADJ 形容詞 If something is **low**, it is close to the ground, to sea level, or to the bottom of something. (位置・高度が) 低い ❑*He bumped his head on the low beams.* 彼は低いはりで頭をぶつけた. ❑*It was late afternoon and the sun was low in the sky.* 夕暮れ時で太陽は沈みかけていた. **3** ADJ 形容詞 When a river is **low**, it contains less water than usual. (水位が) 低い ❑*...pumps that guarantee a constant depth of water even when the supplying river is low.* 水を供給する川の水位が低いときでさえ一定の水量を保証するポンプ **4** ADJ 形容詞 You can use **low** to indicate that something is small in amount or that it is at the bottom of a particular scale. You can use phrases such as **in the low 80s** to indicate that a number or level is less than 85 but not as little as 80. (量が) 少ない ❑*Casualties remained remarkably low.* 犠牲者数はかなり低い数値にとどまった. **2** *They are still having to live on very low incomes.* 彼らは依然としてかなり低所得での生活を強いられている. **5** ADJ 形容詞 **Low** is used to describe people who are not considered to be very important because they are near the bottom of a particular scale or system. (身分・地位が) 低い ❑*She refused to promote Colin above the low rank of "legal adviser."* 彼女は「顧問弁護士」の低階級以上にコリンを昇進することに反対した. **6** N-COUNT 可算名詞 If something reaches a **low** of a particular amount or degree, that is the smallest it has ever been. 最低値 ❑*Prices dropped to a low of about $1.12 in December.* 価格は12月に底値の約1.12ドルまで落ちた. **7** ADJ 形容詞 If the quality or standard of something is **low**, it is very poor. (質・水準が) 低い ❑*A school would not accept low-quality work from any student.* 学校は学生からのレベルの低い提出物を受け付けない. ❑*The inquiry team criticizes staff at the psychiatric hospital for the low standard of care.* 調査団はその精神病院の職員を看護の水準が低いと非難した. **8** ADJ 形容詞 If a food or other substance is **low in** a particular ingredient, it contains only a small amount of that ingredient. 低— [v-link ADJ 'in' n] ❑*They look for foods that are low in calories.* 低カロリーの食べ物を探す. ●COMB IN ADJ 形容詞の複合 **Low** is also a combining form. (連結形で) 低— ❑*...low-sodium tomato sauce.* 低ナトリウムのトマトソース **9** ADJ 形容詞 If you have a **low** opinion of someone or something, you disapprove of them or dislike them. (評価などが) 低い ❑*The majority of sex offenders have a low opinion of themselves.* 性犯罪者の多くは自分に自信がない. **10** ADJ 形容詞 You can use **low** to describe negative feelings and attitudes. (気分・態度が) よくない ❑*We are all very tired and morale is low.* 我々は皆とても疲れていて士気が低い. **11** ADJ 形容詞 If a sound or noise is **low**, it is deep. 低音の ❑*Then suddenly she gave a low, choking moan and began to tremble violently.* そこで突然彼女は低く息がつまるようなうめき声を上げ, ブルブルと震えだした. **12** ADJ 形容詞 If someone's voice is **low**, it is quiet or soft. 静かな, 小さい ❑*Her voice was so low he had to strain to catch it.* 彼女の声があまりにも小さくて彼は懸命に聞き取ろうとした. **13** ADJ 形容詞 A light that is **low** is not bright or strong. 薄暗い ❑*Their eyesight is poor in low light.* 薄暗いところではよく見えない. **14** ADJ 形容詞 If a radio, oven, or light is on **low**, it has been adjusted so that only a small amount of sound, heat, or light is produced. (音量・温度などが) 低い, 暗い ❑*She turned her little kitchen radio on low.* 彼女は台所にある小さなラジオのボリュームを下げた. ❑*Buy a dimmer switch and keep the light on low, or switch it off altogether.* 減光スイッチを購入し照明を暗くするか, 完全に消しなさい. **15** ADJ 形容詞 If you are **low** on something or if a supply of it is **low**, there is not much of it left. 不足している [v-link ADJ] ❑*We're a bit low on bed linen.* ベッドリネンが不足気味だ. **16** ADJ 形容詞 If you are **low**, you are depressed. 落ち込んで [INFORMAL くだけた] ❑*"I didn't ask for this job, you know," he tells friends when he is low.* 「この仕事を望んでいたわけじゃないんだよね。」と, 彼は落ち込むと友達に言う. **17** → see also **lower** **18** to look **high and low** → see **high** **19** low profile → see **profile** **20** to be running **low** → see **run**
→ see **tide**

Thesaurus   *low* また次を参照:

ADJ.	**bottom 1 2** **inferior, second-rate, shoddy 7**

low|er /loʊər/ (lowers, lowering, lowered) **1** ADJ 形容詞 You can use **lower** to refer to the bottom one of a pair of things. 下の方の [ADJ n, 'the' ADJ, 'of' n] □ She bit her lower lip. 彼女は下唇をかんだ. □ ...the lower of the two holes. 2つの穴のうち下の方 **2** ADJ 形容詞 You can use **lower** to refer to the bottom part of something. 下部の, 底部の [ADJ n] □ Use a small cushion to give support to the lower back. 腰のサポートに小さいクッションを使いなさい. **3** ADJ 形容詞 You can use **lower** to refer to people or things that are less important than similar people or things. 下級の [ADJ n, 'the' ADJ] □ Already the awards are causing resentment in the lower ranks of council officers. すでに賞が下級議員の間で不興を買っている. □ The nation's highest court reversed the lower court's decision. 国の最高裁が下級裁の判決を覆した. **4** V-T 他動詞 If you **lower** something, you move it slowly downward. 下げる [他動詞] □ Two reporters had to help lower the coffin into the grave. 2人のレポーターが棺を墓に下ろすのを手伝わなければならなかった. □ Sokolowski lowered himself into the black leather chair. ソコロフスキーは黒いレザーの椅子に身を沈めた. ●**low|er|ing** N-UNCOUNT 不可算名詞 下ろすこと □ ...the extinguishing of the Olympic flame and the lowering of the flag. 聖火の消火と五輪旗を下ろすこと **5** V-T 他動詞 If you **lower** something, you make it less in amount, degree, value, or quality. 減らす, 下げる, 落とす [他動詞] □ The Central Bank has lowered interest rates by 2 percent. 中央銀行は金利を2%下げた. ●**low|er|ing** N-UNCOUNT 不可算名詞 減らすこと, 下げること □ ...a package of social measures which included the lowering of the retirement age. 定年退職年齢の引き下げを含めた一連の社会対策 **6** V-T 他動詞 If someone **lowers** their head or eyes, they look downward, for example, because they are sad or embarrassed. うつむく □ She lowered her head and brushed past photographers as she went back inside. 彼女は中に戻るときうつむいてカメラマンのそばを通り過ぎた. **7** V-T 他動詞 [oft with brd-neg] If you say that you would not **lower yourself** by doing something, you mean that you would not behave in a way that would make you or other people respect you less. 品位を落とす □ Don't lower yourself, don't be the way they are. 自分の品位を落としてあいつらのようにはなるな. **8** V-T/V-I 他動詞/自動詞 If you **lower** your voice or if your voice **lowers**, you speak more quietly. (声を) 落とす [他動詞], (声が) 小さくなる [自動詞] □ The man moved closer, lowering his voice. その男は声をひそめて近寄ってきた. **9** → see also **low**

low|er|case also **lower-case** or **lower case** N-UNCOUNT 不可算名詞 **Lowercase** letters are small letters, not capital letters. 小文字 □ It was printed in lowercase. 小文字で印刷されていた.

low-key ADJ 形容詞 If you say that something is **low-key**, you mean that it is on a small scale rather than involving a lot of activity or being made to seem impressive or important. 控えめな, 小規模の □ The wedding will be a very low-key affair. その結婚式は地味味になるだろう.

low|ly /loʊli/ (lowlier, lowliest) ADJ 形容詞 If you describe someone or something as **lowly**, you mean that they are low in rank, status, or importance. 身分の低い, 下層階級の □ ...lowly bureaucrats pretending to be senators. 上院議員のふりをしている下級官僚

low-paid ADJ 形容詞 If you describe someone or their job as **low-paid**, you mean that their work earns them very little money. 低賃金の □ ...low-paid workers. 低賃金労働者

low-tech /loʊ tɛk/ ADJ 形容詞 **Low-tech** machines or systems are ones that do not use modern or sophisticated technology. ローテクの □ ...a simple form of low-tech electric propulsion. 単純な形式のローテク電気推進

loy|al /lɔɪəl/ ADJ 形容詞 Someone who is **loyal** remains firm in their friendship or support for a person or thing. 忠実な, 忠誠な [APPROVAL 賛成] □ They had remained loyal to the president. 彼らは大統領への忠誠心を維持した. ●**loy|al|ly** ADV 副詞 [ADV with v] 忠誠に □ They have loyally supported their party and their leader. 彼らは忠誠に党と党首を支持してきた.
→ see **hero**

loy|al|ty /lɔɪəlti/ (loyalties) **1** N-UNCOUNT 不可算名詞 **Loyalty** is the quality of staying firm in your friendship or support for someone or something. 忠実さ, 忠誠 □ I have sworn an oath of loyalty to the monarchy. 私は王室への忠誠を宣誓した. **2** N-COUNT 可算名詞 **Loyalties** are feelings of friendship, support, or duty toward someone or something. 忠誠心 □ She had developed strong loyalties to the Manet family. 彼女はマネ家に対して強い忠誠心を抱くようになった.

loy|al|ty card (loyalty cards) N-COUNT 可算名詞 A **loyalty card** is a plastic card that some stores give to regular customers. Each time the customer buys something from the store, points are electronically stored on their card and can be exchanged later for goods or services. ポイントカード

LPG /ɛl pi dʒi/ N-UNCOUNT 不可算名詞 **LPG** is a type of fuel consisting of hydrocarbon gases in liquid form. **LPG** is an abbreviation for "liquefied petroleum gas." 液化石油ガス

lu|bri|cate /lubrɪkeɪt/ (lubricates, lubricating, lubricated) V-T 他動詞 If you **lubricate** something such as a part of a machine, you put a substance such as oil on it so that it moves smoothly.

潤滑油を差す [FORMAL 形式ばった] □ Mineral oils are used to lubricate machinery. 機械を潤滑させるのに鉱物油が使用される. ●**lu|bri|ca|tion** /lubrɪkeɪʃən/ N-UNCOUNT 不可算名詞 潤滑 □ Use a touch of linseed oil for lubrication. 潤滑剤として少量のアマニ油を使いなさい.

Word Link luc ≈ light : hallucinate, lucid, translucent

lu|cid /lusɪd/ **1** ADJ 形容詞 **Lucid** writing or speech is clear and easy to understand. 明快な □ ...a lucid account of the history of mankind. 人類の歴史についての明快な説明 ●**lu|cid|ly** ADV 副詞 [ADV with v] 明快に □ Both of them had the ability to present complex matters lucidly. 2人とも複雑な問題を分かりやすく提起する能力を持っていた. ●**lu|cid|ity** /lusɪdɪti/ N-UNCOUNT 不可算名詞 明快さ □ His writings were marked by an extraordinary lucidity and elegance of style. 彼の作品は並外れた明快さと優美な文体で際立っていた. **2** ADJ 形容詞 If someone is **lucid**, they are thinking clearly again after a period of illness or confusion. 意識が戻った [FORMAL 形式ばった] □ He wasn't very lucid, he didn't quite know where he was. 彼は意識が戻っていなくて, 自分の居場所がよく分からなかった. ●**lu|cid|ity** N-UNCOUNT 不可算名詞 意識清明 □ The pain had lessened in the night, but so had his lucidity. 痛みは夜の間に治まったが, 彼の意識も薄らいだ.

luck /lʌk/ (lucks, lucking, lucked) **1** N-UNCOUNT 不可算名詞 **Luck** or **good luck** is success or good things that happen to you, that do not come from your own abilities or efforts. 運, 幸運 □ I knew I needed a bit of luck to win. 少しの運があれば勝てると分かってたんだ. □ The Sri Lankans have been having no luck with the weather. スリランカチームはこのところ天気に恵まれない. **2** N-UNCOUNT 不可算名詞 **Bad luck** is lack of success or bad things that happen to you, that have not been caused by yourself or other people. 不運 □ I had a lot of bad luck during the first half of this season. 今シーズンの前半はかなりの不運に見舞われた. **3** CONVENTION 慣習表現 If you ask someone the question "**Any luck?**" or "**No luck?**," you want to know if they have been successful in something they were trying to do. どうだった? [INFORMAL くだけた] □ "Any luck?" — "No." 「どうだった?」 「だめだった」 **4** CONVENTION 慣習表現 You can say "**Bad luck**" or "**Hard luck**" to someone when you want to express sympathy to them. 残念, 惜しい [INFORMAL くだけた, FORMULAE 決まり文句] □ Bad luck, man, just bad luck. 残念だね, ホント残念だよ. **5** CONVENTION 慣習表現 If you say "**Good luck**" or "**Best of luck**" to someone, you are telling them that you hope they will be successful in something they are trying to do. がんばって, うまくいきますように [INFORMAL くだけた, FORMULAE 決まり文句] □ He kissed her on the cheek. "Best of luck!" 彼は彼女の頬にキスをして「がんばれよ」と言った. **6** PHRASE 句 You can say someone **is in luck** when they are in a situation where they can have what they want or need. ついている, 運がいい □ You're in luck. The doctor's still in. ついていますね. 医者がまだいますよ. **7** PHRASE 句 If you say that someone **is out of luck**, you mean that they cannot have something which they can normally have. ついていない, 運が悪い □ "What do you want, Roy? If it's money, you're out of luck." 「ロイ, 何が欲しいの? もしお金なら残念だ.」

▶ **luck out** PHRASAL VERB 句動詞 If you **luck out**, you get some advantage or are successful because you have good luck. 運がいい □ Was he born to be successful, or did he just luck out? 彼は成功するように生まれついたのかそれとも単に運がいいのだろうか.

Word Partnership luck は次の語句と使われる:

ADJ.	**dumb** luck, **good** luck, **just** luck, **pure** luck, **sheer** luck **1**
V.	**bring** someone luck, **need a little** luck, **need some** luck, **push** your luck, **try** your luck, **wish** someone luck **1** **have any/bad/better/good/no** luck **1 2**

luck|i|ly /lʌkɪli/ ADV 副詞 You add **luckily** to a statement to indicate that it is good that a particular thing happened or is the case because otherwise the situation would have been difficult or unpleasant. 運よく, 幸いにも [ADV with cl] □ Luckily, we both love football. 幸いにも, 2人ともフットボールが大好きだ.

lucky /lʌki/ (luckier, luckiest) **1** ADJ 形容詞 You say that someone is **lucky** when they have something that is very desirable or when they are in a very desirable situation. ついている, ラッキーな □ I am luckier than most. I have a job. 私はほかの人より恵まれている. 仕事があるもの. □ He is incredibly lucky to be alive. 彼は生きていることが信じられないくらい運がいい. **2** ADJ 形容詞 Someone who is **lucky** seems to always have good luck. 運がいい, 幸運な □ Some people are born lucky aren't they? 生まれつき運がいい人もいるよね. **3** ADJ 形容詞 If you describe an action or experience as **lucky**, you mean that it was good or successful, and that it happened by chance and not as a result of planning or preparation. まぐれの □ They admit they are now desperate for a lucky break. 彼らは今や運が回ってくるのを切望していることを認めている. **4** ADJ 形容詞 A **lucky** object is something that people believe helps them to be successful. 縁起がいい, 幸運をもたら

す ❑*He did not have on his other lucky charm, a pair of green socks.* 彼は縁かつぎの緑の靴下をはいていなかった. **5** PHRASE 句 If you say that someone **will be lucky to** do or get something, you mean that they are very unlikely to do or get it, and will definitely not do or get any more than that. 難しいだろう ❑*You'll be lucky if you get any breakfast.* 朝食にありつくのは難しいだろう. ❑*Those remaining in work will be lucky to get the smallest of pay increases.* 職に残る者は少しでも昇給するのは難しいだろう.

Word Partnership　*lucky* は次の語句と使われる:

V.	be lucky, feel lucky, get lucky, lucky to get *something*, lucky to have *something* **1**
ADV.	lucky enough, pretty lucky, really lucky, so lucky, very lucky **1**
N.	lucky break, lucky guess **3**

lu|cra|tive /lúkrətɪv/ ADJ 形容詞 A **lucrative** activity, job, or business deal is very profitable. 金になる，もうかる ❑*Thousands of ex-army officers have found lucrative jobs in private security firms.* 何千人もの元軍人は民営の警備会社で高給の仕事を見つけた.

lu|di|crous /lúdɪkrəs/ ADJ 形容詞 If you describe something as **ludicrous**, you are emphasizing that you think it is foolish, unreasonable, or unsuitable. ばかばかしい [EMPHASIS 強調] ❑*It was ludicrous to suggest that the visit could be kept secret.* その訪問を秘密にしておくという提案はばかげていた. ● **lu|di|crous|ly** ADV 副詞 ばかばかしいほど ❑*By Western standards the prices are ludicrously low.* 西洋の水準ではばかばかしいほど安かった.

lug /lʌg/ (lugs, lugging, lugged) V-T 他動詞 If you **lug** a heavy or awkward object somewhere, you carry it there with difficulty. 引きずる [INFORMAL くだけた] ❑*Nobody wants to lug around huge suitcases full of clothes.* 服でいっぱいの大きなスーツケースを持ち歩きたい人はいない.

lug|gage /lʌgɪdʒ/ N-UNCOUNT 不可算名詞 **Luggage** is the suitcases and bags that you take with you when you travel. 手荷物 ❑*Leave your luggage in the hotel.* 手荷物はホテルに置いていきなさい.

> **Luggage** is an uncount noun. You can have **a piece of luggage** or **some luggage** but you cannot have "a luggage" or "some luggages." In British English, people normally use **luggage** when they are talking about everything that travelers carry. **Baggage** is a more technical word and is used for example when discussing airports or travel insurance. In American English, **luggage** refers to empty bags and suitcases and **baggage** refers to bags and suitcases with their contents. Both British and American speakers can refer to everything that travelers carry as their **bags**. American speakers can also call an individual suitcase a **bag**.

lug|gage rack (luggage racks) **1** N-COUNT 可算名詞 A **luggage rack** is a shelf for putting luggage on, on a vehicle such as a train or bus. 網棚，手荷物棚 **2** N-COUNT 可算名詞 A **luggage rack** is a metal frame that is fixed on top of a car and used for carrying large objects. ルーフラック [AM 米国英語]

luke|warm /lúkwɔrm/ **1** ADJ 形容詞 Something, especially a liquid, that is **lukewarm** is only slightly warm. 生ぬるい ❑*Wash your face with lukewarm water.* ぬるま湯で顔を洗いなさい. **2** ADJ 形容詞 If you describe a person or their attitude as **lukewarm**, you mean that they are not showing much enthusiasm or interest. やる気がない，いい加減な ❑*Economists have never been more than lukewarm toward him.* 経済学者は彼に対して中途半端な態度しかとってこなかった.

lull /lʌl/ (lulls, lulling, lulled) **1** N-COUNT 可算名詞 A **lull** is a period of quiet or calm in a longer period of activity or excitement. 小休止，途絶え ❑*There was a lull in political violence after the election of the current president.* 現大統領の選挙の後，政治的暴力が途絶えた. **2** V-T 他動詞 If you **are lulled into** feeling safe, someone or something causes you to feel safe at a time when you are not safe. なだめる，うまくなだめ〜にする ❑*It is easy to be lulled into a false sense of security.* うっかり安心してしまいやすい. ❑*I had been lulled into thinking the publicity would be a trivial matter.* 世間の注目なんてどうでもよいと思うようにうまくなだめられた.

lum|ber /lʌmbər/ (lumbers, lumbering, lumbered) **1** N-UNCOUNT 不可算名詞 **Lumber** consists of trees and large pieces of wood that has been roughly cut up. 材木 [mainly AM 主に米国英語] ❑*It was made of soft lumber, spruce by the look of it.* 見たところこぎれいな，柔らかい材木でできていた. **2** V-I 自動詞 If someone or something **lumbers** from one place to another, they move there very slowly and clumsily. のそのそ歩く ❑*He lumbered back to his chair.* 彼は自分のいすへのそのそと戻った.

lu|mi|nous /lúmɪnəs/ ADJ 形容詞 Something that is **luminous** shines or glows in the dark. 光を出す，輝く ❑*The luminous dial on the clock showed five minutes to seven.* 時計の光る文字盤による

と7時5分前だった.

lump /lʌmp/ (lumps, lumping, lumped) **1** N-COUNT 可算名詞 A **lump** of something is a solid piece of it. 塊 ❑*The potter shaped and squeezed the lump of clay into a graceful shape.* 陶工は粘土の塊を優美な形に作り変えた. ❑*...a lump of wood.* 木の塊 **2** N-COUNT 可算名詞 A **lump** on or in someone's body is a small, hard swelling that has been caused by an injury or an illness. しこり ❑*I've got a lump on my shoulder.* 肩にしこりがある. **3** N-COUNT 可算名詞 A **lump** of sugar is a small cube of it. 角砂糖 ❑*...a nugget of pure gold about the size of a lump of sugar.* 角砂糖くらいの大きさの天然の金の塊 **4** → see also **lump sum** **5** PHRASE 句 If you say that you have a **lump in your throat**, you mean that you have a tight feeling in your throat because of a strong emotion such as sorrow or gratitude. のどが詰まる思い，胸がいっぱいになる思い ❑*I stood there with a lump in my throat and tried to fight back tears.* 胸がいっぱいの思いでそこに立ち，必死で涙をこらえた.

▶ **lump together** PHRASAL VERB 句動詞 If a number of different people or things **are lumped together**, they are considered as a group rather than separately. 一緒にする，ひとまとめにする ❑*Policemen and prostitutes, bankers and butchers are all lumped together in the service sector.* 警官，売春婦，銀行員，そして肉屋は皆サービス業として同類に扱われる.

lump sum (lump sums) N-COUNT 可算名詞 A **lump sum** is an amount of money that is paid as a large amount on a single occasion rather than as smaller amounts on several separate occasions. 一括払い（の額）❑*...a tax-free lump sum of $50,000.* 非課税の総額5万ドル
→ see **lottery**

lumpy /lʌmpi/ (lumpier, lumpiest) ADJ 形容詞 Something that is **lumpy** contains lumps or is covered with lumps. 塊が多い，でこぼこの ❑*When the rice isn't cooked properly it goes lumpy and gooey.* ご飯がきちんと炊けていないと固まってネバネバする.

lu|nar /lúnər/ ADJ 形容詞 **Lunar** means relating to the moon. 月の [ADJ n] ❑*The vast volcanic slope was eerily reminiscent of a lunar landscape.* 巨大な火山の丘は不気味なほど月の風景を思い出させる.
→ see **eclipse**

lu|na|tic /lúnətɪk/ (lunatics) **1** N-COUNT 可算名詞 If you describe someone as a **lunatic**, you think they behave in a dangerous, stupid, or annoying way. 頭がおかしい人，変人 [INFORMAL くだけた, DISAPPROVAL 不賛成] ❑*Her son thinks she's an absolute raving lunatic.* 息子は彼女のことを完全に頭がいかれたやつだと思っている. **2** ADJ 形容詞 If you describe someone's behavior or ideas as **lunatic**, you think they are very foolish and possibly dangerous. ばかげた [DISAPPROVAL 不賛成] ❑*...the operation of the market taken to lunatic extremes.* ばかばかしいほどの究極手段がとられた市場捜査 **3** N-COUNT 可算名詞 People who were mentally ill used to be called **lunatics**. 精神異常者，狂人 [OLD-FASHIONED 古風な] ❑*...the lunatics in the Bedlam asylum.* ベドラム精神病院の精神患者

lunch /lʌntʃ/ (lunches, lunching, lunched) **1** N-VAR 可変性名詞 **Lunch** is the meal that you have in the middle of the day. ランチ ❑*Shall we meet somewhere for lunch?* 昼食にどこかで会いましょうか. ❑*He did not enjoy business lunches.* 彼には，ビジネスランチが楽しくなかった. **2** V-I 自動詞 When you **lunch**, you have lunch, especially at a restaurant. 昼食をとる [FORMAL 形式ばった] ❑*Only the extremely rich could afford to lunch at the Mirabelle.* よほどの大金持ちしかミラベルで昼食をとる余裕がない.
→ see **meal**

Word Partnership　*lunch* は次の語句と使われる:

V.	break for lunch, bring *your* lunch, buy *someone* lunch, eat lunch, go *somewhere* for lunch, go to lunch, have lunch, pack a lunch, serve lunch **1**
ADJ.	free lunch, good lunch, hot lunch, late lunch **1**

lunch|eon /lʌntʃən/ (luncheons) N-COUNT 詞 A **luncheon** is a formal lunch, for example, to celebrate an important event or to raise money for charity. 午さん会，昼食会 ❑*Earlier this month, a luncheon for former U.N. staff was held in Vienna.* 今月の初めに元国連職員の午さん会がウィーンで開かれた.

lunch|time /lʌntʃtaɪm/ (lunchtimes) also **lunch time** N-VAR 可変性名詞 **Lunchtime** is the period of the day when people have their lunch. 昼休み ❑*Could we meet at lunchtime?* 昼休みに会えますか?

lung /lʌŋ/ (lungs) N-COUNT 可算名詞 Your **lungs** are the two organs inside your chest which fill with air when you breathe in. 肺 ❑*...a smoker who died of lung cancer.* 肺がんで死亡した喫煙者
→ see **donor, respiratory**

lunge /lʌndʒ/ (lunges, lunging, lunged) V-I 自動詞 If you **lunge** in a particular direction, you move in that direction suddenly and clumsily. 突進する，飛びかかる ❑*He lunged at me, grabbing me violently.* 彼は私に飛びかかり乱暴にひっつかんだ. ● N-COUNT 可算名詞 **Lunge** is also a noun. 突進 ❑*The attacker knocked on their door and made a lunge for Wendy when she answered.* 暴行犯は玄関をノックし，

ウェンディが応答したとき彼女に飛びかかった.

lurch /lɜrtʃ/ (lurches, lurching, lurched) **1** V-I 自動詞 To **lurch** means to make a sudden movement, especially forward, in an uncontrolled way. ガクンと揺れる □ *As the car sped over a pothole she lurched forward.* 車が道路上の穴の上を高速で通り過ぎたとき彼女はガクンと前によろめいた. □ *Henry looked, stared, and lurched to his feet.* ヘンリーは視線を向け, じっと見てよろめいた. ● N-COUNT 可算名詞 **Lurch** is also a noun. 突然の揺れ, よろめき □ *The car took a lurch forward.* 車はガクン前方に揺れた. **2** V-I 自動詞 If you say that a person or organization **lurches from** one thing **to** another, you mean they move suddenly from one course of action or attitude to another in an uncontrolled way. 次々とーに見舞われる [DISAPPROVAL 不賛成] □ *The state government has lurched from one budget crisis to another.* 政府は次々と予算危機に見舞われた. ● N-COUNT 可算名詞 **Lurch** is also a noun. 窮地 □ *The property sector was another casualty of the lurch toward higher interest rates.* 不動産部門も金利の上昇によって被害を受けていた.

lure /lʊər/ (lures, luring, lured) **1** V-T 他動詞 To **lure** someone means to trick them into a particular place or to trick them into doing something that they should not do. 誘惑する □ *He lured her to his home and shot her with his father's gun.* 彼は彼女を家に誘い込み父親の銃で撃った. □ *They did not realize that they were being lured into a trap.* わなに誘い込まれたとは気付いていなかった. **2** N-COUNT 可算名詞 A **lure** is an object which is used to attract animals, especially fish, so that they can be caught. おとり, ルアー **3** N-COUNT 可算名詞 A **lure** is an attractive quality that something has, or something that you find attractive. 魅力 □ *The excitement of hunting big game in Africa has been a lure to Europeans for 200 years.* アフリカで大きな獲物を捕まえる刺激は200年間ヨーロッパ人をひきつけた.

lurid /lʊərɪd/ **1** ADJ 形容詞 If you say that something is **lurid**, you are critical of it because it involves a lot of violence, sex, or shocking detail. 過激な, 生々しい [DISAPPROVAL 不賛成] □ *...lurid accounts of Claire's sexual exploits.* クレアの性的偉業についての生々しい報告 **2** ADJ 形容詞 If you describe something as **lurid**, you do not like it because it is very brightly colored. けばけばしい, どぎつい [DISAPPROVAL 不賛成] □ *She took care to paint her toe nails a lurid red or orange.* 丁寧に足のつめをけばけばしい赤かオレンジ色に塗った.

lurk /lɜrk/ (lurks, lurking, lurked) **1** V-I 自動詞 If someone **lurks** somewhere, they wait there secretly so that they cannot be seen, usually because they intend to do something bad. 待ち伏せす る □ *He thought he saw someone lurking above the chamber during the address.* 演説中にだれかが議場の上で待ち伏せをしているのを見たと思った. **2** V-I 自動詞 If something such as a danger, doubt, or fear **lurks** somewhere, it exists but is not obvious or easily recognized. 潜んでいる □ *Hidden dangers lurk in every family home.* どの家庭にも闇が潜んでいる.

luscious /lʌʃəs/ **1** ADJ 形容詞 If you describe a woman or something about her as **luscious**, you mean that you find her or this thing sexually attractive. 官能的な □ *...a luscious young blonde.* 官能的な若いブロンド女 **2** ADJ 形容詞 **Luscious** food is juicy and very good to eat. おいしい □ *...a small apricot tree which bore luscious fruit.* おいしい実がなる小さなアンズの木

lush /lʌʃ/ (lushes, lusher, lushest) **1** ADJ 形容詞 **Lush** fields or gardens have a lot of very healthy grass or plants. 青々とした □ *...the lush green meadows bordering the river.* 川のそばにある青々とした草原 **2** ADJ 形容詞 If you describe a place or thing as **lush**, you mean that it is very luxurious. 豪華な [v-link ADJ] □ *The Carlton-intercontinental hotel is lush, plush, and very non- backpacker.* カールトン・インターコンチネンタル・ホテルは豪華で高級でバックパッカーには適していない. **3** N-COUNT 可算名詞 If you describe someone as a **lush**, you mean that they drink too much alcohol. のんべえ,

大酒のみ

lust /lʌst/ **1** N-UNCOUNT 不可算名詞 **Lust** is a feeling of strong sexual desire for someone. 強い性欲, 肉欲 □ *His relationship with Angie was the first which combined lust with friendship.* アンジーとは友情と肉欲が混ざり合わさった初めての関係だった. **2** N-UNCOUNT 不可算名詞 A **lust** for something is a very strong and eager desire to have it. 欲望 □ *It was Fred's lust for glitz and glamour that was driving them apart.* 二人を隔てているのはフレッドの華麗な世界への欲望だった.

luxurious /lʌgʒʊəriəs/ **1** ADJ 形容詞 If you describe something as **luxurious**, you mean that it is very comfortable and expensive. 豪華な, ぜいたくな □ *Our honeymoon was two days in Las Vegas at a luxurious hotel called Le Mirage.* 新婚旅行ではラスベガスのレ・ミラージュという豪華ホテルで2泊した. ● **luxuriously** ADV 副詞 豪華に, ぜいたくに □ *The dining-room is luxuriously furnished and carpeted.* ダイニングルームには豪華な家具があり高級カーペットが敷かれていた. **2** ADJ 形容詞 **Luxurious** means feeling or expressing great pleasure and comfort. 満足した □ *Amy tilted her wine in her glass with a luxurious sigh.* エイミーは満足そうなため息をつきながらグラスのワインを傾けた. ● **luxuriously** ADV 副詞 [ADV after v] 満足して □ *Liz laughed, stretching luxuriously.* リズは笑って気持ちよさそうに体を伸ばした.

luxury /lʌkʃəri, lʌgʒə-/ (luxuries) **1** N-UNCOUNT 不可算名詞 **Luxury** is very great comfort, especially among beautiful and expensive surroundings. ぜいたく, 豪勢さ □ *By all accounts he leads a life of considerable luxury.* 皆の話では, 彼は非常にぜいたくな暮らしをしているらしい. **2** N-COUNT 可算名詞 A **luxury** is something expensive which is not necessary but which gives you pleasure. 高級品, ぜいたく □ *A week by the sea is a luxury they can no longer afford.* 海辺で1週間というのは, もはや彼らにとってはかなわない贅沢だ. **3** ADJ 形容詞 A **luxury** item is something expensive which is not necessary but which gives you pleasure. ぜいたくな, 高級な [ADJ n] □ *He could not afford luxury food on his pay.* 彼の給料ではぜいたくな食品は買えなかった. **4** N-SING 単数名詞 A **luxury** is a pleasure which you do not often have the opportunity to enjoy. ぜいたく, 快楽 □ *Hot baths are my favorite luxury.* 熱いお風呂が私のお決まりのぜいたくだ.

Thesaurus	*luxury* また次を参照:
N.	comfort, richness, splendor **1**
	extra, extravagance, nonessential, treat **2 4**

lying /laɪɪŋ/ **Lying** is the present participle of **lie**. lieの現在分詞

lynch /lɪntʃ/ (lynches, lynching, lynched) V-T 他動詞 If an angry crowd of people **lynch** someone, they kill that person by hanging them, without letting them have a trial, because they believe that that person has committed a crime. リンチで殺す, 絞首刑にする □ *They were about to lynch him when reinforcements from the army burst into the room and rescued him.* 陸軍からの増援部隊が部屋に突入し彼を救助したとき, 彼らはまさに彼を絞首刑にするところだった. ● **lynching** (lynchings) N-VAR 可変性名詞 リンチ □ *Some towns found that lynching was the only way to drive away bands of outlaws.* 町によってはリンチが無法者の集団を追い払う唯一の方法だと分かった.

lyric /lɪrɪk/ (lyrics) **1** ADJ 形容詞 **Lyric** poetry is written in a simple and direct style, and usually expresses personal emotions such as love. 叙情的な [ADJ n] □ *...Lawrence's splendid short stories and lyric poetry.* ローレンスの素晴らしい短編と叙情詩 **2** N-COUNT 可算名詞 The **lyrics** of a song are its words. 歌詞 □ *...Kurt Weill's Broadway opera with lyrics by Langston Hughes.* 作詞ラングストン・ヒューズのカート・ワイルのブロードウェイ・オペラ

Mm

M also **m** /ɛm/ (**M's, m's**) N-VAR 可変性名詞 **M** is the thirteenth letter of the English alphabet. 英語アルファベットの第13字

ma'am /mæm/ N-VOC 呼格名詞 People sometimes say **ma'am** as a polite way of addressing a woman whose name they do not know, especially in the American South. 奥様 [mainly AM 主に米国英語, POLITENESS 丁寧さ] ❑ *Would you repeat that please, ma'am?* もう1回言っていただけますか、奥さん.

ma|ca|bre /məkɑbrə/ ADJ 形容詞 You describe something such as an event or story as **macabre** when it is strange and horrible or upsetting, usually because it involves death or injury. 気味の悪い ❑ *Police have made a macabre discovery.* 警察は背筋の凍るような発見をした.

ma|chete /məʃɛti/ (**machetes**) N-COUNT 可算名詞 A **machete** is a large knife with a broad blade. (幅広の大きな) なた

ma|chine /məʃin/ (**machines, machining, machined**)
1 N-COUNT 可算名詞 A **machine** is a piece of equipment that uses electricity or an engine in order to do a particular kind of work. 機械 [also 'by' n] ❑ *I put the coin in the machine and pulled the lever.* 僕はマシンに硬貨を入れてレバーを引いた. **2** N-COUNT 可算名詞 You can use **machine** to refer to a large and well-controlled system or organization. 機構 ❑ *...Nazi Germany's military machine.* ナチドイツの軍事機構. **3** → see also **vending machine** **4** V-T 他動詞 If you **machine** something, you make it or work on it using a machine. 機械で作る, 機械にかける [usu passive] ❑ *The material is machined in a factory.* 原料は工場で機械加工される. ❑ *...machined brass zinc alloy gears.* 機械加工された真ちゅう亜鉛合金のギア
→ see **dairy**

Thesaurus   *machine* また次を参照:

N.	appliance, computer, gadget, mechanism **1**
	organization, structure, system **2**

Word Partnership   *machine* は次の語句と使われる:

V.	**design** a machine, **invent** a machine, **use a** machine **1**
ADJ.	**heavy** machine, **new** machine, machine **washable 1**
N.	machine **oil**, machine **parts**, machine **shop**, Xerox machine **1**

---

ma|chine gun (**machine guns**) N-COUNT 可算名詞 A **machine gun** is a gun which fires a lot of bullets one after the other very quickly. 機関銃 ❑ *Attackers fired machine guns at the convoy.* 襲撃者たちは護衛隊に向かって機関銃を発射した.

ma|chin|ery /məʃinəri/ **1** N-UNCOUNT 不可算名詞 You can use **machinery** to refer to machines in general, or machines that are used in a factory or on a farm. 機械類 ❑ *...quality tools and machinery.* 上質の道具と機械類. **2** N-SING 単数名詞 The **machinery** of a government or organization is the system and all the procedures that it uses to deal with things. 機構 ❑ *The machinery of democracy could be created quickly.* 民主主義の機構は迅速に作ることができた.

ma|chin|ist /məʃinɪst/ (**machinists**) N-COUNT 可算名詞 A **machinist** is a person whose job is to operate a machine, especially in a factory. 機械運転者 ❑ *His father is a machinist in an aerospace plant.* 彼の父親は航空宇宙工場で機械工をしている.

macho /mɑtʃoʊ/ ADJ 形容詞 You use **macho** to describe men who are very conscious and proud of their masculinity. 男っぽい [INFORMAL くだけた] ❑ *...displays of macho bravado.* 男っぽい空威張りの誇示

macke|rel /mækərəl, mækrəl/ (**mackerel**)

Mackerel is both the singular and the plural form.
Mackerel は単数形でも複数形でもある.

N-VAR 可変性名詞 A **mackerel** is a sea fish with a dark, patterned back. サバ ❑ *Almiro's boat had sailed out to the middle of the bay to fish for mackerel.* アルミロの船はサバ漁のため入り江の中央へと出港していた. ● N-UNCOUNT 不可算名詞 **Mackerel** is this fish eaten as food. サバ ❑ *...piles of smoked mackerel.* 燻製のサバの山.

mad /mæd/ (**madder, maddest**) **1** ADJ 形容詞 If you say that

---

someone is **mad**, you mean that they are very angry. 怒った [INFORMAL くだけた] ❑ *You're just mad at me because I don't want to go.* あなたは、私が行きたくないから私に腹を立てているだけよ. **2** ADJ 形容詞 You use **mad** to describe people or things that you think are very foolish. ひどくばかげた [DISAPPROVAL 不賛成] ❑ *You'd be mad to work with him again.* 彼とまた組むなんて君は無謀だ. ● **mad|ness** N-UNCOUNT 不可算名詞 愚行 ❑ *It is political madness.* それは政治的愚行だ. **3** ADJ 形容詞 Someone who is **mad** has a mind that does not work in a normal way, with the result that their behavior is very strange. 気の狂った ❑ *She was afraid of going mad.* 彼女は気が狂うのではないかと心配した. ● **mad|ness** N-UNCOUNT 不可算名詞 狂気 ❑ *He was driven to the brink of madness.* 彼は気が狂う瀬戸際まで追い込まれた. **4** ADJ 形容詞 [v-link ADJ 'about/on' n] If you are **mad about** something or someone, you like them very much. 熱狂した [INFORMAL くだけた] ❑ *She's not as mad about sports as I am.* 彼女は私ほどスポーツ狂ではない. ❑ *He's mad about you.* 彼はあなたに夢中だ. COMB IN ADJ 形容詞の複合 ● **Mad** is also a combining form. 一狂 [mainly BRIT 主に英国英語] ❑ *...his football-mad son.* 彼のフットボール狂の息子. **5** ADJ 形容詞 **Mad** behavior is wild and uncontrolled. 血迷った ❑ *You only have an hour to complete the game so it's a mad dash against the clock.* たった1時間で試合を終了しなければならないから、時間との激しい競争だ. ● **mad|ly** ADV 副詞 [ADV with v] 激しく ❑ *Down in the streets people were waving madly.* 下の街路では人々が激しく手を振っていた. **6** PHRASE 句 If you say that someone or something **drives you mad**, you mean that you find them extremely annoying. 一をいらいら立腹させる [INFORMAL くだけた] ❑ *There are certain things he does that drive me mad.* 彼の行動には私をとても怒らせるものがある. **7** PHRASE 句 If you do something **like mad**, you do it very energetically or enthusiastically. 猛烈に [INFORMAL くだけた] ❑ *He was weight training like mad.* 彼は猛烈にウエイトトレーニングをしていた. **8** → see also **madly**

Thesaurus   *mad* また次を参照:

ADJ.	angry, furious **1**
	crazy, foolish, senseless **2**
	deranged, insane **3**
	crazy **4**

Word Partnership   *mad* は次の語句と使われる:

V.	**get** mad, **make** *someone* mad **1**
	go mad **3**
N.	mad **as hell 1**
	mad **dog**, mad **scientist 3**
	mad **dash**, mad **rush 5**

---

mad|am /mædəm/ also **Madam** N-VOC 呼格名詞 People sometimes say **Madam** as a very formal and polite way of addressing a woman whose name they do not know. For example, a store clerk might address a woman customer as **Madam**. 奥様 [POLITENESS 丁寧さ] ❑ *Try them on, madam.* お客様、お試しください

mad|den /mædⁿn/ (**maddens, maddening, maddened**) V-T 他動詞 To **madden** a person or animal means to make them very angry. 激怒させる ❑ *The deer were maddening farmers by eating their crops.* シカに作物を食べられて農業経営者たちは逆上していた.

mad|den|ing /mædⁿnɪŋ/ ADJ 形容詞 If you describe something as **maddening**, you mean that it makes you feel angry, irritated, or frustrated. ひどく腹立たしい ❑ *Shopping during sales can be maddening.* セールス期間の買い物は頭がおかしくなるほど激烈になることがある. ● **mad|den|ing|ly** ADV 副詞 腹立たしいほどに ❑ *The service is maddeningly slow.* サービスはイライラするほど遅い.

made /meɪd/ **1** **Made** is the past tense and past participle of **make**. make の過去・過去分詞 **2** ADJ 形容詞 If something is **made of** or **made out of** a particular substance, that substance was used to build it. (原料で) 作る [v-link ADJ 'of/out of' n] ❑ *The top of the table is made of glass.* テーブルの天板はガラス製だ. **3** PHRASE 句 If you say that someone **has it made** or **has got it made**, you mean that they are certain to be rich or successful. 成功を確実にしている [INFORMAL くだけた] ❑ *When I was at school, I thought I had it made.* 私は学生時代に成功は確実だと思っていた.

made-up also **made up** 1 ADJ 形容詞 If you are **made up**, you are wearing makeup such as powder or eye shadow. 化粧した [v-link ADJ] □ *She was beautifully made up, beautifully groomed.* 彼女は美しく化粧し、美しく身づくろいをしていた. 2 ADJ 形容詞 A **made-up** word, name, or story is invented, rather than really existing or being true. 作られた □ *It looks like a made-up word.* それは勝手に作られた言葉らしい.

mad|ly /mædli/ ADV 副詞 You can use **madly** to indicate that one person loves another a great deal. 猛烈に □ *She has fallen madly in love with him.* 彼女は彼に熱烈な恋をしている.

mag /mæg/ (**mags**) N-COUNT 可算名詞 A **mag** is the same as a magazine. 雑誌 [INFORMAL くだけた] □ *...a well-known glossy mag.* 有名なグラビア誌.

maga|zine /mægəzin, -zin/ (**magazines**) 1 N-COUNT 可算名詞 A **magazine** is a publication with a paper cover which is issued regularly, usually every week or every month, and which contains articles, stories, photographs, and advertisements. 雑誌 □ *Her face is on the cover of a dozen or more magazines.* 彼女の顔はかなり多くの雑誌の表紙を飾っている. 2 N-COUNT 可算名詞 In an automatic gun, the **magazine** is the part that contains the bullets. 弾倉 □ *The corporal ignored him, sliding the empty magazine from his weapon and replacing it with a fresh one.* 伍長は彼を無視し、自分の武器から空の弾倉を引っ張り出して新しいものと交換した.

→ see **advertising, library**

mag|got /mægət/ (**maggots**) N-COUNT 可算名詞 **Maggots** are creatures that look like very small worms and turn into flies. うじ

mag|ic /mædʒɪk/ 1 N-UNCOUNT 不可算名詞 **Magic** is the power to use supernatural forces to make impossible things happen, such as making people disappear or controlling events in nature. 魔力 □ *They believe in magic.* 彼らは魔力を信じている. □ *...the use of magic to combat any adverse powers or influences.* どのような反対の勢力や影響力とも戦うために呪術の使用 2 N-UNCOUNT 不可算名詞 You can use **magic** when you are referring to an event that is so wonderful, strange, or unexpected that it seems as if supernatural powers have caused it. You can also say that something happens **as if by magic** or **like magic**. 魔法 □ *All this was supposed to work like magic.* これはすべて魔法のように効くはずだった. 3 ADJ 形容詞 You use **magic** to describe something that does things, or appears to do things, by magic. 魔法の [ADJ n] □ *So it's a magic potion?* じゃあ、それは魔法の薬ですか. 4 N-UNCOUNT 不可算名詞 **Magic** is the art and skill of performing mysterious tricks to entertain people, for example by making things appear and disappear. 手品 □ *His secret hobby: performing magic tricks.* 彼のひそかな趣味は手品をすることだ. 5 N-UNCOUNT 不可算名詞 If you refer to **the magic of** something, you mean that it has a special mysterious quality which makes it seem wonderful and exciting to you and which makes you feel happy. 不思議な力 □ *It infected them with some of the magic of a lost age.* それは失われた時代の魔法で彼らを感化した. ● ADJ 形容詞 **Magic** is also an adjective. 不思議な □ *Then came those magic moments in the rose garden.* そして、バラ園であの素晴らしいことが起きる瞬間がやってきた. 6 N-UNCOUNT 不可算名詞 If you refer to a person's **magic**, you mean a special talent or ability that they have, which you admire or consider very impressive. 魅力 □ *The 32-year-old Jamaican-born fighter believes he can still regain some of his old magic.* 32歳のジャマイカ生まれのボクサーは、今でも昔の素晴らしい力を取り戻せると信じている. 7 ADJ 形容詞 You can use expressions such as **the magic number** and **the magic word** to indicate that a number or word is the one which is significant or desirable in a particular situation. 魔法の ['the' ADJ n] □ *...their quest to gain the magic number of 270 electoral votes on Election Day.* 彼らによる、選挙日に270票というマジックナンバー獲得の追求 8 ADJ 形容詞 **Magic** is used in expressions such as **there is no magic formula** and **there is no magic solution** to say that someone will have to make an effort to solve a problem, because it will not solve itself. 魔法の [ADJ n, with neg] □ *There is no magic formula for producing winning products.* 成功する製品をつくる魔法のような手法などありはしない.

Thesaurus *magic* また次を参照:
N. enchantment, illusion, sorcery, witchcraft 1

magi|cal /mædʒɪkəl/ 1 ADJ 形容詞 Something that is **magical** seems to use magic or to be able to produce magic. 魔術的な □ *...the story of Sin-Sin, a little boy who has magical powers.* 魔力を持つ男の子シンシンの物語. ● **magi|cal|ly** /mædʒɪkli/ [ADV with v] 魔法のように □ *During the holiday season the town is magically transformed into a Christmas wonderland.* 休暇シーズンには、町は魔法のようにクリスマスの不思議の国に変貌する. 2 ADJ 形容詞 You can say that a place or object is **magical** when it has a special mysterious quality that makes it seem wonderful and exciting. 不思議な □ *The beautiful island of Bermuda is a magical place to get married.* 美しいバミューダ島は魅惑的な結婚場所だ.

magi|cian /mədʒɪʃən/ (**magicians**) N-COUNT 可算名詞 A **magician** is a person who entertains people by doing magic tricks. 手品師

mag|is|trate /mædʒɪstreɪt/ (**magistrates**) N-COUNT 可算名詞 A **magistrate** is an official who acts as a judge in law courts which deal with minor crimes or disputes. 微罪裁判官 □ *She will face a local magistrate on Tuesday.* 彼女は火曜日に地元の微罪裁判官の裁判を受けることになる.

Word Link   magn ≈ great : **magnate, magnify, magnitude**

mag|nate /mægneɪt, -nɪt/ (**magnates**) N-COUNT 可算名詞 A **magnate** is someone who has earned a lot of money from a particular business or industry. 大事業家 □ *...a multimillionaire shipping magnate.* 大富豪の海運王.

mag|net /mægnɪt/ (**magnets**) 1 N-COUNT 可算名詞 If you say that something is a **magnet** or is like a **magnet**, you mean that people are very attracted by it and want to go to it or look at it. 人を引き付けるもの □ *Prospect Park, with its vast lake, is a magnet for all health freaks.* 広大な湖のあるプロスペクト公園は、すべての健康ファンにとって魅力的だ. 2 N-COUNT 可算名詞 A **magnet** is a piece of iron or other material which attracts iron toward it. 磁石 □ *It's possible to hang a nail from a magnet and then use that nail to pick up another nail.* 釘を磁石から垂らし、その釘で別の釘を拾い上げることが可能だ.

→ see Word Web: **magnet**

mag|net|ic /mægnɛtɪk/ 1 ADJ 形容詞 If something metal is **magnetic**, it acts like a magnet. 磁気を帯びた □ *...magnetic particles.* 磁粉. 2 ADJ 形容詞 You use **magnetic** to describe something that is caused by or relates to the force of magnetism. 磁気の □ *The electrically charged gas particles are affected by magnetic forces.* 帯電気体粒子は磁力の影響を受ける. 3 ADJ 形容詞 You use **magnetic** to describe tapes and other objects which have a coating of a magnetic substance and contain coded information that can be read by computers or other machines. 磁気の □ *...her magnetic-strip ID card.* 彼女の磁気ストライプIDカード. 4 ADJ 形容詞 If you describe something as **magnetic**, you mean that it is very attractive to people because it has unusual, powerful, and exciting qualities. 人を引き付ける □ *...the magnetic effect of the prosperous American economy on would-be immigrants.* 好景気の米国経済の移民希望者を引き付ける効果.

mag|net|ism /mægnɪtɪzəm/ 1 N-UNCOUNT 不可算名詞 Someone or something that has **magnetism** has unusual, powerful, and exciting qualities which attract people to them. 人を引き付ける力 □ *There was no doubting the animal magnetism of the man.* その男性に肉体的魅力があることは疑いなかった. 2 N-UNCOUNT 不可算名詞 **Magnetism** is the natural power of some objects and substances, especially iron, to attract other objects toward them. 磁力 □ *...his research in electricity and magnetism.* 電気および磁力に関する彼の研究

mag|ni|fi|ca|tion /mægnɪfɪkeɪʃən/ (**magnifications**) 1 N-UNCOUNT 不可算名詞 **Magnification** is the act or process of magnifying something. 拡大 □ *The man was tall, his figure shortened by the magnification of Lenny's binoculars.* その男性は背が高かったが、その姿はレニーの双眼鏡の拡大で短く見えていた. 2 N-VAR 可変性名詞 **Magnification** is the degree to which a lens, mirror, or other device can magnify an object, or the degree to which the object is magnified. 倍率 □ *The electron microscope uses a beam of electrons to produce images at high magnifications.* 電子顕微鏡は電子ビームを使用して高倍率の像を出力します.

mag|nifi|cent /mægnɪfɪsənt/ ADJ 形容詞 If you say that

m

Word Web   magnet

Magnets have a north **pole** and a south pole. One side has a **negative charge** and the other side has a **positive** charge. The negative side of a magnet **attracts** the positive side of another magnet. This is where the phrase "opposites attract" comes from. Two sides that have the same charge will **repel** each other. The earth itself is a huge magnet, with a North Pole and a South Pole. A **compass** uses a magnetized needle to indicate directions. The "north" end of the needle always points toward the earth's North Pole.

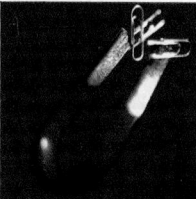

something or someone is **magnificent**, you mean that you think they are extremely good, beautiful, or impressive. すばらしい □...*a magnificent country house in wooded grounds.* 樹木の茂った敷地の素敵なカントリーハウス. ● **mag|nifi|cence** N-UNCOUNT 不可算名詞 壮大さ □ *I shall never forget the magnificence of the Swiss mountains and the beauty of the lakes.* スイスの山々の壮大さと湖の美しさを私は決して忘れないだろう. ● **mag|nifi|cent|ly** ADV 副詞 壮大に □ *The team played magnificently throughout the competition.* そのチームは試合中ずっと立派なプレーをした.

> **Word Link** magn ≈ great : *magnate, magnify, magnitude*

mag|ni|fy /mǽgnɪfaɪ/ (**magnifies, magnifying, magnified**) ■ V-T 他動詞 To **magnify** an object means to make it appear larger than it really is, by means of a special lens or mirror. (レンズなどで) 拡大する □ *This version of the Digges telescope magnifies images 11 times.* ディグス望遠鏡のこの改造版は像を11倍に拡大する. □ *A lens would magnify the picture so it would be like looking at a large TV screen.* レンズは画像を拡大するので, 大型テレビの画面を見ているような感じになるだろう. ■ V-T 他動詞 To **magnify** something means to increase its effect, size, loudness, or intensity. 強める □ *Poverty and human folly magnify natural disasters.* 貧困と人間の愚かさは自然災害を増幅する. ■ V-T 他動詞 If you **magnify** something, you make it seem more important or serious than it really is. 誇張する □ *They do not grasp the broad situation and spend their time magnifying ridiculous details.* 彼らは状況の大筋を把握せず, ばかばかしい細部を誇張して時間を浪費している.

mag|ni|tude /mǽgnɪtud/ ■ N-UNCOUNT 不可算名詞 If you talk about the **magnitude** of something, you are talking about its great size, scale, or importance. 大きさ □ *An operation of this magnitude is going to be difficult.* この規模の運営は困難になるでしょう. ■ PHRASE 句 You can use **order of magnitude** when you are giving an approximate idea of the amount or importance of something. 規模の等級 □ *America and Russia do not face a problem of the same order of magnitude as Japan.* アメリカとロシアは日本と同規模の大きさの問題には直面しない.

mag|pie /mǽgpaɪ/ (**magpies**) N-COUNT 可算名詞 A **magpie** is a large black and white bird with a long tail. カササギ

ma|hoga|ny /məhɒ́gəni/ N-UNCOUNT 不可算名詞 **Mahogany** is a dark reddish brown wood that is used to make furniture. マホガニー □...*mahogany tables and chairs.* マホガニーのテーブルといす.

maid /méɪd/ (**maids**) N-COUNT 可算名詞 A **maid** is a woman who works as a servant in a hotel or private house. お手伝い, メイド □ *A maid brought me breakfast at nine o'clock.* メイドが9時に私に朝食を運んできた.

maid|en /méɪdⁿ/ (**maidens**) ■ N-COUNT 可算名詞 A **maiden** is a young girl or woman. 少女 [LITERARY 文語的] □...*stories of noble princes and their brave deeds on behalf of beautiful maidens.* 高貴な王子たちと, 美しい乙女のために彼らが行った勇敢な行為の物語. ■ ADJ 形容詞 The **maiden** voyage or flight of a ship or aircraft is the first official journey that it makes. 初めての [ADJ n] □ *In 1912, the Titanic sank on her maiden voyage.* 1912年にタイタニック号は処女航海で沈没した.

maid|en name (**maiden names**) N-COUNT 可算名詞 A married woman's **maiden name** is her parents' surname, which she used before she got married and started using her husband's surname. 女性の結婚前の姓 □ *The marriage broke up in 1997 and she took back her maiden name of Boreman.* 結婚は1997年に破綻 (はたん) し, 彼女は結婚前の姓であるボアマンに戻った.

mail /méɪl/ (**mails, mailing, mailed**) ■ N-SING 単数名詞 The **mail** is the public service or system by which letters and packages are collected and delivered. 郵便 ['the' N, also 'by' N] □ *Your check is in the mail.* あなたの小切手は郵便に出しています. ■ N-UNCOUNT 不可算名詞 You can refer to letters and packages that are delivered to you as **mail**. 郵便物 [also 'the' N] □ *There was no mail except the usual junk addressed to the occupant.* 居住者あてのいつもの広告郵便物以外, 郵便物はなかった. ■ V-T 他動詞 If you **mail** a letter or package to someone, you send it to them by putting it in a mailbox or taking it to a post office. 郵送する [mainly AM 主に米国英語] □ *Last year, he mailed the documents to French journalists.* 昨年, 彼はその文書をフランスのジャーナリストに郵送した. □ *He mailed me the contract.* 彼は私に契約書を郵送してきた. ■ V-T 他動詞 To **mail** a message to someone means to send it to them by means of e-mail or a computer network. 電子メールを送る ● N-COUNT 可算名詞 **Mail** is also a noun. メール □ *If you have any problems then send me a mail.* 何か問題があれば, メールをください. ■ → see also **airmail, electronic mail, e-mail, junk mail, mailing, surface mail**

> **Word Partnership** mail は次の語句と使われる:
>
> | | |
> |---|---|
> | PREP. | **by** mail, **in the** mail, **through the** mail ■ |
> | N. | mail **carrier, fan** mail ■ |
> | V. | **deliver** mail, **get** mail, **open** mail, **read** mail, **receive** mail, **send** mail ■ |

mail|box /méɪlbɒks/ (**mailboxes**) ■ N-COUNT 可算名詞 A **mailbox** is a box outside your house where your letters are delivered. 郵便受 □ *The next day there was a letter in her mailbox.* 次の日に彼女の郵便受に手紙が届いていた. ■ N-COUNT 可算名詞 A **mailbox** is a metal box in a public place, where you put letters and small packages to be collected. They are then sorted and delivered. 郵便ポスト [mainly AM 主に米国英語] □ *And with a trembling hand, he dropped the letters into the mailbox.* そして彼は震える手で郵便ポストに手紙を投函した. ■ N-COUNT 可算名詞 On a computer, your **mailbox** is the file where your e-mail is stored. メールボックス □ *The prank crammed his mailbox with computer-delivered electronic junk mail.* 彼のその悪ふざけのせいで彼のメールボックスはコンピュータの配信したジャンクメールでいっぱいになった.

mail|ing /méɪlɪŋ/ (**mailings**) ■ N-UNCOUNT 不可算名詞 **Mailing** is the activity of sending things to people through the postal service. 郵送 [also N ing] □ *The newsletter was printed toward the end of June and ready for mailing July 1.* ニュースレターは6月末にかけて印刷され, 7月1日に郵送の準備が整った. ■ N-COUNT 可算名詞 A **mailing** is something that is sent to people through the postal service. 郵便物 □ *Most of Mahony's expenses were for mass mailings to conservatives across the state.* マホーニーの出費のほとんどは州全体の保守派への大量郵便物だった.

mail|ing list (**mailing lists**) N-COUNT 可算名詞 A **mailing list** is a list of names and addresses that a company or organization keeps, so that they can send people information or advertisements. 郵送先名簿 □ *Place your name on our mailing list now.* 今すぐ当社の郵送先名簿にあなたの名前を入れてください.

mail|man /méɪlmæn/ (**mailmen**) N-COUNT 可算名詞 A **mailman** is a man whose job is to collect and deliver letters and parcels that are sent by mail. 郵便集配人 [AM 米国英語]

mail merge N-UNCOUNT 不可算名詞 **Mail merge** is a word processing procedure which enables you to combine a document with a data file, for example a list of names and addresses, so that copies of the document are different for each person it is sent to. メールマージ [COMPUTING コンピューティング] □ *Using mail-merge software, she makes sure each card goes out on time.* 彼女はメールマージソフトを使ってそれぞれのカードが時間通りに必ず送られるようにする.

mail or|der (**mail orders**) ■ N-UNCOUNT 不可算名詞 **Mail order** is a system of buying and selling goods. You choose the goods you want from a company by looking at their catalog, and the company sends them to you by mail. 通信販売 □ *The toys are available by mail order from Opi Toys.* そのおもちゃはオピトイズからの通信販売でお求めになれます. ■ N-COUNT 可算名詞 **Mail orders** are goods that have been ordered by mail order. 郵便注文 [mainly AM 主に米国英語] □ *I supervise the packing of all mail orders.* 私はすべての郵便注文の梱包を監督している.

maim /méɪm/ (**maims, maiming, maimed**) V-T 他動詞 To **maim** someone means to injure them so badly that part of their body is permanently damaged. 不具にする □ *Mines have been scattered in rice paddies and jungles, maiming and killing civilians.* 地雷が水田やジャングルにばらまかれ, 民間人が不具にされたり, 死亡したりしている.

main /méɪn/ (**mains**) ■ ADJ 形容詞 The **main** thing is the most important one of several similar things in a particular situation. 主要な [det ADJ] □...*one of the main tourist areas of San Francisco.* サンフランシスコの主要遊覧地の1つ □ *My main concern now is to protect the children.* 今私が最も心配しているのはその子供たちの保護だ. ■ PHRASE 句 If you say that something is true **in the main**, you mean that it is generally true, although there may be exceptions. だいたいは □ *Tourists are, in the main, sympathetic people.* 観光客はだいたいは好意的な人たちだ. ■ N-COUNT 可算名詞 The **mains** are the pipes that supply gas or water to buildings, or which take sewage away from them. 主管 □...*the water supply from the mains.* 本管からの給水.

> **Thesaurus** main また次を参照:
>
> | | |
> |---|---|
> | ADJ. | chief, major, primary, principal ■ |

main|frame /méɪnfreɪm/ (**mainframes**) N-COUNT 可算名詞 A **mainframe** or **mainframe computer** is a large, powerful computer which can be used by many people at the same time and which can do very large or complicated tasks. 大型コンピュータ, メインフレーム □ *I downloaded the whole thing into the hospital mainframe before I left work today.* 私は今日, 帰宅する前に, そのすべてを病院のメインフレームにダウンロードした.

main|land /méɪnlænd/ N-SING 単数名詞 You can refer to the largest part of a country or continent as **the mainland** when contrasting it with the islands around it. 本土 □ *She was going to Nanaimo to catch the ferry to the mainland.* 彼女は本土行きのフェリーに乗るためにナナイモに行く途中だった.

main|ly /méɪnli/ ■ ADV 副詞 You use **mainly** when mentioning the main reason or thing involved in something. 主

に □ *The stock market scandal is refusing to go away, mainly because there's still no consensus over how it should be dealt with.* その株式市場のスキャンダルは、それをどう扱うべきかについて意見の一致がいまだに見られないことが主な原因で、なかなか解決されそうにありません. **2** ADV 副詞 You use **mainly** when you are referring to a group and stating something that is true of most of it. 大概は [ADV with group] □ *The African half of the audience was mainly from Senegal or Mali.* 観客の半分を占めるアフリカ人は大概セネガルまたはマリ出身だった.

main road (**main roads**) N-COUNT 可算名詞 A **main road** is an important road that leads from one town or city to another. 幹線道路 □ *Troops had barricaded the main road from the airport.* 軍隊は空港からの幹線道路にバリケードを築いていた.

main|stream /mˈeɪnstrim/ (**mainstreams**) N-COUNT 可算名詞 People, activities, or ideas that are part of the **mainstream** are regarded as the most typical, normal, and conventional because they belong to the same group or system as most others of their kind. 主流 □ *...people outside the economic mainstream.* 経済の本流から外れた人たち.
→ see **culture**

Main Street **1** N-PROPER 固有名詞 In small towns in the United States, the street where most of the stores are is often called **Main Street**. 本通り □ *Almost all the stores and restaurants along Main Street were shut for the season.* その季節には本通りのほとんどすべての店やレストランが閉まっていた. **2** N-UNCOUNT 不可算名詞 **Main Street** is used by journalists to refer to ordinary Americans who live in small towns rather than big cities or are not very rich. 地方都市の生活者 [AM 米国英語] □ *This financial crisis had a much greater impact on Main Street.* この財政危機でより大きな被害を被ったのは地方都市の生活者だった.

main|tain /meɪntˈeɪn/ (**maintains, maintaining, maintained**) **1** V-T 他動詞 If you **maintain** something, you continue to have it, and do not let it stop or grow weaker. 維持する □ *France maintained close contacts with Jordan during the Gulf War.* フランスは湾岸戦争の間ヨルダンとの密接な連絡を維持した. **2** V-T 他動詞 If you say that someone **maintains that** something is true, you mean that they have stated their opinion strongly but not everyone agrees with them or believes them. 主張する, 固執する □ *He has maintained that the money was donated for international purposes.* その金は国際的用途に寄付されたと彼は主張します. □ *"Not all feminism has to be like this," Jo maintains.* 「フェミニズムすべてがこのようなものであるべきではない」とジョーは主張した. **3** V-T 他動詞 If you **maintain** something **at** a particular rate or level, you keep it at that rate or level. 保つ □ *The government was right to maintain interest rates at a high level.* 政府が金利を高いレベルに維持したのは正しかった. **4** V-T 他動詞 If you **maintain** a road, building, vehicle, or machine, you keep it in good condition by regularly checking it and repairing it when necessary. 保守する □ *The house costs a fortune to maintain.* その家の保守には大金がかかる. **5** V-T 他動詞 If you **maintain** someone, you provide them with money and other things that they need. 扶養する □ *...the basic costs of maintaining a child.* 子供の基本的養育費

Thesaurus		*maintain* また次を参照:
V.	carry on, continue; (ant.) neglect **1**	
	keep up, look after, protect, repair **4**	

Word Partnership		*maintain* は次の語句と使われる:
N.	maintain **friendship**, maintain **law**, maintain a **relationship** **1**	
V.	**need to** maintain, **pledge to** maintain, **try to** maintain **1 - 5**	

main|te|nance /mˈeɪntɪnəns/ **1** N-UNCOUNT 不可算名詞 The **maintenance** of a building, vehicle, road, or machine is the process of keeping it in good condition by regularly checking it and repairing it when necessary. 保守 □ *...maintenance work on government buildings.* 政府の建物の保守作業 □ *The window had been replaced last week during routine maintenance.* その窓は先週定期的保守の間に交換されていた. **2** N-UNCOUNT 不可算名詞 **Maintenance** is money that someone gives regularly to another person to pay for the things that the person needs. 生計費 □ *...the government's plan to make absent fathers pay maintenance for their children.* 不在の父親に子供の扶養料を支払わせるという政府の計画 **3** N-UNCOUNT 不可算名詞 If you ensure the **maintenance of** a state or process, you make sure that it continues. 持続 □ *...the maintenance of peace and stability in Asia.* アジアにおける平和と安定の維持

maize /meɪz/ N-UNCOUNT 不可算名詞 **Maize** is the same as **corn**. トウモロコシ [BRIT 英国英語]

ma|jes|tic /mədʒˈestɪk/ ADJ 形容詞 If you describe something or someone as **majestic**, you think they are very beautiful, dignified, and impressive. 威厳のある □ *...a majestic country home*

that once belonged to the Astor family. かつてアスター家所有の堂々たる田舎の邸宅. ● **ma|jes|ti|cal|ly** /mədʒˈestɪkli/ ADV 副詞 堂々と □ *She rose majestically to her feet.* 彼女は堂々と立ち上がった.

maj|es|ty /mˈædʒɪsti/ (**majesties**) **1** N-VOC; PRON 呼格名詞, 代名詞 You use majesty in expressions such as **Your Majesty** or **Her Majesty** when you are addressing or referring to a king or queen. 陛下 [POLITENESS 丁寧さ] [POSS PRON] □ *His Majesty requests your presence in the royal chambers.* 陛下が王宮であなたに謁見を賜ります. **2** N-UNCOUNT 不可算名詞 **Majesty** is the quality of being beautiful, dignified, and impressive. 威厳 □ *...the majesty of the mainland mountains.* 本土の山脈の威厳.

Word Link		*major ≈ larger : major, majority, major league*

ma|jor /mˈeɪdʒər/ (**majors, majoring, majored**) **1** ADJ 形容詞 You use **major** when you want to describe something that is more important, serious, or significant than other things in a group or situation. より重大な [ADJ n] □ *The major factor in the decision to stay or to leave was usually professional.* 残るか去るかを決定する主要な要因は通常専門的なものだった. □ *Drug abuse has long been a major problem for the authorities there.* 薬物乱用は長い間その地の当局にとって主要な問題の1つだった. **2** N-COUNT; N-TITLE; N-VOC 可算名詞, 称号名詞, 呼格名詞 A **major** is an officer who is one rank above captain in the United States Army, Air Force, or Marines. 少佐 □ *I was a major in the war, you know.* 私は戦時には少佐だったんですよ. **3** N-COUNT 可算名詞 At a university or college in the United States, a student's **major** is the main subject that they are studying. 専攻 □ *English majors would be asked to explore the roots of language.* 英語専攻の学生は言語の起源を探究するよう求められるであろう. **4** N-COUNT 可算名詞 At a university or college in the United States, if a student is, for example, a geology **major**, geology is the main subject they are studying. 専攻学生 □ *She was a history major at the University of Oklahoma.* 彼女はオクラホマ大学で歴史学を専攻しました. **5** V-I 自動詞 If a student at a university or college in the United States **majors in** a particular subject, that subject is the main one they study. 専攻する □ *He majored in finance at Claremont Men's College in California.* 彼はカリフォルニア州にあるクレアモント男子大学で財政学を専攻した. **6** ADJ 形容詞 In music, a **major** scale is one in which the third note is two tones higher than the first. 長調 [n ADJ, ADJ n] □ *The orchestra played Mozart's Symphony No. 35 in D Major.* オーケストラはモーツァルトの交響曲35番をニ長調で演奏した. **7** N-PLURAL 複数名詞 The **majors** are groups of professional sports teams that compete against each other, especially in baseball. メジャー [mainly AM 主に米国英語] □ *I knew what I could do in the minor leagues, I just wanted a chance to prove myself in the majors.* 僕はマイナーリーグでやれることは分かっていたが、メジャーで自分を試すチャンスが欲しかっただけなんだ. **8** N-COUNT 可算名詞 A **major** is an important sports competition, especially in golf or tennis. 主要試合 □ *Sarazen became the first golfer to win all four majors.* サラゼンは4つの主要試合すべてで優勝を果たした最初のゴルファーだった.

Thesaurus		*major* また次を参照:
ADJ.	chief, critical, crucial, key, main, principal; (ant.) little, minor, unimportant **1**	

ma|jor|ity /mədʒˈɔrɪti/ (**majorities**) **1** N-SING-COLL 集合的単数名詞 The **majority** of people or things in a group is more than half of them. 大多数, 過半数 □ *The majority of my patients come to me from out of town.* 私の患者の大多数は町外から通院している. ● PHRASE 句 If a group is **in a majority** or **in the majority**, they form more than half of a larger group. 過半数を占める □ *Surveys indicate that supporters of the treaty are still in the majority.* 調査は、その条約の支持者はいまだに過半数を占めていることを示している. **2** N-COUNT 可算名詞 A **majority** is the difference between the number of votes or seats that the winner gets in an election, and the number of votes or seats that the next person or party gets. 得票差 □ *Members of parliament approved the move by a majority of ninety-nine.* 下院議員は99の得票差でその動議を承認しました. **3** ADJ 形容詞 **Majority** is used to describe opinions, decisions, and systems of government that are supported by more than half the people involved. 過半数の [ADJ n] □ *...her continuing disagreement with the majority view.* 大多数の人々の見解と彼女が引き続き示す不一致であること **4** N-UNCOUNT 不可算名詞 **Majority** is the state of legally being an adult. In most states in the United States, people reach their majority at the age of eighteen. 成年 □ *...a citizen of Russia who has reached the age of majority.* 成年に達したロシア市民

Word Partnership		*majority* は次の語句と使われる:
N.	majority **of people**, majority **of the population** **1**	
	majority **leader** **2**	
	majority **opinion**, majority **rule**, majority **vote** **3**	
ADJ.	**overwhelming** majority, **vast** majority **1 2**	

major league (**major leagues**) **1** N-PLURAL 複数名詞 The **major leagues** are groups of professional sports teams that compete against each other, especially in baseball. 大リーグ ❑ *Chandler was instrumental in making Jackie Robinson the first black player in the major leagues.* チャンドラーはジャッキー・ロビンソンが大リーグ初の黒人選手になるのを助けた. **2** ADJ 形容詞 **Major league** means connected with the major leagues in baseball. 大リーグの ❑ *I'm doomed to live in a town with no major league baseball.* 私は大リーグ野球のない町に住むよう運命付けられている. **3** ADJ 形容詞 **Major-league** people or institutions are important or successful. 第1級の ❑ *James Hawes's books have achieved cult status, and his first film boasts major-league stars.* ジェームス・ホーズの本は熱狂的地位を獲得し, 最初の映画は第1級のスターの出演を誇っている. **4** PHRASE 句 If someone **moves into the major league** or **makes it into the major league**, they become very successful in their career. 第1線へ進出する [JOURNALISM ジャーナリズム] ❑ *Once a model has made it into the major league every detail is mapped out by her agency.* モデルが一旦成功を収めると, あらゆる詳細は代理社が入念に計画する.

---

make

❶ CARRYING OUT AN ACTION
❷ CAUSING OR CHANGING
❸ CREATING OR PRODUCING
❹ LINK VERB USES
❺ ACHIEVING OR REACHING
❻ STATING AN AMOUNT OR TIME
❼ PHRASAL VERBS

---

❶ make /meɪk/ (**makes, making, made**)

Make is used in a large number of expressions which are explained under other words in this dictionary. For example, the expression "to make sense" is explained at "sense."

Make はこの辞書の他の単語のもとで説明されている多数の表現に使われる. 例えば, 表現 **to make sense** は **sense** のところで説明されている.

1 V-T 他動詞 You can use **make** with a wide range of nouns to indicate that someone performs an action or says something. For example, if you **make** a suggestion, you suggest something. する ❑ *I'd just like to make a comment.* ちょっとコメントしたいのですが. ❑ *I made a few phone calls.* 私は2, 3人に電話をした. **2** V-T 他動詞 You can use **make** with certain nouns to indicate that someone does something well or badly. For example, if you **make** a success of something, you do it successfully, and if you **make** a mess of something, you do it very badly. する ❑ *Apparently he made a mess of his audition.* 明らかに彼はオーディションを台無しにしてしまった. **3** V-T/V-I 他動詞/自動詞 If you **make as if to** do something or **make to** do something, you behave in a way that makes it seem that you are just about to do it. ようにふるまう [WRITTEN 書き言葉] [他動詞・自動詞] ❑ *Mary made as if to protest, then hesitated.* メリーは抗議するような身振りをしたが, ちゅうちょした. **4** PHRASE 句 If you **make do with** something, you use or have it instead of something else that you do not have, although it is not as good. 間に合わせる ❑ *Why make do with a copy if you can afford the genuine article?* 本物を買う余裕があるなら, なぜコピーで間に合わせるのか.

❷ make /meɪk/ (**makes, making, made**)

⇨ Please look at meaning **10** to see if the expression you are looking for is shown under another headword.

1 V-T 他動詞 If something **makes** you do something, it causes you to do it. させる ❑ *Dirt from the highway made him cough.* 高速道路からのほこりを吸って彼は咳き込んだ. ❑ *The white tips of his shirt collar made him look like a choirboy.* 彼のシャツの襟には白い縁がついていたので, 彼は少年聖歌隊員のように見えた. **2** V-T 他動詞 If you **make** someone do something, you force them to do it. 強制的にさせる ❑ *You can't make me do anything.* 君は私に何も強制的にさせることはできない. **3** V-T 他動詞 You use **make** to talk about causing someone or something to be a particular thing or to have a particular quality. For example, to **make** someone a star means to cause them to become a star, and to **make** someone angry means to cause them to become angry. ーにする ❑ *James Bond, the role that made him a star.* ジェームズ・ボンド, 彼をスターにした役 ❑ *She made life very difficult for me.* 彼女は私を大変生きづらくした. **4** V-T 他動詞 If you say that one thing or person **makes** another seem, for example, small, stupid, or good, you mean that they cause them to seem small, stupid, or good in comparison, even though they are not. させる ❑ *They live in fantasy worlds which make Disneyland seem uninventive.* 彼らはディズニーランドが創意のないものに見えるような空想の世界に住んでいる. **5** V-T 他動詞 If you **make yourself** understood, heard, or known, you succeed in getting people to understand you, hear you, or know that you are there. (人に)してもらう ❑ *He learned enough Spanish to make himself understood.* 彼は自分の意思の疎通ができるくらいまでスペイン語を習った. **6** V-T 他動詞 If you **make** someone something, you appoint them to a

---

particular job, role, or position. 任命する ❑ *He made her a director in his numerous companies.* 彼は彼女を自分の多数の会社の重役に就けた. **7** V-T 他動詞 If you **make** something **into** something else, you change it in some way so that it becomes that other thing. 変える ❑ *We made it into a beautiful home.* 私たちはそれを美しい自宅に改造した. **8** V-T 他動詞 To **make** a total or score a particular amount means to increase it to that amount. (総計を)ーにする ❑ *This makes the total cost of the bulb and energy $27.* これで電球と電気代の総費用は27ドルになる. **9** V-T 他動詞 When someone **makes** a friend or an enemy, someone becomes their friend or their enemy, often because of a particular thing they have done. (味方・敵などに)なる ❑ *Lorenzo was a natural leader who made friends easily.* ロレンゾは生まれついての指導者で, 人と簡単に親しくなれた. **10** to make friends → see friend

❸ make /meɪk/ (**makes, making, made**) **1** V-T 他動詞 To **make** something means to produce, construct, or create it. 作る ❑ *She made her own bread.* 彼女は自分でパンを焼いた. ❑ *Having curtains made professionally can be costly.* 専門家にカーテンを作ってもらうと高くつく場合がある. **2** V-T 他動詞 If you **make** a note or list, you write something down in that form. (注・一覧表などを)付ける ❑ *Mr. Perry made a note in his book.* ペリー氏は自分の本に注を付けた. **3** V-T 他動詞 If you **make** rules or laws, you decide what these should be. 制定する ❑ *The police don't make the laws, they merely enforce them.* 警察は法律を制定しない. それを施行するだけだ. **4** V-T 他動詞 If you **make** money, you get it by working for it, by selling something, or by winning it. (金銭を)手に入れる ❑ *I think every business's goal is to make money.* あらゆるビジネスの目的は金もうけをすることだと思います. **5** V-T 他動詞 If you **make** a case **for** something, you try to establish or prove that it is the best thing to do. (擁護論を)唱える ❑ *You could certainly make a case for this point of view.* 君はたしかにこの見方に賛成の論拠を張ることができた. **6** N-COUNT 可算名詞 The **make** of something such as a car or radio is the name of the company that made it. 型 ❑ *The only car parked outside is a black Saab – a different make.* 外に駐車しているたった1台の車は黒のサーブで, 違うモデルだ.

The **brand** of a product such as jeans, tea, or soap is its name, which can also be the name of the company that makes or sells it. The **make** of a car or electrical appliance such as a radio or washing machine is the name of the company that produces it. If you talk about what **type** of product or service you want, you are talking about its quality and what features it should have. You can also talk about **types** of people or of abstract things. ❑ *...which type of coffeemaker to choose. ...a new type of bank account. ...looking for a certain type of actor.* A **model** of car or of some other devices is a name that is given to a particular **type**, for example, a Ford Escort. Note that **type** can also be used informally to mean either **make** or **model**. For example, if someone asks what **type** of car you have got, you could reply "an SUV," "a Ford," or perhaps "an Escort."

Thesaurus　　　*make* また次を参照:

v.　　build, compose, create, fabricate, produce; (ant.) destroy **❸ 1**

❹ make /meɪk/ (**makes, making, made**) **1** V-LINK 連結動詞 You can use **make** to say that someone or something has the right qualities for a particular task or role. For example, if you say that someone will **make** a good politician, you mean that they have the right qualities to be a good politician. なる ❑ *She'll make a good actress, if she gets the right training.* 適切な訓練を受ければ, 彼女は立派な女優になるだろう. ❑ *You've a very good idea there. It will make a good book.* とても良いアイデアですね. いい本になりますよ. **2** V-LINK 連結動詞 If people **make** a particular pattern such as a line or a circle, they arrange themselves in this way. 構成する ❑ *A group of people made a circle around the Pentagon.* 1群の人たちが国防総省をぐるりと取り囲んだ. **3** V-LINK 連結動詞 You can use **make** to say what two numbers add up to. なる ❑ *Four twos make eight.* 4掛ける2は8になる.

❺ make /meɪk/ (**makes, making, made**) **1** V-T 他動詞 If someone **makes** a particular team or **makes** a particular high position, they do so well that they are put in that team or get that position. 1員になる, 昇進する ❑ *The athletes are just happy to make the team.* 運動選手はチームに入れてただ喜んでいる. **2** V-T 他動詞 If you **make** a place in or by a particular time, you get there in or by that time, often with some difficulty. 間に合う ❑ *The engine is gulping two tons of fuel an hour in order to make New Orleans by nightfall.* 日暮れまでにニューオーリンズに到着するために, 機関車は1時間当たり2トンもの燃料を消費している. **3** PHRASE 句 If you **make it** somewhere, you succeed in getting there, especially in time to do something. 首尾よく到着する ❑ *So you did make it to America, after all.* それで結局アメリカに到着したのですね. ❑ *...the hostages who never made it home.* 帰宅することのかなわなかった人質たち **4** PHRASE 句 If you **make it**, you are successful in achieving

The women of ancient Egypt were among the first to **wear makeup**. They **applied foundation** to lighten their skin and used kohl as eye shadow to darken their eyelids. Greek women used charcoal as an eyeliner and rouge on their cheeks. In 14th century Europe, the most popular **cosmetic** was wheat flour. Women whitened their faces to show their social class. A light **complexion** indicated the woman didn't have to work outdoors. **Cosmetics** containing lead and arsenic sometimes caused illness and death. Makeup use increased in the early 1900s. Suddenly many women could afford mass-produced **lipstick**, **mascara**, and **face powder**.

something difficult, or in surviving through a very difficult period. うまくやり遂げる ❑ I believe I have the talent to make it. 私にはうまくやってのける才能があると信じている. **5** PHRASE 句 If you cannot **make it**, you are unable to attend an event that you have been invited to. 出席する ❑ He hadn't been able to make it to our dinner. 彼は私どもの夕食会に出席することができなかった.

❻ make /meɪk/ (makes, making, made) **1** V-T 他動詞 You use **make it** when saying what you calculate or guess an amount to be. 見積もる ❑ "How many shots has she got left?" — "I make it two." 「彼女にはあと何発残っているだろうか」「2発だと思う」 **2** V-T 他動詞 You use **make it** when saying what time your watch says it is. 思う ❑ I make it nearly nine o'clock. そろそろ9時だと思う.

❼ make /meɪk/ (makes, making, made)
▶ **make for** PHRASAL VERB 句動詞 If you **make for** a place, you move toward it. 〜へ向かう ❑ He rose from his seat and made for the door. 彼はいすから立ち上がって, ドアに向かった. **2** PHRASAL VERB 句動詞 If something **makes for** another thing, it causes or helps to cause that thing to happen or exist. 〜に役に立つ [INFORMAL くだけた] ❑ A happy parent makes for a happy child. 親が幸せなら子供も幸せだ.
▶ **make of** PHRASAL VERB 句動詞 If you ask a person what they **make of** something, you want to know what their impression, opinion, or understanding of it is. 〜を理解する ❑ Nancy wasn't sure what to make of Mick's apology. ナンシーはミックの謝罪をどう理解してよいかさだかでなかった.
▶ **make off** PHRASAL VERB 句動詞 If you **make off**, you leave somewhere as quickly as possible, often in order to escape. 急いで去る ❑ They broke free and made off in a stolen car. 彼らは逃げ出して盗難車で逃走した.
▶ **make off with** PHRASAL VERB 句動詞 If you **make off with** something, you steal it and take it away with you. 持ち逃げする ❑ Otto made off with the last of the brandy. オットーはブランデーの最後のものを持ち逃げした.
▶ **make out 1** PHRASAL VERB 句動詞 If you **make** something **out**, you manage with difficulty to see or hear it. 見分ける, 聞き分ける ❑ I could just make out a tall, pale, shadowy figure tramping through the undergrowth. 私は背の高く青ざめた人影が下生えを歩き回っているのをぼんやりと見分けるのがやっとだった. ❑ She thought she heard a name. She couldn't make it out, though. 彼女は名前を聞いたように思った. だが聞き分けられなかった. **2** PHRASAL VERB 句動詞 If you try to **make** something **out**, you try to understand it or decide whether or not it is true. 理解する, 判読する ❑ I couldn't make it out at all. 私にはぜんぜんわからなかった. ❑ It is hard to make out what criteria are used. どの基準が使われているかはわかりにくい. **3** PHRASAL VERB 句動詞 If you **make out that** something is the case or **make** something **out to** be the case, you try to cause people to believe that it is the case. 立証する ❑ They were trying to make out that I'd actually done it. 彼らは私がそれを実際にやったのだと証明しようとしていた. ❑ I don't think it was as glorious as everybody made it out to be. 私はみんなが言い立てるほどそれが栄誉あるものだったとは思いません. **4** PHRASAL VERB 句動詞 When you **make out** a check, receipt, or order form, you write all the necessary information on it. 記入する ❑ I'll make the check out to you and put it in the mail this afternoon. 私はあなた宛に小切手を切り, 今日の午後に郵送します. **5** PHRASAL VERB 句動詞 If two people **are making out**, they are engaged in sexual activity. 性交する [mainly AM 主に米国英語, INFORMAL くだけた] ❑ ...pictures of the couple making out on the beach. 海岸で性交しているカップルの写真.
▶ **make up 1** PHRASAL VERB 句動詞 The people or things that **make up** something are the members or parts that form that thing. 構成する ❑ The Chinese make up the largest single ethnic group in the city's public classrooms. 中国人はその都市の公立学校で最大の単一民族集団を構成している. ❑ Women officers make up 13 percent of the police force. 女性警官は警察力の13%を構成している. **2** PHRASAL VERB 句動詞 If you **make up** something such as a story or excuse, you invent it, sometimes in order to deceive people. でっち上げる ❑ I think it's very unkind of you to make up stories about him. 彼についての話をでっち上げるなんて, あなたは非常に意地悪だと私は思います. **3** PHRASAL VERB 句動詞 If you **make up** an amount, you add something to it so that it is as large as it should be. 補って完全にする ❑ Less than half of the money that students receive is in the form of grants, and loans have made up the difference. 学生の受け取る金銭の半

分足らずが助成金の形で, 貸付がその差額を補っている. **4** PHRASAL VERB 句動詞 If you **make up** time or hours, you work some extra hours because you have previously taken some time off work. 埋め合わせる ❑ They'll have to make up time lost during the strike. 彼らはストライキ中の遅れを取り戻さなければなりません. **5** PHRASAL VERB 句動詞 If a student **makes up** an examination or course they have failed or missed, they take the examination or course again. 受け直す [AM 米国英語] ❑ Everyone gets a chance to make up tests. 誰もが追試を受けるチャンスがある. **6** PHRASAL VERB 句動詞 If two people **make up** after a quarrel or disagreement, they become friends again. 仲直りする ❑ She came back and they made up. 彼女が戻ってきて, 彼らは仲直りをした. **7** PHRASAL VERB 句動詞 If you **make up** something such as food or medicine, you prepare it by mixing or putting different things together. 作る ❑ Prepare the souffle dish before making up the souffle mixture. スフレの材料を混ぜ合わせる前にスフレの皿を用意しなさい. **8** PHRASAL VERB 句動詞 If you **make up** a bed, you put sheets and blankets on it so that someone can sleep there. 用意する ❑ Her mother made up a bed in her old room. 彼女の母親は彼女の昔の部屋に寝床を整えた.

mak|er /meɪkər/ (makers) **1** N-COUNT 可算名詞 The **maker** of a product is the company that manufactures it. 製造業者 ❑ ...Japan's two largest car makers. 日本で最大の自動車メーカー2社 **2** N-COUNT 可算名詞 You can refer to the person who makes something as its **maker**. 作る人 ❑ ...the makers of news and current affairs programs. ニュースや時事問題番組の制作者

make|shift /meɪkʃɪft/ ADJ 形容詞 **Makeshift** things are temporary and usually of poor quality, but they are used because there is nothing better available. 当座しのぎの ❑ ...the cardboard boxes and makeshift shelters of the homeless. ホームレスのダンボール箱と間に合わせの住まい

make|up /meɪkʌp/ **1** N-UNCOUNT 不可算名詞 **Makeup** consists of things such as lipstick, eye shadow, and powder which some women put on their faces to make themselves look more attractive or which actors use to change or improve their appearance. 化粧 ❑ Normally she wore little makeup, but this evening was clearly an exception. 普段は彼女は薄化粧だが, 今夜は明らかに例外だった. **2** N-UNCOUNT 不可算名詞 Someone's **makeup** is their nature and the various qualities in their character. 気質 ❑ There was some fatal flaw in his makeup, and as time went on he lapsed into long silences or became off-hand. 彼の気質にはある致命的な欠点があり, 時が経つにつれて彼は長い沈黙に陥るか, ぶっきらぼうになるようになった. **3** N-UNCOUNT 不可算名詞 The **makeup** of something consists of its different parts and the way these parts are arranged. 構成 ❑ The ideological makeup of the unions is now radically different from what it had been. 労働組合の思想的な構成は今では過去のものと根本的に異なっている.
→ see Word Web: **makeup**

mak|ing /meɪkɪŋ/ (makings) **1** N-UNCOUNT 不可算名詞 The **making** of something is the act or process of producing or creating it. 制作, 製作 ❑ ...Salomon's book about the making of this movie. この映画の制作に関するサラモンの本. **2** PHRASE 句 If you describe a person or thing as something **in the making**, you mean that they are going to become known or recognized as that thing. 発達中の ❑ Her drama teacher is confident Julie is a star in the making. ジュリーのドラマ教師は彼女がスターの卵だと確信している. **3** PHRASE 句 If something **is the making of** a person or thing, it is the reason that they become successful or become very much better than they used to be. 成功の原因 ❑ This discovery may yet be the making of him. この発見により彼はさらに成功を収めるかもしれない. **4** PHRASE 句 If you say that a person or thing **has the makings of** something, you mean it seems possible or likely that they will become that thing, as they have the necessary qualities. 〜の素質がある ❑ Godfrey had the makings of a successful journalist. ゴドフリーは名ジャーナリストになる素質があった. **5** PHRASE 句 If you say that something such as a problem you have is **of** your own **making**, you mean you have caused or created it yourself. 自身が招いた ❑ Some of the university's financial troubles are of its own making. その大学の財政難の一部は大学自体が招いたものだ.

ma|laria /mələriə/ N-UNCOUNT 不可算名詞 **Malaria** is a serious

disease carried by mosquitoes, which causes periods of fever. マ
ラリア

male /meɪl/ (**males**) **1** ADJ 形容詞 Someone who is **male** is a
man or a boy. 男 ▫ *Many women achievers appear to pose a threat to
their male colleagues.* 多くの女性が成功を遂げ、男性の同僚の地位
は脅かされているようである. ▫ *The company has engaged two male
dancers from the Bolshoi.* そのバレエ団はボリショイから2人の男性ダン
サーを雇った. **2** N-COUNT 可算名詞 Men and boys are sometimes
referred to as **males** when they are being considered as a type. 男
性 ▫ *...the remains of a Caucasian male, aged 65 70.* 65歳から70歳の白
人男性の遺体. **3** ADJ 形容詞 **Male** means relating to, belonging to,
or affecting men rather than women. 男の [ADJ n] ▫ *Massive male
unemployment has diminished the status of men in the family.* 男性の大
量失業は家族における男性の地位を低下させた. ▫ *...male violence.* 男
性による暴力. **4** N-COUNT 可算名詞 You can refer to any creature
that belongs to the sex that cannot lay eggs or have babies as a
male. 雄 ▫ *Males and females take turns brooding the eggs.* 雄と雌は
順番に卵を抱く. ● ADJ 形容詞 **Male** is also an adjective. 雄の ▫ *After
mating, the male wasps tunnel through the sides of their nursery.* 交尾の
あと、雄のスズメバチは育児室の側面にトンネルを掘る.

━━ Word Link ━━ **mal** ≈ bad : *malaria, malfunction, malpractice*

mal|func|tion /mælfʌŋkʃᵊn/ (**malfunctions, malfunctioning,
malfunctioned**) V-I 自動詞 If a machine or part of the body
malfunctions, it fails to work properly. うまく機能しない [FORMAL
形式ばった] ▫ *The radiation can damage microprocessors and computer
memories, causing them to malfunction.* 放射線はマイクロプロセッサ
やコンピュータのメモリを損傷し、誤作動させる. ● N-COUNT 可算名
詞 **Malfunction** is also a noun. 機能不全 ▫ *There must have been a
computer malfunction.* コンピュータの誤動作があったに違いない.

mal|ice /mælɪs/ N-UNCOUNT 不可算名詞 **Malice** is behavior that
is intended to harm people or their reputations, or cause them
embarrassment and upset. 悪意 ▫ *There was a strong current of
malice in many of his portraits.* 彼の肖像画の多くには恨みの強い傾向
が出ていた.

mal|i|cious /məlɪʃəs/ ADJ 形容詞 If you describe someone's
words or actions as **malicious**, you mean that they are intended to
harm people or their reputation, or cause them embarrassment
and upset. 悪意のある ▫ *That might merely have been malicious gossip.*
それは悪意のあるうわさ話に過ぎなかったのかもしれないだろう.
● **mal|i|cious|ly** ADV 副詞 悪意を持って ▫ *...his maliciously accurate
imitation of Hubert de Burgh.* 彼の悪質だが的確なヒューバート・ド・
バラの模写

mal|ig|nant /məlɪgnənt/ **1** ADJ 形容詞 A **malignant** tumor
or disease is out of control and likely to cause death. 悪性の
[MEDICAL 医学の] ▫ *She developed a malignant breast tumor.* 彼女は
乳房に悪性腫瘍 (しゅよう) を発症した. **2** ADJ 形容詞 If you say that
someone is **malignant**, you think they are cruel and like to cause
harm. 敵意に満ちた ▫ *He said that we were evil, malignant, and mean.*
私たちは邪悪で、敵意に満ち、卑劣だと彼は言った.

mall /mɔl/ (**malls**) N-COUNT 可算名詞 A **mall** is a very large,
enclosed shopping area. ショッピングセンター

mal|let /mælɪt/ (**mallets**) N-COUNT 可算名詞 A **mallet** is a
wooden hammer with a square head. 木槌 (きづち)

mal|nu|tri|tion /mælnutrɪʃᵊn/ N-UNCOUNT 不可算名詞 If
someone is suffering from **malnutrition**, they are physically
weak and extremely thin because they have not eaten enough
food. 栄養不良 ▫ *Infections are more likely in those suffering from
malnutrition.* 栄養失調を患う人はより感染しやすい.

mal|prac|tice /mælpræktɪs/ (**malpractices**) N-VAR 可変性
名詞 If you accuse someone of **malpractice**, you are accusing
them of being careless or of breaking the law or the rules of their
profession. 不正行為 [FORMAL 形式ばった] ▫ *There were only one or
two serious allegations of malpractice.* 深刻な責任行為疑惑は1つか2つ
しかなかった.

malt /mɔlt/ (**malts**) **1** N-UNCOUNT 不可算名詞 **Malt** is a

substance made from grain that has been soaked in water
and then dried in a hot oven. Malt is used in the production of
whiskey, beer, and other alcoholic drinks. 麦芽、モルト ▫ *German
beer has traditionally been made from just four ingredients – hops, malt,
yeast, and water.* ドイツのビールは伝統的にホップ、モルト、酵母およ
び水という4種の原料のみから作られている. **2** N-COUNT 可算名詞 A
malt is a drink made from malted milk powder, milk, ice cream,
and sometimes other flavorings. 麦芽乳 [AM 米国英語] ▫ *...a
chocolate malt.* チョコレートモルト.

mam|mal /mæmᵊl/ (**mammals**) N-COUNT 可算名詞 **Mammals**
are animals such as humans, dogs, lions, and whales. In general,
female mammals give birth to babies rather than laying eggs,
and feed their young with milk. 哺乳動物
→ see Word Web: mammal
→ see bat, pet, whale

mam|moth /mæməθ/ (**mammoths**) **1** ADJ 形容詞 You use
mammoth to emphasize that a task or change is very large and
needs a lot of effort to achieve. 巨大な [EMPHASIS 強調] ▫ *...the
mammoth task of relocating the library.* 図書館の移転というとてつも
ない仕事 **2** N-COUNT 可算名詞 A **mammoth** was an animal like
an elephant, with very long tusks and long hair, that lived a long
time ago but no longer exists. マンモス

man /mæn/ (**men, mans, manning, manned**) **1** N-COUNT 可算
名詞 A **man** is an adult male human being. 成人の男性 ▫ *He had
not expected the young man to reappear before evening.* 彼はその若者
が夕方前にまたやってくるとは予想していなかった. ▫ *I have always
regarded him as a man of integrity.* 私は常に彼を人格者だと思ってきた.
2 N-VAR 可変性名詞 **Man** and **men** are sometimes used to refer
to all human beings, including both males and females. Some
people dislike this use. 人 ▫ *The chick initially has no fear of man.* 最
初、ひよこは人間を恐れない. **3** N-COUNT 可算名詞 If you say that
a man is, for example, **a gambling man** or **an outdoors man**, you
mean that he likes gambling or outdoor activities. 一者、一好
き ▫ *Are you a gambling man, Mr. Graham?* グレアムさん、あなたは
賭博好きですか. **4** N-COUNT 可算名詞 If you say that a man is,
for example, **a Harvard man** or **a Yale man**, you mean that he
went to that university. 出身者 ▫ *Stewart, a Yale man, was invited
to stay on and write the script.* エール出身のスチュアートは留まって
脚本を書くよう勧められた. **5** N-COUNT 可算名詞 If you refer to a
particular company's or organization's **man**, you mean a man
who works for or represents that company or organization. 従業
員 [JOURNALISM ジャーナリズム] ▫ *...the Chicago Tribune's man in Abu
Dhabi.* アブダビ駐在のシカゴトリビューン紙の記者 **6** N-SING 単数名
詞 Some people refer to a woman's husband, lover, or boyfriend
as her **man**. 夫、恋人 [INFORMAL くだけた] ▫ *...if they see your man
cuddle you in the kitchen or living room.* あなたの夫が台所や居間であ
なたを抱きしめるのをもし彼らが見たら **7** N-VOC 呼格名詞 In very
informal social situations, **man** is sometimes used as a greeting
or form of address to a man. おい [FORMULAE 決まり文句] ▫ *Hey
wow, man! Where'd you get those boots?* ちょっと、おい！どこでその
ブーツ買ったんだ? **8** V-T 他動詞 If you **man** something such as
a place or machine, you operate it or are in charge of it. 受け持
つ ▫ *French soldiers manned roadblocks in the capital city.* フランス兵
は首都で道路封鎖の任務についた. ▫ *...the person manning the phone
at the complaint department.* 苦情部門で電話を受け持つ人 **9** → see
also **manned, no-man's land** **10** PHRASE 句 If you say that a
man is **man enough** to do something, you mean that he has the
necessary courage or ability to do it. ～する勇気がある ▫ *I told him
that he should be man enough to admit he had done wrong.* 私は間違
いを犯したことを認める勇気を持つべきだと彼に言った. **11** PHRASE
句 If you describe a man as **a man's man**, you mean that he has
qualities which make him popular with other men rather than
with women. 女性よりも男性に好かれる男 ▫ *Very much a man's man,
he enjoyed drinking and jesting with his cronies.* 男性に非常に好かれる
彼は、仲間と飲んだりふざけたりするのを楽しんだ. **12** PHRASE 句 If
you say that a man **is his own man**, you approve of the fact that he
makes his decisions and his plans himself, and does not depend

━━ Word Web ━━ **mammal**

Elephants, dogs, mice, and humans all belong to the class of animals called **mammals**.
Mammals have live babies rather than laying eggs. The females also suckle their **young**
with milk from their bodies. Mammals are **warm-blooded** and usually have hair on
their bodies. Some, such as the brown bear and the raccoon, are omnivorous. Deer and
zebras are herbivorous, living mostly on grass and leaves. Lions and tigers are
carnivorous. They must have a supply of large **game** to survive. Mammals have a variety
of different types of **limbs**. Monkeys have long arms for climbing. Seals have flippers
for swimming.

on other people. 他人の支配を受けない，主体性のある [APPROVAL 賛成] ❏ Be your own man. Make up your own mind. しっかりしなさい. 決心しなさい. **13** PHRASE 句 If you say that a group of men are, do, or think something **to a man**, you are emphasizing that every one of them is, does, or thinks that thing. 1人の例外もなく [EMPHASIS 強調] ❏ To a man, the survivors blamed the government. 生存者は1人残らず政府を非難した.

→ see **age**

man|age /mǽnɪdʒ/ (**manages, managing, managed**) **1** V-T 他動詞 If you **manage** an organization, business, or system, or the people who work in it, you are responsible for controlling them. 管理する ❏ Within two years he was managing the store. 2年の内に，彼はその店を経営するようになった. ❏ There is a lack of confidence in the government's ability to manage the economy. 政府の経済管理能力が信頼されていない. **2** V-T 他動詞 If you **manage** time, money, or other resources, you deal with them carefully and do not waste them. 管理する ❏ In a busy world, managing your time is increasingly important. 多忙な世界では，時間管理がますます重要になる. **3** V-T 他動詞 If you **manage to** do something, especially something difficult, you succeed in doing it. どうにか成し遂げる ❏ Somehow, he'd managed to persuade Kay to buy one for him. なぜか，彼は自分用に1つ購入するようケイをなんとかうまく説得した. ❏ I managed to pull myself up onto a wet, sloping ledge. 私は濡れて傾斜した岩棚の上にかろうじてまっすぐ立った. **4** V-I 自動詞 If you **manage**, you succeed in coping with a difficult situation. 処理する ❏ She had managed perfectly well without medication for three years. 彼女は3年間薬なしで完全にうまく切り抜けた. **5** V-T 他動詞 If you say that you can **manage** an amount of time or money for something, you mean that you can afford to spend that time or money on it. なんとか都合をつける ❏ I try to manage about five hours a week on my bike. 私はなんとかして週に約5時間自転車に乗るようにしている. **6** V-T 他動詞 If you say that someone **managed** a particular response, such as a laugh or a greeting, you mean that it was difficult for them to do it because they were feeling sad or upset. どうにかしてする ❏ He looked dazed as he spoke to reporters, managing only a weak smile. 彼は報道陣に話す際ボーっとしていて，かすかに笑顔をつくるのが精一杯だった. **7** CONVENTION 慣習表現 You say "**I can manage**" or "**I'll manage**" as a way of refusing someone's offer of help and insisting on doing something by yourself. なんとかするよ ❏ I know you mean well, but I can manage by myself. 君が親切に言ってくれているのはわかっているが，自分でなんとかできるよ.

N.　manage **a business/company**, manage **people 1**
　　manage **expenses**, manage **money**, manage
　　resources, manage **time 2**
ADV.　manage **effectively 1 – 4**
V.　manage **to escape**, manage **to survive 3**

man|age|able /mǽnɪdʒəbᵊl/ ADJ 形容詞 Something that is **manageable** is of a size, quantity, or level of difficulty that people are able to deal with. 処理できる ❏ He will now try to cut down the task to a manageable size. 今後彼はその仕事を処理できる大きさに削減するよう努めるでしょう.

man|age|ment /mǽnɪdʒmənt/ (**managements**) **1** N-UNCOUNT 不可算名詞 **Management** is the control and organizing of a business or other organization. 経営 ❏ The zoo needed better management rather than more money. その動物園は，より多くの資金よりもよりよい経営を必要としていました. ❏ The dispute is about wages, working conditions, and the management of the mining industry. 争議の争点は，鉱業における賃金，労働条件および経営だ. **2** N-VAR-COLL 集合的可変性名詞 You can refer to the people who control and organize a business or other organization as the **management**. 経営者側 [BUSINESS 実業] ❏ The management is doing its best to improve the situation. 経営者側は状況の改善に最善を尽くしている. ❏ We need to get more women into top management. 我々は経営陣にもっと女性を加える必要がある. **3** N-UNCOUNT 不可算名詞 **Management** is the way people control different parts of their lives. 管理 ❏ ...her management of her professional life. 彼女の専門家としての生活管理.

N.　**business** management, **crisis** management,
　　management **skills**, management **style**, **waste**
　　management **1**
　　management **team**, management **training 2**
　　anger management, **money** management, **stress**
　　management **3**
ADJ.　**new** management, **senior** management **2**

man|age|ment buy|out (**management buyouts**) N-COUNT 可算名詞 A **management buyout** is the buying of a company by its managers. The abbreviation **MBO** is also used. 経営者による自社株取得 [BUSINESS 実業] ❏ Dozens of company boards are now discreetly sounding out venture capitalists to see if they will support management buyouts. 多数の会社取締役会は現在，マネジメントバイアウトを支持するかどうか投資家に対し慎重な打診を行っている.

man|ag|er /mǽnɪdʒər/ (**managers**) **1** N-COUNT 可算名詞 A **manager** is a person who is responsible for running part of or the whole of a business organization. 経営者 ❏ The chef, staff, and managers are all Chinese. シェフ，従業員および経営者すべてが中国人だ. **2** N-COUNT 可算名詞 The **manager** of a pop star or other entertainer is the person who takes care of their business interests. マネージャー ❏ ...the star's manager and agent, Anne Chudleigh. そのスターのマネージャーかつ代理人であるアン・チャドリー. **3** N-COUNT 可算名詞 The **manager** of a baseball team is the person responsible for training the players and organizing the way they play. In other sports, **coach** is used instead. 監督 ❏ The team expects to name a new manager before spring training. そのチームは春季訓練が始まる前に新監督を迎える予定だ.

→ see **concert, restaurant**

mana|ge|rial /mænɪdʒɪəriəl/ ADJ 形容詞 **Managerial** means relating to the work of a manager. 経営の ❏ ...his managerial skills. 彼の経営手腕. ❏ ...a managerial career. 管理職.

man|ag|ing di|rec|tor (**managing directors**) N-COUNT 可算名詞 The **managing director** of a company is the most important working director, and is in charge of the way the company is managed. 代表取締役，社長 [mainly BRIT 主に英国英語 BUSINESS 実業]

man|date /mǽndeɪt/ (**mandates, mandating, mandated**) **1** N-COUNT 可算名詞 If a government or other elected body has a **mandate** to carry out a particular policy or task, they have the authority to carry it out as a result of winning an election or vote. (政府や選挙で選ばれた団体の) 権限 信任 ❏ The president and his supporters are almost certain to read this vote as a mandate for continued economic reform. 大統領とその支持者たちがこの投票結果を経済改革続投への信任だと捉えることはほぼ間違いない. **2** N-COUNT 可算名詞 If someone is given a **mandate** to carry out a particular policy or task, they are given the official authority to do it. 委任，職権 ❏ How much longer does the independent prosecutor have a mandate to pursue this investigation? その独自の検察官はあとどのくらいこの捜査を続ける職権を持っているのだろう? **3** N-COUNT 可算名詞 You can refer to the fixed length of time that a country's leader or government remains in office as their **mandate**. 任期，就任期間 [FORMAL 形式ばった] ❏ ...his intention to leave politics once his mandate ends. 任期を終えるとすぐに政界を去ろうという彼の意思. **4** V-T 他動詞 When someone **is mandated to** carry out a particular policy or task, they are given the official authority to do it. 職権を与える，委任する [FORMAL 形式ばった] [usu passive] ❏ He'd been mandated by the West African Economic Community to go in and to enforce a ceasefire. 彼は中に入り停戦を実現するように西アフリカ経済共同体から委任されていた. **5** V-T 他動詞 To **mandate** something means to make it mandatory. 義務づける [AM 米国英語] ❏ The proposed initiative would mandate a reduction of carbon dioxide of 40%. その構想案では，二酸化炭素の40パーセント減量が義務づけられることになるだろう. ❏ Sixteen years ago, Quebec mandated that all immigrants send their children to French schools. 16年前にケベック州は，すべての移民に子供を州内のフランスの学校へやるよう義務づけた.

man|da|tory /mǽndətɔri/ **1** ADJ 形容詞 If an action or procedure is **mandatory**, people have to do it, because it is a rule or a law. 義務的な [FORMAL 形式ばった] ❏ ...the mandatory retirement age of 65. 65歳の定年 **2** ADJ 形容詞 If a crime carries a **mandatory** punishment, that punishment is fixed by law for all cases, in contrast to crimes for which the judge or magistrate has to decide the punishment for each particular case. 強制的な [FORMAL 形式ばった] ❏ ...the mandatory life sentence for murder. 殺人に対する強制的な終身刑

mane /meɪn/ (**manes**) N-COUNT 可算名詞 The **mane** on a horse or lion is the long, thick hair that grows from its neck. たてがみ ❏ The horse's mane can be washed at the same time as his body. 馬のたてがみは体を洗う時に一緒に洗える.

ma|neu|ver /mənúvər/ (**maneuvers, maneuvering, maneuvered**) **1** V-T/V-I 他動詞/自動詞 If you **maneuver** something into or out of an awkward position, you skillfully move it there. (難しい所を) 巧みに移動させる うまく操縦する ❏ That will allow them to maneuver the satellite into the shuttle's cargo bay. それにより彼らは衛星をスペースシャトルの貨物室にうまく入れることができるだろう. ❏ I maneuvered my way among the tables to the back corner of the place. 私はテーブルの間をすり抜けて，後ろの隅へ移動した. ● N-VAR 可変性名詞 **Maneuver** is also a noun. 操作，操縦 ❏ The chopper shot upward in a maneuver matched by the other pilot. そのヘリは別のパイロットと同調した操作で上方に飛び上がった. **2** V-T/V-I 他動詞/自動詞 If you **maneuver** a situation,

you change it in a clever and skillful way so that you can benefit from it. (状況を) 巧みに操る　画策する □The president has tried to maneuver the campaign away from himself. 大統領はその運動を自分自身からうまく遠ざけようとした. ●N-COUNT 可算名詞 **Maneuver** is also a noun. 画策, 操作 □The company announced a series of maneuvers to raise cash and reduce debt. その会社は現金を増やし負債を減らす一連の手段を発表した. ❸ N-PLURAL 複数名詞 Military **maneuvers** are training exercises which involve the movement of soldiers and equipment over a large area. 大演習 □Allied troops begin maneuvers tomorrow to show how quickly forces could be mobilized in case of a new invasion. 連合軍部隊は明日, 新たに侵略が起きた場合に軍をどれだけ迅速に動員できるかを示すための大演習する.

man|gle /mǽŋgᵊl/ (mangles, mangling, mangled) V-T 他動詞 If a physical object **is mangled**, it is crushed or twisted very forcefully, so that it is difficult to see what its original shape was. (原形をとどめないほど) めちゃくちゃにする [usu passive] □His body was crushed and mangled beyond recognition. 彼の遺体は識別できないほどに押しつぶされていた.

man|go /mǽŋgoʊ/ (mangoes or mangos) N-VAR 可変化名詞 A **mango** is a large, sweet, yellowish fruit which grows on a tree in hot areas. マンゴー □Peel, stone, and dice the mango. マンゴーの皮をむき, 核を取り出して, さいの目切りにしなさい. ●N-COUNT 可算名詞 A **mango** is the tree that this fruit grows on. マンゴーの木 □...orchards of lime and mango trees. ライムとマンゴーの果樹園

Word Link hood ≈ state, condition : adulthood, childhood, manhood

man|hood /mǽnhʊd/ N-UNCOUNT 不可算名詞 **Manhood** is the state of being a man rather than a boy. 成人男子であること □They were failing lamentably to help their sons grow from boyhood to manhood. 彼らは息子たちが少年から成人になるのを嘆かわしいほど手助けできずにいた.

man-hour (man-hours) N-COUNT 可算名詞 A **man-hour** is the average amount of work that one person can do in an hour. **Man-hours** are used to estimate how long jobs take, or how many people are needed to do a job in a particular time. 人時 (1人1時間の仕事量) □The restoration took almost 4,000 man-hours over four years. その修復工事には4年間にわたりほぼ4千人時が費やされた.

ma|nia /méɪniə/ (manias) ❶ N-COUNT 可算名詞 If you say that a person or group has a **mania for** something, you mean that they enjoy it very much or spend a lot of time on it. 熱狂 □The mania for dinosaurs began in the late 1800s. 恐竜ブームは1800年代後半に始まった. ❷ N-UNCOUNT 不可算名詞 **Mania** is a mental illness which causes the sufferer to become very worried or concerned about something. 躁病 (そうびょう) [also N in pl] □...the treatment of mania. 躁病の治療

ma|ni|ac /méɪniæk/ (maniacs) ❶ N-COUNT 可算名詞 A **maniac** is a crazy person who is violent and dangerous. 狂人 □The cabin looked as if a maniac had been let loose there. その小屋はまるで狂人が解き放たれたかのようだった. ❷ ADJ 形容詞 If you describe someone's behavior as **maniac**, you are emphasizing that it is extremely foolish and uncontrolled. 狂人のような [EMPHASIS 強調] [ADJ n] □He could not maintain his maniac speed for much longer. 彼はその狂人的なスピードをずっと長くは保てなかった. ❸ N-COUNT 可算名詞 If you call someone, for example, a religious **maniac** or a sports **maniac**, you are critical of them because they have such a strong interest in religion or sports. 一狂, 一気違い [DISAPPROVAL 不賛成] □My mom is turning into a religious maniac. 私の母さんは宗教気違いになりつつあるわ.

man|ic /mǽnɪk/ ❶ ADJ 形容詞 If you describe someone as **manic**, you mean that they do things extremely quickly or energetically, often because they are very excited or anxious about something. 熱狂的な, 猛烈な □My job is manic. 私の仕事は本当に熱狂的だった. ●**man|i|cal|ly** /mǽnɪkli/ ADV 副詞 熱狂的に □We cleaned the house manically over the weekend. 私たちは週末に熱狂的に家を清掃した. ❷ ADJ 形容詞 If you describe someone's smile, laughter, or sense of humor as **manic**, you mean that it seems excessive or strange, as if they were insane. 度を越えた, 奇妙な □...a manic grin. 奇妙な笑顔

Word Link cur ≈ caring : curate, curator, manicure

Word Link man ≈ hand : emancipate, manicure, manipulate

mani|cure /mǽnɪkyʊər/ (manicures, manicuring, manicured) V-T 他動詞 If you **manicure** your hands or nails, you care for them by softening your skin and cutting and polishing your nails. (手・爪の) 手入れをする □He was surprised to see how carefully she had manicured her broad hands. 彼は彼女の大きな手がとてもきれいに手入れしてあるのを見て驚いた. ●N-COUNT 可算名詞 **Manicure** is also a noun. 手・爪の手入れ □I have a manicure occasionally. 私は時々マニキュアをしてもらう.

mani|fest /mǽnɪfɛst/ (manifests, manifesting, manifested) ❶ ADJ 形容詞 If you say that something is **manifest**, you mean

that it is clearly true and that nobody would disagree with it if they saw it or considered it. 明白な [FORMAL 形式ばった] □...the manifest failure of the policies. それらの政策の明らかな失敗 ●**mani|fest|ly** ADV 副詞 明白に □She manifestly failed to last the mile-and-a-half of the race. 彼女は明らかにレースの1.5マイルを続けられなかった. ❷ V-T 他動詞 If you **manifest** a particular quality, feeling, or illness, or if it **manifests itself**, it becomes visible or obvious. (特質・感情を) 明らかにする (再帰代名詞を伴い) 現れる [FORMAL 形式ばった] □He manifested a pleasing personality on stage. 彼は魅力的な人柄を舞台で現した. □The virus needs two weeks to manifest itself. そのウィルスが現れるまでには2週間かかる. ●ADJ 形容詞 **Manifest** is also an adjective. 明らかな □The same alarm is manifest everywhere. その同じ警報はどこでも目に付く.

mani|fes|ta|tion /mǽnɪfɛsteɪʃᵊn/ (manifestations) N-COUNT 可算名詞 A **manifestation** of something is one of the different ways in which it can appear. 現れ方 [FORMAL 形式ばった] □Different animals in the colony had different manifestations of the disease. そのコロニーでは動物の種類によって, その病気の症状が異なっていた.

mani|fes|to /mǽnɪfɛstoʊ/ (manifestos or manifestoes) N-COUNT 可算名詞 A **manifesto** is a statement published by a person or group of people, especially a political party, or a government, in which they say what their aims and policies are. (政党・政府などの) 政策表明書 □The Republicans are currently drawing up their election manifesto. 共和党は現在, 選挙公約を作成している.

ma|nipu|late /mənɪpyəleɪt/ (manipulates, manipulating, manipulated) ❶ V-T 他動詞 If you say that someone **manipulates** people, you disapprove of them because they skillfully force or persuade people to do what they want. (人を) 操る [DISAPPROVAL 不賛成] □She's always borrowing my clothes and manipulating me to give her vast sums of money. 彼女はいつも私の服を借りたり, 私が多額のお金を彼女に渡すよう仕向けたりしている. ●**ma|nipu|la|tion** /mənɪpyəleɪʃᵊn/ (manipulations) N-VAR 可変化名詞 巧みな扱い □...repeated criticism or manipulation of our minds. たびたびの批判, もしくは我々の心の操作 ❷ V-T 他動詞 If you say that someone **manipulates** an event or situation, you disapprove of them because they use or control it for their own benefit, or cause it to develop in the way they want. (事件・状況などを) うまく操る [DISAPPROVAL 不賛成] □She was unable, for once, to control and manipulate events. 彼女も今回だけは出来事を管理し操作することができなかった. ●**ma|nipu|la|tion** N-VAR 可変化名詞 (出来事の) 操作 □...accusations of political manipulation. 政治的操作に対する非難 ❸ V-T 他動詞 If you **manipulate** something that requires skill, such as a complicated piece of equipment or a difficult idea, you operate it or process it. (道具などを) 巧みに操作する (考えなどを) うまく処理する □The technology uses a pen to manipulate a computer. その技術はコンピューターを操作するのにペンを使う. ●**ma|nipu|la|tion** N-VAR 可変化名詞 (道具などの) 操作　処理 □...science that requires only the simplest of mathematical manipulations. 最も単純な数学的処理だけを必要とする科学 ❹ V-T 他動詞 If someone **manipulates** your bones or muscles, they skillfully move and press them with their hands in order to push the bones into their correct position or make the muscles less stiff. (骨のズレを) 矯正する (筋肉を) ほぐす □The way he can manipulate my leg has helped my arthritis so much. 彼が私の足を整骨する方法が関節炎を非常に抑えている. ●**ma|nipu|la|tion** N-VAR 可変化名詞 整骨 □A permanent cure will only be effected by acupuncture, chiropractic, or manipulation. 完治させようと思ったら, 針治療か脊柱指圧療法か整骨治療しか効き目がない.

ma|nipu|la|tive /mənɪpyəleɪtɪv, -lətɪv/ ADJ 形容詞 If you describe someone as **manipulative**, you disapprove of them because they skillfully force or persuade people to act in the way that they want. (人を) 操るのがうまい [DISAPPROVAL 不賛成] □He described Mr. Long as cold, calculating, and manipulative. 彼はロング氏のことを冷徹で計算高く人を操るのがうまいと述べた.

man|kind /mǽnkaɪnd/ N-UNCOUNT 不可算名詞 You can refer to all human beings as **mankind** when considering them as a group. Some people dislike this use. 人類 □...the evolution of mankind. 人類の進化

man|ly /mǽnli/ (manlier, manliest) ADJ 形容詞 If you describe a man's behavior or appearance as **manly**, you approve of it because it shows qualities that are considered typical of a man, such as strength or courage. (行動・外見が) 男らしい [APPROVAL 賛成] □He set himself manly tasks and expected others to follow his example. 彼は自分自身に男らしい課題を課し, 他の人たちが彼の例に続くことを期待した. ●**man|li|ness** N-UNCOUNT 不可算名詞 男らしさ □He has no doubts about his manliness. 彼は自分の男らしさを確信している.

man-made also **manmade** ADJ 形容詞 **Man-made** things are created or caused by people, rather than occurring naturally. 人間が作った, 人為の □Man-made and natural disasters have disrupted the government's economic plans. 人為災害と自然災害が政府の経済計画を破たんさせた. □...man-made lakes. 人工湖

manned /mænd/ ❶ ADJ 形容詞 A **manned** vehicle such as a spacecraft has people in it who are operating its controls. （宇宙船などが）有人の ❑ *In thirty years from now the United States should have a manned spacecraft on Mars.* 今から30年後には米国の有人宇宙船が火星にいるはずだ. ❷ → see also **man 8**

man|ner /mænər/ (**manners**) ❶ N-SING 単数名詞 The **manner** in which you do something is the way that you do it. やり方, 方法 ❑ *She smiled again in a friendly manner.* 彼女は再び親しみを込めてほほえんだ. ❑ *I'm a professional and I have to conduct myself in a professional manner.* 私は専門家なので, 専門家らしくふるまわねばならない. ❷ N-SING 単数名詞 Someone's **manner** is the way in which they behave and talk when they are with other people, for example whether they are polite, confident, or bad-tempered. 態度, 物腰 ❑ *His manner was self-assured and brusque.* 彼の態度は自信満々でぞんざいだった. ●**-mannered** COMB IN ADJ 形容詞の複合 行儀が〜の ❑ *Forrest was normally mild-mannered, affable, and untalkative.* フォレストは普段は温厚な物腰で愛想よく寡黙だった. ❸ N-PLURAL 複数名詞 If someone has **good manners**, they are polite and observe social customs. If someone has **bad manners**, they are impolite and do not observe these customs. 礼儀 ❑ *He dressed well and had impeccable manners.* 彼はきちんとした服装をし, 非の打ちどころのないマナーを身につけていた. ❑ *The manners of many doctors were appalling.* 多くの医師のマナーはひどいものだった.

ma|noeu|vre /mənuvər/ → see maneuver

man|power /mænpaʊər/ N-UNCOUNT 不可算名詞 Workers are sometimes referred to as **manpower** when they are being considered as a part of the process of producing goods or providing services. 人材, 労働力 ❑ *...the shortage of skilled manpower in the industry.* その業界の熟練労働者の不足

man|sion /mænʃən/ (**mansions**) N-COUNT 算名詞 A **mansion** is a very large house. 邸宅 ❑ *...an eighteenth-century mansion in New Hampshire.* ニュー・ハンプシャー州にある18世紀の邸宅

man|slaughter /mænslɔtər/ N-UNCOUNT 不可算名詞 **Manslaughter** is the illegal killing of a person by someone who did not intend to kill them. 故殺, 過失致死罪 [LEGAL 法律的] ❑ *A judge accepted her plea that she was guilty of manslaughter, not murder.* 裁判官は, 謀殺ではなく過失致死で有罪だという彼女自身の申し立てを認めた.

mantel|piece /mæntəlpis/ (**mantelpieces**) also **mantlepiece** N-COUNT 可算名詞 A **mantelpiece** is a wood or stone shelf which is the top part of a border around a fireplace. マントルピース（暖炉の上の小さな棚の部分）❑ *On the mantelpiece are a pair of bronze Ming vases.* マントルピースの上には明朝時代の青銅の花瓶が1対ある.

man|tra /mæntrə/ (**mantras**) ❶ N-COUNT 可算名詞 A **mantra** is a word or phrase repeated by Buddhists and Hindus when they meditate, or to help them feel calm. マントラ, 真言 ❷ N-COUNT 可算名詞 You can use **mantra** to refer to a statement or a principle that people repeat very often because they think it is true, especially when you think that it not true or is only part of the truth.（しばしば繰り返される）主張 お題目 ❑ *Listening to customers is now part of the mantra of new management in public services.* 顧客の声に耳を傾けることは今や公益事業の新しい経営管理方針の一部となっている.

manu|al /mænyuəl/ (**manuals**) ❶ ADJ 形容詞 **Manual** work is work in which you use your hands or your physical strength rather than your mind. 手作業の, 体を使った ❑ *...skilled manual workers.* 熟練の肉体労働者 ❷ ADJ 形容詞 **Manual** is used to talk about movements which are made by someone's hands. 手先の [FORMAL 形式ばった] [ADJ n] ❑ *...toys designed to help develop manual dexterity.* 手先の器用さを培うように考案されたおもちゃ ❸ ADJ 形容詞 **Manual** means operated by hand, rather than by electricity or a motor. 手動の [ADJ n] ❑ *There is a manual pump to get rid of the water.* 排水用に手動のポンプがある. ●**manu|al|ly** ADV 副詞 [ADV with v] 手動で ❑ *The device is manually operated, using a simple handle.* その装置は簡単な取っ手を使い手動で動かす. ❹ N-COUNT 可算名詞 A **manual** is a book which tells you how to do something or how a piece of machinery works. 取扱説明書, マニュアル ❑ *...the instruction manual.* 取扱説明書

manu|fac|ture /mænyəfæktʃər/ (**manufactures**, **manufacturing**, **manufactured**) ❶ V-T 他動詞 To **manufacture** something means to make it in a factory, usually in large quantities. 生産する, 製造する [BUSINESS 実業] ❑ *They manufacture the class of plastics known as thermoplastic materials.* 彼らは熱可塑性プラスチック材料として知られるプラスチック類を製造している ❑ *The first three models are being manufactured at the factory in Dayton.* 最初の3つのモデルはデイトンにある工場で生産されている. ●N-UNCOUNT 不可算名詞 **Manufacture** is also a noun. 生産, 製造 ❑ *...the manufacture of nuclear weapons.* 核兵器の製造 ●**manu|fac|tur|ing** N-UNCOUNT 不可算名詞 製造 ❑ *...management headquarters for manufacturing in China.* 中国での製造を担当する経営本部 ❷ N-COUNT 可算名詞 In economics, **manufactures** are goods or products which have been made in a factory.（工場で作られた）製品 [BUSINESS 実業] ❑ *...a long-term rise in the share of manufactures in non-oil exports.* 非石炭株式油輸出品における工場製品の割合の長期にわたる上昇 ❸ V-T 他動詞 If you say that someone **manufactures** information, you are criticizing them because they invent information that is not true.（情報などを）でっち上げる ねつぞうする [DISAPPROVAL 不賛成] ❑ *According to the prosecution, the officers manufactured an elaborate story.* 検察当局によると, その幹部たちは巧妙な作り話をでっち上げていた.

→ see mass production

manu|fac|tur|er /mænyəfæktʃərər/ (**manufacturers**) N-COUNT 可算名詞 A **manufacturer** is a business or company which makes goods in large quantities to sell. 製造業者 [BUSINESS 実業] ❑ *...the world's largest doll manufacturer.* 世界で最大の人形メーカー

→ see industry

ma|nure /mənʊər/ (**manures**) N-MASS 質量名詞 **Manure** is animal feces, sometimes mixed with chemicals, that is spread on the ground in order to make plants grow healthy and strong. 肥料 ❑ *...bags of manure.* 袋入りの肥料

manu|script /mænyəskrɪpt/ (**manuscripts**) N-COUNT 可算名詞 A **manuscript** is a handwritten or typed document, especially a writer's first version of a book before it is published. 原稿 [also 'in' N] ❑ *He had seen a manuscript of the book.* 彼はその本の原稿を見ていた.

many /mɛni/ ❶ DET 限定詞 You use **many** to indicate that you are talking about a large number of people or things. 多くの, たくさんの ❑ *I don't think many people would argue with that.* それに異論を唱える人はそう多くないだろうと思う. ❑ *Not many films are made in Finland.* フィンランドで作られた映画はそう多くはない. ●PRON 代名詞 **Many** is also a pronoun. 多くの人, 多くのもの ❑ *We stood up, thinking through the possibilities. There weren't many.* 私たちは立ち上がり, いろんな可能性をじっくり考えた. そう多くの可能性はなかった. ●QUANT 数量詞 **Many** is also a quantifier. 多くのもの [QUANT 'of' def-pl-n] ❑ *So, once we have cohabited, why do many of us feel the need to get married?* だから, 1度同棲すると, どうしてわたしたちの多くが結婚する必要性を感じるだろうか? ❑ *It seems there are not very many of them left in the sea.* それは海の中にもうあまり残っていないようだ. ●ADJ 形容詞 **Many** is also an adjective. 多くの ❑ *Among his many hobbies was the breeding of fine horses.* 彼の多くの趣味の中に, よい馬を飼育するというのがあった. ❷ ADV 副詞 You use **many** in expressions such as "not many," "not very many," and "too many" when replying to questions about numbers of things or people. あまり多くなく（not many）多すぎるほど（too many）[ADV as reply] ❑ *"How many of the songs that dealt with this theme became hit songs?" — "Not very many."* 「これをテーマにした歌のどれだけがヒットになったの」, 「あまりないね」 ❸ PREDET 前限定詞 You use **many** followed by "a" and a noun to emphasize that there are a lot of people or things involved in something. 幾多の, 数々の（数の多さを強調）[EMPHASIS 強調] ❑ *Many a mother tries to act out her unrealized dreams through her daughter.* 多くの母親が実現できなかった自分の夢を自分の娘を通して実現しようとしている. ❹ DET 限定詞 You use **many** after "how" to ask questions about numbers or quantities. You use **many** after "how" in reported clauses to talk about numbers or quantities. どれほどの（何人の）❑ *How many years have you been here?* もう何年ここにいるのですか. ●PRON 代名詞 **Many** is also a pronoun. どれだけ ['how' PRON] ❑ *How many do you smoke a day?* 1日に何本たばこを吸いますか. ❺ DET 限定詞 You use **many** with "as" when you are comparing numbers of things or people. 〜と同じ数の 〜するだけの数の ❑ *I've always entered as many photo competitions as I can.* 私はいつもできるだけ多くの写真コンクールに参加してきた. ●PRON 代名詞 **Many** is also a pronoun. 同数, 〜するだけの数 ['as' PRON] ❑ *Let the child try on as many as she likes.* その子に好きなだけ試着させてやりなさい. ❻ PRON 代名詞 You use **many** to mean "many people." 多くの人 ❑ *Iris Murdoch was regarded by many as a supremely good and serious writer.* アイリス・マードックは多くの人から最高の純文学作家だとみなされた. ❼ N-SING 単数名詞 The **many** means a large group of people, especially the ordinary people in society, considered as separate from a particular small group. 大衆, 一般人 ❑ *The printing press gave power to a few to change the world for the many.* 印刷機は少数の人々に大衆のために世界を変える力を与えた.

map 656 marinade

You only use **many** to talk about things that can be counted. ❑ *They owned many cars*. You should use **much** if you want to talk about things that cannot be counted. ❑ *...too much water.*

8 PHRASE 句 You use **as many as** before a number to suggest that it is surprisingly large. 一もの多くの [EMPHASIS 強調] ❑ *4 million people watched today's parade.* 400万人もの人々が今日のパレードを見た.

map /mæp/ (**maps, mapping, mapped**) **1** N-COUNT 可算名詞 A **map** is a drawing of a particular area such as a city, a country, or a continent, showing its main features as they would appear if you looked at them from above. 地図 ❑ *He unfolded the map and set it on the floor.* 彼は地図を広げて床に置いた. **2** V-T 他動詞 To **map** an area means to make a map of it. 地図を作る ❑ *...a spacecraft which is using radar to map the surface of Venus.* レーダーを使って金星の表面の地図を作っている宇宙探査機

▶ **map out** PHRASAL VERB 句動詞 If you **map out** something that you are intending to do, you work out in detail how you will do it. 綿密に計画を立てる ❑ *I went home and mapped out my strategy.* 私は家に帰り, 計画を練った. ❑ *I cannot conceive of anybody writing a play by sitting down and mapping it out.* 私は座って計画を練りながら戯曲を書いている人を想像できない.

Word Partnership *map は次の語句と使われる:*

ADJ. **detailed** map **1**
V. **draw** a map, **look at** a map, **open** a map, **read** a map **1**

---

ma|ple /ˈmeɪpəl/ (**maples**) N-VAR 可変性名詞 A **maple** or a **maple tree** is a tree with five-pointed leaves which turn bright red or gold in the fall. カエデ, モミジ ● N-UNCOUNT 不可算名詞 **Maple** is the wood of this tree. カエデ材 ❑ *...a solid maple worktop.* どっしりとしたカエデ材の調理台

mar /mɑr/ (**mars, marring, marred**) V-T 他動詞 To **mar** something means to spoil or damage it. 損なう, 傷つける ❑ *A number of problems marred the smooth running of this event.* たくさんの問題があり, この行事はスムーズに行われなかった.

Mar. Mar. is a written abbreviation for **March**. 3月 (March) の略語

mara|thon /ˈmærəθɒn/ (**marathons**) **1** N-COUNT 可算名詞 A **marathon** is a race in which people run a distance of 26 miles, which is about 42 km. マラソン ❑ *...running in his first marathon.* 彼の初めてのマラソン走行 **2** ADJ 形容詞 If you use **marathon** to describe an event or task, you are emphasizing that it takes a long time and is very tiring. (出来事・任務が) 長く続く [EMPHASIS 強調] [ADJ n] ❑ *People make marathon journeys to buy glass here.* みんなここでガラス製品を買うために遠路はるばるやって来る.

mar|ble /ˈmɑrbəl/ (**marbles**) **1** N-UNCOUNT 不可算名詞 **Marble** is a type of very hard rock which feels cold when you touch it and which shines when it is cut and polished. Statues and parts of buildings are sometimes made of marble. 大理石 ❑ *The house has a superb staircase made from oak and marble.* その家にはオークと大理石からできた豪華な階段がある. **2** N-COUNT 可算名詞 **Marbles** are sculptures made of marble. 大理石の彫刻 ❑ *...marbles and bronzes from the Golden Age of Athens.* アテネ最盛期の大理石とブロンズの像 **3** N-UNCOUNT 不可算名詞 **Marbles** is a children's game played with small balls, usually made of colored glass. You roll a ball along the ground and try to hit an opponent's ball with it. ビー玉遊び ❑ *On the far side of the street, two boys were playing marbles.* 通りの向こう側では2人の男の子がビー玉遊びをしていた. **4** N-COUNT 可算名詞 A **marble** is one of the small balls used in the game of marbles. ビー玉 ❑ *...a glass marble.* ガラスのビー玉

march /mɑrtʃ/ (**marches, marching, marched**) **1** V-T/V-I 他動詞/自動詞 When soldiers **march** somewhere, or when a commanding officer **marches** them somewhere, they walk there with very regular steps, as a group. (兵士を) 行進させる [他動詞], (兵士が) 行進する [自動詞] ❑ *A U.S. infantry battalion was marching down the street.* 米国の歩兵大隊が通りを行進していた. ❑ *Captain Ramirez called them to attention and marched them off to the main camp.* ラミレス大尉は彼らに気をつけの姿勢をとらせ, 本駐屯地まで行進させた. ● N-COUNT 可算名詞 **March** is also a noun. 行進 ❑ *After a short march, the column entered the village.* 短い行進の後, 縦隊はその村に入った. **2** V-I 自動詞 When a large group of people **march** for a cause, they walk somewhere together in order to express their ideas or to protest about something. (抗議デモなどで) 行進する ❑ *The demonstrators then marched through the capital chanting slogans and demanding free elections.* その後, デモ隊はスローガンを繰り返して自由選挙を求めながら首都を行進した. ● N-COUNT 可算名詞 **March** is also a noun. デモ行進 ❑ *Organizers expect up to 300,000 protesters to join the march.* 主催者は最大30万人の抗議者がデモ行進に加わると見込んでいる. ● **march|er** (**marchers**) N-COUNT 可算名詞 デモ参加者 ❑ *Fights between police and marchers lasted for three hours.* 警察とデモ隊との闘争は3時間に及んだ. **3** V-I 自動詞 If you say that someone **marches** somewhere, you mean that they walk there

quickly and in a determined way, for example because they are angry. どんどん歩く ❑ *He marched into the kitchen without knocking.* 彼はノックもせずに台所へずかずかと入って行った. **4** V-T 他動詞 If you **march** someone somewhere, you force them to walk there with you, for example by holding their arm tightly. 無理やり歩かせる ❑ *They were marched through a crocodile-infested area and, if they slowed down, were beaten with sticks.* 彼らはワニが群がる地域を無理やり歩かされ, 歩く速度が遅くなると棒で殴られた. **5** N-SING 単数名詞 The **march** of something is its steady development or progress. (物事の) 進展 進歩 ❑ *It is easy to feel trampled by the relentless march of technology.* 技術の容赦ない進歩に踏みつぶされるように感じるのはたやすい. **6** N-COUNT 可算名詞 A **march** is a piece of music with a regular rhythm that you can march to. 行進曲 ❑ *A military band played Russian marches and folk tunes at the parade last Sunday.* 先週の日曜のパレードで軍楽隊がロシアの行進曲と民俗音楽を演奏した.

March /mɑrtʃ/ (**Marches**) N-VAR 可変性名詞 **March** is the third month of the year in the Western calendar. 3月 ❑ *I flew to Milwaukee in early March.* 私は3月上旬にミルウォーキー市へ飛行機で行った. ❑ *She was born in Austria on March 6, 1920.* 彼女は1920年3月6日にオーストリアで生まれた.

mar|ga|rine /ˈmɑrdʒərɪn/ (**margarines**) N-MASS 質量名詞 **Margarine** is a yellow substance made from vegetable oil that is similar to butter. You spread it on bread or use it for cooking. マーガリン

mar|gin /ˈmɑrdʒɪn/ (**margins**) **1** N-COUNT 可算名詞 A **margin** is the difference between two amounts, especially the difference in the number of votes or points between the winner and the loser in an election or other contest. 差, 票差 ❑ *They could end up with a 50-point winning margin.* 彼らは50票差で当落が決まるかもしれないだろう. **2** N-COUNT 可算名詞 The **margin** of a written or printed page is the empty space at the side of the page. (ページの) 余白 ❑ *She added her comments in the margin.* 彼女は余白にコメントを加えた. **3** N-VAR 可変性名詞 If there is a **margin** for something in a situation, there is some freedom to choose what to do or decide how to do it. (選択などの) 余地 ❑ *The money is collected in a straightforward way with little margin for error.* 資金は誤りの入る余地のほとんどない簡単な方法で集められる. **4** N-COUNT 可算名詞 The **margin** of a place or area is the extreme edge of it. (場所や地域の) 端 ❑ *...the low coastal plain along the western margin.* 西端に沿った低い海岸平野 **5** N-PLURAL 複数名詞 To be **on the margins** of a society, group, or activity means to be among the least typical or least important parts of it. (社会・活動の中で) 重要度の低い部分 ❑ *Students have played an important role in the past, but for the moment, they're on the margins.* 昔は学生が重要な役割を演じたこともあったが, 今のところは, 彼らは影が薄い. **6** → see also **profit margin**

Word Partnership *margin は次の語句と使われる:*

ADJ. **comfortable** margin, **large** margin, **slim** margin **1**
 narrow margin, **wide** margin **1** **2**
N. margin **for error** **3**

---

mar|gin|al /ˈmɑrdʒɪnəl/ **1** ADJ 形容詞 If you describe something as **marginal**, you mean that it is small or not very important. ほんの少しの, 取るに足らない ❑ *This is a marginal improvement on October.* これは10月に比べわずかに向上している **2** ADJ 形容詞 If you describe people as **marginal**, you mean that they are not involved in the main events or developments in society because they are poor or have no power. (人が) 取るに足りない 影響力を持たない ❑ *The tribunals were established for the well-integrated members of society and not for marginal individuals.* それらの裁判所は, 社会のきちんとした成員のためのものであって, 社会の片隅にいる人々のためのものではなかった. **3** ADJ 形容詞 **Marginal** activities, costs, or taxes are not the main part of a business or an economic system, but often make the difference between its success or failure, and are therefore important to control. 限界収益点の [BUSINESS 実業] ❑ *The analysts applaud the cuts in marginal businesses, but insist the company must make deeper sacrifices.* アナリストたちはやっと採算の取れる取引の削減を賞賛するが, 会社がさらに大きな犠牲を払う必要性を主張する.

mar|gin|al|ly /ˈmɑrdʒɪnəli/ ADV 副詞 **Marginally** means to only a small extent. わずかに ❑ *Sales last year were marginally higher than in 1991.* 昨年の売り上げは1991年よりもわずかに多かった.

mari|jua|na /ˌmærɪˈwɑnə/ N-UNCOUNT 不可算名詞 **Marijuana** is a drug which is made from the dried leaves and flowers of the hemp plant, and which can be smoked. マリファナ, 大麻

ma|ri|na /məˈrinə/ (**marinas**) N-COUNT 可算名詞 A **marina** is a small harbor for small boats that are used for leisure. マリーナ (ヨット・ボートの停泊場)

mari|nade /ˌmærɪˈneɪd/ (**marinades, marinading, marinaded**) **1** N-COUNT 可算名詞 A **marinade** is a sauce of oil, vinegar, spices, and herbs, which you pour over meat or fish before you cook it, in order to add flavor, or to make the meat or fish softer. マリネード ❑ *Fish is already tender and moist, so a marinade is just added for*

flavor. 魚はすでに柔らかくしっとりしているので, マリネードは風味のためだけに加える. **2** V-T/V-I 他動詞/自動詞 To **marinade** means the same as to **marinate**. マリネードに漬ける [他動詞], マリネードになる [自動詞] □ *Leave to marinade for 24 hours*. マリネードに24時間漬け込む.

mari|nate /mærɪneɪt/ (**marinates, marinating, marinated**) V-T/V-I 他動詞/自動詞 If you **marinate** meat or fish, or if it **marinates**, you keep it in a mixture of oil, vinegar, spices, and herbs before cooking it, so that it can develop a special flavor. マリネードに漬ける [他動詞], マリネードに漬かる [自動詞] □ *Marinate the chicken for at least 4 hours*. 鶏肉を少なくとも4時間マリネードに漬け込む.

Word Link *mar ≈ sea : marine, maritime, submarine*

---

ma|rine /mərin/ (**marines**) **1** N-COUNT 可算名詞 A **marine** is a member of an armed force, for example the U.S. Marine Corps or the Royal Marines, who is specially trained for military duties at sea as well as on land. 海兵隊員 □ *A small number of Marines were wounded*. 少数の海兵隊員が負傷した. **2** ADJ 形容詞 **Marine** is used to describe things relating to the sea or to the animals and plants that live in the sea. 海の, 海洋動植物の [ADJ n] □ *...breeding grounds for marine life*. 海洋生物の繁殖地 **3** ADJ 形容詞 **Marine** is used to describe things relating to ships and their movement at sea. 船舶の, 航海の [ADJ n] □ *...a lawyer specializing in marine law*. 海法専門の弁護士
→ see **ship**

mari|tal /mærɪtəl/ ADJ 形容詞 **Marital** is used to describe things relating to marriage. 結婚の [ADJ n] □ *Caroline was hoping to make her marital home in Pittsburgh to be near her family*. キャロラインは自分の家族の近くにいるためにピッツバーグに夫婦の家を構えたいと願っていた.

mari|tal sta|tus N-UNCOUNT 不可算名詞 Your **marital status** is whether you are married, single, or divorced. 婚姻状況 [FORMAL 形式ばった] □ *How well off you are in old age is largely determined by race, sex, and marital status*. 老いてからどれだけ裕福かは主に人種・性別・婚姻状況で決まる.

mari|time /mærɪtaɪm/ ADJ 形容詞 **Maritime** is used to describe things relating to the sea and to ships. 海の, 船舶の [ADJ n] □ *...the largest maritime museum of its kind*. その種類では最大の海事博物館

mark /mɑrk/ (**marks, marking, marked**) **1** N-COUNT 可算名詞 A **mark** is a small area of something such as dirt that has accidentally gotten onto a surface or piece of clothing. (染みなどの) 跡 □ *The dogs are always rubbing against the wall and making dirty marks*. その犬たちはいつもその壁に体をこすりつけて汚い跡を残している. **2** V-T/V-I 他動詞/自動詞 If something **marks** a surface, or if the surface **marks**, the surface is damaged by marks or a mark. 跡をつける [他動詞], 跡がつく [自動詞] □ *Leather overshoes were put on the horses' hooves to stop them from marking the turf*. 馬のひづめには芝生に跡をつけないように革のオーバーシューズがはかせられていた. **3** N-COUNT 可算名詞 A **mark** is a written or printed symbol, for example a letter of the alphabet. 記号, 印 □ *He made marks with a pencil*. 彼は鉛筆で記号を書いた. **4** V-T 他動詞 If you **mark** something with a particular word or symbol, you write that word or symbol on it. 記号や文字を書く □ *The bank marks the check "certified."* 銀行は小切手に「保証」と書き込む. □ *Mark them with a symbol*. それらに記号をつけなさい. **5** N-COUNT 可算名詞 A **mark** is a point that is given for a correct answer or for doing something well in an exam or competition. A **mark** can also be a written symbol such as a letter that indicates how good a student's or competitor's work or performance is. (試験・競技の) 得点, 得点を表す記号 □ *...a simple scoring device of marks out of 10, where "1" equates to "Very poor performance."* 10段階で点数をつける簡単な装置で, 点数の1は「非常に悪い成績」というものである. **6** N-PLURAL 複数名詞 If someone gets good or high **marks** for doing something, they have done it well. If they get poor or low **marks**, they have done it badly. 成績, 点数 □ *You have to give her top marks for moral guts*. 彼女の道徳的な勇気に対し, 最高点をつけるべきだ. **7** V-T 他動詞 When a teacher **marks** a student's work, the teacher decides how good it is and writes a number or letter on it to indicate this opinion. 点数をつける □ *He was marking essays in his small study*. 彼は自分の小さな研究室で作文の点数をつけていた. ● **mark|ing** N-UNCOUNT 不可算名詞 採点 □ *For the rest of the lunch break I do my marking*. 私は昼休みの残りは採点をする. **8** N-COUNT 可算名詞 A particular **mark** is a particular number, point, or stage which has been reached or might be reached, especially a significant one. (数などの) 大台 段階 □ *Unemployment is rapidly approaching the one million mark*. 失業者は急速に100万人台に近づきつつある. **9** N-COUNT 可算名詞 The **mark** of something is the characteristic feature that enables you to recognize it. 特徴 □ *The mark of a civilized society is that it looks after its weakest members*. 文明社会の特徴は, 最も弱い立場にある成員の面倒をみることだ. **10** N-SING 単数名詞 If you say that a type of behavior or an event is **a mark of** a particular quality,

feeling, or situation, you mean it shows that that quality, feeling, or situation exists. (性質・感情などの) 表れ □ *It was a mark of his unfamiliarity with Hollywood that he didn't understand that an agent was paid out of his client's share*. 彼の顧客の分け前から代理店に支払われたことを分かっていなかったのは, 彼がハリウッドをよく知らない証拠だった. **11** V-T 他動詞 If something **marks** a place or position, it shows where something else is or where it used to be. (場所・位置を) 示す □ *A huge crater marks the spot where the explosion happened*. 巨大なクレーターは爆発が起こった箇所を示している. **12** V-T 他動詞 An event that **marks** a particular stage or point is a sign that something different is about to happen. (時代の区切りを) 示す □ *The announcement marks the end of an extraordinary period in European history*. その声明はヨーロッパ史上の異常な時代の終わりを告げている. **13** V-T 他動詞 If you do something to **mark** an event or occasion, you do it to show that you are aware of the importance of the event or occasion. 注意を払う, 記念する □ *Hundreds of thousands of people took to the streets to mark the occasion*. その行事を祝うため, 何十万人もの人々が通りに繰り出した. **14** V-T 他動詞 Something that **marks** someone **as** a particular type of person indicates that they are that type of person. 特徴づける □ *Her opposition to abortion and feminism mark her as a convinced traditionalist*. 彼女が妊娠中絶やフェミニズムに反対するのは, 確信的な伝統主義者である印だ. **15** → see also **marked, marking, punctuation mark, question mark 16** PHRASE 句 If someone or something **leaves** their **mark** or **leaves a mark**, they have a lasting effect on another person or thing. 跡を残す, 影響を残す □ *Years of conditioning had left their mark on her, and she never felt inclined to talk to strange men*. 長年にわたる条件づけが彼女に影響していて, 彼女は知らない男性と話したいと思ったことがなかった. **17** PHRASE 句 If you **make** your **mark** or **make a mark**, you become noticed or famous by doing something impressive or unusual. 有名になる, 成功する □ *She made her mark in the film industry in the 1960s*. 彼女は1960年代に映画産業で成功した. **18** PHRASE 句 If something such as a claim or estimate is **wide of the mark**, it is incorrect or inaccurate. 的外れの □ *That comparison isn't as wide of the mark as it seems*. あの比較は見た目ほど的外れではないか.

▶ **mark down** **1** PHRASAL VERB 句動詞 To **mark** an item **down** or **mark** its price **down** means to reduce its price. 値下げする □ *A toy store has marked down the latest computer games*. おもちゃ屋が最新のコンピュータゲームを値下げした. **2** PHRASAL VERB 句動詞 If you **mark** something **down**, you write it down. 書き留める □ *I tend to forget things unless I mark them down*. 私は何でも書いておかないとよく忘れる.

▶ **mark off** PHRASAL VERB 句動詞 If you **mark off** a piece or length of something, you make it separate, for example by putting a line on it or around it. 区分する, 区画する □ *He used a rope to mark off the circle*. 彼はロープを使ってその円を分けた.

▶ **mark up** **1** PHRASAL VERB 句動詞 If you **mark** something **up**, you increase its price. 値上げする □ *You can sell it to them at a set wholesale price, allowing them to mark it up for retail*. 彼らに規定の卸売価格で売って, 彼らが小売用に価格を上乗せできるようにしてやってもよい. **2** → see also **markup**

Thesaurus *mark また次を参照:*

N.	bruise, dot, smudge **1**
	attribute, feature, label, quality, trait **9**
V.	dent, scratch **2**

---

marked /mɑrkt/ ADJ 形容詞 A **marked** change or difference is very obvious and easily noticed. 際立った □ *There has been a marked increase in crimes against property*. 不動産に関する犯罪が著しく増加している. ● **mark|ed|ly** /mɑrkɪdli/ ADV 副詞 際立って, 明らかに □ *The current economic downturn is markedly different from previous recessions*. 現在の経済の沈滞は明らかに前回の不況とは異なる.

mark|er /mɑrkər/ (**markers**) **1** N-COUNT 可算名詞 A **marker** is an object which is used to show the position of something, or is used to help someone remember something. 目印 □ *He put a marker in his book and followed her out*. 彼はしおりを本にはさみ, 彼女について外へ出た. **2** N-COUNT 可算名詞 A **marker** or a **marker pen** is a pen with a thick tip made of felt, which is used for drawing and for coloring things. マーカー □ *Draw your child's outline with a heavy black marker or crayon*. あなたの子供の輪郭を大きな黒のマーカーかクレヨンで書いてください.

mar|ket /mɑrkɪt/ (**markets, marketing, marketed**) **1** N-COUNT 可算名詞 A **market** is a place where goods are bought and sold, usually outdoors. 市場 (いちば) マーケット □ *He sold boots at a market stall*. 彼は市場の出店で長靴を売った. **2** N-COUNT 可算名詞 The **market** for a particular type of thing is the number of people who want to buy it, or the area of the world in which it is sold. 市場 (しじょう) [BUSINESS 実業] □ *The foreign market is increasingly crucial*. 海外市場はますます重要になった. **3** N-SING 単数名詞 The **market** refers to the total amount of a product that is sold each year, especially when you are talking about the competition between the companies who sell that product. 取引量 [BUSINESS

実業 □ *The two big companies control 72% of the market.* その2大会社が年間取引量の72パーセントを押さえている。 **4** ADJ 形容詞 If you talk about a **market** economy, or the **market** price of something, you are referring to an economic system in which the prices of things depend on how many are available and how many people want to buy them, rather than prices being fixed by governments. 自由市場の [BUSINESS 実業] [ADJ n] □ *Their ultimate aim was a market economy for Hungary.* 彼らの究極の目的はハンガリーの自由市場化だった。 □ *He must sell the house for the current market value.* 彼は現行市場価格でその家を売らなければならない。 **5** V-T 他動詞 To **market** a product means to organize its sale, by deciding on its price, where it should be sold, and how it should be advertised. 市場に出す，市販する [BUSINESS 実業] □ *...if you marketed our music the way you market pop music.* 僕たちの音楽をあなたがポピュラー音楽を売るやり方で売り込めば **6** N-SING 単数名詞 **The job market** or the **labor market** refers to the people who are looking for work and the jobs available for them to do. 労働市場 [BUSINESS 実業] □ *Every year, 250,000 people enter the job market.* 毎年25万人が労働市場に参入する。 **7** N-SING 単数名詞 The stock market is sometimes referred to as **the market**. 株式市場，証券取引所 [BUSINESS 実業] □ *The market collapsed last October.* その株式市場は昨年10月に暴落した。 **8** → see also **black market, market forces, open market** **9** PHRASE 句 If you say that it is **a buyer's market**, you mean that it is a good time to buy a particular thing, because there is a lot of it available, so its price is low. If you say that it is **a seller's market**, you mean that very little of it is available, so its price is high. 買い手/売り手市場 [BUSINESS 実業] □ *Don't be afraid to haggle: for the moment, it's a buyer's market.* 値段交渉を怖がらなくてもいいので。今は買い手市場だから。 **10** PHRASE 句 If you are **in the market for** something, you are interested in buying it. 一を買いたいと思って □ *If you're in the market for a new radio, you'll see that the latest models are very different.* もし新しいラジオを買いたかったら，最新の型はぜんぜん違うよ。 **11** PHRASE 句 If something is **on the market**, it is available for people to buy. If it comes **onto the market**, it becomes available for people to buy. 売りに出されて [BUSINESS 実業] □ *...putting more empty offices on the market.* 他にも空いた事務所を売り出し **12** PHRASE 句 If you **price** yourself **out of the market**, you try to sell goods or services at a higher price than other people, with the result that no one buys them from you. 値を高くつけすぎる（その結果，商品が売れ残る）[BUSINESS 実業] □ *At $250,000 for a season, he really is pricing himself out of the market.* ワン・シーズン25万ドルだなんて，彼の値段は本当に高すぎる

→ see **stock market**

Thesaurus
market また次を参照:

N. farmers' market, grocery store, supermarket **1**

mar|ket|able /mɑrkɪtəbᵊl/ ADJ 形容詞 Something that is **marketable** is able to be sold because people want to buy it. 売り物になる，市場性の高い [BUSINESS 実業] □ *What began as an attempt at artistic creation has turned into a marketable commodity.* 芸術的な創作の試みとして始まったものが，売れる品物となった。

mar|ket|eer /mɑrkɪtɪər/ (**marketeers**) N-COUNT 可算名詞 A **marketeer** is the same as a **marketer**. 市場商人 [BUSINESS 実業] **2** → see also **free-marketeer**

mar|ket|er /mɑrkɪtər/ (**marketers**) N-COUNT 可算名詞 A **marketer** is someone whose job involves marketing. 市場商人，マーケティング担当者 [BUSINESS 実業] □ *As a marketer I understood what makes people buy things.* マーケティング担当者として，私は人々が何でものを買うのかよく分かっていた。

mar|ket forces N-PLURAL 複数名詞 When politicians and economists talk about **market forces**, they mean the economic factors that affect the availability of goods and the demand for them, without any help or control by governments. 自由市場方式，市場動向 [BUSINESS 実業] □ *...opening the economy to market forces and increasing the role of private enterprise.* 経済を自由市場方式に開放し，民間企業の役割を増やすこと

mar|ket|ing /mɑrkɪtɪŋ/ N-UNCOUNT 不可算名詞 **Marketing** is the organization of the sale of a product, for example, deciding on its price, the areas it should be supplied to, and how it should be advertised. マーケティング，市場での販売活動 [BUSINESS 実業] □ *...expert advice on production and marketing.* 生産や販売に関する専門家の助言

mar|ket lead|er (**market leaders**) N-COUNT 可算名詞 A **market leader** is a company that sells more of a particular product or service than most of its competitors do. 最大手企業 [BUSINESS 実業] □ *We are becoming one of the market leaders in the fashion industry.* 我々はファッション業界最大手の1つになりつつある。

mar|ket|place /mɑrkɪtpleɪs/ (**marketplaces**) **1** N-COUNT 可算名詞 The **marketplace** refers to the activity of buying and selling products. 商品の売買，市場 [BUSINESS 実業] □ *It's our hope that we will play an increasingly greater role in the marketplace and, therefore, supply more jobs.* 私たちは市場でますます大きな役割を担い，そして

それゆえにより多くの雇用を提供することを望んでいる。 **2** N-COUNT 可算名詞 A **marketplace** is a small area in a town or city where goods are bought and sold, often outdoors. 市場（いちば）□ *The marketplace was jammed with a noisy crowd of buyers and sellers.* 市場は売り買いするにぎやかな人々の群れでごった返していた。

mar|ket re|search N-UNCOUNT 不可算名詞 **Market research** is the activity of collecting and studying information about what people want, need, and buy. 市場調査，マーケット・リサーチ [BUSINESS 実業] □ *A new all-woman market research company has been set up to find out what women think about major news and issues.* 女性が大きなニュースや問題についてどう思うかを調査するために，女性スタッフだけの新しいマーケット・リサーチ会社が設立された。

mar|ket share (**market shares**) N-VAR 可変性名詞 A company's **market share** in a product is the proportion of the total sales of that product that is produced by that company. 市場占有率 [BUSINESS 実業] □ *Ford has been gaining market share this year at the expense of GM and some Japanese car manufacturers.* フォードはGMと日本の自動車製造会社数社を犠牲にして今年の市場シェアを拡大している。

mar|ket test (**market tests, market testing, market tested**) **1** N-COUNT 可算名詞 If a company carries out a **market test**, it asks a group of people to try a new product or service and give their opinions on it. 市場化テスト [BUSINESS 実業] □ *Results from market tests in the U.S. and Europe show little enthusiasm for the product.* 米国と欧州での市場化テストの結果から，その商品はほとんど人気がないことがわかる。 **2** V-T 他動詞 If a new product or service **is market tested**, a group of people are asked to try it and then asked for their opinions on it. 市場化テストをする [BUSINESS 実業] □ *These nuts have been market tested and found to be most suited to the Australian palate.* これらの木の実の市場化テストが行われ，オーストラリア人の味覚に最も合うと分かった。 ● **mar|ket test|ing** N-UNCOUNT 不可算名詞 市場化テスト □ *They learned a lot from the initial market testing exercise.* 彼らは最初に実施した市場化テストから多くを学んだ。

mark|ing /mɑrkɪŋ/ (**markings**) **1** N-COUNT 可算名詞 **Markings** are colored lines, shapes, or patterns on the surface of something, which help to identify it. 印，マーク □ *A plane with Danish markings was over-flying his vessel.* デンマークの印が付いた飛行機が彼の船の上を飛んでいた。 **2** → see also **mark**

mark|up /mɑrkʌp/ (**markups**) N-COUNT 可算名詞 A **markup** is an increase in the price of something, for example the difference between its cost and the price that it is sold for. 値上げ，利幅 □ *We all know that most wine in restaurants is over-priced: a markup of 200 percent on cost is considered normal.* ほとんどのレストランのワインに高い値段がつけられているのは周知のことだ。原価の200パーセントという利幅は当たり前と思われている。

mar|ma|lade /mɑrməleɪd/ (**marmalades**) N-MASS 質量名詞 **Marmalade** is a food made from oranges, lemons, or grapefruit that is similar to jam. It is eaten on bread or toast at breakfast. マーマレード

ma|roon /mərun/ (**maroons, marooning, marooned**) **1** COLOR 色彩語 Something that is **maroon** is dark reddish purple in color. 栗色の，えび茶色の □ *...maroon velvet curtains.* 栗色のビロードのカーテン **2** V-T 他動詞 If someone **is marooned** somewhere, they are left in a place that is difficult for them to escape from. 置き去りにする [usu passive] □ *He was marooned for a year in Jamaica.* 彼はジャマイカに1年間置き去りにされた。

Word Link
age ≈ state of, related to : courage, marriage, patronage

mar|riage /mærɪdʒ/ (**marriages**) **1** N-COUNT 可算名詞 A **marriage** is the relationship between a husband and wife. 婚姻，結婚生活 □ *In a good marriage, both husband and wife work hard to solve any problems that arise.* 良好な婚姻関係では，夫婦の双方が持ち上がるどんな問題も解決しようと努力する。 □ *When I was 35 my marriage broke up.* 35歳の時に，私の結婚生活は破たんした。 **2** N-VAR 可変性名詞 A **marriage** is the act of marrying someone, or the ceremony at which this is done. 結婚，結婚式 □ *I opposed her marriage to Darryl.* 私は彼女がダリルと結婚することに反対した。

→ see **love, wedding**

Do not confuse **marriage** and **wedding**. A **wedding** is a ceremony in which a man and woman get married. It usually includes a meal or other celebration that takes place after the ceremony itself. □ *It wasn't a formal wedding.* This ceremony can also be called a **marriage**. □ *...the day of my marriage.* **Marriage** can also be used to refer to the relationship between a husband and wife. □ *It has been a happy marriage.*

mar|ried /mærid/ **1** ADJ 形容詞 If you are **married**, you have a husband or wife. 結婚した □ *We have been married for 14 years.* 私たちは結婚して14年になる。 □ *She is married to an Englishman.* 彼女は英国人と結婚している。 **2** ADJ 形容詞 **Married** means relating to marriage or to people who are married. 結婚の，夫婦の [ADJ n]

❑*For the first ten years of our married life we lived in a farmhouse.* 私たちは結婚生活の最初の10年間は農家に住んだ. ❸ ADJ 形容詞 If you say that someone is **married** to their work or another activity, you mean that they are very involved with it and have little interest in anything else. 一に専念した [v-link ADJ 'to' n] ❑*"Sam was married to his job," McWhorter said.* 「サムは仕事に夢中だった」とマックホーターが言った.

mar|ry /mǽri/ (**marries, marrying, married**) ❶ V-RECIP 相互動詞 When two people **get married** or **marry**, they legally become husband and wife in a special ceremony. **Get married** is less formal and more commonly used than **marry**. 結婚する ❑*I thought he would change after we got married.* 私たちが結婚すれば彼は変わると私は思っていた. ❑*They married a month after they met.* 彼らは出会って1か月で結婚した. ❑*He wants to marry her.* 彼は彼女と結婚したがっている. ❷ V-T 他動詞 When a priest or official **marries** two people, he or she conducts the ceremony in which the two people legally become husband and wife. （牧師・役人が）結婚式を執り行う ❑*The minister has agreed to marry us in the college chapel.* 牧師は私たちの結婚式を大学の礼拝堂で行うことに同意していた.

marsh /mɑ́rʃ/ (**marshes**) N-VAR 可変性名詞 A **marsh** is a wet, muddy area of land. 湿地, 沼地
→ see **wetland**

mar|shal /mɑ́rʃ⁰l/ (**marshals, marshaling** or **marshalling, marshaled** or **marshalled**) ❶ V-T 他動詞 If you **marshal** people or things, you gather them together and arrange them for a particular purpose. （人・ものを）整列させる 組織する ❑*The company turned its attention to marshaling its creditors' approval.* その会社は債権者の配当順位を整理することに注意を向けた. ❷ N-COUNT 可算名詞 A **marshal** is an official who helps to supervise a public event, especially a sports event. （行事・スポーツの）進行係 ❑*The grand prix is controlled by well-trained marshals.* グランプリはしっかり訓練された進行係が指揮している. ❸ N-COUNT 可算名詞 In the United States and some other countries, a **marshal** is a police officer, often one who is responsible for a particular area. （米国などの）保安官, 警察署長 ❑*A federal marshal was killed in a shoot-out.* 銃撃戦で連邦保安官が1名死亡した. ❹ N-COUNT 可算名詞 A **marshal** is an officer in a fire department. 消防署長 [AM 米国英語] ❑*She was ordered out of her home by a fire marshal because the house next door had an explosion from a leaking gas main.* 隣家でガス本管からのガス漏れ爆発があり, 彼女は消防署長から家を離れるよう指示された.

mart /mɑ́rt/ (**marts**) N-COUNT 可算名詞 A **mart** is a place such as a market where things are bought and sold. 市場（いちば）[AM 米国英語] ❑*...the flower mart.* 花市場

mar|tial /mɑ́rʃ⁰l/ ❶ ADJ 形容詞 **Martial** is used to describe things relating to soldiers or war. 軍隊の, 戦争の [FORMAL 形式ばった] ❑*The paper was actually twice banned under the martial regime.* その新聞は実際に軍事政権の下で2回発行禁止となった. ❷ → see also **court martial**

mar|tial art (**martial arts**) N-COUNT 可算名詞 A **martial art** is one of the methods of fighting, often without weapons, that come from the Far East, for example kung fu, karate, or judo. 格闘技, 武道

mar|tial law N-UNCOUNT 不可算名詞 **Martial law** is control of an area by soldiers, not the police. （軍による）戒厳令 ❑*The military leadership has lifted martial law in several more towns.* 軍指導部はさらに数か所の町で戒厳令を解いた.

mar|tyr /mɑ́rtər/ (**martyrs, martyring, martyred**) ❶ N-COUNT 可算名詞 A **martyr** is someone who is killed or made to suffer greatly because of their religious or political beliefs, and is admired and respected by people who share those beliefs. 殉教者 ❑*...a glorious martyr to the cause of liberty.* 自由という大儀のために輝かしく殉教した者 ❷ V-T 他動詞 If someone **is martyred**, they are killed or made to suffer greatly because of their religious or political beliefs. 殉教者として殺す, 迫害する [usu passive] ❑*St. Pancras was martyred in 304 A.D.* 聖パンクラスは西暦304年に殉教した. ❸ N-COUNT 可算名詞 If you refer to someone as a **martyr**, you disapprove of the fact that they pretend to suffer, or exaggerate their suffering, in order to get sympathy or praise from other people. 殉教者ぶる人 [DISAPPROVAL 不賛成] ❑*When are you going to quit acting like a martyr?* 君はいつ殉教者ぶるのをやめるつもりなんだ? ❹ N-COUNT 可算名詞 If you say that someone is a **martyr to** something, you mean that they suffer as a result of it. 苦しむ人 ❑*Edgar was a martyr to his sense of honor and responsibility.* エドガーは彼の信義と責任感ゆえにひどく苦しんだ.

mar|vel /mɑ́rv⁰l/ (**marvels, marveling** or **marvelling, marveled** or **marvelled**) ❶ V-T/V-I 自動詞 If you **marvel** at something, you express your great surprise, wonder, or admiration. 驚く, 感嘆する ❑*Her fellow members marveled at her seemingly infinite energy.* 仲間たちは彼女の無限の活動力に驚いた. ❑*Sara and I read the story and marveled.* セアラと私はその物語を読み感嘆した. ❷ N-COUNT 可算名詞 You can describe something or someone as a **marvel** to indicate that you think that they are wonderful. 驚嘆すべきもの（人）❑*The whale, like the dolphin, has*

become a symbol of the marvels of creation. イルカと同じく鯨は創造物の素晴らしさの象徴となっている.

mar|vel|ous /mɑ́rvələs/ ADJ 形容詞 If you describe someone or something as **marvelous**, you are emphasizing that they are very good. 素晴らしい, 驚嘆すべき ❑*It's the most marvelous piece of music.* それは最も素晴らしい音楽作品だ. ●**mar|vel|ous|ly** ADV 副詞 素晴らしく, 見事に ❑*We want people to think he's doing marvelously.* 人々には彼が本当によくがんばっていると思ってほしい.

Marx|ism /mɑ́rksɪzəm/ N-UNCOUNT 不可算名詞 **Marxism** is a political philosophy based on the writings of Karl Marx which stresses the importance of the struggle between different social classes. マルクス主義

Marx|ist /mɑ́rksɪst/ (**Marxists**) ❶ ADJ 形容詞 **Marxist** means based on Marxism or relating to Marxism. マルクス主義の ❑*...a Marxist state.* マルクス主義国家 ❷ N-COUNT 可算名詞 A **Marxist** is a person who believes in Marxism or who is a member of a Marxist party. マルクス主義者 ❑*...a 78-year-old former Marxist.* 78歳の元マルクス主義者

mas|cara /mæskǽrə/ (**mascaras**) N-MASS 質量名詞 **Mascara** is a substance used as makeup to make eyelashes darker. マスカラ, まつ毛染め ❑*...water-resistant mascaras.* 耐水性のマスカラ
→ see **makeup**

mas|cot /mǽskɒt/ (**mascots**) N-COUNT 可算名詞 A **mascot** is an animal, toy, or symbol which is associated with a particular organization or event, and which is thought to bring good luck. マスコット ❑*...the official mascot of the Detroit Tigers.* デトロイト・タイガースの公式マスコット

mas|cu|line /mǽskyəlɪn/ ❶ ADJ 形容詞 **Masculine** qualities and things relate to or are considered typical of men, in contrast to women. 男性の ❑*...masculine characteristics like a husky voice and facial hair.* しゃがれ声や顔ひげのような男性的な特徴 ❷ ADJ 形容詞 If you say that someone or something is **masculine**, you mean that they have qualities such as strength or confidence which are considered typical of men. 男らしい ❑*...her aggressive, masculine image.* 彼女の好戦的で男性的なイメージ ❸ ADJ 形容詞 In some languages, a **masculine** noun, pronoun, or adjective has a different form from a feminine or neuter one, or behaves in a different way. （文法）男性の

mas|cu|lin|ity /mǽskyəlɪnɪti/ ❶ N-UNCOUNT 不可算名詞 A man's **masculinity** is the fact that he is a man. 男性であること ❑*...a project on the link between masculinity and violence.* 男であることと暴力行為の関連性についての研究 ❷ N-UNCOUNT 不可算名詞 **Masculinity** means the qualities, especially sexual qualities, which are considered to be typical of men. 男らしさ ❑*The old ideas of masculinity do not work for most men.* 男らしさという古い考え方はほとんどの男性にとって意味がない.

mash /mǽʃ/ (**mashes, mashing, mashed**) V-T 他動詞 If you **mash** food that is solid but soft, you crush it so that it forms a soft mass. つぶして柔らかくする ❑*Mash the bananas with a fork.* フォークでバナナをつぶす.

mask /mǽsk/ (**masks, masking, masked**) ❶ N-COUNT 可算名詞 A **mask** is a piece of cloth or other material, which you wear over your face so that people cannot see who you are, or so that you look like someone or something else. 覆面, 仮面 ❑*The gunman, whose mask had slipped, fled.* 覆面がずり落ちた武装犯人は逃走した. ❷ N-COUNT 可算名詞 A **mask** is a piece of cloth or other material that you wear over all or part of your face to protect you from germs or harmful substances. （菌などを防ぐ）マスク ❑*You must wear goggles and a mask that will protect you against the fumes.* 煙霧から身を守るゴーグルとマスクを必ず着けて下さい. ❸ N-COUNT 可算名詞 If you describe someone's behavior as a **mask**, you mean that they do not show their real feelings or character. （本当の感情・性格を）覆い隠すもの ❑*His mask of detachment cracked, and she saw for an instant an angry and violent man.* 彼の無関心の仮面が割れ, 彼女は一瞬, 怒りに満ちた暴力的な男を見た. ❹ N-COUNT 可算名詞 A **mask** is a thick cream or paste made of various substances, which you spread over your face and leave for some time in order to improve your skin. （美顔に使う）パック ❑*This mask leaves your complexion feeling soft and supple.* この顔パックを使うと肌が柔らかくしなやかな感じになる. ❺ V-T 他動詞 If you **mask** your feelings, you deliberately do not show them in your behavior, so that people cannot know what you really feel. （感情を）隠す ❑*Dina lit a cigarette, trying to mask her agitation.* ダイナは動揺を隠そうとしてたばこに火をつけた. ❻ V-T 他動詞 If one thing **masks** another, it prevents people from noticing or recognizing the other thing. （物を）隠す 見えなくする ❑*He was squinting through the smoke that masked the enemy.* 彼は敵を覆う煙を目を細くして見ていた. ❼ → see also **gas mask**
→ see **football, scuba diving, theater**

masked /mǽskt/ ADJ 形容詞 If someone is **masked**, they are wearing a mask. 覆面をした ❑*Masked youths threw stones and firebombs.* 覆面の若者たちが石や火炎瓶を投げつけた.

m

maso|chism /mæsəkɪzəm/ ■ N-UNCOUNT 不可算名詞
Masochism is behavior in which someone gets sexual pleasure from their own pain or suffering. マゾヒズム, 被虐性愛 □*The tendency toward masochism is however always linked with elements of sadism.* しかし, マゾヒズムの性癖はいつもサディズムの要素と結びついている. ●**maso|chist** (**masochists**) N-COUNT 可算名詞 マゾヒスト, 被虐性愛者 □*...consensual sexual masochists.* 合意に基づいた性的マゾヒストたち ■ N-UNCOUNT 不可算名詞 If you describe someone's behavior as **masochism**, you mean that they seem to be trying to get into a situation which causes them suffering or great difficulty. 自己虐待 □*Once you have tasted life in southern California, it takes a peculiar kind of masochism to return to a British winter.* カリフォルニア州南部で1度生活すると, 英国の冬に戻るのに特有な種類の自虐精神がいる. ●**maso|chist** N-COUNT 可算名詞 自己虐待者 □*Anybody who enjoys this is a masochist.* これを楽しむ人は誰でも自己虐待者だ.

maso|chis|tic /mæsəkɪstɪk/ ■ ADJ 形容詞 **Masochistic** behavior involves a person getting sexual pleasure from their own pain or suffering. 被虐性愛の □*...his masochistic tendencies.* 彼のマゾヒスト的な性癖 ■ ADJ 形容詞 If you describe someone's behavior as **masochistic**, you mean that they seem to be trying to get into a situation which causes them suffering or great difficulty. 自虐的な □*It seems masochistic, somehow.* なぜかそれは自虐的に思える.

ma|son /meɪsⁿn/ (**masons**) N-COUNT 可算名詞 A **mason** is a person who is skilled at making things or building things with stone or bricks. 石工, れんが職人

ma|son|ry /meɪsənri/ N-UNCOUNT 不可算名詞 **Masonry** is bricks or pieces of stone which have been stuck together with cement as part of a wall or building. 石造り, れんが造り □*...a huge blast that sent pieces of masonry flying through the air.* れんがを空中に吹き飛ばした大爆発

mas|quer|ade /mæskəreɪd/ (**masquerades, masquerading, masqueraded**) ■ V-I 自動詞 To **masquerade as** someone or something means to pretend to be that person or thing, particularly in order to deceive other people. (他人・他のものに) なりすます □*He masqueraded as a doctor and fooled everyone.* 彼は医者になりすまし, みんなをだました. ■ N-COUNT 可算名詞 A **masquerade** is an attempt to deceive people about the true nature or identity of something. なりすまし, 見せ掛け □*He told a news conference that the elections would be a masquerade.* 彼は記者会見でそれらの選挙が見せ掛けのものになるだろうと述べた.

mass /mæs/ (**masses, massing, massed**) ■ N-SING 単数名詞 A **mass** of things is a large number of them grouped together. 多数, 集団 □*On his desk is a mass of books and papers.* 彼の机の上には本や書類がたくさん置いてある. ■ N-SING 単数名詞 A **mass of** something is a large amount of it. □*She had a mass of auburn hair.* 彼女はふさふさしたとび色の髪をしていた. ■ QUANT 数量詞 **Masses of** something means a great deal of it. 多量 [INFORMAL くだけた] □*There's masses of work for her to do.* 彼女にはやるべき仕事がたくさんある. ■ ADJ 形容詞 **Mass** is used to describe something which involves or affects a very large number of people. (人の数が) 多数の [ADJ n] □*All the lights went off, and mass hysteria broke out.* すべての明かりが消え, 多くの人がヒステリー状態になった. ■ N-COUNT 可算名詞 A **mass of** a solid substance, a liquid, or a gas is an amount of it, especially a large amount which has no definite shape. (固体・液体・気体の) 大量 □*...before it cools and sets into a solid mass.* それが冷えて固体の塊になる前に ■ N-PLURAL 複数名詞 If you talk about **the masses**, you mean the ordinary people in society, in contrast to the leaders or the highly educated people. 庶民, 一般大衆 □*His music is commercial. It is aimed at the masses.* 彼の音楽は商業的だ. それは一般大衆向けだ. ■ N-SING 単数名詞 The **mass of** people are most of the people in a country, society, or group. 大半, 大部分 □*The 1939-45 world war involved the mass of the population.* 1939年から45年の世界大戦は, 住民の大半を巻き込んだ. ■ V-T/V-I 他動詞/自動詞 When people or things **mass**, or when you **mass** them, they gather together in a large crowd or group. 一固まりにさせる, 集結させる [他動詞], 一固まりになる, 集結する [自動詞] □*Shortly after the workers went on strike, police began to mass at the shipyard.* 労働者がストライキに入るとすぐに警察が造船所に集結し始めた. ■ N-SING 単数名詞 If you say that something is a **mass of** things, you mean that it is covered with them or full of them. いっぱい □*His body was a mass of sores.* 彼は体が傷でいっぱいだった. ■ N-VAR 可変性名詞 In physics, the **mass of** an object is the amount of physical matter that it has. 質量 [TECHNICAL 技術的] □*Astronomers know that Pluto and Triton have nearly the same size, mass, and density.* 天文学者は冥王星とトリトンの大きさ・質量・密度がほぼ同じであることを知っている. ■ N-VAR 可変性名詞 **Mass** is a Christian church ceremony, especially in a Roman Catholic or Orthodox church, during which people eat bread and drink wine in order to remember the last meal of Jesus Christ. ミサ □*She attended a convent school and went to Mass each day.* 彼女は修道院付属の学校に通い, 毎日ミサに出席した. ■ → see also **massed**
→ see **continent**

Word Partnership *mass* は次の語句と使われる:

N.   mass **communication**, mass **destruction**, mass **evacuation**, mass **execution**, mass **exodus**, mass **grave**, mass **hysteria**, mass **killings**, mass **layoffs**, mass **mailing**, mass **migration**, mass **protest**, mass **unemployment** ■
bone mass, muscle mass ■

mas|sa|cre /mæsəkər/ (**massacres, massacring, massacred**) ■ N-VAR 可変性名詞 A **massacre** is the killing of a large number of people at the same time in a violent and cruel way. 大虐殺 □*Maria lost her 62-year-old mother in the massacre.* マリアはその大虐殺で62歳の母を亡くした. ■ V-T 他動詞 If people **are massacred**, a large number of them are attacked and killed in a violent and cruel way. 大虐殺される □*300 civilians are believed to have been massacred by the rebels.* 300人の市民が反政府組織の手によって虐殺されたと見られる.

mas|sage /məsɑʒ/ (**massages, massaging, massaged**) ■ N-VAR 可変性名詞 **Massage** is the action of squeezing and rubbing someone's body, as a way of making them relax or reducing their pain. マッサージ □*Alex asked me if I wanted a massage.* アレックスはマッサージしてほしいかどうかわたしに聞いた. ■ V-T 他動詞 If you **massage** someone or a part of their body, you squeeze and rub their body, in order to make them relax or reduce their pain. マッサージする □*She continued massaging her right foot, which was bruised and aching.* 彼女は打撲して痛みのある右足をマッサージし続けた. ■ V-T 他動詞 If you say that someone **massages** statistics, figures, or evidence, you are criticizing them for changing or presenting the facts in a way that misleads people. ごまかす, 改ざんする [DISAPPROVAL 不賛成] □*Their governments have no reason to "massage" the statistics.* 政府官庁が統計データに「手を加える」理由などありません.

masse /mæs/ → see **en masse**

massed /mæst/ ADJ 形容詞 **Massed** is used to describe a large number of people who have been brought together for a particular purpose. 大勢集まった [ADJ n] □*He could not escape the massed ranks of newsmen who spotted him crossing the lawn.* 彼は芝生を横切るところを大勢の取材陣に見つかり取り囲まれてしまった.

mas|sive /mæsɪv/ ■ ADJ 形容詞 Something that is **massive** is very large in size, quantity, or extent. 巨大な, 膨大な [EMPHASIS 強調] □*There was evidence of massive fraud.* 大規模な詐欺の疑いがあります. □*...massive air attacks.* 大空襲. ●**mas|sive|ly** ADV 副詞 非常に; 大規模に □*...a massively popular game.* 大人気のゲーム. ■ ADJ 形容詞 [ADJ n] If you describe a medical condition as **massive**, you mean that it is extremely serious. 重症の □*He died six weeks later of a massive heart attack.* 彼は重度の心臓発作を起こした6週間後に亡くなった.

mass mar|ket (**mass markets**) ■ N-COUNT 可算名詞 **Mass market** is used to refer to the large numbers of people who want to buy a particular product. 大衆市場 [BUSINESS 実業] □*They now have access to the mass markets of China, Japan and the U.K.* 今や彼らは中国, 日本, イギリスの大衆市場に進出している. ■ ADJ 形容詞 **Mass-market** products are designed and produced for selling to large numbers of people. 大衆向けの [BUSINESS 実業] [ADJ n] □*...mass-market paperbacks.* 文庫本.

mass me|dia N-SING-COLL 集合的単数名詞 You can use the **mass media** to refer to the various ways, especially television, radio, newspapers, and magazines, by which information and news is given to large numbers of people. マスメディア, マスコミ □*...mass media coverage of the issue.* その問題についてのマスコミ報道.

mass-produce (**mass-produces, mass-producing, mass-produced**) V-T 他動詞 If someone **mass-produces** something, they make it in large quantities, usually by machine. This means that the product can be sold cheaply. 大量生産する [BUSINESS 実業] □*...the invention of machinery to mass-produce footwear.* 履物を量産できる機械の発明. ●**mass-produced** ADJ 形容詞 [ADJ n] 大量生産された □*In 1981 it launched the first mass-produced mountain bike.* 1981年会社は初めてマウンテンバイクの量産に乗り出した.

mass pro|duc|tion N-UNCOUNT 不可算名詞 **Mass production** is the production of something in large quantities, especially by machine. 大量生産 [BUSINESS 実業] □*...equipment that would allow the mass production of baby food.* ベビーフードの量産を可能にする設備.

mast /mæst/ (**masts**) ■ N-COUNT 可算名詞 The **masts** of a boat are the tall, upright poles that support its sails. マスト ■ N-COUNT 可算名詞 A radio **mast** is a tall upright structure that is used to transmit radio or television signals. 電波塔

mas|ter /mæstər/ (**masters, mastering, mastered**) ■ N-COUNT 可算名詞 A servant's **master** is the man that he or she works for. 雇い主, 主人 □*My master ordered me not to deliver the message*

except in private. ボスからは必ず伝言は内密に伝えるよう言われていた. **2** N-COUNT 可算名詞 If you say that someone is a **master** of a particular activity, you mean that they are extremely skilled at it. 達人 □ She was a master of the English language. 彼女は英語が堪能だった. ● ADJ 形容詞 **Master** is also an adjective. 熟練した [ADJ n] □ ...a master craftsman. 名匠. **3** N-VAR 可変性名詞 If you are **master** of a situation, you have complete control over it. が自由自在に操れる人 □ Jackson remained calm and always master of his passions. ジャクソンは冷静でいつでも自分の感情を抑えることができた. **4** V-T 他動詞 If you **master** something, you learn how to do it properly or you succeed in understanding it completely. 習得する □ Duff soon mastered the skills of radio production. ダフはすぐにラジオの製作技術を身につけた. **5** V-T 他動詞 If you **master** a difficult situation, you succeed in controlling it. 乗り切る, 打ち勝つ □ When you have mastered one situation you have to go on to the next. 一つの状況を克服してもその次が待っている. **6** → see also **headmaster** **7** N-COUNT 可算名詞 A famous male painter of the past is often called a **master**. 巨匠 □ ...a portrait by the Dutch master, Vincent Van Gogh. オランダの巨匠ヴィンセント・ヴァン・ゴッホの肖像画. **8** ADJ 形容詞 A **master** copy of something, such as a film or a tape recording, is an original copy that can be used to produce other copies. 原本; オリジナルテープ [ADJ n] □ Keep one as a master copy for your own reference and circulate the others. 1部を原本として手元に置き, 残りを配布します. **9** N-SING 単数名詞 A **master's degree** can be referred to as a **master's**. 修士号 □ I've got a master's in economics. 経済学の修士号を持っています.

Thesaurus   master また次を参照:

N.	owner; (ant.) servant, slave **1**
	artist, expert, professional **2**
V.	learn, study, understand **4**

Word Partnership   master は次の語句と使われる:

N.	lord and master, master and slave **1**
	master chef, master craftsman, master criminal, master of disguise, master spy, Zen master **2**
	master a skill **4**
	master drawings **7**

master|mind /mǽstərmaɪnd/ (**masterminds, masterminding, masterminded**) **1** V-T 他動詞 If you **mastermind** a difficult or complicated activity, you plan it in detail and then make sure that it happens successfully. 首謀する □ There are many theories as to who masterminded the attacks. 誰がその攻撃を首謀したかについては多くの説がある. **2** N-COUNT 可算名詞 The **mastermind** behind a difficult or complicated plan, often a criminal one, is the person who is responsible for planning and organizing it. 首謀者 □ He was the mastermind behind the plan to acquire the explosives. 彼こそ爆弾の入手計画の黒幕だろう.

master|piece /mǽstərpis/ (**masterpieces**) **1** N-COUNT 可算名詞 A **masterpiece** is an extremely good painting, novel, movie, or other work of art. 名作 □ His book, I must add, is a masterpiece. 彼の本が傑作だということを付け加えておかなければならない. **2** N-COUNT 可算名詞 An artist's, writer's, or composer's **masterpiece** is the best work that they have ever produced. 代表作 □ "Man's Fate," translated into sixteen languages, is probably his masterpiece. 16か国語に翻訳されている『人間の条件』は彼の代表作といえるだろう. **3** N-COUNT 可算名詞 A **masterpiece** is an extremely clever or skillful example of something. 優れた例, 模範 □ The whole thing was a masterpiece of crowd management. あらゆる点で群集管理の素晴らしいお手本だった.

master plan (**master plans**) N-COUNT 可算名詞 A **master plan** is a thorough plan that is intended to help someone succeed in a very difficult or important task. 基本計画, マスタープラン □ ...the master plan for the reform of the economy. 経済改革の基本計画.

mas|ter's de|gree (**master's degrees**) also **Master's degree** N-COUNT 可算名詞 A **master's degree** is a university degree such as an M.A. or an M.S. which is of a higher level than a bachelor's degree and usually takes one or two years to complete. 修士号 → see **graduation**

mas|tery /mǽstəri/ N-UNCOUNT 不可算名詞 If you show **mastery of** a particular skill or language, you show that you have learned or understood it completely and have no difficulty using it. 熟練, 精通 □ He doesn't have mastery of the basic rules of grammar. 彼は基本的な文法規則すら理解していない.

mas|tur|bate /mǽstərbeɪt/ (**masturbates, masturbating, masturbated**) V-I 自動詞 If someone **masturbates**, they stroke or rub their own genitals in order to obtain sexual pleasure. オナニーする □ Do women masturbate as often as men? 女も男と同じくらいオナニーするのか.

mat /mǽt/ (**mats**) **1** N-COUNT 可算名詞 A **mat** is a small piece of something such as cloth, card, or plastic which you put on a table to protect it from plates or cups. ランチョンマット; コースター □ The food is served on polished tables with mats. 食事はランチョンマットを敷いた光沢のあるテーブルに運ばれる. **2** N-COUNT 可算名詞 A **mat** is a small piece of carpet or other thick material which is put on the floor for protection, decoration, or comfort. マット □ There was a letter on the mat. マットの上に手紙が落ちていた. **3** → see also **matte** → see **gymnastics**

match /mǽtʃ/ (**matches, matching, matched**) **1** N-COUNT 可算名詞 A **match** is an organized game of tennis, soccer, cricket, or some other sport. 試合 □ He was watching a soccer match. 彼はサッカーの試合を観戦していました. **2** N-COUNT 可算名詞 A **match** is a small wooden stick with a substance on one end that produces a flame when you rub it along the rough side of a matchbox or a matchbook. マッチ □ ...a pack of cigarettes and a book of matches. たばこ1箱とブックマッチ1個. **3** V-RECIP 相互動詞 If something of a particular color or design **matches** another thing, they have the same color or design, or have a pleasing appearance when they are used together. 似合う, マッチする □ "The shoes are too tight." —"Well, they do match your dress." 「この靴はきついわ」「それにその服にも似合ってないよ」 ● PHRASAL VERB 句動詞 **Match up** means the same as **match**. 似合う, マッチする □ The pillow cover can match up with the sheets. 枕カバーはシーツと揃えることができる. **4** V-RECIP 相互動詞 If something such as an amount or a quality **matches** another amount or quality, they are both the same or equal. If you **match** two things, you make them the same or equal. 同じである □ Their strengths in memory and spatial skills matched. 彼らの記憶力と空間能力は一致していた. □ Our value system does not match with their value system. 我々の価値観と彼らの価値観は同じではありません. **5** V-RECIP 相互動詞 If one thing **matches** another, they are connected or suit each other in some way. 結びつける □ The students are asked to match the books with the authors. 学生は作品と著者を結びつけるように言われた. □ It can take time and effort to match buyers and sellers. 買い手と売り手をうまく結びつけるには時間と労力を必要とすることがある. ● PHRASAL VERB 句動詞 **Match up** means the same as **match**. 結びつける □ The consultant seeks to match up jobless professionals with small companies in need of expertise. コンサルタントは失業中の専門職者と専門技術を必要とする中小企業とをうまく引き合わせようとしている. □ They compared the fat intake of groups of vegetarians and meat eaters, and matched their diets up with levels of harmful blood fats. 彼らは野菜食と肉食の人たちの脂肪摂取量を比較し, 食事と有害な血中脂質量との関係を明らかにした. **6** N-SING 単数名詞 If a combination of things or people is a good **match**, they have a pleasing effect when placed or used together. ぴったりの組み合わせ □ Helen's choice of lipstick was a good match for her skin tone. ヘレンの選んだ口紅は彼女の肌の色にぴったりだった. **7** V-T 他動詞 If you **match** something, you are as good as it or equal to it, for example in speed, size, or quality. 匹敵する □ They played some fine offensive football, but I think we matched them in every department. 敵は見事な攻めのサッカーを展開したが, 我々もあらゆる点で互角に戦えたと思う. **8** → see also **matched, matching** → see **fire**

Word Partnership   match は次の語句と使われる:

N.	boxing match, chess match, tennis match, wrestling match **1**
V.	strike a match **2**
ADJ.	bad match, good match, perfect match **6**

matched /mǽtʃt/ **1** ADJ 形容詞 If you say that two people are well **matched**, you mean that they have qualities that will enable them to have a good relationship. お似合いの [adv ADJ] □ My parents were not very well matched. 両親はあまり似合いの夫婦ではなかった. **2** ADJ 形容詞 In sports and other competitions, if the two opponents or teams are well **matched**, they are both of the same standard in strength or ability. 互角の [adv ADJ] □ Two well-matched sides conjured up an entertaining game. 両チームの互角のプレーで見ごたえのある試合になった.

match|ing /mǽtʃɪŋ/ ADJ 形容詞 **Matching** is used to describe things that are of the same color or design. よく似合った [ADJ n] □ ...a coat and a matching handbag. コートとそれにお似合いのハンドバッグ.

mate /meɪt/ (**mates, mating, mated**) **1** N-COUNT 可算名詞 Someone's wife, husband, or sexual partner can be referred to as their **mate**. 連れ合い □ He has found his ideal mate. 彼は理想の相手を見つけた. **2** N-COUNT 可算名詞 An animal's **mate** is its sexual partner. つがいの片方 □ The males guard their mates zealously. 雄はつがいの雌を懸命に守る. **3** V-RECIP 相互動詞 When animals **mate**, a male and a female have sex in order to produce young. 交尾する □ This allows the pair to mate properly and stops the hen from staying in the nest. こうして, つがいは無事交尾を果たし, めんどりは巣に留まらずに済むようになる. □ They want the males to mate with wild females. 彼らはこの雄たちが野生の雌と交尾してくれるのを願っている. **4** → see also **classmate, roommate, running mate**

m

Word Web   mathematics

At first prehistoric people **counted** things they could see—for example, four sheep. Later they began to use **numbers** with abstract **quantities** like time—for example, two days. This led to the development of basic **arithmetic**—**addition**, **subtraction**, **multiplication**, and **division**. When people discovered how to use written **numerals**, they could do more complex **mathematical calculations**, **Mathematicians** developed new types of **math** to **measure** land and keep financial records. **Algebra** and **geometry** developed in the Middle East between 2,000 and 3,000 years ago. Algebra uses letters to represent possible quantities. Geometry deals with the relationships among **lines**, **angles**, and **shapes**.

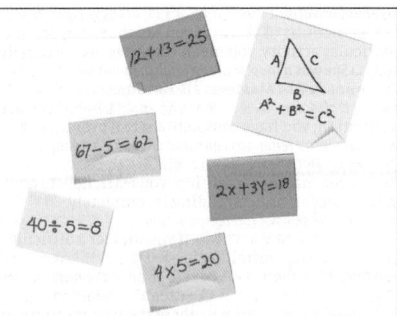

$12 + 13 = 25$

$A^2 + B^2 = C^2$

$67 - 5 = 62$

$2x + 3Y = 18$

$40 \div 5 = 8$

$4 \times 5 = 20$

---

ma|terial /mətɪəriəl/ (**materials**) **1** N-VAR 可変性名詞 A **material** is a solid substance. 物質 □ *...electrons in a conducting material such as a metal.* 金属などの電導性物質内の電子. **2** N-MASS 質量名詞 **Material** is cloth. 生地 □ *...the thick material of her skirt.* 彼女のスカートの厚手の生地. **3** N-PLURAL 複数名詞 **Materials** are the things that you need for a particular activity. 材料 □ *The builders ran out of materials.* 建設業者は材料を使い果たしてしまった. **4** N-UNCOUNT 不可算名詞 Ideas or information that are used as a basis for a book, play, or film can be referred to as **material**. 題材 □ *In my version of the story, I added some new material.* この物語の翻案でわたしは新たな題材をいくつか付け加えた. **5** ADJ 形容詞 **Material** things are related to possessions or money, rather than to more abstract things such as ideas or values. 物質的な □ *Every room must have been stuffed with material things.* どの部屋も物であふれかえっていたに違いない. ● **ma|teri|al|ly** ADV 副詞 物質的に □ *He has tried to help this child materially and spiritually.* 彼はこの子を心身両面にわたって援助しようとしてきた. **6** ADJ 形容詞 [ADJ n] **Material** evidence or information is directly relevant and important in a legal or academic argument. 重大な [FORMAL 形式ばった] □ *The nature and availability of material evidence was not to be discussed.* 重要な証拠とはどのようなものか，またそうした証拠が出せるのかどうか，こうした点については議論しないことになっていた.
→ see **industry**

Word Partnership   material は次の語句と使われる：

ADJ. **genetic** material, **hazardous** material **1**
classified material, **instructional** material, **sensitive** material **1** **6**
new material, **original** material **2** **4**
raw materials **3**

ma|teri|al|ism /mətɪəriəlɪzəm/ **1** N-UNCOUNT 不可算名詞 **Materialism** is the attitude of someone who attaches a lot of importance to money and wants to possess a lot of material things. 物質主義 □ *...the rising consumer materialism in society at large.* 社会全般に広がる消費者の物質主義. **2** N-UNCOUNT 不可算詞 **Materialism** is the belief that only physical matter exists, and that there is no spiritual world. 唯物論 □ *Scientific materialism thus triumphed over ignorance and superstition.* こうして科学的唯物論が無知や迷信に打ち勝った.

ma|teri|al|ize /mətɪəriəlaɪz/ (**materializes, materializing, materialized**) **1** V-I 自動詞 If a possible or expected event does not **materialize**, it does not happen. 実現する [usu with brd-neg] □ *A rebellion by radicals failed to materialize.* 急進派による反乱は現実のものとなりませんでした. **2** V-I 自動詞 If a person or thing **materializes**, they suddenly appear, after they have been invisible or in another place. 姿を現す □ *A moment later Jane materialized, coming in the front door.* すぐにジェーンが姿を現し玄関に入ってきた.

ma|ter|nal /mətɜrnəl/ **1** ADJ 形容詞 **Maternal** is used to describe feelings or actions which are typical of those of a kind mother toward her child. 母親らしい □ *She had little maternal instinct.* 彼女には母性がほとんど欠けていた. **2** ADJ 形容詞 **Maternal** is used to describe things that relate to the mother of a baby. 母親の，妊婦の [ADJ n] □ *Maternal smoking can damage the unborn child.* 妊娠中のたばこはお腹の子に悪影響を及ぼすことがある. **3** ADJ 形容詞 A **maternal** relative is one who is related through a person's mother rather than their father. 母方の [ADJ n] □ *Her maternal grandfather was mayor of Karachi.* 彼女の母方の祖父はカラチの元市長だった.

ma|ter|nity /mətɜrnɪti/ ADJ 形容詞 **Maternity** is used to describe things relating to the help and medical care given to a woman when she is pregnant and when she gives birth. 妊婦の [ADJ n] □ *Your job will be kept open for your return after maternity leave.* 産休から戻られたら元の仕事に復帰できるようにしておきます.

math /mæθ/ N-UNCOUNT 不可算名詞 **Math** is the same as **mathematics**. 数学 [AM 米国英語] □ *He studied math in college.* 彼は大学で数学を学びました.
→ see **mathematics**

math|emati|cal /mæθəmætɪkəl/ **1** ADJ 形容詞 Something that is **mathematical** involves numbers and calculations. 数学的な [ADJ n] □ *...mathematical calculations.* 数学的な計算. ● **math|emati|cal|ly** /mæθəmætɪkli/ ADV 副詞 数学的に □ *...a mathematically complicated formula.* 数学的に複雑な式. **2** ADJ 形容詞 If you have **mathematical** abilities or a **mathematical** mind, you are good at doing calculations or understanding problems that involve numbers. 数学の才能 [ADJ n] □ *...a mathematical genius.* 数学的天才. ● **math|emati|cal|ly** ADV 副詞 [ADV -ed/adj] 数学的に □ *Anyone can be an astrologer as long as they are mathematically minded.* 数学の才能さえあれば誰でも占星術師になれる.
→ see **mathematics**

math|ema|ti|cian /mæθəmətɪʃən/ (**mathematicians**) **1** N-COUNT 可算名詞 A **mathematician** is a person who is trained in the study of numbers and calculations. 数学者 □ *The risks can be so complex that banks hire mathematicians to assess them.* 銀行は複雑化するリスクに対応するため，リスク計算を行う数学者を雇っている. **2** N-COUNT 可算名詞 A **mathematician** is a person who is good at doing calculations and using numbers. 数字に強い人 □ *I'm not a very good mathematician.* 数字にはあまり強くない.
→ see **mathematics, ratio**

math|emat|ics /mæθəmætɪks/ N-UNCOUNT 不可算名詞 **Mathematics** is the study of numbers, quantities, or shapes. 数学 □ *...a professor of mathematics at Boston College.* ボストン大学の数学教授. **2** N-UNCOUNT 不可算名詞 The **mathematics of** a problem are the calculations that are involved in it. 計算 □ *Once you understand the mathematics of debt you can work your way out of it.* 借金の計算のしかたさえ分かったら，そこから抜け出す方法も見つけられる.
→ see Word Web: **mathematics**

maths /mæθs/ N-UNCOUNT 不可算名詞 **Maths** is the same as **mathematics**. 数学; 計算 [BRIT 英国英語]

mati|nee /mætⁿeɪ/ (**matinees**) N-COUNT 可算名詞 A **matinee** is a performance of a play or a showing of a movie which takes place in the afternoon. 昼興行

ma|trix /meɪtrɪks/ (**matrices**) **1** N-COUNT 可算名詞 A **matrix** is the environment or context in which something such as a society develops and grows. 基盤 [FORMAL 形式ばった] □ *...the matrix of their culture.* 彼らの文化的基盤. **2** N-COUNT 可算名詞 In mathematics, a **matrix** is an arrangement of numbers, symbols, or letters in rows and columns which is used in solving mathematical problems. 行列

matte /mæt/ also **matt** or **mat** ADJ 形容詞 A **matte** color, paint, or surface is dull rather than shiny. 光沢のない，つや消しの □ *...a creamy white matte emulsion.* 光沢のない乳白色のエマルション塗料.

mat|ter /mætər/ (**matters, mattering, mattered**) **1** N-COUNT 可算名詞 A **matter** is a task, situation, or event which you have to deal with or think about, especially one that involves problems. 問題 □ *It was clear that she wanted to discuss some private matter.* 間違いなく彼女はプライベートな問題について話したがっていた. □ *Business matters drew him to Louisville.* 彼は仕事でルーイビルに来ることになった. **2** N-PLURAL 複数名詞 You use **matters** to refer to the situation you are talking about, especially when something is affecting the situation in some way. 事態，情勢 [no det] □ *We have no objection to this change, but doubt that it will significantly improve matters.* 今回の変更に反対しないが，それで事態の大きな改善につながるとは考えにくい. □ *If it would facilitate matters, I would be happy to come to New York.* 事態の好転につながるのでしたら喜んでニューヨークへ参ります. **3** N-SING 単数名詞 If you say that a situation is a **matter of** a particular thing, you mean that that is the most important thing to be done or considered when

you are involved in the situation or explaining it. 最も重要なこと ❑ *History is always a matter of interpretation.* 歴史においてはいかに解釈するかが常に重要である. ❑ *Observance of the law is a matter of principle for us.* 法を遵守するかどうかは我々の信条にかかわる問題である. **4** N-UNCOUNT 不可算名詞 Printed **matter** consists of books, newspapers, and other texts that are printed. Reading **matter** consists of things that are suitable for reading, such as books and newspapers. 印刷物, 出版物 ❑ *...the government's plans to place a tax on printed matter.* 印刷物に課税するという政府案. **5** N-UNCOUNT 不可算名詞 **Matter** is the physical part of the universe consisting of solids, liquids, and gases. 物質 ❑ *A proton is an elementary particle of matter that possesses a positive charge.* 陽子は正電荷を持つ素粒子である. **6** N-UNCOUNT 不可算名詞 You use **matter** to refer to a particular type of substance. 物 ❑ *...waste matter from industries.* 産業廃棄物. **7** N-SING 単数名詞 You use **matter** in expressions such as "**What's the matter?**" or "**Is anything the matter?**" when you think that someone has a problem and you want to know what it is. 困ったこと ❑ *Carole, what's the matter? You don't seem happy.* どうかした, キャロル？ 浮かない顔だね. **8** N-SING 単数名詞 You use **matter** in expressions such as "**a matter of weeks**" when you are emphasizing how small an amount is or how short a period of time is. わずか [EMPHASIS 強調] ❑ *Within a matter of days she was back at work.* わずか数日で彼女は仕事に復帰した. **9** V-T/V-I 他動詞/自動詞 If you say that something does not **matter**, you mean that it is not important to you because it does not have an effect on you or on a particular situation. 大したことではない [no cont, usu with brd-neg] ❑ *A lot of the food goes on the floor but that doesn't matter.* 食べ物をたくさんこぼしますが, 気にしないでください. ❑ *As long as staff members are well-groomed, it does not matter how long their hair is.* スタッフは身だしなみさえきちんとしていれば髪は長くても構いません. **10** → see also **subject matter 11** PHRASE 句 If you say that something is **another matter** or a **different matter**, you mean that it is very different from the situation that you have just discussed. 別問題 ❑ *Being responsible for one's own health is one thing, but being responsible for another person's health is quite a different matter.* 自分の健康に責任を持つことと他人の健康に責任を持つことは全く別の話だ. **12** PHRASE 句 If you are going to do something **as a matter of** urgency or priority, you are going to do it as soon as possible, because it is important. すぐに ❑ *Your doctors can help a great deal and you need to talk about it with them as a matter of urgency.* かかりつけ医がいろいろ力になってくれるでしょうから, すぐにでも相談してください. **13** PHRASE 句 If something is **no easy matter**, it is difficult to do. 大変なこと ❑ *Choosing the color for the living-room walls was no easy matter.* リビングの壁を何色にするか, ずいぶん迷った. **14** PHRASE 句 If someone says **that's the end of the matter** or **that's an end to the matter**, they mean that a decision that has been taken must not be changed or discussed any more. この件はこれでおしまいです ❑ *"He's moving in here," Maria said. "So that's the end of the matter."* 「彼がここに越してくることになってる」とマリアは言った. 「もう後には引けないから」 **15** PHRASE 句 You use **the fact of the matter is** or **the truth of the matter is** to introduce a fact which supports what you are saying or which is not widely known, for example because it is a secret. 実のところは ❑ *The fact of the matter is that most people consume far more protein than they actually need.* 実は, 大半の人たちが実際の必要量をはるかに上回るたんぱく質を摂取している. **16** CONVENTION 慣習表現 You say "**it doesn't matter**" to tell someone who is apologizing to you that you are not angry or upset, and that they should not worry. 大丈夫です ❑ *"Did I wake you?" — "Yes, but it doesn't matter."* 「起こしちゃった？」 「そうだけど, 構わないよ」 **17** PHRASE 句 If you say that something **makes matters worse**, you mean that it makes a difficult situation even more difficult. さらに面倒なことになる ❑ *Don't let yourself despair; this will only make matters worse.* 絶望したところでさらに面倒なことになるだけだよ. **18** PHRASE 句 You use **no matter** in expressions such as "**no matter how**" and "**no matter what**" to say that something is true or happens in all circumstances. たとえ…でも ❑ *No matter what your age, you can lose*

weight by following this program. このプログラムに従えば, どの年齢の方でも減量することができます. **19** a matter of **life and death** → see **death 20** as a matter of **course** → see **course 21** as a matter of **fact** → see **fact**
→ see Word Web: matter

matter-of-fact ADJ 形容詞 If you describe a person as **matter-of-fact**, you mean that they show no emotions such as enthusiasm, anger, or surprise, especially in a situation where you would expect them to be emotional. 冷静な ❑ *John was doing his best to give Francis the news in a matter-of-fact way.* ジョンはその知らせをフランシスに落ち着いて伝えようとしていた. ● **matter-of-factly** ADV 副詞 [ADV after v] 冷静に ❑ *"She thinks you're a spy," Scott said matter-of-factly.* 「彼女はお前のことスパイだと思ってる」とスコットは淡々と話した.

mat|tress /mǽtrɪs/ (**mattresses**) N-COUNT 可算名詞 A **mattress** is the large, flat object which is put on a bed to make it comfortable to sleep on. マットレス
→ see **bed**

ma|ture /mətyʊər, -tʊər, -tʃʊər/ (**matures, maturing, matured, maturer, maturest**) **1** V-I 自動詞 When a child or young animal **matures**, it becomes an adult. 大人になる ❑ *You will learn what to expect as your child matures physically.* 子供の身体が成熟していくにつれ, どのような覚悟が必要になってくるのか分かってきます. **2** V-I 自動詞 When something **matures**, it reaches a state of complete development. 成熟する ❑ *When the trees matured they were cut.* 木は十分に成長したところで伐採された. **3** V-I 自動詞 If someone **matures**, they become more fully developed in their personality and emotional behavior. 成長する, 成熟する ❑ *They have matured way beyond their age.* 彼らは年齢よりはるかに成熟している. **4** ADJ 形容詞 If you describe someone as **mature**, you think that they are fully developed and balanced in their personality and emotional behavior. 十分に成長した [APPROVAL 賛成] ❑ *They are emotionally mature and should behave responsibly.* 彼らは精神的に成熟しているので責任のある行動がとれるはずだ. **5** V-T/V-I 他動詞/自動詞 If something such as wine or cheese **matures** or **is matured**, it is left for a time to allow its full flavor or strength to develop. 熟成させる [他動詞], 熟成する [自動詞] ❑ *Unlike wine, brandy matures only in wood, not glass.* ブランデーはワインと違ってびんの中では熟成せず, 樽の中だけで熟成する. **6** ADJ 形容詞 **Mature** cheese or wine has been left for a time to allow its full flavor or strength to develop. 熟成した ❑ *Grate some mature cheddar cheese.* 熟成したチェダーチーズをすりおろします. **7** V-I 自動詞 When an investment such as an insurance policy or bond **matures**, it reaches the stage when the company pays you back the money you have saved, and the interest your money has earned. 満期になる [BUSINESS 実業] ❑ *These bonuses will be paid when your savings plan matures in ten years' time.* 配当金は10年後の満期時に支払われます. **8** ADJ 形容詞 If you say that someone is **mature** or of **mature** years, you are saying politely that they are middle-aged or old. 中年の [POLITENESS 丁寧さ] ❑ *...a man of mature years who had been in the job for longer than most of the members could remember.* ほとんど同僚が思い出せないほど長い間その職に就いている中年男性.

ma|tur|ity /mətyʊ́ərɪti, -tʊər-, -tʃʊər-/ (**maturities**) **1** N-UNCOUNT 不可算名詞 **Maturity** is the state of being fully developed or adult. 成熟 ❑ *Humans experience a delayed maturity; we arrive at all stages of life later than other mammals.* 人間は大人になるまで時間がかかる. 成長のどの段階も他のほ乳類に比べ遅い. **2** N-UNCOUNT 不可算名詞 Someone's **maturity** is their quality of being fully developed in their personality and emotional behavior. 成熟 ❑ *Her speech showed great maturity and humanity.* 彼女の演説には円熟した人間味があふれていた. **3** N-VAR 可変性名詞 When an investment such as an insurance policy or bond reaches **maturity**, it reaches the stage when the company pays you back the money you have saved, and the interest your money has earned. 満期 [BUSINESS 実業] ❑ *Customers are told what their policies will be worth on maturity, not what they are worth today.* 顧

m

Word Web — matter

Matter exists in three states—**solid**, **liquid**, and **gas**. When a solid becomes hot enough, it **melts** and becomes a liquid. When a liquid is hot enough, it **evaporates** into a gas. The process also works the other way around. A gas which becomes very cool will **condense** into a liquid. And a liquid that is cooled enough will freeze and become a solid. Other changes in **state** are possible. Sublimation describes what happens when a solid, dry ice, turns directly into a gas, carbon dioxide. And did you know that glass is actually a liquid, not a solid?

solid   liquid   gas

客が聞かされるのは，現時点の価値ではなく契約が満期になったときの価値である．

Thesaurus　*maturity* また次を参照：

N.　adulthood, manhood, womanhood;
(ant.) immaturity **1**

---

maul /mɔːl/ (**mauls, mauling, mauled**) V-T 他動詞 If you are **mauled** by an animal, you are violently attacked by it and badly injured. 襲われ大けがをする ❑ *He had been mauled by a bear.* 彼は熊に襲われ大けがをしたことがあった．

mav|er|ick /mǽvərɪk/ (**mavericks**) N-COUNT 可算名詞 If you describe someone as a **maverick**, you mean that they are unconventional and independent, and do not think or behave in the same way as other people. 型破りな人 ❑ *He was too much of a maverick ever to hold high office.* 彼は独自の道を進みぜいで一度も高い地位に就くことはありませんでした． ● ADJ 形容詞 **Maverick** is also an adjective. 型破りの [ADJ n] ❑ *...a maverick group of scientists, who oppose the prevailing medical opinion on the disease.* 独自の立場をとる科学者のグループで，その病気に対する医学界の通説に対して異議を唱えている．

max. /mǽks/ ADJ 形容詞 **Max.** is the abbreviation for **maximum**. 最高の，最大の [num ADJ, ADJ n] ❑ *I'll give him eight out of 10, max.* 彼は10点満点で8点ですね．

Word Link　*maxim ≈ greatest : maxim, maximize, maximum*

---

max|im /mǽksɪm/ (**maxims**) N-COUNT 可算名詞 A **maxim** is a rule for good or sensible behavior, especially one in the form of a saying. 格言 ❑ *I believe in the maxim "if it ain't broke, don't fix it."* わたしの座右の銘は「壊れてもいないものを直すな」である．

max|im|ize /mǽksɪmaɪz/ (**maximizes, maximizing, maximized**) **1** V-T 他動詞 If you **maximize** something, you make it as great in amount or importance as you can. 最大にする ❑ *In order to maximize profit, the firm would seek to maximize output.* 最大の収益を得るため，企業は最大限の生産をめざすだろう． **2** V-T 他動詞 If you **maximize** a window on a computer screen, you make it as large as possible. 最大化する ❑ *Click on the square icon to maximize the window.* 四角の印のついたアイコンをクリックしてウィンドウを最大化します．

maxi|mum /mǽksɪməm/ **1** ADJ 形容詞 You use **maximum** to describe an amount which is the largest that is possible, allowed, or required. 最高の，最大の [ADJ n] ❑ *Under planning law the maximum height for a fence or hedge is 6 feet.* 計画法では塀や垣根の高さは最高6フィートと定められている． ● N-SING 単数名詞 **Maximum** is also a noun. 最高，最大 ❑ *The law provides for a maximum of two years in prison.* 法律では最大で2年の刑となります． **2** ADJ 形容詞 You use **maximum** to indicate how great an amount is. 最大限の [ADJ n] ❑ *I need the maximum amount of information you can give me.* 知っている情報はすべて出してください． ❑ *It was achieved with minimum fuss and maximum efficiency.* たいした混乱もなくきわめて円滑に進められた． **3** ADV 副詞 If you say that something is a particular amount **maximum**, you mean that this is the greatest amount it should be or could possibly be, although a smaller amount is acceptable or very possible. 最大で [amount ADV] ❑ *We need an extra 6 grams a day maximum.* 1日当たり最大でさらに6グラム必要だ．

Thesaurus　*maximum* また次を参照：

ADJ.　biggest, greatest, highest, most; (ant.) minimum, lowest **1 2**

Word Partnership　*maximum* は次の語句と使われる：

N.　maximum **benefit**, maximum **charge**, maximum **efficiency**, maximum **fine**, maximum **flexibility**, maximum **height**, maximum **penalty**, maximum **rate**, maximum **sentence**, maximum **speed 1**

---

may /meɪ/

May is a modal verb. It is used with the base form of a verb.

May は法動詞であり，動詞の原型とともに用いられる．

1 MODAL 法動詞 You use **may** to indicate that something will possibly happen or be true in the future, but you cannot be certain. かもしれない，する可能性がある [VAGUENESS あいまいさ] ❑ *We may have some rain today.* 今日は雨が降るかもしれません． ❑ *I may be back next year.* 来年戻るかもしれない． **2** MODAL 法動詞 You use **may** to indicate that there is a possibility that something is true, but you cannot be certain. かもしれない，の可能性がある [VAGUENESS あいまいさ] ❑ *Civil rights officials say there*

may be hundreds of other cases of racial violence. 公民権の担当部署の話では，これ以外にも人種間の暴力事件が数百件起きている可能性があるといいます． **3** MODAL 法動詞 You use **may** to indicate that something is sometimes true or is true in some circumstances. することもある ❑ *A vegetarian diet may not provide enough calories for a child's normal growth.* 野菜中心の食事では子供の正常な成育に必要なカロリーを十分摂取できない場合がある． **4** MODAL 法動詞 You use **may have** with a past participle when suggesting that it is possible that something happened or was true, or when giving a possible explanation for something. だったかもしれない，だった可能性がある [VAGUENESS あいまいさ] ❑ *He may have been to some of those places.* 彼はそれらの場所のいくつかには足を運んだかもしれない． **5** MODAL 法動詞 You use **may** in statements where you are accepting the truth of a situation, but contrasting it with something that is more important. かもしれないが ❑ *I may be almost 50, but there's not much I've forgotten.* もうすぐ50歳になるが，物忘れはあまりひどくない． **6** MODAL 法動詞 You use **may** when you are mentioning a quality or fact about something that people can make use of if they want to. することもできる ❑ *The bag has narrow straps, so it may be worn over the shoulder or carried in the hand.* バッグには細いひもが付いているので肩から掛けることもできるし，ふつうに手で持つこともできる． **7** MODAL 法動詞 You use **may** to indicate that someone is allowed to do something, usually because of a rule or law. You use **may not** to indicate that someone is not allowed to do something. することが許される ❑ *Any two persons may marry provided that both persons are at least 16 years of age on the day of their marriage.* 婚姻日の年齢が男女とも16歳以上であれば婚姻は認められる． **8** MODAL 法動詞 You use **may** when you are giving permission to someone to do something, or when asking for permission. [FORMAL 形式ばった] ❑ *Mr. Hobbs? May we come in?* ホッブズさん？お邪魔してもよろしいですか？ **9** MODAL 法動詞 You use **may** when you are making polite requests. よろしければ [FORMAL 形式ばった, POLITENESS 丁寧さ] ❑ *I'd like the use of your living room, if I may.* よろしければ，居間を使わせてもらえませんか． **10** MODAL 法動詞 You use **may** when you are mentioning the reaction or attitude that you think someone is likely to have to something you are about to say. するかもしれない ❑ *You know, Brian, whatever you may think, I work hard for a living.* なあ，ブライアン，お前がどう思おうが，おれは生活するために一生懸命働いているんだ． **11** MODAL 法動詞 You use **may** so that a particular thing **may** happen, you do it so that there is an opportunity for that thing to happen. できるように ❑ *...the need for an increase in the numbers of surgeons so that patients may be treated as soon as possible.* 患者が速やかな治療を受けられるように外科医を増やす必要性． **12 may as well → see well**

May /meɪ/ (**Mays**) N-VAR 可変性名詞 **May** is the fifth month of the year in the Western calendar. 5月 ❑ *Graduation ceremonies are held in early May.* 卒業式は5月初旬に行われます．

may|be /méɪbi/ **1** ADV 副詞 You use **maybe** to express uncertainty, for example when you do not know that something is definitely true, or when you are mentioning something that may possibly happen in the future in the way you describe. 恐らく，多分 [VAGUENESS あいまいさ] [ADV with cl/group] ❑ *Maybe she is in love.* 多分，彼女は恋しているよ． ❑ *I do think about having children, maybe when I'm 40.* 子供を生むこともちゃんと考えてるわよ．多分40歳ぐらいになったらね． **2** ADV 副詞 You use **maybe** when you are making suggestions or giving advice. **Maybe** is also used to introduce polite requests. できましたら [POLITENESS 丁寧さ] [ADV with cl/group] ❑ *Maybe we can go to the movies or something.* 映画とか見に行きませんか． ❑ *Maybe you'd better tell me what this is all about.* 一体どういうことなのか，話してもらえないですか． **3** ADV 副詞 You use **maybe** to indicate that, although a comment is partly true, there is also another point of view that should be considered. だろうけれども [ADV cl] ❑ *Maybe there is jealousy, but I think the envy is more powerful.* 焼きもちもあるだろうけれど，ねたみのほうが強いんじゃない． **4** ADV 副詞 You can say **maybe** as a response to a question or remark, when you do not want to agree or disagree. もしかしたらね，まあね [ADV as reply] ❑ *"Is she coming back?" — "Maybe. No one hears from her."* 「彼女は帰ってくるの？」「もしかしたらね．誰にも彼女からの連絡がないんだ」 **5** ADV 副詞 You use **maybe** when you are making a rough guess at a number, quantity, or value, rather than stating it exactly. だいたい [VAGUENESS あいまいさ] [ADV amount] ❑ *The men were maybe a hundred feet away and coming closer.* 男たちは100フィートほど向こうからこっちへやって来た． **6** ADV 副詞 People use **maybe** to mean "sometimes," particularly in a series of general statements about what someone does, or about something that regularly happens. 時には [ADV with cl/group] ❑ *They'll come to the bar for a year, or maybe even two, then they'll find another favorite spot.* 彼らはそのバーに1年か，あるいは2年ほど通ってから，次のお気に入りの店にくら替えするわけさ．

may|hem /méɪhɛm/ N-UNCOUNT 不可算名詞 You use **mayhem** to refer to a situation that is not controlled or ordered, when people are behaving in a disorganized, confused, and often

Word Web meal

Mealtime customs vary widely around the world. In the Middle East, popular **breakfast** foods include pita bread, olives and white cheese. In China, favorite **fast food** breakfast items are steamed buns and fried breadsticks. The continental **breakfast** in Europe consists of bread, butter, jam, and a hot drink. In many places **lunch** is a light **meal**, perhaps a **sandwich**. But in Germany, it is the main meal of the day. In most places, **dinner** is the name of the meal eaten in the evening. However, some people say they eat dinner at noon and supper at night.

violent way. 大混乱, パニック ❑ *Their arrival caused mayhem as crowds of refugees rushed towards them.* 彼らが到着すると難民たちがどっと押し寄せて大混乱となりました.

may|on|naise /meɪəneɪz/ N-UNCOUNT 不可算名詞 **Mayonnaise** is a thick, pale sauce made from egg yolks and oil. It is put on food such as salad and sandwiches. マヨネーズ

mayor /meɪər, mɛər/ (**mayors**) N-COUNT 可算名詞 The **mayor** of a town or city is the person who has been elected for a fixed period of time to run its government. 町長, 市長 ❑ *...the new mayor of New York.* ニューヨークの新市長.

maze /meɪz/ (**mazes**) ■ N-COUNT 可算名詞 A **maze** is a complex system of passages or paths between walls or hedges and is designed to confuse people who try to find their way through it, often as a form of amusement. 迷路 ❑ *The palace has extensive gardens, a maze, and tennis courts.* 宮殿には広大な庭園のほか, 迷路やテニスコートがある. ■ N-COUNT 可算名詞 A **maze of** streets, rooms, or tunnels is a large number of them that are connected in a complicated way, so that it is difficult to find your way through them. 迷路のような ❑ *The children lead me through the maze of alleys to the edge of the city.* 子供たちは迷路のような路地を通り抜けて私を街の外れに連れて来た. ■ N-COUNT 可算名詞 You can refer to a set of ideas, topics, or rules as a **maze** when a large number of them are related to each other in a complicated way that makes them difficult to understand. 複雑で理解しがたいもの ❑ *The book tries to steer you through the maze of alternative therapies.* その本では代替医療の複雑な実情に迫っている.

MBO /ɛm bi oʊ/ (**MBOs**) N-COUNT 可算名詞 **MBO** is an abbreviation for **management buyout**. マネジメントバイアウト（現経営権による自社買収）[BUSINESS 実業] ❑ *...the largest MBO ever undertaken by Australian financial investors.* オーストラリアの投資家による最高額のマネジメントバイアウト.

M.D. /ɛm di/ (**M.D.s**) N-COUNT 可算名詞 **M.D.** is an abbreviation for "medical doctor." You can also refer to a person who has this degree as an **M.D.** 医師

me /mi, STRONG mi/ PRON-SING 単数代名詞 A speaker or writer uses **me** to refer to himself or herself. **Me** is a first person singular pronoun. **Me** is used as the object of a verb or a preposition. わたしに, わたしを [v PRON, prep PRON] ❑ *I had to make important decisions that would affect me for the rest of my life.* その後の自分の人生を左右する大きな決断に迫られていた. ❑ *He asked me to go to California with him.* 彼から一緒にカリフォルニアへ行ってくれないかと頼まれた.

mead|ow /mɛdoʊ/ (**meadows**) N-COUNT 可算名詞 A **meadow** is a field which has grass and flowers growing in it. 牧草地, 草地

mea|ger /migər/ ADJ 形容詞 If you describe an amount or quantity of something as **meager**, you are critical of it because it is very small or not enough. わずかな, 不十分な [DISAPPROVAL 不賛成] ❑ *The rations that they gave us were meager and inadequate.* 彼らからの配給は微々たるもので不十分だった.

meal /mil/ (**meals**) ■ N-COUNT 可算名詞 A **meal** is an occasion when people sit down and eat, usually at a regular time. 食事 ❑ *She sat next to him throughout the meal.* 彼女は食事の間じゅう彼の隣に座っていた. ■ N-COUNT 可算名詞 A **meal** is the food you eat during a meal. 食事 ❑ *The waiter offered him red wine or white wine with his meal.* ウェイターに一緒に赤ワインか白ワインはどうですかと勧められた. ■ PHRASE 句 If you have a **square meal**, you have a large, healthy meal. 十分な食事 ❑ *The troops are very tired. They haven't had a square meal for four or five days.* 兵士たちは疲労していた. 4, 5日もまともな食事をとっていなかった.
→ see Word Web: **meal**
→ see **restaurant**

The first meal of the day is called **breakfast**. The most common word for the midday meal is **lunch**, but in some parts of Britain, and in some contexts, **dinner** is used as well. ❑ *He seldom has lunch at all. ...school dinners. ...Christmas dinner.* However, **dinner** is used mainly to refer to a meal in the evening. ❑ *...a celebratory dinner in the evening.* In British English, it may also suggest a formal or special meal. **Supper** and **tea** are sometimes also used to refer to the evening meal, though for some people, **supper** is a snack in the late evening and **tea** is a light meal in the afternoon.

Thesaurus meal また次を参照:

N. breakfast, dinner, lunch, supper ■

Word Partnership meal は次の語句と使われる:

V. enjoy a meal, miss a meal, skip a meal ■
cook a meal, eat a meal, have a meal, order a meal, prepare a meal, serve a meal ■
ADJ. big meal, delicious meal, good meal, hot meal, large meal, simple meal, well-balanced meal ■

m

mean
❶ VERB USES
❷ ADJECTIVE USES
❸ NOUN USES

❶ **mean** /min/ (**means, meaning, meant**)
↪ Please look at meaning ■ to see if the expression you are looking for is shown under another headword. ■ V-T 他動詞 If you want to know what a word, code, signal, or gesture **means**, you want to know what it refers to or what its message is. 意味する [no cont] ❑ *"Credible" means "believable."* credibleは「信じられる」という意味である. ❑ *What does "evidence" mean?* evidenceはどういう意味ですか. ■ V-T 他動詞 If you ask someone what they **mean**, you are asking them to explain exactly what or who they are referring to or what they are intending to say. のつもりで言う [no cont] ❑ *Do you mean me?* わたしのことを言っているの? ❑ *Let me illustrate what I mean with an old story.* 昔話を例にしてわたしの言いたいことを話させてください. ■ V-T 他動詞 If something **means** something to you, it is important to you in some way. 重要性を持つ [no cont] ❑ *The idea that she witnessed this shameful incident meant nothing to him.* 彼女がこの破廉恥な行為を目撃していたことなど, 彼にはどうでもよかった. ■ V-T 他動詞 If one thing **means** another, it shows that the second thing exists or is true. 必ずである [no cont] ❑ *An enlarged prostate does not necessarily mean cancer.* 前立腺が肥大しているからといって全てががんであるわけではない. ■ V-T 他動詞 If one thing **means** another, the first thing leads to the second thing happening. 引き起こす [no cont] ❑ *It would almost certainly mean the end of NATO.* そうなればNATOの終焉（しゅうえん）はほぼ確実である. ■ V-T 他動詞 If doing one thing **means** doing another, it involves doing the second thing. することになる ❑ *Children universally prefer to live in peace and security, even if that means living with only one parent.* 子供は誰でも安全で平穏な生活を望んでいる. そのために片親と暮らすことになってもそれを選ぶだろう. ■ V-T 他動詞 If you say that you **mean** what you are saying, you are telling someone that you are serious about it and are not joking, exaggerating, or just being polite. と本気で言う [no cont] ❑ *He says you're fired if you're not back at work on Friday. And I think he meant it.* 金曜に仕事に戻らないと彼はきみのことを首にすると言ってるけど, それ本気だと思うよ. ■ V-T 他動詞 If you say that someone **meant to** do something, you are saying that they did it deliberately. するつもりである [no cont] ❑ *I didn't mean to hurt you.* きみのこと傷つけるつもりなどなかったんだ. ❑ *If that sounds harsh, it is meant to.* 辛辣（しんらつ）に聞こえたとしたら, まさにそう意図して

いるからだ． **⑨** V-T 他動詞 If you say that someone **did not mean any harm**, offense, or disrespect, you are saying that they did not intend to upset or offend people or to cause problems, even though they may in fact have done so. はなかった [no cont, with brd-neg] ❑ *I'm sure he didn't mean any harm.* 間違いなく彼には悪意はなかったと思う． **⑩** V-T 他動詞 If you **mean to** do something, you intend or plan to do it. するつもりである [no cont] ❑ *Summer is the perfect time to catch up on the new books you meant to read.* 夏は，読もうと思いながら手つかずになっている本を読む絶好の機会だ． **⑪** V-T 他動詞 If you say that something **was meant to** happen, you believe that it was made to happen by God or fate, and did not just happen by chance. する運命にある [usu passive, no cont] ❑ *John was constantly reassuring me that we were meant to be together.* ジョンは2人は結ばれる運命にあるんだと言って，いつもわたしのことを安心させてくれてました． **⑫** PHRASE 句 You say "**I mean**" when making clearer something that you have just said. つまり [口語] ❑ *It was his idea. Gordon's, I mean.* それは彼，つまりゴードンの考えです． **⑬** PHRASE 句 You can use "**I mean**" to introduce a statement, especially one that justifies something that you have just said. というのは [SPOKEN 口語] ❑ *I'm sure he wouldn't mind. I mean, I was the one who asked him.* 彼はきっと気にしないよ．というのは，彼に聞いたのはこの僕なんだから． **⑭** PHRASE 句 You say **I mean** when correcting something that you have just said. いや [SPOKEN 口語] ❑ *It was law or classics – I mean English or classics.* 法律と古典，いや，英語と古典． **⑮** PHRASE 句 If you **know what it means** to do something, you know everything that is involved in a particular activity or experience, especially the effect that it has on you. するということがどんなことかをよく分かる ❑ *I know what it means to lose a child under such tragic circumstances.* あのような痛ましい出来事で子供を失うことがどれほどにつらいことか． **⑯** PHRASE 句 If a name, word, or phrase **means something to** you, you have heard it before and you know what it refers to. 聞いたことがある ❑ *"Oh, Gairdner," he said, as if that meant something to him.* 「ああ，ガードナーか」と，彼はまるでそいつを知っているかのように言った． **⑰** PHRASE 句 You use "**you mean**" in a question to check that you have understood what someone has said. ということですか ❑ *What accident? You mean Christina's?* どの事故？ クリスティーナの事故のこと？ **⑱** → see also **meaning, means, meant ⑲ if you know what I mean** → see **know**

❷ mean /mi̱n/ (meaner, meanest) **①** ADJ 形容詞 If someone is being **mean**, they are being unkind to another person, for example by not allowing them to do something. 意地悪な，思いやりのない ❑ *The little girls had locked themselves in the room because Mack had been mean to them.* マックに意地悪されたので，女の子たちは部屋の中から鍵をかけた． **②** ADJ 形容詞 If you describe a person or animal as **mean**, you are saying that they are very bad-tempered and cruel. 残忍な [mainly AM 主に米国英語] ❑ *The state's former commissioner of prisons once called Leonard the meanest man he'd ever seen.* かつての州の刑務局長がレオナルドのことをこんな残忍な男に出会ったことがないと言ったことがある． **③** ADJ 形容詞 If you describe someone as **mean**, you are being critical of them because they are unwilling to spend much money or to use very much of a particular thing. けちな，金に汚い [BRIT 英国英語, DISAPPROVAL 不賛成] [AM **cheap, stingy** 米国英語 **cheap, stingy**]

Thesaurus *mean* また次を参照：

V.	aim, intend, plan **❶ ⑧ ⑩**
ADJ.	nasty, unfriendly, unkind; (ant.) kind **❷ ①**
	miserly, penny-pinching, stingy, tight-fisted **❷ ③**

❸ mean /mi̱n/ **①** N-SING 単数名詞 The **mean** is a number that is the average of a set of numbers. 平均 ❑ *Take a hundred and twenty values and calculate the mean.* 120個の値から平均を出してください． **②** → see also **means**

me|ander /miæ̱ndər/ (meanders, meandering, meandered) **①** V-I 自動詞 If a river or road **meanders**, it has a lot of bends, rather than going in a straight line from one place to another. 蛇行している ❑ *We took a gravel road that meandered through farmland.* 農地を曲がりくねって走る砂利道を進んだ． ❑ *We crossed a small iron bridge over a meandering stream.* 蛇行した小川にかかる小さな鉄橋を渡った． **②** V-I 自動詞 If you **meander** somewhere, you move slowly and not in a straight line. ぶらぶら歩く ❑ *We meandered through a landscape of mountains, rivers, and vineyards.* 山や川やブドウ畑のある自然の中を散策した．

mean|ing /mi̱nɪŋ/ (meanings) **①** N-VAR 可変性名詞 The **meaning** of a word, expression, or gesture is the thing or idea that it refers to or represents and which can be explained using other words. 意味 ❑ *I hadn't a clue as to the meaning of "activism."* 「アクティビズム」が何のことか全然分からなかった． **②** N-VAR 可変性名詞 The **meaning** of what someone says or of something such as a book or film is the thoughts or ideas that are intended to be expressed by it. 意図，真意 ❑ *Unsure of the meaning of this remark, Ryle chose to remain silent.* 発言の真意がつかめなかったので，ライルは何も言わないことにした． **③** N-UNCOUNT 不可算名詞 If an activity or action

has **meaning**, it has a purpose and is worthwhile. 目的，意義 ❑ *Art has real meaning when it helps people to understand themselves.* 芸術が本来の意味を持つのは人の自己理解に役立つときである．

Word Partnership *meaning* は次の語句と使われる：

N.	meaning **of a term**, meaning **of a word ①**
ADJ.	**literal** meaning **① ②**
	deeper meaning, **new** meaning, **real** meaning, **true** meaning **① - ③**
V.	**explain the** meaning of *something*, **understand the** meaning of *something* **① - ③**

mean|ing|ful /mi̱nɪŋfəl/ **①** ADJ 形容詞 If you describe something as **meaningful**, you mean that it is serious, important, or useful in some way. 重要な，有意義な ❑ *She believes these talks will be the start of a constructive and meaningful dialogue.* 今回の話し合いが建設的で有意義な対話の端緒となるものと彼女は信じています． **②** ADJ 形容詞 A **meaningful** look or gesture is one that is intended to express something, usually to a particular person, without anything being said. 意味ありげな，何かを訴えるような [ADJ n] ❑ *Upon the utterance of this word, Dan and Harry exchanged a quick, meaningful look.* こう言って，ダンとハリーはちらっと意味ありげな視線を交わした． ● **mean|ing|ful|ly** ADV 副詞 意味ありげに ❑ *He glanced meaningfully at the other policeman, then he went up the stairs.* 彼はもう1人の警官に合図するかのように一瞬目を向けると，階段を上っていった．

mean|ing|less /mi̱nɪŋlɪs/ **①** ADJ 形容詞 If something that someone says or writes is **meaningless**, it has no meaning, or appears to have no meaning. 意味のない ❑ *The sentence "kicked the ball the man" is meaningless.* "kicked the ball the man" という文は意味が通じない． **②** ADJ 形容詞 Something that is **meaningless** in a particular situation is not important or relevant. 無価値な，無意味な ❑ *Fines are meaningless to guys earning millions.* 何百万ドルも稼いでいる連中にとって罰金などあってないに等しい． **③** ADJ 形容詞 If something that you do is **meaningless**, it has no purpose and is not at all worthwhile. 目標のない，むなしい ❑ *They seek strong sensations to dull their sense of a meaningless existence.* 彼らは人生の退屈さを紛らわせるために強い刺激を求める．

means /mi̱nz/ **①** N-COUNT 可算名詞 A **means** of doing something is a method, instrument, or process which can be used to do it. **Means** is both the singular and the plural form for this use. 手段，方法 ❑ *The move is a means to fight crime.* 今回の措置は犯罪対策です． ❑ *The army had perfected the use of terror as a means of controlling the population.* 軍は恐怖を武器にして極めて巧妙に人民を統制してきました． **②** N-PLURAL 複数名詞 You can refer to the money that someone has as their **means**. 資産，財産 [FORMAL 形式ばった] ❑ *...a person of means.* 資産家． **③** PHRASE 句 If you do something **by means of** a particular method, instrument, or process, you do it using that method, instrument, or process. を用いて ❑ *This is a two-year course taught by means of lectures and seminars.* これは講義またはセミナー形式で学ぶ2年間のコースです． **④** CONVENTION 慣習表現 You can say "**by all means**" to tell someone that you are very willing to allow them to do something. ぜひどうぞ [FORMULAE 決まり文句] ❑ *"Can I come and have a look at your house?" — "Yes, by all means."* 「お宅を拝見させてもらえますか」「ええ，ぜひどうぞ」

Word Partnership *means* は次の語句と使われる：

| ADJ. | **available** means, **different** means, **diplomatic** means, **legal** means, **military** means, **necessary** means, **other** means **①** |
| N. | means **of communication**, means **of transportation ①** |

meant /me̱nt/ **①** **Meant** is the past tense and past participle of **mean**. mean の過去・過去分詞 **②** ADJ 形容詞 You use **meant to** to say that something or someone was intended to be or do a particular thing, especially when they have failed to be or do it. ―になっている [v-link ADJ to-inf] ❑ *I can't say any more, it's meant to be a big secret.* これ以上は言えないよ．重大な秘密ということになってたんだから． ❑ *Everything is meant to be businesslike.* すべてが効率的に進むようになっている． **③** ADJ 形容詞 If something is **meant for** particular people or for a particular situation, it is intended for those people or for that situation. ―用の，―向けの [v-link ADJ 'for' n] ❑ *Fairy tales weren't just meant for children.* おとぎ話は子供たちばかりのものではありません． ❑ *The seeds were not meant for human consumption.* その種は食用ではなかった． **④** PHRASE 句 If you say that something is **meant to** happen, you mean that it is expected to happen or that it ought to happen. ―することになっている ❑ *The peculiar thing about getting engaged is that you're meant to announce it to everyone.* 婚約で不思議なのは，婚約したらみんなに知らせるものだと思い込んでいることだ． **⑤** PHRASE 句 If you say that something **is meant to** have a particular quality or characteristic, you mean that it has a reputation for being like that. ―だと評判で

ある ❑*The Spurs are meant to be one of the top teams in the league.* スパーズはリーグのトップクラスのチームとして名高い.

mean|time /mi̱ntaɪm/ **1** PHRASE 句 **In the meantime** or **meantime** means in the period of time between two events. 合間 ❑*Eventually your child will leave home to lead her own life, but in the meantime she relies on your support.* いずれ子供は家を巣立って自分の人生を送るようになりますが, それまではあなたの支えが必要です. **2** PHRASE 句 **For the meantime** means for a period of time from now until something else happens. 今のところは, さしあたっては ❑*Some of her stuff is stored for the meantime with her children.* 彼女の持ち物の一部はとりあえず子供たちの元に置いておく.

mean|while /mi̱nwaɪl/ **1** ADV 副詞 **Meanwhile** means while a particular thing is happening. その間に [ADV with cl] ❑*Brush the eggplant with oil, add salt and pepper, and bake till soft. Meanwhile, heat the remaining oil in a heavy pan.* ナスに油を塗って, 塩こしょうを加え, オーブンで柔らかくなるまで焼きます. その間に残りの油を厚手の鍋で熱しておきます. **2** ADV 副詞 **Meanwhile** means in the period of time between two events. 合間 [ADV with cl] ❑*You needn't worry; I'll be ready to greet them. Meanwhile, I'm off to discuss the Fowler's party with Felix.* 心配はいらないよ. 彼らを迎える準備はちゃんとしてあるから. それまで, ファウラーのパーティーのことでフェリックスと話をしてくるね. **3** ADV 副詞 You use **meanwhile** to introduce a different aspect of a particular situation, especially one that is completely opposite to the one previously mentioned. その一方で [ADV with cl] ❑*He had always found his wife's mother a bit annoying. The mother-daughter relationship, meanwhile, was close.* 彼は姑（しゅうとめ）にはいつもいらいらさせられたが, 母と娘のほうは仲がよかった.

mea|sles /mi̱z°lz/ N-UNCOUNT 不可算名詞 **Measles** is an infectious illness that gives you a high temperature and red spots on your skin. はしか [also 'the' N]
→ see **hospital**

meas|ur|able /me̱ʒərəb°l/ **1** ADJ 形容詞 If you describe something as **measurable**, you mean that it is large enough to be noticed or to be significant. 無視できないほどの, 重要な [FORMAL 形式ばった] ❑*Both leaders seemed to expect measurable progress.* 両首脳とも大きな進展を期待している様子でした. **2** ADJ 形容詞 Something that is **measurable** can be measured. 測定できる ❑*Economists emphasize measurable quantities – the number of jobs, the per capita income.* エコノミストは求人数や国民1人当たりの所得といった測定可能な数値を強調します.

meas|ure /me̱ʒər/ (measures, measuring, measured) **1** V-T 他動詞 If you **measure** the quality, value, or effect of something, you discover or judge how great it is. 評価する ❑*I continued to measure his progress against the charts in the doctor's office.* 診察室でカルテと照らし合わせながら彼の回復の経過を見ていった. **2** V-T 他動詞 If you **measure** a quantity that can be expressed in numbers, such as the length of something, you discover it using a particular instrument or device, for example a ruler. 測る ❑*Measure the length and width of the gap.* すき間の長さと幅を測ります. **3** V-T 他動詞 If something **measures** a particular length, width, or amount, that is its size or intensity, expressed in numbers. （長さなどが）ある [no cont] ❑*It measures 20 yards from side to side.* 端から端まで20ヤードある. **4** N-SING 単数名詞 A **measure of** a particular quality, feeling, or activity is a fairly large amount of it. ある程度の [FORMAL 形式ばった] ❑*With the exception of Juan, each attained a measure of success.* ジュアン以外はみんなそこそこうまくやった. **5** N-SING 単数名詞 If you say that one aspect of a situation is **a measure of** that situation, you mean that it shows that the situation is very serious or has developed to a very great extent. 尺度, 目安 ❑*That is a measure of how bad things have become at the bank.* そのことから銀行の現状がいかにひどいかが分かる. **6** N-COUNT 可算名詞 When someone, usually a government or other authority, takes **measures** to do something, they carry out particular actions in order to achieve a particular result. 対策, 施策 [FORMAL 形式ばった] ❑*The government warned that police would take tougher measures to contain the trouble.* 事態収拾に向けて警察による強攻手段も辞さないと, 政府は警告した. **7** N-COUNT 可算名詞 A **measure of** a strong alcoholic drink such as brandy or

whiskey is an amount of it in a glass. In bars, a **measure** is an official standard amount. グラス1杯分 [BRIT 英国英語] ❑*He poured himself another generous measure of whiskey.* 彼はウィスキーをもう1杯なみなみと注いだ. **8** N-COUNT 可算名詞 In music, a **measure** is one of the several short parts of the same length into which a piece of music is divided. 小節 [AM 米国英語] ❑*Malcolm wanted to mix the beginning of a sonata, then add Beethoven for a few measures, then go back to Bach.* マルコムはソナタの冒頭をミキシングして, 数小節ベートーベンを続けてからバッハに戻したかった. **9** → see also **tape measure** **10** PHRASE 句 If you say that something has changed or that it has affected you **beyond measure**, you are emphasizing that it has done this to a great extent. とてつもなく [EMPHASIS 強調] ❑*Mankind's knowledge of the universe has increased beyond measure.* 宇宙に対する人類の知識は飛躍的に増えてきた.
→ see **mathematics**

▶ **measure up** PHRASAL VERB 句動詞 If you do not **measure up to** a standard or to someone's expectations, you are not good enough to achieve the standard or fulfill the person's expectations. 及ばない ❑*It was fatiguing sometimes to try to measure up to her standard of perfection.* 彼女が求める完成の域に達するのは時に大変だった.

Word Partnership		*measure* は次の語句と使われる:
N.		measure **intelligence**, measure **performance**, measure **progress** **1**
		tests measure **1** – **3**
		emergency measure, **safety** measure, **security** measure **6**
V.		**adopt** a measure, **approve** a measure, **support** a measure, **veto** a measure **6**
ADJ.		**drastic** measure, **economic** measure **6**

meas|ure|ment /me̱ʒərmənt/ (measurements) **1** N-COUNT 可算名詞 A **measurement** is a result, usually expressed in numbers, that you obtain by measuring something. 測定値, 寸法 ❑*We took lots of measurements.* いろいろ寸法を測った. **2** N-VAR 可変性名詞 **Measurement** of something is the process of measuring it in order to obtain a result expressed in numbers. 測定, 探寸 ❑*Tests include measurement of height, weight, and blood pressure.* 検査には身長, 体重, 血圧の測定も含まれる. **3** N-VAR 可変性名詞 The **measurement** of the quality, value, or effect of something is the activity of deciding how great it is. 測定 ❑*The measurement of intelligence has been the greatest achievement of twentieth-century scientific psychology.* 知能測定は科学的心理学が20世紀に成し遂げた最大の功績である. **4** N-PLURAL 複数名詞 Your **measurements** are the size of your waist, chest, hips, and other parts of your body, which you need to know when you are buying clothes. 体のサイズ ❑*I know all her measurements and find it easy to buy stuff she likes.* 彼女のサイズはみんな知ってるから, 彼女の好きなものがあったらすぐに買ってあげられるんだ.

meat /mi̱t/ (meats) N-MASS 質量名詞 **Meat** is flesh taken from a dead animal that people cook and eat. 肉 ❑*Meat and fish are relatively expensive.* 肉と魚は高めだ. ❑*...imported meat products.* 輸入ものの肉製品.
→ see Word Web: **meat**
→ see **vegetarian**

meaty /mi̱ti/ (meatier, meatiest) **1** ADJ 形容詞 Food that is **meaty** contains a lot of meat. 肉がたくさん入った ❑*...a pleasant lasagna with a meaty sauce.* ソースに肉がたっぷり入ったおいしいラザニア. **2** ADJ 形容詞 You can describe something such as a piece of writing or a part in a movie as **meaty** if it contains a lot of interesting or important material. 内容の充実した ❑*The short, meaty reports are those he likes best.* 簡潔で内容のあるレポートこそ, 彼が最もよしとするものだ.

me|chan|ic /mɪkæ̱nɪk/ (mechanics) **1** N-COUNT 可算名詞 A **mechanic** is someone whose job is to repair and maintain machines and engines, especially car engines. 機械工; 整備士 ❑*If you smell something unusual (gas fumes or burning, for instance), take the car to your mechanic.* ガソリン臭や焼け焦げるような臭いなど, ふ

Word Web   meat

The English language has different words for animals and the **meat** that comes from them. In the year 1066 AD the Anglo-Saxons of England lost a major battle to the French-speaking Normans. As a result, the Normans became the ruling class and the Anglo-Saxons worked on farms. The Anglo-Saxons tended the animals. They tended **sheep, cows, chickens,** and **pigs** in the fields. The wealthier Normans, who purchased and ate the meat from these animals, used different words. They bought "mouton," which became the word **mutton,** "bouef," which became **beef,** "poulet," which became **poultry,** and "porc," which became **pork.**

だんと違う臭いがしたら，車を整備に出してください. **2** N-PLURAL 複数名詞 The **mechanics of** a process, system, or activity are the way in which it works or the way in which it is done. 仕組み，構造 □ *What are the mechanics of this new process?* この新しい工程はどのような仕組みになっているのですか. **3** N-UNCOUNT 不可算名詞 **Mechanics** is the part of physics that deals with the natural forces that act on moving or stationary objects. 力学 □ *He has not studied mechanics or engineering.* 彼は力学も工学も学んだことがない.

me|chani|cal /mɪkǽnɪkªl/ **1** ADJ 形容詞 A **mechanical** device has parts that move when it is working, often using power from an engine or from electricity. 機械式の □ *a small mechanical device that taps out the numbers.* 数字を打ち出す小型の機械装置. □ *This is the oldest working mechanical clock in the world.* これは動作している機械時計としては世界で最も古い. ● me|chani|cal|ly /mɪkǽnɪkli/ ADV 副詞 [ADV with v] 機械的に □ *The air was circulated mechanically.* 機械によって空気が循環する仕組みになっていた. **2** ADJ 形容詞 **Mechanical** means relating to machines and engines and the way they work. 機械の [ADJ n] □ *...mechanical engineering.* 機械工学. ● me|chani|cal|ly ADV 副詞 [ADV adj/-ed] 機械的に □ *The car was mechanically sound, he decided.* 車は機械的には問題ないと彼は判断した. **3** ADJ 形容詞 If you describe a person as **mechanical**, you mean they are naturally good at understanding how machines work. 機械に強い □ *He was a very mechanical person, who knew a lot about sound.* 彼は機械にはめっぽう強く，音響のことはよく知っていました. ● me|chani|cal|ly ADV 副詞 [ADV -ed] 機械的に □ *I'm not mechanically minded.* 機械には弱い. **4** ADJ 形容詞 If you describe someone's action as **mechanical**, you mean that they do it automatically, without thinking about it. 機械的な □ *It is real prayer, and not mechanical repetition.* それはまさしく本当の祈りで，ただ機械的に繰り返されるものとは違う. ● me|chani|cal|ly ADV 副詞 [ADV with v] 機械的に □ *He nodded mechanically, his eyes fixed on the girl.* 彼はじっと少女を見つめたまま，機械的にうなずいた.

mecha|nism /mɛ́kənɪzəm/ (mechanisms) **1** N-COUNT 可算名詞 In a machine or piece of equipment, a **mechanism** is a part, often consisting of a set of smaller parts, which performs a particular function. 機械装置 □ *...the locking mechanism.* 施錠装置. **2** N-COUNT 可算名詞 A **mechanism** is a special way of getting something done within a particular system. 仕組み □ *There's no mechanism for punishing arms exporters who break the rules.* 規則を守らない武器輸出業者を罰則する仕組みがないのです. **3** N-COUNT 可算名詞 A **mechanism** is a part of your behavior that is automatic and that helps you to survive or to cope with a difficult situation. 機構 □ *...a survival mechanism, a means of coping with intolerable stress.* 生存機構，つまり限度を超えたストレスに対処する機構.

mecha|nize /mɛ́kənaɪz/ (mechanizes, mechanizing, mechanized) V-T 他動詞 If someone **mechanizes** a process, they cause it to be done by a machine or machines, when it was previously done by people. 機械化する □ *Only gradually are technologies being developed to mechanize the task.* 徐々にではあるが，作業の機械化に向かって技術は進展し続けている. ● mecha|ni|za|tion /mɛ̀kənaɪzéɪ^ən/ N-UNCOUNT 不可算名詞 機械化 □ *Mechanization happened years ago on the farms of Islay.* アイラ島の農場が機械化されたのはずっと以前のことである.

med|al /mɛ́dªl/ (medals) N-COUNT 可算名詞 A **medal** is a small metal disk which is given as an award for bravery or as a prize in a sports event. 勲章，メダル □ *Dufour was awarded his country's highest medal for bravery.* デュフールは勇敢な行為に対して与えられた最高位の勲章を受けた.

med|dle /mɛ́dªl/ (meddles, meddling, meddled) V-I 自動詞 If you say that someone **meddles** in something, you are criticizing the fact that they try to influence or change it without being asked. 干渉する [DISAPPROVAL 不賛成] □ *Already some people are asking whether scientists have any right to meddle in such matters.* そうした問題に科学者が介入する権利があるのか疑問視する声が出始めている. □ *If only you hadn't felt compelled to meddle.* 首をつっこまないでほしいんだけどなあ.

Word Link   med ≈ middle : intermediary, media, mediate

me|dia /míːdiə/ **1** N-SING-COLL 集合的単数名詞 You can refer to television, radio, newspapers, and magazines as **the media**. マスメディア，マスコミ □ *It is hard work and not a glamorous job as portrayed by the media.* それは大変な仕事で，マスコミが描くほど華やかな職業ではない. □ *They are wondering whether bias in the news media contributed to the president's defeat.* 偏ったニュース報道が大統領の敗北の一因になったのではないかと彼らは考えています. **2** → see also **mass media, multimedia** **3** **Media** is a plural of **medium**. mediumの複数形
→ see **library**

me|dia cir|cus (media circuses) N-COUNT 可算名詞 If an event is described as a **media circus**, a large group of people from the media are there to report on it and take photographs. 報道合戦 [DISAPPROVAL 不賛成] □ *The couple married in the Caribbean to avoid a media circus.* マスコミの取材攻勢を避けるため，2人はカリブ海で結

婚した.

me|di|aeval /míːdiíːvªl, mɪdíːvªl/ → see **medieval**

me|di|ate /míːdieɪt/ (mediates, mediating, mediated) V-T/V-I 他動詞/自動詞 If someone **mediates** between two groups of people, or **mediates** an agreement **between** them, they try to settle an argument between them by talking to both groups and trying to find things that they can both agree to. 仲裁する，調停する □ *My mom was the one who mediated between Zelda and her mom.* ゼルダとその母親の仲介役になったのはわたしの母だった. □ *United Nations officials have mediated a series of peace meetings between the two sides.* 国連が調停役となって，当事者間の和平交渉が進められています. ● me|dia|tion /míːdiéɪ^ən/ N-UNCOUNT 不可算名詞 仲裁，調停 □ *The agreement provides for United Nations mediation between the two sides.* 協定では国連が両者の調停役となります. ● me|dia|tor (mediators) N-COUNT 可算名詞 仲裁者，調停人 □ *An archbishop has been acting as mediator between the rebels and the authorities.* 大司教が反政府組織と政府との橋渡し役を務めてきました.
→ see **war**

medi|cal /mɛ́dɪkªl/ (medicals) **1** ADJ 形容詞 **Medical** means relating to illness and injuries and to their treatment or prevention. 医療の，医学の [ADJ n] □ *Several police officers received medical treatment for cuts and bruises.* 数名の警察官が切り傷や打撲傷の手当てを受けました. ● medi|cal|ly /mɛ́dɪkli/ ADV 副詞 医学的に □ *Therapists cannot prescribe drugs as they are not necessarily medically qualified.* 療法士には医師の資格は要らないので薬は処方できない. **2** N-COUNT 可算名詞 A **medical** is a thorough examination of your body by a doctor, for example before you start a new job. 健康診断 [mainly BRIT 主に英国英語; AM physical 米国英語 physical]

Word Partnership   *medical* は次の語句と使われる:

N.	medical **advice**, medical **attention**, medical **bills**, medical **care**, medical **center**, medical **doctor**, medical **emergency**, medical **practice**, medical **problems**, medical **research**, medical **science**, medical **supplies**, medical **tests**, medical **treatment** **1**

medi|ca|tion /mɛ̀dɪkéɪ^ən/ (medications) N-VAR 可変性名詞 **Medication** is medicine that is used to treat and cure illness. 薬物 □ *When somebody comes for treatment I always ask them if they are on any medication.* 治療に来た患者には必ず何か飲んでいる薬があるか聞きます.

me|dici|nal /mədísən^əl/ ADJ 形容詞 **Medicinal** substances or substances with **medicinal** effects can be used to treat and cure illnesses. 薬効のある □ *...medicinal plants.* 薬用植物.

medi|cine /mɛ́dɪsɪn/ (medicines) **1** N-UNCOUNT 不可算名詞 **Medicine** is the treatment of illness and injuries by doctors and nurses. 医療，医学 □ *He pursued a career in medicine.* 彼は医学の道に進みました. □ *I was interested in alternative medicine and becoming an aromatherapist.* 代替医療に興味があってアロマセラピストを目指していた. **2** N-MASS 質量名詞 **Medicine** is a substance that you drink or swallow in order to cure an illness. 薬 □ *People in hospitals are dying because of shortages of medicine.* 医薬品の不足で入院患者は死に瀕(ひん)しています.
→ see Word Web: **medicine**

Word Partnership   *medicine* は次の語句と使われる:

V.	**practice** medicine, **study** medicine **1**
	give *someone* medicine, **take** medicine, **use** medicine **2**

me|di|eval /míːdiíːvªl, mɪdíːvªl/ ADJ 形容詞 Something that is **medieval** relates to or was made in the period of European history between the end of the Roman Empire in AD 476 and about AD 1500. 中世の □ *...a medieval castle.* 中世の城.

me|dio|cre /míːdióʊkər/ ADJ 形容詞 If you describe something as **mediocre**, you mean that it is of average quality but you think it should be better. 平凡な，月並みの [DISAPPROVAL 不賛成] □ *His school record was mediocre.* 学校での彼の成績は平凡だった.

me|di|oc|rity /míːdiɒ́krɪti/ N-UNCOUNT 不可算名詞 If you refer to the **mediocrity** of something, you mean that it is of average quality but you think it should be better. 平凡，月並み [DISAPPROVAL 不賛成] □ *...the mediocrity of most contemporary literature.* 現代文学にほぼ共通する新鮮味のなさ.

medi|tate /mɛ́dɪteɪt/ (meditates, meditating, meditated) **1** V-I 自動詞 If you **meditate** on something, you think about it very carefully and deeply for a long time. 深く考える □ *On the day her son began school, she meditated on the uncertainties of his future.* 息子が学校に通い始めた日，彼女は息子の将来に強い不安を感じていた. **2** V-I 自動詞 If you **meditate** you remain in a silent and calm state for a period of time, as part of a religious training or so that you are more able to deal with the problems and difficulties of everyday life. 瞑想する □ *I was meditating, and reached a higher state*

Word Web   medicine

Western **medicine** began in ancient Greece. The Greek philosopher Hippocrates separated medicine from religion and **disease** from supernatural explanations. He is also responsible for the Hippocratic oath which describes a **physician's** duties. During the Middle Ages, Andreas Vesalius helped to advance medicine through his **research** on **anatomy**. Another major step forward was Friedrich Henle's development of **germ** theory. An understanding of germs led to Joseph Lister's demonstrations of the effective use of **antiseptics**, and Alexander Fleming's discovery of the **antibiotic** penicillin.

Important Medical Advances

	1500s Andreas Vesalius anatomy	**1840s** Charles Jackson anesthetic	**1900s** Karl Landsteiner blood type system
400 BC Hippocrates the Hippocratic oath	**1790s** Friedrich Henle germ theory	**1860s** Joseph Lister antiseptic	**1920s** Alexander Fleming antibiotics

400 BC ⟩⟩⟩ 1500 ⟩ 1790 ⟩ 1840 ⟩ 1860 ⟩ 1900 ⟩ 1920

---

of consciousness. 瞑想しているとふだんより高い意識状態に達した．

medi|ta|tion /mɛdɪteɪʃ°n/ N-UNCOUNT 不可算名詞 **Meditation** is the act of remaining in a silent and calm state for a period of time, as part of a religious training, or so that you are more able to deal with the problems of everyday life. 瞑想 ❑ *Many busy executives have begun to practice yoga and meditation.* 多忙な管理職の間でヨガや瞑想を始める人が増えている．

Medi|ter|ra|nean /mɛdɪtəreɪniən/ **1** N-PROPER 固有名詞 **The Mediterranean** is the sea between southern Europe and North Africa. 地中海 ❑ *You have the choice of night fishing in the Mediterranean, or windsurfing on a lake in Switzerland.* 地中海での夜釣りか，スイスの湖でのウィンドサーフィンか，お好きなほうを選んでいただけます． **2** N-PROPER 固有名詞 **The Mediterranean** refers to the southern part of Europe, which is next to the Mediterranean Sea. 地中海沿岸 ❑ *Barcelona has become one of the most dynamic and prosperous cities in the Mediterranean.* バルセロナは地中海沿岸で最も活気のある繁栄した都市の1つになった．

me|dium /miːdiəm/ (**mediums** or **media**)

> The plural of the noun can be either **mediums** or **media** for meanings **4** and **5**. The form **mediums** is the plural for meaning **6**.
>
> 名詞の複数は **mediums** と **media** の意味には **4** か **5** のいずれかである．**mediums** 形は **6** を意味する複数である．

1 ADJ 形容詞 If something is of **medium** size, it is neither large nor small, but approximately halfway between the two. 平均量の ❑ *A medium dose produces severe nausea within hours.* 通常の投薬量でも数時間のうちにひどい吐き気が起こる． **2** ADJ 形容詞 You use **medium** to describe something that is average in degree or amount, or approximately halfway along a scale between two extremes. 中程度の ❑ *Foods that contain only medium levels of sodium are bread, cakes, milk, butter, and margarine.* 中程度のナトリウムを含む食品としては，パン，ケーキ，牛乳，バター，マーガリンなどがある． ● ADV 副詞 **Medium** is also an adverb. 中程度に [ADV adj] ❑ *Toast by stirring in a medium-hot skillet for a few minutes.* 数分間中火のフライパンでよく炒めこんがりと焼きます． **3** COMB IN COLOR 色彩語の複合 If something is of a **medium** color, it is neither light nor dark, but approximately halfway between the two. 普通の明るさの ❑ *Andrea has medium brown hair, gray eyes, and very pale skin.* アンドレアの髪は普通の茶色，目はグレーで，肌はとても白い． **4** N-COUNT 可算名詞 A **medium** is a way or means of expressing your ideas or of communicating with people. 手段 ❑ *In Sierra Leone, English is used as the medium of instruction for all primary education.* シエラレオネでは，全ての初等教育で英語による授業が行われている． **5** N-COUNT 可算名詞 A **medium** is a substance or material which is used for a particular purpose or in order to produce a particular effect. 媒体 ❑ *Blood is the medium in which oxygen is carried to all parts of the body.* 血液は体じゅうに酸素を運ぶ役割を果たす． **6** N-COUNT 可算名詞 A **medium** is a person who claims to be able to contact and speak to people who are dead, and to pass messages between them and people who are still alive. 霊媒 ❑ *Bruce Willis says he has been talking to his dead brother through a medium.* ブルース・ウィリスは，霊媒師を通して亡くなった弟と話しているという． **7** → see also **media**

me|dium term N-SING 単数名詞 The **medium term** is the period of time which lasts a few months or years beyond the present time, in contrast with the short term or the long term. 中期 ❑ *Economists had been arguing that the medium-term economic prospects remained poor.* エコノミストたちは経済の中期見通しは改善していないと主張していました．

meek /miːk/ (**meeker**, **meekest**) ADJ 形容詞 If you describe a person as **meek**, you think that they are gentle and quiet, and likely to do what other people say. おとなしい，従順な ❑ *He was*

a meek, mild-mannered fellow. 彼はおとなしく温和な人でした． ● **meek|ly** ADV 副詞 [ADV with v] おとなしく，従順に ❑ *Most have meekly accepted such advice.* たいていの人がそうした忠告に言われるがままに従っていた．

meet /miːt/ (**meets**, **meeting**, **met**) **1** V-RECIP 相互動詞 If you **meet** someone, you happen to be in the same place as them and start talking to them. You may know the other person, but be surprised to see them, or you may not know them at all. 偶然出会う ❑ *I have just met the man I want to spend the rest of my life with.* ごく最近，生涯の伴侶にしたい男性に出会いました． ❑ *He's the kindest and sincerest person I've ever met.* 彼みたいに優しくて誠実な人，今までいなかった． ● PHRASAL VERB 句動詞 **Meet up** means the same as **meet**. 偶然出会う ❑ *Last night, when he was parking my car, he met up with a buddy he had at Stanford.* 昨日の晩，彼がわたしの車を止めようとしていたら，彼のスタンフォード時代の友人にばったり出会った． **2** V-RECIP 相互動詞 If two or more people **meet**, they go to the same place, which they have earlier arranged to do, so that they can talk or do something together. 会う ❑ *We could meet for a drink after work.* 仕事が終わったら一杯やってもいいけど． ● PHRASAL VERB 句動詞 **Meet up** means the same as **meet**. 会う ❑ *We tend to meet up for lunch once a week.* たいてい週に一度は一緒にお昼をする． **3** V-T 他動詞 If you **meet** someone, you are introduced to them and begin talking to them and getting to know them. 紹介される ❑ *Hey, Terry, come and meet my Dad.* おい，テリー，こっちへ来いよ．おやじを紹介するから． **4** V-T 他動詞 You use **meet** in expressions such as "**Pleased to meet you**" and "**Nice to have met you**" when you want to politely say hello or goodbye to someone you have just met for the first time. 初めまして [FORMULAE 決まり文句] ❑ *"Jennifer," Miss Mallory said, "this is Leigh Taylor." —"Pleased to meet you," Jennifer said.* 「ジェニファー，リー・テイラーさん」とマロリーさんは言った．ジェニファーは「初めまして」とあいさつした． **5** V-T 他動詞 If you **meet** someone at or off their train, plane, or bus, you go to the station, airport, or bus stop in order to be there when they arrive. 出迎える ❑ *Mama met me at the station.* ママが駅で迎えてくれた． ❑ *Lili and my father met me off the boat.* リリと父が船着場まで迎えに来てくれた． **6** V-I 自動詞 When a group of people such as a committee **meet**, they gather together for a particular purpose. 会合を開く ❑ *Officials from the two countries will meet again soon to resume negotiations.* 両国の当局者は近いうちに次の協議を行い交渉を再開する見通しです． **7** V-I 自動詞 If you **meet with** someone, you have a meeting with them. 会う [mainly AM 主に米国英語] ❑ *Most of the lawmakers who met with the president yesterday said they backed the mission.* 昨日，大統領と会談した大半の連邦議員が今回の作戦への支持を表明しました． **8** V-T/V-I 他動詞/自動詞 If something such as a suggestion, proposal, or new book **meets with** or **is met with** a particular reaction, it gets that reaction from people. 見舞われる ❑ *The idea met with a cool response from various quarters.* その案については各方面から冷ややかな反応が寄せられました． ❑ *We hope today's offer will meet with your approval too.* 本日の提案にご賛成いただければうれしいのですが． **9** V-T 他動詞 If something **meets** a need, requirement, or condition, it is good enough to do what is required. 満たす ❑ *He suggested that the current arrangements for the care of severely mentally ill people are inadequate to meet their needs.* 今の介護体制では重度精神障害者の要望が十分満たされていないと，彼は指摘した． **10** V-T 他動詞 If you **meet** something such as a problem or challenge, you deal with it satisfactorily or do what is required. 処理する ❑ *Manufacturing failed to meet the crisis of the 1970s.* 製造業は1970年代の危機に対処できなかった． **11** V-T 他動詞 If you **meet** the cost of something, you provide the money that is needed for it. 負担する ❑ *The government said it will help meet some of the cost of the damage.* 政府は，国が損害の一部を負担することを表明した． **12** V-T 他動詞 If you **meet** a situation, attitude, or problem, you experience it or become aware of it. 直面する ❑ *I honestly don't know how I will react the next*

m

time I meet a potentially dangerous situation. 正直なところ，今度危険を伴うような場面に出会ったら自分がどう反応するのか全然分かりません． **13** V-I 自動詞 You can say that someone **meets with** success or failure when they are successful or unsuccessful. 成功する；失敗する ❏Attempts to find civilian volunteers have met with embarrassing failure. 民間人ボランティアを探す試みは目も当てられない結果に終わった． **14** V-RECIP 相互動詞 When a moving object **meets** another object, it hits or touches it. 触れる ❏He held the lighter so it met the tip of his cigarette. 彼はライターがタバコの先に来るようにした． **15** V-RECIP 相互動詞 If your eyes **meet** someone else's, you both look at each other at the same time. 目が合う [WRITTEN 書き言葉] ❏Nina's eyes met her sisters' across the table. テーブルをはさんでニーナの目が妹の目と合った． **16** V-RECIP 相互動詞 If two areas **meet**, especially two areas of land or sea, they are next to one another. 隣接する ❏It is one of the rare places in the world where the desert meets the sea. そこは砂漠が海に迫っている世界でも珍しい場所です． **17** V-RECIP 相互動詞 The place where two lines **meet** is the place where they join together. 交わる ❏Parallel lines will never meet no matter how far extended. 平行線はどこまで伸ばしても交わることはない． **18** to **make ends meet** → see end **19** to **meet** someone **halfway** → see halfway

▶ **meet up** → meet **meet 1, 2**

Thesaurus		*meet* また次を参照：
v.	bump into, encounter, run into	**1**
	get together	**2**
	gather	**6**
	comply with, follow, fulfill	
	accomplish, achieve, complete, make	**10**

meet|ing /míːtɪŋ/ (**meetings**) **1** N-COUNT 可算名詞 A **meeting** is an event in which a group of people come together to discuss things or make decisions. 会合 ❏Can we have a meeting to discuss that? 集まってそのことを話し合えますか． ●N-SING 単数名詞 You can also refer to the people at a meeting as **the meeting**. 会合の出席者 ❏The meeting decided that further efforts were needed. 会議ではより一層の努力が必要だという結論に至りました． **2** N-COUNT 可算名詞 When you meet someone, either by chance or by arrangement, you can refer to this event as a **meeting**. 出会い ❏In January, 37 years after our first meeting, I was back in the studio with Dennis. デニスと出会って37年目となる1月に彼と再び共演することになった．

Word Partnership	*meeting* は次の語句と使われる：
N.	meeting **agenda**, **board** meeting, **business** meeting **1**
V.	**attend a** meeting, **call a** meeting, **go to a** meeting, **have a** meeting, **hold a** meeting **1**
	plan a meeting, **schedule a** meeting **1 2**

mega|byte /méɡəbaɪt/ (**megabytes**) N-COUNT 可算名詞 In computing, a **megabyte** is one million bytes of data. メガバイト ❏...256 megabytes of memory. 256MBのメモリー．

mel|an|choly /mélənkɒli/ ADJ 形容詞 You describe something that you see or hear as **melancholy** when it gives you an intense feeling of sadness. 物悲しい ❏The only sounds were the distant, melancholy cries of the sheep. 聞こえるのは遠くからする物悲しい羊の声だけだった．

mel|low /méloʊ/ (**mellower, mellowest, mellows, mellowing, mellowed**) **1** ADJ 形容詞 **Mellow** is used to describe things that have a pleasant, soft, rich color, usually red, orange, yellow, or brown. 暖かく柔らかな ❏...the softer, mellower light of evening. 暖かく柔らかに映える夕日． **2** ADJ 形容詞 A **mellow** sound or flavor is pleasant, smooth, and rich. 心地よい，滑らかな ❏His voice was deep and mellow and his speech had a soothing and comforting quality. 低い張りのある声で，人の心を慰め励ますような言葉だった． **3** V-T/V-I 他動詞/自動詞 If someone **mellows** or if something **mellows** them, they become kinder or less extreme in their behavior, especially as a result of growing older. 穏やかにする[他動詞]，穏やかになる[自動詞] ❏He became a taciturn man, a man not easy to live with. Later, when the older children married and had children of their own, he mellowed a little. 彼はむっつりとして一緒に生活しづらい男になっていた．その後，上の子供たちが結婚し孫ができると少し丸みが出てきた． ●ADJ 形容詞 **Mellow** is also an adjective. 穏やかな ❏Is she more mellow and tolerant? 彼女，以前より角がとれて優しくなった？

▶ **mellow out** PHRASAL VERB 句動詞 If someone **mellows out**, they become very relaxed. のんびりくつろぐ [INFORMAL くだけた] ❏Until the moment everyone started telling me to mellow out, I had never been tense for a single moment in my life. みんなからののんびりすればと言われるようになったが，当の本人はそれまで一度だって緊張したことなどなかった．

melo|dra|ma /mélədrɑːmə/ (**melodramas**) N-VAR 可変性名詞 A **melodrama** is a story or play in which there are a lot of exciting or sad events and in which people's emotions are very exaggerated. メロドラマ

melo|dra|mat|ic /mélədrəmǽtɪk/ ADJ 形容詞 **Melodramatic** behavior is behavior in which someone treats a situation as much more serious than it really is. 大げさな ❏"Don't you think you're being slightly melodramatic?" Jane asked. 「自分でもちょっと大げさになってると思わない」とジェーンは聞いた．

melo|dy /mélədi/ (**melodies**) N-COUNT 可算名詞 A **melody** is a tune. メロディー [FORMAL 形式ばった] ❏I whistle melodies from Beethoven and Vivaldi and the more popular classical composers. ベートーベンやビバルディ，さらに人気のあるクラシックの作曲家の旋律を口笛で吹く．

mel|on /mélən/ (**melons**) N-VAR 可変性名詞 A **melon** is a large fruit which is sweet and juicy inside and has a hard green or yellow skin. メロン ❏...some juicy slices of melon. みずみずしい数切れのメロン．

melt /mélt/ (**melts, melting, melted**) **1** V-T/V-I 他動詞/自動詞 When a solid substance **melts** or when you **melt** it, it changes to a liquid, usually because it has been heated. 溶かす [他動詞]，溶ける [自動詞] ❏The snow had melted, but the lake was still frozen solid. 雪は溶けていたが，湖はまだ硬く凍ったままだった． ❏Meanwhile, melt the white chocolate in a bowl suspended over simmering water. その間に，ホワイトチョコレートをボールに入れ熱湯で湯せんして溶かします． **2** V-I 自動詞 If something such as your feelings **melt**, they suddenly disappear and you no longer feel them. 消える [LITERARY 文語的] ❏His anxiety about the outcome melted, only to return later. 結果への彼の不安は消え去ったが，後にその不安が再び戻ることになった． ●PHRASAL VERB 句動詞 **Melt away** means the same as **melt**. 消える ❏When he heard these words, Scot felt his inner doubts melt away. その言葉を耳にしたとき，スコットの心のうちにあった疑いは消えていった． **3** V-I 自動詞 If a person or thing **melts into** something such as darkness or a crowd of people, they become difficult to see, for example because they are moving away from you or are the same color as the background. 溶け込む，紛れ込む [LITERARY 文語的] ❏The youths dispersed and melted into the darkness. 若者たちはばらばらに別れ次第に闇に溶け込んでいった． → see glacier, matter

Thesaurus	*melt* また次を参照：
v.	dissolve, soften, thaw **1**
	disappear, fade **2 3**

melt|down /méltdaʊn/ (**meltdowns**) **1** N-VAR 可変性名詞 If there is **meltdown** in a nuclear reactor, the fuel rods start melting because of a failure in the system, and radiation starts to escape. 炉心溶融，メルトダウン ❏Scientists warned that emergency cooling systems could fail and a reactor meltdown could occur. 科学者たちは，緊急冷却システムが機能せず炉心溶融が発生する危険性があると警告しました． **2** N-UNCOUNT 不可算名詞 The **meltdown** of a company, organization, or system is its sudden and complete failure. 崩壊 [JOURNALISM ジャーナリズム] ❏Urgent talks are going on to prevent the market going into financial meltdown during the summer. 夏場に金融市場が崩壊してしまうのを防ぐため，緊急協議が続けられている．

melt|ing pot (**melting pots**) N-COUNT 可算名詞 A **melting pot** is a place or situation in which people or ideas of different kinds gradually get mixed together. るつぼ ❏The republic is a melting pot of different nationalities. 共和国はまさに人種のるつぼです．

The term **melting pot** is used to picture the mixing of various immigrant traditions together into one American culture. In places where the cultures do not blend but exist intact side by side, this phenomenon has been described as a **mosaic**.

mem|ber /mémbər/ (**members**) **1** N-COUNT 可算名詞 A **member** of a group is one of the people, animals, or things belonging to that group. 一員，メンバー ❏He refused to name the members of staff involved. 彼は関係者の名前を出すのを拒否した． ❏Their lack of training could put members of the public at risk. 彼らの訓練不足によって国民が危険にさらされる可能性がある． **2** N-COUNT 可算名詞 A **member** of an organization such as a club or a political party is a person who has officially joined the organization. 会員 ❏The support of our members is of great importance to the association. 会員の皆さまからのご支援は協会にとって極めて重要です． **3** ADJ 形容詞 A **member country** or **member state** is one of the countries that has joined an international organization or group. 加盟国 [ADJ n] ❏...the member countries of the North American Free Trade Association. 北米自由貿易協定の加盟国． **4** N-COUNT 可算名詞 A **member** or **Member** is a person who has been elected to a legislature or parliament. 議員 ❏He was elected to Parliament as the Member for Leeds. 彼はリーズ選出の下院議員となった．

Mem|ber of Con|gress (**Members of Congress**) N-COUNT 可算名詞 A **Member of Congress** is a person who has been elected to the United States Congress. 連邦下院議員 ❏...the party's only black member of Congress. 党で唯一の黒人下院議員．

Mem|ber of Par|lia|ment (**Members of Parliament**) N-COUNT 可算名詞 A **Member of Parliament** is a person who has been

elected by the people in a particular area to represent them in a country's parliament. The abbreviation **MP** is often used. 下院議員 □ ...the Member of Parliament for Torbay. トーベイ選出の下院議員.

mem|ber|ship /mɛmbərʃɪp/ (**memberships**) **1** N-UNCOUNT 不可算名詞 **Membership** in an organization is the state of being a member of it. 会員であること □ ...his membership in the Communist Party. 彼が共産党員であること. **2** N-VAR-COLL 集合的可変性名詞 The **membership** of an organization is the people who belong to it, or the number of people who belong to it. 会員, 会員数 □ By 1890 the organization had a membership of 409,000. 1890年までに組織は40万9千人の会員を擁するまでになった.

mem|brane /mɛmbreɪn/ (**membranes**) N-COUNT 可算名詞 A **membrane** is a thin piece of skin that connects or covers parts of a person's or animal's body. 皮膜, 薄膜 □ ...inflammation of the thin membrane that lines the heart. 心臓の薄い内膜の炎症.

memo /mɛmoʊ/ (**memos**) N-COUNT 可算名詞 A **memo** is a short official note that is sent by one person to another within the same company or organization. 連絡票 □ He sent out a memo expressing his disagreement with their decisions. 彼はその決定に反対する旨を連絡票で伝えた.

memo|ra|bilia /mɛmərəbɪliə/ N-PLURAL 複数名詞 **Memorabilia** are things that you collect because they are connected with a person or organization in which you are interested. 記念品, 思い出の品 □ ...the country's leading dealer in Beatles memorabilia. ビートルズ関連グッズを扱う国内有数の取扱店.

memo|ra|ble /mɛmərəbəl/ ADJ 形容詞 Something that is **memorable** is worth remembering or likely to be remembered, because it is special or very enjoyable. 記念すべき, 忘れられない □ ...the perfect setting for a nostalgic memorable day. 昔を懐かしむ記念日にぴったりのセッティング.

memo|ran|dum /mɛmərændəm/ (**memoranda** or **memorandums**) **1** N-COUNT 可算名詞 A **memorandum** is a written report that is prepared for a person or committee in order to provide them with information about a particular matter. 覚書 □ ...a memorandum from the Department of Defense on its role. 国防総省がその役割についてまとめた報告書. **2** N-COUNT 可算名詞 A **memorandum** is a short official note that is sent by one person to another within the same company or organization. 回報, 内部文書 [FORMAL 形式ばった] □ ...a memorandum sent to all senior U.N. personnel. 国連の全上級職員に送付された内部文書.

Word Link memor ≈ memory : commemorate, memorial, memory

me|mo|rial /mɪmɔriəl/ (**memorials**) **1** N-COUNT 可算名詞 A **memorial** is a structure built in order to remind people of a famous person or event. 記念館 □ Building a memorial to Columbus has been his lifelong dream. コロンブス記念館の建設は彼の長年の夢でした. **2** ADJ 形容詞 A **memorial** event, object, or prize is in honor of someone who has died, so that they will be remembered. 記念の, 追悼の [ADJ n] □ A memorial service is being held for her at St. Paul's Church. 彼女の追悼式が聖パウロ教会で行われる. **3** N-COUNT 可算名詞 If you say that something will be a **memorial** to someone who has died, you mean that it will continue to exist and remind people of them. 記念物 □ The museum will serve as a memorial to the millions who passed through Ellis Island. 博物館はエリス島を通過した数千万人の移民たちを偲ぶ場所となるでしょう.

Word Link ize ≈ making : finalize, memorize, normalize

memo|rize /mɛməraɪz/ (**memorizes, memorizing, memorized**) V-T 他動詞 If you **memorize** something, you learn it so that you can remember it exactly. 暗記する, 記憶する □ He studied his map, trying to memorize the way to Rose's street. 彼は地図を見ながら, ローズ通りまでの道順を覚えようとした.

memo|ry /mɛmri/ (**memories**) **1** N-VAR 可変性名詞 Your **memory** is your ability to remember things. 記憶力 □ All the details of the meeting are fresh in my memory. 出会ったときのことが克明によみがえってくる. □ But locals with long memories thought this was fair revenge for the injustice of 1961. しかし過去を知る地元住民は, これが1961年の不正に対する当然の仕打ちだと感じた. □ He had a good memory for faces. 彼は人の顔を覚えるのが得意だった. **2** N-COUNT 可算名詞 A **memory** is something that you remember from the past. 思い出 □ She cannot bear to watch the film because of the bad memories it brings back. 彼女はその映画を見ると過去の嫌なことを思い出すので見ていられない. □ Her earliest memory is of singing at the age of four to wounded soldiers. 彼女が最も幼い頃の記憶は, 4歳のときに負傷兵に歌を歌ってあげた記憶である. **3** N-COUNT 可算名詞 A computer's **memory** is the part of the computer where information is stored, especially for a short time before it is transferred to disks or magnetic tapes. メモリー [COMPUTING コンピューティング] □ The data are stored in the computer's memory. データはコンピュータのメモリー上にある. **4** N-SING 単数名詞 If you talk about the **memory** of someone who has died, especially someone who was loved or respected, you are referring to the thoughts, actions, and ceremonies by which they are remembered. 追悼 □ She remained devoted to his memory. 彼女はまだ亡くなった彼のことしか考えられなかった. **5** PHRASE 句 If you say that someone is taking a walk or trip **down memory lane**, you mean that they are talking, writing, or thinking about something that happened to them a long time ago. 思い出をたどる [INFORMAL くだけた] □ His 1998 memoir is a delightful trip down memory lane. 1998年に出た彼の自叙伝は思い出をたどる楽しい旅である. **6** PHRASE 句 If you do something **from memory**, for example speak the words of a poem or play a piece of music, you do it without looking at it, because you know it very well. 記憶をたよりに □ Many members of the church sang from memory. 教会の多くの参列者がそらで歌った. **7** PHRASE 句 If you say that something is, for example, the best, worst, or first thing of its kind **in living memory**, you are emphasizing that it is the only thing of that kind that people can remember. 知っている限り [EMPHASIS 強調] □ The floods are the worst in living memory. 記憶に残るものとしては最もひどい洪水です. **8** PHRASE 句 If you **lose your memory**, you forget things that you used to know. 記憶を失う □ His illness caused him to lose his memory. その病気のせいで彼は記憶を失った. **9** to **commit** something **to memory** → see **commit** → see Word Web: **memory**

Word Partnership memory は次の語句と使われる:

ADJ.	**collective** memory, **conscious** memory, **failing** memory, **fresh in** your memory, **long-/short-term** memory, **poor** memory, **in recent** memory **1** **bad** memory, **good** memory **1 2** **happy** memory, **painful** memory, **sad** memory, **vivid** memory **2**
N.	**computer** memory, **random access** memory, memory **storage 3**

memo|ry card (**memory cards**) N-COUNT 可算名詞 A **memory card** is a type of card containing computer memory that is used in digital cameras and other devices. メモリーカード [COMPUTING]

men /mɛn/ **Men** is the plural of **man**. man の複数形

men|ace /mɛnɪs/ (**menaces, menacing, menaced**) **1** N-COUNT 可算名詞 If you say that someone or something is a **menace** to other people or things, you mean that person or thing is likely to cause serious harm. 脅威となるもの □ In my view, you are a menace to the public. わたしに言わせれば, きみは社会の脅威だよ. **2** N-COUNT 可算名詞 You can refer to someone or something as a **menace** when you want to say that they cause you trouble or annoyance. 厄介者, 厄介ごと [INFORMAL くだけた] □ You're a menace to my privacy, Kenton. ケントン, あなたってほんと私生活に首を突っ込むぎわよね. **3** N-UNCOUNT 不可算名詞 **Menace** is a quality or atmosphere that gives you the feeling that you are in danger or that someone wants to harm you. 脅威 □ There is a pervading sense of menace. 危機感が広がっている. **4** V-T 他動詞 If you say that one thing **menaces** another, you mean that the first thing is likely to cause the second thing serious harm. 脅威を与える □ They seem determined to menace the United States and its allies. 彼らは意を決して

Word Web memory

Scientists divide **memory** into three types. **Short-term** memory holds small amounts of information for a short time. The information is then **forgotten**. Short-term memory lasts from two to thirty seconds. Working memory organizes items in the short-term memory. For example, adding up several numbers in your mind involves working memory. **Long-term** memory can last for years. Several things influence long-term memory. You remember an event with meaningful **associations** better than a routine event. **Rehearsing** the information also helps preserve a long-term memory. In addition, mnemonics can help you **remember** the most important details.

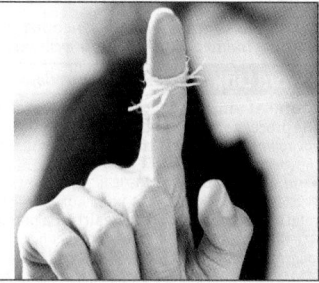

アメリカとその同盟国に脅威を与えようしているようである.

men|ac|ing /mɛnɪsɪŋ/ ADJ 形容詞 If someone or something looks **menacing**, they give you a feeling that they are likely to cause you harm or put you in danger. 脅すような □ *The strong, dark eyebrows give his face an oddly menacing look.* しっかりした濃いまゆ毛のせいでその顔は妙にこわそうである. ●**men|ac|ing|ly** ADV 副詞 脅すように □ *A group of men suddenly emerged from a doorway and moved menacingly forward to block her way.* 突然, 数人の男たちが入口から現れると, 彼女の行く手をさえぎろうと脅すように前に踏み出した.

mend /mɛnd/ (**mends, mending, mended**) ◼ V-T 動詞 If you **mend** a tear or a hole in a piece of clothing, you repair it by sewing it. 繕う □ *Men say that we are only good for cooking their meals and mending their socks.* 男は, 女にできることといえば食事の支度と靴下の修繕ぐらいだという. ◻ V-T/V-I 他動詞/自動詞 If a person or a part of their body **mends** or is **mended**, they get better after they have been ill or have had an injury. 治る □ *I'm feeling a lot better. The cut aches, but it's mending.* だいぶ元気になったよ. 傷は痛むけど, 治ってきてるし. ◼ V-T 他動詞 If you try to **mend** divisions between people, you try to end the disagreements or quarrels between them. 修復する □ *He sent Evans as his personal envoy to discuss ways to mend relations between the two countries.* 両国間の関係修復の打開策を協議するため, 彼はエバンスを自分の特使として派遣した. ◼ V-T 他動詞 If you **mend** something that is broken or not working, you repair it, so that it works properly or can be used. 修理する [mainly BRIT 主に英国英語] □ *They took a long time to mend the roof.* 彼らは屋根を修理するのにずいぶん時間がかかった. ◼ PHRASE 句 If a relationship or situation is on the **mend** after a difficult or unsuccessful period, it is improving. 改善して [INFORMAL くだけた] □ *More evidence that the economy was on the mend was needed.* 景気回復のさらなる裏付けが必要だった. ◼ PHRASE 句 If you are on the **mend** after an illness or injury, you are recovering from it. 回復して [INFORMAL くだけた] □ *The baby had been ill but seemed to be on the mend.* 赤ん坊はずっと病気だったが, 快方に向かっているようだった. ◼ PHRASE 句 If someone who has been behaving badly **mends** their **ways**, they begin to behave well. 改心する □ *He has promised drastic disciplinary action if they do not mend their ways.* 彼らが行いを改めなければ必ず厳しく処罰すると, 彼は言った.

me|nial /miniəl, mɪnyəl/ ADJ 形容詞 **Menial** work is very boring, and the people who do it have a low status and are usually badly paid. 単調な □ *...low-paid menial jobs, such as cleaning and domestic work.* 清掃や家事といった低賃金の単純労働.

Word Link *itis ≈ inflammation : arthritis, hepatitis, meningitis*

men|in|gi|tis /mɛnɪndʒaɪtɪs/ N-UNCOUNT 不可算名詞 **Meningitis** is a serious infectious illness which affects your brain and spinal cord. 髄膜炎

meno|pause /mɛnəpɔz/ N-SING 単数名詞 **Menopause** is the time during which a woman gradually stops menstruating, usually when she is about fifty years old. 更年期 □ *...alternative therapies to fight the symptoms of menopause.* 更年期の症状を緩和する代替療法. ●**meno|pau|sal** ADJ 形容詞 更年期の □ *A menopausal woman of average build and height requires 1600 – 2400 calories daily.* 更年期になると, 平均的な身長と体型の女性で1日1600〜2400cal必要である.

men|strual /mɛnstruəl/ ADJ 形容詞 **Menstrual** means relating to menstruation. 月経の, 生理の [ADJ n] □ *...the menstrual cycle.* 生理周期.

men|stru|ate /mɛnstrueɪt/ V-I 自動詞 When a woman **menstruates**, a flow of blood comes from her uterus. Women menstruate once a month unless they are pregnant or have reached menopause. 生理がある [FORMAL 形式ばった] □ *Lean, hard-training women athletes may menstruate less frequently or not at all.* 運動量の多い筋肉質の女性運動選手の場合, 生理が少なかったり全くなかったりすることがある. ●**men|strua|tion** /mɛnstrueɪʃən/ N-UNCOUNT 不可算名詞 月経, 生理 □ *Menstruation may cease when a woman is anywhere between forty-five and fifty years of age.* 女性は45歳から50歳で閉経になることがある.

mens|wear /mɛnzwɛər/ N-UNCOUNT 不可算名詞 **Menswear** is clothing for men. 紳士服 □ *...the menswear industry.* 紳士服業界

Word Link *ment ≈ mind : dementia, mental, mentality*

men|tal /mɛntəl/ ◼ ADJ 形容詞 **Mental** means relating to the process of thinking. 精神の, 知能の [ADJ n] □ *The intellectual environment has a significant influence on the mental development of the children.* 知的な環境は子供の知能の発達に大きな影響を及ぼす. ●**men|tal|ly** ADV 副詞 精神的に □ *I think you are mentally tired.* 精神的に疲れているんじゃない. ◻ ADJ 形容詞 **Mental** means relating to the state or the health of a person's mind. 精神状態の, 精神衛生の □ *The mental state that had created her psychosis was no longer present.* 彼女は精神障害を引き起こした以前の精神状態とは違っていた. ●**men|tal|ly** ADV 副詞 精神的に, 精神衛生上 □ *...an inmate*

who is mentally disturbed. 精神病を患う収容者 ◼ ADJ 形容詞 [ADJ n] A **mental** act is one that involves only thinking and not physical action. 頭の中でする □ *Practice mental arithmetic when you go out shopping.* 買い物のときには暗算の練習をしましょう. ●**men|tal|ly** ADV 副詞 [ADV with v] 頭の中で □ *This technique will help people mentally organize information.* この方法は頭の中で情報を整理するのに役立つ.
→ see **hypnosis**

men|tal|ity /mɛntælɪti/ (**mentalities**) N-COUNT 可算名詞 Your **mentality** is your attitudes and your way of thinking. 考え方 □ *...a criminal mentality.* 犯罪者の心理

men|tion /mɛnʃən/ (**mentions, mentioning, mentioned**) ◼ V-T 他動詞 If you **mention** something, you say something about it, usually briefly. 触れる, 言及する □ *She did not mention her mother's absence.* 彼女は母親がいないことは言わなかった. □ *I may not have mentioned it to her.* そのことは彼女に何も言わなかったかもしれない. □ *I had mentioned that I didn't really like contemporary music.* 現代音楽があまり好きでないことは前に話したことがある. ◻ N-VAR 可変性名詞 A **mention** is a reference to something or someone. 言及 □ *The statement made no mention of government casualties.* 声明では政府側の死傷者についての言及はありませんでした. ◼ V-T 他動詞 If someone is **mentioned** in writing, a reference is made to them by name, often to criticize or praise something that they have done. 名前が出される [usu passive] □ *I was absolutely outraged that I could be even mentioned in an article of this kind.* この手の記事に自分の名前が出されたことに激怒した. ◼ N-VAR 可変性名詞 A special or honorable **mention** is formal praise that is given for an achievement that is very good, although not usually the best of its kind. 表彰 □ *Two of the losers deserve special mention: Caroline Swaithes, of Kingston, and Maria Pons, of Valley Stream.* 優勝を逃したキングストンのキャロライン・スウェイシス, バリーストリームのマリア・ポンスの2名は特別賞に値する. ◼ CONVENTION 慣習表現 People sometimes say "**don't mention it**" as a polite reply to someone who has just thanked them for doing something. どういたしまして [FORMULAE 決まり文句] □ *"Thank you very much." — "Don't mention it."* 「どうもありがとう」「どういたしまして」

If you **mention** something, you say it, but only briefly, especially when you have not talked about it before. □ *He mentioned that he might go to New York.* If you **comment** on a situation, or make a **comment** about it, you give your opinion on it. □ *Mr. Cook has not commented on these reports… I was wondering whether you had any comments.* If you **remark** on something, or make a **remark** about it, you say what you think or what you have noticed, often in a casual way. □ *Visitors remark on how well the children look… General Sutton's remarks about the conflict.*

Word Partnership mention は次の語句と使われる:

v.	**fail to** mention, **forget to** mention, **neglect to** mention ◼ **make *no*** mention **of** *someone/something* ◻
ADJ.	**honorable** mention, **special** mention ◼

men|tor /mɛntɔr/ (**mentors, mentoring, mentored**) ◼ N-COUNT 可算名詞 A person's **mentor** is someone who gives them help and advice over a period of time, especially help and advice related to their job. 助言者, 先輩 □ *Leon Sullivan was my mentor and my friend.* レオン・サリバンはわたしのよき師であり友人だった. ◻ V-T 他動詞 To **mentor** someone means to give them help and advice over a period of time, especially help and advice related to their job. 助言者となる □ *He had mentored scores of younger doctors.* 彼は多くの若い医師を育てていた.

menu /mɛnyu/ (**menus**) ◼ N-COUNT 可算名詞 In a restaurant or café or at a formal meal, the **menu** is a list of the meals and drinks that are available. メニュー □ *A waiter offered him the menu.* ウェイターは彼にメニューを渡した. ◻ N-COUNT 可算名詞 A **menu** is the food that you serve at a meal. 献立 □ *Try out the menu on a few friends.* その料理を数人の友達に試してもらってください. ◼ N-COUNT 可算名詞 On a computer screen, a **menu** is a list of choices. Each choice represents something that you can do using the computer. メニュー □ *Hold down the shift key and press F7 to display the print menu.* シフトキーを押したままF7を押して, 印刷メニューを表示します.

MEP /ɛm i pi/ (**MEPs**) N-COUNT 可算名詞 An **MEP** is a person who has been elected to the European Parliament. **MEP** is an abbreviation for "Member of the European Parliament." 欧州議会議員 □ *...Tuesday's secret ballot of Europe's 626 MEPs.* 欧州議会議員626名を選ぶ火曜日の無記名投票

mer|ce|nary /mɜrsəneri/ (**mercenaries**) ◼ N-COUNT 可算名詞 A **mercenary** is a soldier who is paid to fight for a country or group that they do not belong to. 傭兵 □ *...the recruitment of foreign mercenaries.* 外国人傭兵の募集 ◻ ADJ 形容詞 If you describe someone as **mercenary**, you are criticizing them because you think that they are only interested in the money that they can

M

get from a particular person or situation. 金目当ての [DISAPPROVAL 不賛成] ❑ *"I hate to sound mercenary," Labane said, "but am I getting paid to be in this play of yours?"*「金目当てだと思われたくないんだけど、きみのこの芝居に出たら報酬は出してもらえるのか」とラバンは言った.

mer|chan|dise /mɜrtʃəndaɪz, -daɪs/ N-UNCOUNT 不可算名詞 **Merchandise** is products that are bought, sold, or traded. 商品, 製品 [FORMAL 形式ばった] ❑ *...a mail-order company that provides merchandise for people suffering from allergies.* アレルギーの人向けの商品を提供する通信販売会社.

mer|chan|dis|er /mɜrtʃəndaɪzər/ (**merchandisers**) N-COUNT 可算名詞 A **merchandiser** is a person or company that sells products to the public. 小売業者, 小売店 [AM 米国英語 BUSINESS 実業] ❑ *In 1979, Liquor Barn thrived as a discount merchandiser.* 1979年, リカー・バーンはディスカウントショップとして成功した.

mer|chan|dis|ing /mɜrtʃəndaɪzɪŋ/ N-UNCOUNT 不可算名詞 **Merchandising** is used to refer to the way stores and businesses organize the sale of their products, for example the way they are displayed and the prices that are chosen. 商品化計画, マーチャンダイジング [mainly AM 主に米国英語 BUSINESS 実業] ❑ *Company executives say revamped merchandising should help Macy's earnings to grow.* 企業の管理職の話では, マーチャンダイジングを見直せばメーシーズの増益につながるといいます. ❷ N-UNCOUNT 不可算名詞 **Merchandising** consists of goods such as toys and clothes that are linked with something such as a movie, sports team, or pop group. キャラクター商品 ❑ *We are selling the full range of World Cup merchandising.* 当店ではワールドカップ関連グッズを幅広く取り揃えております.

mer|chant /mɜrtʃənt/ (**merchants**) ❶ N-COUNT 可算名詞 A **merchant** is a person who buys or sells goods in large quantities, especially one who imports and exports them. 卸売業者; 貿易業者 ❑ *Any knowledgeable wine merchant would be able to advise you.* ワインに詳しい専門の業者に聞けば答えてもらえるでしょう. ❷ N-COUNT 可算名詞 A **merchant** is a person who owns or runs a store, or other business. 小売店主 [AM 米国英語] ❑ *The family was forced to live on credit from local merchants.* 家族は近所の店につけをして生活していくほかなかった. ❸ ADJ 形容詞 **Merchant** seamen or ships are involved in carrying goods for trade. 商業の [ADJ n] ❑ *There's been a big reduction in the size of the merchant fleet in recent years.* 近年, 商船隊の規模は大幅に縮小しています.

mer|chant bank (**merchant banks**) N-COUNT 可算名詞 A **merchant bank** is the same as an **investment bank**. 投資銀行

mer|chant bank|er (**merchant bankers**) N-COUNT 可算名詞 A **merchant banker** is the same as an **investment banker**. 投資銀行の行員

mer|ci|ful|ly /mɜrsɪfəli/ ADV 副詞 You can use **mercifully** to show that you are glad that something good has happened, or that something bad has not happened or has stopped. 幸いにも [FEELINGS 感情] ❑ *Mercifully, a friend came to the rescue.* 幸いにも友人が助けに来てくれた.

mer|ci|less /mɜrsɪlɪs/ ADJ 形容詞 If you describe someone as **merciless**, you mean that they are very cruel or determined and do not show any concern for the effect their actions have on other people. 情け容赦のない ❑ *...the merciless efficiency of a modern police state.* 現代の警察国家における非情なまでの効率重視 ● **mer|ci|less|ly** ADV 副詞 情け容赦なく ❑ *We teased him mercilessly.* 彼のことを手加減せずにからかった.

mer|cu|ry /mɜrkyəri/ N-UNCOUNT 不可算名詞 **Mercury** is a silver-colored liquid metal that is used especially in thermometers and barometers. 水銀

mer|cy /mɜrsi/ (**mercies**) ❶ N-UNCOUNT 不可算名詞 If someone in authority shows **mercy**, they choose not to harm someone they have power over, or they forgive someone they have the right to punish. 情け, 寛大な措置 ❑ *Neither side took prisoners or showed any mercy.* どちらも捕虜をとることも情けをかけることもなかった. ❷ ADJ 形容詞 **Mercy** is used to describe a special journey to help someone in great need, such as people who are sick or made homeless by war. 救援の [JOURNALISM ジャーナリズム] [ADJ n] ❑ *She vanished nine months ago while on a mercy mission to West Africa.* 彼女は9か月前に西アフリカで救援活動に当たっている最中に行方不明になった. ❸ N-COUNT 可算名詞 If you refer to an event or a situation as a **mercy**, you mean that it makes you feel happy or relieved, usually because it stops something unpleasant from happening. 幸い ❑ *It really was a mercy that he'd gone so rapidly at the end.* やつがとっととあの世に行ってくれたおかげで本当に助かった. ❹ PHRASE 句 If one person or thing is **at the mercy of** another, the first person or thing is in a situation where they cannot prevent themselves from being harmed or affected by the second. のなすがままに ❑ *Buildings are left to decay at the mercy of vandals and the weather.* 建物は風雨にさらされ破壊されるがままに放置されている.

mere /mɪər/ (**merest**)

Mere does not have a comparative form. The superlative form **merest** is used to emphasize how small something is, rather than in comparisons.

Mere は比較形がない. 最上級形 **merest** は比較よりもむしろ, ある物がいかに小さいかを強調するのに使われる.

❶ ADJ 形容詞 You use **mere** to emphasize how unimportant or inadequate something is, in comparison to the general situation you are describing. 単なる, ほんの [EMPHASIS 強調] [ADJ n] ❑ *...successful exhibitions which go beyond mere success.* 単なる成功以上の成功を収めた展覧会. ❑ *There is more to good health than the mere absence of disease.* ただ病気をしていなければ健康だというわけではない. ❷ ADJ 形容詞 You use **mere** to indicate that a quality or action that is usually unimportant has a very important or strong effect. ちょっとした [ADJ n] ❑ *The mere mention of food had triggered off hunger pangs.* 食べ物の話を少しでもすると, 空腹で腹が痛くなった. ❸ ADJ 形容詞 You use **mere** to emphasize how small a particular amount or number is. たったの, わずか [EMPHASIS 強調] ['a' ADJ amount] ❑ *Sixty percent of teachers are women, but a mere five percent of women are principals.* 女性の教師は6割を占めるが, うち校長はわずか5%にすぎない.

mere|ly /mɪərli/ ❶ ADV 副詞 You use **merely** to emphasize that something is only what you say and not better, more important, or more exciting. ただのにすぎない [EMPHASIS 強調] ❑ *Michael is now merely a good friend.* マイケルはもうただのよい友人よ. ❑ *Francis Watson was far from being merely a furniture expert.* フランシス・ワトソンは単なる家具のエキスパートにとどまらなかった. ❷ ADV 副詞 You use **merely** to emphasize that a particular amount or quantity is very small. たった, しか [EMPHASIS 強調] [ADV amount] ❑ *The brain accounts for merely three percent of body weight.* 脳の重さは体重のわずか3%にすぎない. ❸ PHRASE 句 You use **not merely** before the less important of two contrasting statements, as a way of emphasizing the more important one. ただではなく [EMPHASIS 強調] ❑ *The team needs players who want to play for Canada, not merely any country that will have them.* チームが求めているのはカナダのために戦ってくれる選手で, ただ雇ってくれればどの国でもよいという選手ではない.

merge /mɜrdʒ/ (**merges, merging, merged**) ❶ V-RECIP 相互動詞 If one thing **merges with** another, or **is merged with** another, they combine or come together to make one whole thing. You can also say that two things **merge**, or **are merged**. 1つになる, 合併する ❑ *Bank of America merged with a rival bank.* バンク・オブ・アメリカはライバル行と合併した. ❑ *The rivers merge just north of a vital irrigation system.* 川の合流地点は重要な灌漑(かんがい)システムのちょうど北に位置しています. ❑ *The two countries merged into one.* 両国は合併した. ❷ V-RECIP 相互動詞 If one sound, color, or object **merges** into another, the first changes so gradually into the second that you do not notice the change. 次第に溶け込む ❑ *Like a chameleon, he could merge unobtrusively into the background.* 彼はカメレオンのように人目につかずに周囲の色に合わせることができた. ❑ *His features merged with the darkness.* 彼の顔は暗闇に消えていった.

mer|ger /mɜrdʒər/ (**mergers**) N-COUNT 可算名詞 A **merger** is the joining together of two separate companies or organizations so that they become one. 合併 [BUSINESS 実業] ❑ *...a merger between two of America's biggest trade unions.* アメリカの二大労働組合の合併.

mer|it /mɛrɪt/ (**merits, meriting, merited**) ❶ N-UNCOUNT 不可算名詞 If something has **merit**, it has good or worthwhile qualities. 価値 ❑ *The argument seemed to have considerable merit.* 有意義な話し合いが行われた模様です. ❷ N-PLURAL 複数名詞 The **merits** of something are its advantages or other good points. 長所, 利点 ❑ *They have been persuaded of the merits of peace.* 彼らは平和の恩恵をずっと信じてきた. ❸ V-T 他動詞 If someone or something **merits** a particular action or treatment, they deserve it. 値する [FORMAL 形式ばった] ❑ *He said he had done nothing wrong to merit a criminal investigation.* 彼は警察の捜査を受けるような悪いことは何もしていないと話しました.

mer|maid /mɜrmeɪd/ (**mermaids**) N-COUNT 可算名詞 In fairy tales and legends, a **mermaid** is a woman with a fish's tail instead of legs, who lives in the sea. 人魚

mer|ri|ly /mɛrɪli/ ❶ ADV 副詞 If you say that someone **merrily** does something, you are critical of the fact that they do it without realizing that there are a lot of problems which they

have not thought about. 無頓着に [DISAPPROVAL 不賛成] [ADV with v] □ *There they were, merrily describing their 16-hour working days while claiming to be happily married.* それで2人は、何気ない調子で日に16時間働くと語り、それでも結婚生活は幸せだと話していた。 **2** ADV 副詞 If you say that something is happening **merrily**, you mean that it is happening fairly quickly, and in a pleasant or satisfactory way. 軽快な [ADV with v] □ *The ferry cut merrily through the water.* フェリーは波を切って颯爽（さっそう）と進んだ。

mer|ry /mɛri/ (**merrier, merriest**) **1** ADJ 形容詞 If you describe someone's character or behavior as **merry**, you mean that they are happy and cheerful. 楽しい、陽気な [OLD FASHIONED 古風な] □ *From the house come bursts of merry laughter.* 家の中からはじけるような楽しい笑い声が聞こえてくる。 ● **mer|ri|ly** ADV 副詞 [ADV after v] 楽しそうに □ *Chris threw back his head and laughed merrily.* クリスは頭をのけぞらせて楽しそうに笑った。 **2** CONVENTION 慣習表現 Just before Christmas and on Christmas Day, people say "**Merry Christmas**" to other people to express the hope that they will have a happy time. メリー・クリスマス [FORMULAE 決まり文句] □ *Merry Christmas, everyone.* みなさん、メリー・クリスマス！

merry-go-round (**merry-go-rounds**) **1** N-COUNT 可算名詞 A **merry-go-round** is a circular platform at a carnival or amusement park on which there are model animals or vehicles for people to ride on as it turns around. メリーゴーランド、回転木馬 **2** N-COUNT 可算名詞 You can refer to a continuous series of activities as a **merry-go-round**. 慌しく続く出来事 [usu sing, oft N 'of' n] □ *...a merry-go-round of parties, dances, musical events, and the like.* パーティー、ダンス、音楽イベントなどがひっきりなしに続く.

mesh /mɛʃ/ (**meshes, meshing, meshed**) **1** N-VAR 可変性名詞 **Mesh** is material like a net made from wire, thread, or plastic. 網 □ *The ground-floor windows are obscured by wire mesh.* 1階の窓は金網で目隠ししている。 **2** V-RECIP 相互動詞 If two things or ideas **mesh** or **are meshed**, they go together well or fit together closely. ぴったり合う □ *Their senses of humor meshed perfectly.* 彼らのユーモアのセンスはぴったり合っていた。 □ *This of course meshes with the economic philosophy of those on the right.* 当然ながらこれは右派の経済哲学とうまく合致する.

mes|mer|ize /mɛzməraɪz/ (**mesmerizes, mesmerizing, mesmerized**) V-T 他動詞 If you **are mesmerized** by something, you are so interested in it or so attracted to it that you cannot think about anything else. 魅了される □ *He was absolutely mesmerized by Pavarotti on television.* 彼はテレビのパバロッティにすっかり魅了された.

mess /mɛs/ (**messes, messing, messed**) **1** N-SING 単数名詞 If you say that something is **a mess** or **in a mess**, you think that it is not neat. 散乱 [also no det] □ *The house is a mess.* 家は散らかっている. **2** N-VAR 可変性名詞 If you say that a situation is **a mess**, you mean that it is full of trouble or problems. You can also say that something is **in a mess**. 混乱 □ *I've made such a mess of my life.* 自分で人生をめちゃくちゃにしてしまった。 □ *...the many reasons why the economy is in such a mess.* このような経済の混乱を招いた多くの原因 **3** N-VAR 可変性名詞 A **mess** is something liquid or sticky that has been accidentally dropped on something. こぼしたもの □ *I'll clear up the mess later.* 汚れたところは後できれいにしておくよ. **4** N-COUNT 可算名詞 The **mess** at a military base or military barracks is the building in which members of the armed forces can eat or relax. 軍隊の食堂 □ *...a party at the officers' mess.* 将校の会食堂でのパーティー.

▶ **mess around** **1** PHRASAL VERB 句動詞 If you **mess around**, you spend time doing things without any particular purpose or without achieving anything. ぶらぶらする □ *We were just messing around playing with paint.* 僕たちは何を描くともなく絵の具をいじって遊んでいた。 **2** PHRASAL VERB 句動詞 If you say that someone **is messing around with** something, you mean that they are interfering with it in a harmful way. の邪魔をする □ *"Don't be stupid," Max snapped. "You don't want to go messing around with bears."* 「何してるんだ。クマにちょっかいを出すとえらいことになるぞ」と、マックスはどなった. **3** PHRASAL VERB 句動詞 If someone **is messing around**, they are behaving in a joking or silly way. ふざける □ *I thought she was messing around.* 彼女はふざけているのだと思った.

▶ **mess up** **1** PHRASAL VERB 句動詞 If you **mess** something **up** or if you **mess up**, you cause something to fail or be spoiled. 台なしにする [INFORMAL くだけた] □ *When politicians mess things up, it is the people who pay the price.* 政治家の失敗のつけを払わされるのは国民である. □ *He had messed up one career.* 彼はずっと続けてきた仕事をだめにしてしまっていた。 **2** PHRASAL VERB 句動詞 If you **mess up** a place or a thing, you make it dirty or not neat. 汚す、散らかす [INFORMAL くだけた] □ *I hope they haven't messed up your video tapes.* やつらがきみのビデオテープをめちゃくちゃにしてなかったらいいんだけど.

▶ **mess with** PHRASAL VERB 句動詞 If you tell someone not to **mess with** a person or thing, you are warning them not to get involved with that person or thing. おせっかいする □ *You are messing with people's religion and they don't like that.* 他人の宗教に首を

突っ込んでくるけど、みんな快く思ってないよ.

V.	clean up a **mess**, leave a **mess**, make a **mess** **1** – **3** get into a **mess** **2**

mes|sage /mɛsɪdʒ/ (**messages, messaging, messaged**) **1** N-COUNT 可算名詞 A **message** is a piece of information or a request that you send to someone or leave for them when you cannot speak to them directly. 伝言、メッセージ □ *I got a message you were trying to reach me.* 連絡をとろうとしてくれていたという伝言をもらいました. **2** N-COUNT 可算名詞 The **message** that someone is trying to communicate, for example in a book or play, is the idea or point that they are trying to communicate. 意図 □ *The report's message was unequivocal.* 報告書の意図は明らかだった. □ *I no longer want to be friends with her but I don't know how to get the message across.* 彼女とはもう友達の縁を切りたいけど、どうやってそれを伝えたらいいものやら. **3** V-T/V-I 他動詞/自動詞 If you **message** someone, you send them a message electronically using a computer or another device such as a cellphone. メッセージを送る □ *People who message a lot feel unpopular if they don't get many back.* たくさんのメッセージを送ると、返事が来ないと自分が嫌われているのではないかと思うようになる.

V.	give *someone* a **message**, leave a **message**, read a **message**, take a **message** **1**
	deliver a **message**, get a **message**, hear a **message**, send a **message** **1** **2**
	get a **message across**, spread a **message** **2**
ADJ.	clear **message**, important **message**, urgent **message** **1** **2**
	powerful **message**, simple **message**, strong **message**, wrong **message** **2**

mes|sag|ing /mɛsɪdʒɪŋ/ N-UNCOUNT 不可算名詞 **Messaging** is the sending of written or spoken messages using a computer or another electronic device such as a cellphone. メッセージング（電子メール・チャットなど） □ *Messaging allows real-time communication by keyboard with up to five people at any one time.* メッセージングを利用すると、一度に最高5人とキーボードを使いリアルタイムのコミュニケーションができる.

mes|sen|ger /mɛsɪndʒər/ (**messengers**) N-COUNT 可算名詞 A **messenger** takes a message to someone, or takes messages regularly as their job. 配達人 [also 'by' N] □ *There will be a messenger at the airport to collect the photographs from our courier.* 空港で使いの者から写真を受け取って誰かが届けてくれるだろう.

messy /mɛsi/ (**messier, messiest**) **1** ADJ 形容詞 A **messy** person or activity makes things dirty or not neat. 汚す、散らかす □ *She was a good, if messy, cook.* 彼女は台所を散らかすけども、料理の腕はよかった. **2** ADJ 形容詞 Something that is **messy** is dirty or not neat. 汚い、散らかった □ *Don't worry if this first coat of paint looks messy.* 下塗りがきれいに塗れてなくても構いません. **3** ADJ 形容詞 If you describe a situation as **messy**, you are emphasizing that it is confused or complicated, and therefore unsatisfactory. 混乱した、やっかいな □ *John had been through a messy divorce himself.* ジョン自身も離婚のごたごたを経験していた.

met /mɛt/ **Met** is the past tense and past participle of **meet**. meet の過去・過去分詞

meta|bol|ic /mɛtəbɒlɪk/ ADJ 形容詞 **Metabolic** means relating to a person's or animal's metabolism. 新陳代謝の [ADJ n] □ *People who have inherited a low metabolic rate will gain weight.* 遺伝的に新陳代謝が低いと肥満になる.

me|tabo|lism /mɪtæbəlɪzəm/ (**metabolisms**) N-VAR 可変性名詞 Your **metabolism** is the way that chemical processes in your body cause food to be used in an efficient way, for example to make new cells and to give you energy. 新陳代謝 □ *If you skip breakfast, your metabolism slows down.* 朝食を抜くと新陳代謝が悪くなる.

met|al /mɛtºl/ (**metals**) N-MASS 質量名詞 **Metal** is a hard substance such as iron, steel, gold, or lead. 金属 □ *...pieces of furniture in wood, metal, and glass.* 木と金属とガラスでできた数点の家具.

→ see Word Web: **metal**
→ see **can, mineral**

me|tal|lic /mətælɪk/ **1** ADJ 形容詞 A **metallic** sound is like the sound of one piece of metal hitting another. 金属的な □ *There was a metallic click and the gates swung open.* カチャという金属的な音を立てて勢いよく門が開いた. **2** ADJ 形容詞 **Metallic** paint or colors shine like metal. 金属光沢のある □ *He had painted all the wood with*

Word Web   metal

In their natural state, most **metals** are not pure. They are usually combined with other materials in mixtures known as **ores**. Almost all metals are **shiny**. Many metals share these special properties–they are ductile, meaning that they can be made into **wire**; they are malleable and can be formed into thin, flat sheets; they are also good **conductors** of heat and electricity. Except for **copper** and **gold**, metals are generally gray or silver in color.

metallic silver paint. 彼は木材全体をメタリックシルバーのペンキで塗っていた. **3** ADJ 形容詞 Something that tastes **metallic** has a bitter, unpleasant taste. 金(かな)臭い □*There was a metallic taste at the back of his throat.* のどの奥のほうで苦い変な味がした. **4** ADJ 形容詞 **Metallic** means consisting entirely or partly of metal. 金属製の □*Even the smallest metallic object, whether a nail file or cigarette lighter, is immediately confiscated.* 爪やすりでもライターでも、金属製のものならどんなに小さいものでもすぐに没収される.

Word Link   *meta ≈ beyond, change : metabolism, metamorphosis, metaphor*

Word Link   *osis ≈ state or condition : hypnosis, metamorphosis, psychosis*

meta|mor|pho|sis /mɛtəmɔrfəsɪs/ (**metamorphoses**) N-VAR 可変性名詞 When a **metamorphosis** occurs, a person or thing develops and changes into something completely different. 大変貌(へんぼう)[FORMAL 形式ばった] □*...his metamorphosis from a Republican to a Democrat.* 彼の共和党員から民主党員への大転身.

meta|phor /mɛtəfər/ (**metaphors**) **1** N-VAR 可変性名詞 A **metaphor** is an imaginative way of describing something by referring to something else which is the same in a particular way. For example, if you want to say that someone is very shy and frightened of things, you might say that they are a mouse. 比喩(ひゆ)例え □*...the avoidance of violent expressions and metaphors like "kill two birds with one stone."* 激しい表現や「一石二鳥」のような比喩は使わないこと. **2** N-VAR 可変性名詞 If one thing is a **metaphor** for another, it is intended or regarded as a symbol of it. 象徴 □*The divided family remains a powerful metaphor for a society that continued to tear itself apart.* その離散家族が分断の続いた社会を今なお如実に象徴している. **3** PHRASE 句 If you **mix** your **metaphors**, you use two conflicting metaphors. People do this accidentally, or sometimes deliberately as a joke. 隠喩(いんゆ)を混用する □*To mix yet more metaphors, you were trying to run before you could walk, and I've clipped your wings.* 変な例えをするなら、お前はまだ歩けないうちから走ろうとしていたから、わたしはお前の羽を切り落として飛べなくしたんだよ.

meta|phori|cal /mɛtəfɔrɪkəl/ ADJ 形容詞 You use the word **metaphorical** to indicate that you are not using words with their ordinary meaning, but are describing something by means of an image or symbol. 比喩的な □*It turns out Levy is talking in metaphorical terms.* レビーは例え話をしていることが分かる. ● **meta|phori|cal|ly** ADV 副詞 比喩的に □*You're speaking metaphorically, I hope.* それって、例えで言ってるんだよね.

mete /mit/ (**metes, meting, meted**)
▸ **mete out** PHRASAL VERB 句動詞 To **mete out** a punishment means to order that someone should be punished in a certain way. 罰を与える [FORMAL 形式ばった] □*His father meted out punishment with a slipper.* 彼の父は部屋ばきでおしおきをした.

me|teor /mitiər/ (**meteors**) N-COUNT 可算名詞 A **meteor** is a piece of rock or metal that burns very brightly when it enters the Earth's atmosphere from space. 流星
→ see Word Web: meteor

Word Link   *ite ≈ mineral, rock : granite, graphite, meteorite*

me|teor|ite /mitiəraɪt/ (**meteorites**) N-COUNT 可算名詞 A **meteorite** is a large piece of rock or metal from space that has landed on earth. 隕石(いんせき)

me|teoro|logi|cal /mitiərəlɒdʒɪkəl/ ADJ 形容詞 **Meteorological** means relating to meteorology. 気象の、気象学の [ADJ n] □*...adverse meteorological conditions.* 悪天候.

me|teor|ol|ogy /mitiərɒlədʒi/ N-UNCOUNT 不可算名詞 **Meteorology** is the study of the processes in the Earth's atmosphere that cause particular weather conditions, especially in order to predict the weather. 気象学 ● **me|teor|olo|gist** /mitiərɒlədʒɪst/ (**meteorologists**) N-COUNT 可算名詞 気象学者 □*Meteorologists have predicted mild rains for the next few days.* ここ数日は穏やかな雨が降り続くでしょう.

Word Link   *meter ≈ measuring : kilometer, meter, perimeter*

me|ter /mitər/ (**meters, metering, metered**) **1** N-COUNT 可算名詞 A **meter** is a device that measures and records something such as the amount of gas or electricity that you have used. メーター □*He was there to read the electricity meter.* 彼はそこで電気のメーターを見ていた. **2** V-T 他動詞 To **meter** something such as gas or electricity means to use a meter to measure how much of it people use, usually in order to calculate how much they have to pay. メーターで計る □*Only a third of these households thought it reasonable to meter water.* これらの世帯で水道の従量制でよいと答えたのは3分の1にとどまった. **3** N-COUNT 可算名詞 A **meter** is the same as a **parking meter**. パーキングメーター **4** N-COUNT 可算名詞 A **meter** is a metric unit of length equal to 100 centimeters. メートル □*She's running the 1,500 meters here.* 彼女は今回1500m走に出場する.

me|thane /mɛθeɪn/ N-UNCOUNT 不可算名詞 **Methane** is a colorless gas that has no smell. Natural gas consists mostly of methane. メタン

meth|od /mɛθəd/ (**methods**) N-COUNT 可算名詞 A **method** is a particular way of doing something. 方法、方式 □*The pill is the most efficient method of birth control.* ピルは最も効果の高い避妊法である.
→ see science

Thesaurus   *method また次を参照 :*

N.	manner, procedure, process, system, technique

Word Partnership   *method は次の語句と使われる :*

ADJ.	**alternative/traditional** method, **best** method, **effective** method, **new** method, **preferred** method, **scientific** method
V.	**develop a** method, **use a** method
N.	method **of payment, teaching** method

me|thodi|cal /məθɒdɪkəl/ ADJ 形容詞 If you describe someone as **methodical**, you mean that they do things carefully,

Word Web   meteor

As an asteroid flies through **space**, small pieces called meteoroids sometimes break off. When a meteoroid enters the earth's **atmosphere**, we call it a **meteor**. As the earth passes through asteroid belts we see spectacular **meteor showers**. Meteors that reach the earth are called meteorites. Scientists believe a huge meteorite struck the earth about 65 million years ago. It left a pit in Mexico called the Chicxulub **Crater**. It's about 150 miles wide. The crash caused earthquakes and tsunamis. It may also have produced a change in the earth's environment. Some believe this event caused the dinosaurs to die out.

thoroughly, and in order. きちょうめんな ❏ *Da Vinci was methodical in his research, carefully recording his observations and theories.* ダ・ヴィンチは丁寧に観察や考察を記録して綿密な研究を行いました. ● me|thodi|cal|ly /məθɒdɪkli/ ADV 副詞 [ADV with v] きちょうめんに ❏ *She methodically put the things into her suitcase.* 彼女はスーツケースにきちんと荷物を詰めた.

meth|od|ol|ogy /mɛθədɒlədʒi/ (methodologies) N-VAR 可変性名詞 A methodology is a system of methods and principles for doing something, for example for teaching or for carrying out research. 方法論, 研究方法 [FORMAL 形式ばった] ❏ *Teaching methodologies vary according to the topic.* 教授法はテーマによって違ってくる. ● meth|odo|logi|cal /mɛθədəlɒdʒɪk^əl/ ADJ 形容詞 方法論の ❏ *...theoretical and methodological issues raised by the study of literary texts.* 文学テクスト研究が提起する理論的かつ方法論的問題.

me|ticu|lous /mətɪkyələs/ ADJ 形容詞 If you describe someone as meticulous, you mean that they do things very carefully and with great attention to detail. 細部にこだわる, 凝り性の ❏ *He was so meticulous about everything.* 彼は何でもきっちりやらないと気が済まない人でした. ● me|ticu|lous|ly ADV 副詞 細部にこだわって ❏ *The flat had been meticulously cleaned.* アパートは隅から隅まで掃除されていた.

me|tre /mitər/ → see meter

met|ric /mɛtrɪk/ ADJ 形容詞 Metric means relating to the metric system. メートル法の ❏ *Around 180,000 metric tons of food aid is required.* およそ18万tの食糧支援が必要である.

met|ro /mɛtroʊ/ (metros) also Metro N-COUNT 可算名詞 The metro is the subway system in some cities, for example in Washington or Paris. 地下鉄 ❏ *A new metro runs under the square, carrying hundreds of thousands who used to cycle to work.* 広場の下を走る新しい地下鉄は, かつて自転車で通勤していた数十万人の乗客を輸送している.
→ see transportation

Word Link poli ≈ city : metropolis, police, policy

me|tropo|lis /mətrɒpəlɪs/ (metropolises) N-COUNT 可算名詞 A metropolis is the largest, busiest, and most important city in a country or region. 大都市 ❏ *Even Lhasa was a small provincial town compared to the bustling metropolis of Chengdu.* 活気に満ちた大都市成都(チョントゥー)から見れば, 拉薩(ラサ)は地方の小都市にすぎなかった.

met|ro|poli|tan /mɛtrəpɒlɪt^ən/ ADJ 形容詞 Metropolitan means belonging to or typical of a large, busy city. 大都市の [ADJ n] ❏ *...the metropolitan district of Miami.* マイアミの市街地 ❏ *...a dozen major metropolitan hospitals.* 大都市にある10前後の大病院

mg mg is a written abbreviation for milligram or milligrams. ミリグラム ❏ *...300 mg of calcium.* カルシウム300mg.

mice /maɪs/ Mice is the plural of mouse. mouseの複数形

Word Link micro ≈ small : microbe, microcosm, microscope

mi|crobe /maɪkroʊb/ (microbes) N-COUNT 可算名詞 A microbe is a very small, living thing, which you can only see if you use a microscope. 微生物; 病原菌 ❏ *...a type of bacteria that include the microbes responsible for tuberculosis and leprosy.* 結核やハンセン病を引き起こす病原菌などと同じバクテリアの一種

micro|chip /maɪkroʊtʃɪp/ (microchips) N-COUNT 可算名詞 A microchip is a very small piece of silicon inside a computer. It has electronic circuits on it and can hold large quantities of information or perform mathematical and logical operations. マイクロチップ

micro|cosm /maɪkrəkɒzəm/ (microcosms) N-COUNT 可算名詞 A microcosm is a small society, place, or activity which has all the typical features of a much larger one and so seems like a smaller version of it. 小世界, 縮図 [FORMAL 形式ばった] [oft N 'of' n, also 'in' n] ❏ *Kitchell says the city was a microcosm of all American culture during the '60s.* キッシェルは, その都市には60年代のアメリカ文化が凝縮されていたと語ります.

micro|cred|it /maɪkroʊkrɛdɪt/ N-UNCOUNT 不可算名詞 Microcredit is credit in the form of small loans offered to local businesses, especially in developing countries. マイクロクレジット(貧困層に対する小額無担保融資) [BUSINESS 実業] ❏ *One tool to fight poverty is the use of microcredit loans.* 貧困と戦う1つの手段がマイクロクレジットの利用である.

micro|fiber /maɪkroʊfaɪbər/ (microfibers) N-VAR 可変性名詞 Microfibers are extremely light, artificial fibers that are used to make cloth. マイクロファイバー ❏ *...woven in great-looking and durable microfiber.* 見た目が美しく耐久性に優れたマイクロファイバーで織った.

micro|organ|ism /maɪkroʊɔrgənɪzəm/ (microorganisms) N-COUNT 可算名詞 A microorganism is a very small living thing which you can only see if you use a microscope. 微生物

Word Link phon ≈ sound : microphone, symphony, telephone

micro|phone /maɪkrəfoʊn/ (microphones) N-COUNT 可算名詞 A microphone is a device that is used to make sounds louder or to record them on a tape recorder. マイク
→ see concert

micro|proc|es|sor /maɪkroʊprɒsɛsər/ (microprocessors) N-COUNT 可算名詞 In a computer, the microprocessor is the main microchip, which controls its most important functions. マイクロプロセッサ [COMPUTING コンピューティング]

Word Link scope ≈ looking : horoscope, microscope, telescope

micro|scope /maɪkrəskoʊp/ (microscopes) N-COUNT 可算名詞 A microscope is a scientific instrument which makes very small objects look bigger so that more detail can be seen. 顕微鏡

micro|scop|ic /maɪkrəskɒpɪk/ ❶ ADJ 形容詞 Microscopic objects are extremely small, and usually can be seen only through a microscope. 微小な, 顕微鏡でしか見えない ❏ *Microscopic fibers of protein were visible.* たんぱく質の微小な繊維が映し出されました. ❷ ADJ 形容詞 A microscopic examination is done using a microscope. 顕微鏡による [ADJ n] ❏ *Microscopic examination of a cell's chromosomes can reveal the sex of the fetus.* 細胞の染色体を顕微鏡で調べると胎児の性別が分かる.

micro|wave /maɪkroʊweɪv/ (microwaves, microwaving, microwaved) ❶ N-COUNT 可算名詞 A microwave or a microwave oven is an oven which cooks food very quickly by electromagnetic radiation rather than by heat. 電子レンジ ❷ V-T 他動詞 To microwave food or drink means to cook or heat it in a microwave oven. 電子レンジで加熱する ❏ *Steam or microwave the vegetables until tender.* 野菜が柔らかくなるまで蒸すか, 電子レンジで加熱します.
→ see cook, wave

mid|air /mɪdɛər/ N-UNCOUNT 不可算名詞 If something happens in midair, it happens in the air, rather than on the ground. 空中, 上空 ❏ *The bird stopped and hovered in mid-air.* 鳥は羽ばたきながら空中で静止した.

mid|day /mɪddeɪ/ ❶ N-UNCOUNT 不可算名詞 Midday is twelve o'clock in the middle of the day. 正午 ❏ *At midday everyone would go down to Reg's Café.* になると, みんなでレグズ・カフェに出かけたものだ. ❷ N-UNCOUNT 不可算名詞 Midday is the middle part of the day, from late morning to early afternoon. 真昼 ❏ *People were beginning to tire in the midday heat.* 日中の暑さにみんな疲れが出始めていました.

mid|dle /mɪd^əl/ (middles) ❶ N-COUNT 可算名詞 The middle of something is the part of it that is farthest from its edges, ends, or outside surface. の真ん中 ❏ *Howard stood in the middle of the room sipping a cup of coffee.* ハワードは部屋の真ん中につっ立ってコーヒーをすすっていた. ❏ *They had a volleyball court in the middle of the courtyard.* 中庭の中央にバレーボールコートがあった. ❷ the middle of nowhere → see nowhere ❸ ADJ 形容詞 The middle object in a row of objects is the one that has an equal number of objects on each side. 真ん中の [ADJ n] ❏ *The middle button of his uniform jacket was strained over his belly.* 彼の制服の真ん中のボタンはお腹の上ではちきれそうになっていた. ❹ N-SING 単数名詞 The middle of an event or period of time is the part that comes after the first part and before the last part. の最中 ❏ *I woke up in the middle of the night and could hear a tapping on the window.* 真夜中に目が覚めると, 窓をコツコツたたく音が聞こえた. ● ADJ 形容詞 Middle is also an adjective. 真ん中の [ADJ n] ❏ *Many classical violinists and pianists become conductors in their middle years.* クラシックのバイオリニストやピアニストが指揮者に転向するのは中年の時期が多い. ❺ PHRASE 句 If you are in the middle of doing something, you are busy doing it. している最中で ❏ *It's a bit hectic. I'm in the middle of cooking for nine people.* ちょっと大変なの. 今9人分の食事を作っている最中なの.
→ see hand

mid|dle age N-UNCOUNT 不可算名詞 Middle age is the period in your life when you are no longer young but have not yet become old. Middle age is usually considered to take place between the ages of 40 and 60. 中年, 中高年 ❏ *Men tend to put on weight in middle age.* 男性は中年期に太る傾向がある.

middle-aged ❶ ADJ 形容詞 If you describe someone as middle-aged, you mean that they are neither young nor old. People between the ages of 40 and 60 are usually considered to be middle-aged. 中年の, 中高年の ❏ *...middle-aged, married businessmen.* 中年の既婚会社員 ❷ ADJ 形容詞 If you describe someone's activities or interests as middle-aged, you are critical of them because you think they are typical of a middle-aged person, for example by being conventional or old-fashioned. 古くさい, 年寄りじみた [DISAPPROVAL 不賛成] ❏ *Her novels are middle-aged and boring.* 彼女の小説は古くさくてつまらない.
→ see age

mid|dle class (middle classes) N-COUNT-COLL 集合可算名詞 The middle class or middle classes are the people in a society who

are not working class or upper class. Business people, managers, doctors, lawyers, and teachers are usually regarded as middle class. 中流階級、中産階級 ● ADJ 形容詞 **Middle class** is also an adjective. 中流階級の、中産階級の ❑ *He is rapidly losing the support of blue-collar voters and of middle-class conservatives.* 彼は、急速に肉体労働者と中流保守層の有権者の支持を失っている。

Mid|dle East N-PROPER 固有名詞 **The Middle East** is the area around the eastern Mediterranean that includes Iran and all the countries in Asia to the west and southwest of Iran. 中東 ❑ *The two great rivers of the Middle East rise in the mountains of Turkey.* 中東の2大河川はトルコ山脈から流れている。

middle|man /mɪdˀlmæn/ (**middlemen**) 1 N-COUNT 可算名詞 A **middleman** is a person or company which buys things from the people who produce them and sells them to the people who want to buy them. 仲介業者、仲買人 [BUSINESS 実業] ❑ *Why don't they cut out the middleman and let us do it ourselves?* どうして仲介業者を断って我々に任せてくれないのだろうか。 2 N-COUNT 可算名詞 A **middleman** is a person who helps in negotiations between people who are unwilling to meet each other directly. 仲介者、仲立ち ❑ *The two sides would only meet indirectly, through middlemen.* 両者は仲介を通して間接的にしか会おうとしない。

mid|dle man|age|ment N-UNCOUNT 不可算名詞 **Middle management** refers to managers who are below the top level of management, and who are responsible for controlling and running an organization rather than making decisions about how it operates. 中間管理職 [BUSINESS 実業] ❑ *The proportion of women in middle management has risen to 40%.* 中間管理職に就く女性の比率が40%上昇した。

middle-of-the-road 1 ADJ 形容詞 If you describe someone's opinions or policies as **middle-of-the-road**, you mean that they are neither left wing nor right wing, and not at all extreme. 中道の、穏健な ❑ *Consensus need not be weak, nor need it result in middle-of-the-road policies.* 世論は弱気である必要はなく、また中道政策に終わる必要もない。 2 ADJ 形容詞 If you describe something or someone as **middle-of-the-road**, you mean that they are ordinary or unexciting. 平凡な ❑ *I actually don't want to be a middle-of-the-road person, married with a mortgage.* 実は、結婚して住宅ローンを抱えるというような平凡な人にはなりたくない。

Word Link	mid ≈ middle : midnight, midst, midweek

mid|night /mɪdnaɪt/ 1 N-UNCOUNT 不可算名詞 **Midnight** is twelve o'clock in the middle of the night. 夜中の12時、午前0時 ❑ *It was well after midnight by the time Anne returned to her apartment.* アンがアパートに戻ったのはとっくに0時を回っていた。 2 ADJ 形容詞 **Midnight** is used to describe something that happens or appears at midnight or in the middle of the night. 午前0時の、真夜中の [ADJ n] ❑ *It is totally out of the question to postpone the midnight deadline.* 午前0時の締め切りを延ばすのは不可能です。 3 PHRASE 句 If someone **is burning the midnight oil**, they are staying up very late in order to study or do some other work. 夜遅くまで勉強する/働く ❑ *Chris is asleep after burning the midnight oil trying to finish his article.* クリスは記事を仕上げようと夜遅くまでがんばったので今は眠っている。

mid-range also **midrange** ADJ 形容詞 You can use **mid-range** to describe products or services which are neither the most expensive nor the cheapest of their type. 中程度の、平均の [ADJ n] ❑ *...the price of a mid-range family car.* 平均的なファミリーカーの値段

midst /mɪdst/ 1 PHRASE 句 If you are **in the midst of** doing something, you are doing it at the moment. 〜の最中で ❑ *We are in the midst of one of the worst recessions for many, many years.* かなり長期にわたる最悪の不景気の真っただ中にいます。 2 PHRASE 句 If something happens **in the midst of** an event, it happens during it. 〜の真っ最中に ❑ *Eleanor arrived in the midst of a blizzard.* エレノアは猛吹雪の真っ最中に到着した。 3 PHRASE 句 If someone or something is **in the midst of** a group of people or things, they are among them or surrounded by them. 〜に囲まれて ❑ *Many were surprised to see him exposed like this in the midst of a large crowd.* 彼がこのように大群衆に囲まれているのを見て驚いた人が多かった。

mid|way /mɪdweɪ/ 1 ADV 副詞 If something is **midway** between two places, it is between them and the same distance from each of them. 中間地点で [ADV prep] ❑ *The studio is midway between his aunt's old home and his cottage.* スタジオはおばの古い家と彼の家の中間点にあった。 ● ADJ 形容詞 **Midway** is also an adjective. 中間地点の [ADJ n] ❑ *Fresno is close to the midway point between LA and San Francisco.* フレズノはロサンゼルスとサンフランシスコの中間付近にある。 2 ADV 副詞 If something happens **midway through** a period of time, it happens during the middle part of it. 半ばで、途中で ❑ *He crashed midway through the race.* 彼はレースの途中で事故にあった。 ● ADJ 形容詞 **Midway** is also an adjective. 途中の [ADJ n] ❑ *They were denied an obvious penalty before the midway point of the first half.* 前半戦の途中で明らかなペナルティーを認められなかった。

mid|week /mɪdwik/ ADJ 形容詞 **Midweek** describes something that happens in the middle of the week. 週の半ばの [ADJ n] ❑ *Enjoy the peace and beauty of midweek walks in the park.* 週半ばの平和で快適な公園の散歩を楽しんでください。 ● ADV 副詞 **Midweek** is also an adverb. 週半ばに ❑ *They'll be able to go up to Washington midweek.* 週の半ばにワシントン州に行けるだろう。

mid|wife /mɪdwaɪf/ (**midwives**) N-COUNT 可算名詞 A **midwife** is a nurse who is trained to deliver babies and to advise pregnant women. 助産婦 ❑ *You don't have to call the midwife as soon as labor starts.* 陣痛が始まったからといってすぐに助産婦を呼ぶ必要はない。

---

might

❶ MODAL USES
❷ NOUN USES

❶ **might** /maɪt/

Might is a modal verb. It is used with the base form of a verb.

Might は法動詞であり、動詞の原型とともに用いられる。

▷ Please look at meaning ⓫ to see if the expression you are looking for is shown under another headword. 1 MODAL 法動詞 You use **might** to indicate that something will possibly happen or be true in the future, but you cannot be certain. 〜かもしれない、〜する可能性がある [VAGUENESS あいまいさ] ❑ *There's a report today that smoking might be banned in most buildings.* 本日、ほとんどの建物で喫煙が禁止される可能性を示した報告書が発表されました。 ❑ *I might well regret it later.* 後で後悔するかもしれない。 2 MODAL 法動詞 You use **might** to indicate that there is a possibility that something is true, but you cannot be certain. 〜かもしれない [VAGUENESS あいまいさ] ❑ *She and Robert's father had not given up hope that he might be alive.* 彼女とロバートの父親は彼が生きているかもしれないという希望を捨てていなかった。 ❑ *You might be right.* あなたが正しいかもしれない。 3 MODAL 法動詞 You use **might** to indicate that something could happen or be true in particular circumstances. 〜かもしれない [VAGUENESS あいまいさ] ❑ *America might sell more cars to the islands if they were made with the steering wheel on the right.* アメリカは右ハンドルの車を生産すればその島への自動車の輸出を増やせるかもしれない。 4 MODAL 法動詞 You use **might have** with a past participle to indicate that it is possible that something happened or was true, or when giving a possible explanation for something. 〜したかもしれない ❑ *I heard what might have been an explosion.* 爆発音らしき音が聞こえた。 5 MODAL 法動詞 You use **might have** with a past participle to indicate that something was a possibility in the past, although it did not actually happen. 〜したかもしれないのに ❑ *If she had had to give up riding she might have taken up sailing competitively.* 乗馬をあきらめていたら、ヨットをもっと真剣に取り組んでいたかもしれないのに。 6 MODAL 法動詞 You use **might** in statements where you are accepting the truth of a situation, but contrasting it with something that is more important. 〜かもしれないが ❑ *They might not have two cents to rub together, but at least they have a kind of lifestyle that is different.* 彼らは無一文かもしれないが、少なくとも独自のライフスタイルがある。 7 MODAL 法動詞 You use **might** when you are saying emphatically that someone ought to do the thing mentioned, especially when you are annoyed because they have not done it. 〜してくれてもよかったのに [EMPHASIS 強調] ❑ *You might have told me that before!* そのことを前に言ってくれてもよかったのに! 8 MODAL 法動詞 You use **might** to make a suggestion or to give advice in a very polite way. 〜したらどうでしょうか [POLITENESS 丁寧さ] ❑ *They might be wise to stop advertising on television.* テレビでの宣伝を止めたほうが賢明だろう。 9 MODAL 法動詞 You use **might** as a polite way of interrupting someone, asking a question, making a request, or introducing what you are going to say next. 〜してもよろしいでしょうか [FORMAL, SPOKEN 形式ばった、口語、POLITENESS 丁寧さ] ❑ *Might I make a suggestion?* 〜してもよろしいでしょうか。 ❑ *Might I ask what you're doing here?* ここで何をなさっているのか伺ってよろしいでしょうか。 10 MODAL 法動詞 You use **might** in expressions such as **I might have known** and **I might have guessed** to indicate that you are not surprised at a disappointing event or fact. 「どうせ〜だろうと思っていたよ」というニュアンスで使われる ❑ *I might have known I'd find you with some little slut.* どうせそこらの尻軽女と一緒になるだろうと思っていたわ。 ⓫ **might as well** → see **well**

❷ **might** /maɪt/ 1 N-UNCOUNT 不可算名詞 **Might** is power or strength. 力、勢力 [FORMAL 形式ばった] ❑ *The might of the army could prove a decisive factor.* 軍力が決定的要因となりうる。 2 PHRASE 句 If you do something **with all** your **might**, you do it using all your strength and energy. 全力で ❑ *She swung the hammer at his head with all her might.* 彼女は全力を使ってハンマーで彼の頭を殴った。

mightn't /maɪtˀnt/ **Mightn't** is a spoken form of "might not." might notの口語での省略形

might've /maɪtəv/ **Might've** is the usual spoken form of "might have," especially when "have" is an auxiliary verb. might haveの短縮形. 特に, might have+過去分詞のときに口語で短縮される.

mighty /maɪti/ (**mightier, mightiest**) **1** ADJ 形容詞 **Mighty** is used to describe something that is very large or powerful. 強力な, 強大な [LITERARY 文語的] ❑ There was a flash and a mighty bang. 閃光(せんこう)がありごう音がした. **2** ADV 副詞 **Mighty** is used in front of adjectives and adverbs to emphasize the quality that they are describing. すごく [mainly AM 主に米国英語, INFORMAL くだけた, EMPHASIS 強調] [ADV adj/adv] ❑ It's something you'll be mighty proud of. すごく自慢に思うようなことだよ. **3** → see also high-and-mighty

migraine /maɪgreɪn/ (**migraines**) N-VAR 可変性名詞 A **migraine** is an extremely painful headache that makes you feel very ill. 片頭痛 ❑ Her mother suffered from migraines. 彼女の母親は片頭痛に悩んだ.

Word Link

migr ≈ moving, changing : emigrant, immigrant, migrant

migrant /maɪgrənt/ (**migrants**) **1** N-COUNT 可算名詞 A **migrant** is a person who moves from one place to another, especially in order to find work. 移住者, 移民 ❑ The government divides asylum seekers into economic migrants and genuine refugees. 政府は避難民を経済難民と真の難民に分類する. **2** N-COUNT 可算名詞 **Migrants** are birds, fish, or animals that migrate from one part of the world to another. 移動動物, 渡り鳥, 回遊魚 ❑ Migrant birds shelter in the reeds. 渡り鳥はアシの茂みに隠れる.

migrate /maɪgreɪt/ (**migrates, migrating, migrated**) **1** V-I 自動詞 If people **migrate**, they move from one place to another, especially in order to find work or to live somewhere for a short time. 移住する, 移動する ❑ People migrate to cities like Jakarta in search of work. 人々は職を求めてジャカルタのような都市に移住する. ●**migration** /maɪgreɪ°n/ (**migrations**) N-VAR 可変性名詞 移動, 移住 ❑ ...the migration of Soviet Jews to Israel. ソビエト系ユダヤ人のイスラエルへの移住 **2** V-I 自動詞 When birds, fish, or animals **migrate**, they move at a particular season from one part of the world or from one part of a country to another, usually in order to breed or to find new feeding grounds. 移動する, 渡る, 回遊する ❑ Most birds have to fly long distances to migrate. 渡り鳥のほとんどは長距離を飛ばなければならない. ●**migration** N-VAR 可変性名詞 移動, 渡り, 回遊 ❑ ...the migration of animals in the Serengeti. セレンゲティに住む動物の移動

mike /maɪk/ (**mikes**) N-COUNT 可算名詞 A **mike** is the same as a **microphone**. マイク [INFORMAL くだけた]

mil /mɪl/ NUM 数詞 **Mil** means the same as **million**. millionの省略形 [INFORMAL くだけた] ❑ Zhamnov, 22, signed for $1.25 mil over three years. ザムノフ, 22歳, 125万ドルで3年契約

mild /maɪld/ (**milder, mildest**) **1** ADJ 形容詞 **Mild** is used to describe something such as a feeling, attitude, or illness that is not very strong or severe. ちょっとした, 軽い ❑ Teddy turned to Mona with a look of mild confusion. テディは少し混乱した様子でモナの方を見た. ●**mildly** ADV 副詞 少し, 軽く ❑ Josephine must have had the disease very mildly as she showed no symptoms. ジョセフィーンは症状がないことから病気が非常に軽かったに違いない. **2** ADJ 形容詞 A **mild** person is gentle and does not get angry easily. 温厚な, 穏やかな ❑ He is a mild man, who is reasonable almost to the point of blandness. 彼は温厚な男性で, 味気ないほどに理性的だ. ●**mildly** ADV 副詞 [ADV after v] 温厚で ❑ "I'm not meddling," Ken said mildly, "I'm just curious." 「おせっかいなんじゃないよ」とケンは穏やかに言った. 「興味があるだけだよ」 **3** ADJ 形容詞 **Mild** weather is pleasant because it is neither extremely hot nor extremely cold. 暖かい, 温暖な ❑ The area is famous for its very mild winter climate. その地域は冬の気候が非常に温暖なので有名だ.

In informal English, if you want to emphasize how hot the weather is, you can say that it is **boiling** or **scorching**. In winter, if the temperature is above average, you can say that it is **mild**. In general, **hot** suggests a higher temperature than **warm**, and **warm** things are usually pleasant. ❑ ...a warm evening.

4 ADJ 形容詞 You describe food as **mild** when it does not taste or smell strong, sharp, or bitter, especially when you like it because of this. まろやかな ❑ This cheese has a soft, mild flavor. このチーズはソフトでまろやかな風味だ. **5** → see also **mildly**

Thesaurus mild また次を参照：

ADJ. slight **1**
friendly, gentle, kind, warm **2**
comfortable, pleasant, warm; (ant.) harsh, severe **3**
weak; (ant.) spicy, strong **4**

mildly /maɪldli/ **1** → see mild **2** PHRASE 句 You use **to put it mildly** to indicate that you are describing something in language

that is much less strong, direct, or critical than what you really think. 控えめに言うと ❑ But not all the money, to put it mildly, has been used wisely. しかし控えめに言っても, 全額が賢明に使われたのではない.

mile /maɪl/ (**miles**) **1** N-COUNT 可算名詞 A **mile** is a unit of distance equal to 1760 yards or approximately 1.6 kilometers. マイル ❑ They drove 600 miles across the desert. 砂漠を600マイル運転した. ❑ She lives just half a mile away. 彼女はほんの半マイル先に住んでいる. **2** N-PLURAL 複数名詞 **Miles** is used, especially in the expression **miles away**, to refer to a long distance. かなりの距離, 遠く ❑ If you enroll at a gym that's miles away, you won't be visiting it as often as you should. 遠くのスポーツクラブに入会すると行く回数が理想を下回るだろう. **3** N-COUNT 可算名詞 **Miles** or a **mile** is used with the meaning "very much" in order to emphasize the difference between two things or qualities, or the difference between what you aimed to do and what you actually achieved. ずっと [INFORMAL くだけた, EMPHASIS 強調] ❑ You're miles better than most of the performers we see nowadays. 君は, 近ごろの役者のほとんどと比べものにならないよ. ❑ With a Democratic candidate in place they won by a mile. 民主党の候補者が決まって圧勝した.

Word Partnership mile は次の語句と使われる：

ADJ. mile **high**, mile **long**, **nautical** mile, **square** mile, mile **wide** **1**

mileage /maɪlɪdʒ/ (**mileages**) **1** N-UNCOUNT 不可算名詞 **Mileage** refers to the distance that you have traveled, measured in miles. 走行距離 ❑ While most of their mileage may be in and around town, they still want highways for longer trips. ほとんどは市内とその周辺を運転するだけだが, それでも長距離用に幹線道路の建設を希望している. **2** N-UNCOUNT 不可算名詞 The **mileage** of a vehicle is the number of miles that it can travel using one gallon or liter of fuel. 燃費 ❑ They are willing to pay up to $500 more for cars that get better mileage. 燃費がよい車には500ドル余分に支払う意欲があります. **3** N-UNCOUNT 不可算名詞 The **mileage** in a particular course of action is its usefulness in getting you what you want. 利点 ❑ It's obviously important to get as much mileage out of the convention as possible. 会議からできるだけ多くを学ぶことが明らかに重要です.

milestone /maɪlstoʊn/ (**milestones**) N-COUNT 可算名詞 A **milestone** is an important event in the history or development of something or someone. 画期的な出来事 ❑ He said the launch of the party represented a milestone in Zambian history. 「新党結成はザンビアの歴史に残る重要な出来事だ」と彼は言った.

milieu /mɪlyu, mil-/ (**milieux** or **milieus**) N-COUNT 可算名詞 Your **milieu** is the group of people or activities that you live among or are familiar with. 環境, 境遇 [FORMAL 形式ばった] ❑ They stayed, safe and happy, within their own social milieu. 自分たちの生活環境内で安全で幸せに暮らした.

militant /mɪlɪtənt/ (**militants**) ADJ 形容詞 You use **militant** to describe people who believe in something very strongly and are active in trying to bring about political or social change, often in extreme ways that other people find unacceptable. 過激な ❑ Militant mine workers in the Ukraine have voted for a one-day stoppage next month. ウクライナの闘争的な鉱炭労働者が来月1日閉鎖をすることに賛成票を投じた. ●N-COUNT 可算名詞 **Militant** is also a noun. 過激派 ❑ Even now we could not be sure that the militants would not find some new excuse to call a strike the following winter. この期に及んでさえ過激派が翌冬にストライキを呼びかける口実を見つけないと確信できない. ●**militancy** N-UNCOUNT 不可算名詞 闘争性 ❑ ...the rise of labor union militancy. 労働組合の闘争性の悪化

Word Link milit ≈ soldier : demilitarize, military, militia

military /mɪlɪteri/ (**militaries**) **1** ADJ 形容詞 **Military** means relating to the armed forces of a country. 軍の, 軍事の ❑ Military action may become necessary. 軍事行動が必要になるかもしれません. ❑ The president is sending in almost 20,000 military personnel to help with the relief efforts. 大統領は救援活動を援助するために兵士ほぼ2万人を派遣します. ●**militarily** /mɪltɛrɪli/ ADV 副詞 軍事的に ❑ They remain unwilling to intervene militarily in what could be an unending war. 終わりのない戦争になりかねない軍事介入には消極的な姿勢を維持しています. **2** N-COUNT-COLL 集合可算名詞 The **military** is the armed forces of a country, especially officers of high rank. 軍, 軍隊 ❑ The bombing has been far more widespread than the military will admit. 爆撃は軍の承認よりもずっと広範囲に及んでいた. **3** ADJ 形容詞 **Military** means well organized, controlled, or neat, in a way that is typical of a soldier. 軍人のような ❑ Your working day will need to be organized with military precision. 仕事の日は軍人のようなきちみつさで計画を立てて物事を行わなければならない. → see army

militia /mɪlɪʃə/ (**militias**) N-COUNT 可算名詞 A **militia** is an organization that operates like an army but whose members are not professional soldiers. 民兵 ❑ The troops will not attempt to

disarm the warring militias. 軍隊は交戦中の民衆から武器を取り上げよ うとはしません.
→ see **army**

milk /mɪlk/ (**milks, milking, milked**) **1** N-UNCOUNT 不可算名詞 **Milk** is the white liquid produced by cows, goats, and some other animals, which people drink and use to make butter, cheese, and yogurt. 乳, 牛乳, ミルク □*He stepped out to buy a quart of milk.* 彼は牛乳を買いに出かけた. **2** V-T 他動詞 If someone **milks** a cow or goat, they get milk from it, using either their hands or a machine. 乳を搾る □*Farm workers milked cows by hand.* 農場労働 者は手で牛の乳搾りをした. **3** N-UNCOUNT 不可算名詞 **Milk** is the white liquid produced by women to feed their babies. 母乳 □*Milk from the mother's breast is a perfect food for the human baby.* ヒトの赤ち ゃんには母乳が完全食だ. **4** N-MASS 質量名詞 Liquid products for cleaning your skin or making it softer are sometimes referred to as **milks**. 乳液 □*Sales of cleansing milks, creams, and gels have doubled over the past decade.* クレンジング乳液・クリーム・ジェルの販売が過 去10年間で倍増した. **5** V-T 他動詞 If you say that someone **milks** something, you mean that they get as much benefit or profit as they can from it, without caring about the effects this has on other people. 搾取する, 食いものにする [DISAPPROVAL 不賛成] □*A few people tried to milk the insurance companies.* 保険会社を搾り取ろう とする人は少ない. **6** → see also **skim milk**
→ see **dairy**

milky /mɪlki/ (**milkier, milkiest**) **1** ADJ 形容詞 If you describe something as **milky**, you mean that it is pale white in color. You can describe other colors as **milky** when they are very pale. 乳白 色の □*A milky mist filled the valley.* 谷間一面が乳白色の霧で覆われて いた. **2** ADJ 形容詞 Drinks or food that are **milky** contain a lot of milk. ミルクがたっぷり入った □*...his big cup of milky coffee.* 大きな カップにミルクがたっぷり入ったコーヒー

mill /mɪl/ (**mills, milling, milled**) **1** N-COUNT 可算名詞 A **mill** is a building in which grain is crushed to make flour. 製粉所 □*There was an old mill that really did grind corn.* 実際に穀粒をひいた古い製粉 所があった. **2** N-COUNT 可算名詞 A **mill** is a small device used for grinding something such as coffee beans or pepper into powder. 粉ひき器 □*...a pepper mill.* コショウひき **3** N-COUNT 可算名詞 A **mill** is a factory used for making and processing materials such as steel, wool, or cotton. 工場 □*...a steel mill.* 製鋼工場 **4** V-T 他動詞 To **mill** something such as wheat or pepper means to grind it in a mill. 製粉する, ひく □*They do not have the capacity to mill the grain.* 穀類を製粉する設備がありません.
▶ **mill around** PHRASAL VERB 句動詞 When a crowd of people **mill around**, they move around within a particular place or area, so that the movement of the whole crowd looks very confused. う ろつく, ぶらぶらする □*Quite a few people were milling around, but nothing was happening.* かなり大勢の人々がうろついていたが, 何事も 起きていなかった.

mil·len·ni·um /mɪlɡniəm/ (**millenniums** or **millennia**) **1** N-COUNT 可算名詞 A **millennium** is a period of one thousand years, especially one which begins and ends with a year ending in "ooo," for example the period from the year 1000 to the year 2000. 千年, 1000年間 □*...the dawn of a new millennium.* 新千年紀の始まり **2** N-SING 単数名詞 Many people refer to the year 2000 as **the Millennium**. ミレニアム □*...the eve of the Millennium.* ミレニアム・イブ

mil·li·gram /mɪlɪɡræm/ (**milligrams**) N-COUNT 可算名詞 A **milligram** is a unit of weight that is equal to a thousandth of a gram. ミリグラム □*...0.5 milligrams of mercury.* 水銀0.5ミリグラム

mil·li·li·ter /mɪlɪlitər/ (**milliliters**) N-COUNT 可算名詞 A **milliliter** is a unit of volume for liquids and gases that is equal to a thousandth of a liter. ミリリットル □*...100 milliliters of blood.* 血 液100ミリリットル

mil·li·me·ter /mɪlɪmitər/ (**millimeters**) N-COUNT 可算名詞 A **millimeter** is a metric unit of length that is equal to a tenth of a centimeter or a thousandth of a meter. ミリメートル □*The creature is a tiny centipede, just 10 millimeters long.* その生物は体長がほんの10ミ リメートルの小さなムカデだ.

mil·lion /mɪlyən/ (**millions**)

The plural form is **million** after a number, or after a word or expression referring to a number, such as "several" or "a few."
複数形は数の後, あるいは **several** や **a few** のような数を指す単 語や表現の後では **million** である.

1 NUM 数詞 A **million** or one **million** is the number 1,000,000. 100万 □*Up to five million people a year visit the county.* 年間最高500

万人がその郡を訪れる. **2** QUANT-PLURAL 複数数量詞 If you talk about **millions of** people or things, you mean that there is a very large number of them but you do not know or do not want to say exactly how many. 何百万もの, たくさんの [QUANT 'of' pl-n] □*The program was viewed on television in millions of homes.* そのテレビ番組は 数百万件で視聴された.

mil·lion·aire /mɪlyənɛər/ (**millionaires**) N-COUNT 可算名詞 A **millionaire** is a very rich person who has money or property worth at least a million dollars. 百万長者, 大金持ち, 大富豪 □*By the time he died, he was a millionaire.* 死亡するまでに彼は百万長者にな っていました.

mil·lionth /mɪlyənθ/ (**millionths**) **1** ORD 序数詞 The **millionth** item in a series is the one you count as number one million. 百 万番目の □*Last year the millionth truck rolled off the assembly line.* 昨 年100万台目のトラックが組立ラインを流れた. **2** FRACTION 端数 A **millionth** of something is one of a million equal parts of it. 100万 分の1 □*The bomb must explode within less than a millionth of a second.* 爆弾は100万分の1秒以内に爆発しなければならない.

mime /maɪm/ (**mimes, miming, mimed**) **1** N-VAR 可変性 名詞 **Mime** is the use of movements and gestures in order to express something or tell a story without using speech. 身ぶ り □*Music, mime, and strong visual imagery play a strong part in the productions.* 音楽・身ぶり・高い視覚的表現力が公演では重要な役割 を果たす. **2** V-T/V-I 他動詞/自動詞 If you **mime** something, you describe or express it using mime rather than speech. 身ぶりで表 現する □*It featured a solo dance in which a woman mimed a lot of dainty housework.* 女性が優美にたくさんの家事を無言で演じるソロダンスが 呼び物だった. **3** V-T/V-I 他動詞/自動詞 If you **mime**, you pretend to be singing or playing an instrument, although the music is in fact coming from a CD or cassette. 口パクをする [BRIT 英国英語; AM lip-synch 米国英語 **lip-synch**]

mim·ic /mɪmɪk/ (**mimics, mimicking, mimicked**) **1** V-T 他動 詞 If you **mimic** the actions or voice of a person or animal, you imitate them, usually in a way that is meant to be amusing or entertaining. 物まねをする, 口まねをする □*He could mimic anybody, and he often reduced Isabel to helpless laughter.* 彼はだれの物 まねもできて, よくイザベルを笑い転がしたものだった. **2** V-T 他 動詞 If someone or something **mimics** another person or thing, they try to be like them. まねる, 模倣する □*The computer doesn't mimic human thought; it reaches the same ends by different means.* コ ンピュータは人間の思考を模倣しない. どんな方法でも同じ結果に 達する. **3** N-COUNT 可算名詞 A **mimic** is a person who is able to mimic people or animals. 物まね上手な人 □*At school I was a good mimic.* 学校時代, 私は物まね上手だった.

min. Min. is a written abbreviation for **minimum**, or for **minutes** or **minute**. minimumの短縮形

mince /mɪns/ (**minces, mincing, minced**) **1** V-T 他動詞 If you **mince** food such as meat or vegetables, you cut or grind it up into very small pieces, usually in a machine. 細かく刻む, みじん切り にする □*Perhaps I'll buy lean meat and mince it myself.* たぶん赤身の肉 を買って自分でミンチにします. **2** N-UNCOUNT 不可算名詞 **Mince** is meat which has been cut or ground up into very small pieces using a machine. ひき肉, ミンチ [BRIT 英国英語; AM **ground beef, hamburger meat** 米国英語 **ground beef, hamburger meat**]
→ see **cut**

mind

❶ NOUN USES
❷ VERB USES

❶ mind /maɪnd/ (**minds**)
⇨ Please look at meaning **39** to see if the expression you are looking for is shown under another headword. **1** N-COUNT 可算名 詞 You refer to someone's **mind** when talking about their thoughts. For example, if you say that something is **in your mind**, you mean that you are thinking about it, and if you say that something is **at the back of your mind**, you mean that you are aware of it, although you are not thinking about it very much. 頭, 心, 精神 □*I'm trying to clear my mind of all this.* このことをすっか り忘れようとしている. □*There was no doubt in his mind that the man was serious.* その男が真剣だということを彼は疑っていなかっ た. **2** N-COUNT 可算名詞 Your **mind** is your ability to think and reason. 思考力, 頭脳 □*You have a good mind.* 君は頭がいい. □*Studying stretched my mind and got me thinking about things.* 勉強す ることで思考力が向上し, 物事について考えるようになっ た. **3** N-COUNT 可算名詞 If you have a particular type of **mind**, you have a particular way of thinking which is part of your character, or a result of your education or professional training. 気質, 独自の考え方 □*Andrew, you have a very suspicious mind.* アンド リュー, とても疑い深いのね. □*The key to his success is his logical mind.* 彼の成功へのかぎは論理的思考だ. **4** N-COUNT 可算名詞 You

can refer to someone as a particular kind of **mind** as a way of saying that they are smart, intelligent, or imaginative. 優れた知性の持ち主 ❑ *She moved to New York, meeting some of the best minds of her time.* 彼女はニューヨークに引っ越し、その頃最も優秀な人々に出会った. **5** → see also **frame of mind, state of mind 6** PHRASE 句 If you tell someone to **bear** something **in mind** or to **keep** something **in mind**, you are reminding or warning them about something important which they should remember. 覚えておく、心に留める ❑ *Bear in mind that gas stations are scarce in the more remote areas.* 辺びな所に行くとガソリンスタンドがあまりないことを覚えておくんだ. **7** PHRASE 句 If you **cast** your **mind back to** a time in the past, you think about what happened then. 以前のことを思い起こす ❑ *Cast your mind back to 1978, when Forest won the title.* フォレストがタイトルを獲得した1978年のことを思い起こそう. **8** PHRASE 句 If you **change** your **mind**, or if someone or something **changes** your **mind**, you change a decision you have made or an opinion that you had. 気が変わる ❑ *I was going to vote for him, but I changed my mind and voted for Reagan.* 彼に投票するつもりだったけれども、気が変わってレーガンに投票しました. **9** PHRASE 句 If something **comes to mind** or **springs to mind**, you think of it without making any effort. 思い浮かぶ ❑ *Integrity and honesty are words that spring to mind when talking of the man.* その男のことを話すと誠実さや正直という言葉が思い浮かぶ. **10** PHRASE 句 If you say that an idea or possibility never **crossed** your **mind**, you mean that you did not think of it. 心をよぎる ❑ *It had never crossed his mind that there might be a problem.* 問題があるかもしれないなんて思いもしなかった. **11** PHRASE 句 If you see something in your **mind's eye**, you imagine it and have a clear picture of it in your mind. 思い浮かべて ❑ *In his mind's eye, he can imagine the effect he's having.* 彼が与えている影響について思い浮かべながら想像ができる. **12** PHRASE 句 If you say that you **have a good mind** to do something or **have half a mind** to do it, you are threatening or announcing that you have a strong desire to do it, although you probably will not do it. 一しようかなと思っている ❑ *He raged on about how he had a good mind to resign.* いかに辞めようと思ったことについて彼は延々とまくし立てた. **13** PHRASE 句 If you ask someone what they **have in mind**, you want to know in more detail about an idea or wish they have. 考えている ❑ *"Maybe we could celebrate tonight."— "What did you have in mind?"* 「もしかすると今夜お祝いをするかもしれない」「何を考えているの」 **14** PHRASE 句 If you do something **with** a particular thing **in mind**, you do it with that thing as your aim or as the reason or basis for your action. 念頭において、考慮して ❑ *These families need support. With this in mind a group of 35 specialists met last weekend.* これらの家族に援助が必要だ. このことを考慮に入れて35人の専門家が先週末に会合した. **15** PHRASE 句 If you say that something such as an illness is **all in the mind**, you mean that it relates to someone's feelings or attitude, rather than having any physical cause. 気の せい ❑ *It could be a virus, or it could be all in the mind.* ウィルスの可能性もあるがすべて気のせいかもしれない. **16** PHRASE 句 If you **know** your **own mind**, you are sure about your opinions, and are not easily influenced by other people. 自分の考えを持っている ❑ *She knows her own mind and won't let anyone talk her into something she doesn't want to do.* 彼女は自分の考えを持っていてだれの言いなりにもならない. **17** PHRASE 句 If you say that someone **is losing their mind**, you think they are becoming mad. 気が狂う ❑ *Sometimes I feel like I'm losing my mind.* ときどき私は気が狂っているのではないかと思うときがある. **18** PHRASE 句 If you **make up** your **mind** or **make** your **mind up**, you decide which of a number of possible things you will have or do. 決心する ❑ *Once he made up his mind to do something, there was no stopping him.* 彼がいったん何かをすると決心したら止めることができない. **19** PHRASE 句 If a number of people are **of one mind, of like mind**, or **of the same mind**, they all agree about something. 同じ意見の ❑ *Contact with other disabled yachtsmen of like mind would be helpful.* 同じ意見を持ったほかのヨット乗りの身障者と連絡を取ると参考になるだろう. **20** PHRASE 句 If you say that something that happens is **a load off** your **mind** or **a weight off** your **mind**, you mean that it causes you to stop worrying, for example because it solves a problem that you had. ホッとして、安心して ❑ *Knowing that she had medical insurance took a great load off her mind.* 彼女は、健康保険があると分かってホッとした. **21** PHRASE 句 If something is **on** your **mind**, you are worried or concerned about it and think about it a lot. 気にかかって ❑ *This game has been on my mind all week.* この試合のことが今週ずっと気になっていた. **22** PHRASE 句 If your **mind is on** something or you **have** your **mind on** something, you are thinking about that thing. 一のことを考えている ❑ *At school I was always in trouble – my mind was never on my work.* 学校で私はいつも困っていた. 勉強が全然頭に入らなかった. **23** PHRASE 句 If you have an **open mind**, you avoid forming an opinion or making a decision until you know all the facts. オープンな姿勢、広い心 ❑ *It's hard to see it any other way, though I'm trying to keep an open mind.* 心を開いているつもりだが、ほかの見方をするのは難しい. **24** PHRASE 句 If something **opens** your **mind** to new ideas or experiences, it makes you more willing to accept them or try them. 進んで考慮する、心を開かせる ❑ *She also stimulated his curiosity and opened his mind*

to other cultures. 彼女は彼の好奇心も刺激しほかの文化に心を開かせた. **25** PHRASE 句 If you say that someone is **out of their mind**, you mean that they are mad or very foolish. 頭がおかしい [DISAPPROVAL 不賛成] ❑ *What are you doing? Are you out of your mind?* 何をしているの?気でも狂ったの? **26** PHRASE 句 If you say that someone is **out of their mind with** a feeling such as worry or fear, you are emphasizing that they are extremely worried or afraid. ひどくして [INFORMAL くだけた, EMPHASIS 強調] ❑ *I was out of my mind with fear. I didn't know what to do.* あまりにも怖くて、どうしたらいいのか分からなかった. **27** PHRASE 句 If you say that someone is, for example, **bored out of** their **mind, scared out of** their **mind**, or **stoned out of** their **mind**, you are emphasizing that they are extremely bored, scared, or affected by drugs. 正気がなくなるほどして [INFORMAL くだけた, EMPHASIS 強調] ❑ *That was one of the most depressing experiences of my life. I was bored out of my mind after five minutes.* あれは私の人生で最も退屈な経験の1つだ. 5分後には退屈で気が狂いそうだった. **28** PHRASE 句 If you **put** your **mind to** something, you start making an effort to do it. 専念する、全力を傾ける ❑ *You could do fine in the world if you put your mind to it.* 全力を尽くせばきっと大丈夫だよ. **29** PHRASE 句 If you can **read** someone's **mind**, you know what they are thinking without them saying anything. 心を読み取る ❑ *Don't expect others to read your mind.* 以心伝心で伝わると思うな. **30** PHRASE 句 To **put** someone's **mind at rest** or **set** their **mind at rest** means to stop them from worrying about something. 安心させる ❑ *It may be advisable to have a blood test to put your mind at rest.* 気休めのためにも血液検査を受けた方がいいだろう. **31** PHRASE 句 If you say that nobody **in their right mind** would do a particular thing, you are emphasizing that it is an irrational thing to do and you would be surprised if anyone did it. 正気の人なら一しないだろう [EMPHASIS 強調] ❑ *No one in his right mind would make such a major purchase without asking questions.* 正気の人なら質問もせずにそんな大きな買い物をしないだろう. **32** PHRASE 句 If you **set** your **mind on** something or **have** your **mind set on** it, you are determined to do it or obtain it. 一しようと決意する、一を熱望する ❑ *When my wife sets her mind on something, she invariably finds a way to achieve it.* 妻が何かをしようと決心するといつも必ず遂げる方法を見つける. **33** PHRASE 句 If something **slips** your **mind**, you forget it. 忘れる ❑ *I was going to mention it, but it slipped my mind.* そのことを言うつもりだったのだが忘れた. **34** PHRASE 句 If you **speak** your **mind**, you say firmly and honestly what you think about a situation, even if this may offend or upset people. 打ち明ける、率直に言う ❑ *Martina Navratilova has never been afraid to speak her mind.* マーティナ・ナブラチロバは自分の意見を言うことを恐れたことがない. **35** PHRASE 句 If something **sticks in** your **mind**, it remains firmly in your memory. 心に焼き付いて離れない ❑ *I've always been fond of poetry and one piece has always stuck in my mind.* 常に詩歌を好んできたが1作がいつも心に焼き付いて離れない. **36** PHRASE 句 If something **takes** your **mind off** a problem or unpleasant situation, it helps you to forget about it for a while. 気を紛らわす ❑ *"How about a game of tennis?" suggested Alan. "That'll take your mind off things."* 「テニスを1試合どう」とアランは提案した. 「それで気を紛らわせるよ」 **37** PHRASE 句 You say or write **to** my **mind** to indicate that the statement you are making is your own opinion. 私の考えでは ❑ *There are scenes in this play which, to my mind, are incredibly violent.* この劇には、私の考えでは、非常に暴力的なシーンがあります. **38** PHRASE 句 If you are **of two minds**, you are uncertain about what to do, especially when you have to choose between two courses of action. 迷っている ❑ *He was of two minds about this plan.* 彼はこの計画について迷っていた. **39** to **give** someone **a piece of** your **mind** → see **piece**

❷ mind /maɪnd/ (**minds, minding, minded**) **1** V-T/V-I 他動詞/自動詞 If you do not **mind** something, you are not annoyed or bothered by it. かまわない、気にしない（否定形で）[usu with brd-neg] ❑ *I don't mind the noise during the day.* 昼間の騒音は気にならない. ❑ *I hope you don't mind me stopping in like this, without an appointment.* お約束なしにこのように立ち寄ってすみません. ❑ *I lit a cigarette and nobody seemed to mind.* タバコに火をつけたがだれも気にしないようだった. **2** V-T/V-I 他動詞/自動詞 You use **mind** in the expressions "**do you mind?**" and "**would you mind?**" as a polite way of asking permission or asking someone to do something. 一してもかまいませんか [POLITENESS 丁寧さ] ❑ *Do you mind if I ask you one more thing?* もう1つお伺いしても構いませんか. ❑ *Would you mind waiting outside for a moment?* 少しの間外で待ってくれませんか. **3** V-T 他動詞 If someone does not **mind** what happens or what something is like, they do not have a strong preference for any particular thing. こだわる [with brd-neg] ❑ *I don't mind what we play, really.* 本当に、何をしようとかまわないです. **4** V-T 他動詞 If you **mind** a child or something such as a store or luggage, you take care of it, usually while the person who owns it or is usually responsible for it is somewhere else. 面倒を見る ❑ *Jim Coulters will mind the store while I'm away.* 私の留守中ジム・クールターが店番をする. **5** PHRASE 句 People use the expression **if you don't mind** when they are rejecting an offer or saying that they do not want

Word Web　mineral

The **extraction** of **minerals** from ore is an ancient process. Neolithic man discovered **copper** around 8000 BC. Using fire and charcoal, they **reduced** the ore to its pure **metal** form. About 4,000 years later, Egyptians learned to pour molten copper into molds and metallurgy was born. **Silver** ore often contains large amounts of copper and **lead**. Silver **refineries** often use the smelting process to remove these impurities. Most **gold** does not exist as an ore. Instead, veins of gold run through the earth. Refiners use solvents such as cyanide to obtain pure gold.

to do something, especially when they are annoyed. よろしければ [FEELINGS 感情] □ "Sit down." — "I prefer standing for a while, if you don't mind." 「座りなさい」 「しばらく立っていたいのです, お構いなければ」 **6** PHRASE 句 You use **mind you** to emphasize a piece of information that you are adding, especially when the new information explains what you have said or contrasts with it. Some people use **mind** in a similar way. 言っておくけど [EMPHASIS 強調] □ They pay full rates. Mind you, they can afford it. 彼らは全額支払うよ. 言っておくけど, それくらいの余裕はあるんだ. **7** CONVENTION 慣習表現 You say **never mind** when you are emphasizing that something is not serious or important, especially when someone is upset about it or is saying they are sorry. 気にしないで, いいよ [EMPHASIS 強調] □ Her voice trembled. "Oh, Sylvia, I'm so sorry." — "Never mind." 彼女の声が震えた. 「ああ, シルビア, ごめんなさい」 「いいよ」 **8** PHRASE 句 You use **never mind** to tell someone that they need not do something or worry about something, because it is not important or because you will do it yourself. 気にしないで, 心配しないで □ "Was his name David?" — "No I don't think it was, but never mind, go on." 「彼の名前はデービッドだった?」 「ううん, 違うと思うけど, 気にしないで, 続けて」 □ Dorothy, come on. Never mind your shoes. They'll soon dry off. ドロシー, おいで. 靴のことは気にしないで. すぐに乾くよ. **9** PHRASE 句 You use **never mind** after a statement, often a negative one, to indicate that the statement is even more true of the person, thing, or situation that you are going to mention next. まして や [EMPHASIS 強調] □ I'm not going to believe it myself, never mind convince anyone else. 自分でも信じられないから, ましてやほかの人を説得するなんて無理だ. **10** PHRASE 句 If you say that you **wouldn't mind** something, you mean that you would quite like it. 欲しい, したい □ I wouldn't mind a coffee. コーヒーをもらえますか. **11** V-T 他動詞 If you tell someone to **mind** something, you are warning them to be careful not to hurt themselves or other people, or damage something. 見ている, 番をする [mainly BRIT 主に英国英語; AM usually **watch** 米国英語では通常 **watch**] **12** V-T 他動詞 You use **mind** when you are reminding someone to do something or telling them to be careful not to do something. 気をつける, 注意する [mainly BRIT 主に英国英語; AM usually **make sure**, **take care** 米国英語では通常 **make sure**, **take care**]

mind|ful /maɪndfəl/ ADJ 形容詞 If you are **mindful of** something, you think about it and consider it when taking action. 意識して, 心に留めて [FORMAL 形式ばった] [v-link ADJ] □ We must be mindful of the consequences of selfishness. 身がってさがもたらす結果を心に留めておかなければならない.

mind|less /maɪndlɪs/ ADJ 形容詞 If you describe a violent action as **mindless**, you mean that it is done without thought and will achieve nothing. 無意識の, 無分別な [DISAPPROVAL 不賛成] □ ...a plot that mixes blackmail, extortion and mindless violence. 脅迫・強奪・無分別な暴力が混ざった策略 **2** ADJ 形容詞 If you describe a person or group as **mindless**, you mean that they are stupid or do not think about what they are doing. 愚かな [DISAPPROVAL 不賛成] □ She wasn't at all the mindless little wife so many people perceived her to be. 彼女は, かなり多くの人々が思ったようなばかな妻ではなかった. ● **mind|less|ly** ADV 副詞 [ADV with v] うっかりと, 愚かに □ I was annoyed with myself for having so quickly and mindlessly lost thirty dollars. あっという間にうっかりと30ドルもなくした自分に腹が立った. **3** ADJ 形容詞 If you describe an activity as **mindless**, you mean that it is so dull that people do it or take part in it without thinking. 頭を使わない [DISAPPROVAL 不賛成] □ ...the mindless repetitiveness of some tasks. ある作業の頭を使わない反復性 ● **mind|less|ly** ADV 副詞 [ADV with v] 頭を使わずに □ I spent many hours mindlessly banging a tennis ball against the wall. 何時間も考えもせずにただテニスボールを壁に打ち続けた.

mine
❶ PRONOUN USE
❷ NOUN AND VERB USES

❶ mine /maɪn/ PRON-POSS 所有代名詞 **Mine** is the first person singular possessive pronoun. A speaker or writer uses **mine** to refer to something that belongs or relates to himself or herself. 私のもの □ Her right hand is inches from mine. 彼女の右手は僕の手から数インチ離れたところにある. □ That wasn't his fault, it was mine. それは彼じゃなくて, 私のせいだった.

❷ mine /maɪn/ (mines, mining, minded) **1** N-COUNT 可算名詞 A **mine** is a place where deep holes and tunnels are dug under the ground in order to obtain a mineral such as coal, diamonds, or gold. 鉱山 □ ...coal mines. 炭鉱 **2** V-T 他動詞 When a mineral such as coal, diamonds, or gold **is mined**, it is obtained from the ground by digging deep holes and tunnels. 採掘する [usu passive] □ The pit is being shut down because it no longer has enough coal that can be mined economically. 経済的な見地から十分な石炭が採掘できなくなり炭鉱は閉鎖された **3** N-COUNT 可算名詞 A **mine** is a bomb which is hidden in the ground or in water and which explodes when people or things touch it. 地雷 **4** V-T 他動詞 If an area of land or water **is mined**, mines are placed there which will explode when people or things touch them. 地雷を敷設する □ The approaches to the garrison have been heavily mined. 駐屯地へ通じる道はかなり多くの地雷が敷設されている. **5** → see also **mining**
→ see **diamond**

mine|field /maɪnfiːld/ (minefields) **1** N-COUNT 可算名詞 A **minefield** is an area of land or water where explosive mines have been hidden. 地雷原 **2** N-COUNT 可算名詞 If you describe a situation as a **minefield**, you are emphasizing that there are a lot of hidden dangers or problems, and people need to behave with care because things could easily go wrong. 危険的な事態, 目に見えない危険区域 [EMPHASIS 強調] □ The whole subject is a political minefield. そのテーマ全体が政治的に難しい問題だ.

min|er /maɪnər/ (miners) N-COUNT 可算名詞 A **miner** is a person who works underground in mines in order to obtain minerals such as coal, diamonds, or gold. 坑夫

min|er|al /mɪnərəl/ (minerals) N-COUNT 可算名詞 A **mineral** is a substance such as tin, salt, or sulfur that is formed naturally in rocks and in the earth. Minerals are also found in small quantities in food and drink. ミネラル, 鉱物
→ see Word Web: **mineral**
→ see **diamond**, **rock**

min|er|al wa|ter (mineral waters) N-MASS 質量名詞 **Mineral water** is water that comes out of the ground naturally and is considered healthy to drink. ミネラルウォーター

min|gle /mɪŋgəl/ (mingles, mingling, mingled) **1** V-RECIP 相互動詞 If things such as sounds, smells, or feelings **mingle**, they become mixed together but are usually still recognizable. 入り交じる □ Now the cheers and applause mingled in a single sustained roar. そして拍手喝采いが交じりあっていつまでも響き渡った. **2** V-RECIP 相互動詞 At a party, if you **mingle with** the other people there, you move around and talk to them. 歓談する □ Go out of your way to mingle with others at the wedding. 披露宴では無理にでもほかの人たちと話をしなさい. □ Guests ate and mingled. 来客は食事をし歓談した.

Word Link　mini ≈ very small : miniature, minibar, minibus

minia|ture /mɪniətʃər, -tʃʊər/ (miniatures) **1** ADJ 形容詞 **Miniature** is used to describe something that is very small, especially a smaller version of something which is normally much bigger. 小型の, ミニチュアの [ADJ n] □ Rosehill Farm has been selling miniature roses since 1979. ローズヒル農場は1979年以来ミニチュアのバラを販売している. **2** PHRASE 句 If you describe one thing as another thing **in miniature**, you mean that it is much smaller in size or scale than the other thing, but is otherwise exactly the same. そっくり小型にした, ミニチュアの □ Ecuador provides a perfect introduction to South America; it's a continent in miniature. エクアドルは小規模な大陸なので, 南アメリカへの第1歩としてはかんぺきだ. **3** N-COUNT 可算名詞 A **miniature** is a very small, detailed painting, often of a person. 細密画

mini|bar /mɪnibɑːr/ (minibars) N-COUNT 可算名詞 In a hotel room, a **minibar** is a small refrigerator containing alcoholic drinks. ミニバー

m

Word Link | mini ≈ very small : miniature, minibar, minibus

mini|bus /mɪnɪbʌs/ (**minibuses**) also **mini-bus** N-COUNT 可算名詞 A **minibus** is a large van which has seats in the back for passengers, and windows along its sides. マイクロバス [also 'by' N] ❑ He was then taken by minibus to the military base. そして彼は基地までマイクロバスで連れて行かれた。

mini|disc /mɪnɪdɪsk/ (**minidiscs**) N-COUNT 可算名詞 商標 A **minidisc** is a small compact disc which you can record music or data on. ミニディスク, MD [TRADEMARK]

mini|dish /mɪnɪdɪʃ/ (**minidishes**) N-COUNT 可算名詞 A **minidish** is a small satellite dish that can receive signals from communications satellites for media such as television programs and the Internet. 受信アンテナ

Word Link | minim ≈ smallest : minimal, minimize, minimum

mini|mal /mɪnɪməl/ ADJ 形容詞 Something that is **minimal** is very small in quantity, value, or degree. 最小限の, 最低の ❑ The cooperation between the two is minimal. 両者間の協力は最小限にとどまっている。

mini|mal|ism /mɪnɪməlɪzəm/ N-UNCOUNT 不可算名詞 **Minimalism** is a style in which a small number of very simple things are used to create a particular effect. ミニマリズム ❑ In her own home, she replaced austere minimalism with cosy warmth and color. 彼女の家では, 簡素なミニマリズムを心地よい暖かさと色に取って代えた。

mini|mal|ist /mɪnɪməlɪst/ (**minimalists**) 1 N-COUNT 可算名詞 A **minimalist** is an artist or designer who uses minimalism. ミニマリスト ❑ He was influenced by the minimalists in the 1970s. 彼は1970年代のミニマリストに影響を受けた。 2 ADJ 形容詞 **Minimalist** is used to describe ideas, artists, or designers that are influenced by minimalism. ミニマリズムの ❑ The two designers settled upon a minimalist approach. 2人の設計士がミニマリズムの方法で落ち着いた。

mini|mize /mɪnɪmaɪz/ (**minimizes, minimizing, minimized**) 1 V-T 他動詞 If you **minimize** a risk, problem, or unpleasant situation, you reduce it to the lowest possible level, or prevent it from increasing beyond that level. 最小限にする ❑ Concerned people want to minimize the risk of developing cancer. 不安に駆られた人々はがん発生のリスクを最小限にとどめたがっている。 2 V-T 他動詞 If you **minimize** something, you make it seem smaller or less significant than it really is. 軽視する ❑ Some have minimized the importance of ideological factors. イデオロギーに関する要素の重要性を軽視した人もいる。 3 V-T 他動詞 If you **minimize** a window on a computer screen, you make it very small, because you do not want to use it. 最小化する ❑ Click the square icon again to minimize the window. ウィンドウを最小化するにはもう1度四角いアイコンをもう1度クリックしなさい。

mini|mum /mɪnɪməm/ 1 ADJ 形容詞 You use **minimum** to describe an amount which is the smallest that is possible, allowed, or required. 最小の, 最低の [ADJ N] ❑ He was only five feet nine, the minimum height for a policeman. 彼の身長はたったの5フィート9インチで, 警察官としての最低身長だ。 ● N-SING 単数名詞 **Minimum** is also a noun. 最小限, 最低限 ❑ This will take a minimum of one hour. これは最低1時間はかかるだろう。 2 ADJ 形容詞 You use **minimum** to state how small an amount is. わずかな [ADJ N] ❑ The basic needs of life are available with minimum effort. 生活必需品はほんの少しの努力で手に入る。 ● N-SING 単数名詞 **Minimum** is also a noun. わずか ❑ With a minimum of fuss, she produced the grandson he had so desperately wished for. 彼女はいとも簡単に, 彼があれほど望んでいた孫を産んだ。 3 ADV 副詞 If you say that something is a particular amount **minimum**, you mean that this is the smallest amount it should be or could possibly be, although a larger amount is acceptable or very possible. 最低でも [amount ADV] ❑ You're talking over a thousand dollars minimum for one course. 1講座につき最低でも1000ドル以上になります。

Word Partnership | minimum は次の語句と使われる:

N.	minimum **age**, minimum **balance**, minimum **payment**, minimum **purchase**, minimum **requirement**, minimum **salary** 1
ADJ.	**absolute** minimum, **bare** minimum 1 2

mini|mum wage N-SING 単数名詞 The **minimum wage** is the lowest wage that an employer is allowed to pay an employee, according to a law or agreement. 最低賃金 ❑ Some of them earn below the minimum wage. 給料が最低賃金に満たない人もいる。
→ see **factory**

min|ing /maɪnɪŋ/ N-UNCOUNT 不可算名詞 **Mining** is the industry and activities connected with getting valuable or useful minerals from the ground, for example coal, diamonds, or gold. 鉱業, 採掘 ❑ ...traditional industries such as coal mining and steel making. 炭鉱業や製鋼業のような伝統的産業
→ see **industry, tunnel**

min|is|ter /mɪnɪstər/ (**ministers**) 1 N-COUNT 可算名詞 A **minister** is a member of the clergy, especially in Protestant churches. 牧師, 聖職者 ❑ His father was a Baptist minister. 彼の父親はバプティスト派の牧師だった。 2 N-COUNT 可算名詞 A **minister** is a person who officially represents their government in a foreign country and has a lower rank than an ambassador. 公使 ❑ He concluded a deal with the Danish minister in Washington. 彼は, ワシントンでデンマーク公使と協定を取り決めた。 3 N-COUNT 可算名詞 In some countries outside the United States, a **minister** is a person who is in charge of a particular government department. 大臣 ❑ When the government came to power, he was named minister of culture. 政府が政権を握ったとき, 彼は文化大臣となった。

min|is|te|rial /mɪnɪstɪəriəl/ ADJ 形容詞 You use **ministerial** to refer to people, events, or jobs that are connected with government ministers. 大臣の, 閣僚の [ADJ N] ❑ The prime minister's initial ministerial appointments haven't pleased all his supporters. 首相の当初の大臣任命に不満を抱く支持者もいる。

min|is|try /mɪnɪstri/ (**ministries**) N-COUNT 可算名詞 In many countries, a **ministry** is a government department which deals with a particular thing or area of activity, for example trade, defense, or transportation. 省 ❑ ...the Ministry of Justice. 法務省

mink /mɪŋk/ (**minks**)

Mink can also be used as the plural form.

Mink は複数形としても使える。

1 N-COUNT 可算名詞 A **mink** is a small animal with highly valued fur. ミンク ❑ ...a proposal for a ban on the hunting of foxes, mink, and hares. キツネ・ミンク・野ウサギの狩猟禁止法の提案 ● N-UNCOUNT 不可算名詞 **Mink** is the fur of a mink. ミンクの毛皮 ❑ ...a mink coat. ミンクのコート 2 N-COUNT 可算名詞 A **mink** is a coat or other garment made from the fur of a mink. ミンクのコート ミンクの衣類 ❑ Some people like to dress up in minks and diamonds. ミンクのコートやダイアモンドで着飾るのが好きな人もいる。

mi|nor /maɪnər/ (**minors**) 1 ADJ 形容詞 You use **minor** when you want to describe something that is less important, serious, or significant than other things in a group or situation. 重要でない ❑ She is known in Italy for a number of minor roles in films. 彼女はイタリアでいくつかの映画の脇役で出演したことで知られている。 2 ADJ 形容詞 A **minor** illness or operation is not likely to be dangerous to someone's life or health. 軽い ❑ Sarah had been plagued continually by a series of minor illnesses since her mid teens. サラは十代の中ごろからずっと一連の軽い病気で悩み続けてきた。 3 N-COUNT 可算名詞 A **minor** is a person who is still legally a child. In most states in the United States, people are minors until they reach the age of eighteen. 未成年 ❑ The approach has virtually ended cigarette sales to minors. その方法により事実上未成年者へのタバコ販売がなくなりました。 4 ADJ 形容詞 A **minor** scale is one in which the third note is three semitones higher than the first. 短調の, 短音階の ❑ ...the unfinished sonata movement in F minor. 未完成のソナタ楽章, へ短調

Thesaurus | minor また次を参照:

ADJ.	insignificant, lesser, small, unimportant; (ant.) important, major, significant 1

Word Partnership | minor は次の語句と使われる:

N.	minor **adjustment**, minor **damage**, minor **detail**, minor **problem** 1 minor **illness**, minor **injury**, minor **operation**, minor **surgery** 2
ADV.	**relatively** minor 1 2

mi|nor|ity /mɪnɒrɪti, maɪ-/ (**minorities**) 1 N-SING 単数名詞 If you talk about a **minority** of people or things in a larger group, you are referring to a number of them that forms less than half of the larger group, usually much less than half. 少数派 ❑ Local authority child-care provision covers only a tiny minority of working mothers. 地方自治体の保育設備はごくわずかの働く母親しか利用できない。 ● PHRASE 句 If people are **in a minority** or **in the minority**, they belong to a group of people or things that form less than half of a larger group. 少数派で ❑ Even in the 1960s, politically active students and academics were in a minority. 1960年代でさえ, 政治に関し活動的な学生や大学教師は少数派だった。 2 N-COUNT 可算名詞 A **minority** is a group of people of the same race, culture, or religion who live in a place where most of the people around them are of a different race, culture, or religion. 少数民族 ❑ ...the region's ethnic minorities. 地域の少数民族

Word Partnership

minority は次の語句と使われる:

N.	minority **leader**, minority **party** 1 minority **applicants**, minority **community**, minority **group**, minority **population**, minority **students**, minority **voters**, minority **women** 2

mint /mɪnt/ (mints, minting, minted) 1 N-UNCOUNT 不可算名詞 **Mint** is an herb with fresh-tasting leaves. ミント、ハッカ □ *Garnish with mint sprigs.* ミントの小枝で飾りなさい. 2 N-COUNT 可算名詞 A **mint** is a candy with a peppermint flavor. Some people suck mints in order to make their breath smell fresher. ハッカあめ □ *She popped a mint into her mouth.* 彼女はハッカあめをポンと口に入れた. 3 N-COUNT 可算名詞 The **mint** is the place where the official coins of a country are made. 造幣局 □ *In 1965 the mint stopped putting silver in dimes.* 1965年に造幣局は10セント硬貨に銀を使用するのをやめました. 4 V-T 他動詞 To **mint** coins or medals means to make them in a mint. 鋳造する □ *...the right to mint coins.* 硬貨を鋳造する権利
→ see **money**

Word Link

min ≈ small, lessen : diminish, minus, minute

mi|nus /maɪnəs/ (minuses) 1 CONJ 接続詞 You use **minus** to show that one number or quantity is being subtracted from another. 差し引いて □ *One minus one is zero.* 1引く1は0. 2 ADJ 形容詞 **Minus** before a number or quantity means that the number or quantity is less than zero. マイナスの、負の [ADJ amount] □ *The aircraft was subjected to temperatures of minus 65 degrees and plus 120 degrees.* 航空機はマイナス65度とプラス120度にさらされました. 3 ADJ 形容詞 Teachers use **minus** in grading work in schools and colleges. "B minus" is not as good as "B," but is a better grade than "C". (成績評価の段階で) マイナス □ *I'm giving him a B minus.* 彼にはBマイナスを出します. 4 PREP 前置詞 To be **minus** something means not to have that thing. ―なしで □ *The film company collapsed, leaving Chris jobless and minus his life savings.* その映画会社は倒産し、クリスは失業し老後の蓄えもなくなった. 5 N-COUNT 可算名詞 A **minus** is a disadvantage. 不利な点 [INFORMAL くだけた] □ *The minuses far outweigh that possible gain.* 不利な点が見込み利益を大幅に上回る.

Thesaurus

minus また次を参照:

PREP.	without 4
N.	deficiency, disadvantage, drawback 5

Word Link

cule ≈ small : minuscule, molecule, ridicule

mi|nus|cule /mɪnɪskyul/ ADJ 形容詞 If you describe something as **minuscule**, you mean that it is very small. 非常に小さい □ *The film was shot in 17 days, a minuscule amount of time.* その映画は17日間という非常に短い期間で撮影された.

minute

❶ NOUN AND VERB USES
❷ ADJECTIVE USE

❶ **mi|nute** /mɪnɪt/ (minutes, minuting, minuted) 1 N-COUNT 可算名詞 A **minute** is one of the sixty parts that an hour is divided into. People often say "**a minute**" or "**minutes**" when they mean a short length of time. 分、少しの時間 □ *The pizza will then take about twenty minutes to cook.* ピザはそれから約20分で焼ける. □ *Bye Mom, see you in a minute.* じゃあ、お母さん、またすぐあとで. 2 N-PLURAL 複数形名詞 The **minutes** of a meeting are the written records of the things that are discussed or decided at it. 議事録 □ *He'd been reading the minutes of the last meeting.* 彼は、前回の会議の議事録を読んでいた. 3 V-T 他動詞 When someone **minutes** something that is discussed or decided at a meeting, they make a written record of it. 議事録に記録する □ *You don't need to minute that.* それは議事録に書かなくていいです. 4 CONVENTION 慣習表現 People often use expressions such as **wait a minute** or **just a minute** when they want to stop you doing or saying something. ちょっと待って □ *Wait a minute, folks, something is wrong here.* ちょっと待って、みんな. ここがおかしい. 5 PHRASE 句 If you say that something will or may happen **at any minute** or **any minute now**, you are emphasizing that it is likely to happen very soon. 今すぐにでも [EMPHASIS 強調] □ *It looked as though it might rain at any minute.* 今にも雨が降り出しそうだった. 6 PHRASE 句 A **last-minute** action is one that is done at the latest time possible. ぎりぎりの □ *He will probably wait until the last minute.* 彼はきっとぎりぎりまで待つだろう. 7 PHRASE 句 If you say that something happens **the minute** something else happens, you are emphasizing that it happens immediately after the other thing. ―するとすぐに [EMPHASIS 強調] □ *The minute you do this, you'll lose control.* これをするとすぐに理性を失う.

❷ **mi|nute** /maɪnut/ (minutest) ADJ 形容詞 If you say that

something is **minute**, you mean that it is very small. 微小の □ *Only a minute amount is needed.* 必要なのはほんの微量だ.

Word Partnership

minute は次の語句と使われる:

V.	take a minute ❶ 1 wait a minute ❶ 4
DET.	a minute or two, another minute, each minute, every minute, half a minute ❶ any minute now, at any minute ❶ 5
N.	minute detail, minute quantity of something ❷

mira|cle /mɪrəkəl/ (miracles) 1 N-COUNT 可算名詞 If you say that a good event is a **miracle**, you mean that it is very surprising and unexpected. 奇跡的なこと、驚くべき出来事 □ *It is a miracle no one was killed.* 死者が出なかったのは奇跡的だ. 2 ADJ 形容詞 A **miracle** drug or product does something that was thought almost impossible. 驚異的、特効 [JOURNALISM ジャーナリズム] [ADJ n] □ *...the miracle drugs that keep his 94-year-old mother healthy.* 94歳の母親の健康を維持する特効薬 3 N-COUNT 可算名詞 A **miracle** is a wonderful and surprising event that is believed to be caused by God. 奇跡 □ *...Jesus's ability to perform miracles.* キリストの奇跡を行う能力

mi|racu|lous /mɪrækyələs/ 1 ADJ 形容詞 If you describe a good event as **miraculous**, you mean that it is very surprising and unexpected. 奇跡的な、驚異的な □ *The horse made a miraculous recovery to finish a close third.* その馬は奇跡的に持ち返しぎりぎり3位に入った. ● **mi|racu|lous|ly** ADV 副詞 奇跡的にも □ *Miraculously, the guards escaped death or serious injury.* 奇跡的にも警備員は死も重傷も免れた. 2 ADJ 形容詞 If someone describes a wonderful event as **miraculous**, they believe that the event was caused by God. 奇跡の、超自然的な □ *...miraculous healing.* 奇跡的回復

mir|ror /mɪrər/ (mirrors, mirroring, mirrored) 1 N-COUNT 可算名詞 A **mirror** is a flat piece of glass which reflects light, so that when you look at it you can see yourself reflected in it. 鏡 □ *He went into the bathroom absent-mindedly and looked at himself in the mirror.* 彼はぼんやりとしながらバスルームに行き鏡に映った姿を見た. 2 V-T 他動詞 If something **mirrors** something else, it has similar features to it, and therefore seems like a copy or representation of it. よく似ている □ *Despite the fact that I have tried to be objective, the book inevitably mirrors my own interests and experiences.* 客観的になろうとしたにもかかわらず、その本は必然的に自分の関心や経験を反映している. 3 V-T 他動詞 If you see something reflected in water, you can say that the water **mirrors** it. 反射する [LITERARY 文語的] □ *...the sudden glitter where a newly flooded field mirrors the sky.* 最近水浸しになった野原に空が反射したところでの突然の輝き
→ see **telescope**

Word Partnership

mirror は次の語句と使われる:

V.	glance in a mirror, look in a mirror, reflect in a mirror, see in a mirror 1
PREP.	in front of a mirror 1
N.	reflection in a mirror 1

mis|be|have /mɪsbɪheɪv/ (misbehaves, misbehaving, misbehaved) V-I 自動詞 If someone, especially a child, **misbehaves**, they behave in a way that is not acceptable to other people. 行儀悪くする □ *When the children misbehaved she was unable to cope.* 子供たちの行儀が悪いとき彼女はうまく対処できなかった.

mis|cal|cu|late /mɪskælkyəleɪt/ (miscalculates, miscalculating, miscalculated) V-T/V-I 他動詞/自動詞 If you **miscalculate**, you make a mistake in judging a situation or in making a calculation. 判断を誤る、計算違いする □ *It's clear that he has badly miscalculated the mood of the people.* 彼が一般の感情をかなり読み違えたのは明らかだ. ● **mis|cal|cu|la|tion** /mɪskælkyəleɪʃən/ (miscalculations) N-VAR 可変性名詞 判断違い、誤算 □ *The coup failed because of miscalculations by the plotters.* クーデターは陰謀者の誤算で失敗に終わった.

mis|car|riage /mɪskærɪdʒ, -kær-/ (miscarriages) N-VAR 可変性名詞 If a pregnant woman has a **miscarriage**, her baby dies and she gives birth to it before it is properly formed. 流産 □ *No one had any idea she had had a miscarriage.* 彼女が流産をしたことはだれも知らなかった.

mis|cel|la|neous /mɪsəleɪniəs/ ADJ 形容詞 A **miscellaneous** group consists of many different kinds of things or people that are difficult to put into a particular category. 雑多な、もろもろの [ADJ n] □ *...a hoard of miscellaneous junk.* さまざまながらくたの宝庫

mis|chief /mɪstʃɪf/ 1 N-UNCOUNT 不可算名詞 **Mischief** is playing harmless tricks on people or doing things you are not supposed to do. It can also refer to the desire to do this. いたずら □ *The little boy was a real handful. He was always up to mischief.* その少年は本当に手に負えなかった. いつもいたずらをしていた. 2 N-UNCOUNT 不可算名詞 **Mischief** is behavior that is

intended to cause trouble for people. It can also refer to the trouble that is caused. 損害, 危害 ❑ *The more sinister explanation is that he is about to make mischief in the Middle East again.* さらに不吉な解釈では, 彼が中東で再び問題を起こそうとしているということだ.

mis|chie|vous /mɪstʃɪvəs/ ■ ADJ 形容詞 A **mischievous** person likes to have fun by playing harmless tricks on people or doing things they are not supposed to. いたずら好きな ❑ *She rocks back and forth on her chair like a mischievous child.* 彼女はいたずらっ子のようにいすを前後にガッタンガッタン揺らしていた. ● **mis|chie|vous|ly** ADV 副詞 いたずらっぽく ❑ *Kathryn winked mischievously.* キャスリンはいたずらっぽくウィンクをした. ■ ADJ 形容詞 A **mischievous** act or suggestion is intended to cause trouble. 嫌がらせの, 悪意のある ❑ *"I have a few mischievous plans," says Zevon.* 「いくつかたくらみがあるんだ」とゼボンは言った. ● **mis|chie|vous|ly** ADV 副詞 悪意を持って ❑ *That does not require "massive" military intervention, as some have mischievously claimed.* それには, 一部の人が悪意を持って主張したような「大規模な」軍事介入は必要がない.

mis|con|cep|tion /mɪskənsɛpʃ⁰n/ (**misconceptions**) N-COUNT 可算名詞 A **misconception** is an idea that is not correct. 誤解 ❑ *It is a misconception that Peggy was fabulously wealthy.* ペギーがとてつもなく裕福だったというのは誤解だ.

mis|con|duct /mɪskɒndʌkt/ N-UNCOUNT 不可算名詞 **Misconduct** is bad or unacceptable behavior, especially by a professional person. 不正行為, 職権乱用 ❑ *A psychologist was found guilty of serious professional misconduct yesterday.* 心理学者が職権乱用の重罪で有罪となった.

mis|de|mean|or /mɪsdɪmiːnər/ (**misdemeanors**) ■ N-COUNT 可算名詞 A **misdemeanor** is an act that some people consider to be wrong or unacceptable. 無作法, 不品行 [FORMAL 形式ばった] ❑ *Paul appeared before the faculty to account for his various misdemeanors.* ポールはさまざまな不品行を説明するために教職会の前に姿を現した. ■ N-COUNT 可算名詞 In the United States and other countries where the legal system distinguishes between very serious crimes and less serious ones, a **misdemeanor** is a less serious crime. 軽罪 [LEGAL 法律的] ❑ *Under state law, it is a misdemeanor to possess a firearm on school premises.* 州法下では学校の敷地内で銃を所持するのは軽罪になる.

mis|er|able /mɪzərəb⁰l/ ■ ADJ 形容詞 If you are **miserable**, you are very unhappy. つらい, 惨めな ❑ *I took a series of badly paid secretarial jobs which made me really miserable.* いくつかの率の悪い秘書系の仕事について本当につらい思いをした. ● **mis|er|ably** /mɪzərəbli/ ADV 副詞 惨めったらしく ❑ *He looked miserably down at his plate.* 彼は惨めったらしく皿を見た. ■ ADJ 形容詞 If you describe a place or situation as **miserable**, you mean that it makes you feel unhappy or depressed. 悲惨な, 不快な ❑ *There was nothing at all in this miserable place to distract him.* この悲惨な場所で彼の気分転換になるようなものは全く何もなかった. ■ ADJ 形容詞 If you describe the weather as **miserable**, you mean that it makes you feel depressed, because it is raining or dull. うっとうしい ❑ *On a gray, wet, miserable day our teams congregated in Port Townsend.* どんよりとした雨模様のうっとうしい日にチームはポートタウンゼンドに集合した. ■ ADJ 形容詞 [ADJ n] If you describe someone as **miserable**, you mean that you do not like them because they are bad-tempered or unfriendly. 無愛想な, 気難しい ❑ *He always was a miserable man. He never spoke to me nor anybody else, not even to pass the time of day.* 彼はいつも無愛想だった. 私にもほかの人にも話しかけたことがなかったっけ, あいさつすらしなかった. ■ ADJ 形容詞 You can describe a quantity or quality as **miserable** when you think that it is much smaller or worse than it ought to be. わずかな, 貧弱な [EMPHASIS 強調] ❑ *Our speed over the ground was a miserable 2.2 knots.* 地上でのスピードはわずか2.2ノットだった. ● **mis|er|ably** ADV 副詞 [ADV adj] わずかに ❑ *...the miserably inadequate supply of books now provided for schools.* 学校に備えられた本の供給があまりにも貧弱なこと ■ ADJ 形容詞 A **miserable** failure is a very great one. 哀れな, ひどい [EMPHASIS 強調] [ADJ n] ❑ *The film was a miserable commercial failure both in Italy and in the United States.* その映画はイタリアでもアメリカでも興行的に大失敗だった. ● **mis|er|ably** ADV 副詞 [ADV with v] ひどく ❑ *Some manage it. Some fail miserably.* なんとか成功する人もいれば, 大失敗する人もいる.

Thesaurus   *miserable* また次を参照:

| ADJ. | unhappy ■ |
| | unfortunate, wretched ■ |

mis|ery /mɪzəri/ (**miseries**) ■ N-VAR 可変性名詞 **Misery** is great unhappiness. 悲惨さ ❑ *All that money brought nothing but sadness and misery and tragedy.* その金は悲哀と苦難と悲劇を生んだだけだった. ■ N-UNCOUNT 不可算名詞 **Misery** is the way of life and unpleasant living conditions of people who are very poor. 貧困 ❑ *A tiny, educated elite profited from the misery of their two million fellow countrymen.* ごく一握りの教養のあるエリートたちが貧困にあえぐ200万人の国民から暴利をむさぼっていた. ■ PHRASE 句 If someone **makes** your **life a misery**, they behave in an unpleasant way

towards you over a period of time and make you very unhappy. 不幸に陥れる ❑ *I would really like living here if it wasn't for the gangs of kids who make our lives a misery.* トラブルを起こすあの非行少年たちさえいなかったら, ここは本当に暮らしやすいところなのに. ■ PHRASE 句 If you **put** someone **out of** their **misery**, you tell them something they are very anxious to know. じらさずに教えてやる [INFORMAL くだけた] ❑ *Please put me out of my misery. How do you do it?* ねえ, じらさないで教えてよ. どうやってするの? ■ PHRASE 句 If you **put** an animal **out of** its **misery**, you kill it because it is sick or injured and cannot be cured or healed. 安楽死させる ❑ *He notes grimly that the Watsons have called the vet to put their dog out of its misery.* ワトソンさんが獣医を呼んで飼犬を安楽死させたと, 彼はぞっとした表情で話す.

mis|fit /mɪsfɪt/ (**misfits**) N-COUNT 可算名詞 A **misfit** is a person who is not easily accepted by other people, often because their behavior is very different from that of everyone else. 場違いな人 ❑ *I have been made to feel a social and psychological misfit for not wanting children.* 子供を望まないことで, 自分はこれまでずっと社会的にも精神的にものけ者扱いされているように感じてきた.

mis|for|tune /mɪsfɔrtʃən/ (**misfortunes**) N-VAR 可変性名詞 A **misfortune** is something unpleasant or unlucky that happens to someone. 不運, 不幸 ❑ *She seemed to enjoy the misfortunes of others.* 彼女はまるで人の不幸を喜んでいるようだった.

mis|giv|ing /mɪsgɪvɪŋ/ (**misgivings**) N-VAR 可変性名詞 If you have **misgivings** about something that is being suggested or done, you feel that it is not quite right, and are worried that it may have unwanted results. 疑い, 不安 ❑ *She had some misgivings about what she was about to do.* 彼女はこれからまさにやろうとしていることに一抹の不安を感じた.

mis|guid|ed /mɪsgaɪdɪd/ ADJ 形容詞 If you describe an opinion or plan as **misguided**, you are critical of it because you think it is based on an incorrect idea. You can also describe people as misguided. 誤解を与える [DISAPPROVAL 不賛成] ❑ *In a misguided attempt to be funny, he manages only offensiveness.* 彼は人を笑わせようとしては誤解され不評を買っている.

mis|han|dle /mɪshænd⁰l/ (**mishandles, mishandling, mishandled**) V-T 他動詞 If you say that someone **has mishandled** something, you are critical of them because you think they have dealt with it badly. 対応を誤る [DISAPPROVAL 不賛成] ❑ *She completely mishandled an important project purely through lack of attention.* 彼女は単なる不注意から重要なプロジェクトを破綻させてしまった. ● **mis|han|dling** N-UNCOUNT 不可算名詞 誤った対応 ❑ *...the government's mishandling of the economy.* 国の経済政策の誤り.

mis|hap /mɪshæp/ (**mishaps**) N-VAR 可変性名詞 A **mishap** is an unfortunate but not very serious event that happens to someone. ちょっとした不幸 ❑ *After a number of mishaps she did manage to get back to Germany.* いろんなハプニングはあったが, 彼女は何とかドイツに戻ることができた.

mis|in|for|ma|tion /mɪsɪnfərmeɪʃ⁰n/ N-UNCOUNT 不可算名詞 **Misinformation** is wrong information which is given to someone, often in a deliberate attempt to make them believe something that is not true. 誤報; 虚偽情報 ❑ *This was a deliberate piece of misinformation.* これは虚偽情報だった.

Word Link mis ≈ bad : *mis*interpret, *mis*leading, *mis*trust

mis|in|ter|pret /mɪsɪntɜrprɪt/ (**misinterprets, misinterpreting, misinterpreted**) V-T 他動詞 If you **misinterpret** something, you understand it wrongly. 誤解する ❑ *He was amazed that he'd misinterpreted the situation so completely.* 状況をそこまで完全に見誤っていたことに彼自身信じられない気持ちだった. ● **mis|in|ter|pre|ta|tion** /mɪsɪntɜrprɪteɪʃ⁰n/ (**misinterpretations**) N-VAR 可変性名詞 誤解 ❑ *...a misinterpretation of the aims and ends of socialism.* 社会主義の目標と最終目的を誤解していたこと.

mis|judge /mɪsdʒʌdʒ/ (**misjudges, misjudging, misjudged**) V-T 他動詞 If you say that someone **has misjudged** a person or situation, you mean that they have formed an incorrect idea or opinion about them, and often that they have made a wrong decision as a result of this. 判断を誤る ❑ *Perhaps I had misjudged him, and he was not so predictable after all.* 彼のことを見損なっていたのかもしれんよ. そんなにありきたりなやつじゃなかった.

mis|lead /mɪslid/ (**misleads, misleading, misled**) V-T 他動詞 If you say that someone or something **has misled** you, you mean that they have made you believe something that is not true, either by telling you a lie or by giving you a wrong idea or impression. 誤解を与える ❑ *It's this legend which has misled scholars.* 学者たちの混乱を招いたのはこの伝説である.

mis|lead|ing /mɪslidɪŋ/ ADJ 形容詞 If you describe something as **misleading**, you mean that it gives you a wrong idea or impression. 誤解を与える ❑ *It would be misleading to say that we were friends.* 2人が友人だったというと誤解を招くかもしれない. ● **mis|lead|ing|ly** ADV 副詞 誤解を与えるように ❑ *The data had been*

presented misleadingly. そのデータの表現は誤解を招くおそれが
あった.

mis|led /mɪslɛd/ **Misled** is the past tense and past participle of
mislead. misleadの過去・過去分詞

mis|man|age /mɪsmænɪdʒ/ (**mismanages, mismanaging,
mismanaged**) V-T 他動詞 To **mismanage** something means to
manage it badly. 対応を誤る □75% of voters think the president has
mismanaged the economy. 有権者の75%が大統領の経済政策は誤ってい
ると答えた.

mis|man|age|ment /mɪsmænɪdʒmənt/ N-UNCOUNT 不可
算名詞 Someone's **mismanagement** of a system or organization
is the bad way they have dealt with it or organized it. 誤った対
応 □His gross mismanagement left the company desperately in need of
restructuring. 彼の放漫経営のせいで会社はリストラを余儀なく
された.

mis|placed /mɪspleɪst/ ADJ 形容詞 If you describe a feeling or
action as **misplaced**, you are critical of it because you think it is
inappropriate, or directed towards the wrong thing or person. 的
外れな [DISAPPROVAL 不賛成] □A telling sign of misplaced priorities is
the concentration on health, not environmental issues. 優先順位の誤り
は、環境ではなく健康のことばかりを問題にしていることにもはっき
りと現れている.

mis|read /mɪsriːd/ (**misreads, misreading**)

> The form **misread** is used in the present tense, and is the past
> tense and past participle, when it is pronounced /mɪsrɛd/.
>
> misread 形は現在時制で使われ、また過去時制と過去分詞でもある
> が、その時は /mɪsrɛd/ と発音される.

1 V-T 他動詞 If you **misread** a situation or someone's behavior,
you do not understand it properly. 見誤る □The administration
largely misread the mood of the electorate. 政府は有権者の意識を大き
く見誤りました. ● **mis|read|ing** (**misreadings**) N-COUNT 可算名
詞 見誤り □...a misreading of opinion in France. フランスの世論の見誤
り. **2** V-T 他動詞 If you **misread** something that has been written
or printed, you look at it and think that it says something that it
does not say. 読み間違える □His chauffeur misread his route and took a
wrong turn. 運転手は道順を誤って間違った角を曲がってしまった.

mis|rep|re|sent /mɪsrɛprɪzɛnt/ (**misrepresents,
misrepresenting, misrepresented**) V-T 他動詞 If someone
misrepresents a person or situation, they give a wrong or
inaccurate account of what the person or situation is like. 誤っ
て伝える □He said that the press had misrepresented him as arrogant
and bullying. 彼は、自分のことを乱暴ないじめ子だと書いた新聞
報道は誤っていると言った. □Hollywood films misrepresented us as
drunks, maniacs, and murderers. ハリウッド映画は我々のことを酔
っ払いや狂人や人殺しのように扱った. ● **mis|rep|re|sen|ta|tion**
/mɪsrɛprɪzɛnteɪʃən/ (**misrepresentations**) N-VAR 可変性名詞 誤っ
て伝えること □I wish to point out your misrepresentation of the facts.
事実を誤って伝えてられる点を指摘しておきたいと思います.

---

miss

❶ USED AS A TITLE OR A FORM OF
ADDRESS
❷ VERB AND NOUN USES

---

❶ Miss /mɪs/ (**Misses**) N-TITLE 称号名詞 You use **Miss** in front of
the name of a girl or unmarried woman when you are speaking
to her or referring to her. さん [FORMAL 形式ばった] □It was nice
talking to you, Miss Ellis. エリスさん、お話できてよかったです.

> In English-speaking countries **Miss** is used in front of the name
> of an unmarried woman when you are speaking or referring
> to her. **Mrs.** is used before the name of a married woman. Some
> women who do not think it is important to let people know
> whether they are married or not, choose to call themselves
> **Ms.** instead. Just like **Mr.**, used for men, Ms. does not tell you
> whether a person is married or single.

❷ miss /mɪs/ (**misses, missing, missed**)
⇨ Please look at meaning **10** to see if the expression you are
looking for is shown under another headword. **1** V-T/V-I 他動
詞/自動詞 If you **miss** something, you fail to hit it, for example
when you have thrown something at it or you have shot a bullet
at it. 的を外す、狙い損なう □She hurled the ashtray across the room,
narrowly missing my head. 彼女が部屋の向こうから投げつけた灰皿
がもう少しで僕の頭に当たるところだった. □When I'd missed a few
times, he suggested I rest the rifle on a rock to steady it. 何度か的を外し
たので、ライフルが動かないように岩の上に置いてはどうかと彼は言
った. ● N-COUNT 可算名詞 **Miss** is also a noun. 的外れ □After more
misses, they finally put two arrows into the lion's chest. さらに射損じ
たが、ついに2本の矢がライオンの胸に命中した. **2** V-T/V-I 他動詞/
自動詞 In sports, if you **miss** a shot, you fail to get the ball in the
goal, net, or hole. 逃す □He scored four of the baskets but missed a free

throw. 彼はフィールドゴールを4回決め、フリースローを1回外した.
□He dived for the ball and missed. 彼はボールに突進したが逃してしま
った. ● N-COUNT 可算名詞 **Miss** is also a noun. 逃すこと □Snow
made his first basket of the game after eight misses. 8回のミスショッ
トが続いたスノーはようやくその試合初のゴールを決めた. **3** V-T 他
動詞 If you **miss** something, you fail to notice it. 見落とす □From
this vantage point he watched, his searching eye never missing a detail.
見晴らしのよいこの場所から彼はじっと眺めた、その鋭い目は何
一つ見逃さなかった. **4** V-T 他動詞 If you **miss** the meaning or
importance of something, you fail to understand or appreciate
it. 理解しそこなう □One ABC correspondent had totally missed the
point of the question. ABCの特派員の1人がその質問の意味を全く取り違
えていた. **5** V-T 他動詞 If you **miss** a chance or opportunity, you
fail to take advantage of it. 逃す □It was too good an opportunity to
miss. それはまたとないチャンスだった. **6** V-T 他動詞 If you **miss**
someone who is no longer with you or who has died, you feel
sad and wish that they were still with you. がいないのを寂しく思
う □Your mama and I are going to miss you at Christmas. ママとわたし
はお前と一緒にクリスマスを過ごせないのが寂しいよ. **7** V-T 他動詞
If you **miss** something, you feel sad because you no longer have
it or are no longer doing or experiencing it. がないのを惜しむ □I
could happily move back into an apartment if it wasn't for the fact that I'd
miss my garden. またアパート暮らしに戻れるのはうれしいんだけど、
庭いじりができなくなることだけが心残りなの. **8** V-T 他動詞 If you
miss something such as a plane or train, you arrive too late to
catch it. 乗り遅れる □He missed the last bus home and had to stay with
a friend. 彼は帰りの最終バスに乗り遅れて、友達に泊めてもらうはめ
になった. **9** V-T 他動詞 If you **miss** something such as a meeting
or an activity, you do not go to it or take part in it. 逃す □It's a pity
Martha and I had to miss our class last week. マーサとわたしが先週のク
ラスに行けなかったのは残念だわ. □You won't be missing much on TV
tonight apart from the usual repeats. 今夜のテレビも再放送ばっかりだ
から、見逃すような番組はあまりないよ. **10** → see also **missing** **11** to
miss the boat → see **boat**

▸ **miss out** **1** PHRASAL VERB 句動詞 If you **miss out on** something
that would be enjoyable or useful to you, you are not involved in it
or do not take part in it. を逃す □We're missing out on a tremendous
opportunity. わたしたちは絶好の機会を逃している. **2** PHRASAL VERB
句動詞 If you **miss out** something or someone, you fail to include
them. 抜かす [BRIT 英国英語; AM 米国英語 **leave out**]

Word Partnership	missは次の語句と使われる:
N.	miss **the point** ❷ **4**
	miss **a chance**, miss **an opportunity** ❷ **5**
	miss **a class**, miss **school** ❷ **9**
ADV.	miss **someone/something terribly** ❷ **6** **7**

Word Link	miss ≈ sending : dis**miss**, **miss**ile, **miss**ionary

mis|sile /mɪsəl/ (**missiles**) **1** N-COUNT 可算名詞 A **missile** is a
tube-shaped weapon that travels long distances through the air
and explodes when it reaches its target. ミサイル □The authorities
offered to stop firing missiles if the rebels agreed to stop attacking civilian
targets. 政府は、反政府側が市民を標的にした攻撃を止めれば、ミサイ
ルの発射を停止する用意があると申し出ました. **2** N-COUNT 可算名詞
Anything that is thrown as a weapon can be called a **missile**. 投
げつけるもの □The football fans began throwing missiles, one of which
hit the referee. サッカーの観客が物を投げ始め、うち1つが審判に命中
しました.

miss|ing /mɪsɪŋ/ **1** ADJ 形容詞 If something is **missing** or has
gone missing, it is not in its usual place, and you cannot find it.
なくなっている □It was only an hour or so later that I discovered that
my gun was missing. 銃がなくなったのにようやく気づいたのは1
時間ぐらい経ってからだった. **2** ADJ 形容詞 If a part of something
is **missing**, it has been removed or has come off, and has not
been replaced. なくなっている □Three buttons were missing from
his shirt. 彼のシャツのボタンが3つとれていました. **3** ADJ 形容詞
If you say that something is **missing**, you mean that it has not
been included, and you think that it should have been. 抜け落
ちている □She had given me an incomplete list. One name was missing
from it. 彼女が渡した名簿には不備があった。1人の名前が抜けてい
た. **4** ADJ 形容詞 Someone who is **missing** cannot be found, and
it is not known whether they are alive or dead. 行方不明の □Five
people died in the explosion and more than one thousand were injured.
One person is still missing. この爆発で5人が死亡、千人以上が負傷しま
した。1人はいまだ行方不明です. **5** PHRASE 句 If a member of the
armed forces is **missing in action**, they have not returned from a
battle, their body has not been found, and they are not thought to
have been captured. 戦地で行方不明になった

Word Partnership

missing は次の語句と使われる:

N.	missing **piece** 1 2
	missing **information**, missing **ingredient** 3
	missing **children**, missing **girl**, missing **people**,
	missing **soldiers** 4
ADV.	**still** missing 1 – 5

mis|sion /mɪʃⁿn/ (missions) **1** N-COUNT 可算名詞 A **mission** is an important task that people are given to do, especially one that involves traveling to another country. 任務 ❑ *Salisbury sent him on a diplomatic mission to North America.* ソールズベリーは彼を外交使節として北アメリカに派遣した. **2** N-COUNT 可算名詞 A **mission** is a group of people who have been sent to a foreign country to carry out an official task. 使節団 ❑ *...a senior member of a diplomatic mission.* 外交使節の上級職員. **3** N-COUNT 可算名詞 A **mission** is a special journey made by a military airplane or spacecraft. 飛行任務, ミッション ❑ *...a bomber that crashed during a training mission in the west Texas mountains.* テキサス州西部の山岳地帯で訓練飛行中に墜落した爆撃機. **4** N-SING 単数名詞 If you say that you have a **mission**, you mean that you have a strong commitment and sense of duty to do or achieve something. 使命 ❑ *He viewed his mission in life as protecting the weak from the evil.* 悪人の手から弱者を守ることこそ, 彼は自分の生涯の使命と考えた. **5** N-COUNT 可算名詞 A **mission** is the activities of a group of Christians who have been sent to a place to teach people about Christianity. 布教活動 ❑ *They say God spoke to them and told them to go on a mission to the poorest country in the Western Hemisphere.* 彼らの話では, 西半球で最も貧しい国へ布教に出かけなさいという神のお告げがあったといいます. **6** N-COUNT 可算名詞 A **mission** is a building or group of buildings in which missionary work is carried out. 伝道所 ❑ *I reside at the mission at St. Michael's.* わたしは聖ミカエル教会の伝道所にいる.

Word Partnership

mission は次の語句と使われる:

ADJ.	**dangerous** mission, **secret** mission, **successful** mission 1
N.	**peacekeeping** mission 1 2
	combat mission, **rescue** mission, **suicide** mission, **training** mission 1 3
V.	**accomplish** a mission, **carry out** a mission 1 3 4

Word Link

miss ≈ sending : dismiss, missile, missionary

mis|sion|ary /mɪʃəneri/ (missionaries) **1** N-COUNT 可算名詞 A **missionary** is a Christian who has been sent to a foreign country to teach people about Christianity. 宣教師 ❑ *My mother would still like me to be a missionary in Africa.* 今でも母はわたしに宣教師としてアフリカで伝道してほしいと思っているだろう. **2** ADJ 形容詞 **Missionary** is used to describe the activities of missionaries. 布教の [ADJ n] ❑ *You should be in missionary work.* あなたは伝道に従事するべきです. **3** ADJ 形容詞 If you refer to someone's enthusiasm for an activity or belief as **missionary** zeal, you are emphasizing that they are very enthusiastic about it. 使命感にあふれた [EMPHASIS 強調] [ADJ n] ❑ *She had a kind of missionary zeal about bringing culture to the masses.* 彼女は使命感に燃えて大衆の教化に力を注いだ.

mis|sion state|ment (mission statements) N-COUNT 可算名詞 A company's or organization's **mission statement** is a document which states what they aim to achieve and the kind of service they intend to provide. ミッションステートメント（企業などの基本方針を述べた文書）[BUSINESS 実業] ❑ *Our mission statement is to be the best design firm in the world.* 当社の社是は世界一の設計会社を目指すことです.

mis|spend /mɪsspend/ (misspends, misspending, misspent) V-T 他動詞 If you say that time or money **has been misspent**, you disapprove of the way in which it has been spent. 無駄遣いする [DISAPPROVAL 不賛成] ❑ *Much of the money was grossly misspent.* あきれたことにその金の多くが無駄遣いされた.

mist /mɪst/ (mists, misting, misted) **1** N-VAR 可変性名詞 **Mist** consists of a large number of tiny drops of water in the air, which make it difficult to see very far. 霧, もや ❑ *Thick mist made flying impossible.* 濃い霧で飛行できなかった. **2** V-T/V-I 他動詞/自動詞 If a piece of glass **mists** or **is misted**, it becomes covered with tiny drops of moisture, so that you cannot see through it easily. 曇る ❑ *The windows misted, blurring the stark streetlight.* 窓が曇っているので, わびしげな街灯がぼんやりと見えた. ● PHRASAL VERB 句動詞 **Mist over** means the same as **mist**. 曇る ❑ *The front windshield was misting over.* フロンドガラスは曇っていた.

mis|take /mɪsteɪk/ (mistakes, mistaking, mistook, mistaken) **1** N-COUNT 可算名詞 If you make a **mistake**, you do something which you did not intend to do, or which produces a result that you do not want. 過ち, 誤り [oft n 'of' -ing, also 'by' n] ❑ *They made the big mistake of thinking they could seize its border with a*

relatively small force. 比較的小さな兵力で国境地帯を奪取できると考えたのは彼らの大きな誤算でした. ❑ *There must be some mistake.* 何かミスがあったに違いない. **2** N-COUNT 可算名詞 A **mistake** is something or part of something that is incorrect or not right. 間違い, 誤り ❑ *Her mother sighed and rubbed out another mistake in the crossword puzzle.* 彼女の母はため息をつくと, クロスワードの間違いをもう1つ消した. **3** V-T 他動詞 If you **mistake** one person or thing for another, you wrongly think that they are the other person or thing. と間違える ❑ *When hay fever first occurs it is often mistaken for a summer cold.* 初めて花粉症にかかったときは, よく夏風邪と間違えられることがある. **4** V-T 他動詞 If you **mistake** something, you fail to recognize or understand it. 誤解する ❑ *The administration completely mistook the feeling of the country.* 政府は全く国民感情を理解していなかった. **5** PHRASE 句 You can say **there is no mistaking** something when you are emphasizing that you cannot fail to recognize or understand it. 間違えようがない [EMPHASIS 強調] ❑ *There's no mistaking the eastern flavor of the food.* その料理が東洋風に味付けされていることはすぐに気づく.

Word Partnership

mistake は次の語句と使われる:

| ADJ. | **fatal** mistake, **honest** mistake, **tragic** mistake 1 **big** mistake, **common** mistake, **costly** mistake, **huge** mistake, **serious** mistake, **terrible** mistake 1 2 |
| V. | **admit** a mistake, **correct** a mistake, **fix** a mistake, **make** a mistake, **realize** a mistake 1 2 |

mis|tak|en /mɪsteɪkən/ **1** ADJ 形容詞 If you are **mistaken about** something, you are wrong about it. を間違えた [v-link ADJ] ❑ *I see I was mistaken about you.* あなたのこと誤解してみたい. **2** PHRASE 句 You use expressions such as **if I'm not mistaken** and **unless I'm very much mistaken** as a polite way of emphasizing the statement you are making, especially when you are confident that it is correct. わたしの思い違いでなければ [EMPHASIS 強調] ❑ *I think Alfred wanted to marry Jennifer, if I am not mistaken.* わたしの思い違いでなければ, 確かにアルフレッドはジェニファーと結婚したかったんですよね. **3** ADJ 形容詞 A **mistaken** belief or opinion is incorrect. 誤った [ADJ n] ❑ *I had a mistaken view of what was happening.* 何が起こっているのかよく分かっていなかった. ● **mis|tak|en|ly** ADV 副詞 [ADV with v] 誤って ❑ *He says they mistakenly believed the standard licenses they held were sufficient.* 彼が言うには, 彼らは自分たちの持っている一般免許で十分だと誤解していたということです.

Word Partnership

mistaken は次の語句と使われる:

| V. | **if I'm not** mistaken 1 2 |
| N. | mistaken **belief**, mistaken **impression**, mistaken **notion** 3 |

mis|ter /mɪstər/ N-VOC 呼格名詞 Men are sometimes addressed as **mister**, especially by children and especially when the person talking to them does not know their name. だんな [INFORMAL くだけた] ❑ *Look, Mister, we know our job, so don't try to tell us what to do.* いいかい, だんな, これはわしらの仕事なんだから, 余計な口出しはやめてくれ.

mis|took /mɪstʊk/ **Mistook** is the past tense and past participle of **mistake**. mistakeの過去・過去分詞

mis|tress /mɪstrɪs/ (mistresses) N-COUNT 可算名詞 A married man's **mistress** is a woman who is not his wife and with whom he is having a sexual relationship. 愛人, 妾（めかけ）[OLD-FASHIONED 古風な] ❑ *Tracy was his mistress for three years.* トレーシーは彼と3年間愛人関係にあった.

Word Link

mis ≈ bad : misinterpret, misleading, mistrust

mis|trust /mɪstrʌst/ (mistrusts, mistrusting, mistrusted) **1** N-UNCOUNT 不可算名詞 **Mistrust** is the feeling that you have toward someone who you do not trust. 不信 ❑ *There was mutual mistrust between the two men.* この2人はお互い相手のことを信用していませんでした. **2** V-T 他動詞 If you **mistrust** someone or something, you do not trust them. 信用しない ❑ *It frequently appears that Bell mistrusts all journalists.* ベルはジャーナリストは誰も信用していないと思えることがよくある.

misty /mɪsti/ ADJ 形容詞 On a **misty** day, there is a lot of mist in the air. 霧の ❑ *It's a little misty this morning.* 今朝は少し霧が出ています.

mis|under|stand /mɪsʌndərstænd/ (misunderstands, misunderstanding, misunderstood) **1** V-T/V-I 他動詞/自動詞 If you **misunderstand** someone or something, you do not understand them properly. 誤解する ❑ *I misunderstood you.* あなたのことを誤解していました. ❑ *They have simply misunderstood what rock and roll is.* 彼らは全くロックンロールが何であるのか分かっていなかった. **2** → see also **misunderstood** **3** CONVENTION 慣習表現 You can say **don't misunderstand me** when you want to correct a wrong impression that you think someone may have gotten about what you are saying. 誤解しないでほしい

mis|under|stand|ing /mɪsʌndərstændɪŋ/ (**misunderstandings**) ■ N-VAR 可変性名詞 A **misunderstanding** is a failure to understand something properly, for example a situation or a person's remarks. 誤解 □ *There has been some misunderstanding of our publishing aims.* 当社の出版目的については幾分誤解されている点がある. ■ N-COUNT 可算名詞 You can refer to a disagreement or slight quarrel as a **misunderstanding**. 不和, いさかい [FORMAL 形式ばった] □ *There was a little misunderstanding with the police and he was arrested.* 彼は警察とひと悶着 (もんちゃく) あって逮捕された.

mis|under|stood /mɪsʌndərstʊd/ ■ **Misunderstood** is the past tense and past participle of **misunderstand**. misunderstand の過去・過去分詞 ■ ADJ 形容詞 If you describe someone or something as **misunderstood**, you mean that people do not understand them and have a wrong impression or idea of them. 誤解された □ *Eric is very badly misunderstood.* エリックはあまりにも誤解されている.

mis|use (**misuses, misusing, misused**)

> The noun is pronounced /mɪsyus/. The verb is pronounced /mɪsyuz/.
>
> 名詞は /mɪsyus/ と発音される. 動詞は /mɪsyuz/ と発音される.

■ N-VAR 可変性名詞 The **misuse** of something is incorrect, careless, or dishonest use of it. 誤用, 悪用 □ *...the misuse of power and privilege.* 権力や特権の乱用 ■ V-T 他動詞 If someone **misuses** something, they use it incorrectly, carelessly, or dishonestly. 誤用する, 悪用する □ *She misused her position in the appointment of 26,000 party supporters to government jobs.* 彼女は職権を乱用し, 2万6千人にのぼる党の支持者を公務員に登用していた. □ *Tess would like a dollar for every time she had heard that word misused by television journalists.* テスはテレビ記者がその言葉を間違って使うたびに1ドルもらいたいと思った.

mite /maɪt/ (**mites**) N-COUNT 可算名詞 **Mites** are very tiny creatures that live on plants, for example, or in animals' fur. ダニ □ *...an itching skin disorder caused by parasitic mites.* 寄生性のダニが原因で起こるかゆみを伴う皮膚病

miti|gate /mɪtɪgeɪt/ (**mitigates, mitigating, mitigated**) V-T 他動詞 To **mitigate** something means to make it less unpleasant, serious, or painful. 和らげる [FORMAL 形式ばった] □ *...ways of mitigating the effects of an explosion.* 爆発の被害を抑えるためのいくつかの方法

miti|gat|ing /mɪtɪgeɪtɪŋ/ ADJ 形容詞 **Mitigating** circumstances or factors make a bad action, especially a crime, easier to understand and excuse, and may result in the person responsible being punished less severely. 軽減する [LEGAL 法律的] [ADJ n] □ *The judge found that in her case there were mitigating circumstances.* 裁判官は彼女の件は軽減事由に該当すると認定した.

mix /mɪks/ (**mixes, mixing, mixed**) ■ V-RECIP 相互動詞 If two substances **mix** or if you **mix** one substance **with** another, you stir or shake them together, or combine them in some other way, so that they become a single substance. 混ざる; 混ぜる □ *Oil and water don't mix.* 油と水は混ざらない □ *A quick stir will mix them thoroughly.* 素早くかき混ぜれば完全に混ざります. □ *Mix the cinnamon with the rest of the sugar.* シナモンを残りの砂糖と混ぜます. ■ V-T 他動詞 If you **mix** something, you prepare it by mixing other things together. 配合する □ *He had spent several hours mixing cement.* 彼は数時間かけてセメントを配合していた. ■ N-VAR 可変性名詞 A **mix** is a powder containing all the substances that you need in order to make something such as a cake or a sauce. の素 (もと) □ *For speed we used packets of pizza dough mix.* 手っ取り早く作るのに, 袋入りのピザ生地ミックスを使った. ■ N-COUNT 可算名詞 A **mix** of different things or people is two or more of them together. の交じり合ったもの □ *The story is a magical mix of fantasy and reality.* 空想と現実が入り混じった不思議な話である. ■ V-RECIP 相互動詞 If two things or activities do not **mix**, it is not a good idea to have them or do them together, because the result would be unpleasant or dangerous. 相容れない [usu with brd-neg] □ *Politics and sports don't mix.* 政治とスポーツは相容れない. □ *Some of these pills don't mix with drink.* これらの薬には服用中に飲酒を避けなければならないものがある. ■ V-RECIP 相互動詞 If you **mix with** other people, you meet them and talk to them. You can also say that people **mix**. 付き合う □ *I ventured the idea that the secret of staying young was to mix with older people.* 若さを保つ秘訣 (ひけつ) は年配の人たちと付き合うことだと, わたしは思い切って言った. □ *People are supposed to mix, do you understand?* 人は互いに交わるものでしょよ, そうじゃない? ■ → see also **mixed** ■ to **mix** your **metaphors** → see **metaphor**

▶ **mix up** ■ PHRASAL VERB 句動詞 If you **mix up** two things or people, you confuse them, so that you think that one of them is the other one. 混同する □ *People often mix me up with other actors.* わたしはよく他の俳優と間違われる. □ *Depressed people may mix up their words.* 気分が沈んだ人は言葉がしどろもどろになることがある. ■ PHRASAL VERB 句動詞 If you **mix up** a number of things,

you put things of different kinds together or place things so that they are not in order. 順序をばらばらにする □ *I like to mix up designer clothes.* デザイナーブランドの服を取り混ぜて着るのが好きだ. □ *Take the cards and mix them up.* トランプを手にとりよく切ります. ■ → see also **mixed up**

Word Partnership mix は次の語句と使われる:

N. mix **ingredients**, mix **with water** ■ ■
ADV. mix **thoroughly**, mix **together** ■ ■

mixed /mɪkst/ ■ ADJ 形容詞 If you have **mixed** feelings about something or someone, you feel uncertain about them because you can see both good and bad points about them. (心境が) 複雑な □ *I came home from the meeting with mixed feelings.* 会合から戻ったわたしは複雑な心境だった. ■ ADJ 形容詞 A **mixed** group of people consists of people of many different types. 様々な人たちがいる □ *I found a very mixed group of individuals, some of whom I could relate to and others with whom I had very little in common.* そこには実に様々な人たちがいて, 自分と似たような人もいれば, ほとんど何も共通点がない人もいた. ■ ADJ 形容詞 **Mixed** is used to describe something that involves people from two or more different races. 異人種の □ *Sally had attended a racially mixed school.* サリーは異人種の生徒が通う学校に行っていた. ■ ADJ 形容詞 **Mixed** education or accommodations are intended for both males and females. 男女共用の □ *Girls who have always been at a mixed school know how to stand up for themselves.* ずっと男女共学できた女子生徒は自分自身を守るにはどうすればよいか知っている. ■ ADJ 形容詞 **Mixed** is used to describe something which includes or consists of different things of the same general kind. ミックスした [ADJ n] □ *...a teaspoon of mixed herbs.* 茶さじ一杯のハーブミックス.

mixed econo|my (**mixed economies**) N-COUNT 可算名詞 A **mixed economy** is an economic system in which some companies are owned by the state and some are not. 混合経済 [BUSINESS 実業] □ *The African National Congress today dropped its doctrine of nationalizing industry in favor of a mixed economy.* アフリカ民族会議は今日, これまでの産業国有化の方針を破棄し, 混合経済を目指すことで一致した.

mixed up ■ ADJ 形容詞 If you are **mixed up**, you are confused, often because of emotional or social problems. 頭が混乱した □ *I think he's a rather mixed up kid.* その子はやや情緒が不安定に思える. ■ ADJ 形容詞 To be **mixed up in** something bad, or **with** someone you disapprove of, means to be involved in it or with them. とかかわり合いになる [v-link ADJ 'in/with' n] □ *Why did I ever get mixed up with you?* なんでお前みたいなやつとかかわってしまったんだろう.

mix|er /mɪksər/ (**mixers**) ■ N-COUNT 可算名詞 A **mixer** is a machine used for mixing things together. ミキサー □ *...an electric mixer.* 電気ミキサー. ■ N-COUNT 可算名詞 A **mixer** is a nonalcoholic drink such as fruit juice or soda that you mix with strong alcohol such as gin. ミキサー (カクテル用のソフトドリンク) □ *At the Tropicana you order ice and mixers from the waiters at the table.* トロピカーナでは氷とミキサーをテーブルに来るウェイターに注文できる. ■ N-COUNT 可算名詞 If you say that someone is a good **mixer**, you mean that they are good at talking to people and making friends. 人付き合いがうまい人 □ *Cooper was a good mixer, he was popular.* クーパーは人付き合いがよく評判もよかった. ■ N-COUNT 可算名詞 A **mixer** is a piece of equipment that is used to make changes to recorded music or film. オーディオミキサー □ *...a three-channel audio mixer.* 3チャンネルオーディオミキサー.

mix|ture /mɪkstʃər/ (**mixtures**) ■ N-SING 単数名詞 A **mixture** of things consists of several different things together. が入り混じったもの □ *They looked at him with a mixture of horror, envy, and awe.* 彼を見る彼らのまなざしには恐怖と羨望 (せんぼう) と畏 (おそ) れが入り混じっていた. ■ N-COUNT 可算名詞 A **mixture** is a substance that consists of other substances which have been stirred or shaken together. 混ぜ合わせたもの □ *...a mixture of water and sugar and salt.* 水と砂糖と塩を混ぜたもの

Thesaurus mixture また次を参照:

N. blend, collection, variety ■
blend, compound, fusion ■

ml ml is a written abbreviation for **milliliter** or **milliliters**. ミリリットル □ *Boil the sugar and 100 ml of water.* 100ℓの水に砂糖を入れて沸騰させます.

mm mm is a written abbreviation for **millimeter** or **millimeters**. ミリ □ *...a 135mm lens.* 135mmレンズ.

moan /moʊn/ (**moans, moaning, moaned**) ■ V-T/V-I 他動詞/自動詞 If you **moan**, you make a low sound, usually because you are unhappy or in pain. うめく □ *Tony moaned in his sleep and then turned over on his side.* トニーは眠ったままうなり声を上げ, 寝返りを打って横向きになった. ● N-COUNT 可算名詞 **Moan** is also a noun. うめき声 □ *Suddenly she gave a low, choking moan and began to*

tremble violently. 彼女は突然息苦しそうに低いうなり声を上げると，激しく震えだした. ② v-ɪ 自動詞 To **moan** means to complain or speak in a way which shows that you are very unhappy. 文句を言う[DISAPPROVAL 不賛成] ❑ *I used to moan if I didn't get at least six hours' sleep at night.* 以前なら最低6時間寝ないとぶつぶつ文句を言ったものだ. ...*moaning about the weather.* 天気のことでぼやいて ③ N-COUNT 可算名詞 A **moan** is a complaint. 不平 [INFORMAL くだけた] ❑ *They have been listening to people's moans and praise.* 彼らはずっと人々の不満や称賛に耳を傾けてきた.

mob /mɒb/ (**mobs, mobbing, mobbed**) ① N-COUNT 可算名詞 A **mob** is a large, disorganized, and often violent crowd of people. 暴徒 ❑ *The inspectors watched a growing mob of demonstrators gathering.* デモの参加者がふくれあがり暴徒化する様子を査察官たちはじっと見守りました. ② N-SING 単数名詞 You can refer to the people involved in organized crime as the **Mob**. マフィア [INFORMAL くだけた] ❑ *He makes ends meet by working as a forger for the Mob.* 彼はマフィアの偽造屋として生計を立てている. ③ N-SING 単数名詞 People sometimes use the **mob** to refer in a disapproving way to the majority of people in a country or place, especially when these people are behaving in a violent or uncontrolled way. 暴徒化した民衆 [mainly BRIT 主に英国英語, DISAPPROVAL 不賛成] ❑ *If they continue like this there is a danger of the mob taking over.* このまま続けば，怒り狂った民衆が権力を奪うことにもなりかねない. ④ V-T 他動詞 If you say that someone **is being mobbed by** a crowd of people, you mean that the people are trying to talk to them or get near them in an enthusiastic or threatening way. ～にもみくちゃにされる [usu passive] ❑ *Her car was mobbed by the media.* 彼女の車に取材陣がどっと押し寄せました.

Word Link mobil ≈ moving : automobile, mobile, mobilize

mobile /moʊbəl/ (**mobiles**) ① ADJ 形容詞 You use **mobile** to describe something large that can be moved easily from place to place. 移動式の，携帯式の ❑ ...*the four-hundred seat mobile theater.* 400席ある移動映画館. ② ADJ 形容詞 If you are **mobile**, you can move or travel easily from place to place, for example because you are not physically disabled or because you have your own transportation. 移動できる ❑ *I'm still very mobile.* まだぴんぴんしてるよ. ● **mobility** /moʊbɪlɪti/ N-UNCOUNT 不可算名詞 移動のしやすさ ❑ *Two cars gave them the freedom and mobility to go their separate ways.* 車が2台あったので，それぞれ好きなところへ自由に行くことができた. ③ ADJ 形容詞 In a **mobile** society, people move easily from one job, home, or social class to another. 流動性のある ❑ *We are a very mobile society and can't resist trying to take everything with us.* 流動社会に生きていると，何もかも持っていきたくなってしまう. ● **mobility** N-UNCOUNT 不可算名詞 流動性 ❑ *Prior to the nineteenth century, there were almost no channels of social mobility.* 19世紀以前の社会では，固定した生活から抜け出す手段はほとんどなかった. ④ N-COUNT 可算名詞 A **mobile** is a decoration that you hang from a ceiling. It usually consists of several small objects which move as the air around them moves. モビール（動く彫刻の一種）⑤ N-COUNT 可算名詞 A **mobile** is the same as a **mobile phone**. 携帯電話 [mainly BRIT 主に英国英語]
→ see **cellphone**

Thesaurus mobile また次を参照：

ADJ. movable, portable ①

Word Partnership mobile は次の語句と使われる：

N. mobile **communications**, mobile **device**, mobile **service** ①

mobile phone (**mobile phones**) N-COUNT 可算名詞 A **mobile phone** is a telephone that you can carry with you and use to make or receive calls wherever you are. 携帯電話 [BRIT 英国英語; AM cellphone, cellular phone 米国英語 cellphone, cellular phone]

mobilize /moʊbɪlaɪz/ (**mobilizes, mobilizing, mobilized**) ① V-T/V-ɪ 他動詞/自動詞 If you **mobilize** support or **mobilize** people to do something, you succeed in encouraging people to take action, especially political action. If people **mobilize**, they prepare to take action. 集結させる [他動詞]，集結する [自動詞] ❑ *The best hope is that we will mobilize international support and get down to action.* 国際的支援を集めて行動を起こすのが我々の最大の望みです. ● **mobilization** /moʊbɪlɪzeɪʃⁿn/ N-UNCOUNT 不可算名詞 集結 ❑ ...*the rapid mobilization of international opinion in support of the revolution.* 革命を支持する急速な国際世論の形成 ② V-T 他動詞 If you **mobilize** resources, you start to use them or make them available for use. 活用する ❑ *If you could mobilize the resources, you could get it done.* 資源を活用できればうまくやれるはずだ. ● **mobilization** N-UNCOUNT 不可算名詞 活用 ❑ ...*the mobilization of resources for education.* 教育資源の活用 ③ V-T/V-ɪ 他動詞/自動詞 If a country **mobilizes**, or **mobilizes** its armed forces, or if its armed forces **mobilize**, they are given orders to prepare for a conflict. 動員する [他動詞] [JOURNALISM OR MILITARY ジャーナリズム，または軍事的] [他動詞]

戦闘準備に入る [自動詞] ❑ *Sudan even threatened to mobilize in response to the ultimatums.* 最終提案に対してスーダンは軍隊を動員すると脅しをかけてきました. ● **mobilization** N-UNCOUNT 不可算名詞 ❑ ...*a demand for full-scale mobilization to defend the republic.* 共和国防衛のために軍隊の総動員を求める強い声

mock /mɒk/ (**mocks, mocking, mocked**) ① V-T 他動詞 If someone **mocks** you, they show or pretend that they think you are foolish or inferior, for example by saying something funny about you, or by imitating your behavior. ばかにする ❑ *I thought you were mocking me.* お前に笑い者にされてると思った. ② ADJ 形容詞 You use **mock** to describe something which is not real or genuine, but which is intended to be very similar to the real thing. 見せかけの [ADJ n] ❑ *"It's tragic!" swoons Jeffrey in mock horror.* 「悲劇だよ！」ジェフリーはショックで倒れるふりをする.

mockery /mɒkəri/ ① N-UNCOUNT 不可算名詞 If someone mocks you, you can refer to their behavior or attitude as **mockery**. ばかにすること ❑ *Was there a glint of mockery in his eyes?* ばかにするような目つきだったか. ② N-SING 単数名詞 If something makes a **mockery** of something, it makes it appear worthless and foolish. ばかにする ❑ *This action makes a mockery of the administration's continuing protestations of concern.* これは強い懸念を表明してきた政府の面目を失わせる行為である.

mocking /mɒkɪŋ/ ADJ 形容詞 A **mocking** expression or **mocking** behavior indicates that you think someone or something is stupid or inferior. あざけるような ❑ *She gave a mocking smile.* 彼女はあざけるように笑った.

modal /moʊdⁿl/ (**modals**) N-COUNT 可算名詞 In grammar, a **modal** or a **modal auxiliary** is a word such as "can" or "would" which is used with a main verb to express ideas such as possibility, intention, or necessity. 法助動詞 [TECHNICAL 技術的]

Word Link mod ≈ measure, manner : mode, model, modern

mode /moʊd/ (**modes**) ① N-COUNT 可算名詞 A **mode** of life or behavior is a particular way of living or behaving. 様式 [FORMAL 形式ばった] ❑ ...*the capitalist mode of production.* 資本家による生産方式 ② N-COUNT 可算名詞 A **mode** is a particular style in art, literature, or dress. 形式 ❑ ...*a slightly more elegant and formal mode of dress.* もう少し華やかでフォーマルなドレス ③ N-COUNT 可算名詞 On some cameras or electronic devices, the different **modes** available are the different programs or settings that you can choose when you use them. モード ❑ ...*when the camera is in manual mode.* カメラがマニュアルモードのときは

model /mɒdⁿl/ (**models, modeling, modeled**) ① N-COUNT 可算名詞 A **model** of an object is a physical representation that shows what it looks like or how it works. 模型 ❑ ...*an architect's model of a wooden house.* 木造住宅の建築模型 ● ADJ 形容詞 **Model** is also an adjective. 模型の [ADJ n] ❑ ...*a model railway.* 鉄道模型 ② N-COUNT 可算名詞 A **model** is a system that is being used and that people might want to copy in order to achieve similar results. 型，モデル [FORMAL 形式ばった] ❑ ...*the Chinese model of economic reform.* 中国型の経済改革 ③ N-COUNT 可算名詞 A **model** of a system or process is a theoretical description that can help you understand how the system or process works, or how it might work. モデル [FORMAL 形式ばった] ❑ *Darwin eventually put forward a model of biological evolution.* ダーウィンはついに生物的進化のモデルを提唱した. ④ V-T 他動詞 If someone such as a scientist **models** a system or process, they make an accurate theoretical description of it in order to understand or explain how it works. モデル化する [FORMAL 形式ばった] ❑ *I have moved from trying to model and understand the distribution and evolution of water vapor.* 水蒸気の分布と発生のモデルを作って解明に努めていましたが，今はそのことから遠ざかっています. ⑤ N-COUNT 可算名詞 If you say that someone or something is **a model of** a particular quality, you are showing approval of them because they have that quality to a large degree. の模範，の手本 [APPROVAL 賛成] ❑ *A model of good manners, he has conquered any inward fury.* 彼は内なる激情を抑え，節度のあるりっぱな態度を示した. ⑥ ADJ 形容詞 You use **model** to express approval of someone when you think that they perform their roles or duties extremely well. 模範となる [APPROVAL 賛成] [ADJ n] ❑ *As a girl she had been a model student.* 学校時代，彼女は模範生だった. ⑦ V-T 他動詞 If one thing is **modeled on** another, the first thing is made so that it is like the second thing in some way. モデルにする ❑ *The quota system was modeled on those operated in America and continental Europe.* その割当制度はアメリカや大陸ヨーロッパで運用されている割当制度をモデルにしたものである. ⑧ V-T 他動詞 If you **model** yourself **on** someone, you copy the way that they do things, because you admire them and want to be like them. 手本にする ❑ *You have been modeling yourself on others all your life.* 君はこれまでずっと人の真似ばかりしてきた. ⑨ N-COUNT 可算名詞 A particular **model** of a machine is a particular version of it. 型，モデル ❑ *To keep the cost down, opt for a basic model.* コストを下げるため，基本モデルを選びます. ⑩ N-COUNT 可算名詞 An artist's **model** is a

person who stays still in a particular position so that the artist can make a picture or sculpture of them. モデル ❑ *...the model for his portrait of Mary Magdalene, the Marchesa Attavanti.* 彼がマグダラのマリアの肖像画のモデルにしたアッタヴァンティ公爵夫人 **11** V-I 自動詞 If someone **models** for an artist, they stay still in a particular position so that the artist can make a picture or sculpture of them. モデルをする ❑ *Tullio has been modeling for Sandra for eleven years.* トゥリオは11年間にわたりサンドラのモデルを務めている. **12** N-COUNT 可算名詞 A fashion **model** is a person whose job is to display clothes by wearing them. ファッションモデル ❑ *...Paris's top fashion model.* パリのトップモデル **13** V-T/V-I 他動詞/自動詞 If someone **models** clothes, they display them by wearing them. モデルをする ❑ *She began modeling in Paris at age 15.* 彼女は15歳のときパリでモデルを始めた. ● **mod|el|ing** N-UNCOUNT 不可算名詞 モデル業 ❑ *She was being offered a modeling contract.* 彼女にはモデルの仕事の話があった. **14** V-T/V-I 他動詞/自動詞 If you **model** shapes or figures, you make them out of a substance such as clay or wood. 型から作る ❑ *There she began to model in clay.* そこで彼女は粘土で作り始めた. **15** → see also **role model** → see **forecast**

The **brand** of a product such as jeans, tea, or soap is its name, which can also be the name of the company that makes or sells it. The **make** of a car or electrical appliance such as a radio or washing machine is the name of the company that produces it. If you talk about what **type** of product or service you want, you are talking about its quality and what features it should have. You can also talk about **types** of people or of abstract things. ❑ *...which type of coffeemaker to choose. ...a new type of bank account. ...looking for a certain type of actor.* A **model** of car or of some other devices is a name that is given to a particular **type**, for example, a Ford Escort. Note that **type** can also be used informally to mean either **make** or **model**. For example, if someone asks what **type** of car you have got, you could reply "an SUV," "a Ford," or perhaps "an Escort."

Word Partnership *model* は次の語句と使われる:

V.	build a model, make a model **11** base *something* on a model, follow a model, serve as a model **11 - 3**
N.	business model **3**
ADJ.	basic model, current model, latest model, new model, standard model **3 9**

mo|dem /móʊdəm, -dɛm/ (modems) N-COUNT 可算名詞 A **modem** is a device which uses a telephone line to connect computers or computer systems. モデム [COMPUTING コンピューティング] [also 'by' N] ❑ *He sent his work to his publishers by modem.* 彼はモデムで作品を出版社に送った.

mod|er|ate (moderates, moderating, moderated)

The adjective and noun are pronounced /mɒdərɪt/. The verb is pronounced /mɒdəreɪt/.

形容詞と名詞は /mɒdərɪt/ と発音される. 動詞は /mɒdəreɪt/ と発音される.

11 ADJ 形容詞 **Moderate** political opinions or policies are not extreme. 穏健な ❑ *He was an easygoing man of very moderate views.* 彼は穏健派の鷹揚(おうよう)な人物だった. **2** ADJ 形容詞 You use **moderate** to describe people or groups who have moderate political opinions or policies. 穏健派の ❑ *...a moderate Democrat.* 民主党の穏健派 ● N-COUNT 可算名詞 A **moderate** is someone with moderate political opinions. 穏健派 ❑ *If he presents himself as a radical he risks scaring off the moderates whose votes he so desperately needs.* 急進的なイメージを示せば, 彼には是が非とも必要な穏健派の票を逃してしまう危険がある. **3** ADJ 形容詞 You use **moderate** to describe something that is neither large nor small in amount or degree. 普通ぐらいの, ほどほどの ❑ *While a moderate amount of stress can be beneficial, too much stress can exhaust you.* 適度なストレスは体によいことがありますが, 過度のストレスは体を消耗させます. ● **mod|er|ate|ly** ADV 副詞 ほどほどに ❑ *Both are moderately large insects, with a wingspan of around four centimeters.* ともにやや大きめの昆虫で, 羽の幅は4cmある. **4** ADJ 形容詞 A **moderate** change in something is a change that is not great. わずかな ❑ *Most drugs offer either no real improvement or, at best, only moderate improvements.* ほとんどの薬で実質的な改善は見られず, 改善が見られた場合でもごくわずかにとどまった. ● **mod|er|ate|ly** ADV 副詞 [ADV after v] わずかに ❑ *Share prices on the Tokyo Exchange declined moderately.* 東証の株価はやや下がりました. **5** V-T/V-I 他動詞/自動詞 If you **moderate** something or if it **moderates**, it becomes less extreme or violent and easier to deal with or accept. 和らげる [他動詞], 和らぐ [自動詞] ❑ *They are hoping that once in office he can be persuaded to moderate his views.* 彼らが望んでいるのは, 彼の就任後にその強硬な姿勢を改めるように促すことです. ● **mod|era|tion** /mɒdəreɪʃ°n/ N-UNCOUNT 不可算名詞 緩和 ❑ *A moderation in food prices helped to offset the first*

increase in energy prices. 食料価格が下がったことで, 初めてのエネルギー価格の上昇を相殺する形になりました.

Word Partnership *moderate* は次の語句と使われる:

N.	moderate **approach**, moderate **position**, moderate **view 11** moderate **amount**, moderate **exercise**, moderate **heat**, moderate **prices**, moderate **speed 3** moderate **growth**, moderate **improvement 4**

mod|era|tion /mɒdəreɪʃ°n/ **11** N-UNCOUNT 不可算名詞 If you say that someone's behavior shows **moderation**, you approve of them because they act in a way that you think is reasonable and not extreme. 節度 [APPROVAL 賛成] ❑ *The United Nations Secretary General called on all parties to show moderation.* 国連事務総長は全ての当事者に対し節度を示すように呼びかけました. ● PHRASE 句 If you say that someone does something such as eat, drink, or smoke **in moderation**, you mean that they do not eat, drink, or smoke too much or more than is reasonable. ほどほどに **2** → see also **moderate**

Word Link *mod ≈ measure, manner : mode, model, modern*

mod|ern /mɒdərn/ **11** ADJ 形容詞 **Modern** means relating to the present time, for example the present decade or present century. 現代の [ADJ n] ❑ *We had a long talk about the problem of materialism in modern society.* 現代社会における物質主義の問題について長時間討議した. **2** ADJ 形容詞 Something that is **modern** is new and involves the latest ideas or equipment. 最新の ❑ *In many ways, it was a very modern school for its time.* さまざまな意味で当時として は先端を行く学校であった. **3** ADJ 形容詞 People are sometimes described as **modern** when they have opinions or ways of behaving that have not yet been accepted by most people in a society. 先進的な ❑ *She is very modern in outlook.* 彼女の考え方はとても先進的である. **4** ADJ 形容詞 **Modern** is used to describe styles of art, dance, music, and architecture that have developed in recent times, in contrast to classical styles. 現代の [ADJ n] ❑ *She'd been a dancer with a modern dance company in New York.* 彼女はニューヨークのモダンダンスカンパニーに所属していたことがあった.

Thesaurus *modern* また次を参照:

ADJ.	contemporary, current, present **11 4** state-of-the-art, up-to-date **2**

Word Partnership *modern* は次の語句と使われる:

N.	modern **civilization**, modern **culture**, modern **era**, modern **life**, modern **science**, modern **society**, modern **times**, modern **warfare 11** modern **conveniences**, modern **equipment**, modern **methods**, modern **techniques**, modern **technology 2** modern **art**, modern **dance**, modern **literature**, modern **music 4**

mod|ern|ize /mɒdərnaɪz/ (modernizes, modernizing, modernized) V-T 他動詞 To **modernize** something such as a system or a factory means to change it by replacing old equipment or methods with new ones. 最新のものにする ❑ *...plans to modernize the refinery.* 精製工場を最新の設備にする計画 ● **mod|erni|za|tion** /mɒdərnɪzeɪʃ°n/ N-UNCOUNT 不可算名詞 最新化 ❑ *...a five-year modernization program.* 近代化5ヵ年計画

mod|est /mɒdɪst/ **11** ADJ 形容詞 A **modest** house or other building is not large or expensive. こぢんまりした, 手ごろな ❑ *They had spent the night at a modest hotel.* その夜, 彼らは小さなホテルに泊まった. **2** ADJ 形容詞 You use **modest** to describe something such as an amount, rate, or improvement which is fairly small. ほどほどの ❑ *Unemployment rose to the still modest rate of 0.7%.* 失業率は0.7%に上昇したが, いまだ低い水準にある. ● **mod|est|ly** ADV 副詞 わずかに ❑ *The nation's balance of payments improved modestly last month.* その国の国際収支は先月わずかに改善しました. **3** ADJ 形容詞 If you say that someone is **modest**, you approve of them because they do not talk much about their abilities or achievements. 謙虚な, 控えめな [APPROVAL 賛成] ❑ *He's modest, as well as being a great player.* 大演奏家であることは言うまでもないが, 彼は謙虚な人でもある. ● **mod|est|ly** ADV 副詞 [ADV with v] 謙虚に ❑ *"You really must be very good at what you do."—"I suppose I am," Kate said modestly.* 「いやほんと, すごくおじょうずですね」「そうですか」とケイトは控えめに答えた.

Word Partnership *modest* は次の語句と使われる:

N.	modest **home/house 11** modest **amount**, modest **fee**, modest **income**, modest **increase 2**

m

mod|es|ty /mɒdɪsti/ ■ N-UNCOUNT 不可算名詞 Someone who shows **modesty** does not talk much about their abilities or achievements. 謙虚 [APPROVAL 賛成] □ *His modesty does him credit, for the food he produces speaks for itself.* 謙虚なのが彼のいいところで，彼の作る料理を味わってみればその素晴らしさがすぐに分かる. ■ N-UNCOUNT 不可算名詞 You can refer to the **modesty** of something such as a place or amount when it is fairly small. 小ささ □ *The modesty of the town itself comes as something of a surprise.* そのこじんまりとした町並みにはちょっと意外に思える. ■ N-UNCOUNT 不可算名詞 If someone, especially a woman, shows **modesty**, they are cautious about the way they dress and behave because they are aware that other people may view them in a sexual way. つましさ □ *There were shrieks of embarrassment, mingled with giggles, from some of the girls as they struggled to protect their modesty.* うち何人かの女の子がくすくすと笑いながらも，恥じらいを見せてキャーと悲鳴を上げた.

modi|fy /mɒdɪfaɪ/ (modifies, modifying, modified) V-T 他動詞 If you **modify** something, you change it slightly, usually in order to improve it. 修正する □ *The club members did agree to modify their recruitment policy.* クラブでは会員規約を改訂することで全会一致しました. ●**modi|fi|ca|tion** /mɒdɪfɪkeɪʃ³n/ (modifications) N-VAR 可変性名詞 修正 □ *Relatively minor modifications were required.* 若干の修正が必要だった.

modu|lar /mɒdʒələr/ ■ ADJ 形容詞 **Modular** means relating to a part of a machine, especially a computer, which performs a particular function. モジュール化した □ *Its modular architecture allows modules to be swapped in and out depending on the processor and operating system.* モジュール設計なので，プロセッサやOSに合わせてモジュールを交換することができる. ■ ADJ 形容詞 In building, **modular** means relating to the construction of buildings in parts called modules. モジュール方式の □ *They ended up buying a modular home on a two-acre lot.* 彼らは2エーカーの敷地に建つモジュラー住宅を買うことにした.

mod|ule /mɒdʒuːl/ (modules) ■ N-COUNT 可算名詞 A **module** is a part of a machine, especially a computer, which performs a particular function. モジュール ■ N-COUNT 可算名詞 A **module** is a part of a spacecraft which can operate by itself, often away from the rest of the spacecraft. モジュール □ *A rescue plan could be achieved by sending an unmanned module to the space station.* 宇宙ステーションに無人モジュールを送り込んで救出するという作戦も考えられます.

moist /mɔɪst/ (moister, moistest) ADJ 形容詞 Something that is **moist** is slightly wet. 湿った □ *The soil is reasonably moist after the September rain.* 9月に降った雨で土壌はほどよく湿っている.

mois|ten /mɔɪs³n/ (moistens, moistening, moistened) V-T 他動詞 To **moisten** something means to make it slightly wet. 湿らす □ *She took a sip of water to moisten her dry throat.* 彼女は水を一口飲み，乾いたのどを潤した.

mois|ture /mɔɪstʃər/ N-UNCOUNT 不可算名詞 **Moisture** is tiny drops of water in the air, on a surface, or in the ground. 湿気，水分 □ *When the soil is dry, more moisture is lost from the plant.* 土壌が乾燥していると植物からさらに水分が失われてしまう.

mois|tur|ize /mɔɪstʃəraɪz/ (moisturizes, moisturizing, moisturized) V-T 他動詞 If you **moisturize** your skin, you rub cream into it to make it softer. If a cream **moisturizes** your skin, it makes it softer. 潤いを与える □ *...products to moisturize, protect, and firm your skin.* 肌を保護し，肌に潤いと張りを与える化粧品.

mold /moʊld/ (molds, molding, molded) ■ N-COUNT 可算名詞 A **mold** is a hollow container that you pour liquid into. When the liquid becomes solid, it takes the same shape as the mold. 型 □ *He makes plastic reusable molds.* 彼は繰り返し使えるプラスチック製の型を作っている. ■ N-COUNT 可算名詞 If a person fits into or is cast in a **mold** of a particular kind, they have the characteristics, attitudes, behavior, or lifestyle that are typical of that type of person. という型にあてはまる □ *He could never be accused of fitting the mold.* 彼がそういうタイプの人間だと非難されることは決してないでしょう. ■ PHRASE 句 If you say that someone **breaks the mold**, you mean that they do completely different things from what has been done before or from what is usually done. 型を破る ■ V-T 他動詞 If you **mold** a soft substance such as plastic or clay, you make it into a particular shape or into an object. 作る □ *He would dampen the clay and begin to mold it into an entirely different shape.* 彼は粘土を湿らせて全く違う形に作り直したものだった. ■ V-T 他動詞 To **mold** someone or something means to change or influence them over a period of time so that they develop in a particular way. の形成に影響を及ぼす □ *It was a very safe, long childhood with Diane, and she really molded my ideas a lot.* 子供時代は何の不安もなく長い間ダイアンと一緒に過ごせたおかげで，ものの考え方という点で彼女から少なからず影響を受けた. ■ V-T/V-I 他動詞/自動詞 When something **molds** to an object or when you **mold** it there, it fits around the object tightly so that the shape of the object can still be seen. ぴったりと合わせる □ *It looked as though the*

plastic wrap was molded to the fruit. ラップは果物にぴったりと密着しているようだった. ■ N-MASS 質量名詞 **Mold** is a soft gray, green, or blue substance that sometimes forms in spots on old food or on damp walls or clothes. カビ □ *She discovered black and green mold growing in her hall closet.* 彼女は玄関のクロゼットにクロカビやアオカビが生えているのを見つけた.

→ see **fungus, laboratory**

mole /moʊl/ (moles) ■ N-COUNT 可算名詞 A **mole** is a natural dark spot or small dark lump on someone's skin. ほくろ □ *Researchers studied moles on those aged between 12 and 50.* 12〜50歳の人たちのほくろを研究した. ■ N-COUNT 可算名詞 A **mole** is a small animal with black fur that lives underground. モグラ ■ N-COUNT 可算名詞 A **mole** is a member of a government or other organization who gives secret information to the press or to a rival organization. スパイ □ *He had been recruited by the Russians as a mole and trained in Moscow.* 彼はロシアのスパイとして雇われ，モスクワで訓練を受けていた.

mo|lecu|lar /məlɛkyələr/ ADJ 形容詞 **Molecular** means relating to or involving molecules. 分子の [ADJ n] □ *...the molecular structure of fuel.* 燃料の分子構造.

Word Link	cule ≈ small : minuscule, molecule, ridicule

mol|ecule /mɒlɪkyuːl/ (molecules) N-COUNT 可算名詞 A **molecule** is the smallest amount of a chemical substance which can exist by itself. 分子 □ *...the hydrogen bonds between water molecules.* 水分子間の水素結合

→ see **element**

mo|lest /məlɛst/ (molests, molesting, molested) V-T 他動詞 A person who **molests** someone, especially a woman or a child, interferes with them in a sexual way against their will. いたずらする □ *He was accused of sexually molesting a female colleague.* 彼は同僚の女性にわいせつな行為をしたとして告訴された.

mol|ten /moʊlt³n/ ADJ 形容詞 **Molten** rock, metal, or glass has been heated to a very high temperature and has become a hot, thick liquid. 溶解した □ *The molten metal is poured into the mold.* 溶けた金属は鋳型に流し込まれる.

→ see **volcano**

mom /mɒm/ (moms) N-FAMILY 家族名詞 Your **mom** is your mother. お母さん，ママ [AM 米国英語, INFORMAL くだけた] □ *We waited for Mom and Dad to get home.* ママとパパが帰ってるのを待ちました.

mo|ment /moʊmənt/ (moments) ■ N-COUNT 可算名詞 You can refer to a very short period of time, for example a few seconds, as a **moment** or **moments**. 瞬間 □ *In a moment he was gone.* すぐに彼は行ってしまった. □ *In a moment, I was asleep once more.* すぐにまた眠りについた. ■ N-COUNT 可算名詞 A particular **moment** is the point in time at which something happens. のとき □ *At this moment a car stopped at the house.* そのとき1台の車が家の前に止まった. ■ PHRASE 句 If you say that something will or may happen **at any moment** or **any moment now**, you are emphasizing that it is likely to happen very soon. 今にも [EMPHASIS 強調] □ *He'll be here to see you any moment now.* もうすぐ彼が会いに来るよ. ■ PHRASE 句 You use expressions such as **at the moment, at this moment,** and **at the present moment** to indicate that a particular situation exists at the time when you are speaking. 今は □ *At the moment, no one is talking to me.* 今は誰も口を聞いてくれない. □ *He's touring South America at this moment in time.* 今ごろ彼は南アフリカを旅行してるよ. ■ PHRASE 句 You use **for the moment** to indicate that something is true now, even if it will not be true in the future. 差し当たり □ *For the moment, a potential crisis appears to have been averted.* 当面の危機は回避されたようだ. ■ PHRASE 句 If you say that someone or something **has** their **moments**, you are indicating that there are times when they are successful or interesting, but that this does not happen very often. うまく行くときもある，見どころもある □ *The film has its moments.* その映画に見せ場がないわけではありません. ■ PHRASE 句 If someone does something **at the last moment**, they do it at the latest time possible. どたん場で □ *They changed their minds at the last moment and refused to go.* 彼らはどたん場になって急に行かないと言い出しました. ■ PHRASE 句 You use the expression **the next moment**, or expressions such as "**one moment** he was there, **the next** he was gone," to emphasize that something happens suddenly, especially when it is very different from what was happening before. 次の瞬間には [EMPHASIS 強調] □ *He is unpredictable, weeping one moment, laughing the next.* 彼は泣いてるかと思うと次の瞬間には笑っていて訳が分からない. ■ PHRASE 句 You use **of the moment** to describe someone or something that is or was especially popular at a particular time, especially when you want to suggest that their popularity is unlikely to last long or did not last long. 今注目されている □ *He's the man of the moment, isn't he?* 彼は時の人なんでしょう？ ■ PHRASE 句 If you say that something happens **the moment** something else happens, you are emphasizing that it happens immediately after the other thing. するとすぐに

[EMPHASIS 強調] ❑ *The moment I closed my eyes, I fell asleep.* 目をつぶったとたん寝入ってしまった. **11 spur of the moment →** see **spur**

Word Partnership	moment は次の語句と使われる:
ADV.	**a moment ago**, **just a** moment **1**
N.	moment **of silence**, moment **of thought 1**
V.	**stop for a** moment, **take a** moment, **think for a** moment, **wait a** moment **1**
ADJ.	**an awkward** moment, **a critical** moment, **the right** moment **1**

mo|men|tari|ly /moʊməntɛərɪli/ **1** ADV 副詞 **Momentarily** means for a short time. 一瞬 ❑ *She paused momentarily when she saw them.* 彼らの姿を見ると彼女は一瞬動作を止めた. **2** ADV 副詞 **Momentarily** means very soon. すぐに [AM 米国英語] ❑ *"My husband will be here momentarily,"* Sophia informed them. 「主人は今すぐ来ます」とソフィアは彼らに知らせた.

mo|men|tary /moʊmənteri/ ADJ 形容詞 Something that is **momentary** lasts for a very short period of time, for example for a few seconds or less. 一瞬の ❑ *...a momentary lapse of concentration.* 一瞬の集中力の低下

mo|men|tous /moʊmɛntəs/ ADJ 形容詞 If you refer to a decision, event, or change as **momentous**, you mean that it is very important, often because of the effects that it will have in the future. 重大な ❑ *...the momentous decision to send in the troops.* 重大な派兵の決定

mo|men|tum /moʊmɛntəm/ **1** N-UNCOUNT 不可算名詞 If a process or movement gains **momentum**, it keeps developing or happening more quickly and keeps becoming less likely to stop. 勢い ❑ *This campaign is really gaining momentum.* この運動は非常な勢いで広がっている. **2** N-UNCOUNT 不可算名詞 In physics, **momentum** is the mass of a moving object multiplied by its speed in a particular direction. 運動量 [TECHNICAL 技術的] **→** see **motion**

Word Partnership	momentum は次の語句と使われる:
V.	**build** momentum, **gain** momentum, **gather** momentum, **have** momentum, **lose** momentum, **maintain** momentum **1 2**

mom|my /mɒmi/ (**mommies**) N-FAMILY 家族名詞 Some people, especially young children, call their mother **mommy**. ママ [AM 米国英語, INFORMAL くだけた] ❑ *Be very good and very quiet and help your mommy.* ねえ, いい子で静かにして, ママのこと手伝ってね.

Mon. Mon. is a written abbreviation for **Monday**. 月曜 ❑ *...Mon., Oct. 19.* 10月19日（月）

Word Link	arch ≒ rule : anarchy, hierarchy, monarch

mon|arch /mɒnərk, -ɑrk/ (**monarchs**) N-COUNT 可算名詞 The **monarch** of a country is the king, queen, emperor, or empress. 君主

mon|ar|chist /mɒnərkɪst/ (**monarchists**) ADJ 形容詞 If someone has **monarchist** views, they believe that their country should have a monarch, such as a king or queen. 君主制支持の ❑ *A monarchist party is running in the forthcoming elections.* 今度の選挙では君主制を支持する政党が名乗りを上げています. ●N-COUNT 可算名詞 A **monarchist** is someone with monarchist views. 君主制支持者 ❑ *The queen's responses to Mr. Chretien will be studied by republicans and monarchists alike here.* 女王がクレティアン氏に示した回答については, 共和制支持者, 君主制支持者ともども十分に検討するだろう.

mon|ar|chy /mɒnərki/ (**monarchies**) **1** N-VAR 可変性名詞 A **monarchy** is a system in which a country has a monarch. 君主制 ❑ *...a serious debate on the future of the monarchy.* 君主制の将来をめぐる真剣な討論 **2** N-COUNT 可算名詞 A **monarchy** is a country that has a monarch. 君主国 ❑ *Britain is a constitutional monarchy.* イギリスは立憲君主国である. **3** N-COUNT 可算名詞 The **monarchy** is used to refer to the monarch and his or her family. 王室 ❑ *The monarchy has to create a balance between its public and private lives.* 王室は公務と私生活を両立させる責務がある.

mon|as|tery /mɒnəsteri/ (**monasteries**) N-COUNT 可算名詞 A **monastery** is a building or collection of buildings in which monks live. 修道院

Mon|day /mʌndeɪ, -di/ (**Mondays**) N-VAR 可変性名詞 **Monday** is the day after Sunday and before Tuesday. 月曜日 ❑ *I went back to work on Monday.* 月曜に仕事に戻った. ❑ *The first meeting of the group took place last Monday.* 先週の月曜日にそのグループの初会合があった.

mon|etar|ism /mɒnɪtərɪzəm/ N-UNCOUNT 不可算名詞 **Monetarism** is an economic policy that involves controlling the amount of money that is available and in use in a country at any one time. マネタリズム（通貨政策を重視する立場）[BUSINESS 実業]

mon|etar|ist /mɒnɪtərɪst/ (**monetarists**) ADJ 形容詞 **Monetarist** policies or views are based on the theory that the amount of money that is available and in use in a country at any one time should be controlled. 通貨政策重視の [BUSINESS 実業] ❑ *...tough monetarist policies.* 厳しい通貨政策. ●N-COUNT 可算名詞 A **monetarist** is someone with monetarist views. マネタリスト ❑ *Such a policy, monetarists claim, encourages steady growth and price stability.* こうした政策によって安定した成長と物価の安定が促されるというのがマネタリストの主張である.

mon|etary /mɒnɪteri/ ADJ 形容詞 **Monetary** means relating to money, especially the total amount of money in a country. 通貨の [BUSINESS 実業] [ADJ n] ❑ *Some countries tighten monetary policy to avoid inflation.* インフレを防ぐため金融を引き締める国もあります.

mon|ey /mʌni/ (**monies** or **moneys**) **1** N-UNCOUNT 不可算名詞 **Money** is the coins or bank notes that you use to buy things, or the sum that you have in a bank account. お金 ❑ *A lot of the money that you pay at the movies goes back to the film distributors.* 映画館で支払うお金の多くが映画の配給元に戻ります. ❑ *Players should be allowed to earn money from advertising.* 選手たちが広告から収入を得られるように認めるべきである. **2** N-PLURAL 複数名詞 **Monies** is used to refer to several separate sums of money that form part of a larger amount that is received or spent. 金額 [FORMAL 形式ばった] ❑ *We drew up a schedule of payments for the rest of the monies owed.* 残金の弁済計画を立てた. **3 →** see also **pocket money 4** PHRASE 句 If you say that someone **has money to burn**, you mean that they have more money than they need, or that they spend their money on things that you think are unnecessary. 金がうなるほどある ❑ *He was a high-earning broker with money to burn.* 彼はブローカーで大もうけし, 金はうなるほどあった. **5** PHRASE 句 If you are **in the money**, you have a lot of money to spend. 金回りがよい [INFORMAL くだけた] ❑ *If you are one of the lucky callers chosen to play, you could be in the money.* 電話で運よく参加者に選ばれたら, 賞金を手にすることができるかもしれません. **6** PHRASE 句 If you **make money**, you obtain money by earning it or by making a profit. 金を稼ぐ ❑ *...the only part of the firm that consistently made money.* その会社でずっと採算がとれていた唯一の部門 **7** PHRASE 句 If you say that you want someone to **put** their **money where their mouth is**, you want them to spend money to improve a bad situation, instead of just talking about improving it. 必要なところに金をつぎ込む ❑ *The government might be obliged to put its money where its mouth is to prove its commitment.* 公約を果たすには政府は資金を投入する以外にないかもしれない. **8** PHRASE 句 If you say that the **smart money** is on a particular person or thing, you mean that people who know a lot about it think that this thing or person will be successful, or this thing will happen. になるに決まっている [JOURNALISM ジャーナリズム] ❑ *With Japan not playing, the smart money was on the Canadians.* 日本が参加しなければ, 勝algesは カナダにあった. **9** PHRASE 句 If you say that **money talks**, you mean that if someone has a lot of money, they also have a lot of power. 金がものを言う ❑ *The formula in Hollywood is simple – money talks.* ハリウッドの常套句は単純明快である. 「金がものを言う」である. **10** PHRASE 句 If you say that someone is **throwing money at** a problem, you are critical of them for trying to improve it by spending money on it, instead of doing more thoughtful and practical things to improve it. 金で片付ける [DISAPPROVAL 不賛成] ❑ *The governor's answer to the problem has been to throw money at it.* 政府はずっとこの問題を金で片付けようとしてきました. **11** PHRASE 句 If you **get** your **money's worth**, you get something which is worth the money that it costs or the effort you have put in. 元がとれる ❑ *The fans get their money's worth.* ファンはお金を払うだけの価値がある. **12** to **give** someone **a run for** their **money →** see **run**
→ see Word Web: **money**
→ see **bank**, **donor**, **lottery**, **salt**

Thesaurus	money また次を参照:
N.	capital, cash, currency, funds, wealth **1**

mon|ey laun|der|ing N-UNCOUNT 不可算名詞 **Money laundering** is the crime of processing stolen money through a legitimate business or sending it abroad to a foreign bank, to hide the fact that the money was illegally obtained. 資金洗浄 ❑ *Investigators are looking at what they believe may be the largest money-laundering scandal in history.* 捜査官は史上最大のマネーロンダリング・スキャンダルかもしれないと考えているものを捜査している.

mon|ey|maker /mʌnimeɪkər/ (**moneymakers**) N-COUNT 可算名詞 If you say that a business, product, or investment is a **moneymaker**, you mean that it makes a big profit. もうけ仕事 [BUSINESS 実業] ❑ *The drug is a big moneymaker for them.* 麻薬は彼らにとって非常に割りのよい仕事だ.

mon|ey mar|ket (**money markets**) N-COUNT 可算名詞 A country's **money market** consists of all the banks and other organizations that deal with short-term loans, capital, and foreign exchange. 金融市場 [BUSINESS 実業] ❑ *On the money markets the dollar was weaker against European currencies.* 金融市場では, ドルは欧州通貨に比較していっそう弱くなっていた.

m

Word Web   money

Early traders used a system of **barter** which didn't involve **money**. For example, a farmer might trade a cow for a wooden cart. In China, India, and Africa, cowrie shells* became a

form of **currency**. The first **coins** were crude lumps of metal. Uniform circular coins appeared in China around 1500 BC. In 1150 AD, the Chinese started using paper bills. In 560 BC, the Lydians (living in what is now Turkey) **minted** three types of coins—a **gold** coin, a **silver** coin, and a mixed metal coin. Their use quickly spread through Asia Minor and Greece.

cowrie shell: a small, shiny, oval shell.

mon|ey or|der (money orders) N-COUNT 可算名詞 A **money order** is a piece of paper representing a sum of money which you can buy at a post office or a bank and send to someone as a way of sending them money by mail. 為替 [AM 米国英語] ❑ *I sent them a money order for $40.* 私は彼らに40ドル分の為替を送った.

mon|ey sup|ply N-UNCOUNT 不可算名詞 The **money supply** is the total amount of money in a country's economy at any one time. 通貨供給量 [BUSINESS 実業] ❑ *They believed that controlling the money supply would reduce inflation.* 彼らは通貨供給量を制御することによりインフレを下げることができると信じていた.

moni|tor /mɒnɪtər/ (monitors, monitoring, monitored) **1** V-T 他動詞 If you **monitor** something, you regularly check its development or progress, and sometimes comment on it. 定期的に監視する, モニターする ❑ *Officials had not been allowed to monitor the voting.* 担当官は投票の監視を許可されていなかった. **2** V-T 他動詞 If someone **monitors** radio broadcasts from other countries, they record them or listen carefully to them in order to obtain information. 聴取する, 傍受する ❑ *Peter Murray is in Washington and has been monitoring reports out of Monrovia.* ピーター・マレーはワシントンに駐在し, モンロビアからの報道を聴取している. **3** N-COUNT 可算名詞 A **monitor** is a machine that is used to check or record things, for example processes or substances inside a person's body. 監視装置 ❑ *The heart monitor shows low levels of consciousness.* 心臓のモニターは意識があまりないことを示している. **4** N-COUNT 可算名詞 A **monitor** is a screen which is used to display certain kinds of information, for example on a computer, in airports, or in television studios. モニター ❑ *He was watching a game of tennis on a television monitor.* 彼はテレビ画面でテニスの試合を見ていた. **5** N-COUNT 可算名詞 You can refer to a person who checks that something is done correctly, or that it is fair, as a **monitor**. 監督者 ❑ *Government monitors will continue to accompany reporters.* 政府の監督者は引き続き報道陣に同伴する.

Word Partnership   *monitor* は次の語句と使われる:

N.	monitor **activity**, monitor **elections**, monitor **performance**, monitor **progress**, monitor a **situation** **1** **color** monitor, **computer** monitor, **video** monitor **4**
ADV.	**carefully** monitor, **closely** monitor **1 2**

monk /mʌŋk/ (monks) N-COUNT 可算名詞 A **monk** is a member of a male religious community that is usually separated from the outside world. 修道士 ❑ *...saffron-robed Buddhist monks.* サフラン色の衣服を着た仏教僧

mon|key /mʌŋki/ (monkeys) **1** N-COUNT 可算名詞 A **monkey** is an animal with a long tail which lives in hot countries and climbs trees. サル **2** N-COUNT 可算名詞 If you refer to a child as a **monkey**, you are saying in an affectionate way that he or she is very lively and naughty. いたずらっ子 [FEELINGS 感情] ❑ *She's such a little monkey.* 彼女はとってもいたずらな子だ.
→ see **primate**

mon|key wrench → see **wrench**

mono /mɒnoʊ/ ADJ 形容詞 **Mono** is used to describe a system of playing music in which all the sound is directed through one speaker only. Compare **stereo**. モノラルの ❑ *This model has a mono soundtrack.* この型はモノラルのサウンドトラックを搭載している.

mo|noga|mous /mənɒɡəməs/ **1** ADJ 形容詞 Someone who is **monogamous** or who has a **monogamous** relationship has a sexual relationship with only one partner. 一夫一婦婚の ❑ *Do you believe that men are not naturally monogamous?* 男性は生来単婚的ではないと思いますか. **2** ADJ 形容詞 **Monogamous** animals have only one sexual partner during their lives or during each mating season. 単婚の ❑ *Only about five percent of mammals are monogamous.* 哺乳動物の内, 単婚なのは約5%だけだ.

Word Link   *mono ≈ one* : *mono*gamy, *mono*logue, *mono*poly

mo|noga|my /mənɒɡəmi/ **1** N-UNCOUNT 不可算名詞 **Monogamy** is used to refer to the state or custom of having a sexual relationship with only one partner. 一夫一婦の性関係 ❑ *People still opt for monogamy and marriage.* 人々は今でも一夫一婦の性関係と結婚を選ぶ. **2** N-UNCOUNT 不可算名詞 **Monogamy** is the state or custom of being married to only one person at a particular time. 一夫一婦制, 単婚 ❑ *In many non-Western societies, however, monogamy has never dominated.* しかし非西洋社会の多くでは, 一夫一婦制が優位を占めたことは決してない.

mono|lith|ic /mɒnəˈlɪθɪk/ ADJ 形容詞 If you refer to an organization or system as **monolithic**, you are critical of it because it is very large and very slow to change, and does not seem to have different parts with different characters. 画一的主義的な [DISAPPROVAL 不賛成] ❑ *...an authoritarian and monolithic system.* 権威主義的で一枚岩的な体制 **2** ADJ 形容詞 If you describe something such as a building as **monolithic**, you do not like it because it is very large and plain with no character. モノリシックな [DISAPPROVAL 不賛成] ❑ *...a huge monolithic concrete building.* 巨大なモノリシック仕上げのコンクリートの建物

mono|logue /mɒnəlɒɡ/ (monologues) also monolog **1** N-COUNT 可算名詞 If you refer to a long speech by one person during a conversation as a **monologue**, you mean that it prevents other people from talking or expressing their opinions. 長談義 ❑ *Morris ignored the question and continued his monologue.* モリスは彼の質問を無視して, 長談義を続けた. **2** N-VAR 可変性名詞 A **monologue** is a long speech which is spoken by one person as an entertainment, or as part of an entertainment such as a play. ひとり芝居, 独白 ❑ *...a monologue based on the writing of Quentin Crisp.* クエンティン・クリスプの作品に基づくひとり芝居

mo|nopo|lize /mənɒpəlaɪz/ (monopolizes, monopolizing, monopolized) **1** V-T 他動詞 If you say that someone **monopolizes** something, you mean that they have a very large share of it and prevent other people from having a share. 独占する ❑ *They are controlling so much cocoa that they are virtually monopolizing the market.* 彼らはあまりに大量のココアを支配しているので, 実質的に市場を独占している. ● **mo|nopo|li|za|tion** /mənɒpəlaɪzeɪʃən/ N-UNCOUNT 不可算名詞 独占 ❑ *...the monopolization of a market by a single supplier.* 単一の供給者による市場の独占 **2** V-T 他動詞 If something or someone **monopolizes** you, they demand a lot of your time and attention, so that there is very little time left for anything or anyone else. ひとり占めする ❑ *He would monopolize her totally, to the exclusion of her brothers and sisters.* 彼は彼女の兄弟姉妹を排除して彼女を完全にひとり占めするだろう.

mo|nopo|ly /mənɒpəli/ (monopolies) **1** N-VAR 可変性名詞 If a company, person, or state has a **monopoly on** something such as an industry, they have complete control over it, so that it is impossible for others to become involved in it. 独占権 [BUSINESS 実業] ❑ *...Russian moves to end a state monopoly on land ownership.* 国家による土地所有の独占権を終焉させようとするロシアの動き **2** N-COUNT 可算名詞 A **monopoly** is a company which is the only one providing a particular product or service. 専売会社 [BUSINESS 実業] ❑ *...a state-owned monopoly.* 国営専売会社. **3** N-SING 単数名詞 If you say that someone does not have a **monopoly** on something, you mean that they are not the only person who has that thing. 独占 ❑ *Women do not have a monopoly on feelings of betrayal.* 裏切られたように感じるのは女性だけではない.

mo|noto|nous /mənɒtʰnəs/ ADJ 形容詞 Something that is **monotonous** is very boring because it has a regular, repeated pattern which never changes. 単調な ❑ *It's monotonous work, like most factory jobs.* それはたいていの工場労働のように退屈な仕事です.

mon|soon /mɒnsuːn/ (monsoons) **1** N-COUNT 可算名詞 The **monsoon** is the season in Southern Asia when there is a lot of very heavy rain. 雨季 ❑ *...the end of the monsoon.* 雨季の終わり **2** N-PLURAL 複数名詞 Monsoon rains are sometimes referred to as **the monsoons**. 雨季に降る雨 ❑ *In Bangladesh, the monsoons have started.* バングラデシュでは雨季が始まりました.
→ see **disaster**

mon|ster /mɒnstər/ (**monsters**) **1** N-COUNT 可算名詞 A **monster** is a large imaginary creature that looks very ugly and frightening. 怪物 ❑ *Both movies are about a monster in the bedroom closet.* 両方とも寝室の押入れにいる怪物についての映画だ. **2** N-COUNT 可算名詞 A **monster** is something which is extremely large, especially something that is difficult to manage or which is unpleasant. 異類に巨大なもの ❑ *the monster which is now the Boston marathon.* 現在はボストンマラソンとなった巨大行事 **3** ADJ 形容詞 **Monster** means extremely and surprisingly large. 巨大な [INFORMAL くだけた, EMPHASIS 強調] [ADJ n] ❑ *...a monster weapon.* 巨大な武器 **4** N-COUNT 可算名詞 If you describe someone as a **monster**, you mean that they are cruel, frightening, or evil. 極悪非道な人 ❑ *Galbraith said that her husband was a depraved monster who threatened and humiliated her.* ガルブレイスは自分の夫を、彼女を脅し侮辱した下劣な人非人だと称した.

mon|strous /mɒnstrəs/ **1** ADJ 形容詞 If you describe a situation or event as **monstrous**, you mean that it is extremely shocking or unfair. 全くひどい ❑ *She endured the monstrous behavior for years.* 彼女は途方もなくひどいふるまいを何年も耐え抜いた. ● **mon|strous|ly** ADV 副詞 [ADV after v] 法外に ❑ *Your husband's family has behaved monstrously.* あなたの夫の家族はひどい振る舞いをした. **2** ADJ 形容詞 If you describe an unpleasant thing as **monstrous**, you mean that it is extremely large in size or extent. 巨大な [EMPHASIS 強調] ❑ *A group of men are erecting a monstrous copper edifice.* 一群の男性が巨大な銅の建物を建築している. ● **mon|strous|ly** ADV 副詞 [ADV adj/-ed] ひどく ❑ *It would be monstrously unfair.* それはとてつもなく不公平だろう. **3** ADJ 形容詞 If you describe something as **monstrous**, you mean that it is extremely frightening because it appears unnatural or ugly. 怪物のような ❑ *...the film's monstrous fantasy figure.* その映画のぞっとするような空想上の人物

month /mʌnθ/ (**months**) **1** N-COUNT 可算名詞 A **month** is one of the twelve periods of time that a year is divided into, for example January or February. 月 ❑ *The trial is due to begin next month.* 裁判は来月開始されることになっている. ❑ *...an exhibition which opens this month at the Guggenheim Museum.* グッゲンハイム美術館で今月始まる展覧会 **2** N-COUNT 可算名詞 A **month** is a period of about four weeks. 1か月 ❑ *She was here for a month.* 彼女はここにひと月滞在した. ❑ *Over the next several months I met most of her family.* その後の数か月の間に私は彼女の家族のほとんどに会った.
→ see **year**

month|ly /mʌnθli/ (**monthlies**) **1** ADJ 形容詞 A **monthly** event or publication happens or appears every month. 月1回の [ADJ n] ❑ *Many people are now having trouble making their monthly house payments.* 多くの人たちが今や毎月の家賃を払えなくなってきています. ❑ *Kidscape runs monthly workshops for teachers.* キッドスケープは教師のためのワークショップを月1回開いている. ● ADV 副詞 **Monthly** is also an adverb. 毎月 [ADV after v] ❑ *In some areas the property price can rise monthly.* 地域によっては不動産価格が月々上昇する可能性がある. **2** N-COUNT 可算名詞 You can refer to a publication that is published monthly as a **monthly**. 月刊刊行物 ❑ *...a satirical monthly.* 風刺的な月刊誌. **3** ADJ 形容詞 **Monthly** quantities or rates relate to a period of one month. 1か月の [ADJ n] ❑ *Consumers are charged a monthly fee above their basic cable costs.* 消費者は基本電信料のほかに月額料金を請求される.

monu|ment /mɒnyəmənt/ (**monuments**) **1** N-COUNT 可算名詞 A **monument** is a large structure, usually made of stone, which is built to remind people of an event in history or of a famous person. 記念建造物 ❑ *...a newly restored monument commemorating a 119-year-old tragedy.* 119年前に起こった悲劇を記念する、新しく復元された記念碑 **2** N-COUNT 可算名詞 A **monument** is something such as a castle or bridge that was built a very long time ago and is regarded as an important part of a country's history. 遺跡 ❑ *...the ancient monuments of Mexico and Peru.* メキシコとペルーの古代遺跡 **3** N-COUNT 可算名詞 If you describe something as a **monument to** someone's qualities, you mean that it is a very good example of the results or effects of those qualities. 記念碑的な仕事 ❑ *By his international achievements he leaves a fitting monument to his beliefs.* 国際的業績により、彼は自分の信念にふさわしい不朽の業績を残している.

monu|men|tal /mɒnyəmɛntəl/ **1** ADJ 形容詞 You can use **monumental** to emphasize the large size or extent of something. 途方もない [EMPHASIS 強調] ❑ *It had been a monumental blunder to give him the assignment.* 彼にその任務を与えたのは途方もない失態だった. **2** ADJ 形容詞 If you describe a book or musical work as **monumental**, you are emphasizing that it is very large and impressive, and is likely to be important for a long time. 記念碑的な [EMPHASIS 強調] ❑ *...his monumental work on Chinese astronomy.* 中国の天文学に関する、彼の不朽の著作 **3** ADJ 形容詞 A **monumental** building or sculpture is very large and impressive. 堂々たる [ADJ n] ❑ *I take no real interest in monumental sculpture.* 非常に大きな彫刻にはあまり興味がない.

mood /mud/ (**moods**) **1** N-COUNT 可算名詞 Your **mood** is the way you are feeling at a particular time. If you are in a good **mood**, you feel cheerful. If you are in a bad **mood**, you feel angry and impatient. 一時的な気分 ❑ *He is clearly in a good mood today.* 今日彼は明らかに機嫌がいい. ❑ *Lily was in one of her aggressive moods.* リリーは攻撃的な気分だった. **2** PHRASE 句 If you say that you are in **the mood for** something, you mean that you want to do it or have it. If you say that you are in no mood to do something, you mean that you do not want to do it or have it. 〜の気になっている ❑ *After a day of air and activity, you should be in the mood for a good meal.* 戸外で活動的に過ごした日のあとは食欲が出るはずだ. **3** N-COUNT 可算名詞 If someone is in a **mood**, the way they are behaving shows that they are feeling angry and impatient. 不機嫌 ❑ *She was obviously in a mood.* 彼女は明らかに機嫌が悪い. **4** N-SING 単数名詞 The **mood** of a group of people is the way that they think and feel about an idea, event, or question at a particular time. 風潮 ❑ *The government seemed to be in tune with the popular mood.* 政府は大衆の風潮に調子を合わせているようだった. **5** N-COUNT 可算名詞 The **mood** of a place is the general impression that you get of it. 雰囲気 ❑ *First set the mood with music.* まず音楽で雰囲気づくりをしなさい.

Word Partnership   *mood* は次の語句と使われる:

ADJ.	bad/good mood, depressed mood, foul mood, positive mood, tense mood **1**
N.	mood change, mood disorder, mood swings **1**
V.	create a mood, set a mood **3** **4**

---

moody /mudi/ (**moodier, moodiest**) **1** ADJ 形容詞 If you describe someone as **moody**, you mean that their feelings and behavior change frequently, and in particular that they often become depressed or angry without any warning. むら気な ❑ *David's mother was unstable and moody.* デビッドの母親は情緒不安定で気分が変わりやすかった. ● **mood|i|ly** ADV 副詞 不機嫌に ❑ *He sat and stared moodily out the window.* 彼は座って窓の外を不機嫌に見つめた. ● **mood|i|ness** N-UNCOUNT 不可算名詞 むら気, 不機嫌 ❑ *His moodiness may have been caused by his poor health.* 彼の不機嫌さは病弱なことが原因だったかもしれない. **2** ADJ 形容詞 If you describe a picture, movie, or piece of music as **moody**, you mean that it suggests particular emotions, especially sad ones. もの悲しげな ❑ *...moody black and white photographs.* もの悲しげな黒白の写真

moon /mun/ (**moons**) **1** N-SING 単数名詞 The **moon** is the object that you can often see in the sky at night. It goes around the earth once every four weeks, and as it does so its appearance changes from a circle to part of a circle. 月 [usu 'the' N, also 'full/new' N] ❑ *the first man on the moon.* 月面に降り立った最初の人 **2** N-COUNT 可算名詞 A **moon** is an object similar to a small planet that travels around a planet. 衛星 ❑ *...Neptune's large moon.* 海王星の大きな衛星
→ see Word Web: **moon**
→ see **astronomer, eclipse, satellite, solar, tide**

A **blue moon** is the name given to the second full moon occurring within one calendar month. It happens at long intervals and so the phrase "Once in a blue moon" means "not often."

moon|light /munlaɪt/ (**moonlights, moonlighting, moonlighted**) **1** N-UNCOUNT 不可算名詞 **Moonlight** is the light that comes from the moon at night. 月光 ❑ *They walked along the road in the moonlight.* 彼らは月光に照らされた道を歩いた. **2** V-I 自動

Word Web   moon

Scientists believe the **moon** is about five billion years old. They think a large asteroid hit the earth. A big piece of the earth broke off. It went flying into **space**. However, Earth's **gravity** caught it and it began to circle the earth. This piece became our moon. The moon orbits the earth once a month. It also **rotates** on its **axis** every thirty days. The moon has no **atmosphere**, so meteoroids constantly crash into it. When a meteoroid hits the surface of the moon, it makes a **crater**. Craters cover the surface of the moon.

詞 If someone **moonlights**, they have a second job in addition to their main job, often without informing their main employers or the tax office. （正規の仕事のほかに）アルバイトをする ❑ ...an engineer who was moonlighting as a taxi driver. タクシーの運転手としてアルバイトをしていた技師

moor /mʊər/ (**moors, mooring, moored**) **1** N-VAR 可変性名詞 A **moor** is an area of open and usually high land with poor soil that is covered mainly with grass and heather. 荒れ地 [mainly BRIT 主に英国英語] ❑ Colliford is higher, right up on the moors. コリフォードはもっと高く、荒野にそびえたっている。 **2** V-T/V-I 他動詞/自動詞 If you **moor**, or **moor** a boat somewhere, you stop and tie it to the land with a rope or chain so that it cannot move away. つなぐ [他動詞・自動詞] ❑ She had moored her barge on the right bank of the river. 彼女ははしけを川の右岸の堤防につないでいた。 ❑ I decided to moor near some tourist boats. 私は観光船のそばに停泊することにした。 **3** N-COUNT 可算名詞 The **Moors** were a Muslim people who established a civilization in North Africa and Spain between the 8th and the 15th centuries A.D. ムーア人 **4** → see also **mooring**

moor|ing /mʊərɪŋ/ (**moorings**) **1** N-COUNT 可算名詞 A **mooring** is a place where a boat can be tied so that it cannot move away, or the object it is tied to. 係留所, 係留 ❑ Free moorings will be available. 無料の係留が利用できるでしょう。 **2** N-PLURAL 複数名詞 **Moorings** are the ropes, chains, and other objects used to moor a boat. 係留装備 ❑ He cut the engine and grabbed the mooring lines. 彼はエンジンを切って係船索をつかんだ。

moor|land /mʊərlænd/ (**moorlands**) N-UNCOUNT 不可算名詞 **Moorland** is land which consists of moors. 荒れ地 [mainly BRIT 主に英国英語] [also N in pl] ❑ ...rugged Yorkshire moorland. 岩だらけのヨークシャーの荒れ地

moose /mus/ (**moose**)

Moose is both the singular and the plural form.

Moose は単数形でも複数形でもある。

N-COUNT 可算名詞 A **moose** is a large type of deer. Moose have big flat horns called antlers and are found in Northern Europe, Asia, and North America. Some people use **moose** to refer to the North American variety of this animal, and **elk** to refer to the European and Asian varieties. ムース

mop /mɒp/ (**mops, mopping, mopped**) **1** N-COUNT 可算名詞 A **mop** is a piece of equipment for washing floors. It consists of a sponge or many pieces of string attached to a long handle. モップ **2** V-T 他動詞 If you **mop** a surface such as a floor, you clean it with a mop. モップでふく ❑ There was a woman mopping the stairs. 階段をモップでふいている女性がいた。 **3** V-T 他動詞 If you **mop** sweat from your forehead or **mop** your forehead, you wipe it with a piece of cloth. （汗などを）ぬぐう ❑ He mopped perspiration from his forehead. 彼は額の汗をぬぐった。

▶ **mop up 1** PHRASAL VERB 句動詞 If you **mop up** a liquid, you clean it with a cloth so that the liquid is absorbed. （こぼれた水などを）ぬぐい取る ❑ A waiter mopped up the mess as best he could. ウェイターは散乱したものをできる限りふき取った。 ❑ When the washing machine spurts out water at least we can mop it up. 洗濯機から水が噴き出した場合、少なくとも水をふき取ることはできる。 **2** PHRASAL VERB 句動詞 If you **mop up** something that you think is undesirable or dangerous, you remove it or deal with it so that it is no longer a problem. 片付ける ❑ The infantry divisions mopped up remaining centers of resistance. 歩兵師団は残った抵抗拠点を掃討した。

mope /moʊp/ (**mopes, moping, moped**) V-I 自動詞 If you **mope**, you feel miserable and do not feel interested in doing anything. ふさぎこむ ❑ Get on with life and don't sit back and mope. 何もせずにふさぎこんでいないで、元気を出せよ。

mo|ped /moʊpɛd/ (**mopeds**) N-COUNT 可算名詞 A **moped** is a small motorcycle which you can also pedal like a bicycle. モーペッド

mor|al /mɒrəl/ (**morals**) **1** N-PLURAL 複数名詞 **Morals** are principles and beliefs concerning right and wrong behavior. 道徳 **2** ...Western ideas and morals. 西洋の思想と道徳。 **2** ADJ 形容詞 **Moral** means relating to beliefs about what is right or wrong. 道徳の [ADJ n] ❑ She describes her own moral dilemma in the film. 彼女はその映画制作に際しての自分自身の道徳上のジレンマを述べている。 ● **mor|al|ly** ADV 副詞 道徳上 ❑ When, if ever, is it morally justifiable to allow a patient to die? もしあるとすれば、いつ患者が死ぬのを許すことが道徳上正当化できるか。 **3** ADJ 形容詞 [ADJ n] **Moral** courage or duty is based on what you believe is right or acceptable, rather than on what the law says should be done. 精神的な ❑ The government had a moral, if not a legal, duty to pay compensation. 法律な義務がなくとも、政府には補償金を支払う精神的な義務がある。 **4** ADJ 形容詞 A **moral** person behaves in a way that is believed by most people to be good and right. 道義をわきまえた ❑ The people who will be on the committee are moral, cultured, competent people. 委員会に参加する人々は道義をわきまえた有能な教養人たちです。 ● **mor|al|ly** ADV 副詞 [ADV with v] 道徳的に ❑ Art is not there to improve you morally. 芸

術は道徳的に人を向上させるためにあるものではない。 **5** ADJ 形容詞 If you give someone **moral** support, you encourage them in what they are doing by expressing approval. 精神的な [ADJ n] ❑ Moral as well as financial support is what the West should provide. 経済的援助のみならず精神的な援助が欧米諸国が提供すべきものだ。 **6** N-COUNT 可算名詞 The **moral** of a story or event is what you learn from it about how you should or should not behave. 教訓 ❑ I think the moral of the story is let the buyer beware. その話の教訓は買い手に用心させることであると思う。 **7** **moral victory** → see **victory** → see **philosophy**

Thesaurus *moral* また次を参照：

| N. | ideology, philosophy, principle, standard **1** |
| ADJ. | moralistic, respectable, upright **2 4** |

Word Partnership *moral* は次の語句と使われる：

N.	moral **dilemma**, moral **sense**, moral **values 2**
	moral **obligation**, moral **responsibility 3**
	moral **behavior**, moral **character 4**
	moral **support 5**

mo|rale /məræl/ N-UNCOUNT 不可算名詞 **Morale** is the amount of confidence and cheerfulness that a group of people have. 士気 ❑ Many pilots are suffering from low morale. 多くのパイロットの士気は低い。

mo|ral|ity /məræliti/ (**moralities**) **1** N-UNCOUNT 不可算名詞 **Morality** is the belief that some behavior is right and acceptable and that other behavior is wrong. 道徳 ❑ ...standards of morality and justice in society. 社会における道徳と正義の基準。 **2** N-COUNT 可算名詞 A **morality** is a system of principles and values concerning people's behavior, which is generally accepted by a society or by a particular group of people. 道徳体系 ❑ ...a morality that is sexist. 性差別的道徳 **3** N-UNCOUNT 不可算名詞 The **morality of** something is how right or acceptable it is. 道義性 ❑ ...the arguments about the morality of blood sports. 流血を伴うスポーツの道義性に関する議論。

mora|to|rium /mɒrətɔriəm/ (**moratoriums** or **moratoria**) N-COUNT 可算名詞 A **moratorium** on a particular activity or process is the stopping of it for a fixed period of time, usually as a result of an official agreement. 一時停止 ❑ The House voted to impose a one-year moratorium on nuclear testing. 下院は1年間の核実験停止を課すことを可決しました。

mor|bid /mɔrbɪd/ ADJ 形容詞 If you describe a person or their interest in something as **morbid**, you mean that they are very interested in unpleasant things, especially death, and you think this is strange. 病的な [DISAPPROVAL 不賛成] ❑ Some people have a morbid fascination with crime. 犯罪に病的に取りつかれている人もいる。 ● **mor|bid|ly** ADV 副詞 病的に ❑ There's something morbidly fascinating about the thought. その考えには何か病的な魅力がある。

more /mɔr/

More is often considered to be the comparative form of **much** and **many**.

More はしばしば **much** と **many** の比較級形であると考えられている。

1 DET 限定詞 You use **more** to indicate that there is a greater amount of something than before or than average, or than something else. You can use "a little," "a lot," "a bit," "far," and "much" in front of **more**. もっと ❑ More and more people are surviving heart attacks. 心臓発作を克服する人の数はますます増えている。 ❑ He spent more time perfecting his dance moves instead of gym work. 彼は体育館での運動よりも、ダンスの動きを完成するのにより多くの時間を費やした。 ● PRON 代名詞 **More** is also a pronoun. いっそう多くの数 ❑ As the level of work increased from light to heavy, workers ate more. 軽労働から重労働に仕事のレベルが増すと、労働者たちはより多くの食事をとった。 ● QUANT 数量詞 **More** is also a quantifier. より多くの量 [QUANT 'of' def-n] ❑ Employees may face increasing pressure to take on more of their own medical costs in retirement. 従業員は、退職後の自分の医療費をより多く負担するという、さらなる圧力に直面することになるかもしれない。 **2** PHRASE 句 You use **more than** before a number or amount to say that the actual number or amount is even greater. ～より以上に ❑ The Afghan authorities say the airport had been closed for more than a year. アフガニスタン当局は、空港は1年以上閉鎖されていたと言っている。 **3** ADV 副詞 You use **more** to indicate that something or someone has a greater amount of a quality than they used to or than is average or usual. より多く [ADV adj/adv] ❑ Prison conditions have become more brutal. 刑務所の環境はより冷酷なものになった。 **4** ADV 副詞 If you say that something is **more** one thing **than** another, you mean that it is like the first thing rather than the second. むしろ ❑ He's more like a movie star than a lifeguard, really. 彼は救助員というよりも映画スターのようだ、ほんとうに。 ❑ Sue screamed, not loudly, more in surprise than terror. スーは恐怖というよりむしろ驚きで大声ではなく叫び声

を上げた。 ⑤ ADV 副詞 If you do something **more** than before or **more** than someone else, you do it to a greater extent or more often. もっと ❑*When we are tired, tense, depressed, or unwell, we feel pain much more.* 私たちは疲れているとき、緊張しているとき、落ち込んでいるとき、具合のわるいときに痛みをずっといっそう強く感じる。 ⑥ ADV 副詞 You can use **more** to indicate that something continues to happen for a further period of time. さらに [ADV after v] ❑*Things might have been different if I'd talked a bit more.* 私がもう少し長く話していたら、状況は違ったかもしれないだろう。 ● PHRASE 句 You can use **some more** to indicate that something continues to happen for a further period of time. もう少し ⑦ ADV 副詞 You use **more** to indicate that something is repeated. For example, if you do something "once more," you do it again once. もう ❑*This train would stop twice more in the suburbs before rolling southeast toward Baltimore.* この列車はバルチモアに向けて南東に走って行く前に、郊外でもう2回停車するだろう。 ⑧ DET 限定詞 You use **more** to refer to an additional thing or amount. You can use "a little," "a lot," "a bit," "far," and "much" in front of **more**. もっと ❑*They needed more time to consider whether to hold an inquiry.* 彼らには調査するか否かを考慮する時間がもう少し必要だった。 ● ADJ 形容詞 **More** is also an adjective. もう [ADJ n] ❑*We stayed in Danville two more days.* 私たちはもう2日ダンビルに滞在した。 ● PRON 代名詞 **More** is also a pronoun. それ以上のこと ❑*Oxfam has appealed to western nations to do more to help the refugees.* オックスファムは難民に対する支援を拡大するよう欧米諸国に訴えている。 ⑨ ADV 副詞 You use **more** in conversations when you want to draw someone's attention to something interesting or important that you are about to say. さらに [ADV adv/adj] ❑*More seriously for him, there are members who say he is wrong on this issue.* さらに彼にとって深刻なことに、この問題について彼は間違っていると言うメンバーがいる。 ⑩ PHRASE 句 You can use **more and more** to indicate that something is becoming greater in amount, extent, or degree all the time. ますます ❑*Her life was heading more and more where she wanted it to go.* 彼女の人生はますます彼女の望みどおりの方向に向かっていた。 ⑪ PHRASE 句 If something is **more or less** true, it is true in a general way, but is not completely true. だいたい [VAGUENESS あいまいさ] ❑*The conference is more or less over.* 会議はだいたい終わった。 ⑫ PHRASE 句 If something is **more than** a particular thing, it has greater value or importance than this thing. より以上のもの ❑*He's more than a coach, he's a friend.* 彼はコーチ以上の者で、友人だ。 ⑬ PHRASE 句 You use **more than** to say that something is true to a greater degree than is necessary or than average. より以上 ❑*The company has more than enough cash available to refinance the loan.* 会社は融資の借り換えに必要以上の現金を持っている。 ⑭ PHRASE 句 You can use **what is more** or **what's more** to introduce an extra piece of information which supports or emphasizes the point you are making. おまけに [EMPHASIS 強調] ❑*Many more institutions, especially banks, were lending to lend money for mortgages, and what was more, banks could lend out more money than they actually held.* より多くの機関、特に銀行が担保をとって金を貸すことを許されており、そのうえ、実際に持っている以上の金を貸すことが可能だった。 ⑮ **all the more** → see **all** ⑯ **any more** → see **any**

more|over /mɔrˈoʊvər/ ADV 副詞 You use **moreover** to introduce a piece of information that adds to or supports the previous statement. そのうえ [FORMAL 形式ばった] ❑*She saw that there was indeed a man immediately behind her. Moreover, he was observing her strangely.* 彼女はすぐ後ろに男が1人たしかにいるのを知った。しかも、男は彼女を変にじろじろ見ていた。

morgue /mɔrg/ (**morgues**) N-COUNT 可算名詞 A **morgue** is a building or a room in a hospital where dead bodies are kept before they are buried or cremated, or before they are identified or examined. 死体保管所

morn|ing /mɔrnɪŋ/ (**mornings**) ⓵ N-VAR 可変性名詞 The **morning** is the part of each day between the time that people usually wake up and 12 o'clock noon or lunchtime. 朝 ❑*During the morning your guide will take you around the city.* 午前中にガイドがあなたに町を案内します。 ❑*On Sunday morning Bill was woken by the telephone.* 日曜日の朝にビルは電話の音で目が覚めた。 ② N-SING 単数名詞 If you refer to a particular time in the **morning**, you mean a time between 12 o'clock midnight and 12 o'clock noon. 午前 ❑*I often stayed up until two or three in the morning.* 私はよく午前2時から3時まで起きていた。 ③ PHRASE 句 If you say that something will happen **in the morning**, you mean that it will happen during the morning of the following day. 午前中に ❑*I'll fly it to St Louis in the morning.* 私は午前中に飛行機でセントルイスに行きます。 ④ PHRASE 句 If you say that something happens **morning, noon and night**, you mean that it happens all the time. 昼夜問わずずっと ❑*You get fit by playing the game, day in, day out, morning, noon and night.* 来る日も来る日も昼夜を問わず試合をすると体の調子がよくなる。

Thesaurus	*morning* また次を参照：
N.	dawn, daybreak, light, sunrise ⓵

mo|rose /məˈroʊs/ ADJ 形容詞 Someone who is **morose** is miserable, bad-tempered, and not willing to talk very much to other people. 陰気な ❑*She was morose, pale, and reticent.* 彼女は陰気で青白く無口だった。 ● **mo|rose|ly** ADV 副詞 陰気に ❑*One elderly man sat morosely at the bar.* 初老の男が1人バーにむっつりと座っていた。

mor|phine /mɔrfin/ N-UNCOUNT 不可算名詞 **Morphine** is a drug used to relieve pain. モルヒネ

mor|sel /mɔrsəl/ (**morsels**) N-COUNT 可算名詞 A **morsel** is a very small amount of something, especially a very small piece of food. ひと口 ❑*...a delicious little morsel of meat.* おいしい肉の小片

mor|tal /mɔrtəl/ (**mortals**) ⓵ ADJ 形容詞 If you refer to the fact that people are **mortal**, you mean that they have to die and cannot live forever. 死ぬべき運命の ❑*A man is deliberately designed to be mortal. He grows, he ages, and he dies.* 人はいつかは死ぬものだ。人は成長し、年を取り、そして死ぬのだ。 ● **mor|tal|ity** /mɔrtæləti/ N-UNCOUNT 不可算名詞 死ぬべき運命 ❑*She has suddenly come face to face with her own mortality.* 彼女は突然自分の死と直面することになった。 ② N-COUNT 可算名詞 You can describe someone as a **mortal** when you want to say that they are an ordinary person. 人間 ❑*Tickets seem unobtainable to the ordinary mortal.* 普通の人にはチケットを手に入れることはできないようだ。 ③ ADJ 形容詞 [ADJ n] You can use **mortal** to show that something is very serious or may cause death. 致命的な ❑*The police were defending themselves and others against mortal danger.* 警察は生死にかかわる危険から自分自身と他の人々を守っていた。 ● **mor|tal|ly** ADV 副詞 致命的に ❑*He falls, mortally wounded.* 彼は致命傷を受け倒れる。 ④ ADJ 形容詞 [ADJ n] You can use **mortal** to emphasize that a feeling is extremely great or severe. はなはだしい [EMPHASIS 強調] ❑*When self-esteem is high, we lose our mortal fear of jealousy.* 自尊心が高いとき、私たちはひどいしっとの恐怖を忘れる。 ● **mor|tal|ly** ADV 副詞 [ADV -ed/adj/adv] ひどく ❑*Candace admits to having been "mortally embarrassed."* キャンディスは「ひどく恥ずかしい思い」をさせられたことを認めている。

mor|tal|ity /mɔrtæləti/ N-UNCOUNT 不可算名詞 The **mortality** in a particular place or situation is the number of people who die. 死亡数 ❑*The nation's infant mortality rate has reached a record low.* 国の乳児死亡率は最低記録に達した。

mor|tar /mɔrtər/ (**mortars**) ⓵ N-COUNT 可算名詞 A **mortar** is a big gun that fires missiles high into the air over a short distance. 迫撃砲 ❑*The two sides exchanged fire with mortars and small arms.* 双方は迫撃砲と小型武器で砲火を交えました。 ② N-UNCOUNT 不可算名詞 **Mortar** is a mixture of sand, water, and cement or lime which is put between bricks to hold them together. しっくい、モルタル ❑*...the mortar between the bricks.* レンガの間に塗られたしっくい ③ N-COUNT 可算名詞 A **mortar** is a bowl in which you can crush things such as herbs, spices, or grain using a rod called a pestle. すり鉢 ❑*Use a mortar and pestle to crush the shells and claws.* すり鉢とすりこぎを使って干羅とはさみをつぶします。

mort|gage /mɔrgɪdʒ/ (**mortgages, mortgaging, mortgaged**) ⓵ N-COUNT 可算名詞 A **mortgage** is a loan of money which you get from a bank or savings and loan association in order to buy a house. (住宅購入の) 借入金 住宅ローン ❑*...an increase in mortgage rates.* 住宅ローン利率の上昇 ② V-T 他動詞 If you **mortgage** your house or land, you use it as a guarantee to a company in order to borrow money from them. 抵当に入れる ❑*They had to mortgage their home to pay the bills.* 彼らは請求書を支払うために、自宅を抵当に入れなければならなかった。 → see **interest rate**

mor|ti|cian /mɔrtɪʃən/ (**morticians**) N-COUNT 可算名詞 A **mortician** is a person whose job is to deal with the bodies of people who have died and to arrange funerals. 葬儀屋 [mainly AM 主に米国英語]

Word Link	mort ≈ death : immortal, mortify, mortuary

mor|tu|ary /mɔrtʃuɛri/ (**mortuaries**) N-COUNT 可算名詞 A **mortuary** is a building or a room in a hospital where dead bodies are kept before they are buried or cremated, or before they are identified or examined. 死体仮置場

mo|sa|ic /moʊzeɪɪk/ (**mosaics**) N-VAR 可変性名詞 A **mosaic** is a design which consists of small pieces of colored glass, pottery, or stone set in concrete or plaster. モザイク ❑*...a Roman villa which once housed a fine collection of mosaics.* かつては立派なモザイクコレクションを収蔵していたローマ風の別荘

Mos|lem /mɒzləm, mʊzlɪm/ → see **Muslim**

mosque /mɒsk/ (**mosques**) N-COUNT 可算名詞 A **mosque** is a building where Muslims go to worship. モスク

mos|qui|to /məskitoʊ/ (**mosquitoes** or **mosquitos**) N-COUNT 可算名詞 **Mosquitos** are small flying insects which bite people and animals in order to suck their blood. カ

moss /mɔs/ (**mosses**) N-MASS 質量名詞 **Moss** is a very small, soft, green plant which grows on damp soil, or on wood or stone. コケ ❑*...ground covered over with moss.* コケにすっかり覆われた地面

most /moʊst/

> **Most** is often considered to be the superlative form of **much** and **many**.

> **Most**はしばしば**much**と**many**の最上級形であると考えられている。

1 QUANT 数量詞 You use **most** to refer to the majority of a group of things or people or the largest part of something. 大部分 [QUANT 'of' def-n] ❑ *Most of the houses in the capital don't have indoor plumbing.* 首都の家屋のほとんどには屋内配管設備がない。 ❑ *By stopping smoking you are undoing most of the damage smoking has caused.* 喫煙をやめたことで，喫煙がもたらした被害の大部分を修復しているのですよ。 ● DET 限定詞 **Most** is also a determiner. 最多数の ❑ *Most people think the queen has done a good job over the last 50 years.* 大方の人は，過去50年にわたって女王は立派な仕事をしたと考えている。 ● PRON 代名詞 **Most** is also a pronoun. 大部分 ❑ *Seventeen civilians were hurt. Most are students who had been attending a twenty-first birthday party.* 一般市民17名が負傷しました。その大部分は21歳の誕生日パーティーに参加していた学生です。 **2** ADJ 形容詞 You use **the most** to mean a larger amount than anyone or anything else, or the largest amount possible. 最大量の ['the' ADJ n] ❑ *The president himself won the most votes.* 大統領自身が最大票を獲得しました。 ● PRON 代名詞 **Most** is also a pronoun. 最大量 ❑ *The most they earn in a day is fifty rubles.* 彼らが得る日給は最高で50ルーブルです。 **3** ADV 副詞 You use **most** to indicate that something is true or happens to a greater degree or extent than anything else. 最も [ADV with v] ❑ *What she feared most was becoming like her mother.* 彼女が最も恐れていたのは自分の母親のようになることだった。 ❑ *...Professor Morris, the person he most hated.* 彼が最も嫌っていた人物，モリス教授 ● PHRASE 句 You use **most of all** to indicate that something happens or is true to a greater extent than anything else. とりわけ **4** ADV 副詞 You use **most** to indicate that someone or something has a greater amount of a particular quality than most other things of its kind. 最も [ADV adj/adv] ❑ *Her children had the best, most elaborate birthday parties in the neighborhood.* 彼女の子供は，近所で最高の非常に凝った誕生日パーティーをした。 ❑ *He was one of the most influential performers of modern jazz.* 彼は最も有力なモダンジャズ演奏家の1人でした。 **5** ADV 副詞 If you do something **the most**, you do it to the greatest extent possible or with the greatest frequency. いちばん ['the' ADV after v] ❑ *What question are you asked the most?* 最もよく聞かれる質問は何ですか。 **6** ADV 副詞 You use **most** in conversations when you want to draw someone's attention to something very interesting or important that you are about to say. とっても [ADV adv/adj] ❑ *Most surprisingly, quite a few said they don't intend to vote at all.* 非常に驚いたことに，かなり多くの人が全然投票するつもりがないと言った。

> Note that you can say "**Most children love candy**," but you cannot say "Most of children love candy." However, when a pronoun is used, you can say "**Most of them love candy**."

7 PHRASE 句 You use **at most** or **at the most** to say that a number or amount is the maximum that is possible and that the actual number or amount may be smaller. 最大限，せいぜい ❑ *Poach the pears in apple juice or water and sugar for ten minutes at most.* 梨をりんごジュースまたは水と砂糖で最大10分ゆでなさい。 **8** PHRASE 句 If you **make the most of** something, you get the maximum use or advantage from it. 〜をできるかぎり利用する ❑ *Happiness is the ability to make the most of what you have.* 幸福とは持っているものをできる限り活用する能力である。

most|ly /moʊstli/

ADV 副詞 You use **mostly** to indicate that a statement is generally true, for example true about the majority of a group of things or people, true most of the time, or true in most respects. たいてい [ADV with cl/group] ❑ *I am working with mostly highly motivated people.* 私は主として非常に意欲的な人と働いている。 ❑ *Cars are mostly metal.* 車の大部分は金属でできている。

mo|tel /moʊtɛl/ (motels)

N-COUNT 可算名詞 A **motel** is a hotel intended for people who are traveling by car. モーテル

moth /mɔθ/ (moths)

N-COUNT 可算名詞 A **moth** is an insect like a butterfly which usually flies around at night. ガ

moth|er /mʌðər/ (mothers, mothering, mothered)

1 N-FAMILY 家族名詞 Your **mother** is the woman who gave birth to you. You can also call someone your **mother** if she brings you up as if she was this woman. 母 ❑ *She sat on the edge of her mother's bed.* 彼女は母のベッドの端に腰掛けた。 ❑ *She's an English teacher and a mother of two children.* 彼女は英語教師であり，2児の母です。 **2** V-T 他動詞 If a woman **mothers** a child, she takes care of it and brings it up, usually because she is its mother. 母として世話する ❑ *Colleen had dreamed of mothering a large family.* コリーンは大家族の母となることを夢見ていた。 **3** V-T 他動詞 If you **mother** someone, you treat them with great care and affection, as if they were a small child. 過保護に扱う ❑ *Stop mothering me.* 母親気取りはやめてくれ。
→ see **family**

moth|er|hood /mʌðərhʊd/

N-UNCOUNT 不可算名詞 **Motherhood** is the state of being a mother. 母であること，母性 ❑ *...women who try to combine work and motherhood.* 仕事と母親の役目の両立を試みる女性たち

mother-in-law (mothers-in-law)

N-COUNT 可算名詞 Someone's **mother-in-law** is the mother of their husband or wife. 義母
→ see **family**

moth|er|ly /mʌðərli/

ADJ 形容詞 **Motherly** feelings or actions are like those of a kind mother. 母親らしい ❑ *It was an incredible display of motherly love and forgiveness.* それは母性愛と寛容さの素晴らしい表示だった。

mo|tif /moʊtif/ (motifs)

N-COUNT 可算名詞 A **motif** is a design which is used as a decoration or as part of an artistic pattern. モティーフ，主模様 ❑ *...a rose motif.* バラのモティーフ

> **Word Link** mot ≈ moving : motion, motivate, promote

mo|tion /moʊʃⁿ/ (motions, motioning, motioned)

1 N-UNCOUNT 不可算名詞 **Motion** is the activity or process of continually changing position or moving from one place to another. 運動 ❑ *...the laws governing light, sound, and motion.* 光，音および運動を支配する法則 ❑ *One group of muscles sets the next group in motion.* ある筋肉群が次の筋肉群を動かす。 **2** N-COUNT 可算名詞 A **motion** is an action, gesture, or movement. 動作 ❑ *He made a neat chopping motion with his hand.* 彼は手で巧みなみじん切りの身振りをした。 **3** N-COUNT 可算名詞 A **motion** is a formal proposal or statement in a meeting, debate, or trial, which is discussed and then voted on or decided on. 動議 ❑ *The conference is now debating the motion and will vote on it shortly.* 会議では現在動議が論議されており，間もなく投票が行われます。 ❑ *Opposition parties are likely to bring a no-confidence motion against the government.* 野党はおそらく政府に対し不信任動議を提出するであろう。 **4** V-T/V-I 他動詞/自動詞 If you **motion** to someone, you move your hand or head as a way of telling them to do something or telling them where to go. 身振りで要求する [他動詞・自動詞] ❑ *She motioned for the locked front doors to be opened.* 彼女は身振りで施錠のかかった玄関のドアを開けるよう求めました。 ❑ *He stood aside and motioned Don to the door.* 彼は脇に寄り，身振りでドンにドアを示した。 **5** → see also **slow motion 6** PHRASE 句 If you say that someone is **going through the motions**, you think they are only saying or doing something because it is expected of them without being interested, enthusiastic, or sympathetic. 形だけやる ❑ *"You really don't care, do you?" she said quietly. "You're just going through the motions."* 「本当に好きじゃないのね」と彼女は静かに言った。「あなたはお義理でやってるだけなんだから」 **7** PHRASE 句 If a process or event is **in motion**, it is happening. If it is **set in motion**, it is starting or beginning to happen. 動いている ❑ *The current chain of events was set in motion by that kidnapping.* 現在の一連の事件はあの誘拐から始まった。 **8** PHRASE 句 If someone **sets the wheels in motion**, they take the necessary action to make something start happening. 事を実行に移す ❑ *I have set the wheels in motion to sell their Arizona ranch.* 私は彼らのアリゾナ州の農場の売却を実行に移した。
→ see Word Web: **motion**

> **Word Web**   motion
>
> Newton's three laws of **motion** describe how **forces** affect the movement of objects. This is the first law: an object at **rest** won't move unless a force makes it move. Similarly, a moving object keeps its **momentum** unless something stops it. The second law describes **acceleration**. The **rate** of acceleration depends on two things: how strong the push on the object is, and how much the object weighs. The third law says that for every **action** there is an equal and opposite **reaction**. When one object **exerts** a force on another, the second object pushes back with an equal force.

Word Partnership motion は次の語句と使われる:

ADJ. **constant** motion, **full** motion, **perpetual** motion 🔟
 circular motion, **smooth** motion 🔟 🔟
 quick motion 🔟
V. **set** *something* **in** motion 🔟 🔟 🔟

mo|tion|less /moʊʃənlɪs/ ADJ 形容詞 Someone or something that is **motionless** is not moving at all. 静止した □ *He has this ability of being able to remain as motionless as a statue, for hours on end.* 彼は何時間も続けて像のように動かないでいることができる能力がある.

motion pic|ture (**motion pictures**) N-COUNT 可算名詞 A **motion picture** is a movie made for movie theaters. 映画 [mainly AM 主に米国英語, FORMAL 形式ばった] □ *It was there that I saw my first motion picture.* 私が最初に映画を見たのはそこでだった.

Word Link ate ≈ causing to be : complicate, humiliate, motivate

Word Link mot ≈ moving : motion, motivate, promote

mo|ti|vate /moʊtɪveɪt/ (**motivates, motivating, motivated**) 🔟 V-T 他動詞 If you **are motivated** by something, especially an emotion, it causes you to behave in a particular way. 動機づけられる □ *They are motivated by a need to achieve.* 彼らを動機づけているのは成功を収めたいという欲求だ. ●**mo|ti|vat|ed** ADJ 形容詞 □ *...highly motivated employees.* 大変意欲的な従業員 ●**mo|ti|va|tion** N-UNCOUNT 不可算名詞 □ *His poor performance may be attributed to lack of motivation rather than to reading difficulties.* 彼の悪い成績は, 読書障害というよりむしろやる気のなさが原因なのかもしれない. 🔟 V-T 他動詞 If someone **motivates** you to do something, they make you feel determined to do it. 動機を与える □ *How do you motivate people to work hard and efficiently?* 人を勤勉に効率よく働かせるにはどのように動機づけしますか. ●**mo|ti|va|tion** N-UNCOUNT 不可算名詞 意欲 □ *Given parental motivation, we are optimistic about the ability of people to change.* 私たちは親としての意欲があれば, 人は変わることができると気楽に考えている.

Word Partnership motivate は次の語句と使われる:

N. motivate **an audience**, motivate **consumers**, motivate **employees**, motivate **people**, motivate **students** 🔟

mo|ti|va|tion /moʊtɪveɪʃən/ (**motivations**) N-COUNT 可算名詞 Your **motivation** for doing something is what causes you to want to do it. 動機づけ □ *Money is my motivation.* 私を動機づけるのは金だ.

mo|tive /moʊtɪv/ (**motives**) N-COUNT 可算名詞 Your **motive** for doing something is your reason for doing it. 動機 □ *Police have ruled out robbery as a motive for the killing.* 警察はその殺人の動機から強盗を除外した.

Word Partnership motive は次の語句と使われる:

PREP. motive **behind** *something*, motive **for** *something*
ADJ. **possible** motive, **primary** motive, **ulterior** motive

mo|tor /moʊtər/ (**motors**) 🔟 N-COUNT 可算名詞 The **motor** in a machine, vehicle, or boat is the part that uses electricity or fuel to provide movement, so that the machine, vehicle, or boat can work. 発動機 □ *She got in and started the motor.* 彼女は乗り込んでモーターを始動させた. 🔟 ADJ 形容詞 **Motor** vehicles and boats have a gasoline or diesel engine. 発動機の [ADJ n] □ *Theft of motor vehicles is up by 15.9%.* 自動車泥棒は15.9%上昇している. 🔟 ADJ 形容詞 **Motor** is used to describe activities relating to vehicles such as cars and buses. 自動車の [mainly BRIT 主に英国英語; AM usually **automotive, automobile** 米国英語では通常 **automotive, automobile**] 🔟 → see also **motoring**
→ see **boat**

motor|bike /moʊtərbaɪk/ (**motorbikes**) N-COUNT 可算名詞 A **motorbike** is a lighter, less powerful motorcycle. 原動機付き自転車 [AM 米国英語]

motor|cycle /moʊtərsaɪkəl/ (**motorcycles**) N-COUNT 可算名詞 A **motorcycle** is a vehicle with two wheels and an engine. オートバイ

motor|cyclist /moʊtərsaɪklɪst/ (**motorcyclists**) N-COUNT 可算名詞 A **motorcyclist** is a person who rides a motorcycle. オートバイ乗り

mo|tor|ing /moʊtərɪŋ/ ADJ 形容詞 **Motoring** means relating to cars and driving. 自動車運転の [mainly BRIT 主に英国英語; AM usually **driving, automobile** 米国英語では通常 **driving, automobile**]

mo|tor|ist /moʊtərɪst/ (**motorists**) N-COUNT 可算名詞 A **motorist** is a person who drives a car. 自動車運転者 □ *Police urged*

motorists to take extra care on the roads. 警察は自動車の運転者にその道路ではくれぐれも気をつけるよう訴えた.

mo|tor|ized /moʊtəraɪzd/ 🔟 ADJ 形容詞 A **motorized** vehicle has an engine. モーターを備えた □ *Around 1910 motorized carriages were beginning to replace horse-drawn cabs.* 1910年頃にはモーター付き車が馬車にとって代わり始めていた. 🔟 ADJ 形容詞 A **motorized** group of soldiers is equipped with motor vehicles. 自動車を備えた □ *...motorized infantry and artillery.* 自動車を備えた歩兵隊と砲兵隊

motor|way /moʊtərweɪ/ (**motorways**) N-VAR 可変性名詞 A **motorway** is a major road that has been specially built for fast travel over long distances. Motorways have several lanes and special places where traffic gets on and leaves. 高速道路 [BRIT 英国英語; AM usually **freeway** or **highway** 米国英語では通常 **freeway** または **highway**]

mot|to /mɒtoʊ/ (**mottoes** or **mottos**) N-COUNT 可算名詞 A **motto** is a short sentence or phrase that expresses a rule for sensible behavior, especially a way of behaving in a particular situation. 標語 □ *"Stay true to yourself" has always been his motto.* 「自分に忠実であれ」は常に彼のモットーだった.

mould /moʊld/ → see **mold**

mound /maʊnd/ (**mounds**) 🔟 N-COUNT 可算名詞 A **mound** of something is a large, rounded pile of it. 山 □ *The bulldozers piled up huge mounds of dirt.* ブルドーザーはごみを巨大な山に盛り上げました. 🔟 N-COUNT 可算名詞 In baseball, the **mound** is the raised area where the pitcher stands when he or she throws the ball. マウンド □ *He went to the mound to talk with a struggling pitcher who spoke only Spanish.* 彼は悪戦苦闘しているスペイン語しか話さないピッチャーと話しにマウンドに行った.
→ see **baseball**

mount /maʊnt/ (**mounts, mounting, mounted**) 🔟 V-T 他動詞 If you **mount** a campaign or event, you organize it and make it take place. 準備する □ *The ANC announced it was mounting a major campaign of mass political protests.* アフリカ民族会議は集団による大きな政治的抗議運動の準備をしていると発表した. 🔟 V-I 自動詞 If something **mounts**, it increases in intensity. 高まる □ *For several hours, tension mounted.* 数時間のあいだ緊張が高まった. 🔟 V-I 自動詞 If something **mounts**, it increases in quantity. 増す □ *The uncollected garbage mounts in city streets.* 市の街路では未収集の生ごみが増している. ●PHRASAL VERB 句動詞 To **mount up** means the same as to **mount**. 増す □ *Her medical bills mounted up.* 彼女の医療費はかさんだ. 🔟 V-T 他動詞 If you **mount** the stairs or a platform, you go up the stairs or go up onto the platform. 上る [FORMAL 形式ばった] □ *Larry was mounting the stairs up into the attic.* ラリーは屋根裏部屋への階段を上っていた. 🔟 V-T 他動詞 If you **mount** a horse or motorcycle, you climb on to it so that you can ride it. 乗る □ *A man in a crash helmet was mounting a motorcycle.* 安全ヘルメットをかぶった男がオートバイに乗ろうとしていた. 🔟 V-T 他動詞 If you **mount** an object on something, you fix it there firmly. 据え付ける □ *Her husband mounts the work on velour paper and makes the frame.* 彼女の夫は作品をベロア紙に貼り, 額を作る. ●**-mounted** COMB IN ADJ 形容詞の複合 □ *She installed a wall-mounted electric fan.* 彼女は壁掛け電気扇風機を取り付けた. 🔟 V-T 他動詞 If you **mount** an exhibition or display, you organize and present it. 開催する □ *The gallery has mounted an exhibition of art by Irish women painters.* その美術館はアイルランドの女性画家たちの美術展を開催している. 🔟 N-IN-NAMES 名称中の名詞 **Mount** is used as part of the name of a mountain. 山 □ *...Mount Everest.* エベレスト山 🔟 → see also **mounted**

moun|tain /maʊntən/ (**mountains**) 🔟 N-COUNT 可算名詞 A **mountain** is a very high area of land with steep sides. 山 □ *Mt. McKinley, in Alaska, is the highest mountain in North America.* アラスカ州にあるマッキンリー山は北米で最も高い山だ. 🔟 QUANT 数量詞 If you talk about a **mountain of** something, or **mountains of** something, you are emphasizing that there is a large amount of it. 山のように多量 [INFORMAL くだけた, EMPHASIS 強調] □ *They are faced with a mountain of bureaucracy.* 彼らは山ほどのお役所仕事に直面している. 🔟 PHRASE 句 If you say that someone has **a mountain to climb**, you mean that it will be difficult for them to achieve what they want to achieve. 達成が困難 [JOURNALISM ジャーナリズム] □ *"We had a mountain to climb after the second goal went in," said Crosby.* 「2つ目のゴールが入ったあと, 我々は窮地に陥った」とクロスビーは言った.
→ see **Picture Dictionary: mountain**

moun|tain bike (**mountain bikes**) N-COUNT 可算名詞 A **mountain bike** is a type of bicycle that is suitable for riding over rough ground. It has a strong frame and thick tires. マウンテンバイク
→ see **bicycle**

Word Link eer ≈ one who does : auctioneer, mountaineer, volunteer

moun|tain|eer /maʊntənɪər/ (**mountaineers**) N-COUNT 可算名詞 A **mountaineer** is a person who is skillful at climbing the steep

Picture Dictionary — mountain

ridge · pass · peak · cliff · summit · glacier

sides of mountains. 登山家

moun|tain|ous /mˈaʊntᵊnəs/ **1** ADJ 形容詞 A **mountainous** place has a lot of mountains. 山の多い □ ...the mountainous region of New Mexico. ニューメキシコ州の山地 **2** ADJ 形容詞 You use **mountainous** to emphasize that something is great in size, quantity, or degree. 山のような [EMPHASIS 強調] [ADJ n] □ The plan is designed to reduce some of the company's mountainous debt. その計画では、会社の巨額債務の1部を削減することを意図している。

moun|tain|side /mˈaʊntᵊnsaɪd/ (mountainsides) N-COUNT 可算名詞 A **mountainside** is one of the steep sides of a mountain. 山腹 □ The couple trudged up the dark mountainside. そのカップルは暗い山腹を重い足取りで歩いた。

mount|ed /mˈaʊntɪd/ **1** ADJ 形容詞 **Mounted** police or soldiers ride horses when they are on duty. 馬に乗った [ADJ n] □ A dozen mounted police rode into the square. 十何人かの騎馬警官が広場に入ってきた。 **2** → see also **mount**

mourn /mˈɔrn/ (mourns, mourning, mourned) **1** V-T/V-I 他動詞/自動詞 If you **mourn** someone who has died or **mourn for** them, you are very sad that they have died and show your sorrow in the way that you behave. 哀悼する [他動詞・自動詞] □ Joan still mourns her father. ジョウンはいまだに父の喪に服している。 □ He mourned for his valiant men. 彼は勇敢な部下に哀悼の意を表した。 **2** V-T/V-I 他動詞/自動詞 If you **mourn** something or **mourn for** it, you regret that you no longer have it and show your regret in the way that you behave. 惜しむ [他動詞・自動詞] □ We mourned the loss of our cities. 私たちは都市を失い嘆き悲しんだ。

mourn|er /mˈɔrnər/ (mourners) N-COUNT 可算名詞 A **mourner** is a person who attends a funeral, especially as a relative or friend of the dead person. 会葬者 □ Weeks after his death, mourners still gather outside the house. 彼の死から数週間がたった後も、哀悼者が家の外に集まっている。
→ see **funeral**

mourn|ful /mˈɔrnfəl/ **1** ADJ 形容詞 If you are **mournful**, you are very sad. 悲しみに沈んだ □ He looked mournful, even near to tears. 彼は悲しげで、泣きそうでさえあった。 ● **mourn|ful|ly** ADV 副詞 悲しみに沈んで □ He stood mournfully at the gate waving bye bye. 彼は悲しげに門にたたずんでさよならの手を振った。 **2** ADJ 形容詞 A **mournful** sound seems very sad. 哀調をおびた □ ...the mournful wail of bagpipes. バグパイプの哀調をおびた、むせぶような音色

mouse /mˈaʊs/ (mice) **1** N-COUNT 可算名詞 A **mouse** is a small, furry animal with a long tail. ネズミ □ ...a mouse running in a wheel in its cage. かごの中の輪の中を走っているネズミ **2** N-COUNT 可算名詞 A **mouse** is a device that is connected to a computer. By moving it over a flat surface and pressing its buttons, you can move the cursor around the screen and do things without using the keyboard. マウス □ Her message had been written; all she had to do was click the mouse. 彼女はすでにメッセージを書いていたので、後はマウスをクリックするだけでよかった。

mouse mat (mouse mats) also **mousemat** N-COUNT 可算名詞 A **mouse mat** is the same as a **mouse pad**. マウスマット [BRIT 英国英語]

mouse pad (mouse pads) also **mousepad** N-COUNT 可算名詞 A **mouse pad** is a flat piece of plastic or some other material that you rest the mouse on while using a computer. マウスパッド [mainly AM 主に米国英語]

mousse /mˈus/ (mousses) **1** N-VAR 可変性名詞 **Mousse** is a sweet, light food made from eggs and cream. It is often flavored with fruit or chocolate. ムース □ ...a rich chocolate mousse. 豪華なチョコレートムース **2** N-MASS 質量名詞 **Mousse** is a soft substance containing a lot of tiny bubbles, for example one that you can put in your hair to make it easier to shape into a particular style. ムース □ He had even put mousse in his hair. 彼は髪にムースまで付けていた。
→ see **dessert**

mous|tache /mˈʌstæʃ/ → see **mustache**

mouth (mouths, mouthing, mouthed)

The noun is pronounced /mˈaʊθ/. The verb is pronounced /mˈaʊð/. The plural of the noun and the third person singular of the verb are both pronounced /mˈaʊðz/.

名詞は /maʊθ/ と発音される。動詞は /maʊð/ と発音される。名詞の複数形と動詞の3人称単数はともに /maʊðz/ と発音される。

1 N-COUNT 可算名詞 Your **mouth** is the area of your face where your lips are, or the space behind your lips where your teeth and tongue are. 口 □ She clamped her hand against her mouth. 彼女は口を手で覆った。 ● **-mouthed** /-mˈaʊðd/ COMB IN ADJ 形容詞の複合 ―な口で □ He straightened up and looked at me, open-mouthed. 彼は背筋を伸ばし、口をぽかんと開けて私を見た。 **2** N-COUNT 可算名詞 You can say that someone has a particular kind of **mouth** to indicate that they speak in a particular kind of way or that they say particular kinds of things. 口のきき方 □ I've always had a loud mouth, I refuse to be silenced. 私はいつも声高にしゃべってきた。沈黙させられるのはいやだ。 ● **-mouthed** COMB IN ADJ 形容詞の複合 ―な口で □ ...Sam, their smart-mouthed teenage son. 生意気な口を利く、彼らの10代の息子、サム **3** N-COUNT 可算名詞 The **mouth** of a cave, hole, or bottle is its entrance or opening. 入り口 □ By the mouth of the tunnel he bent to retie his shoelace. 彼はトンネルの入り口の側でかがんで靴紐を結び直した。 ● **-mouthed** COMB IN ADJ 形容詞の複合 ―口の □ He put the flowers in a wide-mouthed blue vase. 彼は口の広い青い花瓶に花を活けた。 **4** N-COUNT 可算名詞 The **mouth** of a river is the place where it flows into the sea. 河口 □ ...the town at the mouth of the River Fox. フォックス川の河口にある町 **5** V-T 他動詞 If you **mouth** something, you form words with your lips without making any sound. 口をもぐもぐさせる □ I mouthed a goodbye and hurried in behind Momma. 私は声を出さずにさよならを言い、ママの後ろに急いで隠れた。 **6** PHRASE 句 If you have a number of **mouths to feed**, you have the responsibility of earning enough money to feed and take care of that number of people. 扶養家族 □ He had to feed his family on the equivalent of seven hundred dollars a month and, with five mouths to feed, he found this very hard. 彼は月700ドル相当で

族を養わなければならず，5人の扶養家族がいてはこれは非常に困難なことが分かった．**7** PHRASE 句 If you say that someone does not **open** their **mouth**, you are emphasizing that they never say anything at all. 口を開く [EMPHASIS 強調] ❑ *Sometimes I hardly dare open my mouth.* 時々私はほとんど口を利く勇気がなくなる．**8** PHRASE 句 If you **keep** your **mouth shut** about something, you do not talk about it, especially because it is a secret. 秘密を漏らさない ❑ *You wouldn't be here now if she'd kept her mouth shut.* もし彼女が秘密を漏らさなかったら，君が今ここにいるはずはないのだ．**9** to **live hand to mouth** → see hand **10** heart **in** your **mouth** → see heart **11** from the horse's mouth → see horse **12** to put your money where your mouth is → see money **13** shut your mouth → see shut **14** word of mouth → see word
→ see face, respiratory

Word Partnership	*mouth* は次の語句と使われる:
ADJ.	**big** mouth **1** **2**
V.	**close** *your* mouth, **keep** *your* mouth **closed/shut**, **shut** *your* mouth **1** **8**

mouth|ful /ˈmaʊθfʊl/ (**mouthfuls**) **1** N-COUNT 可算名詞 A **mouthful** of drink or food is the amount that you put or have in your mouth. 1口分 ❑ *She gulped down a mouthful of coffee.* 彼女はコーヒーを1口飲み下した．**2** N-SING 単数名詞 If you describe a long word or phrase as **a mouthful**, you mean that it is difficult to say. (言いにくい) 長ったらしい語句 [INFORMAL くだけた] ❑ *It's called the Pan-Caribbean Disaster Preparedness and Prevention Project, which is quite a mouthful.* それは「汎カリビアン災害準備および防災計画」と呼ばれ，かなり長ったらしい名です．

mouth|piece /ˈmaʊθpiːs/ (**mouthpieces**) **1** N-COUNT 可算名詞 The **mouthpiece** of a telephone is the part that you speak into. 送話口 ❑ *He shouted into the mouthpiece.* 彼は送話口に向かって叫んだ．**2** N-COUNT 可算名詞 The **mouthpiece** of a musical instrument or other device is the part that you put into your mouth. マウスピース ❑ *He showed him how to blow into the ivory mouthpiece.* 彼は象牙のマウスピースにどのように息を吹き込むのかを彼に示した．**3** N-COUNT 可算名詞 The **mouthpiece** of an organization or person is someone who informs other people of the opinions and policies of that organization or person. 代弁者 ❑ *Their mouthpiece is the vice president.* 彼らの代弁者は副社長です．
→ see scuba diving

mov|able /ˈmuːvəbəl/ also **moveable** ADJ 形容詞 Something that is **movable** can be moved from one place or position to another. 可動の ❑ *It's a vinyl doll with movable arms and legs.* それは腕と脚が動くビニールの人形です．

move

❶ VERB AND NOUN USES
❷ PHRASES
❸ PHRASAL VERBS

❶ move /muːv/ (**moves, moving, moved**) **1** V-T/V-I 他動詞/自動詞 When you **move** something or when it **moves**, its position changes and it does not remain still. 動かす [他動詞] 動く [自動詞] ❑ *She moved the sheaf of papers into position.* 彼女は紙の束を所定位置に動かした．❑ *A traffic policeman asked him to move his car.* 交通巡査は彼に車を移動するよう頼んだ．❑ *The train began to move.* 列車は動き始めた．**2** V-I 自動詞 When you **move**, you change your position or go to a different place. 動く ❑ *She waited for him to get up, but he didn't move.* 彼女は彼が起き上がるのを待ったが，彼は動かなかった．❑ *He moved around the room, putting his possessions together.* 彼は部屋をあちこち歩き回って，自分の持ち物を集めた．● N-COUNT 可算名詞 **Move** is also a noun. 動き ❑ *The doctor made a move toward the door.* 医師はドアに向かって動いた．**3** V-I 自動詞 If you **move**, you act or you begin to do something. 行動する ❑ *Industrialists must move fast to take advantage of new opportunities in Eastern Europe.* 東欧の新しい機会を利用するためには，企業家は迅速に行動しなければならない．**4** N-COUNT 可算名詞 A **move** is an action that you take in order to achieve something. 処置 ❑ *The one-point cut in interest rates was a wise move.* 公定歩合の1%引き下げは賢明な処置だった．❑ *It may also be a good move to suggest she talks things over.* 彼女に話し合いを提案するのも賢明な策かもしれない．**5** V-I 自動詞 If a person or company **moves**, they leave the building where they have been living or working, and they go to live or work in a different place, taking their possessions with them. 引っ越す ❑ *Two people in love are at home wherever they are, no matter how often they move.* 愛し合う2人はいくら頻繁に引越したとしても，どこででもくつろいでいる．❑ *She had often considered moving to Seattle.* 彼女はシアトルに引っ越すことをしょっちゅう考えた．● N-COUNT 可算名詞 **Move** is also a noun. 移転 ❑ *Modigliani announced his move to Montparnasse in 1909.* モジリアーニはモンパルナスへの転居を1909年に発表した．**6** V-T 他動詞 If people in authority **move** someone, they make that person go from one place or job to another one. 移動させる ❑ *His superiors go from one place or job to another one.*

moved him to another parish. 彼の上司は彼を別の教会区に移動させた．**7** V-I 自動詞 If you **move from** one job or interest **to** another, you change to it. 転職する ❑ *He moved from being a part-time tutor to being a lecturer in social history.* 彼はパートの家庭教師から社会史の講師に転職した．● N-COUNT 可算名詞 **Move** is also a noun. 転職 ❑ *His move to the chairmanship means he will take a less active role in day-to-day management.* 彼の会長就任は日々の経営への参加が減ることを意味する．**8** V-I 自動詞 If you **move to** a new topic in a conversation, you start talking about something different. 移る ❑ *Let's move to another subject, Dan.* ダン，次の話題に移りましょう **9** V-T 他動詞 If you **move** an event or the date of an event, you change the time at which it happens. 変更する ❑ *The club has moved its meeting to Saturday, January 22nd.* クラブはその会合を1月22日土曜日に変更した．**10** V-I 自動詞 If you **move** toward a particular state, activity, or opinion, you start to be in that state, do that activity, or have that opinion. 進む ❑ *The Labour Party has moved to the right and become like your Democratic Party.* 労働党は右寄りになり，あなた方の民主党のようになりました．● N-COUNT 可算名詞 **Move** is also a noun. 動き ❑ *His move to the left was not a sudden leap but a natural working out of ideas.* 彼の左寄りへの動きは突然の変化ではなく，思想から自然に出てきた結果である．**11** V-I 自動詞 If a situation or process is **moving**, it is developing or progressing, rather than staying still. 進展する [usu cont] ❑ *Events are moving fast.* もろもろの出来事は迅速に進展している．**12** V-T 他動詞 If you say that you will not **be moved**, you mean that you have come to a decision and nothing will change your mind. 意見を変えさせる [usu passive] ❑ *Everyone thought I was crazy to go back, but I wouldn't be moved.* 誰もが戻るのは正気の沙汰ではないと思ったが，私の決心は動かなかった．**13** V-T 他動詞 If something **moves** you to do something, it influences you and causes you to do it. 動かして…する気にさせる ❑ *It was punk that first moved him to join a band seriously.* 最初彼が真剣にバンドに入る気になったのはパンクのせいだった．**14** V-T 他動詞 If something **moves** you, it has an effect on your emotions and causes you to feel sadness or sympathy for another person. 心を動かす ❑ *These stories surprised and moved me.* これらの物語は私を驚かせ，感動させた．● **moved** ADJ 形容詞 [v-link ADJ] 感動した ❑ *Those who listened to him were deeply moved.* 彼の話を聞いた人は深く感動した．**15** V-I 自動詞 If you say that someone **moves in** a particular society, circle, or world, you mean that they know people in a particular social class or group and spend most of their time with them. 出入りする ❑ *She moves in high-society circles in Palm Beach.* 彼女はパームビーチの上流社会に出入りしている．**16** V-T/V-I 他動詞/自動詞 At a meeting, if you **move for** something or **move that** something should happen, you formally suggest it so that everyone present can vote on it. 提案する [他動詞・自動詞] ❑ *Somebody needs to move for an adjournment.* 誰かが休会を提案する必要がある．**17** N-COUNT 可算名詞 A **move** is an act of putting a chess piece or other counter in a different position on a board when it is your turn to do so in a game. こまを動かすこと ❑ *With no idea of what to do for my next move, my hand hovered over the board.* 次の手をどう打ったらいいか考えつかぬまま，私の手は盤上をさまよった．

❷ move /muːv/ (**moves, moving, moved**) **1** PHRASE 句 If you say that one **false move** will cause a disaster, you mean that you or someone else must not make any mistakes because the situation is so difficult or dangerous. 間違った行動 ❑ *He knew one false move would end in death.* 彼はちょっとでもミスをしたら死ぬことを知っていた．**2** PHRASE 句 If you **make a move**, you prepare or begin to leave one place and go somewhere else. 出かける ❑ *He glanced at his wristwatch. "I suppose we'd better make a move."* 彼は腕時計をちらっと見て言った．「そろそろ出かけたほうがいいだろう．」**3** PHRASE 句 If you **make a move**, you take a course of action. 行動を起こす ❑ *The week before the deal was supposed to close, fifteen Japanese banks made a move to pull out.* 取引がまとまる予定だった前の週に15の日本の銀行が手を引いた．**4** PHRASE 句 If you are **on the move**, you are going from one place to another. 移動して ❑ *Jack never wanted to stay in one place for very long, so they were always on the move.* ジャックは決して1つの場所に長く居たいと思っていなかったので，彼らはいつも転々と移動していた．**5** to **move the goalposts** → see goalpost **6** to **move a muscle** → see muscle

❸ move /muːv/ (**moves, moving, moved**)
▸ **move in** **1** PHRASAL VERB 句動詞 When you **move in** somewhere, you begin to live there as your home. 新居に引っ越してくる ❑ *Her house was in perfect order when she moved in.* 彼女の家は彼女が引っ越してきた時には完璧な状態だった．❑ *Her husband had moved in with a younger woman.* 彼女の夫はもっと若い女と一緒に住むようになっていた．**2** PHRASAL VERB 句動詞 If police, soldiers, or attackers **move in**, they go toward a place or person in order to deal with or attack them. 襲いかかる ❑ *There were violent and chaotic scenes when police moved in to disperse the crowd.* 警察が群集を追い払うために襲いかかった時には暴力的で混乱した光景があった．**3** PHRASAL VERB 句動詞 If someone **moves in on** an area of activity which was previously only done by a particular group of people, they start becoming involved with it for the first time. 進出する ❑ *I don't want another guy moving in on my territory, you know?*

別の男には私の領域に進出してほしくないのだ.

▶ **move off** PHRASAL VERB 句動詞 When you **move off**, you start moving away from a place. 立ち去る ❑ *Gil waved his hand and the car moved off.* ギルは手を振り, 車は出発した.

▶ **move on** ◼ PHRASAL VERB 句動詞 When you **move on** somewhere, you leave the place where you have been staying or waiting and go there. 転居する ❑ *Mr. Brooke moved on from LA to Phoenix.* ブルック氏はロサンジェルスからフェニックスに移った. ◼ PHRASAL VERB 句動詞 If someone such as a police officer **moves you on**, they order you to stop standing in a particular place and to go somewhere else. 立ち去らせる ❑ *Eventually the police were called to move them on.* 彼らを立ち去らせるために, 結局警察が呼ばれた. ◼ PHRASAL VERB 句動詞 If you **move on**, you finish or stop one activity and start doing something different. 移る ❑ *She ran this shop for ten years before deciding to move on to fresh challenges.* 彼女は新しい努力目標に移ると決心する前にこのお店を10年間経営した.

▶ **move out** PHRASAL VERB 句動詞 If you **move out**, you stop living in a particular house or place and go to live somewhere else. 引っ越して行く ❑ *The harassment had become too much to tolerate and he decided to move out.* 嫌がらせ行為は我慢できないほどどくなったため, 彼は出て行くことに決めた.

▶ **move over** ◼ PHRASAL VERB 句動詞 If you **move over to** a new system or way of doing something, you change to it. 移行する ❑ *The government is having to introduce some difficult changes, particularly in moving over to a market economy.* 政府は特に市場経済への移行の際に, いくつかの困難な変化を導入することを余儀なくされている. ◼ PHRASAL VERB 句動詞 If someone **moves over**, they leave their job or position in order to let someone else have it. 地位を譲る ❑ *Mr. Jenkins should make balanced programs or move over and let someone else who can.* ジェンキンス氏は均衡のとれた計画を作成すべきであり, できなければ地位を譲り, それができる誰か他の人物にさせるべきだ. ◼ PHRASAL VERB 句動詞 If you **move over**, you change your position in order to make room for someone else. 席などを詰めて空ける ❑ *Move over and let me drive.* 席を空けて私に運転させてくれ.

▶ **move up** ◼ PHRASAL VERB 句動詞 If you **move up**, you change your position, especially in order to be nearer someone or to make room for someone else. 席などを詰める ❑ *Move up, John, and let the lady sit down.* ジョン, 席をつめて, その女性を座らせてやって. ◼ PHRASAL VERB 句動詞 If someone or something **moves up**, they go to a higher level, grade, or class. 上昇する ❑ *Share prices moved up.* 株価は上昇した.

move|able /múvəbᵊl/ → see **movable**

Word Link   *ment ≈ state, condition : agreement, management, movement*

Word Link   *mov ≈ moving : movement, movie, unmoved*

---

move|ment /múvmənt/ (**movements**) ◼ N-COUNT 可算名詞 A **movement** is a group of people who share the same beliefs, ideas, or aims. 運動 ❑ *It's part of a broader nationalist movement that's gaining strength throughout the country.* それは国中で強まりつつあるより広い国家主義的運動の一部である. ◼ N-VAR 可変性名詞 **Movement** involves changing position or going from one place to another. 動き ❑ *They actually monitor the movement of the fish going up river.* 彼らは魚が川を遡上する(そじょうする)動きを実際に監視する. ❑ *There was movement behind the window in the back door.* 裏口の窓の後ろに動きがあった. ◼ N-VAR 可変性名詞 A **movement** is a planned change in position that an army makes during a battle or military exercise. 軍隊の移動 ❑ *There are reports of fresh troop movements across the border.* 新たに軍隊が国境を越えて展開しているとの報告がある. ◼ N-VAR 可変性名詞 **Movement** is a gradual development or change of an attitude, opinion, or policy. 進展 ❑ *...the movement toward democracy in Latin America.* ラテンアメリカにおける民主主義への進展. ◼ N-PLURAL 複数名詞 Your **movements** are everything that you do or plan to do during a period of time. 行動 ❑ *I want a full account of your movements the night Mr. Gower was killed.* ガワー氏が殺害された夜のあなたの行動の一部始終を説明してほしい.
→ see **brain**

Word Partnership   *movement は次の語句と使われる:*

N.	**freedom** movement, **labor** movement, **leader of a** movement, **peace** movement, **reform** movement ◼
ADJ.	**environmental** movement, **political** movement ◼ **rapid** movement, **slow** movement, **sudden** movement ◼

mov|er /múvər/ (**movers**) PHRASE 句 The **movers and shakers** in a place or area of activity are the people who have the most power or influence. 有力者 ❑ *It is the movers and shakers of the record industry who will decide which bands make it.* どちらのバンドが成功するのかを決めるのはレコード業界の有力者たちだ.

movie /múvi/ (**movies**) ◼ N-COUNT 可算名詞 A **movie** is a

series of moving pictures that have been recorded so that they can be shown in a theater or on television. A movie tells a story, or shows a real situation. 映画 ❑ *In the first movie Tony Curtis ever made he played a grocery clerk.* トニー・カーティスは初めて出演した映画で食料品店の店員を演じた. ◼ N-PLURAL 複数名詞 You can talk about **the movies** when you are talking about seeing a movie in a movie theater. 映画上映 [mainly AM 主に米国英語] ❑ *He took her to the movies.* 彼は彼女を映画に連れて行った.
→ see **DVD**

An **Oscar** is the nickname for the golden statue given as the prize to those films considered the best each year. Also known as the **Academy Awards**, these prizes also recognize the talent of actors, writers, designers and other crew members. Not only American movies but also foreign films are included.

Word Partnership   *movie は次の語句と使われる:*

ADJ.	**bad/good** movie, **favorite** movie, **new/old** movie, **popular** movie ◼
V.	**go to** a movie, **see** a movie, **watch** a movie ◼
N.	**scene in** a movie, movie **screen**, movie **set**, movie **studio**, **television/TV** movie ◼

movie|goer /múvigoʊər/ (**moviegoers**) N-COUNT 可算名詞 A **moviegoer** is a person who often goes to the movies. 映画ファン [AM 米国英語] ❑ *What is it about Tom Hanks that moviegoers find so appealing?* 映画ファンはトム・ハンクスのどんな所がそんなに魅力的だと思うのか.

movie star (**movie stars**) N-COUNT 可算名詞 A **movie star** is a famous actor or actress who appears in movies. 映画スター [mainly AM 主に米国英語]

movie thea|ter (**movie theaters**) N-COUNT 可算名詞 A **movie theater** is a place where people go to watch movies for entertainment. 映画館 [AM 米国英語]

mov|ing /múvɪŋ/ ◼ ADJ 形容詞 If something is **moving**, it makes you feel an emotion such as sadness, pity, or sympathy very strongly. こころを動かす ❑ *It is very moving to see how much strangers can care for each other.* 見知らぬ人同士がいかにいたわり合いできるかを見て大変こころを動かされる. ● **mov|ing|ly** ADV 副詞 [ADV with v] 感動的に ❑ *You write very movingly of your sister Amy's suicide.* あなたは姉妹のエイミーの自殺についてとても感動的に書いている. ◼ ADJ 形容詞 A **moving** model or part of a machine moves or is able to move. 動いている [ADJ n] ❑ *It also means there are no moving parts to break down.* またそれは動いている部分の故障はないことを意味する.

mow /moʊ/ (**mows, mowing, mowed, mown**)

The past participle can be either **mowed** or **mown**.

過去分詞は **mowed** か **mown** のどちらでもありうる

V-T/V-I 他動詞/自動詞 If you **mow** an area of grass, you cut it using a machine called a lawnmower. 刈る ❑ *He continued to mow the lawn and do other routine chores.* 彼は芝刈りやその他の日常的な仕事をし続けた.

▶ **mow down** PHRASAL VERB 句動詞 If someone **is mowed down**, they are killed violently by a vehicle or gunfire. なぎ倒す, ひき殺す ❑ *She was mowed down on a pedestrian crossing.* 彼女は横断歩道で車にひかれて死んだ.

mow|er /moʊər/ (**mowers**) ◼ N-COUNT 可算名詞 A **mower** is the same as a **lawnmower**. 芝刈り機 ◼ N-COUNT 可算名詞 A **mower** is a machine that has sharp blades for cutting something such as corn or wheat. 刈り取り機

MP3 /ɛm pi θri/ N-UNCOUNT 不可算名詞 **MP3** is a kind of technology that enables you to record and play music from the Internet. MP3

MPEG /ɛmpɛg/ N-UNCOUNT 不可算名詞 **MPEG** is a standard file format for compressing video images so that they can be stored or sent by e-mail more easily. **MPEG** is an abbreviation for "Motion Picture Experts Group." MPEG [COMPUTING コンピューティング]

mph also **m.p.h.** **mph** is written after a number to indicate the speed of something such as a vehicle. **mph** is an abbreviation for "miles per hour." miles per hourの略 ❑ *Inside these zones, traffic speeds are restricted to 20 mph.* これらの地帯内では自動車の最高速度は時速20マイルである.

Mr. /mɪstər/ ◼ N-TITLE 称号名詞 **Mr.** is used before a man's name when you are speaking or referring to him. さん, 氏 ❑ *...Mr. Grant.* グラントさん ❑ *...Mr. Bob Price.* ボブ・プライス氏 ◼ N-VOC 呼格名詞 **Mr.** is sometimes used in front of words such as "president" and "chairman" to address the man who holds the position mentioned. 殿 ❑ *Mr. President, you're aware of the system.* 大統領殿, あなたはその制度にお気づきですね. ◼ → see also **Messrs.**

Mrs. /mɪsɪz/ N-TITLE 称号名詞 **Mrs.** is used before the name of a married woman when you are speaking or referring to her. さん, 夫人 ❑ *Hello, Mrs. Miles.* こんにちわ, マイルズさん ❑ *...Mrs. Anne*

Pritchard. アン・プリチャード夫人

Ms. /mɪz/ N-TITLE 称号名詞 **Ms.** is used, especially in written English, before a woman's name when you are speaking to her or referring to her. If you use **Ms.**, you are not specifying if the woman is married or not. さん □...*Ms. Brown.* ブラウンさん

much /mʌtʃ/ ■ ADV 副詞 You use **much** to indicate the great intensity, extent, or degree of something such as an action, feeling, or change. **Much** is usually used with "so," "too," and "very," and in negative clauses with this meaning. たいそう [ADV after v] □ *She laughs too much.* 彼女は笑いすぎる。□ *Thank you very much.* どうもありがとう。 ■ ADV 副詞 If something does not happen **much**, it does not happen very often. しばしば □ *He said that his father never talked much about the war.* 彼の父親は決して戦争についてあまり語らないと彼は言った。□ *Gwen had not seen her dad all that much, because mostly he worked on the ships.* グウェンの父親はたいてい船上勤務だったので、彼と会うことはまれで滅多になかった。 ■ ADV 副詞 You use **much** in front of "too" or comparative adjectives and adverbs in order to emphasize that there is a large amount of a particular quality. 大いに [EMPHASIS 強調] □ *The skin is much too delicate.* その皮膚はすごくデリケートすぎる。 ■ ADV 副詞 If one thing is **much** the same as another thing, it is very similar to it. だいたい □ *The day ended much as it began.* その日は始まりとだいたい同じように終わった。 ■ DET 限定詞 You use **much** to indicate that you are referring to a large amount of a substance or thing. 多くの □ *They are grown on the hillsides in full sun, without much water.* それらはいっぱいの陽光で大した水なしに丘の中腹で栽培される。□ *Japan has been reluctant to offer much aid to Russia.* 日本はロシアに多くの援助を提供したがらなかった。 ● PRON 代名詞 **Much** is also a pronoun. 多量 □ ...*eating too much and drinking too much.* 食べすぎと飲みすぎ ● QUANT 数量詞 **Much** is also a quantifier. 多量 □ *Much of the time we do not notice that we are solving problems.* 多くの場合、我々は問題を解決していることに気づかない。 ■ ADV 副詞 You use **much** in expressions such as **not much, not very much,** and **too much** when replying to questions about amounts. 大いに [as reply] □ *"Can you hear it where you live?" He shook his head. "Not much."* 「あなたのお住まいからそれは聞えますか」彼は首を振って言った。「大して聞えません」 ■ QUANT 数量詞 If you do not see **much** of someone, you do not see them very often. たびたび [with brd-neg, QUANT 'of' n-proper/pron] □ *I don't see much of Tony nowadays.* 最近トニーとはあまり会っていない。 ■ DET 限定詞 You use **much** in the expression **how much** to ask questions about amounts or degrees, and also in reported clauses and statements to give information about the amount or degree of something. 多くの □ *How much money can I afford?* 私はいくらくらいの金の余裕があるのか。 ● ADV 副詞 **Much** is also an adverb. たくさんに □ *She knows how much this upsets me but she persists in doing it.* 彼女はこれがどれほど私を動揺させるかを知りながら、それを止めようとしない。 ● PRON 代名詞 **Much** is also a pronoun. たくさん ['how' PRON] □ *How much do you earn?* あなたの収入はどのくらいですか。 ■ DET 限定詞 You use **much** in the expression **as much** when you are comparing amounts. 多くの □ *I shall try, with as much patience as is possible, to explain yet again.* 私はできるだけ辛抱強く再び説明してみるつもりだ。□ *Their aim will be to produce as much milk as possible.* 彼らの目的はできるだけ多くの牛乳を生産することであろう。

> You should use **much** if you want to talk about things that cannot be counted. □ ...*too much water.* You only use **many** to talk about things that can be counted. □ *They owned many cars.*

■ PHRASE 句 You use **much as** to introduce a fact which makes something else you have just said or will say rather surprising. ─なのはやまやまなのだが □ *Much as they hope to go home tomorrow, they're resigned to staying on until the end of the year.* 彼らは明日家に帰りたいのはやまやまなのだが、あきらめて年末まで留まるつもりだ。 ■ PHRASE 句 You use **as much** in expressions such as "**I thought as much**" and "**I guessed as much**" after you have just been told something and you want to say that you already believed or expected it to be true. そうだろうと思う □ *You're waiting for a woman – I thought as much.* 君は女性を待っている。私もそうだろうと思った。 ■ PHRASE 句 You use **as much as** before an amount to suggest that it is surprisingly large. ほども [EMPHASIS 強調] □ *The organizers hope to raise as much as $6M for charity.* 組織者達は慈善のために6百万ドルほども集めることを望んでいる。 ■ PHRASE 句 You use **much less** after a statement, often a negative one, to indicate that the statement is more true of the person, thing, or situation that you are going to mention next. いわんや─でない □ *They are always short of water to drink, much less to bathe in.* 彼らはいつも飲み水が不足している。入浴用の水どころではない。 ■ PHRASE 句 If you say that something is not **so much** one thing **as** another, you mean that it is more like the second thing than the first. ではなくむしろ □ *I don't really think of her as a daughter so much as a very good friend.* 私は彼女を娘としてではなくむしろ非常に良い友人としてみている。 ■ PHRASE 句 You use **so much so** to indicate that your previous statement is true to a very great extent, and therefore it has the result mentioned. するほどまでに □ *He himself believed*

in freedom, so much so that he would rather die than live without it. 彼自身、自由なしに生きるくらいなら死んだ方がましだと考えるほど自由を信奉していた。 ■ PHRASE 句 If a situation or action is **too much for** you, it is so difficult, tiring, or upsetting that you cannot cope with it. 手に余る □ *His inability to stay at one job for long had finally proved too much for her.* 彼が1つの職に長い間留まることができないことに彼女はついに耐えられなくなった。 ■ PHRASE 句 You use **very much** to emphasize that someone or something has a lot of a particular quality, or that the description you are about to give is particularly accurate. 非常に [EMPHASIS 強調] □ ...*a man very much in charge of himself.* 非常にしっかりした男 **a bit much → see bit**

muck /mʌk/ N-UNCOUNT 不可算名詞 **Muck** is dirt or some other unpleasant substance. 泥 [INFORMAL くだけた] □ *This congealed muck was interfering with the filter and causing the flooding.* この泥の固まりがフィルターにつまり、水浸しを起こしていた。

mu|cus /myuːkəs/ N-UNCOUNT 不可算名詞 **Mucus** is a thick liquid that is produced in some parts of your body, for example the inside of your nose. 粘液 □ ...*the thin layer of mucus that helps protect the delicate lining of the rectum.* 直腸の繊細な内側を保護するのに役立つ粘液の薄い層

mud /mʌd/ N-UNCOUNT 不可算名詞 **Mud** is a sticky mixture of earth and water. 泥 □ *His uniform was crumpled, untidy, splashed with mud.* 彼の制服はしわくちゃで、だらしなく、泥がはねかかっていた。

mud|dle /mʌdəl/ (muddles, muddling, muddled) ■ N-VAR 可変性名詞 If people or things are **in a muddle**, they are in a state of confusion or disorder. 混乱 □ *My thoughts are all in a muddle.* 私の考えは全て混乱状態だ。□ *We are going to get into a hopeless muddle.* 私たちはひどい混乱状態に陥ろうとしている。 ■ V-T 他動詞 If you **muddle** things or people, you get them mixed up, so that you do not know which is which. 混同する □ *Already, one or two critics have begun to muddle the two names.* 既に1人ふたり批評家がその2つの名前をごっちゃにし始めている。 ● PHRASAL VERB 句動詞 **Muddle up** means the same as **muddle**. 混同する □ *The question muddles up three separate issues.* その質問は3つの別個の問題を混同している。 ● **mud|dled up** ADJ 形容詞 混同した □ *I know that I am getting my words muddled up.* 私は自分の言葉をごっちゃにしているのは知っている。

▶ **muddle through** PHRASAL VERB 句動詞 If you **muddle through**, you manage to do something even though you do not have the proper equipment or do not really know how to do it. なんとか切り抜ける □ *We will muddle through and just play it day by day.* 私たちはなんとか切り抜け、ただ日々それを演奏するだけだ。□ *They may be able to muddle through the next five years like this.* 彼らはこのように今後5年間なんとか切り抜けることができるかもしれない。

▶ **muddle up → see muddle 2**

mud|dled /mʌdəld/ ADJ 形容詞 If someone is **muddled**, they are confused about something. 混乱した □ *I'm afraid I'm a little muddled. I'm not exactly sure where to begin.* 申し訳ないが、私はちょっと混乱している。どこから始めていいか必ずしも分からない。

mud|dy /mʌdi/ (muddier, muddiest, muddies, muddying, muddied) ■ ADJ 形容詞 Something that is **muddy** contains mud or is covered in mud. 泥の多い □ ...*a muddy track.* ぬかるんだ小道 ■ V-T 他動詞 If you **muddy** something, you cause it to be muddy. 泥だらけにする □ *The ground still smelled of rain and they muddied their shoes.* 地面はまだ雨の匂いがし、彼らは靴を泥だらけにした。 ■ V-T 他動詞 If someone or something **muddies** a situation or issue, they cause it to seem less clear and less easy to understand. 混乱させる □ *It's difficult enough without muddying the issue with religion.* 宗教で混乱させなくともそれは十分難しい問題だ。 ● PHRASE 句 If someone or something **muddies the waters**, they cause a situation or issue to seem less clear and less easy to understand. 混乱させる

muf|fle /mʌfəl/ (muffles, muffling, muffled) V-T 他動詞 If something **muffles** a sound, it makes it quieter and more difficult to hear. 消す，鈍くする □ *Blake held his handkerchief over the mouthpiece to muffle his voice.* ブラックはハンカチで送話口を覆い自分の声を殺した。

mug /mʌɡ/ (mugs, mugging, mugged) ■ N-COUNT 可算名詞 A **mug** is a large, deep cup with straight sides and a handle, used for hot drinks. マグ □ *He spooned instant coffee into two of the mugs.* 彼はマグの2個にインスタントコーヒーをスプーンで入れた。 ■ N-COUNT 可算名詞 You can use **mug** to refer to the mug and its contents, or to the contents only. マグ1杯の量 □ *He had been drinking mugs of coffee to keep himself awake.* 彼は眠らないようにマグに入ったコーヒーを何杯も飲んでいた。 ■ N-COUNT 可算名詞 Someone's **mug** is their face. 顔 [INFORMAL くだけた] □ *He managed to get his ugly mug on TV.* 彼はあの醜い顔で首尾よくテレビに出ることができた。 ■ V-T 他動詞 If someone **mugs** you, they attack you in order to steal your money. 襲って強奪する □ *I was walking out to my car when this guy tried to mug me.* 私がこの男に襲われ強奪されようとした時は、車の方に歩いていたところだった。 ● **mug|ging** (muggings) N-VAR 可変性名詞（路上などの）強盗 □ *Bank robberies, burglaries, and muggings are reported almost daily in the press.* 銀行強

盗，押し込み，路上強盗は毎日のように新聞で報道されている．
→ see **dish**

mug|ger /mʌgər/ (**muggers**) N-COUNT 可算名詞 A **mugger** is a person who attacks someone violently in a street in order to steal money from them. 路上強盗 □ ...hiding places for muggers and thieves. 路上強盗や泥棒の隠れ場所

mug|gy /mʌgi/ ADJ 形容詞 **Muggy** weather is unpleasantly warm and damp. 蒸し暑い，うっとうしい □ It was muggy and overcast. うっとうしくどんよりした天気だった．

mule /myul/ (**mules**) ■ N-COUNT 可算名詞 A **mule** is an animal whose parents are a horse and a donkey. ラバ ☑ N-COUNT 可算名詞 A **mule** is a shoe or slipper which is open around the heel. つっかけ式スリッパ

mull /mʌl/ (**mulls, mulling, mulled**) V-T 他動詞 If you **mull** something, you think about it for a long time before deciding what to do. 熟考する [AM 米国用法] □ Last month, a federal grand jury began mulling evidence in the case. 先月，連邦陪審は立ての証拠物件をじっくり調べ始めた．
▸ **mull over** PHRASAL VERB 句動詞 If you **mull** something **over**, you think about it for a long time before deciding what to do. じっくりと考える □ McLaren had been mulling over an idea to make a movie. マクラレンは映画を製作する案をじっくり検討していた．

Word Link *multi = many : multicultural, multimedia, multinational*

multi|cul|tur|al /mʌltikʌltʃərəl/ ADJ 形容詞 **Multicultural** means consisting of or relating to people of many different nationalities and cultures. 多文化の □ ...children growing up in a multicultural society. 多文化社会で育っている子供たち

multi|lat|er|al /mʌltilætərᵊl/ ADJ 形容詞 **Multilateral** means involving at least three different groups of people or nations. 多国間の □ Many want to abandon the multilateral trade talks in Geneva. 多くの国はジュネーブの多国間貿易交渉を放棄している．

multi|me|dia /mʌltimidiə/ ■ N-UNCOUNT 不可算名詞 You use **multimedia** to refer to computer programs and products which involve sound, pictures, and film, as well as text. マルチメディア □ ...the case of an insurance company using multimedia to improve customer service in its branches. マルチメディアを使って支店の顧客サービスを改善する保険会社の場合 ☑ N-UNCOUNT 不可算名詞 In education, **multimedia** is the use of television and other different media in a lesson, as well as books. マルチメディア □ I am making a multimedia presentation for my science project. 私は科学計画のためにマルチメディアのプレゼンテーションを作成中だ．

multi|na|tion|al /mʌltinæʃᵊnᵊl/ (**multinationals**) ■ ADJ 形容詞 A **multinational** company has branches or owns companies in many different countries. 多国籍の ● N-COUNT 可算名詞 **Multinational** is also a noun. 多国籍企業 □ ...multinationals such as Ford and IBM. フォードやIBMなどの多国籍企業 ☑ ADJ 形容詞 **Multinational** armies, organizations, or other groups involve people from several different countries. 多国籍の □ The U.S. troops would be part of a multinational force. 米軍は多国籍軍の一部となるだろう． ☒ ADJ 形容詞 **Multinational** countries or regions have a population that is made up of people of several different nationalities. 多国籍の □ We live in a multinational country. 私たちは多国籍国家に住んでいる．

multi|ple /mʌltipᵊl/ (**multiples**) ■ ADJ 形容詞 You use **multiple** to describe things that consist of many parts, involve many people, or have many uses. 多数の □ He died of multiple injuries. 彼は多数の外傷で死んだ． ☑ N-COUNT 可算名詞 If one number is a **multiple of** a smaller number, it can be exactly divided by that smaller number. 倍数 □ Their numerical system, derived from the Babylonians, was based on multiples of the number six. バビロニア人から受け継いだ彼らの数体系は6の倍数に基づいている．
→ see **copy**

multi|ple choice ADJ 形容詞 In a **multiple choice** test or question, you have to choose the answer that you think is right from several possible answers that are listed on the question paper. 多項式選択の □ The multiple-choice questions must be answered within a strict time limit. 多項式選択の問題は時間制限を厳守して答えなければならない．

multi|pli|ca|tion /mʌltiplikeɪʃᵊn/ ■ N-UNCOUNT 不可算名詞 **Multiplication** is the process of calculating the total of one number multiplied by another. 掛け算 □ There will be simple tests in addition, subtraction, multiplication, and division. 足し算，引き算，掛け算，割り算の簡単なテストが行なわれる予定だ． ☑ N-UNCOUNT 不可算名詞 The **multiplication** of things of a particular kind is the process or fact of them increasing in number or amount. 増加 □ Increasing gravity is known to speed up the multiplication of cells. 重力の増加は細胞の増加を促進することが知られている．
→ see **mathematics**

multi|plic|ity /mʌltiplɪsiti/ QUANT 数量詞 A **multiplicity of** things is a large number or a large variety of them. 多数，多

様 [FORMAL 形式ばった] [QUANT 'of' pl-n] □ ...a writer who uses a multiplicity of styles. 多様の文体を使う作家

multi|ply /mʌltiplaɪ/ (**multiplies, multiplying, multiplied**) ■ V-T/V-I 他動詞/自動詞 When something **multiplies** or when you **multiply** it, it increases greatly in number or amount. 増やす，増える □ Such disputes multiplied in the eighteenth and nineteenth centuries. そうした紛争は18～19世紀に増えた． ☑ V-I 自動詞 When animals and insects **multiply**, they increase in number by giving birth to large numbers of young. 繁殖する □ These creatures can multiply quickly. これらの生物はすばやく繁殖する能力を持っている． ☒ V-T 他動詞 If you **multiply** one number by another, you add the first number to itself as many times as is indicated by the second number. For example 2 multiplied by 3 is equal to 6. 掛ける □ What do you get if you multiply six by nine? 6の9倍は何か．

multi|ra|cial /mʌltireɪʃᵊl/ ADJ 形容詞 **Multiracial** means consisting of or involving people of many different races. 多民族の □ We live in a multiracial society. 私たちは多民族社会に住んでいる．

multi|task|ing /mʌltitæskɪŋ/ N-UNCOUNT 不可算名詞 **Multitasking** is a situation in which a computer or person does more than one thing at the same time. マルチタスキング □ Often women are so good at multitasking that it appears it's all effortless. 女性はしばしばマルチタスキングに長けているのでみな努力を要しないように見える．

multi|tude /mʌltitud/ (**multitudes**) ■ QUANT 数量詞 A **multitude** of things or people is a very large number of them. 多数 [QUANT 'of' pl-n] □ There are a multitude of small, quiet roads to cycle along. サイクリングのための細い静かな道路が多数ある． □ Addiction to drugs can bring a multitude of other problems. 薬物依存は他の問題を多数もたらす可能性がある． ☑ PHRASE 句 If you say that something covers or hides **a multitude of sins**, you mean that it hides something unattractive or does not reveal the true nature of something. 多数のよくないもの ☒ N-COUNT 可算名詞 You can refer to a very large number of people as a **multitude**. 大勢の人 [WRITTEN 書き言葉] □ ...surrounded by a noisy multitude. 騒がしい群集に囲まれて ☒ N-COUNT-COLL 集合可算名詞 You can refer to the great majority of people in a particular country or situation as **the multitude** or **the multitudes**. 一般大衆 □ The hideous truth was hidden from the multitude. ひどい真実は一般大衆から隠されていた．

mum /mʌm/ (**mums**) N-FAMILY 家族名詞 Your **mum** is your mother. 母親 [BRIT 英国英語, INFORMAL くだけた] [AM **mom** 米国英語]

mum|ble /mʌmbᵊl/ (**mumbles, mumbling, mumbled**) V-T/V-I 他動詞/自動詞 If you **mumble**, you speak very quietly and not at all clearly with the result that the words are difficult to understand. ぶつぶつ言う □ Her grandmother mumbled in her sleep. 彼女の祖母はぶつぶつ寝言を言った． □ He mumbled a few words. 彼は1言2言つぶやいた． ● N-COUNT 可算名詞 **Mumble** is also a noun. ぶつぶつ言う声 □ He could hear the low mumble of Navarro's voice. 彼はナバロが低い声でつぶやくのを聞くことができた．

mum|my /mʌmi/ (**mummies**) ■ N-COUNT 可算名詞 A **mummy** is a dead body which was preserved long ago by being rubbed with special oils and wrapped in cloth. ミイラ □ ...an Egyptian mummy. エジプトのミイラ ☑ N-FAMILY 家族名詞 **Mummy** is the same as **mommy**. かあちゃん [BRIT 英国英語, INFORMAL くだけた]

munch /mʌntʃ/ (**munches, munching, munched**) V-T/V-I 他動詞/自動詞 If you **munch** food, you eat it by chewing it slowly, thoroughly, and rather noisily. むしゃむしゃ食べる □ Luke munched the chicken sandwiches. ルークはチキンのサンドイッチをむしゃむしゃ食べた． □ Across the table, his son Benjie munched appreciatively. テーブルの向こうで彼の息子のベンジーは喜んでむしゃむしゃ食べた．

mun|dane /mʌndeɪn/ ADJ 形容詞 Something that is **mundane** is very ordinary and not at all interesting or unusual. 日常的な □ Be willing to do mundane tasks with good grace. 日常的な作業でも進んでやりなさい． ● N-SING 単数名詞 You can refer to mundane things as **the mundane**. 平凡なこと □ It's an attitude that turns the mundane into something more interesting and exciting. 平凡なことをもっと面白く刺激的なことに変えるのは心の持ち様だ．

mu|nic|i|pal /myunɪsɪpᵊl/ ADJ 形容詞 **Municipal** means associated with or belonging to a city or town that has its own local government. 自治都市の，市の [ADJ n] □ The municipal authorities gave the go-ahead for the march. 市当局はデモ行進の許可を与えた． □ ...next month's municipal elections. 来月の市政選挙

mu|nic|i|pal|ity /myunɪsɪpælɪti/ (**municipalities**) N-COUNT 可算名詞 A **municipality** is a city or town that is incorporated and can elect its own government, which is also called a **municipality**. 自治体

mu|ni|tions /myunɪʃᵊnz/ N-PLURAL 複数名詞 **Munitions** are military equipment and supplies, especially bombs, shells, and guns. 軍需品 □ ...the shortage of men and munitions. 兵員と軍需品不足

mu|ral /myʊərᵊl/ (**murals**) N-COUNT 可算名詞 A **mural** is a picture painted on a wall. 壁画 □ ...a mural of San Francisco Bay. サ

ンフランシスコ湾の壁画

mur|der /mɜ́rdər/ (murders, murdering, murdered) **1** N-VAR 可変性名詞 **Murder** is the deliberate and illegal killing of a person. 殺人 ❑ *The three accused, aged between 19 and 20, are charged with attempted murder.* 年齢が19−20歳の3名の容疑者が殺人未遂で逮捕された。 ❑ *She refused to testify, unless the murder charge against her was dropped.* 彼女は殺人の起訴が取り下げられない限り, 宣誓証言することを拒否すると言った。 **2** V-T 他動詞 To **murder** someone means to commit the crime of killing them deliberately. 殺害する ❑ *...a thriller about two men who murder a third to see if they can get away with it.* 見つからずにやりおせるかどうかを見るために3人目の男を殺害する2人の男についての推理小説 **3** PHRASE 句 If you say that someone **gets away with murder**, you are complaining that they can do whatever they like without anyone trying to control them or punish them. なんでもし放題で罰せられない [INFORMAL くだけた, DISAPPROVAL 不賛成] ❑ *His charm and the fact that he is so likeable often allows him to get away with murder.* 彼はその魅力と好感度の高さからしばしば何でも思い通りにできる。

mur|der|er /mɜ́rdərər/ (murderers) N-COUNT 可算名詞 A **murderer** is a person who has murdered someone. 殺人者 ❑ *One of these men may have been the murderer.* こうした男たちの1人はその殺人者だったかもしれない。

murky /mɜ́rki/ (murkier, murkiest) **1** ADJ 形容詞 A **murky** place or time of day is dark and rather unpleasant because there is not enough light. 薄暗く陰気な ❑ *The large lamplit room was murky with wood smoke.* ランプで照明された大きな部屋は蒔きの煙で薄暗く陰気だった。 **2** ADJ 形容詞 **Murky** water or fog is so dark and dirty that you cannot see through it. どんよりした ❑ *...the deep, murky waters of Loch Ness.* ネス湖の深くどんよりした湖水 **3** ADJ 形容詞 If you describe something as **murky**, you mean that the details of it are not clear or that it is difficult to understand. あいまいな ❑ *The law here is a little bit murky.* ここの法律はちょっとはっきりしない。

mur|mur /mɜ́rmər/ (murmurs, murmuring, murmured) **1** V-T 他動詞 If you **murmur** something, you say it very quietly, so that not many people can hear what you are saying. ささやく ❑ *He turned and murmured something to the professor.* 彼は振り返り, 教授に何かをささやいた。 ❑ *"How lovely," she murmured.* 「何て美しいんでしょう」と彼女はささやいた。 **2** N-COUNT 可算名詞 A **murmur** is something that is said but can hardly be heard. ささやき ❑ *They spoke in low murmurs.* 彼らは低い声でささやいた。 **3** N-SING 単数名詞 A **murmur** is a continuous low sound, like the noise of a river or of voices far away. かすかな音 ❑ *The piano music mixes with the murmur of conversation.* ピアノの音楽が人々のささやき声と混じりあう。 **4** N-COUNT 可算名詞 A **murmur of** a particular emotion is a quiet expression of it. ささやき ❑ *The promise of some basic working rights draws murmurs of approval.* ある基礎的の労働権利の約束に賛成のささやき声が起こる。 **5** N-COUNT 可算名詞 A **murmur** is an abnormal sound which is made by the heart and which shows that there is probably something wrong with it. 心雑音 ❑ *The doctor said James had now developed a heart murmur.* 医者はジェームスの心臓に今や雑音が聞こえるようになったと言った。 **6** PHRASE 句 If someone does something **without a murmur**, they do it without complaining. 1言の不平も言わずに ❑ *Then came the bill and my friend paid up without a murmur.* それから請求書が届き, 私の友人は一言も不平も言わずに支払った。

mus|cle /mʌ́səl/ (muscles, muscling, muscled) **1** N-VAR 可変性名詞 A **muscle** is a piece of tissue inside your body that connects two bones and which you use when you make a movement. 筋肉 ❑ *Keeping your muscles strong and in tone helps you to avoid back problems.* 筋肉を強く正常な状態に保つと腰痛になりにくくなる。 **2** N-UNCOUNT 不可算名詞 If you say that someone has **muscle**, you mean that they have power and influence, which enables them to do difficult things. 勢力 ❑ *Eisenhower used his muscle to persuade Congress to change the law.* アイゼンハワーは影響力を使って議会に法律の変更を説得した。 **3** PHRASE 句 If a group, organization, or country **flexes its muscles**, it does something to impress or frighten people, in order to show them that it has power and is considering using it. 力を誇示する ❑ *The Fair Trade Commission has of late been flexing its muscles, cracking down on cases*

of corruption. 公正取引委員会は最近その力を誇示して, 汚職を厳重に取り締まっている。 **4** PHRASE 句 If you say that someone did not **move a muscle**, you mean that they stayed absolutely still. 筋を動かす ❑ *He stood without moving a muscle, unable to believe what his eyes saw so plainly.* 彼はあんなにはっきり見たことを信じられずに身動き1つしないで立っていた。

→ see Word Web: **muscle**

→ see **nervous system**

▶ **muscle in** PHRASAL VERB 句動詞 If someone **muscles in on** something, they force their way into a situation where they have no right to be and where they are not welcome, in order to gain some advantage for themselves. 強引に首を突っ込む [DISAPPROVAL 不賛成] ❑ *Cohen complained that Kravis was muscling in on his deal.* コーエンはクラビスが彼の取引に首を突っ込んできているとこぼした。

Word Partnership	**muscle** は次の語句と使われる:
N.	muscle **aches**, muscle **mass**, muscle **pain**, muscle **tone** **1**
V.	**contract** a muscle, **flex** a muscle, **pull** a muscle **1**

mus|cu|lar /mʌ́skyələr/ **1** ADJ 形容詞 **Muscular** means involving or affecting your muscles. 筋肉の [ADJ n] ❑ *As a general rule, all muscular effort is enhanced by breathing in as the effort is made.* 概して全ての筋肉力はそれを発揮する際に吸い込む呼吸によって高められる。 **2** ADJ 形容詞 If a person or their body is **muscular**, they are very fit and strong, and have firm muscles which are not covered with a lot of fat. 筋肉の発達した ❑ *Like most female athletes, she was lean and muscular.* 大半の女性アスリート同様に彼女は贅肉がなく筋肉が発達していた。

muse /myúz/ (muses, musing, mused) V-T/V-I 他動詞/自動詞 If you **muse** on something, you think about it, usually saying or writing what you are thinking at the same time. 熟考する [WRITTEN 書き言葉] ❑ *Many of the papers muse on the fate of the president.* 多くの新聞は大統領の運命について思いを巡らしている。 ❑ *"As a whole," she muses, "the 'organized church' turns me off."* 「概して私は『組織された教会』には興味がない」と彼女は思いを巡らす。 ● **mus|ing** (musings) N-COUNT 可算名詞 黙想 ❑ *His musings were interrupted by Montagu who came and sat down next to him.* 彼の黙想はやって来て隣に座ったモンターギュによって中断された。

mu|se|um /myuzíəm/ (museums) N-COUNT 可算名詞 A **museum** is a building where a large number of interesting and valuable objects, such as works of art or historical items, are kept, studied, and displayed to the public. 博物館 ❑ *For months Malcolm had wanted to visit the New York art museums.* マルカムは何ヶ月間もニューヨークの美術館に行きたいと思っていた。

→ see **gallery**

mush|room /mʌ́ʃrum/ (mushrooms, mushrooming, mushroomed) **1** N-VAR 可変性名詞 **Mushrooms** are fungi that you can eat. They have short stems and round tops. 茸 ❑ *There are many types of wild mushrooms.* 野生の茸には色々な種類がある。 **2** V-I 自動詞 If something such as an industry or a place **mushrooms**, it grows or comes into existence very quickly. 急速に成長する ❑ *The media training industry has mushroomed over the past decade.* メディア訓練業界は過去10年間に急成長した。

→ see **fungus**

mu|sic /myúzɪk/ **1** N-UNCOUNT 不可算名詞 **Music** is the pattern of sounds produced by people singing or playing instruments. 音楽 ❑ *...classical music.* クラシック音楽 **2** N-UNCOUNT 不可算名詞 **Music** is the art of creating or performing music. 音楽 ❑ *He went on to study music, specializing in the clarinet.* 彼は音楽の勉強を続け, クラリネットを専攻した。 **3** N-UNCOUNT 不可算名詞 **Music** is the symbols written on paper which represent musical sounds. 楽譜 ❑ *He's never been able to read music.* 彼は決して楽譜が読めなかった。 **4** PHRASE 句 If something that you hear is **music to your ears**, it makes you feel very happy. 耳に心地よい [FEELINGS 感情] ❑ *Popular support – it's music to the ears of any politician.* 一般大衆の支援, それはどんな政治家の耳にも心地よいものだ。 **5** PHRASE 句 If you **face the music**, you put yourself in a position where you will be criticized or punished for something

m

There are three types of **muscles** in the body. **Voluntary** or skeletal muscles produce external movements. **Involuntary** or **smooth** muscles provide internal movement within the body. For example, the smooth muscles in the **iris** of the eye adjust the size of the pupil. This controls how much light enters the eye. **Cardiac** muscles are found only in the heart. They work constantly but never get tired. When we **exercise**, voluntary muscles **contract** and then **relax**. With repeated **workouts**, we can **build** these muscles and increase their **strength**. If we don't exercise, these muscles can **atrophy** and become **weak**.

Word Web   music

Wolfgang Amadeus Mozart lived only 35 years (1756-1791). However, he is one of the most important **musicians** in history. Mozart began playing the **piano** at the age of four. A year later he **composed** his first **song**. Since he hadn't yet learned musical notation, his father wrote out the **score** for him. Mozart's father arranged for the boy to play for royalty across Europe. Soon Mozart became known as a gifted **composer**. During his lifetime, he wrote more than 50 **symphonies**. He also composed numerous **operas**, **concertos**, arias, and other musical works.

Notes — Treble Clef: whole, half, quarter, eighth, sixteenth, thirty-second, sixty-fourth
Rests — Bass Clef: whole, half, quarter, eighth, sixteenth, thirty-second, sixty-fourth

you have done. 自分の招いた困難に立ち向かう ❑ *Sooner or later, I'm going to have to face the music.* 遅かれ速かれ，私はその報いを受け入れなければならないだろう．
→ see Word Web: **music**
→ see concert, DVD

Word Partnership   *music* は次の語句と使われる：

ADJ. **live** music, **loud** music, **new** music, **pop**(ular) music **1**
N. **background** music, music **critic**, music **festival** **1** music **business**, music **industry**, music **lesson** **2**
V. **download** music, **hear** music, **listen to** music, **play** music **1** **compose** music, **study** music, **write** music **2**

mu|si|cal /myuːzɪk³l/ (musicals) **1** ADJ 形容詞 You use **musical** to indicate that something is connected with playing or studying music. 音楽の [ADJ n] ❑ *We have a wealth of musical talent in this region.* この地域には音楽の才能を持つ人が多い． ● **mu|si|cal|ly** /myuːzɪkli/ ADV 副詞 音楽的に ❑ *Musically there is a lot to enjoy.* 音楽的には楽しめることがたくさんある． **2** N-COUNT 可算名詞 A **musical** is a play or movie that uses singing and dancing in the story. ミュージカル ❑ *...the smash hit musical, Miss Saigon.* 大当たりのミュージカル，『ミス・サイゴン』 **3** ADJ 形容詞 Someone who is **musical** has a natural ability and interest in music. 音楽の才のある ❑ *I came from a musical family.* 私は音楽的才能のある家庭で育った． **4** ADJ 形容詞 Sounds that are **musical** are light and pleasant to hear. 音調の美しい ❑ *He had a soft, almost musical voice.* 彼は優しくてほとんど音楽的な響きの声をしていた．

mu|si|cal in|stru|ment (musical instruments) N-COUNT 可算名詞 A **musical instrument** is an object such as a piano, guitar, or violin which you play in order to produce music. 楽器 ❑ *The drum is one of the oldest musical instruments.* ドラムは最も古い楽器の1つだった

Word Link   ician ≈ person who works at : electrician, musician, physician

mu|si|cian /myuːzɪʃ³n/ (musicians) N-COUNT 可算名詞 A **musician** is a person who plays a musical instrument as their job or hobby. 器楽演奏家 ❑ *He was a brilliant musician.* 彼は素晴らしい器楽の演奏家だった．
→ see concert, music, orchestra

Mus|lim /mʌzlɪm, mʊs-/ (Muslims) **1** N-COUNT 可算名詞 A **Muslim** is someone who believes in Islam and lives according to its rules. イスラム教徒 **2** ADJ 形容詞 **Muslim** means relating to Islam or Muslims. イスラム教の ❑ *...Iran and other Muslim countries.* イランとその他のイスラム教諸国

mus|lin /mʌzlɪn/ (muslins) N-MASS 質量名詞 **Muslin** is very thin, cotton cloth. モスリン ❑ *...white muslin curtains.* 白いモスリンのカーテン

mus|sel /mʌsªl/ (mussels) N-COUNT 可算名詞 **Mussels** are a kind of shellfish that you can eat from their shells. イガイ

must /məst, STRONG mʌst/ (musts)

The noun is pronounced /mʌst/.
名詞は /mʌst/ と発音される．

Must is a modal verb. It is followed by the base form of a verb.
Must は法動詞であり，動詞の原型に伴われる．

1 MODAL 法動詞 You use **must** to indicate that you think it is very important or necessary for something to happen. You use **must not** or **mustn't** to indicate that you think it is very important or necessary for something not to happen. 〜しなければならない ❑ *What you wear should be stylish and clean, and must definitely fit well.* あなたの着るものはいきで清潔で，そして絶対に体にぴったりしなければならない． ❑ *You are going to have to take a certain amount of criticism, but you must cope with it.* あなたは多少の批判を受けるだろうが，それに対処しなければならない． **2** MODAL 法動詞 You use **must** to indicate that it is necessary for something to happen, usually because of a rule or law. 〜の必要がある ❑ *Candidates must satisfy the general conditions for admission.* 志願者は入学の一般条件を満たす必要がある． ❑ *Mr. Allen must pay Mr. Farnham's legal costs.* アレン氏はファーナム氏の弁護士代を支払わねばならない． **3** MODAL 法動詞 You use **must** to indicate that you are fairly sure that something is the case. 〜に違いない ❑ *At 29 Russell must be one of the youngest ever international referees.* 29歳のラッセルは史上最年少の国際審判員の1人であるに違いない． ❑ *Claire's car wasn't there, so she must have gone to her mother's.* クレアの車はそこになかったので，彼女はお母さんのところに行ったに違いない． **4** MODAL 法動詞 You use **must**, or **must have** with a past participle, to indicate that you believe that something is the case, because of the available evidence. 〜に違いない ❑ *"You must be Emma," said the visitor.* 「あなたはエマでしょう」，と訪問者は言った． ❑ *Miss Holloway had a weak heart. She must have had a heart attack.* ハロウェイさんは心臓が弱かった．彼女は心臓の発作を起こしたに違いない． **5** MODAL 法動詞 If you say that one thing **must** have happened in order for something else to happen, you mean that it is necessary for the first thing to have happened before the second thing can happen. 〜したことが必要である ❑ *In order to take that job, you must leave another job.* あの仕事を始めるためには，別の仕事を辞めていなければならなかった． **6** MODAL 法動詞 You use **must** to express your intention to do something. 〜しなければならない ❑ *I must be getting back.* 私はもうおいとましなければならない． ❑ *I must telephone my parents.* 私は両親に電話しなければならない． **7** MODAL 法動詞 You use **must** to make suggestions or invitations very forcefully. 〜してほしい ❑ *You must see a doctor, Frederick.* フレデリック，是非医者に行ってほしい． **8** MODAL 法動詞 You use **must** in remarks and comments where you are expressing sympathy. きっと〜に違いない ❑ *This must be a very difficult job for you.* これはあなたにとって大変困難な仕事に違いない． **9** MODAL 法動詞 You use **must** in conversation in expressions such as "**I must say**" and "**I must admit**" in order to emphasize a point that you are making. ほんとに [EMPHASIS 強調] ❑ *This came as a surprise, I must say.* これはほんとに意外だった． ❑ *I must admit I like looking feminine.* ほんとに私は女らしく見えるのが好きです． **10** MODAL 法動詞 You use **must** in expressions such as "**it must be noted**" and "**it must be remembered**" in order to draw the reader's or listener's attention to what you are about to say. 〜しなければならない ❑ *It must be noted, however, that not all British and American officers carried out orders.* しかし英国人と米国人の将校全員が命令を遂行したわけではないことは注目されなければならない． **11** MODAL 法動詞 You use **must** in questions to express your anger or irritation about something that someone has done, usually because you do not understand their behavior. あいにく〜する [FEELINGS 感情] ❑ *Why must she interrupt?* どうして彼女は邪魔をしなければならないのか． **12** MODAL 法動詞 You use **must** in exclamations to express surprise or shock. ちがいない [EMPHASIS 強調] ❑ *"Go! Please go."—"You must be joking!"* 「行って，どうか行ってくれ」「冗談でしょう」 ❑ *I really must be quite mad!* 私は本当にどうかしているにちがいない． **13** N-COUNT 可算名詞 If you refer to something as **a must**, you mean that it is absolutely necessary. なくてはならないもの [INFORMAL くだけた] ❑ *Taking out travel insurance may seem an unnecessary expense, but it is a must.* 旅行保険をかけることは不必要な出費に思えるが，それは絶対必要なものだ． **14** PHRASE 句 You say "**if you must**" when you know that you cannot stop someone doing something that you think is wrong or stupid. どうしても〜しなければならないなら ❑ *If you must be in the sunlight, use the strongest sunscreen you can get.* どうしても日光浴したいのなら，できるだけ強い日焼け止めを使いなさい． **15** PHRASE 句 You say "**if you must know**" when you tell someone something that you did not want them to know and you want to suggest that you think they were wrong to ask you about it. どうしても知りたいのなら ❑ *It scared the hell out of her, if you must know. And me, too.* どうしても知りたいのなら言うが，彼女はそれをすごく怖がった．私も怖かった．

mus|tache /mʌstæʃ/ (mustaches) N-COUNT 可算名詞 A man's **mustache** is the hair that grows on his upper lip. If it is very long,

it is sometimes referred to as his **mustaches**. 口ひげ ❑*The thick beard had gone, replaced by a bushy mustache.* 濃いあごひげは消え，ふさふさした口ひげに取り替わった。

mus|tard /mʌstərd/ (**mustards**) **1** N-MASS 質量名詞 **Mustard** is a yellow or brown paste usually eaten with meat. It tastes hot and spicy. マスタード ❑*...a jar of mustard.* マスタードの瓶 **2** COLOR 色彩語 **Mustard** is used to describe things that are brownish yellow in color. からし色 ❑*I sat in my father's chair, a mustard-colored recliner.* 私は父の椅子，からし色のもたれ椅子に座った。 **3** PHRASE 句 If someone does not **cut the mustard**, their work or their performance is not as good as it should be or as good as it is expected to be. いい成績を収める [INFORMAL くだけた] ❑*He just wasn't a good student. He wasn't cutting the mustard and we let him go.* 彼はただ優秀な学生ではなかった。 彼はいい成績を収めなかったので，退学してもらった。

mus|ter /mʌstər/ (**musters, mustering, mustered**) **1** V-T 他動詞 If you **muster** something such as support, strength, or energy, you gather as much of it as you can in order to do something. かき集める ❑*He traveled around West Africa trying to muster support for his movement.* 彼は自分の運動のための支援を集める目的で西アフリカを旅行して回った。 **2** V-T/V-I 他動詞/自動詞 When soldiers **muster** or **are mustered**, they gather together in one place in order to take part in a military action. 召集する，集まる ❑*The men mustered before their clan chiefs.* 男たちは彼らの族長の前に集まった。

mustn't /mʌsənt/ **Mustn't** is the usual spoken form of "must not." must notの縮約形

must've /mʌstəv/ **Must've** is the usual spoken form of "must have," especially when "have" is an auxiliary verb. must haveの縮約形

mu|tant /myutənt/ (**mutants**) N-COUNT 可算名詞 A **mutant** is an animal or plant that is physically different from others of the same species because of a change in its genes. 突然変異体，変種 ❑*New species are merely mutants of earlier ones.* 新しい種類は初期のものの突然変異体にすぎない。

Word Link mut ≈ changing : commute, mutate, mutilate

---

mu|tate /myuteɪt/ (**mutates, mutating, mutated**) **1** V-T/V-I 他動詞/自動詞 If an animal or plant **mutates**, or something **mutates** it, it develops different characteristics as the result of a change in its genes. 突然変異させる，突然変異する ❑*The virus mutates in the carrier's body.* そのウィルスは保菌者の体内で突然変異する。 ❑*HIV has proven to possess an ability to mutate into drug-resistant forms.* HIVは薬が効かない形に突然変異する能力を持っていることが分かった。 ●**mu|ta|tion** /myuteɪʃən/ (**mutations**) N-VAR 可変性名詞 突然変異，突然変異体 ❑*Scientists have found a genetic mutation that appears to be the cause of Huntington's disease.* 科学者はハンティングトン病の原因であると思われる遺伝子の突然変異体を発見した。 **2** V-I 自動詞 If something **mutates into** something different, it changes into that thing. 変化する ❑*Overnight, the gossip begins to mutate into headlines.* 1夜でそのゴシップは重大ニュースに変わり始める。

mute /myut/ (**mutes, muting, muted**) **1** ADJ 形容詞 Someone who is **mute** is silent for a particular reason and does not speak. 無言の ❑*He was mute, distant, and indifferent.* 彼は無言でよそよそしくて無関心だった。 ●ADV 副詞 **Mute** is also an adverb. 無言で [ADV after v] ❑*He could watch her standing mute by the phone.* 彼は彼女が電話のそばに無言で立っているのをじっと見ることができた。 **2** ADJ 形容詞 Someone who is **mute** is unable to speak. 口がきけない ❑*Marianna, the duke's daughter, became mute after a shock.* 公爵の娘のマリアナはショックの後に口がきけなくなった。 **3** V-T 他動詞 If someone **mutes** something such as their feelings or their activities, they reduce the strength or intensity of them. 弱める ❑*The corruption does not seem to have muted the country's prolonged economic boom.* その汚職はその国の長引いた経済ブームを弱めてはいないようだ。 ●**muted** ADJ 形容詞 弱められた ❑*The threat contrasted starkly with his administration's previous muted criticism.* その脅迫は彼の政府が以前に行った穏やかな批判とは全く対照的だった。 **4** V-T 他動詞 If you **mute** a noise or sound, you lower its volume or make it less distinct. 音を弱める ❑*They begin to mute their voices, not be as assertive.* 彼らは強引にならないように彼らは声を弱め始めた。 ●**muted** ADJ 形容詞 弱められた ❑*"Yes," he muttered, his voice so muted I hardly heard his reply.* 「そうだ」と彼はつぶやいたが，その声が余りに弱かったので，その返事はほとんど聞き取れなかったほどだった。

mut|ed /myutɪd/ ADJ 形容詞 **Muted** colors are soft and gentle, not bright and strong. 柔らかな ❑*...painted in subtle, muted colors.* 微妙で柔らかな色彩で描かれた

mu|ti|late /myutəleɪt/ (**mutilates, mutilating, mutilated**) **1** V-T 他動詞 If a person or animal **is mutilated**, their body is severely damaged, usually by someone who physically attacks them. 手足などを切断する ❑*More than 30 horses have been mutilated in the last nine months.* 過去9か月間に30頭以上の馬の脚が切断された。 ❑*He tortured and mutilated six young men.* 彼は6人の若い男を拷問にかけ手足を切断した。 ●**mu|ti|la|tion** /myutəleɪʃən/ (**mutilations**)

N-VAR 可変性名詞 手足切断 ❑*Amnesty International chronicles cases of torture and mutilation.* 国際アムネスティは拷問と手足切断の事例を列挙している。 **2** V-T 他動詞 If something **is mutilated**, it is deliberately damaged or spoiled. 骨抜きにする ❑*Brecht's verdict was that his screenplay had been mutilated.* ブレヒトの判断では彼のシナリオは骨抜きにされた。

mu|ti|ny /myutəni/ (**mutinies, mutinying, mutinied**) **1** N-VAR 可変性名詞 A **mutiny** is a refusal by people, usually soldiers or sailors, to continue obeying a person in authority. 反乱 ❑*A series of coup attempts and mutinies within the armed forces destabilized the regime.* 軍隊内の一連のクーデターの試みと反乱で政権が不安定になった。 **2** V-I 自動詞 If a group of people, usually soldiers or sailors, **mutiny**, they refuse to continue obeying a person in authority. 反乱を起こす ❑*Units stationed around the capital mutinied because they had received no pay for nine months.* 首都周辺に駐屯した部隊は9か月間賃金を受け取らなかったために反乱を起こした。

mut|ter /mʌtər/ (**mutters, muttering, muttered**) V-T/V-I 他動詞/自動詞 If you **mutter**, you speak very quietly so that you cannot easily be heard, often because you are complaining about something. ぼそぼそ言う ❑*"God knows," she muttered, "what's happening in that madman's mind."* 「誰にも分からない」と彼女はつぶやいた。「あの狂人の心に何が起こっているのかは」 ❑*She can hear the old woman muttering about consideration.* 彼女は老女が思いやりについてぶつぶつ言っているのが聞こえる。 ●N-COUNT 可算名詞 **Mutter** is also a noun. ぶつぶつ言うこと ❑*They make no more than a mutter of protest.* 彼らはぶつぶつ抗議するだけだ。 ●**mut|ter|ing** (**mutterings**) N-VAR 可変性名詞 ぶつぶつ言うこと ❑*He heard muttering from the front of the crowd.* 彼は群集の最前列からぶつぶつ言う声がするのを聞いた。

mut|ton /mʌtən/ N-UNCOUNT 不可算名詞 **Mutton** is meat from an adult sheep that is eaten as food. 羊の肉 ❑*...a leg of mutton.* 羊の足肉

→ see Word Web: **meat**

mu|tu|al /myutʃuəl/ **1** ADJ 形容詞 You use **mutual** to describe a situation, feeling, or action that is experienced, felt, or done by both of two people mentioned. 相互の ❑*The East and the West can work together for their mutual benefit and progress.* 東洋と西洋は互恵と進歩のために協力し合うことができる。 ●**mu|tu|al|ly** ADV 副詞 相互に ❑*Attempts to reach a mutually agreed solution had been fruitless.* 相互に合意の解決策に達しようとする試みは無駄だった。 **2** → see exclusive **3** ADJ 形容詞 You use **mutual** to describe something such as an interest which two or more people share. 互いの ❑*They do, however, share a mutual interest in design.* しかし彼らは実際に共にデザインに関心がある。 **4** ADJ 形容詞 [ADJ n] If an insurance company or savings bank has **mutual** status, it is not owned by shareholders but by its customers, who receive a share of the profits. 相互会社組織の [BUSINESS 実業] ❑*...a mutual company based in Columbus, Ohio.* オハイオ州のコロンバスにある相互会社

Word Partnership mutual は次の語句と使われる：

N.	the feeling is mutual, mutual **respect**, mutual **trust**, mutual **understanding 1**
	mutual **agreement**, mutual **friend**, mutual **interest 2**

---

mu|tu|al fund (**mutual funds**) N-COUNT 可算名詞 A **mutual fund** is an organization which invests money in many different kinds of business and which offers units for sale to the public as an investment. 投資信託会社 [AM 米国英語 BUSINESS 実業]

muz|zle /mʌzəl/ (**muzzles, muzzling, muzzled**) **1** N-COUNT 可算名詞 The **muzzle** of an animal such as a dog is its nose and mouth. 鼻口部 ❑*The mongrel presented his muzzle for scratching.* その雑種犬はかいてもらうために鼻口部を出した。 **2** N-COUNT 可算名詞 A **muzzle** is an object that is put over a dog's nose and mouth so that it cannot bite people or make a noise. 口輪 ❑*...dogs like pit bulls, which have to wear a muzzle.* 口輪の着用を義務付けられているピットブル犬などの犬 **3** V-T 他動詞 If you **muzzle** a dog or other animal, you put a muzzle over its nose and mouth. 口輪をはめる ❑*He was convicted of failing to muzzle a pit bull.* 彼はピットブル犬に口輪をはめなかった罪で有罪になった。 **4** V-T 他動詞 If you say that someone **is muzzled**, you are complaining that they are prevented from expressing their views freely. 口封じする [DISAPPROVAL 不賛成] ❑*He complained of being muzzled by the chairman.* 彼は会長に口封じされていると不平を言った。 **5** N-COUNT 可算名詞 The **muzzle** of a gun is the end where the bullets come out when it is fired. 銃口 ❑*Mickey felt the muzzle of a rifle press hard against his neck.* ミッキーはライフルの銃口が彼の首に強く押し付けられるのを感じた。

my /maɪ/

My is the first person singular possessive determiner.

My は1人称単数所有限定詞である。

1 DET 限定詞 A speaker or writer uses **my** to indicate that

Word Web · myth

The scholar Joseph Campbell* believed that **mythologies** explain a **culture's** understanding of their world. **Stories, symbols, rituals,** and **myths** explain the **psychological, social,** cosmological, and **spiritual** parts of life. Campbell also believed that artists and

philosophers are a culture's mythmakers. He explored **archetypal themes** in myths from many different cultures. He showed how these themes are repeated in many different cultures. For example, the **hero's** journey appeared in ancient Greece in *The Odyssey*, and the same theme appears later in England in King Arthur's* search for the Holy Grail*. A 20th-century version shows up in the film *Star Wars*.

Joseph Campbell (1904–1987): an American professor and author.
The Odyssey: an epic poem from ancient Greece.
King Arthur: a legendary king of Great Britain.
Holy Grail: a cup that legends say Jesus used.

something belongs or relates to himself or herself. 私の ❑ *I invited him back to my apartment for coffee.* 私は私のアパートに戻ってコーヒーを飲もうと彼を誘った. **2** DET 限定詞 In conversations or in letters, **my** is used in front of a word like "dear" or "darling" to show affection. 私の [FEELINGS 感情] ❑ *My sweet Freda.* 私の優しいフリーダ **3** DET 限定詞 **My** is used in phrases such as "**My God**" and "**My goodness**" to express surprise or shock. おやまあ [SPOKEN 口語, FEELINGS 感情] ❑ *My God, I've never seen you so nervous.* おやまあ, あなたがそんなにびくびくするのは決して見たことがない.

myri·ad /mɪriəd/ **1** QUANT 数量詞 A **myriad** or **myriads of** people or things is a very large number or great variety of them. 莫大な数の [QUANT 'of' pl-n] ❑ *They face a myriad of problems bringing up children.* 彼らは子供たちの養育で莫大な数の問題に直面する. **2** ADJ 形容詞 **Myriad** means having a large number or great variety. 莫大な数の [ADJ n] ❑ *The magazine has been celebrating pop in all its myriad forms.* その雑誌はすべての膨大な種類のポピュラー音楽を賛美してきた.

my·self /maɪsɛlf/

> **Myself** is the first person singular reflexive pronoun.

> **Myself** は1人称単数再帰代名詞である.

1 PRON-REFL 再帰代名詞 A speaker or writer uses **myself** to refer to himself or herself. **Myself** is used as the object of a verb or preposition when the subject refers to the same person. 私自身 [V PRON, prep PRON] ❑ *I asked myself what I would have done in such a situation.* 私は私だったらどうしただろうかと自問した. **2** PRON-REFL-EMPH 強調的再帰代名詞 You use **myself** to emphasize a first person singular subject. In more formal English, **myself** is sometimes used instead of "me" as the object of a verb or preposition, for emphasis. 私自身 [EMPHASIS 強調] ❑ *I myself enjoy movies, poetry, eating out, and long walks.* 私自身は映画, 詩, 外食, 長い散歩を楽しむ. **3** PRON-REFL-EMPH 強調的再帰代名詞 If you say something such as "**I did it myself**," you are emphasizing that you did it, rather than anyone else. 私自ら [EMPHASIS 強調] ❑ *"Where did you get that embroidery?" — "I made it myself."* 「あの刺繍はどこで手にいれましたか」「私が自分で作りました」

mys·teri·ous /mɪstɪəriəs/ **1** ADJ 形容詞 Someone or something that is **mysterious** is strange and is not known about or understood. 不思議な ❑ *He died in mysterious circumstances.* 彼はなぞめいた状況で死んだ. ❑ *A mysterious illness confined him to bed for over a month.* なぞの病気のせいで彼は1ヶ月以上寝たきりになった. ● **mys·teri·ous·ly** ADV 副詞 不思議なことに ❑ *A couple of messages had mysteriously disappeared.* 2つのメッセージは不思議なことに消えていた. **2** ADJ 形容詞 If someone is **mysterious** about something, they deliberately do not talk much about it, sometimes because they want to make people more interested in it. わけのありそうな ❑ *As for his job – well, there was always mysterious about it.* 彼の仕事に関しては, そうね, 彼はすごくいわくありげだったわ. ● **mys·teri·ous·ly** ADV 副詞 [ADV after v] いわくありげに ❑ *Asked what she meant, she said mysteriously: "Work it out for yourself."* どういう意味かと聞かれた彼女はいわくありげにこたえた. 「自分で考えなさい」

mys·tery /mɪstəri, mɪstri/ (**mysteries**) **1** N-COUNT 可算名詞 A **mystery** is something that is not understood or known about. なぞ ❑ *The source of the gunshots still remains a mystery.* 発砲の源はまだなぞのままだ. **2** N-UNCOUNT 不可算名詞 If you talk about the **mystery** of someone or something, you are talking about how difficult they are to understand or know about, especially when this gives them a rather strange or magical quality. 神秘 ❑ *She's a lady of mystery.* 彼女はなぞめいた女性だ. **3** ADJ 形容詞 A **mystery** person or thing is one whose identity or nature is not known. な

その [ADJ n] ❑ *The mystery hero immediately alerted police after spotting a bomb.* なぞの英雄は爆弾を発見した後すぐに警察に連絡した. **4** N-COUNT 可算名詞 A **mystery** is a story in which strange things happen that are not explained until the end. 推理小説 ❑ *His fourth novel is a murder mystery set in London.* 彼の4作目の小説はロンドンが舞台の殺人推理小説だ.

Word Partnership · mystery は次の語句と使われる:

V.	**remain a** mystery, **unravel a** mystery **1**
	solve a mystery **1** **4**
N.	**murder** mystery, mystery **novel**, mystery **readers** **4**

mys·tic /mɪstɪk/ (**mystics**) **1** N-COUNT 可算名詞 A **mystic** is a person who practices or believes in religious mysticism. 神秘主義者 ❑ *...an Indian mystic known as Bhagwan Shree Rajneesh.* バーグワン・シュリー・ラジニーシュと呼ばれるインド人の神秘家 **2** ADJ 形容詞 **Mystic** means the same as **mystical**. 神秘的な [ADJ n] ❑ *...mystic union with God.* 神との神秘的合一

mys·ti·cal /mɪstɪkᵊl/ ADJ 形容詞 Something that is **mystical** involves spiritual powers and influences that most people do not understand. 神秘的な ❑ *That was clearly a deep mystical experience.* それは明らかに深い神秘的な経験だった.

mys·ti·cism /mɪstɪsɪzəm/ N-UNCOUNT 不可算名詞 **Mysticism** is a religious practice in which people search for truth, knowledge, and closeness to God through meditation and prayer. 神秘主義 ❑ *As a younger man Harrison was intrigued by Indian mysticism.* ハリソンはもっと若い頃, インドの神秘主義に興味をそそられた.

mys·ti·fy /mɪstɪfaɪ/ (**mystifies, mystifying, mystified**) V-T 他動詞 If you **are mystified** by something, you find it impossible to explain or understand. 迷わす ❑ *The audience must have been totally mystified by the plot.* 観客は話の筋が全然わからなかったに違いない. ● **mys·ti·fy·ing** ADJ 形容詞 不可解な ❑ *I find your attitude a little mystifying, Marilyn.* マリリン, 私は君の態度がやや不可解だと思う.

mys·tique /mɪstik/ N-SING 単数名詞 If there is a **mystique** about someone or something, they are thought to be special and people do not know much about them. 神秘性 [also N-UNCOUNT] ❑ *His book destroyed the mystique of monarchy.* 彼の本は君主制の神秘性を破壊した.

myth /mɪθ/ (**myths**) **1** N-VAR 可変性名詞 A **myth** is a well-known story which was made up in the past to explain natural events or to justify religious beliefs or social customs. 神話 ❑ *There is a famous Greek myth in which Icarus flew too near to the Sun.* イカロスが高く飛びすぎた太陽に近づきすぎた有名なギリシア神話がある. **2** N-VAR 可変性名詞 If you describe a belief or explanation as a **myth**, you mean that many people believe it but it is actually untrue. 根拠のない社会通念 ❑ *Contrary to the popular myth, women are not reckless spendthrifts.* 通俗的な社会通念に反して, 女性は向こう見ずな浪費家ではない.
→ see Word Web: **myth**
→ see **fantasy**

Word Partnership · myth は次の語句と使われる:

ADJ.	**ancient** myth, **Greek** myth **1**
	popular myth **2**

mythi·cal /mɪθɪkᵊl/ **1** ADJ 形容詞 Something or someone that is **mythical** exists only in myths and is therefore imaginary. 神話上の ❑ *...the Hydra, the mythical beast that had seven or more heads.* ヒュドラ, 7つかそれ以上の頭を持つ神話上の獣 **2** ADJ 形容詞 If you describe something as **mythical**, you mean that it is untrue or does not exist. 架空の ❑ *...the American West, not the mythical, romanticized West of cowboys and gunslingers, but the real West.* アメリカ西部, カウボーイとガンマンをロマンチック化した架空の西部では

M

なく，真の西部.

my|thol|ogy /mɪθɒlədʒi/ (**mythologies**) **1** N-VAR 可変性名詞 **Mythology** is a group of myths, especially all the myths from a particular country, religion, or culture. 神話 ❑ *In Greek mythology, the god Zeus took the form of a swan to seduce Leda.* ギリシア神話では ゼウスの神は白鳥に姿を変えてレダを誘惑した. ● **mytho|logi|cal** /mɪθəlɒdʒɪkəl/ ADJ 形容詞 神話の ❑ *...the mythological beast that was part lion and part goat.* 半分ライオンで半分ヤギの神話上の獣

2 N-VAR 可変性名詞 You can use **mythology** to refer to the beliefs or opinions that people have about something, when you think that they are false or untrue. 神話的通念 ❑ *Altman strips away the pretense and mythology to expose the film industry as a business like any other, dedicated to the pursuit of profit.* アルトマンは映画産業の仮面と 神話をはぎ取り，この産業が他の産業同様に利益の追求に専念する産業 であることを暴く.

→ see **hero**

m

Nn

N also **n** /ɛn/ (**N's, n's**) N-VAR 可変性名詞 **N** is the fourteenth letter of the English alphabet. 英語アルファベットの第14字

NA also **n/a** CONVENTION 慣習表現 **NA** is a written abbreviation for **not applicable** or **not available**. not applicableの略. 「該当なし」などの意味.

nag /næg/ (**nags, nagging, nagged**) **1** V-T/V-I 他動詞/自動詞 If someone **nags** you, or if they **nag**, they keep asking you to do something you have not done yet or do not want to do. 口うるさく言う, しつこく頼みごとを言う [DISAPPROVAL 不賛成] □ The more Sarah nagged her, the more stubborn Cissie became. サラがしつこく言えば言うほど, シシーは頑固になった. □ My girlfriend nagged me to cut my hair. ガールフレンドが僕に散髪をするようにうるさく言った. ● N-COUNT 可算名詞 A **nag** is someone who nags. 口うるさく言う人 □ Aunt Molly is a nag about regular meals. モリーおばさんは三度三度の食事にうるさい人だ. ● **nagging** N-UNCOUNT 不可算名詞 口うるさく言うこと □ Her endless nagging drove him away from home. 彼女がいつまでも口うるさく言うので彼は家を出た. **2** V-T/V-I 他動詞/自動詞 If something such as a doubt or worry **nags at** you, or **nags** you, it keeps worrying you. 絶えず悩ませる □ He could be wrong about her. The feeling nagged at him. 彼女について彼は誤解していたかもしれない. その気持ちがいつも彼を悩ませた. □ ...the anxiety that had nagged Amy all through lunch. 昼食中にエイミーを悩ませ続けた心配事

nail /neɪl/ (**nails, nailing, nailed**) **1** N-COUNT 可算名詞 A **nail** is a thin piece of metal with one pointed end and one flat end. You hit the flat end with a hammer in order to push the nail into something such as a wall. くぎ □ A mirror hung on a nail above the sink. 鏡が洗面台の上のくぎにかかっていた. **2** V-T 他動詞 If you **nail** something somewhere, you fasten it there using one or more nails. くぎで打ちつける, くぎで固定する □ Frank put the first plank down and nailed it in place. フランクは最初の板を置いて適当な場所にくぎで打ちつけた. □ They nail shut the front door. 玄関のドアをくぎづけして閉めた. **3** N-COUNT 可算名詞 Your **nails** are the thin hard parts that grow at the ends of your fingers and toes. つめ □ Keep your nails short and your hands clean. つめを短く手を清潔に保ちなさい. **4** V-T 他動詞 To **nail** someone means to catch them and prove that they have been breaking the law. 挙げる, 捕まえる [INFORMAL くだけた] □ The prosecution still managed to nail him for robberies at the homes of leading industrialists. それでも検察側は何とか彼を一流の実業家の自宅への強盗罪で検挙した. **5** PHRASE 句 If you say that someone **has hit the nail on the head**, you think they are exactly right about something. 核心を突く, ずばりその通りだ □ "I think it would civilize people a bit more if they had decent conditions." — "I think you've hit the nail on the head." 「まともな状況下なら少しは人々が教化されると思うが」「まさにその通りだと思うよ」

▶ **nail down** **1** PHRASAL VERB 句動詞 If you **nail down** something unknown or uncertain, you find out exactly what it is. 明確にする □ It would be useful if you could nail down the source of this tension. この緊張関係の原因を明確にしてくれると助かる. **2** PHRASAL VERB 句動詞 If you **nail down** an agreement, you manage to reach a firm agreement with a definite result. 合意にこぎつける □ The Secretary of State and his Russian counterpart met to try to nail down the elusive accord. 米国国務長官とロシアの外務大臣が合意が難しい協定を結ぶ目的で会合した.

na|ive /naɪiːv/ also **naïve** ADJ 詞 If you describe someone as **naive**, you think they lack experience and so expect things to be easy or people to be honest or kind. 世間知らずの, うぶな □ It's naive to think that teachers are always tolerant. 教師は常に寛容であると考えるのは浅はかだ. □ Their view was that he had been politically naive. 彼らの意見では, 彼は政治の経験は浅いということだ. ● **na|ive|ly** ADV 副詞 世間知らずにも, 単純に □ ...naively applying Western solutions to Eastern problems. 単純に西洋的な解決策を東洋の問題に応用すること ● **na|ive|ty** /naɪiːvɪti/ N-UNCOUNT 不可算名詞 世間知らず, 単純さ □ I was alarmed by his naivety and ignorance of international affairs. 彼が世間知らずであることと国際問題に関する認識の低さに不安を感じた.

na|ked /neɪkɪd/ **1** ADJ 形容詞 Someone who is **naked** is not wearing any clothes. 裸の □ Her naked body was found wrapped in a sheet in a field. 彼女の裸体が野原でシーツに包まれて発見された. □ They stripped me naked. 彼らは私を裸にした. ● **na|ked|ness** N-UNCOUNT 不可算名詞 裸 □ He had pulled the blanket over his body to hide his nakedness. 裸であることを隠すために毛布を引っ張って体に

かけた. **2** ADJ 形容詞 If an animal or part of an animal is **naked**, it has no fur or feathers on it. (毛や羽が) 生えていない □ The nest contained eight little mice that were naked and blind. 巣には, 毛が生えていなくて目が見えない8匹の小さなネズミがいた. **3** ADJ 形容詞 You can describe an object as **naked** when it does not have its normal covering. 裸の, むきだしの □ ...a naked bulb dangling in a bare room. 空っぽの部屋にぶら下がった裸電球 **4** ADJ 形容詞 [ADJ n] You can use **naked** to describe unpleasant or violent actions and behavior which are not disguised or hidden in any way. 露骨な [JOURNALISM ジャーナリズム] □ Naked aggression and an attempt to change frontiers by force could not go unchallenged. 露骨な敵対行為と国境を軍事力で変更しようという試みは, すんなり受け入れられるはずがなかった. □ ...violence and the naked pursuit of power. 暴力と露骨な権力の追及

Word Partnership	naked は次の語句と使われる:
ADV.	**bare** naked, **completely** naked, **half** naked, **nearly** naked **1**

name /neɪm/ (**names, naming, named**) **1** N-COUNT 可算名詞 The **name** of a person, place, or thing is the word or group of words that is used to identify them. 名前, 名 □ "What's his name?" — "Peter." 「彼の名前は」「ピーター」 □ I don't even know if Sullivan's his real name. サリバンが本当の名前かどうかさえ分からない.

Your **first name** is the name that your parents chose for you. When you are telling someone your name, this comes first in English-speaking countries. Your **last name**, or **surname**, is the name that you share with other members of your family. In between your first name and your last name you may have a **middle name**, a second name that your parents chose for you. It is only usually used in official circumstances such as registering for a course or signing documents.

2 V-T 他動詞 When you **name** someone or something, you give them a name, usually at the beginning of their life. 名をつける □ My mother insisted on naming me Horace. 母は私をホラスと名にしようと言い張った. □ ...a man named John T. Benson. ジョン・T・ベンソンという名の男性 **3** V-T 他動詞 If you **name** someone or something **after** another person or thing, you give them the same name as that person or thing. 〜の名にちなんで名づける □ Why haven't you named any of your sons after yourself? どうして息子に自分の名前を使わなかったんだい? **4** V-T 他動詞 If you **name** someone, you identify them by stating their name. 名前を挙げる □ It's nearly thirty years since a journalist was jailed for refusing to name a source. ジャーナリストが情報筋の名前を挙げるのを拒否したために投獄されてほぼ30年になる. **5** V-T 他動詞 If you **name** something such as a price, time, or place, you say what you want it to be. 希望の値段・時間・場所などを言う □ Call Marty, tell him to name his price. マーティに電話をして, 希望の値段を言うよう指示しなさい. **6** V-T 他動詞 If you **name** the person for a particular job, you say who you want to have the job. 指名する □ The CEO has named a new chief financial officer. 最高経営責任者が新最高財務責任者を指名した. □ When the chairman of Campbell's retired, McGovern was named as his successor. キャンベル社の会長が退職したとき, マクガバンが後継者として指名された. **7** N-COUNT 可算名詞 You can refer to the reputation of a person or thing as their **name**. 評判 □ He had a name for good judgement. 彼は優れた判断力があるという評判だ. **8** N-COUNT 可算名詞 You can refer to someone as, for example, a famous **name** or a great **name** when they are well known. 有名人 [JOURNALISM ジャーナリズム] □ ...some of the most famous names in modeling and show business. モデル業界と芸能界における大物 **9** → see also **brand name, Christian name, first name, maiden name** **10** PHRASE 句 If something is in someone's **name**, it officially belongs to them or is reserved for them. 〜の名義で □ The house is in my husband's name. その家は夫名義だ. **11** PHRASE 句 If someone does something **in the name of** a group of people, they do it as the representative of that group. 〜を代表して □ In the United States the majority governs in the name of the people. 米国では大半が人民を代表して統治している. **12** PHRASE 句 If you do something **in the name of** an ideal or an abstract thing, you do it in order to preserve or promote that thing. 〜の名のもとに □ ...one of those rare occasions in history when a political leader risked his own power in the name of the greater public good. 指導的立場の政治家が公

益のために自分自身の権力を危険にさらしたという歴史的に珍しい出来事 13 PHRASE 句 When you mention someone or something **by name**, or address someone **by name**, you use their name. 名前を呼んで、名前を使って □When he walks down 131st street, he greets most people he sees by name. 131番通りを歩くとき、彼が出会うほとんどの人に名前を呼んであいさつをする。 14 PHRASE 句 You can use **by name** or **by the name of** when you are saying what someone is called. ―という名の [FORMAL 形式ばった] □In 1911 he met up with a young Australian by the name of Harry Busteed. 1911年に彼はハリー・バスティードという名の若いオーストラリア人に出会った。 15 PHRASE 句 If someone **calls** you **names**, they insult you by saying unpleasant things to you or about you. 悪口を言う □At my last school they called me names because I was so slow. 前の学校では私があまりにものろまだったので悪口を言われた。 16 PHRASE 句 If you **make a name for yourself** or **make** your **name as** something, you become well known for that thing. 有名になる □She was beginning to make a name for herself as a portrait photographer. 彼女は肖像写真家として有名になりかけていた。
→ see **Internet**

name|ly /neɪmli/ ADV 副詞 You use **namely** to introduce detailed information about the subject you are discussing, or a particular aspect of it. すなわち、つまり □A district should serve its clientele, namely students, staff, and parents. 地区は顧客、すなわち学生・職員・保護者にサービスを提供するべきだ。

nan|ny /næni/ (**nannies**) N-COUNT 可算名詞 A **nanny** is a woman who is paid by parents to take care of their child or children. ベビーシッター、子守

nap /næp/ (**naps, napping, napped**) 1 N-COUNT 可算名詞 If you take or have a **nap**, you have a short sleep, usually during the day. うたた寝、昼寝 □I might take a little nap. 少し昼寝をするかもしれない。 2 V-I 自動詞 If you **nap**, you sleep for a short period of time, usually during the day. うたた寝をする、昼寝をする □An elderly person may nap during the day and then sleep only five hours a night. 老人の場合、日中にうたた寝をして夜の睡眠は5時間だけという可能性がある。 3 PHRASE 句 If someone **is caught napping**, something happens when they are not prepared for it, although they should have been. ―の不意をつく [INFORMAL くだけた] □The security services were clearly caught napping. 国家保安機関は明らかに不意をつかれた。
→ see **sleep**

nap|kin /næpkɪn/ (**napkins**) N-COUNT 可算名詞 A **napkin** is a square of cloth or paper that you use when you are eating to protect your clothes, or to wipe your mouth or hands. ナプキン □...taking tiny bites of a hot dog and daintily wiping my lips with a napkin. ホットドッグを小口で食べ、ナプキンで優美に唇をふき取ること

nap|py /næpi/ (**nappies**) N-COUNT 可算名詞 A **nappy** is a piece of soft thick cloth or paper which is fastened around a baby's bottom in order to soak up its urine and feces. おむつ [BRIT 英国英語; AM diaper 米国英語 **diaper**]

nar|cot|ic /nɑrkɒtɪk/ (**narcotics**) 1 N-COUNT 可算名詞 **Narcotics** are drugs such as opium or heroin which make you sleepy and stop you from feeling pain. You can also use **narcotics** to mean any kind of illegal drugs. 麻薬、麻酔薬 □He was indicted for dealing in narcotics. 彼は麻薬取引の罪で起訴された。 2 ADJ 形容詞 If something, especially a drug, has a **narcotic** effect, it makes the person who uses it feel sleepy. 眠気を催すような □...hormones that have a narcotic effect on the immune system. 免疫系に麻酔効果のあるホルモン

nar|rate /næreɪt/ (**narrates, narrating, narrated**) 1 V-T 他動詞 If you **narrate** a story, you tell it from your own point of view. 語る [FORMAL 形式ばった] □Each of them narrate the same events from three perspectives. 3人は同じ出来事についてそれぞれの観点から語った。 ● **nar|ra|tion** /næreɪʃ⁰n/ N-UNCOUNT 不可算名詞 話、叙述 □Its story-within-a-story method of narration is confusing. 劇中劇の叙述の方法は分かりにくい。 ● **nar|ra|tor** /næreɪtər/ (**narrators**) N-COUNT 可算名詞 語り手 □Jules, the story's narrator, is an actress in her late thirties. その物語の語り手のジュールズは、30代後半の女優だ。 2 V-T 他動詞 The person who **narrates** a film or program speaks the words which accompany the pictures, but does not appear in it. ナレーションをする □She also narrated a documentary about the Kirov Ballet School. 彼女はキロフ・バレースクールについてのドキュメンタリーのナレーションをした。 ● **nar|ra|tion** N-UNCOUNT 不可算名詞 ナレーション □As soon as the crew gets back from lunch, we can put your narration on it right away. チームが昼食から戻り次第、すぐにナレーションを入れられる。 ● **nar|ra|tor** N-COUNT

可算名詞 (**narrators**) ナレーター □...the narrator of the documentary. ドキュメンタリー番組のナレーター

nar|ra|tive /nærətɪv/ (**narratives**) 1 N-COUNT 可算名詞 A **narrative** is a story or an account of a series of events. 物語、体験談 □...a fast-moving narrative. 話の流れが速い物語 2 N-UNCOUNT 不可算名詞 **Narrative** is the description of a series of events, usually in a novel. 話術 □Neither author was very strong on narrative. どちらの作者も話術に長けていなかった。

nar|row /næroʊ/ (**narrower, narrowest, narrows, narrowing, narrowed**) 1 ADJ 形容詞 Something that is **narrow** measures a very small distance from one side to the other, especially compared to its length or height. 幅が狭い、細い □...through the town's narrow streets. 町の細い通りを抜けて □She had long, narrow feet. 彼女は長く細い足をしていた。 ● **nar|row|ness** N-UNCOUNT 不可算名詞 狭さ □...the narrowness of the river mouth. 河口の狭さ 2 V-I 自動詞 If something **narrows**, it becomes less wide. 狭くなる □The wide track narrows before crossing another stream. 広い道が小川と交差する前に狭くなる。 3 V-T/V-I 他動詞/自動詞 If your eyes **narrow** or if you **narrow** your eyes, you almost close them, for example because you are angry or because you are trying to concentrate on something. 細める [他動詞]、細くなる [自動詞] □Coggins' eyes narrowed angrily. "You think I'd tell you?" コギンズは怒って目を細めた。「君に話すと思うのかい?」 [WRITTEN 書き言葉] 4 ADJ 形容詞 If you describe someone's ideas, attitudes, or beliefs as **narrow**, you disapprove of them because they are restricted in some way, and often ignore the more important aspects of an argument or situation. 限られた、狭い [DISAPPROVAL 不賛成] □...a narrow and outdated view of family life. 狭い考え方は時代遅れで心の狭い考え方 ● **nar|row|ly** ADV 副詞 厳密に □They may define their contribution too narrowly. 彼らは自分たちの貢献を非常に狭い範囲に限定するかもしれない。 ● **nar|row|ness** N-UNCOUNT 不可算名詞 厳密さ □...the narrowness of their mental and spiritual outlook. 精神面での偏狭さ 5 V-T/V-I 他動詞/自動詞 If something **narrows** or if you **narrow** it, its extent or range becomes smaller. 縮める [他動詞]、縮まる [自動詞] □Most recent opinion polls suggest that the gap between the two main parties has narrowed. 最も最近の世論調査によると、主要2党の格差は縮まったという。 ● **nar|row|ing** N-SING 単数名詞 縮小化 □...a narrowing of the gap between rich members and poor. 貧富の格差の縮小化 6 ADJ 形容詞 If you have a **narrow** victory, you succeed in winning but only by a small amount. きわどい、ぎりぎりの □Voters approved the plan by a narrow majority. 投票結果は、その計画はぎりぎりの過半数で通過した。 ● **nar|row|ly** ADV 副詞 ぎりぎり □She narrowly failed to win enough votes. 彼女は小差で落選した。 ● **nar|row|ness** N-UNCOUNT 不可算名詞 差が小さいこと □The narrowness of the victory reflected deep division within the party. つらくも収めた勝利は党内の深い亀裂を反映した。 7 ADJ 形容詞 [ADJ n] If you have a **narrow** escape, something unpleasant nearly happens to you. 間一髪で助かる □Two police officers had a narrow escape when rioters attacked their vehicles. 暴徒がパトカーを攻撃したとき2人の警官は間一髪で逃れた。 ● **nar|row|ly** ADV 副詞 [ADV with v] かろうじて □Five firemen narrowly escaped death when a staircase collapsed beneath their feet. 足元の階段が壊れたとき5人の消防士は九死に一生を得た。 ▶ **narrow down** PHRASAL VERB 句動詞 If you **narrow down** a range of things, you reduce the number of things included in it. 絞る □What's happened is that the new results narrow down the possibilities. どういうことかというと、新しい結果によって可能性が絞られたということだ。

narrow-minded ADJ 形容詞 If you describe someone as **narrow-minded**, you are criticizing them because they are unwilling to consider new ideas or other people's opinions. 心の狭い、偏狭な [DISAPPROVAL 不賛成] □...a narrow-minded bigot. 心の狭い偏屈な人

NASA /næsə/ N-PROPER 固有名詞 **NASA** is a U.S. government organization concerned with spacecraft and space travel. **NASA** is an abbreviation for "National Aeronautics and Space Administration." 米国航空宇宙局

na|sal /neɪz⁰l/ 1 ADJ 形容詞 **Nasal** is used to describe things relating to the nose and the functions it performs. 鼻の [ADJ n] □...inflamed nasal passages. 炎症した鼻くう 2 ADJ 形容詞 If someone's voice is **nasal**, it sounds as if air is passing through their nose as well as their mouth while they are speaking. 鼻声

の、鼻にかかった ❑*Her voice was nasal and penetrating.* 彼女は鼻にかかった甲高い声をしていた.

nas|ty /nǽsti/ (**nastier, nastiest**) ◼ ADJ 形容詞 Something that is **nasty** is very unpleasant to see, experience, or feel. 不愉快な, ひどい ❑...*an extremely nasty murder.* 極悪な殺人事件 ● **nas|ti|ness** N-UNCOUNT 不可算名詞 不快 ❑...*the nastiness of war.* 戦争のむごさ ◼ ADJ 形容詞 If you describe a person or their behavior as **nasty**, you mean that they behave in an unkind and unpleasant way. 意地の悪い ❑*What nasty little snobs you all are.* お前らみんな,意地の悪い気取り屋だ. ❑*The guards looked really nasty.* 警備員はとても意地悪そうだった. ● **nas|ti|ly** ADV 副詞 [ADV after v] 意地悪く ❑*She took the money and eyed me nastily.* 彼女はお金を取り,意地悪そうにこちらを見た. ● **nas|ti|ness** N-UNCOUNT 不可算名詞 意地悪さ ❑*As the years went by his nastiness began to annoy his readers.* 年月が経つうちに,彼の意地の悪さが読者の気に障るようになった. ◼ ADJ 形容詞 If you describe something as **nasty**, you mean it is unattractive, undesirable, or in bad taste. 厄介な, 嫌な ❑*They should put warning labels on those nasty little devices.* あの厄介な器具に警告を貼り付けるべきだ. ◼ ADJ 形容詞 A **nasty** problem or situation is very worrisome and difficult to deal with. 難しい, 始末に終えない ❑*A spokesman said this firm action had defused a very nasty situation.* スポークスマンの発表によると,この断固とした行動により非常に難しい状況が沈静化したという. ◼ ADJ 形容詞 If you describe an injury or a disease as **nasty**, you mean that it is serious or looks unpleasant. ひどい, 重い ❑*My little granddaughter caught her heel in the spokes of her bicycle – it was a very nasty wound.* 幼い孫娘が自転車のスポークにかかとを引っかけて,とてもひどいけがをした.

na|tion /néɪʃªn/ (**nations**) ◼ N-COUNT 可算名詞 A **nation** is an individual country considered together with its social and political structures. 国家,国 ❑*Such policies would require unprecedented cooperation between nations.* そのような政策にはかつてないほどの国家間協力が必要だ.

> **Country** is the most usual word to use when you are talking about the major political units that the world is divided into. **State** is used when you are talking about politics or government institutions. ❑...*the new German state created by the unification process.* ...*Italy's state-controlled telecommunications company.* **State** can also refer to a political unit within a particular country. ❑...*the state of California.* **Nation** is often used when you are talking about a country's inhabitants, and their cultural or ethnic background. ❑*Wales is a proud nation with its own traditions...* *A senior government spokesman will address the nation.* **Land** is a less precise and more literary word, which you can use, for example, to talk about the feelings you have for a particular country. ❑*She was fascinated to learn about this strange land at the edge of Europe.*

◼ N-SING 単数名詞 The **nation** is sometimes used to refer to all the people who live in a particular country, or all the people who belong to a particular ethnic group. 国民,民族 [JOURNALISM ジャーナリズム] ❑*It was a story that touched the nation's heart.* 国民の心の琴線に触れた話だった. ❑...*the former chief of the Cherokee nation.* チェロキー民族のかつての酋長(しゅうちょう)
→ see **country**

→ see country

Thesaurus   *nation* また次を参照:

N.   country, democracy, population, republic, society ◼

---

na|tion|al /nǽʃªnªl/ (**nationals**) ◼ ADJ 形容詞 **National** means relating to the whole of a country or nation rather than to part of it or to other nations. 全国的な,国家の ❑...*major national and international issues.* 重要な国内外の問題 ● **na|tion|al|ly** ADV 副詞 全国的に ❑...*a nationally televised speech.* 全国テレビで放送されたスピーチ ◼ ADJ 形容詞 [ADJ n] **National** means typical of the people or customs of a particular country or nation. 国民的な ❑...*the national characteristics and history of the country.* 国民性と国の歴史 ◼ N-COUNT 可算名詞 You can refer to someone who is legally a citizen of a country as a **national** of that country. 国民,一国籍 ❑...*a Sri-Lankan national.* スリランカ人

na|tion|al|ise /nǽʃªnªlaɪz/ → see **nationalize**

na|tion|al|ism /nǽʃªnªlɪzªm/ ◼ N-UNCOUNT 不可算名詞 You can refer to a person's great love for their nation as **nationalism**. It is often associated with the belief that a particular nation is better than any other nation, and in this case is often used showing disapproval. 国粋主義, ナショナリズム ❑*This kind of fierce nationalism is a powerful and potentially volatile force.* この種の過激な国粋主義は強力で一触即発の勢力になる可能性がある. ◼ N-UNCOUNT 不可算名詞 **Nationalism** is the desire for political independence of people who feel they are historically or culturally a separate group within a country. 民族主義 ❑*The rising tide of Slovak nationalism may also help the party to win representation in parliament.* スロバキア民族主義の上昇気運によりその党が国会議員の当選者を出す可能性がある.

na|tion|al|ist /nǽʃªnªlɪst/ (**nationalists**) ◼ ADJ 形容詞 **Nationalist** means connected with the desire of a group of people within a country for political independence. 民族主義の ❑*The crisis has set off a wave of nationalist feelings in Quebec.* その危機によりケベック州において民族主義の感情が高まった. ● N-COUNT 可算名詞 A **nationalist** is someone with nationalist views. 民族主義者 ❑...*demands by nationalists for an independent state.* 独立国家を求める民族主義者の要求 ◼ ADJ 形容詞 **Nationalist** means connected with a person's great love for their nation. It is often associated with the belief that their nation is better than any other nation, and in this case is often used showing disapproval. 国粋主義的な [ADJ n] ❑*Political life has been infected by growing nationalist sentiment.* 政治生活に高まる国粋的心情が伝わりつつある. ● N-COUNT 可算名詞 A **nationalist** is someone with nationalist views. 国粋主義者 ❑*The parliament is composed mainly of extreme nationalists.* 国会は主に極端な国粋主義者から成り立っている.

na|tion|al|is|tic /nǽʃªnªlɪstɪk/ ◼ ADJ 形容詞 If you describe someone as **nationalistic**, you mean they are very proud of their nation. They also often believe that their nation is better than any other nation, and in this case it is often used showing disapproval. 国粋主義的な ❑*Nationalistic fervor is running high.* 国粋主義的な感情が盛り上がっている.

na|tion|al|ity /nǽʃªnǽlɪti/ (**nationalities**) ◼ N-VAR 可変性名詞 If you have the **nationality** of a particular country, you were born there or have the legal right to be a citizen. 国籍 ❑*Asked his nationality, he said American.* 国籍を聞かれて,アメリカ人と答えた. ◼ N-COUNT 可算名詞 You can refer to people who have the same racial origins as a **nationality**, especially when they do not have their own independent country. 民族 ❑...*the many nationalities that comprise Ethiopia.* エチオピアを構成する多くの民族

na|tion|al|ize /nǽʃªnªlaɪz/ (**nationalizes, nationalizing, nationalized**) V-T 他動詞 If a government **nationalizes** a private company or industry, that company or industry becomes owned by the state and controlled by the government. 国有化する [BUSINESS 実業] ❑*In 1987, Garcia introduced legislation to nationalize Peru's banking and financial systems.* 1987年にガルシアはペルーの銀行組織と金融制度を国有化する法案を提出した. ● **na|tion|ali|za|tion** /nǽʃªnªlɪzéɪʃªn/ N-UNCOUNT 不可算名詞 国有化 ❑...*the campaign for the nationalization of the coal mines.* 炭鉱国有化のキャンペーン

na|tion|al park (**national parks**) N-COUNT; N-IN-NAMES 可算名詞, 名称中の名詞 A **national park** is a large area of land which is protected by the government because of its natural beauty, plants, or animals, and which the public can usually visit. 国立公園 ❑*Roads into Yosemite National Park are closed due to landslides.* ヨセミテ国立公園への道路は山崩れのために閉鎖されている.

Word Link   *wide ≈ extending throughout : nationwide, widespread, worldwide*

---

na|tion|wide /néɪʃªnwàɪd/ ADJ 形容詞 **Nationwide** activities or situations happen or exist in all parts of a country. 全国的な ❑*The rising number of car crimes is a nationwide problem.* 増加の一途をたどる自動車犯罪は全国的な問題だ. ● ADV 副詞 **Nationwide** is also an adverb. 全国的に ❑*The figures show unemployment falling nationwide last month.* 先月の全国的な失業率は低下を示している.

Word Link   *nat ≈ being born : innate, native, prenatal*

---

na|tive /néɪtɪv/ (**natives**) ◼ ADJ 形容詞 Your **native** country or area is the country or area where you were born and brought up. 母国の,故郷の [ADJ n] ❑*It was his first visit to his native country since 1948.* 1948年以来母国を訪れたのは初めてだった. ◼ N-COUNT 可算名詞 A **native** of a particular country or region is someone who was born in that country or region. ～の出身者 ❑*Dr. Aubin is a native of St. Louis.* オーバン先生はセント・ルイスの出身だ. ● ADJ 形容詞 **Native** is also an adjective. 出身の [ADJ n] ❑*Joshua Halpern is a native Northern Californian.* ジョシュア・ハルパーンは北カリフォルニアの出身だ. ◼ N-COUNT 可算名詞 Some European people use **native** to refer to a person living in a non-Western country who belongs to the race or tribe that the majority of people there belong to. This use could cause offense. 土着民,先住民 ❑*They used force to banish the natives from the more fertile land.* 肥沃な土地から先住民を追い出すために武力を用いた. ● ADJ 形容詞 **Native** is also an adjective. 土着の [ADJ n] ❑*Native people were allowed to retain some sense of their traditional culture and religion.* 先住民は伝統文化や宗教を維持することが認められていた. ◼ ADJ 形容詞 Your **native** language or tongue is the first language that you learned to speak when you were a child. 母語の [ADJ n] ❑*She spoke not only her native language, Swedish, but also English and French.* 彼女は母語のスウェーデン語だけでなく英語とフランス語も話した. ◼ ADJ 形容詞 Plants or animals that are **native to** a particular region live or grow there naturally and were not brought there. 原産の [ADJ n, v-link ADJ 'to' n] ❑...*a project to create a 50 acre forest of native Caledonian pines.* カレドニア原産の松で50エーカーの森林を建設するプロジェクト ● N-COUNT 可算名詞 **Native** is also a noun. 原産 ❑*The coconut palm*

is a native of Malaysia. ココヤシの木はマレーシアの原産だ.

Thesaurus   *native* また次を参照:

N.   citizen, resident **2**

Word Partnership   *native* は次の語句と使われる:

N.   native **country**, native **land** **1**
      native **language**, native **tongue** **4**

NATO /ˈneɪtoʊ/ N-PROPER 固有名詞 **NATO** is an international organization which consists of the U.S., Canada, Britain, and other European countries, all of whom have agreed to support one another if they are attacked. **NATO** is an abbreviation for "North Atlantic Treaty Organization." 北大西洋条約機構 ❏ *NATO says it will keep a reduced number of modern nuclear weapons to guarantee peace*. 北大西洋条約機構は, 平和を保証するために近代核兵器の数を削減し維持すると発表した.

natu|ral /ˈnætʃərəl, ˈnætʃrəl/ (**naturals**) **1** ADJ 形容詞 If you say that it is **natural** for someone to act in a particular way or for something to happen in that way, you mean that it is reasonable in the circumstances. 当然の, もっともな ❏ *It is only natural for youngsters to crave the excitement of driving a fast car*. 若者がスピードの出る自動車の運転という刺激を切望するのはもっともだ. ❏ *It is only natural that he should resent you*. 彼が君に怒っているのは当然だ. **2** ADJ 形容詞 **Natural** behavior is shared by all people or all animals of a particular type and has not been learned. 生まれつきの ❏ *...the insect's natural instinct to feed*. えさをとるという昆虫の生まれつきの本能 **3** ADJ 形容詞 Someone with a **natural** ability or skill was born with that ability and did not have to learn it. 天性の ❏ *She has a natural ability to understand the motives of others*. 彼女には他人の動機を理解するという持って生まれた才能がある. **4** N-COUNT 可算名詞 If you say that someone is a **natural**, you mean that they do something very well and very easily. 生まれつき向いている人, 適任者 ❏ *He's a natural with any kind of engine*. 彼は生まれつきエンジンの名人だ. **5** ADJ 形容詞 If someone's behavior is **natural**, they appear to be relaxed and are not trying to hide anything. 自然の, 気取らない ❏ *Bethan's sister was as friendly and natural as the rest of the family*. ベサンの妹は残りの家族と同様に親しみやすくて気取らない人だった. ● **natu|ral|ly** ADV 副詞 自然に ❏ *For pictures of people behaving naturally, not posing for the camera, it is essential to shoot unnoticed*. カメラに向かってポーズをとっている姿ではなく自然にふるまっている人々の写真を撮るには, 気付かれずに撮影しなければならない. ● **natu|ral|ness** N-UNCOUNT 不可算名詞 自然体 ❏ *The critics praised the reality of the scenery and the naturalness of the acting*. 批評家は, 現実的な風景の真実と演技を褒めた. **6** ADJ 形容詞 [ADJ n] **Natural** things exist or occur in nature and are not made or caused by people. 天然の ❏ *The gigantic natural harbor is a haven for boats*. 巨大な自然港湾はボートの避難港だ. ● **natu|ral|ly** ADV 副詞 自然界に ❏ *Nitrates are chemicals that occur naturally in water and the soil*. 硝酸塩は自然の水と土に存在する化学物質だ. **7** PHRASE 句 If someone dies **of** or **from natural causes**, they die because they are ill or old rather than because of an accident or violence. 自然の原因 ❏ *Your brother died of natural causes*. お兄様は自然死でした.

Thesaurus   *natural* また次を参照:

ADJ. normal **1**
      inborn, innate, instinctive **2** **3**
      genuine, sincere, unaffected **5**
      wild; (ant.) artificial **6**

Word Partnership   *natural* は次の語句と使われる:

ADV. **perfectly** natural **1** **2**
N.   natural **reaction**, natural **tendency** **2**
      natural **beauty**, natural **disaster**, natural **food** **6**

---

natu|ral|ist /ˈnætʃərəlɪst, ˈnætʃrəl-/ (**naturalists**) N-COUNT 可算名詞 A **naturalist** is a person who studies plants, animals, insects, and other living things. 博物学者

natu|ral|ly /ˈnætʃərəli, ˈnætʃrəli/ **1** ADV 副詞 You use **naturally** to indicate that you think something is very obvious and not at all surprising under the circumstances. 当然, 言うまでもなく ❏ *When things go wrong, all of us naturally feel disappointed and frustrated*. 物事がうまくいかないと, 当然だれでもがっかりし不満を抱く. ❏ *Naturally these comings and goings excited some curiosity*. 当然, これらの活動はいくらかの好奇心をかき立てた. **2** ADV 副詞 If one thing develops **naturally** from another, it develops as a normal consequence or result of it. 必然的に [ADV after v] ❏ *A study of yoga leads naturally to meditation*. ヨガの勉強は自然に瞑想へとつながる. **3** ADV 副詞 You can use **naturally** to talk about a characteristic of someone's personality when it is the way that they normally act. 生まれつき [ADV adj] ❏ *He has a lively sense of humor and appears naturally confident*. 彼はユーモアのセンスに溢

れ, 生まれつき自信に満ちているようだ. **4** ADV 副詞 If someone is **naturally** good at something, they learn it easily and quickly and do it very well. 生まれながらに [ADV adj] ❏ *Some individuals are naturally good communicators*. 生まれながらにしてコミュニケーションが上手な人がいる. **5** PHRASE 句 If something **comes naturally to** you, you find it easy to do and quickly become good at it. たやすくできる ❏ *Humanitarian work comes naturally to them*. 人道の活動は彼らにとってたやすいことだ. **6** → see also **natural**

natu|ral re|sources N-PLURAL 複数名詞 **Natural resources** are all the land, forests, energy sources and minerals existing naturally in a place that can be used by people. 天然資源 ❏ *Angola was a country rich in natural resources*. アンゴラは天然資源が豊富な国だ.

natu|ral wast|age N-UNCOUNT 不可算名詞 **Natural wastage** is the same as **attrition**. 労働力の自然減 [mainly BRIT 主に英国英語 BUSINESS 実業]

na|ture /ˈneɪtʃər/ (**natures**) **1** N-UNCOUNT 不可算名詞 **Nature** is all the animals, plants, and other things in the world that are not made by people, and all the events and processes that are not caused by people. 自然 ❏ *The most amazing thing about nature is its infinite variety*. 自然について最も驚くべきことは種類が無限にあることだ. ❏ *...grasses that grow wild in nature*. 自然に野生している草

Do not confuse **nature**, **landscape**, **scenery**, and **countryside**. **Nature** includes the landscape, the weather, animals, and plants. ❏ *These creatures roamed the Earth as the finest and rarest wonders of nature*. With **landscape**, the emphasis is on the physical features of the land, while **scenery** includes everything you can see when you look out over an area of land. ❏ *...the landscape of steep woods and distant mountains*. *...unattractive urban scenery*. **Countryside** is land which is away from towns and cities. ❏ *...3,500 acres of mostly flat countryside*.

---

2 N-SING 単数名詞 The **nature** of something is its basic quality or character. 性質 ❏ *Mr. Sharp would not comment on the nature of the issues being investigated*. シャープ氏は, 調査中の問題の特質についてはコメントを拒否した. ❏ *The rise of a major power is both economic and military in nature*. 大国の台頭は経済的また軍事的である. **3** N-SING 単数名詞 Someone's **nature** is their character, which they show by the way they behave. 性格 [with poss, also 'by' N] ❏ *Jeya feels that her ambitious nature made her unsuitable for an arranged marriage*. 野心的な性格のためにお見合い結婚には適していなかったとジェヤは感じている. ❏ *She trusted people. That was her nature*. 彼女は人々を信用した. それが彼女の性格だった. **4** → see also **human nature** **5** PHRASE 句 If you say that something has a particular characteristic **by** its **nature** or **by** its **very nature**, you mean that things of that type always have that characteristic. その性質上 ❏ *Peacekeeping, by its nature, makes pre-planning difficult*. 平和維持活動は, その性質上あらかじめ計画することが難しい. **6** PHRASE 句 If you say that something is **in the nature of things**, you mean that you would expect it to happen in the circumstances mentioned. 当然のことながら, 必然的に ❏ *Of course, in the nature of things, and with a lot of drinking going on, people failed to notice*. 当然のことながら, かなりの飲酒が行われていて人々は気付かなかった. **7** PHRASE 句 If you say that one thing is **in the nature of** another, you mean that it is like the other thing. 一のような ❏ *There is movement toward, I think, something in the nature of a pluralistic system*. 私が思うところでは, 多元的システムのような方向に向かっている. **8** PHRASE 句 If a way of behaving is **second nature** to you, you do it almost without thinking because it is easy for you or obvious to you. 第二の天性, 深く身に付いた習慣 ❏ *Planning ahead had always come as second nature to her*. 前もって計画を立てることは彼女にとっていつも習慣となっていた.

Word Partnership   *nature* は次の語句と使われる:

V.   love nature, **preserve** nature **1**
N.   love of nature, **wonders of** nature **1**
      nature **of life**, nature **of society**, nature **of work** **2**
      nature **and nurture** **3**

---

naugh|ty /ˈnɔti/ (**naughtier, naughtiest**) **1** ADJ 形容詞 If you say that a child is **naughty**, you mean that they behave badly or do not do what they are told. わんぱくな ❏ *Girls, you're being very naughty*. こら, そんなことをしてはいけません. **2** ADJ 形容詞 You can describe books, pictures, or words as **naughty** when they are slightly vulgar or related to sex. 下品な, いやらしい ❏ *You know what little boys are like with naughty words*. 小さい男の子たちがエッチな言葉を聞くとどうなるか分かるでしょう.

nau|sea /ˈnɔziə, -ʒə, -siə, -ʃə/ N-UNCOUNT 不可算名詞 **Nausea** is the condition of feeling sick and the feeling that you are going to vomit. 吐き気 ❏ *I was overcome with a feeling of nausea*. 吐き気でぐったりした.

nau|ti|cal /ˈnɔtɪkəl/ ADJ 形容詞 **Nautical** means relating to ships and sailing. 船の, 航海術の ❏ *...a nautical chart of the region you sail*. 航海する地域の海図

n

Word Web navigation

Early explorers used the **sun** and **stars** to navigate the seas. The sextant allowed later navigators to use these celestial objects to accurately calculate their **position**. By sighting or measuring their position at noon, sailors could determine their latitude. The **compass** helped sailors determine their position at any time of night or day. It also worked in any weather. Today all sorts of travelers use the global positioning system (GPS) to guide their journeys. A GPS receiver is connected to a system of 24 **satellites** that can establish a location within a few feet.

compass   sextant   GPS

Word Link nav ≈ ship : naval, navigate, navy

na|val /ˈneɪvªl/ ADJ 形容詞 **Naval** means belonging to, relating to, or involving a country's navy. 海軍の [ADJ n] ❑ *He was the senior serving naval officer.* 彼は任期中の海軍高官だった.

na|vel /ˈneɪvªl/ (**navels**) N-COUNT 可算名詞 Your **navel** is the small hollow just below your waist at the front of your body. へそ ❑ *...a girl with a ring in her navel.* へそに輪をつけた女の子

navi|gate /ˈnævɪgeɪt/ (**navigates, navigating, navigated**) ■ V-T/V-I 他動詞/自動詞 When someone **navigates** a ship or an aircraft somewhere, they decide which course to follow and steer it there. 誘導する, 操縦する ❑ *Captain Cook was responsible for safely navigating his ship without accident for 100 voyages.* キャプテン・クックは100回の航海中, 無事故で安全に航海することの責任者であった. ❑ *The purpose of the visit was to navigate into an ice-filled fiord.* 訪問の目的は流氷で満ちたフィヨルドに誘導することだった. ● **navi|ga|tion** /ˌnævɪgeɪʃªn/ (**navigations**) N-VAR 可変性名詞 操縦 ❑ *The expedition was wrecked by bad planning and poor navigation.* 遠征はまずい計画と下手な操縦により失敗に終わった. ❷ V-T/V-I 他動詞/自動詞 When a ship or boat **navigates** an area of water, it sails on or across it. 航行する ❑ *...a lock system to allow sea-going craft to navigate the upper reaches of the river.* 外洋船が川の上流を航行できるようにする閘門(こうもん)システム ❑ *Such boats can navigate on the Hudson.* そのようなボートはハドソン川を航行できる. ❸ V-I 自動詞 When someone in a car **navigates**, they decide what roads the car should be driven along in order to get somewhere. 道案内する ❑ *When traveling on fast roads at night it is impossible to drive and navigate at the same time.* 夜間に高速で走っているときに運転しながら同時に道案内をするのは不可能だ. ❑ *...the relief at successfully navigating across the Golden Gate Bridge to arrive here.* 金門橋を越えてここに到着するよううまく道案内できて安心 ❹ V-I 自動詞 When fish, animals, or insects **navigate** somewhere, they find the right direction to go and travel there. 正しい方向を見つける ❑ *In tests, the bees navigate back home after being placed in a field a mile away.* 検証では, ハチは1マイル離れた野原に放されたあと, 元の場所への正しい方向を見つけることができる. ❺ V-T 他動詞 If you **navigate** an obstacle, you move carefully in order to avoid hitting the obstacle or hurting yourself. 通り抜ける ❑ *He's got to learn how to navigate his way around the residence.* あの屋敷を避けて通り抜ける方法を覚えないといけない.
→ see **star**

navi|ga|tion /ˌnævɪgeɪʃªn/ ■ N-UNCOUNT 不可算名詞 You can refer to the movement of ships as **navigation**. 航海術, 航海 ❑ *Pack ice around Iceland was becoming a threat to navigation.* アイスランド周辺の流水は航海への脅威となりつつあった. ❷ → see also **navigate**
→ see Word Web: **navigation**

navi|ga|tor /ˈnævɪgeɪtər/ (**navigators**) N-COUNT 可算名詞 The **navigator** on an aircraft or ship is the person whose job is to work out the direction in which the aircraft or ship should be traveling. 航海士, 操縦者 ❑ *He became a navigator during the war.* 彼は戦時中航海士になった.

navy /ˈneɪvi/ (**navies**) ■ N-COUNT 可算名詞 A country's **navy** consists of the people it employs to fight at sea, and the ships they use. 海軍 ❑ *The operation was organized by the US Navy.* 軍事活動は米国海軍がとりまとめた. ❑ *Her own son was also in the navy.* 彼女自身の息子も海軍にいた. ❷ COLOR 色彩語 Something that is **navy** or **navy-blue** is very dark blue. 濃紺の, ネイビーブルーの ❑ *When I was a fashion editor, I mostly wore white shirts and black or navy trousers.* ファッション・エディターだったころ, たいていは白いシャツを着て黒かネイビーブルーのズボンをはいていた.

Nazi /ˈnɑtsi/ (**Nazis**) ■ N-COUNT 可算名詞 The **Nazis** were members of the right-wing political party, led by Adolf Hitler, which held power in Germany from 1933 to 1945. ナチ党員 ❷ ADJ 形容詞 You use **Nazi** to say that something relates to the Nazis. ナチの ❑ *...the rise of the Nazi Party.* ナチ党の台頭

NB /ˌen ˈbi/ also **N.B.** You write **NB** or **N.B.** to draw someone's attention to what you are about to say or write. 注意, 注 ❑ *NB: The opinions stated in this essay do not necessarily represent those of the Church of God Missionary Society.* 注：このエッセーに記載されている見解は必ずしも聖公会宣教協会を代表しているとは限らない.

near /nɪər/ (**nearer, nearest, nears, nearing, neared**) ■ PREP 前置詞 If something is **near** a place, thing, or person, it is a short distance from them. 近くに ❑ *Don't come near me.* 私の近くに来ないで. ❑ *He drew his chair nearer the fire.* 彼はいすをヒーターの近くに寄せた. ● ADV 副詞 **Near** is also an adverb. 近くで ❑ *He crouched as near to the door as he could.* 彼はできるだけドアの近くでかがんだ. ❑ *She took a step nearer to the barrier.* 彼女は柵の方に一歩近寄った. ● ADJ 形容詞 **Near** is also an adjective. 近くの [ADJ n, 'the' ADJ 'of' n] ❑ *He collapsed into the nearest chair.* 彼は近くのいすに倒れた. ❑ *The nearer of the two barges was perhaps a mile away.* 2隻のはしけのうちの近い方はおそらく1マイル離れたところだった. ❷ PHRASE 句 If someone or something is **near to** a particular state, they have almost reached it. もう少しで ❑ *After the war, the firm came near to bankruptcy.* 戦後, その会社は倒産寸前だった. ❑ *The repairs to the Hafner machine were near to completion.* ハフナー機の修理はほぼ終了していた. ● PREP 前置詞 **Near** means the same as **near to**. もう少しで ❑ *He was near tears.* 彼は泣き出しそうだった. ❑ *For almost a month he lay near death.* ほぼ1か月間彼は瀕死状態で寝込んでいた. ❸ PHRASE 句 If something is similar to something else, you can say that it is **near to** it. 〜のような ❑ *It combined with the resinous cedar smell of the logs to produce a sickening sensation that was near to nausea.* それは丸太の樹脂を含んだスギのにおいと混ざって吐き気のような気分の悪さを引き起こした. ● PREP 前置詞 **Near** means the same as **near to**. 〜のような ❑ *Often her feelings were nearer hatred than love.* しばしば彼女の気持ちは愛情よりも憎しみに近かった. ❹ ADJ 形容詞 You describe the thing most similar to something as **the nearest** thing to it when there is no example of the thing itself. ほぼ等しい ['the' ADJ n 'to' n, 'the' ADJ 'to' n] ❑ *It would appear that the legal profession is the nearest thing to a recession-proof industry.* 法律専門職は景気後退の影響を受けにくい産業にほぼ等しい. ❺ ADV 副詞 If a time or event draws **near**, it will happen soon. 近々 [WRITTEN 書き言葉] ❑ *The time for my departure from Japan was drawing nearer every day.* 日本からの出発のときが日ごとに近づいていた. ❻ PREP 前置詞 If something happens **near** a particular time, it happens just before or just after that time. 〜近く ❑ *Performance is lowest between 3 a.m. and 5 a.m., and reaches a peak near midday.* 効率は午前3時から5時の間が最も低く, 正午近くにピークに達する. ❑ *"Since I retired to this place," he wrote near the end of his life, "I have never been out of these mountains."* 「退職してこの地に来て以来」と彼は寿命が近づいたころに書いた. 「これらの山々から離れたことはなかった」 ❼ PREP 前置詞 You use **near** to say that something is a little more or less than an amount or number stated. 約〜 ❑ *...to increase manufacturing from about 2.5 million cars a year to near 4.75 million.* 年間の自動車生産を250万台から約475万台に増加するには ❽ PREP 前置詞 You can say that someone will **not go near** a person or thing when you are emphasizing that they refuse to see them or go there. 近寄らない [EMPHASIS 強調] [with brd-neg] ❑ *He will absolutely not go near a hospital.* 彼は絶対に病院に行こうとしない. ❾ ADJ 形容詞 **The near** one of two things is the one that is closer. 手前の [det ADJ n] ❑ *...a mighty beech tree on the near side of the little clearing.* 小さな森の空き地の手前側にあるブナの大木 ❿ ADJ 形容詞 You use **near** to indicate that something is almost the thing mentioned. ほとんど [ADJ n] ❑ *She was believed to have died in near poverty.* 彼女はほとんど貧困状態で死亡したと信じられていた. ● ADV 副詞 **Near** is also an adverb. ほぼ [ADV adj] ❑ *...his near fatal accident two years ago.* 2年前の瀕死の(ひんし)事故 ⓫ ADJ 形容詞 In a contest, your **nearest** rival or challenger is the person or team that is most likely to defeat you. 最強の [ADJ n] ❑ *He completed the lengthy course some three seconds faster than his nearest rival, Jonathon Ford.* 彼は長距離コースを最強ライバルのジョナサン・フォードと3秒差で先にゴールした. ⓬ V-T 他動詞 When you **near** a place, you get quite near to it. 近づく, 近寄る [LITERARY 文語的] [no passive] ❑ *As he neared the stable, he slowed the horse and patted it on the neck.* 彼は馬小屋に近づいたとき, 馬のスピードを落とし背中をぽんぽんとたたいた. ⓭ V-T 他動詞 When someone or something **nears** a particular stage or point, they will soon reach that stage or point. 迫る, 近づく [no

passive] *His age was hard to guess – he must have been nearing fifty.* 彼の年齢はよく分からなかった．まもなく50歳というあたりにだったにちがいない．□ *You are nearing the end of your training and you haven't attempted any assessments yet.* 研修の終わりが近づいているがまだ査定を全く受けていない． **14** V-I 自動詞 You say that an important time or event **nears** when it is going to occur quite soon. 近づく，まもなく起こる [LITERARY 文語的] □ *As half time neared, Hardyman almost scored twice.* ハーフタイムが近づいたとき，ハーディマンがもう少しで2回目のゴールを決めた． **15** PHRASE 句 You use **near and far** to indicate that you are referring to a very large area or distance. あちこち，各地 □ *People would gather from near and far.* 人々は各地から集まるだろう． **16** PHRASE 句 If you say that something will happen **in the near future**, you mean that it will happen quite soon. 近いうちに □ *The controversy regarding vitamin C is unlikely to be resolved in the near future.* ビタミンCに関しての論争が近いうちに解決する見込みは低い． **17** PHRASE 句 You use **nowhere near** and **not anywhere near** to emphasize that something is not the case. 程遠い [EMPHASIS 強調] □ *They are nowhere near good enough.* 全くだめだ． □ *It was nowhere near as painful as David had expected.* デービッドの予想に反して全く痛くなかった．

near|by /nɪərbaɪ/ ADV 副詞 If something is **nearby**, it is only a short distance away. 近くの □ *He might easily have been seen by someone who lived nearby.* 彼は近所の人に見られる可能性が高い． □ *The helicopter crashed to earth nearby.* ヘリコプターが近くに墜落した． ● ADJ 形容詞 **Nearby** is also an adjective. 近くの □ *At a nearby table a man was complaining in a loud voice.* 近くのテーブルで男性が大声で苦情を言っていた．

near|ly /nɪərli/ ADV 副詞 **Nearly** is used to indicate that something is not quite the case, or not completely the case. ほぼ □ *Goldsworth stared at me in silence for nearly twenty seconds.* ゴールズワースはほぼ20秒間私をじっと見た． □ *Hunter knew nearly all of this already.* ハンターはすでにこのことをほとんどすべて知っていた． □ *The beach was nearly empty.* 海辺にはほとんどだれもいなかった． **2** ADV 副詞 **Nearly** is used to indicate that something will soon be the case. もう少しで □ *It was already nearly eight o'clock.* すでに8時直前だ． □ *I was nearly asleep.* もう少しで眠るところだった． □ *I've nearly finished the words for your song.* あなたの歌の歌詞をもう少しで書き終えるところだ．

Thesaurus   *nearly* また次を参照：
ADV. almost, approximately **1**

near|sighted /nɪərsaɪtɪd/ also **near-sighted** ADJ 形容詞 Someone who is **nearsighted** cannot see distant things clearly. 近視 □ *As you get older, you may become farsighted or near-sighted.* 年をとるにつれて，遠視か近視になるかもしれない．
→ see **eye**

neat /nit/ (**neater, neatest**) **1** ADJ 形容詞 A **neat** place, thing, or person is organized and clean, and has everything in the correct place. 整とんされた，きちんとした □ *So they left her in the neat little house, alone with her memories.* それで彼らは彼女を思い出と一緒に1人こぎれいな小さな家に残したんだ． □ *Everything was neat and tidy and gleamingly clean.* すべてが整理されていてピカピカだった． ● **neat|ly** ADV 副詞 [ADV with v] きちんと □ *He folded his paper neatly and sipped his coffee.* 彼はきちんと新聞をたたんでコーヒーをすすった． ● **neat|ness** N-UNCOUNT 不可算名詞 きちんとしていること □ *The grounds were a perfect balance between neatness and natural wildness.* その敷地は整然さと自然の状態のちょうどよい釣り合いが取れていた． **2** ADJ 形容詞 Someone who is **neat** keeps their home or possessions organized and clean, with everything in the correct place. きれい好きな □ *"That's not like Alf," he said, "leaving papers muddled like that. He's always so neat."* 「アルフらしくない」と彼は言った．「書類をこんな風にごちゃごちゃにするなんて．彼はいつもとてもきれい好きだ」 ● **neat|ly** ADV 副詞 [ADV with v] きれいに □ *I followed her into that room which her mother had maintained so neatly.* 私は彼女のあとをついて彼女の母親がとてもきれいに片付けているその部屋へ入った． ● **neat|ness** N-UNCOUNT 不可算名詞 整然さ □ *...a paragon of neatness, efficiency and reliability.* 効率性，信頼性の見本 **3** ADJ 形容詞 A **neat** object, part of the body, or shape is quite small and has a smooth outline. こぎれいな，すっきりした □ *...neat handwriting.* きれいな筆跡 **4** ADJ 形容詞 A **neat** movement or action is done accurately and skillfully, with no unnecessary movements. 巧みな □ *"Did you have any trouble?" Byron asked, driving into a small parking lot and changing the subject in the same neat maneuver.* 「どうかしたかい？」とバイロンは小さな駐車スペースに車を入れながら，それと同様にうまく話題を変えて尋ねた． ● **neat|ly** ADV 副詞 [ADV with v] 巧みに □ *He watched her peel and dissect a pear neatly, no mess, no sticky fingers.* 彼は，彼女が手を汚さず上手にナシの皮をむいて切るのを見た． **5** ADJ 形容詞 A **neat** way of organizing, achieving, explaining, or expressing something is clever and convenient. すてきな，素晴らしい □ *It had been such a neat, clever plan.* よくできた巧妙な計画だった． □ *Neat solutions are not easily found to these issues.* このような問題には，よい解決策はなかなか見つからない． ● **neat|ly** ADV 副詞 [ADV with v] うまく

□ *Real people do not fit neatly into these categories.* 現実の人間はこのようなカテゴリーにはうまく当てはまらない． **6** ADJ 形容詞 If you say that something is **neat**, you mean that it is very good. すごくいい [INFORMAL くだけた, APPROVAL 賛成] □ *He thought Mick was a really neat guy.* 彼は，ミックがとてもいいやつだと思った． **7** ADJ 形容詞 When someone drinks strong alcohol **neat**, they do not add a weaker liquid such as water to it. ストレートの（氷や水で割らないで）[mainly BRIT 主に英国英語; AM usually **straight** 米国英語では通常 **straight**]

Thesaurus   *neat* また次を参照：
ADJ. orderly, tidy, uncluttered **1** **2**

nec|es|sari|ly /nɛsɪsɛərɪli/ ADV 副詞 If you say that something is **not necessarily** the case, you mean that it may not be the case or is not always the case. 必ずしも〜ない，〜とはかぎらない [VAGUENESS あいまいさ] □ *Anger is not necessarily the most useful or acceptable reaction to such events.* そのような出来事に対する反応として，怒りが最も効果的とも好ましいともかぎらない． ● CONVENTION 慣習表現 If you reply "**Not necessarily**," you mean that what has just been said or suggested may not be true. そうとはかぎりません □ *"He was lying, of course." — "Not necessarily."* 「もちろん彼はうそをついていたんだ」「そうともかぎらないよ」 **2** ADV 副詞 If you say that something **necessarily** happens or is the case, you mean that it has to happen or be the case and cannot be any different. 必然的に □ *Brookman & Langdon were said to manufacture the most desirable pens and these necessarily command astonishingly high prices.* ブルックマン＆ランドン社は最も望ましいペンを製造するという評判だったので，それらは必然的に驚くべきほどの高額で売れている．

nec|es|sary /nɛsɪsɛri/ **1** ADJ 形容詞 Something that is **necessary** is needed in order for something else to happen. 必要な □ *I kept the engine running because it might be necessary to leave fast.* エンジンを切らなかったのは高速で出発する必要があるかもしれないからだ． □ *Make the necessary arrangements.* 必要な手はずを整えなさい． **2** ADJ 形容詞 A **necessary** consequence or connection must happen or exist, because of the nature of the things or events involved. 必然の [ADJ n] □ *Scientific work is differentiated from art by its necessary connection with the idea of progress.* 科学は，進歩の考えと必然的な関係があるという点で芸術とは異なっている．

Thesaurus   *necessary* また次を参照：
ADJ. essential, mandatory, obligatory, required; (ant.)
     unnecessary **1**
     unavoidable **1**

ne|ces|si|tate /nɪsɛsɪteɪt/ (**necessitates, necessitating, necessitated**) V-T 他動詞 If something **necessitates** an event, action, or situation, it makes it necessary. 必要とする，余儀なくさせる [FORMAL 形式ばった] □ *A prolonged drought had necessitated the introduction of water rationing.* 長期間に及ぶ干ばつのため給水制限の導入が必要となった．

ne|ces|si|ty /nɪsɛsɪti/ (**necessities**) **1** N-UNCOUNT 不可算名詞 The **necessity** of something is the fact that it must happen or exist. 必要性 □ *There is agreement on the necessity of reforms.* 改革の必要性に関して合意がある． □ *As soon as the necessity for action is over the troops must be withdrawn.* 交戦の必要性がなくなり次第，軍隊を撤退させなければならない． PHRASE 句 ● If you say that something is **of necessity** the case, you mean that it is the case because nothing else is possible or practical under the circumstances. 必要に迫られて [FORMAL 形式ばった] □ *...large families where children, of necessity, shared a bed.* 子供たちが必要に迫られてベッドを共にする大家族 **2** N-COUNT 可算名詞 A **necessity** is something that you must have in order to live properly or do something. 必需品 □ *Water is a basic necessity of life.* 水は生活に必要不可欠だ． **3** N-COUNT 可算名詞 A situation or action that is a **necessity** is necessary and cannot be avoided. 不可避 □ *The president pleaded that strong rule from the center was a necessity.* 大統領は中立勢力からの強力な支配が必要だと主張した．

Word Partnership   *necessity* は次の語句と使われる：
ADJ. absolute necessity **1** – **3**
     economic necessity **2** **3**
     political necessity **3**

neck /nɛk/ (**necks**) **1** N-COUNT 可算名詞 Your **neck** is the part of your body which joins your head to the rest of your body. 首 □ *She threw her arms around his neck and hugged him warmly.* 彼女は彼の首に腕を回して優しく抱きしめた． **2** N-COUNT 可算名詞 The **neck** of an article of clothing such as a shirt, dress, or sweater is the part which surrounds your neck. 襟 □ *...the low, ruffled neck of her blouse.* ブラウスの短いフリルつきの襟 **3** N-COUNT 可算名詞 The **neck** of something such as a bottle or a guitar is the long narrow part at one end of it. ネック □ *Catherine gripped the broken neck of the bottle.* キャサリンは壊れた瓶の首をしっかりとつかんで

n

いた． **4** PHRASE 句 If you say that someone **is breathing down your neck**, you mean that they are watching you very closely and checking everything you do. 絶えず付きまとって監視している □ *Most farmers have loan officers breathing down their necks.* ほとんどの農家には融資担当者が絶えず付きまとって監視している． **5** PHRASE 句 In a competition, especially an election, if two or more competitors are **neck and neck**, they are level with each other and have an equal chance of winning. 互角で，接戦で □ *The latest polls indicate that the two main parties are neck and neck.* 最近の世論調査によると2大政党は互角だ． **6** PHRASE 句 If you **stick your neck out**, you bravely say or do something that might be criticized or might turn out to be wrong. 災いを招くようなことをする [INFORMAL くだけた] □ *During my political life I've earned myself a reputation as someone who'll stick his neck out, a bit of a rebel.* 私の政治生活中に私はあえて災いを招くようなことをするちょっとした反抗者だという評判を得た．
→ see **body**

<table>
<tr><td colspan="2">**Word Partnership** *neck*は次の語句と使われる：</td></tr>
<tr><td>N.</td><td>**back/nape of the** neck, **head and** neck, neck **injury** **1**</td></tr>
<tr><td>ADJ.</td><td>**broken** neck, **long** neck, **stiff** neck, **thick** neck **1** **3**</td></tr>
</table>

neck|lace /nɛklɪs/ (**necklaces**) N-COUNT 可算名詞 A **necklace** is a piece of jewelry such as a chain or a string of beads which someone, usually a woman, wears around their neck. ネックレス □ *...a diamond necklace and matching earrings.* ダイアモンドのネックレスとおそろいのイヤリング
→ see **jewelry**

nec|tar|ine /nɛktəriːn/ (**nectarines**) N-COUNT 可算名詞 A **nectarine** is a round, juicy fruit which is similar to a peach but has a smooth skin. ネクタリン

need /niːd/ (**needs, needing, needed**)

> **Need** sometimes behaves like an ordinary verb, for example "She needs to know" and "She doesn't need to know" and sometimes like a modal, for example "No-one need know," "She needn't know," or, in more formal English, "She need not know."
>
> **Need** 々普通動詞のように使われることがある，例えば，**She needs to know** や **She doesn't need to know**．そして時々法動詞のように使われることがある，例えば，**No-one need know** や **She needn't know**．

1 V-T 他動詞 If you **need** something, or **need to** do something, you cannot successfully achieve what you want or live properly without it. 必要とする [no cont] □ *He desperately needed money.* 彼は，お金を切実に必要としていた． □ *I need to make a phone call.* 電話をかける必要がある． □ *I need you to do something for me.* お願いがあるんだけど． □ *I need you here, Wally.* ここにいて欲しいの，ウォリー． ● N-COUNT 可算名詞 **Need** is also a noun. 必要，必要性 □ *Charles has never felt the need to compete with anyone.* チャールズはほかの人と競い合う必要を感じたことがない． □ *...the child who never had his need for attention and importance satisfied.* 認知欲求や自尊心が満たされることのなかった子供 **2** V-T 他動詞 If an object or place **needs** something done to it, that action should be done to improve the object or place. If a task **needs** doing, it should be done to improve a particular situation. 必要がある [no cont] □ *The building needs quite a few repairs.* その建物はかなりの修理が必要だ． □ *...a garden that needs tidying.* 片づけが必要な庭 **3** N-SING 単数名詞 If there is a **need for** something, that thing would improve a situation or something cannot happen without it. 不足，必要性 □ *Mr. Forrest believes there is a need for other similar schools throughout the country.* フォレスト氏は，全国でほかにも同じような学校の必要性があると信じている． □ *"I think we should see a specialist."—"I don't think there's any need for that."* 「専門医に見てもらうべきだと思うよ」「その必要はないと思うな」 **4** V-T 他動詞 If you say that someone does not **need to** do something, you are telling them not to do it, or advising or suggesting that they should not do it. 〜する必要はない，〜しないほうがよい [with neg] □ *Well, for Heaven's sake, you don't need to apologize.* まあ，お願いだから謝ったりしないで． ● MODAL 法動詞 **Need** is also a modal. 〜する必要はない [no cont, with neg] □ *"I'll put the key in the window."—"You needn't bother," he said gruffly.* 「窓にかぎを差し込むよ」「しなくていいよ」とぶっきらぼうに言った． □ *Look, you needn't shout.* いいかい，大声を出すんじゃない． **5** V-T 他動詞 If you tell someone that they don't **need to** do something, or that something need not happen, you are telling them that that thing is not necessary, in order to make them feel better. 〜しなくていいよ [no cont, with neg] □ *He replied, with a reassuring smile, "Oh, you don't need to worry about them."* 彼は心が休まるような笑顔で言った，「ああ，そのことは気にしなくていいよ」 ● MODAL 法動詞 **Need** is also a modal. 〜しなくていいよ [with brd-neg] □ *You needn't worry.* 心配しなくていいよ． □ *We have learned that a market crash need not lead to economic disaster.* 相場の下落が経済的大惨事につながるとはかぎらないことを学んだ． **6** V-T 他動詞 You use **don't need to** when you are giving someone permission not to do something. 〜する必要はない，〜しなくていい [no cont]

□ *You don't need to wait for me.* 私を待つ必要はない． ● MODAL 法動詞 **Need** is also a modal. 〜する必要はない，〜しなくていい [with neg] □ *You needn't come again, if you don't want to.* 来たくなければ，もう来なくてよろしい． **7** MODAL 法動詞 If someone **needn't have** done something, they didn't need to do it. 〜する必要はなかった [with neg] □ *She could have made the sandwich herself; her mother needn't have bothered to do anything.* 彼女は自分でサンドイッチを作れたのに，そうすればお母さんはわざわざ何もする必要はなかった． □ *I was a little nervous when I announced my engagement to Grace, but I needn't have worried.* グレースに婚約のことを話したときちょっと緊張したけど，心配する必要はなかった． **8** V-T 他動詞 If someone **didn't need to** do something, it wasn't necessary or useful for them to do it, although they did it. 〜しなくてよかったのに [no cont, with neg] □ *You didn't need to give me any more money you know, but thank you.* それ以上お金をくれなくてもよかったのに，でも，ありがとう． **9** MODAL 法動詞 You use **need** in expressions such as **I need hardly say** and **I needn't add** to emphasize that the person you are talking to already knows what you are going to say. 言うまでもない [EMPHASIS 強調] □ *I needn't add that if you fail to do as I ask, you will suffer the consequences.* 頼まれた通りにしなければひどい目に会うと付け足すまでもない． ● V-T 他動詞 **Need** is also a verb. 〜するまでもない [no cont] □ *I hardly need to say that I have never lost contact with him.* 彼との連絡が途絶えたことがないと言うまでもない． **10** PHRASE 句 People **in need** do not have enough of essential things such as money, food, or good health. 困って，窮乏して □ *The portable clinic will take doctors to children in need.* 移動診療所で医者が貧窮した子供たちのところへ行く． **11** PHRASE 句 If you are **in need of** something, you need it or ought to have it. 必要としている □ *I was all right but in need of rest.* 大丈夫だけど，休憩が必要だった． □ *He was badly in need of a shave.* 彼はかなりひげが伸びていた． **12** PHRASE 句 If you say that you will do something, especially an extreme action, **if need be**, you mean that you will do it if it is necessary. 必要であれば □ *They will act as my legal advisers if need be.* 必要であれば，彼らが法律顧問を務める．

<table>
<tr><td colspan="2">**Thesaurus** *need* また次を参照：</td></tr>
<tr><td>v.</td><td>demand, must have, require **1**</td></tr>
</table>

nee|dle /niːdəl/ (**needles**) **1** N-COUNT 可算名詞 A **needle** is a small, very thin piece of polished metal which is used for sewing. It has a sharp point at one end and a hole in the other for a thread to go through. 針 □ *He took a needle and thread and sewed it up.* 彼は針と糸を取って縫った． **2** N-COUNT 可算名詞 A **needle** is a thin hollow metal rod with a sharp point, which is part of a medical instrument called a syringe. It is used to put a drug into someone's body, or to take blood out. 注射針 □ *...the transmission of the AIDS virus through dirty needles.* 不潔な注射針を通してエイズウィルスに感染 **3** N-COUNT 可算名詞 Knitting **needles** are thin sticks that are used for knitting. They are usually made of plastic or metal and have a point at one end. 編み棒，編み針 □ *...a pair of knitting needles.* 1組の編み針 **4** N-COUNT 可算名詞 A **needle** is a thin metal rod with a point which is put into a patient's body during acupuncture. (針治療の) 針 □ *I gave Kevin a course of acupuncture using six needles strategically placed on the scalp.* 私はケビンの頭皮に戦略的に6本の針を使って針治療をした． **5** N-COUNT 可算名詞 On an instrument which measures something such as speed or weight, the **needle** is the long strip of metal or plastic on the dial that moves backward and forward, showing the measurement. (計器などの) 針 □ *She kept looking at the dial on the boiler. The needle had reached 250 degrees.* 彼女はボイラーのメモリをしっかりと見ていた．針が250度に達した． **6** N-COUNT 可算名詞 The **needles** of a fir or pine tree are its thin, hard, pointed leaves. (針葉樹の) 針 □ *The carpet of pine needles was soft underfoot.* 松葉のじゅうたんが足の下で柔らかった．

need|less /niːdlɪs/ ADJ 形容詞 Something that is **needless** is completely unnecessary. 無駄な，不必要な □ *But his death was so needless.* しかし彼の死は全く無駄だった． ● **need|less|ly** ADV 副詞 無駄に，不必要に □ *Half a million women die needlessly each year during childbirth.* 毎年，50万人の女性が出産中に不必要に死亡する．

needn't /niːdənt/ **Needn't** is the usual spoken form of "need not." "need not"の短縮形

needy /niːdi/ (**needier, neediest**) ADJ 形容詞 **Needy** people do not have enough food, medicine, or clothing, or adequate houses. 貧窮している，貧困の □ *...a multinational force aimed at ensuring that food and medicine get to needy Somalis.* 貧困しているソマリア族に食料や医薬品を必ず届けるようにすることが目的の多国籍軍 ● N-PLURAL 複数名詞 **The needy** are people who are needy. 貧困者 □ *There will be efforts to get larger amounts of food to the needy.* 貧困者への食糧援助を増加する努力がなされるだろう．

ne|gate /nɪgeɪt/ (**negates, negating, negated**) **1** V-T 他動詞 If one thing **negates** another, it causes that other thing to lose the effect or value that it had. 無効にする [FORMAL 形式ばった] □ *These weaknesses negated his otherwise progressive attitude towards the staff.* これらの弱点により職員に対するそれ以外の前向きな態度が台無しに

なっている. ■ V-T 他動詞 If someone **negates** something, they say that it does not exist. 否定する, 否認する [FORMAL 形式ばった] □ *He warned that to negate the results of elections would only make things worse.* 選挙結果を否認することは事態を悪化させることにしかならないと彼は警告した.

nega|tive /nέgətɪv/ (**negatives**) ■ ADJ 形容詞 A fact, situation, or experience that is **negative** is unpleasant, depressing, or harmful. 不快な, 有害な □ *The news from overseas is overwhelmingly negative.* 海外からのニュースは圧倒的に暗い. ● **nega|tive|ly** ADV 副詞 [ADV with v] 悪く, 有害に □ *This will negatively affect the result over the first half of the year.* これは年の前半の結果に悪影響を及ぼすだろう. ■ ADJ 形容詞 If someone is **negative** or has a **negative** attitude, they consider only the bad aspects of a situation, rather than the good ones. 否定的な □ *When asked for your views about your current job, on no account must you be negative about it.* 現在の仕事についての感想を聞かれたし, 決して否定的なことを言ってはならない. ● **nega|tive|ly** ADV 副詞 否定的に □ *A few weeks later he said that maybe he viewed all his relationships rather negatively.* 数週間後に彼は, 全ての人間関係をやや否定的に考えていたかもしれないと言った. ● **nega|tiv|ity** /nὲgətɪvɪti/ N-UNCOUNT 不可算名詞 否定的な態度 □ *I loathe negativity. I can't stand people who moan.* 否定的な態度が大嫌いだ. 愚痴をこぼす人が我慢できない. ■ ADJ 形容詞 A **negative** reply or decision indicates the answer "no." 否定の, 不同意の □ *Dr. Velayati gave a vague but negative response.* ベラヤチ先生はあいまいだが否定的な回答をした. □ *Upon a negative decision, the applicant loses the protection offered by Belgian law.* 否定判決により, 申請者はベルギーの法律による保護を失う. ● **nega|tive|ly** ADV 副詞 [ADV after v] 否定的に □ *Sixty percent of people answered negatively.* 60％が否定的な回答をした. ■ N-COUNT 可算名詞 A **negative** is a word, expression, or gesture that means "no" or "not." 否定の言葉・表現・しぐさ □ *In the past we have heard only negatives when it came to following a healthy diet.* かつては, 健康食を摂取する話になると否定の言葉しか聞こえなかった. ■ ADJ 形容詞 In grammar, a **negative** clause contains a word such as "not," "never," or "no one." 否定の ■ ADJ 形容詞 If a medical test or scientific test is **negative**, it shows no evidence of the medical condition or substance that you are looking for. 陰性の □ *So far 57 have taken the test and all have been negative.* これまでのところ, 57名が検査を受け全員が陰性だった. ■ HIV **negative** → see HIV ■ N-COUNT 可算名詞 In photography, a **negative** is an image that shows dark areas as light and light areas as dark. Negatives are made from camera film, and are used to print photographs. ネガ, 陰画 □ *...negatives of Diana's wedding dress.* ダイアナ妃のウェディングドレスの写真のネガ ■ ADJ 形容詞 A **negative** charge or current has the same electrical charge as an electron. 負の, マイナスの □ *Stimulate the injury or site of greatest pain with a small negative current.* 傷口や激しい痛みの箇所を弱いマイナス電流で刺激しなさい. ● **nega|tive|ly** ADV 副詞 [ADV -ed] 負に帯電して □ *As these electrons are negatively charged they will attempt to repel each other.* これらの電子が負に帯電しているので互いに反発しようとするだろう. ■ ADJ 形容詞 A **negative** number, quantity, or measurement is less than zero. マイナスの, 負の □ *Difficult texts record a positive score and simple ones score negative numbers.* 難解な文には得点が与えられ, 簡易な文は減点となる. ■ PHRASE 句 If an answer is **in the negative**, it is "no" or means "no." 否定して, 拒否して □ *The Council answered those questions in the negative.* 枢密院はこれらの質問に否定の返答をした.

→ see **lightning, magnet**

ne|glect /nɪglέkt/ (**neglects, neglecting, neglected**) ■ V-T 他動詞 If you **neglect** someone or something, you fail to take care of them properly. 〜の世話をおろそかにする □ *The woman denied that she had neglected her child.* その女性は子供を放ったらかしにしなかったと言った. □ *Feed plants and they grow, neglect them and they suffer.* 植物に肥料を与えると成長するし, なおざりにすると育たない. ● N-UNCOUNT 不可算名詞 **Neglect** is also a noun. 放置 □ *The town's old quayside is collapsing after years of neglect.* 町の古い波止場地帯は長年の放置の末, 崩壊しつつある. ■ V-T 他動詞 If you **neglect** someone or something, you fail to give them the amount of attention that they deserve. 軽視する □ *He'd given too much to his career, worked long hours, neglected her.* 彼は仕事に熱心になりすぎ, 長時間労働をし, 彼女をほったらかしにしていた. ● **ne|glect|ed** ADJ 形容詞 無視された, 忘れ去られた □ *The fact that she is not coming today makes her grandmother feel lonely and neglected.* 彼女が今日来ないためにおばあさんは寂しく孤独を感じた. □ *...a neglected aspect of the city's forgotten history.* 町の忘れられていた歴史の看過されていた1面 ■ V-T 他動詞 If you **neglect to** do something that you ought to

do or **neglect** your duty, you fail to do it. 〜するのを怠る □ *We often neglect to make proper use of our bodies.* しばしば自分の体をきちんと使うのを怠る.

neg|li|gence /nέglɪdʒ³ns/ N-UNCOUNT 不可算名詞 If someone is guilty of **negligence**, they have failed to do something which they ought to do. 過失, 怠慢 [FORMAL 形式ばった] □ *The soldiers were ordered to appear before a disciplinary council on charges of negligence.* 兵士は職務怠慢のために査問委員会への出頭命令が出た.

neg|li|gent /nέglɪdʒ³nt/ ADJ 形容詞 If someone in a position of responsibility is **negligent**, they do not do something which they ought to do. 怠って, 怠慢な □ *The jury determined that the airline was negligent in training and supervising the crew.* 陪審は, その航空会社が乗務員の研修・指導に怠慢であったという判決を下した. ● **neg|li|gent|ly** ADV 副詞 [ADV with v] 怠慢に □ *A manufacturer negligently made and marketed a car with defective brakes.* 製造会社がブレーキに欠陥のある自動車を怠慢に製造し販売した.

neg|li|gible /nέglɪdʒɪb³l/ ADJ 形容詞 An amount or effect that is **negligible** is so small that it is not worth considering or worrying about. 取るに足らない □ *The pay that the soldiers received was negligible.* 兵士が受け取った報酬はごくわずかだった.

ne|go|tiable /nɪgoʊʃiəb³l, -ʃəb³l/ ADJ 形容詞 Something that is **negotiable** can be changed or agreed upon when people discuss it. 交渉の余地がある □ *He warned that his economic program for the country was not negotiable.* 彼は, 国の経済計画には交渉の余地がないことを警告した.

ne|go|ti|ate /nɪgoʊʃieɪt/ (**negotiates, negotiating, negotiated**) ■ V-RECIP 相互動詞 If people **negotiate with** each other or **negotiate** an agreement, they talk about a problem or a situation such as a business arrangement in order to solve the problem or complete the arrangement. 交渉する □ *It is not clear whether the president is willing to negotiate with the Democrats.* 大統領は民主党員と協議する意思があるのかどうかは明らかではありません. □ *When you have two adversaries negotiating, you need to be on neutral territory.* 敵対する2者を交渉させる場合, 中立の立場をとる必要がある. □ *The local government and the army negotiated a truce.* 地方政府と軍隊は停戦の交渉をしました. □ *Western governments have this week urged him to negotiate and avoid force.* 西洋諸国の政府は今週彼に交渉により軍事行動を避けるように要請した. ■ V-T 他動詞 If you **negotiate** an area of land, a place, or an obstacle, you successfully travel across it or around it. うまく通り抜ける □ *Frank Mariano negotiates the desert terrain in his battered pickup.* フランク・マリアノはボロボロのトラックで砂漠地域を乗り越えました. □ *I negotiated the corner on my motorcycle and pulled to a stop.* カーブをオートバイでうまく切り抜け, 停止した.

ne|go|ti|at|ing ta|ble N-SING 単数名詞 If you say that people are at the **negotiating table**, you mean that they are having discussions in order to settle a dispute or reach an agreement. 交渉の席 □ *"We want to settle all matters at the negotiating table," he said.* 「交渉の席で全ての問題に終止符を打ちたい」と彼は言った.

ne|go|tia|tion /nɪgoʊʃieɪʃ³n/ (**negotiations**) N-VAR 可変性名詞 **Negotiations** are formal discussions between people who have different aims or intentions, especially in business or politics, during which they try to reach an agreement. 交渉 □ *Warren said, "We have had meaningful negotiations and I believe we are very close to a deal."* ウォレンはこう言った. 「とても有意義な話し合いが持たれ, 取引成立まであと1歩だと思う」

ne|go|tia|tor /nɪgoʊʃieɪtər/ (**negotiators**) N-COUNT 可算名詞 **Negotiators** are people who take part in political or financial negotiations. 交渉者, 協議者 □ *On Thursday night the rebels' chief negotiator at the peace talks announced that dialogue had gone as far as it could go.* 木曜夜, 和平交渉の場で反乱軍の交渉責任者は話し合いが尽きたと発言した.

neigh|bor /nέɪbər/ (**neighbors**) ■ N-COUNT 可算名詞 Your **neighbor** is someone who lives near you. 隣人, 近所の人 □ *My neighbor spies on me through a crack in the fence.* 隣人が塀の割れ目からのぞき見をしている. ■ N-COUNT 可算名詞 You can refer to the person who is standing or sitting next to you as your **neighbor**. 隣席の人 □ *The woman prodded her neighbor and whispered urgently in his ear.* その女性は隣席の人をつついて切迫した様子で耳元にささや

n

いた。 ❸ N-COUNT 可算名詞 You can refer to something which stands next to something else of the same kind as its **neighbor**. 隣一 ❏...its big oil-rich neighbor. 隣の石油大国

neigh|bor|hood /nˈeɪbərhʊd/ (**neighborhoods**) ❶ N-COUNT 可算名詞 A **neighborhood** is one of the parts of a town where people live. 地区 ❏ There is no neighborhood which is really safe. 本当に安全な地区というのはありません。 ❷ N-COUNT 可算名詞 The **neighborhood** of a place or person is the area or the people around them. 近所、近所の人 ❏...a suburban Boston neighborhood close to where I live. 私が住んでいるところに近いボストン郊外周辺 ❸ PHRASE 句 **In the neighborhood of** a number means approximately that number. 約一 ❏ The album's now sold something in the neighborhood of 2 million copies. そのアルバムはすでに約200万枚ほど売れました。 ❹ PHRASE 句 A place that is **in the neighborhood of** another place is near it. 一の近くに ❏ We went to visit two charming young ladies who lived in the neighborhood of our camp. 我々のテントの近くに住んでいる2人の魅力的な若い女性を訪ねに行った。

neigh|bor|ing /nˈeɪbərɪŋ/ ADJ 形容詞 **Neighboring** places or things are near other things of the same kind. 近くの [ADJ n] ❏ He is on his way back to Beijing after a tour of neighboring Asian capitals. 彼は、近隣のアジア諸国の首都を訪れたあと北京に戻る途中です。

nei|ther /nˈiðər, nˈaɪ-/ ❶ CONJ 接続詞 You use **neither** in front of the first of two or more words or expressions when you are linking two or more things which are not true or do not happen. The other thing is introduced by "nor." 一も一も一ない ❏ Professor Hisamatsu spoke neither English nor German. 久松教授は英語もドイツ語も話さなかった。 ❷ DET 限定詞 You use **neither** to refer to each of two things or people, when you are making a negative statement that includes both of them. どちらの一も一ない ❏ At first, neither man could speak. まず、どちらの男も話せなかった。 ● QUANT-NEG 否定数量詞 **Neither** is also a quantifier. どちらの一も一ない ❏ Neither of us felt like going out. 私たち2人とも出かける気はしなかった。 ● PRON-NEG 否定代名詞 **Neither** is also a pronoun. どちらも一ない ❏ They both smiled; neither seemed likely to be aware of my absence for long. 2人ともにっこりと微笑んだ。どちらも私がいないことにしばらく気付かなかったようだ。 ❸ CONJ 接続詞 If you say that one person or thing does not do something and **neither** does another, what you say is true of all the people or things that you are mentioning. 一もまた一ない ❏ I never learned to swim and neither did they. 私は泳ぎを習ったことがないし、彼らもなかった。 ❹ CONJ 接続詞 You use **neither** after a negative statement to emphasize that you are introducing another negative statement. また一もない [FORMAL 形式ばった] ❏ I can't ever recall Dad hugging me. Neither did I sit on his knee. 父親が私を抱きしめたことなど全然思い出せない。また、父のひざに座ったこともない。

neon /nˈiɒn/ ❶ ADJ 形容詞 **Neon** lights or signs are made from glass tubes filled with neon gas which produce a bright electric light. ネオンの [ADJ n] ❏ In the city squares the neon lights flashed in turn. 街の広場ではネオンの光が交互に点滅した。 ❷ N-UNCOUNT 不可算名詞 **Neon** is a gas which occurs in very small amounts in the atmosphere. ネオン ❏ Inert gases like neon and argon have eight electrons in their outer shell. ネオンやアルゴンのような不活性ガスには最外殻に8つの電子がある。

neph|ew /nˈɛfyu/ (**nephews**) N-COUNT 可算名詞 Someone's **nephew** is the son of their sister or brother. おい ❏ I am planning a 25th birthday party for my nephew. おいの25歳の誕生パーティーを企画している。

nerve /nˈɜrv/ (**nerves**) ❶ N-COUNT 可算名詞 **Nerves** are long thin fibers that transmit messages between your brain and other parts of your body. 神経 ❏...spinal nerves. せき髄神経 ❷ N-PLURAL 複数名詞 If you refer to someone's **nerves**, you mean their ability to cope with problems such as stress, worry, and danger. 神

経 ❏ Jill's nerves are stretched to breaking point. ジルの神経はぎりぎりまで張りつめている。 ❸ N-PLURAL 複数名詞 You can refer to someone's feelings of anxiety or tension as **nerves**. 不安、緊張感 ❏ I just played badly. It wasn't nerves. うまくプレーができなかっただけです。緊張していたんじゃない。 ❹ N-UNCOUNT 不可算名詞 **Nerve** is the courage that you need in order to do something difficult or dangerous. 勇気 ❏ The brandy made him choke, but it restored his nerve. ブランディで彼はむせたが、おかげで勇気を取り戻した。 ❺ PHRASE 句 If someone or something **gets on** your **nerves**, they annoy or irritate you. しゃくに触る、イライラさせる [INFORMAL くだけた] ❏ Lately he hasn't done a thing and it's getting on my nerves. 最近彼は何一つしていなくてしゃくに触るの。 ❻ PHRASE 句 If you say that someone **has a nerve** or **has the nerve** to do something, you are criticizing them for doing something which you feel they had no right to do. 厚かましい、ずうずうしい [INFORMAL くだけた, DISAPPROVAL 不賛成] ❏ He told his critics they had a nerve complaining about him. 批評家が彼について苦情を言うのは厚かましいと彼は言った。 ❼ PHRASE 句 If you **lose** your **nerve**, you suddenly panic and become too afraid to do something that you were about to do. 気後れする ❏ The bomber had lost his nerve and fled. 爆弾テロリストはおじけづいて逃げた。
→ see **ear, eye, nervous system, smell**

nerv|ous /nˈɜrvəs/ ❶ ADJ 形容詞 If someone is **nervous**, they are frightened or worried about something that is happening or might happen, and show this in their behavior. 不安な、神経質になっている ❏ The party has become deeply nervous about its prospects of winning the next election. 党は次回選挙での当選の見込みに関して神経をとがらせてきた。 ● **nerv|ous|ly** ADV 副詞 [ADV with v] 不安そうに ❏ Brunhilde stood up nervously as the men came into the room. 男たちが部屋に入ってくると、ブルンヒルデは不安そうに立ち上がった。 ● **nerv|ous|ness** N-UNCOUNT 不可算名詞 不安 ❏ I smiled warmly so he wouldn't see my nervousness. 私は彼に不安な気持ちを見破られないように優しく微笑んだ。 ❷ ADJ 形容詞 A **nervous** person is very tense and easily upset. 神経質な、心配性な ❏ She was apparently a very nervous woman, and that affected her career. 彼女は明らかにとても神経質な女性で、そのことが仕事に影響した。 ❸ ADJ 形容詞 [ADJ n] A **nervous** illness or condition is one that affects your emotions and your mental state. 神経性の ❏ The number of nervous disorders was rising in the region. 神経症がその地域で増加している。

nerv|ous break|down (**nervous breakdowns**) N-COUNT 可算名詞 If someone has a **nervous breakdown**, they become extremely depressed and cannot cope with their normal life. 神経衰弱、ノイローゼ ❏ His wife would not be able to cope and might suffer a nervous breakdown. 彼の妻はうまくやっていけず、ノイローゼになるかもしれない。

nerv|ous sys|tem (**nervous systems**) N-COUNT 可算名詞 Your **nervous system** consists of all the nerves in your body together with your brain and spinal cord. 神経系 ❏ So it is possible that the symptoms will not finally go until your nervous system is in a better state. そういう訳で、神経系が回復するまで症状が完全には治まらない可能性がある。
→ see Word Web: **nervous system**

nest /nˈɛst/ (**nests, nesting, nested**) ❶ N-COUNT 可算名詞 A bird's **nest** is the home that it makes to lay its eggs in. (鳥の) 巣 ❏ I can see an eagle's nest on the rocks. 岩の上にたかの巣が見える。 ❷ V-I 自動詞 When a bird **nests** somewhere, it builds a nest and settles there to lay its eggs. 巣を作る ❏ Some species may nest in close proximity to each other. 互いに近い場所に巣を作ろうとする種がある。 ❸ N-COUNT 可算名詞 A **nest** is a home that a group of insects or other creatures make in order to live in and give birth to their young in. (昆虫・小動物などの) 巣 ❏ Some solitary bees make their nests in burrows in the soil. 単独性のハチによっては土壌に巣穴を作る。
→ see **bird**

nes|tle /nˈɛsəl/ (**nestles, nestling, nestled**) ❶ V-T/V-I 他動詞/自動詞 If you **nestle** or **are nestled** somewhere, you move into a comfortable position, usually by pressing against someone or against something soft. 心地よく身を落ち着ける ❏ John took one

Word Web   nervous system

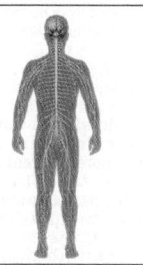

The body's **nervous system** is a two-way road which transmits electrochemical messages to and from various parts of the body. **Sensory neurons** carry information from both inside and outside the body to the **central nervous system** (CNS) which consists of the **brain** and the **spinal cord**. Motor neurons carry impulses from the CNS to **organs** and to **muscles** such as the muscles in the hand, telling them how to move. Sensory and motor neurons are bound together, creating **nerves** that run throughout the body.

---

child into the crook of each arm and let them nestle against him. ジョンはそれぞれの腕に子供を1人ずつ抱き、彼にもたれて休ませた. **2** V-I 自動詞 If something such as a building **nestles** somewhere, it is in that place and seems safe or sheltered. 抱かれている ❏ *Nearby, nestling in the hills, was the children's home.* 近くの丘陵地に囲まれた所に子供たちの家があった.

net
❶ NOUN AND VERB USES
❷ ADJECTIVE AND ADVERB USES

❶ net /nɛt/ (**nets, netting, netted**) **1** N-UNCOUNT 不可算名詞 **Net** is a kind of cloth that you can see through. It is made of fine threads woven together so that there are small equal spaces between them. レース, 網 **2** N-COUNT 可算名詞 A **net** is a piece of netting which is used as a protective covering for something, for example to protect vegetables from birds. (鳥などを防ぐ) 網, ネット ❏ *I threw aside my mosquito net, jumped out of bed and drew up the blind.* 蚊帳を投げ出し, ベッドから飛び出してブラインドを開けた. **3** N-COUNT 可算名詞 A **net** is a piece of netting which is used for catching fish, insects, or animals. (魚・虫・動物などを捕まえる) 網, ネット ❏ *Several fishermen sat on wooden barrels, tending their nets.* 数人の漁夫が木の樽に座り, 漁網の手入れをしていた. **4** V-T 他動詞 If you **net** a fish or other animal, you catch it in a net. 網で捕る ❏ *I'm quite happy to net a fish and then let it go.* 網で魚を捕って逃がしてあげるのが好きだ. **5** V-T 他動詞 If you **net** something, you manage to get it, especially by using skill. 獲得する ❏ *Two fourth-quarter drives netted a grand total of 21 yards.* 第4クォーターでの2回のドライブで合計21ヤード進んだ. **6** V-T 他動詞 If you **net** a particular amount of money, you gain it as profit after all expenses have been paid. 純益を上げる ❏ *He netted profit of $1.85 billion from these large sales of stock.* 彼は株を3回に分けて販売し18億5千万ドルの純益を上げた. **7** N-SING 単数名詞 **The Net** is the same as the **Internet**. インターネット **8** → see also **safety net**
→ see **fish, tennis**

❷ net /nɛt/ **1** ADJ 形容詞 A **net** amount is one which remains when everything that should be subtracted from it has been subtracted. 正味の, 純~ [ADJ n, v-link ADJ 'of' n] ❏ *...a rise in sales and net profit.* 売上高と純利益の増加 ❏ *What you actually receive is net of deductions.* 実際に受け取るのは控除を差し引いた金額だ. ● ADV 副詞 **Net** is also an adverb. 手取りで, 税引き後で ❏ *Balances of $5,000 and above will earn 11 percent gross, 8.25 percent net.* 残高が5000ドル以上の場合, 税込みで11%, 税引き後で8.25%の利率だ. ❏ *They pay him around $2 million net.* 彼の収入は手取りで約200万ドルだ. **2** ADJ 形容詞 The **net** weight of something is its weight without its container or the material that has been used to wrap it. 正味の [ADJ n] ❏ *...350 mg net weight.* 正味重量350mg **3** ADJ 形容詞 A **net** result is a final result after all the details have been considered or included. 最終的な [ADJ n] ❏ *There has been a net gain in jobs in our country.* 当国での最終的な仕事数は増加した.

Word Partnership   net は次の語句と使われる:

N.	**fishing** net ❶ **3**
V.	**access** the Net, **surf** the Net, Net **users** ❶ **7**
N.	net **earnings**, net **income/loss**, net **proceeds**, net **profit**, net **revenue** ❷ **1**
	net **gain**, net **increase**, net **result** ❷ **1 3**

nett /nɛt/ → see **net ❷**

net|tle /nɛtˀl/ (**nettles, nettling, nettled**) **1** N-COUNT 可算名詞 **Nettles** are wild plants which have leaves covered with fine hairs that sting you when you touch them. イラクサ ❏ *The nettles stung their legs.* イラクサに足を刺された. **2** V-T 他動詞 If you **are nettled** by something, you are annoyed or offended by it. いらいらさせる, 怒らせる [他動詞] ❏ *He was nettled by her manner.* 彼は彼女の態度にいらついた.

net|work /nɛtwɜrk/ (**networks, networking, networked**) **1** N-COUNT 可算名詞 A radio or television **network** is a company

or group of companies that broadcast radio or television programs throughout an area. 放送網, ネットワーク ❏ *Los Angeles-based Univision is a Spanish-language broadcast television network.* ロサンゼルスに拠点を置くユニビジョン社はスペイン語放送のテレビ放送網だ. **2** N-COUNT 可算名詞 A **network of** people or institutions is a large number of them that have a connection with each other and work together as a system. つながり, 人脈 ❏ *Distribution of the food is going ahead using a network of local church people and other volunteers.* 地元の教会関係者や他のボランティアの人脈を通じて食料の配給が進んでいる. **3** N-COUNT 可算名詞 A particular **network** is a system of things which are connected and which operate together. For example, a **computer network** consists of a number of computers that are part of the same system. (コンピュータの) ネットワーク ❏ *...a computer network with 154 terminals.* 154機の端末に接続しているコンピュータ・ネットワーク **4** N-COUNT 可算名詞 A **network of** lines, roads, veins, or other long thin things is a large number of them which cross each other or meet at many points. 網状組織, 一網 ❏ *...Strasbourg, with its rambling network of medieval streets.* 中世の道路網が広がるストラスブール **5** V-I 自動詞 If you **network**, you try to meet new people who might be useful to you in your job. ネットワークを作る, 人脈を築く [BUSINESS 実業] ❏ *In business, it is important to network with as many people as possible on a face to face basis.* ビジネスでは, 実際にできるだけ多くの人に会って人脈を築くことが重要だ.
→ see **Internet**

Word Partnership   network は次の語句と使われる:

N.	**broadcast** network, **cable** network, **radio** network, **television/TV** network **1**
	network **administrator**, **computer** network, network **coverage**, network **support** **3**
ADJ.	**extensive** network, **nationwide** network, **vast** network, **worldwide** network **1 – 4**
	wireless network **3**

net|work|ing /nɛtwɜrkɪŋ/ **1** N-UNCOUNT 不可算名詞 **Networking** is the process of trying to meet new people who might be useful to you in your job, often through social activities. ネットワーク作り, 情報交換網 [BUSINESS 実業] ❏ *If executives fail to exploit the opportunities of networking they risk being left behind.* 幹部社員がネットワーキングの機会を利用しそこなったら, 取り残される危険がある. **2** N-UNCOUNT 不可算名詞 You can refer to the things associated with a computer system or the process of establishing such a system as **networking**. ネットワーキング ❏ *Managers have learned to grapple with networking, artificial intelligence, computer-aided engineering and manufacturing.* 経営陣はネットワーキング・人工知能・コンピュータ援用エンジニアリング・製造に取り組むようになった.

Word Link   otic ≈ affecting, causing : erotic, neurotic, patriotic

neu|rot|ic /nʊərɒtɪk/ (**neurotics**) ADJ 形容詞 If you say that someone is **neurotic**, you mean that they are always frightened or worried about things that you consider unimportant. 神経質な, 神経過敏な [DISAPPROVAL 不賛成] ❏ *He was almost neurotic about being followed.* 彼は尾行されていることに関してノイローゼ気味だった. ● N-COUNT 可算名詞 A **neurotic** is someone who is neurotic. 神経症患者, 神経質な人 ❏ *These patients are not neurotics.* これらの患者は神経症ではない.

neu|tral /nᵘtrəl/ (**neutrals**) **1** ADJ 形容詞 If a person or country adopts a **neutral** position or remains **neutral**, they do not support anyone in a disagreement, war, or contest. 中立の ❏ *Let's meet on neutral territory.* 中立地域で会談しよう. ● N-COUNT 可算名詞 A **neutral** is someone who is neutral. 中立者 ❏ *It was a good game to watch for the neutrals.* 中立者が観戦するにはいい試合だった. ● **neu|tral|i|ty** /nᵘtrælɪti/ N-UNCOUNT 不可算名詞 ❏ *...a reputation for political neutrality and impartiality.* 政治的に中立し公平だという評判 **2** ADJ 形容詞 If someone speaks in a **neutral** voice or if the expression on their face is **neutral**, they do not show what they are thinking or feeling. 淡々とした, 感情を表さ

ない ▢*Isabel put her magazine down and said in a neutral voice, "You're very late, darling."* イザベルは雑誌を置いて、淡々とした声で言った. 「あなた、とても遅かったのね」 ●**neu│tral│ity** N-UNCOUNT 不可算名詞 *I noticed, behind the neutrality of his gaze, a deep weariness.* 私は、彼の無感情な視線の陰の深い疲労感に気付いた. ❸ ADJ 形容詞 If you say that something is **neutral**, you mean that it does not have any effect on other things because it lacks any significant qualities of its own, or it is an equal balance of two or more different qualities, amounts, or ideas. 中間の、際立った特徴のない ▢*Three in every five interviewed felt that the budget was neutral and they would be no better off.* インタビューに答えた中で5人に3人は、新予算には際立った特徴がなく暮らし向きがよくなるということはないと感じていた. ❹ N-UNCOUNT 不可算名詞 **Neutral** is the position between the gears of a vehicle such as a car, in which the gears are not connected to the engine. ニュートラル ▢*Graham put the van in neutral and jumped out into the road.* グレハムはバンのギアをニュートラルに入れ、道路に飛び出した. ❺ ADJ 形容詞 In an electrical device or system, the **neutral** wire is one of the three wires needed to complete the circuit so that the current can flow. The other two wires are called the ground wire and the live or positive wire. （電気の）中性の ▢*The ground wire in the house is connected to the neutral wire.* 住宅のアース線は中性線に接続している. ❻ COLOR 色彩語 **Neutral** is used to describe things that have a pale color such as cream or gray, or that have no color at all. 中間の ▢*At the horizon the land mass becomes a continuous pale neutral gray, almost blending with the sky.* 地平線上では、広い陸地が淡い中間的な灰色でどこまでも続き、空と混じり合っているようだ. ❼ ADJ 形容詞 In chemistry, **neutral** is used to describe things that are neither acid nor alkaline. （化学的に）中性の ▢*Pure water is neutral with a pH of 7.* 純水はpH値が7の中性である.
→ see **war**

neu│tral│ize /nʌ́trəlaɪz/ (**neutralizes, neutralizing, neutralized**) ❶ V-T 他動詞 To **neutralize** something means to prevent it from having any effect or from working properly. 無効にする、相殺する ▢*The U.S. is trying to neutralize the resolution in the UN Security Council.* 米国は国連安保理決議を無効にしようとしています. ❷ V-T 他動詞 When a chemical substance **neutralizes** an acid, it makes it less acid. 中和する ▢*Antacids are alkaline and they relieve pain by neutralizing acid in the contents of the stomach.* 制酸剤はアルカリ性で胃酸を中和することにより痛みを和らげる.

nev│er /névər/ ❶ ADV 副詞 **Never** means at no time in the past or at no time in the future. これまで一度もーしたことがない、決してーない ▢*I have never lost the weight I put on in my teens.* 10代の頃に増えた体重を落としたことがない. ▢*Never had he been so free of worry.* 彼にこれほど心配事がないのは初めてだ. ▢*That was a mistake. We'll never do it again.* それは間違いでした. 二度と繰り返しません. ❷ ADV 副詞 **Never** means "not in any circumstances at all." 決してーない ▢*I would never do anything to hurt him.* 決して彼を傷つけるようなことはしない. ▢*Divorce is never easy for children.* 離婚は子供にとって決してたやすくはない. ❸ PHRASE 句 **Never ever** is an emphatic way of saying "never." (neverの強調) 絶対にーない ▢*I never, ever sit around thinking, "What shall I do next?"* 私は、ブラブラしながら「次は何をしようかしら」と考えるようなことは絶対にしない. ❹ ADV 副詞 **Never** is used to refer to the past and means "not." これまでーしたことがない ▢*He never achieved anything.* 彼はこれまで何かを成し遂げたことがない. ▢*I never knew him.* 私は今まで彼のことを知らなかった. ❺ **never mind** → see **mind**

never-ending ADJ 形容詞 If you describe something bad or unpleasant as **never-ending**, you are emphasizing that it seems to last a very long time. 終わりのない[EMPHASIS 強調] ▢*...a never-ending series of scandals rocking the presidency.* 大統領を揺さぶる終わりのないー連のスキャンダル

never│the│less /nèvərðəlés/ ADV 副詞 You use **nevertheless** when saying something that contrasts with what has just been said. それにもかかわらず、[FORMAL 形式ばった][ADV with cl] ▢*Although the market has been flat, residential property costs remain high. Nevertheless, the fall-off in demand has had an impact on resale values.* 市場は低迷しているが、住宅価格は依然として高い. それでも、需要の減少が再販価格に影響を与えた.

new /nu/ (**newer, newest**) ❶ ADJ 形容詞 Something that is **new** has been recently created, built, or invented or is in the process of being created, built, or invented. 新しい、新築の ▢*They've just opened a new hotel in the area.* その地域に新しいホテルをオープンしたばかりだ. ▢*These ideas are nothing new.* これらの考えは全く斬新（ざんしん）さがない. ❷ ADJ 形容詞 Something that is **new** has not been used or owned by anyone. 新しい、新品の ▢*That afternoon she went out and bought a new dress.* その日の午後、彼女は外出し新しいドレスを買った. ▢*There are many boats, new and used, for sale.* 新品、中古を含めて多くのボートが売り出し中だ. ❸ ADJ 形容詞 You use **new** to describe something which has replaced another thing, for example because you no longer have the old one, or it no longer exists, or it is no longer useful. 新しい（従来のものとは違う）▢*Under the new rules, some factories will cut emissions by as much as 90 percent.* 新規定の下では、工場によっては排気ガスを最高90%に

減します. ▢*I had to find somewhere new to live.* 私はどこか新しい住まいを見つけなければならなかった. ▢*Rachel has a new boyfriend.* レイチェルには新しい彼氏がいる. ❹ ADJ 形容詞 **New** is used to describe something that has only recently been discovered or noticed. 新たな、新しい ▢*The new planet is about ten times the size of the earth.* 新たな惑星は地球の約10倍の大きさだ. ❺ ADJ 形容詞 A **new** day or year is the beginning of the next day or year. 新しい、新たに始まる[ADJ n] ▢*The start of a new year is a good time to reflect on the many achievements of the past.* 新年の始まりは、過去の数々の業績を振り返るにちょうどよい. ❻ ADJ 形容詞 **New** is used to describe someone or something that has recently acquired a particular status or position. 新米の、新ー[ADJ n] ▢*...the usual exhaustion of a new mother.* 新米の母親によくある極度の疲労 ❼ ADJ 形容詞 If you are **new to** a situation or place, or if the situation or place is **new to** you, you have not previously seen it or had any experience with it. 目新しい、未経験の [v-link ADJ] ▢*She wasn't new to the company.* 彼女は新入社員ではなかった. ▢*His name was new to me then and it stayed in my mind.* 彼の名前はそのとき初耳で、頭に残った. ❽ ADJ 形容詞 **New** potatoes, carrots, or peas are produced early in the season for such vegetables and are usually small with a sweet flavor. 初物の、新ー[ADJ n] ▢*Serve with a salad and new potatoes.* サラダと新ジャガを添えて出しなさい. ❾ → see also **brand-new** ❿ **as good as new** → see **good**

new blood N-UNCOUNT 不可算名詞 If people talk about bringing **new blood** into an organization or onto a sports team, they are referring to new people who are likely to improve the organization or team. 新勢力、新進気鋭 ▢*We'll get some new blood in there.* 新勢力を入れる予定です.

new│born /núbɔrn/ (**newborns**) ADJ 形容詞 A **newborn** baby or animal is one that has just been born. 生まれたばかりの、新生の ▢*The electronic sensor has been adapted to fit on a newborn baby.* 電子感知器が新生児に取り付けるように改造されました. ● N-PLURAL 複数名詞 **The newborn** are babies or animals who are newborn. 新生児、生まれたばかりの赤ちゃん ▢*Mild jaundice in the newborn is common and often clears without treatment.* 新生児の軽い黄だんはよくあることで、治療なしに治まることが多い.

new│comer /núkʌmər/ (**newcomers**) N-COUNT 可算名詞 A **newcomer** is a person who has recently arrived in a place, joined an organization, or started a new activity. 新人、新入り、新顔 ▢*He must be a newcomer to town and he obviously didn't understand our local customs.* 彼は町の新顔に違いなく、明らかに地元の風習を理解していなかったんだ.

new│found /núfaʊnd/ ADJ 形容詞 A **newfound** quality or ability is one that you have got recently. 新たに得た、新発見の [ADJ n] ▢*His friends have a newfound sense of patriotism.* 彼の友達は新たに愛国心を持ち始めた.

new│ly /núli/ ADV 副詞 **Newly** is used before a past participle or an adjective to indicate that a particular action is very recent, or that a particular state of affairs has very recently begun to exist. 最近、近ごろ [ADV -ed/adj] ▢*She was young at the time, and newly married.* 彼女は当時若くて新婚だった.

news /nuz/ ❶ N-UNCOUNT 不可算名詞 **News** is information about a recently changed situation or a recent event. 知らせ、消息 ▢*We waited and waited for news of him.* 私たちは彼らからの便りを待ち続けた. ▢*They still haven't had any news about when they'll be able to go home.* 彼らがいつ家に帰れるかという知らせは依然としてなかった. ❷ N-UNCOUNT 不可算名詞 **News** is information that is published in newspapers and broadcast on radio and television about recent events in the country or world or in a particular area of activity. ニュース [also 'the' N] ▢*Foreign News is on page 16.* 海外ニュースは16ページに記載. ▢*Those are some of the top stories in the news.* 以上がトップニュースの一部です. ❸ N-SING 単数名詞 **The news** is a television or radio broadcast which consists of information about recent events in the country or the world. ニュース番組 ▢*I heard all about the bombs on the news.* 爆撃についてはすべてニュースで聞いた. ❹ N-UNCOUNT 不可算名詞 If you say that someone or something is **news**, you mean that they are considered to be interesting and important at the moment, and that people want to hear about them on the radio and television and in newspapers. ネタ、興味ある事件 [INFORMAL くだけた] ▢*A murder was big news.* 殺人が大ニュースだった.

Note that, although **news** looks like a plural, it is often in fact an uncount noun. ▢*Good news is always worth waiting for.* You cannot say "a news," but you can say a **piece of news** when you are referring to a particular fact or message. ▢*One of my Dutch colleagues told me a very exciting piece of news.* When you are talking about television and radio news, or newspapers, you can refer to an individual story or report as a **news item**.

5 PHRASE 句 If you say that something is **bad news**, you mean that it will cause you trouble or problems. If you say that something is **good news**, you mean that it will be useful or helpful to you. 悪い知らせ/よい知らせ ❏ *The drop in travel is bad news for the airline industry.* 旅行の減少は航空業界にとっては悪い知らせです. **6** PHRASE 句 If you say that something **is news to** you, you mean that you did not previously know what you have just been told, especially when you are surprised or annoyed about it. 初耳だ ❏ *I'd certainly tell you if I knew anything, but I don't. What you're saying is news to me.* 何か知っていたらちゃんと話すけど、知らないんだ。君が言っていることは初耳なんだ.

Word Partnership   *news* は次の語句と使われる:

ADJ.	**big** news, **grim** news, **sad** news **1**
	latest news **1 2**
V.	**spread** the news, **tell** *someone* the news **1**
	hear the news **1** – **3**
	listen to the news, **watch** the news **3**
N.	news **headlines**, news **media**, news **report**, news **update 2**

news agen|cy (news agencies) N-COUNT 可算名詞 A **news agency** is an organization that gathers news stories from a particular country or from all over the world and supplies them to journalists. 通信社 ❏ *A correspondent for Reuters news agency says he saw a number of demonstrators being beaten.* ロイター通信の特派員によると、多数のデモ参加者が暴行を受けるのを見たという.

news|caster /n<u>u</u>zkæstər/ (newscasters) N-COUNT 可算名詞 A **newscaster** is a person who reads the news on the radio or on television. アナウンサー、ニュースキャスター ❏ *...TV newscaster Barbara Walters.* テレビ・ニュースアナのバーバラ・ウォルターズ

news con|fer|ence (news conferences) N-COUNT 可算名詞 A **news conference** is a meeting held by a famous or important person in which they answer journalists' questions. 記者会見 ❏ *He is due to hold a news conference in about an hour.* 1時間後に記者会見を開く予定です.

news|group /n<u>u</u>zgrup/ (newsgroups) N-COUNT 可算名詞 A **newsgroup** is an Internet site where people can put information and opinions about a particular subject so they can be read by everyone who looks at the site. ニュースグループ ❏ *Surfwatch allows parents to prohibit access to specific web sites, newsgroups, and bulletin boards.* サーフウォッチによって保護者は特定のサイト・ニュースグループ・掲示板へのアクセスを禁止することができる.

news|letter /n<u>u</u>zlɛtər/ (newsletters) N-COUNT 可算名詞 A **newsletter** is one or more printed sheets of paper containing information about an organization that is sent regularly to its members. 会報 ❏ *The organization now has around 18,000 members who receive a quarterly newsletter.* その団体には3か月ごとに会報を受け取る会員が現在1万8千人いる.

news|paper /n<u>u</u>zpeɪpər, n<u>u</u>s-/ (newspapers) **1** N-COUNT 可算名詞 A **newspaper** is a publication consisting of a number of large sheets of folded paper, on which news, advertisements, and other information is printed. 新聞 ❏ *He was carrying a newspaper.* 彼は新聞を持って歩いていた. ❏ *They read their daughter's allegations in the newspaper.* 彼らは娘の申し立てについて新聞で読んだ. **2** N-COUNT 可算名詞 A **newspaper** is an organization that produces a newspaper. 新聞社 ❏ *It is the nation's fastest growing national daily newspaper.* 国内で最も急速に成長している全国日刊紙の出版社だ. **3** N-UNCOUNT 不可算名詞 **Newspaper** consists of pieces of old newspapers, especially when they are being used for another purpose such as wrapping things up. 新聞紙 ❏ *He found two pots, each wrapped in newspaper.* 彼は新聞紙に個別に包まれた鉢を2つ見つけた.
→ see Word Web: **newspaper**
→ see **advertising**

news|print /n<u>u</u>zprɪnt/ **1** N-UNCOUNT 不可算名詞 **Newsprint** is the cheap, fairly rough paper on which newspapers are printed. 新聞印刷用紙 ❏ *...a newsprint warehouse.* 新聞印刷用紙倉庫 **2** N-UNCOUNT 不可算名詞 **Newsprint** is the text that is printed in newspapers. 記事、紙面 ❏ *...the acres of newsprint devoted to Madonna in the past seven days.* この1週間マドンナが紙面をかなりにぎわせた **3** N-UNCOUNT 不可算名詞 **Newsprint** is the ink which is used to print newspapers and magazines. 新聞紙のインク ❏ *They get their hands covered in newsprint.* 彼らの手はインクだらけになる.

news|read|er /n<u>u</u>zridər/ (newsreaders) N-COUNT 可算名詞 A **newsreader** is a person who reads the news on the radio or on television. アナウンサー、ニュースキャスター [BRIT 英国英語; AM newscaster 米国英語 newscaster]

news re|lease (news releases) N-COUNT 可算名詞 A **news release** is a written statement about a matter of public interest which is given to the press by an organization concerned with the matter. プレスリリース [mainly AM 主に米国英語] ❏ *In a news release, the company said it had experienced severe financial problems.* プレスリリースによると、その会社は深刻な財政問題を抱えていたという.

new wave (new waves) N-COUNT 可算名詞 In the arts or in politics, a **new wave** is a group or movement that deliberately introduces new or unconventional ideas instead of using traditional ones. 新傾向、新しい波 ❏ *...the new wave of satirical comedy.* 風刺喜劇の新傾向

New Year **1** N-UNCOUNT 不可算名詞 **New Year** or **the New Year** is the time when people celebrate the start of a year. 新年、正月 [also 'the' N] ❏ *Happy New Year, everyone.* 皆さん、新年おめでとう. ❏ *The restaurant was closed over the New Year.* そのレストランは正月中は閉業していた.

> **New Year's Eve**, the last day of the old year, is known as **Hogmanay** in Scotland, where the festivities are particularly important. Families and friends gather together for the chimes at midnight, and then go "first-footing" – visiting friends and neighbors, and taking along something to drink (often whisky) and a piece of coal which is supposed to bring good luck for the coming year.

2 N-SING 単数名詞 **The New Year** is the first few weeks of a year. 年明け、年初め ❏ *Isabel was expecting their baby in the New Year.* イザベルには年明けに赤ちゃんが生まれる予定だった.

next /n<u>ɛ</u>kst/ **1** ORD 序数詞 The **next** period of time, event, person, or thing is the one that comes immediately after the present one or after the previous one. 次の ❏ *I got up early the next morning.* 翌朝早く起きた. ❏ *...the next available flight.* 次に空いているフライト ❏ *Who will be the next mayor?* 次の市長はだれになるだろうか. **2** DET 限定詞 You use **next** in expressions such as **next Friday**, **next day** and **next year** to refer, for example, to the first Friday, day, or year that comes after the present or previous one. 次の、来ー、翌ー ❏ *Let's plan a big night next week.* 来週、大きな夜のイベントを企画しよう. ❏ *He retires next January.* 彼は来年の1月に退職する. ● ADJ 形容詞 **Next** is also an adjective. 次の、来ー [N ADJ] ❏ *I'll be 26 years old next Friday.* 来週の金曜日に26歳になる. ● PRON 代名詞 **Next** is also a pronoun. 次 ❏ *He predicted that the region's economy would grow by about six percent both this year and next.* 地域の経済は今年と来年ともに約6%成長すると彼は予測した. **3** ADJ 形容詞 The **next** place or person is the one that is nearest to you or that is the first one that you come to. 次の、隣の [det ADJ] ❏ *Grace sighed so heavily that Trish could hear it in the next room.* グレースはあまりにも大きなため息をついたので隣の部屋にいたトリッシュに聞こえた. ❏ *The man in the next chair was asleep.* 隣の席の男性は眠っていた. **4** ADV 副詞 The thing that happens **next** is the thing that happens immediately after something else. 次に、次は ❏ *Next, close your eyes then screw them up tight.* 次に目を閉じ、そして顔にしわがよるほどしっかり閉じなさい. ❏ *I don't know what to do next.* 次に何をすべきか分からない. **5** ADV 副詞 When you **next** do something, you do it for the first time since you last did it. 次に、次回 [ADV before V] ❏ *I next saw him at his house in Vermont.* その次にはバーモント州の彼の家で彼に会った. **6** ADV 副詞 You use **next** to say that something has more of a particular quality than all

n

other things except one. For example, the thing that is **next** best is the one that is the best except for one other thing. 2番目に [ADV adj-superl] ❑ *The one thing he didn't have was a son. I think he's felt that a grandson is the next best thing.* 彼にないものといえば息子だ。その次に欲しいものは孫息子だと感じていると私は思う。 **7** PHRASE 句 You use **after next** in expressions such as **the week after next** to refer to a period of time after the next one. For example, when it is May, the month after next is July. 再来週・再来月など次の次を表す ❑ *...the party's annual conference, to be held the week after next.* 再来週に予定されている党の年次大会 **8** PHRASE 句 If you say that you do something or experience something as much **as the next** person, you mean that you are no different from anyone else in the respect mentioned. だれにも劣らずに [EMPHASIS 強調] ❑ *I enjoy pleasure as much as the next person.* 私はだれにも負けないほど余暇を楽しむ。 **9** PHRASE 句 If one thing is **next to** another thing, it is at the other side of it. 隣に、並んで ❑ *She sat down next to him on the sofa.* 彼女はソファーで彼の隣に座った。 ❑ *...at the southern end of the Gaza Strip next to the Egyptian border.* エジプトとの国境に隣接したガザ地区の南端で **10** PHRASE 句 You use **next to** in order to give the most important aspect of something when comparing it with another aspect. 次には、次いで ❑ *Her children were the number two priority in her life next to her career.* 彼女の人生で仕事に次いで子供が2番目に大切だった。 **11** PHRASE 句 You use **next to** before a negative, or a word that suggests something negative, to mean almost, but not completely. ほとんど ❑ *Johnson still knew next to nothing about tobacco.* ジョンソンは依然としてたばこについてほとんど何も知らなかった。

Word Partnership   *next* は次の語句と使われる：

N.	next **election**, next **generation**, next **level**, next **meeting**, next **move**, next **question**, next **step**, next **stop**, next **time**, next **train** **1** **2** next **day/hour/month/week/year** **1** **2**
V.	come next, go next, happen next **4** **5**

next door

The adjective is usually spelled **next-door**.
形容詞は通常 **next-door** とつづられる。

1 ADV 副詞 If a room or building is **next door**, it is the next one to the right or left. 隣で、隣に ❑ *...I went next door to the bathroom.* 隣の浴室に行った。 ❑ *...the old lady who lived next door.* 隣に住んでいた老婦人 ●ADJ 形容詞 **Next door** is also an adjective. 隣の [ADJ n] ❑ *...a thud like a cellar door slamming shut in a next-door house.* 隣の家で地下室のドアがバタンと閉まったような大きな音 PHRASE 句 If a room or building is **next door to** another one, it is the next one to the left or right. 一の隣の ❑ *The kitchen is right next door to the dining room.* キッチンはダイニングルームのすぐ隣にある。 **2** ADV 副詞 The people **next door** are the people who live in the house or apartment to the right or left of yours. 隣に住む [n ADV] ❑ *The neighbors thought the family next door had moved.* 近所の人々は隣に住む家族が引っ越したと思った。 ●ADJ 形容詞 **Next door** is also an adjective. 隣に住んでいる [ADJ n] ❑ *Even your next-door neighbor didn't see through your disguise.* 隣の住人でさえ君の粉装も見破れなかったよ。 **3** PHRASE 句 If you refer to someone as **the boy next door** or **the girl next door**, you mean that they are pleasant, respectable, and likeable. 感じのいい男の子・好感の持てる女の子 ❑ *He was dependable, straightforward, the boy next door.* 彼は、頼りになる素直な感じのいい男の子だった。

next of kin N-UNCOUNT-COLL 集合的不可算名詞 **Next of kin** is sometimes used to refer to the person who is your closest relative, especially in official or legal documents. 親族 [FORMAL 形式ばった] ❑ *We have notified the next of kin.* 親族に通知しました。

nib|ble /nɪbəl/ (**nibbles, nibbling, nibbled**) **1** V-T/V-I 他動詞/自動詞 If you **nibble** food, you eat it by biting very small pieces of it, for example because you are not very hungry. 少しずつかじる ❑ *Linda lay face down on a living room couch, nibbling popcorn.* リンダは居間のソファーでポップコーンをかじりながらうつぶせに寝転がっていた。 ❑ *She nibbled at a piece of dry toast.* 彼女は、乾いたトーストをかじった。 ●N-COUNT 可算名詞 **Nibble** is also a noun. 一かじり ❑ *We each took a nibble.* 私たちはそれぞれ一口ずつ食べた。 **2** V-T/V-I 他動詞/自動詞 If you **nibble** something, you bite it very gently. そっとかむ ❑ *John found he was kissing and nibbling her ear.* 彼が彼女の耳にキスをしてそっとかんでいるのをジョンは見かけた。 ❑ *Daniel nibbled on his pen.* ダニエルはペンをかんだ。 **3** V-T/V-I 他動詞/自動詞 When an animal **nibbles** something, it takes small bites of it quickly and repeatedly. 少しずつかじる ❑ *A herd of goats was nibbling the turf around the base of the tower.* ヤギの群れが塔のもとの周辺の芝をかじっていた。 ❑ *The birds nibble at the brickwork.* 鳥がれんがの上でえさをついばんでいる。 ●PHRASAL VERB 句動詞 **Nibble away** means the same as **nibble**. 少しずつかじる ❑ *The rabbits nibbled away on the herbaceous plants.* ウサギが草本をかじっていた。 **4** V-I 自動詞 If one thing **nibbles at** another, it gradually

affects, harms, or destroys it. 少しずつ崩していく ❑ *It was all going according to plan, yet small doubts kept nibbling at the edges of his mind.* すべて計画通りに行っていたが、幾つかのささいな疑問が彼の心のどこかに引っかかり続けた。 ●PHRASAL VERB 句動詞 **Nibble away** means the same as **nibble**. 少しずつ崩していく ❑ *Several manufacturers are also nibbling away at Ford's traditional customer base.* 数社の製造会社もフォード社の従来の顧客ベースを少しずつ崩している。

nice /naɪs/ (**nicer, nicest**) **1** ADJ 形容詞 If you say that something is **nice**, you mean that you find it attractive, pleasant, or enjoyable. すてきな、楽しい ❑ *I think silk ties can be quite nice.* シルクのネクタイがとってもよく似合うこともあると思う。 ❑ *It's nice to be here together again.* またここでご一緒できて光栄だ。 ●**nice|ly** ADV 副詞 すてきに、うまく ❑ *He's just written a book, nicely illustrated and not too technical.* 彼は、すてきなイラストが入って専門的すぎない本を書いたところだ。 **2** ADJ 形容詞 If you say that it is **nice of** someone to say or do something, you are saying that they are being kind and thoughtful. This is often used as a way of thanking someone. 優しい、親切な（お礼の表現としても使われる） ❑ *It's awfully nice of you to come all this way to see me.* わざわざ私に会いに来てくれて本当にありがとう。 ❑ *"How are your boys?" — "How nice of you to ask."* 「息子さんはお元気？」「聞いてくれてありがとう」 **3** ADJ 形容詞 If you say that someone is **nice**, you mean that you like them because they are friendly and pleasant. 感じのいい ❑ *I've met your father and he's rather nice.* あなたのお父さんに会ったが感じのいい人だ。 **4** ADJ 形容詞 [v-link ADJ] If you are **nice to** people, you are friendly, pleasant, or polite toward them. 一に優しい ❑ *She met Mr. and Mrs. Ricciardi, who were very nice to her.* 彼女はリチャルディ夫妻に会ったが、2人ともとても親切にしてくれた。 ●**nice|ly** ADV 副詞 [ADV after v] 優しく、親切に ❑ *He treated you very nicely and acted like a decent guy.* 彼はあなたにとても親切にし好青年のようにふるまった。 **5** ADJ 形容詞 When the weather is **nice**, it is warm and pleasant. （天気が）よい ❑ *He nodded to us and said, "Nice weather we're having."* 彼は私たちに向かってうなずきながら「いい天気ですね」と言った。 **6** ADJ 形容詞 You can use **nice** to emphasize a particular quality that you like. ほかの形容詞・副詞の性質を好んでいることを強調して ❑ *With a nice dark color, the wine is medium to full bodied.* いい感じの濃い目の色で、そのワインはミディアムからフルボディの中間だ。 [EMPHASIS 強調] ❑ *I'll explain it nice and simply so you can understand.* 分かるようにきちんと簡単に説明するよ。 **7** ADJ 形容詞 You can use **nice** when you are greeting people. For example, you can say **"Nice to meet you,"** **"Nice to have met you,"** or **"Nice to see you."** 「はじめまして」などのあいさつで使われる ❑ *Good morning. Nice to meet you and thanks for being with us this weekend.* おはようございます。今週末もこの番組を聴いてくださってありがとうございます。 [FORMULAE 決まり文句] ['it' v-link ADJ to-inf] **8** → see also **nicely**

Thesaurus   *nice* また次を参照：

ADJ.	friendly, kind, likable, pleasant, polite; (*ant.*) mean, unpleasant **2** – **4**

Word Partnership   *nice* は次の語句と使われる：

ADJ.	nice **and clean** **1**
V.	look nice, nice to see *someone/something* **1**
N.	nice **clothes**, nice **guy**, nice **people**, nice **place**, nice **smile** **1** **3** nice **day**, nice **weather** **5**

nice|ly /naɪsli/ **1** ADV 副詞 If something is happening or working **nicely**, it is happening or working in a satisfactory way or in the way that you want it to. うまい具合に、満足のいくように [ADV with v] ❑ *She has a bit of private money, so they manage quite nicely.* 彼女にはちょっとした個人資産があって、それで彼らはうまくやっている。 **2** → see also **nice** **3** PHRASE 句 If someone or something **is doing nicely**, they are being successful. 成功している ❑ *...another hotel owner who is doing very nicely.* かなり成功している別のホテル経営者

niche /nɪtʃ, niːʃ/ (**niches**) **1** N-COUNT 可算名詞 A **niche** in the market is a specific area of marketing which has its own particular requirements, customers, and products. ニッチ, 市場のすき間 [BUSINESS 実業] ❑ *I think we have found a niche in the toy market.* おもちゃ市場にニッチを見つけたと思う。 **2** ADJ 形容詞 **Niche** marketing is the practice of dividing the market into specialized areas for which particular products are made. A **niche** market is one of these specialized areas. ニッチー, すき間一 [BUSINESS 実業] [ADJ n] ❑ *Many media experts see such all-news channels as part of a general move towards niche marketing.* ニュース専門局をニッチ戦略に対する一般的な動きの一部とみなすマスコミ専門家が多い。 **3** N-COUNT 可算名詞 A **niche** is a hollow area in a wall which has been made to hold a statue, or a natural hollow part in a hill or cliff. 壁がん、ニッチ ❑ *Above him, in a niche on the wall, sat a tiny veiled Ganesh, the elephant god.* 彼の頭上には、壁のニッチにインド象の神である小さなガネーシャがベールを覆って座っていた。 **4** N-COUNT 可算名詞 Your **niche** is the job or activity which

is exactly suitable for you. 天職, 得意の分野 □ *Simon Lane quickly found his niche as a busy freelance model maker.* サイモン・レーンは早くも多忙なフリーランスのモデル製作者としての天職を見つけた.

nick /nɪk/ (**nicks, nicking, nicked**) **1** V-T 他動詞 If you **nick** something or **nick** yourself, you accidentally make a small cut in the surface of the object or your skin. 軽く傷つける □ *When I pulled out of the space, I nicked the rear bumper of the car in front of me.* 車を出したときに, 前の車のリヤバンパーをあててしまった. □ *A sharp blade is likely to nick the skin and draw blood.* 鋭い刃によって切り傷・出血することがよくある. **2** N-COUNT 可算名詞 A **nick** is a small cut made in the surface of something, usually in someone's skin. 切り傷 □ *The barbed wire had left only the tiniest nick just below my right eye.* 有刺鉄線で右目のすぐ下にほんの小さな切り傷ができた.

nick|el /nɪkəl/ (**nickels**) **1** N-UNCOUNT 不可算名詞 **Nickel** is a silver-colored metal that is used in making steel. ニッケル **2** N-COUNT 可算名詞 In the United States and Canada, a **nickel** is a coin worth five cents. 5セント硬貨 □ *...a large glass jar filled with pennies, nickels, dimes, and quarters.* 1セント硬貨, 5セント硬貨, 10セント硬貨, 25セント硬貨でいっぱいの大きなガラス瓶

nick|name /nɪkneɪm/ (**nicknames, nicknaming, nicknamed**) **1** N-COUNT 可算名詞 A **nickname** is an informal name for someone or something. あだ名, 愛称, ニックネーム □ *Red got his nickname for his red hair.* レッドは赤毛のためにそのあだ名がつけられた. **2** V-T 他動詞 If you **nickname** someone or something, you give them an informal name. あだ名をつける □ *When he got older I nicknamed him Little Alf.* 彼が大きくなってから, 彼にリトル・アルフというあだ名をつけた.

nico|tine /nɪkɪtin/ N-UNCOUNT 不可算名詞 **Nicotine** is the substance in tobacco that people can become addicted to. ニコチン □ *Nicotine produces a feeling of well-being in the smoker.* ニコチンは喫煙者に幸福感をもたらす.

niece /nis/ (**nieces**) N-COUNT 可算名詞 Someone's **niece** is the daughter of their sister or brother. めい □ *...his niece, the daughter of his eldest sister.* 彼のめい, つまり一番上の姉の娘

nig|gle /nɪgəl/ (**niggles, niggling, niggled**) V-T/V-I 他動詞/自動詞 If someone **niggles** you, they annoy you by continually criticizing you for what you think are small or unimportant things. けちをつける, あら探しをする □ *I don't react anymore when opponents try to niggle me.* 反対派が私のあら探しをしようとするときにもう反応しないことにした. ● N-COUNT 可算名詞 **Niggle** is also a noun. あら探し □ *The life we have built together is more important than any minor niggle either of us might have.* 我々が共に築いた人生はお互いが持つささいな不満よりもっと大切だ.

night /naɪt/ (**nights**) **1** N-VAR 可変性名詞 The **night** is the part of each day when the sun has set and it is dark outside, especially the time when people are sleeping. 夜 □ *The fighting began in the late afternoon and continued all night.* けんかは午後遅くに始まり, 夜通し続いた. □ *Finally night fell.* ついに夜のとばりが下りた. **2** N-COUNT 可算名詞 The **night** is the period of time between the end of the afternoon and the time that you go to bed, especially the time when you relax before going to bed. 夕方, 晩 □ *So whose party was it last night?* それでゆうべはだれのパーティだったの? **3** N-COUNT 可算名詞 A particular **night** is a particular evening when a special event takes place, such as a show or a play. タベ □ *The first night crowd packed the building.* 初日の舞台を見に来た観衆で会場はいっぱいだった. **4** PHRASE 句 If it is a particular time **at night**, it is during the time when it is dark and is before midnight. 夜に, 晩に □ *It's eleven o'clock at night in Moscow.* モスクワでは夜の11時だ. **5** PHRASE 句 If something happens **at night**, it happens regularly during the evening or night. 夜間に □ *He was going to college at night, in order to become an accountant.* 彼は会計士になるために夜間大学に通っていた. **6** PHRASE 句 If something happens **day and night** or **night and day**, it happens all the time without stopping. 四六時中, 夜昼なく □ *Dozens of doctors and nurses have been working day and night for weeks.* 何十人もの医者や看護婦が数週間に渡り連日連夜働き続けています. **7** PHRASE 句 If you have **an early night**, you go to bed early. If you have **a late night**, you go to bed late. 早く寝ること; 夜更かしすること □ *I've had a hell of a day, and all I want is an early night.* 今日は一日大変だったから, とにかく早く寝たい. **8 morning, noon, and night →** see **morning → see star**

night|club /naɪtklʌb/ (**nightclubs**) N-COUNT 可算名詞 A **nightclub** is a place where people go late in the evening to drink and dance. ナイトクラブ, ディスコ

night|life /naɪtlaɪf/ N-UNCOUNT 不可算名詞 **Nightlife** is all the entertainment and social activities that are available at night in cities and towns, such as nightclubs and theaters. ナイトライフ, 夜の娯楽 □ *New York's energetic nightlife is second to none.* ニューヨークの活気に満ちたナイトライフはどこの街にも負けない.

night|ly /naɪtli/ ADJ 形容詞 A **nightly** event happens every night. 毎夜の, 毎晩の [ADJ n] □ *I'm sure we watched the nightly news, and then we turned on the movie.* 確かに夜のニュースを見てから映画番組に変えたはずだ. ● ADV 副詞 **Nightly** is also an adverb. 毎夜, 毎晩 □ *She appears nightly on the television news.* 彼女は毎晩テレビニュースに出る.

night|mare /naɪtmeər/ (**nightmares**) **1** N-COUNT 可算名詞 A **nightmare** is a very frightening dream. 悪夢, 怖い夢 □ *All the victims still suffered nightmares.* 被害者全員がまだ悪夢に悩まされていた. **2** N-COUNT 可算名詞 If you refer to a situation as a **nightmare**, you mean that it is very frightening and unpleasant. 悪夢のような状況 □ *The years in prison were a nightmare.* 刑務所にいた年月は悪夢だった. **3** N-COUNT 可算名詞 If you refer to a situation as a **nightmare**, you are saying in a very emphatic way that it is irritating because it causes you a lot of trouble. 非常に面倒なこと □ *Taking my son Peter to a restaurant was a nightmare.* 息子のピーターをレストランに連れて行ったのは最悪だった. [EMPHASIS 強調]

nil /nɪl/ N-UNCOUNT 不可算名詞 If you say that something **is nil**, you mean that it does not exist at all. 無, ゼロ □ *Their legal rights are virtually nil.* 彼らの法律上の権利は事実上皆無です.

nim|ble /nɪmbəl/ (**nimbler, nimblest**) **1** ADJ 形容詞 Someone who is **nimble** is able to move their fingers, hands, or legs quickly and easily. 軽やかな, 器用な □ *Everything had been stitched by Molly's nimble fingers.* モリーの器用な手先のおかげですべてが縫い合わされた. **2** ADJ 形容詞 If you say that someone has a **nimble** mind, you mean they are clever and can think very quickly. 機転の利く □ *A nimble mind backed by a degree in economics gave him a firm grasp of financial matters.* 経済学の学位によって裏付けされた回転の速い頭脳のおかげで, 彼は財政問題をしっかり理解した.

nine /naɪn/ (**nines**) NUM 数詞 **Nine** is the number 9. 9 □ *We still sighted nine yachts.* まだ9隻のヨットが見えた.

911 /naɪn wʌn wʌn/ NUM 数詞 **911** is the number that you call in the United States in order to contact the emergency services. 米国での緊急電話番号, 110番 □ *The women made their first 911 call about a prowler at 12:46 a.m.* 女性たちは午前0時46分に不審者についての最初の緊急通報をした.

nine|teen /naɪntin/ (**nineteens**) NUM 数詞 **Nineteen** is the number 19. 19 □ *They have nineteen days to make up their minds.* 決心をするのに19日残っている.

nine|teenth /naɪntinθ/ ORD 序数詞 The **nineteenth** item in a series is the one that you count as number nineteen. 19番目の □ *...my nineteenth birthday.* 私の19歳の誕生日

nine|ti|eth /naɪntiɪθ/ ORD 序数詞 The **ninetieth** item in a series is the one that you count as number ninety. 90番目の □ *He celebrates his ninetieth birthday on Friday.* 彼は金曜日に90歳の誕生日のお祝いをする.

nine|ty /naɪnti/ (**nineties**) **1** NUM 数詞 **Ninety** is the number 90. 90 □ *It was decided she had to stay another ninety days.* 彼女があと90日滞在しなければならないと決定した. **2** N-PLURAL 複数名詞 When you talk about the **nineties**, you are referring to numbers between 90 and 99. For example, if you are **in your nineties**, you are aged between 90 and 99. If the temperature is **in the nineties**, the temperature is between 90 and 99 degrees. 90代; 90歳代; 90度台 □ *By this time she was in her nineties and needed help more and more frequently.* この頃までには彼女は90代でさらに頻繁に手助けが必要だった. **3** N-PLURAL 複数名詞 The **nineties** is the decade between 1990 and 1999. 90年代 □ *These trends only got worse as we moved into the nineties.* これらの傾向は90年代に入り悪化するだけだった.

ninth /naɪnθ/ (**ninths**) **1** ORD 序数詞 The **ninth** item in a series is the one that you count as number nine. 9番目の □ *...January the ninth.* 1月9日 □ *...students in the ninth grade.* 9年生の学生 **2** FRACTION 端数 A **ninth** is one of nine equal parts of something. 9分の1 □ *The dollar rose by a ninth of a cent.* ドルは9分の1セント上昇しました.

nip /nɪp/ (**nips, nipping, nipped**) **1** V-T 他動詞 If an animal or person **nips** you, they bite you lightly or squeeze a piece of your skin between their finger and thumb. 軽くかむ, つねる □ *I have known cases where dogs have nipped babies.* イヌが赤ちゃんにかみついたケースを知っている. ● N-COUNT 可算名詞 **Nip** is also a noun. かみつくこと, つねること □ *Incidents range from a nip, which fails to break*

the skin or draw blood, to serious injuries. 事件は、つねること（肌を傷つけない、あるいは出血しない）から重傷に及んでいる. **3** N-COUNT 可算名詞 A **nip** is a small amount of a strong alcoholic drink. 一口 □ *She had a habit of taking an occasional nip from a flask of cognac.* 彼女はフラスコに入れたコニャックをたまにちびちびと飲む習慣があった. **3** to **nip** something **in the bud** → see **bud**

nip|ple /nɪpəl/ (**nipples**) **1** N-COUNT 可算名詞 The **nipples** on someone's body are the two small pieces of slightly hard flesh on their chest. Babies suck milk from their mothers' breasts through their mothers' nipples. 乳首 □ *Sore nipples can inhibit the milk supply.* 乳首が痛むと母乳の出が悪くなることがある. **2** N-COUNT 可算名詞 A **nipple** is a piece of rubber or plastic which is attached to the top of a baby's bottle. （ほ乳瓶の）乳首 □ *…a white plastic bottle with a rubber nipple.* ゴム製の乳首がついた白いプラスチックの白

ni|trate /naɪtreɪt/ (**nitrates**) N-MASS 質量名詞 **Nitrate** is a chemical compound that includes nitrogen and oxygen. Nitrates are used as fertilizers in agriculture. 硝酸塩 □ *High levels of nitrate occur in the Midwest because of the heavy use of fertilizers.* 化学肥料の大量使用のためにアメリカ中西部には高レベルの硝酸塩が存在する. → see **firework**

ni|tro|gen /naɪtrədʒən/ N-UNCOUNT 不可算名詞 **Nitrogen** is a colorless element that has no smell and is usually found as a gas. It forms about 78 percent of the Earth's atmosphere, and is found in all living things. 窒素 → see **air**

no /noʊ/ (**noes** or **no's**) **1** CONVENTION 慣習表現 You use **no** to give a negative response to a question. いいえ □ *"Any problems?" — "No, I'm O.K."* 「問題ありますか」「いいえ、大丈夫です」 **2** CONVENTION 慣習表現 You use **no** to say that something that someone has just said is not true. いいえ □ *"We thought you'd emigrated." — "No, no."* 「私たちはあなたが移住したと思っていました」「いいえ、していません」 **3** CONVENTION 慣習表現 You use **no** to refuse an offer or a request, or to refuse permission. いいえ □ *"Here, have mine." — "No, this is fine."* 「さあ、私のをどうぞ」「いや、これで大丈夫です」 □ *Can you just get the message through to Pete for me?" — "No, no I can't."* 「私のためにピーターに伝言を届けてくれますか」「いいえ、それはできません」 **4** EXCLAM 感嘆詞 You use **no** to indicate that you do not want someone to do something. まさか □ *No. I forbid it. You cannot.* だめって、私はそれを許さない. 駄目で. **5** CONVENTION 慣習表現 You use **no** to acknowledge a negative statement or to show that you accept and understand it. ええ □ *"We're not on the main campus." — "No."* 「私たちのいる場所は中央キャンパスではない」「ええ、違います」 □ *"It's not one of my favorite forms of music." — "No."* 「それは私の好きな形式の音楽ではありません」「ええ、違います」 **6** CONVENTION 慣習表現 You use **no** before correcting what you have just said. そうではなく □ *I was twenty-two – no, twenty-one.* 私は22歳、いや21歳だった. **7** EXCLAM 感嘆詞 You use **no** to express shock or disappointment at something you have just been told. なんだって [FEELINGS 感情] □ *"We went with Sarah and the married man that she's currently seeing." — "Oh no."* 「私たちはセイラと彼女が今付き合っている既婚男性と一緒に出かけた」「まさか」 **8** DET 限定詞 You use **no** to mean not any or not one person or thing. 少しの…もない □ *He had no intention of paying the cash.* 彼は現金を支払うつもりは少しもなかった. □ *No job has more influence on the future of the world.* 世界の将来にこれ以上大きく影響する職はない. **9** DET 限定詞 You use **no** to emphasize that someone or something is not the type of thing mentioned. 決して…でない [EMPHASIS 強調] □ *He is no singer.* 彼は歌手どころじゃない. □ *I make it no secret that our worst consultants earn nothing.* 当社で最もひどいコンサルタントは報酬を受けていないことを私は隠さない. **10** ADV 副詞 You can use **no** to make the negative form of a comparative. 少しも [ADV compar] □ *It is to start broadcasting no later than the end of 1994.* それは遅くとも1994年末までに放送を開始する予定だ. □ *Yesterday no fewer than thirty climbers reached the summit.* 昨日は少なくとも30名の登山者が頂上に達した. **11** DET 限定詞 You use **no** in front of an adjective and noun to make the noun group mean its opposite. 決して…でない □ *Sometimes a bit of selfishness, if it leads to greater self-knowledge, is no bad thing.* 多少の自分勝手は自己認識を深めるのに役立つ場合は、悪いことではないこともある. **12** DET 限定詞 **No** is used in notices or instructions to say that a particular activity or thing is forbidden. 一禁止 □ *The captain turned out the "no smoking" signs.* 機長は「禁煙」のサインを消した. □ *No talking after lights out.* 消灯後は話すべからず. **13** N-COUNT 可算名詞 A **no** is a person who has answered "no" to a question or who has voted against something. **No** is also used to refer to their answer or vote. 反対投票者 □ *According to the latest opinion polls, the noes have 50 percent, the yeses 35 percent.* 最近の世論調査によると、反対投票者は50%、賛成投票者は50%である. **14** PHRASE 句 If you say **there is no** doing a particular thing, you mean that it is very difficult or impossible to do that thing. もう…できない [EMPHASIS 強調] □ *There is no going back to the life she had.* 彼女はもう昔の生活に戻ることはできない. **15** not to **take no for an answer** → see **answer 16** no **doubt** → see **doubt 17** no **longer** → see **long 18** in no **way** → see **way 19** there's

no way → see **way 20** no **way** → see **way**

No. (**Nos**) **No.** is a written abbreviation for **number**. number の縮約形 □ *That year he was named the nation's No. 1 college football star.* その年彼はその国1位の大学サッカー選手に指名された.

no|bil|ity /noʊbɪlɪti/ **1** N-SING-COLL 集合的単数名詞 The **nobility** of a society are all the people who have titles and belong to a high social class. 貴族 □ *They married into the nobility and entered the highest ranks of state administration.* 彼らは貴族と姻戚（いんせき）になり、国政の最高階級に入った. **2** N-UNCOUNT 不可算名詞 A person's **nobility** is their noble character and behavior. 気高さ [FORMAL 形式ばった] □ *…his nobility of character, and his devotion to his country.* 彼の人格の気高さと母国への愛着

no|ble /noʊbəl/ (**nobler, noblest**) **1** ADJ 形容詞 If you say that someone is a **noble** person, you admire and respect them because they are unselfish and morally good. 高潔な [APPROVAL 賛成] □ *He was an upright and noble man who was always willing to help in any way he could.* 彼はどんなことにも喜んで手を貸す正直で高潔な男だった. ● **no|bly** ADV 副詞 [ADV with v] 立派に □ *Eric's sister had nobly volunteered to help with the gardening.* エリックの姉妹は園芸を手伝うことを立派に買って出た. **2** ADJ 形容詞 If you say that something is a **noble** idea, goal, or action, you admire it because it is based on high moral principles. 崇高な [APPROVAL 賛成] □ *He had implicit faith in their noble intentions.* 彼は彼らの崇高な意図に絶対の信頼を持っていた. □ *We'll always justify our actions with noble sounding theories.* 我々は常に崇高っぽい理論で自らの行動を正当化することがよくある. **3** ADJ 形容詞 If you describe something as **noble**, you think that its appearance or quality is very impressive, making it superior to other things of its type. 堂々とした □ *…the great parks with their noble trees.* 雄大な樹木のそびえたてる大庭園 **4** ADJ 形容詞 **Noble** means belonging to a high social class and having a title. 貴族階級に属する □ *…rich and noble families.* 裕福な貴族

no|body /noʊbɒdi, -bʌdi/ (**nobodies**) **1** PRON-INDEF-NEG 否定不定代名詞 **Nobody** means not a single person, or not a single member of a particular group or set. 誰も…ない □ *They were shut away in a little room where nobody could overhear.* 彼らは誰も立ち聞きできない小部屋に閉じ込められていた. □ *Nobody realizes how bad things are.* 状況がいかにひどいかを誰も理解していない. **2** N-COUNT 可算名詞 If someone says that a person is a **nobody**, they are saying in an unkind way that the person is not at all important. 名のない人 [DISAPPROVAL 不賛成] □ *A man in my position has nothing to fear from a nobody like you.* 私のような重要な地位にある男は君のような取るに足りない人物を少しも恐れない.

You do not use **nobody** or **no one** in front of **of** to talk about a particular group of people. The word you need is **none**. □ *None of his companions answered.*

noc|tur|nal /nɒktɜrnəl/ **1** ADJ 形容詞 **Nocturnal** means occurring at night. 夜にする □ *The dog's main role will be to accompany me on long nocturnal walks.* その犬の主な役割は私の夜の散歩について来ることになるだろう. **2** ADJ 形容詞 **Nocturnal** creatures are active mainly at night. 夜行性の □ *When there is a full moon, this nocturnal rodent is careful to stay in its burrow.* 満月の時には この夜行性の齧歯（げっし）動物は穴から出ないようにしている. → see **bat**

nod /nɒd/ (**nods, nodding, nodded**) **1** V-T/V-I 他動詞/自動詞 If you **nod**, you move your head downward and upward to show that you are answering "yes" to a question, or to show agreement, understanding, or approval. うなずく [no passive] □ *"Are you okay?" I asked. She nodded and smiled.* 「大丈夫よ」と私は聞いた. 彼女はうなずいて微笑んだ. □ *Jacques tasted one and nodded his approval.* ジャックは1つ味見しうなずいて承認した. ● N-COUNT 可算名詞 **Nod** is also a noun. うなずき □ *She gave a nod and said, "I see."* 彼女はうなずいて「分かりました」と言った. □ *"Probably," agreed Hunter, with a slow nod of his head.* 「多分そうでしょう」とハンターはゆっくりうなずいて合意した. **2** V-I 自動詞 If you **nod** in a particular direction, you bend your head once in that direction in order to indicate something or to give someone a signal. 指し示す [no passive] □ *"Does it work?" he asked, nodding at the piano.* 「それは使えますか」と彼はあごでピアノを指し示しながら聞いた. □ *She nodded toward the dining room. "He's in there."* 彼女はダイニングルームの方向をあごで指し示した. 「彼はそこにいるわ」 **3** V-T/V-I 他動詞/自動詞 If you **nod**, you bend your head once, as a way of saying hello or goodbye. うなずいてあいさつする [no passive] □ *All the girls nodded and said "Hi."* 少女達は全員うなずいて「こんにちは」とあいさつした. □ *Both of them smiled and nodded at friends.* 2人とも微笑みながら友人にうなずいてあいさつした. □ *Tom nodded a greeting.* トムはうなずいてあいさつした.

▶ **nod off** PHRASAL VERB 句動詞 If you **nod off**, you fall asleep, especially when you had not intended to. 居眠りする [INFORMAL くだけた] □ *The judge appeared to nod off yesterday while a witness was being cross-examined.* 判事は昨日証人が反対尋問を受けている最中に居眠りしているようだった.

Word Partnership   nod は次の語句と使われる：

| N. | nod **in agreement**, nod *your* head **1** |
| V. | **give a** nod **1** |

noise /nɔɪz/ (**noises**) **1** N-UNCOUNT 可算名詞 **Noise** is a loud or unpleasant sound. 雑音 ❑ *There was too much noise in the room and he needed peace.* その部屋は騒音がひどく、彼には静けさが必要だった。 ❑ *The noise of bombs and guns was incessant.* 爆弾と銃の音は途絶えることがなかった。 **2** N-COUNT 可算名詞 **A noise** is a sound that someone or something makes. 声 ❑ *Gerald made a small noise in his throat.* ジェラルドは小さくせき払いした。 ❑ *…birdsong and other animal noises.* 鳥のさえずりやその他の動物の声 **3** N-PLURAL 複数名詞 If someone **makes noises** of a particular kind about something, they say things that indicate their attitude to it in a rather indirect or vague way. それとなくほのめかす ❑ *The president took care to make encouraging noises about the future.* 大統領は将来について前向きの姿勢を示すよう気をつけた。 **4** PHRASE 句 If you say that someone **makes the right noises** or **makes all the right noises**, you think that they are showing concern or enthusiasm about something because they feel they ought to rather than because they really want to. もっともらしいことを言う ❑ *But at the annual party conference he always made the right noises.* しかし年次党大会で彼はいつももっともらしいことを言った。

Thesaurus   noise また次を参照：

| N. | boom, crash; (*ant.*) quiet, silence **1** |

Word Partnership   noise は次の語句と使われる：

N.	**background** noise, noise **level**, noise **pollution**, **traffic** noise **1**
ADJ.	**loud** noise **1** **2**
V.	**hear a** noise, **make a** noise **2**

noisy /nɔɪzi/ (**noisier, noisiest**) **1** ADJ 形容詞 A **noisy** person or thing makes a lot of loud or unpleasant noise. うるさい ❑ *…my noisy old typewriter.* うるさい古いタイプライター。 ● **noisily** ADV 副詞 騒々しく ❑ *The students on the grass bank cheered noisily.* 学生達は芝生の土手から騒々しく声援した。 **2** ADJ 形容詞 A **noisy** place is full of a lot of loud or unpleasant noise. 騒々しい ❑ *It's a noisy place with film clips showing constantly on one of the cafe's giant screens.* そのカフェは巨大なスクリーンにひっきりなしに映画を上映する騒々しい場所だ。 ❑ *The baggage hall was crowded and noisy.* 手荷物受取所は混雑して騒々しかった。 **3** ADJ 形容詞 If you describe someone as **noisy**, you are critical of them for trying to attract attention to their views by frequently and forcefully discussing them. 声高の [DISAPPROVAL 不賛成] ❑ *It might, at last, silence the small but noisy intellectual clique.* それはやっと少ないが声高のインテリ派を黙らせるかもしれない。

no|mad|ic /noʊmædɪk/ **1** ADJ 形容詞 **Nomadic** people travel from place to place rather than living in one place all the time. 遊牧の ❑ *…the great nomadic tribes of the Western Sahara.* サハラ西部の偉大な遊牧民族 **2** ADJ 形容詞 If someone has a **nomadic** way of life, they travel from place to place and do not have a settled home. 遊牧民的な ❑ *The daughter of a railroad engineer, she at first had a somewhat nomadic childhood.* 鉄道技師の娘である彼女は最初いくぶん遊牧民的な子供時代を過ごした。

no-man's land **1** N-UNCOUNT 不可算名詞 **No-man's land** is an area of land that is not owned or controlled by anyone, for example the area of land between two opposing armies. 緩衝地帯 ❑ *In Tobruk, leading a patrol in no-man's land, he was blown up by a mortar bomb.* 緩衝地帯で偵察班を引率していた彼はトブルクで迫撃砲で爆死した。 **2** N-SING 単数名詞 If you refer to a situation as a **no-man's land** between different things, you mean that it seems unclear because it does not fit into any of the categories. あいまいな部分 ❑ *The play is set in the dangerous no-man's land between youth and adolescence.* その芝居は青年期と思春期の間の危険であいまいな状態に設定されている。

Word Link   nom ≈ name : denomination, nominal, nominee

nomi|nal /nɒmɪnᵊl/ **1** ADJ 形容詞 You use **nominal** to indicate that someone or something is supposed to have a particular identity or status, but in reality does not have it. 名目だけの ❑ *As he was still not allowed to run a company, his wife became its nominal head.* 彼はまだ会社経営を許されなかったため、彼の妻が名義上の経営者となった。 ● **nominal|ly** ADV 副詞 名目的に ❑ *The sultan was still nominally the chief of staff.* 名目上はスルタンがまだ陸軍参謀総長だった。 ❑ *The road is nominally under the control of UN peacekeeping troops.* その道路は名目上は国連和平軍の管理下にある。 **2** ADJ 形容詞 [ADJ n] A **nominal** price or sum of money is very small in comparison with the real cost or value of the thing that is being bought or sold. 名ばかりの ❑ *I am prepared to sell my shares at a nominal price.* 私はわずかの価格で株を売る心構えがある。 **3** ADJ 形容

詞 In economics, the **nominal** value, rate, or level of something is the one expressed in terms of current prices or figures, without taking into account general changes in prices that take place over time. 名目の [ADJ n] ❑ *Inflation would be lower and so nominal rates would be more attractive in real terms.* インフレ率はより低いため名目比率は実質的にはより魅力的になるだろう。

nomi|nate /nɒmɪneɪt/ (**nominates, nominating, nominated**) **1** V-T 他動詞 If someone **is nominated** for a job or position, their name is formally suggested as a candidate for it. 指名する ❑ *This week one of them will be nominated by the Democratic Party for the presidency of the United States.* 今週彼らの中の1人が民主党から米国大統領候補として指名推薦されるだろう。 ❑ *The Security Council can nominate anyone for secretary-general.* 安全保障理事会は事務総長候補として誰でも指名推薦できる。 **2** V-T 他動詞 If you **nominate** someone to a job or position, you formally choose them to hold that job or position. 任命する ❑ *In 1967 Johnson nominated Thurgood Marshall to the Supreme Court.* 1967年にジョンソンはサーグッド・マーシャルを最高裁判所に任命した。 ❑ *She was nominated by the president as ambassador to Barbados.* 彼女は大統領からバルバドス大使に任命された。 **3** V-T 他動詞 If someone or something such as an actor or a movie **is nominated** for an award, someone formally suggests that they should be given that award. 推薦される ❑ *Practically every movie he made was nominated for an Oscar.* 彼が制作した映画のほとんど全てがアカデミー賞候補となった。

nomi|na|tion /nɒmɪneɪʃᵊn/ (**nominations**) **1** N-COUNT 可算名詞 A **nomination** is an official suggestion of someone as a candidate in an election or for a job. 指名推薦 ❑ *…his candidacy for the Republican presidential nomination.* 共和党の大統領候補者として彼が指名推薦されたこと **2** N-COUNT 可算名詞 A **nomination for** an award is an official suggestion that someone or something should be given that award. 推薦 ❑ *They say he's certain to get a nomination for best supporting actor.* 彼が助演男優賞にノミネートされることは確実らしい。 **3** N-VAR 可変性名詞 The **nomination** of someone to a particular job or position is their appointment to that job or position. 任命 ❑ *…the nomination of Texas Senator Lloyd Bentsen to be treasury secretary.* テキサス州のロイド・ベンツェン上院議員を財務大臣に任命すること

nomi|nee /nɒmɪni/ (**nominees**) N-COUNT 可算名詞 A **nominee** is someone who is nominated for a job, position, or award. 指名推薦された者 ❑ *His nominee for vice president was elected only after a second ballot.* 彼が副大統領に指名推薦した人物は2回目の投票の後でやっと選出された。

non|cha|lant /nɒnʃəlɒnt/ ADJ 形容詞 If you describe someone as **nonchalant**, you mean that they appear not to worry or care about things and that they seem very calm. 無関心な ❑ *Clark's mother is nonchalant about her role in her son's latest work.* クラークの母親は息子の最近の作品における自分の役割について無関心だ。 ❑ *Denis tried to look nonchalant and uninterested.* デニスは無関心を装った。 ● **non|cha|lance** /nɒnʃəlɒns/ N-UNCOUNT 不可算名詞 無関心 ❑ *Affecting nonchalance, I handed her two hundred dollar bills.* 無関心を装いながら私は彼女に200ドルを手渡した。 ● **non|cha|lant|ly** ADV 副詞 無関心そうに ❑ *"Does Will intend to return with us?" Joanna asked as nonchalantly as she could.* 「ウィルは私たちと一緒に戻るつもりですか」とジョアナはできるだけ無関心そうに聞いた。

none /nʌn/ **1** QUANT 数量詞 **None** of something means not even a small amount of it. **None** of a group of people or things means not even one of them. 誰も~ない [QUANT 'of' def-n] ❑ *None of us knew how to treat her.* 私たちはだれも彼女への接し方が分からない。 ● PRON-INDEF-NEG 否定不定代名詞 **None** is also a pronoun. 何も~ない ❑ *I searched bookstores and libraries for information, but found none.* 私は書店や図書館で情報を探したが何も見つからなかった。 ❑ *No one could imagine a great woman painter. None had existed yet.* だれも偉大な女性画家を想像することができなかった。まだだれもいなかった。 **2** PHRASE 句 If you say that someone **will have none of** something, or **is having none of** something, you mean that they refuse to accept it. 受けつけない [INFORMAL くだけた] ❑ *He knew his own mind and was having none of their attempts to keep him at home.* 彼は自分の気持ちを知っており、家にとどめておこうとする彼らの試みを受けつけなかった。 **3** PHRASE 句 You use **none too** in front of an adjective or adverb in order to emphasize that the quality mentioned is not present. 少しも~ない [FORMAL 形式ばった, EMPHASIS 強調] ❑ *He was none too thrilled to hear from me at that hour.* 彼はその時間に私から連絡を受けるのを少しも喜ばなかった。 **4** PHRASE 句 You use **none the** to say that someone or something does not have any more of a particular quality than they did before. 少しも~ではない ❑ *You could end up none the wiser about managing your finances.* あなたは家計の管理について少しも利口にならないかもしれない。 **5 second to none → see second**

Do not confuse **none** and **neither**. You use **none** in negative statements to refer to three or more people or things. □ *None could afford the food.* You use **none of** in the same way, followed by a pronoun or a noun group. □ *None of them had learned anything… None of his companions answered.* You use **neither** in negative statements to refer to two people or things. □ *Neither had close friends in college.* You use **neither of** in the same way, followed by a pronoun or a noun group. □ *Neither of them spoke… Neither of these extremes is desirable.* Note that you can also use **neither** before a singular count noun. □ *Neither side can win.*

Word Partnership   none は次の語句と使われる：

PRON.	none **of that/this/those**, none **of them/us** ■
ADV.	**almost** none, **virtually** none, none **whatsoever** ■
	none **too** ■

none|the|less /nʌnðəlɛs/ ADV 副詞 **Nonetheless** means the same as **nevertheless**. それにもかかわらず [FORMAL 形式ばった] [ADV with cl] □ *There was still a long way to go. Nonetheless, some progress had been made.* まだ長い道のりだった。それにもかかわらず、いくらかの進歩はあった。

non|executive /nɒnɪgzɛkyətɪv/ ADJ 形容詞 Someone who has a **nonexecutive** position in a company or organization gives advice but is not responsible for making decisions or ensuring that decisions are carried out. 非執行の [BUSINESS 実業] [ADJ n] □ *…nonexecutive directors.* 非執行役員

Word Link   non ≈ not : nonexistent, nonprofit, nonstop

non|existent /nɒnɪgzɪstənt/ ADJ 形容詞 If you say that something is **nonexistent**, you mean that it does not exist when you feel that it should. 存在しない □ *Hygiene was nonexistent: no running water, no bathroom.* 衛生は存在しなかった。水道もなければ浴室もなかった。

no-nonsense ■ ADJ 形容詞 If you describe someone as a **no-nonsense** person, you approve of the fact that they are efficient, direct, and quite tough. まじめな [APPROVAL 賛成] □ *She saw herself as a direct, no-nonsense, modern woman.* 彼女は自分自身を率直でまじめで近代的な女性と見た。 ■ ADJ 形容詞 If you describe something as a **no-nonsense** thing, you approve of the fact that it is plain and does not have unnecessary parts. 飾りのない [APPROVAL 賛成] □ *You'll need no-nonsense boots for the jungle.* ジャングルでは飾りのないブーツが必要だろう。

non|payment /nɒnpeɪmənt/ N-UNCOUNT 不可算名詞 **Nonpayment** is a failure to pay a sum of money that you owe. 不払い □ *She faced an end to treatments because of nonpayment of her claim.* 彼女は請求金の不払いのために治療の打ち切りに直面した。

non|profit /nɒnprɒfɪt/ ADJ 形容詞 A **nonprofit** organization is one which is not run with the aim of making a profit. 非営利の [BUSINESS 実業] □ *Most of that money goes to nonprofit organizations that run programs for the poor.* その金の大半は貧困者向けプログラムを提供する非営利団体のものとなる。

non|sense /nɒnsɛns, -səns/ ■ N-UNCOUNT 不可算名詞 If you say that something spoken or written is **nonsense**, you mean that you consider it to be untrue or silly. 役立たないもの [DISAPPROVAL 不賛成] □ *Most orthodox doctors however dismiss this as complete nonsense.* しかしオーソドックスな医者の大半は考えばかげたこととして退ける。 □ *…all that poetic nonsense about love.* あれだけ多くの恋愛についてのロマンチックなたわ言 ■ N-UNCOUNT 不可算名詞 You can use **nonsense** to refer to something that you think is foolish or that you disapprove of. ばかげた行為 [DISAPPROVAL 不賛成] [also 'a' N, usu supp N] □ *Surely it is an economic nonsense to deplete the world of natural resources.* 確かに世界の天然資源を使い果たすことは経済的にばかげた行為だ。 ■ N-UNCOUNT 不可算名詞 You can refer to spoken or written words that do not mean anything because they do not make sense as **nonsense**. ノンセンス詩 □ *…a children's nonsense poem by Charles E Carryl.* チャールズ・E・カリルによる児童向けノンセンス詩 ■ → see also **no-nonsense** ■ PHRASE 句 To **make a nonsense of** something or **make a nonsense of** it means to make it seem ridiculous or pointless. 無意味なものにしてしまう □ *The fighting made a nonsense of peace pledges made last week.* 戦闘は先週の平和の約束を無意味なものにしてしまう。

Thesaurus   nonsense また次を参照：

N.	foolishness, gibberish ■ ■
	absurdity, irrationality, rubbish ■

Word Partnership   nonsense は次の語句と使われる：

ADJ.	**absolute** nonsense, **complete** nonsense, **utter** nonsense ■ - ■
V.	**talk** nonsense ■ ■

non|smoker /nɒnsmoʊkər/ (**nonsmokers**) N-COUNT 可算名詞 A **nonsmoker** is someone who does not smoke. 非喫煙者 □ *It could be fair to nonsmokers to allow smoking in a building with windows that open.* 窓の開く建物で喫煙を許可するのは非喫煙者に不公平だろう。

non|stick /nɒnstɪk/ ADJ 形容詞 **Nonstick** saucepans, frying pans, or baking pans have a special coating on the inside which prevents food from sticking to them. 焦げ付かない □ *Use a shallow nonstick baking pan.* 焦げ付き加工を施した浅いベーキングパンを使いなさい。

non|stop /nɒnstɒp/ ADJ 形容詞 Something that is **nonstop** continues without any pauses or interruptions. 間断のない □ *Many U.S. cities now have nonstop flights to Aspen.* 今やアスペンへの直行便は米国の多くの都市から出ている。 □ *…80 minutes of nonstop music.* 80分の中休みなしの音楽 ● ADV 副詞 **Nonstop** is also an adverb. 途中で一度も中断せずに [ADV after v] □ *Amy and her group had driven nonstop through Spain.* エイミーと彼女のグループは途中どこにも立ち寄らずにスペインをドライブした。

Thesaurus   nonstop また次を参照：

ADJ.	continuous, direct, uninterrupted

noo|dle /nud°l/ (**noodles**) N-COUNT 可算名詞 **Noodles** are long, thin strips of pasta. They are used especially in Chinese and Italian cooking. ヌードル

noon /nun/ ■ N-UNCOUNT 不可算名詞 **Noon** is twelve o'clock in the middle of the day. 正午 □ *The long day of meetings started at noon.* 打ち合わせで構成される長い1日は正午に始まった。 ■ ADJ 形容詞 **Noon** means happening or appearing in the middle part of the day. 真昼の [ADJ n] □ *The noon sun was fierce.* 真昼の太陽は強烈だった。 ■ **morning, noon, and night** → see **morning**

no one PRON-INDEF-NEG 否定不定代名詞 **No one** means not a single person, or not a single member of a particular group or set. だれも~ない □ *Everyone wants to be a hero, but no one wants to die.* だれもが英雄になりたがっているがだれも死にたくはない。

noose /nus/ (**nooses**) N-COUNT 可算名詞 A **noose** is a circular loop at the end of a piece of rope or wire. A noose is tied with a knot that allows it to be tightened, and it is usually used to trap animals or hang people. 輪縄 □ *…a horrifying videotape of a man swinging from a noose.* 男が輪縄にぶら下がっている恐ろしいビデオ

nope /noʊp/ CONVENTION 慣習表現 **Nope** is sometimes used instead of "no" as a negative response. いや [INFORMAL, SPOKEN くだけた、口語] □ *"Is he supposed to work today?" — "Nope, tomorrow."* 「彼女は今日働くことになっていますか」「いや、明日だ」

nor /nɔr/ ■ CONJ 接続詞 You use **nor** after "neither" in order to introduce the second alternative or the last of a number of alternatives in a negative statement. もまた~ない □ *Neither Mr. Rose nor Mr. Woodhead was available for comment yesterday.* 昨日はローズ氏もウッドヘッド氏も質問に応じなかった。 □ *I can give you neither an opinion nor any advice.* 私はあなたに意見も助言も提供することはできない。 ■ CONJ 接続詞 You use **nor** after a negative statement in order to introduce another negative statement which adds information to the previous one. また~でない □ *Cooking up a quick dish doesn't mean you have to sacrifice flavor. Nor does fast food have to be junk food.* 手早く作ったからといって料理がまずいとは限らないし、ファストフードがジャンクフードとは限らない。 ■ CONJ 接続詞 You use **nor** after a negative statement in order to indicate that the negative statement also applies to you or to someone or something else. また~ない □ *"None of us has any idea how long we're going to be here." — "Nor do I."* 「私たちはだれもここにどの位いるか分からない」「私にも分からない」 □ *"If my husband has no future," she said, "then nor do my children."* 「もし私の夫に将来がないなら子供達にも将来はありません」と彼女は言った。

norm /nɔrm/ (**norms**) ■ N-COUNT 可算名詞 **Norms** are ways of behaving that are considered normal in a particular society. 規準 □ *The actions then depart from what she called the commonly accepted norms of democracy.* 取られた行動は通常受け入れられる民主主義の模範と彼女が呼ぶものに反している。 ■ N-SING 単数名詞 If you say that a situation is **the norm**, you mean that it is usual and expected. 典型 □ *Families of six or seven are the norm in Borough Park.* ボロー・パークでは6~7人家族が普通だ。 ■ N-COUNT 可算名詞 A **norm** is an official standard or level that organizations are expected to reach. 平均学力 □ *About 32 percent of students meet national norms in reading.* 学生の約32%は読書力の全国平均学力に達している。

nor|mal /nɔrm°l/ ■ ADJ 形容詞 Something that is **normal** is usual and ordinary, and is what people expect. 正常の □ *The two countries resumed normal diplomatic relations.* 両国は正常の外交関係を再開した。 □ *Her height and weight are normal for her age.* 彼女の身長と体重は彼女の年齢に対して正常だ。 ■ ADJ 形容詞 A **normal** person has no serious physical or mental health problems. 健常な □ *Statistics indicate that depressed patients are more likely to become ill than are normal people.* 統計によると、うつ状態の患者は健常な人より病気になりやすい。

Thesaurus
normal また次を参照：

ADJ.   ordinary, regular, typical, usual **1**

Word Partnership
normal は次の語句と使われる：

N.   normal **conditions**, normal **development**, normal **routine** **1**

V.   **return to** normal **1**

ADV.   **back to** normal **1**
     completely normal, **perfectly** normal **1 2**

nor|mal|ity /nɔrmǽlɪti/ N-UNCOUNT 不可算名詞 **Normality** is a situation in which everything is normal. 正常性 ◻ *A semblance of normality has returned with people going to work and shops reopening.* 人々は仕事場に向い, 店は再開業し, うわべの正常さが戻った.

Word Link
ize ≈ making : finalize, memorize, normalize

nor|mal|ize /nɔrməlaɪz/ (**normalizes, normalizing, normalized**) **1** V-T/V-I 他動詞/自動詞 When you **normalize** a situation or when it **normalizes**, it becomes normal. 正常化する ◻ *Meditation tends to lower or normalize blood pressure.* 瞑想（めいそう）は血圧を下げたり, 正常化にする傾向がある. **2** V-RECIP 相互動詞 If people, groups, or governments **normalize** relations, or when relations **normalize**, they become normal or return to normal. 正常化する ◻ *The two governments were close to normalizing relations.* 両政府は関係の正常化に近づいた ◻ *The United States says they are not prepared to join in normalizing ties with their former enemy.* 米国はかつての敵国との関係正常化に加わるつもりはないと述べている. ● **nor|mali|za|tion** /nɔrməlɪzeɪʃ°n/ N-UNCOUNT 不可算名詞 正常化 ◻ *The two sides would like to see the normalization of diplomatic relations.* 両国は外交関係の正常化を望んでいる.

nor|mal|ly /nɔrməli/ **1** ADV 副詞 If you say that something **normally** happens or that you **normally** do a particular thing, you mean that it is what usually happens or what you usually do. 普通に ◻ *All airports in the country are working normally today.* 今日その国の空港は全て正常に機能している. ◻ *Social progress is normally a matter of struggles and conflicts.* 社会の進歩は通常, 苦労と争いの問題である. **2** ADV 副詞 If you do something **normally**, you do it in the usual or conventional way. 正常に [ADV after v] ◻ *...failure of the blood to clot normally.* 血液が正常に凝固しないこと

north /nɔrθ/ also **North 1** N-UNCOUNT 不可算名詞 The **north** is the direction which is on your left when you are looking toward the direction where the sun rises. 北 [also 'the' N] ◻ *In the north the ground becomes very cold as the winter snow and ice covers the ground.* 北部では冬の雪と氷に覆われて地面は非常に冷たくなる. **2** N-SING 単数名詞 **The north** of a place, country, or region is the part which is in the north. 北部 ◻ *The plan mostly benefits people in the North and Midwest.* その計画は主に北部と中西部の人々のためになる. **3** ADV 副詞 If you go **north**, you travel toward the north. 北へ [ADV after v] ◻ *Anita drove north up Pacific Highway.* アニータはパシフィック・ハイウェーを北にドライブした. **4** ADV 副詞 Something that is **north** of a place is positioned to the north of it. 北方へ ◻ *...a little village a few miles north of Portland.* ポートランドの北方数マイルの小さな村 **5** ADJ 形容詞 The **north** edge, corner, or part of a place or country is the part which is toward the north. 北の [ADJ n] ◻ *...the north side of the mountain.* 山の北側 **6** ADJ 形容詞 "North" is used in the names of some countries, states, and regions in the north of a larger area. 北部の [ADJ n] ◻ *There were demonstrations this weekend in cities throughout North America, Asia and Europe.* 北米, アジア, ヨーロッパ内の都市で今週末デモ行進があった. **7** ADJ 形容詞 A **north** wind is a wind that blows from the north. 北から吹く [ADJ n] ◻ *A bitterly cold north wind.* ひどく冷たい北風 **8** N-SING 単数名詞 **The North** is used to refer to the richer, more developed countries of the world. 先進国 ['the' N] ◻ *Malaysia has emerged as the toughest critic of the North's environmental attitudes.* マレーシアは先進国の環境政策に最も厳しく批評する国であることが明らかになった.
→ see **globe**

north|east /nɔrθist/ **1** N-UNCOUNT 不可算名詞 The **northeast** is the direction which is halfway between north and east. 北東 [also 'the' N] ◻ *...the warm waters of Salt Springs Island to the northeast.* ソルトスプリング島の暖かい海を北東へ **2** N-SING 単数名詞 **The northeast** of a place, country, or region is the part which is in the northeast. 北東部 ◻ *The northeast has been particularly hard hit..* 北東部は特にひどい影響を受けた. **3** ADV 副詞 If you go **northeast**, you travel toward the northeast. 北東へ [ADV after v] ◻ *"We're going northeast," Paula told them, before they started.* 「私たちは北東へ行く予定です」とポーラは出発する前に告げた. **4** ADV 副詞 Something that is **northeast** of a place is positioned to the northeast of it. 北東に [ADV 'of' n] ◻ *This latest attack was at Careysburg, twenty miles northeast of the capital, Monrovia.* この最近の攻撃は首都モンロビアの北東20マイル離れたキャリーズバーグ

で起こった. **5** ADJ 形容詞 The **northeast** edge, corner, or part of a place is the part which is toward the northeast. 北東の [ADJ n] ◻ *...a climate like that of our northeast coast.* 我が国の北東の海岸のような気候

north|eastern /nɔrθistərn/ ADJ 形容詞 **Northeastern** means in or from the northeast of a region or country. 北東部の ◻ *...on the northeastern coast of Florida.* フロリダ北東部の海岸

nor|ther|ly /nɔrðərli/ ADJ 形容詞 A **northerly** point, area, or direction is to the north or toward the north. 北へ向う ◻ *The storm is headed on a northerly path.* 嵐は北に向っている.

north|ern /nɔrðərn/ also **Northern** ADJ 形容詞 **Northern** means in or from the north of a region, state, or country. 北部地方の [ADJ n] ◻ *Their two children were immigrants to Northern Ireland from Pennsylvania.* 彼らの2人の子供達はペニンシルベニアから北アイルランドに移民した.

north|ward /nɔrθwərd/ also **northwards** ADV 副詞 **Northward** or **northwards** means toward the north. 北の方へ ◻ *Tropical storm Marco is pushing northward up Florida's coast.* 熱帯暴風マルコはフロリダの海岸を北方に進んでいる. ● ADJ 形容詞 **Northward** is also an adjective. 北へ向う [ADJ n] ◻ *The northward journey from Jalalabad was no more than 120 miles.* ジャララバードから北に向う旅はせいぜい120マイルだった.

north|west /nɔrθwɛst/ **1** N-UNCOUNT 不可算名詞 The **northwest** is the direction which is halfway between north and west. 北西 [also 'the' N] ◻ *...four miles to the northwest.* 北西に4マイル **2** N-SING 単数名詞 **The northwest** of a place, country, or region is the part which is toward the northwest. 北西部 ◻ *...in the extreme northwest of the country.* その国の北西部の先端 **3** ADV 副詞 If you go **northwest**, you travel toward the northwest. 北西へ [ADV after v] ◻ *Take the narrow lane going northwest parallel with the railroad line.* 鉄道線路と平行して北西に進む細道を取りなさい. **4** ADV 副詞 Something that is **northwest** of a place is positioned to the northwest of it. 北西に [ADV 'of' n] ◻ *Just a couple of hours to the northwest of the capital is the wine-growing area of Hunter Valley.* 首都を北西にほんの数時間行ったところにハンター峡谷のワイン造り地区がある. **5** ADJ 形容詞 The **northwest** part of a place, country, or region is the part which is toward the northwest. 北西にある [ADJ n] ◻ *...the northwest coast of the United States.* 米国北西部の海岸

north|western /nɔrθwɛstərn/ ADJ 形容詞 **Northwestern** means in or from the northwest of a region or country. 北西部地方の ◻ *Virtually every river in northwestern Oregon was near flood stage.* オレゴン州北西部地方の川はほとんど全て高水位に近づいていた.

nose /noʊz/ (**noses, nosing, nosed**) **1** N-COUNT 可算名詞 Your **nose** is the part of your face which sticks out above your mouth. You use it for smelling and breathing. 鼻 ◻ *She wiped her nose with a tissue.* 彼女はティッシュで鼻をふいた. **2** N-COUNT 可算名詞 The **nose** of a vehicle such as an airplane or a boat is the front part of it. 前部 ◻ *They went over to the airplane and stood near its nose.* 彼らは飛行機のところに行き, その前部の近くに立った. **3** N-COUNT 可算名詞 You can refer to your sense of smell as your **nose**. 嗅覚 ◻ *The river that runs through Middlesbrough became ugly on the eye and hard on the nose.* ミドルスパラを流れるその川は見苦しくひどいにおいがするようになった. **4** V-T/V-I 他動詞/自動詞 If a vehicle **noses** in a certain direction or if you **nose** it there, you move it slowly and carefully in that direction. ゆっくり注意深く前進する ◻ *He could not see the driver as the car nosed forward.* 彼は車がゆっくり前進する時に運転者が見えなかった. ◻ *A motorboat nosed out of the mist and nudged into the branches of a tree.* モーターボートはもやの中でゆっくり前進し, 木の枝に接近した. **5** PHRASE 句 If you **keep** your **nose clean**, you behave well and stay out of trouble. 悪事/面倒 にかかわらない [INFORMAL くだけた] ◻ *If you kept your nose clean, you had a job for life.* 悪事にかかわらなかったら一生の職があったのに. **6** PHRASE 句 If you **follow** your **nose** to get to a place, you go straight ahead or follow the most obvious route. まっすぐに進む ◻ *Just follow your nose and in about five minutes you're at the old railway.* まっすぐ進むと約5分後に古い鉄道に着く. **7** PHRASE 句 If you **follow** your **nose**, you do something in a particular way because you feel it should be done like that, rather than because you are following any plan or rules. 直感に頼る ◻ *You won't have to think, just follow your nose.* 考える必要はない, ただ直感に頼りなさい. **8** PHRASE 句 If you say that someone **has a nose for** something, you mean that they have a natural ability to find it or recognize it. かぎつける勘がある ◻ *He had a nose for trouble and a brilliant tactical mind.* 彼には問題をかぎつける勘があり, 駆け引きがひどく上手だった. **9** PHRASE 句 If you say that someone **looks down** their **nose** at something or someone, you mean that they believe they are superior to that person or thing and treat them with disrespect. 見下げる [DISAPPROVAL 不賛成] ◻ *I don't look down my nose at comedy.* 私はコメディを見下げているわけではない. **10** PHRASE 句 If you say that you **paid through the nose** for something, you are emphasizing that you had to pay what you consider too high a price for it. 法外な代金を払う [INFORMAL くだけた, EMPHASIS 強調] ◻ *We don't like paying through the nose for our wine when eating out.* 我々は外食する時にワ

インに法外な代金を払いたくない．**11** PHRASE 句 If someone **pokes** their **nose into** something or **sticks** their **nose into** something, they try to interfere with it even though it does not concern them. おせっかいを焼く [INFORMAL くだけた, DISAPPROVAL 不賛成] ❑ *We don't like strangers who poke their noses into our affairs.* 私たちは見知らぬ人に私たちの問題におせっかいを焼いてもらいたくない． **12** PHRASE 句 To **rub** someone's **nose in** something that they do not want to think about, such as a failing or a mistake they have made, means to remind them repeatedly about it. しつこくなじる [INFORMAL くだけた] ❑ *His enemies will attempt to rub his nose in past policy statements.* 彼の敵は過去の政策声明をしつこくなじろうとするだろう． **13** PHRASE 句 If you **turn up** your **nose at** something, you reject it because you think that it is not good enough for you. ばかにする ❑ *I'm not in a financial position to turn up my nose at several hundred thousand dollars.* 私の家計は数十万ドルの金をばかにする状態ではない． **14** PHRASE 句 If you do something **under** someone's **nose**, you do it right in front of them, without trying to hide it from them. 人の鼻先で ❑ *We've been married 25 years and this carrying on under my nose was the last straw.* 私たちは結婚して25年になるが，すぐ目の前の無責任な振る舞いは限度を超えていた． **15** PHRASE 句 If vehicles are **nose to tail**, the front of one vehicle is close behind the back of another. 数珠つなぎの [mainly BRIT 主に英国英語; AM **bumper-to-bumper** 米国英語 **bumper-to-bumper**] **16** to put someone's **nose out of joint** → see **joint**
→ see **face, respiratory, smell**

▶ **nose around** PHRASAL VERB 句動詞 If you **nose around** a place that belongs to someone else, to see if you can find something interesting. 詮索して回る [INFORMAL くだけた] ❑ *I wondered what else he'd taken and nosed around his bureau.* 彼はその他に何を持ち帰り，机を詮索して回ったのだろうと私は思った． ❑ *He had thought to just nose around, see what he could.* 彼はちょっと詮索して回ろうと考えていた．

Word Partnership   *nose* は次の語句と使われる：

ADJ.	**big** nose, **bloody** nose, **broken** nose, **long** nose, **red** nose, **runny** nose, **straight** nose **1**

nose|dive /**noʊz**daɪv/ (**nosedives, nosediving, nosedived**) also **nose-dive** **1** V-I 自動詞 If prices, profits, or exchange rates **nosedive**, they suddenly fall by a large amount. 暴落する [JOURNALISM ジャーナリズム] ❑ *The value of their shares nosedived by $2.6 billion.* 他の株価は26億ドル暴落した． ● N-SING 単数名詞 **Nosedive** is also a noun. 暴落 ❑ *The bank yesterday revealed a 30 percent nosedive in profits.* 銀行は昨日，利益が30%急減したことを発表した． **2** V-I 自動詞 If something such as someone's reputation or career **nosedives**, it suddenly gets much worse. 急に悪化する [JOURNALISM ジャーナリズム] ❑ *Since the U.S. invasion the president's reputation has nosedived.* 米国の侵略以来，大統領の評判は急激に悪化した． ● N-SING 単数名詞 **Nosedive** is also a noun. 急落 ❑ *He told the tribunal his career had "taken a nosedive" since his dismissal last year.* 彼のキャリアは昨年解雇されてから急に悪化したと彼は裁判所に告げた．

nos|tal|gia /nɒstˈældʒə/ N-UNCOUNT 不可算名詞 **Nostalgia** is an affectionate feeling you have for the past, especially for a particularly happy time. 郷愁 ❑ *He might be influenced by nostalgia for the surroundings of his happy youth.* 彼は幸福な青春時代の環境への郷愁に影響されているのかもしれない．

nos|tal|gic /nɒstˈældʒɪk/ **1** ADJ 形容詞 **Nostalgic** things cause you to think affectionately about the past. 郷愁にふける ❑ *Although we still depict nostalgic snow scenes on Christmas cards, winters are now very much warmer.* 私たちはまだクリスマスカードにノスタルジックな雪の場面を描写するが，冬は今やずっと暖かい． **2** ADJ 形容詞 If you feel **nostalgic**, you think affectionately about experiences you had in the past. ノスタルジックな ❑ *Many people were nostalgic for the good old days.* 多くの人々はよき昔に対してノスタルジアを感じた． ● **nos|tal|gi|cal|ly** /nɒstˈældʒɪkli/ ADV 副詞 ノスタルジックに ❑ *People look back nostalgically on the war period, simply because everyone pulled together.* 人々はだれもが協力したというそれだけの理由で戦時中のことをノスタルジックに思い出す．

nos|tril /nɒstrɪl/ (**nostrils**) N-COUNT 可算名詞 Your **nostrils** are the two openings at the end of your nose. 鼻の穴 ❑ *Keeping your mouth closed, breathe in through your nostrils.* 口を閉じ鼻の穴から呼吸しなさい．

nosy /nˈoʊzi/ (**nosier, nosiest**) also **nosey** ADJ 形容詞 If you describe someone as **nosy**, you mean that they are interested in things which do not concern them. おせっかいな [INFORMAL くだけた, DISAPPROVAL 不賛成] ❑ *He was having to whisper in order to avoid being overheard by their nosy neighbors.* 彼は詮索好きな隣人に立ち聞きされないように小声で話さなければならなかった．

not /nɒt/

Not is often shortened to **n't** in spoken English, and added to the auxiliary or modal verb. For example, "did not" is often shortened to "didn't."

Not はしばしば口語英語では **n't** に短縮され，助動詞または法動詞に付け加えられる．例えば，**did not** はしばしば **didn't** に短縮される．

1 NEG 否定語 You use **not** with verbs to form negative statements. ない ❑ *The sanctions are not working the way they were intended.* 経済制裁は目的どおりには機能していない． ❑ *I don't trust my father anymore.* 私はもう父親を信用しない． **2** NEG 否定語 You use **not** to form questions to which you expect the answer "yes." しない ❑ *Haven't they got enough problems there already?* 彼らはそこで既に十分な問題を抱えているのではないのか． ❑ *Didn't I see you at the party last week?* 僕は先週あなたをパーティーで会いませんでしたか． **3** NEG 否定語 You use **not**, usually in the form **n't**, in questions which imply that someone should have done something, or to express surprise that something is not the case. しない ❑ *Why didn't you do it months ago?* なぜ数か月前にそれをしなかったのですか． ❑ *Why couldn't he listen to her?* なぜ彼は彼女の言うことが聞けなかったのか． **4** NEG 否定語 You use **not**, usually in the form **n't**, in question tags after a positive statement. しない ❑ *It's crazy, isn't it?* それは常識を欠いていますね． ❑ *I've been a great husband, haven't I?* 僕は立派な夫だったよね．私は先週あなたとパーティーで会いませんでしたか． **5** NEG 否定語 You use **not**, usually in the form **n't**, in polite suggestions. `しませんか [POLITENESS 丁寧さ] ❑ *Actually we do have a position in mind. Why don't you fill out our application?* 実のところ心当たりの席があります．願書に記入してみませんか． **6** NEG 否定語 You use **not** to represent the negative of a word, group, or clause that has just been used. 否定の文の省略代用語 ❑ *"Have you found Paula?" — "I'm afraid not, Kate."* 「ポーラは見つかったの」「残念ながら見つかってない，ケイト」 **7** NEG 否定語 You can use **not** in front of "all" or "every" when you want to say something that applies only to some members of the group that you are talking about. 部分否定 ❑ *Not all the money, to put it mildly, has been used wisely.* 控えめに言えば全ての金が賢明に使われたわけではなかった． **8** NEG 否定語 If something is **not** always the case, you mean that sometimes it is the case and sometimes it is not. 部分否定 ❑ *He didn't always win the arguments, but he often was right.* 彼はいつも議論に勝つわけではなかったが彼の言うことはしばしば正しかった． ❑ *She couldn't always afford a babysitter.* 彼女はベビーシッターを雇う金銭的な余裕がいつもあるわけではなかった． **9** NEG 否定語 You can use **not** or **not even** in front of "a" or "one" to emphasize that there is none at all of what is being mentioned. 強意 [EMPHASIS 強調] ❑ *…no office, no phone, not even a shelf on which to put my meager belongings.* 事務所もなければ電話もなく，わずかな所持品を置く棚すらない． ❑ *I sent report after report. But not one word was published.* 私は次々とレポートを送ったが一言も公表されなかった． **10** NEG 否定語 You can use **not** in front of a word referring to a distance, length of time, or other amount to say that the actual distance, time, or amount is less than the one mentioned. `なくもなく [NEG amount] ❑ *The tug crossed our stern not fifty yards away.* 50ヤードも離れていないところでタグボートが私達の船尾を横切った． ❑ *…a large crowd not ten yards away waiting for a bus.* 10ヤードも離れていないところで大勢の人がバスを待っている． **11** NEG 否定語 You use **not** when you are contrasting something that is true with something that is untrue. You use this especially to indicate that people might think that the untrue statement is true. `でない ❑ *He has his place in the Asian team not because he is white but because he is good.* 彼がアジアチームの一員なのは白人だからではなく優秀だからである． ❑ *Training is an investment not a cost.* 研修は経費ではなく投資である． **12** NEG 否定語 You use **not** in expressions such as "not only," "not just," and "not simply" to emphasize that something is true, but it is not the whole truth. `だけでなく [EMPHASIS 強調] ❑ *These movies were not only making money; they were also perceived to be original.* こうした映画はもうかるだけでなく独創的とも見なされた． ❑ *What's it going to cost us, not just in terms of money, but in terms of lives?* 金銭面だけでなく人命の点から見てそれにはどんな犠牲が伴うのか． **13** PHRASE 句 You use **not that** to introduce a negative clause that contradicts something that the previous statement implies. `ということではない ❑ *His death took me a year to get over; not that you're ever really over it.* 彼の死を受け入れるのに1年かかった．そもそも本当に受け入れるというわけではないが． **14** CONVENTION 慣習表現 **Not at all** is an emphatic way of saying "No" or of agreeing that the answer to a question is "No." 全くーでない [EMPHASIS 強調] ❑ *"Sorry. I sound like Abby, don't I?" — "No. Not at all."* 「すみません，私はアビーのように聞こえますね」「いいえ，そんなことはありません」 **15** CONVENTION 慣習表現 **Not at all** is a polite way of acknowledging a person's thanks. どういたしまして [FORMULAE 決まり文句] ❑ *"Thank you very much for speaking with us." — "Not at all."* 「お話ありがとうございます」「どういたしまして」 **16** **not half** → see **half** **17** **if not** → see **if** **18** **more often than not** → see **often**

no|table /nˈoʊtəbəl/ ADJ 形容詞 Someone or something that is **notable** is important or interesting. 注目に値する ❑ *The proposed new structure is notable not only for its height, but for its shape.* 提案された新しい構造は高さだけでなく形が注目に値する． ❑ *Mo did not want to be ruled by anyone and it is notable that she never allowed the men in her life to eclipse her.* モーは誰にも支配されたがらず，彼女が一生のうちで

知り合った男たちに彼女の影を薄くさせなかったことは注目に値する.

noted the building's history of problems. 彼らはその建物の問題の経歴を書きとめていなかった. **12** N-COUNT 可算名詞 You can refer to a banknote as a **note**. 紙幣 [mainly BRIT 主に英国英語; AM usually **bill** 米国英語では通常 **bill**] **13** → see also **noted, promissory note** **14** PHRASE 句 Someone or something that is **of note** is important, worth mentioning, or well-known. 著名な □ ...politicians of note. 著名な政治家 **15** PHRASE 句 If you **take note** of something, you pay attention to it because you think that it is important or significant. よく注意する □ Take note of the weather conditions. 天候状態によく注意する

A **famous** person or thing is known to more people than a **well-known** one. A **notorious** person or thing is famous because they are connected with something bad or undesirable. **Infamous** is not the opposite of **famous**. It has a similar meaning to **notorious**, but is a stronger word. Someone or something that is **notable** is important or interesting.

---

no|tably /nóutəbli/ **1** ADV 副詞 You use **notably** to specify an important or typical example of something that you are talking about. 特に [ADV group/cl] □ The divorce would be granted when more important problems, notably the fate of the children, had been decided. 離婚により重要な問題、とりわけ子供の将来が決まった時に成立するだろう. **2** ADV 副詞 You can use **notably** to emphasize a particular quality that someone or something has. 目立つほどに [EMPHASIS 強調] [ADV adj/adv] □ Old established friends are notably absent, so it's a good opportunity to make new contacts. 旧友は目立つほどに欠席したので新しい知り合いを作る良い機会だ.

notch /nótʃ/ (notches, notching, notched) **1** N-COUNT 可算名詞 You can refer to a level on a scale of measurement or achievement as a **notch**. 段階 [JOURNALISM ジャーナリズム] □ Average earnings in the economy moved up another notch in August. 経済の平均所得は8月にもう一段階上がった. □ In this country the good players are pulled down a notch or two. この国では優秀な選手は一段階か二段階引き下げられる. **2** V-T 他動詞 If you **notch** a success, especially in a sports contest, you achieve it. あげる [JOURNALISM ジャーナリズム] □ "It took longer than we wanted," Clemens said after notching his first victory since June 9. 「思ったより長くかかった」とクレメンスは6月9日以来最初の勝利を得た後に述べた. **3** N-COUNT 可算名詞 A **notch** is a small V-shaped or circular cut in the surface or edge of something. V字型の切れ込み □ It is a myth that gunslingers in the American west cut notches in the handle of their pistol for each man they shot. アメリカ西部のピストルの名人は射殺する毎にピストルの取っ手にV字型の切れ込みを入れるというのは作り話だ.

▶ **notch up** PHRASAL VERB 句動詞 If you **notch up** something such as a score or total, you achieve it. あげる [JOURNALISM ジャーナリズム] □ He had notched up more than 25 victories worldwide. 彼は世界中で25以上の勝利をあげていた.

note /nóut/ (notes, noting, noted) **1** N-COUNT 可算名詞 A **note** is a short letter. 短い手紙 □ Stevens wrote him a note asking him to come to his apartment. スティーブンズは彼をアパートに招く短い手紙を書いた. **2** N-COUNT 可算名詞 A **note** is something that you write down to remind yourself of something. メモ □ I knew that if I didn't make a note I would lose the thought so I asked to borrow a pen or pencil. 私はメモを取らないと発想を失うことが分かっていたのでペンか鉛筆を借りてくれるよう頼んだ. □ She wasn't taking notes on the lecture. 彼女は講義のメモを取っていなかった. **3** N-COUNT 可算名詞 In a book or article, a **note** is a short piece of additional information. 注釈 □ See Note 16 on p. 223. 223ページの注釈16を参照しなさい. **4** N-COUNT 可算名詞 A **note** is a short document that has to be signed by someone and that gives official information about something. 文書 □ Since Mr. Bennett was going to need some time off work, he asked for a sick note. ベネット氏は会社を休まねばならなかったため、彼は病気証明書を求めた. **5** N-COUNT 可算名詞 In music, a **note** is the sound of a particular pitch, or a written symbol representing this sound. 音 □ She has a deep voice and doesn't even try for the high notes. 彼女の声は低く高い音を出そうともしない. **6** N-SING 単数名詞 You can use **note** to refer to a particular quality in someone's voice that shows how they are feeling. 声の調子 □ There is an unmistakable note of nostalgia in his voice when he looks back on the early years of the family business. 家族経営の事業の初期を振り返る時に彼の声は紛れもないノスタルジックな調子を帯びている. **7** N-SING 単数名詞 You can use **note** to refer to a particular feeling, impression, or atmosphere. 雰囲気 □ Yesterday's testimony began on a note of passionate but civilized disagreement. 昨日の証言は熱情的だが礼儀正しい雰囲気で始まった. □ Somehow he tells these stories without a note of horror. どういうわけか彼は恐れる様子もなくこうした話をする. **8** V-T 他動詞 If you **note** a fact, you become aware of it. 気づく □ The White House has noted his promise to support any attack that was designed to enforce the UN resolutions. ホワイトハウスは国連の決議案を実施するための攻撃を支持すると約束したことに気づいた. □ Suddenly, I noted that the rain had stopped. 私は雨がやんだことに突然気づいた. **9** V-T 他動詞 If you tell someone to **note** something, you are drawing their attention to it. 注意する □ Note the statue to Sallustio Bandini, a prominent Sienese. 著名なシエナ人であるサラスチオ・バンディーニの彫像に注意しなさい. **10** V-T 他動詞 If you **note** something, you mention it in order to draw people's attention to it. ～に特に言及する □ The report notes that export and import volumes picked up in leading economies. そのレポートは先進国の輸出入量が増加したことを特筆している. **11** V-T 他動詞 When you **note** something, you write it down as a record of what has happened. 書き留める □ "He has had his tonsils out and has been ill, too," she noted in her diary. 「彼は扁桃腺（へんとうせん）を取ってもらい、体調も崩していた」と彼女は日記に書きとめた. □ They never

▶ **note down** PHRASAL VERB 句動詞 If you **note down** something, you write it down quickly, so that you have a record of it. 書き留める □ She had noted down the names and she told me the story simply and factually. 彼女は名前を書きとめ、手短かつ事実に基づいて私にその話を伝えた. □ If you find a name that's on the list I've given you, note it down. 私のあげた名簿に名前を見つけたらそれを書き留めなさい.

Word Partnership   note は次の語句と使われる:

v.	leave a note, send a note **1**
	find a note, read a note, scribble a note, write a note **1 2**
	make a note **2**
	sound a note, strike a note **5**
	take note of *something* **15**

note|book /nóutbʊk/ (notebooks) **1** N-COUNT 可算名詞 A **notebook** is a small book for writing notes in. 手帳 □ He brought out a notebook and pen from his pocket. 彼はポケットから手帳とペンを取り出した. **2** N-COUNT 可算名詞 A **notebook** computer is a small personal computer. ノートパソコン □ ...a range of notebook computers which allows all your important information to travel safely with you. 重要な情報を全て持ち運べる各種ノートパソコン
→ see **office**

not|ed /nóutɪd/ ADJ 形容詞 To be **noted for** something you do or have means to be well known and admired for it. ～で有名な □ ...a television program noted for its attacks on organized crime. 組織犯罪への攻撃で有名なテレビ番組

noth|ing /nʌ́θɪŋ/ (nothings) **1** PRON-INDEF-NEG 否定不定代詞 **Nothing** means not a single thing, or not a single part of something. 何もない □ I've done nothing much since this morning. 私は今朝からほとんど何もしていない. □ There is nothing wrong with the car. その車には具合の悪いところは何もない. **2** PRON-INDEF-NEG 否定不定代詞 You use **nothing** to indicate that something or someone is not important or significant. 重要でないもの □ Because he had always had money it meant nothing to him. 彼はいつも金銭的に恵まれていたのでそれは彼にとって重要ではなかった. □ Do our years together mean nothing? 私達が一緒に過ごした年月は重要ではないのか. ● N-COUNT 可算名詞 **Nothing** is also a noun. 取るに足りないもの □ It is the picture itself that is the problem; so small, so dull. It's a nothing, really. 問題なのは絵そのものだ. 非常に小さて退屈だ. それは全く取るに足りないものだ. **3** PRON-INDEF-NEG 否定不定代詞 If you say that something cost **nothing** or is worth **nothing**, you are indicating that it cost or is worth a surprisingly small amount of money. 価値のないもの □ The furniture was threadbare; he'd obviously picked it up for nothing. 家具はみすぼらしかった. 彼は明らかにそれをわずかな金額で手に入れたに違いない. **4** PRON-INDEF-NEG 否定不定代詞 You use **nothing** before an adjective or 'to'-infinitive to say that something or someone does not have the quality indicated. 何もない □ Around the lake the countryside generally is nothing special. 湖の周りでカントリーサイドは概してそれほど並外れてはいない. □ There was nothing remarkable about him. 彼にはこれといって顕著な点はなかった. **5** PRON-INDEF-NEG 否定不定代詞 You can use **nothing** before "so" and an adjective or adverb, or before a comparative, to emphasize how strong or great a particular quality is. 何もない [EMPHASIS 強調] □ Youngsters learn nothing so fast as how to beat the system. 若者が制度を打ち負かす方法を覚えるほど早いものはない. □ I consider nothing more important in my life than songwriting. 私の人生で歌謡曲の作詞作曲ほど重要なものはない. **6** PHRASE 句 You can use **all or nothing** to say that either something must be done fully and completely or else it cannot be done at all. 全部か ゼロ □ Either he went through with this thing or he did not; it was all or nothing. 彼がそれをやり通すか、やり通さないかだった. それは全部かゼロかだった. **7** PHRASE 句 If you say that something is **better than nothing**, you mean that it is not what is required, but that it is better to have that thing than to have nothing at all. しないよりまし □ After all, 15 minutes of exercise is better than nothing. やはり15分間の運動は運動しないよりましった. **8** PHRASE 句 You use **nothing but** in front of a noun, an infinitive without "to," or an "-ing" form to mean "only." ～の他は何もない □ All that money brought nothing but sadness and misery and tragedy. あれだけのお金は悲しみと惨めさと悲劇の他に何ももたらさなかった. □ It did nothing but make us ridiculous. それは私たちをこっけいに見せるだけだった. □ He is focused on nothing but winning. 彼は勝つことだけに焦点を当てている. **9** CONVENTION 慣習表現 People

sometimes say "**It's nothing**" as a polite response after someone has thanked them for something they have done. 礼には及びません [FORMULAE 決まり文句] ❑ "*Thank you for the wonderful dinner.*" — "*It's nothing,*" *Sarah said.* 「素晴らしい食事をありがとうございました」「礼には及ばないわ」とセイラは言った。 ⑩ PHRASE 句 If you say about a story or report that there is **nothing to it**, you mean that it is untrue. まったくうそだ ❑ *It's all superstition, and there's nothing to it.* それは全て迷信で、真実ではない。 ⑪ PHRASE 句 If you say about an activity that there is **nothing to it**, you mean that it is extremely easy. 容易なことだ ❑ *If you've shied away from making pancakes in the past, don't be put off – there's really nothing to it!* 今までパンケーキを焼くのをしりごみした人も嫌がらないで。本当に簡単ですよ。 ⑫ PHRASE 句 **Nothing of the sort** is used when strongly contradicting something that has just been said. そのようなものは～ない [EMPHASIS 強調] ❑ "*We're going to talk this over in my office.*" — "*We're going to do nothing of the sort.*" 「私たちはこれを私のオフィスでじっくり話し合うつもりだ」「そのつもりは全くない」 ⑬ **nothing to write home about** → see home ⑭ to **stop at nothing** → see stop ⑮ to **think nothing of** → see think

no|tice /noʊtɪs/ (**notices, noticing, noticed**) ① V-T/V-I 他動詞/自動詞 If you **notice** something or someone, you become aware of them. 気づく ❑ *He stressed that people should not hesitate to contact the police if they've noticed any strangers recently.* 最近見知らぬ人に気づいた場合にはためらわず警察に連絡すべきと彼は強調した。 ❑ *I noticed that most academics were writing papers during the summer.* 私は大学教師の大半が夏に資料を書いていることに気づいた。 ❑ *Luckily, I'd noticed where you left the car.* 幸運にもあなたがどこに車を駐車したかに気づいた。 ❑ *If he thought no one would notice, he's wrong.* 彼がだれも気づいていないと考えたのなら彼は間違っている。 ② N-COUNT 可算名詞 A **notice** is a written announcement in a place where everyone can read it. 掲示 ❑ *Notices in the waiting room requested that you neither smoke nor spit.* 待合室には「禁煙」と「つばを吐くな」という張り紙があった。 ❑ *A few guest houses had "No Vacancies" notices in their windows.* 数件のゲストハウスの窓に「空室なし」の張り紙があった。 ③ N-UNCOUNT 不可算名詞 If you give **notice** about something that is going to happen, you give a warning in advance that it is going to happen. 予告 ❑ *Interest is paid monthly. Three months' notice is required for withdrawals.* 利子は月々支払われます。払い戻しには3ヶ月の予告が必要です。 ❑ *The insured must be given at least 10 days' notice of cancellation.* 被保険者には最低10日間の取り消し予告を与えられなければなりません。 ④ N-COUNT 可算名詞 A **notice** is a formal announcement in a newspaper or magazine about something that has happened or is going to happen. 通報 ❑ *I spotted a notice in a local newspaper.* 私は地元の新聞に通報を見つけた。 ⑤ N-COUNT 可算名詞 A **notice** is one of a number of letters that are similar or exactly the same which an organization sends to people in order to give them information or ask them to do something. 通知 ❑ *Bonus notices were issued each year from head office to local agents.* 毎年ボーナスの通知が本社から地元の代理店に配布された。 ⑥ N-COUNT 可算名詞 A **notice** is a written article in a newspaper or magazine in which someone gives their opinion of a play, movie, or concert. 論評 [BRIT 英国英語; AM review 米国英語review] ⑦ PHRASE 句 **Notice** is used in expressions such as "**on short notice**," "**at a moment's notice**," or "**at twenty-four hours' notice**," to indicate that something can or must be done within a short period of time. すぐに ❑ *There's no one available on such short notice to take her class.* それ程すぐに彼女のクラスを受け持つことのできる人はいません。 ❑ *I live just a mile away, so I can usually be available on short notice.* 私は1マイルしか離れていないところに住んでいるのでたいていすぐに応じられます。 ⑧ PHRASE 句 If a situation is said to exist **until further notice**, it will continue for an uncertain length of time until someone changes it. 追って通知のあるまで ❑ *The bad news was that all flights had been canceled until further notice.* 悪い知らせは追って通知のあるまで全便が欠航になったことだった。 ⑨ PHRASE 句 If an employer **gives** an employee **notice**, the employer tells the employee that he or she must leave his or her job within a short fixed period of time. 解雇を通告する [BUSINESS 実業] ❑ *The next morning I telephoned him and gave him his notice.* 翌朝私は彼に電話し、解雇を通告した。 ⑩ PHRASE 句 If you **give notice** or **hand in notice** you tell your employer that you intend to leave your job soon, within a set period of time. You can also **hand in** your **notice**. 辞表を出す [BUSINESS 実業] ❑ *He handed in his notice at the bank and ruined his promising career.* 彼は銀行に辞表を出し、前途有望な将来を台無しにした。 ⑪ PHRASE 句 If you **take notice of** a particular fact or situation, you behave in a way that shows that you are aware of it. 関心を寄せる ❑ *We want the government to take notice of what we think they should do for single parents.* 我々は政府がシングルペアレントへの対策に関する我々の意見に関心を寄せることを望む。 ⑫ PHRASE 句 If you **take no notice of** someone or something, you do not consider them to be important enough to affect what you think or what you do. 注目されない ❑ *They took no notice of him, he did not stand out, he was in no way remarkable.* 彼が注目されることはなかった。目立たず、注目に値するところは全くなかった。

no|tice|able /noʊtɪsəbəl/ ADJ 形容詞 Something that is **noticeable** is very obvious, so that it is easy to see, hear, or recognize. 明らか ❑ *It is noticeable that women do not have the rivalry that men have.* 女性には男性が持つようなライバル意識がないことは明らかだ。 ● **no|tice|ably** ADV 副詞 著しく ❑ *Standards of living were deteriorating rather noticeably.* 生活水準はかなり著しく悪化していた。

no|tice|board /noʊtɪsbɔrd/ (**noticeboards**) N-COUNT 可算名詞 A **noticeboard** is a board which is usually attached to a wall in order to display notices giving information about something. 掲示板 [mainly BRIT 主に英国英語; AM usually **bulletin board** 米国英語では通常 **bulletin board**]

no|ti|fi|ca|tion /noʊtɪfɪkeɪʃən/ (**notifications**) N-VAR 可変性名詞 If you are given **notification of** something, you are officially informed of it. 通告 ❑ *Names of the dead and injured are being withheld pending notification of relatives.* 死傷者の氏名は親類が通告を受けるまで公表されない。

no|ti|fy /noʊtɪfaɪ/ (**notifies, notifying, notified**) V-T 他動詞 If you **notify** someone of something, you officially inform them about it. 知らせる [FORMAL 形式ばった] ❑ *The skipper notified the coastguard of the tragedy.* 船長は沿岸警備隊に惨事を知らせた。 ❑ *Earlier this year they were notified that their homes were to be cleared away.* 今年のより早い時期に彼らは家が取り払われるとの通知を受けた。

no|tion /noʊʃən/ (**notions**) ① N-COUNT 可算名詞 A **notion** is an idea or belief about something. 概念 ❑ *We each have a notion of just what kind of person we'd like to be.* 私たちは皆理想の人間像がある。 ❑ *I reject absolutely the notion that privatization of our industry is now inevitable.* 私は業界の民営化は今や避けられないという概念を全く否認する。 ② N-PLURAL 複数名詞 **Notions** are small articles for sewing, such as buttons, zips, and thread. 雑貨 [AM 米国英語]

no|to|ri|ety /noʊtəraɪɪti/ N-UNCOUNT 不可算名詞 To achieve **notoriety** means to become well known for something bad. 悪名高いこと ❑ *He achieved notoriety as chief counsel to President Nixon in the Watergate break-in.* 彼はウォーターゲート侵入事件でニクソン大統領の顧問長として有名になった。

no|to|ri|ous /noʊtɔriəs/ ADJ 形容詞 To be **notorious** means to be well known for something bad. 悪名高い ❑ *…an area notorious for drugs, crime and violence.* 麻薬、犯罪、暴力で有名な地区 ● **no|to|ri|ous|ly** ADV 副詞 悪名が知れ渡るほどに ❑ *The train company is overstaffed and notoriously inefficient.* 鉄道会社は必要以上の数の従業員を置き、非効率なことで有名だ。 ❑ *He worked mainly in New York City where living space is notoriously at a premium.* 彼は主に生活の空間が足りないことで有名なニューヨークで働いた。

A **famous** person or thing is known to more people than a **well-known** one. A **notorious** person or thing is famous because they are connected with something bad or undesirable. **Infamous** is not the opposite of **famous**. It has a similar meaning to **notorious**, but is a stronger word. Someone or something that is **notable** is important or interesting.

not|with|stand|ing /nɒtwɪθstændɪŋ, -wɪð-/ PREP 前置詞 If something is true **notwithstanding** something else, it is true in spite of that other thing. ～にもかかわらず [FORMAL 形式ばった] ❑ *He despised William Pitt, notwithstanding the similar views they both held.* 彼は物の見方が似通っていたにもかかわらず、ウィリアム・ピットを軽蔑した。 ● ADV 副詞 **Notwithstanding** is also an adverb. それでも [n ADV] ❑ *His relations with colleagues, differences of opinion notwithstanding, were unfailingly friendly.* 彼の同僚との人間関係は、意

見の相違はあったものの確実に友好的だった.

nought /nɔ̯t/ (noughts) NUM 数詞 **Nought** is the number 0. ゼロ [mainly BRIT 主に英国英語; AM usually **zero** 米国英語では通常 **zero**]

noun /na̯ʊn/ (nouns) **1** N-COUNT 可算名詞 A **noun** is a word such as "car," "love," or "Anne" which is used to refer to a person or thing. 名詞 **2** → see **count noun**, **proper noun**

nour|ish /nɜ̯rɪʃ/ (nourishes, nourishing, nourished) V-T 他動詞 To **nourish** a person, animal, or plant means to provide them with the food that is necessary for life, growth, and good health. 栄養物を与える ◻ The food she eats nourishes both her and the baby. 彼女が食べる食べ物が彼女と赤ん坊の両方の栄養となる. ● **nour|ish|ing** ADJ 形容詞 栄養分の多い ◻ Most of these nourishing substances are in the yolk of the egg. このような滋養物のほとんどが卵の黄身にある.

nour|ish|ment /nɜ̯rɪʃmənt/ **1** N-UNCOUNT 不可算名詞 If something provides a person, animal, or plant with **nourishment**, it provides them with the food that is necessary for life, growth, and good health. 滋養物 ◻ The mother provides the embryo with nourishment and a place to grow. 母親は胚に滋養物と成長する場所をあてがう. **2** N-UNCOUNT 不可算名詞 The action of nourishing someone or something, or the experience of being nourished, can be referred to as **nourishment**. 滋養する ◻ Sugar gives quick relief to hunger but provides no lasting nourishment. 砂糖は空腹感をすぐに和らげるが, 持続的な滋養を与えることにはならない.

Nov. **Nov.** is a written abbreviation for **November**. 11月 (略語) ◻ The first ballot is on Tuesday Nov. 20. 最初の投票は11月20日火曜日である.

Word Link nov ≈ new : innovate, novel, renovate

---

nov|el /nɒ̯vəl/ (novels) **1** N-COUNT 可算名詞 A **novel** is a long written story about imaginary people and events. 小説 ◻ ...a novel by Herman Hesse. ヘルマン・ヘッセの小説 **2** ADJ 形容詞 **Novel** things are new and different from anything that has been done, experienced, or made before. 目新しい ◻ Protesters found a novel way of demonstrating against steeply rising oil prices. 抗議者たちは, 急上昇しているオイル価格に反対する目新しいデモ方法を見つけた.
→ see **library**

nov|el|ist /nɒ̯vəlɪst/ (novelists) N-COUNT 可算名詞 A **novelist** is a person who writes novels. 小説家 ◻ The key to success as a romantic novelist is absolute belief in your story. ロマンティクな小説家としての成功のかぎは, 自分の物語に対する絶対なる確信である.
→ see **fantasy**

nov|el|ty /nɒ̯vəlti/ (novelties) **1** N-UNCOUNT 不可算名詞 **Novelty** is the quality of being different, new, and unusual. 新奇 ◻ In the contemporary western world, rapidly changing styles cater to a desire for novelty and individualism. 現代西洋社会では, 新奇的や個性的であろうとする願望に応じてスタイルが急速に変遷する. **2** N-COUNT 可算名詞 A **novelty** is something that is new and therefore interesting. 新しい物 ◻ Stores really like orange cauliflower because it's a novelty, it's something different. オレンジ色のカリフラワーは新しくて普通とは違うので, 各店でとても好まれている. **3** N-COUNT 可算名詞 **Novelties** are cheap toys, ornaments, or other objects that are sold as presents or souvenirs. 新案商品 ◻ At Easter, we give them plastic eggs filled with small toys, novelties, and coins. イースターの時は, 私たちはプラスチックの卵に小さなおもちゃや目新しい物や硬貨をいっぱい入れて子供たちにやる.

No|vem|ber /no̯ʊvɛmbər/ (Novembers) N-VAR 可変性名詞 **November** is the eleventh month of the year in the Western calendar. 11月 ◻ He arrived in London in November 1939. 彼は1939年11月にロンドンに到着した.

nov|ice /nɒ̯vɪs/ (novices) **1** N-COUNT 可算名詞 A **novice** is someone who has been doing a job or other activity for only a short time and so is not experienced at it. 初心者 ◻ I'm a novice at these things, Lieutenant. You're the professional. 中尉殿, このようなものは私は新米で, あなたがプロです. **2** N-COUNT 可算名詞 In a monastery or convent, a **novice** is a person who is preparing to become a monk or nun. 見習い僧; 尼

now /na̯ʊ/ **1** ADV 副詞 You use **now** to refer to the present time, often in contrast to a time in the past or the future. 現在では ◻ She's a widow now. 彼女は現在未亡人だ. ◻ But we are now a much more fragmented society. しかし, 現在の社会は前よりもいっそうばらばらである. ● PRON 代名詞 **Now** is also a pronoun. 現在 ◻ Now is the time when we must all live as economically as possible. 今こそ全員できる限り倹約して生活しなければならない時代である. **2** ADV 副詞 If you do something **now**, you do it immediately. 今すぐ [ADV after v] ◻ I'm sorry, but I must go now. すみませんが, 私は即刻出かけなければなりません. ● PRON 代名詞 **Now** is also a pronoun. 今 ◻ Now is your chance to talk to him. 今が彼と話すあなたのチャンスだ. **3** CONJ 接続詞 You use **now** or **now that** to indicate that an event has occurred and as a result something else may or will happen. 〜となった今

は ◻ Now you're settled, why don't you take up some serious study? 今はもう落ち着いたので, 何か真剣に勉強を始めるのはどうかい? **4** ADV 副詞 You use **now** to indicate that a particular situation is the result of something that has recently happened. 今では ◻ Mrs. Chandra has received one sweater for each of her five children and says that the winter will not be so hard now. チャンドラ夫人は自分の子供5人用にそれぞれセーターを1枚ずつ受け取ったので, 今では冬もそんなに苦しくはないだろうと言う. ◻ She told me not to repeat it, but now I don't suppose it matters. 繰り返すなと彼女に私は言われたが, 今でそれも問題ではないと思う. **5** ADV 副詞 In stories and accounts of past events, **now** is used to refer to the particular time that is being written or spoken about. 今や ◻ She felt a little better now. そのとき少し気分がよくなった. ◻ It was too late now for Blake to lock his room door. ブレイクが自分の部屋のドアに鍵をかけるには今やすでに遅すぎた. **6** ADV 副詞 You use **now** in statements which specify the length of time up to the present that something has lasted. もう ◻ They've been married now for 30 years. 彼らは結婚してからもう30年になる. ◻ They have been missing for a long time now. 彼らはもう長い間行方不明になっている. **7** ADV 副詞 You say "**Now**" or "**Now then**" to indicate to the person or people you are with that you want their attention, or that you are about to change the subject. これこれ, さて [SPOKEN 口語] [ADV cl] ◻ "Now then," Max said, "to get back to the point." 「さて」とマックスが言った. 「本筋に戻ろと」◻ Now then, what's the trouble? これこれ, どうしたの? **8** ADV 副詞 You use **now** to give a slight emphasis to a request or command. さあ [SPOKEN 口語] [ADV with cl] ◻ Come on now. You know you must be hungry. さあさあ. お腹がすいてるんでしょ. ◻ Come and sit down here, now. さあここに来て座んなさい. **9** ADV 副詞 You can say "**Now**" to introduce information which is relevant to the part of a story or account that you have reached, and which needs to be known before you can continue. さて [SPOKEN 口語] [ADV cl] ◻ My son went to Aspen, in Colorado. Now he and his wife are people who love a quiet vacation. わたしの息子とその妻は静かな休暇が好きな人たちである. さて, 息子とその妻は静かな休暇が好きな人たちである. **10** ADV 副詞 You say "**Now**" to introduce something which contrasts with what you have just said. ところで [SPOKEN 口語] [ADV cl] ◻ Now, if it was me, I'd want to do more than just change the locks. ところで, もし私だったら, 単に錠を取り替える以上のこともしたいと思うだろうよ. **11** PHRASE 句 If you say that something happens **now and then** or **every now and again**, you mean that it happens sometimes but not very often or regularly. 時々 ◻ My father has a collection of magazines to which I return every now and then. 父は雑誌を収蔵していて, 私は時々戻ってそれを読んでいる. **12** PHRASE 句 If you say that something will happen **any day now**, **any moment now**, or **any time now**, you mean that it will happen very soon. いつでも ◻ Jim expects to be sent to Europe any day now. ジムはいつでもヨーロッパに派遣されることを期待している. **13** PHRASE 句 **Just now** means a very short time ago. ついさっき [SPOKEN 口語] ◻ You looked pretty upset just now. あなたはついさっきはひどく動転しているように見えたよ. ◻ I spoke just now of being in love. 僕は恋をしているとついさっき話した. **14** PHRASE 句 You use **just now** when you want to say that a particular situation exists at the time when you are speaking, although it may change in the future. ちょうど今 [SPOKEN 口語] ◻ I'm pretty busy just now. 私はちょうど今すごく忙しい. **15** PHRASE 句 People such as television hosts sometimes use **now** for when they are going to start talking about a different subject or start presenting a new activity. さて今度は [SPOKEN 口語] ◻ And now for something completely different. さて次はまったく違う話題です.

nowa|days /na̯ʊədeɪz/ ADV 副詞 **Nowadays** means at the present time, in contrast with the past. 今日では [ADV with cl] ◻ Nowadays it's acceptable for women to be ambitious. But it wasn't then. このごろは女性が志を抱くことも受け入れられているが, 当時はそうではなかった.

no|where /no̯ʊwɛər/ **1** ADV 副詞 You use **nowhere** to emphasize that a place has more of a particular quality than any other place, or that it is the only place where something happens or exists. どこにもない [EMPHASIS 強調] ◻ Nowhere is language a more serious issue than in Hawaii. ハワイほど言語が重大な問題であるところは他にはない. ◻ This kind of forest exists nowhere else in the world. このような種類の森林は世界中で他にはどこにも存在しない. **2** ADV 副詞 You use **nowhere** when making negative statements to say that a suitable place of the specified kind does not exist. どこにもない ◻ There was nowhere to hide and nowhere to run. 隠れるところも逃げるところもなかった. ◻ I have nowhere else to go, nowhere in the world. 私はどこにも他に行く先がない, 世界中のどこにもない. **3** ADV 副詞 You use **nowhere** to indicate that something or someone cannot be seen or found. どこにもない/いない ◻ Michael glanced anxiously down the corridor, but Wilfred was nowhere to be seen. マイケルは心配そうに廊下をちらっと見たが, ウイルフレッドはどこにも見当たらなかった. ◻ The escaped prisoner was nowhere in sight. 脱走犯はどこにも見当たらなかった. **4** ADV 副詞 You can use **nowhere** to refer in a general way to small, unimportant, or uninteresting places. 何もとりえのないところに ◻ ...endless paths that led nowhere

in particular. 特にこれといった場所には至らない無数の小道 **5** ADV 副詞 If you say that something or someone appears **from nowhere** or **out of nowhere**, you mean that they appear suddenly and unexpectedly. どこからともなく ['from/out of' ADV] *A car came from nowhere, and I had to jump back into the hedge just in time.* 車がどこからともなく来て，私はぎりぎりで生け垣に飛び込まなければならなかった． **6** ADV 副詞 You use **nowhere** to mean not in any part of a text, speech, or argument. どこにもない [EMPHASIS 強調] *He nowhere offers concrete historical background to support his arguments.* 彼は自説を支える具体的な歴史的背景をどこにも提示していない． *Point taken, but nowhere did we suggest that this yacht's features were unique.* 了解しましたが，私どもはこのヨットの特徴がユニークであると言ったことは一切ありません． **7** PHRASE 句 If you say that a place is **in the middle of nowhere**, you mean that it is a long way from other places. 人里はなれたところで *At dusk we pitched camp in the middle of nowhere.* 夕暮れ時に我々はひどくへんぴなところにキャンプした． **8** PHRASE 句 If you use **nowhere near** in front of a word or expression, you are emphasizing that the real situation is very different from, or has not yet reached, the state which that word or expression suggests. まったく〜でない [EMPHASIS 強調] *He's nowhere near recovered yet from his experiences.* 彼はその経験から全然回復していない．

Word Partnership	*nowhere* は次の語句と使われる:
v.	nowhere **to be found**, nowhere **to be seen**, *have* nowhere **to go**, *have* nowhere **to hide**, *have* nowhere **to run 2 3**
	go nowhere **4**

no-win situa|tion (**no-win situations**) N-COUNT 可算名詞 If you are in a **no-win situation**, any action you take will fail to benefit you in any way. 勝つ見込みのない状態 *It was a no-win situation. Either she pretended she hated Ned and felt awful or admitted she loved him and felt even worse!* 八方ふさがりであった．彼女はネッドが嫌いなふりをしているやな思いをするか，さもなければ愛していることを認めてよけいいやな思いをするかであった！

nu|ance /núɑns/ (**nuances**) N-VAR 可変性名詞 A **nuance** is a small difference in sound, feeling, appearance, or meaning. 微妙な違い *We can use our eyes and facial expressions to communicate virtually every subtle nuance of emotion there is.* 我々は目や顔の表情を使って，存在する限りの微妙な感情を実質的にすべて伝えることができる．

nu|clear /núkliər/ **1** ADJ 形容詞 **Nuclear** means relating to the nuclei of atoms, or to the energy released when these nuclei are split or combined. 核の; 原子力の [ADJ n] *...a nuclear power station.* 原子力発電所 *...nuclear energy.* 原子力 **2** ADJ 形容詞 **Nuclear** means relating to weapons that explode by using the energy released when the nuclei of atoms are split or combined. 核兵器の [ADJ n] *They rejected a demand for the removal of all nuclear weapons.* 彼らは核兵器をすべて除去する要求を拒否した．
→ see **energy**

nu|clear re|ac|tor (**nuclear reactors**) N-COUNT 可算名詞 A **nuclear reactor** is a machine which is used to produce nuclear energy or the place where this machine and other related machinery and equipment is kept. 原子炉; 原子炉のある建屋 *The nuclear reactor was not damaged in the lightning storm that struck late last night.* 昨夜遅く襲ってきた雷雨による原子炉の破損はなかった．

nu|cleus /núkliəs/ (**nuclei** /núkliaɪ/) **1** N-COUNT 可算名詞 The **nucleus** of an atom or cell is the central part of it. 原子核; 細胞核 *Neutrons and protons are bound together in the nucleus of an atom.* 原子核では中性子と陽子が一緒に結合している． **2** N-COUNT 可算名詞 The **nucleus** of a group of people or things is the small number of members which form the most important part of the group. 中核 *Matt Cummings and Liko Soules-Ono form the nucleus of the team.* マット・カミングズとリコ・ソールズ・オノはチームの中心である．

nude /núd/ (**nudes**) **1** ADJ 形容詞 A **nude** person is not wearing any clothes. 裸の *The occasional nude bather comes here.* 裸体で時々日光浴をする人がここに来る． ● PHRASE 句 If you do something **in the nude**, you are not wearing any clothes. If you paint or draw someone **in the nude**, they are not wearing any clothes. 裸体で *Sleeping in the nude, if it suits you, is not a bad idea.* 自分に合っていれば，裸で眠ることは悪い考えではない． **2** N-COUNT 可算名詞 A **nude** is a picture or statue of a person who is not wearing any clothes. A **nude** is also a person in a picture who is not wearing any clothes. 裸体画, 裸体像; ヌード写真 *He was one of Australia's most distinguished artists, renowned for his portraits, landscapes, and nudes.* オーストラリアの最も著名な芸術家の1人で，肖像画や風景画や裸体画で有名な人だった．

nudge /nʌdʒ/ (**nudges, nudging, nudged**) **1** V-T 他動詞 If you **nudge** someone, you push them gently, usually with your elbow, in order to draw their attention to something. ひじでそっと突く

I nudged Stan and pointed again. スタンをひじで軽く突き，また指さして示した． ● N-COUNT 可算名詞 **Nudge** is also a noun. ひじなどで軽く突くこと *She slipped her arm under his and gave him a nudge.* 彼女は彼の腕の下に自分の腕を滑り込ませてひじで軽く突いた． **2** V-T 他動詞 If you **nudge** someone or something into a place or position, you gently push them there. そっと押す *Edna Swinson nudged him into the sitting room.* エドナ・スインソンは彼をそっと押して居間に入れた． ● N-COUNT 可算名詞 **Nudge** is also a noun. 軽く押すこと *McKinnon gave the wheel another slight nudge to starboard.* マッキノンは再度かじを軽く右舷にとった． **3** V-T 他動詞 If you **nudge** someone into doing something, you gently persuade them to do it. そっと促す *Bit by bit Bob had nudged Fritz into selling his controlling interest.* 徐々にボブはフリッツに支配持分を売るように促していった． *Foreigners must use their power not simply to punish the country but to nudge it toward greater tolerance.* 単にこれを罰するのではなく，さらなる寛容を促すように，外国人は権力を行使しなければならない． ● N-COUNT 可算名詞 **Nudge** is also a noun. そっと促すこと *I had a feeling that the challenge appealed to him. All he needed was a nudge.* 彼はその挑戦が気に入っているような感じが僕にはした．あとは軽く促しさえすればよかった．

nu|di|ty /núdɪti/ N-UNCOUNT 不可算名詞 **Nudity** is the state of wearing no clothes. 裸であること *...constant nudity and bad language on TV.* テレビの絶え間ない裸体と下品な言葉

nui|sance /núsᵊns/ (**nuisances**) N-COUNT 可算名詞 If you say that someone or something is a **nuisance**, you mean that they annoy you or cause you a lot of problems. やっかいな人／もの *He could be a bit of a nuisance when he was drunk.* 彼は酔っ払っていたときは少々やっかいだった． *Sorry to be a nuisance.* 迷惑をかけてすまない． ● PHRASE 句 If someone **makes a nuisance of** themselves, they behave in a way that annoys other people. 迷惑をかける

null /nʌl/ PHRASE 句 If an agreement, a declaration, or the result of an election is **null and void**, it is not legally valid. 無効で *A spokeswoman said the agreement had been declared null and void.* 女性の代弁者が協定は無効と宣言したと述べた．
→ see **zero**

numb /nʌm/ (**numbs, numbing, numbed**) **1** ADJ 形容詞 If a part of your body is **numb**, you cannot feel anything there. 感覚のない *He could feel his fingers growing numb at their tips.* 彼は指先の感覚がなくなっていくのがわかった． ● **numb|ness** N-UNCOUNT 不可算名詞 無感覚 *I have recently been suffering from pain and numbness in my hands.* 私は最近ずっと両手の痛みと無感覚に悩まされている． **2** ADJ 形容詞 If you are **numb with** shock, fear, or grief, you are so shocked, frightened, or upset that you cannot think clearly or feel any emotion. ぼう然とした *The mother, numb with grief, has trouble speaking.* 悲しみでぼう然としている母親は口を利くことが難しい． ● **numb|ness** N-UNCOUNT 不可算名詞 無感覚 *Many men become more aware of emotional numbness in their 40s.* 40代で感情的な無感覚になっているのにいっそう気づくようになる男が多い． **3** V-T 他動詞 If an event or experience **numbs** you, you can no longer think clearly or feel any emotion. ぼう然とさせる *For a while the shock of Philippe's letter numbed her.* フィリップの手紙に打撃を受け，彼女はしばらくぼう然としていた． ● **numbed** ADJ 形容詞 ぼう然とした *I'm so numbed with shock that I can hardly think.* 私は衝撃であまりにもぼう然として，ほとんど考えることができない． **4** V-T 他動詞 If cold weather, a drug, or a blow **numbs** a part of your body, you can no longer feel anything in it. 感覚を失わせる *The cold numbed my fingers.* 寒さで私の指がかじかんだ． *An injection of local anesthetic is usually given first to numb the area.* 局所麻酔の注射が通常最初にその部分の感覚を麻痺させるためにされる．

num|ber /nʌmbər/ (**numbers, numbering, numbered**) **1** N-COUNT 可算名詞 A **number** is a word such as "two," "nine," or "twelve," or a symbol such as 1, 3, or 47. You use numbers to say how many things you are referring to or where something comes in a series. 数; 数字; 番号 *No, I don't know the room number.* いや，私は部屋の番号は知らない． *Stan Laurel was born at number 3, Argyll Street.* スタン・ローレルはアーガイル通り3番に生まれた． **2** N-COUNT 可算名詞 You use **number** with words such as "large" or "small" to say approximately how many things or people there are. 数 *Quite a considerable number of interviews are going on.* 相当な数の面接が進行中である． *I have had an enormous number of letters from single parents.* 私は片親家庭の親からのものすごい数の手紙を受け取った． **3** N-SING 単数名詞 If there are **a number of** things or people, there are several of them. If there are **any number of** things or people, there is a large quantity of them. 若干; 多数 *I seem to remember that Sam told a number of lies.* サムはいくらかうそを言ったのを私は記憶しているような気がする． **4** N-UNCOUNT 不可算名詞 You can refer to someone's or something's position in a list of the most successful or most popular of a particular type of thing, for example, **number one** or **number two**. 一番 *Martin now faces the world number one, Jansher Khan of Pakistan.* マーティンは今度世界一であるパキスタンのジャンシャ・カーンと対戦する． *Before you knew it, the single was at number 90 in the U.S. singles charts.* そのシングルは，あっという間にアメリカのシングル盤ヒット曲集の第90位になった． **5** V-T 他

動詞 If a group of people or things **numbers** a particular total, that is how many there are. 数に達する ❑ *They told me that their village numbered 100.* 彼らの村では総計100人になると私は聞いた。 **6** N-COUNT 可算名詞 A **number** is the series of numbers that you dial when you are making a telephone call. 電話番号 ❑ *...a list of names and telephone numbers.* 名前と電話番号のリスト ❑ *My number is 414-3925.* 私の電話番号は414-3925です。 **7** N-COUNT 可算名詞 You can refer to a short piece of music, a song, or a dance as a **number**. 曲 ❑ *..."Unforgettable," a number that was written and performed in 1951.* 1951年に作曲され演奏された曲である『アンフォーゲッタブル』 **8** V-T 他動詞 If someone or something **is numbered among** a particular group, they are believed to belong in that group. 含めて数える [FORMAL 形式ばった] ❑ *Lech Walesa and Nelson Mandela are numbered among my personal heroes.* わたしの個人的な英雄の中にはレフ・ワレサとネルソン・マンデラが含まれる。 **9** V-T 他動詞 If you **number** something, you mark it with a number, usually starting at 1. 番号をつける ❑ *He cut his paper up into tiny squares, and he numbered each one.* 紙を小さな四角に切り、それぞれに番号をつけた。 **10** → see also **serial number**
→ see **mathematics, zero**

num|ber one (number ones) **1** ADJ 形容詞 **Number one** means better, more important, or more popular than anything else or anyone else of its kind. 第1級の [INFORMAL くだけた] [ADJ n] ❑ *The economy is the number one issue by far.* 経済ははるかに最優先の問題だ。 **2** N-COUNT 可算名詞 In popular music, the **number one** is the best-selling recording in any one week, or the group or person who has made that recording. ヒット曲第1位の曲 [INFORMAL くだけた] ❑ *Paula is the only artist to achieve four number ones from a debut album.* デビュー曲集で4曲もヒット曲第1位を達成した歌手はポーラだけだ。

num|ber plate (number plates) also **numberplate** N-COUNT 可算名詞 [BRIT 英国英語] A **number plate** is the same as a **license plate**. (車の)ナンバープレート

Word Link	numer ≈ number : in**numer**able, **numer**ical, **numer**ous

nu|meri|cal /nuːmɛrɪkəl/ ADJ 形容詞 **Numerical** means expressed in numbers or relating to numbers. 数の ❑ *Your job is to group them by letter and put them in numerical order.* 君の仕事は文字でグループに分けて、それから番号順にすることだ。 ● **nu|meri|cal|ly** ADV 副詞 数的に ❑ *...a numerically coded color chart.* 数字コード化された色彩表

nu|mer|ous /nuːmərəs/ ADJ 形容詞 If people or things are **numerous**, they exist or are present in large numbers. 多数の ❑ *Sex crimes were just as numerous as they are today.* 性的犯罪は今日と同様に多かった。

Word Partnership	numerous は次の語句と使われる:
N.	numerous **attempts**, numerous **examples**, numerous **occasions**, numerous **problems**, numerous **times**

nun /nʌn/ (nuns) N-COUNT 可算名詞 A **nun** is a member of a female religious community. 修道女 ❑ *Mr. Thomas was taught by the Catholic nuns whose school he attended to work and study hard.* トマス氏はカトリック修道女の学校に通ったが、一生懸命働き勉強することを修道女に教えられた。

nurse /nɜːrs/ (nurses, nursing, nursed) **1** N-COUNT; N-TITLE; N-VOC 可算名詞、称号名詞、呼格名詞 A **nurse** is a person whose job is to care for people who are ill. 看護師 ❑ *She had spent 29 years as a nurse.* 彼女は29年間看護師として過ごした。 **2** V-T 他動詞 If you **nurse** someone, you care for them when they are ill. 看病する ❑ *All the years he was sick my mother had nursed him.* 彼が病気であった何年もの間、ずっと母が看病した。 **3** V-T 他動詞 If you **nurse** an illness or injury, you allow it to get better by resting as much as possible. 養生する ❑ *We're going to go home and nurse our colds.* 私たちは家に帰って風邪を治すつもりだ。 **4** V-T 他動詞 If you **nurse** an emotion or desire, you feel it strongly for a long time. 心に抱く ❑ *Jane still nurses the pain of rejection.* ジェーンはまだ拒絶された痛みを抱いている。

Word Partnership	nurse は次の語句と使われる:
N.	nurse's **aide, visiting** nurse **1**

nurse|ry /nɜːrsəri/ (nurseries) **1** N-COUNT 可算名詞 A **nursery** is a room in a family home in which the young children of the family sleep or play. 子供部屋 ❑ *He has painted murals in his children's nursery.* 彼は子供部屋の壁に絵を描いた。 **2** N-COUNT 可算名詞 A **nursery** is a place where children who are not old enough to go to school are cared for. 保育所 [also 'at/from/to' n] ❑ *She puts her baby in this nursery and then goes back to work.* 彼女は赤ん坊をこの託児所に預けてから仕事に戻る。 **3** N-VAR 可変性名詞 **Nursery** is a school for very young children. 幼稚園 [BRIT 英国英語; AM nursery school, preschool 米国英語 nursery school, preschool] **4** N-COUNT 可算名詞 A **nursery** is a place where plants are grown in order to be sold.

育種場 ❑ *The garden, developed over the past 35 years, includes a nursery.* 過去35年間開発されてきたこの庭園には育種場がある。

nurse|ry school (nursery schools) N-VAR 可変性名詞 A **nursery school** is a school for very young children. 幼稚園 ❑ *She began her professional career as a nursery school teacher.* 彼女は専門職を幼稚園の先生を手始めにした。

nurs|ing /nɜːrsɪŋ/ N-UNCOUNT 不可算名詞 **Nursing** is the profession of caring for people who are ill. 看護 ❑ *She had no aptitude for nursing.* 彼女は看護にぜんぜん向いていなかった。

nurs|ing home (nursing homes) N-COUNT 可算名詞 A **nursing home** is a residence for old or sick people. 老人ホーム、療養所 ❑ *Isaac Binger has died in a nursing home in Florida at the age of 87.* アイザック・ビンガーはフロリダ州の老人ホームで87歳で亡くなった。

nur|ture /nɜːrtʃər/ (nurtures, nurturing, nurtured) **1** V-T 他動詞 If you **nurture** something such as a young child or a young plant, you care for it while it is growing and developing. 養育する [FORMAL 形式ばった] ❑ *Parents want to know the best way to nurture and raise their child to adulthood.* 親は子供を大人に育てる1番いい育て方を知りたいと思っている。 **2** V-T 他動詞 If you **nurture** plans, ideas, or people, you encourage them or help them to develop. 育む [FORMAL 形式ばった] ❑ *She had always nurtured great ambitions for her son.* 彼女は息子のためにいつも大きな野心を抱いていた。 ❑ *...parents whose political views were nurtured in the sixties.* 60年代に政治的見解を育まれた親たち **3** N-UNCOUNT 不可算名詞 **Nurture** is care and encouragement that is given to someone while they are growing and developing. 養育 ❑ *The human organism learns partly by nature, partly by nurture.* 人間という生き物は、一部は天性で、一部は養育で習得する。

nut /nʌt/ (nuts) **1** N-COUNT 可算名詞 The firm shelled fruit of some trees and bushes are called **nuts**. Some nuts can be eaten. 木の実 ❑ *Nuts and seeds are good sources of vitamin E.* 木の実や種はビタミンEのよい源である。 **2** → see also **peanut** **3** N-COUNT 可算名詞 A **nut** is a thick metal ring which you screw onto a metal rod called a bolt. Nuts and bolts are used to hold things such as pieces of machinery together. 留めねじ ❑ *If you want to repair the wheels you just undo the four nuts.* 車輪を修理したいときは、単に留めねじ4個を外す。 **4** N-COUNT 可算名詞 If you describe someone as, for example, a baseball **nut** or a health **nut**, you mean that they are extremely enthusiastic about the thing mentioned. 熱狂的愛好者 [INFORMAL くだけた] ❑ *...Annie, the girlfriend who was a true baseball nut.* 本当に野球狂であったガールフレンドのアニー **5** ADJ 形容詞 If you are **nuts about** something or someone, you like them very much. 熱中している [INFORMAL くだけた, FEELINGS 感情] [v-link ADJ 'about' n] ❑ *They're nuts about the car.* 彼らはその車に夢中になっている。 **6** ADJ 形容詞 If you say that someone goes **nuts** or is **nuts**, you mean that they go crazy or are very foolish. 気が狂った、ばかな [INFORMAL くだけた] [v-link ADJ] ❑ *You guys are nuts.* お前たちは頭がおかしいよ。 **7** PHRASE 句 If someone **goes nuts**, they become extremely angry. 気が狂ったように怒る [INFORMAL くだけた] ❑ *My father would go nuts if he saw bruises on me.* もし僕の打撲傷を見たら父はかっとなるだろう。
→ see **peanut**

nu|tri|ent /nuːtriənt/ (nutrients) N-COUNT 可算名詞 **Nutrients** are substances that help plants and animals to grow. 栄養物 ❑ *In her first book she explained the role of vegetable fibers, vitamins, minerals, and other essential nutrients.* 彼女は最初の本で、野菜繊維、ビタミン、ミネラル、その他の必須栄養分の役割について説明した。
→ see **food**

nu|tri|tion /nuːtrɪʃən/ N-UNCOUNT 不可算名詞 **Nutrition** is the process of taking food into the body and absorbing the nutrients in those foods. 栄養摂取 ❑ *There are alternative sources of nutrition to animal meat.* 動物の肉の代わりになる栄養源がある。

nu|tri|tion|al /nuːtrɪʃənəl/ ADJ 形容詞 The **nutritional** content of food is all the substances that are in it which help you to remain healthy. 栄養分の ❑ *It does sometimes help to know the nutritional content of foods.* 食物の栄養分を知っていることは時々本当に役に立つ。 ● **nu|tri|tion|al|ly** ADV 副詞 栄養上に ❑ *...a nutritionally balanced diet.* 栄養上バランスの取れた日常食

nu|tri|tious /nuːtrɪʃəs/ ADJ 形容詞 **Nutritious** food contains substances which help your body to be healthy. 栄養分のある ❑ *It is always important to choose enjoyable, nutritious foods.* 栄養があって楽しめる食べ物を選ぶことはいつも重要だ。

ny|lon /naɪlɒn/ (nylons) **1** N-UNCOUNT 不可算名詞 **Nylon** is a strong, flexible artificial fiber. ナイロン ❑ *The chair is made of lightweight nylon.* そのいすは軽量ナイロンで作られている。 **2** N-PLURAL 複数名詞 **Nylons** are stockings made of nylon. ナイロンのストッキング [OLD-FASHIONED 古風な] ❑ *She wore a long skirt with pink pumps and black nylons.* 彼女は長いスカートにピンクのパンプスと黒のナイロン靴下をはいていた。
→ see **rope**

O also o /oʊ/ (O's, o's) N-VAR 可変性名詞 O is the fifteenth letter of the English alphabet. 英語アルファベットの第15字

oak /oʊk/ (oaks) N-VAR 可変性名詞 An **oak** or an **oak tree** is a large tree that often grows in forests and has strong, hard wood. オーク □ Many large oaks were felled during the war. 戦争中に大きなオークが多数伐採された. ● N-UNCOUNT 不可算名詞 **Oak** is the wood of this tree. オーク材 □ The cabinet was made of oak and was hand-carved. 飾り棚はオーク材でできていて, 手彫りが施されていた.
→ see **plant**

oar /ɔr/ (oars) N-COUNT 可算名詞 **Oars** are long poles with a wide, flat blade at one end which are used for rowing a boat. オール
→ see **boat**

oasis /oʊeɪsɪs/ (oases /oʊeɪsiz/) **1** N-COUNT 可算名詞 An **oasis** is a small area in a desert where water and plants are found. オアシス **2** N-COUNT 可算名詞 You can refer to a pleasant place or situation as an **oasis** when it is surrounded by unpleasant ones. いこいの場所 □ The immaculately tended gardens are an oasis in the midst of Cairo's urban sprawl. その完璧に手入れされた庭園はカイロの無秩序な膨張の真只中でいこいの場所になっている.
→ see **desert**

oath /oʊθ/ (oaths) **1** N-COUNT 可算名詞 An **oath** is a formal promise, especially a promise to be loyal to a person or country. 誓い □ He took an oath of loyalty to the government. 彼は政府への忠誠を誓った. **2** N-SING 単数名詞 In a court of law, when someone takes **the oath**, they make a formal promise to tell the truth. You can say that someone is **under oath** when they have made this promise. 宣誓 ['the' N, also 'on/under' N] □ His girlfriend had gone into the witness box and taken the oath. 彼の恋人は証人台に進み, 宣誓した. □ Under oath, Andy finally admitted that he had lied. 宣誓した上で, アンディはうそをついていたことをついに認めた.

oat|meal /oʊtmil/ **1** N-UNCOUNT 不可算名詞 **Oatmeal** is a kind of flour made by crushing oats. ひき割りオート麦 [oft N n] □ …oatmeal cookies. オートミールクッキー. **2** N-UNCOUNT 不可算名詞 **Oatmeal** is a thick sticky food made from oats cooked in water or milk and eaten hot, especially for breakfast. オートミールのかゆ [mainly AM 主に米国英語]

oats /oʊts/

The form **oat** is used as a modifier.

oat 形は修飾語として使われる.

N-PLURAL 複数名詞 **Oats** are a cereal crop or its grains, used for making cookies or a food called oatmeal, or for feeding animals. オート麦 □ Oats provide good, nutritious food for horses. オート麦は栄養値の高いおいしい馬のえさになる.
→ see **grain**

obe|di|ent /oʊbidiənt/ ADJ 形容詞 A person or animal who is **obedient** does what they are told to do. 従順な □ He was very respectful at home and obedient to his parents. 彼は家では非常に礼儀正しく, 親の言うことをよく聞く. ● **obe|di|ence** N-UNCOUNT 不可算名詞 従 □ …unquestioning obedience to the law. 法への絶対服従. ● **obe|di|ent|ly** ADV 副詞 [ADV with v] 従順に □ He waited obediently at Keith, waiting for orders. 彼はキースをうやうやしく見て, 命令を待っていた.

obese /oʊbis/ ADJ 形容詞 If someone is **obese**, they are extremely fat. 肥満した □ Obese people tend to have higher blood pressure than lean people. 太り過ぎの人の血圧は, やせた人よりも高い傾向がある. ● **obesity** /oʊbisiti/ N-UNCOUNT 不可算名詞 肥満 □ …the excessive consumption of sugar that leads to problems of obesity. 肥満問題を引き起こす砂糖の取り過ぎ
→ see **diet, sugar**

obey /oʊbeɪ/ (obeys, obeying, obeyed) V-T/V-I 他動詞/自動詞 If you **obey** a person, a command, or an instruction, you do what you are told to do. 従う [他動詞・自動詞] □ Cissie obeyed her mother without question. シィシーは1も2もなく母親に従った. □ Most people obey the law. ほとんどの人は法律に従う. □ It was his duty to obey. 服従することは彼の任務だった.

obitu|ary /oʊbɪtʃuɛri/ (obituaries) N-COUNT 可算名詞 Someone's **obituary** is an account of their life and character which is presented in a newspaper or broadcast soon after they die. 死亡記事 □ His obituary was published in one edition of his own newspaper before it was discovered that he was alive. 彼の死亡記事が彼自身の新聞の1つの版に発表されたが, その後彼が生きていることがわかった.

ob|ject (objects, objecting, objected)

The noun is pronounced /ɒbdʒɪkt/. The verb is pronounced /əbdʒɛkt/.

名詞は /ɒbdʒɪkt/ と発音される. 動詞は /əbdʒɛkt/ と発音される.

1 N-COUNT 可算名詞 An **object** is anything that has a fixed shape or form, that you can touch or see, and that is not alive. 物자 □ He squinted his eyes as though he were studying an object on the horizon. 彼は地平線上の物体を観察しているかのように目を細めた. □ …an object the shape of a coconut. ココナッツ形の物体. **2** N-COUNT 可算名詞 The **object** of what someone is doing is their aim or purpose. 目的 □ The object of the exercise is to raise money for the charity. この行事の目的は慈善事業の資金を集めることです. **3** N-COUNT 可算名詞 The **object** of a particular feeling or reaction is the person or thing it is directed toward or that causes it. 対象 □ The object of her hatred was 24-year-old model Ros French. 彼女の毛嫌いの対象は24歳のモデル, ロス・フレンチだ. □ The object of great interest at the temple was a large marble tower built in memory of Buddha. その寺の大変興味のある見物は, 仏陀を記念して建立された大きな大理石の塔だ. **4** N-COUNT 可算名詞 In grammar, the **object** of a verb or a preposition is the word or phrase which completes the structure begun by the verb or preposition. 目的語 **5** → see also **direct object, indirect object 6** V-T 他動詞 If you **object** to something, you express your dislike or disapproval of it. 反対する [他動詞・自動詞] □ A lot of people will object to the book. 多くの人がその本に反感を持つだろう. □ Cullen objected that his small staff would be unable to handle the added work. カレンは, 彼の少ない職員が追加仕事に対処できないと反対した. **7** PHRASE 句 If you say that **money is no object** or **distance is no object**, you are emphasizing that you are willing or able to spend as much money as necessary or travel whatever distance is required. 金は問題でない [EMPHASIS 強調] □ This was a very impressive program in which money seems to have been no object. これは金をいくら注ぎ込んでも問題でなかったような大変すばらしいプログラムだった.

ob|jec|tion /əbdʒɛkʃən/ (objections) **1** N-VAR 可変性名詞 If you express or raise an **objection to** something, you say that you do not like it or agree with it. 異議 □ Despite objections by the White House, the Senate voted today to cut off aid. ホワイトハウスから異議が唱えられたにもかかわらず, 本日上院は援助の中止に賛成投票をした. **2** N-UNCOUNT 不可算名詞 If you say that you have **no objection to** something, you mean that you are not annoyed or bothered by it. 異存 □ I have no objection to banks making money. 銀行が金をもうけるのに異存は何もない.

V.   **make an** objection, **raise an** objection, **sustain an** objection ■
     have no objection ■

ob|jec|tive /əbdʒɛktɪv/ (**objectives**) ■ N-COUNT 可算名詞 Your **objective** is what you are trying to achieve. 目標 □ *Our main objective was the recovery of the child safe and well.* 我々の主な目的はその子供を安全かつ元気な状態で取り戻すことだ. ② ADJ 形容詞 **Objective** information is based on facts. 客観的 [ADJ n] □ *He had no objective evidence that anything extraordinary was happening.* 彼は何かただならぬことが起きているという客観証拠を何も持っていなかった. ● **ob|jec|tive|ly** ADV 副詞 客観的に □ *We simply want to inform people objectively about events.* 私たちはただ客観的にイベントを人々に紹介したいのだ. ● **ob|jec|tiv|ity** /ˌɒbdʒɛktɪvɪti/ N-UNCOUNT 不可算名詞 客観性 □ *The poll, whose objectivity is open to question, gave the party a 39% share of the vote.* 客観性に疑問の余地がある投票で, その党は39%の得票率を得ました. ③ ADJ 形容詞 If someone is **objective**, they base their opinions on facts rather than on their personal feelings. 客観的な □ *I believe that a journalist should be completely objective.* ジャーナリストは完全に客観的であるべきだと私は思います. ● **ob|jec|tive|ly** ADV 副詞 客観的に □ *Try to view situations more objectively, especially with regard to work.* 特に仕事に関して, 状況をもっと客観的に捉えるようにしなさい. ● **ob|jec|tiv|ity** N-UNCOUNT 不可算名詞 客観性 □ *The psychiatrist must learn to maintain an unusual degree of objectivity.* 精神分析医は異常なまでの客観性を維持することを学ばなければならなければならない.

V.   **achieve an** objective ■
ADJ.   **important** objective, **main** objective, **primary** objective ■

ob|li|ga|tion /ˌɒblɪɡeɪʃⁿn/ (**obligations**) ■ N-VAR 可変性名詞 If you have an **obligation to** do something, it is your duty to do that thing. 義務 □ *When teachers assign homework, students usually feel an obligation to do it.* 教師から宿題を与えられると, 普通学生はやらねばならぬと感じる. ② N-VAR 可変性名詞 If you have an **obligation to** a person, it is your duty to take care of them or protect their interests. 義務 □ *The United States will do that which is necessary to meet its obligations to its own citizens.* 合衆国は自国の市民に対する義務を果たすために必要なことを実行します. ③ PHRASE 句 In advertisements, if a product or a service is available **without obligation**, you do not have to pay for that product or service until you have tried it and are satisfied with it. 責任を負わずに □ *If you are selling your property, why not call us for a free valuation without obligation.* 不動産を売却される場合は当社にお電話の上, 無料評価をお受けください. 当社に義務は一切ありません.

N.   duty, responsibility ■ ②

V.   obligation **to pay** ■
     feel an obligation, **fulfill an** obligation, **meet an** obligation ■ ②
ADJ.   **legal** obligation, **moral** obligation ■ ②
N.   **sense of** obligation ■ ②

ob|liga|tory /əblɪɡətɔri/ ADJ 形容詞 If something is **obligatory**, you must do it because of a rule or a law. 義務的な □ *Most women will be offered an ultrasound scan during pregnancy, although it's not obligatory.* ほとんどの女性は妊娠中に超音波スキャンを勧められるが, ただしこれは必須ではない.

ob|lige /əblaɪdʒ/ (**obliges, obliging, obliged**) ■ V-T 他動詞 If you **are obliged to** do something, a situation, rule, or law makes it necessary for you to do that thing. 義務を負わせられる □ *The storm got worse and worse. Finally, I was obliged to abandon the car and continue on foot.* 嵐はどんどんひどくなり, 私は最後には車を置き去りにして徒歩で進まなくてはならなくなった. ② V-T/V-I 他動詞/自動詞 To **oblige** someone means to be helpful to them by doing what they have asked you to do. 願いを入れる [他動詞・自動詞] □ *Mr. Oakley has always been ready to oblige journalists with information.* オークリー氏はジャーナリストたちに情報を常に進んで与えていた. We called up three economists to ask how to eliminate the deficit and they obliged with very straightforward answers. 我々が3人の経済専門家に赤字の削減方法を電話で質問したところ, 彼らは単刀直入な答えを返してくれました. ③ CONVENTION 慣習表現 If you tell someone that you **would be obliged** or **should be obliged** if they would do something, you are telling them in a polite but firm way that you want them to do it. 恩にきる [FORMAL 形式ばった, POLITENESS 丁

寧さ] □ *I would be obliged if you could read it to us.* それを私たちに読んで聞かせてくださればありがたいのですが.

oblig|ing /əblaɪdʒɪŋ/ ADJ 形容詞 If you describe someone as **obliging**, you think that they are willing and eager to be helpful. 世話好きな [OLD-FASHIONED OR WRITTEN 古風な, または書き言葉, APPROVAL 賛成] □ *He is an extremely pleasant and obliging man.* 彼は非常に愛想のよい親切な男性だ. ● **oblig|ing|ly** ADV 副詞 [ADV with v] 親切に □ *Benedict obligingly held the door open.* ベネディクトは親切にドアを押さえておいた.

oblique /oʊblik/ ADJ 形容詞 If you describe a statement as **oblique**, you mean that it is not expressed directly or openly, making it difficult to understand. 遠まわしの □ *It was an oblique reference to his mother.* それは遠まわしに彼の母親を指していた. ● **oblique|ly** ADV 副詞 [ADV with v] 遠まわしに □ *He obliquely referred to the U.S., Britain and Saudi Arabia.* 彼は遠まわしに米国, 英国およびサウジアラビアに言及した.

oblit|er|ate /əblɪtəreɪt/ (**obliterates, obliterating, obliterated**) ■ V-T 他動詞 If something **obliterates** an object or place, it destroys it completely. 跡形も失くす, 抹殺する □ *Their warheads are enough to obliterate the world several times over.* 彼らの弾頭には世界を何回も抹殺するほどの威力があります. ● **oblit|era|tion** /əblɪtəreɪʃⁿn/ N-UNCOUNT 不可算名詞 抹殺 □ *...the obliteration of three isolated rainforests.* 3つの孤立した熱帯雨林の消滅. ② V-T 他動詞 If you **obliterate** something such as a memory, emotion, or thought, you remove it completely from your mind. 忘却させる □ *There was time enough to obliterate memories of how things once were for him.* 彼には過去の生活の記憶を忘却させるのに十分な時間があった.

obliv|i|on /əblɪviən/ ■ N-UNCOUNT 不可算名詞 **Oblivion** is the state of not being aware of what is happening around you, for example, because you are asleep or unconscious. 忘却 □ *He just drank himself jovially into oblivion.* 彼はただ陽気に酔っ払って記憶をなくした. ② N-UNCOUNT 不可算名詞 **Oblivion** is the state of having been forgotten or of no longer being considered important. 世に忘れられている状態 □ *It seems that the so-called new theory is likely to sink into oblivion.* そのいわゆる新しい理論というものは世に忘れ去られてしまいそうに思える. ③ N-UNCOUNT 不可算名詞 If you say that something is bombed or blasted **into oblivion**, you are emphasizing that it is completely destroyed. 破壊 [EMPHASIS 強調] □ *An entire poor section of town was bombed into oblivion.* 町の貧困区域全体が爆弾で破壊されました.

obliv|i|ous /əblɪviəs/ ADJ 形容詞 If you are **oblivious** to something or **oblivious** of it, you are not aware of it. 気づかずに □ *She lay motionless where she was, oblivious to pain.* 彼女は痛みにも気づかず, その場に動かず横たわった.

ob|nox|ious /əbnɒkʃəs/ ADJ 形容詞 If you describe someone or their behavior as **obnoxious**, you think that they are very unpleasant because of being aggressive, loud, or offensive. 不快な [DISAPPROVAL 不賛成] □ *The people at my table were so obnoxious I had to change my seat.* 同席した人たちはとても不愉快な人たちだったので, 私は席を変えなくてはならなかった.

obo In advertisements, **obo** is used after a price to indicate that the person who is selling something is willing to accept slightly less money than the sum they have mentioned. **obo** is a written abbreviation for "or best offer." 応交渉 [mainly AM 主に米国英語] □ *Family boat. $6,000 obo.* ファミリーボート. 6000ドル, 応交渉
→ see **orchestra**

ob|scene /əbsin/ ■ ADJ 形容詞 If you describe something as **obscene**, you mean it offends you because it relates to sex or violence in a way that you think is unpleasant and shocking. わいせつな □ *I'm not prudish but I think these photographs are obscene.* 私は上品ぶっているわけではないが, これらの写真は卑猥だと思う. ② ADJ 形容詞 In legal contexts, books, pictures, or movies which are judged **obscene** are illegal because they deal with sex or violence in a way that is offensive to the general public. 公序良俗に反する □ *A city magistrate ruled that the novel was obscene and copies should be destroyed.* 市の判事はその小説は公序良俗に反するため印刷部数すべてを廃棄すべきだとの判決を下した. ③ ADJ 形容詞 If you describe something as **obscene**, you disapprove of it very strongly and consider it to be offensive or immoral. 反道徳的な [DISAPPROVAL 不賛成] □ *It was obscene to spend millions producing unwanted food.* 不要な食料を生産するために何百万ものお金を浪費するのは道徳に反する.

ob|scen|ity /əbsɛnɪti/ (**obscenities**) ■ N-UNCOUNT 不可算名詞 **Obscenity** is behavior, art, or language that is sexual and offends or shocks people. わいせつなもの □ *He insisted these photographs were not art but obscenity.* 彼はこれらの写真は芸術ではなくわいせつなものだと主張しました. ② N-VAR 可変性名詞 An **obscenity** is a very offensive word or expression. わいせつ言葉 □ *They shouted obscenities at us and smashed bottles on the floor.* 彼らは私たちに向かってわいせつな言葉を叫んで, 瓶を床に叩きつけて割った.

ob|scure /əbskyʊər/ (**obscurer, obscurest, obscures, obscuring, obscured**) ■ ADJ 形容詞 If something or someone is **obscure**, they

are unknown, or are known by only a few people. よく知られていない □ *The origin of the custom is obscure.* その風習の起源はあまり知られていない. **2** ADJ 形容詞 Something that is **obscure** is difficult to understand or deal with, usually because it involves so many parts or details. 解しがたい □ *The contracts are written in obscure language.* 契約書は意味不明瞭なことばで書かれている. **3** V-T 他動詞 If one thing **obscures** another, it prevents it from being seen or heard properly. 覆い隠す □ *Trees obscured his vision; he couldn't see much of the square's southern half.* 木々が邪魔になって彼は広場の南半分をあまり見ることができなかった. **4** V-T 他動詞 To **obscure** something means to make it difficult to understand. 物事をわかりにくくする □ *…the jargon that frequently obscures educational writing.* 往々にして教育用文章を分かりにくくする専門用語.

ob|scu|ri|ty /əbskyʊ̯ərɪti/ (**obscurities**) **1** N-UNCOUNT 不可算名詞 **Obscurity** is the state of being known by only a few people. 世に知られないこと □ *For the lucky few, there's the chance of being plucked from obscurity and thrown into the glamorous world of modelling.* 幸運な少数の人には、無名から引き上げられて魅惑的なモデルの世界にデビューするチャンスがある. **2** N-VAR 可変性名詞 **Obscurity** is the quality of being difficult to understand. An **obscurity** is something that is difficult to understand. 不明瞭 □ *"How can that be?" asked Hunt, irritated by the obscurity of Henry's reply.* 「どうしてそうなるのか」とヘンリーの返答が不明瞭なのにいらだってハントは聞いた.

ob|ser|vance /əbzɜrvᵊns/ (**observances**) N-VAR 可変性名詞 The **observance** of something such as a law or custom is the practice of obeying or following it. 遵守 □ *County governments should use their powers to ensure strict observance of laws.* 州政府は権力を行使して法律の厳守を保証すべきだ.

ob|ser|vant /əbzɜrvᵊnt/ ADJ 形容詞 Someone who is **observant** pays a lot of attention to things and notices more about them than most people do. 注意深い □ *That's a good description, Mrs. Drummond. You're very observant.* それはよい描写ですね、ドラムンド夫人. あなたはとても観察力が鋭い方ですね.

ob|ser|va|tion /ɒbzərveɪʃᵊn/ (**observations**) **1** N-UNCOUNT 不可算名詞 **Observation** is the action or process of carefully watching someone or something. 観察 □ *…careful observation of the movement of the planets.* 惑星の動きの注意深い観察 **2** N-COUNT 可算名詞 An **observation** is something that you have learned by seeing or watching something and thinking about it. 観察に基づく所見 □ *This book contains observations about the causes of addictions.* この本には依存症の原因に関する所見が含まれている. **3** N-COUNT 可算名詞 If a person makes an **observation**, they make a comment about something or someone, usually as a result of watching how they behave. 所見 □ *Is that a criticism or just an observation?* それは批判ですか、それともただの所見ですか. **4** N-UNCOUNT 不可算名詞 **Observation** is the ability to pay a lot of attention to things and to notice more about them than most people do. 観察力 □ *She has good powers of observation.* 彼女はいい観察力を持っている.
→ see **experiment, forecast, science**

Word Partnership *observation* は次の語句と使われる:

PREP. **by** observation, **through** observation, **under** observation **1**
ADJ. **careful** observation **1**
direct observation **1** – **3**
V. **make an** observation **3**

Word Link *ory ≈ place where something happens : conservatory, factory, observatory*

ob|ser|va|tory /əbzɜrvətɔri/ (**observatories**) N-COUNT 可算名詞 An **observatory** is a building with a large telescope from which scientists study things such as the planets by watching them. 観測所、天文台

Word Link *serv ≈ keeping : conserve, observe, preserve*

ob|serve /əbzɜrv/ (**observes, observing, observed**) **1** V-T 他動詞 If you **observe** a person or thing, you watch them carefully, especially in order to learn something about them. 観察する □ *Olson also studies and observes the behavior of babies.* オルソンは新生児の行動様式も研究・観察している. □ *Are there any classes I could observe?* 私が見学できるクラスはありますか. **2** V-T 他動詞 If you **observe** someone or something, you see or notice them. 気づく、認める [FORMAL 形式ばった] □ *In 1664 Hooke observed a reddish spot on the surface of the planet.* 1664年にフックはその惑星の表面に赤みを帯びた地点があるのを認めた. **3** V-T 他動詞 If you **observe** that something is the case, you make a remark or comment about it, especially when it is something you have noticed and thought about a lot. 述べる [FORMAL 形式ばった] □ *We observe that the first calls for radical transformation did not begin until the period of the industrial revolution.* 私たちは根本的な変化に対する最初の要求は産業革命期まで起こらなかったことだと言っている. **4** V-T 他動

詞 If you **observe** something such as a law or custom, you obey it or follow it. 遵守する □ *Imposing speed restrictions is easy, but forcing drivers to observe them is trickier.* 速度制限を課すのは容易だが、運転者にそれを遵守させるのはいっそう難儀だ. □ *The army was observing a ceasefire.* 軍は休戦を守っていました. **5** V-T 他動詞 If you **observe** an important day such as a holiday or anniversary, you do something special in order to honor or celebrate it. 祝う □ *…where he will observe Thanksgiving with family members.* 彼が家族と感謝祭を祝う場所

Thesaurus *observe* また次を参照:

V. study, watch **1**
detect, notice, spot **2**
celebrate **5**

Word Partnership *observe* は次の語句と使われる:

observe は次の語句と使われる:
N. observe **behavior, opportunity to** observe **1** **2**
observe **guidelines**, observe **rules** **4**
observe **an anniversary** **5**

ob|serv|er /əbzɜrvər/ (**observers**) **1** N-COUNT 可算名詞 You can refer to someone who sees or notices something as an **observer**. 観察者 □ *A casual observer would have taken them to be three men out for an evening stroll.* おざなりに彼らを見た人は宵の散歩に出かけている3人の男性だと思っただろう. **2** N-COUNT 可算名詞 An **observer** is someone who studies current events and situations, especially in order to comment on them and predict what will happen next. 観察者 [JOURNALISM ジャーナリズム] □ *Observers say the events of the weekend seem to have increased support for the opposition.* 週末の出来事で野党の支持が増えたようだと観察者は言っています. **3** N-COUNT 可算名詞 An **observer** is a person who is sent to observe an important event or situation, especially in order to make sure it happens as it should, or to tell other people about it. 監視者 □ *The president suggested that a UN observer should attend the conference.* 大統領は国連監視団が会議に参加するよう提案しました.

Word Partnership *observer* は次の語句と使われる:

observe は次の語句と使われる:
ADJ. **casual** observer **1**
independent observer, **outside** observer **1** – **3**

ob|sess /əbsɛs/ (**obsesses, obsessing, obsessed**) V-T/V-I 他動詞/自動詞 If something **obsesses** you or if you **obsess about** something, you keep thinking about it and find it difficult to think about anything else. 取り付いて悩ます [他動詞] いつも悩む [自動詞] □ *A string of scandals is obsessing America.* 一連の不祥事がアメリカを悩ませている. □ *She stopped drinking but began obsessing about her weight.* 彼女は酒を止めたが、体重を気に病み始めた.

ob|sessed /əbsɛst/ ADJ 形容詞 If someone is **obsessed with** a person or thing, they keep thinking about them and find it difficult to think about anything else. 取りつかれた □ *He was obsessed with gangster movies.* 彼はギャング映画にはまっていた.

ob|ses|sion /əbsɛʃᵊn/ (**obsessions**) N-VAR 可変性名詞 If you say that someone has an **obsession** with a person or thing, you think they are spending too much time thinking about them. 取りつかれていること、強迫観念 □ *She would try to forget her obsession with Christopher.* 彼女はクリストファーへの執着を忘れようと試みるだろう.

ob|ses|sive /əbsɛsɪv/ (**obsessives**) **1** ADJ 形容詞 If someone's behavior is **obsessive**, they cannot stop doing a particular thing or behaving in a particular way. 取りつかれたような □ *Williams is obsessive about motor racing.* ウィリアムズは自動車レースに取りつかれている. ● **ob|ses|sive|ly** ADV 副詞 取りつかれたように □ *He couldn't help worrying obsessively about what would happen.* 彼は何が起こるのか異常なまでに心配せずにいられないだろう. **2** N-COUNT 可算名詞 An **obsessive** is someone who is obsessive about something or who behaves in an obsessive way. 強迫観念に取りつかれた人 □ *Obsessives, in any area, are invariably as boring as their hobbies.* 強迫観念に取りつかれた人は分野にかかわらず、常に彼等の持つ趣味と同じくらい退屈だ.

ob|so|lete /ɒbsəlit/ ADJ 形容詞 Something that is **obsolete** is no longer needed because something better has been invented. すたれた □ *So much equipment becomes obsolete almost as soon as it's made.* 非常に多くの機器はほとんど作製されるや否やすたれていく.

ob|sta|cle /ɒbstəkᵊl/ (**obstacles**) **1** N-COUNT 可算名詞 An **obstacle** is an object that makes it difficult for you to go where you want to go, because it is in your way. 障害 □ *Most competition cars will only roll over if they hit an obstacle.* ほとんどの競争車は障害物に衝突しても転倒するだけだ. **2** N-COUNT 可算名詞 You can refer to anything that makes it difficult for you to do something

as an **obstacle**. じゃま物 ❑ *Overcrowding remains a large obstacle to improving conditions.* 超過密状態は依然として状況改善の大きな障害となっている.

Word Partnership   *obstacle* は次の語句と使われる:

N.	obstacle **course** ◻1
	obstacle **to peace** ◻2
V.	**be an** obstacle, **hit an** obstacle, **overcome an** obstacle ◻1 ◻2
ADJ.	**big/biggest** obstacle, **main** obstacle, **major** obstacle, **serious** obstacle ◻1 ◻2

ob|ste|tri|cian /ɒbstətrɪʃ⁰n/ (**obstetricians**) N-COUNT 可算名詞 An **obstetrician** is a doctor who is specially trained to deal with pregnancy and birth. 産科医 [MEDICAL 医学の] → see **gynecologist**

ob|sti|nate /ɒbstɪnɪt/ ◻1 ADJ 形容詞 If you describe someone as **obstinate**, you are being critical of them because they are very determined to do what they want, and refuse to change their mind or be persuaded to do something else. 頑固な [DISAPPROVAL 不賛成] ❑ *He is obstinate and determined and will not give up.* 彼は強情で決意が固く, あきらめようとしない. ● **ob|sti|nate|ly** ADV 副詞 [ADV with v] 頑固に ❑ *I stayed obstinately in my room, sitting by the telephone.* 私は片意地を張って自分の部屋に留まり, 電話のそばにずっと座っていた. ● **ob|sti|na|cy** N-UNCOUNT1 不可算名詞 頑固 ❑ *I might have become a dangerous man with all that stubbornness and obstinacy built into me.* 私の根深いあのすべての頑固さと強情さをもってすれば, 危険な男になっていたかもしれない. ◻2 ADJ 形容詞 You can describe things as **obstinate** when they are difficult to move, change, or destroy. 根深い ❑ *...rusted farm equipment strewn among the obstinate weeds.* 執拗な雑草の中に散らばった錆びた農機具 ● **ob|sti|nate|ly** ADV 副詞 [ADV with v] 根深く ❑ *...the door of the shop which obstinately stayed closed when he tried to push it open.* 彼が押し開けようとしてもなかなか開かない店のドア

ob|struct /əbstrʌkt/ (**obstructs, obstructing, obstructed**) ◻1 V-T 他動詞 If something **obstructs** a road or path, it blocks it, stopping people or vehicles getting past. 妨げる ❑ *A knot of black and white cars obstructed the intersection.* 白と黒の車の集団が交差点を遮断した. ◻2 V-T 他動詞 To **obstruct** someone or something means to make it difficult for them to move forward by blocking their path. 通行を妨害する ❑ *A number of local people have been arrested for trying to obstruct trucks loaded with logs.* 丸太を積んだトラックの通行を妨害しようとして地元民が数人逮捕された. ◻3 V-T 他動詞 To **obstruct** progress or a process means to prevent it from happening properly. 妨害する ❑ *The authorities are obstructing a United Nations investigation.* 当局は国連の捜査を妨害している. ◻4 V-T 他動詞 If someone or something **obstructs** your view, they are positioned between you and the thing you are trying to look at, stopping you from seeing it completely. さえぎる ❑ *Claire positioned herself so as not to obstruct David's line of sight.* クレアはデイビッドの視線をさえぎらない位置に立った.

ob|struc|tion /əbstrʌkʃ⁰n/ (**obstructions**) ◻1 N-COUNT 可算名詞 An **obstruction** is something that blocks a road or path. 妨害 ❑ *John was irritated by drivers parking near his house and causing an obstruction.* ジョンは彼の家の付近に駐車してじゃまになっている運転者たちにいらいらした. ◻2 N-VAR 可変性名詞 An **obstruction** is something that blocks a passage in your body. 閉塞 ❑ *The boy was suffering from a bowel obstruction.* その少年は腸閉塞症を患っていた. ◻3 N-UNCOUNT 不可算名詞 **Obstruction** is the act of deliberately delaying something or preventing something from happening, usually in business, law, or government. 妨害行為, 議事妨害 ❑ *Mr. Anderson refused to let them in and now faces a criminal charge of obstruction.* アンダーソン氏は彼らの入場を拒否したため, 現在議事妨害の刑事責任を問われている.

ob|tain /əbteɪn/ (**obtains, obtaining, obtained**) V-T 他動詞 To **obtain** something means to get it or achieve it. 得る [FORMAL 形式ばった] ❑ *Evans was trying to obtain a false passport and other documents.* エバンズは偽パスポートやその他の書類を入手しようとしていた.

Word Partnership   *obtain* は次の語句と使われる:

ADJ.	**able to** obtain, **difficult to** obtain, **easy to** obtain, **unable to** obtain
N.	obtain **approval**, obtain **a copy**, obtain **financing**, obtain **help**, obtain **information**, obtain **insurance**, obtain **permission**, obtain **weapons**

ob|tuse /əbtus/ ◻1 ADJ 形容詞 An **obtuse** angle is between 90° and 180°. Compare **acute** angle. 鈍角の [TECHNICAL 技術的] ◻2 ADJ 形容詞 Someone who is **obtuse** has difficulty understanding things, or makes no effort to understand them. 愚鈍な ❑ *I've been waiting for you to ask me the question yourself, and you're being obtuse and slow about it.* 君が自分でその質問をするのを待っていたのだけど, 君は鈍感で時間がかかり過ぎている.

ob|vi|ous /ɒbviəs/ ◻1 ADJ 形容詞 If something is **obvious**, it is easy to see or understand. 明らかな ❑ *...the need to rectify what is an obvious injustice.* 明白な不正を是正する必要性 ◻2 ADJ 形容詞 If you describe something that someone says as **obvious**, you are being critical of it because you think it is unnecessary or shows lack of imagination. 分かりきった [DISAPPROVAL 不賛成] ❑ *Such an explanation seems too simple, and too obvious.* そんな説明は単純すぎて, あまりにも分かりきっている. ● PHRASE 句 If you say that someone **is stating the obvious**, you mean that they are saying something that everyone already knows and understands. 分かりきったことを言う

Thesaurus   *obvious* また次を参照:

ADJ.	noticeable, plain, unmistakable ◻1

Word Partnership   *obvious* は次の語句と使われる:

N.	obvious **answer**, obvious **choice**, obvious **differences**, obvious **example**, obvious **question**, obvious **reasons**, obvious **solution** ◻1 ◻2
ADV.	**fairly** obvious, **immediately** obvious, **less** obvious, **most** obvious, **painfully** obvious, **quite** obvious, **so** obvious ◻1 ◻2

ob|vi|ous|ly /ɒbviəsli/ ◻1 ADV 副詞 You use **obviously** when you are stating something that you expect the person who is listening to know already. 明らかに [EMPHASIS 強調] [ADV with cl] ❑ *Obviously, they've had sponsorship from some big companies.* 彼らは明らかに, 大会社から資金提供を受けていた. ◻2 ADV 副詞 You use **obviously** to indicate that something is easily noticed, seen, or recognized. 明白に [ADV with cl/group] ❑ *They obviously appreciate you very much.* 彼らがあなたに非常に感謝しているのは明らかだ.

oc|ca|sion /əkeɪʒ⁰n/ (**occasions**) ◻1 N-COUNT 可算名詞 An **occasion** is a time when something happens, or a case of it happening. 時 ❑ *I often think fondly of an occasion some years ago in New Orleans.* 私は往々にして数年前にニューオーリンズを訪れた時のことを懐かしく思い出す. ◻2 N-COUNT 可算名詞 An **occasion** is an important event, ceremony, or celebration. 特別な出来事 ❑ *Taking her with me on official occasions has been a challenge.* 公式行事に彼女を同行させるのはやりがいのあることだった. ◻3 N-COUNT 可算名詞 An **occasion** for doing something is an opportunity for doing it. 機会 [FORMAL 形式ばった] ❑ *It is an occasion for all the family to celebrate.* それは家族全員が祝う機会だ. ◻4 PHRASE 句 If you **have occasion to** do something, you have the opportunity to do it or have a need to do it. 機会がある ❑ *Over the next few years many people had occasion to reflect on the truth of his warnings.* その後数年間, 多くの人は彼の警告が真実であったことを反省する機会があった. ◻5 PHRASE 句 If you say that someone **rose to the occasion**, you mean that they did what was necessary to successfully overcome a difficult situation. 難局に対処する ❑ *Colorado rose to the occasion with four players scoring 16 points or more.* コロラドは4人のプレーヤーが16点以上を得点することで難局を切り抜けた.

Word Partnership   *occasion* は次の語句と使われる:

ADJ.	**festive** occasion, **historic** occasion, **rare** occasion, **solemn** occasion, **special** occasion ◻1 ◻2
V.	**mark an** occasion ◻2
	rise to an occasion ◻5

oc|ca|sion|al /əkeɪʒən⁰l/ ADJ 形容詞 **Occasional** means happening sometimes, but not regularly or often. 時折の ❑ *I've had occasional mild headaches all my life.* 私は時折起こる軽い頭痛に一生悩まされている. ● **oc|ca|sion|al|ly** ADV 副詞 ときどき ❑ *He still misbehaves occasionally.* 彼は今でもときどき不作法にふるまう.

oc|cult /əkʌlt, ɒkʌlt/ N-SING 単数名詞 **The occult** is the knowledge and study of supernatural or magical forces. 秘術, オカルト ❑ *Interest in the occult tended toward ceremonial magic rather than witchcraft.* 秘術への興味は魔法よりも儀式魔術に向かう傾向があった. ● ADJ 形容詞 **Occult** is also an adjective. 神秘の [ADJ n] ❑ *...paganism and occult practice.* 異教崇拝と秘術的習慣

oc|cu|pan|cy /ɒkyəpənsi/ N-UNCOUNT 不可算名詞 **Occupancy** is the act of using a room, building, or area of land, usually for a fixed period of time. 占有 [FORMAL 形式ばった] ❑ *Hotel occupancy has been as low as 40%.* ホテル客室利用率は40%まで落ちていた.

Word Link   ant ≈ one who does, has : defend**ant**, deodor**ant**, occup**ant**

oc|cu|pant /ɒkyəpənt/ (**occupants**) ◻1 N-COUNT 可算名詞 The **occupants** of a building or room are the people who live or work there. 占有者 ❑ *Most of the occupants had left before the fire broke out.* 居住者のほとんどは火災発生前に退出していた. ◻2 N-PLURAL 複数名詞 You can refer to the people who are in a place such as a room, vehicle, or bed at a particular time as the **occupants**. 占有者 ❑ *He*

wanted the occupants of the vehicle to get out. 彼は乗員に車から降りて
欲しかった.

oc|cu|pa|tion /ɒkyəpeɪʃn/ (occupations) **1** N-COUNT 可算
名詞 Your **occupation** is your job or profession. 仕事 □I suppose I
was looking for an occupation which was going to be an adventure. 私は
冒険になるような仕事を探していたのだと思う. **2** N-COUNT 可算名
詞 An **occupation** is something that you spend time doing, either
for pleasure or because it needs to be done. する事 □Parachuting
is a dangerous occupation. パラシュートで降下するのは危険なこ
とだ. **3** N-UNCOUNT 不可算名詞 The **occupation** of a country
happens when it is entered and controlled by a foreign army. 占領
□...the occupation of Poland. ポーランドの占領

oc|cu|pa|tion|al /ɒkyəpeɪʃənəl/ ADJ 形容詞 **Occupational**
means relating to a person's job or profession. 職業上の □Some
received substantial occupational assistance in the form of low-interest
loans. 低利融資という形でかなりの職業援助を受けた人もいる.

oc|cu|pi|er /ɒkyəpaɪər/ (occupiers) N-COUNT 可算名詞 The
occupier of a house, apartment, or piece of land is the person who
lives or works there. 居住者 [BRIT 英国英語, FORMAL 形式ばった]
[AM **occupant** 米国英語 **occupant**]

oc|cu|py /ɒkyəpaɪ/ (occupies, occupying, occupied) **1** V-T 他
動詞 The people who **occupy** a building or a place are the people
who live or work there. 居住する, 使用する □There were over 40
tenants, all occupying one wing of the building. 賃貸者は40人以上お
り, 全員が建物の1翼に居住していた. **2** V-T PASSIVE 受動態他動
詞 If a room or something such as a seat is **occupied**, someone is
using it, so that it is not available for anyone else. 占める □The
hospital bed is occupied by his wife. その病院のベッドは彼の妻が使っ
ている. **3** V-T 他動詞 If a group of people or an army **occupies** a
place or country, they move into it, using force in order to gain
control of it. 占領する □U.S. forces now occupy a part of the country.
米軍は現在その国の一部を占領している. **4** V-T 他動詞 If someone
or something **occupies** a particular place in a system, process, or
plan, they have that place. 占める, 就く □Many men still occupy
more positions of power than women. 権力のある地位にはいまだに女性
よりも男性が多く就いている. **5** V-T 他動詞 If something **occupies**
you, or if you **occupy** yourself, your time, or your mind with it,
you are busy doing that thing or thinking about it. (場所や時間
を) とる □Her career occupies all of her time. 彼女の時間はすべて仕
事に取られている. □He occupied himself with packing the car. 彼は車
に荷を積むのに専念していた. ● **oc|cu|pied** ADJ 形容詞 [v-link ADJ]
占められた □Keep the brain occupied. 真剣に考えろよ. **6** V-T 他動
詞 If something **occupies** you, it requires your efforts, attention,
or time. 必要とする □I had other matters to occupy me, during the day
at least. 少なくともその日は他のことで多忙だった. **7** V-T 他動詞 If
something **occupies** a particular area or place, it fills or covers it,
or exists there. 占める □Even small aircraft occupy a lot of space. 飛行
機は小さいものでも広い面積を占める.

Word Partnership occupy は次の語句と使われる:

N. occupy a house, occupy land **1**
occupy a place **1 3 4 7**
occupy a position **3 4**
occupy an area, forces occupy someplace, occupy space,
troops occupy someplace **3 7**

oc|cur /əkɜr/ (occurs, occurring, occurred) **1** V-I 自動詞 When
something **occurs**, it happens. 起こる □If headaches only occur at
night, lack of fresh air and oxygen is often the cause. 頭痛が起こるのが夜
間だけなのなら, 往々にして新鮮な空気や酸素の不足が原因である.
□The crash occurred when the crew shut down the wrong engine. 衝突は
乗組員が間違ったエンジンをシャットダウンしたときに起こった. **2** V-I

自動詞 When something **occurs** in a particular place, it exists or
is present there. 存在する □These snails do not occur on low-lying
coral islands. これらのカタツムリは低地のサンゴ諸島には生息しな
い. **3** V-I 自動詞 If a thought or idea **occurs to** you, you suddenly
think of it or realize it. 心に浮かぶ [no passive, no cont] □It did not
occur to me to check my insurance policy. 保険証書を確認することは私は
思いつかなかった.

Thesaurus occur また次を参照:

v. come about, develop, happen **1**
dawn on, strike **3**

Word Partnership occur は次の語句と使われる:

N. accidents occur, changes occur, deaths occur,
diseases occur, events occur, injuries occur,
problems occur **1**
ADV. frequently occur, naturally occur, normally occur,
often occur, usually occur **1** – **3**

oc|cur|rence /əkɜrəns/ (occurrences) **1** N-COUNT 可算名詞
An **occurrence** is something that happens. できごと [FORMAL 形
式ばった] □Complaints seemed to be an everyday occurrence. 苦情は
毎日起こるできごとであるようだった. **2** N-COUNT 可算名詞 The
occurrence of something is the fact that it happens or is present.
発生 □The greatest occurrence of coronary heart disease is in those over
65. 冠状動脈性心臓病の発生率は65歳以上の人々で最も高い.

Word Partnership occurrence は次の語句と使われる:

ADJ. common occurrence, daily occurrence, everyday
occurrence, frequent occurrence, rare occurrence,
unusual occurrence **1 2**

ocean /oʊʃn/ (oceans) **1** N-SING 単数名詞 The **ocean** is the
sea. 海洋 □There were few sights as beautiful as the calm ocean on
a warm night. 暖かい夜の凪いだ海ほど美しい光景はほとんどな
い. **2** N-COUNT 可算名詞 An **ocean** is one of the five very large
areas of sea on the Earth's surface. 大洋 □They spent many days
cruising the northern Pacific Ocean. 彼らは北太平洋を何日もクルー
ジングしました. **3** N-COUNT 可算名詞 If you say that there is an
ocean of something, you are emphasizing that there is a very
large amount of it. たくさん [INFORMAL くだけた, EMPHASIS 強調]
□I had cried oceans of tears. 私は信じられないくらい泣いて泣きつくし
た. **4** PHRASE 句 If you say that something is **a drop in the ocean**,
you mean that it is a very small amount which is unimportant
compared to the cost of other things or is so small that it has very
little effect on something. 大海の1滴 [EMPHASIS 強調] □His fee is
a drop in the ocean compared with the real cost of broadcasting. 彼の支払
った料金は実際の放送費用に比べるとほんのわずかだった.
→ see Word Web: ocean
→ see beach, earth, river, ship, tide, whale

o'clock /əklɒk/ ADV 副詞 You use **o'clock** after numbers from
one to twelve to say what time it is. For example, if you say that it
is 9 o'clock, you mean that it is nine hours after midnight or nine
hours after noon. 時 [num ADV] □The trouble began just after ten
o'clock last night. その問題は昨夜10時直後に始まった.

Oct. Oct. is a written abbreviation for **October**. 10月の略
□...Tuesday Oct. 25th. 10月25日火曜日

Oc|to|ber /ɒktoʊbər/ (Octobers) N-VAR 可変性名詞 **October** is
the tenth month of the year in the Western calendar. 10月 □Most
seasonal hiring is done in early October. ほとんどの季節雇用は10月初旬
に行われる. □The first plane is due to leave on October 2. 最初の飛行機
は10月2日に出発することになっています.

Word Web ocean

Oceans cover over seventy-five percent of the
earth's surface. These huge bodies of
saltwater are constantly in motion. On the
surface, the wind pushes the water into
waves. At the same time, **currents** under the
surface flow like rivers through the oceans.
These currents are affected by the earth's
rotation. It shifts them to the right in the
northern hemisphere and to the left in the
southern hemisphere. Other forces affect the
oceans as well. For example, the gravitational
pull of the moon and sun cause the **ebb** and
flow of ocean **tides**.

oc|to|pus /ɒktəpəs/ (**octopuses**) N-VAR 可変性名詞 An **octopus** is a soft sea creature with eight long arms called tentacles which it uses to catch food. タコ ● N-UNCOUNT 不可算名詞 **Octopus** is this creature eaten as food. タコ □ ...*plates of octopus.* タコ料理

OD /ou di/ (**OD's, OD'ing, OD'd**) V-I 自動詞 To **OD** means the same as to **overdose**. 麻薬をやり過ぎる [INFORMAL くだけた] □ *His son was a junkie; the kid OD'd a year ago.* 彼の息子は麻薬常習者で、1年前にやりすぎて入院した。 ● N-COUNT 可算名詞 **OD** is also a noun. 麻薬のやりすぎ □ *"I had a friend who died of an OD," she said.* 「私の友人に麻薬のやりすぎで死んだ人がいるの」と彼女は言った。

odd /ɒd/ (**odder, oddest**) **1** ADJ 形容詞 If you describe or something as **odd**, you think that they are strange or unusual. 変な □ *He'd always been odd, but not to this extent.* 彼はいつも風変わりだったけれど、これほどまでではなかった。 □ *What an odd coincidence that he should have known your family.* 彼があなたの家族を知っていたなんて、なんて奇妙な偶然だろう。 ● **odd|ly** 副詞 [ADV with v] 奇妙に □ *...an oddly shaped hill.* 奇妙な形をした丘 **2** ADJ 形容詞 You use **odd** before a noun to indicate that you are not mentioning the type, size, or quality of something because it is not important. 臨時の、雑多な [det ADJ] □ *...moving from place to place where she could find the odd bit of work.* 彼女はあちこちに移動して臨時の仕事を探すことができた。 □ *He had various odd cleaning jobs around the place.* 彼にはその場所で様々な臨時の清掃の仕事があった。 **3** ADV 副詞 You use **odd** after a number to indicate that it is only approximate. 余り [INFORMAL くだけた] [num ADV] □ *How many pages was it, 500 odd?* 何ページありましたか、500余りですか。 □ *He has now appeared in sixty odd films.* 彼はこれで60余りの映画に出たことになる。 **4** ADJ 形容詞 **Odd** numbers, such as 3 and 17, are those which cannot be divided exactly by the number two. 奇数の □ *The odd numbers are on the left as you walk up the street.* 奇数の住居は通りを上って行くと左側にあります。 **5** ADJ 形容詞 You say that two things are **odd** when they do not belong to the same set or pair. 片方の □ *I'm wearing odd socks today by the way.* ところで、私は今日左右違う靴下をはいています。 **6** PHRASE 句 **The odd man out, the odd woman out,** or **the odd one out** in a particular situation is a person who is different from the other people in it. はみだし者、仲間はずれ □ *Azerbaijan has been the odd man out, the one republic not to hold democratic elections.* アゼルバイジャンは民主的選挙を行わない、ただひとつの共和国である点で他と異なっている。 **7** → see also **odds**

Thesaurus   odd また次を参照：

ADJ. | bizarre, different, eccentric, peculiar, strange, unusual, weird; (*ant.*) normal, regular **1**

Word Partnership   odd は次の語句と使われる：

V. | feel odd, look odd, seem odd, sound odd, strike someone as odd, think something odd **1**
N. | odd combination, odd thing **1** | odd job **2**
ADJ. | odd numbered **4**

odd|ity /ɒdɪti/ (**oddities**) N-COUNT 可算名詞 An **oddity** is someone or something that is very strange. 変人、珍奇な物 □ *Losing my hair made me feel an oddity.* 私は禿になって変人のように感じる。

odd|ly /ɒdli/ **1** ADV 副詞 You use **oddly** to indicate that what you are saying is true, but that it is not what you expected. 変に □ *He said no and seemed oddly reluctant to talk about it.* 彼はいいえと言って、それについて話すのを妙に嫌がっているようだった。 □ *Oddly, Emma says she never considered her face to be attractive.* 奇妙にも、エマは自分の顔が決して魅力的だと思ったことはないと言う。 **2** → see also **odd**

odds /ɒdz/ **1** N-PLURAL 複数名詞 You refer to how likely something is to happen as the **odds** that it will happen. 見込み □ *What are the odds of finding a parking space right outside the door?* ドアのすぐ外に駐車場を見つける見込みはどのくらいですか。 **2** N-PLURAL 複数名詞 In betting, **odds** are expressions with numbers such as "10 to 1" and "7 to 2" that show how likely something is thought to be, for example, how likely a particular horse is to lose or win a race. 賭け率 □ *We are offering odds of 6-1 on the fight ending in a knockout.* 我々は試合がノックアウトで終了するには6対1で賭けます。 **3** PHRASE 句 If someone is **at odds** with someone else, or if two people are **at odds**, they are disagreeing or arguing with each other. 不和で □ *He was at odds with the boss.* 彼は上司と仲が悪かった。 **4** PHRASE 句 If you say that **the odds are against** something or someone, you mean that they are unlikely to succeed. 勝ち目がない □ *He reckons the odds are against the plan going ahead.* 彼はその計画が進む可能性は低いと推測している。 **5** PHRASE 句 If something happens **against all odds**, it happens or succeeds although it seemed impossible or very unlikely. どんなに不利な状況になろうとも □ *...families in terrible circumstances, who have stayed together against all odds.* すべ

ての不利な状況にめげず一緒にいた、ひどい状況におかれた諸家族 **6** PHRASE 句 If you say that **the odds are in** someone's **favor,** you mean that they are likely to succeed in what they are doing. 勝ち目がある □ *The troops will only engage in a ground battle when all the odds are in their favor.* 完全に勝ち目がある場合にのみ部隊は地上戦を行うだろう。

→ see **lottery**

Word Partnership   odds は次の語句と使われる：

V. | beat the odds **1 2**
PREP. | the odds of something **1 2** | at odds (with someone) **3** | odds against something **4** | against all odds **5**
N. | odds of winning **1 2** | odds in someone's/something's favor **6**

odor /oudər/ (**odors**) N-VAR 可変性名詞 An **odor** is a particular and distinctive smell. におい □ *...the lingering odor of automobile exhaust.* 車の排気ガスのなかなか消えないにおい

→ see **smell, taste**

of /əv, STRONG ʌv/

In addition to the uses shown below, **of** is used after some verbs, nouns, and adjectives in order to introduce extra information. **Of** is also used in phrasal prepositions such as "because of," "instead of," and "in spite of," and in phrasal verbs such as "make of" and "dispose of."

下記の用法に加えて、**of** は追加の情報を伝えるために、一部の動詞、名詞、形容詞の後に使われる。**Of** はまた **because of, instead of, in spite of** のような句前置詞と共に使われるし、また **make of** や **dispose of** のような句動詞にも使われる。

1 PREP 前置詞 You use **of** to combine two nouns when the first noun identifies the feature of the second noun that you want to talk about. ～の [n PREP n] □ *The average age of the women interviewed was only 21.5.* インタビューを受けて女性の平均年齢はたった21.5歳だった。 □ *...the population of this town.* この町の人口 **2** PREP 前置詞 You use **of** to combine two nouns, or a noun and a present participle, when the second noun or present participle defines or gives more information about the first noun. ～の [n PREP n/-ing] □ *She let out a little cry of pain.* 彼女は痛みで小さな叫び声をあげた。 □ *...the problem of having a national shortage of teachers.* 全国的な教師不足問題 **3** PREP 前置詞 You use **of** after nouns referring to actions to specify the person or thing that is affected by the action or that performs the action. For example, "the kidnapping of the child" refers to an action affecting a child; "the arrival of the next train" refers to an action performed by a train. ～の [n PREP n] □ *It sets targets for reduction of greenhouse-gas emissions.* それは温室効果ガス排出の削減を目標に設定する。 **4** PREP 前置詞 You use **of** after words and phrases referring to quantities or groups of things to indicate the substance or thing that is being measured. ～の □ *...dozens of people.* 多数の人々 □ *...a collection of short stories.* 短編小説集 **5** PREP 前置詞 You use **of** after the name of someone or something to introduce the institution or place they belong to or are connected with. ～の [n PREP n] □ *...the governor of Missouri.* ミズーリ州の知事 **6** PREP 前置詞 You use **of** after a noun referring to a container to form an expression referring to the container and its contents. ～の [n PREP n] □ *...a box of tissues.* 1箱のティッシュペーパー □ *...a roomful of people.* 部屋いっぱいの人々 **7** PREP 前置詞 You use **of** after a countable noun and before an uncountable noun when you want to talk about an individual piece or item. ～の [n PREP n] □ *...a blade of grass.* 1枚の草の葉 □ *Marina ate only one slice of bread.* マリナはパン1枚しか食べなかった。 **8** PREP 前置詞 You use **of** to indicate the materials or things that form something. ～からできた [n PREP n] □ *...local decorations of wood and straw.* 木材とわらでできた地方独特の飾り □ *...loose-fitting garments of linen.* 麻製のゆったりした服 **9** PREP 前置詞 You use **of** after a noun which specifies a particular part of something, to introduce the thing that it is a part of. ～の中で [n PREP n] □ *...the other side of the square.* 広場の向こう側 □ *...the beginning of the year.* 年頭 **10** PREP 前置詞 You use **of** after some verbs to indicate someone or something else involved in the action. ～について □ *He'd been dreaming of her.* 彼は彼女の夢を見ていた。 □ *Listen, I shall be thinking of you always.* いいか、よく聞くんだ。僕は君のことをいつも考えているからね。 **11** PREP 前置詞 You use **of** after some adjectives to indicate the thing that a feeling or quality relates to. ～を [adj PREP n/-ing] □ *I have grown very fond of Alec.* 私はアレックを大変好きになりました。 □ *His father was quite naturally very proud of him.* 彼の父親は全く当然ながら彼を非常に誇りに思っていました。 **12** PREP 前置詞 You use **of** before a word referring to the person who performed an action when saying what you think about the action. ～するとは □ *This has been so nice, so terribly kind of you.* これは大変ご親切にありがとうございました。 **13** PREP 前置詞 If something is **more of** or **less of** a

particular thing, it is that thing to a greater or smaller degree. (もっと多くのもの・より少ないもの) の ['more/less' PREP 'a' n] ❑ *Your extra fat may be more of a health risk than you realize.* 君の余分な脂肪は君が思うよりももっと健康に悪いかもしれない. **14** PREP 前置詞 You use of to indicate a characteristic or quality that someone or something has. の ❑ *...the worth of their music.* 彼らの音楽の価値. ❑ *She is a woman of enviable beauty.* 彼女はうらやむべき美しい女性だ. **15** PREP 前置詞 You use of to specify an amount, value, or age. の [n PREP amount] ❑ *Last Thursday, Nick announced record revenues of $3.4 billion.* 先週木曜日、ニックは34億という記録的収益を発表した. ❑ *...young people under the age of 16 years.* 16歳未満の若者. **16** PREP 前置詞 You use of after a noun such as "month" or "year" to indicate the length of time that some state or activity continues. ～のある [n PREP n/-ing] ❑ *...eight bruising years of war.* 鮮烈な戦争の8年間. **17** PREP 前置詞 You can use of to say what time it is by indicating how many minutes there are before the hour mentioned. ～から [AM 米国英語] ❑ *At about a quarter of eight in the evening Joe Urber calls.* 夜8時15分ごろにジョー・アーバーから電話があります.

of course

1 ADV 副詞 You say of course to suggest that something is normal, obvious, or well-known, and should therefore not surprise the person you are talking to. もちろん [SPOKEN 口語] [ADV with cl] ❑ *Of course there were lots of other interesting things at the exhibition.* もちろん展覧会にはその他にもおもしろいものがたくさんあった. ❑ *"I have read about you in the newspapers of course," Charlie said.* 「あなたのことはもちろん新聞で読んでいますよ」とチャーリーは言った. **2** CONVENTION 慣習表現 You use of course as a polite way of giving permission. もちろん [SPOKEN 口語, FORMULAE 決まり文句] ❑ *"Can I just say something about the game on Saturday?" — "Yes, of course you can."* 「土曜日の試合について1言いっていいかな」「もちろんだよ」 **3** ADV 副詞 You use of course in order to emphasize a statement that you are making, especially when you are agreeing or disagreeing with someone. 当然 [SPOKEN 口語, EMPHASIS 強調] ❑ *"You could be right." — "Of course I'm right!"* 「君が正しいのかもしれない」「当然僕が正しいさ」 ❑ *Of course I'm not afraid!* もちろん私は恐れてなんかいません. **4** CONVENTION 慣習表現 Of course not is an emphatic way of saying no. そうではありません [SPOKEN 口語, EMPHASIS 強調] ❑ *"You're not really seriously considering this thing, are you?" — "No, of course not."* 「君はこの事を本当に真剣に考えているわけじゃないだろうね」「まさか、もちろんそんなことはない」

off

1 AWAY FROM
2 OTHER USES

1 off

The preposition is pronounced /ɔf/. The adverb is pronounced /ɒf/.

前置詞は /ɔf/ と発音される. 副詞は /ɒf/ と発音される.

1 PREP 前置詞 If something is taken off something else or moves off it, it is no longer touching that thing. ～から離れて ❑ *He took his feet off the desk.* 彼は机から両足をどけた. ❑ *I took the key for the room off a rack above her head.* 私は彼女の頭上にある置き棚から部屋の鍵を取った. ● ADV 副詞 Off is also an adverb. 離れて [ADV after v] ❑ *Lee broke off a small piece of orange and held it out to him.* リーは小さなミカンの房をもいで彼に差し出した. **2** PREP 前置詞 When you get off a bus, train, or plane, you come out of it or leave it after you have been traveling on it. ～から降りて ❑ *Don't try to get on or off a moving train!* 動いている列車への乗車下車はおやめください. ● ADV 副詞 Off is also an adverb. 降りて [ADV after v] ❑ *At the next stop the man got off too and introduced himself.* 次の停留所でその男も下車して自己紹介した. **3** PREP 前置詞 If you keep off a street or piece of land, you do not step on it or go there. ～から外れて ❑ *Locking up men does nothing more than keep them off the streets.* 男たちを拘留しても、街をぶらつかせないようにする以外の効果はない. ● ADV 副詞 Off is also an adverb. そして ❑ *...a sign saying "Keep Off."* 「立ち入り禁止」の標識. **4** PREP 前置詞 If something is situated off a place such as a coast, room, or road, it is near to it or next to it, but not exactly in it. ～の沖に ❑ *The boat was anchored off the northern coast of the peninsula.* 船は半島の北海岸の沖合いに停泊していました. ❑ *Lily lives in a penthouse just off Park Avenue.* リリーはパーク街からちょっと外れたペントハウスに住んでいました. **5** ADV 副詞 If you go off, you leave a place. 去って ❑ *He was just about to drive off when the secretary came running out.* 秘書が走り出してきたとき、彼は車で走り去るところだった. ❑ *She was off again, to Kenya.* 彼女はまたケニアに行った. **6** ADV 副詞 When you take off clothing or jewelry that you are wearing, you remove it from your body. 脱ぐ ❑ *He took off his spectacles and rubbed frantically at the lens.* 彼は眼鏡を外して、レンズを必死に拭いていた. **7** ADV 副詞 If you have time off or a particular day off, you do not go to work or school, for example, because you are sick or it is a day when you do not usually work. 休みにして ❑ *The rest of the men had the day off.*

残りの男たちはその日非番だった. ❑ *I'm off tomorrow.* 私は明日休みです. ● PREP 前置詞 Off is also a preposition. ～から離れて ❑ *He could not get time off work to go on vacation.* 彼は仕事から休みを取って休暇に出かけることができなかった. **8** PREP 前置詞 If there is money off something, its price is reduced by the amount specified. ～から値引いて [amount PREP n] ❑ *20 per cent off all jackets this Saturday.* 今度の土曜日はすべての上着が2割引. ● ADV 副詞 Off is also an adverb. 割り引いて ❑ *Take $5 off the regular price of any membership.* どの会員の正規会費から5ドルを値引き. **10** ADV 副詞 If something is a long way off, it is a long distance away from you. 遠くに離れて [n/amount ADV] ❑ *Florida was a long way off.* フロリダ州はずっと遠方だった. **11** ADV 副詞 If something is a long time off, it will not happen for a long time. 隔たって [n/amount ADV] ❑ *An end to the crisis seems a long way off.* 危機はなかなか終わりが見えそうにありません. **12** PREP 前置詞 If you get something off someone, you obtain it from them. ～から [SPOKEN 口語] ❑ *I don't really get a lot of information, and if I do I get it off Mark.* あまりたくさん情報は得ていませんが、得るとしたらマークからです.

2 off

The preposition is pronounced /ɔf/. The adverb is pronounced /ɒf/.

前置詞は /ɔf/ と発音される. 副詞は /ɒf/ と発音される.

1 ADV 副詞 If something such as an agreement or a sports event is off, it is canceled. ～をやめて ❑ *Until Pointon is completely happy, however, the deal's off.* しかし、ポイントンがあらゆる点で満足するまで、契約は解消だ. **2** PREP 前置詞 If someone is off something harmful such as a drug, they have stopped taking or using it. ～を断ち切って ❑ *She felt better and the psychiatrist took her off antidepressants.* 彼女は気分がよくなったので、精神科医は抗うつ剤をやめさせた. **3** PREP 前置詞 If you are off something, you have stopped liking it. ～をやめて ❑ *I'm off coffee at the moment.* 私は今コーヒーを控えています. **4** ADV 副詞 When something such as a machine or electric light is off, it is not functioning or in use. When you switch it off, you stop it from functioning. 止まって ❑ *As he pulled into the driveway, he saw her bedroom light was off.* 彼は私設車道に車を寄せる際、彼女の寝室の明かりが消えているのを見た. ❑ *We used sail power and turned the engine off to save our fuel.* 彼は帆の力を使用し、エンジンを切って燃料を倹約した. **5** ADJ 形容詞 If food has gone off, it tastes and smells bad because it is no longer fresh enough to be eaten. 痛んで [mainly BRIT 主に英国英語; AM usually spoiled, bad 米国英語では通常 spoiled, bad] **6** PREP 前置詞 If you live off a particular kind of food, you eat it in order to live. If you live off a particular source of money, you use it to live. ～を食べて、～で生計を立てて [V PREP n] ❑ *Her husband's memories are of living off roast chicken and drinking whiskey.* 夫の主な思い出はローストチキンを食べ、ウィスキーを飲んで生きていたことだ. **7** PREP 前置詞 If a machine runs off a particular kind of fuel or power, it uses that power in order to function. ～で稼動して [V PREP n] ❑ *The electric armor runs off the tank's power supply.* 電気装甲車はタンクの電源で走行する. **8** PHRASE 句 If something happens on and off, or off and on, it happens occasionally, or only for part of a period of time, not in a regular or continuous way. 断続的に ❑ *I was still working on and off as a waitress to support myself.* 私は生活するために、なおウェイトレスとして時々働いていた.

In addition to the uses shown here, off is used after some verbs and nouns in order to introduce extra information. Off is also used in phrasal verbs such as "get off," "pair off," and "sleep off."

of|fal /ˈɔf﬚l/ **1** N-UNCOUNT 不可算名詞 Offal is the parts of animals' bodies that are thrown away after the animals have been butchered. くず肉 ❑ *...all the blood and offal the butchers shove down in the gutters.* 肉屋たちが溝に捨てる血とくず肉すべて. **2** N-UNCOUNT 不可算名詞 Offal is the internal organs of animals, for example, their hearts and livers, when they are cooked and eaten. 臓物

off-balance also **off balance 1** ADJ 形容詞 If someone or something is **off-balance**, they can easily fall or be knocked over because they are not standing firmly. 平衡を失って [v n ADJ, v-link ADJ] ❑ *He tried to use his own weight to push his attacker off but he was off balance.* 彼は自分の体重で襲撃者を押しのけようとしたが、バランスを崩した. **2** ADJ 形容詞 If someone is caught **off-balance**, they are extremely surprised or upset by a particular event or piece of news that they are not expecting. 不意をつかれて ❑ *Mullins knocked me off-balance with his abrupt change of subject.* マリンズは突然話題の急変で私を狼狽させた.

off-duty ADJ 形容詞 When someone such as a soldier or police officer is **off-duty**, they are not working. 勤務外の ❑ *The place is the haunt of off-duty policemen.* そこは非番の警察官の行きつけの場所だ.

of|fence /əˈfɛns/ → see **offense**

Word Link | *fend ≈ striking : defend, fender, offend*

of|fend /əfɛnd/ (**offends, offending, offended**) ■ V-T/V-I 他動詞／自動詞 If you **offend** someone, you say or do something rude which upsets or embarrasses them. 感情を損なう [他動詞] 不快感を与える [自動詞] ❑ *He apologizes for his comments and says he had no intention of offending the community.* 彼は自分のコメントについて謝罪し、地域社会の感情を害するつもりはなかったのだと言っている。 ❑ *In the great effort not to offend, we end up saying nothing.* 不快感を与えないよう最大の努力をしようとすると、私たちは何も言えなくなる。 ● **of|fend|ed** 形容詞 [v-link ADJ] 感情を害した ❑ *She is terribly offended, angered and hurt by this.* 彼女はこれによりひどく感情を害し、立腹し、傷ついた。 ■ V-I 自動詞 If someone **offends**, they commit a crime. 罪を犯す [FORMAL 形式ばった] [no cont] ❑ *In Western countries girls are far less likely to offend than boys.* 西欧諸国では、少年に比べ少女が罪を犯す確率ははるかに少ない。

of|fend|er /əfɛndər/ (**offenders**) ■ N-COUNT 可算名詞 An **offender** is a person who has committed a crime. 犯罪者 ❑ *The authorities often know that sex offenders will attack again when they are released.* 当局は性犯罪者が出所すると再度暴行に至ることをしばしば知っている。 ■ N-COUNT 可算名詞 You can refer to someone or something which you think is causing a problem as an **offender**. 困り者；物 ❑ *The plant's leaves can often turn brown, and I sometimes cut off the worst offenders.* その植物の葉は頻繁に茶色になることがあるので、私は時々最悪の部分を切り取る。

of|fense /əfɛns/ (**offenses**)

Pronounced /ɔfɛns/ for meaning ■.

/ɔfɛns/の意味では ■ と発音される。

■ N-COUNT 可算名詞 An **offense** is a crime that breaks a particular law and requires a particular punishment. 違反 ❑ *A first offense carries a fine of $1,000.* 最初の違反は1000ドルの罰金に科される。 ■ N-VAR 可変性名詞 **Offense** or an **offense** is behavior that causes people to be upset or embarrassed. 人の感情を害すること、無礼 ❑ *He said he didn't mean to give offense.* 彼は無礼を働く気はなかったのだと言いました。 ■ N-SING 単数名詞 In sports such as football or basketball, the **offense** is the team which has possession of the ball and is trying to score. 攻撃側 [AM 米国英語] ['the' N] ❑ *Between plays the coach was talking to the offense in the huddle.* 試合の合間にコーチはハドルで攻撃側と話をしていた。 ■ CONVENTION 慣習表現 Some people say "**no offense**" to make it clear that they do not want to upset you, although what they are saying may seem rude. 悪く思うな上 [FORMULAE 決まり文句] ❑ *"No offense," she said, "but your sister seems a little gloomy."* 「気を悪くしないでね」と彼女は言った。「でもあなたの妹さんは少し陰気ね」 ■ PHRASE 句 If someone **takes offense at** something you say or do, they feel upset, often unnecessarily, because they think you are being rude to them. 怒る ❑ *Instead of taking offense, the woman smiled.* その女性は怒る代わりに微笑んだ。

Thesaurus | *offense* また次を参照：

N. | crime, infraction, violation, wrongdoing ■
| assault, attack, insult, put-down, snub ■

Word Partnership | *offense* は次の語句と使われる：

ADJ. | **criminal** offense ■
| **serious** offense ■ ■
V. | **commit an** offense ■ ■
| **take** offense ■

of|fen|sive /əfɛnsɪv/ (**offensives**) ■ ADJ 形容詞 Something that is **offensive** upsets or embarrasses people because it is rude or insulting. 無礼な ❑ *Some friends of his found the play horribly offensive.* 彼の友人の幾人かはその劇は非常に侮辱的だと思った。 ■ N-COUNT 可算名詞 A military **offensive** is a carefully planned attack made by a large group of soldiers. 軍事攻勢 ❑ *Its latest military offensive against rebel forces is aimed at re-opening important trade routes.* 最近の反乱軍に対する軍事攻勢は重要な通商路の再開を目的としています。 ■ N-COUNT 可算名詞 If you conduct an **offensive**, you take strong action to show how angry you are about something or how much you disapprove of something. 攻撃 ❑ *Republicans acknowledged that they had little choice but to mount an all-out offensive on the Democratic nominee.* 共和党は、民主党候補に総攻撃をかけるほかに選択の余地がないことを認めた。 ■ PHRASE 句 If you **go on the offensive, go over to the offensive,** or **take the offensive**, you begin to take strong action against people who have been attacking you. 攻撃に出る ❑ *The West African forces went on the offensive in response to attacks on them.* 西アフリカ軍は彼らに対する攻撃に応えて攻勢に出た。

Word Partnership | *offensive* は次の語句と使われる：

N. | **offensive language** ■
| offensive **capability, ground** offensive, offensive **operations,** offensive **weapons** ■
V. | **launch an** offensive, **mount an** offensive ■ ■
| **take the** offensive ■ – ■

of|fer /ɔfər/ (**offers, offering, offered**) ■ V-T 他動詞 If you **offer** something to someone, you ask them if they would like to have it or use it. 提供する ❑ *He has offered seats at the conference table to the Russian leader and the president of Kazakhstan.* 彼は会議用テーブルでロシアの指導者とカザフスタンの大統領に席を提供しました。 ❑ *The number of companies offering them work increased.* 彼らに仕事を提供する会社の数が増えた。 ■ V-T 他動詞 If you **offer to** do something, you say that you are willing to do it. 申し出る ❑ *Peter offered to teach them water-skiing.* ピーターは彼らに水上スキーを教えようと申し出た。 ■ N-COUNT 可算名詞 An **offer** is something that someone says they will give you or do for you. 提供 ❑ *The offer of talks with Moscow marks a significant change from the previous Western position.* モスクワとの対談の申し出は、以前の西側の姿勢から顕著に変化していることを示している。 ❑ *"I ought to reconsider her offer to move in," he mused.* 「彼女の入居申し出を考え直すべきだな」と彼は思い巡らした。 ■ V-T 他動詞 If you **offer** someone information, advice, or praise, you give it to them, usually because you feel that they need it or deserve it. 与える ❑ *They manage a company offering advice on mergers and acquisitions.* 彼らは合併買収に関するアドバイスを提供する会社を経営している。 ❑ *She offered him emotional and practical support in countless ways.* 彼女は数え切れないほどの方法で精神的および実際的な援助を与えた。 ■ V-T 他動詞 If you **offer** someone something such as love or friendship, you show them that you feel that way toward them. 表現する ❑ *The president has offered his sympathy to the Georgian people.* 大統領はジョージア州の住民に同情の念を示しました。 ❑ *It must be better to be able to offer them love and security.* 愛と安全を彼らに与えることができるほうがいいに違いない。 ■ V-T 他動詞 If people **offer** prayers, praise, or a sacrifice to God or a god, they speak to or give something to their god. 捧げる ❑ *Church leaders offered prayers and condemned the bloodshed.* 教会指導者は祈りを捧げ、流血を非難しました。 ● **PHRASAL VERB** 句動詞 **Offer up** means the same as **offer**. 捧げる ❑ *He should consider offering up a prayer to St. Lambert.* 彼は聖ランベルトに祈りをささげることを考慮すべきだ。 ■ V-T 他動詞 If an organization **offers** something such as a service or product, it provides it. 提供する ❑ *We have been successful because we are offering a quality service.* 我々が成功しているのは質の高いサービスを提供しているためだ。 ❑ *The grocery store is offering customers 5 cents for each shopping bag re-used.* 食料雑貨品店は顧客が各買い物袋を再利用するごとに5セントを支払っている。 ■ N-COUNT 可算名詞 An **offer** in a store is a specially low price for a specific product or something extra that you get if you buy a certain product. 特売品の提供 [oft supp N, also 'on' N] ❑ *This month's offers include a pork loin and avocados.* 今月の奉仕品は豚ロース肉とアボガドだ。 ❑ *Today's special offer gives you a choice of three destinations.* 今日の特別提供は、3つの目的地から選べます。 ■ V-T 他動詞 If you **offer** a particular amount of money for something, you say that you will pay that much to buy it. 払おうと申し出る ❑ *He is in a position to offer $825,000 for the bankrupt airline's assets.* 彼は破産した航空会社の資産に825,000ドルの支払いを申し出ることができる。 ❑ *They are offering farmers $2.15 a bushel for corn.* 彼らはトウモロコシ1ブッシェル当たり2.15ドルの支払いを農場経営者たちに申し出ている。 ■ N-COUNT 可算名詞 An **offer** is the amount of money that someone says they will pay to buy something. 申し込み値段 ❑ *The real estate agents say no one else will make me an offer.* 不動産業者は、私に付け値を申し出る業者はその他にいないだろうと言った。 ■ PHRASE 句 If you **have** something **to offer,** you have a quality or ability that makes you important, attractive, or useful. 優れた点が多い ❑ *In your free time, explore all that this incredible city has to offer.* 時間のあるときに、この驚くべき都市の提供する独特の魅力すべてを探索してください。 ■ PHRASE 句 If there is something **on offer,** it is available to be used or bought. 売り物に出て ❑ *They are making trips to check out the merchandise on offer.* 彼らは売りに出されている商品を調べる旅行をしている。 ■ PHRASE 句 If you are **open to offers,** you are willing to do something if someone will pay you an amount of money that you think is reasonable. 交渉に応じる用意がある ❑ *It seems that while the Dodgers are eager to have him, he is still open to offers.* ドジャーズは彼をしきりに獲得したがっているが、彼はまだ様々交渉を受ける気があるようだ。

of|fer|ing /ɔfərɪŋ/ (**offerings**) ■ N-COUNT 可算名詞 An **offering** is something that is being sold. 売り物 ❑ *It was very, very good, far better than vegetarian offerings in many an expensive restaurant.* それはとてもおいしくて、多くの料金の高いレストランの菜食主義料理よりもずっとよかった。 ■ N-COUNT 可算名詞 An **offering** is a gift that people offer to their God or gods as a form of worship. 捧げ物 ❑ *...the holiest of the Shinto rituals, where offerings are made at night to the great Sun.* 夜に天照大神に奉納を行う、神道で最も神聖な儀式。

Picture Dictionary   office

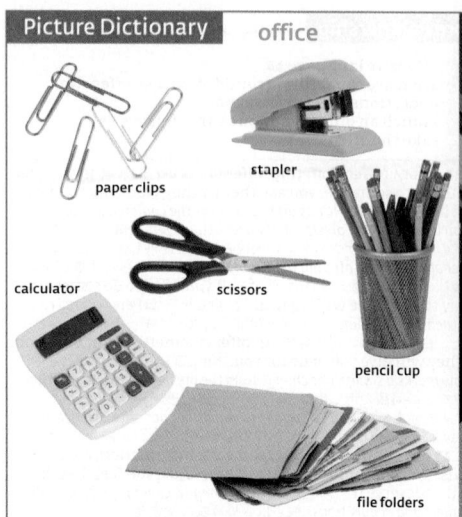
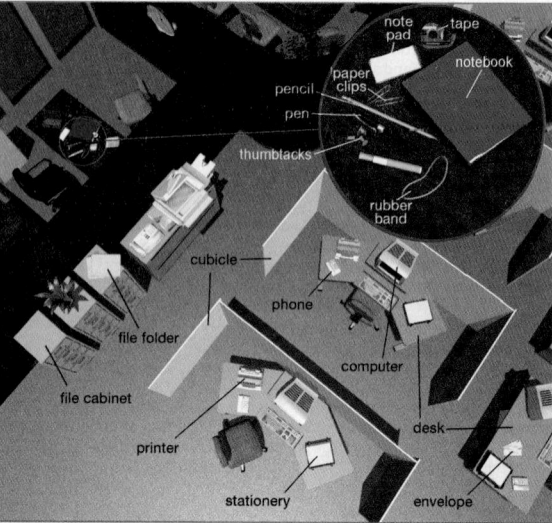

paper clips

stapler

calculator   scissors

pencil cup

file folders

note pad   tape

notebook

paper clips

pencil

pen

thumbtacks

rubber band

cubicle

phone

file folder

computer

file cabinet

desk

printer

stationery   envelope

---

of|fer price (offer prices) **1** N-COUNT 可算名詞 The **offer price** for a particular stock or share is the price that the person selling it says that they want for it. 売出し価格 [BUSINESS 実業] ❑ *The company stunned the technology world by increasing its offer price to $26.* その会社は売出し価格を26ドルまで上げて技術業界に衝撃を与えた. **2** → see also **asking price, bid price**

of|fice /ɔfɪs/ (offices) **1** N-COUNT 可算名詞 An **office** is a room or a part of a building where people work sitting at desks. 事務室 ❑ *By the time Flynn arrived at his office it was 5:30.* フリンが会社に着いたときには5:30だった. ❑ *Telephone their head office for more details.* 詳しくはその本社にお電話ください. **2** N-COUNT 可算名詞 An **office** is a department of an organization, especially the government, where people deal with a particular kind of administrative work. 課, 局 [N-IN-NAMES] ❑ *Thousands have registered with unemployment offices.* 何千もの人が職業あっせん所に登録している. ❑ *...the Congressional Budget Office.* 連邦議会予算事務局 **3** N-COUNT 可算名詞 An **office** is a small building or room where people can go for information, tickets, or a service of some kind. 案内所 ❑ *The tourist office operates a useful room-finding service.* 観光案内所は役に立つ宿探しサービスを行っている. **4** N-COUNT 可算名詞 A doctor's or dentist's **office** is a place where a doctor or dentist sees their patients. 医院 [AM 米国英語] ❑ *The chance of getting AIDS at the doctor's or dentist's office is extremely low.* 医院や歯科医院でAIDSに感染する可能性は極めて低い. **5** N-UNCOUNT 不可算名詞 If someone holds **office** in a government, they have an important job or position of authority. 在任する ❑ *The events to mark the president's four years in office went ahead as planned.* 大統領の在任4年を記念する行事は予定通りに進みました. ❑ *The treasurer shall hold office for five years.* 出納局長の在任期間は5年とします. **6** → see also **box office, post office**
→ see Picture Dictionary: **office**

of|fice hours N-PLURAL 複数名詞 **Office hours** are the times when an office or similar place is open for business. For example, office hours in the United States and Britain are usually between 9 o'clock and 5 o'clock from Monday to Friday. 営業時間 ❑ *If you have any questions, please call Anne Fisher at 555-6203 during office hours.* ご質問がおありの際は, 営業時間内にアン・フィッシャー (555-6203) までお電話ください.

of|fic|er /ɔfɪsər/ (officers) **1** N-COUNT 可算名詞 In the armed forces, an **officer** is a person in a position of authority. 将校 ❑ *...a retired army officer.* 退職した陸軍将校 **2** N-COUNT 可算名詞 Members of the police force can be referred to as **officers**. 警官 ❑ *The officer saw no obvious signs of a break-in.* 警官は明らかな不法侵入の痕跡を見つけることができなかった. ❑ *Officer Montoya was first on the scene.* 現場に最初に現れたのは警官のモントヤだった. **3** N-COUNT 可算名詞 An **officer** is a person who has a responsible position in an organization, especially a government organization. 役人 ❑ *...a local authority education officer.* 地方自治体の教育担当官 **4** → see also **police officer, probation officer**

of|fi|cial /əfɪʃ°l/ (officials) **1** ADJ 形容詞 **Official** means approved by the government or by someone in authority. 公式の ❑ *According to the official figures, more than one thousand people died during the revolution.* 公式数値によると, 革命における死者は千人以上に上りました. ❑ *An official announcement is expected in the next few days.* 公式発表はここ数日の内に行われると期待されます.

● **of|fi|cial|ly** ADV 副詞 公式に ❑ *The election results have still not been officially announced.* 選挙結果はまだ正式に発表されていません. **2** ADJ 形容詞 [ADJ n] **Official** activities are carried out by a person in authority as part of their job. 公の ❑ *The president is in Brazil for an official two-day visit.* 大統領は2日間の公式訪問のためブラジルにいます. **3** ADJ 形容詞 **Official** things are used by a person in authority as part of their job. 公務上の [ADJ n] ❑ *...the official residence of the head of state.* 元首の官邸 **4** ADJ 形容詞 If you describe someone's explanation or reason for something as the **official** explanation, you are suggesting that it is probably not true, but is used because the real explanation is embarrassing. 表向きの, 公式的な [ADJ n] ❑ *They realized that the official explanation left facts unexplained.* 彼らは公的説明では事実が説明されぬままだったことに気づいた. ● **of|fi|cial|ly** ADV 副詞 [ADV with cl/group] 表向きに ❑ *Officially, the guard was to protect us. In fact, they were there to report on our movements.* 公的には, その護衛は私たちを保護するということであったが, 実際には私たちの動きを報告するためにいたのです. **5** N-COUNT 可算名詞 An **official** is a person who holds a position of authority in an organization. 要人 ❑ *A senior UN official hopes to visit Baghdad this month.* 国連の上級幹部が今月バグダッドの訪問を希望している. **6** N-COUNT 可算名詞 An **official** at a sports event is a referee, umpire, or other person who checks that the players follow the rules. 競技役員 ❑ *Officials suspended the game because of safety concerns.* 競技役員は安全上の問題から試合を延期した.

Thesaurus	*official* また次を参照:
ADJ.	authentic, formal, legitimate, valid; (ant.) unauthorized, unofficial **1**
N.	administrator, director, executive, manager **5**

Word Partnership	*official* は次の語句と使われる:
N.	official **documents**, official **language**, official **report**, official **sources**, official **statement** **1** official **duties**, official **visit** **2** **administration** official, **city** official, **government** official, **military** official **5**
ADJ.	**elected** official, **federal** official, **local** official, **senior** official, **top** official **5**

off-licence (off-licences) N-COUNT 可算名詞 An **off-licence** is a store that sells beer, wine, and other alcoholic drinks. 酒類販売免許店 [BRIT 英国英語; AM **liquor store** 米国英語 **liquor store**]

off|line /ɔflaɪn/ **1** ADJ 形容詞 If a computer is **offline**, it is not connected to the Internet. Compare **online**. オフライン [COMPUTING コンピューティング] ❑ *Initially the system was offline for a number of days.* 当初, システムは数日間オフラインになっていた. ● ADV 副詞 **Offline** is also an adverb. オフラインで [ADV with v] ❑ *Most software programs allow you to compose e-mails offline.* ほとんどのソフトウェアプログラムでは, オフラインで電子メールを作成することができる. **2 off line** → see **line 2 8**

off-peak ADJ 形容詞 You use **off-peak** to describe something that happens or that is used at times when there is least demand

offset

for it. Prices at off-peak times are often lower than at other times. ピーク時でない [ADJ n] □ *Callers now pay 33 cents during peak hours and 30 cents during off-peak hours.* 現在、発信者はピーク時には33セントを、オフピーク時には30セントを支払っている. ● ADV 副詞 **Off-peak** is also an adverb. ピーク時でない時に [ADV after v] □ *Each tape lasts three minutes and costs 36 cents per minute off-peak and 48 cents at all other times.* 各テープは3分間続き、1分間当たりオフピーク時は36セント、その他の時間帯は48セントかかる.

off|set /ˈɒfsɛt/ (offsets, offsetting)

The form **offset** is used in the present tense and is the past tense and past participle of the verb.

offset 形は現在時制に使われ、動詞の過去時制と過去分詞でもある.

V-T 他動詞 If one thing **is offset** by another, the effect of the first thing is reduced by the second, so that any advantage or disadvantage is canceled out. 相殺する □ *The increase in pay costs was more than offset by higher productivity.* 給料費用の上昇は、生産性の向上により埋め合わせられる以上のものだった.

off|shoot /ˈɒfʃuːt/ (offshoots) N-COUNT 可算名詞 If one thing is an **offshoot** of another, it has developed from that other thing. 派生物 □ *Psychology began as a purely academic offshoot of natural philosophy.* 心理学は自然哲学の純粋に学術的な支流として始まった.

off|shore /ˈɒfʃɔːr/ ◼ ADJ 形容詞 **Offshore** means situated or happening in the sea, near to the coast. 沖の [ADJ n] □ *...the offshore oil industry.* 海底石油採掘産業 ● ADV 副詞 **Offshore** is also an adverb. 沖に □ *One day a larger ship anchored offshore.* ある日もっと大きな船舶が沖に停泊した. ◼ ADJ 形容詞 **Offshore** investments or companies are located in a place, usually an island, which has fewer tax regulations than most other countries. (税金対策で) 海外に投資・設立された [BUSINESS 実業] [ADJ n] □ *The island offers a wide range of offshore banking facilities.* その島は多岐にわたる税金対策の金融機関を提供します.

off|side /ˈɒfsaɪd/ also **off-side** ◼ ADJ 形容詞 In football, a player is **offside** if they cross the line of scrimmage before a play begins. オフサイドの ◼ ADJ 形容詞 In games such as soccer or hockey, when an attacking player is **offside**, they have broken the rules by being nearer to the goal than a defending player when the ball is passed to them. オフサイドの □ *The goal was disallowed because Wark was offside.* ワークがオフサイドだったので、そのゴールは認められなかった. ● ADV 副詞 **Offside** is also an adverb. オフサイドに [ADV after v] □ *Yoon was standing at least ten yards offside.* ユンは少なくとも10ヤードオフサイドに立っていた. ● N-UNCOUNT 不可算名詞 **Offside** is also a noun. オフサイド □ *Rush had a 45th-minute goal disallowed for offside.* ラッシュはゲーム終了直前にゴールしたが、オフサイドのために認められなかった.

off|spring /ˈɒfsprɪŋ/

Offspring is both the singular and the plural form.

Offspring は単数形でも複数形でもある.

N-COUNT 可算名詞 You can refer to a person's children or to an animal's young as their **offspring**. 子 [FORMAL 形式ばった] □ *Eleanor was now less anxious about her offspring than she had once been.* 今では、エレノアは以前よりも子どもたちのことを心配しなくなった.

of|ten /ˈɒf³n/

Often is usually used before the verb, but it may be used after the verb when it has a word like "less" or "more" before it, or when the clause is negative.

Often は通常動詞の前で用いられるが、その前に **less** または **more** のような語があるとき、あるいは節が否定節であるときは、動詞の後にも使われる可能性がある.

◼ ADV 副詞 If something **often** happens, it happens many times or much of the time. しばしば □ *They often spent Christmas together.* 彼らはたいていクリスマスを一緒に過ごした. □ *That doesn't happen very often.* それはあまり頻繁に起こらない. ◼ ADV 副詞 You use

oil rig

how often to ask questions about frequency. You also use **often** in reported clauses and other statements to give information about the frequency of something. 一回 □ *How often do you brush your teeth?* 1日に何回歯を磨きますか.

You do not use **often** to talk about something that happens several times within a short period of time. You do not say, for example, "I often phoned her yesterday." You say "**I phoned her several times yesterday**" or "**I kept phoning her yesterday**."

◼ PHRASE 句 If something happens **every so often**, it happens regularly, but with fairly long intervals between each occasion. 時々 □ *She's going to come back every so often.* 彼女は時々帰ってくるつもりだ. ◼ PHRASE 句 If you say that something happens **as often as not**, or **more often than not**, you mean that it happens fairly frequently, and that this can be considered as typical. たびたび □ *Yet, as often as not, they find themselves the target of persecution rather than praise.* それでも、彼らはたいてい称賛ではなく虐待の的になっている.

Thesaurus often また次を参照:

ADV. regularly, repeatedly, usually; (*ant.*) never, rarely, seldom ◼

oh /oʊ/ ◼ CONVENTION 慣習表現 You use **oh** to introduce a response or a comment on something that has just been said. ああ [SPOKEN 口語] □ *"Had you seen the car before?" — "Oh yes, it was always in the driveway."* 「その車を見たことはありますか」「ああもちろん、いつも私設車道にあったよ」 ◼ EXCLAM 感嘆詞 You use **oh** to express a feeling such as surprise, pain, annoyance, or happiness. おお [SPOKEN 口語, FEELINGS 感情] □ *"Oh!" Kenny blinked. "Has everyone gone?"* 「あれ」ケニーはまばたきした. 「皆行っちゃったの」 ◼ CONVENTION 慣習表現 You use **oh** when you are hesitating while speaking, for example, because you are trying to estimate something, or because you are searching for the right word. あー [SPOKEN 口語] □ *I've been here, oh, since the end of June.* 私はここに住んでいます、えっと6月の末から.

OHP /oʊ eɪtʃ piː/ (OHPs) N-COUNT 可算名詞 An **OHP** is the same as an **overhead projector**. オーバーヘッドプロジェクター

oil /ɔɪl/ (oils, oiling, oiled) ◼ N-MASS 質量名詞 **Oil** is a smooth, thick liquid that is used as a fuel and for making the parts of machines move smoothly. Oil is found underground. 石油 □ *The company buys and sells about 600,000 barrels of oil a day.* その会社は1日に約60万バレルの石油を売買している. □ *...the rapid rise in prices for oil and gasoline.* 石油とガソリン価格の迅速な上昇. ◼ V-T 他動詞 If you **oil** something, you put oil onto or into it, for example, to make it work smoothly or to protect it. 油を塗る □ *A crew of assistants oiled and adjusted the release mechanism until it worked perfectly.* 助手の乗組員たちがリリースメカニズムに油を差して調整し、うまく機能するようにした. ◼ N-MASS 質量名詞 **Oil** is a smooth, thick liquid made from plants and is often used for cooking. 食用油 □ *Combine the beans, chopped mint, and oil in a large bowl.* 豆、刻んだミントと油を大きなボウルで混ぜ合わせなさい. ◼ N-MASS 質量名詞 **Oil** is a smooth, thick liquid, often with a pleasant smell, that you rub into your skin or add to your bath. オイル □ *Try a hot bath with some relaxing bath oil.* リラックスできるバスオイルを入れた熱い風呂をお試しください. ◼ → see also **crude oil**, **olive oil** ◼ to **burn the midnight oil** → see **midnight** → see Word Web: **oil**

oil paint (oil paints) N-UNCOUNT 不可算名詞 **Oil paint** is a thick paint used by artists. It is made from colored powder and linseed oil. 油絵の具 [also N in pl]

oil paint|ing (oil paintings) N-COUNT 可算名詞 An **oil painting** is a picture which has been painted using oil paints. 油絵 □ *Several magnificent oil paintings adorn the walls.* 堂々たる油絵が何枚か壁を飾っている.

oil rig (oil rigs) N-COUNT 可算名詞 An **oil rig** is a structure on land or in the sea that is used when getting oil from the ground. 油田掘削装置

Word Web oil

There is a great demand for **petroleum** in the world today. Companies are constantly **drilling oil wells** in oilfields on land and on the ocean floor. Some offshore drilling **rigs** or oil platforms sit on a concrete or metal foundation on a man-made island. Others float on a ship. The **crude oil** obtained from these wells goes to **refineries** through **pipelines** or in huge **tanker** ships. At the refinery, the crude oil is processed into a variety of products including **gasoline**, **aviation fuel**, and **plastics**.

oil slick (**oil slicks**) N-COUNT 可算名詞 An **oil slick** is a layer of oil that is floating on the sea or on a lake because it has accidentally come out of a ship or container. 海面に流出した油 □ *The oil slick is now 35 miles long.* 海面に流出した油は現在長さ35マイルまで広がっている.

oily /ˈɔɪli/ (**oilier, oiliest**) **1** ADJ 形容詞 Something that is **oily** is covered with oil or contains oil. 油だらけの □ *He was wiping his hands on an oily rag.* 彼は油だらけのぼろ切れで手を拭いていた. **2** ADJ 形容詞 **Oily** means looking, feeling, tasting, or smelling like oil. 油の □ *...traces of an oily substance.* 油性物質の痕跡

oint|ment /ˈɔɪntmənt/ (**ointments**) **1** N-MASS 質量名詞 An **ointment** is a smooth thick substance that is put on sore skin or a wound to help it heal. 軟膏 □ *A range of ointments and creams is available for the treatment of eczema.* 湿疹の治療には様々な軟膏やクリームが利用できる. **2** PHRASE 句 If you describe someone or something as a **fly in the ointment**, you think they spoil a situation and prevent it from being as successful as you had hoped. ぶちこわし □ *Rachel seems to be the one fly in the ointment of Caroline's smooth life.* レイチェルだけがキャロラインの順調な生活をぶちこわしているようだ.

okay /ˌoʊˈkeɪ/ (**okays, okaying, okayed**) also **OK** or **O.K.** or **ok** **1** ADJ 形容詞 If you say that something is **okay**, you find it satisfactory or acceptable. よろしい [INFORMAL くだけた] □ *...a shooting range where it's OK to use weapons.* 武器の使用が許されている射撃練習場 □ *Is it okay if I come by myself?* 1人で来てもいいですか. ● ADV 副詞 **Okay** is also an adverb. よく [ADV after v] □ *We seemed to manage okay for the first year or so after David was born.* デイビッドが生まれてから最初の1年かそこらは, 私たちは何とかうまくやっていたように思えた. **2** ADJ 形容詞 If you say that someone is **okay**, you mean that they are safe and well. 大丈夫な [INFORMAL くだけた] [v-link ADJ] □ *Check that the baby's okay.* その赤ちゃんが大丈夫か確認せよ. **3** CONVENTION 慣習表現 You can say "**Okay**" to show that you agree to something. 異存はない [INFORMAL くだけた, FORMULAE 決まり文句] □ *"Just tell him I would like to talk to him." — "OK."* 「私が彼と話がしたいと彼に伝えてくれ」「わかった」. **4** CONVENTION 慣習表現 You can say "**Okay?**" to check whether the person you are talking to understands what you have said and accepts it. いいですか [INFORMAL くだけた] □ *We'll get together next week, OK?* 来週会いましょう, いいですか. **5** CONVENTION 慣習表現 You can use **okay** to indicate that you want to start talking about something else or doing something else. よし [INFORMAL くだけた] □ *OK. Now, let's talk some business.* よし, では本題にはいろう. **6** CONVENTION 慣習表現 You can use **okay** to stop someone from arguing with you by showing that you accept the point they are making, though you do not necessarily regard it as very important. わかった [INFORMAL くだけた] □ *Okay, there is a slight difference.* わかった, 若干違いがあるな. **7** V-T 他動詞 If someone in authority **okays** something, they officially agree to it or allow it to happen. 承認する [INFORMAL くだけた] □ *His doctor wouldn't OK the trip.* 彼の医師はその旅行を許可しようとしない. ● N-SING 単数名詞 **Okay** is also a noun. 承認 □ *He gave the okay to issue a new press release.* 彼は報道関係者に新しい発表をだすことを承認した.

old /oʊld/ (**older, oldest**) **1** ADJ 形容詞 Someone who is **old** has lived for many years and is no longer young. 老いた □ *...a white-haired old man.* 白髪の老人 ● N-PLURAL 複数名詞 **The old** are people who are old. 老人たち □ *...providing a caring response for the needs of the old and the handicapped.* 老人および身体障害者の必要に対し介護を提供している **2** ADJ 形容詞 You use **old** to talk about how many days, weeks, months, or years someone or something has lived or existed. 歳の, (年数が) 経った □ *He was abandoned by his father when he was three months old.* 彼は3歳のときに父親に捨てられた. □ *How old are you now?* 今何歳ですか. □ *Bill was six years older than David.* ビルはデイビッドよりも6歳上だった. **3** ADJ 形容詞 Something that is **old** has existed for a long time. 年数を経た □ *She loved the big old house.* 彼女はその大きな古い家が大好きだった. □ *These books must be very old.* これらの本はとても古いに違いない. **4** ADJ 形容詞 Something that is **old** is no longer in good condition because of its age or because it has been used a lot. 古びた, 老朽化した □ *He took a bunch of keys from the pocket of his old corduroy trousers.* 彼は着古したコーデュロイのズボンのポケットから鍵の束を取り出した. **5** ADJ 形容詞 You use **old** to refer to something that is no longer used, that no longer exists, or that has been replaced by something else. 昔の [ADJ n] □ *The old road had disappeared under grass and heather.* 昔の道は雑草とヒースの下に埋もれてしまっていた. **6** ADJ 形容詞 You use **old** to refer to something that used to belong to you, or to a person or thing that used to have a particular role in your life. 以前の [poss ADJ n] □ *I'll make up the bed in your old room.* あなたが以前使っていた部屋にベッドの準備をするわね. □ *I still have affection for my old school.* 私は今でも母校に愛着を感じている. **7** ADJ 形容詞 An **old** friend, enemy, or rival is someone who has been your friend, enemy, or rival for a long time. 年来の [ADJ n] □ *I called my old friend John Horner.* 私は古くからの友人ジョン・ホーナーに電話した. □ *Mr. Brownson, I assure you, King's an old enemy of mine.* ブラウンソンさん, キング氏は確かに私の

年来の敵であります. **8** ADJ 形容詞 You can use **old** to express affection when talking to or about someone you know. 親しい, 一ちゃん [BRIT 英国英語, INFORMAL くだけた, FEELINGS 感情] **9** PHRASE 句 You use **any old** to emphasize that the quality or type of something is not important. If you say that a particular thing is **not any old** thing, you are emphasizing how special or famous it is. どんなーでも [INFORMAL くだけた, EMPHASIS 強調] □ *Any old paper will do.* どんな紙でもいいです. **10** PHRASE 句 **In the old days** means in the past, before things changed. 以前は [In the old days, doctors made housecalls.] 以前は医師が往診してくれた. **11** PHRASE 句 When people refer to **the good old days**, they are referring to a time in the past when they think that life was better than it is now. なつかしい昔 □ *He remembers the good old days when everyone in his village knew you and you could leave your door open at night.* 彼は, 村のだれもが彼を知っており, 夜戸口を開けておけた古き良き時代を思い出す. **12** good old → see good **13** to settle an old score → see score

old age N-UNCOUNT 不可算名詞 Your **old age** is the period of years toward the end of your life. 老年期 □ *They worry about how they will support themselves in their old age.* 彼らは老後にどうやって自活するかを心配している.

old-fashioned **1** ADJ 形容詞 Something such as a style, method, or device that is **old-fashioned** is no longer used, done, or admired by most people, because it has been replaced by something that is more modern. 流行遅れの □ *The house was dull, old-fashioned and in bad condition.* その家は面白みがなく, 流行遅れの上, 荒れていた. **2** ADJ 形容詞 **Old-fashioned** ideas, customs, or values are the ideas, customs, and values of the past. 旧式の □ *She has some old-fashioned values and can be a strict disciplinarian.* 彼女の多少古風な価値観を持ち, しつけが厳しいこともある.

ol|ive /ˈɒlɪv/ (**olives**) **1** N-VAR 可変性名詞 **Olives** are small green or black fruits with a bitter taste. Olives are often pressed to make olive oil. オリーブの実 □ *...a pile of black olives.* 山ほどのブラックオリーブの実 **2** N-COUNT 可算名詞 An **olive tree** is a tree on which olives grow. オリーブの木 □ *Olives look romantic on a hillside in Provence.* プロバンスの丘の中腹に育成するオリーブの木々はロマンティックだ. **3** COLOR 色彩語 Something that is **olive** is yellowish-green in color. オリーブ色 □ *...glowing colors such as deep red, olive, saffron and ocher.* 深紅, オリーブ, サフランおよびオーカーなどの燃えるような色彩. ● COMB IN COLOR 色彩語の複合 **Olive** is also a combining form. オリーブー □ *She wore an olive-green T-shirt.* 彼女はオリーブグリーン色のTシャツを着ていた. **4** ADJ 形容詞 If someone has **olive** skin, the color of their skin is yellowish brown. 褐色の □ *They are handsome with dark, shining hair, olive skin and fine brown eyes.* 彼らはつややかな黒髪, 褐色の皮膚そして美しい茶色の目をしたハンサムだ.

ol|ive oil (**olive oils**) N-MASS 質量名詞 **Olive oil** is oil that is obtained by pressing olives. It is used for putting on salads or in cooking. オリーブ油

Olym|pic /əˈlɪmpɪk/ (**Olympics**) **1** ADJ 形容詞 **Olympic** means relating to the Olympic Games. 国際オリンピック競技の [ADJ n] □ *...the reigning Olympic champion.* 現オリンピックチャンピオン **2** N-PROPER 固有名詞 **The Olympics** are the Olympic Games. 国際オリンピック大会 □ *Have you been watching the Olympics?* オリンピック競技を見ているかい.

Olym|pic Games N-PROPER-COLL 集合的固有名詞 **The Olympic Games** are a set of international sports competitions which take place every four years, each time in a different city. 国際オリンピック大会 □ *At the 1968 Olympic Games she had won gold medals in races at 200, 400, and 800 meters.* 1968年の国際オリンピック大会で, 彼女は200m, 400mおよび800m競技で金メダルを獲得していた.

om|buds|man /ˈɒmbʊdzmən/ (**ombudsmen**) N-COUNT 可算名詞 The **ombudsman** is an independent official who has been appointed to investigate complaints that people make against the government or public organizations. 行政監察官, オンブズマン □ *The leaflet explains how to complain to the banking ombudsman.* この小冊子は銀行オンブズマンに苦情を申し立てる方法を説明している.

ome|let /ˈɒmlɪt, ˈɒmlət/ (**omelets**) also **omelette** N-COUNT 可算名詞 An **omelet** is a type of food made by beating eggs and cooking them in a flat frying pan. オムレツ □ *...a cheese omelet.* チーズオムレツ
→ see **egg**

omen /ˈoʊmɛn/ (**omens**) N-COUNT 可算名詞 If you say that something is an **omen**, you think it indicates what is likely to happen in the future and whether it will be good or bad. 前兆 □ *Her appearance at this moment is an omen of disaster.* この瞬間に彼女が現れたことは災厄の予兆である.

omi|nous /ˈɒmɪnəs/ ADJ 形容詞 If you describe something as **ominous**, you mean that it worries you because it makes you think that something bad is going to happen. 不吉な ▫ *There was an ominous silence at the other end of the phone.* 電話の向こう側には不気味な沈黙があった. ● **omi|nous|ly** ADV 副詞 不吉に ▫ *The bar seemed ominously quiet.* そのバーは不気味なほど静かに思えた.

omis|sion /oʊˈmɪʃ°n/ (**omissions**) **1** N-COUNT 可算名詞 An **omission** is something that has not been included or has not been done, either deliberately or accidentally. 省略 ▫ *He was surprised by his wife's omission from the guest list.* 彼は妻が招待客名簿に入っていないことに驚いた. **2** N-VAR 可変性名詞 **Omission** is the act of not including a particular person or thing or of not doing something. 遺漏 ▫ *…the prosecution's seemingly malicious omission of recorded evidence.* 検察側による証拠記録の一見悪意ある遺漏

omit /oʊˈmɪt/ (**omits, omitting, omitted**) **1** V-T 他動詞 If you **omit** something, you do not include it in an activity or piece of work, deliberately or accidentally. 省略する ▫ *Omit the salt in this recipe.* このレシピの塩は抜かしなさい. **2** V-T 他動詞 If you **omit to** do something, you do not do it. 怠る [FORMAL 形式ばった] ▫ *His new girlfriend had omitted to tell him she was married.* 彼の新しい恋人は既婚であることを彼に言うことを怠っていた.

Thesaurus *omit* また次を参照:

v. forget, leave out, miss; (*ant.*) add, include **1**

---

on

❶ DESCRIBING POSITIONS AND LOCATIONS
❷ TALKING ABOUT HOW OR WHEN SOMETHING HAPPENS
❸ OTHER USES
❹ PHRASES

---

❶ on

The preposition is pronounced /ɒn/. The adverb and the adjective are pronounced /ɒn/.

前置詞は /ɒn/ と発音される. 副詞と形容詞は /ɒn/ と発音される.

1 PREP 前置詞 If someone or something is **on** a surface or object, the surface or object is immediately below them and is supporting their weight. 〜の上に ▫ *He is sitting beside her on the sofa.* 彼はソファに彼女と並んで座っている. ▫ *On top of the cupboards are straw baskets.* 食器棚の一番上にわらのかごがある. **2** PREP 前置詞 If something is **on** a surface or object, it is stuck to it or attached to it. 〜に付いて ▫ *I stared at the peeling paint on the ceiling.* 私は天井の剥げかけた塗料を見つめた. ▫ *The clock on the wall showed one minute to twelve.* 壁に掛かった時計は12時1分前を示していた. ● ADV 副詞 **On** is also an adverb. くっついて [ADV after v] ▫ *I know how to sew a button on.* 私はボタンのつけ方を知っていますよ. **3** PREP 前置詞 If you put, throw, or drop something **on** a surface, you move it or drop it so that it is then supported by the surface. 〜の表面に ▫ *He got his winter jacket from the closet and dropped it on the sofa.* 彼は冬用の上着を押入れから取り出して、ソファに投げかけた. **4** PREP 前置詞 You use **on** to say what part of your body is supporting your weight. 〜をつけて ▫ *He continued to lie on his back and look at clouds.* 彼はあお向けになって空を見続けた. ▫ *He raised himself on his elbows, squinting into the sun.* 彼は両肘をついて起き上がり、目を細めて太陽を見た. **5** PREP 前置詞 You use **on** to say that someone or something touches a part of a person's body. 〜に接して ▫ *He leaned down and kissed her lightly on the mouth.* 彼は体をかがめて彼女にそっとキスした. **6** PREP 前置詞 If someone has a particular expression **on** their face, their face has that expression. 〜に [n PREP n] ▫ *The maid looked at him, a nervous smile on her face.* メイドは、顔に緊張ぎみに微笑んで彼を見た. **7** ADV 副詞 When you put a piece of clothing **on**, you place it over part of your body in order to wear it. If you have it **on**, you are wearing it. 着て [ADV after v] ▫ *He put his coat on while she opened the front door.* 彼女が玄関のドアを開ける間に彼はコートを身に着けた. **8** PREP 前置詞 You can say that you have something **on** you if you are carrying it in your pocket or in a purse. 〜を身につけて [PREP pron] ▫ *I didn't have any money on me.* 私は金の持ち合わせがなかった. **9** PREP 前置詞 If someone's eyes are **on** you, they are looking or staring at you. 〜を凝視して ▫ *Everyone's eyes were fixed on him.* 皆が彼を凝視していた. **10** PREP 前置詞 If you hurt yourself **on** something, you accidentally hit a part of your body against it and that thing causes damage to you. 〜をぶつけて ▫ *Mr. Pendle hit his head on a wall as he fell.* ペンドル氏は、壁に頭をぶつけた. **11** PREP 前置詞 If you are **on** an area of land, you are there. 〜に ▫ *He was able to spend only a few days on the island.* 彼はその島には数日しか滞在することができなかった. ▫ *You lived on the farm until you came back to America?* あなたはアメリカに戻るまでその

農場にいたのですか. **12** PREP 前置詞 If something is situated **on** a place such as a road or coast, it forms part of it or is by the side of it. 〜に ▫ *Bergdorf Goodman has opened a men's store on Fifth Avenue.* バーグドーフ・グッドマンは5番街に紳士服店を開いた. ▫ *The hotel is on the coast.* ホテルは海岸にある. **13** PREP 前置詞 If you get **on** a bus, train, or plane, you go into it in order to travel somewhere. If you are **on** it, you are traveling in it. 〜に乗って ▫ *We waited till twelve and we finally got on the plane.* 私たちは12時まで待って、やっと飛行機に乗りました. ● ADV 副詞 **On** is also an adverb. 乗車して [ADV after v] ▫ *He showed his ticket to the conductor and got on.* 彼は車掌に乗車券を見せて乗車した. **14** PREP 前置詞 If there is something **on** a piece of paper, it has been written or printed there. 〜に書かれて ▫ *The writing on the back of the card was cramped but scrupulously neat.* カードの裏の筆跡は狭苦しかったが、几帳面に整然と書かれていた. **15** PREP 前置詞 If something is **on** a list, it is included in it. 〜に載って ▫ *I've seen your name on the list of deportees.* 被追放者名簿に君の名があった.

❷ on

The preposition is pronounced /ɒn/. The adverb and adjective are pronounced /ɒn/.

前置詞は /ɒn/ と発音される. 副詞と形容詞は /ɒn/ と発音される.

1 PREP 前置詞 You use **on** to introduce the method, principle, or system which is used to do something. 〜で ▫ *…a television that we bought on credit two months ago.* 2か月前にクレジットで買ったテレビ ▫ *They want all groups to be treated on an equal basis.* 彼らは全グループが対等な条件で扱われることを欲しています. **2** PREP 前置詞 If something is done **on** an instrument or a machine, it is done using that instrument or machine. 〜で ▫ *…songs that I could just sit down and play on the piano.* 私がただ座ってピアノで演奏できる歌 **3** PREP 前置詞 If information is, for example, **on** tape or **on** computer, that is the way that it is stored. 〜に記録されて ▫ *We've got her statement on tape.* 私たちはテープに記録された彼女の声明を持っている. **4** PREP 前置詞 If something is being broadcast, you can say that it is **on** the radio or television. 〜に出る ▫ *Every sporting event on television and satellite over the next seven days is listed.* 次の7日間にテレビおよび衛星放送で放送されるスポーツイベントすべてはリストされている. ● ADV 形容詞 **On** is also an adjective. 上演中の [v-link ADJ] ▫ *…teenagers complaining there's nothing good on.* 何も面白いものが放送されていないと文句を言う10代の若者. **5** ADJ 形容詞 When an activity is taking place, you can say that it is **on**. 行われて [v-link ADJ] ▫ *There's an exciting match on at Wimbledon right now.* ウィンブルドンではたった今、ハラハラさせられる試合が行われている. **6** ADV 副詞 You use **on** in expressions such as "**have a lot going on**" and "**not have very much on**" to indicate how busy someone is. 忙しく [SPOKEN 口語] ▫ *I have a lot on in the next week.* 私は来週とても忙しい. **7** PREP 前置詞 You use **on** to introduce an activity that someone is doing, particularly traveling. 〜に従事して ▫ *I've always wanted to go on a cruise.* 私はいつもクルーズに行きたかった. ▫ *We're going on a trip next month.* 私たちは来月旅行にでかける. **8** PREP 前置詞 You can indicate when something happens by saying that it happens **on** a particular day, date, or part of the week. 〜の日時に ▫ *This year's event will take place on June 19th, a week earlier than usual.* 今年のイベントは、例年よりも1週間早く、6月19日に催されるはずだ. ▫ *I was born on Christmas Day.* 私はクリスマスに生まれました. ▫ *The highway is often lined with cars on the weekend.* 週末には高速道路は往々にして渋滞する. **9** PREP 前置詞 You use **on** when mentioning an event that was followed by another one. 〜の直後で [n PREP n/-ing] ▫ *She waited in her hotel to welcome her children on their arrival from Vancouver.* 彼女は子供がバンクーバーから到着するのを歓迎するためホテルで待機した. **10** ADV 副詞 You use **on** to say that someone is continuing to do something. 続けて [ADV after v] ▫ *They walked on in silence for a while.* 彼らはしばらく黙って歩き続けた. ▫ *We worked on into the night.* 彼は夜になっても働き続けた. **11** ADV 副詞 You use **on** in expressions such as **from now on** and **from then on** to indicate that something starts to happen at the time mentioned and continues to happen afterward. 以降 ['from' n ADV] ▫ *Perhaps it would be best not to see much of you from now on.* おそらく、これからはあなたにはあまり会わないのが1番よいでしょう. ▫ *We can expect trouble from this moment on.* この時から困った問題が予想されうる. **12** ADV 副詞 You often use **on** after the adverbs "early," "late," "far," and their comparative forms, especially at the beginning or end of a sentence, or before a preposition. 向かって [adv ADV] ▫ *The market square is a riot of color and animation from early on in the morning.* 市場広場は朝早くから多彩な色彩と活気であふれていた. ▫ *Later on I learned how to read music.* その後になって、私は楽譜の読み方を習った.

❸ on

The preposition is pronounced /ɒn/. The adverb and adjective are pronounced /ɒn/.

前置詞は /ɒn/ と発音される. 副詞と形容詞は /ɒn/ と発音される.

1 PREP 前置詞 Books, discussions, or ideas **on** a particular

subject are concerned with that subject. 〜に関する □ *They offer free counseling on legal matters.* 彼らは法的事項に関する無料カウンセリングを提供している. 彼は大統領選挙に関するいかなる情報の提供も拒否しました. **2** ADV 副詞 When something such as a machine or an electric light is **on**, it is functioning or in use. When you switch it **on**, it starts functioning. かかって, 点いて □ *The light was on and the door was open.* 明かりは点いており, ドアが開いていた. □ *The heating's been turned off. I've turned it on again.* 暖房が切れていたので, 私は再度つけた. **3** PREP 前置詞 If you are **on** a committee or council, you are a member of it. 〜の1員で □ *Claire and Alita were on the organizing committee.* クレアとアリータは組織委員会のメンバーだった. **4** PREP 前置詞 Someone who is **on** a drug takes it regularly. 〜を常用して □ *She was on antibiotics for an eye infection that wouldn't go away.* 彼女はなかなか治らない眼感染症の治療に抗生物質を常用していた. **5** PREP 前置詞 If you live **on** a particular kind of food, you eat it. If a machine runs **on** a particular kind of power or fuel, it uses it in order to function. 〜によって [V PREP n] □ *The caterpillars feed on a wide range of trees, shrubs and plants.* 毛虫は広範な木, 低木, 植物を餌にしている. □ *He lived on a diet of water and canned fish.* 彼は水と缶詰の魚で生きていました. **6** PREP 前置詞 If you are **on** a particular income, that is the income that you have. 〜で生活を立てる [BRIT 英国英語] □ *...young people who are unemployed or on low wages.* 無職または低賃金の若者 □ *He's on three hundred a week.* 彼は週300ドルで暮らしている. **7** PREP 前置詞 Taxes or profits that are obtained from something are referred to as taxes or profits **on** it. 〜に対する [n PREP n] □ *...a general strike to protest a tax on food and medicine.* 食品および医薬品に対する課税に抗議するゼネスト **8** PREP 前置詞 When you buy something or pay for something, you spend money **on** it. (金銭を) 〜に [PREP n/-ing] □ *I resolved not to waste money on a hotel.* 私はホテルに金を浪費しないと決意した. □ *He spent more on feeding the dog than he spent on feeding himself.* 彼は自分の食費よりも, 犬の食費にお金をかけた. **9** PREP 前置詞 When you spend time or energy **on** a particular activity, you spend time or energy doing it. (時間・エネルギーを) 〜に [PREP n/-ing] □ *People complain about how children spend so much time on computer games.* 人々は子供たちがコンピュータゲームに時間を使い過ぎていると不満を漏らしている. □ *You all know why I am here, so I won't waste time on preliminaries.* 皆さん私が出席しているわけをご存知ですので, 前置きは省略させていただきます.

4 on /ɒn/ **1** PHRASE 句 If you say that something happens **on and on**, you mean that it continues to happen for a very long time. 引き続いて □ *...designers, builders, fitters – the list goes on and on.* 設計者, 建築者, 整備工とリストは長々と続く. □ *Lobell drove on and on through the dense and blowing snow.* ロベルは見通しの悪い吹雪の中を運転し続けた. **2** PHRASE 句 If you say that something is **not on** or is **just not on**, you mean that it is unacceptable or impossible. 不可能である, 認められない [BRIT 英国英語, INFORMAL くだけた] **3** on behalf of → see behalf **4** on and off → see off **5** and so on → see so **6** on top of → see top

---

In addition to the uses shown here, **on** is used after some verbs, nouns, and adjectives in order to introduce extra information. **On** is also used in phrasal verbs such as "keep on" and "sign on."

---

once /wʌns/ **1** ADV 副詞 If something happens **once**, it happens one time only. 1度 [ADV with v] □ *I met Miquela once, briefly.* ミケラには1度ちょっとだけあったことがある. □ *Since that evening I haven't once slept through the night.* その夜から, 1晩中眠ったことは1度もない. ●PRON 代名詞 **Once** is also a pronoun. 1度 ['the/'this' PRON] □ *"Have they been to visit you yet?" – "Just the once, yeah."* 「彼らから訪問はありましたか」「ええ, その1度だけ」 **2** ADV 副詞 You use **once** with "a" and words like "day," "week," and "month" to indicate that something happens regularly, one time in each day, week, or month. 1度 [ADV 'a' n] □ *Lung cells die and are replaced about once a week.* 肺細胞は約1週間に1度死んで交換されます. **3** ADV 副詞 If something was **once** true, it was true at some time in the past, but is no longer true. かつて □ *Her parents once ran a store.* 彼女の両親はかつて店を経営していた. □ *I lived there once myself, before I got married.* 私はかつて結婚する前, 私自身そこに住んでいた. **4** ADV 副詞 If someone **once** did something, they did it at some time in the past. かつて [ADV with v] □ *I once went camping at Lake Michigan with a friend.* かつてミシガン湖に友だちとキャンプに行ったことがある. □ *We once walked across the frozen pond at two in the morning.* 私たちは朝2時にその凍った池を横切って歩いて渡った. **5** CONJ 接続詞 If something happens **once** another thing has happened, it happens immediately afterward. 〜するやいなや □ *The decision had taken about 10 seconds once he'd read a market research study.* 彼が市場調査研究を読むやいなや決断は約10秒で下された. **6** PHRASE 句 If something happens **all at once**, it happens suddenly, often when you are not expecting it to happen. 突然に □ *All at once there was someone knocking at the door.* 突然にドアをノックした. **7** PHRASE 句 If you do something **at once**, you do it immediately. ただちに □ *I have to go at once.* 私はすぐに行かなければならない. □ *Remove from the heat, add the parsley, toss and serve at once.* 火から下ろし, パセリを加えて軽くかき混ぜたらすぐに供しなさ

い. **8** PHRASE 句 If a number of different things happen **at once** or **all at once**, they all happen at the same time. 同時に □ *You can't be doing two things at once.* 2つのことを同時にすることはできませ ん. **9** PHRASE 句 **For once** is used to emphasize that something happens on this particular occasion, that it has never happened before, and may never happen again. 1度だけ (は特に) [EMPHASIS 強調] □ *For once, Dad is not complaining.* 今度だけは父が文句を言っていない. **10** PHRASE 句 If something happens **once again** or **once more**, it happens again. もう1度 □ *Amy picked up the hairbrush and brushed her hair once more.* エイミーはヘアブラシを手に取って, もう1度髪にブラシをかけた. **11** PHRASE 句 If something happens **once and for all**, it happens completely or finally. 今度かぎり [EMPHASIS 強調] □ *We have to resolve this matter once and for all.* 私たちはこの問題をきっぱりと解決しなければならない. **12** PHRASE 句 If something happens **once in a while**, it happens sometimes, but not very often. ときたま □ *Your body, like any other machine, needs a full service once in a while.* 君の体は他のどんな機械と同じように時々完全な保守点検を必要とする. **13** PHRASE 句 If you have done something **once or twice**, you have done it a few times, but not very often. 1, 2度 □ *I visited once or twice.* 私は1, 2度訪問した. □ *Once or twice she had caught a flash of interest in William's eyes.* 彼女は1, 2度, ウィリアムの眼に興味のひらめきを認めていた.

---

one

❶ NUMBER
❷ PRONOUN, DETERMINER, AND ADJECTIVE USES
❸ PHRASES

❶ one /wʌn/ (ones) NUM 数詞 **One** is the number 1. 1 □ *They had three sons and one daughter.* 彼らには息子が3人と娘が1人いた. □ *...one thousand years ago.* 千年前に

❷ one /wʌn/ (ones) **1** ADJ 形容詞 If you say that someone or something is the **one** person or thing of a particular kind, you are emphasizing that they are the only person or thing of that kind. ただ1つの [EMPHASIS 強調] [det ADJ] □ *They had alienated the one man who knew the business.* 彼らはその商売を知っていた唯一の男と疎遠になっていた. **2** DET 限定詞 **One** can be used instead of "a" to emphasize the following noun. 1つ [EMPHASIS 強調] □ *There is one thing I would like to know – What is it about Tim that you find so irresistible?* 1つ知りたいことがあります. あなたがティムに否応無しに引き付けられるのはどうしてですか. **3** DET 限定詞 You can use **one** instead of "a" to emphasize the following adjective or expression. とりわけ [くだけた, EMPHASIS 強調] □ *If we ever get married we'll have one terrific wedding.* 私たちがどうせ結婚するのなら, とりわけすごい結婚式を挙げよう. **4** DET 限定詞 You can use **one** to refer to the first of two or more things that you are comparing. つ (いくつかのうちの) □ *Prices vary from one shop to another.* 価格は店によって異なる. ●ADJ 形容詞 **One** is also an adjective. 1つの [det ADJ] □ *The one thing that she accomplished was raising money to update our facilities.* 彼女が達成したことの1つのことは我々の設備をアップデートするための金の工面をしたことだ. ●PRON 代名詞 **One** is also a pronoun. 一方 □ *The twins were dressed differently and one was thinner than the other.* その双子は違う服装をしており, 1人はもう1人よりやせていた. **5** PRON 代名詞 You can use **one** or **ones** instead of a noun when it is clear what type of thing or person you are referring to and you are describing them or giving more information about them. それと同類のもの □ *They are selling their house to move to a smaller one.* 彼らは小さめな家に引っ越すために家を売却している. **6** PRON 代名詞 You use **ones** to refer to people in general. 人 □ *We are the only ones who know.* 知っているのは我々だけだ. **7** PRON 代名詞 You can use **one** instead of a noun group when you have just mentioned something and you want to describe it or give more information about it. それ [PRON 'of' n, PRON 'that'] □ *The issue of land reform was one that dominated Hungary's parliamentary elections.* 土地改革はハンガリーの議会選挙で大きく取り扱われた問題です. **8** DET 限定詞 You can use **one** when you have been talking or writing about a group of people or things and you want to say something about a particular member of the group. 特定の人のうち1人 □ *"A college degree isn't enough," said one honors student.* 「大学の学位では十分じゃない」とある優等生が言った. ●PRON 代名詞 **One** is also a pronoun. 特定の人のうち1人 □ *Some of them couldn't eat a thing. One couldn't even drink.* 彼らの幾人かは食べることができなかったが, 1人は飲むことさえできなかった. **9** QUANT 数量詞 You use **one** in expressions such as "**one of the biggest airports**" or "**one of the most experienced players**" to indicate that something or someone is bigger or more experienced than most other things or people of the same kind. 特定のもののうち1つ [QUANT 'of' adj-superl] □ *Subaru is one of the smallest Japanese car makers.* スバルは最小の日本自動車メーカーの1つだ. **10** DET 限定詞 You can use **one** when referring to a time in the past or in the future. For example, if you say that you did something **one day**, you mean that you did it on a day in the past. ある □ *How would you like to have dinner one night, just you and me?* 君と僕だけでいつか

夕食を共にするのはどうでしょうか. **11 one day** → see **day** **12 PRON** 代名詞 You use **one** to make statements about people in general which also apply to themselves. **One** can be used as the subject or object of a sentence. 人 [FORMAL 形式ばった] ❑ *If one looks at the bigger picture, a lot of positive things are happening.* もっと大局的にみ ると, たくさんよいことが起こっています. ❑ *Where does one go from there?* そこからどこに行くのか.

One or **you** is used when making statements that are true of any individual person. **One** is more formal than **you**. ❑ *I suppose one can't blame him…A crisis can make you stop and take a look at your life.* **People** is used to talk about everyone in general, or about a particular group. ❑ *…the amount of bread people buy… Don't go on about it. People may get embarrassed.*
---

❾ one /wʌn/ **11 PHRASE** 句 You can use **for one** to emphasize that a particular person is definitely reacting or behaving in a particular way, even if other people are not. 個人としては [EMPHASIS 強調] ❑ *I, for one, hope you don't get the job.* 私個人とし ては, あなたはその仕事につかないことを望みます. **21 PHRASE** 句 You can use expressions such as **a hundred and one, a thousand and one**, and **a million and one** to emphasize that you are talking about a large number of things or people. 無数の [EMPHASIS 強調] ❑ *There are a hundred and one ways in which you can raise money.* 君 が資金を調達できる方法は無数にある. **31 PHRASE** 句 You can use **in one** to indicate that something is a single unit, but is made up of several different parts or has several different functions. 1つで かねて ❑ *…a love story and an adventure all in one.* 恋愛物語と冒険す べてが一緒になって. **41 PHRASE** 句 You use **one after the other** or **one after another** to say that actions or events happen with very little time between them. 次々に ❑ *My three guitars broke one after the other.* 私の3台のギターは次々と故障した. **51 PHRASE** 句 **The one and only** can be used in front of the name of an actor, singer, or other famous person when they are being introduced on a show. 唯一無二の ❑ *one of the greatest ever rock performers, the one and only Tina Turner.* 最も偉大なロック演奏家の1人, 天下無二のティナ・ター ナー. **61 PHRASE** 句 You can use **one by one** to indicate that people do things or that things happen in sequence, not all at the same time. 順次に ❑ *We went into the room one by one.* 私たちは1人ずつ部 屋に入った. **71 PHRASE** 句 You use **one or other** to refer to one or more things or people in a group, when it does not matter which particular one or ones are thought of or chosen. `のうちのどれ か ❑ *One or other of the two women was wrong.* 2人の女性のうちどち らかが間違っていた. **81 PHRASE** 句 **One or two** means a few. 1, 2 の, 多少の ❑ *We may make one or two changes.* 私たちはいくらか変更 を加えるかもしれない. ❑ *I've also sold one or two to a publisher.* 私はい くらか出版社にも売った. **91 PHRASE** 句 If you try to **get one up on** someone, you try to gain an advantage over them. 一をリードす る ❑ *…the competitive kind who will see this as the opportunity to be one up on you.* これを君をリードする機会, 勝るだろう競争者たち **10 one another** → see **another** **11 one thing after another** → see **another** **12 of one mind** → see **mind** **13 in one piece** → see **piece**

one-off (**one-offs**) **11 N-COUNT** 可算名詞 You can refer to something as a **one-off** when it is made or happens only once. 1 回限りのもの ❑ *Our survey revealed that these allergies were mainly one-offs.* 私たちの調査により, これらのアレルギー反応は大抵の場合1回 限りであることがわかった. **21 ADJ** 形容詞 A **one-off** thing is made or happens only once. 1回限りの [mainly BRIT 主に英国英語; AM usually **one-time** 米国英語では通常 **one-time**]

on|er|ous /ɒnərəs, oʊnər-/ **ADJ** 形容詞 If you describe a task as **onerous**, you dislike having to do it because you find it difficult or unpleasant. 煩わしい [FORMAL 形式ばった] ❑ *…parents who have had the onerous task of bringing up a very difficult child.* 非常に手の焼け るこどもを育てる厄介な仕事を負った親

one's /wʌnz/ **11 DET** 限定詞 Speakers and writers use **one's** to indicate that something belongs or relates to people in general, or to themselves in particular. 自分の [FORMAL 形式ばった] ❑ *…a feeling of responsibility for the welfare of others in one's community.* 自分 の住む地域社会における他人の福祉に対する責任感 **21 One's** can be used as a spoken form of "one is" or "one has," especially when "has" is an auxiliary verb. one is やone has の省略形 ❑ *No one's going to hurt you.* だれも君を傷つけようとしていない. → see **one**

one|self /wʌnsɛlf/

Oneself is a third person singular reflexive pronoun.

Oneselfは3人称単数の再帰代名詞である.
---

11 PRON-REFL 再帰代名詞 **Oneself** is used to mean "any person in general" as the object of a verb or preposition, when this refers to the same person as the subject of the verb. 自分自身 [FORMAL 形 式ばった] ❑ *One must apply oneself to the present and keep one's eyes firmly fixed on one's future goals.* 人は現在を精一杯生き, 将来の目 標をしっかり見極めなくてはならない. **21 PRON-REFL** 再帰代名詞 **Oneself** is used to mean "any person in general" as the object of a verb or preposition, when "one" is not present but is understood

to be the subject of the verb. 自分自身 [FORMAL 形式ばった] ❑ *The historic feeling of the town makes it a pleasant place to base oneself for summer vacations.* 町はその由緒ある雰囲気により, 夏休みの拠点 にするのに快適な場所となっている.

one-sided 11 ADJ 形容詞 If you say that an activity or relationship is **one-sided**, you think that one of the people or groups involved does much more than the other or is much stronger than the other. 不公平な ❑ *The negotiating was completely one-sided.* その交渉は完全に一方に偏っていた. **21 ADJ** 形容詞 If you describe someone as **one-sided**, you are critical of what they say or do because you think it shows that they have considered only one side of an issue or event. 偏った [DISAPPROVAL 不賛成] ❑ *The organization still believes the government is being one-sided.* その組織は いまだに政府は一方に偏っていると思っている.

one-time also onetime 11 ADJ 形容詞 **One-time** is used to describe something which happened in the past, or something such as a job, position, or role which someone used to have. 前の [JOURNALISM ジャーナリズム] [ADJ n] ❑ *The legislative body had voted to oust the country's onetime rulers.* 立法府はその国の元指導者を追い 出すことを可決していた. **21 ADJ** 形容詞 A **one-time** thing is made or happens only once. 1度だけの [mainly AM 主に米国英語] [ADJ n] ❑ *…a one-time charge.* 手数料の一時払い

one-to-one 11 ADJ 形容詞 In a **one-to-one** relationship, one person deals directly with only one other person. 1対1の [ADJ n] ❑ *…one-to-one training.* 1対1の訓練 ● ADV 副詞 **One-to-one** is also an adverb. 1対1に [ADV after v] ❑ *She would like to talk to people one-to-one.* 彼女は人々と1対1で話すのが好きだ. **21 ADJ** 形容詞 If there is a **one-to-one** match between two sets of things, each member of one set matches a member of the other set. 対応的な [ADJ n] ❑ *In English, there is not a consistent one-to-one match between each written symbol and each distinct spoken sound.* 英語では, それぞれの文字記号とそれぞ れの個別発音との間に首尾一貫した1対1の対応があるわけではない.

one-way 11 ADJ 形容詞 In **one-way** streets or traffic systems, vehicles can only travel along in one direction. 1方通行の [ADJ n] ❑ *…Gotham's maze of one-way streets.* ゴッサムの1方通行路の迷 路 **21 ADJ** 形容詞 **One-way** describes trips which go to just one place, rather than to that place and then back again. 片道の ❑ *The trailers will be rented for one-way trips.* トレーラーは片道旅行のために 借りられるでしょう. **31 ADJ** 形容詞 A **one-way** ticket or fare is for a trip from one place to another, but not back again. 片道の [mainly AM 主に米国英語] ❑ *…a one-way ticket from New York to Los Angeles.* ニューヨークからロスアンゼルスまでの片道切符. ● ADV 副詞 **One-way** is also an adverb. 片道で [ADV after v] ❑ *Unrestricted fares will be increased as much as $80 one-way.* 無制限運賃は最高で片道80ドル で引き上げられます.

on|go|ing /ɒngoʊɪŋ/ **ADJ** 形容詞 An **ongoing** situation has been happening for quite a long time and seems likely to continue for some time in the future. 進行している ❑ *There is an ongoing debate on the issue.* その問題については論議が進行中です.

on|ion /ʌnyən/ (**onions**) **N-VAR** 可変性名詞 An **onion** is a round vegetable with a light brown skin. It has many white layers on its inside which have a strong, sharp smell and taste. タマネギ ❑ *You grind the onion and the raw cranberries together.* タマネギと生のクラン ベリーを一緒にすりつぶす. → see **spice**

on|line /ɒnlaɪn/ also **on-line 11 ADJ** 形容詞 If a company goes **online**, its services become available on the Internet. オン ライン [BUSINESS, COMPUTING 実業, コンピューティング] ❑ *…the first bank to go online.* ウェブサイトを開設した最初の銀行 ❑ *…an online shopping center.* オンラインショッピングセンター **21 ADJ** 形容 詞 If you are **online**, your computer is connected to the Internet. Compare **offline**. オンラインの [COMPUTING コンピューティン グ] ❑ *You can chat to other people who are online.* 他のオンラインの人 たちとチャットすることができます. ● ADV 副詞 **Online** is also an adverb. オンラインで [ADV after v] ❑ *…the cool stuff you find online.* オンラインで見つけるすごい物 **31 on line** → see **line** → see **bank**

on|look|er /ɒnlʊkər/ (**onlookers**) **N-COUNT** 可算名詞 An **onlooker** is someone who watches an event take place but does not take part in it. 傍観者 ❑ *A handful of onlookers stand in the field watching.* 一握りの見物人が競技場に立って見ていた.

---
only

❶ ADVERB AND ADJECTIVE USES
❷ CONJUNCTION
❸ PHRASES
---

❶ only /oʊnli/

In written English, **only** is usually placed immediately before the word it qualifies. In spoken English, however, you can use stress to indicate what **only** qualifies, so its position is not so important.

書き言葉では **only** は通常修飾する語の直前に置かれる．しかし，話し言葉では，**only** が何を修飾するかを示すのに強勢を使えるので，その位置はそれほど重要ではない．

1 ADV 副詞 You use **only** to indicate the one thing that is true, appropriate, or necessary in a particular situation, in contrast to all the other things that are not true, appropriate, or necessary. 唯一の ❑ *Only the president could authorize the use of the atomic bomb.* 原子爆弾の使用を許可できるのは大統領だけだ． ❑ *A business can only be built and expanded on a sound financial base.* 事業は健全な財政基盤の基にのみ作り，拡張できる． **2** ADV 副詞 You use **only** to introduce the thing which must happen before the thing mentioned in the main part of the sentence can happen. だけ [ADV cl/prep] ❑ *The lawyer is paid only if he wins.* 弁護士は勝利したときにのみ支払いを受ける． ❑ *The Bank of England insists that it will cut interest rates only when it is ready.* イングランド銀行は，用意が整ったときにのみ金利を下げると主張する．

When **only** is used as an adverb, its position in the sentence depends on the word or phrase it applies to. If **only** applies to the subject of a clause, you put it in front of the subject. ❑ *Only strong characters can make such decisions.* Otherwise, you normally put it in front of the verb, after the first auxiliary, or after the verb **be**. ❑ *I only want my son back, that is all... He had only agreed to see me because we had met before... I was only able to wash four times in 66 days.* However, some people think it is more correct to put **only** directly in front of the word or phrase it applies to. This is the best position if you want to be quite clear or emphatic. ❑ *It applies only to passengers carrying British passports... She'd done it only because it was necessary.* For extra emphasis, you can put **only** after the word or phrase it applies to. ❑ *The event will be for women only... I'll say this once and once only.*

---

3 ADJ 形容詞 If you talk about **the only** person or thing involved in a particular situation, you mean there are no others involved in it. ただ1人の [det ADJ] ❑ *She was the only woman in Shell's legal department.* シェルの法務部門では，女性は彼女ただ1人だった． **4** ADJ 形容詞 An **only** child is a child who has no brothers or sisters. 1人っ子 [ADJ n] ❑ *The actor, an only child, grew up in the Bronx.* その俳優は1人っ子で，ブロンクスで育った． **5** ADV 副詞 You use **only** to indicate that something is no more important, interesting, or difficult, for example, than you say it is, especially when you want to correct a wrong idea that someone has or may get. だけの ❑ *At the moment it is only a theory.* 現時点では，それは理論に過ぎません． ❑ *"I'm only a sergeant," said Clements.* 「俺は軍曹に過ぎない」とクレメンツは言った． **6** ADV 副詞 You use **only** to emphasize how small an amount is or how short a length of time is. たったしか [EMPHASIS 強調] [ADV n/adv] ❑ *Child car seats only cost about $10 a week to rent.* チャイルドシートの貸借料は週に約10ドルしかかからない． ❑ *...spacecraft guidance systems weighing only a few grams.* たった数グラムの重量しかない宇宙船ガイダンスシステム **7** ADV 副詞 You use **only** to emphasize that you are talking about a small part of an amount or group, not the whole of it. ～だけ [EMPHASIS 強調] [ADV n] ❑ *These are only a few of the possibilities.* これらは可能性のほんの数例です． **8** ADV 副詞 **Only** is used after "can" or "could" to emphasize that it is impossible to do anything except the rather inadequate or limited action that is mentioned. ～だけ [EMPHASIS 強調] [modal ADV inf] ❑ *For a moment I could say nothing. I could only stand and look.* 私はその時点では何も言えない．ただ突っ立って見守ることしかできない． **9** ADV 副詞 You can use **only** in the expressions **I only wish** or **I only hope** in order to emphasize what you are hoping or wishing. ～のみ [EMPHASIS 強調] [ADV before v] ❑ *I only wish he were here now that things are getting better for me.* 私にとって事態がよくなってきている現在彼が今ここに居てくれたらと望むのです． **10** ADV 副詞 You can use **only** before an infinitive to introduce an event which happens immediately after one you have just mentioned, and which is surprising or unfortunate. 結局は [ADV to-inf] ❑ *Ron tried the embassy, only to be told that Hugh was in a meeting.* ロンは大使館を試したが，結局ヒューは会議中だと言われた． **11** ADV 副詞 You can use **only** to emphasize how appropriate a certain course of action or type of behavior is. 全く [EMPHASIS 強調] ❑ *It's only fair to let her know that you intend to apply.* 君が申し込むつもりであることを彼女に知らせるのは全く正しい． **12** ADV 副詞 You can use **only** in front of a verb to indicate that the result of something is unfortunate or undesirable and is likely to make the situation worse rather than better. ただ [ADV before v] ❑ *The embargo would only hurt innocent civilians.* 出入港禁止は罪のない一般市民をただ困らせるだけである．

Thesaurus *only* また次を参照：

ADJ. alone, individual, single, solitary, unique ❶ **3**

---

❷ only /ˈoʊnli/ **1** CONJ 接続詞 **Only** can be used to add a comment which slightly changes or limits what you have just said. ただし [INFORMAL くだけた] ❑ *It's just as dramatic as a movie, only it's real.* それは現実であることを除いては，映画と同じくらいドラ

マチックでした． ❑ *It's a bit like my house, only nicer.* それは少し私の家に似ているけれど，ただしもっとすてきだ． **2** CONJ 接続詞 **Only** can be used after a clause with "would" to indicate why something is not done. がなければ [SPOKEN 口語] ❑ *I'd invite you to come with me, only it's such a long way.* そんなに遠くでなければ，私と一緒に来ていただきたいのだが．

❸ only /ˈoʊnli/ **1** PHRASE 句 If you say you **only have to** do one thing in order to achieve or prove a second thing, you are emphasizing how easily the second thing can be achieved or proved. ～をするだけで [EMPHASIS 強調] ❑ *Any time you want a babysitter, dear, you only have to ask.* ベビーシッターが必要なときは，頼むだけでいいのよ． **2** PHRASE 句 You can say that something has **only just** happened when you want to emphasize that it happened a very short time ago. たった今したばかり [EMPHASIS 強調] ❑ *I've only just arrived.* 私はたった今到着したばかりです． **3** PHRASE 句 You use **only just** to emphasize that something is true, but by such a small degree that it is almost not true at all. かろうじて [EMPHASIS 強調] ❑ *For centuries farmers have only just managed to survive.* その土地の農民は何世紀にもわたって細々と生き延びてきました． ❑ *I am old enough to remember the War, but only just.* 私は戦争を覚えているくらいの年齢ですが，かろうじてです． **4** PHRASE 句 You can use **only too** to emphasize that something is true or exists to a much greater extent than you would expect or like. ただただ [EMPHASIS 強調] ❑ *I know only too well that plans can easily go wrong.* 私は計画というものがもっとすると失敗する可能性があることをわかり過ぎるくらいわかっている． **5** PHRASE 句 You can say that you are **only too** happy to do something to emphasize how willing you are to do it. このうえなく [EMPHASIS 強調] ❑ *I'll be only too pleased to help them out with any questions.* 私はどんな問題でもよろこんで彼らをお助けいたします． **6** **if only** → see **if** **7** **not only** → see **not** **8** **the one and only** → see **one**

on-screen also **onscreen** **1** ADJ 形容詞 **On-screen** means appearing on the screen of a television, movie theater, or computer. 画面上の [ADJ n] ❑ *Read the on-screen lyrics and sing along.* 画面上の歌詞を読んで，一緒に歌いなさい． **2** ADJ 形容詞 **On-screen** means relating to the roles played by film or television actors, in contrast with their real lives. 役者業での [ADJ n] ❑ *...her first on-screen kiss.* 役者としての彼女の最初のキス ● **On-screen** is also an adverb. 役者業で [ADV with cl] ❑ *He was immensely attractive to women, on-screen and off-screen.* 彼は映画上でも現実生活でも女性にとって途方もない魅力があった．

on|set /ˈɒnset/ N-SING 単数名詞 The **onset of** something is the beginning of it, used especially to refer to something unpleasant. 開始 ❑ *Most of the passes have been closed with the onset of winter.* 冬の訪れにより，ほとんどの山道は閉鎖されました．

on|shore /ˈɒnʃɔr/ ADJ 形容詞 **Onshore** means happening on land, rather than at sea. 陸上の ❑ *...Western Europe's biggest onshore oilfield.* 西欧で最大の陸上油田 ● ADV 副詞 **Onshore** is also an adverb. 陸上で [ADV after v] ❑ *They missed the ferry and remained onshore.* 彼らはフェリーに間に合わず，陸に残った．

on|slaught /ˈɒnslɔt/ (**onslaughts**) **1** N-COUNT 可算名詞 An **onslaught** on someone or something is a very violent, forceful attack against them. 猛攻撃 ❑ *The press launched another vicious onslaught on the president.* マスコミは大統領にさらに悪質な猛襲をかけた． **2** N-COUNT 可算名詞 If you refer to an **onslaught** of something, you mean that there is a large amount of it, often so that it is very difficult to deal with. 激しい攻撃 ❑ *...the constant onslaught of ads on TV.* テレビで常時放送される広告の大攻勢

onto /ˈɒntu/

The spelling **on to** is also used.

つづりの **on to** も使われる．

In addition to the uses shown below, **onto** is used in phrasal verbs such as "hold onto" and "latch onto."

下記の用法に加えて，**onto** は hold onto や latch onto のような句動詞に使われる．

---

1 PREP 前置詞 If something moves **onto** or is put **onto** an object or surface, it is then on that object or surface. ～の上へ ❑ *I took my bags inside, lowered myself onto the bed and switched on the TV.* 私はバッグを中に入れ，ベッドに体を落とし，テレビのスイッチをつけた． **2** PREP 前置詞 You can sometimes use **onto** to mention the place or area that someone moves into. ～に ❑ *The players jogged onto the field.* 選手たちはフィールドへゆっくりと走っていった． ❑ *At exactly 5:00 p.m., Marcia drove onto the freeway.* 午後5時ちょうどにマルシアは高速道路に入って行った． **3** PREP 前置詞 You can use **onto** to introduce the place toward which a light or someone's look is directed. ～に ❑ *...the metal part of the door onto which the sun had been shining.* 太陽の光が当たって輝いていたドアの金属部分 ❑ *The colors rotated around on a disc and were reflected onto the wall behind.* その色彩はディスクの上で回転し，後ろの壁に反射された． **4** PREP 前置詞 If a door or room opens **onto** a place, that place

is directly in front of it. 一の方に [v PREP n] ❑ *The door opened onto a well-lit hallway.* 戸口は開けられていて明るく照らされた玄関広間に通じていた. **5** PREP 前置詞 When you change the position of your body, you use **onto** to introduce the part your body which is now supporting you. 一の上へ ❑ *As he stepped backwards she fell onto her knees, then onto her face.* 彼が後ろに下がると, 彼女は膝の上に崩れ折れ, それから, うつぶせに倒れてきた. ❑ *Puffing a little, Mabel shifted her weight onto her feet.* メーベルは1服して, 足に体重をかけた. **6** PREP 前置詞 When you get **onto** a bus, train, or plane, you enter it in order to travel somewhere. 一の上に ❑ *As he got on to the plane, he asked me how I was feeling.* 彼は飛行機に乗ると, 具合はどうかと私に尋ねた. **7** PREP 前置詞 **Onto** is used after verbs such as "hold," "hang," and "cling" to indicate what someone is holding firmly or where something is being held firmly. 一をしっかりと ❑ *The reflector is held onto the sides of the spacecraft with a frame.* 反射体は宇宙船の側面に枠で固定されている. **8** PREP 前置詞 If people who are talking get **onto** a different subject, they begin talking about it. 一に移る ❑ *Let's get on to more important matters.* もっと重要な問題に移りましょう. **9** PREP 前置詞 You can sometimes use **onto** to indicate that something or someone becomes included as a part of a list or system. 一に上がる ❑ *The Macedonian question had failed to get on to the agenda.* マケドニアの質問は議題にならなければませんでした. ❑ *The pill itself has changed a lot since it first came onto the market.* ピルそのものは, 最初に製品化されてから非常な変化を遂げました. **10** PREP 前置詞 If someone **is onto** something important. 一に気づいて [INFORMAL くだけた] ['be' PREP n] ❑ *He leaned across the table and whispered to me, "I'm really onto something."* 彼はテーブル越しに寄りかかって, 「何かとっても臭うんだ」と私にささやいた. **11** PREP 前置詞 If someone **is onto** you, they have discovered that you are doing something illegal or wrong. 一に気づいて [INFORMAL くだけた] ['be' PREP n] ❑ *I had told people what he had been doing, so now the police were onto him.* 私は彼のやっていたことを人々に話したので, 今では警察が彼のことに気づいて調べている.

onus /óunəs/ N-SING 単数名詞 If you say that **the onus is on** someone **to** do something, you mean it is their duty or responsibility to do it. 責任 [FORMAL 形式ばった] ❑ *The onus is on companies and consumers to keep up with anti-virus updates.* ウィルス対策ソフトを更新し続ける責任は会社と利用者にある.

on|ward /ɒnwərd/

The form **onwards** can also be used as an adverb.

onwards 形は副詞としても使える.

1 ADJ 形容詞 **Onward** means moving forward or continuing a journey. 前進して ❑ *American Airlines have two flights a day to Bangkok, and there are onward flights to Phnom Penh.* アメリカン航空にはバンコック行きの便が毎日2便あり, 続けてプノンペンにまで行く便がある. ❑ *The bus continued onward.* バスは走り続けた. **2** ADJ 形容詞 **Onward** means developing, progressing, or becoming more important over a period of time. 前進的な ❑ *...the onward march of progress in the aircraft industry.* 航空機産業の発達の前進 ● ADV 副詞 **Onward** is also an adverb. 前進して [ADV after v] ❑ *From here, it has been onward and upward all the way.* ここからはずっと前進して上昇していくのみだった. **3** ADV 副詞 If something happens from a particular time **onward** or **onwards**, it begins to happen at that time and continues to happen afterward. 先へ ['from' n ADV] ❑ *From the turn of the century onward, she shared the life of the aborigines.* 彼女は世紀の変わり目から先にアボリジニの生活を体験した.

oops /ups, ups/ EXCLAM 感嘆詞 You say "oops" to indicate that there has been a slight accident or mistake, or to apologize to someone for it. おっと [INFORMAL くだけた, FEELINGS 感情] ❑ *Today they're saying, "Oops, we made a mistake."* 今日は彼らは「しまった, 我々は間違いを犯した」と言っている.

ooze /uz/ (oozes, oozing, oozed) **1** V-T/V-I 他動詞/自動詞 When a thick or sticky liquid **oozes** from something or when something **oozes** it, the liquid flows slowly and in small quantities. にじみ出る ❑ *Blood was still oozing from the wound.* 傷口からはまだ血がにじみ出ていた. ❑ *The lava will just ooze gently out of the crater.* 溶岩はただ噴火口から緩やかに流れ出るだろう. **2** V-T/V-I 他動詞/自動詞 If you say that someone or something **oozes** a quality or characteristic, or **oozes** with it, you mean that they show it very strongly. 発散する ❑ *The Southern plantation house oozes charm.* 南部の大農場の家は魅力を発散している.

opaque /oupéik/ **1** ADJ 形容詞 If an object or substance is **opaque**, you cannot see through it. 不透明な ❑ *You can always use opaque glass if you need to block a street view.* 通りの景色を遮断する必要がある場合にはいつでも不透明ガラスを使うことができる. **2** ADJ 形容詞 If you say that something is **opaque**, you mean that it is difficult to understand. 理解しがたい ❑ *...the opaque language of the inspector's reports.* その検査官の報告書の理解しにくい言葉使い

op. cit. /ɒp sɪt/ In reference books, **op. cit.** is used after an

author's name to refer to a book of theirs which has already been mentioned. 前掲書中に [FORMAL 形式ばった] ❑ *...quoted in Iyer, op. cit., p. 332.* イイェル著の前掲書の332ページに引用

OPEC /óupεk/ N-PROPER 固有名詞 **OPEC** is an organization of countries that produce oil. It tries to develop a common policy and system of prices. **OPEC** is an abbreviation for "Organization of Petroleum-Exporting Countries." 石油輸出国機構の略 ❑ *Each member of OPEC would seek to maximize its own production.* 石油輸出国機構の各加盟国はそれ自身の生産を最大限にしようとするだろう.

---

open

❶ DESCRIBING A POSITION OR MOVEMENT
❷ ACCESSIBLE OR AVAILABLE; NOT HIDDEN, BLOCKED, ETC.
❸ BEGIN, START
❹ PHRASES AND PHRASAL VERBS

---

❶ open /óupən/ (opens, opening, opened) **1** V-T/V-I 他動詞/自動詞 If you **open** something such as a door, window, or lid, or if it **opens**, its position is changed so that it no longer covers a hole or gap. 開ける, 開く ❑ *He opened the window and looked out.* 彼は窓を開けて外を眺めた. ● ADJ 形容詞 **Open** is also an adjective. 開いた ❑ *...an open window.* 開いた窓 **2** V-T 他動詞 If you **open** something such as a bottle, box, parcel, or envelope, you move, remove, or cut part of it so you can take out what is inside. 開ける ❑ *I opened the letter.* 私は手紙を開封した. ● ADJ 形容詞 **Open** is also an adjective. 開けた ❑ *...an open bottle of milk.* 開けた牛乳瓶 ● PHRASAL VERB 句動詞 **Open up** means the same as **open**. 開ける ❑ *He opened up a cage and lifted out a 6ft python.* 彼はかごを開け, 6フィートのニシキヘビを取り出した. **3** V-T/V-I 他動詞/自動詞 If you **open** something such as a book, an umbrella, or your hand, or if it **opens**, the different parts of it move away from each other so that the inside of it can be seen. 開く ❑ *He opened the heavy Bible.* 彼は重い聖書を開いた. ❑ *The flower opens to reveal a bee.* 花が開き, ミツバチが見える. ● ADJ 形容詞 **Open** is also an adjective. 開いた ❑ *Without warning, Bardo smacked his fist into his open hand.* バードは警告なしに握りこぶしで手の平をびしゃりと打った. ● PHRASAL VERB 句動詞 **Open out** means the same as **open**. 広げる ❑ *Keith took a map from the dashboard and opened it out on his knees.* キースはダッシュボードから地図を取り出し, 膝の上に広げた. **4** V-T 他動詞 If you **open** a computer file, you give the computer an instruction to display it on the screen. 開く [COMPUTING コンピューティング] ❑ *Double click on the icon to open the file.* そのアイコンをダブルクリックしてファイルを開きなさい.

Note that you do not use **open** as a verb or adjective to talk about electrical devices. If someone causes an electrical device to work by pressing a switch, you say that they **put it on**, **switch it on**, or **turn it on**. ❑ *It's too easy just to switch on the television.* If the device is already working, you say that it **is on**. ❑ *The answering machine is on... He cannot sleep with the light on.*

5 V-T/V-I 他動詞/自動詞 When you **open** your eyes or your eyes **open**, you move your eyelids upward, for example, when you wake up, so that you can see. 開ける, 開く ❑ *When I opened my eyes I saw Melissa standing at the end of my bed.* 目を開けると, メリサが私のベッドの端に立っているのが見えた. ● ADJ 形容詞 **Open** is also an adjective. 開いた ❑ *As soon as he saw that her eyes were open he sat up.* 彼女の目が開いているのを見た途端, 彼は上体を起こした. **6** V-T 他動詞 If you **open** your arms, you stretch them wide apart in front of you, usually in order to put them around someone. 広げる ❑ *She opened her arms and gave me a big hug.* 彼女は両手を広げて私を大きく抱きしめた. **7** V-T 他動詞 If you **open** your shirt or coat, you undo the buttons or pull down the zipper. 広げる ❑ *I opened my coat and let him see the belt.* 私はコートを広げて彼にベルトを見せた. ● ADJ 形容詞 **Open** is also an adjective. 開いた [ADJ n, v-link ADJ] ❑ *The top can be worn buttoned up or open over a T-shirt.* その上着はボタンをかけても, あるいはかけないでTシャツの上に着ることもできる.

❷ open /óupən/ (opens, opening, opened) **1** V-T/V-I 他動詞/自動詞 If people **open** something such as a blocked road or a border, or if it **opens**, people can then pass along it or through it. 開ける, 開く ❑ *The rebels have opened the road from Monrovia to the Ivory Coast.* 反乱軍はモンロビアから象牙海岸への道を開通した. ● ADJ 形容詞 **Open** is also an adjective. 開通した ❑ *We were part of an entire regiment that had nothing else to do but to keep that highway open.* 我々はあの主要道路を開通させておくこと以外に何の任務もない全連隊の一部だった. ● PHRASAL VERB 句動詞 **Open up** means the same as **open**. 開通する ❑ *As rescue workers opened up roads today, it became apparent that some small towns were totally devastated.* 救援隊が今日道路を開通させるにつれて, 一部の小さな町は完全に破壊されたことが明らかになった. **2** V-I 自動詞 If a place **opens into** another, larger place, you can move from one directly into the other. 通じる ❑ *The corridor opened into a low smoky room.* 廊下は天井の低い煙に満ちた部屋に通じていた. ● PHRASAL VERB 句動詞 **Open out** means the same

as **open**. 通じる ❏ *...narrow streets opening out into charming squares.* 魅力的な広場に通じる狭い街路 **3** ADJ 形容詞 An **open** area is a large area that does not have many buildings or trees in it. 広々とした ❏ *Officers will also continue their search of nearby open ground.* 警察官は近くの広々とした土地の捜索も続ける予定だ. **4** ADJ 形容詞 An **open** structure or object is not covered or enclosed. おおいのない [ADJ n] ❏ *Don't leave a child alone in a room with an open fire.* おおいのない暖炉のある部屋に子供を1人だけにしてはならない. **5** V-T/V-I 他動詞/自動詞 When a store, office, or public building **opens** or **is opened**, its doors are unlocked and the public can go in. 開ける, 開く ❏ *Banks closed on Friday afternoon and did not open again until Monday morning.* 銀行は金曜の午後に閉店し, 月曜の朝まで開店しなかった. ❏ *I'd been waiting for him to open the shop.* 私は彼が店を開けるのを待っていた. ❏ ADJ 形容詞 **Open** is also an adjective. 開いた ❏ *The gallery is open Monday through Friday, 9 am to 6 pm.* 美術館の開館時間は月一金の午前9時~午後6時だ. **6** V-T/V-I 他動詞/自動詞 When a public building, factory, or company **opens** or when someone **opens** it, it starts operating for the first time. 開業する, 開店する ❏ *The original station opened in 1954.* 元の駅は1954年に開業した. ❏ *The complex opens to the public tomorrow.* その総合ビルは明日一般公開される. **7** ADJ 形容詞 If a factory or company remains **open**, it continues to operate. 営業中で [v-link ADJ] ❏ *The government says it's no longer willing to spend $170 million a month to keep the pits open.* 政府は毎月1億7000万ドルを投じてはその炭鉱を操業させておく心積もりはないと言う. ❏ *...any operating subsidy required to keep the airline open.* その航空会社を営業させておくための経営補助金 ●**open|ing** (openings) N-COUNT 可算名詞 開幕 ❏ *He was there, though, for the official opening.* でも彼は正式の開幕に参加するためにそこにいた. **8** ADJ 形容詞 If you describe a person or their character as **open**, you mean they are honest and do not want or try to hide anything or to deceive anyone. 隠し立てをしない ❏ *He had always been open with her and she always felt she would know if he lied.* 彼は彼女に隠し立てをしたことがなく, 彼女がうそをつけば分かると彼女はいつも感じていた. ●**open|ness** N-UNCOUNT 不可算名詞 率直 ❏ *...a relationship based on honesty and openness.* 正直で率直さに基づいた関係 **9** ADJ 形容詞 [ADJ n] If you describe a situation, attitude, or way of behaving as **open**, you mean it is not kept hidden or secret. あからさまな ❏ *The action is an open violation of the Vienna Convention.* その行為はウィーン協定のあからさまな違反だ. ●**open|ness** N-UNCOUNT 不可算名詞 公然 ❏ *...the new climate of political openness.* 政治的公然さという新しい風潮 **10** ADJ 形容詞 [v-link ADJ 'to' n] If you are **open to** suggestions or ideas, you are ready and willing to consider or accept them. 受け入れて ❏ *They are open to suggestions on how working conditions might be improved.* 彼らは就業状態を改善する方法についての提案に耳を貸す心構えがある. **11** ADJ 形容詞 If you say that a system, person, or idea is **open to** something such as abuse or criticism, you mean they might receive abuse or criticism because of their qualities, effects, or actions. 招きやすい [v-link ADJ 'to' n] ❏ *The system, though well-meaning, is open to abuse.* その制度は善意から出たものだが, 悪用されやすい. **12** ADJ 形容詞 If you say that a fact or question is **open to** debate, interpretation, or discussion, you mean that people are uncertain whether it is true, what it means, or what the answer is. 招きやすい ❏ *Her interpretation of the facts may be open to doubt.* 彼女のそれらの事実の解釈は疑いを招きやすいかもしれない. **13** ADJ 形容詞 You can use **open** to describe something that anyone is allowed to take part in or accept. 参加自由の ❏ *It's an open meeting, everybody's invited.* それは参加自由の会合なので, 誰でも参加できる. ❏ *...an open invitation.* 誰でも参加できる招待 **14** ADJ 形容詞 If something such as an offer or job is **open**, it is available for someone to accept or apply for. 空いている [v-link ADJ] ❏ *The offer will remain open until further notice.* その申し出は次の通告があるまで有効である. **15** → see also **opening 6** **16** ADJ 形容詞 If an opportunity or your choice is **open to** you, you are able to do a particular thing if you choose to. 利用できる [v-link ADJ 'to' n] ❏ *There are a wide range of career opportunities open to young people.* 若者にはさまざまな種類の職業の可能性がある. **17** V-T 他動詞 To **open** opportunities or possibilities means the same as to **open** them **up**. 開く, 開放する ❏ *The Chief of Naval Operations wants to open opportunities for women in the navy.* 海軍作戦部長は女性に海軍入隊の機会を開放したいと考えている.

Thesaurus	open また次を参照:
v.	crack, reveal, unblock ❶ **1**
	extend, stretch ❶ **3**
ADJ.	friendly, outgoing ❷ **8**

❸ **open** /óupən/ (opens, opening, opened) **1** V-T/V-I 他動詞/自動詞 If something such as a meeting or series of talks **opens**, or if someone **opens** it, it begins. 始める, 始まる ❏ *...an emergency session of the Russian Parliament due to open later this morning.* 今朝後ほど始まる予定のロシア議会の緊急会合 ●**open|ing** N-SING 単数名詞 開始 ❏ *...a statement issued at the opening of the talks.* 協議の始まりに発表された声明 **2** V-T/V-I 他動詞/自動詞 If an event such as a meeting or discussion **opens with** a particular activity, that activity is the first thing that happens or is dealt with. You can also say that someone such as a speaker or singer **opens by** doing a particular thing. 始まる ❏ *The service opened with a hymn.* 礼拝は賛美歌で始まった. ❏ *I opened by saying, "Honey, you look sensational."* 私は「すごく良く似合うじゃない」と開口一番で言った. **3** V-I 自動詞 On the stock exchange, the price at which currencies, shares, or commodities **open** is their value at the start of that day's trading. 取引が始まる [BUSINESS 実業] ❏ *Gold declined $2 in Zurich to open at $385.50.* 金の価格はチューリッヒで2ドル低下し, 385ドル50セントで取引が始まった. **4** V-I 自動詞 When a movie, play, or other public event **opens**, it begins to be shown, be performed, or take place for a limited period of time. 開催される ❏ *A photographic exhibition opens at the Smithsonian on Wednesday.* 写真展が水曜日にスミソニアン研究所で開催される. ●**open|ing** N-SING 単数名詞 'the' N 'of' n] 開会式 ❏ *He is due to attend the opening of the Asian Games on Saturday.* 彼は土曜日にアジア競技会の開会式に参加する予定である. **5** V-T 他動詞 If you **open** an account with a bank or a commercial organization, you begin to use their services. 開設する ❏ *He tried to open an account at the branch of his bank nearest to his workplace.* 彼は勤務先に最も近い銀行の支店で口座を開設しようとした.

❹ **open** /óupən/ (opens, opening, opened) **1** PHRASE 句 If you do something **in the open** or **out in the open**, you do it outdoors rather than in a house or other building. 戸外で ❏ *Many are sleeping in the open because they have no shelter.* 多くの人々は家がないため, 戸外で寝ている. **2** PHRASE 句 If an attitude or situation is **in the open** or **out in the open**, people know about it and it is no longer kept secret. 公然と ❏ *They had advised us to keep it a secret, but we wanted it out in the open.* 彼らはそれを秘密にしておくよう勧めたが, 我々はそれを公表したかった. **3** PHRASE 句 If something is **wide open**, it is open to its full extent. 完全に開いた ❏ *The child had left the inner door wide open.* その子供は内側のドアを開きっぱなしにしていた. **4** PHRASE 句 If you say that a competition, race, or election is **wide open**, you mean that anyone could win it, because there is no competitor who seems to be much better than the others. 決着がどうなるか分からない ❏ *The competition has been thrown wide open by the absence of the world champion.* その試合は世界チャンピオンの不参加により結果の予測がつかなくなっている. **5** **with open arms** → see **arm 6** to **keep** your **eyes open** → see **eye 7** **with** your **eyes open** → see **eye 8** to **open** your **eyes** → see **eye 9** to **open fire** → see **fire 10** to **open** your **heart** → see **heart 11** the **heavens open** → see **heaven 12** an **open mind** → see **mind 13** to **open** your **mind** → see **mind 14** to **keep** your **options open** → see **option**

▶ **open out** → see **open ❶ 3** → see **open ❷ 2**

▶ **open up 1** → see **open ❶ 2** → see **open ❷ 1 2** PHRASAL VERB 句動詞 If a place, economy, or area of interest **opens up**, or if someone **opens** it **up**, more people can go there or become involved in it. 開く ❏ *As the market opens up, I think people are going to be able to spend more money on consumer goods.* 市場が開くと, 人々はより多く消費財を購入することができるようになると思う. ❏ *He said he wanted to see how Albania was opening up to the world.* 彼はアルバニアが世界に開放されている状況を見たいと言った. **3** PHRASAL VERB 句動詞 If something **opens up** opportunities or possibilities, or if they **open up**, they are created. 開く, 開かれる ❏ *It was also felt that the collapse of the system opened up new possibilities.* その体制の崩壊は新しい可能性を開くとも感じられた. **4** PHRASAL VERB 句動詞 When you **open up** a building, you unlock and open the door so that people can get in. 開ける ❏ *Several customers were waiting when I arrived to open up the shop.* 私が店を開けるために到着した時には数人の客が待っていた. **5** PHRASAL VERB 句動詞 If someone **opens up**, they start to say exactly what they think or feel. 心を開く, 打ち解ける ❏ *Lorna found that people were willing to open up to her.* ローナは人々が喜んで彼女に心を開くことを知った.

open-air also **open air** **1** ADJ 形容詞 An **open-air** place or event is outside rather than in a building. 戸外の ❏ *...an open air concert in brilliant sunshine.* 素晴らしい晴天に恵まれた野外コンサート **2** N-SING 単数名詞 If you are **in the open air**, you are outside rather than in a building. 屋外で ❏ *We sleep out under the stars, and eat our meals in the open air.* 私たちは星の下で眠り, 屋外で食事をする.

open-door also **open door** ADJ 形容詞 If a country or organization has an **open-door** policy toward people or goods, it allows them to come freely, without any restrictions. 門戸を開放した [ADJ n] ❏ *...reformers who have advocated an open door economic policy.* 門戸解放経済政策を唱道する改革主義者 ●N-SING 単数名詞 **Open door** is also a noun. 門戸解放 ❏ *...an open door to further foreign investment.* 外国の投資を促進するための門戸解放

open-ended ADJ 形容詞 When people begin an **open-ended** discussion or activity, they do not start with any intention of achieving a particular decision or result. 制限のない ❏ *...an open-ended commitment to the security of the Gulf.* 湾岸の安全に対する全面的な責任

open|ing /óupənɪŋ/ (openings) **1** ADJ 形容詞 The **opening** event, item, day, or week in a series is the first one. 始まりの [ADJ

n] ❑ *They returned to play in the season's opening game.* 彼らは今シーズンの初試合に再び出場した。 **2** N-COUNT 可算名詞 **The opening** of something such as a book, play, or concert is the first part of it. 冒頭 ❑ *The opening of the scene depicts Akhnaten and his family in a moment of intimacy.* 場面の冒頭はアカナテンが家族と親しくしている瞬間を描写している。 **3** N-COUNT 可算名詞 An **opening** is a hole or empty space through which things or people can pass. 穴 ❑ *He squeezed through a narrow opening in the fence.* 彼は塀の小さい穴をかろうじて通った。 **4** N-COUNT 可算名詞 An **opening** in a forest is a small area where there are no trees or bushes. 林間の空き地 [mainly AM 主に米国英語] ❑ *I glanced down at the beach as we passed an opening in the trees.* 私は樹木が途切れた場所を通る時に海岸をちらっと見下ろした。 **5** N-COUNT 可算名詞 An **opening** is a good opportunity to do something, for example, to show people how good you are. 好機 ❑ *Her capabilities were always there; all she needed was an opening to show them.* 彼女はいつも能力があった。必要だったのはそれを示すきっかけだけだった。 **6** N-COUNT 可算名詞 An **opening** is a job that is available. 就職口 ❑ *We don't have any openings now, but we'll call you if something comes up.* 現在は欠員はありませんが、欠員が出来たらご連絡します。 **7** → see also **open**

N.	cut, door, gap, slot, space, window **3**
	clearing, glade **4**
	job, position **6**

opening hours N-PLURAL 複数名詞 **Opening hours** are the times during which a shop, bank, library, or bar is open for business. 営業時間 [mainly BRIT 主に英国英語; AM **business hours** 米国英語 **business hours**]

openly /ˈoʊpənli/ ADV 副詞 If you do something **openly**, you do it without hiding any facts or hiding your feelings. あからさまに ❑ *She openly criticized other athletes.* 彼女は他の競技者たちを公然と批判した。

open market N-SING 単数名詞 Goods that are bought and sold on **the open market** are advertised and sold to anyone who wants to buy them. 公開市場 [BUSINESS 実業] ❑ *On the open market, this would be worth much more.* 公開市場ではこれはもっと高く売れるだろう。

open-minded ADJ 形容詞 If you describe someone as **open-minded**, you approve of them because they are willing to listen to and consider other people's ideas and suggestions. 偏見のない [APPROVAL 賛成] ❑ *He was very open-minded about other people's work.* 彼は他の人々の仕事について全く偏見を持っていなかった。 ● **open-mindedness** N-UNCOUNT 不可算名詞 偏見のなさ ❑ *He was praised for his enthusiasm and his open-mindedness.* 彼は熱心さと偏見のなさを賞された。

open-plan ADJ 形容詞 An **open-plan** building, office, or room has no internal walls dividing it into smaller areas. オープンプランの ❑ *The firm's top managers share the same open-plan office.* その会社の経営幹部たちは同じオープンプランのオフィスを使っている。

Word Link oper ≈ work : cooperate, opera, operation

opera /ˈɒpərə, ˈɒprə/ (**operas**)
Pronounced /ˈɒpərə/ or /ˈoʊpərə/ for meaning **2**.
/ˈoʊpərə/の意味では /ˈoʊpərə/か **2** と発音される。

1 N-VAR 可変性名詞 An **opera** is a play with music in which all the words are sung. オペラ ❑ *...a one-act opera about contemporary women in America.* アメリカの現代女性についての1幕のオペラ ❑ *...an opera singer.* オペラ歌手 **2** → see also **soap opera 3 Opera** is an alternative plural of **opus**. opusの複数形
→ see **music**

operate /ˈɒpəreɪt/ (**operates, operating, operated**) **1** V-T/V-I 他動詞/自動詞 If you **operate** a business or organization, you work to keep it running. If a business or organization **operates**, it carries out its work. 経営する、稼動する ❑ *Until his death in 1986 Greenwood owned and operated an enormous pear orchard.* 1986年に亡くなるまでグリーンウッドは巨大な梨の果樹園を所有し経営していた。 ❑ *...allowing commercial banks to operate in the country.* その国で民間銀行の経営を許して ● **operation** /ˌɒpəˈreɪʃən/ N-UNCOUNT 不可算名詞 経営 ❑ *Company finance is to provide funds for the everyday operation of the business.* 企業財務は事業の日々の経営に資金を提供することである。 **2** V-I 自動詞 The way that something **operates** is the way that it works or has a particular effect. 作動する ❑ *Ceiling and wall lights can operate independently.* 天井と壁の照明は個別に点滅できる。 ❑ *How do accounting records operate?* 会計記録はどのように機能するか。 ● **operation** N-UNCOUNT 不可算名詞 操作 ❑ *No money can be spent on the construction and operation of the streetcar.* 路面電車の建設と運行に使う金は全くありません。 **3** V-T/V-I 他動詞/自動詞 When you **operate** a machine or device, or when it **operates**, you make it work. 操縦する、動く ❑ *A massive rock fall trapped the men as they operated a tunneling machine.* トンネルを掘る機械を操縦

していた時に、作業員たちは巨大な落下岩によって身動きできなくなった。 ● **operation** N-UNCOUNT 不可算名詞 操縦 ❑ *...over 1,000 dials monitoring every aspect of the operation of the airplane.* 航空機操縦のあらゆる局面を監視する1000以上の指示盤 **4** V-I 自動詞 When surgeons **operate on** a patient in a hospital, they cut open a patient's body in order to remove, replace, or repair a diseased or damaged part. 手術を施す ❑ *In March 2005, surgeons operated on Max for a brain aneurysm.* 外科医たちは2005年3月にマックスの脳の動脈瘤（りゅう）を手術した。

V.	function, perform, run, work; (*ant.*) break down, fail **2 3**

Word Partnership *operate* は次の語句と使われる：

N.	operate a business/company, schools operate **1**
	forces operate **1 2**
ADV.	operate efficiently **1**
	operate independently **2**
V.	be allowed to operate, continue to operate **1 2 4**

operatic /ˌɒpəˈrætɪk/ ADJ 形容詞 **Operatic** means relating to opera. オペラの ❑ *...the local amateur operatic society.* 地元のアマチュア・オペラ協会

operating /ˈɒpəreɪtɪŋ/ ADJ 形容詞 **Operating** profits and costs are the money that a company earns and spends in carrying out its ordinary trading activities, in contrast to such things as interest and investment. 営業活動の [BUSINESS 実業] [ADJ n] ❑ *The group made operating profits of $80M before interest.* グループの利払い前営業利益は8000万ドルだった。

operating room (**operating rooms**) N-COUNT 可算名詞 An **operating room** is a special room in a hospital where surgeons carry out medical operations. 手術室

operating system (**operating systems**) N-COUNT 可算名詞 The **operating system** of a computer is its most basic program, which it needs in order to function and run other programs. オペレーティング・システム [COMPUTING コンピューティング] ❑ *...Microsoft's Windows NT operating system.* マイクロソフトのウィンドウNTオペレーティング・システム

operating theatre (**operating theatres**) N-COUNT 可算名詞 An **operating theatre** is the same as an **operating room**. 手術室 [BRIT 英国英語]

operation /ˌɒpəˈreɪʃən/ (**operations**) **1** N-COUNT 可算名詞 An **operation** is a highly organized activity that involves many people doing different things. 作戦 ❑ *The rescue operation began on Friday afternoon.* 救助作戦は金曜の午後に始まった。 ❑ *The soldiers were engaged in a military operation close to the Ugandan border.* 兵隊たちはウガンダ国境近くの軍事作戦に携わっていた。 **2** N-COUNT 可算名詞 A business or company can be referred to as an **operation**. 企業 [BUSINESS 実業] ❑ *Thorn's electronics operation employs around 5,000 people.* ソーンのエレクトロニクス事業の従業員数は約5000人である。 **3** N-COUNT 可算名詞 When a patient has an **operation**, a surgeon cuts open their body in order to remove, replace, or repair a diseased or damaged part. 手術 ❑ *Charles was at the clinic recovering from an operation on his arm.* チャールズは医院で腕の手術から回復中だった。 **4** N-UNCOUNT 不可算名詞 If a system is **in operation**, it is being used. 実施 ❑ *...the free banking system that has been in operation since the early eighties.* 80年代初期から実施されている自由銀行制度 **5** N-UNCOUNT 不可算名詞 If a machine or device is **in operation**, it is working. 稼動 ❑ *There are three ski lifts in operation.* 3つのスキーリフトが稼動中である。 **6** → see also **operative 7** PHRASE 句 When a rule, system, or plan **comes into operation** or you **put** it **into operation**, you begin to use it. 導入される ❑ *The Financial Services Act came into operation four years ago.* 金融サービス法は4年前に導入された。

Word Partnership *operation* は次の語句と使われる：

N.	relief operation, rescue operation **1**
ADJ.	covert operation, massive operation, military operation, undercover operation **1**
	major operation, successful operation **1** – **3**
	emergency operation **1 3**
V.	carry out an operation, plan an operation **1**
	perform an operation **1 3**

operational /ˌɒpəˈreɪʃənəl/ **1** ADJ 形容詞 A machine or piece of equipment that is **operational** is in use or is ready for use. 使用できる ❑ *The whole system will be fully operational by December.* 全システムは12月までに完全に稼動するだろう。 **2** ADJ 形容詞 **Operational** factors or problems relate to the working of a system, device, or plan. 操作上の ❑ *The nuclear industry was required to prove that every operational and safety aspect had been fully researched.* 核産業は操

作と安全の全側面を徹底的に調査したことを証明することが要求された。● op|er|ation|al|ly ADV 副詞 操作上で □ ...goods which are economically or operationally impractical to transport. 経済的あるいは操作上で輸送を実行できない製品

op|er|a|tive /ˈɒpərətɪv, -əreɪtɪv/ (operatives) **1** ADJ 形容詞 A system or service that is **operative** is working or having an effect. 機能的である [FORMAL 形式ばった] □ The commercial telephone service was no longer operative. 商業電話サービスはもはや機能していなかった。 **2** N-COUNT 可算名詞 An **operative** is a worker, especially one who does work with their hands. 工員 [FORMAL 形式ばった] □ In an automated car plant there is not a human operative to be seen. 自動化された自動車工場では工員は1人も見かけられない。 **3** N-COUNT 可算名詞 An **operative** is someone who works for a government agency such as the intelligence service. 秘密情報（ちょうほう）部員 [mainly AM 主に米国英語] □ Naturally the CIA wants to protect its operatives. CIAは当然その諜報部員を保護したがる。 **4** PHRASE 句 If you describe a word as **the operative word**, you want to draw attention to it because you think it is important or exactly true in a particular situation. 重要な意味を持つ語 □ As long as the operative word is "greed," you can't count on people keeping the costs down. 鍵（かぎ）となる言葉が「欲望」である限り，人々が経費を低く抑えておくことは期待できない。

op|er|a|tor /ˈɒpəreɪtər/ (operators) **1** N-COUNT 可算名詞 An **operator** is a person who connects telephone calls at a telephone exchange or in a place such as an office or hotel. 電話交換手 □ He dialed the operator and put in a call to Rome. 彼は交換手に電話してローマに電話をかけた。 **2** N-COUNT 可算名詞 An **operator** is a person who is employed to operate or control a machine. 操作係 □ ...computer operators. コンピュータ操作係 **3** N-COUNT 可算名詞 An **operator** is a person or a company that runs a business. 経営者，事業経営会社 [BUSINESS 実業] □ ...the nation's largest cable TV operator. その国で最大のケーブルテレビ会社 **4** N-COUNT 可算名詞 If you call someone a smooth or shrewd **operator**, you mean that they are skillful at achieving what they want, often in a slightly dishonest way. 抜け目ないやり手 [INFORMAL くだけた] □ He is a smooth operator. Don't underestimate him. 彼は抜け目のないやつだ。やつを見くびるな。

opin|ion /əˈpɪnyən/ (opinions) **1** N-COUNT 可算名詞 Your **opinion** about something is what you think or believe about it. 意見 □ I wasn't asking for your opinion, Mike. マイク，君の意見を聞いているわけではなかった。 □ He held the opinion that a government should think before introducing a tax. 彼は政府が税を導入する前にはよく考えるべきだという意見だった。 **2** N-SING 単数名詞 Your **opinion** of someone is your judgment of their character or ability. 評価 □ That improved Mrs. Goole's already favorable opinion of him. あの結果，グール夫人は彼を従来にも増して高く評価するようになった。 **3** N-UNCOUNT 不可算名詞 You can refer to the beliefs or views that people have as **opinion**. 世論 □ Some, I suppose, might even be in positions to influence opinion. 人によっては世論を左右することがらできるかもしれないと思う。 **4** N-COUNT 可算名詞 An **opinion** from an expert is the advice or judgment that they give you in the subject that they know a lot about. 専門家の意見 □ Even if you have had a regular physical check-up recently, you should still seek a medical opinion. たとえあなたが最近定期的な健康診断を受けていたとしても，なお医者の意見を求めるべきだ。 **5** → see also **public opinion**, **second opinion 6** PHRASE 句 You add expressions such as **"in my opinion"** or **"in their opinion"** to a statement in order to indicate that it is what you or someone else thinks, and is not necessarily a fact. 一の考えでは □ The book is, in Henry's opinion, the best book on the subject. ヘンリーの考えでは，本はその問題について最良の本だ。 **7** PHRASE 句 If someone is **of the opinion that** something is the case, that is what they believe. 一という意見である [FORMAL 形式ばった] □ Frank is of the opinion that Romero should have won. フランクはロメロが勝つべきだったという意見だ。

Thesaurus	opinion また次を参照：
N.	estimation, feeling, judgment, thought, viewpoint **1** – **4**

Word Partnership	opinion は次の語句と使われる：
ADJ.	favorable opinion **1**
	expert opinion, legal opinion, majority opinion, medical opinion **3 4**
V.	express an opinion, give an opinion, share an opinion **1 2**
	ask for an opinion **1 2 4**

opin|ion poll (opinion polls) N-COUNT 可算名詞 An **opinion poll** involves asking people's opinions on a particular subject, especially one concerning politics. 世論調査 □ Nearly three-quarters of people questioned in an opinion poll agreed with the government's decision. 世論調査で質問された人々の4分の3近くが政府の決定に賛成だった。

opium /ˈoʊpiəm/ N-UNCOUNT 不可算名詞 **Opium** is a powerful drug made from the seeds of a type of poppy. Opium is used in medicines that relieve pain or help someone sleep. アヘン

op|po|nent /əˈpoʊnənt/ (opponents) **1** N-COUNT 可算名詞 A politician's **opponents** are other politicians who belong to a different party or who have different aims or policies. 政敵 □ ...Mr. Kennedy's opponent in the leadership contest. 主導権選びにおけるケネディ氏の対抗者 **2** N-COUNT 可算名詞 In a sports contest, your **opponent** is the person who is playing against you. 競争相手 □ Norris twice knocked down his opponent in the early rounds of the fight. ノリスは試合の初期のラウンドで相手を2度ノックダウンした。 **3** N-COUNT 可算名詞 The **opponents of** an idea or policy do not agree with it and do not want it to be carried out. 反対者 □ ...opponents of the spread of nuclear weapons. 核兵器拡散の反対者 → see **chess**

op|por|tun|ist /ˈɒpərtunɪst/ (opportunists) ADJ 形容詞 If you describe someone as **opportunist**, you are critical of them because they take advantage of any situation in order to gain money or power, without considering whether their actions are right or wrong. 日和見主義の [DISAPPROVAL 不賛成] □ ...corrupt and opportunist politicians. 堕落した日和見主義の政治家 ● N-COUNT 可算名詞 An **opportunist** is someone who is opportunist. 日和見主義者 □ Like most successful politicians, Sinclair was an opportunist. シンクレアはたいていの成功した政治家同様に，日和見主義者だった。

op|por|tun|is|tic /ˌɒpərtuˈnɪstɪk/ ADJ 形容詞 If you describe someone's behavior as **opportunistic**, you are critical of them because they take advantage of situations in order to gain money or power, without thinking about whether their actions are right or wrong. 日和見主義の [DISAPPROVAL 不賛成] □ Many of the party's members joined only for opportunistic reasons. 党員の多くは日和見主義的な理由だけで入党した。

op|por|tu|nity /ˌɒpərˈtunɪti/ (opportunities) N-VAR 可変性名詞 An **opportunity** is a situation in which it is possible for you to do something that you want to do. 機会 □ I had an opportunity to go to New York and study. 私にはニューヨークに行って勉強する機会があった。 □ ...equal opportunities in employment. 雇用の均等の機会

Word Partnership	opportunity は次の語句と使われる：
ADJ.	economic opportunity, educational opportunity, equal opportunity, golden opportunity, great opportunity, lost opportunity, rare opportunity, unique opportunity
N.	business opportunity, employment opportunity, investment opportunity
V.	have an opportunity, miss an opportunity, see an opportunity, seize an opportunity, opportunity to speak, take advantage of an opportunity

op|pose /əˈpoʊz/ (opposes, opposing, opposed) V-T 他動詞 If you **oppose** someone or **oppose** their plans or ideas, you disagree with what they want to do and try to prevent them from doing it. 反対する □ Mr. Taylor was not bitter toward those who had opposed him. テイラー氏は彼に反対した人々に憎しみを抱いてはいなかった。

op|posed /əˈpoʊzd/ **1** ADJ 形容詞 If you **are opposed to** something, you disagree with it or disapprove of it. 反対で [v-link ADJ 'to' n/-ing] □ I am utterly opposed to any form of terrorism. 私はどんな種類のテロにもまったく反対だ。 **2** ADJ 形容詞 You say that two ideas or systems are **opposed** when they are opposite to each other or very different from each other. 対立して □ ...people with policies almost diametrically opposed to his own. 彼自身の政策とはほぼ正反対の政策を持つ人々 **3** PHRASE 句 You use **as opposed to** when you want to make it clear that you are talking about one particular thing and not something else. 〜とは対照的に □ We ate in the restaurant, as opposed to the bistro. 我々はビストロではなくそのレストランで食事した。

op|pos|ing /əˈpoʊzɪŋ/ **1** ADJ 形容詞 **Opposing** ideas or tendencies are totally different from each other. 反対の [ADJ n] □ I have a friend who has the opposing view and felt that the war was immoral. 私には，反対の意見を持っていて，その戦争は非道徳的だと感じている友だちがいる。 **2** ADJ 形容詞 **Opposing** groups of people disagree about something or are in competition with one another. 対立する [ADJ n] □ The Georgian leader said in a radio broadcast that he still favored dialogue between the opposing sides. グルジアの指導者はラジオ放送で彼はまだ対立側双方の対話に賛成すると述べた。

op|po|site /ˈɒpəzɪt/ (opposites) **1** PREP 前置詞 If one thing is **opposite** another, it is on the other side of a space from it. 一の反対の位置に □ Jennie had sat opposite her at breakfast. ジェニーは朝食の時に彼女の反対側に座っていた。 ● ADV 副詞 **Opposite** is also an adverb. 反対の位置に □ He looked up at the buildings opposite, but could see no open window. 彼は反対側のビルを見上げたが，開いた窓は見えなかった。 **2** ADJ 形容詞 The **opposite** side or part of something is the side or part that is furthest away from you. 向

こう側の [ADJ n] ❑…*the opposite corner of the room.* 部屋の向こう側の角 ❸ ADJ 形容詞 **Opposite** is used to describe things of the same kind which are completely different in a particular way. For example, north and south are opposite directions, and winning and losing are opposite results in a game. 正反対の ❑*All the cars driving in the opposite direction had their headlights on.* 反対方向に走っている車は全てヘッドライトが点灯されていた。 ❹ N-COUNT 可算名詞 **The opposite of** someone or something is the person or thing that is most different from them. 正反対の人 ❑*Ritter was a very complex man but Marius was the opposite, a simple farmer.* リターはひどく複雑な男だったが、マリウスは正反対で、単純な農夫だった。 ❑*Well, whatever he says you can bet he's thinking the opposite.* いや、彼が何と言おうと、彼は反対のことを考えているに決まっている。

Word Partnership   *opposite* は次の語句と使われる:

ADJ.	**directly** opposite ❶
	exactly (the) opposite, **precisely (the)** opposite, **quite the** opposite ❶ ❸ ❹
	complete opposite, **exact** opposite ❸ ❹
N.	opposite **corner**, opposite **end**, opposite **side** ❷
	opposite **direction**, opposite **effect** ❸
PREP.	**the** opposite **of** *someone/something* ❹

op|po|site sex N-SING 単数名詞 If you are talking about men and refer to **the opposite sex**, you mean women. If you are talking about women and refer to **the opposite sex**, you mean men. 異性 ❑*Body language can also be used to attract members of the opposite sex.* 身体言語は異性を引き付けるのにも使われよう。

op|po|si|tion /ɒpəzɪʃⁿn/ (**oppositions**) ❶ N-UNCOUNT 不可算名詞 **Opposition** is strong, angry, or violent disagreement and disapproval. 反対 ❑*There is bitter opposition from local business to the plan.* その計画には地元の実業界から強い反対がある。 ❷ N-COUNT-COLL 集合可算名詞 **The opposition** is the political parties or groups that are opposed to a government. 野党 ❑*The main opposition parties boycotted the election, saying it would not be conducted fairly.* 主だった野党は公正に行なわれないことを理由に選挙をボイコットした。 ❸ N-COUNT-COLL 集合可算名詞 In countries with a parliament, such as Britain, **the opposition** refers to the politicians or political parties that form part of the parliament, but are not the government. 野党 ❑*…the Leader of the Opposition.* 野党の党首 ❹ N-SING-COLL 集合的単数名詞 **The opposition** is the person or team you are competing against in a sports event. 競争相手 ❑*The coach says his team is not underestimating the opposition.* コーチは彼のチームは相手チームを過小評価はしていないと述べている。

op|press /əpres/ (**oppresses, oppressing, oppressed**) V-T 他動詞 To **oppress** people means to treat them cruelly, or to prevent them from having the same opportunities, freedom, and benefits as others. 迫害する ❑*These people often are oppressed by the governments of the countries they find themselves in.* こうした人々はしばしば住むことになった国の政府の迫害を受ける。

op|pressed /əprest/ 形容詞 People who are **oppressed** are treated cruelly or are prevented from having the same opportunities, freedom, and benefits as others. 抑圧された ❑*Before they took power, they felt oppressed by the white English speakers who controlled things.* 権力を握る前は、彼らは英語を話す白人の支配者に抑圧されていると感じていた。 ● N-PLURAL 複数名詞 **The oppressed** are people who are oppressed. 抑圧されている人々 ❑*…a sense of community with the poor and oppressed.* 貧しくて迫害されている人々の抱く地域社会感

op|pres|sion /əpreʃⁿn/ N-UNCOUNT 不可算名詞 **Oppression** is the cruel or unfair treatment of a group of people. 抑圧、迫害 ❑*…an attempt to escape political oppression.* 政治的迫害から逃げ出す試み

op|pres|sive /əpresɪv/ ❶ ADJ 形容詞 If you describe a society, its laws, or customs as **oppressive**, you think they treat people cruelly and unfairly. 抑圧的な ❑*The new laws will be just as oppressive as those they replace.* 新しい法律は取って代わる法律とちょうど同じくらい抑圧的だろう。 ❷ ADJ 形容詞 If you describe the weather or the atmosphere in a room as **oppressive**, you mean that it is unpleasantly hot and damp. うだるような ❑*The oppressive afternoon heat had tired him out.* うだるような午後の暑さに彼はすっかり疲れてしまった。 ❸ ADJ 形容詞 An **oppressive** situation makes you feel depressed and uncomfortable. 重苦しい ❑*…the oppressive sadness that weighed upon him like a physical pain.* 肉体的苦痛のように彼にのしかかった耐え難い悲しみ

Word Link   *opt ≈ choosing : adopt, opt, optional*

opt /ɒpt/ (**opts, opting, opted**) V-T/V-I 他動詞/自動詞 If you **opt for** something, or **opt to** do something, you choose it or decide to do it in preference to anything else. 選択する ❑*Depending on your circumstances you can opt for one method or the other.* 状況次第で適切な方法を選択できる。

▶ **opt out** PHRASAL VERB 句動詞 If you **opt out of** something, you

choose to be no longer involved in it. 手を引く ❑*The rich can opt out of the public school system.* 富裕層は公立学校制度を利用せずにすむ。

Word Link   *op ≈ eye : optic, optical, optician*

op|tic /ɒptɪk/ ADJ 形容詞 **Optic** means relating to the eyes or to sight. 目の [ADJ n] ❑*The optic nerve is a part of the brain.* 視神経は脳の一部である。
→ see **eye, laser**

op|ti|cal /ɒptɪkəl/ ADJ 形容詞 **Optical** devices, processes, and effects involve or relate to vision, light, or images. 光学の ❑*…optical telescopes.* 光学望遠鏡 ❑*…an optical scanner.* 光学的スキャナー

op|ti|cian /ɒptɪʃⁿn/ (**opticians**) ❶ N-COUNT 可算名詞 An **optician** is someone whose job is to make and sell glasses and contact lenses. 眼鏡商、眼鏡製造業者 ❷ N-COUNT 可算名詞 An **optician** is someone whose job is to test people's eyesight. 検眼士 [BRIT 英国英語; AM **optometrist** 米国英語 **optometrist**] ❸ N-COUNT 可算名詞 An **optician** is a store where you can have your eyes tested and buy glasses and contact lenses. 眼鏡店

op|ti|mal /ɒptɪməl/ → see **optimum**

Word Link   *ism ≈ action or state : communism, optimism, patriotism*

Word Link   *optim ≈ the best : optimism, optimum, optimize*

op|ti|mism /ɒptɪmɪzəm/ N-UNCOUNT 不可算名詞 **Optimism** is the feeling of being hopeful about the future or about the success of something in particular. 楽観主義 ❑*The Indian prime minister has expressed optimism about India's future relations with the U.S.* インドの首相は米国との将来の関係について楽観論を述べた。

op|ti|mist /ɒptɪmɪst/ (**optimists**) N-COUNT 可算名詞 An **optimist** is someone who is hopeful about the future. 楽観主義者 ❑*He has the upbeat manner of an eternal optimist.* 彼の態度は永遠の楽観主義者のように陽気だ。

op|ti|mis|tic /ɒptɪmɪstɪk/ ADJ 形容詞 Someone who is **optimistic** is hopeful about the future or the success of something in particular. 楽観的な ❑*The president says she is optimistic that an agreement can be worked out soon.* 大統領はまもなく合意に達することに楽観的だと言っている。 ● **op|ti|mis|ti|cal|ly** ADV 副詞 [ADV with v] 楽観的に ❑*Both sides have spoken optimistically about the talks.* 両側は話し合いについて楽観的に話した。

op|ti|mize /ɒptɪmaɪz/ (**optimizes, optimizing, optimized**) V-T 他動詞 To **optimize** a plan, system, or machine means to arrange or design it so that it operates as smoothly and efficiently as possible. 最適化する [FORMAL 形式ばった] ❑*The new systems have been optimized for running Microsoft Windows.* 新しいシステムはマイクロソフトのウィンドウズを操作するために最適化されている。

op|ti|mum /ɒptɪməm/ also **optimal** ADJ 形容詞 The **optimum** or **optimal** level or state of something is the best level or state that it could achieve. 最高の [FORMAL 形式ばった] ❑*Try to do some physical activity three times a week for optimum health.* 最高の健康状態を保つために週に3回運動をするようにしなさい。

op|tion /ɒpʃⁿn/ (**options**) ❶ N-COUNT 可算名詞 An **option** is something that you can choose to do in preference to one or more alternatives. 選択肢 ❑*He's argued from the start that the US and its allies are putting too much emphasis on the military option.* 彼は最初から米国と連合国は軍事的選択肢を重視しすぎていると主張してきた。 ❷ N-SING 単数名詞 If you have the **option of** doing something, you can choose whether to do it or not. 選択の自由 ❑*Criminals are given the option of going to jail or facing public humiliation.* 犯罪者は入獄するか公共の場で屈辱を受けるかを選択できる。 ❸ N-COUNT 可算名詞 In business, an **option** is an agreement or contract that gives someone the right to buy or sell something such as property or shares at a future date. オプション [BUSINESS 実業] ❑*Each bank has granted the other an option on 19.9% of its shares.* 各銀行は株式の19.9%へのオプションをお互いに認めた。 ❹ N-COUNT 可算名詞 An **option** is one of a number of subjects which a student can choose to study as a part of his or her course. 選択科目 [mainly BRIT 主に英国英語] ❑*Several options are offered for the student's senior year.* 学生の4学年のために複数の選択科目が提供されている。 ❺ PHRASE 句 If you **keep** your **options open** or **leave** your **options open**, you delay making a decision about something. 選択を保留する ❑*I am keeping my options open; I can decide in a few months.* 私は選択を保留している。数か月後に決められる。

Thesaurus   *option* また次を参照:

N.	alternative, choice, opportunity, preference; *(ant.)* selection ❶ ❷

Word Partnership *option* は次の語句と使われる:

ADJ. **available** option, **best** option, **other** option, **viable** option ① ②
V. **have** an/the option ① ②
choose an option ① ④
option **to buy/purchase**, **exercise** an option ③

Word Link opt ≈ *choosing* : ad*opt*, *opt*, *opt*ional

op|tion|al /ɒpʃənᵊl/ ADJ 形容詞 If something is **optional**, you can choose whether or not you do it or have it. 随意の ❑ *Sex education is a sensitive area for some parents, and thus it should remain optional.* 性教育は一部の親にとって微妙な分野なので、随意のままにしておくべきだ。

Word Link ulent ≈ *full of* : fraud*ulent*, op*ulent*, vir*ulent*

opu|lent /ɒpyələnt/ ADJ 形容詞 **Opulent** things or places look grand and expensive. 豪華な、華やかな [FORMAL 形式ばった] ❑ *Heavy silverplate adds an opulent touch to a formal dinner party.* 重厚な銀の皿は正式なディナーパーティに豪華感を添える。 ● **opu|lence** N-UNCOUNT 不可算名詞 豪華さ ❑ *...the elegant opulence of the embassy.* 大使館のエレガントな華やかさ

or /ər, STRONG ɔːr/ ① CONJ 接続詞 You use **or** to link two or more alternatives. または ❑ *"Tea or coffee?" John asked.* 「紅茶それともコーヒー」とジョンは聞いた。 ② CONJ 接続詞 You use **or** to say soon as he reached the Canary Islands.* 彼はカナリア諸島に到着次第、手紙を書くか電話をかけると言った。 ② CONJ 接続詞 You use **or** to give another alternative, when the first alternative is introduced by "either" or "whether." あるいは ❑ *Items like bread, milk and meat were either unavailable or could be obtained only on the black market.* パン、牛乳、肉などの食品は手に入らないか、闇市場のみで入手できた。

You do not use **or** after **neither**. You use **nor** instead. ❑ *He speaks neither English nor German.*

③ CONJ 接続詞 You use **or** between two numbers to indicate that you are giving an approximate amount. ～かそれとも ❑ *Everyone benefited from limiting their intake of coffee to just one or two cups a day.* コーヒーを1日に1杯か2杯までにしておくことで全員が恩恵を受けた。 ❑ *When I was nine or ten someone explained to me that when you are grown up you have to work.* 私が9歳か10歳の頃、だれかが私に大人になったら働かなければならないと説明してくれた。 ④ CONJ 接続詞 You use **or** to introduce a comment which corrects or modifies what you have just said. いや ❑ *The man was a fool, he thought, or at least incompetent.* その男は馬鹿だ、いや少なくとも無能だと彼は思った。 ⑤ CONJ 接続詞 If you say that someone should do something **or** something bad will happen, you are warning them that if they do not do it, the bad thing will happen. さもないと ❑ *She had to have the operation, or she would die.* 彼女は手術を受ける必要があった。さもないと死んでしまうだろう。 ⑥ CONJ 接続詞 You use **or** to introduce something which is evidence for the truth of a statement you have just made. でなければ ❑ *He must have thought Jane was worth it or he wouldn't have wasted time on her, I suppose.* 彼はジェインにはそれだけの値打ちがあると考えたに違いない。そうでなければ彼女に時間を浪費していなかっただろうと私は思う。 ⑦ PHRASE 句 You use **or not** to emphasize that a particular thing makes no difference to what is going to happen. ～せずとも [EMPHASIS 強調] ❑ *I like it or not, you're in charge.* 好もうと好むまいと君が責任者だ。 ⑧ PHRASE 句 You use **or no** between two occurrences of the same noun in order to say that whether something is true or not makes no difference to a situation. ～せずとも ❑ *The next day, rain or no rain, it was business as usual.* 翌日は雨が降ろうと降るまいと通常通りの商売だった。 ⑨ **or else**→ see **else** ⑩ **or other**→ see **other** ⑪ **or so**→ see **so** ⑫ **or something**→ see **something**

Word Web orchestra

The modern **symphony orchestra** usually has from 60 to 100 **musicians**. The largest group of musicians are in the **string** section. It gives the orchestra its rich, flowing sound. String **instruments** include **violins**, **violas**, **cellos**, and usually **double basses**. **Flutes**, **oboes**, **clarinets**, and **bassoons** make up the woodwind section. The **brass** section is usually quite small. Too much of this sound could overwhelm the more delicate strings. Brass **instruments** include the French horn, **trumpet**, **trombone**, and tuba. The size of the **percussion** section depends on the **composition** being performed. However, there is almost always a timpani player.

oral /ɔːrəl/ (orals) ① ADJ 形容詞 **Oral** communication is spoken rather than written. 口頭の ❑ *...the written and oral traditions of ancient cultures.* 古代文化の文書と口承の伝統 ● **oral|ly** ADV 副詞 [ADV after v] 口頭で ❑ *...their ability to present ideas orally and in writing.* 発想を口頭および文書で発表する彼らの能力 ② N-COUNT 可算名詞 An **oral** is an examination, especially in a foreign language, that is spoken rather than written. 口頭試問 ❑ *I spoke privately to the candidate after the oral.* 私は口頭試問の後でその志願者に個人的に話をした。 ③ ADJ 形容詞 You use **oral** to indicate that something is done with a person's mouth or relates to a person's mouth. 口腔（こうこう）の ❑ *...good oral hygiene.* 良い口腔衛生 ● **oral|ly** ADV 副詞 経口で ❑ *...antibiotic tablets taken orally.* 抗生物質の経口剤

or|ange /ɔːrɪndʒ/ (oranges) ① COLOR 色彩語 Something that is **orange** is of a color between red and yellow. オレンジ色の ❑ *...men in bright orange uniforms.* 鮮やかなオレンジ色の制服姿の男たち ② N-VAR 可変性名詞 An **orange** is a round juicy fruit with a thick, orange-colored skin. オレンジ ❑ *...orange trees.* オレンジの木 → see **color**, **rainbow**

ora|tory /ɔːrətɔːri/ (oratories) ① N-UNCOUNT 不可算名詞 **Oratory** is the art of making formal speeches that strongly affect people's feelings and beliefs. 雄弁、雄弁術 [FORMAL 形式ばった] ❑ *He displayed determination as well as powerful oratory.* 彼は力強い雄弁さと共に決意を示した。 ② N-COUNT 可算名詞 An **oratory** is a room or building where Christians go to pray. 祈祷（きとう）室 [mainly BRIT 主に英国英語]

or|bit /ɔːrbɪt/ (orbits, orbiting, orbited) ① N-COUNT 可算名詞 An **orbit** is the curved path in space that is followed by an object going around and around a planet, moon, or star. 軌道 [also 'in/into' N] ❑ *Mars and Earth have orbits which change with time.* 火星と地球は時の流れとともに変る軌道を持っている。 ② V-T 他動詞 If something such as a satellite **orbits** a planet, moon, or sun, it moves around it in a continuous, curving path. 軌道に乗って回る ❑ *In 1957 the Soviet Union launched the first satellite to orbit the earth.* 1957年にソ連は地球の周りを軌道に乗って回る最初の人工衛星を打ち上げた。 → see **satellite**, **solar**

or|chard /ɔːrtʃərd/ (orchards) N-COUNT 可算名詞 An **orchard** is an area of land on which fruit trees are grown. 果樹園 → see **barn**

or|ches|tra /ɔːrkɪstrə/ (orchestras) ① N-COUNT 可算名詞 An **orchestra** is a large group of musicians who play a variety of different instruments together. Orchestras usually play classical music. オーケストラ ❑ *...the Los Angeles Philharmonic Orchestra.* ロサンジェルス交響楽団 ② → see also **symphony orchestra** ③ N-SING 単数名詞 The **orchestra** or the **orchestra seats** in a theater or concert hall are the seats on the first floor directly in front of the stage. 1等席 [mainly AM 主に米国英語] ❑ *With the balcony blocked off, patrons filled most of the orchestra seats.* バルコニーが使用できないため、聴衆は1等席の大半をふさいだ。 → see Word Web: **orchestra**

or|ches|tral /ɔːrkɛstrəl/ ADJ 形容詞 **Orchestral** means relating to an orchestra and the music it plays. オーケストラの [ADJ n] ❑ *...an orchestral concert.* 管弦楽団のコンサート

or|ches|trate /ɔːrkɪstreɪt/ (orchestrates, orchestrating, orchestrated) V-T 他動詞 If you say that someone **orchestrates** an event or situation, you mean that they carefully organize it in a way that will produce the result that they want. 組織化する ❑ *The colonel was able to orchestrate a rebellion from inside an army jail.* その大佐は軍の留置所内部から反乱を組織化することができた。 ● **or|ches|tra|tion** N-UNCOUNT 不可算名詞 組織化 ❑ *...his skilful orchestration of latent nationalist feeling.* 彼が潜在的な国家主義的感情をうまく組織化したこと

or|ches|tra|tion /ɔːrkɪstreɪʃᵊn/ (orchestrations) N-COUNT 可算

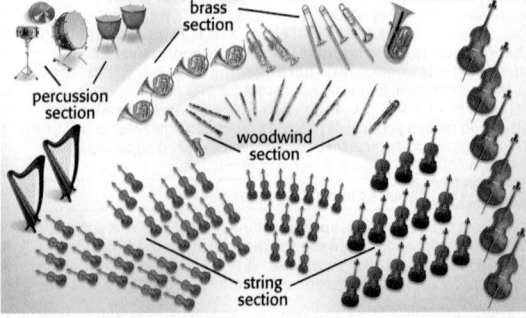
brass section
percussion section
woodwind section
string section

名詞 An **orchestration** is a piece of music that has been rewritten so that it can be played by an orchestra. 管弦楽 ❏ *Mahler's own imaginative orchestration was heard in the same concert.* マーラー独自の想像性に富んだ管弦楽は同じコンサートで聴かれた.

or|chid /ɔrkɪd/ (**orchids**) N-COUNT 可算名詞 **Orchids** are plants with brightly colored, unusually shaped flowers. ラン

or|dain /ɔrdeɪn/ (**ordains, ordaining, ordained**) ① V-T 他動詞 When someone **is ordained**, they are made a member of the clergy in a religious ceremony. 牧師に任命する ❏ *He was ordained a Catholic priest in 1982.* 彼は1982年にカソリックの牧師となった. ❏ *Women have been ordained for many years in the Presbyterian Church.* 長老派教会では女性は永年にわたって牧師に任命されてきた. ② V-T 他動詞 If some authority or power **ordains** something, they decide that it should happen or be in existence. 定める [FORMAL 形式ばった] ❏ *Nehru ordained that socialism should rule.* ネルーは社会主義が支配すべきだと定めた. ❏ *His rule was ordained by heaven.* 彼の支配は天によって定められた.

or|deal /ɔrdil/ (**ordeals**) N-COUNT 可算名詞 If you describe an experience or situation as an **ordeal**, you think it is difficult and stressful. 厳しい試練 ❏ *...the painful ordeal of the last eight months.* 過去8か月間のつらい試練

---

order

❶ SUBORDINATING CONJUNCTION USES

❷ COMMANDS AND REQUESTS

❸ ARRANGEMENTS, SITUATIONS, AND GROUPINGS

---

❶ **or|der** /ɔrdər/ ① PHRASE 句 If you do something **in order to** achieve a particular thing or **in order that** something can happen, you do it because you want to achieve that thing. 〜するために ❏ *Most schools are extremely unwilling to cut down on staff in order to cut costs.* 大半の学校は経費を削減するために職員数を減らすことに非常に消極的だ. ② PHRASE 句 If someone must be in a particular situation **in order to** achieve something they want, they cannot achieve that thing if they are not in that situation. 〜するために ❏ *We need to get rid of the idea that we must be liked all the time in order to be worthwhile.* 我々は値打ちのある人間になるためには常に人に好かれなければならないという考えを捨てる必要がある. ③ PHRASE 句 If something must happen **in order for** something else to happen, the second thing cannot happen if the first thing does not happen. (人・物が)〜するために ❏ *In order for their computers to trace a person's records, they need both the name and address of the individual.* コンピュータで人物の記録を追跡するにはその個人の名前と住所の両方が必要だ.

❷ **or|der** /ɔrdər/ (**orders, ordering, ordered**) ⇨ Please look at meaning ⑫ to see if the expression you are looking for is shown under another headword. ① V-T 他動詞 If a person in authority **orders** someone **to** do something, they tell them to do it. 命じる ❏ *Williams ordered him to leave.* ウィリアムズは彼に出て行くよう命じた. ② V-T 他動詞 If someone in authority **orders** something, they give instructions that it should be done. 命令する ❏ *The president has ordered a full investigation.* 大統領は徹底的な調査を行なうよう命じた. ③ N-COUNT 可算名詞 If someone in authority gives you an **order**, they tell you to do something. 命令 ❏ *The activists were shot when they refused to obey an order to halt.* 活動家たちは止まれという命令に従うのを拒否した時に撃たれた. ❏ *As darkness fell, Clinton gave orders for his men to rest.* 夜が更けたので、クリントンは部下たちが休むよう命令を出した. ④ N-COUNT 可算名詞 A court **order** is a legal instruction stating that something must be done. ❏ *She has decided not to appeal against a court order banning her from keeping animals.* 彼女は動物を飼うのを禁止する裁判所の命令を上訴しないことに決めた. ⑤ V-T/V-I 他動詞/自動詞 When you **order** something that you are going to pay for, you ask for it to be brought to you, sent to you, or obtained for you. 注文する ❏ *The couple ordered a new set of sterling silver rings from Tiffany for $200 each.* そのカップルは１つ200ドルの新しいおそろいの純銀の指輪をティファニーに注文した. ❏ *The waitress arrived. "Are you ready to order?"* ウェイトレスが現われ「ご注文は決まりましたか」と言った. ⑥ N-COUNT 可算名詞 An **order** is a request for something to be brought, made, or obtained for you in return for money. 注文 ❏ *The city is going to place an order for a hundred and eighty-eight buses.* 市は188台のバスを注文しようとしているところだ. ⑦ N-COUNT 可算名詞 Someone's **order** is what they have asked to be brought, made, or obtained for them in return for money. 注文の品 ❏ *The waiter returned with their order and Graham signed the bill.* ウェイターは彼らの注文の品を持って戻り、グレアムは伝票にサインした. ⑧ → see also **mail order**, **postal order** ⑨ PHRASE 句 Something that is **on order** at a store or factory has been asked for but has not yet been supplied. 注文中で ❏ *The airlines still have 2,500 new planes on order.* 航空会社はまだ2500機の新しい航空機を発注中である. ⑩ PHRASE 句 If you do something **to order**, you do it whenever you are asked to do it. 注文に応じて ❏ *She now makes wonderful dried flower arrangements to*

order. 彼女は今や注文に応じて素晴らしいドライフラワーのアレンジをしている. ⑪ PHRASE 句 If you are **under orders to** do something, you have been told to do it by someone in authority. 命令を受けて ❏ *I am under orders not to discuss his mission or his location with anyone.* 私は彼の使命や居場所を誰とも話し合わないようにとの命令を受けている. ⑫ **a tall order** → see **tall**

▶ **order around** PHRASAL VERB 句動詞 If you say that someone is **ordering** you **around**, you mean they are telling you to do things as if they have authority over you, and you dislike this. こき使う ❏ *When we're out he gets really bossy and starts ordering me around.* 私たちが外出する時は、彼は全く威張りくさって私をあれこれとこき使う.

Thesaurus   *order* また次を参照:

V.	charge, command, direct, tell ❷ ①
	buy, request ❷ ⑤
N.	command, direction, instruction ❷ ③ ④

---

❸ **or|der** /ɔrdər/ (**orders, ordering, ordered**) ⇨ Please look at meaning ⑮ to see if the expression you are looking for is shown under another headword. ① N-UNCOUNT 不可算名詞 If a set of things are arranged or done in a particular **order**, they are arranged or done so one thing follows another, often according to a particular factor such as importance. 順序 [also 'a' N] ❏ *Write down (in order of priority) the qualities you'd like to have.* 優先順位に従って自分が持ちたい資質を書きなさい. ❏ *Music shops should arrange their recordings in simple alphabetical order, rather than by category.* 音楽店は種類別ではなく単純なアルファベット順にレコード類を配置すべきだ. ② N-UNCOUNT 不可算名詞 **Order** is the situation that exists when everything is in the correct or expected place, or happens at the correct or expected time. 秩序 ❏ *The wish to impose order upon confusion is a kind of intellectual instinct.* 混乱状態に秩序を押し付けたいという望みはある種の知的本能である. ③ N-UNCOUNT 不可算名詞 **Order** is the situation that exists when people obey the law and do not fight or riot. 治安 ❏ *Troops were sent to the islands to restore order last November.* 昨年の11月にその島々に治安を回復するために軍隊が派遣された. ④ N-SING 単数名詞 When people talk about a particular **order**, they mean the way society is organized at a particular time. 体制, 秩序 ❏ *The end of the Cold War has produced the prospect of a new world order based on international co-operation.* 冷戦の終結は国際協力に基づいた新しい世界秩序の期待を生み出している. ⑤ V-T 他動詞 The way that something **is ordered** is the way that it is organized and structured. 整理する ❏ *...a society which is ordered by hierarchy.* 階級性で構成された社会 ❏ *We know the French order things differently.* 我々はフランス人は物事を異なった方法で整理することを知っている. ⑥ N-COUNT 可算名詞 A religious **order** is a group of monks or nuns who live according to a particular set of rules. 修道会 ❏ *...the Benedictine order of monks.* ベネディクト修道士会 ⑦ → see also **law and order** ⑧ PHRASE 句 If you put or keep something **in order**, you make sure that it is neat or well organized. 整然とした ❏ *Now he has a chance to put his life back in order.* 今や彼は生活を整然としたものに戻す機会だ. ⑨ PHRASE 句 If you think something is **in order**, you think it should happen or be provided. 適切な ❏ *Reforms are clearly in order.* 改革は明らかに適切だ. ⑩ PHRASE 句 You use **in the order of** or **on the order of** when mentioning an approximate figure. 約〜の ❏ *They borrowed something in the order of $10 million.* 彼らは1000万ドルほどの金を借りた. ⑪ PHRASE 句 If something is **in good order**, it is in good condition. 良好な状態で ❏ *The vessel's safety equipment was not in good order.* その船の安全装置は良好な状態ではなかった. ⑫ PHRASE 句 A machine or device that is **in working order** is functioning properly and is not broken. 調子よく動いている ❏ *Only half of the spacecraft's six science instruments are still in working order.* その宇宙船の6つの科学機器の半分だけがまだ調子よく動いている. ⑬ PHRASE 句 A machine or device that is **out of order** is broken and does not work. 故障した ❏ *Their phone's out of order.* 彼らの電話は故障中だ. ⑭ PHRASE 句 If you say that someone or their behavior is **out of order**, you mean that their behavior is unacceptable. 不適切な [INFORMAL くだけた] ❏ *Kent, you're out of order.* ケント、君の態度は不適切だ. ⑮ to **put** your **house in order** → see **house** ⑯ **order of magnitude** → see **magnitude**

or|der book (**order books**) N-COUNT 可算名詞 When you talk about the state of a company's **order book** or **order books**, you are talking about how many orders for their goods the company has. 注文帳 [BRIT 英国英語, BUSINESS 実業]

or|der|ly /ɔrdərli/ (**orderlies**) ① ADJ 形容詞 If something is done in an **orderly** fashion or manner, it is done in a well-organized and controlled way. 規律正しい ❏ *The organizers guided them in an orderly fashion out of the building.* 組織者たちは彼らを混乱なく建物の外に導いた. ② ADJ 形容詞 Something that is **orderly** is neat or arranged in a neat way. 整然とした ❏ *It's a beautiful, clean and orderly city.* それは美しく清潔で整然とした町である. ● **or|der|li|ness** N-UNCOUNT 不可算名詞 整然さ ❏ *A balance is achieved in the painting between orderliness and unpredictability.* その絵画は整然さと意外さの間のバランスが取れている. ③ N-COUNT 可算

名詞 An **orderly** is a person who works in a hospital and does jobs that do not require special medical training. 病院の雑役夫 □*For most of his life, he was a hospital orderly.* 彼は人生の大半を病院の雑役夫として過ごした.

or|di|nance /ˈɔːrdᵊnəns/ (**ordinances**) N-COUNT 可算名詞 An **ordinance** is an official rule or order, especially from a local government. 法令 □ [FORMAL 形式ばった] □ *...ordinances that restrict building development.* 建造物の開発を制限する法令

or|di|nari|ly /ˌɔːrdᵊnˈɛrɪli/ ADV 副詞 If you say what is **ordinarily** the case, you are saying what is normally the case. 通常 □ *The streets would ordinarily have been full of people, but now they were empty.* 通りはどこも通常は人々で一杯だったろうが, 今や空っぱだった.

or|di|nary /ˈɔːrdᵊnɛri/ ■ ADJ 形容詞 **Ordinary** people or things are normal and not special or different in any way. 普通の □ *I strongly suspect that most ordinary people would agree with me.* 大半の普通の人々は私に同意するだろうと私は強く思っている. □ *It has 25 calories less than ordinary ice cream.* それは普通のアイスクリームより25カロリー少ない. ■ PHRASE 句 Something that is **out of the ordinary** is unusual or different. 普通でない □ *The boy's knowledge was out of the ordinary.* その少年の知識は並外れていた.

Thesaurus	*ordinary* また次を参照:
ADJ.	common, everyday, normal, regular, standard, typical, usual; (*ant.*) abnormal, unusual ■

Word Partnership	*ordinary* は次の語句と使われる:
N.	ordinary **Americans**, ordinary **circumstances**, ordinary **citizens**, ordinary **day**, ordinary **expenses**, ordinary **folk**, ordinary **life**, ordinary **people**, ordinary **person** ■
PREP.	**out of the** ordinary ■

or|di|nary shares N-PLURAL 複数名詞 **Ordinary shares** are shares in a company that are owned by people who have a right to vote at the company's meetings and to receive part of the company's profits after the holders of preference shares have been paid. Compare **preference shares**. 普通株 [BRIT 英国英語 BUSINESS 実業] [AM **common stock** 米国英語 **common stock**]

or|di|na|tion /ˌɔːrdᵊnˈeɪʃᵊn/ (**ordinations**) N-VAR 可変化詞 When someone's **ordination** takes place, they are made a minister, priest, or rabbi. 聖職授任 □ *...supporters of the ordination of women.* 女性に聖職位を授与することの支持者

ore /ɔːr/ (**ores**) N-MASS 質量名詞 **Ore** is rock or earth from which metal can be obtained. 鉱石 □ *...a huge iron ore mine.* 巨大な鉄鉱石の炭鉱

→ see **metal**

or|gan /ˈɔːrgən/ (**organs**) ■ N-COUNT 可算名詞 An **organ** is a part of your body that has a particular purpose or function, for example, your heart or lungs. 臓器 □ *...damage to the muscles and internal organs.* 筋肉と内臓への損傷 □ *...the reproductive organs.* 生殖器 ■ N-COUNT 可算名詞 An **organ** is a large musical instrument with pipes of different lengths through which air is forced. It has keys and pedals like a piano. オルガン □ *...the church organ.* 教会のオルガン ■ N-COUNT 可算名詞 You refer to a newspaper or organization as **the organ of** the government or another group when it is used by them as a means of giving information or getting things done. 機関誌 □ *...according to the People's Daily, the official organ of the Chinese communist party.* 中国共産党の公式機関誌である『人民日報』によると

→ see **donor, keyboard, nervous system**

or|gan|ic /ɔːrˈgænɪk/ ■ ADJ 形容詞 **Organic** methods of farming and gardening do not use pesticides, chemical fertilizers, growth hormones, or antibiotics, so that the food produced does not contain toxic chemicals. 有機栽培の □ *Organic farming is expanding everywhere.* 有機農業はいたる所で拡大している. ● **or|gani|cal|ly** ADV 副詞 有機的に □ *...organically grown vegetables.* 有機栽培された野菜

Food that is produced without chemicals is called **organic** or **natural** food. Organic food was once sold only in special shops known as **health food stores** at high prices. These days some of these foods and other low-impact products are sold in ordinary supermarkets.

■ ADJ 形容詞 **Organic** substances are produced by or found in living things. 有機の □ *Incorporating organic material into chalky soils will reduce the alkalinity.* 有機物質を白亜質の土壌に混ぜるとアルカリ度が減少するであろう. ■ ADJ 形容詞 **Organic** change or development happens gradually and naturally rather than suddenly. 系統的な [FORMAL 形式ばった] □ *...to manage the company and supervise its organic growth.* 会社を経営し, その系統的な成長を監督すること

or|gani|sa|tion /ˌɔːrgənaɪˈzeɪʃᵊn/ → see **organization**

or|gani|sa|tion|al /ˌɔːrgənaɪˈzeɪʃᵊnᵊl/ → see **organizational**

or|gan|ise /ˈɔːrgənaɪz/ → see **organize**

or|gan|ism /ˈɔːrgənɪzəm/ (**organisms**) N-COUNT 可算名詞 An **organism** is an animal or plant, especially one that is so small that you cannot see it without using a microscope. 生物, 微生物 □ *Not all chemicals normally present in living organisms are harmless.* 生きている生物に普通存在する化学物質はすべてが無害というわけではない.

or|gan|ist /ˈɔːrgənɪst/ (**organists**) N-COUNT 可算名詞 An **organist** is someone who plays the organ. オルガン奏者

or|gani|za|tion /ˌɔːrgənaɪˈzeɪʃᵊn/ (**organizations**) ■ N-COUNT 可算名詞 An **organization** is an official group of people, for example, a political party, a business, a charity, or a club. 団体 □ *Most of the food for the homeless is provided by voluntary organizations.* ホームレスの人々のための食料は大半がボランティア団体によって提供される. ■ N-UNCOUNT 不可算名詞 The **organization** of an event or activity involves making all the necessary arrangements for it. 組織化 □ *...the exceptional attention to detail that goes into the organization of this event.* この行事を組織するために細部にわたって払われた特別な注意 ■ N-UNCOUNT 不可算名詞 The **organization** of something is the way in which its different parts are arranged or relate to each other. 構成 □ *I am aware that the organization of the book leaves something to be desired.* 私はその本の構成には遺憾な点があることは分かっている.

or|gani|za|tion|al /ˌɔːrgənaɪˈzeɪʃᵊnᵊl/ ■ ADJ 形容詞 **Organizational** abilities and methods relate to the way that work, activities, or events are planned and arranged. 組織の [ADJ n] □ *Evelyn's excellent organizational skills were soon spotted by her employers.* イブリンの雇用者たちはまもなく彼女の素晴らしい組織力に気づいた. ■ ADJ 形容詞 **Organizational** means relating to the structure of an organization. 構成的な [ADJ n] □ *The police now recognize that big organizational changes are needed.* 警察は今や大きな機構的な変化が必要なことを認識している. ■ ADJ 形容詞 **Organizational** means relating to organizations, rather than individuals. 組織の [ADJ n] □ *This problem needs to be dealt with at an organizational level.* この問題は組織的なレベルで取り組む必要がある.

or|gan|ize /ˈɔːrgənaɪz/ (**organizes, organizing, organized**) ■ V-T 他動詞 If you **organize** an event or activity, you make sure that the necessary arrangements are made. 計画する, 準備する □ *In the end, we all decided to organize a concert for Easter.* 結局, 我々は全員復活祭のコンサートを計画することに決めた. □ *...a two-day meeting organized by the United Nations.* 国連が計画した2日間にわたる会議 ■ V-T 他動詞 If you **organize** something that someone wants or needs, you make sure that it is provided. 調達する, 手配する □ *I will organize transportation.* 私が交通を手配します. ■ V-T 他動詞 If you **organize** a set of things, you arrange them in an ordered way or give them a structure. 整理する □ *He began to organize his materials.* 彼は材料をまとめ始めた. □ *She took a hasty cup of coffee and tried to organize her scattered thoughts.* 彼女は急いでコーヒーを飲み, 取り留めのない考えをまとめようとした. ■ V-T 他動詞 If you **organize** yourself, you plan your work and activities in an ordered, efficient way. 切り盛りする □ *...changing the way you organize yourself.* 自分の計画の準備のやり方を変えて □ *Go right ahead, I'm sure you don't need me to organize you.* さあ進めてください. あなたは私なしでも切り盛りできることは分かっています.

Thesaurus	*organize* また次を参照:
V.	coordinate, plan, set up ■ arrange, line up, straighten out ■

or|ga|nized /ˈɔːrgənaɪzd/ ■ ADJ 形容詞 An **organized** activity or group involves a number of people doing something together in a structured way, rather than doing it by themselves. 組織化された [ADJ n] □ *...organized groups of art thieves.* 組織化された美術品泥棒の集団 □ *organized religion.* 組織化された宗教 ■ ADJ 形容詞 Someone who is **organized** plans their work and activities efficiently. 切り盛りの上手な □ *These people are very efficient, very organized, and excellent time managers.* こうした人々は非常に効率的で, 切り盛りがうまく時間を管理するのが上手だ.

or|gan|iz|er /ˈɔːrgənaɪzər/ (**organizers**) ■ N-COUNT 可算名詞 The **organizer** of an event or activity is the person who makes sure that the necessary arrangements are made. 組織者 □ *He became an organizer for the Democratic Party.* 彼は民主党の組織者になった. ■ → see also **personal organizer**

→ see **union**

or|gasm /ˈɔːrgæzəm/ (**orgasms**) N-VAR 可変化名詞 An **orgasm** is the moment of greatest pleasure and excitement in sexual activity. オルガスム □ *...the ability to reach orgasm.* オルガスムに達する能力

orgy /ˈɔːrdʒi/ (**orgies**) N-COUNT 可算名詞 An **orgy** is a party in which people behave in a very uncontrolled way, especially one involving sexual activity. 乱交パーティ □ *It was reminiscent of a*

scene from a Roman orgy. それは古代ローマの乱交パーティを連想させた.

ori|en|tal /ɔːriɛntəl/ ADJ 形容詞 **Oriental** means coming from or associated with eastern Asia, especially China and Japan. 東洋の □ *There were Oriental carpets on the floors.* 床には東洋風のカーペットが敷いてあった.

ori|en|tat|ed /ɔːriɛnteɪtɪd/ **Orientated** means the same as **oriented.,** orientedと同意

ori|en|ta|tion /ɔːriɛnteɪʃən/ (**orientations**) **1** N-VAR 可変性名詞 If you talk about the **orientation** of an organization or country, you are talking about the kinds of aims and interests it has. 方針, 方向付け □ *To a society which has lost its orientation he has much to offer.* 方向性を失った社会に彼は沢山のものを提供できる. **2** N-VAR 可変性名詞 Someone's **orientation** is their basic beliefs or preferences. 志向 □ *...legislation that would have made discrimination on the basis of sexual orientation illegal.* 性的志向に基づく差別を非合法にしていたであろう法律 **3** N-UNCOUNT 不可算名詞 **Orientation** is basic information or training that is given to people starting a new job, school, or course. オリエンテーション □ *They give their new employees a day or two of orientation.* 新社員は1～2日のオリエンテーションを受ける. **4** N-COUNT 可算名詞 The **orientation** of a structure or object is the direction it faces. 方位 □ *Farnese had the orientation of the church changed so that the front would face a square.* ファルネーゼは正面が広場に面するようにその教会の方位を変えさせた.

ori|ent|ed /ɔːriɛntɪd/

> The form **orientated** is also used.
>
> **orientated** 形も使われる.

ADJ 形容詞 If someone **is oriented toward** or **oriented to a** particular thing or person, they are mainly concerned with that thing or person. 志向の [v-link ADJ 'toward/to' n] □ *It seems almost inevitable that North African economies will still be primarily oriented toward Europe.* 北アフリカ諸国の経済がまだ主に欧州志向となることはほぼ避けられないようだ.

ori|gin /ɔːrɪdʒɪn/ (**origins**) **1** N-COUNT 可算名詞 You can refer to the beginning, cause, or source of something as its **origin** or **origins**. 起源 □ *...theories about the origin of life.* 生命の起源に関する諸学説 □ *Their medical problems are basically physical in origin.* 彼らの医療問題は基本的には起源的に肉体的なものである. **2** N-COUNT 可算名詞 When you talk about a person's **origin** or **origins**, you are referring to the country, race, or living conditions of their parents or ancestors. 生まれ, 素性 [usu poss N, also 'of/in' N] □ *Thomas has not forgotten his humble origins.* トマスは貧しい家に生まれたことを忘れたことはない. □ *...people of Asian origin.* アジア系の人々

<table>
<tr><td colspan="2">**Word Partnership**   *origin* は次の語句と使われる:</td></tr>
<tr><td>N.</td><td>origin **of life**, **point of** origin, origin **of the universe 1**
country of origin, **family of** origin **2**</td></tr>
<tr><td>ADJ.</td><td>**unknown** origin **1 2**
ethnic origin, **Hispanic** origin, **national** origin **2**</td></tr>
</table>

origi|nal /ɔːrɪdʒɪnəl/ (**originals**) **1** ADJ 形容詞 You use **original** when referring to something that existed at the beginning of a process or activity, or the characteristics that something had when it began or was made. 最初の [det ADJ] □ *The original plan was to go by bus.* 最初の計画はバスで行く予定だった. **2** N-COUNT 可算名詞 If something such as a document, a work of art, or a piece of writing is an **original**, it is not a copy or a later version. 本物 □ *When you have filled in the questionnaire, copy it and send the original to your employer.* アンケートに記入したらコピーをとり, もとの物をあなたの雇用主に送りなさい. **3** ADJ 形容詞 An **original** document or work of art is not a copy. 本物の □ *...an original movie poster.* 本物の映画ポスター **4** ADJ 形容詞 An **original** piece of writing or music was written recently and has not been published or performed before. 新作の □ *...with catchy original songs by Richard Warner.* リチャード・ワーナーが作曲した覚えやすい新曲 **5** ADJ 形容詞 If you describe someone or their work as **original**, you mean that they are very imaginative and have new ideas. 独創的な [APPROVAL 賛成] □ *It is one of the most original works of imagination in the language.* それはその言語で最も独創的な創作の1つである. ● **origi|nal|ity** /ɔːrɪdʒɪnælɪti/ N-UNCOUNT 不可算名詞 独創性 □ *He was capable of writing things of startling originality.* 彼は驚くほどの独創性に富んだ物事を書くことができた.

<table>
<tr><td colspan="2">**Thesaurus**   *original* また次を参照:</td></tr>
<tr><td>ADJ.</td><td>early, first, initial **1 2**
authentic, genuine **3**
creative, unique **5**</td></tr>
<tr><td>N.</td><td>master; (*ant.*) copy **2**</td></tr>
</table>

origi|nal|ly /ɔːrɪdʒɪnəli/ ADV 副詞 When you say what happened or was the case **originally**, you are saying what happened or was the case when something began or came into existence, often to contrast it with what happened later. 初めは □ *The plane has been kept in service far longer than originally intended.* その航空機は最初の予定よりずっと長期間にわたって就航されている.

origi|nate /ɔːrɪdʒɪneɪt/ (**originates, originating, originated**) V-T/V-I 他動詞/自動詞 When something **originates** or when someone **originates** it, it begins to happen or exist. 始める, 始まる [FORMAL 形式ばった] □ *The disease originated in Africa.* その病気はアフリカで発生した. □ *All carbohydrates originate from plants.* 全ての炭水化物は植物から生じる.

or|na|ment /ɔːrnəmənt/ (**ornaments**) **1** N-COUNT 可算名詞 An **ornament** is an attractive object that you display in your home or in your garden. 装飾品 □ *...a shelf containing a few photographs and ornaments.* 数枚の写真と装飾品が入っている棚 **2** N-UNCOUNT 不可算名詞 Decorations and patterns on a building or a piece of furniture can be referred to as **ornament**. 装飾 [FORMAL 形式ばった] □ *...walls of glass overlaid with ornament.* 装飾の施されたガラスの壁

or|na|men|tal /ɔːrnəmentəl/ ADJ 形容詞 Something that is **ornamental** is attractive and decorative. 装飾用の □ *...an ornamental fountain.* 装飾された噴水.

or|nate /ɔːrneɪt/ ADJ 形容詞 An **ornate** building, piece of furniture, or object is decorated with complicated patterns or shapes. 凝った装飾を施した □ *...an ornate iron staircase.* 凝った装飾を施した鉄製の階段

or|phan /ɔːrfən/ (**orphans, orphaned**) **1** N-COUNT 可算名詞 An **orphan** is a child whose parents are dead. 孤児 □ *...a young orphan girl brought up by peasants.* 農民に育てられた孤児の少女 **2** V-T PASSIVE 受動態他動詞 If a child **is orphaned**, their parents die, or their remaining parent dies. 両親を失う [no cont] □ *...a fifteen-year-old boy left orphaned by the recent disaster.* 最近の大災害で両親を失った15歳の少年

or|phan|age /ɔːrfənɪdʒ/ (**orphanages**) N-COUNT 可算名詞 An **orphanage** is a place where orphans live and are cared for. 孤児院

ortho|dox /ɔːrθədɒks/

> The spelling **Orthodox** is also used for meaning **2** and **3**.
>
> つづりの **Orthodox** は **2** と **3** の意味にも使われる.

1 ADJ 形容詞 **Orthodox** beliefs, methods, or systems are ones which are accepted or used by most people. 正統的な □ *Many of these ideas are now being incorporated into orthodox medical treatment.* こうした考えの多くは現在, 正統的な医療法に組入れられつつある. **2** ADJ 形容詞 If you describe someone as **orthodox**, you mean that they hold the older and more traditional ideas of their religion or party. 正統派の □ *...Orthodox Jews.* 正統派ユダヤ教徒 **3** ADJ 形容詞 The **Orthodox** churches are Christian churches from Eastern Europe which separated from the western church in the eleventh century. 東方正教会の □ *...the Greek Orthodox Church.* ギリシア正教会

<table>
<tr><td colspan="2">**Word Link**   dox ≈ opinion : ortho**dox**y, para**dox**, unortho**dox**</td></tr>
</table>

ortho|doxy /ɔːrθədɒksi/ (**orthodoxies**) **1** N-VAR 可変性名詞 An **orthodoxy** is an accepted view about something. 正統派的見解 □ *These ideas rapidly became the new orthodoxy in linguistics.* こうした考え方は急速に言語学の新しい正統的学説となった. **2** N-UNCOUNT 不可算名詞 The old, traditional beliefs of a religion, political party, or philosophy can be referred to as **orthodoxy**. 正統性 □ *...a conflict between Nat's religious orthodoxy and Rube's belief that his mission is to make money.* ナットの宗教的正統性と金をもうけることが使命というルーブの信念との間の対立

os|ten|ta|tious /ɒstenteɪʃəs/ **1** ADJ 形容詞 If you describe something as **ostentatious**, you disapprove of it because it is expensive and is intended to impress people. けばけばしい [DISAPPROVAL 不賛成] □ *...his house, which, however elaborate, is less ostentatious than the preserves of other Dallas tycoons.* どんなに凝っていてもダラスの他の大物たちの私有地ほど派手ではない彼の家 **2** ADJ 形容詞 If you describe someone as **ostentatious**, you disapprove of them because they want to impress people with their wealth or importance. これ見よがしの [DISAPPROVAL 不賛成] □ *Obviously he had plenty of money and was generous in its use without being ostentatious.* 明らかに彼は大金持ちで, 金を気前よく使ったが, 派手な使い方はしなかった. ● **os|ten|ta|tious|ly** ADV 副詞 □ *Her servants were similarly, if less ostentatiously attired.* 彼女の奉公人たちはそれ程派手ではなかったが, 同じように着飾っていた. **3** ADJ 形容詞 You can describe an action or behavior as **ostentatious** when it is done in an exaggerated way to attract people's attention. 目立つ □ *His wife was fairly quiet but she is not an ostentatious person anyway.* 彼の妻はどちらかというと控えめな女性だった, いずれにせよ彼女は目立ちたがり屋ではない. ● **os|ten|ta|tious|ly** ADV 副詞 これ見よがしに □ *Harry stopped under a street lamp and ostentatiously began inspecting the contents of his bag.* ハリーは街灯の下で立ち止まり, バッグの中身をこれ見よがしに調べ始めた.

os|tra|cize /ɒstrəsaɪz/ (**ostracizes, ostracizing, ostracized**) V-T 他動詞 If someone **is ostracized**, people deliberately behave in an unfriendly way toward them and do not allow them to take part in any of their social activities. 排斥する [usu passive] □ *She claims she's being ostracized by some members of her local community.* 彼女は地元の地域社会の1部の人たちから仲間外れにされていると主張している.

os|trich /ɒstrɪtʃ/ (**ostriches**) N-COUNT 可算名詞 An **ostrich** is a very large, long-necked African bird that cannot fly. ダチョウ

oth|er /ʌðər/ (**others**)

> When **other** follows the determiner **an**, it is written as one word: see **another**.
>
> **other** が限定詞 **an** に従うときは，1語として書かれる．**another**参照．

1 ADJ 形容詞 You use **other** to refer to an additional thing or person of the same type as one that has been mentioned or is known about. 他の [det ADJ, ADJ n] □ *They were just like any other young couple.* 彼らは他の若いカップルとちょうど同じだった. ● PRON 代名詞 **Other** is also a pronoun. 他の人 □ *Four crewmen were killed, one other was injured.* 4名の乗組員が死亡し，残りの1名は負傷した. **2** ADJ 形容詞 You use **other** to indicate that a thing or person is not the one already mentioned, but a different one. 別の [det ADJ, ADJ n] □ *The authorities insist that the discussions must not be linked to any other issue.* 当局は討論をどんな別の問題とも関連付けてはならないと主張する. □ *He would have to accept it; there was no other way.* 彼はそれを容認しなければならないだろう. 他に方法はなかった. ● PRON 代名詞 **Other** is also a pronoun. 別のもの □ *This issue, more than any other, has divided her cabinet.* この問題は他の問題以上に彼女の内閣を分裂させた. **3** ADJ 形容詞 You use **the other** to refer to the second of two things or people when the identity of the first is already known or understood, or has already been mentioned. 反対側の [det ADJ] □ *The captain was at the other end of the room.* 主将は部屋の反対側の端にいた. □ *You deliberately went in the other direction.* あなたはわざと反対の方向に行った. ● PRON-SING 単数代名詞 **The other** is also a pronoun. もう一方のもの ['the' PRON] □ *Almost everybody had a cigarette in one hand and a martini in the other.* ほとんど全員が一方の手にタバコを持ち，他方の手にマティーニを持っていた. **4** ADJ 形容詞 You use **other** at the end of a list or a group of examples, to refer generally to people or things like the ones just mentioned. その他の [det ADJ, ADJ n] □ *The new Station Center will have shops, restaurants and other amenities.* 新しいステーションセンターには商店，レストラン，その他の施設ができます. ● PRON 代名詞 **Other** is also a pronoun. その他のもの；人 □ *Descartes received his stimulus from the new physics and astronomy of Copernicus, Galileo, and others.* デカルトはコペルニクス，ガリレオ，その他の人々の新しい物理学と天文学に刺激された. **5** ADJ 形容詞 You use **the other** to refer to the rest of the people or things in a group, when you are talking about one particular person or thing. 他の [det ADJ] □ *When the other kids were taken to the zoo, he was left behind.* 他の子供たちが動物園に連れて行かれたのに，彼は後に残された. ● PRON 代名詞 **The others** is also a pronoun. 他の人々 ['the' PRON] □ *Aubrey's on his way here, with the others.* オーブリーは他の人々と一緒にこちらに向かっている. **6** ADJ 形容詞 **Other** people are people in general, as opposed to yourself or a person you have already mentioned. 他の [ADJ n] □ *The suffering of other people appalls me.* 他の人々の苦難は私をぞっとさせる. ● PRON-PLURAL 複数代名詞 **Others** means the same as **other people**. 他の人々 □ *His humor depended on contempt for others.* 彼のユーモアは他人に対する軽蔑に依存していた.

> Do not confuse **other** and **another**. You use **other** to refer to more than one type of person or thing. □ *Other boys were arriving now.* When you are talking about two people or things and have already referred to one of them, you refer to the second one as **the other** or **the other one**. When you are talking about several people or things and have already referred to one or more of them, you usually refer to the remaining ones as **the others**. **Another** person or thing means one more person or thing of the same kind. It is usually followed by a singular count noun, "one," "few," or a number larger than one. □ *Rick's got another camera... She had a drink and then another one... I waited another few minutes... They raised another $15,000.*

7 ADJ 形容詞 You use **other** in informal expressions of time such as **the other day**, **the other evening**, or **the other week** to refer to a day, evening, or week in the recent past. せんだっての ['the' ADJ n] □ *I called her the other day and she said she'd like to come over.* 私が彼女に先日電話したら，彼女は遊びにきたいと言った. **8** PHRASE 句 You use expressions like **among other** things or **among others** to indicate that there are several more facts, things, or people like the one or ones mentioned, but that you do not intend to mention them all. 数ある中で [VAGUENESS あいまいさ] □ *He moved to Ohio in 2005 where, among other things, he worked as a journalist.* 彼は2005年にオハイオ州に引越して，そこで中でもジャーナリストとして働いた. □ *His travels took him to Peru, among other places.* 彼は色々な国に旅行したが，中でもペルーに行った. **9** PHRASE 句 If something

happens, for example, **every other day** or **every other month**, there is a day or month when it does not happen between each day or month when it happens. 1日；隔週；隔月おきに **10** □ *Their food is adequate. It includes meat at least every other day, vegetables and fruit.* 彼らの食事は十分だ. 少なくとも1日おきに肉を食べている. **10** PHRASE 句 You use **every other** to emphasize that you are referring to all the rest of the people or things in a group. 他の全ての [EMPHASIS 強調] □ *The same will apply in every other country.* 同じことは他の全ての国に当てはまるだろう. **11** PHRASE 句 You use **nothing other than** and **no other than** when you are going to mention a course of action, decision, or description and emphasize that it is the only one possible in the situation. ～のほかは何も―しない [EMPHASIS 強調] □ *Nothing other than an immediate custodial sentence could be justified.* 正当化できるのは即座の留置刑のみだった. □ *The rebels would not be happy with anything other than the complete removal of the current regime.* 反乱者たちは現政権の完全な除去以外には決して満足しないだろう. **12** PHRASE 句 You use **or other** in expressions like **somehow or other** and **someone or other** to indicate that you cannot or do not want to be more precise about the information that you are giving. ～など [VAGUENESS あいまいさ] □ *I was going to have him called away from the house on some pretext or other.* 私はなんとか口実を設けて彼を家からどこかに呼び出してもらうつもりだった. □ *The foundation is holding a dinner in honor of something or other.* 財団は何かを記念して夕食会を開いている. **13** PHRASE 句 You use **other than** after a negative statement to say that the person, item, or thing that follows is the only exception to the statement. ～以外に □ *She makes no reference to any feminist work other than her own.* 彼女は自分の作品以外にはフェミニスト作品に言及しない. **14** each other → see **each** **15** one after the other → see **one** **16** one or other → see **one** **17** this, that and the other → see **this** **18** in other words → see **word**

> **Word Link** | wise ≈ *in the direction or manner of*: clock*wise*, like*wise*, other*wise*

other|wise /ʌðərwaɪz/ **1** ADV 副詞 You use **otherwise** after mentioning a situation or telling someone to do something, in order to say what the result or consequence would be if the situation did not exist or the person did not do as you say. さもなければ [ADV with cl] □ *Make a note of the questions you want to ask; you will invariably forget some of them otherwise.* 聞きたい質問を書き留めなさい. さもなければ質問のいくつかを忘れることは間違いないだろう. □ *I'm lucky that I'm interested in school work, otherwise I'd go crazy.* 私は勉強に興味があって幸運だ. さもなければ気が狂ってしまうだろう. **2** ADV 副詞 You use **otherwise** before stating the general condition or quality of something, when you are also mentioning an exception to this general condition or quality. もしそうでなければ [ADV group] □ *The decorations for the games have lent a splash of color to an otherwise drab city.* 試合のための飾り付けは，そうでなければさえない町にちょっとした色彩を与えた. **3** ADV 副詞 You use **otherwise** to refer in a general way to actions or situations that are very different from, or the opposite to, your main statement. 違って [WRITTEN 書き言葉] [ADV with v] □ *Take approximately 60 mg up to four times a day, unless advised otherwise by a doctor.* 医者から異なる指示を受けていない場合は，約60ミリグラムを1日に最高4回服用しなさい. □ *There is no way anything would ever happen between us, and believe me I've tried to convince myself otherwise.* 私たちの間に何かが起こるようなことは決してありません. 本当ですよ，私はそうではないと確信しようとしましたが. **4** ADV 副詞 You use **otherwise** to indicate that other ways of doing something are possible in addition to the way already mentioned. 別のやり方で [ADV before v] □ *The studio could punish its players by keeping them out of work, and otherwise controlling their lives.* そのスタジオはその俳優たちを失業状態にしておくか，別のやり方で彼らの生活をコントロールして，彼らを罰することができるだろう. **5** PHRASE 句 You use **or otherwise** or **and otherwise** to mention something that is not the thing just referred to or is the opposite of that thing. ―にせよ，そうでないにせよ □ *It was for the police to assess the validity or otherwise of the evidence.* 証拠が有効であるにせよそうでないにせよ，それを評価するのは警察の仕事だった.

ouch /aʊtʃ/ EXCLAM 感嘆詞 "**Ouch!**" is used in writing to represent the noise that people make when they suddenly feel pain. 痛い □ *She was barefoot and stones dug into her feet. "Ouch, ouch!" she cried.* 彼女ははだしだったので石が両足に食い込んだ. 「あいたた」と彼女は叫んだ.

ought /ɔt/

> **Ought to** is a phrasal modal verb. It is used with the base form of a verb.
>
> **Ought to** は法助詞であり，動詞の原形とともに用いられる.

1 PHRASE 句 You use **ought to** to mean that it is morally right to do a particular thing or that it is morally right for a particular situation to exist, especially when giving or asking for advice or opinions. ―すべきだ □ *Mark, you've got a good wife. You ought to*

take care of her. マーク、君はいい奥さんを持っているね．君は彼女を大切にすべきだ． ❑ *The people who already own a bit of money or land ought to have a voice in saying where it goes.* 既にちょっとした金や土地を持つ人々はその行方について発言権を持つべきだ． **2** PHRASE 句 You use **ought to** when saying that you think it is a good idea and important for you or someone else to do a particular thing, especially when giving or asking for advice or opinions. 一すべきだ ❑ *You don't have to be alone with him and I don't think you ought to be.* あなたは彼と2人だけでいる必要はないし、あなたはそうすべきではないと思う． ❑ *You ought to ask a lawyer's advice.* あなたは弁護士の助言を求めるべきだ． **3** PHRASE 句 You use **ought to** to indicate that you expect something to be true or to happen. きっと一だろう ❑ "*This ought to be fun,*" *he told Alex, eyes gleaming.* 「これはきっと楽しいはずだ」彼は目を輝かせながらアレックスに言った． **4** PHRASE 句 You use **ought to** to indicate that you think that something should be the case, but might not be. 一するはずだ ❑ *They ought to win easily today, but nothing in life is certain.* 彼らは今日は楽勝するはずだが、人生では確実なことは1つもない． **5** PHRASE 句 You use **ought to** to indicate that you think that something has happened because of what you know about the situation, but you are not certain. 一しているはずだ [VAGUENESS あいまいさ] ❑ *He ought to have reached the house some time ago.* 彼はとっくに家に到着しているはずだ． **6** PHRASE 句 You use **ought to have** with a past participle to indicate that something was expected to happen or be the case, but it did not happen or was not the case. 一すべきだった ❑ *Basically the system ought to have worked.* 元来そのシステムは機能すべきだった． **7** PHRASE 句 You use **ought to have** with a past participle to indicate that although it was best or correct for someone to do something in the past, they did not actually do it. 一すればよかった ❑ *I realize I ought to have told you about it.* 私はあなたにそのことについて話しておけばよかった． ❑ *I ought not to have asked you a thing like that. I'm sorry.* 私はあのようなことをあなたに頼むべきではなかった．申し訳ない． **8** PHRASE 句 You use **ought to** when politely telling someone that you should do something, for example, that you must leave. 〜したほうがいい [POLITENESS 丁寧さ] ❑ *I really ought to be getting back now.* 私はもうほんとうに戻りません．

oughtn't /ˈɔːtᵊnt/ **Oughtn't** is a spoken form of "ought not." 口語で用いられるought notの短縮形

ounce /aʊns/ (**ounces**) **1** N-COUNT 可算名詞 An **ounce** is a unit of weight used in the U.S. and Britain. There are sixteen ounces in a pound and one ounce is equal to 28.35 grams. オンス ❑ ...*four ounces of sugar.* 砂糖4オンス **2** N-SING 単数名詞 You can refer to a very small amount of something, such as a quality or characteristic, as an **ounce**. わずか〜 ❑ *If only my father had possessed an ounce of business sense.* 私の父が少しでもビジネス感覚を持っていたならば

our /aʊər/

Our is the first person plural possessive determiner.
Ourは1人称複数所有限定詞である．

1 DET 限定詞 You use **our** to indicate that something belongs or relates both to yourself and to one or more other people. 我々の ❑ *We're expecting our first baby.* 私たちには最初の子供が生まれることになっている． **2** DET 限定詞 A speaker or writer sometimes uses **our** to indicate that something belongs or relates to people in general. 我々の ❑ *We are all entirely responsible for our actions, and for our reactions.* 我々は全員、自分たちの行動と反応に全責任を負う．

ours /aʊərz/

Ours is the first person plural possessive pronoun.
Oursは1人称複数所有代名詞である．

PRON-POSS 所有代名詞 You use **ours** to refer to something that belongs or relates both to yourself and to one or more other people. 我々のもの ❑ *That car is ours.* あの車は私たちの車だ． ❑ *There are few strangers in a town like ours.* 私たちのような町にはよそ者はほとんどいない．

our|selves /aʊərsɛlvz/

Ourselves is the first person plural reflexive pronoun.
Ourselvesは1人称複数再帰代名詞である．

1 PRON-REFL 再帰代名詞 You use **ourselves** to refer to yourself and one or more other people as a group. 我々自身 [V PRON, prep PRON] ❑ *We sat around the fire to keep ourselves warm.* 私たちは体を暖めるために暖炉の周りに座った． **2** PRON-REFL 再帰代名詞 A speaker or writer sometimes uses **ourselves** to refer to people in general. **Ourselves** is used as the object of a verb or preposition when the subject refers to the same people. 我々自身を [V PRON, prep PRON] ❑ *We all know that when we exert ourselves our heart rate increases.* 我々はだれでも力を出すと心拍が増えることを知っている． **3** PRON-REFL-EMPH 強調的再帰代名詞 You use **ourselves** to emphasize a first person plural subject. In more formal English,

ourselves is sometimes used instead of "us" as the object of a verb or preposition, for emphasis. 我々自ら [EMPHASIS 強調] ❑ *Others are feeling just the way we ourselves would feel in the same situation.* 他の人々は同じ状況で我々自身が感じるだろうこととちょうど同じことを感じている． **4** PRON-REFL-EMPH 強調的再帰代名詞 If you say something such as "We did it **ourselves**," you are indicating that the people you are referring to did it, rather than anyone else. 我々自ら ❑ *We villagers built that ourselves, we had no help from anyone.* 私たち村人はそれを自分たちで建てた．だれの手も借りなかった．

oust /aʊst/ (**ousts, ousting, ousted**) **1** V-T 他動詞 If someone is **ousted** from a position of power, job, or place, they are forced to leave it. 追い出す [JOURNALISM ジャーナリズム] ❑ *The leaders have been ousted from power by nationalists.* 指導者たちは国家主義者たちに権力を奪われた． ❑ *The Republicans may oust him in November.* 共和党は11月に彼を追い出すかもしれない． ● **oust|er** (**ousters**) N-COUNT 可算名詞 [usu sing with poss] 追放 [AM 米国英語] ❑ *The group has called for the ouster of the trust's board.* そのグループはトラストの理事会の排除を要求している． ● **oust|ing** N-UNCOUNT 不可算名詞 排除 ❑ *The ousting of his predecessor was one of the most dramatic coups the business world had seen in years.* 彼の前任者の追放は長年ビジネス界で起こった最も劇的なクーデターの1つだった．

out
❶ ADVERB USES
❷ ADJECTIVE AND ADVERB USES
❸ VERB USE
❹ PREPOSITION USES

❶ out /aʊt/

Out is often used with verbs of movement, such as "walk" and "pull," and also in phrasal verbs such as "give out" and "run out."
Outはしばしばwalkや pull のような移動の動詞と共に用いられ、また give out や run out のような句動詞にも用いられる．

1 ADV 副詞 When something is in a particular place and you take it **out**, you remove it from that place. 出して [ADV after v] ❑ *I like the pop you get when you pull out a cork.* 私はコルクを抜く時のパンという音が好きだ． ❑ *He took out his notebook and flipped the pages.* 彼は手帳を取り出し、ページをめくった． **2** ADV 副詞 You can use **out** to indicate that you are talking about the situation outside, rather than inside buildings. 戸外で [ADV after v] ❑ *It's hot out - very hot, very humid.* 外は暑い、非常に蒸し暑い． **3** ADV 副詞 If you are **out**, you are not at home or not at your usual place of work. 外出して ❑ *I tried to get in touch with you yesterday evening, but I think you were out.* 私は昨晩あなたと連絡を取ろうとしたが、あなたは外出中のようだった． **4** ADV 副詞 If you say that someone is **out** in a particular place, you mean that they are in a different place, usually one far away. 離れて [ADV adv/prep] ❑ *The police tell me they've finished their investigations out there.* 警察はあそこでの捜査を終了したと私に言っている． **5** ADV 副詞 When the sea or tide goes **out**, the sea moves away from the shore. 引いて ❑ *The tide was out and they walked among the rock pools.* 潮が引き、彼らは岩の水溜りの間を歩いた． **6** ADV 副詞 If you are **out** a particular amount of money, you have that amount less than you should or than you did. なくなって [mainly AM 主に米国英語, INFORMAL くだけた] [ADV n] ❑ *I'm out ten thousand dollars, with nothing to show for it!* 私は1万ドル使ったが、その成果は見えない．

❷ out /aʊt/ **1** ADJ 形容詞 If a light or fire is **out** or goes **out**, it is no longer shining or burning. 消えて [v-link ADJ] ❑ *All the lights were out in the house.* 家の明かりは全て消えていた． **2** ADJ 形容詞 If flowers are **out**, their petals have opened. 咲いて [v-link ADJ] ❑ *Well, the daffodils are out in the gardens and they're always a beautiful show.* ところで庭園には水仙の花が咲き、それはいつも美しい眺めである． ● ADV 副詞 **Out** is also an adverb. 咲いて [ADV after v] ❑ *I usually put it in my diary when I see the wild flowers coming out.* 私は通常、野の花が咲くのを見るとそれを日記につけている． **3** ADJ 形容詞 If something such as a book or CD is **out**, it is available for people to buy. 発売された [v-link ADJ] ❑ *Their new album is out now.* 彼らの新アルバムは今発売中だ． ● ADV 副詞 **Out** is also an adverb. 発売されて [ADV after v] ❑ *The French edition came out in early 2006.* フランス語版は2006年初期に出版された． **4** ADJ 形容詞 In a game or sport, if someone is **out**, they can no longer take part either because they are unable to or because they have been defeated. 退場になって [v-link ADJ] **5** ADJ 形容詞 In baseball, a player is **out** if they do not reach a base safely. When three players on a team are out in an inning, then the team is **out**. アウトになって **6** ADJ 形容詞 If you say that a proposal or suggestion is **out**, you mean that it is unacceptable. 受け入れられない [v-link ADJ] ❑ *That idea is out, I'm afraid.* その考えは残念ながら受け入れられない． **7** ADJ 形容詞 If you say that a particular thing is **out**, you mean that it is no longer fashionable at the present time. 廃れて [v-link ADJ] ❑ *Romance is making a comeback. Reality is out.* ロマンス小説は返り咲きしている．

写実小説は流行らない. **8** ADJ 形容詞 If you say that a calculation or measurement is **out**, you mean that it is incorrect. はずれて [v-link ADJ] ❏ *When the two ends of the tunnel met in the middle they were only a few inches out.* トンネルの両先端が真ん中で会った際、数インチだけ狂っていた. **9** ADJ 形容詞 If someone is **out** to do something, they intend to do it. しきりに―したがって [INFORMAL くだけた] [v-link ADJ to-inf] ❏ *Most companies these days are just out to make a quick profit.* 近頃は大半の会社がただできるだけ短期間に利益を上げようとしている. **10** ADJ 形容詞 If news or information about something is **out**, information about it has been made public. 世に知られて [v-link ADJ] ❏ *The word is out that she has fled the country.* 彼女は国外に逃亡したという消息が明らかになった.

❸ out /aʊt/ (**outs, outing, outed**) V-T 他動詞 If a group of people **out** a public figure or famous person, they reveal that person's homosexuality against their wishes. 同性愛者であることを暴露する ❏ *The New York gay action group "Queer Nation" recently outed an American Congressman.* ニューヨークの同性愛活動団体「クィア・ネーション」は最近あるアメリカ人国会議員が同性愛者であることを暴露にすること ❏ *The gay and lesbian rights group, Stonewall, sees outing as completely unhelpful.* ゲイとレスビアン権利団体の「ストーンウォール」は同性愛者であることを暴露することは全く役に立たないと考えている. ● **out|ing** N-UNCOUNT 不可算名詞 同性愛者であることを暴露すること

❹ out /aʊt/

> **Out of** is used with verbs of movement, such as "walk" and "pull," and also in phrasal verbs such as "get out of" and "grow out of." **Out** is often used instead of **out of**, for example in "He looked out the window."

> **Out of** はしばしば **walk** や **pull** のような移動の動詞と共に用いられ、また **get out of** や **grow out of** のような句動詞にも用いられる. **Out** はしばしば **out of** の代わりに用いられる、例えば、**He looked out the window.**

1 PHRASE 句 If you go **out of** a place, you leave it. ―の中から外に ❏ *She let him out of the house.* 彼女は彼が家の外に出るのを許した. **2** PHRASE 句 If you take something **out of** the container or place where it has been, you remove it so that it is no longer there. ―の中から外に ❏ *I always took my key out of my bag and put it in my pocket.* 私はいつもバッグから鍵を取り出し、ポケットに入れた. **3** PHRASE 句 If you look or shout **out of** a window, you look or shout away from the room where you are toward the outside. ―の中から外に ❏ *He went on staring out of the window.* 彼は窓から外をじっと眺め続けた. **4** PHRASE 句 If you are **out of** the sun, the rain, or the wind, you are sheltered from it. ―の届かぬところに ❏ *People can keep out of the sun to avoid skin cancer.* 人々は皮膚がんにかからないように日光を避けることができる. **5** PHRASE 句 If someone or something gets **out of** a situation, especially an unpleasant one, they are then no longer in it. If they keep **out of** it, they do not start being in it. ―を脱して ❏ *In the past army troops have relied heavily on air support to get them out of trouble.* 陸軍部隊は以前、困難な事態から脱出させるのに空軍機による援護に大きく頼っていた. ❏ *The economy is starting to climb out of recession.* 経済は景気後退から抜け出し始めている. **6** PHRASE 句 You can use **out of** to say that someone leaves an institution. ―を離れて ❏ *That is precisely what I came out of college thinking I was supposed to do.* この産業は私がカレッジを卒業する時に急に景気がよくなってきていた. **7** PHRASE 句 If you are **out of** range of something, you are beyond the limits of that range. ―の範囲外に ❏ *Shaun was in the bedroom, out of earshot, watching television.* ショーンは寝室でテレビを見ていて聞こえないところにいた. **8** PHRASE 句 You use **out of** to say what feeling or reason causes someone to do something. For example, if you do something **out of** pity, you do it because you pity someone. ―から ❏ *He took up office out of a sense of duty.* 彼は義務感から公職についた. **9** PHRASE 句 If you get something such as information or work **out of** someone, you manage to make them give it to you, usually when they are unwilling to give it. ―から ❏ *"Where is she being held prisoner?" I asked. "Did you get it out of him?"* 「彼女はどこで捕縛になっているのか」と私は尋ねた.「彼からそれを聞いたのか」 **10** PHRASE 句 If you get pleasure or an advantage **out of** something, you get it as a result of being involved with that thing or making use of it. ―から ❏ *Jenkins hasn't let the pressure take the fun out of the sport.* ジェンキンスは重圧でスポーツの楽しみを失うようなことはなかった. **11** PHRASE 句 If you are **out of** something, you no longer have any of it. ―が不足して ❏ *I can't find the sugar – and we're out of milk.* 砂糖が見つからないし、牛乳も切れている. **12** PHRASE 句 If something is made **out of** a particular material, it consists of that material because it has been formed or constructed from it. ―を材料にして ❏ *Would you advise people to make a building out of wood or stone?* あなたは建物を木造で建てることを勧めますか、それとも石造りですか. **13** PHRASE 句 You use **out of** to indicate what proportion of a group of things something is true of. For example, if something is true of one **out of** five things, it is true of one fifth of all things of that kind. ―の中から ❏ *Two out of five thought the business would be sold privately on their retirement or death.* 5人中2人は事業が自分の引

退後あるいは死後に個人的に売却されるだろうと考えた.

out|age /aʊtɪdʒ/ (**outages**) N-COUNT 可算名詞 An **outage** is a period of time when the electricity supply to a building or area is interrupted, for example, because of damage to the cables. 停電 [AM 米国英語] ❏ *A windstorm in Washington is causing power outages throughout the region.* ワシントン州の暴風は全地域で停電を起こしている.

out|back /aʊtbæk/ N-SING 単数名詞 The parts of Australia that are far away from towns are referred to as **the outback**. 奥地 ❏ *Are there many people living in the outback?* 奥地に住んでいる人は多いのか.

out|bid /aʊtbɪd/ (**outbids, outbidding**)

> The form **outbid** is used in the present tense and is the past tense and past participle.

> **outbid** 形は現在時制に使われ、過去時制と過去分詞でもある.

V-T 他動詞 If you **outbid** someone, you offer more money than they do for something that you both want to buy. 競り上げる ❏ *The Museum has antagonized rivals by outbidding them for the world's greatest art treasures.* その美術館は世界で最も偉大な名品に競争相手より高い値をつけて対抗した.

out|bound /aʊtbaʊnd/ ADJ 形容詞 An **outbound** flight is one that is leaving or about to leave a particular place. 出発の ❏ *Airport officials say at least 20 outbound flights were delayed.* 空港職員は少なくとも20の出発便が遅れたと述べている.

out|break /aʊtbreɪk/ (**outbreaks**) N-COUNT 可算名詞 If there is an **outbreak** of something unpleasant, such as violence or a disease, it suddenly starts to happen. 発生 ❏ *The four-day festival ended a day early after an outbreak of violence involving hundreds of youths.* 4日間にわたる祭典は何百人もの若者間で暴力沙汰が起こったため1日早く終わった. ❏ *...an outbreak of chickenpox.* 水疱瘡（ぼうそう）の発生

out|burst /aʊtbɜrst/ (**outbursts**) **1** N-COUNT 可算名詞 An **outburst** of an emotion, especially anger, is a sudden strong expression of that emotion. 爆発、突然のほとばしり ❏ *...a spontaneous outburst of cheers and applause.* 期せずしてどっと湧き上がった歓迎と拍手喝采（かっさい） **2** N-COUNT 可算名詞 An **outburst** of violent activity is a sudden period of this activity. 突発 ❏ *Five people were reported killed today in a fresh outburst of violence.* 本日、新たな暴動の突発で5人が死亡したと伝えられた.

out|cast /aʊtkæst/ (**outcasts**) N-COUNT 可算名詞 An **outcast** is someone who is not accepted by a group of people or by society. のけ者 ❏ *He had always been an outcast, unwanted and alone.* 彼はいつも社会ののけ者で望まれず1人だった.

out|come /aʊtkʌm/ (**outcomes**) N-COUNT 可算名詞 The **outcome** of an activity, process, or situation is the situation that exists at the end of it. 決末 ❏ *Mr. Singh said he was pleased with the outcome.* シン氏は決末に満足していると言った. ❏ *It's too early to know the outcome of her illness.* 彼女の病気の結果を知るのは早すぎる.

out|cry /aʊtkraɪ/ (**outcries**) N-VAR 可変性名詞 An **outcry** is a reaction of strong disapproval and anger shown by the public or media about a recent event. 激しい抗議 ❏ *The killing caused an international outcry.* その殺害事件は国際的な激しい抗議を起こした.

out|dat|ed /aʊtdeɪtɪd/ ADJ 形容詞 If you describe something as **outdated**, you mean that you think it is old-fashioned and no longer useful or relevant to modern life. 時代遅れの ❏ *...outdated and inefficient factories.* 時代遅れで非効率的な工場 ❏ *...outdated attitudes.* 時代遅れの態度

out|do /aʊtdu/ (**outdoes, outdoing, outdid, outdone**) **1** V-T 他動詞 If you **outdo** someone, you are a lot more successful than they are at a particular activity. 打ち勝つ ❏ *It was important for me to outdo them, to feel better than they were.* 私には彼らに打ち勝って、彼らより優れていると感じることが重要だった. **2** PHRASE 句 You use **not to be outdone** to introduce an action which someone takes in response to a previous action. 負けずに ❏ *She wore a lovely tiara but the groom, not to be outdone, had on a very smart embroidered waistcoat.* 彼女は美しいティアラをつけていたが、花婿も負けずに大変気の利いた刺繍入りのチョッキを着ていた.

out|door /aʊtdɔr/ ADJ 形容詞 **Outdoor** activities or things happen or are used outside and not in a building. 戸外の [ADJ n] ❏ *If you enjoy outdoor activities, this is the trip for you.* 野外の活動が好きな人なら、これはぴったりの旅行だ.

out|doors /aʊtdɔrz/ **1** ADV 副詞 If something happens **outdoors**, it happens outside in the fresh air rather than in a building. 野外で ❏ *It was warm enough to be outdoors all afternoon.* 午後じゅう外で過ごせるほど暖かだった. **2** N-SING 単数名詞 You refer to **the outdoors** when talking about activities that take place outside away from buildings. 野外活動 ❏ *I'm a lover of the outdoors.* 私は野外活動が大好きだ.

out|er /aʊtər/ ADJ 形容詞 The **outer** parts of something are the parts which contain or enclose the other parts, and which are furthest from the center. 外の [ADJ n] ❏ *He heard a voice in the outer*

room. 彼は外れの部屋で声がするのを聞いた.

→ see **core**

out|er space N-UNCOUNT 不可算名詞 **Outer space** is the area outside the Earth's atmosphere where the other planets and stars are situated. 宇宙空間 ❑ *In 1957, the Soviets launched Sputnik 1 into outer space.* ソ連は1957年に大気圏外にスプートニク第1号を打ち上げた.

→ see **satellite**

out|fit /aʊtfɪt/ (**outfits**) **1** N-COUNT 可算名詞 An **outfit** is a set of clothes. 服装の1揃い ❑ *She was wearing an outfit she'd bought the previous day.* 彼女は前の日に買った洋服を着ていた. **2** N-COUNT 可算名詞 You can refer to an organization as an **outfit**. 団体 ❑ *He works for a private security outfit.* 彼は民間の警備会社に勤めている.

out|flow /aʊtfloʊ/ (**outflows**) N-COUNT 可算名詞 When there is an **outflow** of money or people, a large amount of money or people move from one place to another. 流出 ❑ *There was a net outflow of about $650m.* 約6億5000万ドルの正味流出額があった.

out|go|ing ⧫ /aʊtgoʊɪŋ/ **1** ADJ 形容詞 **Outgoing** things such as planes, mail, and passengers are leaving or being sent somewhere. 出発する [ADJ n] ❑ *All outgoing flights were grounded.* 出発便は全便離陸を禁じられた. **2** ADJ 形容詞 Someone who is **outgoing** is very friendly and likes meeting and talking to people. 社交性に富んだ ❑ *She's very outgoing.* 彼女は非常に社交性に富んでいる. **3** ADJ 形容詞 You use **outgoing** to describe a person in charge of something who is soon going to leave that position. 辞職する [ADJ n] ❑ *...the outgoing director of the International Folk Festival.* 国際民俗祭の辞職する演出家

out|go|ings /aʊtgoʊɪŋz/ N-PLURAL 複数名詞 Your **outgoings** are the regular amounts of money which you have to spend every week or every month, for example, in order to pay your rent or bills. 出費 [BRIT 英国英語; AM **outlay, expenses** 米国英語 **outlay, expenses**]

out|grow /aʊtgroʊ/ (**outgrows, outgrowing, outgrew, outgrown**) **1** V-T 他動詞 If a child **outgrows** a piece of clothing, they grow bigger, so that it no longer fits them. 大きくなって着られなくなる ❑ *She outgrew her clothes so rapidly that Patsy was always having to buy new ones.* 彼女は成長があまりに速く洋服が合わなく着られなくなるので, パッツィーはしょっちゅう新しい衣服を買わなければならなかった. **2** V-T 他動詞 If you **outgrow** a particular way of behaving or thinking, you change and become more mature, so that you no longer behave or think in that way. 〜から脱却する ❑ *The girl may or may not outgrow her interest in fashion.* 少女は成長して流行への興味を失うかもしれないし, 失わないかもしれない.

out|ing /aʊtɪŋ/ (**outings**) **1** N-COUNT 可算名詞 An **outing** is a short trip, usually with a group of people, away from your home, school, or place of work. 遠足 ❑ *One evening, she made a rare outing to the local night club.* ある晩, 彼女は珍しく地元のナイトクラブに出かけた. **2** → see also **out 3**

out|law /aʊtlɔ/ (**outlaws, outlawing, outlawed**) **1** V-T 他動詞 When something is **outlawed**, it is made illegal. 非合法化する ❑ *In some states gambling was outlawed.* いくつかの州ではギャンブルは非合法化された. ❑ *The German government has outlawed some fascist groups.* ドイツ政府は1部のファシスト団体を非合法化した. **2** N-COUNT 可算名詞 An **outlaw** is a criminal who is hiding from the authorities. 無法者 [OLD-FASHIONED 古風な] ❑ *Jesse was an outlaw, a bandit, a criminal.* ジェシーは無法者, 盗賊, 犯罪人だった.

out|lay /aʊtleɪ/ (**outlays**) N-VAR 可変性名詞 **Outlay** is the amount of money that you have to spend in order to buy something or start a project. 出費 ❑ *Apart from the capital outlay of buying the machine, dishwashers can actually save you money.* 機械の購入代金は別として, 皿洗い機は実際に金の節約になる.

out|let /aʊtlet, -lɪt/ (**outlets**) **1** N-COUNT 可算名詞 An **outlet** is a store or organization which sells the goods made by a particular manufacturer or at a discount price, often direct from the manufacturer. 工場直結の販売店 ❑ *...the largest retail outlet in the city.* その市の最大の小売販売店 ❑ *At the factory outlet you'll find discounted items at up to 75% off regular prices.* 工場の直販店には正価の最高75%引きの割引商品が販売されているでしょう. **2** N-COUNT 可算名詞 If someone has an **outlet for** their feelings or ideas, they have a means of expressing and releasing them. はけ口 ❑ *Her father had found an outlet for his ambition in his work.* 彼女の父は野望のはけ口を仕事に見つけた. **3** N-COUNT 可算名詞 An **outlet** is a hole or pipe through which liquid or air can flow away. 放出口 ❑ *...a warm air outlet.* 温風の排出口 **4** N-COUNT 可算名詞 An **outlet** is a place, usually in a wall, where you can connect electrical devices to the electricity supply. 差し込み口, コンセント [mainly AM 主に米国英語] ❑ *Just plug it into any electric outlet.* それをコンセントに差し込むだけでよい.

out|line /aʊtlaɪn/ (**outlines, outlining, outlined**) **1** V-T 他動詞 If you **outline** an idea or a plan, you explain it in a general way. 概述する ❑ *The mayor outlined his plan to clean up the town's image.* 町長は町のイメージをよくする計画の大要を説明した. **2** N-COUNT

可算名詞 An **outline** is a general explanation or description of something. 大要 [also 'in' N] ❑ *Following is an outline of the survey findings.* 調査決果の大要は以下の通りです. **3** V-T PASSIVE 受動態 他動詞 You say that an object **is outlined** when you can see its general shape because there is light behind it. 輪郭をはっきりさせる ❑ *The Ritz was outlined against the lights up there.* リッツホテルの輪郭はあそこの照明を背景に浮かび上がっていた. **4** N-COUNT 可算名詞 The **outline** of something is its general shape, especially when it cannot be clearly seen. 輪郭 ❑ *He could see only the hazy outline of the goalposts.* 彼にはゴールポストのおぼろげな輪郭しか見えなかった.

Word Partnership	outline は次の語句と使われる:
V.	**write an** outline **1** **2**
N.	**chapter** outline, outline **a paper**, outline **a plan 2**
ADJ.	**broad** outline, **detailed** outline, **general** outline **2** **4**

out|live /aʊtlɪv/ (**outlives, outliving, outlived**) V-T 他動詞 If one person **outlives** another, they are still alive after the second person has died. If one thing **outlives** another thing, the first thing continues to exist after the second has disappeared or been replaced. 〜より長生きする ❑ *I'm sure Rose will outlive many of us.* ローズは我々の多くより長生きすることは確かだ.

out|look /aʊtlʊk/ (**outlooks**) **1** N-COUNT 可算名詞 Your **outlook** is your general attitude toward life. 人生観 [usu sing, with supp, also 'in' N] ❑ *I adopted a positive outlook on life.* 私は前向きな人生観を持った. **2** N-SING 単数名詞 The **outlook** for something is what people think will happen in relation to it. 見通し ❑ *The economic outlook is one of rising unemployment.* 経済的な見通しは失業率が上昇するというものだ.

out|ly|ing /aʊtlaɪɪŋ/ ADJ 形容詞 **Outlying** places are far away from the main cities of a country. 中心から離れた [ADJ n] ❑ *Tourists can visit outlying areas like the Napa Valley Wine Country.* 観光客はナパ渓谷ワイン産地などの中心から離れた場所を訪れることができる.

out|num|ber /aʊtnʌmbər/ (**outnumbers, outnumbering, outnumbered**) V-T 他動詞 If one group of people or things **outnumbers** another, the first group has more people or things in it than the second group. 数で勝る ❑ *...a town where men outnumber women four to one.* 男性が数で女性に対して4対1で勝る町

out of → see **out**

out of date also **out-of-date** ADJ 形容詞 Something that is **out of date** is old-fashioned and no longer useful. 時代遅れの ❑ *The regulations were out of date and confusing.* その規制は時代遅れで混乱のもとだった.

out of touch **1** ADJ 形容詞 Someone who is **out of touch with** a situation is not aware of recent changes in it. 事情にうとくなって [v-link ADJ] ❑ *Washington politicians are out of touch with the American people.* ワシントンの政治家はアメリカ国民の事情にうとい. **2** ADJ 形容詞 If you are **out of touch** with someone, you have not been in contact with them recently and are not familiar with their present situation. 連絡が取れないで [v-link ADJ] ❑ *James and I have been out of touch for years.* 私とジェームズはもう何年も連絡を取りあっていない.

out of work ADJ 形容詞 Someone who is **out of work** does not have a job. 失業して ❑ *...a town where half the men are usually out of work.* 男性の5割が通常失業している町

out|pa|tient /aʊtpeɪʃənt/ (**outpatients**) also **out-patient** N-COUNT 可算名詞 An **outpatient** is someone who receives treatment at a hospital but does not spend the night there. 外来患者 ❑ *...the outpatient clinic.* 外来医院

→ see **hospital**

out|place|ment /aʊtpleɪsmənt/ N-UNCOUNT 不可算名詞 An **outplacement** agency gives advice to managers and other professional people who have recently become unemployed, and helps them find new jobs. 再就職斡旋 [BUSINESS 実業] ❑ *...an outplacement firm in Denver.* デンバー市の再就職斡旋会社

out|post /aʊtpoʊst/ (**outposts**) **1** N-COUNT 可算名詞 An **outpost** is a small group of buildings used for trading or military purposes, either in a distant part of your own country or in a foreign country. 前哨 (ぜんしょう) 地 ❑ *...a remote mountain outpost, linked to the outside world by the poorest of roads.* 最低に劣った道路で外の世界に結ばれている遠隔地の山の前哨地 **2** N-COUNT 可算名詞 An **outpost** is a small settlement or community that is situated in a remote part of a country. 辺境の植民地 ❑ *This rural outpost, 400 miles northeast of Helena, has one stoplight.* ヘレナの北東400マイルのところにあるこの田舎の植民地には停止信号が1つある.

out|put /aʊtpʊt/ (**outputs**) **1** N-VAR 可変性名詞 **Output** is used to refer to the amount of something that a person or thing produces. 生産高 ❑ *Government statistics show the largest drop in industrial output for ten years.* 政府の統計によると工業生産高の減少は10年間で最大だった. **2** N-VAR 可変性名詞 The **output** of a computer or word processor is the information that it displays on a screen or prints on paper as a result of a particular program. 出力, ア

ウトプット □ *You run the software, you look at the output, you make modifications.* あなたはソフトのプログラムを実行し、出力を見て修正を行なう.

out|rage (outrages, outraging, outraged)

The verb is pronounced /autreɪdʒ/. The noun is pronounced /ˈautreɪdʒ/.

動詞は /autreɪdʒ/ と発音される. 名詞は /ˈautreɪdʒ/ と発音される.

1 V-T 他動詞 If you **are outraged** by something, it makes you extremely angry and shocked. 憤慨させる □ *Many people have been outraged by some of the things that have been said.* 多くの人々はその発言のいくつかに激しい怒りを感じた. ● **out|raged** ADJ 形容詞 憤慨した □ *He is truly outraged about what's happened to him.* 彼は身に降りかかったことに心から憤慨している. **2** N-UNCOUNT 不可算名詞 **Outrage** is an intense feeling of anger and shock. 憤慨, 激怒 □ *The decision provoked outrage from women and human rights groups.* その決定は女性や人権団体の憤慨を誘発した. **3** N-COUNT 可算名詞 You can refer to an act or event that angers and shocks you as an **outrage**. 憤慨させるもの □ *The latest outrage was to have been a coordinated gun and bomb attack on the station.* 最近の憤慨させる事件は駅に対する銃と爆弾による協調攻撃であった.

out|ra|geous /autreɪdʒəs/ ADJ 形容詞 If you describe something as **outrageous**, you are emphasizing that it is unacceptable or very shocking. 無法な [EMPHASIS 強調] □ *By diplomatic standards, this was outrageous behavior.* 外交水準から見て, これはけしからぬ行為だ. ● **out|ra|geous|ly** ADV 副詞 並外れて □ *...outrageously expensive skin care items.* べらぼうに高いスキンケア商品

out|right

The adjective is pronounced /ˈautraɪt/. The adverb is pronounced /autraɪt/.

形容詞は /ˈautraɪt/ と発音される. 副詞は /autraɪt/ と発音される.

1 ADJ 形容詞 You use **outright** to describe behavior and actions that are open and direct, rather than indirect. 明白な [ADJ n] □ *Kawaguchi finally resorted to an outright lie.* 川口はついに真っ赤なうそに頼った. ● ADV 副詞 **Outright** is also an adverb. 明白に [ADV after v] □ *Why are you so mysterious? Why don't you tell me outright?* 君はなぜそんなにあいまいに言っているのか. 私にはっきり言ったらどうだ. **2** ADJ 形容詞 **Outright** means complete and total. 完全な [ADJ n] □ *She had failed to win an outright victory.* 彼女は完勝できなかった. ● ADV 副詞 **Outright** is also an adverb. 完全に [ADV after v] □ *The peace plan wasn't rejected outright.* その和平案は完全には拒絶されたわけではなかった. ● PHRASE 句 If someone **is killed outright**, they die immediately, for example, in an accident. 即死する

out|sell /autsɛl/ (outsells, outselling, outsold) V-T 他動詞 If one product **outsells** another product, the first product is sold more quickly or in larger quantities than the second. より多く売れる [BUSINESS 実業] □ *The team's products easily outsell those of other American baseball teams overseas.* そのチームの商品は容易に海外で他のアメリカの野球チームの商品より多く売れる.

out|set /autset/ PHRASE 句 If something happens **at the outset** of an event, process, or period of time, it happens at the beginning of it. If something happens **from the outset** it happens from the beginning and continues to happen. 最初 □ *Decide at the outset what kind of learning program you want to follow.* どのような学習計画に従いたいのかを最初に決めなさい.

out|side /autsaɪd/ (outsides)

The form **outside of** can also be used as a preposition.

outside of 形は前置詞としても使える.

1 N-COUNT 可算名詞 The **outside** of something is the part which surrounds or encloses the rest of it. 外側 □ *...the outside of the building.* 建物の外部 ● ADJ 形容詞 **Outside** is also an adjective. 外側の [ADJ n] □ *...high up on the outside wall.* 外側の壁沿いに高く **2** ADV 副詞 If you are **outside**, you are not inside a building but are quite close to it. 外に □ *I stepped outside and pulled up my collar against the cold mist.* 私は外に出たが, 冷たいもやが出ていて襟を立てた. □ *Outside, the light was fading rapidly.* 外は急に暗くなりつつあった. ● PREP 前置詞 **Outside** is also a preposition. 一の外に □ *The victim was outside a shop when he was attacked.* 被害者は襲われた時に店の外にいた. ● ADJ 形容詞 **Outside** is also an adjective. 外の [ADJ n] □ *...the outside temperature.* 外の気温 **3** PREP 前置詞 If you are **outside** a room, you are not in it but are in the passage or area next to it. 一の外に □ *She'd sent him outside the classroom.* 彼女は彼を教室の外に出した. ● ADV 副詞 **Outside** is also an adverb. 外に □ *They heard voices coming from outside in the corridor.* 彼らは廊下で声が外から来るのを聞いた. **4** ADJ 形容詞 When you talk about the **outside** world, you are referring to things that happen or exist in places other than your own home or community. 外部の [ADJ n] □ *...a side of Morris's character she hid carefully from the outside*

world. 彼女が外部の世界から注意深く隠したモリスの性格の1側面である. ● ADV 副詞 **Outside** is also an adverb. 外部に [ADV after v] □ *The scheme was good for the prisoners because it brought them outside into the community.* その計画は囚人たちを外部に出して地域社会と接触させたので囚人たちのためになった. **5** PREP 前置詞 People or things **outside** a country, town, or region are not in it. [n/-ed PREP n] □ *...an old castle outside Budapest.* ブダペスト市の郊外にある古い城 ● N-SING 単数名詞 **Outside** is also a noun. 外部 ['the' n] □ *Peace cannot be imposed from the outside by the United States or anyone else.* 和平は米国あるいは他のだれによっても外部から押し付けることはできない. **6** ADJ 形容詞 **Outside** people or organizations are not part of a particular organization or group. 外部の [ADJ n] □ *The company now makes much greater use of outside consultants.* その会社は現在では社外のコンサルタントをずっと多く利用している. ● PREP 前置詞 **Outside** is also a preposition. 一の外部で □ *He is hoping to recruit a chairman from outside the company.* 彼は社外から会長をスカウトすることを望んでいる. **7** PREP 前置詞 **Outside** a particular institution or field of activity means in other fields of activity or in general life. 一の外で □ *...the largest merger ever to take place outside the oil industry.* 石油業界の外で起こるこれまで最大の合併 **8** PREP 前置詞 Something that is **outside** a particular range of things is not included within it. 一の範囲外に □ *She is a beautiful boat, but way, way outside my price range.* それは美しいボートだが, 私の予算を大きく大きく上回る. **9** PREP 前置詞 Something that happens **outside** a particular period of time happens at a different time from the one mentioned. 一以外の時に □ *They are open outside normal daily banking hours.* その銀行は日常の営業時間外に営業している.

Thesaurus   outside また次を参照:

ADJ. exterior, outdoor; *(ant.)* inside, interior **1**
PREP. beyond, near; *(ant.)* inside **3 5**

Word Partnership   outside は次の語句と使われる:

N.   the outside **of a building** **1**
      outside **a building**, outside **a car**, outside **a room**, outside **a store** **3**
      outside **interests**, the outside **world** **4**
      outside **a city/town**, outside **a country** **5**
      outside **sources** **6**
ADJ. **cold** outside, **dark** outside **2**
V.   **gather** outside, **go** outside, **park** outside, **sit** outside, **stand** outside, **step** outside, **wait** outside **2 3**

out|sid|er /autsaɪdər/ (outsiders) **1** N-COUNT 可算名詞 An **outsider** is someone who does not belong to a particular group or organization. 部外者 □ *The most likely outcome may be to subcontract much of the work to an outsider.* その仕事の多くを外部の業者に下請けに出すことであろう. **2** N-COUNT 可算名詞 An **outsider** is someone who is not accepted by a particular group, or who feels that they do not belong in it. よそ者 □ *Malone, a cop, felt as much an outsider as any of them.* 警官のマローンは彼らのだれにも負けないほどよそ者であると感じた. **3** N-COUNT 可算名詞 In a competition, an **outsider** is a competitor who is unlikely to win. 勝ち目のない人 □ *He was an outsider in the race to be the new UN Secretary-General.* 彼は新しい国連事務総長への選挙戦で選ばれる可能性はなかった.

out|skirts /autskɜrts/ N-PLURAL 複数名詞 The **outskirts** of a city or town are the parts of it that are farthest away from its center. 郊外, 町外れ □ *Hours later we reached the outskirts of New York.* 数時間後, 我々はニューヨークの郊外に到着した.

out|source /autsɔrs/ (outsources, outsourcing, outsourced) V-T/V-I 他動詞/自動詞 If a company **outsources** work or things, it pays workers from outside the company and often outside the country to do the work or supply the things. 外部から調達する [BUSINESS 実業] □ *...companies that outsource IT functions.* IT業務を外部調達する企業 □ *The company began looking for ways to cut costs, which led to the decision to outsource.* その会社は経費削減手段を探し始めた. そしてその決断は外部調達する決定となった. ● **out|sourc|ing** N-UNCOUNT 不可算名詞 外部調達 □ *The difficulties of outsourcing have been compounded by the increasing resistance of labor unions.* 外部調達の難事は労働組合の抵抗の高まりによっていっそう悪化した.

out|spo|ken /autspoukən/ ADJ 形容詞 Someone who is **outspoken** gives their opinions about things openly and honestly, even if they are likely to shock or offend people. 率直な □ *Some church leaders have been outspoken in their support for political reform in Kenya.* 1部の教会指導者たちは率直にケニアの政治改革を支持してきた. ● **out|spo|ken|ness** N-UNCOUNT 不可算名詞 率直さ □ *Their outspokenness on behalf of civil rights sometimes cost them their jobs.* 彼らは公民権支持の率直な発言のおかげで時に職を失うことがあった.

out|stand|ing /autstændɪŋ/ **1** ADJ 形容詞 If you describe someone or something as **outstanding**, you think that they

are very remarkable and impressive. 傑出した ❏ *Derartu is an outstanding athlete and deserved to win.* デラルチュは傑出したアスリートで勝って当然だった. **2** ADJ 形容詞 Money that is **outstanding** has not yet been paid and is still owed to someone. 未払いの ❏ *The total debt outstanding is $70 billion.* 未払いの債務総額は700億ドルである. **3** ADJ 形容詞 **Outstanding** issues or problems have not yet been resolved. 未解決の ❏ *We still have some outstanding issues to resolve before we'll have a treaty that is ready to sign.* 我々は署名できる協定ができる前に, 解決すべき未解決の問題がまだ若干残っている. **4** ADJ 形容詞 **Outstanding** means very important or obvious. 顕著な ❏ *The company is an outstanding example of a small business that grew into a big one.* その会社は零細企業が大企業に成長した顕著な例だ.

out|stand|ing|ly /aʊtˈstændɪŋli/ ADV 副詞 You use **outstandingly** to emphasize how good, or occasionally how bad, something is. 抜群に [EMPHASIS 強調] [ADV adj/adv] ❏ *Guatemala is an outstandingly beautiful place to visit.* グァテマラは素晴らしく美しい観光地だ.

out|stretched /aʊtˈstrɛtʃt/ ADJ 形容詞 If a part of the body of a person or animal is **outstretched**, it is stretched out as far as possible. 伸びた ❏ *She was staring into the fire muttering, and holding her arms outstretched to warm her hands.* 彼女はぶつぶつ独り言を言いながら火を見つめていて, 手を温めるために両腕を伸ばしていた.

out|strip /aʊtˈstrɪp/ (**outstrips, outstripping, outstripped**) V-T 他動詞 If one thing **outstrips** another, the first thing becomes larger in amount, or more successful or important, than the second thing. より勝る ❏ *In 1989 and 1990 demand outstripped supply, and prices went up by more than a third.* 1989年と1990年に需要は供給を上回り, 価格は3分の1以上上昇した.

out tray (**out trays**) also **out-tray** N-COUNT 可算名詞 An **out tray** is a shallow container used in offices to put letters and documents in when they have been dealt with and are ready to be sent somewhere else. Compare **in tray**. 即決書類入れ [mainly BRIT 主に英国英語; AM usually **out box** 米国英語では通常 **out box**]

out|ward /ˈaʊtwərd/

The form **outwards** can also be used for meanings **3** and **4**.

outwards 形は **3** と **4** の意味にも使える.

1 ADJ 形容詞 The **outward** feelings, qualities, or attitudes of someone or something are the ones they appear to have rather than the ones that they actually have. 外面的な [ADJ n] ❏ *In spite of my outward calm I was very shaken.* 表向きは平静だったが, 私は大変動揺していた. **2** ADJ 形容詞 The **outward** features of something are the ones that you can see from the outside. 外見の [ADJ n] ❏ *Mark was lying unconscious but with no outward sign of injury.* マークは気を失って倒れていたが, 外見は怪我しているようには見えなかった. **3** ADV 副詞 If something moves or faces **outward**, it moves or faces away from the place you are in or the place you are talking about. 外へ [ADV after v] ❏ *The top door opened outward.* 上部の戸は外に開いた. **4** ADV 副詞 If you say that a person or a group of people, such as a government, looks **outward**, you mean that they turn their attention to another group that they are interested in or would like greater involvement with. 国外へ [ADV after v] ❏ *Other poor countries looked outward, strengthening their ties to the economic superpowers.* 他の貧困諸国は国外に注目して, 経済超大国とのつながりを強化した. **5** ADJ 形容詞 An **outward** flight or journey is one that you make away from a place that you are intending to return to later. 外国行きの [ADJ n]

out|ward|ly /ˈaʊtwərdli/ ADV 副詞 You use **outwardly** to indicate the feelings or qualities that a person or situation may appear to have, rather than the ones that they actually have. 見たところは ❏ *They may feel tired, and though outwardly calm, can be irritable.* 彼らは疲れているかも知れない. 見たところは平静だが, 怒りっぽくなっている可能性がある.

out|weigh /aʊtˈweɪ/ (**outweighs, outweighing, outweighed**) **1** V-T 他動詞 If one thing **outweighs** another, the first thing is of greater importance, benefit, or significance than the second thing. より勝さる [FORMAL 形式ばった] ❏ *The advantages of this deal largely outweigh the disadvantages.* この取引の長所は短所を大幅に上回っている. **2** V-T 他動詞 If you **outweigh** someone, you are heavier than them. より重い ❏ *Young outweighed her opponent by about 60 pounds.* ヤングは試合相手より約60ポンド重かった.

out|wit /aʊtˈwɪt/ (**outwits, outwitting, outwitted**) V-T 他動詞 If you **outwit** someone, you use your intelligence or a trick to defeat them or to gain an advantage over them. 裏をかく, 出し抜く ❏ *To win the presidency he first had to outwit his rivals within the Socialist Party.* 大統領の地位を勝ち取るには彼はまず最初に社会党内のライバルを出し抜かねばならなかった.

oval /ˈoʊvəl/ (**ovals**) ADJ 形容詞 **Oval** things have a shape that is like a circle but is wider in one direction than the other. 卵形の, 楕円 (だえん) 形の ❏ *...the small oval framed picture of a little boy.* 小さな男の子の小さな円形の額に入った絵 ● N-COUNT 可算名詞 **Oval** is

also a noun. 卵形 ❏ *Using 2 spoons, form the cheese into small balls or ovals.* スプーンを2本使って, チーズを小さな球か卵形にしなさい.

→ see **circle, shape**

ova|ry /ˈoʊvəri/ (**ovaries**) N-COUNT 可算名詞 A woman's **ovaries** are the two organs in her body that produce eggs. 卵巣 ❏ *...women who have had their ovaries removed.* 卵巣切除した女性.

ova|tion /oʊˈveɪʃən/ (**ovations**) N-COUNT 可算名詞 An **ovation** is a large amount of applause from an audience for a particular performer or speaker. 大かっさい [FORMAL 形式ばった] ❏ *They became civic heroes and received a tumultuous ovation on their appearance in New York City.* 彼らは市民の英雄となり, ニューヨーク市に現れると猛烈な歓迎を受けた.

oven /ˈʌvən/ (**ovens**) N-COUNT 可算名詞 An **oven** is a device for cooking that is like a box with a door. You heat it and cook food inside it. オーブン ❏ *Put the onions and ginger in the oven and let them roast for thirty minutes.* タマネギとショウガをオーブンに入れ, 30分間そのまま焼きなさい.

```
                 over
    ❶ POSITION AND MOVEMENT
    ❷ AMOUNTS AND OCCURRENCES
    ❸ OTHER USES
```

❶ over /ˈoʊvər/

In addition to the uses shown below, **over** is used after some verbs, nouns, and adjectives in order to introduce extra information. **Over** is also used in phrasal verbs such as "hand over" and "glaze over."

下記の用法に加えて, **over** は追加の情報を伝えるために, 1部の動詞, 名詞, 形容詞の後に使われる. **Over** はまた **hand over** や **glaze over** のような句動詞にも使われる.

1 PREP 前置詞 If one thing is **over** another thing or is moving **over** it, the first thing is directly above the second, either resting on it, or with a space between them. ～の上の ❏ *He looked at himself in the mirror over the table.* 彼は自分の姿を机の上の鏡で見た. ● ADV 副詞 **Over** is also an adverb. 上に [ADV after v] ❏ *...planes flying over every 10 or 15 minutes.* 10分か15分おきに頭上を飛ぶ飛行機. **2** PREP 前置詞 If one thing is **over** another thing, it is supported by it and its ends are hanging down on each side of it. ～の上に ❏ *A grey raincoat was folded over her arm.* 灰色のレインコートが折りたたんで彼女の腕にかけられていた. **3** PREP 前置詞 If one thing is **over** another thing, it covers part or all of it. ～の上に ❏ *Mix the ingredients and pour over the mushrooms.* 材料を混ぜ, キノコの上にかけなさい. ❏ *He was wearing a light-grey suit over a shirt.* 彼はシャツの上に淡い灰色の背広を着ていた. ● ADV 副詞 **Over** is also an adverb. 上に [ADV after v] ❏ *Heat this syrup and pour it over.* このシロップを温めて上にかけなさい. **4** PREP 前置詞 If you lean **over** an object, you bend your body so that the top part of it is above the object. ～の上へ, ～の上に押しかぶさって [V PREP n] ❏ *They stopped to lean over a gate.* 彼らは立ち止まり門から身を乗り出した. ● ADV 副詞 **Over** is also an adverb. 上へ [ADV after v] ❏ *Sam leaned over to open the door of the car.* サムは車のドアを開けるため身をかがめた. **5** PREP 前置詞 If you look **over** or talk **over** an object, you look or talk across the top of it. ～を越えて ❏ *I went and stood beside him, looking over his shoulder.* 私は行って彼のそばに立ち, 彼の肩越しに眺めた. **6** PREP 前置詞 If a window has a view **over** an area of land or water, you can see the land or water through the window. ～の全部を [n PREP n, v PREP n] ❏ *...a light and airy bar with a wonderful view over the river.* 川を見渡す景色がすばらしい, 明るくて風通しの良いバー. **7** PREP 前置詞 If someone or something goes **over** a barrier, obstacle, or boundary, they get to the other side of it by going across it, or across the top of it. ～を越えて [V PREP n] ❏ *I stepped over a broken piece of wood.* 私は折れた材木の1片をまたいだ. ❏ *Nearly one million people crossed over the river into Moldavia.* 100万人近くの人たちが河を渡ってモルダヴィアに行った. ● ADV 副詞 **Over** is also an adverb. 越えて [ADV after v] ❏ *I climbed over into the back seat.* 私は後部座席に乗り込んだ. **8** PREP 前置詞 If someone or something moves **over** an area or surface, they move across it, from one side to the other. ～の向こう側へ ❏ *Sam ran swiftly over the lawn to the gate.* 彼女はすばやく芝生を横切り門に走った. **9** PREP 前置詞 If something is on the opposite side of a road or river, you can say that it is **over** the road or river. ～の向こう側に ❏ *...a fashionable neighborhood, just over the river from Manhattan.* マンハッタンのちょうど川向かいにある上流社会地域. **10** ADV 副詞 If you go **over** to a place, you go to that place. 向かって ❏ *I got out the car and drove over to Greg's place.* 私は車を出してグレッグの家に向かった. ❏ *I thought you might have invited her over.* 私はあなたが彼女を招待したのかもしれないと思った. **11** ADV 副詞 You can use **over** to indicate a particular position or place a short distance away from someone or something. 離れて ❏ *He noticed Rolfe standing silently over by the window.* 彼はロルフが無言でぼつんと窓際に立っているのに気づいた. ❏ *John reached over and took Joanna's hand.* ジョンは手を伸ばしてジョアナの手を握った. **12** ADV 副詞 You

use **over** to say that someone or something falls toward or onto the ground, often suddenly or violently. 下に倒れて [ADV after v] ❑ *If he drinks more than two glasses of wine he falls over.* 彼はワインを2杯以上飲んだらぶっ倒れる。 ❑ *She pushed past me, almost knocking me over.* 彼女は私をほとんど突き倒す勢いで押しのけて行った。 **13** ADV 副詞 If something rolls **over** or is turned **over**, its position changes so that the part that was facing upward is now facing downward. さかさまに [ADV after v] ❑ *His car rolled over after a tire was punctured.* タイヤがパンクし、彼の車はひっくり返りました。

Over and **above** are both used to talk about position and height. If something is higher than something else and the two things are imagined as being positioned along a vertical line, you can use either **above** or **over**. ❑ *He opened a cupboard above the sink... She leaned forward until her face was over the basin.* However, if something is higher than something else but the two things are regarded as being wide or horizontal rather than tall or vertical, you have to use **above**. ❑ *The trees rose above the row of houses.* **Above** and **over** are both used to talk about measurements, for example, when you are talking about a point that is higher than another point on a scale. ❑ *Any money earned over that level is taxed. ...everybody above five feet eight inches in height.* You use **over** to say that a distance or period of time is longer than the one mentioned. ❑ *...a height of over twelve thousand feet... Our relationship lasted for over a year.* **Above** and **over** are also both used to talk about people's rank or importance. You use **above** to talk about people who are more important and in a higher position than other people. ❑ *...behaving as if she was in a position above the other staff.* If someone is **over** you, they give orders or instructions to you. ❑ *...an officer in authority over him.*

---

14 PHRASE 句 **All over** a place means in every part of it. いたるところで ❑ *...doctors who work all over the country.* 国中で働いている医者たち **15** PHRASE 句 **Over here** means near you, or in the country you are in. こちらに、こちらでは ❑ *Why don't you come over here tomorrow evening.* 明日の夜家にいらっしゃいよ。 **16** PHRASE 句 **Over there** means in a place a short distance away from you, or in another country. あちらに ❑ *The cafe is just across the road over there.* カフェはちょうど道を渡った向こう側にある。 ❷ **over** /oʊvər/ **1** PREP 前置詞 If something is **over** a particular amount, measurement, or age, it is more than that amount, measurement, or age. ～より以上、～を越えて [PREP amount] ❑ *They say that tobacco will kill over 4 million people worldwide this year.* 今年世界で400万人以上がタバコが原因で死ぬと言われている。 ❑ *His family have accumulated property worth well over $1 million.* 彼の一家は100万ドルを軽く超える資産を蓄えていた。 ● ADV 副詞 **Over** is also an adverb. 超して [amount 'and' ADV] ❑ *...people aged 65 and over.* 65歳以上の人たち **2** PHRASE 句 **Over and above** an amount, especially a normal amount, means more than that amount or in addition to it. ～に加えて、～の上に ❑ *Expenditure on education has gone up by seven point eight per cent over and above inflation.* 教育支出はインフレ率に加えてさらに7.8%上昇した。 **3** ADV 副詞 If you say that you have some food or money **over** or left **over**, you mean that it remains after you have used all that you need. 余分に ❑ *The Larsons pay me well enough, but there's not much left over for luxuries.* ラーソン一家はわたしに十分いい給料をくれるが、さほどの贅沢ができるほどの余裕はない。 **4** ADV 副詞 If you do something **over**, you do it again or start doing it again from the beginning. 繰り返して [AM 米国英語] [ADV after v] ❑ *She said if she had the chance to do it over, she would have hired a press secretary.* 彼女はもう1回やり直すことができたら、報道担当官を雇っただろうと言った。 **5** PHRASE 句 If you say that something happened **twice over, three times over** and so on, you are stating the number of times that it happened and emphasizing that it happened more than once. 2度繰り返して [mainly BRIT 主に英国英語, EMPHASIS 強調] ❑ *James had to have everything spelled out twice over for him.* ジェームズは何ごとも2度繰り返してはっきり説明してもらわないとだめだった。 **6** PHRASE 句 If you do something **over again**, you do it again or start doing it again from the beginning. はじめからもう1度 ❑ *If I could live my life over again, I would do things exactly the same way.* もし人生を始めからやり直しがきくとしても、私は全く同じように生きると思う。 **7** PHRASE 句 If you say that something is happening **all over again**, you are emphasizing that it is happening again, and you are suggesting that it is tiring, boring, or unpleasant. また最初から [EMPHASIS 強調] ❑ *The whole process started all over again.* この行程がすべてまた始めから繰り返された。 **8** PHRASE 句 If you say that something happened **over and over** or **over and over again**, you are emphasizing that it happened many times. 何度も何度も [EMPHASIS 強調] ❑ *He plays the same songs over and over.* 彼は同じ歌を何度も何度も演奏する。

Thesaurus　*over* また次を参照:

PREP. above, beyond, higher than; (ant.) below, under ❶ **1**
ADJ. completed, concluded, done with, ended, finished ❸ **1**

---

❸ **over** /oʊvər/ **1** ADJ 形容詞 If an activity is **over** or **all over**, it is completely finished. 終わって [v-link ADJ] ❑ *Warplanes that have landed there will be kept until the war is over.* そこに着陸した戦闘機は戦争が終わるまでそこに置かれるだろう。 ❑ *I am glad it's all over.* 私はすっかり済んで嬉しい。 **2** PREP 前置詞 If you are **over** an illness or an experience, it has finished and you have recovered from its effects. ～が治って、～が終わって ❑ *I'm glad that you're over the flu.* インフルエンザが治ってよかったわね。 **3** PREP 前置詞 If you have control or influence **over** someone or something, you are able to control them or influence them. ～に対して [n PREP n] ❑ *He's never had any influence over her.* 彼は彼女に全くにらみが効かない。 **4** PREP 前置詞 You use **over** to indicate that a disagreement or feeling relates to or is caused by. ～に関して [n PREP n, v PREP n] ❑ *...concern over recent events in the Dominican Republic.* ドミニカ共和国での最近の出来事に関する懸念 ❑ *Staff at some air and sea ports are beginning to protest over pay.* 一部の空港や海港の従業員は給料について抗議しはじめている。 **5** PREP 前置詞 If something happens **over** a particular period of time or **over** something such as a meal, it happens during that time or during the meal. ～の間、～にわたって ❑ *The number of attacks on the capital had gone down over the past week.* 過去1週間にわたって首都に対する攻撃回数が減っていた。 **6** PREP 前置詞 You use **over** to indicate that you give or receive information using a telephone, radio, or other piece of electrical equipment. ～を使って ❑ *I'm not prepared to discuss this over the telephone.* 私はこれについて電話で話すつもりはない。 ❑ *The head of state addressed the nation over the radio.* 国家元首はラジオで国民に演説しました。 **7** PHRASE 句 The presenter of a radio or television program says "**over to** someone" to indicate the person who will speak next. ～の番です ❑ *With the rest of the sports news, over to Mike Martinez.* 残りのスポーツニュースはマイク・マルティネズからお願いします。 **8** CONVENTION 慣習表現 When people such as the police or the army are using a radio to communicate, they say "**Over**" to indicate that they have finished speaking and are waiting for a reply. 応答どうぞ [FORMULAE 決まり文句]

over|all (overalls)

The adjective and adverb are pronounced /oʊvərɔl/. The noun is pronounced /oʊvərɔl/.

形容詞と副詞は /oʊvərɔl/ と発音される。名詞は /oʊvərɔl/ と発音される。

---

1 ADJ 形容詞 You use **overall** to indicate that you are talking about a situation in general or about the whole of something. 全体的にみた [ADJ n] ❑ *...the overall rise in unemployment.* 全体的にみた失業率の上昇 ● ADV 副詞 **Overall** is also an adverb. 全体的に見て [ADV with cl] ❑ *Overall I was disappointed.* 全体的に見て私はがっかりした。 **2** N-PLURAL 複数名詞 **Overalls** are pants that are attached to a piece of cloth which covers your chest and which has straps going over your shoulders. 胸当て付き作業ズボン [AM 米国英語] [also 'a pair of' N] ❑ *An elderly man dressed in faded overalls took the witness stand.* 色あせたオーバーオールをはいた初老の男性が証言台に立った。 **3** N-PLURAL 複数名詞 **Overalls** consist of a single piece of clothing that combines pants and a jacket. You wear overalls over your clothes in order to protect them while you are working. つなぎ服、上っ張り [also 'a pair of' N]

over|awe /oʊvərɔ/ (overawes, overawing, overawed) V-T 他動詞 If you **are overawed by** something or someone, you are very impressed by them and a little afraid of them. 威圧する [usu passive] ❑ *Don't be overawed by people in authority, however important they are.* 権力を持っている人たちに、たとえ彼らがどんなに重要な人たちでも威圧されるな。

over|board /oʊvərbɔrd/ **1** ADV 副詞 If you fall **overboard**, you fall over the side of a boat into the water. 船外に [ADV after v] ❑ *My sailing instructor fell overboard and nearly drowned during a lesson.* 授業中に私の教官がヨットから落ちて、おぼれそうになった。 **2** PHRASE 句 If you say that someone **goes overboard**, you mean that they do something to a greater extent than is necessary or reasonable. やりすぎる [INFORMAL くだけた] ❑ *Women sometimes damage their skin by going overboard with abrasive cleansers.* 女性は研磨性のクリーナーを使いすぎて皮膚を傷めることもある。

over|came /oʊvərkeɪm/ **Overcame** is the past tense of **overcome.** overcomeの過去形

over|ca|pac|ity /oʊvərkəpæsɪti/ N-UNCOUNT 不可算名詞 If there is **overcapacity** in a particular industry or area, more goods have been produced than are needed, and the industry is therefore less profitable than it could be. 設備過剰 [BUSINESS 実業] ❑ *There is huge overcapacity in the world car industry.* 世界の自動車産業では巨大な設備過剰がある。

over|charge /oʊvərtʃɑrdʒ/ (overcharges, overcharging, overcharged) V-T 他動詞 If someone **overcharges** you, they charge you too much for their goods or services. 高値をふっかける ❑ *If you feel a taxi driver has overcharged you, say so.* もしタクシーの運転手が高い値段を請求したなと思ったら、そう言うように。

over|coat /oʊvərkoʊt/ (overcoats) N-COUNT 可算名詞 An

overcoat is a thick warm coat that you wear in winter. オーバー

over|come /oʊvərkʌm/ (overcomes, overcoming, overcame)

> The form **overcome** is used in the present tense and is also the past participle.
>
> **overcome** 形は現在時制に使われ，過去分詞でもある．

1 V-T 他動詞 If you **overcome** a problem or a feeling, you successfully deal with it and control it. 克服する □ *Molly had fought and overcome her fear of flying.* モリーは飛ぶことに対する恐怖と戦いそれを克服した． **2** V-T 他動詞 If you **are overcome by** a feeling or event, it is so strong or has such a strong effect that you cannot think clearly. 圧倒する □ *The night before the test I was overcome by fear and despair.* 試験の前夜私は不安と絶望感に押しつぶされてしまった． **3** V-T 他動詞 If you **are overcome by** smoke or a poisonous gas, you become very ill or die from breathing it in. 参らせる，窒息させる [usu passive] □ *The residents were trying to escape from the fire but were overcome by smoke.* 住人たちは火災から逃げようとしていたが，煙にまかれてしまった．

Word Partnership overcome は次の語句と使われる：

ADJ.	**difficult to overcome**, **hard to overcome** 1
N.	overcome **difficulties**, overcome **a fear**, overcome **an obstacle/problem**, overcome **opposition** 1
	overcome **by emotion**, overcome **by fear** 2

over|crowd|ed /oʊvərkraʊdɪd/ ADJ 形容詞 An **overcrowded** place has too many things or people in it. 混雑した □ *...a windswept, overcrowded, unattractive beach.* 吹きさらしでひどく混雑していてぱっとしない海岸

over|crowd|ing /oʊvərkraʊdɪŋ/ N-UNCOUNT 不可算名詞 If there is a problem of **overcrowding**, there are more people living in a place than it was designed for. 超過密 □ *Students were protesting at overcrowding in the dorms.* 学生たちは寄宿舎の超過密状態について抗議していた．

over|do /oʊvərdu/ (overdoes, overdoing, overdid, overdone) **1** V-T 他動詞 If someone **overdoes** something, they behave in an exaggerated or extreme way. 度を越す □ *The extent of the rise might indicate that it had been overdone.* その上昇の程度からするとそれは過剰だったのかもしれない． **2** V-T 他動詞 If you **overdo** an activity, you try to do more than you can physically manage. やりすぎる □ *It is important never to overdo new exercises.* 慣れない運動は決してしすぎないことが大切です． □ *It's important to study hard, but don't overdo it.* 一生懸命勉強するのは大切だが，やりすぎはいけない．

over|dose /oʊvərdoʊs/ (overdoses, overdosing, overdosed) **1** N-COUNT 可算名詞 If someone takes an **overdose** of a drug, they take more of it than is safe. 過量，過剰服用 □ *Each year, one in 100 girls ages 15-19 takes an overdose.* 毎年，15歳から19歳の少女100人に1人が薬を過剰服用する． **2** V-I 自動詞 If someone **overdoses on** a drug, they take more of it than is safe. 過剰服用する □ *He'd overdosed on heroin.* 彼はヘロインをやりすぎた． **3** N-COUNT 可算名詞 You can refer to too much of something, especially something harmful, as an **overdose**. やりすぎ □ *An overdose of sun, sea, sand and chlorine can give lighter hair a green tinge.* 比較的明るい色の髪の毛は太陽，海，砂，塩素に過度にさらされると緑色を帯びることがある． **4** V-I 自動詞 You can say that someone **overdoses on** something if they use or do too much of it. やりすぎる □ *The city, he concluded, had overdosed on design.* その市はデザインが過剰だと彼は締めくくった．

over|draft /oʊvərdræft/ (overdrafts) N-COUNT 可算名詞 If you have an **overdraft**, you have spent more money than you have in your bank account, and so you are in debt to the bank. 当座貸し越し □ *Her bank warned that unless she repaid the overdraft she could face legal action.* 銀行は彼女が当座貸し越しを返済しないと法的措置を取られる恐れがあると警告した．

over|drawn /oʊvərdrɔn/ ADJ 形容詞 If you are **overdrawn** or if your bank account is **overdrawn**, you have spent more money than you have in your account, and so you are in debt to the bank. 残高以上引き出した，借り越しの □ *Nick's bank sent him a letter saying he was $500 overdrawn.* ニックの銀行は彼に500ドル超過引き出しがあるとの通知を送った．

over|due /oʊvərdu/ **1** ADJ 形容詞 If you say that a change or an event is **overdue**, you mean that you think it should have happened before now. 遅れた □ *This debate is long overdue.* この討論はとっくに行われているべきものだ． **2** ADJ 形容詞 **Overdue** sums of money have not been paid, even though it is later than the date on which they should have been paid. 未払いの □ *There is a 2% interest charge on overdue balances.* 支払期限を過ぎると差額に2%の利息が付く． **3** ADJ 形容詞 An **overdue** library book has not been returned to the library, even though the date on which it should have been returned has passed. 延滞した □ *...a library book now weeks overdue.* すでに何週間も延滞した図書館の本．

over|eat /oʊvərit/ (overeats, overeating, overate, overeaten) V-I 自動詞 If you say that someone **overeats**, you mean they eat

more than they need to or more than is healthy. 食べ過ぎる □ *If you tend to overeat because of depression, first take steps to recognize the source of your sadness.* 憂うつなため食べ過ぎる傾向がある場合には，まず最初に悲しみの原因が何にあるかを認識するように．

over|es|ti|mate (overestimates, overestimating, overestimated)

> The verb is pronounced /oʊvərɛstɪmeɪt/. The noun is pronounced /oʊvərɛstɪmɪt/.
>
> 動詞は /oʊvərɛstɪmeɪt/ と発音される．名詞は /oʊvərɛstɪmɪt/ と発音される．

1 V-T/V-I 他動詞/自動詞 If you say that someone **overestimates** something, you mean that they think it is greater in amount or importance than it really is. 過大に見積る，過大評価する □ *He was overestimating their desire for peace.* 彼は彼らの和平への望みを過大評価していた． □ *If they overestimate, they lose revenue.* もし見積もりが高すぎると，彼らは収益を失う． • N-COUNT 可算名詞 **Overestimate** is also a noun. 過大評価 □ *Twenty-five thousand turned out to be an overestimate.* 2万5千という見積もりは結局のところ過大すぎた． **2** V-T 他動詞 If you say that something **cannot be overestimated**, you are emphasizing that you think it is very important. 過大評価する [EMPHASIS 強調][with brd-neg] □ *The importance of the media in communicating antidrug messages cannot be overestimated.* 麻薬の使用に反対するメッセージを伝えるに当たって，マスコミの重要性はいくら評価してもしきれないほどだ． **3** V-T 他動詞 If you **overestimate** someone, you think that they have more of a skill or quality than they really have. 買いかぶる □ *I think you overestimate me, Fred.* フレッド，君は私を買いかぶっていると思う．

over|flow (overflows, overflowing, overflowed)

> The verb is pronounced /oʊvərflou/. The noun is pronounced /oʊvərflou/.
>
> 動詞は /oʊvərflou/ と発音される．名詞は /oʊvərflou/ と発音される．

1 V-T/V-I 他動詞/自動詞 If a liquid or a river **overflows**, it flows over the edges of the container or place it is in. あふれる，氾濫する [no passive] □ *Pour in some of the broth, but not all of it, because it will probably overflow.* 全部入れるとあふれると思いますから，ブイヨンの全部ではなく一部だけ入れること． □ *The rivers overflowed their banks.* 河川が氾濫した． **2** V-I 自動詞 If a place or container **is overflowing with** people or things, it is too full of them. あふれる，充満する [usu cont] □ *Schreiber addressed an auditorium overflowing with journalists.* シュライバーはジャーナリストであふれかえる講堂で演説した． **3** N-COUNT 可算名詞 The **overflow** is the extra people or things that something cannot contain or deal with because it is not large enough. 過剰 □ *Tents have been set up next to hospitals to handle the overflow.* 病院の隣にはあふれた患者を収容するのにテントが設置されている． **4** PHRASE 句 If a place or container is filled **to overflowing**, it is so full of people or things that no more can fit in. あふれるほどに □ *The kitchen garden was full to overflowing with fresh vegetables.* 家庭菜園は新鮮な野菜があふれるほどいっぱいだった．

over|grown /oʊvərgroun/ **1** ADJ 形容詞 If a garden or other place is **overgrown**, it is covered with a mass of unruly plants because it has not been cared for. 茂りすぎた □ *We hurried on until we reached a courtyard overgrown with weeds.* 私たちは急いで雑草の生い茂る中庭まで行きました． **2** ADJ 形容詞 If you describe an adult as an **overgrown** child, you mean that their behavior and attitudes are like those of a child, and that you dislike this. 大きくなりすぎた [DISAPPROVAL 不賛成][ADJ n] □ *...a bunch of overgrown kids.* 図体ばかり大きい子供の群れ

over|hang (overhangs, overhanging, overhung)

> The verb is pronounced /oʊvərhæŋ/. The noun is pronounced /oʊvərhæŋ/.
>
> 動詞は /oʊvərhæŋ/ と発音される．名詞は /oʊvərhæŋ/ と発音される．

1 V-T 他動詞 If one thing **overhangs** another, it sticks out over and above it. 張り出す □ *Part of the rock wall overhung the path at one point.* 岩の壁の1部が道に張り出していたところがあった． **2** N-COUNT An **overhang** is the part of something that sticks out over and above something else. 突出部分，張り出し □ *A sharp overhang of rock gave them cover.* 鋭く突き出している岩の下に彼らは避難した．

over|haul (overhauls, overhauling, overhauled)

> The verb is pronounced /oʊvərhɔl/. The noun is pronounced /oʊvərhɔl/.
>
> 動詞は /oʊvərhɔl/ と発音される．名詞は /oʊvərhɔl/ と発音される．

1 V-T 他動詞 If a piece of equipment **is overhauled**, it is cleaned, checked thoroughly, and repaired if necessary. 分解検査する，総点

検する [usu passive] ❑ *They had ensured the plumbing was overhauled a year ago.* 彼らはその配管設備が1年前に分解修理されたことを保証していた。 ●N-COUNT 可算名詞 **Overhaul** is also a noun. 分解検査, 総点検 ❑ *...the overhaul of a cruiser.* クルーザーの分解修理 ❷ V-T 他動詞 If you **overhaul** a system or method, you examine it carefully and make many changes in it in order to improve it. 徹底的に見直す ❑ *...proposals to overhaul bank regulations.* 銀行の規約を徹底的に見直すという提言 ●N-COUNT 可算名詞 **Overhaul** is also a noun. 徹底的見直し ❑ *The study says there must be a complete overhaul of air traffic control systems.* その調査によると、航空管制体制を完全に見直す必要がある。

over|head

The adjective and noun are pronounced /oʊvərhɛd/. The adverb is pronounced /oʊvərhɛd/.
形容詞と名詞は /oʊvərhɛd/ と発音される. 副詞は /oʊvərhɛd/ と発音される.

❶ ADJ 形容詞 You use **overhead** to indicate that something is above you or above the place that you are talking about. 頭上の [ADJ n] ❑ *She turned on the overhead light and looked around the little room.* 彼女は天井の照明を付け, 小さい室内を見回した. ●ADV 副詞 **Overhead** is also an adverb. 頭上に ❑ *...planes passing overhead.* 頭上を通過する飛行機 ❷ N-UNCOUNT 不可算名詞 The **overhead** of a business is its regular and essential expenses, such as salaries, rent, electricity, and telephone bills. 一般経費 [BUSINESS 実業] ❑ *Private insurers spend 27 cents of every dollar on overhead.* 私立の保険会社は1ドルあたり27パーセントを一般経費に使う.

over|head pro|jec|tor (**overhead projectors**) N-COUNT 可算名詞 An **overhead projector** is a machine that has a light inside it and makes the writing or pictures on a sheet of plastic appear on a screen or wall. The abbreviation **OHP** is also used. オーバーヘッドプロジェクター

over|hear /oʊvərhɪər/ (**overhears, overhearing, overheard**) V-T 他動詞 If you **overhear** someone, you hear what they are saying when they are not talking to you and they do not know that you are listening. 立ち聞きする, 盗み聴く ❑ *I overheard two doctors discussing my case.* 2人の医師が私の症例について話し合っているのを立ち聞きした.

over|heat /oʊvərhit/ (**overheats, overheating, overheated**) ❶ V-T/V-I 他動詞/自動詞 If something **overheats** or if you **overheat** it, it becomes hotter than is necessary or desirable. 過熱する, 熱しすぎる ❑ *The engine was overheating and the car was not handling well.* エンジンがオーバーヒートして, 自動車の操作がうまく行かなくなっていた. ●**over|heat|ed** ADJ 形容詞 過熱した ❑ *...that stuffy, overheated apartment.* 風通しの悪い暑すぎるアパート ❷ V-T/V-I 他動詞/自動詞 If a country's economy **overheats** or if conditions **overheat** it, it grows so rapidly that inflation and interest rates rise very quickly. 過熱させる, 過熱する [BUSINESS 実業] ❑ *The private sector is increasing its spending so sharply that the economy is overheating.* 民間部門が支出をあまりにも急速に増加しているために経済が過熱している. ●**over|heat|ed** ADJ 形容詞 過熱した ❑ *...the disastrous consequences of an overheated market.* 過熱した市場のもたらす, 惨たんたる結果

over|heat|ed /oʊvərhitɪd/ ADJ 形容詞 Someone who is **overheated** is very angry about something. 過度に興奮した ❑ *I think the reaction has been a little overheated.* その反応はちょっと興奮しすぎたものだと私は思う.

over|hung /oʊvərhʌŋ/ **Overhung** is the past tense and past participle of **overhang**. overhangの過去・過去分詞

over|joyed /oʊvərdʒɔɪd/ ADJ 形容詞 If you are **overjoyed**, you are extremely happy about something. 狂喜して [v-link ADJ] ❑ *Shelley was overjoyed to see me.* シェリーはわたしに会うと大喜びした.

over|land /oʊvərlænd/ ADJ 形容詞 An **overland** journey is made across land rather than by ship or airplane. 陸路の [ADJ n] ❑ *...an overland journey through Iraq, Turkey, Iran and Pakistan.* イラク, トルコ, イラン, パキスタンを横断する陸路の旅 ●ADV 副詞 **Overland** is also an adverb. 陸路で [ADV after v] ❑ *They're traveling to Baghdad overland.* 彼らは陸路でバグダッドに行くところだ.

over|lap (**overlaps, overlapping, overlapped**)

The verb is pronounced /oʊvərlæp/. The noun is pronounced /oʊvərlæp/.
動詞は /oʊvərlæp/ と発音される. 名詞は /oʊvərlæp/ と発音される.

❶ V-RECIP 相互動詞 If one thing **overlaps** another, or if you **overlap** them, a part of the first thing occupies the same area as a part of the other thing. You can also say that two things **overlap**. 重なる, 重ねる ❑ *When the bag is folded, the bottom overlaps one side.* 袋を畳むと底面は1方の側面に重なります. ❑ *Overlap the slices carefully so there are no gaps.* 薄切りスライスを隙間がないように重ねなさい. ❷ V-RECIP 相互動詞 If one idea or activity **overlaps**

another, or **overlaps** with another, they involve some of the same subjects, people, or periods of time. 一部重なり合う ❑ *Christian Holy Week overlaps with the beginning of the Jewish holiday of Passover.* キリスト教の聖週間はユダヤ教の過ぎ越しの祝いの始まりと一部重り合っている. ❑ *The needs of patients invariably overlap.* 患者たちが必要とすることはいつも重なり合う. ●N-VAR 可変性名詞 **Overlap** is also a noun. 重複 ❑ *...the overlap between civil and military technology.* 民間技術と軍事技術の重複部分

over|leaf /oʊvərlif/ ADV 副詞 **Overleaf** is used in books and magazines to say that something is on the other side of the page you are reading. 裏面に [FORMAL 形式ばった] ❑ *Answer the questionnaire overleaf.* 裏面の質問表に答えなさい.

over|load (**overloads, overloading, overloaded**)

The verb is pronounced /oʊvərloʊd/. The noun is pronounced /oʊvərloʊd/.
動詞は /oʊvərloʊd/ と発音される. 名詞は /oʊvərloʊd/ と発音される.

❶ V-T 他動詞 If you **overload** something such as a vehicle, you put more things or people into it than it was designed to carry. 積みすぎる ❑ *Don't overload the boat or it will sink.* 舟に荷を積みすぎると, さもないと沈んでしまうだろう ●**over|load|ed** ADJ 形容詞 荷を積みすぎた ❑ *Some trains were so overloaded that their suspension collapsed.* 一部の列車は荷を積みすぎていたため懸架装置が壊れた. ❷ V-T 他動詞 To **overload** someone **with** work, problems, or information means to give them more work, problems, or information than they can cope with. 負担をかけすぎる ❑ *...an effective method that will not overload staff with yet more paperwork.* 社員の事務処理をさらに増やして負担をかけすぎないような効果的方法 ●N-UNCOUNT 不可算名詞 **Overload** is also a noun. 負担のかけ過ぎ ❑ *57 percent complained of work overload.* 57%が仕事の負担の多すぎることに文句を言った. ●**over|load|ed** ADJ 形容詞 負担がかかりすぎた ❑ *The bar waiter was already overloaded with orders.* バーのウェイターは注文でもう手一杯だった. ❸ V-T 他動詞 If you **overload** an electrical system, you cause too much electricity to flow through it, and so damage it. 負荷をかけすぎる ❑ *Never overload an electrical outlet.* 絶対にコンセントに負荷をかけすぎるな.

over|look /oʊvərlʊk/ (**overlooks, overlooking, overlooked**) ❶ V-T 他動詞 If a building or window **overlooks** a place, you can see the place clearly from the building or window. 見晴らす ❑ *Pretty and comfortable rooms overlook a flower-filled garden.* きれいで居心地のいい部屋部屋は花でいっぱいの庭を見渡せる. ❷ V-T 他動詞 If you **overlook** a fact or problem, you do not notice it, or do not realize how important it is. 見落とす ❑ *We overlook all sorts of warning signals about our own health.* 自分自身の健康についてのあらゆる種類の危険信号を見落とすものだ. ❸ V-T 他動詞 If you **overlook** someone's faults or bad behavior, you forgive them and take no action. 見逃す ❑ *...satisfying relationships that enable them to overlook each other's faults.* お互いの欠点を大目に見ることのできるような満足できる関係

over|ly /oʊvərli/ ADV 副詞 **Overly** means more than is normal, necessary, or reasonable. 過度に [ADV adj/adv/-ed] ❑ *Employers may become overly cautious about taking on new staff.* 雇用者は新しい社員を雇うのに慎重になりすぎるかもしれない.

over|night /oʊvərnaɪt/ ❶ ADV 副詞 If something happens **overnight**, it happens throughout the night or at some point during the night. 夜のうちに [ADV after v] ❑ *The decision was reached overnight.* 夜のうちにその決定に至りました. ●ADJ 形容詞 **Overnight** is also an adjective. 1泊の [ADJ n] ❑ *Travel and overnight accommodation are included.* 旅行と1泊の宿が含まれている. ❷ ADV 副詞 You can say that something happens **overnight** when it happens very quickly and unexpectedly. 突然に [ADV after v] ❑ *The rules are not going to change overnight.* 規則は急には変わらない. ●ADJ 形容詞 **Overnight** is also an adjective. 突然の [ADJ n] ❑ *In 1970 he became an overnight success in America.* 1970年に彼はアメリカで1夜にして成功者になった. ❸ ADJ 形容詞 **Overnight** bags or clothes are ones that you take when you go and stay somewhere for one or two nights. 短い旅行用の [ADJ n] ❑ *He realized he'd left his overnight bag at Mary's house.* 彼は旅行かばんをメアリーの家に忘れてきたことに気づいた.

over|paid /oʊvərpeɪd/ ADJ 形容詞 If you say that someone is **overpaid**, you mean that you think they are paid more than they deserve for the work they do. 報酬を受けすぎた ❑ *...grossly overpaid corporate lawyers.* 法外な報酬を受けている企業弁護士

over|pass /oʊvərpæs/ (**overpasses**) N-COUNT 可算名詞 An **overpass** is a structure which carries one road over the top of another one. 高架道路 [mainly AM 主に米国英語] ❑ *...a $16 million highway overpass over Route 1.* 1号線を越える1600万ドルの高速高架道路

over|pow|er /oʊvərpaʊər/ (**overpowers, overpowering, overpowered**) ❶ V-T 他動詞 If you **overpower** someone, you manage to take hold of and keep hold of them, although they struggle a lot. 取り押さえる ❑ *It took ten guardsmen to overpower*

him. 州兵10人がかりで彼を取り押さえた. **2** V-T 他動詞 If a feeling **overpowers** you, it suddenly affects you very strongly. 圧倒する, 耐え切れなくする ❑ *A sudden dizziness overpowered him.* 彼は突然のめまいに耐え切れなかった. **3** V-T 他動詞 In a sports match, when one team or player **overpowers** the other, they play much better than the other and beat them easily. 打ち勝つ ❑ *Britain's tennis No 1 yesterday overpowered American Brian Garrow 7-6, 6-3.* 英国のテニスの第1人者は昨日アメリカのブライアン・ギャロウを7-6, 6-3で打ち勝った. **4** V-T 他動詞 If something such as a color or flavor **overpowers** another color or flavor, it is so strong that it makes the second one less noticeable. 圧倒する ❑ *A delicate wine will be overpowered by strong food.* 繊細なワインは味の強い食べ物に押し消されてしまうだろう.

over|pow|er|ing /oʊvərpaʊərɪŋ/ **1** ADJ 形容詞 An **overpowering** feeling is so strong that you cannot resist it. 圧倒的な ❑ *The desire for revenge can be overpowering.* ふくしゅうしたい気持ちは抵抗しがたいことがある. **2** ADJ 形容詞 An **overpowering** smell or sound is so strong that you cannot smell or hear anything else. 強烈な ❑ *There was an overpowering smell of alcohol.* 強烈なアルコールの匂いがした. **3** ADJ 形容詞 An **overpowering** person makes other people feel uncomfortable because they have such a strong personality. 威圧的な ❑ *Mrs. Winter was large and somewhat overpowering.* ウィンター夫人は大柄でちょっと威圧感のある人だった.

over|priced /oʊvərpraɪst/ ADJ 形容詞 If you say that something is **overpriced**, you mean that you think it costs much more than it should. 高すぎる値段の付いた ❑ *I went and had an overpriced cup of coffee in the hotel cafeteria.* 私はホテルのカフェテリアに行って, やたら高いコーヒーを1杯飲んだ.

over|ran /oʊvərræn/ **Overran** is the past tense of **overrun**. overrunの過去形

over|rate /oʊvəreɪt/ (**overrates, overrating, overrated**) also **over-rate** V-T 他動詞 If you say that something or someone is **overrated**, you mean that people have a higher opinion of them than they deserve. 過大評価する ❑ *More men are finding out that the joys of work have been overrated.* 仕事の喜びは過大評価されていたと感じている男性が増えてきている. ● **over|rat|ed** ADJ 形容詞 過大評価された ❑ *Life in the wild is vastly overrated.* 野生的生活は非常に過大評価されている.

over|react /oʊvəriækt/ (**overreacts, overreacting, overreacted**) V-I 自動詞 If you say that someone **overreacts** to something, you mean that they have and show more of an emotion than is necessary or appropriate. 過剰反応する ❑ *I overreact to anything sad.* 私は悲しいことには何にでも過剰な反応を示す.

over|ride (**overrides, overriding, overrode, overridden**)

The verb is pronounced /oʊvəˈraɪd/. The noun is pronounced /oʊvəˈraɪd/.

動詞は /oʊvəˈraɪd/ と発音される. 名詞は /oʊvəˈraɪd/ と発音される.

1 V-T 他動詞 If one thing in a situation **overrides** other things, it is more important than they are. 優先する ❑ *The welfare of a child should always override the wishes of its parents.* 親の希望より子供の福利のほうを常に優先すべきである. **2** V-T 他動詞 If someone in authority **overrides** a person or their decisions, they cancel their decisions. くつがえす ❑ *The president vetoed the bill, and the Senate failed by a single vote to override his veto.* 大統領は法案を拒否し, 上院はたった1票不足したため, 大統領の拒否権を無効にすることができなかった. **3** N-COUNT 可算名詞 An **override** is an attempt to cancel someone's decisions by using your authority over them or by gaining more votes than they do in an election or contest. くつがえすこと [AM 米国英語] ❑ *The bill now goes to the House where an override vote is expected to fail.* 次にその法案はくつがえす得票が得られないと思われている下院にかけられる.

over|rid|ing /oʊvərraɪdɪŋ/ ADJ 形容詞 In a particular situation, the **overriding** factor is the one that is the most important. 最も重要な ❑ *My overriding concern is to raise the standards of state education.* 私にとって最も重要なことは州の教育水準を上げることだ.

over|rule /oʊvərruːl/ (**overrules, overruling, overruled**) V-T 他動詞 If someone in authority **overrules** a person or their decision, they officially decide that the decision is incorrect or not valid. 却下する ❑ *In 1991, the Court of Appeal overruled this decision.* 1991年に控訴裁判所はこの判決をくつがえした.

over|run /oʊvərrʌn/ (**overruns, overrunning, overran**) **1** V-T 他動詞 If an army or an armed force **overruns** a place, area, or country, it succeeds in occupying it very quickly. 一斉に侵略する ❑ *A group of rebels overran the port area and most of the northern suburbs.* 反乱グループが港湾地域と郊外地区北部の大部分を一気に侵略しました. **2** ADJ 形容詞 If you say that a place **is overrun with** things that you consider undesirable, you mean that there are a large number of them there. はびこった [v-link ADJ] ❑ *The hotel has*

been ordered to close because it is overrun by mice and rats. ネズミ類がはびこっているので, そのホテルは閉鎖命令を受けた. **3** V-T/V-I 他動詞/自動詞 If costs **overrun**, they are higher than was planned or expected. 越える, 超過する [BUSINESS 実業] ❑ *We should stop the nonsense of taxpayers trying to finance joint weapons whose costs always overrun hugely.* 見積もりを大きく超過するのを常とする武器の南アフリカ開発の資金を税金から調達するというばかげた話は食い止めるべきだ. ❑ *Costs overran the budget by about 30%.* 予算を約30%超える費用がかかった. ● N-COUNT 可算名詞 **Overrun** is also a noun. 超過 ❑ *He was stunned to discover cost overruns of at least $1 billion.* 彼は少なくとも10億ドルを越える見積もり超過を見つけて気絶せんばかりに驚いた. **4** V-I 自動詞 If an event or meeting **overruns** by, for example, ten minutes, it continues for ten minutes longer than it was intended to. 超過する [BRIT 英国英語]

over|seas /oʊvərsiːz/ **1** ADJ 形容詞 You use **overseas** to describe things that involve or are in foreign countries, usually across a sea or an ocean. 海外の [ADJ n] ❑ *He has returned to South Africa from his long overseas trip.* 彼は長期の海外旅行から南アフリカに帰ってきた. ● ADV 副詞 **Overseas** is also an adverb. 海外へ ❑ *If you're staying for more than three months or working overseas, a full 10-year passport is required.* 海外に3か月以上滞在するか海外で働く場合には10年有効な旅券が必要である. **2** ADJ 形容詞 An **overseas** student or visitor comes from a foreign country, usually across a sea or an ocean. 外国からの ❑ *Every year nine million overseas visitors come to the city.* 毎年外国から900万人の観光客がこの市を訪れる.

over|see /oʊvərsiː/ (**oversees, overseeing, oversaw, overseen**) V-T 他動詞 If someone in authority **oversees** a job or an activity, they make sure that it is done properly. 監督する ❑ *Use a surveyor or architect to oversee and inspect the different stages of the work.* 測量技師あるいは建築家を使って工事のいろいろな段階を監督, 点検させること.

over|shad|ow /oʊvərʃædoʊ/ (**overshadows, overshadowing, overshadowed**) **1** V-T 他動詞 If an unpleasant event or feeling **overshadows** something, it makes it less happy or enjoyable. 影を落とす ❑ *Fears for the president's safety could overshadow his peace-making mission.* 大統領の安全に関する懸念が仲裁の使命に影を落とすす可能性があります. **2** V-T 他動詞 If you **are overshadowed by** a person or thing, you are less successful, important, or impressive than they are. 影を薄くさせる [usu passive] ❑ *Hester is overshadowed by her younger and more attractive sister.* ヘステルはもっと若くてもっと魅力的な妹より見劣りした. **3** V-T 他動詞 If one building, tree, or large structure **overshadows** another, it stands near it, is much taller than it, and casts a shadow over it. 暗くする ❑ *She said stations should be in the open, near housing, not overshadowed by trees or walls.* 彼女は駅は木々や塀などに覆われているべきではなく, 住宅地の近くの広場にあるべきだと言った.

over|sight /oʊvərsaɪt/ (**oversights**) **1** N-COUNT 可算名詞 If there has been an **oversight**, someone has forgotten to do something which they should have done. 見落とし ❑ *William was angered and embarrassed by his oversight.* ウィリアムは自分の手落ちに怒り恥じ入った. **2** ADJ 形容詞 An **oversight** committee or board is responsible for making sure that a process or system works efficiently and correctly. 監視の [ADJ n] ❑ *The bill creates an oversight board with the authority to investigate and punish accounting firms.* その法案は会計事務所を捜査して処罰する権限のある監視委員会を創設する.

over|spend (**overspends, overspending, overspent**)

The verb is pronounced /oʊvərspɛnd/. The noun is pronounced /oʊvərspɛnd/.

動詞は /oʊvərspɛnd/ と発音される. 名詞は /oʊvərspɛnd/ と発音される.

1 V-I 自動詞 If you **overspend**, you spend more money than you can afford to. 金を使いすぎる ❑ *Don't overspend on your home and expect to get the money back when you sell.* 家に金をかけすぎても, 家を売るときに元が取れると思うな. **2** N-COUNT 可算名詞 If an organization or business has an **overspend**, it spends more money than was planned or allowed in its budget. 金の使いすぎ [BRIT 英国英語 BUSINESS 実業] [AM **overrun** 米国英語]

over|state /oʊvərsteɪt/ (**overstates, overstating, overstated**) V-T 他動詞 If you say that someone **is overstating** something, you mean they are describing it in a way that makes it seem more important or serious than it really is. 誇張する ❑ *The authors no doubt overstated their case with a view to catching the public's attention.* 世間の注目を集めるために著者たちはおそらく主張を誇張しただろう.

overt /oʊvɜrt/ ADJ 形容詞 An **overt** action or attitude is done or shown in an open and obvious way. 明白な ❑ *Although there is no overt hostility, black and white students do not mix much.* 明白な敵意はないが, 黒人と白人の生徒はあまり交際しない. ● **overt|ly** ADV 副詞 明白に ❑ *He's written a few overtly political lyrics over the years.* 何年かにわたり彼は明らかに政治的な歌詞をいくつか書いた.

over|take /oʊvərteɪk/ (**overtakes, overtaking, overtook, overtaken**) **1** V-T 他動詞 If someone or something **overtakes**

a competitor, they become more successful than them. 追い越す ❑ Lung cancer has now overtaken breast cancer as a cause of death for women in the U.S. 米国の女性の死因として肺がんは今では乳がんを抜いている. ② V-T 他動詞 If a feeling **overtakes** you, it affects you very strongly. 襲いかかる [LITERARY 文語的] ❑ Something like panic overtook me in a flood. パニックのような何かがいっしきに私を襲った. ③ V-T/V-I 他動詞/自動詞 If you **overtake**, or **overtake** a vehicle or a person that is ahead of you and moving in the same direction, you pass them. 追い越す, 追い越しをする [mainly BRIT 主に英国英語; AM usually **pass** 米国英語では通常 **pass**]

over|throw (overthrows, overthrowing, overthrew, overthrown)

> The verb is pronounced /oʊvərθroʊ/. The noun is pronounced /oʊvərθroʊ/.

> 動詞は /oʊvərθroʊ/ と発音される. 名詞は /oʊvərθroʊ/ と発音される.

V-T 他動詞 When a government or leader is **overthrown**, they are removed from power by force. 倒す ❑ That government was overthrown in a military coup three years ago. あの政府は軍事クーデター で3年前に倒された. ● N-SING 単数名詞 **Overthrow** is also a noun. 打倒 ❑ They were charged with plotting the overthrow of the state. 彼らは国家転覆を計画した罪で告発された.

over|time /oʊvərtaɪm/ ① N-UNCOUNT 不可算名詞 **Overtime** is time that you spend doing your job in addition to your normal working hours. 残業 ❑ He would work overtime, without pay, to finish a job. 彼は仕事を終わらせるために無給で時間外勤務をよくした. ② PHRASE 句 If you say that someone is **working overtime** to do something, you mean that they are using a lot of energy, effort, or enthusiasm trying to do it. 一生懸命にする [INFORMAL くだけた] ❑ We had to battle very hard and our defense worked overtime to keep us in the game. 私たちはとても激しく戦わなければならず, 試合に負けないためにディフェンスは必死だった.

> A salaried worker is paid for a standard number of hours each month. When he or she works **overtime**, instead of additional money the worker is allowed to take time off from the job to compensate for the extra time worked. This is called **comp time** in the U.S., and **time off in lieu** in the U.K.

③ N-UNCOUNT 不可算名詞 **Overtime** is an additional period of time that is added to the end of a sports game in which the score is tied, so that one team can score and win the game. 延長戦 ❑ Denver had won the championship in overtime. デンバーは延長戦で選手権に優勝したことがある.

over|tone /oʊvərtoʊn/ (overtones) N-COUNT 可算名詞 If something has **overtones** of a particular thing or quality, it suggests that thing or quality but does not openly express it. 含み ❑ The strike has taken on overtones of a civil rights campaign. そのストライキは公民権運動のニュアンスを帯びてきている.

over|took /oʊvərtʊk/ **Overtook** is the past tense of **overtake**. overtakeの過去形

over|ture /oʊvərtʃər, -tʃʊər/ (overtures) N-COUNT; N-IN-NAMES 可算名詞, 名称中の名詞 An **overture** is a piece of music, often one that is the introduction to an opera or play. 序曲 ❑ ...Wagner's Mastersingers Overture. ワーグナーのマイスタージンガーの序曲

over|turn /oʊvərtɜrn/ (overturns, overturning, overturned) ① V-T/V-I 他動詞/自動詞 If something **overturns** or if you **overturn** it, it turns upside down or on its side. ひっくり返す, ひっくり返る ❑ The motorcycle veered out of control, overturned and smashed into a wall. 単車はコントロールを失い, ひっくり返って壁に激突した. ❑ Alex jumped up so violently that he overturned his glass of wine. アレックスはあまりに激しく飛び上がったので自分のワイングラスを倒してしまった. ② V-T 他動詞 If someone in authority **overturns** a legal decision, they officially decide that that decision is incorrect or not valid. くつがえす ❑ When the courts overturned his decision, he backed down. 彼の決定を法廷がくつがえすと, 彼は引き下がった.

over|view /oʊvərvyu/ (overviews) N-COUNT 可算名詞 An **overview** of a situation is a general understanding or description of it as a whole. 概観 ❑ The central section of the book is a historical overview of drug use. その本の主要部は薬物使用の歴史的概観である.

over|weight /oʊvərweɪt/ ADJ 形容詞 Someone who is **overweight** weighs more than is considered healthy or attractive. 太りすぎの ❑ Being even moderately overweight increases your risk of developing high blood pressure. さほどでなくても太りすぎは高血圧の危険性を増す.

→ see diet

over|whelm /oʊvərwɛlm/ (overwhelms, overwhelming, overwhelmed) ① V-T 他動詞 If you **are overwhelmed by** a feeling or event, it affects you very strongly, and you do not know how to deal with it. 圧倒する, 感極まらせる ❑ He was overwhelmed by a longing for times past. 彼は過去が懐かしくて胸がいっぱいだった. ● **over|whelmed** ADJ 形容詞 圧倒された ❑ Sightseers may be a little

overwhelmed by the crowds and noise. 観光客たちは人ごみと騒音にちょっと圧倒されるかもしれない. ② V-T 他動詞 If a group of people **overwhelm** a place or another group, they gain complete control or victory over them. 圧倒する ❑ It was clear that one massive Allied offensive would overwhelm the weakened enemy. 連合軍による大規模な攻撃を1回かければ, 弱体化した敵を圧倒できることは明らかだった.

over|whelm|ing /oʊvərwɛlmɪŋ/ ① ADJ 形容詞 If something is **overwhelming**, it affects you very strongly, and you do not know how to deal with it. 圧倒的な, とてもすくわない ❑ The task won't feel so overwhelming if you break it down into small, easy-to-accomplish steps. その課題を小さくて達成しやすい段階に分ければ, それほど手のつけようがないようには感じないでしょう. ● **over|whelm|ing|ly** ADV 副詞 [ADV adj] 圧倒的に ❑ The other women all seemed overwhelmingly confident. 他の女性たちは皆とてもかなわないほど自信があるように見えた. ② ADJ 形容詞 You can use **overwhelming** to emphasize that an amount or quantity is much greater than other amounts or quantities. 圧倒的な [EMPHASIS 強調] ❑ The overwhelming majority of small businesses go broke within the first twenty-four months. 零細企業の圧倒的多数が最初の24か月以内につぶれる. ● **over|whelm|ing|ly** ADV 副詞 圧倒的に ❑ The people voted overwhelmingly for change. 国民は圧倒的に変化を求めて投票した.

Word Partnership	overwhelming は次の語句と使われる:
N.	overwhelming **desire**, overwhelming **response**, overwhelming **responsibility** ① overwhelming **approval**, overwhelming **force**, overwhelming **majority**, overwhelming **odds**, overwhelming **support**, overwhelming **victory** ②

over|work /oʊvərwɜrk/ (overworks, overworking, overworked) V-T/V-I 他動詞/自動詞 If you **overwork** or if someone **overworks** you, you work too hard, and are likely to become very tired or sick. 働きすぎる, 酷使する ❑ He's overworking and has a lot on his mind. 彼は働きすぎて, たくさん心配事を抱えている. ● N-UNCOUNT 不可算名詞 **Overwork** is also a noun. 働きすぎ, 過労 ❑ He died of a heart attack brought on by overwork. 彼は過労のため心臓発作を起こして死んだ. ● **over|worked** ADJ 形容詞 働きすぎの ❑ ...an overworked doctor. 働きすぎの医師

over|worked /oʊvərwɜrkt/ ADJ 形容詞 If you describe a word, expression, or idea as **overworked**, you mean it has been used so often that it no longer has much effect or meaning. 使われすぎている ❑ "Ecological" has become one of the most overworked adjectives among manufacturers of garden supplies. 「エコロジカル」という言葉は園芸用品の製造会社が最も使いすぎている形容詞の1つになっている.

ovu|late /ɒvyəleɪt, oʊv-/ (ovulates, ovulating, ovulated) V-I 自動詞 When a woman or female animal **ovulates**, an egg is produced from one of her ovaries. 排卵する ❑ Some girls may first ovulate even before they menstruate. 中には初潮の前であっても排卵し始める女の子もいる可能性がある. ● **ovu|la|tion** /ɒvyəleɪʃⁿn, oʊv-/ N-UNCOUNT 不可算名詞 排卵 ❑ By noticing these changes, the woman can tell when ovulation is about to occur. このような変化に気づくことにより, 女性は自分が排卵間近なことが分かる.

ow /aʊ/ EXCLAM 感嘆詞 "**Ow!**" is used in writing to represent the noise that people make when they suddenly feel pain. ウッ ❑ Ow! Don't do that! イテッ! やめろよ!

owe /oʊ/ (owes, owing, owed) ① V-T 他動詞 If you **owe** money to someone, they have lent it to you and you have not yet paid it back. 借りている ❑ The company owes money to more than 60 banks. その会社は60以上の銀行から融資を受けている. ❑ Blake already owed him nearly $50. ブレークは彼からすでに50ドル近く借りていた. ② V-T 他動詞 If someone or something **owes** a particular quality or their success **to** a person or thing, they only have it because of that person or thing. おかげである [no passive] ❑ I always suspected she owed her job to her friendship with Roger. 私はずっと彼女が最初の仕事に就いたのは彼女がロジャーと親しかったからなのだと思っていた. ❑ He owed his survival to his strength as a swimmer. 彼は泳ぎがうまかったからこそ生き延びることができたのだ. ③ V-T 他動詞 If you say that you **owe** a great deal to someone or something, you mean that they have helped you or influenced you a lot, and you feel very grateful to them. 感謝している ❑ As a musician I owe much to the radio station in my home town. 音楽家として私の郷里の町のラジオ局にとても感謝している. ④ V-T 他動詞 If you say that something **owes** a great deal to a person or thing, you mean that it exists, is successful, or has its particular form mainly because of them. 負っている ❑ The island's present economy owes a good deal to tourism. その島の現在の経済は観光に負うところが多い. ⑤ V-T 他動詞 If you say that you **owe** someone gratitude, respect, or loyalty, you mean that they deserve it from you. 捧げなければならない ❑ Perhaps we owe these people more respect. 多分私たちはこの人たちをもっと尊敬すべきです. ❑ I owe you an apology; you must have found my attitude very annoying. あなたにあやまらなければなりません. 私の態度にと

ても腹が立ったでしょう． **6** V-T 他動詞 If you say that you **owe it to** someone to do something, you mean that you should do that thing because they deserve it. 義務がある [no passive] ❑ *I can't go; I owe it to him to stay.* 私は帰れません．彼のためにここに居てあげないと． ❑ *You owe it to yourself to get some professional help.* ご自分のことを考えて専門家の助けを受けるべきです． **7** PHRASE 句 You use **owing to** when you are introducing the reason for something. ～の原因で ❑ *Owing to staff shortages, there was no food on the plane.* スタッフ不足のため，飛行機では食べ物が出なかった．

Word Partnership owe は次の語句と使われる：

N.	owe **a debt**, owe **money**, owe **taxes 1**
	owe **a great deal to** *someone* **3 4**
	owe *someone* **an apology 5**

owl /aʊl/ (**owls**) N-COUNT 可算名詞 An **owl** is a bird with a flat face, large eyes, and a small sharp beak. Most owls obtain their food by hunting small animals at night. フクロウ

own /oʊn/ (**owns, owning, owned**) **1** ADJ 形容詞 You use **own** to indicate that something belongs to a particular person or thing. 自分の [poss ADJ] ❑ *My wife decided I should have my own shop.* 私の妻は私が自分の店を持つべきだと心を決めた． ❑ *He could no longer trust his own judgement.* 彼はもはや自分で判断する自信がなかった． ● PRON 代名詞 **Own** is also a pronoun. 自分のもの [poss PRON] ❑ *He saw the major's face a few inches from his own.* 彼は自分の顔から数インチ離れたところにある少佐の顔を見た． **2** ADJ 形容詞 You use **own** to indicate that something is used by, or is characteristic of, only one person, thing, or group. 自分自身の [poss ADJ] ❑ *Jennifer insisted on her own room.* ジェニファーは自分の個室が必要だと主張した． ❑ *Each nation has its own peculiarities when it comes to doing business.* 取引ということになると，すべての国にその国に独特なものがある． ● PRON 代名詞 **Own** is also a pronoun. 独自のもの [poss PRON] ❑ *This young lady has a sense of style that is very much her own.* この若い女性は全く彼女に独特なスタイル感覚を持っている． **3** ADJ 形容詞 You use **own** to indicate that someone does something without any help from other people. 自らの [poss ADJ] ❑ *They enjoy making their own decisions.* 彼らは自分たちで物事を決めるのを楽しんでいる． ● PRON 代名詞 **Own** is also a pronoun. 自らのもの [poss PRON] ❑ *There's no career structure; you have to create your own.* 職業的な組織がないので，自らの道を切り開いてゆかなければならない． **4** V-T 他動詞 If you **own** something, it is your property. 所有する ❑ *His father owns a local video store.* 彼の父親は地元のビデオショップを持っている． **5** PHRASE 句 If you have something you can **call** your **own**, it belongs only to you, rather than being controlled by or shared with someone else. 自分ものだと言う ❑ *I would like a place I could call my own.* 自分だけの場所と言える所が欲しい． **6** PHRASE 句 If someone or something **comes into** their **own**, they become very successful or start to perform very well because the circumstances are right. 本領を発揮する ❑ *Many women have come into their own as teachers, healers, and leaders.* 多くの女性が教師，治療家，指導者として本領を発揮している． **7** PHRASE 句 If you **get** your **own back** on someone, you have your revenge on them because of something bad that they have done to you. 仕返しをする [BRIT 英国英語, INFORMAL くだけた] **8** PHRASE 句 If you say that someone has a particular thing of their **own**, you mean that that thing belongs or relates to them, rather than to other people. 自分自身の ❑ *He set out in search of ideas for starting a company of his own.* 彼は自分自身の会社を設立するためのアイディアを探しに出かけた． **9** PHRASE 句 If someone or something has a particular quality or characteristic **of** their **own**, that quality or characteristic is especially theirs, rather than being shared by other things or people of that type. 独特の ❑ *The cries of the seagulls gave this part of the harbor a fascinating character of its own.* カモメの鳴く声が，港のこの辺りに独特の魅力的な特徴を与えていた． **10** PHRASE 句 When you are **on** your **own**, you are alone. 独りで ❑ *He lives on his own.* 彼は独りで住んでいる． ❑ *I felt pretty lonely last year being on my own.* 私は去年独りぼっちでとても寂しかった． **11** PHRASE 句 If you do something **on** your **own**, you do it without any help from

other people. 独力で ❑ *I work best on my own.* 私は1人で仕事するのが1番効果的だ． **12** to **hold** your **own** → see **hold**

▶ **own up** PHRASAL VERB 句動詞 If you **own up to** something wrong that you have done, you admit that you did it. 自白する ❑ *The teacher is waiting for someone to own up to the graffiti.* 先生は落書きをしたことをだれかが告白するのを待っている．

Thesaurus own また次を参照：

| ADJ. | individual, personal, private **1 2** |
| V. | have, possess **4** |

own brand (**own brands**) N-COUNT 可算名詞 **Own brands** are products which have the trademark or label of the store which sells them, especially a supermarket chain. They are normally cheaper than other popular brands. 自社ブランド [BRIT 英国英語 BUSINESS 実業] [AM store brand 米国英語 **store brand**]

own|er /oʊnər/ (**owners**) N-COUNT 可算名詞 If you are the **owner** of something, it belongs to you. 所有者 ❑ *The owner of the store was sweeping his floor when I walked in.* 私が店の中に入った時，店主が床を掃いていた．

own|er|ship /oʊnərʃɪp/ N-UNCOUNT 不可算名詞 **Ownership** of something is the state of owning it. 所有すること ❑ *On January 23rd, the U.S. decided to relax its rules on the foreign ownership of its airlines.* 1月23日に，米国はアメリカの航空会社を外国人が所有することに関する規則を緩和することを決めた． ❑ *...the growth of home ownership.* 持ち家の増加

own la|bel (**own labels**) N-COUNT 可算名詞 **Own label** is the same as **own brand**. 自社ラベル [BUSINESS 実業] ❑ *People will trade down to own labels which are cheaper.* 人々はより安い自社ラベルの商品を買うでしょう．

ox /ɒks/ (**oxen** /ɒksən/) N-COUNT 可算名詞 An **ox** is a bull that has been castrated. Oxen are used in some countries for pulling vehicles or carrying things. 雄牛

oxy|gen /ɒksɪdʒən/ N-UNCOUNT 不可算名詞 **Oxygen** is a colorless gas that exists in large quantities in the air. All plants and animals need oxygen in order to live. 酸素 ❑ *The human brain needs to be without oxygen for only four minutes before permanent damage occurs.* 人間の脳はたった4分間酸素が欠如しただけで永久的な損傷を受ける．

→ see **air, earth, respiratory**

oys|ter /ɔɪstər/ (**oysters**) **1** N-COUNT 可算名詞 An **oyster** is a large flat shellfish. Some oysters can be eaten and others produce valuable objects called pearls. カキ ❑ *He had two dozen oysters and enjoyed every one of them.* 彼はカキを24個とり，1つ残らず楽しんで食べた． **2** PHRASE 句 If you say that **the world is** someone's **oyster**, you mean that they can do anything or go anywhere that they want to. 世界は一の思いのままだ ❑ *You're young, you've got a lot of opportunity. The world is your oyster.* 君は若くてたくさんのチャンスに恵まれている．世界は君の思いのままだよ．

oz Oz is a written abbreviation for **ounce**. オンス ❑ *Whisk 1 oz of butter into the sauce.* 1オンスのバターをソースに入れかき混ぜよ．

ozone /oʊzoʊn/ N-UNCOUNT 不可算名詞 **Ozone** is a colorless gas which is a form of oxygen. There is a layer of ozone high above the Earth's surface, that protects us from harmful radiation from the sun. オゾン ❑ *What they find could provide clues to what might happen worldwide if ozone depletion continues.* 彼らの発見することは，オゾン量の消耗が続いた場合に世界的に何が起こる可能性があるかを，解明する手掛かりを提供することになるかもしれない．

ozone-friendly ADJ 形容詞 **Ozone-friendly** chemicals, products, or technology do not cause harm to the ozone layer. オゾン層にやさしい ❑ *...ozone-friendly chemicals for fridges and air conditioners.* 冷蔵庫と空調に使われるオゾン層を破壊しない化学物質

ozone lay|er N-SING 単数名詞 **The ozone layer** is the part of the Earth's atmosphere that has the most ozone in it. The ozone layer protects living things from the harmful radiation of the sun. オゾン層 ❑ *...the hole in the ozone layer.* オゾン層の穴

Pp

P also p /piː/ (P's, p's) N-VAR 可変性名詞 **P** is the sixteenth letter of the English alphabet. 英語アルファベットの第16番目の文字

PA /ˌpiː ˈeɪ/ (PAs) N-COUNT 可算名詞 If you refer to the **PA** or the **PA system** in a place, you are referring to the public address system. 拡声装置 [usu "the" N in sing] □ *A voice came booming over the PA.* 拡声装置を通して声がとどろいて来た.

p.a. p.a. is a written abbreviation for **per annum**. 1年につき

pace /peɪs/ (paces, pacing, paced) **1** N-SING 単数名詞 The **pace** of something is the speed at which it happens or is done. 速度、ペース [usu with supp] □ *Many people were not satisfied with the pace of change.* 多くの人たちは変化の速度に満足していなかった。 □ *They could not stand the pace or the workload.* 彼らは仕事のペースや量についていけなかった。 **2** N-SING 単数名詞 Your **pace** is the speed at which you walk. 歩調 [usu with supp] □ *He moved at a brisk pace down the rue St. Antoine.* 彼はきびきびした歩調でサン・アントワーヌ通りを歩いて行った。 **3** N-COUNT 可算名詞 A **pace** is the distance that you move when you take one step. 歩幅 [usu with supp] □ *He'd only gone a few paces before he stopped again.* 彼はほんの数歩行っただけでまた立ち止まった。 **4** V-T/V-I 他動詞/自動詞 If you **pace** a small area, you keep walking up and down in it, because you are anxious or impatient. 歩き続ける、歩き回る □ *As they waited, Kravis paced the room nervously.* 彼らが待つ間、クラビスはそわそわと部屋の中を歩き回った。 □ *He found John pacing around the house, unable to sleep.* ジョンが眠れずに家の中を歩き回っているのに彼は気づいた。 **5** V-T 他動詞 If you **pace yourself** when doing something, you do it at a steady rate. 安定したペースでする □ *It was a tough race and I had to pace myself.* レースはきつく、自分のペースを崩さないようにしなければならなかった。 **6** PHRASE 句 If something **keeps pace with** something else that is changing, it changes quickly in response to it. 歩調をそろえる □ *The earnings of the average American have failed to keep pace with the rate of inflation.* 平均的なアメリカ人の収入はインフレの上昇率についていってない。 **7** PHRASE 句 If you **keep pace with** someone who is walking or running, you succeed in going as fast as them, so that you remain close to them. 後れをとらない □ *With four laps to go, he kept pace with the leaders.* あと4周の時点で彼は先頭集団に後れをとっていなかった。 **8** PHRASE 句 If you do something **at** your **own pace**, you do it at a speed that is comfortable for you. 自分にあった速度で □ *The computer will give students the opportunity to learn at their own pace.* コンピューターは学生たちが本人にあった速度で学ぶ機会をもたらすであろう。 **9 at a snail's pace** → see snail

---

Word Partnership　pace は次の語句と使われる:

N.	pace of change **1**
ADJ.	brisk pace, **fast** pace, record pace, slow pace **1 2**
V.	pick up the pace, set a pace **1 2**
	keep pace with *something* **6**
	keep pace with *someone* **7**

---

paci|fier /ˈpæsɪfaɪər/ (pacifiers) N-COUNT 可算名詞 A **pacifier** is a rubber or plastic object that you give to a baby to suck so that he or she feels comforted. おしゃぶり [AM 米国英語]

paci|fism /ˈpæsɪfɪzəm/ N-UNCOUNT 不可算名詞 **Pacifism** is the belief that war and violence are always wrong. 平和主義 □ *...a leading exponent of pacifism.* 平和主義の指導的な唱道者

paci|fist /ˈpæsɪfɪst/ (pacifists) **1** N-COUNT 可算名詞 A **pacifist** is someone who believes that violence is wrong and refuses to take part in wars. 平和主義者 □ *Many protesters insist they are pacifists, opposed to war in all forms.* 抗議者たちの多くが自分たちは平和主義者であり、あらゆる種類の戦争に反対すると主張する。 **2** ADJ 形容詞 If someone has **pacifist** views, they believe that war and violence are always wrong. 平和主義的な □ *...his mother's pacifist ideals.* 彼の母親の平和主義の理想.

pack /pæk/ (packs, packing, packed) **1** V-T/V-I 他動詞/自動詞 When you **pack** a bag, you put clothes and other things into it, because you are leaving a place or going on vacation. 荷造りする □ *When I was 17, I packed my bags and left home.* 私が17歳のとき荷物をまとめて家を出た。 □ *I began to pack a few things for the trip.* 私はその旅行のためにちょっとした荷造りを始めた。 ● **pack|ing** N-UNCOUNT 不可算名詞 荷造り □ *She left Frances to finish her packing.* 彼女はフランセスが荷造りを済ませるままにした。 **2** V-T 他動詞 When

people **pack** things, for example, in a factory, they put them into containers or boxes so that they can be shipped and sold. 梱包する □ *They offered me a job packing boxes in a warehouse.* 彼らは私に倉庫で箱を梱包する仕事をくれた。 □ *Machines now exist to pack olives in jars.* 今ではオリーブを瓶詰めにする機械がある。 ● **pack|ing** N-UNCOUNT 不可算名詞 梱包 □ *The shipping and packing costs are passed along in the item price.* 運送と梱包の料金は品物の値段に入れられている。 **3** V-T/V-I 他動詞/自動詞 If people or things **pack into** a place or if they **pack** a place, there are so many of them that the place is full. いっぱいに詰め込む、満員になる □ *Hundreds of people packed into the mosque.* 何百もの人々でモスクはいっぱいでした。 **4** N-COUNT 可算名詞 A **pack** of things is a collection of them that is sold or given together in a box or bag. 箱、 1式 □ *The club will send a free information pack.* そのクラブは無料で資料1式を送るだろう。 □ *...a pack of cigarettes.* タバコ1箱 **5** N-COUNT 可算名詞 You can refer to a group of people who go around together as a **pack**, especially when it is a large group that you feel threatened by. 群れ □ *He thus avoided a pack of journalists eager to question him.* 彼はこのようにして彼に質問をしたがっている記者たちの群れを避けました。 **6** N-COUNT 可算名詞 A **pack** of wolves or dogs is a group of them that hunt together. 群れ □ *...a pack of stray dogs.* 野良犬の群れ **7** N-COUNT 可算名詞 A **pack** of playing cards is a complete set of playing cards. 組 [mainly BRIT 主に英国英語; AM usually **deck** 米国英語では通常 **deck**] **8** → see also **packed, packing** **9** PHRASE 句 If you say that an account is **a pack of lies**, you mean that it is completely untrue. うそばっかり □ *You told me a pack of lies.* 君は私に嘘ばっかりついた。 **10** PHRASE 句 If you **send** someone **packing**, you make them go away. ～を追い出す [INFORMAL くだけた] □ *I decided I wanted to live alone and I sent him packing.* 私は独りで生活したいと決心し、彼を追い出した。

pack|age /ˈpækɪdʒ/ (packages, packaging, packaged) **1** N-COUNT 可算名詞 A **package** is something wrapped in paper, in a bag or large envelope, or in a box, usually so that it can be sent to someone by mail. 小包 □ *I tore open the package.* 私は小包を破って開けた。 **2** N-COUNT 可算名詞 A **package** is a small container in which a quantity of something is sold. Packages are either small boxes made of thin cardboard, or bags or envelopes made of paper or plastic. 容器、箱 [mainly AM 主に米国英語] □ *...a package of doughnuts.* ドーナッツ1箱 **3** N-COUNT 可算名詞 A **package** is a set of proposals that are made by a government or organization and that must be accepted or rejected as a group. 一括のもの □ *...a package of measures to help the movie industry.* 映画産業を援助するための一括措置 **4** V-T 他動詞 When a product **is packaged**, it is put into containers to be sold. 詰める [usu passive] □ *The beans are then ground and packaged for sale as ground coffee.* そのあと豆はひかれ、ひいたコーヒー1箱として販売用に袋に詰められる。 **5** V-T 他動詞 If something **is packaged** in a particular way, it is presented or advertised in that way in order to make it seem attractive or interesting. みばをよくする、魅力的に宣伝する [usu passive] □ *A city is like any product, it has to be packaged properly to be attractive to the consumer.* 都市は商品と同様であり、消費者にとって魅力的なようにちゃんとみばをよくしなければならない。 **6** N-COUNT 可算名詞 A **package** tour is a vacation in which your travel and your accommodations are booked for you. パッケージ □ *...package tours to Egypt.* エジプトへのパッケージ旅行

Thesaurus　package また次を参照:

N.	batch, bundle, container, pack, parcel **1**

---

pack|ag|ing /ˈpækɪdʒɪŋ/ N-UNCOUNT 不可算名詞 **Packaging** is the container or covering that something is sold in. 容器、包装 □ *It is selling very well, in part because the packaging is so attractive.* それは1つには包装がとても魅力的なのでとてもよく売れています。

packed /pækt/ **1** ADJ 形容詞 A place that is **packed** is very crowded. 混んだ □ *The place is packed at lunchtime.* あそこはお昼休みは込んでいる。 **2** ADJ 形容詞 Something that is **packed with** things contains a very large number of them. いっぱいで [v-link ADJ "with" n] □ *The encyclopedia is packed with clear illustrations and over 250 recipes.* この百科事典は分かりやすい説明図と250以上もあるレシピでいっぱいです。

pack|et /ˈpækɪt/ (packets) **1** N-COUNT 可算名詞 An information **packet** is a set of information about a particular

subject that is given to people who are interested in that subject. 1式 [AM 米国英語] [with suppl] ❑ *Call us for a free information packet that tells you more.* 詳しい情報1式は電話をいただければお届けします. ❑ *...a 23-page packet of topics to be discussed.* 討論予定の23ページにわたる議題1式. ❷ N-COUNT 可算名詞 A **packet** is a small container in which a quantity of something is sold. Packets are either small boxes made of thin cardboard, or bags or envelopes made of paper or plastic. 容器 [mainly BRIT 主に英国英語] ❑ *...sugar packets.* 砂糖の小袋 ❸ N-COUNT 可算名詞 You can use **packet** to refer to a packet and its contents, or to the contents only. 小包と中身, 小包の中身 [mainly BRIT 主に英国英語; AM usually **pack, package** 米国英語では通常 **pack, package**]

pack|ing /pǽkɪŋ/ ❶ N-UNCOUNT 不可算名詞 **Packing** is the paper, plastic, or other material that is put around things that are being sent somewhere to protect them. 詰め物 ❑ *My fingers shook as I pulled the packing from the box.* 箱から詰め物を取り出す手が震えた. ❷ → see also **pack**

pact /pǽkt/ (**pacts**) N-COUNT 可算名詞 A **pact** is a formal agreement between two or more people, organizations, or governments to do a particular thing or to help each other. 条約 ❑ *Last month he signed a new non-aggression pact with Germany.* 先月彼はドイツとの新しい不可侵条約に調印した.

pad /pǽd/ (**pads, padding, padded**) ❶ N-COUNT 可算名詞 A **pad** is a fairly thick, flat piece of a material such as cloth or rubber. Pads are used, for example, to clean things, to protect things, or to change their shape. 当て物, 詰め物 ❑ *He withdrew the needle and placed a pad of cotton over the spot.* 彼は針を抜いてそこを脱脂綿で覆った. ❑ *...a scouring pad.* たわし ❷ N-COUNT 可算名詞 A **pad** of paper is a number of pieces of paper attached together along the top or the side, so that each piece can be torn off when it has been used. 束 ❑ *She wrote on a pad of paper.* 彼女はメモ用紙に書いた. ❑ *Have a pad and pencil ready and jot down some of your thoughts.* メモ用紙と鉛筆を用意して思いついたことを少し書き留めなさい. ❸ V-I 自動詞 When someone **pads** somewhere, they walk there with steps that are fairly quick, light, and quiet. そっと歩く, 静かに歩く ❑ *Freddy speaks very quietly and pads around in soft velvet slippers.* フレディはとても静かに話し, やわらかいベルベットのスリッパを履いて静かに歩き回る. ❑ *...a dog padding through the streets.* 街路を静かに歩きまわっている犬 ❹ N-COUNT 可算名詞 A **pad** is a platform or an area of flat, hard ground where helicopters take off and land or rockets are launched. 離着陸所, 発射台 ❑ *...a little round helicopter pad.* 小さな丸いヘリコプターの離着陸所 ❑ *...a landing pad on the back of the ship.* 船の後部の着艦区域 ❺ N-COUNT 可算名詞 The **pads** of a person's fingers and toes or of an animal's feet are the soft, fleshy parts of them. 指先, 足 ❑ *Tap your cheeks all over with the pads of your fingers.* ほっぺた全体を指先で軽く叩きなさい. ❻ V-T 他動詞 If you **pad** something, you put something soft in it or over it in order to make it less hard, to protect it, or to give it a different shape. 詰め物をする ❑ *Pad the back of a car seat with a pillow.* 車の座席の背もたれに枕を当てなさい. ● **pad|ded** ADJ 形容詞 詰め物を入れた ❑ *...a padded jacket.* 肩パッドを入れた上着 ❼ V-T 他動詞 If you **pad** or **pad out** a piece of writing or a speech **with** unnecessary words or pieces of information, you include them to make it longer and hide the fact that you do not have very much to say. 引き伸ばす ❑ *Quotations should be used to make points, not to pad the essay.* 引用は主張の正しさを示すために使われるべきであって, 論文を長くするために使われるべきではない. ❑ *The reviewer padded out his review with a lengthy biography of the author.* 書評者はその作家の履歴を長々と書いて書評を引き伸ばした. ❽ V-T 他動詞 If an employee with an expense account **pads** their expenses, they claim that their expenses are greater than they really are in order to get more money from their employer. 水増しする ❑ *She was fired for padding her expenses.* 彼女は経費を水増しして首になった. ❾ → see also **padding**
→ see **skateboarding**
▸ **pad out** PHRASAL VERB 句動詞 → see **pad 7**

pad|ding /pǽdɪŋ/ N-UNCOUNT 不可算名詞 **Padding** is soft material put on something or inside it in order to make it less hard, to protect it, or to give it a different shape. 詰め物 ❑ *...the foam rubber padding on the headphones.* ヘッドフォーンの気泡ゴムの詰め物 ❑ *Players must wear padding to protect them from injury.* 選手は負傷しないようにパッドを付けなければならない.

pad|dle /pǽdᵊl/ (**paddles, paddling, paddled**) ❶ N-COUNT 可算名詞 A **paddle** is a short pole with a wide flat part at one end or at both ends. You hold it in your hands and use it as an oar to move a small boat through water. かい ❑ *We might be able to push ourselves across with the paddle.* かいで押せば向こう岸まで行けるかもしれない. ❷ V-T/V-I 他動詞/自動詞 If you **paddle** a boat, you move it through water using a paddle. こぐ, かいでこぐ ❑ *...the skills you will use to paddle the canoe.* カヌーをこぐのに使うパドラを使う技術 ❸ N-COUNT 可算名詞 A **paddle** is a specially shaped piece of wood that is used for hitting the ball in table tennis. 卓球のラケット [AM 米国英語]
→ see **boat**

pad|dock /pǽdək/ (**paddocks**) N-COUNT 可算名詞 A **paddock** is a small field where horses are kept. 小牧場 ❑ *The family kept horses in the paddock in front of the house.* その1家は馬を家の前の小牧場で飼っていた.

pad|dy /pǽdi/ (**paddies**) N-COUNT 可算名詞 A **paddy** or a **paddy field** is a field that is kept flooded with water and is used for growing rice. 水田 ❑ *...the paddy fields of China.* 中国の水田.

pad|lock /pǽdlɒk/ (**padlocks, padlocking, padlocked**) ❶ N-COUNT 可算名詞 A **padlock** is a lock that is used for fastening two things together. It consists of a block of metal with a U-shaped bar attached to it. One end of the bar is released by turning a key in the lock. 南京錠 ❑ *They had put a padlock on the door of his house.* 彼らは彼の家のドアに南京錠をかけていた. ❷ V-T 他動詞 If you **padlock** something, you lock it or fasten it to something else using a padlock. 南京錠をかける ❑ *Eddie parked his bicycle against a lamppost and padlocked it.* エディーは自転車を街灯柱に立てかけて止めて南京錠をかけた.

pa|gan /péɪɡən/ (**pagans**) ❶ ADJ 形容詞 **Pagan** beliefs and activities do not belong to any of the main religions of the world. They are older, or are believed to be older, than other religions. 土着宗教の ❑ *The Christian church has adapted many pagan ideas over the centuries.* キリスト教教会は何世紀にもわたり土着宗教の考え方を多く取り入れてきている. ❷ N-COUNT 可算名詞 In former times, **pagans** were people who did not believe in Christianity and whom many Christians considered to be inferior people. 異教徒の ❑ *The pagans used torchlight parades and bonfires to celebrate important events.* その異教徒たちはたいまつ行列や焚き火をして重要な行事を祝った.

page /péɪdʒ/ (**pages, paging, paged**) ❶ N-COUNT 可算名詞 A **page** is one side of one of the pieces of paper in a book, magazine, or newspaper. Each page usually has a number printed at the top or bottom. ページ ❑ *Take out your book and turn to page 4.* 本を取り出し4ページを開きなさい. ❑ *...the front page of USA Today.* USA Today紙の第1面. ❷ N-COUNT 可算名詞 The **pages** of a book, magazine, or newspaper are the pieces of paper it consists of. ページ ❑ *He turned the pages of his notebook.* 彼は手帳のページをめくった. ❸ N-COUNT 可算名詞 You can refer to an important event or period of time as a **page** of history. 事件, 時期 [LITERARY 文語的] ❑ *...a new page in the country's political history.* その国の政治史の新局面 ❹ V-T 他動詞 If someone who is in a public place **is paged**, they receive a message, often over a speaker, telling them that someone is trying to contact them. 呼び出す ❑ *He was paged repeatedly as the flight was boarding.* その搭乗便は搭乗中であったので, 彼の名前が何度も呼ばれた. ❺ N-COUNT 可算名詞 A **page** is a young person who takes messages or does small jobs for members of the United States Congress or state legislatures. 議員付きボーイ [AM 米国英語] ❻ N-COUNT 可算名詞 A **page** is a small boy who accompanies the bride at a wedding. 花嫁付き添いの少年
→ see **printing**

pag|eant /pǽdʒənt/ (**pageants**) ❶ N-COUNT 可算名詞 A **pageant** or a **beauty pageant** is a competition in which young women are judged to decide which one is the most beautiful. 美人コンテスト ❑ *...the Miss Universe beauty pageant.* ミス・ユニバース美人コンテスト ❷ N-COUNT 可算名詞 A **pageant** is a colorful public procession, show, or ceremony. Pageants are usually held outdoors and often celebrate events or people from history. 行列 ❑ *...a historical pageant of kings and queens.* 歴代の王と女王の時代行列

pag|er /péɪdʒər/ (**pagers**) N-COUNT 可算名詞 A **pager** is a small electronic device that you can carry around with you and that gives you a number or a message when someone is trying to contact you. ポケットベル ❑ *Scores of messages on his pager have not been answered.* 彼のポケットベルのメッセージには返答していないものが何十件もある.

paid /péɪd/ ❶ **Paid** is the past tense and past participle of **pay**. payの過去・過去分詞 ❷ ADJ 形容詞 **Paid** workers, or people who do **paid** work, receive money for the work that they do. 賃金をもらっている, 有給の [ADJ n] ❑ *Apart from a small team of paid staff, the organization consists of unpaid volunteers.* その団体は少数の有給のスタッフからなるチーム以外は無給のボランティアからなっている. ❸ ADJ 形容詞 If you are given **paid** vacation, you get your wages or salary even though you are not at work. 有給の [ADJ n] ❑ *He agreed to hire her at slightly over minimum wage with two weeks' paid vacation.* 彼は最低賃金をわずかに上まる給料で2週間の有給休暇をつけて彼女を雇うことに合意した. ❹ ADJ 形容詞 If you are well **paid**, you receive a lot of money for the work that you do. If you are badly **paid**, you do not receive much money. 報酬を受けた [adv ADJ] ❑ *...a well-paid accountant.* 高給取りの会計士 ❑ *Travel and tourism employees are among the worst paid in the developed world.* 旅行・観光関係の従業員は先進国では最も低い報酬を受けている部類に入る.

pain /péɪn/ (**pains, pained**) ❶ N-VAR 可変性名詞 **Pain** is the feeling of great discomfort you have, for example, when you have been hurt or when you are ill. 痛み ❑ *...back pain.* 背痛. ❑ *To help*

ease the pain, heat can be applied to the area with a hot water bottle. 痛みを減らすためには、湯たんぽを使って痛む部分を暖めることもできる。❑ *I felt a sharp pain in my lower back.* 私は腰のあたりに鋭い痛みを感じた。● PHRASE 句 If you are **in pain**, you feel pain in a part of your body because you are injured or ill. 痛くて ❑ *She was writhing in pain, bathed in perspiration.* 彼女は痛みにもだえ苦しんで、汗まみれになっていた。 **2** N-UNCOUNT 不可算名詞 **Pain** is the feeling of unhappiness that you have when something unpleasant or upsetting happens. 苦痛 ❑ *...gray eyes that seemed filled with pain.* 苦痛に満ちているよう見えた灰色の目 **3** V-T 他動詞 If a fact or idea **pains** you, it makes you feel upset and disappointed. 苦痛を与える [no cont] ❑ *This public acknowledgement of Ted's disability pained my mother.* テッドの身体障害がこうやって世間に認められたことが私の母にはつらかった。 **4** PHRASE 句 In informal English, if you call someone or something **a pain** or **a pain in the neck**, you mean that they are very annoying or irritating. Expressions such as **a pain in the ass** and **a pain in the butt** are also used, but most people consider them offensive. 不快にさせる・こと、うんざりさせる人・こと [INFORMAL くだけた, DISAPPROVAL 不賛成] ❑ *Getting rid of unwanted applications from your PC can be a real pain.* 不要なアプリケーションをパソコンから取り除くのに本当に苦労することがある。 **5** PHRASE 句 If you **take pains to** do something or **go to great pains to** do something, you try hard to do it, because you think it is important to do it. 骨折って ❑ *He took great pains to see that he got it right.* 彼はそれをちゃんとするように大変骨を折った。

pained /peɪnd/ ADJ 形容詞 If you have a **pained** expression or look, you look upset, worried, or slightly annoyed. 不機嫌な ❑ *Tanya put on a pained look, as though the subject was too delicate to be spoken about.* いかにもそれはとても微妙で話せない話題であるかのように、タニアは不愉快そうな顔をした。

pain|ful /peɪnfəl/ **1** ADJ 形容詞 If a part of your body is **painful**, it hurts because it is injured or because there is something wrong with it. 痛い ❑ *Her glands were swollen and painful.* 彼女はリンパ腺がはれて痛かった。● **pain|ful|ly** ADV 副詞 [ADV with v] 痛んで ❑ *His tooth had started to throb painfully again.* 彼の歯はまたズキズキ痛み出していた。 **2** ADJ 形容詞 If something such as an illness, injury, or operation is **painful**, it causes you a lot of physical pain. 痛い ❑ *...a painful back injury.* 痛い背中の怪我(けが) ● **pain|ful|ly** ADV 副詞 [ADV with v] 痛いほど ❑ *...cracking his head painfully against the cupboard.* 戸棚に頭を思いっきりバシッとぶつけて **3** ADJ 形容詞 Situations, memories, or experiences that are **painful** are difficult and unpleasant to deal with, and often make you feel sad and upset. つらい ❑ *Remarks like that brought back painful memories.* あのような発言がつらい記憶をよみがえらせた。 ❑ *...the painful transition to democracy.* 苦痛を伴う民主主義への歩み ● **pain|ful|ly** ADV 副詞 [ADV with v] つらい思いをして ❑ *...their old relationship, which he had painfully broken off.* 彼がつらい思いをして関係を絶った彼らの昔からの関係

pain|ful|ly /peɪnfəli/ **1** ADV 副詞 You use **painfully** to emphasize a quality or situation that is undesirable. ひどく [EMPHASIS 強調] [ADV adv/adj] ❑ *Things are moving painfully slowly.* 事態の進みがひどく遅い。 ❑ *...a painfully shy young man.* ひどくはにかんだ若い男性 **2** → see also **painful**

pain|killer /peɪnkɪlər/ (**painkillers**) N-COUNT 可算名詞 A **painkiller** is a drug that reduces or stops physical pain. 痛み止め

pain|less /peɪnlɪs/ **1** ADJ 形容詞 If something such as a treatment is **painless**, it causes no physical pain. 無痛の、痛みのない ❑ *Acupuncture treatment is gentle, painless, and relaxing.* 針治療は穏やかで痛みがなく、くつろいだ気分にさせるものだ。 ❑ *The operation itself is a brief, painless procedure.* 手術そのものは短期間で終わり痛みがない。● **pain|less|ly** ADV 副詞 [ADV with v] 痛まずに ❑ *...a technique to eliminate unwanted facial hair quickly and painlessly.* 顔の無駄毛をすばやく痛みなしで除去する技術 **2** ADJ 形容詞 If a process or activity is **painless**, there are no difficulties involved, and you do not have to make a great effort or suffer in any way. たやすい、簡単にできる ❑ *The journey is relatively painless, even with children.* その旅程は子供にとってさえ比較的楽なものです。● **pain|less|ly** ADV 副詞 [ADV with v] たやすく ❑ *...a game for children that painlessly teaches essential pre-reading skills.* 読み書きを習う前に必要な技能を簡単に子供たちに教えるゲーム

pains|taking /peɪnzteɪkɪŋ, peɪnsteɪ-/ ADJ 形容詞 A **painstaking** search, examination, or investigation is done extremely carefully and thoroughly. 骨の折れる ❑ *Forensic experts carried out a painstaking search of the debris.* 残がいの入念な調査を法医学の専門家が実施した。● **pains|taking|ly** ADV 副詞 入念に ❑ *Broken bones were painstakingly pieced together and reshaped.* 折れた骨は入念につなぎ合わされて再形成された。

paint /peɪnt/ (**paints, painting, painted**) **1** N-MASS 質量名詞 **Paint** is a colored liquid that you put onto a surface with a brush in order to protect the surface or to make it look nice, or that you use to produce a picture. ペンキ、絵の具 ❑ *...a can of red paint.* 缶入りの赤い塗料 ❑ *They saw some large letters in white paint.* 彼らは白いペンキで書かれたいくつかの大きな字を見た。 **2** N-SING 単数名詞 On a wall or object, **the paint** is the covering of dried paint on it. ペンキ ❑ *The paint was peeling on the window frames.* 窓枠のペンキがはがれていた。 **3** V-T/V-I 他動詞/自動詞 If you **paint** a wall or an object, you cover it with paint. 塗る、ペンキを塗る ❑ *They started to mend the woodwork and paint the walls.* 彼らは木造部分を修理し壁にペンキを塗り始めた。 ❑ *I had come here to paint.* 私はここにペンキを塗りに来ていたのだ。 **4** V-T 他動詞 If you **paint** something or **paint** a picture of it, you produce a picture of it using paint. 油絵を描く、油絵を描く ❑ *He is painting a huge volcano.* 彼は大きな火山の油絵を描いている。 ❑ *Why do people paint pictures?* なぜ人は絵を描くのでしょうか。 **5** V-T 他動詞 When you **paint** a design or message on a surface, you put it on the surface using paint. ペンキで書く ❑ *...a machine for painting white lines on roads.* 道路に白線を引く機械 ❑ *They went around painting rude slogans on cars.* 彼らは自動車に下品なスローガンを書いてまわった。 **6** V-T 他動詞 If you **paint** a grim or vivid picture of something, you give a description of it that is grim or vivid. 描写する ❑ *The report paints a grim picture of life there.* その報道記事はそこでの厳しい生活の様子を描写している。 **7** → see also **gloss paint, oil paint, painting**
→ see **painting**

paint|brush /peɪntbrʌʃ/ (**paintbrushes**) N-COUNT 可算名詞 A **paintbrush** is a brush that you use for painting. 絵筆、塗料ばけ
→ see **painting**

paint|er /peɪntər/ (**painters**) **1** N-COUNT 可算名詞 A **painter** is an artist who paints pictures. 画家 ❑ *...the French painter Claude Monet.* フランスの画家、クロード・モネ **2** N-COUNT 可算名詞 A **painter** is someone who paints walls, doors, and some other parts of buildings as their job. ペンキ屋 ❑ *...the son of a painter and decorator.* 塗装・室内装飾家の息子

paint|ing /peɪntɪŋ/ (**paintings**) **1** N-COUNT 可算名詞 A **painting** is a picture that someone has painted. 絵、油絵 ❑ *...a large painting of Dwight Eisenhower.* ドワイト・アイゼンハワーの大きな油絵 **2** N-UNCOUNT 不可算名詞 **Painting** is the activity of painting pictures. 絵画 ❑ *...two hobbies she really enjoyed, painting and gardening.* 彼女が心から楽しんだ2つの趣味である絵を描くことと庭いじり **3** N-UNCOUNT 不可算名詞 **Painting** is the activity of painting doors, walls, and some other parts of buildings. ペンキ塗り ❑ *...painting and decorating.* ペンキ塗りと内装
→ see Word Web: **painting**
→ see **art, gallery**

pair /pɛər/ (**pairs, pairing, paired**) **1** N-COUNT 可算名詞 A **pair of** things are two things of the same size and shape that are used together or are both part of something, for example, shoes, earrings, or parts of the body. 対、組 ❑ *...a pair of socks.* 1組の靴下。 ❑ *...earrings that cost $142.50 a pair.* 1組142ドル50セントするイヤリング **2** N-COUNT 可算名詞 Some objects that have two main parts of the same size and shape are referred to as a **pair**, for example, **a pair of pants** or **a pair of scissors**. 着、個 ❑ *...a pair of faded jeans.* 1着の色あせたジーンズ **3** N-SING 単数名詞 You can refer to two people as a **pair** when they are standing or walking together or when they have some kind of relationship with each other. 対、カップル ❑ *A pair of teenage boys were smoking cigarettes.* 10代の男の子が2人でタバコを吸っていた。 ❑ *The pair admitted that their three-year-old marriage was going through "a difficult time."* その夫婦は3年になる結婚が「困難な時期」を体験していると認めた。

The noun **pair** can take either a singular verb or a plural verb, depending on whether it refers to one thing seen as a unit or a collection of two things or people. ❑ *A good, supportive and protective pair of sneakers is essential... The pair are still friends and attend functions together.*

4 V-T 他動詞 If one thing **is paired with** another, it is put with it or considered with it. 組にする [usu passive] ❑ *The trainees will then*

Oil **painting** involves special tools and techniques. Trained artists start by stretching a piece of **canvas** over a wooden **frame**. Then they cover the surface with a **coat** of white **paint**. When it dries, they put it on an **easel**. Most painters use a **palette knife** on a **palette** to mix different **colors** together. They then apply the paint to the canvas using soft bristle **paintbrushes**. When finished, they use turpentine to clean up the brushes and the palette. Three common oil painting styles are the **still life**, the **landscape**, and the **portrait**.

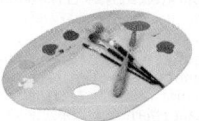

be paired with experienced managers. そのあとで研修生は経験を積んだマネージャーと組まされることになる。 **5** → see also **au pair**

Thesaurus pair また次を参照：

N.　combination, couple, duo, match, two, twosome **1** **3**
V.　combine, join, match up, put together, team **4**

pa|jam|as /pədʒɑːməz/ N-PLURAL 複数名詞 A pair of **pajamas** consists of loose pants and a top that people wear to bed. 寝巻き [also "a" "pair" "of" N] □ I don't want to get out of my pajamas in the morning. 朝は私はパジャマを着替えたくない。

pal /pæl/ (**pals**) N-COUNT 可算名詞 Your **pals** are your friends. 友だち [INFORMAL, OLD-FASHIONED くだけた，古風な] □ They talked like old pals. 彼らは昔からの友だちのように話をした。

pal|ace /pælɪs/ (**palaces**) N-COUNT 可算名詞 A **palace** is a very large impressive house, especially one that is the official home of a king, queen, or president. 宮殿 □ ...Buckingham Palace. バッキンガム宮殿

pal|at|able /pælətəbəl/ **1** ADJ 形容詞 If you describe food or drink as **palatable**, you mean that it tastes pleasant. 味のよい [FORMAL 形式ばった] □ ...flavorings and preservatives, designed to make the food look more palatable. 食品がよりおいしく見えるように意図した調味料と保存料 **2** ADJ 形容詞 If you describe something such as an idea or method as **palatable**, you mean that people are willing to accept it. 受け入れられやすい □ ...a palatable way of firing employees. 従業員の無難な解雇方法

pal|ate /pælɪt/ (**palates**) **1** N-COUNT 可算名詞 Your **palate** is the top part of the inside of your mouth. 口蓋 **2** N-COUNT 可算名詞 You can refer to someone's **palate** as a way of talking about their ability to judge good food or drink. 味覚力 □ ...fresh pasta sauces to tempt more demanding palates. より肥えた舌をその気にさせる新鮮なパスタソース

pale /peɪl/ (**paler, palest, pales, paling, paled**) **1** ADJ 形容詞 If something is **pale**, it is very light in color or almost white. 色の薄い，白っぽい □ Migrating birds filled the pale sky. 白っぽい空は渡り鳥でいっぱいだった。 As we age, our skin becomes paler. 歳をとると皮膚は色あせてくる。 ● COMB IN COLOR 色彩形の複合 **Pale** is also a combining form. 薄い～ □ ...a pale blue sailor dress. 水色のセーラー服 **2** ADJ 形容詞 If someone looks **pale**, their face looks a lighter color than usual, usually because they are ill, frightened, or shocked. 青ざめた □ She looked pale and tired. 彼女は顔色が悪く疲れて見えた。 **3** V-I 自動詞 If one thing **pales** in comparison with another, it is made to seem much less important, serious, or good by it. 見劣りがする □ When someone you love has a life-threatening illness, everything else pales in comparison. 愛する人が命にかかわる病気にかかると、他の事は全てそれほど重要でなくなる。

pal|ette /pælɪt/ (**palettes**) **1** N-COUNT 可算名詞 A **palette** is a flat piece of wood or plastic on which an artist mixes paints. パレット □ The painter's right hand holds the brush, the left the palette. その画家は右手に絵筆を，左手にパレットを握る。 **2** N-COUNT 可算名詞 You can refer to the range of colors that is used by a particular artist or group of artists as their **palette**. 絵の具の範囲 □ He paints from a palette consisting almost exclusively of gray and mud brown. 彼はほとんど灰色と泥のような茶色の絵の具だけで絵を描く。 → see **painting**

palm /pɑːm/ (**palms**) **1** N-COUNT 可算名詞 A **palm** or a **palm tree** is a tree that grows in hot countries. It has long leaves growing at the top, and no branches. ヤシ □ ...golden sands and swaying palms. 金色に輝く砂と風にそよぐヤシの木 **2** N-COUNT 可算名詞 The **palm of** your hand is the inside part of your hand, between your fingers and your wrist. ひら □ Dornberg slapped the table with the palm of his hand. ドーンバーグは手のひらでテーブルをぴしゃりと打った。 **3** PHRASE 句 If you have someone or something **in the palm of** your **hand**, you have control over them. 完全に支配する □ Johnson thought he had the board of directors in the palm of his hand. ジョンソンは重役会議を完全に支配していると思っていた。 → see **desert, hand**

palm|top /pɑːmtɒp/ (**palmtops**) N-COUNT 可算名詞 A **palmtop** is a small computer that you can hold in your hand. パームトップ

pal|pable /pælpəbəl/ ADJ 形容詞 You describe something as **palpable** when it is obvious or intense and easily noticed. 明らかな □ The tension between Amy and Jim is palpable. エミーとジムの間がぴりぴりしているのは歴然としていた。 ● **palpably** /pælpəbli/ ADV 副詞 [ADV with cl/group] 明らかに □ The scene was palpably intense to watch. その情景は目の置き所がないぐらい強烈だった。

pal|try /pɔːltri/ ADJ 形容詞 A **paltry** amount of money or of something else is one that you consider to be very small. 微々たる □ ...a paltry fine of $150. 150ドルの微々たる罰金

pam|per /pæmpər/ (**pampers, pampering, pampered**) V-T 他動詞 If you **pamper** someone, you make them feel comfortable by doing things for them or giving them expensive or luxurious things. よく世話をする，贅沢な思いをさせる □ Why don't you let your mother pamper you for a while? しばらくお母さんによく世話を焼いてもらえば？ □ Pamper yourself with our luxury gifts. 私たちからの豪華な贈り物で贅沢をしてください。 ● **pam|pered** ADJ 形容詞 わがままな，甘やかされた □ ...today's pampered superstars. 現在の甘やかされた大スターたち。

Word Link let ≈ little : booklet, droplet, pamphlet

pam|phlet /pæmflɪt/ (**pamphlets**) N-COUNT 可算名詞 A **pamphlet** is a very thin book with a paper cover that gives information about something. パンフレット □ ...a pamphlet about smoking. 喫煙に関するパンフレット

pan /pæn/ (**pans, panning, panned**) **1** N-COUNT 可算名詞 A **pan** is a round metal container with a long handle, that is used for cooking things in, usually on top of a stove. なべ □ Heat the butter and oil in a large pan. 大きななべでバターと油を熱しなさい。 **2** V-T 他動詞 If something such as a movie or a book is **panned** by journalists, they say it is very bad. こき下ろす [INFORMAL くだけた] [usu passive] □ His first high-budget movie, called "Brain Donors," was panned by the critics. 彼の最初の高予算映画、「大錯乱」は評論家たちにこき下ろされた。 **3** V-T/V-I 他動詞/自動詞 If you **pan** a movie or television camera or if it **pans** somewhere, it moves slowly around so that a wide area is filmed. パンする □ The camera panned along the line of players. カメラは演奏家たちの列に沿ってパンした。 □ A television camera panned the stadium. テレビカメラは球場をパンした。 → see Word Web: **pan**

pana|cea /pænəsiːə/ (**panaceas**) N-COUNT 可算名詞 If you say that something is a **panacea for** a set of problems, you mean that it will solve all those problems. 万能薬 □ Trade is not a panacea for the world's economic or social ills. 通商は世界の経済的あるいは社会的疾患を治す万能薬ではない。

pa|nache /pənæʃ/ N-UNCOUNT 不可算名詞 If you do something **with panache**, you do it in a confident, stylish, and elegant way.

No **saucepan** or **frying pan** is perfect. **Copper pans** conduct heat extremely well. This makes them a popular choice for stovetop cooking. However, copper also reacts with the acid in some foods and wines. For this reason, the best copper pans have a thin layer of **tin** covering the copper. **Cast iron** pans are very heavy and **heat up** slowly. But once hot, they stay hot for a long time. Some people like **stainless steel** pans because they heat up quickly and don't react with chemicals in food. However, the bottom of a stainless pan may not heat up evenly.

堂々とした態度 ❑*The orchestra played with great panache.* そのオーケストラの演奏はとても堂々としていた.

pan|cake /pǽnkeɪk/ (pancakes) N-COUNT 可算名詞 A **pancake** is a thin, flat, circular piece of cooked batter made from milk, flour, and eggs. Pancakes are usually eaten for breakfast, with butter and syrup. パンケーキ

pan|da /pǽndə/ (pandas) N-COUNT 可算名詞 A **panda** or a **giant panda** is a large animal like a bear that has black and white fur and lives in the bamboo forests of China. パンダ
→ see **zoo**

pan|der /pǽndər/ (panders, pandering, pandered) V-I 自動詞 If you **pander to** someone or **to** their wishes, you do everything that they want, often to get some advantage for yourself. こびる [DISAPPROVAL 不賛成] ❑*He has offended the party's traditional base by pandering to the rich and the middle classes.* 彼は金持ち階級や中産階級にこびて党の伝統的支持母体を怒らせた.

pane /peɪn/ (panes) N-COUNT 可算名詞 A **pane** of glass is a flat sheet of glass in a window or door. 枚 ❑*I watch my reflection in a pane of glass.* 私は1枚の窓ガラスに映った自分の姿をじっと見る.

pan|el /pǽnᵊl/ (panels) ■ N-COUNT-COLL 集合可算名詞 A **panel** is a small group of people who are chosen to do something, for example, to discuss something in public or to make a decision. 討論者団, 審査員団 ❑*He assembled a panel of scholars to advise him.* 彼は助言を得るため学者を集めて調査班をつくった. ❑*All the writers on the panel agreed that Quinn's book should be singled out for special praise.* 審査員団に入っている作家は全員, クインの本は特に取り上げて賞賛するに値すると合意しました. ② N-COUNT 可算名詞 A **panel** is a flat rectangular piece of wood or other material that forms part of a larger object such as a door. 鏡板, 羽目板 ❑*the frosted glass panel set in the center of the door.* ドアの中央部にはめ込まれたすりガラス板 ③ N-COUNT 可算名詞 A control **panel** or instrument **panel** is a board or surface that contains switches and controls to operate a machine or piece of equipment. 盤, 板 [n N] ❑*The equipment was extremely sophisticated and was monitored from a central control panel.* その装置は非常に高機能であり, 中央制御盤で監視されていた.

pan|eled /pǽnᵊld/ also **panelled** ■ ADJ 形容詞 A **paneled** room has decorative wooden panels covering its walls. 鏡板張りの, 羽目板張りの ❑*…their cozy paneled den.* 彼らの鏡板張りのこじんまりとした部屋 ● COMB IN ADJ 形容詞の複合 -**paneled** combines with nouns to form adjectives that describe the way a room or wall is decorated or the way a door or window is made. 一の鏡板張りの ❑*…an elegant wood-paneled library.* 木の鏡板を張って装飾してある優雅な図書室 ② ADJ 形容詞 A **paneled** wall, door, or window does not have a flat surface but has square or rectangular areas set into its surface. 鏡板を張った ❑*…an oil landscape on the paneled wall.* 鏡板を張った壁にかけてある風景画油絵

pang /pǽŋ/ (pangs) N-COUNT 可算名詞 A **pang** is a sudden strong feeling or emotion, for example, of sadness or pain. 心の苦しみ ❑*For a moment she felt a pang of guilt about the way she was treating him.* 彼を取り扱っているやり方に彼女は一瞬自責の念に駆られた.

pan|han|dler /pǽnhændlər/ (panhandlers) N-COUNT 可算名詞 A **panhandler** is a person who stops people in the street and asks them for money. 物乞い [mainly AM 主に米国英語, INFORMAL くだけた]

pan|ic /pǽnɪk/ (panics, panicking, panicked) ■ N-VAR 可変性名詞 **Panic** is a very strong feeling of anxiety or fear that makes you act without thinking carefully. 恐慌, パニック ❑*An earthquake has hit the capital, causing damage to buildings and panic among the population.* 首都は地震に襲われ, 建物に被害があり, 住民はパニックに陥りました. ② N-UNCOUNT 不可算名詞 **Panic** or a **panic** is a situation in which people are affected by a strong feeling of anxiety. ろうばい [also a N] ❑*There was a moment of panic as it became clear just how vulnerable the nation was.* その国がいかに攻撃されやすいかが明確になりだすと, あわてふためいた時期があった. ❑*I'm in a panic about getting everything done in time.* 時間内に全部終わらせようと私は泡を食っている状態だ. ③ V-T/V-I 他動詞/自動詞 If you **panic** or if someone **panics** you, you suddenly feel anxious or afraid, and act quickly and without thinking carefully. 恐怖を起こさせる, うろたえる ❑*Guests panicked and screamed when the bomb exploded.* 爆弾が爆発すると客は恐怖におびえ悲鳴を上げた. ❑*The unexpected and sudden memory briefly panicked her.* 意外な突然の思い出に彼女はしばらくうろたえた.

pano|ra|ma /pænərǽmə, -rάːmə/ (panoramas) ■ N-COUNT 可算名詞 A **panorama** is a view in which you can see a long way over a wide area of land, usually because you are on high ground. 全景, パノラマ ❑*Horton looked out over a panorama of fertile valleys and gentle hills.* ホートンは肥沃な谷と緩やかな丘の広がる全景を見渡し

た. ② N-COUNT 可算名詞 A **panorama** is a broad view of a state of affairs or of a constantly changing series of events. 概観 ❑*The play presents a panorama of the history of communism.* その劇は共産主義の歴史の概観を見せる.

pano|ram|ic /pænərǽmɪk/ ADJ 形容詞 If you have a **panoramic** view, you can see a long way over a wide area. 全景の ❑*The terrain's high points provide a panoramic view of Los Angeles.* その地域の高い場所からはロサンジェルスの全景を見渡せる.

pant /pǽnt/ (pants, panting, panted) ■ V-I 自動詞 If you **pant**, you breathe quickly and loudly with your mouth open, because you have been doing something energetic. 息切れする ❑*She climbed rapidly until she was panting with the effort.* 彼女はがんばって息が切れるまで素早く登った. ② → see also **pants**

panties /pǽntiz/ N-PLURAL 複数名詞 **Panties** are short, close-fitting underpants worn by women or girls. パンティー [mainly AM 主に米国英語] ❑*…a pair of white panties.* 白いパンティ1枚

pan|to|mime /pǽntəmaɪm/ N-SING 単数名詞 If you say that a situation or a person's behavior is a **pantomime**, you mean that it is silly or exaggerated and that there is something false about it. 大げさな身振り, 茶番 [mainly BRIT 主に英国英語] ❑*They were made welcome with the usual pantomime of exaggerated smiles and gestures.* 彼らは通例の大げさな笑顔と身振りの茶番で歓迎された.

pants /pǽnts/ ■ N-PLURAL 複数名詞 **Pants** are a piece of clothing that covers the lower part of your body and each leg. ズボン [AM 米国英語] [also "a pair of" N] ❑*She described him as wearing brown corduroy pants and a white cotton shirt.* その男は茶色いコールテンのズボンをはき白い綿のシャツを着ていたと彼女は描写した. ② N-PLURAL 複数名詞 **Pants** are a piece of underwear which have two holes to put your legs through and elastic around the top to hold them up around your waist or hips. パンツ [BRIT 英国英語] [also "a pair of" N] [AM usually **underpants** 米国英語では通常 **underpants**]
→ see also **clothing**

pan|ty|hose /pǽntihoʊz/ also **panty hose** N-PLURAL 複数名詞 **Pantyhose** are a piece of clothing worn by women and girls. They are usually made of flesh-colored nylon and cover the hips, legs and feet. パンティーストッキング [mainly AM 主に米国英語] [also "a pair of" N] ❑*She told him her pantyhose were slipping.* 彼女は自分のパンティーストッキングがずり落ちてきていると彼に言った.

papa /pάːpə/ (papas) N-FAMILY 家族名詞 Some people refer to or address their father as **papa**. パパ [OLD-FASHIONED 古風な] ❑*He was so much older than me, older even than my papa.* 彼は私よりずっと年上で, 私のパパよりも年上だった.

pa|pal /peɪpᵊl/ ADJ 形容詞 **Papal** is used to describe things relating to the Pope. ローマ教皇の [ADJ n] ❑*…the doctrine of papal infallibility.* 教皇不可謬(ふかびゅう)性の教義

pa|per /peɪpər/ (papers, papering, papered) ■ N-UNCOUNT 不可算名詞 **Paper** is a material that you write on or wrap things with. The pages of this book are made of paper. 紙 ❑*He wrote his name down on a piece of paper for me.* 彼は私のために自分の名前を紙に書いてくれた. ❑*…a paper bag.* 紙袋. ② N-COUNT 可算名詞 A **paper** is a newspaper. 新聞 ❑*I might get a paper in the town.* 町で新聞を買うかもしれない. ③ N-COUNT 可算名詞 You can refer to newspapers in general as **the paper** or **the papers**. 新聞 ❑*You can't believe everything you read in the paper.* 新聞に書いてあることを全部は信じられない. ④ N-PLURAL 複数名詞 Your **papers** are sheets of paper with information on them that you might keep in a safe place at home. 書類 ❑*After her death, her papers – including unpublished articles and correspondence – were deposited at the library.* 彼女の死後, 未出版の記事や手紙などの書類は図書館に委託された. ⑤ N-PLURAL 複数名詞 Your **papers** are official documents, such as your passport or identity card, that prove who you are or that give you official permission to do something. 身分証明書 ❑*A young Moroccan stopped by police refused to show his papers.* 警察に呼び止められたモロッコ人の若者は身分証明書を示すことを拒んだ. ⑥ N-COUNT 可算名詞 A **paper** is a long, formal piece of writing about an academic subject. 論文 ❑*He just published a paper in the journal Nature analyzing the fires.* 彼はそれらの火事を分析した論文を『ネイチャー』誌にちょうど発表したところです. ⑦ N-COUNT 可算名詞 A **paper** is an essay written by a student. レポート [mainly AM 主に米国英語] ❑*…the ten common errors that appear most frequently in student papers.* 学生のレポートに最も頻繁に見られる10個の共通の間違い ⑧ N-COUNT 可算名詞 A **paper** prepared by a government or a committee is a report on a question they have been considering or a set of proposals for changes in the law. 提案, 答申 ❑*…a new government paper on electoral reform.* 選挙の改革に関する政府の新案 ⑨ ADJ 形容詞 **Paper** agreements, qualifications, or profits are ones that are stated by official documents to exist, although they may not really be effective or useful. 名目上の [ADJ n] ❑*They expressed deep mistrust of the paper promises.* 彼らは名目上の保証に対する深い不信感を示した. ⑩ V-T 他

Word Web   paper

Around 3000 BC, Egyptians began using the papyrus plant to produce **paper**. They cut the stems of the plant into thin slices and pressed them into **sheets**. A very different Chinese technique developed about the same time. It more closely resembles today's manufacturing process. Chinese paper makers cooked **fiber** made of tree bark. Then they pressed it into molds and let it dry. Around 200 BC, a third technique developed in the Middle East. Craftsmen started using animal skins to make parchment. Today, paper manufacturing destroys millions of trees every year. This has led to **recycling** programs and paperless offices.

動詞 If you **paper** a wall, you put wallpaper on it. 壁紙を張る □ *We papered all four bedrooms.* 私たちは４つの寝室すべてに壁紙を張った. □ *We have papered this bedroom in softest gray.* 私たちはこの寝室には最も淡い灰色の壁紙を張った. **11** PHRASE 句 If you put your thoughts down **on paper**, you write them down. 紙上に □ *It is important to get something down on paper.* なにかを紙に書き止めることが大切です. **12** PHRASE 句 If something seems to be the case **on paper**, it seems to be the case from what you read or hear about it, but it may not really be the case. 理論上では □ *On paper, their country is a multi-party democracy.* 理論上ではその国は複数政党制民主主義国だ.
→ see Word Web: **paper**
→ see **copy**

Word Partnership   *paper* は次の語句と使われる:

ADJ.	**blank** paper, **brown** paper, **colored** paper, **recycled** paper **1** **daily** paper **2**
V.	**fold the** paper **1** **read the** paper **2** **present a** paper, **publish a** paper **6** **draft a** paper, **write a** paper **6** **7**
N.	**morning** paper **2** **research** paper **6** **7**

paper|back /peɪpərbæk/ (**paperbacks**) N-COUNT 可算名詞 A **paperback** is a book with a thin cardboard or paper cover. Compare **hardback**. ペーパーバック [also "in" N] □ *She said she would buy the book when it comes out in paperback.* 彼女はその本がペーパーバックで出版された時に買うと言った.

pa|per clip (**paper clips**) also **paper-clip** or **paperclip** N-COUNT 可算名詞 A **paper clip** is a small piece of bent wire that is used to hold papers together. クリップ
→ see **office**

paper|work /peɪpərwɜrk/ N-UNCOUNT 不可算名詞 **Paperwork** is the routine part of a job that involves writing or dealing with letters, reports, and records. 事務処理 □ *At every stage in the production there will be paperwork — forms to fill in, permissions to obtain, letters to write.* 用紙に記入したり，許可を取ったり，手紙を書いたり，製造の各工程には事務処理がつきものだ.

Pap smear (**Pap smears**) also **Pap test** N-COUNT 可算名詞 A **Pap smear** is a medical test in which cells are taken from a woman's cervix and analyzed to see if any cancer cells are present. パプ塗抹標本 [AM 米国英語]

par /pɑr/ **1** PHRASE 句 If you say that two people or things are **on a par with** each other, you mean that they are equally good or bad, or equally important. 一と同等で □ *The water park will be on a par with some of the best public swim facilities around.* ウォーターパークは現存する最もいい公共水泳施設の一部と肩を並べるものとなるでしょう. **2** N-UNCOUNT 不可算名詞 In golf, **par** is the number of strokes that a good player should take to get the ball into a hole or into all the holes on a particular golf course. パー [N with num, "under/over" N] □ *He was five under par after the first round.* 第1ラウンドを終えた時点で彼は5アンダーパーだった. **3** PHRASE 句 If you say that someone or something is **below par** or **under par**, you are disappointed in them because they are below the standard you expected. 標準以下で □ *Duffy's primitive guitar playing is well below par.* ダフィーの原始的なギターの腕前は全く水準に達していない. □ *A teacher's job is relatively safe, even if they perform under par in the classroom.* 教員の仕事はたとえ授業の水準が低くても比較的安全だ. **4** PHRASE 句 If you say that someone or something is not **up to par**, you are disappointed in them because they are below the standard you expected. 標準に達して □ *It's a constant struggle to try to keep them up to par.* 彼らが常に標準に達するように保つのには絶え間なく苦労している. **5** PHRASE 句 If you **feel below par** or **under par** or **not up to par**, you feel tired and unable to perform as well as you normally do. 体調が優れないで □ *After the birth of her baby she felt generally under par.* 出産後彼女は全般的に体調が優れなかった.

para|ble /pærəbəl/ (**parables**) N-COUNT 可算名詞 A **parable** is a short story, that is told in order to make a moral or religious point, like those in the Bible. たとえ話 □ *...the parable of the Good Samaritan.* 善きサマリア人のたとえ話

para|chute /pærəʃut/ (**parachutes, parachuting, parachuted**) **1** N-COUNT 可算名詞 A **parachute** is a device that enables a person to jump from an aircraft and float safely to the ground. It consists of a large piece of thin cloth attached to your body by strings. パラシュート □ *They fell 41,000 ft. before opening their parachutes.* 彼らはパラシュートを開く前に４万１千フィート落下した. **2** V-T/V-I 他動詞/自動詞 If a person **parachutes** or someone **parachutes** them somewhere, they jump from an aircraft using a parachute. 落下傘で降ろす，落下傘降下する □ *He was a courier for the Polish underground and parachuted into Warsaw.* 彼はポーランドの地下組織の密使で，ワルシャワに落下傘で降下した. **3** V-T 他動詞 To **parachute** something somewhere means to drop it somewhere by parachute. 落下傘で投下する □ *Planes parachuted food, clothing, blankets, medicine, and water into the rugged mountainous border region.* 飛行機は食品，衣料品，毛布，医薬品と水を岩だらけの山岳国境地帯にパラシュートで落とした. **4** V-T/V-I 他動詞/自動詞 If a person **parachutes** into an organization or if they **are parachuted into** it, they are brought in suddenly in order to help it. 緊急援護に現れる，緊急援護に送られる □ *...a consultant who parachutes into corporations and helps provide strategic thinking.* 会社に緊急に来て戦略的考え方を築く援助をするコンサルタント □ *Executives with political influence are parachuted into the company.* 政治的影響力のある重役たちがその会社に送り込まれている.
→ see **fly**

pa|rade /pəreɪd/ (**parades, parading, paraded**) **1** N-COUNT 可算名詞 A **parade** is a procession of people or vehicles moving through a public place in order to celebrate an important day or event. 行列 □ *A military parade marched slowly and solemnly down Pennsylvania Avenue.* ペンシルベニア街を軍事パレードはゆっくり厳かに進行した. **2** V-I 自動詞 When people **parade** somewhere, they walk together in a formal group or a line, usually with other people watching them. 行進する □ *More than four thousand soldiers, sailors, and airmen paraded down the Champs Élysées.* ４千人以上の陸軍兵士，水兵，航空兵が行進した. **3** N-VAR 可変性名詞 **Parade** is a formal occasion when soldiers stand in lines to be seen by an officer or important person, or march in a group. 閲兵式 [oft "on" N] □ *He had them on parade at six o'clock in the morning.* 彼は彼らを朝の６時に閲兵式に出した. **4** V-T 他動詞 If prisoners **are paraded** through the streets of a town or on television, they are shown to the public, usually in order to make the people who are holding them seem more powerful or important. 行進させてさらし者にする [usu passive] □ *Five leading fighter pilots have been captured and paraded before the media.* 戦闘機の有力なパイロット5人が捕えられてマスコミの前にさらし者にされた. **5** V-T 他動詞 If you say that someone **parades** a person, you mean that they show that person to others only in order to gain some advantage for themselves. 連行する [usu passive] □ *Captured prisoners were paraded before television cameras.* 捕えられた捕虜たちがテレビカメラの前に連行されてきました. **6** V-T 他動詞 If people **parade** something, they show it in public so that it can be admired. 見せびらかす □ *Valentino is eager to see celebrities parading his clothes at big occasions.* バレンティーノは主な行事で有名人たちが彼のデザインした服を見せびらかしているのを見たがる. **7** V-T/V-I 他動詞/自動詞 If you say that something **parades as** or **is paraded as** a good or important thing, you mean that some people say that it is good or important but you think it probably is not. まかり通る □ *...all the fashions that parade as modern movements in art.* 現代芸術の動きとしてまかり通っているありとあらゆる流行

para|digm /pærədaɪm/ (**paradigms**) N-VAR 可変性名詞 A **paradigm** is a model for something that explains it or shows how it can be produced. 範例 [FORMAL 形式ばった] □ *...a new paradigm of production.* 生産の新しい典型

para|dise /pærədaɪs/ (**paradises**) **1** N-PROPER 固有名詞 According to some religions, **paradise** is a wonderful place where people go after they die, if they have led good lives. 天国 □ *The Koran describes paradise as a place containing a garden of delight.* コーランには天国は喜びの庭のある場所であると書いてある. **2** N-VAR 可変性名詞 You can refer to a place or situation that seems beautiful

or perfect as **paradise** or **a paradise**. 楽園 ❏ *Bali is one of the world's great natural paradises.* バリは世界でもっともすばらしい自然の楽園の1つである.

| Word Link | dox ≈ opinion : ortho**dox**y, para**dox**, unortho**dox** |

| Word Link | para ≈ beside : **para**dox, **para**medic, **para**llel |

para|dox /pǽrədɒks/ (paradoxes) **1** N-COUNT 可算名詞 You describe a situation as a **paradox** when it involves two or more facts or qualities that seem to contradict each other. パラドックス, 一見矛盾しているように思われる事実 ❏ *The paradox is that the region's most dynamic economies have the most primitive financial systems.* その地域でもっとも活発な経済が最も原始的な金融制度を持っているのは矛盾しているように思える. ❏ *The paradox of exercise is that while using a lot of energy it seems to generate more.* 運動するとたくさんエネルギーを使う一方で, エネルギーをより一層発生しているように思われるのは一見矛盾しているように思われる事実である. **2** N-VAR 可変性名詞 A **paradox** is a statement in which it seems that if one part of it is true, the other part of it cannot be true. パラドックス, 逆説 ❏ *The story contains many levels of paradox.* その話はいろいろな程度の逆説を含んでいる.

para|doxi|cal /pæˈrədɒksɪkᵊl/ ADJ 形容詞 If something is **paradoxical**, it involves two facts or qualities that seem to contradict each other. 逆説的な ❏ *Some sedatives produce the paradoxical effect of making the person more anxious.* 鎮静剤には人をより不安にするという逆説的な効果があるものもある. ● **para|doxi|cal|ly** /pæˈrədɒksɪkli/ ADV 副詞 逆説的に言えば ❏ *Paradoxically, the less you have to do the more you may resent the work that does come your way.* 矛盾するように思われるよ, する仕事量が少なければ少ないほど, 実際に自分に回ってきた仕事を不快に思うものだ.

par|af|fin /pǽrəfɪn/ **1** N-UNCOUNT 不可算名詞 **Paraffin** is a white wax obtained from petroleum or coal. It is used to make candles, to form seals, and in beauty treatments. パラフィン **2** N-UNCOUNT 不可算名詞 **Paraffin** is a strong-smelling liquid which is used as a fuel in heaters, lamps, and engines. 灯油 [mainly BRIT 主に英国英語; AM kerosene 米国英語 **kerosene**]

para|gon /pǽrəgɒn/ (paragons) N-COUNT 可算名詞 If you refer to someone as a **paragon**, you mean that they are perfect or have a lot of a good qualities. 模範, 手本 ❏ *We don't expect candidates to be paragons of virtue.* 私たちは候補者たちが美徳の鑑であることを期待してはいない. ❏ *Our administrator is a paragon of neatness, efficiency, and reliability.* 私たちの管理者は手際がよく能率的で信頼性できる模範的人物だ.

para|graph /pǽrəgræf/ (paragraphs) N-COUNT 可算名詞 A **paragraph** is a section of a piece of writing. A paragraph always begins on a new line and contains at least one sentence. 段落 ❏ *The length of a paragraph depends on the information it conveys.* 段落の長さは伝える情報の量次第である.

par|al|lel /pǽrəlel/ (parallels, paralleling, paralleled) **1** N-COUNT 可算名詞 If something has a **parallel**, it is similar to something else, but exists or happens in a different place or at a different time. If it has **no parallel** or is **without parallel**, it is not similar to anything else. 類似物 ❏ *Readers familiar with military conflict will find a vague parallel to the Vietnam War.* 軍事紛争に精通している読者はベトナム戦争とどことなく類似していることに気付くだろう. ❏ *It's an ecological disaster with no parallel anywhere else in the world.* これは世界のどこにも類を見ない生態学的大惨事です. **2** N-COUNT 可算名詞 If there are **parallels** between two things, they are similar in some ways. 類似点 ❏ *Detailed study of folk music from a variety of countries reveals many close parallels.* いろいろな国の民族音楽を詳しく研究すると, とても類似している点が多く見られる. ❏ *There are significant parallels with the 1980s.* 1980年代と極めて似ている点がある. **3** V-T 他動詞 If one thing **parallels** another, they happen at the same time or are similar, and often seem to be connected. 並行する, 類似する ❏ *Often there are emotional reasons paralleling the financial ones.* 感情的な理由が財政上の理由と並行して存在することが多い. ❏ *His remarks paralleled those of the president.* 彼は大統領と似た発言をした. **4** ADJ 形容詞 **Parallel** events or situations happen at the same time as one another, or are similar to one another. 並行して, 一致して ❏ *...parallel talks between the two countries' foreign ministers.* 両国の外務大臣の間で並行して行われた話し合い ❏ *Their instincts do not always run parallel with ours.* 彼らの直感は必ずしも私たちのものと一致しない. **5** ADJ 形容詞 If two lines, two objects, or two lines of movement are **parallel**, they are the same distance apart along their whole length. 平行な ❏ *...seventy-two ships, drawn up in two parallel lines.* 平行に2列に整列した72隻の船 ❏ *Remsen Street is parallel with Montague Street.* レムゼン通りはモンタギュー通りと平行している. **6** N-COUNT 可算名詞 A **parallel** is an imaginary line round the earth that is parallel to the equator. Parallels are shown on maps. 緯線 [usu "the" ord N] ❏ *...the area south of the 38th parallel.* 38度線の南の地域
→ see **globe, gymnastics**

Thesaurus	*parallel* また次を参照:
N.	analogy, correlation, resemblance, similarity **1** **2**

pa|raly|sis /pərǽləsɪs/ **1** N-UNCOUNT 不可算名詞 **Paralysis** is the loss of the ability to move and feel in all or part of your body. まひ ❏ *...paralysis of the leg.* 下肢のまひ. **2** N-UNCOUNT 不可算名詞 **Paralysis** is the state of being unable to act or function properly. まひ状態 ❏ *The paralysis of the leadership leaves the army without its supreme command.* 指導部がまひ状態になれば, 陸軍はその最高指令がない状態になってしまう.

para|lyze /pǽrəlaɪz/ (paralyzes, paralyzing, paralyzed) **1** V-T 他動詞 If someone **is paralyzed** by an accident or an illness, they have no feeling in their body, or in part of their body, and are unable to move. まひさせる ❏ *She is paralyzed from the waist down.* 彼女は腰から下がまひしている. ● **para|lyzed** ADJ 形容詞 まひした ❏ *A guy with paralyzed legs is not supposed to ride horses.* 両足がまひした男は馬に乗れないことになっている. **2** V-T 他動詞 If a person, place, or organization **is paralyzed by** something, they become unable to act or function properly. まひ状態にする, 無力にする ❏ *The city has been virtually paralyzed by sudden snowstorms.* その市は突然の吹雪でほとんどまひ状態だ. ❏ *She was paralyzed by fear and love.* 彼女は恐怖と愛情で身動きが取れなかった. ● **para|lyzed** ADJ 形容詞 まひした ❏ *He sat in his chair, paralyzed with dread.* 彼は恐れに腰を抜かしていすに座り込んでいた.
→ see **disability**

para|med|ic /pǽrəmedɪk/ (paramedics) N-COUNT 可算名詞 A **paramedic** is a person whose training is similar to that of a nurse and who helps to do medical work. 医療補助員 ❏ *We intend to have a paramedic on every ambulance within the next three years.* この3年以内に救急車すべてに医療補助員を配置するつもりだ.

pa|ram|eter /pərǽmɪtər/ (parameters) N-COUNT 可算名詞 **Parameters** are factors or limits that affect the way something can be done or made. パラメーター, 要因 [FORMAL 形式ばった] ❏ *...some of the parameters that determine the taste of a wine.* ワインの味を決定する要因のいくつか

para|mili|tary /pǽrəmɪliteri/ (paramilitaries) **1** ADJ 形容詞 A **paramilitary** organization is organized like an army and performs either civil or military functions in a country. 準軍事的組織の [ADJ n] ❏ *...Searches by the army and paramilitary forces have continued today.* 陸軍と準軍事的組織の部隊が今日も捜索を続けています. ● N-COUNT 可算名詞 **Paramilitaries** are members of a paramilitary organization. 準軍事的組織の成員 ❏ *Paramilitaries and army recruits patrolled the village.* 準軍事的組織員と陸軍の新兵が村を巡回していた. **2** ADJ 形容詞 A **paramilitary** organization is an illegal group that is organized like an army. 非合法準軍事組織 [ADJ n] ❏ *...a law which said that all paramilitary groups must be disarmed.* 非合法準軍事組織はすべて武装解除されなければならないとする法律 ● N-COUNT 可算名詞 **Paramilitaries** are members of an illegal paramilitary organization. 非合法準軍事組織の成員 ❏ *Paramilitaries were blamed for the shooting.* その狙撃は非合法準軍事組織メンバーの責任だとされた.

para|mount /pǽrəmaʊnt/ ADJ 形容詞 Something that is **paramount** or of **paramount** importance is more important than anything else. 最も重要な ❏ *The children's welfare must be seen as paramount.* 児童の福祉は最も重要視されなければならない.

para|noia /pærənɔ́ɪə/ **1** N-UNCOUNT 不可算名詞 If you say that someone suffers from **paranoia**, you think that they are too suspicious and afraid of other people. 強い疑い, 恐怖 ❏ *The mood is one of paranoia and expectation of war.* 雰囲気は強い懐疑と戦争を予想するものだ. **2** N-UNCOUNT 不可算名詞 In psychology, if someone suffers from **paranoia**, they wrongly believe that other people are trying to harm them, or believe themselves to be much more important than they really are. 偏執症, 妄想症

para|noid /pǽrənɔɪd/ (paranoids) **1** ADJ 形容詞 If you say that someone is **paranoid**, you mean that they are extremely suspicious and afraid of other people. 偏執性の ❏ *I'm not going to get paranoid about it.* 私はこれについて必要以上にこだわるつもりはない. ❏ *...a paranoid politician who saw enemies all around him.* 周りには敵ばかりいると妄想している政治家 **2** ADJ 形容詞 Someone who is **paranoid** suffers from the mental illness of paranoia. 偏執症患者の, 妄想症の ❏ *...paranoid delusions.* 偏執症者の妄想 ● N-COUNT 可算名詞 A **paranoid** is someone who is paranoid. 偏執症患者 ❏ *...these sad, deluded paranoids.* これらの哀れな, 妄想に取りつかれた偏執症患者たち.

para|pher|na|lia /pærəfərnéɪlyə, -féniɫ-/ N-UNCOUNT 不可算名詞 You can refer to a large number of objects that someone has with them or that are connected with a particular activity as **paraphernalia**. 手回り品, 道具類 ❏ *...a large courtyard full of builders' paraphernalia.* 建築業者の道具類でいっぱいの大きな中庭

para|phrase /pǽrəfreɪz/ (paraphrases, paraphrasing, paraphrased) **1** V-T 他動詞 If you **paraphrase** someone or **paraphrase** something that they have said or written, you

express what they have said or written in a different way. 別の言葉で言い換える □*To paraphrase President Bush, we must restore confidence in our economic sector.* ブッシュ大統領の言葉を言い換えると、我々は我々の経済分野に対する信頼を回復しなければならない、となる。 □*Baxter paraphrased the contents of the press release.* バックスターは新聞発表した内容を別の言葉で言い換えた。 **2** N-COUNT 可算名詞 A **paraphrase** of something written or spoken is the same thing expressed in a different way. 言い換え □*The last two clauses were an exact quote rather than a paraphrase of Mr. Forth's remarks.* 最後の2節はフォース氏の発言をそのまま引用したもので、言い換えたものではない。

para|plegic /ˌpærəˈpliːdʒɪk/ (**paraplegics**) N-COUNT 可算名詞 A **paraplegic** is someone who cannot move the lower half of their body, for example, because of an injury to their spine. 下半身不随の人 □*Theoretically, such equipment could help paraplegics regain movement.* 理論的に言って、このような装置は下半身不随の人が動きを取り戻すのに役立つ可能性があるでしょう。 ●ADJ 形容詞 **Paraplegic** is also an adjective. 下半身不随の □*A passenger was injured so badly he will be paraplegic for the rest of his life.* 1名の乗客はとてもひどい怪我を負ったので、今後一生下半身不随でしょう。

para|site /ˈpærəsaɪt/ (**parasites**) **1** N-COUNT 可算名詞 A **parasite** is a small animal or plant that lives on or inside a larger animal or plant, and gets its food from it. 寄生生物、寄生植物 □*Kangaroos harbor a vast range of parasites.* カンガルーは膨大な種類の寄生虫のすみかである。 **2** N-COUNT 可算名詞 If you disapprove of someone because you think that they get money or other things from other people but do not do anything in return, you can call them a **parasite**. 寄食者、たかる人 [DISAPPROVAL 不賛成] □*...a parasite, who produced nothing but lived on the work of others.* 何も生産せず他人の仕事に頼って暮らしていたパラサイト

para|sit|ic /ˌpærəˈsɪtɪk/ also **parasitical** **1** ADJ 形容詞 **Parasitic** diseases are caused by parasites. 寄生虫性の □*Will global warming mean the spread of tropical parasitic diseases?* 地球温暖化が原因で熱帯性寄生虫による病気がまんえんするだろうか。 **2** ADJ 形容詞 **Parasitic** animals and plants live on or inside larger animals or plants and get their food from them. 寄生的な □*...tiny parasitic insects.* 非常に小さな寄生性の昆虫 **3** ADJ 形容詞 If you describe a person or organization as **parasitic**, you mean that they get money or other things from people without doing anything in return. たかり性の、寄生虫のような [DISAPPROVAL 不賛成] □*...a parasitic new middle class of consultants and experts.* コンサルタントや専門家といった寄生性の新しい中産階級

para|troop|er /ˈpærətruːpər/ (**paratroopers**) N-COUNT 可算名詞 **Paratroopers** are soldiers who are trained to be dropped by parachute into battle or into enemy territory. 落下傘兵

par|cel /ˈpɑːrsəl/ (**parcels**) **1** N-COUNT 可算名詞 A **parcel** is something wrapped in paper, in a bag or large envelope, or in a box, usually so that it can be sent to someone by mail. 小包 □*They also sent parcels of food and clothing.* 彼らは食べ物や衣服の小包も送った。 **2** PHRASE 句 If you say that something is **part and parcel of** something else, you are emphasizing that it is involved in or included in it. 重要部分、本質的な部分 [EMPHASIS 強調] □*Learning about life in a new culture is part and parcel of what newcomers to America face.* 新しい文化の中での生活を身につけることが、アメリカへの来たばかりの人が必ず直面することの重要部分だ。

parched /pɑːrtʃt/ **1** ADJ 形容詞 If something, especially the ground or a plant, is **parched**, it is very dry, because there has been no rain. (地面や植物が) 乾燥した □*The clouds gathered and showers poured down upon the parched earth.* 雲がわき起こり、乾いた地面に雨が激しく降った。 **2** ADJ 形容詞 If your mouth, throat, or lips are **parched**, they are unpleasantly dry. (のど・唇などが) からからに乾く □*Her throat was parched, and she was exhausted from all the walking.* 彼女はのどがからからで、長い徒歩の果てに疲れ果てていた。 **3** ADJ 形容詞 If you say that you are **parched**, you mean that you are very thirsty. のどがひどく渇いた [INFORMAL くだけた] [v-link ADJ] □*When I told them I was parched, they went and got me a bottle of mineral water.* 私が、のどが渇いたと言うと、彼らはミネラルウォーターのボトルを買ってきてくれた。

Word Link	don ≈ giving : donate, donor, pardon

par|don /ˈpɑːrdən/ (**pardons, pardoning, pardoned**) **1** CONVENTION 慣習表現 You say **Pardon?**, **I beg your pardon?**, or **Pardon me?** when you want someone to repeat what they have just said because you have not heard or understood it. (聞き返す時に) えっ？、今なんて言われました？ [SPOKEN 口語, FORMULAE 決まり文句] □*"Will you let me open it?"—"Pardon?"—"Can I open it?"* 「私にそれを開けさせてくれる？」「えっ？」「私がそれを開けてもいい？」 **2** CONVENTION 慣習表現 People say **"I beg your pardon?"** when they are surprised or offended by something that someone has just said. (相手の言葉に驚いた時・気分を害した時に) 今、何て言った？ [SPOKEN 口語, FEELINGS 感情] □*"Would you get undressed, please?"—"I beg your pardon?"—"Will you get undressed?"* 「服を脱いでいただけますか？」、「何ですって？」、「服を脱いでくれます

か？」 **3** CONVENTION 慣習表現 You say **"I beg your pardon"** as a way of apologizing for accidentally doing something wrong, such as disturbing someone or making a mistake. (謝る時) すみません [SPOKEN 口語, FORMULAE 決まり文句] □*I beg your pardon. I thought you were someone else.* すみません。あなたが誰か他の人だと思いました。 **4** CONVENTION 慣習表現 Some people say **"Pardon me"** instead of "Excuse me" when they want to politely get someone's attention or interrupt them. (注意を引く時・中断する時) 失礼ですが、すみません [SPOKEN 口語, FORMULAE 決まり文句] □*Pardon me, are you finished, madam?* 失礼ですが、奥さん、もう終わりましたか？ **5** V-T 他動詞 If someone who has been found guilty of a crime is **pardoned**, they are officially allowed to go free and are not punished. 赦免する、無罪放免する [usu passive] □*Hundreds of political prisoners were pardoned and released.* 何百人もの政治犯が赦免され釈放された。 ●N-COUNT 可算名詞 **Pardon** is also a noun. 恩赦、赦免 □*They lobbied the government on his behalf and he was granted a presidential pardon.* 彼らは彼のために政府に働きかけ、彼は大統領恩赦を受けた。

pare /pɛər/ (**pares, paring, pared**) **1** V-T 他動詞 When you **pare** something, or **pare** part of it **off** or **away**, you cut off its skin or its outer layer. 皮をむく □*Pare the brown skin from the meat with a very sharp knife.* よく切れる包丁で肉の茶色い皮をそぎ落とす。 □*He took out a slab of cheese, pared off a slice and ate it hastily.* 彼はチーズの塊を取り出し、一切れ切るや食べた。 **2** V-T 他動詞 If you **pare** something **down** or **back**, or if you **pare** it, you reduce it. 削減する、引き下げる □*The governor's campaign fund could be pared down to $500.* 知事の運動資金は500ドルに引き下げてもいいくらいだろう。 □*The luxury tax won't really do much to pare down the budget deficit.* 奢侈税 (しゃしぜい) は本当に財政赤字の削減にそんなに貢献しないだろう。

par|ent /ˈpɛərənt, ˈpær-/ (**parents**) **1** N-COUNT 可算名詞 Your **parents** are your mother and father. 親 □*Children need their parents.* 子供たちには親が必要だ。 □*This is where a lot of parents go wrong.* これがたくさんの親が間違うところだ。 **2** → see also **single parent** **3** ADJ 形容詞 An organization's **parent** organization is the organization that created it and usually still controls it. (組織の) 母体となる [ADJ n] □*Each unit including the parent company has its own, local management.* 親会社を含め、各構成単位にそれぞれの現地経営陣がいる。
→ see **child**

pa|ren|tal /pəˈrɛntəl/ ADJ 形容詞 **Parental** is used to describe something that relates to parents in general, or to one or both of the parents of a particular child. 親の □*Medical treatment was sometimes given to children without parental consent.* 時々、親の同意なしに子供に治療が施された。

pa|ren|tal leave N-UNCOUNT 不可算名詞 **Parental leave** is time away from work, usually without pay, that parents are allowed in order to care for their children. 育児休暇 [BUSINESS 実業] □*Parents are entitled to 13 weeks' parental leave to be taken during the first five years of a child's life.* 子供が5歳になるまで親は13週の育児休暇を取る権利がある。

pa|ren|the|sis /pəˈrɛnθəsɪs/ (**parentheses** /pəˈrɛnθəsiːz/) N-COUNT 可算名詞 **Parentheses** are a pair of curved marks that you put around words or numbers to indicate that they are additional, separate, or less important. (This sentence is in parentheses.) 丸括弧

par|ent|hood /ˈpɛərənthʊd, ˈpær-/ N-UNCOUNT 不可算名詞 **Parenthood** is the state of being a parent. 親であること □*She may feel unready for the responsibilities of parenthood.* 彼女は親であることの責任に対する心の準備ができていないと感じているのかもしれない。

par|ent|ing /ˈpɛərəntɪŋ, ˈpær-/ N-UNCOUNT 不可算名詞 **Parenting** is the activity of bringing up and taking care of your child. 育児、子育て □*Parenting is not fully valued by society.* 育児は社会によって十分に評価されていない。

par|ish /ˈpærɪʃ/ (**parishes**) **1** N-COUNT 可算名詞 A **parish** is part of a city or town that has its own Catholic church and priest. 教区 □*...Good Shepherd, a parish of about 450 members.* 約450人の教会員を持つ教区であるグッド・シェパード □*...a parish priest.* 教区司祭 **2** N-COUNT 可算名詞 In some parts of the United States, a **parish** is a small region within a state which has its own local government. (米国の1部の州の) 郡 [AM 米国英語] □*...the middle-class parishes of northern Louisiana.* ルイジアナ州北部の中流階級の郡部

par|ity /ˈpærɪti/ N-UNCOUNT 不可算名詞 If there is **parity** between two things, they are equal. 同等、同格 [FORMAL 形式ばった] □*Women have yet to achieve wage or occupational parity in many fields.* 女性はまだまださまざまな分野で賃金や職業の同等性を勝ち取らなければならない。

park /pɑːrk/ (**parks, parking, parked**) **1** N-COUNT 可算名詞 A **park** is a public area of land with grass and trees, usually in a town, where people go in order to relax and enjoy themselves. 公園 □*...Central Park.* 中央公園 □*...a brisk walk with the dog around the park.* 公園の周りを犬と一緒にきびきび散歩 **2** N-COUNT 可算名

In 1858, Central Park* became the first planned urban **park** in the United States. At first only a few wealthy families lived close enough to enjoy it. Today over 20 million visitors of all ages and backgrounds use the park for **recreation** each year. Children love the many **playgrounds**, the **carousel**, and the petting **zoo**. Families spread blankets on the grass for **picnics**. Couples row around the lake in rented rowboats. Seniors **stroll** through the **gardens**. Players fill the **tennis courts** and baseball diamonds all summer. **Cyclists** and **runners** use Central Park Drive* when it's closed to car traffic on weekends.

Central Park: an 843-acre park in New York City.
Central Park Drive: a road in Central Park.

詞 You can refer to a place where a particular activity is carried out as a **park**. (特定の活動用の) 広大な敷地 [supp N] ❑ *...a science and technology park.* 科学技術団地 ❸ V-T/V-I 他動詞/自動詞 When you **park** a vehicle or **park** somewhere, you drive the vehicle into a position where it can stay for a period of time, and leave it there. 駐車させる [他動詞], 駐車する [自動詞] ❑ *Greenfield turned into the next side street and parked.* グリーンフィールドは次のわき道に入り，車をとめた. ❹ V-T 他動詞 If you **park yourself** somewhere, you sit there. (再起形を伴い) 座る [INFORMAL くだけた] ❑ *Every Friday, I would park myself in front of the TV.* 私は毎週金曜日にテレビの前に座ったものだった. ❺ → see also **ballpark, national park**
→ see Word Web: **park**

park|ing /pɑːrkɪŋ/ ❶ N-UNCOUNT 不可算名詞 **Parking** is the action of moving a vehicle into a place in a garage or by the side of the road where it can be left. 駐車 ❑ *In many towns parking is allowed only on one side of the street.* 多くの町で，通りの片側だけに駐車が認められている. ❷ N-UNCOUNT 不可算名詞 **Parking** is space for parking a vehicle in. 駐車場 ❑ *Cars allowed, but parking is limited.* 車の入場可，ただし駐車スペースは限られている.

> Note that you do not use the word "parking" to refer to a place where cars are parked. Instead, you talk about a **parking lot** in American English and a **car park** in British English. **Parking** is used only to refer to the action of parking your car, or to the state of being parked. ❑ *...a "No Parking" sign.* 駐車禁止の標識

park|ing gar|age (parking garages) N-COUNT 可算名詞 A **parking garage** is a building where people can leave their cars. 立体駐車場 [AM 米国英語] ❑ *...a multi-level parking garage.* 多数階の立体駐車場

park|ing lot (parking lots) N-COUNT 可算名詞 A **parking lot** is an area of ground where people can leave their cars. 駐車場，パーキング [AM 米国英語] ❑ *A block up the street I found a parking lot.* その通りをもう1街区行ったところに駐車場を見つけた.

park|ing me|ter (parking meters) N-COUNT 可算名詞 A **parking meter** is a device that you put money into when you park in a parking space. 料金メーター

par|lia|ment /pɑːrləmənt/ (parliaments) also **Parliament** ❶ N-COUNT; N-PROPER 可算名詞, 固有名詞 The **parliament** of some countries is the group of people who make or change its laws, and decide what policies the country should follow. 国会, 議会 ❑ *The Bangladesh Parliament today approved the policy, but it has not yet become law.* バングラデシュ国会は本日その政策を承認したが，まだ法律にはなっていない. ❷ → see also **Member of Parliament** ❸ N-COUNT 可算名詞 A particular **parliament** is a particular period of time in which a parliament is doing its work, between two elections or between two periods of vacation. 国会の会期 ❑ *The legislation is expected to be passed in the next parliament.* その法案は次期国会で通過することが見込まれている.

par|lia|men|ta|ry /pɑːrləmɛntəri/ ADJ 形容詞 **Parliamentary** is used to describe things that are connected with a parliament or with members of parliament. 議会の，議員の [ADJ n] ❑ *He used his influence to make sure she was not selected as a parliamentary candidate.* 彼は彼女が議員候補に絶対選ばれないようにするため自分の影響力を使った.

par|lor /pɑːrlər/ (parlors) N-COUNT 可算名詞 **Parlor** is used in the names of some types of stores that provide a service, rather than selling things. (特にサービス業の) 一店 [n N] ❑ *...a funeral parlor.* 葬儀社

pa|ro|chial /pəroʊkiəl/ ❶ ADJ 形容詞 If you describe someone as **parochial**, you are critical of them because you think they are too concerned with their own affairs and should be thinking about more important things. 偏狭な，視野が狭い [DISAPPROVAL 不賛成] ❑ *When her brother arrives home on a visit from Hong Kong, he*

sneers at her parochial existence. 彼女の弟は香港から帰省してくると，彼女の偏狭な生活をあざける. ❷ ADJ 形容詞 **Parochial** is used to describe things that relate to the parish connected with a particular church. 教区の [ADJ n] ❑ *She was a secretary on the local parochial church council.* 彼女は地元の教会会議の秘書をしていた. ❑ *Their children attend a Jewish parochial school.* 彼らの子供たちはユダヤ教の教区学校に通っている.

paro|dy /pærədi/ (parodies, parodying, parodied) ❶ N-VAR 可変性名詞 A **parody** is a humorous piece of writing, drama, or music that imitates the style of a well-known person or represents a familiar situation in an exaggerated way. パロディ，もじり ❑ *It was like a parody of the balcony scene from Romeo and Juliet.* それは『ロミオとジュリエット』のバルコニー・シーンのパロディのようだった. ❷ V-T 他動詞 When someone **parodies** a particular work, thing, or person, they imitate it in an amusing or exaggerated way. パロディ化する，もじる ❑ *...a sketch parodying the views of Donald Rumsfeld.* ドナルド・ラムズフェルドの見解をもじった寸劇

pa|role /pəroʊl/ (paroles, paroling, paroled) ❶ N-UNCOUNT 不可算名詞 If a prisoner is given **parole**, he or she is released before the official end of their prison sentence and has to promise to behave well. 仮釈放，仮出所 ❑ *Although sentenced to life, he will become eligible for parole after serving 10 years.* 終身刑を宣告されたが，彼は10年服役すれば仮釈放の資格を得るだろう. ❑ *...a parole violation.* 仮釈放違反 ● PHRASE 句 If a prisoner is **on parole**, he or she is released before the official end of their prison sentence and will not be sent back to prison if their behavior is good. 仮釈放中の ❷ V-T 他動詞 If a prisoner **is paroled**, he or she is given parole. 仮釈放する [usu passive] ❑ *He faces at most 12 years in prison and could be paroled after eight years.* 彼は最高12年の刑期に直面しているが，8年服役すれば仮釈放される可能性がある.

par|rot /pærət/ (parrots, parroting, parroted) ❶ N-COUNT 可算名詞 A **parrot** is a tropical bird with a curved beak and brightly-colored or gray feathers. Parrots can be kept as pets. Some parrots are able to copy what people say. オウム ❷ V-T 他動詞 If you disapprove of the fact that someone is just repeating what someone else has said, often without really understanding it, you can say that they **are parroting** it. オウム返しに言う，意味も分からずにまねる [DISAPPROVAL 不賛成] ❑ *Generations of students have learned to parrot the standard explanations.* 代々の学生たちは意味も分からないままお決まりの説明を繰り返すことを学んできた.

pars|ley /pɑːrsli/ N-UNCOUNT 不可算名詞 **Parsley** is a small plant with curly leaves that are used for flavoring or decorating food. パセリ ❑ *...rice with fresh parsley.* 新鮮なパセリを散らしたご飯

pars|nip /pɑːrsnɪp/ (parsnips) N-COUNT 可算名詞 A **parsnip** is a long cream-colored root vegetable. パースニップ (根が食用)

part

❶ NOUN USES, QUANTIFIER USES, AND PHRASES
❷ VERB USES

❶ **part** /pɑːrt/ (parts)
⟳ Please look at meaning ⑯ to see if the expression you are looking for is shown under another headword. ❶ N-COUNT 可算名詞 A **part** of something is one of the pieces, sections, or elements that it consists of. (構成の) 1部 ❑ *I like that part of Cape Town.* 私はケープタウンのその地区が好きだ. ❷ N-COUNT 可算名詞 A **part** for a machine or vehicle is one of the smaller pieces that is used to make it. 部品，パーツ ❑ *...spare parts for military equipment.* 軍用

機器の予備の部品 ❸ QUANT 数量詞 **Part of** something is some of it. 1部の，ある部分 ❏ *It was a very severe accident and he lost part of his foot.* それはとても ひどい事故で，彼は片足の1部を失った． ❏ *Perry spent part of his childhood in Canada.* ペリーは子供時代のある時期をカナダで過ごした． ❹ ADV 副詞 If you say that something is **part** one thing, **part** another, you mean that it is to some extent the first thing and to some extent the second thing. ある部分では，ある意味では ❏ *The television producer today has to be part news person, part educator.* 今日のテレビプロデューサーは，ニュース報道者であり，ある意味では教育者でなければならない． ❺ N-COUNT 可算名詞 You can use **part** when you are talking about the proportions of substances in a mixture. For example, if you are told to use five **parts** water to one **part** paint, the mixture should contain five times as much water as paint. 割合 ❏ *Use turpentine and linseed oil, three parts to two.* テレビン油と亜麻仁油を3対2の割合で使う． ❻ N-COUNT 可算名詞 A **part** in a play or movie is one of the roles in it which an actor or actress can perform. （芝居・映画の）役 ❏ *Alf Sjoberg offered her a large part in the play he was directing.* アルフ・シェーベリは彼が監督をしている劇の大きな役を彼女に提供した． ❼ N-SING 単数名詞 Your **part** in something that happens is your involvement in it. 関与 [poss N "in" n] ❏ *If only he could conceal his part in the accident.* 彼自身がその事故に関与していることを隠すことができさえしたらなあ． ❽ N-UNCOUNT 不可算名詞 If something or someone is **part of** a group or organization, they belong to it or are included in it. （グループ・組織の）成員 [also "a" N, N "of" n] ❏ *Annie had never been part of the in-crowd.* アニーがその排他的集団に属したことは1度もなかった． ❾ N-COUNT 可算名詞 The **part** in someone's hair is the line running from the front to the back of their head where their hair lies in different directions. （髪の）分け目 [AM 米国英語] ❏ *The straight white part in her ebony hair seemed to divide the back of her head in half.* 彼女の黒髪のまっすぐな白い分け目が頭の後ろを2つに分けているようだった． ❿ PHRASE 句 If something or someone **plays** a large or important **part** in an event or situation, they are very involved in it and have an important effect on what happens. 役割を果たす（事件・状況の中で） ❏ *These days work plays an important part in a single woman's life.* 近ごろ仕事が独身女性の人生で重要な役割を担っている． ⓫ PHRASE 句 If you **take part in** an activity, you do it together with other people. 参加する ❏ *Thousands of students have taken part in demonstrations.* 何千人もの学生がデモに参加している． ⓬ PHRASE 句 If you **do** your **part**, you do something that, to a small or limited extent, helps to achieve something. 役割を果たす ❏ *Each of you is going to have to do your part in keeping the community crime-free.* 地域を犯罪のない状態に保つために，あなた方1人ひとりがそれぞれの役割を果たさなくてはならなくなるであろう． ⓭ PHRASE 句 When you are describing people's thoughts or actions, you can say **for** her **part** or **for** my **part**, for example, to introduce what a particular person thinks or does. ～としては [FORMAL 形式ばった] ❏ *For my part, I feel elated and close to tears.* 私としては，有頂天で涙が出そうだ． ⓮ PHRASE 句 If you talk about a feeling or action **on** someone's **part**, you are referring to something that they feel or do. ～にしてみれば，～の方では ❏ *...techniques on their part to keep us from knowing exactly what's going on.* 彼らからすると，一体何が起こっているのかを私たちに知らせないための方法． ❏ *There is no need for any further instructions on my part.* 私の方ではこれ以上の指示の必要は何もない． ⓯ PHRASE 句 You use **in part** to indicate that something exists or happens to some extent but not completely. ある程度 [FORMAL 形式ばった] ❏ *The levels of blood glucose depend in part on what you eat and when you eat.* 血糖値はあなたが何を食べるか，またいつ食べるかにある程度左右される． ⓰ **part and parcel** → see **parcel**

❷ **part** /pɑrt/ (**parts, parting, parted**) ❶ V-T/V-I 他動詞/自動詞 If things that are next to each other **part** or if you **part** them, they move in opposite directions, so that there is a space between them. 分ける [他動詞]，分かれる [自動詞] ❏ *Her lips parted as if she were about to take a deep breath.* 彼女の唇が今まさに深呼吸するかのように開いた． ❷ V-T 他動詞 If you **part** your hair in the middle or at one side, you make it lie in two different directions so that there is a straight line running from the front of your head to the back. （髪を）分ける [FORMAL 形式ばった] ❏ *Picking up a brush, Joanna parted her hair.* ブラシを取り上げて，ジョアンナは髪を分けた． ❸ V-RECIP 相互動詞 When two people **part**, or if one person **parts from** another, they leave each other. （人が）別れる [FORMAL 形式ばった] ❏ *He gave me the envelope and we parted.* 彼は私にその封筒を渡し，私たちは別れた． ❹ V-RECIP 相互動詞 If you **are parted from** someone you love, you are prevented from being with them. 別れさせる，引き離す ❏ *I don't believe Laverne and I will ever be parted.* ラバーンとぼくが別れるなんてあり得ないよ． ❺ → see also **parting**

Thesaurus	*part* また次を参照：
N.	component, fraction, half, ingredient, piece, portion, section; (ant.) entirety, whole ❶ ❺
	role, share ❶ ❻
V.	break up, separate, split, tear ❷ ❸

▶ **part with** PHRASAL VERB 句動詞 If you **part with** something

that is valuable or that you would prefer to keep, you give it or sell it to someone else. ～を手放す ❏ *Buyers might require further assurances before parting with their cash.* 買い手はことによると現金を渡す前にさらに保証を求めるかもしれない．

par|tial /pɑrʃ°l/ ❶ ADJ 形容詞 You use **partial** to refer to something that is not complete or whole. 部分的な，1部の ❏ *He managed to reach a partial agreement with both republics.* 彼はなんとか両共和国から部分的合意を取りつけた． ❏ *...a partial ban on the use of cars in the city.* 市内での車の使用を部分的に禁止 ❷ ADJ 形容詞 If you are **partial to** something, you like it. ～が好きな [v-link ADJ "to" n/-ing] ❏ *He's partial to sporty women with blue eyes.* 彼は青い目の派手な女性が好みだ． ❏ *Mollie confesses she is rather partial to pink.* モリーはピンクがかなり好きなことを認めた． ❸ ADJ 形容詞 Someone who is **partial** supports a particular person or thing, for example, in a competition or dispute, instead of being completely fair. 不公平な，えこひいきをする [v-link ADJ] ❏ *I might be accused of being partial.* 私はえこひいきをしていると非難されるかもしれないだろう．

par|tial|ly /pɑrʃəli/ ADV 副詞 If something happens or exists **partially**, it happens or exists to some extent, but not completely. 部分的に [ADV with cl/group] ❏ *Lisa is deaf in one ear and partially blind.* リサは片方の耳が聞こえず，部分的な視覚障害がある．

par|tici|pant /pɑrtɪsɪpənt/ (**participants**) N-COUNT 可算名詞 The **participants** in an activity are the people who take part in it. （活動などの）参加者 ❏ *40 of the course participants were offered employment with the company.* そのコースの参加者のうちの40名が，その会社への雇用を提示されている．

par|tici|pate /pɑrtɪsɪpeɪt/ (**participates, participating, participated**) V-I 自動詞 If you **participate in** an activity, you take part in it. （活動などに）参加する ❏ *They expected him to participate in the ceremony.* 彼らは彼が式典に出席すると思っていた． ❏ *Over half the population of this country participate in sports.* この国の人口の半分以上がスポーツをしている． ● **par|tici|pa|tion** /pɑrtɪsɪpeɪʃ°n/ N-UNCOUNT 不可算名詞 参加 ❏ *...participation in religious activities.* 宗教活動への参加

Thesaurus	*participate* また次を参照：
V.	compete, cooperate, join in, partake, perform, share; (ant.) observe

par|ti|ci|ple /pɑrtɪsɪp°l/ (**participles**) N-COUNT 可算名詞 In grammar, a **participle** is a form of a verb that can be used in compound tenses of the verb. There are two participles in English: the past participle, which usually ends in "-ed," and the present participle, which ends in "-ing." （過去・現在）分詞

Word Link	cle ≈ small : article, cubicle, particle

par|ti|cle /pɑrtɪk°l/ (**particles**) ❶ N-COUNT 可算名詞 A **particle** of something is a very small piece or amount of it. 小さな粒，微量 ❏ *...a particle of hot metal.* 少量の溶銑（ようせん） ❏ *There is a particle of truth in his statement.* 彼の供述には真実のかけらがある． ❷ N-COUNT 可算名詞 In physics, a **particle** is a piece of matter smaller than an atom such as an electron or a proton. （原子よりも小さい）粒子 [TECHNICAL 技術的] ❏ *...the sub-atomic particles that make up matter.* 物質を構成する素粒子

→ see **lightning**

par|ticu|lar /pərtɪkyələr/ ❶ ADJ 形容詞 You use **particular** to emphasize that you are talking about one thing or one kind of thing rather than other similar ones. 特定の，特有の [EMPHASIS 強調] [ADJ n] ❏ *I remembered a particular story about a mailman who was a murderer.* 私は殺人犯だった郵便配達人についてのある話を覚えている． ❏ *I have to know exactly why it is I'm doing a particular job.* 私はなぜ自分が特定の仕事をしているのかをきちんと知る必要がある． ❷ ADJ 形容詞 If a person or thing has a **particular** quality or possession, it is distinct and belongs only to them. （性質・持ちものが）独自の [ADJ n] ❏ *I have a particular responsibility to ensure I make the right decision.* 私は自分が確実に正しい決断をする特別な責任がある． ❸ ADJ 形容詞 You can use **particular** to emphasize that something is greater or more intense than usual. 格別の，著しい [EMPHASIS 強調] [ADJ n] ❏ *Particular emphasis will be placed on oral language training.* 口頭の言語訓練に特に重点が置かれるだろう． ❹ ADJ 形容詞 If you say that someone is **particular**, you mean that they choose things and do things very carefully, and are not easily satisfied. 細かいところにこだわる，好みがうるさい ❏ *Ted was very particular about the colors he used.* テッドは彼が使う色にとてもこだわった． ❺ → see also **particulars** ❻ PHRASE 句 You use **in particular** to indicate that what you are saying applies especially to one thing or person. 特に，とりわけ ❏ *The situation in Ethiopia in particular is worrisome.* 特にエチオピアの状況はやっかいだ． ❏ *Why should he notice her car in particular?* どうして彼が特に彼女の車に注意を払うべきなのですか．

Thesaurus   particular また次を参照:

ADJ. distinct, precise, specific; (ant.) general ◧ ◨
choosy, finicky, demanding, fussy, picky; (ant.)
easygoing, laidback ◪

par|ticu|lar|ly /pərtɪkyələrli/ ◧ ADV 副詞 You use **particularly** to indicate that what you are saying applies especially to one thing or situation. 特に [ADV with cl/group] ◻ Keep your office space looking good, particularly your desk. あなたの仕事場, 特にあなたの机がきれいにしておきなさい. ◻ More local employment will be created, particularly in service industries. 地元の特にサービス産業で就職口が増えるだろう. ◨ ADV 副詞 **Particularly** means more than usual or more than other things. とりわけ, 著しく [EMPHASIS 強調] [ADV with cl/group] ◻ Progress has been particularly disappointing. 進捗状況はとりわけがっかりするものだった.

par|ticu|lars /pərtɪkyələrz/ N-PLURAL 複数名詞 The **particulars** of something or someone are facts or details about them that are written down and kept as a record. 詳細 ◻ You will find all the particulars in Chapter 9. 第9章にすべての詳細が載っている.

part|ing /pɑrtɪŋ/ (partings) ◧ N-VAR 可変性名詞 **Parting** is the act of leaving a particular person or place. A **parting** is an occasion when this happens. 別れ, 別離 ◻ Parting from any one of you for even a short time is hard. たとえ短い間であっても, お前たちの1人とでも別れるのはつらい. ◨ ADJ 形容詞 Your **parting** words or actions are the things that you say or do as you are leaving a place or person. 別れの [ADJ n] ◻ Her parting words left him feeling empty and alone. 彼女の別れの言葉に, 彼はむなしい孤独な気分になった. ◩ N-COUNT 可算名詞 The **parting** in someone's hair is the line running from the front to the back of their head where their hair lies in different directions. (髪の) 分け目 [BRIT 英国英語; AM part 米国英語]

par|ti|san /pɑrtɪzən/ (partisans) ◧ ADJ 形容詞 Someone who is **partisan** strongly supports a particular person or cause, often without thinking carefully about the matter. (人・大義を) 盲目的に支持する ◻ He is clearly too partisan to be a referee. 彼は審判員になるには明らかに肩入れしすぎる. ◨ N-COUNT 可算名詞 **Partisans** are ordinary people, rather than soldiers, who join together to fight enemy soldiers who are occupying their country. 市民兵 ◻ He was rescued by some Italian partisans. 彼はイタリア人のパルチザンたちに助けられた.

par|ti|tion /pɑrtɪʃⁿn/ (partitions, partitioning, partitioned) ◧ N-COUNT 可算名詞 A **partition** is a wall, screen, or divider that separates one part of a room, vehicle, or other space from another. (部屋などの) 仕切り ◻ ...new offices divided only by glass partitions. ガラスの仕切りで分けられただけの新しいオフィス ◨ V-T 他動詞 If you **partition** a room, you separate one part of it from another by means of a partition. 仕切る ◻ Bedrooms have again been created by partitioning a single larger room. 寝室は再び1つのより大きな部屋を仕切って作っている. ◩ V-T 他動詞 If a country **is partitioned**, it is divided into two or more independent countries. (国などを) 分割する ◻ Korea was partitioned in 1945. 朝鮮半島は1945年に分割された. ◻ ...Churchill's plans to partition the German state. ドイツ国家を分割するというチャーチルの計画 ● N-UNCOUNT 不可算名詞 **Partition** is also a noun. 分割 ◻ ...fighting which followed the partition of India. インド分割の後に起こった戦い

part|ly /pɑrtli/ ADV 副詞 You use **partly** to indicate that something happens or exists to some extent, but not completely. 部分的に, ある程度は [ADV with cl/group] ◻ It's partly my fault. それは私のせいでもある. ◻ I have not worried so much this year, partly because I have had other things to think about. 私は他にも考える事があったりして, 今年はあまり悩まなかった.

part|ner /pɑrtnər/ (partners, partnering, partnered) ◧ N-COUNT 可算名詞 Your **partner** is the person you are married to or are having a romantic or sexual relationship with. 配偶者, 愛人 ◻ Wanting other friends doesn't mean you don't love your partner. 他にも友だちが欲しいといってもあなたが連れ合いを愛していないということではない. ◨ N-COUNT 可算名詞 Your **partner** is the person you are doing something with, for example, dancing with or playing with in a game against two other people. (ダンス・ゲームの) パートナー 相棒 ◻ ...to dance with a partner. パートナーとダンスをすること ◻ Her partner for the game was Venus Williams. その試合の彼女が組む相棒はビーナス・ウィリアムズだった. ◩ N-COUNT 可算名詞 The **partners** in a firm or business are the people who share the ownership of it. 共同経営 (出資) 者 [BUSINESS 実業] ◻ He's a partner in a Chicago law firm. 彼はシカゴの法律事務所のパートナーだ. ◪ N-COUNT 可算名詞 The **partner** of a country or organization is another country or organization with which they work or do business. (国・組織の) 提携者 提携国 ◻ Spain has been one of Cuba's major trading partners. スペインはキューバの主要貿易国の1つとなっている. ◫ V-T 他動詞 If you **partner** someone, you are their partner in a game or in a dance. (ダンス・ゲームの) パートナーとなる ◻ He had partnered the famous Russian ballerina. 彼はあの

有名なロシア人バレリーナと組んだことがある. ◻ He will be partnered by Ian Baker, the defending champion. 彼は前回の優勝者であるイアン・ベイカーと組む予定だ.

part|ner|ship /pɑrtnərʃɪp/ (partnerships) N-VAR 可変性名詞 **Partnership** or a **partnership** is a relationship in which two or more people, organizations, or countries work together as partners. 協力関係, 提携 ◻ ...the partnership between Germany's banks and its businesses. ドイツの銀行と企業の間の提携

part-time

The adverb is also spelled **part time**.

副詞は **part time** ともつづられる.

ADJ 形容詞 If someone is a **part-time** worker or has a **part-time** job, they work for only part of each day or week. パートタイムの, 非常勤の ◻ Many businesses are cutting back by employing lower-paid part-time workers. 多くの企業は賃金の安いパートタイマーを雇うことで経費を削減している. ◻ Part-time work is generally hard to find. 普通, 非常勤の仕事は見つけるのが難しい. ● ADV 副詞 **Part-time** is also an adverb. パートタイムで, 非常勤で [ADV after v] ◻ I want to work part-time. 私はパートタイムの仕事がしたい.

par|ty /pɑrti/ (parties, partying, partied) ◧ N-COUNT 可算名詞 A **party** is a political organization whose members have similar aims and beliefs. Usually the organization tries to get its members elected to the legislature of a country. 政党 ◻ ...a member of the Republican Party. 共和党員 ◻ ...opposition parties. 野党 ◨ N-COUNT 可算名詞 A **party** is a social event, often in someone's home, at which people enjoy themselves doing things such as eating, drinking, dancing, talking, or playing games. パーティー ◻ The couple met at a party. そのカップルはパーティーで出会った. ◻ We threw a huge birthday party. 私たちは盛大な誕生日パーティーを開いた. ◩ V-I 自動詞 If you **party**, you enjoy yourself doing things such as going out to parties, drinking, dancing, and talking to people. パーティーに出かける, パーティーを楽しむ ◻ They come to eat and drink, to swim, to party. 彼らは食べて飲んで, 泳いで, パーティーを楽しむためにやって来る. ◪ N-COUNT 可算名詞 A **party** of people is a group of people who are doing something together, for example, traveling together. 団体, 一行 ◻ They became separated from their party. 彼らは自分の団体から離れてしまった. ◻ ...a party of sightseers. 観光客の一行 ◫ → see also search party ◳ N-COUNT 可算名詞 One of the people involved in a legal agreement or dispute can be referred to as a particular **party**. (契約・紛争の) 当事者 [LEGAL 法律的] ◻ It has to be proved that they are the guilty party. 彼らが有罪者側であることが証明されなければならない. ◻ ...he was the injured party. 彼は被害者だった ◷ PHRASE 句 Someone who is a **party** to or is **party** to an action or agreement is involved in it, and therefore partly responsible for it. 一に関係している, 一に関与している ◻ You were the one that brought up the idea of blackmail. I'd never be a party to such a thing. 脅迫のことを言い出したのはお前だぞ. 僕はそんなことには一切かかわらないよ.

Word Partnership   party は次の語句と使われる:

V.	form a party, join a party, vote for a party ◧
	attend/go to a party, have/host/throw a party, invite someone to a party ◨
N.	party officials, opposition party, party platform ◧
	birthday party, victory party ◩
	wedding party ◪
ADJ.	governing party, political party ◧
	responsible party ◫

---

pass

❶ VERB USES
❷ NOUN USES
❸ PHRASAL VERBS

❶ **pass** /pæs/ (passes, passing, passed) ◧ V-T/V-I 他動詞/自動詞 To **pass** someone or something means to go past them without stopping. 通り過ぎる ◻ As she passed the library door, the telephone began to ring. 彼女が図書館の扉を通り過ぎるとき, 電話が鳴り始めた. ◻ Jane stood aside to let him pass. ジェーンは脇へ寄って, 彼を通した. ◨ V-I 自動詞 When someone or something **passes** in a particular direction, they move in that direction. (ある方向へ) 進む ◻ He passed through the doorway into the kitchen. 彼は戸口を通り抜けて台所の中へ入って行った. ◻ He passed down the tunnel. 彼はトンネルを下って行った. ◩ V-I 自動詞 If something such as a road or pipe **passes** along a particular route, it goes along that route. (一に沿って) 行く ◻ A dirt road passes through the town. 泥道が町の中を通っていた. ◪ V-T 他動詞 If you **pass** something through, over, or around something else, you move or push it through, over, or around that thing. (物を) 通す ◻ She passed the needle through the rough cloth, back and forth. 彼女は粗い布に針を往復させた. ◻ "I don't understand," the detective mumbled, passing a hand through his hair.

「分からん」と探偵は、髪を手ですきながらつぶやいた。 **5** V-T 他動詞 If you **pass** something **to** someone, you take it in your hand and give it to them. （物を人に）渡す □Ken passed the books to Sergeant Wong. ケンはウォン軍曹に本を渡した. **6** V-T/V-I 他動詞/自動詞 If something **passes** or **is passed** from one person to another, the second person then has it instead of the first. 渡す（物を人に）[他動詞], 渡る（物が人に）[自動詞] □His mother's small estate had passed to him after her death. 彼の母が亡くなった後, 彼女の小さな土地は彼の手に渡った. □These powers were eventually passed to municipalities. それらの権限は最終的に地方自治体へ移された. **7** V-T 他動詞 If you **pass** information to someone, you give it to them because it concerns them. （情報を）伝える □Officials failed to pass vital information to their superiors. 職員たちはきわめて重要な情報を上司に伝え損なっていた. ●PHRASAL VERB 句動詞 **Pass on** means the same as **pass**. 伝える □I do not know what to do with the information if I cannot pass it on. 人に伝えてはいけないのなら, 私にはその情報をどう扱っていいか分からない. □From time to time he passed on confidential information to him. 彼は時々, 秘密情報を彼に漏らした. **8** V-T/V-I 他動詞/自動詞 If you **pass**, or **pass** the ball **to** someone on your team in a game such as football or basketball, you throw it to them. （ボールを）パスする □Your partner should then pass the ball back to you. 次にあなたのパートナーはあなたへボールをパスして戻すべきだ. **9** V-I 自動詞 When a period of time **passes**, it happens and finishes. （時が）過ぎる □He couldn't imagine why he had let so much time pass without contacting her. どうしてそんなに長い間, 彼が彼女に連絡を取らずにいたか彼には想像できなかった. □As the years passed he felt trapped by certain realities of marriage. 年月が経つにつれて, 彼は結婚生活のある種の現実にがんじがらめになったように感じた. **10** V-T 他動詞 If you **pass** a period of time in a particular way, you spend it in that way. （時を）過ごす □The children passed the time playing in the streets. 子供たちはその時間を通りで遊んで過ごした. **11** V-I 自動詞 If you **pass through** a stage of development or a period of time, you experience it. 経験する □The country was passing through a grave crisis. その国は重大な危機の中にあった. **12** V-T 他動詞 If an amount **passes** a particular total or level, it becomes greater than that total or level. （合計・程度を）超える □They became the first company in their field to pass the $2 billion turn-over mark. 彼らはその業界で20億ドルの総売り上げ目標を超えた最初の会社となった. **13** V-T 他動詞 If someone or something **passes** a test, they are considered to be of an acceptable standard. （試験に）合格する □Kevin has just passed his driving test. ケビンは運転免許試験に受かったところだ. □...new drugs which have passed early tests to show that they are safe. 安全を示す初期の試験に合格した新薬 **14** V-T 他動詞 If someone in authority **passes** a person or thing, they declare that they are of an acceptable standard or have reached an acceptable standard. 合格にする □Several popular beaches were found unfit for swimming although the government passed them last year. 昨年政府が合格としたにもかかわらず, 人気の海岸のいくつかは水泳に不適格と判定された. **15** V-T 他動詞 When people in authority **pass** a new law or a proposal, they formally agree to it or approve it. （法案を）可決する □The Estonian parliament has passed a resolution declaring the republic fully independent. エストニア議会は共和国の完全独立を宣言する決議案を可決した. **16** V-T 他動詞 When a judge **passes** sentence on someone, he or she says what their punishment will be. （判決を）下す □Passing sentence, the judge said it all had the appearance of a con trick. 裁判官は判決を下し, すべてが信用詐欺の様相を呈していると述べた. **17** V-I 自動詞 If someone or something **passes for** or **passes as** something that they are not, they are accepted as that thing or mistaken for that thing. （—として）通用する □Children's toy guns now look so realistic that they can often pass for the real thing. 最近の子供のおもちゃの銃はとても本物らしくできているので, しばしば本物だと言っても通用する. □It is doubtful whether Ted, even with his fluent French, passed for one of the locals. テッドの流ちょうなフランス語をもってしても, その土地の1人として通るかどうかは疑わしい. **18** V-I 自動詞 If someone makes you an offer or asks you a question and you say that you will **pass on** it, you mean that you do not want to accept or answer it now. やめておく, 次に伝える [INFORMAL くだけた] □I think I'll pass on the swimming. ぼくは水泳はやめておこうと思う. □"You can join us if you like." Brad shook his head. "I'll pass, thanks." 「きみも来たかったら一緒に来ていいよ」ブラッドは首を振った. 「ぼくはやめておく」 **19** V-I 自動詞 In some card games and other games, if you **pass**, you choose not to play at that stage in the game. （トランプ・ゲームで）パスする **20** V-T 他動詞 If you **pass** comment or **pass** a comment, you say something. （意見を）言う [BRIT 英国英語] **21** to **pass the buck** → see buck **22** to **pass judgment** → see judgment

---

Do not confuse **pass** and **spend**. If you do something while you are waiting for something else, you can say you do it to "**pass** the time." □He had brought along a book to pass the time. You can say that time **has passed** in order to show that a period of time has finished. □The first few days passed...The time seems to have passed so quickly. If you **spend** a period of time doing something or **spend** time in a place, you do do that thing or stay in that place for all of the time you are talking about. □I spent three days cleaning our flat. ...a hotel where we could spend the night.

❷ pass /pæs/ (**passes**) **1** N-COUNT 可算名詞 A **pass** in an examination, test, or course is a successful result in it. （試験の）合格 □He's been allowed to re-take the exam, and he's going to get a pass. 彼は追試を受けられることになった. 彼なら合格するだろう. **2** N-COUNT 可算名詞 A **pass** is a document that allows you to do something. 通行証, 許可証 □I got myself a pass into the barracks. 私は兵舎への通行許可証を入手した. **3** N-COUNT 可算名詞 A **pass** in a game such as football or basketball is an act of throwing the ball to someone on your team. （サッカー・バスケットボールの）パス □Hirst rolled a short pass to Merson. ハーストはマーソンに短いパスを送った. **4** N-COUNT; N-IN-NAMES 可算名詞, 名称中の名詞 A **pass** is a narrow path or route between mountains. 山道 □The monastery is in a remote mountain pass. その修道院は人里離れた山道にある.
→ see **mountain**

❸ pass /pæs/ (**passes, passing, passed**)
▶ **pass away** PHRASAL VERB 句動詞 You can say that someone **passed away** to mean that they died, if you want to avoid using the word "die" because you think it might upset or offend people. 亡くなる □He unfortunately passed away last year. 残念ながら, 彼は昨年亡くなった.
▶ **pass off** PHRASAL VERB 句動詞 If an event **passes off** without any trouble, it happens and ends without any trouble. （物事が）無事に終わる [BRIT 英国英語]
▶ **pass off as** PHRASAL VERB 句動詞 If you **pass** something **off as** another thing, you convince people that it is that other thing. —として通す, —だと言い繕う □He passed himself off as a senior psychologist. 彼は古参の心理学者に成り済ました. □I've tried to pass off my accent as a New York one. 私は自分のなまりをニューヨークなまりとして通そうと努力した.
▶ **pass on 1** PHRASAL VERB 句動詞 If you **pass** something **on to** someone, you give it to them so that they have it instead of you. （人に物を）譲る □The winner is passing the money on to her favorite charities. その勝者は賞金を自分の好きなチャリティー団体のいくつかに贈るつもりだ. □The late governor passed on much of his fortune to his daughter. 故知事は財産の多くを彼の娘に残した. **2** PHRASAL VERB 句動詞 You can say that someone **passed on** to mean that they died, if you want to avoid using the word "die" because you think it might upset or offend people. 永眠する □He passed on at the age of 72. 彼は72歳でこの世を去った. **3** → see also pass **❶** 7
▶ **pass out** PHRASAL VERB 句動詞 If you **pass out**, you faint or collapse. 失神する, 意識を失う □He felt sick and dizzy and then passed out. 彼は吐き気を覚えてめまいがし, そして意識を失った.
▶ **pass over 1** PHRASAL VERB 句動詞 If someone **is passed over** for a job or position, they do not get the job or position and someone younger or less experienced is chosen instead. （昇進を）候補から外す 先を越させる □She claimed she was repeatedly passed over for promotion while less experienced white male colleagues were made partners. 彼女は, 自分より経験の浅い白人男性の同僚たちが共同経営者に抜擢されたのに, 繰り返し昇進を見送られたと訴えた. **2** PHRASAL VERB 句動詞 If you **pass over** a topic in a conversation or speech, you do not talk about it. （話題を）避ける □He largely passed over the government's record. 彼は主として政府の業績の話題を避けた.
▶ **pass up** PHRASAL VERB 句動詞 If you **pass up** a chance or an opportunity, you do not take advantage of it. （機会を）逃す 見送る □The official urged the government not to pass up the opportunity that has now presented itself. その役人は政府に今そこに現れた機会を逃さないように強く要請した.

pas|sage /pǽsɪdʒ/ (**passages**) **1** N-COUNT 可算名詞 A **passage** is a long narrow space with walls or fences on both sides, that connects one place or room with another. 通路, 廊下 □Harry stepped into the passage and closed the door behind him. ハリーは廊下に出て, 出てきた部屋のドアを閉めた. **2** N-COUNT 可算名詞 A **passage** in a book, speech, or piece of music is a section of it that you are considering separately from the rest. （本・音楽などの）1節 □He read a passage from Emerson. 彼はエマーソンの1節を読んだ. □...the passage in which the author speaks of the world of imagination. 作者が想像の世界について語る1節 **3** N-COUNT 可算名詞 A **passage** is a long narrow hole or tube in your body, that air or liquid can pass along. （体内の）導管 □...cells that line the air passages. 気道の内側を覆う細胞 **4** N-COUNT 可算名詞 A **passage through** a crowd of people or things is an empty space that allows you to

move through them. (人垣・物の) すき間 ❑*He cleared a passage for himself through the crammed streets.* 彼は混雑した通りを通り抜けて行った. ❺ N-UNCOUNT 不可算名詞 The **passage** of someone or something is their movement from one place to another. (人・物の) 移動 ❑*Germany had not requested Franco's consent for the passage of troops through Spain.* ドイツは軍隊がスペインを通って移動するための許可をフランコに要請していなかった. ❻ N-UNCOUNT 不可算名詞 The **passage** of someone or something is their progress from one situation or one stage in their development to another. (人・物の) 発展 進行 ❑*...to ease their passage to a market economy.* 彼らの市場経済への参入を容易にするために ❼ N-UNCOUNT 不可算名詞 The **passage** of a bill is its progress through Congress so that it can become a law. (法案の) 通過 可決 ❑*...a Medicare bill expected to get final passage in Congress today.* 本日, 議会で最終可決されることが見込まれているメディケア法案 ❽ N-SING 単数名詞 The **passage** of a period of time is its passing. (時間の) 経過 ❑*...an asset that increases in value with the passage of time.* 時の経過と共に価値を増す資産 ❾ N-COUNT 可算名詞 A **passage** is a journey by ship. (船による) 旅行 ❑*We'd arrived the day before after a 10-hour passage from Anchorage.* 私たちはその前日にアンカレッジから船で10時間かけて到着していた. ❿ N-UNCOUNT 不可算名詞 If you are granted **passage** through a country or area of land, you are given permission to go through it. 通行権 ❑*Mr. Thomas would be given safe passage to and from Jaffna.* トマス氏はジャフナを安全に出入りする通行権を与えられるだろう.

passage|way /pǽsɪdʒweɪ/ (**passageways**) N-COUNT 可算名詞 A **passageway** is a long narrow space with walls or fences on both sides, that connects one place or room with another. 通路, 廊下 ❑*Outside, in the passageway, I could hear people moving around.* 私には外の通路で人々が動き回っているのが聞こえた.

pas|sen|ger /pǽsɪndʒər/ (**passengers**) ❶ N-COUNT 名詞 A **passenger** in a vehicle such as a bus, boat, or plane is a person who is traveling in it, but who is not driving it or working on it. 乗客 ❑*Mr. Fullemann was a passenger in the car when it crashed.* 車が衝突した時, フュールマン氏はそれに乗っていた. ❷ ADJ 形容詞 **Passenger** is used to describe something that is designed for passengers, rather than for drivers or freight. 乗客の [ADJ n] ❑*I sat in the passenger seat.* 私は乗客席に座った.
→ see **fly, train**

pass|er|by /pɑsərbaɪ, pǽs-/ (**passersby**) also **passer-by** N-COUNT 可算名詞 A **passerby** is a person who is walking past someone or something. 通行人, 通りがかりの人 ❑*A passerby described what he saw moments after the car bomb had exploded.* ある通行人は, 車爆弾の爆発直後に見たことについて語った.

pass|ing /pǽsɪŋ/ ❶ ADJ 形容詞 A **passing** fashion, activity, or feeling lasts for only a short period of time and is not worth taking very seriously. つかの間の, 一時の [ADJ n] ❑*Hamnett does not believe environmental concern is a passing fad.* ハムネットは, 環境に対する関心が一時的な熱狂だとは思わない. ❷ N-SING 単数名詞 The **passing** of something such as a time or system is the fact of its coming to an end. (時・制度の) 終わり ❑*It was an historic day, yet its passing was not marked by the slightest excitement.* それは歴史に残る日だったにもかかわらず, その日の終わりには興奮のかけらもなかった. ❸ N-SING 単数名詞 You can refer to someone's death as their **passing**, if you want to avoid using the word "death" because you think it might upset or offend people. 逝去 (婉曲表現) ❑*His passing will be mourned by many people.* 彼の逝去は多くの人に嘆き悲しまれるだろう. ❹ N-SING 単数名詞 The **passing** of a period of time is the fact or process of its going by. (時の) 経過 ❑*The passing of time brought a sense of emptiness.* 時が経つにつれ, むなしくなってきた. ❺ ADJ 形容詞 A **passing** mention or reference is brief and is made while you are talking or writing about something else. 大まかな, 思いつきの [ADJ n] ❑*It was just a passing comment, he didn't expand.* それはふとしたコメントに過ぎず, 彼はそこから話を発展させなかった. ❻ → see also **pass** ❼ PHRASE 句 If you mention something **in passing**, you mention it briefly while you are talking or writing about something else. (話の) ついでに ちなみに ❑*The army is only mentioned in passing.* 軍隊についてはただ付随的に触れられている.

pas|sion /pǽʃᵊn/ (**passions**) ❶ N-UNCOUNT 不可算名詞 **Passion** is strong sexual feelings toward someone. 熱情 [also N in pl] ❑*...my passion for a dark-haired, slender boy named Josh.* 黒髪で細身の少年, ジョシュにたいする私の激しい愛情 ❑*...the expression of love and passion.* 愛と激情の表現 ❷ N-UNCOUNT 不可算名詞 **Passion** is a very strong feeling about something or a strong belief in something. 情熱 [also N in pl] ❑*He spoke with great passion.* 彼は大いなる情熱を持って語った. ❸ N-COUNT 可算名詞 If you have a **passion for** something, you have a very strong interest in it and like it very much. (物事に対する) 熱中 ❑*She had a passion for gardening.* 彼女は園芸が大好きだった.

N.　affection, desire, love, lust ❶
　　enthusiasm, fondness, interest ❷ ❸

pas|sion|ate /pǽʃᵊnɪt/ ❶ ADJ 形容詞 A **passionate** person has very strong feelings about something or a strong belief in something. 情熱的な ❑*...his passionate commitment to peace.* 彼の平和に対する情熱的な献身 ❑*He is very passionate about the project.* 彼はその計画にとても熱中している. ●**pas|sion|ate|ly** ADV 副詞 情熱的に, 熱烈に ❑*I am passionately opposed to the death penalty.* 私は死刑に激しく反対している. ❷ ADJ 形容詞 A **passionate** person has strong romantic or sexual feelings and expresses them in their behavior. 情欲的な, 好色な ❑*...a beautiful, passionate woman of twenty-six.* 美しく官能的な26歳の女 ●**pas|sion|ate|ly** ADV 副詞 情欲的に ❑*He was passionately in love with her.* 彼は激しく彼女に恋をしていた.

pas|sive /pǽsɪv/ ❶ ADJ 形容詞 If you describe someone as **passive**, you mean that they do not take action but instead let things happen to them. 受け身の [DISAPPROVAL 不賛成] ❑*His passive attitude made things easier for me.* 彼の受身の姿勢のおかげで私は物事がやりやすかった. ●**pas|sive|ly** ADV 副詞 受け身で ❑*He sat there passively, content to wait for his father to make the opening move.* 彼はそこにおとなしく座り, 父親が口火を切るのを甘んじて待っていた. ❷ ADJ 形容詞 [ADJ n] A **passive** activity involves watching, looking at, or listening to things rather than doing things. 活動的でない ❑*They want less passive ways of filling their time.* 彼らはもっと活動的な方法で時間を過ごしたがる. ❸ ADJ 形容詞 **Passive** resistance involves showing opposition to the people in power in your country by not cooperating with them and protesting in nonviolent ways. 消極的な [ADJ n] ❑*They made it clear that they would only exercise passive resistance in the event of a military takeover.* 彼らはもし軍が支配権を奪うなら消極的な抵抗に出るのみだということを明確にした. ❹ N-SING 単数名詞 In grammar, **the passive** or **the passive voice** is formed using "be" and the past participle of a verb. The subject of a passive clause does not perform the action expressed by the verb but is affected by it. For example, in "He's been murdered," the verb is in the passive. Compare **active**. (文法) 受動態 受身形

pass|port /pǽspɔrt/ (**passports**) N-COUNT 可算名詞 Your **passport** is an official document containing your name, photograph, and personal details, which you need to show when you enter or leave a country. 旅券, パスポート ❑*You should take your passport with you when changing money.* 両替する時には旅券を持っていく必要がある.

pass|word /pǽswɜrd/ (**passwords**) N-COUNT 可算名詞 A **password** is a secret word or phrase that you must know in order to be allowed to enter a place such as a military base, or to be allowed to use a computer system. 合言葉, パスワード ❑*Advance and give the password.* 前に進み, 合言葉を言え.
→ see **Internet**

past /pǽst/ (**pasts**)

> In addition to the uses shown below, **past** is used in the phrasal verb "run past."

> 下記の用法に加えて, **past** は句動詞 **run past** に使われる.

❶ N-SING 単数名詞 **The past** is the time before the present, and the things that have happened. (時間的な) 過去 ❑*In the past, about a third of the babies born to women with diabetes died.* 昔は糖尿病の女性が出産する赤ちゃんの約3分の1は死んだ. ●PHRASE 句 If you accuse someone of **living in the past**, you mean that they think too much about the past or believe that things are the same as they were in the past. 過去に生きる [DISAPPROVAL 不賛成] ❑*What was the point in living in the past, thinking about what had or had not happened?* 何が起こったか起こらなかったかを考えながら, 過去に生きることに何の意味があったのか? ❷ N-COUNT 可算名詞 Your **past** consists of all the things that you have done or that have happened to you. (人の) 過去 ❑*...revelations about his past.* 彼の過去の暴露 ❸ ADJ 形容詞 **Past** events and things happened or existed before the present time. 過去の, 以前の [ADJ n] ❑*I knew from past experience that alternative therapies could help.* 過去の経験から, 私は代替療法が役に立つ場合があることを知っていた. ❑*...a return to the turbulence of past centuries.* 過去の世紀の動乱への回帰 ❹ ADJ 形容詞 You use **past** to talk about a period of time that has just finished. For example, if you talk about the **past five years**, you mean the period of five years that has just finished. 過ぎたばかりの [det ADJ n] ❑*Most stores have remained closed for the past three days.* ここ3日間ほとんどの店が閉まったままだ. ❺ PREP 前置詞 You use **past** when you are stating a time that is thirty minutes or less after a particular hour. For example, if it is **twenty past** six, it is twenty minutes after six o'clock. (時間) —を過ぎて [num PREP num] ❑*It's ten past eleven.* 11時10分だ. ●ADV 副詞 **Past** is also an adverb. 過ぎて [num ADV] ❑*I have my lunch at half past.* 私は12時半にお昼を食べます. ❻ PREP 前置詞 If it is **past** a particular time, it

is later than that time. ーを過ぎて ❑ *It was past midnight.* 真夜中過ぎだった. **7** PREP 前置詞 If you go **past** someone or something, you go near them and keep moving, so that they are then behind you. (人・場所を) 通り過ぎて ❑ *I dashed past him and out of the door.* 私は急いで彼を追い越し, ドアから外に出た. ❑ *A steady procession of people filed past the coffin.* 絶え間ない人々の行列が棺のそばを通り過ぎた. ● ADV 副詞 **Past** is also an adverb. 通り過ぎて ❑ *An ambulance drove past.* 救急車が通り過ぎて行った. **8** PREP 前置詞 If you look or point **past** a person or thing, you look or point at something behind them. ーの後ろの [V PREP n] ❑ *She stared past Christine at the bed.* 彼女はクリスティンの後ろのベッドをじっと見つめた. **9** PREP 前置詞 If something is **past** a place, it is on the other side of it. (ある地点・段階) ーを通り越したところに, ーの先に [v-link PREP n] ❑ *Go north on I-15 to the exit just past Barstow.* I-15を北へ行き, バーストーを越えたばかりところにある出口に行け. **10** PREP 前置詞 If someone or something is **past** a particular point or stage, they are no longer at that point or stage. (ある地点・段階) を越えて ❑ *He was well past retirement age.* 彼は定年をだいぶ過ぎていた.
→ see **history**

pas|ta /pɑstə/ (**pastas**) N-MASS 質量名詞 **Pasta** is a type of food made from a mixture of flour, eggs, and water that is formed into different shapes and then boiled. Spaghetti, macaroni, and noodles are types of pasta. パスタ (スパゲッティ・マカロニなど)

> **Pasta** comes in dozens of shapes and sizes but generally the same recipe is used: water, flour, and sometimes eggs or other flavors. Pasta is cooked in boiling water. Some of the most popular types of pasta are **spaghetti** (long, thin pasta noodles), **macaroni** (short tubes of pasta, often eaten with a cheese sauce), and **lasagne** (flat sheets of pasta, eaten in a dish made of layers of lasagne and meat sauce).

paste /peɪst/ (**pastes, pasting, pasted**) **1** N-MASS 質量名詞 **Paste** is a soft, wet, sticky mixture of a substance and a liquid, that can be spread easily. Some types of paste are used to stick things together. (接着用の) のり ❑ *Blend a little milk with the custard powder to form a paste.* のりを作るには, 少量のミルクをカスタード・パウダーに混ぜる. **2** N-MASS 質量名詞 **Paste** is a soft smooth mixture made of crushed meat, fruit, or vegetables. You can, for example, spread it onto bread or use it in cooking. ペースト ❑ *...tomato paste.* トマト・ペースト **3** V-T 他動詞 If you **paste** something on a surface, you put glue or paste on it and stick it on the surface. (のりなどで) 張る ❑ *...pasting labels on bottles.* ボトルにラベルを張って

pas|tel /pæstɛl/ (**pastels**) ADJ 形容詞 **Pastel** colors are pale rather than dark or bright. パステルカラーの, パステル調の [ADJ n, ADJ color] ❑ *...delicate pastel shades.* 繊細なパステル調の色合い ❑ *...pastel pink, blue, peach, and green.* 淡いピンク, 青, 桃色, そして緑 ● N-COUNT 可算名詞 **Pastel** is also a noun. パステルカラー ❑ *The lobby is decorated in pastels.* ロビーはパステルカラーで塗られている.
→ see **drawing**

pas|time /pæstaɪm/ (**pastimes**) N-COUNT 可算名詞 A **pastime** is something that you do in your spare time because you enjoy it or are interested in it. 娯楽, 気晴らし ❑ *His favorite pastime is golf.* 彼のお気に入りの趣味はゴルフだ.

pas|to|ral /pæstərəl, pæstor-/ **1** ADJ 形容詞 The **pastoral** duties of a priest or other religious leader involve looking after the people he or she has responsibility for, especially by helping them with their personal problems. 牧師の [ADJ n] ❑ *...the pastoral care of the sick.* 病人に対する牧師のケア **2** ADJ 形容詞 A **pastoral** place, atmosphere, or idea is characteristic of peaceful country life and scenery. 田舎の, のどかな [ADJ n] ❑ *...a tranquil pastoral scene.* 静かな田園風景

pas|try /peɪstri/ (**pastries**) **1** N-UNCOUNT 不可算名詞 **Pastry** is a food made from flour, fat, and water that is mixed together, rolled flat, and baked in the oven. It is used, for example, for making pies. ペストリー (小麦粉を練って焼いた食べ物) **2** N-COUNT 可算名詞 A **pastry** is a small cake made with sweet pastry. ペストリー (小麦粉を練った小さなケーキ) ❑ *...a wide range of cakes and pastries.* いろんな種類のケーキやペストリー

pas|ture /pæstʃər/ (**pastures**) N-VAR 可変性名詞 **Pasture** is land with grass growing on it for farm animals to eat. 牧草地 ❑ *The cows are out now, grazing in the pasture.* 雌牛たちは今外に出ていて, 牧草地の草を食べている.
→ see **barn**

pat /pæt/ (**pats, patting, patted**) **1** V-T 他動詞 If you **pat** something or someone, you tap them lightly, usually with your hand held flat. (手の平で) 軽くたたく ❑ *"Don't you worry about any of this," she said patting me on the knee.* 「このことについては心配しなくていいのよ」と彼女は私のひざを軽くたたきながら言った. ❑ *The landlady patted her hair nervously.* 女家主は自分の髪を神経質に軽くたたいた. ● N-COUNT 可算名詞 **Pat** is also a noun. 軽くたたくこと ❑ *He gave her an encouraging pat on the shoulder.* 彼は励ますように彼女の肩を軽くたたいた. **2** N-COUNT 可算名詞 A **pat of** butter

or something else that is soft is a small lump of it. (バターの) 小さな塊 ❑ *Terreano put a pat of butter on his plate.* テリアーノは皿の上に小さなバターの塊を置いた. **3** PHRASE 句 If you give someone **a pat on the back** or if you **pat** them **on the back**, you show them that you think they have done well and deserve to be praised. 称賛, (ほめるために) 背中を軽くたたく [APPROVAL 賛成] ❑ *The players deserve a pat on the back.* その競技者たちは称賛に値する.

patch /pætʃ/ (**patches, patching, patched**) **1** N-COUNT 可算名詞 A **patch** on a surface is a part of it that is different in appearance from the area around it. (表面などの) 他と違って見える部分 ❑ *...the bald patch on the top of his head.* 彼の頭のてっぺんのはげた部分 ❑ *There was a small patch of blue in the gray clouds.* 灰色の雲間に小さな青空が見えた. **2** N-COUNT 可算名詞 A **patch** of land is a small area of land where a particular plant or crop grows. (植物の育つ) 小さな土地 ❑ *...a patch of land covered in forest.* 木々に覆われた小さな土地 ❑ *...the little vegetable patch in her backyard.* 彼女の裏庭の小さな野菜畑 **3** N-COUNT 可算名詞 A **patch** is a piece of material that you use to cover a hole in something. (継ぎの) 当て布 ❑ *...jackets with patches on the elbows.* ひじ当ての付いた上着 **4** N-COUNT 可算名詞 A **patch** is a small piece of material that you wear to cover an injured eye. 眼帯 ❑ *She went to the hospital and found him lying down with a patch over his eye.* 彼女は病院へ行き, 彼が目に眼帯をして横になっているのを見つけた. **5** V-T 他動詞 If you **patch** something that has a hole in it, you repair it by fastening a patch over the hole. 継ぎを当てる, 穴をふさぐ ❑ *He and Walker patched the barn roof.* 彼とウォーカーは納屋の屋根の穴を修理した. ❑ *One of the mechanics took off the damaged tire, and took it back to the station to be patched.* 整備士の1人が損傷したタイヤを取り外し, 修理するため整備場に持ち帰った. **6** N-COUNT 可算名詞 A **patch** is a piece of computer program code written as a temporary solution for dealing with a computer virus and distributed by the makers of the original program. (プログラムの修正用の) パッチ [COMPUTING コンピューティング] ❑ *Older machines will need a software patch to correct the date.* 古い機械は日付を修正するためのソフトウェアパッチが必要になるだろう. **7** PHRASE 句 If you have or go through **a rough patch**, you have a lot of problems for a time. 大変な時期 ❑ *His marriage was going through a rough patch.* 彼の結婚生活は大変な時期にあった.

▶ **patch up** **1** PHRASAL VERB 句動詞 If you **patch up** an argument or relationship, you try to be friendly again and not to argue anymore. 仲直りする ❑ *She has gone on vacation with her husband to try to patch up their marriage.* 彼女は結婚生活を修復しようと, 夫と休暇に出かけている. ❑ *France patched things up with New Zealand.* フランスはニュージーランドと和解した. **2** PHRASAL VERB 句動詞 If you **patch up** something that is damaged, you repair it or patch it. 修理する, 継ぎ当てする ❑ *We can patch up those holes.* 我々はそれらの穴を修理する. **3** PHRASAL VERB 句動詞 If doctors **patch** someone **up** or **patch** their wounds **up**, they treat their injuries. (傷を) 治療する ❑ *...the medical staff who patched her up after the accident.* 事故の後で彼女の治療に当たった医療スタッフ

patch|work /pætʃwɜrk/ ADJ 形容詞 A **patchwork** quilt, cushion, or piece of clothing is made by sewing together small pieces of material of different colors or patterns. パッチワークの [ADJ n] ❑ *...beds covered in patchwork quilts.* パッチワークのキルトで覆われたベッド ● N-UNCOUNT 不可算名詞 **Patchwork** is also a noun. パッチワーク ❑ *For centuries, quilting and patchwork have been popular needlecrafts.* 何世紀もの間キルティングとパッチワークは人気の針仕事となっている.

patchy /pætʃi/ **1** ADJ 形容詞 A **patchy** substance or color exists in some places but not in others, or is thick in some places and thin in others. きれぎれの ❑ *Thick patchy fog and irresponsible driving were to blame.* きれぎれの濃い霧と無責任な運転のせいだった. ❑ *...the brown, patchy grass.* 茶色のまばらな草 **2** ADJ 形容詞 If something is **patchy**, it is not completely reliable or satisfactory because it is not always good. 不完全な, できむらのある ❑ *The evidence is patchy.* 証拠は不完全だ.

pa|tent /pæt³nt/ (**patents, patenting, patented**) **1** N-COUNT 可算名詞 A **patent** is an official right to be the only person or company allowed to make or sell a new product for a certain period of time. 特許 ❑ *P&G applied for a patent on its cookies.* P&Gはクッキーの特許を申請した. ❑ *He held a number of patents for his many innovations.* 彼は彼のたくさんの発明に対する特許を数多く持っていた. **2** V-T 他動詞 If you **patent** something, you obtain a patent for it. 特許を取る ❑ *He patented the idea that the atom could be split.* 彼はその原子は分割できるという考えの特許権を取った. ❑ *The invention has been patented by the university.* その発明は大学が特許を取っている. **3** ADJ 形容詞 You use **patent** to describe something, especially something bad, in order to indicate in an emphatic way that you think its nature or existence is clear and obvious. (悪いことが) 明らかな [EMPHASIS 強調] ❑ *This was patent nonsense.* これはまったくのでたらめだった. ● **pa|tent|ly** ADV 副詞 明らかに ❑ *He made his displeasure patently obvious.* 彼は不快感をあからさまに明示した.

Word Link | pater, patr ≈ father : ex*pater*, *patr*iate, *patr*onize

pa|ter|nal /pətɜrnᵊl/ ■ ADJ 形容詞 **Paternal** is used to describe feelings or actions that are typical of those of a kind father toward his child. 父親らしい □ …*paternal love for his children.* 彼の子供に対する父親らしい愛情 ② ADJ 形容詞 A **paternal** relative is one that is related through a person's father rather than their mother. 父方の [ADJ n] □ …*my paternal grandparents.* 私の父方の祖父母

pa|ter|nity leave /pətɜrniti liv/ N-UNCOUNT 不可算名詞 If a man has **paternity leave**, his employer allows him some time off work because his child has just been born. 父親の育児休暇 [BUSINESS 実業] □ *Paternity leave is rare and, where it does exist, it's unlikely to be for any longer than two weeks.* 父親の育児休暇は珍しく、実際にあるとしても2週間以上は考えられない.

path /pæθ/ (paths) ■ N-COUNT 可算名詞 A **path** is a long strip of ground that people walk along to get from one place to another. 小道 □ *We followed the path along the clifftops.* 私たちはがけの頂上沿いのその小道をたどった. □ *Feet had worn a path in the rock.* 人が通って岩が摩滅して小道となっていた. ② N-COUNT 可算名詞 Your **path** is the space ahead of you as you move along. 進路 □ *A group of reporters blocked his path.* 報道陣が彼の行く手をさえぎった. ③ N-COUNT 可算名詞 The **path** of something is the line that it moves along in a particular direction. 経路 □ *He stepped without looking into the path of a reversing car.* 彼は、逆進してくる車の行き先をよく見ずに足を踏み出した. □ …*people who live near airports or under the flight path of airplanes.* 空港の近く、または飛行機の飛行経路の下に住む人たち ④ N-COUNT 可算名詞 A **path** that you take is a particular course of action or way of achieving something. 行動方針 □ *They appear to have chosen the path of cooperation rather than confrontation.* 彼らは対立ではなく協調の道を選んだようだ.

pa|thet|ic /pəθɛtɪk/ ■ ADJ 形容詞 If you describe a person or animal as **pathetic**, you mean that they are sad and weak or helpless, and they make you feel very sorry for them. 哀れな □ …*a pathetic little dog with a curly tail.* くるんと巻いたしっぽの哀れな子犬 □ *The small group of onlookers presented a pathetic sight.* 人数の少ない観客は哀れな様相を呈していた. ● pa|theti|cal|ly /pəθɛtɪkli/ ADV 副詞 □ *She was pathetically thin.* 彼女は哀れなほどやせていた. ② ADJ 形容詞 If you describe someone or something as **pathetic**, you mean that they make you feel impatient or angry, often because they are weak or not very good. (人が) 救いようのない 情けない [DISAPPROVAL 不賛成] □ *What pathetic excuses.* なんて情けない言い訳だ. □ *Don't be so pathetic.* もうちょっとしっかりしろよ. ● pa|theti|cal|ly ADV 副詞 [ADV adj] 情けないほどに □ *Five women in a group of 18 people is a pathetically small number.* 18人中女性が5人というのは情けないほどに少ない.

patho|logi|cal /pæθəlɒdʒɪkᵊl/ ■ ADJ 形容詞 You describe a person or their behavior as **pathological** when they behave in an extreme and unacceptable way, and have very powerful feelings that they cannot control. (人柄や言動が) 病的な □ *He experiences chronic, almost pathological jealousy.* ほとんど病的なしっとを経験している. □ *He's a pathological liar.* 彼は嘘ばかりついている. ② ADJ 形容詞 **Pathological** means relating to pathology or illness. 病理学の [MEDICAL 医学の] □ …*pathological conditions in animals.* 動物の病理学的状態

pa|thol|ogist /pəθɒlədʒɪst/ (pathologists) N-COUNT 可算名詞 A **pathologist** is someone who studies or investigates diseases and illnesses, or who examines dead bodies in order to find out the cause of death. 病理学者

pa|thol|ogy /pəθɒlədʒi/ N-UNCOUNT 不可算名詞 **Pathology** is the study of the way diseases and illnesses develop. 病理学 [MEDICAL 医学の]

pa|thos /peɪθɒs/ N-UNCOUNT 不可算名詞 **Pathos** is a quality in a situation, movie, or play that makes people feel sadness and pity. 哀れを誘う特質, 哀愁 □ …*the pathos of man's isolation.* 人間の孤独の物悲しさ

path|way /pæθweɪ/ (pathways) ■ N-COUNT 可算名詞 A **pathway** is a path that you can walk along or a route that you can take. 小道, 歩道 □ *Richard was coming up the pathway.* リチャードは小道をやって来ていた. ② N-COUNT 可算名詞 A **pathway** is a particular course of action or a way of achieving something. 方針, (〜に至る) 過程 □ *Diplomacy will smooth your pathway to success.* 外交手腕は成功への道を円滑にする.

pa|tience /peɪʃᵊns/ ■ N-UNCOUNT 不可算名詞 If you have **patience**, you are able to stay calm and not get annoyed, for example, when something takes a long time, or when someone is not doing what you want them to do. 忍耐, 我慢 □ *He doesn't have the patience to wait.* 彼には待つという忍耐力がない. ② PHRASE 句 If someone **tries** your **patience** or **tests** your **patience**, they annoy you so much that it is very difficult for you to stay calm. 忍耐力の限界に挑戦する □ *He tended to stutter whenever he spoke to her, which tried her patience.* 彼は彼女と話をする時にはいつもどもりがちで、それが彼女をいつもいらいらさせた.

pa|tient /peɪʃᵊnt/ (patients) ■ N-COUNT 可算名詞 A **patient** is a person who is receiving medical treatment from a doctor or hospital. A **patient** is also someone who is taken care of by a particular doctor. 患者 □ *The earlier the treatment is given, the better the patient's chances.* 治療が早いほど、患者の回復の可能性が高い. □ *She was tough but wonderful with her patients.* 彼女は厳しい人だったが、患者に対しては素晴らししかった. ② ADJ 形容詞 If you are **patient**, you stay calm and do not get annoyed, for example, when something takes a long time, or when someone is not doing what you want them to do. 辛抱強い, 気長な □ *Please be patient - your check will arrive.* もうしばらくお待ち下さい. あなたの小切手は来ます. ● pa|tient|ly ADV 副詞 [ADV with v] 辛抱強く, 気長に □ *She waited patiently for Frances to finish.* 彼女はフランシスが終わるのをじっと待った.

→ see **diagnosis, illness**

pa|tio /pætiou/ (patios) N-COUNT 可算名詞 A **patio** is an area of flat blocks of stone or concrete next to a house, where people can sit and relax or eat. テラス, 中庭, パティオ

pa|tri|ot /peɪtriət/ (patriots) N-COUNT 可算名詞 Someone who is a **patriot** loves their country and feels very loyal toward it. 愛国者 □ *It has been suggested the founders were not true patriots but men out to protect their own interests.* 創始者たちは真の愛国者ではなく、自分たちの利益を守ろうと躍起になっていた人たちだったことが示唆されている.

Word Link | otic ≈ affecting, causing : er*otic*, neur*otic*, patri*otic*

pat|ri|ot|ic /peɪtriɒtɪk/ ADJ 形容詞 Someone who is **patriotic** loves their country and feels very loyal toward it. 愛国心の強い □ *Winona is fiercely patriotic.* ウィノーラは恐ろしく愛国心が強い.

Word Link | ism ≈ action or state : communism, optim*ism*, patriot*ism*

pat|ri|ot|ism /peɪtriətɪzəm/ N-UNCOUNT 不可算名詞 **Patriotism** is love for your country and loyalty toward it. 愛国心 □ *He was a country boy who had joined the army out of a sense of patriotism and adventure.* 彼は愛国心と冒険心から軍隊に入った田舎の少年だった.

pa|trol /pətroul/ (patrols, patrolling, patrolled) ■ V-T 他動詞 When soldiers, police, or guards **patrol** an area or building, they move around in it in order to make sure that there is no trouble there. (兵士や警察などが) 巡回する 巡視する □ *Prison officers continued to patrol the grounds within the jail.* 看守たちは引き続き刑務所の敷地内を見回った. ● N-COUNT 可算名詞 **Patrol** is also a noun. 巡回, 巡視 □ *He failed to return from a patrol.* 彼は見回りから帰って来られなかった. ② PHRASE 句 Soldiers, police, or guards who are **on patrol** are patrolling an area. 巡回中 □ *The army is now on patrol in Srinagar and a curfew has been imposed.* 軍隊は現在スリナガルを巡回中で、外出禁止令が出されている. ③ N-COUNT 可算名詞 A **patrol** is a group of soldiers or vehicles that are patrolling an area. (軍の) 偵察隊 偵察機 □ *Guerrillas attacked a patrol with hand grenades.* ゲリラが偵察隊を手りゅう弾で襲撃した.

pa|tron /peɪtrən/ (patrons) ■ N-COUNT 可算名詞 A **patron** is a person who supports and gives money to artists, writers, or musicians. (芸術家などの) 後援者 パトロン □ *Catherine the Great was a patron of the arts and sciences.* 女帝エカテリーナは芸術科学の擁護者だった. ② N-COUNT 可算名詞 The **patron** of a charity, group, or campaign is an important person who allows his or her name to be used for publicity. 後援者 (チャリティーやキャンペーンなどの宣伝に名前を使うことを許している人) □ *He has now become one of the patrons of the association.* 現在、彼はその協会の後援者の1人となっている. ③ N-COUNT 可算名詞 The **patrons** of a place such as a bar or hotel are its customers. (バーやホテルなどの) 常連客 □ *Few patrons of a high-priced hotel can be led to expect anything other than luxury service.* 高級ホテルの常連客で、ぜいたくなサービス以外の何かを期待するようになる人はほとんどいない.

Word Link | age ≈ state of, related to : courage, marriage, patron*age*

pat|ron|age /peɪtrənɪdʒ, pæt-/ N-UNCOUNT 不可算名詞 **Patronage** is the support and money given by someone to a person or a group such as a charity. (チャリティーなどへの) 後援 支援金 □ …*government patronage of the arts in Europe.* 政府のヨーロッパにおける芸術への支援

pat|ron|ize /peɪtrənaɪz/ (patronizes, patronizing, patronized) ■ V-T 他動詞 If someone **patronizes** you, they speak or behave toward you in a way that seems friendly, but that shows that they think they are superior to you in some way. 恩着せがましい態度を取る, (人を) 見下した態度を取る [DISAPPROVAL 不賛成] □ *Don't you patronize me!* 恩着せがましい態度は取るな! ② V-T 他動詞 Someone who **patronizes** artists, writers, or musicians supports them and gives them money. (芸術などを) 後援する 擁護する [FORMAL 形式ばった] □ *The Japanese imperial family patronizes the Japanese Art*

Association. 日本の皇室は日本美術協会を後援している. ❸ V-T 他動詞 If someone **patronizes** a place such as a bar, store, or hotel, they are one of its customers. (店などを) ひいきにする ❑ *The ladies of Berne liked to patronize the palace for tea and little cakes.* バーンのご婦人方はお茶と小さなケーキを楽しむためにその宮殿に頻繁に通うのが好きだった.

pat|ron|iz|ing /péɪtrənaɪzɪŋ/ ADJ 形容詞 If someone is **patronizing**, they speak or behave toward you in a way that seems friendly, but that shows that they think they are superior to you. 恩着せがましい, 人を見下した [DISAPPROVAL 不賛成] ❑ *The tone of the interview was unnecessarily patronizing.* その会見の口調は無用に人を見下したものだった.

pat|ter /pǽtər/ (**patters, pattering, pattered**) ❶ V-I 自動詞 If something **patters** on a surface, it hits it quickly several times, making quiet, tapping sounds. パタパタとたたく, パタパタと音を立てる ❑ *Rain pattered gently outside, dripping onto the roof from the pines.* 外では雨が松の木から屋根に落ちて屋根でパラパラと穏やかな音を立てていた. ❷ N-SING 単数名詞 A **patter** is a series of quick, quiet, tapping sounds. パラパラ (パタパタ) という音 ❑ *...the patter of the driving rain on the roof.* 激しい雨が屋根に当たるパラパラという音 ❸ N-SING 単数名詞 Someone's **patter** is a series of things that they say quickly and easily, usually in order to entertain people or to persuade them to buy or do something. 早口のおしゃべり, (芸人や商人の) 早口の口上 ❑ *Women found him charming. It must have been his patter because he's not good-looking.* 女性たちは彼を魅力的だと思った. 彼は美形ではないから, それは彼のおしゃべりのせいだったに違いない.

pat|tern /pǽtərn/ (**patterns**) ❶ N-COUNT 可算名詞 A **pattern** is the repeated or regular way in which something happens or is done. パターン, 傾向 ❑ *All three attacks followed the same pattern.* 3回の襲撃はすべて同じパターンをたどっていた. ❷ N-COUNT 可算名詞 A **pattern** is an arrangement of lines or shapes, especially a design in which the same shape is repeated at regular intervals over a surface. (デザインの) パターン ❑ *...a golden robe embroidered with red and purple thread stitched into a pattern of flames.* 赤と紫の糸で炎のパターンを刺しゅうした金色のローブ ❸ N-COUNT 可算名詞 A **pattern** is a diagram or shape that you can use as a guide when you are making something such as a model or a piece of clothing. 型, 型紙 ❑ *...cutting out a pattern for slacks.* スラックス用の型紙を切り取ること ❑ *Send for our free patterns to knit yourself.* 自分で編むための無料の型紙をお取り寄せください.
→ see **quilt**

Word Partnership   *pattern* は次の語句と使われる:

ADJ.	**familiar** pattern, **normal** pattern, **typical** pattern ❶
	different pattern, **same** pattern, **similar** pattern ❶ ❷
V.	**change** a pattern, **fit** a pattern, **see** a pattern ❶
	follow a pattern ❶ – ❸

pat|terned /pǽtərnd/ ❶ ADJ 形容詞 Something that is **patterned** is covered with a pattern or design. 模様の付いた ❑ *...a plain carpet with a patterned border.* 縁に模様の付いたシンプルなカーペット ❷ V-T PASSIVE 受動態他動詞 If something new **is patterned on** something else that already exists, it is deliberately made so that it has similar features. 模倣された [mainly AM 主に米国英語] ❑ *New York City announced a 10-point policy patterned on the federal bill of rights for taxpayers.* ニューヨーク市は, 連邦政府の納税者に対する権利法案を模倣した10か条政策を発表した.

pause /pɔ́z/ (**pauses, pausing, paused**) ❶ V-I 自動詞 If you **pause** while you are doing something, you stop for a short period and then continue. 休止する, ちょっと止まる ❑ *"It's rather embarrassing," he began, and paused.* 「かなり恥ずかしい話なんだけど」と彼は話を始め, そしてちょっと止まった. ❑ *He talked for two hours without pausing for breath.* 彼は息も切らず2時間話した. ❷ N-COUNT 可算名詞 A **pause** is a short period when you stop doing something before continuing. 休止, ためらい ❑ *After a pause Al said sharply: "I'm sorry if I've upset you."* アルはちょっとためらった後, 一気に言った. 「もし気を悪くしてたらごめん.」

Word Partnership   *pause* は次の語句と使われる:

ADJ.	**awkward** pause, **brief** pause, **long** pause, **short** pause, **slight** pause ❷

pave /péɪv/ (**paves, paving, paved**) V-T 他動詞 If a road or an area of ground **has been paved**, it has been covered with asphalt or concrete, so that it is suitable for walking or driving on. (道や地面を) 舗装する [usu passive] ❑ *The avenue had never been paved, and deep mud made it impassable in winter.* その大通りは一度も舗装されたことがなく, 冬には深いぬかるみで通れなかった.

pave|ment /péɪvmənt/ (**pavements**) ❶ N-COUNT 可算名詞 The **pavement** is the hard surface of a road. 舗装路面 [AM 米国英語] ❑ *The tires of Lenny's bike hissed over the wet pavement.* レニーの自転

車のタイヤが濡れた舗装道路の上でシューと音を立てた. ❷ N-COUNT 可算名詞 A **pavement** is a path with a hard surface, usually by the side of a road. 歩道 [BRIT 英国英語; AM **sidewalk** 米国英語 **sidewalk**]

pa|vil|ion /pəvɪ́lyən/ (**pavilions**) ❶ N-COUNT 可算名詞 A **pavilion** is a large temporary structure such as a tent that is used at outdoor public events. パビリオン, 大型テント ❑ *...heading across the beautiful green lawn toward the International Pavilion.* 美しい緑の芝生を横切り, 国際パビリオンに向かいつつ ❷ N-COUNT 可算名詞 A **pavilion** is an ornamental building in a garden or park. (庭や公園の) あずまや パビリオン ❑ *Despite persistent rain showers, the lawn and pavilion were packed with fans.* なかなかやまない雨にもかかわらず, 芝生やパビリオンはファンでいっぱいだった.

paw /pɔ́/ (**paws, pawing, pawed**) ❶ N-COUNT 可算名詞 The **paws** of an animal such as a cat, dog, or bear are its feet, which have claws for gripping things and soft pads for walking on. (犬や猫など爪のある動物の) 足 手 ❑ *The kitten was black with white front paws and a white splotch on her chest.* 子猫は全身が黒く, 前足と胸が白かった. ❷ V-T 他動詞/自動詞 If an animal **paws** something, or **paws** at it, it draws its foot over it or down it. 足で引っかく, 前足でかく ❑ *Madigan's horse pawed the ground.* マディガンの馬は足で地面を蹴った. ❸ V-T 他動詞/自動詞 If one person **paws** another, or **paws** at them, they touch or stroke them in a way that the other person finds offensive. (手荒く, またはいやらしく) 触る なでる [DISAPPROVAL 不賛成] ❑ *Stop pawing me, Geraldo!* ジェラルド, わたしの体をなでるのはやめて!

pawn /pɔ́n/ (**pawns, pawning, pawned**) ❶ V-T 他動詞 If you **pawn** something that you own, you leave it with a pawnbroker, who gives you money for it and who can sell it if you do not pay back the money before a certain time. 質に入れる ❑ *He is contemplating pawning his watch.* 彼は時計を質に入れることを真剣に考えている. ❷ N-COUNT 可算名詞 In chess, a **pawn** is the smallest and least valuable playing piece. Each player has eight pawns at the start of the game. (チェスの) ポーン (将棋の歩にあたる) ❸ N-COUNT 可算名詞 If you say that someone is using you as a **pawn**, you mean that they are using you for their own advantage. 人の手先 ❑ *It looks as though he is being used as a political pawn by the president.* 彼は大統領に行政の手先として使われているかのようだ.
→ see **chess**
▸ **pawn off** PHRASAL VERB 句動詞 If you **pawn off** something or someone that you do not want **on** another person, you persuade the person to accept them. (人に) 売りつける [DISAPPROVAL 不賛成] ❑ *The factories produce hugely subsidized rubbish they can't pawn off on anybody but the Russians.* 工場では支給される助成金で, ロシア人にしか売れないようながらくたを製造している. ❑ *Are you trying to pawn me off on somebody?* あなたはわたしを誰かに押し付けようとしているの?

pawn|broker /pɔ́nbroʊkər/ (**pawnbrokers**) N-COUNT 可算名詞 A **pawnbroker** is a person who lends people money. People give the pawnbroker something they own, which can be sold if they do not pay back the money before a certain time. 質屋

pay /péɪ/ (**pays, paying, paid**) ❶ V-T/V-I 他動詞/自動詞 When you **pay** an amount of money **to** someone, you give it to them because you are buying something from them or because you owe it to them. When you **pay** something such as a bill or a debt, you pay the amount that you owe. (人に金を) 支払う ❑ *Owners who have already paid for repairs will be reimbursed.* すでに修理代を支払った持ち主には返金される. ❑ *The wealthier may have to pay a little more in taxes.* 収入がより多い人たちには少し増税になるかもしれない. ❷ V-T 他動詞 When you **are paid**, you get your wages or salary from your employer. 給料を支払う ❑ *The lawyer was paid a huge salary.* その弁護士は巨額の給料を受け取った. ❑ *I get paid monthly.* わたしは月に一度, 給料をもらう. ❸ N-UNCOUNT 不可算名詞 Your **pay** is the money that you get from your employer as wages or salary. 給料, 賃金 ❑ *...their complaints about their pay and conditions.* 給料と労働条件に関する彼らの苦情

> When used as a noun, **pay** is a general word which you can use to refer to the money you get from your employer for doing your job. Professional people and office workers receive a **salary**, which is paid monthly. However, when talking about someone's salary, you usually give the annual figure. ❑ *I'm paid a salary of $15,000 a year.* Manual workers are paid **wages**, or a **wage**. The plural is more common than the singular, especially when you are talking about the actual cash that someone receives. ❑ *Every week he handed all his wages in cash to his wife.* Wages are usually paid, and quoted, as an hourly or a weekly sum. ❑ *...a starting wage of five dollars an hour.* Your **income** consists of all the money you receive from all sources, including your pay.

❹ V-T 他動詞 If you **are paid to** do something, someone gives you some money so that you will help them or perform some service for them. 金を払って～させる ❑ *There are people who are paid to sit around and play games.* ぶらぶらしたりゲームをするように金を支給さ

れる人たちがいる． **⑤** V-I 自動詞 If a government or organization makes someone **pay for** something, it makes them responsible for providing the money for it, for example, by increasing prices or taxes. (一の) 費用を支払う □ ...*a legally binding international treaty that establishes who must pay for environmental damage.* 環境破壊に対し誰が費用を支払わなければならないかを定めた法的拘束力のある国際協定. **⑥** V-T/V-I 他動詞/自動詞 If a job, deal, or investment **pays** a particular amount, it brings you that amount of money. (仕事や投資により金が) 支払われる □ *We're stuck in jobs that don't pay very well.* ぼくたちはあまり給料のよくない仕事に縛られているんだ． □ *The banks don't pay interest on those accounts.* 銀行はそれらの口座には利子を払わない． **⑦** V-I 自動詞 If a job, deal, or investment **pays**, it brings you a profit or earns you some money. 賃金を払う □ *There are some agencies now specializing in helping older people to find jobs which pay.* いまや，さらに年配の人たちが有給の仕事を見つけられるよう援助する専門機関がいくつかある． **⑧** V-T/V-I 他動詞/自動詞 If a course of action **pays**, it results in some advantage or benefit for you. 得になる □ *It pays to invest in protective clothing.* 保護服にお金をかけるだけの価値はある． □ *We must demonstrate that aggression will not pay.* わたしたちは攻撃的な行為が何の得にもならないことを示さなければならない． **⑨** V-T/V-I 他動詞/自動詞 If you **pay for** something that you do or have, you suffer as a result of it. 被害を受ける (一のために) 報いを受ける (一の) □ *He was to pay dearly for his lack of resolve.* 彼の決断力のなさの代償は高くついた． □ *Why should I pay the penalty for somebody else's mistake?* 他人の過ちなのに，どうしてわたしが罰を受けないといけないのか？ **⑩** V-T 他動詞 If you **pay** money **down** when you are buying something, you pay only a part of the total cost. You then finish paying for it later, usually by paying a certain amount every month. 頭金を払う [AM 米国英語] □ *We paid $500 down and $100 a month after that.* わたしたちは頭金500ドルを払い，その後は毎月100ドル払った． **⑪** V-T 他動詞 You use **pay** with some nouns, such as in the expressions **pay a visit** or **pay attention**, to indicate that something is given or done. (後に続く動詞の名詞の行為を) 行う □ *Pay us a visit next time you're in Portland.* 今度ポートランドに来たら，わたしたちに会いに来て． □ *He felt a heavy bump, but paid no attention to it.* 彼はドスンとぶつかったのを感じたが，それにまったく注意を払わなかった． **⑫** → see also **paid, sick pay** **⑬** PHRASE 句 If something that you buy or invest in **pays for itself** after a period of time, the money you gain from it, or save because you have it, is greater than the amount you originally spent or invested. 元が取れる □ ...*investments in energy efficiency that would pay for themselves within five years.* 5年内に元が取れるであろうエネルギー効率への投資 **⑭** to **pay dividends** → see **dividend** **⑮** to **pay through the nose** → see **nose**

Do not confuse **pay** and **buy**. If you **pay** someone, **pay** them money, or **pay for** something, you give someone money for something they are selling to you. □ *I paid the taxi driver... I need some money to pay the window cleaner... Some people are forced to pay for their own medicines.* If you **pay** a bill or debt, you pay the amount of money that is owed. □ *He paid his bill and left... We were paying $50 for a single room.* If you **buy** something, you obtain it by paying money for it. □ *Gary's bought a bicycle.*

▶ **pay back** **①** PHRASAL VERB 句動詞 If you **pay back** some money that you have borrowed or taken from someone, you give them an equal sum of money at a later time. 返済する □ *He burst into tears, begging her to forgive him and swearing to pay back everything he had stolen.* 彼は突然泣き出し，彼女に許してくれるよう頼んだ．そして彼が盗んだものすべてを返済すると誓った． **②** PHRASAL VERB 句動詞 If you **pay** someone **back for** doing something unpleasant to you, you take your revenge on them or make them suffer for what they did. (人の不快な行為に) 仕返しをする □ *Some day I'll pay you back for this!* いつかこの仕返しをするからな！

▶ **pay down** PHRASAL VERB 句動詞 If you **pay down** a debt, or **pay down** part of a debt, you give someone part of or all of the money that you owe them. (全額または一部を) 支払う [AM 米国英語] □ *The Treasury plans to pay down about $1.58 billion on the federal debt.* 財務省は連邦政府の負債の支払いに158万ドルを充てる計画だ．

▶ **pay off** **①** PHRASAL VERB 句動詞 If you **pay off** a debt, you give someone all the money that you owe them. (借金を) 全部返す 清算する □ *It would take him the rest of his life to pay off that loan.* 彼がローンを完済するには一生かかるだろう． **②** PHRASAL VERB 句動詞 If an action **pays off**, it is successful or profitable after a period of time. (計画が) うまくいく 成功する (努力が) □ *Sandra was determined to become a doctor and her persistence paid off.* サンドラの医師になるという決意は固く，彼女の粘り強さが報われた． **③** → see also **payoff**

▶ **pay out** PHRASAL VERB 句動詞 If you **pay out** money, usually a large amount, you spend it on something. (多額の金を) 支払う □ *The insurance industry will pay out billions of dollars for damage caused by Hurricane Katrina.* 保険業界はハリケーン・カトリーナの被害に対して何百万ドルもの金を払うだろう． **②** → see also **payout**

▶ **pay up** PHRASAL VERB 句動詞 If you **pay up**, you give the money that you owe them or that they are entitled to, even though you would prefer not to give it. (しぶしぶ) 借金を全額払う

□ *We claimed a refund from the association, but they would not pay up.* わたしたちはその協会に返金を求めたが，彼らは支払いを渋った．

Thesaurus　　　　**pay** また次を参照:

V.	clear, remit, settle **①**
N.	compensation, salary, wages **③**

---

pay|able /peɪəbəl/ **①** ADJ 形容詞 If an amount of money is **payable**, it has to be paid or it can be paid. 支払うべき，支払い可能な [v-link ADJ] □ *The money is not payable until January 31.* そのお金は1月31日まで払えない． **②** ADJ 形容詞 If a check or money order is made **payable to** you, it has your name written on it to indicate that you are the person who will receive the money. (小切手などが) 一あての (小切手などに) [v n ADJ, n ADJ, ADJ "to" n] (toの後に受取人の名前を記入する) □ *Make your check payable to "Stanford Alumni Association."* 小切手は「スタンフォード同窓会」あてにしてください．

pay|back /peɪbæk/ (**paybacks**) **①** N-COUNT 可算名詞 You can use **payback** to refer to the profit or benefit that you obtain from something that you have spent money, time, or effort on. (金や尽力などの投資に対する) 利益 見返り [mainly AM 主に米国英語] □ *There is a substantial payback in terms of employee and union relations.* 従業員と組合のつながりについては，利点が多い． **②** ADJ 形容詞 The **payback** period of a loan is the time in which you are required or allowed to pay it back. 返済 [ADJ n] □ *The payback period can be as short as seven years.* 返済期間は7年という短期でもよい． **③** PHRASE 句 **Payback time** is when someone has to take the consequences of what they have done in the past. You can use this expression to talk about good or bad consequences. 報いを受けるとき (いい意味でも悪い意味でも使う) [INFORMAL くだけた] □ *This was payback time. I've proved once and for all I can become champion.* これは努力が報われた時だった．わたしは自分がチャンピオンになれることをちゃんと証明したのだ．

pay|check /peɪtʃek/ (**paychecks**) N-COUNT 可算名詞 Your **paycheck** is a piece of paper that your employer gives you as your wages or salary, and which you can then cash at a bank. You can also use **paycheck** as a way of referring to your wages or salary. 給料支払い小切手，給料 □ *I just get a small paycheck every month.* わたしは毎月わずかな給料をもらうだけだ． □ *He says his expenses are rising faster than his paycheck.* 彼は給料よりも出費の方がどんどん増えていると言う．

pay|day /peɪdeɪ/ (**paydays**) N-UNCOUNT 不可算名詞 **Payday** is the day of the week or month on which you receive your wages or salary. 給料日 [also N in pl] □ *Until next payday, I was literally without any money.* 次の給料日まで，わたしは文字通り一文無しだった．

Word Link　　ee ≈ one who receives : employ**ee**, pay**ee**, refug**ee**

pay|ee /peɪiː/ (**payees**) N-COUNT 可算名詞 The **payee** of a check or similar document is the person who should receive the money. (小切手などの) 受取人 [FORMAL 形式ばった] □ *On the check, write the name of the payee and then sign your name.* チェックには受取人の名前を書いて，あなたの名前をサインして下さい．

pay en|velope (**pay envelopes**) N-COUNT 可算名詞 Your **pay envelope** is the envelope containing your wages that your employer gives you. 給料袋 [AM 米国英語]

pay|er /peɪər/ (**payers**) **①** N-COUNT 可算名詞 You can refer to someone as a **payer** if they pay a particular kind of bill or fee. For example, a mortgage **payer** is someone who pays a mortgage. 支払人 □ *Lower interest rates pleased millions of mortgage payers.* 住宅ローンを払っている何百万人もの人が低利子率に満足した． **②** → see also **taxpayer** **③** N-COUNT 可算名詞 A **good payer** pays you quickly or pays you a lot of money. A **bad payer** takes a long time to pay you, or does not pay you very much. 金払いのよい (悪い) 人 □ *Small businesses, hit hard by the recession, blame the government, banks, and late payers.* 不況の大打撃を受けた中小企業は，政府や銀行また支払いの遅い人たちを責めている．

pay|ment /peɪmənt/ (**payments**) **①** N-COUNT 可算名詞 A **payment** is an amount of money that is paid to someone, or the act of paying this money. 支払い金額，支払い □ *Thousands of its customers are behind with loans and mortgage payments.* 何千人もの顧客が借金や住宅ローンの支払いを滞らせている． **②** N-UNCOUNT 不可算名詞 **Payment** is the act of paying money to someone or of being paid. 支払い (払う側，受け取る側の両方に使う) □ *He had sought to obtain payment of a sum which he had claimed was owed to him.* 彼は支払われるべきと主張する金額の支払いを要求した． **③** → see also **balance of payments, down payment**

pay|off /peɪɔf/ (payoffs) also **pay-off** ■ N-COUNT 可算名詞 The **payoff from** an action is the advantage or benefit that you get from it. (行為の) 報い 利益 □ If such materials became generally available to the optics industry the payoffs from such a breakthrough would be enormous. もしそのような素材が光学工業界で一般的に利用できるようになると、その発明による利益は莫大なものとなるだろう. ■ N-COUNT 可算名詞 A **payoff** is a payment made to someone, often secretly or illegally, so that they will not cause trouble. 報酬, わいろ □ Soldiers in both countries supplement their incomes with payoffs from drugs exporters. どちらの国の兵士も麻薬の密輸業者からのわいろで収入を補っている. ■ N-COUNT 可算名詞 A **payoff** is a large payment made to someone by their employer when the person has been forced to leave their job. 解雇時の退職金 □ The ousted chairman received a $1.5 million payoff from the loss-making oil company. 解雇された会長は採算の取れない石油会社から150万ドルの退職金を受け取った.

pay|out /peɪaʊt/ (payouts) N-COUNT 可算名詞 A **payout** is a sum of money, especially a large one, that is paid to someone, for example, by an insurance company or as a prize. (特に巨額の) 支払い □ ...long delays in receiving insurance payouts. 保険の支払いを受け取るまでの長い遅延
→ see **lottery**

pay pack|et (pay packets) ■ N-COUNT 可算名詞 Your **pay packet** is the envelope containing your wages that your employer gives you at the end of every week. 給料袋 [BRIT 英国英語; AM **pay envelope** 米国英語 **pay envelope**] ■ N-COUNT 可算名詞 You can refer to someone's wages or salary as their **pay packet**. 給料 [BRIT 英国英語; AM **paycheck, pay** 米国英語 **paycheck, pay**]

pay-per-view N-UNCOUNT 不可算名詞 **Pay-per-view** is a cable or satellite television service in which you pay a fee to watch a particular program. The abbreviation **PPV** is also used. ペイ・パー・ビュー方式 (有料テレビを見た本数だけ支払う方式) □ The match appeared on pay-per-view television. 有料テレビでその試合が放送された.

pay|phone /peɪfoʊn/ (payphones) also **pay phone** N-COUNT 可算名詞 A **payphone** is a telephone that you put coins or a card into before you can make a call. Payphones are usually in public places. 公衆電話

pay|roll /peɪroʊl/ (payrolls) N-COUNT 可算名詞 The people on the **payroll** of a company or an organization are the people who work for it and are paid by it. 給料支払い名簿, 従業員名簿 [BUSINESS 実業] □ They had 87,000 employees on the payroll. 彼らの従業員名簿には8万7千人の従業員が載っていた.

pay|slip /peɪslɪp/ (payslips) also **pay slip** N-COUNT 可算名詞 A **payslip** is the same as a **paystub**. 給料明細 [BRIT 英国英語]

pay|stub /peɪstʌb/ (paystubs) also **pay stub** N-COUNT 可算名詞 A **paystub** is a piece of paper given to an employee when he or she is paid stating how much money has been earned and how much has been taken from that sum for things such as tax. 給与明細票 [AM 米国英語]

PC /piː siː/ (PCs) ■ N-COUNT 可算名詞 A **PC** is a computer that is used by one person at a time in a business, a school, or at home. **PC** is an abbreviation for **personal computer**. の略語、パーソナルコンピュータ □ The price of a PC has fallen by an average of 25% a year since 1982. コンピュータ価格は1982年から平均で1年に25パーセント下がっている. ■ ADJ 形容詞 If you say that someone is **PC**, you mean that they are extremely careful not to offend or upset any group of people in society who have a disadvantage. **PC** is an abbreviation for **politically correct**. 道徳的に正しい, 政治的に正しい (偏見や差別の含まれていない表現に対して使う) □ Certainly, when you're with a group of guys and you're talking about women, you're not PC. 確かに、男のグループといる時に女の話をするのは「政治的に正しくない」ね.

pd. pd. is a written abbreviation for **paid**. It is written on a bill to indicate that it has been paid. paidの略語、領収済み

PDA /piː diː eɪ/ (PDAs) N-COUNT 可算名詞 A **PDA** is a handheld computer, used mainly for storing and accessing personal information such as addresses, telephone numbers, and memos. **PDA** is an abbreviation for **personal digital assistant**. personal digital assistantの略語、電子手帳 □ A typical PDA can function as a cellphone and a personal organizer. 典型的な電子手帳は携帯電話とシステム手帳の機能を果たせる.

pea /piː/ (peas) N-COUNT 可算名詞 **Peas** are round green seeds that grow in long thin cases and are eaten as a vegetable. エンドウ豆

peace /piːs/ ■ N-UNCOUNT 不可算名詞 If countries or groups involved in a war or violent conflict are discussing **peace**, they are talking to each other in order to try to end the conflict. 和平, 和解 □ Peace talks involving other rebel leaders and government representatives broke up without agreement last week, but are due to resume shortly. 先週、他の反体制グループの指導者と政府代表との和平交渉は同意にいたらず解散したが、間もなく再開される予定である. □ Leaders of some rival factions signed a peace agreement last week. いくつかの対抗派閥の指導者は先週、平和協定に署名した. ■ N-UNCOUNT 不可算名詞 If there is **peace** in a country or in the world, there are no wars or violent conflicts going on. 平和 □ The president spoke of a shared commitment to world peace and economic development. 大統領は世界平和と経済開発に対する共有の公約について語った. ■ N-UNCOUNT 不可算名詞 If you disapprove of weapons, especially nuclear weapons, you can use **peace** to refer to campaigns and other activities intended to reduce their numbers or stop their use. 反核兵器 □ ...two peace campaigners accused of causing damage to an F1-11 nuclear bomber. 核爆撃機F1-11に被害を与えたとして訴えられた2人の反核活動家 ■ N-UNCOUNT 不可算名詞 If you have **peace**, you are not being disturbed, and you are in calm, quiet surroundings. 平穏, 平静さ □ All I want is to have some peace and quiet and spend a couple of nice days with my grandchildren. わたしが望むのは、落ち着きと静けさ、そして孫たちと2日間楽しい日々を過ごすことだけだ. ■ N-UNCOUNT 不可算名詞 If you have a feeling of **peace**, you feel contented and calm and not at all worried. You can also say that you are **at peace**. 心の平安 □ I had a wonderful feeling of peace and serenity when I saw my husband. わたしは夫に会った時、すばらしい心の平安と平穏さを感じた. ■ N-UNCOUNT 不可算名詞 If there is **peace** among a group of people, they live or work together in a friendly way and do not argue. You can also say that people live or work **in peace with** each other. 仲むつまじさ, 協調 □ ...a period of relative peace in the country's industrial relations. その国の労使関係における相互協調の時期 ■ PHRASE 句 If someone in authority, such as the army or the police, **keeps the peace**, they make sure that people behave and do not fight or quarrel with each other. 治安を維持する □ ...the first U.N. contingent assigned to help keep the peace in Cambodia. カンボジアの治安維持を支援する任務を受けた国連の第一派遣団 ■ PHRASE 句 If something gives you **peace of mind**, it stops you from worrying about a particular problem or difficulty. 心の平静さ □ The main appeal these bonds hold for individual investors is the safety and peace of mind they offer. 個人投資家にとってのこの公債の主な魅力は安全性と安心感だ.

peace|ful /piːsfʊl/ ■ ADJ 形容詞 **Peaceful** activities and situations do not involve war. 平和な □ He has attempted to find a peaceful solution to the Ossetian conflict. 彼はオセチア紛争の平和的解決策を見つけようとした. ● **peace|ful|ly** ADV 副詞 [ADV with v] 平和的に □ The U.S. military expects the matter to be resolved peacefully. 米軍はその事態が平和的に解決されることを期待している. ■ ADJ 形容詞 **Peaceful** occasions happen without violence or serious disorder. 平穏な □ The farmers staged a noisy but peaceful protest outside the headquarters of the organization. 農民たちは組織の本社の外で騒々しいが非暴力的な抗議を行った. ● **peace|ful|ly** ADV 副詞 [ADV with v] 平穏に □ The governor asked the crowd of protestors to leave peacefully. 知事は群がった抗議者に穏やかに立ち去るよう求めた. ■ ADJ 形容詞 **Peaceful** people are not violent and try to avoid arguing or fighting with other people. 平和を好む、おとなしい □ ...warriors who killed or enslaved the peaceful farmers. 平和を好む農民たちを殺害したり、奴隷にした戦士たち ● **peace|ful|ly** ADV 副詞 [ADV with v] 平和に □ They've been living and working peacefully with members of various ethnic groups. 彼らはさまざまな人種グループの仲間と円満に生活し、働いている. ■ ADJ 形容詞 A **peaceful** place or time is quiet, calm, and free from disturbance. 静かな □ ...a peaceful house in the heart of the Ozarks. オザークの中心にある静かな家 ● **peace|ful|ly** ADV 副詞 [ADV after v] 静かに □ Except for traffic noise the night passed peacefully. 交通の騒音を除けば、その夜は静かに過ぎて行った.

peace|ful|ly /piːsfəli/ ■ ADV 副詞 If you say that someone died **peacefully**, you mean that they suffered no pain or violence when they died. 安らかに [ADV after v] □ He died peacefully on December 10 after a short illness. 彼は短い間いった後、12月10日に安らかに亡くなった. ■ → see also **peaceful**

peach /piːtʃ/ (peaches) ■ N-COUNT 可算名詞 A **peach** is a soft, round, slightly furry fruit with sweet yellow flesh and pinky-orange skin. Peaches grow in warm countries. 桃 ■ COLOR 色彩語 Something that is **peach** is pale pinky-orange in color. 桃色 □ ...a peach silk blouse. 桃色の絹のブラウス

P

Word Web peanut

The **peanut** is not actually a **nut**. It is a legume and grows under the ground. Peanuts originated in South America about 3,500 years ago. Explorers took them to Africa. Later, African slaves introduced the peanut into North America. At first only poor people ate them. However, by 1900 they had become a popular **snack**. You could buy **roasted** peanuts on city streets and at baseball games and circuses. Some scientists believe that roasted peanuts cause more **allergic** reactions than boiled peanuts. George Washington Carver, an African-American scientist, found 325 different uses for peanuts—including **peanut butter**.

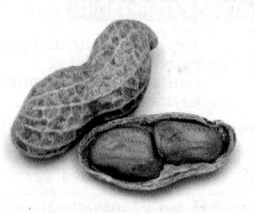

peak /pik/ (peaks, peaking, peaked) **1** N-COUNT 可算名詞 The **peak** of a process or an activity is the point at which it is at its strongest, most successful, or most fully developed. 頂点，最高潮 ❑ The firm has slashed its workforce from a peak of 150,000 in 2000. 企業は従業員総数を2000年の最盛期の15万人から大幅に削減した。 ❑ ...a flourishing career that was at its peak at the time of his death. 彼が亡くなる時に最盛期を迎えていた輝かしいキャリア **2** V-I 自動詞 When something **peaks**, it reaches its highest value or its highest level. 頂点に達する ❑ Temperatures have peaked at over 90 degrees. 気温は90度を越える最高点に達した。 **3** ADJ 形容詞 The **peak** level or value of something is its highest level or value. 最高の [ADJ n] ❑ Today's price is 59% lower than the peak level of $1.5 million. 今日の相場は150万ドルの最高水準より59パーセント低い。 **4** ADJ 形容詞 **Peak** times are the times when there is most demand for something or most use of something. ピークの [ADJ n] ❑ It's always crowded at peak times. そこはピーク時にはいつも混んでいる。 **5** N-COUNT 可算名詞 A **peak** is a mountain or the top of a mountain. 山，山頂 ❑ ...the snow-covered peaks. 雪に覆われた峰々
→ see **mountain**

peal /pil/ (peals, pealing, pealed) **1** V-I 自動詞 When bells **peal**, they ring one after another, making a musical sound. （鐘が）鳴り響く ❑ Church bells pealed at the stroke of midnight. 午前零時ちょうどに教会の鐘が鳴り響いた。 ● N-COUNT 可算名詞 **Peal** is also a noun. 鐘の音 ❑ ...the great peal of the abbey bells. 大修道院のすばらしい鐘の音 **2** N-COUNT 可算名詞 A **peal of** laughter or thunder consists of a long, loud series of sounds. （笑い声や雷の）とどろき ❑ I heard a peal of laughter. 笑い声がとどろきわたるのが聞こえた。

pea|nut /pinʌt, -nət/ (peanuts) N-COUNT 可算名詞 **Peanuts** are small nuts that grow under the ground. Peanuts are often eaten as a snack, especially roasted and salted, and their oil is used in cooking. ピーナツ，落花生 ❑ ...a packet of peanuts. ピーナツ1袋
→ see Word Web: **peanut**

In the early 20th century, African-American scientist George Washington Carver ground **peanuts** into a smooth paste. This food, called **peanut butter**, is used to make sandwiches. Peanut butter and jelly sandwiches are a popular food with American children.

pear /pɛər/ (pears) N-COUNT 可算名詞 A **pear** is a sweet, juicy fruit that is narrow near its stalk, and wider and rounded at the bottom. Pears have white flesh and thin green, yellow, or brown skin. なし

pearl /pɜrl/ (pearls) **1** N-COUNT 可算名詞 A **pearl** is a hard round object that is shiny and creamy white in color. Pearls grow inside the shell of an oyster and are used for making expensive jewelry. 真珠 ❑ She wore a string of pearls at her throat. 彼女は首に真珠のネックレスをつけた。 **2** ADJ 形容詞 **Pearl** is used to describe something that looks like a pearl. 真珠のような ❑ ...tiny pearl buttons. 小さな真珠のようなボタン

peas|ant /pɛzᵊnt/ (peasants) N-COUNT 可算名詞 A **peasant** is a poor person of low social status who works on the land; used to refer to people who live in countries where farming is still a common way of life. 小作人（発展途上国の小作農に対して用いられる） ❑ ...the peasants in the Peruvian highlands. ペルーの山岳地方の小作農たち

peat /pit/ N-UNCOUNT 不可算名詞 **Peat** is decaying plant material that is found under the ground in some cool, wet regions. Peat can be added to soil to help plants grow, or can be burned to produce coal. 泥炭，（燃料用の）ピート ❑ ...a peat fire. 泥炭火災
→ see **wetland**

peb|ble /pɛbᵊl/ (pebbles) N-COUNT 可算名詞 A **pebble** is a small, smooth, round stone which is found on beaches and at the bottom of rivers. 小石（海岸や川底にある小さくて丸いもの）
→ see **beach**

peck /pɛk/ (pecks, pecking, pecked) **1** V-T/V-I 他動詞/自動詞 If a bird **pecks at** something or **pecks** something, it moves its beak forward quickly and bites at it. （くちばしで）つつく ❑ It was winter and the sparrows were pecking at whatever they could find. 冬だった

ので，スズメは見つけられるものすべてをつついていた。 ❑ Chickens pecked in the dust. 鶏がほこりの中をつついた。 ❑ It pecked his leg. それが彼の足をついた。 **2** V-T 他動詞 If you **peck** someone **on the** cheek, you give them a quick, light kiss. （ほおに）軽くキスをする ❑ Elizabeth walked up to him and pecked him on the cheek. エリザベスは彼に歩み寄り，ほおに軽くキスをした。 ● N-COUNT 可算名詞 **Peck** is also a noun. 軽いキス ❑ He gave me a little peck on the cheek. 彼はわたしのほおに軽くキスをした。

pe|cu|liar /pɪkyulyər/ **1** ADJ 形容詞 If you describe someone or something as **peculiar**, you think that they are strange or unusual, sometimes in an unpleasant way. 一風変わった ❑ Mr. Kennet has a rather peculiar sense of humor. ケネット氏のユーモアのセンスはかなり変わっている。 ● pe|cu|liar|ly ADV 副詞 変に ❑ His face had become peculiarly expressionless. 彼の顔は妙に無表情になった。 **2** ADJ 形容詞 If something is **peculiar to** a particular thing, person, or situation, it belongs or relates only to that thing, person, or situation. 特有の，独特の ❑ Punks, soldiers, hippies, and Sumo wrestlers all have distinct hair styles, peculiar to their group. パンク，兵士，ヒッピー，相撲の力士はみな特有の目立つ髪形をしている。 ● pe|cu|liar|ly ADV 副詞 特有に，独特に ❑ ...a peculiarly American conservatism. アメリカ人特有の保守主義

pe|cu|li|ar|ity /pɪkyuliæriti/ (peculiarities) **1** N-COUNT 可算名詞 A **peculiarity** that someone or something has is a strange or unusual characteristic or habit. 風変わりな人，変わっている点 ❑ Joe's other peculiarity was that he was constantly munching hard candy. ジョーのもう1つの変わっているところは，かれがいつも固いキャンディーをかんでいることだった。 **2** N-COUNT 可算名詞 A **peculiarity** is a characteristic or quality that belongs or relates only to one person or thing. 特性，特色 ❑ ...a strange peculiarity of the U.S. system. 米国の制度の奇妙な特色

pe|cu|ni|ary /pɪkyunieri/ ADJ 形容詞 **Pecuniary** means concerning or involving money. 金銭上の [FORMAL 形式ばった] ❑ She denies obtaining a pecuniary advantage by deception. 彼女は詐欺によって金銭的利益を得たことを否定している。

Word Link ped ≈ child : pedagogical, pediatrician, pedophile

peda|gogi|cal /pɛdəgɒdʒɪkᵊl/ ADJ 形容詞 **Pedagogical** means concerning the methods and theory of teaching. 教育学の，教育的な [FORMAL 形式ばった] [ADJ n] ❑ The school district provides training to help teachers improve their pedagogical methods. その学区では教師が教授法を向上できるよう研修を行っている。

Word Link ped ≈ foot : pedal, pedestal, pedestrian

ped|al /pɛdᵊl/ (pedals, pedaling or pedalling, pedaled or pedalled) **1** N-COUNT 可算名詞 The **pedals** on a bicycle are the two parts that you push with your feet in order to make the bicycle move. （自転車の）ペダル **2** V-T/V-I 他動詞/自動詞 When you **pedal** a bicycle, you push the pedals around with your feet to make it move. ペダルを踏む ❑ She climbed on her bike with a feeling of pride and pedaled the five miles home. 彼女は誇らしそうに自転車に乗り，家まで5マイルをこいで帰った。 **3** N-COUNT 可算名詞 A **pedal** in a car or on a machine is a lever that you press with your foot in order to control the car or machine. （車や機械の）フットペダル ❑ ...the brake or accelerator pedals. ブレーキまたはアクセルのペダル
→ see **bicycle**

pe|dan|tic /pɪdæntɪk/ ADJ 形容詞 If you say someone is **pedantic**, you mean that they are too concerned with unimportant details or traditional rules, especially in connection with academic subjects. 学者ぶった，しゃくし定規な [DISAPPROVAL 不賛成] ❑ His lecture was so pedantic and uninteresting. 彼の講義はとても学者ぶったもので面白くなかった。

ped|dle /pɛdᵊl/ (peddles, peddling, peddled) **1** V-T 他動詞 Someone who **peddles** things goes from place to place trying to sell them. 売り歩く ❑ His attempts to peddle his paintings around Laramie's tiny gallery scene proved unsuccessful. ララミーの狭いギャラリー界隈で自分の絵を売り歩こうという彼の試みは不成功に終わった。 **2** V-T 他動詞 Someone who **peddles** drugs sells illegal drugs. （麻薬を）密売する ❑ When a drug pusher offered the Los Angeles youngster $100 to peddle drugs, Jack refused. 麻薬の密売人がロサンゼ

P

ルスの若者に麻薬を売るよう100ドルを差し出した時，ジャックは拒否した．●**peddling** N-UNCOUNT 不可算名詞 密売 ❏ *The war against drug peddling is all about cash.* 麻薬の密売に対する戦いはすべて金次第だ．■ V-T 他動詞 If someone **peddles** an idea or a piece of information, they try to get people to accept it. (間違った考えなどを) 広める [DISAPPROVAL 不賛成] ❏ *They even set up their own news agency to peddle anti-isolationist propaganda.* 彼らは反孤立主義者の宣伝を広めるために独自の報道機関さえ設立した．

ped|es|tal /pɛdɪstᵊl/ (**pedestals**) ■ N-COUNT 可算名詞 A **pedestal** is the base on which something such as a statue stands. (彫刻などの) 台座 ❏ *...a larger than life-sized bronze statue on a granite pedestal.* 御影石の台座に乗せられた実物より大きいブロンズ像 ☑ N-COUNT 可算名詞 If you put someone **on a pedestal**, you admire them very much and think that they cannot be criticized. If someone is knocked **off a pedestal** they are no longer admired. 崇拝の的 ❏ *Since childhood, I put my own parents on a pedestal. I felt they could do no wrong.* 子供の頃からわたしは両親を崇拝していた．彼らは間違いを犯すことなどないと思った．

pe|des|trian /pɪdɛstriən/ (**pedestrians**) ■ N-COUNT 可算名詞 A **pedestrian** is a person who is walking, especially in a town or city, rather than traveling in a vehicle. 歩行者 ❏ *Ingrid was a walker, even in Los Angeles, where a pedestrian is a rare sight.* イングリッドは歩行者がめったに見られないロサンゼルスでさえ歩いていた．☑ ADJ 形容詞 If you describe something as **pedestrian**, you mean that it is ordinary and not at all interesting. ありふれた，平凡な [DISAPPROVAL 不賛成] ❏ *His style is so pedestrian that the book becomes a real bore.* 彼のスタイルは本当にありきたりなので，その本は本当につまらないものとなっている．

pe|dia|tri|cian /pidiətrɪʃᵊn/ (**pediatricians**) N-COUNT 可算名詞 A **pediatrician** is a doctor who specializes in treating children. 小児科医

pe|di|at|rics /pidiætrɪks/

The form **pediatric** is used as a modifier.

pediatric 形は修飾語として使われる．

N-UNCOUNT 不可算名詞 **Pediatrics** is the area of medicine that is concerned with the treatment of children. 小児科 ❏ *...a career in pediatrics.* 小児科での職務
→ see **hospital**

pedi|gree /pɛdɪgri/ (**pedigrees**) ■ N-COUNT 可算名詞 If a dog, cat, or other animal has a **pedigree**, its ancestors are known and recorded. An animal is considered to have a good pedigree when all its known ancestors are of the same type. (動物の) 血統書 ❏ *60 percent of dogs and ten percent of cats have pedigrees.* 60パーセントの犬と10パーセントの猫が血統書付きだ．☑ N-COUNT 可算名詞 Someone's **pedigree** is their background or their ancestors. 素性，家系 ❏ *Hammer's business pedigree almost guaranteed him the acquaintance of presidents.* ハマーの事業経歴なら社長方と知り合いになれることはほぼ約束されていた．

pe|do|phile /pidəfaɪl/ (**pedophiles**) N-COUNT 可算名詞 A **pedophile** is a person, usually a man, who is sexually attracted to children. 小児性愛者

pe|do|phil|ia /pidəfɪliə/ N-UNCOUNT 不可算名詞 **Pedophilia** is sexual activity with children or the condition of being sexually attracted to children. 小児性愛，ペドフィリア ❏ *...allegations of his pedophilia.* 彼の小児性愛疑惑 ❏ *He addressed the clinical aspects of pedophilia and abuse.* 彼は小児性愛と虐待に関する臨床的側面を取り上げた．

peek /pik/ (**peeks, peeking, peeked**) V-I 自動詞 If you **peek at** something or someone, you take a quick look at them, often secretly. ちらっとのぞく，かいま見る ❏ *On two occasions she had peeked at him through a crack in the wall.* 2度ほど彼女は壁の隙間から彼をかいま見た．●N-COUNT 可算名詞 **Peek** is also a noun. のぞき見 ❏ *Companies have been paying outrageous fees for a peek at the technical data.* 企業はその技術データをかいま見るためにとてつもない料金を支払っている．

peel /pil/ (**peels, peeling, peeled**) ■ N-VAR 可変性名詞 The **peel** of a fruit such as a lemon or an apple is its skin. You can also refer to a **peel**. (果物の) 皮 ❏ *...grated lemon peel.* おろしたレモンの皮 ❏ *...a banana peel.* バナナの皮 ☑ V-T 他動詞 When you **peel** fruit or vegetables, you remove their skins. 皮をむく ❏ *She sat down in the kitchen and began peeling potatoes.* 彼女は台所に座ってジャガイモの皮をむき始めた．■ V-T/V-I 他動詞/自動詞 If you **peel off** something

---

that has been sticking to a surface or if it **peels off**, it comes away from the surface. (くっついていたものを) はがす [他動詞]，はがれる [自動詞] ❏ *One of the kids was peeling plaster off the wall.* 子供たちの1人が壁のしっくいをはがしていた．❏ *It took me two days to peel off the labels.* ラベルをはがすのに2日かかった．❏ *Paint was peeling off the walls.* ペンキが壁からはがれかけていた．☑ V-I 自動詞 If a surface **is peeling**, the paint on it is coming away. (表面の塗料が) 落ちる [usu cont] ❏ *Its once-elegant white pillars are peeling.* かつて優美だったその白い柱は色がはげかけている．■ V-I 自動詞 If you **are peeling** or if your skin **is peeling**, small pieces of skin are coming off, usually because you have been burned by the sun. (皮が) むける [usu cont] ❏ *His face was peeling from sunburn.* 彼の顔は日焼けで皮がむけかけていた．
→ see **cut**

peep /pip/ (**peeps, peeping, peeped**) ■ V-I 自動詞 If you **peep**, or **peep at** something, you take a quick look at it, often secretly and quietly. のぞき見する，かいま見る ❏ *Children came to peep at him around the doorway.* 子供たちが彼を入口のまわりからやって来た．●N-SING 単数名詞 **Peep** is also a noun. のぞき見 ["a" N] ❏ *"Fourteen minutes," Chris said, taking a peep at his watch.* 「14分」とクリスはちらっと時計に目をやりながら言った．☑ V-I 自動詞 If something **peeps** out from behind or under something, a small part of it is visible or becomes visible. (体の一部などが) かいま見える 姿を現す ❏ *Purple and yellow flowers peeped up between rocks.* 岩の間から紫と黄色の花が顔を出していた．■ PHRASE 句 If you say that you **don't hear a peep from** someone, you mean that they do not say anything or make any noise. 何の連絡もない，物音も立てない [INFORMAL くだけた] ❏ *You don't hear a peep from her once she's gone to bed.* いったん彼女が布団に入ったら，コトッとも物音がしない．

peer /pɪər/ (**peers, peering, peered**) ■ V-I 自動詞 If you **peer at** something, you look at it very hard, usually because it is difficult to see clearly. じっと見詰める，目を凝らして見る ❏ *I had been peering at a computer print-out that made no sense at all.* わたしは全く意味を成さないコンピュータの印刷を凝視していた．☑ N-COUNT 可算名詞 Your **peers** are the people who are the same age as you or who have the same status as you. 同輩，仲間 ❏ *His engaging personality made him popular with his peers.* 人を引き付ける性格のおかげで彼は友達に人気があった．

peg /pɛg/ (**pegs, pegging, pegged**) ■ N-COUNT 可算名詞 A **peg** is a small piece of wood or metal that is used for fastening something to something else. くぎ，くい ❏ *He builds furniture using wooden pegs instead of nails.* 彼はくぎの代わりに木のくいを使って家具を作る．☑ N-COUNT 可算名詞 A **peg** is a small hook or knob that is attached to a wall or door and is used for hanging things on. (コートなどをかける) フック ❏ *His work jacket hung on the peg in the kitchen.* 彼の作業着が台所のフックにかかっていた．■ N-COUNT 可算名詞 A **peg** is a small device that you use to fasten clothes to a clothes line. 洗濯ばさみ [mainly BRIT 主に英国英語; AM usually **clothespin** 米国英語では通常 **clothespin**] ◗ V-T 他動詞 If you **peg** something somewhere or **peg** it **down**, you fix it there with pegs. くぎ (くい) で固定する ❏ *Peg down netting over the top to keep out leaves.* 落ち葉が入らないようにくぎで上から網を固定する．❏ *...a tent pegged to the ground nearby for the kids.* 子供たちのために近くの地面にくいで固定したテント ◗ V-T 他動詞 If a price or amount of something **is pegged at** a particular level, it is fixed at that level. (価格や数値を) 固定する ❏ *Its currency is pegged to the dollar.* 通貨はドルに決められている．❏ *The Bank wants to peg rates at 9%.* 銀行は利率を9パーセントに固定したがっている．

pel|let /pɛlɪt/ (**pellets**) N-COUNT 可算名詞 A **pellet** is a small ball of paper, mud, lead, or other material. 小粒，丸薬 (小さな球状のもの) を指す) ❏ *He was shot in the head by an air gun pellet.* 彼は空気銃のペレットで頭を撃たれた．

pelt /pɛlt/ (**pelts, pelting, pelted**) ■ N-COUNT 可算名詞 The **pelt** of an animal is its skin, which can be used to make clothing or rugs. (服飾または装飾用の) 動物の皮 ❏ *...a bed covered with beaver pelts.* ビーバーの皮で覆われたベッド ☑ V-T 他動詞 If you **pelt** someone **with** things, you throw things at them. (人に〜を) 投げつける ❏ *Some of the younger men began to pelt one another with snowballs.* 年下の男たちの何人かが雪合戦を始めた．■ V-I 自動詞 If the rain **is pelting down**, it is raining very hard. (雨が) 激しく降る [INFORMAL くだけた] [usu cont] ❏ *The rain now was pelting down.* 雨はいまやどしゃ降りになっていた．

pel|vic /pɛlvɪk/ ADJ 形容詞 **Pelvic** means near or relating to your pelvis. 骨盤の [ADJ n] ❏ *...an inflammation of the pelvic region.* 骨盤部の炎症

pel|vis /pɛlvɪs/ (**pelvises**) N-COUNT 可算名詞 Your **pelvis** is the wide, curved group of bones at the level of your hips. 骨盤

pen /pɛn/ (**pens, penning, penned**) ■ N-COUNT 可算名詞 A **pen** is a long thin object which you use to write in ink. ペン (ボールペン，万年筆等の書くものを指す) ☑ felt-tip pen → see **felt-tip** ■ V-T 他動詞 If someone **pens** a letter, article, or book, they write it. (手紙などを) 書く [FORMAL 形式ばった] ❏ *I really intended to pen*

this letter to you early this morning. わたしは本当は今朝早くにこの手紙をあなたに書くつもりだった。 **4** N-COUNT 可算名詞 A **pen** is also a small area with a fence around it in which farm animals are kept for a short time. （家畜を入れておく）小さなおり **a** *...a holding pen for sheep.* 羊を拘束しておくおり **5** V-T 他動詞 If people or animals **are penned** somewhere or **are penned up**, they are forced to remain in a very small area. 閉じ込める，監禁する [usu passive] **a** *The cattle were penned for the night.* その牛は一晩，狭いおりに入れられた。 **a** *The animals were penned up in cages.* 動物たちはかごに閉じ込められた。
→ see **drawing, office**

Thesaurus	*pen* また次を参照：
N.	cage, coop, corral, enclosure, fence **3**
V.	cage, enclose, shut in **4**

pe|nal /piːnəl/ ADJ 形容詞 **Penal** means relating to the punishment of criminals. 刑罰の **a** *...penal and legal systems.* 刑法制度と法体制

pe|nal|ize /piːnəlaɪz/ (penalizes, penalizing, penalized) V-T 他動詞 If a person or group **is penalized** for something, they are made to suffer in some way because of it. 罰する [usu passive] **a** *Some of the players may, on occasion, break the rules and be penalized.* 選手の何人かは時々，反則をしてペナルティーを科されるかもしれない。

pen|al|ty /penəlti/ (penalties) **1** N-COUNT 可算名詞 A **penalty** is a punishment that someone is given for doing something which is against a law or rule. 刑罰 **a** *One of those arrested could face the death penalty.* 逮捕されたうちの1人は死刑になるかもしれない。 **2** N-COUNT 可算名詞 In sports such as soccer, football, and hockey, a **penalty** is a disadvantage forced on the team that breaks a rule. 罰（スポーツの反則に対する）ペナルティ **a** *Referee Michael Reed had no hesitation in awarding a penalty.* マイケル・リード審判員はペナルティーを科すのに何のためらいもなかった。 **3** N-COUNT 可算名詞 The **penalty** that you pay for something you have done is something unpleasant that you experience as a result. （自分の行い に対する不快な）報い **a** *Why should I pay the penalty for somebody else's mistake?* 他人の過ちなのに，どうしてわたしが報いを受けないといけないのか？

pence /pens/ N-PLURAL 複数名詞 **Pence** is the plural form of penny, a British coin worth one hundredth of a pound. ペンス（pennyの複数形．イギリスの硬貨） **a** *Matches cost only a few pence.* 試合にはわずか数ペンスしかかからなかった。

pen|chant /pentʃɒnt/ N-SING 単数名詞 If someone has a **penchant for** something, they have a special liking for it or a tendency to do it. 好み，傾向 [FORMAL 形式ばった] **a** *...a stylish woman with a penchant for dark glasses.* サングラスが好きなおしゃれな女性

pen|cil /pensəl/ (pencils) N-COUNT 可算名詞 A **pencil** is an object that you write or draw with. It consists of a thin piece of wood with a rod of a black or colored substance through the middle. If you write or draw something **in pencil**, you do it using a pencil. 鉛筆 [also "in" N] **a** *I found a pencil and some blank paper in her desk.* 彼女の机の中に鉛筆1本と何も書いていない紙を見つけた。
→ see **drawing, office**

Word Link	*pend = hanging : appendix, depend, pendant*

pen|dant /pendənt/ (pendants) N-COUNT 可算名詞 A **pendant** is an ornament on a chain that you wear around your neck. ペンダント
→ see **jewelry**

pend|ing /pendɪŋ/ **1** ADJ 形容詞 If something such as a legal procedure is **pending**, it is waiting to be dealt with or settled. 未解決の，審理中の [FORMAL 形式ばった] **a** *She had a libel action against the magazine pending.* 彼女のその雑誌に対する名誉毀損の訴訟は審理中だった。 **a** *In 2006, the court had 600 pending cases.* 2006年に，その裁判所では未解決の訴訟が600件あった。 **2** PREP 前置詞 If something is done **pending** a future event, it is done until that event happens. ～まで [FORMAL 形式ばった] **a** *A judge has suspended the ban pending a full inquiry.* 裁判官はすべての取り調べが終わるまでその禁止令を保留にした。 **3** ADJ 形容詞 Something that is **pending** is going to happen soon. （事が）起ころうとしている [FORMAL 形式ばった] **a** *A growing number of customers have been inquiring about the pending price rises.* ますます多くの顧客が差し迫った値上げに関する問い合わせをしている。

pen|du|lum /pendʒələm/ (pendulums) **1** N-COUNT 可算名詞 The **pendulum** of a clock is a rod with a weight at the end which swings from side to side in order to make the clock work. （時計の）振り子 **2** N-SING 単数名詞 You can use the idea of a **pendulum** and the way it swings regularly as a way of talking about regular changes in a situation or in people's opinions. 趨（すう）勢 定期的に意見が変わる人 **a** *The political pendulum has swung in favor of the liberals.* 政治のなりゆきは自由党に有利に動いた。

pen|etrate /penɪtreɪt/ (penetrates, penetrating, penetrated) **1** V-T 他動詞 If something or someone **penetrates** a physical object or an area, they succeed in getting into it or passing through it. 突き抜ける，貫通する **a** *X-rays can penetrate many objects.* X線はたくさんの物体を通り抜けられる。 ● **pen|etra|tion** /penɪtreɪʃən/ N-UNCOUNT 不可算名詞 [also N in pl] 貫通 **a** *The thick walls prevented penetration by debris from the hurricane.* 厚い壁はハリケーンによる残骸が貫通するのを防いだ。 **2** V-T 他動詞 If someone **penetrates** an organization, a group, or a profession, they succeed in entering it although it is difficult to do so. （組織や職業に）入り込む **a** *...the continuing failure of women to penetrate the higher levels of engineering.* 女性が技術者のより高い地位にずっと進出できないでいること **3** V-T 他動詞 If someone **penetrates** an enemy group or a rival organization, they succeed in joining it in order to get information or cause trouble. （敵などの中に）潜入する 進入する **a** *The CIA had requested our help to penetrate a drug ring operating out of Munich.* CIAはわたしたちにミュンヘン郊外で活動している麻薬組織に潜入するのを手伝うよう要請した。 ● **pen|etra|tion** N-UNCOUNT 不可算名詞 潜入 **a** *...the successful penetration by the KGB of the French intelligence service.* KGBによるフランスの諜報機関への潜入成功 **4** V-T 他動詞 If a company or country **penetrates** a market or area, they succeed in selling their products there. （市場などへ）参入する [BUSINESS 実業] **a** *There have been around 15 attempts from outside Idaho to penetrate the market.* アイダホ外部からその市場に参入しようとする試みが約15件あった。 ● **pen|etra|tion** N-UNCOUNT 不可算名詞 参入 **a** *...import penetration across a broad range of heavy industries.* 重工業の広範囲にわたる重要な市場獲得

pen|etrat|ing /penɪtreɪtɪŋ/ **1** ADJ 形容詞 A **penetrating** sound is loud and usually high-pitched. 突き刺すような，甲高い **a** *Mary heard the penetrating siren of an ambulance.* メアリーは救急車の甲高いサイレンを聞いた。 **2** ADJ 形容詞 If someone gives you a **penetrating** look, it makes you think that they know what you are thinking. 洞察力のある，鋭い **a** *He gazed at me with a sharp, penetrating look that made my heart pound.* 彼がとても鋭い視線でわたしを見つめたので，わたしの心臓はドキドキした。

pen|guin /pengwɪn/ (penguins) N-COUNT 可算名詞 A **penguin** is a type of large black and white sea bird found mainly in the Antarctic. Penguins cannot fly but use their short wings for swimming. ペンギン

peni|cil|lin /penɪsɪlɪn/ N-UNCOUNT 不可算名詞 **Penicillin** is a drug that kills bacteria and is used to treat infections. ペニシリン

Word Link	*insula = island : insular, insulate, peninsula*

pen|in|su|la /pənɪnsələ, -nɪnsyə-/ (peninsulas) N-COUNT 可算名詞 A **peninsula** is a long narrow piece of land that sticks out from a larger piece of land and is almost completely surrounded by water. 半島 **a** *...the political situation in the Korean peninsula.* 朝鮮半島の政治情勢

pe|nis /piːnɪs/ (penises) N-COUNT 可算名詞 A man's **penis** is the part of his body that he uses when he urinates and when he has sex. ペニス，陰茎

pen|ni|less /penɪlɪs/ ADJ 形容詞 Someone who is **penniless** is hardly any money at all. 一文無しの **a** *They'd soon be penniless and homeless if she couldn't find suitable work.* もし彼女がぴったりの仕事を見つけられなかったら，彼らはすぐに一文無しになる

pen|ny /peni/ (pennies, pence) **1** N-COUNT 可算名詞 A **penny** is one cent, or a coin worth one cent. 1ペニー（英国の硬貨で，米国の1セントまた感覚的には1円に相当） [AM 米国英語, INFORMAL くだけた] **a** *Unleaded gasoline rose more than a penny a gallon.* 無鉛ガソリンは1ガロン当たり1ペニー以上も値上がりした。 **2** N-SING 単数名詞 If you say, for example, that you do not have a **penny**, or that something does not cost a **penny**, you are emphasizing that you do not have any money at all, or that something did not cost you any money at all. 小銭，わずかな金 [EMPHASIS 強調] **a** *From the day you arrive at my house, you need not spend a single penny.* わたしの家に着いた日から，あなたは一銭もお金を出さなくていいのよ。

pen|ny stock N-PLURAL 複数名詞 A **penny stock** is a stock whose shares are offered for sale at a very low price. 低位株，ペニー一株 [BUSINESS 実業]

pen|sion /penʃən/ (pensions) N-COUNT 可算名詞 Someone who has a **pension** receives a regular sum of money from a former employer because they have retired or because they are widowed or disabled. 年金，恩給 **a** *...struggling by on a pension.* 年金でなんとか生きている

pen|sion|er /penʃənər/ (pensioners) N-COUNT 可算名詞 A **pensioner** is someone who receives a pension, especially a pension paid by the state to retired people. 年金受給者，年金生活者 [mainly BRIT 主に英国英語]

pen|sion plan (pension plans) N-COUNT 可算名詞 A **pension plan** is an arrangement to receive a pension from an organization such as an insurance company or a former employer in return for making regular payments to them over a number of years. 年金

計画 [BUSINESS 実業] ❏ *I would have been much wiser to start my own pension plan when I was younger.* もっと賢明に若い時から自分の年金計画を始めるべきだった.

Pen|ta|gon /pɛntəgɒn/ N-PROPER 固有名詞 **The Pentagon** is the main building of the U.S. Defense Department, in Washington DC. The U.S. Defense Department is often referred to as **the Pentagon.** ペンタゴン（米国国防総省の建物）米国国防総省 ❏ *...a news conference at the Pentagon.* ペンタゴンでの記者会見

pent|house /pɛnthaʊs/ (**penthouses**) N-COUNT 可算名詞 A **penthouse** or a **penthouse** apartment or suite is a luxurious apartment or set of rooms at the top of a tall building. ペントハウス（ビルの屋上にある高級住宅）ホテルの最上階の部屋 ❏ *...her swanky Manhattan penthouse.* マンハッタンにある彼女のしゃれたペントハウス

pent-up /pɛnt ʌp/ ADJ 形容詞 **Pent-up** emotions, energies, or forces have been held back and not expressed, used, or released. 抑えられた, 閉じ込められた ❏ *He still had a lot of pent-up anger to release.* 彼にはまだ発散させるべきうっせきした怒りがあった.

pe|nul|ti|mate /pɪnʌltɪmɪt/ ADJ 形容詞 The **penultimate** thing in a series of things is the second to the last. 最後から2番目の [FORMAL 形式ば・った] [det ADJ] ❏ *...on the penultimate day of the Asian Games.* アジア競技大会の最後から2日目

peo|ple /piːpəl/ (**peoples, peopling, peopled**) ■ N-PLURAL 複数名詞 **People** are men, women, and children. **People** is normally used as the plural of **person,** instead of "persons." 人々（person の複数形）❏ *Millions of people have lost their homes.* 何百万という人々が家を失った. ❏ *...the people of Angola.* アンゴラの人々 ❷ N-PLURAL 複数名詞 **The people** is sometimes used to refer to ordinary men and women, in contrast to the government or the military. 一般人, 民間人 ❏ *...the will of the people.* 民意 ❸ N-COUNT-COLL 集合可算名詞 A **people** is all the men, women, and children of a particular country or race. 国民, 民族 ❏ *...the native peoples of Central and South America.* 中央・南アメリカの先住民 ❹ V-T 他動詞 If a place or country **is peopled by** a particular group of people, that group of people live there. (場所に人を) 住まわせる [usu passive] ❏ *It was peopled by a fiercely independent race of peace-loving Buddhists.* そこには非常に独立した平和を愛する仏教徒の集団が住んでいた.

pep|per /pɛpər/ (**peppers, peppering, peppered**) ■ N-UNCOUNT 不可算名詞 **Pepper** or **black pepper** is a hot-tasting spice used to flavor food. こしょう ❏ *Season with salt and pepper.* 塩・こしょうで味を調える. ❷ N-COUNT 可算名詞 A **pepper,** or a **bell pepper,** is a hollow green, red, or yellow vegetable with seeds inside it. ピーマン ❏ *2 red or green peppers, sliced.* 薄切りにしたピーマンまたは赤ピーマン2個 ❸ V-T 他動詞 If something **is peppered with** small objects, a lot of those objects hit it. (小さな物体を) 浴びせる [usu passive] ❏ *He was wounded in both legs and severely peppered with shrapnel.* 彼は両足を負傷しており, 榴散 (りゅうさん) 弾を激しく浴びていた.

→ see spice

pepper|mint /pɛpərmɪnt/ (**peppermints**) ■ N-UNCOUNT 不可算名詞 **Peppermint** is a strong, sharp flavoring from the peppermint plant. ペパーミント ❷ N-COUNT 可算名詞 A **peppermint** is a peppermint-flavored piece of candy. ペパーミントのあめ, ペパーミント・キャンディー

pep talk (**pep talks**) also **pep-talk** N-COUNT 可算名詞 A **pep talk** is a speech intended to encourage someone to make more effort or feel more confident. 激励演説, 応援演説 [INFORMAL くだけた] ❏ *Powell and Cheney spent the day giving pep talks to the troops.* パウエルとチェイニーは軍隊に激励演説をしてその日を過ごした.

per /pər, STRONG pɜːr/ ■ PREP 前置詞 You use **per** to express rates and ratios. For example, if something costs $50 **per** year, you must pay $50 each year for it. If a vehicle is traveling at 40 miles **per** hour, it travels 40 miles each hour. 一につき, 一当たり [amount PREP n] ❏ *...$6 per week for lunch.* 週に6ドルの昼食代 ❷ PHRASE **as per** head → see head

per an|num /pər ænəm/ ADV 副詞 A particular amount **per annum** means that amount each year. 1年につき, 1年当たり [amount ADV] ❏ *...a fee of $35 per annum.* 年間35ドルの料金

per cap|i|ta /pər kæpɪtə/ ADJ 形容詞 The **per capita** amount of something is the total amount of it in a country or area divided by the number of people in that country or area. 1人当たりの [ADJ n] ❏ *They have the world's largest per capita income.* 彼らの1人当たりの収入は世界で最も多い. ● ADV 副詞 **Per capita** is also an adverb. 1人につき, 1人当たり [n ADV] ❏ *Ethiopia has almost the lowest oil consumption per capita in the world.* エチオピアの石油消費量はほとんど世界で最も低い.

per|ceive /pərsiːv/ (**perceives, perceiving, perceived**) ■ V-T 他動詞 If you **perceive** something, you see, notice, or realize it,

especially when it is not obvious. 知覚する, 悟る ❏ *Students must perceive for themselves the relationship between success and effort.* 学生たちは成功と努力の関係に自分で気づかなくてはならない. ❷ V-T 他動詞 If you **perceive** someone or something **as** doing or being a particular thing, it is your opinion that they do this thing or that they are that thing. (一と) 一を考える ❏ *Stress is widely perceived as contributing to coronary heart disease.* ストレスは冠状動脈性心臓病の一因だと広く考えられている.

percent /pərsɛnt/ (**percent**) N-COUNT 可算名詞 You use **percent** to talk about amounts. For example, if an amount is 10 percent (10%) of a larger amount, it is equal to 10 hundredths of the larger amount. パーセント ❏ *Sixteen percent of children live in poverty in this country.* この国では子供たちの16パーセントが貧しい生活をしている. ❏ *Sales of new homes fell by 1.4 percent in August.* 新しい住宅の売り上げは8月に1.4パーセント下がった. ● ADJ 形容詞 **Percent** is also an adjective. パーセントの [ADJ n] ❏ *...a 15 percent increase in border patrols.* 国境巡視隊を15パーセント増加 ● ADV 副詞 **Percent** is also an adverb. パーセント（だけ）[ADV with v] ❏ *He predicted sales will fall 2 percent to 6 percent in the second quarter.* 彼は, 第二四半期に売り上げが2パーセント落ち, 6パーセントになると予想した.

per|cent|age /pərsɛntɪdʒ/ (**percentages**) N-COUNT 可算名詞 A **percentage** is a fraction of an amount expressed as a particular number of hundredths of that amount. 割合 ❏ *Only a few vegetable-origin foods have such a high percentage of protein.* 植物が原料の食べ物でたんぱく質の割合がとても多いものはほんのわずかだ.

per|cep|tion /pərsɛpʃən/ (**perceptions**) ■ N-COUNT 可算名詞 Your **perception of** something is the way that you think about it or the impression you have of it. 認識 ❏ *He is interested in how our perceptions of death affect the way we live.* 彼は死に対する認識が人間の生き方にいかに影響するかに興味を持っている. ❷ N-UNCOUNT 不可算名詞 Someone who has **perception** realizes or notices things that are not obvious. 理解力 ❏ *It did not require a lot of perception to realize the interview was over.* インタビューが終わったと気づくのに大した理解力は不要だった. ❸ N-COUNT 可算名詞 **Perception** is the recognition of things using your senses, especially the sense of sight. 鑑識力

per|cep|tive /pərsɛptɪv/ ADJ 形容詞 If you describe a person or their remarks or thoughts as **perceptive,** you think that they are good at noticing or realizing things, especially things that are not obvious. 理解力の鋭い [APPROVAL 賛成] ❏ *He was one of the most perceptive U.S. political commentators.* 彼は米国でも最も鋭い理解力を持つ政治解説者の1人だった.

perch /pɜːrtʃ/ (**perches, perching, perched**)

The form **perch** is used for both the singular and plural in meaning ❻.

perch 形は❻を意味する場合に単複両方に使われる.

■ V-I 自動詞 If you **perch on** something, you sit down lightly on the very edge or tip of it. 腰をかける ❏ *He lit a cigarette and perched on the corner of the desk.* 彼はタバコに火をつけ, 机の角に腰かけた. ❷ V-I 自動詞 To **perch** somewhere means to be on the top or edge of something. 位置を占める ❏ *...the vast slums that perch precariously on top of the hills above which the city was built.* まわりに都市が築かれている丘の上に危なっかしげに存在する巨大なスラム街 ❸ V-T 他動詞 If you **perch** something **on** something else, you put or balance it on the top or edge of that thing. 載せる ❏ *The use of steel and concrete has allowed the builders to perch a light concrete dome on eight slender columns.* 建築業者は鉄鋼とコンクリートを使用して8つの細長い円柱にコンクリートの軽いドームを載せることができた. ❹ V-I 自動詞 When a bird **perches on** something such as a branch or a wall, it lands on it and stands there. 止まり木に止まる ❏ *A blackbird flew down and perched on the parapet outside his window.* クロウタドリが飛び降りてきて窓の外の手すりに止まった. ❺ N-COUNT 可算名詞 A **perch** is a short rod for a bird to stand on. 止まり木 ❏ *A small, yellow bird in a cage sat on its perch outside the house.* 家の外の鳥かごにいる黄色い小鳥は止まり木に止まっていた. ❻ N-COUNT 可算名詞 A **perch** is an edible fish. There are several kinds of perch. パーチ

per|cus|sion /pərkʌʃən/ N-UNCOUNT 不可算名詞 **Percussion** instruments are musical instruments that you hit, such as drums. 打楽器 ❏ *...a large orchestra, with a vast percussion section.* 大がかりな打楽器部を持つ大オーケストラ

→ see drum, orchestra

per diem /pər diːəm, pər/ N-SING 単数名詞 A **per diem** is an amount of money that someone is given to cover their daily expenses while they are working. 旅費日当 [mainly AM 主に米国英語] ❏ *He received a per diem allowance to cover his travel expenses.* 彼は旅行経費を賄うための日当を受け取った.

per|en|nial /pərɛniəl/ (perennials) ■ ADJ 形容詞 You use **perennial** to describe situations or states that keep occurring or that seem to exist all the time; used especially to describe problems or difficulties. 多年的な ❑ ...the perennial urban problems of drugs and homelessness. 麻薬とホームレスという長年の都市問題 ② ADJ 形容詞 A **perennial** plant lives for several years and has flowers each year. 多年生の ❑ ...a perennial herb with greenish-yellow flowers. 黄緑色の花が咲く多年生の薬草 ● N-COUNT 可算名詞 **Perennial** is also a noun. 多年生植物 ❑ ...a low-growing perennial. 低く育つ多年草
→ see **plant**

<blockquote>**Word Link** per ≈ through, thoroughly : perceive, perfect, permit</blockquote>

per|fect (perfects, perfecting, perfected)

The adjective is pronounced /pɜrfɪkt/. The verb is pronounced /pərfɛkt/.

形容詞は /pɜrfɪkt/と発音される. 動詞は /pərfɛkt/と発音される.

■ ADJ 形容詞 Something that is **perfect** is as good as it could possibly be. 完璧な ❑ He spoke perfect English. 彼は完璧な英語を話した. ② ADJ 形容詞 If you say that something is **perfect for** a particular person, thing, or activity, you are emphasizing that it is very suitable for them or for that activity. ぴったりの [EMPHASIS 強調] ❑ The pool area is perfect for entertaining. プールのまわりは人を楽しませるのにうってつけだ. ③ ADJ 形容詞 If an object or surface is **perfect**, it does not have any marks on it, or does not have any lumps, hollows, or cracks in it. 傷のない ❑ Use only clean, Grade A, perfect eggs. 清潔でA等級のキズのない卵のみを使いなさい. ④ ADJ 形容詞 You can use **perfect** to give emphasis to the noun following it. 全くの [EMPHASIS 強調] [ADJ n] ❑ She was a perfect fool. 彼女は全くの愚か者だった. ⑤ V-T 他動詞 If you **perfect** something, you improve it so that it becomes as good as it can possibly be. 完全にする ❑ We perfected a hand-signal system so that he could keep me informed of hazards. 我々は彼が私に常に危険を知らせておけるように手信号システムを完成した.

<blockquote>**Thesaurus** perfect また次を参照 :

ADJ. flawless, ideal; (ant.) defective, faulty ■ ②
complete, undamaged; (ant.) damaged ③</blockquote>

per|fec|tion /pərfɛkʃən/ ■ N-UNCOUNT 不可算名詞 **Perfection** is the quality of being as good as it is possible for something of a particular kind to be. 完全無欠 ❑ His quest for perfection is relentless. 彼の完全無欠の追求は飽くことを知らない. ② N-UNCOUNT 不可算名詞 The **perfection of** something such as a skill, system, or product involves making it as good as it could possibly be. 完成 ❑ Madame Clicquot is credited with the perfection of this technique. クリコ夫人はこの技術を完成させた人だ.

per|fec|tion|ist /pərfɛkʃənɪst/ (perfectionists) N-COUNT 可算名詞 Someone who is a **perfectionist** refuses to do or accept anything that is not as good as it could possibly be. 完全主義者 ❑ He was such a perfectionist that he published only those results that satisfied him completely. 彼は完全主義のあまり完璧に満足した結果しか発表しなかった.

per|fect|ly /pɜrfɪktli/ ■ ADV 副詞 You can use **perfectly** to emphasize an adjective or adverb, especially when you think the person you are talking to might doubt what you are saying. 完全に [EMPHASIS 強調] [ADV adj/adv] ❑ There's no reason why you can't have a perfectly normal child. あなたが完全に正常な子供を持てない理由はない. ❑ You know perfectly well what happened. あなたは何が起こったかを全くもってよく知っている. ② ADV 副詞 If something is done **perfectly**, it is done so well that it could not possibly be done better. 申し分なく [ADV with v] ❑ This ambitious adaptation perfectly captures the spirit of Kurt Vonnegut's acclaimed novel. この野心的な脚色はカート・ヴォネガットの誉れ高い小説の精神を見事にとらえている.

per|form /pərfɔrm/ (performs, performing, performed) ■ V-T 他動詞 When you **perform** a task or action, especially a complicated one, you do it. 行なう ❑ We're looking for people of all ages who have performed outstanding acts of bravery, kindness, or courage. 我々は勇敢, 親切, あるいは勇気で卓越した行為をしたあらゆる年齢の人々を探している. ❑ His council had had to perform miracles on a tiny budget. 彼の評議会はわずかな予算で奇跡を行なわなければならなかった. ② V-T 他動詞 If something **performs** a particular function, it has that function. 果たす ❑ An engine has many parts, each performing a different function. エンジンには数多くの部品があり, それぞれが異なる機能を果たしている. ③ V-T 他動詞 If you **perform** a play, a piece of music, or a dance, you do it in front of an audience. 公演する ❑ Gardiner has pursued relentlessly high standards in performing classical music. ガーディナーはクラシックの演奏で飽くことなく高水準を追求してきた. ❑ This play was first performed in 411 BC. この劇は紀元前411年に初演された. ④ V-I 自動詞 If someone or something **performs well**, they work well or achieve a good result. If they **perform badly**, they work badly or achieve a poor result.

うまくやってのける, 不成功に終わる ❑ He had not performed well in his exams. 彼は試験でよい結果を出していなかった. ❑ State-owned industries will always perform poorly. 国営企業は常に業績がよくないものだ.

<blockquote>**Word Partnership** perform は次の語句と使われる :

N. perform **miracles**, perform **tasks** ■
ADJ. **able to** perform ■ − ③
V. **continue to** perform ■ − ③
ADV. perform **well** ④</blockquote>

<blockquote>**Word Link** ance ≈ quality, state : defiance, performance, resistance</blockquote>

per|for|mance /pərfɔrməns/ (performances) ■ N-COUNT 可算名詞 A **performance** involves entertaining an audience by doing something such as singing, dancing, or acting. 公演 ❑ Inside the theater, they were giving a performance of Bizet's Carmen. 劇場内で彼らはビゼーのカルメンを演奏中だった. ❑ ...her performance as the betrayed Medea. 裏切られたメデイア役の彼女の演技 ② N-VAR 可変性名詞 Someone's or something's **performance** is how successful they are or how well they do something. 実績 ❑ That study looked at the performance of 18 surgeons. その調査は18人の外科医の実績を調べた. ❑ The poor performance has been blamed on the recession and cheaper sports car imports. 業績の悪さは景気後退と安価な輸入スポーツカーが原因とされた. ③ N-SING 単数名詞 The **performance** of a task is the fact or action of doing it. 履行 ❑ He devoted in excess of seventy hours a week to the performance of his duties. 彼は業務の履行に週70時間以上費やした.
→ see **concert, theater**

<blockquote>**Word Partnership** performance は次の語句と使われる :

ADJ. **live** performance ■
good performance, **poor** performance, **strong** performance ■ − ③
academic performance, **economic** performance, **sexual** performance ②
N. performance **appraisal**, **company** performance, **job** performance ②</blockquote>

performance-related pay N-UNCOUNT 不可算名詞 **Performance-related pay** is a rate of pay which is based on how well someone does their job. 能力給 [BUSINESS 実業] ❑ ...plans to introduce performance-related pay for teachers. 教員に能力給を導入する案

per|form|er /pərfɔrmər/ (performers) ■ N-COUNT 可算名詞 A **performer** is a person who acts, sings, or does other entertainment in front of audiences. 公演者 ❑ A performer plays classical selections on the violin. 演奏者がバイオリンでクラシック選集を演奏する. ② N-COUNT 可算名詞 You can use **performer** when describing someone or something in a way that indicates how well they do a particular thing. 成就者 ❑ Until 1987, Canada's industry had been the star performer. カナダの産業は1987年まで特筆すべき実績をあげていた.

per|fume /pɜrfyum, pərfyum/ (perfumes, perfuming, perfumed) ■ N-MASS 質量名詞 **Perfume** is a pleasant-smelling liquid that women put on their skin to make themselves smell nice. 香水 ❑ The hall smelled of her mother's perfume. 玄関は彼女の母親の香水の匂いが漂っていた. ❑ ...a bottle of perfume. 香水一瓶 ② N-MASS 質量名詞 **Perfume** is the ingredient that is added to some products to make them smell nice. 香料 ❑ ...a delicate white soap without perfume. 無香料の快い白い石鹸 ③ V-T 他動詞 If something is used to **perfume** a product, it is added to the product to make it smell nice. 香らせる ❑ The oil is used to flavor and perfume soaps, foam baths, and scents. オイルは石鹸, 入浴剤, 香水の香りづけに使われる.

per|haps /pərhæps, præps/ ■ ADV 副詞 You use **perhaps** to express uncertainty, for example, when you do not know that something is definitely true, or when you are mentioning something that may possibly happen in the future in the way you describe. ことによると [VAGUENESS あいまいさ] [ADV with cl/group] ❑ In the end they lose millions, perhaps billions. 結局彼らは数百万, ことによると数十億を失った. ❑ Perhaps, in time, the message will get through. 教訓はそのうち伝わるかもしれない. ② ADV 副詞 You use **perhaps** in opinions and remarks to make them appear less definite or more polite. あるいは [VAGUENESS あいまいさ] [ADV with cl/group] ❑ Perhaps the most important lesson to be learned is that you simply cannot please everyone. 最も重要な教訓は全員を満足させることはできないということかもしれない. ❑ His very last paintings are perhaps the most puzzling. 彼の絵画の中でも最後のいくつかが最も不可解なものかもしれない. ③ ADV 副詞 You use **perhaps** when you are making suggestions or giving advice. **Perhaps** is also used in formal English to introduce requests. もしかして [POLITENESS 丁

寧さ] [ADV with cl] ❑ *Perhaps I may be permitted a few suggestions.* も しかして多少の質問をしてよろしいでしょうか。❑ *Well, perhaps you'll come and see us at our place?* さて、ひょっとして私達の家に遊びに来て もらえますか。

per|il /pɛrɪl/ (**perils**) N-VAR 可変性名詞 **Perils** are great dangers. 危険 [FORMAL 形式ばった] ❑ *...the perils of the sea.* 海の危険 ❑ *In spite of great peril, I have survived.* 大きな危険にもかかわらず私は生き延びた.

per|il|lous /pɛrɪləs/ ADJ 形容詞 Something that is **perilous** is very dangerous. 危険に満ちた [LITERARY 文語的] ❑ *...a perilous journey across the war zone.* 交戦地帯を横切る危険に満ちた旅 ❑ *The road grew even steeper and more perilous.* その道路は傾斜が急になり、一 段と危険になった. ● **per|il|lous|ly** ADV 副詞 危険に満ちて ❑ *The track snaked perilously upwards.* その小道は危険な感じでうねうねと上り坂 になった.

<table>
<tr><td>Word Link</td><td>meter ≈ measuring : kilometer, meter, perimeter</td></tr>
</table>

<table>
<tr><td>Word Link</td><td>peri ≈ around : perimeter, periodic, periphery</td></tr>
</table>

pe|rim|eter /pərɪmɪtər/ (**perimeters**) N-COUNT 可算名詞 The **perimeter** of an area of land is the whole of its outer edge or boundary. 周囲 ❑ *...the perimeter of the airport.* 空港周辺 → see **area**

pe|ri|od /pɪəriəd/ (**periods**) ◼ N-COUNT 可算名詞 A **period** is a length of time. 期間 ❑ *This crisis might last for a long period of time.* この危機は長期間続くかもしれない. ❑ *...a period of a few months.* 数か月間 ◻ N-COUNT 可算名詞 A **period** in the life of a person, organization, or society is a length of time that is remembered for a particular situation or activity. 時期 ❑ *...a period of economic good health and expansion.* 経済が健康で成長する時期 ❑ *He went through a period of wanting to be accepted.* 彼は認めても らいたい時期を経験した. ◼ N-COUNT 可算名詞 A particular length of time in history is sometimes called a **period**. For example, you can talk about **the Civil War period** or **the Prohibition period** in the U.S. 時代 ❑ *The novel is set in the Roman period.* その小説はローマ時代が舞台である. ❑ *No reference to their existence appears in any literature of the period.* 彼らの存在はその時代のいかなる文献にも言及されていない. ◼ ADJ 形容詞 **Period** costumes, furniture, and instruments were made at an earlier time in history, or look as if they were made then. 時代物の [ADJ n] ❑ *The characters were dressed in full period costume.* 登場人物は時代物の衣服を身にまとっていた. ◼ N-COUNT 可算名詞 Exercise, training, or study **periods** are lengths of time that are set aside for exercise, training, or study. 時間 ❑ *They accompanied him during his exercise periods.* 彼らは体育の時間中に彼に同行した. ◼ N-COUNT 可算名詞 A **period** is the punctuation mark (.) that you use at the end of a sentence when it is not a question or an exclamation. ピリオド [AM 米国英語] ◼ N-COUNT 可算名詞 When a woman has a **period**, she bleeds from her uterus. This usually happens once a month, unless she is pregnant. 月経 ❑ *Can you get pregnant if you have sex during your period?* 生理中にセックスをして妊娠するかい.

<table>
<tr><td>Thesaurus</td><td colspan="2">period また次を参照:</td></tr>
<tr><td>N.</td><td colspan="2">age, course, epoch, era, term, time ◼ – ◼</td></tr>
</table>

pe|ri|od|ic /pɪəriɒdɪk/ ADJ 形容詞 **Periodic** events or situations happen occasionally, at fairly regular intervals. 定期的な ❑ *Periodic checks are taken to ensure that high standards are maintained.* 高い基準を維持するために定期点検が行なわれる.

pe|ri|odi|cal /pɪəriɒdɪkəl/ (**periodicals**) ◼ N-COUNT 可算名詞 **Periodicals** are magazines, especially serious or academic ones, that are published at regular intervals. 定期刊行物 ❑ *The walls would be lined with books and periodicals.* 壁には本や定期刊行物がずらっと並ぶだろう. ◻ ADJ 形容詞 **Periodical** events or situations happen occasionally, at fairly regular intervals. 時おり起こる ❑ *She made periodical visits to her dentist.* 彼女は時おり歯医者に行った. ● **pe|ri|odi|cal|ly** ADV 副詞 [ADV with v] 定期的に ❑ *Meetings are held periodically to monitor progress on the case.* その事件の進展を監督する会合が定期的に開かれる. → see **library**

pe|riph|er|al /pərɪfərəl/ (**peripherals**) ◼ ADJ 形容詞 A **peripheral** activity or issue is one that is not very important compared with other activities or issues. あまり重要でない ❑ *Companies are increasingly eager to contract out peripheral activities like training.* 研修など重要度の低い業務を下請けに出す企業が増えつつある. ◻ ADJ 形容詞 **Peripheral** areas of land are ones that are on the edge of a larger area. 周囲の ❑ *...urban development in the outer peripheral areas of large towns.* 大きな町の周辺地域の都市開発 ◼ N-COUNT 可算名詞 **Peripherals** are devices that can be attached to computers. 周辺装置 [COMPUTING コンピューティング] ❑ *...peripherals to expand the use of our computers.* コンピュータの利用を広げるための周辺装置

pe|riph|ery /pərɪfəri/ (**peripheries**) N-COUNT 可算名詞 If something is on the **periphery** of an area, place, or thing, it

is on the edge of it. 外縁 [FORMAL 形式ばった] ❑ *Taste buds are concentrated at the tip and rear of the tongue and around its periphery.* 味覚芽は舌の先端と後部とその周辺に集まっている.

per|ish /pɛrɪʃ/ (**perishes, perishing, perished**) V-I 自動詞 If people or animals **perish**, they die as a result of very harsh conditions or as the result of an accident. 死ぬ [WRITTEN 書き言葉] ❑ *Most of the butterflies perish in the first frosts of autumn.* 蝶の大半は秋の初霜で死ぬ.

per|jury /pɜrdʒəri/ N-UNCOUNT 不可算名詞 If someone who is giving evidence in a court of law commits **perjury**, they lie. 偽証 [LEGAL 法律的] ❑ *This witness has committed perjury and no reliance can be placed on her evidence.* この証人は偽証罪を犯したため、証言はまったく信用できない.

perk /pɜrk/ (**perks, perking, perked**) N-COUNT 可算名詞 **Perks** are special benefits that are given to people who have a particular job or belong to a particular group. 役職員の特典 ❑ *...a company car, health insurance and other perks.* 社用車、医療保険などの特典 ▶ **perk up** ◼ PHRASAL VERB 句動詞 If something **perks** you **up** or if you **perk up**, you become cheerful and lively, after feeling tired, bored, or depressed. 生き生きとする ❑ *He perks up and jokes with them.* 彼は元気になり彼らと冗談を言う. ◻ PHRASAL VERB 句動詞 If you **perk** something **up**, you make it more interesting. 引き立たせる ❑ *To make the bland taste more interesting, the locals began perking it up with local produce.* 退屈な味を魅力的にするために土地の人が地元で採れたもので味をきわだたせるようにした. ◼ PHRASAL VERB 句動詞 If sales, prices, or economies **perk up**, or if something **perks** them **up**, they begin to increase or improve. 上昇する [JOURNALISM ジャーナリズム] ❑ *House prices could perk up during the fall.* 住宅価格は秋に上昇するかもしれない.

perm /pɜrm/ (**perms, perming, permed**) ◼ N-COUNT 可算名詞 If you have a **perm**, your hair is curled and treated with chemicals so that it stays curly for several months. パーマ ❑ *...a middle-aged lady with a perm.* パーマをかけた中年女性 ◻ V-T 他動詞 When a hairstylist **perms** someone's hair, they curl it and treat it with chemicals so that it stays curly for several months. 髪にパーマをかける ❑ *She had her hair permed.* 彼女はパーマをかけてもらった.

per|ma|nent /pɜrmənənt/ (**permanents**) ◼ ADJ 形容詞 Something that is **permanent** lasts forever. 永続する ❑ *Heavy drinking can cause permanent damage to the brain.* 飲みすぎは脳に一生消えない害を及ぼすことがある. ❑ *...a permanent solution to the problem.* 問題への永久的解決策 ● **per|ma|nent|ly** ADV 副詞 永久的に ❑ *His confidence had been permanently affected by the ordeal.* 彼は苦しい体験をして以来、自信に消えない傷がついた. ● **per|ma|nence** N-UNCOUNT 不可算名詞 永続 ❑ *Anything which threatens the permanence of the treaty is a threat to stability and to peace.* 条約の永続性を脅かすものは全て安定と平和への脅威となる. ◻ ADJ 形容詞 You use **permanent** to describe situations or states that keep occurring or that seem to exist all the time; used especially to describe problems or difficulties. 永続的な ❑ *...a permanent state of tension.* 永続的な緊張状態 ❑ *They feel under permanent threat.* 彼らは永続的に脅かされていると感じている. ● **per|ma|nent|ly** ADV 副詞 永続的に ❑ *...the heavy, permanently locked gate.* 重く、いつも閉ざされたままの門 ◼ ADJ 形容詞 [ADJ n] A **permanent** employee is one who is employed for an unlimited length of time. 終身の ❑ *At the end of the probationary period you will become a permanent employee.* 試用期間後にあなたは正社員となる. ● **per|ma|nent|ly** ADV 副詞 [ADV with v] 永久に ❑ *...permanently employed lifeguards.* 常勤の救助員 ◼ ADJ 形容詞 Your **permanent** home or your **permanent** address is the one at which you spend most of your time or the one that you return to after having stayed in other places. 定住する [ADJ n] ❑ *He had no permanent address.* 彼らには定住所がなかった. ◼ N-COUNT 可算名詞 A **permanent** is a treatment in which a hairstylist curls your hair and treats it with a chemical so that it stays curly for several months. パーマ [AM 米国英語] ❑ *Her hair had had a permanent, but had grown out.* 彼女の髪にはパーマがかかっていたが、伸びてしまった.

<table>
<tr><td>Thesaurus</td><td colspan="2">permanent また次を参照:</td></tr>
<tr><td>ADJ.</td><td colspan="2">constant, continual, everlasting; (ant.) fleeting, temporary ◼</td></tr>
</table>

per|me|ate /pɜrmieɪt/ (**permeates, permeating, permeated**) ◼ V-T 他動詞 If an idea, feeling, or attitude **permeates** a system or **permeates** society, it affects every part of it or is present throughout it. 浸透する ❑ *Bias against women permeates every level of the judicial system.* 女性に対する偏見は司法制度のあらゆるレベルに行き渡っている. ◻ V-T 他動詞 If something **permeates** a place, it spreads throughout it. 広がる ❑ *The smell of roast beef permeated the air.* ローストビーフの匂いが広がった.

per|mis|sible /pərmɪsəbəl/ ADJ 形容詞 If something is **permissible**, it is considered to be acceptable because it does not break any laws or rules. 許される ❑ *Religious practices are permissible under the Constitution.* 宗教の実践は憲法で許されている.

per|mis|sion /pərmɪʃ°n/ N-UNCOUNT 不可算名詞 If someone who has authority over you gives you **permission to** do something, they say that they will allow you to do it. 許可 *He asked permission to leave the room.* 彼は部屋から出る許可を求めた。 *They cannot leave the country without permission.* 彼らは許可なしに出国することはできない。

Word Partnership	*permission* は次の語句と使われる:
V.	**ask (for)** permission, **get** permission, permission **to leave**, **need** permission, **obtain** permission, **receive** permission, **request** permission, **seek** permission
ADJ.	**special** permission, **written** permission

per|mis|sive /pərmɪsɪv/ ADJ 形容詞 A **permissive** person, society, or way of behaving allows or tolerates things that other people disapprove of. 寛大な *The call for law and order replaced the "permissive tolerance" of the 1960s.* 法と秩序への要求が1960年代の「甘い寛容」に取って代わった。 ● **per|mis|sive|ness** N-UNCOUNT 不可算名詞 *Permissiveness and democracy go together.* 寛容さと民主主義は調和する。

Word Link	*per ≈ through, thoroughly : perceive, perfect, permit*

per|mit (permits, permitting, permitted)

The verb is pronounced /pərmɪt/. The noun is pronounced /pɜrmɪt/.

動詞は /pərmɪt/ と発音される。名詞は /pɜrmɪt/ と発音される。

1 V-T 他動詞 If someone **permits** something, they allow it to happen. If they **permit** you to do something, they allow you to do it. 許す [FORMAL 形式ばった] *He can let the court's decision stand and permit the execution.* 彼は法廷の決定に従って死刑執行を許可できる。 *The guards permitted me to bring my camera and tape recorder.* 守衛はカメラとテープレコーダーの持参を許可した。 **2** N-COUNT 可算名詞 A **permit** is an official document which says that you may do something. For example, you usually need a **permit** to work in a foreign country. 許可証 *He has to apply for a permit, and we have to find him a job.* 彼は許可申請を行わなければならず、我々は彼のために職を見つける必要がある。 **3** V-T/V-I 他動詞/自動詞 If a situation **permits** something, it makes it possible for that thing to exist, happen, or be done or it provides the opportunity for it. 許す [FORMAL 形式ばった] *Try to go out for a walk at lunchtime, if the weather permits.* 昼食時間に天気がよければ散歩に出かけるようにしなさい。 *This method of cooking also permits heat to penetrate evenly from both sides.* この調理方法は両側からむらなく熱を浸透させられる。

Thesaurus	*permit* また次を参照:
V.	allow, authorize, let; (ant.) ban, forbid, prohibit **1** **3**
N.	authorization, consent, permission; (ant.) ban **2**

per|ni|cious /pərnɪʃəs/ ADJ 形容詞 If you describe something as **pernicious**, you mean that it is very harmful. 有害な [FORMAL 形式ばった] *I did what I could, but her mother's influence was pernicious.* 私はできるだけのことをしたが彼女の母親の影響は致命的だった。

per|pe|trate /pɜrpɪtreɪt/ (perpetrates, perpetrating, perpetrated) V-T 他動詞 If someone **perpetrates** a crime or any other immoral or harmful act, they commit it. 犯す [FORMAL 形式ばった] *A high proportion of crime in any country is perpetrated by young males in their teens and twenties.* どんな国でも全犯罪の大きな割合が10代と20代の若い男性によって犯されている。 ● **per|pe|tra|tor** (perpetrators) N-COUNT 可算名詞 犯罪者 *The perpetrator of the crime does not have to be traced before you can claim compensation.* 犯人の居所を突き止めなくとも損害賠償を請求できる。

per|pet|ual /pərpɛtʃuəl/ **1** ADJ 形容詞 A **perpetual** feeling, state, or quality is one that never ends or changes. 永久の *...the creation of a perpetual union.* 永遠に続く団結を築き上げること ● **per|pet|ual|ly** ADV 副詞 永久に *They were all perpetually starving.* 彼らは全員永続的に飢えていた。 **2** ADJ 形容詞 A **perpetual** act, situation, or state is one that happens again and again and so seems never to end. 絶え間ない *I thought her perpetual complaints were going to prove too much for me.* 私は彼女ののべつ幕ない不平に耐えられなくなると思った。 ● **per|pet|ual|ly** ADV 副詞 絶え間なく *He perpetually interferes in political affairs.* 彼は絶え間なく政治問題に干渉する。

per|pet|u|ate /pərpɛtʃueɪt/ (perpetuates, perpetuating, perpetuated) V-T 他動詞 If someone or something **perpetuates** a situation, system, or belief, especially a bad one, they cause it to continue. 永続させる *We must not perpetuate the religious divisions of the past.* 我々は過去の宗教的分裂を永続させてはならない。

per|plexed /pərplɛkst/ ADJ 形容詞 If you are **perplexed**, you feel confused and slightly worried by something because you do not understand it. 当惑した *She is perplexed about what to do for her daughter.* 彼女は娘のために何をしていいのか途方に暮れている。

per se /pɜr seɪ, pər-/ ADV 副詞 **Per se** means "by itself" or "in itself," and is used when you are talking about the qualities of one thing considered on its own, rather than in connection with other things. それ自体は *I don't work out per se, but I'm very active physically.* 私はきちんとした運動はしていないが大変活動的に体を動かしている。

per|se|cute /pɜrsɪkyut/ (persecutes, persecuting, persecuted) V-T 他動詞 If someone **is persecuted**, they are treated cruelly and unfairly, often because of their race or beliefs. しいたげられた *Mr. Weaver and his family have been persecuted by the authorities for their beliefs.* ウィーヴァー氏とその家族は自らの信念のために当局から迫害を受けてきた。 *They began by brutally persecuting the Catholic Church.* 彼らはまずカトリック教会を暴力的に迫害した。

per|se|cu|tion /pɜrsɪkyuʃ°n/ (persecutions) N-COUNT 可算名詞 **Persecution** is cruel and unfair treatment of a person or group, especially because of their religious or political beliefs, or their race. 迫害 *...the persecution of minorities.* 少数民族の迫害 *...victims of political persecution.* 政治的迫害の被害者

per|se|ver|ance /pɜrsɪvɪərəns/ N-UNCOUNT 不可算名詞 **Perseverance** is the quality of continuing with something even though it is difficult. 粘り強さ *He has never stopped trying and showed great perseverance.* 彼は努力を怠らず、偉大な粘り強さを示した。

per|se|vere /pɜrsɪvɪər/ (perseveres, persevering, persevered) V-I 自動詞 If you **persevere with** something, you keep trying to do it and do not give up, even though it is difficult. 頑張り通す *This ability to persevere despite obstacles and setbacks is the quality people most admire in others.* 障害や挫折にもかかわらず屈せずにやり通す力は世間が最も賞賛する特性だ。 *...a school with a reputation for persevering with difficult and disruptive children.* 扱いにくい問題児でもうまず努力を続けると評判を持つ学校

per|sist /pərsɪst/ (persists, persisting, persisted) **1** V-I 自動詞 If something undesirable **persists**, it continues to exist. 存続する *Contact your doctor if the cough persists.* 咳が止まない場合は医者に相談しなさい。 **2** V-I 自動詞 If you **persist in** doing something, you continue to do it, even though it is difficult or other people are against it. あくまでやり抜く *Why do people persist in begging for money in the street?* なぜ人々は通りでこじきをし続けるのだろうか。 *He urged the United States to persist with its efforts to bring about peace.* 彼は米国に平和をもたらす努力を続けるよう促した。

per|sis|tence /pərsɪstəns/ **1** N-UNCOUNT 不可算名詞 If you have **persistence**, you continue to do something even though it is difficult or other people are against it. 粘り強さ *Skill comes only with practice, patience, and persistence.* 専門技術は練習、忍耐、粘り強さがあって初めて得られる。 **2** N-UNCOUNT 不可算名詞 The **persistence** of something, especially something bad, is the fact of its continuing to exist for a long time. 永続 *...an expression of concern at the persistence of inflation and high interest rates.* インフレと高金利の長期化に対する懸念の表現

per|sis|tent /pərsɪstənt/ **1** ADJ 形容詞 Something that is **persistent** continues to exist or happen for a long time; used especially about bad or undesirable states or situations. 永続性のある *Her position as national leader has been weakened by persistent fears of another coup attempt.* クーデターが再発するのではないかとの懸念が消えないため国の指導者としての彼女の立場は弱まった。 *His cough grew more persistent until it never stopped.* 彼の咳は一段としつこくなり、やがて止まらなくなった。 **2** ADJ 形容詞 Someone who is **persistent** continues trying to do something, even though it is difficult or other people are against it. 根気強い *...a persistent critic of the president.* 大統領を根気強く批判する人物

per|sis|tent|ly /pərsɪstəntli/ **1** ADV 副詞 If something happens **persistently**, it happens again and again or for a long time. 繰り返して *The allegations have been persistently denied by ministers.* 疑惑は大臣らによって繰り返し否定された。 **2** ADV 副詞 If someone does something **persistently**, they do it with determination even though it is difficult or other people are against it. 粘り強く [ADV with v] *Rachel gently but persistently imposed her will on Doug.* レイチェルはダグに穏やかだが粘り強く自分の意思を押し付けた。

per|son /pɜrs°n/ (people or persons)

The usual word for "more than one person" is **people**. The form **persons** is used as the plural in formal and legal language.

「1人以上」を表す通常の語は **people** である。**persons** 形は形式ばった言葉あるいは法律の言語では複数形として使われる。

1 N-COUNT 可算名詞 A **person** is a man, woman, or child. 人 *At least one person died and several others were injured.* 少なくとも1名が死亡し、数名が負傷した。 *They were both lovely, friendly people.* 彼らは2人とも親切で友好的な人だった。 **2** N-PLURAL 複数名詞 **Persons** is used as the plural of **person** in formal, legal, and technical writing. 人々 *...removal of the right of accused persons to remain silent.* 被告人の黙秘権の剥奪 **3** N-COUNT 可算名詞 If you talk about

someone **as a person**, you are considering them from the point of view of their real nature. 人格 ❑ *Robin didn't feel good about herself as a person.* ロビンは自分の人格が好きでなかった. **4** PHRASE 句 If you do something **in person**, you do it yourself rather than letting someone else do it for you. 本人が直接に ❑ *You must collect the mail in person and take along some form of identification.* 郵便物の受け取りは身分証を持参して本人が出向く必要がある. **5** PHRASE 句 If you meet, hear, or see someone **in person**, you are in the same place as them, rather than, for example, speaking to them on the telephone, writing to them, or seeing them on television. じかに ❑ *It was the first time she had seen him in person.* 彼女がじかに彼に会ったのは初めてだった. **6** N-COUNT 可算名詞 Your **person** is your body. 身体 [FORMAL 形式ばった] ❑ *The suspect had refused to give any details of his identity and had carried no documents on his person.* 容疑者は身元を明かすことを拒否し、身分証も持っていなかった. **7** N-COUNT 可算名詞 In grammar, we use the term **first person** when referring to "I" and "we," **second person** when referring to "you," and **third person** when referring to "he," "she," "it," "they," and all other noun groups. **Person** is also used like this when referring to the verb forms that go with these pronouns and noun groups. 人称

per|so|na /pərsoʊnə/ (**personas** or **personae** /pərsoʊni/) N-COUNT 可算名詞 Someone's **persona** is the aspect of their character or nature that they present to other people, perhaps in contrast to their real character or nature. 本性に対する対外的な態度や性格 [FORMAL 形式ばった] ❑ *The contradictions between her private life and the public persona are not always fully explored.* 彼女の私生活と社会に見せる人格の矛盾はいつも十分に探究されているわけではない.

per|son|al /pərsənəl/ **1** ADJ 形容詞 A **personal** opinion, quality, or thing belongs or relates to one particular person rather than to other people. 個人的な [ADJ n] ❑ *He learned this lesson the hard way – from his own personal experience.* 彼はこの教訓を個人的な経験を通して学んだ. ❑ *That's my personal opinion.* それは私の個人的な意見である. **2** ADJ 形容詞 If you give something your **personal** care or attention, you deal with it yourself rather than letting someone else deal with it. 個人の ❑ *...a business that requires a lot of personal contact.* 人と人のつながりを多大に要する事業 ❑ *...a personal letter from the president's secretary.* 社長秘書からの私信 **3** ADJ 形容詞 **Personal** matters relate to your feelings, relationships, and health. 個人に関する ❑ *...teaching young people about marriage and personal relationships.* 若い人々に結婚や対人関係について教えること ❑ *You never allow personal problems to affect your performance.* 個人の問題を成績に影響させてはならない. **4** ADJ 形容詞 **Personal** comments refer to someone's appearance or character in an offensive way. 特定個人にあてた ❑ *Newspapers resorted to personal abuse.* 新聞は個人攻撃に訴えた. **5** ADJ 形容詞 **Personal** care involves taking care of your body and appearance. 身体の [ADJ n] ❑ *...the new breed of men who take as much time and trouble over personal hygiene as the women in their lives.* 女性と同じくらい身ぎれいさに時間と手間をかける新しいタイプの男性 **6** ADJ 形容詞 A **personal** relationship is one that is not connected with your job or public life. 私人の ❑ *He was a great and valued personal friend whom I've known for many years.* 彼は私が長年付き合ってきた大切な親友だった. **7** ADJ 形容詞 If someone has a **personal** shopper or a **personal** trainer, they employ another person to shop for them or to help them keep fit. 個人用の [ADJ n] ❑ *Another way of escaping the crowds and the changing rooms is to employ a personal shopper.* 人込みと試着室を避けるもう1つの方法はお抱えで買い物をしてくれる人を雇うことだ. ❑ *The best clubs also offer personal trainers to help motivate and ensure that exercises are properly performed.* 最良のクラブには意欲を引き出し運動が適切に行なわれるのを確認するパーソナル・トレーナーもいる. **8** → see also **personals**

per|son|al as|sis|tant (**personal assistants**) N-COUNT 可算名詞 A **personal assistant** is a person who does office work and administrative work for someone. The abbreviation **PA** is also used. 個人秘書 [BUSINESS 実業] ❑ *She was a hard-pressed personal assistant to a frenetic company chairman.* 彼女は猛烈な会社会長について時間に追われる秘書だった.

per|son|al com|put|er (**personal computers**) N-COUNT 可算名詞 A **personal computer** is a computer that is used by one person at a time in a business, a school, or at home. The abbreviation **PC** is also used. パーソナルコンピュータ

per|son|al digi|tal as|sis|tant (**personal digital assistants**) N-COUNT 可算名詞 A **personal digital assistant** is a handheld computer, used mainly for storing and accessing personal information such as telephone numbers, and memos. The abbreviation **PDA** is also used. ❑ *...devices such as cell phones and personal digital assistants.* 携帯電話やPDAなどの装置

per|son|al|ity /pərsənælɪti/ (**personalities**) **1** N-VAR 可変性名詞 Your **personality** is your whole character and nature. 性格 ❑ *She has such a kind, friendly personality.* 彼女は大変親切で友好的な性格だ. ❑ *The contest was as much about personalities as it was about*

politics. 競争は政治と同程度に人格に関するものだった. **2** N-VAR 可変性名詞 If someone has **personality** or is a **personality**, they have a strong and lively character. 人間的魅力 ❑ *...a woman of great personality.* 人間的魅力に溢れた女性 **3** N-COUNT 可算名詞 You can refer to a famous person, especially in entertainment, broadcasting, or sports, as a **personality**. 有名人 ❑ *...the radio and television personality, Johnny Carson.* ラジオとテレビのパーソナリティ、ジョニー・カーソン

per|son|al|ly /pərsənəli/ **1** ADV 副詞 You use **personally** to emphasize that you are giving your own opinion. 自分としては [EMPHASIS 強調] [ADV with cl] ❑ *Personally I think it's a waste of time.* 私としてはそれは時間の無駄だと思う. ❑ *You can disagree about them, and I personally do, but they are great ideas that have made people think.* そうした発想に異論をもっていいし、私としては異論があるが、人に考える機会を与えた偉大な発想だ. **2** ADV 副詞 If you do something **personally**, you do it yourself rather than letting someone else do it. 自ら [ADV with v] ❑ *He is returning to Paris to answer the allegations personally.* 彼は申し立てに自ら答えるためにパリに戻る予定だ. ❑ *When the great man arrived, the club's manager personally escorted him upstairs.* お大尽が到着すると、クラブのマネジャーがじきじきに2階に案内した. **3** ADV 副詞 If you meet or know someone **personally**, you meet or know them in real life, rather than knowing about them or knowing their work. 個人的に [ADV with v] ❑ *He did not know them personally, but he was familiar with their reputation.* 彼は彼らと面識はなかったが評判はよく知っていた. **4** ADV 副詞 You can use **personally** to say that something refers to an individual person rather than to other people. 個人的に ❑ *He was personally responsible for all that people suffered under his rule.* 彼は自らの支配下で苦しんだ全ての人々に個人的に責任を負っていた. **5** ADV 副詞 You can use **personally** to show that you are talking about someone's private life rather than their professional or public life. 個人的に ❑ *This has taken a great toll on me personally and professionally.* これは公私両面で私に大きな打撃を与えた. **6** PHRASE 句 If you **take** someone's remarks **personally**, you are upset because you think that they are criticizing you in particular. 個人に向けられたものとして ❑ *I take everything too personally.* 私は全てのことを自分へのあてつけと取る.

per|son|al or|gan|iz|er (**personal organizers**) N-COUNT 可算名詞 A **personal organizer** is a book containing personal or business information, that you can add pages to or remove pages from to keep the information up-to-date. Small computers with a similar function are also called **personal organizers**. パーソナル・オーガナイザー

per|son|al ste|reo (**personal stereos**) N-COUNT 可算名詞 A **personal stereo** is a small cassette or CD player with very light headphones, that people carry around so that they can listen to music while doing something else. 携帯ステレオプレイヤー

per|soni|fi|ca|tion /pərsɒnɪfɪkeɪʃən/ N-SING 単数名詞 If you say that someone is **the personification of** a particular thing or quality, you mean that they are a perfect example of that thing or that they have a lot of that quality. 象徴 ❑ *Janis Joplin was the personification of the '60s female rock singer.* ジャニス・ジョプリンは60年代の女性ロックシンガーの象徴だった.

per|soni|fy /pərsɒnɪfaɪ/ (**personifies, personifying, personified**) V-T 他動詞 If you say that someone **personifies** a particular thing or quality, you mean that they seem to be a perfect example of that thing, or to have that quality to a very large degree. 象徴する ❑ *She seemed to personify goodness and nobility.* 彼女は善と高潔を象徴するようだった.

per|son|nel /pərsənel/ **1** N-PLURAL 複数名詞 The **personnel** of an organization are the people who work for it. 人員 ❑ *Since 1954 Japan has never dispatched military personnel abroad.* 1954年以降、日本は海外に軍隊を派遣したことがない. ❑ *There has been very little renewal of personnel in higher education.* 高等教育では職員の入れ替えがほとんどなかった. **2** N-UNCOUNT 不可算名詞 **Personnel** is the department in a large company or organization that deals with employees, keeps their records, and helps with any problems they might have. 人事部門 [OLD-FASHIONED 古風な BUSINESS 実業] ❑ *Her first job was in personnel.* 彼の最初の仕事は人事だった.

per|spec|tive /pərspektɪv/ (**perspectives**) **1** N-COUNT 可算名詞 A particular **perspective** is a particular way of thinking about something, especially one that is influenced by your beliefs or experiences. 見方 ❑ *He says the death of his father 18 months ago has given him a new perspective on life.* 彼は18か月前に父親が死んだことで人生に対して新しい見方をするようになったと言う. ❑ *...two different perspectives on the nature of adolescent development.* 青年期の発達の特性に関する2つの異なる見方 **2** PHRASE 句 If you get something **in**

perspective or **into perspective**, you judge its real importance by considering it in relation to everything else. If you get something **out of perspective**, you fail to judge its real importance in relation to everything else. バランスのとれた見方で、偏った見方で □ *Remember to keep things in perspective.* バランスのとれた物の見方をすることを忘れないように。 □ *I let things get out of perspective.* 物事の見方のバランスを失ってしまった。

Thesaurus   *perspective* また次を参照:

N.   attitude, mindset, outlook, viewpoint **1**

---

per|spi|ra|tion /pɜrspɪreɪʃᵊn/ N-UNCOUNT 不可算名詞
Perspiration is the liquid that comes out on the surface of your skin when you are hot or frightened. 汗 [FORMAL 形式ばった]
□ *His hands were wet with perspiration.* 彼の手は汗ばんでいた。
→ see **sweat**

Word Link   suad, suas ≈ urging : dissuade, persuade, persuasive

per|suade /pərsweɪd/ (persuades, persuading, persuaded)
1 V-T 他動詞 If you **persuade** someone **to** do something, you cause them to do it by giving them good reasons for doing it. 説得してさせる □ *My husband persuaded me to come.* 夫は私に来るよう説得した。 □ *We're trying to persuade manufacturers to sell them here.* 我々はそれらをここで販売するようメーカーに説得中である。 **2** V-T 他動詞 If something **persuades** someone **to** take a particular course of action, it causes them to take that course of action because it is a good reason for doing so. 確信して～させる □ *It was the lack of privacy that eventually persuaded us to move after Ben was born.* ベンの誕生後、私達に引越しを決めたのはプライバシーの欠如が原因だった。 **3** V-T 他動詞 If you **persuade** someone that something is true, you say things that eventually make them believe that it is true. 説得する □ *I've persuaded Mrs. Tennant that it's time she retired.* 私はテナント夫人にリタイアする時が来たと説得した。 □ *We had managed to persuade them that it was worth working with us.* 我々は我々と仕事をする価値はあると彼らをやっとのことで説得した。

Thesaurus   *persuade* また次を参照:

V.   cajole, convince, influence, sway, talk into, win over; (*ant.*) discourage, dissuade **1** **3**

Word Partnership   *persuade* は次の語句と使われる:

V.   **attempt to** persuade, **be able to** persuade, **fail to** persuade, **try to** persuade **1** **3**

---

per|sua|sion /pərsweɪʒᵊn/ (persuasions) **1** N-UNCOUNT 不可算名詞 **Persuasion** is the act of persuading someone to do something or to believe that something is true. 説得 □ *Only after much persuasion from Ellis had she agreed to put on a show at all.* エリスが時間をかけて説得した後、やっと彼女はショーを開くことに同意した。 **2** N-COUNT 可算名詞 If you are **of** a particular **persuasion**, you have a particular belief or set of beliefs. 信条 [FORMAL 形式ばった] □ *It is a national movement and has within it people of all political persuasions.* それは全国的運動でその内部にはあらゆる政治的信条を持つ人が含まれる。

per|sua|sive /pərsweɪsɪv/ ADJ 形容詞 Someone or something that is **persuasive** is likely to persuade a person to believe or do a particular thing. 説得力のある □ *What do you think were some of the more persuasive arguments on the other side?* 相手の最も説得力のある議論は何と何だったかと思うか。 □ *I can be very persuasive when I want to be.* 私はその気になれば非常に口がうまくなる。 ● **per|sua|sive|ly** ADV 副詞 [ADV with v] 説得力豊かに □ *...a trained lawyer who can present arguments persuasively.* 説得力たっぷりに弁論を行える弁護士

per|tain /pərteɪn/ (pertains, pertaining, pertained) V-I 自動詞 If one thing **pertains to** another, it relates, belongs, or applies to it. 関連する [FORMAL 形式ばった] □ *...matters pertaining to naval district defense.* 海軍地区防衛に関する事柄

per|ti|nent /pɜrtᵊnənt/ ADJ 形容詞 Something that is **pertinent** is relevant to a particular subject. 関係がある [FORMAL 形式ばった] □ *She had asked some pertinent questions.* 彼女は関係のある質問をした。 □ *...name, address, and other pertinent information.* 氏名、住所およびその他の関連情報

per|vade /pərveɪd/ (pervades, pervading, pervaded) V-T 他動詞 If something **pervades** a place or thing, it is a noticeable feature throughout it. 充満する [FORMAL 形式ばった] □ *The smell of sawdust and glue pervaded the factory.* おがくずと接着剤の匂いが工場に充満していた。

per|va|sive /pərveɪsɪv/ ADJ 形容詞 Something, especially something bad, that is **pervasive** is present or felt throughout a place or thing. 広がる [FORMAL 形式ばった] □ *...the pervasive influence of the army in national life.* 国民生活に広がる軍の影響

per|verse /pərvɜrs/ ADJ 形容詞 Someone who is **perverse** deliberately does things that are unreasonable or that result in

---

harm for themselves. ひねくれた [DISAPPROVAL 不賛成] □ *It would be perverse to stop this healthy trend.* 健康志向を止めるのは流れに逆らうことになるだろう。 □ *He seemed to take a perverse pleasure in being disagreeable.* 彼は無愛想でいることにひねくれた喜びを感じているようだった。 ● **per|verse|ly** ADV 副詞 邪悪に □ *She was perversely pleased to be causing trouble.* 彼女は迷惑をかけていることに人の道を外れた喜びを感じた。

per|ver|sion /pərvɜrʒᵊn, -ʃᵊn/ (perversions) **1** N-VAR 可変性名詞 You can refer to a sexual desire or action that you consider to be abnormal and unacceptable as a **perversion**. 性的な倒錯 [DISAPPROVAL 不賛成] □ *The book was the authority on sexual perversions.* その本は性的倒錯の権威書だった。 **2** N-VAR 可変性名詞 A **perversion of** something is a form of it that is bad or wrong, or the changing of it into this form. 曲解 [DISAPPROVAL 不賛成] □ *Critics say that the system is a dangerous perversion of democracy.* その制度は民主主義の危険な曲解だと言う批判もある。

per|vert (perverts, perverting, perverted)

> The verb is pronounced /pərvɜrt/. The noun is pronounced /pɜrvɜrt/.
>
> 動詞は /pərvɜrt/ と発音される。名詞は /pɜrvɜrt/ と発音される。

1 V-T 他動詞 If you **pervert** something such as a process or society, you interfere with it so that it is not as good as it used to be or as it should be. 誤用する [FORMAL 形式ばった, DISAPPROVAL 不賛成] □ *Any reform will destroy and pervert our constitution.* どんな改革を行っても憲法を破壊し、ゆがめることになるだろう。 **2** N-COUNT 可算名詞 If you say that someone is a **pervert**, you mean that you consider their behavior, especially their sexual behavior, to be immoral or unacceptable. 性倒錯者 [DISAPPROVAL 不賛成] □ *I hope the police track down these perverts and charge them with rape.* 私は警察がこれらの性倒錯者の居所をつき止め、強姦罪で起訴することを望んでいる。

per|vert|ed /pərvɜrtɪd/ **1** ADJ 形容詞 If you say that someone is **perverted**, you mean that you consider their behavior, especially their sexual behavior, to be immoral or unacceptable. 性倒錯の [DISAPPROVAL 不賛成] □ *You've been protecting sick and perverted men.* あなたは異常な性倒錯の男達を保護してきた。 **2** ADJ 形容詞 You can use **perverted** to describe actions or ideas which you think are wrong, unnatural, or harmful. 誤った [DISAPPROVAL 不賛成] □ *...a perverted form of knowledge.* 誤った形態の知識

pes|si|mism /pɛsɪmɪzəm/ N-UNCOUNT 不可算名詞 **Pessimism** is the belief that bad things are going to happen. 悲観 □ *...universal pessimism about the economy.* 経済に関する全般的な悲観

pes|si|mist /pɛsɪmɪst/ (pessimists) N-COUNT 可算名詞 A **pessimist** is someone who thinks that bad things are going to happen. 悲観論者 □ *I'm a natural pessimist; I usually expect the worst.* 私は生まれつき悲観論者だ。たいていは最悪の事態になると思っている。

pes|si|mis|tic /pɛsɪmɪstɪk/ ADJ 形容詞 Someone who is **pessimistic** thinks that bad things are going to happen. 悲観的な □ *Not everyone is so pessimistic about the future.* 誰もが将来についてそれほど悲観的なわけではない。 □ *Hardy has often been criticized for an excessively pessimistic view of life.* ハーディはしばしば人生について過度に悲観的な見方を批判されてきた。

pest /pɛst/ (pests) **1** N-COUNT 可算名詞 **Pests** are insects or small animals that damage crops or food supplies. 害虫 □ *...crops which are resistant to some of the major insect pests and diseases.* 主要な害虫および病気の一部に抵抗力を持つ穀物 □ *Each year ten percent of the crop is lost to a pest called corn rootworm.* 毎年穀物の10%はウリハムシと呼ばれる害虫に食われる。 **2** N-COUNT 可算名詞 You can describe someone, especially a child, as a **pest** if they keep bothering you. 厄介者 [INFORMAL くだけた, DISAPPROVAL 不賛成] □ *He climbed on the table, pulled my hair, and was generally a pest.* 彼はテーブルの上によじ登り私の髪をひっぱり、大概に言って厄介な子だった。
→ see **farm**

pes|ter /pɛstər/ (pesters, pestering, pestered) V-T 他動詞 If you say that someone **is pestering** you, you mean that they keep asking you to do something, or keep talking to you, and you find this annoying. うるさく悩ませる [DISAPPROVAL 不賛成] □ *I thought she'd stop pestering me, but it only seemed to make her worse.* 私は彼女が私につきまとうのを止めるだろうと思ったが、そのことで彼女は余計に悪くなるようだった。 □ *I know he gets fed up with people pestering him for money.* 私は彼が金をせびる人にうんざりするのを知っている。

Word Link   cide ≈ killing : genocide, homicide, pesticide

pes|ti|cide /pɛstɪsaɪd/ (pesticides) N-MASS 質量名詞 **Pesticides** are chemicals that farmers put on their crops to kill harmful insects. 殺虫剤
→ see **pollution**

pet /pɛt/ (pets, petting, petted) **1** N-COUNT 可算名詞 A **pet** is an animal that you keep in your home to give you company and pleasure. ペット □ *It is plainly cruel to keep turtles as pets.* はっきり言ってカメをペットとして飼うのは残酷である。 □ *...a bachelor living*

Word Web — pet

Americans love **pets**. They own more than 51 million **dogs**, 56 million **cats**, 45 million **birds**, 75 million small **mammals** and **reptiles**, and millions of **fish**. Recent studies have shown that adult pet owners are healthier overall than those who don't have **companion animals**. One study (Katcher, 1982) suggests that owning a pet lowers blood pressure. The 2001 German Socio-Economic Panel Survey found that pet owners made fewer doctor visits than others in the group. And a study in the *American Journal of Cardiology* found that male dog owners were less likely to die within a year after a heart attack than people who didn't own dogs.

---

alone in a house with his pet dog. ペットの犬と一軒家に1人で住んでいる独身の男 **2** ADJ 形容詞 Someone's **pet** theory, project, or subject is one that they particularly support or like. 得意の □ *He would not stand by and let his pet project be killed off.* 彼は自分の大切なプロジェクトがつぶされるのを傍観してはいないだろう. **3** V-T 他動詞 If you **pet** a person or animal, you touch them in an affectionate way. なでる □ *The policeman reached down and petted the wolfhound.* 警官は手を伸ばしウルフハウンドをなでた.
→ see Word Web: pet

pet|al /pɛtəl/ (**petals**) N-COUNT 可算名詞 The **petals** of a flower are the thin colored or white parts that together form the flower. 花びら □ *...bowls of dried rose petals.* ドライフラワーのバラの花びらが入った皿

pe|ter /pitər/ (**peters, petering, petered**)
▶ **peter out** PHRASAL VERB 句動詞 If something **peters out**, it gradually comes to an end. しだいに衰えてなくなる □ *The six-month strike seemed to be petering out.* 6か月のストは先細りなってなくなったようだった.

pe|tite /pətit/ ADJ 形容詞 If you describe a woman as **petite**, you are politely saying that she is small and is not fat. 小柄な □ *She was of below average height, petite and slender.* 彼女は平均以下の身長で小柄でほっそりしていた.

pe|ti|tion /pətɪʃ³n/ (**petitions, petitioning, petitioned**)
1 N-COUNT 可算名詞 A **petition** is a document signed by a lot of people that asks a government or other official group to do a particular thing. 嘆願書 □ *People feel so strongly that we recently presented the government with a petition signed by 4,500 people.* 強い民意が存在するので、最近4千5百人の署名入り嘆願書を政府に提出した. **2** N-COUNT 可算名詞 A **petition** is a formal request made to a court of law for some legal action to be taken. 申立書 [LEGAL 法律的] □ *His lawyers filed a petition for all charges to be dropped.* 彼の弁護士は全容疑を取り下げるよう申立書を提出した. **3** V-T/V-I 他動詞/自動詞 If you **petition** someone in authority, you make a formal request to them. 申立てる [LEGAL 法律的] □ *...couples petitioning for divorce.* 離婚を申立てる夫婦 □ *All the attempts to petition Congress had failed.* 議会に申立てを行う試みは全て失敗した.

pet|ri|fied /pɛtrɪfaɪd/ **1** ADJ 形容詞 If you are **petrified**, you are extremely frightened, perhaps so frightened that you cannot think or move. すくむ □ *I've always been petrified of being alone.* 私はいつもひとりでいるのがすごく怖かった. **2** ADJ 形容詞 A **petrified** plant or animal has died and has gradually turned into stone. 石化した [ADJ n] □ *...a block of petrified wood.* 石化した木塊

pet|rol /pɛtrəl/ N-UNCOUNT 不可算名詞 **Petrol** is the same as **gasoline**. ガソリン [BRIT 英国英語]

pe|tro|leum /pətroʊliəm/ N-UNCOUNT 不可算名詞 **Petroleum** is oil that is found under the surface of the earth or under the sea bed. Gasoline and kerosene are obtained from petroleum. 石油
→ see energy, oil

pet|ty /pɛti/ (**pettier, pettiest**) **1** ADJ 形容詞 You can use **petty** to describe things such as problems, rules, or arguments that you think are unimportant or relate to unimportant things. 取るに足りない [DISAPPROVAL 不賛成] □ *He was miserable all the time and fights would start over petty things.* 彼は四六時中気がめいっていて些細なことでよく喧嘩が始まったものだ. □ *...endless rules and petty regulations.* 長々とした規則と大して重要でない規制 **2** ADJ 形容詞 If you describe someone's behavior as **petty**, you mean that they care too much about small, unimportant things and perhaps that they are unnecessarily unkind. 狭量の [DISAPPROVAL 不賛成] □ *He was petty-minded and obsessed with detail.* 彼は心が狭く、細かなことをくよくよ心配した. ● **pet|ti|ness** N-UNCOUNT 不可算名詞 狭量さ □ *Never had she met such spite and pettiness.* 彼女はかつてそのような悪意と狭量さに出会ったことはなかった. **3** ADJ 形容詞 **Petty** is used of people or actions that are less important, serious, or great than others. 小規模の □ *...petty crime, such as purse-snatching and minor break-ins.* ひったくりやちょっとした不法侵入などの軽犯罪

pet|ty cash N-UNCOUNT 不可算名詞 **Petty cash** is money that is kept in the office of a company, for making small payments in cash when necessary. 小口現金 [BUSINESS 実業] □ *After having her expense claims overruled, she took the money from petty cash.* 経費請求が拒否された後、彼女は小口現金からその金を取った.

petu|lant /pɛtʃələnt/ ADJ 形容詞 Someone who is **petulant** is unreasonably angry and upset in a childish way. 短気な □ *His critics say he's just being silly and petulant.* 彼は愚かで怒りっぽくなっているだけだとの批判もある.

pew /pyu/ (**pews**) N-COUNT 可算名詞 A **pew** is a long wooden seat with a back that people sit on in church. 聖堂信者席 □ *Charlene sat in the front pew.* シャーリーンは信徒席の最前列に座った.

pew|ter /pyutər/ N-UNCOUNT 不可算名詞 **Pewter** is a gray metal that is made by mixing tin and lead. Pewter was often used in former times to make ornaments or containers for eating and drinking. しろめ □ *...pewter plates.* しろめの皿

phan|tom /fæntəm/ (**phantoms**) **1** N-COUNT 可算名詞 A **phantom** is a ghost. 幽霊 □ *They vanished down the stairs like two phantoms.* 彼らは2人の幽霊のように階段の下に消えた. **2** ADJ 形容詞 You use **phantom** to describe something that you think you experience but that is not real. 錯覚による [ADJ n] □ *...phantom pregnancies.* 想像妊娠 **3** ADJ 形容詞 **Phantom** is used to describe business organizations, agreements, or goods that do not really exist, but that someone pretends do exist in order to cheat people. 見せかけの [ADJ n] □ *A phantom trading scheme at a Wall Street investment bank went unnoticed for three years.* ウォール街の投資銀行の幽霊取引計画は3年間発覚しなかった.

phar|aoh /fɛəroʊ, færoʊ, feɪ-/ (**pharaohs**) N-COUNT; N-PROPER 可算名詞, 固有名詞 A **pharaoh** was a king of ancient Egypt. ファラオ □ *...Rameses II, Pharaoh of All Egypt.* 古代エジプトのファラオ, ラメス2世

Word Link | *pharma ≈ drug : pharmaceutical, pharmacist, pharmacy*

phar|ma|ceu|ti|cal /fɑrməsutɪkəl/ (**pharmaceuticals**) **1** ADJ 形容詞 **Pharmaceutical** means connected with the industrial production of medicines. 製薬の [ADJ n] □ *...a Swiss pharmaceutical company.* スイスの製薬会社 **2** N-PLURAL 複数名詞 **Pharmaceuticals** are medicines. 医薬 □ *Antibiotics were of no use, neither were other pharmaceuticals.* 抗生物質は役に立たず、他の医薬品も効き目がなかった.

Word Link | *ist ≈ one who practices : artist, chemist, pharmacist*

phar|ma|cist /fɑrməsɪst/ (**pharmacists**) N-COUNT 可算名詞 A **pharmacist** is a person who is qualified to prepare and sell medicines. 薬剤師 □ *Ask your pharmacist for advice.* 薬剤師に助言を求めなさい.

phar|ma|cy /fɑrməsi/ (**pharmacies**) **1** N-COUNT 可算名詞 A **pharmacy** is a store or a department in a store where medicines are sold or given out. 薬局 □ *Pick up the medicine from the pharmacy.* 薬局で薬を受け取りなさい. **2** N-UNCOUNT 不可算名詞 **Pharmacy** is the job or the science of preparing medicines. 薬学 □ *He spent four years studying pharmacy.* 彼は薬学を4年間学んだ.

In American English, the usual way of referring to a store where medicines are sold is a **drugstore**. □ *She went into a drugstore and bought some aspirin.* **Pharmacy** refers specifically to a part of the drugstore where you get prescription medicines. Pharmacies are often located in stores that mainly sell other merchandise, such as supermarkets and discount centers. In Britain, the nearest equivalent of a drugstore is a **chemist's**.

phase /feɪz/ (**phases, phasing, phased**) N-COUNT 可算名詞 A **phase** is a particular stage in a process or in the gradual development of something. 段階 □ *This fall, 6,000 residents will participate in the first phase of the project.* 今秋、6千人の住民がプロジェクトの第一段階に参加する. □ *The crisis is entering a crucial, critical*

P

phase. 危機は重要な段階に入りつつある.
▶ **phase in** PHRASAL VERB 句動詞 If a new way of doing something **is phased in**, it is introduced gradually. 段階的に組み入れる □ *The reforms would be phased in over three years.* 改革は3年間にわたり段階的に導入される.
▶ **phase out** PHRASAL VERB 句動詞 If something **is phased out**, people gradually stop using it. 段階的に除去される □ *They said the present system of military conscription should be phased out.* 彼らは現行の徴兵制度は段階的に廃止されると言った.

Thesaurus
phase また次を参照:
N.   chapter, juncture, period, point, stage, time

Ph.D. /ˌpiː eɪtʃ ˈdiː/ (**Ph.D.s**) also **PhD** **1** N-COUNT 可算名詞 A **Ph.D.** is a degree awarded to people who have done advanced research in a particular subject. **Ph.D.** is an abbreviation for **Doctor of Philosophy**. 博士号 □ *He is more highly educated, with a Ph.D. in chemistry.* 彼は化学の博士号を持ち, さらに高度な教育を受けている. **2 Ph.D.** is written after someone's name to indicate that they have a Ph.D. 博士 □ *...R.D. Combes, Ph.D.* RDコームス博士
→ see **graduation**

pheas|ant /ˈfɛzⁿnt/ (**pheasants**)

Pheasant can also be used as the plural form.

Pheasant は複数形としても使える.

N-COUNT 可算名詞 A **pheasant** is a bird with a long tail. Pheasants are often shot as a sport and then eaten. キジ ● N-UNCOUNT 不可算名詞 **Pheasant** is the flesh of this bird eaten as food. キジの肉 □ *...roast pheasant.* ローストされたキジの肉

phe|nom|enal /fɪˈnɒmɪnⁿl/ ADJ 形容詞 Something that is **phenomenal** is unusually great or good. 驚くべき [EMPHASIS 強調] □ *Exports of Australian wine are growing at a phenomenal rate.* オーストラリア産ワインの輸出は驚異的な比率で拡大している. ● **phe|nom|enal|ly** ADV 副詞 驚くほど □ *Annie, 37, has recently re-launched her phenomenally successful singing career.* 驚異的な人気を集めたアニー (37歳) は最近, 歌手として復帰した.

phe|nom|enon /fɪˈnɒmɪnɒn/ (**phenomena**) N-COUNT 可算名詞 A **phenomenon** is something that is observed to happen or exist. 現象 [FORMAL 形式ばった] □ *...scientific explanations of natural phenomena.* 自然現象の科学的説明
→ see **science experiment**

phi|loso|pher /fɪˈlɒsəfər/ (**philosophers**) **1** N-COUNT 可算名詞 A **philosopher** is a person who studies or writes about philosophy. 哲学者 □ *...the Greek philosopher Plato.* ギリシアの哲学者プラトン **2** N-COUNT 可算名詞 If you refer to someone as a **philosopher**, you mean that they think deeply and seriously about life and other basic matters. 哲人 □ *Carlos was something of a philosopher.* カルロスはちょっとした哲人だった.
→ see **philosophy**

Word Link
soph ≈ wise : philosophical, philosophy, sophisticated

philo|sophi|cal /ˌfɪləˈsɒfɪkⁿl/ **1** ADJ 形容詞 **Philosophical** means concerned with or relating to philosophy. 哲学の □ *He was more accustomed to cocktail party chatter than to political or philosophical discussions.* 彼は政治や哲学の議論よりもカクテルパーティでするようなおしゃべりに慣れていた. ● **philo|sophi|cal|ly** /ˌfɪləˈsɒfɪkli/ ADV 副詞 哲学的に □ *Wilbur says he's not a coward, but that he's philosophically opposed to war.* ウィルバーは臆病 (おくびょう) 者ではないが哲学的に戦争に反対だと言う. **2** ADJ 形容詞 Someone who is **philosophical** does not get upset when disappointing or disturbing things happen. 超然とした [APPROVAL 賛成] □ *Lewis has grown philosophical about life.* ルイスは人生を達観するようになっ

た. ● **philo|sophi|cal|ly** ADV 副詞 [ADV after v] 達観して □ *She says philosophically: "It could have been far worse."* 彼女は達観して言った. 「もっとひどくなっていたかもしれない」

phi|loso|phy /fɪˈlɒsəfi/ (**philosophies**) **1** N-UNCOUNT 不可算名詞 **Philosophy** is the study or creation of theories about basic things such as the nature of existence, knowledge, and thought, or about how people should live. 哲学 □ *He studied philosophy and psychology at Yale.* 彼はエール大学で哲学と心理学を専攻した. **2** N-COUNT 可算名詞 A **philosophy** is a particular set of ideas that a philosopher has. 哲学体系 □ *...the philosophies of Socrates, Plato, and Aristotle.* ソクラテス, プラトン, アリストテレスの哲学体系 **3** N-COUNT 可算名詞 A **philosophy** is a particular theory that someone has about how to live or how to deal with a particular situation. 方針 □ *The best philosophy is to change your food habits to a low-sugar diet.* 最良の方針は糖分の少ない食事の習慣を作ることだ.
→ see Word Web: **philosophy**

Thesaurus
philosophy また次を参照:
N.   attitude, outlook, reasoning **3**

Word Link
phob ≈ fear : homophobic, phobia, xenophobia

pho|bia /ˈfoʊbiə/ (**phobias**) N-COUNT 可算名詞 A **phobia** is a very strong irrational fear or hatred of something. 病的恐怖 □ *The man had a phobia about flying.* その男は飛行機に乗ることに対して病的恐怖を抱いていた.

phone /foʊn/ (**phones, phoning, phoned**) **1** N-SING 単数名詞 The **phone** is an electrical system that you use to talk to someone else in another place, by dialing a number on a piece of equipment and speaking into it. 電話 [usu "the" N, also "by" N] □ *"I didn't tell you over the phone," she said. "I didn't know who might be listening."* 「電話で言わなかったのは誰が聞いているか分からなかったから」と彼女は言った. □ *She looked forward to talking to her daughter by phone.* 彼女は娘と電話で話すのを楽しみにしていた. **2** N-COUNT 可算名詞 The **phone** is the piece of equipment that you use when you dial someone's phone number and talk to them. 電話 □ *Two minutes later the phone rang.* 2分後に電話が鳴った. **3** → see also **cellular phone 4** N-SING 単数名詞 If you say that someone picks up or puts down **the phone**, you mean that they lift or replace the receiver. 受話器 □ *She picked up the phone, and began to dial Maurice's number.* 彼女は受話器を取り上げ, モーリスの番号を回し始めた. **5** V-T/V-I 他動詞/自動詞 When you **phone** someone, you dial their phone number and speak to them by phone. 電話をかける □ *He'd phoned Laura to see if she was better.* 彼はローラの体調がよくなったか聞くために電話をかけた. **6** PHRASE 句 If you say that someone is **on the phone**, you mean that they are speaking to someone by phone. 電話中の □ *She's always on the phone, wanting to know what I've been up to.* 彼女は私のしていることを探るためにいつも電話をしている.
→ see **office**
▶ **phone in 1** PHRASAL VERB 句動詞 If you **phone in** to a radio or television show, you telephone the show in order to give your opinion on a matter that the show has raised. 視聴者が電話で参加する □ *Listeners have been invited to phone in to pick the winner.* 優勝者を決めるためにリスナーの電話参加が呼びかけられた. **2** PHRASAL VERB 句動詞 If you **phone in** to a place, you make a telephone call to that place. 電話を入れる □ *He has phoned in to say he is thinking over his options.* 彼は選択肢を検討中だと伝えるために電話を入れた. **3** PHRASAL VERB 句動詞 If you **phone in** an order for something, you place the order by telephone. 電話で注文する □ *Just phone in your order three or more days prior to departure.* 出発の3日前までに電話で注文してください.
▶ **phone up** PHRASAL VERB 句動詞 When you **phone** someone **up**,

Word Web
philosophy

Philosophy helps us **understand** ourselves and the purpose of our lives. **Philosophers** have studied the same **issues** for thousands of years. The Chinese philosopher Confucius* wrote about personal and **political morals**. He taught that people should love others and honor their parents. They should do what is right, not what is best for themselves. He thought that a ruler who had to use force had already failed as a ruler. The Greek philosopher Plato* wrote about politics and science. Later, Aristotle* outlined a system of **logic** and **reasoning**. He wanted to be absolutely sure what is true and what isn't.

Confucius (551-479 BC)
Plato (427-347 BC)
Aristotle (384-322 BC)

Plato

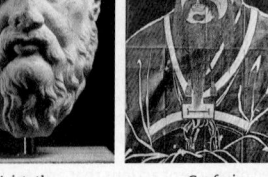
Aristotle

Confucius

you dial their phone number and speak to them by phone. 電話する ❏ *Phone him up and tell him to come and have dinner with you one night.* 彼に電話していつか夕食に招待しなさい。

phone book (**phone books**) N-COUNT 可算名詞 A **phone book** is a book that contains an alphabetical list of the names, addresses, and telephone numbers of the people and businesses in a town or area. 電話帳

phone booth (**phone booths**) ■ N-COUNT 可算名詞 A **phone booth** is a place in a station, hotel, or other public building where there is a public telephone. 公衆電話のある場所 ■ N-COUNT 可算名詞 A **phone booth** is a small shelter outdoors or in a building in which there is a public telephone. 公衆電話ボックス [AM 米国英語]

phone box (**phone boxes**) N-COUNT 可算名詞 A **phone box** is the same as a **phone booth** 公衆電話ボックス [BRIT 英国英語]

phone call (**phone calls**) N-COUNT 可算名詞 If you make a **phone call**, you dial someone's phone number and speak to them by phone. 電話をかけること ❏ *Wait there for a minute. I have to make a phone call.* ちょっとそこで待っていて。電話をかけなきゃならないの。

phone|card /foʊnkɑrd/ (**phonecards**) also **phone card** N-COUNT 可算名詞 A **phonecard** is a plastic card that you can use instead of money to pay for telephone calls in some public telephones. テレフォンカード

phone-in (**phone-ins**) N-COUNT 可算名詞 A **phone-in** is a program on radio or television in which people telephone with questions or opinions and their calls are broadcast. 視聴者が電話で参加する番組 ❏ *She took part in a radio phone-in program.* 彼女は電話でラジオ番組に参加した。

pho|ney /foʊni/ → see **phony**

phos|phate /fɒsfeɪt/ (**phosphates**) N-MASS 質量名詞 A **phosphate** is a chemical compound that contains phosphorus. Phosphates are often used in fertilizers. 燐酸塩

pho|to /foʊtoʊ/ (**photos**) N-COUNT 可算名詞 A **photo** is the same as a **photograph**. 写真 ❏ *Let's take a photo!* 写真を撮ろう。
→ see **photography**

photo|copi|er /foʊtəkɒpiər/ (**photocopiers**) N-COUNT 可算名詞 A **photocopier** is a machine that quickly copies documents onto paper by photographing them. 写真複写機
→ see **copy**

photo|copy /foʊtəkɒpi/ (**photocopies, photocopying, photocopied**) ■ N-COUNT 可算名詞 A **photocopy** is a copy of a document made using a photocopier. 写真複写 ❏ *He was shown a photocopy of the certificate.* 彼は証明書のコピーを見せられた。 ■ V-T 他動詞 If you **photocopy** a document, you make a copy of it using a photocopier. 写真複写する [他動詞] ❏ *Staff photocopied the check before cashing it.* 職員は小切手を現金化する前にコピーした。

photo|graph /foʊtəgræf/ (**photographs, photographing, photographed**) ■ N-COUNT 可算名詞 A **photograph** is a picture that is made using a camera. 写真 ❏ *He wants to take some photographs of the house.* 彼は家の写真を何枚か撮りたがっている。 ■ V-T 他動詞 When you **photograph** someone or something, you use a camera to obtain a picture of them. 撮影する [他動詞] ❏ *She photographed the children.* 彼女は子供たちの写真を撮った。

pho|tog|ra|pher /fətɒgrəfər/ (**photographers**) N-COUNT 可算名詞 A **photographer** is someone who takes photographs as a job or hobby. 写真家 ❏ *…a professional photographer.* プロのカメラマン。
→ see **photography**

photo|graph|ic /foʊtəgræfɪk/ ■ ADJ 形容詞 **Photographic** means connected with photographs or photography. 写真の ❏ *…photographic equipment.* 写真機材 ■ ADJ 形容詞 If you have a **photographic memory**, you are able to remember things in great detail after you have seen them. 詳細な ❏ *He had a photographic memory for maps.* 彼は地図の記憶が抜群だった。

pho|tog|ra|phy /fətɒgrəfi/ N-UNCOUNT 不可算名詞 **Photography** is the skill, job, or process of producing

photographs. 写真術 ❏ *Photography is one of her hobbies.* 写真は彼女の趣味の1つだ。
→ see Word Web: **photography**

photovoltaic /foʊtoʊvɒlteɪk/ ADJ 形容詞 A **photovoltaic** cell or panel is a device that uses sunlight to cause a chemical reaction which produces electricity. 光起電性の [TECHNICAL 技術的] [ADJ n]
→ see **solar system**

phras|al verb /freɪzəl vɜrb/ (**phrasal verbs**) N-COUNT 可算名詞 A **phrasal verb** is a combination of a verb and an adverb or preposition, for example, "shut up" or "knock back," which together have a particular meaning. 句動詞

phrase /freɪz/ (**phrases, phrasing, phrased**) ■ N-COUNT 可算名詞 A **phrase** is a short group of words that people often use as a way of saying something. The meaning of a phrase is often not obvious from the meaning of the individual words in it. 慣用句 ❏ *He used a phrase I hate: "You have to be cruel to be kind."* 彼は「親切であるためには残酷でなければならない」という私の嫌いな成句を使った。 ■ N-COUNT 可算名詞 A **phrase** is a small group of words that forms a unit, either on its own or within a sentence. 句 ❏ *A writer spends many hours going over and over a scene — changing a phrase here, a word there.* 作家は何時間も費やして何度も情景を見直し、ところどころで句や単語を変更する。 ■ V-T 他動詞 If you **phrase** something in a particular way, you express it in words in that way. ことばで表す [他動詞] ❏ *I would have phrased it quite differently.* 私だったらもっと違う表現を使っただろう。 ❏ *The speech was carefully phrased.* 演説は字句を慎重に選んだものだった。 ■ PHRASE 句 If someone has a particular **turn of phrase**, they have a particular way of expressing themselves in words. 言いまわし ❏ *…Schwarzkopf's distinctive turn of phrase.* シュワルツコフの独特な言いまわし。 ■ to **coin a phrase** → see **coin**

physi|cal /fɪzɪkəl/ (**physicals**) ■ ADJ 形容詞 **Physical** qualities, actions, or things are connected with a person's body, rather than with their mind. 身体の ❏ *…the physical and mental problems caused by the illness.* 疾病に起因する身体的および精神的問題 ❏ *Physical activity promotes good health.* 運動は健康を増進する。● **physi|cal|ly** ADV 副詞 肉体的に ❏ *You may be physically and mentally exhausted after a long flight.* 長い飛行機旅で肉体的にも精神的にも疲れて果てているのではありませんか。 ■ ADJ 形容詞 **Physical** things are real things that can be touched and seen, rather than ideas or spoken words. 物質の ❏ *Physical and ideological barriers had come down in Eastern Europe.* 東欧の物質とイデオロギー両面の障害が取り壊された。 ❏ *…physical evidence to support the story.* その話を裏付ける物的証拠 ● **physi|cal|ly** ADV 副詞 物質的に ❏ *…physically cut off from every other country.* 他のすべての国から物質的に疎外された。 ■ ADJ 形容詞 [ADJ n] **Physical** means relating to the structure, size, or shape of something that can be touched and seen. 物地形的な ❏ *…the physical characteristics of the terrain.* 地形の物理的な特徴 ■ ADJ 形容詞 [ADJ n] **Physical** means connected with physics or the laws of physics. 物理学の [ADJ n] ❏ *…the physical laws of combustion and thermodynamics.* 燃焼と熱力学の物理法則 ■ ADJ 形容詞 Someone who is **physical** touches people a lot, either in an affectionate way or in a rough way. 体に触れる ❏ *We decided that in the game we would be physical and aggressive.* 私たちは試合で体を使って攻撃的になることを決心した。 ■ ADJ 形容詞 **Physical** is used in expressions such as **physical love** and **physical relationships** to refer to sexual relationships between people. 肉体の [ADJ n] ❏ *It had been years since they had shared any meaningful form of physical relationship.* 我々が肉体関係といえるようなものを持ってからもう何年も経っていた。 ■ N-COUNT 可算名詞 A **physical** is a medical examination by your doctor to make sure that there is nothing wrong with your health, or a medical examination to make sure you are fit enough to do a particular job. 健康診断 ❏ *Bob failed his physical.* ボブは健康診断が通らなかった。
→ see **diagnosis**

It's easy to **take a picture** with a digital **camera**. You just look through the **viewfinder** and push the **shutter button**. But professional **photographers** need to produce high quality **photos**. So their job is more difficult. First they decide on the correct **film** for the job and **load** the camera. Then they check the **lighting** and carefully **focus** the camera. They usually take several **shots**, one after another. Then it's time to **develop** the film and make **prints**. Sometimes a photographer will **crop** a photo or **enlarge** it to create a more striking **image**.

P

Thesaurus
physical また次を参照：

ADJ. bodily, earthly, mortal, visceral; (ant.) mental **1**
concrete, natural, real, solid, tangible, visible; (ant.)
intangible, theoretical **2**

Word Link
ician ≈ *person who works at* : elect**rician**, mus**ician**,
phys**ician**

phy|si|cian /fɪzɪʃⁿn/ (**physicians**) N-COUNT 可算名詞 A
physician is a medical doctor. 医師 [FORMAL 形式ばった] ❑ *…your
family physician.* あなたの家庭医.
→ see **diagnosis, hospital, medicine**

physi|cist /fɪzɪsɪst/ (**physicists**) N-COUNT 可算名詞 A **physicist**
is a person who does research connected with physics or who
studies physics. 物理学者 ❑ *…a nuclear physicist.* 原子物理学者

phys|ics /fɪzɪks/ N-UNCOUNT 不可算名詞 **Physics** is the
scientific study of forces such as heat, light, sound, pressure,
gravity, and electricity, and the way that they affect objects. 物理
学 ❑ *…the laws of physics.* 物理学的法則.

Word Link
physi ≈ *of nature* : **physi**cal, **physi**cian, **physi**ology

physi|ol|ogy /fɪziɒlədʒi/ **1** N-UNCOUNT 不可算名詞 **Physiology**
is the scientific study of how people's and animals' bodies
function, and of how plants function. 生理学 ❑ *…the Nobel Prize
for Medicine and Physiology.* ノーベル医学・生理学賞 ● **2** N-UNCOUNT
不可算名詞 The **physiology** of a human or animal's body or of a
plant is the way that it functions. 生理機能 ❑ *…the physiology of
respiration.* 呼吸の生理学 ● **physio|logi|cal** /fɪziəlɒdʒɪkⁿl/ ADJ 形
容詞 生理の ❑ *…the physiological effects of stress.* ストレスの生理学
的効果

physio|thera|py /fɪzioʊθɛrəpi/ N-UNCOUNT 不可算名詞
Physiotherapy is the same as **physical therapy**. 物理療法 [BRIT 英
国英語]

phy|sique /fɪzik/ (**physiques**) N-COUNT 可算名詞 Someone's
physique is the shape and size of their body. 体格 ❑ *He has the
physique and energy of a man half his age.* 彼の体格とエネルギーは歳が
半分の人と同じだ.

pia|nist /piænɪst, piɑnɪst/ (**pianists**) N-COUNT 可算名詞 A
pianist is a person who plays the piano. ピアニスト ❑ *She was an
accomplished pianist, a superb swimmer, and a gifted artist.* 彼女は名ピ
アニスト，優れた水泳選手であり，また才能のある芸術家だった.

pi|ano /piænoʊ, pyænoʊ/ (**pianos**) N-VAR 可変性名詞 A **piano**
is a large musical instrument with a row of black and white keys.
When you press these keys with your fingers, little hammers hit
wire strings inside the piano which vibrate to produce musical
notes. ピアノ ❑ *I taught myself how to play the piano.* 私はピアノを独
学した. ❑ *He started piano lessons at the age of 7.* 彼はピアノのレッス
ンを7歳のときに始めた.
→ see **keyboard, music**

pick /pɪk/ (**picks, picking, picked**) **1** V-T 他動詞 If you **pick** a
particular person or thing, you choose that one. 選び取る [他動
詞] ❑ *Mr. Nowell had picked ten people to interview for six sales jobs in
Dallas.* ノウエル氏はダラスにおける6つの営業職の面接に10人の候
補を選んだ. **2** N-SING 単数名詞 You can refer to the best things
or people in a particular group as **the pick of** that group. 精選
物 ❑ *The boys here are the pick of the high school's soccer players.* ここ
にいる少年たちはその高校の選り抜きのサッカー選手だ. **3** V-T
他動詞 When you **pick** flowers, fruit, or leaves, you break them off
the plant or tree and collect them. 摘む [他動詞] ❑ *She used to pick
flowers in the Adirondacks.* 彼女はアディロンダック山地で花を摘んだ
ものだった. **4** V-T 他動詞 If you **pick** something from a place, you
remove it from there with your fingers or your hand. 抜く [他動
詞] ❑ *He picked the napkin from his lap and placed it alongside his plate.*
彼はひざからナプキンを取って皿の横に置いた. **5** V-T 他動詞 If you
pick your **nose** or **teeth**, you remove substances from inside your
nose or between your teeth. ほじる [他動詞] ❑ *Edgar, don't pick your
nose, dear.* エドガー，鼻をほじるのはやめなさい. **6** V-T 他動詞 If
you **pick a fight** with someone, you deliberately cause one. 仕掛
ける [他動詞] ❑ *He picked a fight with a waiter and landed in jail.* 彼は
ウェイターにけんかを仕掛けて刑務所行きになった. **7** V-T 他動詞 If
someone such as a thief **picks** a lock, they open it without a key,
for example, by using a piece of wire. (鍵以外の道具を用いて不法に
錠を) あける [他動詞] ❑ *He picked each lock deftly, and rifled the papers
within each drawer.* 彼は巧みにそれぞれの錠をあけ，引き出しにそれ
ぞれの中にある文書をくまなく捜した. **8** N-COUNT 可算名詞 A **pick** is
the same as a **pickax**. つるはし **9** PHRASE 句 If you are told to **take
your pick**, you can choose any one that you like from a group of
things. 好きなほうを選ぶ ❑ *Accountants can take their pick of company
cars.* 会計士は好きな社用車を選ぶことができる. **10** to **pick holes in**
something → see **hole** **11** to **pick** someone's **pocket** → see **pocket**
▶ **pick on** PHRASAL VERB 句動詞 If someone **picks on** you, they
repeatedly criticize you unfairly or treat you unkindly. いじめる

[INFORMAL くだけた] ❑ *Bullies pick on younger children.* いじめっ子は
幼い子供をいたぶる.
▶ **pick out** **1** PHRASAL VERB 句動詞 If you **pick out** someone or
something, you recognize them when it is difficult to see them,
for example, because they are among a large group. 見つける
❑ *The detective picked out the words with difficulty.* 刑事はやっとのこ
とで単語の意味を理解した. **2** PHRASAL VERB 句動詞 If you **pick out**
someone or something, you choose them from a group of people
or things. 選ぶ ❑ *I have been picked out to represent the whole team.* 私
はチーム全体の代表者に選ばれた.
▶ **pick up** **1** PHRASAL VERB 句動詞 When you **pick** something
up, you lift it up. 持ち上げる ❑ *He picked his cap up from the floor
and stuck it back on his head.* 彼は床から帽子を拾い上げてかぶり直し
た. **2** PHRASAL VERB 句動詞 When you **pick yourself up** after you
have fallen or been knocked down, you stand up rather slowly.
起き上がる ❑ *Tony picked himself up and set off along the track.* トニ
ーは起き上がってトラックを走り出した. **3** PHRASAL VERB 句動詞
When you **pick up** someone or something that is waiting to be
collected, you go to the place where they are and take them away,
often in a car. 受け取る ❑ *She was going over to her parents' house to
pick up some clean clothes for Oskar.* 彼女はオスカーの清潔な衣服を
受け取るために両親の家に行くところだった. **4** PHRASAL VERB 句
動詞 If someone **is picked up** by the police, they are arrested and
taken to a police station. 逮捕連行される ❑ *Rawlings had been picked
up by police at his office.* ローリングスは自分の事務所で警察に逮捕
された. **5** PHRASAL VERB 句動詞 If you **pick up** something such
as a skill or an idea, you acquire it without effort over a period
of time. 自然に身につける [INFORMAL くだけた] ❑ *Where did you
pick up your English?* どこで英語を聞きおぼえたんだい. **6** PHRASAL
VERB 句動詞 If you **pick up** someone you do not know, you talk
to them and try to start a sexual relationship with them. ひっ
かける [INFORMAL くだけた] ❑ *He had picked her up at a nightclub,
where she worked as a singer.* 彼は彼女が歌手として働いているナイト
クラブで彼女をひっかけた. **7** PHRASAL VERB 句動詞 If you **pick up**
an illness, you get it from somewhere or something. ひく（風
邪など）❑ *They've picked up a really nasty infection from something
they've eaten.* 彼らは食べた物でひどい病気に感染した. **8** PHRASAL
VERB 句動詞 If a piece of equipment, for example, a radio or a
microphone, **picks up** a signal or sound, it receives it or detects
it. とらえる ❑ *We can pick up Mexican television.* 私たちはメキシコのテレ
ビを受信できる. **9** PHRASAL VERB 句動詞 If you **pick up** something,
such as a feature or a pattern, you discover or identify it. 理解す
る ❑ *Some groups of consumers are slow to pick up trends in the use of
information technology.* 情報技術の使用トレンドをなかなか理解でき
ない消費者層もある. **10** PHRASAL VERB 句動詞 If someone **picks
up** a point or topic that has already been mentioned, or if they
pick up on it, they refer to it or develop it. 取り上げる ❑ *Can I just
pick up that guy's point?* その男の論点をちょっと取り上げてもいいか
い. **11** PHRASAL VERB 句動詞 If trade or the economy of a country
picks up, it improves. 景気づく ❑ *Industrial production is beginning
to pick up.* 工業生産高は好転し始めています. **12** PHRASAL VERB 句動
詞 If you **pick up** a room or house, you tidy it. 整頓する [AM 米国英
語] ❑ *She decided to start picking up the house from the top down.* 彼女は
その家を上から下まで整理整頓することにした. **13** → see also **pickup**
14 PHRASE 句 When a vehicle **picks up speed**, it begins to move
more quickly. スピードを上げる ❑ *Brian started the engine and pulled
away slowly, but picked up speed once he entered Oakwood Drive.* ブライ
アンはエンジンをかけゆっくり発車したが，オークウッドドライブに入
るとスピードを上げた.

Thesaurus
pick また次を参照：

v. choose, decide on, elect, select **1**
collect, gather, harvest, pull **3**

pick|ax /pɪkæks/ (**pickaxes**) also **pickaxe** N-COUNT 可算名詞 A
pickax is a large tool consisting of a curved, pointed piece of metal
with a long handle attached to the middle. Pickaxes are used for
breaking up rocks or the ground. つるはし

pick|et /pɪkɪt/ (**pickets, picketing, picketed**) **1** V-T/V-I 他動詞/
自動詞 When a group of people, usually labor union members,
picket, or **picket** a place of work, they stand outside in it order
to protest about something, to prevent people from going in, or
to persuade the workers to join a strike. ピケを張る [他動詞] ピ
ケに立つ [自動詞] ❑ *A few dozen employees picketed the company's
headquarters.* 数十人の従業員が本社でピケを張った. ● N-COUNT 可
算名詞 **Picket** is also a noun. ❑ *…forty demonstrators who have
set up a twenty-four hour picket.* 24時間ピケを張った40人のデモ参加者
2 N-COUNT 可算名詞 **Pickets** are people who are picketing a place
of work. ピケ隊員 ❑ *The strikers agreed to remove their pickets and hold
talks with the company.* ストライキ参加者はピケ隊員を退去させ，会社
と折衝を行うことに同意しました.

pick|et line (**picket lines**) N-COUNT 可算名詞 A **picket line** is a
group of pickets outside a place of work. ピケライン ❑ *No one tried
to cross the picket lines.* 誰もピケラインを超えようとはしませんでした.

pick|le /pɪkəl/ (pickles, pickling, pickled) **1** N-PLURAL 複数名詞 **Pickles** are vegetables or fruit, sometimes cut into pieces, which have been kept in vinegar or salt water for a long time so that they have a strong, sharp taste. ピクルス □...a bowl of sliced pickles in lemon juice. ボウル一杯のレモンジュース漬けピクルスの薄切り **2** N-MASS 質量名詞 **Pickle** is a cold spicy sauce with pieces of vegetables and fruit in it. 漬け汁 □...jars of pickle. 漬け汁の入った瓶 **3** V-T 他動詞 When you **pickle** food, you keep it in vinegar or salt water so that it does not go bad and it develops a strong, sharp taste. ピクルスにする [他動詞] □Select your favorite fruit or veg and pickle them while they are still fresh. 好きな果物か野菜を選んで，新鮮なうちにピクルスにする．

pick|led /pɪkəld/ ADJ 形容詞 **Pickled** food, such as vegetables, fruit, and fish, has been kept in vinegar or salt water to preserve it. 漬け物にした □...a jar of pickled fruit. 漬け物にした果物の瓶

pick|pocket /pɪkpɒkɪt/ (pickpockets) N-COUNT 可算名詞 A **pickpocket** is a person who steals things from people's pockets or bags in public places. スリ □Beware of pickpockets, especially when making a purchase. 買い物をするときは特にスリに気をつけなさい．

pick|up /pɪkʌp/ (pickups) **1** N-COUNT 可算名詞 A **pickup** or a **pickup truck** is a small truck with low sides that can be easily loaded and unloaded. ピックアップ・トラック **2** N-SING 単数名詞 A **pickup in** trade or **in** a country's economy is an improvement in it. 好転 □...a pickup in the housing market. 住宅市場の回復 **3** N-COUNT 可算名詞 A **pickup** takes place when someone picks up a person or thing that is waiting to be collected. 拾い上げること □The company had pickup points in most cities. その会社はほとんどの都市に集配拠点を持っていた．

→ see **car**

pic|nic /pɪknɪk/ (picnics, picnicking, picnicked) **1** N-COUNT 可算名詞 When people have a **picnic**, they eat a meal outdoors, usually in a park or a forest, or at the beach. ピクニック □We're going on a picnic tomorrow. 私たちは明日ピクニックに行く． **2** V-I 自動詞 When people **picnic** somewhere, they have a picnic. ピクニックに行く [自動詞] □Afterwards, we picnicked on the riverbank. そのあと私たちは川岸でピクニックをした．

→ see **park**

pic|to|rial /pɪktɔriəl/ ADJ 形容詞 **Pictorial** means using or relating to pictures. 絵画の □...a pictorial history of the Jewish people. 挿絵入りのユダヤ人の歴史書

Word Link

pict ≈ painting : de**pict**, **pict**ure, **pict**uresque

pic|ture /pɪktʃər/ (pictures, picturing, pictured) **1** N-COUNT 可算名詞 A **picture** consists of lines and shapes that are drawn, painted, or printed on a surface and show a person, thing, or scene. 絵 □...drawing a small picture with colored chalk. 色チョークで小さな絵を描く． **2** N-COUNT 可算名詞 A **picture** is a photograph. 写真 □The tourists have nothing to do but take pictures of each other. 観光客は写真を撮りあうことしかすることがない． **3** N-COUNT 可算名詞 Television **pictures** are the scenes that you see on a television screen. 映像 □...heartrending television pictures of human suffering. 人間の受難を映す悲痛なテレビ映像 **4** V-T 他動詞 To be **pictured** somewhere, for example, in a newspaper or magazine, means to appear in a photograph or picture. 写真が載る [usu passive] [他動詞] □The golfer is pictured on many of the front pages, kissing his trophy as he holds it aloft. そのゴルファーがトロフィーを高く持ち上げてキスしている写真が各紙の第1面に掲載された． □...a woman who claimed she had been pictured dancing with a celebrity in a nightclub. ナイトクラブで有名人と踊っているところを写真に撮られたと主張する女性． **5** N-COUNT 可算名詞 You can refer to a movie as a **picture**. 映画 □...a director of epic action pictures. 大作アクション映画の監督 **6** N-COUNT 可算名詞 If you have a **picture** of something in your mind, you have a clear idea or memory of it in your mind as if you were actually seeing it. 心像 □We are just trying to get our picture of the whole afternoon straight. 我々は午後全体の予定をはっきりさせようとしているだけだ． **7** V-T 他動詞 If you **picture** something in your mind, you think of it and have such a clear memory or idea of it that you seem to be able to see it. 想像する [他動詞] □He pictured her with long black braided hair. 彼は黒髪を三つ編みにした彼女を想像した． □He pictured Carrie sitting out in the car, waiting for him. 彼はキャリーが車の座席に座って彼を待っている様子を心に描いた． **8** N-COUNT 可算名詞 A **picture** of something is a description of it or an indication of what it is like. 描写 □I'll try and give you a better picture of what the boys do. 彼らの行為をもっとよくわかるように描写してみます． **9** N-SING 単数名詞 When you refer to the **picture** in a particular place, you are referring to the situation there. 状況 □It's a similar picture across the border in Ethiopia. エチオピア国境の向こう側でも同様の状況だ． **10** PHRASE 句 If you say that someone is **in the picture**, you mean that they are involved in the situation that you are talking about. If you say that they are **out of the picture**, you mean that they are not involved in the situation you are talking about. 事情に通じて，現れて，関係がな

い，いなくなった [v-link PHR, PHR after v] □Meyerson is back in the picture after disappearing in July. メイヤーソンは7月に姿を消したが，復活した． □His dad had been out of the picture since he was eight. 父親は彼が8歳のときにいなくなったままだ． **11** PHRASE 句 If you put someone **in the picture**, you tell them about a situation which they need to know about. 状況を知らせる □Has anyone put you in the picture? 君は誰かに事情を教えてもらったか．

→ see **photography**

Thesaurus

picture また次を参照：

N.	drawing, illustration, image, painting **1**
	photograph **2**
V.	envision, imagine, visualize **7**

Word Partnership

picture は次の語句と使われる：

ADJ.	**pretty as a** picture **1**
	mental picture **6**
	clear picture **6** **8**
	accurate picture, **complete** picture, **different** picture, **larger** picture, **overall** picture, **vivid** picture, **whole** picture **6** **8** **9**
	the big picture **8**

pic|tur|esque /pɪktʃəresk/ **1** ADJ 形容詞 A **picturesque** place is attractive and interesting, and has no ugly modern buildings. 絵のような □...a picturesque mountain village. 絵のような山村 **2** N-SING 単数名詞 You can refer to picturesque things as **the picturesque**. 絵のような物 □...lovers of the picturesque. 美しい物の愛好家

pie /paɪ/ (pies) **1** N-VAR 可変性名詞 A **pie** consists of fruit, meat, or vegetables baked in pastry. パイ □...a slice of apple pie. 一切れのアップルパイ **2** to **eat humble pie** → see **humble**

→ see **dessert**

piece /pis/ (pieces, piecing, pieced) **1** N-COUNT 可算名詞 A **piece of** something is an amount of it that has been broken off, torn off, or cut off. 断片 □...a piece of cake. 一切れのケーキ □Cut the ham into pieces. ハムを切り刻む． **2** N-COUNT 可算名詞 A **piece of** an object is one of the individual parts or sections that it is made of, especially a part that can be removed. 一部分 □...assembling objects out of standard pieces. 標準部品からオブジェクトを組み立てる． **3** N-COUNT 可算名詞 A **piece of** land is an area of land. 一区画 □People struggle to get the best piece of land. 人々は最もよい区画を入手しようと必死になっています． **4** N-COUNT 可算名詞 You can use **piece of** with many uncount nouns to refer to an individual thing of a particular kind. For example, you can refer to some advice as a **piece of advice**. 一つ □When I produced this piece of work, my lecturers were very critical. 私がこの作品を制作したとき，講師たちは非常に批判的だった． □...an interesting piece of information. 興味深い情報 **5** N-COUNT 可算名詞 You can refer to an article in a newspaper or magazine, some music written by someone, a broadcast, or a play as a **piece**. 書かれたもの □She wrote a piece on Gwyneth Paltrow for the New Yorker. 彼女は『ニューヨーカー』にグウィネス・パルトローに関する記事を書いた． □...a vaguely familiar orchestral piece. うっすらと覚えているオーケストラの曲 **6** N-COUNT 可算名詞 You can refer to a work of art as a **piece**. 作品 [FORMAL 形式ばった] □Each piece is unique, an exquisite painting of a real person, done on ivory. 各作品は独特で，この上なく素晴らしい，象牙に描かれた実在の人物の肖像画だ． **7** N-COUNT 可算名詞 You can refer to specific coins as **pieces**. For example, a 5 cent **piece** is a coin that is worth 5 cents. 硬貨 □...lots of 10 cent, 20 cent, and 50 cent pieces. たくさんの10，20および30セント硬貨 **8** N-COUNT 可算名詞 The **pieces** that you use when you play a board game such as chess are the specially made objects that you move around on the board. こま □How many pieces does each player have in backgammon? バックギャモンでは各プレーヤーはこまを何個使いますか． **9** PHRASE 句 If you **give** someone **a piece of** your **mind**, you tell them very clearly that you think they have behaved badly. 人に遠慮なく言う [INFORMAL くだけた] □How very thoughtless. I'll give him a piece of my mind. なんて無分別な．私が彼にはっきり言ってやるわ． **10** PHRASE 句 If someone or something is still **in one piece** after a dangerous journey or experience, they are safe and not damaged or hurt. 無傷で □...providing that my brother gets back alive and in one piece from his mission. 私の弟が生きて無傷で帰ってくるのなら **11** PHRASE 句 You use **to pieces** in expressions such as "smash to pieces," or "take something to pieces," when you are describing how something is broken or comes apart so that it is in separate pieces. こなごなに **12** PHRASE 句 If you **go to pieces**, you are so upset or nervous that you lose control of yourself and cannot do what you should do. 自制心を失う [INFORMAL くだけた] □She's a strong woman, but she nearly went to pieces when Arnie died. 彼女は強い女性だが，アーニーが死んだときは危うく神経衰弱になるところだった． **13** **a piece of the action** → see **action** **14** **bits and pieces** → see **bit**

▶ **piece together** 1 PHRASAL VERB 句動詞 If you **piece together** the truth about something, you gradually discover it. 全貌を知る ❑ *They've pieced together his movements for the last few days before his death.* 彼らは彼が死ぬ前の数日間の行動を総合した。 ❑ *In the following days, Frankie was able to piece together what had happened.* 後日、フランキーは何が起こったのか全貌を知ることができた。 2 PHRASAL VERB 句動詞 If you **piece** something **together**, you gradually make it by joining several things or parts together. 継ぎ合わせる ❑ *This process is akin to piecing together a jigsaw puzzle.* このプロセスはジグソーパズルをつなぎ合わせるのに似ている。
→ see **chess**

Thesaurus	*piece* また次を参照:
N.	bit, fragment, part, portion, section, segment; (ant.) whole 1 2 arrangement, article, creation, production, work 5 6

piece|meal /písmil/ ADJ 形容詞 If you describe a change or process as **piecemeal**, you disapprove of it because it happens gradually, usually at irregular intervals, and is probably not satisfactory. 断片的な [DISAPPROVAL 不賛成] ❑ *These piecemeal solutions won't work.* こういった断片的な問題解決法は役に立たない。 ● ADV 副詞 **Piecemeal** is also an adverb. ばらばらな [ADV after v] ❑ *It was built piecemeal over some 130 years.* それは130年以上をかけて少しずつ建設された。

pie chart (**pie charts**) N-COUNT 可算名詞 A **pie chart** is a circle divided into sections to show the relative proportions of a set of things. 円グラフ

pier /píər/ (**piers**) N-COUNT 可算名詞 A **pier** is a platform sticking out into water that people walk along or use when getting onto or off boats. 桟橋 ❑ *...Chicago's Navy Pier.* シカゴのネイビーピア

pierce /píərs/ (**pierces, piercing, pierced**) 1 V-T 他動詞 If a sharp object **pierces** something, or if you **pierce** something **with** a sharp object, the object goes into it and makes a hole in it. 穴をあける [他動詞] ❑ *One bullet pierced the left side of his chest.* 弾丸が彼の左胸を貫通した。 2 V-T 他動詞 If you have your ears or some other part of your body **pierced**, you have a small hole made through them so that you can wear a piece of jewelry in them. ピアス穴をあける [他動詞] ❑ *I'm having my ears pierced on Saturday.* 土曜日に耳にピアス穴をあけてもらう。 ● **piercing** N-VAR 可変性名詞 (**piercings**) 穴をあけること ❑ *...health risks from needles used in piercing and tattooing.* ピアスや刺青に使用した針に起因する健康上のリスク ❑ *...barefoot girls with braids and piercings.* ピアスをした、髪を三つ編みにしたはだしの少女たち

pierc|ing /píərsɪŋ/ 1 ADJ 形容詞 A **piercing** sound or voice is high-pitched and very sharp and clear in an unpleasant way. 甲高い ❑ *A piercing scream split the air.* 金切り声が空気を引き裂いた。 2 ADJ 形容詞 If someone has **piercing** eyes or a **piercing** stare, they seem to look at you very intensely. 鋭い [WRITTEN 書き言葉] ❑ *...his sandy blond hair and piercing blue eyes.* 彼の薄茶がかったブロンドの髪と鋭い青い眼 3 ADJ 形容詞 A **piercing** wind makes you feel very cold. 身にしみる ❑ *Warm clothing is recommended as the wind can be piercing.* 風が身を切るほど冷たいことがあるので暖かい衣服を着てください。 4 → see **pierce 2**

pi|ety /páɪɪti/ N-UNCOUNT 不可算名詞 **Piety** is strong religious belief, or behavior that is religious or morally correct. 敬虔 ❑ *Known for her piety, she would walk miles to attend communion services in the neighboring villages.* 彼女は敬虔なことで知られており、何マイルも歩いてでも近隣の村の聖餐会に出席する。

pig /píg/ (**pigs, pigging, pigged**) 1 N-COUNT 可算名詞 A **pig** is a pink or black animal with short legs and not much hair on its skin. Pigs are often kept on farms for their meat, which is called pork, ham, or bacon. ブタ ❑ *...the grunting of the pigs.* ブタのブーブーという鳴き声 2 → see also **guinea pig** 3 N-COUNT 可算名詞 If you call someone a **pig**, you think that they are unpleasant in some way, especially that they are greedy or unkind. ブタのような人 [INFORMAL くだけた, DISAPPROVAL 不賛成] ❑ *These guys destroyed the company. They're all a bunch of greedy pigs.* こいつらは会社を破壊した。どいつも貪欲なブタだ。 4 PHRASE 句 If you say "**when pigs fly**" after someone has said that something might happen, you are emphasizing that you think it is very unlikely. そんなことはありえない [HUMOROUS, INFORMAL ユーモアのある、くだけた, EMPHASIS 強調] ❑ *When would they be hired again? Perhaps, as the saying goes, when pigs fly.* 彼らはいつか再雇用されるのか。そんなこと天地がひっくり返りでもしなきゃ、ありえないんじゃないか。 5 PHRASE 句 If you say that someone is **making a pig of themselves**, you are criticizing them for eating a very large amount at one meal. 大食する [INFORMAL くだけた, DISAPPROVAL 不賛成] ❑ *I'm afraid I made a pig of myself at dinner.* 夕食で大食いしてしまったようだ。

▶ **pig out** PHRASAL VERB 句動詞 If you say that people **are pigging out**, you are criticizing them for eating a very large amount at

one meal or over a short period of time. がつがつ食う [INFORMAL くだけた, DISAPPROVAL 不賛成] ❑ *Some are so accustomed to pigging out, they can't cut back.* がつがつ食べることに慣れ切って食事を減らすことのできない人もいる。
→ see **barn, meat**

pi|geon /pɪdʒɪn/ (**pigeons**) N-COUNT 可算名詞 A **pigeon** is a bird, usually gray in color, that has a fat body. Pigeons often live in cities and towns. ハト

pigeon|hole /pɪdʒɪnhoʊl/ (**pigeonholes, pigeonholing, pigeonholed**) also **pigeon-hole** 1 N-COUNT 可算名詞 A **pigeonhole** is one of the sections in a frame on a wall where letters and messages can be left for someone, or one of the sections in a writing desk where you can keep documents. 小仕切りのついた書類入れ 2 V-T 他動詞 To **pigeonhole** someone or something means to decide that they belong to a particular class or category, often without considering all their qualities or characteristics. 分類整理する [他動詞] ❑ *He felt they had pigeonholed him.* 彼は彼らに後回しにされたと感じた。

pig|ment /pɪgmənt/ (**pigments**) N-MASS 質量名詞 A **pigment** is a substance that gives something a particular color. 顔料 [FORMAL 形式ばった] ❑ *The Romans used natural pigments on their fabrics and walls.* ローマ人は生地や壁に自然色素を使用した。

pike /páɪk/ (**pike**)

The plural can also be **pikes**.
複数は **pikes** もある。

N-VAR 可変性名詞 A **pike** is a large fish that lives in rivers and lakes and eats other fish. カワカマス ● N-UNCOUNT 不可算名詞 **Pike** is this fish eaten as food. カワカマス ❑ *...a mousse of pike.* カワカマスのムース

Pilates /pɪlɑ́tiz/ N-UNCOUNT 不可算名詞 **Pilates** is a type of exercise similar to yoga. ピラーテス ❑ *She'd never done Pilates before.* 彼女はそれまでピラーテスをしたことがなかった。

pile /páɪl/ (**piles, piling, piled**) 1 N-COUNT 可算名詞 A **pile of** things is a mass of them that is high in the middle and has sloping sides. の山 ❑ *...a pile of sand.* 砂の山。 ❑ *...a little pile of crumbs.* パン粉の小山 2 N-COUNT 可算名詞 A **pile of** things is a quantity of things that have been put neatly somewhere so that each thing is on top of the one below. 積み重ね ❑ *...a pile of boxes.* 積み重ねられた箱 ❑ *We sat in Sam's study, among the piles of books.* 私たちはサムの書斎で本の山の中に囲まれて座った。

A **pile** of things can be tidy or untidy. ❑ *...a neat pile of clothes.* A **heap** is usually untidy, and often has the shape of a hill or mound. ❑ *Now, the house is a heap of rubble.* A **stack** is usually tidy, and often consists of flat objects placed directly on top of each other. ❑ *...a neat stack of dishes.*

3 V-T 他動詞 If you **pile** things somewhere, you put them there so that they form a pile. 積み重ねる [他動詞] ❑ *He was piling clothes into the suitcase.* 彼はスーツケースに衣服を詰め込んでいた。 4 V-T 他動詞 If something is **piled with** things, it is covered or filled with piles of things. 詰め込まれている [usu passive] [他動詞] ❑ *Tables were piled high with local produce.* テーブルには特産品が山と積まれていた。 5 V-I 自動詞 If a group of people **pile into** or **out of** a vehicle, they all get into it or out of it in a disorganized way. ドヤドヤと入る、ドヤドヤと出る [他動詞] ❑ *They all piled into Jerry's car.* 彼らはみなジェリーの車にドヤドヤと乗り込んだ。 6 N-COUNT 可算名詞 **Piles** are wooden, concrete, or metal posts that are pushed into the ground and on which buildings or bridges are built. Piles are often used in very wet areas so that the buildings do not flood. 杭 ❑ *...settlements of wooden houses, set on piles along the shore.* 海岸に沿って杭を打って建てられた木造住宅の集落 7 N-PLURAL 複数名詞 **Piles** is an informal word meaning **hemorrhoids**. 痔 8 N-SING 単数名詞 The **pile** of a carpet or of a fabric such as velvet is its soft surface. It consists of a lot of little threads standing on end. パイル ❑ *...the carpet's thick pile.* カーペットのぶ厚いパイル 9 PHRASE 句 Someone who is **at the bottom of the pile** is low down in society or low down in an organization. Someone who is **at the top of the pile** is high up in society or high up in an organization. の底辺に、の一番上に [INFORMAL くだけた] ❑ *These workers are fed up with being at the bottom of the pile when it comes to pay.* これらの労働者は最低の賃金にうんざりしている。

▶ **pile up** 1 PHRASAL VERB 句動詞 If you **pile up** a quantity of things or if they **pile up**, they gradually form a pile. 積み重ねる ❑ *Bulldozers piled up huge mounds of dirt.* ブルドーザーが泥を大きな山に積み上げました。 2 PHRASAL VERB 句動詞 If you **pile up** work, problems, or losses or if they **pile up**, you get more and more of them. 積もらせる ❑ *Problems were piling up at work.* 仕事場では問題が山積している。

pil|grim /pɪlgrɪm/ (pilgrims) N-COUNT 可算名詞 **Pilgrims** are people who journey to a holy place for a religious reason. 巡礼者 ❑ *This is where pilgrims to the abbey would pay their first devotions.* ここは教会堂への巡礼者が最初に祈祷を捧げる場所です.

pil|grim|age /pɪlgrɪmɪdʒ/ (pilgrimages) **1** N-COUNT 可算名詞 If you make a **pilgrimage** to a holy place, you go there for a religious reason. 巡礼の旅 ❑ *...the pilgrimage to Mecca.* メッカへの巡礼の旅 **2** N-COUNT 可算名詞 A **pilgrimage** is a trip that someone makes to a place that is very important to them. 参詣 ❑ *...a private pilgrimage to family graves.* 先祖の墓へひっそりと参る.

pill /pɪl/ (pills) **1** N-COUNT 可算名詞 **Pills** are small solid round masses of medicine or vitamins that you swallow without chewing. 丸薬 ❑ *Why do I have to take all these pills?* そうしてこんなたくさんの丸薬を飲まなければならないの. **2** N-SING 単数名詞 If a woman is **on the pill**, she takes a special pill that prevents her from becoming pregnant. ピルを常用する. ❑ *She had been on the pill for three years.* 彼女は3年間ピルを服用していた. **3** PHRASE 句 If a person or group has to accept a failure or an unpleasant piece of news, you can say that it is a **bitter pill** or a **bitter pill to swallow**. 嫌なこと ❑ *You're too old to be given a job. That's a bitter pill to swallow.* あなたは仕事を与えられるには歳を取り過ぎている. それはつらい経験だ. **4** PHRASE 句 If someone does something to **sweeten the pill**, they do it to make some unpleasant news or an unpleasant measure more acceptable. いやなことの苦しみを和らげる ❑ *A few words of praise help to sweeten the pill of criticism.* 少しでも称賛のことばがあれば, 批判がいくらかましに思われる.

pil|lar /pɪlər/ (pillars) **1** N-COUNT 可算名詞 A **pillar** is a tall solid structure that is usually used to support part of a building. 柱 ❑ *...the pillars supporting the roof.* 屋根を支える柱 **2** N-COUNT 可算名詞 If something is the **pillar of** a system or agreement, it is the most important part of it or what makes it strong and successful. 中心となるもの ❑ *The pillar of her economic policy was keeping tight control over money supply.* 彼女の経済政策の柱が, 貨幣供給量を厳しく制御することでした. **3** N-COUNT 可算名詞 If you describe someone as a **pillar** of society or as a **pillar of** the community, you approve of them because they play an important and active part in society or in the community. 中心人物 [APPROVAL 賛成] ❑ *My father is a pillar of the community.* 私の父は地域社会の中心人物だ.

pil|low /pɪloʊ/ (pillows) N-COUNT 可算名詞 A **pillow** is a rectangular cushion that you rest your head on when you are in bed. 枕
→ see **bed, sleep**

pi|lot /paɪlət/ (pilots, piloting, piloted) **1** N-COUNT 可算名詞 A **pilot** is a person who is trained to fly an aircraft. パイロット ❑ *He spent seventeen years as an airline pilot.* 彼は航空会社のパイロットとして17年を費やした. **2** N-COUNT 可算名詞 A **pilot** is a person who steers a ship through a difficult stretch of water, for example, the entrance to a harbor. 水先案内人 ❑ *It seemed that the pilot had another ship to take up the river that evening.* 水先案内人は今夜川を上らせる船がもう一隻あるようだった. **3** V-T 他動詞 If someone **pilots** an aircraft or ship, they act as its pilot. 操縦する [他動詞] ❑ *He piloted his own plane part of the way to Washington.* 彼は自家用機でワシントンに行く途中, 一部自分で操縦した. **4** ADJ 形容詞 A **pilot** plan or a **pilot** project is one that is used to test an idea before deciding whether to introduce it on a larger scale. 試験的な ❑ *The plan is to launch a pilot program next summer.* 試験プログラムを来夏開始する計画である. **5** V-T 他動詞 If a government or organization **pilots** a program or project, they test it, before deciding whether to introduce it on a larger scale. 試験する [他動詞] ❑ *Teachers are piloting a literature-based reading program.* 教師は文学を使用した読書プログラムを試験実施している.

pimp /pɪmp/ (pimps, pimping, pimped) **1** N-COUNT 可算名詞 A **pimp** is a man who gets clients for prostitutes and takes some of the money the prostitutes earn. ポン引き **2** V-I 自動詞 Someone who **pimps** gets clients for prostitutes and takes some of the money the prostitutes earn. ポン引きをする [自動詞] ❑ *He stole, lied, deceived, and pimped his way out of poverty.* 彼は貧困から抜け出すために, 盗み, うそをつき, だまし, ポン引きをした.

pin /pɪn/ (pins, pinning, pinned) **1** N-COUNT 可算名詞 **Pins** are very small thin pointed pieces of metal. They are used in sewing to fasten pieces of material together until they have been sewn. ピン ❑ *...a box of needles and pins.* 針とピンの入った箱 **2** V-T 他動詞 If you **pin** something **on** or **to** something, you attach it with a pin, a safety pin or a thumbtack. ピンで留める [他動詞] ❑ *They pinned a notice to the door.* 彼らは通知をピンでドアに留めました. ❑ *Everyone was supposed to dance with the bride and pin money on her dress.* 誰もが花嫁と踊り, お金を彼女のドレスにピンで留めること

になっていた. **3** V-T 他動詞 If someone **pins** you to something, they press you against a surface so that you cannot move. 押さえておく [他動詞] ❑ *I pinned him against the wall.* 私は彼を壁に押さえつけた. ❑ *I'd try to get away and he'd pin me down, saying he would kill me.* 私は逃げようとしたが, 彼は私を殺すと言いながら押さえつけた. **4** N-COUNT 可算名詞 A **pin** is any long narrow piece of metal or wood that is not sharp, especially one that is used to fasten two things together. ピン ❑ *...the 18-inch steel pin holding his left leg together.* 彼の左脚をつなぎ合わせている18インチのスチールのピン **5** V-T 他動詞 If someone tries to **pin** something on you or to **pin the blame on** you, they say, often unfairly, that you were responsible for something bad or illegal. 人に責任を負わせる ❑ *They're trying to pin it on us.* 彼らは私たちに責任を負わせようとしている. **6** V-T 他動詞 If you **pin** your hopes **on** something or **pin** your faith **on** something, you hope very much that it will produce the result you want. おく（希望, 信頼などを）[他動詞] ❑ *The Democrats are pinning their hopes on the next election.* 民主党は次の選挙に望みを託している. **7** N-COUNT 可算名詞 A **pin** is something worn on your clothing, for example, as jewelry, which is fastened with a pointed piece of metal. ピン付きのブローチ [AM 米国英語] ❑ *...necklaces, bracelets, and pins.* ネックレス, ブレスレット, そしてブローチ **8** → see also **safety pin**
▶ **pin down** **1** PHRASAL VERB 句動詞 If you try to **pin** something **down**, you try to discover exactly what, where, or when it is. 突き止める ❑ *It has taken until now to pin down its exact location.* 正確な場所を突き止めるのに今までかかりました. ❑ *I can only pin it down to between 1936 and 1942.* それは1936年と1942年の間だったとしか言えない. **2** PHRASAL VERB 句動詞 If you **pin** someone **down**, you force them to make a decision or to tell you what their decision is, when they have been trying to avoid doing this. 人に明確な態度を取らせる ❑ *She couldn't pin him down to a date.* 彼女は彼に期日をはっきりさせることができなかった.
→ see **jewelry**

PIN /pɪn/ N-SING 単数名詞 Someone's **PIN** or **PIN number** is a secret number that they can use, for example, with a bank card to withdraw money from a cash machine or ATM. **PIN** is an abbreviation for "personal identification number." 暗証番号 [oft N n] ❑ *To use the service you'll need a PIN number.* そのサービスを利用するには暗証番号が必要だ.

pina|fore /pɪnəfɔr/ (pinafores) N-COUNT 可算名詞 A **pinafore** is a sleeveless dress. It is worn over a blouse or sweater. エプロンドレス

pin|cer /pɪnsər/ (pincers) **1** N-PLURAL 複数名詞 **Pincers** consist of two pieces of metal that are hinged in the middle. They are used as a tool for gripping things or for pulling things out. ペンチ [also "a pair of" N] ❑ *His surgical instruments were a knife and a pair of pincers.* 彼の外科用の器具はナイフとペンチだった. **2** N-COUNT 可算名詞 The **pincers** of an animal such as a crab or a lobster are its front claws. はさみ

pinch /pɪntʃ/ (pinches, pinching, pinched) **1** V-T 他動詞 If you **pinch** a part of someone's body, you take a piece of their skin between your thumb and first finger and give it a short squeeze. つねる [他動詞] ❑ *She pinched his arm as hard as she could.* 彼女は彼の腕をできるだけ強くつねった. ● N-COUNT 可算名詞 **Pinch** is also a noun. つねり ❑ *She gave him a little pinch.* 彼女は彼を軽くつねった. **2** N-COUNT 可算名詞 A **pinch of** an ingredient such as salt is the amount of it that you can hold between your thumb and your first finger. 一つまみ ❑ *Put all the ingredients, including a pinch of salt, into a food processor.* 塩一つまみをはじめすべての材料をフードプロセッサーに入れる. **3** to **take** something **with a pinch of salt** → see **salt** **4** V-T 他動詞 To **pinch** something, especially something of little value, means to steal it. 盗む [INFORMAL くだけた] ❑ *Do you remember when I pinched your glasses?* 私が君のめがねをくすねたときのことを覚えているか. **5** PHRASE 句 If a person or company **is feeling the pinch**, they do not have as much money as they used to, and so they cannot buy the things they would like to buy. 経済的苦境に陥る ❑ *Consumers are spending less and merchants are feeling the pinch.* 消費者支出が低下し, モノを売る企業は苦境に陥っている.

pine /paɪn/ (pines, pining, pined) **1** N-VAR 可変性名詞 A **pine tree** or a **pine** is a tall tree that has very thin, sharp leaves called needles and a fresh smell. Pine trees have leaves all year round. マツの木 ❑ *...high mountains covered in pine trees.* マツの木に覆われた高い山脈 ● N-UNCOUNT 不可算名詞 **Pine** is the wood of this tree. マツ材 ❑ *...a big pine table.* 大きなマツのテーブル. **2** V-I 自動詞 If you **pine for** someone who has died or gone away, you want them to be with you very much and feel sad because they are not there. 悲しみにやつれる [自動詞] ❑ *She'd be sitting at home pining for her lost husband.* 彼女は夫の死を嘆き悲しんで自宅で休んでいる. **3** V-I 自動詞 If you **pine for** something, you want it very much, especially when it is unlikely that you will be able to have it. 思い焦がれる [他動詞] ❑ *I pine for the countryside.* 私は田舎が懐かしくてたまりません.

pine|apple /paɪnæp³l/ (**pineapples**) N-VAR 可変性名詞 A **pineapple** is a large oval fruit that grows in hot countries. It is sweet, juicy, and yellow inside. It has a thick brownish skin. パイナップル

pink /pɪŋk/ (**pinks, pinker, pinkest**) **1** COLOR 色彩語 **Pink** is the color between red and white. ピンク色 □ ...*pink lipstick.* ピンクの口紅 □ ...*white flowers edged in pink.* 縁がピンクの白い花 **2** ADJ 形容詞 **Pink** is used to refer to things relating to or connected with gay people. ゲイの [BRIT 英国英語]

pin|na|cle /pɪnɪk³l/ (**pinnacles**) **1** N-COUNT 可算名詞 A **pinnacle** is a pointed piece of stone or rock that is high above the ground. 頂点 □ *A walker broke his arms, legs, and pelvis yesterday when he plunged 80 feet from a rocky pinnacle.* 昨日、ハイカーが岩のてっぺんから80フィート落下し、腕、脚および骨盤に負傷した. **2** N-COUNT 可算名詞 If someone reaches **the pinnacle of** their career or **the pinnacle of** a particular area of life, they are at the highest point of it. 最高点 □ *She was still at the pinnacle of her career.* 彼女はいまだにキャリアの絶頂期にありました.

pin|point /pɪnpɔɪnt/ (**pinpoints, pinpointing, pinpointed**) **1** V-T 他動詞 If you **pinpoint** the cause of something, you discover or explain it exactly. 正確に示す [他動詞] □ *It was almost impossible to pinpoint the cause of death.* 死因を正確に突き止めることはほとんど不可能だった. □ ...*if you can pinpoint exactly what the anger is about.* 何に対する怒りかを正確に指摘できるなら. **2** V-T 他動詞 If you **pinpoint** something or someone, you discover or show exactly where it is. 正確に位置を示す [他動詞] □ *I could pinpoint his precise location on a map.* 私は彼の正確な位置を地図上で示すことができた.

pin|stripe /pɪnstraɪp/ (**pinstripes**) also **pin-stripe** N-COUNT 可算名詞 **Pinstripes** are very narrow vertical stripes found on certain types of clothing. Businessmen's suits often have pinstripes. ピンストライプ □ *He wore an expensive, dark blue pinstripe suit.* 彼は高価な紺色のピンストライプスーツを身に着けていた.

pint /paɪnt/ (**pints**) N-COUNT 可算名詞 A **pint** is a unit of measurement for liquids. It is equal to 473 cubic centimeters or one eighth of a gallon. パイント □ ...*a pint of ice cream.* 1パイントのアイスクリーム

pin-up (**pin-ups**) also **pinup** N-COUNT 可算名詞 A **pin-up** is an attractive man or woman who appears on posters, often wearing very few clothes. ピンナップ □ ...*pin-up boys.* ピンナップの美少年

pio|neer /paɪənɪ̱ər/ (**pioneers, pioneering, pioneered**) **1** N-COUNT 可算名詞 Someone who is referred to as a **pioneer** in a particular area of activity is one of the first people to be involved in it and develop it. 先駆者 □ ...*one of the leading pioneers of photojournalism.* フォトジャーナリズムの先駆者の1人. **2** V-T 他動詞 Someone who **pioneers** a new activity, invention, or process is one of the first people to do it. 開拓する [他動詞] □ ...*Professor Alec Jeffreys, who invented and pioneered DNA tests.* DNAテストを発明し、先駆者となったアレック・ジェフェリーズ教授 **3** N-COUNT 可算名詞 **Pioneers** are people who leave their own country or the place where they were living, and go and live in a place that has not been lived in before. 開拓者 □ ...*abandoned settlements of early European pioneers.* 初期のヨーロッパ人開拓者の見捨てられた集落

pio|neer|ing /paɪənɪ̱ərɪŋ/ ADJ 形容詞 **Pioneering** work or a **pioneering** individual does something that has not been done before, for example, by developing or using new methods or techniques. 先駆的な □ *The school has won awards for its pioneering work with the community.* その学校は地域社会との先駆的な活動により賞を授与された.

pi|ous /paɪəs/ ADJ 形容詞 Someone who is **pious** is very religious and moral. 敬虔な □ *He was brought up by pious female relatives.* 彼は敬虔な近親者の女性たちに育てられた. ● **pi|ous|ly** ADV 副詞 [ADV with v] □ *Conti kneeled and crossed himself piously.* コンティは敬虔にもひざまずいて神の前で十字を切った.

pipe /paɪp/ (**pipes, piping, piped**) **1** N-COUNT 可算名詞 A **pipe** is a long, round, hollow object, usually made of metal or plastic, through which a liquid or gas can flow. 管 □ *The liquid can't escape into the air, because it's inside a pipe.* 液体はパイプの中に入っているので大気中に漏れることはない. **2** N-COUNT 可算名詞 A **pipe** is an object that is used for smoking tobacco. You put the tobacco into the cup-shaped part at the end of the pipe, light it, and breathe in the smoke through a narrow tube. パイプ □ *Do you smoke a pipe?* パイプを吸いますか. **3** N-COUNT 可算名詞 A **pipe** is a simple musical instrument in the shape of a tube with holes in it. You play a pipe by blowing into it while covering and uncovering the holes with your fingers. 笛 **4** N-COUNT 可算名詞 An **organ pipe** is one of the long hollow tubes in which air vibrates and produces a musical note. （パイプオルガンの）パイプ **5** V-T 他動詞 If liquid or gas is **piped** somewhere, it is transferred from one place to another through a pipe. パイプ輸送される [他動詞] □ *The heated gas is piped through a coil surrounded by water.* 加熱気体は水に囲まれたコイルを通される. □ *The Communists brought electricity to his village and piped in drinking water from the reservoir.* 共産主義者らは彼の村に電気を引き、貯水池から飲み水をパイプで運んだ. **6** → see also **piping** → see **plumbing**

pipe|line /paɪplaɪn/ (**pipelines**) **1** N-COUNT 可算名詞 A **pipeline** is a large pipe that is used for carrying oil or gas over a long distance, often underground. 輸送管路 □ *A consortium plans to build a natural-gas pipeline from Russia to supply eastern Germany.* 共同事業体はドイツ東部に天然ガスを供給するためロシアからパイプラインを建設する予定である. **2** PHRASE 句 If something is **in the pipeline**, it has already been planned or begun. 進行中で □ *Already in the pipeline is a 2.9 percent pay increase for teachers.* すでに教師の給料は2.9%増額の計画がある. → see **oil**

pip|ing /paɪpɪŋ/ N-UNCOUNT 不可算名詞 **Piping** is metal, plastic, or another substance made in the shape of a pipe or tube. 管 □ ...*rolls of bright yellow plastic piping.* 明るい黄色のプラスチック管のロール.

pi|ra|cy /paɪərəsi/ **1** N-UNCOUNT 不可算名詞 **Piracy** is robbery at sea carried out by pirates. 海賊行為 □ *Seven of the fishermen have been formally charged with piracy.* 7人の漁師が海賊行為で正式に起訴された. **2** N-UNCOUNT 不可算名詞 You can refer to the illegal copying of things such as DVDs and computer programs as **piracy**. 著作権侵害 □ ...*protection against piracy of books, films, and other intellectual property.* 書籍、映画、その他の知的財産の侵害に対する保護

pi|rate /paɪərɪt/ (**pirates, pirating, pirated**) **1** N-COUNT 可算名詞 **Pirates** are sailors who attack other ships and steal property from them. 海賊 □ *In the nineteenth century, pirates roamed the seas.* 19世紀には、海賊が大洋を徘徊していた. **2** V-T 他動詞 Someone who **pirates** CDs, DVDs, books, or computer programs copies and sells them when they have no right to do so. 著作権を侵害する [他動詞] □ *Computer crimes include data theft and pirating software.* コンピュータ犯罪にはデータ窃盗およびソフトウェアの著作権侵害が含まれる. ● **pi|rated** ADJ 形容詞 海賊 □ *New technology makes it possible to make pirated copies of music and movies.* 新しい技術は音楽や映画の海賊版の作成を可能にする. **3** ADJ 形容詞 [ADJ n] A **pirate** version of something is an illegal copy of it. 海賊版 □ *Pirate copies of the DVD are already being sold.* そのDVDの海賊版はすでに売られている.

piss /pɪs/ (**pisses, pissing, pissed**) V-I 自動詞 To **piss** means to urinate. 小便 [INFORMAL, VULGAR くだけた、下品な] □ *A man pissed against a wall.* 男は壁に向かって小便をした. ▶ **piss off** **1** PHRASAL VERB 句動詞 If someone or something **pisses** you **off**, they annoy you. いらいらさせる [INFORMAL, VULGAR くだけた、下品な] □ *It pisses me off when they start moaning about going to war.* 彼らが開戦について不平を言いだすと私はうんざりする. ● **pissed off** ADJ 形容詞 怒っている □ *I was really pissed off.* 私は非常に怒っていました. **2** PHRASAL VERB 句動詞 If someone tells a person to **piss off**, they are telling the person in a rude way to go away. 出て行け [INFORMAL, VULGAR くだけた、下品な]

pissed /pɪst/ ADJ 形容詞 If you say that someone is **pissed**, you mean that they are annoyed. 腹を立てて [AM 米国英語, INFORMAL, VULGAR くだけた、下品な] [v-link ADJ] □ *You know Molly's pissed at you.* モリーはあなたに腹を立てているのよ.

piste /piːst/ (**pistes**) N-COUNT 可算名詞 A **piste** is a track of firm snow for skiing on. ピスト □ ...*confident skiers who want to move off the piste.* ピストから外れたがる自信のあるスキーヤー

pis|tol /pɪst³l/ (**pistols**) N-COUNT 可算名詞 A **pistol** is a small gun. ピストル

pis|ton /pɪstən/ (**pistons**) N-COUNT 可算名詞 A **piston** is a cylinder or metal disk that is part of an engine. Pistons slide up and down inside tubes and cause various parts of the engine to move. ピストン

pit /pɪt/ (**pits, pitting, pitted**) **1** N-COUNT 可算名詞 A **pit** is the underground part of a mine, especially a coal mine. 炭坑 **2** N-COUNT 可算名詞 A **gravel pit** or **clay pit** is a very large hole that is left where gravel or clay has been dug from the ground. 採掘場 □ *This area of former farmland was worked as a gravel pit until 1964.* かつて農地だったこの地帯は1964年まで砂利採掘場であった. **3** V-T 他動詞 If two opposing things or people **are pitted against** one another, they are in conflict. 対抗する [usu passive] □ *You will be pitted against two, three, or four people who are every bit as good as you are.* 君は全く同じくらいの能力を持つ相手2人、3人または4人と戦うことになる. **4** N-COUNT 可算名詞 A **pit** is a large hole that is dug in the ground. くぼみ □ *Eric lost his footing and began to slide into the pit.* エリックは足場を無くし、くぼみの中に滑り落ち始めた. **5** N-PLURAL 複数名詞 In auto racing, **the pits** are the areas at the side of the track where drivers stop to get more fuel and to repair their cars during races. ピット □ *He moved quickly into the pits and climbed rapidly out of the car.* 彼はすばやくピットに移動し、車から迅速に降りた. **6** N-COUNT 可算名詞 A **pit** is the large hard seed of a fruit or vegetable. 果物の種 [AM 米国英語] □ ...*cherry pits.* さくらんぼの種 **7** → see also **orchestra pit, pitted** **8** PHRASE 句 If you **pit** your **wits** against someone, you compete with them

in a test of knowledge or intelligence. 知恵比べをする ❑*I'd like to manage at the very highest level and pit my wits against the best.* 私は真に最高のレベルで経営を行い、最高の人たちと戦わせたい. **9** PHRASE 句 If you have a feeling **in the pit of** your **stomach**, you have a tight or sick feeling in your stomach, usually because you are afraid or anxious. 腹の底で ❑*I had a funny feeling in the pit of my stomach.* 私の腹の底におかしな感じを覚えた.
→ see **fruit**

pitch /pɪtʃ/ (**pitches, pitching, pitched**) **1** V-T 他動詞 If you **pitch** something somewhere, you throw it with some force, usually aiming it carefully. 投げる [他動詞] ❑*Simon pitched the empty bottle into the lake.* サイモンは空のボトルを湖に投げ入れた. **2** V-T 他動詞 In the game of baseball, when you **pitch** the ball, you throw it to the batter for them to hit it. 投球する [他動詞] ❑*We passed long, hot afternoons pitching a baseball.* 僕たちは長い暑い午後を野球のピッチングをして過ごした. **3** V-I 他動詞/自動詞 To **pitch** somewhere means to fall forwards suddenly and with a lot of force. 前へ倒れる [他動詞・自動詞] ❑*The movement took him by surprise, and he pitched forward.* その動きは彼の不意を衝き、彼は前に倒れた. ❑*Alan staggered sideways, pitched head-first over the low wall and fell into the lake.* アランは横によろめき、低い壁の上に頭から倒れ、湖に落ちた. **4** V-T 他動詞 If someone **is pitched into** a new situation, they are suddenly forced into it. 状況に陥る [他動詞] ❑*They were being pitched into a new adventure in which they would have to fight the whole world.* 彼らは新しい冒険に巻き込まれ、ありとあらゆるものを相手に戦わなければならなくなった. **5** N-UNCOUNT 不可算名詞 The **pitch** of a sound is how high or low it is. ピッチ ❑*He raised his voice to an even higher pitch.* 彼は声をさらに高くした. **6** V-T 他動詞 If a sound **is pitched at** a particular level, it is produced at the level indicated. 音程を決める [usu passive] [他動詞] ❑*His cry is pitched at a level that makes it impossible to ignore.* 彼は無視できないくらいの高い声で叫んでいる. ❑*His voice was pitched high, the words muffled by his crying.* 彼の声はうわずり言葉は涙声だった. **7** → see also **high-pitched** **8** V-T 他動詞 If something **is pitched at** a particular level or degree of difficulty, it is set at that level. レベルを定める [他動詞] ❑*While this is very important material I think it's probably pitched at too high a level for our students.* これは非常に重要な教材だが、おそらく当校の生徒のレベルよりもかなり高く設定されていると思う. **9** N-SING 単数名詞 If something such as a feeling or a situation rises to a high **pitch**, it rises to a high level. 程度 ❑*The public's feelings were at a high pitch of indignation.* 国民感情はかなりの憤慨を示していた. **10** V-T 他動詞 If someone **pitches** an idea for something such as a new product, they try to persuade people to accept the idea. 売りつける [他動詞] ❑*My agent has pitched the idea to my editor in New York.* 私のエージェントはニューヨークの私の編集者にアイデアを売りつけた. **11** N-COUNT 可算名詞 A **pitch** is an area of ground that is marked out and used for playing a game such as soccer, cricket, or hockey. 競技場 [BRIT 英国英語; AM **field** 米国英語] **12** PHRASE 句 If someone **makes a pitch for** something, they try to persuade people to do or buy it. ことば巧みに売り込む ❑*The president speaks in New York today, making another pitch for his economic program.* 大統領は今日ニューヨークで演説し、自分の経済計画を再度売り込んだ. **13** → see also **sales pitch**

▶ **pitch for** PHRASAL VERB 句動詞 If someone is **pitching for** something, they are trying to persuade other people to give it to them. を狙って売り込む ❑*It was middle-class votes they were pitching for.* 彼らは中流階級の票を狙っていた.

▶ **pitch in** PHRASAL VERB 句動詞 If you **pitch in**, you join in and help with an activity. 貢献する [INFORMAL くだけた] ❑*The agency says international relief agencies also have pitched in.* その機関によると各国際救援機関にも貢献したとのことだ.

pitch|er /pɪtʃər/ (**pitchers**) **1** N-COUNT 可算名詞 A **pitcher** is a cylindrical container with a handle and is used for holding and pouring liquids. 水差し [mainly AM 主に米国英語] ❑*My sister fetched a pitcher of iced water.* 妹は氷水の入った水差しを持ってきた. **2** N-COUNT 可算名詞 In baseball, the **pitcher** is the person who throws the ball to the batter, who tries to hit it. ピッチャー
→ see **baseball**

pit|fall /pɪtfɔl/ (**pitfalls**) N-COUNT 可算名詞 The **pitfalls** involved in a particular activity or situation are the things that may go wrong or may cause problems. 落とし穴 ❑*The pitfalls of working abroad are numerous.* 海外で働くことには数知れぬ落とし穴がある.

piti|ful /pɪtɪfəl/ **1** ADJ 形容詞 Someone or something that is **pitiful** is so sad, weak, or small that you feel pity for them. あわれむべき ❑*He sounded both pitiful and eager to get what he wanted.* 彼は惨めでもあり、欲しいものを手に入れることに熱心でもあるようだ. ● **piti|ful|ly** ADV 副詞 みじめに ❑*His legs were pitifully thin compared to the rest of his bulk.* 彼は本胴体に比べて脚がかわいそうなくらい細かった. **2** ADJ 形容詞 If you describe something as **pitiful**, you mean that it is completely inadequate. くだらない [DISAPPROVAL 不賛成] ❑*The choice is pitiful and the quality of some of the products is very low.* それは話にならぬくらいまずい選択で、一部の製品の質は非常に低い. ● **piti|ful|ly** ADV 副詞 くだらないほど ❑*State help for the mentally handicapped is pitifully inadequate.* 精神的障害者に対する国の援助は話

にならないほど不十分だ.

pit|ted /pɪtɪd/ **1** ADJ 形容詞 **Pitted** fruits have had their pits removed. 種を除いた [ADJ n] ❑*...green and black pitted olives.* 種なしの緑と黒のオリーブ. **2** ADJ 形容詞 If the surface of something is **pitted**, it is covered with a lot of small, shallow holes. あばたのある ❑*Everywhere building facades are pitted with shell and bullet holes.* ビルの正面にはあそこかしこに薬きょうや弾丸で穴があいている.

pity /pɪti/ (**pities, pitying, pitied**) **1** N-UNCOUNT 不可算名詞 If you feel **pity for** someone, you feel very sorry for them. あわれみ ❑*He felt a sudden tender pity for her.* 彼は突然彼女に情け深い同情を感じた. **2** → see also **self-pity** **3** V-T 他動詞 If you **pity** someone, you feel very sorry for them. 気の毒に思う [他動詞] ❑*I don't know whether to hate or pity him.* 彼を嫌うべきか憐れむべきかわからない. **4** N-SING 単数名詞 If you say that it is a **pity** that something is the case, you mean that you feel disappointment or regret about it. 残念だ [FEELINGS 感情] ❑*It is a great pity that all students in the city cannot have the same chances.* 市内の全学生に同じ機会が与えられないのは非常に残念だ. ❑*It's a pity you've arrived so late in the year.* 君がこんな年末になって着いたのは気の毒だ. **5** N-UNCOUNT 不可算名詞 If someone shows **pity**, they do not harm or punish someone they have power over. 同情を示す ❑*Noncommunist forces have some pity toward people here.* 非共産党部隊はここに住む人々にいくらかの同情を示しました. **6** PHRASE 句 If you **take pity on** someone, you feel sorry for them and help them. 気の毒がる ❑*No woman had ever felt the need to take pity on him before.* これまで彼を気の毒がる必要性を感じた女性は皆無だった.

piv|ot /pɪvət/ (**pivots, pivoting, pivoted**) **1** N-COUNT 可算名詞 The **pivot** in a situation is the most important thing that everything else is based on or arranged around. かなめ ❑*Forming the pivot of the exhibition is a large group of watercolors.* 展示会の中心となるのは水彩画の数々だ. **2** V-I 自動詞 If something or someone **pivots**, they balance or turn on a central point. 旋回する ❑*The wheels pivot for easy maneuvering.* 取り回しがいいように車輪が旋回するようになっている. ❑*He pivoted on his heels and walked on down the hall.* 彼はかかとを軸にして回転して、廊下を歩いて行った. **3** N-COUNT 可算名詞 A **pivot** is the pin or the central point on which something balances or turns. 先軸 ❑*The pedal had sheared off at the pivot.* ペダルは先軸のところでねじ切れていた.

piv|ot|al /pɪvətəl/ ADJ 形容詞 A **pivotal** role, point, or figure in something is one that is very important and affects the success of that thing. きわめて重要な ❑*The elections may prove to be pivotal in Colombia's political history.* 選挙はコロンビアの政治史において極めて重要なものとなる可能性がある.

pix|el /pɪksəl/ (**pixels**) N-COUNT 可算名詞 A **pixel** is the smallest area on a computer screen that can be given a separate color by the computer. ピクセル [COMPUTING コンピューティング] ❑*...a display screen that measures one million pixels.* 百万ピクセルの表示画面
→ see **television**

piz|za /pitsə/ (**pizzas**) N-VAR 可変性名詞 A **pizza** is a flat, round piece of dough covered with tomatoes, cheese, and other toppings, and then baked in an oven. ピザ ❑*...the last piece of pizza.* ピザの最後の一切れ

pkg. **Pkg.** is a written abbreviation for **package**. packageの略

plac|ard /plækɑrd, -kərd/ (**placards**) N-COUNT 可算名詞 A **placard** is a large notice that is carried in a march or displayed in a public place. プラカード ❑*The protesters sang songs and waved placards.* 抗議者達は歌を歌いプラカードを振り回した.

Word Link plac ≈ pleasing : compla**c**ent, **plac**ate, **plac**id

pla|cate /pleɪkeɪt/ (**placates, placating, placated**) V-T 他動詞 If you **placate** someone, you do or say something to make them stop feeling angry. なだめる [FORMAL 形式ばった] ❑*He smiled, and made a gesture intended to placate me.* 彼は微笑み、私をなだめるジェスチャーをした.

place
❶ NOUN USES
❷ VERB USES
❸ PHRASES

❶ place /pleɪs/ (**places**) **1** N-COUNT 可算名詞 A **place** is any point, building, area, town, or country. 場所 ❑*We're going to a place called Platoro.* 私達はプラトロという場所に行く. ❑*The pain is always in the same place.* 痛みはいつも同じ所だ. **2** N-SING 単数名詞 You can use **the place** to refer to the point, building, area, town, or country that you have already mentioned. 場所 ❑*Except for the remarkably tidy kitchen, the place was a mess.* 特別よく片付いた台所は別としてその家は散らかり放題だった. **3** N-COUNT 可算名詞 You can refer to somewhere that provides a service, such as a hotel, restaurant, or institution, as a particular kind of **place**. ある目的のための場所 ❑*He found a bed-and-breakfast place.* 彼は宿泊場所を見

つけた. ❑ *My wife and I discovered some superb places to eat.* 妻と私は素晴らしいレストランを発見した. **4** PHRASE 句 When something **takes place**, it happens, especially in a controlled or organized way. 起こる ❑ *The discussion took place in a famous villa on the lake's shore.* 話合いは湖畔の有名な別荘で行なわれた. ❑ *She wanted Randy's wedding to take place quickly.* 彼女はランディの結婚式が早く行なわれることを望んだ. **5** N-SING 単数名詞 **Place** can be used after "any," "no," "some," or "every" to mean "anywhere," "nowhere," "somewhere," or "everywhere." 場所 [mainly AM 主に米国英語, INFORMAL くだけた] ❑ *The poor guy obviously didn't have any place to go for Easter.* 無論, その可哀想な男は復活祭のときに行く場所がなかった. **6** ADV 副詞 If you go **places**, you visit pleasant or interesting places. 遊び回る [mainly AM 主に米国英語] [ADV after v] ❑ *I don't have money to go places.* 私には遊び回る金はない. **7** N-COUNT 可算名詞 You can refer to the position where something belongs, or where it is supposed to be, as its **place**. 本来の場所 ❑ *He returned the album to its place on the shelf.* 彼はアルバムをもともとあった棚の上に返した. **8** N-COUNT 可算名詞 A **place** is a seat or position that is available for someone to occupy. 座席 ❑ *He walked back to the table and sat at the nearest of two empty places.* 彼はテーブルに戻り, 2つの空席の近い方に座った.

> You can use **place** or, more often, **seat** to refer to somewhere where someone can sit. ❑ *The women looked around for a place to sit... There was only one seat free on the train.* More generally, you can refer to a **space** which someone or something can occupy. ❑ *He was clearing a space for her to lie down.* You do not use **place** as an uncount noun to refer to an open or empty area. You should use **room** or **space** instead. **Room** is more likely to be used when you are talking about space inside an enclosed area. ❑ *There's not enough room in the bathroom for both of us... Leave plenty of space between you and the car in front.*

9 N-COUNT 可算名詞 Someone's or something's **place** in a society, system, or situation is their position in relation to other people or things. 地位 ❑ *They want to see more women take their place higher up the corporate or professional ladder.* 彼らはさらに多くの女性が企業や専門職で高い地位につくことを望んでいる. **10** N-COUNT 可算名詞 Your **place** in a race or competition is your position in relation to the other competitors. If you are in first place, you are ahead of all the other competitors. 順位 ❑ *He has risen to second place in the opinion polls.* 彼は世論調査で2位に上がった. **11** N-COUNT 可算名詞 If you get a **place** on a team, on a committee, or in an institution, for example, you are accepted as a member of the team or committee or as a resident of the institution. 所属場所 ❑ *Derek had lost his place on the team.* デレックはチームからはずれた. ❑ *They should be in residential care but there are no places available.* 彼らは居住看護を受けるべきだが, 空きがない. **12** N-SING 単数名詞 A good **place to** do something in a situation or activity is a good time or stage at which to do it. 時機 ❑ *It seemed an appropriate place to end somehow.* とにかくそこで終わるのが適当に思えた. **13** N-COUNT 可算名詞 Your **place** is the house or apartment where you live. 住む場所 [INFORMAL くだけた] ❑ *Let's all go back to my place!* 僕のうちに戻ろうよ. **14** N-COUNT 可算名詞 Your **place in** a book or speech is the point you have reached in reading the book or making the speech. 到達した場所 ❑ *...her finger marking her place in the book.* 読んだところまで示す彼女の指 **15** N-COUNT 可算名詞 If you say how many decimal **places** there are in a number, you are saying how many numbers there are to the right of the decimal point. 桁 (けた) ❑ *A pocket calculator only works to eight decimal places.* 小型計算機は8桁までしか使えない.

→ see **election**, **zero**

❷ place /pleɪs/ (**places, placing, placed**) **1** V-T 他動詞 If you **place** something somewhere, you put it in a particular position, especially in a careful, firm, or deliberate way. 置く ❑ *Brand folded it in his handkerchief and placed it in the inside pocket of his jacket.* ブランドはそれをハンカチで包み, ジャケットの内ポケットに入れた. **2** V-T 他動詞 To **place** a person or thing in a particular state means to cause them to be in it. ある状況に置く ❑ *Widespread protests have placed the president under serious pressure.* 抗議が広がり大統領に大きな重圧を与えた. ❑ *The crisis could well place the relationship at risk.* この危機は関係を危うくする可能性が大いにある. **3** V-T 他動詞 You can use **place** instead of "put" or "lay" in certain expressions where the meaning is carried by the following noun. For example, if you **place emphasis on** something, you emphasize it, and if you **place the blame on** someone, you blame them. 置く ❑ *He placed great emphasis on the importance of family life and ties.* 彼は家族生活と家族間のつながりを大変重視した. ❑ *She seemed to be placing most of the blame on her mother.* 彼女はほとんど母親のせいにしているようだった. **4** V-T 他動詞 If you **place** someone or something in a particular class or group, you label or judge them in that way. 位置づける ❑ *The authorities have placed the drug in Class A, the same category as heroin and cocaine.* 当局はその薬物をヘロインやコカインと同じカテゴリのAクラスに指定した. **5** V-T 他動詞 If a competitor in a race or competition is **placed** first, second, or third, they finish first, second, or third.

If a horse **is placed** in a race, it finishes second. 一位になる [usu passive] ❑ *I had been placed 2nd and 3rd a few times but had never won.* 私は2位と3位になったことはあったが一度も優勝したことはなかった. **6** V-T 他動詞 If you **place an order for** a product or **for** a meal, you ask for it to be sent or brought to you. 注文する ❑ *It is a good idea to place your order well in advance as delivery can often take months rather than weeks.* 配達までに数週間ではなく数か月かかることがしばしばあるので余裕をみて注文を出すのがよい. **7** V-T 他動詞 If you **place an advertisement** in a newspaper, you arrange for the advertisement to appear in the newspaper. 広告を出す ❑ *They placed an advertisement in the local paper for a secretary.* 彼らは秘書募集の広告を地元の新聞に出した. **8** V-T 他動詞 If you **place a bet**, you bet money on something. 賭けをする ❑ *For this race, though, he had already placed a bet on one of the horses.* だが彼はこのレースですでにある馬に賭けをしていた. **9** V-T 他動詞 If an agency or organization **places** someone, it finds them a job or somewhere to live. 世話する ❑ *They managed to place fourteen women in paid positions.* 彼らはどうにかして14人の女性の就職を世話した.

❸ place /pleɪs/ **1** PHRASE 句 If something is happening **all over the place**, it is happening in many different places. そこらじゅう ❑ *Businesses are closing down all over the place.* 至る所で企業が廃業している. **2** PHRASE 句 If things are **all over the place**, they are spread over a very large area, usually in a disorganized way. そこらじゅう ❑ *Our fingerprints are probably all over the place.* 我々の指紋はおそらくそこらじゅうにあると思う. **3** PHRASE 句 If you **change places with** another person, you start being in their situation or role, and they start being in yours. 場所を入れ替える ❑ *With his door key in his hand, knowing Millie and the kids awaited him, he wouldn't change places with anyone.* 玄関の鍵を手にし, ミリーと子供達が自分を待っているのを知りながら, 彼は誰とも入れ替わろうとはしなかった. **4** PHRASE 句 If you have been trying to understand something puzzling and then everything **falls into place** or **clicks into place**, you suddenly understand how different pieces of information are connected and everything becomes clearer. つじつまが合う ❑ *When the reasons behind the decision were explained, of course, it all fell into place.* もちろん決定の理由が説明されたとき全てつじつまが合った. **5** PHRASE 句 If things **fall into place**, events happen naturally to produce a situation you want. 物事が収まる ❑ *Once the decision was made, things fell into place rapidly.* 一旦決定が下された後は急速に事態が収拾した. **6** PHRASE 句 If you say that someone **is going places**, you mean that they are showing a lot of talent or ability and are likely to become very successful. 出世する ❑ *You always knew Barbara was going places, she was different.* バーバラが彼女が成功すると人と違うことはいつも意識していただろう. **7** PHRASE 句 People **in high places** are people who have powerful and influential positions in a government, society, or organization. 高い地位にある ❑ *He had friends in high places.* 彼には社会的地位の高い友人がいた. **8** PHRASE 句 If something is **in place**, it is in its correct or usual position. 適所に ❑ *Gary hastily pushed the drawer back into place.* ギャリーは急いで引き出しを元の場所に押し戻した. **9** PHRASE 句 If something such as a law, a policy, or an administrative structure is **in place**, it is working or able to be used. 実施されている ❑ *Similar legislation is already in place in Utah.* すでに同様の法律がユタ州で実施されている. **10** PHRASE 句 If one thing or person is used or does something **in place of** another, they replace the other thing or person. の代わりに ❑ *Cooked kidney beans can be used in place of French beans.* 調理したインゲン豆はサヤインゲンの代わりに使うことができる. **11** PHRASE 句 If something has particular characteristics or features **in places**, it has them at several points within an area. 場所によっては ❑ *Even now the snow along the roadside was five or six feet deep in places.* 今でも場所によっては道端に5~6フィートの雪がつもっていた. **12** PHRASE 句 If you say what you would have done **in someone else's place**, you say what you would have done if you had been in their situation and had been experiencing what they were experiencing. 立場 ❑ *In her place I wouldn't have been able to resist it.* 私が彼女の立場だったらそれに抵抗はできなかったと思う. **13** PHRASE 句 You say **in the first place** when you are talking about the beginning of a situation or about the situation as it was before a series of events. 第一に ❑ *What brought you to Washington in the first place?* そもそも君はなぜワシントンにやって来たのか. **14** PHRASE 句 You say **in the first place** and **in the second place** to introduce the first and second in a series of points or reasons. **In the first place** can also be used to emphasize a very important point or reason. 第一に, 次に ❑ *In the first place you are not old, Conway. And in the second place, you are a very strong and appealing man.* コンウェイ, まず第一に君は年寄りではない. 第二に君は非常に強くて魅力的な男だ. **15** PHRASE 句 If you say that **it is not** your **place** to do something, you mean that it is not right or appropriate for you to do it, or that it is not your responsibility to do it. する立場ではない ❑ *He says that it is not his place to comment on government commitment to further funds.* 彼は政府が追加資金を約束したことに関して発言する立場にはないと言っている. **16** PHRASE 句 If someone or something seems **out of place** in

a particular situation, they do not seem to belong there or to be suitable for that situation. 不適切な ❑ I felt out of place in my suit and tie. スーツとネクタイ姿の私は場違いに感じた。 **17** PHRASE 句 If you **place** one thing **above**, **before**, or **over** another, you think that the first thing is more important than the second and you show this in your behavior. 優先する ❑ He continued to place security above all other objectives. 彼は他の目的よりも安全を優先し続けた。 **18** PHRASE 句 If you **put** someone **in their place**, you show them that they are less important or clever than they think they are. 身のほどを知らせる ❑ In a few words she had put him in his place. 彼女はわずかな言葉で彼に自分の身のほどを思い知らせた。 **19** PHRASE 句 If you say that someone should **be shown** their **place** or **be kept in** their **place**, you are saying, often in a humorous way, that they should be made aware of their low status. つけ上がらせない ❑ ...an uppity bartender who needs to be shown his place. つけ上がらせてはならない横柄なバーテン **20** PHRASE 句 If one thing **takes second place to** another, it is considered to be less important and is given less attention than the other thing. 次の位置を占める ❑ My personal life has had to take second place to my career. 私の個人的生活は仕事の後回しだった。 **21** PHRASE 句 If one thing or person **takes the place of** another or **takes** another's **place**, they replace the other thing or person. の代わりをする ❑ Optimism was gradually taking the place of pessimism. 楽観主義が次第に悲観主義に取って代わりつつある。

place|ment /pleɪsmənt/ (**placements**) **1** N-UNCOUNT 不可算名詞 The **placement** of something or someone is the act of putting them in a particular place or position. 配置 ❑ The treatment involves the placement of twenty-two electrodes in the inner ear. 治療には内耳に22本の電極を配置することが含まれる。 **2** N-UNCOUNT 不可算名詞 The **placement** of someone in a job, home, or school is the act or process of finding them a job, home, or school. 紹介 ❑ The children were waiting for placement in a foster care home. 子供たちは里親の紹介を待っていた。 **3** N-COUNT 可算名詞 If someone gets a **placement**, they get a job for a short period of time to gain experience. 就業体験 ❑ He spent a year studying Japanese in Tokyo, followed by a six-month work placement with the Japanese government. 彼は東京で1年間日本語を勉強した後、日本政府で6か月の就業体験を行った。

→ see **advertising**

Word Link
plac ≈ pleasing : com**plac**ent, **plac**ate, **plac**id

plac|id /plæsɪd/ **1** ADJ 形容詞 A **placid** person or animal is calm and does not easily become excited, angry, or upset. 穏やかな ❑ She was a placid child who rarely cried. 彼女はほとんど泣かないおとなしい子供だった。 **2** ADJ 形容詞 A **placid** place, area of water, or life is calm and peaceful. 静かな ❑ ...the placid waters of Lake Erie. エリー湖の静かな湖水

pla|gia|rism /pleɪdʒərɪzəm/ N-UNCOUNT 不可算名詞 **Plagiarism** is the practice of using or copying someone else's idea or work and pretending that you thought of it or created it. 剽窃 (ひょうせつ) ❑ Now he's in real trouble. He's accused of plagiarism. 目下彼は大変な窮地に追い込まれている。剽窃 (ひょうせつ) のかどで起訴されたのだ。

Writing a paper entirely or partly composed of the words of others without giving them credit for their work is called **plagiarism**. It is a punishable offense at American colleges and universities where students will be asked to leave. Professional writers who are caught cheating in this way may lose their jobs.

pla|gia|rize /pleɪdʒəraɪz/ (**plagiarizes**, **plagiarizing**, **plagiarized**) V-T 他動詞 If someone **plagiarizes** another person's idea or work, they use it or copy it and pretend that they thought of it or created it. 剽窃 (ひょうせつ) する ❑ The students denied plagiarizing papers. 学生は論文を盗用したことを否定した。

plague /pleɪɡ/ (**plagues**, **plaguing**, **plagued**) **1** N-UNCOUNT 不可算名詞 **Plague** or **the plague** is a very infectious disease that usually results in death. The patient has a severe fever and swellings on his or her body. 疫病 [also "the" N] ❑ ...a fresh outbreak of plague. 疫病の新たな勃発 **2** N-COUNT 可算名詞 A **plague of** unpleasant things is a large number of them that arrive or happen at the same time. 異常発生 ❑ The city is under threat from a plague of rats. 町はネズミの大襲来に脅かされている。 **3** V-T 他動詞 If you **are plagued by** unpleasant things, they continually cause you a lot of trouble or suffering. 悩まされる ❑ She was plagued by weakness, fatigue, and dizziness. 彼女はだるさ、疲労感、めまいに悩まされた。

plaice /pleɪs/ (**plaice**)

Plaice is both the singular and the plural form.

Plaice は単数形でも複数形でもある。

N-VAR 可変性名詞 **Plaice** are a type of flat sea fish. ツノガレイ ● N-UNCOUNT 不可算名詞 **Plaice** is this fish eaten as food. ツノガレイ

plain /pleɪn/ (**plainer**, **plainest**, **plains**) **1** ADJ 形容詞 A **plain** object, surface, or fabric is entirely in one color and has no pattern, design, or writing on it. 無地の ❑ In general, a plain carpet makes a room look bigger. 無地のカーペットというものは部屋を大きく見せる。 ❑ He placed the paper in a plain envelope. 彼は書類を何も印刷されていない封筒に入れた。 **2** ADJ 形容詞 Something that is **plain** is very simple in style. 地味な ❑ It was a plain, gray stone house. それは地味な灰色の石造りの家だった。 ● **plain|ly** ADV 副詞 [ADV -ed] 地味に ❑ He was very tall and plainly dressed. 彼は背が高く地味な服装だった。 **3** ADJ 形容詞 If a fact, situation, or statement is **plain**, it is easy to recognize or understand. 明らかな ❑ It was plain to him that I was having a nervous breakdown. 私がノイローゼにかかっていることは彼にははっきり分かっていた。 **4** ADJ 形容詞 If you describe someone as **plain**, you think they look ordinary and not at all beautiful. 不器量な ❑ ...a shy, rather plain girl with a pale complexion. 青白い顔をした内気で不器量な少女 **5** N-COUNT 可算名詞 A **plain** is a large flat area of land with very few trees on it. 平野 ❑ Once there were 70 million buffalo on the plains. 大平原にはかつて7千万頭の水牛がいた。 **6** PHRASE 句 If a police officer is **in plain clothes**, he or she is wearing ordinary clothes instead of a police uniform. 私服 ❑ Three officers in plain clothes told me to get out of the car. 私服の警官3人が車から出るよう私に命じた。 **7** **plain sailing** → see **sailing**

Thesaurus
plain また次を参照：

ADJ.	bare, common, everyday, modest, ordinary, simple, usual; (ant.) elaborate, fancy **2**
	clear, distinct, evident, transparent **3**

Word Partnership
plain は次の語句と使われる：

N.	plain **style 2**
	plain **English**, plain **language**, plain **speech**, plain **truth 3**

plain|ly /pleɪnli/ **1** ADV 副詞 You use **plainly** to indicate that you believe something is obviously true, often when you are trying to convince someone else that it is true. 明らかに [EMPHASIS 強調] ❑ The judge's conclusion was plainly wrong. 判事の判決は明らかに間違っていた。 ❑ Plainly, a more objective method of description must be adopted. 明らかに、より客観的な描写方法を取り入れる必要がある。 **2** ADV 副詞 You use **plainly** to indicate that something is easily seen, noticed, or recognized. はっきりと ❑ He was plainly annoyed. 彼は明らかに腹を立てていた。 ❑ I could plainly see him turning his head to the right and left. 彼が頭を左右にひねるのがはっきりと見えた。 **3** → see also **plain**

plain|tiff /pleɪntɪf/ (**plaintiffs**) N-COUNT 可算名詞 A **plaintiff** is a person who brings a legal case against someone in a court of law. 原告 ❑ The lead plaintiff of the lawsuit is the University of California. この訴訟の原告団長はカリフォルニア大学だ。

→ see **trial**

plain|tive /pleɪntɪv/ ADJ 形容詞 A **plaintive** sound or voice sounds sad. もの悲しい [LITERARY 文語的] ❑ They lay on the firm sands, listening to the plaintive cry of the seagulls. 彼らはかもめのもの悲しい鳴き声を聞きながら砂の上に横たわった。

plait /pleɪt/ (**plaits**, **plaiting**, **plaited**) **1** V-T 他動詞 If you **plait** three or more lengths of hair, rope, or other material together, you twist them over and under each other to make one thick length. 編む [mainly BRIT 主に英国英語; AM usually **braid** 米国英語では通常 **braid**] **2** N-COUNT 可算名詞 A **plait** is a length of hair that has been plaited. 編んだもの [mainly BRIT 主に英国英語; AM usually **braid** 米国英語では通常 **braid**]

plan /plæn/ (**plans**, **planning**, **planned**) **1** N-COUNT 可算名詞 A **plan** is a method of achieving something that you have worked out in detail beforehand. 計画 ❑ The three leaders had worked out a peace plan. 3人の指導者は和平案を案出した。 ❑ He maintains that everything is going according to plan. 彼は全ては計画通りに進行していると主張する。 **2** V-T/V-I 他動詞/自動詞 If you **plan** what you are going to do, you decide in detail what you are going to do, and you intend to do it. 計画する ❑ If you plan what you're going to eat, you reduce your chances of overeating. 何を食べるかをあらかじめ決めておくと食べ過ぎる機会を減らせる。 ❑ He planned to leave Baghdad on Monday. 彼は月曜日にバグダッドを去る予定にした。 ❑ Moderate Republicans gathered together to plan for the future. 穏健派の共和党員は将来の計画を立てるために集合した。 **3** N-PLURAL 複数名詞 If you have **plans**, you are intending to do a particular thing. 予定 ❑ "I'm sorry," she said. "I have plans for tonight." 「悪いけれど今夜は予定があるの」と彼女は言った。 **4** V-T 他動詞 When you **plan** something that you are going to make, build, or create, you decide what the main parts of it are and do a drawing of how it should be made. 設計する ❑ It is no use trying to plan an 18-hole golf course on a 120-acre site if you have to ruin the environment to do it. それが環境破壊につながるなら120エーカーの敷地に18ホールのゴルフコースを設計しようというのは無駄だ。 **5** N-COUNT 可算名詞 A **plan of** something

that is going to be built or made is a detailed diagram or drawing of it. 設計図 □ ...when you have drawn a plan of the garden. 庭園の設計図を描いたとき ⑥ → see also **planning**

▶ **plan on** PHRASAL VERB 句動詞 If you **plan on** doing something, you intend to do it. つもりである □ They were planning on getting married. 彼らは結婚するつもりだった.

plane /pleɪn/ (planes, planing, planed) ① N-COUNT 可算名詞 A **plane** is a vehicle with wings and one or more engines that can fly through the air. 飛行機 □ He had plenty of time to catch his plane. 彼は飛行機に乗るまでにたっぷり時間があった. □ Her mother was killed in a plane crash. 彼女の母親は飛行機事故で亡くなった. ② N-COUNT 可算名詞 A **plane** is a flat, level surface that may be sloping at a particular angle. 平面 □ ...a building with angled planes. 傾面のある建物 ③ N-SING 単数名詞 If a number of points are in the same **plane**, one line or one flat surface could pass through them all. 平面 □ All the planets orbit the Sun in roughly the same plane, around its equator. 全ての惑星は太陽の赤道のまわりのほぼ同一の平面を公転する. ④ N-COUNT 可算名詞 A **plane** is a tool that has a flat bottom with a sharp blade in it. You move the plane over a piece of wood in order to remove thin pieces of its surface. かんな ⑤ V-T 他動詞 If you **plane** a piece of wood, you make it smaller or smoother by using a plane. かんながけをする □ She watches him plane the surface of a walnut board. 彼女は彼がクルミ材の板にかんながけをするのを見ていた. ⑥ N-COUNT 可算名詞 A **plane** or a **plane tree** is the same as a sycamore. ミズニレ

plan|et /plænɪt/ (planets) N-COUNT 可算名詞 A **planet** is a large, round object in space that moves around a star. The Earth is a planet. 惑星 □ The picture shows six of the nine planets in the solar system. その写真には太陽系の9つの惑星のうち6つが写っている.

→ see **astronomer, galaxy, satellite, solar**

plan|etary /plænɪteri/ ADJ 形容詞 **Planetary** means relating to or belonging to planets. 惑星の [ADJ n] □ Within our own galaxy there are probably tens of thousands of planetary systems. 我々の銀河系にはおそらく何万もの惑星系があると思われる.

plank /plæŋk/ (planks) ① N-COUNT 可算名詞 A **plank** is a long, flat, rectangular piece of wood. 厚板 □ It was very strong, made of three solid planks of wood. それは3枚の木の厚板でできており、非常に頑丈だった. ② N-COUNT 可算名詞 The main **plank** of a particular group or political party is the main principle on which it bases its policy, or its main aim. 政策理念 [JOURNALISM ジャーナリズム] □ The Saudi authorities have made agricultural development a central plank of policy to make the country less dependent on imports. サウジアラビア当局は農業開発を輸入依存を低減する政策の中心とした.

plan|ner /plænər/ (planners) N-COUNT 可算名詞 **Planners** are people whose job is to make decisions about what is going to be done in the future. For example, town planners decide how land should be used and what new buildings should be built. 計画者 □ ...a panel that includes city planners, art experts, and historians. 都市計画、芸術、歴史の専門家を構成メンバーとする委員会

plan|ning /plænɪŋ/ ① N-UNCOUNT 不可算名詞 **Planning** is the process of deciding in detail how to do something before you actually start to do it. 計画を立てること □ The trip needs careful planning. その旅行には慎重な計画が必要だ. ② → see also **family planning** ③ N-UNCOUNT 不可算名詞 **Planning** is control by the local government of the way that land is used in an area and of what new buildings are built there. 建築許可 □ New York City's Planning Commissions rejected the builder's proposals. ニューヨーク市の建築許可委員会は建築業者の提案を退けた.

plant /plænt/ (plants, planting, planted) ① N-COUNT 可算名詞 A **plant** is a living thing that grows in the earth and has a stem, leaves, and roots. 植物 □ Water each plant as often as required. 必要に応じて植物に水をまきなさい. ② V-T 他動詞 When you **plant** a seed, plant, or young tree, you put it into the ground so that it will grow there. 植える □ He says he plans to plant fruit trees and vegetables. 彼は果樹と野菜を植えるつもりだと言っている. ● **plant|ing** N-UNCOUNT 不可算名詞 □ Extensive flooding in the country has delayed planting and many crops are still under water. その国では広範囲に及ぶ洪水のため、作付が遅れ、作物の多くが水につかったままだ. ③ V-T 他動詞 When someone **plants** land **with** a particular type of plant or crop, they put plants, seeds, or young

trees into the land to grow them there. 植える □ They plan to plant the area with grass and trees. その区域に芝生と樹木を植える予定だ. □ Recently much of their energy has gone into planting a large vegetable garden. 最近彼らは大規模な家庭菜園の作付に多大な労力を費やしてきた. ④ N-COUNT 可算名詞 A **plant** is a factory or a place where power is produced. 工場 □ ...Ford's car assembly plants. フォードの自動車組み立て工場 ⑤ N-UNCOUNT 不可算名詞 **Plant** is large machinery that is used in industrial processes. 設備 □ Companies may start to invest in plant and equipment abroad where costs may be lower. 企業はコストの低い外国で生産設備への投資を開始する可能性がある. ⑥ V-T 他動詞 If you **plant** something somewhere, you put it there firmly. しっかり立てる □ She planted her feet wide and bent her knees slightly. 彼女は両足を広げて立ち、膝をちょっと曲げた. ⑦ V-T 他動詞 To **plant** something such as a bomb means to hide it somewhere so that it explodes or works there. 仕掛ける □ So far no one has admitted planting the bomb. 今までのところ誰も爆弾を仕掛けたと認めていない. ⑧ V-T [oft passive] 他動詞 If something such as a weapon or drugs **is planted** on someone, it is put among their possessions or in their house so that they will be wrongly accused of a crime. ひそかに仕掛ける □ He always protested his innocence and claimed that the drugs had been planted to incriminate him. 彼は常に自分が無実だと抗議し、自分を犯罪者に仕立てるため麻薬がこっそり入れられたと主張した. ⑨ V-T 他動詞 If an organization **plants** someone somewhere, they send that person there so that they can get information or watch someone secretly. 潜り込ませる □ Journalists informed police who planted an undercover detective to trap Smith. 記者らはスミスをわなにかけるために覆面捜査官を潜り込ませた警察に情報を伝えた.

→ see **earth, farm, food, plant, tide, tree**

plan|ta|tion /plænteɪʃⁿ/ (plantations) ① N-COUNT 可算名詞 A **plantation** is a large piece of land, especially in a tropical country, where crops such as rubber, coffee, tea, or sugar are grown. 農園 □ ...banana plantations in Costa Rica. コスタリカのバナナ農園 ② N-COUNT 可算名詞 A **plantation** is a large number of trees that have been planted together. 植林地 □ ...a plantation of almond trees. アーモンドの栽培園

plaque /plæk/ (plaques) ① N-COUNT 可算名詞 A **plaque** is a flat piece of metal or stone with writing on it which is fixed to a wall or other structure to remind people of an important person or event. 飾り板 □ The First Lady unveiled a commemorative plaque. 大統領夫人が記念の飾り額のお披露目をした. ② N-UNCOUNT 不可算名詞 **Plaque** is a substance containing bacteria that forms on the surface of your teeth. 歯垢 (しこう) □ Deposits of plaque build up between the tooth and the gum. 歯垢 (しこう) は歯と歯ぐきの間にたまる.

→ see **teeth**

plas|ma /plæzmə/ N-UNCOUNT 不可算名詞 **Plasma** is the clear liquid part of blood that contains the blood cells. 血漿

plas|ma screen (plasma screens) also **plasma display** N-COUNT 可算名詞 A **plasma screen** is a type of thin television screen or computer screen that produces high-quality images. プラズマスクリーン □ ...a 50-inch plasma screen. 50インチのプラズマスクリーン □ ...flat-panel TVs using thin plasma displays. 薄いプラズマディスプレイを使ったフラットパネルテレビ

plas|ter /plæstər/ (plasters, plastering, plastered) ① N-UNCOUNT 不可算名詞 **Plaster** is a smooth paste made of sand, lime, and water that gets hard when it dries. Plaster is used to cover walls and ceilings and is also used to make sculptures. 漆喰 (しっくい) □ There were huge cracks in the plaster, and the green shutters were faded. 漆喰 (しっくい) には大きなひび割れがあり、緑色の雨戸は色あせていた. ② V-T 他動詞 If you **plaster** a wall or ceiling, you cover it with a layer of plaster. 漆喰を塗る □ The ceiling he had just plastered fell in and knocked him off his ladder. 漆喰を塗ったばかりの天井は崩れ落ち、彼ははしごから落ちた. ③ V-T 他動詞 If you **plaster** a surface or a place with something or pictures, you stick a lot of them all over it. べたべた張る □ He has plastered the city with posters proclaiming his qualifications and experience. 彼は自分の資格と経験を声高に訴えるポスターを町に張りつめた. ④ V-T 他動詞 If you **plaster yourself** in some kind of sticky substance, you cover yourself in it. こってり塗りまくる □ She gets sunburned even when she plasters herself from head to toe in factor 7 sun lotion. 彼女は身体中にSPF7の日焼け止めローションをこってり塗っても日焼けする. ⑤ N-COUNT 可算名詞 A **plaster** is a strip of sticky material used for covering small cuts or sores on your body. 絆創膏 (ばんそうこう) [BRIT 英国英語; AM usually **Band-aid** 米国英語では通常 **Band-aid**] ⑥ → see also **plastered**

plas|tered /plæstərd/ ① ADJ 形容詞 If something is **plastered** to a surface, it is sticking to the surface. 一面に張り付いた [v-link ADJ prep/adv] □ His hair was plastered down to his scalp by the rain. 彼の髪は雨で頭皮に張り付いていた. ② ADJ 形容詞 If something or someone is **plastered** with a sticky substance, they are covered with it. まみれた [v-link ADJ] □ My hands, boots, and pants were plastered with mud. 私の手、ブーツ、ズボンは泥にまみれていた. ③ ADJ 形容詞 If a story or photograph is **plastered all over** the front page of a newspaper, it is given a lot of space on the page and made

very noticeable. 大きく掲載される [v-link ADJ prep/adv] ❑*His picture was plastered all over the newspapers.* 彼の写真は新聞にでかでかと載った。 ❹ ADJ 形容詞 If someone gets **plastered**, they get very drunk. ひどく酔っ払った [INFORMAL くだけた] [v-link ADJ] ❑*I decided to get some beer. Seems a good night to get plastered.* 私はビールを買ってくることに決めた。酔っぱらうのにふさわしい夜のようだ。

plas|tic /plǽstɪk/ (**plastics**) ❶ N-MASS 質量名詞 **Plastic** is a material that is produced from oil by a chemical process and that is used to make many objects. It is light in weight and does not break easily. プラスチック ❑*...a wooden crate, sheltered from rain by sheets of plastic.* 雨よけのプラスチックシートで被われた木製の枠箱 ❑*A lot of the plastics that carmakers are using cannot be recycled.* 自動車メーカーの使用するプラスチックの多くは再生処理ができない。 ❷ ADJ 形容詞 If you describe something as **plastic**, you mean that you think it looks or tastes unnatural or not real. 見せかけだけの [DISAPPROVAL 不賛成] ❑*You wanted proper home-cooked meals, you said you had had enough plastic hotel food and airline food.* きみはちゃんとした家庭料理が食べたかった。きみは味気ないホテルや航空会社の食事にはうんざりだと言った。 ❸ N-UNCOUNT 不可算名詞 If you use **plastic** or **plastic money** to pay for something, you pay for it with a credit card instead of using cash. クレジットカードによる支払い [INFORMAL くだけた] ❑*Using plastic to pay for an order is simplicity itself.* 注文の支払いにクレジットカードを使うことは簡単そのものだ。 ❹ ADJ 形容詞 Something that is **plastic** is soft and can easily be made into different shapes. 可塑性の ❑*You can also enjoy mud packs with the natural mud, smooth, gray, soft, and plastic as butter.* 天然の泥、なめらかで灰色でバターのように柔らかく自由な形にできる泥パックも楽しめる。
→ see oil

plas|tic sur|gery N-UNCOUNT 不可算名詞 **Plastic surgery** is the practice of performing operations to repair or replace skin that has been damaged, or to improve people's appearance. 整形手術 ❑*She even had plastic surgery to change the shape of her nose.* 彼女は鼻の形を変えるために整形手術をした。

plas|tic wrap N-UNCOUNT 不可算名詞 **Plastic wrap** is a thin, clear, stretchy plastic that you use to cover food to keep it fresh. 食品包装用フィルム [AM 米国英語]

plate /pleɪt/ (**plates**) ❶ N-COUNT 可算名詞 A **plate** is a round or oval flat dish that is used to hold food. 皿 ❑*Anita pushed her plate away; she had eaten virtually nothing.* アニータはお皿を押しのけた。ほとんど食べていなかった。 ❷ N-COUNT 可算名詞 A **plate of** food is the amount of food on a plate. 料理の一皿 ❑*...a huge plate of bacon and eggs.* ベーコンと卵の大盛り皿 ❸ N-COUNT 可算名詞 A **plate** is a flat piece of metal, especially on machinery or a building. 平板 ❑*...a recess covered by a brass plate.* 真鍮（しんちゅう）の平板で被われたくぼみ ❹ N-COUNT 可算名詞 A **plate** is a small, flat piece of metal with someone's name written on it, which you usually find beside the front door of an office or house. 表札 ❑*...a brass plate by the front door bearing his name.* 玄関脇の彼の名前のついた真鍮（しんちゅう）の表札 ❺ N-PLURAL 複数名詞 On a road vehicle, the **plates** are the panels on the front and back that display the license number. ナンバープレート ❑*...dusty-looking cars with New Jersey plates.* ニュージャージーのナンバーのほこりまみれの自動車 ❻ → see also license plate ❼ N-COUNT 可算名詞 A **plate** in a book is a picture or photograph that takes up a whole page and is usually printed on better quality paper than the rest of the book. 図版 ❑*The book has 55 color plates.* その本には55ページのカラー一刷り図版がある。 ❽ PHRASE 句 If you **have enough on** your **plate** or **have a lot on** your **plate**, you have a lot of work to do or a lot of things to deal with. やるべきことをかかえこんで ❑*We have enough on our plate. There is plenty of work to be done on what we have.* 私達のすべきことは十分ある。手持ちの仕事でやることがたくさんある。
→ see continent, dish, earthquake, rock

plat|eau /plætóʊ/ (**plateaus** or **plateaux**) ❶ N-COUNT 可算名詞 A **plateau** is a large area of high and fairly flat land. 高原 ❑*A broad valley opened up leading to a high, flat plateau of cultivated land.* 広大な低地が開け、そこから耕作された小高い平らな高原に通じていた。 ❷ N-COUNT 可算名詞 If you say that an activity or process has reached a **plateau**, you mean that it has reached a stage where there is no further change or development. 高原状態 ❑*The U.S. heroin market now appears to have reached a plateau.* 米国のヘロイン市場は落ち着いてきたようである。

-plated /-pléɪtɪd/ COMB IN ADJ 形容詞の複合 Something made of metal that is **plated** is covered with a thin layer of another type of metal such as gold and silver. めっきをした ❑*...a gold-plated watch.* 金メッキした時計

plat|form /plǽtfɔːrm/ (**platforms**) ❶ N-COUNT 可算名詞 A **platform** is a flat raised structure, usually made of wood, that people stand on when they make speeches or give a performance. 演壇 ❑*Nick finished what he was saying and jumped down from the platform.* ニックは演説を終え、演壇から飛び降りた。 ❷ N-COUNT 可算名詞 A **platform** is a flat raised structure or area, usually one

that something can stand on or land on. 高台 ❑*They found a spot on a rocky platform where they could pitch their tents.* 彼らは岩だらけの高台にテントを張ることのできる場所を見つけた。 ❸ N-COUNT 可算名詞 A **platform** is a structure built for people to work and live on when drilling for oil or gas at sea, or when extracting it. プラットホーム ❑*The platform began to produce oil in 1994.* そのプラットホームは1994年に石油を産出し始めた。 ❹ N-COUNT 可算名詞 A **platform** in a train or subway station is the area beside the tracks where you wait for or get off a train. プラットホーム ❑*The train was about to leave and I was not even on the platform.* 電車は発車間際だったが私はプラットホームにすら達していなかった。 ❺ N-COUNT 可算名詞 The **platform** of a political party is what they say they will do if they are elected. 政治要綱 ❑*The party has announced a platform of political and economic reforms.* 政党は政治および経済改革の要綱を発表した。 ❻ N-COUNT 可算名詞 If someone has a **platform**, they have an opportunity to tell people what they think or want. 討論の機会 ❑*The demonstration provided a platform for a broad cross-section of speakers.* デモは部門の演説者の幅広いための討論の場を提供した。
→ see skateboarding

plati|num /plǽtɪnəm, plǽtnəm/ N-UNCOUNT 不可算名詞 **Platinum** is a very valuable, silvery-gray metal. It is often used for making jewelry. プラチナ

plati|tude /plǽtɪtjuːd/ (**platitudes**) N-COUNT 可算名詞 A **platitude** is a statement that is considered meaningless and boring because it has been made many times before in similar situations. 陳腐な言葉 [DISAPPROVAL 不賛成] ❑*Why couldn't we say something vital and original instead of just spouting the same old platitudes?* なぜ我々は決まり文句をまくしたてる代わりに重要で独創的なことが言えなかったのか.

pla|ton|ic /plətɒ́nɪk/ ADJ 形容詞 **Platonic** relationships or feelings of affection do not involve sex. プラトニックな ❑*She values the platonic friendship she has had with Chris for ten years.* 彼女は10年間続いたクリスとのプラトニックな友情関係を重んじている。

plat|ter /plǽtər/ (**platters**) ❶ N-COUNT 可算名詞 A **platter** is a large flat plate used for serving food. 大皿 [mainly AM 主に米国英語] ❑*The food was being served on silver platters.* 料理は銀の大皿に盛られて出てきた。 ❷ N-COUNT 可算名詞 A **platter of** food is the amount of food on a platter. 大皿入りの ❑*They were served platters of cheese and fruit.* 彼らは大皿に入れたチーズと果物でもてなされた。 ❸ PHRASE 句 If you say that someone has things **handed to** them **on a platter**, you disapprove of them because they get good things easily. 楽々と手渡す [DISAPPROVAL 不賛成] ❑*Even the presidency was handed to him on a platter.* 大統領の地位ですら彼にやすやすと移譲された。
→ see dish

plau|sible /plɔ́zɪbəl/ ❶ ADJ 形容詞 An explanation or statement that is **plausible** seems likely to be true or valid. 納得できる ❑*A more plausible explanation would be that people are fed up with the administration.* 政府にうんざりしているという説明の方が納得できそうだ。 ● **plau|sibly** /plɔ́zɪbli/ ADV 副詞 [ADV with v] もっともらしく ❑*Having bluffed his way in without paying, he could not plausibly demand his money back.* 彼は代金を支払わずにはったりで中に入ったので、もっともらしく払い戻しを要求することはできなかった。 ● **plau|sibil|ity** /plɔ̀zɪbɪ́lɪti/ N-UNCOUNT 不可算名詞 信憑（ぴょう）性 ❑*...the plausibility of the theory.* その理論の信憑性 ❷ ADJ 形容詞 If you say that someone is **plausible**, you mean that they seem to be telling the truth and to be sincere and honest. もっともらしい ❑*All I can say is that he was so plausible it wasn't just me that he conned.* 私に言えるのは、彼は口先がうまくてペテンにかけられたのが私だけではなかったということだけだ。

play /pleɪ/ (**plays, playing, played**) ❶ V-I 自動詞 When children, animals, or adults **play**, they spend time doing enjoyable things, such as using toys and taking part in games. 遊ぶ ❑*...invite the children over to play.* 子供たちに遊びに来るよう招待する ❑*They played in the little garden.* 彼らは小さな庭で遊んだ。 ● N-UNCOUNT 不可算名詞 **Play** is also a noun. 遊び ❑*...a few hours of play until the babysitter puts them to bed.* ベビーシッターが寝かしつけるまで数時間の遊び ❷ V-RECIP 相互動詞 When you **play** a sport, game, or match, you take part in it. 参加する ❑*While the twins played cards, Leona sat reading.* 双子がトランプをしている間、レオナは座って読書した。 ❑*I used to play basketball.* 私は昔バスケットボールをしていた。 ● N-UNCOUNT 不可算名詞 **Play** is also a noun. プレー ❑*They've got more exciting players and a more exciting style of play.* 選手とプレーのスタイルは彼らの方が刺激的だ。 ❸ V-T/V-I 他動詞/自動詞 When one person or team **plays** another or **plays against** them, they compete against them in a sport or game. 勝負する ❑*Dallas will play Green Bay.* ダラスはグリーンベイと戦う予定だ。 ● N-UNCOUNT 不可算名詞 **Play** is also a noun. 試合 ❑*Fischer won after 5 hours and 41 minutes of play.* フィッシャーは試合開始後5時間41分で勝利した。

4 V-T 他動詞 If you **play** a joke or a trick on someone, you deceive them or give them a surprise in a way that you think is funny, but that often causes problems for them or annoys them. 仕掛ける □ Someone had played a trick on her, and stretched a piece of string at the top of those steps. 誰かが階段の上に1本のひもを張って彼女にいたずらをした。 **5** V-I 自動詞 If you **play with** an object or with your hair, you keep moving it or touching it with your fingers, perhaps because you are bored or nervous. いじくる □ She stared at the floor, idly playing with the strap of her handbag. 彼女は手持ちぶさたにハンドバッグの皮ひもをいじくり回しながら床を見つめた。 **6** N-COUNT 可算名詞 A **play** is a piece of writing performed in a theater, on the radio, or on television. 演劇 □ It's my favorite Shakespeare play. それは私の好きなシェークスピアの劇だ。 **7** V-T 他動詞 If an actor **plays** a role or character in a play or movie, he or she performs the part of that character. 演じる □ …Dr. Jekyll and Mr. Hyde, in which he played Hyde. 彼がハイドの役を演じたジキル博士とハイド氏。 **8** V-LINK 連結動詞 You can use **play** to describe how someone behaves, when they are deliberately behaving in a certain way or like a certain type of person. For example, to **play the innocent**, means to pretend to be innocent, and to **play deaf** means to pretend not to hear something. 役割を務める □ Hill tried to play the peacemaker. ヒルは仲裁人の役割を務めようとした。 □ She was just playing the devoted mother. 彼女は献身的な母親役を務めていただけだ。 **9** V-T 他動詞 You can describe how someone deals with a situation by saying that they **play it** in a certain way. For example, if someone **plays it cool**, they keep calm and do not show much emotion, and if someone **plays it straight**, they behave in an honest and direct way. ふるまう □ Investors are playing it cautious, and they're playing it smart. 投資家は慎重かつ抜け目なくふるまっている。 **10** V-T/V-I 他動詞/自動詞 If you **play** a musical instrument or **play** a tune on a musical instrument, or if a musical instrument **plays**, music is produced from it. 演奏する □ Nina had been playing the piano. ニーナはピアノを弾いていた。 □ He played for me. 彼は私のために演奏した。 **11** V-T/V-I 他動詞/自動詞 If you **play** a record, a CD, or a DVD, you put it into a machine and sound and sometimes pictures are produced. If a record, CD, or DVD **is playing**, sound and sometimes pictures are being produced from it. かける □ She played her records too loudly. 彼女はレコードの音を大きくかけ過ぎた。 □ There is classical music playing in the background. 背景でクラシック音楽が流れている。 **12** V-T/V-I 他動詞/自動詞 If a musician or group of musicians **plays** or **plays** a concert, they perform music for people to listen or dance to. 演奏する □ A band was playing. 楽団が演奏中だった。 **13** PHRASE 句 When something **comes into play** or **is brought into play**, it begins to be used or to have an effect. 効果をあげはじめる □ The real existence of a military option will come into play. 軍事行使という選択肢の実在性が感じられるようになる。 **14** PHRASE 句 If something or someone **plays a part** or **plays a role in** a situation, they are involved in it and have an effect on it. 役割を果たす □ They played a part in the life of their community. 彼らはコミュニティの生活でひとつの役割を果たした。 □ The U.N. would play a major role in monitoring a ceasefire. 国連は停戦の監視で大きな役割を果たすだろう。 **15** to **play ball** → see **ball** □ to **play the fool** → see **fool** **17** to **play to the gallery** → see **gallery** **18** to **play hard to get** → see **hard** **19** to **play havoc** → see **havoc** **20** to **play hooky** → see **hooky** **21** to **play host** → see **host** **22** to **play possum** → see **possum** **23** to **play safe** → see **safe**
→ see DVD, lottery, theater

▶ **play around** **1** PHRASAL VERB 句動詞 If you **play around**, you behave in a silly way to amuse yourself or other people. 遊び回る [INFORMAL くだけた] □ Stop playing around and eat! ふざけたことは止めて食べなさい。 □ There was no doubt he was serious, it wasn't just playing around. 彼が真剣なのは疑いなかった、ばかをやっているだけではなかった。 **2** PHRASAL VERB 句動詞 If you **play around with** a problem or an arrangement of objects, you try different ways of organizing it in order to find the best solution or arrangement. いじくり回す [INFORMAL くだけた] □ I can play around with the pictures in all sorts of ways to make them more eye-catching. 僕は写真をいろいろといじって人目を引くようにできるよ。 **3** PHRASAL VERB 句動詞 If someone **plays around**, they have sex with people other than the person they are married to or having a serious relationship with. 浮気する [INFORMAL くだけた] □ Up to 75 percent of married men may be playing around. 既婚男性の75%までが浮気をしている可能性がある。 □ Robert was playing around with another woman. ロバートは別の女性と浮気をしていた。

▶ **play at** **1** PHRASAL VERB 句動詞 If you say that someone **is playing at** something, you disapprove of the fact that they are doing it casually and not very seriously. 遊び半分にする [DISAPPROVAL 不賛成] [no passive] □ We were still playing at war—dropping leaflets instead of bombs. 我々はまだ爆弾の代わりにビラをまいて戦争ごっこをしていた。 **2** PHRASAL VERB 句動詞 If someone, especially a child, **plays at** being someone or doing something, they pretend to be that person or do that thing as a game. ごっこする [no passive] □ Ed played at being a pirate. エドは海賊の真似をして遊んだ。 **3** PHRASAL VERB 句動詞 If you do not know what someone **is playing at**, you do not understand what they are

doing or what they are trying to achieve. やっている [INFORMAL くだけた] □ She began to wonder what he was playing at. 彼女は彼が何をやっているのかいぶかり始めた。

▶ **play back** PHRASAL VERB 句動詞 When you **play back** a tape or film, you listen to the sounds or watch the pictures after recording them. 再生する □ He bought an answering machine that plays back his messages when he calls. 彼は電話すると伝言を再生する留守番電話を買った。 □ Ted might benefit from hearing his own voice recorded and played back. テッドは自分の声を録音再生して聞くといいかもしれない。

▶ **play down** PHRASAL VERB 句動詞 If you **play down** something, you try to make people believe that it is not particularly important. 軽く扱う □ Western diplomats have played down the significance of the reports. 西側外交官は報告の意味を軽く扱った。

▶ **play on** PHRASAL VERB 句動詞 If you **play on** someone's fears, weaknesses, or faults, you deliberately use them in order to persuade that person to do something, or to achieve what you want. つけ込む □ …a campaign which plays on the population's fear of change. 国民の変化に対する恐怖心につけ込むキャンペーン

▶ **play up** PHRASAL VERB 句動詞 If you **play up** something, you emphasize it and try to make people believe that it is important. 重視する □ The media played up the prospects for a settlement. メディアは和解の見通しを重視した。

play|er /pleɪər/ (**players**) **1** N-COUNT 可算名詞 A **player** in a sport or game is a person who takes part, either as a job or for fun. プレイヤー □ …his greatness as a player. 競技者としての彼の偉大さ □ She was a good golfer and tennis player. 彼女はゴルフとテニスが上手だった。 **2** N-COUNT 可算名詞 You can use **player** to refer to a musician. For example, a **piano player** is someone who plays the piano. 演奏者 □ …a professional trumpet player. プロのトランペット奏者 **3** N-COUNT 可算名詞 If a person, country, or organization is a **player in** something, they are involved in it and important in it. 参加者 □ Big business has become a major player in the art market. 大企業は芸術品市場で重要な位置を占めるようになった。 **4** N-COUNT 可算名詞 You can refer to a person who spends a lot of time enjoying themselves, especially by having a lot of sexual relationships, as a **player**. 遊び人 [AM 米国英語, INFORMAL くだけた] □ He was a ladies' man. A cheater. A player. 彼は女好きの男だった。詐欺師。プレイボーイ。 **5** → see also CD player, record player
→ see chess, football, soccer

play|ful /pleɪfəl/ **1** ADJ 形容詞 A **playful** gesture or person is friendly or humorous. 冗談半分の □ …a playful kiss on the tip of his nose. 彼の鼻先へのおどけたキス ● **play|ful|ly** ADV 副詞 面白半分で □ She pushed him away playfully. 彼女はおどけて彼を押しのけた。 ● **play|ful|ness** N-UNCOUNT 不可算名詞 遊び半分なこと □ …the child's natural playfulness. 子供の自然な陽気さ **2** ADJ 形容詞 A **playful** animal is lively and cheerful. 遊び戯れる □ …a playful puppy. じゃれる子犬

play|ground /pleɪɡraʊnd/ (**playgrounds**) N-COUNT 可算名詞 A **playground** is a piece of land, at school or in a public area, where children can play. 運動場 □ …a seven-year-old boy playing in a school playground. 学校の運動場で遊ぶ7歳の少年
→ see park

play|group /pleɪɡruːp/ (**playgroups**) also **play group** N-COUNT 可算名詞 A **playgroup** is an informal school for very young children, where they learn things by playing. 親子の会 [also prep N]

play|ing card (**playing cards**) N-COUNT 可算名詞 **Playing cards** are thin pieces of cardboard with numbers or pictures printed on them that are used to play various games. トランプ □ …a deck of playing cards. トランプ一組

play|ing field (**playing fields**) **1** N-COUNT 可算名詞 A **playing field** is a large area of grass where people play sports. 競技場 □ Jefferson County has three grass playing fields for 18 varsity football teams. ジェファーソン郡には18校の代表フットボールチームのために芝生の競技場3つがある。 **2** PHRASE 句 You talk about a **level playing field** to mean a situation that is fair, because no competitor or opponent in it has an advantage over another. 公平な競争場 □ American businessmen ask for a level playing field when they compete with foreign companies. アメリカ人の実業家は外国企業と同じ土俵で競争することを求める。

play|list /pleɪlɪst/ (**playlists**) N-COUNT 可算名詞 A **playlist** is a list of songs, albums, and artists that a radio station broadcasts. 放送予定録音表 □ The radio station's playlist is dominated by top-selling youth-orientated groups. ラジオ局の放送予定録音表は上位ランキングの若者志向のグループが優位を占めている。

play|off /pleɪɔf/ (**playoffs**) **1** N-COUNT 可算名詞 A **playoff** is an extra game that is played to decide the winner of a sports competition when two or more people have the same score. プレーオフ □ Nick Faldo was beaten by Peter Baker in a playoff. ニック・ファルドはプレーオフでピーター・ベイカーに敗れた。 **2** N-COUNT 可算名詞 You use **playoffs** to refer to a series of games that are played to decide the winner of a championship. 王座決定戦 □ It's been a long

time since these two teams faced each other in the playoffs. この2つのチームが王座決定戦で対戦するのはしばらくぶりだ。

play|wright /pleɪraɪt/ (**playwrights**) N-COUNT 可算名詞 A **playwright** is a person who writes plays. 劇作家

pla|za /plɑːzə, plæzə/ (**plazas**) ◼ N-COUNT 可算名詞 A **plaza** is an open square in a city. 広場 ❑ Across the busy plaza, vendors sell hot dogs and croissant sandwiches. にぎやかな広場のいたるところにホットドッグやクロワッサン・サンドを売る売り子がいる。 ◻ N-COUNT 可算名詞 A **plaza** is a group of stores or buildings that are joined together or share common areas. ショッピングプラザ [AM 米国英語] ❑ ...a new retail plaza. 新しいショッピングプラザ

plea /pliː/ (**pleas**) ◼ N-COUNT 可算名詞 A **plea** is an appeal or request for something, made in an intense or emotional way. 嘆願 [JOURNALISM ジャーナリズム] ❑ Mr. Nicholas made his emotional plea for help in solving the killing. ニコラス氏は殺人事件解決への援助を求めて感情に訴える嘆願をした。 ◻ N-COUNT 可算名詞 In a court of law, a person's **plea** is the answer that they give when they have been charged with a crime, saying whether or not they are guilty of that crime. 罪状認否 ❑ The judge questioned him about his guilty plea. 判事は彼の有罪の申し立てについて彼に質問した。 ❑ We will enter a plea of not guilty. 我々は無罪の申し立てをするつもりだ。 ◼ N-COUNT 可算名詞 A **plea** is a reason given, to a court of law or to other people, as an excuse for doing something or for not doing something. 抗弁 ❑ Phillips murdered his wife, but got off on a plea of insanity. フィリップスは妻を殺害したが心神喪失の抗弁で刑罰を免れた。

→ see **trial**

plead /pliːd/ (**pleads, pleading, pleaded, pled**) ◼ V-I 自動詞 If you **plead** with someone to do something, you ask them in an intense, emotional way to do it. 嘆願する ❑ The lady pleaded with her daughter to come back home. その女性は家に戻って来るよう娘に懇願した。 ❑ He was kneeling on the floor pleading for mercy. 彼は慈悲を請いながら床にひざまずいた。 ◻ V-I 自動詞 When someone charged with a crime **pleads guilty** or **not guilty** in a court of law, they officially state that they are guilty or not guilty of the crime. 有罪を認める、無罪を主張する ❑ Morris had pleaded guilty to robbery. モリスは強盗罪を認めた。 ◼ V-T 他動詞 If you **plead the case** or **cause** of someone or something, you speak out in their support or defense. 申し立てる ❑ He appeared before the committee to plead his case. 彼は彼の主張を申し立てるために委員会の前に現われた。 ◼ V-T 他動詞 If you **plead** a particular thing as the reason for doing or not doing something, you give it as your excuse. 言い訳にする ❑ Mr. Giles pleads ignorance as his excuse. ジャイルズ氏は無知を言い訳にする。

plead|ing /pliːdɪŋ/ (**pleadings**) ◼ ADJ 形容詞 A **pleading** expression or gesture shows someone that you want something very much. 訴えるような ❑ ...his pleading eyes. 彼の訴えるようなまなざし ❑ ...the pleading expression on her face. 彼の訴えるような表情 ◻ N-UNCOUNT 不可算名詞 **Pleading** is asking someone for something you want very much, in an intense or emotional way. 嘆願すること [also N in pl] ❑ He simply ignored Sid's pleading. 彼はシッドの嘆願を完全に無視した。

pleas|ant /plezənt/ (**pleasanter, pleasantest**) ◼ ADJ 形容詞 Something that is **pleasant** is nice, enjoyable, or attractive. 気持ちのよい ❑ I've got a pleasant little apartment. 私は快適な小さなアパートを持っている。 ● **pleas|ant|ly** ADV 副詞 愉快に ❑ We talked pleasantly of old times. 私達は昔のことを楽しく語り合った。 ◻ ADJ 形容詞 Someone who is **pleasant** is friendly and likeable. 感じの良い ❑ The woman had a pleasant face. その女性は感じの良い顔をしていた。

Thesaurus	pleasant また次を参照:
ADJ.	agreeable, cheerful, delightful, likable, friendly, nice; (ant.) unpleasant ◼

please /pliːz/ (**pleases, pleasing, pleased**) ◼ ADV 副詞 You say **please** when you are politely asking or inviting someone to do something. どうぞ [POLITENESS 丁寧さ] [ADV with cl] ❑ Can you help us please? どうか私達を助けてくれませんか。 ❑ Please come in. どうぞお入りください。 ❑ Can we have the bill please? 伝票をいただけますか。 ◻ ADV 副詞 You say **please** when you are accepting something politely. ぜひ [FORMULAE 決まり文句] ❑ "Tea?"—"Yes, please." 「お茶はどう」「はい、お願いします」 ◼ CONVENTION 慣習表現 You can say **please** to indicate that you want someone to stop doing something or stop speaking. You would say this if, for example, what they are doing or saying makes you angry or upset. お願い [FEELINGS 感情] ❑ Please, Mary, this is all so unnecessary. 頼むわ、メアリー、こんなこと全然しなくていいのに。 ◼ CONVENTION 慣習表現 You can say **please** in order to attract someone's attention politely. すみません [POLITENESS 丁寧さ] ❑ Please, Miss Smith, a moment. すみませんスミスさん、ちょっと。 ◼ V-T/V-I 他動詞/自動詞 If someone or something **pleases** you, they make you feel happy and satisfied. 喜ばせる ❑ More than anything, I want to please you. 何よりも増して私はあなたを喜ばせたい。 ❑ It pleased him to talk to her. 彼は彼女と話すのが好きだった。 ❑ He appeared anxious to please. 彼は喜ばせたがっているよう

だった。 ◼ PHRASE 句 You use **please** in expressions such as **as she pleases, whatever you please,** and **anything he pleases** to indicate that someone can do or have whatever they want. 好むように ❑ Women should be free to dress and act as they please. 女性は自由な服を着て好きに行動するべきだ。 ❑ He does whatever he pleases. 彼は自分の好きなことをする。

pleased /pliːzd/ ◼ ADJ 形容詞 If you are **pleased,** you are happy about something or satisfied with something. 喜んで ❑ Felicity seemed pleased at the suggestion. フェリシティはその提案に満足しているようだった。 ❑ I think he's going to be pleased that we identified the real problems. 私は彼が私達が本当の問題を見極めたことを喜んでくれると思う。 ◻ ADJ 形容詞 If you say you will be **pleased to** do something, you are saying in a polite way that you are willing to do it. 喜んで [POLITENESS 丁寧さ] [v-link ADJ to-inf] ❑ We will be pleased to answer any questions you may have. 我々はどんな質問にも喜んで答えるつもりだ。 ◼ ADJ 形容詞 You can tell someone that you are **pleased with** something they have done in order to express your approval. 満足して [FEELINGS 感情] [v-link ADJ] ❑ I'm pleased with the way things have been going. 私は物事の進行に満足している。 ❑ I am very pleased about the result. 私は結果について大いに喜んでいる。 ❑ We are pleased that the problems have been resolved. 我々は問題が解決されて嬉しい。 ◼ ADJ 形容詞 When you are about to give someone some news that you know will please them, you can say that you are **pleased to** tell them the news or that they will be **pleased to** hear it. 喜んで [v-link ADJ to-inf] ❑ I'm pleased to say that he is now doing well. 幸い彼は現在成功している。 ◼ ADJ 形容詞 In official letters, people often say they will be **pleased to** do something, as a polite way of introducing what they are going to do or inviting people to do something. 喜んで [POLITENESS 丁寧さ] [v-link ADJ to-inf] ❑ We will be pleased to delete the charge from the original invoice. もともとの請求書からその料金を喜んで削除させていただきます。 ◼ PHRASE 句 If someone seems very satisfied with something they have done, you can say that they are **pleased with themselves,** especially if you think they are more satisfied than they should be. 満足した ❑ "Sophie was glad to see you," he said, pleased with himself again for having remembered her name. 「ソフィーは君に会えて喜んでいた」と彼は彼女の名前を覚えていたことに再び満足して言った。 ◼ CONVENTION 慣習表現 You can say "**Pleased to meet you**" as a polite way of greeting someone who you are meeting for the first time. お会いできて光栄です [FORMULAE 決まり文句]

pleas|ing /pliːzɪŋ/ ADJ 形容詞 Something that is **pleasing** gives you pleasure and satisfaction. 楽しい ❑ This area of France has a pleasing climate in August. フランスのこの地域の8月の気候は快い。 ❑ Such a view is pleasing. そのような景色は目を楽しませてくれる。 ● **pleas|ing|ly** ADV 副詞 心地よく ❑ The interior design is pleasingly simple. インテリアデザインは心地よいほどシンプルだ。

pleas|ur|able /plezərəbəl/ ADJ 形容詞 **Pleasurable** experiences or sensations are pleasant and enjoyable. 人を楽しませる ❑ The most pleasurable experience of the evening was the wonderful fireworks display. その晩最も楽しい体験は素晴らしい花火だった。

pleas|ure /plezər/ (**pleasures**) ◼ N-UNCOUNT 不可算名詞 If something gives you **pleasure,** you get a feeling of happiness, satisfaction, or enjoyment from it. 喜び ❑ Watching sports gave him great pleasure. 彼はスポーツ観戦を大変楽しんだ。 ❑ Everybody takes pleasure in eating. 誰でも食べることを楽しいと感じる。 ◻ N-UNCOUNT 不可算名詞 **Pleasure** is the activity of enjoying yourself, especially rather than working or doing what you have a duty to do. 遊び ❑ He mixed business and pleasure in a perfect and dynamic way. 彼は仕事と遊びを完璧でダイナミックな方法で調和させた。 ◼ N-COUNT 可算名詞 A **pleasure** is an activity, experience, or aspect of something that you find very enjoyable or satisfying. 楽しみ ❑ Watching TV is our only pleasure. テレビを見ることが我々の唯一の楽しみだ。 ❑ ...the pleasure of seeing a smiling face. ほほえむ顔を見ることの楽しさ ◼ CONVENTION 慣習表現 If you meet someone for the first time, you can say, as a way of being polite, that it is **a pleasure to meet** them. You can also ask for **the pleasure of** someone's **company** as a polite and formal way of inviting them somewhere. 楽しいもの [POLITENESS 丁寧さ] ❑ "A pleasure to meet you, sir," he said. 「お会いできて幸甚（こうじん）でございます」と彼は言った。 ◼ CONVENTION 慣習表現 You can say "**It's a pleasure**" or "**My pleasure**" as a polite way of replying to someone who has just thanked you for doing something. どういたしまして [FORMULAE 決まり文句] ❑ "Thanks very much anyhow."—"It's a pleasure." 「とにかくどうもありがとう」「どういたしまして」

Word Partnership	pleasureは次の語句と使われる:
ADJ.	**great** pleasure, **intense** pleasure, **simple** pleasure ◼ ◻ **sexual** pleasure ◼

pleat /pliːt/ (**pleats**) N-COUNT 可算名詞 A **pleat** in a piece of clothing is a permanent fold that is made in the cloth by folding one part over the other and sewing across the top end of the fold.

P

プリーツ ❑Her skirt hangs in perfect wide pleats. 彼女のスカートは完璧な幅広のプリーツがついている.

pleat|ed /plitɪd/ ADJ 形容詞 A **pleated** piece of clothing has pleats in it. プリーツのついた ❑...a short white pleated skirt. プリーツのついた短い白のスカート

pledge /plɛdʒ/ (pledges, pledging, pledged) **1** N-COUNT 可算名詞 When someone makes a **pledge**, they make a serious promise that they will do something. 誓約 ❑The meeting ended with a pledge to step up cooperation between the six states of the region. 会合は地域6か国間の協力を強化する誓約をして終わった. **2** V-T 他動詞 When someone **pledges to** do something, they promise in a serious way to do it. When they **pledge** something, they promise to give it. 約束する ❑The Communists have pledged to support the opposition's motion. 共産党は野党の動議を支持すると約束した. ❑Philip pledges support and offers to help in any way that he can. フィリップは支援を約束し, できる限りの援助をすると申し出ている. **3** V-T 他動詞 If you **pledge** a sum of money to an organization or activity, you promise to pay that amount of money to it at a particular time or over a particular period. 寄付を約束する ❑The French president is pledging $150 million in French aid next year. フランス大統領は来年, フランスの援助金の形で1億5千万ドルの提供を約束している. ● N-COUNT 可算名詞 **Pledge** is also a noun. 寄付の約束 ❑...a pledge of forty two million dollars a month. 月々4千2百万ドルの寄付の約束 **4** V-T 他動詞 If you **pledge yourself to** something, you commit yourself to following a particular course of action or to supporting a particular person, group, or idea. 誓約する ❑The president pledged himself to increase taxes for the rich but not the middle classes. 大統領は富裕層には増税するが中産階級にはしないと誓った. **5** V-T 他動詞 If you **pledge** something such as a valuable possession or a sum of money, you leave it with someone as a guarantee that you will repay money that you have borrowed. 抵当として差し出す ❑He asked her to pledge the house as security for a loan. 彼はローンの担保として家を抵当に入れるよう彼女に頼んだ.

Thesaurus	*pledge* また次を参照:
N.	agreement, covenant, guarantee, promise **1**
V.	contract, guarantee, promise, swear, vow **2** **3**

Word Link	*plen ≈ full : plentiful, plenty, replenish*

plen|ti|ful /plɛntɪfəl/ ADJ 形容詞 Things that are **plentiful** exist in such large amounts or numbers that there is enough for people's wants or needs. 豊富な ❑Fish are plentiful in the lake. 湖には魚がたくさんいる.

plen|ty /plɛnti/ QUANT 数量詞 If there is **plenty of** something, there is a large amount of it. If there are **plenty of** things, there are many of them. **Plenty** is used especially to indicate that there is enough of something, or more than you need. 十分の ❑There was still plenty of time to take Jill out for pizza. ジルをピザを食べに連れ出すのに時間はまだ十分あった. ❑Most businesses face plenty of competition. 大半の事業は多くの競争に直面する. ● PRON 代名詞 **Plenty** is also a pronoun. 十分なもの ❑I don't believe in long interviews. Fifteen minutes is plenty. 長い面接が良いとは思わない. 15分で十分だ.

Thesaurus	*plenty* また次を参照:
QUANT.	abundance, capacity, quantity; (ant.) scarcity

pletho|ra /plɛθərə/ N-SING 単数名詞 A **plethora of** something is a large amount of it, especially an amount of it that is greater than you need, want, or can cope with. 過多 [FORMAL 形式ばった] ❑A plethora of new operators will be allowed to enter the market. 極めて多数の新しい事業者が市場参入を許されるだろう.

pli|able /plaɪəbˀl/ ADJ 形容詞 If something is **pliable**, you can bend it easily without cracking or breaking it. 曲げやすい ❑As your baby grows bigger, his bones become less pliable. 赤ちゃんは成長に伴い, 骨の柔軟性を失う.

pli|ers /plaɪərz/ N-PLURAL 複数名詞 **Pliers** are a tool with two handles at one end and two hard, flat, metal parts at the other. Pliers are used for holding or pulling out things such as nails, or for bending or cutting wire. プライヤー [also "a pair of" N]
→ see **tool**

plight /plaɪt/ (plights) N-COUNT 可算名詞 If you refer to someone's **plight**, you mean that they are in a difficult or distressing situation that is full of problems. 苦境 ❑The nation saw the plight of the farmers, whose crops had died. 国民は農産物の不作で農業経営者が陥った苦境を知った.

Thesaurus	*plight* また次を参照:
N.	difficulty, dilemma, problem, situation

plod /plɒd/ (plods, plodding, plodded) **1** V-I 自動詞 If someone **plods**, they walk slowly and heavily. 重い足取りで歩く ❑Crowds of people plodded around in yellow plastic raincoats. 黄色いプラスチ

ックのレインコートを着た人の群れがとぼとぼ歩き回った. **2** V-I 自動詞 If you say that someone **plods on** or **plods along** with a job, you mean that the job is taking a long time. こつこつ働く ❑He is plodding on with negotiations. 彼は交渉をのろのろと進めている.

plot /plɒt/ (plots, plotting, plotted) **1** N-COUNT 可算名詞 A **plot** is a secret plan by a group of people to do something that is illegal or wrong, usually against a person or a government. 陰謀 ❑Security forces have uncovered a plot to overthrow the government. 治安部隊は政府転覆の陰謀を暴露した. **2** V-T 他動詞 If people **plot** to do something or **plot** something that is illegal or wrong, they plan secretly to do it. 陰謀を企てる ❑Prosecutors in the trial allege the defendants plotted to overthrow the government. 裁判で検察官は被告が政府転覆を企んだと立証した. ❑The military were plotting a coup. 軍隊はクーデターをたくらんでいた. **3** V-T 他動詞 When people **plot** a strategy or a course of action, they carefully plan each step of it. 構想を練る ❑Yesterday's meeting was intended to plot a survival strategy for the party. 昨日の打ち合わせは党が生き延びる戦略を練るためのものだった. **4** N-VAR 可変性名詞 The **plot** of a movie, novel, or play is the connected series of events which make up the story. 筋 ❑He began to tell me the plot of his new book. 彼は新刊本の筋書きを私に説明し始めた. **5** N-COUNT 可算名詞 A **plot of** land is a small piece of land, especially one that has been measured or marked out for a special purpose, such as building houses or growing vegetables. 小区画の土地 ❑I thought that I'd buy myself a small plot of land and build a house on it. 私は小さな土地を買ってそこに家を建てようと考えた. **6** V-T 他動詞 When someone **plots** something on a graph, they mark certain points on it and then join the points up. 座標で示す ❑We plotted about eight points on the graph. 我々はグラフに8個ほどの点を示した. **7** V-T 他動詞 When someone **plots** the position or course of a plane or ship, they mark it on a map using instruments to obtain accurate information. プロットする ❑We were trying to plot the course of the submarine. 我々は潜水艦の航路をプロットしようとしていた. **8** V-T 他動詞 If someone **plots** the progress or development of something, they make a diagram or a plan which shows how it has developed in order to give some indication of how it will develop in the future. 記録をつける ❑They used a computer to plot the movements of everyone in the police station on December 24, 1990. 彼らはコンピュータを使って1990年12月24日の警察署の全員の活動記録を作成した.

plow /plaʊ/ (plows, plowing, plowed) **1** N-COUNT 可算名詞 A **plow** is a large farming tool with sharp blades that is pulled across the soil to turn it over, usually before seeds are planted. 鋤(すき) ❑There are new tractors and new plows in the machinery lot. 機械置き場には新しいトラクターと鋤(すき)がある. **2** → see also **snowplow** **3** V-T 他動詞 When someone **plows** an area of land, they turn over the soil using a plow. 鋤で耕す ❑They were no longer using mules and horses to plow their fields. 彼らは鋤で畑を耕すのにラバや馬をもう使っていなかった.
→ see **barn**

▶ **plow back** PHRASAL VERB 句動詞 If profits **are plowed back into** a business, they are used to increase the size of the business or to improve it. 再投資する [BUSINESS 実業] [usu passive] ❑...cash profits that are quickly plowed back into the market. 市場に素早く再投資される現金利益

ploy /plɔɪ/ (ploys) N-COUNT 可算名詞 A **ploy** is a way of behaving that someone plans carefully and secretly in order to gain an advantage for themselves. 策略 ❑Christmas should be a time of excitement and wonder, not a cynical marketing ploy. クリスマスはシニカルなマーケティング戦略ではなく興奮と感嘆のひとときであるべきだ.

pls. **Pls.** is a written abbreviation for **please**. pleaseの縮約形 ❑Have you moved yet? Pls. advise address, phone no., etc. もう引越しは済みましたか. 住所, 電話番号などを知らせてください.

pluck /plʌk/ (plucks, plucking, plucked) **1** V-T 他動詞 If you **pluck** a fruit, flower, or leaf, you take it between your fingers and pull it in order to remove it from its stalk where it is growing. 摘む [WRITTEN 書き言葉] ❑I plucked a lemon from the tree. 私は木からレモンの実を摘んだ. **2** V-T 他動詞 If you **pluck** something from somewhere, you take it between your fingers and pull it sharply from where it is. つかむ [WRITTEN 書き言葉] ❑He plucked the cigarette from his mouth and tossed it out into the street. 彼は口からタバコをつかんで通りに投げ捨てた. ❑He plucked the baby out of my arms. 彼は赤ん坊を私の腕からひったくった. **3** V-T 他動詞 If you **pluck** a guitar or other musical instrument, you pull the strings with your fingers and let them go, so that they make a sound. 爪弾く ❑Nell was plucking a harp. ネルはハープを爪弾いていた. **4** V-T 他動詞 If you **pluck** a chicken or other dead bird, you pull its feathers out to prepare it for cooking. 羽を引き抜く ❑She looked relaxed as she plucked a chicken. 彼女は鶏の羽を引き抜きながらくつろいでいるように見えた. **5** V-T 他動詞 If a woman **plucks** her **eyebrows**, she pulls out some of the hairs using tweezers. まゆ毛を抜く ❑You've plucked your eyebrows at last! あなたはやっとまゆ毛を抜いた. **6** PHRASE 句 If you **pluck up the courage to** do something that you feel nervous about, you make an effort to be brave enough to

Word Web   plumbing

Babylonian* homes of 4,000 years ago had **bathrooms** where people bathed themselves with **water**. The waste water **drained** off through a hole in the floor. At about the same time, the Minoans* in Crete* invented the **flush toilet**. It used rain water held in cisterns. The early Egyptians discovered how to make **pipes** out of clay and **basins** out of **copper**. Some homes in ancient Greece contained latrines that drained into a sewer beneath the street. The Romans were the first to use **lead** for **plumbing** purposes. The word "plumbing" comes from *plumbus*, the Latin word for "lead."

Babylonian: from the ancient city of Babylon.
Minoans (3000 BC – 1100 BC): people who lived on Crete.
Crete: an island in the eastern Mediterranean Sea.

do it. 勇気を奮い起こす ❑ *It took me about two hours to pluck up the courage to call.* 電話をする勇気を奮い起こすのに約2時間かかった.

plug /plʌg/ (**plugs, plugging, plugged**) **1** N-COUNT 可算名詞 A **plug** on a piece of electrical equipment is a small plastic object with two or three metal pins that fit into the holes of an electric outlet and connects the equipment to the electricity supply. プラグ ❑ *I used to go around and take every plug out at night.* 私は夜, 家中のプラグを抜いて回ったものだ. **2** N-COUNT 可算名詞 A **plug** is an electric outlet. ソケット [INFORMAL くだけた] ❑ *Then Bob spotted the problem - the plug in the wall hadn't been switched on.* それからボブが問題を発見した. 壁のソケットはオンになっていなかった. **3** N-COUNT 可算名詞 A **plug** is a thick, circular piece of rubber or plastic that you use to block the hole in a bathtub or sink when it is filled with water. 栓 ❑ *She put the plug in the sink and filled it with cold water.* 彼女は流しに栓をし水を貯めた. **4** N-COUNT 可算名詞 A **plug** is a small, round piece of wood, plastic, or wax that is used to block holes. 詰め物 ❑ *A plug had been inserted in the drill hole.* 穿孔(せんこう)に詰め物が挿入されていた. **5** V-T 他動詞 If you **plug** a hole, you block it with something. ふさぐ ❑ *Crews are working to plug a major oil leak.* 乗組員は大規模な石油流出の穴をふさぐ作業をしているところだ. **6** V-T 他動詞 If someone **plugs** a commercial product, especially a book or a movie, they praise it in order to encourage people to buy it or see it because they have an interest in it doing well. 宣伝する ❑ *We did not want people on the show who are purely interested in plugging a book or movie.* 我々は本や映画の宣伝にしか関心のない人が番組に出演することには反対だった. ● N-COUNT 可算名詞 **Plug** is also a noun. 宣伝 ❑ *Let's do this show tonight and it'll be a great plug, a great promotion.* 今夜このショーをやろうよ, そうすれば大きな宣伝, すごいPRになると思う. **7** PHRASE 句 If someone in a position of power **pulls the plug on** a project or on someone's activities, they use their power to stop them from continuing. おしまいにする ❑ *The banks have the power to pull the plug on the project.* 銀行団にはそのプロジェクトを打ち切る権限がある.

▶ **plug in** or **plug into** **1** PHRASAL VERB 句動詞 If you **plug** a piece of electrical equipment **into** an electricity supply or if you **plug** it **in**, you push its plug into an electric outlet so that it can work. プラグを差し込む ❑ *They plugged in their tape-recorders.* 彼らはテープレコーダーのプラグを差し込んだ. ❑ *I had a TV set but there was no place to plug it in.* テレビはあったが差し込む所がなかった. **2** PHRASAL VERB 句動詞 If you **plug** one piece of electrical equipment **into** another or if you **plug** it **in**, you make it work by connecting the two. 接続する ❑ *They plugged their guitars into amplifiers.* 彼らはギターをアンプに接続した. **3** PHRASAL VERB 句動詞 If one piece of electrical equipment **plugs in** or **plugs into** another piece of electrical equipment, it works by being connected by an electrical cord or lead to an electricity supply or to the other piece of equipment. 接続する ❑ *The device looks like a video recorder and plugs into the home television and stereo system.* その機器はビデオレコーダーにそっくりで, 家庭用テレビとステレオシステムに接続できる. ❑ *They plug into a laptop, desktop, or handheld computer.* それらはラップトップ, デスクトップまたは情報携帯端末に接続する. **4** PHRASAL VERB 句動詞 If you **plug** something **into** a hole, you push it into the hole. 押し込む ❑ *Her instructor plugged live bullets into the gun's chamber.* 彼女の教官は銃の薬室に実弾を詰め込んだ. **5** → see also **plug-in**

plug-and-play ADJ 形容詞 **Plug-and-play** is used to describe computer equipment, for example, a printer, that is ready to use immediately when you connect it to a computer. プラグアンドプレイの [COMPUTING コンピューティング] [ADJ n] ❑ *...a plug-and-play USB camera.* プラグアンドプレイ式USBカメラ

plug-in (**plug-ins**) **1** ADJ 形容詞 A **plug-in** machine is a piece of electrical equipment that is operated by being connected to an electricity supply or to another piece of electrical equipment by means of a plug. 差し込み式の [ADJ n] ❑ *...a plug-in radio.* 差し込み式ラジオ **2** N-COUNT 可算名詞 A **plug-in** is something such as a piece of software that can be added to a computer system to give extra features or functions. プラグイン [COMPUTING コンピ

ューティング] ❑ *Some websites make it seem like you need to download a plug-in or program to access the site.* サイトによってはプラグインやアクセス用プログラムをダウンロードする必要があるように思わせるものもある.

plum /plʌm/ (**plums**) **1** N-COUNT 可算名詞 A **plum** is a small, sweet fruit with a smooth purple, red, or yellow skin and a pit in the middle. 西洋スモモ **2** COLOR 色彩語 Something that is **plum** or **plum-colored** is a dark reddish-purple color. 暗紫色 ❑ *...plum-colored silk.* 暗紫色の絹

plumb|er /plʌmər/ (**plumbers**) N-COUNT 可算名詞 A **plumber** is a person whose job is to connect and repair things such as water and drainage pipes, bathtubs, and toilets. 配管工

plumb|ing /plʌmɪŋ/ **1** N-UNCOUNT 不可算名詞 The **plumbing** in a building consists of the water and drainage pipes, bathtubs, and toilets in it. 配管 ❑ *The wiring and the plumbing were sound but everything else had to be cleaned up.* 配線と配管は問題なかったがそれ以外は全て清浄する必要があった. **2** N-UNCOUNT 不可算名詞 **Plumbing** is the work of connecting and repairing things such as water and drainage pipes, baths, and toilets. 配管工事 ❑ *She learned the rudiments of bricklaying, wiring, and plumbing.* 彼女はレンガ積み, 電気配線, 配管の基礎を学んだ.
→ see Word Web: **plumbing**

plume /plum/ (**plumes**) **1** N-COUNT 可算名詞 A **plume of** smoke, dust, fire, or water is a large quantity of it that rises into the air in a column. もくもく立ち上る煙 ❑ *The rising plume of black smoke could be seen all over Kabul.* もくもく立ち上る黒い煙がカブールの至る所で見られた. **2** N-COUNT 可算名詞 A **plume** is a large, soft bird's feather. 羽 ❑ *...broad straw hats decorated with ostrich plumes.* ダチョウの大羽で飾られた幅広の麦帽子

plum|met /plʌmɪt/ (**plummets, plummeting, plummeted**) V-I 自動詞 If an amount, rate, or price **plummets**, it decreases quickly by a large amount. 急に下がる [JOURNALISM ジャーナリズム] ❑ *In Tokyo share prices have plummeted for the sixth successive day.* 東京の株価は6日間続けて急落した. ❑ *The president's popularity has plummeted to an all-time low in recent weeks.* 大統領の人気はここ数週間, 史上最低のレベルに落ちた.

plump /plʌmp/ (**plumper, plumpest, plumps, plumping, plumped**) **1** ADJ 形容詞 You can describe someone or something as **plump** to indicate that they are somewhat fat or rounded. ふっくらした ❑ *Maria was a pretty little thing, small and plump with a mass of curly hair.* マリアは小柄でふっくらしてふさふさした巻き毛のある美少女だった. ❑ *He pushed a plump little hand toward me.* 彼はふっくらした小さな手を私の方に伸ばした. **2** V-T 他動詞 If you **plump** a pillow or cushion, you shake it and hit it gently so that it goes back into a rounded shape. 膨らませる ❑ *She patted all the seats and plumped all the cushions.* 彼女は全ての椅子をたたき, 全てのクッションを膨らませた. ● PHRASAL VERB 句動詞 **Plump up** means the same as **plump**. 膨らませる ❑ *"You need to rest," she told him reassuringly as she moved to plump up his pillows.* 「あなたは休む必要があります」と彼女は枕を膨らませながら安心させるように彼に言った.

plun|der /plʌndər/ (**plunders, plundering, plundered**) V-T 他動詞 If someone **plunders** a place or **plunders** things **from** a place, they steal things from it. 略奪する [LITERARY 文語的] ❑ *He plundered the palaces and ransacked the treasuries.* 彼は宮殿を荒らし, 宝庫を略奪して回った. ❑ *She faces charges of helping to plunder her country's treasury of billions of dollars.* 彼女は国の資金から何十億ドルをも略奪するのを助けた嫌疑を受けている. ● N-UNCOUNT 不可算名詞 **Plunder** is also a noun. 略奪 ❑ *...a guerrilla group infamous for torture and plunder.* 拷問と略奪で有名なゲリラ団

plunge /plʌndʒ/ (**plunges, plunging, plunged**) **1** V-I 自動詞 If something or someone **plunges** in a particular direction, especially into water, they fall, rush, or throw themselves in that direction. 落ちる ❑ *At least 50 people died when a bus plunged into a river.* バスが川に落下して少なくとも50名の死者が出た. ● N-COUNT 可算名詞 **Plunge** is also a noun. 飛び込み ❑ *...a plunge into cold water.*

冷たい水に飛び込むこと **2** V-T 他動詞 If you **plunge** an object **into** something, you push it quickly or violently into it. 突っ込む ❑ *A soldier plunged a bayonet into his body.* 兵は彼の体に銃剣を突き刺した. ❑ *She plunged her face into a bowl of cold water.* 彼女は冷たい水のはいった容器に顔を沈めた. **3** V-T/V-I 他動詞/自動詞 If a person or thing is **plunged into** a particular state or situation, or if they **plunge into** it, they are suddenly in that state or situation. 突然ある状態に置かれる ❑ *The government's political and economic reforms threaten to plunge the country into chaos.* 政府の政治経済改革は国を混乱状態に追い込む恐れがある. ❑ *Eddy found himself plunged into a world of brutal violence.* エディは自分が残酷な暴力の世界に追い込まれたことを知った. ●N-COUNT 可算名詞 **Plunge** is also a noun. ❑ *That peace often looked like a brief truce before the next plunge into war.* あの平和はしばしば次の戦争に突入する前のつかのまの休戦のように思えた. **4** V-T/V-I 他動詞/自動詞 If you **plunge into** an activity or **are plunged into** it, you suddenly get very involved in it. 急にーし始める ❑ *The two men plunged into discussion.* 2人の男達は急に話し合いを始めた. ❑ *The prince should be plunged into work.* 王子に働かせるべきだ. ●N-COUNT 可算名詞 **Plunge** is also a noun. 首を突っ込むこと ❑ *His sudden plunge into the field of international diplomacy is a major surprise.* 彼が国際外交の分野に関与するようになったのは大変意外だ. **5** V-I 自動詞 If an amount or rate **plunges**, it decreases quickly and suddenly. 急に下がる ❑ *His weight began to plunge.* 彼の体重は急に減り始めた. ❑ *The Peso plunged to a new low on the foreign exchange markets yesterday.* ペソは昨日の外国為替市場で最安値を更新した. ●N-COUNT 可算名詞 **Plunge** is also a noun. 急激な下落 ❑ *Japan's banks are in trouble because of bad loans and the stock market plunge.* 邦銀は不良債権と株価下落で問題を抱えている. **6** PHRASE 句 If you **take the plunge**, you decide to do something that you consider difficult or risky. 思い切ってする ❑ *If you have been thinking about buying mutual funds, now could be the time to take the plunge.* 投資信託の購入を考えているのなら今が思い切って買うときだと思う.

plu|ral /plʊərəl/ (**plurals**) **1** ADJ 形容詞 The **plural** form of a word is the form that is used when referring to more than one person or thing. 複数形の ❑ *"Data" is the Latin plural form of "datum."* Dataはラテン語のdatumの複数形である. **2** N-COUNT 可算名詞 The **plural** of a noun is the form of it that is used to refer to more than one person or thing. 複数形 ❑ *What is the plural of "person"?* personの複数形は何か.

plu|ral|ism /plʊərəlɪzəm/ N-UNCOUNT 不可算名詞 If there is **pluralism** within a society, it has many different groups and political parties. 多元主義 [FORMAL 形式ばった] ❑ *...as the country shifts toward political pluralism.* 国が多元主義に向けて移行するに伴い

plus /plʌs/ (**pluses** or **plusses**) **1** CONJ 接続詞 You say **plus** to show that one number or quantity is being added to another. さらに ❑ *...$5 for a small locker, plus a $3 deposit.* 小さなロッカーは5ドル, その上に3ドルの保証金 **2** ADJ 形容詞 **Plus** before a number or quantity means that the number or quantity is greater than zero. 正数の [ADJ amount] ❑ *The aircraft was subjected to temperatures of minus 65 degrees and plus 120 degrees.* 飛行機はマイナス65度からプラス120度の気温にさらされた. **3** CONJ 接続詞 You can use **plus** when mentioning an additional item or fact. その上に [INFORMAL くだけた] ❑ *There's easily enough room for two adults and three children, plus a dog in the trunk.* 大人2人と子供3人が乗った上, トランクに犬1匹をいれる空間が十分ある. **4** ADJ 形容詞 You use **plus** after a number or quantity to indicate that the actual number or quantity is greater than the one mentioned. より多い [amount ADJ] ❑ *There are only 35 staff to serve 30,000-plus customers.* 3万人以上の顧客に仕える職員は35人しかいない. **5** ADJ 形容詞 Teachers use **plus** in grading work in schools and colleges. "B plus" is a better grade than "B," but it is not as good as "A." の上 **6** N-COUNT 可算名詞 A **plus** is an advantage or benefit. 利点 [INFORMAL くだけた] ❑ *Well-known figures would be a big plus for the new board.* 有名人物が入れば新しい理事会にとって大きな利点となるだろう.

plush /plʌʃ/ (**plusher, plushest**) ADJ 形容詞 If you describe something as **plush**, you mean that it is very comfortable and expensive. 豪華な ❑ *...their plush new training facility.* 彼らの豪華な新しい研修施設

plu|to|nium /pluːtoʊniəm/ N-UNCOUNT 不可算名詞 **Plutonium** is a radioactive element used especially in nuclear weapons and as a fuel in nuclear power stations. プルトニウム

ply /plaɪ/ (**plies, plying, plied**) **1** V-T 他動詞 If you **ply** someone **with** food or drink, you keep giving them more of it. どんどん加える ❑ *Elsie, who had been told that Maria wasn't well, plied her with food.* エルシーはマリアの体調が良くないことを知らされ, どんどん食べ物を彼女に与えた. **2** V-T 他動詞 If you **ply** someone **with** questions, you keep asking them questions. しきりに質問する ❑ *Giovanni plied him with questions and comments with the deliberate intention of prolonging his stay.* ジョバンニは彼を引き止めようとしてしきりに質問した.

ply|wood /plaɪwʊd/ N-UNCOUNT 不可算名詞 **Plywood** is wood that consists of thin layers of wood stuck together. 合板 ❑ *...a sheet of plywood.* 1枚の合板

p.m. /piː em/ also **pm** ADV 副詞 **p.m.** is used after a number to show that you are referring to a particular time between 12 noon and 12 midnight. Compare **a.m.** 午後 [num ADV] ❑ *The spa is open from 7:00 a.m. to 9:00 p.m. every day of the year.* スパは毎日午前7時から午後9時まで営業している.

pneu|mo|nia /numoʊnjə, -moʊniə/ N-UNCOUNT 不可算名詞 **Pneumonia** is a serious disease that affects your lungs and makes it difficult for you to breathe. 肺炎 ❑ *She nearly died of pneumonia.* 彼女は肺炎で死にかけた.

poach /poʊtʃ/ (**poaches, poaching, poached**) **1** V-T/V-I 他動詞/自動詞 If someone **poaches** fish, animals, or birds, they illegally catch them on someone else's property. 密猟する ❑ *Many national parks set up to provide a refuge for wildlife are regularly invaded by people poaching game.* 野生生物の避難所として設立された国立公園の多くには密猟者が定期的に侵入している. ●**poach|er** (**poachers**) N-COUNT 可算名詞 密猟者 ❑ *Security cameras have been installed to guard against poachers.* 密猟者からの保護を目的に防犯カメラが取り付けられた. ●**poach|ing** N-UNCOUNT 不可算名詞 密漁 ❑ *The poaching of elephants for their tusks could start to decline soon.* 牙(きば)を目的とする象の密漁はまもなく減少し始めるかもしれない. **2** V-T 他動詞 If an organization **poaches** members or customers **from** another organization, they secretly or dishonestly persuade them to join them or become their customers. 引き抜く ❑ *Companies sometimes poach employees from one another.* 企業は社員の引き抜き合いをすることがある. ●**poach|ing** N-UNCOUNT 不可算名詞 引き抜くこと ❑ *The union was accused of poaching.* 組合は引き抜きを非難された. **3** V-T 他動詞 If someone **poaches** an idea, they dishonestly or illegally use the idea. 盗む ❑ *They've poached all our best ideas.* 彼らは我々の最良のアイデアをすべて盗んだ. **4** V-T 他動詞 If you **poach** food such as fish, you cook it gently in boiling water, milk, or other liquid. ゆでる ❑ *Poach the chicken until just cooked.* 火が通ったというところまでチキンをゆでなさい. ❑ *...a pear poached in red wine.* 赤ワインで煮たナシ ●**poach|ing** N-UNCOUNT 不可算名詞 煮ること ❑ *You will need a pot of broth for poaching.* 煮るために鍋1杯のだし汁が必要だ.

PO Box /piː oʊ bɒks/ also **P.O. Box** **PO Box** is used before a number as a kind of address. The Post Office keeps letters addressed to the PO Box until they are collected by the person who has paid for the service. 私書箱 ❑ *Send your order and a check to PO Box 2855, Sunnyvale 94087.* 注文書と小切手を私書箱2855, サニーベール94087に送ってください.

pock|et /pɒkɪt/ (**pockets, pocketing, pocketed**) **1** N-COUNT 可算名詞 A **pocket** is a kind of small bag that forms part of a piece of clothing, and that is used for carrying small things such as money or a handkerchief. ポケット ❑ *He took his flashlight from his jacket pocket and switched it on.* 彼はジャケットのポケットから懐中電灯を取り出し, スイッチを入れた. **2** N-COUNT 可算名詞 You can use **pocket** in a lot of different ways to refer to money that people have, get, or spend. For example, if someone gives or pays a lot of money, you can say that they **dig deep into** their **pocket**. If you approve of something because it is very cheap to buy, you can say that it **suits people's pockets**. 資力 ❑ *When you come to choosing a dining table, it really is worth digging deep into your pocket for the best you can afford.* 食卓を選ぶ際にはできる限りで最良の品物を買うために財力を使う価値は大いにある. ❑ *...ladies' fashions to suit all shapes, sizes, and pockets.* あらゆる体型, サイズ, 財力に合わせた女性のファッション **3** ADJ 形容詞 You use **pocket** to describe something that is small enough to fit into a pocket, often something that is a smaller version of a larger item. 小型の [ADJ n] ❑ *...a pocket calculator.* 小型計算機 **4** N-COUNT 可算名詞 A **pocket** of something is a small area where something is happening, or a small area which has a particular quality, and which is different from the other areas around it. 小区域 ❑ *Trapped in a pocket of air, they had only 40 minutes before the tide flooded the chamber.* 彼らは空気のある区域に閉じ込められており, その部屋が潮で水浸しになるまでに40分しかなかった. **5** V-T 他動詞 If someone who is in possession of something valuable such as a sum of money **pockets** it, they steal it or take it for themselves, even though it does not belong to them. 着服する ❑ *Banks have passed some of the savings on to customers and pocketed the rest.* 銀行は利益の一部を顧客に還元し, 残りを利益とした. **6** V-T 他動詞 If you say that someone **pockets** something such as a prize or sum of money, you mean that they win or obtain it, often without needing to make much effort or in a way that seems unfair. 勝ち取る [JOURNALISM ジャーナリズム] ❑ *He pocketed more money from this tournament than in his entire three years as a professional.* 彼はプロとして3年間に稼いだ金額より多くの金をこのトーナメントで稼いだ. **7** V-T 他動詞 If someone **pockets** something, they put it in their pocket, for example, because they want to steal it or hide it. ポケットに入れる ❑ *Anthony snatched his letters and pocketed them.* アンソニーは手紙をつかみ取りポケットに入れた. **8** PHRASE 句 If you say that a person or organization has **deep pockets**, you mean that they have a lot of money with which to pay for something. 十分な資力 ❑ *The church will do anything to avoid scandal – and everyone knows it has deep pockets.* 教会はスキャンダルを回避するためには何でもするだろう. 教会には十分な

資力があることは誰もが知っている。❑…*investors with deep pockets.* 富裕層の投資家 **⑨** PHRASE 句 If you are **out of pocket**, you have less money than you should have or than you intended, for example, because you have spent too much or because of a mistake. 手元になく ❑*Make sure you are not out of pocket for your expenses.* 経費のための金が手元になくならないようにしなさい。 **⑩** PHRASE 句 If someone **picks** your **pocket**, they steal something from your pocket, usually without you noticing. すりを働く ❑*They were more in danger of having their pockets picked than being shot at.* 彼らは撃たれるよりもすりに遭う危険が大きかった。

Word Partnership	*pocket* は次の語句と使われる:
N.	**back** pocket, **hip** pocket, **jacket** pocket, **pants** pocket, **shirt** pocket **1**

pocket|book /pɒkɪtbʊk/ (**pocketbooks**) **1** N-COUNT 可算名詞 You can use **pocketbook** to refer to people's concerns about the money they have or hope to earn. 資力 [AM 米国英語 JOURNALISM ジャーナリズム] ❑*People feel pinched in their pocketbooks and insecure about their futures.* 人々は資力不足のため将来に不安を感じている。 ❑…*the voters' concerns over pocketbook issues.* 資金問題に関する投票者の懸念 **2** N-COUNT 可算名詞 A **pocketbook** is a small bag that a woman uses to carry things such as her money and keys in when she goes out. ハンドバッグ [AM 米国英語]

pocket mon|ey N-UNCOUNT 不可算名詞 **Pocket money** is money for buying small things that you find you want or need. 小遣い銭 ❑*They earned themselves a little pocket money by selling cigarettes.* 彼らはタバコを売って小遣い銭を稼いだ。

pod /pɒd/ (**pods**) N-COUNT 可算名詞 A **pod** is a seed container that grows on plants such as peas or beans. サヤ ❑…*fresh peas in the pod.* サヤに入った新鮮なエンドウ

po|dium /poʊdiəm/ (**podiums**) N-COUNT 可算名詞 A **podium** is a small platform on which someone stands in order to give a lecture or conduct an orchestra. 演壇 ❑*Unsteadily he mounted the podium, adjusted the microphone, coughed, and went completely blank.* 彼はよろめきながら演壇に登り、マイクを調整し、咳をし、言うことをすっかり忘れた。

poem /poʊəm/ (**poems**) N-COUNT 可算名詞 A **poem** is a piece of writing in which the words are chosen for their beauty and sound and are carefully arranged, often in short lines that rhyme. 詩 ❑…*a book of love poems.* 愛の詩の本

poet /poʊɪt/ (**poets**) N-COUNT 可算名詞 A **poet** is a person who writes poems. 詩人 ❑*He was a painter and poet.* 彼は画家で詩人だった。

po|et|ic /poʊetɪk/ **1** ADJ 形容詞 Something that is **poetic** is very beautiful and expresses emotions in a sensitive or moving way. 詩的な ❑*Nikolai Demidenko gave an exciting yet poetic performance.* ニコライ・デミデンコは刺激的だが詩的な演技をした。 **2** ADJ 形容詞 **Poetic** means relating to poetry. 詩の ❑…*Keats' famous poetic lines.* キーツの有名な詩行

po|et|ry /poʊɪtri/ **1** N-UNCOUNT 不可算名詞 Poems, considered as a form of literature, are referred to as **poetry**. 詩歌 ❑…*Russian poetry.* ロシアの詩 **2** N-UNCOUNT 不可算名詞 You can describe something very beautiful as **poetry**. 詩を思わせるようなもの ❑*His music is purer poetry than a poem in words.* 彼の音楽は一編の詩よりも美しい。
→ see genre

poign|ant /pɔɪnyənt/ ADJ 形容詞 Something that is **poignant** affects you deeply and makes you feel sadness or regret. 強く心に訴える ❑…*a poignant combination of beautiful surroundings and tragic history.* 美しい環境と悲劇的な歴史という心に訴えかける組み合わせ ❑…*a poignant love story.* 心に迫る恋愛物語

point
❶ NOUN USES
❷ VERB USES
❸ PHRASES

❶ point /pɔɪnt/ (**points**) **1** N-COUNT 可算名詞 You use **point** to refer to something that someone has said or written. 論点 You disagree with every point she makes. 我々は彼女のすべての論点に反対だ。 ❑*The following account will clearly illustrate this point.* 以下の説明はこの点を明白に示すだろう。 **2** N-SING 単数名詞 If you say that someone **has a point**, or if you **take** their **point**, you mean that you accept that what they have said is important and should be considered. 問題の点 ❑*"If he'd already killed once, surely he'd have killed Sarah?" She had a point there.* 「彼がすでに一度殺人を犯しているのならサラを殺していたはずよ」彼女の言葉には一理あった。 **3** N-SING 単数名詞 **The point** of what you are saying or discussing is the most important part that provides a reason or explanation for the rest. 要点 ❑*"Did I ask you to talk to me?" — "That's not the point."* 「僕はきみに話しかけてくれと言ったか?」「そういう話じゃないんだ」 **4** N-SING 単数名詞 If you ask

what **the point of** something is, or say that there is **no point in** it, you are indicating that a particular action has no purpose or would not be useful. 目的 ❑*What was the point of thinking about him?* 彼について考える意味はなんだったの。 **5** N-COUNT 可算名詞 A **point** is a detail, aspect, or quality of something or someone. 特徴 ❑*Many of the points in the report are correct.* リポートの多くの側面は正しい。 ❑*The most interesting point about the village was its religion.* その村について最も興味深い点は宗教だった。 **6** N-COUNT 可算名詞 A **point** is a particular place or position where something happens. 地点 ❑*I'm sure there's another point we could meet at, but not there.* 私達が落ち合える場所は他にあると思うが、そこはダメだ。 **7** N-SING 単数名詞 You use **point** to refer to a particular time, or a particular stage in the development of something. 時点 ❑*We're all going to die at some point.* 誰もがいずれ死ぬ運命にある。 ❑*It got to the point where he had to leave.* 彼が去らねばならない時が来た。 **8** N-COUNT 可算名詞 The **point** of something such as a pin, needle, or knife is the thin, sharp end of it. 先端 ❑*Put the tomatoes into a bowl and stab each one with the point of a knife.* ボウルにトマトを入れ、ナイフの先で突き刺しなさい。 **9** In spoken English, you use **point** to refer to the dot or mark in a decimal number that separates the whole numbers from the fractions. 小数点 ❑*This is FM stereo one oh three point seven.* こちらはFMステレオ103.7です。 **10** N-COUNT 可算名詞 In some sports, competitions, and games, a **point** is one of the single marks that are added together to give the total score. 得点 ❑*Chamberlain scored 50 or more points four times in the season.* チェンバレンはシーズン中に4回も50点以上を得た。 **11** N-COUNT 可算名詞 The **points of the compass** are directions such as North, South, East, and West. 方位 ❑*Sightseers arrived from all points of the compass.* 観光客はあらゆる方面から到着した。 **12** N-PLURAL 複数名詞 On a railroad track, the **points** are the levers and rails at a place where two tracks join or separate. The points enable a train to move from one track to another. ポイント [BRIT 英国英語; AM 米国英語 **switches**] **13** → see also **breaking point, focal point, point of sale, point of view, sticking point, vantage point**

Thesaurus	**point** また次を参照:
N.	**argument, gist, topic ❶ 3** **location, place, position, spot ❶ 6**

❷ point /pɔɪnt/ (**points, pointing, pointed**) **1** V-I 自動詞 If you **point at** a person or thing, you hold out your finger toward them in order to make someone notice them. 指さす ❑*I pointed at the boy sitting nearest me.* 私は最も近いところに座っている少年を指さした。 ❑*He pointed at me with the stem of his pipe.* 彼はパイプの柄で私の方を指した。 **2** V-T 他動詞 If you **point** something **at** someone, you aim the tip or end of it toward them. 向ける ❑*David pointed his finger at Mary.* デイビッドはメアリーを指さした。 **3** V-I 自動詞 If something **points to** a place or **points** in a particular direction, it shows where that place is or it faces in that direction. 示す ❑*An arrow pointed to the toilets.* 矢印がトイレの場所を示していた。 ❑*He controlled the car until it was pointing forward again.* 彼は車を制御してふたたび直進方向に向かせた。 **4** V-I 自動詞 If something **points to** a particular situation, it suggests that the situation exists or is likely to occur. 指摘する ❑*Earlier reports pointed to students working harder, more continuously, and with enthusiasm.* 以前のリポートは学生が一層の努力を傾け継続的に熱心に勉強していることを指摘した。 **5** V-I 自動詞 If you **point to** something that has happened or that is happening, you are using it as proof that a particular situation exists. 指摘する ❑*George Fodor points to other weaknesses in the campaign.* ジョージ・フォダーはキャンペーンの他の弱みを指摘する。 **6** → see also **pointed**

❸ point /pɔɪnt/ **1** PHRASE 句 If you say that something is **beside the point**, you mean that it is not relevant to the subject that you are discussing. 要点をはずれた ❑*Brian didn't like it, but that was beside the point.* ブライアンはそれが好きではなかったがそれでも関係なかった。 **2** PHRASE 句 When someone **comes to the point** or **gets to the point**, they start talking about the thing that is most important to them. 要点を言う ❑*He came to the point at once. "You did a splendid job on this case."* 彼は直ちに要点を言った。「きみはこの事件を非常にうまくやってのけた」 **3** PHRASE 句 If you **make** your **point** or **prove** your **point**, you prove that something is true, either by arguing about it or by your actions or behavior. 主張を通す ❑*I think you've made your point, dear.* あなたはもう言いたいことをいったでしょう。 ❑*Dr. David McCleland studied one-hundred people, aged eighteen to sixty, to prove the point.* デイビッド・マックランド博士は18歳から60歳までの100人を対象に調査を行ない自説を証明した。 **4** PHRASE 句 If you **make a point of** doing something, you do it in a very deliberate or obvious way. 懸命にする ❑*She made a point of spending as much time as possible away from Oklahoma.* 彼女はできるだけ多くの時間をオクラホマ以外の場所で過ごすようにした。 **5** PHRASE 句 If you are **on the point of** doing something, you are about to do it. の間際に ❑*He was on the point of saying something when the phone rang.* 電話が鳴ったとき、ちょうど彼は何かを言おうとしていた。 **6** PHRASE 句 Something that is **to the point** is relevant to

the subject that you are discussing, or expressed neatly without wasting words or time. 要領を得た ❑ *The description which he had been given was brief and to the point.* 彼が受けた説明は簡潔で要領を得ていた. **7** PHRASE 句 If you say that something is true **up to a point**, you mean that it is partly but not completely true. ある程度までは ❑ *"Was she good?"—"Mmm. Up to a point."* 「彼女はうまかったか」「そうね、ある程度は」 **8 in point of fact** → see **fact** **9** to **point the finger at** someone → see **finger** **10 a sore point** → see **sore**

▶ **point out 1** PHRASAL VERB 句動詞 If you **point out** an object or place, you make people look at it or show them where it is. 指し示す ❑ *They kept standing up to take pictures and point things out to each other.* 彼らは写真を撮り、互いに何かを指し示すために立ち上がり続けた. **2** PHRASAL VERB 句動詞 If you **point out** a fact or mistake, you tell someone about it or draw their attention to it. 指摘する ❑ *I should point out that these estimates cover just the hospital expenditures.* こうした見積りでは病院の支出分しか出ないと指摘する必要がある.

point-blank 1 ADV 副詞 If you say something **point-blank**, you say it very directly or rudely, without explaining or apologizing. ぶっきらぼうに [ADV after v] ❑ *The army apparently refused point-blank to do what was required of them.* 軍は要求されたことをきっぱりと拒絶したようだ. ● **point-blank** Point-blank is also an adjective. そっけない [ADJ n] ❑ *...a point-blank refusal.* そっけない拒絶 **2** ADV 副詞 If someone or something is shot **point-blank**, they are shot when the gun is touching them or extremely close to them. 直射で [ADV after v] ❑ *He put a gun through the open window of the car and fired point-blank at Bernadette.* 彼は車の窓から銃を差し込み、至近距離からバーナデットを撃った. ● ADJ 形容詞 Point-blank is also an adjective. 直射の [ADJ n] ❑ *He had been shot at point-blank range in the back of the head.* 彼は頭の後ろを至近距離から撃たれていた.

point|ed 1 ADJ 形容詞 Something that is **pointed** has a point at one end. 先のとがった ❑ *...a pointed roof.* とがった屋根 **2** ADJ 形容詞 **Pointed** comments or behavior express criticism in a clear and direct way. 鋭い ❑ *I couldn't help notice the pointed remarks slung in my direction.* 私は投げつけられてくる鋭い意見に気づかずにはいられなかった. ● **point|ed|ly** ADV 副詞 明白に ❑ *They were pointedly absent from the news conference.* 彼らはあてつけるように記者会見を欠席した.

point|er /pɔɪntər/ (**pointers**) **1** N-COUNT 可算名詞 A **pointer** is a piece of advice or information that helps you to understand a situation or to find a way of making progress. 助言 ❑ *I hope at least my daughter was able to offer you some useful pointers.* 娘があなたにヒントくらいお教えできていればいいのですが. **2** N-COUNT 可算名詞 A **pointer** is a long stick that is used to point at something such as a large chart or diagram when explaining something to people. 指示棒 ❑ *She tapped on the world map with her pointer.* 彼女は指示棒で世界地図を叩いてくたたいた. **3** N-COUNT 可算名詞 The **pointer** on a measuring instrument is the long, thin piece of metal that points to the numbers. 針 ❑ *A series of levers joined to a pointer shows pressure on a dial.* 一連のレバーが指針盤の圧力を示す針に接合していた.

point|less /pɔɪntlɪs/ ADJ 形容詞 If you say that something is **pointless**, you are criticizing it because it has no sense or purpose. 無意味な [DISAPPROVAL 不賛成] ❑ *Violence is always pointless.* 暴力が効果をもたらすことはない. ❑ *Without an audience the performance is pointless.* 観客なしでは公演は無意味だ. ● **point|less|ly** ADV 副詞 無意味に ❑ *Chemicals were pointlessly poisoning the soil.* 化学物質は無意味に土壌を汚染していた.

point of sale (**points of sale**) **1** N-COUNT 可算名詞 The **point of sale** is the place in a store where a product is passed from the seller to the customer. The abbreviation **POS** is also used. 販売時点 [BUSINESS 実業] ❑ *...information on consumer behavior at the point of sale.* 消費者行動についての販売時点情報 **2** N-UNCOUNT 不可算名詞 **Point-of-sale** is used to describe things that occur or are located or used at the place where you buy something. The abbreviation **POS** is also used. 販売時点情報管理 [BUSINESS 実業] [usu n n] ❑ *Introduction of electronic point-of-sale systems is improving efficiency.* 販売時点情報管理システムの導入は効率性を高めつつある.

point of view (**points of view**) **1** N-COUNT 可算名詞 You can refer to the opinions or attitudes that you have about something as your **point of view**. 考え ❑ *Thanks for your point of view, John.* ジョン、意見を言ってくれてありがとう. **2** N-COUNT 可算名詞 If you consider something **from a particular point of view**, you are using one aspect of a situation in order to judge that situation. 観点 ❑ *Do you think that, from the point of view of results, this exercise was worth the cost?* 結果を見てこれを実行したことには費用に見合う価値があったと思うか.

→ see **history**

poise /pɔɪz/ N-UNCOUNT 不可算名詞 If someone has **poise**, they are calm, dignified, and self-controlled. 落ち着き ❑ *What amazed him even more than her appearance was her poise.* 容姿以上に彼を驚かせたのは彼女の落ち着きだった.

poised /pɔɪzd/ **1** ADJ 形容詞 If a part of your body is **poised**, it

is completely still but ready to move at any moment. 構えた ❑ *He studied the keyboard carefully, one finger poised.* 彼は1本の指を構えたま、キーボードを注意深く調べた. **2** ADJ 形容詞 If someone is **poised to** do something, they are ready to take action at any moment. する構えがとれた [v-link ADJ] ❑ *U.S. forces are poised for a massive air, land, and sea assault.* 米軍は陸海空からの大規模攻撃の態勢がとれている. **3** ADJ 形容詞 If you are **poised**, you are calm, dignified, and self-controlled. 落ち着いた ❑ *She was self-assured, poised, almost self-satisfied.* 彼女は自信たっぷりで落ち着いて、自己満足といってよい態度だった.

poi|son /pɔɪzⁿn/ (**poisons, poisoning, poisoned**) **1** N-MASS 質量名詞 **Poison** is a substance that harms or kills people or animals if they swallow it or absorb it. 毒 ❑ *Poison from the fish causes paralysis, swelling, and nausea.* 魚の毒素は麻痺、腫(は)れ、吐き気を引き起こす. **2** V-T 他動詞 If someone **poisons** another person, they kill the person or make them ill by giving them poison. 毒を与える ❑ *The rumors that she had poisoned him could never be proved.* 彼女が彼を毒殺したという噂は決して立証できなかった. ● **poi|son|ing** N-UNCOUNT 不可算名詞 毒を与えること ❑ *She was sentenced to twenty years' imprisonment for poisoning and attempted murder.* 彼女は毒による殺人未遂で12年間の禁固刑に処された. **3** V-T 他動詞 If you **are poisoned by** a substance, it makes you very ill and sometimes kills you. 害毒を受ける ❑ *Employees were taken to the hospital yesterday after being poisoned by fumes.* 昨日従業員らは煙の毒で被害を受け、病院に運ばれた. ● **poi|son|ing** N-UNCOUNT 不可算名詞 中毒 ❑ *...acute alcohol poisoning.* 急性のアルコール中毒 **4** V-T 他動詞 If someone **poisons** a food, drink, or weapon, they add poison to it so that it can be used to kill someone. 毒を盛る ❑ *If I was your wife I would poison your coffee.* もし私があなたの奥さんだったらコーヒーに毒を入れるだろう. **5** V-T 他動詞 To **poison** water, air, or land means to damage it with harmful substances such as chemicals. 汚染する ❑ *...the textile and fiber industries that taint the air, poison the water, and use vast amounts of natural resources.* 空気や水を汚染し、大量の天然資源を使う繊維業界 ❑ *The land has been completely poisoned by chemicals.* その土地は化学物質で完全に汚染された. **6** V-T 他動詞 Something that **poisons** a good situation or relationship spoils it or destroys it. 毒する ❑ *The whole atmosphere has really been poisoned.* 雰囲気は台無しになった.

poi|son|ous /pɔɪzⁿnəs/ **1** ADJ 形容詞 Something that is **poisonous** will kill you or make you ill if you swallow or absorb it. 有毒な ❑ *All parts of the yew tree are poisonous, including the berries.* イチイの木は実を含むあらゆる部分が有毒である. **2** ADJ 形容詞 An animal that is **poisonous** produces a poison that will kill you or make you ill if the animal bites you. 有害な ❑ *There are hundreds of poisonous spiders and snakes.* 毒を持つクモとヘビは何百種もいる. **3** ADJ 形容詞 If you describe something as **poisonous**, you mean that it is extremely unpleasant and likely to spoil or destroy a good relationship or situation. 悪意のある ❑ *...poisonous comments.* 悪意のある批評 ❑ *...lying awake half the night tormented by poisonous suspicions.* 悪意のある疑惑に悩まされて、ほとんど眠れず

poi|son pill (**poison pills**) N-COUNT 可算名詞 A **poison pill** refers to what some companies do to reduce their value in order to prevent themselves being taken over by another company. 毒薬条項 [BUSINESS 実業] ❑ *Some believe this level of compensation is essentially a poison pill to put off any rival bidders.* この補償水準は本質的に他の買い手を牽制するための毒薬条項だと考える人もいる.

poke /poʊk/ (**pokes, poking, poked**) **1** V-T 他動詞 If you **poke** someone or something, you quickly push them with your finger or with a sharp object. 突く ❑ *Lindy poked him in the ribs.* リンディは彼の横腹をつついた. ● N-COUNT 可算名詞 Poke is also a noun. 突くこと ❑ *John smiled at them and gave Richard a playful poke.* ジョンは彼らに微笑みリチャードを冗談半分につついた. **2** V-T 他動詞 If you **poke** one thing **into** another, you push the first thing into the second thing. 突っ込む ❑ *He poked his finger into the hole.* 彼は指を穴に突っ込んだ. **3** V-I 自動詞 If something **pokes out of** or **through** another thing, you can see part of it appearing from behind or underneath the other thing. 突き出る ❑ *He saw the dog's twitching nose poke out of the basket.* 彼は犬のぴくぴく動く鼻がバスケットからはみ出ているのを見た. **4** V-T/V-I 他動詞/自動詞 If you **poke** your head through an opening or if it **pokes** through an opening, you push it through, often so that you can see something more easily. 突き出す ❑ *Julie tapped on my door and poked her head in.* ジュリーは僕のドアを軽くたたき、顔を中に入れた. **5** to **poke fun at** → see **fun** **6** to **poke** your **nose into** something → see **nose**

pok|er /poʊkər/ (**pokers**) **1** N-UNCOUNT 不可算名詞 **Poker** is a card game that people usually play in order to win money. ポーカー ❑ *Lon and I play in the same weekly poker game.* ロンと私は同じ週一度のポーカーゲームに参加している. **2** N-COUNT 可算名詞 A **poker** is a metal bar that you use to move coal or wood in a stove or fireplace in order to make it burn better. 火かき棒 ❑ *Niigata stirred the wood with a poker, and put another log on.* ニイガタは火かき棒で木をかき回し、まきをもう一本入れた.

po|lar /poʊlər/ **1** ADJ 形容詞 **Polar** means near the North or South Poles. 北極または南極の [ADJ n] ❑ *...the rigors of life in the polar*

regions. 極地の生活の厳しさ ❑ There was a period of excessive warmth which melted some of the polar ice. 北極の氷が溶けるほど極めて暖かい時期があった. ❷ ADJ 形容詞 **Polar** is used to describe things that are completely opposite in character, quality, or type. 正反対の [FORMAL 形式ばった] [ADJ n] ❑ The nomads' lifestyle was the polar opposite of collectivization. 遊牧民の生活様式は集団農場化とは正反対だった.

→ see **Arctic**

po|lar|ize /póʊlərɑɪz/ (**polarizes, polarizing, polarized**) V-T/V-I 他動詞/自動詞 If something **polarizes** people or if something **polarizes**, two separate groups are formed with opposite opinions or positions. 対立させる ❑ Missile deployment did much to further polarize opinion. ミサイルの配備は意見をさらに二極化させた. ❑ As the car rental industry polarizes, business will go to the bigger companies. レンタカー業界の両極化に伴い, 大企業の営業がよくなるだろう. ● **po|lari|za|tion** /póʊlərɪzéɪʃᵊn/ N-UNCOUNT 不可算名詞 両極化 ❑ ...the increasing polarization between rich and poor. 富裕層と貧困層の一層の両極化

pole /póʊl/ (**poles**) ❶ N-COUNT 可算名詞 A **pole** is a long thin piece of wood or metal, used especially for supporting things. 棒 ❑ The truck crashed into a telegraph pole. トラックは電柱に衝突した. ❷ N-COUNT 可算名詞 The Earth's **poles** are the two opposite ends of its axis, its most northern and southern points. 極 ❑ For six months of the year, there is hardly any light at the poles. 極地では1年のうち6か月間は光というものがほとんどない. ❸ N-COUNT 可算名詞 The two **poles** of a magnet are the two ends of the magnet where the magnetic force is strongest. 極 ❑ The important fact is that the two poles of the magnet work in opposite ways. 重要な事実は磁石の2つの極は反対に作用することだ. ❹ N-COUNT 可算名詞 The two **poles** of a range of qualities, opinions, or beliefs are the completely opposite qualities, opinions, or beliefs at either end of the range. 極端 ❑ The two politicians represent opposite poles of the political spectrum. 2人の政治家は政治傾向の両極端を代表している. ❺ PHRASE 句 If you say that two people or things are **poles apart**, you mean that they have completely different beliefs, opinions, or qualities. 正反対だ [EMPHASIS 強調]

→ see **magnet**

po|lem|ic /pəlémɪk/ (**polemics**) N-VAR 可変性名詞 A **polemic** is a very strong written or spoken attack on, or defense of, a particular belief or opinion. 論戦 ❑ ...a polemic against the danger of secret societies. 秘密結社の危険性に抗する議論

Word Link   poli ≈ city : metropolis, **police**, policy

po|lice /pəlís/ (**polices, policing, policed**) ❶ N-SING-COLL 集合的単数名詞 The **police** are the official organization that is responsible for making sure that people obey the law. 警察 ❑ The police are also looking for a second car. 警察は2台目の車も捜索している. ❑ Police say they have arrested twenty people following the disturbances. 警察は騒動の後20人を逮捕したと言っている. ❷ N-PLURAL 複数名詞 **Police** are men and women who are members of the official organization that is responsible for making sure that people obey the law. 警察官 ❑ More than one hundred police have ringed the area. 100人以上の警察官がその区域を取り囲んだ. ❸ V-T 他動詞 If the police or military forces **police** an area or event, they make sure that law and order is preserved in that area or at that event. 警備する ❑ ...the tiny U.N. observer force whose job it is to police the border. 国境警備が任務の小規模な国連監視部隊 ❹ V-T 他動詞 If a person or group in authority **polices** a law or an area of public life, they make sure that what is done is fair and legal. 監視する ❑ ...the self-regulatory body that polices the investment management business. 投資運用を監視する自主規制機関 ❺ → see also **secret police**

po|lice force (**police forces**) N-COUNT 可算名詞 A **police force** is the police organization in a particular country or area. 警察隊 ❑ ...the Wichita police force. ウィチタ警察

police|man /pəlísmən/ (**policemen**) N-COUNT 可算名詞 A **policeman** is a man who is a member of the police force. 警察官

po|lice of|fic|er (**police officers**) N-COUNT 可算名詞 A **police officer** is a member of the police force. 警察官 ❑ ...a meeting of senior police officers. 上級警察官の会合

po|lice sta|tion (**police stations**) N-COUNT 可算名詞 A **police station** is the local office of a police force in a particular area. 警察署 ❑ Two police officers arrested him and took him to Gettysburg police station. 2人の警察官が彼を逮捕し, ゲティスバーグ警察署に連行した.

police|woman /pəlíswʊmən/ (**policewomen**) N-COUNT 可算名詞 A **policewoman** is a woman who is a member of the police force. 婦人警官

poli|cy /pɒ́lɪsi/ (**policies**) ❶ N-VAR 可変性名詞 A **policy** is a set of ideas or plans that is used as a basis for making decisions, especially in politics, economics, or business. 政策 ❑ ...plans that include changes in foreign policy and economic reforms. 対外政策の変更と経済改革を含む計画 ❷ N-COUNT 可算名詞 An official organization's **policy** on a particular issue or toward a country is their attitude and actions regarding that issue or country. 方針

❑ ...the organization's future policy toward South Africa. 南アフリカに対するその機関の将来の方針 ❑ ...the government's policy on repatriation. 本国送還に関する政府の方針 ❸ N-COUNT 可算名詞 An insurance **policy** is a document that shows the agreement that you have made with an insurance company. 保険証書 [BUSINESS 実業] ❑ You are advised to read the small print of homeowner and car insurance policies. 住宅保険と自動車保険の契約内容をお読みください.

Word Partnership   **policy** は次の語句と使われる:

ADJ.	**domestic** policy, **economic** policy, **educational** policy, **foreign** policy, **new** policy, **official** policy, **public** policy ❶
N.	policy **analyst**, **defense** policy, **energy** policy, **immigration** policy ❶ policy **change** (or **change of** policy), policy **objectives**, policy **shift** ❶ ❷ **administration** policy, **government** policy ❷ **insurance** policy ❸

---

policy|holder /pɒ́lɪsihoʊldər/ (**policyholders**) N-COUNT 可算名詞 A **policyholder** is a person who has an insurance policy with an insurance company. 保険契約者 [BUSINESS 実業] ❑ The first 10 percent of legal fees will be paid by the policyholder. 弁護士費用の最初の10%は保険契約者によって支払われる.

po|lio /póʊlioʊ/ N-UNCOUNT 不可算名詞 **Polio** is a serious infectious disease that often makes people unable to use their legs. ポリオ ❑ Gladys was crippled by polio at the age of 3. グラディスは3歳の時にポリオで体が不自由になった.

→ see **hospital**

pol|ish /pɒ́lɪʃ/ (**polishes, polishing, polished**) ❶ N-MASS 質量名詞 **Polish** is a substance that you put on the surface of an object in order to clean it, protect it, and make it shine. 光沢剤 ❑ The still air smelled faintly of furniture polish. 静かな空気にはかすかに家具の光沢剤の匂いがした. ❷ V-T 他動詞 If you **polish** something, you put polish on it or rub it with a cloth to make it shine. 磨く ❑ Each morning he shaved and polished his shoes. 彼は毎朝ひげを剃り, 靴を磨いた. ● N-SING 単数名詞 **Polish** is also a noun. 磨き粉 ❑ He gave his counter a polish with a soft duster. 彼はカウンターを柔らかいぞうきんで磨いた. ● **polished** ADJ 形容詞 磨き上げた ❑ ...a highly polished floor. よく磨かれた床 ❸ N-UNCOUNT 不可算名詞 If you say that a performance or piece of work has **polish**, you mean that it is of a very high standard. 洗練 [APPROVAL 賛成] ❑ The opera lacks the polish of his later work. そのオペラは彼の後期作品のように洗練されたところがない. ❹ V-T 他動詞 If you **polish** your technique, performance, or skill at doing something, you work on improving it. 磨きをかける ❑ They just need to polish their technique. 彼はテクニックにちょっと磨きをかける必要がある. ● PHRASAL VERB 句動詞 **Polish up** means the same as **polish**. 磨きをかける ❑ Polish up your writing skills on a one-week professional course. 1週間の専門コースであなたの文章力を向上させなさい. ❺ → see also **polished**

pol|ished /pɒ́lɪʃt/ ❶ ADJ 形容詞 Someone who is **polished** shows confidence and knows how to behave socially. 教養がある [APPROVAL 賛成] ❑ He is polished, charming, articulate, and an excellent negotiator. 彼は教養があり魅力的で頭脳明晰の上, 交渉上手だ. ❷ ADJ 形容詞 If you describe a performance, ability, or skill as **polished**, you mean that it is of a very high standard. みがきをかけた [APPROVAL 賛成] ❑ ...a very polished performance. みがきにみがかれた演技 ❸ → see also **polish**

po|lite /pəláɪt/ (**politer, politest**) ADJ 形容詞 Someone who is **polite** has good manners and behaves in a way that is socially correct and not rude to other people. 礼儀正しい ❑ Everyone around him was trying to be polite, but you could tell they were all bored. 彼の周囲の人は誰もが礼儀を心がけていたが, どの人も退屈していることが明らかだった. ❑ Gonzales, a quiet and very polite young man, made a favorable impression. 物静かで非常に礼儀正しい若者のゴンザレスは好ましい印象を残した. ● **po|lite|ly** ADV 副詞 礼儀正しく ❑ "Your home is beautiful," I said politely. 「あなたの家はすてきね」と私は丁寧に言った. ● **po|lite|ness** N-UNCOUNT 不可算名詞 礼儀正しさ ❑ She listened to him, but only out of politeness. 彼女は彼の言うことに耳を傾けたが, それは儀礼上のことだった.

Thesaurus   **polite** また次を参照:

ADJ.	considerate, courteous, gracious, respectful, well-mannered; (ant.) brash, impolite, rude

---

po|liti|cal /pəlɪ́tɪkᵊl/ ❶ ADJ 形容詞 **Political** means relating to the way power is achieved and used in a country or society. 政治の ❑ All other political parties have been completely banned. その他の政党はすべて完全に禁止された. ❑ The government is facing another political crisis. 政府はもう1つの政治危機に直面している. ● **po|liti|cal|ly** /pəlɪ́tɪkli/ ADV 副詞 政治的に ❑ They do not believe the killings were politically motivated. 彼らは殺害事件に政治的動機があったとは考えていない. ❷ ADJ 形容詞 Someone who is **political** is interested or involved in politics and holds strong beliefs about

---

Word Web   pollution

Pollution affects all aspects of the **environment**. **Airborne emissions** from industrial plants and vehicle **exhaust** cause air pollution. When these smoky **emissions** combine with fog, the result is **smog**. Airborne pollutants can travel long distances. **Acid rain** caused by factories in the Midwest falls on states to the east. There it damages trees and kills fish in lakes. Chemical waste from factories, **sewage**, and **garbage** have polluted the water and land in many areas. The overuse of **pesticides** and **fertilizers** have added to the problem. These chemicals accumulate in the soil and poison the earth.

---

it. 政治に関心がある ❑ *Oh I'm not political, I take no interest in politics.* いや私は政治的人間ではないし関心は全然ないよ.

→ see **empire, philosophy**

po|li|ti|cal asy|lum N-UNCOUNT 不可算名詞 **Political asylum** is the right to live in a foreign country and is given by the government of that country to people who have to leave their own country for political reasons. 政治亡命者の保護 ❑ *...a university teacher who is seeking political asylum in California.* カリフォルニアで政治亡命を求めている大学教師

po|li|ti|cal econo|my N-UNCOUNT 不可算名詞 **Political economy** is the study of the way in which a government influences or organizes a nation's wealth. 政治経済学

po|li|ti|cal|ly cor|rect ADJ 形容詞 If you say that someone is **politically correct**, you mean that they are extremely careful not to offend or upset any group of people in society who have a disadvantage, or who have been treated differently because of their sex, race, or disability. The abbreviation **PC** is also used. 差別的でない ❑ *...environmentalists and politically correct liberals.* 環境保護主義者と差別表現に慎重な自由主義者 ● N-PLURAL 複数名詞 **The politically correct** are people who are politically correct. 差別的でない人 ["the" N] ❑ *...the hypocrisy of the politically correct.* 差別表現に慎重な人の偽善

poli|ti|cian /pɒlɪtɪʃ⁰n/ (**politicians**) N-COUNT 可算名詞 A **politician** is a person whose job is in politics, especially a member of the government. 政治家 ❑ *They have arrested a number of leading opposition politicians.* 彼らは主要野党の政治家を一斉逮捕した.

poli|tics /pɒlɪtɪks/ 11 N-PLURAL 複数名詞 **Politics** are the actions or activities concerned with achieving and using power in a country or society. The verb that follows **politics** may be either singular or plural. 政治 ❑ *Many people think Nixon transformed American politics.* 多くの人はニクソンがアメリカの政治を変えたと考えている. ❑ *He quickly involved himself in local politics.* 彼はすぐに地方政治に関与するようになった. 2 N-PLURAL 複数名詞 Your **politics** are your beliefs about how a country ought to be governed. 政見 ❑ *My politics are well to the left of center.* 私の政治観は中道派のかなり左寄りだ. 3 N-UNCOUNT 不可算名詞 **Politics** is the study of the ways in which countries are governed. 政治学 ❑ *He began studying politics and medieval history.* 彼は政治学と中世史を勉強し始めた. 4 N-PLURAL 複数名詞 **Politics** can be used to talk about the ways that power is shared in an organization and the ways it is affected by personal relationships between people who work together. The verb that follows **politics** may be either singular or plural. 駆け引き ❑ *You need to understand how office politics influence the working environment.* 従業員間の駆け引きがいかに労働環境に影響するかを理解する必要がある.

poll /poʊl/ (**polls, polling, polled**) 11 N-COUNT 可算名詞 A **poll** is a survey in which people are asked their opinions about something, usually in order to find out how popular something is or what people intend to do in the future. 世論調査 ❑ *Polls show that the European treaty has gained support in Denmark.* 世論調査によると欧州の条約はデンマークで支持を受けていることが示されている. ❑ *We are doing a weekly poll on the president, and clearly his popularity has declined.* 毎週行う世論調査の結果によると, 大統領の人気は明らかに低下している. 2 → see also **opinion poll** 3 V-T 他動詞 If you **are polled** on something, you are asked what you think about it as part of a survey. 世論調査の対象となった [usu passive] ❑ *More than 18,000 people were polled.* 1800人以上が世論調査を受けた. ❑ *Audiences were going to be polled on which of three pieces of contemporary music they liked best.* 観客はアンケートで3曲の現代音楽から最も好きな曲を選ぶことになっていた. 4 N-PLURAL 複数名詞 **The polls** means an election for a country's government, or the place where people go to vote in an election. 投票 ❑ *Incumbent officeholders are difficult to defeat at the polls.* 現職を票で負かすのは難しい. ❑ *Voters are due to go to the polls on Sunday to elect a new president.* 有権者は新大統領を選ぶために日曜に投票所に行く予定だ. 5 V-T 他動詞 If a political party or a candidate **polls** a particular number or percentage of votes, they get that number or percentage of votes in an election. 票を得る ❑ *The result showed he had polled enough votes to force a second*

ballot. 開票結果によると彼は二回目の投票を実施するのに十分な投票を得た. 6 → see also **polling**

pol|len /pɒlən/ (**pollens**) N-MASS 質量名詞 **Pollen** is a fine powder produced by flowers. It fertilizes other flowers of the same species so that they produce seeds. 花粉

poll|ing /poʊlɪŋ/ N-UNCOUNT 不可算名詞 **Polling** is the act of voting in an election. 投票 ❑ *There has been a busy start to polling in today's local elections.* 今日の地方選挙で投票が忙しく始まった.

→ see **election, vote**

pol|lu|tant /pəlut°nt/ (**pollutants**) N-VAR 可変性名詞 **Pollutants** are substances that pollute the environment, especially gases from vehicles and poisonous chemicals produced as waste by industrial processes. 汚染物 ❑ *Industrial pollutants are responsible for a sizable proportion of all cancers.* 産業汚染物は全種類のがんの原因として大きな比率を占めている.

pol|lute /pəlut/ (**pollutes, polluting, polluted**) V-T 他動詞 To **pollute** water, air, or land means to make it dirty and dangerous to live in or to use, especially with poisonous chemicals or sewage. 汚染する ❑ *Heavy industry pollutes our rivers with noxious chemicals.* 重工業は有害な化学物質で川を汚染する. ● **pol|lut|ed** ADJ 形容詞 汚染された ❑ *The police have warned the city's inhabitants not to bathe in the polluted river.* 警察は汚染された川に入らないよう市の住民に警告した.

pol|lu|tion /pəluʃ°n/ 11 N-UNCOUNT 不可算名詞 **Pollution** is the process of polluting water, air, or land, especially with poisonous chemicals. 環境汚染 ❑ *The fine was for the company's pollution of the air near its plants.* 罰金は会社による工場付近の大気汚染に対して課せられた. 2 N-UNCOUNT 不可算名詞 **Pollution** is poisonous or dirty substances that are polluting the water, air, or land somewhere. 汚染物質 ❑ *The level of pollution in the river was falling.* 川の汚染物質のレベルは低下していた.

→ see **Word Web: pollution**

→ see **air, factory, solar system**

polo /poʊloʊ/ N-UNCOUNT 不可算名詞 **Polo** is a game played between two teams of players. The players ride horses and use wooden hammers with long handles to hit a ball. ポロ

poly|es|ter /pɒliɛstər/ (**polyesters**) N-MASS 質量名詞 **Polyester** is a type of synthetic cloth used especially to make clothes. ポリエステル ❑ *...a green polyester shirt.* 緑色のポリエステルのシャツ

poly|eth|yl|ene /pɒliɛθɪlin/ N-UNCOUNT 不可算名詞 **Polyethylene** is a type of plastic made into thin sheets or bags and used especially to keep food fresh or to keep things dry. ポリエチレン [mainly AM 主に米国英語]

poly|thene /pɒlɪθin/ N-UNCOUNT 不可算名詞 **Polythene** is the same as **polyethylene**. ポリエチレン [mainly BRIT 主に英国英語]

pomp /pɒmp/ N-UNCOUNT 不可算名詞 **Pomp** is the use of a lot of ceremony, fine clothes, and decorations, especially on a special occasion. 華やかさ ❑ *I hate all this pomp and ceremony.* このような華々しいことや儀式はすべて大嫌いだ.

pom|pos|ity /pɒmpɒsɪti/ N-UNCOUNT 不可算名詞 **Pomposity** means speaking or behaving in a very serious manner that shows you think you are more important than you really are. 尊大さ [DISAPPROVAL 不賛成] ❑ *Einstein was a scientist who hated pomposity and disliked being called a genius.* アインシュタインは仰々しさが苦手で天才と呼ばれるのを嫌う科学者だった.

pomp|ous /pɒmpəs/ 11 ADJ 形容詞 If you describe someone as **pompous**, you mean that they behave or speak in a very serious way because they think they are more important than they really are. もったいぶった [DISAPPROVAL 不賛成] ❑ *He was somewhat pompous and had a high opinion of his own capabilities.* 彼はどこか思い上がっており, 自分の能力を高く評価していた. ● **pomp|ous|ly** ADV 副詞 もったいぶって ❑ *Robin told me firmly and pompously that he had an important business appointment.* ロビンは重要なビジネスの約束があるともったいぶった態度できっぱりと私に言った. 2 ADJ 形容詞 A **pompous** building or ceremony is very grand and elaborate. 壮大な ❑ *The service was grand without being pompous.* 儀式は仰々しくならない程度に立派だった.

pond /pɒnd/ (ponds) **1** N-COUNT 可算名詞 A **pond** is a small area of water that is smaller than a lake. Ponds are often made artificially. 池 ❑ *She chose a bench beside the duck pond and sat down.* 彼女はカモの池の側のベンチを選んで座った. **2** N-SING 単数名詞 People sometimes refer to the Atlantic Ocean as **the pond**. 大西洋 [MAINLY JOURNALISM 主にジャーナリズム] ❑ *Tourist numbers from across the pond have dropped dramatically.* 北米からの観光客数は大幅に減った.

pon|der /pɒndər/ (ponders, pondering, pondered) V-T/V-I 他動詞/自動詞 If you **ponder** something, you think about it carefully. じっくり考える ❑ *I found myself constantly pondering the question: "How could anyone do these things?"* 私は「一体誰にこんなことができようか」と常に思索していた. ❑ *He pondered over the difficulties involved.* 彼は困難な問題についてじっくり考えた.

pon|der|ous /pɒndərəs/ ADJ 形容詞 **Ponderous** writing or speech is very serious, uses more words than necessary, and is dull. 冗長な [DISAPPROVAL 不賛成] ❑ *He had a dense, ponderous style.* 彼の文体は難解で冗長だった.

pony /poʊni/ (ponies) N-COUNT 可算名詞 A **pony** is a small or young horse. ポニー

pony|tail /poʊniteɪl/ (ponytails) N-COUNT 可算名詞 A **ponytail** is a hairstyle in which someone's hair is tied up at the back of the head and hangs down like a tail. ポニーテール ❑ *Her long, fine hair was swept back in a ponytail.* 彼女の長くて細い髪はポニーテールに束ねられていた.

poo|dle /pudˀl/ (poodles) N-COUNT 可算名詞 A **poodle** is a type of dog with thick curly hair. プードル

pool /pul/ (pools, pooling, pooled) **1** N-COUNT 可算名詞 A **pool** is the same as a **swimming pool**. プール ❑ *...a heated indoor pool.* 屋内式温水プール. **2** N-COUNT 可算名詞 A **pool** is a fairly small area of still water. ため池 ❑ *The pool had dried up and was full of bracken and reeds.* ため池はからからになり, シダやアシで一杯だった. **3** N-COUNT 可算名詞 A **pool** of liquid or light is a small area of it on the ground or on a surface. 液体のたまったところ ❑ *She was found lying in a pool of blood.* 彼女は血の海に横たわっているのを発見された. ❑ *It was raining quietly and steadily and there were little pools of water on the gravel drive.* しとしと雨が降り続き, 砂利を敷いた車道には小さな水たまりがあった. **4** N-COUNT 可算名詞 A **pool** of people, money, or things is a quantity or number of them that is available for an organization or group to use. 予備 ❑ *The available pool of healthy manpower was not as large as military officials had expected.* 予備として使える健康な人員は軍関係者が思っていたほどいなかった. **5** → see also **carpool 6** V-T 他動詞 If a group of people or organizations **pool** their money, knowledge, or equipment, they share it or put it together so that it can be used for a particular purpose. プールする ❑ *We pooled ideas and information.* 我々はアイデアと情報を持ち寄った.

poor /pʊər/ (poorer, poorest) **1** ADJ 形容詞 Someone who is **poor** has very little money and few possessions. 貧しい ❑ *The reason our schools cannot afford better teachers is because people here are poor.* 学校が優れた教師を雇う金銭的な余裕がないのはこの地域の人々が貧しいからである. ● N-PLURAL 複数名詞 **The poor** are people who are poor. 貧乏人 ❑ *Even the poor have their pride.* 貧乏人でも自尊心はある. **2** ADJ 形容詞 The people in a **poor** country or area have very little money and few possessions. 貧しい ❑ *Many countries in the Third World are as poor as they have ever been.* 第三世界の多くの国はこれまでと同じように貧しい. **3** ADJ 形容詞 You use **poor** to express your sympathy for someone. かわいそうな [FEELINGS 感情] [ADJ n] ❑ *I feel sorry for that poor child.* 私はあのかわいそうな子供に同情する. ❑ *It was way too much for the poor guy to overcome.* それは不運な男が克服するにはあんまりだった. **4** ADJ 形容詞 If you describe something as **poor**, you mean that it is of a low quality or standard or that it is in bad condition. 好ましくない ❑ *...the poor state of the economy.* 好ましくない経済状態 ❑ *The gap between the best and poorest childcare provision has widened.* 子供の福祉対策の最良と最悪の間で差が拡大した. ● **poor|ly** ADV 副詞 下手に ❑ *Some are living in poorly built dormitories, even in tents.* 安普請の寮, あるいはテントに住んでいる者すらいる. **5** ADJ 形容詞 If you describe an amount, rate, or number as **poor**, you mean that it is less than expected or less than is considered reasonable. お粗末な ❑ *...poor wages and working conditions.* お粗末な賃金と労働状態 ● **poor|ly** ADV 副詞 不十分に ❑ *During the first week, the evening meetings were poorly attended.* 最初の週は夜の会合の参加者は少なかった. **6** ADJ 形容詞 You use **poor** to describe someone who is not very skillful in a particular activity. 下手な ❑ *He was a poor actor.* 彼は大根役者だった. ● **poor|ly** ADV 副詞 [ADV after v] まずく ❑ *Cheetahs breed very poorly in captivity.* チータは人間に捕えられると繁殖が難しい. **7** ADJ 形容詞 If something is **poor in** a particular quality or substance, it contains very little of the quality or substance. 不十分な [v-link ADJ "in" n] ❑ *Fats and sugar are very rich in energy but poor in vitamins and minerals.* 脂身と砂糖はエネルギーが非常に豊富だがビタミンとミネラルが少ない.

Thesaurus *poor* また次を参照:

ADJ. impoverished, penniless; (*ant.*) rich, wealthy **1 2** inferior **4**

poor|ly /pʊərli/ ADJ 形容詞 If someone is **poorly**, they are ill. 病身の [mainly BRIT 主に英国英語, INFORMAL くだけた]

pop /pɒp/ (pops, popping, popped) **1** N-UNCOUNT 不可算名詞 **Pop** is modern music that usually has a strong rhythm and uses electronic equipment. ポピュラー音楽 ❑ *...the perfect combination of Caribbean rhythms, European pop, and American soul.* カリブ海のリズム, ヨーロッパのポピュラー音楽, アメリカのソウルミュージックの完ぺきな組み合わせ ❑ *...a life-size poster of a pop star.* ポピュラー歌手の等身大ポスター **2** N-UNCOUNT 不可算名詞 You can refer to carbonated drinks such as cola as **pop**. 炭酸飲料 [BRIT 英国英語, INFORMAL くだけた] ❑ *...a can of pop.* 一缶の炭酸飲料 **3** N-COUNT; SOUND 可算名詞, 音声語 **Pop** is used to represent a short sharp sound such as the sound made by bursting a balloon or by pulling a cork out of a bottle. パチンという音 ❑ *Each corn kernel will make a loud pop when cooked.* トウモロコシの粒は火が通るとポンという大きい音を立てます. **4** V-I 自動詞 If something **pops**, it makes a short sharp sound. ポンという音を立てる ❑ *He untwisted the wire off the champagne bottle, and the cork popped and shot to the ceiling.* 彼がシャンパンの瓶から針金をほどくと, コルクがポンという音を立て, 天井に飛んだ. **5** V-I 自動詞 If your eyes **pop**, you look very surprised or excited when you see something. 驚く [INFORMAL くだけた] ❑ *My eyes popped out at the sight of the rich variety of food on show.* 食べ物があまりに多彩だったのでとても驚いた. **6** V-T 他動詞 If you **pop** something somewhere, you put it there quickly. ひょいと入れる [INFORMAL くだけた] ❑ *Marianne got a couple of mugs from the cupboard and popped a teabag into each of them.* マリアンは戸棚からマグを2個取り出し, ティーバッグを放り込んだ. **7** N-FAMILY 家族名詞 Some people call their father **pop**. 父さん [mainly AM 主に米国英語, INFORMAL くだけた] ❑ *I looked at Pop and he had big tears in his eyes.* 私が見るとおやじは目に大きな涙を浮かべていた. **8** to **pop the question** → see **question**

▶ **pop up** PHRASAL VERB 句動詞 If someone or something **pops up**, they appear in a place or situation unexpectedly. ひょこっと現われる [INFORMAL くだけた] ❑ *She was startled when Lisa popped up at the door all smiles.* 彼女はリサが満面微笑んでドアにひょこっと現われたのでびっくりした.

POP /pi oʊ pi/ (POPs) N-COUNT 可算名詞 **POP** is something that proves that you have paid for something. **POP** is an abbreviation for "proof of purchase". 購入証明書

pop|corn /pɒpkɔrn/ N-UNCOUNT 不可算名詞 **Popcorn** is a snack that consists of grains of corn that have been heated until they have burst and become large and light. ポップコーン

pope /poʊp/ (popes) N-COUNT 可算名詞 **The pope** is the head of the Roman Catholic Church. ローマ法王 [usu "the" N; N-TITLE] ❑ *The highlight of the pope's visit will be his message to the people.* ローマ法王の訪問のハイライトは人々へのメッセージになるだろう.

pop|py /pɒpi/ (poppies) N-COUNT 可算名詞 A **poppy** is a plant with a large, delicate flower, usually red in color. The drug opium is obtained from one type of poppy. ケシ ❑ *...a field of poppies.* ケシ畑

Pop|si|cle /pɒpsɪkˀl/ (Popsicles) N-COUNT 商標 A **Popsicle** is a piece of flavored ice on a stick. アイスキャンデー [AM 米国英語, TRADEMARK]

Word Link *popul ≈ people : populace, popular, population*

popu|lace /pɒpyələs/ N-UNCOUNT 不可算名詞 **The populace** of a country is its people. 民衆 [FORMAL 形式ばった] ❑ *...a large proportion of the populace.* 民衆の大部分

popu|lar /pɒpyələr/ **1** ADJ 形容詞 Something that is **popular** is enjoyed or liked by a lot of people. 好かれる ❑ *Chocolate sauce is always popular with youngsters.* チョコレートソースはいつも若者に好かれている. ● **popu|lar|ity** /pɒpyəlærɪti/ N-UNCOUNT 不可算名詞 人気 ❑ *...the growing popularity of Australian wines among consumers.* 消費者間で高まるオーストラリア産ワインの人気 **2** ADJ 形容詞 Someone who is **popular** is liked by most people, or by most people in a particular group. 人気のある ❑ *He remained the most popular politician in Arkansas.* 彼は今でもアーカンソーで最も人気のある政治家でありつづけた. ● **popu|lar|ity** N-UNCOUNT 不可算名詞 人気 ❑ *It is his popularity with ordinary people that sets him apart.* 彼がひときわ輝かせるのは普通の人に人気があることだ. **3** ADJ 形容詞 [ADJ n] **Popular** newspapers, television programs, or forms of art are aimed at ordinary people and not at experts or intellectuals. 大衆向きの ❑ *Once again the popular press in Britain has been rife with stories about their marriage.* またも英国の大衆新聞は彼らの結婚に関する記事でもちきりになっている. ❑ *...one of the classics of modern popular music.* 現代ポピュラー音楽の傑作 **4** ADJ 形容詞 **Popular** ideas, feelings, or attitudes are approved of or held by most people. 一般大衆の間に普及している ❑ *Contrary to popular belief, the oil companies*

can't control the price of crude. 世間で考えられているのとは反対に石油会社は原油価格を左右することができない. ❑ *The military government has been unable to win popular support.* 軍事政府は大衆の支持を得ることができなかった. ● **popu|lar|ity** N-UNCOUNT 不可算名詞 人気 ❑ *Over time, though, Watson's views gained in popularity.* だが時が経ちワトソンの考えは一般に受け入れられるようになった. ⑤ ADJ 形容詞 [ADJ n] **Popular** is used to describe political activities that involve the ordinary people of a country, and not just members of political parties. 一般大衆の ❑ *The late president Ferdinand Marcos was overthrown by a popular uprising in 1986.* 故フェルディナンド・マルコス元大統領は1986年に大衆の反乱により追放された.

→ see **genre**

Word Partnership *popular* は次の語句と使われる:

ADV.	**extremely** popular, **increasingly** popular, **more** popular, **most** popular, **wildly** popular ➊ ➋ ➍
N.	popular **culture**, popular **magazine**, popular **movie**, popular **music**, popular **novel**, popular **restaurant**, popular **show**, popular **song** ➊ ➌

popu|lar|ize /pɒpyələraɪz/ (**popularizes, popularizing, popularized**) V-T 他動詞 To **popularize** something means to make a lot of people interested in it and able to enjoy it. 大衆に広める ❑ *Irving Brokaw, who had studied figure skating in Europe, returned to the U.S. and popularized the new sport.* ヨーロッパでフィギュアスケートを学んだアービング・ブローカフは米国に戻り, この新しいスポーツを大衆に広めた. ● **popu|lari|za|tion** /pɒpyələrɪzeɪʃⁿ/ N-UNCOUNT 不可算名詞 大衆に広めること ❑ *...the popularization of sports through television.* テレビを通じてスポーツを大衆に広めること

popu|lar|ly /pɒpyələrli/ ➊ ADV 副詞 If something or someone is **popularly** known as something, most people call them that, although it is not their official name or title. 一般に [ADV with -ed] ❑ *...the Mesozoic era, more popularly known as the age of dinosaurs.* 一般には恐竜の時代として知られている中生代 ❑ *...an infection popularly called mad cow disease.* 一般に狂牛病と呼ばれる感染症 ➋ ADV 副詞 If something is **popularly** believed or supposed to be the case, most people believe or suppose it to be the case, although it may not be true. 世間では [ADV -ed] ❑ *Schizophrenia is not a "split mind" as is popularly believed.* 精神分裂症は世間で信じられているような「分裂した心」ではない. ➌ ADV 副詞 A **popularly elected** leader or government has been elected by a majority of the people in a country. 一般投票で選ばれた [ADV -ed] ❑ *Walesa was Poland's first popularly elected president.* ワレサはポーランド初めて一般投票で選ばれた大統領だった.

popu|late /pɒpyəleɪt/ (**populates, populating, populated**) ➊ V-T 他動詞 If an area **is populated by** certain people or animals, those people or animals live there, often in large numbers. 住む ❑ *Before all this the island was populated by native American Arawaks.* これ以前はその島にはアメリカ先住民のアラワク族が住んでいた. ● **popu|lat|ed** ADJ 形容詞 [adv ADJ] 住んだで ❑ *The southeast is the most densely populated area.* 南東部は最も人口が密集した地域である. ➋ V-T 他動詞 To **populate** an area means to cause people to live there. 人を居住させる ❑ *Successive regimes annexed the region and populated it with lowland people.* 代々の政府がその地域を併合し, 低地の住民を住まわせた.

Word Link *popul ≈ people : populace, popular, population*

popu|la|tion /pɒpyəleɪʃⁿn/ (**populations**) ➊ N-COUNT 可算名詞 The **population** of a country or area is all the people who live in it. 人口 ❑ *Bangladesh now has a population of about 110 million.* バングラデシュの人口は現在約1億1千万人だ. ❑ *...the annual rate of population growth.* 年間人口増加率 ➋ N-COUNT 可算名詞 If you refer to a particular type of **population** in a country or area, you are referring to all the people or animals of that type there. 全住民 [FORMAL 形式ばった] ❑ *...75.6 percent of the male population over sixteen.* 16歳以上の男性の75.6% ❑ *...areas with a large black population.* 黒人住民の多い地区

→ see Word Web: **population**
→ see **country**

pop-up ➊ ADJ 形容詞 A **pop-up** book, usually a children's book, has pictures that stand up when you open the pages. 開くと飛び出る [ADJ n] ➋ ADJ 形容詞 On a computer screen, a **pop-up** menu or advertisement is a small window containing a menu or advertisement that appears on the screen when you perform particular operations. ポップアップ [COMPUTING] [ADJ n] ❑ *...a program for stopping pop-up ads.* ポップアップ広告を止めるためのプログラム

porce|lain /pɔrsəlɪn, pɔrslɪn/ N-UNCOUNT 不可算名詞 **Porcelain** is a hard, shiny substance made by heating clay. It is used to make delicate cups, plates, and ornaments. 磁器 ❑ *There were lilies everywhere in tall white porcelain vases.* 細長い白い磁器の花瓶に入ったユリがあちらこちらにあった.

→ see **pottery**

porch /pɔrtʃ/ (**porches**) ➊ N-COUNT 可算名詞 A **porch** is a sheltered area at the entrance to a building. It has a roof and sometimes has walls. ポーチ ❑ *She huddled inside the porch as she rang the bell.* ベルを鳴らしながら彼女はポーチの中で体を丸くした. ➋ N-COUNT 可算名詞 A **porch** is a raised platform built along the outside wall of a house and often covered with a roof. ベランダ [AM 米国英語] ❑ *He was standing on the porch, waving as we drove away.* 彼は私達が走り去る時にベランダに立って手を振っていた.

pore /pɔr/ (**pores, poring, pored**) ➊ N-COUNT 可算名詞 Your **pores** are the tiny holes in your skin. 毛穴 ❑ *The size of your pores is determined by the amount of oil they produce.* 毛穴の大きさはそこから発生する油の量によって決まる. ➋ V-I 自動詞 If you **pore over** or **through** information, you look at it and study it very carefully. 熟考する ❑ *We spent hours poring over travel brochures.* 私達は旅行パンフレットを何時間も熟読した.

pork /pɔrk/ N-UNCOUNT 不可算名詞 **Pork** is meat from a pig, usually fresh and not smoked or salted. 豚肉 ❑ *...fried pork chops.* いためたぶつ切り豚肉

→ see **meat**

porn /pɔrn/ N-UNCOUNT 不可算名詞 **Porn** is the same as **pornography**. ポルノ [INFORMAL くだけた] ❑ *...a porn cinema.* ポルノ映画館

por|no|graph|ic /pɔrnəgræfɪk/ ADJ 形容詞 **Pornographic** materials such as movies, DVDs, and magazines are designed to cause sexual excitement by showing naked people or referring to sexual acts. ポルノの [DISAPPROVAL 不賛成] ❑ *I found out he'd been watching pornographic DVDs.* 私は彼がポルノビデオを見ていたのを発見した.

por|nog|ra|phy /pɔrnɒgrəfi/ N-UNCOUNT 不可算名詞 **Pornography** refers to books, magazines, and movies that are designed to cause sexual excitement by showing naked people or referring to sexual acts. ポルノ [DISAPPROVAL 不賛成] ❑ *The country's leading newspaper has called for a new campaign against child pornography.* 国の有力な新聞が児童ポルノ撲滅の新しいキャンペーンを呼びかけた.

po|rous /pɔrəs/ ADJ 形容詞 Something that is **porous** has many small holes in it that water and air can pass through. 小穴の多い ❑ *The local limestone is so porous that all the rainwater immediately sinks below ground.* 地元の石灰石は非常に多孔質のため, 雨はすぐに地下に浸透する.

→ see **pottery**

por|ridge /pɔrɪdʒ/ N-UNCOUNT 不可算名詞 **Porridge** is a thick sticky food made from oats cooked in water or milk and eaten hot, especially for breakfast. かゆ [mainly BRIT 主に英国英語; AM usually **oatmeal** 米国英語では通常 **oatmeal**]

port /pɔrt/ (**ports**) ➊ N-COUNT 可算名詞 A **port** is a town by the sea or on a river that has a harbor. 港 ❑ *...the Mediterranean port of Marseilles.* 地中海のマルセイユ港 ➋ N-COUNT 可算名詞 A **port** is a harbor area where ships load and unload goods or passengers. 港湾 ❑ *...the bridges that link the port area to the rest of the city.* 港湾地域を市内の他地域と結ぶ橋 ➌ N-COUNT 可算名詞 A **port** on a computer is a place where you can attach another piece of equipment such as a printer. ポート [COMPUTING コンピューティング] ❑ *The devices, attached to a PC through standard ports, print bar codes onto envelopes.* 標準ポート経由でパソコンに接続された機

Word Web population

In 1987 the world's **population** was 5 billion. By the year 2000, it had climbed to 6 billion. Demographers predict that the total will top 9 billion by the year 2050. Improvements in medicine, sanitation, and nutrition have caused a decline in **death rates**. At the same time, there has been no overall decrease in **birth rates**. In a few countries, like Japan, the birth rate has dropped dramatically. As Japan's population ages, its workforce shrinks. India has the opposite problem. With its population **trend**, it has more young people wanting to join the workforce than there are jobs available.

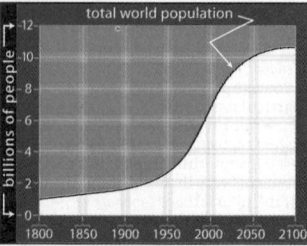

器はバーコードを封筒に印刷する. **4** ADJ 形容詞 In sailing, the **port** side of a ship is the left side when you are on it and facing toward the front. 左舷(げん)の [TECHNICAL 技術的] ❏ *Her official number is carved on the port side of the forecabin.* 船の公認番号は前部船室の左舷側に彫られている. ● N-UNCOUNT 不可算名詞 **Port** is also a noun. 左舷 ❏ *USS Ogden turned to port.* 米軍艦オグデンは左に向った. **5** N-UNCOUNT 不可算名詞 **Port** is a type of strong, sweet red wine. ポートワイン ❏ *He asked for a glass of port after dinner.* 彼は食後に 1 杯のポートワインを頼んだ.

→ see **ship**

| Word Link | able ≈ able to be : incurable, portable, unavoiable |

| Word Link | port ≈ carrying : export, import, portable |

port|able /pɔrtəbəl/ (**portables**) **1** ADJ 形容詞 A **portable** machine or device is designed to be easily carried or moved. 移動式の ❏ *There was a little portable television switched on behind the bar.* カウンターの後ろには小さなポータブルテレビがついていた. **2** N-COUNT 可算名詞 A **portable** is something such as a television, radio, or computer that can be easily carried or moved. 移動できるもの ❏ *We bought a portable for the bedroom.* 我々は寝室用にポータブル機を買った.

por|tal /pɔrtᵊl/ (**portals**) N-COUNT 可算名詞 On the Internet, a **portal** is a website that consists of links to other sites. ポータル [COMPUTING コンピューティング] ❏ *The site acts as a portal for thousands of online dealers.* そのサイトは何千人ものオンラインディーラー向けのポータル役を果たす.

por|ter /pɔrtər/ (**porters**) **1** N-COUNT 可算名詞 A **porter** is a person whose job is to carry things, for example, people's luggage at a train station or in a hotel. ポーター ❏ *Our taxi pulled up at Old Delhi station and a porter sprinted to the door.* 私達のタクシーがオールドデリー駅に止まるとポーターがドアに素早く走り寄った. **2** N-COUNT 可算名詞 In a hospital, a **porter** is someone whose job is to move patients from place to place. 患者や器具を移動させる人 [BRIT 英国英語; AM 米国英語 **orderly**] **3** N-COUNT 可算名詞 A **porter** is a person whose job is to be in charge of the entrance of a building such as a hotel. 玄関番 [BRIT 英国英語; AM **doorman** 米国英語 **doorman**]

port|fo|lio /pɔrtfouliou/ (**portfolios**) **1** N-COUNT 可算名詞 A **portfolio** is a set of pictures by someone, photographs of their work, or examples of their writing, which they use when entering competitions or applying for work. 作品選集 ❏ *After dinner that evening, Edith showed them a portfolio of her own political cartoons.* その晩は夕食後にイーディスが彼らに自分の政治風刺漫画の作品集を見せた. **2** N-COUNT 可算名詞 In finance, a **portfolio** is the combination of investments that a particular person or company owns. ポートフォリオ [BUSINESS 実業] ❏ *...Roger Early, a portfolio manager at Federated Investors Corp.* フェデレイテッド・インベスターズ社のポートフォリオマネジャーのロジャー・アーリー **3** N-COUNT 可算名詞 In politics, a **portfolio** is a high-ranking official's responsibility for a particular area of a government's activities. 大臣の職 ❏ *He has held the defense portfolio since the first free elections in 1990.* 彼は1990年の最初の自由選挙以来, 防衛大臣を務めてきた. **4** N-COUNT 可算名詞 A company's **portfolio** of products or designs is their range of products or designs. 製品ライン [BUSINESS 実業] ❏ *The company has continued to invest heavily in a strong portfolio of products.* その会社は強力な製品ラインに多額の投資を続けてきた.

por|tion /pɔrʃᵊn/ (**portions**) **1** N-COUNT 可算名詞 A **portion** of something is a part of it. 一部 ❏ *Damage was confined to a small portion of the castle.* 損害は城の小さな部分に限定された. ❏ *I have spent a considerable portion of my life here.* 私はここで人生の大部分を過ごした. **2** N-COUNT 可算名詞 A **portion** is the amount of food that is given to one person at a meal. 1人前 ❏ *Desserts can be substituted by a portion of fresh fruit.* デザートは新鮮な果物を一人分でもよい. ❏ *The portions were generous.* 料理はたっぷりあった.

por|trait /pɔrtrit, -treɪt/ (**portraits**) **1** N-COUNT 可算名詞 A **portrait** is a painting, drawing, or photograph of a particular person. 肖像画 ❏ *...badly painted family portraits.* 下手に描かれた家族の肖像画 **2** N-COUNT 可算名詞 A **portrait** of a person, place, or thing is a verbal description of them. 言葉による描写 [usu N of n] ❏ *...this gripping, funny portrait of Jewish life in 1950s Hoboken.* 1950年代のホボケンのユダヤ人の生活の魅力的でおかしみのある描写

→ see **painting**

por|tray /pɔrtreɪ/ (**portrays, portraying, portrayed**) **1** V-T 他動詞 When an actor or actress **portrays** someone, he or she plays that person in a play or movie. 演じる ❏ *In 1975 he portrayed the king in a Los Angeles revival of "Camelot."* 1975年に彼はロサンゼルスでの「キャメロット」の再演で王の役を演じた. **2** V-T 他動詞 When a writer or artist **portrays** something, he or she writes a description or produces a painting of it. 描く ❏ *The film portrays a culture of young people who live in lower Manhattan.* その映画はロワー・マンハッタンに住む若者の文化を描いたものである. **3** V-T 他動詞 If a movie,

book, or television program **portrays** someone in a certain way, it represents them in that way. 描写する ❏ *...complaints about the way women are portrayed in ads.* 広告での女性描写のあり方についての苦情

por|tray|al /pɔrtreɪəl/ (**portrayals**) **1** N-COUNT 可算名詞 An actor's **portrayal of** a character in a play or movie is the way that he or she plays the character. 役を演じること ❏ *Mr. Ying is well-known for his portrayal of a prison guard in the film "The Last Emperor."* イング氏は映画「ラスト・エンペラー」の守衛の役で有名だ. **2** N-COUNT 可算名詞 An artist's **portrayal of** something is a drawing, painting, or photograph of it. 描写されたもの ❏ *...a moving portrayal of St. John the Evangelist by Simone Martini.* シモーネ・マルティーニが聖ヨハネを描いた感動的な絵画 **3** N-COUNT 可算名詞 The **portrayal of** something in a book or movie is the act of describing it or showing it. 描写 ❏ *...an accurate portrayal of family life.* 家庭生活の正確な描写 **4** N-COUNT 可算名詞 The **portrayal of** something in a book, movie, or program is the way that it is made to appear. 描写 ❏ *The media persists in its portrayal of us as muggers, dope sellers, and gangsters.* メディアは我々を強盗, 麻薬販売人, 暴力団員として描写し続ける.

POS /pi ou ɛs/ The **POS** is the place in a store where a product is passed from the seller to the customer. **POS** is an abbreviation for **point of sale**. 販売時点管理 [BUSINESS 実業] ❏ *...a POS system that doubles as an inventory and sales control system.* 在庫管理と販売管理の両方を実現するPOSシステム

pose /pouz/ (**poses, posing, posed**) **1** V-T 他動詞 If something **poses** a problem or a danger, it is the cause of that problem or danger. 提出する ❏ *This could pose a threat to jobs in the coal industry.* これは石炭業界の雇用を脅かす可能性がある. **2** V-T 他動詞 If you **pose** a question, you ask it. If you **pose** an issue that needs considering, you mention the issue. 持ち出す [FORMAL 形式ばった] ❏ *When I finally posed the question, "Why?" he merely shrugged.* 私がやっと質問をしたときに彼は「なぜだ」と肩をすくめただけだった. **3** V-I 自動詞 If you **pose as** someone, you pretend to be that person in order to deceive people. 振りをする ❏ *The team posed as drug dealers to trap the ringleaders.* 一団はリーダーを捕らえるために麻薬取扱業者を装った. **4** V-I 自動詞 If you **pose for** a photograph or painting, you stay in a particular position so that someone can photograph you or paint you. ポーズを取る ❏ *Before going into their meeting the six foreign ministers posed for photographs.* 会合に参加する前に6人の外相は写真撮影のためにポーズを取った. **5** N-COUNT 可算名詞 A **pose** is a particular way that you stand, sit, or lie, for example, when you are being photographed or painted. ポーズを取ること ❏ *We have had several preliminary sittings in various poses.* 私たちは事前にいろいろなポーズで座っていた.

posh /pɒʃ/ (**posher, poshest**) **1** ADJ 形容詞 If you describe something as **posh**, you mean that it is elegant, fashionable, and expensive. 豪華な [INFORMAL くだけた] ❏ *Celebrating a promotion, I took her to a posh hotel for a cocktail.* 昇進を祝って私はカクテルを飲みに彼女を豪華ホテルに連れて行った. **2** ADJ 形容詞 If you describe a person as **posh**, you mean that they belong to or behave as if they belong to the upper classes. 上流階級の [mainly BRIT 主に英国英語, INFORMAL くだけた] ❏ *I wouldn't have thought she had such posh friends.* 彼女にそのような上流階級の友人がいたとは思っていなかった.

po|si|tion /pəzɪʃᵊn/ (**positions, positioning, positioned**) **1** N-COUNT 可算名詞 The **position** of someone or something is the place where they are in relation to other things. 場所 ❏ *The ship was identified, and its name and position were reported to the Coast Guard.* 船が確認され, 名前と所在地が沿岸警備隊に報告された. **2** N-COUNT 可算名詞 When someone or something is in a particular **position**, they are sitting, lying, or arranged in that way. 位置 ❏ *It is crucial that the upper back and neck are held in an erect position to give support for the head.* 頭を支えるためには背中の上部と首を直立位置にすることが大切だ. ❏ *Mr. Dambar had raised himself to a sitting position.* ダンバー氏は起き上がって座った姿勢になった. **3** V-T 他動詞 If you **position** something somewhere, you put it there carefully, so that it is in the right place or position. 置く ❏ *Position the cursor where you want the new margins to begin.* ここから新しいマージンにしたいという場所にカーソルを置く. **4** N-COUNT 可算名詞 Your **position** in society is the role and the importance that you have in it. 地位 ❏ *Adjustment to their changing role and position in society can be painful for some old people.* お年寄りの中には社会における役割と地位の変化に順応するのをつらく感じる人もいる. **5** N-COUNT 可算名詞 A **position** in a company or organization is a job. 職 [FORMAL 形式ばった] ❏ *He left a career in teaching to take up a position with the NEH.* 彼はNEHの仕事を始めるために教師を辞めた. **6** N-COUNT 可算名詞 Your **position** in a race or competition is how well you did in relation to the other competitors or how well you are doing. 位置 ❏ *By the ninth hour the car was running in eighth position.* 9時間経過したころには車は8位で走っていた. **7** N-COUNT 可算名詞 You can describe your situation at a particular time by saying that you are in a particular **position**. 状況 ❏ *He's going to be in a very difficult position if things go badly for him.* もし物事がうまく行かない場合には彼は非常に困難な立場に置かれるだろう. ❏ *Companies*

should be made to reveal more about their financial position. 企業は財務状況に関してより多くの情報を開示することを義務づけられるべきだ。 **8** N-COUNT 可算名詞 Your **position on** a particular matter is your attitude toward it or your opinion of it. 見方 [FORMAL 形式ばった] ❑ *He could be depended on to take a moderate position on most of the key issues.* 彼は主要な問題の大半について穏健な見方をすると思っているだろう。 **9** N-SING 単数名詞 If you are **in a position to** do something, you are able to do it. If you are **in no position to** do something, you are unable to do it. 立場にある。❑ *I am not in a position to comment.* 私は意見を言う立場にない。 **10** PHRASE 句 If someone or something is **in position**, they are in their correct or usual place or arrangement. 所定の場所に ❑ *28,000 U.S. troops are moving into position.* 2万8千人の米軍部隊が配置につくため移動中である。

→ see **navigation**

posi|tive /pɒzɪtɪv/ **1** ADJ 形容詞 If you are **positive about** things, you are hopeful and confident, and think of the good aspects of a situation rather than the bad ones. 前向きの ❑ *Be positive about your future and get on with living a normal life.* 将来について前向きの姿勢を持ち、普通の人生を過ごしていくようにしなさい。 ❑ *Her husband became much more positive and was soon back in full-time employment.* 彼女の夫はずっと前向きになり、まもなく正社員として採用された。 ● **posi|tive|ly** ADV 副詞 [ADV after v] 前向きで ❑ *You really must try to start thinking positively.* 本当に前向きに考え始める必要がある。 **2** ADJ 形容詞 A **positive** fact, situation, or experience is pleasant and helpful to you in some way. 好ましい ❑ *The parting from his sister had a positive effect on John.* 姉と別れたことは John に好ましい影響を与えた。 ● N-SING 単数名詞 The **positive** in a situation is the good and pleasant aspects of it. 肯定的な要素 ["the" n] ❑ *He prefers to focus on the positive.* 彼は肯定的な要素に関心を集中させることを好む。 **3** ADJ 形容詞 If you make a **positive** decision or take **positive** action, you do something definite in order to deal with a task or problem. 絶対的な ❑ *There are positive changes that should be implemented in the rearing of animals.* 動物の飼育に取り入れるべき絶対的な改良がある。 **4** ADJ 形容詞 A **positive** response to something indicates agreement, approval, or encouragement. 肯定的な ❑ *There's been a positive response to the U.N. Secretary-General's recent peace efforts.* 国連事務総長の最近の平和の試みには肯定的な反応があった。 ● **posi|tive|ly** ADV 副詞 [ADV after v] 肯定的に ❑ *He responded positively and accepted the fee of $1,000 I had offered.* 彼は積極的に反応し、私の提供した1000ドルの報酬を受け取った。 **5** ADJ 形容詞 If you are **positive** about something, you are completely sure about it. 確信のある [v-link ADJ] ❑ *"Judith's never late. You sure she said eight?" — "Positive."* 「ジュディスは遅刻したことはない。8時と彼女が言ったのは確かなのか」「間違いない」 **6** ADJ 形容詞 **Positive** evidence gives definite proof of the truth or identity of something. 疑いのない [ADJ n] ❑ *There was no positive evidence that any birth defects had arisen as a result of Vitamin A intake.* ビタミンA摂取が原因で先天性欠損症が発生したという明白な証拠はなかった。 ● **posi|tive|ly** ADV 副詞 [ADV with v] 明白に ❑ *He has positively identified the body as that of his wife.* 彼は遺体が間違いなく妻だと確認した。 **7** ADJ 形容詞 If a medical or scientific test is **positive**, it shows that something has happened or is present. 陽性の ❑ *If the test is positive, a course of antibiotics may be prescribed.* 検査が陽性の場合は1クールの抗生物質が処方されるかもしれない。 **8** HIV positive → see **HIV** **9** ADJ 形容詞 A **positive** number is greater than zero. 正数の [ADJ n] ❑ *It's really a simple numbers game with negative and positive numbers.* これは正数と負数のごく簡単な数のゲームである。 **10** ADJ 形容詞 If something has a **positive** electrical charge, it has the same charge as a proton and the opposite charge to a neutron. 正電荷を持つ [TECHNICAL 技術的]

→ see **lightning**, **magnet**

posi|tive dis|crimi|na|tion N-UNCOUNT 不可算名詞 **Positive discrimination** means making sure that people such as women, members of smaller racial groups, and disabled people get a fair share of the opportunities available. 積極的差別 [BRIT 英国英語; AM **affirmative action** 米国英語 **affirmative action**]

posi|tive|ly /pɒzɪtɪvli/ **1** ADV 副詞 You use **positively** to emphasize that you really mean what you are saying. 確かに [EMPHASIS 強調] [ADV adj-superl] ❑ *This is positively the last chance for the industry to establish such a system.* これは確かに業界がそうしたシステムを確立する最後のチャンスだ。 **2** ADV 副詞 You use **positively** to emphasize that something really is the case, although it may sound surprising or extreme. 決定的に [EMPHASIS 強調] ❑ *Mike's changed since he came back – he seems positively cheerful.* マイクは帰ってきてから変わった。彼はすごく陽気に見える。

pos|sess /pəzes/ **(possesses, possessing, possessed)** V-T 他動詞 If you **possess** something, you have it or own it. 所有する [no passive] ❑ *He was then arrested and charged with possessing an offensive weapon.* 彼はそれから攻撃用の武器を持っていたかどで逮捕され、起訴された。

pos|ses|sion /pəzeʃ°n/ **(possessions)** **1** N-UNCOUNT 不可算名詞 If you are **in possession of** something, you have it, because you have obtained it or because it belongs to you. 所有 [FORMAL 形式ばった] ❑ *Those documents are now in the possession of the Washington Post.* それらの書類は現在ワシントンポスト紙の手中にある。 ❑ *He was also charged with illegal possession of firearms.* また彼は不法な武器の所有で起訴された。 **2** N-COUNT 可算名詞 Your **possessions** are the things that you own or have with you at a particular time. 所有物 ❑ *People had lost their homes and all their possessions.* 人々は家とすべての所有物を失った。

pos|ses|sive /pəzesɪv/ **1** ADJ 形容詞 Someone who is **possessive about** another person wants all that person's love and attention. 独占欲の強い ❑ *Danny could be very jealous and possessive about me.* ダニーは大変やきもち焼きで私を独占したがることがある。 ● **pos|ses|sive|ness** N-UNCOUNT 不可算名詞 独占欲の強さ ❑ *I've ruined every relationship with my possessiveness.* 私は独占欲の強さのためにあらゆる人間関係を駄目にした。 **2** ADJ 形容詞 Someone who is **possessive about** things that they own does not like other people to use them. 所有欲の強い ❑ *People were very possessive about their coupons.* 人々はクーポンをどうしても一人占めしたがった。 **3** ADJ 形容詞 In grammar, a **possessive determiner** or **possessive adjective** is a word such as "my" or "his" that shows who or what something belongs to or is connected with. The **possessive** form of a name or noun has 's added to it, as in "Jenny's" or "cat's." 所有格の

pos|sibil|ity /pɒsɪbɪlɪti/ **(possibilities)** **1** N-COUNT 可算名詞 If you say there is a **possibility that** something is the case or **that** something will happen, you mean that it might be the case or it might happen. 可能性 ❑ *We were not in the least worried about the possibility that candy could rot the teeth.* 私たちはキャンデーで虫歯になるなんて少しも心配していなかった。 **2** N-COUNT 可算名詞 A **possibility** is one of several different things that could be done. 可能性 ❑ *There were several possibilities open to each manufacturer.* 各メーカーにはいくつかの可能性が開けていた。

Note that you do not use **possibility** in sentences like "I had the possibility to do it." The words you need are **opportunity** or **chance**. **Opportunity** is more formal. ❑ *Later Donald had the opportunity of driving the car… The people of Northern Ireland would have the chance to shape their own future.*

pos|sible /pɒsɪb°l/ **(possibles)** **1** ADJ 形容詞 If it is **possible** to do something, it can be done. 可能な ❑ *If it is possible to find out where your brother is, we will.* もしきみの弟さんを見つけることが可能なら、私たちが見つけるよ。 ❑ *Everything is possible if we want it enough.* やる気が十分あれば何でもできる。 **2** ADJ 形容詞 A **possible** event is one that might happen. 起こりうる ❑ *He referred the matter to the attorney general for possible action against several newspapers.* 彼は複数の新聞を訴えることを検討し、その件を法務長官に付託した。 ❑ *One possible solution, if all else fails, is to take legal action.* すべてが失敗した場合に可能な1つの解決策は訴訟を起こすことだ。 **3** ADJ 形容詞 If you say that it is **possible that** something is true or correct, you mean that although you do not know whether it is true or correct, you accept that it might be. あり得る [VAGUENESS あいまいさ] [v-link ADJ] ❑ *It is possible that there's an explanation for all this.* これを全部説明する方法もあり得る。 **4** ADJ 形容詞 If you do something **as** soon **as possible**, you do it as soon as you can. If you get **as** much **as possible** of something, you get as much of it as you can. できるだけ ["as" adv/pron "as" ADJ] ❑ *Please make your decision as soon as possible.* できるだけ早く決めてください。 ❑ *Mrs. Pollard decided to learn as much as possible about the country before going there.* ポラード夫人はその国について訪問前にできるだけ多くを学んでおこうと心に決めた。 **5** ADJ 形容詞 You use **possible** with superlative adjectives to emphasize that something has more or less of a quality than anything else of its kind. 可能な限りの [EMPHASIS 強調] ❑ *They have joined the job market at the worst possible time.* 彼らはこれ以上はないというような最悪の時期に求職活動を始めた。 ❑ *We expressed in the clearest possible way our disappointment, hurt, and anger.* 我々は可能な限りはっきりと落胆、苦悩、怒りを伝えた。 **6** ADJ 形容詞 If you describe someone as, for example, a **possible** governor, you mean that they could be elected as governor. 候補

となる [ADJ n] ❑ *Government sources are now openly speculating about a possible successor for Dr. Lawrence.* 政府筋は現在, ローレンス博士の後継者候補について公然と推測している. ● N-COUNT 可算名詞 **Possible** is also a noun. 候補者 ❑ *Kennedy, who divorced wife Joan in 1982, was tipped as a presidential possible.* 1982年に妻のジョーンと離婚したケネディは大統領候補者として挙げられている. **7** N-SING 単数名詞 **The possible** is everything that can be done in a situation. 可能なこと ❑ *He is a Democrat with the skill, nerve, and ingenuity to push the limits of the possible.* 彼は可能性の限界を押し上げる技能, 勇気, 巧みさを持つ民主党員だ.

pos|sibly /pɒsɪbli/ **1** ADV 副詞 You use **possibly** to indicate that you are not sure whether something is true or might happen. ことによると [VAGUENESS あいまいさ] ❑ *Exercise will not only lower blood pressure but possibly protect against heart attacks.* 運動は血圧を下げるだけでなく心臓の発作を防止するのに役立つかもしれない. ❑ *They were casually dressed; possibly students.* 彼らはカジュアルな格好をしていた. 多分学生だろう. **2** ADV 副詞 You use **possibly** to emphasize that you are surprised, puzzled, or shocked by something that you have seen or heard. とうてい [EMPHASIS 強調] [ADV before v] ❑ *It was the most unexpected piece of news one could possibly imagine.* それは想像しうる最も意外な知らせだった. **3** ADV 副詞 You use **possibly** to emphasize that someone has tried their hardest to do something, or has done it as well as they can. できる限り [EMPHASIS 強調] [ADV before v] ❑ *They've done everything they can possibly think of.* 彼らは思いつく限りのことを全てした. **4** ADV 副詞 You use **possibly** to emphasize that something definitely cannot happen or definitely cannot be done. どうしても [EMPHASIS 強調] [with brd-neg, ADV before v] ❑ *No I really can't possibly answer that!* まあ, 私はそれにはとても答えられません.

---

post
❶ LETTERS, PARCELS, AND INFORMATION
❷ JOBS AND PLACES
❸ POLES

---

❶ **post** /poʊst/ (posts, posting, posted) **1** V-T 他動詞 If you **post** notices, signs, or other pieces of information somewhere, you attach them to a wall or board so that everyone can see them. 張る ❑ *Officials began posting warning notices.* 当局は警告書を張り始めた. ● PHRASAL VERB 句動詞 **Post up** means the same as **post**. 張る ❑ *He has posted a sign up that says "No Fishing."* 彼は「魚釣り禁止」の標識を張った. **2** V-T 他動詞 If you **post** information on the Internet, you make the information available to other people on the Internet. 掲示する [COMPUTING コンピューティング] ❑ *A consultation paper has been posted on the Internet inviting input from users.* 利用者の意見を求める諮問書がインターネットに掲示された. **3** PHRASE 句 If you **keep** someone **posted**, you keep giving them the latest information about a situation that they are interested in. 逐次知らせる ❑ *Keep me posted on your progress.* あなたの進歩について逐次知らせてください. **4** N-UNCOUNT 不可算名詞 You can use **post** to refer to letters and packages that are delivered to you. 郵便 [mainly BRIT 主に英国英語; AM usually **mail**] 米国英語では通常 **mail**] **5** V-T 他動詞 If you **post** a letter or package, you send it to someone by putting it in a mailbox or by taking it to a post office. 投函(とうかん)する [mainly BRIT 主に英国英語; AM usually **mail** 米国英語では通常 **mail**]

❷ **post** /poʊst/ (posts, posting, posted) **1** N-COUNT 可算名詞 A **post** in a company or organization is a job or official position in it, usually one that involves responsibility. 地位 [FORMAL 形式ばった] ❑ *She had earlier resigned her post as President Menem's assistant.* 彼女はその前にメネム大統領の助手の仕事を辞めていた. **2** V-T 他動詞 If you **are posted** somewhere, you are sent there by the organization that you work for and usually work there for several years. 派遣される [usu passive] ❑ *After training she was posted to Biloxi.* 研修の後, 彼女はビロクシに派遣された. **3** V-T 他動詞 If a soldier, guard, or other person **is posted** somewhere, they are told to stand there, in order to supervise an activity or guard a place. 部署につく ❑ *Police have now been posted outside all temples.* 警察は現在すべての寺院の外に配置されている. ❑ *They had to post a signalman at the entrance to the tunnel.* 彼らはトンネルの入り口に信号係を配置しなければならなかった. **4** → see also **posting**

❸ **post** /poʊst/ (posts) **1** N-COUNT 可算名詞 A **post** is a strong upright pole made of wood or metal that is dug into the ground. 柱 ❑ *The device is fixed to a post.* その機器は柱に固定されている. **2** N-COUNT 可算名詞 A **post** is the same as a **goalpost**. ゴールポスト ❑ *Jenkins missed a penalty, hitting the post in the thirteenth minute.* ジェンキンスは13分でボールをゴールポストに当てペナルティゴールを入れ損なった. **3** N-SING 単数名詞 On a horse-racing track, **the**

post is a pole that marks the finishing point. 標柱

post|age /poʊstɪdʒ/ N-UNCOUNT 不可算名詞 **Postage** is the money that you pay for sending letters and packages by mail. 郵便料 ❑ *All prices include postage and handling.* 全ての価格は郵便料と手数料を含む.

post|al /poʊstˀl/ **1** ADJ 形容詞 **Postal** is used to describe things or people connected with the public service of carrying letters and packages from one place to another. 郵便局の [ADJ n] ❑ *Compensation for lost or damaged mail will be handled by the postal service.* 郵便物の紛失または損傷に対する補償は郵便局で処理される. **2** ADJ 形容詞 **Postal** is used to describe activities that involve sending things by mail. 郵便の [ADJ n] ❑ *...free postal delivery.* 無料の郵便配達

post|al or|der (postal orders) N-COUNT 可算名詞 A **postal order** is a piece of paper representing a sum of money which you can buy at a post office and send to someone as a way of sending them money by mail. 郵便為替 [BRIT 英国英語; AM **money order** 米国英語 **money order**]

post|box /poʊstbɒks/ (postboxes) also **post box** N-COUNT 可算名詞 A **postbox** is a metal box in a public place, where you put letters and small parcels to be collected. They are then sorted and delivered. Compare **letterbox**. 郵便受け [BRIT 英国英語; AM **mailbox** 米国英語 **mailbox**]

post|card /poʊstkɑrd/ (postcards) also **post card** N-COUNT 可算名詞 A **postcard** is a thin card, often with a picture on one side, which you can write on and mail to people without using an envelope. 絵葉書

post|code /poʊstkoʊd/ (postcodes) also **post code** N-COUNT 可算名詞 A **postcode** is a short sequence of numbers and letters at the end of an address. 郵便番号 [BRIT 英国英語; AM **zip code** 米国英語 **zip code**]

post|dated /poʊstdeɪtɪd/ ADJ 形容詞 On a **postdated** check, the date is a later one than the date when the check was actually written. You write a postdated check to allow a period of time before the money is taken from your account. 実際より後の日付が書かれた

post|er /poʊstər/ (posters) N-COUNT 可算名詞 A **poster** is a large notice or picture that you stick on a wall or board, often in order to advertise something. ポスター ❑ *I had seen the poster for the jazz festival in Monterey.* 私はモンテレーのジャズフェスティバルのポスターを見た. → see advertising

post|er child (poster children) also **poster boy** also **poster girl** N-COUNT 可算名詞 If someone is a **poster child for** a particular cause, characteristic, or activity, they are seen as a very good or typical example of it. 申し子 [mainly AM 主に米国英語] ❑ *Zidane has become the poster child for a whole generation of French-born youths of North African extraction.* ジダンはフランス生まれの北アフリカ系の若者を代表する時代の申し子となった.

pos|ter|ity /pɒsterɪti/ N-UNCOUNT 不可算名詞 You can refer to everyone who will be alive in the future as **posterity**. 子孫 [FORMAL 形式ばった] ❑ *A photographer recorded the scene on video for posterity.* 写真家は後世のためにその光景をビデオに録画した.

post|gradu|ate /poʊstgrædʒuɪt/ (postgraduates) also **post-graduate** **1** ADJ 形容詞 **Postgraduate** study or research is done by a student who has a bachelor's degree and is studying or doing research at a more advanced level. 大学院生の [ADJ n] **2** N-COUNT 可算名詞 A **postgraduate** or a **postgraduate student** is a student with a first degree from a university who is studying or doing research at a more advanced level. 大学院生 [BRIT 英国英語; AM **graduate student** 米国英語 **graduate student**]

post|ing /poʊstɪŋ/ (postings) **1** N-COUNT 可算名詞 If a member of an armed force gets a **posting** to a particular place, they are sent to live and work there for a period. 任命 ❑ *...awaiting his posting to a field ambulance corps in early 1941.* 1941年はじめに傷病者運搬部隊への任命を待つこと **2** N-COUNT 可算名詞 A **posting** is a message that is placed on the Internet, for example, on a newsgroup or website, for everyone to read. 書き込み [COMPUTING コンピューティング] ❑ *Postings on the Internet can be accessed from anywhere in the world.* インターネットの書き込みは世界中で閲覧できる. **3** N-COUNT 可算名詞 If you get a **posting to** a different town or country, your employers send you to work there, usually for several years. 転勤 [mainly BRIT 主に英国英語; AM usually **assignment** 米国英語では通常 **assignment**]

post|man /poʊstmən/ (postmen) N-COUNT 可算名詞 A **postman** is a man whose job is to collect and deliver letters and packages that are sent by mail. 郵便集配人 [mainly BRIT 主に英国英語; AM usually **letter carrier**, **mailman** 米国英語では通常 **letter carrier**, **mailman**]

P

post|mor|tem /poʊstmɔrtəm/ (postmortems) **1** N-COUNT 可算名詞 A **postmortem** is a medical examination of a dead person's body in order to find out how they died. 検死 □ *A postmortem was carried out to establish the cause of death.* 死亡の原因を確認するために検死が行なわれた. **2** N-COUNT 可算名詞 A **postmortem** is an examination of something that has recently happened, especially something that has failed or gone wrong. 事後の論議 □ *The postmortem on the presidential campaign is under way.* 大統領選挙戦を反省する論議が行われている.

post of|fice (post offices) **1** N-COUNT 可算名詞 A **post office** is a building where you can buy stamps, mail letters and packages, and use other services provided by the national postal service. 郵便局 □ *She rushed to get to the post office before it closed.* 彼女は郵便局が開いているうちにと急いで行った. **2** N-SING 単数名詞 **The Post Office** is sometimes used to refer to the U.S. Postal Service, which operates post offices. 郵政公社 □ *The Post Office has confirmed that up to fifteen thousand jobs could be lost.* 郵政公社は最高1万5千の職が失われることを確認した.

post of|fice box (post office boxes) N-COUNT 可算名詞 A **post office box** is a numbered box in a post office where a person's mail is kept for them until they come to collect it. 私書箱

Word Link post ≈ after : postgraduate, postpone, postwar

---

post|pone /poʊstpoʊn, poʊspoʊn/ (postpones, postponing, postponed) V-T 他動詞 If you **postpone** an event, you delay it or arrange for it to take place at a later time than was originally planned. 延期 □ *He decided to postpone the expedition until the following day.* 彼は翌日まで探検旅行を延期することに決めた.

If you **cancel** or **call off** an arrangement or an appointment, you stop it from happening. □ *His failing health forced him to cancel the meeting...The European Community has threatened to call off peace talks.* If you **postpone** or **put off** an arrangement or an appointment, you make another arrangement for it to happen at a later time. □ *Elections have been postponed until next year...The senate put off a vote on the nomination for one week.* If you **delay** something that has been arranged, you make it happen later than planned. □ *Space agency managers decided to delay the launch of the space shuttle.* If something **delays** you or **holds** you **up**, you start or finish what you are doing later than you planned. □ *He was delayed in traffic...Delivery of equipment had been held up by delays and disputes.*

---

post|pone|ment /poʊstpoʊnmənt, poʊspoʊn-/ (postponements) N-VAR 可変性名詞 The **postponement** of an event is the act of delaying it or arranging for it to take place at a later time than originally planned. 延期 □ *The postponement was due to a dispute over where the talks should be held.* 延期は会談場所についての論争が原因だった.

post|script /poʊstskrɪpt/ (postscripts) **1** N-COUNT 可算名詞 A **postscript** is something written at the end of a letter after you have signed your name. You usually write "P.S." in front of it. 追伸 □ *A brief, handwritten postscript lay beneath his signature.* 短い手書きの追伸が彼の署名の下にあった. **2** N-COUNT 可算名詞 A **postscript** is an addition to a finished story, account, or statement, that gives further information. 後記 □ *Let me add a postscript to this section on diet.* ダイエットに関するこの章に後記を付け足させてください.

pos|tu|late /poʊstʃəleɪt/ (postulates, postulating, postulated) V-T 他動詞 If you **postulate** something, you suggest it as the basis for a theory, argument, or calculation, or assume that it is the basis. 仮定する [FORMAL 形式ばった] □ *He dismissed arguments postulating differing standards for human rights in different cultures and regions.* 彼は異なる文化や地域には異なる人権基準があると仮定する議論を退けた.

pos|ture /poʊstʃər/ (postures, posturing, postured) **1** N-VAR 可変性名詞 Your **posture** is the position in which you stand or sit. 姿勢 □ *You can make your stomach look flatter instantly by improving your posture.* 姿勢を良くすればすぐにお腹を平らに見せることができる. □ *Exercise, fresh air, and good posture are all helpful.* 運動, 新鮮な空気そして良い姿勢はすべて有益である. **2** N-COUNT 可算名詞 A **posture** is an attitude that you have toward something. 態度 [FORMAL 形式ばった] □ *The military machine is ready to change its defensive posture to one prepared for action.* 軍組織は防御姿勢から攻撃姿勢へ変える態勢が整っている. **3** V-I 自動詞 You can say that someone **is posturing** when you disapprove of their behavior because you think they are trying to give a particular impression in order to deceive people. ふりをする [FORMAL 形式ばった, DISAPPROVAL 不賛成] [usu cont] □ *She says the president may just be posturing.* 大統領はポーズを作っているだけかもしれないと彼女は言っている.

→ see **brain**

post|war /poʊstwɔr/ ADJ 形容詞 **Postwar** is used to describe things that happened, existed, or were made in the period immediately after a war, especially World War II, 1939-45. 戦後の □ *Anesthetics and bottle feeding were popular in the early postwar years.* 麻酔薬と哺乳（ほにゅう）瓶で育てることは戦争直後に一般的だった.

---

pot /pɒt/ (pots, potting, potted) **1** N-COUNT 可算名詞 A **pot** is a deep round container used for cooking stews, soups, and other food. 鍋(なべ) □ *...metal cooking pots.* 金属製の料理用鍋. **2** N-COUNT 可算名詞 You can use **pot** to refer to the pot and its contents, or to the contents only. 鍋1杯分 □ *He was stirring a pot of soup.* 彼は鍋1杯のスープをかき回していた. **3** N-COUNT 可算名詞 A **pot** of coffee or tea is an amount of it contained in a pot. ポット1杯分 □ *He spilt a pot of coffee.* 彼はポットに入ったコーヒーをこぼした. **4** N-COUNT 可算名詞 You can use **pot** to refer to a coffeepot or teapot. ポット **4** N-UNCOUNT 不可算名詞 **Pot** is sometimes used to refer to the drug marijuana or the cannabis plant. マリファナ [INFORMAL くだけた] □ *I started smoking pot when I was about eleven.* 私は11歳頃にマリファナを吸い始めた. **5** N-SING 単数名詞 In a card game, **the pot** is the money from all the players which the winner of the game will take as a prize. 賭(か)け金 ["the" N] **6** V-T 他動詞 If you **pot** a young plant, or part of a plant, you put it into a container filled with soil, so it can grow there. 鉢に入れる □ *Pot the cuttings individually.* 切り枝は別々の鉢に入れなさい. ● **pot|ted** ADJ 形容詞 [ADJ n] 鉢植えの □ *...potted plants.* 鉢植えの植物 **7** → see also **melting pot**

po|ta|to /pəteɪtoʊ/ (potatoes) **1** N-VAR 可変性名詞 **Potatoes** are round vegetables with brown or red skins and white insides. They grow under the ground. ジャガイモ **2** PHRASE 句 You can refer to a difficult subject that people disagree on as a **hot potato**. 困難な問題 □ *...a political hot potato such as abortion.* 人工中絶などの政治的な難題.

po|ta|to chip (potato chips) **1** N-COUNT 可算名詞 **Potato chips** are very thin slices of potato that have been fried until they are hard, dry, and crisp. ポテトチップ [AM 米国英語] **2** N-COUNT 可算名詞 **Potato chips** are long, thin pieces of potato fried in oil or fat and eaten hot, usually with a meal. フライドポテト [BRIT 英国英語; AM French fries 米国英語 French fries]

po|ten|cy /poʊtⁿnsi/ **1** N-UNCOUNT 不可算名詞 **Potency** is the power and influence that a person, action, or idea has to affect or change people's lives, feelings, or beliefs. 力 □ *All their songs have a lingering potency.* 彼らの歌はすべて耳に残る. **2** N-UNCOUNT 不可算名詞 The **potency** of a drug, poison, or other chemical is its strength. 有効性 □ *Sunscreen can lose its potency if left over winter in the bathroom cabinet.* 日焼け止めは洗面所の戸棚で冬をこしたら効果がなくなることがある.

Word Link potent ≈ ability, power : impotent, potent, potential

---

po|tent /poʊtⁿnt/ ADJ 形容詞 Something that is **potent** is very effective and powerful. よく効く □ *Their most potent weapon was the Exocet missile.* 彼らの最も効果のある武器はエグゾセ・ミサイルだった.

po|ten|tial /pətɛnʃⁿl/ **1** ADJ 形容詞 You use **potential** to say that someone or something is capable of developing into the particular kind of person or thing mentioned. 潜在的な [ADJ n] □ *The company has identified 60 potential customers.* その会社は60の潜在顧客を見極めた. □ *We are aware of the potential problems and have taken every precaution.* 我々は潜在的な問題を認識しており, あらゆる注意を払った. ● **po|ten|tial|ly** ADV 副詞 [ADV with cl/group] 潜在的に □ *Clearly this is a potentially dangerous situation.* 明らかにこれは潜在的に危険な状況だ. **2** N-UNCOUNT 不可算名詞 If you say that someone or something has **potential**, you mean that they have the necessary abilities or qualities to become successful or useful in the future. 潜在能力 □ *The boy has great potential.* その少年は大きな潜在能力を持っている. □ *The school strives to treat students as individuals and to help each one to achieve their full potential.* 学校は生徒を個人として取扱い, 各人が潜在能力をまっとうできるよう手助けに励む. **3** N-UNCOUNT 不可算名詞 If you say that someone or something has **potential** for doing a particular thing, you mean that it is possible they may do it. If there is **the potential for** something, it may happen. 可能性 □ *John seemed as horrified as I about his potential for violence.* ジョンは自分が暴力を振るう可能性について私と同じくらいぞっとしたようだった. □ *The meeting has the potential to be a watershed event.* その会合は重大な事件となる可能性があった.

po|tion /poʊʃⁿn/ (potions) N-COUNT 可算名詞 A **potion** is a drink that contains medicine, poison, or something that is supposed to have magic powers. 一服 □ *...a magic potion that will make Siegfried forget Brunnhilde and fall in love with Gutrune.* ジークフリードがブリュンヒルデを忘れ, グートルーネに恋をさせる魔法の薬

pot|tery /pɒtəri/ (potteries) **1** N-UNCOUNT 不可算名詞 You can use **pottery** to refer to pots, dishes, and other objects made from clay and then baked in an oven until they are hard. 陶器類 □ *...a fine range of pottery.* 見事な陶器の数々 **2** N-UNCOUNT 不可算名詞 You can use **pottery** to refer to the hard clay that some pots, dishes, and other objects are made of. 陶器 □ *Some bowls were made of pottery and wood.* 一部の鉢は陶器と木材でできていた. **3** N-UNCOUNT 不可算名詞 **Pottery** is the craft or activity

Word Web — pottery

There are three basic types of **pottery**. **Earthenware dishes** are made from **clay** and **fired** at a relatively low temperature. They are **porous** and require a **glaze** in order to hold water. Potters first created earthenware objects about 15,000 years ago. **Stoneware** pieces are heavier and are fired at a higher temperature. They are impermeable even without a glaze. **Porcelain ceramics** are more fragile. They have thin walls and are **translucent**. Stoneware and porcelain are not as old as earthenware. They appeared about 2,000 years ago when the Chinese started building high-temperature kilns. Another name for porcelain is **china**.

---

of making objects out of clay. 陶器製造 ❏ *He became interested in sculpting and pottery.* 彼は彫刻と陶器づくりに関心を持つようになった. **4** N-COUNT 可算名詞 A **pottery** is a factory or other place where pottery is made. 製陶所 ❏ *...the many galleries and potteries which sell pieces by local artists.* 地元芸術家の陶器を販売する多くのギャラリーや窯元.
→ see Word Web: **pottery**

pot|ty /pɒti/ (**potties**) N-COUNT 可算名詞 A **potty** is a deep bowl that a small child uses instead of a toilet. 幼児用便器

pouch /paʊtʃ/ (**pouches**) **1** N-COUNT 可算名詞 A **pouch** is a flexible container like a small bag. 小袋 ❏ *Joe Bob took out his pipe and dug it into a pouch of tobacco.* ジョー・ボブはパイプを取り出し, 袋に入ったタバコに押し込んだ. **2** N-COUNT 可算名詞 The **pouch** of an animal such as a kangaroo or a koala bear is the pocket of skin on its stomach in which its baby grows. 袋 ❏ *...a kangaroo, with a baby in its pouch.* 育児袋に赤ん坊を入れたカンガルー

poul|try /poʊltri/ N-PLURAL 複数名詞 You can refer to chickens, ducks, and other birds that are kept for their eggs and meat as **poultry**. 家禽 (かきん) ❏ *...a poultry farm.* 養禽 (ようきん) 所 ● N-UNCOUNT 不可算名詞 Meat from these birds is also referred to as **poultry**. 鳥肉 ❏ *The menu features roast meats and poultry.* メニューの主な料理は肉と鳥肉のローストだ.
→ see **meat**

pounce /paʊns/ (**pounces, pouncing, pounced**) **1** V-I 自動詞 If someone **pounces on** you, they come up toward you suddenly and take hold of you. 突然襲われる ❏ *He pounced on the photographer, beat him up, and smashed his camera.* 彼は写真家の前に突然現れ, 彼を殴り, 彼のカメラを壊した. **2** V-I 自動詞 If someone **pounces on** something such as a mistake, they quickly draw attention to it, usually in order to gain an advantage for themselves or to prove that they are right. ここぞとばかり責めたてる ❏ *The Democrats are ready to pounce on any Republican failings or mistakes.* 民主党は共和党の失敗を逃さず非難する態度をとっていた. **3** V-I 自動詞 When an animal or bird **pounces**, it jumps on it and holds it, in order to kill it. 突然飛びかかる ❏ *...like a tiger pouncing on its prey.* 突然現われて獲物をさっと捕まえるトラのように

pound /paʊnd/ (**pounds, pounding, pounded**) **1** N-COUNT 可算名詞 A **pound** is a unit of weight used mainly in the U.S., Britain and other countries where English is spoken. One pound is equal to 0.454 kilograms. A **pound** of something is a quantity of it that weighs one pound. ポンド ❏ *Her weight was under ninety pounds.* 彼の体重は90ポンド以下だった. ❏ *...a pound of cheese.* 1ポンドのチーズ **2** N-COUNT 可算名詞 The **pound** is the unit of money which is used in Britain. It is represented by the symbol £. One British pound is divided into a hundred pence. Some other countries, for example, Egypt, also have a unit of money called a **pound**. ポンド ❏ *...multi-million pound profits.* 数百万ポンドの利益 **3** N-SING 単数名詞 The **pound** is used to refer to the British currency system, and sometimes to the currency systems of other countries which use pounds. ポンドの相場 ❏ *The pound is expected to continue to increase against most other currencies.* ポンドの相場は大半の他の通貨に対して上昇し続ける見込みだ. **4** N-COUNT 可算名詞 A **pound** is a place where dogs and cats found wandering in the street are taken and kept until they are claimed by their owners. 動物保護センター ❏ *...cages at the local pound.* 地元の動物保護センターの檻 **5** N-COUNT 可算名詞 A **pound** is a place where cars that have been parked illegally are taken by the police and kept until they have been claimed by their owners. 違法駐車車両の保管場所 ❏ *The car remained in the police pound for a month.* その車は警察の保管場所に1か月間留め置かれていた. **6** V-T/V-I 他動詞/自動詞 If you **pound** something or **pound on** it, you hit it with great force, usually loudly and repeatedly. 何度も強く打つ ❏ *He pounded the table with his fist.* 彼はこぶしでテーブルをドンドンとたたいた. ❏ *Somebody began pounding on the front door.* 誰かが玄関のドアをドンドン たたき始めた. **7** V-T 他動詞 If you **pound** something, you crush it into a paste or a powder or into very small pieces. 砕いて粉々にする ❏ *She pounded the corn kernels.* 彼女はトウモロコシの粒を砕いた. **8** V-I 自動詞 If your heart **is pounding**, it is beating with an unusually

strong and fast rhythm, usually because you are afraid. 激しく鼓動する ❏ *I'm sweating, my heart is pounding. I can't breathe.* 私は汗をかき, 心臓がドキドキしている. 呼吸ができない.

pour /pɔr/ (**pours, pouring, poured**) **1** V-T 他動詞 If you **pour** a liquid or other substance, you make it flow steadily out of a container by holding the container at an angle. 注ぐ ❏ *Pour a pool of sauce on two plates and arrange the meat neatly.* ソースを2枚の皿に注ぎ, きちんと肉を並べる. ❏ *Don poured a generous measure of scotch into a fresh glass.* ドンはたっぷりの量のスコッチを新しいグラスに注いだ. **2** V-T 他動詞 If you **pour** someone a drink, you put some of the drink in a cup or glass so that they can drink it. 注ぐ ❏ *He got up and poured himself another drink.* 彼は立ち上がり, もう1杯注いだ. ❏ *She asked Tillie to pour her a cup of coffee.* 彼女はティリーにコーヒーを注いでくれるよう頼んだ. **3** V-I 自動詞 When a liquid or other substance **pours** somewhere, for example, through a hole, it flows quickly and in large quantities. 流れる ❏ *Blood was pouring from his broken nose.* 骨折した彼の鼻から血が流れていた. ❏ *Tears poured down both our faces.* 私達は二人とも顔に涙がとめどなく流れた. **4** V-I 自動詞 When it rains very heavily, you can say that **it is pouring**. 雨が激しく降る [usu cont] ❏ *It was still pouring outside.* 外はまだどしゃ降りだった. ❏ *The rain was pouring down.* 雨は激しく降った. **5** V-I 自動詞 If people **pour** into or out of a place, they go there quickly and in large numbers. 流れるように移動する ❏ *Any day now, the Northern forces may pour across the new border.* いつ北軍が新しい国境に押し寄せてもおかしくないだろう. ❏ *At six p.m. large groups poured from the numerous offices.* 午後6時に多数のオフィスから人が流れるように出てきた. **6** V-I 自動詞 If something such as information **pours** into a place, a lot of it is obtained or given. 押し寄せる ❏ *Martin, 78, died yesterday. Tributes poured in from around the globe.* マーティンは昨日78歳で亡くなった. 故人をたたえる言葉が世界各国から続々と送られてきた. **7** to **pour cold water on** something → see **water**
→ see **coffee**

▶ **pour out** **1** PHRASAL VERB 句動詞 If you **pour out** a drink, you put some of it in a cup or glass. 注ぐ ❏ *Larry was pouring out four glasses of champagne.* ラリーは4つのグラスにシャンペンを注いでいた. **2** PHRASAL VERB 句動詞 If you **pour out** your thoughts, feelings, or experiences, you tell someone all about them. 吐露する ❏ *I poured my thoughts out on paper in an attempt to rationalize my feelings.* 私は気持ちを整理しようとして紙に思いを書き連ねた.

Word Partnership — pour は次の語句と使われる:

N.   pour **a liquid**, pour **a mixture**, pour **water** **1**
     pour **coffee**, pour **a drink** **2**

pout /paʊt/ (**pouts, pouting, pouted**) V-I 自動詞 If someone **pouts**, they stick out their lips, usually in order to show that they are annoyed or to make themselves sexually attractive. 唇を突き出す ❏ *Like one of the kids, he whined and pouted when he did not get what he wanted.* 彼は ほしいものが手に入らない時には子供のように泣き, 膨れっ面をした. ● N-COUNT 可算名詞 **Pout** is also a noun. 不機嫌 ❏ *She shot me a reproachful pout.* 彼女はとがめるような膨れっ面を私に投げかけた.

pov|er|ty /pɒvərti/ **1** N-UNCOUNT 不可算名詞 **Poverty** is the state of being extremely poor. 貧困 ❏ *According to World Bank figures, 41 percent of Brazilians live in absolute poverty.* 世界銀行のデータによるとブラジル人の41%が絶対的貧困状態にある. **2** N-SING 単数名詞 You can use **poverty** to refer to any situation in which there is not enough of something or its quality is poor. 欠如 [FORMAL 形式ばった] [also adj, N "of" n] ❏ *...a poverty of ideas.* 発想の欠如

pow|der /paʊdər/ (**powders, powdering, powdered**) **1** N-MASS 質量名詞 **Powder** consists of many tiny particles of a solid substance. 粉, 粉末 ❏ *...cocoa powder.* 粉末ココア **2** V-T 他動詞 If a woman **powders** her face or some other part of her body, she puts face powder or talcum powder on it. パウダーをはたく, おしろいをつける ❏ *She powdered her face and applied her lipstick and rouge.* 彼女はおしろいを塗って, 口紅とほお紅をつけた.

pow|dered /paʊdərd/ ADJ 形容詞 A **powdered** substance is one that is in the form of a powder although it can come in a different form. 粉の，粉末状の ❑ *There are only two boxes of powdered milk left.* 粉ミルクが2箱しか残っていない．

pow|er /paʊər/ (powers, powering, powered) **1** N-UNCOUNT 不可算名詞 If someone has **power**, they have a lot of control over people and activities. 権力，支配力 ❑ *In a democracy, power must be divided.* 民主主義においては，権力は分割されなければならない． **2** N-UNCOUNT 不可算名詞 Your **power** to do something is your ability to do it. 能力，才能 ❑ *Human societies have the power to solve the problems confronting them.* 人間社会は直面する問題を解決する能力を持っている． ❑ *Fathers have the power to dominate children and young people.* 父親には子供や若者を支配する能力がある． **3** N-UNCOUNT 不可算名詞 If it is **in** or **within** your **power** to do something, you are able to do it or you have the resources to deal with it. 能力 ❑ *Your debt situation is only temporary, and it is within your power to resolve it.* 借金のある状態というのは一時的に過ぎない．あなたには，それを解決する能力がある． **4** N-UNCOUNT 不可算名詞 If someone in authority has the **power** to do something, they have the legal right to do it. 権限 [also N in pl] ❑ *The police have the power of arrest.* 警察には逮捕権がある． **5** N-UNCOUNT 不可算名詞 If people take **power** or come to **power**, they take charge of a country's affairs. If a group of people are **in power**, they are in charge of a country's affairs. 政権 ❑ *Idi Amin came into power several years later.* イジ・アミンは数年後に政権の座に着いた． ❑ *He first assumed power in 1970.* 彼は1970年に初めて政権に就いた． **6** N-COUNT 可算名詞 You can use **power** to refer to a country that is very rich or important, or has strong military forces. 大国，強国 ❑ *...the emergence of the new major economic power, Japan.* 新しい経済大国，日本の出現 **7** N-UNCOUNT 不可算名詞 The **power** of something is the ability that it has to move or affect things. パワー，馬力 ❑ *The vehicle had better power, better tires, and better brakes.* その車にはパワーがあり，高品質なタイヤ・ブレーキを搭載していた． **8** N-UNCOUNT 不可算名詞 **Power** is energy, especially electricity, that is obtained in large quantities from a fuel source and used to operate lights, heating, and machinery. 電力 ❑ *Nuclear power is cleaner than coal.* 原子力発電は火力発電より低公害だ． ❑ *Power has been restored to most parts that were hit last night by high winds.* 昨夜の強風により被害が出た大半の地域で電力が復旧した． **9** V-T 他動詞 The device or fuel that **powers** a machine provides the energy that the machine needs in order to work. 動力を供給する ❑ *The "flywheel" battery, it is said, could power an electric car for 600 miles on a single charge.* 「フライホイール」電池は1回の充電で電気自動車を600マイル走行可能という． **10** ADJ 形容詞 **Power** tools are operated by electricity. 電動の [ADJ n] ❑ *...large power tools, such as chainsaws.* チェーンソーのような大きい電動式の道具

▶ **power up** PHRASAL VERB 句動詞 When you **power up** something such as a computer or a machine, you connect it to a power supply and switch it on. 始動させる ❑ *Simply power up your laptop and continue work.* 単にラップトップを始動させて仕事を続けなさい．

→ see **electricity, energy, solar system**

Thesaurus power また次を参照:

N. authority, control **1**
   energy, force, intensity, potency, strength **7**

Word Partnership power は次の語句と使われる:

ADJ. divine power, political power **1**
   real power **1** **2**
   tremendous power **1** **2** **7**
   absolute power, power hungry **1** **5**
   economic power, military power **1** **6**
   electric(al) power, nuclear power, solar power **8**
V. exercise power, wield power **1** **4** **5**
   come into power, hold power, maintain power, remain in power, restore to power, rise to power, seize power, share power, take power, transfer power **5**

pow|er bro|ker (power brokers) N-COUNT 可算名詞 A **power broker** is someone who has a lot of influence, especially in politics, and uses it to help other people gain power. 陰の実力者，黒幕 ❑ *Jackson had been a major power broker in the presidential elections.* 大統領選挙においてジャクソンが主な陰の実力者だった．

pow|er cut (power cuts) N-COUNT 可算名詞 A **power cut** is a period of time when the electricity supply to a particular building or area is stopped, sometimes deliberately. 停電 [mainly BRIT 主に英国英語; AM usually **outage** 米国英語では通常 **outage**]

pow|er|ful /paʊərfəl/ **1** ADJ 形容詞 A **powerful** person or organization is able to control or influence people and events. 影響力の強い ❑ *You're a powerful man – people will listen to you.* あなたは影響力の強い人だ．人々はあなたの言うことを聞くだろう． ❑ *...Russia*

and India, two large, powerful countries. ロシアとインド，二つの影響力の強い大国 **2** ADJ 形容詞 You say that someone's body is **powerful** when it is physically strong. たくましい ❑ *Hans flexed his powerful muscles.* ハンスはたくましい力こぶを作った． ● **pow|er|ful|ly** ADV 副詞 [ADV with v] たくましく，力強く ❑ *He is described as a strong, powerfully-built man of 60.* 彼は力強く頑強な体格をした60歳の男性として画かれている． **3** ADJ 形容詞 A **powerful** machine or substance is effective because it is very strong. 馬力のある，強力な ❑ *The more powerful the car, the more difficult it is to handle.* 自動車の馬力が大きいほど運転しにくい． ❑ *...powerful computer systems.* 高性能のコンピュータ・システム ● **pow|er|ful|ly** ADV 副詞 [ADV adj] 強力に ❑ *Crack is a much cheaper, smokable form of cocaine which is powerfully addictive.* クラックは，ずっと安価で喫煙できるタイプの中毒性が強いコカインだ． **4** ADJ 形容詞 A **powerful** smell is very strong. 強烈な ❑ *There was a powerful smell of stale beer.* 気の抜けたビールの強烈なにおいがした． ● **pow|er|ful|ly** ADV 副詞 [ADV after v] 強烈に ❑ *The air smelled powerfully of dry dust.* 空気は強烈に乾いたほこりのにおいがした． **5** ADJ 形容詞 A **powerful** voice is loud and can be heard from a long way away. (声が) 大きい ❑ *At that moment Mrs. Jones's powerful voice interrupted them, announcing a visitor.* その瞬間，訪問者が来たことを知らせるジョーンズ夫人の大声で中断された． **6** ADJ 形容詞 You describe a piece of writing, speech, or work of art as **powerful** when it has a strong effect on people's feelings or beliefs. 説得力のある ❑ *...a powerful 11-part drama about a corrupt city leader.* 不正をしている市の指導者について全11話の説得力のあるドラマ ● **pow|er|ful|ly** ADV 副詞 強烈に ❑ *It's a play – painful, funny, and powerfully acted.* それは，つらくておもしろく，迫力ある演技の劇だ．

pow|er|less /paʊrlɪs/ **1** ADJ 形容詞 Someone who is **powerless** is unable to control or influence events. 無力な ❑ *If you don't have money, you're powerless.* 金がなければ，無力だ． ● **pow|er|less|ness** N-UNCOUNT 不可算名詞 無力さ ❑ *If we can't bring our problems under control, feelings of powerlessness and despair often ensue.* 問題をうまく対処できないと，しばしば無力感や失望感が生じる． **2** ADJ 形容詞 [ADJ to-inf] If you are **powerless to** do something, you are completely unable to do it. 無能な，力がない ❑ *People are being murdered every day and I am powerless to stop it.* 毎日殺人が起きているのに私にはそれを止める力がない．

pow|er line (power lines) N-COUNT 可算名詞 A **power line** is a cable, especially above ground, along which electricity is passed to an area or building. 電線

pow|er plant (power plants) N-COUNT 可算名詞 A **power plant** is the same as a **power station**. 発電所

power-sharing also power sharing N-UNCOUNT 不可算名詞 **Power-sharing** is a political arrangement in which different or opposing groups all take part in government together. 権力分担，連立政権 ❑ *They agreed a power-sharing arrangement, but it collapsed after five months.* 権力分担に合意したが，5か月後に崩壊した．

pow|er sta|tion (power stations) N-COUNT 可算名詞 A **power station** is a place where electricity is produced. 発電所

→ see **electricity**

pow|er steer|ing N-UNCOUNT 不可算名詞 In a vehicle, **power steering** is a system for steering that uses power from the engine so that it is easier for the driver to steer the vehicle. パワーステアリング，パワステ

pp. pp. is the plural of "p." and means "pages." ページ [WRITTEN 書き言葉] ❑ *See chapter 6, pp. 137-41.* 第6章137〜141ページ参照

PR /piːɑːr/ N-UNCOUNT 不可算名詞 **PR** is an abbreviation for **public relations**. 広報 [BUSINESS 実業] ❑ *It will be good PR.* いい宣伝になるだろう．

prac|ti|cable /præktɪkəbəl/ ADJ 形容詞 If a task, plan, or idea is **practicable**, people are able to carry it out. 実行可能な [FORMAL 形式ばった] ❑ *It is not practicable to offer her the original job back.* 彼女を元の仕事に戻すのは無理だ．

prac|ti|cal /præktɪkəl/ **1** ADJ 形容詞 The **practical** aspects of something involve real situations and events, rather than just ideas and theories. 実際的な，実践的な ❑ *...practical suggestions on how to increase the fiber in your daily diet.* 毎日の食事で植物繊維の摂取量を増やす方法についての実際的な提案 **2** ADJ 形容詞 You describe people as **practical** when they make sensible decisions and deal effectively with problems. 分別のある，賢明な [APPROVAL 賛成] ❑ *You were always so practical, Maria.* マリア，あなたはいつもとても賢明だったわ． ❑ *How could she be so practical when he'd just told her something so shattering?* 彼女は，彼からとても衝撃的なことを言われたばかりなのにどうしてそんなに賢明でいられるの？ **3** ADJ 形容詞 **Practical** ideas and methods are likely to be effective or successful in a real situation. 現実的な ❑ *Although the causes of cancer are being uncovered, we do not yet have any practical way to prevent it.* がんの原因は明らかになってきているが，依然として現実的な予防法はない． **4** ADJ 形容詞 You can describe clothes and things in your house as **practical** when they are suitable for a particular purpose rather than just being fashionable or attractive. 実用的な ❑ *...lightweight, practical clothes.* 軽くて実用的な服

Thesaurus practical また次を参照：

ADJ. businesslike, pragmatic, reasonable, sensible, systematic; *(ant.)* impractical **2 3**

prac|ti|cal|ity /præktɪkælɪti/ (**practicalities**) N-VAR 可変性名詞 The **practicalities of** a situation are the practical aspects of it, as opposed to its theoretical aspects. 現実 □ *Decisions about your children should be based on the practicalities of everyday life.* 子供に関する決断は日常生活の現実に基づいているべきだ.

prac|ti|cal|ly /præktɪkli/ **1** ADV 副詞 **Practically** means almost, but not completely or exactly. ほとんど，事実上 [ADV with group/cl] □ *He'd known the old man practically all his life.* 彼は事実上生まれてからずっとその老人を知っていた. **2** ADV 副詞 You use **practically** to describe something that involves real actions or events rather than ideas or theories. 実際的に，現実的に [ADV adj/-ed] □ *The course is more practically based than the master's degree.* その講座は修士課程よりも現実に基づいている.

prac|tice /præktɪs/ (**practices, practicing, practiced**) **1** N-COUNT 可算名詞 You can refer to something that people do regularly as a **practice**. 習慣，慣習 □ *Some firms have reached agreements to cut workers' pay below the level set in their contract, a practice that is illegal in Germany.* ドイツでは違法の慣習だが，契約以下の水準まで減給することに合意した会社がある. **2** N-VAR 可変性名詞 **Practice** means doing something regularly in order to be able to do it better. 練習 □ *She was taking all three of her daughters to basketball practice every day.* 彼女は3人の娘全員を毎日バスケットボールの練習に連れて行っていた. □ *...the hard practice necessary to develop from a learner to an accomplished musician.* 学習者から熟練した音楽家になるために必要な厳しい練習 **3** N-UNCOUNT 不可算名詞 The work done by doctors and lawyers is referred to as the **practice** of medicine and law. People's religious activities are referred to as the **practice** of a religion. 業務，診療，実践 □ *...maintaining or improving his skills in the practice of internal medicine.* 内科診療における彼の技術を維持，あるいは改善すること □ *I eventually realized I had to change my attitude toward medical practice.* 私は，ついに医療行為への姿勢を改めなければいけないことに気づいた. **4** N-COUNT 可算名詞 A doctor's or lawyer's **practice** is his or her business, often shared with other doctors or lawyers. 開業場所 医院，弁護士事務所 □ *The new doctor's practice was miles away from where I lived.* 新しい診療所は私の住んでいるところからずいぶん遠かった. **5** PHRASE 句 What happens **in practice** is what actually happens, in contrast to what is supposed to happen. 実際のところ □ *...the difference between foreign policy as presented to the public and foreign policy in actual practice.* 一般向けに発表された外交政策と実際に行われている外交政策の違い **6** PHRASE 句 If you **put** a belief or method **into practice**, you behave or act in accordance with it. 実行する □ *Now that he is back, the mayor has another chance to put his new ideas into practice.* 彼は復帰したので，市長としてまた新しい考えを実行に移す機会がある. **7** V-T/V-I 他動詞/自動詞 If you **practice**, or **practice** something, you keep doing it regularly in order to be able to do it better. 練習する □ *She practiced the piano in the grade school basement.* 彼女は小学校の地下室でピアノの練習をした. **8** → see also **practiced 9** V-T 他動詞 When people **practice** something such as a custom, craft, or religion, they take part in the activities associated with it. 実践する □ *Her parents had yearned to be free to practice their religion.* 彼女の両親は公然と宗教を実践できることを熱望した. □ *He was brought up in a family that practiced traditional Judaism.* 彼は伝統的なユダヤ教を実践する家族に育てられた. ● **prac|tic|ing** ADJ 形容詞 [ADJ n] 実践している □ *And he was more or less a practicing Muslim throughout his life.* そして彼は生涯を通じておおむね敬虔なイスラム教徒であった. **10** V-T 他動詞 If something cruel is regularly done to people, you can say that it **is practiced on** them. 慣習的に行う [usu passive] □ *Female circumcision is practiced on 2 million girls a year.* 陰核切除は年間2百万人の女子に行われている. **11** V-T/V-I 他動詞/自動詞 Someone who **practices** medicine or law works as a doctor or a lawyer. 開業している □ *He doesn't practice medicine for the money.* 彼はお金のために医業を営んでいるのではない. □ *...the obligations of my license to practice as a lawyer.* 弁護士として開業するための免許の義務

Thesaurus practice また次を参照：

N. custom, habit, method, procedure, system, way **1** . exercise, rehearsal, training, workout **2**

Word Partnership practice は次の語句と使われる：

PREP. **after** practice, **during** practice **2**
ADJ. **clinical** practice, **legal** practice, **medical** practice, **private** practice **3**

prac|ticed /præktɪst/ ADJ 形容詞 Someone who is **practiced at** doing something is good at it because they have had experience

and have developed their skill at it. 経験豊富な，熟練した □ *She worked for years as a bookkeeper, so she's practiced at budgeting.* 彼女は簿記係として何年も働いたので，資金計画には熟練している.

prac|ti|tion|er /præktɪʃənər/ (**practitioners**) N-COUNT 可算名詞 Doctors are sometimes referred to as **practitioners** or **medical practitioners**. 開業医 [FORMAL 形式ばった]

prag|mat|ic /prægmætɪk/ ADJ 形容詞 A **pragmatic** way of dealing with something is based on practical considerations, rather than theoretical ones. A **pragmatic** person deals with things in a practical way. 実際的な，現実的な □ *Robin took a pragmatic look at her situation.* ロビンは彼女の状況について現実的に考えた. ● **prag|mati|cal|ly** /prægmætɪkli/ ADV 副詞 実際的に，現実的に □ *"I can't ever see us doing anything else," stated Brian pragmatically.* 「私たちが以外のことをするなんて想像できない」とブライアンは現実的に言った.

prag|ma|tism /prægmətɪzəm/ N-UNCOUNT 不可算名詞 **Pragmatism** means thinking of or dealing with problems in a practical way, rather than by using theory or abstract principles. 実利主義，現実主義 [FORMAL 形式ばった] □ *She had a reputation for clear thinking and pragmatism.* 彼女は明快な思考と現実主義で評判だった. ● **prag|ma|tist** (**pragmatists**) N-COUNT 可算名詞 現実主義者 □ *He is a political pragmatist, not an idealist.* 彼は政治的現実主義者であり，理想主義者ではない.

prai|rie /prɛəri/ (**prairies**) N-VAR 可変性名詞 A **prairie** is a large area of flat, grassy land in North America. Prairies have very few trees. 大草原，プレーリー

praise /preɪz/ (**praises, praising, praised**) **1** V-T 動詞 If you **praise** someone or something, you express approval for their achievements or qualities. 称賛する，ほめる □ *The American president praised Turkey for its courage.* アメリカ大統領はトルコの勇気を称賛した. □ *Many others praised Sanford for taking a strong stand.* ほかの多くの者はサンフォードが強い姿勢をとったことを称賛しました. **2** N-UNCOUNT 不可算名詞 **Praise** is what you say or write about someone when you are praising them. 称賛，褒め言葉 □ *All the ladies are full of praise for the staff and service they received.* 女性全員がスタッフとサービスのよさを褒めちぎった. □ *I have nothing but praise for the police.* 警察に対して称賛以外に言葉はない.

Thesaurus praise また次を参照：

N. applause, compliment, congratulations; *(ant.)* criticism, insult **2**

pram /præm/ (**prams**) N-COUNT 可算名詞 A **pram** is the same as a **baby carriage**. ベビーカー，乳母車 [BRIT 英国英語]

prank /præŋk/ (**pranks**) N-COUNT 可算名詞 A **prank** is a childish trick. いたずら [OLD-FASHIONED 古風な] □ *Their pranks are amusing at times.* 彼らのいたずらは時には愉快だ.

pray /preɪ/ (**prays, praying, prayed**) **1** V-I 自動詞 When people **pray**, they speak to God in order to give thanks or to ask for his help. 祈る □ *He spent his time in prison praying and studying.* 彼は祈りをささげたり勉強したりと刑務所での時を過ごした. □ *Now all we have to do is help ourselves and pray to God.* 今我々がするべきことは互いに助け合い神に祈ることだけです. **2** V-T 他動詞 When someone is hoping very much that something will happen, you can say that they **are praying** that it will happen. 願う，望む [usu cont] □ *I'm just praying that somebody in Congress will do something before it's too late.* 国会議員のだれかが手遅れにならないうちに行動することをただ祈っています.

→ see **religion**

prayer /prɛər/ (**prayers**) **1** N-UNCOUNT 不可算名詞 **Prayer** is the activity of speaking to God. 祈り □ *They had joined a religious order and dedicated their lives to prayer and good works.* 彼らは教団に入団し，人生を祈りと善行にささげた. **2** N-COUNT 可算名詞 A **prayer** is the words a person says when they speak to God. 祈りの言葉 □ *They should take a little time and say a prayer for the people on both sides.* 彼らは少し時間をとって双方の人々のために祈るべきだ. **3** N-COUNT 可算名詞 You can refer to a strong hope that you have as your **prayer**. 願い，望み □ *This drug could be the answer to our prayers.* この薬で私たちの望みがかなうかもしれない. **4** N-PLURAL 複数名詞 A short religious service at which people gather to pray can be referred to as **prayers**. 礼拝 □ *He promised that the boy would be back at school in time for evening prayers.* 少年が夕方の礼拝に間に合うように学校に戻ると彼は約束した.

preach /priːtʃ/ (**preaches, preaching, preached**) **1** V-T/V-I 他動詞/自動詞 When a member of the clergy **preaches** a sermon, he or she gives a talk on a religious or moral subject during a religious service. 説教する □ *At High Mass the priest preached a sermon on the devil.* 盛大なミサで牧師は悪魔についての説教をした. □ *The bishop preached to a crowd of several hundred local people.* 司教は数百人の地元の人々の群集に説教をした. **2** V-T/V-I 他動詞/自動詞 When people **preach** a belief or a course of action, they try to persuade other people to accept the belief or to take the course of action. 伝道す

る，唱導する □*He said he was trying to preach peace and tolerance to his people.* 彼は，人々に平和と忍耐について唱導しようとしていると言った．□*Health experts are now preaching that even a little exercise is far better than none at all.* 最近健康の専門家は，少しの運動でも全く運動しないよりずっと健康によいことを唱道している．**3** V-I 自動詞 If someone gives you advice in a very serious, boring way, you can say that they **are preaching at** you. (けなして) お説教をする [DISAPPROVAL 不賛成] □*"Don't preach at me," he shouted.* 「お説教はやめてくれ」と彼はどなった．

preach|er /priː**tʃ**ər/ (**preachers**) N-COUNT 可算名詞 A **preacher** is a person, usually a member of the clergy, who preaches sermons as part of a church service. 説教師，伝道者

pre|cari|ous /prɪ**keə**riəs/ **1** ADJ 形容詞 If your situation is **precarious**, you are not in complete control of events and might fail in what you are doing at any moment. 不安定な，心もとない □*Our financial situation had become precarious.* 我々の財政状況は不安定になっていた．● **pre|cari|ous|ly** ADV 副詞 不安定な状態で □*We lived precariously. I suppose I wanted to squeeze as much pleasure from each day as I possibly could.* 我々は不安定な状態で暮らしていた．我々はできる限り楽しみを搾り出そうとしていたと思う．**2** ADJ 形容詞 Something that is **precarious** is not securely held in place and seems likely to fall or collapse at any moment. 落ちそうな，危なっかしい □*They looked really comical as they crawled up precarious ladders.* 彼らが危なっかしいはしごをはい上がるとき本当にこっけいに見えた．● **pre|cari|ous|ly** ADV 副詞 落ちそうで，ぐらぐらして □*One of my grocery bags was still precariously perched on the car bumper.* 買い物袋の1つがまだ車のバンパーに今にも落ちそうな状態で載っかっていた．

| Word Link | | caut ≈ taking care : caution, cautious, precaution |

| Word Link | | pre ≈ before : precaution, precede, prefix |

pre|cau|tion /prɪ**kɔː**ʃ°n/ (**precautions**) N-COUNT 可算名詞 A **precaution** is an action that is intended to prevent something dangerous or unpleasant from happening. 予防措置，予防対策 □*Could he not, just as a precaution, move to a place of safety?* 念のため，彼を安全な場所に移動できますか？

Word Partnership	precaution は次の語句と使われる：
ADV.	**(just) as a** precaution
V.	**take every** precaution

pre|cede /prɪ**siː**d/ (**precedes, preceding, preceded**) **1** V-T 他動詞 If one event or period of time **precedes** another, it happens before it. ～より先に起こる，先行する [FORMAL 形式ばった] □*Intensive negotiations between the main parties preceded the vote.* 選挙の前に主な政党間で集中的な交渉が行われた．□*The earthquake was preceded by a loud roar and lasted 20 seconds.* 轟くようなどろき音に続いて地震が発生し20秒間続きました．**2** V-T 他動詞 If you **precede** someone somewhere, you go in front of them. 先導する [FORMAL 形式ばった] □*He gestured to Alice to precede them from the room.* 彼はアリスに部屋から彼らを先導するように合図した．**3** V-T 他動詞 A sentence, paragraph, or chapter that **precedes** another one comes just before it. ～の前に来る □*Look at the information preceding the paragraph in question.* 問題のパラグラフの前に来る内容を見なさい．

prec|edence /**pres**ɪdəns/ N-UNCOUNT 不可算名詞 If one thing takes **precedence over** another, it is regarded as more important than the other thing. 優先，優位 □*Have as much fun as possible at college, but don't let it take precedence over work.* 大学生活をできるだけ楽しみなさい．だからといって勉強よりも遊びを優先させてはいけません．

prec|edent /**pres**ɪdənt/ (**precedents**) N-VAR 可変性名詞 If there is a **precedent for** an action or event, it has happened before, and this can be regarded as an argument for doing it again. 前例 [FORMAL 形式ばった] □*The trial could set an important precedent for dealing with similar cases.* その裁判は似たようなケースを扱う重要な前例になるかもしれない．

pre|cept /**priː**sept/ (**precepts**) N-COUNT 可算名詞 A **precept** is a general rule that helps you to decide how you should behave in particular circumstances. 教え，教訓 [FORMAL 形式ばった] □*...an electoral process based on the central precept that all people are born equal.* 人は皆平等に生まれたという重要な規範に基づいた選挙過程

pre|cinct /**priː**sɪŋkt/ (**precincts**) N-COUNT 可算名詞 A **precinct** is a part of a city or town that has its own police force. 行政区 [AM 米国英語] □*The shooting occurred in the 34th Precinct.* 襲撃事件は第34区で発生しました．

pre|cious /**pre**ʃəs/ **1** ADJ 形容詞 If you say that something such as a resource is **precious**, you mean that it is valuable and should not be wasted or used badly. 貴重な □*After four months in foreign parts, every hour at home was precious.* 海外で4か月過ごした後なので，母国で過ごす時間はすべて貴重だった．□*A family break allows you to spend precious time together.* 家族旅行をすることで貴重な時間を共に

過ごすことができる．**2** ADJ 形容詞 **Precious** objects and materials are worth a lot of money because they are rare. 高価な □*...jewelry and precious objects belonging to her mother.* 彼女の母親が所有している宝石や高貴な品 **3** ADJ 形容詞 If something is **precious** to you, you regard it as important and do not want to lose it. 大切な □*Her family's support is particularly precious to Josie.* 家族のサポートはジョージーにとって特に大切だ．

pre|cipi|tate (**precipitates, precipitating, precipitated**)

> The verb is pronounced /prɪ**sɪp**ɪteɪt/. The adjective is pronounced /prɪ**sɪp**ɪtɪt/.
>
> 動詞は /prɪ**sɪp**ɪteɪt/ と発音される．形容詞は /prɪ**sɪp**ɪtɪt/ と発音される．

1 V-T 他動詞 If something **precipitates** an event or situation, usually a bad one, it causes it to happen suddenly or sooner than normal. 招く，誘発する [FORMAL 形式ばった] □*The killings in Vilnius have precipitated the worst crisis yet.* ヴィルニアスでの殺りくはこれまでで最悪の危機を誘発した．**2** ADJ 形容詞 A **precipitate** action or decision happens or is made more quickly or suddenly than most people think is sensible. 性急な，軽率な [FORMAL 形式ばった] □*I don't think we should make precipitate decisions.* 軽率な決定を下すべきではないと思う．

pre|cise /prɪ**saɪ**s/ **1** ADJ 詞 You use **precise** to emphasize that you are referring to an exact thing, rather than something vague. まさにその [EMPHASIS 強調] [ADJ n] □*I can remember the precise moment when my daughter came to see me and her new baby brother in the hospital.* 娘が病院に私と生まれたばかりの弟を見に来てくれたさにその瞬間を思い出せる．□*The precise location of the wreck was discovered in 1988.* 難破船の正確な位置が1988年に発見された．**2** ADJ 形容詞 Something that is **precise** is exact and accurate in all its details. 正確な □*They speak very precise English.* 彼らは非常に正確な英語を話す．

pre|cise|ly /prɪ**saɪ**sli/ **1** ADV 副詞 **Precisely** means accurately and exactly. 正確に □*Nobody knows precisely how many people are still living in the camp.* 何人がまだ収容所に住んでいるかをだれも正確に知らない．□*The first bell rang at precisely 10:29 a.m.* 最初のベルは午前10時29分ちょうどに鳴った．**2** ADV 副詞 You can use **precisely** to emphasize that a reason or fact is the only important one there is, or that it is obvious. まさに [EMPHASIS 強調] [ADV with cl/group] □*Children come to zoos precisely to see captive animals.* 子供たちはまさに檻の中の動物を見物するために動物園に来る．**3** ADV 副詞 You can say "**precisely**" to confirm in an emphatic way that what someone has just said is true. その通り [EMPHASIS 強調] [as reply] □*"All I did was write the truth." — "Precisely! Now everyone knows."* 「私は真実を書いただけです」 「その通り！だからみんなが知っているんです」

pre|ci|sion /prɪ**sɪ**ʒ°n/ N-UNCOUNT 不可算名詞 If you do something **with precision**, you do it exactly as it should be done. 正確さ □*The choir sang with precision.* 合唱団は正確に歌った．

pre|clude /prɪ**kluː**d/ (**precludes, precluding, precluded**) **1** V-T 他動詞 If something **precludes** an event or action, it prevents the event or action from happening. 妨げる [FORMAL 形式ばった] □*At 84, John feels his age precludes too much travel.* 84歳でジョンは年齢のためあまりたくさんの旅行ができないと感じる．**2** V-T 他動詞 If something **precludes** you **from** doing something or going somewhere, it prevents you from doing it or going there. 不可能にする [FORMAL 形式ばった] □*A constitutional amendment precludes any president from serving more than two terms.* 憲法改正により大統領は2期以上任期を勤めることができなくなる．

pre|co|cious /prɪ**koʊ**ʃəs/ ADJ 形容詞 A **precocious** child is very clever, mature, or good at something, often in a way that you usually only expect to find in an adult. 早熟な，ませた □*She burst on to the world tennis scene as a precocious 14-year-old.* 彼女は早熟な14歳児として世界のテニス界に突然姿を現した．

pre|con|cep|tion /prɪ**kən**sep**ʃ°n/ (**preconceptions**) N-COUNT 可算名詞 Your **preconceptions** about something are beliefs formed about it before you have enough information or experience. 先入観，偏見 □*Did you have any preconceptions about the sort of people who did computing?* コンピュータを使用するタイプの人々についてなにか先入観を持っていましたか．

pre|con|di|tion /prɪ**kən**dɪ**ʃ°n/ (**preconditions**) N-COUNT 可算名詞 If one thing is a **precondition for** another, it must happen or be done before the second thing can happen or exist. 前提条件 [FORMAL 形式ばった] □*They have demanded the release of three prisoners as a precondition for any negotiation.* 彼らは，交渉の前提条件として3人の囚人の釈放を求めた．

pre|cur|sor /prɪ**kɜː**rsər/ (**precursors**) N-COUNT 可算名詞 A **precursor** of something is a similar thing that happened or existed before it, often something that led to the existence or development of that thing. 先駆者，前触れ □*He said that the deal should not be seen as a precursor to a merger.* 彼は，取引が企業合併への前触れだと見なされるべきではないと言った．

preda|tor /prɛdətər/ (**predators**) 1 N-COUNT 可算名詞 A **predator** is an animal that kills and eats other animals. 捕食動物 ❑With no natural predators on the island, the herd increased rapidly. 島に天敵がいないので、群れは急速に数を増やした. 2 N-COUNT 可算名詞 People sometimes refer to predatory people or organizations as **predators**. 買収をもくろむ企業、相手を食い物にする人 ❑Rumors of a takeover by Hanson are probably far-fetched, but the company is worried about other predators. ハンソン社による乗っ取りのうわさはおそらくありえないが、その会社は他会社による買収を懸念している.
→ see **food, shark**

Word Link ory ≈ relating to : advisory, contradictory, predatory

preda|tory /prɛdətɔri/ 1 ADJ 形容詞 **Predatory** animals live by killing other animals for food. 捕食性の ❑...predatory birds like the eagle. ワシのような捕食鳥 2 ADJ 形容詞 **Predatory** people or organizations are eager to gain something out of someone else's weakness or suffering. 人の弱みに付け込む ❑People will not set up new businesses while they are frightened by the predatory behavior of the banks. 銀行の捕食的な態度に脅かされている間はだれも新しいビジネスを立ち上げようとしない.

pre|de|ces|sor /prɛdɪsɛsər/ (**predecessors**) 1 N-COUNT 可算名詞 Your **predecessor** is the person who had your job before you. 前任者 ❑He maintained that he learned everything he knew from his predecessor. 彼は、知っていることはすべて前任者から学んだと言い張った. 2 N-COUNT 可算名詞 The **predecessor** of an object or machine is the object or machine that came before it in a sequence or process of development. 前作、旧型 ❑Although the car is some 2 inches shorter than its predecessor, its trunk is 20 percent larger. その自動車は前モデルより2インチ短いが、トランクは20%大きい.

pre|dica|ment /prɪdɪkəmənt/ (**predicaments**) N-COUNT 可算名詞 If you are in a **predicament**, you are in an unpleasant situation that is difficult to get out of. 苦境、窮地 ❑Hank explained our predicament. ハンクは我々の苦境について説明した.

Word Link dict ≈ speaking : contradict, dictate, predict

pre|dict /prɪdɪkt/ (**predicts, predicting, predicted**) V-T 他動詞 If you **predict** an event, you say that it will happen. 予測する ❑The latest opinion polls are predicting a very close contest. 最近の世論調査によると激戦が予想される. ❑He predicted that my hair would grow back "in no time." 私の髪は「すぐに」元の長さに伸びると彼は予測した.
→ see **experiment, forecast**

pre|dict|able /prɪdɪktəbl/ ADJ 形容詞 If you say that an event is **predictable**, you mean that it is obvious in advance that it will happen. 予想通りの ❑This was a predictable reaction, given the bitter hostility between the two countries. 2国間の激しい敵意を考慮に入れると、これは予想通りの反応だった. ● **pre|dict|ably** ADV 副詞 予想通りに ❑His article is, predictably, a scathing attack on capitalism. 彼の記事では予想通り資本主義に対する痛烈な非難が書かれている. ● **pre|dict|abil|ity** /prɪdɪktəbɪlɪti/ N-UNCOUNT 不可算名詞 予想通りであること ❑Your mother values the predictability of your Sunday calls. お母さんはあなたが予想通り毎週日曜日に電話をすることを大切に思っている.

pre|dic|tion /prɪdɪkʃən/ (**predictions**) N-VAR 可変性名詞 If you make a **prediction** about something, you say what you think will happen. 予測、予想 ❑He was unwilling to make a prediction for the coming year. 彼は新しい年について予測を立てるのを嫌がった. ❑Weather prediction has never been a perfect science. 天気予報はこれまで科学的にかんぺきだったことがない.
→ see **science**

pre|dis|pose /prɪdɪspoʊz/ (**predisposes, predisposing, predisposed**) 1 V-T 他動詞 If something **predisposes** you to think or behave in a particular way, it makes it likely that you will think or behave in that way. 〜するようになる [FORMAL 形式ばった] ❑They take pains to hire people whose personalities predispose them to serve customers well. 彼らは、客応対が上手にできるような性格の人々を苦心して採用する. ● **pre|dis|posed** ADJ 形容詞 [v-link ADJ] 傾向がある ❑...people who are predisposed to violent crime. 暴力的な犯罪を犯す傾向がある人々 2 V-T 他動詞 If something **predisposes** you **to** a disease or illness, it makes it likely that you will suffer from that disease or illness. （病気に）かかりやすくする [FORMAL 形式ばった] ❑...a gene that predisposes people to alcoholism. アルコール依存症の素因となる遺伝子 ● **pre|dis|posed** ADJ 形容詞 [v-link ADJ] 素因を持っている ❑Some people are genetically predisposed to diabetes. 糖尿病の遺伝的素因を持った人々もいる.

pre|dis|po|si|tion /prɪdɪspəzɪʃən/ (**predispositions**) 1 N-COUNT 可算名詞 If you have a **predisposition to** behave in a particular way, you tend to behave like that because of the kind of person you are or the attitudes you have. 傾向 [FORMAL 形式ばった] ❑There is a thin dividing line between educating the public and creating a predisposition to panic. 国民を啓もうすることとパニックへの傾向を作り出すことは紙一重だ. 2 N-COUNT 可算名詞 If you have a **predisposition to** a disease or illness, it is likely that you will suffer from that disease or illness. 素因 [FORMAL 形式ばった]

❑...a genetic predisposition to lung cancer. 肺がんの遺伝的素因

Word Link dom, domin ≈ rule, master : domain, dominate, predominant

pre|domi|nant /prɪdɒmɪnənt/ ADJ 形容詞 If something is **predominant**, it is more important or noticeable than anything else in a set of people or things. 優勢な、支配的な ❑Mandy's predominant emotion was confusion. マンディの主な感情は当惑だった.

pre|domi|nant|ly /prɪdɒmɪnəntli/ ADV 副詞 You use **predominantly** to indicate which feature or quality is most noticeable in a situation. 主に、大部分は ❑The landscape has remained predominantly rural in appearance. 風景の大部分は外見上は依然として田園風のままだった.

pre|domi|nate /prɪdɒmɪneɪt/ (**predominates, predominating, predominated**) 1 V-I 自動詞 If one type of person or thing **predominates** in a group, there is more of that type of person or thing in the group than of any other. 大勢を占める [FORMAL 形式ばった] ❑In older age groups women predominate because men tend to die younger. 男性のほうが寿命が短い傾向があるため高年齢層では女性が大勢を占める. 2 V-I 自動詞 When a feature or quality **predominates**, it is the most important or noticeable one in a situation. 優位に立っている、優勢である [FORMAL 形式ばった] ❑He wants to create a society where Islamic principles predominate. 彼は、イスラム教原理が優勢な社会を作りたがっています.

pre|emi|nent /priɛmɪnənt/ also **pre-eminent** ADJ 形容詞 If someone or something is **preeminent** in a group, they are more important, powerful, or capable than other people or things in the group. 卓越した、傑出した [FORMAL 形式ばった] ❑...some of the preeminent names in baseball. 野球業界で卓越した選手たち ● **pre|emi|nence** /priɛmɪnəns/ N-UNCOUNT 不可算名詞 卓越、傑出 ❑Europe was poised to reassert its traditional preeminence in Western art. ヨーロッパは、西洋美術において伝統的傑出を再度強調する態勢をとっていました.

pre|empt /priɛmpt/ (**preempts, preempting, preempted**) also **pre-empt** V-T 他動詞 If you **preempt** an action, you prevent it from happening by doing something that makes it unnecessary or impossible. 先手を打つ ❑The law would preempt stronger local rules. その法律は地元のより厳しい規則の先手を打つのだろう. ❑"the survival of the fittest," a slogan that virtually preempted all debate. 事実上すべての議論の先手を打ったスローガン「適者生存」

pre|emp|tive /priɛmptɪv/ also **pre-emptive** ADJ 形容詞 A **preemptive** attack or strike is intended to weaken or damage an enemy or opponent, for example, by destroying their weapons before they can do any harm. 先制の ❑A preemptive strike against a sovereign nation raises moral and legal issues. 主権国家に対する先制攻撃は道徳問題と法律問題を引き起こす.

pref|ace /prɛfɪs/ (**prefaces, prefacing, prefaced**) 1 N-COUNT 可算名詞 A **preface** is an introduction at the beginning of a book that explains what the book is about or why it was written. 前書き、序文 ❑...the preface to Kelman's novel. ケルマンの小説の前書き 2 V-T 他動詞 If you **preface** an action or speech **with** something else, you do or say this other thing first. 前置きをする ❑I will preface what I am going to say with a few lines from Shakespeare. スピーチの前置きとしてシェークスピアから数節引用する.

pre|fer /prɪfɜr/ (**prefers, preferring, preferred**) V-T 他動詞 If you **prefer** someone or something, you like that person or thing better than another, and so you are more likely to choose them if there is a choice. 〜の方が好きだ [no cont] ❑Does he prefer a particular sort of music? 彼は特に好きなタイプの音楽がありますか. ❑I became a teacher because I preferred books and people to politics. 私は、政治よりも本や人のほうが好きなので教師になりました. ❑I prefer to think of peace not war. 私は戦争ではなく平和を思うことの方が好きです. ❑I would prefer him to be with us next season. 来シーズンも彼に当チームに在籍していて欲しいと思っています.

Note that **prefer** can often sound rather formal in ordinary conversation. Verbal expressions such as **like...better** and **would rather** are used more frequently. For example, instead of saying "I prefer football to tennis," you can say "**I like football better than tennis**," instead of "I'd prefer an apple," you can say "**I'd rather have an apple**," and instead of "I'd prefer to walk," you can say "**I'd rather walk**."

pref|er|able /prɛfərəbl, prɛfrə-, prɪfɜrə-/ ADJ 形容詞 If you say that one thing is **preferable to** another, you mean that it is more desirable or suitable. より望ましい ❑A big earthquake a long way off is preferable to a smaller one nearby. 遠隔地での大地震は近隣地での小地震よりましだ. ❑Prevention of a problem is always preferable to trying to cure it. 問題を予防することは治療しようとすることよりも常に望ましい. ● **pref|er|ably** /prɛfərəbli, prɛfrə-, prɪfɜrə-/ ADV 副詞 できれば ❑Do something creative or take exercise, preferably in the fresh air. クリエイティブなことをするか運動をしなさい. できれば新鮮な空気のもとで.

pref|er|ence /ˈprɛfərəns/ (preferences) **1** N-VAR 可変性名詞 If you have a **preference for** something, you would like to have or do that thing rather than something else. 好み，希望 □ *It upset her when men revealed a preference for her sister.* 男性が彼女の妹を好んでいるのが明らかになったとき，彼女は取り乱した． **2** N-UNCOUNT 不可算名詞 If you **give preference to** someone with a particular qualification or feature, you choose them rather than someone else. 優先，優遇 □ *The Pentagon has said it will give preference to companies with which it can do business electronically.* 米国国防総省は，電子的にビジネスを行える会社を優遇すると発表した．

pref|er|ence shares **1** N-PLURAL 複数名詞 **Preference shares** are the same as **preferred stock**. 優先株 [BRIT 英国英語 BUSINESS 実業] **2** → see also **ordinary shares**

pref|er|en|tial /ˌprɛfəˈrɛnʃ°l/ ADJ 形容詞 If you get **preferential** treatment, you are treated better than other people and therefore have an advantage over them. 優遇の □ *Firstborn sons received preferential treatment.* 長男は優遇された．

pre|ferred stock N-UNCOUNT 不可算名詞 **Preferred stock** is the shares in a company that are owned by people who have the right to receive part of the company's profits before the holders of common stock. They also have the right to have their capital repaid if the company fails and has to close. Compare **common stock**. 優先株 [AM 米国英語 BUSINESS 実業]

Word Link	fix ≈ fastening : affix, prefix, suffix

Word Link	pre ≈ before : precaution, precede, prefix

pre|fix /ˈpriːfɪks/ (prefixes) **1** N-COUNT 可算名詞 A **prefix** is a letter or group of letters, for example, "un-" or "multi-," that is added to the beginning of a word in order to form a different word. For example, the prefix "un-" is added to "happy" to form "unhappy." Compare **affix** and **suffix**. 接頭辞 **2** N-COUNT 可算名詞 A **prefix** is one or more numbers or letters added to the beginning of a code number to indicate, for example, what area something belongs to. 識別番号 □ *To telephone from the U.S. use the prefix 011 33 before the numbers given here.* 米国から電話をするには，ここに書いてある番号の前に識別番号の011 33をかけなさい．

preg|nan|cy /ˈprɛgnənsi/ (pregnancies) N-VAR 可変性名詞 **Pregnancy** is the condition of being pregnant or the period of time during which a female is pregnant. 妊娠，妊娠期間 □ *It would be wiser to cut out all alcohol during pregnancy.* 妊娠中はアルコール類を全面的に控える方がよい．

preg|nant /ˈprɛgnənt/ **1** ADJ 形容詞 If a woman or female animal is **pregnant**, she has a baby or babies developing in her body. 妊娠している □ *Lena got pregnant and married.* リーナは妊娠し，結婚した． **2** ADJ 形容詞 A **pregnant** silence or moment has a special meaning that is not obvious but that people are aware of. 意味深長な [ADJ n, v-link ADJ "with" n] □ *There was a long, pregnant silence, which Mrs. Madrigal punctuated by reaching for the check.* 長く意味深長な沈黙があったが，マドリガル夫人が勘定書に手を伸ばして中断した．

Word Partnership	pregnant は次の語句と使われる：
N.	pregnant with a baby/child, pregnant mother, pregnant wife, pregnant woman **1**
V.	be pregnant, become pregnant, get pregnant **1**

pre|heat /ˌpriːˈhiːt/ (preheats, preheating, preheated) V-T 他動詞 If you **preheat** an oven, you switch it on and allow it to reach a certain temperature before you put food inside it. 余熱で温める □ *Preheat the oven to 400 degrees.* オーブンを余熱で400度に温めなさい．

pre|his|tor|ic /ˌpriːhɪˈstɔrɪk/ ADJ 形容詞 **Prehistoric** people and things existed at a time before information was written down. 先史時代の，有史以前の □ *...the famous prehistoric cave paintings of Lascaux.* 有名なラスコーの先史時代の洞くつ壁画

preju|dice /ˈprɛdʒədɪs/ (prejudices, prejudicing, prejudiced) **1** N-VAR 可変性名詞 **Prejudice** is an unreasonable dislike of a particular group of people or things, or a preference for one group of people or things over another. 偏見 □ *There was a deep-rooted racial prejudice long before the two countries went to war.* 2国が戦争を開始するずっと前から根強い人種偏見があった． □ *There is widespread prejudice against workers over 45.* 45歳以上の労働者に対して偏見が広がっている． **2** V-T 他動詞 If you **prejudice** someone or something, you influence them so that they are unfair in some way. 偏見を抱かせる □ *I think your upbringing has prejudiced you.* あなたは育ちのせいで偏見を抱くようになったんだと思う． □ *The report was held back for fear of prejudicing his trial.* 彼の裁判に先入観を与えるのを恐れて，報告書は差し控えられた． **3** V-T 他動詞 If someone **prejudices** another person's situation, they do something that makes it worse than it should be. 害する [FORMAL 形式ばった] □ *Her study was not in any way intended to prejudice the future development of the college.* 彼女の研

究には，大学の未来開発に害を与えるような意図は全くなかった．

Thesaurus	prejudice また次を参照：
N.	bias, bigotry, disapproval, intolerance; (ant.) tolerance **1**

preju|diced /ˈprɛdʒədɪst/ ADJ 形容詞 A person who is **prejudiced** against someone from a different racial group has an unreasonable dislike of them. 偏見を持った □ *Some landlords and landladies are racially prejudiced.* 人種偏見を持った家主もいる．

pre|limi|nary /prɪˈlɪmɪnɛri/ (preliminaries) **1** ADJ 形容詞 **Preliminary** activities or discussions take place at the beginning of an event, often as a form of preparation. 予備的な，仮の □ *Preliminary results show the Republican Party with 11 percent of the vote.* 仮集計結果では，共和党が11%の票を獲得しています． **2** N-COUNT 可算名詞 A **preliminary** is something that you do at the beginning of an activity, often as a form of preparation. 予備段階，下準備 □ *You all know why I am here. So I won't waste time on preliminaries.* 皆さんは，私がここにいる理由を知っています．ですから前置きで時間を無駄にはしません．

prel|ude /ˈprɛljuːd, ˈpreɪluːd/ (preludes) N-COUNT 可算名詞 You can describe an event as a **prelude to** another event or activity when it happens before it and acts as an introduction to it. 前触れ，前兆 □ *For him, reading was a necessary prelude to sleep.* 彼にとっては，就寝前の読書は欠かせない．

prema|ture /ˌpriːməˈtʃʊər/ **1** ADJ 形容詞 Something that is **premature** happens earlier than usual or earlier than people expect. 時期尚早の □ *Accidents are still the number one cause of premature death for Americans.* 交通事故は依然としてアメリカ人若年齢層の死因第1位です． □ *His career was brought to a premature end by a succession of knee injuries.* 彼のキャリアはひざの故障が続いたために時期尚早の終わりとなった． ● **prema|ture|ly** ADV 副詞 □ *The war and the years in the harsh mountains had prematurely aged him.* 戦争と過酷な山々で過ごした年月のために彼は早老した． **2** ADJ 形容詞 You can say that something is **premature** when it happens too early and is therefore inappropriate. 早熟の □ *It now seems their optimism was premature.* 今や彼らの楽観論は早とちりだったようだ． ● **prema|ture|ly** ADV 副詞 早すぎて □ *He was careful not to celebrate prematurely.* 彼はお祝いを急ぎ過ぎないように気をつけた． **3** ADJ 形容詞 A **premature** baby is one that was born before the date when it was expected to be born. 早産の □ *Even very young premature babies respond to their mother's presence.* 超未熟児でさえ母親の存在に反応する． ● **prema|ture|ly** ADV 副詞 [ADV after v] 早産で □ *Danny was born prematurely, weighing only 3lb 3oz.* ダニーは早産で生まれ，体重はほんの3ポンド3オンスだった．

prem|ier /prɪˈmɪər/ (premiers) **1** N-COUNT 可算名詞 The leader of the government of a country is sometimes referred to as the country's **premier**. 首相 □ *...Australian premier Paul Keating.* オーストラリアのポール・キーティング首相 **2** ADJ 形容詞 **Premier** is used to describe something that is considered to be the best or most important thing of a particular type. 最高の，最も重要な [ADJ n] □ *...the country's premier opera company.* その国最高の歌劇団

premi|ere /prɪˈmɪər, prɪˈmjɛər/ (premieres, premiering, premiered) **1** N-COUNT 可算名詞 The **premiere** of a new play or movie is the first public performance of it. 初日，初演，プレミア □ *Four astronauts visited for last week's premiere of the movie Space Station.* 4人の宇宙飛行士が映画「スペース・ステーション」の先週のプレミア上映のために訪れた． **2** V-T/V-I 他動詞/自動詞 When a movie or show **premieres** or is **premiered**, it is shown to an audience for the first time. 封切られる，初演される □ *The documentary premiered at the Jerusalem Film Festival.* そのドキュメンタリー映画はエルサレム映画祭で封切られた．

prem|ier|ship /prɪˈmɪərʃɪp/ N-SING 単数名詞 The **premiership** of a leader of a government is the period of time during which they are the leader. 首相の任期 □ *...the final years of Margaret Thatcher's premiership.* マーガレット・サッチャー首相の任期の最後の数年

prem|ise /ˈprɛmɪs/ (premises) **1** N-PLURAL 複数名詞 The **premises** of a business or an institution are all the buildings and land that it occupies in one place. 敷地，建物 □ *There is a kitchen on the premises.* 建物にはキッチンがある． **2** N-COUNT 可算名詞 A **premise** is something that you suppose is true and that you use as a basis for developing an idea. 前提 [FORMAL 形式ばった] □ *The premise is that schools will work harder to improve if they must compete.* 各学校が競争を強いられれば改善のためにさらに努力をするだろうというのが前提です．

pre|mium /ˈpriːmiəm/ (premiums) **1** N-COUNT 可算名詞 A **premium** is a sum of money that you pay regularly to an insurance company for an insurance policy. 保険料 □ *It is too early to say whether premiums will be affected.* 保険料が影響されるかどうかを発表するには時期尚早だ． **2** N-COUNT 可算名詞 A **premium** is a sum of money that you have to pay for something

in addition to the normal cost. 割増金 □ *Even if customers want "solutions," most are not willing to pay a premium for them.* たとえ客は「解決」を望んでいたとしても、そのために余分な支払いをすることには乗り気でない人がほとんどんだ。 ❸ ADJ 形容詞 **Premium** products are of a higher than usual quality and are often expensive. 高級な [ADJ n] □ *At the premium end of the market, business is booming.* 市場の最高級レベルでは好景気だ。 ❹ PHRASE 句 If something is **at a premium**, it is wanted or needed, but is difficult to get or achieve. 大いに需要があって、品不足で □ *If space is at a premium, choose adaptable furniture that won't fill the room.* スペースに余裕がないなら、部屋がいっぱいにならないような応用の利く家具を選びなさい。 ❺ PHRASE 句 If you buy or sell something **at a premium**, you buy or sell it at a higher price than usual, for example, because it is in short supply. プレミアム価格で □ *He eventually sold the shares back to the bank at a premium.* 彼は最終的にはその株を銀行にプレミアム価格で売り戻した。

premo|ni|tion /priːmənɪʃⁿn, prɛm-/ (**premonitions**) N-COUNT 可算名詞 If you have a **premonition**, you have a feeling that something is going to happen, often something unpleasant. (いやな) 予感 □ *He had an unshakable premonition that he would die.* 死ぬだろうという確かな予感がした。

pre|na|tal /priːneɪtⁿl/ ADJ 形容詞 **Prenatal** is used to describe things relating to the medical care of women during pregnancy. 出生前の □ *I'd met her briefly in a prenatal class.* 私は彼女に母親学級でちらりと会いました。

pre|oc|cu|pa|tion /priːɒkjəpeɪʃⁿn/ (**preoccupations**) ❶ N-COUNT 可算名詞 If you have a **preoccupation with** something or someone, you keep thinking about them because they are important to you. 大きな関心事 □ *Karouzos's poetry shows a profound preoccupation with the Orthodox Church.* カルーゾスの詩は正教会への深い関心を示している。 ❷ N-UNCOUNT 不可算名詞 **Preoccupation** is a state of mind in which you think about something so much that you do not consider other things to be important. 没頭、夢中 □ *The arrest of Senator Pinochet has created a climate of preoccupation among our citizens.* ピノチェト議員の逮捕に国民の気が取られた。

pre|oc|cu|pied /priːɒkjəpaɪd/ ADJ 形容詞 If you are **preoccupied**, you are thinking a lot about something or someone, and so you hardly notice other things. 心を奪われた □ *Tom Banbury was preoccupied with the missing Shepherd child and did not want to devote time to the new murder.* トム・バンベリーはシェパードさんの子が行方不明になっていることで頭がいっぱいで新しい殺人事件に時間を費やしたくなかった。

pre|oc|cu|py /priːɒkjəpaɪ/ (**preoccupies, preoccupying, preoccupied**) V-T 他動詞 If something **is preoccupying** you, you are thinking about it a lot. 夢中にする、心を奪う □ *Crime and the fear of crime preoccupy the community.* 犯罪と犯罪への恐怖で地域社会は悩んでいる。

pre|paid /priːpeɪd/ ADJ 形容詞 **Prepaid** items are paid for in advance, before the time when you would normally pay for them. プリペイド式の、前払いの □ *...prepaid funerals.* 前払い制の葬式

prepa|ra|tion /prɛpəreɪʃⁿn/ (**preparations**) ❶ N-UNCOUNT 不可算名詞 **Preparation** is the process of getting something ready for use or for a particular purpose, or making arrangements for something. 準備、用意 □ *Rub the surface of the wood in preparation for the varnish.* ニス塗りに備えて木の表面をこすりなさい。 □ *Few things distracted the pastor from the preparation of his weekly sermons.* 毎週行っている説教の準備から牧師の気をそらすようなことはほとんどない。 ❷ N-PLURAL 複数名詞 **Preparations** are all the arrangements that are made for a future event. 準備、手はず □ *The United States is making preparations for a large-scale airlift of 1,200 American citizens.* 米国は国民1200名の大規模な空輸に向けて準備を整えている。 ❸ N-COUNT 可算名詞 A **preparation** is a mixture that has been prepared for use as food, medicine, or a cosmetic. (調理した) 食品 (調理した) 薬品、化粧品 □ *...anti-aging creams and sensitive-skin preparations.* 老化防止用クリームと敏感肌用化粧品

pre|para|tory /prɪpærətɔri, prɛpərə-/ ADJ 形容詞 **Preparatory** actions are done before doing something else as a form of preparation or as an introduction. 準備の □ *At least a year's preparatory work will be necessary before building can start.* 建設を開始するまでに少なくとも1年間の準備が必要だ。

pre|pare /prɪpeər/ (**prepares, preparing, prepared**) ❶ V-T 他動詞 If you **prepare** something, you make it ready for something that is going to happen. 準備する □ *Two technicians were preparing a videotape recording of last week's program.* 技術者2人が先週の番組のビデオ撮りの準備をしていた。 □ *On average each report requires 1,000 hours to prepare.* 各報告書には平均1000時間の準備が必要だ。 ❷ V-T/V-I 他動詞/自動詞 If you **prepare for** an event or action that will happen soon, you get yourself ready for it or make the necessary arrangements. 〜のために準備する □ *The party leadership is using management consultants to help prepare for the next election.* 党執行部は次の選挙活動の手助けとして経営コンサルタントを起用している。

□ *He had to go back to his hotel and prepare to catch a train for New York.* 彼はホテルに戻りニューヨーク行きの電車に乗る準備をしなければならなかった。 ❸ V-T 他動詞 When you **prepare** food, you get it ready to be eaten, for example, by cooking it. 調理する □ *She made her way to the kitchen, hoping to find someone preparing dinner.* 彼女は、だれかが夕食の準備をしていることを期待しながら台所に向かった。

pre|pared /prɪpeərd/ ❶ ADJ 形容詞 If you are **prepared to** do something, you are willing to do it if necessary. 覚悟した [v-link ADJ to-inf] □ *Are you prepared to take industrial action?* ストライキをする覚悟はありますか？ ❷ ADJ 形容詞 If you are **prepared for** something that you think is going to happen, you are ready for it. 用意ができた [v-link ADJ "for" n] □ *Police are prepared for large numbers of demonstrators.* 警察は大人数のデモ参加者への備えができています。 ❸ ADJ 形容詞 You can describe something as **prepared** when it has been done or made beforehand, so that it is ready when it is needed. あらかじめ用意された [ADJ n] □ *He ended his prepared statement by thanking the police.* 彼は警察に感謝の意を述べてあらかじめ用意された陳述書を読み終えた。

prepo|si|tion /prɛpəzɪʃⁿn/ (**prepositions**) N-COUNT 可算名詞 A **preposition** is a word such as "by," "for," "into," or "with" that usually has a noun group as its object. 前置詞 □ *There is nothing in the rules of grammar to suggest that ending a sentence with a preposition is wrong.* 文を前置詞で終えるのは誤りだと示す文法の規則は何もない。

pre|pos|ter|ous /prɪpɒstərəs, -trəs/ ADJ 形容詞 If you describe something as **preposterous**, you mean that it is extremely unreasonable and foolish. 非常識な、ばかげた [DISAPPROVAL 不賛成] □ *The whole idea was preposterous.* その考え全体が非常識だった。 ● **pre|pos|ter|ous|ly** ADV 副詞 非常識に □ *Some prices are preposterously high.* 値段によっては非常識なほど高い。

prep school /prɛp skul/ (**prep schools**) ❶ N-VAR 可変性名詞 In the United States, a **prep school** is a private school for students who intend to go to college after they leave. 大学進学予備校、私立進学高校 □ *...an exclusive prep school in Washington.* ワシントン州のレベルの高い予備校 ❷ N-VAR 可変性名詞 In Britain, a **prep school** is a private school where children are educated until the age of 11 or 13. 私立中学校

pre|req|ui|site /priːrɛkwɪzɪt/ (**prerequisites**) N-COUNT 可算名詞 If one thing is a **prerequisite for** another, it must happen or exist before the other thing is possible. 必要条件 □ *Good self-esteem is a prerequisite for a happy life.* 自分に自信を持つことは幸福な生活のための必要条件だ。

pre|roga|tive /prɪrɒgətɪv/ (**prerogatives**) N-COUNT 可算名詞 If something is the **prerogative** of a particular person or group, it is a privilege or a power that only they have. 特権 [FORMAL 形式ばった] □ *It is your prerogative to stop seeing that particular therapist and find another one.* その特定のセラピストの診察をやめてほかのセラピストを探すことはあなたの特権です。

pre|scribe /prɪskraɪb/ (**prescribes, prescribing, prescribed**) ❶ V-T 他動詞 If a doctor **prescribes** medicine or treatment for you, he or she tells you what medicine or treatment to have. 処方する □ *The physician examines the patient then diagnoses the disease and prescribes medication.* 医者は患者の診察を行い、病気の診断をして薬を処方する。 □ *She took twice the prescribed dose of sleeping tablets.* 彼女は処方された服用量の2倍の睡眠薬を飲んだ。 ❷ V-T 他動詞 If a person or set of laws or rules **prescribes** an action or duty, they state that it must be carried out. 定める、規定する [FORMAL 形式ばった] □ *...article II of the constitution, which prescribes the method of electing a president.* 大統領の選出方法を規定する憲法第2条

pre|scrip|tion /prɪskrɪpʃⁿn/ (**prescriptions**) ❶ N-COUNT 可算名詞 A **prescription** is the piece of paper on which your doctor writes an order for medicine and which you give to a pharmacist to get the medicine. 処方せん □ *The new drug will not require a physician's prescription.* その新薬は医者の処方せんを必要としない。 ❷ N-COUNT 可算名詞 A **prescription** is a medicine that a doctor has told you to take. 処方薬 □ *I'm not sleeping even with the prescription Ackerman gave me.* アッカーマンがくれた処方薬を飲んでも眠れない。 ● PHRASE 句 If a medicine is available **by** or **on prescription**, you can only get it from a pharmacist if a doctor gives you a prescription for it. 処方によって ❸ N-COUNT 可算名詞

A **prescription** is a proposal or a plan that gives ideas about how to solve a problem or improve a situation. 提案 ❑ *There's not much difference in the economic prescriptions of Ireland's two main political parties.* アイルランドの主要2党の経済計画にはあまり違いがありません.

pres|ence /prɛzᵊns/ (**presences**) **1** N-SING 単数名詞 Someone's **presence** in a place is the fact that they are there. 存在すること, そこにいること ❑ *They argued that his presence in the town could only stir up trouble.* 彼が町にいることは問題を起こすことにしかならないとは議論した. **2** N-UNCOUNT 不可算名詞 If you say that someone has **presence**, you mean that they impress people by their appearance and manner. 貫禄 [APPROVAL 賛成] ❑ *They do not seem to have the vast, authoritative presence of those great men.* 彼らは, あの偉人たちが持つ偉大で高圧的な貫禄を持っていないようだ. **3** N-COUNT 可算名詞 A **presence** is a person or creature that you cannot see, but that you are aware of. 存在, 霊気 [LITERARY 文語的] ❑ *She started to be affected by the ghostly presence she could feel in the house.* 彼女は家の中で感じる霊気に影響され始めた. **4** N-SING 単数名詞 If a country has a military **presence** in another country, it has some of its armed forces there. 駐留 ❑ *The Philippine government wants the U.S. to maintain a military presence in Southeast Asia.* フィリピン政府は東南アジアでの軍の駐留の維持を望んでいます. **5** N-UNCOUNT 不可算名詞 If you refer to the **presence** of a substance in another thing, you mean that it is in that thing. 存在, 含有 ❑ *The somewhat acid flavor is caused by the presence of lactic acid.* いくらかの酸味があるのは乳酸を含有するためだ. **6** PHRASE 句 If you are **in** someone's **presence**, you are in the same place as that person, and are close enough to them to be seen or heard. ─の面前で ❑ *The talks took place in the presence of a diplomatic observer.* 協議は外交監視員の面前で行われた.

---

present

❶ EXISTING OR HAPPENING NOW
❷ BEING SOMEWHERE
❸ GIFT
❹ VERB USES

---

❶ **pres|ent** /prɛzᵊnt/ **1** ADJ 形容詞 You use **present** to describe things and people that exist now, rather than those that existed in the past or those that may exist in the future. 現在の [ADJ n] ❑ *He has brought much of the present crisis on himself.* 彼は現在の危機の多くを自分でもたらした. ❑ *...the government's present economic difficulties.* 政府の現在の経済問題 **2** N-SING 単数名詞 The **present** is the period of time that we are in now and the things that are happening now. 現在 ❑ *...his struggle to reconcile the past with the present.* 過去と現在との折り合いをつけようとする彼の苦労 ❑ *...continuing right up to the present.* 現在にまで続く権利 **3** PHRASE 句 A situation that exists **at present** exists now, although it may change. 今のところ ❑ *There is no way at present of predicting which individuals will develop the disease.* 現在の段階ではだれが発病するかを予測するのは不可能だ. **4** PHRASE 句 The **present day** is the period of history that we are in now. 現代 ❑ *...Western European art from the period of Giotto to the present day.* ジオットの時代から現代までの西洋美術 **5** PHRASE 句 Something that exists or will be done **for the present** exists now or will continue for a while, although the situation may change later. 差し当たり, 当分は ❑ *The cabinet had expressed the view that sanctions should remain in place for the present.* 制裁措置を差し当たり維持するべきだとの見解を内閣は発表した.

❷ **pres|ent** /prɛzᵊnt/ **1** ADJ 形容詞 If someone is **present at** an event, they are there. 出席している [v-link ADJ] ❑ *The president was not present at the meeting.* 大統領は会議に出席していなかった. ❑ *Nearly 85 percent of men are present at the birth of their children.* 男性の約85%が子供の出産に立ち会う. **2** ADJ 形容詞 If something, especially a substance or disease, is **present in** something else, it exists within that thing. 存在している, 含有している [v-link ADJ] ❑ *This special form of vitamin D is naturally present in breast milk.* この特殊形式のビタミンDはもともと母乳に含有している.

❸ **pres|ent** /prɛzᵊnt/ (**presents**) N-COUNT 可算名詞 A **present** is something that you give to someone, for example, at Christmas or when you visit them. 贈り物, プレゼント ❑ *The carpet was a wedding present from Jack's parents.* そのカーペットはジャックの両親からの結婚祝いだった. ❑ *She bought a birthday present for her mother.* 彼女は母親に誕生祝いのプレゼントを買った.

❹ **pre|sent** /prɪzɛnt/ (**presents, presenting, presented**) **1** V-T 他動詞 If you **present** someone **with** something such as a prize or document, or if you **present** it to them, you formally give it to them. 贈呈する ❑ *The mayor presented him with a gold medal at an official city reception.* 市長は市の公式歓迎会で金メダルを彼に贈呈した. ❑ *Betty will present the prizes to the winners.* ベッティが当選者に賞品を贈呈する. ● **pre|sen|ta|tion** N-UNCOUNT 不可算名詞 贈呈 ❑ *Then came the presentation of the awards by the First Lady.* そのあと大統領夫人による賞の授与が行われた. **2** V-T 他動詞 If something **presents** a difficulty, challenge, or opportunity, it

---

causes it or provides it. もたらす ❑ *This presents a problem for many financial consumers.* これは多くの金融消費者に問題をもたらす. ❑ *The future is going to be one that presents many challenges.* 将来は多くの課題をもたらすものとなるだろう. **3** V-T 他動詞 If an opportunity or problem **presents itself**, it occurs, often when you do not expect it. 生じる ❑ *Their colleagues insulted them whenever the opportunity presented itself.* 機会が生じるごとに同僚が彼らを侮辱した. **4** V-T 他動詞 When you **present** information, you give it to people in a formal way. 公開する, 提示する ❑ *We spend the time collating and presenting the information in a variety of chart forms.* さまざまな図表を使って情報を照合し提示しながら時間を過ごす. ❑ *We presented three options to the unions for discussion.* 労働組合に協議のための3つの選択肢を提示した. ● **pres|en|ta|tion** /prizɛnteɪʃᵊn, prɛzɛnteɪʃᵊn/ (**presentations**) N-VAR 可変性名詞 提示, プレゼンテーション ❑ *...in his first presentation of the theory to the Berlin Academy.* ベルリン・アカデミーに彼が初めてその理論の発表をしたときに ❑ *...a fair presentation of the facts to a jury.* 陪審への公平な事実公開 **5** V-T 他動詞 If you **present** someone or something in a particular way, you describe them in that way. 表す, 説明する ❑ *The government has presented these changes as major reforms.* 政府はこれらの変更を大改革だと説明した. **6** V-T 他動詞 The way you **present yourself** is the way you speak and act when meeting new people. 自己表現をする, ふるまう ❑ *...all those tricks which would help him to present himself in a more confident way in public.* 人前でもっと自信を持って自己表現するのに役立つこれらすべてのコツ **7** V-T 他動詞 If someone or something **presents** a particular appearance or image, that is how they appear or try to appear. (─という)印象を与える ❑ *The small group of onlookers presented a pathetic sight.* 少人数の傍観者は見るも哀れだった. ❑ *Cohen was making an effort to present a kinder, gentler image.* コーヘンはもっと親切で優しい印象を与えようと努力していた. **8** V-T 他動詞 If you **present yourself** somewhere, you officially arrive there, for example, for an appointment. 出頭する ❑ *Get word to him right away that he's to present himself at City Hall by tomorrow afternoon.* 今すぐ彼に, 明日の午後までに市役所に出頭するよう伝えてくれ. **9** V-T 他動詞 If someone **presents** a program on television or radio, they introduce each item in it. 司会する [mainly BRIT 主に英国英語; AM usually **host**, **introduce** 米国英語では通常 host, introduce] **10** V-T 他動詞 When someone **presents** something such as a production of a play or an exhibition, they organize it. 上演する, 企画する ❑ *They threatened to close any theater presenting a play with gay characters.* ゲイが出演する劇を上演している劇場はすべて閉鎖すると脅した. **11** V-T 他動詞 If you **present** someone **to** someone else, often an important person, you formally introduce them. 紹介する ❑ *Fox stepped forward, welcomed him in Malay, and presented him to Jack.* フォックスは前に出て, マレー語で彼に歓迎の言葉を述べ, ジャックに紹介した.

Word Partnership	*present* は次の語句と使われる:
N.	present **century**, present **circumstances**, present **location**, present **position**, present **situation**, present **time** ❶ **1**
	present a **check** ❹ **1**
	present a **challenge**, present a **danger**, present an **opportunity**, present a **problem**, present a **threat** ❹ **2**
	present an **argument**, present **evidence**, present a **plan** ❹ **4**

---

pres|en|ta|tion /prizɛnteɪʃᵊn/ (**presentations**) **1** N-UNCOUNT 不可算名詞 **Presentation** is the appearance of something, that someone has worked to create. 見かけ, 表示 ❑ *We serve traditional French food cooked in a lighter way, keeping the presentation simple.* 当店では盛り付けをシンプルに, 軽く料理をした伝統的なフランス料理を出す. **2** N-COUNT 可算名詞 A **presentation** is a formal event at which someone is given a prize or award. 授与 ❑ *...after receiving his award at a presentation in Kansas City yesterday.* 昨日カンザス市の授与式で賞を受け取ったあと **3** N-COUNT 可算名詞 When someone gives a **presentation**, they give a formal talk, often in order to sell something or get support for a proposal. プレゼンテーション, 発表 ❑ *James Watson, Philip Mayo and I gave a slide and video presentation.* ジェームズ・ワトソン, フィリップ・マヨ, そして私がスライドとビデオを使ったプレゼンテーションを行った. **4** → see also **present**

present-day ADJ 形容詞 **Present-day** things, situations, and people exist at the time in history we are now in. 現代の [ADJ n] ❑ *Even by present-day standards these were large aircraft.* 現代の水準でも, これらは大きい飛行機だった. ❑ *...a huge area of northern India, stretching from present-day Afghanistan to Bengal.* 今日のアフガニスタンからベンガルまで広がるに北インドの広大な地域

pre|sent|er /prɪzɛntᵊr/ (**presenters**) N-COUNT 可算名詞 A radio or television **presenter** is a person who introduces the items in a particular program. 司会者 [mainly BRIT 主に英国英語; AM usually **host**, **anchor** 米国英語では通常 host, anchor]

pres|ent|ly /prɛzᵊntli/ **1** ADV 副詞 If you say that something is **presently** happening, you mean that it is happening now. 現

在 ❑ *She is presently developing a number of projects.* 彼女は現在いくつかのプロジェクトを開発中です. ❑ *The island is presently uninhabited.* その島は現在のところ無人島だ. ❷ ADV 副詞 You use **presently** to indicate that something happened a short time after the time or event that you have just mentioned. 間もなく [WRITTEN 書き言葉] [ADV with cl] ❑ *He was shown to a small office. Presently, a young woman in a white coat came in.* 彼は小さな事務所に案内された. 間もなく, 白いコートを着た若い女性が入ってきた.

pre|serva|tive /prɪzɜːrvətɪv/ (**preservatives**) N-MASS 質量名詞 A **preservative** is a chemical that prevents things from decaying. Some preservatives are added to food, and others are used to treat wood or metal. 防腐剤, 保存剤 ❑ *Nitrates are used as preservatives in food processing.* 硝酸塩は食品加工で防腐剤として使用される.
→ see **salt**

pre|serve /prɪzɜːrv/ (**preserves, preserving, preserved**) ❶ V-T 他動詞 If you **preserve** a situation or condition, you make sure that it remains as it is, and does not change or end. 維持する, 保つ ❑ *We will do everything to preserve peace.* 平和維持のために何でもします. ● **pres|er|va|tion** /prɛzərveɪʃən/ N-UNCOUNT 不可算名詞 維持 ❑ *...the preservation of the status quo.* 現状の維持 ❷ V-T 他動詞 If you **preserve** something, you take action to save it or protect it from damage or decay. 保存する, 保護する ❑ *We need to preserve the forest.* 森林を保護する必要がある. ● **pres|er|va|tion** N-UNCOUNT 不可算名詞 保存, 保護 ❑ *...the preservation of buildings of architectural or historic interest.* 建築学的あるいは歴史的に意義のある建物の保存 ❸ V-T 他動詞 If you **preserve** food, you treat it in order to prevent it from decaying so that you can store it for a long time. 保存する, 防腐する ❑ *I like to make puree, using only enough sugar to preserve the plums.* プラムを保存するのに十分なだけの砂糖を使ってピューレを作りたい. ❹ N-PLURAL 複数名詞 **Preserves** are foods made by cooking fruit with a large amount of sugar so that they can be stored for a long time. ジャム, 砂糖煮 ❑ *She decided to make peach preserves for Christmas gifts.* 彼女は, クリスマスプレゼントにモモの砂糖煮を作ることを決めた. ❺ N-COUNT 可算名詞 If you say that a job or activity is the **preserve** of a particular person or group of people, you mean that they are the only ones who take part in it. 分野, 領分 ❑ *The making and conduct of foreign policy is largely the preserve of the president.* 外交政策の作成と遂行は主に大統領の領分です.
→ see **can**

pre|side /prɪzaɪd/ (**presides, presiding, presided**) V-I 自動詞 If you **preside over** a meeting or an event, you are in charge. 主宰する ❑ *The PM returned to Downing Street to preside over a meeting of his inner cabinet.* 首相は重要閣僚会議を主宰するために官邸に戻った.

presi|den|cy /prɛzɪdənsi/ (**presidencies**) N-COUNT 可算名詞 The **presidency** of a country or organization is the position of being the president or the period of time during which someone is president. 大統領・社長の職・任期, 大統領の職・任期, 社長の職・任期 ❑ *He is a candidate for the presidency of the organization.* 彼は, 組織の長候補です.

presi|dent /prɛzɪdənt/ (**presidents**) ❶ N-TITLE; N-COUNT 称号名詞, 可算名詞 The **president** of a country that has no king or queen is the person who is the head of state of that country. 大統領 [oft "the" N; N-VOC] ❑ *...President Mubarak.* ムバラク大統領 ❷ N-COUNT 可算名詞 The **president** of an organization is the person who has the highest position in it. 社長・会長・頭取・学長など組織の最高職 ❑ *...Alexandre de Merode, the president of the medical commission.* 医学委員長のアレクサンダー・デ・メローデ
→ see **election**

presi|den|tial /prɛzɪdɛnʃəl/ ADJ 形容詞 **Presidential** activities or things relate or belong to a president. 大統領の [ADJ n] ❑ *...campaigning for Peru's presidential election.* ペルーの大統領選に向けた選挙活動
→ see **election**

press /prɛs/ (**presses, pressing, pressed**) ❶ V-T 他動詞 If you **press** something somewhere, you push it firmly against something else. 押しつける ❑ *He pressed his back against the door.* 彼は背中をドアに押し付けた. ❷ V-T 他動詞 If you **press** a button or switch, you push it with your finger in order to make a machine or device work. 押す ❑ *Drago pressed a button and the door closed.* ドラゴがボタンを押すとドアが閉まった. ● N-COUNT 可算名詞 **Press** is also a noun. ❑ *...a TV which rises from a table at the press of a button.* ボタンを押すとテーブルから出てくるテレビ ❸ V-T/V-I 他動詞/自動詞 If you **press** something or **press down on** it, you push hard against it with your foot or hand. 押圧する ❑ *The engine stalled. He pressed the accelerator hard.* エンストした. 彼は, アクセルを強く踏んだ. ❹ V-I 自動詞 If you **press for** something, you try hard to persuade someone to give it to you or to agree to it. 強く要求する, 迫る ❑ *Police might now press for changes in the law.* 次に

警察は法律の変更を強く要求するかもしれない. ❺ V-T 他動詞 If you **press** someone, you try hard to persuade them to do something. 迫る ❑ *Trade unions are pressing him to stand firm.* 労働組合は彼に断固たる態度で臨むように強く求めている. ❑ *Mr. Kurtz seems certain to be pressed for further details.* カーツ氏はきっとさらなる詳細を求められるであろう. ❻ V-T 他動詞 If someone **presses** their claim, demand, or point, they state it in a very forceful way. しつこく主張する ❑ *The protest campaign has used mass strikes and demonstrations to press its demands.* 反対運動では要求を押し付けるために多くのストやデモを行った. ❼ V-T 他動詞 If you **press** something **on** someone, you give it to them and insist that they take it. 押しつける, 強要する ❑ *All I had was money, which I pressed on my reluctant mother.* 私が持っていたのはお金だけだったので, しぶっている彼女の母に押しつけた. ❽ V-T 他動詞 If you **press** clothes, you iron them in order to get rid of the creases. アイロンをかける ❑ *Vera pressed his shirt.* ヴェラはシャツにアイロンをかけた. ❑ *There's a couple of dresses to be pressed.* アイロンがけをしないといけないドレスがいくつかあるんです. ❾ N-SING-COLL 集合的単数名詞 Newspapers are referred to as **the press**. 新聞 ["the" N] ❑ *...interviews in the local and foreign press.* 国内紙と海外の新聞に記載されたインタビュー記事 ❿ N-SING-COLL 集合的単数名詞 報道の自由 Journalists and reporters are referred to as **the press**. 報道陣 ❑ *Christie looked relaxed and calm as she faced the press afterwards.* クリスティは, あとで報道陣に向き合ったというのにリラックスして落ち着いているようだった. ⓫ N-COUNT 可算名詞 A **press** or a **printing press** is a machine used for printing things such as books and newspapers. 印刷機 ⓬ → see also **pressed, pressing** ⓭ PHRASE 句 If someone or something **gets bad press**, they are criticized, especially in the newspapers, on television, or on radio. If they **get good press**, they are praised. 悪評/好評を得る ❑ *...the bad press that career women consistently get in this country.* わが国で相変わらずキャリアウーマンが受ける悪評 ⓮ PHRASE 句 If you **press charges against** someone, you make an official accusation against them that has to be decided in a court of law. 告発する ❑ *I could have pressed charges against him.* 彼を告発することだってできたのですが. ⓯ PHRASE 句 When a newspaper or magazine **goes to press**, it starts being printed. 印刷に回される ❑ *We check prices at the time of going to press.* 印刷に回す段階で価格を確認する.
→ see **newspaper, printing**

press con|fer|ence (**press conferences**) N-COUNT 可算名詞 A **press conference** is a meeting held by a famous or important person in which they answer reporters' questions. 記者会見 ❑ *She gave her reaction to his release at a press conference.* 彼女は記者会見で彼の釈放への感想を述べた.

pressed /prɛst/ ❶ ADJ 形容詞 If you say that you are **pressed for** time or **pressed for** money, you mean that you do not have enough time or money at the moment. (お金が) 足りない (時間に) 追われている [v-link ADJ] ❑ *Are you pressed for time? If not, I suggest we have lunch.* 忙しい？そうでなければ, 一緒にお昼ご飯を食べましょう. ❷ → see also **hard-pressed**

press|ing /prɛsɪŋ/ ❶ ADJ 形容詞 A **pressing** problem, need, or issue has to be dealt with immediately. 差し迫った, 緊急の ❑ *It is one of the most pressing problems facing this country.* それは, この国が直面している最も差し迫った問題の1つです. ❷ → see also **press**

press of|fic|er (**press officers**) N-COUNT 可算名詞 A **press officer** is a person who is employed by an organization to give information about that organization to the press. 広報担当官 ❑ *...the press officer of the Bavarian Government.* バイエルン州政府の広報担当官

press re|lease (**press releases**) N-COUNT 可算名詞 A **press release** is a written statement about a matter of public interest that is given to the press by an organization concerned with the matter. プレスリリース ❑ *The next day, Fox issued a press release saying the show had sold out in 24 hours.* 翌日フォックスは, 入場券は24時間で売り切れたというプレスリリースを行った.

press sec|re|tary (**press secretaries**) N-COUNT 可算名詞 A government's or political leader's **press secretary** is someone who is employed by them to give information to the press. 報道官 ❑ *The press secretary told reporters that a majority of one would be a sufficient mandate.* 報道官は, 1票差で十分な支持となると報道陣に述べた.

press-up (**press-ups**) N-COUNT 可算名詞 **Press-ups** are the same as **push-ups**. 腕立て伏せ [BRIT 英国英語]

pres|sure /prɛʃər/ (**pressures, pressuring, pressured**) ❶ N-UNCOUNT 不可算名詞 **Pressure** is force that you produce when you press hard on something. 押す力 ❑ *She kicked at the*

P

door with her foot, and the pressure was enough to open it. 彼女がド
アを足で蹴ったら、その力でドアが開いた. ❏ The pressure of his
fingers had relaxed. 彼の指の力が緩んだ. **2** N-UNCOUNT 不可算名
詞 The **pressure** in a place or container is the force produced by
the quantity of gas or liquid in that place or container. 気圧, 水
圧 [also N in pl] ❏ The window in the cockpit had blown in and the
pressure dropped dramatically. 操縦席の窓が割れ, 気圧が急激に落ち
た. **3** N-UNCOUNT 不可算名詞 If there is **pressure on** a person,
someone is trying to persuade or force them to do something. 強
要, 圧力 [also N in pl] ❏ He may have put pressure on her to agree. 彼
は, 彼女に同意するよう強要したかもしれない. ❏ A lot of dot-coms
were under pressure from their investors. 多くのインターネット関連企
業に投資家からの圧力がかかっている. **4** N-UNCOUNT 不可算名詞 If
you are experiencing **pressure**, you feel that you must do a lot of
tasks or make a lot of decisions in very little time, or that people
expect a lot from you. プレッシャー, 重圧 [also N in pl] ❏ Can you
work under pressure? プレッシャーに耐えて仕事ができますか? ❏ Even
if I had the talent to play tennis I couldn't stand the pressure. もしテニス
をする才能があったとしても, 重圧に耐えられないだろう. **5** V-T 他
動詞 If you **pressure** someone **to** do something, you try forcefully
to persuade them to do it. 強要する, 圧力をかける ❏ He will never
pressure you to get married. 彼は, 決してあなたに結婚を強要しないだ
ろう. ❏ The Senate should not be pressured into making hasty decisions.
上院は迅速な決定を下すよう強いられるべきではない. ● **pres|sured**
ADJ 形容詞 圧力を受ける, プレッシャーがかかっている ❏ You're likely
to feel anxious and pressured. おそらく不安でプレッシャーを感じるだろ
う. **6** → see also blood pressure
→ see flight, forecast, weather

pres|sure group (pressure groups) N-COUNT 可算名詞 A
pressure group is an organized group of people who are trying to
persuade a government or other authority to do something, for
example, to change a law. 圧力団体 ❏ ...the environmental pressure
group Greenpeace. 環境保護団体のグリーンピース

pres|sur|ized /prɛʃəraɪzd/ ADJ 形容詞 In a **pressurized**
container or area, the pressure inside is different from the
pressure outside. 加圧された ❏ Certain types of foods are also
dispensed in pressurized canisters. 食べ物の種類によっては加圧缶でも
販売されている.

pres|tige /prɛstiʒ, -stidʒ/ **1** N-UNCOUNT 不可算名詞 If a
person, a country, or an organization has **prestige**, they are
admired and respected because of the position they hold or the
things they have achieved. 威信, 名誉 ❏ ...efforts to build up the
prestige of the United Nations. 国連の名誉を築くための努力 ❏ It was
his responsibility for foreign affairs that gained him international prestige.
彼が国際的威信を得たのは外交政策に関する彼の任務だった. **2** ADJ
形容詞 **Prestige** is used to describe products, places, or activities
that people admire because they are associated with being rich or
having a high social position. 高級な [ADJ n] ❏ ...such prestige cars
as Cadillac, Mercedes, Porsche, and Jaguar. キャデラック, メルセデスベ
ンツ, ポルシェ, ジャガーなどの高級車

pres|tig|ious /prɛstidʒəs, -stidʒəs/ ADJ 形容詞 A **prestigious**
institution, job, or activity is respected and admired by people. 一
流の ❏ It's one of the best equipped and most prestigious schools in the
country. それは, 国内で最高の設備が整った名門校の1つだ.

pre|sum|ably /prɪzuməbli/ ADV 副詞 If you say that
something is **presumably** the case, you mean that you think it is
very likely to be the case, although you are not certain. たぶん,
恐らく [VAGUENESS あいまいさ] ❏ The spear is presumably the murder
weapon. やりは恐らく凶器だ.

pre|sume /prɪzum/ (presumes, presuming, presumed) **1** V-T
他動詞 If you **presume that** something is the case, you think that
it is the case, although you are not certain. 推定する, おそらく～だ
と思う ❏ I presume you're here on business. あなたはここに商用でいらっ
しゃるのかと思います. ❏ "Had he been home all week?" — "I presume
so." 「彼は今週ずっと家にいたの?」「たぶんそうだと思う」 **2** V-T
他動詞 If you say that someone **presumes to** do something, you
mean that they do it even though they have no right to do it. 厚か
ましくも～する, でしゃばって～する [FORMAL 形式ばった] ❏ They're
resentful that outsiders presume to meddle in their affairs. 部外者が彼
らの問題に干渉することに憤慨している. **3** V-T 他動詞 If an idea,
theory, or plan **presumes** certain facts, it regards them as true so
that they can be used as a basis for further ideas and theories. 仮
定する [FORMAL 形式ばった] ❏ The legal definition of "know" often
presumes mental control. know（知っている）の法的な定義ではしばし
ば精神正常を仮定する.

pre|sump|tion /prɪzʌmpʃn/ (presumptions) N-COUNT 可算名
詞 A **presumption** is something that is accepted as true but is not
certain to be true. 推測, 仮定 ❏ ...the presumption that a defendant

is innocent until proved guilty. 有罪判決が確定するまでは, 被告人は無
罪だという推定

pre|sump|tu|ous /prɪzʌmptʃuəs/ ADJ 形容詞 If you describe
someone or their behavior as **presumptuous**, you disapprove
of them because they are doing something that they have no
right or authority to do. 厚かましい, でしゃばりの, ずうずうしい
[DISAPPROVAL 不賛成] ❏ It would be presumptuous to judge what the
outcome will be. 結果がどうなるかを裁くのは差し出がましいことで
す.

pre|tax /pritæks/ also **pre-tax** ADJ 形容詞 **Pretax** profits or
losses are the total profits or losses made by a company before tax
has been taken away. 税引き前の, 税込みの [BUSINESS 実業] [ADJ
n] ❏ They announced a fall in pretax profits. 税引き前利益が減少したと
発表された. ● ADV 副詞 **Pretax** is also an adverb. 税引き前に [ADV
after v] ❏ Last year it made $2.5 million pretax. 昨年, 税引き前で250万
ドルの利益があった.

pre|tence /pritɛns, prɪtɛns/ → see pretense

pre|tend /prɪtɛnd/ (pretends, pretending, pretended) **1** V-T
他動詞 If you **pretend that** something is the case, you act in a
way that is intended to make people believe that it is the case,
although in fact it is not. ふりをする, 偽って～する ❏ I pretend that
things are really okay when they're not. 私は, うまくいっていないとき
でも大丈夫なふりをする. ❏ Sometimes the boy pretended to be asleep.
その少年はときどき眠っているふりをした. **2** V-T 他動詞 If children
or adults **pretend that** they are doing something, they imagine
that they are doing it, for example, as part of a game. ふりをする,
ー ごっこをする ❏ She can sunbathe and pretend she's in Cancun. 彼女は
日光浴をしてカンクンにいる気分になれる. **3** V-T 他動詞 If you do
not **pretend that** something is the case, you do not claim that it is
the case. ー というわけではない [with neg] ❏ We do not pretend that
the past six years have been without problems for us. 過去6年間が私たち
に問題がなかったというわけではない.

pre|tense /pritɛns, prɪtɛns/ (pretenses) **1** N-VAR 可変性名詞 A
pretense is an action or way of behaving that is intended to make
people believe something that is not true. ふり, ごまかし ❏ He
goes to the library and makes a pretense of reading some Thorean. 彼は図
書館に行ってトレアンでも読んでいるようなふりをするんだ. ❏ On the
eighth day of questioning, she dropped the pretense that she was Japanese.
尋問8日目に彼女は日本人のふりをするのをやめた. **2** PHRASE
句 If you do something **under false pretenses**, you do it when people
do not know the truth about you and your intentions. 偽って
❏ This interview was conducted under false pretenses. このインタビュー
は真実を偽って行われた.

pre|ten|sion /prɪtɛnʃn/ (pretensions) **1** N-VAR 可変性名詞 If
you say that someone has **pretensions**, you disapprove of them
because they claim or pretend that they are more important than
they really are. 気取り, うぬぼれ [DISAPPROVAL 不賛成] ❏ Her wide-
eyed innocence soon exposes the pretensions of the art world. 彼女の世間
知らずの純情さはまもなく芸術界の虚栄にさらされる. **2** N-PLURAL
不可算名詞 If someone has **pretensions to** something, they claim
to be or do that thing. （真偽かが疑わしい）主張 ❏ The city has
unrealistic pretensions to world-class status. その市は世界で認められた
地位にあるという非現実的な主張をしている.

pre|ten|tious /prɪtɛnʃəs/ ADJ 形容詞 If you say that someone
or something is **pretentious**, you mean that they try to seem
important or significant, but you do not think that they are. う
ぬぼれた [DISAPPROVAL 不賛成] ❏ His response was full of pretentious
nonsense. 彼の反応はうぬぼれたナンセンスに満ちていた.

pre|text /pritɛkst/ (pretexts) N-COUNT 可算名詞 A **pretext** is
a reason that you pretend has caused you to do something. 口実
❏ They wanted a pretext for subduing the region by force. 軍事力でその地
域を制圧するための口実が欲しかった.

pret|ty /prɪti/ (prettier, prettiest) **1** ADJ 形容詞 If you describe
someone, especially a girl, as **pretty**, you mean that they look nice
and are attractive in a delicate way. きれいな, かわいい ❏ She's a
very charming and very pretty girl. 彼女はとても魅力的でとてもきれい
な女の子だ. ● **pret|ti|ly** /prɪtili/ ADV 副詞 きれいに, かわいらしく
❏ She smiled again, prettily. 彼女はかわいらしくまた笑った.

When you are describing someone's appearance, you generally
use **pretty** and **beautiful** to describe women, girls, and babies.
Beautiful is a much stronger word than **pretty**. The equivalent
word for a man is **handsome**. **Good-looking** and **attractive** can
be used to describe people of either sex. **Pretty** can also be used to
modify adjectives and adverbs but is less strong than **very**. In
this sense, **pretty** is informal.

2 ADJ 形容詞 A place or a thing that is **pretty** is attractive and
pleasant, in a charming but not particularly unusual way. すて
きな, 景色がよい ❏ ...a very pretty little town. とてもすてきな小さ
な町 ● **pret|ti|ly** ADV 副詞 すてきに ❏ The living-room was prettily
decorated. リビングルームはきれいに内装が施されていた. **3** ADV 副詞
[ADV adj/adv] You can use **pretty** before an adjective or adverb to
slightly lessen its force. まあまあ [INFORMAL くだけた] ❏ I had a

pretty good idea what she was going to do. 彼女が何をするつもりかだいたいの見当はついていた.

pre|vail /prɪveɪl/ (prevails, prevailing, prevailed) **1** V-I 自動詞 If a proposal, principle, or opinion **prevails**, it gains influence or is accepted, often after a struggle or argument. 普及する, うまく説得する ❑ *We hoped that common sense would prevail.* 常識が広まるといいのですが. ❑ *Rick still believes that justice will prevail.* 正義が普及するとリックは今も信じています. **2** V-I 自動詞 If a situation, attitude, or custom **prevails** in a particular place at a particular time, it is normal or most common in that place at that time. 優勢である, 一般的である ❑ *A similar situation prevails in Canada.* よく似た状況がカナダで一般的だ. ❑ *...the confusion which had prevailed at the time of the revolution.* 革命時に一般化した混乱 **3** V-I 自動詞 If one side in a battle, contest, or dispute **prevails**, it wins. 勝つ ❑ *He appears to have the votes he needs to prevail.* 彼は勝利のために必要な投票数を確保したようです.

preva|lent /prɛvələnt/ ADJ 形容詞 A condition, practice, or belief that is **prevalent** is common. 一般的な ❑ *This condition is more prevalent in women than in men.* この病状は男性よりも女性によくあります. ❑ *Smoking is becoming increasingly prevalent among younger women.* 喫煙は若い女性の間でますます一般化している. ● **preva|lence** N-UNCOUNT 不可算名詞 普及していること ❑ *...the prevalence of cocaine abuse in the 1980s.* 1980年代におけるコカイン乱用の流行

pre|vent /prɪvɛnt/ (prevents, preventing, prevented) **1** V-T 他動詞 To **prevent** something means to ensure that it does not happen. 防ぐ, 防止する ❑ *These methods prevent pregnancy.* これらの方法で妊娠を防ぐことができる. ❑ *Further treatment will prevent cancer from developing.* さらに治療をすることでがんの成長を防ぐだろう. ● **pre|ven|tion** N-UNCOUNT 不可算名詞 予防 ❑ *...the prevention of heart disease.* 心臓病の予防 **2** V-T 他動詞 To **prevent** someone **from** doing something means to make it impossible for them to do it. 防ぐ, 妨げる ❑ *He said this would prevent companies from creating new jobs.* これによって会社が新しい仕事を作りにくくなると彼は言った. ❑ *Its nationals may be prevented from leaving the country.* その国民は国外脱出を阻止されるかもしれない.

pre|ven|ta|tive /prɪvɛntətɪv/ ADJ 形容詞 **Preventative** means the same as **preventive**. 予防の, 防止の

pre|ven|tive /prɪvɛntɪv/ ADJ 形容詞 **Preventive** actions are intended to help prevent things such as disease or crime. 予防の, 防止の ❑ *Too much is spent on curative medicine and too little on preventive medicine.* 治療薬への投資額が多すぎ, 予防薬への投資が足りない.

pre|view /priːvjuː/ (previews) N-COUNT 可算名詞 A **preview** is an opportunity to see something such as a movie, exhibition, or invention before it is open or available to the public. 試写会, 試演会 ❑ *He had gone to see the preview of a play.* 彼は劇の試演会を見に行った.

pre|vi|ous /priːviəs/ **1** ADJ 形容詞 A **previous** event or thing is one that happened or existed before the one that you are talking about. 前の, 以前の [ADJ n] ❑ *She has a teenage daughter from a previous marriage.* 彼女には, 前の夫との10代の娘がいる. **2** ADJ 形容詞 You refer to the period of time or the thing immediately before the one that you are talking about as the **previous** one. 前の, 直前の [det ADJ] ❑ *It was a surprisingly dry day after the rain of the previous week.* その前の週の雨と比べると, 驚くほどの快晴だった.

pre|vi|ous|ly /priːviəsli/ **1** ADV 副詞 **Previously** means at some time before the period that you are talking about. 以前に ❑ *Guyana's railways were previously owned by private companies.* ガイアナの鉄道は以前は民間会社によって経営されていた. ❑ *The contract was awarded to a previously unknown company.* その契約は今まで知られていなかった会社に勝ち取られた. **2** ADV 副詞 You can use **previously** to say how much earlier one event was than another event. 一前に [n ADV] ❑ *He had first entered the House 12 years previously.* 彼が最初に議員になったのは12年前だ.

pre|war /priːwɔːr/ also **pre-war** ADJ 形容詞 **Prewar** is used to describe things that happened, existed, or were made in the period immediately before a war, especially World War II, 1939-45. 戦前の ❑ *...Poland's prewar leader.* ポーランドの戦前の指導者

prey /preɪ/ (preys, preying, preyed) **1** N-UNCOUNT-COLL 集合的不可算名詞 A creature's **prey** are the creatures that it hunts and eats in order to live. えじき, 獲物 ❑ *Electric rays stun their prey with huge electrical discharges.* シビレエイが巨大な発電器官で獲物をまひさせる. **2** V-I 自動詞 A creature that **preys on** other creatures lives by catching and eating them. 捕食する ❑ *The effect was to disrupt the food chain, starving many animals and those that preyed on them.* その作用は, 多くの動物とそれらを捕食する動物を餓死させて食物連鎖を崩壊することだった. **3** N-UNCOUNT 不可算名詞 You can refer to the people who someone tries to harm or trick as their **prey**. えじき, かも ❑ *Police officers lie in wait for the gangs who stalk their prey at night.* 警察官は, 夜えじきをつけまわすギャングを待ち伏せする. **4** V-I 自動詞 If someone **preys on** other people, especially people who are unable to protect themselves, they take advantage of them or harm them in some way. えじきにする, 食い物にする [DISAPPROVAL 不賛成] ❑ *Pam had never learned that there were men who preyed on young runaways.* 若い家出娘を食い物にする男がいることをパムは全く知らなかった. **5** V-I 自動詞 If something **preys on** your mind, you cannot stop thinking and worrying about it. 絶えず悩ませる ❑ *It was a misunderstanding and it preyed on his conscience.* それは誤解で絶えず彼の良心を苦しめた.

→ see **shark**

price /praɪs/ (prices, pricing, priced) **1** N-COUNT 可算名詞 The **price** of something is the amount of money that you have to pay in order to buy it. 値段, 価格 ❑ *...a sharp increase in the price of gas.* ガソリン価格の急上昇 ❑ *They expected house prices to rise.* 住宅価格の上昇が予想された. **2** N-SING 単数名詞 The **price** that you pay for something that you want is an unpleasant thing that you have to do or suffer in order to get it. 代償, 犠牲 ❑ *Slovenia will have to pay a high price for independence.* スロベニアは独立のために高い代価を払わなければならないだろう. ❑ *There may be a price to pay for such relentless activity, perhaps ill health or even divorce.* それほど容赦ない活動のために, おそらく病気やあるいは離婚などの代償を払うことになるかもしれない. **3** V-T 他動詞 If something **is priced at** a particular amount, the price is set at that amount. の値段である ❑ *The bond is currently priced at $900.* 株価は現在900ドルだ. ❑ *Analysts predict that Digital will price the new line at less than half the cost of comparable IBM mainframes.* デジタルは競合製品であるIBM社の大型コンピューターの半分以下の価格で新製品を売り出すだろうとアナリストは予測している. ● **pric|ing** N-UNCOUNT 不可算名詞 価格設定 ❑ *It's hard to maintain competitive pricing.* 競争価格の設定を維持するのは難しい. **4** → see also **retail price index**, **selling price** **5** PHRASE 句 If you want something **at any price**, you are determined to get it, even if unpleasant things happen as a result. どんな代価を払っても, 何としても ❑ *If they wanted a deal at any price, they would have to face the consequences.* もしどうしても取引をしたければ, 責任を取らなければならない. **6** PHRASE 句 If you can buy something that you want **at a price**, it is for sale, but it is extremely expensive. かなりの値段で ❑ *Most goods are available, but at a price.* ほとんどの品物は手に入るが, かなりの高額だ. **7** PHRASE 句 If you get something that you want **at a price**, you get it but something unpleasant happens as a result. かなりの犠牲を払って ❑ *Fame comes at a price.* 名声は相当な犠牲を払って得られる. **8** to **price** yourself **out of the market** → see **market**

The **price** of something is the amount of money that the seller is asking people to pay in order to buy it. ❑ *The price marked on the box was $5.* When you are referring to services, or to things that you pay to use, you usually talk about a **charge** or a **fee**, rather than a **price**. ❑ *There is a one dollar handling charge for telephone reservations. ...$400 in unpaid consulting fees.* The **cost** of something is the amount of money that you actually pay, or would pay, for it. ❑ *The total cost of modernizing the room came to just $800.* See also note at **cost**.

price|less /praɪsləs/ **1** ADJ 形容詞 If you say that something is **priceless**, you are emphasizing that it is worth a very large amount of money, or that it is very important to you although it has little financial value. 非常に高価な, 非常に貴重な [EMPHASIS 強調] ❑ *They are priceless, unique and irreplaceable.* それらは非常に貴重で, 類がなく, かけがえがない. ❑ *Did Mom throw away your priceless Dungeons and Dragons magazine?* お母さんが貴重な『ダンジョンズ＆ドラゴンズ』誌を捨てたの? **2** ADJ 形容詞 If you say that something is **priceless**, you approve of it because it is extremely useful. 非常に役に立つ [APPROVAL 賛成] ❑ *They are a priceless record of a brief period in Colorado history.* それは, コロラドの歴史における短い期間の貴重な記録だ.

price tag (price tags) **1** N-COUNT 可算名詞 If something has a **price tag** of a particular amount, that is the amount that you must pay in order to buy it. 費用, 価格 [WRITTEN 書き言葉] ❑ *The monorail can be completed at the price tag of $1.7 billion.* モノレールは17億ドルで完成できうる. **2** N-COUNT 可算名詞 In a store, the **price**

tag on an article for sale is a small piece of card or paper attached to the article with the price written on it. 値札

price war (**price wars**) N-COUNT 可算名詞 If competing companies are involved in a **price war**, they each try to gain an advantage by lowering their prices as much as possible in order to sell more of their products and damage their competitors financially. 価格競争 [BUSINESS 実業] ❑ *Their loss was partly due to a vicious price war between manufacturers that has cut margins to the bone.* 損失が一部原因は、マージンを徹底的に削減した製造業者間の熾烈(しれつ)な価格競争に一部原因がある。

pricey /ˈpraɪsi/ (**pricier, priciest**) also **pricy** ADJ 形容詞 If you say that something is **pricey**, you mean that it is expensive. (値段が) 高い [INFORMAL くだけた] ❑ *Medical insurance is very pricey.* 医療保険はとても高い。

prick /prɪk/ (**pricks, pricking, pricked**) **1** V-T 他動詞 If you **prick** something or **prick** holes in it, you make small holes in it with a sharp object such as a pin. 小さな穴を開ける ❑ *Prick the potatoes and rub the skins with salt.* ジャガイモにフォークで刺して穴を開け、皮に塩をすりこみなさい。 **2** V-T 他動詞 If something sharp **pricks** you or if you **prick yourself with** something sharp, it sticks into you or presses your skin and causes you pain. ちくりと刺す ❑ *She had just pricked her finger with the needle.* 彼女は、針で指をちくりと刺したところだった。 **3** N-COUNT 可算名詞 A **prick** is a small, sharp pain that you get when something pricks you. ちくっとした痛み ❑ *At the same time she felt a prick on her neck.* 同時に彼女は首にちくっとした痛みを感じた。 **4** N-COUNT 可算名詞 If you call someone a **prick**, you are insulting them because you think they are mean and spiteful or stupid, or you do not like them. ばか、まぬけ [INFORMAL, VERY RUDE くだけた、非常に無作法な, DISAPPROVAL 不賛成] **5** N-COUNT 可算名詞 A man's **prick** is his penis. 肉棒 [INFORMAL, VULGAR くだけた、下品な] [poss N]

prick|ly /ˈprɪkli/ **1** ADJ 形容詞 Something that is **prickly** feels rough and uncomfortable, as if it has a lot of prickles. ちくちくする ❑ *The bunk mattress was hard, the blankets prickly and slightly damp.* 寝台のマットレスは固くて、毛布はちくちくし少し湿っていた。 **2** ADJ 形容詞 Someone who is **prickly** loses their temper or gets upset very easily. 怒りっぽい、キレやすい ❑ *You know how prickly she is.* 彼女がどんなに怒りっぽいか知ってるでしょう。 **3** ADJ 形容詞 A **prickly** issue or subject is one that is rather complicated and difficult to discuss or resolve. 厄介な ❑ *The issue is likely to prove a prickly one.* その問題は厄介のものとなりそうだ。

pricy /ˈpraɪsi/ → see **pricey**

pride /praɪd/ (**prides, priding, prided**) **1** N-UNCOUNT 不可算名詞 **Pride** is a feeling of satisfaction that you have because you or people close to you have done something good or possess something good. 満足感 ❑ *...the sense of pride in a job well done.* 仕事がうまくいったときの満足感 ❑ *We take pride in offering you the highest standards.* 誇りを持って最高水準をお届けしています。 **2** N-UNCOUNT 不可算名詞 **Pride** is a sense of the respect that other people have for you, and that you have for yourself. プライド、自尊心 ❑ *Davis had to salvage his pride.* ディヴィスはプライドを守らなければならなかった。 **3** N-UNCOUNT 不可算名詞 Someone's **pride** is the feeling that they have that they are better or more important than other people. うぬぼれ [DISAPPROVAL 不賛成] ❑ *His pride may still be his downfall.* 彼のごうまんさが依然として失敗の原因となるかもしれない。 **4** V-T 他動詞 If you **pride** yourself **on** a quality or skill that you have, you are very proud of it. 誇りにする、自慢する ❑ *Suarez prides himself on being able to organize his own life.* スアレスは自分の人生のきちんと計画できることを誇りにしている。

Word Partnership	*pride* は次の語句と使われる:
v.	take pride in *something* **1**
	feel pride **1 2**
N.	sense of pride, source of pride **1 – 3**

priest /prist/ (**priests**) **1** N-COUNT 可算名詞 A **priest** is a member of the Christian clergy in the Catholic, Anglican, or Orthodox church. 聖職者、司祭 ❑ *He had trained to be a Catholic priest.* 彼はカトリック教の司祭になると訓練を受けた。 **2** N-COUNT 可算名詞 In many non-Christian religions a **priest** is a man who has particular duties and responsibilities in a place where people worship. 聖職者、僧侶(そうりょ) ❑ *...a New Age priest or priestess.* ニュー・エイジの聖職者

priest|ess /ˈpristɪs/ (**priestesses**) N-COUNT 可算名詞 A **priestess** is a woman in a non-Christian religion who has particular duties and responsibilities in a place where people worship. 女性聖職者 ❑ *...the priestess of the temple.* 神殿のみこ

priest|hood /ˈpristhʊd/ **1** N-UNCOUNT 不可算名詞 **Priesthood** is the position of being a priest or the period of time during which someone is a priest. 司祭職 ❑ *...the early rites of priesthood.* 司祭職の初期の儀式 **2** N-SING 単数名詞 The **priesthood** is all the members of the Christian clergy, especially in a particular church. (集合的にすべての) 聖職者 ❑ *Should the General Synod vote*

women into the priesthood? 総会では女性が聖職者になることを投票決議するべきだろうか。

prim /prɪm/ ADJ 形容詞 If you describe someone as **prim**, you disapprove of them because they behave too correctly and are too easily shocked by anything vulgar. 堅苦しい、取り澄ました [DISAPPROVAL 不賛成] ❑ *We tend to imagine that the Victorians were very prim and proper.* ビクトリア時代の人々はとてもきちょうめんで取り澄ましていたと想像しがちである。 ● **prim|ly** ADV 副詞 [ADV with v] 取り澄まして ❑ *We sat primly at either end of a long bench.* 私たちは長いベンチの両端に取り澄まして座った。

pri|mal /ˈpraɪmᵊl/ ADJ 形容詞 **Primal** is used to describe something that relates to the origins of things or that is very basic. 原始的な、基本的な [FORMAL 形式ばった] ❑ *Jealousy is a primal emotion.* しっとは基本的な感情である。

pri|mari|ly /praɪˈmɛrɪli/ ADV 副詞 You use **primarily** to say what is mainly true in a particular situation. 主に ❑ *...a book aimed primarily at high-energy physicists.* 主に高エネルギー物理学者向けの本 ❑ *Public order is primarily an urban problem.* 社会的秩序は主に都市問題だ。

Word Link	*prim* ≈ *first* : *primary, primate, prime*

pri|ma|ry /ˈpraɪmɛri, -məri/ (**primaries**) **1** ADJ 形容詞 You use **primary** to describe something that is very important. 主要な、第一の [FORMAL 形式ばった] [ADJ n] ❑ *That's the primary reason the company's share price has held up so well.* それが、その会社の株価が高値を維持している主な理由だ。 ❑ *His misunderstanding of language was the primary cause of his other problems.* 彼が言葉を誤解することが他の問題の主な原因だった。 **2** ADJ 形容詞 **Primary** education is the first few years of formal education for children. 初等の [ADJ n] ❑ *The content of primary education should be the same for everyone.* 初等教育の内容は全児童に対して同じようにするべきだ。 ❑ *Ninety-nine percent of primary pupils now have hands-on experience of computers.* 現在では小学生の99%にコンピュータの実体験がある。 **3** ADJ 形容詞 **Primary** is used to describe something that occurs first. 原発性の、一次性の [ADJ n] ❑ *It is not the primary tumor that kills, but secondary growths elsewhere in the body.* 致命的なのは原発性のしゅようではなくて、体内のほかの場所への転移である。 **4** N-COUNT 可算名詞 A **primary** or a **primary election** is an election in an American state in which people vote for someone to become a candidate for a political office. Compare **general election**. 予備選挙 ❑ *...the 1968 New Hampshire primary.* 1968年ニューハンプシャー州予備選挙

pri|ma|ry school (**primary schools**) N-VAR 可変性名詞 A **primary school** is a school for children in the first four or five years of their education. 小学校 [mainly BRIT 主に英国英語; AM usually **elementary school** 米国英語では通常 **elementary school**]

pri|mate /ˈpraɪmeɪt/ (**primates**)

The pronunciation /ˈpraɪmɪt/ is also used for meaning **2**.
2 の意味では発音 /ˈpraɪmɪt/ とも発音される。

1 N-COUNT 可算名詞 A **primate** is a member of the group of mammals that includes humans, monkeys, and apes. 霊長類 ❑ *The woolly spider monkey is the largest primate in the Americas.* ムリキは南北アメリカの霊長類で最も大きい。 **2** N-COUNT 可算名詞 The **Primate of** a particular country or region is the most important priest in that country or region. 主席司教、大司教 ❑ *...the Roman Catholic Primate of All Ireland.* 全アイルランドのローマ・カトリック大主教

→ see Word Web: **primate**

prime /praɪm/ (**primes, priming, primed**) **1** ADJ 形容詞 You use **prime** to describe something that is most important in a situation. 最重要な [ADJ n] ❑ *Political stability, meanwhile, will be a prime concern.* その間、政局安定が最大の関心事だろう。 ❑ *It could be a prime target for guerrilla attack.* それがゲリラ攻撃の第1の標的かもしれない。 **2** ADJ 形容詞 You use **prime** to describe something that is of the best possible quality. 最高の、第一等の [ADJ n] ❑ *The location of these beaches makes them prime sites for development.* これらの海岸の立地条件により、そこが開発に最高の場所となっている。 **3** ADJ 形容詞 You use **prime** to describe an example of a particular kind of thing that is absolutely typical. 典型的な [ADJ n] ❑ *The prime example is Macy's, once the undisputed king of California retailers.* 典型的な例は、かつてだれもが認めたカリフォルニア州小売業界の王者、メーシーズ百貨店だ。 **4** N-UNCOUNT 不可算名詞 If someone or something is in their **prime**, they are at the stage in their existence when they are at their strongest, most active, or most successful. 全盛期で ❑ *Maybe I'm just coming into my prime now.* もしかすると私は今ちょうど全盛期を迎えているところかもしれない。 ❑ *We've had a series of athletes trying to come back well past their prime.* 全盛期をとっくに過ぎているが復帰しようとする選手が続きました。 **5** V-T 他動詞 If you **prime** someone **to do** something, you prepare them to do it, for example by giving them information about it beforehand. あらかじめ用意させる ❑ *Claire wished she'd primed Sarah beforehand.* クレアは前もってサラに用意させればよかったと思った。 ❑ *Marianne had not known until Arnold primed her for*

Word Web   primate

The classification **primate** includes **monkeys, apes,** and **humans.** Scientists have shown that humans and the other primates share some surprising similarities. We used to believe that only humans favor one hand over the other. However, researchers carefully observed a group of 66 **chimpanzees.** They found that chimps are also right-handed and left-handed. Other researchers have learned that chimpanzee groups have different cultures. In 1972 a female **gorilla** named Koko began to learn sign language from a college student. Today Koko understands about 2,000 words and can sign about 500 of them. She makes up sentences using three to six words.

---

her duties that she was to be the sole female. マリアンは、アーノルドが打ち合わせで教えてくれるまで彼女が紅一点となることを知らなかった. ⬛ V-T 他動詞 If someone **primes a bomb** or **a gun,** they prepare it so that it is ready to explode or fire. 火薬を詰める、導火線をつける ❑ He was priming the bomb to go off in an hour's time. 彼は爆弾が1時間後に爆発するように手配した. ❑ He kept a primed shotgun in his office. 彼は、弾を入れた散弾銃を事務所に置いていた。

prime min|is|ter (prime ministers) N-COUNT; N-TITLE 可算名詞, 称号名詞 The leader of the government in some countries is called **the prime minister.** 首相、総理大臣 ❑ ...the former prime minister of Pakistan, Miss Benazir Bhutto. 元パキスタン首相のベナジール・ブット氏

prime rate (prime rates) N-COUNT 可算名詞 A bank's **prime rate** is the lowest rate of interest that it charges at a particular time and that is offered only to certain customers. プライムレート, 最優遇貸出金利 [BUSINESS 実業] ❑ At least one bank cut its prime rate today. 少なくとも1行の銀行が本日プライムレートを下げました。

prime time also **primetime** N-UNCOUNT 不可算名詞 **Prime time** television or radio programs are broadcast when the greatest number of people are watching television or listening to the radio, usually in the evenings. ゴールデンアワー ❑ ...a prime-time television show. ゴールデンアワーのテレビ番組

primi|tive /prɪmɪtɪv/ ⬛ ADJ 形容詞 **Primitive** means belonging to a society in which people live in a very simple way, usually without industries or a writing system. 未開の ❑ ...studies of primitive societies. 未開社会の研究 ➋ ADJ 形容詞 **Primitive** means belonging to a very early period in the development of an animal or plant. 原始の、最初期の ❑ ...primitive whales. 最初期のクジラ ❑ Primitive humans needed to be able to react like this to escape from dangerous animals. 原始人は危険な動物から逃れるために、このように反応できる必要があった. ➌ ADJ 形容詞 If you describe something as **primitive,** you mean that it is very simple in style or very old-fashioned. 原始的な、旧式な ❑ The conditions are primitive by any standards. 環境はどう見ても原始的だ。

prim|rose /prɪmroʊz/ (primroses) N-VAR 可変性名詞 A **primrose** is a wild plant that has pale yellow flowers in the spring. サクラソウ

prince /prɪns/ (princes) ⬛ N-TITLE; N-COUNT 称号名詞, 可算名詞 A **prince** is a male member of a royal family, especially the son of the king or queen of a country. 王子、皇太子 ❑ ...Prince Edward and other royal guests. エドワード王子と他の王家の招待客 ➋ N-TITLE; N-COUNT 称号名詞, 可算名詞 A **prince** is the male royal ruler of a small country or state. 君主、一公 ❑ He was speaking without the prince's authority. 彼は君主の許可なしに話していた。

Word Link   ess ≈ female : actress, heiress, princess

prin|cess /prɪnsɪs, -sɛs/ (princesses) N-TITLE; N-COUNT 称号名詞, 可算名詞 A **princess** is a female member of a royal family, usually the daughter of a king or queen or the wife of a prince. 王女、王妃、皇女 ❑ Princess Anne topped the guest list. アン王女は来賓名簿のトップだった。

prin|ci|pal /prɪnsɪp³l/ (principals) ⬛ ADJ 形容詞 **Principal** means first in order of importance. 主要な [ADJ n] ❑ The principal reason for my change of mind is this. 私の気が変わった主な理由はこれだ. ❑ ...the country's principal source of foreign exchange earnings. その国の貿易黒字の主な財源 ➋ N-COUNT 可算名詞 The **principal** of a school is the person in charge of the school or college. 校長、学長 ❑ Donald King is the principal of Dartmouth High School. ドナルド・キングはダートマス高校の校長です. ➌ N-COUNT 可算名詞 The **principal** of a loan is the original amount of the loan, on which you pay interest. 元金 [FINANCE 財政] [usu sing]
→ see **bank, interest**

prin|ci|pal|ly /prɪnsɪpli/ ADV 副詞 **Principally** means more than anything else. 主に [ADV with cl/group] ❑ This is principally because the major export markets are slowing. これは、主要輸出市場が減速しているのが主な原因です。

prin|ci|ple /prɪnsɪp³l/ (principles) ⬛ N-VAR 可変性名詞 A **principle** is a general belief about the way you should behave, which influences your behavior. 主義、信条 ❑ Buck never allowed himself to be bullied into doing anything that went against his principles. バックはいつも無理やり彼の主義に反することをさせられるということを拒否した. ❑ It's not just a matter of principle. 単なる主義の問題ではありません. ➋ N-COUNT 可算名詞 The **principles** of a particular theory or philosophy are its basic rules or laws. 原理、原則 ❑ ...a violation of the basic principles of Marxism. マルクス主義の基本原理の侵害 ➌ N-COUNT 可算名詞 Scientific **principles** are general scientific laws which explain how something happens or works. 原理、法則 ❑ These people lack all understanding of scientific principles. これらの人々は科学原理を全く理解していない. ➍ PHRASE 句 If you agree with something **in principle,** you agree in general terms to the idea of it, although you do not yet know the details or know if it will be possible. 原則的には ❑ I agree with it in principle but I doubt if it will happen in practice. 原則的には賛成するが、それが実際に起こるとは思わない. ➎ PHRASE 句 If something is possible **in principle,** there is no known reason why it should not happen, even though it has not happened before. 原理上は ❑ Even assuming this to be in principle possible, it will not be achieved soon. これが原理上は可能だと仮定したとしても、近い将来実現することはないだろう. ➏ PHRASE 句 If you refuse to do something **on principle,** you refuse to do it because of a particular belief that you have. 主義として ❑ He would vote against it on principle. 彼の主義として反対票を入れるだろう。

prin|ci|pled /prɪnsɪp³ld/ ADJ 形容詞 If you describe someone as **principled,** you approve of them because they have strong moral principles. 信念を持った [APPROVAL 賛成] ❑ She was a strong, principled woman. 彼女は意志が強く信念を持った女性だった。

print /prɪnt/ (prints, printing, printed) ⬛ V-T 他動詞 If someone **prints** something such as a book or newspaper, they produce it in large quantities using a machine. 印刷する ❑ He started to print his own posters to distribute abroad. 彼は、海外に配送するために自分自身のポスターを印刷し始めた. ❑ Our brochure is printed on environmentally-friendly paper. 当社のカタログは環境に優しい紙に印刷されている. ● PHRASAL VERB 句動詞 In American English, **print up** means the same as **print.** 印刷する ❑ Community workers here are printing up pamphlets for peace demonstrations. 地域のボランティアはここで平和デモのためのパンフレットを印刷しています. ● **print|ing** N-UNCOUNT 不可算名詞 [oft N n] 印刷 ❑ His brother ran a printing and publishing company. 彼の兄は印刷・出版会社を経営していた. ➋ V-T 他動詞 If a newspaper or magazine **prints** a piece of writing, it includes it or publishes it. 掲載する ❑ We can only print letters which are accompanied by the writer's name and address. 著者の住所・氏名が記載されている手紙でなければ掲載できません. ➌ V-T 他動詞 If numbers, letters, or designs **are printed on** a surface, they are put on it in ink or dye using a machine. You can also say that a surface **is printed with** numbers, letters, or designs. 印刷されて ❑ ...the number printed on the receipt. 領収書に印刷されている番号 ❑ The company has for some time printed its phone number on its products. その会社はしばらく製品に電話番号を印刷していました. ➍ N-COUNT 可算名詞 A **print** is a piece of clothing or material with a pattern printed on it. You can also refer to the pattern itself as a **print.** プリント地、プリント柄、模様 ❑ Her mother wore one of her dark summer prints. 彼女の母は濃い夏模様のドレスを着ていた. ❑ In this living room we've mixed glorious floral prints. この居間の室内装飾に見事な花柄を調和した. ➎ V-T 他動詞 When you **print** a photograph, you produce it from a negative. 現像する ❑ Printing a black-and-white negative on to color paper produces a similar monochrome effect. 白黒ネガをカラーペーパーに現像すると同様のモノクロ効果が得られる. ➏ N-COUNT 可算名詞 A **print** is a photograph from a film that has been developed. 写真 ❑ ...black and white prints of Margaret and Jean as children. マーガレットとジーンが子供の頃の白黒写真 ➐ N-COUNT 可算名詞 A **print** is one of a number of copies of a particular picture. It can be either a photograph, something such as a painting, or a picture made

by an artist who puts ink on a prepared surface and presses it against paper. 複製画, 版画 ❏...12 original copper plates engraved by William Hogarth for his famous series of prints. ウィリアム・ホガースが彫刻した数々の有名な版画の12枚の銅製の原版 ◳ N-UNCOUNT 不可算名詞 **Print** is used to refer to letters and numbers as they appear on the pages of a book, newspaper, or printed document. 活字 ❏...columns of tiny print. 小さい活字の欄 ◳ ADJ 形容詞 The **print** media consists of newspapers and magazines, but not television or radio. 活字の [ADJ n] ❏I have been convinced that the print media are more accurate and more reliable than television. 活字メディアのほうがテレビよりも正確で信頼性が高いと思い込んでいた。 ◳ V-T 他動詞 If you **print** words, you write in letters that are not joined together. 活字体で書く ❏Print your name and address on a postcard and send it to us. はがきに住所・氏名を活字で記入し, 当社に郵送してください. ◳ N-COUNT 可算名詞 You can refer to a mark left by someone's foot as a **print**. 足跡 ❏He crawled from print to print, sniffing at the earth, following the scent left in the tracks. その犬は, 足跡に残されたにおいをたどり地面のにおいをかぎながら, 足跡に沿っていった. ◳ N-COUNT 可算名詞 You can refer to oily marks left by someone's fingers as their **prints**. 指紋 ❏Fresh prints of both girls were found in the house. 両方の少女の新しい指紋がその家で発見された. ◳ → see also **printing** ◳ PHRASE 句 If you appear **in print**, or get **into print**, what you say or write is published in a book, newspaper, or magazine. 出版されて, 掲載されて ❏Many of these poets appeared in print only long after their deaths. これらの詩人の多くは彼らの死のずっと後になってやっと出版された. ◳ PHRASE 句 The **small print** or the **fine print** of something such as an advertisement or a contract consists of the technical details and legal conditions, which are often printed in much smaller letters than the rest of the text. 細字部分 ❏I'm looking at the small print; I don't want to sign anything that I shouldn't sign. 細字部分を見ているんだ. 署名するべきでないものには署名したくないから.

→ see **photography**

▶ **print out** ◳ PHRASAL VERB 句動詞 If a computer or a machine attached to a computer **prints** something **out**, it produces a copy of it on paper. プリントアウトする, 印刷する ❏You measure yourself, enter measurements and the computer will print out the pattern. 自分の体を測定し測定値を入力すれば, パソコンが型紙をプリントアウトする. ◳ → see also **printout**

print|er /prɪntər/ (printers) ◳ N-COUNT 可算名詞 A **printer** is a machine that can be connected to a computer in order to make copies on paper of documents or other information held by the computer. プリンター ◳ → see also **laser printer** ◳ N-COUNT 可算名詞 A **printer** is a person or company whose job is printing things such as books. 印刷工, 印刷業者 ❏The manuscript had already been sent off to the printer. 原稿はすでに印刷業者に送られていた.

→ see **office**, **printing**

print|ing /prɪntɪŋ/ (printings) ◳ N-COUNT 可算名詞 If copies of a book are printed and published on a number of different occasions, you can refer to each of these occasions as a **printing**. 一刷 ❏"Cloud Street" is already in its third printing. 『クラウド・ストリート』はすでに第3刷目に入っています. ◳ → see also **print**

→ see Word Web: **printing**

print|out /prɪntaʊt/ (printouts) also **print-out** N-COUNT 可算名詞 A **printout** is a piece of paper on which information from a computer or similar device has been printed. プリントアウト ❏...a computer printout of various financial projections. さまざまな財務予測についてのプリントアウト

pri|or /praɪər/ ◳ ADJ 形容詞 You use **prior** to indicate that something has already happened, or must happen, before another event takes place. 前もっての [ADJ n] ❏He claimed he had no prior knowledge of the protest. 彼は, その抗議についての予備知識が全くなかったと主張した. ❏The Constitution requires the president to seek the prior approval of Congress for military action. 憲法では, 軍事活動を行う前に大統領は議会の承認を求めることが義務付けられている. ◳ ADJ 形容詞 A **prior** claim or duty is more important than other claims or duties and needs to be dealt with first. 優先する, より重要な [ADJ n] ❏The firm I wanted to use had prior commitments. 私が使いたかった会社には先約があった. ◳ PHRASE 句 If something

happens **prior to** a particular time or event, it happens before that time or event. 〜の前に [FORMAL 形式ばった] ❏A death prior to 65 is considered to be a premature death. 65歳より若く死亡した場合, 時期尚早の死とみなされる.

pri|or|itize /praɪɔrɪtaɪz/ (prioritizes, prioritizing, prioritized) ◳ V-T 他動詞 If you **prioritize** something, you treat it as more important than other things. 最優先する ❏Prioritize your own wants rather than constantly thinking about others. 常に人のことを考えるのではなくて, 自分自身にとって必要なことを最優先しなさい. ◳ V-T 他動詞 If you **prioritize** the tasks that you have to do, you decide which are the most important and do them first. 優先順位をつける ❏Make lists of what to do and prioritize your tasks. するべきことをリスト化し, 項目別に優先順位を付けなさい.

pri|or|ity /praɪɔrɪti/ (priorities) ◳ N-COUNT 可算名詞 If something is a **priority**, it is the most important thing you have to do or deal with, or must be done or dealt with before everything else you have to do. 優先すること, 最も重要なこと ❏Being a parent is her first priority. 親であることが彼女にとって最も大切なことだ. ❏The government's priority is to build more power plants. 政府の最優先事項は発電所を増設することだ. ◳ PHRASE 句 If you **give priority to** something or someone, you treat them as more important than anything or anyone else. 優先的に扱う ❏Women are more likely to give priority to child care and education policies. 女性は保育や教育政策を優先的に考える傾向が強い. ◳ PHRASE 句 If something **takes priority** or **has priority over** other things, it is regarded as being more important than them and is dealt with first. 優先させる ❏The fight against inflation took priority over measures to combat the deepening recession. 深まる不況への対応政策よりもインフレとの戦いが優先した.

prise /praɪz/ → see **prize** 5

pris|on /prɪzən/ (prisons) N-VAR 可変性名詞 A **prison** is a building where criminals are kept as punishment. 刑務所 ❏The prison's inmates are being kept in their cells. その刑務所の囚人は独房で収容されている.

pris|on|er /prɪzənər/ (prisoners) ◳ N-COUNT 可算名詞 A **prisoner** is a person who is kept in a prison as a punishment for a crime that they have committed. 囚人 ❏The committee is concerned about the large number of prisoners sharing cells. 委員会は, 大人数の囚人が監房を共有していることについて懸念している. ◳ N-COUNT 可算名詞 A **prisoner** is a person who has been captured by an enemy, for example, in war. 捕虜 [also "hold/take" n N] ❏...wartime hostages and concentration-camp prisoners. 戦時中の人質と強制収容所の捕虜

→ see **war**

pris|tine /prɪstin, prɪstin/ ADJ 形容詞 **Pristine** things are extremely clean or new. 汚れがない, しみ一つない [FORMAL 形式ばった] ❏Now the house is in pristine condition. 今はその家は新築同様だ.

pri|va|cy /praɪvəsi/ N-UNCOUNT 不可算名詞 If you have **privacy**, you are in a place or situation that allows you to do things without other people seeing you or disturbing you. プライバシー ❏He resented the publication of this book, which he saw as an embarrassing invasion of his privacy. 彼はばつの悪いプライバシーの侵害とみなし, この本の出版に憤慨した. ❏Thatched pavilions provide

---

Word Web printing

Before the invention of **printing**, scribes wrote **documents** by hand. The earliest **printers** were the Chinese. They used pieces of wood with rows of **characters** carved into them. Later, they started using **movable type** made of baked clay. They created full **pages** by lining up rows of type. A German named Gutenberg expanded on the idea of movable type. He produced the first metal type. He also introduced the **printing press**. The idea came from the centuries-old wine press. In the 1500s, printed advertisements first appeared in the form of handbills. The earliest newspapers were **published** in the 1600s.

shady retreats for relaxing and reading in privacy. わらぶき屋根のパビリオンは、ひそかにくつろいで読書ができる日陰の休憩所となっている.

pri|vate /praɪvɪt/ (**privates**) **1** ADJ 形容詞 **Private** companies, industries, and services are owned or controlled by individuals or stockholders, rather than by the government or an official organization. 民営の, 私立の [BUSINESS 実業] ❑ *...a joint venture with private industry.* 民間企業との共同事業 ❑ *They sent their children to private schools.* 彼らは子供を私立学校に行かせた. ● **pri|vate|ly** ADV 副詞 [ADV with v] 民営で ❑ *No other European country had so much state ownership and so few privately owned businesses.* 他の欧州諸国でそれほど国有が多くて民間所有のビジネスが少ない国はない. **2** ADJ 形容詞 **Private** individuals are acting only for themselves, and are not representing any group, company, or organization. 私の, 私的の [ADJ n] ❑ *Private individuals with money to lend are more difficult to find than traditional lenders.* 貸出資金を持った私人は従来のながらの金貸しよりも見つけにくい. ❑ *The king was on a private visit to enable him to pray at the tombs of his ancestors.* 国王は先祖の墓参りをするために私的訪問をしていた. **3** ADJ 形容詞 Your **private** things belong only to you, or may only be used by you. 私用の, 個人用の ❑ *They want more state control over private property.* 彼らは私有財産のいっそうの国家管理を望んでいる. **4** ADJ 形容詞 **Private** places or gatherings may be attended only by a particular group of people, rather than by the general public. 内輪の ❑ *673 private golf clubs took part in a recent study.* 内輪のゴルフクラブ673団体が最近の研究に参加した. ❑ *The door is marked "Private".* ドアには「関係者以外立ち入り禁止」の標示がある. **5** ADJ 形容詞 **Private** meetings, discussions, and other activities involve only a small number of people, and very little information about them is given to other people. 内密の ❑ *Don't bug private conversations, and don't buy papers that reprint them.* 密談を盗聴してはいけないし, それが転載される新聞を購入してもいけない. ● **pri|vate|ly** ADV 副詞 内密に ❑ *Few senior figures have issued any public statements but privately the resignation's been welcomed.* 上級官僚で公式声明を出した者はほとんどいないが, 個人的には辞任は歓迎している. **6** ADJ 形容詞 Your **private life** is that part of your life that is concerned with your personal relationships and activities, rather than with your work or business. 私的な, プライベートな ❑ *I've always kept my private and professional life separate.* 私は常に私生活と仕事を分けてきた. **7** ADJ 形容詞 Your **private** thoughts or feelings are ones that you do not talk about to other people. 個人的な ❑ *We all felt as if we were intruding on his private grief.* 私たちは皆, 彼の個人的な悲しみに立ち入っているように感じた. ● **pri|vate|ly** ADV 副詞 個人的に ❑ *Privately, she worries about whether she's really good enough.* 個人的には, 彼女は本当に十分に間に合っているのかと心配した. **8** ADJ 形容詞 If you describe a place as **private**, or as somewhere where you can be **private**, you mean that it is a quiet place and you can be alone there without being disturbed. 人けがなく静かな ❑ *It was the only reasonably private place they could find.* そこが唯一彼らの見つけた人けがなく静かな場所だった. **9** ADJ 形容詞 If you describe someone as a **private** person, you mean that they are very quiet by nature and do not reveal their thoughts and feelings to other people. 引っ込み思案な ❑ *Gould was an intensely private individual.* グールドはひどく内気な人だった. **10** N-COUNT; N-TITLE 可算名詞; 称号名詞 A **private** is a soldier of the lowest rank in an army or the marines. 初等兵, 兵卒 ❑ *He was a private in the U.S. Army.* 彼は米軍で初等兵でした. **11** → see also **privately 12** PHRASE 句 If you do something **in private**, you do it without other people being present, often because it is something that you want to keep secret. 内緒で ❑ *Some of what we're talking about might better be discussed in private.* 私たちが話していることは内緒で話したほうがいいかもしれない.

pri|vate en|ter|prise N-UNCOUNT 不可算名詞 **Private enterprise** is industry and business that is owned by individuals or stockholders, and not by the government or an official organization. 民間企業 [BUSINESS 実業] ❑ *...the encouragement of private enterprise.* 民間企業の促進

pri|vate|ly /praɪvɪtli/ **1** ADV 副詞 If you buy or sell something **privately**, you buy it from or sell it to another person directly, rather than in a store or through a business. 直接に [ADV after v] ❑ *The whole process makes buying a car privately as painless as buying from a garage.* その全過程によって, 自動車を個人から直接購入することが自動車屋から購入するのと同じくらい楽になった. **2** → see also **private**

privately held corporation (**privately held corporations**) N-COUNT 可算名詞 A **privately held corporation** is a company whose shares cannot be bought by the general public. 私会社, 株式非公開会社 [AM 米国英語]
→ see **company**

pri|vate school (**private schools**) N-VAR 可変性名詞 A **private school** is a school that is not supported financially by the government and that parents have to pay for their children to go to. 私立学校 ❑ *...an exclusive private school.* 排他的な私立学校

pri|vate sec|tor N-SING 単数名詞 The **private sector** is the part of a country's economy that consists of industries and commercial companies that are not owned or controlled by the government. 民間部門 [BUSINESS 実業] ❑ *...small firms in the private sector.* 民間部門の子会社

pri|vat|ize /praɪvətaɪz/ (**privatizes, privatizing, privatized**) V-T 他動詞 If a company, industry, or service that is owned by the state **is privatized**, the government sells it and makes it a private company. 民営化する [BUSINESS 実業] ❑ *Many state-owned companies were privatized.* 多くの国有会社が民営化された. ❑ *...a move to privatize prisons.* 刑務所を民営化する動き ● **pri|vati|za|tion** /praɪvətɪzeɪʃ°n/ (**privatizations**) N-VAR 可変性名詞 民営化 ❑ *...the privatization of government services.* 政府サービスの民営化

privi|lege /prɪvɪlɪdʒ, prɪvlɪdʒ/ (**privileges**) **1** N-COUNT 可算名詞 A **privilege** is a special right or advantage that only one person or group has. 特権, 特別扱い ❑ *The Russian Federation has issued a decree abolishing special privileges for government officials.* ロシア連邦は国家公務員の特権を廃止する法令を発布した. **2** N-UNCOUNT 不可算名詞 If you talk about **privilege**, you are talking about the power and advantage that only a small group of people have, usually because of their wealth or their connections with powerful people. 特権, 特典 ❑ *Pironi was the son of privilege and wealth, and it showed.* ピロニは特権と富のある子息で, そのことが明らかだった. **3** N-SING 単数名詞 You can use **privilege** in expressions such as **be a privilege** or **have the privilege** when you want to show your appreciation of someone or something, or to show your respect. 名誉 ❑ *It must be a privilege to know such a man.* そのような男性を知っているとは名誉なことにちがいない.

privi|leged /prɪvɪlɪdʒd, prɪvlɪdʒd/ **1** ADJ 形容詞 Someone who is **privileged** has an advantage or opportunity that most other people do not have, often because of their wealth or connections with powerful people. 特権階級の ❑ *They were, by and large, a very wealthy, privileged elite.* 彼らは概して裕福な特権階級のエリートだった. ● N-PLURAL 複数名詞 The **privileged** are people who are privileged. 特権階級の人々 ❑ *They are only interested in preserving the power of the privileged and the well off.* 彼らは特権階級と裕福層の権利を維持することにしか興味を持っていない. **2** ADJ 形容詞 **Privileged** information is known by only a small group of people, who are not legally required to give it to anyone else. 部外秘の ❑ *The data is privileged information, not to be shared with the general public.* その資料は機密情報であり, 一般市民と共有してはいけません.

prize /praɪz/ (**prizes, prizing, prized**) **1** N-COUNT 可算名詞 A **prize** is money or something valuable that is given to someone who has the best results in a competition or game, or as a reward for doing good work. 賞, 賞金 ❑ *You must claim your prize by telephoning our claims line.* 専用の電話番号にかけて賞金を請求しなければいけません. ❑ *He was awarded the Nobel Prize for Physics in 1985.* 彼は, 1985年にノーベル物理学賞を受賞した. **2** ADJ 形容詞 You use **prize** to describe things that are of such good quality that they win prizes or deserve to win prizes. 受賞した, 受賞に値する [ADJ n] ❑ *...a prize bull.* 入選した雄牛 **3** N-COUNT 可算名詞 You can refer to someone or something as a **prize** when people consider them to be of great value or importance. 素晴らしいもの ❑ *With no lands of his own, he was no great matrimonial prize.* 彼は土地を所有していないので, 結婚相手としては魅力に欠けていた. **4** V-T 他動詞 Something that **is prized** is wanted and admired because it is considered to be very valuable or very good quality. 尊重する [usu passive] ❑ *Military figures made out of lead are prized by collectors.* 鉛製の兵士はコレクターに珍重されている. **5** V-T 他動詞 If you **prize** something **open** or **prize** it away from a surface, you force it to open or force it to come away from the surface. こじ開ける [mainly BRIT 主に英国英語; AM usually **pry** 米国英語では通常 **pry**]

pro /proʊ/ (**pros**) **1** N-COUNT 可算名詞 A **pro** is a professional. プロ [INFORMAL くだけた] ❑ *In the professional theater, there is a tremendous need to prove that you're a pro.* 商業劇場では, 自分がプロであることを証明する必要が極めて高い. **2** ADJ 形容詞 A **pro** player is a professional athlete. You can also use **pro** to refer to sports that are played by professional athletes. プロの [AM 米国英語] [ADJ n] ❑ *...a former college and pro basketball player.* 元大学選手でプロのバスケットボール選手 **3** PREP 前置詞 If you are **pro** a particular course of action or belief, you agree with it or support it. ~に賛成

して □*Americans have always been very pro business, pro competition, pro free market.* アメリカ人は常にビジネス，競争，自由市場を強く支持してきた．**4** PHRASE 句 The **pros and cons** of something are its advantages and disadvantages, which you consider carefully so that you can make a sensible decision. よい点と悪い点，賛否 □*Motherhood has both its pros and cons.* 母親であることには賛否両論ある．

Word Link pro ≈ in front, before : *pro*active, *pro*ceed, *pro*duce

---

pro|ac|tive /prəʊ**æk**tɪv/ ADJ 形容詞 **Proactive** actions are intended to cause changes, rather than just reacting to change. 積極的な，先を見越した □*In order to survive the competition a company should be proactive not reactive.* 競争で生き残るためには，会社は物事が起こってから反応するのではなく先を見越して行動を起こすべきだ．

Word Link prob ≈ testing : *prob*ability, *prob*ation, *prob*e

---

prob|abil|ity /prɒbə**bɪl**ɪti/ (**probabilities**) **1** N-VAR 可変性名詞 The **probability of** something happening is how likely it is to happen, sometimes expressed as a fraction or a percentage. 見込み，公算 □*Without a transfusion, the victim's probability of dying was 100%.* 輸血をしなければ，犠牲者の死亡確率は100%だ．□*The probabilities of crime or victimization are higher with some situations than with others.* 犯罪や虐待の可能性は状況によって高くなる．**2** N-VAR 可変性名詞 You say that there is a **probability that** something will happen when it is likely to happen. 起こりそうなこと [VAGUENESS あいまいさ] □*If you've owned property for several years, the probability is that values have increased.* もし不動産を数年所有すれば，価格が上昇した可能性がある．□*Formal talks are still said to be a possibility, not a probability.* 依然として公式会談の可能性はあるが公算は低いといわれている．**3** PHRASE 句 If you say that something will happen **in all probability**, you mean that you think it is very likely to happen. 恐らく [VAGUENESS あいまいさ] □*The Republicans had better get used to the fact that in all probability, they are going to lose.* 共和党員は恐らく敗北するという現実に向き合った方がよい．

prob|able /**prɒ**bəbᵊl/ **1** ADJ 形容詞 If you say that something is **probable**, you mean that it is likely to be true or likely to happen. ありそうな，可能性が高い [VAGUENESS あいまいさ] □*It is probable that the medication will suppress the symptom without treating the condition.* その薬は治療はせずに症状だけを抑える可能性が高い．**2** ADJ 形容詞 You can use **probable** to describe a role or function that someone or something is likely to have. 予想される [ADJ n] □*...their probable presidential candidate.* 予想される大統領候補者

prob|ably /**prɒ**bəbli/ **1** ADV 副詞 If you say that something is **probably** the case, you think that it is likely to be the case, although you are not sure. 恐らく [VAGUENESS あいまいさ] [ADV with cl/group] □*The White House probably won't make this plan public until July.* 米国政府は恐らくこの計画を7月まで公表しないでしょう．□*Van Gogh is probably the best-known painter in the world.* バン・ゴッホは恐らく世界で最も有名な画家だ．**2** ADV 副詞 You can use **probably** when you want to make your opinion sound less forceful or definite, so that you do not offend people. たぶん [VAGUENESS あいまいさ] [ADV with cl/group] □*What would he think of their story? He'd probably think she and Lenny were both crazy!* 彼はあの話をどう思うだろう．たぶん彼女とレニーは2人ともまともじゃないと思うだろう．

pro|ba|tion /prəʊ**beɪ**ʃᵊn/ **1** N-UNCOUNT 不可算名詞 **Probation** is a period of time during which a person who has committed a crime has to obey the law and be supervised by a probation officer, rather than being sent to prison. 保護観察 □*A young woman admitted three theft charges and was put on probation for two years.* 窃盗罪3件を認めた若い女性は2年間の保護観察を受けた．**2** N-UNCOUNT 不可算名詞 **Probation** is a period of time during which someone is judging your character and ability while you work, in order to see if you are suitable for that type of work. 試用期間 □*Employee appointment to the council will be subject to a term of probation of 6 months.* 自治体職員への任命者へは6か月間の試用期間を受ける必要がある．

pro|ba|tion of|fic|er (**probation officers**) N-COUNT 可算名詞 A **probation officer** is a person whose job is to supervise and help people who have committed crimes and been put on probation. 保護監察官

probe /prəʊb/ (**probes, probing, probed**) **1** V-I 自動詞 If you **probe into** something, you ask questions or try to discover facts about it. 探りを入れる □*The more they probed into his background, the more inflamed their suspicions would become.* 彼の経歴を探れば探るほど，ますます疑惑が炎上するだろう．□*For three years, I have probed for understanding.* 私は3年間理解するために精査してきた．●N-COUNT 可算名詞 **Probe** is also a noun. 調査 □*...a federal grand-jury probe into corruption within the FDA.* 食品医薬品局内の汚職に関する連邦大陪審の調査 **2** V-I 自動詞 If a doctor or dentist **probes**, he or she uses a long instrument to examine part of a patient's body. （探り針で）検査する □*The surgeon would pick up his instruments, probe, repair, and stitch up again.* 執刀医は器具を取り上げ，検査し，修復し，そしてま

た縫合するだろう．□*Dr. Amid probed around the sensitive area.* エィミッド先生は敏感な患部を検査した．**3** N-COUNT 可算名詞 A **probe** is a long thin instrument that doctors and dentists use to examine parts of the body. 探り針 □*...a fiber-optic probe.* 光ファイバーの探り針 **4** V-T 他動詞 If you **probe** a place, you search it in order to find someone or something that you are looking for. 探査する □*A flashlight beam probed the underbrush only yards away from their hiding place.* 懐中電灯の光で彼らの隠れ場所からほんの数ヤード離れたやぶを探査した．

prob|lem /**prɒb**ləm/ (**problems**) **1** N-COUNT 可算名詞 A **problem** is a situation that is unsatisfactory and causes difficulties for people. 問題，困ったこと □*...the economic problems of the inner city.* 都心部の経済問題 □*I do not have a simple solution to the drug problem.* 私には，麻薬問題の簡単な解決策がない．**2** N-COUNT 可算名詞 A **problem** is a puzzle that requires logical thought or mathematics to solve it. （論理学・数学などの）問題 □*With mathematical problems, you can save time by approximating.* 数学の問題では，概算することで時間の節約ができる．

Thesaurus problem また次を参照 :

N. complication, difficulty, hitch **1**
brain-teaser, puzzle, question, riddle **2**

---

prob|lem|at|ic /prɒbləm**æt**ɪk/ ADJ 形容詞 Something that is **problematic** involves problems and difficulties. 問題がある □*Some places are more problematic than others for women traveling alone.* 女性が一人旅をする場合，ほかよりも問題が発生しやすい場所がある．

pro|ce|du|ral /prə**siː**dʒərəl/ ADJ 形容詞 **Procedural** means involving a formal procedure. 手続き上の [FORMAL 形式ばった] □*A Spanish judge rejected the suit on procedural grounds.* スペイン人の判事は手続き上の理由でその訴訟を却下した．

pro|ce|dure /prə**siː**dʒər/ (**procedures**) N-VAR 可変性名詞 A **procedure** is a way of doing something, especially the usual or correct way. 手続き，手順 □*A biopsy is usually a minor surgical procedure.* 生検はふつう簡単な外科手術だ．□*Police insist that Michael did not follow the correct procedure in applying for a visa.* マイケルはビザ申請の正しい手順を踏まなかったと警察は主張した．

Word Partnership procedure は次の語句と使われる :

ADJ. **simple** procedure, **standard (operating)** procedure, **surgical** procedure
V. **follow** a procedure, **perform** a procedure, **use a** procedure

---

Word Link pro ≈ in front, before : *pro*active, *pro*ceed, *pro*duce

---

pro|ceed (**proceeds, proceeding, proceeded**)

The verb is pronounced /prə**siːd**/. The plural noun in meaning **4** is pronounced /**prəʊ**siːdz/.

動詞は /prə**siːd**/と発音される．**4**を意味する複数名詞は /**prəʊ**siːdz/と発音される．

1 V-T 他動詞 If you **proceed to** do something, you do it, often after doing something else first. （次に）ーする □*He proceeded to tell me of my birth.* 次に彼は私の誕生について話してくれた．**2** V-I 自動詞 If you **proceed with** a course of action, you continue with it. 続ける，続行する [FORMAL 形式ばった] □*The group proceeded with a march they knew would lead to bloodshed.* 団体は，流血につながると知りながらも行進を続けた．**3** V-I 自動詞 If an activity, process, or event **proceeds**, it goes on and does not stop. 進行する □*The ideas were not new. Their development had proceeded steadily since the war.* それは新しいアイデアではなかった．戦後着実に進行していた．**4** N-PLURAL 複数名詞 The **proceeds** of an event or activity are the money that has been obtained from it. 収益 □*The proceeds of the concert went to charity.* コンサートの収益はチャリティに寄付された．

pro|ceed|ing /prə**siː**dɪŋ/ (**proceedings**) **1** N-COUNT 可算名詞 Legal **proceedings** are legal action taken against someone. 訴訟手続き [FORMAL 形式ばった] □*...criminal proceedings against the former prime minister.* 前首相に対する刑事訴訟手続き **2** N-COUNT 可算名詞 The **proceedings** are an organized series of events that take place in a particular place. 出来事，成り行き [FORMAL 形式ばった] □*The proceedings of the inquiry will take place in private.* 尋問は内密に行われる．**3** N-PLURAL 複数名詞 You can refer to a written record of the discussions at a meeting or conference as the **proceedings**. 議事録 □*The DOT is to publish the conference proceedings.* 財務省は会議の議事録を出版する予定だ．

pro|cess /**prɒ**ses/ (**processes, processing, processed**) **1** N-COUNT 可算名詞 A **process** is a series of actions which are carried out in order to achieve a particular result. 過程，プロセス □*There was total agreement to start the peace process as soon as possible.* できるだけ早い段階で平和プロセスを開始させるという完

全な合意がありました. ❑ *They decided to spread the building process over three years.* 建設過程を3年間に伸ばすと決定した. **2** N-COUNT 可算名詞 A **process** is a series of things that happen naturally and result in a biological or chemical change. 作用 ❑ *It occurs in elderly men, apparently as part of the aging process.* それは, どうやら老化作用の一部として年配の男性に起こる. **3** V-T 他動詞 When raw materials or foods **are processed**, they are prepared in factories before they are used or sold. 加工処理する ❑ *...fish which are processed by the best methods: from freezing to canning and smoking.* 冷凍, 缶詰, 薫製という最善の方法で加工処理した魚 ❑ *The material will be processed into plastic pellets.* 原料はプラスチック・ペレットに加工される. ● N-COUNT 可算名詞 **Process** is also a noun. ❑ *...the cost of reengineering the production process.* 構造改革と生産工程のコスト ● **pro|cess|ing** N-UNCOUNT 不可算名詞 [usu with supp] 加工処理 ❑ *America sent cotton to England for processing.* 米国は綿花を加工のためにイギリスに輸出した. **4** V-T 他動詞 When people **process** information, they put it through a system or into a computer in order to deal with it. 処理する ❑ *...facilities to process the data, and the right to publish the results.* データを処理するための設備と結果を出版する権利 ● **pro|cess|ing** N-UNCOUNT 不可算名詞 処理 ❑ *...data processing.* データ処理 **5** → see also **word processing** **6** V-T 他動詞 [usu passive] When people **are processed** by officials, their case is dealt with in stages and they pass from one stage of the process to the next. 一定の手順で扱う ❑ *Patients took more than two hours to be processed through the department.* 患者が課の手続きを処理するのに2時間以上かかった. **7** PHRASE 句 If you are **in the process of** doing something, you have started to do it and are still doing it. ～しているところ ❑ *The administration is in the process of drawing up a peace plan.* 政府は和平計画の作成中です. **8** PHRASE 句 If you are doing something and you do something else **in the process**, you do the second thing as part of doing the first thing. その過程で ❑ *You have to let us struggle for ourselves, even if we must die in the process.* たとえその過程で死ななければならなくとも, 自分たちで奮闘させてください.

Word Partnership   process は次の語句と使われる:

ADJ.	**difficult** process, **political** process **1**
	complicated process, **gradual** process, **long** process, **normal** process, **slow** process, **whole** process **1 2**
V.	**participate in a** process **1**
	begin a process, **complete a** process, **control a** process, **describe a** process, **start a** process **1 2**
N.	**application** process, **approval** process, **decision** process, **learning** process, **planning** process **1** process **information 4**

pro|ces|sion /prəsɛʃ³n/ (**processions**) N-COUNT 可算名詞 A **procession** is a group of people who are walking, riding, or driving in a line as part of a public event. 行進, 行列 ❑ *...a funeral procession.* 葬列

pro|ces|sor /prɒsɛsər/ (**processors**) **1** N-COUNT 可算名詞 A **processor** is the part of a computer that interprets commands and performs the processes the user has requested. 処理装置, 加工装置 [COMPUTING コンピューティング] **2** → see also **food processor**, **word processor** **3** N-COUNT 可算名詞 A **processor** is someone or something which carries out a process. 加工業者 ❑ *The frozen-food industry could be supplied entirely by growers and processors outside the country.* 冷凍食品業界は完全に海外の生産者と加工業者により供給されている可能性があります.

pro|claim /prəkleɪm/ (**proclaims, proclaiming, proclaimed**) **1** V-T 他動詞 If people **proclaim** something, they formally make it known to the public. 公表する, 宣言する ❑ *The new government in Venezuela set up its own army and proclaimed its independence.* ベネズエラの新政府は独自の軍を結成し, 独立を宣言した. ❑ *Britain proudly proclaims that it is a nation of animal lovers.* 英国は動物愛好家の国であることを堂々と宣言する. **2** V-T 他動詞 If you **proclaim** something, you state it in an emphatic way. はっきりと言う ❑ *"I think we have been heard today," he proclaimed.* 「今日は我々の意見を聞いてもらえたと思うよ」と彼は声高に言った.

proc|la|ma|tion /prɒkləmeɪʃ³n/ (**proclamations**) N-COUNT 可算名詞 A **proclamation** is a public announcement about something important, often about something of national importance. 宣言, 声明 ❑ *The proclamation of independence was broadcast over the radio.* 独立宣言はラジオで放送された.

pro|cure /prəkyʊər/ (**procures, procuring, procured**) V-T 他動詞 If you **procure** something, especially something that is difficult to get, you obtain it. 入手する, 獲得する [FORMAL 形式ばった] ❑ *It remained very difficult to procure food, fuel, and other daily necessities.* 食べ物, 燃料, その他の日常必需品を入手するのは依然としてかなり難しかった.

pro|cure|ment /prəkyʊərmənt/ N-UNCOUNT 不可算名詞 **Procurement** is the act of obtaining something such as supplies for an army or other organization. 入手 [FORMAL 形式ばった]

❑ *Russia was cutting procurement of new weapons "by about 80 percent,"* he said. ロシアは新兵器の入手を「約80%」削減している, と彼は述べた.

prod /prɒd/ (**prods, prodding, prodded**) **1** V-T 他動詞 If you **prod** someone or something, you give them a quick push with your finger or with a pointed object. つつく ❑ *He prodded Murray with the shotgun.* 彼はマリーを散弾銃でつついた. ❑ *Prod the windowsills to check for signs of rot.* 腐敗の兆しがないかを点検するために窓枠をつつきなさい. ● N-COUNT 可算名詞 **Prod** is also a noun. つつくこと ❑ *He gave the donkey a mighty prod in the backside.* 彼はロバの後部を強くつついた. **2** V-T 他動詞 If you **prod** someone **into** doing something, you remind or persuade them to do it. 駆り立てる, 励ます ❑ *The question is intended to prod students into examining the concept of freedom.* その質問の意図は, 学生を自由の概念について考察するよう駆り立てることです.

pro|di|gious /prədɪdʒəs/ ADJ 形容詞 Something that is **prodigious** is very large or impressive. 巨大な, 並外れた [LITERARY 文語的] ❑ *This business generates cash in prodigious amounts.* この事業は並外れた額の現金をもたらす. ● **pro|di|gious|ly** ADV 副詞 並外れて ❑ *She ate prodigiously.* 彼女は驚くほど食べた.

prod|i|gy /prɒdɪdʒi/ (**prodigies**) N-COUNT 可算名詞 A **prodigy** is someone young who has a great natural ability for something such as music, mathematics, or sports. 天才, 奇才 ❑ *The Russian tennis prodigy is well on the way to becoming the youngest world champion of all time.* ロシアの天才テニス選手はまもなく過去最年少の世界チャンピオンになるだろう.

Word Link   pro ≈ in front, before : **pro**active, **pro**ceed, **pro**duce

pro|duce (**produces, producing, produced**)

The verb is pronounced /prədus/. The noun is pronounced /prɒdus/ or /proʊdus/.

動詞は /prədus/ と発音される. 名詞は /prɒdus/ か /proʊdus/ と発音される.

---

1 V-T 他動詞 To **produce** something means to cause it to happen. (結果を) もたらす ❑ *The drug is known to produce side-effects in women.* その薬は女性に副作用を起こすことが知られている. **2** V-T 他動詞 If you **produce** something, you make or create it. 製造する ❑ *The company produced circuitry for communications systems.* その会社は通信システムの回路を製造した. **3** V-T 他動詞 When things or people **produce** something, it comes from them or slowly forms from them, especially as the result of a biological or chemical process. 生成する ❑ *These plants are then pollinated and allowed to mature and produce seed.* そしてこれらの植物は受粉し, 成長し種がなる. **4** V-T 他動詞 If you **produce** evidence or an argument, you show it or explain it to people in order to make them agree with you. 示す, 説明する ❑ *They challenged him to produce evidence to support his allegations.* 彼らは疑惑を立証するように彼に挑んだ. **5** V-T 他動詞 If you **produce** an object from somewhere, you show it or bring it out so that it can be seen. 提示する ❑ *To rent a car you must produce a passport and a current driver's license.* レンタカーを借りるには, パスポートと有効な運転免許証を提示しなければならない. **6** V-T 他動詞 If someone **produces** something such as a movie, a magazine, or a CD, they organize it and decide how it should be done. 製作する, プロデュースする ❑ *He has produced his own sports magazine.* 彼は自分のスポーツ雑誌を製作した. **7** N-UNCOUNT 不可算名詞 **Produce** is fruit and vegetables that are grown in large quantities to be sold. 生産物, 農産物 ❑ *We manage to get most of our produce in farmers' markets.* なんとか生産物のほとんどを青空市場に出している.

pro|duc|er /prədusər/ (**producers**) **1** N-COUNT 可算名詞 A **producer** is a person whose job is to produce plays, movies, programs, or CDs. プロデューサー, 制作者 ❑ *...a freelance film producer.* フリーランス映画プロデューサー **2** N-COUNT 可算名詞 A **producer** of a food or material is a company or country that grows or manufactures a large amount of it. 生産者, 生産国, 製造会社 ❑ *...Saudi Arabia, the world's leading oil producer.* 世界1の産油国であるサウジアラビア

prod|uct /prɒdʌkt/ (**products**) **1** N-COUNT 可算名詞 A **product** is something that is produced and sold in large quantities, often as a result of a manufacturing process. 製品 ❑ *Try to get the best product at the lowest price.* 最高の製品を最低価格で手に入れてみましょう. **2** N-COUNT 可算名詞 If you say that someone or something is a **product** of a situation or process, you mean that the situation or process has had a significant effect in making them what they are. 結果, 成果 ❑ *We are all products of our time.* 私たちはみな時代のたまものだ.

→ see **advertising, industry, inventor**

pro|duc|tion /prədʌkʃ³n/ (**productions**) **1** N-UNCOUNT 不可算名詞 **Production** is the process of manufacturing or growing something in large quantities. 生産, 製造 ❑ *That model won't go into production before late 2007.* そのモデルは2007年末まで製造されない. **2** N-UNCOUNT 不可算名詞 **Production** is the amount of

goods manufactured or grown by a company or country. 生産高 ❑ *We needed to increase the volume of production.* 生産高を増加する必要があった. **3** N-UNCOUNT 不可算名詞 The **production of** something is its creation as the result of a natural process. 生成 ❑ *These proteins stimulate the production of blood cells.* このたんぱく質が血球生成を完成化する. **4** N-UNCOUNT 不可算名詞 **Production** is the process of organizing and preparing a play, movie, program, or CD, in order to present it to the public. 制作 ❑ *She is head of the production company.* 彼女が制作会社の社長だ. **5** N-COUNT 可算名詞 A **production** is a play, opera, or other show that is performed in a theater. 作品 ❑ *...a critically acclaimed production of Othello.* 絶賛されたオセロの作品 **6** PHRASE 句 When you can do something **on production of** or **on the production of** documents, you need to show someone those documents in order to be able to do that thing. 提示によって ❑ *Entry to the show is free to members on production of their membership cards.* 展覧会への入場は会員証の提示によって会員は無料になる.
→ see **theater**

pro|duc|tion line (**production lines**) N-COUNT 可算名詞 A **production line** is an arrangement of machines in a factory where the products pass from machine to machine until they are finished. 生産ライン ❑ *Honda added a production line this year, hoping to boost domestic sales.* 本田技研は国内販売の促進を期待し, 今年生産ラインを増設した.

pro|duc|tive /prədʌktɪv/ **1** ADJ 形容詞 Someone or something that is **productive** produces or does a lot for the amount of resources used. 生産力のある, 生産性が高い ❑ *Training makes workers highly productive.* 研修により労働者の生産性が非常に高くなる. ❑ *More productive farmers have been able to provide cheaper food.* より低価格で食品を提供することができる生産性の高い農業経営者が増加した. **2** ADJ 形容詞 If you say that a relationship between people is **productive**, you mean that a lot of good or useful things happen as a result of it. 有意義な ❑ *He was hopeful that the next round of talks would also be productive.* 彼は, 次回の協議も有意義なものとなることに期待を寄せていた.

pro|duc|tiv|ity /prɒdʌktɪvɪti/ N-UNCOUNT 不可算名詞 **Productivity** is the rate at which goods are produced. 生産性 ❑ *The third-quarter results reflect continued improvements in productivity.* 第3四半期の結果は生産性の向上が続いていることを反映している.

prod|uct line (**product lines**) N-COUNT 可算名詞 A **product line** is a group of related products produced by one manufacturer, for example, products that are intended to be used for similar purposes or to be sold in similar types of stores. 製品ライン [BUSINESS 実業] ❑ *...the company's most successful product lines.* その会社で最も売れている製品ライン

prod|uct place|ment (**product placements**) N-VAR 可変性名詞 **Product placement** is a form of advertising in which a company has its product placed where it can be clearly seen during a movie or television program. プロダクト・プレースメント [BUSINESS 実業] ❑ *It was the first movie to feature onscreen product placement for its own merchandise.* 映画で自社製品をプロダクト・プレースメントに起用した最初の映画だった.

pro|fess /prəfɛs/ (**professes, professing, professed**) **1** V-T 他動詞 If you **profess to** do or have something, you claim that you do it or have it, often when you do not. 言い張る, 主張する [FORMAL 形式ばった] ❑ *She professed to hate her nickname.* 彼女は自分のあだ名が大嫌いだと言い張った. ❑ *Why do organizations profess that they care?* どうして機関は関心があると装うのだろうか. **2** V-T 他動詞 If you **profess** a feeling, opinion, or belief, you express it. 明言する, 告白する [FORMAL 形式ばった] ❑ *He professed to be content with the arrangement.* 彼は, その取り決めに満足していると述べた. ❑ *Miller professed himself dissatisfied with Broadway theater.* ミラーはブロードウェイの演劇に不満であることを明言した.

pro|fes|sion /prəfɛʃ°n/ (**professions**) **1** N-COUNT 可算名詞 A **profession** is a type of job that requires advanced education or training. 専門職, 職業 [also "by" N] ❑ *Harper was a teacher by profession.* ハーパーは教師だった. **2** N-COUNT-COLL 集合可算名詞 You can use **profession** to refer to all the people who have the same profession. 同業者全体 ❑ *The attitude of the medical profession is very much more liberal now.* 医学界の姿勢は以前に比べるとずっと進歩的になりました.

pro|fes|sion|al /prəfɛʃən°l/ (**professionals**) **1** ADJ 形容詞 **Professional** means relating to a person's work, especially work that requires special training. 専門職の [ADJ n] ❑ *His professional career started at Colgate University.* 彼の職歴はコルゲート大学で始まった. ● **pro|fes|sion|al|ly** ADV 副詞 専門的に ❑ *...a professionally-qualified architect.* 専門の資格を持つ建築家 **2** ADJ 形容詞 [ADJ n] **Professional** people have jobs that require advanced education or training. 専門職に就いた ❑ *...highly qualified professional people like doctors and engineers.* 医者や技術者のようにレベルの高い専門職にある人々 ● N-COUNT 可算名詞 **Professional** is also a noun. 専門職の人 ❑ *My father wanted me to become a professional and have more stability.* 父は私が専門職につきもっと安定した生活を送ることを望ん

でいた. **3** ADJ 形容詞 You use **professional** to describe people who do a particular thing to earn money rather than as a hobby. 玄人の, プロの ❑ *This has been my worst time for injuries since I started as a professional player.* プロ選手として始めて以来負傷に関してここのところ最悪だ. ● N-COUNT 可算名詞 **Professional** is also a noun. プロ, 本職 ❑ *He had been a professional since March 1985.* 彼は1985年3月以来プロとして働いた. ● **pro|fes|sion|al|ly** ADV 副詞 [ADV after v] プロとして ❑ *By age 16 he was playing professionally with bands in Greenwich Village.* 16歳までには, 彼はプロとしてグリニッジビレッジでバンドと演奏した. **4** ADJ 形容詞 **Professional** sports are played for money rather than as a hobby. プロの [ADJ n] ❑ *...an art student who had played professional football for a short time.* 短期間プロのフットボール選手だった画学生 **5** ADJ 形容詞 If you say something that someone does or produces is **professional**, you approve of it because you think that it is of a very high standard. プロ級の, レベルが高い [APPROVAL 賛成] ❑ *They run it with a truly professional but personal touch.* 彼らは非常にプロ意識が高いが親しみのある経営をしている. ● N-COUNT 可算名詞 **Professional** is also a noun. 熟練者 ❑ *...a dedicated professional who worked harmoniously with the cast and crew.* 出演者やスタッフと仲よく仕事をしたひたむきなベテラン ● **pro|fes|sion|al|ly** ADV 副詞 [ADV with v] プロのように ❑ *These tickets have been produced very professionally.* これらのチケットは本格的に制作された.

pro|fes|sion|al|ism /prəfɛʃ°nəlɪzəm/ N-UNCOUNT 不可算名詞 **Professionalism** in a job is a combination of skill and high standards. 専門的技術, プロ意識 [APPROVAL 賛成] ❑ *American companies pride themselves on their professionalism.* 米国企業は専門的技術に誇りを持っている.

pro|fes|sor /prəfɛsər/ (**professors**) **1** N-COUNT; N-TITLE; N-VOC 可算名詞, 称号名詞, 呼格名詞 A **professor** in an American or Canadian university or college is a teacher of the highest rank. 教授 ❑ *Robert Dunn is a professor of economics at George Washington University.* ロバート・ダンはジョージ・ワシントン大学の経済学教授だ. **2** N-TITLE; N-COUNT; N-VOC 称号名詞, 可算名詞, 呼格名詞 A **professor** in a British university is the most senior teacher in a department. 学部長 ❑ *...Professor Cameron.* カメロン学部長
→ see **graduation**

prof|fer /prɒfər/ (**proffers, proffering, proffered**) **1** V-T 他動詞 If you **proffer** something to someone, you hold it toward them so that they can take it or touch it. 差し出す [FORMAL 形式ばった] ❑ *He rose and proffered a silver box full of cigarettes.* 彼は立ち上がって, たばこが詰まった銀の箱を差し出した. **2** V-T 他動詞 If you **proffer** something such as advice to someone, you offer it to them. 与える, 提供する [FORMAL 形式ばった] ❑ *The army has not yet proffered an explanation of how and why the accident happened.* 軍は, 事故が起こった状況と理由をまだ説明していていない.

pro|fi|cien|cy /prəfɪʃ°nsi/ N-UNCOUNT 不可算名詞 If you show **proficiency** in something, you show ability or skill at it. 熟練, たんのう ❑ *Evidence of basic proficiency in English is part of the admissions requirement.* 基礎レベルの英語ができるという証明は, 入学必要条件の一部だ.

pro|fi|cient /prəfɪʃ°nt/ ADJ 形容詞 If you are **proficient in** something, you can do it well. 熟達した, たんのうな ❑ *A great number of Egyptians are proficient in foreign languages.* エジプト人の多くは外国語にたんのうだ.

pro|file /proʊfaɪl/ (**profiles**) **1** N-COUNT 可算名詞 Your **profile** is the outline of your face as it is seen when someone is looking at you from the side. 横顔 ❑ *His handsome profile was turned away from us.* 彼のハンサムな横顔がそっぽを向いてしまった. **2** N-UNCOUNT 不可算名詞 If you see someone **in profile**, you see them from the side. 横顔 ❑ *This picture shows the girl in profile.* この写真では少女を横から見て写している. **3** N-COUNT 可算名詞 A **profile** of someone is a short article or program in which their life and character are described. プロフィール, 簡単な紹介 ❑ *A Washington newspaper published comparative profiles of the candidates' wives.* あるワシントンの新聞社は, 候補者の妻の比較プロフィールを出版した. **4** N-COUNT 可算名詞 If the police make a **profile** of someone they are looking for, they write a description of the sort of person they are looking for. 人物評 [oft N "of" n] ❑ *...the FBI profile of the anthrax killer.* 連邦捜査局が作成した炭そ菌殺人犯の人物評 ● **pro|fil|ing** /proʊfaɪlɪŋ/ N-UNCOUNT 不可算名詞 プロファイリング ❑ *...a former FBI agent who pioneered psychological profiling in the 1970s.* 1970年代に心理学的プロファイリングを始めた元連邦捜査局員 ❑ *DNA profiling would now be added to the struggle against vandalism.* DNA個人識別法がこれから公物の破損との戦いに使用されるだろう. **5** PHRASE 句 If someone has a **high profile**, people notice them and what they do. If you **keep a low profile**, you avoid doing things that will make people notice you. 注目度が高いこと ❑ *...a move that would give Egypt a much higher profile in the upcoming peace talks.* 今度の和平会談でエジプトへの関心度をずっと高めるであろう動き **6** → see also **high-profile**

prof|it /prɒfɪt/ (**profits, profiting, profited**) **1** N-VAR 可変性名詞 A **profit** is an amount of money that you gain when you

are paid more for something than it cost you to make, get, or do it. 利益 ❑ *The bank made pre-tax profits of $6.5 million.* その銀行は650万ドルの税引前利益を出した。 ❑ *You can improve your chances of profit by sensible planning.* 賢明な計画を立てることにより利益を出す可能性を高めることができる。 **2** V-I 自動詞 If you **profit from** something, you earn a profit from it. 利益を得る ❑ *No one was profiting inordinately from the war effort.* 軍需産業から法外な利益を得たものはいなかった。 ❑ *He has profited by selling his holdings to other investors.* 彼は、持ち株を他の投資家に販売することによって利益を得た。 **3** V-T/V-I 他動詞/自動詞 If you **profit from** something, or it **profits** you, you gain some advantage or benefit from it. 得になる、得をする [FORMAL 形式ばった] ❑ *Jennifer wasn't yet totally convinced that she'd profit from a more relaxed lifestyle.* ジェニファーは、もっとのんびりした生活スタイルが得になるとはまだ確信していなかった。 ❑ *So far the French alliance had profited the rebels little.* それまでのところ、フランスの同盟国は反逆者からほとんど得るものはなかった。
→ see **company**

Word Partnership   profit は次の語句と使われる:

N.	**decline in** profit, profit **and loss**, profit **margin**, **operating** profit, profit **sharing** ❶
V.	**make** a profit, **maximize** profit, **post** a profit, **report** a profit, **turn** a profit ❶

prof·it·able /prɒfɪtəbᵊl/ ❶ ADJ 形容詞 A **profitable** organization or practice makes a profit. 収益の上がる ❑ *Drug manufacturing is the most profitable business in the U.S.* 製薬業界が米国で最も収益性の高い業種である。 ● **prof·it·ably** /prɒfɪtəbli/ ADV 副詞 [ADV with v] 利益が出るように ❑ *The 28 French stores are trading profitably.* フランスの28店舗は利益を出して営業している。 ● **prof·it·abil·ity** /ˌprɒfɪtəˈbɪlɪti/ N-UNCOUNT 不可算名詞 収益性 ❑ *Changes were made in operating methods in an effort to increase profitability.* 収益性を上げようという試みで運営方法に変更があった。 **2** ADJ 形容詞 Something that is **profitable** results in some benefit for you. 有益な ❑ *...close collaboration with industry which leads to a profitable exchange of personnel and ideas.* 人材と意見の有益な交換につながる産業との緊密な協力 ● **prof·it·ably** ADV 副詞 [ADV with v] 有益に ❑ *In fact he could scarcely have spent his time more profitably.* 実際彼はほとんど時間を無駄にしていた。

prof·it·eer·ing /ˌprɒfɪˈtɪərɪŋ/ N-UNCOUNT 不可算名詞 **Profiteering** involves making large profits by charging high prices for goods that are hard to get. 不当利益行為 [BUSINESS 実業, DISAPPROVAL 不賛成] ❑ *There's been a wave of profiteering and corruption.* 不当利益行為や汚職が高まっている。

profit-making ❶ ADJ 形容詞 A **profit-making** business or organization makes a profit. 利益を上げている [BUSINESS 実業] ❑ *He wants to set up a profit-making company, owned mostly by the university.* 彼は大部分が大学所有の営利会社を設立したいと思っている。 **2** → see also **nonprofit**

prof·it mar·gin (profit margins) N-COUNT 可算名詞 A **profit margin** is the difference between the selling price of a product and the cost of producing and marketing it. 利ざや [BUSINESS 実業] ❑ *The group had a net profit margin of 30% last year.* その団体は昨年30%の純利益率を出した。

profit-sharing N-UNCOUNT 不可算名詞 **Profit-sharing** is a system by which all the people who work in a company have a share in its profits. 利益分配制 [BUSINESS 実業] ❑ *...the bank's profit-sharing plan.* 銀行の利益分配計画

profit-taking N-UNCOUNT 不可算名詞 **Profit-taking** is the selling of stocks and shares at a profit after their value has risen or just before their value falls. 利食い [BUSINESS 実業] ❑ *The market was held down by profit-taking in the banking sector yesterday.* 昨日の市場は金融部門の利食いのため低迷した。

pro·found /prəˈfaʊnd/ (profounder, profoundest) ❶ ADJ 形容詞 You use **profound** to emphasize that something is very great or intense. 重大な、多大な [EMPHASIS 強調] ❑ *...discoveries which had a profound effect on many areas of medicine.* 医学の多くの分野に多大な影響を与えた発見 ❑ *...profound disagreement.* かなりの食い違い ● **pro·found·ly** ADV 副詞 非常に ❑ *This has profoundly affected my life.* これはかなり私の人生に影響を与えた。 **2** ADJ 形容詞 A **profound** idea, work, or person shows great intellectual depth and understanding. 深みのある ❑ *This is a book full of profound, original, and challenging insights.* これは、深遠で独創的で興味深い洞察に満ちた本だ。

pro·fuse /prəˈfjuːs/ ❶ ADJ 形容詞 **Profuse** sweating, bleeding, or vomiting is sweating, bleeding, or vomiting large amounts. 多量の ❑ *...a remedy that produces profuse sweating.* 多量の発汗を引き起こす治療 ● **pro·fuse·ly** ADV 副詞 [ADV after v] 多量に ❑ *He was bleeding profusely.* 彼は多量に出血していた。 **2** ADJ 形容詞 If you offer **profuse** apologies or thanks, you apologize or thank someone a lot. 心からの ❑ *Then the policeman recognized me, breaking into profuse apologies.* そのあと警察官は私に気づいて、急に平謝りをした。 ● **pro·fuse·ly** ADV 副詞 [ADV after v] 心から ❑ *They were very*

grateful and thanked me profusely. 彼らはとても感謝していて私に心から礼を言ってくれた。

prog·no·sis /prɒgˈnoʊsɪs/ (prognoses /prɒgˈnoʊsiːz/) N-COUNT 可算名詞 A **prognosis** is an estimate of the future of someone or something, especially about whether a patient will recover from an illness. 予後、予測 [FORMAL 形式ばった] ❑ *The doctor's prognosis was that Laurence might walk within 12 months.* 医者の予後によると、ローレンスは12か月以内に歩けるようになるかもしれない。

Word Link   gram ≈ writing : dia*gram*, pro*gram*, tele*gram*

pro·gram /ˈproʊgræm, -grəm/ (programs, programming, programmed) ❶ N-COUNT 可算名詞 A **program** of actions or events is a series of actions or events that are planned to be done. 事業計画 ❑ *The nation's largest training and education program for adults.* 国内最大の成人向け研修・教育プログラム **2** N-COUNT 可算名詞 A television or radio **program** is something that is broadcast on television or radio. 番組 ❑ *...a network television program.* ネットワークテレビ番組 **3** N-COUNT 可算名詞 A theater or concert **program** is a small book or paper that gives information about the play or concert you are attending. プログラム、演目表 ❑ *When you go to concerts, it's helpful to read the program.* コンサートに行くとき、プログラムを読むと参考になる。 **4** V-T 他動詞 When you **program** a machine or system, you set its controls so that it will work in a particular way. 設定する ❑ *Parents can program the machine not to turn on at certain times.* 保護者は一定時間にはスイッチが入らないように設定できる。 **5** N-COUNT 可算名詞 A **program** is a set of instructions that a computer follows in order to perform a particular task. プログラム [COMPUTING コンピューティング] ❑ *The chances of an error occurring in a computer program increase with the size of the program.* コンピュータプログラムでエラーが発生する確率はプログラムのサイズに合わせて上昇する。 **6** V-T 他動詞 When you **program** a computer, you give it a set of instructions to make it able to perform a particular task. プログラムする [COMPUTING コンピューティング] ❑ *He programmed his computer to compare the 1,431 possible combinations of pairs in this population.* 彼は、コンピュータがこの母集団で1431組の組み合わせの可能性を比較するようにプログラムした。 ❑ *...45 million people, about half of whom can program their own computers.* 4千5百万人、このうちの約半分が自分のパソコンをプログラムできる ● **pro·gram·ming** N-UNCOUNT 不可算名詞 プログラミング ❑ *...programming skills.* プログラミング能力
→ see **radio**

Word Partnership   program は次の語句と使われる:

V.	**create** a program, **expand** a program, **implement** a program, **launch** a program, **run** a program ❶ ❺
N.	**computer** program, **software** program ❺ program **a computer** ❻

pro·gramme /ˈproʊgræm/ → see **program**

pro·gram·mer /ˈproʊgræmər/ (programmers) N-COUNT 可算名詞 A computer **programmer** is a person whose job involves writing programs for computers. プログラマー [COMPUTING コンピューティング]

pro·gress (progresses, progressing, progressed)

The noun is pronounced /ˈprɒgrɛs/. The verb is pronounced /prəˈgrɛs/.

名詞は /ˈprɒgrɛs/ と発音される。動詞は /prəˈgrɛs/ と発音される。

1 N-UNCOUNT 不可算名詞 **Progress** is the process of gradually improving or getting nearer to achieving or completing something. 進展 ❑ *The medical community continues to make progress in the fight against cancer.* 医学会はがん撲滅運動で進展を続けている。 **2** N-SING 単数名詞 The **progress** of a situation or action is the way in which it develops. 発展、進歩 ❑ *The president is reported to have been delighted with the progress of the first day's talks.* 大統領は初日の会談の進捗（しんちょく）状況に満足したことを報道されている。 **3** V-I 自動詞 To **progress** means to move over a period of time to a stronger, more advanced, or more desirable state. 進展する、向上する ❑ *He will visit once every two weeks to see how his new employees are progressing.* 彼は、新入社員がどのように向上しているかを確認するため2週間おきに訪問する。 **4** V-I 自動詞 If events **progress**, they continue to happen gradually over a period of time. 進行する ❑ *As the evening progressed, sadness turned to rage.* 夜会が進行するにつれて、悲しみが激しい怒りに変わった。 **5** V-T 他動詞 If you **progress** something, you cause it to develop. 進捗（しんちょく）させる [BRIT 英国英語, FORMAL 形式ばった] [他動詞] **6** PHRASE 句 If something is **in progress**, it has started and is still continuing. 進行中で ❑ *The game was already in progress when we took our seats.* 私たちが席に着いたときには試合はすでに進行中でした。

pro·gres·sion /prəˈgrɛʃᵊn/ (progressions) N-COUNT 可算名詞 A **progression** is a gradual development from one state to another. 進展、進歩 ❑ *Both drugs slow the progression of HIV, but neither cures the disease.* どちらの薬もHIVの進行を遅らせるが、どちらも病気を治療しない。

P

pro|gres|sive /prəgrɛsɪv/ (**progressives**) ◼ ADJ 形容詞
Someone who is **progressive** or has **progressive** ideas has modern ideas about how things should be done, rather than traditional ones. 進歩的な ❑ ...a progressive businessman who had voted for Roosevelt in 1932 and 1936. 1932年と1936年にルーズベルトに投票した進歩的な実業家 ❑ Willan was able to point to the progressive changes he had already introduced. ウィリアムは、自分がすでに導入した進歩的な改革を指摘することができた. ● N-COUNT 可算名詞 A **progressive** is someone who is progressive. 進歩主義者 ❑ The Republicans were deeply split between progressives and conservatives. 共和党は、確信はと保守派の間に深い亀裂があった. ◼ ADJ 形容詞 A **progressive** change happens gradually over a period of time. 徐々に進む, 進行性の ❑ One prominent symptom of the disease is progressive loss of memory. その病気の顕著な症状は進行性記憶喪失である. ● **pro|gres|sive|ly** ADV 副詞 徐々に ❑ Her symptoms became progressively worse. 彼女の症状は徐々に悪化した.

pro|hib|it /prouhɪbɪt/ (**prohibits, prohibiting, prohibited**) V-T 他動詞 If a law or someone in authority **prohibits** something, they forbid it or make it illegal. 禁止する [FORMAL 形式ばった] ❑ ...a law that prohibits tobacco advertising in newspapers and magazines. 新聞や雑誌でのたばこの広告を禁止する法律 ❑ Fishing is prohibited. 魚釣りは禁止されている. ● **pro|hi|bi|tion** N-UNCOUNT 不可算名詞 禁止 ❑ The air force and the navy retain their prohibition of women on air combat missions. 空軍と海軍は女性兵士が空中戦闘任務に就くことへの禁止を維持しています.

pro|hi|bi|tion /prouhɪbɪʃn/ (**prohibitions**) ◼ N-COUNT 可算名詞 A **prohibition** is a law or rule forbidding something. 禁止法 ❑ ...a prohibition on discrimination. 人種差別禁止法 ◼ → see also **prohibit**

pro|hib|i|tive /prouhɪbɪtɪv/ ADJ 形容詞 If the cost of something is **prohibitive**, it is so high that many people cannot afford it. 法外な [FORMAL 形式ばった] ❑ The cost of private treatment can be prohibitive. 私立病院での治療費は法外であることがある. ● **pro|hib|i|tive|ly** ADV 副詞 法外に ❑ Meat and butter were prohibitively expensive. 肉とバターには法外な値段がついていた.

proj|ect (**projects, projecting, projected**)

> The noun is pronounced /prɒdʒɛkt/. The verb is pronounced /prədʒɛkt/.
>
> 名詞は /prɒdʒɛkt/ と発音される. 動詞は /prədʒɛkt/ と発音される.

◼ N-COUNT 可算名詞 A **project** is a task that requires a lot of time and effort. 事業, プロジェクト ❑ Money will also go into local development projects in Vietnam. 資金はベトナムの地方開発計画にも投入される. ❑ ...an international science project. 国際科学プロジェクト ◼ N-COUNT 可算名詞 A **project** is a detailed study of a subject by a student. 研究課題 ❑ Students complete projects for a personal tutor, working at home at their own pace. 学生は家庭教師につき自宅で自分のペースで研究課題を仕上げる. ◼ V-T 他動詞 If something **is projected**, it is planned or expected. 計画する, 予測する ❑ 13% of Americans are over 65; this number is projected to reach 22% by the year 2030. 米国人の13%は65歳を超えているが, この数値は2030年までに22%に達すると予測されている. ❑ The government had been projecting a 5% consumer price increase for the entire year. 政府は1年間で5%の消費者価格上昇を予測していた. ◼ V-T 他動詞 If you **project** someone or something in a particular way, you try to make people see them in that way. If you **project** a particular feeling or quality, you show it in your behavior. 示す, 与える ❑ Bradley projects a natural warmth and sincerity. ブラッドリーには生まれもった温かさと誠実さが現れている. ❑ He just hasn't been able to project himself as the strong leader. 彼は, 単に強力な指導者としてのイメージを与えることができていません. ◼ V-T 他動詞 If you **project** a film or picture **onto** a screen or wall, you make it appear there. 映写する ❑ The team tried projecting the maps with two different projectors onto the same screen. チームは2つの異なる映写機を使って同じスクリーンに地図の映写を試みた. ◼ V-I 自動詞 If something **projects**, it sticks out above or beyond a surface or edge. 突き出る [FORMAL 形式ばった] ❑ ...a narrow ledge that projected out from the bank of the river. 川岸から突き出た狭い出っ張り

> **Word Partnership** project は次の語句と使われる:
>
> V. **approve** a project, **launch** a project ◼
> **complete** a project, **start** a project ◼ ◼
> N. **construction** project, **development** project, project **director/manager** ◼
> **research** project, **science** project, **writing** project ◼ ◼
> ADJ. **involved in** a project, **latest** project, **new** project, **special** project ◼ ◼

pro|jec|tion /prədʒɛkʃn/ (**projections**) ◼ N-COUNT 可算名詞 A **projection** is an estimate of a future amount. 見通し ❑ ...the company's projection of 11 million visitors for the first year. 初年度の訪問者数は1100万人という会社の見通し ◼ N-UNCOUNT 不可算名詞 The **projection** of a film or picture is the act of projecting it onto

a screen or wall. 映写 ❑ They took me into a projection room to see a picture. 彼らは映画を見るために私を映写室に連れて行った.

pro|jec|tor /prədʒɛktər/ (**projectors**) ◼ N-COUNT 可算名詞 A **projector** is a machine that projects films or slides onto a screen or wall. 映写機, プロジェクター ❑ ...a slide projector. スライドプロジェクター ◼ → see also **overhead projector**

pro|lif|er|ate /prəlɪfəreɪt/ (**proliferates, proliferating, proliferated**) V-I 自動詞 If things **proliferate**, they increase in number very quickly. 急増する, 増殖する [FORMAL 形式ばった] ❑ Computerized databases are proliferating fast. 電子化されたデータベースが急増している. ● **pro|lif|era|tion** /prəlɪfəreɪʃn/ N-UNCOUNT 不可算名詞 急増 ❑ ...the proliferation of nuclear weapons. 核兵器の拡散

pro|lif|ic /prəlɪfɪk/ ◼ ADJ 形容詞 A **prolific** writer, artist, or composer produces a large number of works. 多作の ❑ She is a prolific writer of novels and short stories. 彼女は小説やショートストーリーの多作家だ. ◼ ADJ 形容詞 An animal, person, or plant that is **prolific** produces a large number of babies, young plants, or fruit. 繁殖力の強い, 多産の, 実を多くつける ❑ They are prolific breeders, with many hens laying up to six eggs. 彼らは, 多くのめんどりが卵を最高6個産ませている, 生産性の高い畜産家だ.

pro|logue /proulɒg/ (**prologues**) also **prolog** N-COUNT 可算名詞 A **prologue** is a speech or section of text that introduces a play or book. 序文, 前書き ❑ The prologue to the novel is written in the form of a newspaper account. 小説の前書きは新聞記事の形式で書かれています.

pro|long /prəlɒŋ/ (**prolongs, prolonging, prolonged**) V-T 他動詞 To **prolong** something means to make it last longer. 長引かせる ❑ Mr. Chesler said foreign military aid was prolonging the war. 海外への軍事援助が戦争を長引かせているとチェスラー氏が述べた.

pro|longed /prəlɒŋd/ ADJ 形容詞 A **prolonged** event or situation continues for a long time, or for longer than expected. 長期に渡る, 長期の ❑ ...a prolonged period of low interest rates. 長期間に及ぶ低金利

promi|nence /prɒmɪnəns/ N-UNCOUNT 不可算名詞 If someone or something is in a position of **prominence**, they are well-known and important. 著名 ❑ He came to prominence during the World Cup. 彼はワールドカップで名を上げた. ❑ Crime prevention had to be given more prominence. 犯罪防止にもっと関心が寄せられる必要があった.

promi|nent /prɒmɪnənt/ ◼ ADJ 形容詞 Someone who is **prominent** is important and well-known. 著名な, 重要な ❑ ...the children of very prominent or successful parents. とても有名で成功した親を持つ子供たち ◼ ADJ 形容詞 Something that is **prominent** is very noticeable or is an important part of something else. よく目立つ ❑ Here the window plays a prominent part in the design. ここでは窓が設計上よく目立つようになっている. ● **promi|nent|ly** ADV 副詞 [ADV with v] 目立つように ❑ Trade will figure prominently in the second day of talks in Washington. ワシントンでの2日目の会議で貿易が重要な話題となる.

pro|mis|cu|ous /prəmɪskyuəs/ ADJ 形容詞 Someone who is **promiscuous** has sex with many different people. ふしだらな, 淫乱(いんらん)の [DISAPPROVAL 不賛成] ❑ She is perceived as vain, spoiled, and promiscuous. 彼女は, うぬぼれが強くて甘やかされて育ち, ふしだらであるとみなされている. ● **promis|cu|ity** /prɒmɪskyuɪti/ N-UNCOUNT 不可算名詞 乱交, フリーセックス ❑ He has recently urged more tolerance of sexual promiscuity. 彼は最近フリーセックスについてもっと寛容になるよう熱心に説得した.

prom|ise /prɒmɪs/ (**promises, promising, promised**) ◼ V-T/V-I 他動詞/自動詞 If you **promise that** you will do something, you say to someone that you will definitely do it. 約束する ❑ The post office has promised to resume first class mail delivery to the area on Friday. 郵便局は金曜日にその地域への第1種郵便の配達を再開することを約束した. ❑ He had promised that the rich and privileged would no longer get preferential treatment. 彼は, 裕福層や特権階級がもはや優遇されないと約束した. ❑ Promise me you will not waste your time. 時間を無駄にしないと約束して. ❑ I'll call you back, I promise. 後でこちらから電話するよ, 約束する. ◼ V-T 他動詞 If you **promise** someone something, you tell them that you will definitely give it to them or make sure that they have it. ―をあげると約束する ❑ In 1920 the great powers promised them an independent state. 1920年に大国は彼らに独立国家になることを約束した. ◼ N-COUNT 可算名詞 A **promise** is a statement that you make to a person in which you say that you will definitely do something or give them something. 約束 ❑ If you make a promise, you should keep it. 約束をしたら守るべきだ. ◼ V-T 他動詞 If a situation or event **promises to** have a particular quality or **to** be a particular thing, it shows signs that it will have that quality or be that thing. 見込みがある ❑ While it will be fun, the seminar also promises to be most instructive. セミナーは, 楽しめるものでありまた非常にためになりそうだ. ◼ N-UNCOUNT 不可算名詞 If someone or something shows **promise**, they seem likely to be very good or successful. 見込み ❑ The boy first showed promise as an athlete in grade school. その少年はまず小学校で運動選手としての期待を持たせた.

Word Partnership promise は次の語句と使われる：

N.	**campaign** promise 3
V.	**break** a promise, **deliver on** a promise, **keep a** promise, **make a** promise 3
	hold promise, **show** promise 5
ADJ.	**broken** promise, **empty** promise, **false** promise 3
	enormous promise, **great** promise, **real** promise 5

prom|is|ing /prɒmɪsɪŋ/ ADJ 形容詞 Someone or something that is **promising** seems likely to be very good or successful. 有望な ❏ A school has honored one of its brightest and most promising former students. ある学校が最も優秀で有望な元学生の1人の栄誉をたたえた.

prom|is|sory note /prɒmɪsɔri noʊt/ (**promissory notes**) N-COUNT 可算名詞 A **promissory note** is a written, dated promise to pay a specific sum of money to a particular person. 約束手形 [mainly AM 主に米国英語 BUSINESS 実業] ❏ ...a $36.4 million, five-year promissory note. 5年後が支払い期日の3640ドルの約束手形

Word Link mot ≈ moving : motion, motivate, promote

pro|mote /prəmoʊt/ (**promotes, promoting, promoted**) ◼ V-T 他動詞 If people **promote** something, they help or encourage it to happen, increase, or spread. 促進する ❏ You don't have to sacrifice environmental protection to promote economic growth. 経済成長を促進するために環境保護を犠牲にしなくてよい. ● **pro|mo|tion** N-UNCOUNT 不可算名詞 促進 ❏ The government has pledged to give the promotion of democracy higher priority. 政府は民主主義の促進を優先することを約束した. ◼ V-T 他動詞 If a firm **promotes** a product, it tries to increase the sales or popularity of that product. 販売の促進をする, 宣伝する ❏ ...a tour to promote his second solo album. 彼の2枚目のソロアルバムを宣伝するためのツアー ◼ V-T 他動詞 [usu passive] If someone **is promoted**, they are given a more important job or rank in the organization that they work for. 昇進する ❏ I was promoted to editor and then editorial director. 私は編集者に昇進し, そして編集長になった.

Word Partnership promote は次の語句と使われる：

N.	promote **competition**, promote **democracy**, promote **development**, promote **education**, promote **growth**, promote **health**, promote **peace**, promote **stability**, promote **trade**, promote **understanding** 1
	promote **a product** 2

pro|mot|er /prəmoʊtər/ (**promoters**) ◼ N-COUNT 可算名詞 A **promoter** is a person who helps organize and finance an event, especially a sports event. 主催者, 興行主 ❏ ...one of the top boxing promoters in Las Vegas. ラスベガスの一流のボクシング・プロモーターの1人 ◼ N-COUNT 可算名詞 The **promoter** of a cause or idea tries to make it become popular. 推進者, 奨励者 ❏ Aaron Copland was always the most energetic promoter of American music. アーロン・コップランドは常にアメリカ音楽の最も精力的な推進者だった.

→ see **concert**

pro|mo|tion /prəmoʊʃⁿn/ (**promotions**) ◼ N-VAR 可変性名詞 If you are given **promotion** or **a promotion** in your job, you are given a more important job or rank in the organization that you work for. 昇進 ❏ Consider changing jobs or trying for promotion. 転職か昇進を目指すことを考えなさい. ◼ N-VAR 可変性名詞 A **promotion** is an attempt to make a product or event popular or successful, especially by advertising. 販売促進活動, プロモーション [BUSINESS 実業] ❏ Advertising and promotion are what American business does best. 宣伝とプロモーションがアメリカのビジネスが最も得意とするところだ. ◼ → see also **promote**

pro|mo|tion|al /prəmoʊʃənⁿl/ ADJ 形容詞 **Promotional** material, events, or ideas are designed to increase the sales of a product or service. 宣伝用の, プロモーション用の ❏ "Jeans," according to one company's promotional material, "are designed and made to be worn hard." ある会社の宣伝資料によると, 「ジーンズはハードにはきこなすようにデザインし作られている」.

prompt /prɒmpt/ (**prompts, prompting, prompted**) ◼ V-T 他動詞 To **prompt** someone to do something means to make them decide to do it. 促す ❏ Japan's recession has prompted consumers to cut back on buying cars. 日本の景気後退のために消費者は自動車の購入を減らすようになった. ◼ V-T 他動詞 If you **prompt** someone when they stop speaking, you encourage or help them to continue. If you **prompt** an actor, you tell them what their next line is when they have forgotten what comes next. 発言を促す, せりふを教える ❏ "You wouldn't have wanted to bring those people to justice anyway, would you?" Brand prompted him. 「どっちみち, その人たちを法の裁きにかけたかったわけじゃないでしょう」ブランドは彼に先に促した. ◼ ADJ 形容詞 A **prompt** action is done without any delay. 迅速な ❏ It is not too late, but prompt action is needed. 遅すぎるわけではないが, 迅速な行動が必要だ. ◼ ADJ 形容詞 If you are **prompt** to do something, you do it without delay or you are not late. 時間に正確

な, 期限を守った [v-link ADJ] ❏ You have been so prompt in carrying out all these commissions. あなたは, これらのすべての任務を実行するに当たりきっちり期限を守った.

prompt|ing /prɒmptɪŋ/ (**promptings**) N-UNCOUNT 不可算名詞 If you respond to **prompting**, you do what someone encourages or reminds you you to do. 後押し [also N in pl] ❏ The New York team needed little prompting from their coach Bill Parcells. ニューヨークチームはビル・パーセルズ・コーチからのちょっとした後押しが必要だった.

prompt|ly /prɒmptli/ ◼ ADV 副詞 If you do something **promptly**, you do it immediately. 即座に [ADV with v] ❏ Sister Francesca entered the chapel, took her seat, and promptly fell asleep. シスター・フランチェスカは礼拝堂に入り, 席に着き, 即座に眠りに落ちた. ◼ ADV 副詞 If you do something **promptly at** a particular time, you do it at exactly that time. ちょうどに ❏ Promptly at a quarter past seven, we left the hotel. ちょうど7時15分に私たちはホテルを出た.

prone /proʊn/ ◼ ADJ 形容詞 To be **prone to** something, usually something bad, means to have a tendency to be affected by it or to do it. ～にかかりやすい [v-link ADJ] ❏ For all her experience as a television reporter, she was still prone to camera nerves. テレビレポーターとしてあれだけの経験があるにもかかわらず, 彼女はいまだにカメラに向かうと緊張する. ● COMB IN ADJ 形容詞の複合 **-prone** combines with nouns to make adjectives that describe people who are frequently affected by something bad. ～しがちな ❏ ...the most injury-prone rider on the circuit. サーキットで最もけがをしがちなライダー ◼ ADJ 形容詞 If you are lying **prone**, you are lying on your front. うつぶせに [FORMAL 形式ばった] [ADJ after v, ADJ n] ❏ Bob slid from his chair and lay prone on the floor. ボブはいすから滑り落ちて, 床の上でうつぶせになった.

pro|noun /proʊnaʊn/ (**pronouns**) N-COUNT 可算名詞 A **pronoun** is a word that you use to refer to someone or something when you do not need to use a noun, often because the person or thing has been mentioned earlier. Examples are "it," "she," "something," and "myself." 代名詞

Word Link nounce ≈ reporting : announce, denounce, pronounce

pro|nounce /prənaʊns/ (**pronounces, pronouncing, pronounced**) ◼ V-T 他動詞 To **pronounce** a word means to say it using particular sounds. 発音する ❏ Have I pronounced your name correctly? 私は, お名前を正しく発音しましたか? ◼ V-T 他動詞 If you **pronounce** something to be true, you state that it is the case. ～であると断言する [FORMAL 形式ばった] ❏ A specialist has now pronounced him fully fit. 専門医がやっと彼が全快したと判断した.

→ see **trial**

pro|nounced /prənaʊnst/ ADJ 形容詞 Something that is **pronounced** is very noticeable. 顕著な ❏ Most of the art exhibitions have a pronounced Appalachian theme. 美術展のほとんどが顕著なアパラチアのテーマだった.

pro|nounce|ment /prənaʊnsmənt/ (**pronouncements**) N-COUNT 可算名詞 **Pronouncements** are public or official statements on an important subject. 公式発表 ❏ ...the president's latest pronouncements about the protection of minorities. 少数民族保護に関する大統領の最近の公式発表

pro|nun|cia|tion /prənʌnsieɪʃⁿn/ (**pronunciations**) N-VAR 可変性名詞 The **pronunciation** of a word or language is the way it is pronounced. 発音 ❏ She gave the word its French pronunciation. 彼女はその後をフランス語で発音した.

proof /pruf/ (**proofs**) ◼ N-VAR 可変性名詞 **Proof** is a fact, argument, or piece of evidence showing that something is definitely true or definitely exists. 証拠 ❏ You have to have proof of residence in the state of Texas, such as a Texas ID card. テキサス州身分証明書のようなテキサス州での住所を確認できるものが必要です. ❏ This is not necessarily proof that he is wrong. これは, 必ずしも彼が間違っていたという証拠ではない. ◼ ADJ 形容詞 **Proof** is used after a number of degrees or a percentage, when indicating the strength of a strong alcoholic drink such as whiskey. プルーフ（アルコール度数の単位を示す）[amount ADJ] ❏ ...a glass of Wild Turkey bourbon: 101 proof. 101プルーフのワイルド・ターキー・バーボン1杯

Word Partnership proof は次の語句と使われる：

ADJ.	**convincing** proof, **final** proof, **living** proof, proof **positive** 1
V.	**have** proof, **need** proof, **offer** proof, **provide** proof, **require** proof, **show** proof 1

-proof /-pruf/ (**-proofs, -proofing, -proofed**) ◼ COMB IN ADJ 形容詞の複合 **-proof** combines with nouns and verbs to form adjectives indicating that something cannot be damaged or badly affected by the thing or action mentioned. 耐～の, 防～の, ～を通さない ❏ ...a bomb-proof aircraft. 防弾処置を備えた航空機 ❏ In a large microwave-proof dish, melt butter for 20 seconds. 大型の電子レンジ用皿でバターを20秒加熱しなさい. ◼ COMB IN VERB 動詞の複合

-proof combines with nouns to form verbs that refer to protecting something against being damaged or badly affected by the thing mentioned. 耐―にする，防―にする，―を通さなくする □*They recommended that the viaduct be replaced rather than quake-proofed.* その高架橋は耐震性を持たせるよりも建て替えることが勧められている。 **3** → see also **bulletproof, waterproof**

prop /prɒp/ (**props, propping, propped**) **1** V-T 他動詞 If you **prop** an object **on** or **against** something, you support it by putting something underneath it or by resting it somewhere. 立てかける，もたせかける，ぽんと置く □*He rocked back in the chair and propped his feet on the desk.* 彼はいすを後ろに揺り動かして，足を机の上にばんと載せた。 ● PHRASAL VERB 句動詞 **Prop up** means the same as **prop**. もたせかける □*Sam slouched back and propped his elbows up on the bench behind him.* サムはベンチにもたれかかり，ひじをベンチの背にもたせかけた。 **2** N-COUNT 可算名詞 A **prop** is a stick or other object that you use to support something. 支え，つっかい棒 □*Using the table as a prop, he dragged himself to his feet.* テーブルを支えに使いながら，彼は何とか起き上がった。 **3** N-COUNT 可算名詞 To be a **prop** for a system, institution, or person means to be the main thing that keeps them strong or helps them survive. 支えになるもの，頼りになる人 □*The army is one of the main props of the government.* 軍隊は政府の主な柱石の1つだ。 **4** N-COUNT 可算名詞 The **props** in a play or movie are all the objects or pieces of furniture that are used in it. 小道具 □*...the backdrop and props for a stage show.* 舞台用の背景幕と小道具
▶ **prop up 1** PHRASAL VERB 句動詞 To **prop up** something means to support it or help it to survive. 支える，てこ入れする □*Investments in the U.S. money market have propped up the American dollar.* 米国金融市場での投資が米ドルをてこ入れした。 **2** → see **prop 1**

propa|gan|da /ˌprɒpəˈgændə/ N-UNCOUNT 不可算名詞 **Propaganda** is information, often inaccurate information, that a political organization publishes or broadcasts in order to influence people. プロパガンダ，政治宣伝 [DISAPPROVAL 不賛成] □*The party adopted an aggressive propaganda campaign against its rivals.* 党はライバル陣営に対する攻撃的な宣伝攻勢を導入した。

propa|gate /ˈprɒpəgeɪt/ (**propagates, propagating, propagated**) **1** V-T 他動詞 If you **propagate** an idea or piece of information, they spread it and try to make people believe it or support it. 広める，宣伝する [FORMAL 形式ばった] □*They propagated political doctrines that promised to tear apart the fabric of society.* 彼らは社会基盤が崩壊すると約束した政治理論を広めた。 ● **propa|ga|tion** /ˌprɒpəˈgeɪʃən/ N-UNCOUNT 不可算名詞 宣伝，伝道 □*These two countries must work together toward the propagation of true Buddhism.* これらの2国は，真の仏教を布教するために協力しなければならない。 **2** V-T 他動詞 If you **propagate** plants, you grow more of them from the original ones. 繁殖させる [他動詞] □*The easiest way to propagate a vine is to take hardwood cuttings.* つるを繁殖させる手っ取り早い方法は，熟枝挿しをすることだ。 [TECHNICAL 技術的]

Word Link pel ≈ driving, forcing : **compel, expel, propel**

pro|pel /prəˈpɛl/ (**propels, propelling, propelled**) V-T 他動詞 To **propel** something in a particular direction means to cause it to move in that direction. 進ませる [他動詞] □*The tiny rocket is attached to the spacecraft and is designed to propel it toward Mars.* 小さいロケットが宇宙船に接続されていて，火星に誘導するように設計されている。 ● COMB IN ADJ 形容詞の複合 **-propelled** combines with nouns to form adjectives that indicate how something, especially a weapon, is propelled. 一に動かされた，一が推進する □*...rocket-propelled grenades.* 携行ロケット弾

pro|pel|ler /prəˈpɛlər/ (**propellers**) N-COUNT 可算名詞 A **propeller** is a device with blades attached to a boat or aircraft. The engine makes the propeller spin around and causes the boat or aircraft to move. プロペラ □*...a fixed three-bladed propeller.* 固定式の3枚羽プロペラ
→ see **flight**

pro|pen|sity /prəˈpɛnsɪti/ (**propensities**) N-COUNT 可算名詞 A **propensity to** do something or a **propensity for** something is a natural tendency to behave in a particular way. 性癖，性向 [FORMAL 形式ばった] □*Mr. Bint has a propensity to put off decisions to the last minute.* ビント氏は決断をぎりぎりまで延ばす性向がある。

prop|er /ˈprɒpər/ **1** ADJ 形容詞 You use **proper** to describe things that you consider to be real and satisfactory rather than inadequate in some way. 適切な，きちんとした [ADJ n] □*Two out of five people lack a proper job.* 5人中2人はまともな職に就いていない。 **2** ADJ 形容詞 The **proper** thing is the one that is correct or most suitable. 適切な，正しい [ADJ n] □*The Supreme Court will ensure that the proper procedures have been followed.* 最高裁は確実に正しい手順が踏まれるようにするだろう。 **3** ADJ 形容詞 If you say that a way of behaving is **proper**, you mean that it is considered socially acceptable and right. 妥当な，ふさわしい □*In those days it was not thought entirely proper for a woman to be on the stage.* 当時は，女性が舞台に出ることがあまりふさわしくないと思われていた。 **4** ADJ 形

容詞 You can add **proper** after a word to indicate that you are referring to the central and most important part of a place, event, or object and want to distinguish it from other things that are not regarded as being important or central to it. 厳密な意味での，本来の [n ADJ] □*A distinction must be made between archaeology proper and science-based archaeology.* 本来の考古学と科学的アプローチの考古学の区別をつけなければならない。

prop|er|ly /ˈprɒpərli/ **1** ADV 副詞 If something is done **properly**, it is done in a correct and satisfactory way. きちんと，適切に □*You're too thin. You're not eating properly.* あなたはやせすぎよ。きちんと食事を取っていないんでしょ。 **2** ADV 副詞 If someone behaves **properly**, they behave in a way that is acceptable and not rude. ふさわしく，妥当に [ADV after v] □*He's a spoiled brat and it's about time he learned to behave properly.* 彼はだだっ子で，そろそろ行儀を学ぶ時期だ。

prop|er noun (**proper nouns**) N-COUNT 可算名詞 A **proper noun** is the name of a particular person, place, organization, or thing. Proper nouns begin with a capital letter. Examples are "Peggy," "Tuscon," and "the United Nations." Compare **common noun**. 固有名詞

Word Link proper, propr ≈ owning : **property, proprietary, proprietor**

prop|er|ty /ˈprɒpərti/ (**properties**) **1** N-UNCOUNT 不可算名詞 Someone's **property** is all the things that belong to them or something that belongs to them. 所有物 [FORMAL 形式ばった] □*Richard could easily destroy her personal property to punish her for walking out on him.* リチャードは彼女に見捨てられたことの腹いせに彼女の持ち物を壊してしまうことができた。 **2** N-VAR 可変性名詞 A **property** is a building and the land belonging to it. 不動産 [FORMAL 形式ばった] □*Cecil inherited a family property near Stamford.* セシルはスタンフォード近郊の家産を相続した。 **3** N-COUNT 可算名詞 The **properties** of a substance or object are the ways in which it behaves in particular conditions. 特性 □*A radio signal has both electrical and magnetic properties.* 無線信号には電気特性と磁気特性の両方がある。
→ see **element**

proph|ecy /ˈprɒfɪsi/ (**prophecies**) N-VAR 可変性名詞 A **prophecy** is a statement in which someone says they strongly believe that a particular thing will happen. 予言 □*Will the teacher's prophecy be fulfilled?* 先生の予言は的中するだろうか。

proph|esy /ˈprɒfɪsaɪ/ (**prophesies, prophesying, prophesied**) V-T 他動詞 If you **prophesy** that something will happen, you say that you strongly believe that it will happen. 予言する □*He prophesied that within five years his opponent would either be dead or in prison.* 彼は，5年以内に競争相手が死去するか投獄されると予言した。

proph|et /ˈprɒfɪt/ (**prophets**) N-COUNT 可算名詞 A **prophet** is a person who is believed to be chosen by God to say the things that God wants to tell people. 預言者 □*...the sacred name of the Holy Prophet of Islam.* イスラム教の聖なる預言者の神聖な名前

pro|phet|ic /prəˈfɛtɪk/ ADJ 形容詞 If something was **prophetic**, it described or suggested something that did actually happen later. 的中した □*This ominous warning soon proved prophetic.* この不吉な前兆はまもなく予言的中した。

pro|po|nent /prəˈpoʊnənt/ (**proponents**) N-COUNT 可算名詞 If you are a **proponent of** a particular idea or course of action, you actively support it. 支持者，主唱者 [FORMAL 形式ばった] □*Halsey was identified as a leading proponent of the values of progressive education.* ハルシーは進歩的教育の意義についての有力な主唱者として知られていた。

pro|por|tion /prəˈpɔːrʃən/ (**proportions**) **1** N-COUNT 可算名詞 A **proportion of** a group or an amount is a part of it. 部分 [FORMAL 形式ばった] □*A large proportion of the dolphins in that area will eventually die.* その地域のイルカの大部分はいづれ死ぬだろう。 **2** N-COUNT 可算名詞 The **proportion of** one kind of person or thing in a group is the number of people or things of that kind compared to the total number of people or things in the group. 割合 □*The proportion of women in the profession had risen to 17.3%.* その職業に就く女性の割合は17.3%に上昇していた。 **3** N-COUNT 可算名詞 The **proportion of** one amount to another is the relationship between the size of the two amounts. 比率 □*Women's bodies tend to have a higher proportion of fat to water.* 女性の体では脂肪分の比率が水分よりも高い傾向がある。 **4** N-PLURAL 複数名詞 If you refer to the **proportions** of something, you are referring to its size, usually when this is extremely large. 大きさ [WRITTEN 書き言葉] □*In the tropics plants grow to huge proportions.* 熱帯地方では植物はかなり大きく成長する。 **5** PHRASE 句 If one thing increases or decreases **in proportion to** another thing, it increases or decreases to the same degree as that thing. 一に比例して □*The pressure in the cylinders would go up in proportion to the boiler pressure.* シリンダーの気圧はボイラ圧に比例して上昇する。 **6** PHRASE 句 If something is small or large **in proportion to** something else, it is small or large when compared with that thing. 一と比べて □*Children tend to*

have relatively larger heads than adults in proportion to the rest of their body. 子供は成人よりも頭が体のほかの部分と比べて比較的大きい傾向がある。 ◼ PHRASE 句 If you say that something is **out of all proportion** to something else, you think that it is far greater or more serious than it should be. 全く不釣合いで ❑ *The punishment was out of all proportion to the crime.* その刑罰はその犯罪に対して全く不釣合いだった。
→ see **ratio**

pro|por|tion|al /prəpɔrʃən°l/ ADJ 形容詞 If one amount is **proportional to** another, the two amounts increase and decrease at the same rate so there is always the same relationship between them. 釣り合った、比例した [FORMAL 形式ばった] ❑ *Loss of weight is directly proportional to the rate at which the disease is progressing.* 体重減少はその病気の進行速度と正比例する。

pro|por|tion|al rep|re|sen|ta|tion N-UNCOUNT 不可算名詞 **Proportional representation** is a system of voting in which each political party is represented in a legislature or parliament in proportion to the number of people who vote for it in an election. 比例代表制

pro|por|tion|ate /prəpɔrʃ°nɪt/ ADJ 形容詞 **Proportionate** means the same as **proportional**. 釣り合った、比例した ❑ *Republics will have voting rights proportionate to the size of their economies.* 共和国には経済規模に見合った議決権がある。 ● **pro|por|tion|ate|ly** ADV 副詞 相対的に ❑ *We have increased the number of teachers, but the size of the classes hasn't changed proportionately.* 教師の数を増加したが、クラスの規模は相対的に変更していない。

pro|pos|al /prəpoʊz°l/ (proposals) ◼ N-COUNT 可算名詞 A **proposal** is a plan or an idea, often a formal or written one, which is suggested for people to think about and decide upon. 提案、提議 ❑ *The president is to put forward new proposals for resolving the country's constitutional crisis.* 大統領は国の憲法上の危機解決のために新案を提出する予定だ。 ❑ *...the governor's proposal to restrict cigarette sales.* タバコの販売を制限する州知事の提案 ◻ N-COUNT 可算名詞 A **proposal** is the act of asking someone to marry you. プロポーズ、結婚の申し込み ❑ *After a three-weekend courtship, Pam accepted Randy's proposal of marriage.* 3週間の交際後、パムはランディのプロポーズに応じた。

pro|pose /prəpoʊz/ (proposes, proposing, proposed) ◼ V-T 他動詞 If you **propose** something such as a plan or an idea, you suggest it for people to think about and decide upon. 提案する [他動詞] ❑ *Hamilton proposed a change in the traditional debating format.* ハミルトンは従来の議論の方法を変更するよう提案した。 ◻ V-T 他動詞 If you **propose** to do something, you intend to do it. 企てる [他動詞] ❑ *It's still far from clear what action the government proposes to take over the affair.* その問題に対し政府がどんな対策を計画しているかはいまだに全く不明です。 ◼ V-T 他動詞 If you **propose** a motion for debate, or a candidate for election, you begin the debate or the election procedure by formally stating your support for that motion or candidate. 発議する [他動詞] ❑ *He has proposed a resolution limiting the role of U.S. troops.* 彼は米軍の役割を制限する決議案を提出した。 ◻ V-T/V-I 他動詞/自動詞 If you **propose to** someone, or **propose marriage to** them, you ask them to marry you. 結婚を申し込む [自動詞] ❑ *He proposed to his girlfriend over a public-address system.* 彼は拡声装置で恋人に結婚を申し込んだ。

propo|si|tion /prɒpəzɪʃ°n/ (propositions) ◼ N-COUNT 可算名

詞 If you describe something such as a task or an activity as, for example, a difficult **proposition** or an attractive **proposition**, you mean that it is difficult or pleasant to do. 案 ❑ *Making easy money has always been an attractive proposition.* あぶく銭を稼ぐ仕事にはいつもそそられるものだ。 ◻ N-COUNT 可算名詞 A **proposition** is a statement or an idea that people can consider or discuss to decide whether it is true. 命題 [FORMAL 形式ばった] ❑ *The proposition that democracies do not fight each other is based on a tiny historical sample.* 民主主義国は戦火を交えないという命題は極めて小さな歴史的実例に基づいたものである。 ◼ N-COUNT 可算名詞 A **proposition** is a question or statement about an issue of public policy that appears on a voting paper so that people can vote for or against it. 提案 ❑ *Vote Yes on Proposition 136, but No on Propositions 129, 133, and 134.* 提案136号には賛成票を投じるが、提案129、133および134号には反対票を投じること。 ◼ N-COUNT 可算名詞 A **proposition** is an offer or a suggestion that someone makes to you, usually concerning some work or business that you might be able to do together. 提案 ❑ *You came to see me at my office the other day with a business proposition.* 君は先日、事業案を持って私のオフィスに来ましたね。

pro|pri|etary /prəpraɪətɛri/ ADJ 形容詞 **Proprietary** substances or products are sold under a brand name. 登録商標をもつ [FORMAL 形式ばった] ❑ *...some proprietary brands of dog food.* ドッグフードの登録ブランド

pro|pri|etor /prəpraɪətər/ (proprietors) N-COUNT 可算名詞 The **proprietor** of a hotel, store, newspaper, or other business is the person who owns it. 所有者 [FORMAL 形式ばった] ❑ *...the proprietor of a local restaurant.* 地元レストランの経営者。

pro|pri|etress /prəpraɪətrɪs/ (proprietresses) N-COUNT 可算名詞 The **proprietress** of a hotel, store, or business is the woman who owns it. 女性の所有者 [FORMAL 形式ばった] ❑ *The proprietress was alone in the bar.* ママはバーで1人きりだった。

pro ra|ta /proʊ reɪtə/ ADV 副詞 If something is distributed **pro rata**, it is distributed in proportion to the amount or size of something. 比例して [FORMAL 形式ばった] [ADV after v] ❑ *All part-timers should be paid the same, pro rata, as full-timers doing the same job.* パートタイマーは全員常勤者と同じ仕事をした場合、同じ比率で報酬を受けるべきである。 ● ADJ 形容詞 **Pro-rata** is also an adjective. 比例した [ADJ n] ❑ *They are paid their salaries and are entitled to fringe benefits on a pro-rata basis.* 彼らは、案分比例で支払いを受け、付加給付を得る資格がある。

pro|sa|ic /proʊzeɪɪk/ ADJ 形容詞 Something that is **prosaic** is dull and uninteresting. 退屈な [FORMAL 形式ばった] ❑ *His instructor offered a more prosaic explanation for the surge in interest.* 彼の指導者は関心が急速に高まっていることについてもっと月並な説明をした。

prose /proʊz/ N-UNCOUNT 不可算名詞 **Prose** is ordinary written language, in contrast to poetry. 散文 ❑ *Shute's prose is stark and chillingly unsentimental.* シュートの散文は飾り気がなく、冷淡なほど情緒に欠けている。

pros|ecute /prɒsɪkyut/ (prosecutes, prosecuting, prosecuted) ◼ V-T/V-I 他動詞/自動詞 If the authorities **prosecute** someone, they charge them with a crime and put them on trial. 起訴する [他動詞・自動詞] ❑ *The police have decided not to prosecute because the evidence is not strong enough.* 警察は証拠不十分として不起訴を決定した。 ❑ *Photographs taken by roadside cameras will soon be enough to prosecute drivers for speeding.* もうすぐ、道路脇に設置されたカメラで撮影された写真だけで速度違反のドライバーを起訴することができるようになる。 ◻ V-T 他動詞 When a lawyer **prosecutes** a case, he or she tries to prove that the person who is on trial is guilty. 検察官を務める [他動詞・自動詞] ❑ *The attorney who will prosecute the case says he cannot reveal how much money is involved.* その件を告発する検察官は、どのくらいの金額が関与しているかは口外できないと言っています。

pros|ecu|tion /prɒsɪkyuʃ°n/ (prosecutions) ◼ N-VAR 可変性名詞 **Prosecution** is the action of charging someone with a crime and putting them on trial. 起訴 ❑ *Yesterday the head of government called for the prosecution of those responsible for the deaths.* 昨日、政府の首脳は、死に責任のある者を起訴するよう要求しました。 ◻ N-SING 単数名詞 The lawyers who try to prove that a person on trial is guilty are called **the prosecution**. 起訴者側 ❑ *The star witness for the prosecution took the stand.* 検察側の重要証人が証人に立った。

pros|ecu|tor /prɒsɪkyutər/ (prosecutors) N-COUNT 可算名詞 In some countries, a **prosecutor** is a lawyer or official who brings charges against someone or tries to prove in a trial that they are guilty. 検察官

pros|pect /prɒspɛkt/ (prospects, prospecting, prospected) ◼ N-VAR 可変性名詞 If there is some **prospect of** something happening, there is a possibility that it will happen. 見込み ❑ *Unfortunately, there is little prospect of seeing these big questions*

P

answered. 残念ながら、これら大きな問題に対する解答が得られる見込みはほとんどない. ❑ *The prospects for peace in the country's eight-year civil war are becoming brighter.* その国の8年にわたる内戦が収まる見込みが明るくなっています. **2** N-SING 単数名詞 A particular **prospect** is something that you expect or know is going to happen. 予想 ❑ *There was a mixed reaction to the prospect of having new neighbors.* 新しい隣人が来るという予想に人々は様々な反応を示した. **3** N-PLURAL 複数名詞 Someone's **prospects** are their chances of being successful, especially in their career. 成功の見込み ❑ *I chose to work abroad to improve my career prospects.* 私はキャリアで成功する可能性を高めるため、海外で働くことを選択した. **4** V-I 自動詞 When people **prospect for** oil, gold, or some other valuable substance, they look for it in the ground or under the sea. 見込みの有無を調べる [自動詞] ❑ *He had prospected for minerals everywhere from the Gobi Desert to the Transvaal.* 彼は鉱物を求めてゴビ砂漠からトランスバールまであらゆる場所を探鉱した.

Word Partnership   prospect は次の語句と使われる:

V.	prospect **of being** *something*, prospect **of having** *something* **1**
N.	prospect **for/of for peace**, prospect **for/of war** **1**

pro|spec|tive /prəspɛktɪv/ **1** ADJ 形容詞 You use **prospective** to describe someone who wants to be the thing mentioned or who is likely to be the thing mentioned. 見込みのある [ADJ n] ❑ *The story should act as a warning to other prospective buyers.* この話はその他の見込み客に対する警告になるはずだ. **2** ADJ 形容詞 You use **prospective** to describe something that is likely to happen soon. 予期された [ADJ n] ❑ *The terms of the prospective deal are most clearly spelled out in Business Week.* 予期される取引の条件はビジネスウィーク誌に最も明確に詳述されています.

pro|spec|tus /prəspɛktəs/ (**prospectuses**) N-COUNT 可算名詞 A **prospectus** is a detailed document produced by a company, college, or school, which gives details about it. 案内書 ❑ *...a prospectus for a new issue of stock.* 新株発行の目論見書

pros|per /prɒspər/ (**prospers, prospering, prospered**) V-I 自動詞 If people or businesses **prosper**, they are successful and do well. 繁栄する [FORMAL 形式ばった] [自動詞] ❑ *His business continued to prosper.* 彼の事業は引き続き成功した.

Word Link   *sper ≈ hope : desperate, exasperate, prosperity*

pros|per|ity /prɒspɛrɪti/ N-UNCOUNT 不可算名詞 **Prosperity** is a condition in which a person or community is doing well financially. 隆盛 ❑ *...a new era of peace and prosperity.* 新たな平和と繁栄の時代

pros|per|ous /prɒspərəs/ ADJ 形容詞 **Prosperous** people, places, and economies are rich and successful. 繁栄した [FORMAL 形式ばった] ❑ *...the youngest son of a relatively prosperous family.* 比較的裕福な家族の末息子

pros|ti|tute /prɒstɪtut/ (**prostitutes**) N-COUNT 可算名詞 A **prostitute** is a person, usually a woman, who has sex with men in exchange for money. 売春婦 ❑ *He admitted last week he paid for sex with a prostitute.* 先週、彼は売春婦に金を払って性交をしたことを認めた.

pros|ti|tu|tion /prɒstɪtuʃn/ N-UNCOUNT 不可算名詞 **Prostitution** means having sex with people in exchange for money. 売春 ❑ *She eventually drifted into prostitution.* 彼女は最後にはずるずると売春に陥った.

Word Link   *agon ≈ struggling : agonize, antagonist, protagonist*

pro|tago|nist /proʊtægənɪst/ (**protagonists**) **1** N-COUNT 可算名詞 Someone who is a **protagonist** of an idea or movement is a supporter of it. 主唱者 [FORMAL 形式ばった] ❑ *...the main protagonists of their countries' integration into the world market.* 諸国の世界市場への統合を支持するリーダーたち. **2** N-COUNT 可算名詞 A **protagonist** in a play, novel, or real event is one of the main people in it. 主役 [FORMAL 形式ばった] ❑ *...the protagonist of J. D. Salinger's novel "The Catcher in the Rye."* J. D. サリンジャーの小説「ライ麦畑でつかまえて」の主人公

Word Link   *tect ≈ covering : detect, protect, protective*

pro|tect /prətɛkt/ (**protects, protecting, protected**) **1** V-T 他動詞 To **protect** someone or something means to prevent them from being harmed or damaged. 保護する [他動詞] ❑ *So, what can women do to protect themselves from heart disease?* では、女性はどうしたら心臓病を防ぐことができますか. ❑ *A long thin wool coat and a purple headscarf protected her against the wind.* 薄手のウールのロングコートと紫のヘッドスカーフが風から彼女を守った. **2** V-T 他動詞 If an insurance policy **protects** you **against** an event such as death, injury, or theft, the insurance company will give you or your family money if that event happens. 保護する [他動詞] ❑ *Many manufacturers have policies to protect themselves against blackmailers.*

多くの製造業者は脅迫者から身を守るために保険をかけている. → see **hero**

Word Partnership   protect は次の語句と使われる:

N.	protect **against attacks**, protect **children**, protect **citizens**, **duty to** protect, **efforts to** protect, protect **the environment**, **laws** protect, protect **people**, protect **privacy**, protect **women**, protect **workers** **1** protect **property** **1** **2**
ADJ.	**designed to** protect, **necessary to** protect, **supposed to** protect **1** **2**

pro|tec|tion /prətɛkʃən/ (**protections**) **1** N-VAR 可変性名詞 To give or be **protection** against something unpleasant means to prevent people or things from being harmed or damaged by it. 保護 ❑ *Such a diet is widely believed to offer protection against a number of cancers.* こういった食事療法は多くのがんを防ぐと広く信じられている. ❑ *It is clear that the primary duty of parents is to provide protection for our children.* 両親の第一の義務は子供の保護であることは明らかだ. **2** N-UNCOUNT 不可算名詞 If an insurance policy gives you **protection against** an event such as death, injury, fire, or theft, the insurance company will give you or your family money if that event happens. 保護 [oft N "against" n] ❑ *Insurance can be purchased to provide protection against such risks.* こういった危険をカバーするために保険に入ることができる. **3** N-UNCOUNT 不可算名詞 If a government has a policy of **protection**, it helps its own industries by putting a tax on imported goods or by restricting imports in some other way. 保護貿易 [BUSINESS 実業] ❑ *Over the same period trade protection has increased in the rich countries.* 同時期、ゆたかな国々で保護貿易が盛んになった.

pro|tec|tion|ism /prətɛkʃənɪzəm/ N-UNCOUNT 不可算名詞 **Protectionism** is the policy some countries have of helping their own industries by putting a large tax on imported goods or by restricting imports in some other way. 保護貿易主義 [BUSINESS 実業] ❑ *The aim of the current round of talks is to promote free trade and to avert the threat of increasing protectionism.* 今回の会談の目的は、貿易の自由化を促進し、高まる保護貿易主義の脅威を回避することです.

pro|tec|tion|ist /prətɛkʃənɪst/ (**protectionists**) **1** N-COUNT 可算名詞 A **protectionist** is someone who agrees with and supports protectionism. 保護貿易主義の人 [BUSINESS 実業] ❑ *Trade frictions between the two countries had been caused by trade protectionists.* 2国間の貿易摩擦は、保護貿易主義者によって引き起こされた. **2** ADJ 形容詞 **Protectionist** policies, measures, and laws are meant to stop or reduce imports. 保護貿易主義の [BUSINESS 実業] ❑ *The administration may be moving away from free trade and toward more protectionist policies.* 政府は自由貿易から脱却し、保護貿易主義的な政策に移行しているようだ.

pro|tec|tive /prətɛktɪv/ **1** ADJ 形容詞 **Protective** means designed or intended to protect something or someone from harm. 保護用の ❑ *Protective gloves reduce the absorption of chemicals through the skin.* 保護手袋は薬品が皮膚から吸収されるのを防ぐ. **2** ADJ 形容詞 If someone is **protective toward** you, they look after you and show a strong desire to keep you safe. 保護する ❑ *He is very protective toward his mother.* 彼は母親を守ろうとする傾向が強い.

pro|tec|tor /prətɛktər/ (**protectors**) **1** N-COUNT 可算名詞 If you refer to someone as your **protector**, you mean that they protect you from being harmed. 保護者 ❑ *Many mothers see their son as a potential protector and provider.* 母親の多くは、息子がいずれ自分を保護し養ってくれると考えている. **2** N-COUNT 可算名詞 A **protector** is a device that protects someone or something from physical harm. 保護装置 ❑ *He was the only National League umpire to wear an outside chest protector.* 外部チェストプロテクターを着用するナショナルリーグの審判は彼だけだった.

pro|tein /proʊtin/ (**proteins**) N-MASS 質量名詞 **Protein** is a substance found in food and drink such as meat, eggs, and milk. You need protein in order to grow and be healthy. たんぱく質 ❑ *Fish was a major source of protein for the working man.* 労働者の主要なたんぱく質源は魚だった. → see **calorie, diet**

pro|test (**protests, protesting, protested**)

The verb is usually pronounced /prətɛst/. The noun, and sometimes the verb, is pronounced /proʊtɛst/.

動詞は通常 /prətɛst/ と発音される. 名詞と時に動詞は /proʊtɛst/ と発音される.

1 V-T/V-I 他動詞/自動詞 If you **protest** something or **protest against** something, you say or show publicly that you object to it. 異議を申し立てる [他動詞・自動詞] ❑ *They were protesting soaring prices.* 彼らは急騰する物価に抗議していた. **2** N-VAR 可変性名詞 A **protest** is the act of saying or showing publicly that you object to something. 異議申し立て ❑ *The opposition now seems too weak to stage any serious protests against the government.* 野党は現在弱すぎて政府に対して本格的な抗議を行うことができないようだ.

❏ *The Mexican president canceled a trip to Texas in protest at the state's execution of a Mexican national.* メキシコ大統領は, テキサスでの同国人の死刑執行に抗議するため, 同州への訪問を取りやめた. ❸ V-T 他動詞 If you **protest** that something is the case, you insist that it is the case, when other people think that it may not be. 主張する [他動詞] ❏ *When we tried to protest that Mo was beaten up they didn't believe us.* 私たちはモーが散々なぐりつけられたと主張したが, 彼らは信じてくれなかった. ❏ "*I never said any of that to her,*" he protested. 「そんなことを彼女に言ったことはない」と彼は断言した.

Prot|es|tant /prɒtɪstənt/ (**Protestants**) ❶ N-COUNT 可算名詞 A **Protestant** is a Christian who belongs to the branch of the Christian church that separated from the Catholic church in the sixteenth century. プロテスタント ❷ ADJ 形容詞 **Protestant** means relating to Protestants or their churches. プロテスタントの ❏ *Most Protestant churches now have some women ministers.* 現在, プロテスタント教会の大部分に女性聖職者が何人かいる.

pro|test|er /prətɛstər/ (**protesters**) also **protestor** N-COUNT 可算名詞 **Protesters** are people who protest publicly about an issue. 異議を申し立てる者 ❏ *The protesters say the government is corrupt and inefficient.* 抗議者たちは, 政府は腐敗し, 非効率的だと言っています.

pro|to|col /proʊtəkɒl/ (**protocols**) ❶ N-VAR 可変性名詞 **Protocol** is a system of rules about the correct way to act in formal situations. 儀典 ❏ *He has become a stickler for the finer observances of Washington protocol.* 彼はワシントン儀典をさらに厳密に遵守することをうるさく言うようになった. ❷ N-COUNT 可算名詞 A **protocol** is a set of rules for exchanging information between computers. プロトコル [COMPUTING コンピューティング] ❏ *...a computer protocol which could communicate across different languages.* 様々な言語間で通信できるコンピュータプロトコル ❸ N-COUNT 可算名詞 A **protocol** is a written record of a treaty or agreement that has been made by two or more countries. 議定書 [FORMAL 形式ばった] ❏ *...the Montreal Protocol to phase out use and production of CFCs.* フロンガスの使用と生産を段階的に禁止するモントリオール議定書 ❹ N-COUNT 可算名詞 A **protocol** is a plan for a course of medical treatment, or a plan for a scientific experiment. 実験計画案 [AM 米国英語, FORMAL 形式ばった] ❏ *...the detoxification protocol.* 解毒計画案

pro|to|type /proʊtətaɪp/ (**prototypes**) N-COUNT 可算名詞 A **prototype** is a new type of machine or device that is not yet ready to be made in large numbers and sold. 試作品 ❏ *Chris Retzler has built a prototype of a machine called the wave rotor.* クリス・レッツラーはウェイブローターと呼ばれる機械の試作品を製作した.

pro|tract|ed /proʊtræktɪd/ ADJ 形容詞 Something, usually something unpleasant, that is **protracted** lasts a long time, especially longer than usual or longer than you hoped. 長引いた [FORMAL 形式ばった] ❏ *However, after protracted negotiations Ogden got the deal he wanted.* しかし, 長引いた交渉のあとオグデンは望み通りの取引ができた. ❏ *...a protracted civil war.* 長期化した市民戦争

pro|trude /proʊtrud, prə-/ (**protrudes, protruding, protruded**) V-I 自動詞 If something **protrudes from** somewhere, it sticks out. 突き出る [FORMAL 形式ばった] ❏ *...a huge round mass of smooth rock protruding from the water.* 水面から突き出た, 滑らかで巨大な丸い岩

proud /praʊd/ (**prouder, proudest**) ❶ ADJ 形容詞 If you feel **proud**, you feel pleased about something good that you possess or have done, or about something good that a person close to you has done. 誇る ❏ *I felt proud of his efforts.* 私は彼の努力を誇りに思っている. ❏ *They are proud that she is doing well at school.* 彼らは彼女が学校で成績がよいことを自慢に思っている. ● **proud|ly** ADV 副詞 [ADV with v] 誇りをもって ❏ "*That's the first part finished,*" he said proudly. 「最初の部分が完成した」と彼は得意げに言った. ❷ ADJ 形容詞 Your **proudest** moments or achievements are the ones that you are most proud of. 一番誇るに足る [ADJ n] ❏ *This must have been one of the proudest moments of his busy and hard-working life.* これは, 多忙で勤勉な彼の人生でも晴れ舞台だったに違いない. ❸ ADJ 形容詞 Someone who is **proud** has respect for themselves and does not want to lose the respect that other people have for them. 高慢な ❏ *He was too proud to ask his family for help and support.* 彼はあまりにも高慢なために家族に助けや援助を頼めなかった. ❹ ADJ 形容詞 Someone who is **proud** feels that they are better or more important than other people. 尊大な [DISAPPROVAL 不賛成] ❏ *She was said to be proud and arrogant.* 彼女は尊大で傲慢だといわれていた.

prove /pruv/ (**proves, proving, proved, proven**)

The forms **proved** and **proven** can both be used as a past participle.

proved 形と proven 形はどちらも過去分詞として使える

❶ V-LINK 連結動詞 If something **proves to** be true or to have a particular quality, it becomes clear after a period of time that it is true or has that quality. 証明される ❏ *We have been accused of exaggerating before, but unfortunately all our reports proved to be true.* 我々は事実を誇張していると非難されていたが, あいにく我々の全報告書が真実と証明された. ❷ V-T 他動詞 If you **prove that** something is true, you show by means of argument or evidence that it is definitely true. 立証する [他動詞] ❏ *You brought this charge. You prove it!* これを起訴したのはきみだ. きみが立証しなさい. ❏ *The results prove that regulation of the salmon farming industry is inadequate.* その結果により鮭養殖産業の規制が不十分であることが証明された. ❏ *That made me hopping mad and determined to prove him wrong.* 私はそのことで激怒し, 彼の鼻をあかしてやる決心をした. ❸ V-T 他動詞 If you **prove yourself** to have a certain good quality, you show by your actions that you have it. 自分が—であることを証明する [他動詞] ❏ *Margie proved herself to be a good mother.* マギーは良い母親であることを証明した. ❏ *As a composer he proved himself adept at large dramatic forms.* 彼は作曲家として, 大きな劇的形式に熟練していることを証明した.

→ see **science**

prov|erb /prɒvɜrb/ (**proverbs**) N-COUNT 可算名詞 A **proverb** is a short sentence that people often quote, because it gives advice or tells you something about life. ことわざ ❏ *An old Arab proverb says, "The enemy of my enemy is my friend."* 古いアラブのことわざに「敵の敵は味方」というのがあります.

pro|ver|bial /prəvɜrbiəl/ ADJ 形容詞 You use **proverbial** to show that you know the way you are describing something is one that is often used or is part of a popular saying. ことわざにある [ADJ n] ❏ *The limousine sped off down the road in the proverbial cloud of dust.* リムジンは, まさにもうもうたる土煙の中, 道を疾走して行った.

pro|vide /prəvaɪd/ (**provides, providing, provided**) ❶ V-T 他動詞 If you **provide** something that someone needs or wants, or if you **provide** them **with** it, you give it to them or make it available to them. 供給する [他動詞] ❏ *I'll be glad to provide a copy of this.* 喜んで一冊差し上げます. ❏ *They would not provide any details.* 彼らは詳細を全く明かそうとしません. ❏ *They provided him with a car and driver.* 彼らは彼に車と運転手を提供しました. ❷ V-T 他動詞 If a law or agreement **provides that** something will happen, it states that it will happen. 規定する [FORMAL 形式ばった] [他動詞] ❏ *The treaty provides that, by the end of the century, the United States must have removed its bases.* 条約は, 米国が基地を今世紀の終わりまでに撤去することを規定する. ❸ → see also **provided, providing**

▶ **provide for** ❶ PHRASAL VERB 句動詞 If you **provide for** someone, you support them financially and make sure that they have the things that they need. 扶養する ❏ *Elaine wouldn't let him provide for her.* イレーンは彼に生活の援助をさせなかった. ❷ PHRASAL VERB 句動詞 If you **provide for** something that might happen or that might need to be done, you make arrangements to deal with it. 準備する ❏ *Jim had provided for just such an emergency.* ジムはまさにそういった緊急時のために予防手段をとっていた.

pro|vid|ed /prəvaɪdɪd/ CONJ 接続詞 If you say that something will happen **provided** or **provided that** something else happens, you mean that the first thing will happen only if the second thing also happens. の条件で ❏ *The other banks are going to be very eager to help, provided that they see that he has a specific plan.* 彼が具体的な計画を持っていることがわかれば, 他行は非常に意欲的に援助するでしょう.

provi|dence /prɒvɪdəns/ N-UNCOUNT 不可算名詞 **Providence** is God, or a force that is believed by some people to arrange the things that happen to us. 神意 [LITERARY 文語的] ❏ *These women regard his death as an act of providence.* これらの女性は彼の死を神のおぼしめしとみなしている.

pro|vid|ing /prəvaɪdɪŋ/ CONJ 接続詞 If you say that something will happen **providing** or **providing that** something else happens, you mean that the first thing will happen only if the second thing also happens. との条件で ❏ *I do believe in people being able to do what they want to do, providing they're not hurting someone else.* 人は他者を傷つけない限り, 望むことをすればよいと私は信じている.

prov|ince /prɒvɪns/ (**provinces**) **1** N-COUNT 可算名詞 A **province** is a large section of a country that has its own administration. 州 □...the Algarve, Portugal's southernmost province. ポルトガルの最南州であるアルガルベ **2** N-PLURAL 複数名詞 **The provinces** are all the parts of a country except the part where the capital is situated. 地方 □The government plans to transfer some 30,000 government jobs from Paris to the provinces. 政府は約3万の行政職をパリから地方に移転することを計画している. **3** N-SING 単数名詞 If you say that a subject or activity is a particular person's **province**, you mean that this person has a special interest in it, a special knowledge of it, or a special responsibility for it. 範囲 □Tattooing is not just the province of sailors. 入れ墨をするのは水夫に限られてはいない

pro|vin|cial /prəvɪnʃl/ **1** ADJ 形容詞 **Provincial** means connected with the parts of a country away from the capital city. 地方の [ADJ n] □...the Quebec and Ontario provincial police. ケベックおよびオンタリオ州警察. **2** ADJ 形容詞 If you describe someone or something as **provincial**, you disapprove of them because you think that they are old-fashioned and boring. 地方的な [DISAPPROVAL 不賛成] □He decided to revamp the company's provincial image. 彼は会社の田舎じみたイメージを刷新することを決意した.

pro|vi|sion /prəvɪʒn/ (**provisions**) **1** N-UNCOUNT 不可算名詞 The **provision** of something is the act of giving it or making it available to people who need or want it. 供給 [also "a" N] □The department is responsible for the provision of residential care services. その部門は居住看護サービスの供給に責任を負っている. **2** N-VAR 可変性名詞 If you make **provision for** something that might happen or that might need to be done, you make arrangements to deal with it. 用意 □Mr. Kurtz asked if it had ever occurred to her to make provision for her retirement. カーツ氏は, 彼女に退職後の備えを考えたことがあるのかと聞いた. **3** N-UNCOUNT 不可算名詞 If you make **provision for** someone, you support them financially and make sure that they have the things that they need. 糧食を供給する [also N in pl, N "for" n] □Special provision should be made for children. 子供には特別な扶養措置をとるべきだ. **4** N-COUNT 可算名詞 A **provision** in a law or an agreement is an arrangement which is included in it. 規定 □He backed a provision that would allow judges to delay granting a divorce decree in some cases. 彼は場合によっては判事の離婚確定判決を引き延ばすこともできる規定を支持した.

pro|vi|sion|al /prəvɪʒənl/ ADJ 形容詞 You use **provisional** to describe something that has been arranged or appointed for the present, but may be changed in the future. 暫定の □...the possibility of setting up a provisional coalition government. 暫定連立政権を設立する可能性 □These times are provisional and subject to confirmation. これらの時間は暫定的なもので, 確認が必要だ. ● **pro|vi|sion|al|ly** ADV 副詞 [ADV with v] 暫定的に □The U.S. and Japan provisionally agreed to add new chartered flights to serve their major cities. 米国と日本は, 主要都市へ運航する新しいチャーター便を追加することに暫定的に同意しました.

provo|ca|tion /prɒvəkeɪʃn/ (**provocations**) N-VAR 可変性名詞 If you describe a person's action as **provocation** or a **provocation**, you mean that it is a reason for someone else to react angrily, violently, or emotionally. 挑発 □He denies murder on the grounds of provocation. 彼は挑発されたという根拠で殺人罪を否認する.

pro|voca|tive /prəvɒkətɪv/ **1** ADJ 形容詞 If you describe something as **provocative**, you mean that it is intended to make people react angrily or argue against it. 挑発的な □He has made a string of outspoken and sometimes provocative speeches in recent years. 彼は近年, 率直で, ときには挑発的な演説を行った. **2** ADJ 形容詞 If you describe someone's clothing or behavior as **provocative**, you mean that it is intended to make someone feel sexual desire. 性的に挑発的な □Some adolescents might be more sexually mature and provocative than others. 若者の中には人より性的により成熟し, 挑発的な者もいるかもしれない.

pro|voke /prəvoʊk/ (**provokes, provoking, provoked**) **1** V-T 他動詞 If you **provoke** someone, you deliberately annoy them and try to make them behave aggressively. 挑発する [他動詞] □He started beating me when I was about fifteen but I didn't do anything to provoke him. 彼は私が15歳のとき, 私に暴力を振るい始めたが, 私は彼を挑発するようなことは何もしなかった. **2** V-T 他動詞 If something **provokes** a reaction, it causes it. 引き起こす [他動詞] □His election success has provoked a shocked reaction. 彼の選挙での成功は衝撃的反応を引き起こしました.

prow|ess /praʊɪs/ N-UNCOUNT 不可算名詞 Someone's **prowess** is their great skill at doing something. あっぱれな腕前 [FORMAL 形式ばった] □He's always bragging about his prowess as a hunter. 彼は漁師としての腕前をいつも自慢している.

prowl /praʊl/ (**prowls, prowling, prowled**) V-I 自動詞 If an animal or a person **prowls around**, they move around quietly, for example, when they are hunting. うろつく [他動詞] □He prowled around the room, not sure what he was looking for or even why he was there. 彼は何を探しているのか, そこにいるのはなぜかさえわからぬまま部屋の中をうろついた.

Word Link proxim ≈ near : approximate, approximation, proximity

prox|im|ity /prɒksɪmɪti/ N-UNCOUNT 不可算名詞 **Proximity to** a place or person is nearness to that place or person. 近接 [FORMAL 形式ばった] □Part of the attraction is Darwin's proximity to Asia. ダーウィンはアジアに近いことも魅力だ. □He became aware of the proximity of the Afghans. 彼はアフガニスタン人の近接性に気づいた.

proxy /prɒksi/ N-UNCOUNT 不可算名詞 If you do something **by proxy**, you arrange for someone else to do it for you. 代理権 □Those not attending the meeting may vote by proxy. 会議に出席しない人は委任投票をしてよい.

prude /pruːd/ (**prudes**) N-COUNT 可算名詞 If you call someone a **prude**, you mean that they are too easily shocked by things relating to sex. 慎み深さを装う人 [DISAPPROVAL 不賛成] □Caroline was very much a prude. She wouldn't let me see her naked. キャロラインは大変淑女ぶっていた. 彼女は裸を私に見せなかった.

pru|dence /pruːdns/ N-UNCOUNT 不可算名詞 **Prudence** is care and good sense that someone shows when making a decision or taking action. 思慮分別 [FORMAL 形式ばった] □Western businessmen are showing remarkable prudence in investing in the region. 西側の実業家は地域への投資に異例の慎重さを見せている.

pru|dent /pruːdnt/ ADJ 形容詞 Someone who is **prudent** is sensible and careful. 慎重な □It is clearly prudent to take all precautions. あらゆる予防措置をとることは明らかに賢明である. ● **pru|dent|ly** ADV 副詞 慎重に □I believe it is essential that we act prudently. 私たちが慎重に行動することが不可欠だと私は信じています.

prune /pruːn/ (**prunes, pruning, pruned**) **1** N-COUNT 可算名詞 A **prune** is a dried plum. プルーン **2** V-T/V-I 他動詞/自動詞 When you **prune**, or **prune** a tree or bush, you cut off some of the branches so that it will grow better the next year. 刈り込む [他動詞・自動詞] □You have to prune a bush if you want fruit. 実をつけさせたいなら茂みを刈り込まなければならない. ● PHRASAL VERB 句動詞 **Prune back** means the same as **prune**. 刈り込む □Apples, pears, and cherries can be pruned back when they've lost their leaves. リンゴ, 梨, さくらんぼの木は葉が落ちたら余分な枝をおろしてよい. **3** V-T 他動詞 If you **prune** something, you cut out all the parts that you do not need. 余分なものを取り除く [他動詞] □Companies are cutting investment and pruning their product ranges. 企業は投資を削減し, 製品ラインを整理している. ● PHRASAL VERB 句動詞 **Prune back** means the same as **prune**. 余分なものを取り除く □The company has pruned back its workforce by 20,000 since 2003. 2003年以来, その会社は従業員を2万人削減している.

prun|ing shears N-PLURAL 複数名詞 **Pruning shears** are a gardening tool that look like a pair of strong, heavy scissors. Pruning shears are used for cutting the stems of plants. 剪定ばさみ [AM 米国英語]

pry /praɪ/ (**pries, prying, pried**) **1** V-I 自動詞 If someone **pries**, they try to find out about someone else's private affairs, or look at their personal possessions. のぞく [自動詞] □We do not want people prying into our affairs. 私たちの問題を他人にせんさくされたくない. □Imelda might think she was prying. イメルダは彼女がのぞき見していたと思うかもしれない. **2** V-T 他動詞 If you **pry** something **open** or **pry** it away from a surface, you force it open or away from a surface. こじあける [他動詞] □They pried open a sticky can of blue paint. 彼らはくっついていた青ペンキの缶をこじあけた. □They pried the bars apart to free the dog. 彼らはかんぬきをこじあけて犬を解放した.

PS /piː es/ also **P.S.** You write **PS** to introduce something that you add at the end of a letter after you have signed it. 追伸 □PS Please show your friends this letter and the enclosed leaflet. 追伸, この手紙と同封のちらしをお友達にもお見せください.

pseudo|nym /suːdənɪm/ (**pseudonyms**) N-COUNT 可算名詞 A **pseudonym** is a name that someone, usually a writer, uses instead of his or her real name. ペンネーム □Both plays were published under the pseudonym of Philip Dayre. その劇は両方とも, 「フィリップ・デイル」のペンネームで出版された.

Word Link psych ≈ mind : psyche, psychiatrist, psychic

psy|che /saɪki/ (**psyches**) N-COUNT 可算名詞 In psychology, your **psyche** is your mind and your deepest feelings and attitudes. 精神 [TECHNICAL 技術的] □His exploration of the myth brings insight into the American psyche. 彼の神話の探究は, アメリカ精神に洞察を加えるものである.

psyche|del|ic /saɪkədɛlɪk/ **1** ADJ 形容詞 **Psychedelic** means relating to drugs such as LSD that have a strong effect on your mind, often making you see things that are not there. サイケデリックな □...his first real, full-blown psychedelic experience. 彼の初めての極めて本格的なサイケデリック経験. **2** ADJ 形容詞 **Psychedelic** art has bright colors and strange patterns. サイケ調の □...psychedelic patterns. サイケ調のパターン

psy|chi|at|ric /saɪkiˈætrɪk/ **1** ADJ 形容詞 **Psychiatric** means relating to psychiatry. 精神医学の [ADJ n] ❑ *We finally insisted that he seek psychiatric help.* 私たちは最終的に彼は精神科の助けを求めるべきだと主張した。 **2** ADJ 形容詞 **Psychiatric** means involving mental illness. 精神病の [ADJ n] ❑ *About 4% of the prison population have chronic psychiatric illnesses.* 刑務所に服役している人の約4%が慢性的な精神病を患っている。

Word Link	iatr ≈ healing : geriatric, pediatrics, psychiatrist

Word Link	psych ≈ mind : psyche, psychiatrist, psychic

psy|chia|trist /sɪˈkaɪətrɪst/ (**psychiatrists**) N-COUNT 可算名詞 A **psychiatrist** is a doctor who treats people suffering from mental illness. 精神科医

psy|chia|try /sɪˈkaɪətri/ N-UNCOUNT 不可算名詞 **Psychiatry** is the branch of medicine concerned with the treatment of mental illness. 精神医学

psy|chic /ˈsaɪkɪk/ (**psychics**) **1** ADJ 形容詞 If you believe that someone is **psychic** or has **psychic** powers, you believe that they have strange mental powers, such as being able to read the minds of other people or to see into the future. 霊能力を持った ❑ *The woman helped police by using her psychic powers.* その女性は心霊能力で警察を助けた。 ● N-COUNT 可算名詞 A **psychic** is someone who seems to be psychic. 霊能者 ❑ *...her latest role as a psychic who can foretell the future.* 将来を予言できる霊能者としての彼女の最近の役割 **2** ADJ 形容詞 **Psychic** means relating to ghosts and the spirits of the dead. 心霊の ❑ *He declared his total disbelief in psychic phenomena.* 彼は心霊現象を全く信じないと断言した。

psycho|analy|sis /ˌsaɪkoʊəˈnælɪsɪs/ N-UNCOUNT 不可算名詞 **Psychoanalysis** is the treatment of someone who has mental problems by asking them about their feelings and their past in order to try to discover what may be causing their condition. 精神分析

psycho|ana|lyst /ˌsaɪkoʊˈænəlɪst/ (**psychoanalysts**) N-COUNT 可算名詞 A **psychoanalyst** is someone who treats people who have mental problems using psychoanalysis. 精神分析学者

psycho|logi|cal /ˌsaɪkəˈlɒdʒɪkəl/ **1** ADJ 形容詞 **Psychological** means concerned with a person's mind and thoughts. 心理的な ❑ *John received constant physical and psychological abuse from his father.* ジョンは父親から常に身体的、心理的虐待を受けた。 ● **psycho|logi|cal|ly** /ˌsaɪkəˈlɒdʒɪkli/ ADV 副詞 心理的に ❑ *It was very important psychologically for us to succeed.* 私たちにとって成功することは心理的に非常に重要だった。 **2** ADJ 形容詞 [ADJ n] **Psychological** means relating to psychology. 心理学的な ❑ *...psychological testing.* 心理テスト
→ see **myth**

psy|cholo|gist /saɪˈkɒlədʒɪst/ (**psychologists**) N-COUNT 可算名詞 A **psychologist** is a person who studies the human mind and tries to explain why people behave in the way that they do. 心理学者

psy|chol|ogy /saɪˈkɒlədʒi/ **1** N-UNCOUNT 不可算名詞 **Psychology** is the scientific study of the human mind and the reasons for people's behavior. 心理学 ❑ *Professor of Psychology at Haverford College.* ハヴァフォード大学の心理学教授 **2** N-UNCOUNT 不可算名詞 The **psychology of** a person is the kind of mind that they have, which makes them think or behave in the way that they do. 心理 ❑ *...a fascination with the psychology of murderers.* 殺人者の心理に惹かれる気持ち

psycho|path /ˈsaɪkəpæθ/ (**psychopaths**) N-COUNT 可算名詞 A **psychopath** is someone who has serious mental problems and who may act in a violent way without feeling sorry for what they have done. 精神病質者 ❑ *She was abducted by a dangerous psychopath.* 彼女は危険な変質者に拉致された。

Word Link	osis ≈ state or condition : hypnosis, metamorphosis, psychosis

psy|cho|sis /saɪˈkoʊsɪs/ (**psychoses**) N-VAR 可変性名詞 **Psychosis** is mental illness of a severe kind that can make people lose contact with reality. 精神病 [MEDICAL 医学の] ❑ *He may have some kind of neurosis or psychosis later in life.* 彼は晩年に何らかの神経症または精神病を患うかもしれません。

psycho|thera|pist /ˌsaɪkoʊˈθerəpɪst/ (**psychotherapists**) N-COUNT 可算名詞 A **psychotherapist** is a person who treats people who are mentally ill using psychotherapy. 心理療法医

psycho|thera|py /ˌsaɪkoʊˈθerəpi/ N-UNCOUNT 不可算名詞 **Psychotherapy** is the use of psychological methods in treating people who are mentally ill, rather than using physical methods such as drugs or surgery. 心理療法 ❑ *For milder depressions, certain forms of psychotherapy do work well.* 軽微なうつ病には、特定形式の心理療法がよく効きます。

psy|chot|ic /saɪˈkɒtɪk/ ADJ 形容詞 Someone who is **psychotic**

has a type of severe mental illness. 精神異常の [MEDICAL 医学の] ❑ *The man, who police believe is psychotic, is thought to be responsible for eight attacks.* その男は警察が精神異常者とみなしており、8件の暴行事件に関与したと考えられている。

pub /pʌb/ (**pubs**) N-COUNT 可算名詞 A **pub** is a building where people can have drinks, especially alcoholic drinks, and talk to their friends. Many pubs also serve food. 居酒屋 [mainly BRIT 主に英国英語] ❑ *He was in the pub until closing time.* 彼は閉店時間までパブにいた。

During **happy hour** customers in pubs, bars and cafés can buy alcoholic drinks more cheaply than usual. This practice was introduced by owners and managers to entice people into their bars. Happy hour is usually during the late afternoon or early evening, the exact time being chosen by the bar; strangely, it quite often lasts more than an hour.

pu|ber|ty /ˈpyubərti/ N-UNCOUNT 不可算名詞 **Puberty** is the stage in someone's life when their body starts to become physically mature. 思春期 ❑ *Moesha had reached the age of puberty.* モエシャは年ごろになった。

pub|lic /ˈpʌblɪk/ **1** N-SING-COLL 集合的単数名詞 You can refer to people in general, or to all the people in a particular country or community, as **the public**. 公衆 ❑ *The park is now open to the public.* 公園は今一般に公開されている。 ❑ *Pure alcohol is not for sale to the general public.* 純粋なアルコールは一般には売られていない。 **2** N-SING-COLL 集合的単数名詞 You can refer to a set of people in a country who share a common interest, activity, or characteristic as a particular kind of **public**. 人びと ❑ *Market research showed that 93% of the viewing public wanted a hit movie channel.* 市場調査によると、一般視聴者の93%がヒット映画のチャンネルを欲していました。 **3** ADJ 形容詞 **Public** means relating to all the people in a country or community. 公衆の [ADJ n] ❑ *The president is attempting to drum up public support for his economic program.* 大統領は自国の経済計画に対する公衆の支持を獲得しようと躍起になっている。 **4** ADJ 形容詞 **Public** means relating to the government or state, or things that are done for the people by the state. 公共の [ADJ n] ❑ *The social services account for a substantial part of public spending.* 社会サービスは公共支出のかなりの部分を占めている。 ● **pub|lic|ly** ADV 副詞 [ADV -ed] 公的に ❑ *...publicly funded legal services.* 公的資金による法律サービス **5** ADJ 形容詞 **Public** buildings and services are provided for everyone to use. 公共の [ADJ n] ❑ *...the New York Public Library.* ニューヨーク公共図書館 ❑ *The new museum must be accessible by public transportation.* 新しい美術館は公共交通機関が利用できることが条件だ。 **6** ADJ 形容詞 A **public** place is one where people can go about freely and where you can easily be seen and heard. 誰でも出入りできる ❑ *...the heavily congested public areas of international airports.* 国際空港の非常に混雑した公共エリア **7** ADJ 形容詞 If someone is a **public figure** or in **public life**, many people know who they are because they are often mentioned in newspapers and on television. 著名な人物 [ADJ n] ❑ *He hit out at public figures who commit adultery.* 彼は不倫をした有名人を酷評した。 **8** ADJ 形容詞 **Public** is used to describe statements, actions, and events that are made or done in such a way that any member of the public can see them or be aware of them. 公開の [ADJ n] ❑ *...a public inquiry into the most grievous breakdown in security our nation has ever known.* わが国民が経験したことのない重大な公安上の不手際に関する公開調査 ❑ *The comments were the governor's first detailed public statement on the subject.* そのコメントはその件に関して知事が初めて出した詳細な公式声明だった。 ● **pub|lic|ly** ADV 副詞 公に ❑ *He never spoke publicly about the affair.* 彼がその件に関して大っぴらに話すことはなかった。 **9** ADJ 形容詞 [v-link ADJ] If a fact is made **public** or becomes **public**, it becomes known to everyone rather than being kept secret. 知れわたっている ❑ *The facts could cause embarrassment if they ever became public.* それら事実が公にでもなれば、決まりの悪いことになる。 **10** PHRASE 句 If a company **goes public**, it starts selling its shares on the stock exchange. 上場する [BUSINESS 実業] ❑ *The company went public at $21 per share.* その会社は1株21ドルで株を公開した。 **11** PHRASE 句 If you say or do something **in public**, you say or do it when a group of people are present. 人前で ❑ *I probably won't be performing in public much.* 私はおそらくあまり人前では演奏しない。
→ see **library**

pub|li|ca|tion /ˌpʌblɪˈkeɪʃən/ (**publications**) **1** N-UNCOUNT 不可算名詞 The **publication** of a book or magazine is the act of printing it and sending it to stores to be sold. 出版 ❑ *The guide is being translated into several languages for publication near Christmas.* そのガイドはクリスマス近くには出版されるよう様々な言語に翻訳されている。 **2** N-COUNT 可算名詞 A **publication** is a book or magazine that has been published. 出版物 ❑ *They have started legal proceedings against two publications which spoke of an affair.* 彼らは情事に触れた2つの出版物に対する訴訟手続きを開始した。 **3** N-UNCOUNT 不可算名詞 The **publication of** something such as information is the act of making it known to the public, for example, by informing journalists or by publishing

a government document. 公開 □ *A spokesman said: "We have no comment regarding the publication of these photographs."* 広報担当者は「これらの写真が公開されたことについてコメントはありません」と言った.

pub|lic com|pa|ny (**public companies**) N-COUNT 可算名詞 A **public company** is a company whose shares can be bought by the general public. 株式公開会社 [BUSINESS 実業]

pub|li|cist /pʌ́blɪsɪst/ (**publicists**) N-COUNT 可算名詞 A **publicist** is a person whose job involves getting publicity for people, events, or things such as movies or books. 宣伝係 □ ...*Larry Kaplan, a publicist for "Cold Mountain."* 「コールド・マウンテン」の宣伝係を務めるラリー・カプラン.

pub|lic|ity /pʌblɪ́sɪti/ ■ N-UNCOUNT 不可算名詞 **Publicity** is information or actions that are intended to attract the public's attention to someone or something. 広報 □ *Much advance publicity was given to the talks.* その会談の前宣伝はかなり派手に行われた. □ ...*government publicity campaigns.* 政府の宣伝キャンペーン ② N-UNCOUNT 不可算名詞 When the news media and the public show a lot of interest in something, you can say that it is receiving **publicity**. 評判 □ *The case has generated enormous publicity in Brazil.* その事件がブラジルでものすごい話題となりました.

Word Partnership *publicity* は次の語句と使われる:

V.	**generate** publicity ■ ②
	get publicity, **receive** publicity, publicity **surrounding** *someone/something* ②
ADJ.	**bad** publicity, **negative** publicity ②

pub|li|cize /pʌ́blɪsaɪz/ (**publicizes, publicizing, publicized**) V-T 他動詞 If you **publicize** a fact or event, you make it widely known to the public. 公表する [他動詞] □ *The author appeared on television to publicize her latest book.* 著者は最新の本を宣伝するためにテレビ出演した. □ *He never publicized his plans.* 彼が計画を公表したことはない.

pub|lic lim|it|ed com|pa|ny (**public limited companies**) N-COUNT 可算名詞 A **public limited company** is the same as a **public company**. The abbreviation **plc** is used after such companies' names. 株式公開会社 [BRIT 英国英語 BUSINESS 実業]

pub|lic opin|ion N-UNCOUNT 不可算名詞 **Public opinion** is the opinion or attitude of the public regarding a particular matter. 世論 □ *He mobilized public opinion all over the world against hydrogen-bomb tests.* 彼は世界中の世論を動員して水爆試験に反対した.

pub|lic re|la|tions ■ N-UNCOUNT 不可算名詞 **Public relations** is the part of an organization's work that is concerned with obtaining the public's approval for what it does. The abbreviation **PR** is often used. 広報活動 [BUSINESS 実業] □ *The move was good public relations.* その運動はよいPRになった. ② N-PLURAL 複数名詞 You can refer to the opinion that the public has of an organization as **public relations**. 世間の評判 □ *Limiting casualties is important for public relations.* 世評のためには戦争犠牲者を限定することが重要だ.

pub|lic school (**public schools**) ■ N-VAR 可変性名詞 In the United States, Australia, and many other countries, a **public school** is a school that is supported financially by the government and usually provides free education. 公立学校 □ ...*Milwaukee's public school system.* ミルウォーキーの公立学校制度 ② N-VAR 可変性名詞 In Britain, a **public school** is a private school that provides secondary education that parents have to pay for. The students often live at the school during the school term. パブリックスクール □ *He was headmaster of a public school in the West of England.* 彼はイングランド西部のパブリックスクールの校長でした.

pub|lic sec|tor N-SING 単数名詞 The **public sector** is the part of a country's economy which is controlled or supported financially by the government. 公共セクター [BUSINESS 実業] □ ...*Carlos Menem's policy of reducing the public sector and opening up the economy to free-market forces.* 公共部門を縮小し, 経済を自由市場の原理に開放するカルロス・メネムの方針

pub|lic ser|vice (**public services**) ■ N-COUNT 可算名詞 A **public service** is something such as health care, transportation, or the removal of waste, which is organized by the government or an official body in order to benefit all the people in a particular society or community. 公益事業 □ *The money is used by local authorities to pay for public services.* そのお金は地方公共団体による公益事業資金に充てられます. ② N-UNCOUNT 不可算名詞 You use **public service** to refer to activities and jobs that are provided or paid for by a government, especially through the civil service. 公職 [oft N n] □ ...*a distinguished career in public service.* 公職における輝かしい職歴 ③ N-UNCOUNT 不可算名詞 **Public service** activities and types of work are concerned with helping people and providing them with what they need, rather than making a profit. 公共サービス □ ...*the notion of public service and obligation which has been under such attack.* こういった非難を浴びている公共サービスと社会的責任の概念

pub|lic util|ity (**public utilities**) N-COUNT 可算名詞 **Public utilities** are services that are regulated by the government or state, such as the supply of electricity, gas, or water. 公共事業 □ *Officials said water supplies and other public utilities in the capital were badly affected.* 関係筋によると, 首都の水道などの公益事業は著しい影響を受けたとのことだ.

pub|lish /pʌ́blɪʃ/ (**publishes, publishing, published**) ■ V-T 他動詞 When a company **publishes** a book or magazine, it prints copies of it, which are sent to stores to be sold. 刊行する [他動詞] □ *They publish reference books.* 彼らは参考図書を出版する. ② V-T 他動詞 When the people in charge of a newspaper or magazine **publish** a piece of writing or a photograph, they print it in their newspaper or magazine. 発表する [他動詞] □ *Womens' magazines just don't publish articles on the harmful effects of smoking.* 女性誌はとにかく喫煙の有害性に関する記事は載せません. ③ V-T 他動詞 If someone **publishes** a book or an article that they have written, they arrange to have it published. 出版する [他動詞] □ *Walker has published four books of her verse.* ウォーカーは彼女の詩の本を4冊出版したばかりです. ④ V-T 他動詞 If you **publish** information or an opinion, you make it known to the public by having it printed in a newspaper, magazine, or official document. 広める [他動詞] □ *The demonstrators called on the government to publish a list of registered voters.* デモ参加者は政府に登録有権者のリストを公表するよう求めました.

→ see **laboratory, printing**

pub|lish|er /pʌ́blɪʃər/ (**publishers**) N-COUNT 可算名詞 A **publisher** is a person or a company that publishes books, newspapers, or magazines. 発行者 □ *The publishers planned to produce the journal on a weekly basis.* 出版社は週刊新聞の刊行を計画した.

pub|lish|ing /pʌ́blɪʃɪŋ/ N-UNCOUNT 不可算名詞 **Publishing** is the profession of publishing books. 出版業 □ *I had a very high-powered job in publishing.* 私は出版業界で非常に精力的な仕事をしていた.

→ see **newspaper**

pub|lish|ing house (**publishing houses**) N-COUNT 可算名詞 A **publishing house** is a company that publishes books. 出版社

pud|ding /pʊ́dɪŋ/ (**puddings**) N-VAR 可変性名詞 A **pudding** is a cooked sweet food made from ingredients such as milk, sugar, flour, and eggs, and is served either hot or cold. プディング □ ...*a banana vanilla pudding.* バナナ・バニラ・プディング

pud|dle /pʌ́dəl/ (**puddles**) N-COUNT 可算名詞 A **puddle** is a small, shallow pool of liquid that has spread on the ground. 水たまり □ *The road was shiny with puddles, but the rain was at an end.* 道は水たまりで輝いていたが, 雨は止みそうだった.

puff /pʌ́f/ (**puffs, puffing, puffed**) ■ V-I 他動詞 If someone **puffs** on or at a cigarette, cigar, or pipe, they smoke it. 吹かす □ *He lit a cigar and puffed on it twice.* 彼は葉巻に火を点けて, 2回吹かした. ● N-COUNT 可算名詞 **Puff** is also a noun. プッと吹くこと □ *I took a puff on the cigarette and started coughing.* 私はたばこを吹かして咳き込んだ. ② V-T/V-I 他動詞/自動詞 If you **puff** smoke or moisture from your mouth or if it **puffs** from your mouth, you breathe it out. 吹く [他動詞・自動詞] □ *Richard lit another cigarette and puffed smoke toward the ceiling.* リチャードはもう一本たばこに火をつけて天井に向けて煙を吹き出した. ● PHRASAL VERB 句動詞 **Puff out** means the same as **puff**. 吹き出す □ *He drew heavily on his cigarette and puffed out a cloud of smoke.* 彼はたばこを深く吸ってもうもうと煙を吐き出した. ③ V-T 他動詞 If an engine, chimney, or stove **puffs** smoke or steam, clouds of smoke or steam come out of it. 吹く [他動詞] □ *As I completed my 26th lap the Porsche puffed blue smoke.* 26周した後, ポルシェは青い煙を吐いた. ④ N-COUNT 可算名詞 A **puff** of something such as air or smoke is a small amount of it that is blown out from somewhere. 一吹き □ *Wind caught the sudden puff of dust and blew it inland.* 風が一陣のほこりを捕らえ, 陸の方に吹き寄せた. ⑤ V-I 自動詞 If you **are puffing**, you are breathing loudly and quickly with your mouth open because you are out of breath after a lot of physical effort. 息を切らす [usu cont] [自動詞] □ *I know nothing about boxing, but I could see he was unfit, because he was puffing.* ボクシングについては何も知らないが, 彼は息を切らしており不向きであるのがわかる.

pull /pʊ́l/ (**pulls, pulling, pulled**) ■ V-T/V-I 他動詞/自動詞 When you **pull** something, you hold it firmly and use force in order to move it toward you or away from its previous position. 引っ張る [他動詞・自動詞] □ *They have pulled out patients' teeth unnecessarily.* 彼らは抜く必要のない患者の歯を抜いた. □ *Erica pulled at her blonde curls.* エリカは真剣な表情で, ブロンドの巻き毛を引っ張っていた. □ *I helped pull him out of the water.* 私は彼を水中から引き上げるのを助けた. □ *Someone pulled her hair.* 誰かが彼女の髪を引っ張った. ● N-COUNT 可算名詞 **Pull** is also a noun. 引くこと □ *The feather must be removed with a straight, firm pull.* 羽をむしり取るには, まっすぐ, ぐいっと引かなくてはならない. ② V-T 他動詞 When you **pull** an object from a bag, pocket, or cabinet, you put your hand in and bring the object out. 引き抜く [他動詞] □ *Jack pulled the*

slip of paper from his shirt pocket. ジャックはシャツのポケットから紙片を取り出した。 **3** V-T 他動詞 When a vehicle, animal, or person **pulls** a cart or piece of machinery, they are attached to it or hold it, so that it moves along behind them when they move forward. 引く [他動詞] ❑ He pulls a rickshaw, probably the oldest form of human taxi service. 彼は人力車を引いているが、これはおそらく最古の人間タクシーサービスである。 **4** V-T 他動詞 If you **pull yourself** or **pull** a part of your body in a particular direction, you move your body or a part of your body with effort or force. 自力で動かす [他動詞・自動詞] ❑ Hughes pulled himself slowly to his feet. ヒューズは自力でゆっくりと立ち上がった。 ❑ He pulled his arms out of the sleeves. 彼は腕まくりをした。 **5** V-I 自動詞 When a driver or vehicle **pulls** to a stop or a halt, the vehicle stops. 停車する [自動詞] ❑ He pulled to a stop behind a pickup truck. 彼は小型トラックの後ろに車を停めた。 **6** V-I 自動詞 In a race or contest, if you **pull ahead of** or **pull away from** an opponent, you gradually increase the amount by which you are ahead of them. 引き離す [自動詞] ❑ He pulled away, extending his lead to 15 seconds. 彼は二番手を引き離し、リードを15秒に広げた。 **7** V-T 他動詞 If you **pull** something **apart**, you break or divide it into small pieces, often in order to put them back together again in a different way. 引っ張ってばらばらにする [他動詞] ❑ If I wanted to improve the car significantly I would have to pull it apart and start again. 車を著しく改善するには、解体してやり直さなければならないだろう。 **8** V-T 他動詞 To **pull** crowds, viewers, or voters means to attract them. 引き寄せる [INFORMAL くだけた] [他動詞] ❑ The organizers have to employ performers to pull a crowd. 主催者は芸人を雇って観客を集める必要がある。 ● PHRASAL VERB 句動詞 **Pull in** means the same as **pull**. ひきつける ❑ They provided a far better news service and pulled in many more viewers. 彼らははるかに良いニュースサービスを提供し、より多くの視聴者をひきつけた。 **9** N-COUNT 可算名詞 A **pull** is a strong physical force that causes things to move in a particular direction. ひと引き ❑ ...the pull of gravity. 重力の引力 **10** to **pull a face** → see **face** **11** to **pull** someone's **leg** → see **leg** **12** to **pull strings** → see **string** **13** to **pull** your **weight** → see **weight**

▶ **pull away** **1** PHRASAL VERB 句動詞 When a vehicle or driver **pulls away**, the vehicle starts moving forward. 立ち去る ❑ I stood in the driveway and watched him back out and pull away. 私は私道に立って、彼がバックして出て走り去るのをみていた。 **2** PHRASAL VERB 句動詞 If you **pull away from** someone that you have had close links with, you deliberately become less close to them. 離れる ❑ Other daughters, faced with their mother's emotional hunger, pull away. ほかの娘たちは、母親の感情的飢餓に直面し離れていった。

▶ **pull back** **1** PHRASAL VERB 句動詞 If someone **pulls back from** an action, they decide not to do it or continue with it, because it could have bad consequences. 撤回する ❑ They will plead with him to pull back from confrontation. 彼らは対立状態から後に引くよう彼に懇願するだろう。 **2** PHRASAL VERB 句動詞 If troops **pull back** or if their leader **pulls** them **back**, they go some or all of the way back to their own territory. 退却する ❑ They were asked to pull back from their artillery positions around the city. 彼らは都市を囲む砲撃位置から退却するよう要請された。

▶ **pull down** PHRASAL VERB 句動詞 To **pull down** a building or statue means to deliberately destroy it. 取り壊す ❑ They'd pulled the registrar's office down which then left an open space. 彼らは記録係事務所を取り壊し、跡には空き地が残った。

▶ **pull in** **1** PHRASAL VERB 句動詞 When a vehicle or driver **pulls in** somewhere, the vehicle stops there. 停車する ❑ He pulled in at the side of the road. 彼は道路わきに停車した。 **2** → see **pull 8**

▶ **pull into** PHRASAL VERB 句動詞 When a vehicle or driver **pulls into** a place, the vehicle moves into the place and stops there. 寄せて停車する ❑ He pulled into the driveway in front of her garage. 彼は車庫の前の私道に車を止めた。

▶ **pull off** **1** PHRASAL VERB 句動詞 If you **pull off** something very difficult, you succeed in achieving it. 首尾よくやりとげる ❑ The National League for Democracy pulled off a landslide victory. 国民民主連盟は圧倒的な勝利を収めた。 **2** PHRASAL VERB 句動詞 If a vehicle or driver **pulls off** the road, the vehicle stops by the side of the road. 車を道路わきにつける ❑ I pulled off the road at a scenic overlook. 私は景色の良い見渡しがよい所で車を道路わきにつけた。

▶ **pull out** **1** PHRASAL VERB 句動詞 When a vehicle or driver **pulls out**, the vehicle moves out into the road or nearer the center of the road. 道路に入る ❑ She pulled out into the street. 彼女は通りに出た。 **2** PHRASAL VERB 句動詞 If you **pull out of** an agreement, a contest, or an organization, you withdraw from it. 手を引く ❑ The World Bank should pull out of the project. 世界銀行はプロジェクトから手を引くべきだ。 ❑ France was going to pull out of NATO. フランスはNATOから脱退するところだった。 **3** PHRASAL VERB 句動詞 If troops **pull out of** a place or if their leader **pulls** them **out**, they leave it. 立ち去る ❑ The militia in Lebanon has agreed to pull out of Beirut. レバノンに駐在する民兵組織はベイルート撤退に同意した。 ❑ Economic sanctions will be lifted once two-thirds of their forces have pulled out. 部隊の3分の2が撤退すれば経済制裁は解除されます。 **4** PHRASAL VERB 句動詞 If you **pull out of** a bad situation or if someone **pulls** you **out**, you begin to recover from it. 回復する ❑ I pulled out of the depression very quickly with treatment. 私は治療で極めて短期間にう

つ病から立ち直った。 ❑ Sterling has been hit by the economy's failure to pull out of recession. スターリングは不景気が回復しなかったことのあおりを食らった。

▶ **pull over** **1** PHRASAL VERB 句動詞 When a vehicle or driver **pulls over**, or when a police officer **pulls** them **over**, the vehicle moves closer to the side of the road and stops there. 路肩に寄せて停止する ❑ He noticed a man behind him in a blue Ford gesticulating to pull over. 彼は背後の青いフォードに乗った男が車を停めるよう身振りで示しているのに気づいた。 **2** → see also **pullover**

▶ **pull through** PHRASAL VERB 句動詞 If someone with a serious illness or someone in a very difficult situation **pulls through**, they recover. 難局を切り抜ける ❑ Everyone was very concerned whether he would pull through or not. 彼が助かるかどうか誰もが心配していた。 ❑ It is only our determination to fight that has pulled us through. 我々は戦う決意のみで困難を切り抜けた。

▶ **pull together** **1** PHRASAL VERB 句動詞 If people **pull together**, they help each other or work together in order to deal with a difficult situation. 協力して働く ❑ The nation was urged to pull together to avoid a slide into complete chaos. 完全な混乱状態に陥らないよう、国民は互いに協力するよう要請された。 **2** PHRASAL VERB 句動詞 If you are upset or depressed and someone tells you to **pull yourself together**, they are telling you to control your feelings and behave calmly again. 気を取り直す ❑ Pull yourself together, you stupid woman! 落ち着け、このばか者。

▶ **pull up** **1** PHRASAL VERB 句動詞 When a vehicle or driver **pulls up**, the vehicle slows down and stops. 止める ❑ The cab pulled up and the driver jumped out. タクシーが止まり、運転手が飛び出した。 **2** PHRASAL VERB 句動詞 If you **pull up** a chair, you move it closer to something or someone and sit on it. 引き寄せる ❑ He pulled up a chair behind her and put his chin on her shoulder. 彼はいすを彼女の背後に引き寄せてあごを彼女の肩に載せた。

Thesaurus		pull また次を参照:
v.	drag, haul, lug, tow; (ant.) push	**1** **3** **4**
	attract, draw, lure; (ant.) repel	**8**

pull|over /pʊloʊvər/ (pullovers) N-COUNT 可算名詞 A **pullover** is a piece of clothing that covers the upper part of your body and your arms. You put it on by pulling it over your head. プルオーバー

pulp /pʌlp/ (pulps, pulping, pulped) **1** N-SING 単数名詞 If an object is pressed into a **pulp**, it is crushed or beaten until it is soft, smooth, and wet. どろどろしたもの ❑ The olives are crushed to a pulp by stone rollers. オリーブの実は石製のローラーでどろどろにつぶされる。 **2** N-SING 単数名詞 In fruit or vegetables, **the pulp** is the soft part inside the skin. 果肉 ❑ Make maximum use of the whole fruit, including the pulp which is high in fiber. 繊維の多い果肉を含め、果物全部を最大限に使いなさい。 **3** N-UNCOUNT 不可算名詞 Wood **pulp** is material made from crushed wood. It is used to make paper. パルプ **4** ADJ 形容詞 People refer to stories or novels as **pulp** fiction when they consider them to be of poor quality and intentionally shocking or sensational. 安っぽい [ADJ n] ❑ ...lurid '50s pulp novels. 50年代のぞっとするような大衆小説 **5** V-T 他動詞 If vegetables or fruit **are pulped**, they are crushed into a smooth, wet paste. どろどろにする [usu passive] [他動詞] ❑ Onions can be boiled and pulped to a puree. タマネギは煮詰めてすりつぶしてピューレにできる。 **6** V-T 他動詞 If paper, books, or documents **are pulped**, they are destroyed. 廃棄処分する [usu passive] [他動詞] ❑ The first edition had to be pulped because it contained inaccuracies. 第1版は誤りのために廃棄処分しなければなりませんでした。 **7** PHRASE 句 If someone **is beaten to a pulp**, they are hit repeatedly until they are very badly injured. 人をぺしゃんこにやっつける ❑ I tried to talk myself out of a fight and got beaten to a pulp instead by three other boys. 私はけんかを避けようと説得を試みたが、逆に3人の少年にこてんこてんにやっつけられた。

pul|pit /pʊlpɪt, pʌl-/ (pulpits) N-COUNT 可算名詞 A **pulpit** is a small raised platform with a rail or barrier around it in a church, where a member of the clergy stands to speak. 説教壇 ❑ The time came for the sermon and he ascended the pulpit steps. 説教の時間が来たので彼は説教壇の階段を登った。

pul|sate /pʌlseɪt/ (pulsates, pulsating, pulsated) V-I 自動詞 If something **pulsates**, it beats, moves in and out, or shakes with strong, regular movements. 脈動する [自動詞] ❑ The Pole Star appears to be changing from a star that pulsates. 北極星は脈動星から変化しているようだ。

pulse /pʌls/ (pulses, pulsing, pulsed) **1** N-COUNT 可算名詞 Your **pulse** is the regular beating of blood through your body, which you can feel when you touch particular parts of your body, especially your wrist. 脈 ❑ Mahoney's pulse was racing, and he felt confused. マホーニーは脈が非常に早くなって狼狽した。 **2** N-COUNT 可算名詞 In music, a **pulse** is a regular beat, often produced by a drum. 拍子 ❑ ...the repetitive pulse of the music. 音楽の反復的な律動 **3** N-COUNT 可算名詞 A **pulse of** electrical current, light, or sound is a temporary increase in its level. パルス ❑ The switch works by passing a pulse of current between the tip and the surface. スイッチは先端と表面の間に電流パルスを流すことで作動します。 **4** N-SING 単数

名詞 If you refer to **the pulse of** a group in society, you mean the ideas, opinions, or feelings they have at a particular time. 脈動 □ *The White House insists that the president is in touch with the pulse of the black community.* ホワイトハウスは、大統領は黒人社会の脈動を理解していると主張しています。 **5** V-I 自動詞 If something **pulses**, it moves, appears, or makes a sound with a strong regular rhythm. 鼓動する [自動詞] □ *His temples pulsed a little, threatening a headache.* 彼はこめかみが若干脈打っていることから、頭痛が起きそうだと感じた。 **6** N-PLURAL 複数名詞 Some seeds that can be cooked and eaten are called **pulses**, for example, peas, beans, and lentils. 豆類 [mainly BRIT 主に英国英語; AM usually **legumes** 米国英語では通常 **legumes**]

pump /pʌmp/ (**pumps, pumping, pumped**) **1** N-COUNT 可算名詞 A **pump** is a machine or device that is used to force a liquid or gas to flow in a particular direction. ポンプ □ ...*pumps that circulate the fuel around in the engine.* エンジンに燃料を循環させるポンプ □ *There was no water in the building, just a pump in the courtyard.* 建物内は水は引かれておらず、中庭にポンプがあるだけだった。 **2** V-T 他動詞 To **pump** a liquid or gas in a particular direction means to force it to flow in that direction using a pump. ポンプで送り出す [他動詞・自動詞] □ *It's not enough to get rid of raw sewage by pumping it out to sea.* 未処理下水をポンプで海に流して除去するだけでは十分ではありません。 □ *The money raised will be used to dig bore holes to pump water into the dried-up lake.* 調達した資金は水の枯れた湖へ水をポンプで送るための穴を掘るために使われます。 **3** N-COUNT 可算名詞 A fuel or gas **pump** is a machine with a tube attached to it that you use to fill a car with gasoline. ポンプ □ *The average price for all grades of gas at the pump was $3.49 a gallon.* 全等級のガソリンの平均価格は1ガロン当たり3.49ドルである。 **4** V-T 他動詞 If someone **has** their stomach **pumped**, doctors remove the contents of their stomach, for example, because they have swallowed poison or drugs. 胃を洗浄する [usu passive] [他動詞] □ *One woman was rushed to the emergency room to have her stomach pumped.* ある女性が胃洗浄のために救急治療室に緊急搬送された。 **5** N-COUNT 可算名詞 **Pumps** are women's shoes that do not cover the top part of the foot and are usually made of plain leather. パンプス [mainly AM 主に米国英語]

▶ **pump out** PHRASAL VERB 句動詞 To **pump out** something means to produce or supply it continually and in large amounts. 次々と送り出す □ *Japanese companies have been pumping out plenty of innovative products.* 日本企業は革新的な製品を大量に送り出してきた。

▶ **pump up** PHRASAL VERB 句動詞 If you **pump up** something such as a tire, you fill it with air using a pump. 空気をポンプで注入する □ *Pump all the tires up.* すべてのタイヤに空気を入れろ。

pump|kin /pʌmpkɪn/ (**pumpkins**) N-VAR 可変性名詞 A **pumpkin** is a large, round, orange vegetable with a thick skin. カボチャ □ *Quarter the pumpkin and remove the seeds.* カボチャを4等分にして種を除きなさい。

pun /pʌn/ (**puns**) N-COUNT 可算名詞 A **pun** is a clever and amusing use of a word or phrase with two meanings, or of words with the same sound but different meanings. For example, if someone says "The peasants are revolting," this is a pun because it can be interpreted as meaning either that the peasants are fighting against authority, or that they are disgusting. ごろ合わせ □ *He spoke of a hatchet job, which may be a pun on some senator's name.* 彼はいやみな批評をしたが、上院議員の名前をもじったのかもしれない。

punch /pʌntʃ/ (**punches, punching, punched**) **1** V-T 他動詞 If you **punch** someone or something, you hit them hard with your fist. げんこつを食わせる [他動詞] □ *After punching him on the chin she wound up hitting him over the head.* 彼女は彼のあごにパンチを食らわせてから頭を叩いた。 ● N-COUNT 可算名詞 **Punch** is also a noun. パンチ □ *He was hurting Johansson with body punches in the fourth round.* 4ラウンド目、彼はヨハンソンをボディーパンチで痛めつけていました。 ● PHRASAL VERB 句動詞 **Punch out** means the same as **punch**. ぶんなぐる □ *"I almost lost my job today." — "What happened?" — "Oh, I punched out this guy."* 「今日僕は失業するところだった」「どうしたの」「この男をぶんなぐったんだ」 **2** V-T 他動詞 If you **punch** something such as the buttons on a keyboard, you touch them in order to store information on a machine such as a computer or to give the machine a command to do something. 打つ [他動詞] □ *Mrs. Baylor strode to the elevator and punched the button.* ベイラー夫人はエレベーターまで大股で歩きボタンを押した。 **3** V-T 他動詞 If you **punch** holes in something, you make holes in it by pushing or pressing it with something sharp. 穴をあける [他動詞] □ *I took a ballpoint pen and punched a hole in the carton.* 私はボールペンを取り上げてボール紙に穴をあけました。 **4** N-COUNT 可算名詞 A **punch** is a tool that you use for making holes in something. 穴あけ器 □ *Make two holes with a hole punch.* 穴あけ器で穴を2つあけなさい。 **5** N-UNCOUNT 不可算名詞 If you say that something has **punch**, you mean that it has force or effectiveness. 効果 □ *My nervousness made me deliver the vital points of my address without sufficient punch.* 私は緊張していたので演説の肝心なポイントで十分な

パンチを効かせることができなかった。 **6** N-MASS 質量名詞 **Punch** is a drink made from wine, spirits, or fruit juice, mixed with things such as sugar and spices. パンチ □ ...*a bowl of punch.* ボウル一杯のパンチ

▶ **punch in** **1** PHRASAL VERB 句動詞 If you **punch in** a number on a machine or **punch** numbers **into** it, you push the machine's buttons or keys in order to give it a command to do something. (キーなどを叩いてデータを) 入力する □ *You can bank by phone in the U.S., punching in account numbers on the phone.* アメリカでは電話から口座番号を入力することにより銀行取引ができる。 **2** PHRASAL VERB 句動詞 When you **punch in** at work, you arrive there and put a special card into a device to show what time you arrived. タイムレコーダーを押して出勤時刻を記録する □ *He would get up and get ready for work, eat, and punch in at 6 p.m.* 彼は起床して仕事にいく準備をし、食事して、午後6時にタイムレコーダーを押す。

punc|tual /pʌŋktʃuəl/ ADJ 形容詞 If you are **punctual**, you do something or arrive somewhere at the right time and are not late. 時間を守る □ *He's always very punctual. I'll see if he's here yet.* 彼はいつも時間をよく守る。もう来ているか見てみよう。 ● **punc|tu|al|ly** ADV 副詞 時間通りに □ *My guest arrived punctually.* 客は時間通りに来た。

punc|tu|ate /pʌŋktʃueɪt/ (**punctuates, punctuating, punctuated**) V-T 他動詞 If an activity or situation **is punctuated by** particular things, it is interrupted by them at intervals. 何度も中断させる [WRITTEN 書き言葉] [usu passive] □ *The game was punctuated by a series of injuries.* 試合は負傷の連続で何度も中断した。

punc|tua|tion /pʌŋktʃueɪʃən/ **1** N-UNCOUNT 不可算名詞 **Punctuation** is the use of symbols such as periods, commas, or question marks to divide written words into sentences and clauses. 句読点をつけること □ *He was known for his poor grammar and punctuation.* 彼は文法や句読点の使い方がお粗末なことで知られていた。 **2** N-UNCOUNT 不可算名詞 **Punctuation** is the symbols that you use to divide written words into sentences and clauses. 句読点 □ *Jessica had rapidly scanned the lines, none of which boasted a capital letter or any punctuation.* ジェシカはひとくだりをざっと見てみたが、どの行にも大文字や句読点は見当たらなかった。

punc|tua|tion mark (**punctuation marks**) N-COUNT 可算名詞 A **punctuation mark** is a symbol such as a period, comma, or question mark that you use to divide written words into sentences and clauses. 句読記号

punc|ture /pʌŋktʃər/ (**punctures, puncturing, punctured**) **1** N-COUNT 可算名詞 A **puncture** is a small hole in a car tire or bicycle tire that has been made by a sharp object. パンクの穴 □ *Somebody helped me to mend the puncture.* 誰かがパンクを修理するのを手伝ってくれた。 **2** N-COUNT 可算名詞 A **puncture** is a small hole in someone's skin that has been made by or with a sharp object. 小さな穴 □ *An instrument called a trocar makes a puncture in the abdominal wall.* トロカールという器具が腹壁に小さな穴を開ける。 **3** V-T 他動詞 If a sharp object **punctures** something, it makes a hole in it. 穴を開ける □ *The bullet punctured the skull.* 弾丸で頭蓋骨に穴があいた。 **4** V-T/V-I 他動詞/自動詞 If a car tire or bicycle tire **punctures** or if something **punctures** it, a hole is made in the tire. パンクさせる [他動詞]、パンクする [自動詞] □ *His bike's rear tire punctured.* 自転車の後輪がパンクした。

pun|dit /pʌndɪt/ (**pundits**) N-COUNT 可算名詞 A **pundit** is a person who knows a lot about a subject and is often asked to give information or opinions about it to the public. 博学者 □ ...*a well-known political pundit.* 有名な政治学者

pun|gent /pʌndʒ°nt/ ADJ 形容詞 Something that is **pungent** has a strong, sharp smell or taste which is often so strong that it is unpleasant. 刺すように刺激する □ *The more herbs you use, the more pungent the sauce will be.* ハーブを使えば使うほどソースは鋭い風味になる。

pun|ish /pʌnɪʃ/ (**punishes, punishing, punished**) **1** V-T 他動詞 To **punish** someone means to make them suffer in some way because they have done something wrong. 罰する □ *I don't believe that George ever had to punish the children.* ジョージが子供に罰を与えざるを得ない状況はこれまでなかったと思う。 □ *According to present law, the authorities can only punish smugglers with small fines.* 現在の法律によれば、密輸業者に対して当局は少額の罰金処罰しかできない。 **2** V-T 他動詞 To **punish** a crime means to punish anyone who commits that crime. 処罰する □ ...*federal laws to punish crimes such as murder and assault.* 殺人や暴行のような犯罪を処罰する連邦政府の法律

pun|ish|ing /pʌnɪʃɪŋ/ ADJ 形容詞 A **punishing** schedule, activity, or experience requires a lot of physical effort and makes you very tired or weak. へとへとに疲れさせる □ *He claimed his punishing work schedule had made him resort to taking the drug.* 彼は仕

事の過激なスケジュールのため薬物に頼るようになったと主張した.

pun|ish|ment /pʌnɪʃmənt/ (**punishments**) **1** N-UNCOUNT 不可算名詞 **Punishment** is the act of punishing someone or of being punished. 処罰 □ ...a group that campaigns against the physical punishment of children. 子供への体罰反対運動グループ **2** N-VAR 可変性名詞 A **punishment** is a particular way of punishing someone. 懲罰 □ The government is proposing tougher punishments for officials convicted of corruption. 汚職で有罪が確定した公務員に対する罰則強化を政府は提案中である. **3** N-UNCOUNT 不可算名詞 You can use **punishment** to refer to severe physical treatment of any kind. 酷使 □ Don't expect these boots to take the punishment that gardening will give them. このブーツが庭仕事のようなひどい扱いに耐えられると思うな. **4** → see also **capital punishment, corporal punishment**

pu|ni|tive /pyuːnɪtɪv/ ADJ 形容詞 **Punitive** actions are intended to punish people. 懲罰的な [FORMAL 形式ばった] □ ...a punitive bombing raid. 懲罰的爆撃

punk /pʌŋk/ (**punks**) **1** N-UNCOUNT 不可算名詞 **Punk** or **punk rock** is rock music that is played in a fast, loud, and aggressive way and is often a protest against conventional attitudes and behavior. Punk rock was particularly popular in the late 1970s. パンクロック □ I was never really into punk. 本当にパンクロックに夢中になることはなかった. **2** N-COUNT 可算名詞 A **punk** or a **punk rocker** is a young person who likes punk music and dresses in a very noticeable and unconventional way, for example, by having brightly colored hair and wearing metal chains. パンクロック愛好者 □ In the 1970s, punks wore safety pins through their cheeks. 1970年代のパンクは頬に安全ピンをさしていた.

pup /pʌp/ (**pups**) **1** N-COUNT 可算名詞 A **pup** is a young dog. 子犬 □ I'll get you an Alsatian pup for Christmas. クリスマスにはドイツシェパード犬の子犬をあげよう. **2** N-COUNT 可算名詞 The young of some other animals, for example, seals, are called **pups**. アザラシなどの子 □ Two thousand gray seal pups are born there every fall. そこでは毎年秋に2千頭ものゴマフアザラシの子が生まれる.

pu|pil /pyuːpɪl/ (**pupils**) **1** N-COUNT 可算名詞 A **pupil** of a painter, musician, or other expert is someone who studies under that expert and learns his or her skills. 弟子 □ After his education, Goldschmidt became a pupil of the composer Franz Schreker. ゴールドシュミットは教育を終えてから作曲家フランツ・シュレーカーの弟子となった. **2** N-COUNT 可算名詞 The **pupils** of a school are the children who go to it. 生徒 □ ...schools with over 1,000 pupils. 1000人以上生徒がいる学校 **3** N-COUNT 可算名詞 The **pupils** of your eyes are the small, round, black holes in the center of them. ひとみ □ The sick man's pupils were dilated. 病気の男の瞳孔は開いていた. → see **eye**

pup|pet /pʌpɪt/ (**puppets**) **1** N-COUNT 可算名詞 A **puppet** is a doll that you can move, either by pulling strings that are attached to it or by putting your hand inside its body and moving your fingers. 操り人形; 指人形 **2** N-COUNT 可算名詞 You can refer to a person or country as a **puppet** when you mean that their actions are controlled by a more powerful person or government, even though they may appear to be independent. かいらい [DISAPPROVAL 不賛成] □ When the invasion occurred he seized power and ruled the country as a puppet of the occupiers. 侵略があったときに彼は権力を握り, 占領者のかいらいとして国を支配した.

pup|py /pʌpi/ (**puppies**) N-COUNT 可算名詞 A **puppy** is a young dog. 子犬 □ One Sunday he began trying to teach the two puppies to walk on a leash. ある日曜日に, ひもでつないで歩くことを2匹の子犬に教えようとし始めた.

pur|chase /pɜːrtʃɪs/ (**purchases, purchasing, purchased**) **1** V-T 他動詞 When you **purchase** something, you buy it. 購入する [FORMAL 形式ばった] □ He purchased a ticket and went up on the top deck. 切符を購入して上のデッキに上がっていった. ● **pur|chas|er** (**purchasers**) N-COUNT 可算名詞 購入者 □ The broker will get 5% if he finds a purchaser. 購入者が見つかれば仲介人は5%を手にする. **2** N-UNCOUNT 不可算名詞 The **purchase of** something is the act of buying it. 購入 [FORMAL 形式ばった] □ This week he is to visit China to discuss the purchase of military supplies. 今週中国を訪問して軍需品の購入について話し合う予定である. **3** N-COUNT 可算名詞 A **purchase** is something that you buy. 購入品 [FORMAL 形式ばった] □ She opened the tie box and looked at her purchase. It was silk, with maroon stripes. ネクタイの箱を開けて購入した品物を見た. 栗色のしま柄のある絹製であった.

pur|chas|ing pow|er **1** N-UNCOUNT 不可算名詞 The **purchasing power** of a currency is the amount of goods or services that you can buy with it. 貨幣価値 [BUSINESS 実業] □ The real purchasing power of the rouble has plummeted. ルーブルの実質貨幣価値は急落した. **2** N-UNCOUNT 不可算名詞 The **purchasing power** of a person or group of people is the amount of goods or services that they can afford to buy. 購買力 [BUSINESS 実業] □ Wage rates must be maintained in order to maintain the purchasing power of the consumer. 消費者の購買力を維持するために賃金を維持しなければならない.

pure /pyʊər/ (**purer, purest**) **1** ADJ 形容詞 A **pure** substance is not mixed with anything else. 混じりけのない □ ...a carton of pure orange juice. 100%オレンジのジュースの箱 **2** ADJ 形容詞 Something that is **pure** is clean and does not contain any harmful substances. 清純な □ In remote regions, the air is pure and the crops are free of poisonous insecticides. 不便な地方は空気が澄んでいて農作物にも毒になる殺虫剤が使われていない. ● **pu|ri|ty** /pyʊərɪti/ N-UNCOUNT 不可算名詞 [with poss] 清浄 □ They worried about the purity of tap water. 水道の水が清浄かどうか心配した. **3** ADJ 形容詞 If you describe something such as a color, a sound, or a type of light as **pure**, you mean that it is very clear and represents a perfect example of its type. 純粋な □ She was dressed in pure white clothes. 真っ白な衣装を身につけていた. ● **pu|ri|ty** N-UNCOUNT 不可算名詞 純粋さ □ The soaring purity of her voice conjured up the frozen bleakness of the Far North. 高くなっていく彼女の澄んだ声は, 最北地方の凍った荒涼さをまざまざと思わせた. **4** ADJ 形容詞 [ADJ n] **Pure** science or **pure** research is concerned only with theory and not with how this theory can be used in practical ways. 理論的な □ Physics isn't just about pure science with no immediate applications. 物理学とは, すぐには応用されない単なる純粋科学とは. **5** ADJ 形容詞 **Pure** means complete and total. まったくの [EMPHASIS 強調] □ The old man turned to give her a look of pure surprise. 老いた男は彼女の方に向き, まったくびっくりしたという表情をみせた. → see **science**

pu|ree /pyʊreɪ, -riː/ (**purees, pureeing, pureed**) also **purée** **1** N-VAR 性名詞 **Puree** is food that has been crushed or beaten so that it forms a thick, smooth liquid. ピューレ □ ...a can of tomato puree. トマトピューレの缶詰 **2** V-T 他動詞 If you **puree** food, you make it into a puree. ピューレにする □ In a blender, puree the fruit with the orange juice. ミキサーでその果物をオレンジジュースと一緒にピューレにしなさい.

pure|ly /pyʊərli/ ADV 副詞 You use **purely** to emphasize that the thing you are mentioning is the most important feature or that it is the only thing which should be considered. 完全に [EMPHASIS 強調] [ADV with cl/group] □ It is a racing machine, designed purely for speed. それは純粋にスピードのために設計されたレース用の機械だ.

purge /pɜːrdʒ/ (**purges, purging, purged**) **1** V-T 他動詞 To **purge** an organization **of** its unacceptable members means to remove them from it. You can also talk about **purging** people **from** an organization. 追放する □ The leadership voted to purge the party of "hostile and antiparty elements." 指導者たちは党から「敵対的および反党的要素」を一掃することを決した. □ He recently purged the armed forces, sending hundreds of officers into retirement. 彼は最近, 何百人もの士官を退職させて軍の粛正を行った. ● N-COUNT 可算名詞 **Purge** is also a noun. 追放 □ The army have called for a more thorough purge of people associated with the late president. 故大統領の関係者をさらに徹底的に追放せよと陸軍は要求している. **2** V-T 他動詞 If you **purge** something **of** undesirable things, you get rid of them. 捨て去る □ He closed his eyes and lay still, trying to purge his mind of anxiety. 不安感を取り除こうと, 目を閉じて横になったまま静かにしていた.

pu|ri|fy /pyʊərɪfaɪ/ (**purifies, purifying, purified**) V-T 他動詞 If you **purify** a substance, you make it pure by removing any harmful, dirty, or inferior substances from it. 浄化する □ I take wheat and yeast tablets daily to purify the blood. 血液をきれいにするために小麦と酵母菌の錠剤を毎日飲んでいる. ● **pu|ri|fi|ca|tion** /pyʊərɪfɪkeɪʃn/ N-UNCOUNT 不可算名詞 浄化 □ ...a water purification plant. 浄水場

pur|ist /pyʊərɪst/ (**purists**) **1** N-COUNT 可算名詞 A **purist** is a person who wants something to be totally correct or unchanged, especially something they know a lot about. 純粋主義者 □ The new edition of the dictionary carries 7,000 additions to the language, which purists say is under threat. 辞書の新版には7千項目の追加があり, 純粋派は将来が危ないと言っている. **2** ADJ 形容詞 **Purist** attitudes are the kind of attitudes that purists have. 純粋主義者の □ ...a peculiarly purist argument. 特に純正主義者的な議論

pu|ri|tan /pyʊərɪtᵊn/ (**puritans**) **1** N-COUNT 可算名詞 You describe someone as a **puritan** when they live according to strict moral or religious principles, especially when they disapprove of physical pleasures. 厳格主義者 [DISAPPROVAL 不賛成] □ Bykov had forgotten that Malinin was something of a puritan. マリーニンがかなり厳格主義者だったのをブイコフは忘れていた. **2** ADJ 形容詞 **Puritan** attitudes are based on strict moral or religious principles and often involve disapproval of physical pleasures. 清教徒のような [DISAPPROVAL 不賛成] □ Paul was someone who certainly had a puritan streak in him. ポールは確かに清教徒のような傾向のある人だった.

pu|ri|tani|cal /pyʊərɪtænɪkᵊl/ ADJ 形容詞 If you describe someone as **puritanical**, you mean that they have very strict moral principles, and often try to make other people behave in a more moral way. 厳格な [DISAPPROVAL 不賛成] □ He has a puritanical attitude toward sex. 性に関しては厳格な考えを持っている.

pu|ri|ty /pyʊərɪti/ → see **pure**

pur|ple /pɜːrpᵊl/ (**purples**) COLOR 色彩語 Something that is **purple** is of a reddish-blue color. 紫色 □ She wore purple and green silk. 紫と緑の色の絹を着ていた.

P

pur|port /pərpɔrt/ (purports, purporting, purported) V-T 他動詞 If you say that someone or something **purports to** do or be a particular thing, you mean that they claim to do or be that thing, although you may not always believe that claim. 主張する [FORMAL 形式ばった] □ ...a book that purports to tell the whole truth. 真実をすべて語るとされている本

pur|pose /pɜrpəs/ (purposes) ■ N-COUNT 可算名詞 The **purpose** of something is the reason for which it is made or done. 目的 □ The purpose of the occasion was to raise money for medical supplies. その行事の目的は、医療品の資金を集めることであった。□ ...the use of nuclear energy for military purposes. 軍事目的のための原子力使用 ② N-COUNT 可算名詞 Your **purpose** is the thing that you want to achieve. 目的 □ They might well be prepared to do you harm in order to achieve their purpose. 彼らは目的を達成するためなら君に危害を加えるつもりであってもおかしくはない。 ③ N-UNCOUNT 不可算名詞 **Purpose** is the feeling of having a definite aim and of being determined to achieve it. 意図 □ The teachers are enthusiastic and have a sense of purpose. 先生たちは熱心で目的意識を持っている。 ④ PHRASE 句 If you do something **on purpose**, you do it intentionally. わざと □ Was it an accident or did David do it on purpose? 事故だったのか、それともデイビットが故意にしたのか？

Word Partnership	purposeは次の語句と使われる:
V.	**serve** a purpose ■
	accomplish a purpose, **achieve** a purpose ②
ADJ.	**main** purpose, **original** purpose, **primary** purpose, **real** purpose, **sole** purpose ■ – ③

purpose-built ADJ 形容詞 A **purpose-built** building has been specially designed and built for a particular use. 特定用途のために作られた [mainly BRIT 主に英国英語; AM usually **custom-built** 米国英語では通常 **custom-built**]

pur|pose|ful /pɜrpəsfəl/ ADJ 形容詞 If someone is **purposeful**, they show that they have a definite aim and a strong desire to achieve it. 意図を持った □ She had a purposeful air, and it became evident that this was not a casual visit. 意図があるようであり、偶然の訪問でないことが明白になった。 ● **pur|pose|ful|ly** ADV 副詞 決然として □ He strode purposefully toward the barn. 決然として納屋に向かって大またで歩いていった。

purr /pɜr/ (purrs, purring, purred) ■ V-I 自動詞 When a cat **purrs**, it makes a low vibrating sound with its throat because it is contented. 猫がゴロゴロいう □ The kitten had settled comfortably in her arms and was purring enthusiastically. 子猫は気持ちよく彼女の腕の中におさまり、夢中になってゴロゴロとのどを鳴らした。 ② V-I 自動詞 When the engine of a machine such as a car **purrs**, it is working and making a quiet, continuous, vibrating sound. 快調な音を出す □ Both boats purred out of the cave mouth and into open water. 洞穴の中から両方のボートが快調な音を出しながら広々とした水上に出てきた。 ● N-SING 単数名詞 **Purr** is also a noun. 快調な音 □ Carmela heard the purr of a motorcycle coming up the drive. 家の私道に入ってくるオートバイの快調な音がカルメーラに聞こえた。

purse /pɜrs/ (purses, pursing, pursed) ■ N-COUNT 可算名詞 A **purse** is a small bag or a handbag that women carry. ハンドバッグ [AM 米国英語] □ She looked at me and then reached in her purse for cigarettes. 彼女は私を見てから、タバコを取るためハンドバッグに手を差し入れた。 ② N-COUNT 可算名詞 A **purse** is a very small bag that people, especially women, keep their money in. 財布 [mainly BRIT 主に英国英語; AM usually **wallet** 米国英語では通常 **wallet**] ③ N-SING 単数名詞 **Purse** is used to refer to the total amount of money that a country, family, or group has. 資力 □ The money could simply go into the public purse, helping to lower taxes. その金は単純に国庫に入れて、減税に役立てることもできる。 ④ V-T 他動詞 If you **purse** your lips, you move them into a small, rounded shape, usually because you disapprove of something or when you are thinking. 唇をすぼめる □ She pursed her lips in disapproval. 彼女は不満で口をぎゅっと結んだ。

pur|sue /pərsu/ (pursues, pursuing, pursued) ■ V-T 他動詞 If you **pursue** an activity, interest, or plan, you carry it out or follow it. 遂行する [FORMAL 形式ばった] □ He said Japan would continue to pursue the policies laid down at the London summit. 日本はロンドン首脳会談で定められた政策を続行するだろうと彼は言った。 ② V-T 他動詞 If you **pursue** a particular aim or result, you make efforts to achieve it, often over a long period of time. 追い続ける [FORMAL 形式ばった] □ He will pursue a trade policy that protects American workers. アメリカの労働者を保護する貿易政策を追求し続けるだろう。 ③ V-T 他動詞 If you **pursue** a particular topic, you try to find out more about it by asking questions. 追求する [FORMAL 形式ばった] □ If your original request is denied, don't be afraid to pursue the matter. 最初の依頼が拒否されても、その件を追求するのを恐れてはいけない。 ④ V-T 他動詞 If you **pursue** a person, vehicle, or animal, you follow them, usually in order to catch them. 追跡する [FORMAL 形式ばった] □ She pursued the man who had stolen a woman's bag. 彼女は女のバッグを盗んだ男の後を追った。

pur|su|er /pərsuər/ (pursuers) N-COUNT 可算名詞 Your **pursuers** are the people who are chasing or searching for you. 追跡する人 [FORMAL 形式ばった] □ They had shaken off their pursuers. 追跡者たちから逃れ切った。

pur|suit /pərsut/ (pursuits) ■ N-UNCOUNT 不可算名詞 Your **pursuit of** something is your attempts at achieving it. If you do something **in pursuit of** a particular result, you do it in order to achieve that result. 追求 □ ...a young man whose relentless pursuit of excellence is conducted with single-minded determination. ひたむきな決心で飽くなき卓越を追求した若者 ② N-UNCOUNT 不可算名詞 The **pursuit of** an activity, interest, or plan consists of all the things that you do when you are carrying it out. 遂行 □ The vigorous pursuit of policies is no guarantee of success. 方針をいかに精力的に遂行しようとも成功の保証とはならない。 ③ N-UNCOUNT 不可算名詞 Someone who is **in pursuit of** a person, vehicle, or animal is chasing them. 追跡 □ ...a police officer who drove a patrol car at more than 110 mph in pursuit of a motorcycle. オートバイを追いかけてパトカーを時速120マイル以上で運転した警察官 ④ N-COUNT 可算名詞 Your **pursuits** are your activities, usually activities that you enjoy when you are not working. 気晴らし □ They both love outdoor pursuits. 二人とも戸外活動が大好きだ。

pur|vey|or /pərveɪər/ (purveyors) N-COUNT 可算名詞 A **purveyor** of goods or services is a person or company that provides them. 調達者 [FORMAL 形式ばった] □ ...purveyors of gourmet foods. グルメ食品の調達業者

push /pʊʃ/ (pushes, pushing, pushed) ■ V-T/V-I 他動詞/自動詞 When you **push** something, you use force to make it move away from you or away from its previous position. 押して動かす □ The woman pushed back her chair and stood up. 女はいすを後ろに引いて立ち上がった。 □ They pushed him into the car. 彼を車に押し込んだ。 □ ...a pregnant woman pushing a stroller. ベビーカーを押している妊婦 ● N-COUNT 可算名詞 **Push** is also a noun. 押すこと □ He gave me a sharp push. わたしを激しく押した。 ② V-T/V-I 他動詞/自動詞 If you **push through** things that are blocking your way or **push your way through** them, you use force in order to move past them. 押しのけて進む □ I pushed through the crowds and on to the escalator. 人ごみの中を押し分けて進みエスカレーターに乗った。 □ Dix pushed forward carrying a glass. ディックスはグラスを抱えて前に押し進んだ。 ③ V-I 自動詞 If an army **pushes into** a country or area that it is attacking or invading, it moves further into it. 前進する □ One detachment pushed into the eastern suburbs toward the airfield. 分遣隊の一隊が飛行場に向かって東側の郊外に前進して行った。 ● N-COUNT 可算名詞 **Push** is also a noun. 突撃 □ All that was needed was one final push, and the enemy would be vanquished once and for all. 最後の一押しさえあったら十分で、敵は完全に征服できるだろう。 ④ V-T 他動詞 To **push** a value or amount **up** or **down** means to cause it to increase or decrease. 押し上げる；押し下げる □ Any shortage could push up grain prices. 不足があれば穀物価格は上がる可能性がある。 □ The government had done everything it could to push down inflation. インフレーションを押し下げるために政府はできる限りのことをした。 ⑤ V-T 他動詞 If someone or something **pushes** an idea or project in a particular direction, they cause it to develop or progress in a particular way. 押し進める □ China would use its influence to help push forward the peace process. 中国は和平過程を推進するために、影響力を行使するであろう。 ⑥ V-T 他動詞 If you **push** someone **to** do something or **push** them **into** doing it, you encourage or force them to do it. 励ます；強要する □ She thanks her parents for keeping her in school and pushing her to study. 学校に在籍させ、勉強するよう励ましてくれた両親に感謝している。 □ Jason did not push her into stealing the money. ジェイソンは彼女に金を盗むようには強要しなかった。 ● N-COUNT 可算名詞 **Push** is also a noun. 押すこと □ We need a push to take the first step. 最初の一歩を踏み出すのに押しが必要だ。 ⑦ V-I 自動詞 If you **push for** something, you try very hard to achieve it or to persuade someone to do it. 得ようと努力する；強く要求する □ Doctors are pushing for a ban on all cigarette advertising. 医者たちはタバコ宣伝の全面禁止を強く要求している。 ● N-COUNT 可算名詞 **Push** is also a noun. 推進 □ In its push for economic growth it has ignored projects that would improve living standards. 経済成長を推進するあまり、生活水準改善のプロジェクトを無視してきた。 ⑧ V-T 他動詞 If someone **pushes** an idea, a point, or a product, they try in a forceful way to convince people to accept it or buy it. 強引に押しつける □ The commissioners will push the case for opening the plant. 委員たちは工場開設の議論を強引に推し進めるだろう。 ⑨ V-T 他動詞 When someone **pushes** drugs, they sell them illegally. 密売する [INFORMAL くだけた] □ You would be on welfare with your kids pushing drugs to pay the rent. 家賃のために麻薬を密売しながら子供と一緒に生活保護を受けるだろう。 ⑩ → see also **pushed** ⑪ if **push comes to shove** → see **shove**

▶ **push ahead** or **push forward** PHRASAL VERB 句動詞 If you **push ahead** or **push forward** with something, you make progress with it. 推進する □ The government intends to push ahead with its reform program. 政府は改革計画を推し進める意図である。

▶ **push on** PHRASAL VERB 句動詞 When you **push on**, you continue with a trip or task. どんどん進む □ Although the journey

was a long and lonely one, Tumalo pushed on. 旅は長くて寂しかったが，ツマロは突き進んでいった．

▶ **push over** PHRASAL VERB 句動詞 If you **push** someone or something **over**, you push them so that they fall onto the ground. 押し倒す ❑ *We have had trouble with people damaging hedges, uprooting trees and pushing over walls.* 垣根を壊したり，木を引き抜いたり，石塀を押し倒したりする人に困っている．

▶ **push through** PHRASAL VERB 句動詞 If someone **pushes through** a law, they succeed in getting it accepted although some people oppose it. 押して通過させる ❑ *The Democratic majority pushed through a law permitting the sale of arms.* 議会で過半数を占める民主党が武器販売を許可する法律を強引に通過させた．

Thesaurus

push また次を参照：

v.	drive, force, move, pressure, propel, shove, thrust; (ant.) pull 🔳 🔳 encourage, urge 🔳 – 🔳

Word Partnership

push は次の語句と使われる：

N.	push a button, at the push of a button, push a door 🔳 push prices, push rates 🔳 push an agenda, push legislation 🔳 push drugs 🔳

push|chair /pʊʃtʃeər/ (**pushchairs**) N-COUNT 可算名詞 A **pushchair** is a small chair on wheels, in which a baby or small child can sit and be wheeled around. ベビーカー [BRIT 英国英語; AM **stroller** 米国英語 **stroller**]

pushed /pʊʃt/ ADJ 形容詞 If you are **pushed for** something such as time or money, you do not have enough of it. 足りなくて困る [BRIT 英国英語, INFORMAL くだけた] [v-link ADJ] [AM **pressed for** 米国英語 **pressed for**] ❑ *He's going to be a bit pushed for money.* きっと金が足りなくなって少し困るだろう．

push|er /pʊʃər/ (**pushers**) N-COUNT 可算名詞 A **pusher** is a person who sells illegal drugs. 麻薬密売人 [INFORMAL くだけた] ❑ *His father accused him of acting as a carrier for some drug pushers.* 父親は，彼が麻薬密売人の運び屋をしていると責めた．

push-up (**push-ups**) N-COUNT 可算名詞 **Push-ups** are exercises to strengthen your arms and chest muscles. They are done by lying with your face toward the floor and pushing with your hands to raise your body until your arms are straight. 腕立て伏せ ❑ *He did push-ups after games.* 試合の後腕立て伏せをした．

put /pʊt/ (**puts, putting**)

The form **put** is used in the present tense and is the past tense and past participle.

put 形は現在時制に使われ，過去時制と過去分詞でもある．

Put is used in a large number of expressions that are explained under other words in this dictionary. For example, the expression **to put someone in the picture** is explained at **picture**.

Put は多数の表現に使われ，この辞書の他の見出し語の元で説明されている．例えば，表現 **to put someone in the picture** は **picture** のところで説明されている．

🔳 V-T 他動詞 When you **put** something in a particular place or position, you move it into that place or position. 置く ❑ *Leaphorn put the photograph on the desk.* リープホーンは机の上に写真を置いた．❑ *She hesitated, then put her hand on Grace's arm.* 彼女はちゅうちょして，手をグレイスの腕に置いた．🔳 V-T 他動詞 If you **put** someone somewhere, you cause them to go there and to stay there for a period of time. 行かせる ❑ *Rather than put him in the hospital, she had been caring for him at home.* 彼女は彼を入院させる代わりに家でずっと世話をしていた．🔳 V-T 他動詞 To **put** someone or something in a particular state or situation means to cause them to be in that state or situation. させる ❑ *This is going to put them out of business.* これできっと商売ができなくなるだろう．❑ *He was putting himself at risk.* 自分を危険にさらしていた．🔳 V-T 他動詞 To **put** something **on** people or things means to cause them to have it, or to cause them to be affected by it. 与える ❑ *He didn't put any pressure on her.* 彼女には何の圧力もかけないよ．❑ *Be aware of the terrible strain it can put on a child when you expect the best grades.* 最上の成績を期待すると，子供にひどい負担を負わせることがあることに注意してください．🔳 V-T 他動詞 If you **put** your trust, faith, or confidence **in** someone or something, you trust them or have faith or confidence in them. 信頼を寄せる ❑ *He had decided long ago that he would put his trust in socialism when the time came.* 時期が来たら社会主義を信用しようと，何年も前に決心していた．🔳 V-T 他動詞 If you **put** time, strength, or energy **into** an activity, you use it in doing that activity. 投入する ❑ *We're not saying that activists should put all their effort and time into party politics.* 政治活動家は党の政治に

時間と努力のすべてを振り向けるべきであるとは，われわれは言っていない．🔳 V-T 他動詞 If you **put** money **into** a business or project, you invest money in it. 投資する ❑ *Investors should consider putting some money into an annuity.* 投資家は年金に投資することを考慮するべきである．🔳 V-T 他動詞 When you **put** an idea or remark in a particular way, you express it in that way. You can use expressions like **to put it simply** and **to put it bluntly** before saying something when you want to explain how you are going to express it. 言い表す ❑ *I had already met Pete a couple of times through – how should I put it – friends in low places.* ピートとはすでに2回ほど － どういう風に言えばいいかな － 低い地位にいる友人を通して会っていた．❑ *He admitted the security forces might have made some mistakes, as he put it.* 彼の表現だが，治安部隊が何か過ちを犯したかもしれないと認めた．🔳 V-T 他動詞 When you **put a question to** someone, you ask them the question. 質問する ❑ *Is this fair? Well, I put that question today to the mayor.* これは公平だろうか？それで，今日市長にその質問をしたんだ．🔳 V-T 他動詞 If you **put** a case, opinion, or proposal, you explain it and list the reasons why you support or believe it. 提示する ❑ *He always put his point of view with clarity and with courage.* 彼は常に自分の意見を明確にかつ勇気を持って述べた．❑ *He put the case to the Saudi foreign minister.* サウジアラビアの外務大臣にこの件を提起した．🔳 V-T 他動詞 If you **put** something **at** a particular value or **in** a particular category, you consider that it has that value or that it belongs in that category. 評価する ❑ *I would put her age at about 50 or so.* 彼女の年は50歳かそこらだと思う．❑ *All the more technically advanced countries put a high value on science.* 技術的に進んだ国はすべて，科学を高く評価している．🔳 V-T 他動詞 If you **put** written information somewhere, you write, type, or print it there. 記入する ❑ *Mary's family was so pleased that they put an announcement in the local paper to thank them.* メアリーの家族は非常に喜んで，地方紙に彼らに感謝する広告を出した．❑ *I think what I put in that book is now pretty much the agenda for this country.* あの本に書いたことが今だいたいこの国が実践すべき事項になっていると思う．🔳 PHRASE 句 If you **put it to** someone **that** something is true, you suggest that it is true, especially when you think that they will be unwilling to admit this. 事実を提起する ❑ *But I put it to you that they're useless.* でも，あの人たちは役立たずじゃないですか．🔳 PHRASE 句 If you say that something is bigger or better than several other things **put together**, you mean that it is bigger or has more good qualities than all of those other things if they are added together. いっしょにする ❑ *Mary ate more than the rest of us put together.* メアリーはわれわれ全部を合わせたよりもたくさん食べた．

▶ **put across** or **put over** PHRASAL VERB 句動詞 When you **put** something **across** or **put** it **over**, you succeed in describing or explaining it to someone. 理解させる ❑ *He has taken out a half-page advertisement in his local paper to put his point across.* 彼は持論を理解してもらおうと地方紙に半面広告を掲載した．

▶ **put aside** PHRASAL VERB 句動詞 If you **put** something **aside**, you keep it to be dealt with or used at a later time. 取っておく ❑ *Encourage children to put aside some of their allowance to buy Christmas presents.* 小遣いの一部を取っておいてクリスマスのプレゼントを買うことを子供たちに勧めよう．

▶ **put away** PHRASAL VERB 句動詞 If you **put** something **away**, you put it into the place where it is normally kept when it is not being used, for example, in a drawer. 片付ける ❑ *She finished putting the milk away and turned around.* ミルクをしまい終わって，振り返った．❑ *"Yes, Mom," replied Cheryl as she slowly put away her doll.* 人形をのろのろと片付けながら，「はい，かあちゃん」とチェリルが返事をした．

▶ **put back** PHRASAL VERB 句動詞 To **put** something **back** means to delay it or arrange for it to happen later than you previously planned. 遅らせる ❑ *There are always new projects which seem to put the reunion back further.* 再会をさらに遅らせるような新しいプロジェクトがいつも出てくる．

▶ **put down** 🔳 PHRASAL VERB 句動詞 If you **put** something **down** somewhere, you write or type it there. 書き記す ❑ *Never put anything down on paper which might be used in evidence against you at a later date.* 後日不利な証拠として使用されるかもしれないので，絶対紙に何も書き留めるな．❑ *The journalists simply put down what they thought they heard.* 記者たちは聞いたと思ったことを単純に書き記しただけだった．🔳 PHRASAL VERB 句動詞 If you **put down** some money, you pay part of the price of something, and will pay the rest later. 頭金を払う ❑ *He bought an investment property for $100,000 and put down $20,000.* 投資不動産を１０万ドルで買って，２万ドルの頭金を払った．🔳 PHRASAL VERB 句動詞 When soldiers, police, or the government **put down** a riot or rebellion, they stop it by using force. 鎮める ❑ *Soldiers went in to put down a rebellion.* 反乱を鎮圧するために兵隊が出た．🔳 PHRASAL VERB 句動詞 If someone **puts** you **down**, they treat you in an unpleasant way by criticizing you in front of other people or making you appear foolish. けなす ❑ *I know that I do put people down occasionally.* 時々人をこきおろすことがあるのは自分でもわかっている．❑ *Racist jokes come from wanting to put down other kinds of people we feel threatened by.* 人種差別の冗談は，種類が違う人に脅威を感じ，卑しめたいと思う気持ちから出ている．🔳 PHRASAL VERB 句動詞 When an animal **is put down**, it is

P

killed because it is dangerous or very ill. 殺す ❑ *The judge ordered their dog Samson to be put down immediately.* 判事は彼らの犬のサムソンを即殺処分するよう命じた.

▶ **put down to** PHRASAL VERB 句動詞 If you **put** something **down to** a particular thing, you believe that it is caused by that thing. せいであるとする ❑ *You may be a skeptic and put it down to life's inequalities.* きみは懐疑主義者で，それを人生の不平等のせいだと言うかもしれない.

▶ **put forward** PHRASAL VERB 句動詞 If you **put forward** a plan, proposal, or name, you suggest that it should be considered for a particular purpose or job. 提案する；推薦する ❑ *He has put forward new peace proposals.* 新しい和平案を提案した.

▶ **put in** ◼ PHRASAL VERB 句動詞 If you **put in** an amount of time or effort doing something, you spend that time or effort doing it. つぎ込む ❑ *Wade was going to be paid a salary, instead of by the hour, whether he put in forty hours or not.* ウエイドは，40時間働こうが働くまいが，時間給の代わりに月給で払われる予定であった. ❑ *They've put in time and effort to keep the strike going.* ストを続けるために時間と努力をつぎ込んでいる. ◼ PHRASAL VERB 句動詞 If you **put in** a request or **put in for** something, you formally request or apply for that thing. 申請する ❑ *I also put in a request for some overtime.* 残業願いも申請した. ◼ PHRASAL VERB 句動詞 If you **put in** a remark, you interrupt someone or add to what they have said with the remark. 言葉をさしはさむ ❑ *"He was a lawyer before that," Mary Ann put in.* 「その前は弁護士だったわ」とメアリーアンが口をさしはさんだ.

▶ **put off** ◼ PHRASAL VERB 句動詞 If you **put** something **off**, you delay doing it. 延期する ❑ *Women who put off having a baby often make the best mothers.* 出産を延期する女性は最良の母親となることが多い. ◼ PHRASAL VERB 句動詞 If you **put** someone **off**, you make them wait for something that they want. 待たせる ❑ *The old priest tried to put them off, saying that the hour was late.* 年取った神父は，時間が遅すぎると言って彼らを待たせようとした. ◼ PHRASAL VERB 句動詞 If something **puts** you **off** something, it makes you dislike it, or decide not to do or have it. いやにさせる ❑ *The high divorce figures don't seem to be putting people off marriage.* 離婚数が高くても，人は結婚する気がなくなったりしないようだ. ❑ *His personal habits put them off.* 彼の持つ癖で彼らは意欲がなくなった. ◼ PHRASAL VERB 句動詞 If someone or something **puts** you **off**, they take your attention from what you are trying to do and make it more difficult for you to do it. じゃまをして気を散らす ❑ *She asked me to be serious – said it put her off if I laughed.* 彼女は，わたしに本気になるようにと求め - わたしが笑うと気が散ると言った.

▶ **put on** ◼ PHRASAL VERB 句動詞 When you **put on** clothing or makeup, you place it on your body in order to wear it. 身に着ける；化粧する ❑ *She put on her coat and went out.* コートを着て外に出ていった. ❑ *Maximo put on a pair of glasses.* マキシモは眼鏡を掛けた. ◼ PHRASAL VERB 句動詞 When people **put on** a show, exhibition, or service, they perform it or organize it. 催す；手配する ❑ *The band is hoping to put on a show before the end of the year.* 楽団は年末までにはショーを上演したいと望んでいる. ◼ PHRASAL VERB 句動詞 If someone **puts on** weight, they become heavier. 増す ❑ *I can eat what I want but I never put on weight.* 何でも食べたい物を食べることができるが，体重は増えない. ◼ PHRASAL VERB 句動詞 If you **put on** a piece of equipment or a device, you make it start working, for example, by pressing a switch or turning a knob. つける ❑ *I put the radio on.* ラジオをつけた. ◼ PHRASAL VERB 句動詞 If you **put on** a record, tape, or CD **on**, you place it in a record, tape, or CD player and listen to it. かける ❑ *She poured them drinks, and put a record on loud.* 彼らに飲み物をつぎ，レコードを音量を高くしてかけた.

▶ **put out** ◼ PHRASAL VERB 句動詞 If you **put out** an announcement or story, you make it known to a lot of people. 公にする ❑ *No one put out a press release aimed at the public.* 誰も一般向けの公式発表をしなかった. ◼ PHRASAL VERB 句動詞 If you **put out** a fire, candle, or cigarette, you make it stop burning. 消す ❑ *Firemen tried to free the injured and put out the blaze.* 消防員たちは負傷者を解放して，燃え上がる炎を消し止めようとした. ◼ PHRASAL VERB 句動詞 If you **put out** an electric light, you make it stop shining by pressing a switch. 消す ❑ *He crossed to the nightstand and put out the light.* 横切ってサイドテーブルに行き，電気を消した. ◼ PHRASAL VERB 句動詞 If you **put out** things that will be needed, you place them somewhere ready to be used. 出しておく ❑ *Paula had put out her luggage for the bus.* ポーラはバスのために荷物を出しておいた. ◼ PHRASAL VERB 句動詞 If you **put out** your hand, you move it forward, away from your body. 手を差し出す ❑ *He put out his hand to Alfred.* アルフレッドに手を差し出した. ◼ PHRASAL VERB 句動詞 If you **put** someone **out**, you cause them trouble because they have to do something for you. 面倒を掛ける ❑ *It is a very sociable diet to follow because you don't have to put anyone out.* 誰にも面倒をかけないので，つき合いやすいダイエットだ.

▶ **put over** → see **put across**

▶ **put through** ◼ PHRASAL VERB 句動詞 When someone **puts through** someone who is making a telephone call, they make the connection that allows the telephone call to take place. 電話をつ

なぐ ❑ *The operator will put you through.* 交換手が電話をつないでくれるだろう. ◼ PHRASAL VERB 句動詞 If someone **puts** you **through** an unpleasant experience, they make you experience it. 経験させる ❑ *She wouldn't want to put them through the ordeal of a huge ceremony.* 彼女は一大儀式の試練を彼らに体験させたいとは思わないだろう.

▶ **put together** ◼ PHRASAL VERB 句動詞 If you **put** something **together**, you join its different parts to each other so that it can be used. 組み立てる ❑ *He took it apart brick by brick, and put it back together again.* れんがを一つずつ外して，またもとのように組み立てた. ◼ PHRASAL VERB 句動詞 If you **put together** a group of people or things, you form them into a team or collection. 編成する；集める ❑ *It will be able to put together a governing coalition.* 連立政府を編成することができよう. ◼ PHRASAL VERB 句動詞 If you **put together** an agreement, plan, or product, you design and create it. まとめる ❑ *We wouldn't have time to put together an agreement.* 契約書をまとめる時間はなかろう. ❑ *Reports speak of Berlin putting together an aid package for Moscow.* ベルリンがモスクワのために救援計画を今まとめていると報告されている. ◼ → see also **put 14**

▶ **put up** ◼ PHRASAL VERB 句動詞 If people **put up** a wall, building, tent, or other structure, they construct it so that it is upright. 建てる；（テントを）張る ❑ *Protesters have been putting up barricades across a number of major intersections.* いくつかの主要交差点で抗議者たちがバリケードを作っていた. ◼ PHRASAL VERB 句動詞 If you **put up** a poster or notice, you attach it to a wall or board. 掲げる ❑ *They're putting new street signs up.* 通りの名称標識を取り付け中である. ◼ PHRASAL VERB 句動詞 To **put up** resistance to something means to resist it. 示す ❑ *In the end the Kurds surrendered without putting up any resistance.* 最終的にはクルド人は何の抵抗も示さずに降参した. ❑ *He'd put up a real fight to keep you there.* きみがそこにいられるように彼は本気で戦うだろう. ◼ PHRASAL VERB 句動詞 If you **put up** money for something, you provide the money that is needed to pay for it. 提供する ❑ *The state agreed to put up $69,000 to start his company.* 彼の会社を発足させるために，州は6万9千ドルを提供することに同意した. ◼ PHRASAL VERB 句動詞 To **put up** the price of something means to cause it to increase. 上げる ❑ *Their friends suggested they should put up their prices.* 彼らの友達は価格を上げるべきだと提案した. ◼ PHRASAL VERB 句動詞 If a person or hotel **puts** you **up** or if you **put up** somewhere, you stay there for one or more nights. 泊まらせる ❑ *I wanted to know if she could put me up for a few days.* 彼女が数日泊まらせてくれることができるかどうか知りたかった. ❑ *Hundreds of commuters had to be put up in hotel rooms.* 何百人という通勤者がホテルに泊まることになった. ◼ PHRASAL VERB 句動詞 If a political party **puts up** a candidate in an election or if the candidate **puts up**, the candidate takes part in the election. 立候補させる（する）❑ *Barnes put up a candidate of his own for this post.* バーンズはこのポストに対してみずからの候補者を立てた.

▶ **put up with** PHRASAL VERB 句動詞 If you **put up with** something, you tolerate or accept it, even though you find it unpleasant or unsatisfactory. 我慢する ❑ *They had put up with behavior from their son which they would not have tolerated from anyone else.* 彼らは他人であれば耐えられないような息子の行動に我慢した.

put out ADJ 形容詞 If you feel **put out**, you feel annoyed or upset. いらいらさせる [v-link ADJ] ❑ *I did not blame him for feeling put out.* 彼がむっとするのも無理はないと思った.

putt /pʌt/ (putts, putting, putted) ◼ N-COUNT 可算名詞 A **putt** is a stroke in golf that you make when the ball has reached the green in an attempt to get the ball in the hole. パット ❑ *a 5-foot putt.* 5フィートのパット. ◼ V-T/V-I 他動詞/自動詞 In golf, when you **putt**, or **putt** the ball, you hit a putt. パットを打つ ❑ *Turner, however, putted superbly, twice holing from 40 feet.* しかしながらターナーは，40フィートからホールインする素晴らしいパットをふたつ打った.

puz|zle /pʌzᵊl/ (puzzles, puzzling, puzzled) ◼ V-T 他動詞 If something **puzzles** you, you do not understand it and feel confused. 途方にくれさせる ❑ *My sister puzzles me and causes me anxiety.* 姉は私には理解できず心配の種だった. ● **puz|zling** ADJ 形容詞 わけのわからない ❑ *His letter poses a number of puzzling questions.* 彼の手紙にはいくつか首をひねるような質問がある. ◼ V-I 自動詞 If you **puzzle over** something, you try hard to think of the answer to it or the explanation for it. 知恵を絞る ❑ *In rehearsing Shakespeare, I puzzle over the complexities of his verse and prose.* シェークスピアのリハーサルでは，その韻文や散文の複雑さに考え込んでしまう. ◼ N-COUNT 可算名詞 [oft supp N] A **puzzle** is a question, game, or toy that you have to think about carefully in order to answer it correctly or put it together properly. パズル ❑ *a word puzzle.* 言葉のパズル. ◼ → see also **crossword**, **jigsaw** ◼ N-SING 単数名詞 You can describe a person or thing that is hard to understand as a **puzzle**. なぞ ["a" N] ❑ *The rise in accidents remains a puzzle.* 事故の増加は原因不明のままだ.

puz|zled /pʌzᵊld/ ADJ 形容詞 Someone who is **puzzled** is confused because they do not understand something. 途方にくれた ❑ *Critics remain puzzled by the election results.* 選挙の結果について批判者たちは理解に苦しんでいる.

PVC /pi̱ vi si̱/ N-UNCOUNT 不可算名詞 **PVC** is a plastic material that is used for many purposes, for example, to make clothing or shoes or to cover chairs. **PVC** is an abbreviation for "polyvinyl chloride." ポリ塩化ビニール

py|ja|mas /pɪdʒɑ̱məz/ → see **pajamas**

pyra|mid /pɪ̱rəmɪd/ (pyramids) ■ N-COUNT 可算名詞 **Pyramids** are ancient stone buildings with four triangular sloping sides. The most famous pyramids are those built in ancient Egypt to contain the bodies of their kings and queens. ピラミッド ❑ We set off to see the Pyramids and Sphinx. ピラミッドとスフィンクス像を見に出かけた. ❷ N-COUNT 可算名詞 A **pyramid** is a shape, object, or pile of things with a flat base and sloping triangular sides that meet at a point. 角錐 ❑ On a plate in front of him was piled a pyramid of flat white crackers. 彼の前の皿には平たくて白いクラッカーが角錐形に積み上げられていた. ❸ N-COUNT 可算名詞 You can describe something as a **pyramid** when it is organized so that there are fewer people at each level as you go toward the top. ピラミッド状のもの ❑ Traditionally, the Brahmins, or the priestly class, are set at the top of the social pyramid. 伝統的には，聖職者階級であるバラモンは，ピラミッド状社会階級の最高位に据えられている.
→ see **solid, volume**

pyra|mid scheme N-UNCOUNT 不可算名詞 A **Pyramid scheme** is a method of selling in which one person buys a supply of a particular product directly from the manufacturer and then sells it to a number of other people at an increased price. These people sell it on to others in a similar way, but eventually the final buyers are only able to sell the product for less than they paid for it. マルチ商法 [BUSINESS 実業] ❑ The pyramid scheme was marketed through a home page on the World Wide Web. マルチ商法はワールドワイドウエブのホームページを介して売り込まれた.

py|thon /pa̱ɪθɒn, -θən/ (pythons) N-COUNT 可算名詞 A **python** is a large snake that kills animals by squeezing them with its body. ニシキヘビ

P

Qq

Q also **q** /kyu/ (Q's, q's) N-VAR 可変性名詞 **Q** is the seventeenth letter of the English alphabet. キュー（アルファベットの第17文字）

Q & A /kyu ən eɪ/ also **Q and A** N-UNCOUNT 不算名詞 **Q & A** is a situation in which a person or group of people asks questions and another person or group of people answers them. **Q & A** is short for "question and answer." 質疑応答

quad|ru|ple /kwɒdrʌpəl, -druːpəl, kwɒdruːpəl/ (quadruples, quadrupling, quadrupled) **1** V-T/V-I 他動詞/自動詞 If something quadruples an amount or if it quadruples, it becomes four times bigger. 4倍にする [他動詞]、4倍になる [自動詞] □China seeks to quadruple its income in twenty years. 中国は20年間で歳入を4倍にしようと努めている。 **2** PREDET 前限定詞 If one amount is quadruple another amount, it is four times bigger. 4倍の数量 [PREDET det n] □Fifty-nine of its residents have attended graduate school – quadruple the national average. 在籍者の59%が大学院に通っていた – 国内平均の4倍である。 **3** ADJ 形容詞 You use quadruple to indicate that something has four parts or happens four times. 4つの部分からなる；4倍の [ADJ n] □The quadruple murder has replaced property prices as the sole topic of interest. 4重殺人事件が関心ある唯一の話題として不動産価格に取って代わっている。

quaint /kweɪnt/ (quainter, quaintest) ADJ 形容詞 Something that is quaint is attractive because it is old-fashioned. 古風な趣のある □...a small, quaint town with narrow streets and traditional half-timbered houses. 狭い道や伝統的な木骨造りの家のこぢんまりとした古風な町

quake /kweɪk/ (quakes, quaking, quaked) **1** N-COUNT 可算名詞 A quake is the same as an earthquake. 地震 [INFORMAL くだけた] □The quake destroyed mud buildings in many remote villages. 地震のために多数のへんぴな村々で土造りの家が破壊された。 **2** V-I 自動詞 If you quake, you shake, usually because you are very afraid. おののく □I just stood there quaking with fear. 恐ろしさで震えながらただそこに立っていた。 **3** PHRASE 句 If you are quaking in your boots or quaking in your shoes, you feel very nervous or afraid, and may be feeling slightly weak as a result. 足が震える □If you stand up straight, you'll give an impression of self-confidence, even if you're quaking in your boots. まっすぐ背を伸ばして立てば、足が震えていても自信ある印象を与える。

quali|fi|ca|tion /kwɒlɪfɪkeɪʃən/ (qualifications) **1** N-COUNT 可算名詞 Your qualifications are the official documents or titles you have that show you have a required level of education and training. 資格証明書；肩書き □"Do you have any qualifications?" — "Yes, I'm certified to teach high school." 「何か資格証明ありますか？」 – 「はい、高校生を教える免許があります。」 **2** N-UNCOUNT 不算名詞 Qualification is the act of passing the examinations you need to work in a particular profession. 資格取得 □She has met the minimum educational requirements for qualification. 彼女は、資格取得に必要な最低教育条件を満足した。 **3** N-COUNT 可算名詞 The qualifications you need for an activity or task are the qualities and skills that you need to be able to do it. 能力 □Responsibility and reliability are necessary qualifications, as well as a friendly and outgoing personality. 親切で外交的な性格だけでなく、責任感と信頼性があることが必要な能力である。 **4** N-COUNT 可変性名詞 A qualification is a detail or explanation that you add to a statement to make it less strong or less general. 条件 □The empirical evidence considered here is subject to many qualifications. ここで考察される実験上の証拠は多くの条件次第である。 **5** N-COUNT 可算名詞 Your qualifications are the examinations that you have passed. 資格 [BRIT 英国英語] □Lucy Thomson, 16, wants to study theater but needs more qualifications. ルーシー・トムソン（16歳）は演劇を勉強したがっているが、さらなる資格が必要である。

Thesaurus qualification また次を参照：

N.	capability, proficiency, skill **3**
	condition, provision, stipulation **4**

Word Partnership qualification は次の語句と使われる：

N.	qualification for a job, standards for qualification **3**
ADJ.	necessary qualification **3**
PREP.	without qualification **3 4**

---

quali|fied /kwɒlɪfaɪd/ **1** ADJ 形容詞 Someone who is qualified has a certificate, license, diploma or degree in order to work in a particular profession. 資格のある □Demand has far outstripped supply of qualified teachers. 資格のある教師の供給よりも需要の力がはるかにまさっている。 □Are you qualified for this job? この仕事をする資格がありますか？ **2** ADJ 形容詞 If you give someone or something qualified support or approval, your support or approval is not total because you have some doubts. 条件付きの [ADJ n] □The government has in the past given qualified support to the idea of tightening the legislation. 政府は、その法律を強化する考えに対して過去に条件付きのサポートをしたことがある。 **3** PHRASE 句 If you describe something as a qualified success, you mean that it is only partly successful. 制限のある成功 □Even as a humanitarian mission it has been only a qualified success. 人道主義的使命として見ても、制限付きの成功にしか過ぎない。

quali|fi|er /kwɒlɪfaɪər/ (qualifiers) **1** N-COUNT 可算名詞 A qualifier is an early round or match in some competitions. The players or teams who are successful are able to continue to the next round or to the main competition. 予選 □Crew Stadium hosted the U.S.-Mexico qualifier. クルースタジアムはアメリカ合衆国対メキシコの予選を主催した。 **2** → see also qualify

quali|fy /kwɒlɪfaɪ/ (qualifies, qualifying, qualified) **1** V-I 自動詞 If you qualify in a competition, you are successful in one part of it and go on to the next stage. 予選を通過する □We qualified for the final by beating Stanford on Tuesday. 火曜日にスタンフォードを破って決勝戦に出場することになった。 ●qualifier (qualifiers) N-COUNT 可算名詞 □Kenya's Robert Kibe was the fastest qualifier for the 800 meters final. ケニアのロバート・キベは、800メートル決勝戦への一番速い予選通過者であった。 **2** V-T/V-I 他動詞/自動詞 To qualify as something or to be qualified as something means to have all the features that are needed to be that thing. みなす □13 percent of American households qualify as poor, says Mr. Mishel. アメリカ人家庭の13%は貧困とみなされるとミッシェル氏は言う。 **3** V-T 他動詞 If you qualify a statement, you make it less strong or less general by adding a detail or explanation to it. 制限する □I would qualify that by putting it into context. もしわたしだったら、状況の筋道を通して説明するだろう。 □Boyd qualified his opinion, noting that the evidence could be interpreted in other ways. ボイドは、証拠は別の解釈ができるかもしれないことに注目して、自分の意見を修正した。 **4** V-T/V-I 他動詞/自動詞 If you qualify for something or if something qualifies you for it, you have the right to do it or have it. 権限を得る [自動詞]、権限を与える [他動詞] □To qualify for maternity leave you must have worked for the same employer for two years. 出産休暇の権利を得る資格は、同じ雇用主のもとで2年間働いていることである。 □The basic course does not qualify you to practice as a therapist. その基礎コースでは療法士として働く資格は得られない。 **5** V-I 自動詞 When someone qualifies, they receive the certificate, license, diploma, or degree that they need to be able to work in a particular profession. 免状を取る □But when I'd qualified and started teaching it was a different story. 免状を取ってから教え始めたが、事情は全く違っていた。 **6** → see also qualified

---

Word Partnership qualify は次の語句と使われる：

V.	chance to qualify, fail to qualify **1 2 4 5**
PREP.	qualify as something **2**
	qualify for something **4**

---

quali|ta|tive /kwɒlɪteɪtɪv/ ADJ 形容詞 Qualitative means relating to the nature or standard of something, rather than to its quantity. 質的な [FORMAL 形式ばった] □There are qualitative differences in the way children of different ages and adults think. 年齢の違う子ども達や大人達の考え方には質的に相違点がある。

qual|ity /kwɒlɪti/ (qualities) **1** N-UNCOUNT 不算名詞 The quality of something is how good or bad it is. 品質 □Everyone can greatly improve the quality of life. 誰でも人生の質を大いに向上させることができる。 □Other services vary dramatically in quality. その他のサービスは質的に大きく上下がある。 **2** N-UNCOUNT 不算名詞 Something of quality is of a high standard. 良質 □...a college of quality. 質の高い大学 **3** N-COUNT 可算名詞 Someone's qualities are the good characteristics that they have which are part of their nature. 素養 □Sometimes you wonder where your kids get their

good qualities. 自分の子供たちがどこから優れた才能を得るのか時々不思議に思う. ◳ N-COUNT 可算名詞 You can describe a particular characteristic of a person or thing as a **quality**. 特性 ◳ *...a childlike quality.* 子供のような特質

Thesaurus   *quality* また次を参照:

N.	class, kind, position, rank, virtue, worth ◳
	aspect, attribute, characteristic, feature, trait ◳

Word Partnership   *quality* は次の語句と使われる:

N.	**air** quality, quality **of life**, quality **of service**, **water** quality, quality **of work** ◳
ADJ.	**best/better/good** quality, **high/higher/highest** quality, **low** quality, **poor** quality, **top** quality ◳ ◳

qual|ity con|trol N-UNCOUNT 不可算名詞 **Quality control** is the activity of checking that goods or services are of an acceptable standard. 品質管理 [BUSINESS 実業] ◳ *The message is you need better quality control.* もっと良い品質管理が必要であるという教訓である.

qual|ity time N-UNCOUNT 不可算名詞 If people spend **quality time** together, they spend a period of time relaxing or doing things that they both enjoy, and not worrying about work or other responsibilities. 充実した楽しい時間 [APPROVAL 賛成] ◳ *Today I can spend quality time with my family for a change.* 今日はいつもと違って家族と充実した時間を過ごすことができる.

qualm /kwɑːm/ (**qualms**) N-COUNT 可算名詞 If you have no **qualms** about doing something, you are not worried that it may be wrong in some way. 良心のかしゃく ◳ *I have no qualms about recommending the same approach to other doctors.* 他の医者にも同じアプローチを推奨することに少しのためらいもない.

Word Link   quant ≈ how much : *quantify, quantitative, quantity*

quan|ti|fy /kwɒntɪfaɪ/ (**quantifies, quantifying, quantified**) V-T 他動詞 If you try to **quantify** something, you try to calculate how much of it there is. 定量化する [usu with brd-neg] ◳ *It is difficult to quantify an exact figure as firms are reluctant to declare their losses.* 会社は損失を公表したがらないので，正確な数値を出すのは難しい.

quan|ti|ta|tive /kwɒntɪteɪtɪv/ ADJ 形容詞 **Quantitative** means relating to different sizes or amounts of things. 量的な [FORMAL 形式ばった] ◳ *...the advantages of quantitative and qualitative research.* 量的および質的な研究の長所

quan|ti|ty /kwɒntɪti/ (**quantities**) ◳ N-VAR 可変性名詞 A **quantity** is an amount. 量 ◳ *...a small quantity of water.* 少量の水 ◳ N-UNCOUNT 不可算名詞 Things that are produced or available in **quantity** are produced or available in large amounts. 多量 ◳ *After some initial problems, acetone was successfully produced in quantity.* 初期に問題がいくつかあったが，多量のアセトンが順調に生産できた. ◳ N-UNCOUNT 不可算名詞 You can use **quantity** to refer to the amount of something that there is, especially when you want to contrast it with its quality. 分量 ◳ *...the less discerning drinker who prefers quantity to quality.* 質よりも量を好むあまり見識のない酒飲み ◳ PHRASE 句 If you say that someone or something is an **unknown quantity**, you mean that not much is known about what they are like or how they will behave. 未知数 ◳ *She had known Max for some years, but he was still pretty much an unknown quantity.* マックスと知り合ってからもう何年か経ったが，彼女にとってはほとんどまだ真価の予測できない人物であった.
→ see **mathematics**

quan|tum /kwɒntəm/ ◳ ADJ 形容詞 In physics, **quantum** theory and **quantum** mechanics are concerned with the behavior of atomic particles. 量子の [ADJ n] ◳ *Both quantum mechanics and chaos theory suggest a world constantly in flux.* 量子力学とカオス論の両方とも世界が常に流動していることを示唆している. ◳ ADJ 形容詞 A **quantum leap** or **quantum jump** in something is a very great and sudden increase in its size, amount, or quality. 飛躍的進歩 [ADJ n] ◳ *A vaccine which can halt this suffering represents a quantum leap in healthcare in this country.* この苦難を食い止めることができるワクチンは，この国の健康管理の飛躍的進歩を示している.

quar|an|tine /kwɒrəntiːn/ (**quarantines, quarantining, quarantined**) ◳ N-UNCOUNT 不可算名詞 If a person or animal is in **quarantine**, they are being kept separate from other people or animals for a set period of time, usually because they have or may have a disease that could spread. 隔離 ◳ *She was sent home and put in quarantine.* 彼女は家に帰され隔離された. ◳ V-T 他動詞 If people or animals **are quarantined**, they are stopped from having contact with other people or animals. If a place **is quarantined**, people and animals are prevented from entering or leaving it. 隔離する [usu passive] ◳ *Dogs have to be quarantined for six months before they'll let them in.* 犬は入国させる前に6ヶ月間検疫する必要がある.
→ see **illness**

quar|rel /kwɒrəl/ (**quarrels, quarreling** or **quarrelling, quarreled** or **quarrelled**) ◳ N-COUNT 可算名詞 A **quarrel** is an angry argument between two or more friends or family members. 言い争い ◳ *I had a terrible quarrel with my other brothers.* 別の兄弟とひどい口げんかをした. ◳ V-RECIP 相互動詞 When two or more people **quarrel**, they have an angry argument. 口論する ◳ *At one point we quarreled, over something silly.* ある時に何かささいなことで口論した. ◳ N-SING 単数名詞 If you say that you have no **quarrel** with someone or something, you mean that you do not disagree with them. 苦情 ◳ *We have no quarrel with the people of Spain or any other country.* スペインやその他の国の人々に対しては何の文句もない. ◳ N-COUNT 可算名詞 **Quarrels** between countries or groups of people are disagreements, which may be diplomatic or include fighting. 反目 [JOURNALISM ジャーナリズム] ◳ *New Zealand's quarrel with France over the Rainbow Warrior incident was formally ended.* レインボーウォリア事件に関するニュージーランドのフランスに対する不和は正式に終結した.

quar|ry /kwɒri/ (**quarries, quarrying, quarried**) ◳ N-COUNT 可算名詞 A **quarry** is an area that is dug out from a piece of land or the side of a mountain in order to get stone or minerals. 石切り場 ◳ *...an old limestone quarry.* 古い石灰岩採石場 ◳ V-T 他動詞 When stone or minerals **are quarried** or when an area **is quarried** for them, they are removed from the area by digging, drilling, or using explosives. 採石する ◳ *The large limestone caves are also quarried for cement.* 大きな石灰石の洞穴もセメント用に切り出されている.

Word Link   quart ≈ four : *quart, quarter, quarterfinal*

quart /kwɔːrt/ (**quarts**) N-COUNT 可算名詞 A **quart** is a unit of volume that is equal to two pints. There are four quarts in a gallon. The abbreviation **qt.** is also used. クォート〉（液量で約0.95リットル，乾量で約1.1リットル）◳ *Pick up a quart of milk and a loaf of bread.* 1クォートの牛乳と食パンを1個を買う.

quar|ter /kwɔːrtər/ (**quarters, quartering, quartered**) ◳ FRACTION 端数 A **quarter** is one of four equal parts of something. 4分の1 ◳ *A quarter of the residents are over 55 years old.* 居住者の4分の1は55歳を越えている. ◳ *Prices have fallen by a quarter since January.* 価格は1月以降4分の1下がっている. ● PREDET 前限定詞 **Quarter** is also a predeterminer. 4分の1 ◳ *The largest asteroid is Ceres, which is about a quarter the size of the moon.* 一番大きな小惑星はケレスで，月の大きさの4分の1くらいである. ● ADJ 形容詞 **Quarter** is also an adjective. 4分の1の [ADJ n] ◳ *...the past quarter century.* 過去4分の1世紀 ◳ N-COUNT 可算名詞 A **quarter** is an American or Canadian coin that is worth 25 cents. 25セント貨 ◳ *I dropped a quarter into the slot of the pay phone.* 公衆電話の料金差し入れ口に25セントのコインを入れた. ◳ N-COUNT 可算名詞 A **quarter** is a fixed period of three months. Companies often divide their financial year into four quarters. 四半期 ◳ *The group said results for the third quarter are due on October 29.* 第三期四半期の結果は10月29日に出る予定であるとそのグループが言った. ◳ N-UNCOUNT 不可算名詞 When you are telling the time, you use **quarter** to talk about the fifteen minutes before or after an hour. For example, 8:15 is **quarter after** eight and 8:45 is a **quarter of** or a **quarter to** nine. You can also say that 8:15 is **quarter past** eight, and 8:45 is **quarter to** nine. 15分 [also 'a' N] ◳ *It was a quarter to six.* 6時15分前であった. ◳ V-T 他動詞 If you **quarter** something such as a fruit or a vegetable, you cut it into four roughly equal parts. 4つに分ける ◳ *Chop the mushrooms and quarter the tomatoes.* マッシュルームを切り刻んで，トマトを4つに切りなさい. ◳ V-T 他動詞 If the number or size of something **is quartered**, it is reduced to about a quarter of its previous number or size. 4分の1にする [usu passive] ◳ *The doses I suggested for adults could be halved or quartered.* わたしが示した成人服用量は半分にも4分の1にもすることができる. ◳ N-COUNT 可算名詞 A particular **quarter** of a town is a part of the town where a particular group of people traditionally live or work. 区域 ◳ *We wandered through the Chinese quarter.* 中華街を通ってぶらついた. ◳ PHRASE 句 If you do something **at close quarters**, you do it very near to a particular person or thing. 接近して ◳ *You can watch aircraft take off or land at close quarters.* 飛行機が離陸したり着陸したりするのを間近に見ることができる.

Word Partnership   *quarter* は次の語句と使われる:

N.	quarter **(of a) century**, quarter **(of a) pound** ◳
ADJ.	**first/fourth/second/third** quarter ◳
PREP.	**for the** quarter, **in the** quarter ◳
	quarter **after**, quarter **of**, quarter **past**, quarter **to** ◳

quar|ter|final /kwɔːrtərfaɪnⁿl/ (**quarterfinals**) N-COUNT 可算名詞 A **quarterfinal** is one of the four matches in a competition which decides which four players or teams will compete in the semifinal. 準々決勝 ◳ *The very least I'm looking for at the Open is to reach the quarterfinals.* 公開選手権大会では最低でも準々決勝まで到達することを期待している.

q

quar|ter|ly /kwɔːrtərli/ (quarterlies) **1** ADJ 形容詞 A **quarterly** event happens four times a year, at intervals of three months. 年に4回の **2** …the latest Bank of Japan quarterly survey of 5,000 companies. 5,000社を対象とした最新の日本銀行四半期調査 ● ADV 副詞 **Quarterly** is also an adverb. 年4回 [ADV after v] **3** It makes no difference whether dividends are paid quarterly or annually. 配当金の支払いが3か月毎であろうと1年毎であろうと違いはない. **2** N-COUNT 可算名詞 A **quarterly** is a magazine that is published four times a year, at intervals of three months. 季刊誌 **3** The quarterly had been a forum for sound academic debate. その季刊誌はしっかりした学問的討論の場であった.

quar|tet /kwɔːrtɛt/ (quartets) **1** N-COUNT-COLL 集合可算名詞 A **quartet** is a group of four people who play musical instruments or sing together. 四重奏団; 四重唱団 **3** …a string quartet. 弦楽四重奏団 **2** N-COUNT 可算名詞 A **quartet** is a piece of music for four instruments or four singers. 四重奏曲; 四重唱曲 **3** The String Quartet No. 1 is an early work, composed in California in 1941. 第一弦楽四重奏曲は1941年カリフォルニアで作曲された初期の作品である.

quartz /kwɔːrts/ N-UNCOUNT 不可算名詞 **Quartz** is a mineral in the form of a hard, shiny crystal. It is used in making electronic equipment and very accurate watches and clocks. 石英 **3** …a quartz crystal. 水晶結晶板

quash /kwɒʃ/ (quashes, quashing, quashed) **1** V-T 他動詞 If a court or someone in authority **quashes** a decision or judgment, they officially reject it. 破棄する **3** The Appeal Court has quashed the convictions of all eleven people. 上訴裁判所は11人全員に対する有罪判決を破棄した. **2** V-T 他動詞 If someone **quashes** rumors, they say or do something to demonstrate that the rumors are not true. 静める **3** Graham attempted to quash rumors of growing discontent in the dressing room. グラハムは，楽屋につのる不満があるという流言を静めようとした. **3** V-T 他動詞 To **quash** a rebellion or protest means to stop it, often in a violent way. 鎮圧する **3** Troops were displaying an obvious reluctance to get involved in quashing demonstrations. デモ鎮圧に関与することについて，軍隊は明らかなちゅうちょを示していた.

quay /kiː/ (quays) N-COUNT 可算名詞 A **quay** is a long platform beside the sea or a river where boats can be tied up and loaded or unloaded. 埠頭(ふとう) **3** Jack and Stephen were waiting for them on the quay. ジャックとスティーブンは波止場で彼らを待っていた.

queen /kwiːn/ (queens) **1** N-TITLE; N-COUNT 称号名詞, 可算名詞 A **queen** is a woman who rules a country as its monarch. 女王 **3** …Queen Victoria. ビクトリア女王 **2** N-TITLE; N-COUNT 称号名詞, 可算名詞 A **queen** is a woman who is married to a king. 王妃 **3** The king and queen had fled. 国王と王妃は逃避した. **3** N-COUNT 可算名詞 If you refer to a woman as **the queen** of a particular activity, you mean that she is well-known for being very good at it. 花形 **3** …the queen of crime writing. 犯罪小説家の花形 **4** N-COUNT 可算名詞 A **queen** is a male homosexual who dresses and speaks rather like a woman. 女役のホモ [INFORMAL くだけた] **5** N-COUNT 可算名詞 In chess, the **queen** is the most powerful piece. It can be moved in any direction. (チェスの) クイーン **3** Chris will either have to take his queen's knight and lose his own knight, or he'll lose a rook. クリスは相手のクイーンのナイトを取って自分のナイトを失うか，そうでなければルークを失うしかない. **6** N-COUNT 可算名詞 A **queen** is a playing card with a picture of a queen on it. (トランプの) クイーン **3** …the queen of spades. スペードのクイーンの札 **7** N-COUNT 可算名詞 A **queen** or a **queen bee** is a large female bee which can lay eggs. 女王蜂 **3** Glass hives offer a close-up view of the bees at work, with the queen bee in each hive marked by a white dot. ガラス製の蜂の巣箱では，白い点で示されている各巣箱の女王蜂と一緒に，蜂たちが働いている様子を詳細に観察することができる.

→ see **chess**

queer /kwɪər/ (queerer, queerest, queers) **1** ADJ 形容詞 Something that is **queer** is strange. 奇妙な [OLD-FASHIONED 古風な] **3** If you ask me, there's something kind of queer going on. わたしに言わせれば，何か変なことが起こっている **2** N-COUNT 可算名詞 People sometimes call homosexual men **queers**. ホモ [INFORMAL, OFFENSIVE くだけた, 無礼な] ● ADJ 形容詞 **Queer** is also an adjective. ホモの **3** …America's first queer country music star. アメリカ初のホモのカントリーアンドウエスタン歌手

quell /kwɛl/ (quells, quelling, quelled) **1** V-T 他動詞 To **quell** opposition or violent behavior means to stop it. 鎮める **3** Troops eventually quelled the unrest. 軍隊は不穏をついに鎮圧した. **2** V-T 他動詞 If you **quell** an unpleasant feeling such as fear or anger, you stop yourself or other people from having that feeling. 抑える **3** The government is trying to quell fears of a looming oil crisis. 政府は迫るオイル危機の不安を抑えようとしている.

quench /kwɛntʃ/ (quenches, quenching, quenched) V-T 他動詞 If someone who is thirsty **quenches** their **thirst**, they lose their thirst by having a drink. 渇きをいやす **3** He stopped to quench his thirst at a stream. 小川でのどの渇きをいやすために小休止した.

que|ry /kwɪəri/ (queries, querying, queried) **1** N-COUNT 可算名詞 A **query** is a question, especially one that you ask an organization, publication, or expert. 質問 **3** If you have any queries

about this insurance, please contact our call center. この保険について何か質問があれば，当コールセンターまで連絡してください. **2** V-T 他動詞 If you **query** something, you check it by asking about it because you are not sure if it is correct. 問いただす **3** It's got a number you can call to query your bill. 請求書について尋ねるときに電話できる番号が載っている. **3** V-T 他動詞 To **query** means to ask a question. 質問する **3** "Is there something else?" Ray queried as Helen stopped speaking. 「他に何かあるかい？」と，ヘレンが話すのを止めてレイが質問した.

quest /kwɛst/ (quests) **1** N-COUNT 可算名詞 A **quest** is a long and difficult search for something. 探求 [LITERARY OR HUMOROUS 文語的，またはユーモアのある] **3** …the quest for the Holy Grail. 聖杯探求の旅; 絶対達成できない理想の探求 ● PHRASE 句 If you go in **quest** of something, you try to find or obtain it. 求めて **2** V-I 自動詞 If you **are questing for** something, you are searching for it. 捜し求める [LITERARY 文語的] [usu cont] **3** He had been questing for religious belief from an early age. 小さい時から宗教的信念を捜し求めていた. **3** …his questing mind and boundless enthusiasm. 彼の探究心と無限の熱意

ques|tion /kwɛstʃən/ (questions, questioning, questioned) **1** N-COUNT 可算名詞 A **question** is something that you say or write in order to ask a person about something. 質問 **3** They asked a lot of questions about China. 中国について数多くの質問をした. **2** V-T 他動詞 If you **question** someone, you ask them a lot of questions about something. 質問する **3** This led the therapist to question Jim about his parents and their marriage. これは，療法士はジムに両親やその結婚について質問することにつながっていった. ● **ques|tion|ing** N-UNCOUNT 不可算名詞 質問すること **3** The police have detained thirty-two people for questioning. 警察は尋問のために32人を留置中である. **3** V-T 他動詞 If you **question** something, you have or express doubts about whether it is true, reasonable, or worthwhile. 疑う **3** It never occurs to them to question the doctor's decisions. 医者の判断を疑うことなど彼らは考えてもみなかった. **4** N-SING 単数名詞 If you say that there is some **question** about something, you mean that there is doubt or uncertainty about it. If something is **in question** or has been **called into question**, doubt or uncertainty has been expressed about it. 疑いの余地 **3** There's no question about their success. 彼らが成功することは疑いもない. **3** Her political future is in question. 彼女の政治家としての将来が疑われている. **3** My integrity has been called into question by people who have never spoken to me. わたしとぜんぜん話したことのない人たちが，わたしの潔白さに対して異議を唱えている. **5** N-COUNT 可算名詞 A **question** is a problem, matter, or point which needs to be considered. 問題点 **3** But the whole question of aid is a tricky political one. しかし，援助の問題全体が政治的に扱いにくい点だ. **6** N-COUNT 可算名詞 The **questions** on an examination are the problems that test your knowledge or ability. 試験問題 **3** That question did come up on the test. その問題が実際テストで出てきた. **7** → see also **questioning** **8** PHRASE 句 The person, thing, or time **in question** is one which you have just been talking about or which is relevant. 当該の **3** Add up all the income you've received over the period in question. 当該期間に受け取った収入全部を合計しなさい. **9** PHRASE 句 If you say that something is **out of the question**, you are emphasizing that it is completely impossible or unacceptable. 論外の [EMPHASIS 強調] **3** For the homeless, private medical care is simply out of the question. 住所のない浮浪者にとっては個人医療制度はまったく考えられないことである. **10** PHRASE 句 If you **pop the question**, you ask someone to marry you. 求婚する [INFORMAL くだけた] **3** Stuart got serious quickly and popped the question six months later. スチュワートは早々と真剣になり，6か月後に求婚した. **11** PHRASE 句 If you say **there is no question of** something happening, you are emphasizing that it is not going to happen. 疑問の余地はない [EMPHASIS 強調] **3** There was no question of my blaming Janet. 僕がジャネットを責める可能性などまったくない.

Thesaurus	question また次を参照:
N.	query **1**
V.	ask, inquire; (ant.) answer **2**
	doubt **3**

Word Partnership	question は次の語句と使われる:
V.	answer a question, ask a question, beg the question, pose a question, raise a question **1**
N.	answer/response to a question **1**
ADJ.	difficult question, good question, important question **1**

ques|tion|able /kwɛstʃənəbəl/ ADJ 形容詞 If you say that something is **questionable**, you mean that it is not completely honest, reasonable, or acceptable. 疑わしい [FORMAL 形式ばった]

❑ *He has been dogged by allegations of questionable business practices.* 疑わしい事業のやり方に関する申し立てにつきまとわれている.

Thesaurus *questionable* また次を参照:

ADJ. doubtful, dubious, problematic, uncertain

ques|tion|ing /kwɛstʃənɪŋ/ 1 ADJ 形容詞 If someone has a **questioning** expression on their face, they look as if they want to know the answer to a question. 不審そうな [WRITTEN 書き言葉] [ADJ n] ❑ *He raised a questioning eyebrow.* 彼は不審そうに片方の眉を上げた. 2 → see also **question**

ques|tion mark (**question marks**) 1 N-COUNT 可算名詞 A **question mark** is the punctuation mark ? which is used in writing at the end of a question. 疑問符 ❑ *Who invented the question mark?* 誰が疑問符を発明したか? 2 N-COUNT 可算名詞 If there is doubt or uncertainty about something, you can say that there is a **question mark over** it. 疑問の点 ❑ *There are bound to be question marks over his future.* 彼の将来についてはきっと疑問点があるに違いない.

ques|tion|naire /kwɛstʃənɛər/ (**questionnaires**) N-COUNT 可算名詞 A **questionnaire** is a written list of questions which are answered by a lot of people in order to provide information for a report or a survey. アンケート ❑ *Teachers will be asked to fill in a questionnaire.* 先生たちはアンケートに記入するようにと頼まれるでしょう.

→ see **census**

queue /kyu/ (**queues, queuing, queued**)

Queueing can also be used as the continuous form.

Queueing は進行形としても使われる.

1 N-COUNT 可算名詞 A **queue** is a list of computer tasks which will be done in order. 待ち行列 [COMPUTING コンピューティング] ❑ *Your print job has already been sent from your PC to the network print queue.* 印刷作業は, 既にPCからネットワークの印刷待ちに送られました. 2 V-T 他動詞 To **queue** a number of computer tasks means to arrange them to be done in order. 待ち行列に入れる [COMPUTING コンピューティング] 3 N-COUNT 可算名詞 A **queue** is a line of people or vehicles that are waiting for something. 列 [mainly BRIT 主に英国英語; AM usually **line** 米国英語では通常 **line**] 4 N-COUNT 可算名詞 If you say there is a **queue of** people who want to do or have something, you mean that a lot of people are waiting for an opportunity to do it or have it. 行列 [mainly BRIT 主に英国英語; AM usually **line** 米国英語では通常 **line**] 5 V-I 自動詞 When people **queue**, they stand in a line waiting for something. 並んで待つ [mainly BRIT 主に英国英語] ● PHRASAL VERB 句動詞 **Queue up** means the same as **queue**. 並んで待つ [AM usually **stand in line, line up** 米国英語では通常 **stand in line, line up**]

quib|ble /kwɪbəl/ (**quibbles, quibbling, quibbled**) 1 V-RECIP 相互動詞 When people **quibble over** a small matter, they argue about it even though it is not important. ささいなことで口論する ❑ *Lawmakers spent the day quibbling over the final wording of the resolution.* 立法者たちは, 決議の最終的な言い回しについて取るに足らぬ異論を唱えてその日を過ごした. 2 N-COUNT 可算名詞 A **quibble** is a small and unimportant complaint about something. 取るに足らない文句 ❑ *These are minor quibbles.* これらはささいな理屈だ.

quick /kwɪk/ (**quicker, quickest**) 1 ADJ 形容詞 Someone or something that is **quick** moves or does things with great speed. 動きの速い ❑ *You'll have to be quick. The flight leaves in about three hours.* すばやくしなきゃだめだぞ. フライトは3時間くらいで飛び立つから. ● **quick|ly** ADV 副詞 [ADV with v] 急いで ❑ *Cussane worked quickly and methodically.* クセインは急いでかつ順序良く仕事した. ● **quick|ness** N-UNCOUNT 不可算名詞 敏速さ ❑ *...the natural quickness of his mind.* 生来の敏活な思考力 2 ADV 副詞 [ADV after v] **Quicker** is sometimes used to mean "at a greater speed," and **quickest** to mean "at the greatest speed." **Quick** is sometimes used to mean "with great speed." Some people consider this to be non-standard. 早く [INFORMAL くだけた] ❑ *Warm the sugar slightly first to make it dissolve quicker.* より早く溶解させるために最初に砂糖を少し温めなさい. 3 ADJ 形容詞 Something that is **quick** takes or lasts only a short time. 短時間の ❑ *He took one last quick look around the room.* 見納めに部屋全体をさっと見渡した. ● **quick|ly** ADV 副詞 [ADV with v] 短時間に ❑ *You can get in shape quite quickly and easily.* かなり短時間でしかも簡単に体型を整えることができる. 4 ADJ 形容詞 **Quick** means happening without delay or with very little delay. 即座の ❑ *Officials played down any hope for a quick end to the bloodshed.* 当局は流血の早期終結の望みを軽視した. ● **quick|ly** ADV 副詞 [ADV with v] 即座に ❑ *We need to get it back as quickly as possible.* できるだけ早く取り戻す必要がある. 5 ADV 副詞 **Quick** is sometimes used to mean "with very little delay." 迅速に [INFORMAL くだけた] [ADV after v] ❑ *I got away as quick as I could.* できる限り早く逃げた. 6 ADJ 形容詞 If you are **quick to** do something, you do not hesitate to do it. いち早い [v-link ADJ] ❑ *Mark says the ideas are Katie's own, and is quick to praise her talent.* マークはそのアイデアはケイティのもの

であると言い, いち早く彼女の才能を褒めている. 7 ADJ 形容詞 If someone has a **quick temper**, they are easily made angry. 怒りっぽい [ADJ n] ❑ *He readily admitted to the interviewer that he had a quick temper, with a tendency toward violence.* 彼は, 面接する人に自分は怒りっぽく, 暴力を振るいがちだとすぐに認めた. 8 **quick as a flash** → see **flash**

Thesaurus *quick* また次を参照:

ADJ. brisk, fast, rapid, speedy, swift; (*ant.*) slow 1

Word Partnership *quick* は次の語句と使われる:

N.	quick **learner** 1
	quick **glance**, quick **kiss**, quick **look**, quick **question**, quick **smile** 3
	quick **action**, quick **profit**, quick **response**, quick **start**, quick **thinking** 4
V.	**think** quick 5

quick|en /kwɪkən/ (**quickens, quickening, quickened**) V-T/V-I 他動詞/自動詞 If something **quickens** or if you **quicken** it, it becomes faster or moves at a greater speed. 速くなる [自動詞], 速める [他動詞] ❑ *Ann's pulse quickened in alarm.* アンの心拍が驚きで速くなった.

quick fix (**quick fixes**) N-COUNT 可算名詞 If you refer to a **quick fix** to a problem, you mean a way of solving a problem that is easy but temporary or inadequate. その場しのぎ [DISAPPROVAL 不賛成] ❑ *Any tax measures enacted now as a quick fix would only be reversed in a few years when the economy picks up.* 今その場しのぎで制定された税金対策が, 景気が上向きになる数年後にはまた逆戻りになるだけだ.

qui|et /kwaɪɪt/ (**quieter, quietest, quiets, quieting, quieted**) 1 ADJ 形容詞 Someone or something that is **quiet** makes only a small amount of noise. 静かな ❑ *Tania kept the children reasonably quiet and contented.* ターニアは子どもたちをほどよく静かにまた満足させていた. ● **qui|et|ly** ADV 副詞 [ADV with v] 静かに ❑ *"This is goodbye, isn't it?" she said quietly.* 「これはさよならなのね」と彼女は静かに言った. ● **qui|et|ness** N-UNCOUNT 不可算名詞 静けさ ❑ *...the smoothness and quietness of the flight.* フライトの穏やかさと静けさ 2 ADJ 形容詞 If a place is **quiet**, there is very little noise there. ひっそりとした ❑ *She was received in a small, quiet office.* ひっそりとした小さな事務所で応対を受けた. ● **qui|et|ness** N-UNCOUNT 不可算名詞 静寂 ❑ *I miss the quietness of the countryside.* 田舎の静寂が恋しい. 3 ADJ 形容詞 If a place, situation, or time is **quiet**, there is no excitement, activity, or trouble. 動きのない ❑ *...a quiet rural backwater.* 閑散とした田舎のへき地 ● **qui|et|ly** ADV 副詞 [ADV with v] 平穏に ❑ *His most prized time, though, will be spent quietly on his farm.* しかし, 彼が最も重んじている時間は, 農場で穏やかに過ごすときであろう. ● **qui|et|ness** N-UNCOUNT 不可算名詞 平穏 ❑ *He stretched, taking pleasure in the quietness of the morning hour.* 朝方の時間の静けさを楽しみながら背伸びをした. 4 N-UNCOUNT 不可算名詞 **Quiet** is silence. 静寂 ❑ *He called for quiet and announced that the next song was in our honor.* 彼は静かにするように言って, 次はわたしたちに敬意を表した歌だと発表した. 5 ADJ 形容詞 [v-link ADJ] If you are **quiet**, you are not saying anything. 物を言わない ❑ *I told them to be quiet and go to sleep.* 静かにして寝るようにと彼らに言った. ● **qui|et|ly** ADV 副詞 [ADV with v] 黙って ❑ *Amy stood quietly in the doorway watching him.* エミーは彼を見ながら戸口で黙って立っていた. 6 ADJ 形容詞 A **quiet** person behaves in a calm way and is not easily made angry or upset. もの静かな ❑ *He's a nice quiet man.* 落ち着いたいい男だ. 7 V-T/V-I 他動詞/自動詞 If someone or something **quiets** or if you **quiet** them, they become less noisy, less active, or silent. 静かになる [自動詞], 静かにさせる [他動詞] ❑ *The wind dropped and the sea quieted.* 風が落ちて波がないだ. [mainly AM 主に米国英語] 8 V-T 他動詞 To **quiet** fears or complaints means to persuade people that there is no good reason for them. なだめる [mainly AM 主に米国英語] ❑ *Supporters of the constitution had to quiet fears that aristocrats plotted to steal the fruits of the revolution.* 憲法支持者たちは, 貴族が革命の成果を盗もうとたくらむという不安を静めなければならなかった. 9 PHRASE 句 If you **keep quiet about** something or **keep** something **quiet**, you do not say anything about it. 黙っている ❑ *I told her to keep quiet about it.* そのことについては内緒にするようにと彼女に言った. 10 PHRASE 句 If something is done **on the quiet**, it is done secretly or in such a way that people do not notice it. 内密に ❑ *She'd promised to give him driving lessons, on the quiet, when no one could see.* 誰も見てないときにこっそりと運転の練習をみてあげると彼に約束した.

Thesaurus *quiet* また次を参照:

ADJ.	low, placid, silent, soft; (*ant.*) loud 1
	calm, serene, tranquil; (*ant.*) busy 2 3 6
N.	calm, hush, lull 4
V.	calm, hush, soothe; (*ant.*) agitate, excite, stir up 7 8

q

Word Web   quilt

The Hmong* tribes are famous for their colorful **quilts**. Many people think of a quilt as a bed covering. However, these **textiles** feature pictures that tell stories about the people who made them. A favorite story shows how the Hmong fled from China to southeast Asia in the early 1800s. The story sometimes shows the quiltmaker's arrival in a new country. The **seamstress** **sews** small pieces of colorful **fabric** together to make the **design**. The needlework is very elaborate. It includes cross-stitching, **embroidery**, and appliqué. A common border **pattern** is a design that represents mountains—the Hmong's original home.

Hmong: a group of people who live in the mountains of China, Vietnam, Laos, and Thailand.

Word Partnership   *quiet* は次の語句と使われる:

ADV.	**real** quiet, **relatively** quiet, **too** quiet, **very** quiet ■ – ■ ■
V.	**be** quiet, **keep** quiet ■ ■
N.	**peace and** quiet, quiet **neighborhood/street**, quiet **place/spot** ■ ■ quiet **day/evening/night**, quiet **life** ■

qui|et|en /kwaɪɪtⁿn/ → see **quiet 7, 8**

quilt /kwɪlt/ (**quilts, quilting, quilted**) ■ N-COUNT 可算名詞 A **quilt** is a bed cover made by sewing layers of cloth together, usually with different colors sewn together to make a design. キルティングのベットカバー □ ...*an old patchwork quilt.* 古いパッチワークの刺し子ベットカバー ■ N-COUNT 可算名詞 A **quilt** is the same as a **comforter**. 羽根ぶとん [mainly BRIT 主に英国英語] ■ V-T/V-I 他動詞/自動詞 If you **quilt**, or if you **quilt** a piece of fabric, you make a quilt. キルティングにする □ *Maggie knows how to quilt.* マギーはキルティングの仕方を知っている。 □ *Quilting a bed cover can be laborious.* ベットカバーをキルティングするのは時間がかかって骨が折れることもある。

→ see Word Web: **quilt**

quip /kwɪp/ (**quips**) N-COUNT 可算名詞 A **quip** is a remark that is intended be amusing or clever. 気の利いた言い回し [WRITTEN 書き言葉] □ *The commentators make endless quips about the players' appearance.* アナウンサーたちは選手の外見について際限もなく軽口をたたく。

quirk /kwɜrk/ (**quirks**) ■ N-COUNT 可算名詞 A **quirk** is something unusual or interesting that happens by chance. 巡り合わせ □ *By a tantalizing quirk of fate, the pair have been drawn to meet in the first round of the championship.* からかうような運命の気まぐれで、両者は抽選により選手権の第一回戦でぶつかることになった。 ■ N-COUNT 可算名詞 A **quirk** is a habit or aspect of a person's character which is odd or unusual. 奇癖、奇抜さ □ *Brown was always bewildered by the quirks and foibles of people in everyday situations.* ブラウンは、日常場面での人々の奇抜さや変な癖にいつも興味をそそられた。

quirky /kwɜrki/ (**quirkier, quirkiest**) ADJ 形容詞 Something or someone that is **quirky** is odd or unpredictable in their appearance, character, or behavior. 風変わりな; 気まぐれな □ *We've developed a reputation for being quirky and original.* 風変わりで独創的という評判を引き出した。 ● **quirki|ness** N-UNCOUNT 不可算名詞 風変わり; 気まぐれ □ *You will probably notice an element of quirkiness in his behavior.* 彼の行動には風変わりな様子があることに多分気がつくだろう。

quit /kwɪt/ (**quits, quitting**)

> The form **quit** is used in the present tense and is the past tense and past participle.
>
> **quit** 形は現在時制に使われ、過去時制と過去分詞でもある。

■ V-T/V-I 他動詞/自動詞 If you **quit**, or **quit** your job, you choose to leave it. 辞める [INFORMAL くだけた] □ *He quit his job as an office boy.* 彼は使い走りの仕事を辞めた。 ■ V-T 他動詞 If you **quit** an activity or **quit** doing something, you stop doing it. 止める [mainly AM 主に米国英語] □ *A nicotine spray can help smokers quit the habit.* ニコチンスプレーは喫煙者が喫煙の習慣を止めるのに役立つ。 □ *Quit acting like you didn't know.* 知らない振りしてとぼけるな。 □ *Quit it! That hurts!* 止めろ！痛いじゃないか！ ■ V-T 他動詞 If you **quit** a place, you leave it completely and do not go back to it. 立ち退く □ *Science fiction writers have long dreamed that humans might one day quit the earth to colonize other planets.* 空想科学小説家は、人類がある日地球を立ち去り、ほかの惑星に移住することをひさしく夢見ている。 ■ PHRASE 句 If you say that you are going to **call it quits**, you mean that you have decided to stop doing something or being involved in something. 切りあげる □ *They raised $630,000 through*

listener donations, and then called it quits. 聴衆からの寄付を630,000ドル集めて終わりにした。

Thesaurus   *quit* また次を参照:

V.	resign, vacate ■
	break off, cease, discontinue ■
	abandon, leave ■

quite /kwaɪt/ ■ ADV 副詞 You use **quite** to indicate that something is the case to a fairly great extent. **Quite** is less emphatic than "very" and "extremely." かなり [VAGUENESS あいまいさ] □ *I felt quite bitter about it at the time.* あの時はそのことで相当苦々しく思った。 □ *Well, actually it requires quite a bit of work and research.* いえ、実際は作業と研究がかなり必要なんです。 ■ ADV 副詞 You use **quite** to emphasize what you are saying. まったく [EMPHASIS 強調] □ *It is quite clear that we were firing in self defense.* 自己防衛で射撃していたことはまったく明らかだ。 □ *My position is quite different.* わたしの立場は完全に違う。 ■ ADV 副詞 You use **quite** after a negative to make what you are saying weaker or less definite. 完全には〜ではない [VAGUENESS あいまいさ] □ *Something here is not quite right.* ここは何か変だ。 ■ PREDET 前限定詞 You use **quite** in front of a noun group to emphasize that a person or thing is very impressive or unusual. なかなかの [APPROVAL 賛成] [PREDET 'a'n] □ *"Oh, he's quite a character," Sean replied.* 「まあ、彼はなかなかの人物だ」とショーンが答えた。 ■ ADV 副詞 You can say **quite** to express your agreement with someone. 全くそうだ [mainly BRIT 主に英国英語, SPOKEN 口語, FORMULAE 決まり文句] [ADV as reply] □ *"It's your choice, isn't it?" — "Quite."* 「君の選択だろ」—「そのとおりだ。」

Thesaurus   *quite* また次を参照:

ADV.	entirely, extremely, wholly ■

quiv|er /kwɪvər/ (**quivers, quivering, quivered**) ■ V-I 自動詞 If something **quivers**, it shakes with very small movements. 小刻みに震える □ *Her bottom lip quivered and big tears rolled down her cheeks.* 彼女の下唇が震えて、大きな涙がほおを伝って落ちた。 ■ V-I 自動詞 If you say that someone or their voice **is quivering with** an emotion such as rage or excitement, you mean that they are strongly affected by this emotion and show it in their appearance or voice. 震える □ *Cooper arrived, quivering with rage.* クーパーは、怒りでぶるぶる震えながら到着した。 ● N-COUNT 可算名詞 **Quiver** is also a noun. 震え □ *I recognized it instantly and felt a quiver of panic.* すぐにそれと分かり、うろたえて震えを感じた。

quiz /kwɪz/ (**quizzes, quizzing, quizzed**) ■ N-COUNT 可算名詞 A **quiz** is a test, game, or competition in which someone tests your knowledge by asking you questions. クイズ □ *We'll have a quiz at the end of class.* 授業の終わりに簡単なテストをしましょう。 ■ V-T 他動詞 If you **are quizzed** by someone about something, they ask you questions about it. 詳しく質問する □ *He was quizzed about his income, debts, and eligibility for financial aid.* 彼は、収入や借金や金銭支援に適しているかどうか、尋問された。

quo|ta /kwoʊtə/ (**quotas**) ■ N-COUNT 可算名詞 A **quota** is the limited number or quantity of something which is officially allowed. 割り当て □ *The quota of four tickets per person had been reduced to two.* 一人当たり4枚の割り当て券は2枚に減らされた。 ■ N-COUNT 可算名詞 A **quota** is a fixed maximum or minimum proportion of people from a particular group who are allowed to do something, such as come and live in a country or work for the government. 割り当て人数 □ *The bill would force employers to adopt a quota system when recruiting workers.* その法案は、雇用者が労働者を採用する際、強制的に割り当て制度を採用させるものだ。 ■ N-COUNT 可算名詞 Someone's **quota of** something is their expected or deserved share of it. 持ち分 □ *They have the usual quota of human weaknesses, no doubt.* 人間の弱さも、疑いなく並みの人のように持っているさ。

quo|ta|tion /kwoʊteɪʃⁿn/ (**quotations**) **1** N-COUNT 可算名詞 A **quotation** is a sentence or phrase taken from a book, poem, speech, or play, which is repeated by someone else. 引用文（語句） ❑ He illustrated his argument with quotations from Martin Luther King Jr. マーチン・ルーサー・キングの息子からの引用文を挙げて自分の議論を説明した. **2** N-COUNT 可算名詞 When someone gives you a **quotation**, they tell you how much they will charge to do a particular piece of work. 見積もり ❑ Get several written quotations and check exactly what's included in the cost. 見積書をいくつか書面で取り寄せ, コストの中身を正確に確認せよ.

quo|ta|tion mark (**quotation marks**) N-COUNT 可算名詞 **Quotation marks** are punctuation marks that are used in writing to show where speech or a quotation begins and ends. They are usually written or printed as "...". 引用符 ❑ Make sure you have quotation marks at both the beginning and the end of quotes. 引用の始めと終わりに引用符が確実にあるようにしなさい.

quote /kwoʊt/ (**quotes, quoting, quoted**) **1** V-T/V-I 他動詞/自動詞 If you **quote** someone as saying something, you repeat what they have written or said. 引用する ❑ He quoted Mr. Polay as saying that peace negotiations were already underway. ポレイ氏が和平交渉はすでに始まったと言ったと, 彼は引用した. ❑ I gave the letter to the local press and they quoted from it. 地方紙にその手紙を渡し, 新聞社はそれを引用した. **2** N-COUNT 可算名詞 A **quote from** a book, poem, play, or speech is a passage or phrase from it. 引用文（語句） ❑ The paper starts its editorial comment with a quote from an unnamed member of the House. その新聞は, 名を伏せた議員からの引用文で社説を始めている. **3** V-T 他動詞 If you **quote** something such as a law or a fact, you state it because it supports what you are saying. 持ち出す ❑ The Congresswoman quoted statistics saying that the standard of living of the poorest people had fallen. 女性議員は, 最低貧困者の生活レベルは落ちたと言いながら, 統計の例を出した. **4** V-T 他動詞 If someone **quotes** a price **for** doing something, they say how much money they would charge you for a service they are offering or a for a job that you want them to do. 見積もる ❑ A travel agent quoted her $260 for a flight from Boston to New Jersey. 旅行代理店は, ボストンからニュージャージーまでの定期航空便は260ドルだと彼女に言った. **5** N-COUNT 可算名詞 A **quote for** a piece of work is the price that someone says they will charge you to do the work. 見積もり ❑ Always get a written quote for any repairs needed. 必要な修理は全て, いつも書面で見積もりを受け取りなさい. **6** V-T PASSIVE 受動態他動詞 If a company's shares, a substance, or a currency **is quoted** at a particular price, that is its current market price. 相場をつける [BUSINESS 実業] ❑ In early trading in Hong Kong yesterday, gold was quoted at $368.20 an ounce. 昨日香港での取引の初めに, 金は1オンス当り368.20ドルと相場がついた. **7** N-PLURAL 複数名詞 **Quotes** are the same as **quotation marks**. 引用符 [INFORMAL くだけた] ❑ The word "remembered" is in quotes. 「記憶していた」は引用符付きである.

Thesaurus		quote また次を参照:
v.	cite, recite, repeat, retell	**1** **3**
n.	estimate, price	**5**

Quran /kɔrɑn, -ræn, kʊ-/ also **Koran** or **Qur'an** N-PROPER 固有名詞 **The Quran** is the holy book on which the religion of Islam is based. コーラン（イスラム教の経典） ❑ Still a devout Muslim, Lindh reads the Quran and prays every day. 相変わらず信心深いイスラム教徒のリンドハは毎日コーランを読み, 祈りをあげる.

QWER|TY /kwɜrti/ also **Qwerty** or **qwerty** ADJ 形容詞 A **QWERTY** keyboard on a typewriter or computer is the standard English language keyboard, on which the top line of keys begins with the letters q, w, e, r, t, and y. クワーティの [ADJ n] ❑ You can enter text on the QWERTY keyboard or simply write on the screen. テキストはクワーティキーボードで入力するか, ただ単に画面に書くこともできる.

q

Rr

R also **r** /ɑr/ (**R's, r's**) N-VAR 可変性名詞 **R** is the eighteenth letter of the English alphabet. アルファベットの第18字

rab|bi /ræbaɪ/ (**rabbis**) N-COUNT; N-TITLE 可算名詞, 称号名詞 A **rabbi** is a Jewish religious leader, usually one who is in charge of a synagogue, one who is qualified to teach Judaism, or who is an expert on Jewish law. ラビ

rab|bit /ræbɪt/ (**rabbits**) N-COUNT 可算名詞 A **rabbit** is a small, furry animal with long ears. Rabbits are sometimes kept as pets, or live wild in holes in the ground. ウサギ

rab|ble /ræbªl/ N-SING 単数名詞 A **rabble** is a crowd of noisy people who seem likely to cause trouble. やじ馬連 □ *He seems to attract a rabble of supporters more loyal to the man than to the cause.* 彼は，大義よりも人物に忠誠なやじ馬支持者を引き付けるようだ。

ra|bies /reɪbiz/ N-UNCOUNT 不可算名詞 **Rabies** is a serious disease that causes people and animals to go mad and die. 狂犬病

race /reɪs/ (**races, racing, raced**) **1** N-COUNT 可算名詞 A **race** is a competition to see who is the fastest, for example in running, swimming, or driving. 競走 □ *The women's race was won by the only American in the field, Patti Sue Plumer.* 女子の競走では出場していたただ1人のアメリカ人，パティ・スー・プラマーが勝った。 **2** V-T/V-I 他動詞/自動詞 If you **race**, you take part in a race. 競走する [他動詞・自動詞] □ *In the 10 years I raced in Europe, 30 drivers were killed.* 私がヨーロッパで競走した10年間に30名のドライバーが死んだ。 □ *We raced them to the summit.* 私たちは彼らと頂上まで競走した。 **3** N-PLURAL 複数名詞 **The races** are a series of horse races that are held in a particular place on a particular day. People go to watch and to bet on which horse will win. 競馬 □ *The high point of this trip was a day at the races.* この旅行のハイライトは競馬観戦の1日だ。 **4** N-COUNT 可算名詞 A **race** is a situation in which people or organizations compete with each other for power or control. 競争 □ *The race for the White House begins in earnest today.* 米大統領選挙戦は本日本格的に開幕する。 **5** → see also **rat race** **6** N-VAR 可変性名詞 A **race** is one of the major groups which human beings can be divided into according to their physical features, such as the color of their skin. 人種 □ *The college welcomes students of all races, faiths, and nationalities.* この大学は，あらゆる人種，信仰，国籍の学生を受け入れる。 **7** → see also **human race, race relations** **8** V-I 自動詞 If you **race** somewhere, you go there as quickly as possible. 疾走する □ *He raced across town to the State House building.* 彼は街を横切って州議事堂へ疾駆した。 **9** V-I 自動詞 If something **races** toward a particular state or position, it moves very fast toward that state or position. 突進する □ *Do they realize we are racing toward complete economic collapse?* 我々が全面的経済的崩壊に向かって突進していることを彼らは認識しているのだろうか。 **10** V-T 他動詞 If you **race** a vehicle or animal, you prepare it for races and make it take part in races. 出場させる □ *He still raced sports cars as often as he could.* 彼は今でもできるだけ頻繁にスポーツカー競走に出場している。 **11** V-I 自動詞 If your mind **races**, or if thoughts **race** through your mind, you think very fast about something, especially when you are in a difficult or dangerous situation. (考えなどが)頭が巡る □ *I made sure I sounded calm but my mind was racing.* 私はきっと冷静に見えるように努めたが，私の頭の中ではどう対処しようかという思いが駆け巡っていた。 **12** V-I 自動詞 If your heart **races**, it beats very quickly because you are excited or afraid. どきどきする □ *Her heart raced uncontrollably.* 彼女の心臓は抑えきれないほどにどきどきしていた。 **13** → see also **racing** **14** PHRASE 句 You describe a situation as a **race against time** when you have to work very fast in order to do something before a particular time, or before another thing happens. 時間との競走 □ *A spokesman said the rescue operation was a race against time.* スポークスマンは，救済活動は時間との戦いだと言った。

race|course /reɪskɔrs/ (**racecourses**) N-COUNT 可算名詞 A **racecourse** is a track on which horses race. 競馬場 [mainly BRIT 主に英国英語; AM usually **racetrack** 米国英語では通常 **racetrack**]

race|horse /reɪshɔrs/ (**racehorses**) N-COUNT 可算名詞 A **racehorse** is a horse that is trained to run in races. 競走馬

rac|er /reɪsər/ (**racers**) **1** N-COUNT 可算名詞 A **racer** is a person or animal that takes part in races. 競走者，競走馬 □ *Tim Powell is a former champion powerboat racer.* ティム・ポウエルは競艇の前チャンピオンレーサーだ。 **2** N-COUNT 可算名詞 A **racer** is a vehicle

such as a car or bicycle that is designed to be used in races and therefore travels fast. 競走用自動車 □ *...everything from small boats to ocean racers.* 小さなボートから外洋競走用ヨットまですべて

race re|la|tions N-PLURAL 複数名詞 **Race relations** are the ways in which people of different races living together in the same community behave toward one another. 人種関係 □ *...a breakdown in race relations.* 異人種関係の崩壊

race|track /reɪstræk/ (**racetracks**) also **race track** **1** N-COUNT 可算名詞 A **racetrack** is a track on which horses race. 競馬場 [AM 米国英語] □ *...the Breeders' Cup, run Oct. 26 at Arlington racetrack near Chicago.* シカゴ近郊にあるアーリントン競馬場で10月26日に開催されたブリーダーズ・カップ **2** N-COUNT 可算名詞 A **racetrack** is a track for races, for example car or bicycle races. 競走場 □ *...the sound of cars roaring around a racetrack.* 競走路から聞こえるごうごうたる車の音

race|way /reɪsweɪ/ (**raceways**) N-IN-NAMES 名称中の名詞 A **raceway** is a racetrack. 競走場 □ *...the garage area of Pocono Raceway.* ポコノ競走場の車庫地域

ra|cial /reɪʃªl/ ADJ 形容詞 **Racial** describes things relating to people's race. 人種の □ *...the protection of national and racial minorities.* 民族的および人種的少数派の保護 ● **ra|cial|ly** ADV 副詞 人種的に □ *We are both children of racially mixed marriages.* 私たちは2人とも異人種間結婚による子供だ。

rac|ing /reɪsɪŋ/ N-UNCOUNT 不可算名詞 **Racing** refers to races between animals, especially horses, or between vehicles. 競走 □ *Four horse racing tracks operate in Pennsylvania.* ペンシルベニア州では4つの競馬場が運営されている。 → see **bicycle**

rac|ism /reɪsɪzəm/ N-UNCOUNT 不可算名詞 **Racism** is the belief that people of some races are inferior to others, and the behavior which is the result of this belief. 人種差別主義 □ *There is a feeling among some black people that the level of racism is declining.* 黒人の間には，人種差別の程度が低下してきていると感じる人もいます。

rac|ist /reɪsɪst/ (**racists**) ADJ 形容詞 If you describe people, things, or behavior as **racist**, you mean that they are influenced by the belief that some people are inferior because they belong to a particular race. 人種差別的な [DISAPPROVAL 不賛成] □ *You have to acknowledge that we live in a racist society.* 私たちは人種差別社会に住んでいることをきみは受け入れなければなりません。 ● N-COUNT 可算名詞 A **racist** is someone who is racist. 人種差別主義者 □ *He has a hard core of support among white racists.* 彼は白人優位主義者の間に根強い支持がある。

rack /ræk/ (**racks, racking, racked**)

The spelling **wrack** is also used for meanings **2** and **3**.

つづりの **wrack** は **2** と **3** の意味にも使われる。

---

1 N-COUNT 可算名詞 A **rack** is a frame or shelf, usually with bars or hooks, that is used for holding things or for hanging things on. 置き棚 □ *A luggage rack is a sensible option.* 手荷物棚は賢明な選択だ。 **2** V-T 他動詞 If someone **is racked by** something such as illness or anxiety, it causes them great suffering or pain. 苦しめる [usu passive] □ *His already infirm body was racked by high fever.* 彼のすでに弱った体は高熱にさいなまれた。 **3** PHRASE 句 If you **rack your brains**, you try very hard to think of something. 脳みそをしぼる □ *She began to rack her brains to remember what had happened at the nursing home.* 彼女は老人ホームで起こったことを懸命に思い出そうとし始めた。

▶ **rack up** PHRASAL VERB 句動詞 If a business **racks up** profits, losses, or sales, it makes a lot of them. If a sportsman, sportswoman, or team **racks up** wins, they win a lot of games or races. 獲得する [no passive] □ *Lower rates mean that firms are more likely to rack up profits in the coming months.* 一層の低金利は，近い将来，企業が大きな利益を得る可能性がいっそう高くなることを意味する。

rack|et /rǽkɪt/ (**rackets**)

> The spelling **racquet** is also used for meaning **3**.

> つづりの **racquet** は **3** の意味にも使われる.

1 N-SING 単数名詞 A **racket** is a loud, unpleasant noise. 騒音 □ *He makes such a racket I'm afraid he disturbs the neighbors.* 彼はあんなに大騒ぎをしているので、近所迷惑になるのではないかと私は心配している. **2** N-COUNT 可算名詞 You can refer to an illegal activity used to make money as a **racket**. 不正, 密売 [INFORMAL くだけた] □ *I'm sure he'll admit he was in the drug racket in the end.* 彼が薬物密売をしていたことを結局認めると私は確信している. **3** N-COUNT 可算名詞 A **racket** is an oval-shaped bat with strings across it. Rackets are used in tennis, squash, and badminton. ラケット □ *Tennis rackets and balls are provided.* テニスラケットとボールは用意されている.

rack|et|eer|ing /rǽkɪtɪərɪŋ/ N-UNCOUNT 不可算名詞 **Racketeering** is making money from illegal activities such as threatening people or selling worthless, immoral, or illegal goods or services. ゆすり, 詐欺 □ *Edwards was indicted on racketeering charges but never convicted.* エドワードはゆすりで告訴されたが, 決して有罪を宣告されなかった.

racy /rǽɪsi/ (**racier, raciest**) ADJ 形容詞 **Racy** writing or behavior is lively, amusing, and slightly shocking. 活気のある, きわどい □ *He listened to David Bright's racy stories about life in the navy.* 彼はデイビット・ブライトの海軍での生活に関する活気のある話を聞いた.

Word Link   **rad ≈ ray : radar, radial, radius**

ra|dar /rǽɪdɑr/ (**radars**) N-VAR 可変性名詞 **Radar** is a way of discovering the position or speed of objects such as aircraft or ships when they cannot be seen, by using radio signals. レーダー □ *...a ship's radar screen.* 船舶のレーダースクリーン
→ see **bat, forecast**

ra|di|ance /rǽɪdiəns/ **1** N-UNCOUNT 不可算名詞 **Radiance** is great happiness which shows in someone's face and makes them look very attractive. 輝き [also "a" N] □ *She has the vigor and radiance of someone young enough to be her granddaughter.* 彼女は自分の孫でもおかしくないくらいの若者の活力と輝きを持っている. **2** N-UNCOUNT 不可算名詞 **Radiance** is a glowing light shining from something. 発光 [also "a" N] □ *The dim bulb of the bedside lamp cast a soft radiance over his face.* 枕元の薄暗い電球が彼の顔に柔らかい光を投げかけていた.

ra|di|ant /rǽɪdiənt/ **1** ADJ 形容詞 Someone who is **radiant** is so happy that their happiness shows in their face. (幸福などで) 輝く □ *On her wedding day the bride looked truly radiant.* 結婚式の日, 花嫁は実に幸福そうに輝いていた. **2** ADJ 形容詞 Something that is **radiant** glows brightly. さん然たる □ *The evening sun warms the old red brick wall to a radiant glow.* 夕日が古い赤レンガの壁を暖め, さん然と輝かせていた.

ra|di|ate /rǽɪdieɪt/ (**radiates, radiating, radiated**) **1** V-I 自動詞 If things **radiate** out **from** a place, they form a pattern that is like lines drawn from the center of a circle to various points on its edge. 放射状に伸びる □ *Many kinds of woodland can be seen on the various walks which radiate from the Heritage Center.* 遺産センターから四方に広がる様々な遊歩道では, 多種の森林地帯が見られる. **2** V-T/V-I 他動詞/自動詞 If you **radiate** an emotion or quality or if it **radiates from** you, people can see it very clearly in your face and in your behavior. 発散させる [他動詞] □ *She radiates happiness and health.* 彼女は幸せと健康に輝いている. **3** V-T 他動詞 If something **radiates** heat or light, heat or light comes from it. 放射する □ *The metal plate behind my head radiated heat.* 私の頭の後ろの背後にある金属板が熱を放った.

ra|dia|tion /rèɪdiéɪʃən/ **1** N-UNCOUNT 不可算名詞 **Radiation** consists of very small particles of a radioactive substance. Large amounts of radiation can cause illness and death. 放射線 □ *They suffer from health problems and fear the long term effects of radiation.* 彼らは健康障害に苦しんでおり, 放射線の長期的な影響を恐れている. **2** N-UNCOUNT 不可算名詞 **Radiation** is energy, especially heat, that comes from a particular source. 放射エネルギー □ *The $617 million satellite will study energy radiation from the most violent stars in the universe.* 6.17億ドルの衛星は宇宙で最も強烈な星からのエネルギー放射を調査する.
→ see **cancer, greenhouse effect, wave**

Word Partnership   *radiation* は次の語句と使われる:

ADJ.	**nuclear** radiation **1**
N.	radiation **levels**, radiation **therapy/treatment** **1** radiation **damage, effects of** radiation, **exposure to** radiation **1 2**

ra|dia|tor /rǽɪdieɪtər/ (**radiators**) **1** N-COUNT 可算名詞 A **radiator** is a hollow metal device, usually connected by pipes to a central heating system, that is used to heat a room. ラジエーター, 暖房機 **2** N-COUNT 可算名詞 The **radiator** in a car is the part of the engine that is filled with water in order to cool the engine. ラジエーター, エンジン冷却器

radi|cal /rǽdɪkəl/ (**radicals**) **1** ADJ 形容詞 **Radical** changes and differences are very important and great in degree. 根本的な □ *The country needs a period of calm without more surges of radical change.* 国はこれ以上抜本的改革の起こらない穏やかな時期を必要としている. ● **radi|cal|ly** /rǽdɪkli/ ADV 副詞 根本的に □ *...two large groups of people with radically different beliefs and cultures.* 信仰および文化が根本的に異なる人たちで構成される2大グループ **2** ADJ 形容詞 **Radical** people believe that there should be great changes in society and try to bring about these changes. 過激派の □ *...threats by left-wing radical groups to disrupt the proceedings.* 議事を妨害するという左翼過激派グループによる脅し ● N-COUNT 可算名詞 A **radical** is someone who has radical views. 急進論者 □ *Vanessa and I had been student radicals together at Berkeley from 1965 to 1967.* ヴァネッサと私は共に, 1965年から1967年までバークレーの過激派学生だった.

ra|dii /rǽɪdiaɪ/ **Radii** is the plural of **radius**. *radius* の複数形

ra|dio /rǽɪdioʊ/ (**radios, radioing, radioed**) **1** N-UNCOUNT 不可算名詞 **Radio** is the broadcasting of programs for the public to listen to, by sending out signals from a transmitter. ラジオ放送 □ *The last 12 months have been difficult ones for local radio.* 過去12か月は地方のラジオ放送にとって難しい時期だった. **2** N-SING 単数名詞 You can refer to the programs broadcast by radio stations as **the radio**. ラジオ放送番組 □ *A lot of people listen to the radio in the mornings.* 多くの人が朝のラジオ番組を聞いている. **3** N-COUNT 可算名詞 A **radio** is the piece of equipment that you use in order to listen to radio programs. ラジオ受信機 □ *He sat down in the armchair and turned on the radio.* 彼はひじ掛けいすに座ってラジオをつけた. **4** N-UNCOUNT 不可算名詞 **Radio** is a system of sending sound over a distance by transmitting electrical signals. 無線通信 □ *They are in twice daily radio contact with the rebel leader.* 彼らは反乱勢力の指導者と1日に2度無線連絡している. **5** N-COUNT 可算名詞 A **radio** is a piece of equipment that is used for sending and receiving messages. 無線機 □ *Judge Bruce Laughland praised the courage of the young policeman, who managed to raise the alarm on his radio.* ブルース・ラフランド裁判官は, 何とか無線機で警報を発した若い警官の勇気を称賛した. **6** V-T/V-I 他動詞/自動詞 If you **radio** someone, you send a message to them by radio. 無線電信で送る, 無線で通信する □ *The officer radioed for advice.* その警官は無線で助言を求めた.
→ see Word Web: **radio**
→ see **telescope, wave**

radio|ac|tive /rèɪdioʊǽktɪv/ ADJ 形容詞 Something that is **radioactive** contains a substance that produces energy in the form of powerful and harmful rays. 放射性能のある □ *The government has been storing radioactive waste at Fernald for 50 years.* 政府は放射性のある廃棄物を50年間ファナルドに貯蔵してきた. ● **radio|ac|tiv|ity** /rèɪdioʊæktɪvɪti/ N-UNCOUNT 不可算名詞 放射能 □ *...the storage and disposal of solid waste that is contaminated with*

r

Word Web   **radio**

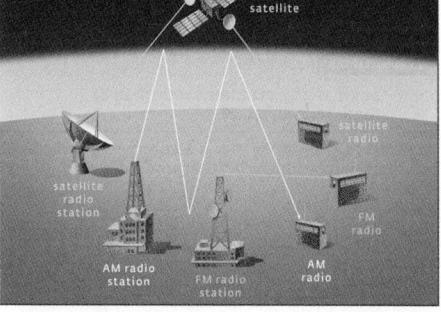

Radio originally provided **communication** between ships at sea. Ships could also contact **stations** on the land. In 1912, the *Titanic* sank in the North Atlantic with over 2,000 people on board. However, a radio call to a nearby ship helped save a third of the passengers. What we call a radio is actually a **receiver**. The **waves** it receives come from a **transmitter**. Radio is an important source of **entertainment**. AM radio carries all kinds of radio **programs**. However, **listeners** often prefer musical programs on the FM waveband or from **satellites** because the sound quality is better.

satellite
satellite radio
satellite radio station
AM radio station
FM radio station
AM radio
FM radio

low levels of radioactivity. 低レベルの放射能に汚染された固形廃棄物
の貯蔵と処分

Word Link *rad ≈ ray : radar, radial, radius*

ra|dius /ˈreɪdiəs/ (radii /ˈreɪdiaɪ/) **1** N-SING 単数名詞 The
radius around a particular point is the distance from it in any
direction. 半径 □ *Nick has searched for work in a ten-mile radius around
his home.* ニックは彼の家から10マイル以内の範囲で仕事を探してきた.
2 N-COUNT 可算名詞 The **radius** of a circle is the distance from
its center to its outside edge. 半径 □ *He indicated a semicircle with a
radius of about thirty miles.* 彼は半径が約30マイルの半円を指し示した.
→ see **area**

raf|fle /ˈræfᵊl/ (raffles, raffling, raffled) **1** N-COUNT 可算名詞 A
raffle is a competition in which you buy tickets with numbers
on them. Afterward some numbers are chosen, and if your ticket
has one of these numbers on it, you win a prize. ラッフル □ *Any
more raffle tickets? Twenty-five cents each or five for a dollar.* 宝くじはも
っといかがですか. 1枚25セントで5枚で1ドルです. **2** V-T 他動詞 If
someone **raffles** something, they give it as a prize in a raffle. ラッ
フルで売る □ *During each show we will be raffling a fabulous prize.* 各シ
ョーの間, 私たちはすばらしい賞品をくじ引きで売ります.

raft /ræft/ (rafts) **1** N-COUNT 可算名詞 A **raft** is a floating
platform made from large pieces of wood or other materials
tied together. いかだ □ *...a river trip on bamboo rafts through dense
rainforest.* 密集した熱帯雨林を通り抜ける竹のいかだでの川旅行
2 N-COUNT 可算名詞 A **raft** is a small rubber or plastic boat that
you blow air into to make it float. 救命いかだ □ *The crew spent two
days and nights in their raft.* 乗組員たちは救命いかだで2昼夜を過ごした.

raft|er /ˈræftər/ (rafters) N-COUNT 可算名詞 **Rafters** are the
sloping pieces of wood that support a roof. 垂木 □ *From the rafters
of the thatched roofs hung strings of dried onions and garlic.* かやぶき屋
根の垂木から, ひも状に束ねられた乾いたタマネギとニンニクが垂れ
下がっている.

rag /ræg/ (rags, ragging, ragged) **1** N-VAR 可変性名詞 A **rag** is
a piece of old cloth which you can use to clean or wipe things. ぼ
ろきれ □ *He was wiping his hands on an oily rag.* 彼は油だらけのぼろ
きれで手をぬぐっていた. **2** N-PLURAL 複数名詞 **Rags** are old torn
clothes. おんぼろの服 □ *There were men, women, and small children,
some dressed in rags.* 男, 女, 小さな子供たちがおり, 中にはおんぼろ
の服を着ている者もいました. **3** N-COUNT 可算名詞 People refer to a
newspaper as a **rag** when they have a poor opinion of it. 三流紙
[INFORMAL くだけた, DISAPPROVAL 不賛成] □ *"This man Tom works
for a local rag," he said.* 「この男, トムは三流地方紙で働いている」と
彼は言った. **4** V-T 他動詞 If someone **rags** you, they tease you in
a friendly way. からかう [INFORMAL くだけた] □ *"They always rag
me about my car," he says.* 「彼らにはいつも僕の車のことでからかわれ
る」と彼は言う.
▶ **rag on** PHRASAL VERB 句動詞 If you **rag on** someone, you speak
angrily to them because they have done something wrong. 一を
しかる [AM 米国英語, INFORMAL くだけた] □ *Ma, quit ragging on
Ruthie.* お母さん, ルーシーをしかるのはやめて.

rage /reɪdʒ/ (rages, raging, raged) **1** N-VAR 可変性名詞 **Rage** is
strong anger that is difficult to control. 激怒 □ *He was red-cheeked
with rage.* 彼のほおは激しい怒りで赤く染まっていた. **2** V-I 自動詞
You say that something powerful or unpleasant **rages** when it
continues with great force or violence. 猛威をふるう □ *Train service
was halted as the fire raged for more than four hours.* 火事が4時間以上
荒れ狂ったために列車の運行は中断された. **3** V-T/V-I 他動詞/自動
詞 If you **rage** about something, you speak or think very angrily
about it. 激怒する, ののしる □ *Monroe was on the phone, raging about
her mistreatment by the brothers.* モンローは電話をかけて, 彼女があ
の兄弟から受けた虐待のことをどなり散らした. **4** N-UNCOUNT 不
可算名詞 You can refer to the strong anger that someone feels in
a particular situation as a particular **rage**, especially when this
results in violent or aggressive behavior. 激情, 暴力ざた □ *Cabin
crews are reporting up to nine cases of air rage a week.* 客室乗務員は1
週間に最高9件の機内暴力を報告しています. **5** → see also **road rage**
6 → see also **raging**
→ see **anger**

Thesaurus *rage* また次を参照:

N.	anger, frenzy, madness, tantrum **1** **4**
V.	fume, scream, yell **3**

rag|ged /ˈrægɪd/ **1** ADJ 形容詞 Someone who is **ragged** looks
messy and is wearing clothes that are old and torn. ぼろを着
た □ *The five survivors eventually reached safety, ragged, half-starved,
and exhausted.* 5人の生存者は, 着ているぼろぼろになり, 半飢餓状態
で, へとへとになってようやく安全な場所にたどり着いた. **2** ADJ 形
容詞 **Ragged** clothes are old and torn. ぼろぼろの □ *...an elderly,
bearded man in ragged clothes.* ぼろぼろの服を着て, あごひげを生やし
た老人 **3** ADJ 形容詞 You can say that something is **ragged** when
it is rough or uneven. でこぼこして □ *O'Brien formed the men into a*

ragged line. オブライエンは男性たちを不規則な線状に並べた.

rag|ing /ˈreɪdʒɪn/ **1** ADJ 形容詞 **Raging** water moves very
forcefully and violently. 荒れ狂う □ *The field trip involved
crossing a raging torrent.* 野外調査旅行には荒れ狂う奔流の横断が含
まれていた. **2** ADJ 形容詞 **Raging** fire is very hot and fierce. 燃え
盛る [ADJ n] □ *As he came closer he saw a gigantic wall of raging flame
before him.* 彼がさらに近寄ると, 猛烈な炎の巨大な壁が彼の前に立
ちはだかった. **3** ADJ 形容詞 **Raging** is used to describe things,
especially bad things, that are very intense. 猛烈な [ADJ n] □ *If
raging inflation returns, then interest rates will shoot up.* 狂乱インフレが
戻ってくると, 金利は急上昇するだろう. **4** → see also **rage**

raid /reɪd/ (raids, raiding, raided) **1** V-T 他動詞 When soldiers
raid a place, they make a sudden armed attack against it, with
the aim of causing damage rather than occupying any of the
enemy's land. 急襲する □ *The guerrillas raided banks and destroyed a
police barracks and an electricity substation.* ゲリラは銀行を急襲し,
警察の建物と変電所を破壊した. ●N-COUNT 可算名詞 **Raid** is also a
noun. 急襲 □ *The rebels attempted a surprise raid on a military camp.*
反逆者たちは軍隊の駐留地への奇襲攻撃を試みた. **2** → see also
air raid **3** V-T 他動詞 If the police **raid** a building, they enter it
suddenly and by force in order to look for dangerous criminals or
for evidence of something illegal, such as drugs or weapons. 手入
れする □ *Police raided their headquarters and other offices.* 警察は彼ら
の本部とその他の事務所を手入れした. ●N-COUNT 可算名詞 **Raid** is
also a noun. 手入れ □ *They were arrested early this morning after a raid
on a house by thirty armed police.* 彼らは本日未明, 30名の武装警官によ
る家宅捜査のあと逮捕されました.

raid|er /ˈreɪdər/ → see **corporate raider**

rail /reɪl/ (rails) **1** N-COUNT 可算名詞 A **rail** is a horizontal bar
attached to posts or around the edge of something as a fence
or support. 横木 □ *They had to walk across an emergency footbridge,
holding onto a rope that served as a rail.* 彼らは手すり代わりのロープ
につかまって, 非常歩道橋を渡らなくてはならなかった. **2** N-COUNT
可算名詞 A **rail** is a horizontal bar that you hang things on. 横棒
□ *This pair of curtains will fit a rail up to 7 ft 6 in wide.* この1対のカー
テンは7フィート6インチの長さのレールに合う. **3** N-COUNT 可算名
詞 **Rails** are the steel bars which trains run on. レール □ *The train
left the rails but somehow forced its way back onto the line.* 列車はレール
を外れたが, なんとか強引に進路に戻った. **4** N-UNCOUNT 不可算名
詞 If you travel or send something **by rail**, you travel or send it on
a train. 鉄道で □ *The president traveled by rail to his home town.* 大統
領は故郷の町へ鉄道で旅行した. **5** PHRASE 句 If something is **back
on the rails**, it is beginning to be successful again after a period
when it almost failed. 再び軌道にのって [mainly BRIT 主に英国英
語 JOURNALISM ジャーナリズム] [AM **back on track** 米国英語 **back
on track**] **6** PHRASE 句 If someone **goes off the rails**, they start to
behave in a way that other people think is unacceptable or very
strange, for example, they start taking drugs or breaking the
law. 常道を外れて [mainly BRIT 主に英国英語] □ *They've got to do
something about these children because clearly they've gone off the rails.*
これらの子供たちは明らかに常軌を逸しているので彼らがなんとかして
やらなければならない.
→ see **skateboarding, train, transportation**

rail|ing /ˈreɪlɪn/ (railings) N-COUNT 可算名詞 A fence made from
metal bars is called a **railing** or **railings**. 柵, 手すり □ *He walked out
on to the balcony where he rested his arms on the railing.* 彼はバルコニー
に出て, 手すりに腕をもたれかけた.

rail|road /ˈreɪlroʊd/ (railroads, railroading, railroaded)
1 N-COUNT 可算名詞 A **railroad** is a route between two places
along which trains travel on steel rails. 鉄道線路 [AM 米国英
語] □ *...railroad tracks that led to nowhere.* どこにも繋がっていな
い鉄道線路 **2** N-COUNT 可算名詞 A **railroad** is a company or
organization that operates railroad routes. 鉄道会社 [AM 米国英
語] □ *The Chicago and Northwestern Railroad wouldn't go along with
that arrangement and said it would shut down completely.* シカゴ・ノ
ースウェスタン鉄道はその取り決めには従おうとせず, 営業を完全に
停止すると言いました. **3** V-T 他動詞 If you **railroad** someone **into**
doing something, you make them do it although they do not
really want to, by hurrying them and putting pressure on them.
せかして一させる □ *He more or less railroaded the rest of Europe into
recognizing the new "independent" states.* 彼は事実上残りの欧州諸国を
せかして新しい「独立」国を承認させた.

rail|way /ˈreɪlweɪ/ (railways) **1** N-COUNT 可算名詞 A **railway**
is the system and network of tracks that trains travel on. 鉄道
[mainly BRIT 主に米国英語] **2** N-COUNT 可算名詞 A **railway** is a
route between two places along which trains travel on steel rails.
鉄道線路 [mainly BRIT 主に英国英語; AM usually **railroad** 米国英語
では通常 **railroad**] **3** N-COUNT 可算名詞 A **railway** is a company or
organization that operates railroad routes. 鉄道会社 [BRIT 英国英
語; AM **railroad** 米国英語 **railroad**]
→ see **train**

rain /reɪn/ (rains, raining, rained) **1** N-UNCOUNT 不可算名詞
Rain is water that falls from the clouds in small drops. 雨 [also

Word Web   rainbow

Sunlight contains all of the colors. When a **ray** of sunlight passes through a prism, it splits into separate colors. This is also what happens when light passes through the drops of water in the air. The light is refracted, and we see a **rainbow**. The colors of the rainbow are **red**, **orange**, **yellow**, **green**, **blue**, indigo, and **violet**. One tradition says that there is a pot of gold at the end of the rainbow. Other myths say that the rainbow is a bridge between Earth and the land of the gods.

"the" N **□** *I hope you didn't get soaked standing out in the rain.* あなたは雨の中で外に立ってびしょぬれになったりしなかったでしょうね. **2** N-PLURAL 複数名詞 In countries where rain only falls in certain seasons, this rain is referred to as **the rains**. 雨季 **□** *...the spring, when the rains came.* 雨季に入る春 **3** V-I 自動詞 When rain falls, you can say that **it is raining**. 雨が降る **□** *It was raining hard, and she didn't have an umbrella.* 雨が激しく降っていたが, 彼女は傘を持っていなかった. **4** V-T/V-I 他動詞/自動詞 If someone **rains** blows, kicks, or bombs **on** a person or place, the person or place is attacked by many blows, kicks, or bombs. You can also say that blows, kicks, or bombs **rain on** a person or place. 雨と降らす [他動詞] 雨と降る [自動詞] **□** *The police, raining blows on rioters and spectators alike, cleared the park.* 警察は暴徒や傍観者に打撃の雨を降らして, 公園から一掃した. ● PHRASAL VERB 句動詞 **Rain down** means the same as **rain**. 雨あられと振りかける **□** *Fighter aircraft rained down high explosives.* 戦闘機は高性能爆発物を雨あられと落とした.
→ see **disaster**, **storm**, **water**

Thesaurus   *rain* また次を参照:

N.   drizzle, precipitation, shower, sleet **1**

rain|bow /ˈreɪnboʊ/ (rainbows) N-COUNT 可算名詞 A **rainbow** is an arch of different colors that you can sometimes see in the sky when it is raining. 虹 **□** *...silk and satin in every shade of the rainbow.* あらゆる虹の色合いをした絹と繻子
→ see Word Web: **rainbow**

rain check PHRASE 句 If you say you will take a **rain check** on an offer or suggestion, you mean that you do not want to accept it now, but you might accept it at another time. (招待などの) 延期 **□** *I was planning to ask you in for a brandy, but if you want to take a rain check, that's fine.* きみをブランデーに誘おうと思っていたが, 別の日がよければそれでもかまわないよ.

rain|coat /ˈreɪnkoʊt/ (raincoats) N-COUNT 可算名詞 A **raincoat** is a waterproof coat. レインコート
→ see **clothing**

rain|drop /ˈreɪndrɒp/ (raindrops) N-COUNT 可算名詞 A **raindrop** is a single drop of rain. 雨滴

rain|fall /ˈreɪnfɔl/ N-UNCOUNT 不可算名詞 **Rainfall** is the amount of rain that falls in a place during a particular period. 降雨量 **□** *There have been four years of below average rainfall.* ここ4年間連続で平均降水量を下回っている.
→ see **erosion**, **storm**

rain for|est (rain forests) also **rainforest** N-VAR 可変性名詞 A **rain forest** is a thick forest of tall trees which is found mainly in tropical areas where there is a lot of rain. 多雨林 **□** *...the destruction of the Amazon rain forest.* アマゾンの熱帯多雨林の破壊

rainy /ˈreɪni/ (rainier, rainiest) ADJ 形容詞 During a **rainy** day, season, or period it rains a lot. 雨の多い **□** *The rainy season in the Andes normally starts in December.* アンデスの雨季は通常12月に始まります.

raise /reɪz/ (raises, raising, raised) **1** V-T 他動詞 If you **raise** something, you move it so that it is in a higher position. 上げる **□** *He raised his hand to wave.* 彼は手を上げて振った. **□** *Milton raised the glass to his lips.* ミルトンはグラスを口に持っていった. **2** V-T 他動詞 If you **raise** a flag, you display it by moving it up a pole or into a high place where it can be seen. (旗を) 揚げる **□** *They had raised the white flag in surrender.* 彼らは白旗を揚げて降参していた. **3** V-T 他動詞 If you **raise** yourself, you lift your body so that you are standing up straight, or so that you are no longer lying flat. 立ち上がらせる **□** *He raised himself into a sitting position.* 彼は起き上がって座った. **4** V-T 他動詞 If you **raise** the rate or level of something, you increase it. 引き上げる **□** *The Federal Reserve Board is expected to raise interest rates.* 連邦準備制度理事会は金利を引き上げると予想されている. **5** V-T 他動詞 To **raise** the standard of something means to improve it. 高める **□** *...a new drive to raise standards of literacy in New York's schools.* ニューヨークの学校における識字能力標準を高める新しい動き **6** V-T 他動詞 If you **raise** your **voice**, you speak more loudly, usually because you are angry. (声を) 張り上げる **□** *Don't you raise your voice to me!* 私に怒鳴りつけないで. **7** N-COUNT 可算

名詞 A **raise** is an increase in your wages or salary. 賃上げ [AM 米国英語] **□** *Within two months Kelly got a raise.* ケリーは2か月経たないうちに昇給した. **8** V-T 他動詞 If you **raise** money **for** a charity or an institution, you ask people for money which you collect on its behalf. (事前などに金を) 集める **□** *...events held to raise money for flood victims.* 洪水の被害者のための募金を行うために開催された行事 **9** V-T 他動詞 If a person or company **raises** money that they need, they manage to get it, for example by selling their property or by borrowing. (資金を) 調達する **□** *They raised the money to buy the house and two hundred acres of land.* 彼らは家と200エーカーの土地を購入するための資金を調達した. **10** V-T 他動詞 If an event **raises** a particular emotion or question, it makes people feel the emotion or consider the question. (ある気持ちを) 起こさせる **□** *The agreement has raised hopes that the war may end soon.* その協定は戦争が間もなく終わるかもしれないという希望を起こさせました. **11** V-T 他動詞 If you **raise** a subject, an objection, or a question, you mention it or bring it to someone's attention. (問題などを) 持ち出す **□** *He had been consulted and had raised no objections.* 彼は相談されましたが, 何ら異議を唱えませんでした. **12** V-T 他動詞 Someone who **raises** a child takes care of it until it is grown up. 育てる **□** *My mother was an amazing woman. She raised four of us kids virtually singlehandedly.* 私の母はすごい女性だった. 私たち4人の子供を事実上1人で育ててくれた. **13** V-T 他動詞 If someone **raises** a particular type of animal or crop, they breed that type of animal or grow that type of crop. 栽培する, 飼養する **□** *He raises 2,000 acres of wheat and hay.* 彼は2000エーカーの土地に小麦とまぐさを栽培しています. **14** to **raise** the **alarm** → see **alarm** **15** to **raise** your **eyebrows** → see **eyebrow** **16** to **raise** a **finger** → see **finger**
→ see **union**

You should be careful not to confuse the verbs **raise** and **rise**. **Raise** is a transitive verb and usually followed by an object, whereas **rise** is an intransitive verb and not followed by an object. **Rise** can also not be used in the passive. **□** *...the government's decision to raise prices... The number of dead is likely to rise.* Both **raise** and **rise** can be used as nouns with meaning pay increase. **Raise** is used in American English, and **rise** is used in British English. **□** *Millions of Americans get a pay raise today. ...a rise of at least 12 percent.*

Thesaurus   *raise* また次を参照:

V.   elevate, hold up, lift **1**
N.   addition, hike, increase **7**

Word Partnership   *raise* は次の語句と使われる:

N.   raise *your hand* **1**
    raise **fares**, raise **interest rates**, raise **the level of** *something*, raise **prices**, raise **taxes** **4**
    raise *your voice* **6**
    pay raise **7**
    raise **money** **8 9**
    raise **capital/revenue** **9**
    raise **awareness**, raise **doubts**, raise **eyebrows**, raise **hopes** **10**
    raise **concerns**, raise **an issue**, raise **questions** **10 11**
    raise **objections** **11**
    raise **a children/family/kids** **12**
    raise **crops** **13**

rai|sin /ˈreɪzən/ (raisins) N-COUNT 可算名詞 **Raisins** are dried grapes. 干しブドウ **□** *...homemade oatmeal with brown sugar and raisins.* 茶色の砂糖と干しぶどう入りの手作りオートミール

rake /reɪk/ (rakes, raking, raked) **1** N-COUNT 可算名詞 A **rake** is a garden tool consisting of a row of metal or wooden teeth attached to a long handle. You can use a rake to make the earth smooth and level before you put plants in, or to gather leaves together. 熊手 **2** V-T 他動詞 If you **rake** a surface, you move a rake across it in order to make it smooth and level. 熊手でかく **□** *Rake*

the soil, press the seed into it, then cover it lightly. 土を熊手でかき，種を押し込んでから土で軽く覆いなさい. **③** V-T 他動詞 If you **rake** leaves or ashes, you move them somewhere using a rake or a similar tool. かいていちにする ❏ I watched the men rake leaves into heaps. 私は男の人たちが葉を熊手で集めて山にするのをじっと見ていた.

▶ **rake in** PHRASAL VERB 句動詞 If you say that someone **is raking in** money, you mean that they are making a lot of money very easily, more easily than you think they should. 荒稼ぎをする [INFORMAL くだけた] ❏ The privatization allowed companies to rake in huge profits. 民営化により会社は巨大な利益を容易に上げることができるようになった.

rake-off (rake-offs) N-COUNT 可算名詞 If someone who has helped to arrange a business deal takes or gets a **rake-off**, they illegally or unfairly take a share of the profits. 不正な取引の上前 [INFORMAL くだけた] ❏ Hall takes a rake-off, often amounting to tens of thousands of dollars on most project deals. ホールはほとんどのプロジェクトの取引でしばしば何万ドルにも上るリベートを取っている.

ral|ly /ráeli/ (rallies, rallying, rallied) **①** N-COUNT 可算名詞 A **rally** is a large public meeting that is held in order to show support for something such as a political party. 集会 ❏ About three thousand people held a rally to mark international human rights day. 約3000人が国際人権日を記念する集会を開いた. **②** V-T/V-I 他動詞/自動詞 When people **rally to** something or when something **rallies** them, they unite to support it. 結集する [他動詞・自動詞] ❏ Her cabinet colleagues have continued to rally to her support. 彼女の同僚の閣僚たちは彼女の支持に結集し続けた. **③** V-I 自動詞 When someone or something **rallies**, they begin to recover or improve after having been weak. 元気を回復する ❏ He rallied enough to thank his doctors. 彼は医者に感謝できるほど十分に元気を回復した. ● N-COUNT 可算名詞 **Rally** is also a noun. 回復 ❏ After a brief rally the shares returned to $2.15. 短期間反発したあと，株は2.15ドルに戻った. **④** N-COUNT 可算名詞 A **rally** in tennis, badminton, or squash is a continuous series of shots that the players exchange without stopping. ラリー ❏ …a long rally. 長いラリー **⑤** N-COUNT 可算名詞 A **rally** is a competition in which vehicles are driven over public roads. ラリー ❏ Carlos Sainz of Spain has won the New Zealand Motor Rally. スペインのカルロス・サインツはニュージーランド自動車ラリーで優勝した.

▶ **rally around** PHRASAL VERB 句動詞 When people **rally around**, they work as a group in order to support someone or something at a difficult time. 味方する／応援に集まってくる ❏ So many people have rallied around to help the family. 非常にたくさんの人たちがその家族の支援に集まってきた.

Word Partnership	rally は次の語句と使われる:
ADJ.	**political** rally **①**
N.	**campaign** rally, **protest** rally, rally **in support of** someone/something **①** **prices/stocks** rally **③**
PREP.	rally **behind** someone/something **②**

ram /ráem/ (rams, ramming, rammed) **①** V-T 他動詞 If a vehicle **rams** something such as another vehicle, it crashes into it with a lot of force, usually deliberately. 激突する ❏ The thieves fled, ramming the policeman's car. 泥棒たちは警察官の車に故意に激突して逃げた. **②** V-T 他動詞 If you **ram** something somewhere, you push it there with great force. 押し込む ❏ He rammed the key into the lock and kicked the front door open. 彼は鍵を錠に押し込み，玄関のドアを蹴り開けた. **③** N-COUNT 可算名詞 A **ram** is an adult male sheep. 雄羊 **④** PHRASE 句 If something **rams home** a message or a point, it makes it clear in a way that is very forceful and that people are likely to listen to. (議論などを) 十分納得させる ❏ The report by the chairman will ram this point home. 委員長による報告書はこの点を強調して徹底させるだろう. **⑤** to **ram** something **down** someone's throat → see **throat**

RAM /ráem/ N-UNCOUNT 不可算名詞 **RAM** is the part of a computer in which information is stored while you are using it. **RAM** is an abbreviation for "Random Access Memory." ラム [COMPUTING コンピューティング] ❏ …a PC with 512 MB RAM. ラムが512MBのパソコン

ram|ble /ráembⁱl/ (rambles, rambling, rambled) **①** N-COUNT 可算名詞 A **ramble** is a long walk in the countryside. 散歩 ❏ …an hour's ramble through the woods. 森の中の1時間の散歩 **②** V-I 自動詞 If you **ramble**, you go on a long walk in the countryside. 漫歩する ❏ …freedom to ramble across the rolling hills. 起伏する丘陵を横切ってあてもなくぶらつく自由 **③** V-I 自動詞 If you say that a person **rambles** in their speech or writing, you mean they do not make much sense because they keep going off the subject in a confused way. とりとめなく話す ❏ Sometimes she spoke sensibly; sometimes she rambled. 彼女は時には分別よく，時には漫然と話した.

rami|fi|ca|tion /ráemɪfɪkéɪʃⁿn/ (ramifications) N-COUNT 可算名詞 The **ramifications** of a decision, plan, or event are all its consequences and effects, especially ones that are not obvious at first. 派生した結果 ❏ The book analyzes the social and political ramifications of AIDS for the gay community. この本はゲイ社会におけるAIDSの社会的および政治的派生効果を分析しています.

ramp /ráemp/ (ramps) N-COUNT 可算名詞 A **ramp** is a sloping surface between two places that are at different levels. 傾斜 ❏ Lillian was coming down the ramp from the museum. リリアンは美術館からの坂道を降りて来るところだった.

→ see **disability, skateboarding, traffic**

ram|page (rampages, rampaging, rampaged)

Pronounced /ráempeɪdʒ/ for meaning **①**, and /raémpeɪdʒ/ for meaning **②**.
① の意味では /ráempeɪdʒ/ と，**②** の意味では /raémpeɪdʒ/ と発音される.

① V-I 自動詞 When people or animals **rampage** through a place, they rush around there in a wild or violent way, causing damage or destruction. 暴れまわる ❏ Hundreds of youths rampaged through the town, smashing store windows and overturning cars. 何百人ものの若者が町を暴れまわって店の窓を叩き壊し，車を転覆させた. **②** PHRASE 句 If people go **on a rampage**, they rush around in a wild or violent way, causing damage or destruction. 暴れまわる ❏ The prisoners went on a rampage destroying everything in their way. 囚人たちは暴れまわって行く手にあるものすべてを破壊しました.

ram|pant /ráempənt/ ADJ 形容詞 If you describe something bad, such as a crime or disease, as **rampant**, you mean that it is very common and is increasing in an uncontrolled way. 手に負えない ❏ Inflation is rampant and industry in decline. インフレが蔓延し，産業界は落ち込んでいる.

ram|shack|le /ráemʃæklⁱl/ ADJ 形容詞 A **ramshackle** building is badly made or in bad condition, and looks as if it is likely to fall down. 倒れそうな ❏ They entered the shop, which was a curious ramshackle building. 彼らはその店に入ったが，それは奇妙な倒れそうな建物であった. **②** ADJ 形容詞 A **ramshackle** system, union, or collection of things has been put together without much thought and is not likely to work very well. がたがたの ❏ They joined with a ramshackle alliance of other rebels. 彼らは他の反乱者たちによる今にもつぶれそうな連合に加わった.

ran /ráen/ **Ran** is the past tense of **run**. run の過去形

ranch /ráentʃ/ (ranches) N-COUNT 可算名詞 A **ranch** is a large farm used for raising animals, especially cattle, horses, or sheep. 牧場 ❏ He lives on a cattle ranch in Texas. 彼はテキサス州にある牛の大牧場に住んでいる.

R & D /ɑːr ən diː/ also **R and D** N-UNCOUNT 不可算名詞 **R & D** refers to the research and development work or department within a large company or organization. **R & D** is an abbreviation for "Research and Development." 研究開発 ❏ Businesses need to train their workers better, and spend more on R & D. 企業は従業員をもっとよく訓練し，研究開発にさらに投資する必要がある.

ran|dom /ráendəm/ **①** ADJ 形容詞 A **random** sample or method is one in which all the people or things involved have an equal chance of being chosen. 無作為の ❏ The survey used a random sample of two thousand people across the Midwest. その調査では中西部地域全域の2千人からの無作為な標本を使用した. ● **ran|dom|ly** ADV 副詞 [ADV with v] 無作為に ❏ …interviews with a randomly selected sample of 30 girls aged between 13 and 18. 無作為に選択された，13歳から18歳の30名の少女の標本との面接 **②** ADJ 形容詞 If you describe events as **random**, you mean that they do not seem to follow a definite plan or pattern. 行き当たりばったりの ❏ …random violence against innocent victims. 何の罪もない犠牲者たちに対する無差別暴力 ● **ran|dom|ly** ADV 副詞 [ADV with v] 行き当たりばったりに ❏ …magazines left scattered randomly around. ところどころ散らかったままの飲み物と雑誌 **③** PHRASE 句 If you choose people or things **at random**, you do not use any particular method, so they all have an equal chance of being chosen. 無作為に ❏ We received several answers, and we picked one at random. 我々は複数の回答を得，その中から無作為に1つを取り上げました. **④** PHRASE 句 If something happens **at random**, it happens without a definite plan or pattern. でたらめに ❏ Three African-Americans were killed by shots fired at random from a minibus. 3名のアフリカ系アメリカ人がマイクロバスから乱射された弾丸により殺されました.

rang /ráeŋ/ **Rang** is the past tense of **ring**. ring の過去形

range /réɪndʒ/ (ranges, ranging, ranged) **①** N-COUNT 可算名詞 A **range of** things is a number of different things of the same general kind. 種類 ❏ A wide range of colors and patterns are available. 広範囲の色とパターンがあります. **②** N-COUNT 可算名詞 A **range** is the complete group that is included between two points on a scale of measurement or quality. 範囲 ❏ The average age range is between 35 and 55. 平均年齢の範囲は35〜55歳だ. **③** N-COUNT 可算名詞 The **range of** something is the maximum area in which it can reach things or detect things. 射程 ❏ The 120mm mortar has a range of 18,000 yards. 120mmの追撃砲の射程は1万8千ヤードだ. **④** V-I 自動詞 If things **range between** two points or **range**

from one point to another, they vary within these points on a scale of measurement or quality. 変動する ❑ *They range in price from $3 to $15.* それらの価格は3ドルから15ドルの間です。 ❑ *...offering merchandise ranging from the everyday to the esoteric.* 日常品から得体の知れない商品まで様々な商品の提供 **5** N-COUNT 可算名詞 A **range** of mountains or hills is a line of them. 山脈 ❑ *...the massive mountain ranges to the north.* 北にある巨大な山脈 **6** N-COUNT 可算名詞 A rifle **range** or a shooting **range** is a place where people can practice shooting at targets. 射撃場 ❑ *It reminds me of my days on the rifle range preparing for duty in Vietnam.* それはベトナムでの任務に備えるためライフル射撃場で過ごした日々を思い出させます。 **7** N-COUNT 可算名詞 A **range** is a large area of open land, especially grazing land in the United States, where cattle are kept. 放牧地 ❑ *He grazed his cattle on the open range.* 彼は広々とした放牧地で牛に草を食べさせた。 **8** N-COUNT 可算名詞 A **range** or **kitchen range** is a large metal device for cooking food using gas or electricity. A range consists of a broiler, an oven, and some gas or electric burners. 料理用のレンジ [AM 米国英語] **9** → see also **free-range** **10** PHRASE 句 If something is **in range** or **within range**, it is near enough to be reached or detected. If it is **out of range**, it is too far away to be reached or detected. 射程内で，射程外で ❑ *Cars are driven through the mess, splashing everyone within range.* 車はぬかるみを走り，あたりの人たちにはね散らす。 **11** PHRASE 句 If you see or hit something **at close range** or **from close range**, you are very close to it when you see it or hit it. If you do something **at a range of** half a mile, for example, you are half a mile away from it when you do it. 近距離から ❑ *He was shot in the head at close range.* 彼は近距離から頭を撃たれた。

→ see **graph**

Word Partnership
range は次の語句と使われる:

ADJ.	**broad** range, **limited** range, **narrow** range, **wide** range **1**
	full range, **normal** range, **whole** range **2**
N.	range **of emotions**, range **of possibilities** **1**
	age range, **price** range, **temperature** range **2**

rang|er /ˈreɪndʒər/ (rangers) N-COUNT 可算名詞 A **ranger** is a person whose job is to take care of a forest or large park. 公園保護官 ❑ *Bill Justice is a park ranger at the Carlsbad Caverns National Park.* ビル・ジャスティスはカールズバード洞窟群国立公園の公園保護官だ。

rank /ræŋk/ (ranks, ranking, ranked) **1** N-VAR 可変性名詞 Someone's **rank** is the position or grade that they have in an organization. 地位 ❑ *He eventually rose to the rank of captain.* 彼は最後には海軍大佐の地位に就いた。 **2** N-VAR 可変性名詞 Someone's **rank** is the social class, especially the high social class, that they belong to. 階級 [FORMAL 形式ばった] ❑ *He must be treated as a hostage of high rank, not as a common prisoner.* 彼は普通の捕虜ではなく高官人質として取り扱わなければならない。 **3** V-T/V-I 他動詞/自動詞 If an official organization **ranks** someone or something 1st, 5th, or 50th, for example, they calculate that the person or thing has that position on a scale. You can also say that someone or something **ranks** 1st, 5th, or 50th, for example. 位置する [他動詞] 位置する [自動詞] ❑ *The report ranks the U.S. 20th out of 22 advanced nations.* その報告書は22の先進国の内，米国を20位にランクしている。 ❑ *...the only Canadian woman to be ranked in the top 50 of the women's world rankings.* 女性の世界ランキングではトップ50内にランクされる唯一のカナダ女性 **4** V-T/V-I 他動詞/自動詞 If you say that someone or something **ranks** high or low on a scale, you are saying how good or important you think they are. 評価する [他動詞・自動詞] ❑ *His prices rank high among those of other contemporary photographers.* 彼の価格はその他の同時代の写真家のものの中でも高い。 ❑ *Investors ranked South Korea high among Asian nations.* 投資家たちはアジア諸国のなかでも韓国を高く評価した。 ❑ *St. Petersburg's night life ranks as more exciting than the capital's.* サンクトペテルスブルグのナイトライフは首都のものよりも刺激的だと評価されている。 **5** N-PLURAL 複数名詞 The **ranks** of a group or organization are the people who belong to it. 組織の全員 ❑ *There were some misgivings within the ranks of the media too.* マスコミの関係者の中にも懸念を示すものがいた。 **6** N-PLURAL 複数名詞 The **ranks** are the ordinary members of an organization, especially of the armed forces. 一般社員，兵卒 ❑ *Most store managers have worked their way up through the ranks.* 店長のほとんどは平社員から出世している。 **7** N-COUNT 可算名詞 A **rank** of people or things is a row of them. 横列 ❑ *Ranks of police in riot gear stood nervously by.* 暴動鎮圧用装備をした警察の横隊は緊張のおももちで待機していた。 **8** N-COUNT 可算名詞 A **taxi rank** is a place on a city street where taxis park when they are available. タクシーの駐車場 [mainly BRIT 主に英国英語; AM **stand** 米国英語 stand] **9** PHRASE 句 If you say that a member of a group or organization **breaks ranks**, you mean that they disobey the instructions of their group or organization. 刃向かう ❑ *Britain appears unlikely to break ranks with other members of the European Union.* 英国が欧州連合の他の加盟国にそむくことはなさそうだ。 **10** PHRASE 句 If you say that the members of a group **close ranks**, you mean that they

are supporting each other only because their group is being criticized. 団結を固める ❑ *Institutions tend to close ranks when a member has been accused of misconduct.* 機関というものは構成員が不正行為で告訴された場合に一致結束する傾向にある。

Thesaurus
rank また次を参照:

N.	class, grade, position, status **1** **2**
V.	assign, place **4**

Word Partnership
rank は次の語句と使われる:

ADJ.	**high** rank, **top** rank **1** **2**
ADV.	rank **above**, rank **below** **3**
	rank **high** **4**

rank and file N-SING 単数名詞 The **rank and file** are the ordinary members of an organization or the ordinary workers in a company, as opposed to its leaders or managers. 下士官兵，平社員 [JOURNALISM ジャーナリズム] ❑ *There was widespread support for him among the rank and file.* 彼は下士官兵に幅広く支持されていた。

ran|sack /ˈrænsæk/ (ransacks, ransacking, ransacked) V-T 他動詞 If people **ransack** a building, they damage things in it or make it very messy, often because they are looking for something in a quick and careless way. かきまわして探す ❑ *Demonstrators ransacked and burned the house where he was staying.* デモ参加者たちは彼が滞在している家をひっかきまわして焼き払いました。

ran|som /ˈrænsəm/ (ransoms, ransoming, ransomed) **1** N-VAR 可変性名詞 A **ransom** is the money that has to be paid to someone so that they will set free a person who has been kidnapped. 身代金 ❑ *Her kidnapper successfully extorted a $250,000 ransom for her release.* 彼女を誘拐した犯人は，彼女の釈放と引き換えに，まんまと25万ドルの身代金をゆすり取った。 **2** V-T 他動詞 If you **ransom** someone who has been kidnapped, you pay the money to set them free. 身代金を払って助け出す ❑ *The same system was used for ransoming or exchanging captives.* 捕虜の身受けまたは交換には同じシステムが使用された。 **3** PHRASE 句 If a kidnapper **is holding** a person **for ransom**, they keep that person prisoner until they are given what they want. 監禁して身代金を要求する ❑ *He is charged with kidnapping a businessman last year and holding him for ransom.* 彼は昨年実業家を誘拐し身代金を要求するために監禁した罪で起訴されている。

rant /rænt/ (rants, ranting, ranted) V-T/V-I 他動詞/自動詞 If you say that someone **rants**, you mean that they talk loudly or angrily, and exaggerate or say foolish things. わめく [他動詞・自動詞] ❑ *As the boss began to rant, I stood up and went out.* 上司が怒鳴り散らし始めたので，私は立ち上がって外に出た。 ❑ *Even their three dogs got bored and fell asleep as he ranted on.* 彼がわめきたて続けると，彼の3匹の犬でさえ退屈して眠ってしまった。 ❑ *"Let's get it over and done with," he ranted.* 「けりをつけてしまおう」と彼はわめいた。 ● N-COUNT 可算名詞 **Rant** is also a noun. わめき声 ❑ *Part I is a rant against organized religion.* 第1部は組織宗教に反対する大言壮語だ。 ● **rant|ing** (rantings) N-VAR 可変性名詞 わめくこと ❑ *He had been listening to Goldstone's rantings all night.* 彼はゴールドストーンのわめき声を1晩中聞いていた。

rap /ræp/ (raps, rapping, rapped) **1** N-UNCOUNT 不可算名詞 **Rap** is a type of music in which the words are not sung but are spoken in a rapid, rhythmic way. ラップ ❑ *Her favorite music was by Run DMC, a rap group.* 彼女の好きな音楽はRun DMCというラップグループのものだった。 **2** V-I 自動詞 Someone who **raps** performs rap music. ラップを歌う ❑ *They rap about life in the inner city.* 彼らは都心の生活に関するラップを歌う。 **3** N-COUNT 可算名詞 A **rap** is a piece of music performed in rap style, or the words that are used in it. ラップの曲 ❑ *Every member contributes to the rap, singing either solo or as part of a rap chorus.* 各メンバーがソロまたはラップコーラス員として歌い，そのラップ曲に貢献している。 **4** V-T/V-I 他動詞/自動詞 If you **rap** on something or **rap** it, you hit it with a series of quick blows. トントン叩く [他動詞・自動詞] ❑ *Mary Ann turned and rapped on Charlie's door.* マリー・アンは振り向いてチャーリーの部屋のドアを叩いた。 ❑ *...rapping the glass with the knuckles of his right hand.* 彼は右手指関節でグラスを叩きながら ● N-COUNT 可算名詞 **Rap** is also a noun. コツンと叩くこと ❑ *There was a sharp rap on the door.* ドアをするどく叩く音が聞こえた。 **5** N-UNCOUNT 不可算名詞 A **rap** is a statement in a court of law that someone has committed a particular crime, or the punishment for committing it. 犯罪容疑，罪 [AM 米国英語, INFORMAL くだけた] ❑ *With that old man dead, you're up against a murder rap.* その老人が死んでしまったので，君は殺人容疑をかけられる。 **6** N-COUNT 可算名詞 A **rap** is an act of criticizing or blaming someone or something. 非難 [JOURNALISM ジャーナリズム] ❑ *Bad corks get the rap for as much as 15 percent of tainted wine.* 不良コルクは汚染ワインの15%までもの原因であると非難される。 **7** V-T 他動詞 If you **rap** someone **for** something, you criticize or blame them for it. 非難する [JOURNALISM ジャーナリズム] ❑ *Water industry chiefs were rapped yesterday for failing their customers.* 水道業界のトップらは昨日，顧客の期待を裏切ったために非難された。 **8** PHRASE 句 If someone in authority **raps**

your **knuckles** or **raps** you **on the knuckles**, they criticize you or blame you for doing something they think is wrong. 一を叱責する [JOURNALISM ジャーナリズム] ❑ *I joined the workers on strike and was rapped on the knuckles.* 私はストライキをする労働者に加わり、叱責された. ❾ PHRASE 句 If you say that someone has gotten **a bum rap**, you mean that they have been treated unfairly or punished unfairly. 無実の罪 [mainly AM 主に米国英語, INFORMAL くだけた] ❑ *She's gotten kind of a bum rap, you know. She's not at all the person she's perceived to be.* 彼女は無実の罪をきせられたのだよ、彼女はそんなことをするような人では絶対ない. ❿ PHRASE 句 If you **take the rap**, you are blamed or punished for something, especially something that is not your fault or for which other people are equally guilty. 人の犯した罪をきる [INFORMAL くだけた] ❑ *When the client was murdered, his wife took the rap, but did she really do it?* 顧客が殺されたとき、彼の妻が罪を背負ったけれど、彼女は本当にやったのか. ⓫ PHRASE 句 If you **beat the rap**, you avoid being blamed for something wrong that you have done. うまく刑罰を免れる [INFORMAL くだけた] ❑ *...an attorney who boasts he can beat any rap, for a $5,000 fee.* 5千ドルの料金でどんな容疑でも無実にできることを自負する弁護士
→ see genre

rape /reɪp/ (rapes, raping, raped) ❶ V-T 他動詞 If someone **is raped**, they are forced to have sex, usually by violence or threats of violence. 強姦する ❑ *A young woman was brutally raped in her own home.* 若い女性が自宅で残忍なやり方で強姦（ごうかん）された. ❷ N-VAR 可変名詞 **Rape** is the crime of forcing someone to have sex. 強姦（ごうかん）❑ *Almost 90 percent of all rapes and violent assaults went unreported.* 全強姦および暴行事件の90％近くが通報されないままだった. ❸ N-COUNT 可算名詞 **Rape** is a plant with yellow flowers which is grown as a crop. Its seeds are crushed to make cooking oil. ナタネ

rap|id /ræpɪd/ ❶ ADJ 形容詞 A **rapid** change is one that happens very quickly. 迅速な ❑ *...the country's rapid economic growth in the 1980s.* 1980年代における今の日の迅速な経済成長 ● **rap|id|ly** ADV 副詞 急速に ❑ *...countries with rapidly growing populations.* 人口が迅速に増大している国々 ❑ *Try to rip it apart as rapidly as possible.* できるだけすばやくばらばらに引き裂いてみなさい. ● **ra|pid|ity** /rəpɪdɪti/ N-UNCOUNT 不可算名詞 迅速 ❑ *...the rapidity with which the weather can change.* 天候が変わりうる迅速さ ❷ ADJ 形容詞 A **rapid** movement is one that is very fast. 敏速な ❑ *He walked at a rapid pace along Charles Street.* 彼はチャールズ通りを急いで歩いた. ● **rap|id|ly** ADV 副詞 [ADV with v] すばやく ❑ *He was moving rapidly around the room.* 彼は部屋の中を早足に歩き回っていた. ● **ra|pid|ity** N-UNCOUNT 不可算名詞 速度 ❑ *The water rushed through the holes with great rapidity.* それらの穴から非常な速さで水がほとばしった.

Thesaurus	*rapid* また次を参照：
ADJ.	fast, speedy, swift; (ant.) slow ❶ ❷

Word Partnership	*rapid* は次の語句と使われる：
N.	rapid **change**, rapid **decline**, rapid **development**, rapid **expansion**, rapid **growth**, rapid **increase**, rapid **progress** ❶ rapid **pace**, rapid **pulse** ❷

rap|ids /ræpɪdz/ N-PLURAL 複数名詞 **Rapids** are a section of a river where the water moves very fast, often over rocks. 急流, 早瀬 ❑ *His canoe was there, on the river below the rapids.* 彼のカヌーは早瀬の下流にあった.

rap|ist /reɪpɪst/ (rapists) N-COUNT 可算名詞 A **rapist** is a man who has raped someone. 強姦（ごうかん）者 ❑ *The convicted murderer and rapist is scheduled to be executed next Friday.* 有罪判決を受けた殺人および強姦事件の犯人は来週金曜日に処刑される予定だ.

rap|per /ræpər/ (rappers) N-COUNT 可算名詞 A **rapper** is a person who performs rap music. ラップ歌手 ❑ *The charts have been dominated by rappers in recent months.* チャートではここ数か月ラップ歌手が優勢である.

rap|port /ræpɔr/ N-SING 単数名詞 If two people or groups have a **rapport**, they have a good relationship in which they are able to understand each other's ideas or feelings very well. 親密な関係 [also no det, oft N "with/between" n] ❑ *The success depends on good rapport between interviewer and interviewee.* 成功は面接者と被面接者がどのくらいうまく意思疎通ができるかにかかっている.

rap|ture /ræptʃər/ N-UNCOUNT 不可算名詞 **Rapture** is a feeling of extreme happiness or pleasure. 狂喜 [LITERARY 文語的] ❑ *The film was shown to gasps of rapture at the Democratic Convention.* その映画が民主党大会で上映され、出席者たちは歓喜のあまり息をのんだ. ❑ *His speech was received with rapture by his supporters.* 彼の演説は支持者たちに歓喜して受け入れられた.

rap|tur|ous /ræptʃərəs/ ADJ 形容詞 A **rapturous** feeling or reaction is one of extreme happiness or enthusiasm. 狂喜した

[JOURNALISM ジャーナリズム] ❑ *The students gave him a rapturous welcome.* 学生たちは彼を熱狂的に歓迎した.

rare /rɛər/ (rarer, rarest) ❶ ADJ 形容詞 Something that is **rare** is not common and is therefore interesting or valuable. 稀有（けう）の ❑ *...the black-necked crane, one of the rarest species in the world.* 世界で最も珍しい種の1つ、黒首鶴 ❷ ADJ 形容詞 An event or situation that is **rare** does not occur very often. まれな ❑ *...on those rare occasions when he did eat alone.* 彼が実際に1人で食事したまれな機会に ❸ ADJ 形容詞 You use **rare** to emphasize an extremely good or remarkable quality. すばらしい [EMPHASIS 強調] [ADJ n] ❑ *Ferris has a rare ability to record her observations on paper.* フェリスは観察結果を紙に記録するすばらしい能力を持っている. ❹ ADJ 形容詞 Meat that is **rare** is cooked very lightly so that the inside is still red. レアの ❑ *Thick tuna steaks are eaten rare, like beef.* 厚いマグロのステーキは牛肉のようにレアで食べる.

Thesaurus	*rare* また次を参照：
ADJ.	incomparable, unique; (ant.) commonplace, ordinary ❶ few, infrequent, uncommon, unusual; (ant.) common, frequent ❷ raw, undercooked; (ant.) well-done ❹

rare|ly /rɛərli/ ADV 副詞 If something **rarely** happens, it does not happen very often. めったに~しない ❑ *They battled against other Indian tribes, but rarely fought with the whites.* 彼らは他のインディアン部族と戦ったが、白人とはめったに戦わなかった.

rar|ity /rɛərɪti/ (rarities) ❶ N-COUNT 可算名詞 If someone or something is a **rarity**, they are interesting or valuable because they are so unusual. 珍しい人, 珍品 [JOURNALISM ジャーナリズム] ❑ *Sontag has always been that rarity, a glamorous intellectual.* ソンタグは常に魅力的なインテリというあのまれな存在だった. ❷ N-UNCOUNT 不可算名詞 The **rarity** of something is the fact that it is very uncommon. まれなこと ❑ *It was a real prize due to its rarity and good condition.* それは非常に珍しいものであり、よい状態だったので本当の貴重なものだった.

rash /ræʃ/ (rashes) ❶ ADJ 形容詞 If someone is **rash** or does **rash** things, they act without thinking carefully first, and therefore make mistakes or behave foolishly. むこうみずの、せっかちな ❑ *It would be rash to rely on such evidence.* そんな証拠に頼るのは軽率だ. ● **rash|ly** ADV 副詞 軽率に ❑ *I made a lot of money, but I rashly gave most of it away.* 私はたくさんの金を稼いだが、軽率にもそのほとんどを散財してしまった. ❷ N-COUNT 可算名詞 A **rash** is an area of red spots that appears on your skin when you are ill or have a bad reaction to something that you have eaten or touched. 発疹 ❑ *He may break out in a rash when he eats these nuts.* 彼はこのナッツを食べると発疹ができることがある. ❸ N-SING 単数名詞 If you talk about a **rash of** events or things, you mean a large number of unpleasant events or undesirable things, which have happened or appeared within a short period of time. 多発 ❑ *...one of the few major airlines left untouched by the industry's rash of takeovers.* その業界で続発した買収の影響をまぬがれた数少ない主要航空会社の1つ

rasp /ræsp/ (rasps, rasping, rasped) ❶ V-T/V-I 他動詞/自動詞 If someone **rasps**, their voice or breathing is harsh and unpleasant to listen to. 耳障りな声で言う [他動詞・自動詞] ❑ *"Where did you put it?" he rasped.* 「どこに置いたんだ」と彼はきしるような声で言った. ● N-SING 単数名詞 **Rasp** is also a noun. 耳障りな声 ❑ *He was still laughing when he heard the rasp of Rennie's voice.* 彼はレニーのしゃがれ声を聞いたときもまだ笑っていた. ❷ V-T/V-I 他動詞/自動詞 If something **rasps** or if you **rasp** it, it makes a harsh, unpleasant sound as it rubs against something hard or rough. きしらせる [他動詞] きしる [自動詞] ❑ *The key rasped in the lock and the door swung open.* 鍵が錠のなかできしり、ドアが前後に揺れながら開いた. ❑ *Frank rasped a hand across his chin.* フランクはあごを手でがりがりとこすった. ● N-SING 単数名詞 **Rasp** is also a noun. きしみ ❑ *...the rasp of something being drawn across the sand.* 何かが砂の中を引かれているような耳障りな音

rasp|berry /ræzberi/ (raspberries) N-COUNT 可算名詞 **Raspberries** are small, soft, red fruit that grow on bushes. キイチゴ

rat /ræt/ (rats, ratting, ratted) ❶ N-COUNT 可算名詞 A **rat** is an animal which has a long tail and looks like a large mouse. ネズミ ❑ *This was demonstrated in a laboratory experiment with rats.* これはネズミを使用した実験室での実験で実証されました. ❷ N-COUNT 可算名詞 If you call someone a **rat**, you mean that you are angry with them or dislike them, often because they have cheated you or betrayed you. 裏切り者 [INFORMAL くだけた, DISAPPROVAL 不賛成] ❑ *What did you do with the gun you took from that little rat Turner?* あの裏切り者ターナーから取り上げた銃をどう処置したのか. ❸ V-I 自動詞 If someone **rats on** you, they tell someone in authority about things that you have done, especially bad things. 密告する [INFORMAL くだけた] ❑ *They were accused of encouraging children to rat on their parents.* 彼らは子供たちに親の告げ口をするような

そのかした罪で告訴された. **4** V-I 自動詞 If someone **rats on** an agreement, they do not do what they said they would do. (協定・約束などを) 破る [INFORMAL くだけた] ❑ *She claims he ratted on their divorce settlement.* 彼女は彼が離婚条件を守らなかったと申し立てている. **5** PHRASE 句 If you **smell a rat**, you begin to suspect or realize that something is wrong in a particular situation, for example that someone is trying to deceive you or harm you. うさん臭く思う ❑ *If I don't send a picture, he will smell a rat.* 私が写真を送らなかったら彼は変に思うだろう.

rate /reɪt/ (rates, rating, rated) **1** N-COUNT 可算名詞 The **rate** at which something happens is the speed with which it happens. 速度 ❑ *The rate at which hair grows can be agonizingly slow.* 髪が伸びる速度は苦痛なほど遅いことがある. **2** N-COUNT 可算名詞 The **rate** at which something happens is the number of times it happens over a period of time. 割合 ❑ *New diet books appear at a rate of nearly one a week.* 新しいダイエットの本はほぼ1週間に1冊の割合で出版される. **3** N-COUNT 可算名詞 A **rate** is the amount of money that is charged for goods or services. 料金 ❑ *A special weekend rate is available from mid-November.* 特別週末料金は11月半ばから利用できる. **4** → see also **exchange rate** **5** N-COUNT 可算名詞 The **rate** of taxation or interest is the amount of tax or interest that needs to be paid. It is expressed as a percentage of the amount that is earned, gained as profit, or borrowed. 率 [BUSINESS 実業] ❑ *The government insisted that it would not be panicked into interest rate cuts.* 政府はうろたえて金利引き下げをすることはないと主張した. **6** V-T/V-I 他動詞/自動詞 If you **rate** someone or something as good or bad, you consider them to be good or bad. You can also say that someone or something **rates** as good or bad. 評価する [no cont] [他動詞] 評価される [自動詞] ❑ *Of all the men in the survey, they rate themselves the least fun-loving and the most responsible.* 調査対象の全男性のうち, 彼らは自分自身を楽しむことを最も好まないが, 最も責任感が強いと評価している. ❑ *Most rated it a hit.* ほとんどの人がそれをヒットだと評価している. ❑ *We rate him as one of the best.* 私たちは彼を一流と評価している. **7** V-T PASSIVE 受動態他動詞 If someone or something **is rated** at a particular position or rank, they are calculated or considered to be in that position on a list. みなす [no cont] ❑ *He is generally rated the country's No. 3 industrialist.* 一般的に彼はこの国でナンバー3の実業家とみなされている. **8** V-T 他動詞 If you say that someone or something **rates** a particular reaction, you mean that this is the reaction you consider to be appropriate. 値する [no cont] ❑ *This is so extraordinary, it rates a medal and a phone call from the president.* これは非常にたぐいまれなので, メダルと大統領からの電話に値する. **9** → see also **rating** **10** PHRASE 句 You use **at any rate** to indicate that what you have just said might be incorrect or unclear in some way, and that you are now being more precise. いずれにしても ❑ *His friends liked her – well, most of them at any rate.* 彼の友人たちは彼女が好きだ. まあ, いずれにしても彼らのほとんどはそうだ. **11** PHRASE 句 If you say that **at this rate** something bad or extreme will happen, you mean that it will happen if things continue to develop as they have been doing. この分では ❑ *At this rate they'd be lucky to get home before eight-thirty or nine.* この分では8時半か9時前に帰宅できたら幸運だろう.
→ see **interest rate, motion**

Word Partnership   rate は次の語句と使われる:

N.   rate **of change** **1**
     birth rate, **crime** rate, **dropout** rate, **heart** rate, **pulse** rate, **survival** rate, **unemployment** rate **2**
     interest rate **4**
ADJ.   **average** rate, **faster** rate, **slow** rate, **steady** rate **1 2**
     high rate, **low** rate **1** – **4**

---

rate of re|turn (rates of return) N-COUNT 可算名詞 The **rate of return** on an investment is the amount of profit it makes, often shown as a percentage of the original investment. 利益率 [BUSINESS 実業] ❑ *High rates of return can be earned on these investments.* これらの投資では高い利益率が稼げる.

ra|ther /rǽðər/ **1** PHRASE 句 You use **rather than** when you are contrasting two things or situations. **Rather than** introduces the thing or situation that is not true or that you do not want. ーよりむしろ ❑ *The problem was psychological rather than physiological.* 問題は生理的なものではなく, むしろ心理的なものだった. ● CONJ 接続詞 **Rather** is also a conjunction. むしろ ❑ *She made students think for themselves, rather than telling them what to think.* 彼女は学生に何を考えるべきか教えるのではなく, 自分で考えさせた. **2** ADV 副詞 You use **rather** when you are correcting something that you have just said, especially when you are describing a particular situation after saying what it is not. それどころか [ADV with cl/group] ❑ *Twenty million years ago, Idaho was not the arid place it is now. Rather, it was warm and damp, populated by dense primordial forest.* 200万年前, アイダホは今のような不毛の地ではありませんでした. それどころか温暖で湿気があり, うっそうとした原始森林が多くありました. **3** PHRASE 句 If you say that you **would rather** do something or you'd **rather** do it, you mean that you would prefer to do it.

If you say that you **would rather not** do something, you mean that you do not want to do it. むしろーをしたほうがよいと思う, むしろーをしないほうがよいと思う ❑ *If it's all the same to you, I'd rather work at home.* きみがどちらでもかまわないのなら, 僕は家で働いたほうがいい. ❑ *Kids would rather play than study.* 子供は勉強するよりも遊びたがるものだ. **4** ADV 副詞 You use **rather** to indicate that something is true to a fairly great extent, especially when you are talking about something unpleasant or undesirable. 相当に ❑ *I grew up in rather unusual circumstances.* 私はかなり異常な環境で育った. ❑ *I'm afraid it's a rather long story.* これは相当長い話になると思います. **5** ADV 副詞 You use **rather** before verbs that introduce your thoughts and feelings, in order to express your opinion politely, especially when a different opinion has been expressed. どちらかと言えば [mainly BRIT 主に英国英語, POLITENESS 丁寧さ] [ADV before v] ❑ *I rather think he was telling the truth.* 私はどちらかと言えば彼が真実を語っているのだと思う.

rati|fi|ca|tion /rætɪfɪkéɪʃ³n/ (ratifications) N-VAR 可変性名詞 The **ratification** of a treaty or written agreement is the process of ratifying it. (条約・協定などの) 批准 ❑ *We welcome this development and we look forward to early ratification of the treaty by China.* 我々はこの進展を歓迎し, 中国が早く条約を批准することを期待する.

rati|fy /rǽtɪfaɪ/ (ratifies, ratifying, ratified) V-T 他動詞 When national leaders or organizations **ratify** a treaty or written agreement, they make it official by giving their formal approval to it, usually by signing it or voting for it. (条約・協定を) 批准する ❑ *The parliaments of Australia and Indonesia have yet to ratify the treaty.* オーストラリアとインドネシアの国会はまだその条約を批准していない.

rat|ing /réɪtɪŋ/ (ratings) **1** N-COUNT 可算名詞 A **rating** of something is a score or measurement of how good or popular it is. 評価, 格付け ❑ *New public opinion polls show the president's approval rating at its lowest point since he took office.* 新しい世論調査によると, 大統領の支持率は就任以来, 最低となっている. **2** → see also **credit rating** **3** N-PLURAL 複数名詞 The **ratings** are the statistics published each week which show how popular each television program is. (テレビの) 視聴率 ❑ *CBS's ratings again showed huge improvement over the previous year.* CBSの視聴率は前年に再び大きく伸びた.

Word Partnership   rating は次の語句と使われる:

N.   **approval** rating **1**
ADJ.   **high** rating, **low** rating, **poor** rating, **top** rating **1 2**

ra|tio /réɪʃoʊ, -ʃioʊ/ (ratios) N-COUNT 可算名詞 A **ratio** is a relationship between two things when it is expressed in numbers or amounts. For example, if there are ten boys and thirty girls in a room, the ratio of boys to girls is 1:3, or one to three. 割合, 比率 ❑ *The adult to child ratio is one to six.* 大人と子供の割合は1対6だ.
→ see Word Web: **ratio**

ra|tion /rǽʃ³n, réɪ-/ (rations, rationing, rationed) **1** N-COUNT 可算名詞 When there is not enough of something, your **ration** of it is the amount that you are allowed to have. 割り当て量, 配給量 ❑ *The meat ration was down to one pound per person per week.* 1人当たりの1週間の肉の配給量は1ポンドに減った. **2** V-T 他動詞 When something **is rationed** by a person or government, you are only allowed to have a limited amount of it, usually because there is not enough of it. (供給を) 配給制にする ❑ *Staples such as bread, rice, and tea are already being rationed.* パンや米やお茶といった必需食料品はすでに配給制になっている. ❑ *The City Council of Moscow has decided that it will begin rationing bread, butter, and meat.* モスクワの市議会は, パンとバターと肉の配給制を始めることを決定した. **3** N-PLURAL 複数名詞 **Rations** are the food that is given to people who do not have enough food or to soldiers. (食料難民・兵士に対する) 食料 ❑ *Aid officials said that the first emergency food rations of wheat and oil sent out here last month.* 先月ここで小麦と油の第1回目の緊急食糧が配給されたことを援助団体の職員が言った. **4** N-COUNT 可算名詞 Your **ration** of something is the amount of it that you normally have. いつもの量 ❑ *...after consuming his ration of junk food and two cigarettes.* 彼がいつもの量のジャンクフードを食べ, 2本のたばこを吸った後 **5** → see also **rationing**

Word Link   ratio ≈ reasoning : **ir**rational, rational, **rationale**

ra|tion|al /rǽʃən³l/ **1** ADJ 形容詞 **Rational** decisions and thoughts are based on reason rather than on emotion. (決断・考えが) 合理的な 道理にかなった ❑ *He's asking you to look at both sides of the case and come to a rational decision.* 彼はきみがその件の両方の立場から検討し, 理にかなった判断をしてくれるよう求めている. ● **ra|tion|al|ly** ADV 副詞 合理的に ❑ *It can be very hard to think rationally when you're feeling so vulnerable and alone.* ひどく弱気で孤独を感じている時に合理的に考えるのはとても難しい場合がある. ● **ra|tion|al|ity** /ræʃənǽlɪti/ N-UNCOUNT 不可算名詞 合理性 ❑ *We live in an era of rationality.* 私たちは合理性の時代に生きている. **2** ADJ

width / length
length
width

形容詞 A **rational** person is someone who is sensible and is able to make decisions based on intelligent thinking rather than on emotion. 分別のある，理性的な □ *Did he come across as a sane, rational person?* 彼が正気で分別ある人のように見えたか.

Word Partnership · rational は次の語句と使われる:

| N. | rational **approach**, rational **choice**, rational **decision**, rational **explanation** 1 |
| | rational **human being**, rational **person** 2 |

Word Link · ratio ≈ reasoning : irrational, rational, rationale

ra|tion|ale /rǽʃənάl, -nǽl/ (rationales) N-COUNT 可算名詞 The rationale for a course of action, practice, or belief is the set of reasons on which it is based. 理論的根拠，根本的理由 [FORMAL 形式ばった] □ *However, the rationale for such initiatives is not, of course, solely economic.* しかし，そうした主導の根本的な理由はもちろん経済的なことだけではない.

ra|tion|al|ist /rǽʃən°lɪst/ 1 ADJ 形容詞 If you describe someone as **rationalist**, you mean that their beliefs are based on reason and logic rather than emotion or religion. 合理主義者の □ *White was both visionary and rationalist.* ホワイトは空想家であり合理主義者でもあった. 2 N-COUNT 可算名詞 If you describe someone as a **rationalist**, you mean that they base their life on rationalist beliefs. 合理主義者 □ *...the rationalists and scientists of the nineteenth century.* 19世紀の合理主義者たちと科学者たち

ra|tion|al|ize /rǽʃən°laɪz/ (rationalizes, rationalizing, rationalized) V-T 他動詞 If you try to **rationalize** attitudes or actions that are difficult to accept, you think of reasons to justify or explain them. 正当化する，合理的に見せようとする □ *He further rationalized his activity by convincing himself that he was actually promoting peace.* 自分は実際に平和を促進していると自分自身を納得させることで，彼は自分の活動をさらに正当化した.

ra|tion|ing /rǽʃənɪŋ/ N-UNCOUNT 不可算名詞 **Rationing** is the system of limiting the amount of food, water, gasoline, or other necessary substances that each person is allowed to have or buy when there is not enough of them. 配給 □ *The municipal authorities here are preparing for food rationing.* ここの市当局は食糧配給制の準備をしている.

rat race N-SING 単数名詞 If you talk about getting out of the **rat race**, you mean leaving a job or way of life in which people compete aggressively with each other to be successful. 激しい出世競争 □ *I had to get out of the rat race and take a look at the real world again.* 私は出世競争の世界を離れて，現実にもう1度目を向けなければならなかった.

rat|tle /rǽt°l/ (rattles, rattling, rattled) 1 V-T/V-I 他動詞/自動詞 When something **rattles** or when you **rattle** it, it makes short, sharp, knocking sounds because it is being shaken or it keeps hitting against something hard. ガタガタ鳴らせる [他動詞]，ガタガタ鳴る [自動詞] □ *She slams the kitchen door so hard I hear dishes rattle.* 彼女は思いきり台所のドアを閉めるので，皿がガチャガチャ鳴るのが聞こえる. ●N-COUNT 可算名詞 **Rattle** is also a noun. ガタガタ鳴る音 □ *There was a rattle of rifle fire.* ライフルを発射するカタカタという音が聞こえた. 2 N-COUNT 可算名詞 A **rattle** is a baby's toy with small, loose objects inside which make a noise when the baby shakes it. ガラガラ 3 V-T 他動詞 If something or someone **rattles** you, they make you nervous. どぎまぎさせる □ *Officials are not normally rattled by any reporter's question.* 役人たちは普通はどんな記者の質問にも動じない. ●**rat|tled** ADJ 形容詞 動揺した，狼狽した □ *He swore in Spanish, an indication that he was rattled.* 彼はスペイン語でののしった. それは彼が動揺したしるしだった.

rau|cous /rɔ́kəs/ ADJ 形容詞 A **raucous** sound is loud, harsh, and rather unpleasant. 耳障りな，騒々しい □ *They heard a bottle being smashed, then more raucous laughter.* ビンが叩き割られる音がし

て，そしてさらに耳障りな笑い声が聞こえた. ●**rau|cous|ly** ADV 副詞 騒々しく □ *They laughed together raucously.* 彼らは一斉にけたたましく笑った.

rav|age /rǽvɪdʒ/ (ravages, ravaging, ravaged) V-T 他動詞 A town, country, or economy that **has been ravaged** is one that has been damaged so much that it is almost completely destroyed. 荒廃させる，ひどく破壊する [usu passive] □ *The country has been ravaged by civil war.* その国は内戦で荒廃している.

rav|ages /rǽvɪdʒɪz/ N-PLURAL 複数名詞 The **ravages of** time, war, or the weather are the damaging effects that they have. 惨害，荒廃 □ *...the ravages of two world wars.* 2つの世界大戦の被害

rave /reɪv/ (raves, raving, raved) 1 V-T/V-I 他動詞/自動詞 If someone **raves**, they talk in an excited and uncontrolled way. わめき散らす □ *She cried and raved for weeks, and people did not know what to do.* 彼女は何週間も泣きわめき，人々はどうしていいか分からなかった. □ *"What is wrong with you, acting like that," she raved.* 「そんな振る舞いをするなんて，どうしたの」と彼女はわめいた. 2 V-T/V-I 他動詞/自動詞 If you **rave about** something, you speak or write about it with great enthusiasm. 夢中になって話す □ *Rachel raved about the new foods she ate while she was there.* レイチェルはそこでの滞在中に食べた新しい食べ物について夢中で語った. □ *"I'd no idea Milan was so wonderful," he raved.* 「ミラノがあんなに素晴らしいなんて思いもよらなかった」と彼はほめちぎった. 3 N-COUNT 可算名詞 A **rave** is a big event at which young people dance to electronic music in a large building or in the open air. Raves are often associated with illegal drugs. レイブ（レイブ音楽にあわせて踊るイベント）□ *...an all-night rave.* 夜通しのレイブ 4 → see also **raving**

ra|ven /reɪv°n/ (ravens) N-COUNT 可算名詞 A **raven** is a large bird with shiny black feathers and a deep harsh call. オオガラス，ワタリガラス

ra|vine /rəvín/ (ravines) N-COUNT 可算名詞 A **ravine** is a very deep, narrow valley with steep sides. 峡谷 □ *The bus overturned and fell into a ravine.* バスはひっくり返り，深い谷間に落ちた.

rav|ing /reɪvɪŋ/ 1 ADJ 形容詞 You use **raving** to describe someone who you think is completely mad. 気が狂った [INFORMAL くだけた] □ *Malcolm looked at her as if she were a raving lunatic.* マルコムはまるで彼女が錯乱した狂人であるかのように見つめた. ●ADV 副詞 **Raving** is also an adverb. すざまじく [ADV adj] □ *I'm afraid Paul has gone raving mad.* 残念だがポールは完全にいかれてしまった. 2 → see also **rave**

raw /rɔ/ (rawer, rawest) 1 ADJ 形容詞 **Raw** materials or substances are in their natural state before being processed or used in manufacturing. 加工していない □ *We import raw materials and energy and export mainly industrial products.* 私たちは原料とエネルギーを輸入し，主に工業製品を輸出している. 2 ADJ 形容詞 **Raw** food is food that is eaten uncooked, that has not yet been cooked, or that has not been cooked enough. （食べ物が）生の 生煮えの □ *...a popular dish made of raw fish.* 生魚を使った人気料理 3 ADJ 形容詞 If a part of your body is **raw**, it is red and painful, perhaps because the skin has come off or has been burned. （皮膚が）赤むけの □ *...the drag of the rope against the raw flesh of my shoulders.* 私の肩の皮がむけてひりひりする部分にロープがこすれること 4 ADJ 形容詞 **Raw** emotions are strong basic feelings or responses which are not weakened by other influences. （感情が）生々しい むき出しの □ *Her grief was still raw and he did not know how to help her.* 彼女の悲しみはまだ生々しく，彼はどう彼女の力になれるか分からなかった. 5 ADJ 形容詞 If you describe something as **raw**, you mean that it is simple, powerful, and real. （物事が）ありのままの 本当の □ *...the raw power of instinct.* 本当の直感力 6 ADJ 形容詞 **Raw** data is facts or information that has not yet been sorted, analyzed, and prepared for use. （データが）未整理の 未処理の □ *Analyses were conducted on the raw data.* 生データが分析された. 7 ADJ 形容詞 If you describe someone in a new job as **raw**, or as a **raw** recruit, you mean that they lack experience in that job. 経験不足の，経験が浅

り □…*replacing experienced men with raw recruits.* 経験に富む男性陣を経験不足の新入社員と入れ替えること **8** ADJ 形容詞 **Raw** weather feels unpleasantly cold. 寒々とした □…*a raw December morning.* 寒々とした12月の朝 **9** ADJ 形容詞 **Raw** sewage is sewage that has not been treated to make it cleaner. （下水が）未処理の [ADJ n] □…*contamination of drinking water by raw sewage.* 未処理の下水による飲料水の汚染 **10** PHRASE 句 If you say that you are getting **a raw deal**, you mean that you are being treated unfairly. 不当な仕打ち, ひどい扱い [INFORMAL くだけた] □ *I think women have a raw deal.* 私は女性が不当な扱いを受けていると思う.

ADJ.	natural **1**
	fresh, uncooked; (ant.) cooked **2**
	scraped, skinned **3**

ray /reɪ/ (**rays**) **1** N-COUNT 可算名詞 **Rays** of light are narrow beams of light. 光線 □ *The sun's rays can penetrate water up to 10 feet.* 太陽の光は水中10フィートの深さまでさし込むことができる. **2** → see also **X-ray** **3** N-COUNT 可算名詞 A **ray of** hope, comfort, or other positive quality is a small amount of it that you welcome because it makes a bad situation seem less bad. （希望などの）光 □ *They could provide a ray of hope amid the general economic gloom.* 全体的な景気沈滞の最中にそれらは希望の光となり得るであろう.

→ see **rainbow, telescope**

ra·zor /reɪzər/ (**razors**) N-COUNT 可算名詞 A **razor** is a tool that people use for shaving. かみそり □…*a plastic disposable razor.* プラスチックの使い捨てかみそり

Rd. also **Rd** **Rd.** is a written abbreviation for **road**. It is used especially in addresses and on maps or signs. 通り（road）の略語 □ *Chicago Botanic Garden, Lake Cook Rd., Glencoe.* グレンコーのレイク・クック通りのシカゴ植物園

re /ri/ PREP 前置詞 You use **re** in documents such as business letters, e-mails, faxes and memos to introduce a subject or item which you are going to discuss or refer to in detail. 〜について〜に関して，（手紙・電子メールなどの冒頭に使う） □ *Dear Mrs. Cox, Re: Homeowners Insurance. We note from our files that we have not yet received your renewal instructions.* コックス様. 住宅所有者保険について. 弊社の書類によりますと，まだお客様への継続通知が届いておりません.

-'re /ər/ **-'re** is the usual spoken form of "are." It is added to the end of the pronoun or noun which is the subject of the verb. For example, "they are" can be shortened to "they're." 口語で用いられるareの短縮形. 動詞の主語である名詞または代名詞の後ろに付く. 例えばthey areはthey'reのように短縮される.

reach /riːtʃ/ (**reaches, reaching, reached**) **1** V-T 他動詞 When someone or something **reaches** a place, they arrive there. （場所に）着く 到着する □ *He did not stop until he reached the door.* 彼はドアにたどり着くまで止まらなかった. **2** V-T 他動詞 If someone or something has **reached** a certain stage, level, or amount, they are at that stage, level, or amount. （レベル・金額などに）達する 到達する □ *The process of political change in South Africa has reached the stage where it is irreversible.* 南アメリカにおける政変の経過は，もう元に戻れないところまで来ている. **3** V-I 自動詞 If you **reach** somewhere, you move your arm and hand to take or touch something. （一に伸ばそう）腕や手を伸ばす □ *Judy reached into her handbag and handed me a small, printed leaflet.* ジュディはハンドバッグに手を突っ込み，小さな印刷のチラシを私に渡した. **4** V-T 他動詞 If you can **reach** something, you are able to touch it by stretching out your arm or leg. （手・足を伸ばして）触れる □ *Can you reach your toes with your fingertips?* 指先で足の指をさわれますか.

You use both **reach** and **arrive** to talk about coming to a particular place. **Reach** is always followed by a noun or pronoun referring to a place, and you can use it to emphasize the effort required to get there. □ *To reach the capital might not be easy.* You can use **arrive** to emphasize being in a place rather than traveling to it. □ *When I arrived in England I was exhausted.* **Arrive at** and **reach** can also be used to say that someone eventually makes a decision or finds the answer to something. □ *It took hours to arrive at a decision… They were unable to reach a decision.*

5 V-T 他動詞 If you try to **reach** someone, you try to contact them, usually by telephone. （人に）連絡を取る □ *Has the doctor told you how to reach him or her in emergencies?* その医師は，緊急時の連絡方法をあなたに教えましたか. **6** V-T/V-I 他動詞/自動詞 If something **reaches** a place, point, or level, it extends as far as that place, point, or level. （場所・レベルに）及ぶ 届く □…*a nightshirt that reached to his knees.* 彼の膝丈まであるナイトシャツ **7** V-T 他動詞 When people **reach** an agreement or a decision, they succeed in achieving it. （同意・結論に）達する □ *A meeting of agriculture ministers has so far failed to reach agreement over farm subsidies.* 農相会議では今のところ農業補助金に関する合意に至っていない. **8** N-UNCOUNT 不可算名詞 Someone's or something's

reach is the distance or limit to which they can stretch, extend, or travel. 届く距離 □ *Isabelle placed a wine cup on the table within his reach.* イザベルはワインカップをテーブル上の彼の手が届くところに置いた. **9** N-UNCOUNT 不可算名詞 If a place or thing is within **reach**, it is possible to have it or get to it. If it is out of **reach**, it is not possible to have it or get to it. 入手可能な範囲, 到達できる範囲 □ *It is located within reach of many important Norman towns, including Bayeux.* それはバイユーを含む多くの重要なノルマンディーの町の近くにある.

v.	arrive, enter, get in **1**
	arrive, succeed **2**
	extend to, hold out, stretch **3**
	call, contact **5**

N.	reach **a destination** **1**
	reach **a goal**, reach **one's potential** **2**
	reach **(an) agreement**, reach **a compromise**, reach **a conclusion**, reach **a consensus**, reach **a decision** **7**

re·act /riækt/ (**reacts, reacting, reacted**) **1** V-I 自動詞 When you **react** to something that has happened to you, you behave in a particular way because of it. （物事に）反応する 対応する □ *They reacted violently to the news.* 彼らはその知らせに激しく反応した. **2** V-I 自動詞 If you **react against** someone's way of behaving, you deliberately behave in a different way because you do not like the way they behave. （一に対して）反発する 反抗する □ *My father never saved money and perhaps I reacted against that.* 私の父は決して貯金をしなかった. 多分わたしはそれに反発したのだ. **3** V-I 自動詞 If you **react to** a substance such as a drug, or **to** something you have touched, you are affected unpleasantly or made ill by it. （薬物などに）反応を示す □ *Someone allergic to milk is likely to react to cheese.* 牛乳にアレルギーがある人は，チーズにアレルギー反応を起こす可能性が高い. **4** V-RECIP 相互動詞 When one chemical substance **reacts with** another, or when two chemical substances **react**, they combine chemically to form another substance. 化学反応を起こす □ *Calcium reacts with water but less violently than sodium and potassium do.* カルシウムは水に化学反応を起こすが，ナトリウムやカリウムほど激しく反応はしない.

ADJ.	**slow to react** **1**
N.	react **to news**, react **to a situation** **1**
ADV.	react **differently**, react **emotionally**, **how to** react, react **negatively**, react **positively**, react **quickly** **1**
	react **strongly**, react **violently** **1 4**

re·ac·tion /riækʃən/ (**reactions**) **1** N-VAR 可変性名詞 Your **reaction to** something that has happened or something that you have experienced is what you feel, say, or do because of it. （物事に対する）反応 □ *Reaction to the visit is mixed.* その訪問に対する反応はさまざまである. **2** N-COUNT 可算名詞 A **reaction against** something is a way of behaving or doing something that is deliberately different from what has been done before. 反動, 反発 □ *All new fashion starts out as a reaction against existing convention.* 新しいはやりはすべて, 既存の習慣に対する反発として始まる. **3** N-SING 単数名詞 If there is a **reaction against** something, it becomes unpopular. 拒否反応 [also no det, N "against" n] □ *Premature moves in this respect might well provoke a reaction against the reform.* この件に関する時期尚早な動きは，改革に対する拒絶反応を引き起こすだろう. **4** N-PLURAL 複数名詞 Your **reactions** are your ability to move quickly in response to something, for example when you are in danger. 反射能力, 反射神経 □ *The sport requires very fast reactions.* その運動は鋭い反射能力を必要とする. **5** N-UNCOUNT 不可算名詞 **Reaction** is the belief that the political or social system of your country should not change. （政治的・社会的変化に対する）反対 反動 [DISAPPROVAL 不賛成] □ *Thus, he aided reaction and thwarted progress.* したがって彼は反動を支援し，発展をはばんだ. **6** N-COUNT 可算名詞 A chemical **reaction** is a process in which two substances combine together chemically to form another substance. （化学）反応 □ *Ozone is produced by the reaction between oxygen and ultraviolet light.* オゾンは酸素と紫外線の化学反応により作り出される. **7** N-COUNT 可算名詞 If you have a **reaction** to a substance such as a drug, or **to** something you have touched, you are affected unpleasantly or made ill by it. （薬物などに対する）反応 □ *Every year, 5,000 people have life-threatening reactions to anesthetics.* 毎年5千人の人が麻酔薬に対し，生死にかかわる反応を起こす.

→ see **motion**

r

Word Partnership   reaction は次の語句と使われる:

ADJ. **mixed** reaction, **negative** reaction, **positive** reaction [1]
emotional reaction, **initial** reaction [1] – [3]
chemical reaction [6]
allergic reaction [7]

re|ac|tion|ary /riˈækʃəneri/ (reactionaries) ADJ 形容詞 A **reactionary** person or group tries to prevent changes in the political or social system of their country. 反動的な [DISAPPROVAL 不賛成] ❑ It became clear to everyone that the chairman was too reactionary, too blinkered. 議長があまりにも反動的であまりにも偏狭であることは、誰の目にも明らかになった。 ● N-COUNT 可算名詞 A **reactionary** is someone with reactionary views. 反動主義者 ❑ Critics viewed him as a reactionary, even a monarchist. 批評家は彼を反動主義者、またきみ主制主義者とさえ見なした。

re|ac|tor /riˈæktər/ (reactors) N-COUNT 可算名詞 A **reactor** is the same as a **nuclear reactor**. 原子炉

read (reads, reading)

The form **read** is pronounced /riːd/ when it is the present tense, and /rɛd/ when it is the past tense and past participle.

read 形はそれが現在時制のときは /riːd/ と発音され、過去時制と過去分詞のときは /rɛd/ と発音される。

[1] V-T/V-I 他動詞/自動詞 When you **read** something such as a book or article, you look at and understand the words that are written there. 読む ❑ Have you read this book? きみはこの本を読んだか。 ❑ I read about it in the paper. それについて私は新聞で読んだ。 ❑ She spends her days reading and watching television. 彼女は本を読んだりテレビを見たりして日々を過ごしている。 ● N-SING 単数名詞 **Read** is also a noun. 読書 ❑ I settled down to have a good read. 私はじっくり読書するために腰を落ち着けた。 [2] V-T/V-I 他動詞/自動詞 When you **read** a piece of writing to someone, you say the words aloud. 読んで聞かせる ❑ Jay reads poetry so beautifully. ジェイはとても見事に詩を朗読する。 ❑ I like it when she reads to us. 私は彼女が私たちに本を読み聞かせてくれるのが好きだ。 [3] V-T/V-I 他動詞/自動詞 People who can **read** have the ability to look at and understand written words. 読んで理解する ❑ He couldn't read or write. 彼は読むことも書くこともできなかった。 ❑ The kid can read words, but did miserably on the test. その子は字を読めるのに、試験のできがひどかった。 [4] V-T 他動詞 If you can **read** music, you have the ability to look at and understand the symbols that are used in written music to represent musical sounds. (楽譜を) 読む ❑ Later on I learned how to read music. その後、私は譜面の読み方を学んだ。 [5] V-T 他動詞 When a computer **reads** a file or a document, it takes information from a disk or tape. (コンピュータがデータを) 読み込む [COMPUTING コンピューティング] ❑ How can I read an Excel file on a computer that only has Word installed? ワードしかインストールされていないコンピュータでどうやってエクセルのファイルを読めるんだ? [6] V-T 他動詞 You can use **read** when saying what is written on something or in something. For example, if a notice **reads** "Entrance," the word "Entrance" is written on it. (─と) 読める 書いてある [no cont] ❑ The sign on the bus read "Private: Not In Service." バスの表示は「私用 乗れません」となっていた。 [7] V-I 自動詞 If you refer to how a piece of writing **reads**, you are referring to its style. (─のように) 認める 書かれている ❑ The book reads like a ballad. その本は民謡のように書かれている。 [8] N-COUNT 可算名詞 If you say that a book or magazine is a good **read**, you mean that it is very enjoyable to read. 読み物 ❑ Ben Okri's latest novel is a good read. ベン・オクリの最新刊はいい読み物だ。 [9] V-T 他動詞 If something **is read** in a particular way, it is understood or interpreted in that way. (─と) 解釈する ❑ The play is being widely read as an allegory of imperialist conquest. その戯曲は帝国主義者の征服を寓話化したものだと広く解釈されている。 [10] V-T 他動詞 If you **read** someone's mind or thoughts, you know exactly what they are thinking without them telling you. (人の心・考えを) 見透かす ❑ From behind her, as if he could read her thoughts, Benny said, "You're free to go any time you like, Madame." 彼女の後ろから、まるで彼女の考えが見透かせるようにベニイは言った。 「奥さん、いつでもお好きな時に行っていいですよ」 [11] V-T 他動詞 If you can **read** someone or you can **read** their gestures, you can understand what they are thinking or feeling by the way they behave or the things they say. (人の考え・感情を) 察する ❑ If you have to work as part of a team, you must learn to read people. あなたがあるチームの中で働かなくてはならないのなら、人の気持ちをくみ取ることを学ばなくてはならない。 [12] V-T 他動詞 When you **read** a measuring device, you look at it to see what the figure or measurement on it is. (計測器を) 読む ❑ It is essential that you are able to read a thermometer. 温度計が読めるということは必須だ。 [13] V-T 他動詞 If a measuring device **reads** a particular amount, it shows that amount. (計測器が数値を) 示す ❑ The thermometer read 105 degrees Fahrenheit. 温度計は華氏105度を指していた。 [14] → see also **reading**

▸ **read into** PHRASAL VERB 句動詞 If you **read** a meaning **into** something, you think it is there although it may not actually be there. ─を─の意味に読み取る ❑ It is dangerous to read too much into one year's figures. 1年の統計からいろんなふうに解釈しすぎるのは危険だ。

▸ **read out** PHRASAL VERB 句動詞 If you **read out** a piece of writing, you say it aloud. 声を出して読む、音読する ❑ He's obliged to take his turn at reading out the announcements. 彼は交代でその知らせを読み上げないといけない。

▸ **read up on** PHRASAL VERB 句動詞 If you **read up on** a subject, you read a lot about it so that you become informed about it. ─について十分に調べる、─を研究する ❑ I've read up on the dangers of all these drugs. 私はこれらの薬すべての危険性を十分に調べた。

Thesaurus   read また次を参照:

V.   scan, skim, study [1]
comprehend; (ant.) sense [1] [3] [4]

Word Partnership   read は次の語句と使われる:

ADV. read **carefully**, read **silently** [1]
V.   **like to** read, **want to** read [1] [2]
listen to someone read [2]
learn (how) to read [3]
N.   read **a book/magazine/(news)paper**, read **a sentence**, read **a sign**, read **a statement** [1] [2]
read **a verdict** [2]
ability to read [3]

read|able /ˈriːdəbəl/ [1] ADJ 形容詞 If you say that a book or article is **readable**, you mean that it is enjoyable and easy to read. 読んで面白い、読みやすい ❑ This is a well researched and very readable book. これはよく調査された、とても面白い本だ。 [2] ADJ 形容詞 A piece of writing that is **readable** is written or printed clearly and can be read easily. (文字・印刷が) 読みやすい 判読可能な ❑ My secretary worked long hours translating my almost illegible writing into a typewritten and readable script. 私の秘書は、私のほとんど判読不能な原稿をタイプライターで打って読みやすい原稿にするため長時間働いた。

read|er /ˈriːdər/ (readers) [1] N-COUNT 可算名詞 The **readers** of a newspaper, magazine, or book are the people who read it. (新聞・本などの) 読者 ❑ These texts give the reader an insight into the Chinese mind. これらの本文は読者に中国人の考えに対する洞察を与える。 ❑ The paper's success is simple: we give our readers what they want. 新聞が成功するのは簡単だ。つまり読者に彼らが求めるものを与えるのだ。 [2] N-COUNT 可算名詞 A **reader** is a person who reads, especially one who reads for pleasure. 読書家 ❑ Thanks to that job I became an avid reader. その仕事のおかげで私は貪欲な読書家になった。

read|er|ship /ˈriːdərʃɪp/ (readerships) N-COUNT 可算名詞 The **readership** of a book, newspaper, or magazine is the number or type of people who read it. 読者数、読者層 ❑ Its readership has grown to over 15,000 subscribers. その読者数は購読者が1万5千人を超えるまでになった。

read|ily /ˈrɛdɪli/ [1] ADV 副詞 If you do something **readily**, you do it in a way which shows that you are very willing to do it. 喜んで、快く [ADV with v] ❑ I asked her if she would allow me to interview her, and she readily agreed. 私が彼女にインタビューしてもいいか尋ねると、彼女は快く引き受けてくれた。 [2] ADV 副詞 You also use **readily** to say that something can be done or obtained quickly and easily. For example, if you say that something can be readily understood, you mean that people can understand it quickly and easily. すぐに、容易に ❑ The components are readily available in hardware stores. 部品は金物店で簡単に手に入る。

Word Partnership   readily は次の語句と使われる:

V.   readily **accept**, readily **admit**, readily **agree** [1]
ADV. readily **apparent** [1]
ADJ. **be** readily **available**, **make** readily **available** [2]

readi|ness /ˈrɛdɪnɪs/ [1] N-UNCOUNT 不可算名詞 If someone is very willing to do something, you can talk about their **readiness to** do it. 喜んですること ❑ ...their readiness to co-operate with the new U.S. envoy. 新しい米国公使に彼らが進んで協力すること [2] N-UNCOUNT 不可算名詞 If you do something **in readiness for** a future event, you do it so that you are prepared for that event. 用意ができていること ❑ Security tightened in the capital in readiness for the president's arrival. 首都では大統領の到着に備えて警備が厳しくなった。

read|ing /ˈriːdɪŋ/ (readings) [1] N-UNCOUNT 不可算名詞 **Reading** is the activity of reading books. 読書、読むこと ❑ I have always loved reading. 私は昔から本を読むのが好きだった。 [2] N-COUNT 可算名詞 A **reading** is an event at which poetry or extracts from books

R

are read to an audience. 朗読, 朗読会 □...*a poetry reading*. 詩の朗読会 ③ N-COUNT 可算名詞 Your **reading of** a word, text, or situation is the way in which you understand or interpret it. 解釈 □*My reading of her character makes me feel that she was too responsible a person to do those things*. 彼女の性格を考えると、彼女はそういうことをするには責任感が強すぎるように私は感じる. ④ N-COUNT 可算名詞 The **reading** on a measuring device is the figure or measurement that it shows. 測定値, 数値 □*The gauge must be giving a faulty reading*. その計測器は数値が間違っているに違いない.

re|adjust /ríːədʒʌst/ (**readjusts, readjusting, readjusted**) ① V-I 自動詞 When you **readjust to** a new situation, usually one you have been in before, you adapt to it. 再適応する □*I can understand why astronauts find it difficult to readjust to life on earth*. 私には、なぜ宇宙飛行士が地上での生活に再適応するのに苦労するのかが分かる. ② V-T 他動詞 If you **readjust** the level of something, your attitude to something, or the way you do something, you change it to make it more effective or appropriate. (水準・態度を) 再調整する 立て直す □*In the end you have to readjust your expectations*. 結局、あなたは自分の予想を見直さないといけない. ③ V-T 他動詞 If you **readjust** something such as a piece of clothing or a mechanical device, you correct or alter its position or setting. (服を) 仕立て直す (機械を) 微調整する □*Readjust your watch. We are now on Moscow time*. 腕時計の時間を直しなさい. もうモスクワ時間です.

re|adjust|ment /ríːədʒʌstmənt/ (**readjustments**) N-VAR 可変性名詞 **Readjustment** is the process of adapting to a new situation, usually one that you have been in before. 再調整, 見直し □*The next few weeks will be a period of readjustment, and will probably not be easy*. 次の数週間は再調整期間となるだろう. そしてそれはたぶん簡単ではないだろう.

ready /rédi/ (**readier, readiest, readies, readying, readied**) ① ADJ 形容詞 If someone is **ready**, they are properly prepared for something. If something is **ready**, it has been properly prepared and is now able to be used. 用意ができて [v-link ADJ] □*It took her a long time to get ready for church*. 彼女は教会へ行く仕度をするのにとても時間がかかった. □*Are you ready to board, Mr. Daly?* ダリーさん、搭乗の準備はできていますか? ② ADJ 形容詞 If you are **ready for** something or **ready to** do something, you have enough experience to do it or you are old enough and sensible enough to do it. 用意ができて [v-link ADJ] □*She says she's not ready for marriage*. 彼女はまだ結婚するには早すぎると言っている. ③ ADJ 形容詞 If you are **ready to** do something, you are willing to do it. 進んで~する, ~もいとわない [v-link ADJ to-inf] □*They were ready to die for their beliefs*. 彼らは信条のために喜んで命を投げ出した. ④ ADJ 形容詞 If you are **ready for** something, you need it or want it. ~が待ち遠しい, ~したい [v-link ADJ "for" n] □*I don't know about you, but I'm ready for bed*. きみはどう知らないけど、僕はもう寝たい. ⑤ ADJ 形容詞 To be **ready to** do something means to be about to do it or likely to do it. 今にも~しそうで [v-link ADJ to-inf] □*She looked ready to cry*. 彼女は今にも泣き出しそうだった. ⑥ ADJ 形容詞 You use **ready** to describe things that are able to be used very quickly and easily. 即座の [ADJ n] □*I didn't have a ready answer for this dilemma*. 私にはこのジレンマに対する即座の解決策が分からなかった. ⑦ V-T 他動詞 When you **ready** something, you prepare it for a particular purpose. 準備する, 用意する [FORMAL 形式ばった] □*John's soldiers were readying themselves for the final assault*. ジョンの兵士たちは最後の襲撃の準備をしていた.

Word Partnership *ready* は次の語句と使われる:

N.	ready **for bed**, ready **for dinner** ①
V.	**get** ready ①
	ready **to begin**, ready **to fight**, ready **to go/leave**, ready **to play**, ready **to start** ①–⑤
	ready **to burst** ⑤
ADV.	**always** ready, **not quite** ready, **not** ready **yet** ①–⑤

ready-made ① ADJ 形容詞 If something that you buy is **ready-made**, you can use it immediately, because the work you would normally have to do has already been done. 既製の, 調理済みの □*We rely quite a bit on ready-made meals – they are so convenient*. 私たちは出来合いの食事に大きく依存している. それらはとても手軽だ. ② ADJ 形容詞 **Ready-made** means extremely convenient or useful for a particular purpose. 都合のいい □*Those wishing to study urban development have a ready-made example on their doorstep*. 都市開発の研究をしたい人たちには、自分の地域におあつらい向きの実例がある.

re|affirm /ríːəfɜrm/ (**reaffirms, reaffirming, reaffirmed**) V-T 他動詞 If you **reaffirm** something, you state it again clearly and firmly. 再び断言する [FORMAL 形式ばった] □*He reaffirmed his commitment to the country's economic reform program*. 彼は国の経済改革綱領の公約を再び明言した.

real /ríːl/ ① ADJ 形容詞 Something that is **real** actually exists and is not imagined, invented, or theoretical. 実在の □*No, it wasn't a dream. It was real*. 違うよ、夢なんかじゃない. 本当にあったんだ. ② ADJ 形容詞 If something is **real** to someone, they

experience it as though it really exists or happens, even though it does not. 現実の, リアルな □*Whitechild's life becomes increasingly real to the reader*. 読者にとってホワイトチャイルドの人生はますます現実味を増している. ③ ADJ 形容詞 A material or object that is **real** is natural or functioning, and not artificial or an imitation. (物質・物が) 本物の 正真正銘の □*...the smell of real leather*. 本皮のにおい ④ ADJ 形容詞 You can use **real** to describe someone or something that has all the characteristics or qualities that such a person or thing typically has. 真の [ADJ n] □*...his first real girlfriend*. 彼の最初の真の女友達 ⑤ ADJ 形容詞 You can use **real** to describe something that is the true or original thing of its kind, in contrast to one that someone wants you to believe is true. 本当の [ADJ n] □*This was the real reason for her call*. これが彼女の訪問の本当の理由だった. ⑥ ADJ 形容詞 You can use **real** to describe something that is the most important or typical part of a thing. 本当の, 真の [ADJ n] □*When he talks, he only gives glimpses of his real self*. 彼は話をする時、本当の自分をチラッとしか見せない. ⑦ ADJ 形容詞 You can use **real** when you are talking about a situation or feeling to emphasize that it exists and is important or serious. 深刻な [EMPHASIS 強調] □*Global warming is a real problem*. 地球温暖化は深刻な問題だ. □*The prospect of civil war is very real*. 内戦の可能性はとても現実味を帯びている. ⑧ ADJ 形容詞 You can use **real** to emphasize a quality that is genuine and sincere. (強調して) 純粋な 心からの [EMPHASIS 強調] [ADJ n] □*You've been drifting from job to job without any real commitment*. きみは仕事に真剣に取り組まずに次々転職してばかりきた. ⑨ ADJ 形容詞 You can use **real** before nouns to emphasize your description of something or someone. (強調して) 本当の [mainly SPOKEN 主に口語, EMPHASIS 強調] □*"You must think I'm a real idiot."* きみは僕が本当に大ばか者だと思っているに違いない. ⑩ ADJ 形容詞 The **real** cost or value of something is its cost or value after other amounts have been added or subtracted and when factors such as the level of inflation have been considered. (費用・価値が) 実質の [ADJ n] □*...the real cost of borrowing*. 実質の借り入れコスト ● PHRASE 句 You can also talk about the cost or value of something **in real terms**. 実質で, 実量で □*In real terms the cost of driving is cheaper than a decade ago*. 実質的に車の運転にかかる費用は10年前よりも安い. ⑪ ADV 副詞 You can use **real** to emphasize an adjective or adverb. 本当に [AM 米国英語, INFORMAL くだけた, EMPHASIS 強調] [ADV adj/adv] □*He is finding prison life "real tough."* 彼は刑務所内の生活を「ほんとにきつい」と感じている. ⑫ PHRASE 句 If you say that someone does something **for real**, you mean that they actually do it and do not just pretend to do it. 本当に, 実際に [INFORMAL くだけた] □*I have gone to premieres in my dreams but I never thought I'd do it for real*. 私は夢で初日に行ったことはあるけど、実際に自分が行くとは決して思わなかった.

> Do not confuse **real** and **actual**. You use **real** to describe things that exist rather than being imagined or theoretical. □*Robert squealed in mock terror, then in real pain*. You use **actual** to emphasize that what you are referring to is real or genuine, for example, the **actual** cost of something is what it costs rather than what you expect it to cost. You can also use **actual** to contrast different aspects of something, for example, the time taken to prepare for something and to do something. □*The actual boat trip takes around forty-five minutes*.

real es|tate ① N-UNCOUNT 不可算名詞 **Real estate** is property in the form of land and buildings, rather than personal possessions. 不動産 [mainly AM 主に米国英語] □*By investing in real estate, he was one of the richest men in the United States*. 不動産に投資することで、彼は米国で最も裕福な人々の1人となった. ② N-UNCOUNT 不可算名詞 **Real estate** businesses and real estate agents sell houses, buildings, and land. 不動産 (業界・業者) [AM 米国英語] □*...the real estate agent who sold you your house*. あなたに家を売った不動産屋

→ see **skyscraper**

re|al|ise /ríːəlaɪz/ → see **realize**

re|al|ism /ríːəlɪzəm/ ① N-UNCOUNT 不可算名詞 When people show **realism** in their behavior, they recognize and accept the true nature of a situation and try to deal with it in a practical way. 現実主義 [APPROVAL 賛成] □*It was time now to show more political realism*. 今や政治的な現実主義をもっと示すべき時だった. ② N-UNCOUNT 不可算名詞 If things and people are presented with **realism** in paintings, stories, or movies, they are presented in a way that is like real life. (芸術の) 写実主義 [APPROVAL 賛成] □*Greene's stories had an edge of realism that made it easy to forget they were fiction*. グリーンの物語は、それらがフィクションであることを容易に忘れそうになるほど写実主義の鋭さを持っていた.

→ see **genre**

re|al|ist /ríːəlɪst/ (**realists**) ① N-COUNT 可算名詞 A **realist** is someone who recognizes and accepts the true nature of a situation and tries to deal with it in a practical way. 現実主義者 [APPROVAL 賛成] □*I see myself not as a cynic but as a realist*. 私は自分自身を皮肉屋ではなく現実主義者だと思っている. ② ADJ 形容詞 A **realist** painter or writer is one who represents things and people

in a way that is like real life. 写実主義の [ADJ n] ❑ *...perhaps the foremost realist painter of our time.* 恐らく現代最高の写実主義画家

re|al|is|tic /ríəlɪstɪk/ ■ ADJ 形容詞 If you are **realistic** about a situation, you recognize and accept its true nature and try to deal with it in a practical way. 現実的な ❑ *Police have to be realistic about violent crime.* 警察は暴力犯罪に現実的に対処しなければならない. ●**re|al|is|ti|cal|ly** ADV 副詞 現実的に ❑ *As an adult, you can assess the situation realistically.* 大人だから，あなたはその状況を現実的に判断できる. ■ ADJ 形容詞 Something such as a goal or target that is **realistic** is one that you can sensibly expect to achieve (目標などが) 実際的な 妥当な ❑ *A more realistic figure is 11 million.* もっと妥当な数は1千百万だ. ■ ADJ 形容詞 You say that a painting, story, or movie is **realistic** when the people and things in it are like people and things in real life. 写実的な，リアルな ❑ *...extraordinarily realistic paintings of Indians.* 驚くほどリアルなインディアンたちを描いた絵 ●**re|al|is|ti|cal|ly** ADV 副詞 写実的に ❑ *The film starts off realistically and then develops into a ridiculous fantasy.* その映画は写実的に始まるが，そこからばかげた空想に発展する.
→ see **art, fantasy**

Word Partnership	*realistic* は次の語句と使われる:
V.	be realistic ■
ADV.	more realistic, very realistic ■ – ■
N.	realistic **assessment**, realistic **expectations**, realistic **view**, realistic **goals** ■

re|al|is|ti|cal|ly /ríəlɪstɪkli/ ■ ADV 副詞 You use **realistically** when you want to emphasize that what you are saying is true, even though you would prefer it not to be true. 現実的に [EMPHASIS 強調] [ADV with cl] ❑ *Realistically, there is never one right answer.* 現実には，正しい答えなど決してないのだ. ■ → see also **realistic**

Word Link	*real ≈ actual* : *reality, realize, really*

re|al|ity /ríælɪti/ (**realities**) ■ N-UNCOUNT 不可算名詞 You use **reality** to refer to real things or the real nature of things rather than imagined, invented, or theoretical ideas. 現実，実物 ❑ *Fiction and reality were increasingly blurred.* 虚構と現実の境界がますますぼやけてきた. ■ → see also **virtual reality** ■ N-COUNT 可算名詞 **The reality of** a situation is the truth about it, especially when it is unpleasant or difficult to deal with. 真実 ❑ *...the harsh reality of top international competition.* 第1線の国際競争の厳しい真実 ■ N-SING 単数名詞 You say that something has become a **reality** when it actually exists or is actually happening. 実在，事実 ❑ *...the whole procedure that made this book become a reality.* この本を実際に世に送り出した行程のすべて ■ PHRASE 句 You can use **in reality** to introduce a statement about the real nature of something, when it contrasts with something incorrect that has just been described. 実際には ❑ *He came across as streetwise, but in reality he was not.* 彼は世慣れた印象を与えたが，実際はそうではなかった.
→ see **fantasy**

Word Partnership	*reality* は次の語句と使われる:
ADJ.	virtual reality ■
V.	distort reality ■
	become a reality ■
N.	reality **of life**, reality **of war** ■
PREP.	in reality ■

re|al|ity TV N-UNCOUNT 不可算名詞 **Reality TV** is a type of television programming that aims to show how ordinary people behave in everyday life, or in situations, often created by the program makers, which are intended to represent everyday life. リアリティーテレビ番組 ❑ *"Storm Warning" is really just typical voyeuristic reality TV.* 『暴風雨警報』はまさに典型的なのぞき見趣味のリアリティーテレビ番組だ.

re|al|iz|able /ríəlaɪzəbᵊl/ ■ ADJ 形容詞 If your hopes or aims are **realizable**, there is a possibility that the things that you want to happen will happen. 現実可能な [FORMAL 形式ばった] ❑ *...the reasonless assumption that one's dreams and desires were realizable.* 人の夢や願望は実現可能だったという筋の通らない仮定 ■ ADJ 形容詞 **Realizable** wealth is money that can be easily obtained by selling something. 換金可能な [FORMAL 形式ばった] ❑ *In many cases this realizable wealth is not realized during the lifetime of the home owner.* 多くの場合，この換金可能な財産は家屋の所有者の存命中には換金されない.

re|al|ize /ríəlaɪz/ (**realizes, realizing, realized**) ■ V-T/V-I 他動詞/自動詞 If you **realize** that something is true, you become aware of that fact or understand it. (事実を) 悟る ❑ *As soon as we realized something was wrong, we moved the children away.* 何かがおかしいと気づくや否や，私たちは子供たちを避難させた. ❑ *People don't realize how serious this recession has actually been.* みんなこの不景気がどれだ

け深刻なものかに気づいてないんだ. ●**re|ali|za|tion** /ríəlɪzeɪʃᵊn/ (**realizations**) N-VAR 可変性名詞 認識，理解 ❑ *There is now a growing realization that things cannot go on like this for much longer.* 今や，こんな事態が長く続くはずがないという認識がだんだん広がりつつある. ■ V-T 他動詞 [usu passive] If your hopes, desires, or fears **are realized**, the things that you hope for, desire, or fear actually happen. (願望・懸念が) 実現する ❑ *All his worst fears were realized.* 彼が恐れていた最悪のことがすべて現実となった. ●**re|ali|za|tion** N-UNCOUNT 不可算名詞 実現 ❑ *In Kravis's venomous tone he recognized the realization of his worst fears.* クラヴィスの悪意に満ちた声の調子から，彼は恐れていた最悪の事態が現実となったことを悟った. ■ V-T 他動詞 When someone **realizes** a design or an idea, they make or organize something based on that design or idea. (デザイン・アイデアを) 形にする [FORMAL 形式ばった] ❑ *I knew the technique that I would have to create in order to realize that structure.* 私はその建築物を建てるためにどんな技術を開発しなければならないかを知っていた. ■ V-T 他動詞 If someone or something **realizes** their potential, they do everything they are capable of doing, because they have been given the opportunity to do so. (可能性を) 実現する ❑ *The support systems to enable women to realize their potential at work are seriously inadequate.* 女性が仕事場で自分の潜在能力を発揮できるよう支援する制度はひどく不十分だ. ■ V-T 他動詞 If something **realizes** a particular amount of money when it is sold, that amount of money is paid for it. (価格で) 売れる [FORMAL 形式ばった] ❑ *A selection of correspondence from P.G. Wodehouse realized 2,000 dollars.* P. G. ウッドハウスの書簡の束が2千ドルで売れた. ●**re|ali|za|tion** N-VAR 可変性名詞 売却 ❑ *...a total cash realization of about $23 million.* 総額約2千3百万ドルの現金での売却

Thesaurus	*realize* また次を参照:
V.	pick up, see, understand ■

Word Partnership	*realize* は次の語句と使われる:
V.	come to realize, make *someone* realize ■
	begin to realize, fail to realize ■ ■
ADV.	suddenly realize ■
	finally realize, fully realize ■ ■
N.	realize a dream ■
	realize your potential ■

real life N-UNCOUNT 不可算名詞 If something happens **in real life**, it actually happens and is not just in a story or in someone's imagination. 実生活，現実 ❑ *In real life men like Richard Gere don't marry hookers.* 現実の世界では，リチャード・ギアのような男性が売春婦と結婚したりしない. ● ADJ 形容詞 **Real life** is also an adjective. 現実の，実生活の [ADJ n] ❑ *...a real-life horror story.* 実際にあった怖い話

re|allo|cate /ríæləkeɪt/ (**reallocates, reallocating, reallocated**) V-T 他動詞 When organizations **reallocate** money or resources, they decide to change the way they spend the money or use the resources. (資金・資材などを) 再配分する 再配置する ❑ *...a cost-cutting program to reallocate people and resources within the company.* 社内で社員と資材を再配置する経費削減計画

re|al|ly /ríəli/ ■ ADV 副詞 You can use **really** to emphasize a statement. (強調して) 本当に [SPOKEN 口語, EMPHASIS 強調] ❑ *I'm very sorry. I really am.* ごめんなさい. 本当にごめんなさい. ■ ADV 副詞 You can use **really** to emphasize an adjective or adverb. (形容詞・副詞を強調) とても [EMPHASIS 強調] [ADV adj/adv] ❑ *It was really good.* それはとてもよかった. ■ ADV 副詞 You use **really** when you are discussing the real facts about something, in contrast to the ones someone wants you to believe. 実際には，実は ❑ *My father didn't really love her.* 父は本当は彼女を愛していなかった. ■ ADV 副詞 People use **really** in questions and negative statements when they want you to answer "no." 本気で (質問・否定形で) [EMPHASIS 強調] [ADV before v] ❑ *Do you really think he would be that stupid?* あなたは彼がそんなにばかだと本気で思っているか. ■ ADV 副詞 If you refer to a time when something **really** begins to happen, you are emphasizing that it starts to happen at that time to a much greater extent and much more seriously than before. 確かに [EMPHASIS 強調] [ADV before v] ❑ *That's when the pressure really started.* それが確かに圧力がひどくなり始めた時だ. ■ ADV 副詞 People sometimes use **really** to slightly reduce the force of a negative statement. (部分否定で) あまり それほど [SPOKEN 口語, VAGUENESS あいまいさ] ❑ *I'm not really surprised.* そんなに驚いてないよ. ■ CONVENTION 慣習表現 You can say **really** to express surprise or disbelief at what someone has said. (驚き・不信を表して) 本当？ うそ！ [SPOKEN 口語, FEELINGS 感情] ❑ *"We discovered it was totally the wrong decision." — "Really?"* 「私たちはそれは完全に間違った決定だということを発見したの」「嘘でしょ！」

Note that **really** and **actually** are both used to emphasize statements. You use **really** in conversation to emphasize something that you are saying. ❏ *I really think he's sick.* Note that when **really** is used in a negative sentence, its position in relation to the verb affects the meaning. For instance, if you say "**I really don't like Richard,**" with **really** in front of the verb, you are emphasizing how much you dislike Richard. However, if you say "**I don't really like Richard,**" with **really** coming after the negative, you are still saying that you dislike Richard, but the feeling is not particularly strong. When you use **really** in front of an adjective or adverb, it has a similar meaning to **very**. ❏ *This is really serious.* **Actually** is used to emphasize what is true or genuine in a situation, often when this is surprising, or a contrast with what has just been said. ❏ *All the characters in the novel actually existed... He actually began to cry.* It can also be used to be precise or to correct someone. ❏ *No one was actually drunk...We couldn't actually see the garden.*

realm /rɛlm/ (realms) ■ N-COUNT 可算名詞 You can use **realm** to refer to any area of activity, interest, or thought. (活動・興味などの) 分野 領域 [FORMAL 形式ばった] ❏ *...the realm of politics.* 政治学の分野 ☑ N-COUNT 可算名詞 A **realm** is a country that has a king or queen. 王国 [FORMAL 形式ばった] ❏ *Defense of the realm is crucial.* 王国の防衛はきわめて重要だ.

real prop|er|ty N-UNCOUNT 不可算名詞 **Real property** is property in the form of land and buildings, rather than personal possessions. 不動産 [AM 米国英語] ❏ *...the owner or tenant of a piece of real property.* 1つの不動産の所有者または借屋人

real-time ADJ 形容詞 **Real-time** processing is a type of computer programming or data processing in which the information received is processed by the computer almost immediately. (データ処理が) リアルタイムの 同時の [COMPUTING コンピューティング] [ADJ n] ❏ *...real-time language translations.* リアルタイムの言語翻訳

Real|tor /rɪəltər, -tɔr/ (Realtors) also **realtor** N-COUNT 可算名詞 商標 A **Realtor** is a person whose job is to sell houses, buildings, and land, and who is a member of the National Association of Realtors. 不動産業者 [AM 米国英語, TRADEMARK] ❏ *When the Realtor showed us this house, we knew we wanted it right way.* 不動産業者がこの家を見せてくれたとき, 私たちはそれが自分たちの求めていた家だとただちに分かった.

real world N-SING 単数名詞 If you talk about **the real world**, you are referring to the world and life in general, in contrast to a particular person's own life, experience, and ideas, which may seem untypical and unrealistic. 現実の世界 ❏ *When they eventually leave the school they will be totally ill-equipped to deal with the real world.* 彼らが最終的に学校を離れる時, 現実に対処する心構えはまったくできていないだろう.

reap /rip/ (reaps, reaping, reaped) V-T 他動詞 If you **reap** the benefits or the rewards of something, you enjoy the good things that happen as a result of it. (利益を) 得る (ほうびを) 受ける ❏ *You'll soon begin to reap the benefits of being fitter.* あなたはじきにいっそう健康であることの利益を得始めるでしょう.

re|appear /riəpɪər/ (reappears, reappearing, reappeared) V-I 自動詞 When people or things **reappear**, they return again after they have been away or out of sight for some time. 再び現れる ❏ *Thirty seconds later she reappeared and beckoned them forward.* 30秒後に彼女は再び現れて, 彼らを前へ招いた.

re|appear|ance /riəpɪərəns/ (reappearances) N-COUNT 可算名詞 The **reappearance** of someone or something is their return after they have been away or out of sight for some time. 再出現 ❏ *His sudden reappearance must have been a shock.* 彼の突然の再出現はショックだったに違いない.

rear /rɪər/ (rears, rearing, reared) ■ N-SING 単数名詞 The **rear** of something such as a building or vehicle is the back part of it. (建物・乗り物の) 後方 後ろ ❏ *He settled back in the rear of the taxi.* 彼はタクシーの後部にもたれて座った. ● ADJ 形容詞 **Rear** is also an adjective. 後方の, 後ろの [ADJ n] ❏ *Manufacturers have been obliged to fit rear seat belts in all new cars.* 製造業者はすべての新車の後部座席にシートベルトを取り付けるよう義務づけられている. ☑ N-SING 単数名詞 If you are at the **rear** of a moving line of people, you are the last person in it. (列の) 最後尾 [FORMAL 形式ばった] ❏ *Musicians played at the front and rear of the procession.* 音楽家たちは行列の最前列と最後尾で演奏した. ☒ N-COUNT 可算名詞 Your **rear** is the part of your body that you sit on. しり, 殿部 (でんぶ) [INFORMAL くだけた] ❏ *I saw him pat a waitress on her rear.* 私は彼がウェイトレスのおしりをなでるのを見た. ◪ V-T 他動詞 If you **rear** children, you take care of them until they are old enough to take care of themselves. (子供を) 育てる 養う ❏ *She reared sixteen children, six her own and ten her husband's.* 彼女は16人の子供たちを育てた. 6人は彼女自身の子供で10人は夫の子供だった. ◧ V-T 他動詞 If you **rear** a young animal, you keep and take care of it until it is old enough to be used for work or food, or until it can look after itself. (動物を) 飼育する

❏ *She spends a lot of time rearing animals.* 彼女は動物の飼育に多くの時間を費やしている. ◨ V-I 自動詞 When a horse **rears**, it moves the front part of its body upward, so that its front legs are high in the air and it is standing on its back legs. (馬が) 後ろ足で立つ ❏ *The horse reared and threw off its rider.* 馬は後ろ足立ちになり, 騎手を振り落とした. ◪ PHRASE 句 If a person or vehicle is **bringing up the rear**, they are the last person or vehicle in a moving line of them. 最後尾につく, しんがりを務める ❏ *...police motorcyclists bringing up the rear of the procession.* 行列のしんがりを務めるオートバイの警察官

re|arrange /riəreɪndʒ/ (rearranges, rearranging, rearranged) ■ V-T 他動詞 If you **rearrange** things, you change the way in which they are organized or ordered. 配置を換える ❏ *When she returned, she found Malcolm had rearranged all her furniture.* 彼女が帰って来た時, マルコムが彼女の家具をすべて配置換えしたのに気づいた. ☑ V-T 他動詞 If you **rearrange** a meeting or an appointment, you arrange for it to take place at a different time from that originally intended. (会合・約束などの) 日程を変更する ❏ *You may cancel or rearrange the appointment.* 予約をキャンセルまたは変更してもよい.

re|arrange|ment /riəreɪndʒmənt/ (rearrangements) N-VAR 可変性名詞 A **rearrangement** is a change in the way that something is arranged or organized. 配置換え, 日程変更 ❏ *...a rearrangement of the job structure.* 職業構造の再編成

rear|view mir|ror /rɪərvyu/ (rearview mirrors) N-COUNT 可算名詞 Inside a car, the **rearview mirror** is the mirror that enables you to see the traffic behind when you are driving. バック・ミラー

rea|son /rizn/ (reasons, reasoning, reasoned) ■ N-COUNT 可算名詞 The **reason for** something is a fact or situation which explains why it happens or what causes it to happen. 起こる重要なことにはすべて理由がある. ❏ *There is a reason for every important thing that happens.* 起こる重要なことにはすべて理由がある. ☑ N-UNCOUNT 不可算名詞 If you say that you have **reason** to believe something or **to** have a particular emotion, you mean that you have evidence for your belief or there is a definite cause of your feeling. 根拠, 証拠 ❏ *They had reason to believe there could be trouble.* 彼らは問題が起こる可能性があると信じる根拠があった. ☒ N-UNCOUNT 不可算名詞 The ability that people have to think and to make sensible judgments can be referred to as **reason**. 理性 ❏ *...a conflict between emotion and reason.* 感情と理性の葛藤 ◪ V-T 他動詞 If you **reason that** something is true, you decide that it is true after thinking carefully about all the facts. (検討して) 判断する ❏ *I reasoned that changing my diet would lower my cholesterol level.* 私は食事を変えることでコレステロール値が下がると判断した. ◧ → see also **reasoned, reasoning** ◨ PHRASE 句 If one thing happens **by reason of** another, it happens because of it. ~という理由で, ~のために [FORMAL 形式ばった] ❏ *The boss retains enormous influence by reason of his position.* 社長はその地位ゆえに多大な影響力を持ち続けている. ◩ PHRASE 句 If you try to make someone **listen to reason**, you try to persuade them to listen to sensible arguments and be influenced by them. 分別ある話に耳を傾ける, 理性的に考える ❏ *The company's top executives had refused to listen to reason.* その会社の経営者たちは道理に耳を傾けようとしていなかった. ◪ PHRASE 句 If you say that something happened or was done **for no reason**, **for no good reason**, or **for no reason at all**, you mean that there was no obvious reason why it happened or was done. 理由もなく ❏ *The guards, he said, would punch them for no reason.* 警備員たちは何の理由もなく彼らを殴る, と彼は話した. ◫ PHRASE 句 If you say that you will do anything **within reason**, you mean that you will do anything that is fair or reasonable and not too extreme. 常識の範囲で ❏ *I will take any job that comes along, within reason.* 私は, 常識の範囲で, 来る仕事はすべて引き受けるつもりだ. ◮ to **see reason** → see **see** ◰ **it stands to reason** → see **stand**

▸ **reason with** PHRASAL VERB 句動詞 If you try to **reason with** someone, you try to persuade them to do or accept something by using sensible arguments. ~を説得する ❏ *He's impossible. I can't reason with him.* 彼はまったく手に負えない. 彼を説得するなんて私にはできない.

Thesaurus	reason また次を参照:
N.	apology, argument, defense, excuse, explanation ■
	analysis, comprehension, intellect, logic ☒

Word Partnership	reason は次の語句と使われる:
ADJ.	**main** reason, **major** reason, **obvious** reason, **only** reason, **primary** reason, **real** reason, **same** reason, **simple** reason ■
	compelling reason, **good** reason, **sufficient** reason ■ ☑

rea|son|able /rizənəbl/ ■ ADJ 形容詞 If you think that someone is fair and sensible you can say that they are **reasonable**. 道理をわきまえた, 分別のある ❏ *He's a reasonable sort of person.* 彼は道理をわきまえた種類の人だ. ● **rea|son|ably** /rizənəbli/ ADV 副詞

道理をわきまえて ❏"I'm sorry, Andrew," she said reasonably. 「アンドリュー、ごめんなさい」と彼女は分別よく言った. ●**rea|son|able|ness** N-UNCOUNT 不可算名詞 道理をわきまえていること ❏"I can understand how you feel," Dan said with great reasonableness. 「きみの気持ちは分かるよ」とダンはとても分別よく言った. **2** ADJ 形容詞 If you say that a decision or action is **reasonable**, you mean that it is fair and sensible. (決断・行動が) 妥当な 分別のある ❏...a perfectly reasonable decision. まったく理にかなった決定 **3** ADJ 形容詞 If you say that an expectation or explanation is **reasonable**, you mean that there are good reasons why it may be correct. (期待・説明が) 筋の通った もっともな ❏It seems reasonable to expect rapid urban growth. 急速な都市の発展を期待するのはもっともなことに思われる. ●**rea|son|ably** ADV 副詞 [ADV with v] 当然 ❏You can reasonably expect your goods to arrive within six to eight weeks. 商品が6から8週間のうちに届くことは当然期待してよい. **4** ADJ 形容詞 If you say that the price of something is **reasonable**, you mean that it is fair and not too high. (値段が) まあまあの 手ごろな ❏You get a good meal for a reasonable price. 手ごろな値段でいい食事が食べられる. ●**rea|son|ably** ADV 副詞 手ごろに ❏...reasonably priced accommodations. 手ごろな値段の宿 **5** ADJ 形容詞 You can use **reasonable** to describe something that is fairly good, but not very good. (質などが) まあまあの そこそこ ❏The boy answered him in reasonable French. その少年はそこそこのフランス語で彼に答えた. ●**rea|son|ably** ADV 副詞 [ADV adj/adv] まあまあ ❏I can dance reasonably well. ダンスはまあまあ上手なほうだ. **6** ADJ 形容詞 A **reasonable** amount of something is a fairly large amount of it. (量が) かなりの ❏They will need a reasonable amount of desk area and good light. 彼らにはかなりの机周りのスペースと明るい照明が必要になるだろう. ●**rea|son|ably** ADV 副詞 [ADV adj/adv] かなり ❏From now on events moved reasonably quickly. 今しがたからさき行事はかなりのテンポで進んだ.

Thesaurus	reasonable また次を参照:
ADJ.	level-headed, rational **1** – **3**
	acceptable, fair, sensible; (ant.) unreasonable **2**
	likely, probable, right **3**
	fair, inexpensive **4**

Word Partnership	reasonable は次の語句と使われる:
N.	reasonable **person 1**
	beyond a reasonable **doubt**, reasonable **expectation**, reasonable **explanation 3**
	reasonable **cost**, reasonable **price**, reasonable **rates 4**
	reasonable **amount 6**
	reasonable **chance**, reasonable **time 5**

rea|soned /ríːzənd/ ADJ 形容詞 A **reasoned** discussion or argument is based on sensible reasons, rather than on an appeal to people's emotions. 筋の通った, 道理に基づいた [APPROVAL 賛成] ❏Their opinions are not based on reasoned argument. 彼らの意見は論理的な議論に基づいたものではない.

rea|son|ing /ríːzənɪŋ/ (reasonings) N-VAR 可変性名詞 **Reasoning** is the process by which you reach a conclusion after thinking about all the facts. (結論に至るまでの) 思考 論証 ❏...the reasoning behind the decision. その結論の背後にある論拠
→ see **philosophy**

re|as|sert /ríːəsɜrt/ (reasserts, reasserting, reasserted) **1** V-T 他動詞 If you **reassert** your control or authority, you make it clear that you are still in a position of power, or you strengthen the power that you had. (支配・権力を) 再主張する ❏...the government's continuing effort to reassert its control in the region. その地方の支配権を再主張しようとする政府の引き続く努力 **2** V-T 他動詞 If something such as an idea or habit **reasserts itself**, it becomes noticeable again. (考え方・習慣を) 盛り返させる ❏His sense of humor was beginning to reassert itself. 彼のユーモアのセンスが再び注目を集め始めていた.

re|as|sess /ríːəsɛs/ (reassesses, reassessing, reassessed) V-T 他動詞 If you **reassess** something, you think about it and decide whether you need to change your opinion about it. 見直す, 再評価する ❏I will reassess the situation when I get home. 家に帰ったら状況を見直す.

re|as|sess|ment /ríːəsɛsmənt/ (reassessments) N-VAR 可変性名詞 If you make a **reassessment** of something, you think about it and decide whether you need to change your opinion about it. 再評価, 再査定 ❏There's a total reassessment of what people want out of life. 人々が人生に何を求めるかについての全体的な見直しがある.

re|as|sur|ance /ríːəʃʊərəns/ (reassurances) **1** N-UNCOUNT 不可算名詞 If someone needs **reassurance**, they are very worried and need someone to help them stop worrying by saying kind or helpful things. 安心, 保証 ❏She needed reassurance that she belonged somewhere. 彼女は自分がどこかに属しているという安心感を必要としていた. **2** N-COUNT 可算名詞 **Reassurances** are things

that you say to help people stop worrying about something. 安心させる言葉 ❏...reassurances that pesticides are not harmful. 殺虫剤が無害であるという保証の言葉

re|as|sure /ríːəʃʊər/ (reassures, reassuring, reassured) V-T 他動詞 If you **reassure** someone, you say or do things to make them stop worrying about something. 安心させる ❏I tried to reassure her, "Don't worry about it. We won't let it happen again." 私は彼女を安心させようとした. 「心配しないで. もう2度とそんなことが起きないようにするから」

Word Partnership	reassure は次の語句と使われる:
N.	reassure **citizens**, reassure **customers**, reassure **investors**, reassure **the public**
V.	seek to **reassure**, try to **reassure**

re|as|sured /ríːəʃʊərd/ ADJ 形容詞 If you feel **reassured**, you feel less worried about something, usually because you have received help or advice. 安心した ❏I feel much more reassured when I've had a physical exam. 私は健康診断を受けたときはもっとずっと安心する.

re|as|sur|ing /ríːəʃʊərɪŋ/ ADJ 形容詞 If someone's words or actions **reassuring**, they make you feel less worried about something. 安心させる, 心強い ❏It was reassuring to hear John's familiar voice. ジョンの聞きなれた声を聞くと心強かった. ●**re|as|sur|ing|ly** ADV 副詞 安心させるように ❏"It's okay now," he said reassuringly. 「もう大丈夫だよ」と彼は安心させるように言った.

re|bate /ríːbeɪt/ (rebates) N-COUNT 可算名詞 A **rebate** is an amount of money which is returned to you after you have paid for goods or services or after you have paid tax or rent. 払い戻し, 割り戻し ❏Citicorp will guarantee its credit card customers a rebate on a number of products. シティコープはクレジットカード利用客に対して, 多くの製品の割り戻しを保証する予定だ.

re|bel (rebels, rebelling, rebelled)

The noun is pronounced /rɛbəl/. The verb is pronounced /rɪbɛl/.

名詞は /rɛbəl/ と発音される. 動詞は /rɪbɛl/ と発音される.

1 N-COUNT 可算名詞 **Rebels** are people who are fighting against their own country's army in order to change the political system there. (政治体制への) 反逆者 ❏...fighting between rebels and government forces. 反乱軍と政府軍の戦い **2** N-COUNT 可算名詞 Politicians who oppose some of their own party's policies can be referred to as **rebels**. (政党内の) 反対派 ❏The rebels want another 1% cut in interest rates. 反対派は金利をあと1パーセント下げることを望んでいる. **3** V-I 自動詞 If politicians **rebel** against one of their own party's policies, they show that they oppose it. (自党の政策に) 反対する ❏Voters rebelled against high property taxes. 有権者は高い資産税に反対した. **4** N-COUNT 可算名詞 You can say that someone is a **rebel** if you think that they behave differently from other people and have rejected the values of society or of their parents. 反逆児 ❏She had been a rebel at school. 彼女は以前は学校の反逆児だった. **5** V-I 自動詞 When someone **rebels**, they start to behave differently from other people and reject the values of society or of their parents. (社会・親に) 反抗する 反発する ❏The child who rebels is unlikely to be overlooked. 反抗する子供は大目に見られにくい.

re|bel|lion /rɪbɛlyən/ (rebellions) **1** N-VAR 可変性名詞 A **rebellion** is a violent organized action by a large group of people who are trying to change their country's political system. 反乱, 暴動 ❏The government soon put down the rebellion. 政府はすぐに反乱を鎮圧した. **2** N-VAR 可変性名詞 A situation in which people show their opposition to the way things have been done in the past can be referred to as **rebellion**. 反抗, 反逆 ❏Women are waging a quiet rebellion against the traditional roles their mothers have played. 女性たちは母親たちが担ってきた従来の役割に静かに反抗している.

re|bel|lious /rɪbɛlyəs/ **1** ADJ 形容詞 If you think someone behaves in an unacceptable way and does not do what they are told, you can say they are **rebellious**. 反抗的な ❏...a rebellious teenager. 反抗的な10代の若者 ●**re|bel|lious|ness** N-UNCOUNT 不可算名詞 反抗性 ❏...the normal rebelliousness of youth. 若者の典型的な反抗性 **2** ADJ 形容詞 [ADJ n] A **rebellious** group of people is a group involved in taking violent action against the rulers of their own country, usually in order to change the system of government there. 反乱を起こした ❏The rebellious officers, having seized the radio station, broadcast the news of the overthrow of the monarchy. 反乱軍の将校たちは, ラジオ放送局を占拠して, きみ主制打倒のニュースを放送した.

re|birth /ríːbɜrθ/ N-UNCOUNT 不可算名詞 You can refer to a change that leads to a new period of growth and improvement in something as its **rebirth**. 再生, 復興 ❏...the rebirth of democracy in Latin America. ラテンアメリカにおける民主主義の復興

re|bound /rɪbaʊnd/ (rebounds, rebounding, rebounded) **1** V-I 自動詞 If something **rebounds** from a solid surface, it bounces

or springs back from it. 跳ね返る ❑His shot in the 21st minute of the game rebounded from a post. 試合開始から21分目に彼のシュートはゴール・ポストから跳ね返った. ❷ V-I 自動詞 If an action or situation **rebounds on** you, it has an unpleasant effect on you, especially when this effect was intended for someone else. (悪い事が) 跳ね返る ❑Mia realized her trick had rebounded on her. ミアは自分の策略が自分に跳ね返ってきたことを悟った.

re|brand /ribrǽnd/ (rebrands, rebranding, rebranded) V-T 他動詞 To **rebrand** a product or organization means to present it to the public in a new way, for example by changing its name or appearance. (商品・企業の) イメージを変える [BUSINESS 実業] ❑There are plans to rebrand many Texas stores. 多くのテキサス店のイメージ変更計画がある.

re|brand|ing /ribrǽndɪŋ/ N-UNCOUNT 不可算名詞 **Rebranding** is the process of giving a product or an organization a new image, in order to make it more attractive or successful. (商品・組織の) イメージ変更 [BUSINESS 実業] ❑A complete rebranding of the school is expected within two years. その学校の完全なイメージ変更は2年以内に行われると予想されている.

re|buff /rɪbʌ́f/ (rebuffs, rebuffing, rebuffed) V-T 他動詞 If you **rebuff** someone or **rebuff** a suggestion that they make, you refuse to do what they suggest. 拒絶する ❑His proposals have already been rebuffed by the governor. 彼の提案はすでに知事によって拒否されている. ● N-VAR 可変性名詞 **Rebuff** is also a noun. 拒絶, 拒否 ❑The results of the poll dealt a humiliating rebuff to Mr. Jones. 世論調査の結果は屈辱的なほどの拒否をジョーンズ氏に示している.

re|build /ri͟bɪ́ld/ (rebuilds, rebuilding, rebuilt) ❶ V-T 他動詞 When people **rebuild** something such as a building or a city, they build it again after it has been damaged or destroyed. (建物・街を) 再建する ❑They say they will stay to rebuild their homes rather than retreat to refugee camps. 彼らは難民キャンプに逃れるよりも, 自分たちの家を再建するために残ると言っている. ❑The old south grandstand must be rebuilt. 古い南側の特別観覧席は建て直さなければならない. ❷ V-T 他動詞 When people **rebuild** something such as an institution, a system, or an aspect of their lives, they take action to bring it back to its previous condition. (制度などを) 再建する 立て直す ❑The president's message was that everyone would have to work hard together to rebuild the economy. 大統領のメッセージは, みんなが経済再建のために共に一生懸命働かなくてはならないというものだった.

re|buke /rɪbyuːk/ (rebukes, rebuking, rebuked) V-T 他動詞 If you **rebuke** someone, you speak severely to them because they have said or done something that you do not approve of. 叱責する, 強く非難する [FORMAL 形式ばった] ❑The president rebuked the House and Senate for not passing those bills within 100 days. 大統領は下院と上院がそれらの法案を100日以内に通過させなかったことを強く非難した. ● N-VAR 可変性名詞 **Rebuke** is also a noun. 叱責, 非難 ❑His statements drew a stinging rebuke from the chairman. 彼の発言は議長から厳しい叱責を買った.

re|call (recalls, recalling, recalled)

> The verb is pronounced /rɪkɔ́l/. The noun is pronounced /ri͟kɔl/.
>
> 動詞は /rɪkɔ́l/ と発音される. 名詞は /ri͟kɔl/ と発音される.

❶ V-T/V-I 他動詞/自動詞 When you **recall** something, you remember it and tell others about it. 思い出す, 思い出を語る ❑Henderson recalled he first met Pollard during a business trip to Washington. ヘンダーソンはワシントンへの出張中にポラードと初めて出会ったことを思い出した. ❑His mother later recalled: "He used to stay up until two o'clock in the morning playing these war games." 彼の母は後で思い出を語った. 「彼はよくこうした戦争ゲームをしながら午前2時まで起きていたわ」 "What was his name?" —"I don't recall." 「彼はなんていう名前だったの?」 「覚えてないなあ」 ❷ N-UNCOUNT 不可算名詞 **Recall** is the ability to remember something that has happened in the past or the act of remembering it. 記憶力 ❑He had a good memory, and total recall of her spoken words. 彼は記憶力がよく, 彼女の言った言葉をすべて覚えていた. ❸ V-T 他動詞 If you **are recalled** to your home, country, or the place where you work, you are ordered to return there. (場所へ) 呼び戻す ❑The U. S. envoy was recalled to Washington. 米国の公使はワシントンへ召還された. ● N-SING 単数名詞 **Recall** is also a noun. 召還 ❑The recall of Ambassador Alan Green is a public signal of America's concern. アラン・グリーン大使の召還はアメリカの懸念を公に表している. ❹ V-T 他動詞 If a company **recalls** a product, it asks the stores or the people who have bought that product to return it because there is something wrong with it. (不良製品を) 回収する リコールする ❑The company said it was recalling one of its drugs and had stopped selling two others. その会社は薬品の1つを回収中で, 他の2薬品は販売を中止しています. ● N-COUNT 可算名詞 **Recall** is also a noun. リコール, 欠陥商品の回収 ❑...a recall of the laptops due to defective supply parts. 欠陥のある供給部品に起因するラップトップ型パソコンの回収

re|cap /ri͟kæp/ (recaps, recapping, recapped) V-T/V-I 他動詞/自動詞 You can say that you are going to **recap** when you want to

draw people's attention to the fact that you are going to repeat the main points of an explanation, argument, or description, as a summary of it. 要点を繰り返す, 要約する ❑To recap briefly, the agreement was rejected 10 days ago. 手短にまとめると, その協定は10日前に拒否された. ❑Can you recap the points included in the proposal? その提案に含まれている点を繰り返してくれませんか. ● N-SING 単数名詞 **Recap** is also a noun. 繰り返し, 要約 ❑Each report starts with a recap of how we did versus our projections. 各報告書は我々の予測に対して実績はどうだったかを要約することから始まっている.

re|capi|tal|ize /rikǽpɪtᵊlaɪz/ (recapitalizes, recapitalizing, recapitalized) V-T/V-I 他動詞/自動詞 If a company **recapitalizes**, it changes the way it manages its financial affairs, for example by borrowing money or reissuing shares. 資本構成を改める [AM 米国英語 BUSINESS 実業] ❑Mr. Warnock resigned as the company abandoned a plan to recapitalize. 会社が資本再構成の計画を断念するとウォーノック氏は辞任した. ❑He plans to recapitalize the insurance fund. 彼は保険資金の資本を再構成するつもりである. ● **re|capi|tali|za|tion** /rikǽpɪtᵊlaɪzeɪʃᵊn/ (recapitalizations) N-COUNT 可算名詞 資本再構成 ❑A substantial thrust of the effort of management is to explore a recapitalization of the company. 経営側の努力は会社の資本再構成の道を探ることに多く注がれている.

re|ca|pitu|late /rikǝpɪ́tʃᵊleɪt/ (recapitulates, recapitulating, recapitulated) V-T/V-I 他動詞/自動詞 You can say that you are going to **recapitulate** the main points of an explanation, argument, or description when you want to draw attention to the fact that you are going to repeat the most important points as a summary. 要点を繰り返す, 要約する ❑Let's just recapitulate the essential points. 重要な点をちょっとまとめてみましょう. ❑It will be put up for sale under the terms already communicated to you, which, to recapitulate, call for a very minimum of publicity. これはあなたにすでにご連絡した条件, つまり, 公表はとにかく最小限に抑えるという条件で売りに出されます. ● **re|ca|pitu|la|tion** /rikǝpɪ́tʃᵊleɪʃᵊn/ N-SING 単数名詞 要約 ❑Chapter nine provides a valuable recapitulation of the material already presented. 第9章にはすでに示した資料を役に立つように要約してある.

re|cap|ture /rikǽptʃᵊr/ (recaptures, recapturing, recaptured) ❶ V-T 他動詞 When soldiers **recapture** an area of land or a place, they gain control of it again from an opposing army who had taken it from them. 奪還する ❑They said the bodies were found when rebels recaptured the area. それらの死体は反乱軍がその地域を奪還した時に見つかったそうだ. ● N-SING 単数名詞 **Recapture** is also a noun. 奪還 ❑...an offensive to be launched for the recapture of the city. その都市を奪還するためにしかける攻撃 ❷ V-T 他動詞 When people **recapture** something that they have lost to a competitor, they get it back again. 取り戻す ❑I believe that he would be the best possibility to recapture the center vote in the upcoming election. 次の選挙で穏健派の票を取り戻すために彼が最も有望だと私は思う. ❸ V-T 他動詞 To **recapture** a person or animal which has escaped from somewhere means to catch them again. 再び捕らえる ❑Police have recaptured Alan Lewis, who escaped from a jail cell in Boston. 警察はボストンの刑務所の監房から脱出したアラン・ルイスを再逮捕した. ● N-SING 単数名詞 **Recapture** is also a noun. 再逮捕 ❑...the recapture of a renegade police chief in Panama. 裏切り者の警察署長のパナマでの再逮捕

re|cede /risi͟d/ (recedes, receding, receded) ❶ V-I 自動詞 If something **recedes** from you, it moves away. 退く, 遠ざかる ❑Luke's footsteps receded into the night. ルークの足音は夜に消えていった. ❑As she receded he waved goodbye. 彼女が遠のくにつれて彼はさよならと手を振った. ❷ V-I 自動詞 When something such as a quality, problem, or illness **recedes**, it becomes weaker, smaller, or less intense. 薄らぐ, 減退する ❑Just as I started to think that I was never going to get well, the illness began to recede. 私はもう治らないのではないだろうかと思い始めたちょうどそのころ, 病気が良くなり始めた. ❸ V-I 自動詞 If a man's hair starts to **recede**, it no longer grows on the front of his head. 生え際が後退する ❑...a youngish man with dark hair just beginning to recede. 髪の毛が黒っぽくってちょっと生え際が後退し始めた, どちらかというと若い男性

re|ceipt /risi͟t/ (receipts) ❶ N-COUNT 可算名詞 A **receipt** is a piece of paper that you get from someone as proof that they have received money or goods from you. 領収書, レシート ❑I wrote her a receipt for the money. 私はその金の領収書を彼女に書いた. ❷ N-PLURAL 複数名詞 **Receipts** are the amount of money received during a particular period, for example by a store or theater. 受領高 ❑He was tallying the day's receipts. 彼はその日の受領高を計算しているところだった. ❸ N-UNCOUNT 不可算名詞 The **receipt** of something is the act of receiving it. 受け取ること [FORMAL 形式ばった] ❑Goods should be supplied within 28 days after the receipt of your order. 品物は注文を受け取ってから28日以内にお届けできるはずです. ❹ PHRASE 句 If you are **in receipt** of something, you have received it or you receive it regularly. 受け取って [FORMAL 形式ばった] ❑We are taking action, having been in receipt of a letter from him. 彼から手紙を受け取り, 我々は措置を講じているところです.

r

re|ceive /rɪsiːv/ (receives, receiving, received) **1** V-T 他動詞 When you **receive** something, you get it after someone gives it to you or sends it to you. 受け取る ❏ *They will receive their awards at a ceremony in Stockholm.* 彼らはストックホルムの式典で賞を受け取るでしょう. **2** V-T 他動詞 You can use **receive** to say that certain kinds of things happen to someone. For example if they are injured, you can say that they **received** an injury. 受ける, 負う ❏ *He received more of the blame than anyone when the plan failed to work.* その計画が失敗したとき彼は誰にも増して非難を受けました. **3** V-T 他動詞 When you **receive** a visitor or a guest, you greet them. 迎える ❏ *The following evening the hotel was again receiving guests.* その翌晩そのホテルは再び宿泊客を迎えていた. **4** V-T 他動詞 If you say that something **is received** in a particular way, you mean that people react to it in that way. 受け入れる [usu passive] ❏ *The resolution had been received with great disappointment within the PLO.* PLOの内部ではその決議は大きな失望で受け取られた. **5** V-T 他動詞 When a radio or television **receives** signals that are being transmitted, it picks them up and converts them into sound or pictures. 受信する ❏ *The reception was a little faint but clear enough for him to receive the signal.* 受信状態は少し弱かったが, その信号を受信するには彼には十分明瞭だった. **6** PHRASE 句 If you **are on the receiving end** or **at the receiving end** of something unpleasant, you are the person that it happens to. 受ける側 ❏ *You saw hate in their eyes and you were on the receiving end of that hate.* あなたは彼らが憎しみに満ちた目をしているのに気づいたが, その憎しみは自分に向けられていた.

Thesaurus   receive また次を参照:

v.   accept, collect, get, take; (ant.) give, present **1**   entertain, take in, welcome **3**

---

re|ceiv|er /rɪsiːvər/ (receivers) **1** N-COUNT 可算名詞 A telephone's **receiver** is the part that you hold near to your ear and speak into. 受話器 ❏ *She picked up the receiver and started to dial.* 彼女は受話器を持ち上げてダイヤルし始めた. **2** N-COUNT 可算名詞 A **receiver** is the part of a radio or television that picks up signals and converts them into sound or pictures. レシーバー ❏ *Auto-tuning VHF receivers are now common in cars.* 今では自動車に自動調整VHFレシーバーはよくあります. **3** N-COUNT 可算名詞 The **receiver** is someone who is appointed by a court of law to manage the affairs of a business, usually when it is facing financial failure. 管財人 [BUSINESS 実業] [usu "the" N] ❏ *...the receivers handling his bankruptcy case.* 彼の破産の件を取り扱っている管財人
→ see **radio, television, tennis**

re|ceiv|er|ship /rɪsiːvərʃɪp/ (receiverships) N-VAR 可変性名詞 If a company goes **into receivership**, it faces financial failure and the administration of its business is handled by the receiver. 管財人による管理 [BUSINESS 実業] ❏ *The company has now gone into receivership with debts of several million.* 数百万の債務がありその会社は今では管財人の管理を受けている.

re|cent /riːsənt/ ADJ 形容詞 A **recent** event or period of time happened only a short while ago. 最近の ❏ *In the most recent attack, one man was shot dead and two others were wounded.* 最も最近の攻撃では男性1名が射殺され, ほか2名が負傷しました.

re|cent|ly /riːsəntli/ ADV 副詞 If you have done something **recently** or if something happened **recently**, it happened only a short time ago. 最近 ❏ *The bank recently opened a branch in Miami.* その銀行は最近マイアミに支店を開いた.

re|cep|tion /rɪsɛpʃən/ (receptions) **1** N-COUNT 可算名詞 A **reception** is a formal party which is given to welcome someone or to celebrate a special event. 歓迎会, レセプション ❏ *At the reception they served smoked salmon.* 歓迎会ではスモークサーモンが出た. **2** N-SING 単数名詞 **Reception** in a hotel is the desk or office that books rooms for people and answers their questions. フロント ["the" N, oft N n, also "at" N] ❏ *Have him bring a car around to reception.* 彼にフロントに車を付けさせなさい. **3** N-SING 単数名詞 **Reception** in an office or hospital is the place where people's appointments and questions are dealt with. 受付 ["the" N, oft N n, also "at" N] ❏ *Wait at reception for me.* 受付で私を待っていなさい. **4** N-COUNT 可算名詞 If someone or something has a particular kind of **reception**, that is the way that people react to them. 歓迎 ❏ *Mr. Mandela was given a warm reception in Washington.* マンデラ氏はワシントンで温かい歓迎を受けた. **5** N-UNCOUNT 不可算名詞 If you get good **reception** from your radio or television, the sound or picture is clear because the signal is strong. If the **reception** is poor, the sound or picture is unclear because the signal is weak. 受信 ❏ *...poor radio reception.* ラジオの悪い受信状況
→ see **wedding**

re|cep|tion|ist /rɪsɛpʃənɪst/ (receptionists) **1** N-COUNT 可算名詞 In an office or hospital, the **receptionist** is the person whose job is to answer the telephone, arrange appointments, and deal with people when they first arrive. 受付係 **2** N-COUNT 可算名詞 In a hotel, the **receptionist** is the person whose job is to reserve rooms for people and answer their questions. フロント係

re|cep|tive /rɪsɛptɪv/ **1** ADJ 形容詞 Someone who is **receptive** to new ideas or suggestions is prepared to consider them or accept them. よく受け入れて ❏ *The voters had seemed receptive to his ideas.* 有権者は彼の意見をよく受け入れたようだった. **2** ADJ 形容詞 If someone who is ill is **receptive to** treatment, they start to get better when they are given treatment. 受容性のある [v-link ADJ "to" n] ❏ *For those patients who are not receptive to treatment, the chance for improvement is small.* 治療に受容性のない患者たちが良くなる可能性は低い.

re|cess /rɪsɛs, riːsɛs/ (recesses, recessing, recessed) **1** N COUNT 可算名詞 A **recess** is a break between the periods of work of an official body such as a committee, a court of law, or a government. 休憩, 休廷 [also "in/from" N] ❏ *The conference broke for a recess, but the 10-minute break stretched to two hours.* 会議は休憩に入りましたが, 10分の休憩の予定が2時間に伸びました. **2** N-VAR 可変性名詞 In a school, **recess** is the period of time between classes when the children are allowed to play. 休み時間 [AM 米国英語] ❏ *She decides to visit the school library during recess.* 彼女は休み時間に学校の図書館に行くことにする. ❏ *...the children's first morning recess.* 子供たちの朝の最初の休み時間 **3** V-I 自動詞 When formal meetings or court cases **recess**, they stop temporarily. 休会する [FORMAL 形式ばった] ❏ *The hearings have now recessed for dinner.* 公聴会は食事のため現在休会している. **4** N-COUNT 可算名詞 In a room, a **recess** is part of a wall which is built further back than the rest of the wall. Recesses are often used as a place to put furniture such as shelves. 壁のへこんだところ ❏ *...a discreet recess next to a fireplace.* 暖炉の横の目立たない壁のへこみ **5** N-COUNT 可算名詞 The **recesses** of something or somewhere are the parts of it that are hard to see because light does not reach them or they are hidden from view. 奥まったところ ❏ *He emerged from the dark recesses of the garage.* 彼はガレージの暗い奥から出てきた. **6** N-COUNT 可算名詞 If you refer to the **recesses** of someone's mind or soul, you are referring to thoughts or feelings they have which are hidden or difficult to describe. 奥底 ❏ *There was something in the darker recesses of his unconscious that was troubling him.* 彼の無意識のさらに暗い奥まったところに彼を悩ませている何かがあった.

re|ces|sion /rɪsɛʃən/ (recessions) N-VAR 可変性名詞 A **recession** is a period when the economy of a country is doing badly, for example because industry is producing less and more people are becoming unemployed. 不景気 ❏ *The oil price increases sent Europe into deep recession.* 原油の価格の上昇のため欧州は深刻な不況に陥りました.

reci|pe /rɛsɪpi/ (recipes) **1** N-COUNT 名詞 A **recipe** is a list of ingredients and a set of instructions that tell you how to cook something. レシピ, 調理法 ❏ *...a traditional recipe for buttermilk biscuits.* バターミルクビスケットの伝統的なレシピ **2** N-SING 単数名詞 If you say that something is **a recipe for** a particular situation, you mean that it is likely to result in that situation. 秘訣, 招く結果となるもの ❏ *Large-scale inflation is a recipe for disaster.* 大規模なインフレは大惨事を招く結果となる.

re|cipi|ent /rɪsɪpiənt/ (recipients) N-COUNT 可算名詞 The **recipient** of something is the person who receives it. 受取り人 [FORMAL 形式ばった] ❏ *...the largest recipient of U.S. foreign aid.* 米国対外援助の最大の被援助国
→ see **donor**

re|cip|ro|cal /rɪsɪprəkəl/ ADJ 形容詞 A **reciprocal** action or agreement involves two people or groups who do the same thing to each other or agree to help each another in a similar way. 相互の, 交換的な [FORMAL 形式ばった] ❏ *They expected a reciprocal gesture before more hostages could be freed.* さらに人質が解放される前に, 交換条件の意思表示があることを予期した.

re|cip|ro|cate /rɪsɪprəkeɪt/ (reciprocates, reciprocating, reciprocated) V-T/V-I 他動詞/自動詞 If your feelings or actions toward someone **are reciprocated**, the other person feels or behaves in the same way toward you as you have felt or behaved toward them. 報いる, 返礼する ❏ *I would like to think the way I treat people is reciprocated.* 私は人の取り扱い方には相応の報いがあると思いたい. ❏ *He needs these people to fulfill his ambitions and reciprocates by bringing out the best in each of them.* 彼が野望を満たすためにはこの人たちが必要で, 彼らのそれぞれの長所を伸ばすことで彼らにお返しをしている.

re|cit|al /rɪsaɪtəl/ (recitals) N-COUNT 可算名詞 A **recital** is a performance of music or poetry, usually given by one person. 独奏会, 独唱会 ❏ *...a solo recital by the harpsichordist Maggie Cole.* ハープシコード奏者マギー・コールの独奏会

re|cite /rɪsaɪt/ (recites, reciting, recited) **1** V-T 他動詞 When someone **recites** a poem or other piece of writing, they say it aloud after they have learned it. 暗唱する ❏ *They recited poetry to one another.* 彼らはお互いに詩を暗唱し合った. **2** V-T 他動詞 If you **recite** something such as a list, you say it aloud. 朗読する ❏ *All he could do was recite a list of government failings.* 彼は政治的失敗のリストを読み上げることしかできなかった.

reck|less /rɛklɪs/ ADJ 形容詞 If you say that someone is **reckless**, you mean that they act in a way which shows that they do not care about danger or the effect their behavior will have on other people. 向こう見ずな □ *He is charged with reckless driving.* 彼は無謀運転で告発された. ● **reck|less|ly** ADV 副詞 向こう見ずに □ *He was leaning recklessly out of the open window.* 彼は向こう見ずにも開いた窓から身を乗り出していた. ● **reck|less|ness** N-UNCOUNT 不可算名詞 無謀さ □ *He felt a surge of recklessness.* 彼は向う見ずな気持ちがこみ上げてくるのを感じた.

reck|on /rɛkən/ (**reckons, reckoning, reckoned**) **1** V-T 他動詞 If you **reckon** that something is true, you think that it is true. 思う [INFORMAL くだけた] □ *Toni reckoned that it must be about three o'clock.* トニーは3時ぐらいに違いないと思った. **2** V-T 他動詞 If something **is reckoned** to be a particular figure, it is calculated to be roughly that amount. 計算する [usu passive] □ *The market is reckoned to be worth $1.4 billion in the U.S. alone.* その市場は米国だけでも14億ドルの価値があると見積もられている. ▶ **reckon with 1** PHRASAL VERB 句動詞 If you say that you had not **reckoned with** something, you mean that you had not expected it and so were not prepared for it. 〜を考慮に入れる、〜を当てにする [with brd-neg] □ *Gary had not reckoned with the strength of Sally's feelings for him.* ゲーリーはサリーがそこまで彼のことを思っているとは考えてもいなかった. **2** PHRASE 句 If you say that there is someone or something **to be reckoned with**, you mean that they must be dealt with and it will be difficult. 〜を入れるべき □ *This act was a signal to his victim's friends that he was someone to be reckoned with.* この行為により彼にやられた犠牲者の友人たちに、彼は侮れない男であることを知らしめた.

reck|on|ing /rɛkənɪŋ/ (**reckonings**) N-VAR 可変性名詞 Someone's **reckoning** is a calculation they make about something, especially a calculation that is not very exact. 推算、推測 □ *By my reckoning we were seven or eight miles from the campground.* 私の推測では私たちはキャンプ場から7マイルか8マイル離れたところにいた.

re|claim /rɪkleɪm/ (**reclaims, reclaiming, reclaimed**) **1** V-T 他動詞 If you **reclaim** something that you have lost or that has been taken away from you, you succeed in getting it back. 取り戻す □ *In 1986, they got the right to reclaim South African citizenship.* 1986年に彼らは南アフリカの市民権を取り戻す権利を得た. **2** V-T 他動詞 If you **reclaim** an amount of money, for example tax that you have paid, you claim it back. 返還要求をする □ *The good news for the industry was that investors don't seem to be in any hurry to reclaim their money.* 産業界にとってよいニュースは、投資家たちが資金の返還要求を少しも急いでいるようすがないことだ. **3** V-T 他動詞 When people **reclaim** land, they make it suitable for a purpose such as farming or building, for example by draining it or by building a barrier against the sea. 干拓する □ *The Netherlands has been reclaiming farmland from water.* オランダは海を干拓して農場を得ている. **4** V-T 他動詞 If a piece of land that was used for farming or building **is reclaimed by** a desert, forest, or the sea, it turns back into desert, forest, or sea. 戻す [usu passive] □ *The diamond towns are gradually being reclaimed by the desert.* ダイアモンドの町々は徐々に砂漠に戻っている.

Word Link *clin ≈ leaning : decline, incline, recline*

re|cline /rɪklaɪn/ (**reclines, reclining, reclined**) **1** V-I 自動詞 If you **recline on** something, you sit or lie on it with the upper part of your body supported at an angle. もたれる、横になる □ *She proceeded to recline on a chaise longue.* 彼女は続いて長いすに横になった. **2** V-T/V-I 他動詞/自動詞 When a seat **reclines** or when you **recline** it, you lower the back so that it is more comfortable to sit in. 背が後ろに倒れる、座席の背もたれを倒す □ *Air France first-class seats recline almost like beds.* エールフランスのファーストクラスの座席はベッドのように背もたれが倒れる. □ *Ramesh had reclined his seat and was lying back smoking.* ラメッシュは彼の座席の背もたれを倒し、タバコを吸いながら横になっていた.

re|cluse /rɪklus, rɛklus/ (**recluses**) N-COUNT 可算名詞 A **recluse** is a person who lives alone and deliberately avoids other people. 世捨て人 □ *His widow became a virtual recluse for the remainder of her life.* 彼の未亡人は残された日々をほとんど世捨て人のように過ごした.

re|clu|sive /rɪklusɪv/ ADJ 形容詞 A **reclusive** person or animal lives alone and deliberately avoids the company of others. 孤独を好む □ *All that neighbors knew about the reclusive man was that he had lived in the building for about 20 years.* 隣人たちがその孤独を好む男について知っていることと言えば、彼はその建物に20年ぐらい住んでいるということだけだった.

rec|og|ni|tion /rɛkəgnɪʃən/ N-UNCOUNT 不可算名詞 **Recognition** is the act of recognizing someone or identifying something when you see it. 見覚え、認知 □ *He searched for a sign of recognition on her face, but there was none.* 彼に見覚えがあるようなしるしが彼女の顔に出ていないか彼は探ったが、全くなかった. **2** N-UNCOUNT 不可算名詞 **Recognition of** something is an understanding and acceptance of it. 認知、認識 □ *Recognition*

of the importance of career development is increasing. 経歴開発が大切だということがより広く認識されてきている. **3** N-UNCOUNT 不可算名詞 When a government gives diplomatic **recognition** to another country, they officially accept that its status is valid. 承認 □ *His government did not receive full recognition by the United States until July.* 7月まで彼の政府は米国に完全には承認されていなかった. **4** N-UNCOUNT 不可算名詞 When a person receives **recognition** for the things that they have done, people acknowledge the value or skill of their work. 認めること □ *At last, her father's work has received popular recognition.* とうとう彼女の父親の業績が一般の人々に認められました. **5** PHRASE 句 If something is done **in recognition of** someone's achievements, it is done as a way of showing official appreciation of them. 〜を認めて □ *...a small plaque in recognition of her contribution to the university.* 大学への彼女の貢献を表彰する小さな記念銘板

Word Partnership *recognition* は次の語句と使われる:

V.	**deserve** recognition, **receive** recognition **2** – **4**
ADJ.	**formal** recognition, **full** recognition **3**
	growing recognition, **special** recognition **4**

rec|og|niz|able /rɛkəgnaɪzəbəl/ ADJ 形容詞 If something can be easily recognized or identified, you can say that it is easily **recognizable**. 認識できる □ *The vault was opened and the body found to be well preserved, his features easily recognizable.* 地下納骨所が開けられ、遺体の保存状態は良好と分かり、容貌が簡単に確認可能であった.

Word Link *cogn ≈ knowing : cognitive, recognize, unrecognizable*

rec|og|nize /rɛkəgnaɪz/ (**recognizes, recognizing, recognized**) **1** V-T 他動詞 If you **recognize** someone or something, you know who that person is or what that thing is. わかる、見覚えがある [no cont] □ *The receptionist recognized him at once.* 受付の人にはすぐに彼がわかった. **2** V-T 他動詞 If someone says that they **recognize** something, they acknowledge that it exists or that it is true. 認める [no cont] □ *I recognize my own shortcomings.* 私は自分の欠点を承知している. **3** V-T 他動詞 If people or organizations **recognize** something as valid, they officially accept it or approve of it. 認める □ *Many doctors recognize homeopathy as a legitimate form of medicine.* 多くの医師がホメオパシーを正当な種類の医学として認めている. □ *France is on the point of recognizing the independence of the Baltic States.* フランスはバルト諸国の独立をまさに承認しようとしている. **4** V-T 他動詞 When people **recognize** the work that someone has done, they show their appreciation of it, often by giving that person an award of some kind. 評価する □ *The army recognized him as an outstandingly able engineer.* 陸軍は彼をずば抜けて能力のある工兵として評価した.

Thesaurus *recognize* また次を参照:

V.	acknowledge, identify, know, notice; (ant.) ignore **1** accept, believe, understand **2 3**

re|coil (**recoils, recoiling, recoiled**)

The verb is pronounced /rɪkɔɪl/. The noun is pronounced /rikɔɪl/.

動詞は /rɪkɔɪl/ と発音される. 名詞は /rikɔɪl/ と発音される.

1 V-I 自動詞 If something makes you **recoil**, you move your body quickly away from it because it frightens, offends, or hurts you. 後ずさりする、ひるむ □ *For a moment I thought he was going to kiss me. I recoiled in horror.* 一瞬彼が私にキスしようとしてると思い、ぞっとして後ずさりした. ● N-UNCOUNT 不可算名詞 **Recoil** is also a noun. 後ずさり □ *...his small body jerking in recoil from the volume of his shouting.* 彼の叫び声の大きさにひるんでけいれんしている彼の小さな体 **2** V-I 自動詞 If you **recoil from** doing something or **recoil at** the idea of something, you refuse to do it or accept it because you dislike it so much. しり込みする □ *People used to recoil from the idea of getting into debt.* 以前は人は借金するという考えにしり込みしたものだった.

rec|ol|lect /rɛkəlɛkt/ (**recollects, recollecting, recollected**) V-T 他動詞 If you **recollect** something, you remember it. 思い出す □ *Ramona spoke with warmth when she recollected the doctor who used to be at the community hospital.* ラモーナは地元の病院に以前いた医師を思い出して温かく話しかけた.

rec|ol|lec|tion /rɛkəlɛkʃən/ (**recollections**) N-VAR 可変性名詞 If you have a **recollection** of something, you remember it. 記憶 □ *Pat has vivid recollections of the trip, and remembers some of the frightening aspects I had forgotten.* パットはその旅行のことをありありと覚えていて、私が忘れていた恐ろしい場面まで記憶している.

rec|om|mend /rɛkəmɛnd/ (**recommends, recommending, recommended**) **1** V-T 他動詞 If someone **recommends** a person or thing to you, they suggest that you would find that person or thing good or useful. 推薦する □ *I just spent a vacation there and would recommend it to anyone.* 私はちょうどそこで休暇を過ごしたとこ

ろで, 誰にでも推薦しますよ. □ *"You're a good worker,"* he told him. *"I'll recommend you for a promotion."* 「きみは良く働く」と彼は彼に言った. 「昇進するようにきみを推薦しよう」 ● **rec|om|mend|ed** ADJ 形容詞 お勧めの □ *Though ten years old, this book is highly recommended.* この本は出版から10年経つが, とてもお勧めだ. **2** V-T 他動詞 If you **recommend** that something is done, you suggest that it should be done. 勧告する □ *The judge recommended that he serve 20 years in prison.* 裁判官は彼は懲役20年の刑に服すよう勧告した. □ *We strongly recommend reporting the incident to the police.* 我々はこの出来事を警察に報告することを強く勧告する. **3** V-T 他動詞 If something or someone has a particular quality to **recommend** them, that quality makes them attractive or gives them an advantage over similar things or people. 魅力的にする □ *La Cucina restaurant has much to recommend it.* ラ・クチーナ食堂はとても魅力がある.

Thesaurus   recommend また次を参照:

V.	endorse, put forward, suggest **1**
	advise, urge **2**

Word Partnership   recommend は次の語句と使われる:

N.	**doctors** recommend, **experts** recommend **1 2**
	recommend **changes 2**
ADV.	**highly** recommend, **strongly** recommend **1 - 3**

rec|om|men|da|tion /rɛkəmɛndeɪʃ°n/ (**recommendations**) **1** N-VAR 可変性名詞 The **recommendations** of a person or a committee are their suggestions or advice on what is the best thing to do. 勧告 □ *The committee's recommendations are unlikely to be made public.* 委員会の勧告は公表されそうにありません. **2** N-VAR 可変性名詞 A **recommendation** of something is the suggestion that someone should have or use it because it is good. 推薦 □ *The best way of finding a lawyer is through personal recommendation.* 弁護士を見つける最もいい方法は個人的な推薦によるものだ.

rec|om|pense /rɛkəmpɛns/ (**recompenses, recompensing, recompensed**) **1** N-UNCOUNT 不可算名詞 If you are given something, usually money, **in recompense**, you are given it as a reward or because you have suffered. 償い [FORMAL 形式ばった] □ *He demands no financial recompense for his troubles.* 彼は自分が迷惑を受けたことに対する金銭的な賠償を求めていない. **2** V-T 他動詞 If you **recompense** someone **for** their efforts or their loss, you give them something, usually money, as a payment or reward. 償う [FORMAL 形式ばった] □ *If they succeed in court, they will be fully recompensed for their loss.* 法廷で彼らが勝てば, 彼らの損失に対して完全に償ってもらえるだろう.

rec|on|cile /rɛkənsaɪl/ (**reconciles, reconciling, reconciled**) **1** V-T 他動詞 If you **reconcile** two beliefs, facts, or demands that seem to be opposed or completely different, you find a way in which they can both be true or both be successful. 和解させる □ *It's difficult to reconcile the demands of my job and the desire to be a good father.* 仕事の負担と良い父親でありたいと思う気持ちをうまく両立させるのは難しい. **2** V-RECIP-PASSIVE 受動態相互動詞 If you **are reconciled with** someone, you become friendly with them again after a quarrel or disagreement. 仲直りさせる □ *He never believed he and Susan would be reconciled.* 彼は彼とスーザンが仲直りするだろうとは決して思っていなかった. **3** V-T 他動詞 If you **reconcile** two people, you make them become friends again after a quarrel or disagreement. 和解させる □ *...my attempt to reconcile him with Toby.* 彼をトービーと仲直りさせる私の試み **4** V-T 他動詞 If you **reconcile yourself to** an unpleasant situation, you accept it, although it does not make you happy to do so. 甘んじさせる □ *She had reconciled herself to never seeing him again.* 彼女はあきらめて彼にはもう2度と会わないことにした. ● **rec|on|ciled** ADJ 形容詞 [v-link ADJ "to" n/-ing] あきらめた □ *She felt, if not grateful for her own situation, at least a little more reconciled to it.* 彼女は自分の置かれている状況に感謝はしなかったが, 少なくとももう少しはあきらめがついたと感じた.

rec|on|cilia|tion /rɛkənsɪlieɪʃ°n/ (**reconciliations**) **1** N-VAR 可変性名詞 **Reconciliation** between two people or countries who have quarreled is the process of their becoming friends again. A **reconciliation** is an instance of this. 和解 □ *...an appeal for reconciliation between Catholics and Protestants.* カトリック教と新教の和解の呼びかけ **2** N-SING 単数名詞 The **reconciliation** of two beliefs, facts, or demands that seem to be opposed is the process of finding a way in which they can both be true or both be successful. 調和 □ *...the ideal of democracy based upon a reconciliation of the values of equality and liberty.* 平等と自由の重要性の調和に基づいた民主主義の理想

re|con|nais|sance /rɪkɒnɪsəns/ N-UNCOUNT 不可算名詞 **Reconnaissance** is the activity of obtaining military information about a place by sending soldiers or planes there, or by the use of satellites. 偵察 □ *The helicopter was returning from a reconnaissance mission.* ヘリコプターは偵察任務から戻ってくるところでした.

re|con|sid|er /rikənsɪdər/ (**reconsiders, reconsidering, reconsidered**) V-T/V-I 他動詞/自動詞 If you **reconsider** a decision or opinion, you think about it and try to decide whether it should be changed. 考え直す, 再考する □ *We want you to reconsider your decision to resign from the board.* あなたが理事会を辞任するという決断を考え直してほしい. □ *If at the end of two years you still feel the same, we will reconsider.* 2年たった後でもあなたの気が変わらないのなら, その時改めて話し合おう.

re|con|struct /rikənstrʌkt/ (**reconstructs, reconstructing, reconstructed**) **1** V-T 他動詞 If you **reconstruct** something that has been destroyed or badly damaged, you build it and make it work again. 建て直す, 再建する □ *The government must reconstruct the shattered economy.* 政府は壊滅状態の経済を再建しなければならない. **2** V-T 他動詞 To **reconstruct** a system or policy means to change it so that it works in a different way. 立て直す, 再建する □ *She actually wanted to reconstruct the state and transform society.* 彼女は現実に国を建て直し社会を変えたいと思っていました. **3** V-T 他動詞 If you **reconstruct** an event that happened in the past, you try to get a complete understanding of it by combining a lot of small pieces of information. 再現する □ *He began to reconstruct the events of December 21, 1988, when flight 103 disappeared.* 103便が姿を消した1988年12月21日の出来事を彼は再現し始めた.

re|con|struc|tion /rikənstrʌkʃ°n/ (**reconstructions**) **1** N-UNCOUNT 不可算名詞 **Reconstruction** is the process of making a country normal again after a war, for example by making the economy stronger and by replacing buildings that have been damaged. 復興 □ *...America's part in the postwar reconstruction of Germany.* 戦後のドイツの復興における米国の役割 **2** N-UNCOUNT 不可算名詞 The **reconstruction** of a building, structure, or road is the activity of building it again, because it has been damaged. 再建, 復旧 □ *Work began on the reconstruction of the road.* 道路の復旧作業が始まった. **3** N-COUNT 可算名詞 The **reconstruction** of a crime or event is when people try to understand or show exactly what happened, often by acting it out. 復元 □ *Mrs. Kerr was too upset to take part in a reconstruction of her ordeal.* カー夫人は動揺しすぎていて彼女の苦しい体験を再現するのには参加できなかった.

re|con|vene /rikənvin/ (**reconvenes, reconvening, reconvened**) V-I 自動詞 If a legislature, court, or conference **reconvenes** or if someone **reconvenes** it, it meets again after a break. 再召集する, 再び集まる □ *The conference might reconvene after its opening session.* 会議は開会式の後, 再び招集がかかるかもしれません.

rec|ord (**records, recording, recorded**)

The noun is pronounced /rɛkərd/. The verb is pronounced /rɪkɔrd/.

名詞は /rɛkərd/ と発音される. 動詞は /rɪkɔrd/ と発音される.

1 N-COUNT 可算名詞 If you keep a **record of** something, you keep a written account or photographs of it so that it can be referred to later. 記録 □ *Keep a record of all the payments.* すべての支払いの記録を残しなさい. **2** V-T 他動詞 If you **record** a piece of information or an event, you write it down, photograph it, or put it into a computer so that in the future people can refer to it. 記録する, 書き留める □ *Her letters record the domestic and social details of diplomatic life in China.* 彼女の手紙には中国での外交官の生活の家庭や社交の詳細が書き留めてある. **3** V-T 他動詞 If you **record** something such as a speech or performance, you make a sound or film so that it can be heard or seen again later. 録音する, 録画する □ *There is nothing to stop viewers from recording the films on videotape.* 視聴者が映画をビデオ録画するのをさえぎるものは何もない. **4** V-T 他動詞 If a musician or performer **records** a piece of music or a television or radio show, they perform it so that it can be put onto CD, tape, or film. 吹き込む, 録音する □ *It took the musicians two and a half days to record their soundtrack for the film.* 音楽家たちが映画のサウンドトラックを吹き込むのには2日半かかった. **5** N-COUNT 可算名詞 A **record** is a round, flat piece of black plastic on which sound, especially music, is stored, and which can be played on a record player. You can also refer to the music stored on this piece of plastic as a **record**. レコード □ *This is one of my favorite records.* これは私のお気に入りのレコードの1つだ. **6** V-T 他動詞 If a dial or other measuring device **records** a certain measurement or value, it shows that measurement or value. 表示する, 示す □ *The test records the electrical activity of the brain.* この検査は脳の電気的活動を示す. **7** N-COUNT 可算名詞 A **record** is the best result that has ever been achieved in a particular sport or activity, for example the fastest time, the farthest distance, or the greatest number of victories. 記録 □ *Roger Kingdom set the world record of 12.92 seconds.* ロジャー・キングダムは12.92秒の世界記録を出した. **8** ADJ 形容詞 You use **record** to say that something is higher, lower, better, or worse than has ever been achieved before. 記録的な [ADJ n] □ *Profits were at record levels.* 記録的な利益率だった. **9** N-COUNT 可算名詞 Someone's **record** is the facts that are known about their

achievements or character. 経歴 ❑ *His record reveals a tough streak.* 彼の経歴から彼には夕フな傾向があることがわかる. **10** N-COUNT 可算名詞 If someone has a criminal **record**, it is officially known that they have committed crimes in the past. 前科 ❑...*a heroin addict with a criminal record going back 15 years.* 15年前にさかのぼる前科のあるヘロイン中毒者 **11** → see also **recording**, **track record** **12** PHRASE 句 If you say that what you are going to say next is **for the record**, you mean that you are saying it publicly and officially and you want it to be written down and remembered. 記録に残すために ❑ *We're willing to state for the record that it has enormous value.* これには膨大な価値があることを記録に残すために私たちは喜んで言う用意があります. **13** PHRASE 句 If you give some information **for the record**, you give it in case people might find it useful at a later time, although it is not a very important part of what you are talking about. とりあえず言うが ❑ *For the record, most Moscow girls leave school at about 18.* とりあえず言っておくが, ほとんどのモスクワの女の子たちは18歳ぐらいで学校を卒業する. **14** PHRASE 句 If something that you say is **off the record**, you do not intend it to be considered as official, or published with your name attached to it. 公式には引用しないで, オフレコで ❑ *May I speak off the record?* オフレコで話して良いですか. **15** PHRASE 句 If you are **on record as** saying something, you have said it publicly and officially and it has been written down. 公表されて, 記録に残っている ❑ *The president is on record as saying that the increase in unemployment is "a price worth paying" to keep inflation down.* インフレが抑えられるなら失業率の上昇という「犠牲を払う価値がある」と大統領が発言したことが記録に残っている. **16** PHRASE 句 If you keep information **on record**, you write it down or store it in a computer so that it can be used later. 記録された ❑ *The practice is to keep on record any analysis of samples.* 慣例ではすべての試料の分析記録を残します.
→ see **diary**, **history**

re|cord|er /rɪkɔrdər/ (**recorders**) **1** N-COUNT 可算名詞 You can refer to a cassette recorder, a tape recorder, or a video recorder as a **recorder**. レコーダー, 録音機 ❑ *Rodney put the recorder on the desk top and pushed the play button.* ロドニーは机の上に録音機を置いて再生ボタンを押した. **2** → see also **tape recorder**, **video recorder** **3** N-VAR 可変性名詞 A **recorder** is a wooden or plastic musical instrument in the shape of a pipe. You play the recorder by blowing into the top of it and covering and uncovering the holes with your fingers. リコーダー **4** N-COUNT 可算名詞 A **recorder** is a machine or instrument that keeps a record of something, for example in an experiment or on a vehicle. 記録装置 ❑ *Data recorders also pinpoint mechanical faults rapidly, reducing repair times.* さらにこのデータ記録装置は機械の故障をすばやく突き止めて修理の時間を短縮する.

re|cord|ing /rɪkɔrdɪŋ/ (**recordings**) **1** N-COUNT 可算名詞 A **recording** of something is a record, CD, tape, or video of it. 録音, 録画 ❑...*a video recording of a police interview.* 警察の事情聴取のビデオ録画 **2** N-UNCOUNT 不可算名詞 **Recording** is the process of making records, CDs, tapes, or videos. レコーディング ❑...*the recording industry.* レコード産業

re|cord play|er (**record players**) N-COUNT 可算名詞 A **record player** is a machine on which you can play a record in order to listen to the music or other sounds on it. レコード・プレーヤー ❑ *His parents had no record player or television.* 彼の両親はレコード・プレーヤーもテレビも持っていなかった.

re|count (**recounts**, **recounting**, **recounted**)

The verb is pronounced /rɪkaʊnt/. The noun is pronounced /rikaʊnt/.
動詞は /rɪkaʊnt/ と発音される. 名詞は /rikaʊnt/ と発音される.

1 V-T 他動詞 If you **recount** a story or event, you tell or describe it to people. 物語る, 詳しく話す [FORMAL 形式ばった] ❑ *He then recounted the story of the interview for his first job.* 彼はその後の最初の仕事のインタビューの話を詳しく話した. **2** N-COUNT 可算名詞 A **recount** is a second count of votes in an election when the result is very close. 数え直し ❑ *She wanted a recount. She couldn't believe that I got more votes than she did.* 彼女は数え直しを希望した. 私のほうが彼女より得票が多かったとは彼女には信じられなかった.

re|coup /rɪkup/ (**recoups**, **recouping**, **recouped**) V-T 他動詞 If you **recoup** a sum of money that you have spent or lost, you get it back. 取り戻す ❑ *Insurance companies are trying to recoup their losses*

by increasing premiums. 保険会社は掛け金を値上げして損失を取り戻そうとしている.

re|course /rikɔrs/ N-UNCOUNT 不可算名詞 If you achieve something without **recourse to** a particular course of action, you succeed without carrying out that action. To have **recourse to** a particular course of action means to have to do that action in order to achieve something. 頼ること [FORMAL 形式ばった] ❑ *It enabled its members to settle their differences without recourse to war.* これにより加盟国間では戦争しないで意見の違いを解決することが可能になった.

re|cov|er /rɪkʌvər/ (**recovers**, **recovering**, **recovered**) **1** V-I 自動詞 When you **recover from** an illness or an injury, you become well again. 回復する ❑ *He is recovering from a knee injury.* 彼はひざの怪我から回復しかけている.

Recover is a fairly formal word. In conversation, you usually say that someone **gets better**. ❑ *Qualified nurses help patients get better more quickly.*

2 V-I 自動詞 If you **recover from** an unhappy or unpleasant experience, you stop being upset by it. 立ち直る ❑...*a tragedy from which he never fully recovered.* 彼が決して完全には立ち直らなかった悲惨な出来事 **3** V-I 自動詞 If something **recovers from** a period of weakness or difficulty, it improves or gets stronger again. 立ち直る, 挽回する ❑ *He recovered from a 4-2 deficit to reach the quarter-finals.* 彼は4対2で負けていたのを挽回し準々決勝に達した. **4** V-T 他動詞 If you **recover** something that has been lost or stolen, you find it or get it back. 取り戻す ❑ *Police raided five houses in Brooklyn and recovered stolen goods.* 警察はブルックリンで5軒の家を捜索して盗品を回収した. **5** V-T 他動詞 If you **recover** a mental or physical state, it comes back again. For example, if you **recover** consciousness, you become conscious again. 取り戻す, 元通りになる ❑ *She had a severe attack of asthma and it took an hour to recover her breath.* 彼女は重篤な喘息の発作に襲われ, 普通に呼吸ができるまで回復するのに1時間以上かかった. **6** V-T 他動詞 If you **recover** money that you have spent, invested, or lent to someone, you get the same amount back. 取り戻す ❑ *Legal action is being taken to recover the money.* その金を取り戻すために訴訟をしている.

re|cov|ery /rɪkʌvəri/ (**recoveries**) **1** N-VAR 可変性名詞 If a sick person makes a **recovery**, he or she becomes well again. 回復 ❑ *He made a remarkable recovery from a shin injury.* 彼はすねの怪我から目を見張るほど回復した. **2** N-VAR 可変性名詞 When there is a **recovery** in a country's economy, it improves. 回復 ❑ *Interest-rate cuts have failed to bring about economic recovery.* 金利の切り下げは経済の回復をもたらさなかった. **3** N-UNCOUNT 不可算名詞 You talk about the **recovery** of something when you get it back after it has been lost or stolen. 取り戻すこと ❑ *A substantial reward is being offered for the recovery of a painting by Turner.* ターナー作の絵画を取り戻すために多額の報酬が用意されている. **4** N-UNCOUNT 不可算名詞 You talk about the **recovery** of someone's physical or mental state when they return to this state. 取り戻すこと ❑...*the abrupt loss and recovery of consciousness.* 意識を突然失いそして取り戻すこと **5** PHRASE 句 If someone is **in recovery**, they are being given a course of treatment to help them recover from something such as a drug habit or mental illness. リハビリ治療中の ❑...*Carole, a compulsive pot smoker and alcoholic in recovery.* マリファナとアルコール中毒のリハビリ治療を受けているキャロル

re|cre|ate /rikrieɪt/ (**recreates**, **recreating**, **recreated**) V-T 他動詞 If you **recreate** something, you succeed in making it exist or seem to exist in a different time or place from its original time or place. 再現する ❑ *I am trying to recreate family life far from home.* 私は家から遠く離れたところで家族生活を再現しようとしています.

rec|rea|tion (**recreations**)

Pronounced /rɛkrieɪʃᵊn/ for meaning **1**. Pronounced /rikrieɪʃᵊn/ and hyphenated re|cre|a|tion for meaning **2**.
1 の意味では /rɛkrieɪʃᵊn/ と発音される. **2** の意味では /rikrieɪʃᵊn/ と発音されて, re|cre|a|tion とハイフンで結ばれる.

1 N-VAR 可変性名詞 **Recreation** consists of things that you do in your spare time to relax. 娯楽, 気晴らし ❑ *Saturday afternoon is for recreation and outings.* 土曜の午後は娯楽と外出の時間だ. **2** N-COUNT 可算名詞 A **recreation** of something is the process of making it exist or seem to exist again in a different time or place. 再現すること ❑ *They are planning to build a faithful recreation of the original frontier town.* 彼らは昔の辺境の町を忠実に再現したものを建てようと計画している.
→ see **park**

rec|rea|tion|al /ˌrɛkrieɪʃənəl/ ADJ 形容詞 **Recreational** means relating to things people do in their spare time to relax. 娯楽の □ ...parks and other recreational facilities. 公園その他の娯楽施設

rec|rea|tion|al drug (recreational drugs) N-COUNT 可算名詞 **Recreational drugs** are illegal drugs such as cannabis or cocaine that people take occasionally for enjoyment, especially when they are spending time socially with other people. 気晴らしのための麻薬 □ Society largely turns a blind eye to recreational drug use. 社会は気晴らしのために麻薬を使用することは見て見ぬふりをすることが多い.

re|crim|i|na|tion /rɪˌkrɪmɪneɪʃən/ (recriminations) N-UNCOUNT 不可算名詞 **Recriminations** are accusations that two people or groups make about each other. 非難をし返すこと [also N in pl] □ The bitter arguments and recriminations have finally ended the relationship. 辛らつな口論と非難のし合いの末結局別れた.

re|cruit /rɪkruːt/ (recruits, recruiting, recruited) ■ V-T 他動詞 If you **recruit** people for an organization, you select them and persuade them to join it or work for it. 募集する □ The police are trying to recruit more black and Hispanic officers. 警察は黒人やヒスパニック系の警官を募集し採用しようとしている. □ She set up her stand to recruit students to the Anarchist Association. 無政府主義者連合に学生を募集するために, 彼女は自分のスタンドを立てた. ●**re|cruit|ing** N-UNCOUNT 不可算名詞 募集すること □ A bomb exploded at an army recruiting office. 陸軍徴兵事務所で爆弾が爆発しました. ■ N-COUNT 可算名詞 A **recruit** is a person who has recently joined an organization or an army. 新兵, 新人 □ ...a new recruit to the LA Police Department. LA警察の新米

re|cruit|ment /rɪkruːtmənt/ N-UNCOUNT 不可算名詞 The **recruitment** of workers, soldiers, or members is the act or process of selecting them for an organization or army and persuading them to join. 募集 □ ...the examination system for the recruitment of civil servants. 公務員募集の試験制度

Word Link rect ≈ right, straight : correct, rectangle, rectify

rec|tan|gle /ˈrɛktæŋgəl/ (rectangles) N-COUNT 可算名詞 A **rectangle** is a four-sided shape whose corners are all ninety-degree angles. Each side of a rectangle is the same length as the one opposite to it. 長方形
→ see ratio, shape, volume

rec|tan|gu|lar /rɛktæŋgyələr/ ADJ 形容詞 Something that is **rectangular** is shaped like a rectangle. 長方形の □ ...a rectangular table. 長方形のテーブル

rec|ti|fy /ˈrɛktɪfaɪ/ (rectifies, rectifying, rectified) V-T 他動詞 If you **rectify** something that is wrong, you change it so that it becomes correct or satisfactory. 直す, 是正する □ Only an act of Congress could rectify the situation. その状態を是正するには議会で法を制定する必要があるでしょう.

re|cu|per|ate /rɪkuːpəreɪt/ (recuperates, recuperating, recuperated) V-I 自動詞 When you **recuperate**, you recover your health or strength after you have been ill or injured. 療養の □ I went away to the country to recuperate. 私は回復するために田舎に行った. ●**re|cu|pera|tion** /rɪkuːpəreɪʃən/ N-UNCOUNT 不可算名詞 回復 □ Leonard was very pleased with his powers of recuperation. レナードは自分の回復力にとても喜んでいた.

re|cur /rɪkɜːr/ (recurs, recurring, recurred) V-I 自動詞 If something **recurs**, it happens more than once. 繰り返される, 再発する □ ...a theme that was to recur frequently in his work. 彼の作品に頻繁に繰り返されるはずだった主題

re|cur|rence /rɪkɜːrəns/ (recurrences) N-VAR 可変性名詞 If there is a **recurrence** of something, it happens again. 再発 □ Police are out in force to prevent a recurrence of the violence. 警察は暴力の再発を防ぐため大挙出動している.

re|cur|rent /rɪkɜːrənt/ ADJ 形容詞 A **recurrent** event or feeling happens or is experienced more than once. 繰り返し起こる □ Race is a recurrent theme in the work. その作品の中では人種が主題として繰り返し取り上げられている.

re|cy|cle /riːsaɪkəl/ (recycles, recycling, recycled) V-T 他動詞 If you **recycle** things that have already been used, such as bottles or sheets of paper, you process them so that they can be used again. 再生利用する □ The objective would be to recycle 98 percent of domestic waste. 目標は一般廃棄物の98パーセントを再生利用することであろう. ●**re|cy|cling** N-UNCOUNT 不可算名詞 再生利用 □ ...a recycling plan. 再生利用計画
→ see dump, paper

> **Recycling** has become so common in North America that many communities have special procedures for sorting and collecting the trash. Glass, metal, paper and plastic can be separated and used again. In some places, residents must pay a fine if they do not recycle.

red /rɛd/ (reds, redder, reddest) ■ COLOR 色彩語 Something that is **red** is the color of blood or fire. 赤 □ ...a bunch of red roses.

赤いバラの花束 ■ ADJ 形容詞 If you say that someone's face is **red**, you mean that it is redder than its normal color, because they are embarrassed, angry, or out of breath. 赤い □ With a bright red face I was forced to admit that I had no real idea. 顔を真っ赤にして, 私にはしっかりした見当がつかないことを認めざるを得なかった. ■ ADJ 形容詞 You describe someone's hair as **red** when it is between red and brown in color. 赤毛の □ ...a girl with red hair. 赤毛の少女 ■ N-MASS 質量名詞 You can refer to red wine as **red**. 赤ワイン □ The spicy flavors in these dishes call for reds rather than whites. これらの料理は香辛料が効いているので白ワインより赤が向いている. ■ ADJ 形容詞 If a U.S. state is described as **red**, it means that the majority of its residents vote for the Republican Party in elections, especially in the presidential elections. 共和党支持者が過半数の □ ...policies that could guarantee her enough support in red states to win the White House in 2008. 2008年に彼女が米国大統領の職を勝ち取るのに十分な支持を共和党支持者が過半数の州で保障できるような政策 ■ PHRASE 句 If a person or company is **in the red** or if their bank account is **in the red**, they have spent more money than they have in their account and therefore they owe money to the bank. 赤字を出して □ The theater is $500,000 in the red. その劇場は50万ドルの赤字を出している. ■ PHRASE 句 If you **see red**, you suddenly become very angry. かっとなる □ I didn't mean to break his nose. I just saw red. 彼の鼻柱を折るつもりはなかったんだ. かっとなっただけだ.
→ see color, rainbow

red card (red cards) N-COUNT 可算名詞 In soccer, if a player is shown the **red card**, the referee holds up a red card to indicate that the player must leave the field for breaking the rules. レッドカード □ He was shown a red card for a rough tackle. 荒っぽいタックルをしたために彼はレッドカードを示された.

red|dish /ˈrɛdɪʃ/ ADJ 形容詞 **Reddish** means slightly red in color. 赤っぽい □ He had reddish brown hair. 彼は赤茶色の髪の毛をしていた.

re|deem /rɪdiːm/ (redeems, redeeming, redeemed) ■ V-T 他動詞 If you **redeem yourself** or your reputation, you do something that makes people have a good opinion of you again after you have behaved or performed badly. 取り戻す, 名誉を挽回する □ He realized the mistake he had made and wanted to redeem himself. 彼は犯した間違いに気づき名誉挽回したいと思った. ■ V-T 他動詞 When something **redeems** an unpleasant thing or situation, it prevents it from being completely bad. 救う □ Work is the way that people seek to redeem their lives from futility. 仕事は人が人生を無意味さから救おうとする方法である. ■ V-T 他動詞 If you **redeem** a debt or money that you have promised to someone, you pay money that you owe or that you promised to pay. 弁済する [FORMAL 形式ばった] □ The amount required to redeem the mortgage was $358,587. 住宅ローンを償還するのは358,587ドル必要だった. ■ V-T 他動詞 In religions such as Christianity, to **redeem** someone means to save them by freeing them from sin and evil. 救う, あがなう □ ...a new female spiritual force to redeem the world. 世界を救う新しい女性の霊能力

re|deem|able /rɪdiːməbəl/ ADJ 形容詞 If something is **redeemable**, it can be exchanged for a particular sum of money or for goods worth a particular sum. 換金できる, 商品に換えられる □ Their full catalog costs $5, redeemable against a first order. 彼らの総合カタログは5ドルで, それは初めて注文するときに商品に換えられる.

re|demp|tion /rɪdɛmpʃən/ (redemptions) ■ N-VAR 可変性名詞 **Redemption** is the act of redeeming something or of being redeemed by something. あがない, 償還 [FORMAL 形式ばった] □ He craves redemption for his sins. 彼は彼の罪のあがないを切望している. □ ...redemption of the loan. 融資の返済 ■ PHRASE 句 If you say that someone or something is **beyond redemption**, you mean that they are so bad it is unlikely that anything can be done to improve them. 救いようがない □ No man is beyond redemption. 救いようがない人などいない.

re|devel|op|ment /riːdɪvɛləpmənt/ N-UNCOUNT 不可算名詞 When **redevelopment** takes place, the buildings in one area of a town are knocked down and new ones are built in their place. 再開発 □ The group's intention is to clear the site for redevelopment. そのグループはその跡を再開発のために平地にするつもりだ.

red-hot ■ ADJ 形容詞 **Red-hot** metal or rock has been heated to such a high temperature that it has turned red. 赤熱した □ ...red-hot iron. 赤熱した鉄 ■ ADJ 形容詞 A **red-hot** object is too hot to be touched safely. 赤熱の □ In the main rooms red-hot radiators were left exposed. 主要な部屋では赤熱の暖房器がむき出しになったままだった. ■ ADJ 形容詞 **Red-hot** is used to describe a person or thing that is very popular, especially someone who is very good at what they do or something that is new and exciting. 話題の [JOURNALISM ジャーナリズム] □ Some traders are already stacking the red-hot book on their shelves. 業者によってはすでにその注目の的の本を棚に並べ始めている.

re|di|rect /riːdɪrɛkt, -daɪ-/ (redirects, redirecting, redirected) ■ V-T 他動詞 If you **redirect** your energy, resources, or ability, you begin doing something different or trying to achieve something

different. 方向性を変える ❑ *Controls were used to redistribute or redirect resources.* 資源を再分配したり方向性を変えたりするのに規制が適用された. **2** V-T 他動詞 If you **redirect** someone or something, you change their course or destination. 向きを変える ❑ *She redirected them to the men's department.* 彼女は彼らに男性用品売り場の方に行くように示した.

re|dis|trib|ute /ridɪstrɪbyut/ (redistributes, redistributing, redistributed) V-T 他動詞 If something such as money or property **is redistributed**, it is shared among people or organizations in a different way from the way that it was previously shared. 再分配する ❑ *Wealth was redistributed more equitably among society.* 富は社会にもっと平等に分配されるようになりました. ●**re|dis|tri|bu|tion** /ridɪstrɪbyuⁿn/ N-UNCOUNT 不可算名詞 再分配 ❑ *One of government's primary duties is the redistribution of income, so that the better off can help the worse off out of poverty.* 政府の本来の務めの1つは、裕福な人たちが貧乏な人たちを貧困から助け出せるように所得を再分配することだ.

re|dress /rɪdrɛs/ (redresses, redressing, redressed)

The noun is also pronounced /ri̱drɛs/ in American English.

名詞は米語では /ri̱drɛs/ とも発音される.

1 V-T 他動詞 If you **redress** something such as a wrong or a complaint, you do something to correct it or to improve things for the person who has been badly treated. 是正する [FORMAL 形式ばった] ❑ *More and more victims turn to litigation to redress wrongs done to them.* ますます多くの被害者たちが自分たちが被った不正を是正するために訴訟という手段に訴える. **2** V-T 他動詞 If you **redress** the balance or the imbalance between two things that have become unfair or unequal, you make them fair and equal again. 正す, 取り戻す [FORMAL 形式ばった] ❑ *So we're trying to redress the balance and to give teachers a sense that both spoken and written language are equally important.* そこで私たちは均衡を取り戻そうとして, 話し言葉も書き言葉も同様に重要なのだという感覚を教員が持つようにしようとしています. **3** N-UNCOUNT 不可算名詞 **Redress** is money that someone pays you because they have caused you harm or loss. 補償 [FORMAL 形式ばった] ❑ *They are continuing their legal battle to seek some redress from the government.* 彼らは政府からいくらかでも補償してもらうことを求めて法廷闘争を続けている.

red tape N-UNCOUNT 不可算名詞 You refer to official rules and procedures as **red tape** when they seem unnecessary and cause delay. 複雑な手続き [DISAPPROVAL 不賛成] ❑ *The little money that was available was tied up in bureaucratic red tape.* 利用できるわずかな資金は官僚的な複雑な手続きに使い道を拘束されていた.

re|duce /rɪdu̱s/ (reduces, reducing, reduced) **1** V-T 他動詞 If you **reduce** something, you make it smaller in size or amount, or less in degree. 減らす ❑ *It reduces the risks of heart disease.* それは心臓疾患の危険性を減らす. **2** V-T 他動詞 If someone **is reduced to** a weaker or inferior state, they become weaker or inferior as a result of something that happens to them. 陥らせる [usu passive] ❑ *They were reduced to extreme poverty.* 彼らは極端な貧困状態に陥っていた. **3** V-T 他動詞 If you say that someone **is reduced to** doing something, you mean that they have to do it, although it is unpleasant or embarrassing. 余儀なくさせる [usu passive] ❑ *He was reduced to begging for a living.* 彼は生活のため物乞いをする羽目になった. **4** V-T 他動詞 If something is changed to a different or less complicated form, you can say that it **is reduced to** that form. 変える [usu passive] ❑ *All the buildings in the town have been reduced to rubble.* その町の建物はすべてがれきの山と化している. **5** V-T/V-I 他動詞/自動詞 If you **reduce** liquid when you are cooking, or if it **reduces**, it is boiled in order to make it less in quantity and thicker. 煮詰める, 煮詰まる ❑ *Boil the liquid in a small saucepan to reduce it by half.* 半分に煮詰まるまで小さななべで汁を煮なさい. **6** PHRASE 句 If something or someone **reduces you to tears**, they make you feel so unhappy that you cry. 泣かせる ❑ *The attentions of the media reduced her to tears.* メディアの注目を浴び彼女は泣いてしまった.

→ see **mineral**

re|duc|tion /rɪdʌkⁿn/ (reductions) **1** N-COUNT 可算名詞 When there is a **reduction in** something, it is made smaller. 減少 ❑ *...a future reduction in interest rates.* 今後の金利引き下

げ. **2** N-UNCOUNT 不可算名詞 **Reduction** is the act of making something smaller in size or amount, or less in degree. 削減 ❑ *...a new strategic arms reduction agreement.* 新しい戦略兵器削減の合意
→ see **dump**

re|dun|dan|cy /rɪdʌndənsi/ (redundancies) **1** N-UNCOUNT 不可算名詞 **Redundancy** means being made redundant. 余剰従業員の解雇 [BUSINESS 実業] ❑ *Thousands of bank employees are facing redundancy as their employers cut costs.* 銀行が費用削減するのに伴い何千もの銀行職員が余剰解雇に直面している. **2** N-COUNT 可算名詞 When there are **redundancies**, an organization tells some of its employees to leave because their jobs are no longer necessary or because the organization can no longer afford to pay them. 余剰人員 [BRIT 英国英語 BUSINESS 実業] [AM **dismissals, layoffs** 米国英語 **dismissals, layoffs**]

re|dun|dant /rɪdʌndənt/ **1** ADJ 形容詞 Something that is **redundant** is unnecessary, for example, because it is no longer needed or because its job is being done by something else. 不必要な ❑ *Changes in technology may mean that once-valued skills are now redundant.* 技術の変化により以前は尊重されていた技術が今では不必要になっている可能性がある. **2** ADJ 形容詞 If you are made **redundant**, your employer tells you to leave because your job is no longer necessary or because your employer cannot afford to keep paying you. 余剰人員の, 余剰解雇の [BRIT 英国英語 BUSINESS 実業] [AM **be dismissed, be laid off** 米国英語 **be dismissed, be laid off**]

reed /ri̱d/ (reeds) **1** N-COUNT 可算名詞 **Reeds** are tall plants that grow in large groups in shallow water or on ground that is always wet and soft. They have strong, hollow stems that can be used for making things such as mats or baskets. アシ **2** N-COUNT 可算名詞 A **reed** is a small piece of cane or metal inserted into the mouthpiece of a woodwind instrument. The reed vibrates when you blow through it and makes a sound. リード

reef /ri̱f/ (reefs) N-COUNT 可算名詞 A **reef** is a long line of rocks or sand, the top of which is just above or just below the surface of the sea. 礁 ❑ *An unspoiled coral reef encloses the bay.* 手付かずのさんご礁が入り江を囲んでいる.

reek /ri̱k/ (reeks, reeking, reeked) **1** V-I 自動詞 To **reek of** something, usually something unpleasant, means to smell very strongly of it. 悪臭を放つ ❑ *Your breath reeks of stale cigar smoke.* あなたの息は古い葉巻の煙のような悪臭を放っている. ●N-SING 単数名詞 **Reek** is also a noun. 悪臭 ❑ *He smelled the reek of whiskey.* 彼はウィスキーの臭いをぷんぷんさせていた. **2** V-I 自動詞 If you say that something **reeks of** unpleasant ideas, feelings, or practices, you disapprove of it because it gives a strong impression that it involves ideas, feelings, or practices. くさい, 気味がある [DISAPPROVAL 不賛成] ❑ *The whole thing reeks of hypocrisy.* 丸ごと全部偽善の臭いがする.

reel /ri̱l/ (reels, reeling, reeled) **1** N-COUNT 可算名詞 A **reel** is a cylindrical object around which you wrap something such as movie film, magnetic tape, or fishing line. 巻き枠, リール ❑ *...a 30-meter reel of cable.* 30mのケーブル1巻き **2** V-I 自動詞 If someone **reels**, they move about in an unsteady way as if they are going to fall. よろめく ❑ *He was reeling a little. He must be very drunk.* 彼は少しよろめいていた. とっても酔っ払っていたに違いない. **3** V-I 自動詞 If you **are reeling** from a shock, you are feeling extremely surprised or upset because of it. 動揺する [usu cont] ❑ *I'm still reeling from the shock of hearing about it.* 私はそれを聞いた衝撃でまだ動揺しています. **4** V-I 自動詞 If you say that your brain or your mind **is reeling**, you mean that you are very confused because you have too many things to think about. くらくらする ❑ *His mind reeled at the question.* その質問に彼の頭はくらくらした.

▶ **reel off** PHRASAL VERB 句動詞 If you **reel off** information, you repeat it from memory quickly and easily. すらすら話す, 並べ立てる ❑ *She reeled off the titles of a dozen or so of the novels.* 彼女はその12作近くの小説の題名を並べ立てました.

re|elect /ri̱ɪlɛkt/ (reelects, reelecting, reelected) also **re-elect** V-T 他動詞 When someone such as a politician or an official who has been elected **is reelected**, they win another election and are therefore able to continue in their position as, for example, president, or an official in an organization. 再選する ❑ *He needs 51 percent to be reelected.* 彼の再選には51%の票が必要だ. ❑ *James Rhodes was reelected governor of Ohio.* ジェームズ・ローズはオハイオ州知事に再選された. ●**re|elec|tion** /ri̱ɪlɛkʃⁿn/ N-UNCOUNT 不可算名詞 再選 ❑ *He is heavily favored to win reelection.* 彼は再選を果たすと強く見込まれている.

re|ex|am|ine /ri̱ɪgzæmɪn/ (reexamines, reexamining, reexamined) also **re-examine** V-T 他動詞 If a person or group of people **reexamines** their ideas, beliefs, or attitudes, they think

about them carefully because they are no longer sure if they are correct. 再点検する ❑ *The marriage will cause Drew to reexamine his life.* その結婚をきっかけにしてドリューは人生を見つめ直すだろう. ● **re|ex|ami|na|tion** /ˌriːɪɡzæmɪˈneɪʃ°n/ (**reexaminations**) N-VAR 可変性名詞 再点検 ❑ *The issue has led to a reexamination of censorship rules.* この問題がもとで検閲の規定が再点検されることになった.

ref /rɛf/ (**refs**) **1** **Ref.** is an abbreviation for **reference**. It is written in front of a code at the top of business letters and documents. The code refers to a file where all the letters and documents about the same matter are kept. 参照 [BUSINESS 実業] ❑ *Our Ref: JAH/JW.* 当方参照番号: JAH/JW. **2** N-COUNT 可算名詞 The **ref** in a sports game, such as football, soccer, or boxing, is the same as the **referee**. 審判 [INFORMAL くだけた] ❑ *The ref said it was a fumble.* 審判がそれはファンブルだと言った.

re|fer /rɪˈfɜːr/ (**refers, referring, referred**) **1** V-I 自動詞 If you **refer to** a particular subject or person, you talk about them or mention them. 言及する ❑ *In his speech, he referred to a recent trip to Canada.* 演説で彼は最近のカナダ旅行について触れた. **2** V-I 自動詞 If you **refer to** someone or something **as** a particular thing, you use a particular word, expression, or name to mention or describe them. 呼ぶ ❑ *Marcia had referred to him as a dear friend.* マーシャは彼を親友と呼んでいた. **3** V-I 自動詞 If a word **refers to** a particular thing, situation, or idea, it describes it in some way. 示す ❑ *The term electronics refers to electrically induced action.* エレクトロニクスという用語は電気的に誘発される作用をいう. **4** V-T 他動詞 If a person who is ill **is referred to** a hospital or a specialist, they are sent there by a doctor in order to be treated. (病院などに) 紹介する [usu passive] ❑ *She was referred to the hospital by a neighborhood clinic.* 彼女は近所の医院でその病院に紹介してもらった. **5** V-T 他動詞 If you **refer** a task or a problem **to** a person or an organization, you formally tell them about it, so that they can deal with it. 委ねる, 持ち込む ❑ *He could refer the matter to the high court.* 彼はこの件を高裁に持ち込むことができるでしょう. **6** V-T 他動詞 If you **refer** someone **to** a person or organization, you send them there for the help they need. 差し向ける ❑ *Now and then I referred a client to him.* 折に触れ私は依頼者を彼に回した. **7** V-I 自動詞 If you **refer to** a book or other source of information, you look at it in order to find something out. 参照する ❑ *He referred briefly to his notebook.* 彼はチラッと手帳を見た. **8** V-T 他動詞 If you **refer** someone **to** a source of information, you tell them the place where they will find the information they need or that you think will interest them. 参照させる ❑ *Mr. Bryan also referred me to a book by the American journalist Anthony Scaduto.* ブライアンさんは米国の記者アンソニー・スカデュトの書いた本も見てみるように言った.

ref|eree /ˌrɛfəˈriː/ (**referees, refereeing, refereed**) **1** N-COUNT 可算名詞 The **referee** is the official who controls a sports event such as a football game or a boxing match. 審判 **2** V-I 自動詞 When someone **referees** a sports event or contest, they act as referee. 審判をする ❑ *Vautrot has refereed in two World Cups.* ヴォートロはワールドカップの2つの大会で審判を務めたことがあります. **3** N-COUNT 可算名詞 A **referee** is a person who gives you a reference, for example when you are applying for a job. 身元保証人 [BRIT 英国英語; AM **reference** 米国英語 **reference**]
→ see **football, tennis**

ref|er|ence /ˈrɛfərəns, ˈrɛfrəns/ (**references**) **1** N-VAR 可変性名詞 **Reference** to someone or something is the act of talking about them or mentioning them. A **reference** is a particular example of this. 言及 ❑ *He made no reference to any agreement.* 彼はどんな合意にも少しも触れなかった. **2** N-UNCOUNT 不可算名詞 **Reference** is the act of consulting someone or something in order to get information or advice. 参考, 照会 ❑ *Please keep this sheet in a safe place for reference.* 参考のためのこのプリントをなくさずに取っておいてください. **3** ADJ 形容詞 **Reference** books are ones that you look at when you need specific information or facts about a subject. 参照用の [ADJ n] ❑ *...a useful reference work for teachers.* 教師にとって便利な参考書 **4** N-COUNT 可算名詞 A **reference** is a word, phrase, or idea which comes from something such as a book, poem, or play and which you use when making a point about something. 引用 ❑ *...a reference from the Koran.* コーランからの引用文 **5** N-COUNT 可算名詞 A **reference** is something such as a number or a name that tells you where you can obtain the information you want. 参照 ❑ *Make a note of the reference number shown on the form.* 用紙の参照番号を覚えておくこと. **6** N-COUNT 可算名詞 A **reference** is a letter that is written by someone who knows you and which describes your character and abilities. When you apply for a job, an employer might ask for **references**. 推薦状, 証明書 ❑ *The firm offered to give her a reference.* その会社は彼女に証明書を書いてあげると申し出た. **7** N-COUNT 可算名詞 A **reference** is a person who gives you a reference, for example when you are applying for a job. 身元保証人 [mainly AM 主に米国語] ❑ *The official at the American embassy asked me for two references.* アメリカ大使館の職員は身元保証人を2人用意するようにと言った. **8** PHRASE 句 You use **with reference to** or **in reference to** in order to indicate what something relates to. 関連して ❑ *I am writing with reference to your*

article on salaries for scientists. 科学者の給料に関するあなたの記事についてお便りします. **9** → see also **cross-reference**

ref|er|en|dum /ˌrɛfəˈrɛndəm/ (**referendums** or **referenda** /ˌrɛfəˈrɛndə/) N-COUNT 可算名詞 If a country holds a **referendum** on a particular policy, they ask the people to vote on the policy and show whether or not they agree with it. 国民投票 ❑ *Estonia said today it too plans to hold a referendum on independence.* 本日エストニア政府も独立について国民投票を行う計画があると発表した.

re|fer|ral /rɪˈfɜːrəl/ (**referrals**) N-VAR 可変性名詞 **Referral** is the act of officially sending someone to a person or authority that is qualified to deal with them. A **referral** is an instance of this. 差し向け, 差し向けられた人 ❑ *Legal Aid can often provide referral to other types of agencies.* 法律扶助協会がしばしば異なる種類の機関に人を差し向けることができる.

re|fill (**refills, refilling, refilled**)

The verb is pronounced /riːˈfɪl/. The noun is pronounced /ˈriːfɪl/.

動詞は /riːˈfɪl/ と発音される. 名詞は /ˈriːfɪl/ と発音される.

1 V-T 他動詞 If you **refill** something, you fill it again after it has been emptied. 補充する ❑ *I refilled our wine glasses.* 私はみんなのグラスにワインを注ぎ足した. ● **Refill** is also a noun. お代わり [INFORMAL くだけた] ❑ *Max held out his cup for a refill.* マックスはお代わりするためコップを差し出した. **2** N-COUNT 可算名詞 A **refill** of a particular product is a quantity of that product sold in a cheaper container than the one it is usually sold in. You use a refill to fill the more permanent container when it is empty. 詰め替え品 ❑ *Refill packs are cheaper and lighter.* 詰め替えパックはもっと安くて軽い.

re|fi|nance /ˌriːfɪˈnæns, riːˈfaɪnæns/ (**refinances, refinancing, refinanced**) V-T/V-I 他動詞/自動詞 If a person or a company **refinances** a debt or if they **refinance**, they borrow money in order to pay the debt. 借り換える, 借り換えをする [BUSINESS 実業] ❑ *A loan was arranged to refinance existing debt.* すでにある借金を借り換えるためにローンが組まれた.

re|fine /rɪˈfaɪn/ (**refines, refining, refined**) **1** V-T 他動詞 When a substance **is refined**, it is made pure by having all other substances removed from it. 精製する [usu passive] ❑ *Oil is refined to remove naturally occurring impurities.* 油は自然含有不純物を除去するために精製される. ● **refining** N-UNCOUNT 不可算名詞 精製 ❑ *...oil refining.* 油の精製 **2** V-T 他動詞 [usu passive] If something such as a process, theory, or machine **is refined**, it is improved by having small changes made to it. 改良する ❑ *Surgical techniques are constantly being refined.* 外科の技術は常に改良されている.
→ see **sugar**

re|fined /rɪˈfaɪnd/ **1** ADJ 形容詞 A **refined** substance has been made pure by having other substances removed from it. 精製された ❑ *...refined sugar.* 精糖 **2** ADJ 形容詞 If you say that someone is **refined**, you mean that they are very polite and have good manners and good taste. 上品な ❑ *...refined and well-dressed ladies.* 上品で身なりのよい婦人たち **3** ADJ 形容詞 If you describe a machine or a process as **refined**, you mean that it has been carefully developed and is therefore very efficient or elegant. 精密な ❑ *This technique is becoming more refined and more acceptable all the time.* この技術は, 常により精密でより満足のいくものに進化し続けている.

re|fine|ment /rɪˈfaɪnmənt/ (**refinements**) **1** N-VAR 可変性名詞 **Refinements** are small changes or additions that you make to something in order to improve it. **Refinement** is the process of making refinements. 改良 ❑ *Older cars inevitably lack the latest safety refinements.* 当然ながら旧モデル車には最新の安全装置はついていない. **2** N-UNCOUNT 不可算名詞 **Refinement** is politeness and good manners. 洗練

re|fin|ery /rɪˈfaɪnəri/ (**refineries**) N-COUNT 可算名詞 A **refinery** is a factory where a substance such as oil or sugar is refined. 精製所 ❑ *...an oil refinery.* 精油所
→ see **industry, mineral, oil**

re|fit (**refits, refitting, refitted**)

The verb is pronounced /riːˈfɪt/. The noun is pronounced /ˈriːfɪt/.

動詞は /riːˈfɪt/ と発音される. 名詞は /ˈriːfɪt/ と発音される.

V-T 他動詞 When a ship **is refitted**, it is repaired or is given new parts, equipment, or furniture. 修理する, 改修する [usu passive]

❑ *During the war, navy ships were refitted here.* 戦時中, 海軍の軍艦はここで再整備されていた. ● N-COUNT 可算名詞 **Refit** is also a noun. 修理, 改修 ❑ *The ship finished an extensive refit last year.* その船は昨年大幅な改修を終えた.

Word Link　　re ≈ back, again : reflect, repay, restate

re|flect /rɪflɛkt/ (reflects, reflecting, reflected) **1** V-T 他動詞 If something **reflects** an attitude or situation, it shows that the attitude or situation exists or it shows what it is like. 反映する, 表す ❑ *A newspaper report seems to reflect the view of most members of Congress.* 新聞報道というものには大半の国会議員の見方が反映されているようだ. **2** V-T/V-I 他動詞/自動詞 When light, heat, or other rays **reflect** off a surface or when a surface **reflects** them, they are sent back from the surface and do not pass through it. 反射する ❑ *The sun reflected off the snow-covered mountains.* 太陽の光が雪を頂いた山々に反射していた. **3** V-T 他動詞 When something **is reflected** in a mirror or in water, you can see its image in the mirror or in the water. 映す [usu passive] ❑ *His image was reflected many times in the mirror.* 彼の姿はその鏡に何度も映った. **4** V-I 自動詞 When you **reflect on** something, you think deeply about it. 思案する ❑ *We should all give ourselves time to reflect.* 全員がじっくりと考える時間を持つべきだ. **5** V-T 他動詞 You can use **reflect** to indicate that a particular thought occurs to someone. 思い起こす ❑ *Things were very much changed since before the war, he reflected.* 何もかも戦前とはずいぶん変わってしまった, と彼は思った. **6** V-I 自動詞 If an action or situation **reflects** in a particular way **on** someone or something, it gives people a good or bad impression of them. 影響をもたらす ❑ *The affair hardly reflected well on the president.* その事件は大統領にほとんどよい影響を与えなかった.
→ see **echo, telescope**

re|flec|tion /rɪflɛkʃ°n/ (reflections) **1** N-COUNT 可算名詞 A **reflection** is an image that you can see in a mirror or in glass or water. 映った像 ❑ *Meg stared at her reflection in the bedroom mirror.* メグは寝室の鏡に映った姿を見つめた. **2** N-UNCOUNT 不可算名詞 **Reflection** is the process by which light and heat are sent back from a surface and do not pass through it. 反射 ❑ *...the reflection of a beam of light off a mirror.* 鏡に反射した光線 **3** N-COUNT 可算名詞 If you say that something is a **reflection of** a particular person's attitude or **of** a situation, you mean that it is caused by that attitude or situation and therefore reveals something about it. 反映 ❑ *Inhibition in adulthood seems to be a reflection of a person's experiences as a child.* 成人の心理的抑制は, 子供の頃の経験を反映するようだ. **4** N-SING 単数名詞 If something is a **reflection** or a **sad reflection** on a person or thing, it gives a bad impression of them. 悪いことの表れ ❑ *Infection with head lice is no reflection on personal hygiene.* アタマジラミの感染は個人の衛生状態の表れではない. **5** N-UNCOUNT 不可算名詞 **Reflection** is careful thought about a particular subject. Your **reflections** are your thoughts about a particular subject. 熟慮 [also N in pl] ❑ *After days of reflection she decided to write back.* 何日かよく考えた末, 彼女は返事を書くことにした. ● PHRASE 句 If someone admits or accepts something **on reflection**, they admit or accept it after having thought carefully about it. よく考えてみると ❑ *While the news at first shocked me, on reflection it made perfect sense.* 最初はその情報にはショックを受けたが, よく考えると完全に筋が通ったものだった.
→ see **echo**

re|flec|tive /rɪflɛktɪv/ **1** ADJ 形容詞 If you are **reflective**, you are thinking deeply about something. 思索にふけって [WRITTEN 書き言葉] ❑ *I walked on in a reflective mood to the car, thinking about the poor honeymooners.* 私はあの気の毒な新婚旅行者のことを思案しながら車の方に歩いていった. **2** ADJ 形容詞 If something is **reflective of** a particular situation or attitude, it is typical of that situation or attitude, or is a consequence of it. 反映している [v-link ADJ "of" n] ❑ *The German government's support of the U.S. is not entirely reflective of German public opinion.* ドイツ政府の米国支持は, 国民の世論をすっかり反映したものではない. **3** ADJ 形容詞 A **reflective** surface or material sends back light or heat. 反射する [FORMAL 形式ばった] ❑ *Avoid using pans with a shiny, reflective base as the heat will be reflected back.* 熱を反射するため, 底面が光沢のある反射素材のなべは使わないようにしてください.

Word Link　　flex ≈ bending : flex, flexible, reflex

re|flex /rɪflɛks/ (reflexes) **1** N-COUNT 可算名詞 A **reflex** or a **reflex action** is something that you do automatically and without thinking, as a habit or as a reaction to something. くせ ❑ *Walt fumbled in his pocket, a reflex from his smoking days.* 喫煙していたころのくせで, ウォルトはポケットをまさぐった. **2** N-COUNT 可算名詞 A **reflex** or a **reflex action** is a normal, uncontrollable reaction of your body to something that you feel, see, or experience. 反射 ❑ *...tests for reflexes, like tapping the knee or the heel with a rubber hammer.* ひざやかかとをゴム製ハンマーでとんとんたたく反射試験 **3** N-PLURAL 複数名詞 Your **reflexes** are your ability to react quickly with your body when something unexpected happens, for example when you are involved in sports or when you are

driving a car. 反射神経 ❑ *It takes great skill, cool nerves, and the reflexes of an athlete.* 優れた技能, 冷静沈着さ, 運動選手並みの反射神経が求められる.

re|form /rɪfɔrm/ (reforms, reforming, reformed) **1** N-VAR 可変性名詞 **Reform** consists of changes and improvements to a law, social system, or institution. A **reform** is an instance of such a change or improvement. 改革 ❑ *The party embarked on a program of economic reform.* 党は経済改革計画の実行に乗り出した. **2** V-T 他動詞 If someone **reforms** something such as a law, social system, or institution, they change or improve it. 改革する ❑ *...his plans to reform the country's economy.* 国の経済改革を目指す彼の計画 **3** V-T/V-I 他動詞/自動詞 When someone **reforms** or when something **reforms** them, they stop doing things that society does not approve of, such as breaking the law or drinking too much alcohol. 改心させる [他動詞], 改心する [自動詞] ❑ *When his court case was coming up, James promised to reform.* ジェームズは自分の裁判が近づくと, 改心すると約束した. ● **re|formed** ADJ 形容詞 改心した ❑ *...a reformed alcoholic.* アルコール依存症を克服した人

Word Partnership　　reform は次の語句と使われる:

ADJ.	**economic** reform, **political** reform **1**
N.	**education** reform, **election** reform, **health care** reform, reform **movement**, **party** reform, **prison** reform, **tax** reform **1**

re|form|er /rɪfɔrmər/ (reformers) N-COUNT 可算名詞 A **reformer** is someone who tries to change and improve something such as a law or a social system. 改革者 ❑ *How could he be a reformer and a defender of established interests at the same time?* 彼が改革者でもあり同時に既得権の擁護者でもあるなんてありえないよ.

re|frain /rɪfreɪn/ (refrains, refraining, refrained) **1** V-I 自動詞 If you **refrain from** doing something, you deliberately do not do it. 控える ❑ *Mrs. Hardie refrained from making any comment.* ハーディー夫人はいかなるコメントも差し控えた. **2** N-COUNT 可算名詞 A **refrain** is a short, simple part of a song, which is repeated many times. リフレイン ❑ *...a refrain from an old song.* 昔の歌のリフレイン **3** N-COUNT 可算名詞 A **refrain** is a comment or saying that people often repeat. 決まり文句 ❑ *Rosa's constant refrain is that she doesn't have a life.*「生きがいがないの」がローサの決まり文句です.

re|fresh /rɪfrɛʃ/ (refreshes, refreshing, refreshed) **1** V-T 他動詞 If something **refreshes** you when you are hot, tired, or thirsty, it makes you feel cooler or more energetic. すがすがしい気分にする ❑ *The lotion cools and refreshes the skin.* このローションは肌に清涼感と爽快（そうかい）感を与えます. ● **re|freshed** ADJ 形容詞 さわやかな気分で ❑ *He awoke feeling completely refreshed.* 彼はとてもさわやかな気分で目覚めた. **2** V-T 他動詞 If you **refresh** something old or dull, you make it as good as it was when it was new. 新たにする ❑ *Many view these meetings as an occasion to share ideas and refresh friendship.* 多くの人々はこれらの会合を意見交換と友情を新たにする場だとみている. **3** V-T 他動詞 If someone **refreshes** your memory, they tell you something that you had forgotten. 呼び起こす ❑ *He walked on the opposite side of the street to refresh his memory of the building.* その建物の記憶を呼び起こすため, 彼は通りの反対側を歩いた. **4** V-T 他動詞 If you **refresh** a web page, you click a button in order to get the most recent version of the page. 更新する [COMPUTING コンピューティング] ❑ *I've refreshed the page a few times and still see no comments.* 何回かページを更新してみたけれど, それでも何のコメントも来なかったのだ.

re|fresh|er course (refresher courses) N-COUNT 可算名詞 A **refresher course** is a training course in which people improve their knowledge or skills and learn about new developments that are related to the job that they do. 再教育講座

re|fresh|ing /rɪfrɛʃɪŋ/ **1** ADJ 形容詞 You say that something is **refreshing** when it is pleasantly different from what you are used to. すがすがしい, 胸のすくような ❑ *It's refreshing to hear somebody speaking common sense.* 良識ある意見を聞くのは気分がいいな. ● **re|fresh|ing|ly** ADV 副詞 さわやかに ❑ *He was refreshingly honest.* 彼はすがすがしいほど正直だ. **2** ADJ 形容詞 A **refreshing** bath or drink makes you feel energetic or cool again after you have been tired or hot. 清涼感のある ❑ *Herbs have been used for centuries to make refreshing drinks.* ハーブは何世紀も清涼飲料の原料として使われてきた.

re|fresh|ment /rɪfrɛʃmənt/ (refreshments) **1** N-PLURAL 複数名詞 **Refreshments** are drinks and small amounts of food that are provided, for example, during a meeting or a trip. 茶菓 ❑ *Lunch and refreshments will be provided.* 昼食と茶菓が出ます. **2** N-UNCOUNT 不可算名詞 You can refer to food and drink as **refreshment**. 軽い飲食物 [FORMAL 形式ばった] ❑ *May I offer you some refreshment?* 何か軽いものをお出ししましょうか.

re|frig|er|ate /rɪfrɪdʒəreɪt/ (refrigerates, refrigerating, refrigerated) V-T 他動詞 If you **refrigerate** food, you make it cold

Word Web — refrigerator

Refrigerators and **freezers cool** and **freeze** food, but how do they work? A gas passes through coils inside the walls of the refrigerator or freezer. As it does so, it absorbs heat and **chills** the interior. Then a pump compresses the gas, which raises its **temperature**. It pushes the gas through coils on the outside of the refrigerator. There it expands and becomes a liquid. At the same time, it gives off heat into the surrounding air. The liquid then flows through a valve into a low pressure area. There it becomes a gas again. Then the cycle repeats itself.

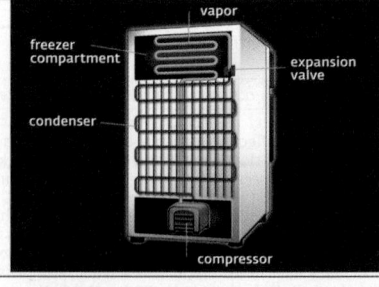

vapor
freezer compartment
expansion valve
condenser
compressor

by putting it in a refrigerator, usually in order to preserve it. 冷蔵する ❏ *Refrigerate the dough overnight.* 生地を一晩冷蔵してください.
→ see **dairy**

re|frig|era|tor /rɪfrɪdʒəreɪtər/ (**refrigerators**) N-COUNT 可算名詞 A **refrigerator** is a large container which is kept cool inside, usually by electricity, so that the food and drink in it stays fresh. 冷蔵庫
→ see Word Web: **refrigerator**

re|fu|el /rifyuəl/ (**refuels, refueling** or **refuelling, refueled** or **refuelled**) V-T/V-I 他動詞/自動詞 When an aircraft or other vehicle **refuels** or when someone **refuels** it, it is filled with more fuel so that it can continue its journey. 燃料を補給する ❏ *His plane stopped in Hawaii to refuel.* 彼の乗った飛行機は給油のためハワイに立ち寄った. ● **re|fu|el|ing** N-UNCOUNT 不可算名詞 燃料補給 ❏ *...nighttime refueling of vehicles.* 夜間の燃料補給

ref|uge /rɛfyudʒ/ (**refuges**) ◼ N-UNCOUNT 不可算名詞 If you take **refuge** somewhere, you try to protect yourself from physical harm by going there. 避難 ❏ *They took refuge in a bomb shelter.* 彼らは防空ごうに避難した. ◾ N-COUNT 可算名詞 A **refuge** is a place where you go for safety and protection, for example from violence or from bad weather. 避難所 ❏ *Eventually Suzanne fled to a refuge for battered women.* スザンヌはたまりかねて暴行を受けた女性のための避難施設に逃げ込んだ. ◼ N-UNCOUNT 不可算名詞 If you take **refuge** in a particular way of behaving or thinking, you try to protect yourself from unhappiness or unpleasantness by behaving or thinking in that way. 逃げ場 ❏ *All too often, they get bored and seek refuge in drink and drugs.* あまりにもしばしば彼らは退屈して, 酒や麻薬に逃げる.

Word Link — *ee = one who receives : employee, payee, refugee*

refu|gee /rɛfyudʒi/ (**refugees**) N-COUNT 可算名詞 **Refugees** are people who have been forced to leave their homes or their country, either because there is a war there, because of their political or religious beliefs, or because of natural disaster. 避難民 ❏ *A political refugee from Cameroon has moved into our neighborhood.* カメルーンからの政治難民が近所に越してきた.

re|fund (**refunds, refunding, refunded**)

> The noun is pronounced /rifʌnd/. The verb is pronounced /rifʌnd/.
>
> 名詞は /rifʌnd/ と発音される. 動詞は /rifʌnd/ と発音される.

◼ N-COUNT 可算名詞 A **refund** is a sum of money that is returned to you, for example because you have paid too much or because you have returned goods to a store. 払戻金 ❏ *Face it – you'll just have to take those cowboy boots back and ask for a refund.* よく見てみろよ. とにかくそのカウボーイブーツは返品して払い戻しを受けるべきだよ. ◾ V-T 他動詞 If someone **refunds** your money, they return it to you, for example because you have paid too much or because you have returned goods to a store. 払い戻す ❏ *We guarantee to refund your money if you're not delighted with your purchase.* お買い上げになった商品がお気に召さない場合は返金させていただきます.

Thesaurus — *refund* また次を参照:

N.	payment, reimbursement ◼
V.	give back, pay back, reimburse ◾

re|fund|able /rifʌndəbəl/ ADJ 形容詞 A **refundable** payment will be paid back to you in certain circumstances. 払い戻し可能の ❏ *A refundable deposit is payable on arrival.* 払い戻し可能保証金は到着時払いです.

re|fur|bish /rifɜrbɪʃ/ (**refurbishes, refurbishing, refurbished**) V-T 他動詞 To **refurbish** a building or room means to clean it and decorate it and make it more attractive or better equipped. 改装する ❏ *We have spent money on refurbishing the offices.* 我々は事務所の改装に金を使った.

re|fus|al /rifyuzəl/ (**refusals**) ◼ N-VAR 可変性名詞 Someone's **refusal to** do something is the fact of them showing or saying that they will not do it, allow it, or accept it. 拒否 ❏ *Her country suffered through her refusal to accept change.* 国は女王が変化を受け入れようとしないため苦しんだ. ◾ PHRASE 句 If someone has **first refusal** on something that is being sold or offered, they have the right to decide whether or not to buy it or take it before it is offered to anyone else. 第一先買権 ❏ *A tenant may have a right of first refusal if a property is offered for sale.* 不動産が売りに出される場合, テナントは第一先買権を持つものとする.

re|fuse (**refuses, refusing, refused**)

> The verb is pronounced /rifyuz/. The noun is pronounced /rɛfyus/ and is hyphenated ref|use.
>
> 動詞は /rifyuz/ と発音される. 名詞は /rɛfyus/ と発音され, refluseとハイフンで結ばれる.

◼ V-T/V-I 他動詞/自動詞 If you **refuse to** do something, you deliberately do not do it, or you say firmly that you will not do it. 拒否する ❏ *He refused to comment after the trial.* 彼は裁判後にコメントすることを拒否した. ❏ *I could hardly refuse, could I?* 断れそうにないってことですね. ◾ V-T 他動詞 If someone **refuses** something, they do not give it to you or do not allow you to have it. 与えない ❏ *The United States has refused him a visa.* 米国は彼に査証を発給しなかった. ◼ V-T 他動詞 If you **refuse** something that is offered to you, you do not accept it. 断る ❏ *The patient has the right to refuse treatment.* 患者には治療を拒む権利がある. ◼ N-UNCOUNT 不可算名詞 **Refuse** consists of the trash and all the things that are not wanted in a house, store, or factory, and that are regularly thrown away; used mainly in official language. ごみ ❏ *The town made a weekly collection of refuse.* その町では毎週ごみを収集した.
→ see **dump**

> Do not confuse **refuse** and **deny**. If you **refuse** to do something, you deliberately do not do it, or you say firmly that you will not do it. ❏ *...people who refuse to change their opinions... He refused to condemn them.* You can **refuse** something that someone offers you. ❏ *The patient has the right to refuse treatment.* If someone does not allow you to have something you ask for, or to do something you have asked to do, you can say that they **refuse** you. ❏ *He can run to Dad for money if I refuse him.* If you **deny** something, you say that it is not true. ❏ *The allegation was denied by government spokesmen.* If someone **denies** you something, they do not allow you to have it. ❏ *I never denied her anything.*

Thesaurus — *refuse* また次を参照:

V.	decline, reject, turn down; (*ant.*) accept ◼ ◼
N.	garbage, rubbish, trash ◼

Word Partnership — *refuse* は次の語句と使われる:

V.	refuse **to answer**, refuse **to cooperate**, refuse **to go**, refuse **to participate**, refuse **to pay** ◼ refuse **to allow**, refuse **to give** ◼ ◾ refuse **to accept** ◼ ◼

re|fute /rifyut/ (**refutes, refuting, refuted**) ◼ V-T 他動詞 If you **refute** an argument, accusation, or theory, you prove that it is wrong or untrue. 誤りを証明する [FORMAL 形式ばった] ❏ *It was the kind of rumor that it is impossible to refute.* 誤りを証明するのは不可能だという説が一種のうわさになった. ◾ V-T 他動詞 If you **refute** an argument or accusation, you say that it is not true. 論破する [FORMAL 形式ばった] ❏ *Isabelle is quick to refute any suggestion of intellectual snobbery.* イザベルは知性を鼻にかけるような提案はすぐに論破する.

re|gain /rigeɪn/ (**regains, regaining, regained**) V-T 他動詞 If you **regain** something that you have lost, you get it back again. 取り戻す ❏ *Troops have regained control of the city.* 部隊はその都市の支配権を取り戻した.

Word Link reg ≈ rule : regal, regime, regulation

re|gal /ríːgʰl/ ADJ 形容詞 If you describe something as **regal**, you mean that it is suitable for a king or queen, because it is very impressive or beautiful. 王者らしい □ He sat with such regal dignity. 彼は堂々たる王者の威厳をもって着席した.

re|gard /rɪɡɑrd/ (regards, regarding, regarded) **1** V-T 他動詞 If you **regard** someone or something **as** being a particular thing or **as** having a particular quality, you believe that they are that thing or have that quality. みなす □ He was regarded as the most successful president of modern times. 彼は現代で最も成功した大統領だと考えられていた. **2** V-T 他動詞 If you **regard** something or someone **with** a feeling such as dislike or respect, you have that feeling toward them. 一な目で見る □ He regarded drug dealers with loathing. 彼は麻薬の売人たちを嫌悪の目で眺めた. **3** N-UNCOUNT 不可算名詞 If you have **regard for** someone or something, you respect them and care about them. If you hold someone **in high regard**, you have a lot of respect for them. 敬意 □ I have a very high regard for him and what he has achieved. 私は彼の人となりと業績を非常に高く評価しています. **4** N-PLURAL 複数名詞 **Regards** are greetings. You use **regards** in expressions such as **best regards** and **with kind regards** as a way of expressing friendly feelings toward someone, especially in a letter. 手紙の結語で「敬具」や「〜によろしく」という意味で用いる. □ Give my regards to your family. ご家族の皆さんによろしく. [FORMULAE 決まり文句] **5** PHRASE 句 You can use **as regards** to indicate the subject that is being talked or written about. 〜に関しては □ As regards the war, Haig believed in victory at any price. その戦いについては，どうあってもヘイグは勝てると信じていた. **6** PHRASE 句 You can use **with regard to** or **in regard to** to indicate the subject that is being talked or written about. 〜に関しては □ The department is reviewing its policy with regard to immunization. 局は予防接種の方針を見直しているところだ.

Word Partnership regardは次の語句と使われる:

PREP. regard as **1**
regard with **2**
regard for **3**
in/with regard to, with/without regard **6**

re|gard|ing /rɪɡɑrdɪŋ/ PREP 前置詞 You can use **regarding** to indicate the subject that is being talked or written about. 〜について □ He refused to divulge any information regarding the man's whereabouts. 彼はその男の所在に関するどんな情報も明かそうとしなかった.

re|gard|less /rɪɡɑrdlɪs/ **1** PHRASE 句 If something happens **regardless of** something else, it is not affected or influenced at all by that other thing. 〜にかかわらず □ It takes in people regardless of religion, color, or creed. そこは宗教，人種，信条を問わず誰でも受け入れてくれる. **2** ADV 副詞 If you say that someone did something **regardless**, you mean that they did it even though there were problems or factors that could have stopped them. それでも [ADV after v] □ Despite her recent surgery she has been carrying on regardless. 彼女は最近手術を受けましたが，それでも働き続けている.

re|gen|er|ate /rɪdʒɛnəreɪt/ (regenerates, regenerating, regenerated) **1** V-T 他動詞 To **regenerate** something means to develop and improve it to make it more active, successful, or important, especially after a period when it has been getting worse. 再生する □ The government will continue to try to regenerate inner-city areas. 政府は都心部の再生の努力を続行するようです. ● **re|gen|era|tion** /rɪdʒɛnəreɪʃʰn/ N-UNCOUNT 不可算名詞 再生 □ ...the physical and economic regeneration of the area. その地区の物理的，経済的再生. **2** V-T/V-I 他動詞/自動詞 If organs or tissues **regenerate** or if something **regenerates** them, they heal and grow again after they have been damaged. 再生する □ Nerve cells have limited ability to regenerate if destroyed. 神経細胞は破壊されても限られた範囲でなら再生できる. ● **re|gen|era|tion** N-UNCOUNT 不可算名詞 再生 □ Vitamin B assists in red-blood-cell regeneration. ビタミンBは赤血球の再生を助ける.

reg|gae /rɛɡeɪ/ N-UNCOUNT 不可算名詞 **Reggae** is a kind of West Indian popular music with a very strong beat. レゲエ音楽 □ Many people will remember Bob Marley for giving them their first taste of reggae music. ボブ・マーレーは最初にレゲエ音楽を知らしめた人物として多くの人々に記憶されるでしょう.

re|gime /rəʒiːm, reɪ-/ (regimes) **1** N-COUNT 可算名詞 If you refer to a government or system of running a country as a **regime**, you are critical of it because you think it is not democratic and uses unacceptable methods. 政体，体制 [DISAPPROVAL 不賛成] □ ...the collapse of the Fascist regime at the end of the war. 戦争末期のファシズム政権の崩壊. **2** N-COUNT 可算名詞 A **regime** is the way that something such as an institution, company, or economy is run, especially when it involves tough or severe action. 管理体制 □ The authorities moved him to the less rigid regime of an open prison. 当局は，

彼を管理がより緩やかな開放的な刑務所に移した. **3** N-COUNT 可算名詞 A **regime** is a set of rules about food, exercise, or beauty that some people follow in order to stay healthy or attractive. 養生規則 □ He has a new fitness regime to strengthen his back. 彼は背筋強化用の新しい訓練メニューを取り入れている.

regi|ment /rɛdʒɪmənt/ (regiments) **1** N-COUNT 可算名詞 A **regiment** is a large group of soldiers that is commanded by a colonel. 連隊 **2** N-COUNT 可算名詞 A **regiment of** people is a large number of them. 大勢の □ ...robust food, good enough to satisfy a regiment of hungry customers. 空腹を抱えた大勢の客を満足させるに十分なよい，しっかりとした食事

regi|men|tal /rɛdʒɪmɛntʰl/ ADJ 形容詞 **Regimental** means belonging to a particular regiment. 連隊の [ADJ n] □ Mills was regimental colonel. ミルズは連隊長だった.

re|gion /riːdʒʰn/ (regions) **1** N-COUNT 可算名詞 A **region** is a large area of land that is different from other areas of land, for example because it is one of the different parts of a country with its own customs and characteristics, or because it has a particular geographical feature. 地域 □ ...Barcelona, capital of the autonomous region of Catalonia. カタルーニャ自治州の州都，バルセロナ **2** N-COUNT 可算名詞 You can refer to a part of your body as a **region**. 部位 □ ...the pelvic region. 骨盤部位 **3** PHRASE 句 You say **in the region of** to indicate that an amount that you are stating is approximate. およそ〜くらいで [VAGUENESS あいまいさ] □ The plan will cost in the region of six million dollars. その計画はおよそ600万ドルの費用がかかるでしょう.

re|gion|al /riːdʒʰnʰl/ ADJ 形容詞 **Regional** is used to describe things which relate to a particular area of a country or of the world. 地域の □ The Garden's menu is based on Hawaiian regional cuisine. ガーデンのメニューはハワイの地域料理をベースにしている.

reg|is|ter /rɛdʒɪstər/ (registers, registering, registered) **1** N-COUNT 可算名詞 A **register** is an official list or record of people or things. 登記簿 □ ...registers of births, deaths, and marriages. 出生，死亡，婚姻の登記簿 **2** V-T/V-I 他動詞/自動詞 If you **register** to do something, you put your name on an official list, in order to be able to do that thing or to receive a service. 登録する □ Have you come to register at the school? 入学手続きに来られたのですか. □ Thousands lined up to register to vote. 選挙登録するために何千人もが列を作りました. **3** V-T 他動詞 If you **register** something, such as the name of a person who has just died or information about something you own, you have these facts recorded on an official list. 登記する □ In order to register a car in Japan, the owner must have somewhere to park it. 日本で車両を登録するには，所有者は駐車場を確保しなければならない. **4** V-T/V-I 他動詞/自動詞 When something **registers** on a scale or measuring instrument, it shows on the scale or instrument. 示す，記録する □ It will only register on sophisticated X-ray equipment. それは精巧なX線装置でのみ記録されるでしょう. □ The earthquake registered 5.7 on the Richter scale. その地震はリヒタースケールでマグニチュード5.7を記録した. **5** V-T 他動詞 If you **register** your feelings or opinions about something, you do something that makes them clear to other people. 表す □ Voters wish to register their dissatisfaction with the ruling party. 有権者は与党への不満を表明したいと望んでいる. **6** V-I 自動詞 If a feeling **registers on** someone's face, their expression shows clearly that they have that feeling. 表れる □ Surprise again registered on Rodney's face. ロドニーはまた驚きの表情を浮かべた. **7** V-T/V-I 他動詞/自動詞 If a piece of information does not **register** or if you do not **register** it, you do not really pay attention to it, and so you do not remember it or react to it. 心に銘記する，印象に残る □ It wasn't that she couldn't hear me, it was just that what I said sometimes didn't register in her brain. 彼女に私の言葉が聞こえなかったのではなく，ただ私の言うことが時々彼女の印象に残らなかっただけだ. **8** → see also **cash register** → see **bank**

Word Partnership registerは次の語句と使われる:

N. voters register **1**
V. register to vote **2**

reg|is|trar /rɛdʒɪstrɑr/ (registrars) N-COUNT 可算名詞 A **registrar** is an administrative official in a college or university who is responsible for student records. 学籍係

reg|is|tra|tion /rɛdʒɪstreɪʃʰn/ N-UNCOUNT 不可算名詞 The **registration** of something such as a person's name or the details of an event is the recording of it in an official list. 登録 □ They have campaigned strongly for compulsory registration of dogs. 彼らは畜犬登録の義務化を断固として訴えてきました. □ With the high voter registration, many will be voting for the first time. 選挙人登録数が伸びていますが，多くの人が初めて投票を行うようです.

reg|is|tra|tion num|ber → see **license number**

reg|is|try /rɛdʒɪstri/ (registries) N-COUNT 可算名詞 A **registry** is a collection of all the official records relating to something, or the place where they are kept. 記録，記録保管所 □ There is no

international registry of stolen art. 盗難美術品の国際的な記録保管所はありません。

re|gress /rɪɡrɛs/ (**regresses, regressing, regressed**) V-I 自動詞 When people or things **regress**, they return to an earlier and less advanced stage of development. 後戻りする [FORMAL 形式ばった] ❑ If your child regresses to babyish behavior, all you know for certain is that the child is under stress. 子供が赤ちゃん期への退行行動を示す場合、確かなのはその子にストレスがかかっているということです。 ● **re|gres|sion** /rɪɡrɛʃ³n/ (**regressions**) N-VAR 可変性名詞 退行 ❑ Calderdale accepts that this can cause regression in a student's learning process. コールダーデールは、このことで生徒の学習過程が退行することがありうると認めている。

re|gret /rɪɡrɛt/ (**regrets, regretting, regretted**) ■ V-T 他動詞 If you **regret** something that you have done, you wish that you had not done it. 後悔する ❑ I simply gave in to him, and I've regretted it ever since. 僕は彼にあっさり降参したが、それ以来ずっと後悔している。 ❑ Ellis seemed to be regretting that he had asked the question. エリスはその質問をしたことを後悔しているようだった。 ■ N-VAR 可変性名詞 **Regret** is a feeling of sadness or disappointment, which is caused by something that has happened or something that you have done or not done. 後悔 ❑ Larry said he had no regrets about retiring. ラリーは引退について全く後悔していないと述べた。 ■ V-T 他動詞 You can say that you **regret** something as a polite way of saying that you are sorry about it. You use expressions such as **I regret to say** or **I regret to inform you** to show that you are sorry about something. 残念に思う [POLITENESS 丁寧さ] ❑ "I very much regret the injuries he sustained," he said. 「私は彼が負傷されたことを大変お気の毒に思っています」と彼は言った。 ❑ I regret that the United States has added its voice to such protests. 米国がそのような抗議に賛成意見を加えたのは残念です。

Word Partnership	regret は次の語句と使われる:
N.	regret **a decision**, regret **a loss** ■
V.	**come to** regret ■
	express regret ■

re|gret|table /rɪɡrɛtəb³l/ ADJ 形容詞 You describe something as **regrettable** when you think that it is bad and that it should not happen or have happened. 残念な [FORMAL 形式ばった、FEELINGS 感情] ❑ The army said it had started an investigation into what it described as a regrettable incident. 陸軍は彼らが言うところの「遺憾な出来事」に対する調査を開始したと発表した。 ● **re|gret|tably** ADV 副詞 遺憾ながら ❑ Regrettably we could find no sign of the man and the search was terminated. 遺憾ながら、我々はその男の足跡をたどることができず、捜索は打ち切られた。

re|group /riɡrup/ (**regroups, regrouping, regrouped**) V-T/V-I 他動詞/自動詞 When people, especially soldiers, **regroup**, or when someone **regroups** them, they form an organized group again, in order to continue fighting. 再結成する ❑ Now the rebel army has regrouped and reorganized. 今や反乱軍は再結成され、再編成された。

regu|lar /rɛɡyələr/ (**regulars**) ■ ADJ 形容詞 **Regular** events have equal amounts of time between them, so that they happen, for example, at the same time each day or each week. 定期的な ❑ Get regular exercise. 定期的に運動をしなさい。 ❑ We're going to be meeting there on a regular basis. 我々はそこで定期的に会合をする予定です。 ● **regu|lar|ly** ADV 副詞 [ADV with v] 定期的に ❑ He also writes regularly for "International Management" magazine. 彼は定期的に『国際経営』誌にも寄稿しています。 ● **regu|lar|ity** N-UNCOUNT 不可算名詞 規則正しさ ❑ The overdraft arrangements had been generous because of the regularity of the half-yearly payments. 当座貸し越しの取り決めは、半年ごとの定期的な支払いのために寛大なものであった。 ■ ADJ 形容詞 **Regular** events happen often. たびたびの ❑ Although it may look unpleasant, this condition is harmless and usually clears up with regular shampooing. 見た目はよくないかもしれませんが、この状態は害はありませんし、普通は繰り返しシャンプーすることできれいになります。 ● **regu|lar|ly** ADV 副詞 [ADV with v] しばしば ❑ Fox, badger, and weasel are regularly seen here. ここではキツネ、アナグマ、イタチがよく見られる。 ● **regu|lar|ity** N-UNCOUNT 不可算名詞 不変なこと ❑ Closures and job losses are again being announced with monotonous regularity. 休業や失業が再びおきそうな単調さで発表されつつある。 ■ ADJ 形容詞 [ADJ n] If you are, for example, a **regular** customer at a store or a **regular** visitor to a place, you go there often. 常連の ❑ She has become a regular visitor to Houghton Hall. 彼女はホートン・ホールをたびたび訪れている。 ■ N-COUNT 可算名詞 The **regulars** at a place or on a team are the people who often go to the place or are often on the team. 常連、レギュラー選手 ❑ Regulars at his local bar have set up a fund to help out. 彼の地元のバーの常連客が支援基金を設立した。 ■ ADJ 形容詞 You use **regular** when referring to the thing, person, time, or place that is usually used by someone. For example, someone's **regular** place is the place where they usually sit. いつもの [det ADJ n] ❑ The man shook his hand and then sat at his regular table near the windows. その男性は手を振り、窓際のいつもの席に着いた。 ■ ADJ 形容詞 A **regular**

rhythm consists of a series of sounds or movements with equal periods of time between them. 規則正しい ❑ ...a very regular beat. とても規則正しい拍子。 ● **regu|lar|ly** ADV 副詞 [ADV with v] 規則正しく ❑ Remember to breathe regularly. 規則正しく呼吸をすることを忘れないでください。 ● **regu|lar|ity** N-UNCOUNT 不可算名詞 規則性 ❑ Experimenters have succeeded in controlling the rate and regularity of the heartbeat. 実験者たちは、心拍周期とその規則性をコントロールすることに成功した。 ■ ADJ 形容詞 [ADJ n] **Regular** is used to mean "normal." 普通の [mainly AM 主に米国英語] ❑ The product looks and burns like a regular cigarette. その製品は見た目も燃え方も普通のたばこに似ている。 ■ ADJ 形容詞 In some restaurants, a **regular** drink or quantity of food is of medium size. レギュラーサイズの [mainly AM 主に米国英語] [ADJ n] ❑ ...a cheeseburger and regular fries. チーズバーガーとポテトフライのレギュラー ■ ADJ 形容詞 A **regular** pattern or arrangement consists of a series of things with equal spaces between them. 一定な、均等な ❑ The village was laid out in regular patterns. その村は一定間隔の整然とした配置だった。 ■ ADJ 形容詞 If something has a **regular** shape, both halves are the same and it has straight edges or a smooth outline. 等辺の ❑ ...some regular geometrical shape. ある等辺の幾何学的形状 ● **regu|lar|ity** N-UNCOUNT 不可算名詞 等辺性 ❑ ...the chessboard regularity of their fields. チェス盤のように等辺的に広がる畑。 ■ ADJ 形容詞 In grammar, a **regular** verb, noun, or adjective inflects in the same way as most verbs, nouns, or adjectives in the language. (屈折変化が) 規則的な

Word Partnership	regular は次の語句と使われる:
N.	regular **basis**, regular **checkups**, regular **exercise**, regular **meetings**, regular **schedule**, regular **visits** ■ ■
	regular **customer**, regular **visitor** ■
	regular **coffee**, regular **guy**, regular **hours**, regular **mail**, regular **season** ■
	regular **verbs** ■

regu|late /rɛɡyəleɪt/ (**regulates, regulating, regulated**) V-T 他動詞 To **regulate** an activity or process means to control it, especially by means of rules. 規制する ❑ Under such a plan, the government would regulate competition among insurance companies so that everyone gets care at lower cost. そのような案では、誰もがより低い保険料で手当て受けられるように、政府は保険会社間の競争を規制するみたいだ。

Word Link	regu ≈ rule : regal, regime, regulation

regu|la|tion /rɛɡyəleɪʃ³n/ (**regulations**) ■ N-COUNT 可算名詞 **Regulations** are rules made by a government or other authority in order to control the way something is done or the way people behave. 規定 ❑ The European Union has proposed new regulations to control the hours worked by its employees. 欧州連合は職員の労働時間を調整する新規定を提案した。 ■ N-UNCOUNT 不可算名詞 **Regulation** is the controlling of an activity or process, usually by means of rules. 規制 ❑ Some in the market now want government regulation in order to reduce costs. 今や市場では経費を削減するために政府の規制が求める人もいる。 → see **factory**

Word Partnership	regulation は次の語句と使われる:
ADJ.	**new** regulation ■
	federal regulation, **financial** regulation, **strict** regulation ■ ■
N.	**banking** regulation, **government** regulation, **industry** regulation ■ ■

regu|la|tor /rɛɡyəleɪtər/ (**regulators**) N-COUNT 可算名詞 A **regulator** is a person or organization appointed by a government to regulate an area of activity such as banking or industry. 調整者 ❑ An independent regulator will be appointed to ensure fair competition. 公正な競争を確保するために第3者の調整者が任命される予定だ。 ● **regu|la|tory** /rɛɡyələtɔri/ ADJ 形容詞 調整の ❑ ...the U.S.'s financial regulatory system. 米国の金融調整制度

re|hab /rihæb/ (**rehabs, rehabbing, rehabbed**) ■ N-UNCOUNT 不可算名詞 **Rehab** is the process of helping someone to lead a normal life again after they have been ill, or when they have had a drug or alcohol problem. **Rehab** is short for **rehabilitation**. リハビリテーション [INFORMAL くだけた] ❑ ...a hospital rehab program. 病院のリハビリプログラム ■ V-T 他動詞 If you **rehab** an old building, you repair and improve it and get it back into good condition. 修復する [AM 米国英語、INFORMAL くだけた] ❑ People are improving and rehabbing homes throughout the city. その市のいたるところで家屋の改修や修復が行われている。

re|ha|bili|tate /rihəbɪliteɪt/ (**rehabilitates, rehabilitating, rehabilitated**) V-T 他動詞 To **rehabilitate** someone who has been ill or in prison means to help them to live a normal life again. To

rehabilitate someone who has a drug or alcohol problem means to help them stop using drugs or alcohol. リハビリを施す，更正させる ☐ *Considerable efforts have been made to rehabilitate patients who have suffered in this way.* こういった状態に苦しむ患者のリハビリに相当な努力が払われてきた。 ●**re|ha|bili|ta|tion** /rihəbɪlɪteɪʃᵊn/ N-UNCOUNT 不可算名詞 リハビリテーション，更正 ☐ *A number of other techniques are now being used by psychologists in the rehabilitation of young offenders.* 心理学者は，若い犯罪者を更生する他の手法も現在いくつか適用している。

re|hears|al /rɪhɜrsᵊl/ (**rehearsals**) **1** N-VAR 可変性名詞 A **rehearsal** of a play, dance, or piece of music is a practice of it in preparation for a performance. リハーサル ☐ *The band was scheduled to begin rehearsals for a concert tour.* そのバンドはコンサートツアーに向けたリハーサルを始める予定だった。 **2** → see also **dress rehearsal** **3** N-COUNT 可算名詞 You can describe an event or object that is a preparation for a more important event or object as a **rehearsal for** it. 予行演習 ☐ *Daydreams may seem to be rehearsals for real-life situations, but we know they are not.* 白日夢は現実にこれから起ることの予兆のように思えるかもしれないが，そうではないことがわかっている。

re|hearse /rɪhɜrs/ (**rehearses, rehearsing, rehearsed**) **1** V-T/V-I 他動詞/自動詞 When people **rehearse** a play, dance, or piece of music, they practice it in order to prepare for a performance. リハーサルをする ☐ *In his version, a group of actors are rehearsing a play about Joan of Arc.* 彼の脚色で，一群の俳優たちはジャンヌダルクの劇のリハーサルを行っている。 ☐ *Tens of thousands of people have been rehearsing for the opening ceremony in the new stadium.* 何万人もが新しい競技場の開会式典のリハーサルを行ってきた。 **2** V-T 他動詞 If you **rehearse** something that you are going to say or do, you silently practice it by imagining that you are saying or doing it. あらかじめ思い描く ☐ *Anticipate any tough questions and rehearse your answers.* 厳しい質問を想定して，答え方をあらかじめ考えておきなさい。 → see **memory**

reign /reɪn/ (**reigns, reigning, reigned**) **1** V-I 自動詞 If you say, for example, that silence **reigns** in a place or confusion **reigns** in a situation, you mean that the place is silent or the situation is confused. (雰囲気が) 行き渡る [WRITTEN 書き言葉] ☐ *Last night confusion reigned about how the debate, which continues today, would end.* 昨夜はその議論が，実は今日も続いているのだが，どのように終わるのかについて混乱を呈していた。 **2** V-I 自動詞 When a king or queen **reigns**, he or she rules a country. 統治する ☐ *...Henry II, who reigned from 1154 to 1189.* 1154年から1189年まで王位にあったヘンリー二世 ●N-COUNT 可算名詞 **Reign** is also a noun. 統治 ☐ *...Queen Victoria's reign.* ビクトリア女王の治世

re|im|burse /riɪmbɜrs/ (**reimburses, reimbursing, reimbursed**) V-T 他動詞 If you **reimburse** someone for something, you pay them back the money that they have spent or lost because of it. 返済する [FORMAL 形式ばった] ☐ *I'll be happy to reimburse you for any expenses you've had.* あなたが支払ったどんな経費も喜んで払い戻しさせていただきます。

re|im|burse|ment /riɪmbɜrsmənt/ (**reimbursements**) N-VAR 可変性名詞 If you receive **reimbursement for** money that you have spent, you get your money back, for example because the money should have been paid by someone else. 返済 [FORMAL 形式ばった] ☐ *She is demanding reimbursement for medical and other expenses.* 彼女は医療費やその他の費用の返済を要求している。

rein /reɪn/ (**reins, reining, reined**) **1** N-PLURAL 複数名詞 **Reins** are the thin leather straps attached around a horse's neck which are used to control the horse. 手綱 ☐ *Cord held the reins while the stallion tugged and snorted.* コードは雄馬が鼻息を荒げて引っ張る手綱を握っていた。 **2** N-PLURAL 複数名詞 Journalists sometimes use the expression **the reins** or **the reins of power** to refer to the control of a country or organization. 支配 ☐ *He was determined to see the party keep a hold on the reins of power.* 彼はその党が権力の座を守り続けるのを見て取ろうと決心した。 **3** PHRASE 句 If you **give free rein to** someone, you give them a lot of freedom to do what they want. 一に自由にさせる ☐ *The government continued to believe it should give free rein to the private sector in transportation.* 政府は運輸業では民間セクターに自由に任せるべきという考えを持ち続けた。 **4** PHRASE 句 If you **keep a tight rein on** someone, you control them firmly. 一を厳しく管理する ☐ *Her parents kept her on a tight rein with their narrow and inflexible views.* 彼女の両親は偏狭で，頑固な考え方で彼女を厳しく管理していた。

▶ **rein back** PHRASAL VERB 句動詞 To **rein back** something such as spending means to control it strictly. 一を抑える ☐ *He promised that between now and the end of the year the government would try to rein back inflation.* 彼は今から年末の間に政府がインフレの抑制に努めると約束した。

▶ **rein in** PHRASAL VERB 句動詞 To **rein in** something means to control it. 一を抑える ☐ *Many people have begun looking for long-term ways to rein in spending.* 多くの人は長期的に消費を抑える方法を模索し始めていた。

re|incar|na|tion /riːɪnkɑrneɪʃᵊn/ (**reincarnations**) **1** N-UNCOUNT 不可算名詞 If you believe in **reincarnation**, you believe that you will be reincarnated after you die. 霊魂再生 ☐ *Many African tribes believe in reincarnation.* アフリカの部族の多くは，霊魂再生を信じている。 **2** N-COUNT 可算名詞 A **reincarnation** is a person or animal whose body is believed to contain the spirit of a dead person. 生まれ変わり ☐ *Another little girl, believed to be the reincarnation of her grandmother, was obsessed with sewing.* また別の少女は，おばあさんの生まれ変わりだと考えられていたのですが，裁縫に執着していたのです。

rein|deer /reɪndɪər/ (**reindeer**)

Reindeer is both the singular and the plural form.

Reindeer は単数形でも複数形でもある。

N-COUNT 可算名詞 A **reindeer** is a deer with large horns called antlers that lives in northern areas of Europe, Asia, and America. トナカイ ☐ *...a herd of reindeer.* トナカイの1群れ

re|inforce /riɪnfɔrs/ (**reinforces, reinforcing, reinforced**) **1** V-T 他動詞 If something **reinforces** a feeling, situation, or process, it makes it stronger or more intense. 強める ☐ *I hope this will reinforce Indonesian determination to deal with this kind of threat.* これがきっかけとなり，インドネシアがこのような脅威に対処する決意を強化してくれることを私は望んでいる。 **2** V-T 他動詞 If something **reinforces** an idea or point of view, it provides more evidence or support for it. 強固にする ☐ *The delegation hopes to reinforce the idea that human rights are not purely internal matters.* 代表団は人権問題は純粋に国内の問題ではないという考えを強化できればと思っている。 **3** V-T 他動詞 To **reinforce** an object means to make it stronger or harder. 補強する ☐ *Eventually, they had to reinforce the walls with exterior beams.* 結局，彼らは壁を外側のはりで補強せざるを得なくなった。 **4** V-T 他動詞 To **reinforce** an army or police force means to make it stronger by increasing its size or providing it with more weapons. To **reinforce** a position or place means to make it stronger by sending more soldiers or weapons. 拡充する ☐ *Both sides have been reinforcing their positions after yesterday's fierce fighting.* 昨日の激しい戦闘の後に両陣営は軍備を拡充しています。

re|inforce|ment /riɪnfɔrsmənt/ (**reinforcements**) **1** N-PLURAL 複数名詞 **Reinforcements** are soldiers or police officers who are sent to join an army or group of police in order to make it stronger. 援軍 ☐ *Mr. Vlok promised new measures to protect residents, including the dispatch of police and troop reinforcements.* ヴロック氏は，警察や部隊の増援隊の派遣を含む新しい住民保護政策を約束した。 **2** N-VAR 可変性名詞 The **reinforcement** of something is the process of making it stronger. 強化 ☐ *I am sure that this meeting will contribute to the reinforcement of peace and security all over the world.* この会談によって世界中の平和と安全はより確かなものになることを私は確信している。

re|instate /riɪnsteɪt/ (**reinstates, reinstating, reinstated**) **1** V-T 他動詞 If you **reinstate** someone, you give them back a job or position that had been taken away from them. 復職させる ☐ *The governor is said to have agreed to reinstate five senior workers who were dismissed.* 知事は解任された上級職5名の復職に合意したようです。 **2** V-T 他動詞 To **reinstate** a law, facility, or practice means to start having it again. 復活させる ☐ *She says the public response was a factor in the decision to reinstate the grant.* 彼女は，大衆の声が助成金再開を決めた要因の1つだった，と述べている。

re|instate|ment /riɪnsteɪtmənt/ **1** N-UNCOUNT 不可算名詞 **Reinstatement** is the act of giving someone back a job or position that has been taken away from them. 復職 ☐ *Parents campaigned in vain for her reinstatement.* 親は彼女の復職に向けた運動をしたが不成功に終わった。 **2** N-UNCOUNT 不可算名詞 The **reinstatement** of a law, facility, or practice is the act of causing it to exist again. 復活 ☐ *He welcomed the reinstatement of the 10 percent bank base rate.* 彼は銀行基準金利が再び10パーセントになったことを歓迎した。

re|it|er|ate /riɪtəreɪt/ (**reiterates, reiterating, reiterated**) V-T 他動詞 If you **reiterate** something, you say it again, usually in order to emphasize it. 繰り返し述べる [FORMAL 形式ばった JOURNALISM ジャーナリズム] ☐ *He reiterated his opposition to the creation of a central bank.* 彼は中央銀行創設には反対だと繰り返し述べた。

re|ject (rejects, rejecting, rejected)

The verb is pronounced /rɪdʒɛkt/. The noun is pronounced /rɪ́dʒɛkt/.

動詞は /rɪdʒɛkt/ と発音される. 名詞は /rɪ́dʒɛkt/ と発音される.

1 V-T 他動詞 If you **reject** something such as a proposal, a request, or an offer, you do not accept it or you do not agree to it. 却下する ❑ *The government is expected to reject the idea of state subsidy for a new high-speed railroad.* 政府は新しい高速鉄道への国家補助金を拒否する模様です. ● re|jec|tion /rɪdʒɛ́kʃn/ (rejections) N-VAR 可変性名詞 ❑ *The rejection of such initiatives by no means indicates that voters are unconcerned about the environment.* そういった発案の拒否は, 決して有権者が環境問題に無関心だということを示しているわけではない. **2** V-T 他動詞 If you **reject** a belief or a political system, you refuse to believe in it or to live by its rules. 受け入れない, 拒絶する ❑ *...the children of Eastern European immigrants who had rejected their parents' political and religious beliefs.* 両親の政治・宗教思想を受け入れなかった東欧移民の子供たち ● re|jec|tion N-VAR 可変性名詞 拒絶 ❑ *His rejection of our values is far more complete than that of D. H. Lawrence.* 彼はD・H・ロレンスよりはるかに徹底して私たちの価値観を拒絶している. **3** V-T 他動詞 If someone **is rejected** for a job or course of study, it is not offered to them. 不合格にする ❑ *One of my most able students was rejected by another university.* 最もよくできる生徒の1人が別の大学に不合格だった. ● re|jec|tion N-COUNT 可算名詞 不合格 ❑ *Be prepared for lots of rejections before you land a job.* 就職するまでに何社も不採用になることを覚悟しなさい. **4** V-T 他動詞 If someone **rejects** another person who expects affection from them, they are cold and unfriendly toward them. 断る ❑ *...people who had been rejected by their lovers.* 恋人に振られた経験を持つ人々 ● re|jec|tion N-VAR 可変性名詞 拒絶 ❑ *These feelings of rejection and hurt remain.* このような拒絶されて傷ついた気持ちは消えない. **5** V-T 他動詞 If a person's body **rejects** something such as a new heart that has been transplanted into it, it tries to attack and destroy it. 拒絶反応を示す ❑ *It was feared his body was rejecting a kidney he received in a transplant four years ago.* 彼の体が4年前に移植された腎臓に拒絶反応を示していると懸念されていました. ● re|jec|tion N-VAR 可変性名詞 拒絶反応 ❑ *...a special drug which stops rejection of transplanted organs.* 移植された臓器の拒絶反応を抑える特別な薬 **6** N-COUNT 可算名詞 A **reject** is a product that has not been accepted for use or sale, because there is something wrong with it. 不良品 ❑ *The check shirt is a reject - too small.* このチェックのシャツは不良品だ. 小さすぎるよ.

Thesaurus

reject また次を参照:

V. decline, refuse, turn down; (ant.) accept **1**

Word Partnership

reject は次の語句と使われる:

V. **vote** to reject **1**
N. reject **an offer**, reject **a plan**, reject **a proposal**, **voters** reject **1**
reject **an idea 1 2**
reject **an application 3**

re|joice /rɪdʒɔ́ɪs/ (rejoices, rejoicing, rejoiced) V-T/V-I 他動詞/自動詞 If you **rejoice**, you are very pleased about something and you show it in your behavior. 喜ぶ ❑ *Garbo plays the queen, rejoicing in the love she has found with Antonio.* ガルボが演じるのは, アントニオへの愛に気づいた喜びに満ちた女王の役です. ● re|joic|ing N-UNCOUNT 不可算名詞 喜び ❑ *There was general rejoicing at the news.* そのニュースは一般の人々に歓迎されました.

re|ju|venate /rɪdʒúːvəneɪt/ (rejuvenates, rejuvenating, rejuvenated) **1** V-T 他動詞 If something **rejuvenates** you, it makes you feel or look young again. 若返らせる ❑ *Shelley was advised that the Italian climate would rejuvenate him.* シェリーは, イタリアの気候のもとでなら元気を回復するだろうと助言された. **2** V-T 他動詞 If you **rejuvenate** an organization or system, you make it more lively and more efficient, for example by introducing new ideas. 活性化させる ❑ *The government pushed through plans to rejuvenate the inner cities.* 政府は都心部の活性化計画を推し進めた.

re|kin|dle /riːkɪ́ndl/ (rekindles, rekindling, rekindled) **1** V-T 他動詞 If something **rekindles** an interest, feeling, or thought that you used to have, it makes you think about it or feel it again. 再びかきたてる ❑ *Ben Brantley's article on Sir Ian McKellen rekindled many memories.* ベン・ブラントレーによるイアン・マッケラン卿の記事は多くの記憶をよみがえらせた. **2** V-T 他動詞 If something **rekindles** an unpleasant situation, it makes the unpleasant situation happen again. 再燃させる ❑ *There are fears that the series could rekindle animosity between the two countries.* そのシリーズによってこ とによると2か国間の敵意が再燃する恐れがある.

re|lapse /rɪlǽps/ (relapses, relapsing, relapsed)

The noun can be pronounced /rɪlǽps/ or /ríːlæps/.

名詞は /rɪlǽps/ と /ríːlæps/ のどちらでも発音できる.

1 V-I 自動詞 If you say that someone **relapses into** a way of behaving that is undesirable, you mean that they start to behave in that way again. 再び陥る ❑ *"I wish I did," said Phil Jordan, relapsing into his usual gloom.* いつもの暗い調子に陥って「やればいいんだけどさ」とフィル・ジョーダンは言った. ● N-COUNT 可算名詞 **Relapse** is also a noun. 逆戻り ❑ *...a relapse into the nationalism of the nineteenth century.* 19世紀の国家主義への逆戻り **2** V-I 自動詞 If a sick person **relapses**, their health suddenly gets worse after it had been improving. 再発する ❑ *In 90 percent of cases the patient will relapse within six months.* 90パーセントの患者は6か月以内に再発するだろう. ● N-VAR 可変性名詞 **Relapse** is also a noun. 再発 ❑ *The treatment is usually given to women with a high risk of relapse after surgery.* この治療は, 通常は手術後の再発リスクが高い女性に適用される.

re|late /rɪléɪt/ (relates, relating, related) **1** V-I 自動詞 If something **relates to** a particular subject, it concerns that subject. 関係する ❑ *Other recommendations relate to the details of how such data is stored.* 他に提案されているのは, このようなデータの保存方法の詳細についてです. **2** V-RECIP 相互動詞 The way that two things **relate**, or the way that one thing **relates to** another, is the sort of connection that exists between them. 関connect する ❑ *I don't think he understood the dynamics of how the police and the city administration relate.* 彼が警察と市政がいかに関係しているかという力学を理解しているようには思えません. ❑ *Trainees should be invited to relate new ideas to their past experiences.* 新しい考えを過去の経験に関連づけるように訓練生に促すべきだ. **3** V-RECIP 相互動詞 If you can **relate to** someone, you can understand how they feel or behave so that you are able to communicate with them or deal with them easily. 心が通う ❑ *He is unable to relate to other people.* 彼は他の人たちとうまくつきあえない.

re|lat|ed /rɪléɪtɪd/ **1** ADJ 形容詞 If two or more things are **related**, there is a connection between them. 関連した ❑ *The philosophical problems of chance and of free will are closely related.* 偶然性と自由意志という哲学的な問題は密接に関連している. **2** ADJ 形容詞 People who are **related** belong to the same family. 親族の [v-link ADJ] ❑ *The children, although not related to us by blood, had become as dear to us as our own.* その子たちは私どもと血はつながっていませんが, 実の子と同じようにいとしい存在になっていました. **3** ADJ 形容詞 If you say that different types of things, such as languages, are **related**, you mean that they developed from the same language. 同族の ❑ *He recognized that Sanskrit, the language of India, was related very closely to Latin, Greek, and the Germanic and Celtic languages.* 彼は, インドの言語のサンスクリット語はラテン語, ギリシャ語, ゲルマン語系やケルト語系の諸語などにとても近い同族語だと気づいた.

-related /-rɪléɪtɪd/ COMB IN ADJ 形容詞の複合 **-related** combines with nouns to form adjectives with the meaning "connected with the thing referred to by the noun." 一に関係した ❑ *More than 50 arrests were made, mostly for drug-related offenses.* 50件以上の検挙があったが, そのほとんどが麻薬関連の犯罪だった.

re|la|tion /rɪléɪʃn/ (relations) **1** N-COUNT 可算名詞 **Relations** between people, groups, or countries are contacts between them and the way in which they behave toward each other. 関係 ❑ *Greece has established full diplomatic relations with Israel.* ギリシアはイスラエルと完全な外交関係を樹立した. **2** → see also **industrial relations**, **public relations**, **race relations** **3** N-COUNT 可算名詞 If you talk about the **relation** of one thing to another, you are talking about the ways in which they are connected. 関係 ❑ *It is a question of the relation of ethics to economics.* それは倫理と経済の関係の問題だ. **4** N-COUNT 可算名詞 Your **relations** are the members of your family. 親族 ❑ *...visits to friends and relations.* 友人や親戚への訪問 **5** PHRASE 句 You can talk about something **in relation to** something else when you want to compare the size, condition, or position of the two things. 一と比較して ❑ *The money he'd been ordered to pay was minimal in relation to his salary.* 彼に命じられた支払額は, 彼の給与からするとごく小額だった. **6** PHRASE 句 If something is said or done **in relation to** a subject, it is said or done in connection with that subject. 一に関係して ❑ *...a question that has been asked many times in relation to Irish affairs.* アイルランド問題に関して何度もされた質問

Word Partnership

relation は次の語句と使われる:

PREP. relation **between** *someone/something* **and** *someone/something* **1**
relation **of** *something* **to** *something* **2**
in relation **to** *something* **4 5**
V. **bear a** relation **2**

re|la|tion|ship /rɪléɪʃnʃɪp/ (relationships) **1** N-COUNT 可算名詞 The **relationship** between two people or groups is the way in which they feel and behave toward each other. 関係 ❑ *...the friendly relationship between France and Britain.* フランスと英国の友好

的な関係 **2** N-COUNT 可算名詞 A **relationship** is a close friendship between two people, especially one involving romantic or sexual feelings. 恋愛関係 ❑ *We had been together for two years, but both of us felt the relationship wasn't really going anywhere.* 私たちは2年間交際を続けていましたが、どちらもこれ以上関係が進むことはないと感じていました。 **3** N-COUNT 可算名詞 The **relationship** between two things is the way in which they are connected. 関連性 ❑ *A number of small-scale studies have already indicated that there is a relationship between diet and cancer.* すでに小規模な研究の多くが、日常の飲食物とがんに関連性があることを示唆している。

Word Partnership   relationship は次の語句と使われる:

ADJ.	**professional** relationship, **working** relationship **1**
	abusive relationship, **good** relationship, **healthy** relationship, **loving** relationship **1 2**
	close relationship, **intimate** relationship **1** – **3**
	romantic relationship, **sexual** relationship **1 2**
V.	**develop a** relationship, **end a** relationship, **have a** relationship, **maintain a** relationship **1 2**
	establish a relationship **1** – **3**

rela|tive /rɛlətɪv/ (relatives) **1** N-COUNT 可算名詞 Your **relatives** are the members of your family. 親族 ❑ *Get a relative to look after the children.* 親戚の誰かにその子たちの面倒を頼みなさい。 **2** ADJ 形容詞 You use **relative** to say that something is true to a certain degree, especially when compared with other things of the same kind. 比較上の [ADJ n] ❑ *The fighting resumed after a period of relative calm.* 比較的平穏な時期を経て戦闘が再開された。 **3** ADJ 形容詞 You use **relative** when you are comparing the quality or size of two things. 相対的な [ADJ n] ❑ *They chatted about the relative merits of London and Paris as places to live.* 彼らは居住地としてのロンドンとパリの相対的な長所を話していた。 **4** PHRASE 句 **Relative to** something means with reference to it or in comparison with it. 〜に対して ❑ *Japanese interest rates rose relative to America's.* 日本の金利は米国と比べて上がった。 **5** ADJ 形容詞 If you say that something is **relative**, you mean that it needs to be considered and judged in relation to other things. 相対的な ❑ *Fitness is relative; one must always ask "Fit for what?"* 適性とは相対的なものだ。つまり、「何に対して適しているのか」が常に求められるのである。 **6** N-COUNT 可算名詞 If one animal, plant, language, or invention is a **relative of** another, they have both developed from the same type of animal, plant, language, or invention. 同族 ❑ *The pheasant is a close relative of the guinea hen.* キジはホロホロチョウの近親種だ。

Word Partnership   relative は次の語句と使われる:

ADJ.	**close** relative, **distant** relative **1**
N.	**friend and** relative **1**
	relative **calm**, relative **ease**, relative **safety**, relative **stability 2**

rela|tive clause (relative clauses) N-COUNT 可算名詞 In grammar, a **relative clause** is a subordinate clause which specifies or gives information about a person or thing. Relative clauses come after a noun or pronoun and, in English, often begin with a relative pronoun such as "who," "which," or "that." 関係詞節

rela|tive|ly /rɛlətɪvli/ ADV 副詞 **Relatively** means to a certain degree, especially when compared with other things of the same kind. 比較的に [ADV adj/adv] ❑ *The sums needed are relatively small.* 必要金額は比較的小さい。

re|launch /rilɔntʃ/ (relaunches, relaunching, relaunched) V-T 他動詞 To **relaunch** something such as a company, a product, or a program means to start it again or to produce it in a similar way. 再出発させる ❑ *He is hoping to relaunch his film career with a remake of the 1971 British thriller.* 彼は1971年の英国スリラーのリメイク版で映画人としてのキャリアを再開したいと思っている。 ● N-COUNT 可算名詞 **Relaunch** is also a noun. 再出発 ❑ *Relaunches are often simply a way of boosting sales.* 再出発は販売促進の手段にすぎないことが多い。

Word Link   lax ≈ allowing, loosening : lax, laxative, relax

re|lax /rɪlæks/ (relaxes, relaxing, relaxed) **1** V-T/V-I 他動詞/自動詞 If you **relax** or if something **relaxes** you, you feel more calm and less worried or tense. くつろがせる [他動詞]、くつろぐ [自動詞] ❑ *I ought to relax and stop worrying about it.* 私はくつろいでそのことを心配するのは止めなければならない。 **2** V-T/V-I 他動詞/自動詞 When a part of your body **relaxes**, or when you **relax** it, it becomes less stiff or firm. 和らげる [他動詞]、和らぐ [自動詞] ❑ *Massage is used to relax muscles, relieve stress and improve the circulation.* マッサージは筋肉をほぐしたり、ストレスを解放したり、血行をよくするために行われます。 **3** V-T 他動詞 If you **relax** your grip or hold on something, you hold it less tightly than before. 緩める ❑ *He gradually relaxed his grip on the arms of the chair.* 彼はひじ掛けを握る手を徐々に緩め

た。 **4** V-T/V-I 他動詞/自動詞 If you **relax** a rule or your control over something, or if it **relaxes**, it becomes less firm or strong. 緩める [他動詞]、緩くなる [自動詞] ❑ *Rules governing student conduct have relaxed somewhat in recent years.* 学生の行為を管理する規則は、近年いくぶん緩くなった。 **5** → see also **relaxed, relaxing**
→ see **muscle**

Thesaurus   relax また次を参照:

V.	calm down, rest, unwind **1**
	ease off, loosen **3 4**

Word Partnership   relax は次の語句と使われる:

V.	**sit back and** relax **1**
	begin to relax, **try to** relax **1 2**
N.	**time to** relax **1**
	relax *your body*, **muscles** relax **2**

Word Link   ation ≈ state of : celebration, elevation, relaxation

re|laxa|tion /rilækseɪʃⁿn/ **1** N-UNCOUNT 不可算名詞 **Relaxation** is a way of spending time in which you rest and feel comfortable. くつろぎ ❑ *You should be able to find the odd moment for relaxation.* きみは合間にくつろぐ時間を取れるようにならないといけないよ。 **2** N-UNCOUNT 不可算名詞 If there is **relaxation** of a rule or control, it is made less firm or strong. 緩和 ❑ *The relaxation of travel restrictions means they are free to travel and work.* 旅行規制の緩和により、彼らは自由に旅行して仕事することができるようになる。

re|laxed /rɪlækst/ **1** ADJ 形容詞 If you are **relaxed**, you are calm and not worried or tense. くつろいだ、安らいだ ❑ *As soon as I had made the final decision, I felt a lot more relaxed.* 最終決断をしたらすぐに気持ちがずっと安らいだ。 **2** ADJ 形容詞 If a place or situation is **relaxed**, it is calm and peaceful. 和やかな ❑ *The atmosphere at lunch was relaxed.* 昼食の雰囲気は和やかだった。

re|lax|ing /rɪlæksɪŋ/ ADJ 形容詞 Something that is **relaxing** is pleasant and helps you to relax. くつろいだ気分にさせる ❑ *I find cooking very relaxing.* 料理が気晴らしになるのよ。

re|lay (relays, relaying, relayed)

The noun is pronounced /rileɪ/. The verb is pronounced /rɪleɪ/.

名詞は /rileɪ/ と発音される。動詞は /rɪleɪ/ と発音される。

1 N-COUNT 可算名詞 A **relay** or a **relay race** is a race between two or more teams, for example teams of runners or swimmers. Each member of the team runs or swims one section of the race. リレー ❑ *Britain's prospects of beating the United States in the relay looked poor.* リレーで英国が米国を破るという見込みは薄そうだった。 **2** V-T 他動詞 To **relay** television or radio signals means to send them or broadcast them. 中継する ❑ *The satellite will be used mainly to relay television programs.* その衛星は主にテレビ番組の中継に使われるでしょう。 **3** V-T 他動詞 If you **relay** something that has been said to you, you repeat it to another person. 取り次ぐ [FORMAL 形式ばった] ❑ *She relayed the message, then frowned.* 彼女は伝言を取り次ぎ、それから顔をしかめた。

re|lease /rɪlis/ (releases, releasing, released) **1** V-T 他動詞 If a person or animal is **released** from somewhere where they have been locked up or cared for, they are set free or allowed to go. 解き放す [usu passive] ❑ *He was released from custody the next day.* 彼は翌日に監禁を解かれた。 **2** N-COUNT 可算名詞 When someone is released, you refer to their **release**. 解放 [with supp] ❑ *He called for the immediate release of all political prisoners.* 彼は直ちにすべての政治犯を釈放するよう要求した。 **3** V-T 他動詞 If someone or something **releases** you **from** a duty, task, or feeling, they free you from it. 解く [FORMAL 形式ばった] ❑ *Divorce releases both the husband and wife from all marital obligations to each other.* 離婚によって男女双方とも夫婦間の義務から解放される。 ● N-UNCOUNT 不可算名詞 **Release** is also a noun. 解放 [also "a" N, oft N "from" N] ❑ *Our therapeutic style offers release from stored tensions, traumas, and grief.* 我々の治療スタイルで、蓄積した緊張、トラウマ、悲しみが解放されます。 **4** V-T 他動詞 To **release** feelings or abilities means to allow them to be expressed. 表す ❑ *Expressing your own person releases your creativity.* 人が自立すると創造性が発揮される。 ● N-UNCOUNT 不可算名詞 **Release** is also a noun. 発現 ❑ *She felt the sudden sweet release of her own tears.* 彼女は心地よい涙が流れるのを感じた。 **5** V-T 他動詞 If someone in authority **releases** something such as a document or information, they make it available. 発表する ❑ *They're not releasing any more details yet.* 彼らはそれ以上の詳細は明らかにしないようです。 ● N-COUNT 可算名詞 **Release** is also a noun. 発表 ❑ *Action had been taken to speed up the release of checks.* 小切手の発行を早める措置が取られていた。 **6** V-T 他動詞 If you **release** someone or something, you stop holding them. 解放する [FORMAL 形式ばった] ❑ *He stopped and faced her, releasing her wrist.* 彼は立ち止まって彼女の方を向き、手首を離した。 **7** V-T 他動詞 If something **releases** gas, heat, or a substance, it causes it to leave its container or

the substance that it was part of and enter the surrounding atmosphere or area. 放出する ❑ *...a weapon that releases toxic nerve gas.* 有毒な神経ガスを放出する武器 ● N-COUNT 可算名詞 **Release** is also a noun. 放出 ❑ *Under the agreement, releases of cancer-causing chemicals will be cut by about 80 percent.* その合意により，発がん性化学物質の放出は約80パーセント削減されるでしょう. ⑧ V-T 他動詞 When an entertainer or company **releases** a new CD, DVD, or movie, it becomes available so that people can buy it or see it. 発売する，封切りする ❑ *He is releasing an album of love songs.* 彼はラブソングのアルバムをリリースする予定だ. ⑨ N-COUNT 可算名詞 A new **release** is a new CD, DVD, or movie that has just become available for people to buy or see. 新盤，封切り映画 ❑ *Of the new releases that are out there now, which do you think are really good?* 今出ている新盤ではどれが本当にいいと思う？ ⑩ → see also **press release**

rel|egate /rɛlɪgeɪt/ (**relegates, relegating, relegated**) V-T 他動詞 If you **relegate** someone or something to a less important position, you give them this position. 降格させる ❑ *Might it not be better to relegate the king to a purely ceremonial function?* 王を単なる儀式のための存在に下げるほうがいいのではないでしょうか.

re|lent /rɪlɛnt/ (**relents, relenting, relented**) V-I 自動詞 If you **relent**, you allow someone to do something that you had previously refused to allow them to do. 折れる ❑ *Finally his mother relented and gave permission for her youngest son to marry.* 結局は母親が折れて，末息子の結婚を許した.

re|lent|less /rɪlɛntlɪs/ ❶ ADJ 形容詞 Something bad that is **relentless** never stops or never becomes less intense. 情け容赦なく続く ❑ *The pressure now was relentless.* 今やその重圧は容赦なく続いていた. ● **re|lent|less|ly** ADV 副詞 情け容赦もなく続いて ❑ *The sun is beating down relentlessly.* 日差しが情け容赦なく照り続けている. ❷ ADJ 形容詞 Someone who is **relentless** is determined to do something and refuses to give up, even if what they are doing is unpleasant or cruel. 容赦のない ❑ *Relentless in his pursuit of quality, his technical ability was remarkable.* 彼の品質への追求はあくなきもので，腕も素晴らしかった. ● **re|lent|less|ly** ADV 副詞 容赦なく ❑ *She always questioned me relentlessly.* 彼女はいつも私に容赦ない質問を投げかけた.

rel|evance /rɛləvəns/ N-UNCOUNT 不可算名詞 Something's **relevance to** a situation or person is its importance or significance in that situation or to that person. 関連性 ❑ *Politicians' private lives have no relevance to their public roles.* 政治家の私生活は公共の役割とは何ら関係はない.

rel|evant /rɛləvənt/ ADJ 形容詞 Something that is **relevant to** a situation or person is important or significant in that situation or to that person. 意味のある ❑ *Is socialism still relevant to people's lives?* 社会主義は今も人々の生活に意味を持っていますか.

re|li|able /rɪlaɪəbəl/ ❶ ADJ 形容詞 People or things that are **reliable** can be trusted to work well or to behave in the way that you want them to. 信頼できる ❑ *She was efficient and reliable.* 彼女は有能で信頼できる人だった. ● **re|li|ably** /rɪlaɪəbli/ ADV 副詞 たのもしく ❑ *It's been working reliably for years.* それは何年もよく動いてきた. ● **re|li|abil|ity** /rɪlaɪəbɪlɪti/ N-UNCOUNT 不可算名詞 信頼性 ❑ *He's not at all worried about his car's reliability.* 彼は自分の車の信頼性をまったく疑っていなかった. ❷ ADJ 形容詞 Information that is **reliable** or that is from a **reliable** source is very likely to be correct. 信頼できる ❑ *There is no reliable information about civilian casualties.* 民間人の犠牲者についての確かな情報は何もありません. ● **re|li|ably** ADV 副詞 信頼できる筋からの ❑ *Sonia, we are reliably informed, loves her family very much.* 確かな情報ですが，ソニアは家族をとても愛しています. ● **re|li|abil|ity** N-UNCOUNT 不可算名詞 信頼性 ❑ *Both questioned the reliability of recent opinion polls.* 両者は最近の世論調査の信頼性を疑問視していた.

re|li|ance /rɪlaɪəns/ N-UNCOUNT 不可算名詞 A person's or thing's **reliance on** something is the fact that they need it and often cannot live or work without it. 依存 ❑ *...the country's increasing reliance on foreign aid.* その国の外国の援助への増大する依存

re|li|ant /rɪlaɪənt/ ADJ 形容詞 A person or thing that is **reliant on** something needs it and often cannot live or work without it. 頼っている [v-link ADJ "on/upon" n] ❑ *These people are not wholly reliant on Western charity.* これらの人々は西洋諸国の義援金に全面的に頼っているわけではない.

rel|ic /rɛlɪk/ (**relics**) ❶ N-COUNT 可算名詞 If you refer to

something or someone as a **relic of** an earlier period, you mean that they belonged to that period but have survived into the present. 遺物 ❑ *Germany's asylum law is a relic of an era in European history that has passed.* ドイツの難民保護法はヨーロッパ史の過ぎ去った一時代の名残だ. ❷ N-COUNT 可算名詞 A **relic** is something which was made or used a long time ago and which is kept for its historical significance. 記念物 ❑ *...a museum of war relics.* 戦争記念物博物館

re|lief /rɪliːf/ (**reliefs**) ❶ N-UNCOUNT 不可算名詞 If you feel a sense of **relief**, you feel happy because something unpleasant has not happened or is no longer happening. 安心 [also "a" N] ❑ *I breathed a sigh of relief.* 安堵（あんど）のため息をついた. ❷ N-UNCOUNT 不可算名詞 If something provides **relief** from pain or distress, it stops the pain or distress. 除去，軽減 ❑ *...a self-help program which can give lasting relief from the torment of hay fever.* 花粉症の苦しみを長く和らげることができる自助プログラム ❸ N-UNCOUNT 不可算名詞 **Relief** is money, food, or clothing that is provided for people who are very poor, or who have been affected by war or a natural disaster. 救援物資，救援金 ❑ *Relief agencies are stepping up efforts to provide food, shelter, and agricultural equipment.* 救援機関は食品，避難所，農業用具の供給にますます力をいれている. ❹ N-COUNT 可算名詞 A **relief** worker is someone who does your work when you go home, or who is employed to do it instead of you when you are sick. 交代者 ❑ *No relief drivers were available.* 代わりのドライバーは都合がつかなかった.

re|lieve /rɪliːv/ (**relieves, relieving, relieved**) ❶ V-T 他動詞 If something **relieves** an unpleasant feeling or situation, it makes it less unpleasant or causes it to disappear completely. 和らげる，解放する ❑ *Drugs can relieve much of the pain.* 薬でその痛みはかなり和らげられます. ❷ V-T 他動詞 If someone or something **relieves** you **of** an unpleasant feeling or difficult task, they take it from you. 取り除く ❑ *A part-time bookkeeper will relieve you of the burden of chasing unpaid invoices.* パートタイムの簿記係を採用すれば未払いの請求書を追いかけることもなくなるでしょう. ❸ V-T 他動詞 If you **relieve** someone, you take their place and continue to do the job or duty that they have been doing. 交代する ❑ *At seven o'clock the night nurse came in to relieve her.* 7時に夜勤の看護師がやって来て彼女と交代した. ❹ V-T 他動詞 If someone **is relieved of** their duties or **is relieved of** their post, they are no longer required to continue in their job. 解任する [FORMAL 形式ばった] [usu passive] ❑ *The officer involved was relieved of his duties because he had violated strict guidelines.* その関係した将校は厳格な指針を破ったため解任された.

re|lieved /rɪliːvd/ ADJ 形容詞 If you are **relieved**, you feel happy because something unpleasant has not happened or is no longer happening. 安心した ❑ *We are all relieved to be back home.* 私たちはみんな祖国に帰ることができてほっとしています.

re|li|gion /rɪlɪdʒən/ (**religions**) ❶ N-UNCOUNT 不可算名詞 **Religion** is belief in a god or gods and the activities that are connected with this belief, such as praying or worshiping in a building such as a church or temple. 信仰 ❑ *...his understanding of Indian philosophy and religion.* インドの哲学と信仰に関する彼の理解 ❷ N-COUNT 可算名詞 A **religion** is a particular system of belief in a god or gods and the activities that are connected with this system. 宗教 ❑ *...the Christian religion.* キリスト教 → see Word Web: **religion**

re|li|gious /rɪlɪdʒəs/ ❶ ADJ 形容詞 You use **religious** to describe things that are connected with religion or with one particular religion. 宗教の [ADJ n] ❑ *Religious groups are now able to meet quite openly.* 宗教団体は今ではとても堂々と集会を行うことができます. ❷ ADJ 形容詞 Someone who is **religious** has a strong belief in a god or gods. 信心深い ❑ *They are both very religious and felt it was a gift from God.* 彼らはどちらも信心深く，それは神からの贈り物だと考えた.

re|lin|quish /rɪlɪŋkwɪʃ/ (**relinquishes, relinquishing, relinquished**) V-T 他動詞 If you **relinquish** something such as power or control, you give it up. 放棄する [FORMAL 形式ばった] ❑ *He does not intend to relinquish power.* 彼は権力を手放すつもりはない.

rel|ish /rɛlɪʃ/ (**relishes, relishing, relished**) V-T 他動詞 If you **relish** something, you get a lot of enjoyment from it. 楽しむ ❑ *I relish the challenge of doing jobs that others turn down.* 私は他の人が断

Word Web · religion

Today the world's population is about 33% **Christian**, 21% **Islamic**, 16% **agnostic**, and 14% **Hindu**. Christians believe in one **god**, but they also **pray** to his son, Jesus Christ. Followers of **Islam** believe in a single god, Allah, and follow the teachings of the prophet Muhammad. Their **divine scripture** is the Koran. They also honor parts of the **Jewish** and **Christian Bible**. Hinduism recognizes a single **deity** along with other **gods** and **goddesses**. **Buddhism** developed after Hinduism in India and does not include a god figure. All religions seem to share one traditional **belief**—the idea of treating others the way we wish to be treated.

Buddhism Christianity Judaism

Hinduism

るような仕事をするという挑戦を楽しんでいる. ●N-UNCOUNT 不可算名詞 **Relish** is also a noun. 楽しむこと ❑ The three men ate with relish. その3人の男は食事をたんのうした.

re|live /riːlɪv/ (relives, reliving, relived) V-T 他動詞 If you **relive** something that has happened to you in the past, you remember it and imagine that you are experiencing it again. (心の中で) 再び体験する ❑ There is no point in reliving the past. 過去を思い起こしても意味はない.

re|lo|cate /riːloʊkeɪt/ (relocates, relocating, relocated) V-T/V-I 他動詞/自動詞 If people or businesses **relocate** or if someone **relocates** them, they move to a different place. 移動させる [他動詞], 移動する [自動詞] ❑ If the company was to relocate, most employees would move. もし会社が移転するなら, ほとんどの従業員も移動するだろう. ●re|lo|ca|tion /riːloʊkeɪʃⁿn/ (relocations) N-UNCOUNT 不可算名詞 移転 ❑ The company says the cost of relocation will be negligible. 同社によると, 移転コストはごくわずかだろうとのことだ.

re|lo|ca|tion ex|penses N-PLURAL 複数名詞 **Relocation expenses** are a sum of money that a company pays to someone who moves to a new area in order to work for the company. The money is to help them pay for moving their belongings. 移転手当 [BUSINESS 実業] ❑ Relocation expenses were paid to encourage senior staff to move to the region. 年長の職員がその地域に異動するのを奨励するために移転手当が支払われた.

re|luc|tant /rɪlʌktənt/ ADJ 形容詞 If you are **reluctant to** do something, you are unwilling to do it and hesitate before doing it, or do it slowly and without enthusiasm. 気が進まない ❑ Mr. Spero was reluctant to ask for help. スペロ氏は支援を求めるのは気が進まなかった. ●re|luc|tant|ly ADV 副詞 しぶしぶ ❑ We have reluctantly agreed to let him go. 我々は彼を行かせることをしぶしぶ承諾した. ●re|luc|tance N-UNCOUNT 不可算名詞 気が進まないこと ❑ Committee members have shown extreme reluctance to explain their position to the media. 委員会の面々は, メディアに対して彼らの立場を説明することに極端な難色を示してきました.

Thesaurus · reluctant また次を参照:

ADJ. hesitant, unwilling; (ant.) eager, willing

rely /rɪlaɪ/ (relies, relying, relied) ■ V-I 自動詞 If you **rely on** someone or something, you need them and depend on them in order to live or work properly. 頼る ❑ They relied heavily on the advice of their professional advisers. 彼らは専門家の顧問の助言を非常に頼りにしていた. ■ V-I 自動詞 If you can **rely on** someone to work well or to behave as you want them to, you can trust them to do this. 信頼する ❑ I know I can rely on you to sort it out. きみにならその問題の解決を任せられるよ.

re|main /rɪmeɪn/ (remains, remaining, remained) ■ V-LINK 連結動詞 If someone or something **remains** in a particular state or condition, they stay in that state or condition and do not change. (ある状態の) ままである ❑ The three men remained silent. その男性3人は黙ったままだった. ■ V-I 自動詞 If you **remain** in a place, you stay there and do not move away. とどまる ❑ They have asked the residents to remain in their homes. 彼らはその住人たちに家から出ないように頼んでいる. ■ V-I 自動詞 You can say that something **remains** when it still exists. 残る ❑ The wider problem remains. より広範囲な問題が残っている. ■ V-LINK 連結動詞 If something **remains to be** done, it has not yet been done and still needs to be done. (やり残された) ままである ❑ Major questions remain to be answered about his work. 彼の業績についての主要な疑問はまだ答えられていない. ■ N-PLURAL 複数名詞 The **remains of** something are the parts of it that are left after most of it has been taken away or destroyed. 残りの物 ❑ They were cleaning up the remains of their picnic. 彼らはピクニックの残り物を片付けていた. ■ N-PLURAL 複数名詞 The **remains of** a person or animal are the parts of their body that are left after they have died, sometimes after they have been dead for a long time. 遺体 ❑ The unrecognizable remains of a man had been found. 男性の見分けの付かない遺体が発見されていた. ■ → see also **remaining**

Thesaurus · remain また次を参照:

v. last, linger, stay; (ant.) depart, leave ■

re|main|der /rɪmeɪndər/ QUANT 数量詞 The **remainder of** a group are the things or people that still remain after the other things or people have gone or have been dealt with. 残留者, 残留物 [QUANT "of" def-n] ❑ He gulped down the remainder of his coffee. 彼は残ったコーヒーを飲み干した. ●PRON 代名詞 **Remainder** is also a pronoun. 残り ❑ Only 5.9 percent of the area is now covered in trees. Most of the remainder is farmland. 今はその地域の5.9パーセントしか木々で覆われていなくて, 残りの大部分は農地である.

re|main|ing /rɪmeɪnɪŋ/ ■ ADJ 形容詞 The **remaining** things or people out of a group are the things or people that still exist, are still present, or have not yet been dealt with. 残った [ADJ n] ❑ The three parties will meet next month to work out remaining differences. その3党は未合意事項を解決するために来月会合を持つ予定です. ■ → see also **remain**

re|mand /rɪmænd/ (remands, remanding, remanded) ■ V-T 他動詞 If a person who is accused of a crime **is remanded** in custody, they are kept in prison until their trial begins. If a person **is remanded on bail**, they are told to return to the court at a later date, when their trial will take place. 再拘留する [usu passive] ❑ Carter was remanded in custody for seven days. カーターは7日間再拘留された. ■ N-UNCOUNT 不可算名詞 **Remand** is used to refer to the process of remanding someone in custody or on bail, or to the period of time until their trial begins. 再拘留 ❑ The remand hearing is often over in three minutes. 再拘留の審問はしばしば3分で終わる.

re|mark /rɪmɑrk/ (remarks, remarking, remarked) ■ V-T/V-I 他動詞/自動詞 If you **remark** that something is the case, you say that it is the case. 述べる ❑ I remarked that I would go shopping that afternoon. 午後は買い物に行く予定だ, と私は言いました. ❑ On several occasions she remarked on the boy's improvement. 彼女は何度かその少年の上達について述べていた. ■ N-COUNT 可算名詞 If you make a **remark** about something, you say something about it. 意見 ❑ She has made outspoken remarks about the legalization of marijuana. 彼女はマリファナの合法化について率直な意見を述べた.

If you **remark** on something, or make a **remark** about it, you say what you think or what you have noticed, often in a casual way. ❑ Visitors remark on how well the children look... General Sutton's remarks about the conflict. If you **comment** on a situation, or make a **comment** about it, you give your opinion on it. ❑ Mr. Cook has not commented on these reports... I was wondering whether you had any comments. If you **mention** something, you say it, but only briefly, especially when you have not talked about it before. ❑ He mentioned that he might go to New York.

Word Partnership · remark は次の語句と使われる:

ADJ. casual remark, offhand remark ■
v. hear a remark, make a remark ■

re|mark|able /rɪmɑrkəbⁿl/ ADJ 形容詞 Someone or something that is **remarkable** is unusual or special in a way that makes people notice them and be surprised or impressed. 注目すべき ❑ He was a remarkable man. 彼は注目に値する人物だった. ●re|mark|ably /rɪmɑrkəbli/ ADV 副詞 著しく ❑ Herbal remedies are remarkably successful in treating eczema. 薬草療法は湿疹 (しっしん) の治療に非常に効果がある.

re|match /riːmætʃ/ (rematches) ■ N-COUNT 可算名詞 A **rematch** is a second game that is played between two people or teams, for example because their first match was a draw or because there was a dispute about some aspect of it. 再試合 ❑ Duff said he would be demanding a rematch. ダフは再試合を要求するつもりだと言った. ■ N-COUNT 可算名詞 A **rematch** is a second game or contest between two people or teams who have already faced

each other. 再戦 [mainly AM 主に米国英語] ❑ *Stanford will face UCLA in a rematch.* スタンフォードはUCLAと再び対戦するでしょう.

re|medial /rɪmiːdiəl/ ❶ ADJ 形容詞 **Remedial** action is intended to correct something that has been done wrong or that has not been successful. 改善の, 救済的な [FORMAL 形式ばった] ❑ *Some authorities are now having to take remedial action.* 今では改善策を講じるをえなくなってきている官庁もある. ❷ ADJ 形容詞 **Remedial** education is intended to improve a person's ability to read, write, or do mathematics, especially when they find these things difficult. 補習の ❑ *...children who required remedial education.* 補習教育が必要だった子供たち.

rem|edy /rɛmədi/ (remedies, remedying, remedied) ❶ N-COUNT 可算名詞 A **remedy** is a successful way of dealing with a problem. 改善策, 救済策 ❑ *The remedy lies in the hands of the government.* 改善策は政府の手の内にある. ❷ N-COUNT 可算名詞 A **remedy** is something that is intended to cure you when you are ill or in pain. 治療法 ❑ *There are many different kinds of natural remedies to help overcome winter infections.* 冬場の伝染病の克服を助ける多種多様な自然療法がある. ❸ V-T 他動詞 If you **remedy** something that is wrong or harmful, you correct it or improve it. 改善する, 救済する ❑ *A great deal has been done internally to remedy the situation.* その状況を改善するために内部で多くの事が試みられてきた.

re|mem|ber /rɪmɛmbər/ (remembers, remembering, remembered) ❶ V-T/V-I 他動詞/自動詞 If you **remember** people or events from the past, you still have an idea of them in your mind and you are able to think about them. 覚えている ❑ *You wouldn't remember me. I was in another group.* きみは僕のことを覚えていないだろう. 別のグループだったからね. ❑ *I remembered that we had made the last of the coffee the day before.* 私は私たちが前日にコーヒーを使い切ったことを覚えていた. ❑ *What a day that was, do you remember?* あれはどんな日だったか, 覚えてる？ ❷ V-T 他動詞 If you **remember** that something is the case, you become aware of it again after a time when you did not think about it. 思い出す ❑ *She remembered that she was going to the club that evening.* 彼女は, その夜クラブに行くところだったことを思い出した. ❸ V-T/V-I 他動詞/自動詞 If you cannot **remember** something, you are not able to bring it back into your mind when you make an effort to do so. 覚える [usu with brd-neg] ❑ *If you can't remember your number, write it in code in an appointment book.* 自分の番号を覚えられないなら, 自分にしか分からない形で手帳に書きとめればよい. ❑ *I can't remember what I said.* 私は何を言ったか思い出せないよ. ❑ *Don't tell me you can't remember.* 覚えてないなんて言わないでよ. ❹ V-T 他動詞 If you **remember to** do something, you do it when you intend to. 忘れずに～する ❑ *Please remember to enclose a stamped self-addressed envelope when writing.* 手紙には, ご自身の住所が記載し切手を貼った返信用封筒を忘れずに同封してください. ❺ V-T 他動詞 You tell someone to **remember that** something is the case when you want to emphasize its importance. 覚えている, 忘れないでいる [EMPHASIS 強調] ❑ *It is important to remember that each person reacts differently.* 反応は人によって異なるということを忘れないことが大切だ.

→ see **memory**

Do not confuse **remember** and **remind**. If you **remember** something, you are able to bring it back into your mind. ❑ *He remembers everything that happened... I could not remember her name.* If you **remember** to do something, you do what you are meant to do without forgetting or needing to be told to do it. ❑ *He remembered to turn the gas off... Remember to put all your tools away.* If someone **reminds** you of someone or something, they make you think about that person or thing. ❑ *He reminds me of Maurice Fitzgerald... The pink dress reminds me of when I was a chauffeur in New York.* You cannot use 'remember' in this way. You can use **remember** with the 'to' infinitive or the '-ing' form of the verb, but note that they have different meanings. If you **remember** to do something, you do it when you intend to. ❑ *He remembered to buy his wife chocolates.* If you **remember** doing something, you are thinking back to the past. ❑ *I remember reading the newspaper aloud to my father at five.*

Thesaurus   *remember* また次を参照:

V.   look back, recall, think back; (ant.) forget ❶ ❸

Word Partnership   *remember* は次の語句と使われる:

CONJ.	remember **what**, remember **when**, remember **where**, remember **why** ❶ – ❸
ADJ.	**easy to** remember, **important to** remember ❶ ❷ ❹ ❺
ADV.	remember **clearly**, remember **correctly**, remember **exactly**, **still** remember, remember **vividly** ❶ ❸ **always** remember ❶ ❹ ❺

re|mem|brance /rɪmɛmbrəns/ N-UNCOUNT 不可算名詞 If

you do something **in remembrance of** a dead person, you do it as a way of showing that you want to remember them and that you respect them. 追悼 [FORMAL 形式ばった] ❑ *They wore black in remembrance of those who had died.* 亡くなった人々をしのんで彼らは黒い服を着た.

re|mind /rɪmaɪnd/ (reminds, reminding, reminded) ❶ V-T 他動詞 If someone **reminds** you of a fact or event that you already know about, they say something which makes you think about it. 思い出させる ❑ *So she simply welcomed Tim and reminded him of the last time they had met.* だから彼女は実際にティムを歓迎し, 彼と最後に会った時を思い出すようにしむけたのよ. ❷ V-T 他動詞 You use **remind** in expressions such as **Let me remind you that** and **May I remind you that** to introduce a piece of information that you want to emphasize. It may be something that the hearer already knows about or a new piece of information. Sometimes these expressions can sound unfriendly. 思い出させるために言う [SPOKEN 口語, EMPHASIS 強調] ❑ *"Let me remind you," said Marianne, "that Milwaukee is also my home town."* マリアンヌは「申し上げておきたいのですが, ミルウォーキー市もまた私のふるさとなのです」と言った. ❸ V-T 他動詞 If someone **reminds** you to do a particular thing, they say something which makes you remember to do it. (忘れずに～をするように) 注意する ❑ *Can you remind me to buy a bottle of wine?* 忘れずにワイン1本を買うように私に注意してもらえますか. ❹ V-T 他動詞 If you say that someone or something **reminds** you of another person or thing, you mean that they are similar to the other person or thing and that they make you think about them. (～に似ていて) 連想させる ❑ *She reminds me of the wife of the pilot who used to work for you.* 彼女はきみの元で働いていたパイロットの奥さんを思い出させるよ.

Do not confuse **remind** and **remember**. If someone **reminds** you **of** someone or something, they make you think about that person or thing. ❑ *He reminds me of Maurice Fitzgerald... The pink dress reminds me of when I was a chauffeur in New York.* If you **remember** something, you are able to bring it back into your mind. ❑ *He remembers everything that happened... I could not remember her name.* If you **remember to** do something, you do what you are meant to do without forgetting or needing to be told to do it. ❑ *He remembered to turn the gas off... Remember to put all your tools away.*

Word Partnership   *remind* は次の語句と使われる:

PREP.	remind *someone* of *something* ❶ remind *you* of *someone/something* ❹
V.	**let me** remind *you*, **may I** remind *you* ❷

re|mind|er /rɪmaɪndər/ (reminders) ❶ N-COUNT 可算名詞 Something that serves as a **reminder of** another thing makes you think about the other thing. 思い出させる物 [WRITTEN 書き言葉] ❑ *The last thing you'd want is a constant reminder of a bad experience.* あなたが最もごめん被りたいのは, 嫌な体験を絶えず連想させるものでしょう. ❷ N-COUNT 可算名詞 A **reminder** is a letter or note that is sent to tell you that you have not done something such as pay a bill or return library books. 督促状 ❑ *...the final reminder for the gas bill.* ガス代の最終督促状

remi|nisce /rɛmɪnɪs/ (reminisces, reminiscing, reminisced) V-I 自動詞 If you **reminisce** about something from your past, you write or talk about it, often with pleasure. 思い出を語る [FORMAL 形式ばった] ❑ *I don't like reminiscing because it makes me feel old.* 思い出話をするのは年を取った気がするから好きじゃない.

remi|nis|cence /rɛmɪnɪsəns/ (reminiscences) N-VAR 可変性名詞 Someone's **reminiscences** are things that they remember from the past, and which they talk or write about. **Reminiscence** is the process of remembering these things and talking or writing about them. 回想 [FORMAL 形式ばった] ❑ *Here I am boring you with my reminiscences.* 私ったら, 思い出話をしすぎるね.

remi|nis|cent /rɛmɪnɪsənt/ ADJ 形容詞 If you say that one thing is **reminiscent of** another, you mean that it reminds you of it. 連想させる [FORMAL 形式ばった] [v-link ADJ "of" n] ❑ *We drank from wax-coated paper cups reminiscent of a visit to the dentist.* 私たちは, 歯医者での治療を連想させるようなろうをひいた紙コップで飲んだ.

re|mis|sion /rɪmɪʃᵊn/ (remissions) N-VAR 可変性名詞 If someone who has had a serious disease such as cancer is **in remission** or if the disease is **in remission**, the disease has been controlled so that they are not as ill as they were. 薄らぐこと, 軽減 ❑ *Brain scans have confirmed that the disease is in remission.* 脳スキャンで病状が軽減していることが確かめられた.

re|mit /rɪmɪt/ (remits, remitting, remitted) V-T 他動詞 If you **remit** money to someone, you send it to them. (金を) 送る [FORMAL 形式ばった] ❑ *Many immigrants regularly remit money to their families.* 多くの移民は定期的に家族に送金する.

re|mit|tance /rɪmɪtᵊns/ (remittances) N-VAR 可変性名詞 A **remittance** is a sum of money that you send to someone. 送金額

[FORMAL 形式ばった] ❑ *Please enclose your remittance, making checks payable to Valley Technology Services.* 受取人をバレー・テクノロジー・サービスに指定した代金分の小切手を封書でお送りください.

rem|nant /rɛmnənt/ (**remnants**) N-COUNT 可算名詞 The **remnants of** something are small parts of it that are left over when the main part has disappeared or has been used or destroyed. 残り ❑ *Beneath the present church were remnants of Roman flooring.* 今建っている教会の下にはローマ時代の床材が残っていた.

re|morse /rɪmɔrs/ N-UNCOUNT 不可算名詞 **Remorse** is a strong feeling of sadness and regret about something wrong that you have done. 自責の念 ❑ *He was full of remorse and asked Beatrice what he could do to make amends.* 彼は深い自責の念にかられ、ベアトリスにどうすれば償えるかと尋ねた.

re|mote /rɪmoʊt/ (**remoter, remotest, remotes**) **1** ADJ 形容詞 **Remote** areas are far away from cities and places where most people live, and are therefore difficult to get to. 遠隔の ❑ *Landslides have cut off many villages in remote areas.* 山崩れでへき地の多くの村への交通が遮断されています. **2** ADJ 形容詞 The **remote** past or **remote** future is a time that is many years distant from the present. 遠い ❑ *Slabs of rock had slipped sideways in the remote past and formed this hole.* 遠い昔、岩板が横すべりを起こしてこの穴ができた. **3** ADJ 形容詞 If something is **remote from** a particular subject or area of experience, it is not relevant to it because it is very different. かけ離れた ❑ *This government depends on the wishes of a few who are remote from the people.* この政府は国民からは遠い存在である数人の意向に左右されている. **4** ADJ 形容詞 If you say that there is a **remote** possibility or chance that something will happen, you are emphasizing that there is only a very small chance that it will happen. とても起こりそうにない [EMPHASIS 強調] ❑ *I use sunscreen whenever there is even a remote possibility that I will be in the sun.* 私は日光を浴びる可能性がほとんどなくても日焼け止めを使う. **5** ADJ 形容詞 If you describe someone as **remote**, you mean that they behave as if they do not want to be friendly or closely involved with other people. よそよそしい ❑ *She looked so beautiful, and at the same time so remote.* 彼女はすごく美人に見えたが、同時にとてもそっけない感じだった. **6** N-COUNT 可算名詞 A **remote** is the same as a **remote control**. リモコン ❑ *He flipped through the channels with the remote.* 彼はリモコンでチャンネルを次々と変えた.

re|mote ac|cess N-UNCOUNT 不可算名詞 **Remote access** is a system that allows you to gain access to a particular computer or network using a separate computer. リモートアクセス [COMPUTING コンピューティング] ❑ *The diploma course would offer remote access to course materials via the Internet's world wide web.* 免状取得コースではインターネットのワールド・ワイド・ウェブ経由でコース教材にリモートアクセスできます.

re|mote con|trol (**remote controls**) **1** N-UNCOUNT 不可算名詞 **Remote control** is a system of controlling a machine or a vehicle from a distance by using radio or electronic signals. 遠隔操作 ❑ *The bomb was detonated by remote control.* その爆弾は遠隔操作で爆発された. **2** N-COUNT 可算名詞 The **remote control** for a television or other equipment is the device that you use to control the machine from a distance, by pressing the buttons on it. リモコン ❑ *Richard picked up the remote control and turned on the television.* リチャードはリモコンを手に取りテレビをつけた.

re|mote|ly /rɪmoʊtli/ **1** ADV 副詞 You use **remotely** with a negative statement to emphasize the statement. 全然（〜でない）[EMPHASIS 強調] ❑ *We had never seen anything remotely like it before.* 我々はそのようなものは以前全く見たことがなかった. **2** ADV 副詞 If someone or something is **remotely** placed or situated, they are a long way from other people or places. 遠く離れたところに [ADV -ed] ❑ *...the remotely situated, five bedroom house.* へんぴな所に建つ、寝室5部屋を備えた家

re|mov|al /rɪmuvəl/ (**removals**) **1** N-UNCOUNT 不可算名詞 The **removal** of something is the act of removing it. 除去 ❑ *What they expected to be the removal of a small lump turned out to be major surgery.* 小さなはれ物を除去するはずのものが、大手術になりました. **2** N-VAR 可変性名詞 **Removal** is the process of transporting furniture or equipment from one building to another. 移動、引越し [BRIT 英国英語; AM moving 米国英語 moving]

re|move /rɪmuv/ (**removes, removing, removed**) **1** V-T 他動詞 If you **remove** something from a place, you take it away. 取り去る [WRITTEN 書き言葉] ❑ *As soon as the cake is done, remove it from the oven.* ケーキが焼けたら、すぐにオーブンから取り出してください. **2** V-T 他動詞 If you **remove** clothing, you take it off. 脱ぐ [WRITTEN 書き言葉] ❑ *He removed his jacket.* 彼は上着を脱いだ. **3** V-T 他動詞 If you **remove** a stain from something, you make the stain disappear by treating it with a chemical or by washing it. 落とす ❑ *This treatment removes the most stubborn stains.* この処理でどうしても取れないようなシミが落ちます. **4** V-T 他動詞 If people **remove** someone **from** power or **from** something such as a committee, they stop them from being in power or being a member of the committee. 解任する ❑ *The student senate voted to remove Fuller from office.* 学生評議会はフラーの解任を可決した. **5** V-T

他動詞 If you **remove** an obstacle, a restriction, or a problem, you get rid of it. 除去する ❑ *The agreement removes the last serious obstacle to the signing of the arms treaty.* その合意が成立すると軍備条約締結への最後の重大な障害が除去される.

Thesaurus	**remove** また次を参照:
v.	take away, take out **1**
	take off, undress **2**

re|moved /rɪmuvd/ ADJ 形容詞 If you say that an idea or situation is far **removed from** something, you mean that it is very different from it. かけ離れた [v-link ADJ "from" n] ❑ *Central office was too far removed from operating decisions at the department level.* 本部は部門レベルの意思を決定するにはあまりにもかけ離れすぎていた.

re|mu|ner|ate /rɪmyunəreɪt/ (**remunerates, remunerating, remunerated**) V-T 他動詞 If you **are remunerated** for work that you do, you are paid for it. 報酬を出す [FORMAL 形式ばった] [usu passive] ❑ *You will be remunerated and so will your staff.* あなたにも報酬は出ますし、スタッフにも出ます.

re|mu|nera|tion /rɪmyunəreɪ°n/ (**remunerations**) N-VAR 可変性名詞 Someone's **remuneration** is the amount of money that they are paid for the work that they do. 報酬 [FORMAL 形式ばった] ❑ *...the continuing marked increases in the remuneration of the company's directors.* 会社の役員報酬の顕著な増加傾向

re|nais|sance /rɛnɪsɑns/ **1** N-PROPER 固有名詞 The **Renaissance** was the period in Europe, especially Italy, in the 14th, 15th, and 16th centuries, when there was a new interest in art, literature, science, and learning. ルネサンス時代 ❑ *...the Renaissance masterpieces in London's galleries.* ロンドンの美術館にあるルネサンス時代の名作. **2** N-SING 単数名詞 If something experiences a **renaissance**, it becomes popular or successful again after a time when people were not interested in it. 復興 ❑ *Popular art is experiencing a renaissance.* 大衆芸術が復興しつつある.

ren|der /rɛndər/ (**renders, rendering, rendered**) V-T 他動詞 You can use **render** with an adjective that describes a particular state to say that someone or something is changed into that state. For example, if someone or something makes a thing harmless, you can say that they **render** it harmless. （ある状態に）する ❑ *It contained so many errors as to render it worthless.* それは価値がなくなるくらい多くの間違いが含まれていた.

ren|dez|vous /rɒndeɪvu/ (**rendezvousing, rendezvoused**)

The form **rendezvous** is pronounced /rɒndeɪvuz/ when it is the plural of the noun or the third person singular of the verb.

rendezvous形はそれが名詞の複数形か動詞の3人称単数形のときは/rɒndeɪvuz/と発音される.

1 N-COUNT 可算名詞 A **rendezvous** is a meeting, often a secret one, that you have arranged with someone for a particular time and place. （約束された）会合 ❑ *I had almost decided to keep my rendezvous with Tony.* 私はあやうくトニーと会い続けるところだった. **2** N-COUNT 可算名詞 A **rendezvous** is the place where you have arranged to meet someone, often secretly. 会合場所 ❑ *Their rendezvous would be the Plaza Hotel.* 彼らの会合場所はプラザホテルだろう. **3** V-RECIP 相互動詞 If you **rendezvous with** someone or if the two of you **rendezvous**, you meet them at a time and place that you have arranged. 待ち合わせる ❑ *The plan was to rendezvous with him on Sunday afternoon.* 計画では、日曜の午後に彼と待ち合わせることになっていた.

ren|egade /rɛnɪgeɪd/ (**renegades**) N-COUNT 可算名詞 A **renegade** is a person who abandons the religious, political, or philosophical beliefs that he or she used to have, and accepts opposing or different beliefs. 改宗者、変節者 ❑ *He has shown himself to be a renegade without respect for the rule of law.* 彼は法規を守らない変節者だという正体を現しました.

re|nege /rɪnɪg/ (**reneges, reneging, reneged**) V-I 自動詞 If someone **reneges on** a promise or an agreement, they do not do what they have promised or agreed to do. 背く ❑ *He reneged on a promise to leave his wife.* 彼は妻と別れるという約束を破った.

re|new /rɪnu/ (**renews, renewing, renewed**) **1** V-T 他動詞 If you **renew** an activity, you begin it again. 再開する ❑ *He renewed his attack on government policy toward Europe.* 彼は政府の対ヨーロッパ政策への攻撃を再開しました. **2** V-RECIP 相互動詞 If you **renew** a relationship **with** someone, you start it again after you have not seen them or have not been friendly with them for some time. 復活させる ❑ *When the two men met again after the war they renewed their friendship.* その2人の男性は戦後に再会し、親交を取り戻しました. **3** V-T 他動詞 When you **renew** something such as a license or a contract, you extend the period of time for which it is valid. 更新する ❑ *Larry's landlord threatened not to renew his lease.* ラリーの大家は契約を更新しないと彼を脅した. **4** V-T 他動詞 You can say that something **is renewed** when it grows again or is replaced after it has been destroyed or lost. 復活させる [usu passive] ❑ *Nature's*

repair process is slow and steady, with cells being constantly renewed. 自然の修復過程は細胞が再生を続けていて，ゆっくりと着実に進行する.

Thesaurus *renew* また次を参照：

v.   continue, resume, revive **1** – **4**

---

re|new|able /rɪnjuːəbəl/ **1** ADJ 形容詞 **Renewable** resources are natural ones such as wind, water, and sunlight which are always available. 再生可能な □ ...*renewable energy sources.* 再生可能なエネルギー資源 **2** ADJ 形容詞 If a contract or agreement is **renewable**, it can be extended when it reaches the end of a fixed period of time. 更新できる □ *A formal contract is signed which is renewable annually.* 1年ごとに更新できる正式な契約が結ばれる.

re|new|al /rɪnjuːəl/ (**renewals**) **1** N-SING 単数名詞 If there is a **renewal of** an activity or a situation, it starts again. 再開 □ *They will discuss the possible renewal of diplomatic relations.* 彼らは国交再開の見込みについて話し合いを行う予定です. **2** N-VAR 可変性名詞 The **renewal** of a document such as a license or a contract is an official increase in the period of time for which it remains valid. 期限の延長 □ *His contract came up for renewal.* 彼の契約は延長の対象となった. **3** N-UNCOUNT 不可算名詞 **Renewal** of something lost, dead, or destroyed is the process of it growing again or being replaced. 復興，再開発 □ ...*a political lobbyist concentrating on urban renewal and regeneration.* 都市の再開発と再生に専心する政治的ロビイスト

re|nounce /rɪnaʊns/ (**renounces, renouncing, renounced**) V-T 他動詞 If you **renounce** a belief or a way of behaving, you decide and declare publicly that you no longer have that belief or will no longer behave in that way. 捨てる □ *After a period of imprisonment she renounced terrorism.* 懲役期間を終えて彼女はテロ行為をやめた.

Word Link *nov ≈ new : in*novate, *novel, reno*vate

---

reno|vate /rɛnəveɪt/ (**renovates, renovating, renovated**) V-T 他動詞 If someone **renovates** an old building, they repair and improve it and get it back into good condition. 改装する □ *The couple spent thousands renovating the house.* 夫婦は家の改装に数千の費用をかけた. ● **reno|va|tion** /rɛnəveɪʃən/ (**renovations**) N-VAR 可変性名詞 改装 □ ...*a property which will need extensive renovation.* 大がかりな改修が必要となりそうな不動産

re|nown /rɪnaʊn/ N-UNCOUNT 不可算名詞 A person of **renown** is well known, usually because they do or have done something good. 有名な □ *She used to be a singer of some renown.* 彼女は昔はある程度の知れた歌手でした.

re|nowned /rɪnaʊnd/ ADJ 形容詞 A person or place that is **renowned for** something, usually something good, is well known because of it. 有名な □ *The area is renowned for its Romanesque churches.* そこはロマネスク様式の教会群で有名な地区です.

rent /rɛnt/ (**rents, renting, rented**) **1** V-T 他動詞 If you **rent** something, you regularly pay its owner a sum of money in order to be able to have it and use it yourself. 借りる □ *She rents a house with three other girls.* 彼女は他の3人の女性と一緒に家を借りている. **2** V-T 他動詞 If you **rent** something **to** someone, you let them have it and use it in exchange for a sum of money which they pay you regularly. 賃貸する □ *She rented rooms to university students.* 彼女は大学生たちに部屋を貸した. ● PHRASAL VERB 句動詞 **Rent out** means the same as **rent**. 賃貸する □ *Last summer Brian Williams rented out his house and went camping.* 去年の夏，ブライアン・ウィリアムスは自分の家を賃貸に出して，キャンプに出かけた. **3** N-VAR 可変性名詞 **Rent** is the amount of money that you pay regularly to use a house, apartment, or piece of land. 賃貸料 □ *She worked to pay the rent while I went to college.* 私が大学に行っている間，彼女は家賃を払うために働いた. **4** PHRASE 句 If something is **for rent**, it is available for you to use in exchange for a sum of money. 貸し出し用の [mainly AM 主に米国英語] □ *Helmets will be available for rent at all Vail Resort ski areas.* ベイル・リゾートでは，どのスキー場でもレンタルヘルメットが利用できるようです.

Do not confuse **rent**, **hire**, and **let**. If you make a series of payments to use something for a long time, you say that you **rent** it. □ ...*the apartment he had rented... He rented a TV.* You can say that you **rent** or **rent out** a house or room to someone when they pay you money to live there. □ *We rented our house to a college professor.* In British English, it is more common to say that you **let** it. □ *They were letting a room to a school teacher.* Americans also use **rent** when you pay a sum of money to use something for a short time. □ *He rented a car for the weekend.* In British English, if you pay a sum of money to use something for a short time, you usually say that you **hire** it. □ *He was unable to hire another car.*

rent|al /rɛntəl/ (**rentals**) **1** N-UNCOUNT 不可算名詞 The **rental** of something such as a car or piece of equipment is the activity or process of renting it. レンタル [also N n in pl] □ *We can arrange car rental from Chicago's O'Hare Airport.* シカゴ・オヘア空港からレンタカーが手配できます. **2** N-COUNT 可算名詞 The **rental** is the amount of money that you pay when you rent something such as a car,

property, or piece of equipment. 賃貸料 □ *It has been let at an annual rental of $393,000.* そこは年39万3千ドルで貸し出されてきた. **3** ADJ 形容詞 You use **rental** to describe things that are connected with the renting out of goods, properties, and services. レンタルの [ADJ n] □ *A friend drove her to Atlanta, where she picked up a rental car.* 友人が彼女をアトランタまで乗せて行き，そこで彼女はレンタカーを借りた.

re|or|gan|ize /riɔːrgənaɪz/ (**reorganizes, reorganizing, reorganized**) V-T/V-I 他動詞/自動詞 To **reorganize** something means to change the way in which it is organized, arranged, or done. 再編成する □ *It is the mother who is expected to reorganize her busy schedule.* 過密なスケジュールを組み直す必要があるのはまさしく母親である. □ *Four thousand troops have been reorganized into a fighting force.* 4千人の部隊が1戦闘部隊に再編成されました. ● **re|or|gani|za|tion** /riɔːrgənaɪzeɪʃən/ (**reorganizations**) N-VAR 可変性名詞 再編成 □ ...*the reorganization of the legal system.* 法制度の再編成.

rep /rɛp/ (**reps**) **1** N-COUNT 可算名詞 A **rep** is a person whose job is to sell a company's products or services, especially by traveling around and visiting clients. **Rep** is short for **representative**. 外交員 □ *I'd been working as a sales rep for a photographic company.* 写真会社の販売外交員として勤めていました. **2** N-COUNT 可算名詞 A **rep** is a person who acts as a representative for a group of people, usually a group of people who work together. 代表者 □ *Contact the health and safety rep at your union.* 加入している組合の健康安全担当の代表者に連絡してください.

re|paid /rɪpeɪd/ **Repaid** is the past tense and past participle of **repay**. repayの過去・過去分詞

re|pair /rɪpɛər/ (**repairs, repairing, repaired**) **1** V-T 他動詞 If you **repair** something that has been damaged or is not working properly, you fix it. 修理する □ *Goldsmith has repaired the roof to ensure the house is windproof.* ゴールドスミスは確実に家を風防にするために屋根を修理した. ● **re|pair|er** (**repairers**) N-COUNT 可算名詞 修理人 □ ...*services provided by builders, plumbers, and TV repairers.* 建築業者，配管工，テレビ修理工が提供するサービス **2** V-T 他動詞 If you **repair** a relationship or someone's reputation after it has been damaged, you do something to improve it. 回復する □ *The administration continued to try to repair the damage caused by the secretary's interview.* 政府はその長官のインタビューで傷ついた評判を回復しようと努力を続けていた. **3** N-VAR 可変性名詞 A **repair** is something that you do to mend a machine, building, piece of clothing, or other thing that has been damaged or is not working properly. 修理 □ *Many women know how to make repairs on their cars.* 女性の多くは自分の車の修理方法を知っている.

Word Partnership *repair* は次の語句と使われる：

N.   repair a chimney, repair equipment, repair parts, repair a roof **1**
      repair damage **1** **2**
      repair a relationship **2**
      auto repair, car repair, home repair, road repair, repair service, repair shop **3**

---

re|pat|ri|ate /ripeɪtrieɪt/ (**repatriates, repatriating, repatriated**) **1** V-T 他動詞 If a country **repatriates** someone, it sends them back to their home country. 送還する □ *It was not the policy of the government to repatriate genuine refugees.* 真の難民を送還するのは政府の方針ではなかった. ● **re|pat|ria|tion** /ripeɪtrieɪʃən/ (**repatriations**) N-VAR 可変性名詞 送還 □ *Today they begin the forced repatriation of Vietnamese boat people.* 本日，ベトナムのボート難民の強制送還が始められる. **2** V-T 他動詞 If someone **repatriates** money that is invested in another country, they change their investments so that the money is invested in their own country. 本国へ送り帰す

Word Link *re ≈ back, again : re*flect, *re*pay, *re*state

---

re|pay /rɪpeɪ/ (**repays, repaying, repaid**) **1** V-T 他動詞 If you **repay** a loan or a debt, you pay back the money that you owe to the person who you borrowed or took it from. 返済する □ *He advanced funds of his own to his company, which was unable to repay him.* 彼は会社に手持ちの資金を融資したが，会社は彼に返済することができなかった. **2** V-T 他動詞 If you **repay** a favor that someone did for you, you do something for them in return. 報いる □ *It was very kind. I don't know how I can ever repay you.* なんてご親切に．いったいどのようにお返しすればいいのでしょう.

re|pay|able /rɪpeɪəbəl/ ADJ 形容詞 A loan that is **repayable** within a certain period of time must be paid back within that time. 払い戻しすべき [mainly BRIT 主に英国英語; AM usually **payable** 米国英語では通常 **payable**]

re|pay|ment /rɪpeɪmənt/ (**repayments**) **1** N-COUNT 可算名詞 **Repayments** are amounts of money which you pay at regular intervals to a person or organization in order to repay a debt. 返済

金 [mainly BRIT 主に英国英語; AM usually **payment** 米国英語では通常 **payment**] **2** N-UNCOUNT 不可算名詞 The **repayment** of money is the act or process of paying it back to the person you owe it to. 返済 ❑ *He failed to meet last Friday's deadline for repayment of a $114 million loan.* 彼は先週金曜日が期日だった1億1400万ドルの返済ができなかった.

re|peal /rɪpiːl/ (repeals, repealing, repealed) V-T 他動詞 If the government **repeals** a law, it officially ends it, so that it is no longer valid. 廃止する ❑ *The government has just repealed the law segregating public facilities.* 政府は公共施設を人種別に分ける法律を廃止したところです. ● N-UNCOUNT 不可算名詞 Repeal is also a noun. 廃止 ❑ *Next year will be the 60th anniversary of the repeal of Prohibition.* 来年は禁酒法撤廃60周年に当たる.

re|peat /rɪpiːt/ (repeats, repeating, repeated) **1** V-T 他動詞 If you **repeat** something, you say or write it again. You can say **I repeat** to show that you feel strongly about what you are repeating. 繰り返す ❑ *He repeated that he had been misquoted.* 彼は誤った引用をされたのだと繰り返し述べました. ❑ *She repeated her call yesterday for an investigation into the incident.* 昨日彼女はその事件の調査を何度も要求しました. **2** V-T 他動詞 If you **repeat** something that someone else has said or written, you say or write the same thing, or tell it to another person. 反復する ❑ *She had an irritating habit of repeating everything I said to her.* いらいらすることに, 彼女は私の言うことを何でもまた伝える癖があった. ❑ *I trust you not to repeat that to anyone else.* あなたはそのことを他の誰にも言わないって私は信じているからね. **3** V-T 他動詞 If you **repeat yourself**, you say something which you have said before, usually by mistake. (再帰形を伴う) 同じことを繰り返し言う ❑ *He spoke well to begin with, but then started rambling and repeating himself.* 出だしは順調だった彼の話は, 次第にまとまりがなく同じことの繰り返しになり始めた. **4** V-T/V-I 他動詞/自動詞 If you **repeat** an action, you do it again. 繰り返す ❑ *The next day I repeated the procedure.* 私は翌日もその手順を繰り返した. ❑ *Move the leg up and down several times and rotate the foot. Repeat on the right leg.* 片足を数回上げ下げして足先を回してください. 右足も繰り返しなさい. **5** V-T 他動詞 If an event or series of events **repeats itself**, it happens again. (再帰形を伴い) 繰り返し起こる ❑ *The UN will have to work hard to stop history from repeating itself.* 歴史を繰り返させないために国連には非常な努力が求められるでしょう. **6** N-COUNT 可算名詞 If there is a **repeat of** an event, usually an undesirable event, it happens again. 繰り返し ❑ *There were fears that there might be a repeat of last year's campaign of strikes.* 昨年のストライキ運動がまた繰り返されるのではと懸念されていました. **7** ADJ 形容詞 If a company gets **repeat** business or **repeat** customers, people who have bought their goods or services before buy them again. 再注文の, 再び訪れる [BUSINESS 実業] [ADJ n] ❑ *Nearly 60% of our bookings come from repeat business and personal recommendation.* 予約の約60パーセントはリピーターか口コミでいらしたお客様です. **8** N-COUNT 可算名詞 A **repeat** is a television or radio program that has been broadcast before. 再放送 ❑ *There's nothing except sports and repeats on TV.* スポーツ番組と再放送ぐらいしかやってない.

Thesaurus repeat また次を参照:

V.	reiterate, restate, retell **1** **2**
N.	encore, rerun **8**

re|peat|ed /rɪpiːtɪd/ ADJ 形容詞 **Repeated** actions or events are ones that happen many times. 繰り返しの [ADJ n] ❑ *Mr. Lawssi apparently did not return the money, despite repeated reminders.* ローシ氏はどうやら, 繰り返しの督促にもかかわらずお金を返さなかったようです.

re|peat|ed|ly /rɪpiːtɪdli/ ADV 副詞 If you do something **repeatedly**, you do it many times. 繰り返して [ADV with v] ❑ *Both men have repeatedly denied the allegations.* 男性は2人とも申し立てを繰り返し否定しました.

re|pel /rɪpɛl/ (repels, repelling, repelled) **1** V-T 他動詞 When an army **repels** an attack, they successfully fight and drive back soldiers from another army who have attacked them. 撃退する [FORMAL 形式ばった] ❑ *They have fifty thousand troops along the border ready to repel any attack.* 彼らはいかなる攻撃も撃退できるように国境沿いに5万人の部隊を配備している. **2** V-T 他動詞 If something **repels** you, you find it horrible and disgusting. 不快にする [no cont] ❑ *...a violent excitement that frightened and repelled her.* 彼女をおびえさせ, 不快にさせた過激な興奮状態 ● **re|pelled** ADJ 形容詞 嫌悪感を抱いた ❑ *She was very striking but in some way I felt repelled.* 彼女はとても目立っていたが, なぜか私は嫌悪感を覚えた. **3** V-RECIP 相互動詞 When a magnetic pole **repels** another magnetic pole, it gives out a force that pushes the other pole away. You can also say that two magnetic poles **repel** each other or that they **repel**. 反発する [TECHNICAL 技術的] → see **magnet**

re|pel|lent /rɪpɛlənt/ (repellents) also **repellant** **1** ADJ 形容詞 If you think that something is horrible and disgusting you can say that it is **repellent**. 不快な [FORMAL 形式ばった] ❑ *...a very*

large, very repellent toad. とても大きくて, とても気持悪いヒキガエル **2** N-MASS 質量名詞 **Insect repellent** is a product containing chemicals that you spray into the air or on your body in order to keep insects away. 防虫剤 ❑ *...mosquito repellent.* 蚊よけ剤.

re|pent /rɪpɛnt/ (repents, repenting, repented) V-I 自動詞 If you **repent**, you show or say that you are sorry for something wrong you have done. 悔やむ ❑ *Those who refuse to repent, he said, will be punished.* 「悔い改めようとしない人々は, 罰せられるであろう」と彼は言った.

re|pent|ance /rɪpɛntəns/ N-UNCOUNT 不可算名詞 If you show **repentance** for something wrong that you have done, you make it clear that you are sorry for doing it. 後悔 ❑ *They showed no repentance during their trial.* 公判中彼らはまったく改悛 (しゅん) の様子を見せなかった.

re|pent|ant /rɪpɛntənt/ ADJ 形容詞 Someone who is **repentant** shows or says that they are sorry for something wrong they have done. 後悔している ❑ *He was feeling guilty and depressed, repentant and scared.* 彼は罪の意識にさいなまれ, 落ち込み, 後悔し, おびえていた.

rep|er|toire /rɛpərtwɑr/ (repertoires) N-COUNT 可算名詞 A performer's **repertoire** is all the plays or pieces of music that he or she has learned and can perform. レパートリー ❑ *Meredith D'Ambrosio has thousands of songs in her repertoire.* メレディス・ダンブロジオのレパートリーは何千曲にも上ります.

rep|er|tory /rɛpərtɔri/ N-UNCOUNT 不可算名詞 A **repertory** company is a group of actors and actresses who perform a small number of plays for just a few weeks at a time. They work in a **repertory** theater. レパートリー劇団 [usu N n] ❑ *...a well-known repertory company in Boston.* ボストンの有名なレパートリー劇団

rep|eti|tion /rɛpɪtɪʃən/ (repetitions) **1** N-VAR 可変性名詞 If there is a **repetition** of an event, usually an undesirable event, it happens again. 繰り返し ❑ *Today the city government has taken measures to prevent a repetition of last year's confrontation.* 市役所は昨年の対立を繰り返させないためにあれこれ手段を講じています. **2** N-VAR 可変性名詞 **Repetition** means using the same words again. 反復 ❑ *He could also have cut much of the repetition and thus saved many pages.* 彼はまた反復箇所の多くを削除して, そうしてかなりのページを削減することもできたでしょうに.

re|peti|tive /rɪpɛtɪtɪv/ **1** ADJ 形容詞 Something that is **repetitive** involves actions or elements that are repeated many times and is therefore boring. 繰り返しの多い [DISAPPROVAL 不賛成] ❑ *...factory workers who do repetitive jobs.* 反復作業に従事する工場労働者 **2** ADJ 形容詞 **Repetitive** movements or sounds are repeated many times. 反復の ❑ *This technique is particularly successful where problems occur as the result of repetitive movements.* 反復運動の結果生じた問題には, この手法が特に有効です.

re|place /rɪpleɪs/ (replaces, replacing, replaced) **1** V-T 他動詞 If one thing or person **replaces** another, the first is used or acts instead of the second. 取って代わる ❑ *One species of tree replaces another as a forest ages.* 森が古くなるにつれて, ある種の木が別の種の木に取って代わる. ❑ *...the lawyer who replaced Robert as chairman of the company.* ロバートに代わり会社の会長に就任した弁護士 **2** V-T 他動詞 If you **replace** one thing or person **with** another, you put something or someone else in their place to do their job. 取り替える ❑ *I clean out all the grease and replace it with oil so it works better in very low temperatures.* グリースをすっかりふき取って, 代わりにオイルを塗ったから, 気温が非常に低くてもいっそうよく作用します. **3** V-T 他動詞 If you **replace** something that is broken, damaged, or lost, you get a new one to use instead. 差し替える ❑ *The shower that we put in a few years back has broken and we cannot afford to replace it.* 数年前に取り付けたシャワーが壊れてしまったが, 新しいのに付け替える金がないんだ. **4** V-T 他動詞 If you **replace** something, you put it back where it was before. 元の位置に戻す ❑ *Replace the caps on the bottles.* 口金をみな元のビンにはめなさい.

re|place|ment /rɪpleɪsmənt/ (replacements) **1** N-UNCOUNT 不可算名詞 If you refer to the **replacement** of one thing by another, you mean that the second takes the place of the first. 交代 [with supp] ❑ *...the replacement of damaged or lost books.* 傷んだり無くなったりした本の差し替え **2** N-COUNT 可算名詞 Someone who takes someone else's place in an organization, government, or team can be referred to as their **replacement**. 後任 ❑ *Taylor has nominated Adams as his replacement.* テイラーはアダムズを自分の後任に指名した.

re|play (replays, replaying, replayed)

> The verb is pronounced /riːpleɪ/. The noun is pronounced /riːpleɪ/.
>
> 動詞は /riːpleɪ/ と発音される. 名詞は /riːpleɪ/ と発音される.

1 V-T 他動詞 If a game or match between two sports teams **is replayed**, the two teams play it again, because neither team won the first time, or because the game was stopped because of bad weather. 再試合を行う [usu passive] ❑ *The game had to be replayed*

at the end of the season. その試合はシーズン末にやり直さなければ ならなかった. ● N-COUNT 可算名詞 You can refer to a game that is replayed as a **replay**. 再試合 □ *If there has to be a replay we are confident of victory.* もし再試合になったら、我々は勝つ自身がありま す. ② V-T 他動詞 If you **replay** something that you have recorded on film or tape, you play it again in order to watch it or listen to it. 再生する □ *He stopped the machine and replayed the message.* 彼は機械 を止め、メッセージを再生した. ● N-COUNT 可算名詞 **Replay** is also a noun. 再生 □ *I watched a slow-motion videotape replay of his fall.* 彼 の落下をビデオのスロー再生で見た. ③ V-T 他動詞 If you **replay** an event in your mind, you think about it again and again. (頭の中 で) 再現する □ *She spends her nights lying in bed, replaying the fire in her mind.* 彼女はベッドに横たわり、あの火事を何度も思い浮かべなが ら夜を過ごす.

re|plen|ish /rɪplɛnɪʃ/ (replenishes, replenishing, replenished) V-T 他動詞 If you **replenish** something, you make it full or complete again. 補充する [FORMAL 形式ばった] □ *Three hundred thousand tons of cereals are needed to replenish stocks.* 在庫を補充する には30万トンの穀物が必要です.

rep|li|ca /rɛplɪkə/ (replicas) N-COUNT 可算名詞 A **replica** of something such as a statue, building, or weapon is an accurate copy of it. 複製 □ *...a human-sized replica of the Statue of Liberty.* 自由 の女神像の人間大のレプリカ

re|ply /rɪplaɪ/ (replies, replying, replied) ① V-T/V-I 他動詞/ 自動詞 When you **reply to** something that someone has said or written to you, you say or write an answer to them. 返答する □ *"That's a nice dress," said Michael. "Thanks," she replied solemnly.* 「素 敵なドレスだね」とマイケルが言った.「ありがとう」と彼女は真顔 で答えた. □ *He replied that this was absolutely impossible.* これは絶 対に不可能ですよ、と彼は答えた. □ *He never replied to the letters.* 彼 はそれらの手紙には返事を決して出さなかった. ② N-COUNT 可算名 詞 A **reply** is something that you say or write when you answer someone or answer a letter or advertisement. 返事 [oft N "to/ from" n, also "in" N] □ *I called out a challenge, but there was no reply.* かかってこいと叫んだが、返答はなかった. □ *He said in reply that the question was unfair.* その質問はフェアじゃない、と彼は答えて言っ た. ③ V-I 自動詞 If you **reply** to something such as an attack **with** violence or **with** another action, you do something in response. 応酬する □ *During a number of violent incidents farmers threw eggs and empty bottles at police, who replied with tear gas.* 一連の暴力沙汰 (ざ た) の間に、農民は卵や空き瓶を警察に投げつけ、警察は催涙ガスで 応酬した.

re|port /rɪpɔrt/ (reports, reporting, reported) ① V-T 他動 詞 If you **report** something that has happened, you tell people about it. 報告する □ *I reported the theft to the police.* 私は警察に盗難 届けを出した. □ *The officials also reported that two more ships were apparently heading for Malta.* また官辺筋は、さらに2隻の船がマルタ に向かったようだと伝えた. □ *"He seems to be all right now," reported a relieved Taylor.* 「かれはもう大丈夫そうだ」とテイラーはほっとし た顔で伝えた. □ *She reported him missing the next day.* 次の日に彼 女は彼が行方不明だと報告した. ② V-I 自動詞 If you **report on** an event or subject, you tell people about it, because it is your job or duty to do so. 報道する □ *Many journalists based outside of Sudan have been refused visas to enter the country to report on political affairs.* ス ーダン国外に拠点を置く多くのジャーナリストが、政治問題を報道す る目的での入国査証の発給を拒否されました. ③ N-COUNT 可算名詞 A **report** is a news article or broadcast which gives information about something that has just happened. 報道 □ *According to a report in the newspaper, he still has control over the remaining shares.* 新 聞報道によると、彼は依然としてその残りの株式の支配権を持ってい る. ④ N-COUNT 可算名詞 A **report** is an official document which a group of people issue after investigating a situation or event. 調 査報告書 □ *The education committee will today publish its report on the supply of teachers for the next decade.* 教育委員会は今日、今後10年間の 教員供給に関する調査報告書を公表する予定です. ⑤ N-COUNT 可算名 詞 If you give someone a **report** on something, you tell them what has been happening. 報告 □ *She came back to give us a progress report on how the project is going.* 彼女は私たちにその計画の進捗状況を報告 するために戻ってきました. ⑥ N-COUNT 可算名詞 If you say that there are **reports** that something has happened, you mean that some people say it has happened but you have no direct evidence of it. うわさ [VAGUENESS あいまいさ] □ *There are unconfirmed reports*

that two people have been shot in the neighboring town of Springfield. ス プリングフィールドの隣町で2人が撃たれたとの未確認情報があります. ⑦ V-T 他動詞 If someone **reports** you **to** a person in authority, they tell that person about something wrong that you have done. 訴え出る □ *His ex-wife reported him to police a few days later.* 彼の元妻 が数日後に彼を警察に訴えた. ⑧ V-I 自動詞 If you **report to** a person or place, you go to that person or place and say that you are ready to start work or say that you are present. 出頭する □ *Mr. Ashwell has to surrender his passport and report to the police every five days.* アシ ュウェル氏はパスポートを引き渡して、5日ごとに警察に出頭しなけれ ばなりません. ⑨ V-I 自動詞 If you say that one employee **reports to** another, you mean that the first employee is told what to do by the second one and is responsible to them. 監督下にある [FORMAL 形式ばった] [no cont] □ *He reported to a section chief, who reported to a division chief, and so on up the line.* 彼は課長の監督下にあり、課長は部 長の監督下にあり、さらに上に行っても同様な管理形態になっていまし た. ⑩ → see also **reporting**

re|port card (report cards) ① N-COUNT 可算名詞 A **report card** is an official written account of how well or how badly a student has done during the term or year that has just finished. 成績表 [AM 米国英語] □ *The only time I got their attention was when I brought home straight A's on my report card.* 私が彼らの注目をあびたのは、オ ールAの成績表を持ち帰ったときだけだった. ② N-COUNT 可算名詞 A **report card** is a report on how well a person, organization, or country has been doing recently. 報告書 [AM 米国英語 JOURNALISM ジャーナリズム] □ *The president today issued his final report card on the state of the economy.* 本日、大統領は経済状態に関する最終報告書を発 表しました.

re|port|ed|ly /rɪpɔrtɪdli/ ADV 副詞 If you say that something is **reportedly** true, you mean that someone has said that it is true, but you have no direct evidence of it. 伝えられたところで は [FORMAL 形式ばった、VAGUENESS あいまいさ] □ *More than two hundred people have reportedly been killed in the past week's fighting.* 伝 えられたところによると、過去1週間の戦闘で死者は200名を越えた.

re|port|er /rɪpɔrtər/ (reporters) N-COUNT 可算名詞 A **reporter** is someone who writes news articles or who broadcasts news reports. 報道記者 □ *...a TV reporter.* テレビレポーター

re|port|ing /rɪpɔrtɪŋ/ N-UNCOUNT 不可算名詞 **Reporting** is the presenting of news in newspapers, on radio, and on television. 報 道 □ *This newspaper has achieved a reputation for honest and impartial political reporting.* この新聞社は、公正かつ偏らない報道という評価を 受けてきました.

re|posi|tory /rɪpɑzɪtɔri/ (repositories) N-COUNT 可算名詞 A **repository** is a place where something is kept safely. 保管場所 [FORMAL 形式ばった] □ *A church in Moscow became a repository for police files.* とあるモスクワの教会が警察書類の保管場所になりまし た.

re|pos|sess /rɪpəzɛs/ (repossesses, repossessing, repossessed) V-T 他動詞 If your car or house **is repossessed**, the people who supplied it take it back because they are still owed money for it. 取り返す、引き揚げる [usu passive] □ *His car was repossessed by the company.* 彼の車はその会社に引き揚げられた.

re|pos|ses|sion /rɪpəzɛʃən/ (repossessions) N-VAR 可変 性名詞 The **repossession** of someone's house or car is the act of repossessing it. 回収、引き揚げ □ *...the problem of home repossessions.* 家屋差し押さえの問題

rep|re|sent /rɛprɪzɛnt/ (represents, representing, represented) ① V-T 他動詞 If someone such as a lawyer or a politician **represents** a person, a group of people, or a place, they act on behalf of that person, group, or place. 代表する □ *...the politicians we elect to represent us.* 我々の代表として選出する政治家 □ *...Richard Bolling, a Democrat who represented Missouri in Congress.* リチャード・ボーリング、ミズーリ州選出の民主党議員 ② V-T 他 動詞 If you **represent** a person or group at an official event, you go there on their behalf. 代理をする □ *The general secretary may represent the president at official ceremonies.* 公式行事で書記長が大統領 の代行を務める場合があります. ③ V-T 他動詞 If you **represent** your country or city in a competition or sports event, you take part in it on behalf of the country or city where you live. 代表を務める □ *My only aim is to represent the United States at the Olympics.* 私のただ1つの 目標は、アメリカ代表でオリンピックに出ることです. ④ V-T PASSIVE 受動態他動詞 If a group of people or things is well **represented** in a particular activity or in a particular place, a lot of them can be found there. 多く見られる □ *Women are already well represented in the area of TV drama.* 多くの女性がすでにテレビドラマ界に進出し

ている. **5** V-T 他動詞 If a sign or symbol **represents** something, it is accepted as meaning that thing. 表す [no cont] ❏ *...a black dot in the middle of the circle is supposed to represent the source of the radiation.* 円中央の黒い点は，放射線源を表すものとする **6** V-T 他動詞 To **represent** an idea or quality means to be a symbol or an expression of that idea or quality. 象徴する [no cont, no passive] ❏ *New York represents everything that's great about America.* ニューヨークはアメリカの偉大さをあらゆる点で象徴している. **7** V-T 他動詞 If you **represent** a person or thing **as** a particular thing, you describe them as being that thing. 描写する ❏ *The popular press tends to represent him as an environmental guru.* 大衆紙は彼を環境問題の権威者として扱う傾向にある.

rep|re|sen|ta|tion /rɛprɪzɛnteɪʃ³n/ (representations) **1** N-UNCOUNT 不可算名詞 If a group or person has **representation** in a legislature or on a committee, someone in the legislature or on the committee supports them and makes decisions on their behalf. 代表 ❏ *Puerto Ricans are U.S. citizens but they have no representation in Congress.* プエルトリコ人はアメリカ国民ですが，彼らは議会に代表を出していない. **2** → see also **proportional representation 3** N-COUNT 可算名詞 You can describe a picture, model, or statue of a person or thing as a **representation** of them. 肖像 [FORMAL 形式ばった] ❏ *...a lifelike representation of Christ.* キリストの真に迫った肖像画

rep|re|senta|tive /rɛprɪzɛntətɪv/ (representatives) **1** N-COUNT 可算名詞 A **representative** is a person who has been chosen to act or make decisions on behalf of another person or a group of people. 代表者 ❏ *...labor union representatives.* 労働組合の代表者たち **2** N-COUNT 可算名詞 A **representative** is a person whose job is to sell a company's products or services, especially by traveling around and visiting other companies. 外交員 [FORMAL 形式ばった] ❏ *She had a stressful job as a sales representative.* 彼女は販売外交員というストレスの多い仕事をしていた. **3** N-COUNT 可算名詞 In the United States, a **representative** is a member of the House of Representatives, the less powerful of the two parts of Congress. 米国下院議員 ❏ *...a Republican representative from Wyoming.* ワイオミング州選出の共和党下院議員 **4** ADJ 形容詞 A **representative** group consists of a small number of people who have been chosen to make decisions on behalf of a larger group. 代表の [ADJ n] ❏ *The new head of state should be an 87-member representative council.* 新国家元首は87名からなる代表評議会によって選出されるべきです. **5** ADJ 形容詞 Someone who is typical of the group to which they belong can be described as **representative**. 典型的な ❏ *He was in no way representative of dog trainers in general.* 彼は決して犬の訓練士全般の典型的な人物ではなかった. **6** → see also **House of Representatives**

re|press /rɪprɛs/ (represses, repressing, repressed) **1** V-T 他動詞 If you **repress** a feeling, you make a deliberate effort not to show or have this feeling. 抑える ❏ *It is anger that is repressed that leads to violence and loss of control.* 抑えられると暴力に発展し制御できなくなるのが怒りだ. **2** V-T 他動詞 If you **repress** a smile, sigh, or moan, you try hard not to smile, sigh, or moan. こらえる ❏ *He repressed a smile.* 彼は笑いをこらえた. **3** V-T 他動詞 If a section of society **is repressed**, their freedom is restricted by the people who have authority over them. 抑圧する [DISAPPROVAL 不賛成] ❏ *...a UN resolution banning him from repressing his people.* 彼に民衆への圧政を禁じる国連の決議

re|pressed /rɪprɛst/ ADJ 形容詞 A **repressed** person is someone who does not allow themselves to have natural feelings and desires, especially sexual ones. 抑圧された ❏ *Some have charged that the Puritans were sexually repressed.* 一部の人たちは清教徒たちは性的に抑圧されていたと非難している.

re|pres|sion /rɪprɛʃ³n/ (repressions) **1** N-UNCOUNT 不可算名詞 **Repression** is the use of force to restrict and control a society or other group of people. 弾圧 [DISAPPROVAL 不賛成] ❏ *...a society conditioned by violence and repression.* 暴力と弾圧に慣らされた社会 **2** N-UNCOUNT 不可算名詞 **Repression** of feelings, especially sexual ones, is a person's unwillingness to allow themselves to have natural feelings and desires. 抑圧 ❏ *Much of the anger he's felt during his life has stemmed from the repression of his feelings about men.* 彼がこれまでの人生で覚えた怒りの多くは，男性への感情を抑えることから生じている.

re|pres|sive /rɪprɛsɪv/ ADJ 形容詞 A **repressive** government is one that restricts people's freedom and controls them by using force. 弾圧的な [DISAPPROVAL 不賛成] ❏ *The military regime in power was unpopular and repressive.* 軍事政権は評判も悪く，弾圧的だった.

re|prieve /rɪpriv/ (reprieves, reprieving, reprieved) **1** V-T 他動詞 If someone who has been sentenced in a court **is reprieved**, their punishment is officially delayed or canceled. 執行を猶予する [no cont] ❏ *Fourteen people, waiting to be hanged for the murder of a former prime minister, have been reprieved.* 前大統領を殺害のかどで絞首刑が確定していた14名の執行が延期された. ● N-VAR 可変性名詞 **Reprieve** is also a noun. 執行猶予 ❏ *A man awaiting death by lethal injection has been saved by a last-minute reprieve.* 薬物注射による死刑が

確定していた男は，執行寸前の延期で救われた. **2** N-COUNT 可算名詞 A **reprieve** is a delay before a very unpleasant or difficult situation which may or may not take place. 一時的猶予 ❏ *It looked as though the college would have to shut, but this week it was given a reprieve.* 大学は閉校せざるをえないように見えたが，今週は猶予を与えられた.

rep|ri|mand /rɛprɪmænd/ (reprimands, reprimanding, reprimanded) V-T 他動詞 If someone **is reprimanded**, they are spoken to angrily or seriously for doing something wrong, usually by a person in authority. 叱責する [FORMAL 形式ばった] ❏ *He was reprimanded by a teacher for talking in the corridor.* 彼は廊下での私語を先生に叱られた. ● N-VAR 可変性名詞 **Reprimand** is also a noun. 叱責 ❏ *He has been fined five thousand dollars and given a severe reprimand.* 彼は罰金5千ドルを科せられ，厳しい叱責を受けた.

re|print (reprints, reprinting, reprinted)

The verb is pronounced /riprɪnt/. The noun is pronounced /riprɪnt/.

動詞は /riprɪnt/ と発音される. 名詞は /riprɪnt/ と発音される.

1 V-T 他動詞 If a book **is reprinted**, further copies of it are printed when all the other ones have been sold. 増刷する [usu passive] ❏ *It remained an exceptionally rare book until it was reprinted in 1918.* 1918年に復刻されるまで，それは非常に希少な本だった. **2** N-COUNT 可算名詞 A **reprint** is a process in which new copies of a book or article are printed because all the other ones have been sold. 増刷 ❏ *Demand picked up and a reprint was required last November.* 需要が伸び，昨年の11月に増刷が必要となった. **3** N-COUNT 可算名詞 A **reprint** is a new copy of a book or article, printed because all the other ones have been sold or because minor changes were made to the original. 再版 ❏ *...a reprint of a 1962 novel.* 1962年の小説の再版

re|pris|al /rɪpraɪz³l/ (reprisals) N-VAR 可変性名詞 If you do something to a person **in reprisal**, you hurt or punish them because they have done something violent or unpleasant to you. 報復 ❏ *There were fears that some of the Western hostages might be killed in reprisal.* 西洋人の人質の何人かが報復として殺されるのでは，という恐れがありました.

re|proach /rɪproʊtʃ/ (reproaches, reproaching, reproached) **1** V-T 他動詞 If you **reproach** someone, you say or show that you are disappointed, upset, or angry because they have done something wrong. 責める ❏ *She is quick to reproach anyone who doesn't live up to her own high standards.* 彼女はすぐに自分自身の高い標準に達しない人を非難する. **2** N-VAR 可変性名詞 If you look at or speak to someone with **reproach**, you show or say that you are disappointed, upset, or angry because they have done something wrong. 非難 ❏ *He looked at her with reproach.* 彼は非難がましく彼女を見た. **3** V-T 他動詞 If you **reproach yourself**, you think with regret about something you have done wrong. （再帰形を伴い）自分を責める ❏ *You've no reason to reproach yourself, no reason to feel shame.* きみは自分を責めたり，恥じたりすることは何もない.

re|pro|duce /riprədus/ (reproduces, reproducing, reproduced) **1** V-T 他動詞 If you try to **reproduce** something, you try to copy it. 再現する ❏ *The effect has proved hard to reproduce.* 効果を再び出すのは難しいと分かった. **2** V-T 他動詞 If you **reproduce** a picture, speech, or piece of writing, you make a photograph or printed copy of it. 複製する ❏ *We are grateful to you for permission to reproduce this article.* この記事の翻刻をお許しくださりありがとうございます. **3** V-T 他動詞 If you **reproduce** an action or an achievement, you repeat it. 再現する ❏ *If we can reproduce the form we have shown in the last couple of months we will be successful.* ここ2か月で示してきた形を再現できれば成功するだろう. **4** V-T/V-I 他動詞/自動詞 When people, animals, or plants **reproduce**, they produce young. 繁殖させる [他動詞]，繁殖する [自動詞] ❏ *...a society where women are defined by their ability to reproduce.* 女性が生殖能力で定義される社会 ❏ *We are reproducing ourselves at such a rate that our numbers threaten the ecology of the planet.* 人口は地球の生態系を脅かす勢いで増え続けている. ● **re|pro|duc|tion** /riprədʌkʃ³n/ N-UNCOUNT 不可算名詞 生殖 ❏ *Treatments using assisted reproduction techniques jumped 30 percent.* 生殖補助医療技術による処置は30パーセントも伸びた.

re|pro|duc|tion /riprədʌkʃ³n/ (reproductions) **1** N-COUNT 可算名詞 A **reproduction** is a copy of something such as a piece of furniture or a work of art. 複製品 ❏ *...a reproduction of a popular religious painting.* 有名な宗教画の複製品 **2** → see also **reproduce** → see **flower**

re|pro|duc|tive /riprədʌktɪv/ ADJ 形容詞 **Reproductive** processes and organs are concerned with the reproduction of living things. 生殖の ❏ *...the female reproductive system.* 女性の生殖器官

rep|tile /rɛptaɪl, -tɪl/ (reptiles) N-COUNT 可算名詞 **Reptiles** are a group of cold-blooded animals which lay eggs and have skins covered with small, hard plates called scales. Snakes, lizards, and crocodiles are reptiles. 爬虫（はちゅう）類 → see **pet**

re|pub|lic /rɪpʌblɪk/ (republics) N-COUNT 可算名詞 A **republic** is a country where power is held by the people or the representatives that they elect. Republics have presidents who are elected, rather than kings or queens. 共和国 ❑ *In 1918, Austria became a republic.* 1918年にオーストリアは共和国になった。 ❑ *...the Baltic republics.* バルト諸国の共和国

re|pub|li|can /rɪpʌblɪkən/ (republicans) ◼ ADJ 形容詞 **Republican** means relating to a republic. In **republican** systems of government, power is held by the people or the representatives that they elect. 共和制の ❑ *...the nations that had adopted the republican form of government.* 共和制の政治形態を採用していた国々 ◼ ADJ 形容詞 If someone is **Republican**, they belong to or support the Republican Party. 共和党の ❑ *Lower taxes made Republican voters happier with their party.* 減税により、共和党支持の有権者は党への満足度を高めた。 ● N-COUNT 可算名詞 A **Republican** is someone who supports or belongs to the Republican Party. 共和党員, 共和党支持者 ❑ *What made you decide to become a Republican, as opposed to a Democrat?* あなたはなぜ民主党員ではなく、共和党員になると決めたのですか。

re|pu|di|ate /rɪpyudieɪt/ (repudiates, repudiating, repudiated) V-T 他動詞 If you **repudiate** something or someone, you show that you strongly disagree with them and do not want to be connected with them in any way. 拒絶する, 拒否する [FORMAL OR WRITTEN 形式ばった、または書き言葉] ❑ *Leaders urged people to turn out in large numbers to repudiate the violence.* 指導者たちはその暴力事件に抗議するために大勢の市民に結集を呼びかけました。 ● **re|pu|dia|tion** /rɪpyudieɪʃ⁰n/ (repudiations) N-VAR 可変性名詞 拒絶, 拒否 ❑ *He believes his public repudiation of the conference decision will enhance his standing as a leader.* 公の場で会議の決定を拒絶したことで、彼は自らの指導者としての立場が強まるものと考えている。

re|pul|sive /rɪpʌlsɪv/ ADJ 形容詞 If you describe something or someone as **repulsive**, you mean that they are horrible and disgusting and you want to avoid them. 気持ち悪い ❑ *...repulsive, fat, white slugs.* 気持ちの悪い丸々とした白いナメクジ

repu|table /rɛpyətəb⁰l/ ADJ 形容詞 A **reputable** company or person is reliable and can be trusted. 評判のよい ❑ *You are well advised to buy your car through a reputable dealer.* 車を購入するときは評判のよいディーラーから買うことをお勧めする。

repu|ta|tion /rɛpyəteɪʃ⁰n/ (reputations) ◼ N-COUNT 可算名詞 To have a **reputation for** something means to be known or remembered for it. …という評判 ❑ *Alice Munro has a reputation for being a very depressing writer.* アリス・マンローは非常に暗い作風で知られている。 ◼ N-COUNT 可算名詞 Something's or someone's **reputation** is the opinion that people have about how good they are. If they have a good reputation, people think they are good. 評判 ❑ *This college has a good academic reputation.* この大学は学術機関として高い評価を得ている。 ◼ PHRASE 句 If you know someone **by reputation**, you have never met them but you have heard about their reputation. うわさで ❑ *She was by reputation a good organizer.* 聞くところでは彼女は腕利きのまとめ役らしい。

Word Partnership reputation は次の語句と使われる:

V.	**acquire** a reputation, **build** a reputation, **damage** someone's reputation, **earn** a reputation, **establish** a reputation, **gain** a reputation, **have** a reputation, **ruin** someone's reputation, **tarnish** someone's reputation ◼ ◼
ADJ.	**bad** reputation, **good** reputation ◼ ◼

re|put|ed /rɪpyutɪd/ V-T PASSIVE 受動態他動詞 If you say that something **is reputed to** be true, you mean that people say it is true, but you do not know if it is definitely true. 評判である [FORMAL 形式ばった, VAGUENESS あいまいさ] ❑ *He was reputed to be a fine cook.* 彼の料理はうまいと評判だった。 ● **re|put|ed|ly** /rɪpyutɪdli/ ADV 副詞 評判によれば ❑ *He reputedly earns two million dollars a year.* うわさでは彼は年に200万ドルも稼ぐそうです。

re|quest /rɪkwɛst/ (requests, requesting, requested) ◼ V-T 他動詞 If you **request** something, you ask for it politely or formally. 依頼する [FORMAL 形式ばった] ❑ *Mr. Dennis said he had requested access to a telephone.* デニスさんの話では、彼は電話を使わせてほしいと頼んだそうです。 ◼ V-T 他動詞 If you **request** someone **to do** something, you politely or formally ask them to do it. …に…してほしいと依頼する [FORMAL 形式ばった] ❑ *Students are requested to park at the rear of the building.* 学生は建物の裏側に駐車してください。 ◼ N-COUNT 可算名詞 If you make a **request**, you politely or formally ask someone to do something. 依頼 ❑ *France had agreed to his request for political asylum.* フランス政府は彼の政治亡命の申請を認めていました。 ◼ PHRASE 句 If you do something **at** someone's **request**, you do it because they have asked you to. …の依頼で ❑ *The evacuation is being organized at the request of the United Nations Secretary General.* 国連事務総長からの要請で避難の準備が進められています。 ◼ PHRASE 句 If something is given or done **on request**, it is given or done whenever you ask for it. 依頼に応じて ❑ *Details are available on request.* ご要望がありましたら詳細をお送りします。

Word Partnership request は次の語句と使われる:

N.	request **aid**, request **a hearing**, request **information**, request **permission**, request **a response** ◼
V.	**agree to** a request, **consider** a request, **deny** a request, **grant** a request, **make** a request, **refuse** a request, **reject** a request, **respond to** a request, **send** a request, **submit** a request ◼

re|quire /rɪkwaɪər/ (requires, requiring, required) ◼ V-T 他動詞 If you **require** something or if something **is required**, you need it or it is necessary. 必要とする [FORMAL 形式ばった] ❑ *If you require further information, you should consult the registrar.* 詳しくは教務課にお問い合わせください。 ❑ *This isn't the kind of crisis that requires us to drop everything else.* ほかのすべてを中止すべきほどの危機ではありません。 ◼ V-T 他動詞 If a law or rule **requires** you **to** do something, you have to do it. 義務づける [FORMAL 形式ばった] ❑ *The rules also require employers to provide safety training.* 規則では雇用者は安全教育も行うことになっています。 ❑ *At least 35 manufacturers have flouted a law requiring prompt reporting of such malfunctions.* 少なくとも35社がこうした事故の速やかな報告を義務づける法律に従っていません。

re|quire|ment /rɪkwaɪərmənt/ (requirements) ◼ N-COUNT 可算名詞 A **requirement** is a quality or qualification that you must have in order to be allowed to do something or to be suitable for something. 要件 ❑ *Its products met all legal requirements.* その企業の製品は法律の基準をすべて満たしていた。 ◼ N-COUNT 可算名詞 Your **requirements** are the things that you need. 必要なもの [FORMAL 形式ばった] ❑ *Variations of this program can be arranged to suit your requirements.* 当プログラムはご要望に応じたカスタマイズが可能です。

Word Partnership requirement は次の語句と使われる:

ADJ.	**legal** requirement, **minimum** requirement ◼
V.	**meet** a requirement ◼

requi|site /rɛkwɪzɪt/ (requisites) ◼ ADJ 形容詞 You can use **requisite** to indicate that something is necessary for a particular purpose. 必要な [FORMAL 形式ばった] ❑ *She filled in the requisite paperwork.* 彼女は必要書類に記入した。 ◼ N-COUNT 可算名詞 A **requisite** is something that is necessary for a particular purpose. 必要なもの [FORMAL 形式ばった] ❑ *An understanding of accounting techniques is a requisite for the work of the analysts.* アナリストとして仕事をするには会計知識が必須である。

re|sale /riseɪl/ N-UNCOUNT 不可算名詞 The **resale** price of something that you own is the amount of money that you would get if you sold it. 転売, 再販 ❑ *...a well-maintained used car with a good resale value.* 行き届いた整備で高値がついた中古車

re|sched|ule /riʃkɛdʒul, -dʒuəl/ (reschedules, rescheduling, rescheduled) ◼ V-T 他動詞 If someone **reschedules** an event, they change the time at which it is supposed to happen. …の日程を変更する ❑ *Since I'll be away, I'd like to reschedule the meeting.* 留守をしますので会議の日程を変更していただきたいのですが。 ◼ V-T 他動詞 To **reschedule** a debt means to arrange for the person, organization, or country that owes money to pay it back over a longer period because they are in financial difficulty. 繰り延べる ❑ *...companies that have gone bust or had to reschedule their debts.* 倒産企業や繰り延べ返済が必要な企業

res|cue /rɛskyu/ (rescues, rescuing, rescued) ◼ V-T 他動詞 If you **rescue** someone, you get them out of a dangerous or unpleasant situation. 救う ❑ *Helicopters rescued nearly 20 people from the roof of the burning building.* 炎上している建物の屋上にいた20人近くがヘリコプターで救出されました。 ● **res|cu|er** (rescuers) N-COUNT 可算名詞 救助する人 ❑ *It took rescuers 90 minutes to reach the trapped men.* 救助隊が閉じ込められていた男性を救出するまで90分かかった。 ◼ N-UNCOUNT 不可算名詞 **Rescue** is help which gets someone out of a dangerous or unpleasant situation. 救出 ❑ *A big rescue operation has been launched for a trawler missing in the North Atlantic.* 北大西洋で行方不明になったトロール船の大規模な捜索活動が始まっています。 ◼ N-COUNT 可算名詞 A **rescue** is an attempt to save someone from a dangerous or unpleasant situation. 救出 ❑ *A major air-sea rescue is under way.* 海と空からの大規模な捜索が行なわれています。 ◼ PHRASE 句 If you **go to** someone's **rescue** or **come to** their **rescue**, you help them when they are in danger or difficulty. 助けに行く ❑ *The 23-year-old's screams alerted a passerby who went to her rescue.* 通りがかった人がその23歳の女性の叫び声に気づいて助けに駆けつけた。

Word Partnership　　rescue は次の語句と使われる:

N.　firefighters rescue, rescue **a hostage**, rescue **miners**,
　rescue **people**, **police** rescue, **volunteers** rescue,
　rescue **wildlife** ■
　rescue **attempt**, rescue **crews**, rescue **effort**, rescue
　mission, rescue **operation**, rescue **teams**, rescue
　workers ■

re|search /rɪsɜːrtʃ, rɪsɜːrt/ (researches, researching,
researched) ■ N-UNCOUNT 不可算名詞 **Research** is work that
involves studying something and trying to discover facts about
it. 研究，調査 [also N in pl] □ *Sixty-five percent of the 1987 budget
went for nuclear weapons research and production.* 1987年の予算の65%
が核兵器の研究と製造に充てられた. ■ V-T 他動詞 If you **research**
something, you try to discover facts about it. 研究する，調査す
る □ *She spent two years in South Florida researching and filming her
documentary.* 彼女は南フロリダで2年にわたり記録映画の調査と撮影に
あたりました. ● **re|search|er** (researchers) N-COUNT 可算名詞 研
究者，調査員 □ *He chose to join the company as a market researcher.* 彼
は市場調査員としてその企業に入社することにした.
→ see **hospital, inventor, laboratory, medicine, science, zoo**

Word Partnership　　research は次の語句と使われる:

N.　**animal** research, **cancer** research, research **and
development**, research **facility**, research **findings**,
laboratory research, research **methods**, research
paper, research **project**, research **report**, research
results, research **scientist** ■

ADJ.　**biological** research, **clinical** research, **current**
research, **experimental** research, **medical** research,
recent research, **scientific** research ■

re|sell /rɪsɛl/ (resells, reselling, resold) V-T/V-I 他動詞/自動詞 If
you **resell** something that you have bought, you sell it again. 転
売する，再版する □ *Storekeepers buy them in bulk and resell them for
$150 each.* 店主たちはそれを大量に仕入れて1個150ドルで販売する.
□ *It makes sense to buy at dealer prices so you can maximize your profits
if you resell.* 転売したときにできるだけ大きな儲けが出るように卸値で
買うのがいい.

re|sem|blance /rɪzɛmbləns/ (resemblances) N-VAR 可変性名
詞 If there is a **resemblance** between two people or things, they
are similar to each other. 似ていること □ *There was a remarkable
resemblance between him and Pete.* 彼とピートは驚くほどそっくりだ
った.

re|sem|ble /rɪzɛmbəl/ (resembles, resembling, resembled) V-T
他動詞 If one thing or person **resembles** another, they are similar
to each other. 似ている [no cont] □ *Some of the commercially produced
venison resembles beef in flavor.* 市販されているシカ肉の中には牛肉の
味にそっくりなものがある.

re|sent /rɪzɛnt/ (resents, resenting, resented) V-T 他動詞 If you
resent someone or something, you feel bitter and angry about
them. 恨む □ *She resents her mother for being so tough on her.* 彼女は母
親が自分にとても厳しいので恨んでいる.

re|sent|ful /rɪzɛntfəl/ ADJ 形容詞 If you are **resentful**, you feel
resentment. 恨んで □ *At first I felt very resentful and angry about
losing my job.* 最初のうちは失業したことに大きな憤りと怒りを感じ
た.

re|sent|ment /rɪzɛntmənt/ (resentments) N-UNCOUNT 不
可算名詞 **Resentment** is bitterness and anger that someone
feels about something. 恨み，憤り [also N in pl] □ *She expressed
resentment at being interviewed by a social worker.* 彼女は民生委員から
面接を受けたことに腹を立てた.

res|er|va|tion /rɛzərveɪʃən/ (reservations) ■ N-VAR 可変性名詞
If you have **reservations about** something, you are not sure that it
is entirely good or right. 疑い，懸念 □ *I told him my main reservation
about his film was the ending.* きみの映画で特に気になるのは結末の
部分だと，わたしは彼に言った. ■ N-COUNT 可算名詞 If you make
a **reservation**, you arrange for something such as a table in a
restaurant or a room in a hotel to be kept for you. 予約 □ *He went
to the desk to inquire and make a reservation.* 彼は予約できるよう窓口に開
きに行った. ■ N-COUNT 可算名詞 A **reservation** is an area of land
that is set separate for a particular group of people to live in. 保
留地 □ *Seventeen thousand Indians live in Arizona on a reservation.* アリ
ゾナ州では1万7千人の先住民が保留地で生活しています.
→ see **hotel**

re|serve /rɪzɜːrv/ (reserves, reserving, reserved) ■ V-T 他動
詞 If something **is reserved for** a particular person or purpose,
it is kept specially for that person or purpose. 取っておく [usu
passive] □ *A double room with a balcony overlooking the sea had been
reserved for him.* バルコニーから海が見渡せるダブルの部屋が彼の
ために取ってあった. ■ V-T 他動詞 If you **reserve** something
such as a table, ticket, or magazine, you arrange for it to be kept

specially for you, rather than sold or given to someone else. 予約
する □ *I'll reserve a table for five.* 5人で予約しておくよ. ■ N-COUNT
可算名詞 A **reserve** is a supply of something that is available for
use when it is needed. 蓄え □ *The Persian Gulf has 65 percent of the
world's oil reserves.* ペルシャ湾は全世界の原油の埋蔵量の65%を占めて
います. ■ N-COUNT 可算名詞 A nature **reserve** is an area of land
where the animals, birds, and plants are officially protected. 保
護区 [mainly BRIT 主に英国英語; AM **preserve** 米国英語 **preserve**]
■ N-UNCOUNT 不可算名詞 If someone shows **reserve**, they keep
their feelings hidden. 遠慮 □ *I hope that you'll overcome your reserve
and let me know.* どうぞご遠慮なくお話しください. ■ PHRASE 句 If
you have something **in reserve**, you have it available for use when
it is needed. 予備の □ *He poked around the top of his cabinet for the
bottle of whiskey that he kept in reserve.* 彼はしまっておいたウィスキー
をとろうと戸棚の一番上を捜し回った. ■ **to reserve judgment** → see
judgment ■ **to reserve the right** → see **right**

Thesaurus　　reserve また次を参照:

V.　hold, save, set aside ■ ■
N.　stock, store, supply ■

re|served /rɪzɜːrvd/ ■ ADJ 形容詞 Someone who is **reserved**
keeps their feelings hidden. 控えめな □ *He was unemotional, quiet,
and reserved.* 彼は感情を表に出さない，もの静かで控えめな人だっ
た. ■ ADJ 形容詞 A table in a restaurant or a seat in a theater that
is **reserved** is being kept for someone rather than given or sold to
anyone else. 予約の □ *Seats, or sometimes entire tables, were reserved.*
予約が入って，時には全席が予約で埋まることもあった.

res|er|voir /rɛzərvwɑːr/ (reservoirs) ■ N-COUNT 可算名詞
A **reservoir** is a lake that is used for storing water before it is
supplied to people. 貯水池 ■ N-COUNT 可算名詞 A **reservoir of**
something is a large quantity of it that is available for use when
needed. 貯蔵 □ *...the huge oil reservoir beneath the Kuwaiti desert.* ク
ウェート砂漠の地下に眠る莫大（ばくだい）な石油
→ see **dam**

Word Link　　sid ≈ sitting : pre**sid**e, pre**sid**ent, re**sid**e

re|side /rɪzaɪd/ (resides, residing, resided) ■ V-I 自動詞 If
someone **resides** somewhere, they live there or are staying there.
居住する；駐在する [FORMAL 形式ばった] □ *Margaret resides with
her invalid mother in a Seattle suburb.* マーガレットは病弱な母とシ
アトル郊外で暮らしている. ■ V-I 自動詞 If a quality **resides in**
something, the thing has that quality. …にある [FORMAL 形式ばっ
た] [no cont] □ *Happiness does not reside in strength or money.* 力や金
があっても幸せにはなれない.

resi|dence /rɛzɪdəns/ (residences) ■ N-COUNT 可算名詞 A
residence is a house where people live. 住宅 [FORMAL 形式ばった]
□ *The house is currently run as a country inn, but could easily convert back
into a private residence.* 現在その家屋は旅館として使われているが，改
装すればすぐに住宅に戻すことができる. ■ N-UNCOUNT 不可算名詞
Your place of **residence** is the place where you live. 居住 [FORMAL
形式ばった] □ *There were significant differences among women based on
age, place of residence, and educational levels.* 女性においては，年齢，
居住地，教育水準によって大きな違いが見られた. ■ N-UNCOUNT 不
可算名詞 Someone's **residence** in a particular place is the fact that
they live there or that they are officially allowed to live there.
在住 □ *They had entered the country and had applied for permanent
residence.* 彼らは入国して永住権を申請していました. ■ → see
also **residence hall** ■ PHRASE 句 If someone is **in residence** in
a particular place, they are living there. 居住して □ *The king and
queen of Jordan are in residence.* ヨルダン国王夫妻が住まわれている.

resi|dence hall (residence halls) N-COUNT 可算名詞 **Residence
halls** are buildings with rooms or apartments, usually built by
universities or colleges, in which students live during the
school year. 学生寮 [AM 米国英語] □ *A freshman adviser lives in each
residence hall.* 新入生指導員が各寮に1名ずつ住み込みで指導に当たっ
ている.

Word Link　　ent ≈ one who does, has : depend**ent**, resid**ent**, superintend**ent**

resi|dent /rɛzɪdənt/ (residents) ■ N-COUNT 可算名詞 The
residents of a house or area are the people who live there. 住
人，住民 □ *The archbishop called on the government to build more low
cost homes for local residents.* 大主教は政府に対し，地元住民のた
めの安価な住宅をさらに建設するよう求めました. ■ ADJ 形容詞
Someone who is **resident in** a country or a town lives there. 居住
して [v-link ADJ] □ *He moved to the United States in 1990 to live with
his son, who had been resident in Baltimore since 1967.* 1990年に彼は
アメリカに移り，1967年からバルティモアで暮らしている息子の元
へ行った. ■ N-COUNT 可算名詞 A **resident** or a **resident** doctor
is a doctor who is receiving a period of specialized training in a
hospital after completing his or her internship. 研修医 [AM 米国
英語] □ *Many resident doctors complain that they are assigned too many*

r

duties that are usually not performed by physicians. 多くの研修医が不満に思っているのは、ふつう医者がやらないような仕事が多すぎることだ.

→ see **country, hospital**

resi|den|tial /rɛzɪdɛnʃ°l/ ① ADJ 形容詞 A **residential** area contains houses rather than offices or factories. 住宅地の □ ...a posh residential area 20 minutes from the White House ホワイトハウスから20分の高級住宅地 ② ADJ 形容詞 A **residential** institution is one where people live while they are studying there or being cared for there. 寮制の □ Training involves a two-year residential course. 教育課程には2年間の全寮制コースが含まれる.

re|sid|ual /rɪzɪdʒuəl/ ADJ 形容詞 **Residual** is used to describe what remains of something when most of it has gone. 残留した □ ...residual radiation from nuclear weapons testing. 核実験の残留放射線

resi|due /rɛzɪdu, -dyu/ (residues) N-COUNT 可算名詞 A **residue** of something is a small amount that remains after most of it has gone. 残留物 □ Always using the same shampoo means that a residue can build up on the hair. 同じシャンプーをずっと使い続けると、髪に残留物がたまる恐れがある.

re|sign /rɪzaɪn/ (resigns, resigning, resigned) ① V-T/V-I 他動詞/自動詞 If you **resign** from a job or position, you formally announce that you are leaving it. 辞職する、辞任する □ A hospital administrator has resigned over claims he lied to get the job. 就任の際に事実を偽ったとして病院の理事が辞任した. □ Mr Robb resigned his position last month. ロブ氏は先月辞任した. ② V-T 他動詞 If you **resign yourself** to an unpleasant situation or fact, you accept it because you realize that you cannot change it. あきらめる □ Pat and I resigned ourselves to yet another summer without a boat. パットとわたしは今年の夏もボートなしで我慢することにした. ③ → see also **resigned**

Do not confuse **resign** and **retire**. If someone **resigns** from their job, they leave it after saying that they do not want to do it any more. He hasn't decided whether he will resign. You can **resign** from your job at any age, and perhaps start another job soon afterward. When someone **retires**, they leave their job and stop working, often because they have reached the age when they can get a pension. He had been planning for some time to retire at around age 60. When professional athletes stop playing sport as their job, you can also say that they **retire**, even if they are fairly young. A heart attack at the age of 36 forced him to retire from tennis.

Thesaurus *resign* また次を参照:

v.　leave, quit, step down ①

res|ig|na|tion /rɛzɪgneɪʃ°n/ (resignations) ① N-VAR 可変性名詞 Your **resignation** is a formal statement of your intention to leave a job or position. 辞職、辞任 □ Bob Morgan has offered his resignation and it has been accepted. ボブ・モーガンは辞任を申し入れて了承された. ② N-UNCOUNT 不可算名詞 **Resignation** is the acceptance of an unpleasant situation or fact because you realize that you cannot change it. あきらめ □ He sighed with profound resignation. 彼は心底あきらめのため息をついた.

re|signed /rɪzaɪnd/ ADJ 形容詞 If you are **resigned to** an unpleasant situation or fact, you accept it without complaining because you realize that you cannot change it. あきらめて □ He is resigned to the noise, the mess, the constant upheaval. うるさくて、散らかるし、次々と大事件が持ち上がるけども、彼はしかたないとあきらめている.

re|sili|ent /rɪzɪlyənt/ ADJ 形容詞 Something that is **resilient** is strong and not easily damaged by being hit, stretched, or squeezed. 弾力性のある □ ...an armchair of some resilient plastic material. 弾力性に富んだプラスチック素材でできたひじ掛け椅子 ● **re|sili|ence** N-UNCOUNT 不可算名詞 [also "a" N] 弾力性 □ Do you feel that your muscles do not have the strength and resilience that they should have? 筋肉の力や弾力が今ひとつでないと感じますか. ② ADJ 形容詞 People and things that are **resilient** are able to recover easily and quickly from unpleasant or damaging events. 立ち直りの早い、回復力のある □ When the U.S. stock market collapsed in October 1987, the Japanese stock market was the most resilient. 1987年10月にアメリカの株式市場が急落したときに、日本市場の回復が最も早かった. ● **re|sili|ence** N-UNCOUNT 不可算名詞 [also "a" N] 立ち直りの早さ、回復力 □ ...the resilience of human beings to fight after they've been attacked. やられたらやり返すという人間の底力

res|in /rɛzɪn/ (resins) ① N-MASS 質量名詞 **Resin** is a sticky substance that is produced by some trees. 樹脂 □ ...a tropical tree that is bled regularly for its resin. 樹脂を集めるために定期的に樹液を採取する熱帯樹木 ② N-MASS 質量名詞 **Resin** is a substance that is produced chemically and used to make plastics. 合成樹脂 □ The plastic resin is used in a wide range of products, including electrical wire insulation. プラスチック樹脂は電線の絶縁体などの広範囲の用途がある.

re|sist /rɪzɪst/ (resists, resisting, resisted) ① V-T 他動詞 If you **resist** something such as a change, you refuse to accept it and try to prevent it. 抵抗する、反対する □ They resisted our attempts to modernize the distribution of books. 彼らは書籍の流通を革新しようとする我々の試みに反対した. ② V-T/V-I 他動詞/自動詞 If you **resist** someone or **resist** an attack by them, you fight back against them. 抵抗する □ The man was shot outside his house as he tried to resist arrest. 男は逮捕の際に抵抗し家の外で撃たれました. □ When she attempted to cut his nails he resisted. 彼女がつめを切ろうとすると彼は嫌がった. ③ V-T 他動詞 If you **resist** doing something, or **resist** the temptation to do it, you stop yourself from doing it although you would like to do it. 我慢する [oft with neg] □ Congress should resist the temptation to try quick economic fixes. 議会は安易な経済政策に走るべきではない. ④ V-T 他動詞 If someone or something **resists** damage of some kind, they are not damaged. 耐える □ ...bodies trained and toughened to resist the cold. 寒さに耐えられるように訓練して鍛えた体

Word Link | *ance* ≈ quality, state : *defiance, performance, resistance*

---

re|sist|ance /rɪzɪstəns/ (resistances) ① N-UNCOUNT 不可算名詞 **Resistance** to something such as a change or a new idea is a refusal to accept it. 反対 □ The U.S. wants big cuts in European agricultural export subsidies, but this is meeting resistance. アメリカはEUの輸出補助金の大幅な削減を求めていますが、EU側の抵抗にあっています. ② N-UNCOUNT 不可算名詞 **Resistance** to an attack consists of fighting back against the people who have attacked you. 抵抗 □ A CBS correspondent in Colombo says the troops are encountering stiff resistance. コロンボ在駐のCBS特派員によれば、軍は激しい抵抗にあっている模様です. ③ N-UNCOUNT 不可算名詞 The **resistance** of your body to germs or diseases is its power to remain unharmed or unaffected by them. 抵抗力 □ This disease is surprisingly difficult to catch, as most people have a natural resistance to it. 意外にもこの病気にはかかりにくい. ほとんどの人が生まれつきこの病気に対する耐性を持っているためである. ④ N-UNCOUNT 不可算名詞 Wind or air **resistance** is a force which slows down a moving object or vehicle. 抵抗 □ The design of the bicycle reduces the effects of wind resistance and drag. この自転車は空気抵抗を減らすように設計されている. ⑤ N-VAR 可変性名詞 In electrical engineering or physics, **resistance** is the ability of a substance or an electrical circuit to stop the flow of an electrical current through it. 抵抗 □ The salt reduces the electrical resistance of the water. 食塩を加えると水の電気抵抗は小さくなります.

→ see **bicycle, flight**

re|sist|ant /rɪzɪstənt/ ① ADJ 形容詞 Someone who is **resistant** to something is opposed to it and wants to prevent it. 抵抗する □ Some people are very resistant to the idea of exercise. 運動と聞いただけで非常に抵抗を感じる人がいる. ② ADJ 形容詞 If something is **resistant** to a particular thing, it is not harmed by it. 抵抗力がある □ ...how to improve plants to make them more resistant to disease. 耐病性に優れた品種に改良する方法

re|skill /riskɪl/ (reskills, reskilling, reskilled) V-T/V-I 他動詞/自動詞 If you **reskill**, or if someone **reskills** you, you learn new skills, so that you can do a different job or do your old job in a different way. 再教育する [BRIT 英国英語 BUSINESS 実業] [他動詞] 新しい技能を身につける [自動詞] [AM retrain 米国英語 retrain]

reso|lute /rɛzəlut/ ADJ 形容詞 If you describe someone as **resolute**, you approve of them because they are very determined not to change their mind or not to give up a course of action. 毅然（きぜん）とした [FORMAL 形式ばった] □ Voters perceive him as a decisive and resolute international leader. 彼らを決断力のある毅然とした国際的な指導者と考えている. ● **reso|lute|ly** ADV 副詞 断固として □ He resolutely refused to speak English unless forced to. 彼はやむを得ない場合を除けば決して英語を話そうとはしなかった.

reso|lu|tion /rɛzəluʃ°n/ (resolutions) ① N-COUNT 可算名詞 A **resolution** is a formal decision made at a meeting by means of a vote. 決議 □ He replied that the UN had passed two major resolutions calling for a complete withdrawal. 国連はすでに完全撤退を求める2つの主要決議案を可決している、と彼は答えました. ② N-COUNT 可算名詞 If you make a **resolution**, you decide to try very hard to do something. 決心 □ They made a resolution to lose all the weight gained during the Christmas holidays. 彼はクリスマス休暇で増えてしまった体重を元に戻すことにした. ③ N-UNCOUNT 不可算名詞 **Resolution** is determination to do something or not do something. 決意 □ "I think I'll try a hypnotist," I said with sudden resolution. 「催眠術でも試してみようかな」と、私はとっさにそう決めて言った. ④ N-SING 単数名詞 The **resolution** of a problem or difficulty is the final solving of it. 解決 [FORMAL 形式ばった] □ ...the successful resolution of a dispute involving UN inspectors in Baghdad. バグダッドに派遣した国連査察団をめぐる問題がうまく妥結したこと

re|solve /rɪzɒlv/ (resolves, resolving, resolved) ① V-T 他動詞 To **resolve** a problem, argument, or difficulty means to find a solution to it. 解決する [FORMAL 形式ばった] □ We must find a way

to resolve these problems before it's too late. 手遅れになる前にこうした問題の解決策を見つける必要があります. **2** V-T 他動詞 If you **resolve to** do something, you make a firm decision to do it. …しようと決心する [FORMAL 形式ばった] □ She resolved to report the matter to the hospital's nursing supervisor. 彼女はこの件を病院の看護責任者に報告することにした. **3** N-VAR 可変性名詞 **Resolve** is determination to do what you have decided to do. 決意 [FORMAL 形式ばった] □ So you're saying this will strengthen the American public's resolve to go to war if necessary? そうすると, 必要なら戦争も辞さないというアメリカ国民の決意だと言われるだろうということなわけですね.

re|solved /rɪzɒlvd/ ADJ 形容詞 If you are **resolved to** do something, you are determined to do it. …しようと決心して [FORMAL 形式ばった] [v-link ADJ to-inf] □ Most people with property to lose were resolved to defend it. 財産を失う恐れのある人の大半が自分の財産を守ろうした.

reso|nance /rɛzənəns/ (resonances) **1** N-VAR 可変性名詞 If something has a **resonance for** someone, it has a special meaning or is particularly important to them. 共鳴 □ The ideas of order, security, family, religion and country had the same resonance for them as for Michael. 秩序, 安全, 家庭, 宗教, 国家に関する信念に対しては, 彼らもマイケルと同じように共鳴した. **2** N-UNCOUNT 不可算名詞 If a sound has **resonance**, it is deep, clear, and strong. 響き □ His voice had lost its resonance; it was tense and strained. その声は響きを失い, 緊張して震えていた.

reso|nant /rɛzənənt/ ADJ 形容詞 A sound that is **resonant** is deep and strong. よく響く □ His voice sounded oddly resonant in the empty room. 彼の声はがらんとした部屋に異様に響き渡った.

Word Link

son ≈ sound : resonate, sonata, supersonic

reso|nate /rɛzəneɪt/ (resonates, resonating, resonated) **1** V-I 自動詞 If something **resonates**, it vibrates and produces a deep, strong sound. 鳴り響く □ The bass guitar began to thump so loudly that it resonated in my head. やかましくなり始めたベースの音が頭の中でこだました. **2** V-I 自動詞 You say that something **resonates** when it has a special meaning or when it is particularly important to someone. 共感を与える □ What are the issues resonating with voters? 有権者が特に関心を寄せる問題は何でしょうか.

re|sort /rɪzɔrt/ (resorts, resorting, resorted) **1** V-I 自動詞 If you **resort to** a course of action that you do not really approve of, you adopt it because you cannot see any other way of achieving what you want. やむなく頼る □ His punishing work schedule had made him resort to drugs. 過酷な仕事のスケジュールのせいで彼は麻薬に手を出してしまった. **2** N-UNCOUNT 不可算名詞 If you achieve something without **resort to** a particular course of action, you succeed without carrying out that action. To have **resort to** a particular course of action means to have to do that action in order to achieve something. やむなく頼ること □ Congress has a responsibility to ensure that all peaceful options are exhausted before resort to war. 議会は, 武力行使に出る前に平和的な解決の余地がないかを十分に確認する責任を負っています. **3** PHRASE 句 If you do something **as a last resort**, you do it because you can find no other way of getting out of a difficult situation or of solving a problem. 最後の手段として □ Nuclear weapons should be used only as a last resort. 核兵器はあくまで最終手段として使うべきです. **4** N-COUNT 可算名詞 A **resort** is a place where a lot of people spend their vacation. 行楽地 □ The ski resorts are expanding to meet the growing number of skiers that come here. 年々増加するスキー客に対応するため, スキー場は拡大を続けている.

re|sound|ing /rɪzaʊndɪŋ/ **1** ADJ 形容詞 A **resounding** sound is loud and clear. 響き渡る □ There was a resounding slap as Andrew struck him violently across the face. アンドリューが彼の横っ面をぴしゃりとたたく音が響き渡った. **2** ADJ 形容詞 You can refer to a very great success as a **resounding** success. 全くの [EMPHASIS 強調] □ The good weather helped to make the occasion a resounding success. 好天候も大成功の一因だった.

re|source /rɪsɔrs/ (resources) **1** N-COUNT 可算名詞 The **resources** of an organization or person are the materials, money, and other things that they have and can use in order to function properly. 財貨, 資産 □ Some families don't have the resources to feed themselves adequately. 十分養っていけるだけの資産がない家族もいます. **2** N-COUNT 可算名詞 A country's **resources** are the things that it has and can use to increase its wealth, such as coal, oil, or land. 資源 □ …resources like coal, tungsten, oil, and copper. 石炭, タングステン, 石油, 銅などの資源.

re|source|ful /rɪsɔrsfəl/ ADJ 形容詞 Someone who is **resourceful** is good at finding ways of dealing with problems. 機転の利く □ He was amazingly inventive and resourceful, and played a major role in my career. 彼は驚くほど創意に富み機転が利く人で, 仕事の面でわたしの大きな支えとなってくれた. ● re|source|ful|ness N-UNCOUNT 不可算名詞 機転の利くこと □ Because of his adventures, he is a person of far greater experience and resourcefulness. 修羅場をくぐり抜けてきた彼のほうが, はるかに経験豊富で才覚あふれた人である.

re|spect /rɪspɛkt/ (respects, respecting, respected) **1** V-T 他動詞 If you **respect** someone, you have a good opinion of their character or ideas. 敬意を払う □ I want him to respect me as a career woman. わたしが仕事に生きる女性だということを彼に分かってほしい. **2** N-UNCOUNT 不可算名詞 If you have **respect for** someone, you have a good opinion of them. 尊敬する □ I have tremendous respect for Dean. ディーンのことは非常に尊敬している. **3** → see also self-respect **4** V-T 他動詞 If you **respect** someone's wishes, rights, or customs, you avoid doing things that they would dislike or regard as wrong. 尊重する □ Finally, trying to respect her wishes, I said I'd leave. 結局, 彼女の望みを尊重して, わたしが出て行こうと言った. **5** N-UNCOUNT 不可算名詞 If you show **respect for** someone's wishes, rights, or customs, you avoid doing anything they would dislike or regard as wrong. 尊重 □ They will campaign for respect for aboriginal rights and customs. 彼らはアボリジニの権利と風習を守る運動を起こすことにしています. **6** V-T 他動詞 If you **respect** a law or moral principle, you agree not to break it. 守る □ It is about time tour operators respected the law and their own code of conduct. そろそろ旅行会社は法律や社内法規を遵守すべき時ではないか. ● N-UNCOUNT 不可算名詞 **Respect** is also a noun. 遵守 □ …respect for the law and the rejection of the use of violence. 法律を守り決して暴力を振るわないこと. **7** PHRASE 句 You can say **with all due respect** when you are politely disagreeing with someone or criticizing them. お言葉を返すようですが [POLITENESS 丁寧さ] □ With all due respect, I hardly think that's the point. 失礼ですが, わたしにはとてもそれが問題の核心だとは思えませんが. **8** PHRASE 句 If you **pay** your **respects to** someone, you go to see them or speak to them. You usually do this to be polite, and not necessarily because you want to do it. あいさつに伺う [FORMAL 形式ばった] □ Carl had asked him to visit the hospital and to pay his respects to Francis. カールは病院にフランシスのお見舞いに行ってもらえないかと彼に頼んでいた. **9** PHRASE 句 You use expressions like **in this respect** and **in many respects** to indicate that what you are saying applies to the feature you have just mentioned or to many features of something. この点では; いろんな点で □ Within the Department of Justice are several drug-fighting agencies. The lead agency in this respect is the DEA. 司法省には麻薬を取り締まるいくつかの機関がある. その先頭に立つのが麻薬取締局である. **10** PHRASE 句 You use **with respect to** to say what something relates to. …について [FORMAL 形式ばった] □ Parents often have little choice with respect to the way their child is medically treated. 親は子供が受ける治療について ほとんど選択の余地のないことが多い. **11** → see also respected

Thesaurus

respect また次を参照:

v.	admire, esteem **1**
N.	consideration, courtesy, esteem **4**

Word Partnership

respect は次の語句と使われる:

v.	deserve respect, earn respect, gain respect **2** lack respect for someone/something, show respect for someone/something, treat someone/something with respect **2** **4** **5**
N.	lack of respect **2** **4** **5** respect someone's privacy, respect someone's rights, respect someone's wishes **3** respect the law **6**

re|spect|able /rɪspɛktəbəl/ **1** ADJ 形容詞 Someone or something that is **respectable** is approved of by society and considered to be morally correct. まともな, きちんとした □ He came from a perfectly respectable middle-class family. 彼はまさに堅実な中流階級の出だ. ● re|spect|abil|ity /rɪspɛktəbɪlɪti/ N-UNCOUNT 不可算名詞 体面 □ If she divorced Tony, she would lose the respectability she had as Mrs. Tony Tatterton. 彼女がトニーと離婚するとしたら, トニー・タタートンの妻という地位を失うことになる. **2** ADJ 形容詞 You can say that something is **respectable** when you mean that it is good enough or acceptable. 相当な, かなりの □ …investments that offer respectable and highly attractive rates of return. 十分な利回りを提供する極めて魅力的な投資先.

re|spect|ed /rɪspɛktɪd/ ADJ 形容詞 Someone or something that is **respected** is admired and considered important by many people. 評価の高い □ He is highly respected for his novels and plays as well as his translations of American novels. 彼はアメリカ小説の翻訳はもちろん, 自身の小説や戯曲でも極めて高い評価を得ています.

re|spect|ful /rɪspɛktfəl/ ADJ 形容詞 If you are **respectful**, you show respect for someone. 敬意を払う □ The children in our family are always respectful to their elders. うちの子供たちはいつも年上の人に礼儀正しい. ● re|spect|ful|ly ADV 副詞 敬意を払って □ "You are an artist," she said respectfully. 「芸術家でいらっしゃるのですか」と彼女は丁重に言った.

re|spec|tive /rɪspɛktɪv/ ADJ 形容詞 **Respective** means relating or belonging separately to the individual people you have just mentioned. それぞれの [ADJ n] □ Steve and I were at very different

Word Web   respiratory system

Respiration moves **air** in and out of the **lungs**. Air comes in through the **nose** or **mouth**. Then it travels down the windpipe and into the **lungs**. In the lungs **oxygen** absorbs into the bloodstream. Blood carries oxygen to the heart and other organs. The lungs also remove **carbon dioxide** from the blood. This **gas** is then **exhaled** through the mouth. During inhalation the **diaphragm** moves downward and the lungs fill with air. During exhalation the diaphragm relaxes and air flows out. Adult humans **breathe** about six liters of air each minute.

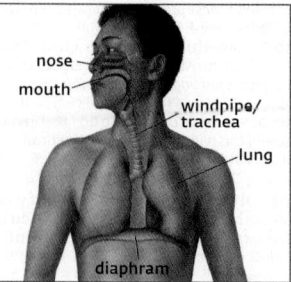

nose
mouth
windpipe/
trachea
lung
diaphram

---

stages in our respective careers. スティーブとわたしではそれぞれがやっている仕事のレベルが全然違っていた.

re|spec|tive|ly /rɪspɛktɪvli/ ADV 副詞 **Respectively** means in the same order as the items that you have just mentioned. それぞれ [ADV with cl/group] ❏ Their sons were three and six respectively. 彼らの息子はそれぞれ3歳と6歳だった.

Word Link   spir ≈ breath : aspire, inspire, respiratory

res|pira|tory /rɛspərətɔri/ ADJ 形容詞 **Respiratory** means relating to breathing. 呼吸器の [MEDICAL 医学の] [ADJ n] ❏ ...people with severe respiratory problems. 重度の呼吸障害のある人
→ see Word Web: **respiratory system**

res|pite /rɛspɪt/ **1** N-SING 単数名詞 A **respite** is a short period of rest from something unpleasant. 小休止 [FORMAL 形式ばった] [also no det, oft N "from" n] ❏ It was some weeks now since they'd had any respite from shellfire. ここ数週間、砲撃は休みなく続いている. **2** N-SING 単数名詞 A **respite** is a short delay before a very unpleasant or difficult situation which may or may not take place. 猶予 [FORMAL 形式ばった] [also no det] ❏ Devaluation would only give the economy a brief respite. 通貨を切り下げても経済に与える効果は一時的なものだろう.

re|spond /rɪspɒnd/ (responds, responding, responded) **1** V-T/V-I 他動詞/自動詞 When you **respond** to something that is done or said, you react to it by doing or saying something yourself. 対応する; 返答する ❏ They are likely to respond positively to the president's request for aid. 彼らは大統領の援助の要請に対して前向きの回答を示す模様です. ❏ "I have no idea," she responded. 「分からない」と彼女は答えた. **2** V-I 自動詞 When you **respond to** a need, crisis, or challenge, you take the necessary or appropriate action. 対処する ❏ This modest group size allows our teachers to respond to the needs of each student. このように少人数のグループにしていますので、教師は一人ひとりの生徒の要望に応えることができます. **3** V-I 自動詞 If a patient or their injury or illness **is responding to** treatment, the treatment is working and they are getting better. 効果を示す ❏ I'm pleased to say that he is now doing well and responding to treatment. 喜ばしいことに彼は治療効果が現れて順調に回復している.

re|sponse /rɪspɒns/ (responses) N-COUNT 可算名詞 Your **response** to an event or to something that is said is your reply or reaction to it. 反応; 回答 [oft N "to/from" n, also "in" N] ❏ There has been no response to his remarks from the government. 今のところ彼の発言に対する政府の回答はありません.

Word Partnership   response は次の語句と使われる:

ADJ.	**correct** response, **enthusiastic** response, **immediate** response, **military** response, **negative/positive** response, **overwhelming** response, **quick** response, **written** response

re|sponse time (response times) **1** N-COUNT 可算名詞 The **response time** of an emergency service such as the police or the fire department is the length of time it takes them to arrive at an incident such as a crime or a fire after it has been reported to them. 緊急車の到着所要時間 ❏ Kyle says the average 911 response time is about 9.2 minutes. カイルによれば、緊急車が現場に到着するまでに平均して9.2分ほどかかるという. **2** N-COUNT 可算名詞 **Response time** is the time taken for a computer to do something after you have given an instruction. 応答時間 [COMPUTING コンピューティング] ❏ The only flaw is the slightly slow response times when you press the buttons. 1つ問題なのはボタンを押してから応答するまで少し時間がかかる点である.

re|spon|sibil|ity /rɪspɒnsɪbɪliti/ (responsibilities) **1** N-UNCOUNT 不可算名詞 If you have **responsibility** for something or someone, or if they are your **responsibility**, it is your job or duty to deal with them and to make decisions relating to them. 責任, 担当 ❏ Each manager had responsibility for just under 600 properties. 1人の責任者が担当する物件数は600件を少々下回る程度だった. **2** N-UNCOUNT 不可算名詞 If you accept **responsibility**

---

for something that has happened, you agree that you were to blame for it or you caused it. 責任 ❏ No one admitted responsibility for the attacks. 攻撃を認める犯行声明はなかった. **3** N-PLURAL 複数名詞 Your **responsibilities** are the duties that you have because of your job or position. 業務, 任務 ❏ I am told that he handled his responsibilities as a counselor in a highly intelligent and caring fashion. 彼はカウンセラーとしての職務を的確にしかも相手の身になって果たしたと聞いています. **4** N-UNCOUNT 不可算名詞 If someone is given **responsibility**, they are given the right or opportunity to make important decisions or to take action without having to get permission from anyone else. 責任 ❏ She would have loved to have a better-paying job with more responsibility. 彼女はもっと給料が高い責任ある仕事を望んでいただろう. **5** N-SING 単数名詞 If you think that you have a **responsibility to** do something, you feel that you ought to do it because it is morally right to do it. ...する責任 ❏ The court feels it has a responsibility to ensure that customers are not misled. 裁判所は、消費者がだまされないようにするのは司法の責任と感じている. **6** N-SING 単数名詞 If you think that you have a **responsibility to** someone, you feel that it is your duty to take action that will protect their interests. 責任 ❏ She had decided that as a doctor she had a responsibility to her fellow creatures. 彼女は同じ生命をもつ動物に対して医者としての責任があると考えていた.

Word Partnership   responsibility は次の語句と使われる:

V.	**assume** responsibility, **bear** responsibility, **share** responsibility, **take** responsibility **1** – **4** **have (a)** responsibility **1** **4** **5** **6** **accept** responsibility, **claim** responsibility **2** **be given** responsibility **4**
ADJ.	**financial** responsibility, **personal** responsibility **1** – **4** **moral** responsibility **5**

re|spon|sible /rɪspɒnsɪbəl/ **1** ADJ 形容詞 If someone or something is **responsible for** a particular event or situation, they are the cause of it or they can be blamed for it. 責任のある [v-link ADJ] ❏ He still felt responsible for her death. 彼女が死んだのは自分のせいだと思っていた. **2** ADJ 形容詞 If you are **responsible for** something, it is your job or duty to deal with it and make decisions relating to it. 担当の [v-link ADJ] ❏ ...the cabinet member responsible for the environment. 環境担当閣僚 **3** ADJ 形容詞 If you are **responsible to** a person or group, they have authority over you and you have to report to them about what you do. 報告義務がある [v-link ADJ "to" n] ❏ I'm responsible to my board of directors. 理事会に報告する義務がある. **4** ADJ 形容詞 **Responsible** people behave properly and sensibly, without needing to be supervised. 責任のある ❏ He feels that the media should be more responsible in what they report. マスコミは報道内容に対しもっと責任を持つべきだと彼は感じている. ● **re|spon|sibly** ADV 副詞 [ADV with v] 責任を持って ❏ He urged everyone to act responsibly. 彼は全員に責任のある行動をとるように命じました. **5** ADJ 形容詞 **Responsible** jobs involve making important decisions or carrying out important tasks. 重責の [ADJ n] ❏ You are too young for such a responsible position. このような重責を担うにはきみはまだ若すぎる.

re|spon|sive /rɪspɒnsɪv/ **1** ADJ 形容詞 A **responsive** person is quick to react to people or events and to show emotions such as pleasure and affection. 反応のよい ❏ Harriet was an easy, responsive little girl. ハリエットは愛想がよくはきはきした女の子だ. ● **re|spon|sive|ness** N-UNCOUNT 不可算名詞 反応性 ❏ This condition decreases sexual desire and responsiveness. この病気にかかると性欲が減退し反応が鈍くなる. **2** ADJ 形容詞 If someone or something is **responsive**, they react quickly and favorably. すぐに対応する ❏ With an election coming soon, your representative should be very responsive to your request. 選挙の間際になると、議員は有権者の要望を親身になって聞くようになる. ● **re|spon|sive|ness** N-UNCOUNT 不可算名詞 対応の速さ ❏ Such responsiveness to public pressure is extraordinary. 世論の圧力に対してこうした素早い対応をとるのは異例のことです.

Word Web   restaurant

There are over 900,000 **restaurants** in the United States. These include traditional sit-down eateries as well as **coffee shops, cafeterias,** and **takeout** places. Here are some more key statistics. Forty percent of American adults have worked in a restaurant at some point in their lives. Only the government employs more people than the food service business. The restaurant industry has more minority **managers** than any other industry. In 2005, the average **tip** received by a **waiter** or **waitress** was 18%. The average **meal** cost $31.51. The most popular **cuisine** was Italian (31% preferred it), followed by Asian (25%).

---

rest

❶ QUANTIFIER USES
❷ VERB AND NOUN USES

❶ rest /rɛst/ **1** QUANT 数量詞 **The rest** is used to refer to all the parts of something or all the things in a group that remain or that you have not already mentioned. 残り [QUANT "of" def-n] ❑ *It was an experience I will treasure for the rest of my life.* それは一生大切にしたい経験でした. ● PRON 代名詞 **Rest** is also a pronoun. 残り ❑ *The first payment was made yesterday, and the rest will be paid next month.* 昨日最初の支払いがあり、残りは来月に支払われる. **2** PHRASE 句 You can add **and the rest** or **all the rest of it** to the end of a statement or list when you want to refer in a vague way to other things that are associated with the ones you have already mentioned. …などなど [SPOKEN 口語, VAGUENESS あいまいさ] ❑ *...a man with nice clothes, an SUV, and the rest.* いかした服でSUVを乗り回すという感じの男

> If you are talking about an uncountable noun, for example "food," the verb following **rest** is singular. ❑ *The rest of the food was delicious.* If you are talking about a countable noun, such as "boys," the verb is plural. ❑ *The rest of the boys were delighted.*

❷ rest /rɛst/ (rests, resting, rested)
↷ Please look at meaning **14** to see if the expression you are looking for is shown under another headword. **1** V-T/V-I 他動詞/自動詞 If you **rest** or if you **rest** your body, you do not do anything active for a time. 休める [他動詞] [自動詞] ❑ *He's tired and exhausted, and has been advised to rest for two weeks.* 彼は過労で2週間の休養をとるように言われている. **2** N-VAR 可変性名詞 If you get some **rest** or have a **rest,** you do not do anything active for a time. 休息、休憩 ❑ *"You're worn out, Laura," he said. "Go home and get some rest."* 「ローラ、ひどく疲れてるようだし、うちに帰って休みなさい」と彼は言った. **3** V-I 自動詞 If something such as a theory or someone's success **rests on** a particular thing, it depends on that thing. …に基づいている [FORMAL 形式ばった] ❑ *Such a view rests on a number of incorrect assumptions.* このような見解は数々の間違った思い込みに基づいている. **4** V-I 自動詞 If authority, a responsibility, or a decision **rests with** you, you have that authority or responsibility, or you are the one who will make that decision. …にかかっている [FORMAL 形式ばった] ❑ *The final decision rested with the president.* 最終決定は大統領の手に委（ゆだ）ねられた. **5** V-T 他動詞 If you **rest** something somewhere, you put it there so that its weight is supported. 置く、載せる ❑ *He rested his arms on the back of the chair.* 彼は椅子の背に腕をのせた. **6** V-T/V-I 他動詞/自動詞 If something **is resting** somewhere, or if you **are resting** it there, it is in a position where its weight is supported. 載せる；もたれる ❑ *His head was resting on her shoulder.* 彼は頭を彼女の肩にもたれかけていた. **7** V-I 自動詞 If you **rest** on or against someone or something, you lean on them so that they support the weight of your body. 寄りかかる ❑ *He rested on his pickax for a while.* しばらく彼はつるはしに寄りかかっていた. **8** N-COUNT 可算名詞 A **rest** is an object that is used to support something, especially your head, arms, or feet. 支え ❑ *When you are sitting, keep your elbow on the armrest.* 座っている間はひじをひじ掛にのせておきなさい. **9** V-I 自動詞 If your eyes **rest on** a particular person or object, you look directly at them, rather than somewhere else. …に留まる [WRITTEN 書き言葉] ❑ *As she spoke, her eyes rested on her husband's face.* 彼女が話している間、その目はずっと夫の顔に向けられていた. **10** → see also **rested 11** PHRASE 句 When an object that has been moving **comes to rest,** it finally stops. 止まる [FORMAL 形式ばった] ❑ *The plane had plowed a path through a patch of forest before coming to rest in a field.* 飛行機は森林の樹木をなぎ倒しながらようやく野原で止まった. **12** PHRASE 句 If someone refuses to **let** a subject **rest,** they refuse to stop talking about it, especially after they have been talking about it for a long time. …について話すのをやめる ❑ *I am not prepared to let this matter rest.* この件についてここで切り上げるつもりはありません. **13** PHRASE 句 To **put** someone's **mind**

at rest or **set** their **mind at rest** means to tell them something that stops them from worrying. 安心させる ❑ *A brain scan last Friday finally set his mind at rest.* 先週の金曜に頭部CTの結果を聞いて彼はようやく安心した. **14** rest assured → see assured **15** to rest on your laurels → see laurel
→ see motion, sleep

Thesaurus   rest また次を参照:

v.	lie down, relax ❷ **1**

rest area (rest areas) N-COUNT 可算名詞 A **rest area** is a place beside a highway where you can buy gas and other things, use a toilet or have a meal. サービスエリア [mainly AM 主に米国英語] ❑ *...a freeway rest area in Texas Canyon.* テキサスキャニオンの高速道路のサービスエリア

Word Link   re ≈ back, again : **re**flect, **re**pay, **re**state

re|state /riːsteɪt/ (restates, restating, restated) V-T 他動詞 If you **restate** something, you say it again in words or writing, usually in a slightly different way. 言い直す [FORMAL 形式ばった] ❑ *He continued throughout to restate his opposition to violence.* 彼は暴力に反対する自分の立場を終始繰り返しました.

res|tau|rant /rɛstərənt, -tərɑnt, -trɑnt/ (restaurants) N-COUNT 可算名詞 A **restaurant** is a place where you can eat a meal and pay for it. In restaurants, your food is usually served to you at your table by a waiter or waitress. レストラン、料理店 ❑ *They ate in an Italian restaurant in Forth Street.* 彼らは四番街のイタリアンレストランで食事をとった.
→ see Word Web: **restaurant**
→ see city

> The **salad bar** is a popular feature of American restaurants, and allows the customer to choose what kind of and how much salad to eat for a set price. Salad bars may offer bread, soup, or dessert as well.

rest|ed /rɛstɪd/ ADJ 形容詞 If you feel **rested,** you feel more energetic because you have just had a rest. 休養した [v-link ADJ] ❑ *He looked tanned and well rested after his vacation.* 休暇明けの彼は日焼けして十分休養したようだった.

rest|less /rɛstlɪs/ ADJ 形容詞 If you are **restless,** you are bored, impatient, or dissatisfied, and you want to do something else. 退屈でじっとしていられない ❑ *By 1982, she was restless and needed a new impetus for her talent.* 1982年には彼女は現状に満足できず、才能を伸ばすための新しい刺激を求めていた. ● **rest|less|ness** N-UNCOUNT 不可算名詞 退屈でじっとしていられないこと ❑ *From the audience came increasing sounds of restlessness.* 退屈した観客のざわめき声が大きくなった. **2** ADJ 形容詞 If someone is **restless,** they keep moving around because they find it difficult to keep still. 落ち着かない ❑ *My father seemed very restless and excited.* 父はそわそわして全く落ち着かない様子だった. ● **rest|less|ness** N-UNCOUNT 不可算名詞 落ち着きのなさ ❑ *Karen complained of hyperactivity and restlessness.* カレンは多動と落ち着きのなさを訴えた. ● **rest|less|ly** ADV 副詞 落ち着かない様子で ❑ *He paced up and down restlessly, trying to put his thoughts in order.* 彼は落ちつかない様子で行ったり来たりしながら、考えをまとめようとしていた.

re|stock /riːstɒk/ (restocks, restocking, restocked) V-T/V-I 他動詞/自動詞 If you **restock** something such as a shelf, refrigerator, or store, you fill it with food or other goods to replace what you have used or sold. 補充する ❑ *I have to restock the freezer.* 冷凍庫のものを補充しておかないと. ❑ *Manufacturers are testing a system that tracks products leaving the shelves and alerts employees to restock.* メーカーでは、棚からなくなった製品を探知して従業員に補充するように知らせるシステムの実験を行っている.

re|store /rɪstɔr/ (restores, restoring, restored) **1** V-T 他動詞 To **restore** a situation or practice means to cause it to exist again. 回復する ❑ *The army has recently been brought in to restore order.* 治

r

安を回復するため，最近軍隊が投入されました．●res|to|ra|tion /rɛstəreɪʃ°n/ N-UNCOUNT 不可算名詞 回復 ❑His visit is expected to lead to the restoration of diplomatic relations. 彼の訪問を機に国交回復につながることが期待されています． 2 V-T 他動詞 To restore someone or something to a previous condition or place means to cause them to be in that condition or place once again. もり戻す ❑We will restore her to health but it may take time. 彼女が健康を取り戻せるようにやってみます．時間はかかるかもしれませんが．●res|to|ra|tion N-UNCOUNT 不可算名詞 取り戻すこと ❑I owe the restoration of my hearing to this remarkable new technique. わたしが聴力を回復できたのはこの素晴らしい新しい治療法のおかげである．3 V-T 他動詞 When someone restores something such as an old building, painting, or piece of furniture, they repair and clean it, so that it looks like it did when it was new. 修復する ❑...experts who specialize in examining and restoring ancient parchments. 古代の羊皮紙を綿密に調査し修復する専門家 ●res|to|ra|tion (restorations) N-VAR 可変性名詞 修復 ❑I specialized in the restoration of old houses. わたしの専門は古民家の修復だった．●re|stored /rɪstɔrd/ ADJ 形容詞 修復された ❑The restored building helps people understand the historic significance of our neighborhood. この修復された建造物がこの地域の歴史的な重要性を知ってもらう上で役に立つ．4 V-T 他動詞 [usu passive] If something that was lost or stolen is restored to its owner, it is returned to them. 戻る [FORMAL 形式ばった] ❑The following day their horses and goods were restored to them. 翌日，馬と品物が彼の元へ戻った．

re|strain /rɪstreɪn/ (restrains, restraining, restrained) 1 V-T 他動詞 If you restrain someone, you stop them from doing what they intended or wanted to do, usually by using your physical strength. 引き止める ❑Wally gripped my arm, partly to restrain me and partly to reassure me. ウォリーはわたしの腕をしっかりつかんだが，それはわたしを引き止めたい気持ちと安心させたい気持ちからだった．2 V-T 他動詞 If you restrain an emotion or you restrain yourself from doing something, you prevent yourself from showing that emotion or doing what you wanted or intended to do. 抑える，我慢する ❑She was unable to restrain her desperate anger. 彼女に抑えようもない怒りが込み上げてきた．3 V-T 他動詞 To restrain something that is growing or increasing means to prevent it from getting too large. 抑制する ❑The radical 500-day plan was very clear on how it intended to try to restrain inflation. 500日徹底プランではインフレ抑制の方法が明快に示されていました．

re|strained /rɪstreɪnd/ 1 ADJ 形容詞 Someone who is restrained is very calm and unemotional. 控えめな ❑Under the circumstances, he felt he'd been very restrained. あのような状況でよく自制できたのだと彼は我ながら感心した．2 ADJ 形容詞 If you describe someone's clothes or the decorations in a house as restrained, you mean that you like them because they are simple and not too brightly colored. 地味な [APPROVAL 賛成] ❑Her black suit was restrained and expensive. 彼女の黒いスーツは落ち着いた風合いで高価なものだった．

re|straint /rɪstreɪnt/ (restraints) 1 N-VAR 可変性名詞 Restraints are rules or conditions that limit or restrict someone or something. 制限 ❑The president is calling for spending restraints in some areas. 大統領は数分野での支出制限を求めてる．2 N-UNCOUNT 不可算名詞 Restraint is calm, controlled, and unemotional behavior. 慎み，控えめ ❑They behaved with more restraint than I'd expected. 彼らの振る舞いはわたしが予想していたより控えめだった．

re|strict /rɪstrɪkt/ (restricts, restricting, restricted) 1 V-T 他動詞 If you restrict something, you put a limit on it in order to reduce it or prevent it from becoming too great. 制限する ❑There is talk of raising the admission requirements to restrict the number of students on campus. キャンパスの学生数を制限するため，入学要件を厳しくするという話があります．●re|stric|tion /rɪstrɪkʃ°n/ N-UNCOUNT 不可算名詞 制限 ❑Since the costs of science were rising faster than inflation, some restriction on funding was necessary. 科学研究費の上昇がインフレ上昇分を上回ったため，何らかの予算の制限が必要だった．2 V-T 他動詞 To restrict the movement or actions of someone or something means to prevent them from moving or acting freely. 制限する ❑The government imprisoned dissidents, forbade travel, and restricted the press. 政府は反体制派を投獄し，旅行を禁止し，報道規制を敷いた．●re|stric|tion N-UNCOUNT 不可算名詞 制限 ❑...the justification for this restriction of individual liberty. こうした個人の自由の制限を正当化する根拠 3 V-T 他動詞 If you restrict someone or their activities to one thing, they can only do, have, or deal with that thing. If you restrict them to one place, they cannot go anywhere else. 限定する ❑For the first two weeks, patients are restricted to the grounds. 最初の2週間，患者は敷地の外に出ることはできない．4 V-T 他動詞 If you restrict something to a particular group, only that group can do it or have it. If you restrict something to a particular place, it is allowed only in that place. 限定する ❑Trustees had decided to restrict university entry to about 30 percent of applicants. 理事会は大学入学者を出願者の約30％に抑えることを決定していた．

re|strict|ed /rɪstrɪktɪd/ 1 ADJ 形容詞 Something that is

restricted is quite small or limited. 制限された 2 ❑...the monotony of a heavily restricted diet. 厳しい制限食の味気なさ 2 ADJ 形容詞 If something is restricted to a particular group, only members of that group have it. If it is restricted to a particular place, it exists only in that place. 限定された [v-link ADJ "to" n] ❑Discipline problems are by no means restricted to children in families dependent on benefits. しつけの問題は何も生活保護世帯の子供に限られたものではない．3 ADJ 形容詞 A restricted area is one that only people with special permission can enter. 立入禁止の ❑...a highly restricted area close to the old naval airfield. 旧海軍飛行場に隣接する立ち入りが厳重に制限されている区域

re|stric|tion /rɪstrɪkʃ°n/ (restrictions) 1 N-COUNT 可算名詞 A restriction is an official rule that limits what you can do or that limits the amount or size of something. 制限 ❑...the lifting of restrictions on political parties and the news media. 政党と報道機関に対する制限の解除 2 N-COUNT 可算名詞 You can refer to anything that limits what you can do as a restriction. 制限 ❑His parents are trying to make up to him for the restrictions of urban living. 両親は何とか彼を都会生活の束縛から解放してやりたいと思っている．3 → see also restrict

re|stric|tive /rɪstrɪktɪv/ ADJ 形容詞 Something that is restrictive prevents people from doing what they want to do, or from moving freely. 制限する ❑The state will adopt a more restrictive policy on arms sales. 州は銃器販売の取り締まりの強化に乗り出します．

rest|room /rɛstrum, -rʊm/ (restrooms) also rest room N-COUNT 可算名詞 In a restaurant, theater, or other public place, a restroom is a room with a toilet for customers to use. 手洗い，トイレ [AM 米国英語]

re|struc|ture /ristrʌktʃər/ (restructures, restructuring, restructured) V-T 他動詞 To restructure an organization or system means to change the way it is organized, usually in order to make it work more effectively. 再構築する，構造改革をする ❑The president called on educators and politicians to help him restructure American education. 大統領はアメリカの教育制度改革に向けて教育者や政治家に協力を呼びかけました．●re|struc|tur|ing (restructurings) N-VAR 可変性名詞 再構築，構造改革 ❑The company is to lay off 1,520 workers as part of a restructuring. 会社はリストラ策の一環として1520人の従業員を解雇することにしている．

re|sult /rɪzʌlt/ (results, resulting, resulted) 1 N-COUNT 可算名詞 A result is something that happens or exists because of something else that has happened. 結果 ❑Compensation is available for people who have developed asthma as a direct result of their work. 仕事が直接の原因でぜんそくにかかった患者には補償金が支給されている．2 V-I 自動詞 If something results in a particular situation or event, it causes that situation or event to happen. …の結果に終わる ❑Fifty percent of road accidents result in head injuries. 頭部外傷につながるケースが交通事故の半数に及ぶ．3 V-I 自動詞 If something results from a particular event or action, it is caused by that event or action. 原因で起こる ❑Many hair problems result from what you eat. 髪のトラブルは食事が原因で起こることが多い．4 N-COUNT 可算名詞 A result is the situation that exists at the end of a contest. 結果 ❑The final election results will be announced on Friday. 最終的な開票結果は金曜日に発表されます．5 N-COUNT 可算名詞 A result is the number that you get when you do a calculation. 計算結果 ❑They found their computers producing different results from exactly the same calculation. 計算式は全く同じなのにコンピュータによって計算結果がまちまちであるに彼らは気づいた．6 N-COUNT 可算名詞 Your results are the marks or grades that you get for examinations you have taken. 成績 [mainly BRIT 主に英国英語; AM usually scores 米国英語では通常 scores]

Thesaurus	result また次を参照：
N.	by-product, consequence 1
V.	come about, produce, turn out, wind up 3

re|sult|ant /rɪzʌltənt/ ADJ 形容詞 Resultant means caused by the event just mentioned. 結果として生じる [FORMAL 形式ばった] [ADJ n] ❑At least a quarter of a million people have died in the fighting and the resultant famines. 戦いとそれに伴う食糧難で少なくとも25万人が死亡しました．

re|sume /rɪzum/ (resumes, resuming, resumed) 1 V-T/V-I 他動詞/自動詞 If you resume an activity or if it resumes, it begins again. 再開する [FORMAL 形式ばった] [他動詞] 再開される [自動詞] ❑After the war he resumed his duties at Wellesley College. 戦争が終わると彼はウェルズリー大学の職に復帰した．●re|sump|tion /rɪzʌmpʃ°n/ N-UNCOUNT 不可算名詞 再開 ❑It is premature to speculate about the resumption of negotiations. 今のところ交渉再開のめどは立っていない．2 V-T 他動詞 If you resume your seat or position, you return to the seat or position you were in before you moved. 戻る [FORMAL 形式ばった] ❑"I changed my mind," Blanche said, resuming her seat. 「わたし，気が変わったわ」ブランチはこう言うと自分の席に戻った．

re|sur|gence /rɪsɜ́rdʒ³ns/ N-SING 単数名詞 If there is a **resurgence of** an attitude or activity, it reappears and grows. 復活，再燃 [FORMAL 形式ばった] [also no det, oft N "of" n] ❑ *Police say drugs traffickers are behind the resurgence of violence.* 警察によれば，暴力が再発している背後には麻薬取引が絡んでいるようです.

res|ur|rect /rɛ̀zərɛ́kt/ (**resurrects, resurrecting, resurrected**) V-T 他動詞 If you **resurrect** something, you cause it to exist again after it had disappeared or ended. 復活させる ❑ *Attempts to resurrect the ceasefire have already failed once.* 再び停戦に持ち込むための協議はこれまでにも一度決裂しています. ● **res|ur|rec|tion** /rɛ̀zərɛ́kʃ³n/ N-UNCOUNT 不可算名詞 復活 ❑ *This is a resurrection of an old story from the mid-70s.* これは70年代半ばの古い話を持ち出したものです.

re|sus|ci|tate /rɪsʌ́sɪteɪt/ (**resuscitates, resuscitating, resuscitated**) ◻ V-T 他動詞 If you **resuscitate** someone who has stopped breathing, you cause them to start breathing again. 蘇生（そせい）させる ❑ *A policeman and then a paramedic tried to resuscitate her.* まず警察官が彼女に蘇生処置を行い，続いて救急隊員が行なった. ● **re|sus|ci|ta|tion** /rɪsʌ̀sɪteɪʃ³n/ N-UNCOUNT 不可算名詞 蘇生 ❑ *They must even now be rushing her to the hospital for resuscitation and treatment.* 救命治療のため，今なお彼女を病院に急送しているところに違いない. ◻ V-T 他動詞 If you **resuscitate** something, you cause it to become active or successful again. 復興させる ❑ *He has submitted a bid to resuscitate the weekly magazine, which closed in April with losses of $1 million a year.* 1年間100万ドルの年間赤字を出して4月に廃刊した週刊誌を復刊しようと買収を申し入れた. ● **re|sus|ci|ta|tion** N-UNCOUNT 不可算名詞 復興 ❑ *The economy needs vigorous resuscitation.* 力強く経済を再生させる必要がある.

re|tail /rí:teɪl/ (**retails, retailing, retailed**) ◻ N-UNCOUNT 不可算名詞 **Retail** is the activity of selling products direct to the public, usually in small quantities. Compare **wholesale**. 小売り [BUSINESS 実業] ❑ *Retail stores usually count on the Christmas season to make up to half of their annual profits.* 小売店は一般的に年間収益の半分をクリスマスシーズンの売り上げに期待しています. ◻ ADV 副詞 If something is sold **retail**, it is sold in ordinary stores direct to the public. 小売りで [BUSINESS 実業] [ADV after v] ❑ *We sell wholesale to several chains that sell retail to the public.* 当社は消費者に小売りしているいくつかのチェーンに卸しています. ◻ V-I 自動詞 If an item in a store **retails at** or **for** a particular price, it is for sale at that price. 小売される [BUSINESS 実業] ❑ *It originally retailed at $23.50.* 当初は23ドル50セントで売られていた. ◻ → see also **retailing**

re|tail|er /rí:teɪlər/ (**retailers**) N-COUNT 可算名詞 A **retailer** is a person or business that sells goods to the public. 小売業者 [BUSINESS 実業] ❑ *Furniture and carpet retailers are among those reporting the sharpest annual decline in sales.* 家具やカーペットの小売業もここ1年で売り上げが激減した業種である.

re|tail|ing /rí:teɪlɪŋ/ N-UNCOUNT 不可算名詞 **Retailing** is the activity of selling products direct to the public, usually in small quantities. Compare **wholesaling**. 小売り [BUSINESS 実業] ❑ *She spent fourteen years in retailing.* 彼女は14年間小売りの仕事をした.

re|tail park (**retail parks**) N-COUNT 可算名詞 A **retail park** is a large, specially built area, usually at the edge of a town or city, where there are a lot of large stores and sometimes other facilities such as movie theaters and restaurants. ショッピングモール [BRIT 英国英語; AM **shopping mall** 米国英語 **shopping mall**]

re|tail price in|dex N-PROPER 固有名詞 The **retail price index** is a list of the prices of typical goods which shows how much the cost of living changes from one month to the next. 小売物価指数 [BRIT 英国英語 BUSINESS 実業]

re|tain /rɪteɪn/ (**retains, retaining, retained**) V-T 他動詞 To **retain** something means to continue to have that thing. 保つ [FORMAL 形式ばった] ❑ *The interior of the shop still retains a nineteenth-century atmosphere.* 船内には今も19世紀の雰囲気が漂っている.

Thesaurus		**retain** また次を参照:
v.		hold, keep, maintain, remember, save; (*ant.*) give up, lose

re|tain|er /rɪteɪnər/ (**retainers**) N-COUNT 可算名詞 A **retainer** is a fee that you pay to someone in order to make sure that they will be available to do work for you if you need them to. 依頼料，着手金 ❑ *I'll need a five-hundred-dollar retainer.* 依頼料として500ドルいただきます.

re|tali|ate /rɪtǽlieɪt/ (**retaliates, retaliating, retaliated**) V-I 自動詞 If you **retaliate** when someone harms or annoys you, you do something which harms or annoys them in return. 仕返しをする，報復する ❑ *I was sorely tempted to retaliate.* 仕返しをしてやりたい気持ちでいっぱいだった. ❑ *The company would retaliate against employees who joined a union.* 会社は組合に入った従業員に対し報復するだろう. ● **re|talia|tion** /rɪtæ̀liéɪʃ³n/ N-UNCOUNT 不可算名詞 報復 ❑ *Police said they believed the attack was in retaliation for the death of the drug trafficker.* 警察の発表では，今回の攻撃を麻薬密売者の死に対する報復

と見ているようです.

re|ten|tion /rɪténʃ³n/ N-UNCOUNT 不可算名詞 The **retention of** something is the keeping of it. 保持 [FORMAL 形式ばった] ❑ *The Citizens' Forum supported special powers for Quebec but also argued for the retention of a strong central government.* 市民フォーラムはケベック州に特別な権限を与えることを支持したが，同時に強力な中央政府の維持にも賛成した.

re|think /ri:θɪ́ŋk/ (**rethinks, rethinking, rethought**) ◻ V-T 他動詞 If you **rethink** something such as a problem, a plan, or a policy, you think about it again and change it. ❑ *Both major political parties are having to rethink their policies.* 主要政党はともに政策を見直す必要があります. ◻ N-SING 単数名詞 If you have a **rethink** of a problem, a plan, or a policy, you think about it again and change it. 再考 [JOURNALISM ジャーナリズム] ❑ *There must be a rethink of government policy toward this vulnerable group.* こうした弱者に対する政府の政策は見直すべきである.

reti|cent /rɛ́tɪsənt/ ADJ 形容詞 Someone who is **reticent** does not tell people about things. 口の重い ❑ *She is so reticent about her achievements.* 彼女は自分の功績についてあまり話したがらない. ● **reti|cence** N-UNCOUNT 不可算名詞 無口 ❑ *Pearl didn't mind his reticence; in fact she liked it.* パールには彼の無口は気にならなかった。実はそんな彼が好きだった.

reti|na /rɛ́tɪnə/ (**retinas**) N-COUNT 可算名詞 Your **retina** is the area at the back of your eye. It receives the image that you see and then sends the image to your brain. 網膜 ❑ *Bruno had to have eye surgery on a torn retina two years ago.* ブルーノは2年前に網膜剥離（はくり）で目の手術をした.

→ see **eye**

re|tire /rɪtaɪ́ər/ (**retires, retiring, retired**) ◻ V-I 自動詞 When older people **retire**, they leave their job and usually stop working completely. 退職する ❑ *At the age when most people retire, he is ready to face a new career.* ほとんどの人が退職するような年齢になって，彼は新しい仕事に挑戦しようとしている. ◻ V-I 自動詞 When an athlete **retires from** their sport, they stop playing in competitions. When they **retire from** a race or a game, they stop competing in it. 引退する ❑ *I have decided to retire from Formula One racing at the end of the season.* 今シーズン限りでF1レースから引退することにしました. ◻ V-I 自動詞 When a jury in a court of law **retires**, the members of it leave the court in order to decide whether someone is guilty or innocent. 退廷する ❑ *The jury will retire to consider its verdict today.* 陪審員は本日退廷して評議を行なう見通しである. ◻ → see also **retired**

Do not confuse **retire** and **resign**. When someone **retires**, they leave their job and stop working, often because they have reached the age when they can get a pension. ❑ *He had been planning for some time to retire at around age 60.* When professional sportsmen and women stop playing sport as their job, you can also say that they **retire**, even if they are fairly young. ❑ *A heart attack at the age of 36 forced him to retire from tennis.* If someone **resigns** from their job, they leave it after saying that they do not want to do it any more. ❑ *He hasn't decided whether he will resign.* You can **resign** from your job at any age, and perhaps start another job soon afterward.

Thesaurus		**retire** また次を参照:
v.		finish, leave, stop, quit ◻

re|tired /rɪtaɪ́ərd/ ◻ ADJ 形容詞 A **retired** person is an older person who has left his or her job and has usually stopped working completely. 引退した ❑ *...a seventy-three-year-old retired teacher from Florida.* フロリダ出身の73歳の元教師 ◻ → see also **retire**

re|tire|ment /rɪtaɪ́ərmənt/ (**retirements**) ◻ N-VAR 可変性名詞 **Retirement** is the time when a worker retires. 定年 ❑ *The proportion of the population who are over retirement age has grown tremendously in the past few years.* ここ数年で定年後の人の割合が急増している. ◻ N-UNCOUNT 不可算名詞 A person's **retirement** is the period in their life after they have retired. 退職後の生活，老後 ❑ *"Growing Older" considered the needs of the elderly for financial support during retirement.* 『老い』は老後を送る人たちへの経済的支援の必要性を訴えている.

re|tort /rɪtɔ́rt/ (**retorts, retorting, retorted**) ◻ V-T 他動詞 To **retort** means to reply angrily to someone. 言い返す，切り返す [WRITTEN 書き言葉] ❑ *"You can't smoke in here," Shaw said. — "Don't worry, it's not tobacco," he retorted.* 「ここは禁煙だぞ」とショーが言うと，「心配ご無用。タバコじゃない」と彼は言い返した. ● N-COUNT 可算名詞 **Retort** is also a noun. 応答 ❑ *His sharp retort clearly made an impact.* 彼のとげとげしい返事は明らかに衝撃を与えました.

re|trace /rɪtréɪs/ (**retraces, retracing, retraced**) ◻ V-T 他動詞 If you **retrace** your steps or **retrace** your way, you return to the place you started from by going back along the same route. 引き返す，後戻りする ❑ *He retraced his steps to the spot where he'd left the case.* 彼はスーツケースを置き忘れた場所まで引き返した.

re|tract /rɪtrækt/ (retracts, retracting, retracted) **1** V-T/V-I 他動詞/自動詞 If you **retract** something that you have said or written, you say that you did not mean it. 撤回する [FORMAL 形式ばった] □ Mr. Smith hurriedly sought to retract the statement, but it had just been broadcast on national radio. スミス氏は慌てて発言を撤回しようとしたが、ちょうどラジオで全国に放送されたところだった。 □ He's hoping that if he makes me feel guilty, I'll retract. わたしに悪かったと思わせて言ったことを取り消してほしいと彼は願っている。 ● **re|trac|tion** /rɪtrækʃ°n/ (retractions) N-COUNT 可算名詞 撤回 □ Miss Pearce said she expected an unqualified retraction of his comments within twenty-four hours. 24時間以内に彼が発言をすべて撤回することを期待していると、ピアースさんは語りました。 **2** V-T/V-I 他動詞/自動詞 When a part of a machine or a part of a person's body **retracts** or is **retracted**, it moves inward or becomes shorter. 引っ込める [FORMAL 形式ばった] [他動詞] 引っ込む [自動詞] □ Torn muscles retract and lose strength, structure, and tightness. 筋肉が断裂すると、筋肉の力や組織や張りが失われてしまう。

re|train /riːtreɪn/ (retrains, retraining, retrained) V-T/V-I 他動詞 If you **retrain**, or if someone **retrains** you, you learn new skills, especially in order to get a new job. 再訓練する [他動詞] 新しい技能を身につける [自動詞] □ Look at what you can do to retrain for a job that will make you happier. 技能を身につけてやりがいの仕事を見つけるために何ができるかよく考えなさい。 ● **re|train|ing** N-UNCOUNT 不可算名詞 再訓練 □ ...measures such as the retraining of the workforce at their place of work. 職場における従業員の再教育などの対策

re|treat /rɪtriːt/ (retreats, retreating, retreated) **1** V-I 自動詞 If you **retreat**, you move away from something or someone. 引き下がる □ "I've already got a job," I said quickly, and retreated from the room. 「わたしにはすでにやるべき仕事があります」とわたしは急いでそう言うと、部屋から出ていった。 **2** V-I 自動詞 When an army **retreats**, it moves away from enemy forces in order to avoid fighting them. 撤退する □ The French, suddenly outnumbered, were forced to retreat. いきなり増兵した敵軍に圧倒され、フランス軍は撤退を余儀なくされた。 ● N-VAR 可変性名詞 **Retreat** is also a noun. 撤退 □ In June 1942, the British 8th Army was in full retreat. 1942年6月、イギリス第8陸軍は完全撤退した。 **3** V-I 自動詞 If you **retreat from** something such as a plan or a way of life, you give it up, usually in order to do something safer or less extreme. 退く □ She retreated from public life. 彼女は公務から退いた。 ● N-VAR 可変性名詞 **Retreat** is also a noun. 退却 □ The president's remarks appear to signal that there will be no retreat from his position. 大統領の発言からは辞任する意思のないことがうかがわれます。 **4** N-COUNT 可算名詞 A **retreat** is a quiet, isolated place that you go to in order to rest or to do things in private. 静養所 □ He spent yesterday hidden away in his country retreat. 彼は昨日人目を避けて郊外の静養先で過ごした。

re|trench /rɪtrentʃ/ (retrenches, retrenching, retrenched) V-I 自動詞 If a person or organization **retrenches**, they spend less money. 支出を削減する [FORMAL 形式ばった] □ Shortly afterwards, cuts in defense spending forced the aerospace industry to retrench. その後まもなく、防衛費の削減によって航空宇宙産業は事業の縮小を余儀なくされた。

re|tri|bu|tion /rɛtrɪbyuːʃ°n/ N-UNCOUNT 不可算名詞 **Retribution** is punishment for a crime, especially punishment that is carried out by someone other than the official authorities. 報復 [FORMAL 形式ばった] □ He didn't want any further involvement for fear of retribution. 報復を恐れた彼はそれ以上かかわり合おうとしなかった。

re|triev|al /rɪtriːv°l/ **1** N-UNCOUNT 不可算名詞 The **retrieval** of information from a computer is the process of getting it back. 検索 □ ...electronic storage and retrieval systems. 電子データ保管検索システム **2** N-UNCOUNT 不可算名詞 The **retrieval** of something is the process of getting it back from a particular place, especially from a place where it should not be. 回収 □ Its real purpose is the launching and retrieval of small airplanes in flight. 真の目的は飛行中の機体から小型機を発射し回収することである。

re|trieve /rɪtriːv/ (retrieves, retrieving, retrieved) **1** V-T 他動詞 If you **retrieve** something, you get it back from the place where you left it. 回収する □ The men were trying to retrieve weapons left when the army abandoned the island. その人たちは軍隊が島から撤退するときに放置していった武器の回収に取り組んでいました。 **2** V-T 他動詞 If you manage to **retrieve** a situation, you succeed in bringing it back into a more acceptable state. 打開する □ He, the one man who could retrieve that situation, might receive the call. 彼は状況を打開することのできる人物なので、彼のところに電話があるかもしれない。 **3** V-T 他動詞 To **retrieve** information from a computer or from your memory means to get it back. 検索する □ Computers can instantly retrieve millions of information bits. コンピュータを使えば、大量の情報を即座に検索できる。

ret|ro /rɛtroʊ/ ADJ 形容詞 **Retro** clothes, music, and objects are based on the styles of the past. レトロの [JOURNALISM ジャーナリズム] □ ...clothing stores where original versions of many of today's retro looks can be found for a fraction of the price. 今のレトロなファッションのもとになった古着が安い値段で見つかる洋服店

retro|spect /rɛtrəspɛkt/ PHRASE 句 When you consider something **in retrospect**, you think about it afterward, and often have a different opinion about it from the one that you had at the time. 振り返ってみると □ In retrospect, I wish that I had thought about alternative courses of action. 今にして思えば、いざというときの行動を考えておけばよかった。

retro|spec|tive /rɛtrəspɛktɪv/ (retrospectives) **1** N-COUNT 可算名詞 A **retrospective** is an exhibition or showing of work done by an artist over many years, rather than his or her most recent work. 回顧展 □ ...a retrospective of the films of Judy Garland. ジュディー・ガーランドを回顧する上映会 **2** ADJ 形容詞 **Retrospective** feelings or opinions concern things that happened in the past. 過去を振り返る □ Afterwards, retrospective fear of the responsibility would make her feel almost faint. 後になって振り返ったときに彼女はその責任の重さを痛いほど感じるだろう。 ● **retro|spec|tive|ly** ADV 副詞 振り返ってみれば □ Retrospectively, it seems as if they probably were negligent. 今から思えば、たぶん彼らは怠慢だったのだろう。 **3** ADJ 形容詞 **Retrospective** laws or legal actions take effect from a date before the date when they are officially approved. 遡(そ)及的な [mainly BRIT 主に英国英語; AM **retroactive** 米国英語では **retroactive**]

re|turn /rɪtɜːrn/ (returns, returning, returned) **1** V-I 自動詞 When you **return to** a place, you go back there after you have been away. 戻る □ There are unconfirmed reports that Aziz will return to Moscow within hours. 未確認ですが、アジズが数時間のうちにモスクワに戻るという情報があります。 **2** N-SING 単数名詞 Your **return** is your arrival back at a place where you had been before. 戻ること □ Kenny explained the reason for his sudden return to Dallas. ケニーは突然ダラスに舞い戻ってきた訳を話した。 **3** V-T 他動詞 If you **return** something that you have borrowed or taken, you give it back or put it back. 返す □ I enjoyed the book and said so when I returned it. その本は面白かった。返すときにもそう言った。 ● N-SING 単数名詞 **Return** is also a noun. 返却 □ The main demand of the Indians is for the return of one-and-a-half-million acres of forest to their communities. 特に先住民が要求しているのは150万エーカーの森林の返還です。 **4** V-T 他動詞 If you **return** something somewhere, you put it back where it was. 戻す □ He returned the notebook to his jacket. 彼はジャケットに手帳を戻した。 **5** V-T 他動詞 If you **return** someone's action, you do the same thing to them as they have just done to you. If you **return** someone's feelings, you feel the same way toward them as they feel toward you. 応える □ Back at the station the chief inspector returned the call. 警部は署に戻ると電話をかけ直した。 **6** V-I 自動詞 If a feeling or situation **returns**, it comes back or happens again after a period when it was not present. 戻る、よみがえる □ Official reports in Algeria suggest that calm is returning to the country. アルジェリア政府の発表によれば、国内は平穏を取り戻しつつあるようです。 ● N-SING 単数名詞 **Return** is also a noun. 戻ること □ It was like the return of his youth. 彼に戻ったような気分だった。 **7** V-I 自動詞 If you **return to** a state that you were in before, you start being in that state again. 戻る □ Life has improved and returned to normal. 生活は改善してふだんの状態に戻った。 ● N-SING 単数名詞 **Return** is also a noun. 戻ること □ He made an uneventful return to normal health. 彼は順調に健康を取り戻していった。 **8** V-I 自動詞 If you **return to** a subject that you have mentioned before, you begin talking about it again. 立ち返る □ The power of the church is one theme all these writers return to. 教会の権力はこれらの作家がすべて再び取り上げるテーマである。 **9** V-I 自動詞 If you **return to** an activity that you were doing before, you start doing it again. 復帰する □ At that stage he will be 52, young enough to return to politics if he wishes to do so. その頃には彼は52歳になるが、政界に戻ろうと思えば戻ることのできる年齢である。 ● N-SING 単数名詞 **Return** is also a noun. 復帰 □ He has not ruled out the shock possibility of a return to football. 彼はサッカー界に復帰する可能性を否定していない。 **10** V-T 他動詞 When a judge or jury **returns** a verdict, they announce whether they think the person on trial is guilty or not. 言い渡す □ They returned a verdict of not guilty. 彼らは無罪の判決を下した。 **11** ADJ 形容詞 A **return** ticket is a ticket for a trip from one place to another and then back again. 往復の [mainly BRIT 主に英国英語; AM usually **round trip** 米国英語では通常 **round trip**] **12** ADJ 形容詞 The **return** trip is the part of a trip that takes you back to where you started from. 帰りの [ADJ] □ Buy an extra ticket for the return trip. 帰りの切符もあわせて買うようにね。 **13** N-COUNT 可算名詞 The **return on** an investment is the profit that you get from it. 収益 [BUSINESS 実業] □ Profits have picked up this year but the return on capital remains tiny. 本年度に入って収益は上向いたものの、資本収益率は依然として極めて低い。 **14** PHRASE 句 If you do something **in return** for what someone else has done for you, you do it because they did that thing for you. お返しとして、報酬として □ You pay regular premiums and in return the insurance company will pay out a lump sum. 定期的に保険料を払い続けた見返りとして、保険会社から多額の払い戻しがある。 **15** to **return fire** → see **fire**
→ see **library**

return また次を参照:

Thesaurus

return また次を参照:

v.   come again, come back, go back, reappear **1**
      give back, hand back, pay back; (ant.) keep **3**
N.   arrival, homecoming; (ant.) departure **2**

Word Partnership

return は次の語句と使われる:

v.   **decide to** return, **plan to** return, **want to**
      return **1 3 4 5 9**
N.   return **a (phone) call 5**
      return **to work 9**
      return **trip 12**
      return **on an investment, rate of** return **13**

re|uni|fi|ca|tion /riyunɪfɪkeɪʃ³n/ N-UNCOUNT 不可算名詞 The **reunification** of a country or city that has been divided into two or more parts for some time is the joining of it together again. 再統合 [with supp] □ ...the reunification of East and West Beirut in 1991. 1991年の東西ベイルートの再統合

re|union /riyunɪ̃ən/ (reunions) **1** N-COUNT 可算名詞 A **reunion** is a party attended by members of the same family, school, or other group who have not seen each other for a long time. 再会, 親睦会 □ The association holds an annual reunion. 協会は毎年親睦会を開いています. **2** N-VAR 可変性名詞 A **reunion** is a meeting between people who have been separated for some time. 再会 □ The children weren't allowed to see her for nearly a week. It was a very emotional reunion. 子供たちは1週間近く彼女との面会を許されていなかったので, 熱烈な再会となった.

re|unite /riyunaɪt/ (reunites, reuniting, reunited) **1** V-T 他動詞 If people **are reunited**, or if they **reunite**, they meet each other again after they have been separated for some time. 再会する □ She and her youngest son were finally allowed to be reunited with their family. 彼女と末息子はようやく家族との再会を許されました. **2** V-T/V-I 他動詞/自動詞 If a divided organization or country **is reunited**, or if it **reunites**, it becomes one united organization or country again. 再統合する □ As of this evening, Germany is reunited. In Berlin they're celebrating. 今夜, ドイツは統一を果たしました. ベルリンでは市民が統一を祝っています. □ His first job will be to reunite the army. 彼の最初の仕事は軍隊の再編になるだろう.

re|value /rivælyu/ (revalues, revaluing, revalued) **1** V-T 他動詞 When a country **revalues** its currency, it increases the currency's value so that it can buy more foreign currency than before. 切り上げる □ Countries enjoying surpluses will be under no pressure to revalue their currencies. 貿易黒字国は通貨切り上げの圧力を受けることはないだろう. **2** V-T 他動詞 To **revalue** something means to increase the amount that you calculate it is worth so that its value stays roughly the same in comparison with other things, even if there is inflation. 再評価する □ It is now usual to revalue property assets on a more regular basis. 短期間ごとに不動産を再評価することは今や当たり前となっている.

re|vamp /rivæmp/ (revamps, revamping, revamped) **1** V-T 他動詞 If someone **revamps** something, they make changes to it in order to try and improve it. 見直す □ All the country's political parties have accepted that it is time to revamp the system. 国のどの政党も制度を見直すべき時期に来ていることを認めている. ● N-SING 単数名詞 **Revamp** is also a noun. 見直し □ The revamp includes replacing the old navy uniform with a crisp blue and white cotton outfit. 見直しの中には, これまでの紺の制服をやめてさわやかな青と白の木綿の制服にすることも含まれている.

re|veal /rivil/ (reveals, revealing, revealed) **1** V-T 他動詞 To **reveal** something means to make people aware of it. 知らせる □ She has refused to reveal the whereabouts of her daughter. 彼女は娘の居場所を一切明かそうとしない. □ A survey of the American diet has revealed that a growing number of people are overweight. アメリカ人の食生活に関する調査によれば, 肥満人口が増加していることが明らかになりました. **2** V-T 他動詞 If you **reveal** something that has been out of sight, you uncover it so that people can see it. 見せる □ In the principal room, a gray carpet was removed to reveal the original pine floor. 最も主要な部屋ではグレーのカーペットをはがしてもとの松材の床が見えるようにした.

re|veal|ing /riviliŋ/ ADJ 形容詞 A **revealing** statement, account, or action tells you something that you did not know, especially about the person doing it or making it. 啓発するような □ ...a revealing interview. はっとさせられる対談

rev|el /rɛv³l/ (revels, reveling or revelling, reveled or revelled) V-I 自動詞 If you **revel in** a situation or experience, you enjoy it very much. とても喜ぶ □ Annie was smiling and laughing, clearly reveling in the attention. アニーはほほえんだり笑ったりして, 見るからに注目を引いてご満悦の様子だった.

rev|ela|tion /rɛvəleɪʃ³n/ (revelations) **1** N-COUNT 可算名詞 A **revelation** is a surprising or interesting fact that is made known to people. 新事実 □ ...the seemingly everlasting revelations

about his private life. とめどなく明かされる彼の私生活についての新事実 **2** N-VAR 可変性名詞 The **revelation of** something is the act of making it known. 暴露 □ ...following the revelation of his affair with a former secretary. 元秘書との不倫が発覚した後に **3** N-SING 単数名詞 If you say that something you experienced was **a revelation**, you are saying that it was very surprising or very good. 新発見 □ Degas's work had been a revelation to her. ドガの作品はまさしく彼女にとって発見であった.

re|venge /rivɛndʒ/ (revenges, revenging, revenged) **1** N-UNCOUNT 不可算名詞 **Revenge** involves hurting or punishing someone who has hurt or harmed you. 報復, 復讐 (ふくしゅう) □ The attackers were said to be taking revenge on the 14-year-old, claiming he was a school bully. 話によれば, 暴行した生徒たちはこの14歳の生徒からいじめを受けてその仕返しをしたという. **2** V-T 他動詞 If you **revenge** yourself on someone who has hurt you, you hurt them in return. 報復する, 復讐する [WRITTEN 書き言葉] □ The paper accused her of trying to revenge herself on her former lover. 新聞記事によれば, 彼女は昔の恋人に復讐しようとしていたという.

rev|enue /rɛvənyu/ (revenues) **1** N-UNCOUNT 不可算名詞 **Revenue** is money that a company, organization, or government receives from people. 収入; 歳入 [BUSINESS 実業] [also N in pl] □ ...a boom year at the movies, with record advertising revenue and the highest ticket sales since 1980. 記録的な広告収入と1980年以降最高の興行収入でブームに沸いた映画界の1年 **2** → see also Internal Revenue Service

re|ver|ber|ate /rivɜrbəreɪt/ (reverberates, reverberating, reverberated) **1** V-I 自動詞 When a loud sound **reverberates** through a place, it echoes through it. 鳴り響く □ Day in and day out, the flat crack of the tank guns reverberates through the little Bavarian town. 来る日も来る日もドーンという戦車砲の鈍い砲声がバパリアの小さな町に響き渡る. **2** V-I 自動詞 You can say that an event or idea **reverberates** when it has a powerful effect which lasts a long time. 反響が広がる □ The controversy surrounding the takeover yesterday continued to reverberate around the television industry. 昨日は買収をめぐる議論でテレビ業界に大きな波紋が広がった.

Word Link

vere ≈ fear, awe : irreverent, revere, reverence

re|vere /rivɪər/ (reveres, revering, revered) V-T 他動詞 If you **revere** someone or something, you respect and admire them greatly. あがめる [FORMAL 形式ばった] □ The Chinese revered corn as a gift from heaven. 中国人は穀物を天からの贈り物としてあがめた. ● **revered** ADJ 形容詞 あがめられる □ ...some of the country's most revered institutions. 国で最もおそれられているいくつかの機関

rev|er|ence /rɛvərəns/ N-UNCOUNT 不可算名詞 **Reverence for** someone or something is a feeling of great respect for them. 崇敬 [FORMAL 形式ばった] □ We stand together now in mutual support and in reverence for the dead. 今我々はみんな力を合わせ, 亡くなった方々に敬意を払います.

Rev|er|end /rɛvərənd/ N-TITLE 称号名詞 **Reverend** is a title used before the name or rank of an officially appointed Christian religious leader. The abbreviation **Rev.** is also used. 一師 □ The service was led by the Reverend Jim Simons. 儀式はジム・サイモンズ師が執り行ないました.

re|ver|sal /rivɜrs³l/ (reversals) **1** N-COUNT 可算名詞 A **reversal** of a process, policy, or trend is a complete change in it. 大転換 □ The paper says the move represents a complete reversal of previous U.S. policy. 新聞報道では, 今回の措置はアメリカの従来の政策が180度転換したことを示していると伝えています. **2** N-COUNT 可算名詞 When there is a role **reversal** or a **reversal** of roles, two people or groups exchange their positions or functions. 逆転 □ When children end up taking care of their parents, it is a strange role reversal indeed. 子供のほうが親の面倒をみるようになるというのは全く奇妙な役割の逆転である.

re|verse /rivɜrs/ (reverses, reversing, reversed) **1** V-T 他動詞 When someone or something **reverses** a decision, policy, or trend, they change it to the opposite decision, policy, or trend. 覆す □ They have made it clear they will not reverse the decision to increase prices. 彼らは価格引き上げの決定を覆す考えはないことを明らかにしています. **2** V-T 他動詞 If you **reverse** the order of a set of things, you arrange them in the opposite order, so that the first thing comes last. 逆にする □ Because the normal word order is reversed in passive sentences, they are sometimes hard to follow. 受動態の文では普通と語順が逆になるので理解しにくいことがある. **3** V-T 他動詞 If you **reverse** the positions or functions of two things, you change them so that each thing has the position or function that the other one had. 入れ替える □ He reversed the position of the two stamps. 彼は2枚の切手を入れ替えた. **4** V-T/V-I 他動詞/自動詞 When a car **reverses** or when you **reverse** it, the car is driven backward. バックさせる [mainly BRIT 主に英国英語] [他動詞] バックする [自動詞] [AM usually back up] 米国英語では通常 **back up**] **5** N-UNCOUNT 不可算名詞 If your car is **in reverse**, you have changed gears so that you can drive it backward. バック □ He lurched the car in reverse along the ruts to the access road. 彼が車をバ

ックさせると侵入路に通じるわだちにとられて車が傾いた. **6** ADJ 形容詞 **Reverse** means opposite from what you expect or to what has just been described. 逆の, 反対の □ *The wrong attitude will have exactly the reverse effect.* やり方を誤れば全く逆効果になるだろう. **7** N-SING 単数名詞 If you say that one thing is **the reverse** of another, you are emphasizing that the first thing is the complete opposite of the second thing. 逆, 反対 □ *He was not at all jolly. Quite the reverse.* 彼は決して上機嫌ではなかった. いや, 全くその反対だった. **8** N-SING 単数名詞 **The reverse** or **the reverse side** of a flat object which has two sides is the less important or the other side. 裏面 □ *A chart on the reverse of this letter highlights your savings.* 本状の裏面にお客様の預金残高をまとめた表がございます. **9** PHRASE 句 If something happens **in reverse** or goes **into reverse**, things happen in the opposite way from what usually happens or from what has been happening. 逆に □ *Amis tells the story in reverse, from the moment the man dies.* エイミスはその男の死の瞬間から話を過去にさかのぼって物語ります. **10** PHRASE 句 If you **reverse the charges** when you make a telephone call, the person who you are phoning pays the cost of the call and not you. コレクトコールする [mainly BRIT 主に英国英語; AM usually **call collect** 米国英語では通常 **call collect**]

Word Link

vert ≈ turning : convert, invert, revert

re|vert /rɪvɜ́rt/ (**reverts, reverting, reverted**) **1** V-I 自動詞 When people or things **revert to** a previous state, system, or type of behavior, they go back to it. 戻る □ *Jackson said her boss became increasingly depressed and reverted to smoking heavily.* ジャクソンの話では, 彼女の上司はますますふさぎ込んで, 以前のヘビースモーカーに戻ってしまったという. **2** V-I 自動詞 When someone **reverts to** a previous topic, they start talking or thinking about it again. 戻る [WRITTEN 書き言葉] □ *In the car she reverted to the subject uppermost in her mind. "You know, I really believe what Grandma told you."* 車の中で彼女は最も気になっている話に戻した. 「ねえ, わたしはおばあちゃんがあなたに言ったこと, 本当だと思うわ」 **3** V-I 自動詞 If property, rights, or money **revert to** someone, they become that person's again after someone else has had them for a period of time. 復帰する [LEGAL 法律的] □ *When the lease ends, the property reverts to the owner.* 賃貸契約期間が終了すると, 建物とその敷地の権利は所有者に復帰する.

re|view /rɪvyú/ (**reviews, reviewing, reviewed**) **1** N-COUNT 可算名詞 A **review** of a situation or system is its formal examination by people in authority. This is usually done in order to see whether it can be improved or corrected. 再検討 [oft N "of" n, also prep N] □ *The president ordered a review of U.S. economic aid to Jordan.* 大統領はヨルダンへのアメリカの経済援助を見直すよう指示しました. **2** V-T 他動詞 If you **review** a situation or system, you consider it carefully to see what is wrong with it or how it could be improved. 検討する □ *The president reviewed the situation with his cabinet yesterday.* 大統領は昨日, 閣僚と共に情勢の検討を行ないました. **3** N-COUNT 可算名詞 A **review** is a report in the media in which someone gives their opinion of something such as a new book or movie. 批評 □ *We've never had a good review in the music press.* 今まで音楽雑誌で好意的に評価されたことは一度もない. **4** V-T 他動詞 If someone **reviews** something such as a new book or movie, they write a report or give a talk on television or radio in which they express their opinion of it. 批評を書く □ *Richard Coles reviews all the latest video releases.* リチャード・コールズは最新リリースのビデオを全作品にわたって批評する. **5** V-T/V-I 他動詞/自動詞 When you **review for** an examination, you read things again and make notes in order to be prepared for the examination. 復習する [AM 米国英語] □ *Reviewing for exams gives you a chance to bring together all the individual parts of the course.* 試験勉強すれば, 教科の内容のそれぞれの関連が分かってくる. □ *Review all the notes you need to cover for each course.* どの教科も範囲となるところは講義ノートですべて復習しておきます. ● N-COUNT 可算名詞 **Review** is also a noun. 復習 □ *If you have to cover 12 chapters in American history, begin by planning on three two-hour reviews with four chapters per session.* アメリカ史の範囲が12章にわたるのなら, 1回に4章分ずつ2時間で復習し, 3回に分けてやるように計画すればよい.

Thesaurus

review また次を参照 :

N.	analysis, evaluation, inspection, study **1**
V.	prepare, read, study **5**

Word Partnership

review は次の語句と使われる :

N.	**performance** review **1**
	review **a case**, review **evidence** **2**
	book review, **film/movie** review, **restaurant** review **3**
	review **questions** **5**

re|view|er /rɪvyúər/ (**reviewers**) N-COUNT 可算名詞 A **reviewer** is a person who reviews new books, movies, television programs,

---

CDs, plays, or concerts. 批評家 □ *...the reviewer for Atlantic Monthly.* 米誌『アトランティック・マンスリー』に寄稿する批評家

re|vise /rɪváɪz/ (**revises, revising, revised**) **1** V-T 他動詞 If you **revise** the way you think about something, you adjust your thoughts, usually in order to make them better or more suited to how things are. 変える □ *With time he came to revise his opinion of the profession.* 時が経つとともにその職業に対する彼の見方は変わっていった. **2** V-T 他動詞 If you **revise** a price, amount, or estimate, you change it to make it more fair, realistic, or accurate. 変える □ *They realized that some of their prices were higher than their competitors' and revised prices accordingly.* 競争企業よりも価格の高い製品があることが分かり, 会社は値下げに踏み切った. **3** V-T 他動詞 When you **revise** an article, a book, a law, or a piece of music, you change it in order to improve it, make it more modern, or make it more suitable for a particular purpose. 校訂する ; 校正する □ *Three editors handled the work of revising the articles for publication.* 出版にあたっては編集者3名が記事の編集に当たった. **4** V-I 自動詞 When you **revise for** an examination, you read things again and make notes in order to be prepared for the examination. 復習する [BRIT 英国英語; AM **review** 米国英語 **review**]

re|vi|sion /rɪvíʒ³n/ (**revisions**) **1** N-VAR 可変性名詞 To make a **revision** of something that is written or something that has been decided means to make changes to it in order to improve it, make it more modern, or make it more suitable for a particular purpose. 改訂 ; 校正 □ *The phase of writing that is actually most important is revision.* 執筆で実は最も重要なのが校正作業である. **2** N-UNCOUNT 不可算名詞 When people who are studying do **revision**, they read things again and make notes in order to prepare for an examination. 復習 [BRIT 英国英語; AM **review** 米国英語 **review**]

re|vis|it /rivízɪt/ (**revisits, revisiting, revisited**) **1** V-T 他動詞 If you **revisit** a place, you return there for a visit after you have been away for a long time, often after the place has changed a lot. 再訪する □ *In the summer, when we returned to Canada, we revisited this lake at dawn.* 夏になってカナダに戻ったわたしたちは明け方にこの湖に再び足を運んだ. **2** V-T 他動詞 If you **revisit** a subject or topic, you discuss it again or consider it again. 再び扱う, 再検討する □ *The committee agreed to revisit the issue at their next meeting.* 委員会は次回にその問題をもう一度話し合うことで一致した.

Word Link

vita ≈ life : revitalize, vital, vitality

re|vi|tal|ize /rivάɪt³lάɪz/ (**revitalizes, revitalizing, revitalized**) V-T 他動詞 To **revitalize** something that has lost its activity or its health means to make it active or healthy again. 活力を与える, よみがえらせる □ *This hair conditioner is excellent for revitalizing dry, lifeless hair.* このヘアコンディショナーはぱさついてつやのない髪を見事によみがえらせます.

Word Link

viv ≈ living : revival, survive, vivacious

re|viv|al /rivάɪv³l/ (**revivals**) **1** N-COUNT 可算名詞 When there is a **revival** of something, it becomes active or popular again. 復活 □ *This return to realism has produced a revival of interest in a number of artists.* こうしたリアリズムへの回帰は, 多くのアーティストたちの間に再び関心を巻き起こすことになった. **2** N-COUNT 可算名詞 A **revival** is a new production of a play, an opera, or a ballet. 再上演 □ *...John Clement's revival of Chekhov's "The Seagull".* ジョン・クレメントによるチェーホフ作『かもめ』の再上演 **3** N-UNCOUNT 不可算名詞 A **revival** meeting is a public religious event that is intended to make people more interested in Christianity. 信仰復興 □ *He toured the country organizing revival meetings.* 彼は全国を回ってリバイバル集会を組織した.

re|vive /rivάɪv/ (**revives, reviving, revived**) **1** V-T/V-I 他動詞/自動詞 When something such as the economy, a business, a trend, or a feeling **is revived** or when it **revives**, it becomes active, popular, or successful again. [他動詞] 復興する [自動詞] □ *...an attempt to revive the economy.* 経済を復興させる試み **2** V-T 他動詞 When someone **revives** a play, opera, or ballet, they present a new production of it. 再上演する □ *His plays continue to be revived both here and abroad.* 彼の劇は国内外で再上演が続いている. **3** V-T/V-I 他動詞/自動詞 If you **revive** someone who has fainted or if they **revive**, they become conscious again. 意識を回復させる [他動詞] 意識を取り戻す □ *She and a neighbor tried in vain to revive him.* 彼女は近所の人と懸命に彼の意識を回復させようとしたが, 意識が戻ることはなかった.

re|voke /rivóʊk/ (**revokes, revoking, revoked**) V-T 他動詞 When people in authority **revoke** something such as a license, a law, or an agreement, they cancel it. 取り消す, 無効にする [FORMAL 形式ばった] □ *The government revoked her husband's license to operate migrant labor crews.* 政府は彼女の夫が所持していた季節労働者を雇用するための免許を取り消しました.

re|volt /rivóʊlt/ (**revolts, revolting, revolted**) **1** N-VAR 可変性名詞 A **revolt** is an illegal and often violent attempt by a group of people to change their country's political system. 暴動 □ *It was*

undeniably a revolt by ordinary people against their leaders. それは紛れもなく一般民衆が指導者に対して起こした暴動であった. **2** V-I 自動詞 When people **revolt**, they make an illegal and often violent attempt to change their country's political system. 暴動を起こす ❑ In 1375 the townspeople revolted. 1375年，町の住民は立ち上がった. **3** N-VAR 可変性名詞 A **revolt** by a person or group against someone or something is a refusal to accept the authority of that person or thing. 抵抗 ❑ Conservative Republicans had led the revolt against the budget package. 保守的な共和党議員が予算案反対の先陣を切っていた. **4** V-I 自動詞 When people **revolt against** someone or something, they reject the authority of that person or reject that thing. 抵抗する ❑ In 1978 California taxpayers revolted against higher taxes. 1978年，カリフォルニアの納税者は税金の引き上げに反対した.

re|volt|ing /rɪvˈoʊltɪŋ/ ADJ 形容詞 If you say that something or someone is **revolting**, you mean that you think they are horrible and disgusting. むかむかさせる ❑ The smell in the cell was revolting. 独房はむかつくようなにおいがした.

revo|lu|tion /rɛvəlˈuʃⁿ/ (**revolutions**) **1** N-COUNT 可算名詞 A **revolution** is a successful attempt by a large group of people to change the political system of their country by force. 革命 ❑ The period since the revolution has been one of political turmoil. 革命後は政治の混乱が続いています. **2** N-COUNT 可算名詞 A **revolution** in a particular area of human activity is an important change in that area. 大変革 ❑ The nineteenth century witnessed a revolution in ship design and propulsion. 19世紀になると，船舶の設計と推進力において著しい進歩が見られた.

revo|lu|tion|ary /rɛvəlˈuʃənɛri/ (**revolutionaries**) **1** ADJ 形容詞 **Revolutionary** activities, organizations, or people have the aim of causing a political revolution. 革命の，急進的な ❑ Do you know anything about the revolutionary movement? その革命運動のことで何か知ってることはあるか. **2** N-COUNT 可算名詞 A **revolutionary** is a person who tries to cause a revolution or who takes an active part in one. 革命家 ❑ The revolutionaries laid down their arms and their leaders went into voluntary exile. 革命に参加した者たちは降伏し，指導者は自ら亡命した. **3** ADJ 形容詞 **Revolutionary** ideas and developments involve great changes in the way that something is done or made. 革命的な ❑ Invented in 1951, the rotary engine is a revolutionary concept in internal combustion. 1951年に発明されたロータリーエンジンは内燃機関の概念を打ち破るものだった.

revo|lu|tion|ize /rɛvəlˈuʃənaɪz/ (**revolutionizes, revolutionizing, revolutionized**) V-T 他動詞 When something **revolutionizes** an activity, it causes great changes in the way that it is done. 革命をもたらす ❑ Over the past forty years plastics have revolutionised the way we live. 過去40年間以上にわたり，プラスチックは我々の生活に革命をもたらしてきました.

re|volve /rɪvˈɒlv/ (**revolves, revolving, revolved**) **1** V-I 自動詞 If you say that one thing **revolves around** another thing, you mean that the second thing is the main feature or focus of the first thing. 〜を中心に回る ❑ Since childhood, her life has revolved around tennis. 子供の頃からずっと彼女の生活はテニスである. **2** V-I 自動詞 If a discussion or conversation **revolves around** a particular topic, it is mainly about that topic. 〜を中心に展開する ❑ The debate revolves around specific accounting techniques. 個々の会計手法をめぐって議論は進められる. **3** V-I 自動詞 If one object **revolves around** another object, the first object turns in a circle around the second object. 回転する ❑ The satellite revolves around the earth once every hundred minutes. 人工衛星は100分で1回地球の周りを回っています. **4** V-T/V-I 他動詞/自動詞 When something **revolves** or when you **revolve** it, it moves or turns in a circle around a central point or line. 回転する ❑ Overhead, the fan revolved slowly. 頭上では扇風機がゆっくりと回っていた.

re|volv|er /rɪvˈɒlvər/ (**revolvers**) N-COUNT 可算名詞 A **revolver** is a kind of hand gun. Its bullets are kept in a revolving cylinder in the gun. リボルバー，回転式拳銃（けんじゅう）

re|vue /rɪvjˈu/ (**revues**) N-COUNT 可算名詞 A **revue** is a theatrical performance consisting of songs, dances, and jokes about recent events. レビュー

re|vul|sion /rɪvˈʌlʃⁿn/ N-UNCOUNT 不可算名詞 Someone's **revulsion** at something is the strong feeling of disgust or disapproval they have toward it. 強い嫌悪 ❑ ...their revulsion at the act of desecration. 神を冒涜（ぼうとく）する行為に対する強い反感

re|ward /rɪwˈɔrd/ (**rewards, rewarding, rewarded**) **1** N-COUNT 可算名詞 A **reward** is something that you are given, for example because you have behaved well, worked hard, or provided a service to the community. 褒美 ❑ A bonus of up to five percent can be added to a student's final exam score as a reward for good spelling, punctuation, and grammar. 綴（つづ）りや句読点や文法が正しく書けていると，褒美として期末試験で最高5%の得点が加算される. **2** N-COUNT 可算名詞 A **reward** is a sum of money offered to anyone who can give information about lost or stolen property, a missing person, or someone who is wanted by the police. 謝礼金，報奨金 ❑ The firm last night offered a $10,000 reward for information leading to the conviction of the killer. 会社は昨夜，殺人犯の有罪判決に

つながった情報に対して1万ドルの謝礼金を提供した. **3** V-T 他動詞 If you do something and **are rewarded** with a particular benefit, you receive that benefit as a result of doing that thing. 報われる ❑ Make the extra effort to impress the buyer and you will be rewarded with a quicker sale at a better price. 購入者に好印象を与えるようにしっかり努力すれば，素早く高値で販売することができるだろう. **4** N-COUNT 可算名詞 The **rewards** of something are the benefits that you receive as a result of doing or having that thing. 報酬 ❑ The company is just starting to reap the rewards of long-term investments. 会社は長期的投資の恩恵をちょうど受け始めたところである.

Thesaurus   reward また次を参照：

N.   bonus, prize; (ant.) punishment **1**

Word Partnership   reward は次の語句と使われる：

N.   reward **for good behavior**, **risk** and reward **1**
     reward **for information 2**
V.   **give** someone a reward, **offer** a reward **1 2**

re|ward|ing /rɪwˈɔrdɪŋ/ ADJ 形容詞 An experience or action that is **rewarding** gives you satisfaction or brings you benefits. やりがいのある ❑ ...a career that she found stimulating and rewarding. 彼女が刺激的でやりがいがあると感じた仕事

re|wind /riwˈaɪnd/ (**rewinds, rewinding, rewound**) V-T/V-I 他動詞/自動詞 When the tape in a video or tape recorder **rewinds** or when you **rewind** it, the tape goes backwards so that you can play it again. Compare **fast forward**. 巻き戻す ❑ Wendy rewound the tape and played the message again. ウェンディはテープを巻き戻しもう一度メッセージを再生した.

re|work /riwˈɜrk/ (**reworks, reworking, reworked**) V-T 他動詞 If you **rework** something such as an idea or a piece of writing, you reorganize it and make changes to it in order to improve it or bring it up to date. 作り直す ❑ See if you can rework your schedule and come up with practical ways to reduce the number of hours you're on call. 予定を組み直して待機時間を減らせる現実的な方法がないか検討します.

re|write /riraɪt/ (**rewrites, rewriting, rewrote, rewritten**) **1** V-T 他動詞 If someone **rewrites** a piece of writing such as a book, an article, or a law, they write it in a different way in order to improve it. 書き直す ❑ Following this critique, students rewrite their papers and submit them for final evaluation. この指導を受けると，学生はレポートを書き直して提出し最終評価を受けます. **2** V-T 他動詞 If you accuse someone such as a government of **rewriting** history, you are criticizing them for selecting and presenting particular historical events in a way that suits their own purposes. 書き換える [DISAPPROVAL 不賛成] ❑ We have always been an independent people, no matter how they rewrite history. 彼らがどのように歴史を書き換えようとも，我々が独立心にあふれる民族であり続けてきたことに変わりはない.

rhet|o|ric /rˈɛtərɪk/ **1** N-UNCOUNT 不可算名詞 If you refer to speech or writing as **rhetoric**, you disapprove of it because it is intended to convince and impress people but may not be sincere or honest. 美辞麗句 [DISAPPROVAL 不賛成] ❑ The change is largely cosmetic, a matter of acceptable political rhetoric rather than social reality. 変化はほとんどが表面的なもので，社会の現実というよりは許容された政治的なレトリックの話である. **2** N-UNCOUNT 不可算名詞 **Rhetoric** is the skill or art of using language effectively. 修辞法 [FORMAL 形式ばった] ❑ ...the noble institutions of political life, such as political rhetoric, public office, and public service. 政治雄弁術，公職，公務などの政治生活の由緒ある伝統

rhe|tori|cal /rɪtˈɔrɪkⁿl/ **1** ADJ 形容詞 A **rhetorical** question is one that is asked in order to make a statement rather than to get an answer. 修辞的な ❑ He grimaced slightly, obviously expecting no answer to his rhetorical question. 彼は少し顔をしかめ，反語的な問いに返事は無用だと言わんばかりだった. ● **rhe|tori|cal|ly** /rɪtˈɔrɪkli/ ADV 副詞 [ADV with v] 修辞的に ❑ "Do these kids know how lucky they are?" Jackson asked rhetorically. 「この子たちはどんなに自分たちが恵まれているか分かってるのか」とジャクソンは反語として言った. **2** ADJ 形容詞 **Rhetorical** language is intended to be grand and impressive. 大げさな [FORMAL 形式ばった] ❑ These arguments may have been used as a rhetorical device to argue for a perpetuation of a United Nations role. こうした主張は国連の役割の恒久性を認めるための便利な表現として使われてきたふしがある. ● **rhe|tori|cal|ly** ADV 副詞 大げさに ❑ Suddenly, the narrator speaks in his most rhetorically elevated mode. 突然，尊大で誇張した語り口に変わった.

rhi|no /rˈaɪnoʊ/ (**rhinos**) N-COUNT 可算名詞 A **rhino** is the same as a **rhinoceros**. サイ [INFORMAL くだけた]

rhi|noc|er|os /raɪnˈɒsərəs/ (**rhinoceroses**) N-COUNT 可算名詞 A **rhinoceros** is a large Asian or African animal with thick, gray skin and a horn, or two horns, on its nose. サイ

rhyme /raɪm/ (**rhymes, rhyming, rhymed**) **1** V-RECIP 相互動詞 If one word **rhymes with** another or if two words **rhyme**, they

have a very similar sound. Words that rhyme with each other are often used in poems. 韻を踏む ❑*June always rhymes with moon in old love songs.* 昔の恋愛詩では*June*は必ず*moon*と踏む。 ❑*...the sort of people who give their children names that rhyme: Donnie, Ronnie, Connie.* ドニー、ロニー、コニーのように子供の名前を同じ韻にするような人たち ❷ V-I 自動詞 If a poem or song **rhymes**, the lines end with words that have very similar sounds. 韻を用いる ❑*In his efforts to make it rhyme, he seems to have chosen the first word that came into his head.* 彼は同じ韻の言葉を探そうとして最初に浮かんだ言葉を選んだようである。 ❸ N-COUNT 可算名詞 A **rhyme** is a word which rhymes with another word, or a set of lines which rhyme. 同韻語 ❑*The one rhyme for passion is fashion.* passionの同韻語の1つにfashionがある。 ❹ N-COUNT 可算名詞 A **rhyme** is a short poem which has rhyming words at the ends of its lines. 押韻（おういん）詩 ❑*He was teaching Helen a little rhyme.* 彼はヘレンに短い押韻詩を教えているところだった。 ❺ N-UNCOUNT 不可算名詞 **Rhyme** is the use of rhyming words as a technique in poetry. If something is written in **rhyme**, it is written as a poem in which the lines rhyme. 押韻 ❑*The plays are in rhyme.* その戯曲は押韻を用いている。

rhythm /rɪðəm/ (**rhythms**) ❶ N-VAR 可変性名詞 A **rhythm** is a regular series of sounds or movements. リズム ❑*His music of that period fused the rhythms of Jazz with classical forms.* 当時の彼の音楽はジャズのリズムとクラシックの形式を融合したものした。 ❷ N-COUNT 可算名詞 A **rhythm** is a regular pattern of changes, for example changes in your body, in the seasons, or in the tides. 周期 ❑*Begin to listen to your own body rhythms.* 自分の体のリズムに耳を傾けてみましょう。

rhyth|mic /rɪðmɪk/ also **rhythmical** /rɪðmɪkᵊl/ ADJ 形容詞 A **rhythmic** movement or sound is repeated at regular intervals, forming a regular pattern or beat. リズミカルな ❑*Good breathing is slow, rhythmic and deep.* ゆっくりと深い規則的な呼吸がよい呼吸である。 ●**rhyth|mi|cal|ly** /rɪðmɪkli/ ADV 副詞 [ADV after v] リズミカルに ❑*She stood, swaying her hips, moving rhythmically.* 彼女は腰を左右に振りながらリズムをとっていた。

rib /rɪb/ (**ribs**) ❶ N-COUNT 可算名詞 Your **ribs** are the 12 pairs of curved bones that surround your chest. ろっ骨 ❑*Her heart was thumping against her ribs.* 彼女の胸はろっ骨に響くほど高鳴った。 ❷ N-COUNT 可算名詞 A **rib** of meat such as beef or pork is a piece that has been cut to include one of the animal's ribs. あばら肉 ❑*...a rib of beef.* 牛のあばら肉 ❑*...pork ribs.* 豚のあばら肉

rib|bon /rɪbən/ (**ribbons**) ❶ N-VAR 可変性名詞 A **ribbon** is a long, narrow piece of cloth that you use for tying things together or as a decoration. リボン ❑*She had tied back her hair with a peach satin ribbon.* 彼女はピーチ色のサテンのリボンで髪を束ねていた。 ❷ N-COUNT 可算名詞 A typewriter or printer **ribbon** is a long, narrow piece of cloth containing ink and is used in a typewriter or printer. インクリボン

rice /raɪs/ (**rices**) N-MASS 質量名詞 **Rice** consists of white or brown grains taken from a cereal plant. You cook rice and usually eat it with meat or vegetables. 米 ❑*...a meal consisting of chicken, rice, and vegetables.* とり肉、米、野菜の食事
→ see Word Web: **rice**
→ see **grain**, **rice**

rich /rɪtʃ/ (**richer, richest, riches**) ❶ ADJ 形容詞 A **rich** person has a lot of money or valuable possessions. 金持ちの ❑*You're going to be a very rich man.* お前は大金持ちになるよ。 ●N-PLURAL 複数名詞 **The rich** are rich people. 金持ち ❑*This is a system in which the rich are taken care of and the poor are left to suffer.* この制度では金持ちが優遇され弱者は切り捨てられる。 ❷ N-PLURAL 複数名詞 **Riches** are valuable possessions or large amounts of money. 財産、富 ❑*An Olympic gold medal can lead to untold riches for an athlete.* オリンピックの金メダルをとれば、選手にとってとてつもない財産になりうる。 ❸ ADJ 形容詞 A **rich** country has a strong economy and produces a lot of wealth, so many people who live there have a high standard of living. 豊かな ❑*There is hunger in many parts of the world, even in rich countries.* 飢えは世界の多くの地域にあり、先進国にすら存在します。 ❹ N-PLURAL 複数名詞 If you talk about the Earth's **riches**, you are referring to things that exist naturally in large quantities and that are useful and valuable, for example minerals, wood, and oil. 資源 ❑*...Russia's vast natural riches.* ロシアの膨大な天然

資源 ❺ ADJ 形容詞 If something is **rich in** a useful or valuable substance or is a **rich source of** it, it contains a lot of it. 〜が豊かな [v-link ADJ "in" n, ADJ n] ❑*Liver and kidneys are particularly rich in vitamin A.* レバーと腎臓（じんぞう）はとりわけビタミンAが豊富である。 ❻ ADJ 形容詞 **Rich** food contains a lot of fat or oil. 脂肪分の多い ❑*Additional cream would make it too rich.* さらにクリームを加えるとこってりしすぎてしまうだろう。 ●**rich|ness** N-UNCOUNT 不可算名詞 脂肪分が高いこと ❑*A squeeze of fresh lime juice cuts the richness of the avocado.* 新鮮なライムを絞って加えるとアボカドのしつこさが消える。 ❼ ADJ 形容詞 **Rich** soil contains large amounts of substances that make it good for growing crops or flowers. 肥えた ❑*Farmers grow rice in the rich soil.* 農民は肥沃（ひよく）な土地で稲作している。 ❽ ADJ 形容詞 A **rich** deposit of a mineral or other substance is a large amount of it. 豊富な ❑*...the country's rich deposits of the metal lithium.* その国のリチウムを豊富に産出する鉱床 ●**rich|ness** N-UNCOUNT 不可算名詞 豊富さ ❑*...the richness of Tibet's mineral deposits.* チベットの鉱産資源の豊かさ ❾ ADJ 形容詞 [ADJ n] If you say that something is a **rich** vein or source of something such as humor, ideas, or information, you mean that it can provide a lot of that thing. 豊かな ❑*The director discovered a rich vein of sentimentality.* ディレクターはとばしる感情を感じ取った。 ❿ ADJ 形容詞 **Rich** smells are strong and very pleasant. **Rich** colors and sounds are deep and very pleasant. 豊かな ❑*...a rich and luxuriously perfumed bath essence.* 豊かでぜいたくな香りのバスエッセンス ●**rich|ness** N-UNCOUNT 不可算名詞 豊かさ ❑*His musicals were infused with richness of color and visual detail.* 彼のミュージカルは色彩に富んでいて細部まで目が行き届いている。 ⓫ ADJ 形容詞 A **rich** life or history is one that is interesting because it is full of different events and activities. 豊かな ❑*A rich and varied cultural life is essential for this couple.* この夫婦には豊かで変化に富んだ文化的な生活が何より欠かせない。 ●**rich|ness** N-UNCOUNT 不可算名詞 豊かさ ❑*It all adds to the richness of human life.* それはまさに人間の生活を一層豊かなものにする。 ⓬ ADJ 形容詞 A **rich** collection or mixture contains a wide and interesting variety of different things. 豊かな ❑*Visitors can view a rich and colorful array of aquatic plants and animals.* そこを訪れれば、さまざまな水生の動植物を楽しむことができる。 ●**rich|ness** N-UNCOUNT 不可算名詞 豊かさ ❑*...a huge country, containing a richness of culture and diversity of landscape.* 豊かな文化と変化に富んだ自然に恵まれたスケールの大きい国

Thesaurus rich また次を参照：

ADJ. affluent, wealthy; (ant.) poor ❶

Word Partnership rich は次の語句と使われる：

ADJ. rich **and beautiful**, rich **and famous**, rich **and powerful** ❶
V. **become** rich, **get** rich **(quick)** ❶
N. rich **kids**, rich **man/people**, rich **and poor** ❶
rich **country/nation** ❸
rich **in natural resources** ❺
rich **diet**, rich **food** ❻
rich **color** ❿
rich **culture**, rich **heritage**, rich **history**, rich **tradition** ⓫

rich|ly /rɪtʃli/ ❶ ADV 副詞 If something is **richly** colored, flavored, or perfumed, it has a pleasantly strong color, flavor, or perfume. 豊かに ❑*...Renaissance masterpieces, so richly colored and lustrous.* 色彩と輝きに満ちたルネサンス期の傑作。 ❷ ADV 副詞 If something is **richly** decorated, patterned, or furnished, it has a lot of elaborate and beautiful decoration, patterns, or furniture. ぜいたくに ❑*Coffee steamed in the richly decorated silver pot.* 豪華な装飾のほどこされた銀のポットからコーヒーが湯気を立てていた。 ❸ ADV 副詞 If you say that someone **richly** deserves an award, success, or victory, you approve of what they have done and feel very strongly that they deserve it. 十分に [FEELINGS 感情] ❑*He achieved the success he so richly deserved.* 彼が成功を果たしたのはしごく当然だ。 ❹ ADV 副詞 If you are **richly** rewarded for doing something, you get something very valuable or pleasant in return for doing

Word Web rice

An ancient Chinese myth says that an animal gave humans the gift of **rice**. Once a large flood destroyed all the crops. When the people returned from the hills, they saw a dog. It had bunches of rice **seeds** in its tail. They planted this new **grain** and were never hungry again. In many Asian countries the words for rice and **food** are identical. Rice has many non-food uses. It is the main ingredient in some kinds of laundry **starch**. The Japanese make a liquor called saké from it. And in Thailand, rice **straw** is made into hats and shoes.

it. 十分に ❏ *It is a difficult book to read, but it richly rewards the effort.* 読みにくさはあるが，読みごたえのある本である．

rick|ety /rɪkiti/ ADJ 形容詞 A **rickety** structure or piece of furniture is not very strong or well made, and seems likely to collapse or break. 壊れそうな ❏ *Mona climbed the rickety wooden stairs.* モナはがたがたする木の階段を上った．

rid /rɪd/ (rids, ridding)

> The form **rid** is used in the present tense and is the past tense and past participle of the verb.
>
> rid 形は現在時制に使われ，動詞の過去時制と過去分詞でもある．

1 PHRASE 句 When you **get rid of** something that you do not want or do not like, you take action so that you no longer have it or suffer from it. 取り除く；抜け出す ❏ *The owner needs to get rid of the car for financial reasons.* 車の持ち主は経済的な理由で車を売り払う必要がある． **2** PHRASE 句 If you **get rid of** someone who is causing problems for you or who you do not like, you do something to prevent them from affecting you anymore, for example by making them leave. 追い払う ❏ *He believed that his manager wanted to get rid of him for personal reasons.* 経営者が個人的な理由で自分を厄介払いしようとしていると彼は思っていた． **3** V-T 他動詞 If you **rid** a place or person **of** something undesirable or unwanted, you succeed in removing it completely from that place or person. 〜から〜を取り除く ❏ *The proposals are an attempt to rid the country of political corruption.* 計画はこの国から政治腐敗をなくするための試みです． **4** V-T 他動詞 If you **rid yourself of** something you do not want, you take action so that you no longer have it or are no longer affected by it. 抜け出す ❏ *Why couldn't he ever rid himself of those thoughts, those worries?* どうして彼はそうした思いや不安から抜け出すことができなかったのか． **5** ADJ 形容詞 If you **are rid of** someone or something that you did not want or that caused problems for you, they are no longer with you or causing problems for you. 解放される [v-link ADJ "of" n] ❏ *The family had sought a way to be rid of her and the problems she had caused them.* 家族はどうすれば彼女自身と彼女が引き起こした問題から解放されるのかずっと考えていた．

rid|den /rɪdᵊn/ **Ridden** is the past participle of **ride**. ride の過去分詞

-ridden /-rɪdᵊn/ COMB IN ADJ 形容詞の複合 **-ridden** combines with nouns to form adjectives that describe something as having a lot of a particular undesirable thing or quality, or suffering very much because of it. 〜に悩まされた ❏ *…the debt-ridden economies of Latin America.* 債務に苦しむ中南米経済．

rid|dle /rɪdᵊl/ (riddles, riddling, riddled) **1** N-COUNT 可算名詞 A **riddle** is a puzzle or joke in which you ask a question that seems to be nonsense but which has a clever or amusing answer. なぞなぞ ❏ *All comers to the Sphinx were asked a riddle, and failure to solve it meant death.* スフィンクスに出会った旅人はみんななぞを問いかけられ，解けないときは殺された． **2** N-COUNT 可算名詞 You can describe something as a **riddle** if people have been trying to understand or explain it but have not been able to. なぞ ❏ *Scientists claimed yesterday to have solved the riddle of the birth of the universe.* 昨日，宇宙誕生のなぞを解明したという科学者の発表があった． **3** V-T 他動詞 If someone **riddles** something **with** bullets or bullet holes, they fire a lot of bullets into it. 穴だらけにする ❏ *Unknown attackers riddled two homes with gunfire.* 正体不明の武装グループの銃撃で2軒の家が穴だらけになった．

rid|dled /rɪdᵊld/ **1** ADJ 形容詞 If something is **riddled with** bullets or bullet holes, it is full of bullet holes. 〜で穴だらけになった ❏ *The bodies of four people were found riddled with bullets.* 銃弾で穴だらけになった4人の遺体が発見されました． **2** ADJ 形容詞 If something is **riddled with** undesirable qualities or features, it is full of them. 〜で満ちた [v-link ADJ "with" n] ❏ *They were the principal shareholders in a bank riddled with corruption.* 彼らは汚職で腐敗しきった銀行の大株主でした．

ride /rɑɪd/ (rides, riding, rode, ridden) **1** V-T/V-I 他動詞/自動詞 When you **ride** a horse, you sit on it and control its movements. 乗る ❏ *I saw a girl riding a horse.* 少女が馬に乗っているのを見た． ❏ *Can you ride?* 馬には乗れるか． **2** V-T/V-I 他動詞/自動詞 When you **ride** a bicycle or a motorcycle, you sit on it, control it, and travel along on it. 乗る ❏ *Riding a bike is great exercise.* 自転車に乗るといい運動になる． ❏ *Two men riding on motorcycles opened fire on him.* 単車に乗った2人組が彼に発砲した． **3** V-I 自動詞 When you **ride** in a vehicle such as a car, you travel in it. 乗る ❏ *He prefers traveling on the subway to riding in a limousine.* 彼はリムジンに乗るよりも地下鉄に乗るほうが好きである． **4** N-COUNT 可算名詞 A **ride** is a trip on a horse or bicycle, or in a vehicle. 乗っていくこと ❏ *She took some friends for a ride in the family car.* 彼女は友人数人を連れてドライブに行った． **5** N-COUNT 可算名詞 In an amusement park, a **ride** is a large machine that people ride on for fun. 遊園地の乗り物 ❏ *…roller coasters or other thrill rides at amusement parks.* ジェットコースターのようなスリル満点の遊園地の乗り物 **6** V-I 自動詞 If you say that one thing **is riding on** another, you mean that the first thing

depends on the second thing. 〜次第である [oft cont] ❏ *Billions of dollars are riding on the outcome of the election.* 何十億ドルもの金が選挙の行方にかかっている． **7** → see also **riding**

> When you want to say that someone is controlling a horse, bicycle, or motorbike, you can use **ride** as a transitive verb, with the object coming immediately after it. ❏ *Whether you ride a motorbike, scooter or moped, get yourself properly trained.* However, if you want to say that someone is a passenger in a vehicle, **ride** must be followed by a preposition. ❏ *I was riding on the back of a friend's bicycle…We are still letting our children ride in the front seat of our cars.* If **ride** is used without an object, a preposition, or any other phrase that specifies the context, it usually refers to the activity of riding a horse. ❏ *"Do you ride?"—"No, I've never been on a horse."*

8 PHRASE 句 If you say that someone faces **a rough ride**, you mean that things are going to be difficult for them because people will criticize them a lot or treat them badly. ひどい目 [INFORMAL くだけた] ❏ *The president could face a rough ride unless the plan works.* 計画がうまくいかなければ，大統領は厳しい批判にさらされる可能性がある． **9** PHRASE 句 If you describe something as **a free ride**, you mean that things are going to be very easy and that people will take advantage of this. 丸もうけ [INFORMAL くだけた] ❏ *I've had an opponent every time. I've never had a free ride. I've had to fight.* 毎回敵がいた．やすやすと勝ったことはなく，いつも戦いだった． **10** PHRASE 句 If you say that someone **has been taken for a ride**, you mean that they have been deceived or cheated. だまされる [INFORMAL くだけた] ❏ *You got taken for a ride. Why did you give him five thousand dollars?* うまく乗せられたんだよ．なんでやつに5千ドル渡したんだ． **11** PHRASE 句 If someone **rides herd on** other people or their actions, they supervise them or watch them closely. 見張る [AM 米国英語] [PHR n] ❏ *…state efforts to ride herd on the oil companies.* 石油会社を監督する州の取り組み ❏ *…Hank, who often stayed late riding herd on the day-to-day business of the magazine.* ハンクは雑誌の日常業務についてあれこれ指示し，残業で遅くなることがたびたびあった． **12** PHRASE 句 Someone who **rides the rails** travels by train, especially over a long period of time and without buying a ticket. 無賃乗車する [AM 米国英語] ❏ *It is 1933, the height of the Great Depression, and the hobos are busy riding the rails.* 大恐慌真っ只中の1933年で，渡り者の労働者は貨物列車にただ乗りしてせわしなく移動した．

▶ **ride out** PHRASAL VERB 句動詞 If someone **rides out** a storm or a crisis, they manage to survive a difficult period without suffering serious harm. 乗り切る ❏ *The Republicans think they can ride out the political storm.* 共和党はこの難しい政局をうまく乗り切れると見ている．

Word Partnership	ride は次の語句と使われる：	
N.	bus/car/subway/train ride, ride home ❹	
V.	give *someone* a ride, go for a ride, offer *someone* a ride ❹	
ADJ.	long ride, scenic ride, short ride, smooth ride ❹ ❺	

rid|er /rɑɪdər/ (riders) N-COUNT 可算名詞 A **rider** is someone who rides a horse, a bicycle, or a motorcycle as a hobby or job. You can also refer to someone who is riding a horse, a bicycle, or a motorcycle as a **rider**. 乗る人 ❏ *She is a very good and experienced rider.* 彼女は手綱さばきのうまい乗馬のベテランである．

ridge /rɪdʒ/ (ridges) **1** N-COUNT 可算名詞 A **ridge** is a long, narrow piece of raised land. 山の背 ❏ *…a high road along a mountain ridge.* 尾根伝いの本道 **2** N-COUNT 可算名詞 A **ridge** is a raised line on a flat surface. 細長い隆起 ❏ *…the bony ridge of the eye socket.* 眼窩（がんか）の骨の隆起 → see **mountain**

Word Link	cule ≈ small : minuscule, molecule, ridicule

Word Link	rid, ris ≈ laughing : deride, derision, ridicule

ridi|cule /rɪdɪkyul/ (ridicules, ridiculing, ridiculed) **1** V-T 他動詞 If you **ridicule** someone or **ridicule** their ideas or beliefs, you make fun of them in an unkind way. ばかにする ❏ *I admired her all the more for allowing them to ridicule her and never striking back.* 彼女に一層感心したのは，彼らにばかにされても何一つ言い返さなかったことである． **2** N-UNCOUNT 不可算名詞 If someone or something is an object of **ridicule** or is held up to **ridicule**, someone makes fun of them in an unkind way. ばかにすること ❏ *As a heavy child, she became the object of ridicule from classmates.* 太っていたせいで彼女は同級生からいつも笑い者にされた．

Thesaurus	ridicule また次を参照：	
V.	humiliate, mimic, mock; (ant.) praise ❶	

ri|dicu|lous /rɪdɪkyələs/ ADJ 形容詞 If you say that something or someone is **ridiculous**, you mean that they are very foolish. ばかげた ❏ *It is ridiculous to suggest we are having a romance.* 2人のことを

r

恋人みたいに言うなんてとんでもない.

ri|dicu|lous|ly /rɪdɪkyələsli/ ADV 副詞 You use **ridiculously** to emphasize the fact that you think something is unreasonable or very surprising. ばかばかしいほど，信じられないほど [EMPHASIS 強調] □ *Dana bought rolls of silk that seemed ridiculously cheap.* デーナが絹地が信じられないほど安かったので何巻か買った.

rid|ing /raɪdɪŋ/ N-UNCOUNT 不可算名詞 **Riding** is the activity or sport of riding horses. 乗馬 □ *The next morning we went riding again.* 次の朝も乗馬に行った.

rife /raɪf/ ADJ 形容詞 If you say that something, usually something bad, is **rife** in a place or that **the place is rife with** it, you mean that it is very common. 広まって [v-link ADJ] □ *Speculation is rife that he will be fired.* 彼が首になるという憶測が飛び交っています.

ri|fle /raɪfᵊl/ (rifles, rifling, rifled) ■ N-COUNT 可算名詞 A **rifle** is a gun with a long barrel. ライフル銃 □ *They shot him at point blank range with an automatic rifle.* 彼らは彼を至近距離から自動小銃で撃ちました. ■ V-T/V-I 他動詞/自動詞 If you **rifle through** things or **rifle** them, you make a quick search among them in order to find something or steal something. くまなく捜す □ *I discovered my husband rifling through the filing cabinet.* 夫がファイリングキャビネットをくまなく捜しているのを見つけた.

rift /rɪft/ (rifts) ■ N-COUNT 可算名詞 A **rift** between people or countries is a serious quarrel or disagreement that stops them from having a good relationship. 対立 □ *The interview reflected a growing rift between the president and Congress.* インタビューは大統領と議会との溝が深まっていることを表しています. ■ N-COUNT 可算名詞 A **rift** is a split that appears in something solid, especially in the ground. 溝 □ *The earth convulsed uncontrollably, a rift opened suddenly and, with a horrid sucking sound, swallowed the entire pool.* 地面が激しく揺れ，突然亀裂が走ったかと思うと，恐ろしい轟音（ごうおん）を立ててプールごと地面に吸い込まれていった.

rig /rɪg/ (rigs, rigging, rigged) ■ V-T If someone **rigs** an election, a job appointment, or a game, they dishonestly arrange it to get the result they want or to give someone an unfair advantage. 不正に操作する □ *She accused her opponents of rigging the vote.* 彼女は対立陣営が不正投票を行なったと非難しました. ■ N-COUNT 可算名詞 A **rig** is a large structure that is used for looking for oil or gas and for taking it out of the ground or the sea bed. 掘削装置 □ *...a supply vessel for oil rigs in the Gulf of Mexico.* メキシコ湾の石油掘削施設で使う補給船. ■ N-COUNT 可算名詞 A **rig** is a truck that is made in two or more sections which are joined together by metal bars, so that the vehicle can turn more easily. トレーラートラック [AM 米国英語] □ *An inspection of his rig showed that three of the brakes were faulty.* 彼のトレーラートラックを点検すると，ブレーキ3箇所に問題があることが判明した. → see oil

rig|ging /rɪgɪŋ/ ■ N-UNCOUNT 不可算名詞 Vote or ballot **rigging** is the act of dishonestly organizing an election to get a particular result. 不正操作 [usu supp N] □ *She was accused of corruption, of vote rigging on a massive scale.* 彼女は大々的な買収と不正投票を行なった罪で起訴されました. ■ N-UNCOUNT 不可算名詞 On a ship, the **rigging** is the ropes which support the ship's masts and sails. 索具（さくぐ）□ *...the howling of the wind in the rigging.* 帆でうなる風の音.

right

❶ CORRECT, APPROPRIATE, OR ACCEPTABLE
❷ DIRECTION AND POLITICAL GROUPINGS
❸ ENTITLEMENT
❹ DISCOURSE USES
❺ USED FOR EMPHASIS

❶ right /raɪt/ (rights, righting, righted)
↻ Please look at meaning ■ to see if the expression you are looking for is shown under another headword. ■ ADJ 形容詞 If something is **right**, it is correct and agrees with the facts. 正しい □ *That's absolutely right.* 全くその通りです. □ *Clocks never told the right time.* 時計が正しい時を告げたことはこれまでなかった. ● ADV 副詞 **Right** is also an adverb. 正しく [ADV after v] □ *He guessed right about some things.* 彼の推測どおりだったこともいくつかあった. ■ ADJ 形容詞 If you do something in the **right** way or in the **right** place, you do it as or where it should be done or was planned to be done. 正しい □ *Walking, done in the right way, is a form of aerobic exercise.* ウォーキングも正しく行なえば一種の有酸素運動になる. □ *They have computerized systems to ensure delivery of the right pizza to the right place.* 彼らは注文を受けたピザを確実に注文先に配達するためにコンピュータシステムを導入した. ● ADV 副詞 **Right** is also an adverb. 正しく [ADV after v] □ *To make sure I did everything right, I bought a fat instruction book.* すべてがうまくやれているか確かめるた

め，分厚い解説書を買った. ■ ADJ 形容詞 If you say that someone is seen in **all the right** places or knows **all the right** people, you mean that they go to places that are socially acceptable or know people who are socially acceptable. 適切な □ *He was always to be seen in the right places.* 彼の姿をいかがわしい場所で見かけるようなことは全然なかった. ■ ADJ 形容詞 If someone is **right about** something, they are correct in what they say or think about it. 正しい □ *Ron has been right about the result of every general election but one.* ロンの総選挙の予測は1度予想が外れただけがその他はいつも当たっている. ■ ADJ 形容詞 If something such as a choice, action, or decision is the **right** one, it is the best or most suitable one. 正しい □ *She'd made the right choice in leaving New York.* ニューヨークを離れるという彼女の選択は間違っていなかった. ■ ADJ 形容詞 If something is **not right**, there is something unsatisfactory about the situation or thing that you are talking about. 満足のいかない [v-link ADJ, with brd-neg] □ *Ratatouille doesn't taste right with any other oil.* ほかの油だとラタトゥイユの味がうまく出ない. ■ ADJ 形容詞 If you think that someone was **right** to do something, you think that there were good moral reasons why they did it. 正しい [v-link ADJ] □ *You were right to do what you did, under the circumstances.* ああいう状況だったからきみのやったことは間違ってないよ. ■ ADJ 形容詞 **Right** is used to refer to activities or actions that are considered to be morally good and acceptable. 正しい [v-link ADJ, oft with brd-neg] □ *It's not right, leaving her like this.* 彼女をこんなふうに見捨ててしまうのは考えものだ. ● N-UNCOUNT 不可算名詞 **Right** is also a noun. 正しい行為 □ *At least he knew right from wrong.* 彼でもやっていいことと悪いことぐらいは分かっていた. ● **right|ness** N-UNCOUNT 不可算名詞 正しさ □ *Many people have very strong opinions about the rightness or wrongness of abortion.* 妊娠中絶の是非をめぐってははっきりした意見を持つ人が多い. ■ V-T 他動詞 If you **right** something or if it **rights itself**, it returns to its normal or correct state, after being in an undesirable state. 正常な状態に戻す □ *They recognize the urgency of righting the economy.* 彼らは経済の建て直しが急務であることを認識している. ■ V-T 他動詞 If you **right** a wrong, you do something to make up for a mistake or something bad that you did in the past. 正す □ *We've made progress in righting the wrongs of the past.* 過去の過ちを正す取り組みは成果を上げています. ■ V-T 他動詞 If you **right** something that has fallen or rolled over, or if it **rights itself**, it returns to its normal upright position. 立て直す □ *He righted the yacht and continued the race.* 彼は倒れたヨットを起こしレースを続けた. ■ ADJ 形容詞 [ADJ n] The **right** side of a material is the side that is intended to be seen and that faces outward when it is made into something. 表の □ *Trim off excess fabric and turn the right side out.* 余分な生地を切って表（おもて）の面が外側にくるようにします. ■ PHRASE 句 If you say that things **are going right**, you mean that your life or a situation is developing as you intended or expected and you are pleased with it. 順調に進む □ *I can't think of anything in my life that's going right.* 僕の人生でうまくいっていることなんて1つもないよ. ■ PHRASE 句 If you **put** something **right**, you correct something that was wrong or that was causing problems. 正す □ *We've discovered what went wrong and are going to put it right.* どこが間違っていたか分かったのでこれから正していきます. ■ **heart in the right place** → see heart ■ **it serves you right** → see serve

❷ right /raɪt/

The spelling **Right** is also used for meaning ❸.
つづりの **Right** は ❸ の意味にも使われる.

■ N-SING 単数名詞 The **right** is one of two opposite directions, sides, or positions. If you are facing north and you turn to the right, you will be facing east. In the word "to," the "o" is to the right of the "t." 右 □ *Ahead of you on the right will be a lovely garden.* 前方の右に美しい庭がある. ● ADV 副詞 **Right** is also an adverb. 右に [ADV after v] □ *Turn right into the street.* 右に曲がって通りに出てください. ■ ADJ 形容詞 Your **right** arm, leg, or ear, for example, is the one which is on the right side of your body. Your **right** shoe or glove is the one which is intended to be worn on your right foot or hand. 右の [ADJ n] □ *She shattered her right leg in a fall.* 彼女は転落して右足を粉砕骨折した. ■ N-SING-COLL 集合的単数名詞 You can refer to people who support the political ideals of capitalism and conservatism as **the right**. They are often contrasted with **the left**, who support the political ideals of socialism. 右派 □ *The Republican Right despise him.* 共和党右派は彼を毛嫌いしている.

Thesaurus	*right* また次を参照：
ADJ.	appropriate, correct, just, true; (ant.) unjust, wrong ❶
	conservative, right-wing; (ant.) left, liberal ❷ ❸

❸ right /raɪt/ (rights) ■ N-PLURAL 複数名詞 Your **rights** are what you are morally or legally entitled to do or to have. 権利 □ *They don't know their rights.* 彼らは自分たちにどんな権利があるのか知らない. ■ N-SING 単数名詞 If you have a **right to** do or to have something, you are morally or legally entitled to do

it or to have it. 権利 ❏ ...*a woman's right to choose.* 女性が中絶を選ぶ権利. **3** N-PLURAL 複数名詞 If someone has **the rights to** a story or book, they are legally allowed to publish it or reproduce it in another form, and nobody else can do so without their permission. 版権 ❏ *An agent bought the rights to his life.* あるエージェントが彼の伝記の版権を得た. **4** PHRASE 句 If something is not the case but you think that it should be, you can say that **by rights** it should be the case. 本来ならば ❏ *She did work which by rights should be done by someone else.* 彼女は本来ならばほかの人がすべき仕事までこなした. **5** PHRASE 句 If someone is a successful or respected person **in their own right**, they are successful or respected because of their own efforts and talents rather than those of the people they are closely connected with. 人に頼らずに ❏ *Although now a celebrity in her own right, actress Lynn Redgrave knows the difficulties of living in the shadow of her famous older sister.* 女優リン・グレーブは今では自力でスターの座を手にしたが, 有名な姉をもつ妹として生きていく難しさを痛感している. **6** PHRASE 句 If you say that you **reserve the right** to do something, you mean that you will do it if you feel that it is necessary. 権利を保有する ❏ *He reserved the right to change his mind.* 彼は最終的な態度を保留しています. **7** PHRASE 句 If you say that someone is **within** their **rights to** do something, you mean that they are morally or legally entitled to do it. 〜する権利がある ❏ *You were quite within your rights to refuse to cooperate with him.* あなたは彼への協力を断る当然の権利があった.

❹ **right** /raɪt/ **1** ADV 副詞 You use **right** in order to attract someone's attention or to indicate that you have dealt with one thing so you can go on to another. では, じゃあ [SPOKEN 口語] [ADV cl] ❏ *Right, I'll be back in a minute.* では, すぐに戻ります. **2** CONVENTION 慣習表現 You can use **right** to check whether what you have just said is correct. 〜でしょう, 〜ね [SPOKEN 口語] ❏ *They have a small plane, right?* あの人たちは小型飛行機を持っているよね. **3** ADV 副詞 You can say "**right**" to show that you are listening to what someone is saying and that you accept it or understand it. そうだね, わかった [SPOKEN 口語] [ADV as reply] ❏ *"It was probably much harder for older people. Don't you think?"—"Right."* 「きっと年配者にはずっと難しかったんだ. そう思わない?」「そうだね」 **4** → see also **all right**

❺ **right** /raɪt/ **1** ADV 副詞 You can use **right** to emphasize the precise place, position, or time of something. ちょうど [EMPHASIS 強調] [ADV adv/prep] ❏ *The back of a car appeared right in front of him.* 車の後部がいきなり彼の目の前に現れた. **2** ADV 副詞 You can use **right** to emphasize how far something moves or extends or how long it continues. 〜までずっと [EMPHASIS 強調] [ADV prep/adv] ❏ ...*the highway that runs through the neutral zone right to the army positions.* 軍の陣地までずっと続く中立帯を通り抜ける幹線道路. **3** ADV 副詞 You can use **right** to emphasize that an action or state is complete. すっかり, 完全に [EMPHASIS 強調] [ADV adv/prep] ❏ *The candle had burned right down.* ろうそくがすっかり燃え尽きた. **4** ADV 副詞 If you say that something happened **right after** a particular time or event or **right before** it, you mean that it happened immediately after or before it. すぐ, 直〜 [EMPHASIS 強調] [ADV prep/adv] ❏ *All of a sudden, right after the summer, Mother gets married.* 何の前触れもなく夏が終わるとすぐに, 母が結婚する. **5** ADV 副詞 If you say **I'll be right there** or **I'll be right back**, you mean that you will get to a place or get back to it in a very short time. すぐに, あっという間に [EMPHASIS 強調] [ADV adv] ❏ *I'm going to get some water. I'll be right back.* ちょっとお水を飲んでくる. すぐに戻るよ. **6** PHRASE 句 If you do something **right away**, you do it immediately. すぐに [INFORMAL くだけた, EMPHASIS 強調] ❏ *He wants to see you right away.* 彼はきみに今すぐ会いたがっています. **7** PHRASE 句 You can use **right now** to emphasize that you are referring to the present moment. たった今 [INFORMAL くだけた, EMPHASIS 強調] ❏ *Right now I'm feeling very excited.* 今とてもワクワクしているんです.

right an|gle (**right angles**) **1** N-COUNT 可算名詞 A **right angle** is an angle of ninety degrees. A square has four right angles. 直角 **2** PHRASE 句 If two things are **at right angles**, they are situated so that they form an angle of 90° where they touch each other. You can also say that one thing is **at right angles to** another. 〜と直角に ❏ ...*two lasers at right angles.* 直角に交わるレーザー光線

right-click (**right-clicks, right-clicking, right-clicked**) V-I 自動詞 To **right-click** or to **right-click on** something means to press the right-hand button on a computer mouse. 右クリックする [COMPUTING コンピューティング] ❏ *All you have to do is right-click on the desktop and select New Folder.* デスクトップで右クリックして「新しいフォルダ」を選択するだけでいい.

right|eous /raɪtʃəs/ ADJ 形容詞 If you think that someone behaves or lives in a way that is morally good, you can say that they are **righteous**. People sometimes use **righteous** to express their disapproval when they think someone is only behaving in this way so that others will admire or support them. 道徳的な, 偽善な [FORMAL 形式ばった] ❏ *Aren't you afraid of being seen as a righteous crusader?* 正義の活動家だとみなされるのを恐れていないのですか?

right|ful /raɪtfəl/ ADJ 形容詞 If you say that someone or something has returned to its **rightful** place or position, they have returned to the place or position that you think they should have. 正当な [ADJ n] ❏ *We have restored Hamill to his rightful place as editor.* ハミルを編集者という彼に適切な職場に復帰させました. ● **right|ful|ly** ADV 副詞 [ADV group] 正当に ❏ *Jealousy is the feeling that someone else has something that rightfully belongs to you.* しっととは本来自分が所有すべきものを他の人が持っているという感情である.

right-hand ADJ 形容詞 If something is on the **right-hand** side of something, it is positioned on the right of it. 右側の, 右手の [ADJ n] ❏ ...*a church on the right-hand side of the road.* 道路の右手にある教会

right-handed ADJ 形容詞 Someone who is **right-handed** uses their right hand rather than their left hand for activities such as writing and sports, and for picking things up. 右利きの ● ADV 副詞 **Right-handed** is also an adverb. 右利きで [ADV after v] ❏ *I batted left-handed and bowled right-handed.* 僕は左で打って右で投げてました.

right-hand man (**right-hand men**) N-COUNT 可算名詞 Someone's **right-hand man** is the person who acts as their chief assistant and helps and supports them a lot in their work. 右腕, 腹心 ❏ *He is Rupert Murdoch's right-hand man at News International.* 彼はニュースインターナショナル社でルパート・マードックの右腕だ.

right tri|an|gle (**right triangles**) N-COUNT 可算名詞 A **right triangle** has one angle that is a right angle. 直角三角形 [AM 米国英語]
→ see **shape**

right-wing

> The spelling **right wing** is also used for meaning **2**.

> つづりの **right wing** は **2** の意味にも使われる.

1 ADJ 形容詞 A **right-wing** person or group has conservative or capitalist views. 右派の, 保守派の ❏ ...*a right-wing government.* 右翼政権 **2** N-SING 単数名詞 The **right wing** of a political party consists of the members who have the most conservative or the most capitalist views. 右派, 保守派 ❏ ...*the right wing of the Republican Party.* 共和党の右派

right-winger (**right-wingers**) N-COUNT 可算名詞 If you think someone has views which are more right-wing than most other members of their party, you can say they are a **right-winger**. 右派の人 ❏ *Across Europe, hard-line right-wingers are gaining power.* ヨーロッパ全域で強硬な右派が台頭している.

rig|id /rɪdʒɪd/ **1** ADJ 形容詞 Laws, rules, or systems that are **rigid** cannot be changed or varied, and are therefore considered to be rather severe. 融通の利かない [DISAPPROVAL 不賛成] ❏ *Several colleges in our study have rigid rules about student conduct.* 当研究部門には学生の品行について厳格な規則を設けた大学がある. ● **rigid|ity** /rɪdʒɪdɪti/ N-UNCOUNT 不可算名詞 厳格さ ❏ ...*the rigidity of government policy.* 政府の方針の厳格さ ● **rig|id|ly** ADV 副詞 [ADV with v] 厳格に ❏ *The caste system was so rigidly enforced that non-Hindus were not even allowed inside a Hindu home.* カースト制は非常に厳格に遵守されていて非ヒンズー教徒はヒンズー教徒の家に入ることさえ認められなった. **2** ADJ 形容詞 If you disapprove of someone because you think they are not willing to change their way of thinking or behaving, you can describe them as **rigid**. 頑固な [DISAPPROVAL 不賛成] ❏ *She was a fairly rigid person who had strong religious views.* 彼女は宗教的見解を持ったかなり頑固な人だった. **3** ADJ 形容詞 A **rigid** substance or object is stiff and does not bend, stretch, or twist easily. 硬い, 硬直した ❏ ...*rigid plastic containers.* 硬質プラスチックの容器 ● **rigid|ity** N-UNCOUNT 不可算名詞 硬さ, 硬直性 ❏ ...*the strength and rigidity of glass.* ガラスの強度と硬直性

rig|or /rɪgər/ (**rigors**) **1** N-PLURAL 複数名詞 If you refer to **the rigors** of an activity or job, you mean the difficult, demanding, or unpleasant things that are associated with it. 厳しさ, 過酷さ ❏ *They're accustomed to the rigors of army life.* 彼らは軍隊生活の厳しさに慣れています. **2** N-UNCOUNT 不可算名詞 If something is done with **rigor**, it is done in a strict, thorough way. 厳密さ ❏ *The prince had performed his social duties with professional rigor.* 王子は専門職的な厳密さで社会義務を行った.

rig|or|ous /rɪgərəs/ **1** ADJ 形容詞 A test, system, or procedure that is **rigorous** is very thorough and strict. 厳密な ❏ *The selection process is based on rigorous tests of competence and experience.* 選考過程は厳格な適性検査と経験に基づいている. ● **rig|or|ous|ly** ADV 副詞 厳密に ❏ ...*rigorously conducted research.* 厳密に行われた調査 **2** ADJ 形容詞 If someone is **rigorous** in the way that they do something, they are very careful and thorough. 厳しい, 厳格な ❏ *He is rigorous in his control of expenditure.* 彼は出費管理に厳しい.

rim /rɪm/ (**rims**) **1** N-COUNT 可算名詞 The **rim** of a container such as a cup or glass is the edge that goes all the way around the top. 縁, へり ❏ *She looked at him over the rim of her glass.* 彼女は眼鏡の縁越しに彼を見た. **2** N-COUNT 可算名詞 The **rim** of a circular object is its outside edge. 周辺, 縁 ❏ ...*a round mirror with white*

r

metal rim. 白い金属製のフレームがついた丸い鏡

rind /raɪnd/ (rinds) **1** N-VAR 可変性名詞 The rind of a fruit such as a lemon or orange is its thick outer skin. (レモン・オレンジなどの) 皮 □ ...grated lemon rind. おろしたレモンの皮 **2** N-VAR 可変性名詞 The rind of cheese or bacon is the hard outer edge which you do not usually eat. (チーズ・ベーコンなどの) 皮 □ ...a cream cheese with a soft rind. 柔らかい皮のついたクリームチーズ

ring
❶ TELEPHONING OR MAKING A SOUND
❷ SHAPES AND GROUPS

❶ ring /rɪŋ/ (rings, ringing, rang, rung)
↪ Please look at meaning **8** to see if the expression you are looking for is shown under another headword. **1** V-I 自動詞 When a telephone rings, it makes a sound to let you know that someone is phoning you. 鳴る □ As soon as he got home, the phone rang. 彼が家に着くとすぐに電話が鳴った. ● N-COUNT 可算名詞 Ring is also a noun. 呼び出し音、コール音 □ After at least eight rings, an ancient-sounding maid answered the phone. 少なくとも8回の呼び出し音の後で、年老いた声をしたメイドが電話に出た. ● ringing N-UNCOUNT 不可算名詞 鳴ること □ She was jolted out of her sleep by the ringing of the telephone. 彼女は電話の音にびっくりして目が覚めた. **2** V-T/V-I 他動詞/自動詞 When you ring someone, you telephone them. 電話をかける [mainly BRIT 主に英国英語; AM usually call 米国英語では通常 call] ● PHRASAL VERB 句動詞 Ring up means the same as ring. 電話をかける **3** V-T/V-I 他動詞/自動詞 When you ring a bell or when a bell rings, it makes a sound. 鳴らす [他動詞]、鳴る [自動詞] □ He heard the school bell ring. 彼はチャイムが鳴るのが聞こえた. ● N-COUNT 可算名詞 Ring is also a noun. 鳴る音 □ There was a ring of the bell. ベルの音がした. ● ringing N-UNCOUNT 不可算名詞 鳴り響く音 □ ...the ringing of church bells. 教会の鳴り響く音 **4** V-I 自動詞 If you say that a place is ringing with sound, usually pleasant sound, you mean that the place is completely filled with that sound. 鳴り響く [LITERARY 文語的] □ The whole place was ringing with music. その場所全体に音楽が鳴り響いていた. **5** N-SING 単数名詞 You can use ring to describe a quality that something such as a statement, discussion, or argument seems to have. For example, if an argument has a familiar ring, it seems familiar. 感じ、響き □ His proud boast of leading "the party of low taxation" has a hollow ring. 「軽税の党」を第一とした彼の自信に溢れた演説には空疎な響きがあった. **6** PHRASE 句 If you give someone a ring, you phone them. 電話をかける [mainly BRIT 主に英国英語, INFORMAL くだけた] [AM usually call 米国英語では通常 call] □ We'll give him a ring as soon as we get back. 戻り次第彼に電話をします. **7** PHRASE 句 If a statement rings true, it seems to be true or genuine. If it rings hollow, it does not seem to be true or genuine. 真実味がある/ないする □ Joanna's denial rang true. ジョアンナの否定の仕方には真実味があった. **8** → see also ringing **9** to ring a bell → see bell

▸ **ring back** PHRASAL VERB 句動詞 [no passive] If you ring someone back, you phone them either because they phoned you earlier and you were not there or because you did not finish an earlier telephone conversation. 折り返し電話をする、かけ直す [BRIT 英国英語; AM call back 米国英語 call back]

▸ **ring in** PHRASAL VERB 句動詞 If you ring in, you phone a place, such as the place where you work. 電話を入れる [BRIT 英国英語; AM call in 米国英語 call in]

▸ **ring off** PHRASAL VERB 句動詞 When you ring off, you put down the receiver at the end of a telephone call. 電話を切る [BRIT 英国英語; AM hang up 米国英語 hang up]

▸ **ring round** or **ring around** PHRASAL VERB 句動詞 If you ring round or ring around, you phone several people, usually when you are trying to organize something or to find some information. 何件か電話をする [BRIT 英国英語; AM call around 米国英語 call around]

▸ **ring up** **1** → see ring **❶** **2** PHRASAL VERB 句動詞 If a store clerk rings up a sale on a cash register, he or she presses the keys in order to record the amount that is being spent. レジに打つ □ She was ringing up her sale on an ancient cash register. 彼女は売上を古びたレジに打ち込んでいた. **3** PHRASAL VERB 句動詞 If a company rings up an amount of money, usually a large amount of money, it makes that amount of money in sales or profits. 達成する □ The advertising agency rang up 1.4 billion dollars in yearly sales. その広告会社は14億ドルの年間売り上げを達成した.

❷ ring /rɪŋ/ (rings, ringing, ringed) **1** N-COUNT 可算名詞 A ring is a small circle of metal or other substance that you wear on your finger as jewelry. 指輪 □ ...a gold wedding ring. 金の結婚指輪 **2** N-COUNT 可算名詞 An object or substance that is in the shape of a circle can be described as a ring. 輪状のもの、リング □ Frank took a large ring of keys from his pocket. フランクはポケットからかぎのついた大きなリングを取り出した. **3** N-COUNT 可算名詞 A group of people or things arranged in a circle can be described as a ring.

丸、輪 □ They then formed a ring around the square. そして彼らは広場の辺りで輪になった. **4** N-COUNT 可算名詞 At a boxing or wrestling match or a circus, the ring is the place where the contest or performance takes place. It consists of an enclosed space with seats around it. リング、土俵 □ He will never again be allowed inside a boxing ring. 彼はボクシングのリング内には2度と入場を認められないだろう. **5** N-COUNT 可算名詞 You can refer to an organized group of people who are involved in an illegal activity as a ring. 一団 □ Police are investigating the suspected drug ring at the school. 警察はその学校の麻薬問題で容疑のかかっている集団について調査している. **6** N-COUNT 可算名詞 → see burner **7** V-T 他動詞 If a building or place is ringed with or by something, it is surrounded by it. 取り囲む [BRIT 英国英語] [usu passive] □ The areas are sealed off and ringed by troops. その地域は閉鎖されて軍隊に取り囲まれている. → see circle, hand, jewelry

ring bind|er (ring binders) N-COUNT 可算名詞 A ring binder is a file with hard covers, which you can insert pages into. The pages are held in by metal rings on a bar attached to the inside of the file. リングバインダー

ring|ing /rɪŋɪŋ/ **1** ADJ 形容詞 A ringing sound is loud and can be heard very clearly. 鳴り響く、響き渡る [ADJ n] □ He hit the metal steps with a ringing crash. 彼は鉄の階段でガラガラガッチャンと音を立てて墜落した. **2** ADJ 形容詞 A ringing statement or declaration is one that is made forcefully and is intended to make a powerful impression. 力強い、明確な [ADJ n] □ ...the party's 14th congress, which gave a ringing endorsement to capitalist-style economic reforms. 資本主義的経済改革に力強い支持を示した第14回党大会

ring tone (ring tones) N-COUNT 可算名詞 The ring tone is the sound made by a telephone, especially a cell phone, when it rings. 着信音、リングトーン □ They offer 70 hours' standby time, 2hr. 50min. talk time, and 15 ring tones. 連続待受時間が70時間、通話時間が2時間50時間、そして15種類のリングトーンを搭載している.

rink /rɪŋk/ (rinks) N-COUNT 可算名詞 A rink is a large area covered with ice where people go to ice-skate, or a large area of concrete where people go to roller-skate. リンク □ The other skaters were ordered off the rink. スケートをしていたほかの人たちはリンクから出るように命じられた.

rinse /rɪns/ (rinses, rinsing, rinsed) **1** V-T 他動詞 When you rinse something, you wash it in clean water in order to remove dirt or soap from it. すすぐ、さっと洗う □ It's important to rinse the rice to remove the starch. ヌカを落とすために米を研ぐことが大切です. ● N-COUNT 可算名詞 Rinse is also a noun. すすぎ洗い □ Clean skin means plenty of lather followed by a rinse with water. 清潔な肌というのはたくさんのせっけんの泡の後に水洗いをすることです. **2** V-T 他動詞 If you rinse your mouth, you clean it by filling your mouth with water or with a liquid that kills germs, then spitting it out. うがいをする □ Use a toothbrush on your tongue as well, and rinse your mouth frequently. 舌にも歯ブラシを使い、頻繁にうがいをしなさい. ● PHRASAL VERB 句動詞 Rinse out means the same as rinse. うがいをする □ After her meal she invariably rinsed out her mouth. 彼女は食後に必ずうがいをする. ● N-MASS 質量名詞 Rinse is also a noun. うがい □ ...mouth rinses with fluoride. フッ化物入りの口内洗浄剤

riot /raɪət/ (riots, rioting, rioted) **1** N-COUNT 可算名詞 When there is a riot, a crowd of people behave violently in a public place, for example they fight, throw stones, or damage buildings and vehicles. 暴動 □ Twelve inmates have been killed during a riot at the prison. 刑務所で起きた暴動で囚人12名が死亡した. **2** V-I 自動詞 If people riot, they behave violently in a public place. 暴動を起こす □ Last year 600 inmates rioted, starting fires and building barricades. 昨年は600名の囚人が、放火をしたりバリケードを築いたりなどの暴動を起こした. ● ri|ot|er (rioters) N-COUNT 可算名詞 暴徒 □ The militia dispersed the rioters. 民兵は暴徒を追い散らした. ● ri|ot|ing N-UNCOUNT 不可算名詞 暴動 □ At least fifteen people are now known to have died in three days of rioting. 3日間続いた暴動において現段階で少なくとも15名が死亡したと伝えられている. **3** N-SING 単数名詞 If you say that there is a riot of something pleasant such as color, you mean that there is a large amount of various types of it. 多彩さ [APPROVAL 賛成] □ It would be a riot of color, of poppies and irises and flowers of every kind. ケシやアヤメなどの各種の花で色とりどりだろう. **4** PHRASE 句 If someone in authority reads you the riot act, they tell you that you will be punished unless you start behaving yourself. 止めるように命ずる、厳しくしかる □ I'm glad you read the riot act to Billy. He's still a kid and still needs to be told what to do. ビリーにきつく言ってくれて助かったよ. 彼はまだ子供でどうしたらいいか言われなければ分からないんだ. **5** PHRASE 句 If people run riot, they behave in a wild and uncontrolled manner. 騒ぎまわる □ Rampaging prisoners ran riot through the jail. たけり狂った囚人が刑務所で騒ぎ回った. **6** PHRASE 句 If something such as your imagination runs riot, it is not limited or controlled, and produces ideas that are new or exciting, rather than sensible. 次々とわき出る □ She dressed strictly for comfort and economy, but let her imagination run riot with costume jewelry. 彼女は快適で経済的な服のみを身につけたが、アクセサリーには想像力を生かした.

rip /rɪp/ (rips, ripping, ripped) **1** V-T/V-I 他動詞/自動詞 When something **rips** or when you **rip** it, you tear it forcefully with your hands or with a tool such as a knife. 引き裂く, びりっと破る □ I felt the banner rip as we were pushed in opposite directions. 私たちが反対方向に押されたとき垂れ幕がびりっと破れたのを感じた. **2** N-COUNT 可算名詞 A **rip** is a long cut or split in something made of cloth or paper. 裂け目, 破れ目 □ Looking at the rip in her new dress, she flew into a rage. 彼女は新しいドレスが破れているのを見て激怒した. **3** V-T 他動詞 If you **rip** something away, you remove it quickly and forcefully. はぎ取る □ He ripped away a wire that led to the alarm button. 彼は, 警報ボタンにつながっている線をむしり取った. **4** V-I 自動詞 If something **rips** into someone or something or **rips** through them, it enters that person or thing so quickly and forcefully that it often goes completely through them. 通り抜ける □ A volley of bullets ripped into the facing wall. 弾丸の一斉射撃により外装壁を通り抜けた. **5** PHRASE 句 If you **let it rip**, you do something forcefully and without trying to control yourself. 成り行きに任せる, ほうっておく [INFORMAL くだけた] □ Turn the guitars up full and let it rip. ギターの音量を全開にして音の流れに任せなさい.

▶ **rip off** PHRASAL VERB 句動詞 If someone **rips** you **off**, they cheat you by charging you too much money for something or by selling you something that is broken or damaged. ぼる, ぼったくる [INFORMAL くだけた] □ The bigger, more reputable online casinos are not going to rip you off. より大手の信頼のできるオンライン・カジノではぼられない. → see also **rip-off**

▶ **rip up** PHRASAL VERB 句動詞 If you **rip** something **up**, you tear it into small pieces. びりびりに破る □ If we wrote, I think he would rip up the letter. もし私たちが手紙を書けば, 彼はその手紙をびりびりに破ると思う.

→ see **cut**

ripe /raɪp/ (riper, ripest) **1** ADJ 形容詞 **Ripe** fruit or grain is fully grown and ready to eat. 熟した □ Always choose firm, but ripe fruit. 常に身が締まって熟した果物を選びなさい. **2** ADJ 形容詞 If a situation is **ripe for** a particular development or event, you mean that development or event is likely to happen soon. 一の時を迎えようとしている, 機が熟している [v-link ADJ "for" n/-ing] □ A hospital consultant said conditions were ripe for an outbreak of cholera and typhoid. これらが腸チフスの発生に十分な条件がそろっていると医師が述べた. **3** PHRASE 句 If someone lives to a **ripe old age**, they live until they are very old. 高齢 □ He lived to the ripe old age of 95. 彼は95歳という高齢まで長生きした.

rip|en /raɪpən/ (ripens, ripening, ripened) V-T/V-I 他動詞/自動詞 When crops **ripen** or when the sun **ripens** them, they become ripe. 熟する □ I'm waiting for the apples to ripen. リンゴが熟するのを待っているんだ.

rip-off (rip-offs) N-COUNT 可算名詞 If you say that something that you bought was a **rip-off**, you mean that you were charged too much money or that it was of very poor quality. ぼったくり [INFORMAL くだけた] □ The service charge is a rip-off, but I'm willing to pay if I'm guaranteed a seat. サービス料は不当に高いが席を確保できるなら喜んで支払います.

rip|ple /rɪpᵊl/ (ripples, rippling, rippled) **1** N-COUNT 可算名詞 **Ripples** are little waves on the surface of water caused by the wind or by something moving in or on the water. さざ波 □ Gleaming ripples cut the lake's surface. きらきらしたさざ波が湖面を切り刻んだ. **2** V-T/V-I 他動詞/自動詞 When the surface of an area of water **ripples** or when something **ripples** it, a number of little waves appear on it. さざ波を立てる [他動詞], さざ波が立つ [自動詞] □ You throw a pebble in a pool and it ripples. 小石を水に投げると さざ波が立つ. **3** V-I 自動詞 If something such as a feeling **ripples** over someone's body, it moves across it or through it. さざ波のように伝わる [LITERARY 文語的] □ A chill shiver rippled over his skin. 寒くてブルブルっと震えた. **4** N-COUNT 可算名詞 If an event causes **ripples**, its effects gradually spread, causing several other events to happen one after the other. 連鎖反応, 波紋 □ If Brazil defaults on its foreign debt, it will cause ripples throughout the world. ブラジルが外債の履行を怠ると世界中に波紋が広がる.

rise /raɪz/ (rises, rising, rose, risen) **1** V-I 自動詞 If something **rises**, it moves upward. 昇る, 上がる □ Wilson's ice-cold eyes watched the smoke rise from his cigarette. ウィルソンは氷のように冷たい目つきでたばこから煙が立ち昇るのを見ていた. ● PHRASAL VERB 句動詞 **Rise up** means the same as **rise**. 昇る, 上がる □ Spray rose up from the surface of the water. しぶきが水面から吹き出た. **2** V-I 自動詞 When you **rise**, you stand up. 立ち上がる [FORMAL 形式ばった] □ Luther rose slowly from the chair. ルターはゆっくりといすから立ち上がった. ● PHRASAL VERB 句動詞 **Rise up** means the same as **rise**. 立ち上がる □ The only thing I wanted was to rise up from the table and leave this house. 私はただ席を立ってこの家から出たかった. **3** V-I 自動詞 When you **rise**, you get out of bed. 起床する, 起きる [FORMAL 形式ばった] □ Tony had risen early and gone to the cottage to work. トニーは早起きをしてコテージに仕事に行った. **4** V-I 自動詞 When the sun or moon **rises**, it appears in the sky. 昇る, 出る □ He wanted to be over the line of the ridge before the sun had risen. 彼は日の出前に尾根の向こうに行きたがっていた. **5** V-I 自動詞 You can say that

something **rises** when it appears as a large, tall shape. そびえる [LITERARY 文語的] □ The building rose before him, tall and stately. その建物が彼の目の前に高く堂々とそびえていた. ● PHRASAL VERB 句動詞 **Rise up** means the same as **rise**. そびえる □ The White Mountains rose up before me. ホワイト山脈が前にそびえていた. **6** V-I 自動詞 If the level of something such as the water in a river **rises**, it becomes higher. (水かさなどが) 増す (水位が) 上がる □ The waters continue to rise as more than 1,000 people are evacuated. 水面は上昇を続けており, 100人以上の住民が避難しています. **7** V-I 自動詞 If land **rises**, it slopes upward. 上り坂になる □ He looked up the slope of land that rose from the house. 彼はその家から始まる上り坂を見上げた. **8** V-T/V-I 他動詞/自動詞 If an amount **rises**, it increases. 増加する, 上昇する □ Interest rates rise from 4% to 5%. 金利が4%から5%に上昇した. □ Tourist trips of all kinds rose by 10.5% between 1977 and 1987. 1977年から1987年までの期間に観光旅行全体が10.5%増加した. □ Exports rose 23%. 輸出が23%増加した. **9** N-COUNT 可算名詞 A **rise** in the amount of something is an increase in it. 増加 □ …the expectation of a rise in interest rates. アメリカでさらに上昇する見通し **10** N-SING 単数名詞 The **rise of** a movement or activity is an increase in its popularity or influence. 台頭, 高まり □ The rise of racism in America is a serious concern. アメリカでの人種差別の台頭は深刻な問題だ. **11** N-COUNT 可算名詞 A **rise** is an increase in your wages or your salary. 昇給, 賃上げ [BRIT 英国英語; AM **raise** 米国英語 **raise**] □ If the level of something rises, it becomes stronger. 強まる □ The wind was still rising, approaching a force nine gale. 風は依然として強まっており, 風力9の強風になる勢いだった. **13** V-I 自動詞 If a sound **rises** or if someone's voice **rises**, it becomes louder or higher. 大きくなる, 高くなる □ "Bernard?" Her voice rose hysterically. 「バーナード?」彼女の声が興奮して高くなった. **14** V-I 自動詞 When the people in a country **rise**, they try to defeat the government or army that is controlling them. 反乱を起こす □ President Bush had encouraged the Panamanian military to rise against General Noriega. ブッシュ大統領はパナマ軍がノリエガ将軍に対して反乱を起こすよう促した. ● PHRASAL VERB 句動詞 **Rise up** means the same as **rise**. 反乱を起こす □ He warned that if the government moved against him the people would rise up. 彼は, 政府が彼に逆らうと国民が反乱を起こすだろうと警告した. **15** V-I 自動詞 If someone **rises to** a higher position or status, they become more important, successful, or powerful. 昇進する, 出世する □ She is a strong woman who has risen to the top of a deeply sexist organization. 彼女は性差別がひどい組織のトップにまで昇進した強い女性だ. ● PHRASAL VERB 句動詞 **Rise up** means the same as **rise**. 昇進する □ I started with Hoover 26 years ago in sales and rose up through the ranks. 私は26年前フーバー社のセールス担当で入社し, 出世の階段を上った. **16** N-SING 単数名詞 The **rise** of someone is the process by which they become more important, successful, or powerful. 昇進, 出世 □ Haig's rise was fueled by an all-consuming sense of patriotic duty. ヘーグの昇進は熱心な愛国者としての義務感に支えられた. **17** PHRASE 句 If something **gives rise to** an event or situation, it causes that event or situation to happen. 引き起こす □ Low levels of choline in the body can give rise to high blood pressure. 体内のコリン値が低いと高血圧を引き起こすことがある. **18** to **rise to the challenge** → see **challenge** **19** to **rise to the occasion** → see **occasion**

> You should be careful not to confuse the verbs **rise** and **raise**. **Rise** is an intransitive verb and cannot be followed by an object, whereas **raise** is a transitive verb and is usually followed by an object. **Rise** can also not be used in the passive. □ The number of dead is likely to rise. …the government's decision to raise prices. Both **raise** and **rise** can be used as nouns with meaning pay increase. **Raise** is used in American English, and **rise** is used in British English. □ Millions of Americans get a pay raise today. …a rise of at least 12 per cent.

▶ **rise above** PHRASAL VERB 句動詞 If you **rise above** a difficulty or problem, you manage not to let it affect you. 克服する □ It tells the story of an aspiring young man's attempt to rise above the squalor of the street. それは街路の汚らしい生活からはい出ようとした意欲的な若者の話だ.

▶ **rise up** → see **rise** 1, 2, 5, 14, 15

risk /rɪsk/ (risks, risking, risked) **1** N-VAR 可変性名詞 If there is a **risk of** something unpleasant, there is a possibility that it will happen. 危険性 □ There is a small risk of brain damage from the procedure. 治療処置により脳損傷を起こす危険性が少しある. **2** N-COUNT 可算名詞 If something that you do is a **risk**, it might have unpleasant or undesirable results. リスク, 危険 □ You're taking a big risk showing this to Kravis. これをクラビスに見せるなんて大きな危険を冒しているよ. **3** N-COUNT 可算名詞 If you say that something or someone is a **risk**, you mean they are likely to cause harm. 危険, 害 □ It's being obese that constitutes a health risk. 健康に害を及ぼすのは肥満であることだ. **4** N-COUNT 可算名詞 If you are considered a good **risk**, a bank or store thinks that it is safe to lend you money or let you have goods without paying for them at the time. 信用できる顧客 □ Before providing the cash, they will have to decide whether you are a good or bad risk. 現金を渡す前に, 信用できる顧客かどうかを判断しなければならない. **5** V-T 他動詞 If

you **risk** something unpleasant, you do something which might result in that thing happening or affecting you. 〜という結果になる可能性がある ❑ *Those who fail to register risk severe penalties.* 登録をし忘れる者には厳しい処罰が行われる可能性がある. **6** V-T 他動詞 If you **risk** doing something, you do it, even though you know that it might have undesirable consequences. 危険を冒す ❑ *The skipper was not willing to risk taking his ship through the straits until he could see where he was going.* 船長は行き先が見えるようになるまでは船で海峡を通る危険を冒したくなかった. **7** V-T 他動詞 If you **risk** your life or something else important, you behave in a way that might result in it being lost or harmed. 〜を失う覚悟で〜する ❑ *She risked her own life to help a disabled woman.* 彼女は死を覚悟で障害のある女性を助けた. **8** PHRASE 句 To be **at risk** means to be in a situation where something unpleasant might happen. 危険にさらされて ❑ *Up to 25,000 jobs are still at risk.* 最高2万5千の職がなお危険にさらされている. **9** PHRASE 句 If you do something **at the risk of** something unpleasant happening, you do it even though you know that the unpleasant thing might happen as a result. 〜を覚悟で ❑ *At the risk of being repetitive, I will say again that statistics are only a guide.* 繰り返しになるのを覚悟で再度申し上げますが, 統計は単なる手引きにすぎません. **10** PHRASE 句 If you tell someone that they are doing something **at their own risk**, you are warning them that, if they are harmed, it will be their own responsibility. 自分の責任で ❑ *Those who wish to come here will do so at their own risk.* ここに来ることを希望する者は各自自分の責任で行ってください. **11** PHRASE 句 If you **run** the **risk of** doing or experiencing something undesirable, you do something knowing that the undesirable thing might happen as a result. 危険を冒す ❑ *The officers had run the risk of being dismissed.* 将校は解雇処分になる危険を冒した.

Thesaurus	*risk* また次を参照:
N.	danger, gamble, hazard; (ant.) safety **2 3**
V.	chance, endanger, gamble, jeopardize **5** – **7**

risk man|age|ment N-UNCOUNT 不可算名詞 **Risk management** is the skill or job of deciding what the risks are in a particular situation and taking action to prevent or reduce them. 危機管理, リスクマネジメント ❑ *Good risk management and higher sales can both boost profits.* 効果的なリスクマネジメントや売上増加により利益を上げることができる.

risky /rɪski/ (riskier, riskiest) ADJ 形容詞 If an activity or action is **risky**, it is dangerous or likely to fail. 危険な, 冒険的な ❑ *Investing in airlines is a very risky business.* 航空会社への投資は非常に危険性が高い.

rite /raɪt/ (rites) N-COUNT 算名詞 A **rite** is a traditional ceremony that is carried out by a particular group or within a particular society. 儀式 ❑ *Most traditional societies have transition rites at puberty.* ほとんどの伝統社会では思春期に移行儀式を行う.

ritu|al /rɪtʃuəl/ (rituals) **1** N-VAR 可変性名詞 A **ritual** is a religious service or other ceremony which involves a series of actions performed in a fixed order. 儀式, 儀礼 ❑ *This is the most ancient, and holiest of the Shinto rituals.* これが神道の最も古くて神聖な儀式だ. **2** ADJ 形容詞 **Ritual** activities happen as part of a ritual

or tradition. 儀式の [ADJ n] ❑ *...fasting and ritual dancing.* 断食と儀式的な踊り **3** N-VAR 可変性名詞 A **ritual** is a way of behaving or a series of actions that people regularly carry out in a particular situation, because it is their custom to do so. 習慣 ❑ *The whole Italian culture revolves around the ritual of eating.* イタリア文化全体が食習慣を中心に展開する. **4** ADJ 形容詞 You can describe something as a **ritual** action when it is done in exactly the same way whenever a particular situation occurs. 習慣的な, 形式的な [ADJ n] ❑ *I realized that here the conventions required me to make the ritual noises.* ここではしきたりに従って形式的なことを言わなければならないと気づいた.
→ see **myth**

ri|val /raɪvəl/ (rivals, rivaling, rivaled) **1** N-COUNT 可算名詞 Your **rival** is a person, business, or organization who you are competing or fighting against in the same area or for the same things. ライバル, 競争相手 ❑ *The world champion finished more than two seconds ahead of his nearest rival.* 世界チャンピオンは最強ライバルに2秒差でゴールした. **2** N-COUNT 可算名詞 If you say that someone or something has **no rivals** or is **without rival**, you mean that it is best of its type. 匹敵するものがない, 最高だ ❑ *The area is famous for its wonderfully fragrant wine which has no rivals in the Rhone.* この地域は, ローヌ地方で最高の香り高いワインで有名だ. **3** V-T 他動詞 If you say that one thing **rivals** another, you mean that they are both of the same standard or quality. 張り合う, 匹敵する ❑ *Cassette recorders cannot rival the sound quality of CDs.* カセットレコーダーはCDの音質にかなわない.

ri|val|ry /raɪvəlri/ (rivalries) N-VAR 可変性名詞 **Rivalry** is competition or fighting between people, businesses, or organizations who are in the same area or want the same things. 競争 ❑ *The rivalry between the Inkatha and the ANC has resulted in violence in the black townships.* インカタとアフリカ民族会議の間の競争は黒人居住区に暴動を引き起こした.

riv|er /rɪvər/ (rivers) N-COUNT 可算名詞 A **river** is a large amount of fresh water flowing continuously in a long line across the land. 川 ❑ *...a chemical plant on the banks of the river.* 川岸にある化学工場
→ see Picture Dictionary: **river**

river|side /rɪvərsaɪd/ N-SING 単数名詞 The **riverside** is the area of land by the banks of a river. 川岸, 川辺 ❑ *They walked back along the riverside.* 彼らは川岸に沿って歩いて帰った.

riv|et /rɪvɪt/ (rivets, riveting, riveted) V-T 他動詞 If you **are riveted** by something, it fascinates you and holds your interest completely. くぎづけにする ❑ *As a child I remember being riveted by my grandfather's appearance.* 子供の頃, 祖父が現れるとくぎづけになったことを覚えている. ❑ *He was riveted to the John Wayne movie.* 彼はジョン・ウェインの映画にくぎづけになった.

riv|et|ing /rɪvɪtɪŋ/ ADJ 形容詞 If you describe something as **riveting**, you mean that it is extremely interesting and exciting, and that it holds your attention completely. とても面白い, 心を奪うような ❑ *...Jeffrey Wolf's riveting new novel.* ジェフリー・ウルフの新しく出た夢中になる小説

roach /roʊtʃ/ (roaches) N-COUNT 可算名詞 A **roach** is the same as a **cockroach**. ゴキブリ [mainly AM 主に米国英語] ❑ *He found his*

Picture Dictionary

river
spring
lake
stream
gorge
valley
river
ocean
delta

brother in a seedy, roach-infested apartment. 彼は弟がみすぼらしくてゴキブリだらけのアパートにいるのを見つけた.

road /roʊd/ (roads) ■ N-COUNT 可算名詞 A **road** is a long piece of hard ground that is built between two places so that people can drive or ride easily from one place to the other. 道路 □ There was very little traffic on the roads. 道路の交通はとても少なかった. □ We just go straight up the Boston Post Road. ボストン・ポスト・ロードをまっすぐ行くだけです. ■ N-COUNT 可算名詞 The **road to** a particular result is the means of achieving it or the process of achieving it. 〜への道, 過程 □ We are bound to see some ups and downs along the road to recovery. 回復への過程で何度か回復と悪化を繰り返すことになるだろう. ■ PHRASE 句 If you say that someone is **on the road to** something, you mean that they are likely to achieve it. 〜に向かっている □ The government took another step on the road to political reform. 政府は, 政治改革に向かってさらに1歩進んだ. ■ **the end of the road** → see **end**
→ see **traffic**

road rage N-UNCOUNT 不可算名詞 **Road rage** is anger or violent behavior caused by someone else's bad driving or the stress of being in heavy traffic. 交通渋滞でのイライラ 運転中の怒り □ Two women were being hunted by police after a road rage attack on a male motorist. 2人の女性が男性ドライバーに激怒して攻撃した後, 警察に追われていた.

road|side /roʊdsaɪd/ (roadsides) N-COUNT 可算名詞 The **roadside** is the area at the edge of a road. 道路沿い, 道端 □ Bob was forced to leave the car at the roadside and run for help. ボブは道路わきに車を置き, 走って助けを求めざるを得なかった.

road|work /roʊdwɜrk/ N-UNCOUNT 不可算名詞 **Roadwork** is repairs or other work being done on a road. 道路工事 □ The traffic was stationary due to three sets of roadwork in less than a mile. 1マイル未満のところで3か所道路工事があるため交通は止まっていた.

roam /roʊm/ (roams, roaming, roamed) V-T/V-I 他動詞/自動詞 If you **roam** an area or **roam around** it, you wander or travel around it without having a particular purpose. うろうろする, 放浪する □ Barefoot children roamed the streets. 素足の子供たちが通りでうろうろしていた. □ I spent a couple of years roaming around the countryside. 私は数年間, 地方を放浪して過ごした.

roam|ing /roʊmɪŋ/ N-UNCOUNT 不可算名詞 **Roaming** refers to the service provided by a cellphone company which makes it possible for you to use your cellphone when you travel. ローミング □ Ignorance of roaming call charges is common. ローミング料金を知らない人が多い.

roar /rɔr/ (roars, roaring, roared) ■ V-I 自動詞 If something, usually a vehicle, **roars** somewhere, it goes there very fast, making a loud noise. ごう音を立てて走る [WRITTEN 書き言葉] □ A police car roared past. パトカーがごう音を立てて走り去った. ■ V-I 自動詞 If something **roars**, it makes a very loud noise. ごう音を立てる, とどろく [WRITTEN 書き言葉] □ The engine roared, and the vehicle leapt forward. エンジンがごう音を立て, 車が急発進した. ● N-COUNT 可算名詞 **Roar** is also a noun. ごう音, とどろき □ ...the roar of traffic. 交通のごう音. ■ V-I 自動詞 If someone **roars with** laughter, they laugh in a very noisy way. 爆笑する □ Max threw back his head and roared with laughter. マックスは頭をのけぞらせて大爆笑した. ● N-COUNT 可算名詞 **Roar** is also a noun. 爆笑 □ There were roars of laughter as he stood up. 彼が立ち上がると大爆笑が起こった. ■ V-T/V-I 他動詞/自動詞 If someone **roars**, they shout something in a very loud voice. どなる [WRITTEN 書き言葉] □ "I'll kill you for that," he roared. 「そのことで殺してやる」と彼はどなった. □ During the playing of the national anthem the crowd roared and whistled. 国歌が流れている間, 群衆は声を上げ, 口笛を吹いた. ● N-COUNT 可算名詞 **Roar** is also a noun. 大きな声 □ There was a roar of approval. 賛成のどよめきがあった. ■ V-I 自動詞 When a lion **roars**, it makes the loud sound that lions typically make. ほえる □ The lion roared once, and sprang. ライオンは1度うなると跳び上がった. ● N-COUNT 可算名詞 **Roar** is also a noun. うなり声 □ ...the roar of lions in the distance. 遠くから聞こえるライオンのうなり声

roar|ing /rɔrɪŋ/ ■ ADJ 形容詞 A **roaring** fire has large flames and sends out a lot of heat. ぼうぼうと燃えている [ADJ n] □ ...nighttime beach parties, with a roaring fire. 火をぼうぼうと燃やしながらの夜のビーチパーティ ■ ADJ 形容詞 If something is a **roaring** success, it is extremely successful. かなりの, 大〜 [ADJ n] □ The government's first effort to privatize a company has been a roaring success. 民営化のための政府の最初の試みは大成功だった. ■ → see also **roar**

roast /roʊst/ (roasts, roasting, roasted) ■ V-T 他動詞 When you **roast** meat or other food, you cook it by dry heat in an oven or over a fire. 焼く, ローストする □ I personally would rather roast a chicken whole. 個人的にはチキンを丸焼きにする方が好きだ. ■ ADJ 形容詞 **Roast** meat has been cooked by roasting. 焼いた, ローストした [ADJ n] □ They serve the most delicious roast beef. その店はとてもおいしいローストビーフを出す. ■ N-COUNT 可算名詞 A **roast** is a piece of meat that is cooked by roasting. ロースト □ Come into the kitchen. I've got to put the roast in. キッチンに来てちょうだい. ロース

トをオーブンに入れなくっちゃ.
→ see **cook, peanut**

rob /rɒb/ (robs, robbing, robbed) ■ V-T 他動詞 If someone is **robbed**, they have money or property stolen from them. 強奪する, 盗む □ Mrs. Yacoub was robbed of her designer watch at her Westchester home. ヤクーブ夫人はウェチェスターの自宅でデザイナー時計を盗まれた. ■ V-T 他動詞 If someone is **robbed of** something that they deserve, have, or need, it is taken away from them. 奪う □ When Miles Davis died jazz was robbed of its most distinctive voice. マイルズ・デイビスが亡くなったとき, ジャズ界は最も特徴のある歌声を失った.

Do not confuse **rob** and **steal**. If someone **robs** someone or somewhere, they take something, often violently, from that person or place without asking and without intending to give it back. □ They planned to rob an old widow... They joined forces to rob a factory. You can also say that someone **robs** you of something when referring to what has been taken. □ The two men were robbed of more than $700. If someone **steals** something, for example, money or a car, they take it without asking and without intending to give it back. □ My car was stolen on Friday evening. Note that you cannot say that someone **steals** someone.

rob|ber /rɒbər/ (robbers) N-COUNT 可算名詞 A **robber** is someone who steals money or property from a bank, store, or vehicle, often by using force or threats. 強盗犯, 盗賊 □ Armed robbers broke into a jeweler's through a hole in the wall. 武装強盗犯が壁の穴を通って宝石商に侵入した.

Anyone who steals can be called a **thief**. A **robber** often uses violence or the threat of violence to steal things from places such as banks or businesses. A **burglar** breaks into houses or other buildings and steals things.

rob|bery /rɒbəri/ (robberies) N-VAR 可変性名詞 **Robbery** is the crime of stealing money or property from a bank, store, or vehicle, often by using force or threats. 強盗 □ The gang members committed dozens of armed robberies over the past year. 暴力団員は過去1年間で数十件の武装強盗を犯した.

robe /roʊb/ (robes) ■ N-COUNT 可算名詞 A **robe** is a loose piece of clothing that covers all of your body and reaches the ground. You can describe someone as wearing a **robe** or as wearing **robes**. 礼服, 式服 [FORMAL 形式ばった] □ Pope John Paul II knelt in his white robes before the simple altar. ヨハネ・パウロ2世は白い礼服を着て質素な祭壇の前にひざまずいた. ■ N-COUNT 可算名詞 A **robe** is a piece of clothing, usually made of toweling, which people wear in the house, especially when they have just gotten up or taken a bath. ガウン, バスローブ □ Kyle put on a robe and went down to the kitchen. カイルはバスローブを着て台所に下りて行った.

ro|bot /roʊbət, -bɒt/ (robots) N-COUNT 可算名詞 A **robot** is a machine that is programmed to move and perform certain tasks automatically. ロボット □ ...very lightweight robots that we could send to the moon for planetary exploration. 惑星探査の目的で月に送ることができる非常に軽量なロボット
→ see **mass production**

ro|bust /roʊbʌst, roʊbʌst/ ■ ADJ 形容詞 Someone or something that is **robust** is very strong or healthy. 頑健な, たくましい □ He was always the robust one, physically strong and mentally sharp. 彼は, 力強くて頭が切れ常にたくましい人だった. ■ ADJ 形容詞 **Robust** views or opinions are strongly held and forcefully expressed. 断固とした □ The Secretary of State has made a robust defense of the agreement. 国務長官はその協定の断固たる擁護をした.

rock /rɒk/ (rocks, rocking, rocked) ■ N-UNCOUNT 不可算名詞 **Rock** is the hard substance which the earth is made of. 岩 □ The hills above the valley are bare rock. 谷間の上の丘には岩肌が見えている. ■ N-COUNT 可算名詞 A **rock** is a large piece of rock that sticks up out of the ground or the sea, or that has broken away from a mountain or a cliff. 岩 □ She sat cross-legged on the rock. 彼女は岩の上で足を組んで座った. ■ N-COUNT 可算名詞 A **rock** is a piece of rock that is small enough for you to pick up. 石 □ She bent down, picked up a rock, and threw it into the trees. 彼女はかがんで石を拾い, 林の中に投げた. ■ V-T/V-I 他動詞/自動詞 When something **rocks** or when you **rock** it, it moves slowly and regularly backward and forward or from side to side. 揺らぐ [他動詞], 揺れる [自動詞] □ His body rocked from side to side with the train. 彼の体が電車で左右に揺れた. ■ V-T 他動詞/自動詞 If an explosion or an earthquake **rocks** a building or an area, it causes the building or area to shake. (爆発・地震などが) 揺らす [JOURNALISM ジャーナリズム] [他動詞], 揺れる [自動詞] □ Three people were injured yesterday when an explosion rocked the factory. 昨日地震で工場が揺れたとき3名が負傷した. □ In Taipei buildings rocked back and forth. 台北では建物が前後に揺れた. ■ V-T 他動詞 If an event or a piece of news **rocks** a group or society, it shocks them or makes them feel less secure. 動揺を与える [JOURNALISM ジャーナリズム] □ His death rocked the fashion business. 彼の死でファッション界に動揺が広がった. ■ N-UNCOUNT 不可算名詞 **Rock** is loud music with a strong beat that is usually

Word Web · rock

Rocks are made of **minerals**. They may consist of a single **element**. However, they usually contain **compounds** of several elements. Each type of rock also has a unique **crystal** structure. Rock is constantly in the process of changing. When **lava erupts** from a **volcano**, it forms igneous rock. Wind, water, and ice **erode** this type of rock. The resulting **sediment** collects in rivers. As these layers of particles build up, they form sedimentary rock. When tectonic plates move around, they create heat and pressure. This melting and crushing changes sedimentary rock into metamorphic rock.

 **igneous**    **sedimentary**    **metamorphic**

played and sung by a small group of people using instruments such as electric guitars and drums. ロック（ミュージック）❏...a rock concert. ロックコンサート
→ see Word Web: **rock**
→ see **crystal, earth, fossil, genre**

rock and roll also **rock'n'roll** N-UNCOUNT 不可算名詞 **Rock and roll** is a kind of popular music developed in the 1950s which has a strong beat and is played on electrical instruments. ロックンロール ❏...Elvis Presley – the King of Rock and Roll. ロックンロールの王、エルビス・プレスリー.

rock bot|tom also **rock-bottom** ◆ N-UNCOUNT 不可算名詞 If something has reached **rock bottom**, it is at such a low level that it cannot go any lower. どん底 ❏Morale in the armed forces was at rock bottom. 軍隊の士気は最低だった. ◆ ADJ 形容詞 A **rock-bottom** price or level is a very low one, mainly in advertisements. 最低の [APPROVAL 賛成] ❏Why did they do offer is a good product at a rock-bottom price. その店はよい製品を底値で売っている.

rock|et /rɒkɪt/ (rockets, rocketing, rocketed) ◆ N-COUNT 可算名詞 A **rocket** is a space vehicle that is shaped like a long tube. ロケット ❏...the Apollo 12 rocket that took astronauts to the moon. 宇宙飛行士の月面着陸を成功させたアポロ12号 ◆ N-COUNT 可算名詞 A **rocket** is a missile containing explosives that is powered by gas. ロケット弾 ❏There has been a renewed rocket attack on the capital. 新たに首都へのロケット弾攻撃があった. ◆ N-COUNT 可算名詞 A **rocket** is a firework that quickly goes high into the air and then explodes. ロケット花火、打ち上げ花火 ◆ V-I 自動詞 If things such as prices or social problems **rocket**, they increase very quickly and suddenly. 急騰する、急上昇する ❏ [JOURNALISM ジャーナリズム] ❏Fresh food is so scarce that prices have rocketed. 新鮮な食品が非常に限られていて値段が急騰した. ◆ V-I 自動詞 If something such as a vehicle **rockets** somewhere, it moves there very quickly. 突進する ❏A train rocketed by, shaking the walls of the row houses. 電車が連なった家々の壁を揺らしながら、猛烈な速さで通り過ぎた. ◆ N-UNCOUNT 不可算名詞 **Rocket** is the same as **arugula**. キバナスズシロ、ルッコラ [BRIT 英国英語]

rocky /rɒki/ (rockier, rockiest) ◆ ADJ 形容詞 A **rocky** place is covered with rocks or consists of large areas of rock and has nothing growing on it. 岩だらけの ❏The paths are often very rocky so strong boots are advisable. その道は岩だらけのところが多いのでしっかりした靴を履いたほうがよい. ◆ ADJ 形容詞 A **rocky** situation or relationship is unstable and full of difficulties. 不安定な、難しい ❏They had gone through some rocky times together when Ann was first married. アナが最初に結婚した時、いろいろと問題があった.

rod /rɒd/ (rods) N-COUNT 可算名詞 A **rod** is a long, thin, metal or wooden bar. 棒、さお ❏...a 15-foot thick roof that was reinforced with steel rods. 鋼棒で補強された厚さ15フィートの屋根

rode /roʊd/ **Rode** is the past tense of **ride**. rideの過去形

ro|dent /roʊdⁿt/ (rodents) N-COUNT 可算名詞 **Rodents** are small mammals which have sharp front teeth. Rats, mice, and squirrels are rodents. （一般的に）ネズミ（リスやネズミなどの）げっし動物

ro|deo /roʊdioʊ, roʊdeɪoʊ/ (rodeos) N-COUNT 可算名詞 A **rodeo** is a public entertainment event in which cowboys show different skills, including riding wild horses and catching cattle with ropes. ロデオ

rogue /roʊg/ (rogues) ◆ N-COUNT 可算名詞 A **rogue** is a man who behaves in a dishonest or criminal way. ごろつき ❏Mr. Ward wasn't a rogue at all. ウォードは少しも悪漢ではなかった. ◆ N-COUNT 可算名詞 If a man behaves in a way that you do not approve of but you still like him, you can refer to him as a **rogue**. ワル [FEELINGS 感情] ❏...Falstaff, the lovable rogue. 憎めないワル、フォルスタッフ ◆ ADJ 形容詞 A **rogue** element is someone or something that behaves differently from others of its kind, often causing damage. 逸脱した [ADJ n] ❏Computer systems throughout the country are being affected by a series of mysterious rogue programs, known as viruses. 全国のコンピュタシステムがウィルスとして知られる一連の不可解で異常なプログラムに影響されている.

role /roʊl/ (roles) ◆ N-COUNT 可算名詞 If you have a **role** in a situation or in society, you have a particular position and function in it. 役割、役目 ❏Until now scientists had very little clear evidence about the drug's role in preventing even more serious effects of infection. 現在に至るまで科学者には、伝染病がさらに深刻な影響を及ぼすことを防止することにおける薬の役割について明らかな証拠はほとんどなかった. ◆ N-COUNT 可算名詞 A **role** is one of the characters that an actor or singer can play in a movie, play, or opera. 役 ❏She has just landed the lead role in their latest production. 彼女は最新公演での主役をちょうど手に入れたところだった.
→ see **theater**

Word Partnership · role は次の語句と使われる:

N.	**leadership** role, role **reversal** ◆ **lead** role ◆ ◆
ADJ.	**active** role, **key** role, **parental** role, **positive** role, **significant** role, **traditional** role, **vital** role ◆ **bigger/larger** role, **leading** role, **major** role ◆ ◆ **starring** role ◆
V.	**play** a role, **take on** a role ◆ ◆

role mod|el (role models) N-COUNT 可算名詞 A **role model** is someone you admire and try to imitate. お手本、ロールモデル ❏Five out of the ten top role models for teenagers are black. ティンエイジャーのロールモデル上位10人のうち5人が黒人だ.

roll /roʊl/ (rolls, rolling, rolled) ◆ V-T/V-I 他動詞/自動詞 When something **rolls** or when you **roll** it, it moves along a surface, turning over many times. 転がす [他動詞]、転がる [自動詞] ❏The ball rolled into the net. ボールは転がってネットに入った. ◆ V-I 自動詞 If you **roll** somewhere, you move on a surface while lying down, turning your body over and over, so that you are sometimes on your back, sometimes on your side, and sometimes on your front. （人が）転がる ❏When I was a little kid I rolled down a hill and broke my leg. 小さい頃、丘を転がり落ちって足を骨折した. ◆ V-I 自動詞 When vehicles **roll** along, they move along slowly. ゆっくり動く ❏The truck quietly rolled forward and demolished all the old wooden fencing. トラックが静かに前進し古い木の柵をすべて破壊した. ◆ V-I 自動詞 If a machine **rolls**, it is operating. 作動する ❏He slipped and fell on the step as the cameras rolled. カメラが回っているとき彼は滑って段で転んだ. ◆ V-I 自動詞 If drops of liquid **roll** down a surface, they move quickly down it. 流れる ❏She looks at Ginny and tears rolled down her cheeks. 彼女はジニーの方を見ると涙がほおを伝った. ◆ V-T 他動詞 If you **roll** something flexible **into** a cylinder or a ball, you form it into a cylinder or a ball by wrapping it several times around itself or by shaping it between your hands. 丸める ❏He took off his sweater, rolled it into a pillow, and lay down on the grass. 彼はセーターを脱ぎ、丸めて枕にし、草の上に寝転がった. ● PHRASAL VERB 句動詞 **Roll up** means the same as **roll**. 丸める ❏Stein rolled up the paper bag with the money inside. スタインはお金が入った紙袋を丸めた. ◆ N-COUNT 可算名詞 A **roll** of paper, plastic, cloth, or wire is a long piece of it that has been wrapped many times around itself or around a tube. 1巻 ❏The photographers had already shot a dozen rolls of film. カメラマンはすでに十数本のフィルムを撮った. ◆ V-T 他動詞 If you **roll up** something such as a car window or a blind, you cause it to move upward by turning a handle. If you **roll it down**, you cause it to move downward by turning a handle. 開ける/閉める ❏In mid-afternoon, shopkeepers began to roll down their shutters. 昼下がりに小売店主らがシャッターを閉め始めた. ◆ V-T/V-I 他動詞/自動詞 If you **roll** your eyes or if your eyes **roll**, they move around and upward. People sometimes roll their eyes when they are frightened, bored, or annoyed. 目を白黒させる、目をむく [WRITTEN 書き言葉] ❏People may roll their eyes and talk about overprotective, interfering grandmothers. 人々は目をむきながら過保護で干渉しがちな祖母について話すかもしれない. ◆ N-COUNT 可算名詞 A **roll** is a small piece of bread that is round or long and is made to be eaten by one person. Rolls are often eaten plain, with butter, or with a filling. ロールパン ❏He sipped at his coffee and spread butter and marmalade on a roll. 彼はコーヒーをすすり、ロールパンにバターとマーマレードをつけた. ◆ N-COUNT 可算名詞 A **roll of** drums is a long, low, fairly loud sound made by drums. ドーンドンという音 ❏As

the town clock struck two, they heard the roll of drums. 町の時計が2時を打つと，太鼓のとどろきが聞こえてきた。 **12** N-COUNT 可算名詞 A **roll** is an official list of people's names. 名簿 □ Pro-democracy activists say a new electoral roll should be drawn up. 民主化運動活動家は新しい選挙人名簿を作成するべきだと述べた。 **13** → see also **rolling, rock and roll** **14** PHRASE 句 If something is several things **rolled into one**, it combines the main features or qualities of those things. 合わさって1つになった □ This is our kitchen, living room, and dining room all rolled into one. ここは，キッチン，リビング，ダイニングが1つになった部屋だ。 **15** **heads will roll** → see **head**

▶ **roll back** PHRASAL VERB 句動詞 To **roll back** prices, taxes, or benefits means to reduce them. 引き下げる [mainly AM 主に米国英語] □ One provision of the law was to roll back taxes to the 1975 level. その法律の条項によると税金を1975年の水準まで引き下げるとのことです。

▶ **roll in** PHRASAL VERB 句動詞 If something such as money **is rolling in**, it is appearing or being received in large quantities. 転がり込む [INFORMAL くだけた] □ Don't forget, I have always kept the money rolling in. 私にはいつも腐るほどお金が入ってきたってことを忘れないで。

▶ **roll out** PHRASAL VERB 句動詞 If a company **rolls out** a new product or service, or if the product or service **rolls out**, it is made available to the public. 発売する □ On Thursday Microsoft rolls out its new operating system. 木曜日にマイクロソフト社は新しいOSを発売する。 □ Northern Telecom says its products will roll out over 18 months beginning early next year. ノーザン・テレコム社は来年明けから18か月間に及び製品を販売する。

▶ **roll over** **1** PHRASAL VERB 句動詞 If you are lying down and you **roll over**, you turn your body so that a different part of you is facing upward. 寝返りを打って再び眠りについた □ I rolled over and went back to sleep. 寝返りを打って再び眠りについた。 **2** PHRASAL VERB 句動詞 If a moving vehicle such as a car **rolls over**, it turns over many times, usually because it has crashed. 転倒する □ Those kinds of vehicles are more likely to roll over than passenger cars. そのタイプの車は乗用車よりも転倒しやすい。 **3** PHRASAL VERB 句動詞 If you say that someone **rolls over**, you mean that they stop resisting someone and do what the other person wants them to do. 言いなりになる □ That's why most people and organizations just roll over and give up when they're challenged or attacked by the I.R.S. そういうわけで，国税庁に説明を求められたり非難されたりするとたいていの人々や組織は言われた通りにするんだ。 **4** PHRASAL VERB 句動詞 If you **roll over** a loan or other financial arrangement, you extend it, for example by adding it to another loan. 延期する，先送りする [BUSINESS 実業] □ There seems to be no way to spread out the tax or roll over the cash into another pension plan. 税金の支払い期間を延ばしたり資金を別の年金プランに繰り越すことはできないようだ。 **5** → see also **rollover** **6** PHRASAL VERB 句動詞 In lotteries and similar games, if a jackpot **rolls over**, it is not won by anyone and the money is added to the prize money for the next lottery. 次回へ繰り越される □ If the jackpot isn't won this week it will roll over again to next week. もし特賞が今週当たらなければ来週に再度繰り越される。 **7** → see also **rollover**

▶ **roll up** **1** PHRASAL VERB 句動詞 If you **roll up** your sleeves or pant legs, you fold the ends back several times, making them shorter. まくる □ The jacket was too big for him so he rolled up the cuffs. その上着は大きすぎたので，彼はそで口をまくり上げた。 **2** PHRASAL VERB 句動詞 If people **roll up** somewhere, they arrive there, especially in a car and often late. 姿を現す，遅れて来る [INFORMAL くだけた] □ They eventually rolled up two hours late. 2時間遅れでやっと到着した。 □ They rolled up two hours late. 2時間遅れで到着した。 **3** → see also **roll 6**

roll|er /roʊlər/ (rollers) **1** N-COUNT 可算名詞 A **roller** is a cylinder that turns around in a machine or device. ローラー **2** N-COUNT 可算名詞 **Rollers** are hollow tubes that women roll their hair round in order to make it curly. カーラー □ She gets up every morning and puts her hair in rollers. 彼女は毎朝起きるとカーラーで髪を巻く。

Roll|er|blade /roʊlərbleɪd/ (Rollerblades) N-COUNT 可算名詞 商標 **Rollerblades** are a type of roller skates with a single line of wheels along the bottom. ローラーブレード [TRADEMARK]，インラインスケート ● **roll|er|blad|ing** N-UNCOUNT 不可算名詞 ローラーブレードをすること □ Rollerblading is great for all ages. インラインスケートは年齢に関わりなく楽しむことができる。

roll|er coast|er (roller coasters) **1** N-COUNT 可算名詞 A **roller coaster** is a small railroad at an amusement park that goes up and down steep slopes fast and that people ride on for pleasure or excitement. ジェットコースター □ It's great to go on the roller coaster five times and not be sick. ジェットコースターに5回乗って気分が悪くならないのは素晴らしい。 **2** N-COUNT 可算名詞 If you say that someone or something is on a **roller coaster**, you mean that they go through many sudden or extreme changes in a short time. 波乱万丈 [JOURNALISM ジャーナリズム] □ I've been on an emotional roller coaster since I've been here. ここに来て以来，波乱万丈が続いている。

roller skate (roller skates, roller-skates, roller-skating, roller-skated) **1** N-COUNT 可算名詞 **Roller skates** are shoes with four

small wheels on the bottom. ローラースケート靴 □ A boy of about ten came up on roller skates. 10歳ぐらいの少年がローラースケート靴 **2** V-I 自動詞 If you **roller-skate**, you move over a flat surface wearing roller skates. ローラースケートをする □ On the day of the accident, my son Gary was roller-skating outside our house. 事故のあった日，息子のギャリーは家の前でローラースケートをしていた。

roll|ing /roʊlɪŋ/ ADJ 形容詞 **Rolling** hills are small hills with gentle slopes that extend a long way into the distance. 起伏している，ゆるやかにうねった [ADJ n] □ ...the rolling countryside of southwestern France. フランス南西地方のなだらかに起伏している田園地方

ROM /rɒm/ **1** N-UNCOUNT 不可算名詞 **ROM** is the permanent part of a computer's memory. The information stored there can be read but not changed. **ROM** is an abbreviation for "read-only memory." ROM [COMPUTING コンピューティング] 読み出し専用記憶媒体 □ It's got 256 megabytes of ROM and 512 megabytes of RAM. 256メガバイトのROMと512メガバイトのRAMを内蔵している。 **2** → see also **CD-ROM**

| Word Link | an, ian ≈ one of, relating to : Christian, pedestrian, Roman |

Ro|man /roʊmən/ (Romans) **1** ADJ 形容詞 **Roman** means related to or connected with ancient Rome and its empire. 古代ローマの，ローマ帝国の □ ...the fall of the Roman Empire. ローマ帝国の滅亡 ● N-COUNT 可算名詞 A **Roman** was a citizen of ancient Rome or its empire. 古代ローマ人 □ When they conquered Britain, the Romans brought this custom with them. 古代ローマ人が英国を征服したとき，この習慣を持ち込んだ。 **2** ADJ 形容詞 **Roman** means related to or connected with modern Rome. ローマの □ ...a Roman hotel room. ローマ風のホテルルーム ● N-COUNT 可算名詞 A **Roman** is someone who lives in or comes from Rome. ローマ人 □ ...soccer-mad Romans. サッカー狂のローマ人

Ro|man Catho|lic (Roman Catholics) **1** ADJ 形容詞 The **Roman Catholic** Church is the same as the **Catholic** Church. ローマカトリック教会の □ ...a Roman Catholic priest. ローマカトリック教会の司祭 **2** N-COUNT 可算名詞 A **Roman Catholic** is the same as a **Catholic**. ローマカトリック信者 □ Like her, Maria was a Roman Catholic. 彼女と同様に，マリアはカトリック信者だった。

ro|mance /roʊmæns, roʊmæns/ (romances) **1** N-COUNT 可算名詞 A **romance** is a relationship between two people who are in love with each other but who are not married to each other. 恋愛関係 □ After a whirlwind romance the couple announced their engagement in July. 目まぐるしい恋愛のあと，2人は7月に婚約発表をした。 **2** N-UNCOUNT 不可算名詞 **Romance** refers to the actions and feelings of people who are in love, especially behavior that is very caring or affectionate. 恋愛，恋 □ He still finds time for romance by cooking candlelit dinners for his girlfriend. 彼は今でも恋愛のための時間を見つけて彼女のためにろうそくをともした食事を作る。 **3** N-UNCOUNT 不可算名詞 You can refer to the pleasure and excitement of doing something new or exciting as **romance**. 冒険 □ We want to recreate the romance and excitement that used to be part of rail journeys. 鉄道旅行の一環として冒険的でエキサイティングな雰囲気を再現したい。 **4** N-COUNT 可算名詞 A **romance** is a novel or movie about a love affair. 恋愛もの □ Her taste in fiction was for chunky historical romances. 彼女の小説の好みは分厚い歴史的恋愛小説だ。 → see **love**

Ro|man nu|mer|al /roʊmən nuːmərəl/ (Roman numerals) N-COUNT 可算名詞 **Roman numerals** are the letters used by the ancient Romans to represent numbers, for example I, IV, VIII, and XL, which represent 1, 4, 8, and 40. Roman numerals are still sometimes used today. ローマ数字 [usu pl] → see Picture Dictionary: **Roman numerals**

ro|man|tic /roʊmæntɪk/ (romantics) **1** ADJ 形容詞 Someone who is **romantic** or does **romantic** things says and does things that make their wife, husband, girlfriend, or boyfriend feel special and loved. ロマンチックな，愛情を示した □ When we're together, all he talks about is business. I wish he were more romantic. 私たちが一緒のとき，彼が話すのは仕事のことだけ。もっとロマンチックだったらいいのに。 **2** ADJ 形容詞 **Romantic** means connected with sexual love. 恋愛に [ADJ n] □ He was not interested in a romantic relationship with Ingrid. 彼はイングリッドとの恋愛関係の興味がなかった。 ● **ro|man|ti|cal|ly** ADV 副詞 恋愛感情を持って □ We are not romantically involved. 私たちは恋愛関係にはない。 **3** ADJ 形容詞 [ADJ n] A **romantic** play, movie, or story describes or represents a love affair. 恋愛もの，ロマンスの □ It is a lovely romantic comedy, well worth seeing. それは素敵な恋愛コメディで，見る価値が十分にある。 **4** ADJ 形容詞 If you say that someone has a **romantic** view or idea of something, you are critical of them because their view of it is unrealistic and they think that thing is better or more exciting than it really is. 非現実的な，理想化した [DISAPPROVAL 不賛成] □ He has a romantic view of rural society. 彼は農村社会について非現実的な考えを持っている。 ● N-COUNT 可算名詞 A **romantic**

Picture Dictionary

Roman numerals

I	1	XI	11	XXI	21	XL	40
II	2	XII	12	XXII	22	L	50
III	3	XIII	13	XXIII	23	LX	60
IV	4	XIV	14	XXIV	24	LXX	70
V	5	XV	15	XXV	25	LXXX	80
VI	6	XVI	16	XXVI	26	XC	90
VII	7	XVII	17	XXVII	27	C	100
VIII	8	XVIII	18	XXVIII	28	D	500
IX	9	XIX	19	XXIX	29	M	1000
X	10	XX	20	XXX	30	MMVIII	2008

is a person who has romantic views. 夢想家 ❏ *You're a hopeless romantic.* きみは救いようのない夢想家だ. **5** ADJ 形容詞 Something that is **romantic** is beautiful in a way that strongly affects your feelings. ロマンチックな，素敵な ❏ *It is considered one of the most romantic restaurants in the city.* そこは，街で最もロマンチックなレストランのうちの1つとみなされている. ● **ro|man|ti|cal|ly** ADV 副詞 ロマンチックに，素敵に ❏ *...the romantically named, but very muddy, Cave of the Wild Horses.* ロマンチックに名称付けられているが，泥だらけのワイルドホースの洞窟

→ see **love**

romp /rɒmp/ (**romps, romping, romped**) **1** V-I 自動詞 Journalists use **romp** in expressions like **romp home, romp in**, or **romp to victory**, to say that a person or horse has won a race or competition very easily. 楽勝する ❏ *Mr. Foster romped home with 141 votes.* フォスター氏はあっさりと141票獲得した. **2** V-I 自動詞 When children or animals **romp**, they play noisily and happily. はしゃぐ ❏ *Dogs and little children romped happily in the garden.* イヌと小さな子供たちが庭で楽しそうにはしゃぎ回った.

roof /ruːf/ (**roofs**)

The plural can be pronounced /ruːfs/ or /ruːvz/.

名詞は /ruːfs/ または /ruːvz/ と発音できる.

1 N-COUNT 可算名詞 The **roof** of a building is the covering on top of it that protects the people and things inside from the weather. (建物の) 屋根 ❏ *...a small stone cottage with a red slate roof.* 赤いスレート屋根の小さな石造りのコテージ **2** N-COUNT 可算名詞 The **roof** of a car or other vehicle is the top part of it, which protects passengers or goods from the weather. (車の) 屋根，ルーフ ❏ *The car rolled onto its roof, trapping him.* 自動車が逆さに転倒し，彼は中に閉じ込められた. **3** N-COUNT 可算名詞 The **roof** of your mouth is the highest part of the inside of your mouth. 上あご，口蓋 (こうがい) ❏ *She clicked her tongue against the roof of her mouth.* 彼女は舌打ちをした. **4** PHRASE 句 If the level of something such as the price of a product or the rate of inflation **goes through the roof**, it suddenly increases very rapidly indeed. べらぼうに上がる，うなぎ登りだ [INFORMAL くだけた] ❏ *Prices for Korean art have gone through the roof.* 韓国の芸術作品の価格が急騰した. **5** PHRASE 句 If you **hit the roof** or **go through the roof**, you become very angry, and usually show your anger by shouting at someone. 頭にくる，キレる [INFORMAL くだけた] ❏ *Sergeant Long will hit the roof when I tell him you've gone off.* きみが逃げたことを伝えたら軍曹はカンカンに怒るだろう. **6** PHRASE 句 If a number of things or people are **under one roof** or **under the same roof**, they are in the same building. 一つ屋根の下で，同じ屋根の下で ❏ *The firms intend to open either together under one roof or alongside each other in shopping malls.* その会社は同じビル内かあるいはショッピングモールで隣に並んで開業する方針だ.

Word Partnership   *roof* は次の語句と使われる:

N.	roof **of a building/house, metal** roof, **rain on a** roof, **slate** roof, **tin** roof 1
V.	roof **collapses**, roof **leaks, repair a** roof 1
ADJ.	**retractable** roof 1 2

rookie /rʊki/ (**rookies**) **1** N-COUNT 可算名詞 A **rookie** is someone who has just started doing a job and does not have much experience, especially someone who has just joined the army or police force. 新米，新入り [mainly AM 主に米国英語, INFORMAL くだけた] ❏ *I don't want to have another rookie to train.* また新米を養成するのは嫌だ. **2** N-COUNT 可算名詞 A **rookie** is someone who has been competing in a professional sport for less

than a year. 新人選手，ルーキー [AM 米国英語] ❏ *...the oldest rookie on the European Tour.* ヨーロッパツアーで最高齢の新人選手

room /ruːm/ (**rooms, rooming, roomed**) **1** N-COUNT 可算名詞 A **room** is one of the separate sections or parts of the inside of a building. Rooms have their own walls, ceilings, floors, and doors, and are usually used for particular activities. You can refer to all the people who are in a room as **the room**. 部屋，部屋にいる人たち ❏ *A minute later he excused himself and left the room.* 少しして彼は断ってから部屋を出た. ❏ *The largest conference room could seat 5,000 people.* 一番大きい会議室には5千人が収容できます. **2** N-COUNT 可算名詞 If you talk about your **room**, you are referring to the room that you alone use, especially your bedroom at home or your office at work. (個人の) 部屋 オフィス ❏ *If you're running upstairs, go to my room and bring down my sweater, please.* 2階に上がるなら，私の部屋に行ってセーターを取ってきて. **3** N-COUNT 可算名詞 A **room** is a bedroom in a hotel. (ホテルの) 部屋 ❏ *Toni reserved a room in a hotel not far from Arzfeld.* トニーはアルズフェルドから程遠くないところにホテルの部屋を予約した. **4** V-I 自動詞 If you **room** with someone, you share a rented room, apartment, or house with them, for example when you are a student. 同居する，ルームシェアする [AM 米国英語] ❏ *I had roomed with him in New Haven when we were both at Yale Law School.* エール大学法学部に在学中，ニューヘーブンで彼と同居した. **5** N-UNCOUNT 不可算名詞 If there is **room** somewhere, there is enough empty space there for people or things to be fitted in, or for people to move freely or do what they want to. スペース ❏ *There is usually room to accommodate up to 80 visitors.* 通常，最高80名のゲストを収容するスペースがある. **6** N-UNCOUNT 不可算名詞 If there is **room for** a particular kind of behavior or action, people are able to behave in that way or to take that action. 余地 ❏ *The intensity of the work left little room for personal grief or anxiety.* 仕事が厳しかったので感傷に浸る余地はほとんどなかった. **7** → see also **chat room, dining room, drawing room, emergency room, living room, restroom**

You should use **room** or **space** to refer to an open or empty area. You do not use **place** as an uncount noun in this sense. **Room** is more likely to be used when you are talking about space inside an enclosed area. ❏ *There's not enough room in the bathroom for both of us... Leave plenty of space between you and the car in front.*

room|mate /ruːmmeɪt/ (**roommates**) N-COUNT 可算名詞 Your **roommate** is the person you share a room, apartment, or house with, for example when you are in college. ルームメイト，同居人 [AM 米国英語] ❏ *Derek and I are close; we were roommates for two years.* デリクと私は親しくて2年間同居した.

room ser|vice N-UNCOUNT 不可算名詞 **Room service** is a service in a hotel by which meals or drinks are provided for guests in their rooms. ルームサービス ❏ *The hotel did not normally provide room service.* そのホテルは通常ルームサービスがなかった.

→ see **hotel**

roomy /ruːmi/ (**roomier, roomiest**) ADJ 形容詞 If you describe a place as **roomy**, you mean that you like it because it is large inside and you can move around freely and comfortably. 広々とした [APPROVAL 賛成] ❏ *The car is roomy and a good choice for anyone who needs to carry equipment.* その車は中が広くて，機材を運ぶ必要がある人に適している.

roost /ruːst/ (**roosts, roosting, roosted**) **1** N-COUNT 可算名詞 A **roost** is a place where birds or bats rest or sleep. ねぐら，止まり木 ❏ *Something disturbed the bird on its roost.* 何かがねぐらにいる鳥をじゃました. **2** V-I 自動詞 When birds or bats **roost** somewhere, they rest or sleep there. ねぐらにする ❏ *The peacocks roost in nearby shrubs.* クジャクが近くの低木をねぐらにしている. **3** PHRASE 句

rooster

If bad or wrong things that someone has done in the past **have come home to roost**, or if their **chickens have come home to roost**, they are now experiencing the unpleasant effects of these actions. 付けが回る，罰が当たる □*Appeasement has come home to roost.* 妥協策に付けが回ってきた． **4** PHRASE 句 If you say that someone **rules the roost** in a particular place, you mean that they have control and authority over the people there. 牛耳る [INFORMAL くだけた] □*Today the country's nationalists rule the roost and hand out the jobs.* 今ではその国の国粋主義者が政権を取り仕事を分配している．

→ see **bat**

roost|er /rúːstər/ (**roosters**) N-COUNT 可算名詞 A **rooster** is an adult male chicken. おんどり [AM 米国英語]

root /rúːt/ (**roots, rooting, rooted**) **1** N-COUNT 可算名詞 The **roots** of a plant are the parts of it that grow under the ground. 根，根っこ □*...the twisted roots of an apple tree.* リンゴの木のねじれた根 **2** V-T/V-I 他動詞/自動詞 If you **root** a plant or cutting or if it **roots**, roots form on the bottom of its stem and it starts to grow. 根づかせる [他動詞]，根づく [自動詞] □*Most plants will root in about six to eight weeks.* ほとんどの植物は6から8週間で根づく． **3** ADJ 形容詞 **Root** vegetables or **root** crops are grown for their roots, which are large and can be eaten. 根菜の [ADJ n] □*...root crops such as carrots and potatoes.* ニンジンやジャガイモなどの根菜類 **4** N-COUNT 可算名詞 The **root** of a hair or tooth is the part of it that is underneath the skin. 毛根，歯根 □*...decay around the roots of teeth.* 歯根あたりの虫歯 **5** N-PLURAL 複数名詞 You can refer to the place or culture that a person or their family comes from as their **roots**. ルーツ □*I am proud of my Brazilian roots.* 私はブラジル人の血を引いていることに誇りを持っている． **6** N-COUNT 可算名詞 You can refer to the cause of a problem or of an unpleasant situation as **the root of** it or **the roots of** it. 根源，根本 □*We got to the root of the problem.* 問題の根源に達した． **7** V-I 自動詞 If you **root through** or **in** something, you search for something by moving other things around. かき回して探す □*She rooted through the bag, found what she wanted, and headed toward the door.* 彼女はバックをかき回し，探していたものを見つけ，ドアの方に向かった． **8** → see also **rooted, grassroots, square root** **9** PHRASE 句 If someone **puts down roots**, they make a place their home, for example by taking part in activities there or by making a lot of friends there. 落ち着く，根を下ろす □*When they got to Montana, they put down roots and built a life.* 彼らがモンタナに行ったとき，そこに落ち着いて生活を築いた． **10** PHRASE 句 If an idea, belief, or custom **takes root**, it becomes established among a group of people. 定着する □*Time would be needed for democracy to take root.* 民主主義が定着するには時間がかかるだろう．

▶ **root out 1** PHRASAL VERB 句動詞 If you **root out** a person, you find them and force them from the place they are in, usually in order to punish them. 捜し出す □*The generals have to root out traitors.* 大将は反逆者を探し出さなければならない． **2** PHRASAL VERB 句動詞 If you **root out** a problem or an unpleasant situation, you find out who or what is the cause of it and put an end to it. 根絶する，一掃する □*There would be a major drive to root out corruption.* 腐敗を一掃するのはかなりの活動になるだろう．

Word Partnership	*root* は次の語句と使われる：
N.	**tree** root **1**
	root **canal 4**
	root **cause of** *something*, root **of a problem 6**
V.	**take** root **10**

root|ed /rúːtɪd/ **1** ADJ 形容詞 If you say that one thing is **rooted in** another, you mean that it is strongly influenced by it or has developed from it. 根ざしている，根源がある [v-link ADJ "in" n] □*The crisis is rooted in deep rivalries between the two groups.* 危機は2グループ間の深い対立関係に根源がある． **2** ADJ 形容詞 If someone has deeply **rooted** opinions or feelings, they believe or feel something

extremely strongly and are unlikely to change. 根深い，定着した □*Racism is a deeply rooted prejudice which has existed for thousands of years.* 人種差別は何千年間も存在し深く定着した偏見だ． **3** PHRASE 句 If you are **rooted to the spot**, you are unable to move because you are very frightened or shocked. くぎづけになって □*We just stopped there, rooted to the spot.* 私たちはくぎづけになって，ただそこに立ち止まった．

rope /róʊp/ (**ropes, roping, roped**) **1** N-VAR 可変性名詞 A **rope** is a thick cord or wire that is made by twisting together several thinner cords or wires. Ropes are used for jobs such as pulling cars, tying up boats, or tying things together. ロープ，縄 □*He tied the rope around his waist.* 彼は彼女の腰の周りにロープを結んだ． **2** V-T 他動詞 If you **rope** one thing **to** another, you tie the two things together with a rope. ロープで縛る □*I roped myself to the chimney.* 私は自分の体を煙突にロープで縛ったんです． **3** PHRASE 句 If you **give** someone **enough rope to hang themselves**, you give them the freedom to do a job in their own way because you hope that their attempts will fail and that they will look foolish. 自由にさせて自滅させる □*The king has merely given the politicians enough rope to hang themselves.* 王はただ政治家を自由にさせて自滅に陥れたに過ぎない． **4** PHRASE 句 If you **are learning the ropes**, you are learning how a particular task or job is done. やり方を覚える [INFORMAL くだけた] □*He tried hiring more salesmen to push his radio products, but they took too much time to learn the ropes.* 彼は無線機の販売促進のためにセールスマンの数を増やしてみたが，仕事を覚えるのに時間がかかりすぎた． **5** PHRASE 句 If you **know the ropes**, you know how a particular job or task should be done. やり方を知っている [INFORMAL くだけた] □*The moment she got to know the ropes, there was no stopping her.* 彼女はやり方がわかった途端，だれも彼女を止めることはできなかった． **6** PHRASE 句 If you **show** someone **the ropes**, you show them how to do a particular job or task. やり方を教える [INFORMAL くだけた] □*We had a patrol out on the border, breaking in some young soldiers, showing them the ropes.* 国境付近にパトロール隊を置き，若い兵士を慣れさせながら，仕事を教えている．

▶ **rope in** PHRASAL VERB 句動詞 If you say that you **were roped in to** do a particular task, you mean that someone persuaded you to help them do that task. 引き込んで〜させる [INFORMAL くだけた] □*Visitors were roped in for potato picking and harvesting.* 観光客はジャガイモ取りに引きずりこまれた．

→ see Word Web: **rope**

rose /róʊz/ (**roses**) **1** **Rose** is the past tense of **rise**. riseの過去形 **2** N-COUNT 可算名詞 A **rose** is a flower, often with a pleasant smell, which grows on a bush with stems that have sharp points called thorns on them. バラの花 □*She bent to pick a red rose.* 彼女はかがんで赤いバラを取った． **3** N-COUNT 可算名詞 A **rose** is bush that roses grow on. バラの枝 □*Prune rambling roses when the flowers have faded.* バラの花が色あせたら，あちこちに伸びた枝を切りなさい． **4** COLOR 色彩語 Something that is **rose** is reddish pink in color. バラ色の [LITERARY 文語的] □*...the rose and violet hues of a twilight sky.* バラ色とスミレ色がかった夕焼け空 **5** PHRASE 句 If you say that a situation is not **a bed of roses**, you mean that it is not as pleasant as it seems, and that there are some unpleasant aspects to it. いいこと，楽しいこと □*We all knew that life was unlikely to be a bed of roses back in Nebraska.* ネブラスカ州に戻ってからの生活はいいことばかりじゃないだろうとみんな分かっていた．

→ see **plant**

Word Link	ette ≈ small : *cigarette, diskette, rosette*

ro|sette /roʊzét/ (**rosettes**) N-COUNT 可算名詞 A **rosette** is a large, circular decoration made from colored ribbons which is given as a prize in a competition, or is worn to show support for a political party or sports team. (バラ形の) 花飾り □*Marjorie stood on the porch with a big yellow rosette tied around the post.* 柱に大きくて黄色い花飾り装飾されたベランダに，マージョリーは立った．

Word Web	rope

Rope consists of a number of **threads**, **strands**, or **fiber**. A machine twists the strands around one another in such a way that they won't **unravel**. Natural materials like hemp and synthetic ones like **nylon** are used. Rope has played a central role in the history of humanity. The Egyptians used it to help build the pyramids. The ships Columbus* discovered America with required rope to raise the sails. Early mountain climbers used thick **cords** to reach high peaks. Using rope always involves making **knots**. The square knot and clove hitch are two of the most common knots.

square knot   clove hitch

Christopher Columbus (1451-1506): an Italian explorer.

ros|ter /rɒstər/ (**rosters**) **1** N-COUNT 可算名詞 A **roster** is a list which gives details of the order in which different people have to do a particular job. 当番表 ❑ *The next day he put himself first on the new roster for domestic chores.* 翌日彼は家事の新しい当番表の一番上に自分の名前を書いた. **2** N-COUNT 可算名詞 A **roster** is a list, especially of the people who work for a particular organization or are available to do a particular job. It can also be a list of the athletes who are available for a particular team. 勤務表, 選手名簿 [mainly AM 主に米国英語] ❑ *The Amateur Softball Association's roster of umpires has declined to 57,000.* アマチュアソフトボール教会の審判員名簿の登録数は5万7千人に減少した.

ros|y /roʊzi/ (**rosier, rosiest**) **1** ADJ 形容詞 If you say that someone has a **rosy** face, you mean that they have pink cheeks and look very healthy. バラ色の, 顔色がいい ❑ *Bethan's round, rosy face seemed hardly to have aged at all.* ベサンのバラ色の丸顔は昔と変わりがなかった. **2** ADJ 形容詞 If you say that a situation looks **rosy** or that the picture looks **rosy**, you mean that the situation seems likely to be good or successful. バラ色の, (未来が) 明るい ❑ *The job prospects for those graduating in engineering are far less rosy now than they used to be.* 工学部の卒業生の就職の見通しは一昔に比べるとかなり暗い.

rot /rɒt/ (**rots, rotting, rotted**) **1** V-T/V-I 他動詞/自動詞 When food, wood, or another substance **rots**, or when something **rots** it, it becomes softer and is gradually destroyed. 腐る, 腐敗する ❑ *If we don't unload it soon, the grain will start rotting in the silos.* すぐに荷降ろしをしないと, 穀物がサイロで腐り始める. **2** N-UNCOUNT 不可算名詞 If there is **rot** in something, especially something that is made of wood, parts of it have decayed and fallen apart. 腐朽 ❑ *Investigations had revealed extensive rot in the beams under the ground floor.* 調査により1階の床のはりの腐敗が広範囲に及んでいることが明らかになった. **3** N-SING 単数名詞 You can use **the rot** to refer to the way something gradually gets worse. For example, if you are talking about the time when **the rot set in**, you are talking about the time when a situation began to get steadily worse and worse. 状況の悪化 ❑ *In many schools, the rot is beginning to set in. Standards are falling all the time.* 多くの学校で状況が悪化している. 道徳基準がどんどん下がっている. **4** V-I 自動詞 If you say that someone is being left to **rot** in a particular place, especially in a prison, you mean that they are being left there and their physical and mental condition is being allowed to get worse and worse. 堕落する ❑ *Most governments simply leave the long-term jobless to rot.* 長期失業者を単に堕落させる政府がほとんどだ.

> **Word Link**   rot ≈ turning : rotary, rotate, rotation

ro|ta|ry /roʊtəri/ **1** ADJ 形容詞 **Rotary** means turning or able to turn around a fixed point. 回転する [ADJ n] ❑ *...turning linear into rotary motion.* 直線運動を回転運動に変えること **2** ADJ 形容詞 **Rotary** is used in the names of some machines that have parts that turn around a fixed point. 回転式の, ロータリー [ADJ n] ❑ *...a rotary engine.* ロータリーエンジン

ro|tate /roʊteɪt/ (**rotates, rotating, rotated**) **1** V-T/V-I 他動詞/自動詞 When something **rotates** or when you **rotate** it, it turns with a circular movement. 回転させる [他動詞], 回転する [自動詞] ❑ *The earth rotates around the sun.* 地球は太陽の周りを公転する. **2** V-T/V-I 他動詞/自動詞 If people or things **rotate**, or if someone **rotates** them, they take turns to do a particular job or serve a particular purpose. 交替する ❑ *The members of the club can rotate and one person can do all the preparation for the evening.* クラブの会員が持ちまわり制で担当でき, 1人でミーティングの準備をすべてできる.

→ see **moon**

ro|ta|tion /roʊteɪʃən/ (**rotations**) **1** N-VAR 可変性名詞 **Rotation** is circular movement. A **rotation** is the movement of something through one complete circle. 回転 ❑ *...the daily rotation of the earth upon its axis.* 毎日の地球の自転 **2** N-UNCOUNT 不可算名詞 The **rotation** of a group of things or people is the fact of them taking turns to do a particular job or serve a particular purpose. If people do something **in rotation**, they take turns to do it. 交替制, 持ち回り ❑ *He grew a different crop on the same field five years in a row, what researchers call crop rotation.* 彼は異なった穀物を同じ畑に5年連続で栽培しましたが, それを専門家は転作と呼びます.

rot|ten /rɒt³n/ **1** ADJ 形容詞 If food, wood, or another substance is **rotten**, it has decayed and can no longer be used. 腐った, 腐敗した ❑ *The smell outside this building is overwhelming – like rotten eggs.* このビルの外のにおいは半端じゃなくて, まるで腐った卵のようです. **2** ADJ 形容詞 If you describe something as **rotten**, you think it is very unpleasant or of very poor quality. 最悪な, 最低な [INFORMAL くだけた] ❑ *I personally think it's a rotten idea.* 個人的には, 私の考えは最低だと思う. **3** ADJ 形容詞 If you feel **rotten**, you feel bad, either because you are ill or because you are sorry about something. 気が重い [INFORMAL くだけた] ❑ *I had rheumatic fever and spent that year feeling rotten.* リューマチ熱にかかってその年は暗い気持ちで過ごした.

> **Thesaurus**   rotten また次を参照:
>
> ADJ.   decomposed, spoiled; (ant.) fresh **1**

rough /rʌf/ (**rougher, roughest**) **1** ADJ 形容詞 If a surface is **rough**, it is uneven and not smooth. ざらざらした ❑ *His hands were rough and callused, from years of karate practice.* 何年間も空手の練習をしたせいで, 彼の手はざらざらでたこができていた. ● **rough|ness** N-UNCOUNT 不可算名詞 ざらざら ❑ *She rested her cheek against the roughness of his jacket.* 彼女は彼の上着のざらざらしたところに首をもたれかけた. **2** ADJ 形容詞 You say that people or their actions are **rough** when they use too much force and not enough care or gentleness. 乱暴な, 荒っぽい ❑ *Football's a rough game at the best of times.* フットボールは順調なときでも荒っぽいスポーツだ. ● **rough|ly** ADV 副詞 乱暴に ❑ *They roughly pushed her forward.* 彼らは彼女を手荒く前へ押した. ● **rough|ness** N-UNCOUNT 不可算名詞 乱暴さ ❑ *He regretted his roughness.* 彼は乱暴にしたことを後悔した. **3** ADJ 形容詞 A **rough** area, city, school, or other place is unpleasant and dangerous because there is a lot of violence or crime there. 治安の悪い ❑ *It was quite a rough part of our town.* そこはこの町でもかなり治安の悪い地域だった. **4** ADJ 形容詞 If you say that someone has had a **rough** time, you mean that they have had some difficult or unpleasant experiences. つらい ❑ *All women have a rough time in our society.* 私たちの社会では女性の生活は皆大変だ. **5** ADJ 形容詞 A **rough** calculation or guess is approximately correct, but not exact. おおよその, 約～ ❑ *We were only able to make a rough estimate of how much fuel would be required.* 燃料の必要量に関して概算の見積もりしか出せませんでした. ● **rough|ly** ADV 副詞 [ADV with cl/group] おおよそ ❑ *Gambling and tourism pay roughly half the entire state budget.* ギャンブルと観光業で州予算全体の約半分を賄っています. **6** ADJ 形容詞 If you give someone a **rough** idea, description, or drawing of something, you indicate only the most important features, without much detail. 大まかな ❑ *I've got a rough idea of what he looks like.* 彼の外見についてだいたい見当がついた. ● **rough|ly** ADV 副詞 大まかに ❑ *He knew roughly what was about to be said.* 彼はこれから言われることについてだいたい分かっていた. **7** ADJ 形容詞 You can say that something is **rough** when it is not neat and well made. 粗雑な ❑ *The bench had a rough wooden table in front of it.* そのベンチの前には粗削りな木製テーブルがあった. ● **rough|ly** ADV 副詞 [ADV with v] 粗く ❑ *Roughly chop the tomatoes and add them to the casserole.* トマトをざく切りにしキャセロールに加えなさい. **8** ADJ 形容詞 If the sea or the weather at sea is **rough**, the weather is windy or stormy and there are very big waves. 荒れた ❑ *A fishing vessel and a cargo ship collided in rough seas.* 漁船と貨物船が荒海で衝突した. **9** PHRASE 句 If you have to **rough it**, you have to live without the possessions and comforts that you normally have. 不便な生活をする [INFORMAL くだけた] ❑ *There is a campsite but, if you prefer not to rough it, the Lake Hotel is nearby.* キャンプ場があるが, 不便な生活を好まなければ, レイク・ホテルが近くにある. **10 rough justice** → see **justice**

▶ **rough up** PHRASAL VERB 句動詞 If someone **roughs** you **up**, they attack you and hit or beat you. 暴力を振るう [INFORMAL くだけた] ❑ *They threw him in a cell and roughed him up a bit.* 彼らは監房で彼を投げ, 少し痛い目にあわせた. ❑ *He was fired from his job after roughing up a colleague.* 彼は同僚に暴力を振るったあと解雇された.

> **Thesaurus**   rough また次を参照:
>
> ADJ.   coarse, harsh; (ant.) smooth **1**
>   approximate, estimated, vague; (ant.) exact **5 6**

rou|lette /ruːlɛt/ N-UNCOUNT 不可算名詞 **Roulette** is a gambling game in which a ball is dropped onto a wheel with numbered holes in it while the wheel is spinning around. The players bet on which hole the ball will be in when the wheel stops spinning. ルーレット ❑ *I had been playing roulette at the casino.* カジノでルーレットをしたことがある.

> **round**
> **❶** PHRASE
> **❷** NOUN USE
> **❸** ADJECTIVE USES
> **❹** VERB USES

❶ round /raʊnd/

> **Round** is used mainly in British English. See **around**.

> **Round** は主として英国英語で用いられる. **around** 参照.

PHRASE 句 If something happens **all year round**, it happens throughout the year. 1年中 ❑ *Many of these plants are evergreen, so you can enjoy them all year round.* これらの植物の多くは常緑樹なので年間を通して楽しめる.

❷ round /raʊnd/ (**rounds**) **1** N-COUNT 可算名詞 A **round of** events is a series of related events, especially one which comes

after or before a similar series of events. 1回（一連の行事・出来事などの）❑ *It was agreed that another round of preliminary talks would be held in Beijing.* 北京で予備交渉を再度行うことが合意された. **2** N-COUNT 可算名詞 In sports, a **round** is a series of games in a competition. The winners of these games go on to play in the next round, and so on, until only one player or team is left. 一回戦 ❑ *...in the third round of the Ryder Cup.* ライダー・カップの3回戦 **3** N-COUNT 可算名詞 In a boxing or wrestling match, a **round** is one of the periods during which the boxers or wrestlers fight. （ボクシング・レスリングの）ラウンド ❑ *He was declared the victor in the 11th round.* 彼は11ラウンドで勝利を決めた. **4** N-COUNT 可算名詞 A **round** of golf is one game, usually including 18 holes. （ゴルフの）ラウンド ❑ *...two rounds of golf.* ゴルフの2ラウンド **5** N-COUNT 可算名詞 If you do your **rounds** or your **round**, you make a series of visits to different places or people, for example as part of your job. 巡回 ❑ *The doctors still did their morning rounds.* それでも医者は朝の回診をした. **6** N-COUNT 可算名詞 If you buy a **round** of drinks, you buy a drink for each member of the group of people that you are with. 酒をおごる番 ❑ *They sat on the clubhouse terrace, downing a round of drinks.* 彼らは，クラブハウスのテラスに座って酒をごくごく飲んでいた. **7** N-COUNT 可算名詞 A **round** of ammunition is the bullet or bullets released when a gun is fired. 1発分 ❑ *...firing 1,650 rounds of ammunition during a period of ten minutes.* 10分間で1650発分の弾薬を発射すること **8** N-COUNT 可算名詞 If there is a **round of applause**, everyone claps their hands to welcome someone or to show that they have enjoyed something. ひとしきりの（拍手）❑ *Sue got a sympathetic round of applause.* スーは好意的な拍手を浴びた. **9** PHRASE 句 If you **make the rounds** or **do the rounds**, you visit a series of different places. 次々に回る ❑ *After school, I had picked up Nick and Ted and made the rounds of the dry cleaner and the food stores.* 放課後，ニックとテッドを迎えに行って，クリーニング屋とスーパーを次々に回った.

❸ round /raʊnd/ (**rounder, roundest**) **1** ADJ 形容詞 Something that is **round** is shaped like a circle or ball. 丸い ❑ *She had small feet and hands and a flat, round face.* 彼女の手足は小さくて，のっぺりとした丸顔だった. **2** ADJ 形容詞 A **round** number is a multiple of 10, 100, 1,000, and so on. Round numbers are used instead of precise ones to give the general idea of a quantity or proportion. 端数のない，切りのいい [ADJ n] ❑ *I asked how much silver could be bought for a million dollars, which seemed a suitably round number.* 100万ドルでどのくらいの銀が買えるかを聞いたのは，適当に切りのいい額のようだったからだ.

❹ round /raʊnd/ (**rounds, rounding, rounded**) **1** V-T 他動詞 If you **round** a place or obstacle, you move in a curve past the edge or corner of it. 曲がる ❑ *The house disappeared from sight as we rounded a corner.* 角を曲がるとその家が見えなくなった. **2** V-T 他動詞 If you **round** an amount **up** or **down**, or if you **round** it **off**, you change it to the nearest whole number or nearest multiple of 10, 100, 1000, and so on. 切り上げる／切り下げる，丸める ❑ *We needed to do decimals to round up and round down numbers.* 小数は四捨五入しなければならない. ❑ *The fraction was then multiplied by 100 and rounded to the nearest half or whole number.* 分数に100を掛け，最も近い整数か1/2の数に切り上げた. **3** → see also **rounded**

▶ **round up 1** PHRASAL VERB 句動詞 If the police or army **round up** a number of people, they arrest or capture them. 一斉逮捕する ❑ *The police rounded up a number of suspects.* 警察は多数の容疑者を一斉逮捕した. **2** PHRASAL VERB 句動詞 If you **round up** animals or things, you gather them together. 寄せ集める ❑ *He had sought work as a cowboy, rounding up cattle.* 彼はカウボーイとして牛を追う仕事を探した. **3** → see also **round ❹ 2 4** → see also **roundup**

round|about /ˈraʊndəbaʊt/ (**roundabouts**) **1** ADJ 形容詞 If you go somewhere by a **roundabout** route, you do not go there by the shortest and quickest route. 遠回りの ❑ *He left today on a roundabout route for Jordan and is also due soon in Egypt.* 彼は今日ヨルダンに向けて遠回りのルートで出発し，まもなくエジプトにも到着予定だ. **2** ADJ 形容詞 If you do or say something in a **roundabout** way, you do not do or say it in a simple, clear, and direct way. 遠回しな ❑ *We made a little fuss in a roundabout way.* 私たちは遠回しに少し文句を言った. **3** N-COUNT 可算名詞 A **roundabout** is a circular structure in the road at a place where several roads meet. You drive around it until you come to the road that you want. ロータリー [BRIT 英国英語; AM **traffic circle, rotary** 米国英語 **traffic circle, rotary**] **4** N-COUNT 可算名詞 A **roundabout** at an amusement park is a large, circular mechanical device with seats, often in the shape of animals or cars, on which children sit and go around and around. メリーゴーラウンド，回転木馬 [BRIT 英国英語; AM **merry-go-round, carousel** 米国英語 **merry-go-round, carousel**] **5** N-COUNT 可算名詞 A **roundabout** in a park or school play area is a circular platform that children sit or stand on. People push the platform to make it spin around. 回転遊具 [BRIT 英国英語; AM **merry-go-round** 米国英語 **merry-go-round**] **6** **round about** → see **round**

round|ed /ˈraʊndɪd/ **1** ADJ 形容詞 Something that is **rounded** is curved in shape, without any points or sharp edges. 丸い，丸

みを帯びた ❑ *...a low, rounded hill.* 低くなだらかな丘 **2** ADJ 形容詞 You describe something or someone as **rounded** when you are expressing approval of them because they have a personality which is fully developed in all aspects. 成熟した，人間的な丸みのある [APPROVAL 賛成] ❑ *...his carefully organized narrative, full of rounded, believable, and interesting characters.* 円熟でもっともらしくて面白い登場人物がたくさん登場する，彼の慎重にまとめられた話

round trip (**round trips**) **1** N-COUNT 可算名詞 If you make a **round trip**, you travel to a place and then back again. 往復 ❑ *The train operates the 2,400-mile round trip once a week.* その列車は週に1度往復2400マイルの距離を走行する. **2** ADJ 形容詞 A **round-trip** ticket is a ticket for a train, bus, or plane that allows you to travel to a particular place and then back again. 往復の [AM 米国英語] [ADJ n] ❑ *Mexicana Airlines has announced cheaper round-trip tickets between Los Angeles and cities it serves in Mexico.* メキシコ航空は，ロサンゼルス市—メキシコ国内の都市間の格安往復チケットの案内をした.

round|up /ˈraʊndʌp/ (**roundups**) N-COUNT 可算名詞 In journalism, especially television or radio, a **roundup** of news is a summary of the main events that have happened. まとめ，ダイジェスト ❑ *First, we have this roundup of the day's news.* まず，1日のニュースのまとめをお送りします.

rouse /raʊz/ (**rouses, rousing, roused**) **1** V-T/V-I 他動詞/自動詞 If someone **rouses** you when you are sleeping or if you **rouse**, you wake up. （眠りから）起こす [LITERARY 文語的] [他動詞]，目を覚ます [自動詞] ❑ *Hilton roused him at eight-thirty by rapping on the door.* ヒルトンは8時半に戸をこつこつ叩いて彼を起こした. **2** V-T 他動詞 If you **rouse yourself**, you stop being inactive and start doing something. 奮起する ❑ *She seemed to be unable to rouse herself to do anything.* 彼女は奮起して事に当たるということができないようだった. **3** V-T 他動詞 If something or someone **rouses** you, they make you very emotional or excited. かきたてる ❑ *He did more to rouse the crowd there than anybody else.* 彼はほかのだれよりもそこにいた群衆をかきたてるようなことをしました. ● **rous|ing** ADJ 形容詞 鼓舞する，励ましの ❑ *...a rousing speech to the convention in support of the president.* 大会で大統領を支持する熱弁 **4** V-T 他動詞 If something **rouses** a feeling in you, it causes you to have that feeling. 駆り立てる ❑ *It roused a feeling of rebellion in him.* それは彼に反感を駆り立てた.

→ see **dream**

rout /raʊt/ (**routs, routing, routed**) V-T 他動詞 If an army, sports team, or other group **routs** its opponents, it defeats them completely and easily. 圧勝する ❑ *...the Battle of Hastings at which the Norman army routed the English opposition.* ノルマン軍が敵のイングランドに圧勝したヘイスティングズの戦い ● N-COUNT 可算名詞 **Rout** is also a noun. 完敗 ❑ *One after another the Italian bases in the desert fell as the retreat turned into a rout.* 撤退が敗北に変わるにつれて砂漠のイタリア基地が次々に陥落した.

route /ruːt/ (**routes, routing, routed**) **1** N-COUNT 可算名詞 A **route** is a way from one place to another. ルート，道筋 ❑ *...the most direct route to the center of town.* 町の中心部への最短ルート **2** N-COUNT 可算名詞 A bus, air, or shipping **route** is the way between two places along which buses, planes, or ships travel regularly. 路線，航路 ❑ *...the main shipping routes to Japan.* 日本への主な航路 **3** N-IN-NAMES 名称中の名詞 In the United States, **Route** is used in front of a number in the names of main roads between major cities. 一号線 ❑ *From San Francisco take the freeway to the Broadway-Webster exit on Route 580.* サンフランシスコから高速道路にのって580号線が通っているブロードウェイ・ウェブスター出口で下りなさい. **4** N-COUNT 可算名詞 Your **route** is the series of visits you make to different people or places, as part of your job. 巡回 [mainly AM 主に米国英語] ❑ *He began cracking open big blue tins of butter cookies and feeding the dogs on his route.* 彼は，巡回の途中でバタークッキーの大きくて青い缶をブシップシッと開けてイヌに食べさせ始めた. **5** N-COUNT 可算名詞 You can refer to a way of achieving something as a **route**. 方法 ❑ *Researchers are trying to get at the same information through an indirect route.* 研究者は間接的な方法で同じ情報を得ようとしています. **6** V-T 他動詞 If vehicles, goods, or passengers **are routed** in a particular direction, they are made to travel in that direction. 送る [usu passive] ❑ *Trains are taking a lot of freight that used to be routed via trucks.* かつてはトラックによって輸送されていた多くの荷物が電車で輸送されている. **7** PHRASE 句 **En route to** a place means on the way to that place. **En route** is sometimes spelled **on route** in nonstandard English. 〜に行く途中で ❑ *They have arrived in London en route to the United States.* 彼らは米国に行く途中でロンドンに到着しました. **8** PHRASE 句 Journalists sometimes use **en route** when they are mentioning an event that happened as part of a longer process or before another event. 途中で ❑ *The German set three tournament records and equaled two others en route to grabbing golf's richest prize.* そのドイツ選手は，ゴルフ界最高の賞金を得る過程で3つの部門でトーナメント新記録を出し，2部門でタイの成績を出した.

r

Thesaurus *route* また次を参照：

N. path, road, trail 1 2

Word Partnership *route* は次の語句と使われる：

N. **escape** route, **parade** route 1
ADJ. **scenic** route 1
main route 1 2
alternative route, **shortest** route 1 2 5
different route, **direct** route 1 6

rou|tine /rutin/ (**routines**) 1 N-VAR 可変性名詞 A **routine** is the usual series of things that you do at a particular time. A **routine** is also the practice of regularly doing things in a fixed order. 日課，習慣 ❑ *The players had to change their daily routine and lifestyle.* 選手は日課と生活スタイルを変えなければならなかった． 2 ADJ 形容詞 You use **routine** to describe activities that are done as a normal part of a job or process. 定期的な，一般的な ❑ *...a series of routine medical tests including X-rays and blood tests.* レントゲン検査及び血液検査を含む一連の定期健診 3 ADJ 形容詞 A **routine** situation, action, or event is one which seems completely ordinary, rather than interesting, exciting, or different. 平凡な，退屈な [DISAPPROVAL 不賛成] ❑ *So many days are routine and uninteresting, especially in winter.* 退屈で面白くない日が，特に冬に，あまりにも多い． 4 N-VAR 可変性名詞 You use **routine** to refer to a way of life that is uninteresting and ordinary, or hardly ever changes. 平凡 [DISAPPROVAL 不賛成] ❑ *...the mundane routine of her life.* 彼女の平々凡々な生活 5 N-COUNT 可算名詞 A **routine** is a computer program, or part of a program, that performs a specific function. ルーチン [COMPUTING コンピューティング] ❑ *...an installation routine.* インストールルーチン 6 N-COUNT 可算名詞 A **routine** is a short sequence of jokes, remarks, actions, or movements that forms part of a longer performance. 決まり文句，お決まりの演技，決まった型 ❑ *...an athletic dance routine.* アスレチックダンスの決まったステップ

Word Partnership *routine* は次の語句と使われる：

N. **exercise** routine, **work** routine 1
morning routine 1 4
routine **maintenance**, routine **tests** 2
routine **day** 3
comedy routine, **dance** routine 6
ADJ. **daily** routine, **normal** routine, **regular** routine, **usual** routine 1 2

rou|tine|ly /rutinli/ 1 ADV 副詞 If something is **routinely** done, it is done as a normal part of a job or process. 通常，一般的に ❑ *Vitamin K is routinely given in the first week of life to prevent bleeding.* 出血予防のため通常生後1週間以内にビタミンKを投与する． 2 ADV 副詞 If something happens **routinely**, it happens repeatedly and is not surprising, unnatural, or new. 日常的に，当たり前に [ADV with v] ❑ *Any outside criticism is routinely dismissed as interference.* 外部の批判はすべて妨害であるとみなされ規定通りに却下される．

rov|ing /roʊvɪŋ/ ADJ 形容詞 You use **roving** to describe a person who travels around, rather than staying in a fixed place. 放浪する [ADJ n] ❑ *He is to join NBC to cover the Olympic Games in Barcelona next month as a roving reporter.* 彼は，移動記者として来月バルセロナでオリンピック大会を報道するためにNBC社に入社する予定だ．

R

row
❶ ARRANGEMENT OR SEQUENCE
❷ MAKING A BOAT MOVE

❶ **row** /roʊ/ (**rows**) 1 N-COUNT 可算名詞 A **row of** things or people is a number of them arranged in a line. 列 ❑ *...a row of pretty little cottages.* かわいい小さな家の並び 2 N-IN-NAMES 名称中の名詞 **Row** is sometimes used in the names of streets. 一通り ❑ *...the house at 236 Larch Row.* ラーチ通り236番地にある家 3 → see also **death row** 4 PHRASE 句 If something happens several times **in a row**, it happens that number of times without a break. If something happens several days **in a row**, it happens on each of those days. 連続して ❑ *They have won five championships in a row.* 彼らは5回連続優勝した．

❷ **row** /roʊ/ (**rows, rowing, rowed**) 1 V-T/V-I 他動詞/自動詞 When you **row**, you sit in a boat and make it move through the water by using oars. If you **row** someone somewhere, you take them there in a boat, using oars. （人を）ボートに乗せて連れて行く [他動詞]，ボートをこぐ [自動詞] ❑ *He rowed as quickly as he could to the shore.* 彼は岸に着くようできるだけ早くこいだ． ❑ *The boatman refused to row him back.* 船頭は彼を帰りのボートに乗せるのを断った． ● N-COUNT 可算名詞 **Row** is also a noun. ボートこぎ ❑ *I took Daniel for a row.* ダニエルをボートこぎに連れて行った． 2 → see also **rowing**

row|dy /raʊdi/ (**rowdier, rowdiest**) ADJ 形容詞 When people are **rowdy**, they are noisy, rough, and likely to cause trouble. 騒々しい，けんかっ早い ❑ *He has complained to the police about rowdy neighbors.* 彼は騒々しい隣人を警察に訴えた．

row house (**row houses**) N-COUNT 可算名詞 A **row house** is one of a row of similar houses that are joined together by both of their side walls. 長屋建て住宅，テラスハウス [AM 米国英語] ❑ *...a city block of row houses.* テラスハウスの街区

row|ing /roʊɪŋ/ N-UNCOUNT 不可算名詞 **Rowing** is a sport in which people or teams race against each other in boats with oars. 漕艇（そうてい） ❑ *...competitions in rowing, swimming, and water skiing.* 漕艇（そうてい），水泳，水上スキーのレース

Word Link *roy ≈ king : royal, royalist, royalty*

roy|al /rɔɪəl/ (**royals**) 1 ADJ 形容詞 **Royal** is used to indicate that something is connected with a king, queen, or emperor, or their family. A **royal** person is a king, queen, or emperor, or a member of their family. 国王の，天皇の，王室の ❑ *...an invitation to a royal garden party.* 王室のガーデンパーティへの招待 2 ADJ 形容詞 **Royal** is used in the names of institutions or organizations that are officially appointed or supported by a member of a royal family. 王立の，ロイヤルー [ADJ n] ❑ *...the Royal Academy of Music.* 英国王立音楽院 3 N-COUNT 可算名詞 Members of the royal family are sometimes referred to as **royals**. 王室の一員 [INFORMAL くだけた] ❑ *The royals have always been patrons of charities pulling in large donations.* 王室家の人々はいつもチャリティの後援者として多額の寄付金を集めてきた．

roy|al|ist /rɔɪəlɪst/ (**royalists**) N-COUNT 可算名詞 A **royalist** is someone who supports their country's royal family or who believes that their country should have a king or queen. 王政主義者 ❑ *He was hated by the royalists and mistrusted by the communists.* 彼は王政主義者に嫌われて共産主義者には信用されなかった．

roy|al|ty /rɔɪəlti/ (**royalties**) 1 N-UNCOUNT 不可算名詞 The members of royal families are sometimes referred to as **royalty**. 王族 ❑ *Royalty and government leaders from all around the world are gathering in Japan.* 世界各国からの王族と政府首脳が日本に集合している． 2 N-PLURAL 複数名詞 **Royalties** are payments made to authors and musicians when their work is sold or performed. They usually receive a fixed percentage of the profits from these sales or performances. 印税 ❑ *I lived on about $5,000 a year from the royalties on my book.* 年間5千ドルの拙著の印税で生活を立てた． 3 N-COUNT 可算名詞 Payments made to someone whose invention, idea, or property is used by a commercial company can be referred to as **royalties**. 特許権使用料 ❑ *The royalties enabled the inventor to re-establish himself in business.* 特許権使用料のおかげでその発明家は事業を再建することができた．

RSI /ɑr ɛs aɪ/ N-UNCOUNT 不可算名詞 People who suffer from **RSI** have pain in their hands and arms as a result of repeating similar movements over a long period of time, usually as part of their job. **RSI** is an abbreviation for **repetitive strain injury**. けんしょう炎，反復運動過多損傷 ❑ *The women developed painful RSI because of poor working conditions.* 劣悪な作業環境のために女性らは有痛性のけんしょう炎にかかった．

RSVP /ɑr ɛs vi pi/ also **R.S.V.P.** **RSVP** is an abbreviation for "répondez s'il vous plaît," which means "please reply." It is written on the bottom of a card inviting you to a party or special occasion. ご返事お待ちしています [FORMAL 形式ばった]

When **RSVP** appears on an invitation, the sender needs to know whether or not the guest will come to the event. The guest should answer in plenty of time so the host can make plans. If the note **BYOB** also appears, it means the host wants the guest to "Bring Your Own Bottle" if they wish to drink alcoholic drinks.

rub /rʌb/ (**rubs, rubbing, rubbed**) 1 V-T/V-I 他動詞/自動詞 If you **rub** a part of your body or if you **rub at** it, you move your hand or fingers backward and forward over it while pressing firmly. こする，さする ❑ *He rubbed his arms and stiff legs.* 彼は腕と筋肉が張った足をさすった． 2 V-T/V-I 他動詞/自動詞 If you **rub against** a surface or **rub** a part of your body **against** a surface, you move it backward and forward while pressing it against the surface. こすりつける ❑ *A cat was rubbing against my leg.* ネコが私の両脚に体をこすりつけていた． 3 V-T/V-I 他動詞/自動詞 If you **rub** an object or a surface or you **rub at** it, you move a cloth backward and forward over it in order to clean or dry it. ふく，磨く ❑ *She took off her glasses and rubbed them hard.* 彼女は眼鏡を外してゴシゴシふいた． 4 V-T 他動詞 If you **rub** a substance **into** a surface or **rub** something such as dirt **from** a surface, you spread it over the surface or remove it from the surface using your hand or something such as a cloth. 塗る，擦り込む，擦りつける ❑ *He rubbed oil into my back.* 彼は私の背中にオイルを塗った． 5 V-T/V-I 他動詞/自動詞 If you **rub** two things **together** or if they **rub together**, they move backward and forward, pressing against each other. こすり合わせる ❑ *He*

rubbed his hands together a few times. 彼は数回手をこすり合わせた。 **6** V-I 自動詞 If something you are wearing or holding **rubs**, it makes you sore because it keeps moving backward and forward against your skin. こすれて痛い、すりむく □It should be comfortable against the skin without rubbing, chafing, or cutting into anything. それはこすったり、すりむいたり、切れたりすることなく肌に優しいはずだ。 **7** N-COUNT 可算名詞 A massage can be referred to as a **rub**. もむこと、マッサージ □She sometimes asks if I want a back rub. 彼女はときどき私に背中をもんで欲しいかと聞く。 **8** PHRASE 句 If you **rub shoulders with** famous people, you meet them and talk to them. You can also say that you **rub elbows with** someone. 近づきになる □He regularly rubbed shoulders with the likes of Elizabeth Taylor and Kylie Minogue. 彼は定期的にエリザベス・テイラーやカイリー・ミノーグのような人物とお近づきになる。 **9** PHRASE 句 If you **rub** someone **the wrong way**, you offend or annoy them without intending to. (人の) 神経を逆なでする [INFORMAL くだけた] □What are you going to get out of him if you rub him the wrong way? 彼の神経を逆なでして何を求めているんだい? 彼 **10** to **rub** someone's **nose in it → see nose**
▶ **rub out** PHRASAL VERB 句動詞 If you **rub out** something that you have written on paper or a board, you remove it using an eraser. 消しゴムで消す [BRIT 英国英語; AM erase 米国英語 erase]

Word Partnership	rub は次の語句と使われる:
PREP.	rub **against 2**
	rub **off**, rub **with 2**
ADV.	rub **together 5**

rub|ber /rʌbər/ (rubbers) **1** N-UNCOUNT 不可算名詞 **Rubber** is a strong, waterproof, elastic substance made from the juice of a tropical tree or produced chemically. It is used for making tires, boots, and other products. ゴム □...the smell of burning rubber. ゴムを燃やすにおい **2** N-COUNT 可算名詞 A **rubber** is a condom. コンドーム [AM 米国英語, INFORMAL くだけた] **3** N-COUNT 可算名詞 A **rubber** is a small piece of rubber or other material that is used to remove mistakes that you have made while writing, drawing, or typing. 消しゴム [BRIT 英国英語; AM eraser 米国英語 eraser]

rub|ber band (rubber bands) N-COUNT 可算名詞 A **rubber band** is a thin circle of very elastic rubber. You put it around things such as papers in order to keep them together. 輪ゴム
→ see office

rub|ber stamp (rubber stamps, rubber stamping, rubber stamped) also **rubber-stamp 1** N-COUNT 可算名詞 A **rubber stamp** is a small device with a name, date, or symbol on it. You press it onto an ink pad and then on to a document in order to show that the document has been officially dealt with. ゴム印 □In post offices, virtually every document that's passed across the counter is stamped with a rubber stamp. 郵便局では事実上カウンターを越えた書類すべてにゴム印が押されている。 **2** V-T 他動詞 When someone in authority **rubber-stamps** a decision, plan, or law, they agree to it without thinking about it much. めくら判を押す □The board's job is to rubber-stamp his decisions. 理事会の仕事は彼の決断にめくら版を押すことだ。

rub|bish /rʌbɪʃ/ (rubbishes, rubbishing, rubbished) **1** N-UNCOUNT 不可算名詞 **Rubbish** consists of unwanted things or waste material such as used paper, empty cans and bottles, and waste food. ごみ [mainly BRIT 主に英国英語; AM usually garbage, trash 米国英語では通常 garbage, trash] **2** N-UNCOUNT 不可算名詞 If you think that something is of very poor quality, you can say that it is **rubbish**. しょうもないもの [mainly BRIT 主に英国英語, INFORMAL くだけた] **3** V-T 他動詞 If you **rubbish** a person, their ideas or their work, you say they are of little value. けなす、こき下ろす [BRIT 英国英語, INFORMAL くだけた] [AM trash 米国英語 trash]

In British English, **rubbish** is the word most commonly used to refer to waste material that is thrown away. In American English, the words **garbage** and **trash** are more usual. □...the smell of rotting garbage... She threw the bottle into the trash. **Garbage** and **trash** are sometimes used in British English, but only informally and metaphorically. □I don't have to listen to this garbage... The book was trash.

rub|ble /rʌbəl/ **1** N-UNCOUNT 不可算名詞 When a building is destroyed, the pieces of brick, stone, or other materials that remain are referred to as **rubble**. 瓦礫 (がれき) □Thousands of bodies are still buried under the rubble. 何千もの死体が依然として瓦礫 (がれき) の下に埋まっている。 **2** N-UNCOUNT 不可算名詞 **Rubble** is used to refer to the small pieces of bricks and stones that are used as a bottom layer on which to build roads, paths, or houses. 基礎、土台 □Brick rubble is useful as the base for paths and patios. れんがの土台は小道やテラスの基礎に便利だ。

ruby /rubi/ (rubies) **1** N-COUNT 可算名詞 A **ruby** is a dark red jewel. ルビー □...a ruby and diamond ring. ルビーとダイアモンドの指輪 **2** COLOR 色彩語 Something that is **ruby** is dark red in color. ルヴィー色 □...a glass of ruby-red Cabernet Sauvignon. ルヴィー色のカベルネ・ソーヴィニヨンを1杯

ruck|sack /rʌksæk/ (rucksacks) N-COUNT 可算名詞 A **rucksack** is a bag with straps that go over your shoulders, so that you can carry things on your back, for example when you are walking or climbing. リュックサック [BRIT 英国英語; AM usually backpack, knapsack, pack 米国英語では通常 backpack, knapsack, pack]

rud|der /rʌdər/ (rudders) **1** N-COUNT 可算名詞 A **rudder** is a device for steering a boat. It consists of a vertical piece of wood or metal at the back of the boat. かじ **2** N-COUNT 可算名詞 An airplane's **rudder** is a vertical piece of metal at the back which is used to make the plane turn to the right or to the left. 方向舵

rud|dy /rʌdi/ (ruddier, ruddiest) ADJ 形容詞 If you describe someone's face as **ruddy**, you mean that their face is a reddish color, usually because they are healthy or have been working hard, or because they are angry or embarrassed. 血色のいい、赤らんだ □He had a naturally ruddy complexion, even more flushed now from dancing. 彼は生まれつき顔色がよかったが、踊ったあとなのでさらに紅潮していた。

rude /rud/ (ruder, rudest) **1** ADJ 形容詞 When people are **rude**, they act in an impolite way toward other people or say impolite things about them. 失礼な、無礼な □He's rude to her friends and obsessively jealous. 彼は彼女の友達に無愛想で異常なほどにしっと深い。 ● **rude|ly** ADV 副詞 失礼に □I could not understand why she felt compelled to behave so rudely to a friend. どうして彼女が友達にそれほど失礼に振るまわざるを得なかったのか理解できなかった。 ● **rude|ness** N-UNCOUNT 不可算名詞 失礼、無礼な態度 □I was annoyed at Caleb's rudeness, but I can forgive it. 母はキャレブの無礼さにイライラしていたが、私は許せる。 **2** ADJ 形容詞 **Rude** is used to describe words and behavior that are likely to embarrass or offend people, because they relate to sex or to body functions. 下品な、いやらしい、すけべな □Fred keeps cracking rude jokes with the guests. フレッドは客に下ネタジョークを飛ばしてばかりだ。 **3** ADJ 形容詞 [ADJ n] If someone receives a **rude** shock, something unpleasant happens unexpectedly. 突然の □It will come as a rude shock when their salary or income-tax refund cannot be cashed. 給料や所得税の返還を現金化できないような突然の衝撃として表面化するだろう。 ● **rude|ly** ADV 副詞 [ADV with v] 突然に、いきなり □People were rudely awakened by a siren just outside their window. 窓のすぐ外から聞こえるサイレンでいきなり起こされた。 **4** rude awakening → see awakening

Thesaurus	rude また次を参照:
ADJ.	disrespectful, impolite, vulgar; (ant.) polite **1 2**

ru|di|men|ta|ry /rudɪmɛntəri, -tri/ ADJ 形容詞 **1** **Rudimentary** things are very basic or simple and are therefore unsatisfactory. 原始的な [FORMAL 形式ばった] □The earth surface of the courtyard extended into a kind of rudimentary kitchen. 中庭の地表が原始的な台所のようなところに広がっていた。 **2** ADJ 形容詞 **Rudimentary** knowledge includes only the simplest and most basic facts. 初歩的な、基本的な [FORMAL 形式ばった] □He had only a rudimentary knowledge of French. 彼はフランス語の基本的な知識しかなかった。

ruf|fle /rʌfəl/ (ruffles, ruffling, ruffled) **1** V-T 他動詞 If you **ruffle** someone's hair, you move your hand backward and forward through it as a way of showing your affection toward them. クシャクシャにする □"Don't let that get you down," he said, ruffling Ben's dark curls. 「あまり気にするなよ」と彼はベンのくせのある栗毛をクシャクシャにしながら言った。 **2** V-T 他動詞 When the wind **ruffles** something such as the surface of the sea, it causes it to move gently in a wavelike motion. 波立てる [LITERARY 文語的] □The evening breeze ruffled the pond. 夕風が池にさざ波を立てた。 **3** V-T 他動詞 If something **ruffles** someone, it causes them to panic and lose their confidence or to become angry or upset. 動揺させる、いら立たせる □I could tell that my refusal to allow him to ruffle me infuriated him. 私が冷静に対処したことで彼が激怒したことが明らかだった。 **4** V-T/V-I 他動詞/自動詞 If a bird **ruffles** its feathers or if its feathers **ruffle**, they stand out on its body, for example when it is cleaning itself or when it is frightened. 逆立てる [他動詞], 逆立つ [自動詞] □Tame birds, when approached, will stretch out their necks and ruffle their neck feathering. 飼いならされた鳥は、誰かが近づくと、首を伸ばして首の羽を逆立てる。 **5** N-COUNT 可算名詞 **Ruffles** are folds of cloth at the neck or the ends of the arms of a piece of clothing, or sometimes sewn on things as a decoration. フリル、ひだ飾り □...a white blouse with ruffles at the neck and cuffs. 襟ぐりと袖口にフリルがついた白いブラウス **6** PHRASE 句 To **ruffle** someone's **feathers** means to cause them to become very angry, nervous, or upset. 怒らせる □His direct, often abrasive approach will doubtless ruffle a few feathers. 彼の率直で無神経なやり方によって間違いなく感情を害する人がいるだろう。

ruf|fled /rʌfəld/ ADJ 形容詞 Something that is **ruffled** is no longer smooth or neat. しわくちゃの □Her short hair was oddly ruffled and then flattened around her head. 彼女に短い髪は妙にくにゃくにゃでしかも部分的にペタンコになっていた。

rug /rʌg/ (**rugs**) **1** N-COUNT 可算名詞 A **rug** is a piece of thick material that you put on a floor. It is like a carpet but covers a smaller area. 敷物，マット □ *A Persian rug covered the hardwood floors.* ペルシアじゅうたんが木製のフロアに敷かれていた. **2** N-COUNT 可算名詞 A **rug** is a small blanket which you use to cover your shoulders or your knees to keep them warm. 肩掛け，ひざ掛け [mainly BRIT 主に英国英語] □ *The old lady was seated in her chair at the window, a rug over her knees.* 老婦人がひざ掛けをして窓際のいすに座っていた. **3** PHRASE 句 If someone **pulls the rug from under** a person or thing or **pulls the rug from under** someone's **feet**, they stop giving their help or support. 援助を打ち切る，足元をすくう □ *If the banks opt to pull the rug from under the ill-fated project, it will go into liquidation.* 銀行がその不運な事業の援助を打ち切ることを選べば，倒産するだろう. **4** to **sweep** something **under the rug** → see **sweep**

rug|by /ˈrʌgbi/ N-UNCOUNT 不可算名詞 **Rugby** or **rugby football** is a game played by two teams using an oval ball. Players try to score points by carrying the ball to their opponents' end of the field, or by kicking it over a bar fixed between two posts. ラグビー

rug|ged /ˈrʌgɪd/ **1** ADJ 形容詞 A **rugged** area of land is uneven and covered with rocks, with few trees or plants. 起伏の多い，ゴツゴツした [LITERARY 文語的] □ *We left the rough track and bumped our way over a rugged mountainous terrain.* 我々はでこぼこ道を去り，ガタガタと荒涼とした山岳地帯をはるか遠くに越えた. **2** ADJ 形容詞 If you describe a man as **rugged**, you mean that he has strong, masculine features. いかつい [LITERARY 文語的, APPROVAL 賛成] □ *A look of pure disbelief crossed Shankly's rugged face.* 全く信じられないという表情がシャンクリーのいかつい顔を横切った. **3** ADJ 形容詞 If you describe someone's character as **rugged**, you mean that they are strong and determined, and have the ability to cope with difficult situations. たくましい [APPROVAL 賛成] □ *Rugged individualism forged America's frontier society.* 徹底した個人主義がアメリカのフロンティア社会を築いた. **4** ADJ 形容詞 A **rugged** piece of equipment is strong and is designed to last a long time, even if it is treated roughly. 頑丈な □ *The camera combines rugged reliability with unequaled optical performance and speed.* そのカメラは頑丈で信頼性が高く，光学性能と速度において無敵だ.

ruin /ˈruːɪn/ (**ruins, ruining, ruined**) **1** V-T 他動詞 To **ruin** something means to severely harm, damage, or spoil it. 台なしにする，だめにする □ *My wife was ruining her health through worry.* 妻は心配性のため健康を損なっていた. **2** V-T 他動詞 To **ruin** someone means to cause them to no longer have any money. 破産させる □ *She accused him of ruining her financially with his taste for the high life.* 彼女は，彼のぜいたく性のために経済的に破滅したことで彼を非難した. **3** N-UNCOUNT 不可算名詞 **Ruin** is the state of no longer having any money. 破産 □ *The farmers said that recent inflation has driven them to the brink of ruin.* 農場経営者は，最近のインフレのために破産寸前までいったと述べた. **4** N-UNCOUNT 不可算名詞 **Ruin** is the state of being severely damaged or spoiled, or the process of reaching this state. 崩壊，廃退 □ *The vineyards were falling into ruin.* ブドウ園は荒れ果てていた. **5** N-PLURAL 複数名詞 The **ruins of** something are the parts of it that remain after it has been severely damaged or weakened. 遺跡，廃虚 □ *The new Turkish republic he helped to build emerged from the ruins of a great empire.* 彼が建国の手助けをした新トルコ共和国は，偉大な帝国の遺跡から現れた. **6** N-COUNT 可算名詞 The **ruins** of a building are the parts of it that remain after the rest has fallen down or been destroyed. 跡地 □ *One dead child was found in the ruins almost two hours after the explosion.* 爆発のほぼ2時間後に子供が1人跡地で見つかった. **7** → see also **ruined** **8** PHRASE 句 If something is **in ruins**, it is completely spoiled. ぼろぼろで □ *Its heavily subsidized economy is in ruins.* 大幅に援助された経済はぼろぼろだ. **9** PHRASE 句 If a building or place is **in ruins**, most of it has been destroyed and only parts of it remain. 廃墟と化して □ *The abbey was in ruins.* 教会堂は廃墟となっていました.

▶ **Thesaurus** *ruin* また次を参照:

V.	destroy, smash, wreck **1**

ruined /ˈruːɪnd/ ADJ 形容詞 A **ruined** building or place has been very badly damaged and has gradually fallen down because no one has taken care of it. 荒れ果てた [ADJ n] □ *...a ruined church.* 荒れ果てた教会

rule /ruːl/ (**rules, ruling, ruled**) **1** N-COUNT 可算名詞 **Rules** are instructions that tell you what you are allowed to do and what you are not allowed to do. 規則，ルール □ *...a thirty-two-page pamphlet explaining the rules of basketball.* バスケットボールのルールを説明した全32ページのパンフレット. **2** N-COUNT 可算名詞 A **rule** is a statement telling people what they should do in order to achieve success or a benefit of some kind. 原則，するべきこと □ *An important rule is to drink plenty of water during any flight.* 大事なことは飛行中にたくさんの水分をとることです. **3** N-COUNT 可算名詞 The **rules** of something such as a language or a science are statements that describe the way that things usually happen in a particular situation. 規則，法則 □ *...according to the rules*

of quantum theory. 量子論の法則によると **4** N-SING 単数名詞 If something is **the rule**, it is the normal state of affairs. 通例 □ *However, for many Americans today, weekend work has unfortunately become the rule rather than the exception.* しかしながら，今日のアメリカ人の多くにとって，週末に働くことは残念ながら例外というよりはむしろ通例になりました. **5** V-T/V-I 他動詞/自動詞 The person or group that **rules** a country controls its affairs. 支配する，統治する □ *For four centuries, he says, foreigners have ruled Angola.* 4世紀に渡って外国人がアンゴラを支配したと彼は述べた. □ *He ruled for eight months.* 彼は8か月間支配した. ● N-UNCOUNT 不可算名詞 **Rule** is also a noun. 支配 □ *...demands for an end to one-party rule.* 一党支配終焉（しゅうえん）に対する要求 **6** V-T 他動詞 If something **rules** your life, it influences or restricts your actions in a way that is not good for you. 支配する，左右する □ *Scientists have always been aware of how fear can rule our lives and make us ill.* 科学者は，いかに恐れが生活に影響を与え病気を引き起こすかについて常に認識してきた. **7** V-T/V-I 他動詞/自動詞 When someone in authority **rules** that something is true or should happen, they state that they have officially decided that it is true or should happen. 裁定を下す，宣告する [FORMAL 形式ばった] □ *The court ruled that laws passed by the assembly remained valid.* 裁判所は議会を通過した法律は依然として有効であるという判決を下した. □ *The Israeli court has not yet ruled on the case.* イスラエルの裁判所はまだその訴訟の判決を下していない. **8** V-T 他動詞 If you **rule** a straight line, you draw it using something that has a straight edge. 直線を引く □ *...a ruled grid of horizontal and vertical lines.* 縦横の直線が引かれた升目 **9** → see also **golden rule, ground rule, ruling** **10** PHRASE 句 If you say that something happens **as a rule**, you mean that it usually happens. 一般に，概して □ *As a rule, however, such attacks have been aimed at causing damage rather than taking life.* しかしながら，一般的にはその ような攻撃は殺戮（さつりく）のためというよりはむしろ被害を及ぼすのが目的で行われてきた. **11** PHRASE 句 If someone in authority **bends the rules** or **stretches the rules**, they do something even though it is against the rules. 規則を曲げる □ *There happens to be a particular urgency in this case, and it would help if you could bend the rules.* この件はたまたま特別緊急を要するので，もし規則を曲げられると助かります. **12** PHRASE 句 A **rule of thumb** is a rule or principle that you follow which is not based on exact calculations, but rather on experience. 経験則，大ざっぱに言えること □ *A good rule of thumb is that a broker must generate sales of ten times his salary if his employer is to make a profit.* 経験から言って，雇用者が利益を上げるには仲介者は給料の10倍の売上を上げければならない.

▶ **rule out** **1** PHRASAL VERB 句動詞 If you **rule out** a course of action, an idea, or a solution, you decide that it is impossible or unsuitable. 不可能/不適切だと判断する □ *The Treasury Department has ruled out using a weak dollar as the main solution for the country's trade problems.* 財務省は，国の貿易問題の主な解決策としてドル安を利用することが不適切だと判断した. **2** PHRASAL VERB 句動詞 If something **rules out** a situation, it prevents it from happening or from being possible. 未然に防ぐ □ *A serious car accident in 1986 ruled out a permanent future for him in farming.* 1986年に深刻な交通事故にあったため彼は一生農業に就くことができなくなった.

▶ **Thesaurus** *rule* また次を参照:

N.	guideline, law, standard **1** **2**
	authority, leadership **5**
V.	command, dictate, govern **5** **6**

▶ **Word Partnership** *rule* は次の語句と使われる:

V.	break a **rule**, change a **rule**, follow a **rule** **1**
N.	gag **rule** **1**
	exception to a **rule** **1** – **4**
	majority **rule**, minority **rule** **5**
	courts **rule**, judges **rule** **7**
	rule of thumb **12**
PREP.	against a **rule**, under a **rule** **1**
	rule over something **1**

rul|er /ˈruːlər/ (**rulers**) **1** N-COUNT 可算名詞 The **ruler** of a country is the person who rules the country. 支配者 □ *The former military ruler of Lesotho has been placed under house arrest.* 元軍指導者のレソト氏が軟禁下に置かれている. **2** N-COUNT 可算名詞 A **ruler** is a long, flat piece of wood, metal, or plastic with straight edges marked in or inches or centimeters. Rulers are used to measure things and to draw straight lines. 定規，物差し □ *...a twelve-inch ruler.* 12インチの定規

rul|ing /ˈruːlɪŋ/ (**rulings**) **1** ADJ 形容詞 The **ruling** group of people in a country or organization is the group that controls its affairs. 支配している，政権を握っている [ADJ n] □ *...the Mexican voters' growing dissatisfaction with the ruling party.* メキシコ有権者の与党に対する不満の高まり **2** N-COUNT 可算名詞 A **ruling** is an official decision made by a judge or court. 判決 □ *Goodwin tried to have the court ruling overturned.* グッドウィンは裁判所の判決を覆そう

とした. **3** ADJ 形容詞 Someone's **ruling** passion or emotion is the feeling they have most strongly, which influences their actions. 支配的な [ADJ で] ❑ *Even my love of literary fame, my ruling passion, never soured my temper.* 私が最も情熱を感じていた文名に対する熱い思いでさえ決して私を気短な性格に変えたりはしなかった.

rum /rʌm/ (**rums**) N-MASS 質量名詞 **Rum** is an alcoholic drink made from sugar. ラム酒 ❑...*a bottle of rum.* ラム酒を1本

rum|ble /rʌmbªl/ (**rumbles, rumbling, rumbled**) **1** N-COUNT 可算名詞 A **rumble** is a low, continuous noise. ゴロゴロという音 ❑ *The silence of the night was punctuated by the distant rumble of traffic.* 遠くから聞こえる交通の騒音で夜の静けさが破られた. **2** V-I 自動詞 If a vehicle **rumbles** somewhere, it moves slowly forward while making a long, continuous noise. ガタゴトと進む ❑ *A bus rumbled along the road.* バスが道路をガタガタ走った. **3** V-I 自動詞 If something **rumbles**, it makes a low, continuous noise. ゴロゴロと鳴る ❑ *The sky, swollen like a black bladder, rumbled and crackled.* 黒い風船のように膨らんだ空がゴロゴロ, バリバリと音を立てた. **4** V-I 自動詞 If your stomach **rumbles**, it makes a vibrating noise, usually because you are hungry. グーグー鳴る ❑ *Her stomach rumbled. She hadn't eaten any breakfast.* 彼女のおなかがグーグーとなった. 朝ごはんを食べていなかったのだ.

rum|bling /rʌmblɪŋ/ (**rumblings**) **1** N-COUNT 可算名詞 A **rumbling** is a low, continuous noise. 低いうなり ❑...*the rumbling of an empty stomach.* 空腹のためおなかが鳴る音 **2** N-COUNT 可算名詞 **Rumblings** are signs that a bad situation is developing or that people are becoming annoyed or unhappy. 不満の声 ❑ *Even Baldwin had become aware that there were rumblings of discontent within the ranks.* 職員の間で不満の声があることをボールドウィンでさえ気づいていた.

rum|mage /rʌmɪdʒ/ (**rummages, rummaging, rummaged**) V-I 自動詞 If you **rummage through** something, you search for something you want by moving things around in a careless or hurried way. かき回して捜す ❑ *They rummage through piles of secondhand clothes for something that fits.* 彼らは積み上げられた古着をかき回して自分にサイズが合うものを捜した. ●N-SING 単数名詞 **Rummage** is also a noun. かき回して捜すこと ❑ *A brief rummage will provide several pairs of gloves.* ちょっとかき回して捜せば手袋が何枚か見つかるだろう. ●PHRASAL VERB 句動詞 **Rummage around** means the same as **rummage**. かき回して捜す ❑ *I opened the fridge and rummaged around.* 冷蔵庫を開けてくまなく探した.

People trying to raise funds for charity, for a school (for example, to buy a computer), or for a church (to repair the roof, perhaps) may come up with the idea of holding a **rummage sale** (or **jumble sale** in the UK) in the school or church hall. Items such as clothing, toys, books, and household goods are donated by people who no longer need them, and shoppers come along in the hope of finding a second-hand bargain.

ru|mor /rumər/ (**rumors**) N-VAR 可変性名詞 A **rumor** is a story or piece of information that may or may not be true, but that people are talking about. うわさ ❑ *U.S. officials are discounting rumors of a coup.* 米国高官はクーデターのうわさを否定している.

Word Partnership *rumor*は次の語句と使われる:

ADJ.	**false** rumor
V.	**hear** a rumor, **spread** a rumor, **start** a rumor

ru|mored /rumərd/ V-T PASSIVE 受動態他動詞 If something **is rumored** to be the case, people are suggesting that it is the case, but they do not know for certain. うわさされている ❑ *The company is rumored to be a takeover target.* その会社が買収の対象だといううわさが流れている.

rump /rʌmp/ (**rumps**) **1** N-COUNT 可算名詞 An animal's **rump** is its rear end. しり, 殿部 ❑ *The cows' rumps were marked with their owner's initials and a number.* 牛の殿部には飼い主のイニシャルと番号が記入されている. **2** N-UNCOUNT 不可算名詞 **Rump** or **rump steak** is meat cut from the rear end of a cow. しり肉, ランプステーキ ❑...*a pound of rump.* しり肉1ポンド **3** N-SING 単数名詞 The **rump** of a group, organization, or country consists of the members who remain in it after the rest have left. 残った人々 [mainly BRIT 主に英国英語] ❑ *The rump of the party does in fact still have considerable assets.* 残留した党員は実は今なお非常に貴重だ.

run

❶ VERB USES
❷ NOUN USES
❸ PHRASES
❹ PHRASAL VERBS

❶ run /rʌn/ (**runs, running, ran**)

The form **run** is used in the present tense and is also the past participle of the verb.

run 形は現在時制に使われ, 動詞の過去分詞でもある.

1 V-T/V-I 他動詞/自動詞 When you **run**, you move more quickly than when you walk, for example because you are in a hurry to get somewhere, or for exercise. 走る ❑ *I excused myself and ran back to the telephone.* 私は断ってから電話の方に駆け足で戻った. ❑ *He ran the last block to the White House with two cases of gear.* 彼は最後のブロックをホワイトハウスまで道具を2箱持って走った. **2** V-T/V-I 他動詞/自動詞 When someone **runs** in a race, they run in competition with other people. 出場する ❑...*when I was running in the New York Marathon.* ニューヨークマラソンに出場したとき ❑ *He ran a tremendous race.* 彼はレースで素晴らしい走りをした. **3** V-T/V-I 他動詞/自動詞 When a horse **runs** in a race or when its owner **runs** it, it competes in a race. 競馬に出場させる [他動詞], 競馬に出場する [自動詞] ❑ *The sky was overruled by the owner, Peter Bolton, who insisted on Cool Ground running in the Gold Cup.* オーナーのピータ・ボルトンはゴールドカップでのクール・グラウンドの出場を主張し, 彼の意見を却下した. **4** V-I 自動詞 If you say that something long, such as a road, **runs** in a particular direction, you are describing its course or position. You can also say that something **runs** the length or width of something else. 延びている, 走っている ❑...*the sun-dappled trail which ran through the beech woods.* ブナの森を通って延びている木漏れ日の差す小道 **5** V-T 他動詞 If you **run** a wire or tube somewhere, you attach it or pull it from, to, or across a particular place. 通す, 延ばす ❑ *Our host ran a long extension cord out from the house and set up a screen and a projector.* ホストは家から長い延長コードを延ばしてモニターとプロジェクターを設置した. **6** V-T 他動詞 If you **run** your hand or an object **through** something, you move your hand or the object through it. さっと通す ❑ *He laughed and ran his fingers through his hair.* 彼は笑って髪に指をすっと通した. **7** V-T 他動詞 If you **run** something through a machine, process, or series of tests, you make it go through the machine, process, or tests. 実行する ❑ *They have gathered the best statistics they can find and run them through their own computers.* できる範囲で最高の統計データを集め各自のパソコンで処理した. **8** V-I 自動詞 If someone **runs for** office in an election, they take part as a candidate. 立候補する, 出馬する ❑ *It was only last February that he announced he would run for president.* 彼が大統領選への出馬表明をしたのは今年の2月にすぎない. ❑ *It is no easy job to run against John Glenn, Ohio's Democratic senator.* オハイオ州の民主党議員のジョン・グレンに対抗して立候補するのは簡単ではない. **9** V-T 他動詞 If you **run** something such as a business or an activity, you are in charge of it or you organize it. 経営する, 開催する ❑ *His stepfather ran a prosperous paint business.* 彼の義父は繁盛している塗装事業を経営している. ❑...*a well-run, profitable organization.* 経営状態がよく採算の取れている組織 **10** V-I 自動詞 If you talk about how a system, an organization, or someone's life **is running**, you are saying how well it is operating or progressing. 順調に進んでいく [usu cont] ❑ *Officials in charge of the camps say the system is now running extremely smoothly.* 収容所の係官によると, 組織は現在とても順調に運営されているという. **11** V-T/V-I 他動詞/自動詞 If you **run** an experiment, computer program, or other process, or start it **running**, you start it and let it continue. 行う ❑ *He ran a lot of tests and it turned out I had an infection called mycoplasma.* 彼はかなりの検査を行い, 私はマイコプラズマという感染症にかかっていることが分かった. **12** V-T/V-I 他動詞/自動詞 When a machine **is running** or when you **are running** it, it is switched on and is working. 作動する [usu cont] ❑ *We told him to wait out front with the engine running.* 私たちは彼にエンジンをかけたまま外で待つように言った. **13** V-I 自動詞 A machine or equipment that **runs on** or **off** a particular source of energy functions using that source of energy. (燃料で) 動く ❑ *The buses run on diesel.* そのバスはディーゼル油で走っている. **14** V-I 自動詞 When you say that vehicles such as trains and buses **run** from one place to another, you mean they regularly travel along that route. 運行する ❑ *A shuttle bus runs frequently between the inn and the country club.* シャトルバスがその宿とカントリー・クラブ間を頻繁に運行している. **15** V-T 他動詞 If you **run** someone somewhere in a car, you drive them there. 車で送る [INFORMAL くだけた] ❑ *Could you run me up to Baltimore?* バルチモアまで乗せていってくれない? **16** V-I 自動詞 If you **run** over or down to a place that is quite near, you drive there. 車で行く [INFORMAL くだけた] ❑ *I'll run over to Short Mountain and check on Mrs. Adams.* ちょっとショート・マウンテンまで行ってアダムズさんの様子を見てくるよ. **17** V-I 自動詞 If a liquid **runs** in a particular direction, it flows in that direction. 流れる ❑ *Tears were running down her cheeks.* 涙が彼女のほおを流れ落ちた. **18** V-T 他動詞 If you **run** water, or if you **run** a faucet or a bath, you cause water to flow from a faucet. (蛇口から水を) 出す ❑ *She went to the sink and ran water into her empty glass.* 彼女は流しに行って空のコップに水を入れた. **19** V-I 自動詞 If a faucet or a bath **is running**, water is coming out of a faucet. 水が出る [only cont] ❑ *The kitchen sink had been stopped up and the faucet left running, so water spilled over onto the floor.* 流し台に栓がしてあり, 蛇口の水が出しっぱなしになっていたので, 水が床にあふれ出た. **20** V-I 自動詞 If your nose **is running**, liquid is flowing out of it, usually because you have a cold. 鼻水を垂らす [usu cont] ❑ *Timothy was crying, mostly from exhaustion, and his nose was running.* ティモシーは

疲れが主な原因で泣いていて，鼻水を垂らしていた．**21** V-I 自動詞 If a surface **is running with** a liquid, that liquid is flowing down it. 滴る [usu cont] *After an hour he realized he was completely running with sweat.* 1時間後に彼は汗だくになっていることに気づいた．**22** V-T/V-I 他動詞/自動詞 When you **run** a cassette or videotape or when it **runs**, it moves through the machine as the machine operates. 再生する *Leaphorn pushed the play button again, ran the tape, pushed stop, pushed rewind.* リーフォーンは再生ボタンを押してテープを聴き，停止を押し，巻き戻しを押した．**23** V-I 自動詞 If the dye in some cloth or the ink on some paper **runs**, it comes off or spreads when the cloth or paper gets wet. にじむ *The ink had run on the wet paper.* インクが濡れた紙ににじんだ．**24** V-I 自動詞 If a feeling **runs through** your body or a thought **runs through** your mind, you experience it or think it quickly. 体の中を走る，頭をよぎる *She felt a surge of excitement run through her.* 彼女は興奮の高まりが全身に走るのを感じた．**25** V-I 自動詞 If a feeling or noise **runs through** a group of people, it spreads among them. 広がる *A buzz of excitement ran through the crowd.* 興奮したざわめきが群衆の間に広がった．**26** V-I 自動詞 If a theme or feature **runs through** something such as someone's actions or writing, it is present in all of it. 一貫している *Another thread running through this series is the role of doctors in the treatment of the mentally ill.* このシリーズに一貫して流れている別の特徴は精神疾患の治療に当たる医者の役目だ．**27** V-T/V-I 他動詞/自動詞 When newspapers or magazines **run** a particular item or story or if it **runs**, it is published or printed. 掲載する [他動詞], 掲載される [自動詞] *The New Orleans Times-Picayune ran a series of four scathing editorials entitled "The Choice of Our Lives."* ニュー・オーリンズ・タイムズ・ピキューン紙は「人生の選択」という痛烈な社説を4部作で掲載した．**28** V-I 自動詞 If an amount **is running** at a particular level, it is at that level. 達している *Today's figures show inflation running at 10.9 percent.* 今日の数字ではインフレ率は10．9％に達している．**29** V-I 自動詞 If a play, event, or legal contract **runs** for a particular period of time, it lasts for that period of time. 上演される，有効である *It pleased critics but ran for only three months on Broadway.* それは評判はよかったが，ブロードウェイで3か月しか上演されなかった．*The contract was to run from 1992 to 2020.* その契約は1992年から2020年まで有効という予定だった．**30** V-I 自動詞 If someone or something **is running** late, they have taken more time than had been planned. If they **are running** on time or ahead of time, they have taken the time planned or less than had been planned. late, on time, ahead of timeなどの副詞・副詞句を伴って「遅れている」「予定通り進んでいる」「予定より早く進んでいる」など進行状況を表す *Tell her I'll call her back later, I'm running late again.* 彼女に後で電話すると伝えて．また遅れているの．[usu cont] V-T 他動詞 If you **are running** a temperature or a fever, you have a high temperature because you are ill. 熱がある *The little girl is running a fever and she needs help.* その小さな少女は熱があり助けが必要だ．→ see also **running**

❷ **run** /rʌn/ (runs) 1 N-COUNT 可算名詞 A **run** is a time when you move somewhere on foot more quickly than when you walk, usually for exercise. 走ること *After a six-mile run, Jackie returns home for a substantial breakfast.* 6マイル走ってから，ジャッキーはたっぷりと朝食をするため家に戻った．**2** N-SING 単数名詞 A **run** for office is an attempt to be elected to office. 立候補 [mainly AM 主に米国英語] [N "for" n] *He was already preparing his run for the presidency.* 彼は早くも大統領選の準備にとりかかっていた．**3** N-COUNT 可算名詞 A **run** is a trip somewhere. 車でちょっと出かけること *...doing the morning school run.* 朝，学校まで車で一走りする．**4** N-COUNT 可算名詞 A **run** of a play or television program is the period of time during which performances are given or programmes are shown. 連続公演 *The show will transfer to Broadway on October 9, after a month's run in Philadelphia.* ショーはフィラデルフィアで1か月公演してから，10月9日にはブロードウェイに舞台を移す．**5** N-SING 単数名詞 A **run** of successes or failures is a series of successes or failures. 連続 *The team is haunted by a run of low scores.* チームはここのところなかなか得点に結びつけることができない．**6** N-COUNT 可算名詞 A **run** of a product is the amount that a company or factory decides to produce at one time. 1回の生産量 *Wayne plans to increase the print run to 1,000.* ウェインは1回の印刷部数を1000枚に増やす計画である．**7** N-COUNT 可算名詞 In baseball or cricket, a **run** is a score of one, which is made by players running between marked places on the field after hitting the ball. 得点 *The Padres scored four runs off Terry Adams in the last 2 innings.* パドレスは最終2回でテリー・アダムズ投手から4点を奪った．**8** N-SING 単数名詞 If someone gives you **the run of** a place, they give you permission to go where you like in it and use it as you wish. 使用許可 *He had the run of the house and the pool.* 彼は家とプールを自由に使うことができた．**9** N-SING 単数名詞 If there is

a **run on** something, a lot of people want to buy it or get it at the same time. 好調な売れ行き *A run on the dollar has killed off hopes of a rate cut.* ドル買いが進んだことで金利引下げの望みはなくなった．**10** N-COUNT 可算名詞 A **run** is a hole or torn part in a woman's stocking or pantyhose, where some of the vertical threads have broken, leaving only the horizontal threads. 伝線 *I had a run in my stocking.* ストッキングが伝線した．**11** N-COUNT 可算名詞 A ski **run** or bobsled **run** is a course or route that has been designed for skiing or for riding in a bobsled. コース *...an avalanche on Colorado's highest ski run.* コロラド州で最も標高の高いスキーコースでの雪崩（なだれ）事故．

❸ **run** /rʌn/ (runs, running, ran)

> The form **run** is used in the present tense and is also the past participle of the verb.

> run 形は現在時制に使われ，動詞の過去分詞でもある．

1 PHRASE 句 If you **run** someone **a close second**, or **run a close second**, you almost beat them in a race or competition. 僅差で2位につける *While "Nightly" has led in the ratings all season, "World News Tonight" is running a close second.* 全期間にわたって『ナイトリー』が視聴率のトップを走り，そのすぐ後を『ワールド・ニュース・トゥナイト』が追っている．**2** PHRASE 句 If a river or well **runs dry**, it no longer has any water in it. If an oil well **runs dry**, it no longer produces any oil. 干上がる *Streams had run dry for the first time in memory.* 小川が枯れたのは記憶する限りそれが初めてだった．**3** PHRASE 句 If a source of information or money **runs dry**, no more information or money can be obtained from it. 尽きる *Three days into production, the kitty had run dry.* 生産3日目にして資金が底をついてしまった．**4** PHRASE 句 If a characteristic **runs in** someone's **family**, it often occurs in members of that family, in different generations. 代々伝わる *The insanity which ran in his family haunted him.* 自分の血に流れる狂気に彼は苦しんだ．**5** PHRASE 句 If you **make a run for it** or if you **run for it**, you run away in order to escape from someone or something. 一目散に逃げる *A helicopter hovered overhead as one of the gang made a run for it.* 一味の1人が逃亡を図り，ヘリコプターが上空から追跡した．**6** PHRASE 句 If people's feelings **are running high**, they are very angry, concerned, or excited. 高ぶっている *Feelings there have been running high in the wake of last week's killing.* 先週の殺人事件以来，人々の感情は高ぶっています．**7** PHRASE 句 If you talk about what will happen **in the long run**, you are saying what you think will happen over a long period of time in the future. If you talk about what will happen **in the short run**, you are saying what you think will happen in the near future. 長い目で見れば，短期的に見れば *Sometimes expensive drugs or other treatments can be economical in the long run.* 薬などの治療費が高くついても，長い目で見ればそのほうが経済的なこともある．**8** PHRASE 句 If you say that someone could **give** someone else **a run for** their **money**, you mean you think they are almost as good as the other person. 互角である *...a youngster who even now could give Meryl Streep a run for her money.* 千その歳でメリル・ストリープの演技に負けない子役．**9** PHRASE 句 If someone is **on the run**, they are trying to escape or hide from someone such as the police or an enemy. 逃走中で *Fifteen-year-old Danny is on the run from a juvenile detention center.* 15歳のダニーは少年鑑別所から脱走し今なお逃走中である．**10** PHRASE 句 If someone is **on the run**, they are being severely defeated in a contest or competition. 追い詰められて *I knew I had him on the run.* 彼を追い詰めているのが分かった．**11** PHRASE 句 If you **are running short of** something or **running low on** something, you do not have much of it left. If a supply of something **is running short** or **running low**, there is not much of it left. 不足する *Government forces are running short of ammunition and fuel.* 政府軍は弾薬と燃料が底をつきかけている．**12** to **run deep** → see **deep** **13** to **run an errand** → see **errand** **14** to **run the gauntlet** → see **gauntlet** **15** to **run riot** → see **riot** **16** to **run a risk** → see **risk** **17** to **run wild** → see **wild**

❹ **run** /rʌn/ (runs, running, ran)

> The form **run** is used in the present tense and is also the past participle of the verb.

> run 形は現在時制に使われ，動詞の過去分詞でもある．

▶ **run across** PHRASAL VERB 句動詞 If you **run across** someone or something, you meet them or find them unexpectedly. 偶然出会う；偶然見つける *We ran across some old friends in the village.* 村で昔なじみとばったり出会った．

▶ **run around** PHRASAL VERB 句動詞 If you **run around**, you go to a lot of places and do a lot of things, often in a rushed or disorganized way. 忙しく動き回る *We had been running around cleaning up.* 掃除でばたばたしていた． *Jessica was running around with the camera snapping pictures.* ジェシカはカメラを手にして忙しく動き回って写真を撮っていた． *I will not have you running around the countryside without my authority.* わたしが許可しない限り，お前に自由に田舎を動き回らせることはしないよ．

▶ **run away** **1** PHRASAL VERB 句動詞 If you **run away** from a

place, you leave it because you are unhappy there. 逃げる □*I ran away from home when I was sixteen.* 16歳のときに家出をした。 □*After his beating, Colin ran away and hasn't been heard of since.* コリンは彼に殴られて逃げ出したが、その後の消息は分かっていない。 **2** PHRASAL VERB 句動詞 If you **run away** with someone, you secretly go away with them in order to live with them or marry them. 駆け落ちする □*She ran away with a man called McTavish last year.* 彼女は去年マクタビッシュという男と駆け落ちした。 **3** PHRASAL VERB 句動詞 If you **run away from** something unpleasant or new, you try to avoid dealing with it or thinking about it. 避ける □*They run away from the problem, hoping it will disappear of its own accord.* 彼らはその問題に触れようとはせず、問題が自然に解消してくれることを願っている。 **4** → see also **runaway**

▶ **run away with** PHRASAL VERB 句動詞 If you let your imagination or your emotions **run away with** you, you fail to control them and cannot think sensibly. 自制心を失わせる □*You're letting your imagination run away with you.* きみは妄想に駆られているよ。

▶ **run by** PHRASAL VERB 句動詞 If you **run** something **by** someone, you tell them about it or mention it, to see if they think it is a good idea, or can understand it. 一に一について意見を聞く □*I'm definitely interested, but I'll have to run it by Larry Estes.* 確かに興味はあるけど、ラリー・エステスが何というか聞いてみないと。

▶ **run down** **1** PHRASAL VERB 句動詞 If you **run** people or things **down**, you criticize them strongly. けなす □*I'm always running myself down.* いつも自己嫌悪に陥っています。 **2** PHRASAL VERB 句動詞 If a vehicle or its driver **runs** someone **down**, the vehicle hits them and injures them. ひく □*Lozano claimed that motorcycle driver Clement Lloyd was trying to run him down.* オートバイを運転していたクレメント・ロイドが自分をはねようとしたと、ロザノは証言しました。 **3** PHRASAL VERB 句動詞 If a machine or device **runs down**, it gradually loses power or works more slowly. 動力が落ちる □*The batteries are running down.* 電池が切れかかっている。 **4** PHRASAL VERB 句動詞 If people **run down** an industry or an organization, they deliberately reduce its size or the amount of work that it does. 縮小する □*The government is cynically running down Sweden's welfare system.* 皮肉なことに政府はスウェーデンの福祉制度を縮小しているのである。 **5** PHRASAL VERB 句動詞 If someone **runs down** an amount of something, they reduce it or allow it to decrease. 減らす □*But the survey also revealed firms were running down stocks instead of making new products.* しかし調査によると、企業は新しく製品を製造する代わりに在庫を減らしていることも明らかになった。 **6** → see also **run-down**

▶ **run into** **1** PHRASAL VERB 句動詞 If you **run into** problems or difficulties, you unexpectedly begin to experience them. 陥る □*Wang agreed to sell IBM Systems last year after it ran into financial problems.* 昨年ワンは資金難に陥っていたIBMシステムを売却することで同意した。 **2** PHRASAL VERB 句動詞 If you **run into** someone, you meet them unexpectedly. 偶然出会う □*He ran into Krettner in the corridor a few minutes later.* 数分してから廊下でクレットナーにばったり出会った。 **3** PHRASAL VERB 句動詞 If a vehicle **runs into** something, it accidentally hits it. 一に突っ込む □*The driver failed to negotiate a bend and ran into a tree.* ドライバーは角を曲がりそこなって木に衝突した。 **4** PHRASAL VERB 句動詞 You use **run into** when indicating that the cost or amount of something is very great. 一に達する □*He said companies should face punitive civil penalties running into millions of dollars.* 企業は何百万ドルにも達する懲罰的賠償金を直視すべきだと、彼は言う。

▶ **run off** **1** PHRASAL VERB 句動詞 If you **run off** with someone, you secretly go away with them in order to live with them or marry them. 駆け落ちする □*The last thing I'm going to do is run off with somebody's husband.* 人のだんなと駆け落ちするなんてありっこない。 **2** PHRASAL VERB 句動詞 If you **run off** copies of a piece of writing, you produce them using a machine. 印刷する □*If you want to run off a copy sometime today, you're welcome to.* 今日コピーをとるのでしたら、どうぞご遠慮なく。 **3** PHRASE 句 If you say that someone **is running off at the mouth**, you are criticizing them for talking too much. 余計なことをいう [DISAPPROVAL 不賛成] [v inflects] □*That was when she really started running off at the mouth. I'll bet she hasn't shut up yet.* さっきちょうど彼女がおしゃべりを始めたころでね。きっと今もペラペラしゃべっているよ。

▶ **run out** **1** PHRASAL VERB 句動詞 If you **run out of** something, you have no more of it left. なくなる □*They have run out of ideas.* 彼らはアイデアが尽きてしまいました。 □*We're running out of time.* 時間がなくなりそうだ。 **2** to **run out of steam** → see **steam** **3** PHRASAL VERB 句動詞 If something **runs out**, it becomes used up so that there is no more left. 尽きる □*Conditions are getting worse and supplies are running out.* 状況は悪化し、蓄えも底をつきかけています。 **4** PHRASAL VERB 句動詞 When a legal document **runs out**, it stops being valid. 失効する □*When the lease ran out the family moved to Cleveland.* 賃貸の期限が切れたので一家はクリーブランドに移った。

▶ **run over** PHRASAL VERB 句動詞 If a vehicle or its driver **runs** a person or animal **over**, it knocks them down or drives over them. ひく □*You can always run him over and make it look like an accident.* いつでも車で彼をひいて事故に見せかけることができる。

▶ **run through** **1** PHRASAL VERB 句動詞 If you **run through** a list of items, you read or mention all the items quickly. ざっと見る □*I ran through the options with him.* どんなオプションがあるのか彼と一緒に目を通した。 **2** PHRASAL VERB 句動詞 If you **run through** a performance or a series of actions, you practice it. 全体を練習する □*Doug stood still while I ran through the handover procedure.* わたしが引き継ぎの手順を確認している間、ダグはじっと立っていた。

▶ **run up** **1** PHRASAL VERB 句動詞 If someone **runs up** bills or debts, they acquire them by buying a lot of things or borrowing money. かさむ □*She managed to run up a credit card debt of $60,000.* ばかなことに彼女はクレジットカードで6万ドルもの借金を抱え込んでしまった。 **2** → see also **run-up**

▶ **run up against** PHRASAL VERB 句動詞 If you **run up against** problems, you suddenly begin to experience them. 出くわす □*I ran up against the problem of getting taken seriously long before I became a writer.* 作家になるずっと以前に、真剣に受け取ってもらえないという問題にぶつかっていました。

run|away /rʌnəweɪ/ (**runaways**) **1** ADJ 形容詞 You use **runaway** to describe a situation in which something increases or develops very quickly and cannot be controlled. とどめのない [ADJ n] □*Our June sale was a runaway success.* 6月の売り上げは上々であった。 **2** N-COUNT 可算名詞 A **runaway** is someone, especially a child, who leaves home without telling anyone or without permission. 家出人 □*...a teenage runaway.* 家出した10代の子。 **3** ADJ 形容詞 A **runaway** vehicle or animal is moving forward quickly, and its driver or rider has lost control of it. 暴走した [ADJ n] □*The runaway car careered into a bench, hitting an elderly couple.* 暴走した車はベンチに突っ込んで年配の夫婦をはねた。

run-down

The spelling **rundown** is also used. The adjective is pronounced /rʌn daʊn/. The noun is pronounced /rʌn daʊn/.

つづりの **rundown** も使われる。形容詞は /rʌn daʊn/ と発音され、名詞は /rʌn daʊn/ と発音される。

1 ADJ 形容詞 If someone is **run-down**, they are tired or slightly ill. 疲れた、調子が悪い [INFORMAL くだけた] □*When 23-year-old Marilyn Brown started to feel run-down last December, it never occurred to her that she could have tuberculosis.* 去年の12月に23歳のマリリン・ブラウンさんは体の不調を感じ始めた。そのときはまさか結核にかかるとは夢にも思っていなかった。 **2** ADJ 形容詞 A **run-down** building or area is in very poor condition. 荒廃した □*They have put substantial funds into rebuilding one of the most run-down areas.* 最も荒廃したひどい地域の1つを復興するため、巨額な資金を投入してきた。 **3** ADJ 形容詞 A **run-down** place of business is not as active as it used to be or does not have many customers. 業績不振の □*...a run-down slate quarry.* 寂れたスレート採石場。 **4** N-SING 単数名詞 If you give someone a **rundown** of a group of things or a **rundown** on something, you give them details about it. 詳細な報告 [INFORMAL くだけた] □*Here's a rundown of the options.* オプションの詳細は次のとおり。

rung /rʌŋ/ (**rungs**) **1** **Rung** is the past participle of **ring**. ring の過去分詞 **2** N-COUNT 可算名詞 The **rungs** on a ladder are the wooden or metal bars that form the steps. はしごの段 □*I swung myself onto the ladder and felt for the next rung.* はしごにぶら下がって足で次の段を探した。 **3** N-COUNT 可算名詞 If you reach a particular **rung** in your career, in an organization, or in a process, you reach that level in it. 地位 □*I first worked with him in 1971 when we were both on the lowest rung of our careers.* 1971年に彼と初めて仕事をした頃は2人とも下積み時代であった。

run-in (**run-ins**) N-COUNT 可算名詞 A **run-in** is an argument or quarrel with someone. 口げんか [INFORMAL くだけた] □*I had a monumental run-in with him a couple of years ago.* 2年ほど前に彼とひどい口げんかをした。

run|ner /rʌnər/ (**runners**) **1** N-COUNT 可算名詞 A **runner** is a person who runs, especially for sport or pleasure. 走る人 □*...a marathon runner.* マラソンランナー。 **2** N-COUNT 可算名詞 The **runners** in a horse race are the horses taking part. 出走馬 □*There are 18 runners in the top race of the day.* 今日のトップレースの出走馬は18頭である。 **3** N-COUNT 可算名詞 A drug **runner** or gun **runner** is someone who illegally takes drugs or guns into a country. 密輸人 □*...a gang of evil gun runners.* 暗躍する銃の密輸組織。 **4** N-COUNT 可算名詞 Someone who is a **runner** for a particular person or company is employed to take messages, collect money, or do other small tasks for them. 使い走り □*...a bookie's runner.* 馬券屋の使い走り。 **5** N-COUNT 可算名詞 **Runners** are thin strips of wood or metal underneath something which help it to move smoothly. 滑走面 □*...the runners of his sled.* そりのランナー。 → see **park**

runner-up (**runners-up**) N-COUNT 可算名詞 A **runner-up** is someone who has finished in second place in a race or competition. 2位の選手 □*The ten runners-up will receive a case of wine.* 2位となった10名の方にはワイン1ケースを差し上げます。

run|ning /rʌnɪŋ/ **1** N-UNCOUNT 不可算名詞 **Running** is the activity of moving fast on foot, especially as a sport. 競

走 ❏We chose to do cross-country running. クロスカントリー走を選んだ. **2** N-SING 単数名詞 **The running of** something such as a business is the managing or organizing of it. 経営 ❏...the committee in charge of the day-to-day running of the party. 党の日常業務を行う委員会 **3** ADJ 形容詞 You use **running** to describe things that continue or keep occurring over a period of time. 長い間続く [ADJ n] ❏He also began a running feud with Dean Acheson. 彼とディーン・アチソンとの長年にわたる確執も始まった. **4** ADJ 形容詞 A **running** total is a total which changes because numbers keep being added to it as something progresses. 現在の [ADJ n] ❏He kept a running tally of who had called him, who had visited, who had sent flowers. 電話をくれたのはだれか, 訪れたのはだれか, 花を送ってきたのはだれか, 逐一記録した. **5** ADV 副詞 You can use **running** when indicating that something keeps happening. For example, if something has happened every day for three days, you can say that it has happened for the third day **running** or for three days **running**. 一連続で [n ADV] ❏He said drought had led to severe crop failure for the second year running. 彼の話では, 干ばつで2年続けて深刻な不作に見舞われたという. **6** ADJ 形容詞 **Running** water is water that is flowing rather than standing still. 流れている [ADJ n] ❏The forest was filled with the sound of running water. 森は流れる水の音にあふれていた. **7** ADJ 形容詞 If a house has **running** water, it is supplied to the house through pipes and faucets. 水道の [ADJ n] ❏...a house without electricity or running water in a tiny African village. アフリカの小さな村の電気も水道もない家 **8** PHRASE 句 If someone is **in the running for** something, they have a good chance of winning or obtaining it. If they are **out of the running for** something, they have no chance of winning or obtaining it. 勝算のある/勝算のない ❏Until this week he appeared to have ruled himself out of the running because of his age. 今週に入るまで彼は年齢のせいで勝算はないと見ていたようです. **9** PHRASE 句 If something such as a system or place is **up and running**, it is operating normally. 作動して ❏We're trying to get the medical facilities up and running again. 医療設備が元どおりに使えるよう懸命に努力しています.

run|ning costs N-PLURAL 複数名詞 The **running costs** of a business are the amount of money that is regularly spent on things such as salaries, heating, lighting, and rent. 維持費 [BRIT 英国英語 BUSINESS 実業] [AM **overhead** 米国英語 **overhead**]

run|ning mate (**running mates**) N-COUNT 可算名詞 In an election campaign, a candidate's **running mate** is the person that they have chosen to help them in the election. If the candidate wins, the running mate will become the second most important person after the winner. 副一候補 [mainly AM 主に米国英語] ❏...Clinton's selection of Al Gore as his running mate. アル・ゴアを副大統領候補にしたクリントンの選択

run|ny /rʌni/ (**runnier, runniest**) **1** ADJ 形容詞 Something that is **runny** is more liquid than usual or than was intended. とろっとした ❏Warm the honey until it becomes runny. ハチミツをとろとろになるまで温めます. **2** ADJ 形容詞 If someone has a **runny** nose or **runny** eyes, liquid is flowing from their nose or eyes. 鼻水の出る; 涙目の ❏Symptoms are streaming eyes, a runny nose, headache, and a cough. 涙目, 鼻水, 頭痛, せきなどの症状が現れる.

run time (**run times**) N-COUNT 可算名詞 **Run time** is the time during which a computer program is running. 起動時間 [COMPUTING コンピューティング] ❏With run time for most applications lasting days or weeks, the queue fills up quickly. アプリケーションの大半は実行に数日から数週間を要するため, すぐに待ち行列が一杯になってしまう.

run-up (**run-ups**) N-SING 単数名詞 The **run-up to** an event is the period of time just before it. 直前の時期 [mainly BRIT 主に英国英語] ❏The company believes the products will sell well in the run-up to Christmas. 製品はクリスマス期間中順調に売れるだろうと, 会社では見ている.

run|way /rʌnweɪ/ (**runways**) N-COUNT 可算名詞 At an airport, the **runway** is the long strip of ground with a hard surface which an airplane takes off from or lands on. 滑走路 ❏The plane started taxiing down the runway. 飛行機は滑走路に向かって誘導路を移動し始めた.

rup|ture /rʌptʃər/ (**ruptures, rupturing, ruptured**) **1** N-COUNT 可算名詞 A **rupture** is a severe injury in which an internal part of your body tears or bursts open, especially the part between the bowels and the abdomen. 破裂 ❏He died of an abdominal infection caused by a rupture of his stomach. 彼は胃破裂による腹部内感染で亡くなった. **2** V-T/V-I 他動詞/自動詞 If a person or animal **ruptures** a part of their body or if it **ruptures**, it tears or bursts open. 裂く [他動詞], 破裂する [自動詞] ❏His stomach might rupture from all the acid. その酸のせいで彼の胃は破裂する恐れがある. ❏While playing badminton, I ruptured my Achilles tendon. バトミントンをしているときにアキレス腱を切ってしまった. **3** V-T 他動詞 If you **rupture yourself**, you rupture a part of your body, usually because you have lifted something heavy. ヘルニアになる ❏He ruptured himself playing football. 彼はサッカーをしているときにヘルニアになっ

た. **4** V-T/V-I 他動詞/自動詞 If an object **ruptures** or if something **ruptures** it, it bursts open. 破裂する [自動詞], 破裂させる [他動詞] ❏Certain gasoline tanks in trucks can rupture and burn in a collision. トラックのガソリンタンクの中には, 衝突時に破裂して炎上するものがあります. **5** N-COUNT 可算名詞 If there is a **rupture** between people, relations between them get much worse or end completely. 仲たがい; 断絶 ❏The incidents have not yet caused a major rupture in the political ties between countries. 今のところ, この事件によって国家間の政治的関係が決裂するような事態には至っていません. **6** V-T 他動詞 If someone or something **ruptures** relations between people, they damage them, causing them to become worse or to end. 不和を招く; 決裂させる ❏Brutal clashes between squatters and police yesterday ruptured the city's governing coalition. 昨日起こった不法占拠者と警察との激しい衝突は市の与党会派の分裂を招いた.
→ see **crash**

ru|ral /rʊərəl/ **1** ADJ 形容詞 **Rural** places are far away from large towns or cities. 田舎の ❏These plants have a tendency to grow in the more rural areas. こうした植物は田舎のほうが生育しやすい. **2** ADJ 形容詞 **Rural** means having features which are typical of areas that are far away from large towns or cities. 田舎風の [ADJ n] ❏...the old rural way of life. 昔ながらの田舎暮らし.

ruse /ruz, rus/ (**ruses**) N-COUNT 可算名詞 A **ruse** is an action or plan which is intended to deceive someone. 策略 [FORMAL 形式ばった] ❏It is now clear that this was a ruse to divide them. これが彼らの仲を裂くための計略だったことは今や明らかです.

rush /rʌʃ/ (**rushes, rushing, rushed**) **1** V-T/V-I 他動詞/自動詞 If you **rush** somewhere, you go there quickly. 大急ぎで行く ❏A schoolgirl rushed into a burning apartment to save a man's life. 女子生徒が男性を助け出そうと燃えているアパートの部屋に飛び込んだ. ❏I've got to rush. Got a meeting in a few minutes. 大急ぎで行かないと. 数分で会議が始まるんだ. ❏I rushed to get the 7:00 a.m. train. 朝の7時の電車に乗ろうと急いで出かけた. **2** V-T 他動詞 If people **rush to do something**, they do it as soon as they can, because they are very eager to do it. 急いで…する ❏Russian banks rushed to buy as many dollars as they could. ロシアの銀行は慌てて買えるだけのドルを買った. **3** N-SING 単数名詞 A **rush** is a situation in which you need to go somewhere or do something very quickly. 慌しさ ❏The men left in a rush. 男たちは慌しく出発した. **4** N-SING 単数名詞 If there is a **rush for** something, many people suddenly try to get it or do it. 殺到 ❏Record stores are expecting a huge rush for the single. レコード店ではシングル盤を買い求める客が殺到すると見ている. **5** N-SING 単数名詞 The **rush** is a period of time when many people go somewhere or do something. 混雑期 ❏The store's opening coincided with the Christmas rush. 店のオープンがちょうどクリスマスの繁忙期と重なった. **6** V-T/V-I 他動詞/自動詞 If you **rush** something, you do it in a hurry, often too quickly and without much care. 慌ててする ❏You can't rush a search. 性急に捜査してはならない. ❏Instead of rushing at life, I wanted something more meaningful. 慌しい人生よりももっと有意義なものを求めていた. ●**rushed** ADJ 形容詞 慌しい ❏The report had all the hallmarks of a rushed job. 報告書にはあちらこちらに急いでまとめられた形跡が見られた. **7** V-T 他動詞 If you **rush** someone or something to a place, you take them there quickly. 急いで連れて行く; 急いで運ぶ ❏They had rushed him to a hospital for a lifesaving operation. 救命手術のため, 彼を急いで病院に運んでいた. **8** V-T/V-I 他動詞/自動詞 If you **rush into** something or **are rushed into** it, you do it without thinking about it for long enough. 慌ててする ❏He will not rush into any decisions. 彼は軽はずみな判断はしないでしょう. ❏They had rushed into it without adequate appreciation of the task. 彼らは仕事の内容をよく理解しないまま, 事を急いでしまった. ●**rushed** ADJ 形容詞 慌しい ❏At no time did I feel rushed or under pressure. 慌しいとか, せかされているとか感じたことは全くなかった. **9** V-T/V-I 他動詞/自動詞 If you **rush** something or someone, or **rush at** them, you move quickly and forcefully at them, often in order to attack them. 突入する ❏They rushed the entrance and forced their way in. 彼らは入口から強引に突入した. ❏Reporters rushed at him and he ran back inside. 記者たちが押し寄せてきたので彼は走って中に戻った. **10** V-I 自動詞 If air or liquid **rushes** somewhere, it flows there suddenly and quickly. 勢いよく流れる ❏Water rushes out of huge tunnels. 巨大なトンネルから水が勢いよく流れ出る. ●N-COUNT 可算名詞 **Rush** is also a noun. 勢いよく流れること ❏A rush of air on my face woke me. 突然顔に吹いてくる風で目が覚めた. **11** N-COUNT 可算名詞 If you experience a **rush of** a feeling, you suddenly experience it very strongly. 激しい感情 ❏A rush of pure affection swept over him. 突然, 彼の中に純粋な愛情が激しく湧き上がった.

Word Partnership	rushは次の語句と使われる:
ADJ.	**mad** rush **3** **4**
	sudden rush **3** **4** **10** **11**
N.	**evening** rush, **morning** rush **5**
	rush **to judgment** **6**
	rush **of air**, rush **of water** **10**
	rush **of adrenaline** **11**

R

rush hour (**rush hours**) N-COUNT 可算名詞 The **rush hour** is one of the periods of the day when most people are traveling to or from work. ラッシュアワー [also "at/during" N] ❑ *During the evening rush hour it was often solid with vehicles.* 夕方のラッシュ時は車が途切れないことが多かった.

rust /rʌst/ (**rusts, rusting, rusted**) **1** N-UNCOUNT 不可算名詞 **Rust** is a brown substance that forms on iron or steel, for example when it comes into contact with water. さび ❑ *...a decaying tractor, red with rust.* 赤さびが出てぼろぼろになったトラクター **2** V-I 自動詞 When a metal object **rusts**, it becomes covered in rust and often loses its strength. さびる ❑ *Copper nails are better than iron nails because the iron rusts.* 鉄のくぎはさびるので銅のくぎのほうがよい. **3** COLOR 色彩語 **Rust** is sometimes used to describe things that are reddish brown in color. さび色 ❑ *...rust and gold leaves from the maples.* もみじの赤褐色や黄色の葉

rus|tic /rʌstɪk/ ADJ 形容詞 You can use **rustic** to describe things or people that you approve of because they are simple or unsophisticated in a way that is typical of the countryside. 素朴な, ひなびた [APPROVAL 賛成] ❑ *...the rustic charm of a country lifestyle.* 質素な田舎暮らしの魅力

rus|tle /rʌsᵊl/ (**rustles, rustling, rustled**) V-T/V-I 他動詞/自動詞 When something thin and dry **rustles** or when you **rustle** it, it makes soft sounds as it moves. サラサラと音をたてる, カサカサと音をたてる [自動詞], サラサラと音をさせる, カサカサと音をさせる [他動詞] ❑ *The leaves rustled in the wind.* 風に揺られて葉がさらさらと音を立てた. ❑ *She rustled her papers impatiently.* 彼女はいらいらして紙をガサガサと鳴らした. ● N-COUNT 可算名詞 **Rustle** is also a noun. サラサラいう音, カサカサいう音 ❑ *She sat perfectly still, without even a rustle of her frilled petticoats.* 彼女はじっと座ったまま, フリルのついたペチコートのきぬずれの音さえ立てなかった. ● **rus|tling** (**rustlings**) N-VAR 可変性名詞 サラサラいう音, カサカサいう音 ❑ *We were all terrified by a rustling sound coming from beneath one of the seats.* 1つの座席の下からカサカサという音がしたのでみんな怖くなった.

▶ **rustle up** PHRASAL VERB 句動詞 If you **rustle up** something to eat or drink, you make or prepare it quickly, with very little planning. 急いで支度する ❑ *Let's see if somebody can rustle up a cup of coffee.* すぐにコーヒーを入れてくれる人がいないか捜してみよう.

rusty /rʌsti/ (**rustier, rustiest**) **1** ADJ 形容詞 A **rusty** metal object such as a car or a machine is covered with rust, which is a brown substance that forms on iron or steel when it comes into contact with water. さびた ❑ *...a rusty iron gate.* さびた鉄の門扉 **2** ADJ 形容詞 If a skill that you have or your knowledge of something is **rusty**, it is not as good as it used to be, because you have not used it for a long time. 腕が鈍った, 下手になった ❑ *You may be a little rusty, but past experience and teaching skills won't have been lost.* 多少鈍っているかもしれないが, 過去の経験や指導能力は失われていないでしょう.

rut /rʌt/ (**ruts**) **1** N-COUNT 可算名詞 If you say that someone is **in a rut**, you disapprove of the fact that they have become fixed in their way of thinking and doing things, and find it difficult to change. You can also say that someone's life or career is **in a rut**. 型にはまっていること [DISAPPROVAL 不賛成] ❑ *I don't like being in a rut – I like to keep moving on.* 型にはまるのは好きじゃない. いつも前に進みたい. **2** N-COUNT 可算名詞 A **rut** is a deep, narrow mark made in the ground by the wheels of a vehicle. わだち ❑ *Our driver slowed up as we approached the ruts in the road.* 道路にわだちがある場所に近づいたので運転手は車の速度を落とした.

ruth|less /ruːθlɪs/ **1** ADJ 形容詞 If you say that someone is **ruthless**, you mean that you disapprove of them because they are very harsh or cruel, and will do anything that is necessary to achieve what they want. 冷酷な [DISAPPROVAL 不賛成] ❑ *The president was ruthless in dealing with any hint of internal political dissent.* 内部に少しでも反する者がいれば, 大統領は容赦なく処分しました. ● **ruth|less|ly** ADV 副詞 [ADV with v] 冷酷に ❑ *The party has ruthlessly crushed any sign of organized opposition.* 党は少しでも反対派が組織だった動きを見せると容赦なく弾圧してきた. ● **ruth|less|ness** N-UNCOUNT 不可算名詞 冷酷 ❑ *...a powerful political figure with a reputation for ruthlessness.* 冷酷なことで知られる政界の重鎮 **2** ADJ 形容詞 A **ruthless** action or activity is done forcefully and thoroughly, without much concern for its effects on other people. 徹底的な, 断固とした ❑ *Her lawyers have been ruthless in thrashing out a divorce settlement.* 彼女の弁護士は離婚協議をまとめようと躍起になっている. ● **ruth|less|ly** ADV 副詞 徹底的に, 断固として ❑ *Gloria showed signs of turning into the ruthlessly efficient woman her father wanted her to be.* グロリアは非情なまでの辣腕 (らつわん) ぶりを見せ始めていたが, それはまさに父親が望むところであった. ● **ruth|less|ness** N-UNCOUNT 不可算名詞 徹底ぶり ❑ *...a woman with a brain and business acumen and a certain healthy ruthlessness.* 頭がよくビジネス感覚に優れ, 徹底してやるが度をわきまえている女性

RV /ɑːr viː/ (**RVs**) N-COUNT 可算名詞 An **RV** is a van that is equipped with such things as beds and cooking equipment, so that people can live in it, usually while they are on vacation. **RV** is an abbreviation for **recreational vehicle**. キャンピングカー [mainly AM 主に米国英語] ❑ *...a group of RVs pulled over on the side of the highway.* 高速道路の路肩に停まったキャンピングカーの一団.

rye /raɪ/ **1** N-UNCOUNT 不可算名詞 **Rye** is a cereal grown in cold countries. Its grains can be used to make flour, bread, or other foods. ライ麦 ❑ *One of the first crops that I grew when we came here was rye.* こちらに来て初めて育てた穀物の1つがライ麦でした. **2** N-UNCOUNT 不可算名詞 **Rye** is bread made from rye. ライ麦パン [AM 米国英語] ❑ *I was eating ham and Swiss cheese on rye.* ライ麦パンにハムとスイスチーズをのせて食べていた.

r

Ss

S also **s** /ɛs/ (**S's, s's**) N-VAR 可変性名詞 **S** is the nineteenth letter of the English alphabet. 英語アルファベットの第19字

Sab|bath /sǽbəθ/ N-PROPER 固有名詞 **The Sabbath** is the day of the week when members of some religious groups do not work. The Jewish Sabbath is on Saturday and the Christian Sabbath is on Sunday. 安息日 □...a deeply religious man who will not discuss politics on the Sabbath. 安息日に政治の話はしようとしない信仰のあつい男.

sab|bat|i|cal /səbǽtɪkᵊl/ (**sabbaticals**) N-COUNT 可算名詞 A **sabbatical** is a period of time during which someone such as a university teacher can leave their ordinary work and travel or study. 研究休暇 [also "on" N] □He took a year's sabbatical from teaching to write a book. 彼は本を執筆するために, 教職から1年間の研究休暇を取った.

sabo|tage /sǽbətɑʒ/ (**sabotages, sabotaging, sabotaged**) **1** V-T 他動詞 If a machine, railroad line, or bridge **is sabotaged**, it is deliberately damaged or destroyed, for example, in a war or as a protest. 故意に破壊する [usu passive] □The main pipeline supplying water was sabotaged by rebels. 主要な給水パイプラインは反乱軍によって故意に破壊された. ●N-UNCOUNT 不可算名詞 **Sabotage** is also a noun. 破壊行為 □The bombing was a spectacular act of sabotage. その爆撃は目を見張るような破壊行為でした. **2** V-T 他動詞 If someone **sabotages** a plan or a meeting, they deliberately prevent it from being successful. 故意に妨害する □He accused the opposition of doing everything they could to sabotage the election. 彼はあらゆる手を尽くして選挙を妨害しているとして反対派を非難した.

sa|chet /sæʃéɪ/ (**sachets**) N-COUNT 可算名詞 A **sachet** is a small soft bag containing a perfumed powder or other substance placed in drawers to give clothing a pleasant smell. におい袋 [AM 米国英語] □a lilac sachet. ライラックのにおい袋.

sack /sǽk/ (**sacks, sacking, sacked**) **1** N-COUNT 可算名詞 A **sack** is a large bag made of thick paper or rough material. Sacks are used to carry or store things such as food or groceries. 大袋 □...a sack of potatoes. 大袋1つのジャガイモ **2** V-T 他動詞 If your employers **sack** you, they tell you that you can no longer work for them because you have done something that they did not like or because your work was not good enough. 首にする [mainly BRIT 主に英国英語, INFORMAL くだけた] [AM usually **fire** 米国英語では通常 **fire**] ●N-SING 単数名詞 **Sack** is also a noun. 解雇

sack|ing /sǽkɪŋ/ (**sackings**) **1** N-UNCOUNT 不可算名詞 **Sacking** is rough woven material that is used to make sacks. 粗麻布 □...a piece of sacking. 1切れのズック. **2** N-COUNT 可算名詞 A **sacking** is when an employer tells a worker to leave their job. 解雇 [mainly BRIT 主に英国英語, INFORMAL くだけた] [AM usually **firing** 米国英語では通常 **firing**]

sa|cred /séɪkrɪd/ **1** ADJ 形容詞 Something that is **sacred** is believed to be holy and to have a special connection with God. 神聖な □The owl is sacred for many Californian Indian people. カリフォルニア州のインディアンの人々の多くにとってフクロウは神聖なものである. **2** ADJ 形容詞 Something connected with religion or used in religious ceremonies is described as **sacred**. 宗教上の [ADJ n] □...sacred art. 宗教芸術. **3** ADJ 形容詞 You can describe something as **sacred** when it is regarded as too important to be changed or interfered with. 尊重すべき, 不可侵の □My memories are sacred. 私の思い出は何物にも代えがたい大切なものだ.

sac|ri|fice /sǽkrɪfaɪs/ (**sacrifices, sacrificing, sacrificed**) **1** V-T 他動詞 To **sacrifice** an animal or person means to kill them in a special religious ceremony as an offering to a god. いけにえにして供する □The priest sacrificed a chicken. 司祭は鶏をいけにえにして捧げた. ●N-COUNT 可算名詞 **Sacrifice** is also a noun. いけにえ □...animal sacrifices to the gods. 神に捧げられた動物のいけにえ. **2** V-T 他動詞 If you **sacrifice** something that is valuable or important, you give it up, usually to obtain something else for yourself or for other people. 犠牲にする □She sacrificed family life to her career. 彼女は家庭生活を仕事の犠牲にした. ●N-VAR 可変性名詞 **Sacrifice** is also a noun. 犠牲 □She made many sacrifices to get Anita a good education. アニータによい教育を受けさせるため, 彼女は多くの犠牲を払った.

sac|ri|fi|cial /sǽkrɪfɪʃᵊl/ ADJ 形容詞 **Sacrificial** means connected with or used in a sacrifice. いけにえの [ADJ n] □...the sacrificial altar. いけにえの祭壇.

sad /sǽd/ (**sadder, saddest**) **1** ADJ 形容詞 If you are **sad**, you feel unhappy, usually because something has happened that you do not like. 悲しい □The relationship had been important to me and its loss left me feeling sad and empty. その関係は私にとって大切なものだったので, それを失くしたとき私は悲しく, むなしかった. □I'm sad that Julie's marriage is on the verge of splitting up. ジュリーの結婚が離婚に瀕していることを私はとても悲しく思う. ●**sad|ly** ADV 副詞 悲しんで □...a gallant man who will be sadly missed by all his comrades. 同僚の誰からもいなくなればさびしがられるだろう勇敢な男性. ●**sad|ness** N-UNCOUNT 不可算名詞 悲しみ □It is with a mixture of sadness and joy that I say farewell. 私がさよならを告げるのは悲しみと喜びが入り混じった気持です. **2** ADJ 形容詞 **Sad** stories and **sad** news make you feel sad. 悲しむべき □...a desperately humorous, impossibly sad novel. 猛烈にユーモラスで, どうしようもなく悲しい小説 **3** ADJ 形容詞 A **sad** event or situation is unfortunate or undesirable. 嘆かわしい □It's a sad truth that children are the biggest victims of passive smoking. 子供たちが間接喫煙の最大の被害者であることは嘆かわしい真実だ. ●**sad|ly** ADV 副詞 痛ましく □Sadly, bamboo plants die after flowering. 痛ましいことに, 竹は花を咲かせたあと枯れてしまう. **4** ADJ 形容詞 If you describe someone as **sad**, you do not have any respect for them and think their behavior or ideas are ridiculous. けしからぬ [INFORMAL くだけた, DISAPPROVAL 不賛成] □...sad bikers and youngsters who think that Jim Morrison is God. ジム・モリソンは神だと信じている, いまいましい例のバイカーや若者たち
→ see **cry, emotion**

Thesaurus
sad また次を参照:

ADJ.	depressed, down, gloomy, unhappy; (*ant.*) cheerful, happy **1**
	miserable, tragic, unhappy **3**

Word Partnership
sad は次の語句と使われる:

V.	feel sad, seem sad **1**
	look sad **1 4**
ADV.	kind of sad, a little sad, really sad, so sad, too sad, very sad **1** – **4**
N.	sad news, sad story **2**
	sad day, sad eyes, sad face, sad fact, sad truth **3**

sad|den /sǽdᵊn/ (**saddens, saddened**) V-T 他動詞 If something **saddens** you, it makes you feel sad. 悲しませる [no cont] □The cruelty in the world saddens me incredibly. 世界にはびこる残酷な行為は私を途方もなく悲しみに沈ませる. ●**sad|dened** ADJ 形容詞 [v-link ADJ] 悲しんだ □He was disappointed and saddened that legal argument had stopped the trial. 法律上の主張により裁判が中止されたことで彼は失望し, 悲しんでいる.

sad|dle /sǽdᵊl/ (**saddles, saddling, saddled**) **1** N-COUNT 可算名詞 A **saddle** is a leather seat that you put on the back of an animal so that you can ride the animal. 鞍 **2** V-T 他動詞 If you **saddle** a horse, you put a saddle on it so that you can ride it. 馬に鞍をつける □Why don't we saddle a couple of horses and go for a ride? 2頭の馬に鞍をつけてひと乗りしに出掛けないか. ●PHRASAL VERB 句動詞 **Saddle up** means the same as **saddle**. 馬に鞍を置く □I want to be gone from here as soon as we can saddle up. 私は馬に鞍を置いたらできるだけ早くここから出たい. **3** N-COUNT 可算名詞 A **saddle** is a seat on a bicycle or motorcycle. サドル
→ see **horse**

sad|ism /séɪdɪzəm, sǽd-/ N-UNCOUNT 不可算名詞 **Sadism** is a type of behavior in which a person obtains pleasure from hurting other people and making them suffer physically or mentally. サディズム □Psychoanalysts tend to regard both sadism and masochism as arising from childhood deprivation. 精神分析学者はサディズムとマゾヒズムの両方ともが, 小児期の喪失に起因するとみなす傾向がある. ●**sad|ist** /séɪdɪst, sǽd-/ N-COUNT 可算名詞 (**sadists**) サディスト □The man was a sadist who tortured animals and people. その男は動物や人間を拷問にかけるサディストだった.

sa|dis|tic /sədɪstɪk/ ADJ 形容詞 A **sadistic** person obtains pleasure from hurting other people and making them suffer physically or mentally. サディスト的な □The prisoners rioted against mistreatment by sadistic guards. 囚人たちはサディスト的な守衛たちによる虐待に対して暴動を起こした.

s.a.e. /ɛs eɪ iː/ (**s.a.e.s**) N-COUNT 可算名詞 An **s.a.e.** is the same as an SASE. 切手を張った返信用封筒 [BRIT 英国英語]

sa|fa|ri /səfɑːri/ (**safaris**) N-COUNT 可算名詞 A **safari** is a trip to observe or hunt wild animals, especially in East Africa. サファリ [also "on" N] □ He'd like to go on safari to photograph snakes and tigers. 彼はヘビやトラの写真を撮るためにサファリに行きたがっている。

safe /seɪf/ (**safer, safest, safes**) ◼ ADJ 形容詞 Something that is **safe** does not cause physical harm or danger. 安全な □ Officials arrived to assess whether it is safe to bring emergency food supplies into the city. 緊急用食料をその都市に運んでも安全かどうかを見極めるために役人が到着しました。 □ Most foods that we eat are safe for birds. 私たちが食べる食物のほとんどは鳥にとって安全だ。 ◼ ADJ 形容詞 If a person or thing is **safe from** something, they cannot be harmed or damaged by it. 被害の心配がない [v-link ADJ] □ They are safe from the violence that threatened them. 彼らは彼らを脅かす暴力から被害を受けることはない。 ◼ ADJ 形容詞 If you are **safe**, you have not been harmed, or you are not in danger of being harmed. 無事な [v-link ADJ] □ Where is Sophy? Is she safe? ソフィーはどこにいるの。無事なの。 ● **safe|ly** ADV 副詞 [ADV with v] □ All 140 guests were brought out of the building safely by firemen. 消防士により、140人の客全員がその建物から無事に連れ出された。 ◼ ADJ 形容詞 A **safe** place is one where it is unlikely that any harm, damage, or unpleasant things will happen to the people or things that are there. 危険のない □ The continuing tension has prompted more than half the inhabitants of the refugee camp to flee to safer areas. 緊張感が継続したため、難民キャンプの居住者の半分以上がいっそう安全な場所に逃げ出しました。 ● **safe|ly** ADV 副詞 [ADV after v] 安全に □ The banker keeps the money tucked safely under his bed. 銀行家は安全なベッドの下にその金をしまい込んでいる。 ◼ ADJ 形容詞 If people or things have a **safe** trip, they reach their destination without harm, damage, or unpleasant things happening to them. 無事な [ADJ n] □ I told him good night, come back any time, and have a safe trip home. 私は彼に、おやすみ、いつでもまたいらっしゃい、そして無事に帰宅してくださいと言った。 ● **safe|ly** ADV 副詞 無事に □ The space shuttle returned safely today from a 10-day mission. スペースシャトルは10日間の任務から本日無事に帰還した。 ◼ ADJ 形容詞 [ADJ n] If you are at a **safe** distance from something or someone, you are far enough away from them to avoid any danger, harm, or unpleasant effects. 危険の心配のない □ I shall conceal myself at a safe distance from the battlefield. 私は戦場から安全な距離にそっと身を隠します。 ◼ ADJ 形容詞 If something you have or expect to obtain is **safe**, you cannot lose it or be prevented from having it. 確実な □ We as consumers need to feel confident that our jobs are safe before we will spend spare cash. 私たちは消費者として、余分な現金を使う前に、失業の心配がないことを確信する必要がある。 ◼ ADJ 形容詞 A **safe** course of action is one in which there is very little risk of loss or failure. 手堅い □ Electricity shares are still a safe investment. 電力株はいまだに手堅い投資である。 ● **safe|ly** ADV 副詞 手堅く □ We reveal only as much information as we can safely risk at a given time. 我々は所定の時に支障なく危険を冒せるだけの情報しか口外しない。 ◼ ADJ 形容詞 If **it is safe to** say or assume something, you can say it with very little risk of being wrong. 間違いない □ I think it is safe to say that very few students expend the effort to do quality work in school. 学校で質の高い研究をしようと努力する学生はほとんどいないといっても過言ではないと思う。 ● **safe|ly** ADV 副詞 [ADV before v] 間違いなく □ I think you can safely say that he will not be appearing in another of my films. 彼女は私の映画には もう2度と出ることはないと言っても間違いないと思う。 ◼ N-COUNT 可算名詞 A **safe** is a strong metal cabinet with special locks, in which you keep money, jewelry, or other valuable things. 金庫 □ The files are now in a safe to which only he has the key. ファイルは今、彼しか鍵を持たない金庫に入っています。 ◼ → see also **safely** ◼ PHRASE 句 If you say that a person or thing is **in safe hands**, or is **safe in** someone's **hands**, you mean that they are being taken care of by a reliable person and will not be harmed. 保護されて □ I had a huge responsibility to ensure these packets remained in safe hands. 私は、これらの小包を常に確実に安全であるようにする膨大な責任を負っていた。 ◼ PHRASE 句 If you **play safe** or **play it safe**, you do not take any risks. 安全第1にふるまう □ If you want to play safe, cut down on the amount of salt you eat. あなた方が安全第1にしたいなら、塩の摂取量を減らしなさい。 ◼ PHRASE 句 If you say you are doing something **to be on the safe side**, you mean that you are doing it in case something undesirable happens, even though this may be unnecessary. 大事をとって □ You might still want to go for an X-ray, however, just to be on the safe side. しかし、あなたはただ大事をとってX線をやはりやったほうがよいでしょう。 ◼ PHRASE 句 If you say "**it's better to be safe than sorry**," you are advising someone to take action in order to avoid possible unpleasant consequences later, even if this seems unnecessary. 後で後悔するより安全策をとったほうがよい □ Don't be afraid to have this checked by a doctor – better safe than sorry! これを医者に診てもらうことを恐れないで。後で後悔するよりいいわよ。 ◼ PHRASE 句 You say that someone is **safe and sound** when they are still alive or unharmed after being in danger. 無事安全に □ All I'm hoping for is that wherever Trevor is he will come home safe and sound. トレヴァーがどこにいようと、私が望むのは彼が無事安

全に帰ってくることだけだ。

全に帰ってくることだけだ。

	Word Partnership *safe* は次の語句と使われる:
N.	safe **drinking water**, safe **operation** ◼ **children/kids are** safe, safe **at home** ◼ safe **environment**, safe **neighborhood**, safe **place**, safe **streets** ◼ safe **bet**, safe **investment** ◼
ADV.	**completely** safe, **perfectly** safe, **reasonably** safe, **relatively** safe ◼◼◼

safe de|pos|it box (**safe deposit boxes**) N-COUNT 可算名詞 A **safe deposit box** is a small box, usually kept in a special room in a bank, in which you can store valuable objects. 貸金庫

safe|guard /seɪfgɑːrd/ (**safeguards, safeguarding, safeguarded**) ◼ V-T 他動詞 To **safeguard** something or someone means to protect them from being harmed, lost, or badly treated. 保護する [FORMAL 形式ばった] □ They will press for international action to safeguard the ozone layer. オゾン層を保護するために彼らは国際的行動を強く求めるつもりです。 ◼ N-COUNT 可算名詞 A **safeguard** is a law, rule, or measure intended to prevent someone or something from being harmed. 保障条項 □ As an additional safeguard against weeds you can always use an underlay of heavy duty polyethylene. さらなる雑草の予防手段として、頑丈なポリエチレンの下張りはいつでも使える。

safe ha|ven (**safe havens**) ◼ N-COUNT 可算名詞 If part of a country is declared a **safe haven**, people who need to escape from a dangerous situation such as a war can go there and be protected. 安全な避難所 □ Countries overwhelmed by the human tide of refugees want safe havens set up at once. 潮のように押し寄せる難民に閉口している国々は、早急に安全な避難所の構築を望んでいる。 ◼ N-UNCOUNT 不可算名詞 If a country provides **safe haven** for people from another country who have been in danger, it allows them to stay there under its official protection. 避難先 [AM 米国英語] □ Some Democrats support granting the Haitians temporary safe haven in the U.S. 民主党員の中には、アメリカにおける一時避難先をハイチ人に提供することを支持している者もいる。 ◼ N-COUNT 可算名詞 A **safe haven** is a place, a situation, or an activity which provides people with an opportunity to escape from things that they find unpleasant or worrying. 避難所 □ ...the idea of the family as a safe haven from the brutal outside world. 残忍な外界からの安全な隠れ場所としての家族という考え

safe|ly /seɪfli/ ◼ ADV 副詞 If something is done **safely**, it is done in a way that makes it unlikely that anyone will be harmed. 安全に □ The waste is safely locked away until it is no longer radioactive. 廃棄物は放射性がなくなるまで鍵をかけて安全に保管される。 □ "Drive safely," he said and waved goodbye. 「安全運転でね」と彼は言って、さよならの手を振った。 ◼ ADV 副詞 You also use **safely** to say that there is no risk of a situation being changed. 間違いなく □ Once events are safely in the past, this idea seems to become less alarming. いったん出来事が間違いなく過去のものとなってしまえば、この考えもあまり憂慮すべきものとは思われなくなるようだ。 ◼ → see also **safe**

safe sex also **safer sex** N-UNCOUNT 不可算名詞 **Safe sex** is sexual activity in which people protect themselves against the risk of AIDS and other diseases, usually by using condoms. 安全なセックス □ You must practice safe sex and know your partner well. あなたは安全なセックスを行い、パートナーをよく知らなければならない。

safe|ty /seɪfti/ ◼ N-UNCOUNT 不可算名詞 **Safety** is the state of being safe from harm or danger. 安全 □ The report goes on to make a number of recommendations to improve safety on aircraft. さらに、このレポートは航空機の安全性を改善する勧告を多く行っている。 ◼ N-UNCOUNT 不可算名詞 If you reach **safety**, you reach a place where you are safe from danger. 安全な場所 □ He stumbled through smoke and fumes to pull her to safety. 彼は煙や蒸気の中をよろめきながら彼女を安全な場所に連れ出した。 □ People scurried for safety as the firing started. 発砲が始まったので、人々は安全な場所を求めてあわてて走った。 ◼ N-SING 単数名詞 If you are concerned about the **safety** of something, you are concerned that it might be harmful or dangerous. 安全性 □ ...consumers are showing growing concern about the safety of the food they buy. 消費者は自分たちが購入する食品の安全性に益々関心を見せている。 ◼ N-SING 単数名詞 If you are concerned for someone's **safety**, you are concerned that they might be in danger. 安全 □ There is grave concern for the safety of witnesses. 証人の安全には深刻な懸念がある。 ◼ ADJ 形容詞 **Safety** features or measures are intended to make something less dangerous. 安全な [ADJ n] □ The built-in safety device compensates for a fall in water pressure. 内蔵安全装置が水圧の降下を埋め合わせる。

Word Partnership　safety は次の語句と使われる:

v.	improve safety, provide safety 1
	ensure safety 1 3 4
	fear for *someone's* safety 4
N.	child safety, fire safety, health and safety, highway/
	traffic safety, safety measures, public safety, safety
	regulations, safety standards, workplace safety 1
	safety concerns, food safety 3
	safety device, safety equipment 5

safe|ty belt (safety belts) also **safety-belt** N-COUNT 可算名詞 A **safety belt** is a strap attached to a seat in a car or airplane. You fasten it around your body and it stops you from being thrown forward if there is an accident. 安全ベルト □ *Please return to your seats and fasten your safety belts.* お席にお戻りになり、安全ベルトをお締めください。

safe|ty net (safety nets) 1 N-COUNT 可算名詞 A **safety net** is something that you can rely on to help you if you get into a difficult situation. 安全策 □ *Welfare is the only real safety net for low-income workers.* 福祉は低収入労働者が唯一頼れる安全策です。 2 N-COUNT 可算名詞 In a circus, a **safety net** is a large net that is placed below performers on a high wire or trapeze in order to catch them and prevent them being injured if they fall off. 安全ネット

safe|ty of|fic|er (safety officers) N-COUNT 可算名詞 The **safety officer** in a company or an organization is the person who is responsible for the safety of the people who work or visit there. 安全管理者 □ *Organizers had consulted widely with police and safety officers to ensure tight security.* 主催者は厳密な警備を確保するため、警察や安全管理者に広く助言を求めていた。

safe|ty pin (safety pins) N-COUNT 可算名詞 A **safety pin** is a bent metal pin used for fastening things together. The point of the pin has a cover so that when the pin is closed it cannot hurt anyone. 安全ピン □ *...trousers which were held together with safety pins.* 安全ピンでつなぎ合わされたズボン。

sag /sǽg/ (sags, sagging, sagged) V-I 自動詞 When something **sags**, it hangs down loosely or sinks downward in the middle. たるむ □ *The shirt's cuffs won't sag and lose their shape after washing.* 洗濯してもそのシャツのそで口はたるんだり、形くずれしたりしない。

saga /sɑ́gə/ (sagas) 1 N-COUNT 可算名詞 A **saga** is a long story, account, or sequence of events. 長編歴史物語 □ *...a 600-page saga about 18th-century slavery.* 18世紀の奴隷制度に関する600ページの長編歴史物語。 2 N-COUNT 可算名詞 A **saga** is a long story composed in medieval times in Norway or Iceland. サガ □ *...a Nordic saga of giants and trolls.* 巨人とトロールに関する北欧のサガ。

sage /séɪdʒ/ N-UNCOUNT 不可算名詞 **Sage** is a herb used in cooking. セージ

said /sɛ́d/ **Said** is the past tense and past participle of **say**.

sail /séɪl/ (sails, sailing, sailed) 1 N-COUNT 可算名詞 **Sails** are large pieces of material attached to the mast of a ship. The wind blows against the sails and pushes the ship along. 帆 □ *The white sails billow with the breezes they catch.* 白い帆は風を捕らえて膨らむ。 2 V-I 自動詞 You say a ship **sails** when it moves over the sea. 帆走する □ *The trawler had sailed from the port of Zeebrugge.* トロール漁船はゼーブリュッへ港から出帆していた。 3 V-T/V-I 他動詞/自動詞 If you **sail** a boat or if a boat **sails**, it moves across water using its sails. 帆走させる [他動詞] 帆走する [自動詞] □ *His crew's job is to sail the boat.* 彼の乗組員の仕事は船を帆走させることだ。 □ *I'd buy a big boat and sail around the world.* 私は大きなボートを買って世界一周の船旅に出る。 4 → see also **sailing** 5 PHRASE 句 When a ship **sets sail**, it leaves a port. 出帆する □ *He loaded his vessel with another cargo and set sail.* 彼は船にもう1つ貨物を積んで、出帆した。

▶ **sail through** PHRASAL VERB 句動詞 If someone or something **sails through** a difficult situation or experience, they deal with it easily and successfully. 〜を楽々と成し遂げる □ *While she sailed through her exams, he struggled.* 彼女は試験に楽々と受かったが、彼は苦戦した。

sail|ing /séɪlɪŋ/ (sailings) 1 N-UNCOUNT 不可算名詞 **Sailing** is the activity or sport of sailing boats. 帆走、ヨット競技 □ *There was swimming and sailing down on the lake.* 湖では水泳や帆走が行われていた。 2 N-COUNT 可算名詞 **Sailings** are trips made by a ship carrying passengers. 航海 □ *Ferry companies are providing extra sailings from Calais.* フェリーの会社はカレーから臨時便を運行している。 3 PHRASE 句 If you say that a task was not all **plain sailing**, you mean that it was not very easy. とんとん拍子 □ *Pregnancy wasn't all plain sailing and once again there were problems.* 妊娠はすべて順調というわけには行かず、前と同じようにいろいろ問題があった。

→ see **boat**

sail|or /séɪlər/ (sailors) N-COUNT 可算名詞 A **sailor** is someone who works on a ship or sails a boat. 船乗り □ *...sailors, marines and Coast Guard personnel.* 水兵、海兵隊員および沿岸警備隊員

saint /séɪnt/ (saints) 1 N-COUNT; N-TITLE 可算名詞、称号名詞 A **saint** is someone who has died and been officially recognized and honored by the Christian church because his or her life was a perfect example of the way Christians should live. 聖人 □ *Every parish was named after a saint.* 教会区それぞれには聖人にちなんだ名前が付けられた。 2 N-COUNT 可算名詞 If you refer to a living person as a **saint**, you mean that they are extremely kind, patient, and unselfish. 聖者 [APPROVAL 賛成] □ *My girlfriend Geraldine is a saint to put up with me.* 私の恋人ジェラルディンは私を我慢してくれる聖者のような人だ。

saint|ly /séɪntli/ ADJ 形容詞 A **saintly** person behaves in a very good or very holy way. 高徳な [APPROVAL 賛成] □ *She has been saintly in her self-restraint.* 彼女は気高く自制している。

sake /séɪk/ (sakes) 1 PHRASE 句 If you do something **for the sake of** something, you do it for that purpose or in order to achieve that result. You can also say that you do it **for** something's **sake**. 〜のために □ *Let's assume for the sake of argument that we manage to build a satisfactory database.* 議論上、私たちはなんとか満足なデータベースを構築すると仮定しよう。 □ *For the sake of historical accuracy, please permit us to state the true facts.* 歴史的正確さを期すために、我々に事実を述べさせてください。 2 PHRASE 句 If you do something **for its own sake**, you do it because you want to, or because you enjoy it, and not for any other reason. You can also talk about, for example, **art for art's sake** or **sport for sport's sake**. 自身のために □ *Economic change for its own sake did not appeal to him.* 彼は経済変化それ自体には関心がなかった。 3 PHRASE 句 When you do something **for someone's sake**, you do it in order to help them or make them happy. 〜のために □ *I trust you to do a good job for Stan's sake.* 君がスタンのためにがんばってくれることを私は信頼している。 4 PHRASE 句 Some people use expressions such as **for God's sake**, **for heaven's sake**, **for goodness' sake**, or **for Pete's sake** in order to express annoyance or impatience, or to add force to a question or request. The expressions "for God's sake" and "for Christ's sake" could cause offense. とんでもない、後生だから [INFORMAL くだけた、FEELINGS 感情] □ *For goodness' sake, why didn't you call me?* あきれた、どうして私に電話してくれなかったの。

sal|ad /sǽləd/ (salads) N-VAR 可変性名詞 A **salad** is a mixture of cold foods such as lettuce, tomatoes, or cold cooked potatoes, cut up and mixed with a dressing. It is often served with other food as part of a meal. サラダ □ *...a salad of tomato, onion and cucumber.* トマト、タマネギときゅうりのサラダ

→ see **dish**

sala|ried /sǽlərid/ ADJ 形容詞 **Salaried** people receive a salary from their job. 俸給を受けている [BUSINESS 実業] □ *...salaried employees.* サラリーマン。

sala|ry /sǽləri/ (salaries) N-VAR 可変性名詞 A **salary** is the money that someone earns each month or year from their employer. 給与 [BUSINESS 実業] □ *The lawyer was paid a huge salary.* その弁護士はすごい高給取りでした。

→ see **salt**

Professional people and office workers receive a **salary**, which is paid monthly. However, when talking about someone's salary, you usually give the annual figure. □ *I'm paid a salary of $29,000 a year.* **Pay** is a general noun which you can use to refer to the money you get from your employer for doing your job. Manual workers are paid **wages**, or a **wage**. The plural is more common than the singular, especially when you are talking about the actual cash that someone receives. □ *Every week he handed all his wages in cash to his wife.* Wages are usually paid, and quoted, as an hourly or a weekly sum. □ *...a starting wage of five dollars an hour.* Your **income** consists of all the money you receive from all sources, including your pay.

sale /séɪl/ (sales) 1 N-SING 単数名詞 The **sale** of goods is the act of selling them for money. 販売 □ *Efforts were made to limit the sale of alcohol.* アルコール販売を制限する努力がなされた。 2 N-PLURAL 複数名詞 The **sales** of a product are the quantity of it that is sold. 売上げ高 □ *The newspaper has sales of 1.72 million.* その新聞の売上げは172万部だ。 □ *...the huge Christmas sales of computer games.* コンピュータゲームのクリスマスでの莫大な売上高 3 N-PLURAL 複数名詞 The part of a company that deals with **sales** deals with selling the company's products. 営業 □ *Until 1983 he worked in sales and marketing.* 1983年まで彼は営業とマーケティングで働いていた。 4 N-COUNT 可算名詞 A **sale** is an occasion when a store sells things at less than their normal price. 特売 □ *...a pair of jeans bought half-price in a sale.* 特売で半額で買ったジーパン 5 N-COUNT 可算名詞 A **sale** is an event when goods are sold to the person who offers the highest price. 競売 □ *The Old Master was bought by dealers at the Christie's sale.* その巨匠の作品はクリスティーの競売で業者に買い取られた。 6 PHRASE 句 If something is **for sale**, it is being offered to people to buy. 売りに出した □ *The yacht is for sale at a price of 1.7 million dollars.* そのヨットは170万ドルの値段で売りに出されている。 7 PHRASE 句 If products in a store are **on sale**, they can be

bought for less than their normal price. 特価で売りに出て ❑ *A good shopper doesn't just buy things because they're on sale.* 賢い買い物客は、特価だからという理由だけで物を買わない. **8** PHRASE 句 Products that are **on sale** can be bought. 売りに出て ❑ *English textbooks and dictionaries are on sale everywhere.* 英語の教科書や辞書はどこでも売られている. ❑ *Tickets go on sale this week.* チケットは今週発売される. **9** PHRASE 句 If a property or company is **up for sale**, its owner is trying to sell it. 売りに出して ❑ *The mansion has been put up for sale.* その大邸宅は売りに出されている.

sales|clerk /ˈseɪlzklɜrk/ (**salesclerks**) also **sales clerk** N-COUNT 可算名詞 A **salesclerk** is a person who works in a store selling things to customers and helping them to find what they want. 店員 [AM 米国英語]

sales force (**sales forces**) also **salesforce** N-COUNT 可算名詞 A company's **sales force** is all the people that work for that company selling its products. 販売員 [BUSINESS 実業] ❑ *His sales force is signing up schools at the rate of 25 a day.* 彼の販売員たちは1日に25校の割合で学校に購入契約をさせている.

sales|man /ˈseɪlzmən/ (**salesmen**) N-COUNT 可算名詞 A **salesman** is a man whose job is to sell things, especially directly to stores or other businesses on behalf of a company. 販売外交員 ❑ *...an insurance salesman.* 保険販売員

sales|person /ˈseɪlzpɜrsən/ (**salespeople** or **salespersons**) N-COUNT 可算名詞 A **salesperson** is a person who sells things, either in a store or directly to customers on behalf of a company. 販売員 [BUSINESS 実業] ❑ *They will usually send a salesperson out to measure your bathroom.* その会社は通常、販売員を派遣して浴室の寸法を測ります.

sales pitch (**sales pitches**) N-COUNT 可算名詞 A salesperson's **sales pitch** is what they say in order to persuade someone to buy something from them. 売込み口上 ❑ *His sales pitch was smooth and convincing.* 彼の売込み口上は滑らかで, 説得力がありました.

sales slip (**sales slips**) N-COUNT 可算名詞 A **sales slip** is a piece of paper that you are given when you buy something in a store, which shows when you bought it and how much you paid. 売上伝票, レシート [AM 米国英語]

sales tax (**sales taxes**) N-VAR 可変性名詞 The **sales tax** on things that you buy is the percentage of money that you pay to the local or state government. 売上げ税 [BUSINESS 実業] ❑ *The state's unpopular sales tax on snacks has ended.* その国の菓子類にかけられる不人気な売上げ税は撤廃された.

sales|wom|an /ˈseɪlzwʊmən/ (**saleswomen**) N-COUNT 可算名詞 A **saleswoman** is a woman who sells things, either in a store or directly to customers on behalf of a company. 女性販売員 [BUSINESS 実業] ❑ *...an insurance saleswoman.* 女性保険販売員.

sa|li|ent /ˈseɪliənt, ˈseɪlyənt/ ADJ 形容詞 The **salient** points or facts of a situation are the most important ones. 顕著な [FORMAL 形式ばった] ❑ *He read the salient facts quickly.* 彼は顕著な諸事実をさっと読んだ.

sa|li|va /səˈlaɪvə/ N-UNCOUNT 不可算名詞 **Saliva** is the watery liquid that forms in your mouth and helps you to chew and digest food. 唾液 ❑ *He noticed a lot of saliva settling in his mouth.* 彼は口の中につばが大量にたまるのに気づいた.

salm|on /ˈsæmən/ (**salmon**)

> **Salmon** is both the singular and the plural form.
>
> **Salmon** は単数形でも複数形でもある.

N-COUNT 可算名詞 A **salmon** is a large silver-colored fish. サケ ● N-UNCOUNT 不可算名詞 **Salmon** is the orangey-pink flesh of this fish which is eaten as food. It is often smoked and eaten raw. サケの肉 ❑ *He gave them a splendid lunch of smoked salmon.* 彼は彼らに豪華なスモークサーモンの昼食をふるまった.

sa|lon /səˈlɒn/ (**salons**) N-COUNT 可算名詞 A **salon** is a place where people have their hair cut or colored, or have beauty treatments. 美容院 ❑ *...a new hair salon.* 新しいヘアサロン.

sa|loon /səˈluːn/ (**saloons**) N-COUNT 可算名詞 A **saloon** is a place where alcoholic drinks are sold and drunk. 酒場, バー [AM 米国英語, OLD-FASHIONED 古風な] ❑ *In the saloon, he drank whiskey and let* his eyes become accustomed to the dimness. バーで彼はウィスキーを飲み, 薄暗さに目を慣れさせた.

salt /sɔlt/ (**salts, salting, salted**) **1** N-UNCOUNT 不可算名詞 **Salt** is a strong-tasting substance, in the form of white powder or crystals, which is used to improve the flavor of food or to preserve it. Salt occurs naturally in sea water. 塩 ❑ *Season lightly with salt and pepper.* 塩と胡椒で軽く味付けしなさい. **2** V-T 他動詞 When you **salt** food, you add salt to it. 塩で味をつける ❑ *Salt the stock to your taste and leave it simmering very gently.* 煮出し汁に好みに応じて塩で味つけし, とろ火で煮詰めなさい. ● **salt|ed** ADJ 形容詞 塩味の ❑ *Put a pan of salted water on to boil.* 鍋に塩水を入れて沸騰させなさい. **3** N-COUNT 可算名詞 **Salts** are substances that are formed when an acid reacts with an alkali. 塩 ❑ *The rock is rich in mineral salts.* その岩には鉱塩分が多く含まれている. **4** PHRASE 句 If you **take** something **with a grain of salt**, you do not believe that it is completely accurate or true. ～を割り引いて受け取る ❑ *You have to take these findings with a grain of salt because respondents tend to give the answers they feel they should.* 回答者は期待されると思う回答をしているので, これらの結果は控えめに受け取る必要がある. **5** PHRASE 句 If you say, for example, that any doctor **worth** his or her **salt** would do something, you mean that any doctor who was good at his or her job or who deserved respect would do it. 有能な ❑ *No golf teacher worth his salt would ever recommend that you grip the club tightly.* 有能なゴルフインストラクターなら誰も決してクラブの握りを固くするように勧めたりしないだろう.

→ see Word Web: **salt**
→ see **crystal, ocean, sweat**

Word Partnership	saltは次の語句と使われる:
V.	add salt, season with salt, sprinkle salt, taste salt **1**
N.	salt air, salt and pepper, pinch of salt, teaspoon of salt **1**

salty /ˈsɔlti/ (**saltier, saltiest**) ADJ 形容詞 Something that is **salty** contains salt or tastes of salt. 塩気のある ❑ *...salty foods such as ham and bacon.* ハムやベーコンなどの塩を含む食品.
→ see **taste**

sa|lute /səˈluːt/ (**salutes, saluting, saluted**) **1** V-T/V-I 他動詞/自動詞 If you **salute** someone, you greet them or show your respect with a formal sign. Soldiers usually salute officers by raising their right hand so that their fingers touch their forehead. 敬礼する [他動詞・自動詞] ❑ *One of the company stepped out and saluted the General.* 中隊の1人が歩み出て, 将軍に敬礼した. ● N-COUNT 可算名詞 **Salute** is also a noun. 敬礼 [also "in" N] ❑ *He gave his salute and left.* 彼は敬礼して立ち去った. **2** V-T 他動詞 To **salute** a person or their achievements means to publicly show or state your admiration for them. ほめたたえる ❑ *I salute the governor for the leadership role that he is taking.* 私は知事に対して発揮している指導者の役割に敬意を表します.

sal|vage /ˈsælvɪdʒ/ (**salvages, salvaging, salvaged**) **1** V-T 他動詞 If something **is salvaged**, someone manages to save it, for example, from a ship that has sunk, or from a building that has been damaged. 引き揚げる [usu passive] ❑ *The team's first task was to decide what equipment could be salvaged.* そのチームの最初の仕事は, どの機器を引き揚げるかを決めることだった. **2** N-UNCOUNT 不可算名詞 **Salvage** is the act of salvaging things from somewhere such as a damaged ship or building. 救出 ❑ *The salvage operation went on.* 引き揚げ作業は続いた. **3** N-UNCOUNT 不可算名詞 The **salvage** from somewhere such as a damaged ship or building is the things that are saved from it. 救助された貨物 ❑ *They climbed up on the rock with their salvage.* 彼らは救出した財貨を持って岩を登った. **4** V-T 他動詞 If you manage to **salvage** a difficult situation, you manage to get something useful from it so that it is not a complete failure. 救う ❑ *Officials tried to salvage the situation.* 役人たちはその状況を救おうと試みた. **5** V-T 他動詞 If you **salvage** something such as your pride or your reputation, you manage to keep it even though it seems likely you will lose it, or you get it back after losing it. 救う ❑ *We definitely wanted to salvage some pride for American tennis.* 私たちはもちろんアメリカのテニス界のプライドを多少とも守りたかった.

S

Word Web   salt

Since prehistoric times, **salt** has been used for a **seasoning**, a **preservative**, and even **money**. A book about salt published in China around 2700 BC describes methods of producing salt that are strikingly similar to current methods. The ancient Greeks exchanged salt for slaves, giving rise to the expression, "not worth his salt." Roman soldiers received *salarium argentum* (salt money), which is the source of the English word *salary*. And salt has altered the course of history. For example, the salt tax was one major cause of the French Revolution.

sal|va|tion /sælveɪʃ³n/ ◼ N-UNCOUNT 不可算名詞 In Christianity, **salvation** is the fact that Christ has saved a person from evil. 救い ❑ *The church's message of salvation has changed the lives of many.* 教会の救いのメッセージは多くの人々の人生を変えた。 ◻ N-UNCOUNT 不可算名詞 The **salvation** of someone or something is the act of saving them from harm, destruction, or an unpleasant situation. 救済 ❑ *...those whose marriages are beyond salvation.* 救いようのない結婚の危機を迎えた夫婦 ◻ N-SING 単数名詞 If someone or something is your **salvation**, they are responsible for saving you from harm, destruction, or an unpleasant situation. 救済手段 ❑ *The country's salvation lies in forcing through democratic reforms.* この国の救済手段は、民主主義改革を推し進めることにかかっている。

same /seɪm/ ◼ ADJ 形容詞 If two or more things, actions, or qualities are **the same**, or if one is **the same as** another, they are very like each other in some way. 同様の ❑ *The houses were all the same – square, close to the street, needing paint.* 家はどれも同じで、正方形で、街路に近く、塗装が必要だ。 ❑ *People with the same experience in the job should be paid the same.* 仕事で同じ経験を持つ人々には、同額の給料を支払うべきだ。 ◻ PHRASE 句 If something is happening **the same as** something else, the two things are happening in a way that is similar or exactly the same. 一と同じ ❑ *I mean, the same as a marriage is a relationship.* 結婚が関係であるのと同じで、それは関係なのよ。 ◻ ADJ 形容詞 You use **same** to indicate that you are referring to only one place, time, or thing, and not to different ones. 同一の ❑ *Bernard works at the same institution as Arlette.* バーナードはアーレットと同一の機関で働いている。 ❑ *It's impossible to get everybody together at the same time.* 全ての人を同時に集めるのは不可能だ。 ◻ ADJ 形容詞 Something that is still **the same** has not changed in any way. 同じ、変わらない ["the" ADJ] ❑ *Taking ingredients from the same source means the beers stay the same.* 同一の供給元からの材料を使うことで、ビールの味が一定になる。 ◻ PRON 代名詞 You use **the same** to refer to something that has previously been mentioned or suggested. 同様のこと ["the" PRON] ❑ *We made the decision which was right for us. Other parents must do the same.* 私たちは私たちにとって正しい決定をした。他の親も同様にする必要がある。 ❑ *In the United States small bookstores survive quite well. The same applies to small publishers.* アメリカでは小規模書店がかなりうまく生き残っている。小規模出版社にも同じことが当てはまる。 ● ADJ 形容詞 **Same** is also an adjective. 同様の ["the" ADJ] ❑ *He's so effective. I admire Ginny for pretty much the same reason.* 彼はとても効率的だ。これとほとんど同じ理由でジニーはとてもすごいと思う。 ◻ CONVENTION 慣習表現 You say "**same here**" in order to suggest that you feel the same way about something as the person who has just spoken to you, or that you have done the same thing. こっちも同じだ [INFORMAL, SPOKEN くだけた、口語、FORMULAE 決まり文句] ❑ *"Nice to meet you," said Michael. "Same here," said Mary Ann.* 「お会いできてうれしいです」とミッシェルが言った。「全く同感です」とメリー・アンが言った。 ◻ CONVENTION 慣習表現 You say "**same to you**" in response to someone who wishes you well with something. ご同様に [INFORMAL, SPOKEN くだけた、口語、FORMULAE 決まり文句] ❑ *"Have a nice Easter." — "And the same to you Bridie."* 「よいイースターを」「プライディー、あなたも」 ◻ PHRASE 句 You say "**same again**" when you want to order another drink of the same kind as the one you have just had. 同じのをもう一杯 [INFORMAL, SPOKEN くだけた、口語] ❑ *Give Roger another pint, Imogen, and I'll have the same again.* イモジェン、ロジャーにもう一杯やってくれ、僕にはまた同じのをくれ。 ◻ PHRASE 句 You can say **all the same** or **just the same** to introduce a statement which indicates that a situation or your opinion has not changed, in spite of what has happened or what has just been said. それでも、やはり ❑ *I arranged to pay him the dollars when he got there, a purely private arrangement. All the same, it was illegal.* 私は彼がそこについたらドルで金を支払うよう手配した。それは全くの個人的な取り決めだった。やはり不法だった。 ◻ PHRASE 句 If you say "**It's all the same to me,**" you mean that you do not care which of several things happens or is chosen. どうでもいい [mainly SPOKEN 主に口語] ❑ *Whether I've got a mustache or not it's all the same to me.* 口ひげを生やすかどうか、僕はどちらでも構わない。 ◻ **at the same time** → see **time**

Thesaurus *same* また次を参照：

ADJ.	alike, equal, identical; (ant.) different ◼
	constant, unchanged; (ant.) different ◻

sam|ple /sæmp³l/ (**samples, sampling, sampled**) ◼ N-COUNT 可算名詞 A **sample** of a substance or product is a small quantity of it that shows you what it is like. 見本 ❑ *You'll receive samples of paint, curtains and upholstery.* あなたにペンキ、カーテンと室内装飾材料の見本をお送りします。 ❑ *We're giving away 2,000 free samples.* 我が社は2千個のサンプルを無料で進呈している。 ◻ N-COUNT 可算名詞 A **sample** of a substance is a small amount of it that is examined and analyzed scientifically. 試料 ❑ *They took samples of my blood.* 彼らは私の血液試料を採った。 ◻ N-COUNT 可算名詞 A **sample** of

people or things is a number of them chosen out of a larger group and then used in tests or used to provide information about the whole group. 標本 ❑ *We based our analysis on a random sample of more than 200 males.* 私たちは200人以上の男性の無作為標本を元に分析を行った。 ◻ V-T 他動詞 If you **sample** food or drink, you taste a small amount of it in order to find out if you like it. 試食する ❑ *We sampled a selection of different bottled waters.* 私たちは様々な瓶詰めの水を選んで試飲した。 ◻ V-T 他動詞 If you **sample** a place or situation, you experience it for a short time in order to find out about it. 試す ❑ *...the chance to sample a different way of life.* 別の生き方を試すチャンス
→ see **DVD, laboratory**

Thesaurus *sample* また次を参照：

N.	bit, piece, portion, specimen ◼ ◻
V.	experience, taste, try ◻ ◻

sanc|tion /sæŋkʃ³n/ (**sanctions, sanctioning, sanctioned**) ◼ V-T 他動詞 If someone in authority **sanctions** an action or practice, they officially approve of it and allow it to be done. 認可する ❑ *He may now be ready to sanction the use of force.* 彼はこれで武力行使を裁可する準備ができたようです。 ● N-UNCOUNT 不可算名詞 **Sanction** is also a noun. 認可 ❑ *...a newspaper run by citizens without the sanction of the government.* 政府の認可を受けずに市民が経営している新聞。 ◻ N-PLURAL 複数名詞 **Sanctions** are measures taken by countries to restrict trade and official contact with a country that has broken international law. 制裁 ❑ *The continued abuse of human rights has now led the United States to impose sanctions against the regime.* 相次ぐ人権侵害は、今や米国がその政権に制裁を加える結果となった。

Word Partnership *sanction* は次の語句と使われる：

PREP.	sanction **against, without** sanction ◼
V.	**impose** a sanction, **lift** a sanction ◼
ADJ.	**legal** sanction, **official** sanction, **proposed** sanction ◼

sanc|tity /sæŋktɪti/ N-UNCOUNT 不可算名詞 If you talk about **the sanctity of** something, you mean that it is very important and must be treated with respect. 神聖さ ❑ *...the sanctity of human life.* 人間の命の尊厳

sanc|tu|ary /sæŋktʃueri/ (**sanctuaries**) ◼ N-COUNT 可算名詞 A **sanctuary** is a place where people who are in danger from other people can go to be safe. 避難所 ❑ *His church became a sanctuary for thousands of people who fled the civil war.* 彼の教会は内戦を逃れた何千もの人たちの避難所になった。 ◻ N-UNCOUNT 不可算名詞 **Sanctuary** is the safety provided in a sanctuary. 庇護 ❑ *Some of them have sought sanctuary in the church.* 彼らのうちの何名かは教会に庇護を求めた。 ◻ N-COUNT 可算名詞 A **sanctuary** is a place where birds or animals are protected and allowed to live freely. 保護区域 ❑ *...a bird sanctuary.* 鳥類保護区

sand /sænd/ (**sands, sanding, sanded**) ◼ N-UNCOUNT 不可算名詞 **Sand** is a substance that looks like powder, and consists of extremely small pieces of stone. Some deserts and many beaches are made up of sand. 砂 ❑ *They all walked barefoot across the damp sand to the water's edge.* 彼らはみんな裸足で湿った砂の上を波打ち際まで歩いた。 ◻ N-PLURAL 複数名詞 **Sands** are a large area of sand, for example, a beach. 砂原 ❑ *...miles of golden sands.* 何マイルも続く金色の砂浜。 ◻ V-T 他動詞 If you **sand** a wood or metal surface, you rub sandpaper over it in order to make it smooth or clean. 紙やすりで磨く ❑ *Sand the surface softly and carefully.* 表面に優しく、慎重に紙やすりをかけなさい。 ● PHRASAL VERB 句動詞 **Sand down** means the same as **sand**. 紙やすりで磨く ❑ *I was going to sand down the chairs and repaint them.* 私は椅子を紙やすりで磨いて、ペンキを塗り直すつもりだった。
→ see **beach, desert, erosion, glass**

san|dal /sænd³l/ (**sandals**) N-COUNT 可算名詞 **Sandals** are light shoes that you wear in warm weather, which have straps instead of a solid part over the top of your foot. サンダル ❑ *...a pair of old sandals.* 1足の古いサンダル

S & L /ɛs ən ɛl/ (**S & Ls**) N-COUNT 可算名詞 S & L is an abbreviation for **savings and loan**. 貯蓄貸付協会 [BUSINESS 実業]

sand|paper /sændpeɪpər/ N-UNCOUNT 不可算名詞 **Sandpaper** is strong paper that has a coating of sand on it. It is used for rubbing wood or metal surfaces to make them smoother. 紙やすり ❑ *...a piece of sandpaper.* 1枚の紙やすり

sand|stone /sændstoʊn/ (**sandstones**) N-MASS 質量名詞 **Sandstone** is a type of rock which contains a lot of sand. It is often used for building houses and walls. 砂岩 ❑ *...the reddish sandstone walls.* 赤みがかった砂岩でできた壁。

sand|wich /sænwɪtʃ, sænd-/ (**sandwiches, sandwiching, sandwiched**) ◼ N-COUNT 可算名詞 A **sandwich** usually consists of two slices of bread with a layer of food such as cheese or

meat between them. サンドイッチ ❑…*a ham sandwich.* ハムサンド. **2** V-T 他動詞 If you **sandwich** two things **together** with something else, you put that other thing between them. If you **sandwich** one thing between two other things, you put it between them. サンドイッチにする ❑*Carefully split the sponge ring, then sandwich the two halves together with whipped cream.* リング型スポンジケーキ慎重に2枚割りにして，間にホイップクリームを挟みなさい.

→ see **meal**

sandy /sǽndi/ (**sandier, sandiest**) ADJ 形容詞 A **sandy** area is covered with sand. 砂状の ❑…*long, sandy beaches.* 長い砂浜.

| Word Link | san ≈ health : insane, sane, sanitation |

sane /seɪn/ (**saner, sanest**) **1** ADJ 形容詞 Someone who is **sane** is able to think and behave normally and reasonably, and is not mentally ill. 正気の *He seemed perfectly sane.* 彼は完全に正気に見えた. **2** ADJ 形容詞 If you refer to a **sane** person, action, or system, you mean one that you think is reasonable and sensible. 健全な ❑*No sane person wishes to see conflict or casualties.* まっとうな人は紛争や死傷者を見ることを望んだりしない.

sang /sæŋ/ **Sang** is the past tense of **sing**.

sani|tary /sǽnɪtɛri/ **1** ADJ 形容詞 **Sanitary** means concerned with keeping things clean and healthy, especially by providing a sewage system and a clean water supply. 衛生の [ADJ n] ❑*Sanitary conditions are appalling.* 衛生状態はひどいものだ. **2** ADJ 形容詞 If you say that a place is not **sanitary**, you mean that it is not very clean. 清潔な ❑*It's not the most sanitary place one could swim.* それは泳げる場所としてはあまり衛生的ではない.

sani|tary nap|kin (**sanitary napkins**) N-COUNT 可算名詞 A **sanitary napkin** is a pad of thick soft material which women wear to absorb the blood during their periods. 生理用ナプキン [AM 米国英語]

sani|tary tow|el (**sanitary towels**) N-COUNT 可算名詞 A **sanitary towel** is the same as a **sanitary napkin**. 生理用ナプキン [BRIT 英国英語]

sani|ta|tion /sǽnɪteɪ˄ən/ N-UNCOUNT 不可算名詞 **Sanitation** is the process of keeping places clean and healthy, especially by providing a sewage system and a clean water supply. 公衆衛生 ❑…*the hazards of contaminated water and poor sanitation.* 汚染された水と粗末な下水設備の危険

san|ity /sǽnɪti/ N-UNCOUNT 不可算名詞 A person's **sanity** is their ability to think and behave normally and reasonably. 正気 ❑*He and his wife finally had to move from their apartment just to preserve their sanity.* 彼とその妻は，とうとう，正気を保つためにだけのために，アパートから引っ越さなければならなかった.

sank /sæŋk/ **Sank** is the past tense of **sink**.

sap /sæp/ (**saps, sapping, sapped**) **1** V-T 他動詞 If something **saps** your strength or confidence, it gradually weakens or destroys it. 活力を失わせる ❑*I was afraid the sickness had sapped my strength.* 私は病気で活力を失ってしまったのではないかと心配だった. **2** N-UNCOUNT 不可算名詞 **Sap** is the watery liquid in plants and trees. 液汁 ❑*The leaves, bark and sap are also common ingredients of local herbal remedies.* 葉，樹皮および樹液も地元の薬草療法の普通の材料だ.

sap|phire /sǽfaɪər/ (**sapphires**) **1** N-VAR 可変性名詞 A **sapphire** is a precious stone which is blue in color. サファイア ❑…*a sapphire engagement ring.* サファイアの婚約指輪 **2** COLOR 色彩語 Something that is **sapphire** is bright blue in color. サファイア色 [LITERARY 文語的] ❑…*white snow and sapphire skies.* 白い雪とサファイア色の空.

sar|casm /sɑ́rkæzəm/ N-UNCOUNT 不可算名詞 **Sarcasm** is speech or writing which actually means the opposite of what it seems to say. Sarcasm is usually intended to mock or insult someone. 皮肉 ❑*Sarcasm and demeaning remarks have no place in parenting.* 子育てでは皮肉や侮辱的な発言が出る幕はない.

sar|cas|tic /sɑrkǽstɪk/ ADJ 形容詞 Someone who is **sarcastic** says or does the opposite of what they really mean in order to mock or insult someone. 皮肉な ❑*She poked fun at people's shortcomings with sarcastic remarks.* 彼女は皮肉なものの言い様で人々の欠点をからかった. ● **sar|cas|ti|cal|ly** /sɑrkǽstɪkli/ ADV 副詞 皮肉たっぷりに ❑*"What a surprise!" Caroline murmured sarcastically.* 「何とまあ」キャロラインは皮肉たっぷりにつぶやいた.

sar|dine /sɑrdín/ (**sardines**) N-COUNT 可算名詞 **Sardines** are a kind of small sea fish, often eaten as food. イワシ ❑*They opened a can of sardines.* 彼らはイワシの缶詰を開けた.

sar|don|ic /sɑrdɒnɪk/ ADJ 形容詞 If you describe someone as **sardonic**, you mean their attitude to people or things is humorous but rather critical. 冷笑的な ❑*He was a big, sardonic man, who intimidated even the most self-confident students.* 彼は，最も自信のある学生でさえおびえさせる，冷笑的な大男だった.

SASE /ɛs eɪ ɛs í/ (**SASEs**) N-SING 単数名詞 An **SASE** is an envelope to which you have stuck a stamp and written your own name and address. You send it to a person or organization so that they can reply to you in it. **SASE** is an abbreviation for "self-addressed stamped envelope." 切手を貼った返信用封筒 [AM 米国英語]

sash /sǽʃ/ (**sashes**) N-COUNT 可算名詞 A **sash** is a long piece of cloth which people wear around their waist or over one shoulder, especially with formal or official clothes. 飾り帯 ❑*She wore a white dress with a thin blue sash.* 彼女は細い青色の腰帯のついた白いドレスを着ていた.

sas|sy /sǽsi/ ADJ 形容詞 If an older person describes a younger person as **sassy**, they mean they are disrespectful in a lively, confident way. 生意気な [AM 米国英語, INFORMAL くだけた] ❑*Are you that sassy with your parents, young lady?* 君は自分の親にそんな生意気な口をきくのかね，お嬢さん.

sat /sæt/ **Sat** is the past tense and past participle of **sit**.

SAT /ɛs eɪ tí/ (**SATs**) N-PROPER 固有名詞 The **SAT** is a set of examinations which are usually taken by students who wish to enter a college or university. 大学進学適性テスト [AM 米国英語] ❑*The average SAT score among 2004's freshman class was 1,200.* 2004年度の新入生クラスの平均SATスコアは1200だった.

Sat. **Sat.** is a written abbreviation for **Saturday**. 土曜日の省略形

Satan /seɪt˄n/ N-PROPER 固有名詞 In the Christian religion, **Satan** is the Devil, a powerful evil being who is the chief opponent of God. 魔王

sa|tan|ic /sətǽnɪk, seɪ-/ ADJ 形容詞 Something that is **satanic** is considered to be caused by or influenced by Satan. 魔王の ❑…*satanic cults.* 邪悪な狂信的教団

sat|el|lite /sǽt˄laɪt/ (**satellites**) **1** N-COUNT 可算名詞 A **satellite** is an object which has been sent into space in order to collect information or to be part of a communications system. Satellites move continually around the Earth or around another planet. 人工衛星 [also "by" N] ❑*The rocket launched two communications satellites.* ロケットは通信衛星2基を打ち上げた. **2** ADJ 形容詞 **Satellite** television is broadcast using a satellite. 衛星放送の [ADJ n] ❑*They have four satellite channels.* 彼らは衛星放送チャンネルが4つある. **3** N-COUNT 可算名詞 A **satellite** is a natural object in space that moves around a planet or star. 衛星 ❑…*the satellites of Jupiter.* 木星の衛星. **4** N-COUNT 可算名詞 You can refer to a country, area, or organization as a **satellite** when it is controlled by or depends on a larger and more powerful one. 衛星国，衛星都市 ❑*Some companies are outfitting their satellite offices with wireless LANs.* 衛星オフィスにワイヤレスLANを備えている会社もある.

→ see Word Web: **satellite**

→ see **astronomer, forecast, navigation, radio, television**

sat|el|lite dish (**satellite dishes**) N-COUNT 可算名詞 A **satellite dish** is a piece of equipment which people have on their house in order to receive satellite television. 衛星放送用パラボラアンテナ

| Word Web | satellite |

The **moon** is the earth's best-known **satellite**. However, humans began **launching** other objects into **space** starting in 1957. That's when the first artificial satellite, Sputnik, began to **orbit** the earth. Today, hundreds of satellites circle the **planet**. The largest of these is the International **Space Station**. It completes an orbit about every 90 minutes and sometimes can be seen from the earth. Others, such as the Hubble Telescope, help us learn more about **outer space**. The NOAA 12 monitors the earth's climate. Most TV weather forecasts feature images taken from satellites. Today, many TV programs are also broadcast by satellite.

sat|in /sˈæt²n/ (satins) ■ N-MASS 質量名詞 **Satin** is a smooth, shiny kind of cloth, usually made from silk. しゅす □...*a peach satin ribbon.* 桃色のしゅすのリボン. ② ADJ 形容詞 If something such as paint, wax, or cosmetic gives something a **satin** finish, it reflects light to some extent but is not very shiny. しゅすのような [ADJ n] □ *The final stage of waxing left it with a satin sheen.* ワックスがけの最終段階によりそれにしゅすのような光沢が与えられた.

sat|ire /sˈætaɪər/ (satires) ■ N-UNCOUNT 不可算名詞 **Satire** is the use of humor or exaggeration in order to show how foolish or wicked some people's behavior or ideas are. 風刺 □ *The commercial side of the Christmas season is an easy target for satire.* クリスマスシーズンの商業的な面は格好の風刺の的です. ② N-COUNT 可算名詞 A **satire** is a play, movie, or novel in which humor or exaggeration is used to criticize something. 風刺文学 □...*a sharp satire on the American political process.* アメリカの政治過程を鋭く風刺する作品

sa|tiri|cal /sətˈɪrɪk²l/ ADJ 形容詞 A **satirical** drawing, piece of writing, or comedy show is one in which humor or exaggeration is used to criticize something. 風刺的な □...*a satirical novel about New York life in the late 80s.* 80年代後期のニューヨーク生活に関する風刺小説

sat|is|fac|tion /sˌætɪsfˈækʃ²n/ ■ N-UNCOUNT 不可算名詞 **Satisfaction** is the pleasure that you feel when you do something or get something that you wanted or needed to do or get. 満足感 □ *She felt a small glow of satisfaction.* 彼女はちょっとした満足感の高まりを感じた. □ *Both sides expressed satisfaction with the progress so far.* 両側ともこれまでの進歩に満足を表明した. ② N-UNCOUNT 不可算名詞 If you get **satisfaction** from someone, you get money or an apology from them because you have been treated badly. 賠償 □ *If you can't get any satisfaction, complain to the park owner.* 何も賠償してもらえないのなら, 公園の所有者に苦情を申し込みなさい. ③ PHRASE 句 If you do something **to** someone's **satisfaction**, they are happy with the way that you have done it. 満足のいくように □ *She never could seem to do anything right or to his satisfaction.* 彼女には適切なことや彼が満足するようなことをすることが決してできないように見えた.

sat|is|fac|tory /sˌætɪsfˈæktəri/ ADJ 形容詞 Something that is **satisfactory** is acceptable to you or fulfills a particular need or purpose. 満足な □ *I never got a satisfactory answer.* 私は決して満足のいく答えをもらったことはない.

sat|is|fied /sˈætɪsfaɪd/ ■ ADJ 形容詞 If you are **satisfied with** something, you are happy because you have gotten what you wanted or needed. 満足した □ *We are not satisfied with these results.* 私たちはこれらの結果には不満足だ. ② ADJ 形容詞 If you are **satisfied that** something is true or has been done properly, you are convinced about this after checking it. 得心した [v-link ADJ] □ *People must be satisfied that the treatment is safe.* 人々は治療が安全であることを納得しているにちがいない.

Word Link *sat, satis ≈ enough : dis*satis*faction, in*satia*ble,* satis*fy*

sat|is|fy /sˈætɪsfaɪ/ (satisfies, satisfying, satisfied) ■ V-T 他動詞 If someone or something **satisfies** you, they give you enough of what you want or need to make you pleased or contented. 満足させる □ *The pace of change has not been quick enough to satisfy everyone.* 変化の速度は鈍くて全ての人々を満足させるわけにはいきませんでした. ② V-T 他動詞 To **satisfy** someone **that** something is true or has been done properly means to convince them by giving them more information or by showing them what has been done. 納得させる □ *He has to satisfy the environmental lobby that real progress will be made to cut emissions.* 排気量削減において実際に進展がみられるであろうことを, 彼は環境活動団体に納得してもらわなければなりません. ③ V-T 他動詞 If you **satisfy** the requirements for something, you are good enough or have the right qualities to fulfill these requirements. 満たす (条件を) □ *The executive committee recommends that the procedures should satisfy certain basic requirements.* 執行委員会は, その手順が特定の基本要件を満たすべきだと勧告した.

Word Partnership *satisfy* は次の語句と使われる:

N.	satisfy an **appetite**, satisfy **demands**, satisfy a **desire** ■
	satisfy a **need** ■ ③
	satisfy **critics**, satisfy someone's **curiosity** ②

sat|is|fy|ing /sˈætɪsfaɪɪŋ/ ADJ 形容詞 Something that is **satisfying** makes you feel happy, especially because you feel you have achieved something. 満足な □ *I found wood carving satisfying.* 私は木彫りにやりがいを見つけた.

satu|rate /sˈætʃəreɪt/ (saturates, saturating, saturated) ■ V-T 他動詞 If people or things **saturate** a place or object, they fill it completely so that no more can be added. いっぱいにする □ *In the last days before the vote, both sides are saturating the airwaves.* 投票前の

最後の数日は両陣営とも放送電波を飽和状態にしている. ② V-T 他動詞 If someone or something **is saturated**, they become extremely wet. 浸す, ずぶぬれにする □ *If the filter has been saturated with motor oil, it should be discarded and replaced.* フィルターにモーターオイルがいっぱいに浸み込んでいる場合, 破棄して交換しなければならない.

satu|ra|tion /sˌætʃərˈeɪʃ²n/ ■ N-UNCOUNT 不可算名詞 **Saturation** is the process or state that occurs when a place or thing is filled completely with people or things, so that no more can be added. 飽和 □ *Japanese car makers have been equally blind to the saturation of their markets at home and abroad.* 日本の自動車メーカーも同様に, 国内および海外の市場が飽和状態に達していることがわかっていない. ② ADJ 形容詞 **Saturation** is used to describe a campaign or other activity that is carried out very thoroughly, so that nothing is missed. 集中 [ADJ n] □ *The concept of saturation marketing makes perfect sense.* 集中マーケティングの概念は, まったく道理にかなっている.

Sat|ur|day /sˈætərdeɪ, -di/ (Saturdays) N-VAR 可変性名詞 **Saturday** is the day after Friday and before Sunday. 土曜日 □ *He called her on Saturday morning at the studio.* 土曜日の朝に彼はスタジオにいる彼女に電話をかけた. □ *Every Saturday dad made a beautiful pea and ham soup.* 毎週土曜日に父はすばらしい豆とハムのスープを作ってくれた.

sauce /sˈɔːs/ (sauces) N-MASS 質量名詞 A **sauce** is a thick liquid which is served with other food. ソース □...*pasta cooked in a sauce of garlic, tomatoes, and cheese.* ニンニク, トマト, チーズのソースをからめたパスタ

sauce|pan /sˈɔːspæn/ (saucepans) N-COUNT 可算名詞 A **saucepan** is a deep metal cooking pot, usually with a long handle and a lid. 片手鍋 □ *Place the potatoes and parsnips in a large saucepan, cover with cold water and bring to the boil.* ジャガイモとカブを大きなソースパンに入れ, ひたひたになるまで冷水を入れて沸騰させなさい. → see **pan**

sau|cer /sˈɔːsər/ (saucers) N-COUNT 可算名詞 A **saucer** is a small curved plate on which you stand a cup. 受け皿 □ *Rae's coffee cup clattered against the saucer as she picked it up.* レイがコーヒーカップを持ち上げた時, カップが受け皿に当たってカチャカチャと音をたてた. → see **dish**

saucy /sˈɔːsi/ (saucier, sauciest) ADJ 形容詞 Someone or something that is **saucy** refers to sex in a light-hearted, amusing way. わいせつな, いかがわしい □...*a saucy joke.* いかがわしいジョーク

sau|na /sˈɔːnə/ (saunas) ■ N-COUNT 可算名詞 If you have a **sauna**, you sit or lie in a room that is so hot that it makes you sweat. People have saunas in order to relax and to clean their skin thoroughly. サウナ □ *Every month I have a sauna.* 私は毎月サウナに入る. ② N-COUNT 可算名詞 A **sauna** is a room or building where you can have a sauna. サウナ浴場 □ *The hotel has a sauna, solarium and heated indoor swimming pool.* そのホテルはサウナ浴場, サンルームおよび屋内温水プールを備えている.

saun|ter /sˈɔːntər/ (saunters, sauntering, sauntered) V-I 自動詞 If you **saunter** somewhere, you walk there in a slow, casual way. ぶらぶら散歩する □ *We watched our fellow students saunter into the building.* 私たちは学友たちが建物にぶらぶらと歩いて入っていくのを見つめていた.

sau|sage /sˈɔːsɪdʒ/ (sausages) N-VAR 可変性名詞 A **sausage** consists of minced meat, usually pork, mixed with other ingredients and is contained in a tube made of skin or a similar material. ソーセージ □...*sausages and fries.* ソーセージとフライドポテト

sau|té /sˈoʊteɪ/ (sautés, sautéing, sautéed) V-T 他動詞 When you **sauté** food, you fry it quickly in hot oil or butter. ソテーにする □ *Sauté the chicken until golden brown.* キツネ色になるまで鶏肉をソテーにしなさい.

sav|age /sˈævɪdʒ/ (savages, savaging, savaged) ■ ADJ 形容詞 Someone or something that is **savage** is extremely cruel, violent, and uncontrolled. 残忍な □ *This was a savage attack on a defenseless young girl.* これは無防備の少女に対する残忍な攻撃だった. □...*the savage wave of violence that swept the country in November 1987.* 1987年11月に全国を激しく吹き荒れた残忍な暴力の波 ● **sav|age|ly** ADV 副詞 残忍に □ *He was savagely beaten.* 彼は残忍に殴られた. ② N-COUNT 可算名詞 If you refer to people as **savages**, you dislike them because you think that they do not have an advanced society and are violent. 野蛮人 [DISAPPROVAL 不賛成] □...*their conviction that the area was a frozen desert peopled with uncouth savages.* その地域は粗野な野蛮人の住む凍結した砂漠だという彼らの確信 ③ V-T 他動詞 [usu passive] If someone **is savaged** by a dog or other animal, the animal attacks them violently. 噛む □ *The animal then turned on him and he was savaged to death.* そして, その動物は彼に襲いかかり, 彼は噛まれて死んだ.

sav|age|ry /sˈævɪdʒri/ N-UNCOUNT 不可算名詞 **Savagery** is extremely cruel and violent behavior. 蛮行 □...*the sheer savagery of war.* 戦争の全くの残忍さ

save /seɪv/ (**saves, saving, saved**) **1** V-T 他動詞 If you **save** someone or something, you help them to avoid harm or to escape from a dangerous or unpleasant situation. 救う ❑ *...an austerity program designed to save the country's failing economy.* 国の後退しつつある経済を救うために策定された財政緊縮策 ❑ *The meeting is an attempt to mobilize nations to save children from death by disease and malnutrition.* その会議は子供たちを疾病や栄養失調による死から救うために, 諸国家を動員する試みである. **2** V-T/V-I 他動詞/自動詞 If you **save**, you gradually collect money by spending less than you get, usually in order to buy something that you want. 貯蓄する [他動詞・自動詞] ❑ *The majority of people intend to save, but find that by the end of the month there is nothing left.* 大部分の人たちは貯金しようとするが, 月末には何も残っていないことに気づく. ❑ *Tim and Barbara are now saving for a house in the suburbs.* ティムとバーバラは, 現在郊外に家を買おうと貯金している. ❑ *I was trying to save money to go to college.* 私は大学に行くために貯金しようと試みていた. ● PHRASAL VERB 句動詞 **Save up** means the same as **save**. 貯蓄する ❑ *Julie wanted to put some of her money aside for holidays or save up for something special.* ジュリーは休暇のためにお金を取っておいたり, 何か特別なものを買うために貯金したりしたかった. **3** V-T/V-I 他動詞/自動詞 If you **save** something such as time or money, you prevent the loss or waste of it. 節約する [他動詞・自動詞] ❑ *It saves time in the kitchen to have things you use a lot within reach.* 台所では, よく使うものを手の届くところにおいておくと時間を節約できる. ❑ *I'll try to save him the expense of a flight from Perth.* 私はパースからの航空費用を彼のために節約するように努めよう. ❑ *A new filter can save on energy bills.* 新しいフィルターを使用すると, 光熱費を節約することができる. **4** V-T 他動詞 If you **save** something, you keep it because it will be needed later. 取っておく ❑ *Drain the beans thoroughly and save the stock for soup.* 豆の水気を完全に切って, スープ種はスープ用に取っておきなさい. **5** V-T 他動詞 If someone or something **saves** you **from** an unpleasant action or experience, they change the situation so that you do not have to do it or experience it. 救う ❑ *The scanner will reduce the need for exploratory operations which will save risk and pain for patients.* スキャナーは試験手術の必要性を削減し, 患者の危険や苦痛をなくす. ❑ *She was hoping that something might save her from having to make a decision.* 彼女は, 何かが起こって決断を下さなくてもよくなればと願っていた. **6** V-T/V-I 他動詞/自動詞 If you **save** data in a computer, you give the computer an instruction to store the data on a tape or disk. 保存する [COMPUTING コンピューティング] [他動詞・自動詞] ❑ *Try to get into the habit of saving your work regularly.* 作業を定期的に保存する習慣をつけるようにしなさい. ❑ *Save frequently when you are creating graphics.* グラフィックスの作成時には頻繁に保存しなさい. **7** V-T/V-I 他動詞/自動詞 If a goalkeeper **saves**, or **saves** a shot, they succeed in preventing the ball from going into the goal. ゴールを守る [他動詞] [自動詞] ❑ *He saved one shot when the ball hit him on the head.* 彼はボールが頭に当たったために, シュートがゴールするのを防げた. ● N-COUNT 可算名詞 **Save** is also a noun. 敵の得点を防ぐこと ❑ *The goalie made some great saves.* ゴールキーパーは何度かとてもうまくゴールを守った. **8** to **save the day** → see **day 9** to **save face** → see **face**
▶ **save up** → see **save 2**

Thesaurus		*save* また次を参照:
v.	defend, protect, rescue **1**	
	conserve, economize, hoard; *(ant.)* waste **2** – **4**	

sav|er /seɪvər/ (**savers**) N-COUNT 可算名詞 A **saver** is a person who regularly saves money, especially by paying it into a bank account. 貯蓄家 ❑ *Low interest rates are bad news for savers, who have seen their income halved over the last year.* 低金利は過去1年で収入が半減するのを経験した貯蓄家にとって悪い知らせだ.

sav|ing /seɪvɪŋ/ (**savings**) **1** N-COUNT 可算名詞 A **saving** is a reduction in the amount of time or money that is saved or needed. 節約 ❑ *You can enjoy a year's membership for just $28 – a saving of $7 off the regular rate.* あなたは正規の料金より7ドル安いたった28ドルの会費で1年間会員になれます. **2** N-PLURAL 複数名詞 Your **savings** are the money that you have saved, especially in a bank or a building society. 預金 ❑ *Her savings were in the First National Bank.* 彼女の貯金はファースト・ナショナル銀行に預けてあった.
→ see **bank**

sav|ings and loan (**savings and loans**) N-COUNT 可算名詞 A **savings and loan** association is a business where people save money to earn interest, and which lends money to savers to buy houses. Compare **building society**. 貯蓄貸付 [mainly AM 主に米国英語 BUSINESS 実業]

sav|ior /seɪvyər/ (**saviors**) N-COUNT 可算名詞 A **savior** is a person who saves someone or something from danger, ruin, or defeat. 救助者 ❑ *...the savior of his country.* 救国者

sa|vor /seɪvər/ (**savors, savoring, savored**) **1** V-T 他動詞 If you **savor** an experience, you enjoy it as much as you can. 楽しむ ❑ *She savored her newfound freedom.* 彼女は新しく手に入れた自由を満喫した. **2** V-T 他動詞 If you **savor** food or drink, you eat or drink it slowly in order to taste its full flavor and to enjoy it properly. 味わう ❑ *Just relax, eat slowly and savor the full flavor of your food.* ゆったりとして, ゆっくり食べてお料理の味を十分味わいなさい.

Word Link	*vor ≈ eating : herbivorous, savory, voracious*

sa|vory /seɪvəri/ ADJ 形容詞 **Savory** food has a salty or spicy flavor rather than a sweet one. 塩味の, 辛味の ❑ *...all sorts of sweet and savory breads.* あらゆる種類の甘いパンや塩味のパン

saw /sɔ/ (**saws, sawing, sawed, sawed** or **sawn**) **1** **Saw** is the past tense of **see**. **2** N-COUNT 可算名詞 A **saw** is a tool for cutting wood, which has a blade with sharp teeth along one edge. Some saws are pushed backward and forward by hand, and others are powered by electricity. のこぎり **3** V-T/V-I 他動詞/自動詞 If you **saw** something, you cut it with a saw. のこぎりで切る ❑ *He escaped by sawing through the bars of his cell.* 彼は独房の金属棒をのこぎりで切って脱走した.
→ see **cut, tool**

saw|dust /sɔdʌst/ N-UNCOUNT 不可算名詞 **Sawdust** is dust and very small pieces of wood which are produced when you saw wood. おがくず ❑ *...a layer of sawdust.* おがくずの層

sawn /sɔn/ **Sawn** is the past participle of **saw**. [mainly BRIT 主に英国英語]

sax /sæks/ (**saxes**) N-COUNT 可算名詞 A **sax** is the same as a **saxophone**. サクソホーン [INFORMAL くだけた]

saxo|phone /sæksəfoʊn/ (**saxophones**) N-VAR 可変性名詞 A **saxophone** is a musical instrument in the shape of a curved metal tube with a narrower part that you blow into and keys that you press. サクソホーン

sax|opho|nist /sæksəfoʊnɪst/ (**saxophonists**) N-COUNT 可算名詞 A **saxophonist** is someone who plays the saxophone. サクソホーン奏者

say

❶ VERB AND NOUN USES
❷ PHRASES AND CONVENTIONS

❶ say /seɪ/ (**says** /sɛz/, **saying, said** /sɛd/) **1** V-T 他動詞 When you **say** something, you speak words. 言う ❑ *"I'm sorry," he said.* 「すみません」と彼は言った. ❑ *She said they were very impressed.* 彼女は彼らが非常に良い印象を受けていたと言った. ❑ *Forty-one people are said to have been seriously hurt.* 41人が重傷を負ったと言われている. **2** V-T 他動詞 You use **say** in expressions such as **I would just like to say** to introduce what you are actually saying, or to indicate that you are expressing an opinion or admitting a fact. If you state that you **can't say** something or you **wouldn't say** something, you are indicating in a polite or indirect way that it is not the case. 言う ❑ *I would just like to say that this is the most hypocritical thing I have ever heard in my life.* これほど偽善的な話はこれまでに聞いたことがないと私は言いたい. ❑ *I must say that rather shocked me, too.* それは私にも相当に衝撃を与えたと言わせてもらいたい. **3** V-T 他動詞 You can mention the contents of a piece of writing by mentioning what it **says** or what someone **says** in it. 書いてある ❑ *The report says there is widespread and routine torture of political prisoners in the country.* そのレポートには, その国では政治犯の拷問が幅広く日常的に行なわれていると書いてある. ❑ *You can't have one without the other, as the song says.* 歌にあるように片方だけを持つことはできない. **4** V-T 他動詞 If you **say** something **to yourself**, you think it. 思う ❑ *Perhaps I'm still dreaming, I said to myself.* 多分私はまだ夢をみているのだと私は思った. **5** N-SING 単数名詞 If you have a **say** in something, you have the right to give your opinion and influence decisions relating to it. 発言権 [usu "a" N, also "more/some" N] ❑ *You can get married at sixteen, and yet you haven't got a say in the running of the country.* 16歳で結婚することはできるが, 国の運営には発言権はない. **6** V-T 他動詞 You indicate the information given by something such as a clock, dial, or map by mentioning what it **says**. 示す ❑ *The clock said four minutes past eleven when we set off.* 私たちが出発した時, 時計の針は11時4分を指していた. **7** V-T 他動詞 If something **says** something **about** a person, situation, or thing, it gives important information about them. 示す ❑ *I think that says a lot about how well Safin is playing.* それはサフィンがどれほどうまくやっているかを多く示していると思う. **8** V-T 他動詞 If something **says** a lot **for** a person or thing, it shows that this person or thing is very good or has a lot of good qualities. 示す ❑ *That the Escort is still the nation's bestselling car in 1992 says a lot for the power of Ford's marketing people.* エスコートが1992年も国内の販売台数でまだ1位であることは, フォード社のマーケティング担当者の能力について多くを示している. **9** V-T 他動詞 You use **say** in expressions such as **I'll say that for them** and **you can say this for them** after or before you mention a good quality that someone has, usually when you think they do not have many good qualities. 断言する ❑ *He's usually well-dressed, I'll say that for him.* 彼は普段きちんとした身なりをしている. それだけは断言で

きる. 10 V-T 他動詞 You can use **say** when you want to discuss something that might possibly happen or be true. 仮定する [only imper] ❑ *Say you were buying a new car, would your discussion begin and end with the monthly payment?* 新しい車を買うとした場合には、話合いは初めから終わりまで月々の支払いのことになるか. 11 PHRASE 句 You can use **say** or **let's say** when you mention something as an example. 例えば ❑ *To see the problem here more clearly, let's look at a different biological system, say, an acorn.* ここで問題をよりはっきりと知るために、異なる生物学的体系、例えばどんぐりを調べてみよう.

Note that, with the verb **say**, if you want to mention the person who is being addressed, you should use the preposition **to**. "What did she say you?" is wrong. "**What did she say to you?**" is correct. The verb **tell**, however, is usually followed by a direct object indicating the person who is being addressed. ❑ *He told Alison he was suffering from leukemia…What did she tell you?* "What did she tell to you?" is wrong. **Say** is the most general verb for reporting the words that someone speaks. **Tell** is used to report information that is given to someone. ❑ *The manufacturer told me that the product did not contain corn.* **Tell** can also be used with a "to" infinitive to report an order or instruction. ❑ *My mother told me to shut up and eat my dinner.*

Thesaurus

say また次を参照:

v. announce, communicate, declare, speak ❶ 1

❷ **say** /seɪ/ (**says** /sɛz/, **saying**, **said** /sɛd/) 1 PHRASE 句 If you say that something **says it all**, you mean that it shows you very clearly the truth about a situation or someone's feelings. はっきり示す ❑ *This is my third visit in a week, which says it all.* これが1週間に3度目の私の訪問ですが、これでお分かりでしょう. 2 CONVENTION 慣習表現 You can use "**You don't say**" to express surprise at what someone has told you. People often use this expression to indicate that in fact they are not surprised. ほんとですか [FEELINGS 感情] ❑ *"I'm a writer." — "You don't say. What kind of book are you writing?"* 「私は作家です」「ほおー、どんな種類の本を書いていますか」 3 PHRASE 句 If you say there is a lot **to be said for** something, you mean you think it has a lot of good qualities or aspects. 一にはそれなりのいい点が ❑ *There's a lot to be said for being based in the country.* その国に駐屯しているのにはそれなりのいい点が多い. 4 PHRASE 句 If someone asks **what** you **have to say for yourself**, they are asking what excuse you have for what you have done. 一はどんな弁解することがあるか ❑ *"Well," she said eventually, "what have you to say for yourself?"* 「それで」と彼女はようやく口を開いた.「あなたの弁解は何ですか」 5 PHRASE 句 If something **goes without saying**, it is obvious. 言うまでもないことである ❑ *It goes without saying that if someone has lung problems they should not smoke.* 肺疾患を持つ人間が禁煙すべきなのは言うまでもないことだ. 6 PHRASE 句 When one of the people or groups involved in a discussion **has** their **say**, they give their opinion. 自分の言いたいことを言う ❑ *Voters were finally having their say today.* 投票者は今日やっと自分の意見を言っていた. 7 CONVENTION 慣習表現 You use "**I wouldn't say no**" to indicate that you would like something, especially something that has just been offered to you. 喜んで [INFORMAL くだけた, FORMULAE 決まり文句] ❑ *I wouldn't say no to a drink.* 飲み物は喜んでいただきます. 8 PHRASE 句 You use **that is to say** or **that's to say** to indicate that you are about to express the same idea more clearly or precisely. 換言すると [FORMAL 形式ばった] ❑ *That would mean voting no, that is to say, using the veto.* それは反対票を投じること、すなわち拒否権を行使することを意味するだろう. 9 CONVENTION 慣習表現 You can use "**You can say that again**" to express strong agreement with what someone has just said. 全くそのとおり [INFORMAL くだけた, EMPHASIS 強調] ❑ *"You are in enough trouble already." — "You can say that again," sighed Richard.* 「あなたは既に十分問題を抱えている」「全くその通りです」

say|ing /seɪɪŋ/ (**sayings**) N-COUNT 可算名詞 A **saying** is a sentence that people often say and that gives advice or information about human life and experience. ことわざ ❑ *We also realize the truth of that old saying: Charity begins at home.* また、私たちは昔からのことわざ、「愛は家庭に始まる」が真実であることを実感している.

scab /skæb/ (**scabs**) N-COUNT 可算名詞 A **scab** is a hard, dry covering that forms over the surface of a wound. かさぶた ❑ *The area can be very painful until scabs form after about ten days.* その部分は10日ほどしてからかさぶたができるまでかなり痛くなるかもしれない.

scaf|fold /skæfəld, -oʊld/ (**scaffolds**) 1 N-COUNT 可算名詞 A **scaffold** was a raised platform on which criminals were hanged or had their heads cut off. 処刑台 ❑ *Ascending the shaky ladder to the scaffold, More addressed the executioner.* ぐらぐらする処刑台へのはしごを登りながら、モアは処刑人に話しかけた. 2 N-COUNT 可算名詞 A **scaffold** is a temporary raised platform on which workers stand to paint, repair, or build high parts of a building. 足場 ❑ *They were standing on top of a giant scaffold.* 彼らは巨大な足場のてっぺんに立っていた.

scaf|fold|ing /skæfəldɪŋ/ N-UNCOUNT 不可算名詞 **Scaffolding** consists of poles and boards made into a temporary framework that is used by workers when they are painting, repairing, or building high parts of a building, usually outside. 足場 ❑ *Workers have erected scaffolding around the base of the tower below the roadway.* 作業員は道路の下にある塔の基部の周りに足場を建てた.

Word Link cal, caul ≈ hot, heat : calorie, cauldron, scald

scald /skɔld/ (**scalds, scalding, scalded**) 1 V-T 他動詞 If you **scald yourself**, you burn yourself with very hot liquid or steam. やけどをする（再帰形を伴なって）❑ *A patient jumped into a bath being prepared by a member of staff and scalded herself.* 患者は職員の1人が沸かした風呂に飛び込み、やけどをした. 2 N-COUNT 可算名詞 A **scald** is a burn caused by very hot liquid or steam. やけど ❑ *Scalds, burns and poisoning can all be life-threatening.* 熱湯のやけど、火傷、中毒は全て致命的となりうる.

Word Link scal, scala ≈ ladder, stairs : escalate, escalator, scale

scale /skeɪl/ (**scales, scaling, scaled**) 1 N-SING 単数名詞 If you refer to the **scale** of something, you are referring to its size or extent, especially when it is very big. 規模 ❑ *However, he underestimates the scale of the problem.* しかし、彼は問題の大きさを過小評価している. ❑ *The break-down of law and order could result in killing on a massive scale.* 法と秩序が崩壊した場合には、大規模な殺人が起こりうるだろう. 2 → see also **full-scale, large-scale, small-scale** 3 N-COUNT 可算名詞 A **scale** is a set of levels or numbers which are used in a particular system of measuring things or are used when comparing them. 目盛り ❑ *...an earthquake measuring 5.5 on the Richter scale.* リヒター・スケールが5.5の地震 ❑ *The patient rates the therapies on a scale of zero to ten.* 患者はその治療をゼロから10までの尺度で評価する. 4 → see also **timescale** 5 N-COUNT 可算名詞 A pay **scale** or **scale** of fees is a list that shows how much someone should be paid, depending, for example, on their age or what work they do. 等級表、賃金表 ❑ *...those on the high end of the pay scale.* 給料の等級表の高い部分の人たち 6 N-COUNT 可算名詞 The **scale** of a map, plan, or model is the relationship between the size of something in the map, plan, or model and its size in the real world. 縮尺比 ❑ *The map, on a scale of 1:10,000, shows over 5,000 individual paths.* 1万分の1のその地図は5000以上の小道を示している. 7 → see also **full-scale, large-scale** 8 ADJ 形容詞 A **scale** model or **scale** replica of a building or object is a model of it which is smaller than the real thing but has all the same parts and features. 縮尺型[ADJ n] ❑ *Franklin made his mother an intricately detailed scale model of the house.* フランクリンは彼の家の手の込んだ詳細な縮尺模型を母親のために作った. 9 N-COUNT 可算名詞 In music, a **scale** is a fixed sequence of musical notes, each one higher than the next, which begins at a particular note. 音階 ❑ *...the scale of C major.* ハ調長音階 10 N-COUNT 可算名詞 The **scales** of a fish or reptile are the small, flat pieces of hard skin that cover its body. うろこ ❑ *Remove any excess scales from the fish skin.* 魚の皮膚から余分なうろこを削り落としなさい. 11 N-COUNT 可算名詞 A **scale** is a piece of equipment used for weighing things, for example, for weighing amounts of food that you need in order to make a particular meal. はかり [usu pl] ❑ *...a pair of kitchen scales.* 台所のはかり ❑ *...a bathroom scale.* 体重計 12 V-T 他動詞 If you **scale** something such as a mountain or a wall, you climb up it or over it. 登る [WRITTEN 書き言葉] ❑ *...Rebecca Stephens, the first British woman to scale Everest.* 英国人女性で初めてエベレストに登ったレベッカ・スチーブンス 13 PHRASE 句 If something is **out of scale with** the things near it, it is too big or too small in relation to them. 釣り合いがとれない ❑ *The tiny church was out of scale with the new banks and offices around it.* そのちっぽけな教会は周囲に新しくできた銀行や事務所と釣り合いがとれなかった. 14 PHRASE 句 If the different parts of a map, drawing, or model are **to scale**, they are the right size in relation to each other. 一定の比率で ❑ *...a miniature garden, with little pagodas and bridges all to scale.* 小さな塔や橋が全て一定の比率で縮小されたミニチュア庭園

→ see **graph**

▶ **scale down** PHRASAL VERB 句動詞 If you **scale down** something, you make it smaller in size, amount, or extent than it used to be. 縮小する ❑ *One factory has had to scale down its workforce from six hundred to only six.* ある工場は労働力を600名からたったの6名に圧縮しなければならなかった.

▶ **scale up** PHRASAL VERB 句動詞 If you **scale up** something, you make it greater in size, amount, or extent than it used to be. 拡大する ❑ *...a major push to scale up treatment programs for people in poor countries.* 貧困国の国民のための治療プログラムを拡大しようとする大きな努力

scalp /skælp/ (**scalps, scalping, scalped**) 1 N-COUNT 可算名詞 Your **scalp** is the skin under the hair on your head. 頭皮 ❑ *He smoothed his hair back over his scalp.* 彼は頭皮を覆うように髪の毛をなでつけた. 2 V-T 他動詞 If someone **scalps** tickets, they sell them outside a sports stadium or theater, usually for more than their original value. プレミア付きで売る [AM 米国英語] ❑ *He was trying to*

pick up some cash scalping tickets. 彼はチケットをプレミア付きで売って金を稼ごうとしていた.
→ see **hair**

scal|pel /skǽlpᵊl/ (**scalpels**) N-COUNT 可算名詞 A **scalpel** is a knife with a short, thin, sharp blade. Scalpels are used by surgeons during operations. 外科用メス

scalp|er /skǽlpər/ (**scalpers**) N-COUNT 可算名詞 A **scalper** is someone who sells tickets outside a sports stadium or theater, usually for more than their original value. ダフ屋 [AM 米国英語] ❑ *Another scalper said he'd charge $1,000 for a $125 ticket.* もう1人のダフ屋は1000ドルで125枚のチケットを売ると言った.

scam /skǽm/ (**scams, scamming, scammed**) ■ V-T 他動詞 If someone **scams** a person or organization, they deceive them in order to get something valuable from them, especially money. だます [INFORMAL くだけた] ❑ *When I told them they were being scammed, they couldn't believe it.* 私が彼らにだまされていると告げた時, 彼らはそれを信じることができなかった. ❑ *Ryan's campaign fund allegedly scammed the state out of a million dollars.* 申立てによると, ライアンのキャンペーン資金組織は州から百万ドルだまし取った ❑ *...a prisoner who scammed his way out of court.* だまして裁判を免れた囚人 ■ N-COUNT 可算名詞 A **scam** is an illegal trick, usually with the purpose of getting money from people or avoiding paying tax. 信用詐欺 [INFORMAL くだけた] ❑ *They believed they were participating in an insurance scam, not a murder.* 彼らは殺人ではなく保険詐欺に参加していると思い込んでいた.

scamp|er /skǽmpər/ (**scampers, scampering, scampered**) V-I 自動詞 When people or small animals **scamper** somewhere, they move there quickly with small, light steps. 慌てて走る ❑ *Children scampered off the yellow school bus and into the playground.* 子供たちは黄色のスクールバスから降りて, 運動場に駆け込んだ.

scan /skǽn/ (**scans, scanning, scanned**) ■ V-T/V-I 他動詞/自動詞 When you **scan** written material, you look through it quickly in order to find important or interesting information. 走り読みする ❑ *She scanned the advertisement pages of the newspapers.* 彼女は新聞の広告欄を走り読みした. ● N-SING 単数名詞 **Scan** is also a noun. 走り読み ❑ *I just had a quick scan through your book again.* 私は再びあなたの本を走り読みしたところだ. ■ V-T/V-I 他動詞/自動詞 When you **scan** a place or group of people, you look at it carefully, usually because you are looking for something or someone. じっと見る [no passive] ❑ *The officer scanned the room.* その警官は部屋を入念に調べた. ❑ *She was nervous and kept scanning the crowd for Paul.* 彼女は神経質にポールを捜して群集をくまなく見渡し続けた. ❸ V-T 他動詞 If people **scan** something such as luggage, they examine it using a machine that can show or find things inside it that cannot be seen from the outside. スキャンする ❑ *Their approach is to scan every checked-in bag with a bomb detector.* 彼らの方法は預けられた手荷物を全て爆弾探知機でスキャンすることだ. ❹ V-T 他動詞 If a computer disk **is scanned**, a program on the computer checks the disk to make sure that it does not contain a virus. 走査する [COMPUTING コンピューティング] ❑ *Not all ISPs are equipped to scan for viruses.* 全てのプロバイダーがウィルス走査の機能を備えているとは限らない. ❺ V-T 他動詞 If a picture or document **is scanned** into a computer, a machine passes a beam of light over it to make a copy of it in the computer. スキャンする [COMPUTING コンピューティング] [usu passive] ❑ *The entire paper contents of all libraries will eventually be scanned into computers.* 全ての図書館の全ての紙の内容は最終的にはコンピュータに収められるだろう. ❻ V-T 他動詞 If a radar or sonar machine **scans** an area, it examines or searches it by sending radar or sonar beams over it. 走査する ❑ *The ship's radar scanned the sea ahead.* その船のレーダーは前方の海を走査した. ❼ N-COUNT 可算名詞 A **scan** is a medical test in which a machine sends a beam of X-rays over a part of your body in order to check that it is healthy. 走査 ❑ *A brain scan revealed the blood clot.* 脳のスキャンにより血栓が見つかった.

scan|dal /skǽndᵊl/ (**scandals**) ■ N-COUNT 可算名詞 A **scandal** is a situation or event that is thought to be shocking and immoral and that everyone knows about. 不祥事 ❑ *...a financial scandal.* 金融機関の不祥事 ❷ N-UNCOUNT 不可算名詞 **Scandal** is talk about the shocking and immoral aspects of someone's behavior or something that has happened. スキャンダル ❑ *He loved gossip and scandal.* 彼はゴシップとスキャンダルが大好きだった.

scan|dal|ous /skǽndᵊləs/ ■ ADJ 形容詞 **Scandalous** behavior or activity is considered immoral and shocking. 恥ずべき ❑ *They would be sacked for criminal or scandalous behavior.* 彼らは犯罪的または恥ずべき行動により解雇されるだろう. ● **scan|dal|ous|ly** ADV 副詞 [ADV with v] ❑ *He asked only that Ingrid stop behaving so scandalously.* 彼はイングリッドにそれ程の醜態をさらすのだけは止めるよう頼んだ. ❷ ADJ 形容詞 **Scandalous** stories or remarks are concerned with the immoral and shocking aspects of someone's behavior or something that has happened. 中傷的な ❑ *Newspaper columns were full of scandalous tales.* 新聞の欄は中傷的な記事でいっぱいだった.

scan|dal sheet (**scandal sheets**) N-COUNT 可算名詞 You can refer to newspapers and magazines which print mainly stories about sex and crime as **scandal sheets**. ゴシップ紙, ゴシップ誌 [AM 米国英語] ❑ *What if someone sells the story to the scandal sheets?* もし誰かがその話をゴシップ紙に売ったらどうなるか.

scan|ner /skǽnər/ (**scanners**) ■ N-COUNT 可算名詞 A **scanner** is a machine which is used to examine, identify, or record things, for example by using a beam of light, sound, or X-rays. スキャナー ❑ *...brain scanners.* 脳のスキャナー ❷ N-COUNT 可算名詞 A **scanner** is a piece of computer equipment that you use for copying a picture or document into a computer. スキャナー [COMPUTING コンピューティング] ❑ *...a color printer and scanner.* カラー印刷機兼用スキャナー
→ see **laser**

scant /skǽnt/ ADJ 形容詞 You use **scant** to indicate that there is very little of something or not as much of something as there should be. 不足気味の ❑ *She began to berate the police for paying scant attention to the theft from her car.* 彼女は自分の車の窃盗に十分注意を払わなかったことに対して警察をひどく非難し始めた.

scape|goat /skéɪpgoʊt/ (**scapegoats, scapegoating, scapegoated**) ■ N-COUNT 可算名詞 If you say that someone is made a **scapegoat** for something bad that has happened, you mean that people blame them and may punish them for it although it may not be their fault. 身代わり ❑ *I don't think I deserve to be made the scapegoat for a couple of bad results.* 私は2回ほどの悪い決果の責任を負わされるに値しないと思う. ❷ V-T 他動詞 To **scapegoat** someone means to blame them publicly for something bad that has happened, even though it was not their fault. 罪を転嫁する ❑ *...a climate where ethnic minorities are continually scapegoated for the lack of jobs and housing problems.* 失業と住宅問題の責任が絶えず少数民族に転嫁される風潮

scar /skɑ́r/ (**scars, scarring, scarred**) ■ N-COUNT 可算名詞 A **scar** is a mark on the skin which is left after a wound has healed. 傷跡 ❑ *He had a scar on his forehead.* 彼の額には傷跡があった. ❷ V-T 他動詞 If your skin **is scarred**, it is badly marked as a result of a wound. 傷跡を残す [usu passive] ❑ *He was scarred for life during a fight.* 彼は喧嘩で一生残る傷跡ができた. ❸ V-T 他動詞 If a surface **is scarred**, it is damaged and there are ugly marks on it. 跡を残す [usu passive] ❑ *The arena was scarred by deep muddy ruts.* 競技場は深い泥の車の跡をとどめていた. ❹ N-COUNT 可算名詞 If an unpleasant physical or emotional experience leaves a **scar** on someone, it has a permanent effect on their mind. 心の傷 ❑ *The early years of fear and the hostility left a deep scar on the young boy.* 幼い頃の恐怖感と敵対感はその少年の心に深い傷を残した. ❺ V-T 他動詞 If an unpleasant physical or emotional experience **scars** you, it has a permanent effect on your mind. 傷を残す ❑ *This is something that's going to scar him forever.* これは彼の心に永久に傷跡を残すものだろう.

scarce /skérs/ (**scarcer, scarcest**) ■ ADJ 形容詞 If something is **scarce**, there is not enough of it. 不十分な ❑ *Food was scarce and expensive.* 食料は不足し, 高価だった. ❑ *Jobs are becoming increasingly scarce.* 職は益々不足している. ❷ PHRASE 句 If you **make yourself scarce**, you quickly leave the place you are in, usually in order to avoid a difficult or embarrassing situation. 姿を消す [INFORMAL くだけた] ❑ *It probably would be a good idea if you made yourself scarce.* おそらく君は姿を消した方がいいだろうと思う.

scarce|ly /skérsli/ ■ ADV 副詞 You use **scarcely** to emphasize that something is only just true or only just the case. やっと [EMPHASIS 強調] ❑ *He could scarcely breathe.* 彼はかろうじて呼吸できた. ❑ *I scarcely knew him.* 私は彼をほとんど知らなかった. ❷ ADV 副詞 You can use **scarcely** to say that something is not true or is not the case, in a humorous or critical way. まさか…でない ❑ *It can scarcely be coincidence.* まさか偶然とは思えない. ❸ ADV 副詞 If you say **scarcely had** one thing happened when something else happened, you mean that the first event was followed immediately by the second. ～するかしないうちに [ADV before v] ❑ *Scarcely had the votes been counted, when the telephone rang.* 投票結果が集計されるやいなや電話が鳴った.

scar|city /skérsɪti/ (**scarcities**) N-VAR 可変性名詞 If there is a **scarcity of** something, there is not enough of it for the people who need it or want it. 不足 [FORMAL 形式ばった] ❑ *...an ever-increasing scarcity of water.* どこまでもとどまることをしらない水不足

scare /skér/ (**scares, scaring, scared**) ■ V-T 他動詞 If something **scares** you, it frightens or worries you. 怖がらせる ❑ *You're scaring me.* あなたが私は怖い. ❑ *The prospect of failure scares me rigid.* 私は失敗の見込みをひどく恐れている. ❷ PHRASE 句 If you want to emphasize that something scares you a lot, you can say that it **scares the hell out of you** or **scares the life out of you**. ～をひどく怖がらせる [INFORMAL くだけた, EMPHASIS 強調] ❸ N-SING 単数名詞 If a sudden unpleasant experience gives you a **scare**, it frightens you. 恐怖 ❑ *Don't you realize what a scare you've given us all?* あなたは私たち全員をどんなに怖がらせたのが分からないのか. ❹ N-COUNT 可算名詞 A **scare** is a situation in which many people are afraid or worried because they think something dangerous

is happening which will affect them all. 恐れ騒ぐこと ❑ *The news set off a continent-wide health scare.* その報道の決失、大陸じゅうで健康問題にびくびくし始めた。 **5** N-COUNT 可算名詞 A **bomb scare** or a **security scare** is a situation in which there is believed to be a bomb in a place. 恐れ騒ぐこと ❑ *Despite many recent bomb scares, no one has yet been hurt.* 最近多くの爆弾騒ぎがあったが、まだ負傷人は1人も出ていない。 **6** → see also **scared**

▶ **scare away** → see **scare off** 1

▶ **scare off** **1** PHRASAL VERB 句動詞 If you **scare off** or **scare away** a person or animal, you frighten them so that they go away. 脅かして追い払う ❑ *...an alarm to scare off an attacker.* 攻撃者を追い払うための警報器 **2** PHRASAL VERB 句動詞 If you **scare someone off**, you accidentally make them unwilling to become involved with you. 敬遠させる ❑ *I don't think that revealing your past to your boyfriend scared him off.* 過去のことを話したからあなたのボーイフレンドがあなたから遠ざかったわけではないと思う。

scare|crow /sk**ɛə**rkroʊ/ (**scarecrows**) N-COUNT 可算名詞 A **scarecrow** is an object in the shape of a person, which is put in a field where crops are growing in order to frighten birds away. かかし

scared /sk**ɛə**rd/ **1** ADJ 形容詞 If you are **scared of** someone or something, you are frightened of them. 怖がった ❑ *I'm certainly not scared of him.* 私は確かに彼を怖いとは思っていない。 ❑ *I was too scared to move.* 私は怖くて動けなかった。 **2** ADJ 形容詞 If you are **scared that** something unpleasant might happen, you are nervous and worried because you think that it might happen. びくびくして ❑ *I was scared that I might be sick.* 私は病気ではないかとひやひやした。

scare|monger|ing /sk**ɛə**rmʌŋgərɪŋ, -mɒŋ-/ N-UNCOUNT 不可算名詞 If one person or group accuses another person or group of **scaremongering**, they accuse them of deliberately spreading worrying stories to try and frighten people. 危険なデマを飛ばすこと ❑ *The government yesterday accused Greenpeace of scaremongering.* 政府は昨日、危険なデマを飛ばしているとグリーンピースを非難した。

scarf /sk**ɑ**rf/ (**scarfs** or **scarves**) N-COUNT 可算名詞 A **scarf** is a piece of cloth that you wear around your neck or head, usually to keep yourself warm. スカーフ ❑ *He reached up to loosen the scarf around his neck.* 彼は手を伸ばして首に巻きつけたスカーフを緩めた。

scar|let /sk**ɑ**rlɪt/ (**scarlets**) COLOR 色彩語 Something that is **scarlet** is bright red. 鮮紅色の ❑ *...her scarlet lipstick.* 彼女の真っ赤な口紅

scarves /sk**ɑ**rvz/ **Scarves** is a plural of **scarf**.

scary /sk**ɛə**ri/ (**scarier, scariest**) ADJ 形容詞 Something that is **scary** is rather frightening. 怖い [INFORMAL くだけた] ❑ *I think prison is going to be a scary thing for Harry.* 刑務所はハリーにとって怖いものになると思う。 ❑ *There's something very scary about him.* 彼はどこか大変薄気味悪いところがある。

scath|ing /sk**eɪ**ðɪŋ/ ADJ 形容詞 If you say that someone is being **scathing** about something, you mean that they are being very critical of it. 痛烈な ❑ *Republican senators were scathing in their criticism of today's hearing.* 共和党上院議員は今日の公聴会を痛烈に批判した。

scat|ter /sk**æ**tər/ (**scatters, scattering, scattered**) **1** V-T 他動詞 If you **scatter** things over an area, you throw or drop them so that they spread all over the area. ばらまく ❑ *She tore the rose apart and scattered the petals over the grave.* 彼女はバラをちぎって花びらを墓石の上にまき散らした。 ❑ *They've been scattering toys everywhere.* 彼らは至る所におもちゃをまき散らしていた。 **2** V-T/V-I 他動詞/自動詞 If a group of people **scatter** or if you **scatter** them, they suddenly separate and move in different directions. 追い散らす、四散する ❑ *After dinner, everyone scattered.* 食後は全員が散り散りになった。 **3** → see also **scattered, scattering**

scat|tered /sk**æ**tərd/ **1** ADJ 形容詞 **Scattered** things are spread over an area in an untidy or irregular way. 散らかった [ADJ n] ❑ *He picked up the scattered toys.* 彼は散らかっているおもちゃを拾いあげた。 ❑ *Tomorrow there will be a few scattered showers.* 明日はにわか雨が少し散発的に降るでしょう。 **2** ADJ 形容詞 If something is **scattered** with a lot of small things, they are spread all over it. ばらまかれて [v-link ADJ "with" n] ❑ *Every surface is scattered with photographs.* あらゆる表面に写真がばらまかれている。

scat|ter|ing /sk**æ**tərɪŋ/ (**scatterings**) N-COUNT 可算名詞 A **scattering of** things or people is a small number of them spread over an area. 散在する程度の数 ❑ *...the scattering of houses east of the village.* 村の東部に散在する住宅

scav|enge /sk**æ**vɪndʒ/ (**scavenges, scavenging, scavenged**) V-T/V-I 他動詞/自動詞 If people or animals **scavenge for** things, they collect them by searching among waste or unwanted objects. あさる ❑ *Many are orphans, their parents killed as they scavenged for food.* 多くは孤児で、彼らの両親は食べ物をあさっている最中に殺された。 ❑ *Children scavenge through garbage.* 子供たちがごみあさりをする。 ● **scav|en|ger** N-COUNT 可算名詞 (**scavengers**) 清掃動物 ❑ *...scavengers such as rats.* ネズミなどの清掃動物

sce|nario /sɪn**ɛə**rioʊ/ (**scenarios**) N-COUNT 可算名詞 If you talk about a likely or possible **scenario**, you are talking about the way in which a situation may develop. 筋書き ❑ *The conflict degenerating into civil war is everybody's nightmare scenario.* 紛争が内戦につながることは誰にとっても悪夢のような筋書きだ。

scene /s**i**n/ (**scenes**) **1** N-COUNT 可算名詞 A **scene** in a play, movie, or book is part of it in which a series of events happen in the same place. 場 ❑ *...the opening scene of "A Christmas Carol."* 『クリスマスキャロル』の第1場 ❑ *...Act I, scene 1.* 第1幕、第1場 **2** N-COUNT 可算名詞 You refer to a place as a **scene** when you are describing its appearance and indicating what impression it makes on you. 現場 ❑ *It's a scene of complete devastation.* それは完全な破壊の現場だ。 ❑ *Thick black smoke billowed over the scene.* 濃い黒煙がその現場に逆巻いた。 **3** N-COUNT 可算名詞 You can describe an event that you see, or that is broadcast or shown in a picture, as a **scene** of a particular kind. 場面 ❑ *There were emotional scenes as the refugees enjoyed their first breath of freedom.* 難民が最初の自由を満喫した際に感動的な場面があった。 ❑ *Television broadcasters were warned to exercise caution over depicting scenes of violence.* テレビ局のキャスターは暴力の場面の描写には慎重を期するよう警告された。 **4** N-COUNT 可算名詞 The **scene of** an event is the place where it happened. 現場 ❑ *The area has been the scene of fierce fighting for three months.* その地区は3か月間の激戦の現場だった。 ❑ *...traces left at the scene of a crime.* 犯罪の現場に残された痕跡 **5** N-SING 単数名詞 You can refer to an area of activity as a particular type of **scene**. 活動分野 ❑ *Sandman's experimentation has made him something of a cult figure on the local music scene.* サンドマンの実験は地元の音楽界で彼をちょっとしたカルト的人物にした。 **6** N-COUNT 可算名詞 If you make a **scene**, you embarrass people by publicly showing your anger about something. 大騒ぎ ❑ *I'm sorry I made such a scene.* 私はあんなに騒ぎ立てて申し訳ない。 **7** PHRASE 句 If something is done **behind the scenes**, it is done secretly rather than publicly. こっそりと ❑ *But behind the scenes Mr. Cain will be working quietly to try to get a deal done.* しかし裏面ではケイン氏は取引をまとめようとそっと動いているだろう。 **8** PHRASE 句 If you refer to what happens **behind the scenes**, you are referring to what happens during the making of a movie, play, or radio or television program. 舞台裏で ❑ *It's an exciting opportunity to learn what goes on behind the scenes.* 舞台裏で何が起こるかを知るのはわくわくするような機会だ。 **9** PHRASE 句 If you have a **change of scene**, you go somewhere different after being in a particular place for a long time. 環境の変化 ❑ *What you need is a change of scene. Why not go on a cruise?* あなたに必要なのは転地だ。クルーズの旅に出てはどうですか。 **10** PHRASE 句 Something that **sets the scene for** a particular event creates the conditions in which the event is likely to happen. 一に道を開く ❑ *An improving economy helped set the scene for his re-election.* 経済の改善は彼の再選の布石となった。 **11** PHRASE 句 When a person or thing appears **on the scene**, they come into being or become involved in something. When they disappear **from the scene**, they are no longer there or are no longer involved. 現場に（現れる） ❑ *He could react jealously when and if another child comes on the scene.* 彼は他の子供がその場に現れるとやきもちを焼くことがある。

→ see **animation, drawing**

Word Partnership	*scene* は次の語句と使われる:		
N.	movie scene, sex scene **1**		
	scene of an accident, crime scene, scene of a murder, scene of a shooting **4**		
	music scene **5**		
ADJ.	final scene, first/opening scene, nude scene **1**		
	political scene **5**		
V.	describe a scene **2 3**		
	arrive at a scene, leave a scene, rush to a scene **4**		

scen|ery /s**i**nəri/ **1** N-UNCOUNT 不可算名詞 The **scenery** in a country area is the land, water, or plants that you can see around you. 景色 ❑ *...the island's spectacular scenery.* その島の壮大な風景 **2** N-UNCOUNT 不可算名詞 In a theater, the **scenery** consists of the structures and painted backgrounds that show where the action in the play takes place. 背景 ❑ *Instead of stagehands, the actors will move the scenery right in front of the audience.* 舞台係の代わりに俳優が観客の目の前で背景を動かす予定だ。

Do not confuse **scenery, landscape, countryside,** and **nature.** With **landscape,** the emphasis is on the physical features of the land, while **scenery** includes everything you can see when you look out over an area of land. ❑ *...the landscape of steep woods and distant mountains. ...unattractive urban scenery.* **Countryside** is land which is away from towns and cities. ❑ *...3,500 acres of mostly flat countryside.* **Nature** includes the landscape, the weather, animals, and plants, which are not created by man. ❑ *These creatures roamed the Earth as the finest and rarest wonders of nature.*

3 PHRASE 句 If you have a **change of scenery**, you go somewhere different after being in a particular place for a long time. 転地 ❑ *A*

change of scenery might do you good. 転地して風景が変わればひよとする とあなたのためになるかもしれない.

sce|nic /síːnɪk/ **1** ADJ 形容詞 A **scenic** place has attractive scenery. 風光明媚な ❑ *This is an extremely scenic part of America.* ここ はアメリカの非常に風光明媚な場所だ. **2** ADJ 形容詞 A **scenic** route goes through attractive scenery and has nice views. 景色のよい ❑ *It was even marked on the map as a scenic route.* それは景色のよい自 動車道として地図に印さえあった.

scent /sɛnt/ (**scents, scenting, scented**) **1** N-COUNT 可算名 詞 The **scent** of something is the pleasant smell that it has. 芳香 ❑ *Flowers are chosen for their scent as well as their look.* 花は見かけだけ でなく香りでも選ばれる. **2** V-T 他動詞 If something **scents** a place or thing, it makes it smell pleasant. かおらせる ❑ *Jasmine flowers scent the air.* ジャスミンの花の香りが空中に漂う. **3** N-MASS 質量名 詞 **Scent** is a liquid which women put on their necks and wrists to make themselves smell nice. 香水 ❑ *She dabbed herself with scent.* 彼女は香水を軽くたたいてつけた. **4** N-VAR 可変性名詞 The **scent** of a person or animal is the smell that they leave and that other people sometimes follow when looking for them. 臭跡 ❑ *A police dog picked up the murderer's scent.* 警察犬は殺人犯の臭いをかぎつけ た. **5** V-T 他動詞 When an animal **scents** something, it becomes aware of it by smelling it. かぎつける [no cont] ❑ *...dogs which scent the hidden birds.* 隠れた鳥の居場所をかぎつける犬
→ see **flower**

scent|ed /sɛntɪd/ ADJ 形容詞 **Scented** things have a pleasant smell, either naturally or because perfume has been added to them. 香りのよい ❑ *The white flowers are pleasantly scented.* その白い 花はよい香りがする.

scep|tic /skɛptɪk/ → see **skeptic**

scep|ti|cal /skɛptɪkəl/ → see **skeptical**

scep|ti|cism /skɛptɪsɪzəm/ → see **skepticism**

sched|ule /skɛdʒul, -uəl/ (**schedules, scheduling, scheduled**) **1** N-COUNT 可算名詞 A **schedule** is a plan that gives a list of events or tasks and the times at which each one should happen or be done. 予定表 ❑ *He has been forced to adjust his schedule.* 彼は自 分の予定表の調整を余儀なくされた. **2** N-UNCOUNT 不可算名詞 You can use **schedule** to refer to the time or way something is planned to be done. For example, if something is completed **on schedule**, it is completed at the time planned. 予定 ❑ *The jet arrived in Johannesburg two minutes ahead of schedule.* そのジェット機は予定よ り2分早くヨハネスブルグに到着した. ❑ *Everything went according to schedule.* 全ては予定通りに進行した. **3** V-T 他動詞 If something **is scheduled** to happen at a particular time, arrangements are made for it to happen at that time. 予定する [usu passive] ❑ *The space shuttle had been scheduled to blast off at 04:38.* スペースシャトル は4時38分に発射されるように予定されていた. ❑ *A presidential election was scheduled for last December.* 大統領選挙は昨年12月に予定されて いた. **4** N-COUNT 可算名詞 A **schedule** is a written list of things, for example, a list of prices, details, or conditions. 表 ❑ *Ticket plans and a pricing schedule will not be released until later this year.* チ ケット計画と料金表は本年末まで発表されないだろう. **5** N-COUNT 可算名詞 A **schedule** is a list of all the times when trains, boats, buses, or aircraft are supposed to arrive at or leave a particular place. 時刻表 [mainly AM 主に米国英語] ❑ *...a bus schedule.* バスの 時刻表. **6** N-COUNT 可算名詞 In a school or college, a **schedule** is a diagram that shows the times in the week at which particular subjects are taught. 時間割 [AM 米国英語] ❑ *He began college with a schedule that included biology, calculus and political science.* 彼の大学教 育は生物学, 微積分学, 政治学を含む時間割で始まった.

Word Partnership *schedule* は次の語句と使われる:

ADJ. **busy** schedule, **hectic** schedule **1**
regular schedule **1 5**

N. **change of** schedule, schedule **of events**, **payment** schedule, **playoff** schedule, **work** schedule **1 4**
bus schedule, **train** schedule **5**

PREP. **according to** schedule, **ahead of** schedule, **behind** schedule, **on** schedule **2**

---

scheme /skim/ (**schemes, scheming, schemed**) **1** N-COUNT 可算名詞 A **scheme** is someone's plan for achieving something, especially something that will bring them some benefit. 計画 ❑ *...a quick money-making scheme to get us through the summer.* 夏を 切り抜けるための素早く金を稼ぐもくろみ ❑ *They would first have to work out some scheme for getting the treasure out.* 彼らはまずその財 宝を取り出す案を練り上げる必要があるだろう. **2** V-T/V-I 他 動詞/自動詞 If you say that people **are scheming**, you mean that they are making secret plans in order to gain something for themselves. たくらむ [DISAPPROVAL 不賛成] [oft cont] ❑ *Everyone's always scheming and plotting.* 誰もが終始策巧みをし, 陰謀を企ててい る. ❑ *The bride's family were scheming to prevent a wedding.* 花嫁の家 族は結婚式を妨害しようとたくらんでいた. **3** N-COUNT 可算名詞 A **scheme** is a plan or arrangement involving many people which

is made by a government or other organization. 計画 [BRIT 英 国英語; AM **plan, program** 米国英語 **plan, program**] ❑ *...a private pension scheme.* 民間の年金計画 **4** PHRASE 句 When people talk about **the scheme of things** or **the grand scheme of things**, they are referring to the way that everything in the world seems to be organized. 物事の成り立ち ❑ *We realize that we are infinitely small within the scheme of things.* 私たちは物事の成り立ちから言って非常に 小さい存在であることは分かっている.

Thesaurus *scheme* また次を参照:

N. design, plan, strategy **1**

Word Link *schis, schiz ≈ cutting, splitting : schism, schizoid, schizophrenia*

schizo|phre|nia /skɪtsəfríniə/ N-UNCOUNT 不可算名詞 **Schizophrenia** is a serious mental illness. People who suffer from it are unable to relate their thoughts and feelings to what is happening around them and often withdraw from society. 統 合失調症

schizo|phren|ic /skɪtsəfrɛnɪk/ (**schizophrenics**) N-COUNT 可算名詞 A **schizophrenic** is a person who is suffering from schizophrenia. 統合失調症の患者 ❑ *He was diagnosed as a paranoid schizophrenic.* 彼は妄想型統合失調症と診断された. ● ADJ 形容詞 **Schizophrenic** is also an adjective. 統合失調症の ❑ *...a schizophrenic patient.* 統合失調症の患者

Word Link *schol ≈ school : scholar, scholarship, scholastic*

schol|ar /skɒlər/ (**scholars**) N-COUNT 可算名詞 A **scholar** is a person who studies an academic subject and knows a lot about it. 学者 [FORMAL 形式ばった] ❑ *The library attracts thousands of scholars and researchers.* 何千人もの学者や研究者がその図書館を利用する.
→ see **history**

schol|ar|ly /skɒlərli/ **1** ADJ 形容詞 A **scholarly** person spends a lot of time studying and knows a lot about academic subjects. 学 究的な ❑ *He was an intellectual, scholarly man.* 彼は知性があり, 学究的 な男だった. **2** ADJ 形容詞 A **scholarly** book or article contains a lot of academic information and is intended for academic readers. 専門的な ❑ *...the more scholarly academic journals.* より専門的な学術誌 **3** ADJ 形容詞 **Scholarly** matters and activities involve people who do academic research. 学者の ❑ *This has been the subject of intense scholarly debate.* これは学者間で激しく討論されてきた主題だった.

schol|ar|ship /skɒlərʃɪp/ (**scholarships**) **1** N-COUNT 可算名詞 If you get a **scholarship** to a school or university, your studies are paid for by the school or university or by some other organization. 奨学金 ❑ *He got a scholarship to the Pratt Institute of Art.* 彼はプラ ット美術学校への奨学金を獲得した. **2** N-UNCOUNT 不可算名詞 **Scholarship** is serious academic study and the knowledge that is obtained from it. 学問 ❑ *I want to take advantage of your lifetime of scholarship.* 私はあなたの生涯の学問を利用したい.

scho|las|tic /skəlæstɪk/ ADJ 形容詞 Your **scholastic** achievement or ability is your academic achievement or ability while you are at school. 学校の [FORMAL 形式ばった] [ADJ n] ❑ *...the values which encouraged her scholastic achievement.* 彼女の学業 成績を上げることを励ました価値観

school /skul/ (**schools, schooling, schooled**) **1** N-VAR 可変性 名詞 A **school** is a place where children are educated. You usually refer to this place as **school** when you are talking about the time that children spend there and the activities that they do there. 学 校 ❑ *...a boy who was in my class at school.* 学校で同級生だった男の子 ❑ *Even the good students say homework is what they most dislike about school.* 優秀な生徒ですら, 宿題が学校で一番嫌いなものだと言う. ❑ *...a school built in the Sixties.* 60年代に建てられた学校

In public education in the United States, most schools are **co-educational** or **coed**, that is they allow both male and female students to enroll. Schools that are not coed are usually private schools.

2 N-COUNT-COLL 集合可算名詞 A **school** is the students or staff at a school. 全校 (教師と生徒全体) ❑ *Deirdre, the whole school's going to hate you.* デアドレ, あなたは全校に憎まれると思う. **3** N-COUNT; N-IN-NAMES 可算名詞, 名称中の名詞 A privately-run place where a particular skill or subject is taught can be referred to as a **school**. 学校, 教習所 ❑ *...a riding school.* 乗馬学校 **4** N-VAR; N-IN-NAMES 可変性名詞, 名称中の名詞 A university, college, or university department specializing in a particular type of subject can be referred to as a **school**. 学部 ❑ *...a lecturer in the school of veterinary medicine at the University of Pennsylvania.* ペンシルベニア大学獣医 学部の講師 **5** N-UNCOUNT 不可算名詞 **School** is used to refer to college. 大学 [AM 米国英語] ❑ *Jack eventually graduated from school, got married, and got his first real job.* ジャックはやがて大学を卒業し, 結婚し, 初めての仕事に就いた. **6** N-COUNT-COLL 集合可算名詞 A particular **school of** writers, artists, or thinkers is a group of them

whose work, opinions, or theories are similar. 流派，学派 [usu with supp] ❑ ...the Chicago school of economists. シカゴ経済学者学派 **7** V-T 他動詞 If you **school** someone **in** something, you train or educate them to have a certain skill, type of behavior, or way of thinking. 教える [WRITTEN 書き言葉] ❑ Many mothers schooled their daughters in the myth of female inferiority. 多くの母親は女性の劣等性という誤った通念を娘に教えた. **8** → see also **boarding school, grade school, graduate school, grammar school, high school, nursery school, prep school, primary school, private school, public school, schooling, state school**

school board (**school boards**) N-COUNT-COLL 集合可算名詞 A **school board** is a committee in charge of education in a particular city or area, or in a particular school, especially in the United States. 教育委員会 [AM 米国英語] ❑ Colonel Richard Nelson served on the school board until this year. リチャード・ネルソン大佐は今年まで教育委員会の委員を務めていた.

school|boy /skʊlbɔɪ/ (**schoolboys**) N-COUNT 可算名詞 A **schoolboy** is a boy who goes to school. 男子生徒 ❑ ...a group of ten-year-old schoolboys. 10歳の男子生徒の1集団

school|child /skʊltʃaɪld/ (**schoolchildren**) N-COUNT 可算名詞 **Schoolchildren** are children who go to school. 学童 ❑ Last year I had an audience of schoolchildren and they laughed at everything. 昨年私は学童と話す機会があったが、彼らはどんなことにも笑った.

school|days /skʊldeɪz/ also **school days** N-PLURAL 複数名詞 Your **schooldays** are the period of your life when you were at school. 学生時代 ❑ He was happily married to a girl he had known since his schooldays. 彼は学生時代以来知っていた女性と幸せな結婚生活をしていた.

school friend (**school friends**) also **schoolfriend** N-COUNT 可算名詞 A **school friend** is a friend of yours who is at the same school as you, or who used to be at the same school when you were children. 学生時代の友達 ❑ I spent the evening with an old school friend. 私は昔の学生時代の友人と一緒に夕方を過ごした.

school|girl /skʊlgɜrl/ (**schoolgirls**) N-COUNT 可算名詞 A **schoolgirl** is a girl who goes to school. 女子生徒 ❑ ...half a dozen giggling schoolgirls. くすくす笑う6人の女子生徒

school|ing /skʊlɪŋ/ N-UNCOUNT 不可算名詞 **Schooling** is education that children receive at school. 学校教育 ❑ His formal schooling continued erratically until he reached the age of eleven. 彼の正式な学校教育は中断しながら11歳になるまで続いた.

school|teach|er /skʊltitʃər/ (**schoolteachers**) N-COUNT 可算名詞 A **schoolteacher** is a teacher in a school. 学校教師

Word Link	sci ≈ knowing : conscience, science, unconscious

sci|ence /saɪəns/ (**sciences**) **1** N-UNCOUNT 不可算名詞 **Science** is the study of the nature and behavior of natural things and the knowledge that we obtain about them. 科学 ❑ The best discoveries in science are very simple. 科学の最善の発見物は非常にシンプルだ. **2** N-COUNT 可算名詞 A **science** is a particular branch of science such as physics, chemistry, or biology. 自然科学 ❑ Physics is the best example of a science which has developed strong, abstract theories. 物理学は強力で抽象的な理論を発展させた自然科学の最もいい例だ. **3** N-COUNT 可算名詞 A **science** is the study of some aspect of human behavior, for example, sociology or anthropology. 人文系科学 ❑ ...the modern science of psychology. 近代心理学 **4** → see also **social science**

→ see Word Web: **science**

sci|ence fic|tion N-UNCOUNT 不可算名詞 **Science fiction** consists of stories in books, magazines, and movies about events that take place in the future or in other parts of the universe. 空想科学小説

sci|en|tif|ic /saɪəntɪfɪk/ **1** ADJ 形容詞 **Scientific** is used to describe things that relate to science or to a particular science. 科学的な ❑ Scientific research is widely claimed to be the source of the high standard of living in the U.S. 米国の高い生活水準の源は科学的研究であると広く主張されている. ❑ ...the use of animals in scientific experiments. 科学的実験に動物を利用すること ● **sci|en|tif|i|cally**

/saɪəntɪfɪkli/ ADV 副詞 科学的に ❑ ...scientifically advanced countries. 科学的に進歩した国々 **2** ADJ 形容詞 If you do something in a **scientific** way, you do it carefully and thoroughly, using experiments or tests. 科学的原理に従った ❑ It's not a scientific way to test their opinions. それは彼らの意見を調べる科学的な方法ではない. ● **sci|en|tif|i|cally** ADV 副詞 科学的に ❑ Efforts are being made to research it scientifically. それを科学的に研究するよう努力がなされている.

sci|en|tist /saɪəntɪst/ (**scientists**) N-COUNT 可算名詞 A **scientist** is someone who has studied science and whose job is to teach or do research in science. 科学者 ❑ Scientists say they've already collected more data than had been expected. 科学者たちは予想以上のデータを既に収集したと言っている.

sci-fi /saɪ faɪ/ N-UNCOUNT 不可算名詞 **Sci-fi** is short for **science fiction**. 空想科学小説の [INFORMAL くだけた] ❑ ...a two-and-a-half hour sci-fi film. 2時間半のSF映画

scis|sors /sɪzərz/ N-PLURAL 複数名詞 **Scissors** are a small cutting tool with two sharp blades that are screwed together. You use scissors for cutting things such as paper and cloth. はさみ [also "a pair of" N] ❑ He told me to get some scissors. 彼は私にはさみを持ってくるよう命じた.
→ see office

scoff /skɒf/ (**scoffs, scoffing, scoffed**) V-I 自動詞 If you **scoff at** something, you speak about it in a way that shows you think it is ridiculous or inadequate. あざ笑う ❑ At first I scoffed at the notion. 最初は私はその考えをあざ笑った.

scold /skoʊld/ (**scolds, scolding, scolded**) V-T 他動詞 If you **scold** someone, you speak angrily to them because they have done something wrong. しかる [FORMAL 形式ばった] ❑ If he finds out, he'll scold me. 彼に見つかったら、僕はしかられるだろう. ❑ Later she scolded her daughter for having talked to her father like that. 後で彼女は父親にあのような話し方をしたことに対して娘をしかった.

scoop /skuːp/ (**scoops, scooping, scooped**) **1** V-T 他動詞 If you **scoop** something from a container, you remove it with something such as a spoon. すくう ❑ ...the sound of a spoon scooping dog food out of a can. 缶詰のドッグフードをスプーンですくう音 **2** N-COUNT 可算名詞 A **scoop** is an object like a spoon which is used for picking up a quantity of a food such as ice cream or an ingredient such as flour. しゃくし **3** N-COUNT 可算名詞 You can use **scoop** to refer to an exciting news story which is reported in one newspaper or on one television program before it appears anywhere else. 特だね ❑ ...one of the biggest scoops in the history of newspapers. 新聞史上最大の特だねの1つ **4** V-T 他動詞 If you **scoop** a person or thing somewhere, you put your hands or arms under or around them and quickly move them there. 抱き上げる ❑ Michael knelt next to her and scooped her into his arms. マイケルは彼女の横にひざまずいて、彼女を両腕に抱き上げた.
▶ **scoop up** PHRASAL VERB 句動詞 If you **scoop** something **up**, you put your hands or arms under it and lift it in a quick movement. かき集める ❑ Use both hands to scoop up the leaves. 両手で落ち葉をかき集めなさい.

scoot|er /skuːtər/ (**scooters**) **1** N-COUNT 可算名詞 A **scooter** is a small light motorcycle which has a low seat. スクーター **2** N-COUNT 可算名詞 A **scooter** is a type of child's bicycle which has two wheels joined by a wooden board and a handle on a long pole attached to the front wheel. The child stands on the board with one foot, and uses the other foot to move forward. 片足スケート

scope /skoʊp/ **1** N-UNCOUNT 不可算名詞 If there is **scope** for a particular kind of behavior or activity, people have the opportunity to behave in this way or do that activity. 場 ❑ He believed in giving his staff scope for initiative. 彼は社員にイニシアティブを取る場を与えることが大切だと思っていた. **2** N-SING 単数名詞 The **scope of** an activity, topic, or piece of work is the whole area which it deals with or includes. 範囲 ❑ Mr. Dobson promised to widen the organization's scope of activity. ドブソン氏は組織の活動範囲を広げることを約束した.

Word Web	science

Science is the study of the laws that govern the natural world. It uses **research** and **experiments** to try to explain various **phenomena**. Scientists follow the **scientific method** which begins with **observation** and measurement. Then they state a **hypothesis**, which is a possible explanation for the observations and measurements. Next, scientists make a **prediction**, which is a logical **deduction** based on the hypothesis. The last step is to conduct experiments which **prove** or **disprove** the hypothesis. Scientists construct and modify **theories** based on **empirical findings**. Pure science deals only with theories, while **applied** science has practical applications.

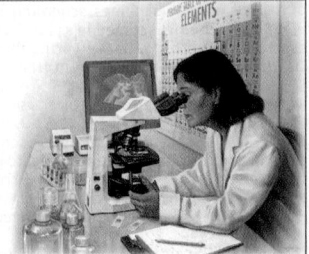

scorch /skɔrtʃ/ (scorches, scorching, scorched) **1** V-T 他動詞 To **scorch** something means to burn it slightly. 焦がす □ The bomb scorched the side of the building. 爆弾は建物の側面を焦がした。● scorched ADJ 形容詞 焦げた □ ...scorched black earth. 焦げた黒い地面 **2** V-T/V-I 他動詞/自動詞 If something **scorches** or **is scorched**, it becomes marked or changes color because it is affected by too much heat or by a chemical. 焦げる，焦がす □ The leaves are inclined to scorch in hot sunshine. その葉は暑い日光で焦げやすい。

scorch|ing /skɔrtʃɪŋ/ ADJ 形容詞 **Scorching** or **scorching hot** weather or temperatures are very hot indeed. 焼けつくような [INFORMAL くだけた，EMPHASIS 強調] □ That race was run in scorching weather. あのレースは焼けつくような天候で行なわれた。

> In informal English, if you want to emphasize how hot the weather is, you can say that it is **boiling** or **scorching**. In winter, if the temperature is above average, you can say that it is **mild**. In general, **hot** suggests a higher temperature than **warm**, and **warm** things are usually pleasant. □ ...a warm evening.

score /skɔr/ (scores, scoring, scored)

> In meaning **9**, the plural form is **score**.
>
> **9**を意味する場合は複数形は**score**。

1 V-T/V-I 他動詞/自動詞 In a sport or game, if a player **scores** a goal or a point, they gain a goal or point. 得点する □ Patten scored his second touchdown of the game. パッテンはその試合の2度目のタッチダウンで得点した。□ He scored late in the third quarter to cut the gap to 10 points. 彼は第3クォーターの後半に得点し，格差を10点に縮めた。 **2** V-T/V-I 他動詞/自動詞 If you **score** a particular number or amount, for example, as a mark in a test, you achieve that number or amount. 得点する □ Kelly had scored an average of 147 on three separate IQ tests. ケリーは3つの別々のIQテストで平均147点を取っていた。□ Congress scores low in public opinion polls. 議会は世論調査で低く評価されている。 **3** N-COUNT 可算名詞 Someone's **score** in a game or test is a number, for example, a number of points or runs, which shows what they have achieved or what level they have reached. 得点 □ The U.S. Open golf tournament was won by Ben Hogan, with a score of 287. 全米オープンゴルフトーナメントは287点のスコアでベン・ホーガンが優勝した。□ He won this year's title with a score of 9,687. 彼は今年の選手権を9,687のスコアで獲得した。 **4** N-COUNT 可算名詞 The **score** in a game is the result of it or the current situation, as indicated by the number of goals, runs, or points obtained by the two teams or players. 得点 □ 4-1 was the final score. 最終得点は4対1だった。□ They beat the Giants by a score of 7 to 3. 彼らは7対0でジャイアンツを破った。 **5** V-T 他動詞 If you **score** a success, a victory, or a hit, you are successful in what you are doing. 勝ち取る [WRITTEN 書き言葉] □ His abiding passion was ocean racing, at which he scored many successes. 彼の持ち続ける情熱は海のレースであったが，それで彼は多くの成功を勝ち取った。 **6** N-COUNT 可算名詞 The **score** of a movie, play, or similar production is the music which is written or used for it. 背景音楽 □ The dance is accompanied by an original score by Henry Torgue. 踊りはヘンリー・トーグのオリジナル版の伴奏付きだ。 **7** N-COUNT 可算名詞 The **score** of a piece of music is the written version of it. 楽譜 □ He recognizes enough notation to be able to follow a score. 彼は楽譜を読むのに十分な記譜法を知っている。 **8** QUANT 数量詞 If you refer to **scores of** things or people, you are emphasizing that there are very many of them. 多数の [WRITTEN 書き言葉，EMPHASIS 強調] [QUANT "of" pl-n] □ Campaigners lit scores of bonfires in ceremonies to mark the anniversary. 運動家たちは記念日を祝う式典で多数のかがり火をつけた。 **9** NUM 数詞 A **score** is twenty or approximately twenty. 20 [WRITTEN 書き言葉] □ A score of countries may be either producing or planning to obtain chemical weapons. 20か国ほどが化学兵器を生産しているかまたはその取得を計画している可能性がある。 **10** V-T 他動詞 If you **score** a surface with something sharp, you cut a line or number of lines in it. 切り傷を入れる □ Lightly score the surface of the steaks with a sharp cook's knife. 鋭い包丁でステーキの表面に軽く切り目を入れなさい。 **11** PHRASE 句 If you **keep score** of the number of things that are happening in a certain situation, you count them and record them. 回数を記録する □ You can keep score of your baby's movements before birth by recording them on a kick chart. 赤ちゃんの胎動をキックチャートに記録して出生前の動きの回数を記録することができる。 **12** PHRASE 句 If you **know the score**, you know what the real facts of a situation are and how they affect you, even though you may not like them. 真相を知る [SPOKEN 口語] □ I don't feel sorry for Carl. He knew the score, he knew what he had to do and couldn't do it. 私はカールには同情しない。彼は内幕を知っていて，何をすべきかが知っていたのにできなかった。 **13** PHRASE 句 You can use **on that score** or **on this score** to refer to something that has just been mentioned, especially an area of difficulty or concern. その/この点では □ I became pregnant easily. At least I've had no problems on that score. 私は簡単に妊娠した。少なくともその点では問題は何もなかった。 **14** PHRASE 句 If you **settle a score** or **settle an old score with** someone, you take revenge on them for something they have done in the past. 恨みを晴らす □ The groups had historic scores to settle with each other. それらのグループは互いに晴らしたい歴史的な恨みを持っていた。

→ see **music**

score|board /skɔrbɔrd/ (scoreboards) N-COUNT 可算名詞 A **scoreboard** is a large board, for example, at a sports arena or stadium, which shows the score in a game or competition. 得点表示板 □ The figures flash up on the scoreboard. 得点は得点表示板にさっと表示される。

scor|er /skɔrər/ (scorers) **1** N-COUNT 可算名詞 In football, hockey, and many other sports and games, a **scorer** is a player who scores a goal, runs, or points. 得点者 □ ...David Hirst, the scorer of 11 goals this season. 今シーズン11のゴールを得点したデイビッド・ハースト **2** N-COUNT 可算名詞 A **scorer** is an official who writes down the score of a game or competition as it is being played. 記録係

scorn /skɔrn/ (scorns, scorning, scorned) **1** N-UNCOUNT 不可算名詞 If you treat someone or something **with scorn**, you show contempt for them. 軽べつ，さげすみ □ Researchers greeted the proposal with scorn. 研究者たちはその提案を一笑に付した。 **2** V-T 他動詞 If you **scorn** someone or something, you feel or show contempt for them. 軽べつする，さげすむ □ Several leading officers have quite openly scorned the peace talks. 数人の高官は和平会談を全くあからさまに軽べつした。 **3** V-T 他動詞 If you **scorn** something, you refuse to have it or accept it because you think it is not good enough or suitable for you. 拒絶する □ ...people who scorned traditional methods. 従来の方法を拒絶した人々

scorn|ful /skɔrnfəl/ ADJ 形容詞 If you are **scornful of** someone or something, you show contempt for them. 軽べつ的な □ He is deeply scornful of politicians. 彼は政治家を深く軽べつしている。

scotch /skɒtʃ/ (scotches, scotching, scotched) V-T 他動詞 If you **scotch** a rumor, plan, or idea, you put an end to it before it can develop any further. もみ消す，つぶす □ They have scotched rumors that they are planning a special show. 彼らは特別なショーを企画中だといううわさをもみ消した。

Scotch /skɒtʃ/ (Scotches) N-MASS 質量名詞 **Scotch** or **Scotch whisky** is whiskey made in Scotland. スコッチウィスキー □ ...a bottle of Scotch. 1瓶のスコッチウィスキー ● N-COUNT 可算名詞 A **Scotch** is a glass of Scotch. グラス1杯のスコッチウィスキー □ He poured himself a Scotch. 彼はグラスにスコッチウィスキーを注いだ。

scot-free /skɒt fri/ ADV 副詞 If you say that someone got away **scot-free**, you are emphasizing that they escaped punishment for something that you believe they should have been punished for. 罪を免れて [EMPHASIS 強調] [ADV after v] □ Others who were guilty were being allowed to get off scot-free. 有罪のその他の人々は無罪放免になることを許されつつあった。

scour /skaʊər/ (scours, scouring, scoured) **1** V-T 他動詞 If you **scour** something such as a place or a book, you make a thorough search of it to try to find what you are looking for. 徹底的に調査する □ Rescue crews had scoured an area of 30 square miles. 救助隊は30平方マイルの地区をくまなく調べていた。 **2** V-T 他動詞 If you **scour** something such as a sink, floor, or pan, you clean its surface by rubbing it hard with something rough. こすって洗う □ He decided to scour the sink. 彼は流しをこすって洗うことにした。

scourge /skɜrdʒ/ (scourges, scourging, scourged) **1** N-COUNT 可算名詞 A **scourge** is something that causes a lot of trouble or suffering to a group of people. 大きな悩みの種 [oft N "of" n] □ ...the best chance in 20 years to end the scourge of terrorism. テロリズムという大きな悩みの種を終わらせる20年間における最良の機会 **2** V-T 他動詞 If something **scourges** a place or group of people, it causes great pain and suffering to people. 大いに苦しめる □ Economic anarchy scourged the post-war world. 経済の混乱状態が戦後世界を大いに苦しめた。

scout /skaʊt/ (scouts, scouting, scouted) **1** N-COUNT 可算名詞 A **scout** is someone who is sent to an area of countryside to find out the position of an enemy army. 偵察兵 □ They set off, two men out in front as scouts, two behind in case of any attack from the rear. 彼らは前方に偵察兵として2名，後方にもう2名を後方からの攻撃に備えて配置し，出発した。 **2** V-T/V-I 他動詞/自動詞 If you **scout** somewhere **for** something, you go through that area searching for it. 捜す □ I wouldn't have time to scout the area for junk. 私にはその地区でガラクタを捜す時間はないだろう。□ A team of four was sent to scout for a nuclear test site. 4名の1団が核実験の場所を捜しに派遣された。

scowl /skaʊl/ (scowls, scowling, scowled) V-I 自動詞 When someone **scowls**, an angry or hostile expression appears on their face. 顔をしかめる □ He scowled, and slammed the door behind him. 彼は顔をしかめ，ドアをばたんと閉めてしまった。● N-COUNT 可算名詞 **Scowl** is also a noun. しかめっ面 □ Chris met the remark with a scowl. クリスはその意見を聞いて顔をしかめた。

scram|ble /skræmbəl/ (scrambles, scrambling, scrambled) **1** V-I 自動詞 If you **scramble** over rocks or up a hill, you move quickly over them or up it using your hands to help you. よじ登る

❑ *Tourists were scrambling over the rocks looking for the perfect camera angle.* 観光客たちは完璧な写真撮影場所を探して岩をよじ登っていた。 **2** V-I 自動詞 If you **scramble** to a different place or position, you move there in a hurried, awkward way. はって進む ❑ *Ann threw back the covers and scrambled out of bed.* アンはベッドカバーを引きはがし、ベッドからはい出た。 **3** V-T 他動詞/自動詞 If a number of people **scramble for** something, they compete energetically with each other for it. 奪い合う ❑ *More than three million fans are expected to scramble for tickets.* 3百万人以上のファンが先を争ってチケットを購入すると思われる ●N-COUNT 可算名詞 **Scramble** is also a noun. 奪い合い ❑ *...the scramble for jobs.* 職の奪い合い **4** V-T 他動詞 If you **scramble** eggs, you break them, mix them together and then cook them in butter. かき混ぜながら焼く ❑ *Make the toast and scramble the eggs.* トーストとスクランブルエッグを作りなさい。 ●**scram|bled** ADJ 形容詞 かき混ぜて焼いた ❑ *...scrambled eggs and bacon.* スクランブルエッグとベーコン **5** V-T 他動詞 If a device **scrambles** a radio or telephone message, it interferes with the sound so that the message can only be understood by someone with special equipment. スクランブルする ❑ *The system lets you encrypt or scramble the data that's sent between machines.* そのシステムには機器間で送信されたデータの暗号化とスクランブルの機能がある。

→ see **egg**

scrap /skr**æ**p/ (**scraps, scrapping, scrapped**) **1** N-COUNT 可算名詞 A **scrap of** something is a very small piece or amount of it. 小片 ❑ *A crumpled scrap of paper was found in her handbag.* くしゃくしゃの紙切れが彼女のハンドバッグに見つかった。 **2** N-PLURAL 複数名詞 **Scraps** are pieces of unwanted food which are thrown away or given to animals. 食べ残し ❑ *...the scraps from the Sunday dinner table.* 日曜の夕食の食べ残し **3** V-T 他動詞 If you **scrap** something, you get rid of it or cancel it. 廃棄する [JOURNALISM ジャーナリズム] ❑ *President Hussein called on all countries in the Middle East to scrap nuclear or chemical weapons.* フセイン大統領は核・化学兵器を廃棄するよう全ての中東諸国に呼びかけた。 **4** ADJ 形容詞 **Scrap** metal or paper is no longer wanted for its original purpose, but may have some other use. くずの [ADJ n] ❑ *There's always tons of scrap paper in Dad's office.* お父さんの事務所にはいつも数トンの紙くずがある。 **5** N-UNCOUNT 不可算名詞 **Scrap** is metal from old or damaged machinery or cars. くず鉄、金属くず ❑ *Thousands of tanks, artillery pieces and armored vehicles will be cut up for scrap.* 数千台の戦車、大砲、装甲車が細かく切断され、くず鉄屑になるだろう。 **6** N-COUNT 不可算名詞 You can refer to a fight or a quarrel as a **scrap**, especially if it is not very serious. つかみ合い、けんか [INFORMAL くだけた] ❑ *He had suffered a mild concussion in a scrap for a loose ball.* 彼はキープされていないボールの奪い合いで軽い脳震盪または脳しんとうを起こしていた。 ●V-I 自動詞 **Scrap** is also a verb. つかみ合いをする ❑ *Our guys scrapped and competed and went right to the wire.* 我々の男たちは殴りあい、競い合い、最後まで競り合った。

scrap|book /skr**æ**pbʊk/ (**scrapbooks**) N-COUNT 可算名詞 A **scrapbook** is a book with empty pages on which you can stick things such as pictures or newspaper articles in order to keep them. スクラップブック ❑ *...a large scrapbook of press clippings and photographs.* 新聞の切り抜きと写真を集めた大きなスクラップブック。

scrape /skr**eɪ**p/ (**scrapes, scraping, scraped**) **1** V-T 他動詞 If you **scrape** something from a surface, you remove it, especially by pulling a sharp object over the surface. こすり落とす [他動詞] ❑ *She went around the car scraping the frost off the windows.* 彼女は車の回りを歩きながら窓についた霜をこそげ落とした。 **2** V-T/V-I 他動詞/自動詞 If something **scrapes** against something else, it rubs against it, making a noise or causing slight damage. こすって音をたてる [他動詞・自動詞] ❑ *The only sound is that of knives and forks scraping against china.* 聞こえるのはナイフとフォークが陶器をこする音だけだ。 ❑ *The car hurtled past us, scraping the wall and screeching to a halt.* 車が私たちの前を猛烈なスピードで走り去り、壁をこすり、キーッと音をたてて止まった。 **3** V-T 他動詞 If you **scrape** a part of your body, you accidentally rub it against something hard and rough, and damage it slightly. すりむく [他動詞] ❑ *She stumbled and fell, scraping her palms and knees.* 彼女はつまずいてころび、手のひらとひざをすりむいた。

▶ **scrape through** PHRASAL VERB 句動詞 If you **scrape through** an examination, you just succeed in passing it. If you **scrape through** a competition or a vote, you just succeed in winning it. かろうじて通過する ❑ *He was a poor student, barely scraping through his final year.* 彼はできの悪い学生で、最終学年をやっとのことで終了した。

▶ **scrape together** PHRASAL VERB 句動詞 If you **scrape together** an amount of money or a number of things, you succeed in obtaining it with difficulty. かき集める ❑ *They only just managed to scrape the money together.* 彼らはやっとのことでお金をかき集めた。

scrap|heap /skr**æ**phip/ also **scrap heap** **1** N-SING 単数名詞 If you say that someone has been thrown on the scrapheap, you mean that they have been forced to leave their job by an uncaring employer and are unlikely to get other work. 解雇を強いられる ❑ *Thousands of miners have been thrown on the scrapheap with no jobs*

and no prospects. 何千人もの鉱山労働者が、仕事も将来の見込みもないまま強制的に解雇された。 **2** N-SING 単数名詞 If things such as machines or weapons are thrown on the scrapheap, they are thrown away because they are no longer needed. 廃棄処分にする ❑ *Thousands of Europe's tanks and guns are going to the scrap heap.* 何千もの欧州の戦車や銃が廃棄処分にされる。

scratch /skr**æ**tʃ/ (**scratches, scratching, scratched**) **1** V-T/V-I 他動詞/自動詞 If you **scratch yourself**, you rub your fingernails against your skin because it is itching. (痒いところなどを) かく [他動詞・自動詞] ❑ *He scratched himself under his arm.* 彼はわきの下をかいた。 ❑ *The old man lifted his cardigan to scratch his side.* その老人はカーディガンを持ち上げて横腹をかいた。 **2** V-T 他動詞 If a sharp object **scratches** someone or something, it makes small shallow cuts on their skin or surface. 引っかく [他動詞] ❑ *The branches tore at my jacket and scratched my hands and face.* 枝が私のジャケットを引き裂き、手と顔を引っかいた。 **3** N-COUNT 可算名詞 **Scratches** on someone or something are small shallow cuts. かすり傷 ❑ *The seven-year-old was found crying with scratches on his face and neck.* その7歳児は顔と首に引っかき傷を負い、泣いているところを発見された。 **4** PHRASE 句 If you do something **from scratch**, you do it without making use of anything that has been done before. 初めから ❑ *Building a home from scratch can be both exciting and challenging.* 家をゼロから建てるのは、心躍るものでも、困難なものでもある。 **5** PHRASE 句 If you say that someone is **scratching** their **head**, you mean that they are thinking hard and trying to solve a problem or puzzle. 懸命に考える、困惑する ❑ *The Institute spends a lot of time scratching its head about how to boost American productivity.* その協会は米国の生産性をどのように促進したらよいか、何時間も頭を悩ませている。

scratch card (**scratch cards**) also **scratchcard** N-COUNT 可算名詞 A **scratch card** is a card with hidden words or symbols on it. You scratch the surface off to reveal the words or symbols and find out if you have won a prize. スクラッチカード

scrawl /skr**ɔ**l/ (**scrawls, scrawling, scrawled**) **1** V-T 他動詞 If you **scrawl** something, you write it in a careless and messy way. なぐり書きする [他動詞] ❑ *He scrawled a hasty note to his wife.* 彼は大急いで妻宛のメモをなぐり書きした。 ❑ *Someone had scrawled "Scum" on his car.* 誰かが彼の車に「人間のくず」と走り書きした。 **2** N-VAR 可変性名詞 You can refer to writing that looks careless and messy as a **scrawl**. なぐり書き ❑ *The letter was handwritten, in a hasty, barely decipherable scrawl.* 手紙は、大急ぎで走り書きされ、かろうじて解読できるものだった。

scrawny /skr**ɔ**ni/ (**scrawnier, scrawniest**) ADJ 形容詞 If you describe a person or animal as **scrawny**, you mean that they look unattractive because they are so thin. 骨ばった [DISAPPROVAL 不賛成] ❑ *...a scrawny woman with dyed black hair.* 髪を黒く染めたやせた女性。

scream /skr**i**m/ (**screams, screaming, screamed**) **1** V-I 自動詞 When someone **screams**, they make a very loud, high-pitched cry, for example, because they are in pain or are very frightened. 叫び声をあげる [自動詞] ❑ *Women were screaming; some of the houses nearest the bridge were on fire.* 女性たちが金切り声をあげていた。橋に最も近い家のいくつかが火事になっていた。 ●N-COUNT 可算名詞 **Scream** is also a noun. 絶叫 ❑ *Hilda let out a scream.* ヒルダは悲鳴をあげた。 **2** V-T 他動詞 If you **scream** something, you shout it in a loud, high-pitched voice. 金切り声で言う [他動詞] ❑ *"Brigid!" she screamed. "Get up!"* 「ブリジッド、起きなさい」と彼女は声を張りあげた。

screech /skr**i**tʃ/ (**screeches, screeching, screeched**) **1** V-I 自動詞 When a vehicle **screeches** somewhere or if its tires **screech**, its tires make an unpleasant high-pitched noise on the road. キーキー鳴る [自動詞] ❑ *A black Mercedes screeched to a halt beside the helicopter.* 黒いメルセデスが鋭い音をたててヘリコプターの横に止まった。 **2** V-T/V-I 他動詞/自動詞 When you **screech** something, you shout it in a loud, unpleasant, high-pitched voice. 金切り声で叫ぶ [他動詞・自動詞] ❑ *"Get me some water, Jeremy!" I screeched.* 「水もってきてよ、ジェレミー」と私は金切り声で叫んだ。 ●N-COUNT 可算名詞 **Screech** is also a noun. 金切り声 ❑ *The figure gave a screech.* その人影は鋭い叫び声をあげた。 **3** V-I 自動詞 When a bird, animal, or thing **screeches**, it makes a loud, unpleasant, high-pitched noise. キーキー鳴る [自動詞] ❑ *A macaw screeched at him from its perch.* コンゴウインコは止まり木から彼に向かってキーキー鳴んだ。 ●N-COUNT 可算名詞 **Screech** is also a noun. かん高い耳障りな叫び声 ❑ *He heard the screech of brakes.* 彼はブレーキのキキーッという音を聞いた。

screen /skr**i**n/ (**screens, screening, screened**) **1** N-COUNT 可算名詞 A **screen** is a flat vertical surface on which pictures or words are shown. Television sets and computers have screens, and movies are shown on a screen in movie theaters. 画面 **2** → see also **widescreen** **3** N-SING 単数名詞 You can refer to movies or television as **the screen**. 映画、テレビ ["the" N, also "on/off" N] ❑ *Many viewers have strong opinions about violence on the screen.* 多くの視聴者は、テレビで放送される暴力に対し強固な意見をもって

います. ❹ V-T 他動詞 When a movie or a television program **is screened**, it is shown in the movie theater or broadcast on television. 上映する ❏ *The series is likely to be screened in January.* そのシリーズはおそらく1月に放送される. ● **screen|ing** N-COUNT 可算名詞 (**screenings**) 上映 ❏ *The film-makers will be present at the screenings to introduce their works.* 映画制作者は, 作品を紹介するために上映会に出席する. ❺ N-COUNT 可算名詞 A **screen** is a vertical panel which can be moved around. It is used to keep cold air away from part of a room, or to create a smaller area within a room. ついたて ❏ *They put a screen in front of me so I couldn't see what was going on.* 彼らは私の前についたてを置いたので, その向こうで何が起こっているのかわからなかった. ❻ V-T 他動詞 [usu passive] If something **is screened by** another thing, it is behind it and hidden by it. おおい隠す [他動詞] ❏ *Most of the road behind the hotel was screened by an apartment block.* ホテルの背後にある道のほとんどは団地で人目からさえぎられていた. ❼ V-I 自動詞 To **screen for** a disease means to examine people to make sure that they do not have it. 検査する [自動詞] ❏ *...a quick saliva test that would screen for people at risk of tooth decay.* 虫歯の危険性のある人を検査する迅速な唾液検査. ● **screen|ing** N-VAR 可変性名詞 検査 ❏ *Our country has an enviable record on breast screening for cancer.* わが国は胸部癌検査でうらやましいほどの記録を持っている. ❽ V-T/V-I 他動詞/自動詞 When an organization **screens** people who apply to join it, it investigates them to make sure that they are not likely to cause problems. 審査する [他動詞・自動詞] ❏ *They will screen all their candidates.* 彼らは候補者全員を審査します. ❾ V-T 他動詞 To **screen** people or luggage means to check them using special equipment to make sure they are not carrying a weapon or a bomb. 検査する [他動詞] ❏ *The airline had not been searching unaccompanied baggage by hand, but only screening it on X-ray machines.* その航空会社は, 別送手荷物検査は手作業では行っておらず, X線機器でのみスクリーニングしています. → see **computer, television**

screen|play /skrɪnpleɪ/ (**screenplays**) N-COUNT 可算名詞 A **screenplay** is the words to be spoken in a movie, and instructions about what will be seen in it. 映画脚本

screen|saver /skrɪnseɪvər/ (**screensavers**) also **screen saver** N-COUNT 可算名詞 A **screensaver** is a moving picture which appears or is put on a computer screen when the computer is not used for a while. スクリーンセーバー [COMPUTING コンピューティング]

screen|writer /skrɪnraɪtər/ (**screenwriters**) N-COUNT 可算名詞 A **screenwriter** is a person who writes screenplays. 映画台本作家

screw /skru/ (**screws, screwing, screwed**) ❶ N-COUNT 可算名詞 A **screw** is a metal object similar to a nail, with a raised spiral line around it. You turn a screw using a screwdriver so that it goes through two things, for example, two pieces of wood, and fastens them together. ねじ ❏ *Each bracket is fixed to the wall with just three screws.* 各ブラケットはねじ3つだけで壁に固定される. ❷ V-T/V-I 他動詞/自動詞 If you **screw** something somewhere or if it **screws** somewhere, you fix it in place by means of a screw or screws. ねじで取り付ける [他動詞・自動詞] ❏ *I had screwed the shelf on the wall myself.* 私は自分で棚を壁に取り付けた. ❏ *Screw down any loose floorboards.* 緩んだ床板があればねじで留める. ❸ ADJ 形容詞 A **screw** lid or fitting is one that has a raised spiral line on the inside or outside of it, so that it can be fixed in place by twisting. ねじる [ADJ n] ❏ *...an ordinary jam jar with a screw lid.* スクリューキャップの付いた普通のジャムの瓶. ❹ V-T/V-I 他動詞/自動詞 If you **screw** something somewhere or if it **screws** somewhere, you fix it in place by twisting it around and around. ねじ込む [他動詞・自動詞] ❏ *"Yes, I know that," Kelly said, screwing the silencer onto the pistol.* 「ああ, わかってる」 サイレンサーをピストルにねじ込みながらケリーは言った. ❏ *Screw down the lid fairly tightly.* ふたをねじり回してかなりきつく締める. ❺ V-T 他動詞 If you **screw** something such as a piece of paper **into** a ball, you squeeze it or twist it tightly so that it is in the shape of a ball. 丸める [他動詞] ❏ *He screwed the paper into a ball and tossed it into the fire.* 彼は紙を丸めて火にくべた. ❻ V-T 他動詞 If you **screw** your face or your eyes **into** a particular expression, you tighten the muscles of your face to form that expression, for example, because you are in pain or because the light is too bright. ゆがめる [他動詞] ❏ *He screwed his face into an expression of mock pain.* 彼はふざけて苦痛を見せかけた. ❼ V-RECIP 相互動詞 If someone **screws** someone else or if two people **screw**, they have sex together. 性交する [INFORMAL, VULGAR くだけた, 下品な] ❏ *"Are you screwing her?" she said.* 「あなた彼女と寝てるの」 彼女は聞いた. ❽ V-T 他動詞 Some people use **screw** in expressions such as **screw you** or **screw that** to show that they are not concerned about someone or something or that they feel contempt for them. こんちきしょう [INFORMAL, VULGAR くだけた, 下品な, FEELINGS 感情] [only imper] [他動詞] ❏ *Something inside me snapped. "Well, screw you then!"* 私の堪忍袋の緒が切れた. 「はあん, ふざけんじゃねーよ」 ❾ V-T 他動詞 If someone **screws** something, especially money, **out of** you, they get it from you by putting pressure on you. むりに奪う [INFORMAL くだけた] [他動詞] ❏ *After decades of rich nations screwing money out of poor nations, it's about time some went the*

other way. 何十年にもわたって富裕国は貧困国からお金を搾取してきたが, そろそろ, その逆が起こるべきだ.

▶ **screw up** ❶ PHRASAL VERB 句動詞 If you **screw up** your eyes or your face, you tighten your eye or face muscles, for example, because you are in pain or because the light is too bright. 目を細める, 顔をゆがめる ❏ *She had screwed up her eyes, as if she found the sunshine too bright.* 彼女は, 日光がまぶしく過ぎるかのように目を細めた. ❏ *Close your eyes and screw them up tight.* 目を閉じて, しっかりつぶりなさい. ❷ PHRASAL VERB 句動詞 If you **screw up** a piece of paper, you squeeze it tightly so that it becomes very creased and no longer flat, usually when you are throwing it away. くしゃくしゃにする ❏ *He would start writing to his family and would screw the letter up in frustration.* 彼は家族へ手紙を書き始めるが, いらいらして手紙をくしゃくしゃにする. ❸ PHRASAL VERB 句動詞 To **screw** something **up**, or to **screw up**, means to cause something to fail or be spoiled. 大へまをしてだいなしにする [INFORMAL くだけた] ❏ *You can't open the window because it screws up the air conditioning.* エアコンが効かなくなるから窓を開けてはなりません. ❏ *Get out. Haven't you screwed things up enough already, you idiot!* 出て行け. もう十分だいなしにしただろう, この大ばか.

screw|driver /skrudraɪvər/ (**screwdrivers**) N-COUNT 可算名詞 A **screwdriver** is a tool that is used for turning screws. It consists of a metal rod with a flat or cross-shaped end that fits into the top of the screw. ドライバー → see **tool**

screwed up ADJ 形容詞 If you say that someone is **screwed up**, you mean that they are very anxious or worried, or that they have psychological problems. 混乱した [INFORMAL くだけた] ❏ *He was really screwed up with his emotional problems.* 彼は情緒障害で非常に混乱していた.

Word Link scrib ≈ writing : in**scrib**e, **scrib**ble, tran**scrib**e

scrib|ble /skrɪbəl/ (**scribbles, scribbling, scribbled**) ❶ V-T/V-I 他動詞/自動詞 If you **scribble** something, you write it quickly and roughly. ぐんぐん書く [他動詞・自動詞] ❏ *She scribbled a note to tell Mom she'd gone out.* 彼女は, 出かけると母に伝えるためにメモを走り書きした. ❷ V-I 自動詞 To **scribble** means to make meaningless marks or rough drawings using a pencil or pen. 落書きする [自動詞] ❏ *When Caroline was five she scribbled on a wall.* キャロラインは5歳のとき, 壁に落書きした. ❸ N-VAR 可変性名詞 **Scribble** is something that has been written or drawn quickly and roughly. 走り書き ❏ *I'm sorry what I wrote was such a scribble.* すみません, こんな悪文を書いてしまって.

scrip /skrɪp/ (**scrips**) N-COUNT 可算名詞 A **scrip** is a certificate which shows that an investor owns part of a share or stock. 仮株権 [BUSINESS 実業] ❏ *The cash or scrip would be offered as part of a pro rata return of capital to shareholders.* 案文資本配当の一部として, 現金か仮株権が供与される.

script /skrɪpt/ (**scripts, scripting, scripted**) ❶ N-COUNT 可算名詞 The **script** of a play, movie, or television program is the written version of it. 台本 ❏ *Jenny's writing a film script.* ジェニーは映画の台本を書いている. ❷ V-T 他動詞 The person who **scripts** a movie or a radio or television play writes it. スクリプトを書く [他動詞] ❏ *...James Cameron, who scripted and directed both films.* 両方の映画の台本と監督を受け持ったジェームズ・キャメロン. ❸ N-VAR 可変性名詞 You can refer to a particular system of writing as a particular **script**. 書記法 [usu adj N] ❏ *...a text in the Malay language but written in Arabic script.* マレー語だが, アラビア文字で書かれた文章. ❹ N-VAR 可変性名詞 **Script** is handwriting in which the letters are joined together. 筆記文字 ❏ *When you're writing in script, there are four letters of the alphabet that you can't complete in one stroke.* アルファベットを筆記体で書く際, 1筆でかけない文字が4つある. → see **animation**

Word Link script ≈ writing : manu**script**, **script**ure, tran**script**

scrip|ture /skrɪptʃər/ (**scriptures**) N-VAR 可変性名詞 **Scripture** or **the scriptures** refers to writings that are regarded as holy in a particular religion, for example, the Bible in Christianity. 聖書 ❏ *...a quote from scripture.* 聖書からの引用. → see **religion**

scroll /skroʊl/ (**scrolls, scrolling, scrolled**) ❶ N-COUNT 可算名詞 A **scroll** is a long roll of paper or a similar material with writing on it. 巻物 ❏ *Ancient scrolls were found in caves by the Dead Sea.* 死海のそばの洞窟で古代書簡が発見されました. ❷ N-COUNT 可算名詞 A **scroll** is a painted or carved decoration made to look like a scroll. 渦巻き形の装飾 ❏ *...a handsome suite of chairs incised with Grecian scrolls.* ギリシャの渦巻模様が彫刻された美しい椅子一組. ❸ V-I 自動詞 If you **scroll** through text on a computer screen, you move the text up or down to find the information that you need. スクロールする [COMPUTING コンピューティング] [自動詞] ❏ *I scrolled down to find "United States of America."* 私は下方向にスクロールして, 「アメリカ合衆国」 を検索した. → see **book**

S

scroll bar (**scroll bars**) N-COUNT 可算名詞 On a computer screen, a **scroll bar** is a long thin box along one edge of a window, which you click on with the mouse to move the text up, down, or across the window. スクロールバー [COMPUTING コンピューティング]

scrounge /skraʊndʒ/ (**scrounges, scrounging, scrounged**) V-T/V-I 他動詞/自動詞 If you say that someone **scrounges** something such as food or money, you disapprove of them because they get it by asking for it, rather than by buying it or earning it. たかる [INFORMAL くだけた, DISAPPROVAL 不賛成] □*We managed to scrounge every piece of gear you requested.* 私たちは君が要求した周辺機器すべてをなんとかせしめた.

scrub /skrʌb/ (**scrubs, scrubbing, scrubbed**) ■ V-I 他動詞 If you **scrub** something, you rub it hard in order to clean it, using a stiff brush and water. ごしごし洗う [他動詞] □*Surgeons began to scrub their hands and arms with soap and water before operating.* 外科医は手と腕を石鹸と水でごしごし洗い始めた. ● N-SING 単数名詞 Scrub is also a noun. ごしごしこすり磨くこと □*The walls needed a good scrub.* 壁はよくこすって洗う必要がある. ■ V-T 他動詞 If you **scrub** dirt or stains **off** something, you remove them by rubbing hard. ごしごしこすって洗い落とす [他動詞] □*I started to scrub off the dirt.* 私は汚れをごしごしこすって落とし始めた. ■ N-UNCOUNT 不可算名詞 Scrub consists of low trees and bushes, especially in an area that has very little rain. 低木林 □*There is an area of scrub and woodland beside the railroad.* 鉄道のそばには低木林や森林地帯がある. ■ N-PLURAL 複数名詞 Scrubs are the protective clothes that surgeons and other hospital staff wear in operating rooms. 手術着 [mainly AM 主に米国英語, INFORMAL くだけた] □*...a man wearing blue hospital scrubs.* 青い病院着を着た男.

scruffy /skrʌfi/ (**scruffier, scruffiest**) ADJ 形容詞 Someone or something that is **scruffy** is dirty and messy. うすぎたない □*...a young man, pale, scruffy and unshaven.* 無精ひげを生やしたきたならしい, 顔の青白い若い男.

scrunch /skrʌntʃ/ (**scrunches, scrunching, scrunched**)
▶ **scrunch up** PHRASAL VERB 句動詞 If you **scrunch** something **up**, you squeeze it or bend it so that it is no longer in its natural shape and is often crushed. もみくしゃにする □*She scrunched up three pages of notes and threw them in the bin.* 彼女は3枚のメモをもみくしゃにしてごみ箱に入れた.

scruple /skruːpəl/ (**scruples**) N-VAR 可変性名詞 Scruples are moral principles or beliefs that make you unwilling to do something that seems wrong. 良心のとがめ □*...a man with no moral scruples.* 平気で悪いことをする人.

scrupulous /skruːpjʊləs/ ■ ADJ 形容詞 Someone who is **scrupulous** takes great care to do what is fair, honest, or morally right. 実直な [APPROVAL 賛成] □*You're being very scrupulous, but to what end?* 君は非常に良心的だが, 何が狙いなのかね. □*I have been scrupulous about telling them the dangers.* 私は細心の注意をもって彼らに危険を伝えてきた. ■ ADJ 形容詞 Scrupulous means thorough, exact, and careful about details. 周到な □*Both readers commend Knutson for his scrupulous attention to detail.* 読者は双方とも, 徹底して詳細に注意を払うナトソンを称賛した.

scrutinize /skruːtənaɪz/ (**scrutinizes, scrutinizing, scrutinized**) V-T 他動詞 If you **scrutinize** something, you examine it very carefully, often to find out some information from it or about it. 細かに調べる [他動詞] □*Her purpose was to scrutinize his features to see if he was an honest man.* 彼女の目的は, 彼の特性を綿密に調べ, 彼が正直な人かどうかを知ることでした.

scrutiny /skruːtəni/ N-UNCOUNT 不可算名詞 If a person or thing is under **scrutiny**, they are being studied or observed very carefully. 監視されて □*His private life came under media scrutiny.* 彼の私生活はマスコミに注視されるようになった.

scuba diving /skuːbədaɪvɪŋ/ N-UNCOUNT 不可算名詞 Scuba diving is the activity of swimming underwater using special breathing equipment. The equipment consists of cylinders of air which you carry on your back and which are connected to your mouth by rubber tubes. スキューバダイビング
→ see Picture Dictionary: **scuba diving**

scuffle /skʌfəl/ (**scuffles, scuffling, scuffled**) ■ N-COUNT 可算名詞 A **scuffle** is a short, disorganized fight or struggle. 乱闘 □*Violent scuffles broke out between rival groups demonstrating for and against independence.* 独立賛成派と反対派の対抗グループ間で, 激しい乱闘が勃発しました. ■ V-RECIP 相互動詞 If people **scuffle**, they fight for a short time in a disorganized way. 取っ組み合いをする □*Police scuffled with some of the protesters.* 警察は抗議者数人ともみ合いになりました.

sculpt /skʌlpt/ (**sculpts, sculpting, sculpted**) ■ V-T/V-I 他動詞/自動詞 When an artist **sculpts** something, they carve or shape it out of a material such as stone or clay. 彫刻する [他動詞・時動詞] □*An artist sculpted a full-size replica of her head.* アーチストは自分の頭の等身大レプリカを彫りました. ■ V-T 他動詞 If something **is sculpted**, it is made into a particular shape. 形にされる [他動詞] □*More familiar landscapes have been sculpted by surface erosion.* 地表侵食で, より見慣れた景観が形成された.

sculptor /skʌlptər/ (**sculptors**) N-COUNT 可算名詞 A **sculptor** is someone who creates sculptures. 彫刻家

sculpture /skʌlptʃər/ (**sculptures**) ■ N-VAR 可変性名詞 A **sculpture** is a work of art that is produced by carving or shaping stone, wood, clay, or other materials. 彫刻作品 □*...stone sculptures of figures and animals.* 人物や動物の石の彫刻. ■ N-UNCOUNT 不可算名詞 Sculpture is the art of creating sculptures. 彫刻術 □*Both studied sculpture.* 2人とも彫塑を学んだ.
→ see **gallery**

scum /skʌm/ ■ N-PLURAL 複数名詞 If you refer to people as **scum**, you are expressing your feelings of dislike and disgust for them. 人間のくず [INFORMAL くだけた, DISAPPROVAL 不賛成] □*She never would have even spoken to scum like him when Mom was alive.* ママが生きていたころ, 彼女は彼のような人間のくずとは話すことさえなかった. ■ N-UNCOUNT 不可算名詞 Scum is a layer of a dirty or unpleasant-looking substance on the surface of a liquid. 浮きかす □*...scum marks around the bath.* 浴槽のまわりについた浮きかすの跡.

scurry /skɜri/ (**scurries, scurrying, scurried**) V-I 自動詞 When people or small animals **scurry** somewhere, they move there quickly and hurriedly, especially because they are frightened. あわてて走る [WRITTEN 書き言葉] [自動詞] □*The attack began, sending residents scurrying for cover.* 攻撃が開始し, 居住者は避難所を求めて疾走しました.

scuttle /skʌtəl/ (**scuttles, scuttling, scuttled**) ■ V-I 自動詞 When people or small animals **scuttle** somewhere, they run there with short quick steps. 急いで行く [自動詞] □*Two very small children scuttled away in front of them.* 2人の幼児が彼らの前をあわてて走り去っていった. ■ V-T 他動詞 To **scuttle** a plan or a proposal means to make it fail or cause it to stop. (計画などを) やめる [他動詞] □*Such threats could scuttle the peace conference.* こういった脅しは平和会議をおじゃんにしかねません.

sea /si/ (**seas**) ■ N-SING 単数名詞 The **sea** is the salty water that covers about three-quarters of the Earth's surface. 海 ["the" N, also "by" N] □*Most of the kids have never seen the sea.* 子供たちのほとんどは海を見たことがなかった. ■ N-PLURAL 複数名詞 You use **seas** when you are describing the sea at a particular time or in a particular area. 海 [LITERARY 文語的] □*He drowned after 30 minutes in the rough seas.* 彼は荒海で30分後におぼれた. ■ N-COUNT; N-IN-NAMES 可算名詞, 名称中の名詞 A **sea** is a large area of salty water that is part of an ocean or is surrounded by land. 大洋 □*...the North Sea.* 北海. ■ PHRASE 句 **At sea** means on or under the sea, far away from land. 陸地の見えない海上で □*The boats remain at sea for an average of ten days at a time.* 船の平均航海日数は10日間である. ■ PHRASE 句 If you go or look out **to sea**, you go or look across the sea. 海に出る □*...fishermen who go to sea for two weeks at a time.* 1回に2週間航海に出る漁師.

Picture Dictionary — scuba diving

scuba mask

air tank

pressure gauge

hose
mouthpiece
diver

Word Partnership *sea* は次の語句と使われる:

PREP.	**above the** sea, **across the** sea, **below the** sea, **beneath the** sea, **by** sea, **from the** sea, **into the** sea, **near the** sea, **over the** sea [1]
N.	sea **air**, sea **coast**, **land and** sea, sea **voyage** [1]
ADJ.	**calm** sea, **deep** sea [1]

sea|bed /síːbɛd/ also **sea bed** N-SING 単数名詞 The **seabed** is the ground under the sea. 海底 ◻ *The wreck was raised from the seabed in June 2000.* 難破船は2000年6月に海底から引き上げられた.

sea change (**sea changes**) N-COUNT 可算名詞 A **sea change** in someone's attitudes or behavior is a complete change. 著しい変貌 ◻ *A sea change has taken place in young people's attitudes to their parents.* 親に対する若者の態度の著しい変化.

sea|food /síːfuːd/ N-UNCOUNT 不可算名詞 **Seafood** is shellfish such as lobsters, mussels, and crabs, and sometimes other sea creatures that you can eat. 海産食物 ◻ *...a seafood restaurant.* シーフードレストラン.

sea|front /síːfrʌnt/ (**seafronts**) N-COUNT 可算名詞 The **seafront** is the part of a seaside town that is nearest to the sea. It usually consists of a road with buildings that face the sea. 海岸通り ◻ *They decided to meet on the seafront.* 彼らは海岸通りで会うことにした.

sea|gull /síːgʌl/ (**seagulls**) N-COUNT 可算名詞 A **seagull** is a common kind of bird with white or gray feathers. カモメ

seal
❶ CLOSING
❷ ANIMAL

❶ **seal** /síːl/ (**seals, sealing, sealed**) [1] V-T 他動詞 When you **seal** an envelope, you close it by folding part of it over and sticking it down, so that it cannot be opened without being torn. 封をする [他動詞] ◻ *He sealed the envelope and put on a stamp.* 彼は封筒に封をして切り離手を貼った. ◻ *Write your letter and seal it in a blank envelope.* 手紙を書いて, 宛名の書いてない封筒に入れなさい. [2] V-T 他動詞 If you **seal** a container or an opening, you cover it with something in order to prevent air, liquid, or other material from getting in or out. If you **seal** something **in** a container, you put it inside and then close the container tightly. 密閉する [他動詞] ◻ *She filled the containers, sealed them with a cork, and stuck on labels.* 彼女は容器を満たし, コルクで密閉してラベルを貼った. ◻ *A woman picks them up and seals them in plastic bags.* その女性はそれらを拾い上げて, ポリ袋に密閉しました. [3] N-COUNT 可算名詞 The **seal** on a container or opening is the part where it has been sealed. シール ◻ *When assembling the pie, wet the edges where the two crusts join, to form a seal.* パイを作る際は, 2枚のパイ皮の端をぬらして合わせ, しっかり閉じる. [4] N-COUNT 可算名詞 A **seal** is a device or a piece of material, for example, in a machine, which closes an opening tightly so that air, liquid, or other substances cannot get in or out. 封 [oft N "on" n] ◻ *Check seals on fridges and freezers regularly.* 冷蔵庫と冷凍庫の充填材を定期的に検査する. [5] N-COUNT 可算名詞 A **seal** is something such as a piece of sticky paper or wax that is fixed to a container or door and must be broken before the container or door can be opened. シール [oft N "on" n] ◻ *The seal on the box broke when it fell from its hiding-place.* 箱のシールは, 隠し場所から落ちたときに破れた. [6] N-COUNT 可算名詞 A **seal** is a special mark or design, for example, on a document, representing someone or something. It may be used to show that something is genuine or officially approved. 印章 ◻ *...a supply of note paper bearing the presidential seal.* 大統領の印章が付いた便箋の供給. [7] V-T 他動詞 If someone in authority **seals** an area, they stop people entering or passing through it, for example, by placing barriers in the way. 封じる [他動詞] ◻ *The soldiers were deployed to help paramilitary police seal the border.* 兵士は準憲兵隊が国境を封鎖するのを援助するために配備されました. ▸ PHRASAL VERB 句動詞 **Seal off** means the same as **seal**. 立入り禁止にする ◻ *Police and troops sealed off the area after the attack.* 攻撃のあと, 警察と軍隊はその地域を立入り禁止にした. [8] V-T 他動詞 To **seal** something means to make it definite or confirm how it is going to be. 決定する [WRITTEN 書き言葉] [他動詞] ◻ *McLaren are close to sealing a deal with Renault.* マクレーンはルノーとの契約に調印する寸前だ. ◻ *A general election will be held which will seal his destiny one way or the other.* どっちみち, 総選挙が行われ, 彼の運命が決定される.

→ see **Arctic, can**

▸ **seal off** [1] PHRASAL VERB 句動詞 If one object or area is **sealed off** from another, there is a physical barrier between them, so that nothing can pass between them. 閉鎖する ◻ *Windows are usually sealed off.* 窓は通常閉鎖されている. [2] → see **seal ❶ 7**

❷ **seal** /síːl/ (**seals**) N-COUNT 可算名詞 A **seal** is a large animal with a rounded body and flat legs called flippers. Seals eat fish

and live in and near the sea, usually in cold parts of the world. アザラシ

sea lev|el also **sea-level** N-UNCOUNT 不可算名詞 **Sea level** is the average level of the sea with respect to the land. The height of mountains or other areas is calculated in relation to **sea level**. 海水面 ◻ *The stadium was 5,000 feet above sea level.* 競技場の海抜は5000フィートだった. ◻ *The whole place is at sea level.* その場所全体が海抜ゼロだ.

→ see **glacier**

seam /síːm/ (**seams**) [1] N-COUNT 可算名詞 A **seam** is a line of stitches which joins two pieces of cloth together. 縫い目 ◻ *The skirt ripped along a seam.* スカートは縫い目にそって破れた. [2] N-COUNT 可算名詞 A **seam** of coal is a long, narrow layer of it underneath the ground. 層 ◻ *The average coal seam here is three feet thick.* ここの平均石炭層厚は3フィートだ. [3] PHRASE 句 If something **is coming apart at the seams** or **is falling apart at the seams**, it is no longer working properly and may soon stop working completely. だめになる ◻ *Our university system is in danger of falling apart at the seams.* 我々の大学のシステムは崩壊の危険に瀕しています. [4] PHRASE 句 If a place is very full, you can say that it is **bursting at the seams**. はちきれそうになる ◻ *The hotels of Warsaw, Prague and Budapest were bursting at the seams.* ワルシャワ, プラハおよびブダペストのホテルはすごい込みようである.

sea|man /síːmən/ (**seamen**) N-COUNT 可算名詞 A **seaman** is a sailor, especially one who is not an officer. 水夫 ◻ *The men emigrate to work as seamen.* 男性は移住し, 水夫として働く.

seam|less /síːmlɪs/ ADJ 形容詞 You use **seamless** to describe something that has no breaks or gaps in it or which continues without stopping. とぎれのない ◻ *It was a seamless procession of wonderful electronic music.* すばらしい電子音楽がとぎれなく演奏された. ● **seam|less|ly** ADV 副詞 [ADV with v] とぎれなく ◻ *It's a class move, allowing new and old to blend seamlessly.* それは新しいものと古いものをシームレスに融合する一流映画です.

search /sɜːrtʃ/ (**searches, searching, searched**) [1] V-I 自動詞 If you **search for** something or someone, you look carefully for them. 捜す [自動詞] ◻ *The Turkish security forces have started searching for the missing men.* トルコの保安部隊は, 行方不明者の捜索を開始しました. ◻ *They searched for a spot where they could sit on the floor.* 彼らは地べたに座れる場所を探した. [2] V-T/V-I 他動詞/自動詞 If you **search** a place, you look carefully for something or someone there. 捜索して求める [他動詞・自動詞] ◻ *Armed troops searched the hospital yesterday.* 昨日, 武装した軍隊が病院を捜索しました. ◻ *She searched her desk for the necessary information.* 彼女は必要な情報が自分の机にないか捜した. ◻ *Relief workers are still searching through collapsed buildings.* 難民救済ワーカーはいまだに崩壊した建物を捜索している. [3] N-COUNT 可算名詞 A **search** is an attempt to find something or someone by looking for them carefully. 捜索 ◻ *There was no chance of him being found alive and the search was abandoned.* 彼が生きて発見される可能性はなかったので, 捜索は断念された. [4] V-T 他動詞 If a police officer or someone else in authority **searches** you, they look carefully to see whether you have something hidden on you. 捜査する [他動詞] ◻ *The man took her suitcase from her and then searched her.* その男は彼女からスーツケースを取り上げ, 彼女の身体捜査をした. [5] V-I 自動詞 If you **search for** information on a computer, you give the computer an instruction to find that information. 検索する [COMPUTING コンピューティング] [自動詞] ◻ *You can use a directory service to search for people on the Internet.* あなたはインターネットで電話番号案内を使用して, 人を検索することができる. ● N-COUNT 可算名詞 **Search** is also a noun. 検索 ◻ *He came across this story while he was doing a computer search of local news articles.* 彼はコンピュータで検索を行っていたときにこの物語を偶然見つけた. [6] → see also **searching** [7] PHRASE 句 If you go **in search of** something or someone, you try to find them. 捜し求めて ◻ *Miserable, and unexpectedly lonely, she went in search of Jean-Paul.* 彼女は惨めで, 思った以上に寂しくなって, ジョン・ポールを捜しに出かけた. [8] CONVENTION 慣習表現 You say **"search me"** when someone asks you a question and you want to emphasize that you do not know the answer. 知らん [INFORMAL くだけた, EMPHASIS 強調] ◻ *"So why did he get interested all of a sudden?" — "Search me."* 「ではなぜ彼は突然興味を持ったのかい」「わからんね」

Thesaurus *search* また次を参照:

V.	hunt, inspect, look for, seek [1] [2]
N.	exploration, hunt, inspection, quest [3]

Word Partnership　*search* は次の語句と使われる:

N.	search **for a job**, **talent** search, search **for the truth** 1
	search **an area**, search **for clues** 1 2
	search **for information** 1 2 5
	investigators search, **police** search, search **suspects** 4
	computer search, search **criteria**, search **the Internet**, **online** search 5
V.	**conduct a** search 3

search en|gine (**search engines**) N-COUNT 可算名詞 A **search engine** is a computer program that searches for documents containing a particular word or words on the Internet. 検索エンジン [COMPUTING コンピューティング]

search|ing /sɜ́rtʃɪŋ/ ADJ 形容詞 A **searching** question or look is intended to discover the truth about something. 探るような □ *They asked her some searching questions on moral philosophy and logic.* 彼らは倫理学と論理について彼女に鋭い質問をした.

search|light /sɜ́rtʃlaɪt/ (**searchlights**) N-COUNT 可算名詞 A **searchlight** is a large powerful light that can be turned to shine a long way in any direction. サーチライト □ *Helicopters threw searchlights over the meadows and the lake.* ヘリコプターは牧草地や湖をサーチライトで照らした.

search par|ty (**search parties**) N-COUNT 可算名詞 A **search party** is an organized group of people who are searching for someone who is missing. 捜査隊

search war|rant (**search warrants**) N-COUNT 可算名詞 A **search warrant** is a special document that gives the police permission to search a house or other building. 捜索令状 □ *Officers armed with a search warrant entered the apartment.* 捜索令状を持った警官がアパートに乗り込んだ.

sear|ing /sɪ́ərɪŋ/ 1 ADJ 形容詞 **Searing** is used to indicate that something such as pain or heat is very intense. 強く焼きつくような [ADJ n] □ *She woke to feel a searing pain in her feet.* 彼女は足に焼きつくような痛みを感じて目を覚ました. 2 ADJ 形容詞 A **searing** speech or piece of writing is very critical. きびしい [ADJ n] □ *There's a searing column in today's paper about the president's decision.* 本日の新聞には、大統領の決断に関する、辛らつなコラムが掲載されている.

sea|shore /síʃɔr/ (**seashores**) N-COUNT 可算名詞 The **seashore** is the part of a coast where the land slopes down into the sea. 海岸 □ *She takes her inspiration from shells and stones she finds on the seashore.* 彼女は、海岸で見つける貝殻や石から発想を得ている.

sea|sick /síːsɪk/ ADJ 形容詞 If someone is **seasick** when they are traveling in a boat, they vomit or feel sick because of the way the boat is moving. 船酔いの □ *It was quite rough at times, and she was seasick.* 時として非常に荒れていたので、彼女は船に酔った. ● **sea|sick|ness** N-UNCOUNT 不可算名詞 船酔い □ *He was very prone to seasickness and already felt queasy.* 彼は船酔いになりやすく、すでに吐き気がしていた.

sea|side /síːsaɪd/ N-SING 単数名詞 You can refer to an area that is close to the sea, especially one where people go for their vacation, as **the seaside**. 海辺 □ *I went to spend a few days at the seaside.* 私は海辺で数日を過ごしに出かけた.

sea|son /síːzⁿn/ (**seasons, seasoning, seasoned**) 1 N-COUNT 可算名詞 The **seasons** are the main periods into which a year can be divided and which each have their own typical weather conditions. 季節 □ *Fall is my favorite season.* 秋は私の大好きな季節だ. □ *...the only region of Brazil where all four seasons are clearly defined.* 四季すべてが明確に特徴づけられる、ブラジルで唯一の地域. 2 N-COUNT 可算名詞 You can use **season** to refer to the period during each year when a particular activity or event takes place. For example, the planting **season** is the period when a particular plant or crop is planted. 流行期 □ *...birds arriving for the breeding season.* 繁殖期に到着する鳥. 3 N-COUNT 可算名詞 You can use **season** to refer to the period when a particular fruit, vegetable, or other food is ready for eating and is widely available. 旬 [N N, also "in/out of" N] □ *The plum season is about to begin.* ウメの旬がはじまろうとしている. 4 N-COUNT 可算名詞 You can use **season** to refer to a fixed period during each year when a particular sport is played or when a particular activity is allowed. シーズン □ *...the baseball season.* 野球シーズン. □ *Deer hunting season is only a couple of weeks long.* 鹿の狩猟期はたった数週間しかない. 5 N-COUNT 可算名詞 A **season** is a period in which a play or show, or a series of plays or shows, is performed in one place. シーズン □ *...a season of three new plays.* 新しい芝居3作品のシーズン. 6 N-COUNT 可算名詞 A **season** of movies is several of them shown as a series because they are connected in some way. 映画祭 □ *...a brief season of films in which Artaud appeared.* アルトーが出演する短期間の映画祭. 7 N-COUNT 可算名詞 The vacation **season** is the time when most people take their vacation. シーズン [usu sing, usu supp N, also "in/out of" N] □ *...the peak vacation season.* 休暇シーズンのピーク. 8 V-T 他動詞 If you **season** food with salt, pepper, or spices,

you add them to it in order to improve its flavor. 調味する [他動詞] □ *Season the meat with salt and pepper.* 塩とこしょうで肉に味付けする. 9 → see also **seasoned, seasoning** 10 PHRASE 句 If a female animal is **in season**, she is in a state where she is ready to have sex. さかりがついている □ *There are a few ideas around on how to treat fillies and mares in season.* さかりのついた雌の子馬や雄馬の扱い方に関するアイデアはないことはない.

→ see **plant**

sea|son|al /síːzⁿnl/ ADJ 形容詞 A **seasonal** factor, event, or change occurs during one particular time of the year. 季節の [ADJ n] □ *The figures aren't adjusted for seasonal variations.* 数値は季節変動に対して調整されていません. ● **sea|son|al|ly** ADV 副詞 季節的に □ *The seasonally adjusted unemployment figures show a rise of twelve-hundred.* 季節調整後の失業者数は1200人の増加を示している.

sea|soned /síːzⁿnd/ ADJ 形容詞 You can use **seasoned** to describe a person who has a lot of experience of something. For example, a **seasoned** traveler is a person who has traveled a lot. 訓練を積んだ □ *The author is a seasoned academic.* 著者は経験豊かな研究者だ.

sea|son|ing /síːzⁿnɪŋ/ (**seasonings**) N-MASS 質量名詞 **Seasoning** is salt, pepper, or other spices that are added to food to improve its flavor. 調味料 □ *Mix the meat with the onion, carrot, and some seasoning.* 肉をタマネギ、ニンジン、多少の調味料と混ぜる.

→ see **salt**

sea|son tick|et (**season tickets**) N-COUNT 可算名詞 A **season ticket** is a ticket that you can use repeatedly during a certain period, without having to pay each time. You can buy **season tickets** for things such as buses, trains, regular sports events, or theater performances. 定期券 □ *We went to renew our monthly season ticket.* 私たちは1か月定期券の更新に行った.

seat /síːt/ (**seats, seating, seated**) 1 N-COUNT 可算名詞 A **seat** is an object that you can sit on, for example, a chair. 席 □ *Stephen returned to his seat.* スティーブンは自分の席に戻った. 2 N-COUNT 可算名詞 The **seat** of a chair is the part that you sit on. 座部 □ *The stool had a torn, red plastic seat.* スツールには破れた赤いプラスチックの座部がついていた. 3 V-T 他動詞 If you **seat yourself** somewhere, you sit down. 座る [WRITTEN 書き言葉] [他動詞] □ *He waved toward a chair, and seated himself at the desk.* 彼はいすを手で示して、着席した. 4 V-T 他動詞 A building or vehicle that **seats** a particular number of people has enough seats for that number. 収容する [他動詞] □ *The theater seats 570.* その劇場は570人を収容する. 5 N-SING 単数名詞 The **seat** of a piece of clothing is the part that covers your bottom. 衣服の尻部 [usu "the" N "of" n] □ *Then he got up, brushed off the seat of his jeans, and headed slowly down the slope.* そして、彼は立ち上がってジーンズの尻をブラシで払って、坂をゆっくり下りていった. 6 N-COUNT 可算名詞 When someone is elected to a legislature you can say that they, or their party, have won a **seat**. 議席 □ *Independent candidates won the majority of seats on the local council.* 無所属候補が地方自治体で議席の過半数を勝ち取りました. 7 N-COUNT 可算名詞 If someone has a **seat** on the board of a company or on a committee, they are a member of it. 取締役の地位 □ *He has been unsuccessful in his attempt to win a seat on the board of the company.* 彼は、会社の取締役の地位を得ようとしたが失敗した. 8 N-COUNT 可算名詞 The **seat** of an organization, a wealthy family, or an activity is its base. 所在地 □ *Gunfire broke out early this morning around the seat of government in Lagos.* 今朝未明に、ラゴスの政府所在地で砲撃が起こりました. 9 → see also **deep-seated** 10 PHRASE 句 If you **take a back seat**, you allow other people to have all the power and to make all the decisions. 目立たない立場になる □ *You need to take a back seat and think about both past and future.* 君は過去と未来の両方を熟考することを第一に考える必要がある. 11 PHRASE 句 If you **take a seat**, you sit down. 着席する [FORMAL 形式ばった] □ *"Take a seat," he said in a bored tone.* 「どうぞお座りください」彼は退屈そうな声で言った.

Word Partnership　*seat* は次の語句と使われる:

ADJ.	**back** seat, **empty** seat, **front** seat 1
	vacant seat, **vacated** seat 1 6 7
	congressional seat 6
N.	**car** seat, **child** seat, **driver's** seat, **passenger** seat, seat **at a table**, **theater** seat, **toilet** seat 1
	seat **in the House/Senate** 6
	seat **on the board** 7

seat belt (**seat belts**) also **seatbelt** N-COUNT 可算名詞 A **seat belt** is a strap attached to a seat in a car or an aircraft. You fasten it across your body in order to prevent yourself being thrown out of the seat if there is a sudden movement or stop. シートベルト □ *The fact I was wearing a seat belt saved my life.* 私はシートベルトを付けていたために助かった.

→ see **car**

S

Laws have been passed in most of the U.S. requiring motorists and their passengers to wear **seat belts** while in a moving vehicle. For small children's safety, **car seats** especially designed with belts to fit them must be used. Those caught not using seat belts are liable for a heavy fine.

seat|ing /síːtɪŋ/ **1** N-UNCOUNT 不可算名詞 You can refer to the seats in a place as the **seating**. 収容力 ❑ *The stadium has been fitted with seating for over eighty thousand spectators.* スタジアムは8万人以上の観客を収容する能力がありました. **2** N-UNCOUNT 不可算名詞 The **seating** at a public place or a formal occasion is the arrangement of where people will sit. 座席の配置 ❑ *She made a mental note to check the seating arrangements before the guests filed into the dining-room.* 彼女は, 客がダイニングルームに列を成す前に座席の配置をチェックすることを心に留めた.

sea|weed /síːwiːd/ (**seaweeds**) N-MASS 質量名詞 **Seaweed** is a plant that grows in the sea. There are many kinds of seaweed. 海草 ❑ *...seaweed washed up on a beach.* 海岸に打ち上げられた海草.

sec /sɛk/ (**secs**) N-COUNT 可算名詞 If you ask someone to wait a **sec**, you are asking them to wait for a very short time. ちょっとの間 [INFORMAL くだけた] ❑ *Can you just hang on a sec?* ちょっと待ってくれないか.

sec. /sɛk/ (**secs**) **Sec.** is a written abbreviation for **second** or **seconds**. secondまたはsecondsの略 ❑ *The first woman to finish was Grete Waitz of Norway, with a time of 2 hrs, 29 min., 30 sec.* 最初にゴールした女性は, 2時間29分30秒のタイムで, ノルウェーのグレテ・ワイツだった.

se|clud|ed /sɪklúːdɪd/ ADJ 形容詞 A **secluded** place is quiet and private. 隠遁した ❑ *We were tucked away in a secluded corner of the room.* 私たちは部屋の奥まった隅に押し込まれた.

se|clu|sion /sɪklúːʒən/ N-UNCOUNT 不可算名詞 If you are living **in seclusion**, you are in a quiet place away from other people. 隠遁 ❑ *She lived in seclusion with her husband on their farm in Panama.* 彼女はパナマの農場で夫と隠遁生活を送りました.

---

second

❶ PART OF A MINUTE

❷ COMING AFTER SOMETHING ELSE

---

❶ **sec|ond** /sɛkənd/ (**seconds**) N-COUNT 可算名詞 A **second** is one of the sixty parts that a minute is divided into. People often say "**a second**" or "**seconds**" when they simply mean a very short time. 秒 ❑ *For a few seconds nobody said anything.* しばらくの間, 誰も何も言わなかった. ❑ *It only takes forty seconds.* 40秒しかかからない.

❷ **sec|ond** /sɛkənd/ (**seconds, seconding, seconded**) ➪ **Please look at category ⓬ to see if the expression you are looking for is shown under another headword. 1** ORD 序数詞 The **second** item in a series is the one that you count as number two. 第2の ❑ *...the second day of his visit to Delhi.* 彼のデリー訪問の2日目. ❑ *...their second child.* 彼らの第2子. ❑ *...the Second World War.* 第2次世界大戦. **2** ORD 序数詞 **Second** is used before superlative adjectives to indicate that there is only one thing better or larger than the thing you are referring to. 第2の [ORD adj-superl] ❑ *The party is still the second strongest in Italy.* その政党はそれでもイタリアで第2番目に力があります. **3** ADV 副詞 You say **second** when you want to make a second point or give a second reason for something. 2番目の [ADV cl] ❑ *First, the weapons should be intended for use only in retaliation after a nuclear attack. Second, the possession of the weapons must be a temporary expedient.* 第1に, 武器は核攻撃後の報復でのみ使用されるべきだ. 第2に, 武器の所持は臨時措置である必要がある. **4** N-PLURAL 複数名詞 If you have **seconds**, you have a second helping of food. お代わり [INFORMAL くだけた] ❑ *There's seconds if you want them.* お望みでしたらお代わりもありますよ. **5** N-COUNT 可算名詞 **Seconds** are goods that are sold cheaply in stores because they have slight faults. 二級品 ❑ *These are not seconds, or unbranded goods, but first-quality products.* これらは二級品でも無印商品でもなく, 一級商品だ. **6** V-T 他動詞 If you **second** a proposal in a meeting or debate, you formally express your agreement with it so that it can then be discussed or voted on. (動議などに) 賛成する [他動詞] ❑ *...Bryan Sutton, who seconded the motion against fox hunting.* キツネ狩りに反対する動議に賛成したブライアン・サットン. **7** V-T 他動詞 If you **second** what someone has said, you say that you agree with them or say the same thing yourself. 支持する [他動詞] ❑ *The U.N. secretary-general seconded the appeal for peace.* 国連事務総長は平和への訴えを支持した. **8** PHRASE 句 If you experience something **at second hand**, you are told about it by other people rather than experiencing it yourself. また聞きで ❑ *Most of them, after all, had not been at the battle and had only heard of the massacre at second hand.* 結局, ほとんどの人は戦闘に行ったことはなく, 大虐殺については間接的に聞いたことがあるだけだった. **9** → see also **secondhand 10** PHRASE 句 If you say that something is **second to none**, you are emphasizing that it is very good indeed or the best that there is. 何ものにも劣らない [EMPHASIS 強調] ❑ *Our scientific research is second to none.* 我々の科学研究は何者にも劣らない. **11** PHRASE 句 If you say that something is **second only to** something else, you mean that only that thing is better or greater than it. 次いで ❑ *As a major health risk hepatitis is second only to tobacco.* 主要な健康上のリスクとして, 肝臓炎はタバコに次いで第2位です. **12** **second nature** → see **nature 13** **in the second place** → see **place**

sec|ond|ary /sɛkənderi/ **1** ADJ 形容詞 If you describe something as **secondary**, you mean that it is less important than something else. 副の ❑ *The street erupted in a huge explosion, with secondary explosions in the adjoining buildings.* その通りで大爆発が起こり, 隣接する建物で派生的な爆発が起こった. ❑ *They argue that human rights considerations are now of only secondary importance.* 人権の配慮はもはや第2次的に重要なものに過ぎなくなったと論じている. **2** ADJ 形容詞 **Secondary** diseases or infections happen as a result of another disease or infection that has already happened. 2次の ❑ *These patients had been operated on for the primary cancer but there was evidence of secondary tumors.* これらの患者は原発性癌で手術を受けましたが, 二次性腫瘍の兆候が見られました. **3** ADJ 形容詞 **Secondary** education is given to students between the ages of 11 or 12 and 17 or 18. 中等 ❑ *Examinations are taken after about five years of secondary education.* 約5年間の中等教育のあと, 試験が行われます.

sec|ond|ary school (**secondary schools**) N-VAR 可変性名詞 A **secondary school** is a school for students between the ages of 11 or 12 and 17 or 18. 中学校 ❑ *She taught history at a secondary school.* 彼女は中等学校で歴史を教えた.

sec|ond best also **second-best 1** ADJ 形容詞 **Second best** is used to describe something that is not as good as the best thing of its kind but is better than all the other things of that kind. 次位の ❑ *He put on his second-best suit.* 彼は2番目に良いスーツを着込んだ. **2** ADJ 形容詞 You can use **second best** to describe something that you have to accept even though you would have preferred something else. 次善の ❑ *...a messy, second-best solution.* 面倒くさい次善のソリューション. ● N-SING 単数名詞 **Second best** is also a noun. 次位のもの ❑ *Oatmeal is a good second best.* オートミールは1位と大差のない2位だ.

second-class also **second class 1** ADJ 形容詞 If someone treats you as a **second-class** citizen, they treat you as if you are less valuable and less important than other people. 第2級の [ADJ n] ❑ *Too many airlines treat our children as second-class citizens.* 子供を第2級市民として扱う航空会社が多すぎる. **2** ADJ 形容詞 If you describe something as **second-class**, you mean that it is of poor quality. 2流の ❑ *I am not prepared to see children in some parts of this country having to settle for a second-class education.* 私は, 2流教育で妥協しなければならない, この国の特定地域の子供たちに会う覚悟ができていない. **3** ADJ 形容詞 The **second-class** accommodations on a train or ship are the ordinary accommodations, which are cheaper and less comfortable than the first-class accommodations. 2等の [ADJ n] ❑ *He sat in the corner of a second-class compartment.* 彼は2等客室の隅に座った. ❑ *Seven second-class passengers prepared to disembark.* 7人の2等客は上陸の準備をした. ● ADV 副詞 **Second class** is also an adverb. 2等で [ADV after v] ❑ *I recently traveled second class from Pisa to Ventimiglia.* 最近私はピサからベンティミリアまで2等の乗り物で旅行した. ● N-UNCOUNT 不可算名詞 **Second-class** is second-class accommodations on a train or ship. 2等 ❑ *"Is there any chance of a compartment to myself?"—"Not in second class."* 「個室をもらえる可能性はありますか」「2等ではないね」 **4** ADJ 形容詞 **Second-class** postage is a slower and cheaper type of postage. 第2種 [BRIT 英国英語] [ADJ n]

second|hand /sɛkəndhænd/ also **second-hand 1** ADJ 形容詞 **Secondhand** things are not new and have been owned by someone else. 中古の ❑ *They could afford a secondhand car, she thought.* 中古車なら彼らでも買えると彼女は思った. ● ADV 副詞 **Secondhand** is also an adverb. 古物で [ADV after v] ❑ *Household appliances were bought secondhand and are outdated.* 家庭電化製品は中古で購入され, 流行遅れだった. **2** ADJ 形容詞 A **secondhand** store sells secondhand goods. 中古品売買の [ADJ n] ❑ *...lovingly restored old pieces bought from a secondhand store.* 古物商で買った, 丹精に修復された古い作品. **3** ADJ 形容詞 **Secondhand** stories, information, or opinions are those you learn about from other people rather than directly or from your own experience. また聞きの ❑ *He urged the committee to discount any secondhand knowledge or hearsay.* 彼はまた聞きの知識やうわさすべては無視するよう委員会を熱心に説得した. ● ADV 副詞 **Secondhand** is also an adverb. また聞きで [ADV after v] ❑ *I only heard about it secondhand.* 私はまた聞きしただけだ. **4** **at second hand** → see **second**

sec|ond lan|guage (**second languages**) N-COUNT 可算名詞 Someone's **second language** is a language which is not their native language but which they use at work or at school. 第2外国語 ❑ *Lucy teaches English as a second language.* ルーシーは第2言語として英語を教えている.

sec|ond|ly /sɛkəndli/ ADV 副詞 You say **secondly** when you want to make a second point or give a second reason for something. 第2に □ *It makes you look firstly how you're treated and secondly how you treat everybody else.* それは、第1にあなたがどんな待遇を受けるか、第2にあなたがそのほかの人たちをどう取り扱うかに注意を向けさせる.

sec|ond opin|ion (second opinions) N-COUNT 可算名詞 If you get a **second opinion**, you ask another qualified person for their opinion about something such as your health. 別の医師の意見 □ *I would like to see a specialist for a second opinion on my doctor's diagnosis.* 私の医師の診断に関して、専門家に意見を聞きたい.

second-rate ADJ 形容詞 If you describe something as **second-rate**, you mean that it is of poor quality. 劣った □ *...second-rate restaurants.* 2流のレストラン.

sec|ond thought (second thoughts) **1** N-SING 単数名詞 If you do something without **a second thought**, you do it without thinking about it carefully, usually because you do not have enough time or you do not care very much. 考え直し □ *This murderous lunatic could kill them both without a second thought.* この残忍な精神障害者は、一も二もなく両者ともを殺してしまうかもしれない. **2** N-PLURAL 複数名詞 If you have **second thoughts about** a decision that you have made, you begin to doubt whether it was the best thing to do. 再考 □ *I had never had second thoughts about my decision to leave the company.* 私は、退職する決意を翻したことはなかった. **3** PHRASE 句 You can say **on second thoughts** or **on second thought** when you suddenly change your mind about something that you are saying or something that you have decided to do. 考え直してみると □ *"Wait there!" Kathryn rose. "No, on second thought, follow me."* 「待って」キャスリンは立ち上がった. 「やめた、やっぱり私について来て」

se|cre|cy /sɪkrəsi/ N-UNCOUNT 不可算名詞 **Secrecy** is the act of keeping something secret, or the state of being kept secret. 秘密厳守 □ *The government has thrown a blanket of secrecy over the details.* 政府は詳細を秘密のベールに包んでいる.

se|cret /sɪkrɪt/ (secrets) **1** ADJ 形容詞 If something is **secret**, it is known about by only a small number of people, and is not told or shown to anyone else. 秘密の □ *Soldiers have been training at a secret location.* 兵士は秘密の場所で訓練をしてきました. ● **se|cret|ly** ADV 副詞 ひそかに □ *He wore a hidden microphone to secretly tape-record conversations.* 彼は、内緒で会話をテープに録音するために隠しマイクを着用しました. **2** → see also **top secret** **3** N-COUNT 可算名詞 A **secret** is a fact that is known by only a small number of people, and is not told to anyone else. 機密 □ *I think I enjoyed keeping our love a secret.* 彼は私たちの恋愛を秘密にしておくのを楽しんだと、私は思う. **4** N-SING 単数名詞 If you say that a particular way of doing things is **the secret of** achieving something, you mean that it is the best or only way to achieve it. 極意 □ *The secret of success is honesty and fair dealing.* 成功の秘訣は誠実さと公正な取引だ. **5** N-COUNT 可算名詞 Something's **secrets** are the things about it which have never been fully explained. 謎 □ *We have an opportunity now to really unlock the secrets of the universe.* 私たちは今、宇宙の謎を実際に解き明かす機会を得ました. **6** PHRASE 句 If you do something **in secret**, you do it without anyone else knowing. 内緒で □ *Dan found out that I had been meeting my ex-boyfriend in secret.* ダンは、私が昔の彼氏と内緒で会っていたのに気づいた. **7** PHRASE 句 If you say that someone can **keep a secret**, you mean that they can be trusted not to tell other people a secret that you have told them. 秘密を守る □ *Tom was utterly indiscreet, and could never keep a secret.* トムは全くもって軽率で、秘密を守れたことはありませんでした. **8** PHRASE 句 If you **make no secret** of something, you tell others about it openly and clearly. 秘密にしない □ *His wife made no secret of her hatred for the formal occasions.* 彼の妻は公式の場に対する嫌悪を隠さなかった.

Thesaurus secret また次を参照:

ADJ. hidden, private, unknown; (ant.) known **1**

---

sec|re|tar|ial /sɛkrɪtɛəriəl/ ADJ 形容詞 **Secretarial** work is the work done by a secretary in an office. 秘書の [ADJ n] □ *I was doing temporary secretarial work.* 私は臨時で秘書の仕事をしていた.

sec|re|tari|at /sɛkrɪtɛəriət/ (secretariats) N-COUNT 可算名詞 A **secretariat** is a department that is responsible for the administration of an international political organization. 事務局 □ *...the U.N. secretariat.* 国連事務局.

sec|re|tary /sɛkrɪtɛri/ (secretaries) **1** N-COUNT 可算名詞 A **secretary** is a person who is employed to do office work, such as typing letters, answering phone calls, and arranging meetings. 秘書 **2** N-COUNT 可算名詞 The **secretary** of a company is the person who has the legal duty of keeping the company's records. 事務官 **3** N-COUNT; N-TITLE 可算名詞, 称号名詞 **Secretary** is used in the titles of high officials who are in charge of main government departments. 長官 □ *...a former Venezuelan foreign secretary.* ベネズエラの前外務大臣.

secretary-general (secretaries-general) also Secretary General N-COUNT 可算名詞 The **secretary-general** of an international political organization is the person in charge of its administration. 事務局長 □ *...the United Nations Secretary-General.* 国連事務総長.

Sec|re|tary of State (Secretaries of State) N-COUNT 可算名詞 In the United States, **the Secretary of State** is the head of the government department which deals with foreign affairs. 国務長官

se|crete /sɪkriːt/ (secretes, secreting, secreted) **1** V-T 他動詞 If part of a plant, animal, or human **secretes** a liquid, it produces it. 分泌する [他動詞] □ *The sweat glands secrete water.* 汗腺は水を分泌する [他動詞]. **2** V-T 他動詞 If you **secrete** something somewhere, you hide it there so that nobody will find it. 隠す [LITERARY 文語的] [他動詞] □ *She secreted the gun in the kitchen cabinet.* 彼女は台所の食器戸棚に銃を隠した.

se|cre|tion /sɪkriːʃən/ (secretions) **1** N-UNCOUNT 不可算名詞 **Secretion** is the process by which certain liquid substances are produced by parts of plants or from the bodies of people or animals. 分泌 □ *...the secretion of adrenaline.* アドレナリンの分泌. **2** N-PLURAL 複数名詞 **Secretions** are liquid substances produced by parts of plants or bodies. 分泌液 □ *...gastric secretions.* 胃液分泌.

se|cre|tive /sɪkrətɪv, sɪkriːt/ ADJ 形容詞 If you are **secretive**, you like to have secrets and to keep your knowledge, feelings, or intentions hidden. 秘密主義の □ *Billionaires are usually fairly secretive about the exact amount that they're worth.* 典型的に、億万長者はその正確な財産高についてはかなり秘密主義を通す.

se|cret po|lice N-UNCOUNT 不可算名詞 The **secret police** is a police force in some countries that works secretly and deals with political crimes committed against the government. 秘密警察 [also "the" N] □ *...former members of the secret police.* 秘密警察の元メンバー.

se|cret ser|vice (secret services) **1** N-COUNT 可算名詞 A country's **secret service** is a secret government department whose job is to find out enemy secrets and to prevent its own government's secrets from being discovered. 諜報部 □ *...French secret service agents.* フランスの大統領護衛官. **2** N-COUNT 可算名詞 **The Secret Service** is the government department in the United States which protects the president, the vice president, and their families. 財務省（秘密）検察局 [AM 米国英語] □ *He finished his career as head of the Secret Service team assigned to President Reagan.* 彼は、レーガン大統領に配属された検察局の長官としてその職業人生を終えた.

sect /sɛkt/ (sects) N-COUNT 可算名詞 A **sect** is a group of people that has separated from a larger group and has a particular set of religious or political beliefs. 分派

sec|tar|ian /sɛktɛəriən/ ADJ 形容詞 **Sectarian** means resulting from the differences between different religions. 分派の □ *He was the fifth person to be killed in sectarian violence last week.* 彼は先週の派閥暴力で殺害された5人目の被害者でした. □ *The police said the murder was sectarian.* 殺人は宗教がらみだと警察は言いました.

Word Link sect ≈ cutting : dissect, intersect, section

---

sec|tion /sɛkʃən/ (sections, sectioning, sectioned) **1** N-COUNT 可算名詞 A **section** of something is one of the parts into which it is divided or from which it is formed. 部分 □ *He said it was wrong to single out any section of society for AIDS testing.* エイズの試験に社会の任意グループを選び出すのは間違っていると彼は言った. □ *...the Georgetown section of Washington, D.C.* ワシントンDCのジョージタウン地区. **2** → see also **cross-section** **3** V-T 他動詞 If something is **sectioned**, it is divided into sections. 区分する [usu passive] [他動詞] □ *It holds vegetables in place while they are being peeled or sectioned.* それは皮を剥いたり、分割したりする時、野菜を所定場所に保持する. **4** N-COUNT 可算名詞 A **section** is a diagram of something such as a building or a part of the body. It shows how the object would appear to you if it were cut from top to bottom and looked at from the side. 切断面 □ *For some buildings a vertical section is more informative than a plan.* 建物によっては、平面図よりも垂直断面のほうが有益である.

Word Partnership section は次の語句と使われる:

N.	section **of a city**, section **of a coast**, **rhythm** section, **sports** section **1**
ADJ.	**main** section, **new** section, **thin** section **1** **special** section **1 3**

---

sec|tor /sɛktər/ (sectors) **1** N-COUNT 可算名詞 A particular **sector** of a country's economy is the part connected with that specified type of industry. 部門 □ *...the nation's manufacturing sector.* 国の製造部門. **2** → see also **private sector, public sector** **3** N-COUNT 可算名詞 A **sector** of a large group is a smaller group which is part of it. 部門 □ *Workers who went to the Gulf came from the poorest sectors of Pakistani society.* ペルシャ湾に行った労働者はパキス

タン社会の最貧困地域の出身でした. **4** N-COUNT 可算名詞 A **sector** is an area of a city or country which is controlled by a military force. 戦闘地区 ❑ *Officers were going to retake sectors of the city.* 将校 は町の戦闘地区を奪回するつもりでした.

secu|lar /sɛkyələr/ ADJ 形容詞 You use **secular** to describe things that have no connection with religion. 非宗教的な ❑ *He spoke about preserving the country as a secular state.* 彼は国を非宗教的 な国として持続させることについて話しました.

se|cure /sɪkyʊər/ (**secures, securing, secured**) **1** V-T 他動詞 If you **secure** something that you want or need, you obtain it, often after a lot of effort. 確保する [FORMAL 形式ばった] [他動詞] ❑ *Federal leaders continued their efforts to secure a ceasefire.* 連邦の指 導者たちは休戦を保障する努力を継続しました. **2** V-T 他動詞 If you **secure** a place, you make it safe from harm or attack. 安全にす る [FORMAL 形式ばった] [他動詞] ❑ *Staff withdrew from the main part of the prison but secured the perimeter.* 職員は刑務所の主要部からは撤 退しましたが, 周辺の安全は確保しました. **3** ADJ 形容詞 A **secure** place is tightly locked or well protected, so that people cannot enter it or leave it. 安全な ❑ *We'll make sure our home is as secure as possible from now on.* これからは家庭ができる限り安全に保たれるよ う私たちは保証する. ● **se|cure|ly** ADV 副詞 安全に ❑ *He locked the heavy door securely and kept the key in his pocket.* 彼は重いドアをしっか りと閉めて, 鍵をポケットに入れた. **4** V-T 他動詞 If you **secure** an object, you fasten it firmly to another object. しっかり留める [他 動詞] ❑ *He helped her close the cases up, and then he secured the canvas straps as tight as they would go.* 彼は彼女がケースを閉じるのを手伝 ってから, キャンバスストラップでできるだけきつく締めた. **5** ADJ 形容詞 If an object is **secure**, it is fixed firmly in position. 固定 して ❑ *Check that joints are secure and the wood is sound.* 接合部が固 定され, 木材が正常であることを確認する. ● **se|cure|ly** ADV 副詞 [ADV with v] しっかりと ❑ *Ensure that the frame is securely fixed to the ground with bolts.* フレームをボルトでしっかり確実に地面に固定する. **6** ADJ 形容詞 If you describe something such as a job as **secure**, it is certain not to change or end. 安定した ❑ *...demands for secure wages and employment.* 安定した賃金と雇用に対する要求. ❑ *Senior citizens long for a more predictable and secure future.* 高齢者はより予想 外のことは起こらない, 安定した未来を望んでいる. **7** ADJ 形容詞 A **secure** base or foundation is strong and reliable. ゆるぎない ❑ *He was determined to give his family a secure and solid base.* 彼は家族に揺る ぎない確かな基盤を与えると決意していた. **8** ADJ 形容詞 If you feel **secure**, you feel safe and happy and are not worried about life. 安 心な ❑ *She felt secure and protected when she was with him.* 彼女は彼と いるときは, 安心で, 守られていると感じた. **9** V-T 他動詞 If a loan **is secured**, the person who lends the money may take property such as a house from the person who borrows the money if they fail to repay it. 担保付 [BUSINESS 実業] [usu passive] [他動詞] ❑ *The loan is secured against your home.* ローンは自宅を担保に貸し付けられ ている.

Thesaurus   *secure* また次を参照:

V.	catch, get, obtain; (*ant.*) lose **1**
	attach, fasten **4**
ADJ.	safe, sheltered **8**
	locked, tight **5**

se|cu|rity /sɪkyʊərɪti/ (**securities**) **1** N-UNCOUNT 不可算名 詞 **Security** refers to all the measures that are taken to protect a place, or to ensure that only people with permission enter it or leave it. 警備態勢 ❑ *They are now under a great deal of pressure to tighten their airport security.* 空港警備強化というずいぶんと大きな 圧力が現在かかっている. ❑ *Strict security measures are in force in the capital.* 首都では厳しい警備対策がしかれている. **2** N-UNCOUNT 不 可算名詞 A feeling of **security** is a feeling of being safe and free from worry. 安心 ❑ *He loves the security of a happy home life.* 幸せな 家庭生活がもたらす安心感を大事にする. ❑ *If an alarm gives you that feeling of security, then it's worth carrying.* 警報器があることで安心する のであれば, 携帯する価値はある. ● PHRASE 句 If something gives

you **a false sense of security**, it makes you believe that you are safe when you are not. 誤った安心感 **3** N-UNCOUNT 不可算名詞 If something is **security** for a loan, you promise to give that thing to the person who lends you money, if you fail to pay the money back. 担保 [BUSINESS 実業] ❑ *The central bank will provide special loans, and the banks will pledge the land as security.* 中央銀行は特別貸 し付けを用意し, 諸銀行は土地を担保とするだろう. **4** N-PLURAL 複 数名詞 **Securities** are stocks, shares, bonds, or other certificates that you buy in order to earn regular interest from them or to sell them later for a profit. 有価証券 [BUSINESS 実業] ❑ *National banks can package their own mortgages and underwrite them as securities.* 国 立銀行は自身の抵当を一括して, 有価証券として保証することができ る. **5** → see also **Social Security**

se|cu|rity cam|era (**security cameras**) N-COUNT 可算名詞 A **security camera** is a video camera that records people's activities in order to detect and prevent crime. 防犯カメラ

Se|cu|rity Coun|cil N-PROPER 固有名詞 The **Security Council** is the committee which governs the United Nations. It has permanent representatives from the United States, Russia, China, France, and the United Kingdom, and temporary representatives from some other countries. 安全保障理事会

se|cu|rity guard (**security guards**) N-COUNT 可算名詞 A **security guard** is someone whose job is to protect a building or to collect and deliver large amounts of money. 警備員, 護衛

se|cu|rity risk (**security risks**) N-COUNT 可算名詞 If you describe someone as a **security risk**, you mean that they may be a threat to the safety of a country or organization. 危険人物 ❑ *Individuals considered a security risk will have to report to immigration authorities within 30 days.* 危険人物と考えられた個人は, 30日以内に移 民局に出頭しなければならないだろう.

se|dan /sɪdæn/ (**sedans**) N-COUNT 可算名詞 A **sedan** is a car with seats for four or more people, a fixed roof, and a trunk that is separate from the part of the car that you sit in. セダン型自動車 [AM 米国英語] → see **car**

se|date /sɪdeɪt/ (**sedates, sedating, sedated**) **1** ADJ 形容詞 If you describe someone or something as **sedate**, you mean that they are quiet and rather dignified, though perhaps a bit dull. 平 静な ❑ *She took them to visit her sedate, elderly cousins.* 彼女は物静か な初老のいとこたちに会いに, 彼らを連れて行った. ❑ *Her life was sedate, almost mundane.* 彼女の人生は平静で, ほとんど平凡なもの であった. **2** ADJ 形容詞 If you move along at a **sedate** pace, you move slowly, in a controlled way. ゆっくりと ❑ *We set off again at a more sedate pace.* 私たちはもっとゆっくりとした歩調で再び出発し た. **3** V-T 他動詞 If someone **is sedated**, they are given a drug to calm them or to make them sleep. 鎮静剤を与える ❑ *The patient is sedated with intravenous use of sedative drugs.* その患者は静脈経由の鎮 静剤で安静にしている.

se|da|tion /sɪdeɪʃən/ N-UNCOUNT 不可算名詞 If someone is **under sedation**, they have been given medicine or drugs in order to calm them or make them sleep. 鎮静状態 ❑ *His mother was under sedation after the boy's body was brought back from Germany.* 少年の遺 体がドイツから運ばれてきてからその子の母親は鎮静剤を与えられた 状態であった.

seda|tive /sɛdətɪv/ (**sedatives**) N-COUNT 可算名詞 A **sedative** is a medicine or drug that calms you or makes you sleep. 鎮静剤 ❑ *They use opium as a sedative, rather than as a narcotic.* アヘンを麻薬と してではなく鎮静剤として使用している.

sed|en|tary /sɛdənteri/ ADJ 形容詞 Someone who has a **sedentary** lifestyle or job sits down a lot of the time and does not do much exercise. ほとんど座ってばかりいる ❑ *Obesity and a sedentary lifestyle has been linked with an increased risk of heart disease.* 肥満と座ってばかりいる生活様式は, 心臓病の危険が増大することに つながりがある.

sedi|ment /sɛdɪmənt/ (**sediments**) N-VAR 可変性名詞 **Sediment** is solid material that settles at the bottom of a liquid, especially earth and pieces of rock that have been carried along and then left somewhere by water, ice, or wind. 沈殿物 ❑ *Many organisms that die in the sea are soon buried by sediment.* 海中で死ぬ生 物の多くは, じきに沈殿物で埋められる. → see **rock**

se|duce /sɪdus/ (**seduces, seducing, seduced**) **1** V-T 他動詞 If something **seduces** you, it is so attractive that it makes you do something that you would not otherwise do. 引き付ける ❑ *The view of lake and plunging cliffs seduces visitors.* 湖や急な絶壁の景色が 訪問客を魅惑する. ● **se|duc|tion** /sɪdʌkʃən/ N-VAR 可変性名詞 (**seductions**) 魅惑 ❑ *...the seduction of words.* 言葉の魅惑. **2** V-T 他 動詞 If someone **seduces** another person, they use their charm to persuade that person to have sex with them. 口説く ❑ *She has set out to seduce Stephen.* 彼女はスティーブンを誘惑しようと試みている. ● **se|duc|tion** N-VAR 可変性名詞 くどき ❑ *Her methods of seduction are subtle.* 彼女の誘惑方法は巧妙である.

se|duc|tive /sɪdʌktɪv/ **1** ADJ 形容詞 Something that is **seductive** is very attractive or makes you want to do something that you would not otherwise do. 魅惑的な ❏ *It's a seductive argument.* 人の気を引く議論だ ● **se|duc|tive|ly** ADV 副詞 魅惑的に ❏ *...his seductively simple assertion.* 魅惑的なほど単純な彼の主張 **2** ADJ 形容詞 A person who is **seductive** is very attractive sexually. 色気のある ❏ *...a seductive woman.* 色っぽい女 ● **se|duc|tive|ly** ADV 副詞 色っぽく ❏ *...looking seductively over her shoulder.* 誘惑するように肩越しに見ながら

---

see

❶ VERB USES
❷ EXPRESSIONS, PHRASES AND CONVENTIONS
❸ PHRASAL VERBS

---

❶ see /siː/ (**sees, seeing, saw, seen**) **1** V-T/V-I 他動詞/自動詞 When you **see** something, you notice it using your eyes. 見える [no cont] ❏ *You can't see colors at night.* 夜は色が見えない。❏ *She can see, hear, touch, smell, and taste.* 彼女は見ること、聞くこと、触ること、匂いをかぐことができ、味が分かる。**2** V-T 他動詞 If you **see** someone, you visit them or meet them. 会う ❏ *I saw him yesterday.* 昨日彼に会った。❏ *Mick wants to see you in his office right away.* ミックが今すぐ彼の事務所で君に会いたいそうだ。**3** V-T 他動詞 If you **see** an entertainment such as a play, movie, concert, or sports game, you watch it. 見る、見物する [no cont] ❏ *I haven't been to see a movie in 10 years.* 私はもう10年も映画を見に行っていない。**4** V-T/V-I 他動詞/自動詞 If you **see** that something is true or exists, you realize by observing that it is true or exists. 見て知る [no cont] ❏ *I could see she was lonely.* 私は彼女が寂しいのがわかった。❏ *...a lot of people saw what was happening but did nothing about it.* 何が起こっているのか見てわかっている人は多くいたが、誰も何もしなかった。❏ *My taste has changed a bit over the years as you can see.* ご覧のように、年月を重ねるにつれて私の好みが少し変わっている。**5** V-T 他動詞 If you **see** what someone means or **see** why something happened, you understand what they mean or understand why it happened. 理解する [no cont, no passive] ❏ *Oh, I see what you're saying.* はあ、おっしゃることはわかります。❏ *I really don't see any reason for changing it.* 変更する理由が私には全くわからない。**6** V-T 他動詞 If you **see** someone or something **as** a certain thing, you have the opinion that they are that thing. みなす ❏ *She saw him as a visionary, but her father saw him as a man who couldn't make a living.* 彼女は彼を空想家とみなしたが、彼女の父親は生活能力がない男とみなした。❏ *Others saw it as a betrayal.* 他の人はそれを裏切りとみなした。❏ *As I see it, Steve has three choices open to him.* 私の考えでは、スティーブには選択肢が3つある。**7** V-T 他動詞 If you **see** a particular quality in someone, you believe they have that quality. If you ask what someone **sees** in a particular person or thing, you want to know what they find attractive about that person or thing. 認める [no cont, no passive] ❏ *Frankly, I don't know what Paul sees in her.* 正直に言って、ポールが彼女のどこがいいと思っているのかわからない。**8** V-T 他動詞 If you **see** something happening in the future, you imagine it, or predict that it will happen. 想像する;予測する [no cont] ❏ *A good idea, but can you see Taylor trying it?* いい考えだけど、テーラーがやってみると思うかい? **9** V-T 他動詞 If a period of time or a person **sees** a particular change or event, it takes place during that period of time or while that person is alive. 目撃する [no passive] ❏ *Yesterday saw the resignation of the chief financial officer.* 昨日首席財務担当官が辞任した。❏ *He had worked with the general for three years and was sorry to see him go.* 彼は3年間その将軍付きで働いていたが、彼が退任するのを見るのを残念に思った。**10** V-T 他動詞 If you **see that** something is done or if you **see to it that** it is done, you make sure that it is done. 取り計らう ❏ *See that you take care of him.* しっかりと彼の世話をしてくれ。**11** V-T 他動詞 If you **see** someone to a particular place, you accompany them to make sure that they get there safely, or to show politeness. 見送る ❏ *He didn't offer to see her to her car.* 彼女を車まで見送ろうとはしなかった。**12** V-T 他動詞 If you **see** a lot **of** someone, you often meet each other or visit each other. 会う、会いに行く ❏ *We used to see quite a lot of his wife, Carolyn.* 彼の妻のキャロリンとよく会っていたものだった。**13** V-T 他動詞 If you **are seeing** someone, you spend time with them socially, and are having a romantic or sexual relationship. 交際する ❏ *My husband was still seeing her and he was having an affair with her.* 私の夫はまだ彼女と付き合っていて、情事を重ねていた。**14** V-T 他動詞 **See** is used in books to indicate to readers that they should look at another part of the book, or at another book, because more information is given there. 参照する [only imper] ❏ *Surveys consistently find that men report feeling safe on the street after dark. See, for example, Hindelang and Garofalo (1978, p.127).* 調査では一貫して、男は暗くなっても通りは安全と感じていると報告している。例として、ヒンデラングとガロファロ（1978年、127ページ）を参照。

Thesaurus	*see* また次を参照:
v.	glimpse, look, observe, watch **❶ 1**
	grasp, observe, understand **❶ 5**

❷ see /siː/ (**sees, seeing, saw, seen**) **1** V-T 他動詞 You can use **see** in expressions to do with finding out information. For example, if you say "**I'll see what's happening**," you mean that you intend to find out what is happening. 調べる ❏ *Let me just see what the next song is.* 次の歌は何かちょっと見てみよう。❏ *Every time we asked our mother, she said, "Well, see what your father says."* 母に尋ねる度ごとに、母は「さあね、お父さんが何と言うか聞いてみてよ」と言った。**2** V-T 他動詞 You can use **see** in expressions in which you promise to try and help someone. For example, if you say "**I'll see if I can do it**," you mean that you will try to do the thing concerned. 見てみる ❏ *I'll see if I can call her for you.* 君のために彼女を呼んであげるかやってみよう。**3** V-T 他動詞 Some writers use **see** in expressions such as **we saw** and **as we have seen** to refer to something that has already been explained or described. 読む ❏ *We saw in Chapter 16 how annual cash budgets are produced.* 年間の現金予算がどのようにして生み出されるかを第16章でみた。❏ *Laws are often not clear, as we saw in Chapter 1.* 第1章で見たように、法律はしばしば明確でないことがある。**4** PHRASE 句 You can use **seeing that** or **seeing as** to introduce a reason for what you are saying. 〜であることを考えると [INFORMAL, SPOKEN くだけた、口語] ❏ *Seeing as Mr. Moreton is a doctor, I assume he is reasonably intelligent.* モレトン氏は医者であるから、それなりに聡明であると思う。**5** CONVENTION 慣習表現 You can say "**I see**" to indicate that you understand what someone is telling you. なるほど [SPOKEN 口語, FORMULAE 決まり文句] ❏ *"He came home in my car." — "I see."* 「彼は私の車で家に帰ってきた」「なるほど」 **6** CONVENTION 慣習表現 People say "**I'll see**" or "**We'll see**" to indicate that they do not intend to make a decision immediately, and will decide later. 考えておこう ❏ *We'll see. It's a possibility.* 考えておこう。それは可能性の1つだ。**7** CONVENTION 慣習表現 People say "**let me see**" or "**let's see**" when they are trying to remember something, or are trying to find something. ええと ❏ *Let's see, they're six – no, make that five hours ahead of us.* ええと、彼らは我々より6時間、いや違う、5時間進んでいる。**8** PHRASE 句 If you try to make someone **see sense** or **see reason**, you try to make them realize that they are wrong or are being stupid. 道理が分かる ❏ *He was hopeful that by sitting together they could both see sense and live as good neighbors.* 彼は一緒に座って話すことで彼らは共に物の道理がわかり、近所同士としてうまくやっていけると希望を持っていた。**9** CONVENTION 慣習表現 You can say "**you see**" when you are explaining something to someone, to encourage them to listen and understand. ねえ [SPOKEN 口語] ❏ *Well, you see, you shouldn't really feel that way about it.* まあ、だって、実はそのことについてそんなふうに感じるべきじゃないんです。**10** CONVENTION 慣習表現 "**See you**," "**be seeing you**," and "**see you later**" are ways of saying goodbye to someone when you expect to meet them again soon. じゃあまた [INFORMAL, SPOKEN くだけた、口語, FORMULAE 決まり文句] ❏ *"Talk to you later." – "All right. See you, love."* 「後でじゃまた後で」「うん。じゃあね、あなた」 **11** CONVENTION 慣習表現 You can say "**You'll see**" to someone if they do not agree with you about what you think will happen in the future, and you believe that you will be proved right. いまに分かる ❏ *The thrill wears off after a few years of marriage. You'll see.* 結婚して数年経つとスリルが消えていくから。いまに分かる。**12** to **have seen better days →** see **day** **13** to **be seen dead →** see **dead** **14** as **far as the eye can see →** see **eye** **15** to **see eye to eye →** see **eye** **16** as **far as I can see →** see **far** **17** to **see fit →** see **fit** **18** to **see red →** see **red** **19** **wait and see →** see **wait**

You use **see** to talk about things that you are aware of because a visual impression reaches your eyes. You often use **can** in this case. ❏ *I can see the fax here on the desk.* If you want to say that someone is paying attention to something they can see, you say that they **are looking at** it or **are watching** it. In general, you **look at** something that is not moving, while you **watch** something that is moving or changing. ❏ *I asked him to look at the picture above his bed... He watched Blake run down the stairs.*

❸ see /siː/ (**sees, seeing, saw, seen**)
▶ **see about** PHRASAL VERB 句動詞 When you **see about** something, you arrange for it to be done or provided. 手配をする ❏ *Tony announced it was time to see about lunch.* 昼ご飯を用意する時間だとトニーが知らせた。
▶ **see off** PHRASAL VERB 句動詞 When you **see** someone **off**, you go with them to the station, airport, or port that they are leaving from, and say goodbye to them there. 見送る ❏ *Ben had planned a steak dinner for himself after seeing Jackie off on her plane.* ジャッキーが飛行機に乗るのを見送ったあと、ベンは1人でステーキの食事をするつもりであった。
▶ **see out** PHRASAL VERB 句動詞 If you **see out** a period of time, you continue to do what you are doing until that period of time is

over. 最後までする □ *The lease runs for 21 years, and they are committed to seeing out that time.* 賃借期間は21年間であるが，彼らは期限まで続ける覚悟でいる.

▶ **see through** 1 PHRASAL VERB 句動詞 If you **see through** someone or their behavior, you realize what their intentions are, even though they are trying to hide them. 見抜く □ *I saw through your little ruse from the start.* 私は取るに足りないお前のたくらみは最初から見抜いていた. 2 → see also **see-through**

▶ **see to** PHRASAL VERB 句動詞 If you **see to** something that needs attention, you deal with it. 処置をする □ *While Franklin saw to the luggage, Sara took Eleanor home.* フランクリンが荷物の処理をしている間に，セアラはエレナを家に連れて帰った.

seed /síːd/ (**seeds, seeding, seeded**) 1 N-VAR 可変название名詞 A **seed** is the small, hard part of a plant from which a new plant grows. 種 □ *I sow the seed in pots of soil-based compost.* 土壌を基にした堆肥を入れた鉢にその種をまく. 2 V-T 他動詞 If you **seed** a piece of land, you plant seeds in it. 種をまく □ *Men mowed the wide lawns and seeded them.* 男どもは広い芝地を刈って種をまいた. □ *The primroses should begin to seed themselves down the steep hillside.* 急な丘の斜面でサクラソウが種を落とし始めるころだ. 3 N-PLURAL 複数名詞 You can refer to the **seeds of** something when you want to talk about the beginning of a feeling or process that gradually develops and becomes stronger or more important. 根源 [LITERARY 文語的] □ *He raised questions meant to plant seeds of doubts in the minds of jurors.* 彼は陪審員の心に疑惑の種を植え付けることを意図した質問をした. 4 N-COUNT 可算名詞 In sports such as tennis or badminton, a **seed** is a player who has been ranked according to his or her ability. シード選手 □ ...*Roger Federer, Wimbledon's top seed and the world No.1.* ウインブルドンのトップシード選手であり，世界一であるロジャー・フェデラー. 5 V-T 他動詞 When a player or a team is **seeded** in a sports competition, they are ranked according to their ability. シードする [usu passive] □ *The Longhorns have won a national title and are seeded first overall.* ロングホーンズチームは全国選手権で優勝し，総合で第1シードとなった. □ *He is seeded second, behind Brad Beven.* ブラッド・ベーヴェンの後に続いて，第2シードされた. 6 PHRASE 句 If vegetable plants **go to seed**, they produce flowers and seeds as well as leaves. 種ができる □ ...*plants that had long since flowered, gone to seed, and died.* とっくの昔に花が咲き，種ができ，枯れた植物 7 PHRASE 句 If you say that someone or something **has gone to seed**, you mean that they have become much less attractive, healthy, or efficient. 盛りが過ぎる □ *He says the economy has gone to seed.* 経済は衰えてしまったと彼は言う. □ ...*a retired cop who has gone to seed.* 盛りの過ぎてしまった退職警官
→ see **flower, fruit, plant, rice**

seed capi|tal N-UNCOUNT 不可算名詞 **Seed capital** is an amount of money that a new company needs to pay for the costs of producing a business plan so that they can raise further capital to develop the company. 種子資本 [BUSINESS 実業] □ *I am negotiating with financiers to raise seed capital for my latest venture.* 私の最も新しい投機事業について種子資本を集めるために，私は金融業者たちと交渉中である.

seed|ling /síːdlɪŋ/ (**seedlings**) N-COUNT 可算名詞 A **seedling** is a young plant that has been grown from a seed. 苗

seed mon|ey N-UNCOUNT 不可算名詞 **Seed money** is money that is given to someone to help them start a new business or project. 着手資金 [BUSINESS 実業] □ *The government will give seed money to the project.* 政府はその計画に着手金を与えるだろう.

seedy /síːdi/ (**seedier, seediest**) ADJ 形容詞 If you describe a person or place as **seedy**, you disapprove of them because they look dirty and messy, or they have a bad reputation. みすぼらしい [DISAPPROVAL 不賛成] □ *Frank ran errands for a seedy local villain.* フランクは怪しげな田舎の悪党の走り使いをした. □ *We were staying in a seedy hotel close to the red light district.* 風俗街に近いいかがわしいホテルに宿泊中であった.

See|ing Eye dog (**Seeing Eye dogs**) also **Seeing-Eye dog** N-COUNT 可算名詞 商標 A **Seeing Eye dog** is a dog that has been trained to lead a blind person. 盲導犬 [AM 米国英語, TRADEMARK]
→ see **disability**

seek /síːk/ (**seeks, seeking, sought**) 1 V-T 他動詞 If you **seek** something such as a job or a place to live, you try to find one. 探す [FORMAL 形式ばった] □ *They have had to seek work as laborers.* 肉体労働者としての仕事を探さなければならなかった. □ *Four people who sought refuge in the Italian embassy have left voluntarily.* イタリア大使館に保護を求めた4名は自発的に立ち去った. 2 V-T 他動詞 When someone **seeks** something, they try to obtain it. 要求する [FORMAL 形式ばった] □ *The prosecutors have warned they will seek the death penalty.* 検察官側は死刑を要求する意思であると警告している. 3 V-T 他動詞 If you **seek** someone's help or advice, you contact them in order to ask for it. 求める [FORMAL 形式ばった] □ *Always seek professional legal advice before entering into any agreement.* どんな契約を結ぶ前にも常に専門法律家の助言を求めてください. □ *On important issues, they seek a second opinion.* 重要な件については，別の意見も求める. 4 V-T 他動詞 If you **seek to** do something, you try to do it.

しようと努める [FORMAL 形式ばった] □ *He also denied that he would seek to annex the country.* その国を併合しようとすることも否定した.

▶ **seek out** PHRASAL VERB 句動詞 If you **seek out** someone or something or **seek** them **out**, you keep looking for them until you find them. 探し出す □ *Now is the time for local companies to seek out business opportunities in Europe.* いまこそ地元の会社がヨーロッパでの事業チャンスを探し出すときである.

Word Partnership *seek* は次の語句と使われる:

N.   seek **asylum**, seek **election**, seek **employment**, seek **shelter** 1 2
     seek **justice**, seek **revenge** 2
     seek **advice**, seek **approval**, seek **assistance/help**, seek **counseling**, seek **permission**, seek **protection**, seek **support** 3

---

seek|er /síːkər/ (**seekers**) 1 N-COUNT 可算名詞 A **seeker** is someone who is looking for or trying to get something. 探求者 □ *I am a seeker after truth.* 私は真実を追求する者である. 2 → see also **asylum seeker**

seem /síːm/ (**seems, seeming, seemed**) 1 V-LINK 連結動詞 You use **seem** to say that someone or something gives the impression of having a particular quality, or of happening in the way you describe. 思われる [no cont] □ *The explosions seemed quite close by.* 爆発はたいそう近くのように思われた. □ *To everyone who knew them, they seemed an ideal couple.* 彼らを知っている人の誰にとっても，彼らは理想的なカップルのように見えた. □ *The calming effect seemed to last for about ten minutes.* 気を静める効果は10分くらい続くように思えた. □ *It seems that the attack was carefully planned.* その攻撃は細心に計画されたもののように見えた. □ *It seemed as if she'd been gone forever.* まるで彼女が永遠に去っていったように思えた. 2 V-LINK 連結動詞 You use **seem** when you are describing your own feelings or thoughts, or describing something that has happened to you, in order to make your statement less forceful. 気がする [VAGUENESS あいまいさ] [no cont] □ *I seem to have lost all my self-confidence.* 私は自信が全くなくなってしまったような気がする. □ *I seem to remember giving you very precise instructions.* 私はあなたに非常に正確な指示をしたのを覚えているような気がする. 3 PHRASE 句 If you say that you **cannot seem** or **could not seem to** do something, you mean that you have tried to do it and were unable to. どうしてもできないようだ □ *No matter how hard I try I cannot seem to catch up on all the bills.* どんなに頑張ってみても，請求書の全部には支払いができないようだ.

seem|ing /síːmɪŋ/ ADJ 形容詞 **Seeming** means appearing to be the case, but not necessarily the case. For example, if you talk about someone's **seeming** ability to do something, you mean that they appear to be able to do it, but you are not certain. 外見上の [FORMAL 形式ばった, VAGUENESS あいまいさ] [ADJ n] □ *Wall Street analysts have been highly critical of the company's seeming inability to control costs.* ウォールストリート分析家たちは，その会社の一見無能なコスト管理を酷評している.

seem|ing|ly /síːmɪŋli/ 1 ADV 副詞 If something is **seemingly** the case, you mean that it appears to be the case, even though it may not really be so. 一見したところ [ADV adj/adv] □ *A seemingly endless line of trucks waits in vain to load up.* 一見したところ終わりなく続くトラックの列が，積荷できずむなしく待っている. 2 ADV 副詞 You use **seemingly** when you want to say that something seems to be true. どうやら―のようで [VAGUENESS あいまいさ] □ *He has moved to Spain, seemingly to enjoy a slower style of life.* 彼はどうやらゆったりした生活様式を楽しむためにスペインに引っ越していった.

seen /síːn/ **Seen** is the past participle of **see**.

seep /síːp/ (**seeps, seeping, seeped**) 1 V-I 自動詞 If something such as liquid or gas **seeps** somewhere, it flows slowly and in small amounts into a place where it should not go. しみ出る □ *Radioactive water had seeped into underground reservoirs.* 放射性の水が地下の貯水池にしみ込んでいた. □ *The gas is seeping out of the rocks.* ガスが岩からしみ出している. ● N-COUNT 可算名詞 **Seep** is also a noun. 滲出(しんしゅつ)する □ ...*an oil seep.* 石油のしみ出るところ 2 V-I 自動詞 If something such as information or an emotion **seeps** into or out of a place, it enters or leaves it gradually. 漏れる □ *Many of us thrive on competition, but it can seep into areas of our lives where we do not want it.* 競走が生きがいである人が多いが，競走したくない人生の領域にもそれが忍び込んでくることがある.

see|saw /síːsɔː/ (**seesaws**) also **see-saw** N-COUNT 可算名詞 A **seesaw** is a long board which is balanced in the middle. To play on it, a child sits on each end, and when one end goes up, the other goes down. シーソー □ *There was a sandpit, a seesaw and a swing in the playground.* 遊び場には砂場とシーソーとぶらんこがあった.

seethe /síːð/ (**seethes, seething, seethed**) V-I 自動詞 When you **are seething**, you are very angry about something but do not express your feelings about it. 怒りで煮えくり返る □ *She took it calmly at first but under the surface was seething.* 彼女は最初は落ち着

いてそれを受け止めていたが，内心は煮えくり返っていた．❏*She put a hand on her hip, grinning derisively, while I seethed with rage.* 私が怒りで煮えくり返っている間，彼女は腰に片手を当ててあなどり笑いしていた．

see-through /ˌ/ ADJ 形容詞 **See-through** clothes are made of thin cloth, so that you can see a person's body or underwear through them. 透けて見える ❏*She was wearing a white, see-through blouse, a red bra showing beneath.* 彼女は赤いブラジャーが下に透けて見える，白いブラウスを着ていた．

seg|ment /ˈsɛɡmənt/ (**segments**) **1** N-COUNT 可算名詞 A **segment of** something is one part of it, considered separately from the rest. 部分 ❏*...the poorer segments of society.* 社会のより貧しい層 **2** N-COUNT 可算名詞 A **segment** of fruit such as an orange or grapefruit is one of the sections into which it is easily divided. 袋 ❏*Peel all the fruit except the lime and separate into segments.* ライムを除いて果物は全部皮をむいて，1つ1つの袋に分けてください **3** N-COUNT 可算名詞 A **segment** of a circle is one of the two parts into which it is divided when you draw a straight line through it. 弓形 ❏*The other children stood around the circle, one in each segment.* 円の弓形の中に1人ずつ立ち，他の子どもたちは円の周りに立った．

seg|re|gate /ˈsɛɡrɪɡeɪt/ (**segregates, segregating, segregated**) V-T 他動詞 To **segregate** two groups of people or things means to keep them physically apart from each other. 分離する ❏*A large detachment of police was used to segregate the two rival camps of protesters.* 相対立する2つの抗議デモ陣営を分離するするために，大規模な警官の派遣隊が使われた．

seg|re|gat|ed /ˈsɛɡrɪɡeɪtɪd/ ADJ 形容詞 **Segregated** buildings or areas are kept for the use of one group of people who are the same race, sex, or religion, and no other group is allowed to use them. 分離された ❏*...racially segregated schools.* 人種的に分離された学校

seg|re|ga|tion /ˌsɛɡrɪˈɡeɪʃən/ N-UNCOUNT 不可算名詞 **Segregation** is the official practice of keeping people apart, usually people of different sexes, races, or religions. 分離，隔離 ❏*The Supreme Court unanimously ruled that racial segregation in schools was unconstitutional.* 最高裁判所は全員一致で，学校での人種隔離は憲法違反であると裁決した．

seis|mic /ˈsaɪzmɪk/ **1** ADJ 形容詞 **Seismic** means caused by or relating to an earthquake. 地震の [ADJ n] ❏*Earthquakes produce two types of seismic waves.* 地震には2種類の地震波がある． **2** ADJ 形容詞 A **seismic** shift or change is a very sudden or dramatic change. とてつもない [usu ADJ n] ❏*I have never seen such a seismic shift in public opinion in such a short period of time.* こんなに短期間で大衆の意見がこれほど劇的に変化したのは今までに全く見たことがない．

→ see **earthquake**

seize /siz/ (**seizes, seizing, seized**) **1** V-T 他動詞 If you **seize** something, you take hold of it quickly, firmly, and forcefully. つかみ取る ❏*"Leigh," he said seizing my arm to hold me back.* 私を引きもどそうと腕をつかんで「リー」と彼は言った． **2** V-T 他動詞 When a group of people **seize** a place or **seize** control of it, they take control of it quickly and suddenly, using force. 占領する，奪う ❏*Troops have seized the airport and railroad terminals.* 部隊は空港の発着ロビーと鉄道の終着駅を占領した． **3** V-T 他動詞 If a government or other authority **seize** someone's property, they take it from them, often by force. 没収する ❏*Police were reported to have seized all copies of this morning's edition of the newspaper.* その新聞の今日の朝刊の発行部数は全て警察が没収したと伝えられた． **4** V-T 他動詞 When someone **is seized**, they are arrested or captured. 捕らえる ❏*U.N. officials say two military observers were seized by the Khmer Rouge yesterday.* 国連当局者は，昨日ク国軍監視要員2名がクメール・ルージュに捕らえられたと言っている． **5** V-T 他動詞 When you **seize** an opportunity, you take advantage of it and do something that you want to do. 逃さずつかむ ❏*During the riots hundreds of people seized the opportunity to steal property.* 暴動中に何百という人が機会を逃さず財物を盗んだ．

▶ **seize on** PHRASAL VERB 句動詞 If you **seize on** something or **seize upon** it, you show great interest in it, often because it is useful to you. 飛びつく ❏*Newspapers seized on the results as proof that global warming wasn't really happening.* 各新聞社は，地球温暖化は実際は起こっていないという証拠としてその結果に飛びついた．

▶ **seize up** **1** PHRASAL VERB 句動詞 If a part of your body **seizes up**, it suddenly stops working, because you have strained it or because you are getting old. 動かなくなる ❏*After two days' exertions, it's the arms and hands that seize up, not the legs.* 2日間ほど激しく活動したら，動かなくなるのは腕や手であり，足ではない． **2** PHRASAL VERB 句動詞 If something such as an engine **seizes up**, it stops working, because it has not been properly cared for. 止まる ❏*She put diesel fuel, instead of gasoline, into the tank causing the motor to seize up.* 彼女がガソリンではなくディーゼル燃料をタンクに入れたので，モーターが動かなくなった．

sei|zure /ˈsiʒər/ (**seizures**) **1** N-COUNT 可算名詞 If someone has a **seizure**, they have a sudden violent attack of an illness,

especially one that affects their heart or brain. 発作 ❏*...a mild cardiac seizure.* 軽い心臓発作 **2** N-COUNT 可算名詞 If there is a **seizure of** power or a **seizure of** an area of land, a group of people suddenly take control of the place, using force. 強奪，占領 ❏*...the seizure of territory through force.* 武力行使による領地占領 **3** N-COUNT 可算名詞 When an organization such as the police or customs makes a **seizure of** illegal goods, they find them and take them away. 没収 ❏*Police have made one of the biggest seizures of heroin there's ever been.* 警察はヘロインのいままでで最大規模の押収の1つを成し遂げた．

sel|dom /ˈsɛldəm/ ADV 副詞 If something **seldom** happens, it happens only occasionally. めったにない ❏*They seldom speak.* めったに話をしない ❏*I've seldom felt so happy.* 私はこれほど幸せに感じたことはめったにない．

se|lect /sɪˈlɛkt/ (**selects, selecting, selected**) **1** V-T 他動詞 If you **select** something, you choose it from a number of things of the same kind. 選ぶ ❏*Voters are selecting candidates for both U.S. Senate seats and for 52 congressional seats.* 投票者たちは，米国上院の議席と下院の52議席の両方の候補者を選択しているところである． ❏*With a difficult tee shot, select a club which will keep you short of the trouble.* ティーショットが難しい時は，問題に至らないようなクラブを選んでください． **2** V-T 他動詞 If you **select** a file or a piece of text on a computer screen, you click on it so that it is marked in a different color, usually in order for you to give the computer an instruction relating to that file or piece of text. 選択する [COMPUTING コンピューティング] ❏*I selected a file and pressed the delete key.* 私はファイルを1つ選択して削除のキーを押した． **3** ADJ 形容詞 A **select** group is a small group of some of the best people or things of their kind. 選び抜かれた [ADJ n] ❏*...a select group of French cheeses.* えり抜きのフランス産チーズ各種 **4** ADJ 形容詞 If you describe something as **select**, you mean it has many desirable features, but is available only to people who have a lot of money or who belong to a high social class. 高級な ❏*Christian Lacroix is throwing a very lavish and very select party.* クリスチャン・ラクロワは非常にぜいたくで非常に高級なパーティーを開催予定だ．

Thesaurus	**select** また次を参照：
V.	choose, pick out, take **1**
ADJ.	best, exclusive **3** **4**

se|lec|tion /sɪˈlɛkʃən/ (**selections**) **1** N-UNCOUNT 不可算名詞 **Selection** is the act of selecting one or more people or things from a group. 選抜 ❏*...Darwin's principles of natural selection.* ダーウィンの自然淘汰の原理 ❏*Dr. Sullivan's selection to head the Department of Health was greeted with satisfaction.* サリバン博士が保健省の長として選ばれたことは満足の意を持って迎えられた． **2** N-COUNT 可算名詞 A **selection** of people or things is a set of them that have been selected from a larger group. 選ばれた人（もの）❏*...this selection of popular songs.* この流行歌集 **3** N-COUNT 可算名詞 The **selection of** goods in a store is the particular range of goods that it has available and from which you can choose what you want. 品ぞろえ ❏*It offers the widest selection of antiques of every description in a one-day market.* 1日限りの市では，さまざまなたぐいの骨董品が幅広く取りそろえられている． **4** N-COUNT 可算名詞 In computing, a **selection** is an area of the screen that you have highlighted, for example because you want to copy it to another file. 選択 [COMPUTING コンピューティング]

se|lec|tive /sɪˈlɛktɪv/ **1** ADJ 形容詞 A **selective** process applies only to a few things or people. 精選された [ADJ n] ❏*Selective breeding may result in a greyhound running faster and seeing better than a wolf.* グレイハウンド犬の品種改良は，狼よりも速く走ることができ，視力も上回る結果となるかもしれない． ●**se|lec|tive|ly** ADV 副詞 精選して ❏*Within the project, trees are selectively cut on a 25-year rotation.* その計画内においては，木々は25年回転で選択伐採される． **2** ADJ 形容詞 When someone is **selective**, they choose things carefully, for example, the things that they buy or do. 選択眼のある ❏*Sales still happen, but buyers are more selective.* 安売りはいまだにあるが，買手はいっそう選びかたようになってきている． ●**se|lec|tive|ly** ADV 副詞 [ADV with v] 注意深く選んで ❏*...people on small incomes who wanted to shop selectively.* 物を注意深く選んで買物したいと思っていた低所得の人たち **3** ADJ 形容詞 If you say that someone has a **selective** memory, you disapprove of the fact that they remember certain facts about something and deliberately forget others, often because it is convenient for them to do so. 都合のいいものだけを選ぶ，えり好みの [DISAPPROVAL 不賛成] ❏*We seem to have a selective memory for the best bits of the past.* 我々は過去の最もよかったところを選択的に記憶するようだ． ●**se|lec|tive|ly** ADV 副詞 [ADV with v] 都合のいいものを選択している ❏*...a tendency to remember only the pleasurable effects of the drug and selectively forget all the adverse effects.* 麻薬の楽しいききめだけを覚えていて，悪影響は全て意識的に忘れるという傾向

self /sɛlf/ (**selves**) **1** N-COUNT 可算名詞 Your **self** is your basic personality or nature, especially considered in terms of what you are really like as a person. 自分 ❏*You're looking more like your

usual self. いつもの君に戻ってきているよ. **2** N-COUNT 可算名詞 A person's **self** is the essential part of their nature which makes them different from everyone and everything else. 自分自身 □ *I want to explore and get in touch with my inner self.* 自分自身の心をもっと探って理解したい. □ *The face is the true self visible to others.* 顔は, 自分の本質が他人に見えるところだ.

self-adhesive ADJ 形容詞 Something that is **self-adhesive** is covered on one side with a sticky substance like glue, so that it will stick to surfaces. 接着性の □ *...self-adhesive labels.* 接着ラベル.

self-assured ADJ 形容詞 Someone who is **self-assured** shows confidence in what they say and do because they are sure of their own abilities. 自信のある □ *He's a self-assured, confident negotiator.* 彼は自信と度胸のある交渉者だ.

self-centered ADJ 形容詞 Someone who is **self-centered** is only concerned with their own wants and needs and never thinks about other people. 自己中心の [DISAPPROVAL 不賛成] □ *It's very self-centered to think that people are talking about you.* 人々が自分のうわさをしていると思うのは非常に自己中心的である.

self-confessed ADJ 形容詞 If you describe someone as a **self-confessed** murderer or a **self-confessed** romantic, for example, you mean that they admit openly that they are a murderer or a romantic. 自認している [ADJ n] □ *The self-confessed drug addict was arrested 13 months ago.* その自称麻薬中毒者は13か月前に逮捕された.

self-confidence N-UNCOUNT 不可算名詞 If you have **self-confidence**, you behave confidently because you feel sure of your abilities or value. 自信 □ *With the end of my love affair, I lost all the self-confidence I once had.* 私の恋愛の終結とともに, 私はかつて持っていた自信を全て失ってしまった.

self-confident ADJ 形容詞 Someone who is **self-confident** behaves confidently because they feel sure of their abilities or value. 自信のある □ *She'd blossomed into a self-confident young woman.* 彼女は自信のある若い女性に開花していた.

self-conscious ADJ 形容詞 Someone who is **self-conscious** is easily embarrassed and nervous because they feel that everyone is looking at them and judging them. 自意識過剰な □ *I felt a bit self-conscious in my bikini.* 私はビキニなので少し人前が気になった.

self-contained **1** ADJ 形容詞 You can describe someone or something as **self-contained** when they are complete and separate and do not need help or resources from outside. 自己充足の □ *He seems completely self-contained and he doesn't miss you when you're not there.* 彼は全く自己充足的な男のようで, 君がいなくてもさびしがりはしない. **2** ADJ 形容詞 **Self-contained** accommodations such as an apartment have all their own facilities, so that a person living there does not have to share rooms such as a kitchen or bathroom with other people. 各戸独立式の □ *Her family lives in a self-contained three-bedroom suite in the back of the main house.* 彼女の家族は, 主家の裏にある, 独立完備した3寝室のアパートに住んでいる.

self-control N-UNCOUNT 不可算名詞 **Self-control** is the ability to not show your feelings or not do the things that your feelings make you want to do. 自制心 □ *His self-control, reserve and aloofness were almost inhuman.* 彼の自制心, 遠慮, よそよそしさはほとんど非人間的だった.

self-defense **1** N-UNCOUNT 不可算名詞 **Self-defense** is the use of force to protect yourself against someone who is attacking you. 自己防衛 □ *The women acted in self-defense after years of abuse.* その女性たちは長年虐待された後に自己防衛の行動を取った. **2** N-UNCOUNT 不可算名詞 **Self-defense** is the action of protecting yourself against something bad. 護身 □ *Tai Chi is an ancient form of self-defense.* 太極拳は大昔からの護身術である.

self-determination N-UNCOUNT 不可算名詞 **Self-determination** is the right of a country to be independent, instead of being controlled by a foreign country, and to choose its own form of government. 民族自決権 □ *...Lithuania's right to self-determination.* リトアニアの民族自決の権利

self-employed ADJ 形容詞 If you are **self-employed**, you organize your own work and taxes and are paid by people for a service you provide, rather than being paid a regular salary by a person or a firm. 自営の [BUSINESS 実業] □ *There are no paid holidays or sick leave if you are self-employed.* もし自営業者であれば, 有給休暇も病気休暇もない. ● N-PLURAL 複数名詞 The **self-employed** are people who are self-employed. 自営業者たち □ *We want more support for the self-employed.* 我々は自営業者に対する支持がもっと欲しい.

self-esteem N-UNCOUNT 不可算名詞 Your **self-esteem** is how you feel about yourself. For example, if you have low self-esteem, you do not like yourself, you do not think that you are a valuable person, and therefore you do not behave confidently. 自尊心 □ *Poor self-esteem is at the center of many of the difficulties we experience in our relationships.* 我々が人間関係で経験する困難な問題は, 自尊心が乏しいことが問題の中心であることが多い.

self-evident ADJ 形容詞 A fact or situation that is **self-evident** is so obvious that there is no need for proof or explanation. わかりきった □ *It is self-evident that we will never have enough resources to meet the demand.* 需要を満足させるだけの資源は決して充分にはありえない, ということは自明である.

self-explanatory ADJ 形容詞 Something that is **self-explanatory** is clear and easy to understand without needing any extra information or explanation. 自明の □ *I hope the graphs on the following pages are self-explanatory.* 次ページ以降のグラフは見れば分かると思います.

self-help N-UNCOUNT 不可算名詞 **Self-help** consists of people providing support and help for each other in an informal way, rather than relying on the government, authorities, or other official organizations. 自助 □ *She set up a self-help group for parents with overweight children.* 彼女は肥満児を持つ両親のための助け合いグループを作った.

self-image (**self-images**) N-COUNT 可算名詞 Your **self-image** is the set of ideas you have about your own qualities and abilities. 自己像 □ *Children who have a positive self-image are less likely to present behavior and discipline problems.* 肯定的な自己像を持つ子どもたちは, 行動や規律の問題を起こすことがいっそう少ない.

self-important ADJ 形容詞 If you say that someone is **self-important**, you disapprove of them because they behave as if they are more important than they really are. 尊大な [DISAPPROVAL 不賛成] □ *He was self-important, vain and ignorant.* 彼はうぬぼれが強く, 見えを張り, 無知であった. ● **self-importance** N-UNCOUNT 不可算名詞 尊大 □ *Many visitors complained of his bad manners and self-importance.* 訪問客の多くが彼の行儀の悪さや尊大な態度に苦情を言った.

self-imposed ADJ 形容詞 A **self-imposed** restriction, task, or situation is one that you have deliberately created or accepted for yourself. 自ら自分に課した □ *He returned home after eleven years of self-imposed exile.* 彼は11年間の自主亡命の後に故国に戻った.

self-indulgence (**self-indulgences**) N-VAR 可変性名詞 **Self-indulgence** is the act of allowing yourself to have or do the things that you enjoy very much. 放縦 □ *He prayed to be saved from self-indulgence.* 彼は自堕落から救われるように祈った.

self-indulgent ADJ 形容詞 If you say that someone is **self-indulgent**, you mean that they allow themselves to have or do the things that they enjoy very much. 放縦な, わがままな □ *Why give publicity to this self-indulgent, adolescent oaf?* なぜこのわがままな思春期のまぬけの宣伝をするのか?

self-inflicted ADJ 形容詞 A **self-inflicted** wound or injury is one that you do to yourself deliberately. 自ら傷つけた □ *He is being treated for a self-inflicted gunshot wound.* 彼は自分で発砲した弾丸による負傷の治療中である.

self-interest N-UNCOUNT 不可算名詞 If you accuse someone of **self-interest**, you disapprove of them because they always want to do what is best for themselves rather than for anyone else. 私利 [DISAPPROVAL 不賛成] □ *Their current protests are motivated purely by self-interest.* 彼らの現在の抗議は純粋に私利が動機である.

selfish /sɛlfɪʃ/ ADJ 形容詞 If you say that someone is **selfish**, you mean that he or she cares only about himself or herself, and not about other people. 利己的な [DISAPPROVAL 不賛成] □ *I think I've been very selfish. I've been mainly concerned with myself.* 今まで非常に身勝手だったと思う. 主に自分のことしか考えていなかった. ● **selfishly** ADV 副詞 利己的に □ *Someone has selfishly emptied the cookie jar.* 誰かが勝手にビスケットの入った瓶を空にしてしまった. ● **selfishness** N-UNCOUNT 不可算名詞 自己本位 □ *The arrogance and selfishness of different interest groups never ceases to amaze me.* さまざまな利益団体の横柄さや自己本位にはいつもびっくり仰天させられる.

selfless /sɛlflɪs/ ADJ 形容詞 If you say that someone is **selfless**, you approve of them because they care about other people more than themselves. 無私無欲の [APPROVAL 賛成] □ *She was a wonderful companion and her generosity to me was entirely selfless.* 彼女はすばらしい友であり, 私に対する寛大な行為は全く無私なものだった.

self-pity N-UNCOUNT 不可算名詞 **Self-pity** is a feeling of unhappiness that you have about yourself and your problems, especially when this is unnecessary or greatly exaggerated. 自分に対するあわれみ [DISAPPROVAL 不賛成] □ *I was unable to shake off my self-pity.* 私は自己憐憫 (れんびん) を断ち切れなかった.

self-portrait (**self-portraits**) N-COUNT 可算名詞 A **self-portrait** is a drawing, painting, or written description that you do of yourself. 自画像

self-regulation N-UNCOUNT 不可算名詞 **Self-regulation** is the controlling of a process or activity by the people or organizations that are involved in it rather than by an outside organization such as the government. 自主規制 □ *Competition between companies is too fierce for self-regulation to work.* 自主規制が機能するには, 会社間の競争があまりにも激しすぎる.

S

self-respect N-UNCOUNT 不可算名詞 **Self-respect** is a feeling of confidence and pride in your own ability and worth. 自尊心 ❑ *They have lost not only their jobs, but their homes, their self-respect and even their reason for living.* 彼らは仕事だけでなく，家庭，自尊心，それに生きる目的さえも失っている.

self-righteous ADJ 形容詞 If you describe someone as **self-righteous**, you disapprove of them because they are convinced that they are right in their beliefs, attitudes, and behavior and that other people are wrong. 独りよがりの [DISAPPROVAL 不賛成] ❑ *He is critical of the monks, whom he considers narrow-minded and self-righteous.* 彼は修道士たちが，了見が狭く独善的と考えているので，修道士に対しては批判的だ. ●**self-righteousness** N-UNCOUNT 不可算名詞 ❑ *Her aggressiveness and self-righteousness caused prickles of anger at the back of his neck.* 彼女の攻撃的な性格と独りよがりに彼はむらむらと怒りがこみ上げてきた.

self-service ADJ 形容詞 A **self-service** store, restaurant, or garage is one where you get things for yourself rather than being served by another person. セルフサービス式の ❑ *...a self-service cafeteria with a wide choice.* 幅広い選択のあるセルフサービスの食堂

> Gasoline stations in North America offer **full-service** and **self-service**. In **self-service** gas stations, the customer pumps his own gasoline and pays the attendant. Self-serve gasoline is cheaper than gas pumped by the attendant.

self-study N-UNCOUNT 不可算名詞 **Self-study** is study that you do on your own, without a teacher. 独学 ❑ *Individuals can enrol on self-study courses in the university's language institute.* 個人が大学の言語研究所の独学コースに受講登録ができる.

self-styled ADJ 形容詞 If you describe someone as a **self-styled** leader or expert, you disapprove of them because they claim to be a leader or expert but they do not actually have the right to call themselves this. 自称の [DISAPPROVAL 不賛成] [ADJ n] ❑ *Two of those arrested are said to be self-styled area commanders.* 逮捕されたうちの2人は自称地域指揮官と名乗っている.

self-sufficiency /sɛlf səfɪʃ°nsi/ N-UNCOUNT 不可算名詞 **Self-sufficiency** is the state of being self-sufficient. 自給自足

self-sufficient 🔟 ADJ 形容詞 If a country or group is **self-sufficient**, it is able to produce or make everything that it needs. 自給自足の ❑ *This enabled the country to become self-sufficient in sugar.* これによって国が砂糖の自給自足ができるようになった. 🔟 ADJ 形容詞 Someone who is **self-sufficient** is able to live happily without anyone else. 自立できる ❑ *Although she had various boyfriends, Madeleine was, and remains, fiercely self-sufficient.* マデリンにはさまざまな男友だちがいたが，彼女には激しいほどの自立心があったし今もある.

sell /sɛl/ (sells, selling, sold) 🔟 V-T/V-I 他動詞/自動詞 If you **sell** something that you own, you let someone have it in return for money. 売る ❑ *Catlin sold the paintings to Philadelphia industrialist Joseph Harrison.* カトリンはフィラデルフィアの大実業家ジョセフ・ハリソンに絵を売った. ❑ *The directors sold the business for $14.8 million.* 取締役たちはその事業を1480万ドルで売った. ❑ *When is the best time to sell?* 売る時期はいつが1番良いか? 🔟 V-T 他動詞 If a store **sells** a particular thing, it is available for people to buy there. 販売する ❑ *It sells everything from hair ribbons to oriental rugs.* 髪飾りのリボンから東洋の敷物まで何でも売っている. 🔟 V-I 自動詞 If something **sells for** a particular price, that price is paid for it. 売れる ❑ *Unmodernized property can sell for up to 40 percent of its modernized market value.* 最新式でない不動産は，その不動産を最新式にしたときの市場価格の最高40%で売ることができる. 🔟 V-I 自動詞 If something **sells**, it is bought by the public, usually in fairly large quantities. 売れ行きがいい ❑ *Even if this album doesn't sell and the critics don't like it, we wouldn't ever change.* たとえこの曲集が売れなくても，評論家たちが気に入らなくても，私たちは絶対に変わらない. 🔟 V-T/V-I 他動詞/自動詞 Something that **sells** a product makes people want to buy the product. 売れ行きを促進する ❑ *It is only the sensational that sells news magazines.* 時事週刊誌が売れるのは扇情的なものだけである. ❑ *...the maxim that safety doesn't sell.* 安全は売れないという格言 🔟 V-T 他動詞 If you **sell** someone an idea or proposal, or **sell** someone **on** an idea, you convince them that it is a good one. 売り込む ❑ *She tried to sell me the idea of buying my own paper shredder.* 彼女は自分用の紙裁断機を買うという考えを僕に吹き込もうとした. ❑ *She is hoping she can sell the idea to clients.* 彼女はその案を顧客に売り込むことができるようにと願っている. 🔟 PHRASE 句 If someone **sells** their **body**, they have sex for money. 体を売る ❑ *85 percent said they would rather not sell their bodies for a living.* 85パーセントができれば生活のために売春はしたくないと言った. 🔟 PHRASE 句 If you talk about someone **selling** their **soul** in order to get something, you are criticizing them for abandoning their principles. 魂まで売る [DISAPPROVAL 不賛成] ❑ *...a man who would sell his soul for political viability.* 政治的生存のためには魂までも売る男

▶ **sell off** 🔟 PHRASAL VERB 句動詞 If you **sell** something **off**, you sell it because you need the money. 売り払う ❑ *The company is*

selling off some sites and concentrating on cutting debts. 会社は拠点のいくつかを売り払い，負債を削減することに専念中である. 🔟 → see also **sell-off**

▶ **sell on** PHRASAL VERB 句動詞 If you buy something and then **sell** it **on**, you sell it to someone else soon after buying it, usually in order to make a profit. 売り渡す ❑ *Mr. Farrier bought cars at auctions and sold them on.* ファリヤー氏は競売で車を買い，それらを転売した.

▶ **sell out** 🔟 PHRASAL VERB 句動詞 If a store **sells out** of something, it sells all its stocks of it, so that there is no longer any left for people to buy. 売り尽くす ❑ *Hardware stores have sold out of water pumps and tarpaulins.* あちこちの金物屋は水揚げポンプと防水シートを売り尽くした. 🔟 PHRASAL VERB 句動詞 If a performance, sports event, or other entertainment **sells out**, all the tickets for it are sold. 切符が売り切れる ❑ *Football games often sell out well in advance.* フットボールの試合はしばしば切符が早くから売り切れる. 🔟 PHRASAL VERB 句動詞 When things **sell out**, all of them are available are sold. 売り切れる ❑ *Sleeping bags sold out almost immediately.* 寝袋はほとんどすぐに売り切れた. 🔟 PHRASAL VERB 句動詞 If you accuse someone of **selling out**, you disapprove of the fact that they do something which used to be against their principles, or give in to an opposing group. 変節する; 売り切る [DISAPPROVAL 不賛成] ❑ *You don't have to sell out and work for some corporation.* 君は変節してどこかの会社の仕事をする必要はない. 🔟 PHRASAL VERB 句動詞 If you **sell out**, you sell everything you have, such as your house or your business, because you need the money. 店じまいする ❑ *I'll have a going out of business sale. I'll sell out and move out of here.* 私は閉店売り出しをして，店じまいをしてここを立ち退こうと思う. 🔟 → see also **sell-out, sold out**

Thesaurus		*sell* また次を参照:
v.		barter, exchange, retail; (*ant.*) buy 🔟 🔟

sell-by date (**sell-by dates**) N-COUNT 可算名詞 The **sell-by date** on a food container is the date by which the food should be sold or eaten before it starts to decay. 賞味期限 ❑ *...a piece of cheese four weeks past its sell-by date.* 4週間も賞味期限を過ぎたチーズの1片

Word Link	*ar, er ≈ one who acts as :* buyer, liar, **seller**

sell|er /sɛlər/ (**sellers**) 🔟 N-COUNT 可算名詞 A **seller** of a type of thing is a person or company that sells that type of thing. 販売人 ❑ *...a flower seller.* 花売り 🔟 N-COUNT 可算名詞 In a business deal, the **seller** is the person who is selling something to someone else. 売り手 ❑ *In theory, the buyer could ask the seller to have a test carried out.* 理論的には，買い手は売り手にテストをしてもらうよう依頼することも可能である. 🔟 N-COUNT 可算名詞 If you describe a product as, for example, a big **seller**, you mean that large numbers of it are being sold. 売れ行き ❑ *The gift store's biggest seller is a photo of Nixon meeting Presley.* その土産店で最高に売れているものは，ニクソンがプレスリーと会っている写真である. 🔟 → see also **bestseller**

sel|ler's mar|ket N-SING 単数名詞 When there is a **seller's market** for a particular product, there are fewer of the products for sale than people who want to buy them, so buyers have little choice and prices go up. 売り手市場 [BUSINESS 実業] ❑ *It's a seller's market, and no one is forced to discount to remain competitive.* 売り手市場なので，誰も競争力を維持するために値引きを強いられることはない.

sell|ing point (**selling points**) N-COUNT 可算名詞 A **selling point** is a desirable quality or feature that something has which makes it likely that people will want to buy it. 商品の目玉 [BUSINESS 実業] ❑ *A garden is one of the biggest selling points with house-hunters.* 家探しの1番大きな目玉の中には庭がある.

sell|ing price (**selling prices**) N-COUNT 可算名詞 The **selling price** of something is the price for which it is sold. 売値 [BUSINESS 実業] ❑ *Palm said the average selling price of its devices was $183.* パームはその機器の平均売価は183ドルだと言った.

sell-off (**sell-offs**) also **selloff** N-COUNT 可算名詞 The **sell-off** of something, for example, an industry owned by the state or a company's shares, is the selling of it. 売り出し [BUSINESS 実業] ❑ *The privatization of the electricity industry was the biggest sell-off of them all.* 電気産業の民営化がそのうちで1番大きかった売り出しであった.

sell-out (**sell-outs**) also **sellout** 🔟 N-COUNT 可算名詞 If a play, sports event, or other entertainment is a **sell-out**, all the tickets for it are sold. 売り切れ ❑ *Their concert there was a sell-out.* そこでの演奏会は大入り満員であった. 🔟 N-COUNT 可算名詞 If you describe someone's behavior as a **sell-out**, you disapprove of the fact that they have done something which used to be against their principles, or given in to an opposing group. 変節; 裏切り行為 [DISAPPROVAL 不賛成] ❑ *For some, his decision to become a Socialist candidate at Sunday's election was simply a sell-out.* 日曜日の選挙では社会党の候補者になるという彼の決断は，一部の人にとっては絶対に裏切り行為であった.

selves /sɛlvz/ Selves is the plural of self.

se|man|tics /sɪmæntɪks/

> The form **semantic** is used as a modifier.

> semantic 形は修飾語として使われる.

N-UNCOUNT 不可算名詞 **Semantics** is the branch of linguistics that deals with the meanings of words and sentences. 意味論

sem|blance /sɛmbləns/ N-UNCOUNT 不可算名詞 If there is a **semblance of** a particular condition or quality, it appears to exist, even though this may be a false impression. 外観, 見せかけ [FORMAL 形式ばった] ❑ *At least a semblance of normality has been restored to parts of the country.* その国の各地域では少なくともうわべは正常に戻っている.

se|men /siːmən/ N-UNCOUNT 不可算名詞 **Semen** is the liquid containing sperm that is produced by the sex organs of men and male animals. 精液

se|mes|ter /sɪmɛstər/ (semesters) N-COUNT 可算名詞 In colleges and universities in some countries, a **semester** is one of the two main periods into which the year is divided. 2学期制の学期 ❑ *...February 22nd when most of their students begin their spring semester.* 彼らのほとんどの学生にとって春学期が始まる2月22日

semi /sɛmi, sɛmaɪ/ (semis) **1** N-COUNT 可算名詞 In a sports competition, **the semis** are the semifinals. 準決勝 [INFORMAL くだけた] ❑ *He reached the semis after beating Nadal in the quarterfinal.* 彼は準々決勝でナダルを打ち負かして準決勝に進んだ. **2** N-COUNT 可算名詞 A **semi** is the same as a **tractor-trailer**. トレーラートラック [AM 米国英語]

Word Link **semi** ≈ half : semicircle, semiconductor, semifinal

semi|cir|cle /sɛmisɜrkəl, sɛmaɪ-/ (semicircles) also **semicircle** N-COUNT 可算名詞 A **semicircle** is one half of a circle, or something having the shape of half a circle. 半円, 半円形 ❑ *They sit cross-legged in a semicircle and share stories.* 彼らはあぐらをかいて半円形に座り, お互いに物語を語り合う.

semi|co|lon /sɛmikoʊlən/ (semicolons) N-COUNT 可算名詞 A **semicolon** is the punctuation mark ; which is used in writing to separate different parts of a sentence or list or to indicate a pause. セミコロン

semi|con|duc|tor /sɛmikəndʌktər, sɛmaɪ-/ (semiconductors) N-COUNT 可算名詞 A **semiconductor** is a substance used in electronics whose ability to conduct electricity increases with greater heat. 半導体
→ see solar system

semi-detached /sɛmidɪtætʃt, sɛmaɪ-/ also **semidetached** ADJ 形容詞 A **semi-detached** house is a house that is joined to another house on one side by a shared wall. 2軒建ての家屋の [mainly BRIT 主に英国英語; AM usually duplex 米国英語では通常 duplex] ● N-SING 単数名詞 **Semi-detached** is also a noun. 2軒連続住宅

semi|fi|nal /sɛmifaɪn³l, sɛmaɪ-/ (semifinals) N-COUNT 可算名詞 A **semifinal** is one of the two games or races in a competition that are held to decide who will compete in the final. 準決勝 ❑ *We want to go into the semifinal, no matter who the rival is.* 対抗者が誰であろうと, 我々は準決勝に進みたい. ● N-PLURAL 複数名詞 **The semifinals** is the round of a competition in which these two games or races are held. 準決勝 ❑ *Team USA reached the semifinals by defeating New Zealand in the second round.* アメリカチームは第2回戦でニュージーランドを破り準決勝に達した.

semi|nal /sɛmɪn³l/ ADJ 形容詞 **Seminal** is used to describe things such as books, works, events, and experiences that have a great influence in a particular field. 影響力の大きい [FORMAL 形式ばった] ❑ *...author of the seminal book "Animal Liberation."* 画期的な本である『動物の開放』の著者

semi|nar /sɛmɪnɑr/ (seminars) **1** N-COUNT 可算名詞 A **seminar** is a meeting where a group of people discuss a problem or topic. 討論会 ❑ *...a series of half-day seminars to help businessmen get the best value from investing in information technology.* 情報技術投資から最大限の価値が得られるように事業家を援助する半日講習会シリーズ **2** N-COUNT 可算名詞 A **seminar** is a class at a college or university in which the teacher and a small group of students discuss a topic. 演習 ❑ *Students are asked to prepare material in advance of each weekly seminar.* 学生は毎週のゼミに前もって資料を準備するように言われている.

semi|skilled /sɛmiskɪld, sɛmaɪ-/ ADJ 形容詞 A **semiskilled** worker has some training and skills, but not enough to do specialized work. 半熟練な [BUSINESS 実業]

Sen|ate /sɛnɪt/ (Senates) **1** N-PROPER-COLL 集合的固有名詞 **The Senate** is the smaller and more important of the two parts of the legislature in some U.S. states and in some countries, for example, the United States and Australia. 上院 ❑ *The Senate is expected to pass the bill shortly.* 上院はまもなくその法案を可決するも

のと期待されている. **2** N-PROPER-COLL 集合的固有名詞 **The Senate** is the governing council at some universities. 評議会 ❑ *By the time I was vice chancellor, the Senate had become a much larger and a much more democratic body.* 私が副総長になるころには, 評議会はずっと大きくなりずっと民主的になっていた.

Word Link **sen** ≈ old : senator, senile, senior

sena|tor /sɛnɪtər/ (senators) N-COUNT; N-TITLE 可算名詞, 称号名詞 A **senator** is a member of a political Senate, for example, in the United States or Australia. 上院議員 ❑ *...Texas' first black senator.* テキサス州の最初の黒人上院議員

send /sɛnd/ (sends, sending, sent) **1** V-T 他動詞 When you **send** someone something, you arrange for it to be taken and delivered to them, for example, by mail. 送る ❑ *Myra Cunningham sent me a note thanking me for dinner.* マイラ・カニンガムは夕食会の謝礼を述べた短信を私に送ってくれた. ❑ *I sent a copy to the school principal.* 私は写しを学校長に送った. **2** V-T 他動詞 If you **send** someone somewhere, you tell them to go there. 行かせる ❑ *Inspector Banbury came up to see her, but she sent him away.* バンベリー警部が彼女に会いに来たが, 彼女は追い払った. ❑ *...the government's decision to send troops to the region.* その地域に部隊を派遣するという政府の決定 ❑ *I suggested that he rest, and sent him for an X-ray.* 彼に休養するように勧め, レントゲン写真を撮りに行かせた. **3** V-T 他動詞 If you **send** someone **to** an institution such as a school or a prison, you arrange for them to stay there for a period of time. 入れる ❑ *It's his parents' choice to send him to a boarding school, rather than a convenient day school.* 便利な通学学校ではなく全寮制の学校に彼を入れるのは, 彼の両親の選択である. **4** V-I 他動詞 To **send** a signal means to cause it to go to a place by means of radio waves or electricity. 送信する ❑ *The transmitters will send a signal automatically to a local base station.* 伝達装置は地方の基地局に自動的に信号を送信する. **5** V-T 他動詞 If something **sends** things or people in a particular direction, it causes them to move in that direction. させる ❑ *The explosion sent shrapnel flying through the sides of cars on the crowded highway.* 爆発で榴散弾 (りゅうさんだん) が飛び, 混雑した高速道路を走る諸車の横側を貫通していった. ❑ *A left hook sent him reeling.* 左フックでくらい彼はよろよろした. **6** V-T 他動詞 To **send** someone or something **into** a particular state means to cause them to go into or be in that state. (一の状態に) させる ❑ *My attempt to fix it sent Lawrence into fits of laughter.* 私の修理のやり方を見てローレンスは笑い転げた. ❑ *...before civil war and famine sent the country plunging into anarchy.* 内戦や飢えで国が無制制に陥る前 **7** to **send** someone **packing** → see **pack**

▶ **send away for** → see **send for 2**

▶ **send for** **1** PHRASAL VERB 句動詞 If you **send for** someone, you send them a message asking them to come and see you. 来るように頼む ❑ *I've sent for the doctor.* 私はその医者を呼びにやった. **2** PHRASAL VERB 句動詞 If you **send for** something, or **send away for**, or **send off for** it, you write and ask for it to be sent to you. 取り寄せる ❑ *Send for your free catalog today.* 無料の商品目録を本日ご注文ください.

▶ **send in** **1** PHRASAL VERB 句動詞 If you **send in** something such as a competition entry or a letter applying for a job, you mail it to the organization concerned. 提出する ❑ *Applicants are asked to send in a résumé and a cover letter.* 志願者は履歴書と添え状を送付してください. **2** PHRASAL VERB 句動詞 When a government **sends in** troops or police officers, it orders them to deal with a crisis or problem somewhere. 投入する ❑ *He has asked the government to send in troops to end the fighting.* 彼は戦闘を終結させるために部隊を投入するように政府に求めている.

▶ **send off** **1** PHRASAL VERB 句動詞 When you **send off** a letter or package, you send it somewhere by mail. 発送する ❑ *He sent off copies to various people for them to read and make comments.* 彼は読んで論評してもらうため, いろいろな人に本を送った. **2** PHRASAL VERB 句動詞 If a soccer player **is sent off**, the referee makes them leave the field during a game, as a punishment for seriously breaking the rules. 退場させる [mainly BRIT 主に英国英語; AM eject 米国英語 eject]

▶ **send off for** → see **send for 2**

▶ **send out** **1** PHRASAL VERB 句動詞 If you **send out** things such as letters or bills, you send them to a large number of people at the same time. 送付する ❑ *She had sent out well over four hundred invitations that afternoon.* その日の午後, 彼女は400通は優に超える招待状を送付した. **2** PHRASAL VERB 句動詞 To **send out** a signal, sound, light, or heat means to produce it. 発する ❑ *The crew did not send out any distress signals.* 乗組員は何の遭難信号も発信しなかった.

▶ **send out for** PHRASAL VERB 句動詞 If you **send out for** food, for example, pizza or sandwiches, you phone and ask for it to be delivered to you. 出前を注文する ❑ *Let's send out for a pizza.* ピザの出前を頼もう.

Thesaurus	send また次を参照 :
v.	issue, mail, ship, transmit; (ant.) receive **1**

S

send|er /sɛndər/ (**senders**) N-COUNT 可算名詞 **The sender of** a letter, package, or radio message is the person who sent it. 送り主 ❑ *The sender of the best letter every week will win a check for $50.* 毎週最優秀の手紙の差出人は50ドルの小切手を獲得するであろう.

Word Link *sen ≈ old : senator, senile, senior*

se|nile /siːnaɪl/ ADJ 形容詞 If old people become **senile**, they become confused, can no longer remember things, and are unable to take care of themselves. 老人性認知症の ● **se|nil|ity** /sɪnɪlɪti/ N-UNCOUNT 不可算名詞 老人性認知症 ❑ *The old man was forced to resign after showing unmistakable signs of senility.* 間違えようもないもうろく症状が見られた後, その老人は強制的に引退させられた.

sen|ior /siːnyər/ (**seniors**) ❶ ADJ 形容詞 The **senior** people in an organization or profession have the highest and most important jobs. 幹部の [ADJ n] ❑ *...senior officials in the Israeli government.* イスラエル政府の高官たち ❑ *...the company's senior management.* 会社の重役たち ❷ ADJ 形容詞 If someone is **senior to** you in an organization or profession, they have a higher and more important job than you or they are considered to be superior to you because they have worked there for longer and have more experience. 上司の ❑ *The position had to be filled by an officer senior to Haig.* その地位の補充はヘイグよりも上の将校でなければならなかった. ● N-PLURAL 複数名詞 Your **seniors** are the people who are senior to you. 上司 ❑ *He was described by his seniors as a model officer.* 上官たちは彼を模範的な士官であると評した. ❸ N-SING 単数名詞 **Senior** is used when indicating how much older one person is than another. For example, if someone is ten years your **senior**, they are ten years older than you. 年上の者 ❑ *She became involved with a married man many years her senior.* 彼女は何歳も年上の既婚男性と関係するようになった. ❹ N-COUNT 可算名詞 **Seniors** are students in a high school, university, or college who are in their fourth year of study. 最上級生 [AM 米国英語] ❑ *...the number of high school seniors who go on to college.* 大学に進む高校最終学年の学生数 ❺ N-COUNT 可算名詞 A **senior** is the same as a **senior citizen**. 老齢者 ❑ *Tickets at the gate are $10, $7 for seniors (age 55 and up).* 入場時購入の切符は10ドルで, 老齢者 (55歳以上) は7ドルである. ❻ ADJ 形容詞 If you take part in a sport at **senior** level, you take part in competitions with adults and people who have reached a high degree of achievement in that sport. 最上級の [ADJ n] ❑ *This will be his fifth international championship and his third at senior level.* これは彼の5回目の国際選手権で, 最上級レベルでは3回目になろう.

sen|ior citi|zen (**senior citizens**) N-COUNT 可算名詞 A **senior citizen** is an older person who has retired or receives social security benefits. 年金生活者の老人 ❑ *...services for senior citizens.* お年寄りのための公的便宜

→ see **age**

sen|ior|ity /siːniɒrɪti/ N-UNCOUNT 不可算名詞 A person's **seniority** in an organization is the importance and power that they have compared with others, or the fact that they have worked there for a long time. 年功 ❑ *He has said he will fire editorial employees without regard to seniority.* 彼は年功にかかわらず編集員をくびにすると言っている.

Word Link *sens ≈ feeling : sensation, senseless, sensitive*

sen|sa|tion /sɛnseɪʃ°n/ (**sensations**) ❶ N-COUNT 可算名詞 A **sensation** is a physical feeling. 知覚 ❑ *Floating can be a very pleasant sensation.* 浮かぶことは時に大変気持ちがいいこともある. ❷ N-UNCOUNT 不可算名詞 **Sensation** is your ability to feel things physically, especially through your sense of touch. 感覚 ❑ *The pain was so bad that she lost all sensation.* 彼女は痛みが全てなくなるほど痛みが激しかった. ❸ N-COUNT 可算名詞 You can use **sensation** to refer to the general feeling or impression caused by a particular experience. 感じ ❑ *It's a funny sensation to know someone's talking about you in a language you don't understand.* 理解できない言語で誰かが私の話をしていると分かることは, おかしな感じがするものだ. ❹ N-COUNT 可算名詞 If a person, event, or situation is a **sensation**, it causes great excitement or interest. 大評判となっている人 (こと) ❑ *...the film that turned her into an overnight sensation.* 彼女が1夜にして大評判となった映画 ❺ N-SING 単数名詞 If a person, event, or situation causes **a sensation**, they cause great interest or excitement. 大評判 ❑ *She was just 14 when she caused a sensation at the Montreal Olympics.* モントリオールオリンピック大会で大評判になったとき, 彼女はわずか14歳であった.

→ see **taste**

sen|sa|tion|al /sɛnseɪʃən°l/ ❶ ADJ 形容詞 A **sensational** result, event, or situation is so remarkable that it causes great excitement and interest. 衝撃的な ❑ *The world champions suffered a sensational defeat.* 世界チャンピオンは衝撃的な敗北を喫した. ● **sen|sa|tion|al|ly** ADV 副詞 驚くべきことに ❑ *The rape trial was sensationally halted yesterday.* 驚くべきことにレイプ事件の裁判は昨日中止されました. ❷ ADJ 形容詞 You can describe stories or reports as **sensational** if you disapprove of them because they present facts in a way that is intended to cause feelings of shock, anger, or

excitement. 扇情的な [DISAPPROVAL 不賛成] ❑ *...sensational tabloid newspaper reports.* 扇情的なタブロイド紙の報道. ❸ ADJ 形容詞 You can describe something as **sensational** when you think that it is extremely good. とても素晴らしい ❑ *Her voice is sensational.* 彼女の声はとても素晴らしい. ● **sen|sa|tion|al|ly** ADV 副詞 飛び抜けて ❑ *...sensationally good food.* とびきりおいしい料理.

sense /sɛns/ (**senses, sensing, sensed**) ❶ N-COUNT 可算名詞 Your **senses** are the physical abilities of sight, smell, hearing, touch, and taste. 感覚 ❑ *She stared at him again, unable to believe the evidence of her senses.* 彼女は自分が見聞きした証拠が信じられず, 再び彼を見つめた. ❷ V-T 他動詞 If you **sense** something, you become aware of it or you realize it, although it is not very obvious. 感知する ❑ *She probably sensed that I wasn't telling her the whole story.* 彼女はたぶん, 私が全てを話そうとしていないと感じ取っていただろう. ❑ *He looks about him, sensing danger.* 彼は危険を感じて周囲を見回す. ❸ N-SING 単数名詞 If you have a **sense that** something is the case, you think that it is the case, although you may not have firm, clear evidence for this belief. 勘 ❑ *Suddenly you got this sense that people were drawing themselves away from each other.* 突然, あなたは人々がお互いに距離を置こうとしているというこの直感的な勘を覚えたのです. ❹ N-SING 単数名詞 If you have a **sense** of guilt or relief, for example, you feel guilty or relieved. 意識 ❑ *When your child is struggling for life, you feel this overwhelming sense of guilt.* 子供が生死の境をさまよっている場合, このような抗し難い罪の意識にさいなまれるのです. ❺ N-SING 単数名詞 If you have a **sense of** something such as duty or justice, you are aware of it and believe it is important. 観念 ❑ *My sense of justice was offended.* 私の正義感が踏みにじられた. ❑ *We must keep a sense of proportion about all this.* 私たちはこの件すべてにおいて平衡感覚を保たなければなりません. ❻ N-SING 単数名詞 Someone who has a **sense** of timing or style has a natural ability with regard to timing or style. You can also say that someone has a bad **sense** of timing or style. センス [N "of" n, also n n] ❑ *He has an impeccable sense of timing.* 彼のタイミングを読むセンスはとても鋭い. ❑ *Her dress sense is appalling.* 彼女の服装センスはひどいものだ. ❼ → see also **sense of humor** ❽ N-UNCOUNT 不可算名詞 **Sense** is the ability to make good judgments and to behave sensibly. 判断力 ❑ *...when he was younger and had a bit more sense.* 彼がもっと若くて, もう少し判断力があったとき ❑ *When that doesn't work they sometimes have the sense to seek help.* それがうまくいかないときは, 彼らは助けを求める判断力がある. ❾ → see also **common sense** ❿ N-SING 単数名詞 If you say that there is no **sense** or little **sense in** doing something, you mean that it is not a sensible thing to do because nothing useful would be gained by doing it. 意義 ❑ *There's no sense in pretending this doesn't happen.* こんなことは起らない, と取り繕っても意味はないよ. ⓫ N-COUNT 可算名詞 A **sense** of a word or expression is one of its possible meanings. 意味 ❑ *...a noun which has two senses.* 2通りの意味を持つ名詞. ⓬ PHRASE 句 **Sense** is used in several expressions to indicate how true your statement is. For example, if you say that something is true **in a sense**, you mean that it is partly true, or true in one way. If you say that something is true **in a general sense**, you mean that it is true in a general way. ある意味で ❑ *In a sense, both were right.* ある意味, どちらも正しかった. ❑ *Though his background was modest, it was in no sense deprived.* 彼は裕福な出ではないが, 決して困窮していたわけではない. ⓭ PHRASE 句 If something **makes sense**, you can understand it. 意味をなす ❑ *He was sitting there saying, "Yes, the figures make sense."* 彼はそこに座って「ああ. その数字には納得できるな」と言った. ⓮ PHRASE 句 When you **make sense of** something, you succeed in understanding it. 一の意味を理解する ❑ *Provided you didn't try to make sense of it, it sounded beautiful.* 君がその意味を理解しようとしなかったら, それは美しく聞こえたのに. ⓯ PHRASE 句 If a course of action **makes sense**, it seems sensible. 理にかなった ❑ *It makes sense to look after yourself.* 自分を大事にするのは理にかなっている. ❑ *The project should be re-appraised to see whether it made sound economic sense.* その計画は経済的に健全かどうかを見るために再評価すべきだ. ⓰ PHRASE 句 If you say that someone has **come to** their **senses** or **has been brought to** their **senses**, you mean that they have stopped being foolish and are being sensible again. 分別を取り戻す ❑ *Eventually the world will come to its senses and get rid of them.* 最終的に世界は分別を取り戻し, それらを廃止するだろう. ⓱ PHRASE 句 If you say that someone **talks sense**, you mean that what they say is sensible. もっともなことを言う ❑ *When he speaks, he talks sense.* 彼は話すときはもっともなことを言う. ⓲ PHRASE 句 If you **have a sense that** something is true or you **get a sense that** something is true, you think that it is true. 一だと実感する [mainly SPOKEN 主に口語] ❑ *Do you have the sense that you are loved by the public?* 一般大衆に愛されていると感じていますか. ⓳ to see **sense** → see **see**

→ see **smell**

Thesaurus	*sense* また次を参照:
V.	notice, perceive, realize ❷
N.	feeling, sensation ❷
	awareness, feeling, perception ❸ – ❻

sense|less /sɛnslɪs/ ■ ADJ 形容詞 If you describe an action as **senseless**, you think it is wrong because it has no purpose and produces no benefit. 無意味な ❑ ...people whose lives have been destroyed by acts of senseless violence. 愚かな暴力行為で命を奪われた人々. ■ ADJ 形容詞 If someone is **senseless**, they are unconscious. 意識の無い ❑ They were knocked to the ground, beaten senseless and robbed of their wallets. 彼らは地面にたたきつけられ、気を失うまで殴られ、財布を奪われた.

sense of hu|mor N-SING 単数名詞 Someone who has a **sense of humor** often finds things amusing, rather than being serious all the time. ユーモアのセンス ❑ She seems to have a good sense of humor. 彼女にはユーモアのいいセンスがありそうだ.

sen|sibil|ity /sɛnsɪbɪlɪti/ (**sensibilities**) ■ N-UNCOUNT 不可算名詞 Sensibility is the ability to experience deep feelings. 感性 ❑ Everything he writes demonstrates the depth of his sensibility. 彼が書くどの文章にも感性の深さが現れている. ■ N-VAR 可変性名詞 Someone's **sensibility** is their tendency to be influenced or offended by things. 繊細な感受性 ❑ He was unable to control his sensibility. 彼はあふれてくる感情を抑えることができなかった.

sen|sible /sɛnsɪbᵊl/ ■ ADJ 形容詞 Sensible actions or decisions are good because they are based on reasons rather than emotions. 賢明な ❑ It might be sensible to get a lawyer. 弁護士に頼むのが賢明かもしれないよ. ❑ The sensible thing is to leave them alone. 賢明なのは、彼らをそっとしておくことだよ. ● **sen|sibly** /sɛnsɪbli/ ADV 副詞 賢明にも ❑ He sensibly decided to lie low for a while. 彼は賢明にもしばらく目立たないようにしていることにした. ■ ADJ 形容詞 Sensible people behave in a sensible way. 分別のある ❑ She was a sensible girl and did not panic. その少女は聡明で、パニックには陥らなかった. ❑ Oh come on, let's be sensible about this. おいおい、このことについては冷静になろうよ. ■ ADJ 形容詞 Sensible shoes or clothes are practical and strong rather than fashionable and attractive. 実用本位の ❑ Wear loose clothing and sensible footwear. 楽な服と履きやすい靴を着用してください. ● **sen|sibly** ADV 副詞 実用的に ❑ They were not sensibly dressed. 彼らの服装は実用的なものではなかった.

> Take care not to confuse **sensible** and **sensitive**. You do not use **sensible** to describe someone whose feelings or emotions are strongly affected by their experiences. The word you need is **sensitive**. ❑ ...a highly sensitive artist.

Word Link sens ≈ feeling : sensation, senseless, sensitive

sen|si|tive /sɛnsɪtɪv/ ■ ADJ 形容詞 If you are **sensitive to** other people's needs, problems, or feelings, you show understanding and awareness of them. 敏感な [APPROVAL 賛成] ❑ The classroom teacher must be sensitive to a child's needs. 担任教師は子供のニーズに敏感でなければならない. ● **sen|si|tive|ly** ADV 副詞 敏感に ❑ The abuse of women needs to be treated seriously and sensitively. 女性虐待問題には真剣かつ細やかな対応が必要だ. ● **sen|si|tiv|ity** /sɛnsɪtɪvɪti/ N-UNCOUNT 不可算名詞 [oft N "for" n] 敏感さ ❑ A good relationship involves concern and sensitivity for each other's feelings. 良い関係を築くには、互いの感情を配慮し、理解することが求められる. ■ ADJ 形容詞 If you are **sensitive about** something, you are easily worried and offended when people talk about it. 一を気にする ❑ Young people are very sensitive about their appearance. 若い人たちは非常に外見を気にするものだ. ● **sen|si|tiv|ity** N-VAR 可変性名詞 (**sensitivities**) 過敏さ ❑ ...people who suffer extreme sensitivity about what others think. 他人がどう思うかを極度に気にする人たち ■ ADJ 形容詞 A **sensitive** subject or issue needs to be dealt with carefully because it is likely to cause disagreement or make people angry or upset. 慎重を要する ❑ Employment is a very sensitive issue. 雇用問題は非常に慎重さが求められる問題だ. ● **sen|si|tiv|ity** N-UNCOUNT 不可算名詞 [oft N "of" n] 微妙さ ❑ Due to the obvious sensitivity of the issue he would not divulge any details. その問題がデリケートなのは明白ですから、彼はいかなる点も明らかにはしようとしなかった. ■ ADJ 形容詞 **Sensitive** documents or reports contain information that needs to be kept secret and dealt with carefully. 機密の ❑ He instructed staff to shred sensitive documents. 彼はスタッフに機密書類をシュレッダーにかけるよう指示した. ■ ADJ 形容詞 Something that is **sensitive to** a physical force, substance, or treatment is easily affected by it and often harmed by it. 過敏な ❑ ...a chemical which is sensitive to light. 光に敏感な化学物質 ● **sen|si|tiv|ity** N-UNCOUNT 不可算名詞 感度 ❑ ...the sensitivity of cells to damage by chemotherapy. 化学療法による損傷に対する細胞の感受性. ■ ADJ 形容詞 A **sensitive** piece of scientific equipment is capable of measuring or recording very small changes. 感度のよい ❑ ...an extremely sensitive microscope. 超高感度顕微鏡. ● **sen|si|tiv|ity** N-UNCOUNT 不可算名詞 感度 ❑ ...the sensitivity of the detector. 探知機の感度.

Thesaurus sensitive また次を参照:

ADJ. conscious, perceptive, understanding; (ant.) insensitive ■
emotional, irritable, touchy ■

Word Partnership sensitive は次の語句と使われる:

N.	sensitive **areas**, sensitive **issue** ■
	sensitive **information**, sensitive **material** ■
	heat sensitive, **light** sensitive, sensitive **skin** ■
	sensitive **equipment** ■
ADV.	**overly** sensitive, **so** sensitive, **too** sensitive ■ ■
	highly sensitive, **very** sensitive ■ – ■
	politically sensitive ■
	environmentally sensitive ■

sen|sor /sɛnsər/ (**sensors**) N-COUNT 可算名詞 A **sensor** is an instrument which reacts to certain physical conditions or impressions such as heat or light, and which is used to provide information. センサー ❑ The latest Japanese vacuum cleaners contain sensors that detect the amount of dust and type of floor. 最新の日本製掃除機には、ほこりの量と床の材質を検知するセンサーがついている.

sen|so|ry /sɛnsəri/ ADJ 形容詞 **Sensory** means relating to the physical senses. 感覚の [FORMAL 形式ばった] [ADJ n] ❑ Almost all sensory information from the trunk and limbs passes through the spinal cord. 胴体および手足で得られた知覚情報のほぼすべてが脊髄を通って伝達される.

→ see **nervous system, smell**

sen|sual /sɛnʃuəl/ ■ ADJ 形容詞 Someone or something that is **sensual** shows or suggests a great liking for physical pleasures, especially sexual pleasures. 肉欲的な ❑ He was a very sensual person. 彼はとても好色な男です. ❑ ...the sensual curve of her lips. 肉感的な彼女の唇のカーブ. ● **sen|su|al|ity** /sɛnʃuælɪti/ N-UNCOUNT 不可算名詞 肉感的さ ❑ The wave and curl of her blonde hair gave her sensuality and youth. ウェーブのかかったブロンドの巻き毛が、彼女をセクシーで若く見せた. ■ ADJ 形容詞 Something that is **sensual** gives pleasure to your physical senses rather than to your mind. 官能的な ❑ It was an opera, very glamorous and very sensual. それは非常に魅惑的で非常に官能的なオペラだった. ● **sen|su|al|ity** N-UNCOUNT 不可算名詞 官能性 ❑ These perfumes have warmth and sensuality. これらの香水は温もりのある官能的な香りがします.

sen|su|ous /sɛnʃuəs/ ■ ADJ 形容詞 Something that is **sensuous** gives pleasure to the mind or body through the senses. 感覚的な ❑ The film is ravishing to look at and boasts a sensuous musical score. その映画は映像が魅惑的だし、感覚的な背景音楽も誇りである. ● **sen|su|ous|ly** ADV 副詞 感覚に訴えるように ❑ She lay in the deep bath for a long time, enjoying its sensuously perfumed water. 彼女はお湯の感覚的な香りを楽しみながら長い間深い浴槽につかっていた. ■ ADJ 形容詞 Someone or something that is **sensuous** shows or suggests a great liking for sexual pleasure. 官能的な ❑ ...his sensuous young mistress, Marie-Therese. 彼の官能的な若い愛人、マリー・テレーズ. ❑ ...wide sensuous lips. 大きく官能的な唇. ● **sen|su|ous|ly** ADV 副詞 官能的に ❑ The nose was straight, the mouth sensuously wide and full. 鼻はまっすぐで、口は肉感的に大きくふっくらとしていた.

sent /sɛnt/ **Sent** is the past tense and past participle of **send**.

sen|tence /sɛntəns/ (**sentences, sentencing, sentenced**) ■ N-COUNT 可算名詞 A **sentence** is a group of words which, when they are written down, begin with a capital letter and end with a period, question mark, or exclamation mark. Most sentences contain a subject and a verb. 文 ❑ Here we have several sentences incorrectly joined by commas. コンマで不適切につながれた文がいくつかあります. ■ N-VAR 可変性名詞 In a law court, a **sentence** is the punishment that a person receives after they have been found guilty of a crime. 判決 ❑ They are already serving prison sentences for their part in the assassination. 彼らは暗殺に加わったかどで既に服役中だ. ❑ He was given a four-year sentence. 彼は4年の刑を宣告されました. ❑ The court is expected to pass sentence later today. 法廷は今日遅くに判決を言い渡すようです. ■ → see also **death sentence** ■ V-T 他動詞 When a judge **sentences** someone, he or she states in court what their punishment will be. 判決を下す ❑ A military court sentenced him to death in his absence. 軍法会議は欠席裁判で彼に死刑を宣告した. ❑ She was sentenced to nine years in prison. 彼女は9年の刑を宣告された.

→ see **trial**

sen|ti|ment /sɛntɪmənt/ (**sentiments**) ■ N-VAR 可変性名詞 A **sentiment** that people have is an attitude which is based on their thoughts and feelings. 感情 ❑ Public sentiment rapidly turned anti-American. 世論は急速に反米に傾いた. ❑ He's found growing sentiment for military action. 彼は軍事行動への感情が高まっていくのを気づいた. ■ N-COUNT 可算名詞 A **sentiment** is an idea or feeling that someone expresses in words. 意見、感想 ❑ I must agree with the sentiments expressed by John Prescott. 私はジョン・プレスコットの意見に賛成せざるを得ません. ■ N-UNCOUNT 不可算名詞 **Sentiment** is feelings such as pity or love, especially for things in the past, and may be considered exaggerated and foolish. 感傷 ❑ Laura kept that letter out of sentiment. ローラはその手紙を感傷から取っておいた.

sen|ti|men|tal /sɛntɪmɛntᵊl/ ■ ADJ 形容詞 Someone or something that is **sentimental** feels or shows pity or love,

sometimes to an extent that is considered exaggerated and foolish. 感傷的な ❑ I'm trying not to be sentimental about the past. 私は過ぎたことには感傷的にならないようにしている. ● sen|ti|men|tal|ly ADV 副詞 ❑ Childhood had less freedom and joy than we sentimentally attribute to it. 感傷的に子供時代は自由と喜びにあふれていると考えられているが, 実際はそれほどでもなかった. ● sen|ti|men|tal|ity /sɛntɪmɛntælɪti/ N-UNCOUNT 不可算名詞 感傷的なこと ❑ In this book there is no sentimentality. この本にはお涙ちょうだいの要素はありません. ② ADJ 形容詞 Sentimental means relating to or involving feelings such as pity or love, especially for things in the past. 思い出の ❑ Our paintings and photographs are of sentimental value only. 私どもの油絵や写真は価値はありませんが思い出深いものなのです.

sen|try /sɛntri/ (**sentries**) N-COUNT 可算名詞 A **sentry** is a soldier who guards a camp or a building. 番兵 ❑ The sentry would not let her enter. 見張り番は彼女を中に入れようとしなかった.

sepa|rate (**separates**, **separating**, **separated**)

The adjective and noun are pronounced /sɛpərɪt/. The verb is pronounced /sɛpəreɪt/.

形容詞と名詞は /sɛpərɪt/ と発音される. 動詞は /sɛpəreɪt/ と発音される.

■ ADJ 形容詞 If one thing is **separate from** another, there is a barrier, space, or division between them, so that they are clearly two things. 別個の ❑ They are now making plans to form their own separate party. 彼らは今自分達で別個の党を作ろうと計画している. ❑ Business bank accounts were kept separate from personal ones. 事業用の銀行口座は個人口座とは分けておかれた. ② ADJ 形容詞 If you refer to **separate** things, you mean several different things, rather than just one thing. 個々の ❑ Use separate chopping boards for raw meats, cooked meats, vegetables and salads. まな板は, 生肉, 調理済みの肉, 野菜やサラダなどのように用途別に専用のものを使いなさい. ❑ Men and women have separate exercise rooms. 男性と女性それぞれに専用のトレーニングルームがある. ③ V-RECIP 相互動詞 If you **separate** people or things that are together, or if they **separate**, they move apart. 分ける; 分かれる ❑ Police moved in to separate the two groups. 警察は2組を引き離すために介入した. ❑ The pans were held in both hands and swirled around to separate gold particles from the dirt. 選鉱なべを両手で持ち, 砂金を泥から分けるためにぐるぐる回された. ❑ The front end of the car separated from the rest of the vehicle. その車の前部はその他の部分と分かれている. ④ V-RECIP 相互動詞 If you **separate** people or things that have been connected, or if one **separates from** another, the connection between them is ended. 分ける; 分かれる ❑ They want to separate teaching from research. 彼らは授業と研究を分けたいと思っている. ❑ It's very possible that we may see a movement to separate the two parts of the country. 国の2つの部分を分離しようとする動きが見られるのはほぼ確実でしょう. ⑤ V-RECIP 相互動詞 If a couple who are married or living together **separate**, they decide to live apart. 分かれる ❑ Her parents separated when she was very young. 彼女の両親は彼女が幼いときに離婚した. ⑥ V-T 他動詞 An object, obstacle, distance, or period of time which **separates** two people, groups, or things exists between them. 隔てる ❑ ...the white-railed fence that separated the yard from the paddock. 小牧場と牧草地を隔てる白いレールの柵. ❑ They had undoubtedly made progress in the six years that separated the two periods. 彼らはその6年間で以前とは見違えるほど明らかな進歩を見せていた. ⑦ V-T 他動詞 If you **separate** one idea or fact from another, you clearly see or show the difference between them. 区別する ❑ It is difficult to separate legend from truth. 伝説か実話かを区別するのは難しい. ❑ ...learning how to separate real problems from imaginary illnesses. 症状が実際のものか心因性かを区別する方法を学んで ● PHRASAL VERB 句動詞 **Separate out** means the same as **separate**. ❑ How can one ever separate out the act from the attitudes that surround it? 人は, いかにして周りの人々の態度に影響されずに行動することができるのだろうか. ⑧ V-T 他動詞 A quality or factor that **separates** one thing from another is the reason why the two things are different from each other. 分かつ ❑ The single most important factor that separates ordinary photographs from good photographs is the lighting. よい写真を普通の写真と分ける唯一最大の要因は, ライティングである. ⑨ V-T 他動詞 If a particular number of points **separate** two teams or competitors, one of them is winning or has won by that number of points. (得点で) 離す ❑ In the end only three points separated the two teams. 結局, 両チームの得点差はたった3点だった. ⑩ V-T/V-I 他動詞/自動詞 If you **separate** a group of people or things into smaller elements, or if a group **separates**, it is divided into smaller elements. 分割する [他動詞], 分かれる [自動詞] ❑ The police wanted to separate them into smaller groups. 警察は彼らをより小さい集団に分割したいと思っていた. ❑ Let's separate into smaller groups. もっと少人数のグループに分かれよう. ● PHRASAL VERB 句動詞 **Separate out** means the same as **separate**. 分割する ❑ If I prepared many hours ahead, the mixture may separate out. 十分な時間をかければ, その混合物は分離するかもしれない. ⑪ N-PLURAL 複数名詞 **Separates** are clothes such as skirts, pants, and shirts which cover just the top half or the bottom half of your body. セ

パレーツ ❑ She wears coordinated separates instead of a suit. 彼女はスーツではなく, セパレーツをコーディネートして着ている. ⑫ → see also **separated** ⑬ PHRASE 句 When two or more people who have been together for some time **go** their **separate ways**, they go to different places or end their relationship. それぞれの道を行く ❑ Sue was 27 when she and her husband decided to go their separate ways. スーが夫と別々の道を歩むと決めたのは27歳のときだった.

▶ **separate out** PHRASAL VERB 句動詞 If you **separate out** something from the other things it is with, you take it out. 取り出す ❑ The ability to separate out reusable elements from other waste is crucial. 再利用可能なものを不用品と判別できることが非常に大切なのです. ② → see also **separate 7, 10**

sepa|rat|ed /sɛpəreɪtɪd/ ■ ADJ 形容詞 Someone who is **separated** from their wife or husband lives apart from them, but is not divorced. 別居している [v-link ADJ] ❑ Most single parents are either divorced or separated. 1人で子育てをしている親は, 大半が離婚したか別居をしている. ② ADJ 形容詞 If you are **separated** from someone, for example, your family, you are not able to be with them. 離れ離れの ❑ The idea of being separated from him, even for a few hours, was torture. 彼と離れ離れになるなんて, ほんの数時間でも耐え難いわ.

sepa|rate|ly /sɛpərɪtli/ ADV 副詞 If people or things are dealt with **separately** or do something **separately**, they are dealt with or do something at different times or places, rather than together. 別々に ❑ Cook each vegetable separately until just tender. 野菜はそれぞれ別に少し柔らかくなるまで火を通してください.

sepa|ra|tion /sɛpəreɪʃən/ (**separations**) ■ N-VAR 可変性名詞 The **separation** of two or more things or groups is the fact that they are separate or become separate, and are not linked. 分離 [oft N "of/from/between" n] ❑ He believes in the separation of the races. 彼は人種分離主義者です. ② N-VAR 可変性名詞 During a **separation**, people who usually live together are not together. 離れていること ❑ She wondered if Harry had been unfaithful to her during this long separation. 彼女がハリーと長らく離れていた間に彼が自分を裏切っていたのではないかしらと思った. ③ N-VAR 可変性名詞 If a couple who are married or living together have a **separation**, they decide to live apart. 別居 ❑ They agreed to a trial separation. 彼らは別居してみることに同意した.

sepa|ra|tism /sɛpərətɪzəm/ N-UNCOUNT 不可算名詞 **Separatism** is the beliefs and activities of separatists. 分離主義 ❑ ...a doctrine of racial separatism. 人種分離主義の教義.

sepa|ra|tist /sɛpərətɪst/ (**separatists**) ■ ADJ 形容詞 **Separatist** organizations and activities within a country involve members of a group of people who want to establish their own separate government or are trying to do so. 分離主義の [ADJ n] ❑ Spanish police say they have arrested ten people suspected of being members of the Basque separatist movement. スペイン警察は, バスク分離派の活動メンバーの容疑で10名を逮捕したと述べている. ② N-COUNT 可算名詞 **Separatists** are people who want their own separate government or are involved in separatist activities. 分離主義者 ❑ The army has come under attack by separatists. 軍隊が分離主義者による攻撃を受けている.

Sept. Sept. is a written abbreviation for **September**. 9月 ❑ I've booked it for Thurs. Sept. 8th. 予約しているのは9月8日, 木曜日です.

Sep|tem|ber /sɛptɛmbər/ (**Septembers**) N-VAR 可変性名詞 **September** is the ninth month of the year in the Western calendar. 9月 ❑ Her son, Jerome, was born in September. 彼女の息子, ジェロームは9月に生まれた. ❑ We didn't make the original September 30 release date. 我々は当初の発行予定日であった9月30日に間に合わせることができなかった.

sep|tic /sɛptɪk/ ADJ 形容詞 If a wound or a part of your body becomes **septic**, it becomes infected. 細菌に感染した, 敗血症の ❑ A flake of plaster from the ceiling fell into his eye, which became septic. 天井から石膏のかけらが落ちて彼の目の中に入り, 目が敗血症になった.

se|quel /sikwəl/ (**sequels**) N-COUNT 可算名詞 A book or movie which is a **sequel to** an earlier one continues the story of the earlier one. 続編 ❑ She is currently writing a sequel to Daphne du Maurier's "Rebecca." 彼女は現在ダフネ・デュ・モーリアの『レベッカ』の続編を執筆中だ.

se|quence /sikwəns/ (**sequences**) ■ N-COUNT 可算名詞 A **sequence** of events or things is a number of events or things that come one after another in a particular order. 連続 ❑ ...the sequence of events which led to the murder. 殺人事件に発展した一連の出来事 ② N-COUNT 可算名詞 A particular **sequence** is a particular order in which things happen or are arranged. 順序 ❑ ...the color

sequence yellow, orange, purple, blue, green and white. 黄, オレンジ, 紫, 青, 緑, 白という配色.

se|quin /síːkwɪn/ (**sequins**) N-COUNT 可算名詞 **Sequins** are small, shiny disks that are sewn on clothes to decorate them. シークイン, スパンコール ❑ *The frocks were covered in sequins, thousands of them.* フロックには何千個ものスパンコールが付けられていた.

se|rene /sɪríːn/ ADJ 形容詞 Someone or something that is **serene** is calm and quiet. 静かな ❑ *She looked as calm and serene as she always did.* 彼女はいつものようにとても静かで冷静に見えた. ❑ *He didn't speak much, he just smiled with that serene smile of his.* 彼はあまりしゃべらず, 彼特有の静かな笑みを浮かべるだけだった. ● **se|rene|ly** ADV 副詞 静かに ❑ *We sailed serenely down the river.* 我々は静かに舟で川を下った. ❑ *She carried on serenely sipping her gin and tonic.* 彼女は穏やかにジントニックを飲み続けた. ● **se|ren|ity** /sɪrénɪti/ N-UNCOUNT 不可算名詞 平静 ❑ *I had a wonderful feeling of peace and serenity when I saw my husband.* 私は夫の姿を見たら, 安らかで穏やかな, すばらしい気持ちになった.

ser|geant /sɑ́ːrdʒ^ənt/ (**sergeants**) ❶ N-COUNT; N-TITLE; N-VOC 可算名詞, 称号名詞, 呼格名詞 A **sergeant** is a non-commissioned officer of middle rank in the army, marines, or air force. 軍曹 ❑ *A sergeant with a detail of four men came into view.* 4人の分遣隊を引き連れた軍曹が現れた. ❷ N-COUNT; N-TITLE; N-VOC 可算名詞, 称号名詞, 呼格名詞 A **sergeant** is an officer with the rank immediately below a captain. 巡査部長 ❑ *A police sergeant patrolling the area spotted flames at the store.* その地域を巡回中の巡査部長がその店が燃えているのを発見した.

ser|geant ma|jor (**sergeant majors**) also **sergeant-major** N-COUNT; N-TITLE; N-VOC 可算名詞, 称号名詞, 呼格名詞 A **sergeant major** is a noncommissioned army or marine officer of the highest rank. 上級曹長

se|rial /síəriəl/ (**serials**) ❶ N-COUNT 可算名詞 A **serial** is a story which is broadcast on television or radio or is published in a magazine or newspaper in a number of parts over a period of time. 連続番組, 連載物 ❑ *...one of television's most popular serials.* 最も人気の高い連続番組の1つ ❷ ADJ 形容詞 **Serial** killings or attacks are a series of killings or attacks committed by the same person. This person is known as a **serial** killer or attacker. 連続の [ADJ n] ❑ *...serial murders.* 連続殺人.

se|rial|iza|tion /sìəriəlaɪzéɪ^ʃn/ (**serializations**) ❶ N-UNCOUNT 不可算名詞 **Serialization** is the act of serializing a book. 連載 ❑ *It was first written for serialization in a magazine.* それは最初, 雑誌の連載用に書かれたものだった. ❷ N-COUNT 可算名詞 A **serialization** is a story, originally written as a book, which is being published or broadcast in a number of parts. 連載化, 連続放送化 ❑ *...the serialization of Jane Austen's Pride and Prejudice.* ジェーン・オースティンの『プライドと偏見』の連続ドラマ化

se|rial|ize /síəriəlaɪz/ (**serializes, serializing, serialized**) V-T 他動詞 If a book **is serialized**, it is broadcast on the radio or television or is published in a magazine or newspaper in a number of parts over a period of time. 連載する, 連続放送する [usu passive] ❑ *Attention was first drawn to the book when a condensed version was serialized in The New Yorker.* 初めてその本が注目されたのは, 雑誌『ニューヨーカー』に縮刷版が連載されたときだった.

se|rial num|ber (**serial numbers**) ❶ N-COUNT 可算名詞 The **serial number** of an object is a number on that object which identifies it. 通し番号 ❑ *...the gun's serial number.* その拳銃の通し番号 ❑ *...your bike's serial number.* あなたの自転車の製造番号. ❷ N-COUNT 可算名詞 The **serial number** of a member of the United States military forces is a number which identifies them. 認識番号 ❑ *He could never ever give any responses to his captor other than name, rank, serial number and date of birth.* 彼は捕らわれても, 氏名, 階級, 認識番号, 生年月日以外の情報は一切答えることができなかった.

se|rial port (**serial ports**) N-COUNT 可算名詞 A **serial port** on a computer is a place where you can connect the computer to a device such as a modem or a mouse. シリアルポート [COMPUTING コンピューティング]

se|ries /síəriz/ (**series**)

Series is both the singular and the plural form.

Series は単数形でも複数形でもある.

❶ N-COUNT 可算名詞 A **series of** things or events is a number of them that come one after the other. 一連 ❑ *...a series of meetings with students and political leaders.* 学生と政治指導者の一連の会談. ❷ N-COUNT 可算名詞 A radio or television **series** is a set of programs of a particular kind which have the same title. シリーズ ❑ *...Captain Kirk's chair from the TV series "Star Trek."* テレビシリーズ『スタートレック』のカーク船長のいす.

se|ri|ous /síəriəs/ ❶ ADJ 形容詞 **Serious** problems or situations are very bad and cause people to be worried or afraid. 深刻な ❑ *Crime is an increasingly serious problem in Russian society.* ロシアでは犯罪がますます深刻な社会問題になっている. ❑ *The government*

still face very serious difficulties. 政府はまだ非常に重大な困難に直面している. ● **se|ri|ous|ly** ADV 副詞 深刻に ❑ *If this ban was to come in it would seriously damage my business.* この禁止令が発令されたら, 私の事業は深刻なダメージを受けるだろう. ● **se|ri|ous|ness** N-UNCOUNT 不可算名詞 [oft N "of" n] 深刻さ ❑ *...the seriousness of the crisis.* その危機の深刻さ ❷ ADJ 形容詞 **Serious** matters are important and deserve careful and thoughtful consideration. 重大な ❑ *I regard this as a serious matter.* 私はこれを重大事項ととらえています. ❑ *Don't laugh boy. This is serious.* 笑ってはいけないよ, お前. これは大変なことなんだ. ❸ ADJ 形容詞 When important matters are dealt with in a **serious** way, they are given careful and thoughtful consideration. 真剣な ❑ *My parents never really faced up to my drug use in any serious way.* 両親はおれが薬物を使用しているという事実に何ら真剣に向き合わなかったのさ. ❑ *It was a question which deserved serious consideration.* それは真剣に考慮すべき問題だった. ● **se|ri|ous|ly** ADV 副詞 [ADV with v] 真剣に ❑ *The management will have to think seriously about their positions.* 経営陣は自分たちの地位を真剣に考えなければならなくなるだろう. ❹ ADJ 形容詞 **Serious** music or literature requires concentration to understand or appreciate it. 固い, 芸術本位の [ADJ n] ❑ *...serious classical music.* 芸術的なクラッシック音楽. ❺ ADJ 形容詞 If someone is **serious about** something, they are sincere about what they are saying, doing, or intending to do. 本気の ❑ *You really are serious about this, aren't you?* あなたは本当にこのことは本気なのね. ● **se|ri|ous|ly** ADV 副詞 本気で ❑ *Are you seriously jealous of Erica?* あなたは本気でエリカにしっとしてるの? ● **se|ri|ous|ness** N-UNCOUNT 不可算名詞 [oft N "of" n] 本気 ❑ *In all seriousness, there is nothing else I can do.* 冗談抜きで, 僕ができることは他に何もないよ. ❻ ADJ 形容詞 **Serious** people are thoughtful and quiet, and do not laugh very often. まじめな ❑ *He's quite a serious person.* 彼は本当にまじめな人です. ● **se|ri|ous|ly** ADV 副詞 [ADV with v] まじめに ❑ *They spoke to me very seriously but politely.* 彼らは神妙かつ礼儀正しく私に話しかけてきました.

<table>
<tr><td colspan="2">**Thesaurus**　　　　serious また次を参照:</td></tr>
<tr><td>ADJ.</td><td>crucial, important, significant; (ant.) unimportant ❶ ❷
businesslike, humorless, solemn; (ant.) cheerful ❻</td></tr>
</table>

<table>
<tr><td colspan="2">**Word Partnership**　　serious は次の語句と使われる:</td></tr>
<tr><td>N.</td><td>serious **accident**, serious **condition**, serious **crime**, serious **danger**, serious **harm**, serious **illness**, serious **injury**, serious **mistake**, serious **problem**, serious **threat**, serious **trouble** ❶
serious **matter**, serious **situation** ❶ ❷
serious **business**, serious **question** ❷
serious **consideration**, serious **doubts** ❸
serious **expression**, serious **face** ❻</td></tr>
<tr><td>ADV.</td><td>potentially serious ❶ ❷
extremely serious, more serious, quite serious, really serious, very serious ❶ – ❸ ❺ ❻
deadly serious ❷ ❺ ❻</td></tr>
</table>

se|ri|ous|ly /síəriəsli/ ❶ ADV 副詞 You use **seriously** to indicate that you are not joking and that you really mean what you say. 本当のところ [ADV with cl] ❑ *Seriously, I only smoke in the evenings.* 実は晩にばかこを吸いません. ❷ CONVENTION 慣習表現 You say "**seriously**" when you are surprised by what someone has said, as a way of asking them if they really mean it. 本当に [SPOKEN 口語, FEELINGS 感情] ❑ *"I tried to chat him up at the general store." He laughed. "Seriously?"* 「雑貨屋で彼に話しかけようとしたのさ」彼は笑った. 「本当かい?」 ❸ → see also **serious** ❹ PHRASE 句 If you **take** someone or something **seriously**, you believe that they are important and deserve attention. ～を真剣に考える ❑ *It's hard to take them seriously in their pretty gray uniforms.* かわいいグレーの制服を着た女の子なんて本気にはなれないよ.

ser|mon /sɑ́ːrmən/ (**sermons**) N-COUNT 可算名詞 A **sermon** is a talk on a religious or moral subject that is given by a member of the clergy as part of a church service. 説教 ❑ *Cardinal Murphy will deliver the sermon on Sunday.* マーフィー枢機卿は日曜日に説教を行います.

ser|pent /sɑ́ːrpənt/ (**serpents**) N-COUNT 可算名詞 A **serpent** is a snake. ヘビ [LITERARY 文語的] ❑ *...the serpent in the Garden of Eden.* エデンの園のヘビ.

se|rum /síərəm/ (**serums**) ❶ N-VAR 可変性名詞 A **serum** is a liquid that is injected into someone's blood to protect them against a poison or disease. 血清 ❑ *...painful injections of anti-cancer serum.* 抗癌性血清の苦痛を伴う注射. ❷ N-UNCOUNT 不可算名詞 **Serum** is the watery, pale yellow part of blood. 漿液 (しょうえき) ❑ *The strip, which accepts blood, serum or plasma, is inserted into the analyzer.* 血液, 漿液, もしくは血漿 (けっしょう) が入っている小片を分析器に挿入します.

S

serv|ant /ˈsɜːrvᵊnt/ (servants) **1** N-COUNT 可算名詞 A **servant** is someone who is employed to work at another person's home, for example, as a cleaner or a gardener. 使用人 □...a large Victorian family with several servants. 数名の使用人を抱えたビクトリア時代の大家族. **2** N-COUNT 可算名詞 You can use **servant** to refer to someone or something that provides a service for people or can be used by them. 奉仕者 □ Like any other public servants, police must respond to public demand. 他の公務員同様、警察は人々の要求にこたえなくてはならない. **3** → see also civil **servant**

serve /sɜːrv/ (serves, serving, served) **1** V-T 他動詞 If you **serve** your country, an organization, or a person, you do useful work for them. 仕える □ It is unfair to soldiers who have served their country well for many years. それは何年も国によく仕えてきた軍人に対して不公平だ. **2** V-I 自動詞 If you **serve** in a particular place or as a particular official, you perform official duties, especially in the armed forces, as a civil servant, or as a politician. 勤務する □ During the second world war he served with 92nd Airborne. 第2次世界大戦中、彼は第92空挺(くうてい)師団に所属していた. □ They have both served on the school board. 彼らはどちらも教育委員会のメンバーである. **3** V-T/V-I 他動詞/自動詞 If something **serves as** a particular thing or **serves** a particular purpose, it performs a particular function, which is often not its intended function. 役割を果たす □ She ushered me into the front room, which served as her office. 彼女は自分の事務室にしている表側の部屋に私を通してくれた. □ I really do not think that an inquiry would serve any useful purpose. 私は本当に、問い合わせをしても何の役にも立たないだろうと思う. **4** V-T 他動詞 If something **serves** people or an area, it provides them with something that they need. 必要を満たす □ This could mean the closure of thousands of small businesses which serve the community. このことで、地域社会の必要を満たしている何千社もの小企業が閉鎖することになりかねない. □ ...improvements in the public water-supply system serving the Nairobi area. ナイロビ地区の公共給水設備の改善 **5** V-T 動詞 Something that **serves** someone's interests benefits them. 役に立つ □ The economy should be organized to serve the interests of all the people. 経済は全ての人の利益にかなうように計画されるべきだ. **6** V-T/V-I 他動詞/自動詞 When you **serve** food and drinks, you give people food and drinks. (飲食物を)出す □ Serve it with French bread. それにはフランスパンをつけてお出ししてね. □ Serve the cakes warm. ケーキは温めて出してください. □ Refrigerate until ready to serve. 食卓に出すまでは冷蔵してください. ● PHRASAL VERB 句動詞 **Serve up** means the same as **serve**. (飲食物を)出す □ After all, it is no use serving up TV dinners if the kids won't eat them. 結局、子供たちに食べる気がないならテレビディナーを出しても無駄ですよ. **7** V-T 他動詞 **Serve** is used to indicate how much food a recipe produces. For example, a recipe that **serves** six provides enough food for six people. 一人分である [no cont] □ Garnish with fresh herbs. Serves 4. 生のハーブを添えましょう. これで4人分です. **8** V-T/V-I 他動詞/自動詞 Someone who **serves** customers in a store or a bar helps them and provides them with what they want to buy. 応対する □ They wouldn't serve me in any bars because I looked too young. 私は幼く見えたから、どこのバーでもお客として扱われなかったのよ. **9** V-T 他動詞 When the police or other officials **serve** someone **with** a legal order or **serve** an order on them, they give or send the legal order to them. 送達する、執行する [LEGAL 法律的] □ Immigration officers tried to serve her with a deportation order. 入国管理官は彼女に退去命令を送達しようとした. **10** V-T 他動詞 If you **serve** something such as a prison sentence or an apprenticeship, you spend a period of time doing it. 務める □ ...Leo, who is currently serving a life sentence for murder. 現在殺人罪で終身刑に服しているレオ **11** V-T/V-I 他動詞/自動詞 When you **serve** in games such as tennis and badminton, you throw up the ball or shuttlecock and hit it to start play. サーブする □ He served 17 double faults. 彼は17回のダブルフォールトを犯した. ● N-COUNT 可算名詞 **Serve** is also a noun. サーブ □ His second serve clipped the net. 彼のセカンドサーブはネットした. **12** N-COUNT 可算名詞 When you describe someone's **serve**, you are indicating how well or how fast they serve a ball or shuttlecock. サーブ □ His powerful serve was too much for the defending champion. 彼の力強いサーブには前回優勝者もかないませんでした. **13** → see also serving **14** PHRASE 句 If you say **it serves** someone **right** when something unpleasant happens to them, you mean that it is their own fault and you have no sympathy for them. 自業自得である [FEELINGS 感情] □ Serves her right for being so stubborn. あんなに強情だったのだから彼女の自業自得よ.

▶ **serve up** → see **serve** 6

Word Partnership *serve* は次の語句と使われる:

N.	serve **a community**, serve **the public** **1** **4**
	serve **a purpose** **3**
	serve **someone's needs** **5**
	serve **cake**, serve **food** **6**

---

serv|er /ˈsɜːrvər/ (servers) **1** N-COUNT 可算名詞 In computing, a **server** is part of a computer network which does a particular task, such as storing or processing information, for all or part of the network. サーバー [COMPUTING コンピューティング] **2** N-COUNT 可算名詞 A **server** is a person who works in a restaurant, serving people with food and drink. 給仕 [AM 米国英語] □ A server came by balancing a tray of wineglasses. 給仕がワイングラスを載せたトレーの平衡を保って通り過ぎた. **3** N-COUNT 可算名詞 In tennis and badminton, the **server** is the player whose turn it is to hit the ball or shuttlecock to start play. サーバー □ ...the fastest server in tennis. 最速のテニスサーバー.

→ see **Internet, tennis**

---

service

❶ NOUN AND ADJECTIVE USES
❷ VERB USES
❸ PHRASES

---

❶ **ser|vice** /ˈsɜːrvɪs/ (services) **1** N-COUNT 可算名詞 A **service** is something that the public needs, such as transportation, communications facilities, hospitals, or energy supplies, which is provided in a planned and organized way by the government or an official body. 公益事業 □ The postal service has been trying to cut costs. 郵便事業はコスト削減を試みてきた. □ We have started a campaign for better nursery and school services. 我々は、より良い保育所、学校サービスに向けての運動を始めました. **2** N-COUNT 可算名詞 You can sometimes refer to an organization or private company as a particular **service** when it provides something for the public or acts on behalf of the government. 部門 □ The Agriculture Department has ultimate control over the Forest Service. 農務省は林野部に対して最高の権限を持つ. **3** N-COUNT 可算名詞 If an organization or company provides a particular **service**, they can do a particular job or a type of work for you. サービス □ The kitchen maintains a twenty-four hour service and can be contacted via reception. 厨房は24時間サービスです. ご要望がございましたらフロントへお申し付けください. **4** N-PLURAL 複数名詞 **Services** are activities such as tourism, banking, and selling things which are part of a country's economy, but are not concerned with producing or manufacturing goods. サービス産業 □ Mining rose by 9.1%, manufacturing by 9.4% and services by 4.3%. 鉱業は9.1、製造業は9.4、サービス業は4.3パーセント上昇した. **5** N-UNCOUNT 不可算名詞 The level or standard of **service** provided by an organization or company is the amount or quality of the work it can do for you. サービス □ Taking risks is the only way employees can provide effective and efficient customer service. リスクを負うことが、従業員が顧客に効果的で効率の良いサービスを提供する唯一の方法です. **6** N-COUNT 可算名詞 A bus or train **service** is a route or regular trip that is part of a transportation system. 運行便 □ The local bus service is well run and extensive. 地方のバス便は本数も多く、広範囲をカバーしています. **7** N-PLURAL 複数名詞 Your **services** are the things that you do or the skills that you use in your job, which other people find useful and are usually willing to pay you for. サービス □ I have obtained the services of a top photographer to take our pictures. 私は自分たちの写真は一流の写真家に撮ってもらってきました. **8** N-UNCOUNT 不可算名詞 If you refer to someone's **service** or **services to** a particular organization or activity, you mean that they have done a lot of work for it or spent a lot of their time on it. 従事 [also N in pl, oft N "to" n] □ You've given a lifetime of service to athletics. あなたはこれまでずっと陸上競技にあけてきたのよ. □ Most employees had long service with the company and were familiar with our products. 従業員の大半は当社での勤続年数が長く、当社の製品に明るかった. **9** N-COUNT 可算名詞 The **Services** are the army, the navy, the air force and the marines. 陸海空軍 □ Some of the money could be spent on persuading key specialists to stay in the Services. 重要な熟練兵を軍に残るように促すのに、その資金の一部が投入されるだろう. **10** N-UNCOUNT 不可算名詞 **Service** is the work done by people or equipment in the army, navy, or air force, for example, during a war. 軍務 □ Units are being called up today for service in the Gulf. 部隊が今日湾岸地区での軍務に召集される. **11** N-UNCOUNT 不可算名詞 When you receive **service** in a restaurant, hotel, or store, an employee asks you what you want or gives you what you have ordered. サービス □ Service was attentive and the meal proceeded at a leisurely pace. サービスは行き届いており、食事もゆったりと進みました. **12** N-COUNT 可算名詞 A **service** is a religious ceremony that takes place in a church or synagogue. 礼拝 [also no det] □ After the hour-long service, his body was taken to a cemetery in the south of the city. 1時間の礼拝の後、彼の遺体は市の南部の共同墓地へ運ばれた. **13** N-COUNT 可算名詞 If a vehicle or machine has a **service**, it is examined, adjusted, and cleaned so that it will keep working efficiently and safely. 点検 [also no det] □ The car needs a service. その車は修理が必要だ. **14** N-COUNT 可算名詞 A **dinner service** or a **tea service** is a complete set of plates, cups, saucers, and other pieces of china. 一式 □ ...a 60-piece dinner service. 60点一式のディナー用食器類. **15** N-COUNT 可算名詞 In tennis, badminton, and some other sports, when it is your **service**, it is your turn to serve. サーブ権 □ She conceded just three points on her service during the first set. 第1セットで彼女が自分のサービスゲ

ームで許した得点は3点だけだった. ⓰ ADJ 形容詞 **Service** is used to describe the parts of a building or structure that are used by the staff who clean, repair, or take care of it, and are not usually used by the public. 業務用の [ADJ n] ❑ I went out through the kitchen and down the service elevator. 私は調理場から出て, 業務用エレベータ ーで下りました. ⓱ → see also **civil service, community service, emergency services, in-service, public service, room service** → see **dry-cleaning, economics, industry, library**

❷ **ser|vice** /sɜ͟ːvɪs/ (services, servicing, serviced) ❶ V-T 他 動詞 If you have a vehicle or machine **serviced**, you arrange for someone to examine, adjust, and clean it so that it will keep working efficiently and safely. 保守点検する ❑ I had my car serviced at the local garage. 私は車を地元の整備工場で保守点検 してもらった. ❷ V-T 他動詞 If someone or something **services** an organization, a project, or a group of people, they provide it with the things that it needs in order to function properly or effectively. サービスを提供する ❑ There are now 400 staff at headquarters, servicing our regional and overseas work. 今本社では400名 のスタッフが, 地域および海外のサービスを担当しています.

❸ **ser|vice** /sɜ͟ːvɪs/ ❶ PHRASE 句 If you **do** someone **a service**, you do something that helps or benefits them. ～の手助けを する, ～の役に立つ ❑ You are doing me a great service, and I'm very grateful to you. 私のためによく尽くしてくださって, あなたにはとて も感謝しています. ❷ PHRASE 句 If a piece of equipment or type of vehicle is **in service**, it is being used or is able to be used. If it is **out of service**, it is not being used, usually because it is not working properly. 稼働中の, 休止中の ❑ Cuts in funding have meant that equipment has been kept in service long after it should have been replaced. 資金が削減された結果, 設備が取替え時期を過ぎた後もずっと使い続 けることになった. ❑ In 1882, the city's first electric tram cars went into service. 1882年, 市内で初めて路面電車が運行を開始した.

ser|vice charge (**service charges**) N-COUNT 可算名詞 A **service charge** is an amount that is added to your bill in a restaurant to pay for the work of the person who comes and serves you. サービ ス料 ❑ Most restaurants add a 10 percent service charge to the bill. ほと んどのレストランでは勘定書きに10パーセントのサービス料を加える.

ser|vice in|dus|try (**service industries**) N-COUNT 可算名詞 A **service industry** is an industry such as banking or insurance that provides a service but does not produce anything. サービス産業 ❑ Seventy-two percent of people now work in service industries. 今では72 パーセントの人々がサービス産業で働いている.

ser|vice|man /sɜ͟ːvɪsmən/ (**servicemen**) N-COUNT 可算名 詞 A **serviceman** is a man who is in the army, navy, air force, or marines. 軍人 ❑ He was an American serviceman based in Vietnam during the war. 彼はベトナム戦争では現地に駐屯したアメリカ軍人だ った.

ser|vice pro|vid|er (**service providers**) N-COUNT 可算名詞 A **service provider** is a company that provides a service, especially an Internet service. プロバイダー [COMPUTING コンピューティング]

ser|vice sta|tion (**service stations**) N-COUNT 可算名詞 A **service station** is a place that sells things for vehicles such as gas, oil, and spare parts. Service stations often sell food, drinks, and other products. ガソリンスタンド

serv|ing /sɜ͟ːvɪŋ/ (**servings**) ❶ N-COUNT 可算名詞 A **serving** is an amount of food that is given to one person at a meal. 1人 分 ❑ Quantities will vary according to how many servings of soup you want to prepare. 分量は何人分のスープを用意するかによって変わり ます. ❷ ADJ 形容詞 A **serving** spoon or dish is used for giving out food at a meal. 給仕用の [ADJ n] ❑ Pile the potatoes into a warm serving dish. そのジャガイモは温めておいた給仕用のお皿に盛ってく ださい.

ses|sion /se͟ʃ⁰n/ (**sessions**) ❶ N-COUNT 可算名詞 A **session** is a meeting of a court, legislature, or other official group. 会合 [also "in" N] ❑ After two late-night sessions, the Security Council has failed to reach agreement. 夜遅くの2回の会合が持たれましたが, 安全保障 理事会は合意には至りませんでした. ❑ The Arab League is meeting in emergency session today. アラブ連盟は本日緊急の会合を開いて いる. ❷ N-COUNT 可算名詞 A **session** is a period during which the meetings of a court, legislature, or other official group are regularly held. 会期 [also "in" N] ❑ From September until December, Congress remained in session. 9月から12月まで議会は開会してい た. ❸ N-COUNT 可算名詞 A **session** of a particular activity is a period of that activity. 期間 ❑ The two leaders emerged for a photo session. その2人の指導者が写真撮影の時間のために現れました.

---

set

❶ NOUN USES
❷ VERB AND ADJECTIVE USES

---

❶ **set** /se͟t/ (**sets**) ❶ N-COUNT 可算名詞 A **set of** things is a number of things that belong together or that are thought of as a group. 一式 ❑ There must be one set of laws for the whole of the country. 国全体として一連の法律がなくてはならない. ❑ The mattress and base are normally bought as a set. 普通, マットレスとベッド本体はセット で購入されている. ❑ ...a chess set. チェスセット. ❷ N-COUNT 可 算名詞 In tennis, a **set** is one of the groups of six or more games that form part of a match. セット ❑ Graf was leading 5-1 in the first set. 第1セットではグラフは5‐1でリードしていた. ❸ N-COUNT 可算 名詞 In mathematics, a **set** is a group of mathematical quantities that have some characteristic in common. 集合 ❑ ...the field of set theory. 集合論の分野. ❹ N-COUNT 可算名詞 The **set** for a play, movie, or television show is the furniture and scenery that is on the stage when the play is being performed or in the studio where filming takes place. セット [also "on/off" N] ❑ From the first moment he got on the set, he wanted to be a director too. セットに 立ったその瞬間から, 彼は監督もやってみたいと思ったのです. ❑ He achieved fame for his stage sets for the Folies Bergères. 彼はフォリー・ ベルジェールの舞台セットで名声を得た. ❺ N-COUNT 可算名詞 A **set** is an appliance that receives television or radio signals. For example, a television set is a television. 装置 ❑ Children spend so much time in front of the television set. 子供たちはテレビの前でとても 長い時間を費やしている.

❷ **set** /se͟t/ (**sets, setting**)

The form **set** is used in the present tense and is the past tense and past participle of the verb.

set 形は現在時制に使われ, 動詞の過去時制と過去分詞でもある.

➭ Please look at category ㉒ to see if the expression you are looking for is shown under another headword. ❶ V-T 他動詞 If you **set** something somewhere, you put it there, especially in a careful or deliberate way. 設置する ❑ He took the case out of her hand and set it on the floor. 彼は彼女の手からケースを取って床に置 いた. ❷ ADJ 形容詞 If something is **set** in a particular place or position, it is in that place or position. ～にある [v-link ADJ prep/ adv] ❑ The castle is set in 25 acres of beautiful grounds. 城は25エーカ ーの美しい敷地に建っている. ❸ ADJ 形容詞 If something is **set into** a surface, it is fixed there and does not stick out. 埋め込まれ た [v-link ADJ prep/adv] ❑ The man unlocked a gate set in a high wall and let me through. その男は高い壁に埋め込まれた門の錠を開け, 私 を通してくれた. ❹ V-T 他動詞 You can use **set** to say that a person or thing causes another person or thing to be in a particular condition or situation. For example, to **set** someone free means to cause them to be free, and to **set** something going means to cause it to start working. (ある状態に) させる ❑ Set the kitchen timer going. キッチンタイマーをオンにしてください. ❑ Dozens of people have been injured and many vehicles set on fire. 負傷者は数十人 にも上り, 何台もの車が炎上しました. ❺ V-T 他動詞 When you **set** a clock or control, you adjust it to a particular point or level. セ ットする ❑ Set the volume as high as possible. 音量を最大にセットし てください. ❻ V-T 他動詞 If you **set** a date, price, goal, or level, you decide what it will be. 決める ❑ The conference chairman has set a deadline of noon tomorrow. 議長は期限を明日の正午に定めた. ❑ A date will be set for a future meeting. 今後の会議日程が設定される でしょう. ❼ V-T 他動詞 If you **set** a certain value **on** something, you think it has that value. 評価を与える ❑ She sets a high value on autonomy. 彼女は自治を重要視している. ❽ V-T 他動詞 If you **set** something such as a record, an example, or a precedent, you do something that people will want to copy or try to achieve. つく り出す ❑ Legal experts said her case would not set a precedent because it was an out-of-court settlement. 法律の専門家によれば, 示談が成 立したから彼女のケースは先例にはならないだろう, とのことだっ た. ❾ V-T 他動詞 If someone **sets** you a task or aim or if you **set** yourself a task or aim, you need to succeed in doing it. 課す ❑ I have to plan my academic work very rigidly and set myself clear objectives. 私は, 厳格に学業計画を立て, 自身に明確な目標を課さなければな らないのです. ❿ ADJ 形容詞 You use **set** to describe something which is fixed and cannot be changed. 定められた ❑ A set period of fasting is supposed to bring us closer to godliness. 一定期間断食する と私たちはより信心深くなると考えられている. ⓫ ADJ 形容詞 A **set** book must be studied by students taking a particular course. 指定 の [BRIT 英国英語] [ADJ n] [AM required 米国英語 required] の. ⓬ ADJ 形 容詞 If a play, movie, or story is **set** in a particular place or period of time, the events in it take place in that place or period. (舞 台や場面が) 設定された [v-link ADJ prep/adv] ❑ The play is set in a small Midwestern town. その芝居は中西部の小さな町が舞台になってい る. ⓭ ADJ 形容詞 If you are **set to** do something, you are ready to do it or are likely to do it. If something is **set to** happen, it is about to happen or likely to happen. ～の用意が整って [v-link ADJ to-inf] ❑ Roberto Baggio was set to become one of the greatest players of all time. ロベルト・バッジオは史上最高のプレーヤーの1人になろうとしてい た. ⓮ ADJ 形容詞 If you are **set on** something, you are strongly determined to do or have it. If you are **set against** something, you are strongly determined not to do or have it. 決意した [v-link ADJ "on/against" n/-ing] ❑ She was set on going to an all-girls school. 彼 女は女子校に行こうと決めていた. ⓯ V-I 自動詞 When something such as jelly, melted plastic, or cement **sets**, it becomes firm or hard. 固まる ❑ You can add ingredients to these desserts as they begin

to set. デザートが固まり始めたら具材を加えることができる. **16** V-I 自動詞 When the sun **sets**, it goes below the horizon. 沈む □ They watched the sun set behind the distant dales. 彼らは遠くの谷に日が沈むのをじっと眺めた. **17** V-T 他動詞 To **set** a trap means to prepare it to catch someone or something. 仕掛ける □ He seemed to think I was setting some sort of trap for him. 彼は私が彼を落としいれようとしていると思っているようだった. **18** V-T 他動詞 When someone **sets** the table, they prepare it for a meal by putting plates and flatware on it. (食卓を) 整える □ One would shop and cook, another would set the table and another would wash up. 買い物と調理, 配膳, 洗い物の係りを1人ずつで担当する予定でした. **19** V-T 他動詞 If someone **sets** a poem or a piece of writing to music, they write music for the words to be sung to. (曲を) つける □ He has attracted much interest by setting ancient religious texts to music. 昔の宗教的文章に曲をつけたことで彼に大きな関心が寄せられた. **20** → see also **setting** **21** PHRASE 句 If someone **sets the scene** or **sets the stage for** an event to take place, they make preparations so that it can take place. 〜のおぜん立てをする □ The Democratic convention has set the scene for a ferocious election campaign this fall. 民主党大会は, この秋の熾烈 (しれつ) な選挙戦への準備を整えた. **22** to **set fire to** something → see **fire** **23** to **set foot** somewhere → see **foot** **24** to **set your heart on** something → see **heart** **25** to **set sail** → see **sail** **26** to **set to work** → see **work**

Thesaurus

set また次を参照:

N.	bunch, group **①** **1**
	scene **①** **4**
V.	arrange, place **②** **1** **2**
	decide, fix **②** **6** **7**
ADJ.	established **②** **10**

▶ **set aside** **1** PHRASAL VERB 句動詞 If you **set** something **aside** for a special use or purpose, you keep it available for that use or purpose. 取っておく □ Some doctors advise setting aside a certain hour each day for worry. 毎日悩むための時間を設けるように助言する医者もいる. **2** PHRASAL VERB 句動詞 If you **set aside** a belief, principle, or feeling, you decide that you will not be influenced by it. 無視する □ He urged the participants to set aside minor differences for the sake of achieving peace. 彼は参加者に, 平和実現のためにはわずかな相違点は無視してほしいと要請しました.

▶ **set back** **1** PHRASAL VERB 句動詞 If something **sets** you **back** or **sets** a project or plan, it causes a delay. 遅らせる □ It has set us back in so many respects that I'm not sure how long it will take for us to catch up. そのことによってあまりにも多くの点で進行が滞ってしまったので, 遅れを取り戻すのにどのくらいかかるか私には見当がつきません. **2** PHRASAL VERB 句動詞 If something **sets** you **back** a certain amount of money, it costs you that much money. 費用がかかる [INFORMAL くだけた] □ A bottle of imported beer will set you back $7. 輸入ビールは1瓶7ドルするでしょう. **3** → see also **setback**

▶ **set down** **1** PHRASAL VERB 句動詞 If a committee or organization **sets down** rules for doing something, it decides what they should be and officially records them. 定める □ I like to make suggestions rather than setting down laws and forcing people to follow them. 私は法律を定めて人々にそれを強いるのではなく, 提案をしたいのです. **2** PHRASAL VERB 句動詞 If you **set down** your thoughts or experiences, you write them all down. 書き留める □ Old Walter is setting down his memories of village life. ウォルター老人は村の生活の思い出を書きつづっている.

▶ **set in** PHRASAL VERB 句動詞 If something unpleasant **sets in**, it begins and seems likely to continue or develop. (好ましくないことが) 始まる □ Winter is setting in and the population is facing food and fuel shortages. 冬が始まり, 住民は食糧と燃料不足に直面しています.

▶ **set off** **1** PHRASAL VERB 句動詞 When you **set off**, you start a journey. 出発する □ Nichols set off for his remote farmhouse in Connecticut. ニコルスはコネチカット州のへんぴなところにある別荘に出かけた. □ The president's envoy set off on another diplomatic trip. 大統領特使が次の外交訪問に出発した. **2** PHRASAL VERB 句動詞 If something **sets off** something such as an alarm or a bomb, it makes it start working so that, for example, the alarm rings or the bomb explodes. 作動させる □ Any escape, once it's detected, sets off the alarm. いかなる逃亡も検知されれば警報が作動する. □ Someone set off a fire extinguisher. 誰かが消火器を放射した. **3** PHRASAL VERB 句動詞 If something **sets off** an event or a series of events, it causes it to start happening. 引き起こす □ The arrival of the charity van set off a minor riot as villagers scrambled for a share of the aid. 救援物資輸送車が到着すると, 援助物資を分けてもらおうと村人が押しかけ, 小競り合いが起こった.

▶ **set out** **1** PHRASAL VERB 句動詞 When you **set out**, you start a journey. 出発する □ When setting out on a long walk, always wear suitable boots. 長い散歩に出かけるときは, 必ずそれに適した靴をはきなさい. **2** PHRASAL VERB 句動詞 If you **set out** to do something, you start trying to do it. 〜し始める □ He has achieved what he set out to do three years ago. 彼は3年前にし始めたことをようやく成し遂げた. **3** PHRASAL VERB 句動詞 If you **set** things **out**, you arrange or display them somewhere. 並べる □ Set out the cakes attractively,

using lacy doilies. レースのドイリーを敷いて, ケーキを見栄えよく並べなさい. **4** PHRASAL VERB 句動詞 If you **set out** a number of facts, beliefs, or arguments, you explain them in writing or speech in a clear, organized way. 明確に述べる, 明確に書く □ He has written a letter to The Times setting out his views. 彼は自分の考えを明確に記した手紙を『タイムズ』紙に投稿した.

▶ **set up** **1** PHRASAL VERB 句動詞 If you **set** something **up**, you create or arrange it. 設置する □ The two sides agreed to set up a commission to investigate claims. 双方が要求を調査する委員会を設立することに同意した. □ ...an organization which sets up meetings about issues of interest to women. 女性に関心のある問題についての会合を設ける組織. ● **setting up** N-UNCOUNT 不可算名詞 設立 □ The government announced the setting up of a special fund. 政府は特別基金の設立を発表しました. **2** PHRASAL VERB 句動詞 If you **set up** a temporary structure, you place it or build it somewhere. 築く □ They took to the streets, setting up roadblocks of burning tires. 彼らは街頭に出て, 火をつけたタイヤで道路にバリケードを築いた. **3** PHRASAL VERB 句動詞 If you **set up** a device or piece of machinery, you do the things that are necessary for it to be able to start working. 据え付ける □ Setting up the camera can be tricky. カメラの設置には注意を要する場合がある. **4** PHRASAL VERB 句動詞 If you **set up** somewhere or **set yourself up** somewhere, you establish yourself in a new business or new area. (事業などを) 設立する □ The mayor's plan offers incentives to firms setting up in lower Manhattan. 市長の計画には, マンハッタン南端部での事業設立に対する奨励措置が盛り込まれている. □ He worked as a dance instructor in London before setting himself up in Bucharest. ブカレストで身を立てるまで彼はロンドンでダンスの教師をしていた. □ Grandfather set them up in a printing business. 祖父は彼らに印刷業を始めさせた. **5** PHRASAL VERB 句動詞 If you **set up** house or home or **set up** shop, you buy a house or business of your own and start living or working there. (家・店舗を) 構える □ They married, and set up home in Atlanta. 彼らは結婚し, アトランタに家を構えた. **6** PHRASAL VERB 句動詞 If you **are set up** by someone, they make it seem that you have done something wrong when you have not. はめる [INFORMAL くだけた] □ He claimed yesterday that he had been set up after drugs were discovered at his home. 彼は昨日, 自宅で麻薬が発見されてから, 自分ははめられたのだと主張した. **7** → see also **setup**

set|back /sɛtbæk/ (**setbacks**) N-COUNT 可算名詞 A **setback** is an event that delays your progress or reverses some of the progress that you have made. 後退 [oft N "for/in/to" n] □ The move represents a setback for the Middle East peace process. その運動は中東和平プロセスの後退を表している.

set|tee /sɛti/ (**settees**) N-COUNT 可算名詞 A **settee** is a long comfortable seat with a back and arms, which two or more people can sit on. ソファー

set|ting /sɛtɪŋ/ (**settings**) **1** N-COUNT 可算名詞 A particular **setting** is a particular place or type of surroundings where something is or takes place. 環境 □ Rome is the perfect setting for romance. ローマは恋愛に最適な場所です. **2** N-COUNT 可算名詞 A **setting** is one of the positions to which the controls of a device such as a stove or heater can be adjusted. (機械・装置などの) 調節 □ You can boil the fish fillets on a high setting. 魚の切り身は高温でゆでてもいいです.

set|tle /sɛtᵊl/ (**settles, settling, settled**) **1** V-T 他動詞 If people **settle** an argument or problem, or if something **settles** it, they solve it, for example, by making a decision about who is right or about what to do. 解決する □ They agreed to try to settle their dispute by negotiation. 彼らは争議を話し合いによって解決するよう試みることに同意した. **2** V-T/V-I 他動詞/自動詞 If people **settle** a legal dispute or if they **settle**, they agree to end the dispute without going to a court of law, for example, by paying some money or by apologizing. 示談する, 和解する □ In an attempt to settle the case, Molken has agreed to pay restitution. その訴訟で和解を成立させるために, モルケンは賠償金を支払うことに同意した. □ She got much less than she would have done if she had settled out of court. 彼女は裁判所で和解を成立させた場合に比べてずっと少ない額しか受け取っていない. **3** V-T/V-I 他動詞/自動詞 If you **settle** a bill or debt, you pay the amount that you owe. 支払う, 清算する □ I settled the bill for my coffee and his two glasses of wine. 私は, 自分のコーヒーと彼が飲んだワイン2杯分の勘定を済ませた. □ She has now settled with her landlord. 彼女はもう家賃の支払いを済ませた. **4** V-T 他動詞 If something **is settled**, it has all been decided and arranged. 決める, 決着をつける [usu passive] □ As far as we're concerned, the matter is settled. 私たちの目から見れば, その問題は決着がついている. **5** V-T/V-I 他動詞/自動詞 When people **settle** a place or in a place, or when a government **settles** them there, they start living there permanently. 移住させる [他動詞], 定住する [自動詞] □ Refugees settling in a new country suffer from a number of problems. 新しい国に移住している難民はあらゆる問題を抱えている. □ He visited Paris and eventually settled there. 彼はパリを訪れて, 結局はそこに移り住みました. **6** V-T/V-I 他動詞/自動詞 If you **settle yourself** somewhere or **settle** somewhere, you sit down or make yourself comfortable. 座ってくつろぐ □ Albert settled himself on the sofa. ア

ルパートはソファーに腰を下ろしてくつろいだ。 **7** V-T/V-I 他動詞/自動詞 If something **settles** or if you **settle** it, it sinks slowly down and becomes still. 積もらせる，沈殿させる [他動詞]，積もる，沈殿する [自動詞] □A black dust settled on the walls. 黒いほこりが壁に積もった。 □Once its impurities had settled, the oil could be graded. いったんその不純物が沈殿すれば，油を選別できる。 **8** V-I 自動詞 If your eyes **settle on** or **upon** something, you stop looking around and look at that thing for some time. (目が) くぎづけになる □The man let his eyes settle upon Blume's face. その男の目がブルーンの顔にくぎづけになっていた。 **9** V-I 自動詞 When birds or insects **settle on** something, they land on it from above. 留まる □Moths flew in front of it, eventually settling on the rough painted metal. ガがその前を飛び，結局ペンキ塗りのざらざらの金属の上に留まった。 **10** → see also **settled 11** when the dust settles → see dust **12** to settle a score → see score

▶ **settle down 1** PHRASAL VERB 句動詞 When someone **settles down**, they start living a quiet life in one place, especially when they get married or buy a house. 落ち着く □One day I'll want to settle down and have a family. いつか結婚して身を固めたいと思っています。 **2** PHRASAL VERB 句動詞 If a situation or a person that has been going through a lot of problems or changes **settles down**, they become calm. 落ち着く，解決する □It'd be fun, after the situation in Europe settles down, to take a trip to France. ヨーロッパの情勢が落ち着いたらフランスに旅行に行くと楽しいだろう。 **3** PHRASAL VERB 句動詞 If you **settle down to** do something or **to** something, you prepare to do it and concentrate on it. 本腰を入れて取りかかる □He got his coffee, came back and settled down to listen. 彼はコーヒーを持って戻り，聞くことに集中した。 **4** PHRASAL VERB 句動詞 If you **settle down** for the night, you get ready to lie down and sleep. 寝支度を整える □They put up their tents and settled down for the night. 彼らはテントを張って寝支度を整えた。

▶ **settle for** PHRASAL VERB 句動詞 If you **settle for** something, you choose or accept it, especially when it is not what you really want but there is nothing else available. 一でよしとする，一で我慢する □Virginia was a perfectionist. She was just not prepared to settle for anything mediocre. バージニアは完ぺき主義者だった。月並みなもので我慢する気は全然なかった。

▶ **settle in** PHRASAL VERB 句動詞 If you **settle in**, you become used to living in a new place, doing a new job, or going to a new school. 慣れる □I enjoyed school enormously once I'd settled in. いったん慣れると，学校生活がとっても楽しかった。

▶ **settle on** PHRASAL VERB 句動詞 If you **settle on** a particular thing, you choose it after considering other possible choices. 決定する □I finally settled on a Mercedes. It's the ideal car for me. やっとベンツに決めた。それが僕には理想的な車だ。

▶ **settle up** PHRASAL VERB 句動詞 When you **settle up**, you pay a bill or a debt. 勘定を払う，清算する □I'll have to settle up what I owe for the phone. 私は電話代を清算しないといけない。

Word Partnership	settleは次の語句と使われる:
N.	settle **differences**, settle **things** ☐
	settle **a dispute**, settle **a matter** ☐ ☐
	settle **a case**, settle **a claim**, settle **a lawsuit/suit** ☐
V.	**agree** to settle, **decide to** settle ☐ – ☐

set|tled /sɛtˀld/ **1** ADJ 形容詞 If you have a **settled** way of life, you stay in one place, in one job, or with one person, rather than moving around or changing. 安定した □He decided to lead a more settled life with his partner. 彼はパートナーともっと安定した生活を送るように決めた。 **2** ADJ 形容詞 A **settled** situation or system stays the same all the time. 安定した，変化のない □There has been a period of settled weather. しばらく安定した天気が続いている。

set|tle|ment /sɛtˀlmənt/ (**settlements**) **1** N-COUNT 可算名詞 A **settlement** is an official agreement between two sides who were involved in a conflict or argument. 和解，合意 □Our objective must be to secure a peace settlement. 我々の目的は和平調停を確実にすることであるべきだ。 **2** N-COUNT 可算名詞 A **settlement** is an agreement to end a disagreement or dispute without going to a court of law, for example, by offering someone money. 示談 □She accepted an out-of-court settlement of $40,000. 彼女は4万ドルの示談金に承諾した。 **3** N-UNCOUNT 不可算名詞 The **settlement** of a debt is the act of paying back money that you owe. 決済，清算 □...ways to delay the settlement of debts. 借金返済を遅らせる方法 **4** N-COUNT 可算名詞 A **settlement** is a place where people have come to live and have built homes. 集落 □The village is a settlement of just fifty houses. その村はたった50軒の集落だ。

set|tler /sɛtlər, sɛtˀl-/ (**settlers**) N-COUNT 可算名詞 **Settlers** are people who go to live in a new country. 移住者，開拓者 □The first German village in southwestern Siberia was founded a century ago by settlers from the Volga region. 南西シベリアでの最初のドイツ村落はボルガ地方からの移住者によって100年前に形成された。

set-top box (**set-top boxes**) N-COUNT 可算名詞 A **set-top box** is a piece of equipment that rests on top of your television and receives digital television signals. セットトップボックス

set|up /sɛtʌp/ (**setups**) also **set-up 1** N-COUNT 可算名詞 A particular **setup** is a particular system or way of organizing something. [INFORMAL くだけた] □It appears to be an idyllic domestic setup. のどかな家庭のようだ。 **2** N-COUNT 可算名詞 If you describe a situation as a **setup**, you mean that people have planned it in order to deceive you or to make it look as if you have done something wrong. わな [INFORMAL くだけた] □He was asked to pick somebody up and bring them to a party, not realizing it was a setup. 彼は人を迎えに行ってパーティに連れて来るように頼まれたのですが，それがわなだとは気づきませんでした。 **3** N-SING 単数名詞 The **setup** of computer hardware or software is the process of installing it and making it ready to use. セットアップ [COMPUTING コンピューティング] □The worst part of the setup is the poor instruction manual. セットアップで最悪なのは取扱説明書が分かりにくいことだ。

sev|en /sɛvˀn/ (**sevens**) NUM 数詞 **Seven** is the number 7. 7 □Sarah and Ella have been friends for seven years. サラとエラは親しくなって7年になる。

Word Link	teen ≈ plus ten, from 13-19 : eighteen, seventeen, teenager

sev|en|teen /sɛvˀntin/ (**seventeens**) NUM 数詞 **Seventeen** is the number 17. 17 □Jenny is seventeen years old. ジェニーは17歳だ。

sev|en|teenth /sɛvˀntinθ/ (**seventeenths**) **1** ORD 序数詞 The **seventeenth** item in a series is the one that you count as number seventeen. 17番目の □She gave birth to Annabel just after her seventeenth birthday. 彼女は17歳の誕生日の直後にアナベルを出産した。 **2** FRACTION 端数 A **seventeenth** is one of seventeen equal parts of something. 17分の1

sev|enth /sɛvˀnθ/ (**sevenths**) **1** ORD 序数詞 The **seventh** item in a series is the one that you count as number seven. 7番目の □I was the seventh child in the family. 私は家族で7番目の子供だった。 **2** FRACTION 端数 A **seventh** is one of seven equal parts of something. 7分の1 □A million people died, a seventh of the population. 人口の7分の1に当たる100万人が死亡した。

sev|en|ti|eth /sɛvˀntiəθ/ (**seventieths**) **1** ORD 序数詞 The **seventieth** item in a series is the one that you count as number seventy. 70番目の □...the seventieth anniversary of the discovery of Tutankhamun's tomb. ツタンカーメンの墓の発見70周年記念祭 **2** FRACTION 端数 A **seventieth** is one of seventy equal parts of something. 70分の1

sev|en|ty /sɛvˀnti/ (**seventies**) **1** NUM 数詞 **Seventy** is the number 70. 70 □Seventy people were killed. 70人が死亡した。 **2** N-PLURAL 複数名詞 When you talk about the **seventies**, you are referring to numbers between 70 and 79. For example, if you are in your **seventies**, you are aged between 70 and 79. If the temperature is in the **seventies**, it is between 70 and 79. 70代，70度台 □I thought it was a long way to go for two people in their seventies, but Sylvia loved the idea. 70代の2人が行くには遠すぎると思ったが，シルビアは乗り気だった。 **3** N-PLURAL 複数名詞 The **seventies** is the decade between 1970 and 1979. 70年代 □In the late Seventies, things had to be new, modern, revolutionary. 70年代の終わりごろは，何でも新しく現代的で画期的でなければならなかった。

Word Link	sever ≈ separating : sever, several, severance

sev|er /sɛvər/ (**severs, severing, severed**) **1** V-T 他動詞 To **sever** something means to cut through it or to cut it completely off. 切断する [FORMAL 形式ばった] □Richardson severed his right foot in a motorcycle accident. リチャードソンはオートバイ事故で右足を切断した。 **2** V-T 他動詞 If you **sever** a relationship or connection that you have with someone, you end it suddenly and completely. 断絶する [FORMAL 形式ばった] □She severed her ties with her homeland. 彼女は母国とのつながりを断ち切った。

sev|er|al /sɛvrəl/ DET 限定詞 **Several** is used to refer to a number of people or things that is not large but is greater than two. いくつかの，何人かの □I had lived two doors away from this family for several years. 私はこの家族の2軒隣で数年間暮らした。 □Several blue plastic boxes under the window were filled with CDs. 窓の下に置かれたいくつかの青いプラスチックの箱にはCDが詰められていた。 ●QUANT 数量詞 **Several** is also a quantifier. いくつか，何人か [QUANT "of" pl-n] □The building was picketed by demonstrators, several of whom were well-known actors. デモ参加者がそのビルでピケを張っていたが，その中には有名な俳優もいた。 ●PRON 代名詞 **Several** is also a pronoun. 数人 □No one drug will suit or work for everyone and sometimes several may have to be tried. 1種類の薬が全員に適するわけでも効くわけでもなく，ときには数種類を試すことが必要かもしれない。

sev|er|ance /sɛvrəns, -ərəns/ ADJ 形容詞 **Severance** pay is a sum of money that a company gives to its employees when it has to stop employing them. 解雇手当，退職金 [BUSINESS 実業] [ADJ n] □We were offered 13 weeks' severance pay. 13週間分の給料を退職金として提示された。

S

se|vere /sɪvɪər/ (severer, severest) ■ ADJ 形容詞 You use **severe** to indicate that something bad or undesirable is great or intense. 深刻な □ *...a business with severe cash flow problems.* 深刻な資金難を抱えた会社 □ *Shortages of professional staff are very severe in some places.* 専門的な職員の不足は地域によっては非常に深刻だ. ● **se|vere|ly** ADV 副詞 深刻に □ *The U.N. wants to send food aid to 10 countries in Africa severely affected by the drought.* 国連は干ばつで大被害を受けたアフリカの10カ国に食糧援助を行うことを希望しています. □ *An aircraft overshot the runway and was severely damaged.* 飛行機が滑走路をオーバーランし, かなり破損した. ● **se|ver|ity** /sɪvɛrɪti/ N-UNCOUNT 不可算名詞 [usu with supp] 深刻さ □ *Several drugs are used to lessen the severity of the symptoms.* 数種類の薬が症状を和らげるために使用された. ■ ADJ 形容詞 **Severe** punishments or criticisms are very strong or harsh. 厳しい □ *This was a dreadful crime and a severe sentence is necessary.* これは恐ろしい犯罪で厳罰が必要だ. ● **se|vere|ly** ADV 副詞 [ADV with v] 厳しく □ *...a campaign to try to change the law to punish dangerous drivers more severely.* 危険な運転をするドライバーをもっと厳しく罰するよう法律改正を求めるキャンペーン ● **se|ver|ity** N-UNCOUNT 不可算名詞 [usu with supp] 厳重さ □ *He was sickened by the severity of the sentence.* 彼は判決の厳しさに腹を立てた.

Thesaurus severe また次を参照:

ADJ. critical, extreme, intense, tough ■ ■

Word Partnership severe は次の語句と使われる:

N. severe **consequences**, severe **depression**, severe **disease/illness**, severe **drought**, severe **flooding**, severe **injuries**, severe **pain**, severe **problem**, severe **symptoms**, severe **weather** ■
severe **penalty**, severe **punishment** ■
ADV. **less/more/most** severe, **very** severe ■ ■

---

sew /soʊ/ (sews, sewing, sewed, sewn) V-T/V-I 他動詞/自動詞 When you **sew** something such as clothes, you make them or repair them by joining pieces of cloth together by passing thread through them with a needle. 縫う □ *She sewed the dresses on the sewing machine.* 彼女はミシンでドレスを縫った. □ *Anyone can sew on a button, including you.* あなたを含めて誰でもボタンの縫い付けができる. → see **quilt**

sew|age /suɪdʒ/ N-UNCOUNT 不可算名詞 **Sewage** is waste matter such as feces or dirty water from homes and factories, which flows away through sewers. 下水 □ *...treatment of raw sewage.* 下水処理 → see **pollution**

sew|er /suər/ (sewers) N-COUNT 可算名詞 A **sewer** is a large underground channel that carries waste matter and rain water away, usually to a place where it is treated and made harmless. 下水管, 下水道 □ *...the city's sewer system.* 市の下水道

sew|ing /soʊɪŋ/ ■ N-UNCOUNT 不可算名詞 **Sewing** is the activity of making or mending clothes or other things using a needle and thread. 裁縫, 針仕事 □ *Her mother had always done all the sewing.* 彼女の母がいつもすべての針仕事をした. ■ N-UNCOUNT 不可算名詞 **Sewing** is clothes or other things that are being sewn. 衣類, 服 □ *We all got out our own sewing and sat in front of the log fire.* 私たちはみんな服を脱いで暖炉の前に座った.

sewn /soʊn/ **Sewn** is the past participle of **sew**. sewの過去分詞

sex /sɛks/ (sexes, sexing, sexed) ■ N-COUNT 可算名詞 The two **sexes** are the two groups, male and female, into which people and animals are divided according to the function they have in producing young. 男性, 女性 □ *...a movie star who appeals to all ages and both sexes.* すべての年齢層と男性・女性両方に人気の映画スター □ → see also **opposite sex** ■ N-COUNT 可算名詞 The **sex** of a person or animal is their characteristic of being either male or female. 性 □ *She continually failed to gain promotion because of her sex.* 彼女は女性であるためになかなか昇進できなかった. □ *The new technique has been used to identify the sex of fetuses.* 胎児の性を識別するために新技術が使用されてきた. ■ N-UNCOUNT 不可算名詞 **Sex** is the physical activity by which people can produce young. 性交, セックス □ *He was very open in his attitudes about sex.* 彼はセックスに対する考え方がとてもオープンだった. □ *The entire film revolves around drugs, sex and violence.* その映画全体が麻薬, セックス, そして暴力を中心に展開する. ■ PHRASE 句 If two people **have sex**, they perform the act of sex. セックスする □ *Have you ever thought about having sex with someone other than your husband?* 夫以外の人とセックスすることを考えたことがありますか?

▶ **sex up** PHRASAL VERB 句動詞 To **sex** something **up** means to make it seem more attractive or interesting than it actually is. いっそう魅力的に見せかける, セクシーにする [INFORMAL くだけた] □ *Nintendo is sexing up its U.S. advertising to launch the new handheld device.* 任天堂は, 新しい携帯ゲームの販売のために米国での広告を派手に行っている.

---

sex|ism /sɛksɪzəm/ N-UNCOUNT 不可算名詞 **Sexism** is the belief that the members of one sex, usually women, are less intelligent or less capable than those of the other sex and need not be treated equally. It is also the behavior which is the result of this belief. 性差別主義 □ *Groups like ours are committed to eradicating homophobia, racism and sexism.* 私たちのような団体は同性愛嫌悪, 人種差別そして性差別をなくすことに尽力している.

sex|ist /sɛksɪst/ (sexists) ADJ 形容詞 If you describe people or their behavior as **sexist**, you mean that they are influenced by the belief that the members of one sex, usually women, are less intelligent or less capable than those of the other sex and need not be treated equally. 性差別的な [DISAPPROVAL 不賛成] □ *Old-fashioned sexist attitudes are still common.* 時代遅れの性差別的な態度は依然としてよく見られる. ● N-COUNT 可算名詞 A **sexist** is someone with sexist views or behavior. 性差別主義者 □ *It's got nothing to do with sexism. You know I'm not a sexist.* それは性差別とは全く関係ない. 私が性差別をしないのは知っているだろう.

sex symbol (sex symbols) N-COUNT 可算名詞 A **sex symbol** is a famous person, especially an actor or a singer, who is considered by many people to be sexually attractive. セックスシンボル, セクシーな有名人 □ *...Hollywood sex symbols of the Forties.* ハリウッドの40年代のセックスシンボル

sex|ual /sɛkʃuəl/ ■ ADJ 形容詞 **Sexual** feelings or activities are connected with the act of sex or with people's desire for sex. 性の, 性的な □ *This was the first sexual relationship I'd had.* これは私の初めての肉体関係でした. ● **sexu|al|ly** ADV 副詞 □ *...sexually transmitted diseases.* 性感染症 ■ ADJ 形容詞 **Sexual** means relating to the differences between male and female people. 性別の, 性差の □ *Women's groups denounced sexual discrimination.* 女性団体が性差別を公然と非難した. ● **sexu|al|ly** ADV 副詞 [ADV with v] 性的に □ *If you're sexually harassed, you ought to do something about it.* セクハラにあった場合は何らかの手を打つべきです. ■ ADJ 形容詞 **Sexual** means relating to the differences between heterosexuals and homosexuals. 性的指向の □ *...couples of all sexual persuasions.* あらゆる性的指向を持ったカップル ■ ADJ 形容詞 **Sexual** means relating to the biological process by which animals and people produce young. 有性の, 生殖の □ *Girls generally reach sexual maturity two years earlier than boys.* 女子は男子よりも一般的に2年早く性的に成熟する. ● **sexu|al|ly** ADV 副詞 男女別に □ *The first organisms that reproduced sexually were free-floating plankton.* 最初に有性生殖をした生物は浮遊性のプランクトンだった.

sex|ual abuse N-UNCOUNT 不可算名詞 If a child or other person suffers **sexual abuse**, someone forces them to take part in sexual activity with them, often regularly over a period of time. 性的虐待 □ *...victims of sexual abuse.* 性的虐待の被害者

sex|ual har|ass|ment N-UNCOUNT 不可算名詞 **Sexual harassment** is repeated and unwelcome sexual comments, looks, or physical contact at work, usually a man's actions that offend a woman. セクハラ, 性的嫌がらせ □ *Sexual harassment of women workers by their bosses is believed to be widespread.* 上司による女性社員へのセクハラは広範囲に及ぶとみられる.

sex|ual inter|course N-UNCOUNT 不可算名詞 **Sexual intercourse** is the physical act of sex between two people. 性交 [FORMAL 形式ばった] □ *I have never had sexual intercourse with her and that is the truth.* 私は彼女と性交を行ったことは1度もなく, それは事実だ.

sexu|al|ity /sɛkʃuælɪti/ ■ N-UNCOUNT 不可算名詞 A person's **sexuality** is their sexual feelings. 性衝動, 性衝動 □ *...the growing discussion of women's sexuality.* 女性の性行動に関して高まる論議 ■ N-UNCOUNT 不可算名詞 You can refer to a person's **sexuality** when you are talking about whether they are sexually attracted to people of the same sex or a different sex. 性的指向 □ *He believes he has been discriminated against because of his sexuality.* 彼は自分の性的指向のために差別されていると思っている.

sexy /sɛksi/ (sexier, sexiest) ADJ 形容詞 You can describe people and things as **sexy** if you think they are sexually exciting or sexually attractive. セクシーな, 色っぽい □ *She was one of the sexiest women I had seen.* 彼女は僕が今までに出会った中で最もセクシーな女性の1人だった.

sh /ʃ/ → see **shh**

shab|by /ʃæbi/ (shabbier, shabbiest) ADJ 形容詞 **Shabby** things or places look old and in bad condition. ボロボロの, みすぼらしい □ *His clothes were old and shabby.* 彼の服はボロボロでみすぼらしかった.

shack /ʃæk/ (shacks, shacking, shacked) N-COUNT 可算名詞 A **shack** is a simple hut built from tin, wood, or other materials. 掘っ立て小屋

▶ **shack up** PHRASAL VERB 句動詞 If someone **has shacked up with** someone else or two people **have shacked up** together, they have started living together as lovers. 同棲(どうせい)する [INFORMAL くだけた] □ *...the deserters who had shacked up with local women.* 地元の女性と同棲(どうせい)した脱走兵 □ *Young people are afraid to get*

married, so they shack up. 若者たちは結婚するのを恐れて，それで同棲（どうせい）する．

shade /ʃeɪd/ (shades, shading, shaded) **1** N-COUNT 可算名詞 A **shade of** a particular color is one of its different forms. For example, emerald green and olive green are shades of green. 色調 ▫ In the mornings the sky appeared a heavy shade of mottled gray. 午前中の空はところどころどんよりと暗かった． ▫ The walls were painted in two shades of green. 壁は2種類の緑の色調で塗られていた． **2** N-UNCOUNT 不可算名詞 **Shade** is an area of darkness under or next to an object such as a tree, where sunlight does not reach. 日陰 ▫ Temperatures in the shade can reach forty-eight degrees Celsius at this time of year. 日陰の気温はこの時期には摂氏48度に達することがある． ▫ Alexis walked up the coast, and resumed his reading in the shade of an overhanging cliff. アレクシスは海岸を歩き，突き出たがけの日陰で再び読書を始めた． **3** V-T 他動詞 If you say that a place or person **is shaded** by objects such as trees, you mean that the place or person cannot be reached, harmed, or bothered by strong sunlight because those objects are in the way. 陰にする ▫ ...a health resort whose beaches are shaded by palm trees. ビーチにヤシの木で日陰になっている保養地 **4** V-T 他動詞 If you **shade** your eyes, you put your hand or an object partly in front of your face in order to prevent a bright light from shining into your eyes. (目を) 日ざしから守る ▫ You can't look directly into it; you've got to shade your eyes or close them altogether. 直接それを見込んではいけない．目に手をかざすか，しっかり両目を閉じなさい． **5** N-UNCOUNT 不可算名詞 **Shade** is darkness or shadows as they are shown in a picture. 陰影，陰 ▫ ...Rembrandt's skillful use of light and shade to create the atmosphere of movement. 動作の雰囲気を作り出すためにレンブラントが明暗を巧みに用いて **6** N-COUNT 可算名詞 The **shades of** something abstract are its many, slightly different forms. 微妙な違い ▫ ...the capacity to convey subtle shades of meaning. 微妙な意味合いを伝える能力 **7** N-COUNT 可算名詞 A **shade** is a piece of stiff cloth or heavy paper that you can pull down over a window as a covering. ブラインド [AM 米国英語] ▫ Nancy left the shades down and the lights off. ナンシーはブラインドを下ろして電気をつけていなかった．

shad|ow /ʃædoʊ/ (shadows, shadowing, shadowed) **1** N-COUNT 可算名詞 A **shadow** is a dark shape on a surface that is made when something stands between a light and the surface. 影，影法師 ▫ An oak tree cast its shadow over a tiny round pool. オークの木が小さな丸い水たまりに影を投げかけた． ▫ Nothing would grow in the shadow of the gray wall. 灰色の塀の影には何も育たないだろう． **2** N-UNCOUNT 不可算名詞 **Shadow** is darkness in a place caused by something preventing light from reaching it. 影，暗がり ▫ Most of the lake was in shadow. 湖のほとんどは陰になっていた． **3** V-T 他動詞 If something **shadows** a thing or place, it covers it with a shadow. 陰にする ▫ The hood shadowed her face. フードで彼女の顔が陰になっていた． **4** V-T 他動詞 If someone **shadows** you, they follow you very closely wherever you go. 尾行する，後をつける ▫ The president is constantly shadowed by bodyguards. 大統領には常にボディガードが後をつけている． **5** ADJ 形容詞 A British Member of Parliament who is a member of the **shadow** cabinet or who is a **shadow** cabinet minister belongs to the main opposition party and takes a special interest in matters which are the responsibility of a particular government minister. 影の [ADJ n] ▫ ...the shadow chancellor. 影の大蔵大臣 ● N-COUNT 可算名詞 **Shadow** is also a noun. 影の大臣 ▫ Clarke swung at his shadow the accusation that he was "a tabloid politician." クラークは，「タブロイド紙を騒がせる政治家」と非難されたことで影の大臣をうまくかわした． **6** PHRASE 句 If you say that something is true **without a shadow of a doubt** or **without a shadow of doubt**, you are emphasizing that there is no doubt at all that it is true. 少しの疑いもなく [EMPHASIS 強調] ▫ It was without a shadow of a doubt the best we've played. 間違いなく今までで最高のプレーだった． **7** PHRASE 句 If you live **in the shadow of** someone or in their **shadow**, their achievements and abilities are so great that you are not noticed or valued. 陰に隠れて，目立たずに ▫ He has always lived in the shadow of his brother. 彼はいつも兄の陰に隠れて暮らしてきた．

Word Partnership	shadow は次の語句と使われる:
N.	someone's shadow **1**
	shadow of something **1** **2** **6**
V.	cast a shadow **1** **2**
	live in the shadow **7**

shad|ow|y /ʃædoʊi/ **1** ADJ 形容詞 A **shadowy** place is dark or full of shadows. 陰になった ▫ I watched him from a shadowy corner. 私は陰になった角から彼を監視した． **2** ADJ 形容詞 A **shadowy** figure or shape is someone or something that you can hardly see because they are in a dark place. ぼんやりとした，まぼろしのような [ADJ n] ▫ ...a tall, shadowy figure silhouetted against the pale wall. 淡い色の壁に映った背が高くてぼんやりとした人影 **3** ADJ 形容詞 You describe activities and people as **shadowy** when very little is known about them. なぞに包まれた ▫ ...the shadowy world of spies.

スパイのなぞに包まれた世界

shady /ʃeɪdi/ (shadier, shadiest) **1** ADJ 形容詞 You can describe a place as **shady** when you like the fact that it is sheltered from bright sunlight, for example, by trees or buildings. 日陰の ▫ After flowering, place the pot in a shady spot in the garden. 花が咲いた後は，庭の日陰の場所に鉢を置きなさい． **2** ADJ 形容詞 You can describe activities as **shady** when you think that they might be dishonest or illegal. You can also use **shady** to describe people who are involved in such activities. うさんくさい，怪しい [DISAPPROVAL 不賛成] ▫ In the 1980s, the company was notorious for shady deals. 1980年代にその会社はいかがわしい取引をすることで知られていた．

shaft /ʃæft/ (shafts) **1** N-COUNT 可算名詞 A **shaft** is a long vertical passage, for example, for an elevator. シャフト（垂直の空間）▫ The fire began in an elevator shaft and spread to the roof. 火事はエレベーターのシャフトで発生し，屋根まで広がった． **2** N-COUNT 可算名詞 In a machine, a **shaft** is a rod that turns around continually in order to transfer movement in the machine. 軸，シャフト ▫ ...a drive shaft. ドライブシャフト **3** N-COUNT 可算名詞 A **shaft** is a long thin piece of wood or metal that forms part of a spear, ax, golf club, or other object. 柄，シャフト ▫ ...golf clubs with steel shafts. スチールシャフトのゴルフクラブ **4** N-COUNT 可算名詞 A **shaft** of light is a beam of light, for example, sunlight shining through an opening. 一筋 ▫ A brilliant shaft of sunlight burst through the doorway. 一筋の明るい太陽の光が戸口から急に差し込んできた．

shag|gy /ʃægi/ (shaggier, shaggiest) ADJ 形容詞 **Shaggy** hair or fur is long and messy. ぼさぼさの，もじゃもじゃの ▫ Tim, who still has longish, shaggy hair, used to turn up at official dinners in jeans and T-shirt. ティムは今でもぼさぼさの長髪だが，以前は公式の晩餐会にもジーンズとTシャツで現れたものだった．

shake /ʃeɪk/ (shakes, shaking, shook, shaken) **1** V-T 他動詞 If you **shake** something, you hold it and move it quickly backward and forward or up and down. You can also **shake** a person, for example, because you are angry with them or because you want them to wake up. 振る，揺さぶる ▫ The nurse took the thermometer, shook it, and put it under my armpit. 看護婦は体温計を手に取って振り，私のわきの下に入れた． ● N-COUNT 可算名詞 **Shake** is also a noun. ▫ She picked up the bag of salad and gave it a shake. 彼女はサラダが入った袋を取って，振った． **2** V-T 他動詞 If you **shake yourself** or your body, you make a lot of quick, small, repeated movements without moving from the place where you are. ブルブルッと体を震わせる ▫ As soon as he got inside, the dog shook himself. その犬は中に入るとすぐにブルブルッと体を震った． ● N-COUNT 可算名詞 **Shake** is also a noun. 体を震わせること ▫ Take some slow, deep breaths and give your body a bit of a shake. ゆっくり深呼吸をして体を少し揺すりなさい． **3** V-T 他動詞 If you **shake** your head, you turn it from side to side in order to say "no" or to show disbelief or sadness. 首を横に振る ▫ "Anything else?" Chris asked. Kathryn shook her head wearily. 「ほかに何か?」とクリスが尋ねた．キャスリンは疲れた様子で首を横に振った． ● N-COUNT 可算名詞 **Shake** is also a noun. 首を横に振ること ▫ "The elm trees are all dying," said Palmer, with a sad shake of his head. 「ニレの木が全部枯れかかっているよ」とパーマーは悲しそうに首を横に振りながら言った． **4** V-I 自動詞 If you **are shaking**, or a part of your body **is shaking**, you are making quick, small movements that you cannot control, for example, because you are cold or afraid. (体が) 震える ▫ He roared with laughter, shaking in his chair. 彼はいすに座って体を揺さぶるように爆笑をした． ▫ My hand shook so much that I could hardly hold the microphone. 私の手があまりに震えていたのでマイクを持つのがやっとだった． **5** V-T 他動詞 If you **shake** your fist or an object such as a stick **at** someone, you wave it in the air in front of them because you are angry with them. 振りかざす ▫ The colonel rushed to Earle and shook his gun at him. 大佐はアールのいるところに駆け上がり，銃を彼に向かって振りかざした． **6** V-T/V-I 他動詞/自動詞 If a force **shakes** something, or if something **shakes**, it moves from side to side or up and down with quick, small, but sometimes violent movements. 揺らし，震動させる [他動詞]，揺れる，震動する [自動詞] ▫ ...an explosion that shook buildings several kilometers away. 何キロも離れたところにある建物を揺らした爆発 **7** V-T 他動詞 To **shake** something into a certain place or state means to bring it into that place or state by moving it quickly up and down or from side to side. 振ってかける ▫ She shook some pepper onto her sandwich. 彼女はコショウを振ってサンドイッチにかけた． **8** V-I 自動詞 If your voice **is shaking**, you cannot control it properly and it sounds very unsteady, for example, because you are nervous or angry. (声が) 震える ▫ His voice shaking with rage, he asked how the committee could keep such a report from the public. 怒りで声を震わせながら，彼はどのようにして委員会がそのような報告書を一般から隠すことができたのかを尋ねました． **9** V-T 他動詞 If an event or a piece of news **shakes** you, or **shakes** your confidence, it makes you feel upset and unable to think calmly. 動揺させる [他動詞] ▫ There was no doubt that the news of Tandy's escape had shaken them all. タンディが逃げたという知らせに皆が動揺したのは間違いがなかった． **10** V-T 他動詞 If an event **shakes** a group of people or their beliefs, it causes great uncertainty and makes them question their beliefs. 揺るがす，ぐらつかせる ▫ The

five years she spent as a news correspondent in Moscow were five years that shook the world. 彼女が新聞通信記者としてモスクワで過ごした5年間は世界を揺るがした5年間だった. **11** PHRASE 句 If you **shake** someone's **hand** or **shake** someone **by the hand**, you shake hands with them. 一と握手する ❏ *I said congratulations and walked over to him and shook his hand.* 私はお祝いの言葉を述べて, 彼の方に歩み寄り握手した. **12** PHRASE 句 If you **shake hands with** someone, you take their right hand in your own for a few moments, often moving it up and down slightly, when you are saying hello or goodbye to them, congratulating them, or agreeing on something. You can also say that two people **shake hands**. 握手する ❏ *He nodded greetings to Mary Ann and Michael and shook hands with Burke.* 彼はマリアンとマイケルに会釈をし, バークと握手した.

▶ **shake down** **11** PHRASAL VERB 句動詞 If someone **shakes** you **down**, they use threats or search you physically in order to obtain something from you. ゆする, 恐喝する [AM 米国英語] ❏ *He accused the lawyer of shaking him down.* 彼は弁護士を恐喝の罪で告発した. ❏ ...*crooks who had tried to shake down other hotels.* 他のホテルを巻き上げようとした詐欺師 **2** → see also **shakedown**

▶ **shake off** **11** PHRASAL VERB 句動詞 If you **shake off** something that you do not want such as an illness or a bad habit, you manage to recover from it or get rid of it. 治す ❏ *Businessmen are frantically trying to shake off the bad habits learned under six decades of a protected economy.* 実業家たちは60年間続いた保護経済の下で身に付いた悪い癖を必死でぬぐおうとしている. **2** PHRASAL VERB 句動詞 If you **shake off** someone who is following you, you manage to get away from them, for example, by running faster than them. まく, 逃げる ❏ *Although I could pass him I could not shake him off.* 彼を追い越すことはできたがまくことはできなかった.

▶ **shake out** PHRASAL VERB 句動詞 If you wonder how something will **shake out**, you wonder how it will develop and what the outcome will be. 収まる [AM 米国英語] ❏ *We don't know how this situation will shake out.* この状況がどのように収まるか見当がつかない.

▶ **shake up** **11** PHRASAL VERB 句動詞 If someone **shakes up** something such as an organization, an institution, or a profession, they make major changes to it. 変革する ❏ *The government wanted to accelerate the reform of the institutions, to find new ways of shaking up the country.* 国を変革する新しい方法を探し出すために, 政府は制度の改革を促進することを求めていた. **2** → see also **shakeup**

Thesaurus   *shake* また次を参照:

V.	jerk, move, ruffle, swing **11** **2**

Word Partnership   *shake* は次の語句と使われる:

V.	**begin to** shake **11** – **7**
N.	shake *your* head **3**
	shake *someone's* confidence **9**
	shake *someone's* hand **11**
	shake hands (with *someone*) **12**

shake|up /ˈʃeɪkʌp/ (**shakeups**) N-COUNT 可算名詞 A **shakeup** is a major set of changes in an organization or a system. 大刷新, 大改革 [JOURNALISM ジャーナリズム] ❏ *Community leaders say a complete departmental shakeup is needed.* 地域社会の指導者は, 徹底的な省単位での大改革が必要だと述べています.

shaky /ˈʃeɪki/ (**shakier, shakiest**) **11** ADJ 形容詞 If you describe a situation as **shaky**, you mean that it is weak or unstable, and seems unlikely to last long or be successful. 不安定な ❏ *A shaky ceasefire is holding after three days of fighting between rival groups.* 対抗グループ間の開争が3日間続いた後不安定な停戦が持続している. **2** ADJ 形容詞 If your body or your voice is **shaky**, you cannot control it properly and it shakes, for example, because you are ill or nervous. ぶるぶる震えている ❏ *We have all had a shaky hand and a dry mouth before speaking in public.* 人前で話す前は, 私たちは皆手が震えてのどが渇く.

shall /ʃəl, STRONG ʃæl/

Shall is a modal verb. It is used with the base form of a verb.

Shall は法動詞であり, 動詞の原型とともに用いられる.

11 MODAL 法動詞 You use **shall** with "I" and "we" in questions in order to make offers or suggestions, or to ask for advice. 一しましょうか ❏ *Shall I get the keys?* かぎを取ってきましょうか. ❏ *Well, shall we go?* じゃあ, 行きましょうか. ❏ *Let's have a nice little stroll, shall we?* ちょっと散歩にでも行きましょうか. **2** MODAL 法動詞 You use **shall**, usually with "I" and "we," when you are referring to something that you intend to do, or when you are referring to something that you are sure will happen to you in the future. 一する予定である [FORMAL 形式ばった] ❏ *We shall be landing in Paris in sixteen minutes, exactly on time.* 定刻通り16分後にパリに到着の予定だ. ❏ *I shall know more next month, I hope.* 来月にはもう少し詳しいことが分かるはずだ. **3** MODAL 法動詞 You use **shall** with "I" or "we"

during a speech or piece of writing to say what you are going to discuss or explain later. 一します [FORMAL 形式ばった] ❏ *In Chapter 3, I shall describe some of the documentation that I gathered.* 第3章では私が集めた書類の一部について説明します. **4** MODAL 法動詞 You use **shall** to indicate that something must happen, usually because of a rule or law. You use **shall not** to indicate that something must not happen. 一すべし ❏ *The president shall hold office for five years.* 大統領は5年間在職すべし. **5** MODAL 法動詞 You use **shall**, usually with "you," when you are telling someone that they will be able to do or have something they want. 一してよい ❏ *Very well, if you want to go, you go you shall.* よろしい, 行きたいのなら行ってもいい.

shal|low /ˈʃæloʊ/ (**shallower, shallowest**) **11** ADJ 形容詞 A **shallow** container, hole, or area of water measures only a short distance from the top to the bottom. 浅い ❏ *Put the milk in a shallow dish.* 浅皿に牛乳を入れなさい. **2** ADJ 形容詞 If you describe a person, piece of work, or idea as **shallow**, you disapprove of them because they do not show or involve any serious or careful thought. 浅はかな [DISAPPROVAL 不賛成] ❏ *I think he is shallow, vain and untrustworthy.* 彼は浅はかでうぬぼれが強くて信用できないと思う. **3** ADJ 形容詞 If your breathing is **shallow**, you take only a very small amount of air into your lungs at each breath. (呼吸が) 浅い ❏ *She began to hear her own taut, shallow breathing.* 彼女は自分自身の緊張した浅い呼吸が聞こえ始めた.

sham /ʃæm/ (**shams**) N-COUNT 可算名詞 Something that is a **sham** is not real or is not really what it seems to be. いんちき [DISAPPROVAL 不賛成] ❏ *The government's promises were exposed as a hollow sham.* 政府の約束は無意味なごまかしだったことが暴かれた.

sham|bles /ˈʃæmbəlz/ N-SING 単数名詞 If a place, event, or situation is **a shambles** or is **in a shambles**, everything is in disorder. めちゃくちゃ, 大混乱 ❏ *The ship's interior was an utter shambles.* その船の内装は全くめちゃくちゃだった.

shame /ʃeɪm/ (**shames, shaming, shamed**) **11** N-UNCOUNT 不可算名詞 **Shame** is an uncomfortable feeling that you get when you have done something wrong or embarrassing, or when someone close to you has. 恥ずかしい思い, 羞恥 (しゅうち) 心 ❏ *She felt a deep sense of shame.* 彼女はとても後ろめたく感じた. ❏ *Her father and her brothers would die of shame.* 彼女の父親と兄弟は羞恥 (しゅうち) 心のために命を落とすだろう. **2** N-UNCOUNT 不可算名詞 If someone brings **shame** on you, they make other people lose their respect for you. 恥, 不面目 ❏ *I don't want to bring shame on the family name.* 私は家族の面目をつぶしたくない. **3** V-T 他動詞 If something **shames** you, it causes you to feel shame. 恥をかかせる ❏ *Her son's affair had humiliated and shamed her.* 彼女は息子の件で屈辱を感じ恥ずかしかった. **4** V-T 他動詞 If you **shame** someone **into** doing something, you force them to do it by making them feel ashamed not to. 辱めて一させる ❏ *He would not let neighbors shame him into silence.* 彼は, 辱めて黙らせようとする隣人に抵抗している. **5** N-SING 単数名詞 If you say that something is **a shame**, you are expressing your regret about it and indicating that you wish it had happened differently. 残念 [FEELINGS 感情] ❏ *It's a crying shame that police have to put up with these mindless attacks.* 警察がこれらの愚かな攻撃に耐えなければならないのは非常に残念だ. **6** CONVENTION 慣習表現 You can use **shame** in expressions such as **shame on you** and **shame on him** to indicate that someone ought to feel shame for something they have said or done. 恥知らずめ [FEELINGS 感情] ❏ *He tried to deny it. Shame on him!* 彼はそれを否定しようとした. みっともない限りだ. **7** PHRASE 句 If someone **puts** you **to shame**, they make you feel ashamed because they do something much better than you do. 一に恥ずかしい思いをさせる ❏ *His playing really put me to shame.* 彼の演奏は本当に素晴らしくて自分が恥ずかしくなる.

→ see emotion

Word Partnership   *shame* は次の語句と使われる:

V.	**experience** shame, **feel** shame **11**
N.	**feelings of** shame, **sense of** shame **11**

shame|ful /ˈʃeɪmfəl/ ADJ 形容詞 If you describe a person's action or attitude as **shameful**, you think that it is so bad that the person ought to be ashamed. 恥ずべき, けしからぬ [DISAPPROVAL 不賛成] ❏ ...*the most shameful episode in U.S. naval history.* 米国海軍の歴史の中で最も恥ずべき出来事 ● **shame|ful|ly** ADV 副詞 恥ずかしいほど ❏ *At times they have been shamefully neglected.* 時には, 彼らは恥ずかしいほどなおざりにされてきた.

shame|less /ˈʃeɪmləs/ ADJ 形容詞 If you describe someone as **shameless**, you mean that they should be ashamed of their behavior, which is unacceptable to other people. ずうずうしい, 恥知らずの [DISAPPROVAL 不賛成] ❏ ...*a shameless attempt to stifle democratic debate.* 民主主義的な議論を鎮圧させようとする恥知らずな試み ● **shame|less|ly** ADV 副詞 ずうずうしく ❏ ...*a shamelessly lazy week-long trip.* ずうずうしいほどに怠惰な1週間の旅

sham|poo /ʃæmˈpu/ (**shampoos, shampooing, shampooed**) **11** N-MASS 質量名詞 **Shampoo** is a soapy liquid that you use for

washing your hair. シャンプー ❑…*a bottle of shampoo.* シャンプーのボトル ❷ V-T 他動詞 When you **shampoo** your hair, you wash it using shampoo. シャンプーする，洗髪する ❑*Shampoo your hair and dry it.* 髪を洗って乾かしなさい。
→ see **hair**

shan't /ʃænt/ **Shan't** is the usual spoken form of "shall not." shall not の短縮形

shape /ʃeɪp/ (**shapes, shaping, shaped**) ❶ N-COUNT 可算名詞 The **shape of** an object, a person, or an area is the appearance of their outside edges or surfaces, for example, whether they are round, square, curved, or fat. 形，体形 [oft N "of" N, also "in" N] ❑*Each mirror is made to order and can be designed to almost any shape or size.* 各鏡はオーダーメードでほぼ希望通りの形や大きさにデザインできる。❑…*little pens in the shape of baseball bats.* 野球のバットの形をした小さなペン ❑…*sofas and chairs of contrasting shapes and colors.* 対照的な形と色をしたソファーやいす ❷ N-COUNT 可算名詞 You can refer to something that you can see as a **shape** if you cannot see it clearly, or if its outline is the clearest or most striking aspect of it. 物影 ❑*The great gray shape of a tank rolled out of the village.* 巨大な戦車の灰色の影がその村から現れた。❸ N-COUNT 可算名詞 A **shape** is a space enclosed by an outline, for example, a circle, a square, or a triangle. (描かれた) 形 ❑*Imagine a sort of a kidney shape.* 腎臓の形のようなものを思い浮かべてください。❹ N-SING 単数名詞 The **shape of** something that is planned or organized is its structure and character. 形態，性格 ❑*The last two weeks have seen a lot of talk about the future shape of Europe.* 過去2週間で将来のヨーロッパのあり方についてたくさんの論議がなされた。❺ V-T 他動詞 Someone or something that **shapes** a situation or an activity has a very great influence on the way it develops. 決定づける，方向づける ❑*Like it or not, our families shape our lives and make us what we are.* いやが応でも，家族が人生を方向づけ自分そのものを作り上げる。❻ V-T 他動詞 If you **shape** an object, you give it a particular shape, using your hands or a tool. 形作る ❑*Cut the dough in half and shape each half into a loaf.* パン生地を半分に切り，それぞれを1つのパンにしなさい。❼ → see also **shaped** ❽ PHRASE 句 If you say, for example, that you will not accept something **in any shape or form**, or **in any way, shape or form**, you are emphasizing that you will not accept it in any circumstances. 少しも—ない [EMPHASIS 強調] ❑*I don't condone violence in any shape or form.* 私は決して暴力を大目に見ることはありません。❾ PHRASE 句 If someone or something is **in shape**, or **in good shape**, they are in a good state of health or in a good condition. If they are **in bad shape**, they are in a bad state of health or in a bad condition. 体調がよくて/悪くて ❑…*the Fatburner Diet Book, a comprehensive guide to getting in shape.* 体調を整えるための総合的な手引書である『ザ・ファットバーナー・ダイエット・ブック』 ❑*He was still in better shape than many young men.* それでも彼ほど体調のよくない若者がたくさんいる。❿ PHRASE 句 If you **lick, knock,** or **whip** someone or something **into shape**, you use whatever methods are necessary to change or improve them so that they are in the condition that you want them to be in. 厳しく鍛え上げる，しごく ❑*You'll have four months in which to lick the recruits into shape.* 新社員をしごき上げるのに4か月ある。⓫ PHRASE 句 If something is **out of shape**, it is no longer in its proper or original shape, for example, because it has been damaged or wrongly handled. 形が崩れて ❑*Once most wires are bent out of shape, they don't return to the original position.* いったんほとんどの針金が折れて形が崩れると，元の状態に戻ることはない。⓬ PHRASE 句 When you are **out of shape**, you are unhealthy and unable to do a lot of physical activity without getting tired. 体調が悪くて ❑*I weighed 245 pounds and was out of shape.* 私は体重が245ポンドで体調不調だ。⓭ PHRASE 句 When something **takes shape**, it develops or starts to appear in such a way that it becomes fairly clear what its final form will be. 具体化する ❑*In 1912 women's events were added, and the modern Olympic program began to take shape.* 1912年に女性の競技が追加され，現代のオリンピックのプログラムがはっきりした形をとり始めた。

▸ **shape up** ❶ PHRASAL VERB 句動詞 If something **is shaping up**, it is starting to develop or seems likely to happen. 展開する ❑*There are also indications that a major tank battle may be shaping up for tonight.* 大規模な戦車戦が今夜展開する兆しもあります。❷ PHRASAL VERB 句動詞 If you ask how someone or something **is shaping up**, you want to know how well they are doing in a particular situation or activity. —となる ❑*I did have a few worries about how Hugh and I would shape up as parents.* ヒューと私がどんな親になるか少し心配でした。❸ PHRASAL VERB 句動詞 If you tell someone to **shape up**, you are telling them to start behaving in a sensible and responsible way. 行いを正す，しっかりする ❑*They were given a year to shape up or risk losing their scholarships.* 彼らは行いを正すために1年与えられ，さもなければ奨学金を失う危険がある。
→ see Picture Dictionary: **shapes**
→ see **circle, mathematics**

Word Partnership	*shape* は次の語句と使われる:
V.	**change** shape ❶
	change the shape **of** *something* ❹
	get in shape ❾
ADJ.	**dark** shape ❷
	(pretty) bad/good/great shape, **better/worse** shape, **physical** shape, **terrible** shape ❾

shaped /ʃeɪpt/ ADJ 形容詞 Something that is **shaped** like a particular object or in a particular way has the shape of that object or a shape of that type. —の形をした [v-link ADJ] ❑*A new perfume from Russia came in a bottle shaped like a tank.* ロシア製の新しい香水は戦車の形をした瓶に入っていた。

share /ʃɛər/ (**shares, sharing, shared**) ❶ N-COUNT 可算名詞 A company's **shares** are the many equal parts into which its ownership is divided. Shares can be bought by people as an investment. 株，株式 [BUSINESS 実業] ❑*People in China are eager to buy shares in new businesses.* 中国に住む人々は新しい企業の株の購入に熱心だ。❷ V-RECIP 相互動詞 If you **share** something **with** another person, you both have it, use it, or occupy it. You can also say that two people **share** something. 共用する，一緒に使う，分け合う ❑…*the small income he had shared with his brother from his father's estate.* 彼が兄と分け合った父親の不動産からのささやかな収入 ❑*Two Americans will share this year's Nobel Prize for Medicine.* 2人のアメリカ人が今年のノーベル医学賞を共同受賞するでしょう。❸ V-RECIP 相

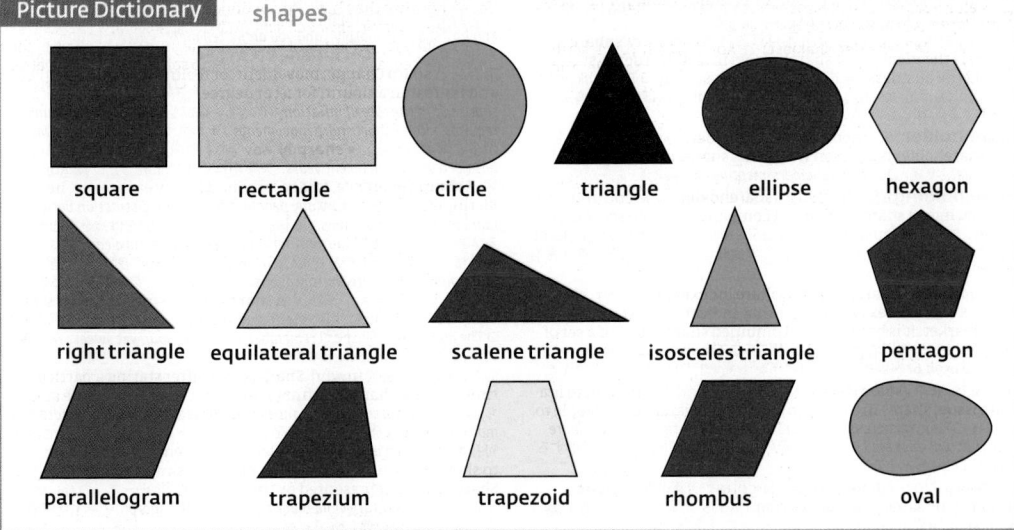

Picture Dictionary　　shapes

square

rectangle

circle

triangle

ellipse

hexagon

right triangle

equilateral triangle

scalene triangle

isosceles triangle

pentagon

parallelogram

trapezium

trapezoid

rhombus

oval

S

Word Web   shark

Sharks are different from other **fish**. The **skeleton** of a shark is made of **cartilage**, not bone. The flexibility of cartilage allows this **predator** to maneuver around its **prey** easily. Sharks also have several gill **slits** with no flap covering them. Its scales are also much smaller and harder than fish scales. And its teeth are special too. Sharks grow new teeth when they lose old ones. It's almost impossible to escape from a shark. Some of them can swim up to 44 miles per hour. But sharks only kill 50 to 75 people each year worldwide.

互助詞 If you **share** a task, duty, or responsibility **with** someone, you each carry out or accept part of it. You can also say that two people **share** something. 分担する ❑ *You can find out whether they are prepared to share the cost of the flowers with each other.* 彼らが花代を君と分担するつもりがあるのかどうか確かめてみたら. ⁴ V-RECIP 相互動詞 If you **share** an experience **with** someone, you have the same experience, often because you are with them at the time. You can also say that two people **share** something. 分かち合う ❑ *Yes, I want to share my life with you.* ええ，あなたと人生を分かち合いたいわ. ⁵ V-T 他動詞 If you **share** someone's opinion, you agree with them. 賛成する，同意する [no cont] ❑ *The forum's members share his view that business can be a positive force for change in developing countries.* フォーラムのメンバーは，ビジネスが開発途上国において肯定的な勢力となりうるという彼の見解に同意した. ⁶ V-RECIP 相互動詞 If one person or thing **shares** a quality or characteristic **with** another, they have the same quality or characteristic. You can also say that two people or things **share** something. 同じ一を持っている，共有する [no cont] ❑ *La Repubblica and El Pais are politically independent newspapers which share similar characteristics.* ラ・レプブリカ紙とエル・パイス紙はよく似た特徴を持つ政治的に独立した新聞社だ. ⁷ V-T/V-I 他動詞/自動詞 If you **share** something that you have with someone, you give some of it to them or let them use it. (自分のものを) 分ける，共有する ❑ *He shared his food with the family.* 彼は自分の食べ物を家族と分けた. ❑ *Scientists now have to compete for funding, and do not share information among themselves.* 科学者はこれからは研究費のために張り合わなければならず，互いに情報交換をしない. ❑ *I wanted everybody to share.* 私はみんなに自分のものを分け合って欲しかった. ⁸ V-T 他動詞 If you **share** something personal such as a thought or a piece of news **with** someone, you tell them about it. 伝える ❑ *It can be beneficial to share your feelings with someone you trust.* 信用する人に自分の気持ちを伝えることで気持ちが楽になるかもしれない. ⁹ N-COUNT 可算名詞 If something is divided or distributed among a number of different people or things, each of them has, or is responsible for, a **share** of it. 取り分，分担 ❑ *Sara also pays a share of the gas, electricity and phone bills.* サラもガス・電気・電話代の一部を負担している. ¹⁰ N-COUNT 可算名詞 If you have or do your **share** of something, you have or do an amount that seems reasonable to you, or to other people. 妥当な量 ❑ *Women must receive their fair share of training for good-paying jobs.* 女性は高給与の仕事に必要となるための適度な研修を受けなければなりません. ¹¹ → see also **lion's share, market share, power-sharing**
→ see **company**

▶ **share out** PHRASAL VERB 句動詞 If you **share out** an amount of something, you give each person in a group an equal or fair part of it. 平等に分ける，山分けする

share capi|tal N-UNCOUNT 不可算名詞 A company's **share capital** is the money that shareholders invest in order to start or expand the business. 株式資本金 [BUSINESS 実業] ❑ *The bank has a share capital of almost 100 million dollars.* その銀行はほぼ1億ドルの株式資本金を所有している.

share|holder /ʃɛərhoʊldər/ (**shareholders**) N-COUNT 可算名詞 A **shareholder** is a person who owns shares in a company. 株主 [BUSINESS 実業] ❑ *...a shareholder's meeting.* 株主総会

share|holding /ʃɛərhoʊldɪŋ/ (**shareholdings**) N-COUNT 可算名詞 If you have a **shareholding** in a company, you own some of its shares. 株式保有 [BUSINESS 実業] ❑ *She will retain her very significant shareholding in the company.* 彼女はその会社のかなりの比率の株式保有を維持するだろう.

share in|dex (**share indices** or **share indexes**) N-COUNT 可算名詞 A **share index** is a number that indicates the state of a stock market. It is based on the combined share prices of a set of companies. 株価指数 [BUSINESS 実業] ❑ *The share index was up 16.4 points to 1,599.6.* 株価指数は16.4ポイント高い1,599.6で取引を終えた.

share is|sue (**share issues**) N-COUNT 可算名詞 When there is a **share issue**, shares in a company are made available for people to buy. 株式発行 [BUSINESS 実業] ❑ *The deal will be financed by a share issue that will raise $128.9 million.* その取引は1億2890万ドルを調達する株式発行を財源とするだろう.

share op|tion (**share options**) N-COUNT 可算名詞 A **share option** is the same as a **stock option**. ストックオプション，株式購入権 [BRIT 英国英語 BUSINESS 実業]

share shop (**share shops**) N-COUNT 可算名詞 A **share shop** is a store or Internet website where members of the public can buy shares in companies. 株式販売会社，株式販売サイト [BUSINESS 実業]

share|ware /ʃɛərwɛər/ N-UNCOUNT 不可算名詞 **Shareware** is computer software that you can try before deciding whether or not to buy the legal right to use it. シェアウェア [COMPUTING コンピューティング] ❑ *...a shareware program.* シェアウェアプログラム

shark /ʃɑrk/ (**shark**)

The plural can also be **sharks**.

複数は **sharks** もある.

N-VAR 可変性名詞 A **shark** is a very large fish. Some sharks have very sharp teeth and may attack people. サメ
→ see Word Web: **shark**

sharp /ʃɑrp/ (**sharps, sharper, sharpest**) ¹ ADJ 形容詞 A **sharp** point or edge is very thin and can cut through things very easily. A **sharp** knife, tool, or other object has a point or edge of this kind. 鋭い，とがった ❑ *With a sharp knife, make diagonal slashes in the chicken breast.* よく切れる包丁でにわとりの胸肉にはすかいに切り目を入れなさい. ² ADJ 形容詞 You can describe a shape or an object as **sharp** if part of it or one end of it comes to a point or forms an angle. とがった，角張った ❑ *His nose was thin and sharp.* 彼の鼻は細くてとがっていた. ³ ADJ 形容詞 A **sharp** bend or turn is one that changes direction suddenly. 急な，鋭い ❑ *I was approaching a fairly sharp bend that swept downhill to the left.* 左に緩やかに下っているかなり急なカーブに近づいているところでした. ● ADV 副詞 **Sharp** is also an adverb. 急な角度に [ADV adv] ❑ *Do not cross the bridge but turn sharp left to go down on to the towpath.* 橋を渡らず左に急角度で曲がって引き船道に下りて行きなさい. ● **sharp|ly** ADV 副詞 [ADV after v] 急角度で ❑ *Room number nine was at the far end of the corridor where it turned sharply to the right.* 部屋番号9は急角度で右に曲がっている廊下の突き当たりにあった. ⁴ ADJ 形容詞 If you describe someone as **sharp**, you are praising them because they are quick to notice, hear, understand, or react to things. 頭の切れる，鋭敏な [APPROVAL 賛成] ❑ *He is very sharp, a quick thinker and swift with repartee.* 彼は非常に鋭敏で頭の回転が速く当意即妙の受け答えをする. ⁵ ADJ 形容詞 If someone says something in a **sharp** way, they say it suddenly and rather firmly or angrily, for example, because they are warning or criticizing you. しんらつな，とげとげしい ❑ *"Don't contradict your mother," was Charles's sharp reprimand.* 「お母さんに反抗するのはやめなさい」とチャールズは厳しくしかった. ● **sharp|ly** ADV 副詞 厳しく，とげとげしく ❑ *"You've known," she said sharply, "and you didn't tell me?"* 「あなたは知っていたくせに私に言わなかったのね」と彼女はとげとげしく言った. ⁶ ADJ 形容詞 A **sharp** change, movement, or feeling occurs suddenly, and is great in amount, force, or degree. 急激な ❑ *There's been a sharp rise in the rate of inflation.* インフレ率が急上昇した. ❑ *Tennis requires a lot of short sharp movements.* テニスでは短時間の急な動きが多く求められる. ● **sharp|ly** ADV 副詞 急激に ❑ *Unemployment has risen sharply in recent years.* 失業率は近年急上昇した. ⁷ ADJ 形容詞 A **sharp** difference, image, or sound is very easy to see, hear, or distinguish. 明確な ❑ *Many people make a sharp distinction between humans and other animals.* ヒトと他の動物との区別をはっきりとつける人々が多い. ❑ *All the footmarks are quite sharp and clear.* すべての足跡はかなりはっきりとしている. ● **sharp|ly** ADV 副詞 はっきりと ❑ *Opinions on this are sharply divided.* これについての意見ははっきりと分かれている. ⁸ ADJ 形容詞 A **sharp** taste or smell is rather strong or bitter, but is often also clear and fresh. ピリッとする，酸っぱい ❑ *The apple tasted just as I remembered – sharp, sour, yet sweet.* そのリンゴは，ピリッと酸っぱいけども甘さもあって，ちょうど懐かしい味がした. ⁹ ADV 副詞 [n ADV] **Sharp** is used after stating a particular time to show that something happens at exactly the time stated. ちょうど，きっかり ❑ *She planned to unlock the store at 8:00 sharp this morning.* 彼女は今朝8時きっかりに開店する予定だった. ¹⁰ N-COUNT 可算名詞 **Sharp** is used after a letter representing a musical note to show that the note should be played or sung half a tone higher. **Sharp** is often represented by the symbol ♯. シャープ (の音) 嬰音 (えいおん) ❑ *A solitary viola plucks a lonely, soft F sharp.* ヴィオラ奏者が1人で寂しく静かな嬰 (えい) ヘ長調を弾いている.

sharp|en /ʃɑrpən/ (sharpens, sharpening, sharpened) 1 V-T/V-I 他動詞/自動詞 If your senses, understanding, or skills **sharpen** or **are sharpened**, you become better at noticing things, thinking, or doing something. 鋭くする [他動詞]，鋭くなる [自動詞] ❑ *Her gaze sharpened, as if she had seen something unusual.* 彼女は何か珍しいものでも見たかのように視線が鋭くなった. ❑ *He will need to sharpen his diplomatic skills in order to work with Congress.* 彼は連邦議会と協力していくためには外交手腕を磨く必要があるだろう. 2 V-T 他動詞 If you **sharpen** an object, you make its edge very thin or you make its end pointed. 削る，研ぐ ❑ *He started to sharpen his knife.* 彼はナイフを研ぎ始めた.

sharp|en|er /ʃɑrpənər/ (sharpeners) N-COUNT 可算名詞 A **sharpener** is a tool or machine used for sharpening pencils or knives. 削り器，鉛筆削り ❑ *...a pencil sharpener.* 鉛筆削り

shat /ʃæt/ **Shat** is the past tense and past participle of **shit**. shit の過去形・過去分詞

shat|ter /ʃætər/ (shatters, shattering, shattered) 1 V-T/V-I 他動詞/自動詞 If something **shatters** or **is shattered**, it breaks into a lot of small pieces. 割れる ❑ *safety glass that won't shatter if it's broken.* 割れても粉々にならない安全ガラス ❑ *The car shattered into a thousand burning pieces in a 200 mph crash.* その自動車は時速200マイルで遭った交通事故で粉々になって炎上した. ● **shat|ter|ing** N-UNCOUNT 不可算名詞 ❑ *...the shattering of glass.* 粉々に割れたガラス 2 V-T 他動詞 If something **shatters** your dreams, hopes, or beliefs, it completely destroys them. 打ち砕く ❑ *A failure would shatter the hopes of many people.* 失敗は多くの人々の希望を打ち砕くだろう. 3 V-T 他動詞 If someone **is shattered** by an event, it shocks and upsets them very much. (精神的に) 打ちのめす ❑ *He had been shattered by his son's death.* 彼は息子の死によって精神的にすっかり参っていた. 4 → see also **shattered, shattering** → see **crash, glass**

shat|tered /ʃætərd/ ADJ 形容詞 If you are **shattered** by something, you are extremely shocked and upset about it. ずたずたになった，落ち込んだ ❑ *It is desperately sad news and I am absolutely shattered to hear it.* 本当に悲しい知らせで，それを聞いてすっかり落ち込んでいる.

shave /ʃeɪv/ (shaves, shaving, shaved) 1 V-T/V-I 他動詞/自動詞 When a man **shaves**, he removes the hair from his face using a razor or shaver so that his face is smooth. ひげをそる，毛をそる [自動詞] ❑ *He took a bath and shaved before dinner.* 彼は夕食の前に風呂に入りひげをそった. ❑ *He had shaved his face until it was smooth.* 彼はスベスベになるまでひげをそった. ● N-COUNT 可算名詞 **Shave** is also a noun. ひげをそること ❑ *He never seemed to need a shave.* 彼はひげをそる必要がなさそうだった. ● **shav|ing** N-UNCOUNT 不可算名詞 ❑ *...a range of shaving products.* さまざまなシェービング用製品 2 V-T 他動詞 If you **shave off** part of a piece of wood or other material, you cut very thin pieces from it. 削り取る ❑ *I set the log on the ground and shaved off the bark.* 丸太を地面に置いて樹皮を削り取った. 3 V-T 他動詞 If you **shave** a small amount **off** something such as a record, cost, or price, you reduce it by that amount. 短縮する，下げる ❑ *She's already shaved four seconds off the national record for the mile.* 彼女はすでに1マイル走で全国記録を4秒縮めている. 4 → see also **shaving** 5 PHRASE 句 If you describe a situation as a **close shave**, you mean that there was nearly an accident or a disaster but it was avoided. 危機一髪 ❑ *I can't quite believe the close shaves I've had just recently.* つい最近あった危機一髪の出来事がちょっと信じられない.

shav|er /ʃeɪvər/ (shavers) N-COUNT 可算名詞 A **shaver** is an electric device, used for shaving hair from the face and body. シェーバー，電気かみそり ❑ *...men's electric shavers.* 男性用電気かみそり

shav|ing /ʃeɪvɪŋ/ (shavings) 1 N-COUNT 可算名詞 **Shavings** are small very thin pieces of wood or other material which have been cut from a larger piece. かんなくず，削りくず ❑ *The floor was covered with shavings from his wood carvings.* 床は彼の彫刻の削りくずでいっぱいだった. 2 → see also **shave**

shawl /ʃɔl/ (shawls) N-COUNT 可算名詞 A **shawl** is a large piece of woolen cloth which a woman wears over her shoulders or head, or which is wrapped around a baby to keep it warm. ショール，肩掛け → see **clothing**

she /ʃɪ, STRONG ʃi/

> **She** is a third person singular pronoun. **She** is used as the subject of a verb.
>
> **She** は3人称単数の代名詞である. **She** は動詞の主語として用いられる.

1 PRON-SING 単数代名詞 You use **she** to refer to a woman, girl, or female animal who has already been mentioned or whose identity is clear. 彼女 ❑ *When Ann arrived home that night, she found Brian in the house watching TV.* アンがその晩帰宅すると，ブライアンが家でテレビを見ていたんです. ❑ *She was seventeen and she had no education or employment.* 彼女は17歳で教育も受けていないし仕事にも就いていませんでした. 2 PRON-SING 単数代名詞 Some writers may use **she** to refer to a person who is not identified as either male or female. They do this because they wish to avoid using the pronoun "he" all the time. Some people dislike this use and prefer to use "he or she" or "they." 既出の人の性別が不明の場合，常にheで受けるのを避けて用いられる ❑ *The student may show signs of feeling the strain of responsibility and may give up.* 学生は責任感に負担に感じる兆候を見せ，あきらめるかもしれない. 3 PRON-SING 単数代名詞 **She** is sometimes used to refer to a country or nation. 既出の国を指して用いられる ❑ *The country needs new leadership if she is to play a role in future development.* その国は未来開発で一翼を担うつもりなら，新しい指導者が必要だ. 4 PRON-SING 単数代名詞 Some people use **she** to refer to a car or machine. People who sail often use **she** to refer to a ship or boat. 既出の車・機会・船を指して用いられる ❑ *The Seaflower was being repaired, but soon she was fit to sail again.* シーフラワーは修理中だったが，すぐにまた航海出来るようになった.

shear /ʃɪər/ (shears, shearing, sheared, sheared or shorn) 1 V-T 他動詞 To **shear** a sheep means to cut its wool off. 毛を刈る ❑ *Competitors have six minutes to shear four sheep.* 出場者は4頭のヒツジの毛を刈るのに6分間与えられる. ● **shear|ing** N-UNCOUNT 不可算名詞 毛を刈ること ❑ *...a display of sheep shearing.* ヒツジの毛刈り 2 N-PLURAL 複数名詞 A pair of **shears** is a garden tool like a very large pair of scissors. Shears are used especially for cutting hedges. 大ばさみ ❑ *Trim the shrubs with shears.* 低木を大ばさみで切りそろえなさい.

sheath /ʃiθ/ (sheaths) N-COUNT 可算名詞 A **sheath** is a covering for the blade of a knife. さや

shed /ʃɛd/ (sheds, shedding)

> The form **shed** is used in the present tense and in the past tense and past participle of the verb.
>
> **shed** 形は動詞の現時制および過去時制と過去分詞として使われる.

1 N-COUNT 可算名詞 A **shed** is a small building that is used for storing things such as garden tools. 物置小屋 ❑ *...a garden shed.* 庭の物置小屋 2 N-COUNT 可算名詞 A **shed** is a large shelter or building, for example, at a train station, port, or factory. 車庫，倉庫 ❑ *...a vast factory shed.* 巨大な工場の倉庫 3 V-T 他動詞 When a tree **sheds** its leaves, its leaves fall off in the autumn. When an animal **sheds** hair or skin, some of its hair or skin drops off. (葉を) 落とす 毛皮を切りする，角質が落ちる ❑ *Some of the trees were already beginning to shed their leaves.* すでに葉を落とし始めている木々もあった. 4 V-T 他動詞 To **shed** something means to get rid of it. 削減する，削除する [FORMAL 形式ばった] ❑ *The firm is to shed 700 jobs.* その会社は700人を解雇する予定だ. 5 V-T 他動詞 If you **shed** tears, you cry. (涙を) 流す ❑ *They will shed a few tears at their daughter's wedding.* 公開花嫁は少し涙を流すだろう. 6 V-T 他動詞 To **shed** blood means to kill people in a violent way. If someone **sheds** their blood, they are killed in a violent way, usually when they are fighting in a war. (血を) 流す 殺害する (さつがい)する [FORMAL 形式ばった] ❑ *...young warriors, eager to shed blood.* 流血戦を熱望している若い兵士たち 7 to **shed light on** something → see **light** → see **cry**

she'd /ʃɪd, ʃid/ 1 **She'd** is the usual spoken form of "she had," especially when "had" is an auxiliary verb. she had の短縮形 ❑ *She'd been to clubs all over the world.* 彼女は世界中のクラブに行っていた. 2 **She'd** is a spoken form of "she would." she would の短縮形 ❑ *She'd do anything for a bit of money.* 彼女はちょっとしたお金のためならなんでもする.

sheen /ʃin/ N-SING 単数名詞 If something has a **sheen**, it has a smooth and gentle brightness on its surface. つや，光沢 ❑ *The carpet had a silvery sheen to it.* カーペットは銀色に光っていた.

sheep /ʃip/ (**sheep**)

Sheep is both the singular and the plural form.

Sheep は単数形でも複数形でもある.

N-COUNT 可算名詞 A **sheep** is a farm animal which is covered with thick curly hair called wool. Sheep are kept for their wool or for their meat. 羊 ❑ ...grassland on which a flock of sheep were grazing. 羊の群れが草を食(は)んでいた草原.
→ see **barn**, **meat**

sheep|ish /ʃipɪʃ/ ADJ 形容詞 If you look **sheepish**, you look slightly embarrassed because you feel foolish or you have done something silly. 決まりが悪い ❑ I asked him why. He looked a little sheepish when he answered. 彼に訳を聞いてみると少しばつが悪そうに答えた.

sheer /ʃɪər/ (**sheerer, sheerest**) **1** ADJ 形容詞 You can use **sheer** to emphasize that a state or situation is complete and does not involve or is not mixed with anything else. 全くの [EMPHASIS 強調] [ADJ n] ❑ His music is sheer delight. 彼の音楽はこの上なく素晴らしい. ❑ Sheer chance quite often plays an important part in sparking off an idea. 全くの偶然が大きく作用してアイデアが浮かぶことは少なくありません. **2** ADJ 形容詞 A **sheer** cliff or drop is extremely steep or completely vertical. 険しい ❑ There was a sheer drop just outside my window. 窓の外はすぐ急斜面になっていた. **3** ADJ 形容詞 **Sheer** material is very thin, light, and delicate. 極薄の ❑ ...sheer black tights. 極薄の黒いタイツ.

Word Partnership	sheer は次の語句と使われる:
N.	sheer **delight**, sheer **force**, sheer **luck**, sheer **number**, sheer **pleasure**, sheer **power**, sheer **size**, sheer **strength**, sheer **terror**, sheer **volume** **1**

sheet /ʃit/ (**sheets**) **1** N-COUNT 可算名詞 A **sheet** is a large rectangular piece of cotton or other cloth that you sleep on or cover yourself with in a bed. シーツ ❑ Once a week, a maid changes the sheets. 週に1度メードがシーツを交換してくれる. **2** N-COUNT 可算名詞 A **sheet** of paper is a rectangular piece of paper. 一枚 ❑ ...a sheet of newspaper. 新聞紙1枚. **3** N-COUNT 可算名詞 You can use **sheet** to refer to a piece of paper which gives information about something. パンフレット ❑ ...information sheets on each country in the world. 世界各国ごとにその国の情報をまとめたパンフレット. **4** N-COUNT 可算名詞 A **sheet** of glass, metal, or wood is a large, flat, thin piece of it. 薄板 ❑ ...a cracked sheet of glass. ひびの入ったガラス板. ❑ Overhead cranes were lifting giant sheets of steel. 頭上ではクレーンが巨大な鋼板を引き上げていた. **5** N-COUNT 可算名詞 A **sheet** of something is a thin wide layer of it over the surface of something else. 一面に薄く広がったもの ❑ ...a sheet of ice. 一面に張った氷. **6** → see also **balance sheet**, **broadsheet**, **fact sheet**, **spreadsheet**, **worksheet**
→ see **bed**, **glass**, **paper**

sheikh /ʃik, ʃeɪk/ (**sheikhs**) N-TITLE; N-COUNT 称号名詞, 可算名詞 A **sheikh** is a male Arab chief or ruler. 族長, 長老 ❑ ...Sheikh Khalifa. 族長ハリーファ.

shelf /ʃɛlf/ (**shelves**) **1** N-COUNT 可算名詞 A **shelf** is a flat piece of wood, metal, or glass which is attached to a wall or to the sides of a cabinet. Shelves are used for keeping things on. 棚 ❑ He took a book from the shelf. 彼は棚から1冊の本をとった. **2** PHRASE 句 If you buy something **off the shelf**, you buy something that is not specially made for you. 市販で ❑ Lower-priced jewelry will be sold off the shelf by this fall. 低価格のアクセサリーが今秋発売される.

shell /ʃɛl/ (**shells, shelling, shelled**) **1** N-COUNT 可算名詞 The **shell** of a nut or egg is the hard covering which surrounds it. 殻 ❑ They cracked the nuts and removed their shells. 彼らは木の実を割って殻をとった. ●N-UNCOUNT 不可算名詞 **Shell** is the substance that a shell is made of. 殻 ❑ ...beads made from ostrich egg shell. ダチョウの卵の殻で作ったビーズ. **2** N-COUNT 可算名詞 The **shell** of an animal such as a tortoise, snail, or crab is the hard protective covering that it has around its body or on its back. 甲羅; 殻 ❑ ...the spiral form of a snail shell. らせん形をしたカタツムリの殻. **3** N-COUNT 可算名詞 **Shells** are hard objects found on beaches. They are usually pink, white, or brown and are the coverings which used to surround small sea creatures. 貝殻 ❑ I collect shells and interesting seaside items. 貝殻や海辺で拾った面白いものを集めている. **4** V-T 他動詞 If you **shell** nuts, peas, shrimp, or other food, you remove their natural outer covering. 殻をとる ❑ She shelled and ate a few nuts. 彼女は少しだけ木の実の殻をむいて食べました. **5** N-COUNT 可算名詞 If someone comes out of their **shell**, they become more friendly and interested in other people and less quiet, shy, and reserved. 殻 ❑ Her normally shy son had come out of his shell. いつもは恥ずかしがる彼女の息子が打ち解けていた. **6** N-COUNT 可算名詞 The **shell** of a building, boat, car, or other structure is the outside frame of it. 骨組み, 骨格 ❑ ...the shells of burned buildings. 焼けた建物の骨組み. **7** N-COUNT 可算名詞 A **shell** is a weapon consisting of a metal container filled with explosives that can be fired from a large gun over long distances. 砲弾 ❑ Tanks fired shells at the house. 戦車はその家に砲弾を発射した. **8** V-T 他動詞 To **shell** a place means to fire explosive shells at it. 砲撃する ❑ The rebels shelled the densely-populated suburbs near the port. 反政府軍は港の近くの人口が集中する近郊地域に砲撃を行ないました. ●**shell|ing** N-VAR 可変性名詞 (**shellings**) 砲撃 ❑ Out on the streets, the shelling continued. 市街では砲撃が続きました.
▸ **shell out** PHRASAL VERB 句動詞 If you **shell out for** something, you spend a lot of money on it. 大金を出す [INFORMAL くだけた] ❑ You won't have to shell out a fortune for it. そんなものに大金を出すことはない. ❑ ...an insurance policy which saves you from having to shell out for repairs. 修理費用をまかなってくれる保険.

she'll /ʃil, ʃɪl/ **She'll** is the usual spoken form of "she will." ❑ Sharon was a wonderful lady and I know she'll be greatly missed. シャロンさんは素晴らしい方でしたから, その死を悼む人たちは多いでしょう.

shell com|pa|ny (**shell companies**) **1** N-COUNT 可算名詞 A **shell company** is a company that another company takes over in order to use its name to gain an advantage. シェル・カンパニー (企業買収の受け皿となる会社) [BUSINESS 実業] ❑ The U.S. shell company was set up to mount a bid for Kingston Communications. そのアメリカのシェル・カンパニーはキングストン・コミュニケーションズの買収を目的に設立された. **2** N-COUNT 可算名詞 A **shell company** is a company which does not conduct legitimate business but which has been officially registered, so that it can be used for fraud. ダミー会社 [BUSINESS 実業]

shell|fish /ʃɛlfɪʃ/ (**shellfish**)

Shellfish is both the singular and the plural form.

Shellfish は単数形でも複数形でもある.

N-VAR 可変性名詞 **Shellfish** are small creatures that live in the sea and have a shell. 甲殻類 ❑ Fish and shellfish are the specialties. 名物は魚や甲殻類である.

shell pro|gram (**shell programs**) N-COUNT 可算名詞 A **shell program** is a basic computer program that provides a framework within which the user can develop the program to suit their own needs. シェル [COMPUTING コンピューティング]

shel|ter /ʃɛltər/ (**shelters, sheltering, sheltered**) **1** N-COUNT 可算名詞 A **shelter** is a small building or covered place which is made to protect people from bad weather or danger. 避難所 ❑ The city's bomb shelters were being prepared for possible air raids. 市内では万一の空襲に備えて防空壕が作られていた. **2** N-UNCOUNT 不可算名詞 If a place provides **shelter**, it provides you with a place to stay or live, especially when you need protection from bad weather or danger. 避難 ❑ The number of families seeking shelter rose by 17 percent. 避難を希望する家族は17%増加しました. ❑ Although horses do not generally mind the cold, shelter from rain and wind is important. 馬は一般的に寒さには強いが, 雨風からは保護してやることが大切である. **3** N-COUNT 可算名詞 A **shelter** is a building where homeless people can sleep and get food. 収容施設 ❑ ...a shelter for homeless women. 女性のホームレスのための収容施設. **4** V-I 自動詞 If you **shelter** in a place, you stay there and are protected from bad weather or danger. 避難する ❑ ...a man sheltering in a doorway. 入口の近くにじっと潜んでいる男. **5** V-T 他動詞 If a place or thing **is sheltered**, it is protected by that thing from wind and rain. 雨風から守る [usu passive] ❑ ...a wooden house, sheltered by a low pointed roof. 低くとがった屋根で風雨をしのいでいる木造の家. **6** V-T 他動詞 If you **shelter** someone, usually someone who is being hunted by police or other people, you provide them with a place to stay or live. かくまう ❑ A neighbor sheltered the boy for seven days. 近所の人が少年を7日間かくまっていました.

Word Partnership	shelter は次の語句と使われる:
N.	**bomb** shelter **1**
	shelter **and clothing**, **emergency** shelter, **food and** shelter **2**
	homeless shelter **3**
ADJ.	**temporary** shelter **1** – **3**
V.	**find** shelter, **provide** shelter, **seek** shelter **2**

shel|tered /ʃɛltərd/ **1** ADJ 形容詞 A **sheltered** place is protected from wind and rain. 風雨にさらされない ❑ ...a shallow-sloping beach next to a sheltered bay. 入り江の横にある遠浅の海岸. **2** ADJ 形容詞 If you say that someone has led a **sheltered** life, you mean that they have been protected from difficult or unpleasant experiences. 庇護された ❑ Perhaps I've just led a really sheltered life. 私は今まで恵まれすぎていたのかもしれない. **3** ADJ 形容詞 **Sheltered** accommodations or work is designed for old or disabled people. It allows them to be independent but also allows them to get help when they need it. 養護の [ADJ n] ❑ Call the family service agencies to find out if they sponsor this kind of sheltered housing. こうした養護施設に補助が出るのかどうか, 福祉課に電話で問い合わせてください. **4** → see also **shelter**

shelve /ʃɛlv/ (**shelves, shelving, shelved**) **1** V-T 他動詞 If someone **shelves** a plan or project, they decide not to continue with it, either for a while or permanently. 棚上げにする ❑ *King County has shelved plans to build a driving range.* キング郡はゴルフ練習場の建設計画を棚上げした. **2** **Shelves** is the plural of **shelf**.

shep|herd /ʃɛpərd/ (**shepherds, shepherding, shepherded**) **1** N-COUNT 可算名詞 A **shepherd** is a person, especially a man, whose job is to take care of sheep. 羊飼い **2** V-T 他動詞 If you **are shepherded** somewhere, someone takes you there to make sure that you arrive at the right place safely. 案内される [usu passive] ❑ *She was shepherded by her guards up the rear ramp of the aircraft.* 彼女は護衛に誘導されて航空機の後部タラップを上った.

sher|iff /ʃɛrɪf/ (**sheriffs**) N-COUNT; N-TITLE 可算名詞, 称号名詞 In the United States, a **sheriff** is a person who is elected to make sure that the law is obeyed in a particular county. 保安官 ❑ *...the local sheriff.* 地元の保安官.

sher|ry /ʃɛri/ (**sherries**) N-MASS 質量名詞 **Sherry** is a type of strong wine that is made in southwestern Spain. It is usually drunk before a meal. シェリー酒 ❑ *I poured us a glass of sherry.* グラスにシェリー酒をついだ.

she's /ʃiz, ʃɪz/ **1** **She's** is the usual spoken form of "she is." ❑ *She's an exceptionally good cook.* 彼女の料理の腕前は抜群である. **2** **She's** is a spoken form of "she has," especially when "has" is an auxiliary verb. ❑ *She's been married for seven years and has two daughters.* 彼女は結婚7年で2人の娘がいる.

shh /ʃ/ also **sh** CONVENTION 慣習表現 You can say "**Shh**!" to tell someone to be quiet. しっ, 静かに [INFORMAL, SPOKEN くだけた, 口語] ❑ *Shh, don't wake Danny.* しっ, ダニーを起こさないで.

shield /ʃild/ (**shields, shielding, shielded**) **1** N-COUNT 可算名詞 Something or someone which is a **shield** against a particular danger or risk provides protection from it. 保護するもの; 保護者 ❑ *He used his left hand as a shield against the reflecting sunlight.* 彼は左手で反射する日の光を遮った. **2** V-T 他動詞 If something or someone **shields** you **from** a danger or risk, they protect you from it. 〜から〜を保護する ❑ *He shielded his head from the sun with an old sack.* 彼は古い布袋を頭にかぶって暑さをしのいだ. **3** V-T 他動詞 If you **shield** your eyes, you put your hand above your eyes to protect them from direct sunlight. 保護する ❑ *He squinted and shielded his eyes.* 彼は目を細め, 手をかざして日光を遮った. **4** N-COUNT 可算名詞 A **shield** is a large piece of metal or leather which soldiers used to carry to protect their bodies while they were fighting. 盾 ❑ *He clanged his sword three times on his shield.* 彼は剣を盾に3回打ち付けた. **5** N-COUNT 可算名詞 A **shield** is a sports prize or badge that is shaped like a shield. 優勝盾
→ see **army**

shift /ʃɪft/ (**shifts, shifting, shifted**) **1** V-T/V-I 他動詞/自動詞 If you **shift** something or if it **shifts**, it moves slightly. 少し動かす [他動詞]; 少し動く [自動詞] ❑ *He stopped, shifting his cane to his left hand.* 彼は立ち止まってステッキを左右に持ち替えた. ❑ *He shifted from foot to foot.* 彼は落ち着きなく体を左右に揺すった. **2** V-T/V-I 他動詞/自動詞 If someone's opinion, a situation, or a policy **shifts** or **is shifted**, it changes slightly. 少し変わる ❑ *Attitudes to mental illness have shifted in recent years.* 最近になって, 精神病に対する見方が少し変わってきた. ● N-COUNT 可算名詞 **Shift** is also a noun. 変化 [usu N prep] ❑ *...a shift in government policy.* 国の政策の変化. **3** V-T 他動詞 If someone **shifts** the responsibility or blame for something onto you, they unfairly make you responsible or make people blame you for it, instead of them. なすりつける [DISAPPROVAL 不賛成] ❑ *It was a vain attempt to shift the responsibility for the murder to somebody else.* 殺人の責任を他人になすりつけようとしたが無駄だった. **4** V-T 他動詞 If you **shift** gears in a car, you put the car into a different gear. 変える [AM 米国英語] ❑ *He shifts gears and pulls away slowly.* 彼はギアを変えてゆっくりと引き離す. **5** N-COUNT 可算名詞 If a group of factory workers, nurses, or other people work **shifts**, they work for a set period before being replaced by another group, so that there is always a group working. Each of these set periods is called a **shift**. You can also use **shift** to refer to a group of workers who work together on a particular shift. 交替制の勤務時間 ❑ *His father worked shifts in a steel mill.* 彼の父は交替制で製鉄所で働いていた.

	Word Partnership shift は次の語句と使われる:
N.	shift *your* weight **1**
	shift *your* position **1 2**
	shift *your* attention, shift in focus, policy shift, shift in/of power, shift in priorities **2**
	shift blame **3**
	shift gears **4**
	shift change, night shift **5**
ADJ.	dramatic shift, major shift, significant shift **2**

shim|mer /ʃɪmər/ (**shimmers, shimmering, shimmered**) V-I 自動詞 If something **shimmers**, it shines with a faint, unsteady

light or has an unclear, unsteady appearance. ちらちらと光る ❑ *The lights shimmered on the water.* 明かりが水面にゆらゆらと揺らいでいた. ● N-SING 単数名詞 **Shimmer** is also a noun. ちらちらした光 ❑ *...a shimmer of starlight.* ちらちら光る星明かり.

shin /ʃɪn/ (**shins**) N-COUNT 可算名詞 Your **shins** are the front parts of your legs between your knees and your ankles. 向うずね ❑ *She punched him on the nose and kicked him in the shins.* 彼女はげんこつで彼の鼻を殴って向うずねをけった.

shine /ʃaɪn/ (**shines, shining, shined** or **shone**) **1** V-I 自動詞 When the sun or a light **shines**, it gives out bright light. 輝く ❑ *It is a mild morning and the sun is shining.* 穏やかな朝で太陽が輝いている. **2** V-T 他動詞 If you **shine** a flashlight or other light somewhere, you point it there, so that you can see something when it is dark. 照らす ❑ *One of the men shone a torch in his face.* 連中の1人が懐中電灯で彼の顔を照らした. ❑ *The man walked slowly toward her, shining the flashlight.* 男は懐中電灯を照らしながら彼女に向かってゆっくりと歩いた. **3** V-I 自動詞 Something that **shines** is very bright and clear because it is reflecting light. (反射して) 輝く ❑ *Her blue eyes shone and caught the light.* 彼女の青い瞳が輝きその光をとらえた. ❑ *...a pair of patent leather shoes that shone like mirrors.* 鏡のように輝くエナメル靴. **4** N-SING 単数名詞 Something that has a **shine** is bright and clear because it is reflecting light. 光沢 ❑ *This gel gives a beautiful shine to the hair.* このジェルは髪に美しいつやを与えます. **5** V-I 自動詞 Someone who **shines** at a skill or activity does it extremely well. 異彩を放つ ❑ *Did you shine at school?* 学校ではすごく勉強ができたの？ **6** → see also **shining**
→ see **light**

shin|gle /ʃɪŋgəl/ (**shingles**) **1** N-UNCOUNT 不可算名詞 **Shingle** is a mass of small rough pieces of stone on the shore of a sea or a river. 小石 ❑ *...a beach of sand and shingle.* 砂と小石が混じった海岸. **2** N-UNCOUNT 不可算名詞 **Shingles** is a disease in which painful red spots spread in bands over a person's body, especially around their waist. 帯状疱疹 (ほうしん) **3** N-COUNT 可算名詞 **Shingles** are thin pieces of wood or another material which are fixed in rows to cover a roof or wall. 屋根板 [usu pl] ❑ *The roofs had shingles missing.* 屋根板に屋根板がなかった. **4** N-COUNT 可算名詞 A **shingle** is a small sign that is hung outside a building, such as the place where a doctor or lawyer works. 看板 [AM 米国英語] **5** PHRASE 句 If you **hang out** your **shingle** or **hang out a shingle**, you start your own business. 看板を出す [AM 米国英語] [v and n inflect] ❑ *She hung out her shingle under the name Designs by Pamela.* 彼女は「デザイン・バイ・パメラ」という屋号で開業した. ❑ *The industry isn't regulated, so anybody can hang out a shingle.* この業界には規制がないので誰でも開業できる.

shin|ing /ʃaɪnɪŋ/ **1** ADJ 形容詞 A **shining** achievement or quality is a very good one which should be greatly admired. 卓越した ❑ *She is a shining example to us all.* 彼女はみんなの素晴らしい手本である. **2** → see also **shine**

shiny /ʃaɪni/ (**shinier, shiniest**) ADJ 形容詞 **Shiny** things are bright and reflect light. 輝く ❑ *Her blonde hair was shiny and clean.* 彼女の金髪はつややかで美しかった.
→ see **metal**

ship /ʃɪp/ (**ships, shipping, shipped**) **1** N-COUNT 可算名詞 A **ship** is a large boat which carries passengers or cargo. 船 [also "by" N] ❑ *Within ninety minutes the ship was ready for departure.* 90分以内で船は出航の準備が整った. ❑ *We went by ship over to America.* 船ではるばるアメリカに渡った. **2** V-T 他動詞 If people, supplies, or goods **are shipped** somewhere, they are sent there on a ship or by some other means of transportation. 輸送される [usu passive] ❑ *We'll ship your order to the address we print on your checks.* ご注文の品は小切手に書かれたご住所にお送りいたします. ❑ *Food is being shipped to drought-stricken Southern Africa.* 干ばつに襲われたアフリカ南部に食料が輸送されています. **3** → see also **shipping**
→ see Word Web: **ship**

	Word Partnership ship は次の語句と使われる:
V.	board a ship, build a ship, ship docks, jump ship, sink a ship **1**
N.	bow of a ship, captain of a ship, cargo ship, ship's crew **1**

ship|ment /ʃɪpmənt/ (**shipments**) **1** N-COUNT 可算名詞 A **shipment** is an amount of a particular kind of cargo that is sent to another country on a ship, train, airplane, or other vehicle. 発送 ❑ *After that, food shipments to the port could begin in a matter of weeks.* それから数週間ほどでその港への食料の出荷が始まるだろう. **2** N-UNCOUNT 不可算名詞 The **shipment** of a cargo or goods somewhere is the sending of it there by ship, train, airplane,

Word Web   ship

Large **ocean-going vessels** remain an important way of transporting people and **cargo**. **Oil tankers** and **container ships** are a common sight in many **ports**. **Ocean liners** serve as both transportation and hotel for tourists. Some of these **ships** are several stories tall. The **captain** steers a **cruise ship** from the **bridge**, while passengers enjoy themselves on the promenade deck. Huge **warships** carry thousands of soldiers to battlefields around the world. **Aircraft carriers** include a flight deck where planes can take off and land. **Ferries, barges,** fishing **craft**, and research **boats** are also an important part of the **marine** industry.

or some other vehicle. 発送 □ *Bananas are packed before being transported to the docks for shipment overseas.* バナナは梱包してから船積港に運ばれ海外に輸出される.

ship|ping /ˈʃɪpɪŋ/ ■ N-UNCOUNT 不可算名詞 **Shipping** is the transportation of cargo or goods as a business, especially on ships. 海運業 [usu with supp] □ *...the international shipping industry.* 国際海運業界. □ *...a coupon for free shipping of your catalog order.* カタログ注文時の送料無料クーポン. ❷ N-UNCOUNT 不可算名詞 You can refer to the amount of money that you pay to a company to transport cargo or goods as **shipping**. 送料 □ *It is $39.95 plus $3 shipping.* 代金は39.95ドルおよび送料です.

ship|wreck /ˈʃɪprɛk/ (shipwrecks, shipwrecked) ■ N-VAR 可変性名詞 If there is a **shipwreck**, a ship is destroyed in an accident at sea. 遭難船 □ *He was drowned in a shipwreck off the coast of Spain.* 彼はスペイン沖で船が遭難し溺死した. ❷ N-COUNT 可算名詞 A **shipwreck** is a ship which has been destroyed in an accident at sea. 難破船 □ *More than 1,000 shipwrecks litter the coral reef ringing the islands.* 島々を取り囲むサンゴ礁には1000隻以上の難破船があちこちに沈んでいる. ❸ V-T PASSIVE 受動態他動詞 If someone **is shipwrecked**, their ship is destroyed in an accident at sea but they survive and manage to reach land. 遭難する □ *He was shipwrecked after visiting the island.* その島を訪れた後, 彼の船は遭難した.

ship|yard /ˈʃɪpjɑrd/ (shipyards) N-COUNT 可算名詞 A **shipyard** is a place where ships are built and repaired. 造船所 □ *The Queen Mary 2 is currently docked at the shipyard.* クィーンメアリー2号は入渠 (にゅうきょ) 中である.

shirt /ˈʃɜrt/ (shirts) ■ N-COUNT 可算名詞 A **shirt** is a piece of clothing that you wear on the upper part of your body. Shirts have a collar, sleeves, and buttons down the front. シャツ ❷ → see also **sweatshirt, T-shirt** → see **clothing**

shit /ˈʃɪt/ (shits, shitting, shat) ■ N-UNCOUNT 不可算名詞 Some people use **shit** to refer to solid waste matter from the body of a human being or animal. くそ, うんこ [INFORMAL くだけた, 下品な] □ *...a pile of dog shit.* 大量の犬のうんち. (ふん) ❷ V-I 自動詞 To **shit** means to get rid of solid waste matter from the body. うんこする [INFORMAL, VULGAR くだけた, 下品な] □ *...his memories of the yellow dog shitting on the stairs.* 階段でうんこしていた薄茶色の犬の思い出. ❸ N-SING 単数名詞 To have a **shit** means to get rid of solid waste matter from the body. うんこ [INFORMAL, VULGAR くだけた, 下品な] □ *Before dying he confesses that he hasn't taken a shit in weeks.* 死ぬ間際になって, 彼は何週間もうんこが出ていないんだと明かす. ❹ N-UNCOUNT 不可算名詞 People sometimes refer to things that they do not like as **shit**. くだらないもの [INFORMAL, VULGAR くだけた, 下品な, DISAPPROVAL 不賛成] □ *This is a load of shit.* 実にくだらない.

shiv|er /ˈʃɪvər/ (shivers, shivering, shivered) V-I 自動詞 When you **shiver**, your body shakes slightly because you are cold or frightened. 震える □ *He shivered in the cold.* 彼は寒さで震えた. ● N-COUNT 可算名詞 **Shiver** is also a noun. 震え □ *The emptiness here sent shivers down my spine.* ここは人けがなくて背筋がぞっとした.

Word Partnership   shiver は次の語句と使われる:

V.   **feel** a shiver, shiver **goes/runs down your spine,** *something* **makes you** shiver, *something* **sends a** shiver **down your spine**

shoal /ˈʃoʊl/ (shoals) N-COUNT 可算名詞 A **shoal** of fish is a large group of them swimming together. 群れ □ *Among them swam shoals of fish.* その中には魚の群れも泳いでいた.

shock /ˈʃɒk/ (shocks, shocking, shocked) ■ N-COUNT 可算名詞 If you have a **shock**, something suddenly happens which is unpleasant, upsetting, or very surprising. 衝撃的なこと □ *The extent of the violence came as a shock.* 暴力の残虐さは衝撃を与えました. □ *He has never recovered from the shock of your brother's death.* お前の兄さんが亡くなってからというもの, あいつはショックから

立ち直れないでいるんだ. ❷ N-UNCOUNT 不可算名詞 **Shock** is a person's emotional and physical condition when something very frightening or upsetting has happened to them. ショック □ *The little boy was speechless with shock.* 男の子はびっくりして口が開けなかった. ❸ N-UNCOUNT 不可算名詞 If someone is **in shock**, they are suffering from a serious physical condition in which their blood is not flowing around their body properly, for example, because they have had a bad injury. ショック状態 □ *He was found beaten and in shock.* 彼は殴られてショック状態でいるところを発見された. ❹ V-T 他動詞 If something **shocks** you, it makes you feel very upset, because it involves death or suffering and because you had not expected it. 衝撃を与える □ *After forty years in the police force nothing much shocks me.* 40年も警察に勤めていると少々のことでは驚かないよ. ● **shocked** ADJ 形容詞 衝撃を受けた □ *This was a nasty attack and the woman is still very shocked.* これは卑劣な暴行事件で, 女性はまだショックから抜け出せないでいる. ❺ V-T/V-I 他動詞/自動詞 If someone or something **shocks** you, it upsets or offends you because you think it is vulgar or morally wrong. あきれさせる □ *You can't shock me.* お前がどんなばかなことをしようと驚かないよ. □ *They were easily shocked in those days.* その頃彼らはちょっとしたことでもショックを受けた. □ *...the desire to shock.* 相手をあっと言わせたい願望. ● **shocked** ADJ 形容詞 びっくりする □ *Don't look so shocked.* そんなにびっくりしないで. ❻ N-VAR 可変性名詞 A **shock** is the force of something suddenly hitting or pulling something else. 衝撃 □ *Steel barriers can bend and absorb the shock.* 鉄柵 (てつさく) は折れ曲がって衝撃を吸収することができる. ❼ N-COUNT 可算名詞 A **shock** is the same as an **electric shock**. 電気ショック, 感電 ❽ → see also **electric shock**

Word Partnership   shock は次の語句と使われる:

V.   **come as a** shock ■
    send a shock ■ ❼
    express shock, **feel** shock ❷
N.   **in a state of** shock, shock **value** ❷

shock|ing /ˈʃɒkɪŋ/ ■ ADJ 形容詞 You can say that something is **shocking** if you think that it is very bad. ひどい [INFORMAL くだけた] □ *The media coverage was shocking.* マスコミ報道はひどいものでした. ● **shock|ing|ly** ADV 副詞 [ADV adj/adv] ひどく □ *His memory was becoming shockingly bad.* 彼の記憶力はめっきり衰えていった. ❷ ADJ 形容詞 You can say that something is **shocking** if you think that it is morally wrong. けしからぬ, とんでもない □ *It is shocking that nothing was said.* 言葉の1つもなかったのはあきれるばかりである. ● **shock|ing|ly** ADV 副詞 驚くほど □ *Shockingly, this useless and dangerous surgery did not end until the 1930s.* 信じがたいことに, この不要で危険な手術が1930年代まで行なわれていたのである. ❸ → see also **shock**

shock wave (shock waves) also **shockwave** ■ N-COUNT 可算名詞 A **shock wave** is an area of very high pressure moving through the air, earth, or water. It is caused by an explosion or an earthquake, or by an object traveling faster than sound. 衝撃波 □ *The shock waves yesterday were felt from Las Vegas to San Diego.* 昨日の地震の衝撃はラスベガスからサンディエゴまで感じられた. ❷ N-COUNT 可算名詞 A **shock wave** is the effect of something surprising, such as a piece of unpleasant news, that causes strong reactions when it spreads through a place. 衝撃 □ *The crime sent shock waves throughout the country.* 事件は全国を震撼させた. → see **sound**

shod|dy /ˈʃɒdi/ (shoddier, shoddiest) ADJ 形容詞 **Shoddy** work or a **shoddy** product has been done or made carelessly or badly. 粗雑な, 粗悪な □ *I'm normally quick to complain about shoddy service.* サービスの対応が悪いときはたいていすぐに苦情をいう. ● **shod|di|ly** ADV 副詞 粗雑に □ *These products are shoddily produced.* これらの製品は粗悪品である.

shoe /ˈʃu/ (shoes, shoeing, shoed or shod) ■ N-COUNT 可算名詞 **Shoes** are objects which you wear on your feet. They cover most of your foot and you wear them over socks or stockings. 靴 □ *...a pair of shoes.* 靴1足. □ *Low-heeled comfortable shoes are best.* かか

との低い履きやすい靴が一番よい. **2** N-COUNT 可算名詞 A **shoe** is the same as a **horseshoe**. 蹄鉄 (ていてつ) **3** V-T 他動詞 When a blacksmith **shoes** a horse, they attach horseshoes onto their feet. 蹄鉄を打つ □ *Blacksmiths spent most of their time repairing tools and shoeing horses.* 鍛冶屋は道具の修理と蹄鉄の打ち付けに大半の時間を費やした. **4** PHRASE 句 If you **fill** someone's **shoes** or **step into their shoes**, you take their place by doing the job they were doing. ー の後任となる □ *No one has been able to fill his shoes.* 彼の後任を果たせる者は誰もいません. **5** PHRASE 句 If you talk about being **in** someone's **shoes**, you talk about what you would do or how you would feel if you were in their situation. ー の立場になって □ *I wouldn't want to be in his shoes.* 彼のような立場に立たされるのはごめんだね.

→ see **clothing**

shoe|string /ʃuːstrɪŋ/ **1** ADJ 形容詞 A **shoestring** budget is one where you have very little money to spend. ごくわずかな [ADJ n] □ *The movie was made on a shoestring budget.* その映画はわずかな予算で制作された. **2** PHRASE 句 If you do something or make something **on a shoestring**, you do it using very little money. わずかな金で □ *The theater will be run on a shoestring.* 劇場はわずかな資金で運営される見通しである.

shone /ʃɒn/ **Shone** is the past tense and past participle of **shine**.

shook /ʃʊk/ **Shook** is the past tense of **shake**.

shoot /ʃuːt/ (**shoots, shooting, shot**) **1** V-T 他動詞 If someone **shoots** a person or an animal, they kill them or injure them by firing a bullet or arrow at them. 撃つ □ *The police had orders to shoot anyone who attacked them.* 警察官は攻撃してきた者には発砲してもよいと指示されていた. □ *The man was shot dead by the police during a raid on his house.* 警察が男の自宅に強制捜査に入った際に男は射殺された. **2** V-I 自動詞 To **shoot** means to fire a bullet from a weapon such as a gun. 発砲する □ *He taunted armed officers by pointing to his head, as if inviting them to shoot.* ほら撃ったらどうぞと, 彼は自分の頭を指さしながら銃を持った警官を挑発した. □ *The police came around the corner and they started shooting at us.* 警官は曲がり角のところから来るとこっちに発砲し始めた. **3** V-I 自動詞 If someone or something **shoots** in a particular direction, they move in that direction quickly and suddenly. 素早く動く □ *They had almost reached the boat when a figure shot past them.* もうすぐボートに着くというときに彼らの前を人影がさっと通り過ぎた. **4** V-T/V-I 他動詞/自動詞 If you **shoot** something somewhere or if it **shoots** somewhere, it moves there quickly and suddenly. 素早く動かす [他動詞] 素早く動く [自動詞] □ *Masters shot a hand across the table and gripped his wrist.* マスターズはテーブル越しにいきなり手を伸ばし彼の手首をつかんだ. □ *As soon as she got close, the old woman's hand shot out.* 老婆が近づいてきたかと思うと素早くその手が伸びた. **5** V-T 他動詞 If you **shoot** a look at someone, you look at them quickly and briefly, often in a way that expresses your feelings. 一瞬向ける □ *Mary Ann shot him a rueful look.* メアリー・アンは彼に悔やんでいるような表情を見せた. **6** V-I 自動詞 If someone **shoots to fame**, they become famous or successful very quickly. 躍進する □ *Alina Reyes shot to fame a few years ago with her extraordinary first novel.* アリーナ・レイェスは数年前に異色のデビュー作で一躍有名になった. **7** V-T 他動詞 When people **shoot** a movie or **shoot** photographs, they make a movie or take photographs using a camera. 撮影する □ *He'd love to shoot his film in Cuba.* 彼はぜひキューバで映画を撮りたいと思っている. ● N-COUNT 可算名詞 **Shoot** is also a noun. 撮影 □ *...a barn presently being used for a video shoot.* ビデオ撮影で現在使っている納屋. **8** N-COUNT 可算名詞 **Shoots** are plants that are beginning to grow, or new parts growing from a plant or tree. 新芽 □ *Prune established plants annually as new shoots appear.* 植物が根づいたら, 毎年新芽が出る頃に剪定します. **9** V-I 自動詞 In sports such as soccer or basketball, when someone **shoots**, they try to score by kicking or throwing the ball toward the goal or hoop. シュートする □ *Spencer scuttled away from Singh to shoot wide when he should have scored.* スペンサーはシンから急いで離れたせいで大きくシュートを外して得点のチャンスを逃した. **10** → see also **shooting, shot 11** to **shoot from the hip** → see **hip**

▶ **shoot down** PHRASAL VERB 句動詞 **1** If someone **shoots down** an airplane, a helicopter, or a missile, they make it fall to the ground by hitting it with a bullet or missile. 撃ち落す □ *They claimed to have shot down one incoming missile.* 彼らの主張によれば, 飛んできたミサイル1基を撃墜したという. **2** PHRASAL VERB 句動詞 If one person **shoots down** another, they shoot them with a gun. 撃ち合う □ *He was prepared to suppress rebellion by shooting down protesters.* 抗議する群衆に発砲してでも彼は暴動を鎮圧する覚悟でした.

▶ **shoot up** PHRASAL VERB 句動詞 If something **shoots up**, it grows or increases very quickly. 急に伸びる □ *Sales shot up by 9% last month.* 先月の売り上げは9%も急増しました.

shoot|ing /ʃuːtɪŋ/ (**shootings**) **1** N-COUNT 可算名詞 A **shooting** is an occasion when someone is killed or injured by being shot with a gun. 銃撃 □ *Two more bodies were found nearby after the shooting.* 銃撃後に現場付近でさらに2人の遺体が見つかった. **2** N-UNCOUNT 不可算名詞 **Shooting** is hunting animals with a gun as a leisure activity. 狩猟 □ *Grouse shooting begins in August.* ライチョウ狩りは8月に解禁されます. **3** N-UNCOUNT 不可算名詞 The **shooting** of a movie is the act of filming it. 撮影 □ *Ingrid was busy learning her lines for the next day's shooting.* イングリッドは翌日の撮影のせりふを覚えるのに余念がなかった. **4** N-UNCOUNT 不可算名詞 In sports such as basketball and soccer, a player's **shooting** is their ability to score points or goals. シュート力 □ *When asked whether the injury affected his shooting, Iverson said: "Not at all."* このけがでシュート力は大丈夫かという問いに, アイバーソンは「全く問題ない」と答えた.

shop /ʃɒp/ (**shops, shopping, shopped**) **1** N-COUNT 可算名詞 A **shop** is a small store that sells one type of merchandise. ー店 □ *...a gift shop.* ギフトショップ. □ *He and his wife run their own antiques shop.* 彼は妻と一緒に骨董 (こっとう) 店を営んでいる. **2** N-COUNT 可算名詞 A **shop** is a building or part of a building where things are sold. 店 [mainly BRIT 主に英国英語; AM usually **store** 米国英語では通常 **store**]

3 V-I 自動詞 When you **shop**, you go to stores or shops and buy things. 買い物をする □ *He always shopped at the co-op.* 彼はいつも生協の店で買い物していた. □ *...some advice that's worth bearing in mind when shopping for a new carpet.* 新しいじゅうたんを購入するときに知っておくとよいポイント. ● **shop|per** N-COUNT 可算名詞 (**shoppers**) 買い物客 □ *...crowds of Christmas shoppers.* クリスマスの買い物客の人ごみ. **4** N-COUNT 可算名詞 You can refer to a place where a particular service is offered as a particular type of **shop**. ー店 □ *...the barber shop where Rodney sometimes had his hair cut.* ロドニーがときどき散髪に行った理髪店. □ *...betting shops.* 場外馬券売場. **5** → see also **coffee shop, shopping 6** PHRASE 句 If you say that people **are talking shop**, you mean that they are talking about their work, and this is boring for other people who do not do the same work. 仕事の話をする □ *Although I get on well with my colleagues, if you hang around together all the time you just end up talking shop.* 私も同僚とは仲がいいが, いつも一緒にいるとついつい仕事の話になってしまいますよね.

▶ **shop around** PHRASAL VERB 句動詞 If you **shop around**, you go to different stores or companies in order to compare the prices and quality of goods or services before you decide to buy them. 店を回ってみる □ *Prices may vary so it's well worth shopping around before you buy.* 店によって値段が違うかもしれないので買う前に店を回ってみるのがよい.

shop as|sis|tant (**shop assistants**) N-COUNT 可算名詞 A **shop assistant** is a person who works in a store selling things to customers. 店員 [mainly BRIT 主に英国英語; AM usually **sales clerk** 米国英語では通常 **sales clerk**]

shop floor also **shop-floor** or **shopfloor** N-SING 単数名詞 The **shop floor** is used to refer to all the ordinary workers in a factory or the area where they work, especially in contrast to the people who are in charge. 現場 □ *Cost must be controlled, not just on the shop floor but in the boardroom too.* コスト削減は生産現場だけでなく経営者側でも必要である.

shop|keep|er /ʃɒpkiːpər/ (**shopkeepers**) N-COUNT 可算名詞 A **shopkeeper** is a person who owns or manages a shop. 店主

shop|lift /ʃɒplɪft/ (**shoplifts, shoplifting, shoplifted**) V-T/V-I 他動詞/自動詞 If someone **shoplifts**, they steal goods from a store by hiding them in a bag or in their clothes. 万引きする □ *He openly shoplifted from a supermarket.* 彼はスーパーなどで堂々と万引きした. ● **shop|lifter** N-COUNT 可算名詞 (**shoplifters**) 万引きする人 □ *A*

persistent shoplifter has been banned from every store in town. 万引きの常習者が町のすべての店から締め出されることになった.

shop|lifting /ʃɒplɪftɪŋ/ N-UNCOUNT 不可算名詞 **Shoplifting** is stealing from a store by hiding things in a bag or in your clothes. 万引き □ *The grocer accused her of shoplifting and demanded to look in her bag.* 食料雑貨店の店主は彼女が万引きしていたと言って, かばんの中を見せるように求めました.

shop|ping /ʃɒpɪŋ/ **1** N-UNCOUNT 不可算名詞 When you do the **shopping**, you go to the stores or shops and buy things. 買い物 □ *I'll do the shopping this afternoon.* 午後から買い物に行くつもりだ. **2** N-UNCOUNT 不可算名詞 Your **shopping** is the things that you have bought from stores, especially food. 買った物 [mainly BRIT 主に英国英語; AM usually **groceries** 米国英語では通常 **groceries**]

Word Partnership   *shopping* は次の語句と使われる:

N.	shopping **bag, Christmas** shopping, shopping **district, food** shopping, **grocery** shopping, **holiday** shopping, **online** shopping, shopping **spree 1**

shop|ping cen|ter (**shopping centers**) N-COUNT 可算名詞 A **shopping center** is a specially built area containing a lot of different stores. ショッピングセンター □ *They met in the parking lot at the new shopping center.* 彼らは新しいショッピングセンターの駐車場で会った.

shop|ping chan|nel (**shopping channels**) N-COUNT 可算名詞 A **shopping channel** is a television channel that broadcasts programs showing products that you can buy over the phone or online. ショッピングチャンネル

shop|ping mall (**shopping malls**) N-COUNT 可算名詞 A **shopping mall** is a specially built covered area containing stores and restaurants which people can walk between, and where cars are not allowed. ショッピングモール

shore /ʃɔːr/ (**shores, shoring, shored**) N-COUNT 可算名詞 The **shores** or the **shore** of a sea, lake, or wide river is the land along the edge of it. Someone who is **on shore** is on the land rather than on a ship. 岸 [also prep N] □ *They walked down to the shore.* 彼らは歩いて海岸に下りた. □ *...elephants living on the shores of Lake Kariba.* カリバ湖岸で暮らす象.

You can use **beach, coast,** and **shore** to talk about the piece of land beside a stretch of water. The **shore** is the area of land along the edge of the ocean, a lake, or a wide river. The **coast** is the area of land that lies alongside the ocean. You may be referring just to the land close to the ocean, or to a wider area that extends further inland. A **beach** is a flat area of sand or pebbles next to the ocean.

▶ **shore up** PHRASAL VERB 句動詞 If you **shore up** something that is weak or about to fail, you do something in order to strengthen it or support it. 支える □ *The democracies of the West may find it hard to shore up their defenses.* 欧米の民主主義諸国は防衛力強化の難しさを知ることになるかもしれない.

shore|line /ʃɔːrlaɪn/ (**shorelines**) N-COUNT 可算名詞 A **shoreline** is the edge of a sea, lake, or wide river. 海岸線 □ *...the rocks along the shoreline.* 海岸線に続く岩場.

shorn /ʃɔːrn/ **Shorn** is the past participle of **shear**.

short
❶ ADJECTIVE AND ADVERB USES
❷ NOUN USES

❶ short /ʃɔːrt/ (**shorter, shortest**)
↪ **Please look at category 16 to see if the expression you are looking for is shown under another headword.** **1** ADJ 形容詞 If something is **short** or lasts for a **short** time, it does not last very long. 短い □ *The announcement was made a short time ago.* 発表はつい先ほどありました. □ *Kemp gave a short laugh.* ケンプは一瞬笑った. **2** ADJ 形容詞 A **short** speech, letter, or book does not have many words or pages in it. 短い □ *They were performing a short extract from Shakespeare's Two Gentlemen of Verona.* 彼らはシェイクスピアの『ヴェローナの二紳士』のごく一部を演じた. **3** ADJ 形容詞 Someone who is **short** is not as tall as most people are. 背の低い □ *I'm tall and thin and he's short and fat.* 私は背が高くやせているが, かれのほうは背が低くて太っている. □ *...a short, elderly woman with gray hair.* 背の低い白髪まじりの年配の女性. **4** ADJ 形容詞 Something that is **short** measures only a small amount from one end to the other. 短い □ *The restaurant is only a short distance away.* レストランはすぐ近くだ. □ *A short flight of steps led to a grand doorway.* 階段を少し上ったところに立派な玄関があった. **5** ADJ 形容詞 If you are **short** of something or if it is **short**, you do not have enough of it. If you are running **short** of something or if it is running **short**, you do not have much of it left. 一不足で [v-link ADJ] □ *Her father's illness left the family short of money.* 父親の

病気になったせいで家族がお金に困るようになった. □ *Government forces are running short of ammunition and fuel.* 政府軍は弾薬と燃料が底をつきかけています. **6** ADJ 形容詞 If someone or something is or stops **short of** a place, they have not quite reached it. If they are or fall **short of** an amount, they have not quite achieved it. 一に届かない [v-link ADJ] □ *He stopped a hundred yards short of the building.* 彼は建物の百ヤード手前で止まった. **7** PHRASE 句 **Short of** a particular thing means except for that thing or without actually doing that thing. 一以外に □ *Short of gagging the children, there was not much he could do about the noise.* さるぐつわでもはめない限り, 彼には子供たちを黙らせる手段はほとんどなかった. **8** ADV 副詞 If something is **cut short** or **stops short**, it is stopped before people expect it to or before it has finished. 中断される [ADV after v] □ *His glittering career was cut short by a heart attack.* 彼は心臓発作で突然光り輝かしい生涯を閉じた. **9** ADJ 形容詞 If a name or abbreviation is **short for** another name, it is the short version of that name. 一の省略形で [v-link ADJ "for" n] □ *Her friend Kes (short for Kesewa) was in tears.* 彼女の友達のケス（本名ケセワ）は涙を流していた. **10** ADJ 形容詞 If you have a **short** temper, you get angry very easily. (気が) 短い □ *...an awkward, self-conscious woman with a short temper.* 取っ付きにくい自意識過剰で短気な女. **11** ADJ 形容詞 If you are **short with** someone, you speak briefly and rather rudely to them, because you are impatient or angry. そっけない [v-link ADJ] □ *She seemed nervous or tense, and she was definitely short with me.* 彼女は緊張してピリピリしていたようで, ほんとにそっけなくされた. **12** PHRASE 句 If a person or thing is called something **for short**, that is the short version of their name. 略して □ *Opposite me was a woman called Jasminder (Jazzy for short).* 向かい側にはジャスミンダー（愛称ジャジー）という女性がいた. **13** PHRASE 句 You use **in short** when you have been giving a lot of details and you want to give a conclusion or summary. 要するに □ *Try tennis, badminton or windsurfing. In short, anything challenging.* テニスでも, バトミントンでも, ウインドサーフィンでもやってみなさい. 要は何かに挑戦すること. **14** PHRASE 句 If someone or something **is short on** a particular good quality, they do not have as much of it as you think they should have. 一が不十分である [DISAPPROVAL 不賛成] □ *The proposals were short on detail.* 提案は具体性に欠けていた. **15** PHRASE 句 If someone **stops short of** doing something, they come close to doing it but do not actually do it. 一するのを思いとどまる □ *He stopped short of explicitly criticizing the government.* 彼は政府をあからさまに批判するのは避けました. **16 short of breath → see breath 17 on short notice → see notice 18 to draw the short straw → see straw 19 in short supply → see supply 20 in the short term → see term**

Thesaurus   *short* また次を参照:

ADJ.	brief, quick; *(ant.)* long ❶ **1 2** petite, slight, small; *(ant.)* tall ❶ **3**

❷ short /ʃɔːrt/ (**shorts**) **1** N-PLURAL 複数名詞 **Shorts** are pants with very short legs, that people wear in hot weather or for taking part in sports. 半ズボン [also "a pair of" N] □ *...two women in bright cotton shorts and tee shirts.* 派手な綿のショートパンツとTシャツ姿の2人の女性. **2** N-PLURAL 複数名詞 **Shorts** are men's underpants with short legs. 男性用の下着のパンツ [mainly AM 主に米国英語] [also "a pair of" N] **3** N-COUNT 可算名詞 A **short** is a short film, especially one that is shown before the main film at the cinema. 短編映画

short|age /ʃɔːrtɪdʒ/ (**shortages**) N-VAR 可変性名詞 If there is a **shortage of** something, there is not enough of it. 不足 □ *A shortage of funds is preventing the U.N. from monitoring relief.* 資金不足のせいで国連は救援活動が監視できない. □ *Vietnam is suffering from food shortage.* ベトナムは食糧難に陥っています.

short-change (**short-changes, short-changing, short-changed**) **1** V-T 他動詞 If someone **short-changes** you, they do not give you enough change after you have bought something from them. 釣り銭を少なく渡す □ *The cashier made a mistake and short-changed him.* レジ係は間違って彼に釣り銭を少なく渡した. **2** V-T 他動詞 If you **are short-changed**, you are treated unfairly or dishonestly, often because you are given less of something than you deserve. 不当な扱いを受ける [usu passive] □ *Women are in fact still being short-changed in the press.* 報道において は, 女性は実際今でも公正な扱いを受けていない.

short|coming /ʃɔːrtkʌmɪŋ/ (**shortcomings**) N-COUNT 可算名詞 Someone's or something's **shortcomings** are the faults or weaknesses which they have. 欠点, 短所 □ *Marriages usually break down as a result of the shortcomings of both partners.* 一般に結婚生活は双方の欠点が原因で破綻する.

short|cut /ʃɔːrtkʌt/ (**shortcuts**) **1** N-COUNT 可算名詞 A **shortcut** is a quicker way of getting somewhere than the usual route. 近道 □ *I tried to take a shortcut and got lost.* 近道をしようとしていたら道に迷ってしまった. **2** N-COUNT 可算名詞 A **shortcut** is a method of achieving something more quickly or more easily than if you use the usual methods. 手っ取り早い方法 □ *Fame can*

be a shortcut to love and money. 名声があれば恋人も富も簡単に手に入る. **3** N-COUNT 可算名詞 On a computer, a **shortcut** is an icon on the desktop that allows you to go immediately to a program or document. ショートカット [COMPUTING コンピューティング] ❑ *There are any number of ways to move or copy icons or create shortcuts in Windows.* Windowsでは, アイコンの移動やコピー, ショートカットの作成の方法がいくつも用意されている. **4** N-COUNT 可算名詞 On a computer, a **shortcut** is a keystroke or a combination of keystrokes that allows you to give commands without using the mouse. ショートカットキー [COMPUTING コンピューティング] ❑ *There is a handy keyboard shortcut to save you having to scroll up to the top of the screen.* 画面の最上部までスクロールする手間を省く便利なショートカットキーがある.

short|en /ˈʃɔːrtən/ (**shortens, shortening, shortened**) **1** V-T/V-I 他動詞/自動詞 If you **shorten** an event or the length of time that something lasts, or if it **shortens**, it does not last as long as it would otherwise do or as it used to do. 短くする [他動詞] 短くなる [自動詞] ❑ *Smoking can shorten your life.* 喫煙は寿命を縮める恐れがある. ❑ *The trading day is shortened in observance of the Labor Day holiday.* レイバーデーのため, 取引時間が短縮される. **2** V-T/V-I 他動詞/自動詞 If you **shorten** an object or if it **shortens**, it becomes smaller in length. 短くする [他動詞] 短くなる [自動詞] ❑ *Her father paid $5,000 for an operation to shorten her nose.* 彼女の父は鼻を小さくする手術に5000ドル支払った. **3** V-T 他動詞 If you **shorten** a name or other word, you change it by removing some of the letters. 縮める ❑ *Originally called Lili, she eventually shortened her name to Lee.* 初めのうち彼女はリリーと呼ばれていたが, そのうちリーとつづめるようになった.

short|fall /ˈʃɔːrtfɔːl/ (**shortfalls**) N-COUNT 可算名詞 If there is a **shortfall in** something, there is less of it than you need. 不足分 ❑ *The government has refused to make up a $30,000 shortfall in funding.* 政府は財源の不足分3万ドルの拠出を拒否している.

short|hand /ˈʃɔːrthænd/ **1** N-UNCOUNT 不可算名詞 **Shorthand** is a quick way of writing and uses signs to represent words or syllables. Shorthand is sometimes used by secretaries and journalists to write down what someone is saying. 速記 ❑ *Ben took notes in shorthand.* ベンは速記でメモを取った. **2** N-UNCOUNT 不可算名詞 You can use **shorthand** to mean a quick or simple way of referring to something. 簡潔な言い方 [also "a" N] ❑ *Laslett uses the shorthand of "second age" for the group of younger people who are creating families.* ラスレットは子供をもうける若い人たちを簡単に「第2世代」と呼んでいる.

short-haul ADJ 形容詞 **Short-haul** is used to describe things that involve transporting passengers or goods over short distances. Compare **long-haul**. 短距離輸送の [ADJ n] ❑ *...short-haul flights, for example Chicago to Philadelphia.* シカゴ・フィラデルフィア間などの短距離便.

short list /ˈʃɔːrtlɪst/ (**shortlists, shortlisting, shortlisted**) also **short list** **1** N-COUNT 可算名詞 If someone is on a **shortlist**, for example, for a job or a prize, they are one of a small group of people who have been chosen from a larger group. The successful person is then chosen from the small group. 最終選考リスト ❑ *If you've been asked for an interview you are probably on a shortlist for no more than six.* 面接に呼ばれたのなら, おそらく最終選考リストの6名以内に入っているはずだ. **2** V-T 他動詞 If someone or something **is shortlisted** for a job or a prize, they are put on a shortlist. 最終選考に残る [usu passive] ❑ *He was shortlisted for the Nobel Prize for literature several times.* 彼はノーベル文学賞の最終選考に残ったことが数回あった.

short-lived ADJ 形容詞 Something that is **short-lived** does not last very long. つかの間の ❑ *Any hope that the speech would end the war was short-lived.* その演説によって戦争が終結するという望みはすぐについえた.

short|ly /ˈʃɔːrtli/ ADV 副詞 If something happens **shortly** after or before something else, it happens not long after or before it. If something is going to happen **shortly**, it is going to happen soon. まもなく ❑ *Their trial will shortly begin.* 彼らの裁判はまもなく始まる見通しです. ❑ *Shortly after moving into her apartment, she found a job.* アパートに引越してすぐに彼女は仕事を見つけた.

short|sight|ed /ˌʃɔːrtˈsaɪtɪd/ also **short-sighted** **1** ADJ 形容詞 If someone is **shortsighted** about something, or if their ideas are **shortsighted**, they do not make proper or careful judgments about the future. 近視眼的な ❑ *Environmentalists fear that this is a shortsighted approach to the problem of global warming.* 環境団体からは姑息な温暖化対策ではないかという懸念が出ています. **2** ADJ 形容詞 If you are **short-sighted**, you cannot see things properly when they are far away, because there is something wrong with your eyes. 近視の [mainly BRIT 主に英国英語; AM usually **nearsighted** 米国英語では通常 **nearsighted**]

short-term ADJ 形容詞 **Short-term** is used to describe things that will last for a short time, or things that will have an effect soon rather than in the distant future. 短期的な ❑ *Investors weren't concerned about short-term profits over the next few years.* 投資家は今後

数年間の短期的利益については懸念していなかった. ❑ *The company has 90 staff, almost all on short-term contracts.* 同社には90名の社員がいるが, ほとんどが短期契約社員である.

→ see **memory**

shot /ʃɒt/ (**shots**) **1** **Shot** is the past tense and past participle of **shoot**. **2** N-COUNT 可算名詞 A **shot** is an act of firing a gun. 発砲 ❑ *He had murdered Perceval at point blank range with a single shot.* 彼はパーシバルを至近距離からの一発で射殺していた. **3** N-COUNT 可算名詞 Someone who is a good **shot** can shoot well. Someone who is a bad **shot** cannot shoot well. 撃ち手 ❑ *He was not a particularly good shot because of his eyesight.* 彼は視力が弱かったので特に射撃がうまいわけではなかった. **4** N-COUNT 可算名詞 In sports such as soccer, golf, or tennis, a **shot** is an act of kicking, hitting, or throwing the ball, especially in an attempt to score a point. ショット, シュート ❑ *He had only one shot at goal.* 彼は一度だけシュートした. **5** N-COUNT 可算名詞 A **shot** is a photograph or a particular sequence of pictures in a movie. 写真 ❑ *I decided to try for a more natural shot of a fox peering from the bushes.* 茂みの中からキツネがのぞいている写真をもっと自然に撮ってみることにした. **6** N-COUNT 可算名詞 If you have a **shot at** something, you attempt to do it. 試み [INFORMAL くだけた] ❑ *The heavyweight champion will be given a shot at Holyfield's world title.* ヘビー級チャンピオンはホリーフィールドの持つ世界タイトルに挑戦する. **7** N-COUNT 可算名詞 A **shot of** a drug is an injection of it. 注射 ❑ *He administered a shot of Nembutal.* 彼はネンブタールを注射した. **8** N-COUNT 可算名詞 A **shot of** a strong alcoholic drink is a small glass of it. 一杯 ❑ *...a shot of vodka.* ウォッカ1杯. **9** PHRASE 句 If you **give** something your **best shot**, you do it as well as you possibly can. 全力を尽くす [INFORMAL くだけた] ❑ *I don't expect to win. But I am going to give it my best shot.* 勝つことは考えていませんが, 全力で挑むつもりです. **10** PHRASE 句 The person who **calls the shots** is in a position to tell others what to do. 支配する ❑ *The directors call the shots and nothing happens without their say-so.* 重役は采配(さいはい)を振るうもので, 彼らの指示なしには何も前に進まない. **11** PHRASE 句 If you do something **like a shot**, you do it without any delay or hesitation. すぐに [INFORMAL くだけた] ❑ *I heard the key turn in the front door and I was out of bed like a shot.* 玄関の鍵を開ける音が聞こえたのですぐベッドから飛び起きた. **12** PHRASE 句 If you describe something as **a long shot**, you mean that it is unlikely to succeed, but is worth trying. 一か八かの賭け ❑ *The deal was a long shot, but Bagley had little to lose.* 取引は大きな賭けだったが, バグリーが失うものはほとんどなかった. **13** PHRASE 句 People sometimes use the expression **by a long shot** to emphasize the opinion they are giving. 決して [EMPHASIS 強調] ❑ *The missile-reduction treaty makes sweeping cuts, but the arms race isn't over by a long shot.* ミサイル削減条約によって大幅な削減が実現するが, これで軍拡競争が終わることは断じてありません.

→ see **photography**

Word Partnership	shot は次の語句と使われる:
V.	**fire** a shot, **hear** a shot **2**
	miss a shot **2 4**
	take a shot **2 4 - 8**
	block a shot, **hit** a shot **4**
	get a shot, **give** *someone* a shot **6 7**
ADJ.	**single** shot, **warning** shot **2**
	good shot **2 3**
	winning shot **4**

shot|gun /ˈʃɒtɡʌn/ (**shotguns**) N-COUNT 可算名詞 A **shotgun** is a gun used for shooting birds and animals which fires a lot of small metal balls at one time. 散弾銃

should /ʃəd, STRONG ʃʊd/

Should is a modal verb. It is used with the base form of a verb.

Should は法動詞であり, 動詞の原型とともに用いられる.

1 MODAL 法動詞 You use **should** when you are saying what would be the right thing to do or the right state for something to be in. 一したほうがよい, 一すべきである ❑ *I should exercise more.* 私はもっと運動したほうがいい. ❑ *He's never going to be able to forget it. And I don't think he should.* 彼はそのことを決して忘れることはできないだろう. また, 忘れるべきでないと思う. ❑ *Should our children be taught to swim at school?* 学校で子供たちに水泳を教えたほうがよいか. **2** MODAL 法動詞 You use **should** to give someone an order to do something, or to report an official order. 一する義務がある ❑ *18-year-olds are sent reminders that they should register to vote.* 18歳になると有権者登録を求める通知が送られてくる. **3** MODAL 法動詞 If you say that something **should have** happened, you mean that it did not happen, but that you wish it had. If you say that something **should not have** happened, you mean that it did happen, but that you wish it had not. 一すべきだった ❑ *I should have gone this morning but I was feeling a bit ill.* 今朝行っておけばよかったのに, ちょっと調子が悪かった. ❑ *You should have written to the area manager again.* もう一度地域統括者に手紙を書いておくべきだった. **4** MODAL 法動詞 You

use **should** when you are saying that something is probably the case or will probably happen in the way you are describing. If you say that something **should have** happened by a particular time, you mean that it will probably have happened by that time. 一の はずである □ *You should have no problem with reading this language.* 君 なら問題なくこの言語を読めるはずだ. □ *The doctor said it will take six weeks and I should be fine by then.* 医者の話では，全治6週間，その 頃までにはよくなるだろうということだった. **5** MODAL 法動詞 You use **should** in questions when you are asking someone for advice, permission, or information. 一したほうがよいでしょうか □ *Should I take out a loan?* ローンを組んだほうがよいでしょうか. □ *What should I do?* 私はどうしたらいいの. **6** MODAL 法動詞 You say "**I should,**" usually with the expression "if I were you," when you are giving someone advice by telling them what you would do if you were in their position. [mainly BRIT 主に英国英語, FORMAL 形式ばった] □ *I should look out if I were you!* もし私があなただったら用 心するだろうね. **7** MODAL 法動詞 You use **should** in conditional clauses when you are talking about things that might happen. 仮に [FORMAL 形式ばった] □ *If you should be fired, your health and pension benefits will not be automatically cut off.* 仮に解雇されてと しても，医療保険と年金給付がそのまま打ち切られてしまうことは ない. **8** MODAL 法動詞 You use **should** in "that" clauses after certain verbs, nouns, and adjectives when you are talking about a future event or situation. 一するように □ *He raised his glass and indicated that I should do the same.* 彼はグラスを持ち上げて，私にも同 じことをするように合図した. □ *I insisted that we should have a look at every car.* 私はすべての車を調べるべきだと言った. **9** MODAL 法動詞 You use **should** in expressions such as **I should think** and **I should imagine** to indicate that you think something is true but you are not sure. 一でしょう [VAGUENESS あいまいさ] □ *I should think it's going to rain soon.* すぐにでも雨が降ってきそうだけど. **10** MODAL 法動詞 You use **should** in expressions such as **You should have seen us** and **You should have heard him** to emphasize how funny, shocking, or impressive something that you experienced was. 一すればよかったのに [SPOKEN 口語, EMPHASIS 強調] □ *You should have heard him last night!* 彼が昨夜何て言ったか，聞かせてあげたか ったよ.

shoul|der /ʃoʊldər/ (**shoulders, shouldering, shouldered**) **1** N-COUNT 可算名詞 Your **shoulders** are between your neck and the tops of your arms. 肩 □ *She led him to an armchair, with her arm round his shoulder.* 彼女は彼をひじ掛け椅子まで連れ ていった. **2** N-PLURAL 複数名詞 When you talk about someone's problems or responsibilities, you can say that they carry them **on** their **shoulders.** 一の肩にのしかかって □ *No one suspected the anguish he carried on his shoulders.* 彼の背負った大変な苦労を疑う者 はいなかった. **3** V-T 他動詞 If you **shoulder** the responsibility or the blame for something, you accept it. 引き受ける □ *He has had to shoulder the responsibility of his father's mistakes.* 彼は父の過ちの責 任を背負い込むはめになった. **4** V-T 他動詞/自動詞 If you **shoulder** someone **aside** or if you **shoulder** your **way** somewhere, you push past people roughly using your shoulder. 肩で押す □ *The policemen rushed past him, shouldering him aside.* 警察官は彼を肩で押しのける にして走り過ぎた. □ *She could do nothing to stop him as he shouldered his way into the house.* 彼が家の中に押し入ろうとするのを彼女は制止 することができなかった. **5** N-VAR 可変性名詞 A **shoulder** is a cut of meat from the upper part of the front leg of an animal. 肩肉 □ *...shoulder of lamb.* 子羊の肩肉. **6** N-COUNT 可算名詞 On a busy road such as a freeway, the **shoulder** is the area at the side of the road where vehicles are allowed to stop in an emergency. 路肩 [AM 米国英語] **7** PHRASE 句 If someone offers you **a shoulder to cry on** or is **a shoulder to cry on,** they listen sympathetically as you talk about your troubles. 親身になって悩みを聞いてくれる人 □ *Mrs. Barrantes longs to be at her daughter's side to offer her a shoulder to cry on.* バランテスさんは娘の味方になって悩みを聞いてやりたいと思って いる. **8** PHRASE 句 If you say that someone or something stands **head and shoulders above** other people or things, you mean that they are a lot better than them. ずば抜けて □ *The two candidates stood head and shoulders above the rest.* 2人は他の候補より断然優 れていた. **9** PHRASE 句 If two or more people stand **shoulder to shoulder,** they are next to each other, with their shoulders touching. 肩を並べて □ *They fell into step, walking shoulder to shoulder with their heads bent against the rain.* 彼らは肩を寄せ合ってうつむ いて雨の中を歩き始めた. **10** PHRASE 句 If people work or stand **shoulder to shoulder,** they work together in order to achieve something, or support each other. 力を合わせて □ *They could fight shoulder-to-shoulder against a common enemy.* 彼らは共通の敵に対し一 致団結して戦えるはずである. **11** to **rub shoulders with** → see **rub** → see **body**

Word Partnership *shoulder* は次の語句と使われる:

ADJ.	**bare** shoulder, **broken** shoulder, **dislocated** shoulder, **left/right** shoulder **1**
N.	**head on** *someone's* shoulder **1** shoulder **a burden 3**
V.	**look over** *your* shoulder, **tap** *someone* on the shoulder **1** **cry on** *someone's* shoulder **7**

shouldn't /ʃʊdᵊnt/ **Shouldn't** is the usual spoken form of "should not."

should've /ʃʊdəv/ **Should've** is the usual spoken form of "should have," especially when "have" is an auxiliary verb.

shout /ʃaʊt/ (**shouts, shouting, shouted**) V-T/V-I 他動詞/自動 詞 If you **shout,** you say something very loudly, usually because you want people a long distance away to hear you or because you are angry. 大声を出す □ *He had to shout to make himself heard above the wind.* 彼は風の音にかき消されないように大声を出さなければなら なかった. □ *"She's alive!" he shouted triumphantly.* 「あいつ，生きて る！」と彼は歓声をあげた. □ *Andrew rushed out of the house, shouting for help.* アンドリューは大声で助けを求めながら家の外に走り出た. ● N-COUNT 可算名詞 **Shout** is also a noun. 叫び声 □ *The decision was greeted with shouts of protest from the crowd.* 決定に対して群集から抗 議の声が沸き起こりました. ▶ **shout out** PHRASAL VERB 句動詞 If you **shout** something **out,** you say it very loudly so that people can hear you clearly. 大声で言 う □ *They shouted out the names of those detained.* 彼らは拘留者の名前 を大声で読み上げました. □ *I shouted out "I'm OK!"* 「大丈夫だ」と大 きな声で言った.

Word Partnership *shout* は次の語句と使われる:

PREP.	shout **at** *someone*
V.	**hear** a/*someone* shout, **want to** shout

shove /ʃʌv/ (**shoves, shoving, shoved**) **1** V-T/V-I 他動詞/自動詞 If you **shove** someone or something, you push them with a quick, violent movement. 乱暴に押す □ *He shoved her out of the way.* 彼は 彼女を乱暴に押しのけていった. □ *He's the one who shoved me.* 乱暴 に押したのは彼だ. ● N-COUNT 可算名詞 **Shove** is also a noun. 押 すこと □ *She gave Gracie a shove toward the house.* 彼女はグレーシー を家の方向にぐいと押した. **2** V-T 他動詞 If you **shove** something somewhere, you push it there quickly and carelessly. 押し込む □ *We shoved a copy of the newsletter beneath their door.* ドアの下に会 報をぎゅっと押し込んだ. **3** PHRASE 句 If you talk about what you think will happen **if push comes to shove,** you are talking about what you think will happen if a situation becomes very bad or difficult. いざとなったら [INFORMAL くだけた] □ *If push comes to shove, if you should lose your case in the court, what will you do?* 最悪の場 合，つまり裁判に負けたらどうするつもりですか.

Word Partnership *shove* は次の語句と使われる:

ADV.	shove *someone* **down 1**
V.	**give** *someone/something* a shove **1**
PREP.	shove *someone/something* **into** *someone/something* **1**

shov|el /ʃʌvᵊl/ (**shovels, shoveling** or **shovelling, shoveled** or **shovelled**) **1** N-COUNT 可算名詞 A **shovel** is a tool with a long handle that is used for lifting and moving earth, coal, or snow. シャベル □ *...a coal shovel.* 石炭用シャベル. **2** V-T 他動詞 If you **shovel** earth, coal, or snow, you lift and move it with a shovel. シ ャベルですくう □ *He has to get out and shovel snow.* 彼は外に出て雪か きをしなければなりません. **3** V-T 他動詞 If you **shovel** something somewhere, you push a lot of it quickly into that place. 大量にほ うり込む □ *There was silence, except for Randall, who was obliviously shoveling food into his mouth.* みんな黙っていたが，ランダルが気ま めずに食べ物を口にかき込む音だけがしていた.

show

❶	VERB USES
❷	NOUN AND ADJECTIVE USES
❸	PHRASAL VERBS

❶ show /ʃoʊ/ (**shows, showing, showed, shown**) **1** V-T 他 動詞 If something **shows that** a state of affairs exists, it gives information that proves it or makes it clear to people. 示す □ *Research shows that young people still look to parents as their main source for health information.* 調査によれば，若者が今でも主に両親か ら健康に関する情報を得ていることが明らかになった. □ *These figures show an increase of over one million in unemployment.* この数値から失 業者が百万人以上増加したことが分かる. **2** V-T 他動詞 If a picture,

chart, movie, or piece of writing **shows** something, it represents it or gives information about it. 描かれている □*Figure 4.1 shows the respiratory system.* 図4.1は呼吸器系を示している. □*The cushions, shown left, measure 20 x 12 inches and cost $39.95.* 左にあるクッションは20×12インチの大きさで、価格は39.95ドルである. □*Much of the film shows the painter simply going about his task.* ほぼ全編にわたって仕事に打ち込む画家の姿が描き出されている. ☑ V-T 他動詞 If you **show** someone something, you give it to them, take them to it, or point to it, so that they can see it or know what you are referring to. 見せる □*Cut out this article and show it to your boss.* この記事を切り抜いて上司に見せなさい. □*He showed me the apartment he shares with Esther.* 彼はエスターと一緒に間借りしているアパートを見せてくれた. ☑ V-T 他動詞 If you **show** someone to a room or seat, you lead them there. 案内する □*It was very good of you to come. Let me show you to my study.* よく来てくれたね. 書斎に案内しよう. □*Milton was shown into the office.* ミルトンはオフィスに通された. ☑ V-T 他動詞 If you **show** someone how to do something, you do it yourself so that they can watch you and learn how to do it. 教える □*Claire showed us how to make a chocolate cake.* クレアはチョコレートケーキの作り方を教えてくれた. □*There are seasoned professionals who can teach you and show you what to do.* どうすればよいか指導してくれるベテランの専門家が揃っています. ☑ V-T/V-I 他動詞/自動詞 If something **shows** or if you **show** it, it is visible or noticeable. 見せる [他動詞] 見える [自動詞] □*When he smiled he showed a row of strong white teeth.* ほほえんだときに彼の健康そうな白い歯が見えた. □*Faint glimmers of daylight were showing through the trees.* 木の間から日光がかすかに洩れていた. ☑ V-T/V-I 他動詞/自動詞 If you **show** a particular attitude, quality, or feeling, or if it **shows**, you behave in a way that makes this attitude, quality, or feeling clear to other people. 表に出す [他動詞] 明らかに示す [自動詞] □*She showed no interest in her children.* 彼女はわが子に無関心だった. □*Ferguson was unhappy and it showed.* ファーガソンは悲しかった. 周りからもはっきりと分かった. □*You show me respect.* 私に敬意を示しなさい. ☑ V-T 他動詞 If something **shows** a quality or characteristic or if that quality or characteristic **shows itself**, it can be noticed or observed. 示す □*The story shows a strong narrative gift and a vivid eye for detail.* 物語は迫力ある語りの才能と細部まで及ぶ鮮やかな描写力が印象的である. □*Her popularity clearly shows no sign of waning.* 彼女の人気は全く衰える気配がない. ☑ V-T 他動詞 If a company **shows** a profit or a loss, its accounts indicate that it has made a profit or a loss. 示す □*It is the only one of the three companies expected to show a profit for the quarter.* これら3社のうちで四半期での黒字が見込まれるのはこの1社だけです. ☑ V-I 自動詞 If a person you are expecting to meet does not **show**, they do not arrive at the place where you expect to meet them. 現われる [mainly AM 主に米国英語] □*There was always a chance he wouldn't show.* 彼が姿を見せない恐れはいつもあった. ● PHRASAL VERB 句動詞 **Show up** means the same as **show**. 現われる □*We waited until five o'clock, but he did not show up.* 5時まで待ったが彼は姿を見せなかった. ☑ V-T/V-I 他動詞/自動詞 If someone **shows** a film or television program, it is broadcast or appears on television or in the theater. 上映する □*The TV news showed the same film clip.* テレビのニュースでも同じ予告クリップが流れた. □*The movie is now showing at theaters around the country.* この映画は全国の映画館で上映中である. ☑ V-T 他動詞 To **show** things such as works of art means to put them in an exhibition where they can be seen by the public. 展示する □*50 dealers will show oils, watercolors, drawings and prints from 1900 to 1992.* 50人の画商が集まって、1900年から1992年までに制作された油絵、水彩画、デッサン、版画を展示する. ☑ PHRASE 句 If you **have** something **to show for** your efforts, you have achieved something as a result of what you have done. これまでの成果があがる □*I'm nearly 31 and it's about time I had something to show for my time in my job.* もうすぐ31歳になる. これまでの仕事の成果がそろそろ出てきてもよい頃だ. ☑ PHRASE 句 If you say **it just goes to show** or **it just shows** that something is the case, you mean that what you have just said or experienced demonstrates that it is the case. 一ということがよく分かる □*I forgot all about the ring. Which just goes to show that getting good grades in school doesn't mean you're clever.* その指輪のことはすっかり忘れてしまっていた. つまりこれは、学校の成績がよくても頭がいいとは限らないということだ. ☑ to **show** someone the **door** → see **door** ☑ to **show** your **face** → see **face** → see **concert, laser, theater**

② show /ʃoʊ/ (shows) ☑ N-COUNT 可算名詞 A **show of** a feeling or quality is an attempt by someone to make it clear that they have that feeling or quality. 示すこと [usu "a" N "of" n] □*Miners gathered in the center of Bucharest in a show of support for the government.* 鉱山労働者はブカレスト市街に集まって政府への支持を表明しました. ☑ N-UNCOUNT 不可算名詞 If you say that something is **for show**, you mean that it has no real purpose and is done just to give a good impression. 見せかけ □*The change in government is more for show than for real.* 政府の変化は本物というより見せかけである. ☑ N-COUNT 可算名詞 A television or radio **show** is a program on television or radio. 番組 □*I had my own TV show.* 自分のテレビ番組を持っていた. □*...a popular talk show on a Cuban radio station.* キューバのラジオ局の人気トーク番組. ☑ N-COUNT 可算名詞 A **show**

in a theater is an entertainment or concert, especially one that includes different items such as music, dancing, and comedy. ショー □*How about going shopping and seeing a show?* 買い物してショーを見るのはどうだ? ☑ N-COUNT 可算名詞 A **show** is a public exhibition of things, such as works of art, fashionable clothes, or things that have been entered in a competition. 展覧会, 展示会 [also "on" n] □*Currently, the show is in Boston.* 展示会はボストンで開催中です. □*It plans about 30 such fashion shows this fall in department stores.* 今秋、こうしたファッションショーを30回程度デパートを会場にして開催する予定である.

Thesaurus	*show* また次を参照:
v.	demonstrate, display, exhibit, present ❶ ☑
n.	act, entertainment, production, program ❷ ☑ ☑
	demonstration, display, presentation ❷ ☑

❸ show /ʃoʊ/ (shows, showing, showed, shown)
▶ **show off** ☑ PHRASAL VERB 句動詞 If you say that someone **is showing off**, you are criticizing them for trying to impress people by showing in a very obvious way what they can do or what they own. いい格好をする. [DISAPPROVAL 不賛成] □*All right, there's no need to show off.* いいよ、格好はつけなくていいんだ. ☑ PHRASAL VERB 句動詞 If you **show off** something that you have, you show it to a lot of people or make it obvious that you have it, because you are proud of it. 見せびらかす □*Naomi was showing off her engagement ring.* ネイオーミは婚約指輪を自慢げに見せていた. ☑ → see also **show-off**
▶ **show up** ☑ PHRASAL VERB 句動詞 If something **shows up** or if something **shows** it **up**, it can be seen or noticed. 目立つ □*You may have some strange disease that may not show up for 10 or 15 years.* あなたは奇病にかかっているかも知れません. その病気は発病までに10年から15年もかかる場合があります. □*The orange color shows up well against most backgrounds.* オレンジ色はどんな背景色でもたいてい目立つ. ☑ PHRASAL VERB 句動詞 If someone or something **shows** you **up**, they make you feel embarrassed or ashamed of them. 恥をかかせる □*He wanted to teach her a lesson for showing him up in front of Leonov.* 彼はレオーノフの前で恥をかかされたので彼女を懲らしめてやろうと思った. ☑ → see also **show ❶ ☑**

show busi|ness N-UNCOUNT 不可算名詞 **Show business** is the entertainment industry of movies, theater, and television. 芸能界、ショービジネス □*He started his career in show business by playing the saxophone and singing.* 彼はサックス奏者兼歌手としてショービジネスにデビューしました.

show|down /ʃoʊdaʊn/ (showdowns) N-COUNT 可算名詞 A **showdown** is a big argument or conflict which is intended to settle a dispute that has lasted for a long time. 最終決着 □*They may be pushing the president toward a final showdown with his party.* 大統領が自らの党と最終決着を図るように彼らは仕向けている可能性がある.

show|er /ʃaʊər/ (showers, showering, showered) ☑ N-COUNT 可算名詞 A **shower** is a device for washing yourself. It consists of a pipe which ends in a flat cover with a lot of holes in it so that water comes out in a spray. シャワー □*She heard him turn on the shower.* 彼女はシャワーを出す音が聞こえた. ☑ N-COUNT 可算名詞 A **shower** is a small enclosed area containing a shower. シャワー室 □*Do you sing in the shower?* シャワーしているときに歌いますか. ☑ N-COUNT 可算名詞 The **showers** or the **shower** in a place such as a gym is the area containing showers. シャワー室 □*The showers are a mess.* シャワー室は汚かった. ☑ N-COUNT 可算名詞 If you take a **shower**, you wash yourself by standing under a spray of water from a shower. シャワー □*I think I'll take a shower before dinner.* 夕食前にシャワーを浴びようかな. ☑ V-I 自動詞 If you **shower**, you wash yourself by standing under a spray of water from a shower. シャワーを浴びる □*There wasn't time to shower or change clothes.* シャワーを浴びたり着替えたりしている暇はなかった. ☑ N-COUNT 可算名詞 A **shower** is a short period of rain, especially light rain. にわか雨 □*There'll be bright or sunny spells and scattered showers this afternoon.* 午後はしばらく晴天が続き、その後にわか雨が降るでしょう. ☑ N-COUNT 可算名詞 You can refer to a lot of things that are falling as a **shower** of them. 降り注いでくるもの □*Showers of sparks flew in all directions.* 火花が雨のようにあちらこちらに飛び散った. ☑ V-T 他動詞 If you **are showered with** a lot of small objects or pieces, they are scattered over you. 一を浴びる [usu passive] □*They were showered with rice in the traditional manner.* 2人は伝統的なライスシャワーの祝福を受けました. ☑ N-COUNT 可算名詞 A **shower** is a party or celebration at which the guests bring gifts. お祝い贈呈パーティー [mainly AM 主に米国英語] □*...a baby shower.* ベビーシャワー.
→ see **meteor, soap, wedding**

shown /ʃoʊn/ **Shown** is the past participle of **show**.

show-off (show-offs) also **showoff** N-COUNT 可算名詞 If you say that someone is a **show-off**, you are criticizing them for trying to impress people by showing in a very obvious way what

they can do or what they own. 見せびらかす人 [INFORMAL くだけた, DISAPPROVAL 不賛成] ❑ *Many jet ski riders are big show-offs who stick around populated areas so everyone can see their turns and maneuvers.* ジェットスキーに乗る人は、ターンや操縦ぶりをみんなに見せびらかそうと人の集まる場所で乗り回す人が多い.

show|piece /ʃoʊpis/ (**showpieces**) also **show-piece** N-COUNT 可算名詞 A **showpiece** is something that is admired because it is the best thing of its type, especially something that is intended to be impressive. 優れた手本 ❑ *The factory was to be a showpiece of Western investment in the East.* 工場は旧共産圏での西側資本の成功例となるはずでした.

show|room /ʃoʊrum/ (**showrooms**) N-COUNT 可算名詞 A **showroom** is a store in which goods are displayed for sale, especially goods such as cars or electrical or gas appliances. ショールーム ❑ *...a car showroom.* 車のショールーム.

shrank /ʃræŋk/ **Shrank** is the past tense of **shrink**.

shrap|nel /ʃræpnəl/ N-UNCOUNT 不可算名詞 **Shrapnel** consists of small pieces of metal which are scattered from exploding bombs and shells. 爆弾の破片 ❑ *He was hit by shrapnel from a grenade.* 炸裂した手榴弾(しゅりゅうだん)の破片が彼に当たりました.

shred /ʃred/ (**shreds, shredding, shredded**) ◼ V-T 他動詞 If you **shred** something such as food or paper, you cut it or tear it into very small, narrow pieces. 細長く切る；千切りにする ❑ *They may be shredding documents.* 彼らは書類を裁断している可能性があります. ◼ N-COUNT 可算名詞 If you cut or tear food or paper **into shreds**, you cut or tear it into small, narrow pieces. 細長い断片 ❑ *Cut the cabbage into fine long shreds.* キャベツを千切りにします. ◼ N-COUNT 可算名詞 If there is not a **shred** of something, there is not even a small amount of it. 一は一切ない ❑ *He said there was not a shred of evidence to support such remarks.* 彼によれば、そうした発言を裏付ける証拠は一切ないといいます. ❑ *There is not a shred of truth in the story.* その話には真実のかけらもなかった.

shrewd /ʃrud/ (**shrewder, shrewdest**) ADJ 形容詞 A **shrewd** person is able to understand and judge a situation quickly and to use this understanding to their own advantage. 抜け目のない ❑ *She's a shrewd businesswoman.* 彼女はやり手の実業家である.

shriek /ʃrik/ (**shrieks, shrieking, shrieked**) V-I 自動詞 When someone **shrieks**, they make a short, very loud cry, for example, because they are suddenly surprised, are in pain, or are laughing. 金切り声を上げる ❑ *She shrieked and leapt from the bed.* 彼女は悲鳴を上げてベッドから飛び起きた. ● N-COUNT 可算名詞 **Shriek** is also a noun. 金切り声 ❑ *Sue let out a terrific shriek and leapt out of the way.* スーは恐ろしい悲鳴を上げてすぐにその場を離れた.

shrill /ʃrɪl/ (**shriller, shrillest**) ADJ 形容詞 A **shrill** sound is high-pitched and unpleasant. 金切り声の ❑ *Shrill cries and startled oaths flew up around us as pandemonium broke out.* 辺りは大混乱に陥り、甲高い悲鳴や驚きの罵声が沸き起こった. ❑ *...the shrill whistle of the engine.* エンジンの高くうなるような音.

shrimp /ʃrɪmp/ (**shrimp**)

The plural can also be **shrimps**.

複数形は **shrimps** もある.

N-COUNT 可算名詞 **Shrimps** are small shellfish with long tails and many legs. 小エビ ❑ *Add the shrimp and cook for 30 seconds.* 小エビを加えて30秒ほど加熱します.

shrimp cock|tail (**shrimp cocktails**) N-VAR 可変性名詞 A **shrimp cocktail** is a dish that consists of shrimp and a sauce. It is usually eaten at the beginning of a meal. 小エビのカクテル [mainly AM 主に米国英語]

shrine /ʃraɪn/ (**shrines**) ◼ N-COUNT 可算名詞 A **shrine** is a place of worship which is associated with a particular holy person or object. 聖堂、礼拝堂；（日本の）神社 ❑ *...the holy shrine of Mecca.* メッカのカアバ神殿. ◼ N-COUNT 可算名詞 A **shrine** is a place that people visit and treat with respect because it is connected with a dead person or with dead people that they want to remember. 霊場、巡礼地 ❑ *The monument has been turned into a shrine to the dead and the missing.* 今では記念碑は死者や行方不明者を偲ぶ場所になりました.

shrink /ʃrɪŋk/ (**shrinks, shrinking, shrank, shrunk**) ◼ V-I 自動詞 If cloth or clothing **shrinks**, it becomes smaller in size, usually as a result of being washed. 縮む ❑ *People were short in those days – or else those military uniforms all shrank in the wash!* 当時の人が小さかったのか、それとも洗濯して軍服が縮んでしまったのか. ◼ V-T/V-I 他動詞/自動詞 If something **shrinks** or something else **shrinks** it, it becomes smaller. 縮む [自動詞] 縮ませる [他動詞] ❑ *The vast forests of West Africa have shrunk.* 西アフリカの広大な森林が消失している. ◼ V-I 自動詞 If you **shrink away** from someone or something, you move away from them because you are frightened, shocked, or disgusted by them. 後ずさりする ❑ *One child shrinks away from me when I try to talk to him.* 1人の子供に話しかけようとしたら後ずさ

りします. ◼ V-I 自動詞 If you do not **shrink from** a task or duty, you do it even though it is unpleasant or dangerous. ひるむ [usu with neg] ❑ *He is decisive and won't shrink from a fight.* 彼は決断力に優れ、戦いにひるむようなことはない. ◼ N-COUNT 可算名詞 A **shrink** is a psychiatrist. 精神科医 [INFORMAL くだけた] ❑ *I've seen a shrink already.* 精神科医には診てもらっている. ◼ **no shrinking violet →** see **violet**

shriv|el /ʃrɪvəl/ (**shrivels, shriveling** or **shrivelling, shriveled** or **shrivelled**) V-T/V-I 他動詞/自動詞 When something **shrivels** or when something **shrivels** it, it becomes dryer and smaller, often with lines in its surface, as a result of losing the water it contains. しなびる [自動詞] しなびさせる [他動詞] ❑ *The plant shrivels and dies.* 植物はしなびて枯れる. ● PHRASAL VERB 句動詞 **Shrivel up** means the same as **shrivel**. しなびる ❑ *The leaves started to shrivel up.* 葉はしなび始めました. ● **shriv|eled** ADJ 形容詞 しなびた ❑ *...a shriveled chestnut.* 干からびた栗の実.

shroud /ʃraʊd/ (**shrouds, shrouding, shrouded**) ◼ N-COUNT 可算名詞 A **shroud** is a cloth which is used for wrapping a dead body. 死装束(しにしょうぞく)；埋葬するときに着せる白衣. ◼ V-T 他動詞 If something **has been shrouded in** mystery or secrecy, very little information about it has been made available. ベールに包まれている ❑ *For years the teaching of acting has been shrouded in mystery.* 長年にわたって演技指導は秘密のベールに包まれてきた. ◼ V-T 他動詞 If darkness, fog, or smoke **shrouds** an area, it covers it so that it is difficult to see. 覆う ❑ *Mist shrouded the hilltops.* 丘の頂に霧がかかった.

shrub /ʃrʌb/ (**shrubs**) N-COUNT 可算名詞 **Shrubs** are plants that have several woody stems. 低木 ❑ *...flowering shrubs.* 花の咲く木.

shrug /ʃrʌg/ (**shrugs, shrugging, shrugged**) V-T/V-I 他動詞/自動詞 If you **shrug**, you raise your shoulders to show that you are not interested in something or that you do not know or care about something. 肩をすくめる ❑ *I shrugged, as if to say, "Why not?"* どうしてなの、とでも言うつもりで肩をすくめた. ● N-COUNT 可算名詞 **Shrug** is also a noun. 肩をすくめること ❑ *"I suppose so," said Anna with a shrug.* 「そうね」とアンは肩をすくめた.
▶ **shrug off** PHRASAL VERB 句動詞 If you **shrug** something **off**, you ignore it or treat it as if it is not really important or serious. 無視する ❑ *He shrugged off the criticism.* 彼は批判を一蹴しました.

shrunk /ʃrʌŋk/ **Shrunk** is the past participle of **shrink**.

shud|der /ʃʌdər/ (**shudders, shuddering, shuddered**) ◼ V-I 自動詞 If you **shudder**, you shake with fear, horror, or disgust, or because you are cold. 震える ❑ *Lloyd had urged her to eat caviar. She had shuddered at the thought.* ロイドはキャビアを食べてみるよう強く勧めたが、彼女は考えるだけでもぞっとした. ● N-COUNT 可算名詞 **Shudder** is also a noun. 身震い [usu sing] ❑ *She gave a violent shudder.* 彼女は激しく身震いした. ◼ V-I 自動詞 If something such as a machine or vehicle **shudders**, it shakes suddenly and violently. ガタガタ揺れる ❑ *The train began to pull out of the station – then suddenly shuddered to a halt.* 列車は駅から出ようとしたところ、突然ガタガタと揺れて停まった. ◼ N-COUNT 可算名詞 If something sends a **shudder** or **shudders** through a group of people, it makes them worried or afraid. 戦慄 ❑ *The next crisis sent a shudder of fear through the U.N. community.* その次の危機では国連加盟国に恐怖の戦慄が走った.

shuf|fle /ʃʌfəl/ (**shuffles, shuffling, shuffled**) ◼ V-I 自動詞 If you **shuffle** somewhere, you walk there without lifting your feet properly off the ground. 足を引きずって歩く ❑ *Moira shuffled across the kitchen.* モイラは足をひきずって台所の反対側へ行った. ● N-SING 単数名詞 **Shuffle** is also a noun. 足をひきずって歩くこと ❑ *She noticed her own proud walk had become a shuffle.* 自分の歩き方には自信があった彼女だが、それが今では引きずって歩いていることに気づいた. ◼ V-T/V-I 他動詞/自動詞 If you **shuffle around**, you move your feet about while standing or you move your bottom about while sitting, often because you feel uncomfortable or embarrassed. もぞもぞ動かす [他動詞] もぞもぞする [自動詞] ❑ *He shuffles around in his chair.* 彼は椅子に座ってもぞもぞする. ◼ V-T 他動詞 If you **shuffle** playing cards, you mix them up before you begin a game. 切る ❑ *There are various ways of shuffling and dealing the cards.* トランプの切り方や配り方はいろいろある.

shun /ʃʌn/ (**shuns, shunning, shunned**) V-T 他動詞 If you **shun** someone or something, you deliberately avoid them or keep away from them. 避ける ❑ *From that time forward everybody shunned him.* それからというもの、みんな彼を避けるようになった.

shunt /ʃʌnt/ (**shunts, shunting, shunted**) V-T 他動詞 If a person or thing **is shunted** somewhere, they are moved or sent there, usually because something finds them inconvenient. 追いやられる [DISAPPROVAL 不賛成] [usu passive] ❑ *He has spent most of his life being shunted between his mother, father and various foster families.* 彼はこれまでほとんどずっと母親や父親やいろんな里親の間を転々としながら暮らしてきました.

shut /ʃʌt/ (shuts, shutting)

The form **shut** is used in the present tense and is the past tense and past participle.

shut 形は現在時制に使われ、過去時制と過去分詞でもある。

1 V-T/V-I 他動詞/自動詞 If you **shut** something such as a door or if it **shuts**, it moves so that it fills a hole or a space. 閉める [他動詞] 閉まる [自動詞] ❑ *Just make sure you shut the gate.* ちゃんと門を閉めたかちょっと見てください。 ●ADJ 形容詞 **Shut** is also an adjective. 閉じた [v-link ADJ] ❑ *They have warned residents to stay inside and keep their doors and windows shut.* 家の外に出ないでドアや窓を閉めておくように住民に呼びかけた。 **2** V-T 他動詞 If you **shut** your eyes, you lower your eyelids so that you cannot see anything. 閉じる ❑ *Lucy shut her eyes so she wouldn't see it happen.* ルーシーは目を閉じて、それが起こるところを見ないようにした。 ●ADJ 形容詞 **Shut** is also an adjective. 閉じた [v-link ADJ] ❑ *His eyes were shut and he seemed to have fallen asleep.* 彼は目を閉じて眠っているようだった。 **3** V-T/V-I 他動詞/自動詞 If your mouth **shuts** or if you **shut** your mouth, you place your lips firmly together. 閉じる ❑ *Daniel's mouth opened, and then shut again.* ダニエルは口を開けたと思ったら、また閉じた。 ●ADJ 形容詞 **Shut** is also an adjective. 閉じた [v-link ADJ] ❑ *She was silent for a moment, lips tight shut, eyes distant.* 彼女はしばらく口をつぐんで遠くを見ながら黙っていた。 **4** V-T/V-I 他動詞/自動詞 When a store, bar, or other public building **shuts** or when someone **shuts** it, it is closed and you cannot use it until it is open again. 閉店する ❑ *There is a tendency to shut museums or shops at a moment's notice.* 博物館や店舗は時間になったらすぐに閉まることが多い。 ❑ *Stores usually shut from noon to 3pm, and stay open late.* 店はたいてい正午から午後3時まで閉まり、夜は遅くまでやっている。 ●ADJ 形容詞 **Shut** is also an adjective. 閉じた [v-link ADJ] ❑ *Make sure you have food to tide you over when the local shop may be shut.* 近くの店が閉まっているかもしれないので、食料は十分用意しておこう。 **5** PHRASE 句 If someone tells you to **keep** your **mouth shut** about something, they are telling you not to let anyone else know about it. 口外しない ❑ *I don't have to tell you how important it is for you to keep your mouth shut about all this.* 言うまでもないが、このことを少しでも外に漏らしたらどうなるか分かってるよな。 **6** PHRASE 句 If you **keep** your **mouth shut**, you do not express your opinions about something, even though you would like to. 我慢して黙っている ❑ *If she had kept her mouth shut she would still have her job now.* 我慢して黙っていたら、彼女は仕事を失わずに済んだだろうに。

▶ **shut down** **1** PHRASAL VERB 句動詞 If a factory or business **shuts down** or if someone **shuts** it **down**, work there stops or it is no longer in business. 一時休業する；廃業する ❑ *It is required by law to shut down banks which it regards as chronically short of capital.* 法律では、銀行が慢性的な資金難に陥った場合は廃業することになっている。 **2** → see also **shutdown**

▶ **shut in** **1** PHRASAL VERB 句動詞 If you **shut** someone or something **in** a room, you close the door so that they cannot leave it. 閉じ込める ❑ *The door enables us to shut the birds in the shelter in bad weather.* 悪天候のときはドアを閉めれば、鳥をシェルターにかくまってやることができる。 **2** → see also **shut-in**

▶ **shut off** **1** PHRASAL VERB 句動詞 If you **shut off** something such as an engine or an electrical item, you turn it off to stop it from working. 止める ❑ *They pulled over and shut off the engine.* 彼らは車を路肩に寄せてエンジンを切った。 **2** PHRASAL VERB 句動詞 If you **shut yourself off**, you avoid seeing other people, usually because you are feeling depressed. 引きこもる ❑ *Billy tends to keep things to himself more and shut himself off.* ビリーは言いたいこともだんだん言わなくなり、自分の殻に閉じこもるようになっている。 **3** PHRASAL VERB 句動詞 If an official organization **shuts off** the supply of something, they no longer send it to the people they supplied in the past. 止める ❑ *The State Water Project has shut off all supplies to farmers.* 州の水利事業局は農業用水の供給をすべて停止している。

▶ **shut out** **1** PHRASAL VERB 句動詞 If you **shut** something or someone **out**, you prevent them from getting into a place, for example, by closing the doors. 締め出す ❑ *"I shut him out of the bedroom," says Maureen.* 「彼を寝室から締め出してやったわ」とモーリーンは言う。 **2** PHRASAL VERB 句動詞 If you **shut out** a thought or a feeling, you prevent yourself from thinking or feeling it. 追い出す ❑ *I shut out the memory which was too painful to dwell on.* いつまでもよくよく考えたところでつらいだけだから、そのことは思い出さないようにした。 **3** PHRASAL VERB 句動詞 If you **shut** someone **out** of something, you prevent them from having anything to do with it. 締め出す ❑ *She is very reclusive, to the point of shutting me out of her life.* 彼女はほんとに人を寄せ付けなくなった。この私も彼女の人生から締め出されてしまった。 **4** PHRASAL VERB 句動詞 In sports such as football and hockey, if one team **shuts out** the team they are playing against, they win and prevent the opposing team from scoring. シャットアウトする ❑ *Harvard shut out Yale, 14-0.* ハーバード大はエール大を14対0で完封した。 **5** → see also **shutout**

▶ **shut up** PHRASAL VERB 句動詞 If someone **shuts up** or if someone **shuts** them **up**, they stop talking. You can say **"shut up"** as an impolite way to tell a person to stop talking. 黙る；黙らせる ❑ *Just shut up, will you?* ちょっと黙っててくれない？

Thesaurus　　shut また次を参照：

V.　close, fasten, secure; (ant.) open **1**

Word Partnership　　shut は次の語句と使われる：

N.　shut **a door**, shut **a gate**, shut **a window** **1**
V.　force *something* shut, pull *something* shut, push *something* shut, slam *something* shut **1**
ADV.　shut **tight/tightly** **1** – **3**
　　shut **temporarily** **4**

shut|down /ʃʌtdaʊn/ (shutdowns)

N-COUNT 可算名詞 A **shutdown** is the closing of a factory, store, or other business, either for a short time or forever. 一時休業；廃業 ❑ *The shutdown is the latest in a series of painful budget measures.* 緊縮予算による影響が相次ぐなか、新たに今回の廃業が起こりました。

shut|ter /ʃʌtər/ (shutters)

1 N-COUNT 可算名詞 **Shutters** are wooden or metal covers fitted on the outside of a window. They can be opened to let in the light, or closed to keep out the sun or the cold. 雨戸 ❑ *She opened the shutters and gazed out over village roofs.* 彼女は雨戸を開けて、村の家々の屋根を眺めた。 **2** N-COUNT 可算名詞 The **shutter** in a camera is the part which opens to allow light through the lens when a photograph is taken. シャッター ❑ *There are a few things you should check before pressing the shutter release.* シャッターボタンを押す前に確認しておくことがいくつかある。

→ see **photography**

shut|tle /ʃʌtl/ (shuttles, shuttling, shuttled)

1 N-COUNT 可算名詞 A **shuttle** is the same as a **space shuttle**. スペースシャトル **2** N-COUNT 可算名詞 A **shuttle** is a plane, bus, or train which makes frequent trips between two places. 定期往復便 ❑ *There is a free 24-hour shuttle between the airport terminals.* 両空港のターミナル間は、無料のシャトルバスが24時間運行されています。 **3** V-T/V-I 他動詞/自動詞 If someone or something **shuttles** or **is shuttled** from one place to another place, they frequently go from one place to the other. 往復する ❑ *He and colleagues have shuttled back and forth between the three capitals.* 彼は同僚と一緒に3つの首都の間を何度も行き来しました。

shy /ʃaɪ/ (shyer, shyest, shies, shying, shied)

1 ADJ 形容詞 A **shy** person is nervous and uncomfortable in the company of other people. 内気な ❑ *She was a shy, quiet girl.* 彼女は恥ずかしがりの無口な子だった。 ❑ *She was a shy and retiring person off-stage.* 私生活の彼女は内気で人見知りする人だった。 ●**shy|ly** ADV 副詞 恥ずかしそうに ❑ *The children smiled shyly.* 子供たちは恥ずかしそうに微笑みました。 ●**shy|ness** N-UNCOUNT 不可算名詞 ❑ *Eventually he overcame his shyness.* やがて彼は内気な性格を克服した。 **2** ADJ 形容詞 If you are **shy about** or **shy of** doing something, you are unwilling to do it because you are afraid of what might happen. ～したがらない ❑ *They feel shy about showing their feelings.* 彼らは感情を表に出そうとしらがらない。

▶ **shy away from** PHRASAL VERB 句動詞 If you **shy away from** doing something, you avoid doing it, often because you are afraid or not confident enough. ～にしり込みする ❑ *We frequently shy away from making decisions.* なかなか決断に踏み切れないことがよくある。

Thesaurus　　shy また次を参照：

ADJ.　nervous, quiet, sheepish, uncomfortable; (ant.) confident **1**

sib|ling /sɪblɪŋ/ (siblings)

N-COUNT 可算名詞 Your **siblings** are your brothers and sisters. きょうだい [FORMAL 形式ばった] ❑ *His siblings are in their twenties.* 彼のきょうだいは20代である。

Note that there is no common English word that can refer to both a brother and a sister. You simply have to use both words. ❑ *She has 13 brothers and sisters.* The word **sibling** exists, but it is very formal. Some Americans use **sib** as an informal substitute for **sibling**. ❑ *All my sibs were home for Thanksgiving.*

sick /sɪk/ (sicker, sickest)

1 ADJ 形容詞 If you are **sick**, you are ill. **Sick** usually means physically ill, but it can sometimes be used to mean mentally ill. 病気の ❑ *He's very sick. He needs medication.* 彼の具合、とても悪いんだ。薬がいるよ。 ❑ *She found herself with two small children, a sick husband, and no money.* 気がついたら、彼女は2人の子供と病気の夫を抱え、その上お金もなかった。 ●N-PLURAL 複数名詞 The **sick** are people who are sick. 病人 ❑ *There were no doctors to treat the sick.* 病人の治療にあたる医師がいませんでした。 **2** ADJ 形容詞 If you are **sick**, the food that you have eaten comes up from your stomach and out of your mouth. If you **feel sick**, you feel as if you are going to be sick. 吐く；吐き気のする [v-link ADJ] ❑ *She got up and was sick in the sink.* 彼女は起き上がって流し台に吐いた。

❏ *The very thought of food made him feel sick.* 食べ物のことを考える
だけでも吐き気がした. ❸ ADJ 形容詞 If you say that you are **sick
of** something or **sick and tired of** it, you are emphasizing that
you are very annoyed by it and want it to stop. ～に嫌気がさし
て [INFORMAL くだけた, EMPHASIS 強調] [v-link ADJ "of" n/-ing]
❏ *I am sick and tired of hearing all these people moaning.* この連中から
あれこれ愚痴を聞かされるのはもううんざりしている. ❹ ADJ 形容
詞 If you describe something such as a joke or story as **sick**, you
mean that it deals with death or suffering in an unpleasantly
humorous way. 悪趣味な [DISAPPROVAL 不賛成] ❏ *...a sick joke
about a cat.* 猫に関する悪趣味なユーモア. ❺ PHRASE 句 If you say
that something or someone **makes** you **sick**, you mean that they
make you feel angry or disgusted. むかつかせる [INFORMAL くだ
けた] ❏ *It makes me sick that this wasn't disclosed.* むかつくのはこれが
明かされなかったことだ. ❻ PHRASE 句 If you are **out sick**, you are
not at work because you are sick. 病欠して [usu v-link PHR] ❏ *That
afternoon she was fired from her job as a nurse, because she'd been out
sick so much.* その日の午後, 看護師をしていた彼女はクビになった.
病気欠勤が多すぎたせいだった. ❼ PHRASE 句 If you say that you
are **worried sick**, you are emphasizing that you are extremely
worried. ひどく心配して [INFORMAL くだけた, EMPHASIS 強調]
❏ *He was worried sick about what our mothers would say.* 彼は私たちの
母親たちがどういうか気が気でならなかった.

The words **ill** and **sick** are very similar in meaning, but are
used in slightly different ways. **Ill** is generally not used before
a noun, and can be used in verbal expressions such as **fall ill**
and **be taken ill**. ❏ *He fell ill shortly before Christmas... One of the
jury members was taken ill.* **Sick** is often used before a noun. ❏ *...
sick children.* In British English, **ill** is a slightly more polite, less
direct word than **sick**. **Sick** often suggests the actual physical
feeling of being ill, for example nausea or vomiting. ❏ *I spent the
next 24 hours in bed, groaning and being sick.* In American English,
sick is often used where British people would say **ill**. ❏ *Some
people get hurt in accidents or get sick.*

Word Partnership *sick は次の語句と使われる:*

N.	sick **children**, sick **mother**, sick **patients**, sick **people**, sick **person** ❶
ADV.	**really** sick, **very** sick ❶
V.	**care for** the sick ❶
	become sick, feel sick, get sick ❶ ❷
ADJ.	**worried** sick ❼

sick|en /sɪkən/ (**sickens, sickening, sickened**) V-T 他動詞 If
something **sickens** you, it makes you feel disgusted. うんざりさ
せる ❏ *The notion that art should be controlled by intellectuals sickened
him.* 芸術は知識人が統制すればよいという考えに彼は憤りを感じた.

sick|en|ing /sɪkənɪŋ/ ADJ 形容詞 You describe something
as **sickening** when it gives you feelings of horror or disgust, or
makes you feel sick. いまわしい, おぞましい ❏ *...the sickening rise in
the number of suicide bombings.* おぞましいほどの自爆テロの増加.

sick leave N-UNCOUNT 不可算名詞 **Sick leave** is the time that a
person spends away from work because of illness or injury. 病気
休暇 [BUSINESS 実業] ❏ *I have been on sick leave for seven months with
depression.* うつ病で病気休暇をとって7か月になる.

sick|ly /sɪkli/ (**sicklier, sickliest**) ❶ ADJ 形容詞 A **sickly** person
or animal is weak, unhealthy, and often ill. 病弱な ❏ *He had been a
sickly child.* 子供の頃, 彼は病弱だった. ❷ ADJ 形容詞 A **sickly** smell
or taste is unpleasant and makes you feel slightly sick, often
because it is extremely sweet. むかむかする ❏ *...the sickly smell of
rum.* ラム酒のむかつくようなにおい.

sick|ness /sɪknɪs/ (**sicknesses**) ❶ N-UNCOUNT 不可算名詞
Sickness is the state of being ill or unhealthy. 病気 ❏ *In fifty-two
years of working he had one week of sickness.* 52年間働いて, 彼が病気
をしたのはたった1週間だった. ❷ N-UNCOUNT 不可算名詞 **Sickness**
is the uncomfortable feeling that you are going to vomit. 吐き
気 ❏ *After a while, the sickness gradually passed and she struggled to
the mirror.* しばらくすると吐き気は治まってきたので, 彼女は何とか
鏡のところまで行こうとした. ❸ N-VAR 可変性名詞 A **sickness** is a
particular illness. 病気 ❏ *More than 930 local people are registered as
suffering from radiation sickness.* 930人を超える周辺住民が放射能障害
の認定を受けている.

sick pay N-UNCOUNT 不可算名詞 When you are ill and unable
to work, **sick pay** is the money that you get from your employer
instead of your normal wages. (雇用者が支払う) 傷病手当
[BUSINESS 実業] ❏ *They are not eligible for sick pay.* 彼らは病気休職し
ても手当は出ない.

---

side

❶ A SURFACE, POSITION, OR PLACE
❷ ONE ASPECT OR ONE POINT
   OF VIEW
❸ PHRASES

---

❶ **side** /saɪd/ (**sides**) ❶ N-COUNT 可算名詞 The **side of**
something is a position to the left or right of it, rather than in
front of it, behind it, or on it. 側面 ❏ *On one side of the main entrance
there's a red plaque.* 正面玄関横に赤い銘板が飾られています. ❏ *...a
photograph with Joe and Ken on each side of me.* ジョーとケンに挟まれて
撮った写真. ❷ N-COUNT 可算名詞 The **side** of an object, building,
or vehicle is any of its flat surfaces which is not considered to be
its front, its back, its top, or its bottom. 面, 側 ❏ *We put a notice
on the side of the box.* 箱の側面に注意書きを貼った. ❸ N-COUNT 可
算名詞 The **sides** of a hollow or a container are its inside vertical
surfaces. 内側 ❏ *The rough rock walls were like the sides of a deep canal.*
荒々しい岩の壁面は深い水路の側面のようだった. ❏ *Line the base of
the dish with greaseproof paper and lightly grease the sides.* 皿の底にワ
ックスペーパーを敷いて, 内側に油を薄く塗ります. ❹ N-COUNT 可
算名詞 The **sides** of an area or surface are its edges. 端 ❏ *Park on
the side of the road.* 道路わきの公園. ❏ *...a small beach on the north
side of the peninsula.* 半島の北端にある小さな浜辺. ❺ N-COUNT 可
算名詞 The two **sides** of an area, surface, or object are its two
halves. 一側 ❏ *She turned over on her stomach on the other side of the
bed.* 彼女は寝返りしてベッドの反対側にうつぶせになった. ❏ *The
major center for language is in the left side of the brain.* 言語を主につか
さどるのは左脳です. ❻ N-COUNT 可算名詞 The two **sides** of a road
are its two halves on which traffic travels in opposite directions.
車線 ❏ *It had gone on to the wrong side of the road and hit a car coming
in the other direction.* それは対向車線に入り, 反対方向から走ってき
た車と衝突した. ❼ N-COUNT 可算名詞 If you talk about the other
side of a town, a country, or the world, you mean a part of the
town, the country, or the world that is very far from where you
are. 向こう ❏ *He lives the other side of town.* 彼は町の向こうに住んで
いる. ❽ N-COUNT 可算名詞 Your **sides** are the parts of your body
between your front and your back, from under your arms to your
hips. わき腹 ❏ *His arms were limp at his sides.* 彼の腕は両わきにだら
っと垂れていた. ❾ N-COUNT 可算名詞 If someone is **by** your
side or **at** your **side**, they stay near you and give you comfort or
support. ～の味方 ❏ *He was constantly at his wife's side.* 彼はいつも妻
の肩をもった. ❿ N-COUNT 可算名詞 The two **sides** of something
flat, for example, a piece of paper, are its two flat surfaces. You
can also refer to one side of a piece of paper filled with writing as
one **side** of writing. 面 ❏ *The new copiers only copy onto one side of the
paper.* 新しいコピー機は用紙の片面だけに複写する. ❏ *Fry the chops
until brown on both sides.* チョップの両面がキツネ色になるまで炒めま
す. ⓫ N-COUNT 可算名詞 One **side** of a tape or record is what you
can hear or record if you play the tape or record from beginning to
end without turning it over. 一面 ❏ *We want to hear side A.* A面を聴
きたい. ⓬ ADJ 形容詞 **Side** is used to describe things that are not
the main or most important ones of their kind. 主要でない [ADJ n]
❏ *She slipped in and out of the theater by a side door.* 彼女は劇場の通用口
からこっそり出入りした.

❷ **side** /saɪd/ (**sides, siding, sided**) ❶ N-COUNT 可算名詞 The
different **sides** in a war, argument, or negotiation are the groups
of people who are opposing each other. 一側 ❏ *Both sides appealed
for a new ceasefire.* 双方とも新たな停戦を求めた. ❷ N-COUNT 可算
名詞 The different **sides of** an argument or deal are the different
points of view or positions involved in it. 側面 ❏ *His words drew
sharp reactions from people on both sides of the issue.* 彼の発言に対して
は, 意見の対立する双方に厳しい反応が出されました. ❸ V-I 自動詞
If one person or country **sides with** another, they support them in
an argument or a war. If people or countries **side against** another
person or country, they support each other against them. 味方す
る ❏ *There has been much speculation that they might be siding with the
rebels.* 彼らが反政府側につくかもしれないという憶測が広まっていま
す. ❹ N-COUNT 可算名詞 In sports, a **side** is a team. チーム [BRIT
英国英語] ❺ N-COUNT 可算名詞 A particular **side** of something
such as a situation or someone's character is one aspect of it. 側
面 ❏ *He is in charge of the civilian side of the U.N. mission.* 彼はその国連
活動の民事部門を担当している. ❻ N-COUNT 可算名詞 The **mother's
side** and the **father's side** of your family are your mother's
relatives and your father's relatives. 母方; 父方 ❏ *So was your
father's side more well off?* それじゃ, 父方はもっと裕福なの?

❸ **side** /saɪd/ (**sides**) ❶ PHRASE 句 If two people or things are
side by side, they are next to each other. 並んで ❏ *We sat side by
side on two wicker seats.* 私たちは2脚の籐(とう)椅子に並んで座っ
た. ❷ PHRASE 句 If people work or live **side by side**, they work or
live closely together in a friendly way. 協力して ❏ *...areas where
different nationalities have lived side by side for centuries.* 異なる民族が
何世紀にもわたって力を合わせて暮らしてきた地域. ❸ PHRASE 句 If
something moves **from side to side**, it moves repeatedly to the left

and to the right. 左右に ❑ *She was shaking her head from side to side.* 彼女は頭を左右に振っていた。 **4** PHRASE 句 If you are **on** someone's **side**, you are supporting them in an argument or a war. ～に味方して ❑ *He has the Democrats on his side.* 彼は民主党を味方につけている。 **5** PHRASE 句 If something is **on** your **side** or if you have it **on** your **side**, it helps you when you are trying to achieve something. 味方して ❑ *The weather is rather on our side.* 天候はむしろこっちの味方をしている。 **6** PHRASE 句 If you say that something is **on the small side**, you are saying politely that you think it is slightly too small. If you say that someone is **on the young side**, you are saying politely that you think they are slightly too young. ちょっと～めで [POLITENESS 丁寧さ] ❑ *He's quiet and a bit on the shy side.* 彼は無口で少し内気なところがあります。 **7** PHRASE 句 If someone does something **on the side**, they do it in addition to their main work. 副業で ❑ *...ways of making a little bit of money on the side.* 副業でちょっと稼ぐ方法。 **8** PHRASE 句 If you **put** something **to one side** or put it **on one side**, you temporarily ignore it in order to concentrate on something else. とりあえずおいて置く ❑ *He can now concentrate on a project he'd originally put to one side.* 手つかずのままにしていた企画にようやく彼は本腰を入れることができる。 **9** PHRASE 句 If you **take** someone **to one side** or draw them **to one side**, you speak to them privately, usually in order to give them advice or a warning. わきに連れ出す ❑ *He took Sabrina to one side and told her about the safe.* 彼はサブリナをわきに連れ出して，金庫のことを話した。 **10** PHRASE 句 If you **take sides** or **take someone's side** in an argument or war, you support one of the sides against the other. 味方をする ❑ *We cannot take sides in a civil war.* 内戦ではどちらにも味方できない。 **11** **the other side of the coin** → see **coin** **12** **to err on the side of** something → see **err** **13** **to be on the safe side** → see **safe** **14** someone's **side of the story** → see **story**

side-effect (**side-effects**) also **side effect** **1** N-COUNT 可算名詞 The **side-effects** of a drug are the effects, usually bad ones, that the drug has on you in addition to its function of curing illness or pain. 副作用 ❑ *Side-effects include nausea, tiredness, and dizziness.* 副作用としては，吐き気，だるさ，目まいなどが挙げられる。 **2** N-COUNT 可算名詞 A **side-effect of** a situation is something unplanned and usually unpleasant that happens in addition to the main effects of that situation. 思わぬ結果 ❑ *One side effect of modern life is stress.* 現代生活に避けて通れないのがストレスです。

side|line (**sidelines, sidelining, sidelined**) **1** N-COUNT 可算名詞 A **sideline** is something that you do in addition to your main job in order to earn extra money. 副業 ❑ *It was quite a lucrative sideline.* 実にもうかる副業だった。 **2** N-PLURAL 複数名詞 The **sidelines** are the lines marking the long sides of the playing area, for example, on a football field or tennis court. サイドライン **3** N-PLURAL 複数名詞 If you are **on the sidelines** in a situation, you do not influence events at all, either because you have chosen not to be involved, or because other people have not involved you. 傍観して ❑ *France no longer wants to be left on the sidelines when critical decisions are made.* 重大な決定がなされるときにもはやフランスは手をこまねいてはいない。 **4** V-T 他動詞 If someone or something **is sidelined,** they are made to seem unimportant and not included in what people are doing. 実戦から外されて [usu passive] ❑ *For months he had been under pressure to resign and was about to be sidelined anyway.* 何か月にもわたって辞任の圧力を受けていた彼は，どちらにせよ一線から退くのは目に見えていた。

→ see **football, soccer, tennis**

side road (**side roads**) N-COUNT 可算名詞 A **side road** is a road which leads off a busier, more important road. わき道

side|step /sáɪdstep/ (**sidesteps, sidestepping, sidestepped**) also **side-step** V-T 他動詞 If you **sidestep** a problem, you avoid discussing it or dealing with it. 回避する ❑ *Rarely, if ever, does he sidestep a question.* 彼が質問を受け流すようなことはたとえあったにせよめったにない。

side street (**side streets**) N-COUNT 可算名詞 A **side street** is a quiet, often narrow street which leads off a busier street. わき道，横丁

side|walk /sáɪdwɔk/ (**sidewalks**) N-COUNT 可算名詞 A **sidewalk** is a path with a hard surface by the side of a road. 歩道 [AM 米国英語] ❑ *Two men and a woman were walking briskly down the sidewalk toward him.* 男2人と女1人が早足で歩道を歩いて彼に向かってきた。

side|ways /sáɪdweɪz/ **1** ADV 副詞 **Sideways** means from or toward the side of something or someone. 横向きに [ADV after v] ❑ *Piercey glanced sideways at her.* ピアシーは横目でちらっと彼女を見た。 ❑ *The ladder blew sideways.* はしごは風で横向きに倒れた。 ● ADJ 形容詞 **Sideways** is also an adjective. 横向きの [ADJ n] ❑ *Alfred shot him a sideways glance.* アルフレッドは横目でちらっと彼を見た。 **2** ADV 副詞 If you are moved **sideways** at work, you move to another job at the same level as your old job. 横滑りで異動する [ADV after v] ❑ *He would be moved sideways, rather than demoted.* 彼は降格ではなく横滑りになるだろう。 ● ADJ 形容詞 **Sideways** is also an adjective. 横向きの [ADJ n] ❑ *...her recent sideways move.* 最近あった彼女の横滑り人事。

siege /sídʒ/ (**sieges**) **1** N-COUNT 可算名詞 A **siege** is a military or police operation in which soldiers or police surround a place in order to force the people there to come out or give up control of the place. 包囲 [also "under" N] ❑ *We must do everything possible to lift the siege.* 包囲網の解除に向けてありとあらゆる努力が必要である。 **2** PHRASE 句 If police, soldiers, or journalists **lay siege to** a place, they surround it in order to force the people there to come out or give up control of the place. 包囲する ❑ *The rebels laid siege to the governor's residence.* 反体制派は州知事公邸を包囲しました。

Word Partnership siege は次の語句と使われる:

PREP.	**after a** siege, **during a** siege, **under** siege **1**
V.	**end a** siege, **lift a** siege **1**

sieve /sív/ (**sieves, sieving, sieved**) **1** N-COUNT 可算名詞 A **sieve** is a tool used for separating solids from liquids or larger pieces of something from smaller pieces. It consists of a metal or plastic ring with a wire or plastic net underneath, which the liquid or smaller pieces pass through. ざる，こし器； ふるい ❑ *Press the raspberries through a fine sieve to form a puree.* ラズベリーを目の細かいざるで裏ごししてピューレにします。 **2** V-T 他動詞 When you **sieve** a substance, you put it through a sieve. 裏ごしする； ふるいがける ❑ *Cream the margarine in a small bowl, then sieve the powdered sugar into it.* マーガリンを小さなボウルでクリーム状にしたら，粉砂糖をふるいかけます。

sift /síft/ (**sifts, sifting, sifted**) **1** V-T 他動詞 If you **sift** a powder such as flour or sand, you put it through a sieve in order to remove large pieces or lumps. ふるいにかける ❑ *Sift the flour and baking powder into a medium-sized mixing bowl.* 小麦粉とベーキングパウダーをふるいにかけて，中サイズのミキシングボウルに入れます。 **2** V-T/V-I 他動詞/自動詞 If you **sift through** something such as evidence, you examine it thoroughly. 精査する ❑ *Police officers have continued to sift through the wreckage following yesterday's bomb attack.* 昨日の爆撃事件を受けて，警察は残骸を詳しく調べています。

sigh /sáɪ/ (**sighs, sighing, sighed**) **1** V-I 自動詞 When you **sigh**, you let out a deep breath, as a way of expressing feelings such as disappointment, tiredness, or pleasure. ため息をつく ❑ *Michael sighed wearily.* マイケルは疲れてため息をついた。 ❑ *Roberta sighed with relief.* ロバータはほっとしてため息をついた。 ● N-COUNT 可算名詞 **Sigh** is also a noun. ため息 ❑ *She kicked off her shoes with a sigh.* 彼女はため息をつきながら靴を振り飛ばして脱いだ。 **2** PHRASE 句 If people breathe or heave a **sigh of relief**, they feel happy that something unpleasant has not happened or is no longer happening. 安堵のため息 ❑ *With monetary mayhem now retreating into memory, European countries can breathe a collective sigh of relief.* 通貨統合の混乱の記憶もようやく薄らぎ，EU加盟国はみな安堵の胸をなで下ろしている。

Word Partnership sigh は次の語句と使われる:

ADJ.	**collective** sigh, **deep** sigh, **long** sigh **1**
V.	**breathe a** sigh, **give a** sigh, **hear a** sigh, **heave a** sigh, **let out a** sigh **1** **2**

sight /sáɪt/ (**sights, sighting, sighted**) **1** N-UNCOUNT 不可算名詞 Someone's **sight** is their ability to see. 視力 ❑ *My sight is failing, and I can't see to read any more.* 視力が衰えてきて，もう本が読めなくなった。 **2** N-SING 単数名詞 The **sight of** something is the act of seeing it or an occasion on which you see it. 見ること ❑ *I faint at the sight of blood.* 血を見ると失神する。 **3** N-COUNT 可算名詞 A **sight** is something that you see. 光景 ❑ *The practice of hanging clothes across the street is a common sight in many parts of the city.* 道路の上を渡すように洗濯物を干す習慣が，その都市のあちこちでよく見られる光景である。 **4** V-T 他動詞 If you **sight** someone or something, you suddenly see them, often briefly. 見かける ❑ *The security forces sighted a group of young men that had crossed the border.* 治安部隊は国境を越えてきた若い男たちの集団を目撃しました。 **5** N-PLURAL 複数名詞 The **sights** are the places that are interesting to see and that are often visited by tourists. 観光地 ❑ *We'd toured the sights of Paris.* パリの観光地を回った。 **6** → see also **sighting** **7** PHRASE 句 If you **catch sight of** someone, you suddenly see them, often briefly. ～を見かける ❑ *Then he caught sight of her small black velvet hat in the crowd.* すると，彼は人込みの中に彼女の小さい黒いベルベットの帽子を見つけた。 **8** PHRASE 句 If you say that something seems to have certain characteristics **at first sight**, you mean that it appears to have the features you describe when you first see it but later it is found to be different. 一見して ❑ *The theory is not as simple as you might think at first sight.* この理論は一見単純そうだが，それほど単純ではない。 **9** PHRASE 句 If something is **in sight** or within sight, you can see it. If it is **out of sight**, you cannot see it. 見えるところに；見えないところに ❑ *The sandy beach was in sight.* 砂浜は見えるところにあった。 ❑ *The Atlantic coast is within sight of the hotel.* ホテルからは大西洋の海岸が見える。 **10** PHRASE 句 If a result or a decision is **in sight** or **within sight**, it is likely to

happen within a short time. 目前で ❑*An agreement on many aspects of trade policy was in sight.* 通商政策の数多い分野での合意が目前に迫っていた. **11** PHRASE 句 If you **lose sight of** an important aspect of something, you no longer pay attention to it because you are worrying about less important things. 見失う ❑*In some cases, U.S. industry has lost sight of customer needs in designing products.* アメリカ企業は，商品の企画段階で消費者のニーズを見失っていることがある. **12** PHRASE 句 If someone is ordered to do something **on sight**, they have to do it without delay, as soon as a person or thing is seen. 見たらすぐに ❑*Troops shot anyone suspicious on sight.* 軍は不審者を見つけたらすぐに発砲した. **13** PHRASE 句 If you **set** your **sights on** something, you decide that you want it and try hard to get it. ねらいを定める ❑*They have set their sights on the world record.* 彼らは世界記録をねらっている. **14** PHRASE 句 If you **have** something **in** your **sights**, you are trying hard to achieve it, and you have a good chance of success. If you **have** someone **in** your **sights**, you are determined to catch, defeat, or overcome them. 〜を目指す，〜をねらう ❑*The Giants' slugger also has fourth place in his sights, needing 13 homers to move past Frank Robinson's 586.* ジャイアンツの主砲も歴代4位をねらっている. フランク・ロビンソンの持つ586本の記録まであとホームラン13本である. ❑*Is this knowledge of yours the reason the murderer now has you in his sights?* このことを知っているせいで，君は殺人犯から次の標的にされているというのか.

Word Partnership *sight* は次の語句と使われる：

ADJ.	**common** sight, **familiar** sight, **welcome** sight **3** **in plain** sight **9** **the end is in** sight **10**
V.	**catch** sight of *someone/something* **7** **come into** sight, **keep** *someone/something* in sight **7 9 10** **drop out of** sight, **lose** sight of *something* **11**

sight|ing /sáɪtɪŋ/ (**sightings**) N-COUNT 可算名詞 A **sighting of** something, especially something unusual or unexpected is an occasion on which it is seen. 目撃 ❑*...the sighting of a rare sea bird at Lundy Island.* ランディー島での珍しい海鳥の観察.

sight|see|ing /sáɪtsiːɪŋ/ N-UNCOUNT 不可算名詞 If you go **sightseeing** or do some **sightseeing**, you travel around visiting the interesting places that tourists usually visit. 観光 ❑*...a day's sightseeing in Venice.* ベニスの1日観光.
→ see **city**

sign /sáɪn/ (**signs, signing, signed**) **1** N-COUNT 可算名詞 A **sign** is a mark or shape that always has a particular meaning, for example, in mathematics or music. 記号，符号 ❑*Equations are generally written with an equal sign.* 等式ではふつう等号を使う. **2** N-COUNT 可算名詞 A **sign** is a movement of your arms, hands, or head which is intended to have a particular meaning. 合図 ❑*They gave Lavalle the thumbs-up sign.* 彼らはラバージェにOKの合図を出した. **3** V-T 他動詞 If you **sign**, you communicate with someone using sign language. If a program or performance **is signed**, someone uses sign language so that deaf people can understand it. 手話で話す ❑*All programs will be either "signed" or subtitled.* 番組にはすべて手話か字幕が付くことになっている. **4** N-COUNT 可算名詞 A **sign** is a piece of wood, metal, or plastic with words or pictures on it. Signs give you information about something, or give you a warning or an instruction. 標識，看板 ❑*...a sign saying that the highway was closed because of snow.* 幹線道路が雪で通行止めになっていることを知らせる標示. **5** N-VAR 可変名詞 If there is a **sign of** something, there is something which shows that it exists or is happening. 様子 ❑*They are prepared to hand back a hundred prisoners of war a day as a sign of goodwill.* 彼らは善意のしるしとして，1日に100人ずつ戦争捕虜を送還してもいいと伝えました. ❑*His face and movements rarely betrayed a sign of nerves.* 彼は心配していても，めったに顔や態度に出さなかった. **6** V-T 他動詞 When you **sign** a document, you write your name on it, usually at the end or in a special space. You do this to indicate that you have written the document, that you agree with what is written, or that you were present as a witness. 署名する，調印する ❑*World leaders are expected to sign a treaty pledging to increase environmental protection.* 各国の指導者は環境保護の推進を誓う条約に調印する見通しです. **7** V-T/V-I 他動詞/自動詞 If an organization **signs** someone or if someone **signs** for an organization, they sign a contract agreeing to work for that organization for a specified period of time. 契約する ❑*The Minnesota Vikings signed Herschel Walker from the Dallas Cowboys.* ミネソタ・バイキングズはダラス・カウボーイズのハーシェル・ウォーカーと契約した. **8** N-COUNT 可算名詞 In astrology, a **sign** or a **sign of the zodiac** is one of the twelve areas into which the heavens are divided. 星座宮（きゅう） ❑*The new moon takes place in your opposite sign of Libra on the 15th.* 15日に真反対のてんびん座で新月になる. **9** → see also **signing** **10** PHRASE 句 If you say that there is **no sign of** someone, you mean that they have not yet arrived, although you are expecting them to come. 兆しがない ❑*The train was on time, but there was no sign of my Finnish*

friend. 列車は定刻に到着したが，フィンランドの友人が姿を見せる気配はなかった.

▶ **sign for** PHRASAL VERB 句動詞 If you **sign for** something, you officially state that you have received it, by signing a form or book. 受け取りのサインをする ❑*When the letter carrier delivers your order, check the carton before signing for it.* 注文が届いたときは，箱の中身を確認してから受け取りのサインをします.

▶ **sign in** PHRASAL VERB 句動詞 If you **sign in**, you officially indicate that you have arrived at a hotel or club by signing a book or form. チェックインのサインをする ❑*I signed in and crunched across the gravel to my room.* チェックインのサインをして，自分の部屋まで砂利道をざくざく歩いた.

▶ **sign over** PHRASAL VERB 句動詞 If you **sign** something **over**, you sign documents that give someone else property, possessions, or rights that were previously yours. 〜を譲渡する ❑*Two years ago, he signed over his art collection to the New York Metropolitan Museum of Art.* 2年前，彼は自分の美術コレクションをニューヨークのメトロポリタン美術館に譲渡した.

▶ **sign up** PHRASAL VERB 句動詞 If you **sign up** for an organization or if an organization **signs** you **up**, you sign a contract officially agreeing to do a job or course of study. 参加する；就業契約する ❑*He signed up as a flight attendant with Korean Air.* 彼は大韓航空の客室乗務員として雇われた.

Thesaurus *sign* また次を参照：

N.	nod, signal, wave **2**
V.	authorize, autograph, endorse **6**

Word Partnership *sign* は次の語句と使われる：

V.	**give a** sign **2** **hang a** sign, **read a** sign **4** **see a** sign **4 5** **show no** sign of *something* **5** **refuse to** sign **6** **see no** sign of *someone/something* **10**
N.	sign **on a door**, sign **over an entrance**, **neon** sign, **stop** sign, sign **in a window** **4** sign **an agreement**, sign **an autograph**, sign **a contract**, sign **legislation**, sign *your* **name**, sign a **petition**, sign a **treaty** **6**
ADJ.	**bad/good** sign, **encouraging** sign, **positive** sign, **a sure** sign, **warning** sign **5**
PREP.	sign **of progress**, sign **of the times**, sign **of trouble**, sign **of weakness** **5**

sig|nal /sígnəl/ (**signals, signaling** or **signalling, signaled** or **signalled**) **1** N-COUNT 可算名詞 A **signal** is a gesture, sound, or action which is intended to give a particular message to the person who sees or hears it. 合図；信号 ❑*They fired three distress signals.* 彼らは遭難信号を3回発射した. ❑*As soon as it was dark, Mrs. Evans gave the signal.* エバンス夫人は暗くなるとすぐに合図した. **2** V-T/V-I 他動詞/自動詞 If you **signal** to someone, you make a gesture or sound in order to send them a particular message. 合図する；信号を送る ❑*Mandy started after him, signaling to Jesse to follow.* マンディは彼のあとを追い，ジェシーについて来るように合図した. ❑*She signaled to Ted that she was moving forward.* 彼女は自分が前に進んでいることをテッドに合図した. **3** N-COUNT 可算名詞 If an event or action is a **signal** of something, it suggests that this thing exists or is going to happen. しるし；前触れ ❑*Kurdish leaders saw the visit as an important signal of support.* クルド人指導者はこの訪問を重要な支援の意思表示と受け取った. **4** V-T 他動詞 If someone or something **signals** an event, they suggest that the event is happening or likely to happen. ほのめかす；前兆となる ❑*He seemed to be signaling important shifts in U.S. government policy.* アメリカ政府が重要な政策転換を図ることを彼は暗に示したものと思われる. **5** N-COUNT 可算名詞 A **signal** is a piece of equipment beside a railroad, which indicates to train drivers whether they should stop the train or not. 信号機 ❑*A signal failure contributed to the crash.* 信号機の故障が衝突事故の一因となった. **6** N-COUNT 可算名詞 A **signal** is a series of radio waves, light waves, or changes in electrical current which may carry information. 信号波 ❑*...high-frequency radio signals.* 高周波無線信号.
→ see **cellphone, television**

Word Partnership *signal* は次の語句と使われる：

V.	**give a** signal **1 3** **send a** signal **1 3 6**
ADJ.	**wrong** signal **1 3** **clear** signal, **strong** signal **1 3 6** **important** signal **3**

sig|na|tory /sígnətɔri/ (**signatories**) N-COUNT 可算名詞 The **signatories** of an official document are the people, organizations,

or countries that have signed it. 署名者, 署名国 [FORMAL 形式ば
った] ❑ *Both countries are signatories to the Nuclear Non-Proliferation Treaty.* 両国とも核拡散防止条約の加盟国です.

sig|na|ture /sɪgnətʃər, -tʃʊər/ (**signatures**) N-COUNT 可算名詞
Your **signature** is your name, written in your own characteristic way, often at the end of a document to indicate that you wrote the document or that you agree with what it says. 署名, サイン ❑ *I was writing my signature at the bottom of the page.* ページの一番下にサインしていた.

sig|nifi|cance /sɪgnɪfɪkəns/ N-UNCOUNT 不可算名詞 The **significance** of something is the importance that it has, usually because it will have an effect on a situation or shows something about a situation. 重要性 ❑ *Ideas about the social significance of religion have changed over time.* 宗教の社会的重要性をどのように考えるかは時代と共に変化してきた.

Word Partnership	*significance* は次の語句と使われる:
ADJ.	**cultural** significance, **great** significance, **historic**/ **historical** significance, **political** significance, **religious** significance
V.	**downplay** the significance of *something*, **explain** the significance of *something*, **understand** the significance of *something*

sig|nifi|cant /sɪgnɪfɪkənt/ ■ ADJ 形容詞 A **significant** amount or effect is large enough to be important or affect a situation to a noticeable degree. かなりの ❑ *Most 11-year-olds are not encouraged to develop reading skills; a small but significant number are illiterate.* 11歳児の大半が読解力を伸ばす指導を受けておらず, 読み書きできない子供も少ないものの相当数いる. ● **sig|nifi|cant|ly** ADV 副詞 かなり ❑ *The number of Senators now supporting him had increased significantly.* 彼を支持する上院議員は相当数にのぼっていました. ② ADJ 形容詞 A **significant** fact, event, or thing is one that is important or shows something. 意義深い ❑ *I think it was significant that he never knew his own father.* 彼が実の父親を知らなかったことは重要だと考える. ● **sig|nifi|cant|ly** ADV 副詞 重要なことは ❑ *Significantly, the company recently opened a huge store in Atlanta.* 重要なのは, 同社が最近アトランタに超大型店を出店したことである.

Thesaurus	*significant* また次を参照:
ADJ.	big, important, large; (*ant.*) insignificant, minor, small ■

sig|ni|fy /sɪgnɪfaɪ/ (**signifies, signifying, signified**) ■ V-T 他動詞 If an event, a sign, or a symbol **signifies** something, it is a sign of that thing or represents that thing. 意味する ❑ *These were not*

the only changes that signified the end of boyhood. 少年期の終わりを示す変化はこれだけに限られなかった. ② V-T 他動詞 If you **signify** something, you make a sign or gesture in order to communicate a particular meaning. 示す ❑ *Two jurors signified their dissent.* 陪審員2名が反対意見を出した.

sign|ing /saɪnɪŋ/ (**signings**) ■ N-UNCOUNT 不可算名詞 The **signing** of a document is the act of writing your name to indicate that you agree with what it says or to say that you have been present to witness other people writing their signature. 署名, 調印 ❑ *Spain's top priority is the signing of the treaty.* スペインが最優先事項としているのがその条約への調印である. ② N-COUNT 可算名詞 A **signing** is someone who has recently signed a contract agreeing to play for a sports team or work for a record company. 契約者 [usu with supp] ❑ *...the salary paid to the club's latest signing.* クラブの新規契約選手に支払われる給与. ③ N-UNCOUNT 不可算名詞 The **signing** of a player by a sports team or a group by a record company is the act of drawing up a legal document setting out the length and terms of the association between them. 契約 ❑ *The ranks of professional tennis swelled with the signing of Bobby Riggs.* ボビー・リッグズが契約したことで…. ④ N-UNCOUNT 不可算名詞 **Signing** is the use of sign language to communicate with someone who is deaf. 手話を使うこと ❑ *The two deaf actors converse solely in signing.* 耳の不自由な2人の俳優はもっぱら手話で会話する.

sign lan|guage (**sign languages**) N-VAR 可変性名詞 **Sign language** is movements of your hands and arms used to communicate. There are several official systems of sign language, used, for example, by deaf people. Movements are also sometimes invented by people when they want to communicate with someone who does not speak the same language. 手話 ❑ *Her son used sign language to tell her what happened.* 彼女の息子は手話を使って何が起こったかを彼女に伝えました.
→ see Picture Dictionary: **sign language**

Sikh /siːk/ (**Sikhs**) N-COUNT 可算名詞 A **Sikh** is a person who follows the Indian religion of Sikhism. シーク教徒 ❑ *The rise of racism concerns Sikhs because they are such a visible minority.* シーク教徒は人種差別の高まりを警戒しているが, それは自分たちが少数派で姿を見ればすぐに分かるからである. ❑ *...a Sikh temple.* シーク教寺院.

Sikh|ism /siːkɪzəm/ N-UNCOUNT 不可算名詞 **Sikhism** is an Indian religion which separated from Hinduism in the sixteenth century and which teaches that there is only one God. シーク教

si|lence /saɪləns/ (**silences, silencing, silenced**) ■ N-VAR 可変性名詞 If there is **silence**, nobody is speaking. 沈黙 ❑ *They stood in silence.* 彼らは黙って立っていた. ❑ *He never lets those long silences develop during dinner.* 夕食の時にそうした長い沈黙が続くのを彼は絶対に許さない. ② N-UNCOUNT 不可算名詞 Someone's **silence**

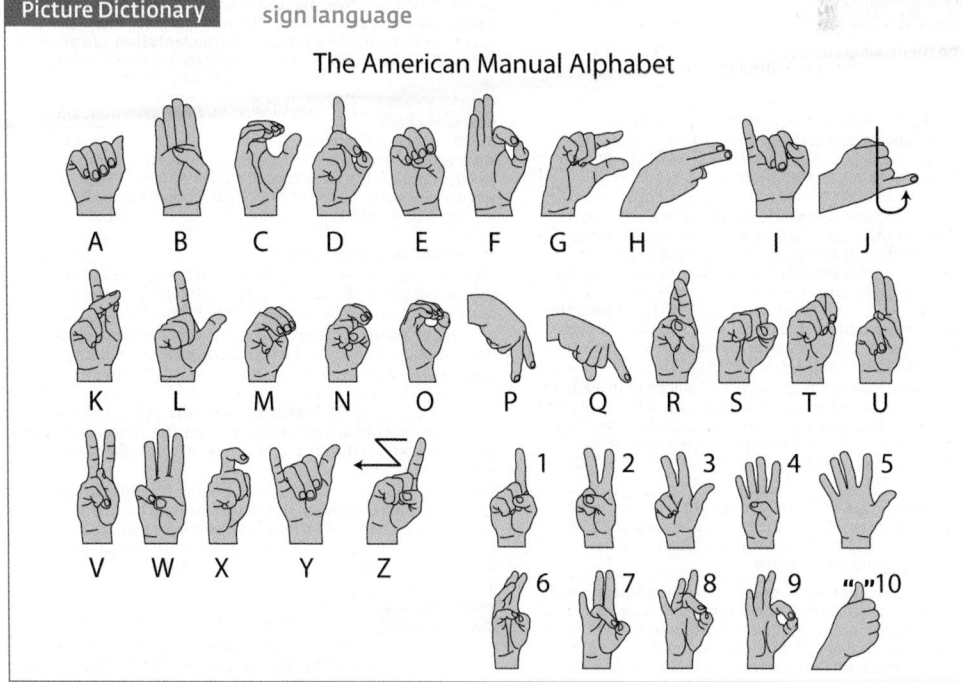

Picture Dictionary　　sign language

The American Manual Alphabet

A B C D E F G H I J

K L M N O P Q R S T U

V W X Y Z　　1 2 3 4 5

6 7 8 9 ""10

about something is their failure or refusal to speak to other people about it. 無言 □ *The district court ruled that Popper's silence in court today should be entered as a plea of not guilty.* 今日の法廷でポッパーが黙秘したことについて，裁判所はこれを無罪の答弁とみなす判断をしました。 ● PHRASE 句 If someone **breaks** their **silence** about something, they talk about something that they have not talked about before or for a long time. 沈黙を破る ❸ V-T 他動詞 If someone **silences** you, they stop you from expressing opinions that they do not agree with. 黙らせる □ *Like other tyrants, he tried to silence anyone who spoke out against him.* 彼も暴君の例に漏れず，誰であれ盾突く者の口を封じた。

Word Partnership   silence は次の語句と使われる:

ADJ.	**awkward** silence, **complete** silence, **long** silence, **sudden** silence, **total** silence ❶
V.	silence **falls**, **listen** in silence, **observe** a silence, **sit** in silence, **watch** *something* in silence ❶ **break** a/*your* silence ❷

---

si|lent /saɪlənt/ ❶ ADJ 形容詞 Someone who is **silent** is not speaking. 黙っている，無言の [v-link ADJ] □ *Trish was silent because she was reluctant to put her thoughts into words.* トリッシュは自分の思いを口にしたくなかったので黙っていた。 □ *He spoke no English and was completely silent during the visit.* 彼は英語を全く話さないので，訪問している間ずっと黙っていた。 ● **si|lent|ly** ADV 副詞 [ADV with v] 黙って □ *She and Ned sat silently for a moment, absorbing the peace of the lake.* 彼女とネッドは湖の静けさに浸りながらしばらく黙って座っていた。 ❷ ADJ 形容詞 A place that is **silent** is completely quiet, with no sound at all. Something that is **silent** makes no sound at all. 静まり返った □ *The room was silent except for the TV.* 部屋は静まり返り，聞こえるのはテレビの音だけだった。 ● **si|lent|ly** ADV 副詞 [ADV with v] 静かに □ *Strange shadows moved silently in the almost permanent darkness.* 永遠に続くと思えるような暗闇の中を不審な影が音も立てずに移動した。 ❸ ADJ 形容詞 A **silent** movie has pictures usually accompanied by music but does not have the actors' voices or any other sounds. 無声の [ADJ n] □ *...one of the famous silent films of Charlie Chaplin.* チャーリー・チャップリンの有名な無声映画のうちの1作品。 ❹ PHRASE 句 If you **give** someone **the silent treatment**, you do not speak to them for a period of time because you are annoyed at something they have done. 口を聞かない □ *He fully expected his mother to give him the silent treatment.* 彼は母親が口を聞いてくれなくなることは十分覚悟していた。

Thesaurus   silent また次を参照:

ADJ.	hushed, mute, speechless ❶ noiseless, quiet ❷

Word Partnership   silent は次の語句と使われる:

V.	**go** silent, **keep** silent, **remain** silent, **sit** silent ❶
N.	silent **prayer**, silent **reading** ❶

---

si|lent part|ner (silent partners) N-COUNT 可算名詞 A **silent partner** is a person who provides some of the capital for a business but who does not take an active part in managing the business. 匿名組合員 [AM 米国英語 BUSINESS 実業] □ *...firms run by his friends in which he was a silent partner.* 友人たちが経営し彼が匿名組合員になっていたいくつかの会社。

sil|hou|ette /sɪluɛt/ (silhouettes) ❶ N-COUNT 可算名詞 A **silhouette** is the solid dark shape that you see when someone or something has a bright light or pale background behind them. シルエット □ *The dark silhouette of the castle ruins stood out boldly against the fading light.* 城跡の暗いシルエットが薄れゆく光を背景にくっきりと見えた。 ❷ N-COUNT 可算名詞 The **silhouette** of something is the outline that it has, which often helps you to recognize it. 輪郭 □ *...the distinctive silhouette of the Manhattan skyline.* マンハッタンのスカイラインの個性的な輪郭。

sili|con /sɪlɪkən/ N-UNCOUNT 不可算名詞 **Silicon** is an element that is found in sand and in minerals such as quartz and granite. Silicon is used to make parts of computers and other electronic equipment. ケイ素，シリコン □ *The new chip will be made from a piece of silicon about the size of a postage stamp.* 新しい半導体チップは切手大ほどのシリコン1枚から作られる。

> **Silicon Valley** is an area in the U.S., near San Francisco, where the computer industry dominates the local economy. These days the name may also be given to other locations where computer companies are gathered.

sili|con chip (silicon chips) N-COUNT 可算名詞 A **silicon chip** is a very small piece of silicon inside a computer. It has electronic circuits on it and can hold large quantities of information or perform mathematical or logical operations. シリコンチップ □ *Today's silicon chip-based computers can't come close.* 今のシリコンベースのコンピュータでは到底及ばない。

sili|cone /sɪlɪkoʊn/ N-UNCOUNT 不可算名詞 **Silicone** is a tough artificial substance made from silicon, which is used to make polishes, and also used in cosmetic surgery and plastic surgery. シリコン（ケイ素系合成樹脂）□ *...women who suffered health problems from silicone breast implants that leak.* 豊胸用のシリコンが漏れて健康障害をきたした女性たち。

silk /sɪlk/ (silks) N-MASS 質量名詞 **Silk** is a substance which is made into smooth fine cloth and sewing thread. You can also refer to this cloth or thread as **silk**. 絹 □ *They continued to get their silks from China.* 彼らは中国から絹を買い続けた。 □ *Pauline wore a silk dress with a strand of pearls.* ポーリーンは絹のドレスに真珠のネックレスをしていた。

silky /sɪlki/ (silkier, silkiest) ADJ 形容詞 If something has a **silky** texture, it is smooth, soft, and shiny, like silk. 絹のような □ *...dresses in seductively silky fabrics.* セクシーな絹のような素材でできたドレス。

sill /sɪl/ (sills) N-COUNT 可算名詞 A **sill** is a shelf along the bottom edge of a window, either inside or outside a building. 窓台，下枠 □ *Whitlock was perched on the sill of the room's only window.* ホイットロックは部屋に1つだけある窓台に腰をかけていた。

sil|ly /sɪli/ (sillier, silliest) ADJ 形容詞 If you say that someone or something is **silly**, you mean that they are foolish, childish, or ridiculous. 愚かな □ *Jean-Pierre told me that I am silly to be upset about this.* こんなことで気分を害するなんてばかじゃない，と親友は言う。 □ *I thought it would be silly to be too rude at that stage.* その程度のことであまり無礼な態度をとるのは愚かだろうと思った。

silt /sɪlt/ N-UNCOUNT 不可算名詞 **Silt** is fine sand, soil, or mud which is carried along by a river. 沈泥 □ *The lake was almost solid with silt and vegetation.* 湖は沈泥と植物ばかりでほとんど枯れていた。 → see **erosion**

sil|ver /sɪlvər/ (silvers) ❶ N-UNCOUNT 不可算名詞 **Silver** is a valuable pale gray metal that is used for making jewelry and ornaments. 銀 □ *...a hand-crafted brooch made from silver.* 手作りの銀のブローチ。 □ *...amber earrings set in silver.* シルバーの台に琥珀（こはく）を埋め込んだイヤリング。 ❷ N-UNCOUNT 不可算名詞 **Silver** consists of coins that are made from silver or that look like silver. 銀貨 □ *...the basement where $150,000 in silver was buried.* 15万ドル相当の銀貨が埋められた地下室。 ❸ N-UNCOUNT 不可算名詞 You can use **silver** to refer to all the things in a house that are made of silver, especially the flatware and dishes. 銀器；銀食器 [also "the" N] □ *He beat the rugs and polished the silver.* 彼は敷物のほこりをたたいて，銀食器を磨いた。 ❹ COLOR 色彩語 **Silver** is used to describe things that are shiny and pale gray in color. 銀色 □ *He had thick silver hair which needed cutting.* 彼は銀色の濃い髪を散髪してもいいほど伸ばしていた。 → see **mineral, money, silverware**

sil|ver med|al (silver medals) N-COUNT 可算名詞 If you win a **silver medal**, you come second in a competition, especially a sports contest, and are given a medal made of silver as a prize. 銀メダル □ *Gillingham won the silver medal in the 200 meters at Seoul.* ギリンガムはソウルオリンピックの200mで銀メダルを獲得した。

Word Link   ware ≈ merchandise : hardware, silverware, software

sil|ver|ware /sɪlvərwɛər/ N-UNCOUNT 不可算名詞 You can use **silverware** to refer to all the things in a house that are made of silver, especially the flatware and dishes. 銀製品，銀食器 □ *There was a serving spoon missing when Nina put the silverware back in its box.* ニーナが銀食器を箱に戻したとき給仕用のスプーンが見当たらなかった。 → see Word Web: **silverware**

sil|very /sɪlvəri/ ADJ 形容詞 **Silvery** things look like silver or are the color of silver. 銀のような，銀色の □ *My father is a small, intense man with silvery hair.* 私の父は銀髪で小柄で情熱的な人だ。

sim /sɪm/ (sims) N-COUNT 可算名詞 A **sim** is a computer game that simulates an activity such as playing a sport or flying an aircraft. SLG, SIM, シミュレーションゲーム [COMPUTING コンピューティング]

SIM card /sɪm kɑrd/ (SIM cards) N-COUNT 可算名詞 A **SIM card** is a microchip in a cellphone that connects it to a particular phone network. **SIM** is an abbreviation for "Subscriber Identity Module." SIMカード

simi|lar /sɪmɪlər/ ADJ 形容詞 If one thing is **similar to** another, or if two things are **similar**, they have features that are the same. 似ている □ *...a savory cake with a texture similar to that of carrot cake.* ニンジンケーキとよく似た食感のある風味のあるケーキ。 □ *The accident was similar to one that happened in 1973.* その事故は1973年に発生した事故と似ていた。

Word Link   simil ≈ similar : assimilate, dissimilar, similarity

simi|lar|ity /sɪmɪlærɪti/ (similarities) ❶ N-UNCOUNT 不可算名詞 If there is a **similarity between** two or more things, they are similar to each other. 類似，似ていること □ *...the astonishing*

Word Web   silverware

Anthropologists tell us that the first knives were simple cutting instruments made from flint that were first used about two million years ago. The first modern knife with a metal **blade** and wooden **handle** appeared about 1000 years BC. During the Middle Ages, people carried their own eating knives with them because no one provided knives for guests. The earliest **spoons** were made from scooped-out bones or shells tied to the end of sticks. Later the Romans introduced bronze and **silver** spoons. The earliest **forks** had only two tines and were used only for carving and serving meat.

butter knife · dessert spoon · dessert fork · soup spoon · dinner knife · dinner fork · salad fork

---

similarity between my brother and my first-born son. 私の兄と長男の驚くほど似ていること ❑ There was a very basic similarity in our philosophy. 私たちの人生観には非常に基本的な類似性がある。 ❷ N-COUNT 可算名詞 **Similarities** are features that things have which make them similar to each other. 類似点 ❑ There were significant similarities between mother and son. 母と息子には著しい類似点があった。

sim|lar|ly /sɪmɪlɑrli/ ❶ ADV 副詞 You use **similarly** to say that something is similar to something else. 同じように ❑ Most of the men who now gathered around him again were similarly dressed. 彼の周りにまた集まった男たちはほとんど同じような格好をしていた。 ❷ ADV 副詞 You use **similarly** when mentioning a fact or situation that is similar to the one you have just mentioned. 同様に [ADV with cl] ❑ Same-sex marriages are not recognized. Similarly, marriages of close relatives are not legal. 同性間の結婚は認められていない。 同様に近親者間の結婚も違法である。

sim|mer /sɪmər/ (simmers, simmering, simmered) ❶ V-T/V-I 他動詞/自動詞 When you **simmer** food or when it **simmers**, you cook it by keeping it at boiling point or just below boiling point. ことこと煮る ❑ Make an infusion by boiling and simmering the rhubarb and camomile together. ルバーブとカムミールを一緒に沸騰させたと弱火でことこと煮て煎じなさい。 ●N-SING 単数名詞 **Simmer** is also a noun. ことこと煮ること ❑ Combine the stock, whole onion and peppercorns in a pan and bring to a simmer. 鍋に煮出しと丸ごとのタマネギとコショウの実を入れてことこと煮なさい。 ❷ V-I 自動詞 If a conflict or a quarrel **simmers**, it does not actually happen for a period of time, but eventually builds up to the point where it does. (くすぶっていた感情が)今にも爆発する ❑ ...bitter divisions that have simmered for more than half a century. 半世紀以上もくすぶってきたむごい分裂

sim|ple /sɪmpªl/ (simpler, simplest) ❶ ADJ 形容詞 If you describe something as **simple**, you mean that it is not complicated, and is therefore easy to understand. 簡単な, 分かりやすい ❑ ...simple pictures and diagrams. 分かりやすい図表 ❑ ...pages of simple advice on filling in your tax form. 納税申告用紙の記入について の簡単なアドバイスが書かれているページ ●**sim|ply** ADV 副詞 [ADV with v] ❑ When applying for a visa extension state simply and clearly the reasons why you need an extension. ビザの延長を申請する際には申請理由を明確に記入すること。 ❷ ADJ 形容詞 If you describe people or things as **simple**, you mean that they have all the basic or necessary things they require, but nothing extra. 純朴な, 簡素な ❑ He ate a simple dinner of rice and beans. 彼はご飯と豆だけの簡素な食事をした。 ❑ ...the simple pleasures of childhood. 子供の頃の素朴な喜び ●**sim|ply** ADV 副詞 [ADV after v] 簡素に ❑ The living room is furnished simply with white wicker furniture and blue-and-white fabrics. 居間は, 白い枝編みの家具と青と白の布地の簡素な家具を備え付けていた。 ❸ ADJ 形容詞 If a problem is **simple** or if its solution is **simple**, the problem can be solved easily. 簡単な, 解きやすい ❑ Some puzzles look difficult but are actually quite simple. 難しそうに見えるが実は非常に簡単なパズルもある。 ❹ ADJ 形容詞 A **simple** task is easy to do. 簡単な, しやすい ❑ The job itself had been simple enough. その仕事そのものは簡単だった。 ●**sim|ply** ADV 副詞 [ADV after v] たやすく ❑ We can do things that were not possible before, and they can be done simply. 以前は不可能だったことができるようになり, しかもたやすくできる。 ❺ ADJ 形容詞 You use **simple** to emphasize that the thing you are referring to is the only important or relevant reason for something. 単なる [EMPHASIS 強調] ❑ His refusal to talk was simple stubbornness. 彼が話し合いを拒否しているのは単に頑固なだけだった。 ❻ ADJ 形容詞 In grammar, **simple** tenses are ones which are formed without an auxiliary verb "be," for example "I dressed and went for a walk" and "This tastes nice." **Simple** verb groups are used especially to refer to completed actions, regular actions, and situations. Compare **continuous**. 単文の ❼ → see also **simply**

Thesaurus   simple また次を参照:

ADJ. clear, easy, understandable; (ant.) complicated ❶ ❸ ❹ plain ❷

Word Partnership   simple は次の語句と使われる:

N. simple **concept**, simple **explanation**, simple **instructions**, simple **language**, simple **message**, simple **procedure**, simple **steps** ❶
    simple **life**, simple **pleasure** ❷
    simple **answer**, simple **question** ❸
    simple **matter**, simple **task**, simple **test** ❸ ❹
    simple **fact** ❺
ADV. **rather** simple ❶ – ❸
    fairly simple, **pretty** simple, **quite** simple, **really** simple, **relatively** simple, **very** simple ❶ – ❹
    simple **enough**, so simple ❶ ❸ ❹

sim|ple in|ter|est N-UNCOUNT 不可算名詞 **Simple interest** is interest that is calculated on an original sum of money and not also on interest which has previously been added to the sum. Compare **compound interest**. 単利 [BUSINESS 実業] ❑ ...an investment that pays only simple interest. 単利のみがつく投資

sim|plic|ity /sɪmplɪsɪti/ N-UNCOUNT 不可算名詞 The **simplicity** of something is the fact that it is not complicated and can be understood or done easily. 単純さ ❑ The apparent simplicity of his plot is deceptive. 一見単純に見える彼の策略には誰もひっかかりやすい。

sim|pli|fi|ca|tion /sɪmplɪfɪkeɪªn/ (simplifications) ❶ N-COUNT 可算名詞 You can use **simplification** to refer to the thing that is produced when you make something simpler or when you reduce it to its basic elements. 簡略化されたもの, 単純化されたもの ❑ Like any such diagram, it is a simplification. このタイプのほかの図表と同様に, それは簡略化したものだ。 ❷ N-UNCOUNT 不可算名詞 **Simplification** is the act or process of making something simpler. 簡略化, 単純化 ❑ Everyone favors the simplification of court procedures. 誰もが裁判手続きの簡略化に賛成だ。

sim|pli|fy /sɪmplɪfaɪ/ (simplifies, simplifying, simplified) V-T 他動詞 If you **simplify** something, you make it easier to understand or you remove the things which make it complex. 簡略化する, 単純化する ❑ Our aim is to simplify the complex social security system. 我々の目的は複雑な社会保障制度を簡略化することだ。

sim|plis|tic /sɪmplɪstɪk/ ADJ 形容詞 A **simplistic** view or interpretation of something makes it seem much simpler than it really is. 単純化した, 短絡的な ❑ He has a simplistic view of the treatment of eczema. 彼はアトピーの治療について短絡的な意見を持っている。

sim|ply /sɪmpli/ ❶ ADV 副詞 You use **simply** to emphasize that something consists of only one thing, happens for only one reason, or is done in only one way. 単に–だけ [EMPHASIS 強調] ❑ The table is simply a chipboard circle on a base. そのテーブルは単に台に丸いチップボードが載っているだけだ。 ❑ Most of the damage that's occurred was simply because of fallen trees. 発生した被害のほとんどは単に倒木が原因でした。 ❷ ADV 副詞 You use **simply** to emphasize what you are saying. 全く [EMPHASIS 強調] ❑ This sort of increase simply cannot be justified. この種の増加は全く正当化できない。 ❸ → see also **simple**

simu|late /sɪmyəleɪt/ (simulates, simulating, simulated) ❶ V-T 他動詞 If you **simulate** an action or a feeling, you pretend that you are doing it or feeling it. 装う, –するふりをする ❑ They rolled about on the Gilligan Road, simulating a bloodthirsty fight. 彼らは残虐な喧嘩をしているふりをしてギリ崎ロードの路上を転げまわった。 ❷ V-T 他動詞 If you **simulate** a set of conditions, you create

s

them artificially, for example, in order to conduct an experiment. シミュレートする，模擬で行う ❏ *The scientist developed one model to simulate a full year of the globe's climate.* その科学者は1年間の地球の気候をシミュレートするモデルを開発した．

simu|la|tion /sɪmyəleɪʃ°n/ (**simulations**) N-VAR 可変性名詞 **Simulation** is the process of simulating something or the result of simulating it. シミュレーション ❏ *Training includes realistic simulation of casualty procedures.* 研修には事故が起きた場合の手順に関する現実的なシミュレーションが含まれている．

simul|ta|neous /saɪməlteɪniəs/ ADJ 形容詞 Things which are **simultaneous** happen or exist at the same time. 同時に起こる，同時の ❏ *...the simultaneous release of the book and the CD.* 本とCDの同時発売 ● **simul|ta|neous|ly** ADV 副詞 ❏ *The two guns fired almost simultaneously.* 2丁の銃がほぼ同時に発砲した．

sin /sɪn/ (**sins, sinning, sinned**) **1** N-VAR 可変性名詞 **Sin** or a **sin** is an action or type of behavior which is believed to break the laws of God. (宗教上の) 罪 ❏ *The Vatican's teaching on abortion is clear: it is a sin.* 妊娠中絶に関するローマ法王の教えは明確で，それは罪である． **2** V-I 自動詞 If you **sin**, you do something that is believed to break the laws of God. 罪を犯す ❏ *The Spanish Inquisition charged him with sinning against God and man.* スペインの異端審問は彼が神と人に対する罪を犯したことで告発した． ● **sin|ner** /sɪnər/ N-COUNT 可変名詞 (**sinners**) 罪人 ❏ *I was shown that I am a sinner, that I needed to repent of my sins.* 私は，自分が罪人で罪を悔やむ必要があることを示された． **3** N-COUNT 可算名詞 A **sin** is any action or behavior that people disapprove of or consider morally wrong. (道徳上の) 罪 過ち ❏ *...the sin of arrogant hard-heartedness.* 傲慢な冷酷さという過ち

Word Partnership *sin* は次の語句と使われる：

PREP. **without** sin **1**
V. **commit a** sin **1**
　　 live in sin **3**
ADJ. **unpardonable** sin **1** **3**
N. **sin taxes** **3**

since /sɪns/ **1** PREP 前置詞 You use **since** when you are mentioning a time or event in the past and indicating that a situation has continued from then until now. 一以来ずっと ❏ *He's been in exile in India since 1959.* 彼は1959年以来インドに亡命中です． ❏ *She had a sort of breakdown some years ago, and since then she has been very shy.* 彼女は数年前にちょっと神経が参ってしまって，それ以来ずっと内気になった． ● ADV 副詞 **Since** is also an adverb. それ以来ずっと [ADV with v] ❏ *They worked together in the 1960s, and have kept in contact ever since.* 彼らは1960年代に同僚として働き，それ以来ずっと連絡を取り続けている． ● CONJ 接続詞 **Since** is also a conjunction. 一して以来ずっと ❏ *I've earned my own living since I was seven, doing all kinds of jobs.* 7歳のときからありとあらゆる仕事をしながら自分の生活費を稼いできた． **2** PREP 前置詞 You use **since** to mention a time or event in the past when you are describing an event or situation that has happened after that time. 一以来，一後 ❏ *The percentage increase in reported crime this year is the highest since the war.* 今年届け出のあった犯罪の増加率は戦後で最高だ． ● CONJ 接続詞 **Since** is also a conjunction. 一して以来，一してから ❏ *So much has changed in the sport since I was a teenager.* 私が十代だった頃からスポーツ界はずいぶん変わった． ❏ *Since I have become a mother, the sound of children's voices has lost its charm.* 母親になってから子供の声に魅力を感じなくなった． **3** ADV 副詞 When you are talking about an event or situation in the past, you use **since** to indicate that another event happened at some point later in time. それ以来，その後 [ADV with v] ❏ *About six thousand people were arrested, several hundred of whom have since been released.* 約6000人が逮捕され，そのうちの数百人はその後釈放された． **4** CONJ 接続詞 You use **since** to introduce reasons or explanations. 一なので ❏ *I'm forever on a diet, since I put on weight easily.* 私は太りやすい体質なのでいつもダイエット中だ．

sin|cere /sɪnsɪər/ ADJ 形容詞 If you say that someone is **sincere**, you approve of them because they really mean the things they say. You can also describe someone's behavior and beliefs as **sincere**. 誠実な，裏表がない [APPROVAL 賛成] ❏ *He's sincere in his views.* 彼は自分の意見に忠実だ． ● **sin|cer|ity** /sɪnserɪti/ N-UNCOUNT 不可算名詞 誠実さ ❏ *I was impressed with his deep sincerity.* 私は彼の心からの誠実さに感心した．

sin|cere|ly /sɪnsɪərli/ **1** ADV 副詞 If you say or feel something **sincerely**, you really mean or feel it, and are not pretending. 心から，本当に ❏ *"Congratulations," he said sincerely.* 「おめでとう」と彼は心から言った． ❏ *...sincerely-held religious beliefs.* 心から抱いている宗教的信条 **2** CONVENTION 慣習表現 People write "**Sincerely yours**" or "**Sincerely**" before their signature at the end of a formal letter when they have addressed it to someone by name. People sometimes write "**Yours sincerely**" instead. 敬具 ❏ *Sincerely yours, Robbie Weinz.* 敬具 ロビー・ワインツ

sin|ful /sɪnfəl/ ADJ 形容詞 If you describe someone or something as **sinful**, you mean that they are wicked or immoral. 罪深い，不道徳な ❏ *"I am a sinful man, Magda," he said quietly.* 「私は

罪深い男だ，マグダ」と彼は静かに言った． ❏ *This is a sinful world.* この世は罪深い世界だ． ● **sin|ful|ness** N-UNCOUNT 不可算名詞 罪深さ ❏ *...the sinfulness of apartheid.* アパルトヘイトの罪深さ

sing /sɪŋ/ (**sings, singing, sang, sung**) **1** V-T/V-I 他動詞/自動詞 When you **sing**, you make musical sounds with your voice, usually producing words that fit a tune. 歌う ❏ *I can't sing.* 私は歌が下手だ． ❏ *I sing about love most of the time.* 私はほとんどの場合ラブソングを歌います． ❏ *They were all singing the same song.* 彼らはみんな同じ歌を歌っていた． **2** → see also **singing**

▶ **sing along** PHRASAL VERB 句動詞 If you **sing along with** a piece of music, you sing it while you are listening to someone else perform it. 一に合わせて歌う ❏ *We listen to children's shows on the radio, and Janey can sing along with the tunes.* ラジオで子供番組を聞いているとジェイニーがすべての曲に合わせて歌うことができる． ❏ *Would-be Elvis Presleys can sing along to "Jailhouse Rock," "Love me Tender," and "Blue Suede Shoes."* 自称エルビス・プレスリーは『ジェイルハウス・ロック』『ラブ・ミー・テンダー』『ブルー・スエード・シューズ』に合わせて歌うことができる．

Thesaurus *sing* また次を参照：

V. chant, hum **1**

Word Partnership *sing* は次の語句と使われる：

V. **begin** to sing, **can/can't** sing, **dance and** sing, **hear someone, like** to sing **1**
N. **birds** sing, sing **someone's praises**, sing **a song 1**

sing|er /sɪŋər/ (**singers**) N-COUNT 可算名詞 A **singer** is a person who sings, especially as a job. 歌手，シンガー ❏ *My mother was a singer in a dance band.* 私の母はダンスバンドのシンガーだった． → see **concert**

sing|ing /sɪŋɪŋ/ N-UNCOUNT 不可算名詞 **Singing** is the activity of making musical sounds with your voice. 歌うこと，歌唱 ❏ *...a people's carnival, with singing and dancing in the streets.* 通りで歌って踊る民族のカーニバル ❏ *...the singing of a traditional hymn.* 伝統的な賛美歌の合唱

sin|gle /sɪŋgəl/ (**singles, singling, singled**) **1** ADJ 形容詞 You use **single** to emphasize that you are referring to one thing, and no more than one thing. たった1つの [EMPHASIS 強調] [ADJ n] ❏ *A single shot rang out.* たった1回の銃声が鳴った． ❏ *Over six hundred people were wounded in a single day.* たった1日で600人以上が負傷した． **2** ADJ 形容詞 You use **single** to indicate that you are considering something on its own and separately from other things like it. every を強調して用いる ❏ *Every single house in town had been damaged.* 町中の家という家すべてが破損しました． [EMPHASIS 強調] [det ADJ] **3** ADJ 形容詞 Someone who is **single** is not married. You can also use **single** to describe someone who does not have a girlfriend or boyfriend. 独身の，恋人がいない ❏ *Is it difficult being a single mother?* 片親での子育ては大変ですか． **4** ADJ 形容詞 A **single** room is a room intended for one person to stay or live in. シングルの，1人用の ❏ *Each guest has her own single room, or shares, on request, a double room.* 客は各自シングルルームあるいは希望に応じてダブルルームを相部屋で宿泊する． ● N-COUNT 可算名詞 **Single** is also a noun. シングルルーム，1人部屋 ❏ *It's $65 for a single, $98 for a double and $120 for an entire suite.* シングルが65ドル，ダブルが98ドル，そしてスイートルームが120ドルだ． **5** ADJ 形容詞 A **single** bed is wide enough for one person to sleep in. シングルの，1人で寝るための [ADJ n] ❏ *...his bedroom with its single bed.* シングルベッドを置いている彼の部屋 **6** ADJ 形容詞 A **single** ticket is a ticket for a trip from one place to another but not back again. 片道の [BRIT 英国英語] ❏ *I'd like a single to Edinburgh, please.* エディンバラまでの片道切符を1枚お願いします． ● N-COUNT 可算名詞 **Single** is also a noun. [AM **one-way** 米国英語 **one-way**] **7** N-COUNT 可算名詞 A **single** is a small record which has one song on each side. A **single** is also a CD which has a few short songs on it. You can also refer to the main song on a record or CD as a **single**. シングル盤 ❏ *The winners will pocket a cash sum and get a chance to release their debut CD single.* 入賞者は賞金を受け取り，デビューシングルの販売のチャンスがある． **8** N-UNCOUNT 不可算名詞 **Singles** is a game of tennis or badminton in which one player plays another. The plural **singles** can be used to refer to one or more of these matches. シングルス ❏ *Lleyton Hewitt won the men's singles.* レイトン・ヒューイットが男子シングルスで優勝した． **9** → see also **single-** **10** **in single file** → see **file** → see **hotel, tennis**

▶ **single out** PHRASAL VERB 句動詞 If you **single** someone **out** from a group, you choose them and give them special attention or treatment. 取り上げる ❏ *The gunman had singled Debilly out and waited for him.* 武装した犯人はデビリーを選び出し，彼を待った． ❏ *His immediate manager has singled him out for a special mention.* 彼の直属の上司は彼を選んで特別に触れた．

single- /sɪŋgəl-/ COMB IN ADJ 形容詞の複合 **single-** is used to form words which describe something that has one part or feature, rather than having two or more of them. シングルの，

単一 ❑ *The single-engine plane landed in western Arizona.* 単発飛行機がアリゾナ州西部に着陸した.

single-handed also **single-handedly** ADV 副詞 If you do something **single-handed**, you do it on your own, without help from anyone else. 単独で [ADV after v] ❑ *I brought up my seven children single-handed.* 私は自分一人で7人の子供を育てた.

single-minded ADJ 形容詞 Someone who is **single-minded** has only one aim or purpose and is determined to achieve it. ひたむきな, いちずな ❑ *They were effective politicians, ruthless and single-minded in their pursuit of political power.* 彼らは政治権力追求において冷酷でいちずで有能な政治家だった.

sin|gle par|ent (**single parents**) N-COUNT 可算名詞 A **single parent** is someone who is bringing up a child on their own, because the other parent is not living with them. 片親, シングルマザー, シングルファーザー ❑ *I was bringing up my three children as a single parent.* 私はシングルマザーとして3人の子供を育てました. ❑ *...single-parent families.* 片親の家族

sin|gle sup|plement (**single supplements**) also **single person supplement** N-COUNT 可算名詞 A **single supplement** is an additional sum of money that a hotel charges for one person to stay in a room meant for two people. 一人部屋の追加料金 ❑ *You can avoid the single supplement by agreeing to share a twin room.* ツインルームの相部屋に同意すると一人部屋の追加料金を払わなくてよい.

sin|gu|lar /sɪŋgyələr/ ❶ ADJ 形容詞 The **singular** form of a word is the form that is used when referring to one person or thing. 単数形の ❑ *...the fifteen case endings of the singular form of the Finnish noun.* フィンランド語の名詞単数形の15種類の格語尾 ❷ N-SING 単数名詞 The **singular** of a noun is the form of it that is used to refer to one person or thing. 単数形 ❑ *The inhabitants of the Arctic are known as the Inuit. The singular is Inuk.* 北極圏の居住者はInuit（イヌイット族）として知られている. 単数形はInukである.

sin|is|ter /sɪnɪstər/ ADJ 形容詞 Something that is **sinister** seems evil or harmful. 不吉な, 不気味な, 有害な ❑ *There was something sinister about him that she found disturbing.* 彼には何か不気味なところがあって彼女は不安に駆られた.

sink /sɪŋk/ (**sinks, sinking, sank, sunk**) ❶ N-COUNT 可算名詞 A **sink** is a large fixed container in a kitchen or bathroom, with faucets to supply water. In the kitchen, it is used for washing dishes, and in the bathroom it is used to wash your hands and face. 流し, 洗面台 ❑ *The sink was full of dirty dishes.* 台所の流し台は汚れた皿で一杯だった. ❑ *The bathroom is furnished with 2 toilets, 2 showers, and 2 sinks.* バスルームにはトイレが2つ, シャワーが2つ, 洗面台が2つあった. ❷ V-T/V-I 他動詞/自動詞 If a boat **sinks** or if someone or something **sinks** it, it disappears below the surface of a mass of water. 沈める, 沈没させる [他動詞], 沈む, 沈没する [自動詞] ❑ *In a naval battle your aim is to sink the enemy's ship.* 海戦での目的は敵の船を沈没させることだ. ❑ *The boat was beginning to sink fast.* そのボートはどんどん沈み始めた. ❸ V-I 自動詞 If something **sinks**, it disappears below the surface of a mass of water. （水面下に）沈む ❑ *A fresh egg will sink and an old egg will float.* 新鮮な卵は水に沈み古い卵は浮く. ❹ V-I 自動詞 If something **sinks**, it moves slowly downward. (下方に)沈む ❑ *Far off to the west the sun was sinking.* 遠く西に太陽が沈みかかっていた. ❺ V-I 自動詞 If something **sinks to** a lower level or standard, it falls to that level or standard. 低下する ❑ *Share prices would have sunk – hurting small and big investors.* 株価が低下し, 大口・小口投資家が損を出すところだった. ❑ *Pay increases have sunk to around seven percent.* 昇給率は約7%に低下した. ❻ V-I 自動詞 If your heart or your spirits **sink**, you become depressed or lose hope. (気が)沈む ❑ *My heart sank because I thought he was going to dump me for another girl.* 彼が他の女の子のために私と別れるつもりだと思ったので私の気分は沈んだ. ❼ V-T/V-I 他動詞/自動詞 If something sharp **sinks** or **is sunk into** something solid, it goes deeply into it. はめこむ ❑ *I sank my teeth into a peppermint cream.* 私はペパーミントクリームにがぶりと食いついた. ❽ V-T 他動詞 If someone **sinks** a well, mine, or other large hole, they make a deep hole in the ground, usually by digging or drilling. 掘る ❑ *...the site where Stephenson sank his first mineshaft.* スティーブンソンが最初の坑道を掘った場所 ❾ V-T 他動詞 If you **sink** money into a business or project, you spend money on it in the hope of making more money. つぎ込む, 投資する ❑ *He has already sunk $25 million into the project.* 彼はすでにその事業に2500万ドルをつぎ込んだ. ❿ → see also **sinking, sunk** ⓫ PHRASE 句 If you say that someone will have to **sink or swim**, you mean that they will have to succeed through their own efforts, or fail. のるかそるか, いちかばちか ❑ *I think athletes sink or swim depending on how they motivate themselves.* 運動選手はいかにやる気を起こすかによって成功するかどうかが決まると思う. ⓬ **without trace** → see **trace**

▶ **sink in** PHRASAL VERB 句動詞 When a statement or fact **sinks in**, you finally understand or realize it fully. 実感する, やっと理解する ❑ *The implication took a while to sink in.* 含意をちゃんと理解するのにしばらくかかった.

| N. | bathroom sink, dishes in a sink, kitchen sink ❶ |
| | sink a ship ❷ |

sip /sɪp/ (**sips, sipping, sipped**) ❶ V-T/V-I 他動詞/自動詞 If you **sip** a drink or **sip at** it, you drink by taking just a small amount at a time. ちびちび飲む ❑ *Jessica sipped her drink thoughtfully.* ジェシカは思いにふけりながらちびちびと飲んだ. ❑ *He sipped at the glass and then put it down.* 彼はグラスからちびちびと飲んで, 下に置いた. ❷ N-COUNT 可算名詞 A **sip** is a small amount of drink that you take into your mouth. 一口 ❑ *Harry took a sip of bourbon.* ハリーはバーボンを一口飲んだ.

si|phon /saɪfən/ (**siphons, siphoning, siphoned**) also **syphon** ❶ V-T 他動詞 If you **siphon** liquid from a container, you make it come out through a tube and down into a lower container by enabling the pressure of the air on it to push it out. （サイフォンで）吸い上げる ❑ *He told police someone had tried to siphon gas from his car.* 彼は, 何者かが彼の車からガソリンを吸い上げようとしたと警察に通報した. ● PHRASAL VERB 句動詞 **Siphon off** means the same as **siphon**. 吸い上げる ❑ *Surgeons siphoned off fluid from his left lung.* 外科医は彼の左肺から液体を吸い上げた. ❷ N-COUNT 可算名詞 A **siphon** is a tube that you use for siphoning liquid. サイフォン, 吸い上げ管 ❸ V-T 他動詞 If you **siphon** money or resources from something, you cause them to be used for a purpose for which they were not intended. 流用する ❑ *He siphoned $1.2 billion from his companies to prop up his crumbling media empire.* 彼は会社から12億ドルを流用し彼の崩れかけたメディア王国のてこ入れに使った. ● PHRASAL VERB 句動詞 **Siphon off** means the same as **siphon**. 流用する ❑ *He had siphoned off a small fortune in aid money from the United Nations.* 彼は国連の援助金から大金を流用しました.

sir /sɜr/ (**sirs**) ❶ N-VOC 呼格名詞 People sometimes say **sir** as a polite way of addressing a man whose name they do not know, or an older man. For example, a store clerk might address a male customer as **sir**. 名前を知らない男性に対する敬意を込めた呼びかけ ❑ *Excuse me sir, but would you mind telling me what sort of car that is?* すみませんが, それがどの種の車だったかを話していただけませんか? [POLITENESS 丁寧さ] ❷ N-TITLE 称号名詞 **Sir** is the title used in front of the name of a knight or baronet. ナイト爵や準男爵に付ける敬称 ❑ *She introduced me to Sir Tobias and Lady Clarke.* 彼女は私にサー・トビアスとレイディー・クラークを紹介してくれた. ❸ CONVENTION 慣習表現 You use the expression **Dear Sir** at the beginning of a formal letter or a business letter when you are writing to a man. 各位 ❑ *Dear Sir, Enclosed is a copy of my résumé for your consideration.* 各位, 履歴書を同封しておりますので, ご検討の方よろしくお願いします.

si|ren /saɪrən/ (**sirens**) N-COUNT 可算名詞 A **siren** is a warning device which makes a long, loud noise. Most fire engines, ambulances, and police cars have sirens. サイレン, 警報 ❑ *It sounds like an air raid siren.* 空襲警報のように聞こえる.

sis|ter /sɪstər/ (**sisters**) ❶ N-COUNT 可算名詞 Your **sister** is a girl or woman who has the same parents as you. 姉のきょうだい, 姉, 妹 [oft poss N] ❑ *His sister Sarah helped him.* 姉のサラが彼を手伝った. ❑ *...Vanessa Bell, the sister of Virginia Woolf.* バージニア・ウルフの妹, バネッサ・ベル ❷ → see also **half sister, stepsister**

Note that there is no common English word that can refer to both a brother and a sister. You simply have to use both words. ❑ *She has 13 brothers and sisters.* The word **sibling** exists, but it is very formal. Some Americans use **sib** as an informal substitute for **sibling**. ❑ *All my sibs were home for Thanksgiving.*

❸ N-COUNT; N-TITLE; N-VOC 可算名詞, 称号名詞, 呼格名詞 **Sister** is a title given to a woman who belongs to a religious community. 修道女, シスター ❑ *Sister Francesca entered the chapel.* シスター・フランチェスカが礼拝堂に入った. ❹ N-COUNT 可算名詞 You can describe a woman as your **sister** if you feel a connection with her, for example, because she belongs to the same race, religion, country, or profession. 同胞, 同士 ❑ *Modern woman has been freed from many of the duties that befell her sisters in times past.* 現代の女性は, 昔の女性に降りかかった多くの義務から解放されている. ❺ ADJ 形容詞 You can use **sister** to describe something that is of the same type or is connected in some way to another thing you have mentioned. 姉妹— [ADJ n] ❑ *...the International Monetary Fund and its sister organization, the World Bank.* 国際通貨基金とその姉妹機関の世界銀行
→ see **family**

sister-in-law (**sisters-in-law**) N-COUNT 可算名詞 Someone's **sister-in-law** is the sister of their husband or wife, or the woman who is married to their brother. 義理の姉, 義理の妹
→ see **family**

S

sit /sɪt/ (sits, sitting, sat) **1** V-I 自動詞 If you **are sitting** somewhere, for example, in a chair, your bottom is resting on the chair and the upper part of your body is upright. 座っている ▫ *Mother was sitting in her chair in the kitchen.* 母は台所のいすに座っていました. ▫ *They had been sitting watching television.* 彼らは座っててテレビを見ていました. **2** V-I 自動詞 When you **sit** somewhere, you lower your body until you are sitting on something. 座る ▫ *He set the cases against a wall and sat on them.* 彼は壁の横に箱を置いてその上に座った. ▫ *Eva pulled over a chair and sat beside her husband.* エバはいすを引いて夫の隣に座った. ● PHRASAL VERB 句動詞 **Sit down** means the same as **sit**. 座る ▫ *I sat down, stunned.* 私はぼう然として腰を下ろしました. **3** V-T 他動詞 If you **sit** someone somewhere, you tell them to sit there or put them in a sitting position. 座らせる [他動詞] ▫ *He used to sit me on his lap.* 彼は昔、私をひざの上に座らせてくれたものでした. ● PHRASAL VERB 句動詞 To **sit** someone **down** somewhere means to **sit** there. 座らせる ▫ *She helped him out of the water and sat him down on the rock.* 彼女は彼を川から助け出し岩の上に座らせた. **4** V-I 自動詞 If you **sit on** a committee or other official group, you are a member of it. 役員を務める [no cont] ▫ *He was asked to sit on numerous committees.* 彼は数々の委員会の役員を務めるように依頼された. **5** V-I 自動詞 When a legislature, court, or other official body **sits**, it officially carries out its work. 開会する、開廷する [FORMAL 形式ばった] ▫ *The court sits under tight security in a former museum.* 裁判所は元美術館で厳重な警備の下で開会した. **6** PHRASE 句 If you **sit tight**, you remain in the same place or situation and do not take any action, usually because you are waiting for something to happen. 動かない、しっかり腰を据える ▫ *Sit tight. I'll be right back.* 動かないで. すぐに戻るから. **7** to **sit on the fence** → see **fence**

▸ **sit back** PHRASAL VERB 句動詞 If you **sit back** while something is happening, you relax and do not become involved in it. のんびりする [INFORMAL くだけた] ▫ *They didn't have to do anything except sit back and enjoy life.* 彼らはのんびりとして人生を楽しむ以外は何もしなくてよかった.

▸ **sit in on** PHRASAL VERB 句動詞 If you **sit in on** a lesson, meeting, or discussion, you are present while it is taking place but do not take part in it. 聴講する、傍聴する ▫ *Will they permit you to sit in on a few classes as an observer?* いくつかの講義に聴講者として参加することを認められますか.

▸ **sit on** PHRASAL VERB 句動詞 If you say that someone **is sitting on** something, you mean that they are delaying dealing with it. 手をつけない [INFORMAL くだけた] ▫ *He had been sitting on the document for at least two months.* 彼は少なくとも2か月間はその書類に手をつけないでいた.

▸ **sit out** PHRASAL VERB 句動詞 If you **sit** something **out**, you wait for it to finish, without taking any action. 終わるまでじっと待つ ▫ *The only thing I can do is keep quiet and sit this one out.* 私ができることは静かにこれが終わるまでじっと待つことだけだ.

▸ **sit through** PHRASAL VERB 句動詞 If you **sit through** something such as a movie, lecture, or meeting, you stay until it is finished although you are not enjoying it. (我慢して) 終わりまで待つ ▫ *...movies so bad you can hardly bear to sit through them.* 最後まで見るに耐えないひどい映画.

▸ **sit up** **1** PHRASAL VERB 句動詞 If you **sit up**, you move into a sitting position when you have been leaning back or lying down. 起き上がる ▫ *Her head spins dizzily as soon as she sits up.* 彼女が起き上がるとすぐに頭がクラクラした. **2** PHRASAL VERB 句動詞 If you **sit** someone **up**, you move them into a sitting position when they have been leaning back or lying down. (人を) 起き上がらせる ▫ *She sat him up and made him comfortable.* 彼女は彼を起き上がらせて座り心地をよくしました. **3** PHRASAL VERB 句動詞 If you **sit up**, you do not go to bed although it is very late. 夜更かしする ▫ *We sat up drinking and talking.* 私たちは飲んだりしゃべったりしながら夜更かしをした. **4** → see also **sit-up**

Thesaurus *sit* また次を参照 :

V. perch, rest, settle **1** – **3**

Word Partnership *sit* は次の語句と使われる :

ADV. sit alone, sit back, sit comfortably, sit quietly, sit still **1**

PREP. sit in a circle, sit on the porch, sit on the sidelines **1** sit on a bench, sit in a chair, sit on the floor, sit on *someone's* lap, sit around/at a table **1 2**

V. sit and eat, sit and enjoy, sit and listen, sit and talk, sit and wait, sit and watch (or sit watching) **1** sit down to dinner/eat, sit down and relax **1 2**

site /saɪt/ (sites, siting, sited) **1** N-COUNT 可算名詞 A **site** is a piece of ground that is used for a particular purpose or where a particular thing happens. 敷地、現場 ▫ *I was working as a foreman on a building site.* 私は建設現場で現場監督として働いていた. **2** N-COUNT 可算名詞 **The site of** an important event is the place where it happened. 跡、場所 ▫ *Scientists have described the Aral sea as the site of the worst ecological disaster on earth.* 科学者はアラル海を地球上で最悪の生態学的惨事があった場所だと説明した. **3** N-COUNT 可算名詞 A **site** is a piece of ground where something such as a statue or building stands or used to stand. 跡地、遺跡 ▫ *...the site of Moses' tomb.* モーゼの墓の遺跡 **4** N-COUNT 可算名詞 A **site** is the same as a **website**. サイト **5** V-T 他動詞 If something **is sited** in a particular place or position, it is put there or built there. 設置する、ある [usu passive] ▫ *He said chemical weapons had never been sited in Germany.* 彼は、ドイツでは化学兵器が設置されたことがないと述べた. ● **siting** N-SING 単数名詞 設置 ▫ *...controls on the siting of gas storage vessels.* ガス貯蔵船設置の規制 **6** PHRASE 句 If someone or something is **on site**, they are in a particular area or group of buildings where people work, study, or stay. 現地に、その場に ▫ *It is cheaper to have extra building work done when the builder is on site, rather than bringing him back for a small job.* 建設業者が現地にいる間に追加工事を依頼する方があとで少しの作業のために呼び戻すよりも安く仕上がる. **7** PHRASE 句 If someone or something is **off site**, they are away from a particular area or group of buildings where people work, study, or stay. 現場を離れて ▫ *There is ample car parking off site.* 敷地外に大きな駐車場がある.

sit-in (sit-ins) N-COUNT 可算名詞 A **sit-in** is a protest in which people go to a public place and stay there for a long time. 座り込み ▫ *The campaigners held a sit-in outside the Supreme Court.* 活動家たちが最高裁の前で座り込みをした.

sit|ting room (sitting rooms) also **sitting-room** N-COUNT 可算名詞 A **sitting room** is a room in a house where people sit and relax. 居間 [OLD-FASHIONED 古風な]

situ|at|ed /sɪtʃueɪtɪd/ ADJ 形容詞 If something **is situated** in a particular place or position, it is in that place or position. 位置している ▫ *His hotel is situated in one of the loveliest places on the Loire.* 彼のホテルはロワールで最も素敵な場所の1つにある.

Word Link *site, situ ≈ position, location : campsite, situation, website*

situa|tion /sɪtʃueɪʃⁿn/ (situations) N-COUNT 可算名詞 You use **situation** to refer generally to what is happening in a particular place at a particular time, or to refer to what is happening to you. 状況、事態 ▫ *Army officers said the situation was under control.* 陸軍士官は、事態が収拾されたと述べた. ▫ *And now for a look at the travel situation in the rest of the country.* では次に、国内の他の地域の交通状況をご覧ください.

Thesaurus *situation* また次を参照 :

N. circumstances, condition, plight, position, state

Word Partnership *situation* は次の語句と使われる :

ADJ. bad situation, complicated situation, current situation, dangerous situation, difficult situation, economic situation, financial situation, political situation, present situation, same situation, tense situation, terrible situation, unique situation, unusual situation, whole situation

V. describe a situation, discuss a situation, handle a situation, improve a situation, understand a situation

sit-up (sit-ups) also **situp** N-COUNT 可算名詞 **Sit-ups** are exercises that you do to strengthen your stomach muscles. They involve sitting up from a lying position while keeping your legs straight on the floor. 腹筋運動 ▫ *He does 100 sit-ups each day.* 彼は1日腹筋運動を100回する.

six /sɪks/ (sixes) NUM 数詞 **Six** is the number 6. 6 ▫ *...a glorious career spanning more than six decades.* 60年以上に及ぶ華々しいキャリア

six|teen /sɪkstin/ (sixteens) NUM 数詞 **Sixteen** is the number 16. 16 ▫ *...exams taken at the age of sixteen.* 16歳で受験する試験 ▫ *He worked sixteen hours a day.* 彼は1日16時間働いた.

six|teenth /sɪkstinθ/ (sixteenths) **1** ORD 序数詞 The **sixteenth** item in a series is the one that you count as number sixteen. 第16の ▫ *...the sixteenth century AD.* 西暦16世紀 **2** FRACTION 端数 A **sixteenth** is one of sixteen equal parts of something. 16分の1 ▫ *...a sixteenth of a second.* 16分の1秒

sixth /sɪksθ/ (sixths) **1** ORD 序数詞 The **sixth** item in a series is the one that you count as number six. 第6の ▫ *...the sixth round of the World Cup.* ワールドカップ第6ラウンド **2** FRACTION 端数 A **sixth** is one of six equal parts of something. 6分の1 ▫ *The company yesterday shed a sixth of its workforce.* その会社は昨日従業員の6分の1を解雇した.

sixth form (sixth forms) also **sixth-form** N-COUNT 可算名詞
The **sixth form** in a British school consists of students aged 16 to 18, usually studying for A levels. (大学進学を目指す生徒が多い) 高等学校

six|ti|eth /sɪkstiəθ/ (sixtieths) **1** ORD 序数詞 The **sixtieth** item in a series is the one that you count as number sixty. 第60の ❑ He is to retire on his sixtieth birthday. 彼は60歳の誕生日に退職する予定だ。 **2** FRACTION 端数 A **sixtieth** is one of sixty equal parts of something. 60分の1

six|ty /sɪksti/ (sixties) **1** NUM 数詞 **Sixty** is the number 60. 60 ❑ ...the sunniest April for more than sixty years. 過去60年以上で最高の日照時間を記録した4月 **2** N-PLURAL 複数名詞 When you talk about the **sixties**, you are referring to numbers between 60 and 69. For example, if you are **in** your **sixties**, you are aged between 60 and 69. If the temperature is **in the sixties**, it is between 60 and 69 degrees. 60代、60度代 ❑ ...a lively widow in her sixties. 60歳代の元気な未亡人 **3** N-PLURAL 複数名詞 The **sixties** is the decade between 1960 and 1969. 60年代 ❑ In the sixties there were the deaths of the two Kennedy brothers and Martin Luther King. 60年代にはケネディ兄弟2人やマーチン・ルーサー・キングが死亡した。

siz|able /saɪzəbᵊl/ also **sizeable** ADJ 形容詞 **Sizable** means fairly large. かなり大きい ❑ Harry inherited the house and a sizable piece of land that surrounds it. ハリーは家とその周辺のかなりの土地を相続した。

size /saɪz/ (sizes, sizing, sized) **1** N-VAR 可変性名詞 The **size** of something is how big or small it is. Something's size is determined by comparing it to other things, counting it, or measuring it. 大きさ、規模 ❑ In 1970 the average size of a French farm was 19 hectares. 1970年のフランス農場の平均規模は19ヘクタールだった。 ❑ ...shelves containing books of various sizes. 様々なサイズの本が置かれている棚 **2** N-UNCOUNT 不可算名詞 The **size of** something is the fact that it is very large. 〜の大きさ ❑ He knows the size of the task. 彼はその仕事の規模を分かっている。 **3** N-COUNT 可算名詞 A **size** is one of a series of graded measurements, especially for things such as clothes or shoes. サイズ、寸法 ❑ My sister is the same height but only a size 12. 妹は身長は同じだけど服のサイズはたった の12号だ。

▶ **size up** PHRASAL VERB 句動詞 If you **size up** a person or situation, you carefully look at the person or think about the situation, so that you can decide how to act. 見極める [INFORMAL くだけた] ❑ Some U.S. manufacturers have been sizing up the UK as a possible market for their clothes. 米国の製造業者には英国をアパレル市場の候補として考慮している会社もある。

ADJ.	**average** size, **full** size **1**
	sheer size **2**
	mid-size, **right** size, size **large/medium/small 3**
N.	**bite** size, **class** size, **family** size, **life** size, **pocket** size **1**
	size **chart**, **king/queen** size **3**
V.	**double in** size, **increase in** size, **vary in** size **1**
	a size fits 3

size|able /saɪzəbᵊl/ → see **sizable**

siz|zle /sɪzᵊl/ (sizzles, sizzling, sizzled) V-I 自動詞 If something such as hot oil or fat **sizzles**, it makes hissing sounds. ジュージューと音を立てる ❑ The sausages and burgers sizzled on the barbecue. ソーセージやハンバーグがバーベキューでジュージューと音を立てた。

skate /skeɪt/ (skates, skating, skated) **1** N-COUNT 可算名詞 **Skates** are ice-skates. アイススケート靴 **2** N-COUNT 可算名詞 **Skates** are roller-skates. ローラースケート靴 **3** V-I 自動詞 If you **skate**, you move around wearing ice-skates or roller-skates. アイススケートをする、ローラースケートをする ❑ I actually skated, and despite some teetering I did not fall on the ice. 実際にスケートをしたよ。ちょっとぐらついたけど氷の上でこけなかったよ。 ● **skat|ing** N-UNCOUNT 不可算名詞 スケート、スケートをすること ❑ They all went skating together in the winter. 彼らは皆冬には一緒にスケートをしに行った。 ● **skat|er** N-COUNT 可算名詞 (skaters) スケートをする人 ❑ West Lake, an outdoor ice-skating rink, attracts skaters during the day and night. 屋外アイススケート場のウェスト・レイクは連日連夜スケート客でにぎわっている。

skate|board /skeɪtbɔrd/ (skateboards) N-COUNT 可算名詞 A **skateboard** is a narrow board with wheels at each end, which people stand on and ride for pleasure. スケートボード
→ see **skateboarding**

skate|board|ing /skeɪtbɔrdɪŋ/ N-UNCOUNT 不可算名詞 **Skateboarding** is the activity of riding on a skateboard. スケートボード (をすること) ❑ ...a skateboarding competition. スケートボード大会
→ see Picture Dictionary: **skateboarding**

skel|etal /skɛlɪtᵊl/ **1** ADJ 形容詞 **Skeletal** means relating to the bones in your body. 骨格の [ADJ n] ❑ ...the skeletal remains of seven adults. 大人7人の白骨化した遺体 **2** ADJ 形容詞 A **skeletal** person is so thin that you can see their bones through their skin. やせこけた、骨と皮だけの ❑ ...a hospital filled with skeletal children. やせこけた子供たちで一杯の病院
→ see **muscle**

skel|eton /skɛlɪtᵊn/ (skeletons) **1** N-COUNT 可算名詞 Your **skeleton** is the framework of bones in your body. 骨格、がい

Picture Dictionary **skateboarding**

elbow pad

helmet

knee pad

skateboard

platform

wheel

ramp

S

骨 ❏...a human skeleton. 人間のがい骨 ❷ ADJ 形容詞 A **skeleton** staff is the smallest number of staff necessary in order to run an organization or service. 必要最小限の [ADJ n] ❏Only a skeleton staff remains to show anyone interested around the site. 必要最小限の職員だけが残って現場に興味のある人を案内している. ❸ N-COUNT 可算名詞 The **skeleton** of something such as a building or a plan is its basic framework. 骨組み, 骨子 ❏The town of Rudbar had ceased to exist, with only skeletons of buildings remaining. ルードバルの町は建物の骨組みだけを残して消滅した.
→ see **shark**

skep|tic /skɛptɪk/ (skeptics) N-COUNT 可算名詞 A **skeptic** is a person who has doubts about things that other people believe. 疑い深い人, 懐疑論者 ❏He is a skeptic who tries to keep an open mind. 彼は, 先入観を持たないようにしているが疑い深い.

skep|ti|cal /skɛptɪkᵊl/ ADJ 形容詞 If you are **skeptical about** something, you have doubts about it. 疑い深い, 懐疑的な ❏Others here are more skeptical about the chances for justice being done. ここにいるほかの人たちは法の裁きが下される可能性についてさらに疑いを持っています.

skep|ti|cism /skɛptɪsɪzəm/ N-UNCOUNT 不可算名詞 **Skepticism** is great doubt about whether something is true or useful. 懐疑, 疑念 ❏A survey reflects business skepticism about the strength of the economic recovery. 調査は景気回復力へのビジネス界の懐疑を反映している.

sketch /skɛtʃ/ (sketches, sketching, sketched) ❶ N-COUNT 可算名詞 A **sketch** is a drawing that is done quickly without a lot of details. Artists often use sketches as a preparation for a more detailed painting or drawing. スケッチ, 素描 ❏...a sketch of a soldier by Orpen. オーペンによる軍人のスケッチ ❷ V-T/V-I 他動詞/自動詞 If you **sketch** something, you make a quick, rough drawing of it. スケッチする ❏Clare and David Astor are sketching a view of far Spanish hills. ディビッド・クレア・アスター夫妻が遠く離れたスペインの丘の風景をスケッチしている. ❸ N-COUNT 可算名詞 A **sketch** of a situation, person, or incident is a brief description of it without many details. 手短な説明, 概略 ❏...thumbnail sketches of heads of state and political figures. 国の指導者と政界実力者の簡単な説明 ❹ V-T 他動詞 If you **sketch** a situation or incident, you give a short description of it, including only the most important facts. 概略を述べる ❏Cross sketched the story briefly, telling the facts just as they had happened. クロスはその話を手短に, 発生したとおりの事実を話した. ● PHRASAL VERB 句動詞 **Sketch out** means the same as **sketch**. 概略を述べる ❏He sketched out plans to give consumers more affordable choices. 彼は消費者がさらに買い求めやすい商品を販売する計画について簡単に説明した. ❺ N-COUNT 可算名詞 A **sketch** is a short humorous piece of acting, usually forming part of a comedy show. 寸劇 ❏...a five-minute sketch about a folk singer. フォークシンガーに関する5分間の寸劇
→ see **animation, drawing**

sketchy /skɛtʃi/ (sketchier, sketchiest) ADJ 形容詞 **Sketchy** information about something does not include many details and is therefore incomplete or inadequate. 大ざっぱな, 不十分な ❏Details of what actually happened are still sketchy. 実際に起きたことについての詳細は依然として不明だ.

skew /skyu/ (skews, skewing, skewed) V-T 他動詞 If something is **skewed**, it is changed or affected to some extent by a new or unusual factor, and so is not correct or normal. ねじ曲げる, 歪曲(わいきょく)する ❏The arithmetic of nuclear running costs has been skewed by the fall in the cost of other fuels. 原子力発電所の運営費の計算は他の燃料費の低下により歪曲(わいきょく)されている.

skew|er /skyuər/ (skewers) N-COUNT 可算名詞 A **skewer** is a long pin made of wood or metal that is used to hold pieces of food together during cooking. くし

ski /ski/ (skis, skiing, skied) ❶ N-COUNT 可算名詞 **Skis** are long, flat, narrow pieces of wood, metal, or plastic that are fastened to boots so that you can move easily on snow or water. スキー板 ❏...a pair of skis. スキー板1組 ❷ V-I 自動詞 When people **ski**, they move over snow or water on skis. スキーをする ❏They surf, ski and ride. 彼らはサーフィンをし, スキーをし乗馬をする. ● **ski|er** /skiər/ N-COUNT 可算名詞 (skiers) スキーヤー スキーをする人 ❏He is an enthusiastic skier. 彼はスキーに熱心だ. ● **ski|ing** N-UNCOUNT 不可算名詞 スキーをすること ❏My hobbies were skiing and scuba diving. 趣味はスキーとスキューバダイビングだった. ❸ ADJ 形容詞 [ADJ n] You use **ski** to refer to things that are concerned with skiing. スキーの ❏...the Swiss ski resort of Klosters. スイスのスキー場, クロスターズ ❏...a private ski instructor. 個人指導のスキーインストラクター

skid /skɪd/ (skids, skidding, skidded) V-I 自動詞 If a vehicle **skids**, it slides sideways or forward while moving, for example, when you are trying to stop it suddenly on a wet road. 横滑りする, スキッドする ❏The car pulled up too fast and skidded on the dusty shoulder of the road. その車は急停止をしほこりっぽい路肩でスキップした. ● N-COUNT 可算名詞 **Skid** is also a noun. 横滑り, スキップ ❏I slammed the brakes on and went into a skid. 急ブレーキをかけると横滑りした.

skil|ful /skɪlfəl/ → see **skillful**

skill /skɪl/ (skills) ❶ N-COUNT 可算名詞 A **skill** is a type of work or activity which requires special training and knowledge. 技能, 技術 ❏Most of us will know someone who is always learning new skills, or studying new fields. 私たちのほとんどは常に新しい技術を習得している, あるいは新しい分野の学習をしている人を知っているだろう. ❷ N-UNCOUNT 不可算名詞 **Skill** is the knowledge and ability that enables you to do something well. 熟練, うまさ ❏The cut of a diamond depends on the skill of its craftsman. ダイアモンドのカットは職人の技量によって決まる.

Thesaurus	skill また次を参照:
N.	ability, proficiency, talent ❶ ❷

skilled /skɪld/ ❶ ADJ 形容詞 Someone who is **skilled** has the knowledge and ability to do something well. 熟練した ❏Few doctors are actually trained, and not all are skilled, in helping their patients make choices. 患者が治療の選択をする手助けをできるように実際に訓練を受けた医者はほとんどいなくて, それを上手にできない医者もいる. ❷ ADJ 形容詞 **Skilled** work can only be done by people who have had some training. 特殊技能を要する ❏New industries demanded skilled labor not available locally. 新産業は地元では見つからないような特殊な技術を持つ労働力を必要とした.

skill|ful /skɪlfəl/ ADJ 形容詞 Someone who is **skillful** at something does it very well. 上手な, 熟練した ❏He actually is quite a skillful campaigner. 彼は実はとても熟練した運動家だった. ● **skill|ful|ly** ADV 副詞 [ADV with v] 上手に, 巧みに ❏The city's rulers skillfully played both powers off against each other. その市の指導者たちはうまく互いの権力を交じ合いました.

skim /skɪm/ (skims, skimming, skimmed) ❶ V-T 他動詞 If you **skim** something **from** the surface of a liquid, you remove it. 取り除く ❏Rough seas today prevented specially equipped ships from skimming oil off the water's surface. 本日は海が荒れていたため特別装備をした船による海面から油を取り除く作業ができませんでした. ❷ V-T/V-I 他動詞/自動詞 If something **skims** a surface, it moves quickly along just above it. 滑る, 滑走する ❏...seagulls skimming the waves. 波をかすめて飛ぶカモメ ❸ V-T/V-I 他動詞/自動詞 If you **skim** a piece of writing, you read through it quickly. さっと読む, 目を通す ❏He skimmed the pages quickly, then read them again more carefully. 彼は書類にさっと目を通し, そのあとじっくり再読した.
▶ **skim off** PHRASAL VERB 句動詞 If someone **skims off** the best part of something, or money which belongs to other people, they take it for themselves. 取る, 自分のものにする ❏The regime was able to skim off about $10 billion in illegal revenue. その政権は不法収入から約100億ドル取り上げることができた. ❏She admitted she skimmed cash off the top of the fees she collected. 彼女は自分で集めた手数料から現金をかすみ取ったことを認めた.

skim milk N-UNCOUNT 不可算名詞 **Skim milk** is milk from which the cream has been removed. スキムミルク

skimpy /skɪmpi/ (skimpier, skimpiest) ADJ 形容詞 Something that is **skimpy** is too small in size or quantity. 小さすぎる, 少なすぎる ❏...skimpy underwear. 露出度の高い下着

skin /skɪn/ (skins, skinning, skinned) ❶ N-VAR 可変性名詞 Your **skin** is the natural covering of your body. 皮膚, 肌 ❏His skin is clear and smooth. 彼の肌は透明感があってスベスべだ. ❏There are three major types of skin cancer. 皮膚癌には主に3種類ある. ❷ N-VAR 可変性名詞 An **animal skin** is skin which has been removed from a dead animal. Skins are used to make things such as coats and rugs. (動物の) 皮 ❏That was real crocodile skin. それは本物のワニ皮でした. ❸ N-VAR 可変性名詞 The **skin** of a fruit or vegetable is its outer layer or covering. (果物・野菜の) 皮 ❏The outer skin of the orange is called the "zest." オレンジの外皮はzestと呼ばれる. ❹ N-SING 単数名詞 If a **skin** forms on the surface of a liquid, a thin, fairly solid layer forms on it. 膜 ❏Stir the custard occasionally to prevent a skin forming. 膜が張らないようにカスタードをときどき混ぜなさい. ❺ V-T 他動詞 If you **skin** a dead animal, you remove its skin. 皮をはぐ ❏...with the expertise of a chef skinning a rabbit. シェフのウサギの皮をはぐ特別な技術
→ see Word Web: **skin**

Word Partnership	skin は次の語句と使われる:
ADJ.	**dark** skin, **dry** skin, **fair** skin, **oily** skin, **pale** skin, **sensitive** skin, **smooth** skin, **soft** skin ❶
N.	skin and bones, skin cancer, skin cells, skin color (or color of someone's skin), skin cream, skin problems, skin type ❶ leopard skin ❷

skin|ny /skɪni/ (skinnier, skinniest) ADJ 形容詞 A **skinny** person is extremely thin, often in a way that you find unattractive. ガリガリの [INFORMAL くだけた] ❏He was quite a skinny little boy. 彼はガリガリの小さい子だった.

Word Web   skin

What is the best thing you can do for your **skin**? Stay out of the sun. When skin **cells** grow normally, the skin remains smooth and firm. However, the sun's **ultraviolet** rays sometimes cause damage. This can lead to **sunburn**, **wrinkles**, and skin cancer. The damage may not be apparent for several years. However, doctors have discovered that even a light **suntan** can be dangerous. **Sunlight** makes the melanin in skin turn dark. This is the body's attempt to protect itself from the ultraviolet radiation. Dermatologists recommend limiting exposure to the sun and always using a **sunscreen**.

skip /skɪp/ (**skips, skipping, skipped**) **1** V-I 自動詞 If you **skip** along, you move almost as if you are dancing, with a series of little jumps from one foot to the other. スキップする ❑ *They saw the man with a little girl skipping along behind him.* 彼らは男性とその後をついてスキップしている小さな女の子を見た. ❑ *We went skipping down the street arm in arm.* 私たちは腕を組んでスキップしながら町を歩いた. ● N-COUNT 可算名詞 **Skip** is also a noun. スキップ ❑ *The boxer gave a little skip as he came out of his corner.* ボクサーはコーナーから出てくるとき少しスキップした. **2** V-T 他動詞 When someone **skips rope**, they jump up and down over a rope which they or two other people are holding at each end and turning around and around. 縄跳びをする ❑ *They skip rope and play catch, waiting for the bell.* 彼らはベルが鳴るまで縄跳びをしたり, キャッチボールをします. ● **skip|ping** N-UNCOUNT 不可算名詞 縄跳び ❑ *We did rope skipping and things like that.* 私たちは縄跳びとかの遊びをしました. **3** V-T 他動詞 If you **skip** something that you usually do or something that most people do, you decide not to do it. 抜く, しない ❑ *It is important not to skip meals.* 食事を抜かないことは大切だ. **4** V-T/V-I 他動詞/自動詞 If you **skip** or **skip over** a part of something you are reading or a story you are telling, you miss it out or pass over it quickly and move on to something else. 抜かす, とばす ❑ *You might want to skip the exercises in this chapter.* この章の練習問題はとばしてもよい. **5** V-I 自動詞 If you **skip from** one subject or activity to another, you move quickly from one to the other, although there is no obvious connection between them. とぶ, 次々と話題が変わる ❑ *She kept up a continuous chatter, skipping from one subject to the next.* 彼女は次から次へと話題を変えながらしゃべり続けた. **6** N-COUNT 可算名詞 A **skip** is a large, open, metal container which is used to hold and take away large unwanted items and trash. 廃棄物コンテナ [BRIT 英国英語; AM **Dumpster** 米国英語 **Dumpster**]

skip|per /skɪpər/ (**skippers**) N-COUNT; N-VOC 可算名詞, 呼格名詞 You can use **skipper** to refer to the captain of a ship or boat. 船長 ❑ *...the skipper of an English fishing boat.* 英国の漁船の船長

skir|mish /skɜrmɪʃ/ (**skirmishes, skirmishing, skirmished**) **1** N-COUNT 可算名詞 A **skirmish** is a minor battle. 小競り合い ❑ *Border skirmishes between India and Pakistan were common.* インドとパキスタンの国境争いはよく起こった. **2** V-RECIP 相互動詞 If people **skirmish**, they fight. 小競り合いをする ❑ *They were skirmishing close to the minefield now.* 彼らは今度は地雷原の近くで争っていた.

skirt /skɜrt/ (**skirts, skirting, skirted**) **1** N-COUNT 可算名詞 A **skirt** is a piece of clothing worn by women and girls. It fastens at the waist and hangs down around the legs. スカート **2** V-T 他動詞 Something that **skirts** an area is situated around the edge of it. ぐるっと囲む ❑ *We raced across a large field that skirted the slope of a hill.* 私たちは丘の斜面をぐるっと囲む大きな野原の周りを競争した. **3** V-T/V-I 他動詞/自動詞 If you **skirt** a problem or question, you avoid dealing with it. 避ける ❑ *He skirted the hardest issues, concentrating on areas of possible agreement.* 彼は難題への言及を避けて, 合意可能な分野に集中した.
→ see **clothing**

skull /skʌl/ (**skulls**) N-COUNT 可算名詞 Your **skull** is the bony part of your head which encloses your brain. 頭がい骨 ❑ *Her husband was later treated for a fractured skull.* 彼女の夫は後に頭がい骨骨折で治療を受けた.

sky /skaɪ/ (**skies**) N-VAR 可変性名詞 The **sky** is the space around the earth which you can see when you stand outside and look upward. 空 ❑ *The sun is already high in the sky.* 太陽はすでに天高く昇っている. ❑ *...warm sunshine and clear blue skies.* 暖かい太陽の光とよく晴れた青い空
→ see **star**

Word Partnership   sky は次の語句と使われる:

ADV.	sky **above, the** sky **overhead, up in the** sky
ADJ.	**black** sky, **blue** sky, **bright** sky, **clear** sky, **cloudless** sky, **dark** sky, **empty** sky, **high in the** sky

sky|line /skaɪlaɪn/ (**skylines**) N-COUNT 可算名詞 The **skyline** is the line or shape that is formed where the sky meets buildings or the land. スカイライン, 空を背景にした建物の輪郭 ❑ *The village church dominates the skyline.* 村の教会がそびえ立っていた.

sky|scraper /skaɪskreɪpər/ (**skyscrapers**) N-COUNT 可算名詞 A **skyscraper** is a very tall building in a city. 超高層ビル
→ see Word Web: **skyscraper**
→ see **city**

slab /slæb/ (**slabs**) N-COUNT 可算名詞 A **slab of** something is a thick, flat piece of it. 厚板, 平板 [with supp] ❑ *...slabs of stone.* 石板

slack /slæk/ (**slacker, slackest, slacks, slacking, slacked**) **1** ADJ 形容詞 Something that is **slack** is loose and not firmly stretched or tightly in position. 緩んだ, たるんだ ❑ *The boy's jaw went slack.* 少年のあごが緩んだ. **2** ADJ 形容詞 A **slack** period is one in which there is not much work or activity. 低調な ❑ *The workload can be evened out, instead of the shop having busy times and slack periods.* 店に繁盛期と閑散期があるのではなくて, 仕事量を安定化することができる. **3** ADJ 形容詞 Someone who is **slack** in their work does not do it properly. いいかげんな [DISAPPROVAL 不賛成] ❑ *Many publishers have simply become far too slack.* 単にいいかげんになりすぎた出版社が多い. **4** V-I 自動詞 If someone **is slacking**, they are not working as hard as they should. 手を抜く [DISAPPROVAL 不賛成] [only cont] ❑ *He had never let a foreman see him slacking.* 彼は監督にサボっているところを見られたことがなかった. ● PHRASAL VERB 句動詞 **Slack off** means the same as **slack**. 手を抜く ❑ *If someone slacks off, Bill comes down hard.* 手を抜く者がいればビルは厳しく処罰する.

slack|en /slækən/ (**slackens, slackening, slackened**) **1** V-T/V-I 他動詞/自動詞 If something **slackens** or if you **slacken** it, it becomes slower, less active, or less intense. 不振にする, 弱める [他動詞], 不振になる, 弱まる [自動詞] ❑ *Inflationary pressures continued to slacken last month.* 先月はインフレ圧力のため引き続き景気が後退した. **2** V-T/V-I 他動詞/自動詞 If your grip or a part of your body **slackens** or if you **slacken** your grip, it becomes looser or more relaxed. 緩める [他動詞], 緩む [自動詞] ❑ *Her grip slackened on Arnold's arm.* アーノルドの腕を握る彼女の力が緩んだ.

slam /slæm/ (**slams, slamming, slammed**) **1** V-T/V-I 他動詞/自動詞 If you **slam** a door or window or if it **slams**, it shuts noisily and with great force. バタンと閉める [他動詞], バタンと閉まる [自動詞] ❑ *She slammed the door and locked it behind her.* 彼女はドアをバタンと閉めて後ろ手でかぎをかけた. ❑ *I was relieved to hear the front door slam.* 玄関のドアがバタンと閉まる音を聞いてほっとした. **2** V-T 他動詞 If you **slam** something **down**, you put it there quickly and with

Word Web   skyscraper

Large American **cities** were expanding rapidly in the early 1900s. As this happened, **land** became scarce and expensive. **Real estate developers** soon felt the need for taller **buildings** and the **skyscraper** was born. Two things made these buildings possible—mass-produced steel and the invention of the **elevator**. The **construction** of the Empire State Building set two important records. At 102 **stories**, it was the tallest building in the world for 41 years. And 3,000 workers completed it in only 14 months. To accomplish this, they worked day and night, seven days a week, including holidays.

S

great force. 乱暴に置く ❏ *She listened in a mixture of shock and anger before slamming the phone down.* 彼女はショックと怒りを感じながら聞いて、受話器をガチャンと置いた. **3** V-T 他動詞 To **slam** someone or something means to criticize them very severely. 激しく非難する、こき下ろす [JOURNALISM ジャーナリズム] ❏ *The famed filmmaker slammed the claims as "an outrageous lie."* その有名映画制作者はその話を「真っ赤なうそ」だとこき下ろした. **4** V-T/V-I 他動詞/自動詞 If one thing **slams** into or against another, it crashes into it with great force. 激突する ❏ *The plane slammed into the building after losing an engine shortly after take-off.* その飛行機は離陸直後にエンジン1機を無くしビルに激突した.

Word Partnership   *slam* は次の語句と使われる:

N.	slam **a door** **1**
V.	hear *something* slam **1**
ADV.	slam *(something)* **shut** **1**

slan|der /slǽndər/ (**slanders, slandering, slandered**) **1** N-VAR 可変性名詞 **Slander** is an untrue spoken statement about someone which is intended to damage their reputation. Compare **libel**. 名誉毀損 ❏ *Dr. Bach is now suing the company for slander.* バッハ博士は現在その会社を名誉毀損で訴えています. **2** V-T 他動詞 To **slander** someone means to say untrue things about them in order to damage their reputation. 中傷する ❏ *He accused me of slandering him and trying to undermine his position.* 彼は私が彼を中傷し彼の立場を不利にしようとしていると非難した.

slang /slǽŋ/ N-UNCOUNT 不可算名詞 **Slang** consists of words, expressions, and meanings that are informal and are used by people who know each other very well or who have the same interests. 俗語、スラング ❏ *Archie liked to think he kept up with current slang.* アーチーは流行のスラングを知っていると思っていたかった.

slant /slǽnt/ (**slants, slanting, slanted**) **1** V-I 自動詞 Something that **slants** is sloping, rather than horizontal or vertical. 傾く ❏ *The morning sun slanted through the glass roof.* ガラスの屋根を通して朝日が差し込んだ. **2** N-SING 単数名詞 If something is on a **slant**, it is in a slanting position. 傾き ❏ *... long pockets cut on the slant.* 長い斜めポケット **3** V-T 他動詞 If information or a system is **slanted**, it is made to show favor toward a particular group or opinion. 偏る [usu passive] ❏ *The program was deliberately slanted to make the home team look good.* その番組はわざと地元チームびいきで制作されていた. **4** N-SING 単数名詞 A particular **slant** on a subject is a particular way of thinking about it, especially one that is unfair. 偏見 ❏ *The political slant at Focus can be described as center-right.* フォーカスに対する政治的偏見は中道右派だといえる.

slap /slǽp/ (**slaps, slapping, slapped**) **1** V-T 他動詞 If you **slap** someone, you hit them with the palm of your hand. 平手で打つ ❏ *He would push or slap her once in a while.* 彼はたまに彼女を押したり平手打ちしたりする. ❏ *I slapped him hard across the face.* 私は彼に思いきりびんたを食らわした. ●N-COUNT 可算名詞 **Slap** is also a noun. 平手打ち ❏ *He reached forward and gave her a slap.* 彼は前に手を伸ばして彼女にびんたを食らわした. **2** V-T 他動詞 If you **slap** something **onto** a surface, you put it there quickly, roughly, or carelessly. ドンと置く ❏ *He emptied his drink and slapped the money on the bar.* 彼は酒を飲み干してカウンターに金をたたきつけた. **3** V-T 他動詞 If journalists say that the authorities **slap** something such as a tax or a ban **on** something, they think it is unreasonable or put on without careful thought. 不当に課す、巻き上げる [INFORMAL くだけた, DISAPPROVAL 不賛成] ❏ *The government slapped a ban on the export of unprocessed logs.* 政府は未処理の木材の輸出禁止措置を取った.

Word Partnership   *slap* は次の語句と使われる:

N.	a slap **on the back,** a slap **in the face,** a slap **on the wrist** **1**

slash /slǽʃ/ (**slashes, slashing, slashed**) **1** V-T 他動詞 If you **slash** something, you make a long, deep cut in it. ざっくり切る ❏ *He came within two minutes of bleeding to death after slashing his wrists.* 彼は手首を切ったあと2分以内に出血多量で死亡した. ●N-COUNT 可算名詞 **Slash** is also a noun. 切りつけること ❏ *Make deep slashes in the meat and push in the spice paste.* 肉に深い切り目を入れてスパイスペーストを塗りこみなさい. **2** V-I 自動詞 If you **slash** at a person or thing, you quickly hit at them with something such as a knife. 切りつける ❏ *He slashed at her, aiming carefully.* 彼は慎重に彼女を目掛けて切りつけた. **3** V-T 他動詞 To **slash** something such as costs or jobs means to reduce them by a large amount. 大幅に削減する [JOURNALISM ジャーナリズム] ❏ *Car makers could be forced to slash prices.* 自動車メーカーは大幅に価格を引下げざるをえないかもしれない. **4** N-COUNT 可算名詞 You say **slash** to refer to a sloping line that separates letters, words, or numbers. For example, if you are giving the number 340/2/K you say "Three four zero, slash two, slash K." 斜線、スラッシュ [SPOKEN 口語]

slate /sleɪt/ (**slates, slating, slated**) **1** N-UNCOUNT 不可算名詞 **Slate** is a dark gray rock that can be easily split into thin layers. Slate is often used for covering roofs. 粘板岩 ❏ *a stone-built cottage, with a traditional slate roof.* 伝統的な粘板岩の屋根がある石造りの家 **2** N-COUNT 可算名詞 A **slate** is one of the small flat pieces of slate that are used for covering roofs. スレート ❏ *Thieves had stolen the slates from the roof.* どろぼうが屋根からスレートを盗んだ. **3** V-T PASSIVE 受動態他動詞 If something **is slated to** happen, it is planned to happen at a particular time or on a particular occasion. 予定している [mainly AM 主に米国英語] ❏ *Bromfield was slated to become U.S. Secretary of Agriculture.* ブロムフィールドは米国農務官になる予定だった. **4** PHRASE 句 If you start **with a clean slate**, you do not take account of previous mistakes or failures and make a fresh start. 白紙の状態 ❏ *The proposal is to pay everything you owe, so that you can start with a clean slate.* その提案は、一から出直しができるよう借金をすべて清算することだ.

slaugh|ter /slɔ́tər/ (**slaughters, slaughtering, slaughtered**) **1** V-T 他動詞 If large numbers of people or animals **are slaughtered**, they are killed in a way that is cruel or unnecessary. 虐殺する [usu passive] ❏ *Thirty four people were slaughtered while lining up to cast their votes.* 投票するために列に並んでいる間に34人が虐殺された. ●N-UNCOUNT 不可算名詞 **Slaughter** is also a noun. 虐殺 ❏ *This was only a small part of a war where the slaughter of civilians was commonplace.* これは民間人の虐殺が一般的に行われていた戦争のほんの一部に過ぎなかった. **2** V-T 他動詞 To **slaughter** animals such as cows and sheep means to kill them for their meat. 解体処理する、食肉処理する ❏ *Lack of chicken feed means that chicken farms are having to slaughter their stock.* ニワトリのえさが不足しているためニワトリ農場は解体処理せざるをえない状態になっている. ●N-UNCOUNT 不可算名詞 **Slaughter** is also a noun. 食肉処理 ❏ *More than 491,000 sheep were exported for slaughter last year.* 49万1000頭以上のヒツジが昨年食肉処理のために輸出された.

slave /sleɪv/ (**slaves, slaving, slaved**) **1** N-COUNT 可算名詞 A **slave** is someone who is the property of another person and has to work for that person. 奴隷 ❏ *The state of Liberia was formed a century and a half ago by freed slaves from the United States.* リベリア国は米国から解放された奴隷によって150年前に建国された. **2** N-COUNT 可算名詞 You can describe someone as a **slave** when they are completely under the control of another person or of a powerful influence. (比ゆ的に) 奴隷 ❏ *She may no longer be a slave to the studio system, but she still has a duty to her fans.* 彼女はもはやスタジオ・システムの奴隷ではないかもしれないが、今なおファンに対する義務はある. **3** V-I 自動詞 If you say that a person **is slaving over** something or is **slaving for** someone, you mean that they are working very hard. あくせく働く ❏ *When you're busy all day the last thing you want to do is spend hours slaving over a hot stove.* 忙しい1日を過ごしたあと、せっせと料理に何時間も費やすのだけは避けたいやだ. ●PHRASAL VERB 句動詞 **Slave away** means the same as **slave**. せっせと働く ❏ *He stares at the hundreds of workers slaving away in the intense sun.* 彼は、強烈な太陽の光の下でせっせと働く何百人もの労働者を見つめた.

slav|ery /sleɪvəri, sleɪvri/ N-UNCOUNT 不可算名詞 **Slavery** is the system by which people are owned by other people as slaves. 奴隷制度 ❏ *My people have survived 400 years of slavery.* 我が国民は400年間の奴隷制度を生き延びました.

sleaze /sliz/ N-UNCOUNT 不可算名詞 You use **sleaze** to describe activities that you consider immoral, dishonest, or not respectable, especially in politics, business, journalism, or entertainment. 低俗さ、いかがわしさ [INFORMAL くだけた, DISAPPROVAL 不賛成] ❏ *She claimed that an atmosphere of sleaze and corruption now surrounded the government.* 不道徳な雰囲気と汚職が今の政府を取り巻いていると彼女は主張した.

slea|zy /slizi/ (**sleazier, sleaziest**) **1** ADJ 形容詞 If you describe a place as **sleazy**, you dislike it because it looks dirty and badly cared for, and not respectable. いかがわしい、安っぽい [INFORMAL くだけた, DISAPPROVAL 不賛成] ❏ *... sleazy bars.* いかがわしいバー **2** ADJ 形容詞 If you describe something or someone as **sleazy**, you disapprove of them because you think they are not respectable and are rather disgusting. 品がない、いかがわしい [INFORMAL くだけた, DISAPPROVAL 不賛成] ❏ *The accusations are making the government's conduct appear increasingly sleazy.* その告発により政府の品行がますます怪しくなってきた.

sled /slɛd/ (**sleds, sledding, sledded**) **1** N-COUNT 可算名詞 A **sled** is an object used for traveling over snow. It consists of a framework which slides on two strips of wood or metal. そり [AM 米国英語] ❏ *I saw her pulling three children through the snow on a sled.* 彼女が雪の中3人の子供をそりに乗せて引いているのを見た. **2** V-I 自動詞 If you **sled** or go **sledding**, you ride on a sled. そりで滑る [AM 米国英語] ❏ *We got home and went sledding on the small hill in our back yard.* 家に帰り、裏庭にある小さな丘でそり滑りにでかけた.

sledge /slɛdʒ/ (**sledges, sledging, sledged**) **1** N-COUNT 可算名詞 A **sledge** is the same as a **sled**. そり [BRIT 英国英語] **2** V-I 自動詞 If you **sledge** or go **sledging**, you ride on a sledge. そりで滑る [BRIT 英国英語]

sleek /sli̱k/ (**sleeker, sleekest**) **1** ADJ 形容詞 **Sleek** hair or fur is smooth and shiny and looks healthy. 滑らかでつやのある ❏ ...*sleek black hair.* つやのある黒髪 **2** ADJ 形容詞 If you describe someone as **sleek**, you mean that they look rich and stylish. おしゃれな ❏ *Lord White is as sleek and elegant as any other millionaire businessman.* ホワイト卿はほかの大実業家と同様におしゃれで上品だ。 **3** ADJ 形容詞 **Sleek** vehicles, furniture, or other objects look smooth, shiny, and expensive. かっこいい，ピカピカで高級な ❏ ...*a sleek white BMW.* かっこいい白いBMW

sleep /sli̱p/ (**sleeps, sleeping, slept**) **1** N-UNCOUNT 不可算名詞 **Sleep** is the natural state of rest in which your eyes are closed, your body is inactive, and your mind does not think. 眠り，睡眠 ❏ *They were exhausted from lack of sleep.* 彼らは睡眠不足で疲れ切っていた。 ❏ *Be quiet and go to sleep.* おしゃべりはやめて眠りなさい。 **2** V-I 自動詞 When you **sleep**, you rest with your eyes closed and your mind and body inactive. 眠る ❏ *During the drive, the baby slept.* 運転中，赤ちゃんは眠っていた。 ❏ *I've not been able to sleep for the last few nights.* ここ数日眠れないの。 **3** N-COUNT 可算名詞 A **sleep** is a period of sleeping. 睡眠時間 ❏ *I think he may be ready for a sleep soon.* そろそろ彼の寝る時間だと思う。 **4** V-T 他動詞 If a building or room **sleeps** a particular number of people, it has beds for that number of people. 一人宿泊できる [不 cont, no passive] ❏ *The villa sleeps 10.* 別荘には10人泊まれる。 **5** → see also **sleeping** **6** PHRASE 句 If you cannot **get to sleep**, you are unable to sleep. 眠る ❏ *I can't get to sleep with all that singing.* あの歌声がうるさくて眠れない。 **7** PHRASE 句 If you say that you didn't **lose** any **sleep over** something, you mean that you did not worry about it at all. 気掛かりで眠れない ❏ *I didn't lose too much sleep over that investigation.* あの調査が気掛かりで不眠になったわけじゃない。 **8** PHRASE 句 If you are trying to make a decision and you say that you will **sleep on it**, you mean that you will delay making a decision on it until the following day, so you have time to think about it. よく考える ❏ *I need more time to sleep on it. It's a big decision and I want to make the right one.* もう少し考える時間が必要だ。重大な決断だから正しい決断を出したい。 **9** PHRASE 句 If a sick or injured animal **is put to sleep**, it is killed by a vet in a way that does not cause it pain. 安楽死させる ❏ *I'm going take the dog down to the vet's and have her put to sleep.* イヌを獣医に連れて行って安楽死させるつもりです。 **10** to **sleep rough** → see **rough**
→ see Word Web: **sleep**
→ see **dream**

> There are several verbal expressions in English using the noun **sleep** which refer to the moment when you start to sleep. When you go to bed at night, you normally **go to sleep** or **fall asleep**. When you **go to sleep**, it is usually a deliberate action. ❏ *He didn't want to go to sleep.* You can **fall asleep** by accident, or at a time when you should be awake. ❏ *I've seen doctors fall asleep in the operating room.* If you have difficulty sleeping, you can say that you cannot **get to sleep**. ❏ *Sometimes the fever prevents the child from getting to sleep.*

▶ **sleep around** PHRASAL VERB 句動詞 If you say that someone **sleeps around**, you disapprove of them because they have sex with a lot of different people. いろんな人と寝る（肉体関係を持つ）[INFORMAL くだけた, DISAPPROVAL 不賛成] ❏ *I don't sleep around.* 誰とでも寝るわけじゃない。

▶ **sleep in** PHRASAL VERB 句動詞 If you **sleep in**, you stay asleep in the morning for longer than you usually do. 朝寝坊す ❏ *Yesterday, few players turned up because most slept in.* 昨日、ほとんどの選手が朝寝坊をしたので参加者はほとんどいなかった。

▶ **sleep off** PHRASAL VERB 句動詞 If you **sleep off** the effects of too much traveling, drink, or food, you recover from it by sleeping. 眠って治す ❏ *It's a good idea to spend the first night of your vacation sleeping off the jet lag.* 休暇の初日は時差ぼけを治すのにしっかり眠るといいだろう。

▶ **sleep over** PHRASAL VERB 句動詞 If someone, especially a child, **sleeps over** in a place such as a friend's home, they stay there for one night. 人の家に泊まる ❏ *She said his friends could sleep over.* 彼女は、彼の友達が泊まりに来てもいいと言った。

▶ **sleep together** PHRASAL VERB 句動詞 If two people **are sleeping together**, they are having a sexual relationship, but are not usually married to each other. （肉体）関係を持つ ❏ *I'm pretty sure*

they slept together before they were married. あの2人は婚前交渉を持っていたと確信している。

▶ **sleep with** PHRASAL VERB 句動詞 If you **sleep with** someone, you have sex with them. 一と寝る，一とセックスする ❏ *He was old enough to sleep with a girl and make her pregnant.* 彼は女の子と寝て妊娠させてもおかしくない年齢だった。

┌───┐
│ **Thesaurus**   *sleep* また次を参照： │
├───┤
│ N.   nap, rest, slumber **1** **3** │
│ V.   doze, rest, snooze; (*ant.*) awaken, wake **2** │
└───┘

┌───┐
│ **Word Partnership**   *sleep* は次の語句と使われる： │
├───┤
│ V.   **can't/couldn't** sleep, **drift off to** sleep, **get enough** sleep, **get some** sleep, **go to** sleep, **need** sleep **1** │
│ N.   sleep **deprivation**, sleep **disorder**, sleep **on the floor**, **hours of** sleep, **lack of** sleep, sleep **nights** **1** │
│ ADJ.   **deep** sleep **1** **good** sleep **3** │
└───┘

sleep|er /sli̱pər/ (**sleepers**) N-COUNT 可算名詞 You can use **sleeper** to indicate how well someone sleeps. For example, if someone is a light **sleeper**, they are easily woken up. 「眠りが浅い人」「眠りが深い人」などの表現で用いる ❏ *I'm a very light sleeper and I can hardly get any sleep at all.* 私はとても眠りが浅くて、ほとんど全然眠れないの。

sleep|ing bag (**sleeping bags**) N-COUNT 可算名詞 A **sleeping bag** is a large deep bag with a warm lining, used for sleeping in, especially when you are camping. 寝袋

sleep|ing part|ner (**sleeping partners**) N-COUNT 可算名詞 A **sleeping partner** is the same as a **silent partner**. 匿名社員 [BRIT 英国英語 BUSINESS 実業]

sleep|less /sli̱pləs/ **1** ADJ 形容詞 A **sleepless** night is one during which you do not sleep. 眠れない（夜）❏ *I have sleepless nights worrying about her.* 彼女のことが心配で眠れない夜がある。 **2** ADJ 形容詞 Someone who is **sleepless** is unable to sleep. 眠れない、不眠症の ❏ *A sleepless baby can seem to bring little reward.* あまり眠らない赤ちゃんからはあまり子育ての喜びを得られないようだ。

sleep|over /sli̱pou̱vər/ (**sleepovers**) also **sleep-over** N-COUNT 可算名詞 A **sleepover** is an occasion when someone, especially a child, sleeps for one night in a place such as a friend's home. 外泊，友達の家に泊まること ❏ *Emily couldn't ask a friend for a sleepover until she cleaned her room.* エミリーは自分の部屋を片付けるまで友達に泊まりに来るよう誘えなかった。

sleep|walk /sli̱pwɔ̱k/ (**sleepwalks, sleepwalking, sleepwalked**) V-I 自動詞 If someone **is sleepwalking**, they are walking around while they are asleep. 眠ったまま歩き回る、夢中歩行する ❏ *He once sleepwalked to the middle of the road outside his home at 1 a.m.* 彼は一度午前1時に家の前の道の真ん中まで夢中歩行した。

sleepy /sli̱pi/ (**sleepier, sleepiest**) **1** ADJ 形容詞 If you are **sleepy**, you are very tired and are almost asleep. 眠い、眠そうな ❏ *I was beginning to feel amazingly sleepy.* だんだん信じられないくらい眠くなってきた。 ● **sleep|ily** ADV 副詞 [ADV with v] 眠そうに ❏ *Joanna sat up, blinking sleepily.* ジョアンナは起き上がって眠そうにまばたきした。 **2** ADJ 形容詞 A **sleepy** place is quiet and does not have much activity or excitement. 眠ったような、静かで活気がない ❏ *Valence is a sleepy little town just south of Lyon.* バランスはリヨンのすぐ南にある小さな眠ったような町だ。

sleet /sli̱t/ N-UNCOUNT 不可算名詞 **Sleet** is rain that is partly frozen. みぞれ ❏ *...blinding snow, driving sleet and wind.* 目を開けていられないような雪、みぞれ混じりの暴風雨
→ see **water**

sleeve /sli̱v/ (**sleeves**) **1** N-COUNT 可算名詞 The **sleeves** of a coat, shirt, or other item of clothing are the parts that cover your arms. そで ❏ *His sleeves were rolled up to his elbows.* 彼のそではひじまでまくり上げられていた。 **2** N-COUNT 可算名詞 A record **sleeve** is the stiff cover in which a record is kept. ジャケット [mainly BRIT 主に英国英語] ❏ *...an album sleeve.* アルバムのジャケット **3** PHRASE 句 If you have something **up** your **sleeve**, you have an idea or plan which you have not told anyone about. You can also say that

S

┌───┐
│ **Word Web**   sleep │
├───┤
│ Do you ever go to **bed** and then discover you can't **fall asleep**? You start **yawning** and you feel **tired**. But somehow your body isn't ready for a good night's **rest**. You **toss and turn** and pound the **pillow** for hours. After a while you may start to **doze**, but then five minutes later you're **wide awake**. The scientific name for this condition is **insomnia**. There are many causes for sleeplessness like this. If you **nap** too late in the day it may interrupt your normal sleep cycle. Health and job-related worries can also affect sleep patterns. │
└───┘

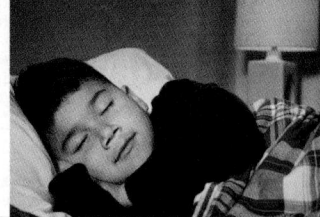

someone has **an ace, card,** or **trick up** their **sleeve**. ひそかに用意している □*He wondered what tricks Shearson had up his sleeve.* 彼はシアソンがひそかにどんな裏技を隠し持っているのかなと思った.

sleigh /sleɪ/ (**sleighs**) N-COUNT 可算名詞 A **sleigh** is a vehicle which can slide over snow. Sleighs are usually pulled by horses. (馬車の) そり

slen|der /slɛndər/ ◼ ADJ 形容詞 A **slender** person is attractively thin and graceful. すらりとした, スマートな [WRITTEN 書き言葉, APPROVAL 賛成] □*She was slender, with delicate wrists and ankles.* 彼女はきゃしゃな手首と足首をして, すらりとしていた. □*...a tall, slender figure in a straw hat.* 麦わら帽子をかぶってすらりと背が高い人影 ◼ ADJ 形容詞 You can use **slender** to describe a situation which exists but only to a very small degree. わずかな [WRITTEN 書き言葉] □*The United States held a slender lead.* 米国がわずかに首位を維持した.

slept /slɛpt/ **Slept** is the past tense and past participle of **sleep**. sleepの過去・過去分詞

slice /slaɪs/ (**slices, slicing, sliced**) ◼ N-COUNT 可算名詞 A **slice** of bread, meat, fruit, or other food is a thin piece that has been cut from a larger piece. 薄切り □*Try to eat at least four slices of bread a day.* 少なくともパンを1日4切れ食べるようにしなさい. ◼ V-T 他動詞 If you **slice** bread, meat, fruit, or other food, you cut it into thin pieces. 薄く切る, 切り分ける □*Helen sliced the cake.* ヘレンはケーキを切り分けた. ● PHRASAL VERB 句動詞 **Slice up** means the same as **slice**. 薄く切る, 切り分ける □*I sliced up an onion.* タマネギを薄切りにしました. ◼ N-COUNT 可算名詞 You can use **slice** to refer to a part of a situation or activity. 部分 □*Fiction takes up a large slice of the publishing market.* フィクションは出版市場のかなりの部分を占める. ◼ **slice of the action** → see **action** → see **cut**

> **Word Partnership** slice は次の語句と使われる:
>
> | | |
> |---|---|
> | ADJ. | **small** slice, **thin** slice ◼ |
> | N. | slice **of bread**, slice **of pie**, slice **of pizza** ◼ |
> | | slice **a cake** ◼ |
> | | slice **of life** ◼ |
> | PREP. | slice **into**, slice **off**, slice **through** ◼ |

slick /slɪk/ (**slicker, slickest**) ◼ ADJ 形容詞 A **slick** performance, production, or advertisement is skillful and impressive. 素晴らしい □*There's a big difference between an amateur video and a slick Hollywood production.* アマチュアのビデオと本格的なハリウッドの製作には大きな違いがある. ◼ ADJ 形容詞 A **slick** action is done quickly and smoothly, and without any obvious effort. 滑らかな, 無駄のない □*They were outplayed by the Colombians' slick passing and decisive finishing.* 彼らはコロンビアチームに無駄のないパスと決定的なシュートで負けた. ◼ ADJ 形容詞 A **slick** person speaks easily in a way that is likely to convince people, but is not sincere. 口先がうまい [DISAPPROVAL 不賛成] □*Don't be fooled by slick politicians.* 口先がうまい政治家にだまされてはいけません. ◼ N-COUNT 可算名詞 A **slick** is the same as an **oil slick**. 油膜 □*Experts are trying to devise ways to clean up the huge slick.* 専門家は, その巨大な油膜の清掃方法を考案中です.

slide /slaɪd/ (**slides, sliding, slid**) ◼ V-T/V-I 他動詞/自動詞 When something **slides** somewhere or when you **slide** it there, it moves there smoothly over or against something. 滑らせる [他動詞], 滑る [自動詞] □*She slid the door open.* 彼女はドアをするすると開けた. □*I slid the wallet into his pocket.* 私は財布を彼のポケットに滑り込ませた. ◼ V-I 自動詞 If you **slide** somewhere, you move there smoothly and quietly. こっそり動く □*He slid into the driver's seat.* 彼はそっと運転席に滑り込んだ. ◼ V-I 自動詞 To **slide into** a particular mood, attitude, or situation means to gradually start to have that mood, attitude, or situation often without intending to. 陥る □*She had slid into a depression.* 彼女はうつ状態に陥った. ◼ V-T/V-I 他動詞/自動詞 If currencies or prices **slide**, they gradually become worse or lower in value. 下がる, 下落する [JOURNALISM ジャーナリズム] □*The dollar continued to slide.* ドルが下落し続けました. ● N-COUNT 可算名詞 **Slide** is also a noun. 下落 □*...the dangerous slide in oil prices.* 原油価格の危険な下落 ◼ N-COUNT 可算名詞 A **slide** is a small piece of photographic film which you project onto a screen so that you can see the picture. スライド □*...a slide show.* スライドショー ◼ N-COUNT 可算名詞 A **slide** is a piece of glass on which you put something that you want to examine through a microscope. スライドガラス, スライド □*...a drop of blood on a slide.* スライドに落とした1滴の血液 ◼ N-COUNT 可算名詞 A **slide** is a piece of playground equipment that has a steep slope for children to go down for fun. 滑り台 □*...two young children playing on a slide.* 滑り台で遊んでいる2人の小さな子供たち

> **Word Partnership** slide は次の語句と使われる:
>
> | | |
> |---|---|
> | V. | **begin to** slide, **continue to** slide ◼ – ◼ |
> | ADJ. | **downward** slide, **recent** slide, **steep** slide ◼ |

slight /slaɪt/ (**slighter, slightest, slights, slighting, slighted**) ◼ ADJ 形容詞 Something that is **slight** is very small in degree or quantity. わずかな □*Doctors say he has made a slight improvement.* 医者は, 彼がわずかに回復したと述べている. □*He's not the slightest bit worried.* 彼はちっとも心配していません. ◼ ADJ 形容詞 A **slight** person has a fairly thin and delicate looking body. きゃしゃな □*She is smaller and slighter than Christie.* 彼女はクリスティーよりも小柄できゃしゃだ. ● **slight|ly** ADV 副詞 [ADV -ed] きゃしゃな体つきの □*...a slightly built man.* きゃしゃな体つきの男 ◼ V-T 他動詞 If you **are slighted**, someone does or says something that insults you by treating you as if your views or feelings are not important. 軽んじる, 侮辱する [usu passive] □*They felt slighted by not being adequately consulted.* 彼らは十分に相談を受けなかったことで侮辱されたように感じました. ● N-COUNT 可算名詞 **Slight** is also a noun. 軽視, 侮辱 □*It's difficult to persuade my husband that it isn't a slight on him that I enjoy my evening class.* 私が夜間講座を楽しんでいるのは夫に対する侮辱ではないことを説得するのは難しい. ◼ PHRASE 句 You use **in the slightest** to emphasize a negative statement. 少しも [EMPHASIS 強調] □*That doesn't interest me in the slightest.* 私はそれには全く興味がない.

slight|ly /slaɪtli/ ADV 副詞 **Slightly** means to some degree but not to a very large degree. わずかに □*His family then moved to a slightly larger house.* 彼の家族はそのあと少し大き目の家に引っ越した. □*Each person learns in a slightly different way.* 各自わずかに異なった方法で学習する.

slim /slɪm/ (**slimmer, slimmest, slims, slimming, slimmed**) ◼ ADJ 形容詞 A **slim** person has an attractively thin and well-shaped body. ほっそりした, スリムな [APPROVAL 賛成] □*The young woman was tall and slim.* その若い女性は背が高くすらりとしていた. ◼ ADJ 形容詞 A **slim** book, wallet, or other object is thinner than usual. 薄い □*The slim booklets describe a range of services and facilities.* その薄い小冊子には一連のサービスと施設について説明されている. ◼ ADJ 形容詞 A **slim** chance or possibility is a very small one. わずかな □*There's still a slim chance that he may become president.* 彼が大統領になる可能性はわずかに残っている. ◼ V-T 他動詞 If an organization **slims** its products or workers, it reduces the number of them that it has. 縮小する, 削減する [BUSINESS 実業] □*The company recently slimmed its product line.* その会社は最近製品ラインを縮小しました.

▶ **slim down** ◼ PHRASAL VERB 句動詞 If you **slim down**, you lose weight and become thinner. 減量する, やせる □*His family will lose weight when they slim down with a friend.* 友達とダイエットをすると減量できるだろう. ◼ PHRASAL VERB 句動詞 If a company or other organization **slims down** or is **slimmed down**, it employs fewer people, in order to save money or become more efficient. リストラする, 規模縮小する [BUSINESS 実業] □*Many firms have had little choice but to slim down.* リストラ以外にほとんど選択肢がない会社が多い.

> **Word Partnership** slim は次の語句と使われる:
>
> | | |
> |---|---|
> | ADJ. | **tall and** slim ◼ |
> | ADV. | **pretty** slim, **very** slim ◼ ◼ |
> | N. | slim **chance**, slim **lead**, slim **margin** ◼ |

slime /slaɪm/ N-UNCOUNT 不可算名詞 **Slime** is a thick, wet substance which covers a surface or comes from the bodies of animals such as snails. 粘液 ぬるぬる, ねばねばするもの □*He swam down and retrieved his glasses from the muck and slime at the bottom of the pond.* 彼は潜って, どろどろでぬるぬるした池の底から眼鏡を取ってきた.

slimy /slaɪmi/ (**slimier, slimiest**) ADJ 形容詞 **Slimy** substances are thick, wet, and unpleasant. **Slimy** objects are covered in a slimy substance. ぬるぬるした, ねばねばした □*His feet slipped in the slimy mud.* 彼の足がぬるぬるした泥に滑り込んだ.

sling /slɪŋ/ (**slings, slinging, slung**) ◼ V-T 他動詞 If you **sling** something somewhere, you throw it there carelessly. ほうり投げる □*Marla was recently seen slinging her shoes at Trump.* マーラは最近彼女の靴をトランプにほうり投げるのを見られた. ◼ V-T 他動詞 If you **sling** something over your shoulder or over something such as a chair, you hang it there loosely. ぶら下げる □*She slung her coat over her desk chair.* 彼女はコートをいすに掛けた. □*He had a small green backpack slung over one shoulder.* 彼は, 片方の肩に小さな緑色のバックパックを掛けていた. ◼ V-T 他動詞 If a rope, blanket, or other object **is slung** between two points, someone has hung it loosely between them. つるす [usu passive] □*...two long poles with a blanket slung between them.* 毛布を間につるした2本の長い棒 ◼ N-COUNT 可算名詞 A **sling** is an object made of ropes, straps, or cloth that is used for carrying things. つり網, つり革 □*They used slings of rope to lower us from one set of arms to another.* 彼らは, 私たちを腕から腕に渡すのに縄網を使った. ◼ N-COUNT 可算名詞 A **sling** is a piece of cloth which supports someone's broken or injured arm and is tied around their neck. 三角きん, つり包帯 □*She was back at work with her arm in a sling.* 彼女は三角きんに腕をつって仕事に復帰した.

sling|shot /slɪŋʃɒt/ (slingshots) N-COUNT 可算名詞 A slingshot is a device for shooting small stones. It is made of a Y-shaped stick with a piece of elastic tied between the two top posts. パチンコ [AM 米国英語]

slip /slɪp/ (slips, slipping, slipped) **1** V-I 自動詞 If you **slip**, you accidentally slide and lose your balance. 足を滑らせる □He had slipped on an icy pavement. 彼は凍った歩道で足を滑らせた. **2** V-I 自動詞 If something **slips**, it slides out of place or out of your hand. 滑る, 滑り落ちる □His glasses had slipped. 彼の眼鏡が滑り落ちた. **3** V-I 自動詞 If you **slip** somewhere, you go there quickly and quietly. そっと行く, こっそり行く □Amy slipped downstairs and out of the house. エイミーはこっそり1階に降りて家を出た. **4** V-T 他動詞 If you **slip** something somewhere, you put it there quickly in a way that does not attract attention. さっと置く □I slipped a note under Louise's door. 私はルイーズのドアの下にメモをさっと差し込んだ. □He found a coin in his pocket and slipped it into her hand. 彼はポケットの中にコインを見つけたのですっと彼女の手に渡した. **5** V-T 他動詞 If you **slip** something **to** someone, you give it to them secretly. こっそり渡す □Robert had slipped her a note in school. ロバートは学校で彼女にこっそりメモを手渡した. **6** V-I 自動詞 To **slip into** a particular state or situation means to pass gradually into it, in a way that is hardly noticed. (うっかりーという状態に) なっていく, はまる □It amazed him how easily one could slip into a routine. 彼は, 人がいかに習慣にはまりやすいかに驚いた. **7** V-T/V-I 他動詞/自動詞 If something **slips to** a lower level or standard, it goes to that level or standard. 低下する, 下落する □Shares slipped to $1.17. 株価は1.17ドルまで低下した. □In June, producer prices slipped 0.1% from May. 6月には生産者物価指数が前月比0.1%低下した. ●N-SING 単数名詞 **Slip** is also a noun. 低下 □...a slip in consumer confidence. 消費者の信頼が低下 **8** V-T/V-I 他動詞/自動詞 If you **slip into** or **out of** clothes or shoes, you put them on or take them off quickly and easily. さっと着る/はく/脱ぐ □She slipped out of the jacket and tossed it on the couch. 彼女はさっと上着を脱いでソファーの上にぽんと置いた. **9** N-COUNT 可算名詞 A **slip** is a small or unimportant mistake. ちょっとしたミス □We must be well prepared; there must be no slips. ミスのないようにしっかりと準備しなければならない. **10** N-COUNT 可算名詞 A **slip** of paper is a small piece of paper. 紙片 □...little slips of paper he had torn from a notebook. 彼がノートから破った小さな紙片 □I put her name on the slip. 私は紙片に彼女の名前を書いた. **11** N-COUNT 可算名詞 A **slip** is a thin piece of clothing that a woman wears under her dress or skirt. スリップ **12** PHRASE 句 If you **let slip** information, you accidentally tell it to someone, when you wanted to keep it secret. うっかり口を滑らせる □I bet he let slip that I'd gone to America. きっと彼は私がアメリカに行ったことをうっかりもらしたに違いない. **13** PHRASE 句 If something **slips** your **mind**, you forget about it. うっかり忘れる □The reason for my visit had obviously slipped his mind. 彼は, 私が訪れた理由を明らかに忘れたようだ.

▶ **slip up** PHRASAL VERB 句動詞 If you **slip up**, you make a small or unimportant mistake. うっかりミスをする □There were occasions when we slipped up. 私たちはうっかりミスをしたこともある.

Thesaurus	slip また次を参照:
V.	fall, slide, trip **1**
N.	blunder, failure, flub, foul-up, mistake **9**
	leaf, page, paper, sheet **10**

Word Partnership	slip は次の語句と使われる:
ADJ.	slip **resistant** **1**
N.	slip **of paper**, **sales** slip **10**
V.	**let** (something) slip **12**

slip|page /slɪpɪdʒ/ (slippages) N-VAR 可変性名詞 **Slippage** is a failure to maintain a steady position or rate of progress, so that a particular target or standard is not achieved. ずれ, 低下 □...a substantial slippage in the value of sterling. 英国ポンド価値のかなりの下落

slip|per /slɪpər/ (slippers) N-COUNT 可算名詞 **Slippers** are loose, soft shoes that you wear at home. 室内履き, スリッパ □...a pair of old slippers. 古いスリッパ1足

slip|pery /slɪpəri/ **1** ADJ 形容詞 Something that is **slippery** is smooth, wet, or oily and is therefore difficult to walk on or to hold. つるつるした, 滑りやすい □The tiled floor was wet and slippery. タイルの床は濡れていて滑りやすかった. **2** ADJ 形容詞 You can describe someone as **slippery** if you think that they are dishonest in a clever way and cannot be trusted. 当てにならない, ずるい [DISAPPROVAL 不賛成] □He is a slippery customer, and should be carefully watched. 彼は横着な客だから気をつけて監視するべきだ. **3** PHRASE 句 If someone is on a **slippery slope**, they are involved in a course of action that is difficult to stop and that will eventually lead to failure or trouble. 危険な坂道 □The company started down the slippery slope of believing that they knew better than the customer. その会社は, 客よりもわきまえていると信じて危険な下り坂を下り始めた.

slit /slɪt/ (slits, slitting)

The form **slit** is used in the present tense and is the past tense and past participle.

slit 形は現在時制に使われ, 過去時制と過去分詞でもある.

1 V-T 他動詞 If you **slit** something, you make a long narrow cut in it. 細長く切れ目を入れる □They say somebody slit her throat. 誰かが彼女ののどをかき切ったらしい. □He began to slit open each envelope. 彼は封筒を1枚ずつ切って開け始めた. **2** N-COUNT 可算名詞 A **slit** is a long narrow cut. 細長い切り込み, スリット □Make a slit in the stem about half an inch long. 茎に約半インチの切込みを入れなさい. **3** N-COUNT 可算名詞 A **slit** is a long narrow opening in something. すき間 □She watched them through a slit in the curtains. 彼女はカーテンのすき間から彼らを見た.
→ see shark

slith|er /slɪðər/ (slithers, slithering, slithered) **1** V-I 自動詞 If you **slither** somewhere, you slide along in an uneven way. ずるずる滑る □Robert lost his footing and slithered down the bank. ロバートは足を踏み外して土手をずるずると滑り落ちた. **2** V-I 自動詞 If an animal such as a snake **slithers**, it moves along in a curving way. にょろにょろはう, するするする □The snake slithered into the water. ヘビがするすると水の中へはって行った.

sliv|er /slɪvər/ (slivers) N-COUNT 可算名詞 A **sliver of** something is a small thin piece or amount of it. 窓があった場所にはガラスの破片1つありませんでした. □Not a sliver of glass remains where the windows were. 窓があった場所にはガラスの破片1つありませんでした.

slog /slɒg/ (slogs, slogging, slogged) **1** V-T/V-I 他動詞/自動詞 If you **slog through** something, you work hard and steadily through it. コツコツと癒ばる [INFORMAL くだけた] □They secure their degrees by slogging through an intensive 11-month course. 彼らは11か月集中講座をコツコツと癒ばって学位を確保する. ●PHRASAL VERB 句動詞 **Slog away** means the same as slog. コツコツと癒ばる □Edward slogged away, always learning. エドワードはいつも学びながらコツコツと癒ばった. **2** N-SING 単数名詞 If you describe a task as a **slog**, you mean that it is tiring and requires a lot of effort. 苦難, 大変 [INFORMAL くだけた] [also no det] □There is little to show for the two years of hard slog. 2年間の大変な努力の成果を見せるものはほとんどない.

slo|gan /sloʊgən/ (slogans) N-COUNT 可算名詞 A **slogan** is a short phrase that is easy to remember. Slogans are used in advertisements and by political parties and other organizations who want people to remember what they are saying or selling. スローガン, 標語, キャッチコピー □They could campaign on the slogan "We'll take less of your money." 「We'll take less of your money (安さでは負けません)」というキャッチコピーでキャンペーンができる.

slop /slɒp/ (slops, slopping, slopped) V-T/V-I 他動詞/自動詞 If liquid **slops** from a container or if you **slop** liquid somewhere, it comes out over the edge of the container, usually accidentally. こぼれる □A little cognac slopped over the edge of the glass. コニャックが少しグラスの縁からこぼれた.

slope /sloʊp/ (slopes, sloping, sloped) **1** N-COUNT 可算名詞 A **slope** is the side of a mountain, hill, or valley. 斜面 □Saint-Christo is perched on a mountain slope. 聖クリストファー像が山の斜面に置かれている. **2** N-COUNT 可算名詞 A **slope** is a surface that is at an angle, so that one end is higher than the other. 坂 □The street must have been on a slope. その通りは坂になっていたに違いない. **3** V-I 自動詞 If a surface **slopes**, it is at an angle, so that one end is higher than the other. 傾斜する □The bank sloped down sharply to the river. 岸は川の方に急な傾斜をしていた. ●**slop|ing** ADJ 形容詞 傾斜した □...a brick building, with a sloping roof. 傾斜した屋根のレンガ造りの建物 **4** V-I 自動詞 If something **slopes**, it leans to the right or to the left rather than being upright. 傾く □The writing sloped backwards. その筆跡は右上がりだった. **5** N-COUNT 可算名詞 The **slope** of something is the angle at which it slopes. 傾斜 □The slope increases as you go up the curve. カーブを上るにつれて傾斜が増す. **6** slippery slope → see slippery

slop|py /slɒpi/ (sloppier, sloppiest) ADJ 形容詞 If you describe someone's work or activities as **sloppy**, you mean they have been done in a careless and lazy way. ずさんな [DISAPPROVAL 不賛成] □He has little patience for sloppy work from colleagues. 彼は同僚のずさんな仕事にはほとんど我慢ができない.

slot /slɒt/ (slots, slotting, slotted) **1** N-COUNT 可算名詞 A **slot** is a narrow opening in a machine or container, for example, a hole that you put coins in to make a machine work. 挿入口 □He dropped a coin into the slot and dialed. 彼はコインを投入口に入れて電話した. **2** V-T/V-I 他動詞/自動詞 If you **slot** something into something else, or if it **slots** into it, you put it into a space where it fits. 差し込む, はめ込む □He was slotting a CD into a CD player. 彼はCDをCDプレーヤーに入れていた. □The car seat belt slotted into place easily. その車のシートベルトははめやすかった. **3** N-COUNT 可算名詞 A **slot** in a schedule or program is a place in it where an activity can take place. 時間枠 □Visitors can book a time slot a week or more in advance. 観光客は1週間以上前から予約ができる.

slouch /slaʊtʃ/ (**slouches, slouching, slouched**) V-I 自動詞 If someone **slouches**, they sit or stand with their shoulders and head bent so they look lazy and unattractive. 前かがみになる（だらっとした姿勢）❑ *Try not to slouch when you are sitting down.* 座っているときは前かがみにならないようにしなさい。

slow /sloʊ/ (**slower, slowest, slows, slowing, slowed**) ◼ ADJ 形容詞 Something that is **slow** moves, happens, or is done without much speed. （スピードが）遅い❑ *The traffic is heavy and slow.* 交通量が多くてなかなか進みません。❑ *Electric whisks should be used on a slow speed.* 電気泡立て器を遅いスピードで使うべきだ。● **slow|ly** ADV 副詞 [ADV with v] ゆっくりと❑ *He spoke slowly and deliberately.* 彼はゆっくりと意図的に話した。● **slow|ness** N-UNCOUNT 不可算名詞 遅さ❑ *She lowered the glass with calculated slowness.* 彼女は意図的にゆっくりとグラスを下げた。◼ ADV 副詞 [ADV after v] In informal English, **slower** is used to mean "at a slower speed" and **slowest** is used to mean "at the slowest speed." In nonstandard English, **slow** is used to mean "with little speed." ゆっくりと❑ *I began to walk slower and slower.* 歩く速度がだんだんと遅くなった。◼ ADJ 形容詞 Something that is **slow** takes a long time. 時間がかかる❑ *The distribution of passports has been a slow process.* パスポート発行には時間がかかっている。● **slow|ly** ADV 副詞 [ADV with v] 徐々に、だんだんと❑ *My resentment of her slowly began to fade.* 彼女に対する怒りはだんだんと薄れてきた。● **slow|ness** N-UNCOUNT 不可算名詞 時間がかかること❑ *...the slowness of political and economic progress.* 政治的また経済的進歩に時間がかかること◼ ADJ 形容詞 [v-link ADJ] If someone is **slow** to do something, they do it after a delay. 遅れてーする❑ *The world community has been slow to respond to the crisis.* 国際社会はこの危機への対処が遅れています。◼ V-T/V-I 他動詞/自動詞 If something **slows** or if you **slow** it, it starts to move or happen more slowly. 速度を落とさせる、鈍化させる [他動詞]、速度を落とす、遅くなる [自動詞]❑ *The rate of bombing has slowed considerably.* 爆撃の速度がかなり遅くなりました。❑ *She slowed the car and began driving up a narrow road.* 彼女は車のスピードを落とし、細い道に入った。◼ ADJ 形容詞 Someone who is **slow** is not very clever and takes a long time to understand things. （理解・のみ込みが）遅い❑ *He got hit on the head and he's been a bit slow since.* 彼は頭を打ってからちょっと遅くなった。◼ ADJ 形容詞 If you describe a situation, place, or activity as **slow**, you mean that it is not very exciting. 活気がない❑ *Don't be faint-hearted when things seem a bit slow or boring.* 少しぐらい沈滞気味だったりつまらないからといってやる気をなくすな。◼ ADJ 形容詞 If a clock or watch is **slow**, it shows a time that is earlier than the correct time. 遅れている❑ *The clock is about two and a half minutes slow.* その時計は約2分半遅れている。◼ **slowly but surely** → see **surely**

▶ **slow down** ◼ PHRASAL VERB 句動詞 If something **slows down** or if something **slows** it **down**, it starts to move or happen more slowly. 速度を落とす❑ *The bus slowed down for the next stop.* そのバスは次のバス停で止まるために速度を落とした。❑ *There is no cure for the disease, although drugs can slow down its rate of development.* その病気の進行速度を落とす薬はあるが治療薬はない。◼ PHRASAL VERB 句動詞 If someone **slows down** or if something **slows** them **down**, they become less active. のんびりする❑ *You will need to slow down for a while.* しばらくの間のんびりする必要がある。◼ → see also **slowdown**

▶ **slow up** PHRASAL VERB 句動詞 **Slow up** means the same as **slow down** 1. 速度を落とす❑ *Sales are slowing up.* 売上が落ちている。

Word Partnership	slow は次の語句と使われる:
ADJ.	slow **acting**, slow **moving** ◼ slow **but steady** ◼ ◼
N.	slow **movements**, slow **speed**, slow **traffic** ◼ slow **death**, slow **growth**, slow **pace**, slow **process**, slow **progress**, slow **recovery**, slow **response**, slow **sales**, slow **start**, slow **stop** ◼

slow|down /sloʊdaʊn/ (**slowdowns**) ◼ N-COUNT 可算名詞 A **slowdown** is a reduction in speed or activity. 減速❑ *There has been a sharp slowdown in economic growth.* 経済成長が急に減速している。◼ N-COUNT 可算名詞 A **slowdown** is a protest in which workers deliberately work slowly and cause problems for their employers. サボタージュ、怠業 [AM 米国英語 BUSINESS 実業]❑ *It's impossible to assess how many officers are participating in the slowdown.* サボへの参加者数を見積もるものは不可能です。

slow mo|tion also **slow-motion** N-UNCOUNT 不可算名詞 When film or television pictures are shown **in slow motion**, they are shown much more slowly than normal. スローモーション❑ *It seemed almost as if he were falling in slow motion.* まるで彼がスローモーションで落ちているようだった。

sludge /slʌdʒ/ (**sludges**) N-VAR 可変性名詞 **Sludge** is thick mud, sewage, or industrial waste. 汚泥、ヘどろ❑ *More than a million gallons of sludge has seeped into the water.* 100万ガロン以上の汚泥が水に浸透しました。

slug /slʌg/ (**slugs**) ◼ N-COUNT 可算名詞 A **slug** is a small slow-moving creature with a long soft body and no legs, like a snail

without a shell. ナメクジ◼ N-COUNT 可算名詞 If you take a **slug of** an alcoholic drink, you take a large mouthful of it. 一口分 [INFORMAL くだけた]❑ *Edgar took a slug of his drink.* エドガーはごくんと一口飲んだ。

slug|gish /slʌgɪʃ/ ADJ 形容詞 You can describe something as **sluggish** if it moves, works, or reacts much slower than you would like or is normal. 不振な、不調な❑ *The economy remains sluggish.* 経済は依然として低迷しています。❑ *Circulation is much more sluggish in the feet than in the hands.* 血液循環は手よりも足の方がずっと悪い。

slum /slʌm/ (**slums**) N-COUNT 可算名詞 A **slum** is an area of a city where living conditions are very bad and where the houses are in bad condition. スラム街、貧民街❑ *...a slum area of St. Louis.* 聖ルイスの貧民地区

slum|ber /slʌmbər/ (**slumbers, slumbering, slumbered**) N-VAR 可変性名詞 **Slumber** is sleep. 眠り [LITERARY 文語的]❑ *He had fallen into exhausted slumber.* 彼は疲れて眠りこけた。● V-I 自動詞 **Slumber** is also a verb. 眠る❑ *The older three girls are still slumbering peacefully.* 上の3人の女の子たちはまだ安らかに眠っている。

slum|ber par|ty (**slumber parties**) N-COUNT 可算名詞 A **slumber party** is an occasion when a group of young friends spend the night together at the home of one of the group. お泊り会、パジャマパーティ [mainly AM 主に米国英語]❑ *I'm having a slumber party for my birthday.* 誕生日にはお泊りパーティをする。

slump /slʌmp/ (**slumps, slumping, slumped**) ◼ V-I 自動詞 If something such as the value of something **slumps**, it falls suddenly and by a large amount. 急落する❑ *Net profits slumped by 41%.* 純利益が41%急落した。● N-COUNT 可算名詞 **Slump** is also a noun. 急落❑ *The council's land is now worth much less than originally hoped because of a slump in property prices.* 自治体所有地の地価は、不動産価格が急落したため今では当初の期待をかなり下回る。◼ N-COUNT 可算名詞 A **slump** is a time when many people in a country are unemployed and poor. 不況❑ *...the slump of the early 1980s.* 1980年代初めの不況◼ V-T/V-I 他動詞/自動詞 If you **slump** somewhere, you fall or sit down there heavily, for example, because you are very tired or you feel ill. 倒れ込む、座り込む❑ *She slumped into a chair.* 彼女はいすに座り込んだ。

slung /slʌŋ/ **Slung** is the past tense and past participle of **sling**. sling の過去形・過去分詞

slur /slɜr/ (**slurs, slurring, slurred**) ◼ N-COUNT 可算名詞 A **slur** is an insulting remark which could damage someone's reputation. 中傷❑ *This is yet another slur on the integrity of the police.* これは警察の品位に対するまた新たな中傷だ。◼ V-T/V-I 他動詞/自動詞 If someone **slurs** their speech or if their speech **slurs**, they do not pronounce each word clearly, because they are drunk, ill, or sleepy. ろれつが まわらない、分かりにくい話し方をする❑ *He repeated himself and slurred his words more than usual.* 彼はいつもより話がくどくて分かりにくかった。

slurp /slɜrp/ (**slurps, slurping, slurped**) ◼ V-T/V-I 他動詞/自動詞 If you **slurp** a liquid, you drink it noisily. 音を立ててすする❑ *He blew on his soup before slurping it off the spoon.* 彼はスープをフウフウ吹いてスプーンからジュルジュルとすすった。◼ N-COUNT 可算名詞 A **slurp** is a noise that you make with your mouth when you drink noisily, or a mouthful of liquid that you drink noisily. すする音❑ *He takes a slurp from a cup of black coffee.* 彼はブラックコーヒーを1口すすって飲んだ。

slush /slʌʃ/ N-UNCOUNT 不可算名詞 **Slush** is snow that has begun to melt and is therefore very wet and dirty. 解けかけの雪❑ *Front-drive cars work better in the snow and slush.* 雪やぬかるみの中では前輪駆動車の方が走りやすい。

slush fund (**slush funds**) N-COUNT 可算名詞 A **slush fund** is a sum of money collected to pay for an illegal activity, especially in politics or business. 不正資金❑ *He's accused of misusing $17.5 million from a secret government slush fund.* 彼は政府の秘密の不正資金から1750万ドルを悪用したことで告発されています。

sly /slaɪ/ ◼ ADJ 形容詞 A **sly** look, expression, or remark shows that you know something that other people do not know or that was meant to be a secret. 隠し立てのあるような❑ *His lips were spread in a sly smile.* 彼の唇に隠し立てをしたような笑いが浮かんでいた。● **sly|ly** ADV 副詞 隠し立てがあるように❑ *Anna grinned slyly.* アナはきまり悪そうに笑った。◼ ADJ 形容詞 If you describe someone as **sly**, you disapprove of them because they keep their feelings or intentions hidden and are clever at deceiving people. ずる賢い [DISAPPROVAL 不賛成]❑ *She is devious and sly and manipulative.* 彼女はこうかつでずる賢く、人を操るのが上手だ。

smack /smæk/ (**smacks, smacking, smacked**) ◼ V-T 他動詞 If you **smack** someone, you hit them with your hand. 平手打ちする❑ *She smacked me on the side of the head.* 彼女は私の側頭を平手打ちした。● N-COUNT 可算名詞 **Smack** is also a noun. 平手打ち❑ *Sometimes he just doesn't listen and I end up shouting at him or giving him a smack.* ときどき彼はただ話を聞かないので、結局は大声でどなったり、平手打ちを食らわしたりしてしまいます。◼ V-T 他動詞 If

you **smack** something somewhere, you put it or throw it there so that it makes a loud, sharp noise. パシッとたたきつける ❑ He smacked his hands down on his knees. 彼はひざに両手をパンとたたきつけた. ❸ V-I 自動詞 If one thing **smacks of** another thing that you consider bad, it reminds you of it or is like it. ～じみたところがある, ～気味である ❑ The engineers' union was unhappy with the motion, saying it smacked of racism. 技術系社員の組合が, その提案が人種差別的であるといって不満だった. ❹ ADV 副詞 Something that is **smack** in a particular place is exactly in that place. ちょうど [INFORMAL くだけた] [ADV prep] ❑ In part that's because industry is smack in the middle of the city. 1つには産業がちょうど町の中心地にあるのが理由です. ❺ N-UNCOUNT 不可算名詞 **Smack** is heroin. ヘロイン [INFORMAL くだけた] ❑ ...a smack addict. ヘロイン中毒者 ❻ PHRASE 句 If you **smack** your **lips**, you open and close your mouth noisily, especially before or after eating, to show that you are eager to eat or enjoyed eating. 舌鼓を打つ ❑ "I really want some dessert," Keaton says, smacking his lips. 「すごくデザートが食べたい」とキートンは舌鼓を打ちながら言った.

small /smɔl/ (smaller, smallest) ❶ ADJ 形容詞 A **small** person, thing, or amount of something is not large in physical size. 小さい ❑ She is small for her age. 彼女は年齢の割には背が低いです. ❑ Stick them on using a small amount of glue. 少量ののりを使って貼り付けなさい. ❷ ADJ 形容詞 A **small** group or quantity consists of only a few people or things. 少ない ❑ A small group of students meets regularly to learn Japanese. 学生の小グループが日本語の学習のために定期的に集まっています. ❸ ADJ 形容詞 A **small** child is a very young child. 幼い ❑ I have a wife and two small children. 妻と幼い子供が2人います. ❹ ADJ 形容詞 You use **small** to describe something that is not significant or great in degree. ささやかな ❑ It's quite easy to make quite small changes to the way that you work. 仕事の仕方をほんの少し変えることはたやすい. ❑ No detail was too small to escape her attention. どのような細かい点も彼女に気づかれずに済むということはなかった. ❺ ADJ 形容詞 **Small** businesses or companies employ a small number of people and do business with a small number of clients. 小規模な ❑ ...shops, restaurants and other small businesses. 店, レストラン, その他の小企業. ❻ ADJ 形容詞 If someone makes you look or feel **small**, they make you look or feel stupid or ashamed. 肩身が狭い, 恥ずかしい [v-link ADJ] ❑ This may just be another of her schemes to make me look small. これは単に私に恥をかかせるための彼女の別策略かもしれない. ❼ N-SING 単数名詞 **The small of** your **back** is the bottom part of your back that curves in slightly. 腰のくびれ部分, ウエスト ❑ Place your hands on the small of your back and breathe in. 両手を腰に置いて息を吸いなさい. ❽ **the small hours** → see hour ❾ **small wonder** → see wonder

> You can use the adjective **small** rather than **little** to draw attention to the fact that something is small. For instance, you cannot say "The town is little" or "I have a very little car," but you can say "**The town is small**" or "**I have a very small car**." **Little** is a less precise word than **small**, and may be used to suggest the speaker's feelings or attitude toward the person or thing being described. For that reason, **little** is often used after another adjective. ❑ What a nice little house you've got here!... ❑ Shut up, you horrible little boy!

Thesaurus

small また次を参照:

ADJ. little, minute, petite, slight; (ant.) big, large ❶
young ❸
insignificant, minor; (ant.) important, major, significant ❹

---

small print N-UNCOUNT 不可算名詞 **The small print** of a contract or agreement is the part of it that is written in very small print. You refer to it as **the small print** especially when you think that it might include unfavorable conditions which someone might not notice or understand. 細字部分 ❑ Read the small print in your contract to find out exactly what you are insured for. 保険対象が何かを正確に理解するために契約書の細字部分を読みなさい.

small-scale ADJ 形容詞 A **small-scale** activity or organization is small in size and limited in extent. 小規模の ❑ ...the small-scale production of farmhouse cheeses in Vermont. バーモント州で小規模生産されている農家手作りチーズ

smart /smɑrt/ (smarter, smartest, smarts, smarting, smarted) ❶ ADJ 形容詞 You can describe someone who is clever or intelligent as **smart**. 頭がいい ❑ He thinks he's smarter than Sarah is. 彼は, 自分がサラよりも頭がいいと思っている. ❷ ADJ 形容詞 **Smart** people and things are pleasantly neat and clean in appearance. きちんとした格好の, スマートな [mainly BRIT 主に英国英語] ❑ He was smart and well groomed but not good looking. 彼はスマートで身だしなみがよいがハンサムではなかった. ❑ I was dressed in a smart navy blue suit. 私は, おしゃれなネービーブルーのスーツを着ていた. ● **smart|ly** ADV 副詞 [ADV with v] おしゃれに, スマートに ❑ He dressed very smartly, which was important in those days. 彼はきちんとした服装をしていたが, それは当時大切だった. ❸ ADJ 形容詞 A **smart**

place or event is connected with wealthy and fashionable people. 上流の, あかぬけした [mainly BRIT 主に英国英語] ❑ ...smart dinner parties. 洗練されたディナーパーティ ❹ V-I 自動詞 If a part of your body or a wound **smarts**, you feel a sharp stinging pain in it. ずきずき痛む ❑ My eyes smarted from the smoke. 煙で目が痛かった. ❺ V-I 自動詞 If you **are smarting** from something such as criticism or failure, you feel upset about it. 憤慨する [JOURNALISM ジャーナリズム] [usu cont] ❑ The Americans were still smarting from their defeat in the Vietnam War. アメリカ人はベトナム戦争での敗戦になお憤慨していた.

smart card (smart cards) N-COUNT 可算名詞 A **smart card** is a plastic card which looks like a credit card and can store and process computer data. スマートカード ❑ We encourage the use of smart cards for online payments. オンラインでの支払いにスマートカードの使用を奨励している.

smart|en /smɑrtⁿn/ (smartens, smartening, smartened)
▸ **smarten up** PHRASAL VERB 句動詞 If you **smarten** yourself or a place **up**, you make yourself or the place look neater and tidier. 見栄えをよくする, きれいにする ❑ ...a 10-year program to smarten up the city. 町の外観を向上させるための10年計画 ❑ She had wisely smartened herself up. 彼女は抜け目なく身なりを整えていた.

smash /smæʃ/ (smashes, smashing, smashed) ❶ V-T/V-I 他動詞/自動詞 If you **smash** something or if it **smashes**, it breaks into many pieces, for example, when it is hit or dropped. 粉々に壊す [他動詞], 粉々に壊れる [自動詞] ❑ Someone smashed a bottle. 誰かが瓶を粉々に割った. ❑ A crowd of youths started smashing windows. 若者の群衆が窓を割り始めました. ❷ V-T/V-I 他動詞/自動詞 If you **smash** through a wall, gate, or door, you get through it by hitting and breaking it. 打ち砕く [他動詞], 打ち砕ける [自動詞] ❑ The demonstrators used trucks to smash through embassy gates. デモ隊はトラックを使って大使館の門を打ち砕いた. ❸ V-T/V-I 他動詞/自動詞 If something **smashes** or **is smashed** against something solid, it moves very fast and with great force against it. 激突する ❑ The bottle smashed against a wall. 瓶が壁にガッシャーンと当たった. ❹ V-T 他動詞 To **smash** a political group or system means to deliberately destroy it. 打倒する [INFORMAL くだけた] ❑ Their attempts to clean up politics and smash the power of party machines failed. 政治を浄化し党の勢力を打倒しようという彼らの試みは失敗した.
▸ **smash up** ❶ PHRASAL VERB 句動詞 If you **smash** something **up**, you completely destroy it by hitting it and breaking it into many pieces. めちゃくちゃに壊す ❑ She took revenge on her ex-boyfriend by smashing up his home. 彼女は元恋人の家をめちゃくちゃに壊して復讐をした. ❷ PHRASAL VERB 句動詞 If you **smash up** your car, you damage it by crashing it into something. ぶつけて壊す ❑ All you told me was that he'd smashed up yet another car. あなたが話してくれたのは, 彼がまた別の車をぶつけて壊したということだけだった.

smear /smɪr/ (smears, smearing, smeared) ❶ V-T 他動詞 If you **smear** a surface **with** an oily or sticky substance or **smear** the substance onto the surface, you spread a layer of the substance over the surface. 塗りつける ❑ My sister smeared herself with suntan oil and slept by the swimming pool. 姉は日焼け用オイルを体に塗りつけてプール脇で眠った. ❷ N-COUNT 可算名詞 A **smear** is a dirty or oily mark. 汚れ, 油汚れ ❑ There was a smear of gravy on his chin. 彼のあごにはグレービーソースが付いていた. ❸ V-T 他動詞 To **smear** someone means to spread unpleasant and untrue rumors or accusations about them in order to damage their reputation. 中傷する [JOURNALISM ジャーナリズム] ❑ They planned to smear him by publishing information about his private life. 彼の私生活についての情報を出版して彼を中傷する計画を立てた. ❹ N-COUNT 可算名詞 A **smear** is an unpleasant and untrue rumor or accusation that is intended to damage someone's reputation. 中傷 [JOURNALISM ジャーナリズム] ❑ He puts all the accusations down to a smear campaign by his political opponents. 彼は非難のすべてはライバル政治家による組織的中傷であると判断している. ❺ N-COUNT 可算名詞 A **smear** or a **smear test** is a medical test in which a few cells are taken from a woman's cervix and examined to see if any cancer cells are present. パパニコロー検査, パップスメア検査 [BRIT 英国英語; AM **Pap smear**, **Pap test** 米国英語 **Pap smear**, **Pap test**]

smell /smɛl/ (smells, smelling, smelled) ❶ N-COUNT 可算名詞 The **smell** of something is a quality it has which you become aware of when you breathe in through your nose. におい ❑ ...the smell of freshly baked bread. 焼きたてのパンの香り ❑ ...horrible smells. 悪臭 ❷ N-UNCOUNT 不可算名詞 Your sense of **smell** is the ability that your nose has to detect things. 嗅覚 (きゅうかく) ❑ ...people who lose their sense of smell. 嗅覚 (きゅうかく) を失う人々 ❸ V-LINK 連結動詞 If something **smells** a particular way, it has a quality which you become aware of through your nose, においがする ❑ The room smelled of lemons. その部屋はレモンのにおいがした. ❑ It smells delicious. おいしそうなにおいがします. ❹ V-I 自動詞 If you say that something **smells**, you mean that it smells unpleasant. 臭い ❑ Ma threw that out. She said it smelled. マーはそれを捨てた. 臭かったと言っていた. ❺ V-T 他動詞 If you **smell** something, you become aware of it when you breathe in through your nose. ～の

Word Web   smell

Scientists believe that the average person can recognize about 10,000 separate **odors**. Until recently, however, the **sense** of smell was a mystery. We now know that most substances release odor molecules into the air. They enter the body through the **nose**. When they reach the **nasal cavity**, they attach to **sensory** cells. The olfactory **nerve** carries the information to the brain and we identify the smell. The eyes, mouth, and throat also contain **receptors** that add to the olfactory experience. Interestingly, our sense of smell is more accurate later in the day than it is in the morning.

においがする ❑*As soon as we opened the front door we could smell the gas.* 玄関を開けるとすぐに、ガス漏れのにおいがした. **6** V-T 他動詞 If you **smell** something, you put your nose near it and breathe in, so that you can discover its smell. においをかぐ ❑*I took a fresh rose out of the vase on our table, and smelled it.* テーブルの上の花瓶からバラを1本取って、そのにおいをかいだ. **7** to smell a rat → see rat
→ see Word Web: smell
→ see taste

Thesaurus   smell また次を参照:

N.	aroma, fragrance, odor, scent **1**
V.	reek, stink **4**
	breathe, inhale, sniff **5**

smelly /smɛli/ (**smellier, smelliest**) ADJ 形容詞 Something that is **smelly** has an unpleasant smell. 臭い ❑*He had extremely smelly feet.* 彼の足はすごく臭かった.

smile /smaɪl/ (**smiles, smiling, smiled**) **1** V-I 自動詞 When you **smile**, the corners of your mouth curve up and you sometimes show your teeth. People smile when they are pleased or amused, or when they are being friendly. ほほえむ, にっこり笑う ❑*When he saw me, he smiled and waved.* 彼は私を見て, にっこり笑って手を振ってくれた. ❑*He rubbed the back of his neck and smiled ruefully at me.* 彼は首の後ろをさすって私に悲しそうにほほえんだ. **2** N-COUNT 可算名詞 A **smile** is the expression that you have on your face when you smile. ほほえみ, 笑顔 ❑*She gave a wry smile.* 彼女は苦笑いをした. ❑*"There are some sandwiches if you're hungry," she said with a smile.* 「おなかがすいているのならサンドイッチがありますよ」と彼女は笑顔で言った.

Word Partnership   smile は次の語句と使われる:

V.	smile and laugh, make *someone* smile, smile and nod, see *someone* smile, try to smile **1**
	smile fades, flash a smile, give *someone* a smile **2**
ADJ.	big/little/small smile, broad smile, friendly smile, half smile, sad smile, shy smile, warm smile, wide smile, wry smile **2**

smiley /smaɪli/ (**smileys**) **1** ADJ 形容詞 A **smiley** person smiles a lot or is smiling. にこにこした [INFORMAL くだけた] [usu ADJ n] ❑*Two smiley babies are waiting for their lunch.* ニコニコ笑顔の赤ちゃんが2人昼食を待っている. **2** N-COUNT 可算名詞 A **smiley** or a **smiley face** is a symbol used in e-mail to show how someone is feeling. :-) is a smiley showing happiness. スマイリー, スマイルマーク [COMPUTING コンピューティング]

smirk /smɜrk/ (**smirks, smirking, smirked**) V-I 自動詞 If you **smirk**, you smile in an unpleasant way, often because you believe that you have gained an advantage over someone else or know something that they do not know. にやにや笑う ❑*Two men standing nearby looked at me, nudged each other and smirked.* 近くに立っていた男が2人私を見て, お互いを軽く押し合ってにやにや笑った.

smog /smɒg/ (**smogs**) N-VAR 可変性名詞 **Smog** is a mixture of fog and smoke which occurs in some busy industrial cities. スモッグ ❑*Cars cause pollution, both smog and acid rain.* 自動車は, スモッグと酸性雨の両方の公害を引き起こします.
→ see pollution

smoke /smoʊk/ (**smokes, smoking, smoked**) **1** N-UNCOUNT 不可算名詞 **Smoke** consists of gas and small bits of solid material that are sent into the air when something burns. 煙 ❑*A cloud of black smoke blew over the city.* もうもうとした黒煙が町の空に流れている. **2** V-I 自動詞 If something **is smoking**, smoke is coming from it. 煙を出す ❑*The chimney was smoking fiercely.* 煙突から猛烈に煙が出ていた. **3** V-T/V-I 他動詞/自動詞 When someone **smokes** a cigarette, cigar, or pipe, they suck the smoke from it into their mouth and blow it out again. If you regularly smoke cigarettes, cigars, or a pipe. (たばこなどを) 吸う [他動詞], 喫煙する [自動詞] ❑*He was sitting alone, smoking a big cigar.* 彼は大きな葉巻を吸いながら1人で座っていた. ● N-SING 単数名詞 **Smoke** is also a noun. 喫煙 ❑*Someone came out for a smoke.* 一服するために誰かが

出てきた. **4** V-T 他動詞 If fish or meat **is smoked**, it is hung over burning wood so that the smoke preserves it and gives it a special flavor. 薫製にする [usu passive] ❑*...the grid where the fish were being smoked.* 魚を載せて薫製にしている焼き網 **5** → see also smoking **6** PHRASE 句 If someone says **where there's smoke there's fire**, they mean that there are rumors or signs that something is true so it must be at least partly true. 火のないところに煙は立たない ❑*A lot of the stuff in the story is not true, but I have to say that where there's smoke there's fire.* その話の多くは事実ではないが, 火のないところに煙は立たないとも言えます. **7** PHRASE 句 If something **goes up in smoke**, it is destroyed by fire. 煙と消える ❑*The crew were able to put out the fire after only 25 acres had gone up in smoke.* ほんの25エーカーが炎上したあと消防士は火事を消し止めることができた. **8** PHRASE 句 If something that is very important to you **goes up in smoke**, it fails or ends without anything being achieved. はかなく消える ❑*I was afraid you'd say no, and my dream would go up in smoke.* だめだと言われて夢がはかなく消えるものだと思っていた.
→ see fire

Word Partnership   smoke は次の語句と使われる:

ADJ.	black smoke, dense smoke, heavy smoke, secondhand smoke, thick smoke **1**
N.	cigarette smoke, cloud of smoke, smoke damage, smoke from a fire, smoke inhalation, smell of smoke, tobacco smoke **1** smoke a cigar/cigarette, smoke tobacco **3**
V.	see smoke, smell smoke **1** smoke and drink **3**

smok|ing /smoʊkɪŋ/ **1** N-UNCOUNT 不可算名詞 **Smoking** is the act or habit of smoking cigarettes, cigars, or a pipe. 喫煙 ❑*Smoking is now banned in many places of work.* 最近では職場の多くが禁煙となっている. **2** ADJ 形容詞 A **smoking** area is intended for people who want to smoke. 喫煙用の [ADJ n] ❑*California no longer allows smoking areas in restaurants.* カリフォルニア州ではもはやレストランに喫煙席が認められない. **3** → see also smoke

Word Partnership   smoking は次の語句と使われる:

V.	ban smoking, quit smoking, stop smoking **1**
N.	ban on smoking, dangers of smoking, smoking and drinking, effects of smoking, smoking habits, risk of smoking **1** (no) smoking section **2**

smoky /smoʊki/ (**smokier, smokiest**) also **smokey** **1** ADJ 形容詞 A place that is **smoky** has a lot of smoke in the air. 煙たい ❑*His main problem was the extremely smoky atmosphere at work.* 彼の主な問題は職場が非常に煙たいことだ. **2** ADJ 形容詞 You can use **smoky** to describe something that looks like smoke, for example, because it is slightly blue or gray or because it is not clear. くすんだ, 曇ったような [ADJ n, ADJ color] ❑*At the center of the dial is a piece of smoky glass.* 文字盤の真ん中にはくすんだガラスがある. **3** ADJ 形容詞 Something that has a **smoky** flavor tastes as if it has been smoked. いぶしたような, スモーキーな ❑*The fish had just the right amount of smoky flavor for my taste.* その魚は私の好みにぴったりのいぶしたような風味があった.

smol|der /smoʊldər/ (**smolders, smoldering, smoldered**) **1** V-I 自動詞 If something **smolders**, it burns slowly, producing smoke but not flames. くすぶる, 煙る ❑*The wreckage was still smoldering several hours after the crash.* 残骸 (ざんがい) は事故から数時間後も依然としてくすぶっていた. **2** V-I 自動詞 If a feeling such as anger or hatred **smolders** inside you, you continue to feel it but do not show it. くすぶる, 内攻する ❑*...the guilt that had so long smoldered in her heart.* 彼女の心に長い間くすぶっていた罪悪感 **3** V-I 自動詞 If you say that someone **smolders**, you mean that they are sexually attractive, usually in a mysterious or very intense way. 性的魅力がある ❑*He was good-looking, with dark eyes which could smolder with just the right intimation of passion.* 彼は情熱を感じさせる魅力的な黒い瞳をしていてかっこよかった.
→ see fire

S

smooth /smuːð/ (smoother, smoothest, smooths, smoothing, smoothed) **1** ADJ 形容詞 A **smooth** surface has no roughness, lumps, or holes. すべすべした、平らな ❑ *...a rich cream that keeps skin soft and smooth.* 肌を柔らかくスベスベに保つ高級クリーム **2** ADJ 形容詞 A **smooth** liquid or mixture has been mixed well so that it has no lumps. 滑らかな ❑ *Continue whisking until the mixture looks smooth and creamy.* ミックスが滑らかでクリーム上になるまでかき混ぜ続けなさい. **3** ADJ 形容詞 If you describe a drink such as wine, whiskey, or coffee as **smooth**, you mean that it is not bitter and is pleasant to drink. 口当たりのよい、まろやかな ❑ *This makes the whiskeys much smoother.* これでウィスキーの口当たりがよくなる. **4** ADJ 形容詞 A **smooth** line or movement has no sudden breaks or changes in direction or speed. スムーズな ❑ *This exercise is done in one smooth motion.* この運動は1つながりのスムーズな動きで行う. ● **smooth|ly** ADV 副詞 [ADV with v] スムーズに ❑ *Make sure that you execute all movements smoothly and without jerking.* 必ずすべての動きをスムーズにぎくしゃくせずに行いなさい. **5** ADJ 形容詞 A **smooth** ride, flight, or sea crossing is very comfortable because there are no unpleasant movements. 快適な ❑ *The active suspension system gives the car a very smooth ride.* アクティブサスペンションシステムのための自動車の乗り心地がとてもよい. **6** ADJ 形容詞 You use **smooth** to describe something that is going well and is free of problems or trouble. 円滑な ❑ *Political hopes for a swift and smooth transition to democracy have been dashed.* 民主主義への迅速で円滑な移行に対する政治的期待は打ち砕かれた. ● **smooth|ly** ADV 副詞 [ADV with v] 円滑に ❑ *So far, talks at GM have gone smoothly.* これまでのところGMでの会議は順調です. **7** ADJ 形容詞 If you describe a man as **smooth**, you mean that he is extremely smart, confident, and polite, often in a way that you find rather unpleasant. 調子のいい、口先がうまい ❑ *Twelve extremely good-looking, smooth young men have been picked as finalists.* 12名の非常にルックスがよくて如才ない若者が最終選考に残った. **8** V-T 他動詞 If you **smooth** something, you move your hands over its surface to make it smooth and flat. しわを延ばす ❑ *She stood up and smoothed down her frock.* 彼女は立ち上がってドレスのしわを延ばした.

→ see **muscle**

▶ **smooth out** PHRASAL VERB 句動詞 If you **smooth out** a problem or difficulty, you solve it, especially by talking to the people concerned. 解決する ❑ *Baker was smoothing out differences with European allies.* ベイカーはヨーロッパ同盟国間の相違を取り除いていました.

▶ **smooth over** PHRASAL VERB 句動詞 If you **smooth over** a problem or difficulty, you make it less serious and easier to deal with, especially by talking to the people concerned. 丸く治める、解決の方向に進める ❑ *...an attempt to smooth over the violent splits that have occurred.* 最近起きた激しい対立を解決の方向に進める試み ❑ *The president is trying to smooth things over.* 大統領は事態の改善に努めている.

smoth|er /smʌðər/ (smothers, smothering, smothered) **1** V-T 他動詞 If you **smother** a fire, you cover it with something in order to put it out. 消す ❑ *The girl's parents were also burned as they tried to smother the flames.* 少女の両親も炎を消そうとしてやけどした. **2** V-T 他動詞 To **smother** someone means to kill them by covering their face with something so that they cannot breathe. 窒息死させる ❑ *He tried to smother me with a pillow.* 彼は枕で私を窒息死させようとした. **3** V-T 他動詞 Things that **smother** something cover it completely. 覆う ❑ *Once the shrubs begin to smother the little plants, we have to move them.* 低木が背の低い草を覆い始めたら移植する必要がある. **4** V-T 他動詞 If you **smother** someone, you show your love for them too much and protect them too much. (あまりの愛情で)息苦しくさせる ❑ *She loved her own children, almost smothering them with love.* 彼女は子供たちを愛しすぎて、あまりの愛情で子供たちは息が詰まるほどだった. **5** V-T 他動詞 If you **smother** an emotion or a reaction, you control it so that people do not notice it. 抑える ❑ *She tried to smother her anger and help them resolve their conflicts.* 彼女は怒りをこらえ、彼らが争いを解決できるように力になろうとした.

smoul|der /smoʊldər/ → see **smolder**

SMS /ɛs ɛm ɛs/ N-UNCOUNT 不可算名詞 **SMS** is a way of sending short written messages from one cellphone to another. **SMS** is an abbreviation for **short message system** or **short message service**. ショートメッセージサービス

smudge /smʌdʒ/ (smudges, smudging, smudged) **1** N-COUNT 可算名詞 A **smudge** is a dirty mark. 汚れ、しみ ❑ *There was a dark smudge on his forehead.* 彼の額には黒っぽいしみがあった. **2** V-T 他動詞 If you **smudge** a substance such as ink, paint, or make-up that has been put on a surface, you make it less neat by touching or rubbing it. 汚す ❑ *She rubbed her eyes, smudging her make-up.* 彼女は目をこすったので化粧がくずれた. **3** V-T 他動詞 If you **smudge** a surface, you make it dirty by touching it and leaving a substance on it. 汚す ❑ *She kissed me, careful not to smudge me with her fresh lipstick.* 彼女は塗ったばかりの口紅がつかないようにそっとキスした.

→ see **drawing**

smug /smʌg/ ADJ 形容詞 If you say that someone is **smug**, you are criticizing the fact they seem very pleased with how good, clever, or lucky they are. 独りよがりの、うぬぼれの強い [DISAPPROVAL 不賛成] ❑ *Thomas and his wife looked at each other in smug satisfaction.* トマスと妻は満足げに見つめ合った.

smug|gle /smʌgᵊl/ (smuggles, smuggling, smuggled) V-T 他動詞 If someone **smuggles** things or people into a place or out of it, they take them there illegally or secretly. 密輸する ❑ *My message is "If you try to smuggle drugs you are stupid."* 私が言いたいのは「麻薬の密輸など、ばかのすることだ」ということである. ❑ *Police have foiled an attempt to smuggle a bomb into Belfast airport.* 警察はベルファスト空港に爆弾を持ち込む計画を事前に阻止しました. ● **smug|gling** N-UNCOUNT 不可算名詞 密輸 ❑ *An air hostess was arrested and charged with drug smuggling.* 女性客室乗務員が麻薬密輸で逮捕、起訴された.

smug|gler /smʌglər/ (smugglers) N-COUNT 可算名詞 **Smugglers** are people who take goods into or out of a country illegally. 密輸業者 ❑ *...drug smugglers.* 麻薬密輸業者.

snack /snæk/ (snacks, snacking, snacked) **1** N-COUNT 可算名詞 A **snack** is a simple meal that is quick to cook and to eat. 軽食 ❑ *Lunch was a snack in the fields.* お昼は野原での軽食だった. **2** N-COUNT 可算名詞 A **snack** is something such as a chocolate bar that you eat between meals. スナック ❑ *Do you eat sweets, cakes or sugary snacks?* お菓子やケーキや何か甘いものを間食しますか. **3** V-I 自動詞 If you **snack**, you eat snacks between meals. 間食する ❑ *Instead of snacking on crisps and chocolate, nibble on celery or carrot.* ポテトチップやチョコレートを間食するのをやめて、セロリやニンジンをかじりなさい.

→ see **peanut**

snack bar (snack bars) N-COUNT 可算名詞 A **snack bar** is a place where you can buy drinks and simple meals such as sandwiches. 軽食堂

snag /snæg/ (snags, snagging, snagged) **1** N-COUNT 可算名詞 A **snag** is a small problem or disadvantage. 障害 ❑ *A police clampdown on car thieves hit a snag when villains stole one of their cars.* 警察が自動車窃盗団の取り締まりを強化していたところ、警察車両1台が窃盗団に盗まれるという思わぬ事態が発生した. **2** V-T/V-I 他動詞/自動詞 If you **snag** part of your clothing on a sharp or rough object or if it **snags**, it gets caught on the object and tears. 引っかけて破く [他動詞] 引っかけて破れる [自動詞] ❑ *She snagged a heel on a root and tumbled to the ground.* 彼女は靴のかかとを根に引っかけて地面に倒れた. ❑ *Brambles snagged his suit.* キイチゴに引っかけてスーツが破れた.

snail /sneɪl/ (snails) **1** N-COUNT 可算名詞 A **snail** is a small animal with a long, soft body, no legs, and a spiral-shaped shell. Snails move very slowly. カタツムリ **2** PHRASE 句 If you say that someone does something **at a snail's pace**, you are emphasizing that they are doing it very slowly, usually when you think it would be better if they did it much more quickly. のろのろと [EMPHASIS 強調] ❑ *The train was moving now at a snail's pace.* そのとき電車はのろのろと進んでいた.

snail mail N-UNCOUNT 不可算名詞 Some computer users refer to the postal system as **snail mail**, because it is very slow in comparison with e-mail. 郵便

snake /sneɪk/ (snakes, snaking, snaked) **1** N-COUNT 可算名詞 A **snake** is a long, thin reptile without legs. ヘビ **2** V-I 自動詞 Something that **snakes** in a particular direction goes in that direction in a line with a lot of bends. くねって進む [LITERARY 文語的] ❑ *The road snaked through forested mountains.* 木々が生い茂る山間を縫うように道はうねうねと続いた.

→ see **desert**

snap /snæp/ (snaps, snapping, snapped) **1** V-T/V-I 他動詞/自動詞 If something **snaps** or if you **snap** it, it breaks suddenly, usually with a sharp cracking noise. ポキンと折る [他動詞] ポキンと折れる [自動詞] ❑ *He shifted his weight and a twig snapped.* 彼が体重を移動させると小枝がポキンと折れた. ❑ *The brake pedal had just snapped off.* そのときちょうどブレーキペダルがポキンと折れた. ● N-SING 単数名詞 **Snap** is also a noun. ポキンと折れる音 ❑ *Every minute or so I could hear a snap, a crack and a crash as another tree went down.* ほぼ1分間隔で木が倒れるたびに、バシン、メリメリ、ドシーンという音が聞こえました. **2** V-T/V-I 他動詞/自動詞 If you **snap** something into a particular position, or if it **snaps** into that position, it moves quickly into that position, with a sharp sound. パチンと音を立ててある状態にする [他動詞] パチンと音を立ててある状態になる [自動詞] ❑ *He snapped the cap on his ballpoint.* 彼はボールペンのキャップをパチンとつけた. ● N-SING 単数名詞 **Snap** is also a noun. パチンという音 ❑ *He shut the book with a snap and stood up.* 彼は本をパシンと閉じると立ち上がった. **3** V-T 他動詞 If you **snap your fingers**, you make a sharp sound by moving your middle finger quickly across your thumb, for example, in order to accompany music or to order someone to do something. 指を鳴らす ❑ *She had millions of listeners snapping their fingers to her first single.* 何百万人もの人が彼女の初シ

ングルを聞きながら指を鳴らしました. □*He snapped his fingers, and Wilson produced a sheet of paper.* 彼が指を鳴らすと、ウィルソンは1枚の紙を取り出した. ●N-SING 単数名詞 **Snap** is also a noun. 指を鳴らすこと [N "of" n] □*I could obtain with the snap of my fingers anything I chose.* 指をパチンと鳴らすことで選んだものは何でも手に入れることができた. **4** V-T/V-I 他動詞/自動詞 If someone **snaps at** you, they speak to you in a sharp, unfriendly way. ぶっきらぼうに言う □*"Of course I don't know her,"* Roger snapped. 「彼女のことを知っているわけないだろ」とロジャーは乱暴に言った. **5** V-I 自動詞 If someone **snaps**, or if something **snaps** inside them, they suddenly stop being calm and become very angry because the situation has become too tense or too difficult for them. かっとなる □*He finally snapped when she prevented their children from visiting him one weekend.* ある週末に子供たちが彼に会いに来れないように彼女がしたので、彼はついにかっとなった. **6** V-I 自動詞 If an animal such as a dog **snaps at** you, it opens and shuts its jaws quickly near you, as if it were going to bite you. かみつこうとする □*His teeth clicked as he snapped at my ankle.* 私の足首にかみつこうとしたら、その歯がカチンと鳴った. **7** ADJ 形容詞 A **snap** decision or action is one that is taken suddenly, often without careful thought. 性急な [ADJ n] □*I think this is too important for a snap decision.* これはとても大切なことなので性急に判断しないほうがよいと思う. **8** N-COUNT 可算名詞 A **snap** is the same as a **snap fastener**. スナップ [AM 米国英語] **9** N-COUNT 可算名詞 A **snap** is a photograph. スナップ写真 [INFORMAL くだけた] □*...a snap my mother took last year.* 母が去年撮ったスナップ写真.
▶ **snap up** PHRASAL VERB 句動詞 If you **snap** something **up**, you buy it quickly because it is cheap or is just what you want. 先を争って買う □*...a millionaire ready to snap them up at the premium price of $200 a gallon.* 1ガロン200ドルという高値でも先を争って買おうとする大金持ち.

snap|shot /snǽpʃɒt/ (**snapshots**) **1** N-COUNT 可算名詞 A **snapshot** is a photograph that is taken quickly and casually. スナップ写真 □*Let me take a snapshot of you guys, so friends back home can see you.* みんなのスナップ写真、撮らせてよ. 故郷の友達に見せてあげたいから. **2** N-COUNT 可算名詞 If something provides you with a **snapshot** of a place or situation, it gives you a brief idea of what that place or situation is like. 寸描 [usu sing, usu N "of" n] □*The interviews present a remarkable snapshot of Britain in these dark days of recession.* 対談からは暗い不況期にあったイギリスの様子を十分うかがい知ることができる.

snare /snéǝr/ (**snares, snaring, snared**) **1** N-COUNT 可算名詞 A **snare** is a trap for catching birds or small animals. It consists of a loop of wire or rope which pulls tight around the animal. わな □*I felt like an animal caught in a snare.* わなにかかった動物の気分だった. **2** N-COUNT 可算名詞 If you describe a situation as a **snare**, you mean that it is a trap from which it is difficult to escape. わな、落とし穴 [FORMAL 形式ばった] □*Given data which are free from bias there are further snares to avoid in statistical work.* たとえ偏りのないデータであっても、統計処理ではさらに回避しなければならない落とし穴がある. **3** V-T 他動詞 If someone **snares** an animal, they catch it using a snare. わなにかける □*He'd snared a rabbit earlier in the day.* 彼はその日早くウサギを1匹わなにかけていた.

snarl /snɑ́ːrl/ (**snarls, snarling, snarled**) V-I 自動詞 When an animal **snarls**, it makes a fierce, rough sound in its throat while showing its teeth. 歯をむき出してうなる □*He raced ahead up into the bush, barking and snarling.* それはほえたりうなったりしながら茂みの中に突っ走っていった. ●N-COUNT 可算名詞 **Snarl** is also a noun. うなること □*With a snarl, the second dog made a dive for his heel.* 2番目の犬がうなりながら彼のかかとに飛びかかってきた.

snatch /snǽtʃ/ (**snatches, snatching, snatched**) **1** V-T/V-I 他動詞/自動詞 If you **snatch** something or **snatch at** something, you take it or pull it away quickly. つかみ取る □*Mick snatched the cards from Archie's hand.* ミックはアーチーの手からカードを奪い取った. □*He snatched up the telephone.* 彼はいきなり受話器を取り上げた. **2** V-T 他動詞 If something **is snatched** from you, it is stolen, usually using force. If a person **is snatched**, they are taken away by force. ひったくられる [usu passive] □*If your bag is snatched, let it go.* かばんをひったくられても後を追ってはいけない. **3** V-T 他動詞 If you **snatch** an opportunity, you take it quickly. If you **snatch** something to eat or a rest, you have it quickly in between doing other things. 急いで〜する □*I snatched a glance at the mirror.* 私はチラッと鏡を見た. **4** V-T 他動詞 If you **snatch** victory in a competition, you defeat your opponent by a small amount or just before the end of the contest. もぎ取る □*The American came from behind to snatch victory by a mere eight seconds.* 後続にいたアメリカ人選手がわずか8秒の差で優勝を奪い取った. **5** N-COUNT 可算名詞 A **snatch** of a conversation or a song is a very small piece of it. 一部 □*I heard snatches of the conversation.* 会話の一部を耳にした.

sneak /sníːk/ (**sneaks, sneaking, sneaked** or **snuck**)

The form **snuck** is informal.

snuck 形はくだけた語である.

1 V-I 自動詞 If you **sneak** somewhere, you go there very

quietly on foot, trying to avoid being seen or heard. そっと歩く □*Sometimes he would sneak out of his house late at night to be with me.* 彼は私に会うためにときどき夜中に家からこっそり抜け出していた. **2** V-T 他動詞 If you **sneak** something somewhere, you take it there secretly. こっそりと持ち込む □*He smuggled papers out each day, photocopied them, and snuck them back.* 彼は毎日書類をこっそり持ち出しては、コピーをとってこっそりと元に戻しました. **3** V-T 他動詞 If you **sneak** a look at someone or something, you secretly have a quick look at them. こっそり見る □*You sneak a look at your watch to see how long you've got to wait.* あとどれくらい待つのか、こっそりと時計を見る.

sneak|er /sníːkǝr/ (**sneakers**) N-COUNT 可算名詞 **Sneakers** are casual shoes with rubber soles that people wear often for running or other sports. スニーカー [mainly AM 主に米国英語] [usu pl] □*...a new pair of sneakers.* 新品のスニーカー1足.
→ see **clothing**

Athletic shoes have many names. The simplest name is **sneakers**. Other names may specify where the shoe was designed to be worn: **tennis shoe**, **gym shoe**, **basketball shoe**, **running shoe** and so on. In the UK, the term **trainers** is usually used.

sneer /sníǝr/ (**sneers, sneering, sneered**) V-T/V-I 他動詞/自動詞 If you **sneer at** someone or something, you express your contempt for them by the expression on your face or by what you say. ばかにする □*Most critics have sneered at the movie, calling it dull and cheaply made.* ほとんどの評論家がその映画を退屈な三流映画として一笑に付した. □*"I don't need any help from you,"* he sneered. 「お前なんかに助けてもらう必要ないよ」と彼は見下すように言った. ●N-COUNT 可算名詞 **Sneer** is also a noun. ばかにすること □*Canete's mouth twisted in a contemptuous sneer.* カニエテは口元をゆがめてせら笑った.

sneeze /sníːz/ (**sneezes, sneezing, sneezed**) **1** V-I 自動詞 When you **sneeze**, you suddenly take in your breath and then blow it down your nose noisily without being able to stop yourself, for example, because you have a cold. くしゃみをする □*What exactly happens when we sneeze?* くしゃみをしたとき実際には何が起こっているのだろう. ●N-COUNT 可算名詞 **Sneeze** is also a noun. くしゃみ □*Coughs and sneezes spread infections.* せきやくしゃみで感染症が広がる. **2** PHRASE 句 If you say that something is **not to be sneezed at**, you mean that it is worth having. ばかにできない [INFORMAL くだけた] □*The money's not to be sneezed at.* その金はばかにならない.

sniff /snɪf/ (**sniffs, sniffing, sniffed**) **1** V-I 自動詞 When you **sniff**, you breathe in air through your nose hard enough to make a sound, for example, when you are trying not to cry, or in order to show disapproval. 鼻を鳴らして息を吸う；鼻をすする □*She wiped her face and sniffed loudly.* 彼女は顔をふくと、大きな音を立てて鼻をすすった. ●N-COUNT 可算名詞 **Sniff** is also a noun. 鼻を鳴らすこと □*At last the sobs ceased, to be replaced by sniffs.* ようやく泣き声が治まったら、今度は鼻をすする音になった. **2** V-T/V-I 他動詞/自動詞 If you **sniff** something or **sniff at** it, you smell it by sniffing. においをかぐ □*Suddenly, he stopped and sniffed the air.* 突然彼は立ち止まり、空気のにおいをかいだ. **3** V-T 他動詞 You can use **sniff** to indicate that someone says something in a way that shows their disapproval or contempt. ばかにして言う □*"Tourists!"* she sniffed. 「観光客め！」と彼女はののしるように言った. **4** V-T/V-I 他動詞/自動詞 If you say that something is **not to be sniffed at**, you think it is very good or worth having. If someone **sniffs at** something, they do not think it is good enough, or they express their contempt for it. ばかにできない；ばかにする [usu passive, usu with brd-neg] □*The salary was not to be sniffed at either.* 給料もばかにならなかった. **5** V-T 他動詞 If someone **sniffs** a substance such as glue, they deliberately breathe in the substance or the gases from it as a drug. 鼻から吸う □*He felt light-headed, as if he'd sniffed glue.* 彼はシンナーを鼻から吸ったみたいにくらくらした.
▶ **sniff out** **1** PHRASAL VERB 句動詞 If you **sniff out** something, you discover it after some searching. かぎつける [INFORMAL くだけた] □*...journalists who are trained to sniff out scandal.* スキャンダルをかぎつける訓練を受けたジャーナリスト. **2** PHRASAL VERB 句動詞 When a dog used by a group such as the police **sniffs out** hidden explosives or drugs, it finds them using its sense of smell. かぎ分ける □*...a police dog trained to sniff out explosives.* 爆発物をかぎ分ける訓練を受けた警察犬.

snig|ger /snɪ́gǝr/ (**sniggers, sniggering, sniggered**) V-I 自動詞 If someone **sniggers**, they laugh quietly in a disrespectful way, for example at something rude or unkind. くすくす笑う □*Suddenly, three schoolkids sitting near me started sniggering.* 隣に座っていた3人の小学生が突然くすくす笑い始めた. ●N-COUNT 可算名詞 **Snigger** is also a noun. くすくす笑い □*...trying to suppress a snigger.* くすくす笑うのを抑えようとして.

snip /snɪp/ (**snips, snipping, snipped**) V-T/V-I 他動詞/自動詞 If you **snip** something, or if you **snip at** or **through** something, you cut it quickly using sharp scissors. チョキンと切る □*He has now*

begun to snip away at the piece of paper. それから彼は1枚の紙をチョキチョキと切り始めた.

snipe /snaɪp/ (snipes, sniping, sniped) **1** V-I 自動詞 If someone **snipes at** you, they criticize you. 非難する ❑ The media were still sniping at the president's adviser yesterday. マスコミは昨日も依然として大統領補佐官をこき下ろしていた. **2** V-I 自動詞 To **snipe at** someone means to shoot at them from a hidden position. 狙撃する ❑ Gunmen have repeatedly sniped at U.S. Army positions. 米軍の陣地への狙撃が繰り返されています.

snip|er /snaɪpər/ (snipers) N-COUNT 可算名詞 A **sniper** is someone who shoots at people from a hidden position. 狙撃者 ❑ ...a sniper attack. 狙撃.

snip|pet /snɪpɪt/ (snippets) N-COUNT 可算名詞 A **snippet** of something is a small piece of it. 断片 ❑ ...snippets of popular classical music. 大衆向けのクラシックの小曲.

snob /snɒb/ (snobs) N-COUNT 可算名詞 If you call someone a **snob**, you disapprove of them because they behave as if they are superior to other people because of their intelligence, taste, or social status. 上流気取りの人 [DISAPPROVAL 不賛成] ❑ She was an intellectual snob. 彼女は学者ぶる人だった.

snob|bery /snɒbəri/ N-UNCOUNT 不可算名詞 **Snobbery** is the attitude of a snob. 上流気取り ❑ There has often been an element of snobbery in golf. ゴルフにはある種の上流気取りのところが多分にある.

snook|er /snʊkər/ N-UNCOUNT 不可算名詞 **Snooker** is a game involving balls on a large table. The players use a long stick to hit a white ball, and score points by knocking colored balls into the pockets at the sides of the table. スヌーカー ❑ ...a game of snooker. スヌーカーの試合.

snoop /snup/ (snoops, snooping, snooped) **1** V-I 自動詞 If someone **snoops** around a place, they secretly look around it in order to find out things. かぎ回る ❑ Ricardo was the one she'd seen snooping around Kim's hotel room. 彼女はキムの客室の周囲をかぎ回る男を目撃していたが, それがリカルドだった. ● N-COUNT 可算名詞 **Snoop** is also a noun. かぎ回ること ❑ The second house that Grossman had a snoop around contained "strong simple furniture." グロスマンのぞいた2軒目の家には「丈夫で質素な」家具が置いてあった. ● **snoop|er** N-COUNT 可算名詞 (snoopers) かぎ回る人 ❑ Even if the information is intercepted by a snooper, it is impossible for them to decipher it. たとえこの情報がスパイに傍受されたとしても解読は不可能である. **2** V-I 自動詞 If someone **snoops on** a person, they watch them secretly in order to find out things about their life. ひそかに監視する ❑ Governments have been known to snoop on and harass innocent citizens in the past. 国家は過去において罪のない市民をひそかに監視して悩ましてきたことで知られる.

snooze /snuz/ (snoozes, snoozing, snoozed) **1** N-COUNT 可算名詞 A **snooze** is a short, light sleep, especially during the day. うたた寝 [INFORMAL くだけた] ❑ I lay down on the bed with my shoes off to have a snooze. 少し寝ようと靴を脱いでベッドに横になった. **2** V-I 自動詞 If you **snooze**, you sleep lightly for a short period of time. うたた寝する [INFORMAL くだけた] ❑ Mark snoozed in front of the television. マークはテレビの前でうとうとした.

snore /snɔr/ (snores, snoring, snored) **1** V-I 自動詞 When someone who is asleep **snores**, they make a loud noise each time they breathe. いびきをかく ❑ His mouth was open, and he was snoring. 彼は口を開けていびきをかいていました. ● N-COUNT 可算名詞 **Snore** is also a noun. いびき ❑ Uncle Arthur, after a loud snore, woke suddenly. アーサーおじさんは自分の大きないびきで急に目が覚めた.

snor|kel /snɔrkəl/ (snorkels, snorkeling, snorkeled) **1** N-COUNT 可算名詞 A **snorkel** is a tube through which a person swimming just under the surface of the sea can breathe. シュノーケル **2** V-I 自動詞 When someone **snorkels**, they swim under water using a snorkel. シュノーケルで潜る ❑ Swim off the side of the ship and snorkel in some of the clearest waters imaginable. 船の側面から泳ぎ出して, 想像を絶するほど澄み切った海でシュノーケリングをします.

snort /snɔrt/ (snorts, snorting, snorted) **1** V-I 自動詞 When people or animals **snort**, they breathe air noisily out through their noses. People sometimes snort in order to express disapproval or amusement. 鼻を鳴らす ❑ Harrell snorted with laughter. ハレルは鼻の先でせせら笑った. ● N-COUNT 可算名詞 **Snort** is also a noun. 鼻を鳴らすこと ❑ ...snorts of laughter. せせら笑い. **2** V-T 他動詞 To **snort** a drug such as cocaine means to breathe it in quickly through your nose. 鼻から吸う ❑ He died of cardiac arrest after snorting cocaine at a party. 彼はパーティーでコカインを吸引した後に心停止で亡くなりました.

snow /snoʊ/ (snows, snowing, snowed) **1** N-UNCOUNT 不可算名詞 **Snow** consists of a lot of soft white pieces of frozen water that fall from the sky in cold weather. 雪 ❑ Six inches of snow blocked roads. 6インチの積雪で道路は通行できなくなった. **2** V-I 自動詞 When **it snows**, snow falls from the sky. 雪が降る ❑ It had been snowing all night. 夜通し雪が降っていた.

→ see **Arctic, storm, water**

snow|ball /snoʊbɔl/ (snowballs, snowballing, snowballed) **1** N-COUNT 可算名詞 A **snowball** is a ball of snow. Children often throw snowballs at each other. 雪玉 **2** V-I 自動詞 If something such as a project or campaign **snowballs**, it rapidly increases and grows. 雪だるま式に大きくなる ❑ From those early days the business has snowballed. 開設当初から事業は急成長してきた.

snow|board /snoʊbɔrd/ (snowboards) N-COUNT 可算名詞 A **snowboard** is a narrow board that you stand on in order to slide quickly down snowy slopes as a sport or for fun. スノーボード

snow|board|ing /snoʊbɔrdɪŋ/ N-UNCOUNT 不可算名詞 **Snowboarding** is the sport or activity of traveling down snowy slopes using a snowboard. スノーボーディング ❑ New snowboarding facilities should attract more people. 新しいスノーボード場にはこれまで以上の客が訪れるだろう.

snow|plow /snoʊplaʊ/ (snowplows) N-COUNT 可算名詞 A **snowplow** is a vehicle which is used to push snow off roads or railroad tracks. 除雪車

snowy /snoʊi/ (snowier, snowiest) ADJ 形容詞 A **snowy** place is covered in snow. A **snowy** day is a day when a lot of snow has fallen. 雪の積もった; 雪の降る ❑ ...the snowy peaks of the Bighorn Mountains. ビッグホーン山脈の雪に覆われた峰々.

snub /snʌb/ (snubs, snubbing, snubbed) **1** V-T 他動詞 If you **snub** someone, you deliberately insult them by ignoring them or by behaving or speaking rudely toward them. 侮辱する ❑ He snubbed her in public and made her feel an idiot. 彼は人前で彼女に乱暴な態度をとって, 彼女をばか者扱いした. **2** N-COUNT 可算名詞 If you snub someone, your behavior or your remarks can be referred to as a **snub**. 侮辱 ❑ Ryan took it as a snub. ライアンは侮辱されたと感じた.

snuck /snʌk/ **Snuck** is a past tense and past participle of **sneak**. [INFORMAL くだけた]

snuff /snʌf/ (snuffs, snuffing, snuffed) N-UNCOUNT 不可算名詞 **Snuff** is powdered tobacco which people take by breathing in quickly through their nose. かぎたばこ ❑ ...the old man's habit of taking snuff. その老人のかぎたばこを吸う習慣.

▶ **snuff out** PHRASAL VERB 句動詞 To **snuff out** something such as a disagreement means to stop it, usually in a forceful or sudden way. 押しつぶす ❑ Every time a new flicker of resistance appeared, the government snuffed it out. 新たな抵抗の兆しが現れるたびに政府はもみ消した.

snug /snʌg/ (snugger, snuggest) **1** ADJ 形容詞 If you feel **snug** or are in a **snug** place, you are very warm and comfortable, especially because you are protected from cold weather. 居心地のよい ❑ They lay snug and warm amid the blankets and watched their sister hard at work. 彼らは心地よく毛布に包まって横になり, 姉さんが精を出して仕事をするのを見ていた. **2** ADJ 形容詞 Something such as a piece of clothing that is **snug** fits very closely or tightly. ぴったり合う ❑ ...a snug black T-shirt and skin-tight black jeans. 体にぴったり合った黒のTシャツと黒のジーンズ.

snug|gle /snʌgəl/ (snuggles, snuggling, snuggled) V-I 自動詞 If you **snuggle** somewhere, you settle yourself into a warm, comfortable position, especially by moving closer to another person. 居心地のよい場所に移動する; すり寄る ❑ Jane snuggled up against his shoulder. ジェインは彼の肩に寄り添った.

so /soʊ/

Usually pronounced /soʊ/ for meanings **1**, **6**, **7**, **8**, **13** and **16**.
1, **6**, **7**, **8**, **15**, **16** および /soʊ/ の意味には通常 と発音される.

1 ADV 副詞 You use **so** to refer back to something that has just been mentioned. そう, そのように [ADV after v] "Do you think that made much of a difference to the family?" — "I think so." 「それは家族にとって大きなことだったと思いますか」「そう思います」 ❑ If you can't play straight, then say so. 正直になれないんだったら, そう言えば. **2** ADV 副詞 You use **so** when you are saying that something which has just been said about one person or thing is also true of another one. 同様に [ADV cl] ❑ I enjoy Ann's company and so does Martin. 私はアンと一緒にいると楽しいし, マーティンも同じだ. ❑ They had a wonderful time and so did I. 彼らはとても楽しんだし, 私も楽しかった. **3** CONJ 接続詞 You use the structures as...so and just as...so when you want to indicate that two events or situations are similar in some way. 一と同じように ❑ As computer systems become even more sophisticated, so too do the methods of those who exploit the technology. コンピュータシステムがさらに高度化すると, その技術を利用する方法も同じように高度化します. ❑ Just as John has changed, so has his wife. ジョンも変わったが, 妻も変わった. **4** ADV 副詞 If you say that a state of affairs is **so**, you mean that it is the way it has been described. そうである [v-link ADV] ❑ In those days English dances as well as songs were taught at school, but that seems no longer to be so. 当時, 学校ではイギリスの歌だけでなくダンスも教えていたが, 今はそういうことはないようだ. ❑ It is strange to think that he held strong views on many things, but it

must have been so. 彼がいろんなことに対してはっきりした考えを持っていたと思うとおかしな気がするが、そうだったに違いない。 **5** ADV 副詞 You can use **so** with actions and gestures to show a person how to do something, or to indicate the size, height, or length of something. そのように [ADV after v] □ *Clasp the chain like so.* そのようにチェーンを留めなさい。 **6** CONJ 接続詞 You use **so** and **so that** to introduce the result of the situation you have just mentioned. だから、そのため □ *I am not an emotional type and so cannot bring myself to tell him I love him.* 私は感情的なタイプではないので、彼に愛していると口に出して言う気になれない。 □ *People are living longer than ever before, so even people who are 65 or 70 have a surprising amount of time left.* 以前より長生きするようになったので、65歳や70歳の人でもずいぶん老い先が長くなりました。 **7** CONJ 接続詞 You use **so, so that**, and **so as** to introduce the reason for doing the thing that you have just mentioned. ~するように、~するために □ *Come to my suite so I can tell you all about this wonderful play I saw in Boston.* 私のスイートに来ませんか。そしたら、ボストンで見たこの素晴らしい芝居のことを全部お話しできますよ。 □ *He took her arm and hurried her upstairs so that they wouldn't be overheard.* 盗み聞きされないように、彼は彼女の腕を引っぱって急いで上の階に上がらせた。 **8** ADV 副詞 You can use **so** in conversations to introduce a new topic, or to introduce a question or comment about something that has been said. それで [ADV cl] □ *So how was your day?* それで今日はどうだった？ □ *So you're a runner, huh?* それじゃ、あなたはランナーなんですね。 □ *So as for your question, Miles, the answer still has to be no.* マイルズ、それで君の質問なんだが、答えは依然としてノーのままだ。 **9** ADV 副詞 You can use **so** in conversations to show that you are accepting what someone has just said. そのとおり [ADV cl] □ *"It makes me feel, well, important." — "And so you are."* 「何か偉くなったような気分がするよ」「そのとおりだよ」 □ *"You can't possibly use this word." — "So I won't."* 「こんな言葉、使っちゃいけませんよ」「分かった。使わないよ」 **10** CONVENTION 慣習表現 You say "**So?**" and "**So what?**" to indicate that you think that something that someone has said is unimportant. それがどうしたというのですか [INFORMAL くだけた] □ *"My name's Bruno." — "So?"* 「僕はブルーノだ」「それがどうだっていうんだ」 **11** ADV 副詞 You can use **so** in front of adjectives and adverbs to emphasize the quality that they are describing. とても、非常に [EMPHASIS 強調] [ADV adj/adv] □ *He was surprised they had married – they had seemed so different.* 彼は2人が結婚したことにびっくりした。2人が正反対のように思えたからだ。 **12** ADV 副詞 You can use **so...that** and **so...as** to emphasize the degree of something by mentioning the result or consequence of it. とても~なので [EMPHASIS 強調] □ *The tears were streaming so fast she could not see.* 涙がとめどなくあふれすぎて目が見えなかった。 □ *He's not so stupid as to listen to rumors.* 彼はうわさに耳を貸すほどばかじゃない。 **13** → see also **insofar as** **14** PHRASE 句 You use **and so on** or **and so forth** at the end of a list to indicate that there are other items that you could also mention. ~など □ *...the government's policies on such important issues as health, education, tax, and so on.* 医療、教育、税金などの重要懸案に対する政府の方針。 **15** PHRASE 句 You use **so much** and **so many** when you are saying that there is a definite limit to something but you are not saying what this limit is. 限られた~ □ *There is only so much time in the day for answering letters.* 1日のうちに手紙の返事が書ける時間は限られている。 □ *There is only so much fuel in the tank and if you burn it up too quickly you are in trouble.* タンクの燃料は限りがあるので、あまり早く使い切ってしまうと面倒なことになる。 **16** PHRASE 句 You use the structures **not...so much** and **not so much...as** to say that something is one kind of thing rather than another kind. ~ほどでない □ *I did not really object to Will's behavior so much as his personality.* ウィルの性格は嫌だけど、彼の態度はそれほどでもない。 **17** PHRASE 句 You use **or so** when you are giving an approximate amount. ~かそのくらい [VAGUENESS あいまいさ] □ *Though rates are heading down, they still offer real returns of 8% or so.* 金利は下がっているものの、依然として実質8%前後の利回りがある。 **18** **so much the better** → see **better** **19** **so far so good** → see **far** **20** **so long** → see **long** **21** **so much so** → see **much** **22** **every so often** → see **often** **23** **so there** → see **there**

So, very, and **too** can all be used to intensify the meaning of an adjective, an adverb, or a word like **much** or **many**. However, they are not used in the same way. **Very** is the simplest intensifier. It has no other meaning beyond that. **So** can suggest an emotional reaction on the part of the speaker, such as pleasure, surprise, or disappointment. □ *John makes me so angry!...* □ *Oh thank you so much!* **So** can also refer forward to a result clause introduced by **that**. □ *The procession was forced to move so slowly that he arrived three hours late.* **Too** suggests an excessive or undesirable amount, often so much that a particular result does not or cannot happen. □ *She does wear too much make-up at times... He was too late to save her.*

soak /soʊk/ (**soaks, soaking, soaked**) **1** V-T/V-I 他動詞/自動詞 If you **soak** something or leave it to **soak**, you put it into a liquid and leave it there. 浸す、つける □ *Soak the beans for 2 hours.* 豆を2時間ほど水に浸します。 **2** V-T 他動詞 If a liquid **soaks** something or if you **soak** something **with** a liquid, the liquid makes the thing very wet. びしょびしょにする □ *The water had soaked his jacket and shirt.* その水で彼のジャケットとシャツはびしょ濡れになった。 **3** V-I 自動詞 If a liquid **soaks through** something, it passes through it. しみ込む □ *There was so much blood it had soaked through my boxer shorts.* かなりの出血でボクサーパンツは血に染まっていた。 **4** V-I 自動詞 If someone **soaks**, they spend a long time in a hot bath, because they enjoy it. つかる □ *What I need is to soak in a hot tub.* どうしたいかといえば、熱い風呂につかりたい。 ● N-COUNT 可算名詞 **Soak** is also a noun. つかること □ *I was having a long soak in the bath.* ゆっくりと風呂につかっていました。 **5** → see also **soaked, soaking**
▶ **soak up** **1** PHRASAL VERB 句動詞 If a soft or dry material **soaks up** a liquid, the liquid goes into the substance. 吸い込む □ *The cells will promptly start to soak up moisture.* 細胞はすぐに水分を吸収し始める。 **2** PHRASAL VERB 句動詞 If you **soak up** the atmosphere in a place that you are visiting, you observe or get involved in the way of life there, because you enjoy it or are interested in it. 楽しむ [INFORMAL くだけた] □ *Keaton comes here once or twice a year to soak up the atmosphere.* キートンはこの雰囲気に浸るために年に1、2度ここを訪れる。 **3** PHRASAL VERB 句動詞 If something **soaks up** something such as money or other resources, it uses a great deal of money or other resources. 使い果たす □ *Defense soaks up 40 percent of the budget.* 国防費は国家予算の40%にも及んでいます。

soaked /soʊkt/ ADJ 形容詞 If someone or something gets **soaked** or **soaked through**, water or some other liquid makes them extremely wet. ずぶぬれの □ *I have to check my tent – it got soaked last night in the storm.* テントが大丈夫か見ておかないとね。昨夜の大雨でずぶぬれになったから。 □ *We got soaked to the skin.* 私たちはずぶぬれになった。

soak|ing /soʊkɪŋ/ ADJ 形容詞 If something is **soaking** or **soaking wet**, it is very wet. ずぶぬれの □ *My face and raincoat were soaking wet.* 顔もレーンコートもびしょびしょだった。

so-and-so PRON-SING 単数代名詞 You use **so-and-so** instead of a word, expression, or name when you are talking generally rather than giving a specific example of a particular thing. これこれしかじか [INFORMAL くだけた] □ *It would be a case of "just do so-and-so and here's your cash."* これは「これこれしかじかのことをしてくれ。ほら礼はここにある」というようなケースだろう。

soap /soʊp/ (**soaps**) **1** N-MASS 質量名詞 **Soap** is a substance that you use with water for washing yourself or sometimes for washing clothes. せっけん □ *...a bar of lavender soap.* ラベンダーのせっけん1個。 □ *...a large box of soap powder.* 粉せっけんの大箱1箱。 **2** N-COUNT 可算名詞 A **soap** is the same as a **soap opera**. ソープオペラ [INFORMAL くだけた]
→ see Word Web: **soap**

soap op|era (**soap operas**) N-COUNT 可算名詞 A **soap opera** is a popular television drama series about the daily lives and problems of a group of people who live in a particular place. ソープオペラ、連続メロドラマ

soar /sɔr/ (**soars, soaring, soared**) **1** V-I 自動詞 If the amount, value, level, or volume of something **soars**, it quickly increases by a great deal. 急に上がる [JOURNALISM ジャーナリズム] □ *Shares soared on the New York stock exchange.* ニューヨーク証券取引所で株価

S

Word Web soap

Soap is an important part of everyday life. We **wash** our hands before we eat. We lather up with a **bar** of soap in the **shower** or tub. We use liquid **detergent** to **clean** our dishes. We use **laundry** detergent to get our clothes clean. But why do we use soap? How does it work? It works almost like a magnet. Only instead of attracting and repelling metal, soap attracts dirt and grease. It makes a **bubble** around the dirt, and water washes it all away.

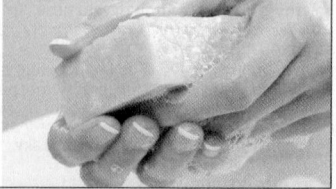

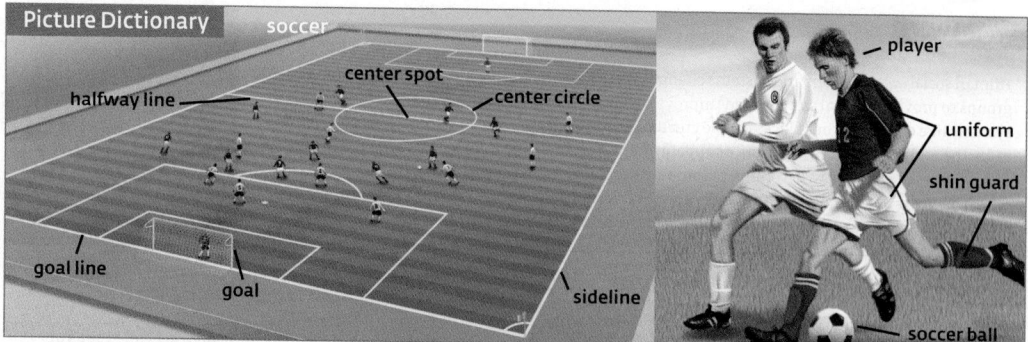

Picture Dictionary soccer

halfway line · center spot · center circle · player · uniform · shin guard · goal line · goal · sideline · soccer ball

が急騰した. ② V-I 自動詞 If something such as a bird **soars** into the air, it goes quickly up into the air. 空高く舞い上がる [LITERARY 文語的] ❑ If you're lucky, a splendid golden eagle may soar into view. 運がよければ, 空高く舞い上がるイヌワシの壮麗な姿が見られるかもしれない.

sob /spb/ (**sobs, sobbing, sobbed**) ■ V-I 自動詞 When someone **sobs**, they cry in a noisy way, breathing in short breaths. むせび泣く, 泣きじゃくる ❑ She began to sob again, burying her face in the pillow. 彼女は枕に顔をうずめて, また泣きじゃくり始めた. ● **sob|bing** N-UNCOUNT 不可算名詞 むせび泣き ❑ The room was silent except for her sobbing. 部屋は静まり返り, ただ彼女のむせび泣く声だけがしていた. ② N-COUNT 可算名詞 A **sob** is one of the noises that you make when you are crying. むせび泣く音 ❑ Her sobs grew louder. 彼女のむせび泣く声がだんだん激しくなった.

so|ber /soʊbər/ (**sobers, sobering, sobered**) ■ ADJ 形容詞 When you are **sober**, you are not drunk. 酔っていない, しらふの ❑ He'd been drunk when I arrived. Now he was sober. 私が来たとき彼は酔っていたが, そのときにはもう酔いがさめていた. ② ADJ 形容詞 A **sober** person is serious and thoughtful. まじめな ❑ We are now far more sober and realistic. 今では以前よりずっとまじめで現実的になった. ❑ It was a room filled with sad, sober faces. 部屋は悲しく重苦しい雰囲気に包まれていた. ● **so|ber|ly** ADV 副詞 まじめに ❑ "There's a new development," he said soberly. 「新たな進展がある」と彼は真剣な表情で言った. ③ ADJ 形容詞 **Sober** colors and clothes are plain and rather dull. 地味な ❑ He dresses in sober gray suits. 彼は地味なグレーのスーツを着ている. ● **so|ber|ly** ADV 副詞 [ADV with v] 地味に ❑ She saw Ellis, soberly dressed in a well-cut dark suit. 彼女はエリスを見かけたが, 仕立てのよい黒っぽいスーツ姿で控えめだった. ④ → see also **sobering**

▶ **sober up** PHRASAL VERB 句動詞 If someone **sobers up**, or if something **sobers** them **up**, they become sober after being drunk. 酔いがさめる; 酔いをさます ❑ He was left to sober up in a police cell. 彼は酔いがさめるまで警察の留置場に入れられた.

so|ber|ing /soʊbərɪŋ/ ADJ 形容詞 You say that something is a **sobering** thought or has a **sobering** effect when a situation seems serious and makes you become serious and thoughtful. 目を覚ますような ❑ It is a sobering thought that in the 17th century she could have been burned as a witch. これがもし17世紀だったら彼女は魔女として火あぶりにされていたかもしれないと考えるとぞっとする.

so-called also **so called** ■ ADJ 形容詞 You use **so-called** to indicate that you think a word or expression used to describe someone or something is in fact wrong. 俗にいう [ADJ n] ❑ These are the facts that explode their so-called economic miracle. これらは俗にいう「経済の奇跡」を否定する事実である. ② ADJ 形容詞 You use **so-called** to indicate that something is generally referred to by the name that you are about to use. いわゆる [ADJ n] ❑ ...a summit of the world's seven leading market economies, the so-called G-7. 世界の経済先進7か国サミット, いわゆるG7サミット.

soc|cer /spkər/ N-UNCOUNT 不可算名詞 **Soccer** is a game played by two teams of eleven players using a round ball. Players kick the ball to each other and try to score goals by kicking the ball into a large net. Outside the United States, this game is also referred to as **football**. サッカー ❑ ...a soccer match. サッカーの試合. → see Picture Dictionary: soccer

soc|cer play|er /spkər pleɪər/ (**soccer players**) N-COUNT 可算名詞 A **soccer player** is a person who plays soccer, especially as a profession. サッカー選手. [AM 米国英語]

so|cia|ble /soʊʃəb^эl/ ADJ 形容詞 **Sociable** people are friendly and enjoy talking to other people. 社交的な ❑ She was, and remained, extremely sociable, enjoying dancing, golf, tennis, skating, and bicycling. 彼女は昔からずっと人付き合いがよく, ダンスにゴルフ, テニスにスケートにサイクリングと楽しみが多かった.

Word Link soci ≈ companion : **associate, social, sociology**

so|cial /soʊʃ^эl/ ■ ADJ 形容詞 **Social** means relating to society or to the way society is organized. 社会の [ADJ n] ❑ ...the worst effects of unemployment, low pay, and other social problems. 失業, 低賃金といった社会問題を生む最悪の結果. ❑ ...long-term social change. 長期的な社会の変化. ❑ ...changing social attitudes. 変化する社会の態度. ● **so|cial|ly** ADV 副詞 社会的に ❑ Let's face it – drinking is a socially acceptable habit. 現実に向き合おうじゃないか. 飲酒は社会的に認められた習慣だ. ② ADJ 形容詞 **Social** means relating to the status or rank that someone has in society. 社会の [ADJ n] ❑ Higher education is unequally distributed across social classes. 高等教育は階級間の格差がある. ● **so|cial|ly** ADV 副詞 社会的に ❑ For socially ambitious couples this is a problem. 世俗的な成功を望むカップルにとってこれは問題である. ③ ADJ 形容詞 [ADJ n] **Social** means relating to leisure activities that involve meeting other people. つきあいの ❑ We ought to organize more social events. もっと親睦活動をやっていくべきだ. ● **so|cial|ly** ADV 副詞 つきあいで ❑ We have known each other socially for a long time. 我々は長いつきあいがある. → see **kiss, myth, society**

so|cial|ism /soʊʃəlɪzəm/ N-UNCOUNT 不可算名詞 **Socialism** is a set of political principles whose general aim is to create a system in which everyone has an equal opportunity to benefit from a country's wealth. Under socialism, the country's main industries are usually owned by the state. 社会主義

so|cial|ist /soʊʃəlɪst/ (**socialists**) ■ ADJ 形容詞 **Socialist** means based on socialism or relating to socialism. 社会主義の ❑ ...members of the ruling Socialist Party. 与党社会党の党員. ② N-COUNT 可算名詞 A **socialist** is a person who believes in socialism or who is a member of a socialist party. 社会主義者; 社会党員 ❑ Esperanto has always been popular among socialists. エスペラントはこれまでずっと社会主義者たちの間で広く使われてきました.

so|cial|ize /soʊʃəlaɪz/ (**socializes, socializing, socialized**) V-I 自動詞 If you **socialize**, you meet other people socially, for example at parties. つきあう ❑ ...an open meeting, where members socialized and welcomed any new members. 新会員との交流の場となった自由参加の歓迎会.

so|cial sci|ence (**social sciences**) ■ N-UNCOUNT 不可算名詞 **Social science** is the scientific study of society. 社会学 ❑ The research methods of social science generate two kinds of data. 社会学の研究方法によって2種類のデータが生み出される. ② N-COUNT 可算名詞 The **social sciences** are the various types of social science, for example sociology and politics. 社会科学 ❑ ...a degree in a social science. 社会科学の学位.

So|cial Se|cu|rity N-UNCOUNT 不可算名詞 **Social Security** is a system by which workers and employers in the U.S. have to pay money to the government, which gives money to people who are retired, who are disabled, or who cannot work. 社会保障 ❑ My mother never worked, so she's not eligible for Social Security. 母は勤めたことがないので社会保障を受ける資格はない. ❑ Future retirees are expected to get smaller Social Security benefits than promised. 今後退職する人については, 社会保障の年金支給額は当初予定よりも減額される見込みである.

So|cial Se|cu|rity num|ber (**Social Security numbers**) N-COUNT 可算名詞 A **Social Security** number is a nine-digit number that is given to U.S. citizens and to people living in the U.S. You need it to get a job, collect Social Security benefits and receive some government services. 社会保障番号 ❑ Questions such as date of birth and Social Security number are straightforward. 生年月日や社会保障番号などの質問ならば簡単に分かる.

so|cial ser|vices N-PLURAL 複数名詞 **Social services** in a district are the services provided by the local authority or government to help people who have serious family problems or financial problems. 社会福祉 ❑ Schools and social services are also struggling to

Word Web   society

Human **social** organizations and **customs** change over time. Early humans established **hunter-gatherer** groups to provide mutual support and improve survival. Later, people in some areas formed family systems like **clans**. In other places people created multi-family groups, or **tribes**. Here leadership came through inheritance, election, or appointment. Some groups were led by women, but these matriarchies are rare today. According to some anthropologists, many societies today are patriarchies where power is held by men. **Feminism** is a societal response seeking to balance power in society. Societies continue to evolve to meet the needs of the people who live within them.

absorb the influx. 学校や社会福祉課も押し寄せる人たちの対応に追われている.

so|cial work N-UNCOUNT 不可算名詞 **Social work** is work which involves giving help and advice to people with serious family problems or financial problems. 社会福祉業務

so|cial work|er (social workers) N-COUNT 可算名詞 A **social worker** is a person whose job is to do social work. ソーシャルワーカー, 民生委員

so|ci|e|ty /səsaɪɪti/ (societies) **1** N-UNCOUNT 不可算名詞 **Society** is people in general, thought of as a large organized group. 社会 □ *This reflects attitudes and values prevailing in society.* これは社会に浸透している態度や価値観を反映している. **2** N-VAR 可変性名詞 A **society** is the people who live in a country or region, their organizations, and their way of life. 社会 □ *We live in a capitalist society.* 我々は資本主義社会に生きている. **3** N-COUNT 可算名詞 A **society** is an organization for people who have the same interest or aim. 一協会 □ *...the Atlanta Horticultural Society.* アトランタ園芸協会. **4** N-UNCOUNT 不可算名詞 **Society** is the rich, fashionable people in a particular place who meet on social occasions. 上流社会 □ *The couple quickly became a fixture in society.* 2人はすぐに社交界に溶け込んでいった.
→ see Word Web: **society**

so|cio|eco|nom|ic /soʊsiʊɛkənɒmɪk, -ikə-/ ADJ 形容詞 **Socioeconomic** circumstances or developments involve a combination of social and economic factors. 社会経済的な [ADJ n] □ *The age, education, and socioeconomic status of these young mothers led to less satisfactory child care.* こうした若い母親は, 年齢や教育, 社会経済的な地位が障害となって, 十分な子育てができなかった.

Word Link   *soci ≈ companion : as**soci**ate, **soci**al, **soci**ology*

so|ci|ol|o|gy /soʊsiɒlədʒi/ N-UNCOUNT 不可算名詞 **Sociology** is the study of society or of the way society is organized. 社会学 ● **so|cio|logi|cal** /soʊsiəlɒdʒɪkªl/ ADJ 形容詞 社会学的な □ *Psychological and sociological studies were emphasizing the importance of the family.* 心理学や社会学の研究では家族の重要性を強調していた. ● **so|ci|olo|gist** N-COUNT 可算名詞 (sociologists) 社会学者 □ *By the 1950s some sociologists were confident that they had identified the key characteristics of capitalist society.* 1950年代までには, 一部の社会学者は資本主義社会の主要な特徴を解明したと信じていた.

so|cio|po|liti|cal /soʊsioʊpəlɪtɪkªl/ ADJ 形容詞 **Sociopolitical** systems and problems involve a combination of social and political factors. 社会政治的な [ADJ n] □ *...contemporary sociopolitical issues such as ecology, human rights, and nuclear arms.* 生態系, 人権, 核兵器など, 現代の社会政治上の問題.

sock /sɒk/ (socks, socking, socked) **1** N-COUNT 可算名詞 **Socks** are pieces of clothing which cover your foot and ankle and are worn inside shoes. 靴下, ソックス □ *a pair of knee-high socks.* ハイソックス1足. **2** V-T 他動詞 If you **sock** someone or something, you hit them hard. 殴る [INFORMAL くだけた] □ *Once, after a boy made a comment, she socked him.* 彼女は以前1度, 男の子が何か言ったのでその子を殴ったことがあった. **3** V-T 他動詞 If someone **is socked with** something bad, it happens to them. 降りかかってくる □ *Phil got socked with a bill for nearly $1,000.* フィルのところに突然1000ドル近い請求書が送りつけられてきた.
→ see **clothing**

sock|et /sɒkɪt/ (sockets) **1** N-COUNT 可算名詞 A **socket** is a device on a piece of electrical equipment into which you can put a bulb or plug. ソケット □ *On the stairway to the basement, he took the light bulb out of the socket.* 地下室に下りる階段で彼はソケットから電球をはずした. **2** N-COUNT 可算名詞 A **socket** is a device or point in a wall where you can connect electrical equipment to the power supply. コンセント [mainly BRIT 主に英国英語; AM usually **outlet** 米国英語では通常 **outlet**] **3** N-COUNT 可算名詞 You can refer to any hollow part or opening in a structure which another part fits into as a **socket**. 肩の関節を5回回します. □ *Rotate the shoulders in their sockets five times.* 肩の関節を5回回します.

soda /soʊdə/ (sodas) **1** N-MASS 質量名詞 **Soda** is a sweet carbonated drink. 炭酸飲料 [AM 米国英語] □ *...a glass of diet soda.* グラス1杯のダイエット炭酸飲料. ● N-COUNT 可算名詞 A **soda** is a

bottle of soda. 1瓶の炭酸飲料 □ *They had liquor for the adults and sodas for the children.* 大人にはお酒, 子供には炭酸飲料が出されました.

> Carbonated drinks containing no alcohol are called **soda** or **soda pop**. They are usually very sweet. Another name is **soft drinks**, and this is the term usually used in the UK.

2 N-UNCOUNT 不可算名詞 **Soda** is the same as **soda water**. ソーダ水 **3** → see also **baking soda, club soda**

soda pop (soda pops) N-UNCOUNT 不可算名詞 **Soda pop** is a sweet carbonated drink. 炭酸飲料 [AM 米国英語] □ *Beer and soda pop are served before the bus departs.* バスが出発する前にビールや炭酸飲料が出される. ● N-COUNT 可算名詞 A **soda pop** is a bottle or a glass of soda pop. コップ1杯の炭酸飲料 □ *He bought me a soda pop.* 彼は炭酸飲料を1杯おごってくれた.

soda wa|ter also **soda-water** N-UNCOUNT 不可算名詞 **Soda water** is carbonated water and is often used for mixing with alcoholic drinks and fruit juice. ソーダ水

sod|den /sɒdªn/ ADJ 形容詞 Something that is **sodden** is extremely wet. びしょぬれの □ *We stripped off our sodden clothes.* びしょぬれの服を脱いだ.

so|dium /soʊdiəm/ N-UNCOUNT 不可算名詞 **Sodium** is a silvery white chemical element which combines with other chemicals. Salt is a sodium compound. ナトリウム □ *The fish or seafood is heavily salted with pure sodium chloride.* 魚介類は不純物の含まない食塩をたっぷり使って塩漬けされる.

sofa /soʊfə/ (sofas) N-COUNT 可算名詞 A **sofa** is a long, comfortable seat with a back and usually with arms, which two or three people can sit on. ソファー

soft /sɒft/ (softer, softest) **1** ADJ 形容詞 Something that is **soft** is pleasant to touch, and not rough or hard. しなやかな □ *Regular use of a body lotion will keep the skin soft and supple.* 日頃からボディーローションを使うと, すべすべしたしなやかな肌になります. □ *When it's dry, brush the hair using a soft, nylon baby brush.* 髪が乾いたら, 赤ちゃん用の柔らかいナイロンブラシで髪をとかしてあげます. ● **soft|ness** N-UNCOUNT 不可算名詞 しなやかさ □ *The sea air robbed her hair of its softness.* 海風にさらされて, 彼女の髪はしなやかさを失った. **2** ADJ 形容詞 Something that is **soft** changes shape or bends easily when you press it. 柔らかな □ *She lay down on the soft, comfortable bed.* 彼女は柔らかで心地よいベッドに横になった. □ *Add enough milk to form a soft dough.* 生地が柔らかくなるように牛乳を十分加えます. **3** ADJ 形容詞 Something that has a **soft** appearance has smooth curves rather than sharp or distinct edges. 優しい □ *This is a smart, yet soft and feminine look.* おしゃれで, しかも優しく女性らしいファッションだ. ● **soft|ly** ADV 副詞 [ADV with v] 心地よく □ *She wore a softly tailored suit.* 彼女は優しい感じのスーツを着ていた. **4** ADJ 形容詞 Something that is **soft** is very gentle and has no force. For example, a **soft** sound or voice is quiet and not harsh. A **soft** light or color is pleasant to look at because it is not bright. 穏やかな □ *There was a soft tapping on my door.* ドアを軽くたたく音がした. ● **soft|ly** ADV 副詞 [ADV with v] 穏やかに □ *She crossed the softly lit room.* 彼女は柔らかな照明の部屋を通り抜けた. **5** ADJ 形容詞 If you are **soft on** someone, you do not treat them as strictly or severely as you should. 甘い [DISAPPROVAL 不賛成] □ *The president says the measure is soft and weak on criminals.* 大統領によれば, この処置は犯罪者に甘く手ぬるいと言います. **6** ADJ 形容詞 If you say that someone has a **soft heart**, you mean that they are sensitive and sympathetic toward other people. 人に優しい [APPROVAL 賛成] □ *Her rather tough and worldly exterior hides a very soft and sensitive heart.* たくましくて如才ない外見とは裏腹に, 彼女には人に優しい隠れた一面がある. **7** ADJ 形容詞 You use **soft** to describe a way of life that is easy and involves very little work. 楽な □ *...a soft life and easy living.* 楽な人生と楽な暮らし. **8** ADJ 形容詞 **Soft** water does not contain much of the mineral calcium and so makes bubbles easily when you use soap. 軟水の □ *an area where the water is very soft.* 軟水度の高い地域. **9** ADJ 形容詞 **Soft** drugs are drugs, such as cannabis, which are illegal but which many people do not consider to be strong or harmful. 中毒性の弱い [mainly BRIT 主に英国英語] [ADJ n] [AM **recreational** 米国英語 **recreational**]

Word Web   solar

solar collector

photovoltaic cells

Traditional **fossil fuel energy** sources are becoming scarce and expensive. They also cause environmental **pollution**. Recently scientists have turned to alternative sources of energy such as **solar power**. There are two ways of using the **sun's energy**. **Thermal** systems produce heat. **Photovoltaic** systems generate electricity. Thermal systems use a **solar collector**. This is an insulated box with a transparent cover. It stores the sun's energy for use in household air or water heating systems. Photovoltaic systems use thin layers of **semiconductor** materials to change the sun's heat into electricity. They are commonly used to power calculators and solar-powered watches.

Thesaurus   *soft* また次を参照：

ADJ.   fluffy, silky; (*ant.*) firm, hard, rough **1**
     malleable **2**
     faint, gentle, light, low; (*ant.*) clear, strong **4**

soft drink (**soft drinks**) N-COUNT 可算名詞 A **soft drink** is a cold, nonalcoholic drink such as lemonade or fruit juice, or a carbonated drink. ソフトドリンク, 清涼飲料

sof|ten /sɔ́fᵊn/ (**softens, softening, softened**) **1** V-T/V-I 他動詞/自動詞 If you **soften** something or if it **softens**, it becomes less hard, stiff, or firm. 柔らかくする [他動詞] 柔らかくなる [自動詞] □ *Soften the butter mixture in a small saucepan.* バターを混ぜたものを小さな鍋で溶かします. **2** V-T 他動詞 If one thing **softens** the damaging effect of another thing, it makes the effect less severe. 和らげる □ *There were also pledges to soften the impact of the subsidy cuts on the poorer regions.* 財政的に厳しい地域には補助金削減の影響を緩和するという公約もあった. **3** V-T/V-I 他動詞/自動詞 If you **soften** your position, if your position **softens**, or if you **soften**, you become more sympathetic and less hostile or critical. 軟化させる [他動詞] 軟化する [自動詞] □ *The letter shows no sign that the Germans have softened their position.* 手紙からはドイツが態度を軟化させた様子はうかがえません. □ *His party's policy has softened a lot in recent years.* 近年, 彼の党は穏健路線に転換してきた. **4** V-T/V-I 他動詞/自動詞 If your voice or expression **softens** or if you **soften** it, it becomes more gentle and friendly. 和らげる [他動詞] 和らぐ [自動詞] □ *All at once, Mick's serious expression softened into a grin.* 一瞬にしてミックの深刻な表情が笑顔に変わった. **5** V-T 他動詞 If you **soften** something such as light, a color, or a sound, you make it less bright or harsh. 和らげる □ *We wanted to soften the light without destroying the overall effect of space.* 空間の全体的な感じはそのまま残して照明を和らげたかった. **6** V-T 他動詞 Something that **softens** your skin makes it very smooth and pleasant to touch. すべすべにする □ *...products designed to moisturize and soften the skin.* 肌に潤いとしなやかさを与える化粧品.

soft land|ing (**soft landings**) N-COUNT 可算名詞 In economics, a **soft landing** is a situation in which the economy stops growing but this does not produce a recession. 軟着陸 □ *...the belief that the economy is on course for a so-called soft landing.* 経済がいわゆる軟着陸に向かっているという見方.

soft loan (**soft loans**) N-COUNT 可算名詞 A **soft loan** is a loan with a very low interest rate. Soft loans are usually made to developing countries or to businesses in developing countries. ソフトローン [BUSINESS 実業]

soft sell also **soft-sell** N-SING 単数名詞 A **soft sell** is a method of selling or advertising that involves persuading people in a gentle way rather than putting a lot of pressure on people to buy things. 穏やかな売り込み [BUSINESS 実業] □ *I think many customers probably prefer a soft sell.* 穏やかな売り込みを好む消費者のほうが多いだろう.

Word Link   *ware ≈ merchandise : hardware, silverware, software*

soft|ware /sɔ́ftwɛər/ N-UNCOUNT 不可算名詞 Computer programs are referred to as **software**. Compare **hardware**. ソフト

ウエア [COMPUTING コンピューティング] □ *...the people who write the software for big computer projects.* 大規模なコンピュータプロジェクトのソフトウエアを開発する人たち.
→ see **computer**

sog|gy /sɔ́gi/ (**soggier, soggiest**) ADJ 形容詞 Something that is **soggy** is unpleasantly wet. じめじめした □ *...soggy cheese sandwiches.* べったりしたチーズサンド.

soil /sɔ́ɪl/ (**soils**) N-MASS 質量名詞 **Soil** is the substance on the surface of the earth in which plants grow. 土 □ *We have the most fertile soil in the Midwest.* アメリカでは中西部の土壌が最も肥沃である.
→ see **farm**

sol|ace /sɔ́lɪs/ N-UNCOUNT 可算名詞 **Solace** is a feeling of comfort that makes you feel less sad. 慰め [FORMAL 形式ばった] □ *I found solace in writing when my father died three years ago.* 3年前に父を亡くしたとき, ものを書くことが心の慰めになった.

so|lar /sóʊlər/ **1** ADJ 形容詞 **Solar** is used to describe things relating to the sun. 太陽の □ *A total solar eclipse is due to take place some time tomorrow.* 明日, 皆既日食が起こります. **2** ADJ 形容詞 **Solar** power is obtained from the sun's light and heat. 太陽熱発電の □ *...the financial savings from solar energy.* 太陽熱発電による経費節減.
→ see Word Web: **solar**
→ see **energy, greenhouse effect, solar system**

so|lar sys|tem (**solar systems**) N-COUNT 可算名詞 The **solar system** is the sun and all the planets that go around it. 太陽系 □ *Saturn is the second biggest planet in the solar system.* 土星は太陽系で2番目に大きい惑星です.
→ see Word Web: **solar system**
→ see **galaxy**

sold /sóʊld/ **Sold** is the past tense and past participle of **sell**.

sol|dier /sóʊldʒər/ (**soldiers**) N-COUNT 可算名詞 A **soldier** is a member of an army, especially a person who is not an officer. 兵士
→ see **war**

sold out **1** ADJ 形容詞 If a performance, sports event, or other entertainment is **sold out**, all the tickets for it have been sold. 売り切れの [v-link ADJ] □ *The premiere on Monday is sold out.* 月曜の初日のチケットは完売した. **2** ADJ 形容詞 If a store is **sold out of** something, it has sold all of it that it had. 品切れになっている [v-link ADJ] □ *The stores are sometimes sold out of certain groceries.* 店では一部の食料雑貨が品切れになっているところがあります. **3** → see **also sell out**

sole /sóʊl/ (**soles**) **1** ADJ 形容詞 The **sole** thing or person of a particular type is the only one of that type. 唯一の [ADJ n] □ *Their sole aim is to destabilize the Indian government.* 彼らの唯一の目的はインドの政権を弱体化することです. **2** ADJ 形容詞 If you have **sole** charge or ownership of something, you are the only person in charge of it or who owns it. ただ一人の [ADJ n] □ *Many women are left as the sole providers in families after their husband has died.* 女性の多くは夫が亡くなると一人で家族を支えることになります. **3** N-COUNT 可算名詞 The **sole** of your foot or of a shoe or sock

Word Web   solar system

The **sun** formed when a **nebula** turned into a star almost 5 billion years ago. All the **planets**, **comets**, and asteroids in our **solar system** started out in this nebula. Today they all **orbit** around the sun. The four planets closest to the sun are small and rocky. The next four consist mostly of **gases**. The outermost planet, Pluto, is a dwarf planet. It is composed of rock and ice. Many of the planets have **moons** orbiting them. Most asteroids are irregularly shaped and covered with **craters**. Only about 200 asteroids have diameters of over 100 kilometers.

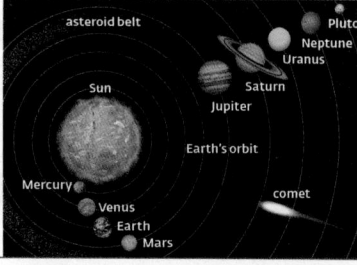

is the underneath surface of it. 足底 ❑ *...shoes with rubber soles.* ゴム底の靴.
→ see **fish, foot**

sole|ly /soʊlli/ ADV 副詞 If something involves **solely** one thing, it involves only this thing and no others. もっぱら ❑ *Too often we make decisions based solely upon what we see in the magazines.* 雑誌に書かれたことだけで判断してしまうことが多すぎる.

sol|emn /sɒləm/ **1** ADJ 形容詞 Someone or something that is **solemn** is very serious rather than cheerful or humorous. 厳粛な ❑ *His solemn little face broke into smiles.* 彼のまじめくさった小さな顔から突然笑みがこぼれた. ● **sol|emn|ity** /səlɛmnɪti/ N-UNCOUNT 不可算名詞 厳粛さ ❑ *The setting for this morning's signing ceremony matched the solemnity of the occasion.* 今朝の署名式の会場は厳粛な式典にふさわしい場所でした. **2** ADJ 形容詞 A **solemn** promise or agreement is one that you make in a very formal, sincere way. 真剣な ❑ *She made a solemn promise to him when they became engaged that she would give up cigarettes for good.* 婚約するときに彼女が彼に堅く約束したのは, たばこは金輪際吸わないということだった.

so|lic|it /səlɪsɪt/ (solicits, soliciting, solicited) **1** V-T 他動詞 If you **solicit** money, help, support, or an opinion **from** someone, you ask them for it. 要請する [FORMAL 形式ばった] ❑ *He's already solicited their support on health care reform.* 彼はすでに彼らに対して医療改革について支援してくれるように要請しています. **2** V-I 自動詞 When prostitutes **solicit**, they offer to have sex with people in return for money. 客引きする ❑ *Prostitutes were forbidden to solicit on public roads and in public places.* 公道や人目のつく場所で売春の客引きをすることは禁じられた. ● **so|lic|it|ing** N-UNCOUNT 不可算名詞 売春の客引き ❑ *Girls could get very heavy sentences for soliciting – nine months or more.* 少女たちは売春勧誘罪で9ヶ月以上の重い刑を受ける恐れがある.

so|lic|ita|tion /səlɪsɪteɪʃⁿn/ (solicitations) N-VAR 可変性名詞 **Solicitation** is the act of asking someone for money, help, support, or an opinion. 懇願 [mainly AM 主に米国英語] ❑ *Republican leaders are making open solicitation of the Italian-American vote.* 共和党の指導者たちは公然とイタリア系アメリカ人有権者に支持を呼びかけている.

so|lici|tor /səlɪsɪtər/ (solicitors) N-COUNT 可算名詞 In the United States, a **solicitor** is the chief lawyer in a government or city department. 法務官

sol|id /sɒlɪd/ (solids) **1** ADJ 形容詞 A **solid** substance or object stays the same shape whether it is in a container or not. 固体の ❑ *...the potential of greatly reducing our solid waste problem.* 大幅に固体廃棄物を減らせる可能性. **2** N-COUNT 可算名詞 A **solid** is a substance that stays the same shape whether it is in a container or not. 固体 ❑ *Solids turn to liquids at certain temperatures.* 固体は決まった温度になると液体に変わる. **3** ADJ 形容詞 A substance that is **solid** is very hard or firm. 硬い ❑ *The snow had melted, but the lake was still frozen solid.* 雪は解けていたが, 湖はまだ硬く凍っていた. **4** ADJ 形容詞 A **solid** object or mass does not have a space inside it, or holes or gaps in it. ぎっしり詰まった ❑ *...a tunnel carved through 50 ft of solid rock.* 50フィートの硬い岩盤を掘り抜いたトンネル. ❑ *The train station was packed solid with people.* 駅は押すな押すなの大混雑だった. **5** ADJ 形容詞 If an object is made of **solid** gold or **solid** wood, for example, it is made of gold or wood all the way through, rather than just on the outside. 純粋の [ADJ n] ❑ *The faucets appeared to be made of solid gold.* 蛇口は純金製のようだった. ❑ *...solid wood doors.* 無垢 (むく) 板のドア. **6** ADJ 形容詞 A structure that is **solid** is strong and is not likely to collapse or fall over. 頑丈な ❑ *Banks are built to look solid to reassure their customers.* 銀行は顧客に安心感を与えるために頑丈にできている. ● **sol|id|ly** ADV 副詞 [ADV with v] 頑丈に ❑ *Their house, which was solidly built, resisted the main shock.* 彼らの家は頑丈に建てられていたので一番大きな衝撃にも耐えた. ● **so|lid|ity** /səlɪdɪti/ N-UNCOUNT 不可算名

詞 頑丈さ ❑ *...the solidity of walls and floors.* 壁や床の頑丈さ. **7** ADJ 形容詞 If you describe someone as **solid**, you mean that they are very reliable and respectable. 堅実な [APPROVAL 賛成] ❑ *You want a husband who is solid and stable, someone who will devote himself to you.* 堅実で頼りがいがあって, 自分に尽くしてくれるような人を夫にしたいだろう. ● **sol|id|ly** ADV 副詞 堅実に ❑ *Graham is so solidly consistent.* グレアムはとても堅実で頼りがいがある. ● **so|lid|ity** N-UNCOUNT 不可算名詞 堅実なこと ❑ *He had the proverbial solidity of the English.* 彼はいわゆるイギリス人の堅実さを持ち合わせていた. **8** ADJ 形容詞 **Solid** evidence or information is reliable because it is based on facts. 信頼できる ❑ *We don't have good solid information on where the people are.* その人たちの居場所については確かな情報がありません. **9** ADJ 形容詞 You use **solid** to describe something such as advice or a piece of work which is useful and reliable. 有益な ❑ *The organization provides churches with solid advice on a wide range of subjects.* 団体は教会に対して広範にわたる有益な助言を提供している. ● **sol|id|ly** ADV 副詞 [ADV with v] ぶっ通しで ❑ *She's played solidly throughout the spring.* 彼女はこの春ずっと休みなく演奏してきました. **10** ADJ 形容詞 You use **solid** to describe something such as the basis for a policy or support for an organization when it is strong, because it has been developed carefully and slowly. 強固な ❑ *...a Democratic nominee with solid support within the party and broad appeal beyond.* 党内からは確固たる支持を受け, 党外でも幅広い人気を集める民主党指名候補. ● **sol|id|ly** ADV 副詞 The Los Alamos district is solidly Republican. ロスアラモス選挙区は共和党の厚い地盤である. ● **so|lid|ity** N-UNCOUNT 不可算名詞 強固さ ❑ *...doubts over the solidity of European backing for the American approach.* ヨーロッパがアメリカのやり方をどこまで本気で支持しているのかという疑問. **11** ADJ 形容詞 [ADJ n, -ed ADJ] If you do something for a **solid** period of time, you do it without any pause or interruption throughout that time. ぶっ通しの ❑ *We had worked together for two solid years.* 2年間ぶっ通しで一緒に働きました. ● **sol|id|ly** ADV 副詞 [ADV with v] ぶっ通しで ❑ *People who had worked solidly since Christmas enjoyed the chance of a Friday off.* クリスマスからずっと働き詰めだった人たちはこの金曜日の休みを楽しんだ.
→ see Picture Dictionary: **solids**
→ see **dump, matter**

soli|dar|ity /sɒlɪdærɪti/ N-UNCOUNT 不可算名詞 If a group of people show **solidarity**, they show support for each other or for another group, especially in political or international affairs. 連帯 ❑ *Supporters want to march tomorrow to show solidarity with their leaders.* 支持者は指導者との連帯を示すため, 明日行進をしたがっています.

so|lidi|fy /səlɪdɪfaɪ/ (solidifies, solidifying, solidified) **1** V-T/V-I 他動詞/自動詞 When a liquid **solidifies** or **is solidified**, it changes into a solid. 凝固する [他動詞・自動詞] ❑ *The thicker lava would have taken two weeks to solidify.* より厚い溶岩が凝固するには2週間かかるだろう. ❑ *The Energy Department plans to solidify the deadly waste in a high-tech billion-dollar factory.* エネルギー部門は極めて有害な廃棄物を10億ドルのハイテク工場で凝固する計画です. **2** V-T/V-I 他動詞/自動詞 If something such as a position or opinion **solidifies**, or if

---

Picture Dictionary   solids

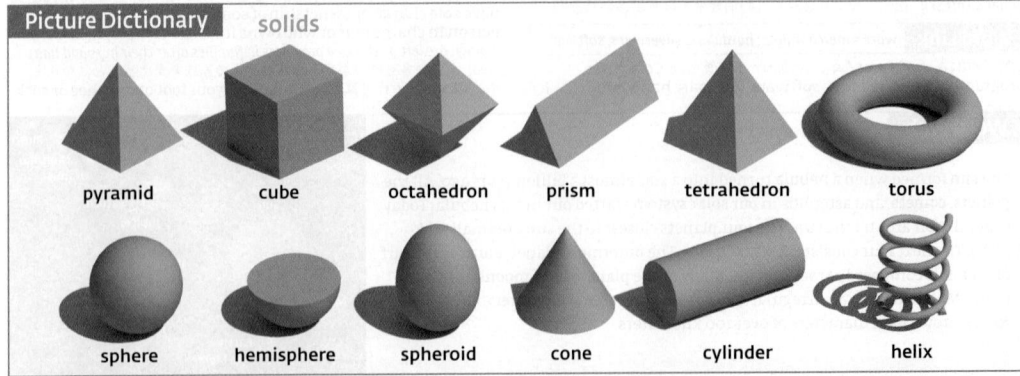

pyramid   cube   octahedron   prism   tetrahedron   torus

sphere   hemisphere   spheroid   cone   cylinder   helix

something **solidifies** it, it becomes firmer and more definite and unlikely to change. 固まる [他動詞・自動詞] ❑ *Her attitudes solidified through privilege and habit.* 彼女の態度は特権と習慣によって強固になった. ❑ *...his attempt to solidify his position as chairman.* 委員長としての地位を固める彼の試み.

soli|tary /sɒlɪtɛri/ **1** ADJ 形容詞 A person or animal that is **solitary** spends a lot of time alone. ひとりぼっちの ❑ *Paul was a shy, pleasant, solitary man.* ポールは内気だけど、愛想の良い、ひとり暮らしの男性だった. **2** ADJ 形容詞 A **solitary** activity is one that you do alone. 単独の [ADJ n] ❑ *His evenings were spent in solitary drinking.* 彼は1人酒で夜を過ごした. **3** ADJ 形容詞 A **solitary** person or object is alone, with no others near them. 人里離れた [ADJ n] ❑ *You could see the occasional solitary figure making a study of wildflowers or grasses.* 野草や草を調べる世捨て人を時折垣間見ることができる.

soli|tude /sɒlɪtud/ N-UNCOUNT 不可算名詞 **Solitude** is the state of being alone, especially when this is peaceful and pleasant. 孤独 ❑ *He enjoyed his moments of solitude before the pressures of the day began in earnest.* 彼はその日、重圧が本格的にのしかかってくる前の孤独な時間を満喫した.

solo /soʊloʊ/ (**solos**) **1** ADJ 形容詞 You use **solo** to indicate that someone does something alone rather than with other people. ソロの ❑ *He had just completed his final solo album.* 彼はちょうど、最後のソロアルバムを完成したところだ. ❑ *...Daniel Amokachi's spectacular solo goal.* ダニエル・アモカチの見事な単独ゴール. ● ADV 副詞 **Solo** is also an adverb. 単独で [ADV after v] ❑ *Charles Lindbergh became the very first person to fly solo across the Atlantic.* チャールズ・リンドバーグは、世界で初めて大西洋単独横断飛行をした. **2** N-COUNT 可算名詞 A **solo** is a piece of music or a dance performed by one person. 独奏 ❑ *The original version featured a guitar solo.* ギターソロを呼び物にしたオリジナルバージョン.

so|lo|ist /soʊloʊɪst/ (**soloists**) N-COUNT 可算名詞 A **soloist** is a musician or dancer who performs a solo. 独奏者 ❑ *...the relationship between soloist and orchestra.* 独唱者とオーケストラの関係.

sol|uble /sɒlyəbəl/ **1** ADJ 形容詞 A substance that is **soluble** will dissolve in a liquid. 溶ける ❑ *Uranium is soluble in sea water.* ウラニウムは海水に溶ける. **2** COMB IN ADJ 形容詞の複合 If something is **water-soluble** or **fat-soluble**, it will dissolve in water or in fat. 水に溶ける ❑ *The red dye on the leather is water-soluble.* 皮革の赤い染料は水に溶ける.

so|lu|tion /səluʃən/ (**solutions**) **1** N-COUNT 可算名詞 A **solution** to a problem or difficult situation is a way of dealing with it so that the difficulty is removed. 解法 ❑ *Although he has sought to find a peaceful solution, he is facing pressure to use greater military force.* 彼は平和的解決を見つけようと努めましたが、兵力を増強せよという圧力に直面しています. **2** N-COUNT 可算名詞 The **solution to** a puzzle is the answer to it. 解答 ❑ *We invited readers who completed the puzzle to send in their solutions.* 彼はパズルを解いた読者に解答を送るよう求めた. **3** N-COUNT 可算名詞 A **solution** is a liquid in which a solid substance has been dissolved. 溶液 [also "in" N] ❑ *...a warm solution of liquid detergent.* 液体洗剤の暖かい溶液.

Word Partnership	*solution* は次の語句と使われる:
ADJ.	**best** solution, **peaceful** solution, **perfect** solution, **possible** solution, **practical** solution, **temporary** solution **1**
	easy solution, **obvious** solution, **simple** solution **1** **2**
N.	solution **to a conflict**, solution **to a crisis** **1** **2** solution **to a problem** **1** **2**
V.	**propose** a solution, **reach** a solution, **seek** a solution **1** **2** **find** a solution **1** **2**

solve /sɒlv/ (**solves, solving, solved**) V-T 他動詞 If you **solve** a problem or a question, you find a solution or an answer to it. 解く [他動詞] ❑ *Their domestic reforms did nothing to solve the problem of unemployment.* 彼らの国内改革は、全く失業問題の解決にならなかった.

Word Partnership	*solve* は次の語句と使われる:
N.	**ability to** solve *something*, solve **a crisis**, solve **a mystery**, solve **a problem**, solve **a puzzle**, **way to** solve *something*
V.	**attempt/try to** solve *something*, **help** solve *something*

sol|ven|cy /sɒlvənsi/ N-UNCOUNT 不可算名詞 A person's or organization's **solvency** is their ability to pay their debts. 支払い能力 [BUSINESS 実業] ❑ *...unsound investments that could threaten the company's solvency.* 会社の支払い能力を脅かす可能性のある不健全投資.

sol|vent /sɒlvənt/ (**solvents**) **1** ADJ 形容詞 If a person or a company is **solvent**, they have enough money to pay all their debts. 支払い能力のある [BUSINESS 実業] ❑ *They're going to have*

to show that the company is now solvent. 彼らは会社が今では支払い能力があることを示さなければなりません. **2** N-MASS 質量名詞 A **solvent** is a liquid that can dissolve other substances. 溶剤 ❑ *...a small amount of cleaning solvent.* 少量の洗濯用溶剤.

→ see **dry-cleaning**

som|ber /sɒmbər/ **1** ADJ 形容詞 If someone is **somber**, they are serious or sad. 陰気な ❑ *Spencer cried as she described the somber mood of her co-workers.* スペンサーは彼女が同僚たちの憂鬱な気持ちを語るのを聞いて泣いた. **2** ADJ 形容詞 **Somber** colors and places are dark and dull. 薄暗い ❑ *His room was somber and dark.* 彼の部屋は地味で薄暗い.

some /səm, STRONG sʌm/ **1** DET 限定詞 You use **some** to refer to a quantity of something or to a number of people or things, when you are not stating the quantity or number precisely. 多少の ❑ *Robin opened some champagne.* ロビンはシャンペンを何本か開けた. ❑ *He went to fetch some books.* 彼は本を何冊か取りにいった. ● PRON 代名詞 **Some** is also a pronoun. いくらか ❑ *This year all the apples are all red. My niece and nephew are going out this morning with step-ladders to pick some.* 今年、リンゴはすべて赤くなった. 私の姪と甥は、今朝はしごを持って出かけてボールを拾う. **2** DET 限定詞 You use **some** to emphasize that a quantity or number is fairly large. For example, if an activity takes **some** time, it takes quite a lot of time. かなりの [EMPHASIS 強調] ❑ *I have discussed this topic in some detail.* 私はこの件についてかなり詳細に話し合った. ❑ *He remained silent for some time.* 彼は最前から黙ったままだ. **3** DET 限定詞 You use **some** to emphasize that a quantity or number is fairly small. For example, if something happens to **some** extent, it happens a little. 若干の数 [EMPHASIS 強調] ❑ *"Isn't there some chance that William might lead a normal life?" asked Jill.* 「ウィリアムが普通の生活を送れる可能性はいくらかありますか」ジルは聞いた. ❑ *All mothers share to some extent in the tension of a wedding.* どの母親も結婚式の緊張感についてある程度同意する. **4** QUANT 数量詞 If you refer to **some of** the people or things in a group, you mean a few of them but not all of them. If you refer to **some of** a particular thing, you mean a part of it but not all of it. いくらかの ❑ *Some of the people already in work will lose their jobs.* すでに仕事についている人たちの一部は職を失う. ❑ *Remove the cover and spoon some of the sauce into a bowl.* カバーを取り外し、ソースを少しスプーンですくってボールに入れる. ● PRON 代名詞 **Some** is also a pronoun. 一部 ❑ *When the chicken is cooked I'll freeze some.* 鶏肉が煮えたら、私は一部を冷凍する.

> You use **not any** instead of **some** in negative sentences. ❑ *There isn't any money.*

5 DET 限定詞 If you refer to **some** person or thing, you are referring to that person or thing but in a vague way, without stating precisely which person or thing you mean. ある [VAGUENESS あいまいさ] ❑ *If you are worried about some aspect of your child's health, call us.* 子供の健康面で何か心配がある場合は私どもにお電話ください. **6** ADV 副詞 You can use **some** in front of a number to indicate that it is approximate. およそ [VAGUENESS あいまいさ] [ADV num] ❑ *I have kept birds for some 30 years.* 私はおよそ30年間鳥を飼った. **7** ADV 副詞 **Some** is used to mean to a small extent or degree. いくぶん [AM 米国英語] [ADV after v] ❑ *If Susanne is off somewhere, I'll kill time by looking around some.* スーザンがどこかに行っているのなら、私は少しあたりを見て回って時間をつぶす. **8** DET 限定詞 You can use **some** in front of a noun in order to express your approval or disapproval of the person or thing you are mentioning. なかなかの [INFORMAL くだけた, FEELINGS 感情] ❑ *"Some party!" — "Yep. One hell of a party."* 「たいしたパーティだな」「うん. ものすごいパーティーだ」

some|body /sʌmbɒdi, -bədi/ PRON-INDEF 不定代名詞 **Somebody** means the same as **someone**. 誰か

> You use **not anybody** instead of **somebody** in negative sentences. ❑ *There isn't anybody here.*

some|how /sʌmhaʊ/ **1** ADV 副詞 You use **somehow** to say that you do not know or cannot say how something was done or will be done. なんとかして ❑ *We'll manage somehow, you and me. I know we will.* 君と私はなんとかやっていけるさ. そう信じてる. ❑ *Somehow Karin managed to cope with the demands of her career.* カリンはどうにか仕事の要請をこなした. **2** **somehow or other** → see **other**

some|one /sʌmwʌn/

> The form **somebody** is also used.

> **somebody** 形も使われる.

1 PRON-INDEF 不定代名詞 You use **someone** or **somebody** to refer to a person without saying exactly who you mean. 誰か ❑ *Her father was shot by someone trying to rob his small retail store.* 彼女の父は、彼の小さな小売店で強盗を働こうとしていた誰かに撃たれた. ❑ *I need someone to help me.* 誰か助けてくれる人が欲しい. **2** PRON-INDEF 不定代名詞 If you say that a person is **someone** or **somebody in** a particular kind of work or **in** a particular place,

you mean that they are considered to be important in that kind of work or in that place. 何某といわれる偉い人 □*"Before she came around," she says, "I was somebody in this town."* 「彼女が現れる前はね」彼女は言う、「私はこの町ではひとかどの人物だったのよ」

> You use **not anyone** instead of **someone** in negative sentences. □*There isn't anyone here.*

some|place /sʌmpleɪs/ ADV 副詞 **Someplace** means the same as **somewhere**. どこかに [AM 米国英語] [ADV after v] □*Maybe if we could go someplace together, just you and I.* 君と僕だけでどこかに行こうか。

som|er|sault /sʌmərsɔlt/ (somersaults, somersaulting, somersaulted) ■ N-COUNT 可算名詞 If someone or something does a **somersault**, they turn over completely in the air. 宙返り □*Trained dogs did somersaults on a man's shoulders.* 訓練された犬は男の肩の上で宙返りをした。 ② V-I 自動詞 If someone or something **somersaults**, they perform one or more somersaults. 宙返りをする [自動詞] □*His boat hit a wave and somersaulted.* 彼の船は波に突き当たって、とんぼ返りをした。

some|thing /sʌmθɪŋ/ ■ PRON-INDEF 不定代名詞 You use **something** to refer to a thing, situation, event, or idea, without saying exactly what it is. 何か □*He realized right away that there was something wrong.* 何かがおかしいことに彼はすぐさま気がついた。 □*There was something vaguely familiar about him.* 彼は何かどことなく見たことがある感じがした。 □*"You said there was something you wanted to ask me," he said politely.* 「何か私に聞きたいことがあるとおっしゃいましたね」彼は礼儀正しく言った。 ② PRON-INDEF 不定代名詞 You can use **something** to say that the description or amount that you are giving is not exact. やや [PRON prep] □*Clive made a noise, something like a grunt.* クリーブは不満のような声を出した。 □*Their membership seems to have risen to something over 10,000.* 彼らの会費は1万強に値上がりしたようだ。 ③ PRON-INDEF 不定代名詞 If you say that a person or thing is **something** or is really **something**, you mean that you are very impressed by them. たいしたもの [INFORMAL くだけた] □*You're really something.* 君は本当にたいしたものだ。 ④ PRON-INDEF 不定代名詞 You can use **something** in expressions like **"that's something"** when you think that a situation is not very good but is better than it might have been. 無視できないもの □*Well, at least he was in town. That was something.* ふうむ、少なくとも彼は街にいたんだ。それはすごいな。 ⑤ PRON-INDEF 不定代名詞 If you say that a thing is **something of** a disappointment, you mean that it is quite disappointing. If you say that a person is **something of** an artist, you mean that they are quite good at art. ちょっとした [PRON "of" n] □*The city proved to be something of a disappointment.* その都市はなんともがっかりだった。 ⑥ PRON-INDEF 不定代名詞 If you say that there is **something** in an idea or suggestion, you mean that it is quite good and should be considered seriously. 相当なもの [PRON "in" n] □*Could there be something in what he said?* 彼が言ったことは重要なのか。 ⑦ PRON-INDEF 不定代名詞 You use **something** in expressions such as **"or something"** and **"or something like that"** to indicate that you are referring to something similar to what you have just mentioned but you are not being exact. かなにか [VAGUENESS あいまいさ] □*This guy, his name was Briarly or Beardly or something.* 名前がブラーリーとかビアドリーとかなんとかいった、この男は。

⑧ **something like** → see **like**

> You use **not anything** instead of **something** in negative sentences. □*There isn't anything here.*

some|time /sʌmtaɪm/ ADV 副詞 You use **sometime** to refer to a time in the future or the past that is unknown or that has not yet been decided. いつか □*The sales figures won't be released until sometime next month.* 売り上げ高は来月のいつかにならないと公表されません。 □*Why don't you come and see me sometime.* 近々会いに来ませんか。

some|times /sʌmtaɪmz/ ADV 副詞 You use **sometimes** to say that something happens on some occasions rather than all the time. 時々 □*During the summer, my skin sometimes gets greasy.* 夏の間、私の肌は油っぽくなることがある。 □*Sometimes I think he dislikes me.* 時々、彼は私を嫌いなんじゃないかと思う。

some|what /sʌmwʌt, -wɒt/ ADV 副詞 You use **somewhat** to indicate that something is the case to a limited extent or degree. やや [FORMAL 形式ばった] [ADV with cl/group] □*He concluded that Oswald was somewhat abnormal.* オズワルドは少々異常だと彼は結論しました。 □*He explained somewhat unconvincingly that the company was paying for everything.* 彼は会社がすべてを支払っていたのだとやや説得力を欠く説明をした。

some|where /sʌmwɛər/ ■ ADV 副詞 You use **somewhere** to refer to a place without saying exactly where you mean. どこかに □*I've got a feeling I've seen him before somewhere.* 以前どこかで彼を見たことがあると感じた。 □*I'm not going home yet. I have to go somewhere else first.* まだ家には帰らないわ。その前に寄るところがあるの。 □*I needed somewhere to live.* 私は住むところが必要だった。 ② ADV

副詞 You use **somewhere** when giving an approximate amount, number, or time. ほぼ [ADV prep] □*He is believed to be worth somewhere between seven million and ten million dollars.* 彼の財産は7百万から1千万ドルくらいだといわれています。 □*Caray is somewhere between 73 and 80 years of age.* カレイの年齢は73歳から80歳の間です。 ③ PHRASE 句 If you say that you **are getting somewhere**, you mean that you are making progress toward achieving something. うまくいく □*At last they were agreeing, at last they were getting somewhere.* 少なくとも彼らは同意しようとしていた、何はともあれ効果があったのだ。

> You use **not anywhere** instead of **somewhere** in negative sentences. □*He isn't going anywhere.* Informally, Americans also use the forms **someplace** and **anyplace**.

son /sʌn/ (sons) ■ N-COUNT 可算名詞 Someone's **son** is their male child. 息子 □*He shared a pizza with his son Laurence.* 彼はピザを息子のローレンスと分けました。 □*Sam is the seven-year-old son of Eric Davies.* サムは、エリック・デイビスの7歳の息子だ。 ② N-COUNT 可算名詞 A man, especially a famous man, can be described as a **son** of the place he comes from. 住人 [JOURNALISM ジャーナリズム] □*...New Orleans's most famous son, Louis Armstrong.* ニューオーリンズで最も有名な人、ルイス・アームストロング ③ N-VOC 呼格名詞 Some people use **son** as a form of address when they are showing kindness or affection to a boy or a man who is younger than them. きみ [INFORMAL くだけた, FEELINGS 感情] □*Don't be frightened by failure, son.* 失敗を恐れるんじゃないよ、坊や。
→ see **child**

so|na|ta /sənɑtə/ (sonatas) N-COUNT 可算名詞 A **sonata** is a piece of classical music written either for a single instrument, or for one instrument and a piano. ソナタ

song /sɔŋ/ (songs) ■ N-COUNT 可算名詞 A **song** is words and music sung together. 歌 □*...a voice singing a Spanish song.* スペインの歌を歌う声。 ② N-UNCOUNT 不可算名詞 **Song** is the art of singing. 声楽 □*...dance, music, mime, and song.* 踊り、音楽、マイムと声楽。 ③ N-COUNT 可算名詞 A bird's **song** is the pleasant, musical sounds that it makes. さえずる声 □*It's been a long time since I heard a blackbird's song in the evening.* 夕方にクロウタドリの鳴く声を聞いたのはずいぶん前だ。 ④ PHRASE 句 If someone **bursts into song** or **breaks into song**, they start singing. 歌いだす □*I feel as if I should break into song.* 私は歌いだしたくなった。
→ see **concert, music**

Word Partnership   song は次の語句と使われる：

ADJ.	**beautiful** song, **favorite** song, **old** song, **popular** song ■
V.	**hear** a song, **play** a song, **record** a song, **sing** a song, **write** a song ■
N.	**hit** song, **love** song, song **lyrics**, song **music**, **pop** song, **rap** song, song **title**, **theme** song, **words of** a song ■ **bird's** song ③

son|ic /sɒnɪk/ ADJ 形容詞 **Sonic** is used to describe things related to sound. 音の [TECHNICAL 技術的] [ADJ n] □*...the sonic boom of enemy fighter-bombers.* 敵の戦闘爆撃機の衝撃音。
→ see **sound**

son-in-law (sons-in-law) N-COUNT 可算名詞 Someone's **son-in-law** is the husband of their daughter. 娘の夫。

son|net /sɒnɪt/ (sonnets) N-COUNT 可算名詞 A **sonnet** is a poem that has 14 lines. Each line has 10 syllables, and the poem has a fixed pattern of rhymes. ソネット

son of a bitch (sons of bitches) also **son-of-a-bitch** N-COUNT 可算名詞 If someone is very angry with another person, or if they want to insult them, they sometimes call them a **son of a bitch**. 畜生 [INFORMAL, OFFENSIVE, VULGAR くだけた、無礼な、下品な、DISAPPROVAL 不賛成]

soon /sun/ (sooner, soonest) ■ ADV 副詞 If something is going to happen **soon**, it will happen after a short time. If something happened **soon** after a particular time or event, it happened a short time after it. 間もなく □*You'll be hearing from us very soon.* 近いうちに連絡します。 ② PHRASE 句 If you say that something happens **as soon as** something else happens, you mean that it happens immediately after the other thing. するとすぐに □*As soon as relations improve they will be allowed to go.* 彼らは、関係が改善したらすぐに帰宅を許される。 ③ PHRASE 句 If you say that you **would just as soon** do something or you'**d just as soon** do it, you mean that you would prefer to do it. したい □*These people could afford to retire to Florida but they'd just as soon stay put.* これらの人たちはフロリダで定年生活をする余裕があったにもかかわらず、どこにもいかなかった。 □*I'd just as soon not have to make this public.* これは公にしたくありません。

soot /sʊt, suːt/ N-UNCOUNT 不可算名詞 **Soot** is black powder which rises in the smoke from a fire and collects usually on the inside of chimneys. すす ❑ ...a wall blackened by soot. すすで黒くなった壁.

soothe /suːð/ (soothes, soothing, soothed) ◼ V-T 他動詞 If you **soothe** someone who is angry or upset, you make them feel calmer. なだめる [他動詞] ❑ He would take her in his arms and soothe her. 彼は彼女を腕に抱いて、なだめたかった. ●**sooth|ing** ADJ 形容詞 慰めるような ❑ Put on some nice soothing music. 何か、心が和らぐようなよい音楽をかけてください. ◼ V-T 他動詞 Something that **soothes** a part of your body where there is pain or discomfort makes the pain or discomfort less severe. （苦痛などを）和らげる [他動詞] ❑ ...body lotion to soothe dry skin. 乾いた肌を鎮めるボディーローション. ●**sooth|ing** ADJ 形容詞 和らげる ❑ Cold tea is very soothing for burns. 冷たいお茶は火傷の痛みの緩和に非常によく効く.

Word Link soph ≈ wise : *philo*soph*ical, philo*soph*y, *sophi*sticated*

---

so|phis|ti|cat|ed /səfɪstɪkeɪtɪd/ ◼ ADJ 形容詞 A **sophisticated** machine, device, or method is more advanced or complex than others. 精巧な ❑ Honeybees use one of the most sophisticated communication systems of any insect. ミツバチは昆虫の中では最も複雑な通信システムを使用している. ◼ ADJ 形容詞 Someone who is **sophisticated** is comfortable in social situations and knows about culture, fashion, and other matters that are considered socially important. 洗練された ❑ Claude was a charming, sophisticated companion. クラウドは魅力的で洗練された仲間だった. ◼ ADJ 形容詞 A **sophisticated** person is intelligent and knows a lot, so that they are able to understand complicated situations. 見識のある ❑ These people are very sophisticated observers of the foreign policy scene. これらの人たちは大変見識のある、外交政策の監視団です.

Word Partnership sophisticated は次の語句と使われる:

ADJ.	advanced, complex, elaborate, intricate ◼ cultured, experienced, refined, worldly; (ant.) backward, crude ◼

---

so|phis|ti|ca|tion /səfɪstɪkeɪʃ⁰n/ N-UNCOUNT 不可算名詞 The **sophistication** of people, places, machines, or methods is their quality of being sophisticated. 洗練 ❑ It would take many decades to build up the level of education and sophistication required. 必要とされる高レベルの教育と知識を蓄積するには何世紀もかかるだろう.

so|pra|no /səprænoʊ, -prɑːn-/ (sopranos) N-COUNT 可算名詞 A **soprano** is a woman, girl, or boy with a high singing voice. ソプラノ ❑ She was the main soprano at the Bolshoi theatre. 彼女はボルショイ劇場の主演ソプラノでした.

sor|did /sɔːrdɪd/ ◼ ADJ 形容詞 If you describe someone's behavior as **sordid**, you mean that it is immoral or dishonest. 卑しい [DISAPPROVAL 不賛成] ❑ He sat with his head buried in his hands as his sordid double life was revealed. 彼の強欲な二重生活が暴露される間、彼は手に頭を埋めて座っていた. ◼ ADJ 形容詞 If you describe a place as **sordid**, you mean that it is dirty, unpleasant, or depressing. 不潔な [DISAPPROVAL 不賛成] ❑ ...the attic windows of their sordid little rooms. 彼らのみすぼらしい小さな屋根裏部屋の窓.

sore /sɔːr/ (sorer, sorest, sores) ◼ ADJ 形容詞 If part of your body is **sore**, it causes you pain and discomfort. ちょっと触れても痛い ❑ It's years since I've had a sore throat like I did last night. 私が昨日夜のようなのどの痛みを味わったのは何年かぶりだ. ◼ ADJ 形容詞 If you are **sore** about something, you are angry and upset about it. 怒っている [mainly AM 主に米国英語, INFORMAL くだけた] [v-link ADJ] ❑ The result is that they are now all feeling very sore at you. その結果、彼らみんなが今、君に対して非常に憤慨している. ◼ N-COUNT 可算名詞 A **sore** is a painful place on the body where the skin is infected. 皮膚の破れた箇所 ❑ Our backs and hands were covered with sores and burns from the ropes. 僕たちの背中と手には、ロープで傷とやけどがいっぱいできた. ◼ PHRASE 句 If something is a **sore point with** someone, it is likely to make them angry or embarrassed if you try to discuss it. 痛いところ ❑ The continuing presence of American troops on Korean soil remains a very sore point with these students. 韓国の国土に米軍が駐在し続けることは、これらの学生にとってはいまだに大きな不満の種だ.

sore|ly /sɔːrli/ ADV 副詞 **Sorely** is used to emphasize that a feeling such as disappointment or need is very strong. 激しく [EMPHASIS 強調] ❑ If for one was sorely disappointed. 少なくとも僕はひどく失望した. ❑ He will be sorely missed. 彼は大変惜しまれるだろう.

sor|row /sɒroʊ, sɔː-/ N-UNCOUNT 不可算名詞 **Sorrow** is a feeling of deep sadness or regret. 悲しみ ❑ Words cannot express my sorrow. 私の悲哀は言葉では表現できない.

sor|rows /sɒroʊz, sɔː-/ ◼ N-PLURAL 複数名詞 **Sorrows** are events or situations that cause deep sadness. 悲しみの種 ❑ ...the joys and sorrows of everyday living. 日常生活の喜びと悲しみ. ◼ to **drown** one's **sorrows** → see **drown**

sor|ry /sɒri, sɔː-/ (sorrier, sorriest) ◼ CONVENTION 慣習表現 You say "**Sorry**" or "**I'm sorry**" as a way of apologizing to someone for something that you have done which has upset them or caused them difficulties, or when you bump into them accidentally. どうもすいません [FORMULAE 決まり文句] ❑ "We're all talking at the same time." — "Yeah. Sorry." 「皆同時に話していますよ」「あ、すいません」❑ Sorry I took so long. お待たせしました. ❑ I'm really sorry if I said anything wrong. 何かまずいことを言ったのなら申し訳ありません. ◼ ADJ 形容詞 If you are **sorry** about a situation, you feel regret, sadness, or disappointment about it. 後悔する [v-link ADJ] ❑ She was very sorry about all the trouble she'd caused. 彼女はこのような問題を起こして大変後悔していた. ❑ I'm sorry he's gone. 彼が行ってしまったことは残念だ. ◼ CONVENTION 慣習表現 You use **I'm sorry** or **sorry** as an introduction when you are telling a person something that you do not think they will want to hear, for example when you are disagreeing with them or giving them bad news. 残念ながら ❑ No, I'm sorry, I can't agree with you. いいえ、残念ながら、同意しかねます. ❑ "I'm sorry," he told the real estate agent, "but we really must go now." 「残念ですが」彼は不動産業者に告げた、「でも、本当にもう行かなくてはならないのです」 ◼ PHRASE 句 You use the expression **I'm sorry to say** to express regret together with disappointment or disapproval. あいにくですが [FEELINGS 感情] ❑ I've only done half of it, I'm sorry to say. 半分しかやってないんだけど、悪いけど. ◼ CONVENTION 慣習表現 You say "**I'm sorry**" to express your regret and sadness when you hear sad or unpleasant news. 気の毒 [FEELINGS 感情] ❑ "I'm afraid he's ill." 「彼は病気じゃないかと思う」「それはお気の毒に」 ◼ ADJ 形容詞 If you feel **sorry** for someone who is unhappy or in an unpleasant situation, you feel sympathy and sadness for them. 同情する [v-link ADJ] "for" n] ❑ I felt sorry for him and his colleagues - it must have been so frustrating for them. 彼とその同僚に同情した. 大変いらだたしかったことだろう. ◼ ADJ 形容詞 You say that someone is feeling **sorry for themselves** when you disapprove of the fact that they keep thinking unhappily about their problems, rather than trying to be cheerful and positive. すっかりしょげて [DISAPPROVAL 不賛成] [v-link ADJ] ❑ What he must not do is to sit around at home feeling sorry for himself. 彼は家でぶらぶら過ごしてしょげ返っている場合ではないのだ. ◼ CONVENTION 慣習表現 You say "**Sorry?**" when you have not heard something that someone has said and you want them to repeat it. 今なんとおっしゃいましたか [FORMULAE 決まり文句] ❑ Once or twice I heard her muttering, but when I said, "Sorry? What did you say?" she didn't respond. 1, 2度彼女がぼそぼそいっている のが聞こえたが、私が「今なんとおっしゃいましたか」と聞いても彼女は応えなかった. ◼ CONVENTION 慣習表現 You use **sorry** when you correct yourself and use different words to say what you have just said, especially when what you say the second time does not use the words you would normally choose to use. 失礼 ❑ Barcelona will be hoping to bring the trophy back to Spain (sorry, Catalonia) for the first time. バルセロナは、トロフィーを初めてスペイン（失礼、カタロニア）に持ち帰ることを望んでいることだろう. ◼ ADJ 形容詞 If someone or something is in a **sorry** state, they are in a bad state, mentally or physically. ひどい [ADJ n] ❑ The fire left Kuwait's oil industry in a sorry state. 火事により、クウェートの石油産業は遺憾な状態に陥った. ◼ **better safe than sorry** → see **safe**

sort /sɔːrt/ (sorts, sorting, sorted) ◼ N-COUNT 可算名詞 If you talk about a particular **sort** of something, you are talking about a class of things that have particular features in common and that belong to a larger group of related things. 種類 ❑ What sort of school did you go to? どのような種類の学校にいきましたか. ❑ There are so many different sorts of mushrooms available these days. この頃は非常に多様なきのこが出回っている. ❑ A dozen trees of various sorts were planted. 様々な種類の木がたくさん植えられた. ◼ N-SING 単数名詞 You describe someone as a particular **sort** when you are describing their character. 性質 [with supp] ❑ He seemed to be just the right sort for the job. 彼はこの仕事にぴったりのようだ. ❑ She was a very vigorous sort of person. 彼女は大変活発な性格の人だった. ◼ V-T/V-I 他動詞/自動詞 If you **sort** things, you separate them into different classes, groups, or places, for example so that you can do different things with them. 分類する [他動詞・自動詞] ❑ He sorted the materials into their folders. 彼は材料をフォルダに分類した. ❑ He unlatched the box and sorted through the papers. 彼は箱の掛け金を外して、書類をより分けた. ◼ PHRASE 句 **All sorts of** things or people means a large number of different things or people. あらゆる種類の ❑ There are all sorts of animals, including bears, pigs, kangaroos, and penguins. クマ、ブタ、カンガルー、ペンギンを含むあらゆる種類の動物. ❑ It was used by all sorts of people. それはあらゆる種類の人に使用されていた. ◼ PHRASE 句 If you describe something as a thing **of sorts** or as a thing **of a sort**, you are suggesting that the thing is of a rather poor quality or standard. その種としては不十分な ❑ He made a living of sorts selling encyclopedias door-to-door. 彼は、百科事典の訪問販売でまがりなりに生計を立てていた. ◼ PHRASE 句 You use **sort of** when you want to say that your description of something is not very accurate. いわば [INFORMAL くだけた, VAGUENESS あいまいさ] ❑ You could even order windows from a catalogue – a sort of mail

order stained glass service. カタログ，いわば通信販売のステンドガラスサービスから窓を注文することさえできます。 **7** **nothing of the sort** → see **nothing**

▶ **sort out 1** PHRASAL VERB 句動詞 If you **sort out** a group of things, you separate them into different classes, groups, or places, for example so that you can do different things with them. 区別する ❑ Sort out all your bills, receipts, invoices, and expenses as quickly as possible and keep detailed accounts. 請求書，領収書，送り状および経費すべてをできるだけ迅速に整理して，明細な帳簿をつけなさい。 ❑ Davina was sorting out scraps of material. ダビナは材料のくずを選別していた。 **2** PHRASAL VERB 句動詞 If you **sort out** a problem or the details of something, you do what is necessary to solve the problem or organize the details. 解決する ❑ India and Nepal have sorted out their trade and security dispute. インドとネパールは貿易および安全保障争議を解決しました。 **3** PHRASAL VERB 句動詞 If you **sort yourself out**, you organize yourself or calm yourself so that you can act effectively and reasonably. 整える ❑ We're in a state of complete chaos here and I need a little time to sort myself out. 私たちは今完全な混乱状態にあり，私には体制を整える時間が少し必要だ。

sor|tie /sɔ́rti/ (**sorties**) N-COUNT 可算名詞 If a military force makes a **sortie**, it leaves its own position and goes briefly into enemy territory to make an attack. 出撃 [FORMAL 形式ばった] ❑ His men made a sortie to Guazatan and took a prisoner. 彼の部下はGuazatanに出撃し，捕虜を取った。

SOS /ɛ́s oʊ ɛ́s/ N-SING 単数名詞 An **SOS** is a signal which indicates to other people that you are in danger and need help quickly. 遭難信号 ❑ The ferry did not even have time to send out an SOS. フェリーには遭難信号を送信する時間さえありませんでした。

sought /sɔ́t/ **Sought** is the past tense and past participle of **seek**. seekの過去・過去分詞形

sought-after ADJ 形容詞 Something that is **sought-after** is in great demand, usually because it is rare or of very good quality. 需要の多い ❑ An Olympic gold medal is the most sought-after prize in world sport. オリンピック金メダルは，世界のスポーツで最も珍重される賞である。

soul /soʊl/ (**souls**) **1** N-COUNT 可算名詞 Your **soul** is the part of you that consists of your mind, character, thoughts, and feelings. Many people believe that your soul continues existing after your body is dead. 魂 ❑ She went to pray for the soul of her late husband. 彼女は今は亡き主人の冥福を祈りに行った。 **2** N-COUNT 可算名詞 You can refer to someone as a particular kind of **soul** when you are describing their character or condition. 精神 ❑ He's a jolly soul. 彼は陽気な精神の持ち主です。 **3** N-SING 単数名詞 You use **soul** in negative statements like **not a soul** to mean nobody at all. ひとっこひとりとして ❑ I've never harmed a soul in my life. 私は人生で誰一人として傷つけたことはない。 **4** N-UNCOUNT 不可算名詞 **Soul** is the same as **soul music**. ソウル ❑ ...American soul singer Anita Baker. アメリカのソウルシンガー，アニタ・ベーカー。 **5** to **bare** one's **soul** → see **bare** **6** **body and soul** → see **body**

sound

❶ NOUN AND VERB USES
❷ ADJECTIVE USES

❶ sound /saʊnd/ (**sounds, sounding, sounded**)
⟳ **Please look at category 11 to see if the expression you are looking for is shown under another headword.** **1** N-COUNT 可算名詞 A **sound** is something that you hear. 音 ❑ Peter heard the sound of gunfire. ピーターは発砲の音を聞いた。 ❑ Liza was so frightened she couldn't make a sound. ライザはあまりにも脅えていて，声さえ立てられなかった。 **2** N-UNCOUNT 不可算名詞 **Sound** is energy that travels in waves through air, water, or other substances, and can be heard. 音 ❑ The airplane will travel at twice the speed of sound. 飛行機は音速の2倍の速さで飛びます。 **3** N-SING 単数名詞 **The sound** on a television, radio, or CD player is what you hear coming from

the machine. Its loudness can be controlled. 音声 ❑ She went and turned the sound down. 彼女は音量を下げに行った。 **4** N-COUNT 可算名詞 A singer's or band's **sound** is the distinctive quality of their music. サウンド ❑ They have started showing a strong soul element in their sound. 彼らはそのサウンドに強いソウルの要素を見せ始めた。 **5** V-T/V-I 他動詞/自動詞 If something such as a horn or a bell **sounds** or if you **sound** it, it makes a noise. 鳴らす [他動詞] 音がでる [自動詞] ❑ The buzzer sounded in Daniel's office. ダニエルのオフィスでブザーが鳴った。 **6** V-T 他動詞 If you **sound** a warning, you publicly give it. If you **sound** a note of caution or optimism, you say publicly that you are cautious or optimistic. （警報などを）発する [他動詞] ❑ The archbishop has sounded a warning to world leaders on third world debt. 大司教は第三世界の債務について各国指導者に警告を発しました。 **7** V-LINK 連結動詞 When you are describing a noise, you can talk about the way it **sounds**. 音がする ❑ They heard what sounded like a huge explosion. 彼らは巨大な爆発のような音を聞きました。 ❑ The creaking of the hinges sounded very loud in that silence. ヒンジのきしみとその静寂の中で非常に大きく響いた。 **8** V-LINK 連結動詞 When you talk about the way someone **sounds**, you are describing the impression you have of them when they speak. 聞こえる ❑ She sounded a bit worried. 彼女は少し心配しているように聞こえた。 ❑ Murphy sounds like a child. マーフィーは子供のようだ。 **9** V-LINK 連結動詞 When you are describing your impression or opinion of something you have heard about or read about, you can talk about the way it **sounds**. 思われる ❑ It sounds like a wonderful idea to me. Does it really work? すばらしいアイデアのように私には思われますが，本当にうまくいくのかしら。 ❑ It sounds as if they might have made a dreadful mistake. 彼らは恐ろしい間違いを犯したように思われる。 **10** N-SING 単数名詞 You can describe your impression of something you have heard about or read about by talking about **the sound of** it. 印象 ❑ It was a new idea we liked the sound of. これが私たちがいい印象を受けた新しいアイデアだ。 ❑ I don't like the sound of Toby Osborne. 私はトビー・オズボーンのスタイルが気に入らない。 **11** to **sound the alarm** → see **alarm** **12** **safe and sound** → see **safe**

→ see Word Web: **sound**
→ see **concert, ear, echo**

▶ **sound out** PHRASAL VERB 句動詞 If you **sound** someone **out**, you question them in order to find out what their opinion is about something. 探る ❑ He is sounding out Middle Eastern governments on ways to resolve the conflict. 彼は中東政府が扮装を解決する方法を探っています。

❷ sound /saʊnd/ (**sounder, soundest**) **1** ADJ 形容詞 If a structure, part of someone's body, or someone's mind is **sound**, it is in good condition or healthy. 堅実な ❑ When we bought the house, it was structurally sound. 僕たちが家を購入した時，その構造はしっかりしていた。 ❑ Although the car is basically sound, I was worried about certain areas. 車は基本的に正常だが，一部の機能については心配があった。 **2** ADJ 形容詞 **Sound** advice, reasoning, or evidence is reliable and sensible. 堅実な ❑ They are trained nutritionists who can give sound advice on diets. 彼らは，食餌療法について信頼できるアドバイスを与えられる，訓練を受けた栄養士だ。 ❑ Buy a policy only from an insurance company that is financially sound. 保険は，財政的に健全な保険会社からのみ購入しなさい。 **3** ADJ 形容詞 If you describe someone's ideas as **sound**, you mean that you approve of them and think they are correct. 論理的に正しい [APPROVAL 賛成] ❑ I am not sure that this is sound democratic practice. これが正統な民主的実践だと確信している。 **4** ADJ 形容詞 If someone is in a **sound** sleep, they are sleeping very deeply. ぐっすりした [ADJ n] ❑ She had woken me out of a sound sleep. 彼女は深い眠りから私を起こした。 ● ADV 副詞 **Sound** is also an adverb. ぐっすり [ADV adj] ❑ He was lying in bed, sound asleep. 彼はベッドに横たわって，ぐっすり眠っていた。 **5** → see also **soundly**

Word Web   sound

Sound is the only form of energy we can hear. It consists of **vibrating** molecules of air. Rapid vibrations called high **frequencies** produce high-pitched sounds. Slower vibrations produce lower frequencies. Sound vibrations travel in waves, just like **waves** in water. Each wave has a **crest** and a **trough**. Amplitude is a measure of how high above the medium line a sound wave moves. When a **sound wave** bounces off an object, it produces an **echo**. When an airplane reaches **supersonic** speed, it generates **shock waves**. As these waves move toward the ground, a sonic boom occurs.

amplitude   crest

medium line   wave height

trough   wavelength

sound|card /saʊndkɑrd/ (soundcards) also sound card
N-COUNT 可算名詞 A **soundcard** is a piece of equipment which can be put into a computer so that the computer can produce music or other sounds. サウンドカード [COMPUTING コンピューティング]

sound|ly /saʊndli/ ❶ ADV 副詞 If someone is **soundly** defeated or beaten, they are defeated or beaten thoroughly. 徹底的に [ADV -ed] ❑ Needing just a point from their match at St. Helens, they were soundly beaten, going down by 35 points to 10. 聖ヘレンズでの試合で欲しかったのは1点だけだったのに、彼らは35点対10点で完敗した。 ❷ ADV 副詞 If a decision, opinion, or statement is **soundly** based, there are sensible or reliable reasons behind it. 力強く [APPROVAL 賛成] [ADV -ed] ❑ Changes must be soundly based in economic reality. 変化は経済的実態にしっかり基づいたものでなければならない。 ❸ ADV 副詞 If you sleep **soundly**, you sleep deeply and do not wake during your sleep. ぐっすり ❑ How can he sleep soundly at night? He's the one responsible for all those crimes. 彼はどうして夜ぐっすり眠れるのだろうか。これら犯罪すべての責任は彼にあるのに。

sound sys|tem (sound systems) N-COUNT 可算名詞 A **sound system** is a set of equipment for playing recorded music, or for making a band's music able to be heard by everyone at a concert. ステレオセット

sound|track /saʊndtræk/ (soundtracks) also sound track
N-COUNT 可算名詞 The **soundtrack** of a movie is its sound, speech, and music. It is used especially to refer to the music. サウンドトラック ❑ ...the soundtrack to a movie called "Judgment Night." 「審判の夜」という題名の映画のサウンドトラック.

soup /sup/ (soups) N-MASS 質量名詞 **Soup** is liquid food made by boiling meat, fish, or vegetables in water. スープ ❑ ...home-made chicken soup. 手作りのチキンスープ.

sour /saʊər/ (sours, souring, soured) ❶ ADJ 形容詞 Something that is **sour** has a sharp, unpleasant taste like the taste of a lemon. 酸っぱい ❑ The stewed apple was sour even with honey. とろ火で煮たリンゴははちみつをつけても酸っぱかった。 ❷ ADJ 形容詞 **Sour** milk is milk that has an unpleasant taste because it is no longer fresh. 酸敗した ❑ The milk had gone sour. 牛乳が酸っぱくなった。 ❸ ADJ 形容詞 Someone who is **sour** is bad-tempered and unfriendly. 意地の悪い ❑ She made a sour face in his direction. 彼女は彼のいる方向に向かって不愉快な顔をした。 ● **sour|ly** ADV 副詞 [ADV with v] 不機嫌に ❑ "Leave my mother out of it," he said sourly. 「母は巻き込まないでくれ」彼は不機嫌に言った。 ❹ ADJ 形容詞 If a situation or relationship **turns sour** or **goes sour**, it stops being enjoyable or satisfactory. まずいことになる ❑ Everything turned sour for me there. そこでは、私にとってすべてがうまくいかなくなった。 The American dream is beginning to turn sour. アメリカの夢は実現不可能なものになりつつある。 ❺ V-T/V-I 他動詞/自動詞 If a friendship, situation, or attitude **sours** or if something **sours** it, it becomes less friendly, enjoyable, or hopeful. 不愉快にする [他動詞] 不愉快になる [自動詞] ❑ If anything sours the relationship, it is likely to be real differences in their world-views. 彼らの関係をだめにするものがあるとすれば、それは世界観における実質的な違いだろう。
→ see fruit, taste

source /sɔrs/ (sources, sourcing, sourced) ❶ N-COUNT 可算名詞 The **source** of something is the person, place, or thing which you get it from. 源 ❑ ...over 40 percent of adults use television as their major source of information about the arts. 大人の40%以上が芸術の主要情報源としてテレビを使用している。 ❑ Renewable sources of energy must be used. エネルギー再生可能資源を使用する必要がある。 ❷ V-T 他動詞 In business, if a person or firm **sources** a product or a raw material, they find someone who will supply it. 調達する [BUSINESS 実業] [他動詞] ❑ Together they travel the world, sourcing clothes for the small, privately-owned company. 彼らは、小規模な私企業のために衣類を調達しながら、世界を一緒に旅した。 ❸ N-COUNT 可算名詞 A **source** is a person or book that provides information for a news story or for a piece of research. 情報源 ❑ Military sources say the boat was heading south at high speed. 軍情報源によると、船は高速で南に向かっていました。 ❹ N-COUNT 可算名詞 The **source of** a difficulty is its cause. 原因 ❑ This gave me a clue as to the source of the problem. これは問題の原因の糸口を私に与えてくれた。 ❺ N-COUNT 可算名詞 The **source** of a river or stream is the place where it begins. 源泉 ❑ ...the source of the Tiber. テベレ川の源泉.
→ see diary, history

south /saʊθ/ also South ❶ N-UNCOUNT 不可算名詞 The **south** is the direction which is on your right when you are looking toward the direction where the sun rises. 南 [also "the" N] ❑ The

town lies ten miles to the south of here. その街はここから10マイル南にある。 ❷ N-SING 単数名詞 The **south of** a place, country, or region is the part which is in the south. 南部 [usu "the" N, oft N "of" n] ❑ ...vacations in the south of Mexico. メキシコ南部での休暇. ❸ ADV 副詞 If you go **south**, you travel toward the south. 南へ [ADV after v] ❑ I drove south on Highway 9. 私は高速9号を南に走った。 ❹ ADV 副詞 Something of a place is positioned to the south of it. 南にある [ADV "of" n] ❑ They now own and operate a farm 50 miles south of Rochester. 彼らは今では、ロチェスターから50マイル南にある牧場を所有し、経営している。 ❺ ADJ 形容詞 The **south** edge, corner, or part of a place or country is the part which is toward the south. 南部の [ADJ n] ❑ ...the south coast of Long Island. ロングアイランドの南沿岸. ❻ ADJ 形容詞 "**South**" is used in the names of some countries, states, and regions in the south of a larger area. 南部 ❑ Next week the president will visit five South American countries in six days. 来週、大統領は6日間で南米の5か国を訪問します。 ❼ ADJ 形容詞 A **south** wind is a wind that blows from the south. 南からの ❑ ...a mild south wind. 南からの微風. ❽ N-SING 単数名詞 The **South** is used to refer to the poorer, less developed countries of the world. 発展途上国 ["the" N] ❑ The debate will pit the industrial North against developing countries in the South. その論争では工業の発展した北側先進諸国と南側発展途上国が対抗することになる。
→ see globe

south|east /saʊθist/ ❶ N-UNCOUNT 不可算名詞 The **southeast** is the direction which is halfway between south and east. 南東 [also "the" N] ❑ It shook buildings as far away as Galveston, 90 miles to the southeast. それは、南東90マイルにあるガルベストンに至るまで建物を揺るがした。 ❷ N-SING 単数名詞 The **southeast of** a place, country, or region is the part which is in the southeast. 南東部 ❑ Record levels of rainfall fell over the southeast of the country. 国の南東部で最高レベルの降水量が記録された。 ❸ ADV 副詞 If you go **southeast**, you travel toward the southeast. 南東へ [ADV after v] ❑ I know we have to go southeast, more or less. 大体南東へ行かなくてはならないのは分かっている。 ❹ ADV 副詞 Something is **southeast of** a place is positioned to the south-east of it. 南東にある [ADV "of" n] ❑ ...a vessel that is believed to have sunk 500 miles southeast of Nova Scotia. ノバスコシア州の南東500マイルに沈没したと考えられている船. ❺ ADJ 形容詞 The **southeast** part of a place, country, or region is the part which is toward the southeast. 南東の [ADJ n] ❑ ...rural southeast Kansas. カンザス州の南東にある農村部. ❑ ...Southeast Asia. 東南アジア. ❻ ADJ 形容詞 A **southeast** wind is a wind that blows from the southeast. 南東からの [ADJ n] ❑ Thick clothes kept the chill southeast wind from freezing his bones. 彼は厚着をしていたので、南東からの冷たい風でも骨まで凍ることはなかった。

south|eastern /saʊθistərn/ ADJ 形容詞 **Southeastern** means in or from the southeast of a region or country. 南東の ❑ ...this city on the southeastern edge of the United States. 米国の南東部のはずれにあるこの都市.

south|er|ly /sʌðərli/ ❶ ADJ 形容詞 A **southerly** point, area, or direction is to the south or toward the south. 南の ❑ We set off in a southerly direction. 私たちは南方向に出発した。 ❷ ADJ 形容詞 A **southerly** wind is a wind that blows from the south. 南からの ❑ ...a strong southerly wind. 強い南風.

south|ern /sʌðərn/ also Southern ADJ 形容詞 **Southern** means in or from the south of a region, state, or country. 南にある [ADJ n] ❑ The Everglades National Park stretches across the southern tip of Florida. エバーグレイド国立公園はフロリダの南端に広がっています.

south|ern|er /sʌðərnər/ (southerners) N-COUNT 可算名詞 A **southerner** is a person who was born in or lives in the south of a country. 南部地方の人 ❑ Bob Wilson is a southerner, from Texas. ボブ・ウィルソンはテキサス州出身の南部出身だ.

south|ward /saʊθwərd/ also southwards ADV 副詞 **Southward** or **southwards** means toward the south. 南方へ [ADV after v] ❑ They drove southward. 彼らは南方へ走った。 ● ADV 副詞 **Southward** is also an adjective. 南方の ❑ Instead of her normal southward course towards Alexandria and home, she headed west. 彼女はアレキサンドリアと自宅に向かういつもの南方へのコースを取らずに、西に向かった。

south|west /saʊθwest/ ❶ N-UNCOUNT 不可算名詞 The **southwest** is the direction which is halfway between south and west. 南西 [also "the" N] ❑ ...some 500 kilometers to the southwest of Johannesburg. ヨハネスブルグからおよそ500キロメートル南西. ❷ N-SING 単数名詞 The **southwest of** a place, country, or region is the part which is toward the southwest. 南西部 ❑ ...the southwest of France. フランスの南西部. ❸ ADV 副詞 If you go **southwest**, you travel toward the southwest. 南西へ [ADV after v] ❑ We took a plane southwest across the Anatolian plateau to Cappadocia. 私たちは、アナトリア高原を越えてカッパドキアへと南西へ向かう飛行機に乗った。 ❹ ADV 副詞 Something of a place is positioned to the southwest of it. 南西にある [ADV "of" n] ❑ It's some 65 miles southwest of Houston. それはヒューストンから約65マイル南西にある。 ❺ ADJ 形容詞 The **southwest** part of a place, country, or region is the part which is toward the southwest. 南西の [ADJ n] ❑ ...a Labor

Day festival in southwest Louisiana. ルイジアナ州南西部で催されるレイバーデー祭り. **6** ADJ 形容詞 A **southwest** wind is a wind that blows from the southwest. 南西からの [ADJ n] □ *Then the southwest wind began to blow.* そして、南西から風が吹き始めた.

south|western /sa͟ʊθwe̱stərn/ ADJ 形容詞 **Southwestern** means in or from the southwest of a region or country. 南西の □ *...remote areas in the southwestern part of the country.* 国の南西部にある辺ぴな地域.

sou|venir /su͟ːvənɪər/ (**souvenirs**) N-COUNT 可算名詞 A **souvenir** is something which you buy or keep to remind you of a vacation, place, or event. みやげ □ *...a souvenir of the summer of 1992.* 1992年夏の思い出.

sov|er|eign /so̱vrɪn/ (**sovereigns**) **1** ADJ 形容詞 A **sovereign** state or country is independent and not under the authority of any other country. 独立の □ *Lithuania and Armenia signed a treaty in Vilnius recognizing each other as independent sovereign states.* リトアニアとアルメニアは、お互いを独立した主権国と認める協定をヴィルニアスで調印した. **2** ADJ 形容詞 **Sovereign** is used to describe the person or institution that has the highest power in a country. 最上の □ *Sovereign power will continue to lie with the Supreme People's Assembly.* 主権は最高人民会議にあり続けるでしょう. **3** N-COUNT 可算名詞 A **sovereign** is a king, queen, or other royal ruler of a country. 君主 □ *In March 1889, she became the first British sovereign to set foot on Spanish soil.* 1889年3月、彼女はスペインの地に足を踏み入れた、最初の英国女王となった.

sov|er|eign|ty /so̱vrɪnti/ N-UNCOUNT 不可算名詞 **Sovereignty** is the power that a country has to govern itself or another country or state. 主権 □ *Concern to protect national sovereignty is far from new.* 国家主権の保護に関する懸念は今に始まったことではありません.

SOW

❶ VERB USES
❷ NOUN USE

---

❶ sow /so͟ʊ/ (**sows, sowing, sowed, sown**) **1** V-T 他動詞 If you **sow** seeds or **sow** an area of land **with** seeds, you plant the seeds in the ground. 種子をまく [他動詞] □ *Sow the seed in a warm place in February/March.* 2月または3月に、暖かい場所に種子をまく. **2** V-T 他動詞 If someone **sows** an undesirable feeling or situation, they cause it to begin and develop. 植え付ける [他動詞] □ *He cleverly sowed doubts into the minds of his rivals.* 彼はライバルの心に疑いの種を巧妙に植え付けた. **3** PHRASE 句 If one thing **sows the seeds of** another, it starts the process which leads eventually to the other thing. 種をまく □ *Rich industrialized countries have sown the seeds of global warming.* 豊かな産業国は、地球温暖化の種を植え付けた.

❷ sow /sa͟ʊ/ (**sows**) N-COUNT 可算名詞 A **sow** is an adult female pig. 雌豚

spa /spɑ͟ː/ (**spas**) **1** N-COUNT 可算名詞 A **spa** is a place where water with minerals in it comes out of the ground. People drink the water or go in it in order to improve their health. 温泉 □ *...Fiuggi, a spa town famous for its water.* 水で有名な温泉町フィウッジ. **2** N-COUNT 可算名詞 A health **spa** is a kind of hotel where people go to exercise and have special treatments in order to improve their health. 保養地ホテル □ *There's also an excellent spa with a large pool, steam room, and sauna.* 大型プール、蒸し風呂、サウナの設備があるすばらしい温泉場ホテルもある. **3** N-COUNT 可算名詞 A **spa** is a type of bathtub that can send out jets of water to massage your body. スパ □ *...a large bathroom with a shower and a spa.* シャワーとスパの付いた大きな浴室.
→ see **hotel**

space /spe͟ɪs/ (**spaces, spacing, spaced**) **1** N-VAR 可変性名詞 You use **space** to refer to an area that is empty or available. The area can be any size. For example, you can refer to a large area outside as a large open **space** or to a small area between two objects as a small **space**. 空間 □ *...cutting down yet more trees to make space for houses.* 住宅用の土地を造るために、さらに木を伐採する. □ *I had plenty of space to write and sew.* 私は執筆や裁縫をするための広い場所を持っていた. □ *The space underneath could be used as a storage area.* 下のスペースは保管地域として使用できる.

> You should use **space** or **room** to refer to an open or empty area. You do not use **place** as an uncount noun in this sense. **Room** is more likely to be used when you are talking about space inside an enclosed area. □ *There's not enough room in the bathroom for both of us... Leave plenty of space between you and the car in front.*

2 N-VAR 可変性名詞 A particular kind of **space** is the area that is available for a particular activity or for putting a particular kind of thing in. スペース □ *...the high cost of office space.* 高い事務所スペース費用. □ *You don't want your living space to look like a bedroom.* あなたは生活空間を寝室のように見せたくないでしょう. **3** N-UNCOUNT 不可算名詞 If a place gives a feeling of **space**, it gives an impression of being large and open. 空間 □ *Large paintings can*

enhance the feeling of space in small rooms. 大きな絵画を飾ると、小さな部屋の空間感を増すことができます. **4** N-UNCOUNT 不可算名詞 If you give someone **space** to think about something or to develop as a person, you allow them the time and freedom to do this. 時間 □ *You need space to think everything over.* 君にはすべてをよく考える時間が必要だ. **5** N-UNCOUNT 不可算名詞 The amount of **space** for a topic to be discussed in a document is the number of pages available to discuss the topic. 紙面 □ *We can't promise to publish a reply as space is limited.* 紙面が限られているので、返答を発行する約束はできない. **6** N-SING 単数名詞 A **space of** time is a period of time. 期間 □ *They've come a long way in a short space of time.* 短期間のうちに彼らは大いに出世した. **7** N-UNCOUNT 不可算名詞 **Space** is the area beyond the Earth's atmosphere, where the stars and planets are. 宇宙 □ *The six astronauts on board will spend ten days in space.* 機内の6人の宇宙飛行士が宇宙で10日を過ごします. □ *...launching satellites into space.* サテライトの宇宙への打ち上げ. **8** N-UNCOUNT 不可算名詞 **Space** is the whole area within which everything exists. 空間 □ *She felt herself transcending time and space.* 彼女は時間と空間を越えているかのように感じた. **9** V-T 他動詞 If you **space** a series of things, you arrange them so that they are not all together but have gaps or intervals of time between them. 間隔をおく [他動詞] □ *Women once again are having fewer children and spacing them further apart.* 女性が産む子供の数はさらに減り、その出産間隔はより長くなっている. ● PHRASAL VERB 句動詞 **Space out** means the same as **space**. 間隔をあける □ *He talks quite slowly and spaces his words out.* 彼はかなりゆっくり、語間をあけて話します. ● **spacing** N-UNCOUNT 不可算名詞 間隔をとること □ *Generous spacing gives healthier trees and better crops.* 間隔を広くとると、木がより健康になり、収穫高が上がる. **10** → see also **airspace, breathing space, outer space, spacing** **11** PHRASE 句 If you are staring **into space**, you are looking straight in front of you, without actually looking at anything in particular, for example because you are thinking or because you are feeling shocked. 虚空を □ *He just sat in the dressing room staring into space.* 彼は楽屋にただ座って虚空を見つめた.
→ see **meteor, moon, satellite**

space|craft /spe͟ɪskræft/ (**spacecraft**)

> **Spacecraft** is both the singular and the plural form.

> **Spacecraft** は単数形でも複数形でもある.

N-COUNT 可算名詞 A **spacecraft** is a rocket or other vehicle that can travel in space. 宇宙船 □ *...the world's largest and most expensive unmanned spacecraft.* 世界最大かつ最も高価な無人の宇宙船.

space|ship /spe͟ɪsʃɪp/ (**spaceships**) N-COUNT 可算名詞 A **spaceship** is a spacecraft that carries people through space. 宇宙船 □ *...an alien spaceship.* 未確認の宇宙船.

space shut|tle (**space shuttles**) N-COUNT 可算名詞 A **space shuttle** or a **shuttle** is a spacecraft that is designed to travel into space and back to Earth several times. スペースシャトル

space sta|tion (**space stations**) N-COUNT 可算名詞 A **space station** is a place built for astronauts to live and work in, which is sent into space and then keeps going around the Earth. 宇宙ステーション

spac|ing /spe͟ɪsɪŋ/ **1** N-UNCOUNT 不可算名詞 **Spacing** refers to the way that typing or printing is arranged on a page, especially in relation to the amount of space that is left between words or lines. 間隔をあけること □ *Single spacing is used within paragraphs, double spacing between paragraphs.* 段落内ではシングルスペース、段落間ではダブルスペースが使用される. **2** → see also **spacing**

spa|cious /spe͟ɪʃəs/ ADJ 形容詞 A **spacious** room or other place is large in size or area, so that you can move around freely in it. 広々とした □ *The house has a spacious kitchen and dining area.* その家には広々とした台所とダイニングがある.

spade /spe͟ɪd/ (**spades**) **1** N-COUNT 可算名詞 A **spade** is a tool used for digging, with a flat metal blade and a long handle. 手鋤 □ *...a garden spade.* 園芸用手鋤. **2** N-UNCOUNT-COLL 集合的不可算名詞 **Spades** is one of the four suits in a deck of playing cards. Each card in the suit is marked with one or more black symbols: ♠. スペード □ *...the ace of spades.* スペードのエース. **3** N-COUNT 可算名詞 A **spade** is a playing card of this suit. スペードの札 □ *He would have done better to play a spade now.* 彼には、今スペードを出すよりももっと良い手があったろうに.

spa|ghet|ti /spəge̱ti/ N-UNCOUNT 不可算名詞 **Spaghetti** is a type of pasta. It looks like long pieces of string and is usually served with a sauce. スパゲッティ

spam /spæ̱m/ (**spams, spamming, spammed**) V-T 他動詞 In computing, to **spam** people or organizations means to send unwanted e-mail to a large number of them, usually as advertising. スパムを送る [COMPUTING コンピューティング] [他動詞] □ *...programs that let you spam the newspapers.* 新聞会社宛にスパムを送らせるプログラム. ● N-VAR 可変性名詞 **Spam** is also a noun. スパム □ *...a small group of people fighting the spam plague.* スパムの異常発生と戦う人たちの小さなグループ. ● **spam|mer** /spæ̱mər/

span N-COUNT 可算名詞 (spammers) スパム送信者 ❑ *The real culprits are the spammers.* 実際の犯人はスパム発信者だ.

→ see **advertising**

span /spæn/ (spans, spanning, spanned) ❶ N-COUNT 可算名詞 A **span** is the period of time between two dates or events during which something exists, functions, or happens. 期間 ❑ *The batteries had a life span of six hours.* 電池の寿命は6時間だった. ❷ N-COUNT 可算名詞 Your concentration **span** or your attention **span** is the length of time you are able to concentrate on something or be interested in it. 短い時間 ❑ *His ability to absorb information was astonishing, but his concentration span was short.* 彼が情報を吸収する能力は驚くべきものだったが, 彼の集中力は長続きしなかった. ❸ V-T 他動詞 If something **spans** a long period of time, it lasts throughout that period of time or relates to that whole period of time. わたる [no passive] [他動詞] ❑ *His professional career spanned 16 years.* 彼の職歴は16年にわたった. ❹ V-T 他動詞 If something **spans** a range of things, all those things are included in it. 広がる [no passive] [他動詞] ❑ *Bernstein's compositions spanned all aspects of music, from symphonies to musicals.* バーンスタインは, 交響曲からミュージカルまで, 音楽のあらゆるジャンルで作曲を行った. ❺ N-COUNT 可算名詞 The **span** of something that extends or is spread out sideways is the total width of it from one end to the other. 範囲 [usu with supp] ❑ *It is a very pretty butterfly, with a 2-inch wing span.* それは, 翼幅が2インチの非常に美しいチョウです. ❻ V-T 他動詞 A bridge or other structure that **spans** something such as a river or a valley stretches right across it. かかる [他動詞] ❑ *Travelers get from one side to the other by walking across a footbridge that spans a little stream.* 旅行者は, 一方の側から他方へ, 小川にかかった歩道橋を歩いて渡る.

→ see **bridge**

Word Partnership span は次の語句と使われる:

ADJ.	brief span ❶ short span ❶ ❺
N.	life span, time span ❶ attention span ❷ span years ❸

spank /spæŋk/ (spanks, spanking, spanked) V-T 他動詞 If someone **spanks** a child, they punish them by hitting them on the bottom several times with their hand. 尻を平手でぶつ ❑ *When I used to do that when I was a kid, my mom would spank me.* 子供のときそれをしていたとき, ママは私のお尻をひっぱたいたものでした.

span|ner /spænər/ (spanners) N-COUNT 可算名詞 A **spanner** is the same as a **wrench**. スパナ [mainly BRIT 主に英国英語]

spar /spɑr/ (spars, sparring, sparred) V-RECIP 相互動詞 If you **spar with** someone, you box using fairly gentle blows instead of hitting your opponent hard, either when you are training or when you want to test how quickly your opponent reacts. スパークリングする ❑ *He entered the ring to spar a few one-minute rounds with an old friend.* 彼はリングに上がり, 旧友と1分ラウンドのスパークリングを数回行った.

spare /spɛər/ (spares, sparing, spared) ❶ ADJ 形容詞 You use **spare** to describe something that is the same as things that you are already using, but that you do not need yet and are keeping ready in case another one is needed. 予備の ❑ *If possible keep a spare pair of glasses accessible in case your main pair is broken or lost.* できれば, 通常使用している眼鏡が壊れたり, 損失したりした場合に備えて, スペアの眼鏡を用意しなさい. ❑ *He could have taken a spare key.* 彼はスペアキーを取ったかもしれない. ● N-COUNT 可算名詞 **Spare** is also a noun. スペア ❑ *Give me the trunk key and I'll get the spare.* トランクの鍵をください, スペアキーを作るから. ❷ ADJ 形容詞 You use **spare** to describe something that is not being used by anyone, and is therefore available for someone to use. 余分の ❑ *They don't have a lot of spare cash.* 彼らは余分の現金はあまり持ち合わせていない. ❑ *The spare bedroom is on the second floor.* 客用の寝室は2階にある. ❸ V-I 自動詞 If you have something such as time, money, or space **to spare**, you have some extra time, money, or space that you have not used or which you do not need. 倹約する [only to-inf] [自動詞] ❑ *You got here with ninety seconds to spare.* 君がここで割ける時間は90秒だ. ❹ V-T 他動詞 If you **spare** time or another resource **for** a particular purpose, you make it available for that purpose. 取って置く [他動詞] ❑ *She said that she could only spare 35 minutes for our meeting.* 彼女は私たちの会議には35分しか割けないと言った. ❺ V-T 他動詞 If a person or a place **is spared**, they are not harmed, even though other people or places have been. 助命される [LITERARY 文語的] [usu passive] [他動詞] ❑ *We have lost everything, but thank God, our lives have been spared.* 私たちはすべてを失ったが, 私たちの命は助かってよかった. ❻ V-T 他動詞 If you **spare** someone an unpleasant experience, you prevent them from suffering it. 容赦する [他動詞] ❑ *I wanted to spare Frances the embarrassment of discussing this subject.* 私はこの件を話し合ってフランシスにきまり悪い思いをさせたくなかった. ❑ *Prisoners are spared the indignity*

of wearing uniforms. 囚人はユニフォームを着るという屈辱を免れる. ❼ → see also **sparing** ❽ PHRASE 句 If you **spare a thought for** an unfortunate person, you make an effort to think sympathetically about them and their bad luck. 考えてやる ❑ *Spare a thought for the nation's shopkeepers – consumer sales slid again in May.* わが国の小売店主のことを考えてくれ, 消費者売り上げは5月にまたもや下落したんだ.

Thesaurus spare また次を参照:

ADJ.	additional, backup, emergency, extra, reserve ❶ ❷

Word Partnership spare は次の語句と使われる:

N.	spare change, spare equipment ❶ spare bedroom ❷ a moment to spare, time to spare ❸ spare someone's life ❺

spare part (spare parts) N-COUNT 可算名詞 **Spare parts** are parts that you can buy separately to replace old or broken parts in a piece of equipment. They are usually parts that are designed to be easily removed or fitted. スペアパーツ ❑ *In the future the machines will need spare parts and maintenance.* 将来, 機械はスペアパーツとメンテナンスが必要になる.

spare time N-UNCOUNT 不可算名詞 Your **spare time** is the time during which you do not have to work and you can do whatever you like. 余暇 ❑ *In her spare time she read books on cooking.* 彼女は余暇に料理の本を読んだ.

spar|ing /spɛərɪŋ/ ADJ 形容詞 Someone who is **sparing with** something uses it or gives it only in very small quantities. 倹約な ❑ *I'm never sparing with the garlic.* 私はニンニクは常にたっぷり使う. ● **spar|ing|ly** ADV 副詞 [ADV after v] 倹約して ❑ *Medication is used sparingly.* 医薬品は控えめに使われる.

spark /spɑrk/ (sparks, sparking, sparked) ❶ N-COUNT 可算名詞 A **spark** is a tiny bright piece of burning material that flies up from something that is burning. 火の粉 ❑ *The fire gradually got bigger and bigger. Sparks flew off in all directions.* 火事はどんどん大きくなり, 火の粉があちこちに飛散した. ❷ N-COUNT 可算名詞 A **spark** is a flash of light caused by electricity. It often makes a loud sound. 火花 ❑ *He passed an electric spark through a mixture of gases.* 彼は混合気体の中に放電した. ❸ V-I 自動詞 If something **sparks**, sparks of fire or light come from it. 火花を散らす ❑ *The wires were sparking above me.* 私の頭上で電線から火花が散っていました. ❹ V-T 他動詞 If a burning object or electricity **sparks** a fire, it causes a fire. 発火させる ❑ *A dropped cigarette may have sparked the fire.* 1本のポイ捨てたばこが火事の原因だったのかもしれない. ❺ N-COUNT 可算名詞 A **spark of** a quality or feeling, especially a desirable one, is a small but noticeable amount of it. 生気 ❑ *His music lacked that vital spark of imagination.* 彼の音楽に欠けていたのは, 沸き立つ想像力だ. ❻ V-T 他動詞 If one thing **sparks** another, the first thing cause the second thing to start happening. 誘発する ❑ *My teacher organized a unit on space exploration that really sparked my interest.* 先生は宇宙研究グループを作ったが, 僕はそれにすごく興味をかきたてられた. ● PHRASAL VERB 句動詞 **Spark off** means the same as **spark**. 誘発する ❑ *That incident sparked it off.* あの事件が引き起こした. ❼ PHRASE 句 If **sparks fly** between people, they discuss something in an excited or angry way. 火花が散る ❑ *They are not afraid to tackle the issues or let the sparks fly when necessary.* 彼らはそれらの問題に取り組み, 必要があれば議論を戦わせることをためらってはいない.

→ see **engine, fire**

Word Partnership spark は次の語句と使われる:

N.	spark from a fire ❶ spark conflict, spark debate, spark interest, spark a reaction ❻
V.	ignite a spark, provide a spark ❺

spar|kle /spɑrk°l/ (sparkles, sparkling, sparkled) ❶ V-I 自動詞 If something **sparkles**, it is clear and bright and shines with a lot of very small points of light. 輝く ❑ *The jewels on her fingers sparkled.* 彼女の指で宝石が輝いていた. ❑ *His bright eyes sparkled.* 彼の明るい瞳が輝いた. ● N-UNCOUNT 不可算名詞 **Sparkle** is also a noun. 輝き ❑ *...the sparkle of colored glass.* 色ガラスのきらめき. ❷ N-COUNT 可算名詞 **Sparkles** are small points of light caused by light reflecting off a clear bright surface. きらめき ❑ *...sparkles of light.* 光のきらめき. ❸ V-I 自動詞 Someone who **sparkles** is lively, intelligent, and witty. (才気が) 輝く [APPROVAL 賛成] ❑ *She sparkles, and has as much zest as a person half her age.* 彼女は才気にあふれ, 歳が半分くらいの人と同じくエネルギッシュです. ● N-UNCOUNT 不可算名詞 **Sparkle** is also a noun. 才気 ❑ *There was little sparkle in their performance.* 彼の演技にはほとんど才気らしきものはありませんでした. ● **spar|kling** ADJ 形容詞 才気ある ❑ *He is sparkling and versatile in front of the camera.* カメラを前にして彼は才気と万能さを発揮している.

S

spar|kling /spɑrklɪŋ/ **1** ADJ 形容詞 **Sparkling** drinks are slightly carbonated. 発泡性の □ ...a glass of sparkling wine. グラス1杯のスパークリングワイン. **2** → see also **sparkle**

spar|row /spærov/ (**sparrows**) N-COUNT 可算名詞 A **sparrow** is a small brown bird that is very common in the United States. スズメ

sparse /spɑrs/ (**sparser, sparsest**) ADJ 形容詞 Something that is **sparse** is small in number or amount and spread out over an area. まばらな □ Many slopes are rock fields with sparse vegetation. 多くの斜面は草木のまばらな岩場です. □ He was a tubby little man in his fifties, with sparse hair. 彼は50代で, 小柄ですんぐりした体型で, 髪も薄かった. ● **sparse|ly** ADV 副詞 まばらに □ ...the sparsely populated interior region, where there are few roads. 人口のまばらな内陸部で, 道路もほとんどありません.

spar|tan /spɑrtᵊn/ ADJ 形容詞 A **spartan** lifestyle or existence is very simple or strict, with no luxuries. 質素な □ Their spartan lifestyle prohibits a fridge or a phone. 彼らが採用する質素な生活様式では, 冷蔵庫や電話も使わない.

spasm /spæzəm/ (**spasms**) N-VAR 可変性名詞 A **spasm** is a sudden tightening of your muscles, which you cannot control. けいれん □ A muscular spasm in the coronary artery can cause a heart attack. 冠状動脈の筋肉のけいれんが心臓発作に至る場合がある.

spat /spæt/ **Spat** is a past tense and past participle of **spit**.

spate /speɪt/ (**spates**) N-COUNT 可算名詞 A **spate** of things, especially unpleasant things, is a large number of them that happen or appear within a short period of time. 大量 □ ...the recent spate of attacks on horses. 最近の馬への相次ぐ攻撃.

spa|tial /speɪʃᵊl/ **1** ADJ 形容詞 **Spatial** is used to describe things relating to areas. 空間の [ADJ n] □ ...the spatial distribution of black employment and population in South Africa. 南アフリカにおける黒人雇用と人口の分布. **2** ADJ 形容詞 Your **spatial** ability is your ability to see and understand the relationships between shapes, spaces, and areas. 空間把握の [ADJ n] □ His manual dexterity and fine spatial skills were wasted on routine tasks. 定型業務では, 彼は手先の器用さや優れた空間把握力を発揮できなかった.

spat|ter /spætər/ (**spatters, spattering, spattered**) V-T/V-I 他動詞/自動詞 If a liquid **spatters** a surface or you **spatter** a liquid over a surface, drops of the liquid fall on an area of the surface. 跳ねかける, 跳ねかかる □ He stared at the rain spattering on the glass. 彼はガラスにパラパラと当たる雨を見つめていた. □ Gently turn the fish, being careful not to spatter any hot butter on yourself. 熱くなったバターが自分に飛ばないように注意して, 魚をそっと裏返してください.

speak /spik/ (**speaks, speaking, spoke, spoken**) **1** V-I 自動詞 When you **speak**, you use your voice in order to say something. 話す □ He tried to speak, but for once, his voice had left him. 彼は話そうと試みたが, 今度ばかりは, 声がでなかった. □ I rang the hotel and spoke to Louie. 私はホテルに電話し, ルーイと話した. □ She cried when she spoke of Oliver. オリバーの話をしたとき彼女は泣いた. ● **spo|ken** ADJ 形容詞 [ADJ n] 口語の □ ...a marked decline in the standards of written and spoken English. 文語英語と口語英語の水準の顕著な低下. **2** V-I 自動詞 When someone **speaks to** a group of people, they make a speech. 演説する □ When speaking to the seminar Mr. Franklin spoke of his experience, gained on a recent visit to Trinidad. セミナーの講演で, フランクリン氏は最近訪問したトリニダードでの体験について話した. □ He's determined to speak at the Democratic Convention. 彼は民主党大会での演説を決めました. **3** V-I 自動詞 If you **speak for** a group of people, you make their views and demands known, or represent them. 代弁する □ He said it was the job of the Church to speak for the underprivileged. 恵まれない人を代弁するのは教会の務めだ, と彼は発言した. □ I speak for all 7,000 members of our organization. 当社7千名の社員を代表して申し上げます. **4** V-T 他動詞 If you **speak** a foreign language, you know the language and are able to have a conversation in it. 話す □ He doesn't speak English. 彼は英語を話しません. **5** V-I 自動詞 People sometimes mention something that has been written by saying what the author **speaks of**. 書き表す □ Throughout the book Liu speaks of the abuse of Party power. リューは本の全編で党の職権乱用について述べています. **6** V-RECIP 相互動詞 If two people **are not speaking**, they no longer talk to each other because they have argued. 口をきかない [with neg] □ He is not speaking to his mother because of her friendship with his ex-wife. 彼が母親と口をきかないのは, 彼女が自分の先妻と仲が良いからだ. **7** V-I 自動詞 If you say that something **speaks for itself**, you mean that its meaning or quality is so obvious that it does not need explaining or pointing out. それ自体が物語る [no cont] □ ...the figures speak for themselves – bleak prospects at home and a worsening outlook for exports. その数字から明らかなのは–国内産業の不振, 輸出の悪化という暗い見通しだ. **8** PHRASE 句 If a person or thing is **spoken for** or **has been spoken for**, someone has claimed them or asked for them, so no one else can have them. 予約済みである □ She'd probably drop some comment about her "fiancé" into the conversation so that he'd think she was already spoken for. 女がその会話の中で「婚約者」について触れたのは, 彼女には決まった相手がいるということを彼に思わ

せたいからでしょう. **9** PHRASE 句 If you **speak well of** someone or **speak highly of** someone, you say good things about them. If you **speak ill of** someone, you criticize them. 一をほめる, 一を悪く言う □ Both spoke highly of the Russian president. 両者ともロシア大統領を高く評価しました. **10** PHRASE 句 You use **so to speak** to draw attention to the fact that you are describing or referring to something in a way that may be amusing or unusual rather than completely accurate. いわば □ I ought not to tell you but I will, since you're in the family, so to speak. 君はいわば家族の一員なんだから, 言うべきではないんだけどあえて言うよ. **11** to **speak** your **mind** → see **mind** to **speak volumes** → see **volume**

There are some differences in the way the verbs **speak** and **talk** are used. When you **speak**, you could, for example, be addressing someone or making a speech. **Talk** is more likely to be used when you are referring to a conversation or discussion. □ I talked about it with my family at dinner... Sometimes we'd talk all night. **Talk** can also be used to emphasize the activity of saying things, rather than the words that are spoken. □ She thought I talked too much.

▶ **speak out** PHRASAL VERB 句動詞 If you **speak out** against something or in favor of something, you say publicly that you think it is bad or good. はっきりと言う □ As tempers rose, he spoke out strongly against some of the radical ideas for selling off state-owned property. 感情が高まると, 彼は国営財産を売却するという過激な案にきっぱりと反対を表明しました.

▶ **speak up** **1** PHRASAL VERB 句動詞 If you **speak up**, you say something, especially to defend a person or protest about something, rather than just saying nothing. はっきりと言う □ Uncle Herbert never argued, never spoke up for himself. ハーバートおじさんは, 口論したり自分の考えを主張したりする人ではない. **2** PHRASAL VERB 句動詞 If you ask someone to **speak up**, you are asking them to speak more loudly. 大きな声で話す [no cont] □ I'm quite deaf – you'll have to speak up. 私はずいぶん耳が遠いのでね. もっと大きな声で話してもらわないと.

Thesaurus	speak また次を参照:
v.	articulate, communicate, declare, talk **1**

Word Partnership	speak は次の語句と使われる:
ADV.	speak **clearly**, speak **directly**, speak **louder**, speak **slowly** speak **freely**, speak **publicly** **1 2**
N.	**chance to** speak, **opportunity to** speak, speak **the truth 1 2** speak **English/French/Spanish**, speak **a (foreign) language 4**

-speak /-spik/ COMB IN N-UNCOUNT 不可算名詞の複合 **-speak** is used to form nouns which refer to the kind of language used by a particular person or by people involved in a particular activity. You use **-speak** when you disapprove of this kind of language because it is difficult for other people to understand. 一用語 [DISAPPROVAL 不賛成] □ Team building, motivation, and performance feature widely in modern business-speak. チームビルディング, モチベーション, パフォーマンスといった語は, ビジネス用語でよく使われる.

speak|er /spikər/ (**speakers**) **1** N-COUNT 可算名詞 A **speaker** at a meeting, conference, or other gathering is a person who is making a speech or giving a talk. 演説者 □ Among the speakers at the gathering was Treasury Secretary Nicholas Brady. その集会の講演者にはニコラス・ブレイディも含まれていました. □ Bruce Wyatt will be the guest speaker at next month's meeting. 来月の会合では, ブルース・ワイアットが来賓演説を行う予定です. **2** N-COUNT 可算名詞 A **speaker of** a particular language is a person who speaks it, especially one who speaks it as their first language. (言語の) 話者 □ ...in the Ukraine, where a fifth of the population are Russian speakers. ウクライナでは国民の5分の1がロシア語話者です. **3** N-PROPER; N-VOC 固有名詞, 呼格名詞 In the legislature or parliament of many countries, the **Speaker** is the person who is in charge of meetings. 議長 □ ...the Speaker of the House. 議会議長 **4** N-COUNT 可算名詞 A **speaker** is a person who is speaking. 話し手 □ From a simple gesture or the speaker's tone of voice, the Japanese listener gleans the whole meaning. 日本人は, 話し手の単純な身振りや声の調子からその人が意図するところを探ります. **5** N-COUNT 可算名詞 A **speaker** is a piece of electrical equipment, for example part of a radio or set of equipment for playing CDs or tapes, through which sound comes out. スピーカー □ For a good stereo effect, the speakers should not be too wide apart. 良いステレオ効果を得るには, スピーカー位置を離しすぎてはいけません.

speak|ing /spikɪŋ/ **1** N-UNCOUNT 不可算名詞 **Speaking** is the activity of giving speeches and talks. 話すこと □ It would also train women union members in public speaking and decision-making. そのことは女性組合員にとって演説や意思決定のよい訓練にもなるでしょう. **2** PHRASE

句 You can say "**speaking as** a parent" or "**speaking as** a teacher," for example, to indicate that the opinion you are giving is based on your experience as a parent or as a teacher. 一の立場で言えば □ *Well, speaking as a journalist I'm dismayed by the amount of pressure there is for pictures of combat.* ジャーナリストの立場から言わせてもいますと、これらの戦闘の写真に対する圧力の大きさに驚いています. ③ PHRASE 句 You use **speaking** in expressions such as **generally speaking** and **technically speaking** to indicate which things or which particular aspect of something you are talking about. 一に言えば □ *Generally speaking there was no resistance to the idea.* 概して言えば、その案への反対はありませんでした.

spear /spɪər/ (**spears, spearing, speared**) ① N-COUNT 可算名詞 A **spear** is a weapon consisting of a long pole with a sharp metal point attached to the end. やり ② V-T 他動詞 If you **spear** something, you push or throw a pointed object into it. 突く □ *Spear a piece of fish with a carving fork and dip it in the batter.* 大きなフォークで魚の身を刺して、衣用の生地につけてください.
→ see **army**

spear|head /spɪərhɛd/ (**spearheads, spearheading, spearheaded**) V-T 他動詞 If someone **spearheads** a campaign or an attack, they lead it. 先頭に立つ [JOURNALISM ジャーナリズム] □ *She is spearheading a nationwide campaign against domestic violence.* 彼女は家庭内暴力防止の全国キャンペーンを指揮しています.

spec /spɛk/ (**specs**) ① N-COUNT 可算名詞 The **spec** for something, especially a machine or vehicle, is its design and the features included in it. 仕様 [INFORMAL くだけた] □ *The standard spec includes stainless steel holding tanks.* 標準仕様にはステンレス製の貯蔵タンクが含まれる. ② N-PLURAL 複数名詞 Someone's **specs** are their glasses. 眼鏡 [INFORMAL くだけた] [also "a pair of" N] □ *...a young businessman in his specs and suit.* 眼鏡をかけたスーツ姿の若いビジネスマン. ③ PHRASE 句 If you do something **on spec**, you do it hoping to get something that you want, but without being asked or without being certain to get it. いちかばちかで [INFORMAL くだけた] □ *When searching for a job Adrian favors networking and writing letters on spec.* エイドリアンは、人脈を頼みにいちかばちかで応募書類を出すというやり方で求職活動を行っている.

spe|cial /spɛʃ°l/ (**specials**) ① ADJ 形容詞 Someone or something that is **special** is better or more important than other people or things. 特別な □ *You're very special to me, darling.* あなたは私にとって、とても大切な人なのよ. □ *My special guest will be Jerry Seinfeld.* 特別ゲストにジェリー・サインフェルドをお迎えする予定です. ② ADJ 形容詞 **Special** means different from normal. 特殊な [ADJ n] □ *In special cases, a husband can deduct the travel expenses of his wife who accompanies him on a business trip.* 特別として、夫が出張で妻を同伴する場合に妻の旅費を控除できる. □ *So you didn't notice anything special about him?* それで彼に別段変わった様子はなかったのかい？ ③ ADJ 形容詞 You use **special** to describe someone who is officially appointed or who has a particular position specially created for them. 特別一 [ADJ n] □ *Due to his wife's illness, he returned to the State Department as special adviser to the president.* 妻の病気が理由で、彼は大統領の特別顧問として国務省に戻った. ④ ADJ 形容詞 You use **special** to describe something that relates to one particular person, group, or place. 特有の □ *Every anxious person will have his or her own special problems or fears.* 不安症の人は、それぞれに特有の問題や心配事を抱えている場合が多い. ⑤ N-COUNT 可算名詞 A **special** is a product, program, or meal which is not normally available, or which is made for a particular purpose. 限定版 □ *...complaints about the Halloween special, "Ghostwatch."* ハロウィーン限定版「ゴーストウォッチ」に対するクレーム. □ *Grocery stores have to offer enough specials to bring people into the store.* 食料品店は客寄せ用に限定品を十分に用意する必要がある.

Thesaurus	special また次を参照:
ADJ.	distinctive, exceptional, unique; (ant.) ordinary ①②④

spe|cial ef|fect (**special effects**) N-COUNT 可算名詞 In a movie, **special effects** are unusual pictures or sounds that are created by using special techniques. 特殊効果 □ *...a Hollywood horror film with special effects that are not for the nervous.* 臆病な人には耐えられないような特殊効果を用いたハリウッド版ホラー映画.

spe|cial|ise /spɛʃəlaɪz/ → see **specialize**

spe|cial|ist /spɛʃəlɪst/ (**specialists**) N-COUNT 可算名詞 A **specialist** is a person who has a particular skill or knows a lot about a particular subject. 専門家 □ *Peckham, himself a cancer specialist, is well aware of the wide variations in medical practice.* ペッカム自身は癌の専門医だが、治療行為の選択肢の多さは十分認識している.

spe|cial|ity /spɛʃiælɪti/ (**specialities**) N-COUNT 可算名詞 A **speciality** is the same as a **specialty**. 専門 [mainly BRIT 主に英国英語]

spe|cial|ize /spɛʃəlaɪz/ (**specializes, specializing, specialized**) V-I 自動詞 If you **specialize in** a thing, you know a lot about it and concentrate a great deal of your time and energy on it, especially in your work or when you are studying or training. You also use **specialize** to talk about a restaurant which concentrates on a particular type of food. 専門とする □ *...a University professor who specializes in the history of the Russian empire.* ロシア帝国の歴史を専門にする大学教授. ● spe|cial|iza|tion /spɛʃəlɪzeɪʃ°n/ N-VAR 可変性名詞 (**specializations**) 専門化 □ *This degree offers a major specialization in social policy alongside a course in sociology.* この学位では社会学のコースと平行して社会政策の専門学位が取得できます.

spe|cial|ized /spɛʃəlaɪzd/ ADJ 形容詞 Someone or something that is **specialized** is trained or developed for a particular purpose or area of knowledge. 専門化した □ *Cocaine addicts get specialized support from knowledgeable staff.* コカイン中毒患者は治療に精通したスタッフの専門的な支援を受ける.

spe|cial|ly /spɛʃəli/ ① ADV 副詞 If something has been done **specially for** a particular person or purpose, it has been done only for that person or purpose. 特別に □ *...a soap specially designed for those with sensitive skin.* 敏感肌用に特別に作られたせっけん. □ *Patrick needs to use specially adapted computer equipment.* パトリックが使いたいのは専用のコンピューター機器である. ② ADV 副詞 **Specially** is used to mean more than usually or more than other things. 特に [INFORMAL くだけた] □ *Stay in bed extra late or get up specially early.* とことん遅い時間まで寝るか、とことん早起きしなさい.

spe|cial of|fer (**special offers**) N-COUNT 可算名詞 A **special offer** is a product, service, or program that is offered at reduced prices or rates. 特別奉仕品 □ *Ask about special offers on our new 2-week vacations.* 今後2週間の休暇向け特別奉仕品は要チェック.

spe|cial|ty /spɛʃəlti/ (**specialties**) ① N-COUNT 可算名詞 Someone's **specialty** is a particular type of work that they do most or do best, or a subject that they know a lot about. 専門 [AM 米国英語] □ *His specialty is international law.* 彼の専門は国際法です. ② N-COUNT 可算名詞 A **specialty** of a particular place is a special food or product that is always very good there. 名物 [AM 米国英語] □ *...seafood, paella, and other specialties.* シーフード、パエリア、その他の名物料理.

spe|cies /spiʃiz/ (**species**)

Species is both the singular and the plural form.

Species は単数形でも複数形でもある.

N-COUNT 可算名詞 A **species** is a class of plants or animals whose members have the same main characteristics and are able to breed with each other. 種 □ *Pandas are an endangered species.* パンダは絶滅危惧（きぐ）種です.
→ see **plant, zoo**

spe|cif|ic /spɪsɪfɪk/ ① ADJ 形容詞 You use **specific** to refer to a particular exact area, problem, or subject. 特定の [ADJ n] □ *Massage may help to increase blood flow to specific areas of the body.* マッサージで体の特定部位の血行が促進されることがある. ② ADJ 形容詞 If someone is **specific**, they give a description that is precise and exact. You can also use **specific** to describe their description. 明確な □ *She declined to be more specific about the reasons for the separation.* 彼女は、別居の原因についてこれ以上具体的に述べることを拒否しました. ③ ADJ 形容詞 Something that is **specific to** a particular thing is connected with that thing only. 特有の □ *Send your resume with a cover letter that is specific to that particular job.* 履歴書と、応募職種に特化した職歴を記載したカバーレターをご送付ください. ● COMB IN ADJ 形容詞の複合 **Specific** is also used after nouns. 一特有の □ *Most studies of trade have been country-specific.* これまでの商業研究はほとんどが各国ごとに行われていました.

spe|cifi|cal|ly /spɪsɪfɪkli/ ① ADV 副詞 You use **specifically** to emphasize that something is given special attention and considered separately from other things of the same kind. 特に [EMPHASIS 強調] [ADV with v] □ *...the first nursing home designed specifically for people with AIDS.* 初めてのエイズ患者専用の養護施設. □ *We haven't specifically targeted schoolchildren.* 特に学童を対象にしてきたわけではありません. ② ADV 副詞 You use **specifically** to add something more precise or exact to what you have already said. 具体的に言えば [ADV with group] □ *Death frightens me, specifically my own death.* 死、つまりは自分の死が怖いのです. □ *...the Christian, and specifically Protestant, religion.* キリスト教、具体的にはプロテスタント. ③ ADV 副詞 You use **specifically** to indicate that something has a restricted nature, as opposed to being more general in nature. 特有に [ADV adj] □ *...a specifically female audience.* 女性ばかりの聴衆. ④ ADV 副詞 If you state or describe something **specifically**, you state or describe it precisely and clearly. 明確に [ADV with v] □ *I specifically asked for this steak rare.* ステーキの焼き方はレアで、とははっきりお願いしましたよ.

speci|fi|ca|tion /spɛsɪfɪkeɪʃ°n/ (**specifications**) N-COUNT 可算名詞 A **specification** is a requirement which is clearly stated, for example about the necessary features in the design of something. 指定条件 □ *I'd like to buy some land and have a house built to my specification.* 土地を買って自分の希望通りの家を建てたいな.

S

spe|cif|ics /spɪsɪfɪks/ N-PLURAL 複数名詞 The **specifics** of a subject are the details of it that need to be considered. 詳細事項 ❑ *Things improved when we got down to the specifics.* 私たちが詳細事項に取り掛かかると事態は好転した。

speci|fy /spɛsɪfaɪ/ (**specifies, specifying, specified**) ◼ V-T 他動詞 If you **specify** something, you give information about what is required or should happen in a certain situation. 指定する ❑ *They specified a spacious entrance hall.* 彼らは広いエントランスホールを指定した。 ◼ V-T 他動詞 If you **specify** what should happen or be done, you explain it in an exact and detailed way. 具体的に述べる ❑ *Each recipe specifies the size of egg to be used.* 使用する卵のサイズはレシピに具体的に記してあります。 ❑ *A new law specified that houses must be a certain distance back from the water.* 新しい法律は、家は水際から一定距離を置いて建てることを定めている。

speci|men /spɛsɪmɪn/ (**specimens**) ◼ N-COUNT 可算名詞 A **specimen** is a single plant or animal which is an example of a particular species or type and is examined by scientists. 標本 [usu with supp] ❑ *200,000 specimens of fungus are kept at the Komarov Botanical Institute.* 20万種の菌類の標本がコマロフ植物研究所に保管されている。 ◼ N-COUNT 可算名詞 A **specimen of** something is an example of it which gives an idea of what the whole of it is like. 見本 [usu with supp] ❑ *Job applicants have to submit a specimen of handwriting.* 求職者は手書きの見本を提出しなければなりません。 ◼ N-COUNT 可算名詞 A **specimen** is a small quantity of someone's urine, blood, or other body fluid which is examined in a medical laboratory, in order to find out if they are ill or if they have been drinking alcohol or taking drugs. 検体 ❑ *He refused to provide a specimen.* 彼は検体の提供を拒んだ。

speck /spɛk/ (**specks**) ◼ N-COUNT 可算名詞 A **speck** is a very small stain, mark, or shape. 小さなしみ [oft N "of" n] ❑ *He has even cut himself shaving. There is a speck of blood by his ear.* 彼はひげをそって肌を切ったみたいだ。耳の側に血が少しついているんだ。 ◼ N-COUNT 可算名詞 A **speck** is a very small piece of a powdery substance. 小さな粒 [oft N "of" n] ❑ *Billy leaned forward and brushed a speck of dust off his shoes.* ビリーは前かがみになって、靴についたほこりを払った。

specs /spɛks/ → see **spec**

Word Link spect ≈ looking : spectacle, spectacular, spectator

spec|ta|cle /spɛktək°l/ (**spectacles**) ◼ N-COUNT 可算名詞 A **spectacle** is a strange or interesting sight. 光景 ❑ *It was a spectacle not to be missed.* それは見逃せない光景だったよ。 ◼ N-VAR 可変性名詞 A **spectacle** is a grand and impressive event or performance. ショー ❑ *Ninety-four thousand people turned up for the spectacle.* 9万4千人がそのショーに来場した。 ◼ N-PLURAL 複数名詞 Glasses are sometimes referred to as **spectacles**. 眼鏡 [OLD-FASHIONED 古風な] [also "a pair of" n] ❑ *He looked at me over the tops of his spectacles.* 彼は眼鏡フレームの上から私を見た。

spec|tacu|lar /spɛktækyələr/ (**spectaculars**) ◼ ADJ 形容詞 Something that is **spectacular** is very impressive or dramatic. 目を見張るような ❑ *...spectacular views of the Sugar Loaf Mountain.* シュガー・ローフ・マウンテンの壮大な景色。 ● **spec|tacu|lar|ly** ADV 副詞 My turnover increased spectacularly. 売り上げは驚くほど伸びた。 ◼ N-COUNT 可算名詞 [usu n n] A **spectacular** is a show or performance which is very grand and impressive. 豪華ショー ❑ *...a television spectacular.* テレビの豪華番組。

Word Link ator ≈ one who does : creator, innovator, spectator

spec|ta|tor /spɛkteɪtər/ (**spectators**) N-COUNT 可算名詞 A **spectator** is someone who watches something, especially a sports event. 観客 ❑ *Thirty thousand spectators watched the final game.* 3万人が決勝戦を観戦した。

spec|ter /spɛktər/ (**specters**) N-COUNT 可算名詞 If you refer to the **specter** of something unpleasant, you are referring to something that you are frightened might occur. 恐ろしいもの [usu "the" N "of" n] ❑ *The arrests raised the specter of revenge attacks.* 一連の逮捕劇によって報復攻撃への不安が高まった。

spec|trum /spɛktrəm/ (**spectra** or **spectrums**) ◼ N-SING 単数名詞 The **spectrum** is the range of different colors which is produced when light passes through a glass prism or through a drop of water. A rainbow shows the colors in the spectrum. スペクトル ◼ N-COUNT 可算名詞 A **spectrum** is a range of a particular type of thing. 範囲 ❑ *She'd seen his moods range across the emotional spectrum.* 彼女は、彼の気分が感情次第で変わるのを見てきた。 ❑ *Politicians across the political spectrum have denounced the act.* 政治家たちは党派によらず今の行為を非難した。

specu|late /spɛkyəleɪt/ (**speculates, speculating, speculated**) ◼ V-T/V-I 他動詞/自動詞 If you **speculate** about something, you make guesses about its nature or identity, or about what might happen. 推測する ❑ *Critics of the project speculate about how many hospitals could be built instead.* プロジェクトの反対派が、その代わりに病院が何棟建てられるかを試算する。 ❑ *The doctors speculate that he died of a cerebral hemorrhage caused by a blow on the head.* 医者は

彼の死因は頭部強打による脳内出血だと見ている。 ● **specu|la|tion** /spɛkyəleɪʃ°n/ N-VAR 可変性名詞 (**speculations**) 推測 ❑ *The president has gone out of his way to dismiss speculation about the future of the economy.* 大統領は今後の経済に関する憶測を払拭(ふっしょく)するのに骨を折ってきました。 ◼ V-I 自動詞 If someone **speculates** financially, they buy property, stocks, or shares, in the hope of being able to sell them again at a higher price and make a profit. 投資する ❑ *The banks made too many risky loans which now can't be repaid, and they speculated in property whose value has now dropped.* 銀行は危険な融資を重ね、不動産に投機しましたが、今では融資は焦げ付き、不動産価値も下落したのです。

Word Partnership speculate は次の語句と使われる:

N. analysts speculate, speculate **about** a game, speculate **about** an outcome ◼

specu|la|tive /spɛkyələɪtɪv, -lətɪv/ ◼ ADJ 形容詞 A piece of information that is **speculative** is based on guesses rather than knowledge. 推測の ❑ *The papers ran speculative stories about the mysterious disappearance of Eddie Donagan.* 各新聞社がエディ・ドナー癌のなぞめいた失踪(しっそう)に関する憶測記事を掲載した。 ◼ ADJ 形容詞 **Speculative** is used to describe activities which involve buying goods or shares, or buildings and properties, in the hope of being able to sell them again at a higher price and make a profit. 投機の ❑ *Thousands of retirees were persuaded to mortgage their homes to invest in speculative bonds.* 何千人もの年金生活者が自宅を担保に投機的な債券に投資するようしむけられた。

specu|la|tor /spɛkyələɪtər/ (**speculators**) N-COUNT 可算名詞 A **speculator** is a person who speculates financially. 投資家 ❑ *He sold the contracts to another speculator for a profit.* 利益を得ようとして彼はそれらの約定を他の投資家に売った。

sped /spɛd/ **Sped** is a past tense and past participle of **speed**.

speech /spitʃ/ (**speeches**) ◼ N-UNCOUNT 不可算名詞 **Speech** is the ability to speak or the act of speaking. 発話 ❑ *...the development of speech in children.* 子供の発話能力の発達。 ❑ *Intoxication interferes with speech and coordination.* 中毒症状では発話と協調運動に支障を来たす。 ◼ N-SING 単数名詞 Your **speech** is the way in which you speak. 話し方 ❑ *His speech became increasingly thick and nasal.* 彼はますます不明瞭で鼻にかかるような話し方をするようになった。 ◼ N-UNCOUNT 不可算名詞 **Speech** is spoken language. 口語 ❑ *He could imitate in speech or writing most of those he admired.* 彼は自分が尊敬する人の話し方や書き方をほとんどまねることができた。 ◼ N-COUNT 可算名詞 A **speech** is a formal talk which someone gives to an audience. 演説 ❑ *She is due to make a speech on the economy next week.* 彼女は来週経済について講演する予定である。 ❑ *He delivered his speech in French.* 彼は演説をフランス語で行った。 ◼ → see also **direct speech, indirect speech** → see **election**

Word Partnership speech は次の語句と使われる:

ADJ. slurred speech ◼
free speech ◼
famous speech, major speech, political speech, recent speech ◼
N. acceptance speech, campaign speech, keynote speech, speech writing ◼
V. deliver a speech, give a speech, make a speech, prepare a speech ◼

speech|less /spitʃlɪs/ ADJ 形容詞 If you are **speechless**, you are temporarily unable to speak, usually because something has shocked you. 言葉を失って ❑ *Alex was almost speechless with rage and despair.* アレックスは怒りと落胆のあまりほとんど口が利けなかった。

speed /spid/ (**speeds, speeding, sped** or **speeded**)

The form of the past tense and past participle is **sped** in meaning ◼ but **speeded** for the phrasal verb.

過去時制と過去分詞の形は **sped** を意味する場合は ◼ であるが、句動詞のためには **speeded** である。

◼ N-VAR 可変性名詞 The **speed** of something is the rate at which it moves or travels. 速度 ❑ *He drove off at high speed.* 彼は高速で走り去った。 ❑ *Wind speeds reached force five.* 風速は風力5レベルに達した。 ◼ N-COUNT 可算名詞 The **speed** of something is the rate at which it happens or is done. 速さ ❑ *In the late 1850s the speed of technological change quickened.* 1850年代後半、技術の進歩は加速した。 ◼ N-UNCOUNT 不可算名詞 **Speed** is very fast movement or travel. スピード ❑ *Speed is the essential ingredient of all athletics.* スピードは全ての運動競技に欠かせない要素である。 ❑ *He put on a burst of speed.* 彼は一気に加速した。 ◼ N-UNCOUNT 不可算名詞 **Speed** is a very fast rate at which something happens or is done. 速さ ❑ *I was amazed at his speed of working.* 私は彼の仕事の速さに驚いた。 ◼ V-I 自動詞 If you **speed** somewhere, you move or travel

there quickly, usually in a vehicle. 疾走する □ *Trains will speed through the tunnel at 186 mph.* 列車は時速186マイルでトンネルを抜けるだろう. **6** V-I 自動詞 Someone who **is speeding** is driving a vehicle faster than the legal speed limit. スピード違反をする [usu cont] □ *This man was not qualified to drive and was speeding.* この男は無免許でスピードを犯していた. ● **speed|ing** N-UNCOUNT 不可算名詞 スピード違反 □ *He was fined for speeding last year.* 彼は去年スピード違反で罰金を科せられた. **7** N-UNCOUNT 不可算名詞 **Speed** is an illegal drug such as amphetamine which some people take to increase their energy and excitement. 覚せい剤 [INFORMAL くだけた] **8** to **pick up speed** → see **pick**

▶ **speed up** **1** PHRASAL VERB 句動詞 When something **speeds up** or when you **speed** it **up**, it moves or travels faster. 速める, 速まる □ *You notice that your breathing has speeded up a bit.* あなたは自分の呼吸が少し早まったことに気づく. **2** PHRASAL VERB 句動詞 When a process or activity **speeds up** or when something **speeds** it **up**, it happens at a faster rate. スピードアップする □ *Job losses are speeding up.* 失業が急増している. □ *I had already taken steps to speed up a solution to the problem.* 問題解決のスピードアップする手はすでに打っておいた.

speed dial (**speed dials**) N-VAR 可変性名詞 **Speed dial** is a facility on a telephone that allows you to call a number by pressing a single button rather than by dialing the full number. 短縮ダイヤル □ *Who's at the top of your speed-dial list?* 短縮ダイヤルリストの最初は誰ですか.

speed lim|it (**speed limits**) N-COUNT 可算名詞 The **speed limit** on a road is the maximum speed at which you are legally allowed to drive. 制限速度 □ *I was fined $158 for exceeding the speed limit by 15 mph.* 制限速度15マイル超過で158ドルの罰金を取られた.

speed|om|eter /spidɒmɪtər/ (**speedometers**) N-COUNT 可算名詞 A **speedometer** is the instrument in a vehicle which shows how fast the vehicle is moving. 速度計

speedy /spidi/ (**speedier, speediest**) ADJ 形容詞 A **speedy** process, event, or action happens or is done very quickly. 迅速な □ *We wish Bill a speedy recovery.* 私たちはビルの速やかな回復を祈っています.

spell /spɛl/ (**spells, spelling, spelled** or **spelt**) **1** V-T 他動詞 When you **spell** a word, you write or speak each letter in the word in the correct order. 綴る □ *He gave his name and then helpfully spelled it.* 彼は名前を言って, 親切にそのつづりも教えてくれた. □ *How do you spell "potato?"* 「ポテト」はどうつづるのですか. ● PHRASAL VERB 句動詞 **Spell out** means the same as **spell**. つづる □ *If I don't know a word, I ask them to spell it out for me.* もし単語が分からないときは, 彼らに頼んでつづってもらいます. **2** V-T/V-I 他動詞/自動詞 Someone who can **spell** knows the correct order of letters in words. 正しくつづる [no cont] □ *It's shocking how students can't spell these days.* 近頃は生徒がいかに正しくつづれないかにがく然とします. □ *He can't even spell his own name.* 彼は自分の名前さえ正しく書けなかった. **3** V-T 他動詞 If something **spells** a particular outcome, often an unpleasant one, it suggests that this will be the result. 意味する [no cont] □ *If the irrigation plan goes ahead, it could spell disaster for the birds.* かんがい計画が進行すれば, 鳥に大きな被害もたらすことになる. **4** N-COUNT 可算名詞 A **spell** of a particular type of weather or a particular activity is a short period of time during which this type of weather or activity occurs. 一続きの期間 □ *There has been a long spell of dry weather.* 長らく雨が降らない天気が続いている. **5** N-COUNT 可算名詞 A **spell** is a situation in which events are controlled by a magical power. 魔法 □ *They say she died after a witch cast a spell on her.* 彼女は魔女に魔法をかけられて死んだとされている. **6** → see also **spelling**

▶ **spell out** **1** PHRASAL VERB 句動詞 If you **spell** something **out**, you explain it in detail or in a very clear way. 詳しく説明する □ *Be assertive and spell out exactly how you feel.* 堂々と, 自分が感じたままを詳しく述べなさい. **2** → see **spell 1**

Thesaurus *spell* また次を参照:

N. period, phase **4**

Word Partnership *spell* は次の語句と使われる:

N. spell **a name/word** **1**
spell **the end** of *something*, spell **trouble** **3**
V. **can/can't** spell *something* **2**
break a spell, **cast a** spell **5**

spell-check (**spell-checks, spell-checking, spell-checked**) also **spell check** **1** V-T 他動詞 If you **spell-check** something you have written on a computer, you use a special program to check whether you have made any spelling mistakes. スペルをチェックする [COMPUTING コンピューティング] □ *This model allows you to spell-check over 100,000 different words.* このモデルには10万語のスペルチェック機能がついています. **2** N-COUNT 可算名詞 If you run

a **spell-check** over something you have written on a computer, you use a special program to check whether you have made any spelling mistakes. スペルチェック機能 [COMPUTING コンピューティング]

spell-checker (**spell-checkers**) also **spell checker** N-COUNT 可算名詞 A **spell-checker** is a special program on a computer which you can use to check whether something you have written contains any spelling mistakes. スペルチェック機能 [COMPUTING コンピューティング]

spell|ing /spɛlɪŋ/ (**spellings**) **1** N-COUNT 可算名詞 A **spelling** is the correct order of the letters in a word. スペル □ *In most languages adjectives have slightly different spellings for masculine and feminine.* 多くの言語では, 形容詞の男性形と女性形はスペルが少し異なります. **2** N-UNCOUNT 不可算名詞 **Spelling** is the ability to spell words in the correct way. It is also an attempt to spell a word in the correct way. スペリング能力 □ *His spelling is very bad.* 彼のスペリング能力はとても低い. **3** → see also **spell**

spelt /spɛlt/ **Spelt** is a past tense and past participle form of **spell**. [mainly BRIT 主に英国英語]

spend /spɛnd/ (**spends, spending, spent**) **1** V-T 他動詞 When you **spend** money, you pay money for things that you want or need. 使う □ *By the end of the vacation I had spent all my money.* 休暇が終わるまでに私は所持金を全部使い果たした. □ *Businessmen spend enormous amounts advertising their products.* 実業家は自社製品の広告に莫大な費用をかける. **2** V-T 他動詞 If you **spend** time or energy doing something, you use your time or effort doing it. 費やす □ *Engineers spend much time and energy developing brilliant solutions.* 技術者は優れた解決方法を探るのに多くの時間と労力を費やす. **3** V-T 他動詞 If you **spend** a period of time in a place, you stay there for a period of time. 過ごす □ *We spent the night in a hotel.* 私たちはその晩はホテルで過ごした.

Do not confuse **spend** and **pass**. If you **spend** a period of time doing something or **spend** time in a place, you do that thing or stay in that place for all of the time you are talking about. □ *I spent three days cleaning our apartment. ...a hotel where we could spend the night.* If you do something while you are waiting for something else, you can say you do it to "**pass** the time." □ *He had brought along a book to pass the time.* You can say that time **has passed** in order to show that a period of time has finished. □ *The first few days passed... The time seems to have passed so quickly.*

Word Partnership *spend* は次の語句と使われる:

N. spend **billions/millions, companies** spend, **consumers** spend, spend **money** **1**
spend **an amount** **1** **2**
spend **energy**, spend **time** **2**
spend **a day**, spend **hours/minutes**, spend **months/weeks/years**, spend **a night**, spend **a weekend** **3**
V. **afford to** spend, **expect to** spend, **going to** spend, **plan to** spend **1** – **3**

spend|er /spɛndər/ (**spenders**) N-COUNT 可算名詞 If a person or organization is a **big spender** or a compulsive **spender**, for example, they spend a lot of money or are unable to stop themselves from spending money. お金を使う人 □ *The Swiss are Europe's biggest spenders on food.* スイス人の食費への支出はヨーロッパで最も多い.

spent /spɛnt/ **Spent** is the past tense and past participle of **spend**.

sperm /spɜrm/ (**sperms**)

Sperm can also be used as the plural form.

Sperm は複数形としても使える.

1 N-COUNT 可算名詞 A **sperm** is a cell which is produced in the sex organs of a male animal and can enter a female animal's egg and fertilize it. 精子 □ *Conception occurs when a single sperm fuses with an egg.* 受精は1個の精子が卵子と合体して成立する. **2** N-UNCOUNT 不可算名詞 **Sperm** is used to refer to the liquid that contains sperm when it is produced. 精液 □ *...a sperm donor.* 精子提供者.

spew /spyu/ (**spews, spewing, spewed**) V-T/V-I 他動詞/自動詞 When something **spews** out a substance or when a substance **spews** from something, the substance flows out quickly in large quantities. 噴出する □ *The volcano spewed out more scorching volcanic ashes, gases, and rocks.* 火山はさらに高温の灰, ガス, 石を噴出しました.

Word Link *sphere* ≈ *ball : atmosphere, hemisphere, sphere*

sphere /sfɪər/ (**spheres**) **1** N-COUNT 可算名詞 A **sphere** is an object that is completely round in shape like a ball. 球 □ *Because the Earth spins, it is not a perfect sphere.* 地球は自転しているため, 完

Word Web spice

While researching the use of **spices** in cooking, scientists discovered that many of them have strong disease-prevention properties. Bacteria can grow quickly on food and cause a variety of serious illnesses in humans. The researchers found that many spices are extremely antibacterial. For example, **garlic**, **onion**, allspice, and oregano kill almost all common germs. **Cinnamon**, tarragon, cumin, and **chili peppers** also eliminate about 75% of bacteria. And even common, everyday **black pepper** destroys about 25% of all microbes. The research also found a connection between hot climates and **spicy** food and cold climates and **bland** food.

garlic onion chili pepper

ginger black pepper cinnamon cloves

全な球形ではない. **2** N-COUNT 可算名詞 A **sphere of** activity or interest is a particular area of activity or interest. 領域 □ ...the sphere of international politics. 国際政治の領域.
→ see solid, volume

spice /spaɪs/ (spices, spicing, spiced) **1** N-MASS 質量名詞 A **spice** is a part of a plant, or a powder made from that part, which you put in food to give it flavor. Cinnamon, ginger, and paprika are spices. スパイス □ ...herbs and spices. 香草とスパイス. **2** V-T 他動詞 If you **spice** something that you say or do, you add excitement or interest to it. 趣を添える □ They spiced their conversations and discussions with intrigue. 彼らは会話や議論を計画的に面白くした. ● PHRASAL VERB 句動詞 **Spice up** means the same as **spice**. 趣を添える □ Her publisher wants her to spice up her stories with sex. 出版社は彼女に性的な趣向を書き添えるよう求めている.
→ see Word Web: spice

spiced /spaɪst/ ADJ 形容詞 Food that is **spiced** has had spices or other strong-tasting foods added to it. スパイスが使われた □ Every dish was served heavily spiced. どの料理にも多量のスパイスが使われていた.

spicy /spaɪsi/ (spicier, spiciest) ADJ 形容詞 **Spicy** food is strongly flavored with spices. 香辛料の効いた □ Thai food is hot and spicy. タイ料理は辛みと香辛料が強い.
→ see spice

spi|der /spaɪdər/ (spiders) N-COUNT 可算名詞 A **spider** is a small creature with eight legs. Most types of spiders make structures called webs in which they catch insects for food. クモ

spike /spaɪk/ (spikes) N-COUNT 可算名詞 A **spike** is a long piece of metal with a sharp point. 大くぎ □ ...a 15-foot wall topped with iron spikes. 上部に忍び返しが打ち込まれた高さ15フィートの塀.

spike heels N-PLURAL 複数名詞 **Spike heels** are the same as **stilettos**. スパイクヒール ((高くてとがったヒール)) の靴 [AM 米国英語] [also "a pair of" n]

spiky /spaɪki/ ADJ 形容詞 Something that is **spiky** has one or more sharp points. とがった □ Her short spiky hair is damp with sweat. 彼女の短くつんつんした髪が汗でにっとりしている.

spill /spɪl/ (spills, spilling, spilled or spilt) **1** V-T/V-I 他動詞/自動詞 If a liquid **spills** or if you **spill** it, it accidentally flows over the edge of a container. あふれさせる, あふれる □ Seventy thousand tons of oil spilled from the tanker. 7万トンもの石油がタンカーから流出した. □ He always spilled the drinks. 彼はいつも飲み物をこぼしていた. **2** N-COUNT 可算名詞 A **spill** is an amount of liquid that has spilled from a container. 流出物 □ She wiped a spill of milkshake off the counter. 彼女はカウンターにこぼれたミルクセーキをふき取った. **3** V-T/V-I 他動詞/自動詞 If the contents of a bag, box, or other container **spill** or **are spilled**, they come out of the container onto a surface. こぼす, こぼれる □ A number of bags had split and were spilling their contents. 何点かのバッグが裂けて中身が出てきていた. **4** V-I 自動詞 If people or things **spill** out of a place, they come out of it in large numbers. あふれ出る □ Tears began to spill out of the boy's eyes. 少年の目からは涙があふれ出した.

spill|age /spɪlɪdʒ/ (spillages) N-VAR 可変性名詞 If there is a **spillage**, a substance such as oil escapes from its container. **Spillage** is also used to refer to the substance that escapes. 流出 □ ...an oil spillage off the coast of Texas. テキサス沖での石油の流出.

spin /spɪn/ (spins, spinning, spun) **1** V-T/V-I 他動詞/自動詞 If something **spins** or if you **spin** it, it turns quickly around a central point. 回す, 回る □ The latest disks, used for small portable computers, spin 3,600 times a minute. 小型携帯コンピュータ用の最新のディスクは, 1分間に3千6百回転する. □ He spun the wheel sharply and made a U turn in the middle of the road. 彼は道路の真ん中で急ハンドルを切ってUターンした. ● N-VAR 可変性名詞 **Spin** is also a noun. 回転 □ This

driving mode allows you to move off in third gear to reduce wheel-spin in icy conditions. この走行モードだと, 凍った路面でもサードギヤでホイールスピンを抑えながら発進できます. **2** V-I 自動詞 If your head **is spinning**, you feel unsteady or confused, for example because you are drunk, ill, or excited. (頭が) ぐらぐらする □ My head was spinning from the wine. ワインで頭がくらくらしていた. **3** N-SING 単数名詞 If someone puts a certain **spin** on an event or situation, they interpret it and try to present it in a particular way. 偏った解釈 [INFORMAL くだけた] □ He interpreted the vote as support for the constitution and that is the spin his supporters are putting on the results today. 彼は投票結果は憲法支持の表れだと解釈しました. そして彼の支持者も今日の結果をそのように偏って解釈しようとしています. **4** N-UNCOUNT 不可算名詞 In politics, **spin** is the way in which political parties try to present everything they do in a positive way to the public and the media. (政治的な) 情操操作 □ The public is sick of spin and tired of promises. 人々はゆがめられた情報や公約にへきえきしている. **5** N-SING 単数名詞 If you go for a **spin** or take a car for a **spin**, you make a short trip in a car just to enjoy yourself. 一走りする □ Tom Wright celebrated his 99th birthday by going for a spin in his sporty Mazda. トム・ライトはマツダのスポーツカーで一走りして自分の99歳の誕生日を祝った. **6** V-T 他動詞 When people **spin**, they make thread by twisting together pieces of a fiber such as wool or cotton using a device or machine. 紡ぐ □ Michelle will also spin a customer's wool fleece to specification at a cost of $2.25 an ounce. ミシェルはまた, 羊の毛を1オンス当たり2ドル25セントで紡いでくれます. **7** N-UNCOUNT 不可算名詞 In a game such as tennis or baseball, if you put **spin** on a ball, you deliberately make it spin rapidly when you hit or throw it. 回転 □ He threw it back again, putting a slight spin on the ball. 彼は, ボールに少し回転をかけて再び投げ返した.
▶ **spin off** PHRASAL VERB 句動詞 To **spin off** something such as a company means to create a new company that is separate from the original organization. 分離独立させる [BUSINESS 実業] □ He rescued the company and later spun off its textile division into a separate entity. 彼はその会社を救済し, 後に繊維部門を分離し別会社にした.
▶ **spin out** PHRASAL VERB 句動詞 If you **spin** something **out**, you make it last longer than it normally would. 引き延ばす □ My wife's lawyer was anxious to spin things out for as long as possible. 妻の弁護士はできるだけ事を長引かせようとしていた.

Word Partnership spin は次の語句と使われる:

N.	spin **a wheel** **1**
ADJ.	**positive** spin **3** **4**

spin|ach /spɪnɪtʃ/ N-UNCOUNT 不可算名詞 **Spinach** is a vegetable with large dark green leaves. ほうれんそう

spi|nal /spaɪn²l/ ADJ 形容詞 **Spinal** means relating to your spine. せき髄の [ADJ n] □ ...spinal fluid. 脊髄 (せきずい) 液.
→ see brain, nervous system

spin doc|tor (spin doctors) N-COUNT 可算名詞 In politics, a **spin doctor** is someone who is skilled in public relations and who advises political parties on how to present their policies and actions. 政治活動顧問 [INFORMAL くだけた] □ ...two spin doctors in the majority leader's office. 多数党総務の2名の政治活動顧問.

spine /spaɪn/ (spines) **1** N-COUNT 可算名詞 Your **spine** is the row of bones down your back. 背骨 □ ...injuries to his spine. 彼の背骨の損傷. **2** N-COUNT 可算名詞 The **spine** of a book is the narrow stiff part which the pages and covers are attached to. (本の) 背 □ ...a book with "Lifestyle" on the spine. 背に「ライフスタイル」と印刷された本. **3** N-COUNT 可算名詞 **Spines** are also long, sharp points on an animal's body or on a plant. とげ □ An adult hedgehog can

boast 7,500 spines. ハリネズミの成獣には7千5百本ものとげを持つものがいる.

spin|off /spɪnɒf/ (**spinoffs**) **1** N-COUNT 可算名詞 A **spinoff** is an unexpected but useful or valuable result of an activity that was designed to achieve something else. 副次的効果 ❑ *The company put out a report on commercial spinoffs from its research.* その企業は自社研究による商業的波及効果についてのレポートを発表した. **2** N-COUNT 可算名詞 A **spinoff** is a book, film, or television series that comes after and is related to a successful book, film, or television series. 続編 ❑ *The film is a spinoff from the TV series "Sabrina The Teenage Witch."* その映画は連続テレビドラマ「サブリナ」の続編です.

spi|ral /spaɪrəl/ (**spirals, spiraling** or **spiralling, spiraled** or **spiralled**) **1** N-COUNT 可算名詞 A **spiral** is a shape which winds around and around, with each curve above or outside the previous one. らせん ❑ *The maze is actually two interlocking spirals.* その迷路は実は2本のらせんの組み合わせになっている. ● ADJ 形容詞 **Spiral** is also an adjective. らせん状の [ADJ n] ❑ *...a spiral staircase.* らせん階段. **2** V-T/V-I 他動詞/自動詞 If something **spirals** or is **spiraled** somewhere, it grows or moves in a spiral curve. らせん状に動く ❑ *Vines spiraled upward toward the roof.* つるは屋根に向かってらせん状に伸びた. ❑ *The aircraft began spiraling out of control.* 飛行機は操縦不能となりきりもみ状態になった. ● N-COUNT 可算名詞 **Spiral** is also a noun. らせん状の動き ❑ *Larks were rising in spirals from the ridge.* ヒバリが尾根かららせん状になって飛び立っていった. **3** V-I 自動詞 If an amount or level **spirals**, it rises quickly and at an increasing rate. 急上昇する ❑ *Production costs began to spiral.* 製造コストは急に膨らみ出した. ● N-SING 単数名詞 **Spiral** is also a noun. 急上昇 ❑ *...an inflationary spiral.* 悪性インフレ. **4** V-I 自動詞 If an amount or level **spirals** downward, it falls quickly and at an increasing rate. 急降下する ❑ *House prices will continue to spiral downwards.* 住宅価格はこれからも下降の勢いが止まらないだろう. ● N-SING 単数名詞 **Spiral** is also a noun. 急降下 ❑ *...a spiral of debt.* 負債の悪循環.
→ see **circle**

spire /spaɪər/ (**spires**) N-COUNT 可算名詞 The **spire** of a building such as a church is the tall pointed structure on the top. 尖塔 ❑ *...a church spire poking above the trees.* 木立の上に突き出している教会の尖塔.

spir|it /spɪrɪt/ (**spirits**) **1** N-SING 単数名詞 Your **spirit** is the part of you that is not physical and that consists of your character and feelings. 精神 ❑ *The human spirit is virtually indestructible.* 人間の精神は事実上不滅である. **2** N-COUNT 可算名詞 A person's **spirit** is the nonphysical part of them that is believed to remain alive after their death. 魂 ❑ *His spirit has left him and all that remains is the shell of his body.* 彼の魂は体を離れ, 残っているのは抜け殻となった体だけだ. **3** N-COUNT 可算名詞 A **spirit** is a ghost or supernatural being. 霊 ❑ *In the Middle Ages branches were hung outside country houses as a protection against evil spirits.* 中世では, 悪霊を寄せ付けないために地主の屋敷の外には枝がぶら下げられていた. **4** N-UNCOUNT 不可算名詞 **Spirit** is the courage and determination that helps people to survive in difficult times and to keep their way of life and their beliefs. 勇気 ❑ *She was a very brave girl and everyone who knew her admired her spirit.* 少女はとても勇気があり, 彼女を知る誰もがその勇気をたたえていた. **5** N-UNCOUNT 不可算名詞 **Spirit** is the liveliness and energy that someone shows in what they do. 快活さ ❑ *They played with spirit.* 彼らは生き生きと演奏した. **6** N-SING 単数名詞 The **spirit** in which you do something is the attitude you have when you are doing it. 気持ち ❑ *Their problem can only be solved in a spirit of compromise.* 譲り合う気持ちがなければ彼らの問題は解決しないだろう. **7** N-UNCOUNT 不可算名詞 A particular kind of **spirit** is the feeling of loyalty to a group that is shared by the people who belong to the group. 忠誠心 ❑ *There is a great sense of team spirit in the squad.* その小隊には大いなる団結心があった. **8** N-SING 単数名詞 A particular kind of **spirit** is the set of ideas, beliefs, and aims that are held by a group of people. 精神 ❑ *...the real spirit of the anti-war movement.* 反戦運動の真の精神. **9** N-SING 単数名詞 The **spirit** of something such as a law or an agreement is the way that it was intended to be interpreted or applied. 精神 ❑ *The requirement for work permits violates the spirit of the 1950 treaty.* その労働許可の要件は1950年の条約の精神に反するものです. **10** N-COUNT 可算名詞 You can refer to a person as a particular kind of **spirit** if they show a certain characteristic or if they show a lot of enthusiasm in what they are doing. 一な人 ❑ *I like to think of myself as a free spirit.* 私は自分が自由人だと思いたい. **11** N-PLURAL 複数名詞 Your **spirits** are your feelings at a particular time, especially feelings of happiness or unhappiness. 気分 ❑ *At supper, everyone was in high spirits.* 夕食のとき, 皆の気分は高揚していた. **12** N-PLURAL 複数名詞 **Spirits** are strong alcoholic drinks such as whiskey and gin. 蒸留酒 ❑ *The only problem here is that they don't serve beer - only wine and spirits.* この店の唯一の難点はビールを置いていないことだ. ワインや蒸留酒しかないのさ.

N.	**human** spirit **1** **2**
	evil spirit **3**
	team spirit **7**
ADJ.	**free** spirit, **independent** spirit **5** **10**
	competitive spirit, **generous** spirit **6**

spir|it|ed /spɪrɪtɪd/ **1** ADJ 形容詞 A **spirited** action shows great energy and courage. 活発な ❑ *This television program provoked a spirited debate.* このテレビ番組が活発な議論を招いた. **2** ADJ 形容詞 A **spirited** person is very active, lively, and confident. 快活な ❑ *He was by nature a spirited little boy.* 彼はもともと快活な少年だった.

spir|itu|al /spɪrɪtʃuəl/ **1** ADJ 形容詞 **Spiritual** means relating to people's thoughts and beliefs, rather than to their bodies and physical surroundings. 精神の ❑ *She lived entirely by spiritual values, in a world of poetry and imagination.* 彼女は詩歌や想像の世界の中で生きていた. ● **spir|itu|al|ly** ADV 副詞 精神的に ❑ *Our whole program is spiritually oriented but not religious.* 我々の全プログラムは, 精神性を重視したものだが, 宗教性はない. ● **spir|itu|al|ity** /spɪrɪtʃuælɪti/ N-UNCOUNT 不可算名詞 精神性 ❑ *...the peaceful spirituality of Japanese culture.* 日本文化の平和を好む精神性. **2** ADJ 形容詞 **Spiritual** means relating to people's religious beliefs. 宗教上の ❑ *He is the spiritual leader of the world's Catholics.* 彼は世界のカトリック教徒の宗教的指導者である.
→ see **myth**

spit /spɪt/ (**spits, spitting, spit** or **spat**) **1** N-UNCOUNT 不可算名詞 **Spit** is the watery liquid produced in your mouth. You usually use **spit** to refer to an amount of it that has been forced out of someone's mouth. だ液 ❑ *A trickle of spit collected at the corner of her mouth.* つばが彼女の口の端にたまっていた. **2** V-I 自動詞 If someone **spits**, they force an amount of liquid out of their mouth, often to show hatred or contempt. つばを吐く ❑ *The gang thought of hitting him too, but decided just to spit.* その一味は彼を殴ってやろうとも思ったが, つばを吐きかけるだけにした. ❑ *They spat at me and taunted me.* 彼らは私につばを吐き, 悪口を浴びせた. **3** V-T 他動詞 If you **spit** liquid or food somewhere, you force a small amount of it out of your mouth. 吐き出す ❑ *Spit out that gum and pay attention.* ガムを口から出して, 集中しなさい. **4** N-COUNT 可算名詞 A **spit** is a long rod which is pushed through a piece of meat and hung over an open fire to cook the meat. 焼きぐし ❑ *She roasted the meat on a spit.* 彼女は肉をくしに刺してあぶった. **5** PHRASE 句 If you say that one person is **the spitting image of** another, you mean that they look very similar. そっくりな [INFORMAL くだけた] ❑ *Nina looks the spitting image of Sissy Spacek.* ニーナはシシー・スペイセクにそっくりだ.

spite /spaɪt/ **1** PHRASE 句 You use **in spite of** to introduce a fact which makes the rest of the statement you are making seem surprising. 一にもかかわらず ❑ *Josef Krips at the State Opera hired her in spite of the fact that she had never sung on stage.* 国立オペラのジョセフ・クリップスは, 彼女には舞台経験がないのに採用した. **2** PHRASE 句 If you do something **in spite of yourself**, you do it although you did not really intend to or expect to. その気はないのに ❑ *The blunt comment made Richard laugh in spite of himself.* そのあけすけなコメントを聞いてリチャードは思わず笑ってしまった. **3** N-UNCOUNT 不可算名詞 If you do something cruel out of **spite**, you do it because you want to hurt or upset someone. 悪意 ❑ *I refused her a divorce, out of spite I suppose.* 私が彼女との離婚を拒否したのは, 腹いせからだったと思う. **4** V-T 他動詞 If you do something cruel **to spite** someone, you do it in order to hurt or upset them. 意地悪をする [only to-inf] ❑ *Pantelaras was giving his art collection away for nothing, to spite Marie and her husband.* パンテララスは自分の美術品を無料で寄贈していたが, それはマリーと彼女の夫へのいやがらせからだった.

splash /splæʃ/ (**splashes, splashing, splashed**) **1** V-I 自動詞 If you **splash around** or **splash about** in water, you hit or disturb the water in a noisy way, causing some of it to fly up into the air. (水を) 飛び散らす ❑ *A lot of people were in the water, swimming or simply splashing about.* 多くの人が水の中で泳いだり, バチャバチャと水を飛ばしたりしていた. ❑ *She could hear the voices of her friends as they splashed in a nearby rock pool.* 友達が近くの潮溜まりで水遊びをしていて, 彼女にはその声が聞こえた. **2** V-T/V-I 他動詞/自動詞 If you **splash** a liquid somewhere or if it **splashes**, it hits someone or something and scatters in a lot of small drops. はねかかる ❑ *He closed his eyes tight, and splashed the water on his face.* 彼はぎゅっと目を閉じて, 顔に水をバシャッとかけた. ❑ *A little wave, the first of many, splashed in my face.* 小さな波が, それはつぎつぎに寄せてくる波の先頭だったが, 私の顔にかかった. **3** N-SING 単数名詞 A **splash** is the sound made when something hits water or falls into it. 水がはねる音 ❑ *There was a splash and something fell clumsily into the water.* ザブンという音とともに, 何かがそこにも水に落ちた. **4** N-COUNT 可算名詞 A **splash** of a liquid is a small quantity of it that falls on something or is added to something. 飛沫 (ひまつ) ❑ *Wallcoverings and floors should be able to withstand*

steam and splashes. 壁紙と床面は蒸気や水滴をはじくものにすべきで
す. **5** N-COUNT 可算名詞 A **splash** of color is an area of a bright
color which contrasts strongly with the colors around it. 彩り
❑ ...shady walks punctuated with splashes of color. ところどころ彩色され
た日があたらない歩道. **6** V-T 他動詞 If a magazine or newspaper
splashes a story, it prints it in such a way that it is very
noticeable. 派手に書きたてる ❑ The newspapers splashed the story all
over their front pages. それらの新聞社は第1面全面でその話を書きた
てた. **7** PHRASE 句 If you **make a splash**, you become noticed or
become popular because of something that you have done. 注目を
集める ❑ Now she's made a splash in the television show "Civil Wars." 今
や彼女はテレビドラマ「男の証言・女の証言」で注目を集めている.

splat|ter /splǽtər/ (**splatters, splattering, splattered**) V-T/V-I
他動詞/自動詞 If a thick wet substance **splatters** on something or
is **splattered** on it, it drops or is thrown over it. はねかける, はねか
かる ❑ The rain splattered against the windows. 雨が窓にはねかかって
いた. ❑ "Sorry Edward," I said, splattering the cloth with jam. 私はジャ
ムをナプキンに飛ばしてしまい「ごめん, エドワード」と謝った.

splen|did /splɛ́ndɪd/ ADJ 形容詞 If you say that something is
splendid, you mean that it is very good. 素晴らしい ❑ The book
includes a wealth of splendid photographs. その本には素晴らしい写真が
たくさん載っている. ● **splen|did|ly** ADV 副詞 [ADV with v] 素晴らし
く ❑ I have heard him tell people that we get along splendidly. 私たちが
てもうまくいっていると彼が他の人に話すのを耳にした.

splen|dor /splɛ́ndər/ (**splendors**) **1** N-UNCOUNT 不可算名
詞 The **splendor** of something is its beautiful and impressive
appearance. 素晴らしさ ❑ She gazed down upon the nighttime
splendor of the city. 彼女は素晴らしい街の夜景をじっと見下ろし
た. **2** N-PLURAL 複数名詞 The **splendors** of a place or way of life
are its beautiful and impressive features. 素晴らしいもの ❑ ...such
splendors as the Acropolis and the Parthenon. アクロポリスやパルテノ
ン神殿のような素晴らしい遺跡.

splin|ter /splɪ́ntər/ (**splinters, splintering, splintered**)
1 N-COUNT 可算名詞 A **splinter** is a very thin, sharp piece of wood,
glass, or other hard substance, which has broken off from a
larger piece. 破片 ❑ ...splinters of glass. ガラスの破片. **2** V-T/V-I 他
動詞/自動詞 If something **splinters** or **is splintered**, it breaks into
thin, sharp pieces. 粉々にする, 粉々になる ❑ The ruler cracked and
splintered into pieces. ものさしが割れて粉々になった.

split /splɪ́t/ (**splits, splitting**)

The form **split** is used in the present tense and is the past tense
and past participle of the verb.

split 形は現在時制に使われ, 動詞の過去時制と過去分詞でもある.

1 V-T/V-I 他動詞/自動詞 If something **splits** or if you **split** it, it is
divided into two or more parts. 割れる ❑ In a severe gale the
ship split in two. ひどい強風で船は真二つになった. ❑ If the chicken
is fairly small, you may simply split it in half. もし鶏肉がかなり小さけ
れば, 二つに切るだけでいいですよ. **2** V-T/V-I 他動詞/自動詞 If an
organization **splits** or **is split**, one group of members disagree
strongly with the other members, and may form a group of their
own. 分裂させる, 分裂する ❑ Yet it is feared the Republican leadership
could split over the agreement. しかし, その合意をめぐって共和党
指導部が分裂することが懸念されている. ● ADJ 形容詞 **Split** is also
an adjective. 分裂した ❑ The Kremlin is deeply split in its approach to
foreign policy. 対外政策への取り組みに関してロシア政府内に深い溝
ができています. **3** N-COUNT 可算名詞 A **split** in an organization
is a disagreement between its members. 分裂 ❑ They accused
both radicals and conservatives of trying to provoke a split in the party.
彼らは急進派と保守派の双方を党内の分裂をはかったとして非難し
た. **4** N-SING 単数名詞 A **split** between two things is a division or
difference between them. 相違 ❑ ...a split between what is thought
and what is felt. 思考と感情の相違. **5** V-T/V-I 他動詞/自動詞 If
something such as wood or a piece of clothing **splits** or **is split**, a
long crack or tear appears in it. 裂く, 裂ける ❑ The seat of his gray
pants split. 彼のグレーのパンツがお尻の所で裂けた. **6** N-COUNT 可
算名詞 A **split** is a long crack or tear. 裂け目 ❑ The plastic-covered
seat has a few small splits around the corners. ビニール製の座席の角
に少しひび割れが生じている. **7** V-T 他動詞 If two or more people
split something, they share it between them. 分ける ❑ I would
rather pay for a meal than watch nine friends pick over and split a bill. 9人
が割り勘ですったもんだするくらいだったら僕が払うよ.
▶ **split up 1** PHRASAL VERB 句動詞 If two people **split up**,
or if someone or something **splits** them **up**, they end their
relationship or marriage. 別れる ❑ Research suggests that children
whose parents split up are more likely to drop out of high school. 離婚家
庭の子供は高校で落ちこぼれやすい傾向にあるという調査結果が出て
いる. ❑ I was beginning to think that nothing could ever split us up. 私は
自分たちを分かつものは何もないと考え始めていた. **2** PHRASAL VERB
句動詞 If a group of people **split up** or **are split up**, they go away
in different directions. 分かれる ❑ Did the two of you split up in the
woods? 君たち2人は森で分かれたのかい？ ❑ This situation has split up
the family. この件で家族はばらばらになった. **3** PHRASAL VERB 句

動詞 If you **split** something **up**, or if it **splits up**, you divide it so
that it is in a number of smaller separate sections. 分割する ❑ Any
thought of splitting up the company was unthinkable, they said. その会
社を分割することなど一切考えられないな, と彼らは言った. ❑ Even
though museums have begged to borrow her collection, she could never
split it up. 美術館が彼女のコレクションの借用を懇願し続けても, 彼女
は決してそれを分割しないだろう.

Thesaurus split また次を参照:

V. break, divide, part, separate; (ant.) combine **1 2 5**
N. crack, tear **5 6**
separation **6**

Word Partnership split は次の語句と使われる:

PREP. split into **1**
split over something **1**
split between **4 7**
split among **7**
N. split shares, split wood **1**
split in a party **3**
ADV. split apart **1 2**

---

split sec|ond also **split-second** N-SING 単数名詞 A **split
second** is an extremely short period of time. 一瞬間 ❑ Her gaze
met Michael's for a split second. 彼女のじっと見つめる目がマイケルの
目と一瞬合った. ❑ In law enforcement, we have to make split-second
decisions. 法を執行する時, 即座に判断しなければならない.

splut|ter /splʌ́tər/ (**splutters, spluttering, spluttered**)
1 V-T/V-I 他動詞/自動詞 If someone **splutters**, they make short
sounds and have difficulty speaking clearly, for example because
they are embarrassed or angry. せき込んで話す ❑ "But it cannot
be," he spluttered. 「でも, そんなはずはない」と彼はせき込んで早口
に言った. **2** V-I 自動詞 If something **splutters**, it makes a series
of short, sharp sounds. パチパチ音を立てる ❑ Suddenly the engine
coughed, spluttered, and died. 突然エンジンがせき込んでパチパチと音
がし, 動かなくなった.

spoil /spɔ́ɪl/ (**spoils, spoiling, spoiled** or **spoilt**) **1** V-T 他動詞
If you **spoil** something, you prevent it from being successful or
satisfactory. 台なしにする ❑ It's important not to let mistakes spoil
your life. 失敗で人生を台なしにしないようにすることは重要であ
る. **2** V-T 他動詞 If you **spoil** children, you give them everything
they want or ask for. This is considered to have a bad effect on a
child's character. 甘やかしてダメにする ❑ Grandparents are often
tempted to spoil their grandchildren whenever they come to visit. 祖父母
は孫たちが会いに来るたびに甘やかしたがることが多い. **3** V-T 他動
詞 If you **spoil yourself** or another person, you give yourself
or them something nice as a treat or do something special for
them. 特別扱いにする ❑ Spoil yourself with a new perfume this summer.
今年の夏は新しい香水で自分に特別サービスしましょう. **4** V-T/V-I
他動詞/自動詞 If food **spoils** or if it **is spoiled**, it is no longer fit to
be eaten. 食べ物が悪くなる ❑ We all know that fats spoil by becoming
rancid. 脂肪は腐ったようなにおいがすると傷んでいることは誰にも分
かる. **5** PHRASE 句 If you say that someone is **spoiled for choice**
or **spoilt for choice**, you mean that they have a great many things
of the same type to choose from. 選ぶのに困る [mainly BRIT 主に
英国英語]

spoilt /spɔ́ɪlt/ **Spoilt** is a past participle and past tense of **spoil**.
[BRIT 英国英語]

spoke /spóʊk/ **1 Spoke** is the past tense of **speak**. **2** N-COUNT
可算名詞 The **spokes** of a wheel are the bars that connect the
outer ring to the center. スポーク [usu pl]
→ see **bicycle**, **wheel**

spo|ken /spóʊkən/ **Spoken** is the past participle of **speak**.

spokes|man /spóʊksmən/ (**spokesmen**) N-COUNT 可算名詞 A
spokesman is a male spokesperson. 男性代弁者 ❑ A U.N. spokesman
said that the mission will carry 20 tons of relief supplies. 国連代弁者はこ
の特別任務で20トンの救援資材を運ぶだろうと述べた.

spokes|person /spóʊkspɜrsən/ (**spokespersons** or
spokespeople) N-COUNT 可算名詞 A **spokesperson** is a person
who speaks as the representative of a group or organization. 代弁
者 ❑ A spokesperson for Amnesty, Norma Johnston, describes some cases.
アムネスティ団体の代弁者であるノーマ・ジョンストンがいくつか実例
を描写している.

spokes|woman /spóʊkswʊmən/ (**spokeswomen**) N-COUNT
可算名詞 A **spokeswoman** is a female spokesperson. 女性代弁者
❑ A United Nations spokeswoman in New York said the request would be
considered. ニューヨークの国際連合代弁者は, その依頼を考慮すると
述べた.

sponge /spʌ́ndʒ/ (**sponges, sponging, sponged**) **1** N-COUNT
可算名詞 **Sponge** is a very light soft substance with lots of little
holes in it, which can be either artificial or natural. It is used to
clean things or as a soft layer. スポンジ ❑ ...a sponge mattress. ス

ポンジのマットレス **2** N-COUNT 可算名詞 A **sponge** is a piece of sponge that you use for washing yourself or for cleaning things. スポンジ ❑ *He wiped off the table with a sponge.* スポンジでテーブルをふいた。 **3** V-T 他動詞 If you **sponge** something, you clean it by wiping it with a wet sponge. きれいにふく ❑ *Fill a bowl with water and gently sponge your face and body.* ボウルに水を満たしてスポンジを濡らし、やさしく顔や体をふいてください。 ● PHRASAL VERB 句動詞 **Sponge down** means the same as **sponge**. ふく ❑ *If your child's temperature rises, sponge her down gently with tepid water.* 子供の熱が上がれば、ぬるま湯でやさしく体をふいてやる。 **4** V-I 自動詞 If you say that someone **sponges off** other people or **sponges on** them, you mean that they regularly get money from other people when they should be trying to support themselves. たかる [INFORMAL くだけた, DISAPPROVAL 不賛成] ❑ *He should just get an honest job and stop sponging off the rest of us!* ともかくちゃんとした仕事を得て、私たちみんなに頼るのを止めるべきだ。 **5** N-VAR 可変性名詞 A **sponge** is a light cake or pudding made from flour, eggs, sugar, and sometimes shortening. スポンジケーキ [BRIT 英国英語; AM **sponge cake** 米国英語 **sponge cake**]

spon|sor /spɒnsər/ (**sponsors, sponsoring, sponsored**) **1** V-T 他動詞 If an organization or an individual **sponsors** something such as an event or someone's training, they pay some or all of the expenses connected with it, often in order to get publicity for themselves. 資金援助する ❑ *Dozens of companies, including Hewlett-Packard, are sponsoring the event.* ヒューレット-パッカード社も含めて多数の会社がその行事の資金援助をしている。 **2** V-T 他動詞 If you **sponsor** someone who is doing something to raise money for charity, for example trying to walk a certain distance, you agree to give them a sum of money for the charity if they succeed in doing it. 募金の出資者となる ❑ *Please could you sponsor me for my school's campaign for Help the Aged?* 老人援助団体のため僕の学校が活動中ですが、どうぞ僕の募金出資者となっていただけますか？ **3** V-T 他動詞 If you **sponsor** a proposal or suggestion, you officially put it forward and support it. 提案する ❑ *Eight senators sponsored legislation to stop the military funding.* 8人の上院議員が軍事財源を止める法律制定を提案した。 **4** V-T 他動詞 When a country or an organization such as the United Nations **sponsors** negotiations between countries, it suggests holding the negotiations and organizes them. 発起人となる ❑ *Given the strength of pressure on both sides, the superpowers may well have difficulties sponsoring negotiations.* 両者の圧力の強さを考慮すれば、超大国が交渉の発起人となるのはたぶん難しいだろう。 **5** V-T 他動詞 If one country accuses another of **sponsoring** attacks on it, they mean that the other country does not do anything to prevent the attacks, and may even encourage them. 後援する ❑ *We have to make the states that sponsor terrorism pay a price.* テロ主義支援に報いを受けるという国を作らなければならない。 **6** V-T 他動詞 If a company or organization **sponsors** a television program, they pay to have a special advertisement shown at the beginning and end of the program, and at each commercial break. 番組提供者となる ❑ *The company plans to sponsor television programs as part of its marketing strategy.* 会社は販売戦略の一環としてテレビ番組の提供者となる計画を立てている。 **7** N-COUNT 可算名詞 A **sponsor** is a person or organization that sponsors something or someone. 後援する ❑ *Race officials announced a handful of new sponsors on Tuesday.* 競馬職員は火曜日に少数の新しい後援者を発表した。

spon|sor|ship /spɒnsərʃɪp/ N-UNCOUNT 不可算名詞 **Sponsorship** is financial support given by a sponsor. 資金支援 [also N in pl] ❑ *Campbell is one of an ever-growing number of skiers in need of sponsorship.* 資金支援者を必要とするスキー選手は増え続けており、キャンベルはその一人である。

spon|ta|neity /spɒntəniiti, -neɪ-/ N-UNCOUNT 不可算名詞 **Spontaneity** is spontaneous, natural behavior. 自然さ ❑ *He had the spontaneity of a child.* 子供の自然さを持っていた。

spon|ta|neous /spɒnteɪniəs/ **1** ADJ 形容詞 **Spontaneous** acts are not planned or arranged, but are done because someone suddenly wants to do them. 自発的な ❑ *Diana's house was crowded with happy people whose spontaneous outbursts of song were accompanied by lively music.* ダイアナの家は幸せそうな人でいっぱいで、自然に沸き起こる歌は生き生きとした音楽の伴奏があった。 ● **spon|ta|neous|ly** ADV 副詞 自発的に ❑ *Many people spontaneously stood up and cheered.* 多くの人が自ら立ち上がりかっさいした。 **2** ADJ 形容詞 A **spontaneous** event happens because of processes within something rather than being caused by things outside it. 自然に発生する ❑ *I had another spontaneous miscarriage at around the 16th to 18th week.* 第16週から第18週ころにまた自然流産した。 ● **spon|ta|neous|ly** ADV 副詞 [ADV after v] 自然に発生して ❑ *Usually a woman's breasts produce milk spontaneously after the birth.* 通常女性の乳房は出産後に自然と乳が出る。

spooky /spuki/ (**spookier, spookiest**) ADJ 形容詞 A place that is **spooky** has a frightening atmosphere, and makes you feel that there are ghosts around. 幽霊の出そうな [INFORMAL くだけた] ❑ *The whole place has a slightly spooky atmosphere.* その場所全体に少々気味の悪い雰囲気が漂っている。

spool /spul/ (**spools**) N-COUNT 可算名詞 A **spool** is a round object onto which thread, tape, or film can be wound, especially before it is put into a machine. 糸巻き；巻軸 ❑ *...the hissing of a tape rewinding on its spool.* テープが巻軸に巻き戻されているシューという音。

spoon /spun/ (**spoons, spooning, spooned**) **1** N-COUNT 可算名詞 A **spoon** is an object used for eating, stirring, and serving food. One end of it is shaped like a shallow bowl and it has a long handle. さじ ❑ *He stirred his coffee with a spoon.* さじでコーヒーを混ぜた。 **2** V-T 他動詞 If you **spoon** food into something, you put it there with a spoon. さじですくう ❑ *He spooned instant coffee into two of the mugs.* インスタントコーヒーをさじですくってマグカップの2つに入れた。

→ see silverware

spo|rad|ic /spəræedɪk/ ADJ 形容詞 **Sporadic** occurrences of something happen at irregular intervals. 散発的な ❑ *...a year of sporadic fighting in the north of the country.* その国の北部で散発的な戦いが続いた一年間。 ● **spo|rad|ical|ly** ADV 副詞 [ADV with v] 散発的に ❑ *The distant thunder from the coast continued sporadically.* 海岸の方から遠く聞こえる雷が散発的に続いた。

sport /spɔrt/ (**sports**) N-VAR 可変性名詞 **Sports** are games such as football and basketball and other competitive leisure activities which need physical effort and skill. スポーツ ❑ *I chose boxing because it is my favorite sport.* ボクシングは好きなスポーツなので選んだ。 ❑ *She excels at sports.* スポーツに秀でている。

sport|ing /spɔrtɪŋ/ ADJ 形容詞 **Sporting** means relating to sports or used for sports. スポーツの ❑ *...major sporting events, such as the U.S. Open and the World Series.* 全米オープンゴルフ選手権や全米プロ野球選手権などのような大きなスポーツ行事

sports car (**sports cars**) N-COUNT 可算名詞 A **sports car** is a low, fast car, usually with room for only two people. スポーツカー → see car

sports|man /spɔrtsmən/ (**sportsmen**) N-COUNT 可算名詞 A **sportsman** is a man who takes part in sports. 男性スポーツ家

sports|woman /spɔrtswʊmən/ (**sportswomen**) N-COUNT 可算名詞 A **sportswoman** is a woman who takes part in sports. 女性スポーツ家

sporty /spɔrti/ (**sportier, sportiest**) **1** ADJ 形容詞 You can describe a car as **sporty** when it performs like a racing car but can be driven on normal roads. スポーツカー的な ❑ *The steering and braking are exactly what you want from a sporty car.* 操縦とブレーキは、スポーツカー的な車に欲しいものそのものである。 **2** ADJ 形容詞 Someone who is **sporty** likes playing sports. 運動好きな ❑ *I'm an outdoor, sporty type and don't want to sit behind a desk all day.* 戸外や運動が好きなタイプであり、一日中デスクに座っていたくない。

spot /spɒt/ (**spots, spotting, spotted**) **1** N-COUNT 可算名詞 **Spots** are small, colored areas on a surface. 斑点 (はんてん) ❑ *The leaves have yellow areas on the top and underneath are powdery orange spots.* 葉は上側に黄色い部分があり、裏には粉っぽいオレンジ色のまだらがある。 **2** N-COUNT 可算名詞 **Spots** on a person's skin are small lumps or marks. 吹き出物；ほくろ [AM usually **pimples** 米国英語では通常 **pimples**] **3** N-COUNT 可算名詞 You can refer to a particular place as a **spot**. 地点 ❑ *They stayed at several of the island's top tourist spots.* 島の最良観光地点の数か所に泊まった。 **4** N-COUNT 可算名詞 A **spot** in a television or radio show is a part of it that is regularly reserved for a particular performer or type of entertainment. 出番 ❑ *Unsuccessful at screen writing, he got a spot on a CNN show.* 脚色家としてうまくいかず、CNNのショーに出演できた。 **5** V-T 他動詞 If you **spot** something or someone, you notice them. 見つける ❑ *Vicenzo failed to spot the error.* ビセンゾは間違いを見落とした。 **6** N-COUNT 可算名詞 A **spot of** a liquid is a small amount of it. 少しの [mainly BRIT 主に英国英語] ❑ *Spots of rain had begun to fall.* 雨がぽつぽつと降り始めた。 **7** PHRASE 句 If you do something **on the spot**, you do it immediately. その場で ❑ *James was called to see the producer and got the job on the spot.* ジェームズは制作者に会うように呼び出され、その場で仕事を得た。 **8** **rooted to the spot** → see rooted

spot|less /spɒtlɪs/ ADJ 形容詞 Something that is **spotless** is completely clean. しみのない ❑ *Each morning cleaners make sure everything is spotless.* 毎朝、掃除担当者が全て確実に一点のしみもないようにしている。 ● **spot|less|ly** ADV 副詞 [ADV adj] 清浄に ❑ *The house had huge, spotlessly clean rooms.* 家には大きくて非のうちどころもないほど清潔な部屋があった。

spot|light /spɒtlaɪt/ (**spotlights, spotlighting, spotlighted**) **1** N-COUNT 可算名詞 A **spotlight** is a powerful light, for example in a theater, which can be directed so that it lights up a small

S

area. スポットライト ② V-T 他動詞 If something **spotlights** a particular problem or situation, it makes people notice it and think about it. 注目を集めさせる ☐ *The budget crisis also spotlighted a weakening economy.* 予算危機や，弱まる経済にもまた注目が当てられた. ③ PHRASE 句 Someone or something that is **in the spotlight** is getting a great deal of public attention. 注目を集めて ☐ *Webb is back in the spotlight.* ウエブはまた注目を集めている.
→ see concert

spouse /spaʊs/ (**spouses**) N-COUNT 可算名詞 Someone's **spouse** is the person they are married to. 配偶者 ☐ *You, or your spouse, must be at least 60 to participate.* 参加するためには，本人か偶者が少なくとも60歳でなければならない.

spout /spaʊt/ (**spouts, spouting, spouted**) ① V-T/V-I 他動詞/自動詞 If something **spouts** liquid or fire, or if liquid or fire **spout** out of something, it comes out very quickly with a lot of force. 噴出する ☐ *He replaced the boiler when the last one began to spout flames.* 前のボイラーが炎を吹き出し始めたときに取り替えた. ☐ *The main square has a fountain that spouts water 40 feet into the air.* 大広場には水を40フィート空中に噴き上げる噴水がある. ② V-T 他動詞 If you say that someone **spouts** something, you disapprove of them because they say something which you do not agree with or which you think do not honestly feel. べらべらまくし立てる [DISAPPROVAL 不賛成] ☐ *My mother would go red in the face and spout bitter recriminations.* 母はきっと顔を真っ赤にして激しく非難し返すだろう. ③ N-COUNT 可算名詞 A **spout** is a long, hollow part of a container through which liquids can be poured out easily. 注ぎ口 ☐ *She lifted the kettle a little and tilted its spout over the tea-pot.* やかんを少し持ち上げてきゅうすの上で注ぎ口を傾けた.

sprain /spreɪn/ (**sprains, spraining, sprained**) ① V-T 他動詞 If you **sprain** a joint such as your ankle or wrist, you accidentally damage it by twisting it or bending it violently. くじく ☐ *He fell and sprained his ankle.* 転んで足首をくじいた. ② N-COUNT 可算名詞 A **sprain** is the injury caused by spraining a joint. ねんざ ☐ *Rubin suffered a right ankle sprain when she rolled over on her ankle.* ルービンは右足首で転倒したときに足首のねんざをした.

sprang /spræŋ/ **Sprang** is the past tense of **spring**.

sprawl /sprɔl/ (**sprawls, sprawling, sprawled**) ① V-I 自動詞 If you **sprawl** somewhere, you sit or lie down with your legs and arms spread out in a careless way. 大の字に寝そべる ☐ *She sprawled on the bed as he had left her, not even moving to cover herself up.* 彼が出て行ったときのまま，彼女はベットに寝に掛け物をかけようともせず大の字になっていた. ● PHRASAL VERB 句動詞 **Sprawl out** means the same as **sprawl**. 大の字に寝そべる ☐ *He would take two aspirin and sprawl out on his bed.* アスピリンを2錠飲んでからベットに体を投げ出して横になったものだった. ② V-I 自動詞 If you say that a place **sprawls**, you mean that it covers a large area of land. 不規則に広がる ☐ *The State Recreation Area sprawls over 900 acres on the southern tip of Key Biscayne.* 州立憩いの場はキービスケーン島の南端にあり，900エーカー以上に広がっている. ③ N-UNCOUNT 不可算名詞 You can use **sprawl** to refer to an area where a city has grown outward in an uncontrolled way. 無計画に広がる ☐ *The whole urban sprawl of Ankara contains over 2.6 million people.* アンカラの都市膨張の全域には260万以上の人が含まれる.

spray /spreɪ/ (**sprays, spraying, sprayed**) ① N-VAR 可変性名詞 **Spray** is a lot of small drops of water which are being thrown into the air. 水煙 ☐ *The moon was casting a rainbow through the spray from the waterfall.* 滝の水煙に月が虹をかけていた. ② N-MASS 質量名詞 A **spray** is a liquid kept under pressure in a can or other container, which you can force out in very small drops. 噴霧液 ☐ *...hair spray.* ヘアスプレー. ③ V-T/V-I 他動詞/自動詞 If you **spray** a liquid somewhere or if it **sprays** somewhere, drops of the liquid cover a place or shower someone. しぶきを飛ばす [他動詞]，しぶきをたてる [自動詞] ☐ *A sprayer hooked to a tractor can spray five gallons onto ten acres.* トラクターに鍵で留めた散布器は5リットルを10エーカーに散布することができる. ☐ *Inmates thrown bricks at prison officers who were spraying them with a hose.* ホースでしぶきを飛ばしている看守たちに向かって囚人たちはレンガを投げつけた. ④ V-T/V-I 他動詞/自動詞 If a lot of small things **spray** somewhere or if something **sprays** them, they are scattered somewhere with a lot of force. 飛び散る [自動詞]，飛び散らす [他動詞] ☐ *A shower of mustard seeds sprayed into the air and fell into the grass.* カラシナの種が空中に飛び散って草の中に落ちた. ☐ *The intensity of the blaze shattered windows, spraying glass on the streets below.* 強烈な炎が窓ガラスをこなごなに割り，破片が下の通りに飛び散っていった. ⑤ V-T 他動詞 If someone **sprays** bullets somewhere, they fire a lot of bullets at a group of people or things. 浴びせかける ☐ *He ran to the top of the building, spraying bullets into shoppers below.* 下にいる買い物客に銃弾を浴びせかけながら建物の上まで駆け上がった. ⑥ V-T 他動詞 If something **is sprayed**, it is painted using paint kept under pressure in a container. スプレーでペンキを塗る [usa 自動詞] ☐ *The bare metal was sprayed with several coats of primer.* 地の金属に下塗り用のペンキをスプレーで数回塗った. ⑦ V-T/V-I 他動詞/自動詞 When someone **sprays** against insects, they cover plants or crops with a chemical which prevents insects from feeding on them. 散布する ☐ *He*

doesn't spray against pests or diseases. 有害虫や植物の病気に対して散布しない. ☐ *Confine the use of insecticides to the evening and do not spray plants that are in flower.* 殺虫剤は夕方のみに使用し，開花している植物には散布しないでください. ⑧ N-COUNT 可算名詞 A **spray** is a piece of equipment for spraying water or another liquid, especially over growing plants. 噴霧器 ☐ *Farmers can use the spray to kill weeds without harming the soy crop.* 農夫は噴霧器を使用して大豆作物に害を与えずに雑草を除くことができる.

Word Partnership		*spray* は次の語句と使われる:
N.	spray **bottle, bug** spray, spray **can, hair** spray, **pepper** spray ②	
	spray **with water** ③	

spread /sprɛd/ (**spreads, spreading, spread**) ① V-T 他動詞 If you **spread** something somewhere, you open it out or arrange it over a place or surface, so that all of it can be seen or used easily. 広げる ☐ *She spread a towel on the sand and lay on it.* 砂の上にタオルを広げ，その上に横になった. ● PHRASAL VERB 句動詞 **Spread out** means the same as **spread**. 広げる ☐ *He extracted several glossy prints and spread them out on a low coffee table.* いくつもの光沢写真を取り出して低いテーブルの上いっぱいに広げた. ② V-T 他動詞 If you **spread** your arms, hands, fingers, or legs, you stretch them out until they are far apart. 伸ばす ☐ *Sitting on the floor, spread your legs as far as they will go without overstretching.* 床に座って，伸ばし過ぎない程度に足を広がる限り開いてください. ● PHRASAL VERB 句動詞 **Spread out** means the same as **spread**. 伸ばす ☐ *David made a gesture, spreading out his hands as if he were showing that he had no explanation to make.* デイビットは，まるで何の説明もできないことを示すように両手を広げた. ③ V-T 他動詞 If you **spread** a substance on a surface or **spread** the surface **with** the substance, you put a thin layer of the substance over the surface. 薄く塗る ☐ *Spread the mixture in the cake pan and bake for 30 minutes.* 混ぜ合わせたものをケーキ焼き型に入れて広げ，30分間オーブンで焼いてください. ④ V-T/V-I 他動詞/自動詞 If something **spreads** or **is spread** by people, it gradually reaches or affects a larger and larger area or more and more people. 流布する ☐ *The industrial revolution, which started a couple of hundred years ago in Europe, is now spreading across the world.* 200年前にヨーロッパで始まった産業革命は現在世界中に広まってきている. ☐ *...the sense of fear spreading in residential neighborhoods.* 近隣住宅地に広がっていく恐怖感. ● N-SING 単数名詞 **Spread** is also a noun. 流布 ☐ *The greatest hope for reform is the gradual spread of information.* 改革のための一番大きな望みは，徐々に情報が広まることである. ⑤ V-T/V-I 他動詞/自動詞 If something **spreads** or **is spread**, such as a liquid, gas, or smoke **spreads** or **is spread**, it moves outward in all directions so that it covers a larger area. 広がる [自動詞]，広げる [他動詞] ☐ *Fire spread rapidly after a chemical truck exploded.* 化学薬品トラックが爆発してから火事が急速に広がった. ☐ *A dark red stain was spreading across his shirt.* 彼のシャツに赤黒いしみが広がっていった. ● N-SING 単数名詞 **Spread** is also a noun. 広がること ☐ *The situation was complicated by the spread of a serious forest fire.* 深刻な山火事の拡大で状況は複雑であった. ⑥ V-T 他動詞 If you **spread** something **over** a period of time, it takes place regularly or continuously over that period, rather than happening at one time. 一にわたってする ☐ *There seems to be little difference whether you eat all your calorie allowance at once, or spread it over the day.* カロリーの一日相当量を一度で全部食べてしまうのも，一日にわたって取るのも，ほとんど差はないように見える. ⑦ V-T 他動詞 If you **spread** something such as wealth or work, you distribute it evenly or equally. 分散する ☐ *...policies that spread the state's wealth more evenly.* 州の富をさらに平等に分散させる方針. ● N-SING 単数名詞 **Spread** is also a noun. 分散 ☐ *There are easier ways to encourage the even spread of wealth.* 富の平等分散を奨励するさらに簡単な方法がある. ⑧ N-SING 単数名詞 A **spread of** ideas, interests, or other things is a wide variety of them. 広がり ☐ *A topic-based approach can be hard to assess in schools with a typical spread of ability.* 典型的な能力の広がりのある学校では，題目を基にした取り組みは評価が難しいことがある. ⑨ N-COUNT 可算名詞 A **spread** is two pages of a book, magazine, or newspaper that are opposite each other when you open it at a particular place. 見開き ☐ *There was a double-page spread of a dinner for 46 people.* 46人用の食事が見開きページの二つ分あった. ⑩ N-SING 単数名詞 **Spread** is used to refer to the difference between the price that a seller wants someone to pay for a particular stock or share and the price that the buyer is willing to pay. 値幅 [BUSINESS 実業] ☐ *Market makers earn their livings from the spread between buying and selling prices.* 株式の仕手は，買値と売値の差から生計を立てている. ⑪ **to spread your wings** → see wing

▶ **spread out** ① PHRASAL VERB 句動詞 If people, animals, or vehicles **spread out**, they move apart from each other. 分散する ☐ *Felix watched his men move like soldiers, spreading out into two teams.* フェリックスは，自分の部下が兵隊のように動いて二つのチームに分かれるのを見ていた. ② PHRASAL VERB 句動詞 If something such as a city or forest **spreads out**, it gets larger and gradually begins to cover a larger area. 広がる ☐ *Cities such as Tokyo are spreading out.* 東

京のような都市は広がりつつある. **3** → see **spread 1, 2**

Thesaurus
spread また次を参照:

V.	arrange, disperse, prepare **1**
N.	range, variety **8**

Word Partnership
spread は次の語句と使われる:

ADV.	spread **evenly** **1 3 5 7**
	spread **quickly**, spread **rapidly**, spread **widely** **1 4 5**
N.	spread **an epidemic**, spread **fear**, **fires**, spread **an infection**, spread **a message**, spread **news**, spread **rumors**, spread **technology**, spread **a virus** **4**
V.	continue to **spread**, **prevent/stop the spread of** *something* **4 5**

spread out ADJ 形容詞 If people or things are **spread out**, they are a long way apart. 散らばっている □ *The Kurds are spread out across five nations.* クルド族は5か国にわたって分散している.

spread|sheet /sprɛdʃiːt/ (**spreadsheets**) N-COUNT 可算名詞 A **spreadsheet** is a computer program that is used for displaying and dealing with numbers. Spreadsheets are used mainly for financial planning. 表計算シート [COMPUTING コンピューティング]

spree /spriː/ (**sprees**) N-COUNT 可算名詞 If you spend a period of time doing something in an excessive way, you can say that you are going **on** a particular kind of **spree**. 派手にやること □ *Some people went on a spending spree in December to beat the new tax.* 新しい課税に先んじて12月に派手に買い物をした人もいた.

spring /sprɪŋ/ (**springs, springing, sprang, sprung**) **1** N-VAR 可変性名詞 **Spring** is the season between winter and summer when the weather becomes warmer and plants start to grow again. 春 □ *They are planning to move house next spring.* 来年の春に家を引っ越すことを計画している. **2** N-COUNT 可算名詞 A **spring** is a spiral of wire which returns to its original shape after it is pressed or pulled. ばね □ *Unfortunately, as a standard mattress wears, the springs soften and so do not support your spine.* 残念ながら、標準マットレスを使い古すにつれてばねが弱くなり、背骨を支えられなくなる. **3** N-COUNT 可算名詞 A **spring** is a place where water comes up through the ground. It is also the water that comes from that place. 泉; 泉の水 □ *To the north are the hot springs.* 北の方には温泉がある. **4** V-I 自動詞 When a person or animal **springs**, they jump upward or forward suddenly or quickly. 跳び上がる □ *He sprang to his feet, grabbing his keys off the coffee table.* 低いテーブルからキーをひっつかみながら突然立ち上がった. □ *The lion roared once and sprang.* ライオンは一声吠えて飛びかかった. **5** V-I 自動詞 If something **springs** in a particular direction, it moves suddenly and quickly. 勢いよく〜する □ *Sadly when the lid of the trunk sprang open, it was empty.* 不幸にもトランクのふたがぱっと開いたとき、中は空だった. **6** V-I 自動詞 If one thing **springs from** another thing, it is the result of it. 生じる □ *Ethiopia's art springs from its early Christian as well as its Muslim heritage.* エチオピアの芸術は、早期キリスト教およびイスラム教伝統から生じている. **7** V-T 他動詞 If you **spring** some news or a surprise **on** someone, you tell them something that they did not expect to hear, without warning them. 急に持ち出す □ *McLaren sprang a new idea on him.* マクラーレンは突然新しい考えを彼に持ち出した. **8** to **spring to mind** → see **mind**
→ see **river**

▶ **spring up** PHRASAL VERB 句動詞 If something **springs up**, it suddenly appears or begins to exist. 現われる □ *New theaters and arts centers sprang up all over the country.* 新しい劇場や芸術センターが全国各地に出現した.

Word Partnership
spring は次の語句と使われる:

ADJ.	**early** spring, **last** spring, **late** spring, **next** spring **1** **cold** spring, **hot** spring, **warm** spring **1 3**
N.	spring **day**, spring **flowers**, spring **rains**, spring **semester**, spring **training**, spring **weather** **1** spring **water** **3**

spring|board /sprɪŋbɔːrd/ (**springboards**) **1** N-COUNT 可算名詞 If something is a **springboard for** something else, it makes it possible for that thing to start or happen. 出発点 □ *The 1981 budget was the springboard for an economic miracle.* 1981年度予算は経済奇跡の出発点であった. **2** N-COUNT 可算名詞 A **springboard** is a flexible board from which you jump into a swimming pool or onto a piece of gymnastic equipment. 跳躍板

sprin|kle /sprɪŋkᵊl/ (**sprinkles, sprinkling, sprinkled**) **1** V-T 他動詞 If you **sprinkle** a thing **with** something such as a liquid or powder, you scatter the liquid or powder over it. 振りかける □ *Sprinkle the meat with salt and place in the pan.* 肉に塩を振りかけて鍋に入れてください. □ *At the festival, candles are blessed and sprinkled with holy water.* 祭りの時は、ろうそくを祝福して聖なる水を振りかける. **2** V-T 他動詞 If something **is sprinkled with** particular

---

things, it has a few of them throughout it and they are far apart from each other. 点在させる □ *Unfortunately, the text is sprinkled with errors.* 残念ながら、本文は間違いが散在している.

sprint /sprɪnt/ (**sprints, sprinting, sprinted**) **1** N-SING 単数名詞 The **sprint** is a short, fast running race. 短距離競走 □ *Rob Harmeling won the sprint in Bordeaux.* ロブ・ハーメリングはボルドーの短距離競走に優勝した. **2** N-COUNT 可算名詞 A **sprint** is a short race in which the competitors run, drive, ride, or swim very fast. 短距離競技 □ *Lewis will compete in both sprints in Stuttgart.* ルイスはシュツットガルトで両方の短距離競技に参加するだろう. **3** N-SING 単数名詞 A **sprint** is a fast run that someone does, either at the end of a race or because they are in a hurry. 全力疾走 □ *Gilles Delion, of France, won the Tour of Lombardy in a sprint finish at Monza yesterday.* フランスのジル・デリョンは昨日モンツァでのロンバルディアツアーをラストスパートで優勝した. **4** V-I 自動詞 If you **sprint**, you run or ride as fast as you can over a short distance. 全速力で走る □ *Sergeant Horne sprinted to the car.* ホーン巡査部長は車に向かって全速力で走った.

sprint|er /sprɪntər/ (**sprinters**) N-COUNT 可算名詞 A **sprinter** is a person who takes part in short, fast races. 短距離競技者

sprout /spraʊt/ (**sprouts, sprouting, sprouted**) **1** V-I 自動詞 When plants, vegetables, or seeds **sprout**, they produce new shoots or leaves. 芽を出す □ *It only takes a few days for beans to sprout.* 豆はたった数日で芽が出る. **2** V-I 自動詞 When leaves, shoots, or plants **sprout** somewhere, they grow there. 生え始める □ *Leaf-shoots were beginning to sprout on the hawthorn.* サンザシに若葉がもえ始めていた. **3** V-T/V-I 他動詞/自動詞 If something such as hair **sprouts** from a person or animal, or if they **sprout** it, it grows on them. 生える [自動詞], 生やす [他動詞] □ *She is very old now, with little, round, wire-rimmed glasses and whiskers sprouting from her chin.* 今はたいそう年寄りで、金属枠の小さくて丸い眼鏡をかけており、あごからはひげが生えている. [no passive] **4** N-COUNT 可算名詞 **Sprouts** are vegetables that look like tiny cabbages. They are also called **brussels sprouts**. 芽キャベツ [usu pl]
→ see **tree**

spruce /spruːs/ (**spruces, sprucing, spruced**)

Spruce is both the singular and the plural form.

Spruce は単数形でも複数形でもある.

1 N-VAR 可変性名詞 A **spruce** is a kind of evergreen tree. トウヒ □ *Trees such as spruce, pine, and oak have been planted.* トウヒ、マツ、オークなどの木々が植えられた. □ *...a young blue spruce.* 若いアオトウヒ **2** ADJ 形容詞 Someone who is **spruce** is very neat and clean in appearance. こぎれいな □ *Chris was looking spruce in his stiff-collared black shirt and new short hair cut.* クリスは新しく髪を短く切り、堅い襟の黒ワイシャツを着ていて、しゃれて見えた.

▶ **spruce up** PHRASAL VERB 句動詞 If something **is spruced up**, its appearance is improved. If someone **is spruced up**, they have made themselves look very smart. こぎれいにする □ *Many buildings have been spruced up.* 建物が多数こぎれいになっている.

sprung /sprʌŋ/ **Sprung** is the past participle of **spring**.

spun /spʌn/ **Spun** is the past tense and past participle of **spin**.
→ see **wheel**

spur /spɜːr/ (**spurs, spurring, spurred**) **1** V-T 他動詞 If one thing **spurs** you **to** do another, it encourages you to do it. 拍車をかける □ *It's the money that spurs these fishermen to risk a long ocean journey in their flimsy boats.* このような漁師がもろい船で海洋に長く出航する危険をおかすのを駆り立てているのは、金である. ● PHRASAL VERB 句動詞 **Spur on** means the same as **spur**. 拍車をかける □ *Their attitude, rather than holding him back, only seemed to spur Philip on.* 彼らの態度が、フィリップを抑制するよりもかえって拍車をかけているように思えた. **2** V-T 他動詞 If something **spurs** a change or event, it makes it happen faster or sooner. 駆り立てる [JOURNALISM ジャーナリズム] □ *The administration may put more emphasis on spurring economic growth.* その行政管理は、経済の成長をいっそう刺激するかもしれない. **3** N-COUNT 可算名詞 Something that acts as a **spur to** something else encourages a person or organization to do that thing or makes it happen more quickly. 激励 □ *...a belief in competition as a spur to efficiency.* 効率を刺激するものとして競争を信じること **4** PHRASE 句 If you do something **on the spur of the moment**, you do it suddenly, without planning it beforehand. その時のはずみで □ *They admitted they had taken a vehicle on the spur of the moment.* とっさに車を取ってしまったと認めた.

Word Partnership
spur は次の語句と使われる:

N.	spur **demand**, spur **development**, spur **economic growth**, spur **the economy**, spur **interest**, spur **investment**, spur **sales** **2**

spu|ri|ous /spyʊəriəs/ **1** ADJ 形容詞 Something that is **spurious** seems to be genuine, but is false. 似て非なる [DISAPPROVAL 不賛成] □ *He was arrested in 1979 on spurious corruption*

S

charges. 1979年にまことしやかな汚職罪で逮捕された. **2** ADJ 形容詞 A **spurious** argument or way of reasoning is incorrect, and so the conclusion is probably incorrect. 偽の [DISAPPROVAL 不賛成] ❑ *...a spurious framework for analysis.* いかがわしい分析枠組み

spurn /spɜrn/ (**spurns, spurning, spurned**) V-T 他動詞 If you **spurn** someone or something, you reject them. はねつける ❑ *He spurned the advice of management consultants.* 経営顧問の助言を鼻にあしらった.

spurt /spɜrt/ (**spurts, spurting, spurted**) **1** V-T/V-I 他動詞/自動詞 When liquid or fire **spurts** from somewhere, it comes out quickly in a thin, powerful stream. 噴出する ❑ *He hit her on the head, causing her to spurt blood.* 彼が彼女の頭を打ったので, 血がほとばしり出た. ❑ *I saw flames spurt from the roof.* 屋根から炎がほとばしり出るのを見た. ● PHRASAL VERB 句動詞 **Spurt out** means the same as **spurt**. 噴出する ❑ *When the washing machine spurts out water at least we can mop it up.* 洗濯機から水がほとばしり出たら, 少なくともモップで拭くことはできる. **2** N-COUNT 可算名詞 A **spurt** of liquid is a stream of it which comes out of something very forcefully. 噴出 ❑ *A spurt of diesel came from one valve and none from the other.* ディーゼル重油が片方の弁から噴出して, 他方からは全然出なかった. **3** N-COUNT 可算名詞 A **spurt of** activity, effort, or emotion is a sudden, brief period of intense activity, effort, or emotion. 全力投入; 激発 ❑ *The average boy of 14 years old is only beginning his adolescent growth spurt.* 平均的な14歳の少年は, 思春期の急成長が始まったばかりである. **4** V-I 自動詞 If someone or something **spurts** somewhere, they suddenly increase their speed for a short while in order to get there. 全速力で走る ❑ *The back wheels spun and the van spurted up the last few feet.* 後輪が回転し, ライトバンは最後の数フィートを力走した. **5** PHRASE 句 If something happens in **spurts**, there are periods of activity followed by periods in which it does not happen. 時々思い出したように ❑ *The deals came in spurts: three in 1977, none in 1978, three more in 1979.* 取引は思い出したように来た: 1977年に3件, 1978年はゼロ, 1979年にはさらに3件.

spy /spaɪ/ (**spies, spying, spied**) **1** N-COUNT 可算名詞 A **spy** is a person whose job is to find out secret information about another country or organization. 諜報(ちょうほう)部員 ❑ *He was jailed for five years as an alleged spy.* スパイと申し立てられて5年間の拘禁となった. **2** ADJ 形容詞 A **spy** satellite or **spy** plane obtains secret information about another country by taking photographs from the sky. 偵察の [ADJ n] ❑ *...pictures from unmanned spy planes operated by the U.S. military.* 米国軍隊が操作する無人偵察飛行機からの写真 **3** V-I 自動詞 Someone who **spies for** a country or organization tries to find out secret information about another country or organization. スパイを働く ❑ *The agent spied for East Germany for more than twenty years.* その秘密情報員は東ドイツのために20年以上スパイをした. ❑ *East and West are still spying on one another.* いまだにお互いをひそかに見張っている東西 ● **spying** N-UNCOUNT 不可算名詞 スパイ活動 ❑ *...a ten-year sentence for spying.* スパイ活動に対して10年の判決 **4** V-I 自動詞 If you **spy on** someone, you watch them secretly. ひそかに見張る ❑ *That day he spied on her while pretending to work on the shrubs.* その日は潅木の手入れをしている振りをしながら彼女をひそかに見張った.

sq. **sq.** is used as a written abbreviation for **square** when you are giving the measurement of an area. 平方の ❑ *The building provides about 25,500 sq. ft. of air-conditioned offices.* そのビルには25,500平方フィートのエアコン付き事務所がある.

squab|ble /skwɒbəl/ (**squabbles, squabbling, squabbled**) V-RECIP 相互動詞 When people **squabble**, they quarrel about something that is not really important. つまらないことでけんかする ❑ *Mother is devoted to Dad although they squabble all the time.* 母はとうちゃんを熱愛しているが, 二人ともいつもささいなことでけんかをしている. ❑ *The children were squabbling over the remote-control for the television.* 子供たちはテレビのリモコンの取り合いをしていた. ● **squab|bling** N-UNCOUNT 不可算名詞 つまらないけんかすること ❑ *In recent months its government has been paralyzed by political squabbling.* ここ数か月間は, 政府はつまらない政治論争のために麻痺している. ● N-COUNT 可算名詞 **Squabble** is also a noun. つまらないけんか ❑ *There have been minor squabbles about phone bills.* 電話の請求書でささいな口論があった.

squad /skwɒd/ (**squads**) **1** N-COUNT 可算名詞 A **squad** is a section of a police force that is responsible for dealing with a particular type of crime. 警察の特別分隊 ❑ *The building was evacuated and the bomb squad called.* ビルから人が避難し, 爆弾処理部隊が呼び出された. **2** N-COUNT 可算名詞 A **squad** is a group of players from which a sports team will be chosen. 選手団 ❑ *The American squad has pulled out of the four-day basketball tournament.* アメリカ選手団は4日間のバスケットボール勝ち抜き試合から抜けた.

squad|ron /skwɒdrən/ (**squadrons**) N-COUNT-COLL 集合可算名詞 A **squadron** is a section of one of the armed forces, especially the air force. 飛行大隊 ❑ *A squadron of F-15 fighters is on its way home.* F-15戦闘機大隊が帰路についている.

squal|id /skwɒlɪd/ ADJ 形容詞 A **squalid** place is dirty, untidy, and in bad condition. むさくるしい ❑ *The early industrial cities were*

squalid and unhealthy places. 早期産業都市は薄汚くて不健康な場所であった.

squal|or /skwɒlər/ N-UNCOUNT 不可算名詞 You can refer to very dirty, unpleasant conditions as **squalor**. むさ苦しさ ❑ *He was out of work and living in squalor.* 失業しており, むさ苦しい生活をしていた.

squan|der /skwɒndər/ (**squanders, squandering, squandered**) V-T 他動詞 If you **squander** money, resources, or opportunities, you waste them. 無駄にする ❑ *Hobbs didn't squander his money on flashy cars or other vices.* ホッブズは派手な車や他の悪行に金を浪費しなかった.

square /skwɛər/ (**squares, squaring, squared**) **1** N-COUNT 可算名詞 A **square** is a shape with four sides that are all the same length and four corners that are all right angles. 正方形 ❑ *Serve the cake warm or at room temperature, cut in squares.* ケーキは温めるか室温にして, 四角に切って出してください. ❑ *There was a calendar on the wall, with large squares around the dates.* 壁には日付が大きな四角で囲まれたカレンダーが一つあった. **2** N-COUNT; N-IN-NAMES 可算名詞, 名称中の名詞 In a town or city, a **square** is a flat open place, often in the shape of a square. 広場 ❑ *The house is located in one of the city's prettiest squares.* 家は市でも最もきれいな広場に入る場所にあった. **3** ADJ 形容詞 Something that is **square** has a shape the same as a square or similar to a square. 正方形の ❑ *Round tables seat more people in the same space as a square table.* 同じスペースでも, 丸いテーブルは四角いテーブルよりも人が多く座れる. **4** ADJ 形容詞 **Square** is used before units of length when referring to the area of something. For example, if something is three feet long and two feet wide, its area is six square feet. 平方の [ADJ n] ❑ *The new complex will provide 10 million square feet of office space.* 新しい総合ビルは1000万平方フィートの事務所用の広さがあるだろう. **5** ADJ 形容詞 **Square** is used after units of length when you are giving the length of each side of something that is square in shape. 一辺がーの正方形の [amount ADJ] ❑ *...a linen cushion cover, 45 cm. square.* 一辺が45cm四角の亜麻布のクッションカバー **6** V-T 他動詞 To **square** a number means to multiply it by itself. For example, **3** squared is 3 x 3, or 9. **3 squared** is usually written as 3². 2乗する ❑ *Take the time in seconds, square it, and multiply by 5.12.* 時間を秒にして, それを2乗し, さらに5.12を掛けてください. **7** N-COUNT 可算名詞 The **square** of a number is the number produced when you multiply that number by itself. For example, the square of 3 is 9. 2乗 ❑ *...the square of the speed of light, an exceedingly large number.* 光の速さの2乗である非常に大きな数値 **8** V-T/V-I 他動詞/自動詞 If you **square** two different ideas or actions **with** each other or if they **square with** each other, they fit or match each other. 一致させる [他動詞], 一致する [自動詞] ❑ *That explanation squares with the facts, doesn't it?* その説明は事実と適合しますね. **9** V-T 他動詞 If you **square** something **with** someone, you ask their permission or check with them that what you are doing is acceptable. 了解させる ❑ *I squared it with Dan, who said it was all right so long as I was back next Monday morning.* ダンと了解は取っており, ダンは次の月曜日の朝までに戻って来さえすれば大丈夫だと言った. **10** → see also **squarely** **11** PHRASE 句 If you are **back to square one**, you have to start dealing with something from the beginning again because the way you were dealing with it has failed. 振り出しに戻って ❑ *If your complaint is not upheld, you may feel you are back to square one.* 不満の訴えが支持されなければ, 振り出しに戻ったような気がするかもしれない. **12** **fair and square** → see **fair**
→ see **shape**

square|ly /skwɛərli/ **1** ADV 副詞 **Squarely** means directly or in the middle, rather than indirectly or at an angle. 真正面に [ADV with v] ❑ *I kept the gun aimed squarely at his eyes.* 銃でまともに彼の目を狙い続けた. **2** ADV 副詞 If something such as blame or responsibility lies **squarely** with someone, they are definitely the person responsible. はっきりと [ADV with v] ❑ *The president put the blame squarely on his opponent.* 大統領は対抗者をまっこうから非難した.

square root (**square roots**) N-COUNT 可算名詞 The **square root** of a number is another number which produces the first number when it is multiplied by itself. For example, the square root of 16 is 4. 平方根

squash /skwɒʃ/ (**squashes, squashing, squashed**) **1** V-T 他動詞 If someone or something **is squashed**, they are pressed or crushed with such force that they become injured or lose their shape. 押しつぶす ❑ *Robert was lucky to escape with just a broken foot after being squashed against a fence by a car.* ロバートは車で塀に押しつぶされ, 片足の骨折だけでまぬがれたのは幸運だった. ❑ *Whole neighborhoods have been squashed flat by shelling.* 砲撃で近隣は全てがれきの原となっている. **2** ADJ 形容詞 If people or things are **squashed into** a place, they are put or pushed into a place where there is not enough room for them to be. 詰め込まれた [v-link ADJ "into" n] ❑ *There were 2,000 people squashed into her recent show.* 彼女の最近のショーに2,000人が詰めかけた. **3** V-T 他動詞 If you **squash** something that is causing you trouble, you put a stop

to it, often by force. 鎮圧する ❑ *The troops would stay in position to squash the first murmur of trouble.* 少しでも問題のきざしがあればすぐに鎮圧できるように軍隊は持ち場にいたものだった. ❹ N-VAR 可算性名詞 A **squash** is one of a family of vegetables that have thick skin and soft or firm flesh inside. かぼちゃ ❺ N-UNCOUNT 不可算名詞 **Squash** is a game in which two players hit a small rubber ball against the walls of a court using rackets. スカッシュ ❑ *I also play squash.* スカッシュもする. ❻ N-SING 単数名詞 If you say that getting a number of people into a small space is **a squash**, you mean that it is only just possible for them all to get into it. ぎゅうぎゅう詰め [BRIT 英国英語, INFORMAL くだけた] [AM **squeeze** 米国英語 **squeeze**]

squat /skwɒt/ (**squats, squatting, squatted**) ❶ V-I 自動詞 If you **squat**, you lower yourself toward the ground, balancing on your feet with your legs bent. しゃがむ ❑ *We squatted beside the pool and watched the diver sink slowly down.* プールのそばにしゃ癌で, 飛び込み選手がゆっくりと沈んでいくのを見ていた. ● PHRASAL VERB 句動詞 **Squat down** means the same as **squat**. しゃがむ ❑ *Albert squatted down and examined it.* アルバートはしゃがみ込んでそれを調べた. ● N-SING 単数名詞 **Squat** is also a noun. しゃがむこと ❑ *He bent to a squat and gathered the puppies on his lap.* しゃ癌だ姿勢になって子犬をひざにかき抱いた. ❷ ADJ 形容詞 If you describe someone or something as **squat**, you mean they are short and thick, usually in an unattractive way. ずんぐりした ❑ *Eddie was a short squat fellow in his forties with thinning hair.* エディーは40歳代の髪がはげかかっている, 背の低いずんぐりしたやつであった. ❸ V-I 他動詞/自動詞 People who **squat** occupy an unused building or unused land without having a legal right to do so. 無断で居座る ❑ *You can't simply wander around squatting on other people's property.* 他人の持ち家に無断で居座り歩くなんてことは絶対にしてはいけない.

squat|ter /skwɒtər/ (**squatters**) N-COUNT 可算名詞 A **squatter** is someone who lives in an unused building without having a legal right to do so and without paying any rent or any property tax. 無断居住者 ❑ *...another violent clash as police evicted squatters from empty buildings.* 空きビルから無断居住者たちを警察が立ち退かせた, 同様な激しい衝突

squeak /skwiːk/ (**squeaks, squeaking, squeaked**) V-I 自動詞 If something or someone **squeaks**, they make a short, high-pitched sound. きしる ❑ *My boots squeaked a little as I walked.* 歩くにつれてブーツがきしった. ❑ *The door squeaked open.* ドアがきしんで開いた. ● N-COUNT 可算名詞 **Squeak** is also a noun. きしる音 ❑ *He gave an outraged squeak.* 激怒して金切り声を上げた.

squeal /skwiːl/ (**squeals, squealing, squealed**) V-I 自動詞 If someone or something **squeals**, they make a long, high-pitched sound. キーキーいう ❑ *Jennifer squealed with delight and hugged me.* ジェニファーは喜びで歓声を上げて私を しっかりと抱いた. ● N-COUNT 可算名詞 **Squeal** is also a noun. 甲高い音 ❑ *At that moment there was a squeal of brakes and the angry blowing of a car horn.* その時ブレーキのきしる甲高い音がし, 車の警笛が怒ったように鳴った.

squeam|ish /skwiːmɪʃ/ ADJ 形容詞 If you are **squeamish**, you are easily upset by unpleasant sights or situations. すぐに気分が悪くなる ❑ *I'm terribly squeamish. I can't bear gory films.* いつもすぐに吐き気がするし, 血みどろの映画には耐えられない.

squeeze /skwiːz/ (**squeezes, squeezing, squeezed**) ❶ V-T 他動詞 If you **squeeze** something, you press it firmly, usually with your hands. ぎゅっと握る ❑ *He squeezed her arm reassuringly.* 安心させるように彼女の腕を軽く押さえた. ● N-COUNT 可算名詞 **Squeeze** is also a noun. ぎゅっと握ること ❑ *I liked her way of reassuring you with a squeeze of the hand.* 手を軽く握って安心させる彼女のやり方が好きだった. ❷ V-T 他動詞 If you **squeeze** a liquid or a soft substance out of an object, you get the liquid or substance out by pressing the object. 絞る ❑ *Joe put the plug in the sink and squeezed some detergent over the dishes.* ジョーは流しに栓をして, 皿の上に洗剤を少し絞って出した. ❸ V-T/V-I 他動詞/自動詞 If you **squeeze** a person or thing somewhere or if they **squeeze** there, they manage to get through or into a small space. 詰め込む [他動詞], 割り込む [自動詞] ❑ *They lowered him gradually into the cockpit. Somehow they squeezed him in the tight space, and strapped him in.* 徐々に彼を運転席に降ろし, なんとか狭い空間に押し込んでシートベルトをつけた. ❹ N-SING 単数名詞 If you say that getting a number of people into a small space is **a squeeze**, you mean that it is only just possible for them all to get into it. ぎっしり詰めること [INFORMAL くだけた] ❑ *It was a squeeze in the car with five of them.* 車に5人乗ってぎゅうぎゅう詰めだった.

squid /skwɪd/ (**squids**)

Squid can also be used as the plural form.
Squid は複数形としても使える.

N-COUNT 可算名詞 A **squid** is a sea creature with a long soft body and many soft arms called tentacles. イカ ❺ N-UNCOUNT 不可算名詞 **Squid** is pieces of this creature eaten as food. イカの身 ❑ *Add the prawns and squid and cook for 2 minutes.* エビとイカを加えて2分間煮てください.

squint /skwɪnt/ (**squints, squinting, squinted**) ❶ V-I 自動詞

If you **squint at** something, you look at it with your eyes partly closed. 目を細めて見る ❑ *The girl squinted at the photograph.* 少女は目を細めて写真を見た. ❑ *The bright sunlight made me squint.* 明るい太陽の光に目を細めた. ❷ N-COUNT 可算名詞 If someone has a **squint**, their eyes look in different directions from each other. 斜視 ❑ *...a pimple-faced man with a squint.* 斜視でにきび面の男

squirm /skwɜːrm/ (**squirms, squirming, squirmed**) ❶ V-I 自動詞 If you **squirm**, you move your body from side to side, usually because you are nervous or uncomfortable. のたくる ❑ *He had squirmed and wriggled and screeched when his father had washed his face.* 父親が彼の顔を洗った時, 体をのたくったり, くねらせたり, 金切り声で叫んだりした. ❑ *He gave a feeble shrug and tried to squirm free.* かすかに肩をすくめ, もがいて自由になろうとした. ❷ V-I 自動詞 If you **squirm**, you are very embarrassed or ashamed. もじもじする ❑ *Mentioning religion is a sure way to make him squirm.* 宗教を話に出すと, 必ず彼はきまりわるがる.

squir|rel /skwɜːrəl/ (**squirrels**) N-COUNT 可算名詞 A **squirrel** is a small animal with a long furry tail. Squirrels live mainly in trees. リス

squirt /skwɜːrt/ (**squirts, squirting, squirted**) ❶ V-T/V-I 他動詞/自動詞 If you **squirt** a liquid somewhere or if it **squirts** somewhere, the liquid comes out of a narrow opening in a thin fast stream. ほとばしらせる [他動詞], ほとばしる [自動詞] ❑ *Norman cut open his pie and squirted tomato sauce into it.* ノーマンはパイを切って開き, その中にケチャップを浴びせかけた. ● N-COUNT 可算名詞 **Squirt** is also a noun. 噴出 ❑ *It just needs a little squirt of oil.* 少々オイルを吹きかけさえすればいい. ❷ V-T 他動詞 If you **squirt** something **with** a liquid, you squirt the liquid at it. 吹きかける ❑ *They squirted each other with soapy water.* せっけん水をお互いに浴びせかけ合った.

St.

The form **SS** is used as the plural for meaning ❷.
SS 形は ❷ を意味する複数として使われる.

❶ **St.** is a written abbreviation for **Street**. 通りの略語 ❑ *...116 Princess St.* プリンセス通り116番 ❷ **St.** is a written abbreviation for **Saint**. 聖人の略語 ❑ *...St. Thomas.* 聖人トマス

stab /stæb/ (**stabs, stabbing, stabbed**) ❶ V-T 他動詞 If someone **stabs** you, they push a knife or sharp object into your body. 突き刺す ❑ *Somebody stabbed him in the stomach.* 誰かが彼の腹を突き刺した. ❑ *Dean tried to stab him with a screwdriver.* ディーンは彼をねじ回しで刺そうとした. ❷ V-T/V-I 他動詞/自動詞 If you **stab** something or **stab at** it, you push at it with your finger or with something pointed that you are holding. 指でつつく; 突き刺す ❑ *Bess stabbed a slice of cucumber.* ベスはきゅうりの薄切りを突き刺した. ❑ *Goldstone flipped through the pages and stabbed his thumb at the paragraph he was looking for.* ゴールドストーンはページをぱらぱらとめくり, 探していた段落を親指で突いた. ❸ N-SING 単数名詞 If you have a **stab** at something, you try to do it. 試み [INFORMAL くだけた] ❑ *Several tennis stars have had a stab at acting.* かなり多くのテニスの花形が演劇をやってみた. ❹ N-SING 単数名詞 You can refer to a sudden, usually unpleasant feeling as a **stab of** that feeling. 突然の鋭い痛み [LITERARY 文語的] ❑ *...a stab of pain just above his eye.* 片目のすぐ上に刺すような痛み ❺ PHRASE 句 If you say that someone **has stabbed you in the back**, you mean that they have done something very harmful to you when you thought that you could trust them. You can refer to an action of this kind as a **stab in the back**. だまし討ち; だまし討ち ❑ *She felt betrayed, as though her daughter had stabbed her in the back.* まるで自分の娘に背後から一突きされたように, 裏切られた気持ちであった. ❻ **a stab in the dark** → see **dark**

stab|bing /stæbɪŋ/ (**stabbings**) ❶ N-COUNT 可算名詞 A **stabbing** is an incident in which someone stabs someone else with a knife. 刺傷 ❑ *...the victim of a stabbing.* 刺傷の被害者 ❷ ADJ 形容詞 A **stabbing** pain is a sudden sharp pain. 刺すような [ADJ 1] ❑ *He was struck by a stabbing pain in his midriff.* 胴の中央部に刺すような鋭い痛みに襲われた.

sta|bil|ity /stəbɪlɪti/ → see **stable**

sta|bi|lize /steɪbɪlaɪz/ (**stabilizes, stabilizing, stabilized**) V-T/V-I 他動詞/自動詞 If something **stabilizes**, or **is stabilized**, it becomes stable. 安定する [自動詞], 安定させる [他動詞] ❑ *Although her illness is serious, her condition is beginning to stabilize.* 病気は重いが, 病状は安定し始めてきている. ● **sta|bi|li|za|tion** /steɪbɪlaɪzeɪʃən/ N-UNCOUNT 不可算名詞 安定化 ❑ *...the stabilization of property prices.* 不動産価格の安定化

sta|ble /steɪbəl/ (**stabler, stablest, stables**) ❶ ADJ 形容詞 If something is **stable**, it is not likely to change or come to an end suddenly. 安定した ❑ *The price of oil should remain stable for the rest of 1992.* 石油価格は1992年中は安定したままと思われる. ● **sta|bil|ity** /stəbɪlɪti/ N-UNCOUNT 不可算名詞 安定性 ❑ *It was a time of political stability and progress.* 政治的な安定と進歩の時期であった. ❷ ADJ 形容詞 If someone has a **stable** personality, they are calm and

reasonable and their mood does not change suddenly. しっかりした ❑*Their characters are fully formed and they are both very stable children.* 二人とも性格は完全に形成されており、共にそいそうしっかりした子供である。 ❸ ADJ 形容詞 You can describe someone who is seriously ill as **stable** when their condition has stopped getting worse. 変わらない ❑*The injured man was in a stable condition.* 負傷した男の病状は安定していた。 ❹ ADJ 形容詞 Chemical substances are described as **stable** when they tend to remain in the same chemical or atomic state. 簡単に分解しない [TECHNICAL 技術的] ❑*The less stable compounds were converted into a compound called Delta-A THC.* あまり安定性のない化合物は、デルタ-A THCと呼ばれる化合物に転換された。 ❺ ADJ 形容詞 If an object is **stable**, it is firmly fixed in position and is not likely to move or fall. 強固な ❑*This structure must be stable.* この構造は強固に違いない。 ❻ N-COUNT 可算名詞 A **stable** or **stables** is a building in which horses are kept. 馬小屋 ❼ N-COUNT 可算名詞 A **stable** or **stables** is an organization that breeds and trains horses for racing. 競馬訓練所 ❑*Miss Curling won on two horses from Mick Trickey's stable.* カーリング嬢はミック・トリッキーのきゅう舎の馬2頭に掛けて当たった。

stack /stæk/ (**stacks, stacking, stacked**) ❶ N-COUNT 可算名詞 A **stack** of things is a pile of them. 積み重ねた山 ❑*There were stacks of books on the bedside table and floor.* 寝台用テーブルの上や床のあちこちに積み上げた本の山があった。 ❷ V-T 他動詞 If you **stack** a number of things, you arrange them in neat piles. 積み重ねる ❑*Mrs. Cathiard was stacking the clean bottles in crates.* キャシアード夫人は箱の中にきれいな瓶を積み重ねていた。 ● PHRASAL VERB 句動詞 **Stack up** means the same as **stack**. ❑*He ordered them to stack up pillows behind his back.* 彼の背に枕を積み重ねるように彼らに命令した。 ❸ N-PLURAL 複数名詞 If you say that someone has **stacks of** something, you mean that they have a lot of it. 多量 [INFORMAL くだけた] ❑*If the job's that good, you'll have stacks of money.* もしその仕事がそんないいのなら、金もたくさんもうかるだろう。 ❹ PHRASE 句 If you say that **the odds are stacked against** someone, or that particular factors **are stacked against** them, you mean that they are unlikely to succeed in what they want to do because the conditions are not favorable. 大変不利な立場におかれている ❑*The odds are stacked against civilians getting a fair trial.* 公平な裁判をしてもらうことに対しては一般市民は大変不利な立場におかれている。

A **stack** of things is usually tidy, and often consists of flat objects placed directly on top of each other. ❑*...a neat stack of dishes.* A **heap** of things is usually untidy, and often has the shape of a hill or mound. ❑*Now, the house is a heap of rubble.* A **pile** can be tidy or untidy. ❑*...a neat pile of clothes.*

---

sta|dium /steɪdiəm/ (**stadiums** or **stadia**) /steɪdiə/ N-COUNT; N-IN-NAMES 可算名詞, 名称中の名詞 A **stadium** is a large sports field with rows of seats all around it. 競技場 ❑*...a baseball stadium.* 野球場

staff /stæf/ (**staffs, staffing, staffed**) ❶ N-COUNT-COLL 集合可算名詞 The **staff** of an organization are the people who work for it. 職員 ❑*The staff were very good.* 職員はたいへん良かった。 ❑*The outpatient program has a staff of six people.* 外来課程は6人の職員がいる。 ❑*...staff members.* 職員メンバー ➜ see also **chief of staff** ❷ N-PLURAL 複数名詞 People who are part of a particular staff are often referred to as **staff**. 部員 ❑*10 staff were allocated to the task.* その作業に10人が配置された。 ❸ V-T 他動詞 If an organization is **staffed by** particular people, they are the people who work for it. 人を配置する [usu passive] ❑*They are staffed by volunteers.* 仕事をする人が配置されている。 ● **staffed** ADJ 形容詞 [adv ADJ] 人が配置された ❑*The house allocated to them was pleasant and spacious, and well staffed.* 割り当てられた家は広くて感じがよく、充分に職員が配置されていた。

staff|ing /stæfɪŋ/ N-UNCOUNT 不可算名詞 **Staffing** refers to the number of workers employed to work in a particular organization or building. 職員数 [BUSINESS 実業] ❑*Staffing levels in prisons are too low.* 刑務所の職員レベルは低すぎる。

stag /stæg/ (**stags**) N-COUNT 可算名詞 A **stag** is an adult male deer belonging to one of the larger species of deer. Stags usually have large branch-like horns called antlers. 雄鹿

stage /steɪdʒ/ (**stages, staging, staged**) ❶ N-COUNT 可算名詞 A **stage** of an activity, process, or period is one part of it. 段階 ❑*The way children talk about or express their feelings depends on their age and stage of development.* 子供が自分の気持ちについて話したり、表現したりする方法は、子供の年齢や発育段階に依存する。 ❷ N-COUNT 可算名詞 In a theater, the **stage** is an area where actors or other entertainers perform. 舞台 [also "on" N] ❑*The road crew needed more than 24 hours to move and rebuild the stage after a concert.* 巡業団員は演奏会の後、舞台を運んで、再度組み立てるのに24時間以上必要であった。 ❸ V-T 他動詞 If someone **stages** a play or other show, they organize and present a performance of it. 上演する ❑*Maya Angelou first staged the play "And I Still Rise" in the late 1970s.* マヤ・アンジェローは、1970年代終わりに『それでもなお立ち上がる』の劇を始めて上演した。 ❹ V-T 他動詞 If you **stage** an event or ceremony, you organize it and usually take part in it. 催す ❑*Russian workers*

have staged a number of strikes in protest at the republic's declaration of independence. ロシア人労働者は、共和国の独立宣言に抗議してストライキを何度も催した。 ❺ N-SING 単数名詞 You can refer to a particular area of activity as a particular **stage**, especially when you are talking about politics. 政治活動の舞台 ❑*He was finally forced off the political stage last year by the deterioration of his physical condition.* 健康状況が悪化して、去年とうとう政治舞台から強制的に退かされた。 ❻ to **set the stage** ➜ see **set** ➜ see **concert**

Word Partnership *stage* は次の語句と使われる:

ADJ.	**advanced** stage, **critical** stage, **crucial** stage, **early** stage, **final** stage, **late/later** stage ❶
V.	**reach a** stage ❶ **leave the** stage, **take the** stage ❷
N.	stage **of development**, stage **of a disease**, stage **of a process** ❶ **actors on** stage, **center** stage, **concert** stage, stage **fright**, stage **manager** ❷

---

stag|fla|tion /stægfleɪʃⁿn/ N-UNCOUNT 不可算名詞 If an economy is suffering from **stagflation**, inflation is high but there is no increase in the demand for goods or in the number of people who have jobs. スタグフレーション [BUSINESS 実業] ❑*Many of the industrialized economies would be pushed into a cycle of stagflation.* 多数の先進工業諸国の経済がスタグフレーション周期に押し込まれるだろう。

stag|ger /stægər/ (**staggers, staggering, staggered**) ❶ V-I 自動詞 If you **stagger**, you walk very unsteadily, for example because you are ill or drunk. よろよろ歩く ❑*He lost his balance, staggered back against the rail and toppled over.* 体の平衡を失い、よろよろと後ずさりして手すりにぶつかり前にのめった。 ❷ V-T 他動詞 If something **staggers** you, it surprises you very much. めんくらわせる ❑*The whole thing staggers me.* そのことは全部がびっくりだった。 ● **stag|gered** ADJ 形容詞 [v-link ADJ] びっくりした ❑*I was simply staggered by the heat of the Argentinian high-summer.* アルジェンチンの盛夏の暑さにまったくぼうぜんとした。 ❸ V-T 他動詞 To **stagger** things such as people's vacations or hours of work means to arrange them so that they do not all happen at the same time. 重ならないようにずらす ❑*During the past few years the university has staggered the summer vacation periods for students.* 過去数年間大学は学生の夏期休暇を時差休暇にした。

stag|ger|ing /stægərɪŋ/ ADJ 形容詞 Something that is **staggering** is very surprising. 驚くべき ❑*...a staggering $900 million in short- and long-term debt.* 9億ドルというあぜんとするほどの長短期負債

stag|nant /stægnənt/ ❶ ADJ 形容詞 If something such as a business or society is **stagnant**, there is little activity or change. 沈滞した [DISAPPROVAL 不賛成] ❑*...advice on how to revive the stagnant economy.* 景気沈滞の回復方法についての助言を求めていた。 ❷ ADJ 形容詞 **Stagnant** water is not flowing, and therefore often smells unpleasant and is dirty. よどんだ ❑*...a stagnant pond.* よどんだ池

stag|nate /stægneɪt/ (**stagnates, stagnating, stagnated**) V-I 自動詞 If something such as a business or society **stagnates**, it stops changing or progressing. 沈滞する [DISAPPROVAL 不賛成] ❑*Industrial production is stagnating.* 工業生産が沈滞中である。 ● **stag|na|tion** /stægneɪʃⁿn/ N-UNCOUNT 不可算名詞 沈滞 ❑*...the stagnation of the steel industry.* 鋼鉄産業の沈滞

staid /steɪd/ ADJ 形容詞 If you say that someone or something is **staid**, you mean that they are serious, dull, and rather old-fashioned. 生真面目な ❑*...a staid seaside resort.* 古風な海辺の保養地

stain /steɪn/ (**stains, staining, stained**) ❶ N-COUNT 可算名詞 A **stain** is a mark on something that is difficult to remove. しみ ❑*Remove stains by soaking in a mild solution of bleach.* 薄い漂白溶液に漬けてしみを落としてください。 ❷ V-T 他動詞 If a liquid **stains** something, the thing becomes colored or marked by the liquid. 変色する ❑*Some foods can stain the teeth, as of course can smoking.* 食べ物の中には、もちろん喫煙もそうだが、歯を変色させるものがある。 ● **stained** ADJ 形容詞 しみのついた ❑*His clothing was stained with mud.* 服は泥の跡で汚れていた。 ● **-stained** COMB IN ADJ 形容詞の複合 ❑*...ink-stained fingers.* インクで汚れた指 ➜ see **dry-cleaning**

stained glass also **stained-glass** N-UNCOUNT 不可算名詞 **Stained glass** consists of pieces of glass of different colors which are fitted together to make decorative windows or other objects. ステンドグラス ❑*...the stained glass window in St. John's Cathedral.* 聖ジョン大聖堂のステンドグラスの窓

stain|less steel /steɪnlɪs stiːl/ N-UNCOUNT 不可算名詞 **Stainless steel** is a metal made from steel and chromium which does not rust. ステンレス ❑*...a stainless steel sink.* ステンレスの流し ➜ see **pan**

stair /steər/ (**stairs**) N-PLURAL 複数名詞 **Stairs** are a set of

steps inside a building which go from one floor to another. 階段 ❑ *Nancy began to climb the stairs.* ナンシーは階段を上り始めた. ❑ *We walked up a flight of stairs.* 私達は一続きの階段を上った.

stair|case /ˈstɛərkeɪs/ (**staircases**) N-COUNT 可算名詞 A **staircase** is a set of stairs inside a building. 階段 ❑ *They walked down the staircase together.* 彼らは一緒に階段を降りた.
→ see **house**

stair|way /ˈstɛərweɪ/ (**stairways**) N-COUNT 可算名詞 A **stairway** is a staircase or a flight of steps, inside or outside a building. 階段 ❑ *...the stairway leading to the top floor.* 最上階に続く階段

stake /steɪk/ (**stakes, staking, staked**) **1** PHRASE 句 If something is **at stake**, it is being risked and might be lost or damaged if you are not successful. 危うくなって ❑ *The tension was naturally high for a game with so much at stake.* 非常に多くのものを失う危険のある試合では当然、緊張感は高かった. **2** N-PLURAL 複数名詞 The **stakes** involved in a contest or a risky action are the things that can be gained or lost. 賞金 ❑ *The game was usually played for high stakes between two large groups.* その競技は通常、2つの大きなグループ間で高額の賞金目当てで行なわれた. **3** V-T 他動詞 If you **stake** something such as your money or your reputation **on** the result of something, you risk your money or reputation on it. 賭ける ❑ *He has staked his political future on an election victory.* 彼は政治家としての前途を選挙の勝利に賭けた. **4** N-COUNT 可算名詞 If you have a **stake in** something such as a business, it matters to you, for example because you own part of it or because its success or failure will affect you. 利害関係 ❑ *He was eager to return to a more entrepreneurial role in which he had a big financial stake in his own efforts.* 彼は自らの努力が財務に大きく関与する起業家的役割に戻りたがっていた. **5** N-PLURAL 複数名詞 You can use **stakes** to refer to something that is like a contest. For example, you can refer to the choosing of a leader as the **leadership stakes**. 競争 ❑ *We are lagging behind in the childcare stakes.* 我々は育児競争で遅れを取っている. **6** N-COUNT 可算名詞 A **stake** is a pointed wooden post which is pushed into the ground, for example in order to support a young tree. 杭(くい) ❑ *His arms were tied to wooden stakes to hold him flat.* 彼の腕は平らにしておくために木の杭に縛り付けられていた. **7** PHRASE 句 If you **stake a claim**, you say that something is yours or that you have a right to it. 権利を主張する ❑ *Jane is determined to stake her claim as an actress.* ジェインは女優としての権利を主張する決意がある.

Word Partnership	*stake* は次の語句と使われる:
N.	**interests** at stake, **issues** at stake **1** stake **lives** on *something* **3** stake **in a company/firm**, **majority/minority** stake **4**
ADJ.	**controlling** stake, **personal** stake **4**

stake|hold|er /ˈsteɪkhoʊldər/ (**stakeholders**) N-COUNT 可算名詞 **Stakeholders** are people who have an interest in a company's or organization's affairs. 投資者 [BUSINESS 実業] ❑ *...the Delaware River Port Authority, a major stakeholder in Penn's Landing.* Penn's Landing社の主要投資者であるDelaware River Port Authority

stale /steɪl/ (**staler, stalest**) **1** ADJ 形容詞 **Stale** food is no longer fresh or good to eat. 新鮮でない ❑ *Their daily diet consisted of a lump of stale bread, a bowl of rice, and stale water.* 彼らの毎日の食事は一塊の干からびたパン、1杯のご飯、よどんだ水だった. **2** ADJ 形容詞 **Stale** air or smells are unpleasant because they are no longer fresh. よどんだ ❑ *...the smell of stale sweat.* むっとする汗のにおい **3** ADJ 形容詞 If you say that a place, an activity, or an idea is **stale**, you mean that it has become boring because it is always the same. 新鮮さを失った [DISAPPROVAL 不賛成] ❑ *Her relationship with Mark has become stale.* 彼女とマークとの関係は新鮮さを失った.

stale|mate /ˈsteɪlmeɪt/ (**stalemates**) N-VAR 可変性名詞 **Stalemate** is a situation in which neither side in an argument or contest can win or in which no progress is possible. 行き詰まり ❑ *The proportional representation system was widely blamed for two inconclusive election results and a year of political stalemate.* 比例代表制は2度の不確定な選挙結果と1年間の政治的行き詰まりの原因と広く非難された.

stalk /stɔk/ (**stalks, stalking, stalked**) **1** N-COUNT 可算名詞 The **stalk** of a flower, leaf, or fruit is the thin part that joins it to the plant or tree. 茎 ❑ *A single pale blue flower grows up from each joint on a long stalk.* 長い茎の節(ふし)から1本の水色の花が育つ. **2** V-T 他動詞 If you **stalk** a person or a wild animal, you follow them quietly in order to kill them, catch them, or observe them carefully. こっそり追跡する ❑ *He stalks his victims like a hunter after a deer.* 彼はシカを追う狩猟者のように被害者をこっそり追跡する. **3** V-T 他動詞 If someone **stalks** someone else, especially a famous person or a person they used to have a relationship with, they keep following them or contacting them in an annoying and frightening way. ひそかに追跡する ❑ *Even after their divorce he continued to stalk and*

threaten her. 離婚した後ですら彼は彼女の後をひそかに追い、脅かし続けた.

stalk|er /ˈstɔkər/ (**stalkers**) N-COUNT 可算名詞 A **stalker** is someone who keeps following or contacting someone else, especially a famous person or a person they used to have a relationship with, in an annoying and frightening way. ストーカー ❑ *She had been followed and then trapped by a stalker.* 彼女はストーカーに追跡され、わなにかけられた.

stall /stɔl/ (**stalls, stalling, stalled**) **1** V-T/V-I 他動詞/自動詞 If a process **stalls**, or if someone or something **stalls** it, the process stops but may continue at a later time. 止まる、止める ❑ *The Social Democratic Party has vowed to try to stall the bill until the current session ends.* 社会民主党は現在の会議が終わるまで法案を阻止すると誓った. ❑ *...but the peace process stalled.* だが和平プロセスは行き詰った. **2** V-I 自動詞 If you **stall**, you try to avoid doing something until later. 回避する ❑ *Thomas had spent all week stalling over his decision.* トマスは1週間ずっと決断を避けた. **3** V-T 他動詞 If you **stall** someone, you prevent them from doing something until a later time. 引き止める ❑ *The store manager stalled the man until the police arrived.* 店長は警察官が到着するまでその男を引き止めた. **4** V-T/V-I 他動詞/自動詞 If a vehicle **stalls** or if you accidentally **stall** it, the engine stops suddenly. 止まる、止ねる ❑ *The engine stalled.* エンジンが止まった. **5** N-COUNT 可算名詞 A **stall** is a large table on which you put goods that you want to sell, or information that you want to give people. 屋台 ❑ *...market stalls selling local fruits.* 地元の果物を売る市場の屋台 **6** N-PLURAL 複数名詞 The **stalls** in a theater or concert hall are the seats on the ground floor directly in front of the stage. 劇場の一階前方の席 [mainly BRIT 主に英国英語; AM orchestra 米国英語 **orchestra**] **7** N-COUNT 可算名詞 A **stall** is a small enclosed area in a room which is used for a particular purpose, for example a shower. 小仕切り [AM 米国英語] ❑ *She went into the shower stall, turned on the water, and grabbed the soap.* 彼女はシャワー室に行き、栓をひねって水を出し、石鹸をつかんだ.
→ see **traffic**

stal|lion /ˈstælyən/ (**stallions**) N-COUNT 可算名詞 A **stallion** is a male horse, especially one kept for breeding. 種馬

stal|wart /ˈstɔlwərt/ (**stalwarts**) N-COUNT 可算名詞 A **stalwart** is a loyal worker or supporter of an organization, especially a political party. 不動の党人 ❑ *His free-trade policies aroused suspicion among party stalwarts.* 彼の自由貿易政策は意志強固な党人の間で疑惑を生んだ.

stami|na /ˈstæmɪnə/ N-UNCOUNT 不可算名詞 **Stamina** is the physical or mental energy needed to do a tiring activity for a long time. スタミナ ❑ *You have to have a lot of stamina to be a top-class dancer.* 一流のダンサーでいるためにはスタミナが必要だ.

stam|mer /ˈstæmər/ (**stammers, stammering, stammered**) **1** V-T/V-I 他動詞/自動詞 If you **stammer**, you speak with difficulty, hesitating and repeating words or sounds. どもる ❑ *Five percent of children stammer at some point.* 子供の5%はどもった経験がある. ❑ *"Forgive me," I stammered.* 「すみません」と私はどもった. ● **stam|mer|ing** N-UNCOUNT 不可算名詞 どもり ❑ *Of all speech impediments stammering is probably the most embarrassing.* 全ての言語障害でどもりはおそらく最もきまりの悪いものだと思う. **2** N-SING 単数名詞 Someone who has a **stammer** tends to stammer when they speak. どもり ❑ *A speech therapist cured his stammer.* スピーチセラピストは彼のどもりを治した.

stamp /stæmp/ (**stamps, stamping, stamped**) **1** N-COUNT 可算名詞 A **stamp** or a **postage stamp** is a small piece of paper which you lick and stick on an envelope or package before you mail it to pay for the cost of the postage. 切手 ❑ *...a book of stamps.* 1綴(つづ)りの切手 ❑ *As of February 3rd, the price of a first class stamp will go up to 29 cents.* 2月3日から第一種切手の値段は29セントに引き上げられる. **2** N-COUNT 可算名詞 A **stamp** is a small block of wood or metal which has a pattern or a group of letters on one side. You press it onto a pad of ink and then onto a piece of paper in order to produce a mark on the paper. The mark that you produce is also called a **stamp**. 刻印 ❑ *...a date stamp and an ink pad.* 日付印と印肉 **3** V-T 他動詞 If you **stamp** a mark or word on an object, you press the mark or word onto the object using a stamp or other device. 刻印する ❑ *Car manufacturers stamp a vehicle identification number at several places on new cars to help track down stolen vehicles.* 自動車メーカーは盗難車を追跡するために新車に自動車身元確認番号を刻印する. **4** V-T/V-I 他動詞/自動詞 If you **stamp** or **stamp** your foot, you lift your foot and put it down very hard on the ground, for example because you are angry or because your feet are cold. 踏みつける ❑ *Often he teased me till my temper went and I stamped and screamed, feeling furiously helpless.* 彼はしばしば私がとても無力に感じながら怒ってじだんだを踏み、大声を上げるまで私をからかった. ❑ *His foot stamped down on the accelerator.* 彼の足はアクセルを踏みつけた. ● **Stamp** is also a noun. ❑ *...hearing the creak of a door and the stamp of cold feet.* ドアのキーキー鳴る音と冷たい足の踏みつける音を聞くこと **5** V-I 自動詞 If you **stamp** somewhere, you walk there putting your feet down very

hard on the ground because you are angry. 足を踏み鳴らす □*"I'm going before things get any worse!" he shouted as he stamped out of the bedroom.* 「これ以上悪化する前に出かける」と彼は荒々しく寝室から出て行った. ⓺ V-I 自動詞 **If you stamp on** something, you put your foot down on it very hard. 踏みつける □*He received the original ban last week after stamping on the referee's foot during the final.* 彼は先週, 最終戦中に審判員の足を踏みつけ, 最初の禁止を受けた. ⓻ N-SING 単数名詞 If something bears **the stamp of** a particular quality or person, it clearly has that quality or was done by that person. しるし □*Most of us want to make our home a familiar place and put the stamp of our personality on its walls.* 私達の大半は家を見慣れた場所にし, 壁に個性のしるしをつけたいと思う. ⓼ → see also **rubber stamp**

▶ **stamp out** PHRASAL VERB 句動詞 **If you stamp** something **out**, you put an end to it. 撲滅する □*Dr. Muffett stressed that he was opposed to bullying in schools and that action would be taken to stamp it out.* マフェット博士は学校のいじめを撲滅するための行動が取る必要があると強調した.

stamp·ed ad|dressed en|ve·lope (stamped addressed envelopes) N-COUNT 可算名詞 A **stamped addressed envelope** is the same as an **SASE**. 返信用切手を貼った封筒 [BRIT 英国英語]

stam·pede /stæmpíːd/ (stampedes, stampeding, stampeded) ⓵ N-COUNT 可算名詞 If there is a **stampede**, a group of people or animals run in a wild, uncontrolled way. どっと押し寄せること □*There was a stampede for the exit.* 出口に人々がどっと押し寄せた. ⓶ V-T/V-I 他動詞/自動詞 If a group of animals or people **stampede** or if something **stampedes** them, they run in a wild, uncontrolled way. どっと逃げ出す □*The crowd stampeded and many were crushed or trampled underfoot.* 群衆はどっと逃げ出し, 多くの人々は押しつぶされたり, 踏みつけられた. □*...a herd of stampeding cattle.* どっと逃げ出す牛の群れ ⓷ N-COUNT 可算名詞 If a lot of people all do the same thing at the same time, you can describe it as a **stampede**. 衝動的な大衆行動 □*...a stampede of consumers rushing to buy merchandise at bargain prices.* 割引価格で商品を急いで買おうとする消費者の衝動的な大衆行動

stance /stæns/ (stances) ⓵ N-COUNT 可算名詞 Your **stance** on a particular matter is your attitude to it. 姿勢 □*Congress had agreed to reconsider its stance on the armed struggle.* 議会は武力紛争についての姿勢を再考することに合意した. ⓶ N-COUNT 可算名詞 Your **stance** is the way that you are standing. 足の構え [FORMAL 形式ばった] □*Take a comfortably wide stance and flex your knees a little.* 足を広げ, ひざを少し曲げなさい.

stand

❶ VERB USES AND PHRASES
❷ NOUN USES
❸ PHRASAL VERBS

❶ **stand** /stænd/ (stands, standing, stood) ⓵ V-I 自動詞 When you **are standing**, your body is upright, your legs are straight, and your weight is supported by your feet. 立っている □*She was standing beside my bed staring down at me.* 彼女は私を見つめながらベッドの側に立っていた. □*They told me to stand still and not to turn round.* 彼らは私にじっと立ったまま, 振り返らないよう命じた. ● PHRASAL VERB 句動詞 **Stand up** means the same as **stand**. 立つ □*We waited, standing up, for an hour.* 私達は1時間立って待っていた. ⓶ V-I 自動詞 When someone who is sitting **stands**, they change their position so that they are upright and on their feet. 立ち上がる □*Becker stood and shook hands with Ben.* ベッカーは立ち上がりベンと握手した. ● PHRASAL VERB 句動詞 **Stand up** means the same as **stand**. 立ち上がる □*When I walked in, they all stood up and started clapping.* 私が中に入ると彼らは全員立ち上がり, 拍手をし始めた. ⓷ V-I 自動詞 If you **stand aside** or **stand back**, you move a short distance sideways or backward, so that you are standing in a different place. わきに寄る □*I stood aside to let her pass me.* 私は彼女が通れるようにわきに寄った. ⓸ V-I 自動詞 If something such as a building or a piece of furniture **stands** somewhere, it is in that position, and is upright. 立っている [WRITTEN 書き言葉] □*The house stands alone on top of a small hill.* その家は小さな丘の上にぽつんと立っている. ⓹ V-I 自動詞 You can say that a building **is standing** when it remains after other buildings around it have fallen down or been destroyed. 元のままである □*The palace, which* was damaged by bombs in World War II, still stood. 第二次世界大戦中に爆弾の被害を受けた宮殿はまだ原形をとどめている. ⓺ V-T 他動詞 If you **stand** something somewhere, you put it there in an upright position. まっすぐ立てる □*Stand the plant in the open in a sunny, sheltered place.* 陽のあたる保護された広々とした場所で植物をまっすぐ立てなさい. ⓻ V-I 自動詞 If you leave food or a mixture of something **to stand**, you leave it without disturbing it for some time. そのままにしておく □*The salad improves if made in advance and left to stand.* サラダは事前に作りそのままにしておくと味がよくなる. ⓼ V-I 自動詞 If you ask someone **where** or **how** they **stand** on a particular issue, you are asking them what their attitude or view is. 態度を取る □*The amendment will force senators to show where they stand on the issue of sexual harassment.* 改正案により議員はセクハラ問題に対する姿勢を明らかにせざるをえなくなるだろう. ⓽ V-I 自動詞 If you do not know **where** you **stand with** someone, you do not know exactly what their attitude to you is. 評価されている □*No one knows where they stand with him; he is utterly unpredictable.* 彼にどう思われているか知る者はいない. 彼は全く何をしでかすか分からない男だ. ⓾ V-LINK 連結動詞 You can use **stand** instead of "be" when you are describing the present state or condition of something or someone. ある □*The alliance stands ready to do what is necessary.* 同盟は必要なことを行う覚悟がある. ⑪ V-I 自動詞 If a decision, law, or offer **stands**, it still exists and has not been changed or canceled. 有効である □*Although exceptions could be made, the rule still stands.* 例外も出てくるだろうがその規則は今も有効である. ⑫ V-I 自動詞 If something that can be measured **stands at** a particular level, it is at that level. ある □*The inflation rate now stands at 3.6 percent.* インフレ率は現在, 3.6%である. ⑬ V-T 他動詞 If something can **stand** a situation or a test, it is good enough or strong enough to experience it without being damaged, harmed, or shown to be inadequate. 持ちこたえる □*These are the first machines that can stand the wear and tear of continuously crushing glass.* これらは継続的にガラスを粉砕するのに耐えられる最初の機械である. ⑭ V-T 他動詞 If you cannot **stand** something, you cannot bear it or tolerate it. 我慢する □*I can't stand any more. I'm going to run away.* もう我慢できない. 私は家出するつもりだ. □*Stoddart can stand any amount of personal criticism.* ストダートはどんなに個人的批判を受けてもびくともしない. ⑮ V-T 他動詞 If you cannot **stand** someone or something, you dislike them very strongly. 我慢する [INFORMAL くだけた] □*I can't stand that man and his arrogance.* 私はあの男の傲慢さが我慢ならない. ⑯ V-T 他動詞 If you **stand to gain** something, you are likely to gain it. If you **stand to lose** something, you are likely to lose it. 得る立場にある, 失う立場にある □*The management group would stand to gain millions of dollars if the company were sold.* 経営陣は会社が売却された場合には何百万ドルもの金額を取得する立場に置かれる. ⑰ V-I 自動詞 If you **stand in** an election, you are a candidate in it. 立候補する [BRIT 英国英語; AM **run** 米国英語 **run**] ⑱ → see also **standing** ⑲ PHRASE 句 If you say **it stands to reason** that something is true or likely to happen, you mean that it is obvious. 理にかなっている □*It stands to reason that if you are considerate and friendly to people you will get a lot more back.* 思慮深く友好的であれば多くのものを得られることは当然である. ⑳ PHRASE 句 If you **stand in the way of** something or **stand in a person's way**, you prevent that thing from happening or prevent that person from doing something. いく手をふさいでいる □*The administration would not stand in the way of such a proposal.* 行政機関はそのような提案を妨害することはないだろう. ㉑ to **stand a chance** → see **chance** ㉒ to **stand firm** → see **firm** ㉓ to **stand on your own two feet** → see **foot** ㉔ to **stand your ground** → see **ground** ㉕ to **stand** someone **in good stead** → see **stead** ㉖ to **stand trial** → see **trial**

❷ **stand** /stænd/ (stands) ⓵ N-COUNT 可算名詞 If you take or make a **stand**, you do something or say something in order to make it clear what your attitude to a particular thing is. 立場 □*He felt the need to make a stand against racism in South Africa.* 彼は南アフリカの人種差別に反対の立場を取る必要を感じた. ⓶ N-COUNT 可算名詞 A **stand** is a small store or stall, outdoors or in a large public building. 屋台 □*He ran a newspaper stand outside the American Express office.* 彼はアメリカンエクスプレスの事務所の外で新聞売り場をやっていた. ⓷ N-PLURAL 複数名詞 The **stands** at a sports stadium or arena are a large structure where people sit or stand to watch what is happening. 観客席 □*The people in the stands at Candlestick Park are standing and cheering with all their might.* キャンドルスティック・パークの観覧席の人々は立って力いっぱい応援している. ● N-COUNT 可算名詞 In British English, **stand** is used with the same meaning. 観客席 □*I was sitting in the stand for the first game.* 私は最初の試合のために観客席に座っていた. ⓸ N-COUNT 可算名詞 A **stand** is an object or piece of furniture that is designed for supporting or holding a particular kind of thing. 台 □*The teapot came with a stand to catch the drips.* ティーポットにはしたたりを受け止める台が付いていた. ⓹ N-COUNT 可算名詞 A **stand** is an area where taxis or buses can wait to pick up passengers. 駐車場 □*Luckily there was a taxi stand nearby.* 幸いタクシー乗り場が近くにあった. ⓺ N-SING 単数名詞 In a law court, **the stand** is the place

where a witness sits to answer questions. 証人席 ❑*When the father took the stand today, he contradicted his son's testimony.* 父親が今日証人席に立った時、彼は息子の証言に反対の陳述をした。

❸ **stand** /stænd/ (**stands, standing, stood**)

▶ **stand aside** PHRASAL VERB 句動詞; AM **stand down** 米国英語 **stand down**

▶ **stand back** PHRASAL VERB 句動詞 If you **stand back** and think about a situation, you think about it as if you were not involved in it. 距離を置いてものを考える [BRIT 英国英語] ❑*Stand back and look objectively at the problem.* 距離を置き、問題を客観的に見なさい。

▶ **stand by** ■ PHRASAL VERB 句動詞 If you **are standing by,** you are ready and waiting to provide help or to take action. 待機する ❑*British and American warships are standing by to evacuate their citizens if necessary.* 英国と米国の戦艦は必要であれば国民を後送するために待機中である。 ② → see also **standby** ③ PHRASAL VERB 句動詞 If you **stand by** and let something bad happen, you do not do anything to stop it. 傍観する [DISAPPROVAL 不賛成] ❑*The Secretary of Defense has said that he would not stand by and let democracy be undermined.* 防衛長官は民主主義が傷つくのを傍観するつもりはないと述べた。 ④ PHRASAL VERB 句動詞 If you **stand by** someone, you continue to give them support, especially when they are in trouble. 支援する [APPROVAL 賛成] ❑*I wouldn't break the law for a friend, but I would stand by her if she did.* 私は友人のために法律を破るつもりはないが、彼女が法律違反を犯した場合には支援するだろう。 ⑤ PHRASAL VERB 句動詞 If you **stand by** an earlier decision, promise, or statement, you continue to support it or keep it. 守る ❑*The decision has been made and I have got to stand by it.* 決定は下され、私はそれを守り通さねばならない。

▶ **stand down** PHRASAL VERB 句動詞 If someone **stands down,** they resign from an important job or position, often in order to let someone else take their place. 身を引く ❑*Four days later, the despised leader finally stood down, just 17 days after taking office.* 4日後、ひどく嫌われた指導者は就任後たった17日でついに身を引いた。

▶ **stand for** ■ PHRASAL VERB 句動詞 If you say that a letter **stands for** a particular word, you mean that it is an abbreviation for that word. 意味する ❑*AIDS stands for Acquired Immune Deficiency Syndrome.* AIDSは後天性免疫不全症のことである。 ② PHRASAL VERB 句動詞 The ideas or attitudes that someone or something **stands for** are the ones that they support or represent. 象徴する ❑*The party is trying to give the impression that it alone stands for democracy.* その党は民主主義を象徴するのは我が党だけであるという印象を与えようとしている。 ③ PHRASAL VERB 句動詞 If you will **not stand for** something, you will not allow it to happen or continue. 我慢しない [with neg] ❑*It's outrageous, and we won't stand for it any more.* それはひどい。もうそれはたくさんだ。

▶ **stand in** ■ PHRASAL VERB 句動詞 If you **stand in for** someone, you take their place or do their job, because they are sick or away. 代役を務める ❑*I had to stand in for her on Tuesday when she didn't show up.* 私は彼女が現われなかった火曜日に彼女の代役を務めなければならなかった。 ② → see also **stand-in**

▶ **stand out** ■ PHRASAL VERB 句動詞 If something **stands out,** it is very noticeable. 目立つ ❑*Every tree, wall and fence stood out against dazzling white fields.* あらゆる木、壁そして塀はまばゆいばかりの白い野原を背景にひときわ目立った。 ② PHRASAL VERB 句動詞 If something **stands out** from a surface, it rises up from it. 突き出る ❑*His tendons stood out like rope beneath his skin.* 彼のアキレス腱は皮膚の下のロープのように突き出た。

▶ **stand up** ■ → see **stand** ❶, 2 ② PHRASAL VERB 句動詞 If something such as a claim or a piece of evidence **stands up,** it is accepted as true or satisfactory after being carefully examined. 信じられる ❑*He made wild accusations that did not stand up.* 彼は信じられないような途方もない告発をした。 ③ PHRASAL VERB 句動詞 If a boyfriend or girlfriend **stands** you **up,** they fail to keep an arrangement to meet you. 待ちぼうけを食わせる [INFORMAL くだけた] ❑*We were to have had dinner together yesterday evening, but he stood me up.* 私達は昨夜一緒に食事をするはずだったのに彼は私をすっぽかした。

▶ **stand up for** PHRASAL VERB 句動詞 If you **stand up for** someone or something, you defend them and make your feelings or opinions very clear. 弁護する [APPROVAL 賛成] ❑*They stood up for what they believed to be right.* 彼らは正しいと信じることを弁護した。

▶ **stand up to** ■ PHRASAL VERB 句動詞 If something **stands up to** bad conditions, it is not damaged or harmed by them. もつ ❑*Is this building going to stand up to the strongest gales?* このビルは強風に耐えるだろうか。 ② PHRASAL VERB 句動詞 If you **stand up to** someone, especially someone more powerful than you are, you defend yourself against their attacks or demands. 恐れず立ち向かう ❑*He hit me, so I hit him back – the first time in my life I'd stood up to him.* 彼は私を殴ったので私は殴り返した。生まれて初めて立ち向かった。

stand-alone ■ ADJ 形容詞 A **stand-alone** business or organization is independent and does not receive financial support from another organization. 独立した [BUSINESS 実業] [ADJ

n] ❑*They plan to relaunch it as a stand-alone company.* 彼らは独立した会社として着手し直す予定である。 ② ADJ 形容詞 A **stand-alone** computer is one that can operate on its own and does not have to be part of a network. 独立型の [COMPUTING コンピューティング] [ADJ n] ❑*...an operating system that can work on networks and stand-alone machines.* ネットワークおよび独立型機器に使えるオペレーティングシステム

stand|ard /stændərd/ (**standards**) ■ N-COUNT 可算名詞 A **standard** is a level of quality or achievement, especially a level that is thought to be acceptable. 水準 ❑*The standard of professional cricket has never been lower.* プロのクリケットの水準がこれほど低かったことはない。 ② N-COUNT 可算名詞 A **standard** is something that you use in order to judge the quality of something else. 標準 ❑*...systems that were by later standards absurdly primitive.* 後の標準と比べるとひどく旧式なシステム ③ N-PLURAL 複数名詞 **Standards** are moral principles which affect people's attitudes and behavior. 道徳的な規範 ❑*My father has always had high moral standards.* 私の父は常に高い道徳の規範を持ってきた。 ④ ADJ 形容詞 You use **standard** to describe things which are usual and normal. 普通の ❑*It was standard practice for untrained clerks to advise in serious cases such as murder.* 殺人などの深刻な事件でも訓練を受けていない職員が助言をするのは普通だった。 ⑤ ADJ 形容詞 A **standard** work or text on a particular subject is one that is widely read and often recommended. 定評ある [ADJ n] ❑*At twenty he translated Euler's standard work on algebra into English.* 20歳で彼は数学に関するオイラーの定評ある作品を英訳した。

Word Partnership	*standard* は次の語句と使われる:
V.	become a standard, maintain a standard, meet a standard, raise a standard, set a standard, use a standard ■ ②
N.	standard of excellence, industry standard ■ ②, standard English, standard equipment, standard practice, standard procedure ④

stand|ard|ize /stændərdaɪz/ (**standardizes, standardizing, standardized**) V-T 他動詞 To **standardize** things means to change them so that they all have the same features. 標準化する ❑*There is a drive both to standardize components and to reduce the number of models.* 品名を標準化し、モデル数を減らす欲求がある。 ● **stand|ard|i|za|tion** /stændərdaɪzeɪʃⁿ/ N-UNCOUNT 不可算名詞 標準化 ❑*...the standardization of working hours.* 労働時間の標準化
→ see **mass production**

stand|ard of liv|ing (**standards of living**) N-COUNT 可算名詞 Your **standard of living** is the level of comfort and wealth which you have. 生活水準 ❑*We'll continue to fight for a decent standard of living for our members.* 我々は会員のまともな生活水準のために闘い続けるつもりだ。

stand|ard time N-UNCOUNT 不可算名詞 **Standard time** is the official local time of a region or country. 標準時 ❑*Tonight the nation switches from daylight-saving time to standard time.* 今夜、夏時間から標準時に変わる。

stand|by /stændbaɪ/ (**standbys**) also **stand-by** ■ N-COUNT 可算名詞 A **standby** is something or someone that is always ready to be used if they are needed. 代物 ❑*Canned varieties of beans and peas are a good standby.* 缶詰の豆やグリーンピースはよい代物である。 ② PHRASE 句 If someone or something is **on standby,** they are ready to be used if they are needed. 待機して ❑*Five ambulances are on standby at the port.* 港では5台の救急車が待機している。 ③ ADJ 形容詞 A **standby** ticket for something such as the theater or a plane trip is a cheap ticket that you buy just before the performance starts or the plane takes off, if there are still some seats left. キャンセル待ちの [ADJ n] ❑*He bought a standby ticket to New York at 5:30 a.m. the following morning and flew to JFK airport six hours later.* 彼は翌朝5時半にニューヨーク行きのキャンセル待ち航空券を買い、6時間後にJFK空港行きの便に乗った。 ● ADV 副詞 **Standby** is also an adverb. キャンセル待ちで [ADV after v] ❑*Magda was going to fly standby.* マグダはキャンセル待ちで飛行機に乗る予定だった。

stand-in (**stand-ins**) N-COUNT 可算名詞 A **stand-in** is a person who takes someone else's place or does someone else's job for a while, for example because the other person is sick or away. 代役 ❑*He was a stand-in for my regular doctor.* 彼は私の通常の医者の代診だった。

stand|ing /stændɪŋ/ (**standings**) ■ N-UNCOUNT 不可算名詞 Someone's **standing** is their reputation or status. 立派な地位 ❑*...an artist of international standing.* 国際的な名声のあるアーティスト ❑*He has improved his country's standing abroad.* 彼は海外での彼の母国の評判を高めた。 ② N-COUNT 可算名詞 A party's or person's **standing** is their popularity. 人気 ❑*But, as the opinion poll shows, the party's standing with the people at large has never been so low.* しかし世論調査が示しているように、一般の人々の間でその政党の人気はかつてないほど低下した。 ③ ADJ 形容詞 You use **standing** to describe something which is permanently in existence. 常備の [ADJ n]

S

Word Web   star

North Star

Astronomy is the oldest science. It is the study of **stars** and other objects in the **night sky**. People sometimes confuse astronomy and **astrology**. Astrology is the belief that the stars influence people's lives. Long ago people named groups of stars after gods, heroes, and imaginary animals. One of the most famous of these **constellations** is the Big Dipper. Its original name meant "the big bear." It is easy to find and it points toward the North Star*. For centuries sailors have used the North Star to **navigate**. The best-known star in our **galaxy** is the **sun**.

North Star: the star that the earth's northern axis points toward.

Big Dipper

❑ *Israel has a relatively small standing army and its strength is based on its reserves.* イスラエルの常備軍は比較的小規模で、その強さは予備軍に基づいている. **5** → see also **long-standing**

stand|off /stǽndɔf/ (**standoffs**) N-COUNT 可算名詞 A **standoff** is a situation in which neither of two opposing groups or forces will make a move until the other one does something, so nothing can happen until one of them gives way. 行き詰まり ❑ *There is no sign of an end to the standoff between Mohawk Indians and the Quebec provincial police.* モホーク族とケベック州警察間の行き詰まりが終わる兆しはなかった.

stand|point /stǽndpɔɪnt/ (**standpoints**) N-COUNT 可算名詞 **From** a particular **standpoint** means looking at an event, situation, or idea in a particular way. 観点 ❑ *He believes that from a military standpoint, the situation is under control.* 彼は軍の観点からは万時順調だと考えている.

stand|still /stǽndstɪl/ N-SING 単数名詞 If movement or activity comes **to** or is brought **to** a **standstill**, it stops completely. 停止 ❑ *Abruptly the group ahead of us came to a standstill.* 我々の前方のグループは突然停止した.

stand-up also **standup** (**stand-ups**) **1** ADJ 形容詞 A **stand-up** comic or comedian stands alone in front of an audience and tells jokes. 立ったままでジョークを連発して客を笑わせる [ADJ n] ❑ *He does all kinds of accents, he can do jokes – he could be a stand-up comic.* 彼はあらゆる種類のなまりを真似したり、ジョークを飛ばす. 彼はスタンドアップコメディアンになれるだろう. **2** N-UNCOUNT 不可算名詞 **Stand-up** is stand-up comedy. スタンドアップコメディ ❑ *...likability, professionalism and the kind of nerve you need to do stand-up.* 好感が持てること、プロ意識そしてスタンドアップコメディに必要な神経 **3** N-COUNT 可算名詞 A **stand-up** is a stand-up comedian. スタンドアップコメディアン ❑ *...one of the worst stand-ups alive.* この上なくひどいスタンドアップコメディアンの1人

stank /stǽŋk/ **Stank** is the past tense of **stink**. stinkの過去形

sta|ple /stéɪpᵊl/ (**staples, stapling, stapled**) **1** ADJ 形容詞 A **staple** food, product, or activity is one that is basic and important in people's everyday lives. 基本的な [ADJ n] ❑ *Rice is the staple food of more than half the world's population.* 米は世界の人口の半分以上の基本食品である. ❑ *The Chinese also eat a type of pasta as part of their staple diet.* また中国人は基本食品の一部としてある種のパスタを食べる. ● N-COUNT 可算名詞 **Staple** is also a noun. 基本食品 ❑ *Fish is a staple in the diet of many Africans.* 魚は多くのアフリカ人の基本食品である. **2** N-COUNT 可算名詞 A **staple** is something that forms an important part of something else. 主要な要素 ❑ *Political reporting has become a staple of American journalism.* 政治報道はアメリカのジャーナリズムの主要な要素となっている. **3** N-COUNT 可算名詞 **Staples** are small pieces of bent wire that are used mainly for holding sheets of paper together firmly. ホッチキスの針 **4** V-T 他動詞 If you **staple** something, you fasten it to something else or fix it in place using staples. ホッチキスで留める ❑ *Staple some sheets of paper together into a book.* 数枚の紙をホッチキスで留めてノートにしなさい.

sta|pler /stéɪplər/ (**staplers**) N-COUNT 可算名詞 A **stapler** is a device used for putting staples into sheets of paper. ホッチキス → see **office**

star /stɑr/ (**stars, starring, starred**) **1** N-COUNT 可算名詞 A **star** is a large ball of burning gas in space. Stars appear to us as small points of light in the sky on clear nights. 星 ❑ *The nights were pure with cold air and lit with stars.* 夜空は冷え冷えと澄みわたり、星が輝いていた. **2** N-COUNT 可算名詞 You can refer to a shape or an object as a **star** when it has four, five, or more points sticking out of it in a regular pattern. 星形のもの ❑ *Children at school receive colored stars for work well done.* 良い成績を取った生徒には色つきの星形が与えられる. **3** N-COUNT 可算名詞 You can say how many **stars** something such as a hotel or restaurant has as a way of talking about its quality, which is often indicated by a number of star-shaped symbols. The more stars something has, the better it is. 星印 ❑ *...five star hotels.* 5つ星ホテル **4** N-COUNT 可算名詞 Famous actors, musicians, and sports players are often referred

to as **stars**. 人気者 ❑ *...star of the TV series Scrubs.* テレビの連続番組Scrubsの人気者 ❑ *By now Murphy is Hollywood's top male comedy star.* 現在までにマーフィーはハリウッドで最も人気のある男のコメディアンだった. **5** V-I 自動詞 If an actor or actress **stars in** a play or movie, he or she has one of the most important parts in it. 主役を務める ❑ *The previous year Adolphson had starred in a play in which Ingrid had been an extra.* 前の年にアドルフソンはイングリッドがエクストラを務めた劇で主役を務めた. **6** V-T 他動詞 If a play or movie **stars** a famous actor or actress, he or she has one of the most important parts in it. 主役にする ❑ *...a Hollywood movie, "The Secret of Santa Vittoria," directed by Stanley Kramer and starring Anthony Quinn.* スタンリー・クレイマー監督、アントニー・クィン主演のハリウッド映画 The Secret of Santa Vittoria **7** N-PLURAL 複数名詞 Predictions about people's lives which are based on astrology and appear regularly in a newspaper or magazine are sometimes referred to as **the stars**. 星占い ❑ *There was nothing in my stars to say I'd have travel problems!* 星占いには旅行のトラブルに出会うとは全く出ていなかった.

→ see Word Web: **star**
→ see **galaxy, navigation**

Word Partnership   starは次の語句と使われる:

ADJ.	**bright** star **1 4**
	big star, **former** star, **rising** star **4**
N.	**bronze** star, **gold** star **2**
	all-star cast/game, basketball/football/tennis star, **guest** star, **film/movie** star, **pop/rap** star, **porn** star, **TV** star **4**
	star **in a film/movie/show 5**

star|board /stɑ́rbərd, -bɔrd/ ADJ 形容詞 The **starboard** side of a ship or an aircraft is the right side when you are on it and facing toward the front. 右舷(げん)の [TECHNICAL 技術的] ❑ *He detected a ship moving down the starboard side of the submarine.* 彼は潜水艦の右側に降りる船を探知した. ● N-UNCOUNT 不可算名詞 **Starboard** is also a noun. 右側 ❑ *I could see the fishing boat to starboard.* 右側に漁船が見えた.

starch /stɑrtʃ/ (**starches**) **1** N-MASS 質量名詞 **Starch** is a substance that is found in foods such as bread, potatoes, pasta, and rice and gives you energy. でんぷん ❑ *She reorganized her eating so that she was taking more fruit and vegetables and less starch, salt, and fat.* 彼女は果物や野菜を増やして、でんぷん、塩、脂肪を減らす食生活に変えた. **2** N-UNCOUNT 不可算名詞 **Starch** is a substance that is used for making cloth stiffer, especially cotton and linen. 糊(のり)❑ *He never puts enough starch in my shirts.* 彼は私のシャツにつける糊はいつも足りない.
→ see **rice**

star|dom /stɑ́rdəm/ N-UNCOUNT 不可算名詞 **Stardom** is the state of being very famous, usually as an actor, musician, or athlete. スターの地位 ❑ *In 1929 she shot to stardom on Broadway in a Noel Coward play.* 彼女は1929年にノエル・カワードの劇でブロードウェイのスターの地位にのし上がった.

stare /steər/ (**stares, staring, stared**) **1** V-I 自動詞 If you **stare** at someone or something, you look at them for a long time. じっと見つめる ❑ *Tamara stared at him in disbelief, shaking her head.* タマラは首を降りながら信じられないという様子をじっと見つめた. ❑ *Ben continued to stare out the window.* ベンは窓の外をじっと見続けた. ● N-COUNT 可算名詞 **Stare** is also a noun. じっと見つめること ❑ *Hlasek gave him a long, cold stare.* フラセキは彼を長いこと冷たい目で凝視した. **2** PHRASE 句 If a situation or the answer to a problem **is staring** you **in the face**, it is very obvious, although you may not be immediately aware of it. 明白である [INFORMAL くだけた] ❑ *Then the answer hit me. It had been staring me in the face ever since Lullington.* それから答えを思いついた. それはラリントン以来、明白だった.

S

The verbs **stare** and **gaze** are both used to talk about looking at something for a long time. If you **stare at** something or someone, it is often because you think they are strange or shocking. ❑ *Various families came out and stared at us.* If you **gaze at** something, it is often because you think it is marvelous or impressive. ❑ *A fresh-faced little girl gazes in wonder at the bright fairground lights.*

Word Partnership   stare は次の語句と使われる:

| ADJ. | **blank** stare ❶ |
| V. | **continue** to stare, **turn** to stare ❶ |

stark /stɑrk/ (starker, starkest) ❶ ADJ 形容詞 **Stark** choices or statements are harsh and unpleasant. 動かしがたい ❑ *Companies face a stark choice if they want to stay competitive.* 競争力を維持したい企業は逃れられない選択を行なわねばならない. ● **stark|ly** ADV 副詞 容赦なく ❑ *That issue is presented starkly and brutally by Bob Graham and David Cairns.* その問題はボブ・グレアムとディビッド・ケアーンズによって情け容赦なく提示された. ❷ ADJ 形容詞 If two things are in **stark** contrast to one another, they are very different from each other in a way that is very obvious. 際立った ❑ *...secret cooperation between London and Washington that was in stark contrast to official policy.* 公式の政策とは著しい対照的だった英米間の秘密の協力 ❑ *Angus's child-like paintings contrast starkly with his adult subject matter in these portraits.* アンガスの子供のような絵画はこうした肖像画の成人向けのテーマと著しく対照をなす. ❸ ADJ 形容詞 Something that is **stark** is very plain in appearance. きわめて簡素な ❑ *...the stark white, characterless fireplace in the drawing room.* 居間にある簡素な白の特徴のない暖炉 ● **stark|ly** ADV 副詞 きわめて簡素に ❑ *The room was starkly furnished.* その部屋にはきわめて簡素な家具が置かれていた.

start /stɑrt/ (starts, starting, started) ❶ V-T 他動詞 If you **start** to do something, you do something that you were not doing before and you continue doing it. 始める ❑ *John then unlocked the front door and I started to follow him up the stairs.* ジョンはそれから玄関のドアの錠を開き, 私は彼に続いて階段を上がり始めた. ❑ *It was 1956 when Susanna started the work on the garden.* スザンナが庭造りを始めたのは1956年のことだった. ● N-COUNT 可算名詞 **Start** is also a noun. 開始 ❑ *After several starts, she read the report properly.* 数回読み始めた後, 彼女はきちんとリポートを読んだ. ❷ V-T/V-I 他動詞/自動詞 When something **starts**, or if someone **starts** it, it takes place from a particular time. 始まる ❑ *The fire is thought to have started in an upstairs room.* 火事は上階の部屋で起きたと考えられている. ❑ *All of the passengers started the day with a swim.* 全ての乗客は水泳で1日を開始した. ● N-SING 単数名詞 **Start** is also a noun. 始まり ❑ *...1918, four years after the start of the Great War.* 1918年, 第一次世界大戦が始まった4年後 ❸ V-I 自動詞 If you **start by** doing something, or if you **start with** something, you do that thing first in a series of actions. 取り掛かる ❑ *I started by asking how many day-care centers were located in the United States.* 私は米国にはいくつの老人福祉センターがあるのかという質問で始めた. ❹ V-I 自動詞 You use **start** to say what someone's first job was. For example, if their first job was that of a factory worker, you can say that they **started as** a factory worker. ...から始める ❑ *Betty started as a shipping clerk at the clothes factory.* ベティは洋服工場の発送係として働き始めた. ● PHRASAL VERB 句動詞 **Start off** means the same as **start**. 始める ❑ *Mr. Dambar had started off as an assistant to Mrs. Spear's husband.* ダンバー氏はスペアー夫人の夫のアシスタントとして働き始めた. ❺ V-T 他動詞 When someone **starts** something such as a new business, they create it or cause it to begin. 設立する ❑ *George Granger has started a health center and I know he's looking for qualified staff.* ジョージ・グレンジャーは医療センターを設立し, 私は彼が資格のあるスタッフを探しているのを知っている. ● PHRASAL VERB 句動詞 **Start up** means the same as **start**. 操業を開始する ❑ *The cost of starting up a day-care center for children ranges from $150,000 to $300,000.* 託児所の操業を開始する費用は15万ドルから30万ドルの間である. ❻ → see also **startup** ❼ V-T/V-I 他動詞/自動詞 If you **start** an engine, car, or machine, or if it **starts**, it begins to work. 始動させる, 始動する ❑ *He started the car, which hummed smoothly.* 彼が始動させた車は低い持続音を出した. ● PHRASAL VERB 句動詞 **Start up** means the same as **start**. 始動させる ❑ *He waited until they went inside the building before starting up the car and driving off.* 彼は彼らが建物の中に入るのを見届けてから車を始動させ, 走り去った. ❑ *Put the key in the ignition and turn it to start the car up.* 鍵を点火装置に入れ, それを回して車を始動させなさい. ❽ V-I 自動詞 If you **start**, your body suddenly moves slightly as a result of surprise or fear. びくっと動く ❑ *She put the bottle on the coffee table beside him, banging it down hard. He started at the sound, his concentration broken.* 彼女は彼の側のコーヒーテーブルに瓶をドンと置いた. 彼は物音にびくっとする こと ❑ *Sylvia woke with a start.* シルビアははっとして目を覚ました. ❾ → see also **false start, head start** ❿ PHRASE 句 You use **for a start** or **to start with** to introduce the first of a number of things or reasons that you want to mention or could mention. まず第一

に ❑ *You must get her name and address, and that can be a problem for a start.* 彼女の名前と住所を手に入れる必要があるが, それはまず第一に難しいかもしれない. ⓫ PHRASE 句 **To start with** means at the very first stage of an event or process. 初めは ❑ *To start with, the pressure on her was very heavy, but it's eased off a bit now.* 初めは彼女への重圧は非常に大きかったが, 今はやや弱まった. ⓬ to **get off to a flying start** → see **flying**

Start, begin, and commence all have a similar meaning, although commence is more formal and is not normally used in conversation. ❑ *The meeting is ready to begin... He tore the list up and started a fresh one... The space probe commenced taking a series of photographs.* Note that begin, start, and commence can all be followed by an -ing form or a noun, but only begin and start can be followed by a "to" infinitive.

▶ **start off** ❶ PHRASAL VERB 句動詞 If you **start off by** doing something, you do it as the first part of an activity. 始める ❑ *She started off by accusing him of blackmail but he more or less ignored her.* 彼女は彼を恐喝のかどで非難し始めたが, 彼は多かれ少なかれ彼女を無視した. ❷ PHRASAL VERB 句動詞 To **start** someone **off** means to cause them to begin doing something. 始めさせる ❑ *Her mother started her off acting in children's theater.* 彼女の母親は彼女に子供劇団で演技を始めさせた. ❸ PHRASAL VERB 句動詞 To **start** something **off** means to cause it to begin. 始めさせる ❑ *He became more aware of the things that started that tension off.* 彼はその緊張状態を始めさせた事柄に気づくようになった. ❹ → see **start 4**
▶ **start on** PHRASAL VERB 句動詞 If you **start on** something that needs to be done, you start dealing with it. 取り掛かる ❑ *Before you start on these chapters, clear your head.* この章に取り掛かる前に頭をすっきりさせなさい.
▶ **start out** ❶ PHRASAL VERB 句動詞 If someone or something **starts out as** a particular thing, they are that thing at the beginning although they change later. 始める ❑ *Daly was a fast-talking Irish-American who had started out as a salesman.* デイリーはセールスマンとして仕事を始めた口車のうまいアイルランド系アメリカ人だった. ❷ PHRASAL VERB 句動詞 If you **start out by** doing something, you do it at the beginning of an activity. 始める ❑ *I'm careful to start out by saying clearly what I want.* 私は望むことをはっきりと言うことで始めるようにしている.
▶ **start over** PHRASAL VERB 句動詞 If you **start over** or **start** something **over**, you begin something again from the beginning. やり直す [mainly AM 主に米国英語] ❑ *...moving the kids to some other schools, closing them down and starting over with a new staff.* 子供達を別の学校に移し, それらを閉鎖し, 新しい職員とやり直すこと
▶ **start up** → see **start 5, 6**

Thesaurus   start また次を参照:

| V. | begin, commence, originate ❶ ❷ establish, found, launch ❺ |
| N. | beginning, onset ❶ ❷ jump, scare, shock ❼ |

start|er /stɑrtər/ (starters) N-COUNT 可算名詞 A **starter** is a small quantity of food that is served as the first course of a meal. 前菜 [mainly BRIT 主に英国英語; AM usually **appetizer** 米国英語では通常 **appetizer**]

start|ing point (starting points) also **starting-point** ❶ N-COUNT 可算名詞 Something that is a **starting point** for a discussion or process can be used to begin it or act as a basis for it. 起点 ❑ *These proposals represent a realistic starting point for negotiation.* こうした提案は交渉の現実的な起点である. ❷ N-COUNT 可算名詞 When you make a journey, your **starting point** is the place from which you start. 出発点 ❑ *They had already walked a couple of miles or more from their starting point.* 彼らは既に出発点から2マイル以上歩いていた.

star|tle /stɑrt³l/ (startles, startling, startled) V-T 他動詞 If something sudden and unexpected **startles** you, it surprises and frightens you slightly. どきりとさせる ❑ *The telephone startled him.* 彼は電話の音にどきりとした. ● **star|tled** ADJ 形容詞 びっくりした ❑ *Martha gave her a startled look.* マーサは彼女を見てびっくりした表情をした.

star|tling /stɑrtlɪŋ/ ADJ 形容詞 Something that is **startling** is so different, unexpected, or remarkable that people react to it with surprise. 驚くべき ❑ *Sometimes the results may be rather startling.* 時には驚くべき結果が得られることがある.

start|up /stɑrtʌp/ (startups) ❶ ADJ 形容詞 The **startup** costs of something such as a new business or new product are the costs of starting to run or produce it. 新事業を開始する際の [BUSINESS 実業] [ADJ n] ❑ *That is enough to pay the startup costs for fourteen research projects.* それは14のリサーチプロジェクトの新事業開始費用を支払うのに十分だ. ❷ ADJ 形容詞 A **startup** company is a small business that has recently been started by someone. 操業開始の [BUSINESS 実業] [ADJ n] ❑ *Thousands and thousands of startup firms have poured into the computer market.* 操業開始した何千もの企業がコンピュータ市

場に押し寄せた. ●N-COUNT 可算名詞 **Startup** is also a noun. 操業開始したばかりの会社 ❏ *For now the only bright spots in the labor market are small businesses and high-tech startups.* 今のところ, 労働市場の唯一の明るい場所は小規模事業と操業開始したばかりのハイテク企業だ.

star|va|tion /stɑːrveɪʃⁿn/ N-UNCOUNT 不可算名詞 **Starvation** is extreme suffering or death, caused by lack of food. 餓死 ❏ *Over three hundred people have died of starvation since the beginning of the year.* 年初以来, 3百人以上の人が餓死した.

starve /stɑːrv/ (**starves, starving, starved**) **1** V-I 自動詞 If people **starve**, they suffer greatly from lack of food which sometimes leads to their death. 餓えに苦しむ ❏ *A number of the prisoners we saw are starving.* 我々の会った数人の囚人は餓えている. ❏ *In the 1930s, millions of Ukrainians starved to death or were deported.* 1930年代には何百万ものウクライナ人が餓死するか国外追放となった. **2** V-T 他動詞 To **starve** someone means not to give them any food. 餓えさせる ❏ *He said the only alternative was to starve the people, and he said this could not be allowed to happen.* 彼は唯一の残された選択は国民を餓えさせることだが, これは起きてはならないことだと言った. **3** V-T 他動詞 If a person or thing is **starved of** something that they need, they are suffering because they are not getting enough of it. 不足を感じる ❏ *The electricity industry is not the only one to have been starved of investment.* 投資不足なのは電力会社だけではなかった.

starv|ing /stɑːrvɪŋ/ ADJ 形容詞 If you say that you are **starving**, you mean that you are very hungry. 死ぬほど空腹である [INFORMAL くだけた] [v-link ADJ] ❏ *Apart from anything else I was starving.* 他のことはともかく私は死ぬほどお腹が空いていた.

stash /stæʃ/ (**stashes, stashing, stashed**) **1** V-T 他動詞 If you **stash** something valuable in a secret place, you store it there to keep it safe. しまっておく [INFORMAL くだけた] ❏ *We went for the bottle of whiskey that we had stashed behind the bookcase.* 我々は本棚の後ろに隠しておいた1瓶のウィスキーを取りに行った. **2** N-COUNT 可算名詞 A **stash of** something valuable is a secret store of it. 隠したもの [INFORMAL くだけた] ❏ *A large stash of drugs had been found aboard the yacht.* そのヨットに大量の麻薬が隠されているのが発見された.

state /steɪt/ (**states, stating, stated**) **1** N-COUNT 可算名詞 You can refer to countries as **states**, particularly when you are discussing politics. 国 ❏ *Mexico is a secular state and does not have diplomatic relations with the Vatican.* メキシコは非宗教的な国でバチカンとは外交関係を結んでいない.

Country is the most usual word to use when you are talking about the major political units that the world is divided into. **State** is used when you are talking about politics or government institutions. ...*the new German state created by the unification process.* ...*Italy's state-controlled telecommunications company.* **State** can also refer to a political unit within a particular country. ...*the state of California.* **Nation** is often used when you are talking about a country's inhabitants, and their cultural or ethnic background. ❏ *Wales is a proud nation with its own traditions.* ...*A senior government spokesman will address the nation.* **Land** is a less precise and more literary word, which you can use, for example, to talk about the feelings you have for a particular country. ❏ *She was fascinated to learn about this strange land at the edge of Europe.*

---

2 N-COUNT 可算名詞 Some large countries such as the U.S. are divided into smaller areas called **states**. 州 ❏ *Leaders of the Southern states are meeting in Louisville.* 南部の州の指導者がルイビルで会合を行なう予定だ. **3** N-PROPER 固有名詞 The U.S. is sometimes referred to as **the States**. 米国 [INFORMAL くだけた] ❏ *She bought it last year in the States.* 彼女はそれを昨年, アメリカで買った. **4** N-SING 単数名詞 You can refer to the government of a country as **the state**. 政府 ❏ *The state does not collect enough revenue to cover its expenditure.* 政府の歳出は歳入を超過している. **5** ADJ 形容詞 **State** industries or organizations are financed and organized by the government rather than private companies. 政府の [ADJ n] ❏ ...*reform of the state social-security system.* 国の社会保障制度の改革 **6** → see **state school** **7** ADJ 形容詞 A **state** occasion is a formal one involving the head of a country. 公式用の [ADJ n] ❏ *The president of the Czech Republic is in Washington on a state visit.* チェコ共和国の大統領はワシントンを公式訪問中である. **8** N-COUNT 可算名詞 When you talk about the **state of** someone or something, you are referring to the condition they are in or what they are like at a particular time. 状態 ❏ *For the first few months after Daniel died, I was in a state of clinical depression.* ダニエルが死んでから最初の数ヶ月間私はうつ病だった. **9** V-T 他動詞 If you **state** something, you say or write it in a formal or definite way. 述べる ❏ *Clearly state your address and telephone number.* 住所と電話番号をはっきりと述べなさい. ❏ *The police report stated that he was arrested for allegedly assaulting his wife.* 警察の報告書によると, 彼は妻を暴行した容疑で逮捕された. **10** → see also **head of state, welfare state** **11** PHRASE 句 If you say that someone **is not in a fit state to** do something, you mean that they are too upset or ill to do it. 適さない状態 ❏ *When*

you left our place, you weren't in a fit state to drive. あなたが私達の家を出た時にあなたは運転に適した状態ではなかった. **12** PHRASE 句 If you are **in a state** or if you get **into a state**, you are very upset or nervous about something. 極度の緊張状態 ❏ *I was in a terrible state because nobody could understand why I had this illness.* 私がこの病気にかかった理由を誰も理解できなかったため, 私はひどい状態にいた. **13** PHRASE 句 If the dead body of an important person **lies in state**, it is publicly displayed for a few days before it is buried. 公式に安置される ❏ ...*the 30,000 people who filed past the cardinal's body while it lay in state last week.* 先週公式に安置された枢機卿の遺体を弔問した3万人の人々
→ see **matter**

State De|part|ment N-PROPER 固有名詞 In the United States, the **State Department** is the government department that is concerned with foreign affairs. 国務省 ❏ *Officials at the State Department say the issue is urgent.* 国務省の職員はその問題が緊急を要すると言っている.

state|ment /steɪtmənt/ (**statements**) **1** N-COUNT 可算名詞 A **statement** is something that you say or write which gives information in a formal or definite way. 述べたこと ❏ *Andrew now disowns that statement, saying he was depressed when he made it.* アンドリューは今, 気が滅入っていたことを理由に言ったことを取り消している. **2** N-COUNT 可算名詞 A **statement** is an official or formal announcement that is issued on a particular occasion. 声明 ❏ *The statement by the military denied any involvement in last night's attack.* 軍は昨夜の攻撃への関与を否定する声明を発表した. **3** N-COUNT 可算名詞 You can refer to the official account of events which a suspect or a witness gives to the police as a **statement**. 陳述 ❏ *The 350-page report was based on statements from witnesses to the events.* 350ページの報告書は事件の証人による陳述に基づいていた. **4** N-COUNT 可算名詞 If you describe an action or thing as a **statement**, you mean that it clearly expresses a particular opinion or idea that you have. 主張 ❏ *The following recipe is a statement of another kind - food is fun!* 次のレシピは「食べ物は楽しい」という別の種類の主張である. **5** N-COUNT 可算名詞 A printed document showing how much money has been paid into and taken out of a bank or investment account is called a **statement**. 口座収支報告書 ❏ ...*the address at the top of your monthly statement.* 毎月の口座収支報告書の上部の住所
→ see **bank**

state of af|fairs N-SING 単数名詞 If you refer to a particular **state of affairs**, you mean the general situation and circumstances connected with someone or something. 情勢 ❏ *Some say this state of affairs just can't last.* この情勢は続かないと言う人もいる.

state of mind (**states of mind**) N-COUNT 可算名詞 Your **state of mind** is your mood or mental state at a particular time. 精神状態 ❏ *I want you to get into a whole new state of mind.* 私はあなたに全く新しい精神状態になってもらいたい.

state-of-the-art ADJ 形容詞 If you describe something as **state-of-the-art**, you mean that it is the best available because it has been made using the most modern techniques and technology. 最新式の ❏ ...*the production of state-of-the-art military equipment.* 最新技術を結集した軍の設備
→ see **technology**

state school (**state schools**) **1** N-COUNT 可算名詞 In the United States, a **state school** is a college or university that is part of the public education system provided by the state government. 州立学校 ❏ *At all 14 state schools, tuition and fees are going up this fall by an average of about 10 percent.* 州立学校全14校の学費は今秋平均して約10%引き上げられる. **2** N-COUNT 可算名詞 A **state school** is the same as a **public school**. 公立学校 [BRIT 英国英語]

states|man /steɪtsmən/ (**statesmen**) N-COUNT 可算名詞 A

statesman is an important and experienced politician, especially one who is widely known and respected. 政治家 ❑*Hamilton is a great statesman and political thinker.* ハミルトンは偉大な政治的な思想家である と共に偉大な政治家であった.

state troop|er (**state troopers**) N-COUNT 可算名詞 In the U.S., a **state trooper** is a member of the police force in one of the states. 州警察の警官 [AM 米国英語] ❑*State troopers said the truck driver was going too fast when he lost control.* 州警察の警官はハンドル を切り損ねた時、トラックの運転手はスピードを出しすぎていたと述 べた.

state uni|ver|sity (**state universities**) N-COUNT 可算名詞 A **state university** is the same as a **state school**. 州立大学 [AM 米国 英語] ❑*He was a professor at the local state university.* 彼は地元の州立 大学の教授だった.

stat|ic /stǽtɪk/ **1** ADJ 形容詞 Something that is **static** does not move or change. ほとんど変化しない ❑*The number of young people obtaining qualifications has remained static or decreased.* 資格を取得する若者の数はほとんど変化しないか、減少した. **2** N-UNCOUNT 不可算名詞 **Static** or **static electricity** is electricity which can be caused by things rubbing against each other and which collects on things such as your clothes or metal objects. 静電気 ❑*When the weather turns cold and dry, my clothes develop a static problem.* 寒くて乾燥している時には洋服に静電気が起こ る. **3** N-UNCOUNT 不可算名詞 If there is **static** on the radio or television, you hear a series of loud noises which spoils the sound. 空電による雑音 ❑*After only a minute an authoritative voice came through the static on the radio.* ほんの1分後に権威ぶった声がラジ オの雑音越しに聞こえた.

sta|tion /stéɪʃ^ən/ (**stations, stationing, stationed**) **1** N-COUNT 可算名詞 A **station** or a **train station** is a building by a railroad track where trains stop so that people can get on or off. 駅 ❑*Ingrid went with him to the train station to see him off.* イングリッドは彼 を鉄道駅まで見送った. **2** N-COUNT 可算名詞 A **bus station** is a building, usually in a town or city, where buses stop, usually for a while, so that people can get on or off. 停留所 ❑*I walked the two miles back to the bus station and bought a ticket home.* 私はバス の停留所まで2マイル戻り、家までの切符を買った. **3** N-COUNT 可算名詞 If you talk about a particular radio or television **station**, you are referring to the company that broadcasts programs. 放送局 ❑*...an independent local radio station.* 独立した地元のラジオ局. **4** V-T PASSIVE 受動態他動詞 If soldiers or officials **are stationed** in a place, they are sent there to do a job or to work for a period of time. 駐屯する ❑*Reports from the capital, Lome, say troops are stationed on the streets.* 首都ロメからの報告によると、軍隊は街路に 駐屯している. **5** → see also **gas station, police station, power station, service station, space station** → see **cellphone, radio, satellite, television**

sta|tion|ary /stéɪʃəneri/ ADJ 形容詞 Something that is **stationary** is not moving. 静止している ❑*Stationary cars in traffic jams cause a great deal of pollution.* 渋滞で動かない車は大量の大気汚 染の原因となる.

sta|tion|ery /stéɪʃəneri/ N-UNCOUNT 不可算名詞 **Stationery** is paper, envelopes, and other materials or equipment used for writing. 文房具 ❑*...envelopes and other office stationery.* 封筒など の文房具 → see **office**

sta|tion wag|on (**station wagons**) N-COUNT 可算名詞 A **station wagon** is a car with a long body, a door at the rear, and space behind the back seats. ステーションワゴン [AM 米国英語] → see **car**

sta|tis|tic /stətístɪk/ (**statistics**) **1** N-COUNT 可算名 詞 **Statistics** are facts which are obtained from analyzing information expressed in numbers, for example information about the number of times that something happens. 統計 ❑*Official statistics show real wages declining by 24%.* 公式の統計によ ると、実質賃金は24%減少した. **2** N-UNCOUNT 不可算名詞 **Statistics** is a branch of mathematics concerned with the study of information that is expressed in numbers. 統計学 ❑*...a professor of mathematical statistics.* 数理統計学の教授

sta|tis|ti|cal /stətístɪk^əl/ ADJ 形容詞 **Statistical** means relating to the use of statistics. 統計の ❑*The report contains a great deal of statistical information.* そのリポートには大量の統計的情報が含まれ ている. ●**sta|tis|ti|cal|ly** /stətístɪkli/ ADV 副詞 統計的に ❑*The results are not statistically significant.* 決果は統計的には重要ではない.

stat|ue /stǽtʃu/ (**statues**) N-COUNT 可算名詞 A **statue** is a large sculpture of a person or an animal, made of stone or metal. 彫像 ❑*...a bronze statue of an Arabian horse.* アラブ馬のブロンズの 彫像

stat|ure /stǽtʃər/ **1** N-UNCOUNT 不可算名詞 Someone's **stature** is their height. 身長 ❑*It's more than his physical stature that makes him remarkable.* 彼が目立つ理由は身長だけではない. ❑*Mother was of very small stature, barely five feet tall.* 母の身長は5フィートにや っと達するくらいで、大変小柄だった. **2** N-UNCOUNT 不可算名詞 The **stature** of a person is the importance and reputation that they have. 才能 ❑*Who can deny his stature as the world's greatest cellist?* 世 界で最も偉大なチェロ演奏者としての彼の才能を誰が否定できようか.

sta|tus /stéɪtəs, stǽt-/ **1** N-UNCOUNT 不可算名詞 Your **status** is your social or professional position. 地位 ❑*People of higher status tend to use certain drugs.* 高い地位を持つ人々は特定の麻薬を使う 傾向がある. ❑*...women and men of wealth and status.* 財産家で重要人 物の男女 **2** N-UNCOUNT 不可算名詞 **Status** is the importance and respect that someone has among the public or a particular group. 信望 ❑*Nurses are undervalued, and they never enjoy the same status as doctors.* 看護婦は過小評価されており、医者と同じ信望を享受すること は決してない. **3** N-UNCOUNT 不可算名詞 The **status** of something is the importance that people give it. 重要性 ❑*Those things that can be assessed by external tests are being given unduly high status.* 外部のテ ストで評価される事柄は過度に重視されている. **4** N-UNCOUNT 不可 算名詞 A particular **status** is an official description that says what category a person, organization, or place belongs to, and gives them particular rights or advantages. 地位 ❑*The Snoqualmie tribe regained its status as a federally recognized tribe.* スノークアルミー族は 連邦政府に認可された民族としての地位を取り戻した. **5** N-UNCOUNT 不可算名詞 The **status** of something is its state of affairs at a particular time. 状態 ❑*The council unanimously directed city staff to prepare a status report on the project.* 協議会は満場一致で市の職員にそ のプロジェクトの情勢リポートを作成するよう指示した.

sta|tus quo /stéɪtəs kwóʊ, stǽt-/ N-SING 単数名詞 The **status quo** is the state of affairs that exists at a particular time, especially in contrast to a different possible state of affairs. 現状 ❑*By 492 votes to 391, the federation voted to maintain the status quo.* 連 邦政府は492対391で現状を維持することに投票した.

stat|ute /stǽtʃut/ (**statutes**) N-VAR 可変性名詞 A **statute** is a rule or law which has been made by a government or other organization and formally written down. 制定法 ❑*The new statute covers the care for, raising, and protection of children.* 新しい制定法には 子供の養育と保護が含まれる.

statu|tory /stǽtʃutɔri/ ADJ 形容詞 **Statutory** means relating to rules or laws which have been formally written down. 制定 法の [FORMAL 形式ばった] ❑*The FCC has no statutory authority to regulate the Internet.* FCCにはインターネットを規制する制定法による 権限はない.

staunch /stɔntʃ/ (**stauncher, staunchest**) ADJ 形容 詞 A **staunch** supporter or believer is very loyal to a person, organization, or set of beliefs, and supports them strongly. 忠実 な ❑*He's a staunch supporter of controls on government spending.* 彼は 政府支出の管理を忠実に支援している. ●**staunch|ly** ADV 副詞 揺るぎ なく ❑*He was staunchly opposed to a public confession.* 彼は人前での告 白に断固反対した.

stay /stéɪ/ (**stays, staying, stayed**) **1** V-I 自動詞 If you **stay** where you are, you continue to be there and do not leave. とどま る ❑*"Stay here," Trish said. "I'll bring the car down the drive to take you back."* 「ここにいて」とトリッシュは言った. 「あなたを送るために私 道に車を動かすから」 **2** V-I 自動詞 If you **stay** in a town, or hotel, or at someone's house, you live there for a short time. 滞在す る ❑*Gordon stayed at The Park Hotel, Milan.* ゴードンはミラノのパー クホテルに泊まった. ❑*Can't you stay a few more days?* あと数日滞在 できませんか. ● N-COUNT 可算名詞 **Stay** is also a noun. ❑*An experienced Indian guide is provided during your stay.* 経験豊富なインド 人のガイドがあなたの滞在中にお世話します. **3** V-LINK 連結動詞 If someone or something **stays** in a particular state or situation, they continue to be in it. とどまる ❑*The Republican candidate said he would "work like crazy to stay ahead."* 共和党の候補者は「前方にとど まるために夢中になって働く」だろうと言った. ❑*...community care networks that offer classes on how to stay healthy.* 健康を維持する方法 についてのコースを提供する地域社会ケアネットワーク **4** V-I 自動 詞 If you **stay away from** a place, you do not go there. 離れている ❑*Management also stayed away from work during the strike.* 経営陣もス

トライキ中に作業に携わらなかった. **5** V-I 自動詞 If you **stay out of** something, you do not get involved in it. 干渉しない □ *In the past, the U.N. has stayed out of the internal affairs of countries unless invited in.* 国連は以前, 招待されない限り国の内部情勢に干渉しなかった. **6** PHRASE 句 If you **stay put**, you remain somewhere. 動かずにい る □ *He was forced by his condition to stay put and remain out of politics.* 彼は病気のために動かずに政治から離れていることを余儀なくされた. **7** PHRASE 句 If you **stay the night** in a place, you sleep there for one night. 泊まる □ *They had invited me to come to supper and stay the night.* 彼らは泊りがけで夕食に来るよう私を誘った.

▶ **stay in** PHRASAL VERB 句動詞 If you **stay in** during the evening, you remain at home and do not go out. 家にいる □ *If I stay in, my boyfriend cooks a wonderful lasagne or chicken or steak.* 外出しない時は私のボーイフレンドが美味しいラザニアまたはチキンまたはステーキを作ってくれる.

▶ **stay on** PHRASAL VERB 句動詞 If you **stay on** somewhere, you remain there after other people have left or after the time when you were going to leave. 残る □ *He had managed to arrange to stay on in Adelaide.* 彼はアデレードに残ることをどうにかして手配した.

▶ **stay out** PHRASAL VERB 句動詞 If you **stay out** at night, you remain away from home, especially when you are expected to be there. 家に帰らない □ *That was the first time Elliot stayed out all night.* それはエリオットが初めて一晩中家に帰らなかった時だった.

▶ **stay up** PHRASAL VERB 句動詞 If you **stay up**, you remain out of bed at a time when most people have gone to bed or at a time when you are normally in bed yourself. 寝ずに起きている □ *I used to stay up late with my mom and watch movies.* 私はよくお母さんと一緒に夜遅くまで映画を見ていたものだ.

stead /stɛd/ □ PHRASE 句 If you say that something will **stand** someone **in good stead**, you mean that it will be very useful to them in the future. 大いに役に立つ □ *These two games here will stand them in good stead for the future.* これらの2つのゲームは将来役に立つだろう.

stead|fast /stɛdfæst/ ADJ 形容詞 If someone is **steadfast in** something that they are doing, they are convinced that what they are doing is right and they refuse to change it or to give up. 断固とした □ *He remained steadfast in his belief that he had done the right thing.* 彼は自分がしたことは正しいという信念を貫いた.

stead|y /stɛdi/ (**steadier, steadiest, steadies, steadying, steadied**) □ ADJ 形容詞 A **steady** situation continues or develops gradually without any interruptions and is not likely to change quickly. 徐々の, 安定した □ *Despite the steady progress of building work, the campaign against it is still going strong.* 建設が徐々に進んでいるにもかかわらず, 反対運動は依然として活発だ. □ *The improvement in standards has been steady and persistent, but has attracted little comment from educationalists.* 教育水準の改善は安定して持続してきたが, 教育専門家からの批判はほとんどない. ● **stead|i|ly** /stɛdɪli/ ADV 副詞 [ADV with v] 徐々に, 安定して □ *Relax as much as possible and keep breathing steadily.* できるだけリラックスをして安定した呼吸を続けなさい. **2** ADJ 形容詞 If an object is **steady**, it is firm and does not shake or move around. 安定した, ぐらつかない □ *Get as close to the subject as you can and hold the camera steady.* 被写体にできるだけ近づいてカメラをしっかりと持ちなさい. **3** ADJ 形容詞 If you look at someone or speak to them in a **steady** way, you look or speak in a calm, controlled way. 落ち着いた □ *"Well, go on," said Camilla, her voice fairly steady.* 「じゃあ, 続けて」とカミラはかなり落ち着いた声で言った. ● **stead|i|ly** ADV 副詞 [ADV after v] 落ち着いて □ *He moved back a little and stared steadily at Elaine.* 彼は少し後ろに下がってイレインを落ち着いて見つめた. **4** ADJ 形容詞 If you describe a person as **steady**, you mean that they are sensible and reliable. 頼りになる □ *He was firm and steady unlike other men she knew.* 彼女が知っているほかの男性と違って, 彼はしっかりしていて頼りがいがあった. **5** V-T/V-I 他動詞/自動詞 If you **steady** something or if it **steadies**, it stops shaking or moving around. 安定させる, しっかりと支える [他動詞] □ *Get up* 安定する, 動かなくなる [自動詞] □ *Two men were on the bridge-deck, steadying a ladder.* 2人の男が船橋楼甲板ではしごをしっかり支えていた. **6** V-T 他動詞 If you **steady yourself**, you control your voice or expression, so that people will think that you are calm and not nervous. 落ち着かせる □ *Somehow she steadied herself and murmured, "Have you got a cigarette?"* 彼女はどうにか落ち着きを取り戻して小声で言った. 「たばこはある?」

Thesaurus steady また次を参照:

ADJ. consistent, continuous, uninterrupted **1**
constant, fixed, stable **2**
calm, cool, reserved, sedate **3**

S

Word Partnership steady は次の語句と使われる:

N. steady **decline/increase**, steady **diet**, steady **growth**, steady **improvement**, steady **income**, steady **progress**, steady **rain**, steady **rate**, steady **supply** **1**
V. **remain** steady **1 4**
hold/keep something steady **2**
hold steady **5**

steak /steɪk/ (**steaks**) □ N-VAR 可変性名詞 A **steak** is a large flat piece of beef without much fat on it. You cook it by grilling or frying it. ステーキ, ビーフステーキ □ *a steak sizzling on the grill.* グリルでジュージューと焼けているステーキ **2** N-COUNT 可算名詞 A fish **steak** is a large piece of fish that contains few bones. 切り身 □ *...fresh salmon steaks.* 新鮮なサケの切り身

steal /stiːl/ (**steals, stealing, stole, stolen**) □ V-T/V-I 他動詞/自動詞 If you **steal** something **from** someone, you take it away from them without their permission and without intending to return it. 盗む □ *He was accused of stealing a small boy's bicycle.* 彼は小さな男の子の自転車を盗んだと非難された. □ *People who are drug addicts come in and steal.* 麻薬中毒者がやってきて盗みを働く. ● **sto|len** ADJ 形容詞 盗まれた □ *We have now found the stolen car.* すでに盗難車を発見した. **2** V-T 他動詞 If you **steal** someone else's ideas, you pretend that they are your own. 盗用する □ *A writer is suing director Steven Spielberg for allegedly stealing his film idea.* 作家がスティーブン・スピルバーグ監督を映画の原案を盗用したという罪で訴えている.

Do not confuse **steal** and **rob**. If someone **steals** something, for example, money or a car, they take it without asking and without intending to give it back. □ *My car was stolen on Friday evening.* Note that you cannot say that someone **steals** someone. If someone **robs** someone or somewhere, they take something, often violently, from that person or place without asking and without intending to give it back. □ *They planned to rob an old widow... They joined forces to rob a factory.* You can also say that someone **robs** you of something when referring to what has been taken. □ *The two men were robbed of more than $700.*

Thesaurus steal また次を参照:

V. burglarize, embezzle, swipe, take **1**

steam /stiːm/ (**steams, steaming, steamed**) □ N-UNCOUNT 不可算名詞 **Steam** is the hot mist that forms when water boils. **Steam** vehicles and machines are operated using steam as a means of power. 蒸気 □ *In an electric power plant the heat converts water into high-pressure steam.* 発電所では熱が水を高圧蒸気に変える. **2** V-I 自動詞 If something **steams**, it gives off steam. 蒸気を上げる □ *...restaurants where coffee pots steamed on their burners.* コーヒーポットから湯気が出ているレストラン **3** V-T/V-I 他動詞/自動詞 If you **steam** food or if it **steams**, you cook it in steam rather than in water. 蒸す □ *Steam the carrots until they are just beginning to be tender.* ニンジンがちょうど柔らかくなりかけるまで蒸しなさい. □ *Leave the vegetables to steam over the rice for the 20 minutes' cooking time.* 野菜を米の上に載せたまま20分間蒸しなさい. **4** PHRASE 句 If something such as a plan or a project goes **full steam ahead**, it progresses quickly. 全力で □ *The administration was determined to go full steam ahead with its reform program.* 政府は改革計画を全力で推し進める意思を固くしていた. **5** PHRASE 句 If you **run out of steam**, you stop doing something because you have no more energy or enthusiasm left. 力尽きる, 嫌になる [INFORMAL くだけた] □ *I decided to paint the bathroom ceiling but ran out of steam halfway through.* お風呂の天井のペンキ塗りをすると決めたが, 途中で嫌になった.

→ see cook, train

▶ **steam up** PHRASAL VERB 句動詞 When a window, mirror, or pair of glasses **steams up**, it becomes covered with steam or mist. 湯気で曇る □ *...the irritation of living with lenses that steam up when you come in from the cold.* 寒いところから中に入るとレンズが曇るのを我慢するいらだち

Word Partnership steam は次の語句と使われる:

N. steam **bath**, clouds of steam, steam **engine**, steam **locomotive**, steam **pipes**, steam **turbine** **1**
ADJ. steam **powered**, **rising** steam **1**

steamy /stiːmi/ □ ADJ 形容詞 **Steamy** means involving exciting sex. 熱々の, ホットな [INFORMAL くだけた] □ *He'd had a steamy affair with an office colleague.* 彼は会社の同僚と熱々の不倫関係を持った. **2** ADJ 形容詞 A **steamy** place has hot, wet air. 湯気でもうもうとした □ *...a steamy cafe.* 湯気が立ち込めているカフェ

steel /stiːl/ (**steels, steeling, steeled**) □ N-MASS 質量名詞 **Steel** is a very strong metal which is made mainly from iron. Steel is

used for making many things, for example, bridges, buildings, vehicles, and flatware. 鋼鉄，スチール ❏ ...steel pipes. 鋼管 ❏ ...the iron and steel industry. 鉄鋼業 ❷ → see also **stainless steel** ❸ V-T 他動詞 If you **steel yourself**, you prepare to deal with something unpleasant. 覚悟を決める ❏ Those involved are steeling themselves for the coming battle. 関係者は来るべき戦いへの覚悟を決めている.
→ see **bridge, train**

steely /stíːli/ ADJ 形容詞 **Steely** is used to emphasize that a person is strong and determined. 決然とした [EMPHASIS 強調] ❏ Clad in their black sweatsuits, the Maryland players had a steely determination. 黒のスウェットスーツを身につけて，メリーランドの選手たちは決然としていた.

steep /stíːp/ (**steeper, steepest**) ❶ ADJ 形容詞 A **steep** slope rises at a very sharp angle and is difficult to go up. 急な，険しい ❏ San Francisco is built on 40 hills and some are very steep. サンフランシスコは40の丘の上に建設されていてとても急な坂もある.
● **steep|ly** ADV 副詞 [ADV with v] 急（角度）に ❏ The road climbs steeply, with good views of Orvieto through the trees. 道は急勾配（こうばい）の上り坂で，木々の間から見えるオルビエトの町の景観がすてきだ. ❏ ...steeply terraced valleys. 急傾斜で段々になっている谷間 ❷ ADJ 形容詞 A **steep** increase or decrease in something is a very big increase or decrease. 急な，大幅な ❏ Consumers are rebelling at steep price increases. 消費者は物価高騰に反逆しています.
● **steep|ly** ADV 副詞 急に，大幅に ❏ Unemployment is rising steeply. 失業率が急増している. ❸ ADJ 形容詞 If you say that the price of something is **steep**, you mean that it is expensive. 高い [INFORMAL くだけた] ❏ The annual premium can be a little steep, but will be well worth it if your dog is injured. 年間保険料はやや高いが，飼い犬がけがをした場合十分に価値がある.

steeped /stíːpt/ ADJ 形容詞 If a place or person is **steeped in** a quality or characteristic, they are surrounded by it or deeply influenced by it. 包まれている，染まっている [v-link ADJ "in" n] ❏ The castle is steeped in history and legend. その城には歴史と伝説が染み込んでいる.

steer /stíər/ (**steers, steering, steered**) ❶ V-T 他動詞 When you **steer** a car, boat, or plane, you control it so that it goes in the direction that you want. 操縦する ❏ What is it like to steer a ship this size? このサイズの船を操縦するのはどのような感じですか? ❷ V-T 他動詞 If you **steer** people toward a particular course of action or attitude, you try to lead them gently in that direction. 一の方向に導く ❏ The new government is seen as one that will steer the country in the right direction. 新政府は国を正しい方向に導くものだと見なされている. ❸ V-T 他動詞 If you **steer** someone in a particular direction, you guide them there. 案内する ❏ Nick steered them into the nearest seats. ニックは彼らを最も近い席に案内した. ❹ PHRASE 句 If you **steer clear of** someone or something, you deliberately avoid them. 一を避ける，一に近づかないようにする ❏ I think a lot of people, women in particular, steer clear of these sensitive issues. 多くの人々が，特に女性は，このようなデリケートな問題を避けると思う.

steer|ing wheel (**steering wheels**) N-COUNT 可算名詞 In a car or other vehicle, the **steering wheel** is the wheel which the driver holds when he or she is driving. ハンドル

stem /stém/ (**stems, stemming, stemmed**) ❶ V-I 自動詞 If a condition or problem **stems from** something, it was caused originally by that thing. 一に由来する ❏ All my problems stem from drink. 私のすべての問題は本を正せば飲酒が原因だ. ❷ V-T 他動詞 If you **stem** something, you stop it spreading, increasing, or continuing. 食い止める，抑える [FORMAL 形式ばった] ❏ Austria has sent three army battalions to its border with Hungary to stem the flow of illegal immigrants. オーストリアは不法入国者の流入を食い止めるために陸軍大隊3団をハンガリーとの国境に派遣した. ❸ N-COUNT 可算名詞 The **stem** of a plant is the thin, upright part on which the flowers and leaves grow. 茎 ❏ He stooped down, cut the stem for her with his knife and handed her the flower. 彼は前かがみになって自分のナイフで彼女のために茎を切り，花を彼女に渡した.

Word Partnership	stem は次の語句と使われる:
N.	charges stem from *something*, problems stem from *something* ❶
	stem the flow of *something*, stem losses, stem the tide of *something* ❷

stem cell (**stem cells**) N-COUNT 可算名詞 A **stem cell** is a type of cell that can produce other cells which are able to develop into any kind of cell in the body. 幹細胞 ❏ Stem cell research is supported by many doctors. 幹細胞研究は多くの医者に支持されている.

stench /sténtʃ/ (**stenches**) N-COUNT 可算名詞 A **stench** is a strong and very unpleasant smell. 悪臭 ❏ The stench of burning rubber was overpowering. ゴムを焼却する悪臭がすごかった.

sten|cil /sténsəl/ (**stencils, stenciling** or **stencilling, stenciled**

or **stencilled**) ❶ N-COUNT 可算名詞 A **stencil** is a piece of paper, plastic, or metal which has a design cut out of it. You place the stencil on a surface and paint it so that paint goes through the holes and leaves a design on the surface. ステンシル ❷ V-T 他動詞 If you **stencil** a design or if you **stencil** a surface **with** a design, you put a design on a surface using a stencil. ステンシルで刷る ❏ He then stenciled the ceiling with a moon and stars motif. そして彼はステンシルで天井に月や星のモチーフを刷った.

step /stép/ (**steps, stepping, stepped**) ❶ N-COUNT 可算名詞 If you take a **step**, you lift your foot and put it down in a different place, for example when you are walking. 1歩 ❏ I took a step toward him. 私は彼の方に1歩近寄った. ❏ She walked on a few steps. 彼女は数歩歩いた. ❷ V-I 自動詞 If you **step on** something or **step in** a particular direction, you put your foot on the thing or move your foot in that direction. 踏む，踏み出す ❏ This was the moment when Neil Armstrong became the first man to step on the Moon. これが，人類で初めてニール・アームストロングが月面に踏み立つ瞬間だった. ❏ She accidentally stepped on his foot on a crowded commuter train. 彼女は込み合った通勤電車の中でうっかり彼の足を踏んづけた. ❸ N-COUNT 可算名詞 **Steps** are a series of surfaces at increasing or decreasing heights, on which you put your feet in order to walk up or down to a different level. 段，階段 ❏ This little room was along a passage and down some steps. その小さい部屋は通路を抜けて行から数段下りたところにあった. ❹ N-COUNT 可算名詞 A **step** is a raised flat surface in front of a door. （戸口の）上がり段 ❏ A little girl was sitting on the step of the end house. 小さな女の子がテラスハウスの端の家の戸口で座っていた. ❺ → see also **doorstep** ❻ N-COUNT 可算名詞 A **step** is one of a series of actions that you take in order to achieve something. 措置，一歩 ❏ He greeted the agreement as the first step toward peace. 彼は和平に向けての第一歩として合意を歓迎した. ❼ N-COUNT 可算名詞 A **step** in a process is one of a series of stages. 段階 ❏ The next step is to put the theory into practice. 次の段階は理論を実行に移すことだ. ❽ N-COUNT 可算名詞 The **steps** of a dance are the sequences of foot movements which make it up. ステップ ❏ She was a better dancer than Gordon. At least she knew the steps. 彼女のダンスはゴードンよりも上手だった. 少なくとも彼女はステップを知っていた. ❾ N-SING 単数名詞 Someone's **step** is the way they walk. 足取り，歩き方 ❏ He quickened his step. 彼は足取りを早めた. ❿ PHRASE 句 If you stay **one step ahead of** someone or something, you manage to achieve more than they do or avoid competition or danger from them. 一の一歩先 ❏ Successful travel is partly a matter of keeping one step ahead of the crowd. よい旅行とはある程度は他の観光客より一歩先んずることだ. ⓫ PHRASE 句 If people who are walking or dancing are **in step**, they are moving their feet forward at exactly the same time as each other. If they are **out of step**, their feet are moving forward at different times. 足並みをそろえて/外して ❏ They were almost the same height and they moved perfectly in step. 彼らはほぼ同じ身長で完全に足並みをそろえていた. ⓬ PHRASE 句 If people are **in step with** each other, their ideas or opinions are the same. If they are **out of step with** each other, their ideas or opinions are different. 考えが一致して/一致しないで ❏ Moscow is anxious to step in step with Washington. モスクワはワシントンと歩調を合わせることを切望している. ⓭ PHRASE 句 If you do something **step by step**, you do it by progressing gradually from one stage to the next. 着実に，一歩一歩 ❏ I am not rushing things and I'm taking it step by step. 慌ててするのではなくて一歩一歩進めている. ⓮ PHRASE 句 If someone tells you to **watch** your **step**, they are warning you to be careful about how you behave or what you say so that you do not get into trouble. 慎重にふるまう ❏ He said I'd come to a bad end, if I didn't watch my step. 気をつけて慎重にふるまわなければひどいことになると，彼は私に警告した.

▸ **step aside** → see **stand down**
▸ **step back** PHRASAL VERB 句動詞 If you **step back** and think about a situation, you think about it as if you were not involved in it. 一歩引く ❏ I stepped back and analyzed the situation. 私は一歩引いて状況を分析した.
▸ **step down** or **step aside** PHRASAL VERB 句動詞 If someone **steps down** or **steps aside**, they resign from an important job or position, often in order to let someone else take their place. 辞任する ❏ Judge Ito said that if his wife was called as a witness, he would step down as trial judge. 伊藤判事は，妻が証人として呼び出されるなら第一審裁判官を辞任すると述べた.
▸ **step in** PHRASAL VERB 句動詞 If you **step in**, you get involved in a difficult situation because you think you can or should help with it. 介入する ❏ If no agreement was reached, the army would step in. もし合意に達しなければ軍が介入するだろう.
▸ **step up** PHRASAL VERB 句動詞 If you **step up** something, you increase it or increase its intensity. 強化する ❏ He urged donors to step up their efforts to send aid to Somalia. 彼は，ソマリアに援助を送るため寄贈者により一層の努力をするよう促した.

Word Partnership

step は次の語句と使われる:

ADV.	step **outside** 2 step **ahead**, step **backward**, step **closer**, step **forward** 2 5 6
N.	step **in a process** 6
ADJ.	**big** step, **bold** step, **giant** step, **the right** step **critical** step, **important** step, **positive** step 5 6

step|brother /stɛpbrʌðər/ (**stepbrothers**) also **step-brother**
N-COUNT 可算名詞 Someone's **stepbrother** is the son of their stepfather or stepmother. 継父/継母の息子

step|daughter /stɛpdɔtər/ (**stepdaughters**) also **step-daughter** N-COUNT 可算名詞 Someone's **stepdaughter** is a daughter that was born to their husband or wife during a previous relationship. まま娘，(女の)連れ子

step|family /stɛpfæmɪli, -fæm/ (**stepfamilies**) N-COUNT 可算名詞 A **stepfamily** is a family that consists of a husband and wife and one or more children from a previous marriage or relationship. 再婚家族 □ Stepfamilies are rapidly becoming the norm, not the exception. 再婚家族は急速に例外ではなく一般的になりつつある。

Word Link

step ≈ related by remarriage : step**father**, step**mother**, step**sister**

step|father /stɛpfɑðər/ (**stepfathers**) also **step-father**
N-COUNT 可算名詞 Someone's **stepfather** is the man who has married their mother after the death or divorce of their father. 継父

step|mother /stɛpmʌðər/ (**stepmothers**) also **step-mother** N-COUNT 可算名詞 Someone's **stepmother** is the woman who has married their father after the death or divorce of their mother. 継母

step|ping stone (**stepping stones**) also **stepping-stone** or **steppingstone** 1 N-COUNT 可算名詞 You can describe a job or event as a **stepping stone** when it helps you to make progress, especially in your career. 足掛かり，布石 □ It is just another stepping stone to bigger and better things. それは，単にさらに大きくさらによいものへの新たな足掛かりに過ぎない。 2 N-COUNT 可算名詞 **Stepping stones** are a line of large stones which you can walk on in order to cross a shallow stream or river. 飛び石

step|sister /stɛpsɪstər/ (**stepsisters**) also **step-sister** N-COUNT 可算名詞 Someone's **stepsister** is the daughter of their stepfather or stepmother. 継父・継母の娘

step|son /stɛpsʌn/ (**stepsons**) also **step-son** N-COUNT 可算名詞 Someone's **stepson** is a son born to their husband or wife during a previous relationship. まま息子，(男の)連れ子

ste|reo /stɛrioʊ, stɪər-/ (**stereos**) 1 ADJ 形容詞 **Stereo** is used to describe a sound system in which the sound is played through two speakers. Compare **mono**. ステレオ □ ...loudspeakers that give all-around stereo sound. オールラウンドなステレオサウンドを出すスピーカー 2 N-COUNT 可算名詞 A **stereo** is a CD player with two speakers. ステレオ

ste|reo|type /stɛriətaɪp, stɪər-/ (**stereotypes, stereotyping, stereotyped**) 1 N-COUNT 可算名詞 A **stereotype** is a fixed general image or set of characteristics that people believe represent a particular type of person or thing. 固定観念，定型イメージ □ There's always a stereotype about successful businessmen. 成功するビジネスマンについて常に定型イメージがあった。 2 V-T 他動詞 If someone **is stereotyped** as something, people form a fixed general idea or image of them, so that it is assumed that they will behave in a particular way. 固定観念で見る [usu passive] □ He was stereotyped by some as a renegade. 彼は裏切り者だと決めつける人もいた。

ste|reo|typi|cal /stɛriətɪpɪkᵊl, stɪər-/ ADJ 形容詞 A **stereotypical** idea of a type of person or thing is a fixed general idea that a lot of people have about it, that may be false in many cases. 典型的な，固定観念的な □ These are men whose masculinity does not conform to stereotypical images of the unfeeling male. これらの男性は，冷酷だという典型的な男性のイメージに合わないタイプだ。

ster|ile /stɛrəl/ 1 ADJ 形容詞 Something that is **sterile** is completely clean and free from germs. 無菌の □ He always made sure that any cuts were protected by sterile dressings. 彼は，切り傷は必ず消毒ガーゼで保護するようにした。 ● **ste|ril|ity** /stərɪləti/ N-UNCOUNT 不可算名詞 無菌状態 □ ...the antiseptic sterility of the hospital. 病院の完璧なほどの無菌状態 2 ADJ 形容詞 A person or animal that is **sterile** is unable to have or produce babies. 不妊の，子供を生めない □ George was sterile. ジョージは無精子だ。 ● **ste|ril|ity** N-UNCOUNT 不可算名詞 不妊 □ This disease causes sterility in both males and females. この病気は男性・女性ともに不妊症の原因となる。

steri|lize /stɛrɪlaɪz/ (**sterilizes, sterilizing, sterilized**) 1 V-T 他動詞 If you **sterilize** a thing or a place, you make it completely clean and free from germs. 殺菌する □ Sulfur is also used to sterilize equipment. 硫黄も器具の殺菌に使用される。 ● **steri|li|za|tion** /stɛrɪlɪzeɪᵊn/ N-UNCOUNT 不可算名詞 殺菌 □ ...the pasteurization and sterilization of milk. 牛乳の低温殺菌と高温殺菌 2 V-T 他動詞 [usu passive] If a person or an animal **is sterilized**, they have a medical operation that makes it impossible for them to have or produce babies. 避妊手術を施す □ My wife was sterilized after the birth of her fourth child. 妻は4人目の子供の出産後に避妊手術を受けた。 ● **steri|li|za|tion** N-VAR 可変性名詞 (**sterilizations**) 避妊手術 □ In some cases, a sterilization is performed through the vaginal wall. 場合によっては，避妊手術は膣壁から行われる。

ster|ling /stɜrlɪŋ/ 1 ADJ 形容詞 **Sterling** means very good in quality; used to describe someone's work or character. すばらしい，優秀な [FORMAL 形式ばった, APPROVAL 賛成] □ Those are sterling qualities to be admired in anyone. それらは称賛されるべき紛れもない資質だ。 2 N-UNCOUNT 不可算名詞 **Sterling** is the money system of Great Britain. 英貨 □ The stamps had to be paid for in sterling. 切手は英貨で支払わなければならなかった。

stern /stɜrn/ (**sterner, sternest**) 1 ADJ 形容詞 **Stern** words or actions are very severe. 厳しい，重大な □ Mr. Monroe issued a stern warning to those who persist in violence. モンロー氏は暴力に固執する者に対して厳重な警告を出した。 ● **stern|ly** ADV 副詞 厳しく □ "We will take the necessary steps," she said sternly. 「我々は必要な措置を講じます」と彼女は厳格に述べた。 2 ADJ 形容詞 Someone who is **stern** is very serious and strict. いかめしい，厳しい □ Her father was stern and hard to please. 彼女の父親はいかめしくて気難しかった。

ster|oid /stɪrɔɪd, stɛr-/ (**steroids**) N-COUNT 可算名詞 A **steroid** is a type of chemical substance found in your body. Steroids can be artificially introduced into the bodies of athletes to improve their strength. ステロイド

stew /stu/ (**stews, stewing, stewed**) 1 N-VAR 可変性名詞 A **stew** is a meal which you make by cooking meat and vegetables in liquid at a low temperature. シチュー □ She served him a bowl of beef stew. 彼女は彼にビーフシチューを出した。 2 V-T 他動詞 When you **stew** meat, vegetables, or fruit, you cook them slowly in liquid in a covered pot. とろ火で煮込む □ Stew the apple and blackberries to make a thick pulp. リンゴとブラックベリーをどろどろになるまでとろ火で煮込みなさい。

stew|ard /stuərd/ (**stewards**) 1 N-COUNT 可算名詞 A **steward** is a man who works on a ship, plane, or train, taking care of passengers and serving meals to them. 男性客室乗務員 2 N-COUNT 可算名詞 A **steward** is a man or woman who helps to organize a race, march, or other public event. 世話役，幹事 □ The steward at the march stood his ground while the rest of the marchers decided to run. 行進の幹事は，残りの行進者が逃げると決めても1人行進を続けた。

stew|ard|ess /stuərdɪs/ (**stewardesses**) N-COUNT 可算名詞 A **stewardess** is a woman who works on a ship, plane, or train, taking care of passengers and serving meals to them. 女性客室乗務員，スチュワーデス

stick

❶ NOUN USES
❷ VERB USES

❶ **stick** /stɪk/ (**sticks**) 1 N-COUNT 可算名詞 A **stick** is a thin branch which has fallen off a tree. 小枝 □ ...people carrying bundles of dried sticks to sell for firewood. 薪として売るために枯れた枝の束を抱えている人々 2 N-COUNT 可算名詞 A **stick** is a long thin piece of wood which is used for a particular purpose. 棒 □ ...lollipop sticks. ペロペロキャンディの棒 □ ...drum sticks. ドラムスティック 3 N-COUNT 可算名詞 Some long thin objects that are used in sports are called **sticks**. スティック □ ...lacrosse sticks. ラクロスのスティック □ ...hockey sticks. ホッケーのスティック 4 N-COUNT 可算名詞 A **stick** of something is a long thin piece of it. 棒状のもの □ ...a stick of celery. セロリスティック 5 N-COUNT 可算名詞 A **stick** is a long thin piece of wood which is used for supporting someone's weight or for hitting people or animals. つえ [BRIT 英国英語; AM cane 米国英語 cane] 6 PHRASE 句 If someone **gets the wrong end of the stick** or **gets hold of the wrong end of the stick**, they do not understand something correctly and get the wrong idea about it. すっかり勘違いする [INFORMAL くだけた] □ I think someone has got the wrong end of the stick. They should have established the facts before speaking out. 誰かが勘違いしたんだと思う。声を上げる前に事実を確認するべきだった。
→ see **drawing**

❷ **stick** /stɪk/ (**sticks, sticking, stuck**) 1 V-T 他動詞 If you **stick** something somewhere, you put it there in a rather casual way. 置く，突っ込む [INFORMAL くだけた] □ He folded the papers and stuck them in his desk drawer. 彼はその書類を折って机の引き出しに突っ込んだ。 2 V-T/V-I 他動詞/自動詞 If you **stick** a pointed object **in**

something, or if it **sticks in** something, it goes into it or through it by making a cut or hole. 刺す [他動詞], 刺さる [自動詞] ❑ *They sent in loads of male nurses and stuck a needle in my back.* 何人もの看護士が来て背中に針を刺したんだ. ❸ V-I 自動詞 If something **is sticking out** from a surface or object, it extends up or away from it. If something **is sticking into** a surface or object, it is partly in it. 出ている, 刺さっている ❑ *They lay where they had fallen from the crane, sticking out of the water.* クレーンから落ちたところにころがって, 水から出ている. ❹ V-T 他動詞 If you **stick** one thing to another, you attach it using glue, Scotch tape, or another sticky substance. 張る, くっつける ❑ *Don't forget to clip the token and stick it on your card.* トークンを切り抜いてはがきに張るのを忘れないように. ❺ V-I 自動詞 If one thing **sticks to** another, it becomes attached to it and is difficult to remove. くっつく ❑ *The soil sticks to the blade and blocks the plow.* 土が刃にくっついてすきが詰まる. ❑ *Peel away the waxed paper if it has stuck to the bottom of the cake.* ケーキの底にパラフィン紙がくっついていれば, それをはがしなさい. ❻ V-I 自動詞 If something **sticks in** your mind, you remember it for a long time. 頭から離れない ❑ *The incident stuck in my mind because it was the first example I had seen of racism in that country.* その国で見た人種差別の最初の例としてその事件は頭から離れなかった. ❼ V-I 自動詞 If something which can usually be moved **sticks**, it becomes fixed in one position. 動かなくなる ❑ *The needle on the dial went right around to fifty feet, which was as far as it could go, and there it stuck.* 指針盤の針が50フィート辺りまで回り, それ以上は動かなくなった. ❽ → see also **stuck**

Word Partnership	*stick* は次の語句と使われる:
PREP.	stick out ❷ ❸
	stick to *something* ❷ ❺
ADV.	stick together ❷ ❺

▶ **stick around** PHRASAL VERB 句動詞 If you **stick around**, you stay where you are, often because you are waiting for something. もうちょっといる [INFORMAL くだけた] ❑ *Stick around a while and see what develops.* もうちょっといて様子を見よう.

▶ **stick by** ❶ PHRASAL VERB 句動詞 If you **stick by** someone, you continue to give them help or support. 支えとなる ❑ *...friends who stuck by me during the difficult times.* つらいときに私を支えてくれた友達 ❷ PHRASAL VERB 句動詞 If you **stick by** a promise, agreement, decision, or principle, you do what you said you would do, or do not change your mind. 貫く, 実行する ❑ *But I made my decision then and stuck by it.* しかし私はそのとき決心をして, それを実行した.

▶ **stick out** ❶ PHRASAL VERB 句動詞 If you **stick out** part of your body, you extend it away from your body. 突き出す ❑ *She made a face and stuck out her tongue at him.* 彼女はおどけた顔をして彼に向かって舌を出した. ❷ to **stick** your **neck out** → see **neck** ❸ PHRASAL VERB 句動詞 If something **sticks out**, it is very noticeable because it is unusual. 目立つ ❑ *What had Cutter done to make him stick out from the crowd?* カッターは群衆から目立つために何をしたんだ? ❹ PHRASE 句 If someone in an unpleasant or difficult situation **sticks it out**, they do not leave or give up. がまんする, 癪り続ける ❑ *I really didn't like New York, but I wanted to stick it out a little bit longer.* あまりニューヨークは好きではなかったが, もう少し癪り続けたかった.

▶ **stick to** ❶ PHRASAL VERB 句動詞 If you **stick to** something or someone when you are traveling, you stay close to them. 一から離れない ❑ *Let's stick to the road we know.* 知っている道を行こう. ❷ PHRASAL VERB 句動詞 If you **stick to** something, you continue doing, using, saying, or talking about it, rather than changing to something else. 続ける ❑ *Perhaps he should have stuck to writing.* おそらく彼は執筆を続けるべきでした. ❸ PHRASAL VERB 句動詞 If you **stick to** a promise, agreement, decision, or principle, you do what you said you would do, or do not change your mind. やり通す, 貫く ❑ *Immigrant support groups are waiting to see if he sticks to his word.* 移民支援団体は, 彼が約束を守るかどうかを見守っています. ❹ to **stick to** your **guns** → see **gun**

▶ **stick together** PHRASAL VERB 句動詞 If people **stick together**, they stay with each other and support each other. 支え合う ❑ *If we all stick together, we ought to be okay.* 私たちみんなが協力し合えば, きっと大丈夫だ.

▶ **stick up for** PHRASAL VERB 句動詞 If you **stick up for** a person or a principle, you support or defend them forcefully. 味方をする ❑ *You would think my own father would stick up for me once in a while.* 実の父親ならたまには私をかばってくれると思うでしょう.

▶ **stick with** ❶ PHRASAL VERB 句動詞 If you **stick with** something, you do not change to something else. 続ける ❑ *If you're in a job that keeps you busy, stick with it.* 忙しい仕事に就いているなら, それを続けなさい. ❷ PHRASAL VERB 句動詞 If you **stick with** someone, you stay close to them. 一のそばについている, 一と一緒にいる ❑ *Tugging the woman's arm, she pulled her to her side saying: "You just stick with me, dear."* 彼女はその女性の腕をグイッと引っ張ってそばに引き寄せて言った. 「私のそばから離れちゃだめよ」

stick|er /stɪkər/ (stickers) N-COUNT 可算名詞 A **sticker** is a

small piece of paper or plastic, with writing or a picture on one side, that you can stick onto a surface. ステッカー, シール ❑ *...a bumper sticker that said, Flowers Make Life Lovelier.* 「花は人生を華やかにする」と書いてある車のステッカー

stick|er price (sticker prices) N-COUNT 可算名詞 The **sticker price** of an item, especially a car, is the price at which it is advertised. 表示価格 [AM 米国英語] ❑ *This model carries a sticker price of nearly $27,000.* このモデルは表示価格が2万7千ドル近くだ.

stick|er shock N-UNCOUNT 不可算名詞 **Sticker shock** is the shock you feel when you find out how expensive something is. 値札ショック [AM 米国英語] ❑ *Get over the sticker shock and invest in good kitchen knives.* 値札ショックから立ち直って, 良質の包丁に投資しなさい.

stick|ing point (sticking points) N-COUNT 可算名詞 A **sticking point** in a discussion or series of negotiations is a point on which the people involved cannot agree and which may delay or stop the talks. A **sticking point** is also one aspect of a problem which you have trouble dealing with. 障害, 支障 ❑ *The main sticking point was the question of taxes.* 主な障害は税の問題だ.

stick shift (stick shifts) N-COUNT 可算名詞 A **stick shift** is the lever that you use to change gear in a car or other vehicle. シフトレバー, ギヤ [mainly AM 主に米国英語] ❑ *I'm having trouble with this stick shift because I'm left-handed.* 左利きなのでこのシフトレバーにてこずっている.

sticky /stɪki/ (stickier, stickiest) ❶ ADJ 形容詞 A **sticky** substance is soft, or thick and liquid, and can stick to other things. Sticky things are covered with a sticky substance. ねばねばする ❑ *...sticky toffee.* ネバネバのタフィー ❑ *If the dough is sticky, add more flour.* 生地がネバネバしていれば, 小麦粉を加えなさい. ❷ ADJ 形容詞 **Sticky** weather is unpleasantly hot and damp. 蒸し暑い ❑ *...four desperately hot, sticky days in the middle of August.* 8月中旬の耐え難いほど蒸し暑い4日間 ❸ ADJ 形容詞 A **sticky** situation involves problems or is embarrassing. 面倒な, 厄介な [INFORMAL くだけた] ❑ *Inevitably the transition will yield some sticky moments.* 当然移行により面倒なことが起きるだろう.

stiff /stɪf/ (stiffer, stiffest) ❶ ADJ 形容詞 Something that is **stiff** is firm or does not bend easily. 硬い ❑ *The furniture was stiff, uncomfortable, too delicate, and too neat.* その家具は硬くて使い心地が悪く, ちみつすぎてきれいすぎた. ❑ *His gabardine trousers were brand new and stiff.* 彼の作業ズボンは新品で硬かった. ● **stiff|ly** ADV 副詞 硬く ❑ *Moira sat stiffly upright in her straight-backed chair.* モイラは背のまっすぐないすに体をこわばらせてまっすぐに座っていた. ❷ ADJ 形容詞 Something such as a door or drawer that is **stiff** does not move as easily as it should. 開けにくい ❑ *Train doors have handles on the inside. They are stiff so that they cannot be opened accidentally.* 列車のドアは内側にハンドルがある. 誤ってドアが開かないようにハンドルは回しにくくなっている. ❸ ADJ 形容詞 If you are **stiff**, your muscles or joints hurt when you move, because of illness or because of too much exercise. 凝った, 筋肉痛がある ❑ *The mud bath is particularly recommended for relieving tension and stiff muscles.* 泥風呂は緊張感や筋肉痛を和らげるのに効果的とされている. ● **stiff|ly** ADV 副詞 ぎこちなく ❑ *He climbed stiffly from the Volkswagen.* 彼はフォルクスワーゲンからぎこちなく下りた. ❹ ADJ 形容詞 **Stiff** behavior is rather formal and not very friendly or relaxed. よそよそしい ❑ *They always seemed a little awkward with each other, a bit stiff and formal.* 彼らはいつも少しよそよそしくて, 改まっていて, お互いに少しぎこちなさそうでした. ● **stiff|ly** ADV 副詞 よそよそしく ❑ *"Why don't you borrow your sister's car?" said Cassandra stiffly.* 「お姉さんの車を借りたら?」とカッサンドラはよそよそしく言った. ❺ ADJ 形容詞 **Stiff** can be used to mean difficult or severe. 厳しい ❑ *She faces stiff competition in the Best Actress category.* 彼女は最優秀女優部門で厳しい競争に直面する. ❻ ADV 副詞 [adj ADV] If you are bored **stiff**, worried **stiff**, or scared **stiff**, you are extremely bored, worried, or scared. すっごく [INFORMAL くだけた, EMPHASIS 強調] ❑ *Anna tried to look interested. Actually, she was bored stiff.* アナは興味があるふりをした. 実際はひどく退屈していた. ● ADJ 形容詞 **Stiff** is also an adjective. かなり [v n ADJ] ❑ *Even if he bores you stiff, it is good manners not to let him know it.* たとえ彼があなたをすっかり退屈させたとしても, それを彼に知らせないのが礼儀だ.

stiff|en /stɪfən/ (stiffens, stiffening, stiffened) ❶ V-I 自動詞 If you **stiffen**, you stop moving and stand or sit with muscles that are suddenly tense, for example because you feel afraid or angry. こわばる ❑ *Ada stiffened at the sound of his voice.* アダは彼の声を聞いて体が硬直した. ❷ V-T/V-I 自動詞 If your muscles or joints **stiffen**, or if something **stiffens** them, they become difficult to bend or move. 凝る, 張る ❑ *The blood supply to the skin is reduced when muscles stiffen.* 筋肉が張ると皮膚への血液の供給が低下する. ● PHRASAL VERB 句動詞 **Stiffen up** means the same as **stiffen**. 凝る, 張る ❑ *These clothes restrict your freedom of movement and stiffen up the whole body.* これらの服を着ると自由に動きにくくなり, 体全体がこわばる. ❸ V-T 他動詞 If something such as cloth **is stiffened**, it is made firm so that it does not bend easily. ぱりっとさせる [usu passive] ❑ *This special paper was actually thin, soft Sugiwara paper that*

had been stiffened with a kind of paste. この特別の紙は実はパリッとするようなのりが使われている薄くて柔らかい杉原紙だ.

sti|fle /staɪf^əl/ (**stifles, stifling, stifled**) **1** V-T 他動詞 If someone **stifles** something you consider to be a good thing, they prevent it from continuing. 妨害する [DISAPPROVAL 不賛成] □*Regulations on children stifled creativity.* 子供に対する規制が創造性を妨げる. **2** V-T 他動詞 If you **stifle** a yawn or laugh, you prevent yourself from yawning or laughing. こらえる □*She makes no attempt to stifle a yawn.* 彼女は全くあくびをこらえようとしない. **3** V-T 他動詞 If you **stifle** your natural feelings or behavior, you prevent yourself from having those feelings or behaving in that way. 抑える □*It is best to stifle curiosity and leave birds' nests alone.* 好奇心を抑えて鳥の巣をそっとしておきなさい.

sti|fling /staɪflɪŋ/ **1** ADJ 形容詞 **Stifling** heat is so intense that it makes you feel uncomfortable. You can also use **stifling** to describe a place that is extremely hot. 暑苦しい □*The stifling heat of the little room was beginning to make me nauseous.* その小さな部屋が暑苦しくて気分が悪くなりかけていた. **2** ADJ 形容詞 If a situation is **stifling**, it makes you feel uncomfortable because you cannot do what you want. 息が詰まりそうな □*Life at home with her parents and two sisters was stifling.* 両親と2人の姉妹との家での生活は息が詰まりそうだった. **3** → see also **stifle**

stig|ma /stɪgmə/ (**stigmas**) N-VAR 可変性名詞 If something has a **stigma** attached to it, people think it is something to be ashamed of. 汚名 □*There is still a stigma attached to cancer.* いまだに癌に伴う汚名はある.

stig|ma|tize /stɪgmətaɪz/ (**stigmatizes, stigmatizing, stigmatized**) V-T 他動詞 If someone or something **is stigmatized**, they are unfairly regarded by many people as being bad or having something to be ashamed of. 汚名を着せる □*Children in single-parent families must not be stigmatized.* 片親家族の子供が非難されてはならない.

sti|let|to /stɪletoʊ/ (**stilettos**) N-COUNT 可算名詞 **Stilettos** are women's shoes that have high, very narrow heels. スティレットヒール, スティレット □*Off came her sneakers and on went a pair of stilettos.* スニーカーを脱いでスティレットヒールを履いた.

---

still

❶ ADVERB USES

❷ NOT MOVING OR MAKING A NOISE

❸ EQUIPMENT

---

❶ still /stɪl/ **1** ADV 副詞 If a situation that used to exist **still** exists, it has continued and exists now. まだ, いまだに □*I still dream of home.* 今でも実家の夢を見ます. □*Brian's toe is still badly swollen and he cannot put on his shoe.* ブライアンの足の指はいまだにかなりはれていて靴を履けない. **2** ADV 副詞 If something that has not yet happened could **still** happen, it is possible that it will happen. If something that has not yet happened is **still to** happen, it will happen at a later time. これからでも, まだ [ADV before v] □*Big money could still be made if the crisis keeps oil prices high.* 危機が原油の高い値を維持すればこれからでも大金が稼げるかもしれない. □*We could still make it, but we won't get there till three.* なんとか行けそうですが, 到着は3時以降になります. **3** ADV 副詞 If you say that there **is still** an amount of something left, you are emphasizing that there is that amount left. 依然として, まだ ["be" ADV n] □*There are still some outstanding problems.* 依然として未解決問題が残っている. **4** ADV 副詞 You use **still** to emphasize that something remains the case or is true in spite of what you have just said. けれども, しかしそれでも [ADV before v] □*I'm average for my height. But I still feel I'm fatter than I should be.* 私は身長に対して平均的な体重だ. しかしそれでも太りすぎのように感じる. **5** ADV 副詞 You use **still** to indicate that a problem or difficulty is not really worth worrying about. それにもかかわらず [ADV with cl] □*Their luck had simply run out. Still, never fear.* 単に運が尽きたんだ. だけど心配は無用だ. **6** ADV 副詞 You use **still** in expressions such as **still further, still another,** and **still more** to show that you find the number or quantity of things you are referring to surprising or excessive. さらに, より一層 [EMPHASIS 強調] [ADV n/adv] □*We look forward to strengthening still further our already close co-operation with the police.* 我々はすでに密接な警察との協力関係をさらに強化することを期待している. **7** ADV 副詞 You use **still** with comparatives to indicate that something has even more of a quality than something else. (比較級を強調して) さらに [EMPHASIS 強調] [ADV with compar] □*Formula One motor car racing is supposed to be dangerous. "Indycar" racing is supposed to be more dangerous still.* F1レースは危険だということになっているが, 「インディカー」レースはさらにもっと危険らしい.

If you say that something is **still** happening or is **still** the case, you are usually emphasizing your surprise that it has been happening or has been the case for so long. □*She was still looking at me...There are still plenty of horses around here.* **Already** is often used to add emphasis or to suggest that it is surprising that something has happened so soon. □*They were already eating their lunch.* You use **yet** in negative sentences and in questions. It is often used to add emphasis, to suggest surprise that something has not happened, or to say that it will happen later. □*Have you seen it yet?...The troops could not yet see the shore... It isn't dark yet.*

❷ still /stɪl/ (**stiller, stillest, stills**) **1** ADJ 形容詞 If you stay **still**, you stay in the same position and do not move. じっとしている, 静止した [ADJ v] □*David had been dancing about like a child, but suddenly he stood still and looked at Brad.* デービッドは子供のように踊りまわっていたが, 突然立ち止まって, ブラッドの方を見た. **2** ADJ 形容詞 If air or water is **still**, it is not moving. 風がない, 水の流れがない □*The night air was very still.* 夜風は全くなかった. **3** ADJ 形容詞 If a place is **still**, it is quiet and shows no sign of activity. 静かな, しいんとした □*In the room it was very still.* 部屋の中は静まりかえっていた. ● **still|ness** N-UNCOUNT 不可算名詞 静けさ □*Four deafening explosions shattered the stillness of the night air.* 4回の耳をつんざくような爆音が夜のしじまが完全に失われた. **4** ADJ 形容詞 Drinks that are **still** do not contain any bubbles of carbon dioxide. 無炭酸の, 炭酸の入っていない □*...a glass of still water.* 水を1杯 **5** N-COUNT 可算名詞 A **still** is a photograph taken from a movie which is used for publicity purposes. スチール写真 □*...stills from the James Bond movie series.* ジェームズ・ボンド映画シリーズからのスチール写真

❸ still /stɪl/ (**stills**) N-COUNT 可算名詞 A **still** is a piece of equipment used to make strong alcoholic drinks by a process called distilling. 蒸留器

still|born /stɪlbɔrn/ ADJ 形容詞 A **stillborn** baby is dead when it is born. 死産の □*It was a miracle that she survived the birth of her stillborn baby.* 彼女が死産児の出産を生き延びたのは奇跡だった.

still life (**still lifes**) N-VAR 可変性名詞 A **still life** is a painting or drawing of an arrangement of objects such as flowers or fruit. **Still life** refers to this type of painting or drawing. 静物画 □*...a still life by one of France's finest artists.* フランスの最も優秀な芸術家の1人が描いた静物画 → see **painting**

stimu|lant /stɪmyələnt/ (**stimulants**) N-COUNT 可算名詞 A **stimulant** is a drug that makes your body work faster, often increasing your heart rate and making you less likely to sleep. 興奮剤, 刺激物 □*It is not a good idea to fight fatigue by taking stimulants.* 興奮剤を飲んで疲労と戦うのはよくない.

stimu|late /stɪmyəleɪt/ (**stimulates, stimulating, stimulated**) **1** V-T 他動詞 To **stimulate** something means to encourage it to begin or develop further. 刺激する, 活気づける □*America's priority is rightly to stimulate its economy.* アメリカの優先事項は当然経済の活性化だ. ● **stimu|la|tion** /stɪmyəleɪʃ^ən/ N-UNCOUNT 不可算名詞 刺激, 活性化 □*...an economy in need of stimulation.* 活性化を必要とする経済 **2** V-T 他動詞 [usu passive] If you **are stimulated by** something, it makes you feel full of ideas and enthusiasm. かきたてる, 刺激する □*Bill was stimulated by the challenge.* ビルは難題によってやる気が出た. ● **stimu|lat|ing** ADJ 形容詞 刺激的な, 興味をかきたてる □*It is a complex yet stimulating book.* それは複雑だが刺激的な本だ. ● **stimu|la|tion** N-UNCOUNT 不可算名詞 刺激, 興奮 □*Many enjoy the mental stimulation of a challenging job.* やりがいのある仕事による精神的な刺激を楽しむ人が多い. **3** V-T 他動詞 If something **stimulates** a part of a person's body, it causes it to move or start working. 刺激する, 施す □*Exercise stimulates the digestive and excretory systems.* 運動は消化器官と排せつ期間を刺激する. ● **stimu|lat|ing** ADJ 形容詞 刺激性の, 促進性の □*...the stimulating effect of adrenaline.* アドレナリンの刺激効果 ● **stimu|la|tion** N-UNCOUNT 不可算名詞 [usu with supp] 刺激, 促進 □*...physical stimulation.* 肉体的刺激

stimu|la|tive /stɪmyəleɪtɪv/ ADJ 形容詞 If a government policy has a **stimulative** effect on the economy, it encourages the economy to grow. 刺激的な, 活力を与える □*It is possible that a tax cut might have some stimulative effect.* 減税に刺激的効果がある可能性があります.

stimu|lus /stɪmyələs/ (**stimuli** /stɪmyəlaɪ/) N-VAR 可変性名詞 A **stimulus** is something that encourages activity in people or things. 刺激, 励み □*Interest rates could fall soon and be a stimulus to the U.S. economy.* 金利がまもなく下がり米国経済への刺激となる可能性がある.

sting /stɪŋ/ (**stings, stinging, stung**) **1** V-T/V-I 他動詞/自動詞 If a plant, animal, or insect **stings** you, a sharp part of it, usually covered with poison, is pushed into your skin so that you feel a sharp pain. 刺す □*The nettles stung their legs.* イラクサに足を刺された. **2** N-COUNT 可算名詞 The **sting** of an insect or animal is the part that stings you. 針 □*Remove the bee sting with tweezers.* ハチ

の針をピンセットで抜きなさい。 3 N-COUNT 可算名詞 If you feel a **sting**, you feel a sharp pain in your skin or other part of your body. チクっとした痛み ❏ *This won't hurt – you will just feel a little sting.* これは痛くはないよ、ちょっとチクっとするだけだ。 4 V-T/V-I 他動詞/自動詞 If a part of your body **stings**, or if a substance **stings** it, you feel a sharp pain there. チクッと痛む、ヒリヒリと痛む ❏ *His cheeks were stinging from the icy wind.* 彼のほおは冷たい風のせいでヒリヒリしていた。 5 V-T 他動詞 If someone's remarks **sting** you, they make you feel hurt and annoyed. (精神的に) 傷つける [no cont] ❏ *Some of the criticism has stung him.* その批評の一部は彼を傷つけた。

stin|gy /stɪndʒi/ (**stingier, stingiest**) ADJ 形容詞 If you describe someone as **stingy**, you are criticizing them for being unwilling to spend money. けちな [INFORMAL くだけた, DISAPPROVAL 不賛成] ❏ *The West is stingy with aid.* 西側は救援を渋っている。

stink /stɪŋk/ (**stinks, stinking, stank, stunk**) 1 V-I 自動詞 To **stink** means to smell very bad. 悪臭を放つ ❏ *We all stank and nobody minded.* 僕らはみんなとても臭かったが、誰も気にしなかった。 ● N-SING 単数名詞 **Stink** is also a noun. 悪臭 ❏ *He was aware of the stink of stale beer on his breath.* 彼は自分の息が気の抜けたビールでぷんぷんにおうのに気づいていた。 2 V-I 自動詞 If you say that something **stinks**, you mean that you disapprove of it because it involves ideas, feelings, or practices that you do not like. 最悪である [INFORMAL くだけた, DISAPPROVAL 不賛成] ❏ *I think their methods stink.* 彼らのやり方は最低だと思う。 3 N-SING 単数名詞 If someone makes a **stink** about something they are angry about, they show their anger in order to make people take notice. いちゃもん [INFORMAL くだけた] ❏ *The family's making a hell of a stink.* その家族はすごいいちゃもんをつけている。

stint /stɪnt/ (**stints**) N-COUNT 可算名詞 A **stint** is a period of time which you spend doing a particular job or activity or working in a particular place. 期間、任期 ❏ *He is returning to this country after a five-year stint in Hong Kong.* 彼は香港での5年の任期を終えたら帰国する。

stipu|late /stɪpyuleɪt/ (**stipulates, stipulating, stipulated**) V-T 他動詞 If you **stipulate** a condition or **stipulate that** something must be done, you say clearly that it must be done. 明記する ❏ *She could have stipulated that she would pay when she collected the computer.* 彼女はコンピュータを受け取るときに支払いをすると明確にしておくこともできたのに。 ● **stipu|la|tion** /stɪpyuleɪʃ°n/ N-COUNT 可算名詞 (**stipulations**) 条件 ❏ *Clifford's only stipulation is that his clients obey his advice.* クリフォードの唯一の条件はクライアントが彼のアドバイスに従うことだ。

stir /stɜr/ (**stirs, stirring, stirred**) 1 V-T 他動詞 If you **stir** a liquid or other substance, you move it around or mix it in a container using something such as a spoon. かき回す、かき混ぜる ❏ *Stir the soup for a few seconds.* スープを数秒間かき回しなさい。 ❏ *There was Mrs. Bellingham, stirring sugar into her tea.* ベリンガムさんが紅茶に入れた砂糖をかき混ぜていた。 2 V-I 自動詞 If you **stir**, you move slightly, for example because you are uncomfortable or beginning to wake up. 身動きする、もじもじする [WRITTEN 書き言葉] ❏ *Eileen shook him, and he started to stir.* エイリーンが彼を揺するど、彼はもぞもぞ動き出した。 3 V-I 自動詞 If you do not **stir from** a place, you do not move from it. 出る [WRITTEN 書き言葉] [usu with brd-neg] ❏ *She had not stirred from the house that evening.* 彼女はその晩ずっと家にいた。 4 V-T/V-I 他動詞/自動詞 If something **stirs** or if the wind **stirs** it, it moves gently in the wind. 動かす [他動詞]、かすかに動く [自動詞] ❏ *Palm trees stir in the soft Pacific breeze.* ヤシの木が太平洋のそよ風でゆらゆら揺れる。 [WRITTEN 書き言葉] 5 V-T/V-I 他動詞/自動詞 If a particular memory, feeling, or mood **stirs** or **is stirred** in you, you begin to think about it or feel it. 呼び起こす [他動詞]、沸き起こる [自動詞] ❏ *Then a memory stirs in you and you start feeling anxious.* そして思い出が自分の中に沸き起こり、心配になる。 [WRITTEN 書き言葉] ❏ *Amy remembered the anger he had stirred in her.* エイミーは、彼にかき立てられた怒りを思い出した。 6 N-SING 単数名詞 If an event causes a **stir**, it causes great excitement, shock, or anger among people. 騒ぎ ❏ *His movie has caused a stir.* 彼の映画は騒ぎを起こした。 7 → see also **stirring**

▸ **stir up** 1 PHRASAL VERB 句動詞 If something **stirs up** dust or **stirs up** mud in water, it causes it to rise up and move around. 舞い上げる ❏ *They saw first a cloud of dust and then the car that was stirring it up.* 彼らはまず砂ぼこりを、そしてそれを舞い上げていた自動車を見た。 2 PHRASAL VERB 句動詞 If you **stir up** a particular mood or situation, usually a bad one, you cause it. 巻き起こす、かき立てる [DISAPPROVAL 不賛成] ❏ *As usual, Harriet is trying to stir up trouble.* いつも通り、ハリエットは問題を起こそうとしている。

Word Partnership stir は次の語句と使われる：

| N. | stir **a mixture**, stir **in sugar** 1 |
| V. | **cause** a stir, **create** a stir 6 |

stir|ring /stɜrɪŋ/ (**stirrings**) 1 ADJ 形容詞 A **stirring** event, performance, or account of something makes people very excited

or enthusiastic. 感動的な ❏ *The president made a stirring speech.* 大統領は感動的な演説をした。 2 N-COUNT 可算名詞 A **stirring of** a feeling or thought is the beginning of one. 兆し [usu N "of" n] ❏ *I feel a stirring of curiosity.* 好奇心の芽生えを感じる。

stitch /stɪtʃ/ (**stitches, stitching, stitched**) 1 V-T/V-I 他動詞/自動詞 If you **stitch** cloth, you use a needle and thread to join two pieces together or to make a decoration. (布を) 縫う ❏ *Fold the fabric and stitch the two layers together.* 布を折って2枚を縫い合わせなさい。 ❏ *We stitched incessantly.* 私たちは休みなく裁縫を続けた。 2 N-COUNT 可算名詞 **Stitches** are the short pieces of thread that have been sewn in a piece of cloth. 一針、縫い目 ❏ *...a row of straight stitches.* まっすぐな縫い目の列 3 N-COUNT 可算名詞 In knitting and crochet, a **stitch** is a loop made by one turn of wool around a knitting needle or crochet hook. 一編み、編み目 ❏ *Her mother counted the stitches on her knitting needles.* 彼女の母親が編み棒の編み目を数えた。 4 N-UNCOUNT 不可算名詞 If you sew or knit something in a particular **stitch**, you sew or knit in a way that produces a particular pattern. 一編み ❏ *The design can be worked in cross stitch.* そのデザインはクロスステッチが合うかもしれない。 5 V-T 他動詞 When doctors **stitch** a wound, they use a special needle and thread to sew the skin together. (傷口を) 縫う ❏ *Jill washed and stitched the wound.* ジルは傷口を洗浄して縫合した。 6 N-COUNT 可算名詞 A **stitch** is a piece of thread that has been used to sew the skin of a wound together. (傷口を縫う) 一針 ❏ *He had six stitches in a head wound.* 彼は頭の傷で6針縫った。 7 N-SING 単数名詞 A **stitch** is a sharp pain in your side, usually caused by running or laughing a lot. わき腹の痛み ❏ *One of them was laughing so much he got a stitch.* 彼らのうちの1人は笑いすぎてわき腹が痛くなった。

stock /stɒk/ (**stocks, stocking, stocked**) 1 N-COUNT 可算名詞 **Stocks** are shares in the ownership of a company, or investments on which a fixed amount of interest will be paid. 株、株券 [BUSINESS 実業] ❏ *...the buying and selling of stocks and shares.* 株の売買 2 N-UNCOUNT 不可算名詞 A company's **stock** is the amount of money which the company has through selling shares. 総株価 [BUSINESS 実業] ❏ *Two years later, when Compaq went public, their stock was valued at $38 million.* 2年後、コンパック社が上場したとき、総株価は3800万ドルの価値がついた。 3 V-T 他動詞 If a store **stocks** particular products, it keeps a supply of them to sell. 在庫を置く [no cont] ❏ *The store stocks everything from cigarettes to recycled paper.* その店はたばこからリサイクル紙まであらゆるものを店に置いている。 4 N-UNCOUNT 不可算名詞 A store's **stock** is the total amount of goods which it has available to sell. 在庫 ❏ *When a nearby store burned down, our stock was ruined by smoke.* 近くの店が全焼したとき、当社の在庫が煙で台なしになった。 5 V-T 他動詞 If you **stock** something such as a cupboard, shelf, or room, you fill it with food or other things. 置く、蓄える ❏ *I worked stocking shelves in a grocery store.* 食料品店の棚並べをして働いた。 ❏ *Some families stocked their cellars with food and water.* 地階貯蔵室に食べ物や水を蓄えた家族もあります。 ● PHRASAL VERB 句動詞 **Stock up** means the same as **stock**. 置く、蓄える ❏ *I had to stock the boat up with food.* ボートに食糧を積み込まなければならなかった。 6 N-COUNT 可算名詞 If you have a **stock** of things, you have a supply of them stored in a place ready to be used. 蓄え ❏ *I keep a stock of cassette tapes describing various relaxation techniques.* さまざまなリラクセーション療法について説明しているカセットテープをたくさん持っている。 7 ADJ 形容詞 A **stock** answer, expression, or way of doing something is one that is very commonly used, especially because people cannot be bothered to think of something new. お決まりの [ADJ n] ❏ *My boss had a stock response – "If it ain't broke, don't fix it!"* 上司はお決まりの反応だった。「壊れてねえなら直すな！」 8 N-MASS 質量名詞 **Stock** is a liquid, usually made by boiling meat, bones, or vegetables in water, that is used to give flavor to soups and sauces. 煮出し汁、ストック ❏ *Finally, add the beef stock.* 最後にビーフストックを加えなさい。 9 → see also **stocking** 10 PHRASE 句 If goods are in **stock**, a store has them available to sell. If they are **out of stock**, it does not. 在庫がある/品切れで ❏ *Check that your size is in stock.* あなたのサイズの在庫があるかを確認しなさい。 11 PHRASE 句 If you **take stock**, you pause to think about all the aspects of a situation or event before deciding what to do next. 検討する ❏ *It was time to take stock of the situation.* 状況を検討するときだった。 12 **lock, stock, and barrel** → see **barrel**

▸ **stock up** 1 → see **stock** 5 2 PHRASAL VERB 句動詞 If you **stock up on** something, you buy a lot of it, in case you cannot get it later. 買い込む、まとめ買いをする ❏ *The authorities have urged people to stock up on fuel.* 当局は人々に燃料を買い込むようにせき立てた。 → see **company, stock market**

stock|broker /stɒkbroʊkər/ (**stockbrokers**) N-COUNT 可算名詞 A **stockbroker** is a person whose job is to buy and sell stocks and shares for people who want to invest money. 株式仲買人 [BUSINESS 実業]

stock|broking /stɒkbroʊkɪŋ/ N-UNCOUNT 不可算名詞 **Stockbroking** is the professional activity of buying and selling stocks and shares for clients. 株式仲買 [BUSINESS 実業] ❏ *His*

S

Word Web   stock market

The Dutch established the first **stock exchange** in Amsterdam in 1611. Its purpose was to raise **capital** to **invest** in the spice trade with the Far East. It also **traded** in metals and grains such as wheat and rye. The Dutch also experienced the world's first **stock market crash**. Tulips were an important **commodity** in seventeenth century Holland. By 1636 a single tulip bulb sold for the equivalent of $76,000. However, **confidence** in the tulip market suddenly dropped. Soon a tulip bulb was worth only $1. **Commerce** in Holland did not recover for many years.

stockbroking firm was hit by the 1987 crash. 彼の株式仲買会社は1987年の暴落であおりを受けた.

stock con|trol N-UNCOUNT 不可算名詞 **Stock control** is the activity of making sure that a company always has exactly the right amount of goods available to sell. 在庫管理 [BUSINESS 実業] ❑ *Better stock control helped Wal-Mart to reduce its expenses by $2 billion in 1997.* 効率的な在庫管理によって1997年にはウォールマートは経費を20億ドル削減した.

stock ex|change (stock exchanges) N-COUNT 可算名詞 A **stock exchange** is a place where people buy and sell stocks and shares. **The stock exchange** is also the trading activity that goes on there and the trading organization itself. 株式売買, 株取引 [BUSINESS 実業] ❑ *The shortage of good stock has kept some investors away from the stock exchange.* 良い銘柄が不足しているために株取引を控えている投資家もいる.

→ see **stock market**

stock|holder /stɒkhoʊldər/ (stockholders) N-COUNT 可算名詞 A **stockholder** is a person who owns shares in a company. 株主 [AM 米国英語 BUSINESS 実業] ❑ *He was a stockholder in a hotel corporation.* 彼はホテルの株主だった.

stock|ing /stɒkɪŋ/ (stockings) N-COUNT 可算名詞 **Stockings** are items of women's clothing which fit closely over their feet and legs. Stockings are usually made of nylon and are held in place by garters. ストッキング ❑ *...a pair of nylon stockings.* ナイロンストッキング1足

stock mar|ket (stock markets) N-COUNT 可算名詞 The **stock market** consists of the general activity of buying stocks and shares, and the people and institutions that organize it. 株式取引, 株式市場 [BUSINESS 実業] ❑ *He's been studying and playing the stock market since he was 14.* 彼は14歳のときから株式取引について勉強し株取引をしてきた.

→ see Word Web: **stock market**

→ see **company**

stock op|tion (stock options) N-COUNT 可算名詞 A **stock option** is an opportunity for the employees of a company to buy shares at a special price. 株式購入権, ストックオプション [AM 米国英語 BUSINESS 実業] ❑ *He made a huge profit from the sale of shares purchased in January under the company's stock option program.* 彼は会社の自社株購入制度の下1月に購入した株の販売でかなりの利益を得た.

stock|pile /stɒkpaɪl/ (stockpiles, stockpiling, stockpiled) **1** V-T 他動詞 If people **stockpile** things such as food or weapons, they store large quantities of them for future use. 備蓄する, 貯蔵する ❑ *People are stockpiling food for the coming winter.* 人々は今度の冬に備えて食料を貯蔵している. **2** N-COUNT 可算名詞 A **stockpile** of things is a large quantity of them that have been stored for future use. 備蓄, 貯蔵 ❑ *The two leaders also approved treaties to cut stockpiles of chemical weapons.* 2人の指導者は化学兵器の備蓄を削減する協定も承認した.

stock|taking /stɒkteɪkɪŋ/ N-UNCOUNT 不可算名詞 **Stocktaking** is the same as doing an **inventory**. 棚卸し, 在庫調べ [mainly BRIT 主に英国英語 BUSINESS 実業]

stocky /stɒki/ (stockier, stockiest) ADJ 形容詞 A **stocky** person has a body that is broad, solid, and often short. がっしりした ❑ *...a short stocky man in his forties.* 40代で小柄でがっしりした男性

stoke /stoʊk/ (stokes, stoking, stoked) **1** V-T 他動詞 If you **stoke** a fire, you add coal or wood to it to keep it burning. 燃料を補給する ❑ *She was stoking the stove with sticks of maple.* 彼女はストーブにカエデの枝を薪として足していた. ● PHRASAL VERB 句動詞 **Stoke up** means the same as **stoke**. 燃料を補給する ❑ *He stoked up the fire in the hearth.* 彼は暖炉の火に燃料を補給した. **2** V-T 他動詞 If you **stoke** something such as a feeling, you cause it to be felt more strongly. かき立てる ❑ *These demands are helping to stoke fears of civil war.* これらの要求は内戦への恐怖心をかき立てる一役を買っている. ● PHRASAL VERB 句動詞 **Stoke up** means the same as **stoke**. かき立てる ❑ *He has sent his proposals in the hope of stoking up interest for the idea.* 彼はその案への関心をかき立てることを期待して提案書を送った.

stole /stoʊl/ **Stole** is the past tense of **steal**. steal の過去形

sto|len /stoʊlᵊn/ **Stolen** is the past participle of **steal**. steal の過去分詞

stom|ach /stʌmək/ (stomachs, stomaching, stomached) **1** N-COUNT 可算名詞 Your **stomach** is the organ inside your body where food is digested before it moves into the intestines. 胃 ❑ *He had an upset stomach.* 彼は胃がもたれる. **2** N-COUNT 可算名詞 You can refer to the front part of your body below your waist as your **stomach**. 腹, おなか ❑ *The children lay down on their stomachs.* 子供たちはうつぶせになっていた. **3** N-COUNT 可算名詞 If the front part of your body below your waist feels uncomfortable because you are feeling worried or frightened, you can refer to it as your **stomach**. 胸, おなか ❑ *His stomach was in knots.* 彼のおなかがきりきりした. **4** N-COUNT 可算名詞 If you say that someone has a strong **stomach**, you mean that they are not disgusted by things that disgust most other people. 太い神経, 度胸 ❑ *Surgery often demands actual physical strength, as well as the possession of a strong stomach.* 医者はしばしば度胸だけでなく体力そのものも要求する. **5** V-T 他動詞 If you cannot **stomach** something, you cannot accept it because you dislike it or disapprove of it. 耐える, 認める [with brd-neg] ❑ *I could never stomach the cruelty involved in the wounding of animals.* 動物を傷つけることに関わる残酷さには決して耐えられなかった. **6** PHRASE 句 If you do something **on an empty stomach**, you do it without having eaten. すき腹に, 空腹のときに ❑ *Avoid drinking on an empty stomach.* 空腹のときはアルコールを飲まないように.

stomp /stɒmp/ (stomps, stomping, stomped) V-I 自動詞 If you **stomp** somewhere, you walk there with very heavy steps, often because you are angry. どしんどしんと歩く ❑ *He turned his back on them and stomped off up the hill.* 彼はそいつらに背を向けて丘をどしんどしんと登っていった.

stone /stoʊn/ (stones, stoning, stoned) **1** N-MASS 質量名詞 **Stone** is a hard solid substance found in the ground and often used for building houses. 石, 石材 ❑ *He could not tell whether the floor was wood or stone.* 彼には床が木材か石材のどちらを使っているのかわからなかった. ❑ *People often don't appreciate that marble is a natural stone.* 大理石が天然石であるという値打ちを分からない人が多い. **2** N-COUNT 可算名詞 A **stone** is a small piece of rock that is found on the ground. 小石, 石ころ ❑ *He removed a stone from his shoe.* 彼は靴から小石を取り除いた. **3** N-COUNT 可算名詞 A **stone** is a large piece of stone put somewhere in memory of a person or event, or as a religious symbol. 記念碑, 石碑 ❑ *The monument consists of a circle of gigantic stones.* その記念碑は巨大な石碑の円でできている. **4** N-UNCOUNT 不可算名詞 **Stone** is used in expressions such as **set in stone** and **tablets of stone** to suggest that an idea or rule is firm and fixed, and cannot be changed. 確固たる考え ❑ *He is merely throwing the idea forward for discussion; it is not cast in stone.* 彼は確固たる考えなしにただ単に議論のために案をぶつけているだけだ. **5** N-COUNT 可算名詞 You can refer to a jewel as a **stone**. 宝石 ❑ *...a diamond ring with three stones.* 3つの宝石がついたダイアモンドの指輪 **6** N-COUNT 可算名詞 A **stone** is a small hard ball of minerals and other substances which sometimes forms in a person's kidneys or gallbladder. 結石 ❑ *He had kidney stones.* 彼にはじん臓結石がありました. **7** N-COUNT 可算名詞 The **stone** in a plum, cherry, or other fruit is the large hard seed in the middle of it. 種 [mainly BRIT 主に英国英語; AM usually **pit** 米国英語では通常 **pit**] **8** V-T 他動詞 If people **stone** someone or something, they throw stones at them. 石を投げる ❑ *Youths burned cars and stoned police.* 若者が自動車を燃やし, 警察に石を投げた. **9** → see also **stepping stone, stoned**

→ see **fruit**

stoned /stoʊnd/ ADJ 形容詞 If someone is **stoned**, their mind is greatly affected by a drug such as marijuana. (マリファナなどで) ハイになって ラリって [INFORMAL くだけた] ❑ *Half of them were so stoned they couldn't even see.* 半数は麻薬であまりにもハイになっていて視覚さえ衰えていた.

stony /stoʊni/ (stonier, stoniest) **1** ADJ 形容詞 **Stony** ground is rough and contains a lot of stones. 石の多い, 石だらけの ❑ *The steep, stony ground is well drained.* 急勾配(こうばい)で石の多い土地が

S

水はけは良い. [2] ADJ 形容詞 A **stony** expression or attitude does not show any sympathy or friendliness. 無表情な ❏ She gave me the stoniest look I ever got. 彼女は, 私がいままでで見たこともないほど冷たい視線を投げかけた.

stood /stʊd/ **Stood** is the past tense and past participle of **stand**. stand の過去形/過去分詞

stool /stul/ (**stools**) N-COUNT 可算名詞 A **stool** is a seat with legs but no support for your arms or back. スツール, 丸いす ❏ O'Brien sat on a bar stool and leaned his elbows on the counter. オブライエンはバーのスツールに腰掛け, ひじをカウンターについていた.

stoop /stup/ (**stoops, stooping, stooped**) [1] V-I 自動詞 If you **stoop**, you stand or walk with your shoulders bent forward. 猫背である ❏ She was taller than he was and stooped slightly. 彼女は彼よりも背が高く少し猫背だった. ● N-SING 単数名詞 **Stoop** is also a noun. 猫背 ❏ He was a tall, thin fellow with a slight stoop. 彼は背が高くて少し猫背のやせた男だった. [2] V-I 自動詞/自動詞 If you **stoop**, you bend your body forward and downward. かがむ ❏ He stooped to pick up the carrier bag of groceries. 彼は食料品の入った買い物袋を取り上げるのにかがだ. ❏ Two men in shirt sleeves stooped over the car. ワイシャツ姿の男性 2人が車の上に前かがみになった. [3] V-I 自動詞 If you say that a person **stoops to** doing something, you are criticizing them because they do something wrong or immoral that they would not normally do. ーするまで落ちぶれる, ーというみっともないことをする [DISAPPROVAL 不賛成] ❏ He had not, until recently, stooped to personal abuse. 彼は最近まで人身攻撃をするまでは落ちぶれていなかった.

stop /stɒp/ (**stops, stopping, stopped**) [1] V-T/V-I 他動詞/自動詞 If you have been doing something and then you **stop** doing it, you no longer do it. ーするのを止める [他動詞], やめる, 中断する [自動詞] ❏ Stop throwing those stones! 石を投げるのをやめなさい! ❏ Does either of the parties want to stop the fighting? どちら側も争いをやめたくはないのでしょうか? ❏ She stopped in mid-sentence. 彼女は言いかけてやめた. [2] V-T 他動詞 If you **stop** something from happening, or you **stop** something happening, you prevent it from happening or prevent it from continuing. 妨げる ❏ He proposed a new diplomatic initiative to try to stop the war. 彼は戦争を回避するために新たな外交政策を提案しました. ❏ He would do what he must to stop her from destroying him. 彼は, 彼女が彼の人生をぶち壊すのを防ぐために必要なことをするだろう. [3] V-I 自動詞 If an activity or process **stops**, it is no longer happening. やむ [自動詞] ❏ The rain had stopped and a star or two was visible over the mountains. 雨がやみ, 星が1つ2つ山の上に現れた. ❏ The system overheated and filming had to stop. システムがオーバーヒートしたので撮影を中止しなければならなかった. [4] V-T/V-I 他動詞/自動詞 If something such as machine **stops** or **is stopped**, it is no longer moving or working. 止める [他動詞], 止まる [自動詞] ❏ The clock stopped at 11:59 Saturday night. 時計が土曜の夜11時59分に止まりました. ❏ Arnold stopped the engine and got out of the car. アーノルドはエンジンを止めて車から出た. [5] V-T/V-I 他動詞/自動詞 When a moving person or vehicle **stops** or **is stopped**, they no longer move and they remain in the same place. 停止する ❏ The car failed to stop at an army checkpoint. その自動車は軍の検問所で停止しそこなった. ❏ He stopped and let her catch up with him. 彼は立ち止まって彼女を待った. [6] N-SING 単数名詞 If something that is moving comes **to a stop** or is brought **to a stop**, it slows down and no longer moves. 停止 ❏ People often wrongly open doors before the train has come to a stop. 電車が停止する前に誤ってドアを開ける人が多い. [7] V-T/V-I 他動詞/自動詞 If someone does not **stop to** think or **to** explain, they continue with what they are doing without taking any time to think about or explain it. 落ち着いてーする ❏ She doesn't stop to think about what she's saying. 彼女は何を言おうとしているのか落ち着いて考えません. ❏ There is something rather strange about all this if one stops to consider it. 落ち着いて考えてみるとこの件には何かがおかしい. [8] V-I 自動詞 If you say that a quality or state **stops** somewhere, you mean that it exists or is true up to that point, but no further. 終わる ❏ The cafe owner has put up the required "no smoking" signs, but thinks his responsibility stops there. 喫茶店のオーナーは必須の「禁煙」の標識を掲げたが, 彼の責任はそこまでだと思っている. [9] N-COUNT 可算名詞 A **stop** is a place where buses or trains regularly stop so that people can get on and off. バス停, 停車駅 ❏ The closest subway stop is Houston Street. 最寄の地下鉄の駅はヒューストン・ストリートだ. [10] V-I 自動詞 If you **stop** somewhere on a journey, you stay there for a short while. しばらくとどまる ❏ He insisted we stop at a small restaurant just outside of Atlanta. 彼は, アトランタ郊外の小さなレストランに寄ろうと言い張った. [11] N-COUNT 可算名詞 A **stop** is a time or place at which you stop during a journey. 滞在先, 立ち寄り先 ❏ The last stop in Mr. Robinson's lengthy tour was Paris. ロビンソン氏の長旅の最後の滞在地はパリだった. [12] PHRASE 句 If you say that someone will **stop at nothing to** get something, you are emphasizing that they are willing to do things that are extreme, wrong, or dangerous in order to get it. 何があってもやめない, 手段を選ばない [EMPHASIS 強調] ❏ Their motive is money, and they will stop at nothing to get it. 彼らの動機はお金で, 金を得るためには手段を選ばない. [13] PHRASE 句 If you **put a stop to** something that you do not like or approve

of, you prevent it from happening or continuing. ーを終わらせる ❏ His daughter should have stood up and put a stop to all these rumors. 彼の娘は立ち上がってこれらのうわさに終止符を打つべきだった. [14] PHRASE 句 If you say that someone does not **know when to stop**, you mean that they do not control their own behavior very well and so they often annoy or upset other people. 行動をわきまえる ❏ Like many politicians before him, Mr. Bentley did not know when to stop. 彼以前の多くの政治家と同様に, ベントリー氏は行動をわきまえていなかった. [15] to **stop dead** → see **dead** [16] to **stop short of** → see **short** [17] to **stop** someone **in** their **tracks** → see **track**

> When an action comes to an end or **stops**, you can say that someone **stops doing** it. ❏ She stopped reading and closed the book. However, if you say that someone **stops to do** something, you mean that they interrupt their movement or another activity in order to do that thing. The "to" infinitive indicates purpose. ❏ I stopped to read the notices on the bulletin board.

▶ **stop by** or **stop in** PHRASAL VERB 句動詞 If you **stop by** somewhere, you make a short visit to a person or place. 立ち寄る, ちょっと寄る [INFORMAL くだけた] ❏ Perhaps I'll stop by the hospital. おそらく病院に立ち寄るだろう.

▶ **stop off** PHRASAL VERB 句動詞 If you **stop off** somewhere, you stop for a short time in the middle of a trip. 立ち寄る, 短期滞在する ❏ The president stopped off in Poland on his way to Munich for the economic summit. 大統領は経済サミットのためにミュンヘンに行く道中にポーランドに立ち寄りました.

stop|light /stɒplaɪt/ (**stoplights**) also **stop light** N-COUNT 可算名詞 A **stoplight** is a set of colored lights which controls the flow of traffic on a road. (交通) 信号 [AM 米国英語] ❏ Holly waited at a stoplight, impatient for the signal to change. ホリーは信号が青に変わるのをじりじりしながら待った.

stop|over /stɒpoʊvər/ (**stopovers**) N-COUNT 可算名詞 A **stopover** is a short stay in a place in between parts of a trip. 一時滞在, ストップオーバー ❏ The Sunday flights will make a stopover in Paris. 日曜日のフライトはパリでストップオーバーする.

stop|page /stɒpɪdʒ/ (**stoppages**) [1] N-COUNT 可算名詞 When there is a **stoppage**, people stop working because of a disagreement with their employers. ストライキ [BUSINESS 実業] ❏ Mineworkers in the Ukraine have voted for a one-day stoppage next month. ウクライナの鉱山労働者は来月1日ストライキをすることを決めた. [2] N-COUNT 可算名詞 A **stoppage** is the same as **time out**. 中断 [mainly BRIT 主に英国英語]

stop|watch /stɒpwɒtʃ/ (**stopwatches**) also **stop-watch** N-COUNT 可算名詞 A **stopwatch** is a watch with buttons which you press at the beginning and end of an event, so that you can measure exactly how long it takes. ストップウォッチ

stor|age /stɔrɪdʒ/ N-UNCOUNT 不可算名詞 If you refer to the **storage** of something, you mean that it is kept in a special place until it is needed. 保管, 貯蔵 ❏ ...the storage of toxic waste. 有害廃棄物の保管 ❏ Some of the space will at first be used for storage. スペースの一部はまずは収納用に使われる.

store /stɔr/ (**stores, storing, stored**) [1] N-COUNT 可算名詞 A **store** is a building or part of a building where things are sold. 店, 商店 ❏ They are selling them for $10 apiece at a few stores in Texas and Oklahoma. テキサス州とオクラホマ州のいくつかの店で1個10ドルで販売しています. ❏ ...grocery stores. 食料品店 [2] V-T 他動詞 When you **store** things, you put them in a container or other place and leave them there until they are needed. 保管する, 貯蔵する ❏ Store the cookies in an airtight tin. 密封した缶にクッキーを保管しなさい. ● PHRASAL VERB 句動詞 **Store away** means the same as **store**. 保管する, 貯蔵する ❏ He simply stored the tapes away. 彼はただそのテープをとっておいた. [3] V-T 他動詞 When you **store** information, you keep it in your memory, in a file, or in a computer. 記憶させる ❏ Where in the brain do we store information about colors? 脳のどの部分にヒトは色彩についての情報を記憶するのだろうか? [4] N-COUNT 可算名詞 A **store of** things is a supply of them that you keep somewhere until you need them. 蓄積, 保存 ❏ I handed over my secret store of chocolate. 私は取っておきのチョコレートを手渡した. [5] N-COUNT 可算名詞 A **store** is a place where things are kept while they are not being used. 倉庫, 貯蔵庫 ❏ ...a store for spent fuel from submarines. 潜水艦の使用済み燃料の保管場所 [6] → see also **department store** [7] PHRASE 句 If something is **in store for** you, it is going to happen at some time in the future. 待ち構えて ❏ Surprises were also in store for me. 意外なことも私に起きるところだった.

→ see **city**

▶ **store away** → see **store 2**

▶ **store up** PHRASAL VERB 句動詞 If you **store** something **up**, you keep it until you think that the time is right to use it. 蓄える ❏ Investors were storing up a lot of cash in anticipation of disaster. 投資家は大暴落を予想して大金をためこんでいました.

S

Word Web storm

Here's how to protect yourself and your property when a severe **storm** hits. Listen for warnings from the **weather** service. Strong **wind** may blow trash cans around and **hail** may damage your car. Both should go into the garage. If you are outdoors when a storm strikes, get under cover. If you are in the open, **lightning** could hit you. Heavy **rainfall** can cause **flooding**. After the **rain** has passed, do not drive on flooded roads. The water may be deeper than you think. Be sure to buy food and batteries before a **blizzard** since **snow** may clog the roads.

Thesaurus store また次を参照:

N.	business, market, shop **1**
	collection, reserve, stock **4**
V.	accumulate, keep, save **2** **3**

store|card /stɔrkard/ (**storecards**) also **store card** N-COUNT 可算名詞 A **storecard** is a plastic card that you use to buy goods on credit from a particular store or group of stores. ストアカード [mainly BRIT 主に英国英語; AM usually **charge card** 米国英語では通常 **charge card**]

store|keeper /stɔrkipər/ (**storekeepers**) N-COUNT 可算名詞 A **storekeeper** is a shopkeeper. 店主 [mainly AM 主に米国英語]

sto|rey /stɔri/ → see **story**

storm /stɔrm/ (**storms, storming, stormed**) **1** N-COUNT 可算名詞 A **storm** is very bad weather, with heavy rain, strong winds, and often thunder and lightning. あらし □...the violent storms which whipped the East Coast. 東海岸を荒らした激しい暴風雨 **2** N-COUNT 可算名詞 If something causes a **storm**, it causes an angry or excited reaction from a large number of people. 騒動 □The photos caused a storm when they were first published. その写真が最初に出版されたとき大騒動が起きた. **3** N-COUNT 可算名詞 A **storm** of applause or other noise is a sudden loud amount of it made by an audience or other group of people in reaction to something. 大きなー, あらしのような □His speech was greeted with a storm of applause. 彼の演説はあらしのような拍手かっさいで迎えられた. **4** V-I 自動詞 If you **storm into** or **out of** a place, you enter or leave it quickly and noisily, because you are angry. 怒ってどたばたと入る/出る □After a bit of an argument, he stormed out. 少し口論をしたあと, 彼は怒って出て行った. **5** V-T 他動詞 If a place that is being defended **is stormed**, a group of people attack it, usually in order to get inside it. 襲撃する □Government buildings have been stormed and looted. 政府の建物が襲撃され略奪された. ● **storm|ing** N-UNCOUNT 不可算名詞 襲撃 □...the storming of the Bastille. バスティーユの襲撃 **6** PHRASE 句 If someone or something **takes** a place **by storm**, they are extremely successful. 大成功を収める □Kenya's long-distance runners have taken the athletics world by storm. ケニアの長距離ランナーは陸上競技会で大成功を収めた.
→ see Word Web: **storm**
→ see **disaster, forecast, hurricane, weather**

Word Partnership storm は次の語句と使われる:

ADJ.	**tropical** storm **1**
	gathering storm, **heavy** storm, **severe** storm **1** **2**
N.	storm **clouds**, storm **damage, ice/rain/snow** storm, storm **warning**, storm **winds**
	center of a storm, **eye of a** storm **1** **2**
	storm **a building** **5**
V.	**hit by a** storm, **weather the** storm **1** **2**
	cause a storm **2**

stormy /stɔrmi/ (**stormier, stormiest**) **1** ADJ 形容詞 If there is **stormy** weather, there are strong winds and heavy rain. あらしの, 荒れ模様の □It had been a night of stormy weather, with torrential rain and high winds. 集中豪雨と暴風が吹き荒れる荒天の夜だった. **2** ADJ 形容詞 **Stormy** seas have very large strong waves because there are strong winds. しけた, 荒れた □They make the treacherous journey across stormy seas. 彼らは荒れた海を横切る危険な旅をする. **3** ADJ 形容詞 If you describe a situation as **stormy**, you mean it involves a lot of angry argument or criticism. 激しい □The letter was read at a stormy meeting. その手紙は大荒れの会議で読まれた.

sto|ry /stɔri/ (**stories**) **1** N-COUNT 可算名詞 A **story** is a description of imaginary people and events, which is written or told in order to entertain. 物語, 話 □The second story in the book is titled "The Scholar." その本の2番目の物語は『学者』という題目だ. □I shall tell you a story about four little rabbits. 4羽のかわいいウサギについての話をしよう. **2** N-COUNT 可算名詞 A **story** is a description of an event or something that happened to someone, especially a spoken description of it. 話, 話題 □The parents all shared interesting stories about their children. 親は皆子供についての面白い話を語り合った. **3** N-COUNT 可算名詞 The **story of** something is a description of all the important things that have happened to it since it began. 歴史, 経歴 □...the story of the women's movement. 女性運動の歴史 **4** N-COUNT 可算名詞 If someone invents a **story**, they give a false explanation or account of something. 作り話 □He invented some story about a cousin. 彼はいとこについての作り話をした. **5** N-COUNT 可算名詞 A news **story** is a piece of news in a newspaper or in a news broadcast. 記事 □Those are some of the top stories in the news. 以上が本日の主なニュースでした. □They'll do anything for a story. 彼らはネタのためなら何でもする. **6** N-COUNT 可算名詞 A **story** of a building is one of its different levels, which is situated above or below other levels. 階 □...long brick buildings, two stories high. 2階建ての長いれんが造りの建物 **7** PHRASE 句 You use **a different story** to refer to a situation, usually a bad one, which exists in one set of circumstances when you have mentioned that it does not exist in another set of circumstances. 事情が違う □Where Marcella lives, the rents are fairly cheap, but a little further north it's a different story. マーセラが住んでいるところでは家賃は割と安いのですが, 少し北に行くと事情が異なります. **8** PHRASE 句 If you say that **it's the same old story** or **it's the old story**, you mean that something unpleasant or undesirable seems to happen again and again. よくあることだ, また同じような話だ □It's the same old story. They want one person to do three people's jobs. また同じ状況だ. 1人の従業員に3人分の仕事をしてもらいたいと思っている. **9** PHRASE 句 If you say that something is **only part of the story** or is **not the whole story**, you mean that the explanation or information given is not enough for a situation to be fully understood. それがすべてではない □This may be true but it is only part of the story. これは本当かもしれないが, 話の一部でしかない. **10** PHRASE 句 If someone tells you their **side of the story**, they tell you why they behaved in a particular way and why they think they were right, when other people think that person behaved wrongly. 一方の言い分 □He had already made up his mind before even hearing her side of the story. 彼は彼女の言い分を聞く前にすでに決心をしていた.
→ see **myth**
→ see **skyscraper**

Thesaurus story また次を参照:

N.	epic, fable, fairy tale, romance, saga, tale **1**
	account, report **2**
	fabrication, lie, untruth **4**
	article, feature **5**

Word Partnership story は次の語句と使われる:

N.	**character in a** story, story **hour**, story **line**, **narrator of a** story, **title of a** story, story **writer** **1**
	beginning of a story, **end of a** story, **horror** story, **version of a** story **1** - **5**
	life story **2**
	front page story, **news** story **5**
V.	**hear a** story, **tell a** story **1** - **4**
	publish a story, **read a** story, **write a** story **1** **5**
ADJ.	**classic** story, **compelling** story, **funny** story, **good** story, **interesting** story **1** - **5**
	familiar story **2** - **5**
	the full story, **untold** story **2** **3** **5**
	the whole story **2** **3** **5** **9**
	big story, **related** story, **top** story **5**

stout /staut/ (**stouter, stoutest**) **1** ADJ 形容詞 A **stout** person is rather fat. かっぷくがよい, でっぷりとした □He was a tall, stout man with gray hair. 彼は背が高くてでっぷりとした白髪交じりの男性だった. **2** ADJ 形容詞 **Stout** shoes, branches, or other objects are thick and strong. 頑丈な □I hope you've both got stout shoes. 2人とも丈夫な靴を持っているといいのだが.

stove /stoʊv/ (**stoves**) N-COUNT 可算名詞 A **stove** is a piece of equipment which provides heat, either for cooking or for heating a room. レンジ，こんろ，ストーブ ❑ *She put the kettle on the gas stove.* 彼女はガスこんろでやかんの湯を沸かした。

stow /stoʊ/ (**stows, stowing, stowed**) V-T 他動詞 If you **stow** something somewhere, you carefully put it there until it is needed. しまい込む ❑ *Luke stowed his camera bags into the trunk.* ルークはカメラケースをトランクにしまい込んだ。

stow|away /stoʊəweɪ/ (**stowaways**) N-COUNT 可算名詞 A **stowaway** is a person who hides in a ship, airplane, or other vehicle in order to make a journey secretly or without paying. 密航者 ❑ *The crew discovered the stowaway about two days into their voyage.* 乗務員は航海の約2日目に密航者を発見した。

strad|dle /stræd³l/ (**straddles, straddling, straddled**) 1 V-T 他動詞 If you **straddle** something, you put or have one leg on either side of it. またぐ，足を広げる ❑ *He looked at her with a grin and sat down, straddling the chair.* 彼はにっこりと彼女の方を見て，いすにまたがって座った。 2 V-T 他動詞 If something **straddles** a river, road, border, or other place, it stretches across it or exists on both sides of it. またがっている ❑ *A small wooden bridge straddled the dike.* 小さな木橋が堤防にまたがっていた。 3 V-T 他動詞 Someone or something that **straddles** different periods, groups, or fields of activity exists in, belongs to, or takes elements from them all. また ぐ，及ぶ ❑ *He straddles two cultures, having been brought up in the United States and later converted to Islam.* 彼は米国で育ち後にイスラム 教徒になったので2つの文化をまたいでいる。

straight /streɪt/ (**straighter, straightest, straights**) 1 ADJ 形 容詞 A **straight** line or edge continues in the same direction and does not bend or curve. まっすぐな，一直線の ❑ *Keep the boat in a straight line.* ボートをまっすぐなままにしなさい。 ❑ *His teeth were perfectly straight.* 彼の歯は完璧なほどまっすぐに生えていた。 ● ADV 副詞 **Straight** is also an adverb. まっすぐに，一直線に [ADV after v] ❑ *Stand straight and stretch the left hand to the right foot.* まっす ぐに立って左手を右足の方に伸ばしなさい。 2 ADJ 形容詞 **Straight** hair has no curls or waves in it. 直毛の，ストレートの ❑ *Grace had long straight dark hair which she wore in a bun.* グレースは長くてスト レートの黒髪で巻き髪にしていた。 3 ADV 副詞 You use **straight** to indicate that the way from one place to another is very direct, with no changes of direction. 直接，まっすぐに [ADV prep/adv] ❑ *...squirting the medicine straight to the back of the child's throat.* 薬 を子供ののどの奥に直接吹きかけること ❑ *He finished his conversation and stood up, looking straight at me.* 彼は会話を終えて立ち上がり，ま っすぐに私のほうを見た。 4 ADV 副詞 If you go **straight** to a place, you go there immediately. すぐに [ADV prep/adv] ❑ *As always, we went straight to the experts for advice.* いつも通り，私たちはすぐに専門 家のアドバイスを求めに行った。 5 ADJ 形容詞 If you give someone a **straight** answer, you answer them clearly and honestly. 率直 な [ADJ n] ❑ *What a shifty arguer he is, refusing ever to give a straight answer to a straight question.* 彼は率直な質問にいつも率直に答えるの を避けて，なんてごまかしが多いのだろう。 ● ADV 副詞 **Straight** is also an adverb. 率直に [ADV after v] ❑ *I lost my temper and told him straight that I hadn't been looking for any job.* 私はカッとなって，仕事 なんて探していなかったと彼に率直に言った。 6 ADJ 形容詞 **Straight** means following one after the other, with no gaps or intervals. 連続した [ADJ n] ❑ *They'd won 12 straight games before they lost.* 敗戦 するまでに12連勝した。 ● ADV 副詞 **Straight** is also an adverb. 連続して [n ADV] ❑ *He called from Washington, having been there for 31 hours straight.* 彼はワシントンに31時間ずっといて，そこから電話して きた。 7 ADJ 形容詞 A **straight** choice or a **straight** fight involves only two people or things. 二者択一の，一対一の [ADJ n] ❑ *It's a straight choice between low-paid jobs and no jobs.* 低給職か無職かの 二者択一だ。 8 ADJ 形容詞 If you describe someone as **straight**, you mean that they are normal and conventional, for example in their opinions and in the way they live. まっとうな ❑ *Dorothy was described as a very straight woman, a very strict Christian who was married to her job.* ドロシーは仕事に没頭している非常に敬虔なキリ スト教徒でとてもまっとうな女性として描かれていた。 9 ADJ 形容 詞 If you describe someone as **straight**, you mean that they are heterosexual rather than homosexual. ストレートの，同性愛でな い [INFORMAL くだけた] ❑ *His sexual orientation was a lot more gay than straight.* 彼の性的指向はストレートというよりかなりゲイだっ た。 ● N-COUNT 可算名詞 **Straight** is also a noun. ストレート，異性 愛の人，のんけ ❑ *...a standard of sexual conduct that applies equally to gays and straights.* ゲイとストレートの人に同様に当てはまる性行為の 基準 10 PHRASE 句 If you **get** something **straight**, you make sure that you understand it properly or that someone else does. はっき りさせる [SPOKEN 口語] ❑ *You need to get your facts straight.* 事実をは っきりさせることが必要です。 11 **a straight face** → see **face**

Word Partnership *straight* は次の語句と使われる：

N. straight **line**, straight **nose** 1
second/third straight **loss/victory/win**, second/ third straight **season/year** 6

V. **drive** straight, **keep going** straight, **look** straight, **point** straight 3

straight ar|row (**straight arrows**) N-COUNT 可算名詞 A **straight arrow** is someone who is very traditional, honest, and moral. まじめ人間，堅物 [mainly AM 主に米国英語] [oft N n] ❑ *...a well-scrubbed, straight-arrow group of young people.* きれい好きで堅物 の若者のグループ

straight away also **straightaway** ADV 副詞 If you do something **straight away**, you do it immediately and without delay. 直ちに，今すぐに [ADV with v] ❑ *I should go and see a doctor straight away.* 今すぐ医者に見てもらうべきだ。

straight|en /streɪt³n/ (**straightens, straightening, straightened**) 1 V-T 他動詞 If you **straighten** something, you make it neat or put it in its proper position. 片付ける，まっす ぐにする ❑ *She sipped her coffee and straightened a picture on the wall.* 彼女はコーヒーをすすって壁にかかっている絵をまっすぐにし た。 ● PHRASAL VERB 句動詞 **Straighten up** means the same as **straighten**. 片付ける，まっすぐにする ❑ *This is my job, to straighten up, to file things.* これが私の仕事で，整理整とん，ファイリングをす る。 2 V-I 自動詞 If you are standing in a relaxed or slightly bent position and then you **straighten**, you make your back or body straight and upright. 姿勢を正す ❑ *The three men straightened and stood waiting.* 3人の男は背筋を伸ばし，立ちながら待った。 ● PHRASAL VERB 句動詞 **Straighten up** means the same as **straighten**. 姿勢 を正す ❑ *He straightened up and slipped his hands in his pockets.* 彼は 姿勢を正しポケットに手を入れた。 3 V-T/V-I 他動詞/自動詞 If you **straighten** something, or it **straightens**, it becomes straight. ま っすぐに伸ばす [他動詞]，まっすぐに伸びる [自動詞] ❑ *Straighten both legs until they are fully extended.* 両足が完全に伸びるまでまっす ぐに伸ばしなさい。 ● PHRASAL VERB 句動詞 **Straighten out** means the same as **straighten**. まっすぐに伸ばす ❑ *No one would dream of straightening out the church's knobbly spire.* 教会ので凸凹こぼこした先塔を まっすぐにしようなどと思いつくものは誰もいない。
▶ **straighten out** PHRASAL VERB 句動詞 If you **straighten out** a confused situation, you succeed in getting it organized and cleaned up. 解決する ❑ *He would make an appointment with him to straighten out a couple of things.* 彼は，いくつかのことを解決するため に彼と会う約束をするだろう。 2 → see **straighten** 3
▶ **straighten up** → see **straighten** 1, 2

straight|forward /streɪtfɔrwərd/ 1 ADJ 形容詞 If you describe something as **straightforward**, you approve of it because it is easy to do or understand. 簡単な，明快な [APPROVAL 賛 成] ❑ *Disposable diapers are fairly straightforward to put on.* 紙おむ つはまあまあまあ簡単だ。 ❑ *The question seemed straightforward enough.* その質問は十分に分かりやすかったようだ。 2 ADJ 形容詞 If you describe a person or their behavior as **straightforward**, you approve of them because they are honest and direct, and do not try to hide their feelings. 率直な，誠実な [APPROVAL 賛成] ❑ *She is very blunt, very straightforward, and very honest.* 彼女はとても素直で， 誠実で率直だ。

strain /streɪn/ (**strains, straining, strained**) 1 N-VAR 可変性 名詞 If **strain** is put **on** an organization or system, it has to do more than it is able to do. 重圧，負担 ❑ *The prison service is already under considerable strain.* 刑務所業務はすでにかなりの重圧を受けてい る。 2 V-T 他動詞 To **strain** something means to make it do more than it is able to do. 無理をさせる，負担をかける ❑ *The volume of scheduled flights is straining the air traffic control system.* 定期便の量 は航空管制システムに負担をかけています。 3 N-UNCOUNT 不可算 名詞 **Strain** is a state of worry and tension caused by a difficult situation. ストレス [also N in pl] ❑ *She was tired and under great strain.* 彼女は疲れていてかなりのストレスがたまっていた。 4 N-SING 単数名詞 If you say that a situation is **a strain**, you mean that it makes you worried and tense. 重荷 ❑ *I sometimes find it a strain to be responsible for the mortgage.* ときどき住宅ローンへの責任を重荷に 感じる。 5 N-UNCOUNT 不可算名詞 **Strain** is a force that pushes, pulls, or stretches something in a way that may damage it. 力 ❑ *Place your hands under your buttocks to take some of the strain off your back.* 両手をおしりの下に置き背中の力を抜きなさい。 6 N-VAR 可 変性名詞 **Strain** is an injury to a muscle in your body, caused by using the muscle too much or twisting it. 筋違い，体を痛めるこ と ❑ *Avoid muscle strain by warming up with slow jogging.* ゆっくりジ ョギングをしてウォーミングアップをすることで筋肉痛を防ぎなさ い。 7 V-T 他動詞 If you **strain** a muscle, you injure it by using it too much or twisting it. 痛める [他動詞] ❑ *He strained his back during a practice session.* 彼は練習中に腰を痛めた。 8 V-T 他動詞 If you **strain to** do something, you make a great effort to do it when it is difficult to do. 精いっぱい努力する ❑ *I had to strain to hear.* 精いっぱ い耳を澄まさなければならなかった。 9 V-T 他動詞 When you **strain**

food, you separate the liquid part of it from the solid parts. こす ❑ *Strain the stock and put it back into the pane.* 煮出し汁をこして鍋に戻しなさい. 🔟 N-COUNT 可算名詞 A **strain** of a germ, plant, or other organism is a particular type of it. 種類, 品種 ❑ *Every year new strains of influenza develop.* 毎年新種のインフルエンザが発生する.

Word Partnership strain は次の語句と使われる:

ADJ.	**great** strain 🔟 🔞 🔢
	virulent strain 🔟
N.	**stress and** strain 🔞
	muscle strain, strain **a muscle** 🔟 🔢
	strain **of bacteria/virus** 🔟

strained /streɪnd/ 🔟 ADJ 形容詞 If someone's appearance, voice, or behavior is **strained**, they seem worried and nervous. こわばった, 心配そうな ❑ *She looked a little pale and strained.* 彼女は少し青ざめて心配そうだった. 🔢 ADJ 形容詞 If relations between people are **strained**, those people do not like or trust each other. 緊迫した, ぎくしゃくした ❑ *...a period of strained relations between the mayor and his deputy.* 市長と副市長の緊迫関係が続いた期間

strait /streɪt/ (**straits**) 🔟 N-COUNT; N-IN-NAMES 可算名詞, 名称中の名詞 You can refer to a narrow strip of sea which joins two large areas of sea as a **strait** or **the straits**. 海峡 ❑ *An estimated 1,600 vessels pass through the strait annually.* 年間で約1600隻の船がその海峡を通過する. 🔢 N-PLURAL 複数名詞 If someone is **in** dire or desperate **straits**, they are in a very difficult situation, usually because they do not have much money. 窮地に陥って [adj N] ❑ *The company's closure has left many small businessmen in desperate financial straits.* その会社の倒産は多くの小企業経営者を経済的窮地に追い込んだ.

strait|jacket /streɪtdʒækɪt/ (**straitjackets**) 🔟 N-COUNT 可算名詞 A **straitjacket** is a special jacket used to tie the arms of a violent person tightly around their body. 拘束衣 ❑ *Occasionally his behavior became so uncontrollable that he had to be placed in a straitjacket.* たまに彼の行動があまりにも手に負えなくなるので, 拘束衣を身につけなければならなかった. 🔢 N-COUNT 可算名詞 If you describe an idea or a situation as a **straitjacket**, you mean that it is very limited and restricting. 束縛 ❑ *...the ideological straitjacket of religious fundamentalism.*

strand /strænd/ (**strands, stranding, stranded**) 🔟 N-COUNT 可算名詞 A **strand** of something such as hair, wire, or thread is a single thin piece of it. 1本 ❑ *She tried to blow a gray strand of hair from her eyes.* 彼女は目にかかっている白髪を吹き飛ばそうとした. 🔢 V-T 他動詞 If you **are stranded**, you are prevented from leaving a place, for example because of bad weather. 立ち往生する ❑ *The climbers had been stranded by a storm.* 登山家たちはあらしのために立ち往生した.
→ see **rope**

strange /streɪndʒ/ (**stranger, strangest**) 🔟 ADJ 形容詞 Something that is **strange** is unusual or unexpected, and makes you feel slightly nervous or afraid. 奇妙な, 変な ❑ *Then a strange thing happened.* そして奇妙なことが起こった. ❑ *There was something strange about the flickering blue light.* そのチカチカする青い光はどこか奇妙だった. ● **strange|ly** ADV 副詞 妙に ❑ *She noticed he was acting strangely.* 彼女は, 彼の行動が奇妙なことに気づいた. ● **strange|ness** N-UNCOUNT 不可算名詞 奇妙なこと ❑ *...the breathy strangeness of the music.* 息が混じって変な音楽 🔢 ADJ 形容詞 [ADJ n] A **strange** place is one that you have never been to before. A **strange** person is someone that you have never met before. 見知らぬ ❑ *I ended up alone in a strange city.* 見知らぬ町で結局1人になってしまった. 🔞 → see also **stranger**

Thesaurus strange また次を参照:

| ADJ. | bizarre, different, eccentric, idiosyncratic, odd, peculiar, unusual, weird; (ant.) ordinary, usual 🔟 |
| | exotic, foreign, unfamiliar 🔢 |

strange|ly /streɪndʒli/ 🔟 ADV 副詞 You use **strangely** to emphasize that what you are saying is surprising. 不思議なことに [EMPHASIS 強調] [ADV with cl] ❑ *Strangely, they hadn't invited her to join them.* 不思議なことに, 彼らは彼女を仲間に入るよう誘わなかった. 🔢 → see also **strange**

stran|ger /streɪndʒər/ (**strangers**) 🔟 N-COUNT 可算名詞 A **stranger** is someone you have never met before. 見知らぬ人 ❑ *Telling a complete stranger about your life is difficult.* 赤の他人に自分の人生について語るのは難しい. 🔢 N-PLURAL 複数名詞 If two people are **strangers**, they do not know each other. 見ず知らずの人, 他人同士 ❑ *The women knew nothing of the dead girl. They were strangers.* その女性たちは死亡した少女のことを何も知らなかった. お互い顔見知りではなかった. 🔞 N-COUNT 可算名詞 If you are a **stranger to** something, you have had no experience of it or do not understand

it. 新参者 ❑ *He is no stranger to controversy.* 彼は論争には慣れている. 🔢 → see also **strange**

> You do not use **stranger** to talk about someone who comes from a country which is not your own. You can refer to him or her as a **foreigner**, but this word can sound rather rude. It is better to say specifically where someone comes from. ❑ *He's Egyptian... She's from Finland.*

stran|gle /stræŋgᵊl/ (**strangles, strangling, strangled**) 🔟 V-T 他動詞 To **strangle** someone means to kill them by squeezing their throat tightly so that they cannot breathe. 絞殺する ❑ *He tried to strangle a border policeman and steal his gun.* 彼は国境警備員を絞殺し銃を盗もうとした. 🔢 V-T 他動詞 To **strangle** something means to prevent it from succeeding or developing. (成功・発展を) 妨げる ❑ *The country's economic plight is strangling its scientific institutions.* その国の経済苦境が科学機関の発展を妨げている.

strangle|hold /stræŋgᵊlhoʊld/ N-SING 単数名詞 To have a **stranglehold on** something means to have control over it and prevent it from being free or from developing. 完全支配 ❑ *These companies are determined to keep a stranglehold on the banana industry.* これらの会社はバナナ産業の完全支配を維持するつもりでいる.

strap /stræp/ (**straps, strapping, strapped**) 🔟 N-COUNT 可算名詞 A **strap** is a narrow piece of leather, cloth, or other material. Straps are used to carry things, fasten things together, or to hold a piece of clothing in place. ひも, バンド ❑ *Nancy gripped the strap of her beach bag.* ナンシーはビーチバッグのひもをしっかりとつかんだ. ❑ *She pulled the strap of her nightgown onto her shoulder.* 彼女はネグリジェのひもを引いて肩にかけた. 🔢 V-T 他動詞 If you **strap** something somewhere, you fasten it there with a strap. ひもで縛る ❑ *She strapped the baby seat into the car.* 彼女はベビーシートをシートベルトで固定した.

stra|tegic /strətiːdʒɪk/ 🔟 ADJ 形容詞 **Strategic** means relating to the most important, general aspects of something such as a military operation or political policy, especially when these are decided in advance. 戦略的 ❑ *...the new strategic thinking which NATO leaders produced at the recent London summit.* 北大西洋条約機構の指導者らが最近のロンドンサミットで製作した新戦略的思考 ● **stra|tegi|cal|ly** /strətiːdʒɪkli/ ADV 副詞 ❑ *...strategically important roads, bridges and buildings.* 戦略的に重要な道路, 橋, 建物 🔢 ADJ 形容詞 **Strategic** weapons are very powerful missiles that can be fired only after a decision to use them has been made by a political leader. 戦略— ❑ *...strategic nuclear weapons.* 戦略核兵器 🔞 ADJ 形容詞 If you put something in a **strategic** position, you place it cleverly in a position where it will be most useful or have the most effect. 巧みな戦略の, 効果的な ❑ *...the marble benches Eve had placed at strategic points throughout the gardens, where the views were spectacular.* イヴが庭中の効果的な場所に置いた大理石のベンチ, そこからの景色は素晴らしい ● **stra|tegi|cal|ly** ADV 副詞 うまく ❑ *We had kept its presence hidden with a strategically placed chair.* うまくいすを置いてそれを隠した.

Word Partnership strategic は次の語句と使われる:

N.	strategic **decisions**, strategic **forces**, strategic **interests**, strategic **planning**, strategic **targets**, strategic **thinking** 🔟
	strategic **missiles**, strategic **nuclear weapons** 🔢
	strategic **location**, strategic **position** 🔞

strat|egist /strætədʒɪst/ (**strategists**) N-COUNT 可算名詞 A **strategist** is someone who is skilled in planning the best way to gain an advantage or to achieve success, especially in war. 戦略家 ❑ *Military strategists had devised a plan that guaranteed a series of stunning victories.* 軍事戦略家が連戦圧勝を保証する計画を考案した.

strat|egy /strætədʒi/ (**strategies**) 🔟 N-VAR 可変性名詞 A **strategy** is a general plan or set of plans intended to achieve something, especially over a long period. 戦略 ❑ *The energy secretary will present the strategy tomorrow afternoon.* エネルギー庁長官が明日の午後戦略を発表します. 🔢 N-UNCOUNT 不可算名詞 **Strategy** is the art of planning the best way to gain an advantage or achieve success, especially in war. 作戦, 計画 ❑ *I've just been explaining the basic principles of strategy to my generals.* ちょうど軍司令官に作戦の基本方針を説明していたところだ.

Thesaurus strategy また次を参照:

| N. | plan, policy, tactics 🔟 |

straw /strɔ:/ (**straws**) **1** N-UNCOUNT 不可算名詞 Straw consists of the dried, yellowish stalks from crops such as wheat or barley. わら □ *The barn was full of bales of straw.* 納屋はわら俵でいっぱいだった。 □ *I stumbled through mud to a yard strewn with straw.* 私はつまづきながらぬかるみを越えてわらの散らばった作業場に出た。 **2** N-COUNT 可算名詞 A straw is a thin tube of paper or plastic, which you use to suck a drink into your mouth. ストロー □ *...a bottle of lemonade with a straw in it.* ストローが入ったレモネードのボトル **3** PHRASE 句 If you **are clutching at straws** or **grasping at straws**, you are trying unusual or extreme ideas or methods because other ideas or methods have failed. わらにも（何にでも）すがろうとする □ *...a badly thought-out plan from an administration clutching at straws.* わらにもすがる思いでいる経営陣が頭をひねって考え出した苦策 **4** PHRASE 句 If an event is **the last straw** or **the straw that broke the camel's back**, it is the latest in a series of unpleasant or undesirable events, and makes you feel that you cannot tolerate a situation any longer. 限界, 我慢の限度を越えさせるもの □ *For him the Church's decision to allow the ordination of women had been the last straw.* 彼にとっては教会が女性の聖職任命を認めた決定は我慢の限度を越えていた。 **5** PHRASE 句 If you **draw the short straw**, you are chosen from a number of people to perform a job or duty that you will not enjoy. はずれくじを引く □ *...if a few of your guests have drawn the short straw and agreed to drive others home after your summer barbecue.* もしゲストのうちの何人かがはずれくじを引いて, バーベキューの後に他のゲストを家に送ることを承知したのなら → see **rice**

straw|berry /strɔ:beri/ (**strawberries**) N-COUNT 可算名詞 A strawberry is a small red fruit which is soft and juicy and has tiny yellow seeds on its skin. イチゴ □ *...strawberries and cream.* 生クリームをかけたイチゴ

stray /streɪ/ (**strays, straying, strayed**) **1** V-I 自動詞 If someone strays somewhere, they wander away from where they are supposed to be. はぐれる □ *Tourists often get lost and stray into dangerous areas.* 観光客はよく道に迷って危険な地域に迷い込む。 **2** ADJ 形容詞 A stray dog or cat has wandered away from its owner's home. 迷子の, のら— [ADJ n] □ *A stray dog came up to him.* 迷子のイヌが彼の方にやって来た。 ● N-COUNT 可算名詞 Stray is also a noun. 迷子（のイヌ・ネコ）野良犬/野良猫 □ *The dog was a stray which had been adopted.* そのイヌは拾われた野良犬だった。 **3** V-I 自動詞 If your mind or your eyes stray, you do not concentrate on or look at one particular subject, but start thinking about or looking at other things. （気が）散る（視線が）それる □ *Even with the simplest cases I find my mind straying.* とても単純な訴訟でさえ, よそごとを考えてしまう。 **4** ADJ 形容詞 You use stray to describe something that exists separated from other similar things. はぐれた [ADJ n] □ *An 8-year-old boy was killed by a stray bullet.* 8歳の少年が流れ弾に当たって死亡した。

streak /stri:k/ (**streaks, streaking, streaked**) **1** N-COUNT 可算名詞 A streak is a long stripe or mark on a surface which contrasts with the surface because it is a different color. 筋, しま □ *There are these dark streaks on the surface of the moon.* 月面にこれらのしま模様がある。 **2** V-T 他動詞 If something streaks a surface, it makes long stripes or marks on the surface. 筋をつける □ *Rain had begun to streak the windowpanes.* 雨の滴が窓ガラスに筋をひき始めた。 **3** N-COUNT 可算名詞 If someone has a streak of a particular type of behavior, they sometimes behave in that way. 傾向 [usu sing, with supp] □ *We're both alike – there is a streak of madness in us both.* 私たち2人はよく似ている。どちらも狂ったところがある。 **4** V-I 自動詞 If something or someone streaks somewhere, they move there very quickly. さっと動く □ *A meteorite streaked across the sky.* いん石がさっと空を横切りました。 **5** N-COUNT 可算名詞 A winning streak or a lucky streak is a continuous series of successes, for example in gambling or sports. A losing streak or an unlucky streak is a series of failures or losses. —続き □ *The casinos had better watch out since I'm obviously on a lucky streak!* どう考えても僕には幸運が続いているからカジノは用心した方がいいぞ。

stream /stri:m/ (**streams, streaming, streamed**) **1** N-COUNT 可算名詞 A stream is a small narrow river. 小川 □ *There was a small stream at the end of the garden.* 庭の端には小さな小川があった。 **2** N-COUNT 可算名詞 A stream of smoke, air, or liquid is a narrow moving mass of it. 流れ □ *He breathed out a stream of cigarette smoke.* 彼はふうっとタバコの煙を吐いた。 **3** N-COUNT 可算

名詞 A stream of vehicles or people is a long moving line of them. 長い列 □ *There was a stream of traffic behind him.* 彼の後ろにはかなり車が並んでいた。 **4** N-COUNT 可算名詞 A stream of things is a large number of them occurring one after another. 連続 □ *The discovery triggered a stream of readers' letters.* その発見により読者からの便りが跡を絶たなかった。 □ *...a never-ending stream of jokes.* 延々と続くジョーク **5** V-I 自動詞 If a liquid streams somewhere, it flows or comes out in large amounts. 流れ出る □ *Tears streamed down their faces.* 涙が彼らのほおを流れ落ちた。 **6** V-I 自動詞 If your eyes are streaming, liquid is coming from them, for example because you have a cold. You can also say that your nose is streaming. 涙が出る, 鼻水を垂らす [usu cont] □ *Her eyes were streaming now from the wind.* 風のせいで彼女の目から涙が出ていた。 **7** V-I 自動詞 If people or vehicles stream somewhere, they move there quickly and in large numbers. どんどん押し寄せる □ *Refugees have been streaming into Travnik for months.* 難民が何か月にも渡りトラブニクにどんどん押し寄せています。 **8** V-I 自動詞 When light streams into or out of a place, it shines strongly into or out of it. 差し込む □ *Sunlight was streaming into the courtyard.* 日光が中庭にさし込んでいた。 **9** PHRASE 句 If something such as a new factory or a new system comes on stream or is brought on stream, it begins to operate or becomes available. 操業に入って, 開始して □ *As new mines come on stream, Chile's share of world copper output will increase sharply.* 新しい鉱山が操業開始するので, 銅生産の世界市場におけるチリの占有率は急上昇するだろう。 → see **river**

stream|line /stri:mlaɪn/ (**streamlines, streamlining, streamlined**) V-T 他動詞 To streamline an organization or process means to make it more efficient by removing unnecessary parts of it. 合理化する □ *They're making efforts to streamline their normally cumbersome bureaucracy.* 通常は面倒なお役所手続きを合理化しようと努力しています。 → see **mass production**

stream|lined /stri:mlaɪnd/ ADJ 形容詞 A streamlined vehicle, animal, or object has a shape that allows it to move quickly or efficiently through air or water. 合理化された □ *...these beautifully streamlined and efficient cars.* これらの素晴らしく合理化された効率的な自動車

street /stri:t/ (**streets**) **1** N-COUNT; N-IN-NAMES 可算名詞, 名称中の名詞 A street is a road in a city, town, or village, usually with houses along it. 通り □ *He lived at 66 Bingfield Street.* 彼はビングフィールド通り66番地に住んでいた。 **2** N-COUNT 可算名詞 You can use street or streets when talking about activities that happen out of doors in a city or town rather than inside a building. 街頭 □ *Changing money on the street is illegal – always use a bank.* 街頭での両替は違法なので常に銀行を利用しなさい。 □ *Their aim is to raise a million dollars to get the homeless off the streets.* 彼らの目的は, 100万ドルの募金を集めてホームレスを街頭から一掃することだ。 **3** → see also **Downing Street, Main Street, Wall Street**

street|car /stri:tkɑ:r/ (**streetcars**) N-COUNT 可算名詞 A streetcar is an electric vehicle for carrying people which travels on rails in the streets of a city or town. 路面電車 [AM 米国英語] → see **transportation**

strength /strɛŋkθ, strɛŋθ/ (**strengths**) **1** N-UNCOUNT 不可算名詞 Your strength is the physical energy that you have, which gives you the ability to perform various actions, such as lifting or moving things. 力, 体力 □ *She has always been encouraged to swim to build up the strength of her muscles.* 彼女は筋力を鍛えるために水泳をするよう勧められてきた。 □ *He threw it forward with all his strength.* 彼はそれを全力で前に投げた。 **2** N-UNCOUNT 不可算名詞 Someone's strength in a difficult situation is their confidence or courage. 勇気, 強さ [also "a" N] □ *Something gave me the strength to overcome the difficulty.* 何かが私にその困難を乗り越える勇気を与えてくれた。 □ *He copes incredibly well. His strength is an inspiration to me in my life.* 彼は信じられないほどうまく対処する。彼の強さに私は生涯感化されている。 **3** N-UNCOUNT 不可算名詞 The strength of an object or material is its ability to be treated roughly, or to carry heavy weights, without being damaged or destroyed. 強度, 耐久性 [also N in pl] □ *He checked the strength of the cables.* 彼はケーブルの強度を確認した。 **4** N-UNCOUNT 不可算名詞 The strength of a person, organization, or country is the power or influence that they have. 勢力 [also N in pl] □ *America values its economic leadership, and the political and military strength that goes with it.* 米国は経済的指導力とそれに伴う政治力と軍事力を重視する。 □ *The alliance, in its first show of strength, drew a hundred thousand-strong crowd to a rally.* その同盟は最初の力の誇示として何十万人もの強力な群衆を集会に引き寄せた。 **5** N-UNCOUNT 不可算名詞 If you refer to the strength of a feeling, opinion, or belief, you are talking about how deeply it is felt or believed by people, or how much they are influenced by

it. 強さ，深さ ❑ *He was surprised at the strength of his own feeling.* 彼は自分自身の感情の強さに驚いた．**6** N-VAR 可変名詞 Someone's **strengths** are the qualities and abilities that they have which are an advantage to them, or which make them successful. 長所 ❑ *Take into account your own strengths and weaknesses.* 自分自身の長所と短所を考慮に入れなさい．❑ *Tact was never Mr. Moore's strength.* 気配りは決してモアー氏の強みではなかった．**7** N-UNCOUNT 不可算名詞 If you refer to the **strength** of a currency, economy, or industry, you mean that its value or success is steady or increasing. 強さ，競争力 ❑ *...the long-term competitive strength of the economy.* 長期間に及ぶ経済の競争力 **8** N-UNCOUNT 不可算名詞 The **strength** of a group of people is the total number of people in it. 人数 [also N in pl] ❑ *...elite forces, comprising about one-tenth of the strength of the army.* 陸軍兵士の約10分の1を構成している精鋭軍 **9** N-UNCOUNT 不可算名詞 The **strength** of a wind, current, or other force is its power or speed. 力，強さ [also N in pl] ❑ *Its oscillation depends on the strength of the gravitational field.* 振動は重力場の強さによる．**10** N-UNCOUNT 不可算名詞 The **strength** of a drink, chemical, or drug is the amount of the particular substance in it that gives it its particular effect. 濃度 [also N in pl] ❑ *It is very alcoholic, sometimes near the strength of port.* それはときてアルコール度が強くて，ポートワインと同程度のことがある．**11** PHRASE 句 If a person or organization **goes from strength to strength**, they become more and more successful or confident. ますます力をつける ❑ *A decade later, the company has gone from strength to strength.* 10年後，その会社は成功を重ねた．**12** PHRASE 句 If a team or army is at **full strength**, all the members that it needs or usually has are present. 全員そろって ❑ *He needed more time to bring U.S. forces there up to full strength.* 彼には米国の駐屯部隊を全員呼ぶための時間がもう少し必要だった．**13** PHRASE 句 If one thing is done **on the strength of** another, it is done because of the influence of that other thing. 〜の力によって ❑ *He was elected to power on the strength of his charisma.* 彼は持ち合わせたカリスマ性によって政権の座に就いた．

→ see **muscle**

strength|en /strɛŋθə³n/ (strengthens, strengthening, strengthened) **1** V-T 他動詞 If something **strengthens** a person or group or if they **strengthen** their position, they become more powerful and secure, or more likely to succeed. 強化する ❑ *Giving the president the authority to go to war would strengthen his hand for peace.* 大統領に武力行使の決定権を与えることは彼の和平への権限を強化するだろう．**2** V-T 他動詞 If something **strengthens** a case or argument, it supports it by providing more reasons or evidence for it. 裏付ける，支持する ❑ *He does not seem to be familiar with research which might have strengthened his own arguments.* 彼は，自分の議論の裏づけになる可能性のある研究について熟知していないようだ．**3** V-T/V-I 他動詞/自動詞 If a currency, economy, or industry **strengthens**, or if something **strengthens** it, it increases in value or becomes more successful. 好転する，改善する ❑ *The dollar strengthened against most other currencies.* ほとんどの通貨に対してドル高になった．**4** V-T 他動詞 If something **strengthens** you or **strengthens** your resolve or character, it makes you more confident and determined. 鍛える，丈夫にする ❑ *Any experience can teach and strengthen you, but particularly the more difficult ones.* どのような経験からも学び，鍛えられるが，特により大変な経験から ❑ *This merely strengthens our resolve to win the pennant.* これによってリーグ戦優勝への決意が強まった．**5** V-T/V-I 他動詞/自動詞 If something **strengthens** a relationship or link, or if it **strengthens**, it makes it closer and more likely to last for a long time. 深める [他動詞]，深まる [自動詞] ❑ *It will draw you closer together, and it will strengthen the bond of your relationship.* それによってお互いがより身近になり絆が強まるだろう．**6** V-T/V-I 他動詞/自動詞 If something **strengthens** an impression, feeling, or belief, or if it **strengthens**, it becomes greater or affects more people. 強める [他動詞]，強まる [自動詞] ❑ *His speech strengthens the impression he is the main power in the organization.* 彼のスピーチにより彼が組織の中心人物であるという印象が強くなった．❑ *Every day of sunshine strengthens the feelings of optimism.* 連日の日光によって楽観的感情が高まる．**7** V-T 他動詞 If something **strengthens** your body or a part of your body, it makes it healthier, often in such a way that you can move or carry heavier things. (体を) 鍛える ❑ *Cycling is good exercise. It strengthens all the muscles of the body.* サイクリングはよい運動で，体全体の筋肉を鍛える．**8** V-T 他動詞 If something **strengthens** an object or structure, it makes it able to be treated roughly or able to support heavy weights, without being damaged or destroyed. 補強する ❑ *The builders will have to strengthen the existing joists with additional timber.* 建設業者は現在の根太に木材を追加して補強しなければならない．

strenu|ous /strɛnyuəs/ ADJ 形容詞 A **strenuous** activity or action involves a lot of energy or effort. 激しい，懸命な ❑ *Avoid strenuous exercise in the evening.* 夜は激しい運動を避けなさい．❑ *Strenuous efforts had been made to improve conditions in the jail.* 刑務所の環境を改善するために懸命の努力がなされた．

stress /strɛs/ (stresses, stressing, stressed) **1** V-T 他動詞 If you **stress** a point in a discussion, you put extra emphasis on

it because you think it is important. 強調する ❑ *The spokesman stressed that the measures did not amount to an overall ban.* その法案は要するに全面禁止ということにはならなかったことをスポークスマンは強調した．❑ *China's leaders have stressed the need for increased co-operation between Third World countries.* 中国の首脳陣は，第三世界各国間のさらなる協力の必要性を強調した．● N-VAR 可変名詞 **Stress** is also a noun. 強調，重視 ❑ *Japanese car makers are laying ever more stress on overseas sales.* 日本の自動車メーカーは海外での販売をこれまで以上に重視している．**2** N-VAR 可変名詞 If you feel under **stress**, you feel worried and tense because of difficulties in your life. ストレス ❑ *Katy could think clearly when not under stress.* ケイティはストレスを受けていないときにははっきりと考えられるのに．**3** V-T 他動詞 If you **stress** a word or part of a word when you say it, you put emphasis on it so that it sounds slightly louder. 強勢を置く，強めて言う ❑ *She stresses the syllables as though teaching a child.* 彼女は子供に教えているかのように音節に強勢を置く．● N-VAR 可変名詞 **Stress** is also a noun. 強勢，アクセント ❑ *...the misplaced stress on the first syllable of this last word.* この最後の言葉の最初の音節に誤って付けられたアクセント

→ see **emotion**

Word Partnership	*stress* は次の語句と使われる:
N.	stress **the importance of** *something* **1** **anxiety and** stress, **effects of** stress, **job/work-related** stress, stress **management**, stress **reduction**, **response to** stress, **symptoms of** stress, stress **test 2**
V.	**cause** stress, **cope with** stress, **deal with** stress, **experience** stress, **induce** stress, **reduce** stress, **relieve** stress **2**
ADJ.	**emotional** stress, **excessive** stress, **high** stress, **physical** stress, stress **related**, **severe** stress **2**

stressed /strɛst/ ADJ 形容詞 If you are **stressed**, you feel tense and anxious because of difficulties in your life. ストレスのたまった ❑ *Work out what situations or people make you feel stressed and avoid them.* どのような状況や人々がストレスを与えているのかを考え，それを避けなさい．

stressed out ADJ 形容詞 If someone is **stressed out**, they are very tense and anxious because of difficulties in their life. ストレスで参っている [INFORMAL くだけた] ❑ *I can't imagine sitting in traffic, getting stressed out.* 交通渋滞に巻き込まれてイライラするなんて想像できない．

stress|ful /strɛsfəl/ ADJ 形容詞 If a situation or experience is **stressful**, it causes the person involved to feel stress. ストレスの多い ❑ *I think I've got one of the most stressful jobs there is.* 私は，最もストレスが多いタイプの仕事についていると思う．

stretch /strɛtʃ/ (stretches, stretching, stretched) **1** V-I 自動詞 Something that **stretches** over an area or distance covers or exists in the whole of that area or distance. 伸びる，続く [no cont] ❑ *The procession stretched for several miles.* その行列は何マイルも続いていた．**2** N-COUNT 可算名詞 A **stretch of** road, water, or land is a length or area of it. 区間 ❑ *It's a very dangerous stretch of road.* そこはとても危険な区間だ．**3** V-T/V-I 他動詞/自動詞 When you **stretch**, you put your arms or legs out straight and tighten your muscles. 伸ばす [他動詞]，伸びをする [自動詞] ❑ *He yawned and stretched.* 彼はあくびをして伸びをした．❑ *Try stretching your legs and pulling your toes upwards.* 足を伸ばして足の指を上に上げてみなさい．● N-COUNT 可算名詞 **Stretch** is also a noun. ストレッチ，伸び ❑ *At the end of a workout spend time cooling down with some slow stretches.* 運動の終わりには，ゆっくりとストレッチをしながらクールダウンを行いなさい．**4** N-COUNT 可算名詞 A **stretch of** a period of time. 期間 ❑ *...after an 18-month stretch in the army.* 陸軍で1年半過ごしたあと **5** V-I 自動詞 If something **stretches from** one time to another, it begins at the first time and ends at the second, which is longer than expected. 及ぶ，続く ❑ *...a working day that stretches from seven in the morning to eight at night.* 朝の7時から夜の8時にまで及ぶ勤務日 **6** V-I 自動詞 If a group of things **stretch from** one type of thing **to** another, the group includes a wide range of things. 及ぶ，含む ❑ *...a trading empire, with interests that stretched from chemicals to sugar.* 薬品から砂糖に至るまで関心を抱いている超大手商社 **7** V-T/V-I 他動詞/自動詞 When something soft or elastic **stretches** or **is stretched**, it becomes longer or bigger as well as thinner, usually because it is pulled. 伸ばす [他動詞]，伸びる [自動詞] ❑ *The cables are designed not to stretch.* ケーブルは伸びないようにデザインされている．**8** V-T/V-I 他動詞/自動詞 If you **stretch** an amount of something or if it **stretches**, you make it last longer than it usually would by being careful and not wasting any of it. もたせる [他動詞]，もつ [自動詞] ❑ *They're used to stretching their budgets.* 彼らは予算をもたせるのに慣れています．**9** V-T 他動詞 If something **stretches** your money or resources, it uses them up so you have hardly enough for your needs. (使って) 足りなくなる ❑ *The drought there is stretching resources.* そこでは干ばつのため資源が足りなくなってきています．**10** V-T 他動詞 If you say that a job or task **stretches** you, you mean that you like it because it makes

you work hard and use all your energy and skills so that you do not become bored or achieve less than you should.（自分の能力を）伸ばす [APPROVAL 賛成] ❑ I'm trying to move on and stretch myself with something different. 私は生活を改めて何か違うことをして自分を伸ばそうとしている. **11** PHRASE 句 If you say that something is not true or possible **by any stretch of the imagination**, you are emphasizing that it is completely untrue or absolutely impossible. どう考えても~ない [EMPHASIS 強調] ❑ Her husband was not a womanizer by any stretch of the imagination. 彼女の夫はどう考えても女たらしではなかった.

▶ **stretch out** **1** PHRASAL VERB 句動詞 If you **stretch out** or **stretch yourself out**, you lie with your legs and body in a straight line. 手足を伸ばす ❑ The bathtub was too small to stretch out in. バスタブは小さすぎて手足を伸ばせられなかった. **2** PHRASAL VERB 句動詞 If you **stretch out** a part of your body, you hold it out straight. まっすぐ伸ばす ❑ He was about to stretch out his hand to grab me. 彼は手を伸ばして私をつかむところだった.

Word Partnership
stretch は次の語句と使われる:

PREP.	stretch **across** **1** **3**
	during a stretch **3** **4**
	at a stretch **3**
N.	stretch **of highway/road**, stretch **of a river**, **along a** stretch **of road**, **down the road a** stretch **2**
	stretch **your legs** **3**

stretch|er /strɛtʃər/ (stretchers, stretchered) **1** N-COUNT 可算名詞 A **stretcher** is a long piece of canvas with a pole along each side, which is used to carry an injured or sick person. 担架, ストレッチャー ❑ The two ambulance attendants quickly put Plover on a stretcher and got him into the ambulance. 2人の救急隊員が手早くプローバーを担架に載せ, 救急車に乗せた. **2** V-T PASSIVE 受動態他動詞 If someone **is stretchered** somewhere, they are carried there on a stretcher. 担架で運ばれる ❑ I was close by as Lester was stretchered into the ambulance. レスターが救急車に運ばれたとき私は近くにいた.

strewn /struːn/ ADJ 形容詞 If a place is **strewn with** things, they are lying scattered there. 散乱している [v-link ADJ "with" n] ❑ The front room was strewn with books and clothes. 居間は本や服で散らかっていた. ● COMB IN ADJ 形容詞の複合 **Strewn** is also a combining form. ~で散らかった ❑ ...a litter-strewn street. ごみが散乱している通り

strick|en /strɪkən/ **1** **Stricken** is the past participle of some meanings of **strike**. strike の過去分詞 **2** ADJ 形容詞 If a person or place is **stricken by** something such as an unpleasant feeling, an illness, or a natural disaster, they are severely affected by it. 打ちひしがれた, 襲われた ❑ ...a family stricken by genetically-inherited cancer. 遺伝性の癌に見舞われた家族 ● COMB IN ADJ 形容詞の複合 **Stricken** is also a combining form. ~に見舞われた ❑ ...a leukemia-stricken child. 白血病に見舞われた子供

strict /strɪkt/ (stricter, strictest) **1** ADJ 形容詞 A **strict** rule or order is very clear and precise or severe and must always be obeyed completely. 厳しい, 絶対的な ❑ The officials had issued strict instructions that we were not to get out of the jeep. 関係者は, ジープから出てはいけないと言う厳しい指示を出した. ❑ French privacy laws are very strict. フランスのプライバシー法は非常に厳しい. ● **strict|ly** ADV 副詞 [ADV with v] 厳しく ❑ The acceptance of new members is strictly controlled. 新入会員の承認は厳しく管理されている. **2** ADJ 形容詞 If a parent or other person in authority is **strict**, they regard many actions as unacceptable and do not allow them. 厳しい, 厳格な ❑ My parents were very strict. 私の両親はとても厳しかった. ● **strict|ly** ADV 副詞 厳格に ❑ My own mother was brought up very strictly and correctly. 私自身の母はとても正しくしつけられた. **3** ADJ 形容詞 [ADJ n] If you talk about the **strict** meaning of something, you mean the precise meaning of it. 厳密な ❑ It's not quite peace in the strictest sense of the word, rather the absence of war. 厳密に言えば, 平和というわけではなくて, むしろ戦争がないことだ. ● **strict|ly** ADV 副詞 [ADV adj] 厳密に ❑ Actually, that is not strictly true. 実は, それは厳密には本当じゃない. **4** ADJ 形容詞 You use **strict** to describe someone who never does things that are against their beliefs. 厳格な, ストリクトな [ADJ n] ❑ Millions of Americans are now strict vegetarians. 最近は何百万人ものアメリカ人が厳格なベジタリアンだ.

strict|ly /strɪktli/ ADV 副詞 You use **strictly** to emphasize that something is of one particular type, or intended for one particular thing or person, rather than any other. ただ~だけ [EMPHASIS 強調] [ADV group] ❑ He seemed fond of her in a strictly professional way. 彼は彼女をただ仕事の面でだけ気に入っているようだった.

stride /straɪd/ (strides, striding, strode) **1** V-I 自動詞 If you **stride** somewhere, you walk there with quick, long steps. 大またで歩く, どんどん歩く ❑ They were joined by a newcomer who came striding across a field. 野原をどんどん歩いてきた新入りが彼らに加わった. **2** N-COUNT 可算名詞 A **stride** is a long step which you take

when you are walking or running. 大またの1歩 ❑ With every stride, runners hit the ground with up to five times their body-weight. ランナーは, 1足ごとに体重の最高5倍の重さで地面を踏む. **3** N-COUNT 可算名詞 If you **make strides** in something that you are doing, you make rapid progress in it. 進歩 ❑ The country has made enormous strides politically but not economically. その国は政治的にはかなりの進歩を遂げたが, 経済的にはそうではない. **4** PHRASE 句 If you **get into** your **stride** or **hit** your **stride**, you start to do something easily and confidently, after being slow and uncertain. 調子が出る ❑ The campaign is just getting into its stride. キャンペーンはちょうど本調子になりかけている. **5** PHRASE 句 If you **take** a problem or difficulty **in stride**, you deal with it calmly and easily. うまく切り抜ける ❑ He took the ridiculous accusation in stride. 彼はばかげた言いがかりをうまく切り抜けた.

Word Partnership
stride は次の語句と使われる:

V.	**break** (your) stride, **lengthen** your stride **2**
ADJ.	**long** stride **2**
	in full stride **5**

stri|dent /straɪdənt/ ADJ 形容詞 If you use **strident** to describe someone or the way they express themselves, you mean that they make their feelings or opinions known in a very strong way that perhaps makes people uncomfortable. しつこい, 執拗（しつよう）な [DISAPPROVAL 不賛成] ❑ She was increasingly seen as a strident feminist. 彼女はますます執拗（しつよう）なフェミニストと見なされている.

strife /straɪf/ N-UNCOUNT 不可算名詞 **Strife** is strong disagreement or fighting. 紛争, 抗争 [FORMAL 形式ばった] ❑ Money is a major cause of strife in many marriages. 金銭に関することが多くの結婚問題の主な原因だ.

strike

❶ NOUN USES
❷ VERB USES AND PHRASES
❸ PHRASAL VERBS

❶ strike /straɪk/ (strikes) **1** N-COUNT 可算名詞 When there is a **strike**, workers stop doing their work for a period of time, usually in order to try to get better pay or conditions for themselves. ストライキ [BUSINESS 実業] [also "on" n] ❑ Air traffic controllers have begun a three-day strike in a dispute over pay. 航空管制官が賃金に関する論争で, 3日間のストライキを開始した. ❑ Staff at the hospital went on strike in protest at the incidents. 病院の職員がその事故に抗議をしてストライキに入った. **2** N-COUNT 可算名詞 A **military strike** is a military attack, especially an air attack. 攻撃 ❑ ...a punitive air strike. 過酷な空襲 **3** → see also **hunger strike**
→ see **union**

❷ strike /straɪk/ (strikes, striking, struck, stricken)

The form **struck** is the past tense and past participle. The form **stricken** can also be used as the past participle for meanings **5** and **13**.

struck 形は過去時制と過去分詞である. stricken 形は **5** と **13** を意味する過去分詞としても使える.

1 V-I 自動詞 When workers **strike**, they go on strike. ストライキをする [BUSINESS 実業] ❑ ...their recognition of the workers' right to strike. 労働者がストライキをする権利の承認 ❑ They shouldn't be striking for more money. 昇給を求めてストライキをするべきではない. ● **strik|er** N-COUNT 可算名詞 (strikers) ストライキ参加者 ❑ The strikers want higher wages, which state governments say they can't afford. ストライキ参加者は賃上げを求めているが, 州政府は不可能だと述べています. **2** V-T 他動詞 If you **strike** someone or something, you deliberately hit them. 殴る [FORMAL 形式ばった] ❑ She took two quick steps forward and struck him across the mouth. 彼女は前にさっと2歩進んで, 彼の口のあたりを殴った. ❑ It is impossible to say who struck the fatal blow. 誰が決定的打撃を与えたかを述べるのは不可能だ. **3** V-T 他動詞 If something that is falling or moving **strikes** something, it hits it. 落ちる, 当たる [FORMAL 形式ばった] ❑ His head struck the bottom when he dived into the 6 ft end of the pool. プールの端の6フィートの深さのところに飛び込んだとき, 彼は頭をプールの底に当たった. ❑ One 16-inch shell struck the control tower. 16インチの弾丸が管制塔に落ちた. **4** V-T/V-I 他動詞/自動詞 If you **strike** one thing against another, or if one thing **strikes** against another, the first thing hits the second thing. 衝突する [FORMAL 形式ばった] ❑ Wilde fell and struck his head on the stone floor. ウィルでは転んで, 頭を石のフロアにぶつけた. **5** V-T/V-I 他動詞/自動詞 If something such as an illness or disaster **strikes**, it suddenly happens. 襲う ❑ Fed officials continued to insist that the dollar would soon return to stability but disaster struck. 連邦政府はドルがまもなく安定状態に戻ると主張し続けたが, 大暴落が起こった. ❑ A moderate earthquake struck the northeastern United States early on Saturday. 中度の地震が土曜日の早朝に米国北東部を襲った. **6** V-I 自

動詞 To **strike** means to attack someone or something quickly and violently. 攻撃する，襲撃する ❑ *He was the only cabinet member out of the country when the terrorists struck.* テロ攻撃があったとき，彼だけが国外にいる官僚でした． ⁊ V-T 他動詞 [no cont] If an idea or thought **strikes** you, it suddenly comes into your mind. 心に浮かぶ ❑ *A thought struck her. Was she jealous of her mother, then?* ある考えが彼女の心に浮かんだ．じゃあ，彼女は母親にしっとしていたのだろうか？ ⁸ V-T 他動詞 If something **strikes** you **as** being a particular thing, it gives you the impression of being that thing. 〜と考える ❑ *He struck me as a very serious but friendly person.* 彼はとてもまじめだが，気さくな人だという印象を与えた． ⁹ V-T 他動詞 If you **are struck** by something, you think it is very impressive, noticeable, or interesting. 感動する ❑ *She was struck by his simple, spellbinding eloquence.* 彼女は彼の単純で魅惑的な雄弁さに感動した． ¹⁰ V-RECIP 相互動詞 If you **strike** a deal or a bargain with someone, you come to an agreement with them. （契約を）結ぶ ❑ *They struck a deal with their paper supplier, getting two years of newsprint on credit.* 紙の供給業者と2年間分の新聞印刷用紙を売り掛けで購入するという契約を結んだ． ❑ *The two struck a deal in which Rendell took half of what a manager would.* 2者は，レンデルが通常のマネージャーの半額を受け取るという契約を結んだ． ¹¹ V-T 他動詞 If you **strike** a balance, you do something that is halfway between two extremes. （バランスを）取る ❑ *At times like that you have to strike a balance between sleep and homework.* そのようなときには，睡眠と宿題のバランスを取らなければならない． ¹² V-T 他動詞 If you **strike** a pose or attitude, you put yourself in a particular position, for example when someone is taking your photograph. （ポーズを） ❑ *She struck a pose, one hand on her hip and the other waving an imaginary cigarette.* 彼女は，片手を腰に置き，もう一方の手でたばこを吸っているふりをしてポーズをとった． ¹³ V-T 他動詞 If something **strikes** fear **into** people, it makes them very frightened or anxious. 引き起こす [LITERARY 文語的] ❑ *If there is a single subject guaranteed to strike fear in the hearts of parents, it is drugs.* もし必ず親心に恐怖心を引き起こすテーマがひとつあるとすれば，それは麻薬だ． ¹⁴ V-T/V-I 他動詞/自動詞 When a clock **strikes**, its bells make a sound to indicate what the time is. 打つ [他動詞] 時を打つ [自動詞] ❑ *The clock struck nine.* 時計が9時を打った． ¹⁵ V-T 他動詞 If you **strike** words **from** a document or an official record, you remove them. 削除する，抹消する [FORMAL 形式ばった] ❑ *Strike that from the minutes.* それを議事録から抹消しなさい． ● PHRASAL VERB 句動詞 **Strike out** means the same as **strike**. 削除する，抹消する ❑ *The censor struck out the next two lines.* 検閲官が次の2行を削除した． ¹⁶ V-T 他動詞 When you **strike** a match, you make it produce a flame by moving it quickly against something rough. 擦る ❑ *Robina struck a match and held it to the crumpled newspaper in the grate.* ロビーナはマッチを擦って，暖炉にある丸めた新聞紙につけた． ¹⁷ V-T 他動詞 If someone **strikes** oil or gold, they discover it in the ground as a result of mining or drilling. 掘り当てる，発見する ❑ *Oil industry sources say that Marathon Oil Company has struck oil in Syria.* 石油産業の業界筋によるとマラトン石油会社がシリアで油脈を掘り当てたということです． ¹⁸ → see also **stricken**, **striking** ¹⁹ to **strike** a chord → see **chord** ²⁰ to **strike home** → see **home**

❸ **strike** /straɪk/ (strikes, striking, struck, stricken)

▶ **strike down** PHRASAL VERB 句動詞 If someone **is struck down**, especially by an illness, they are killed or severely harmed. 命を落とす [WRITTEN 書き言葉] ❑ *Frank had been struck down by a massive heart attack.* フランクは重度の心臓発作で命を落としてしまった．

▶ **strike out** PHRASAL VERB 句動詞 ¹ In baseball, if a batter **strikes out**, they fail three times to hit the ball and end their turn. If a pitcher **strikes out**, they throw three balls that the batter fails to hit, and end the batter's turn. 三振する ❑ *Trachsel has struck Bonds out on seven occasions.* トラクセルはボンズを7回三振に仕留めた． ❑ *The third baseman struck out four times.* 三塁手は4回三振になった． ❑ *The Marlin pitcher struck out the first batter he faced.* マーリンの投手は最初に迎えた打者を三振に仕留めた． ² PHRASAL VERB 句動詞 If you **strike out**, you begin to do something different, often because you want to become more independent. 自立する ❑ *She wanted me to strike out on my own, buy a business.* 彼女は僕に事業を始めて，自立することを望んでいた． ³ PHRASAL VERB 句動詞 If you **strike out** at someone, you hit, attack, or speak angrily to them. 当り散らす ❑ *He seemed always ready to strike out at anyone and for any cause.* 彼はいつでも誰にでもどんな理由でも当り散らしそうだった． ⁴ → see also **strike ❷ 15**

▶ **strike up** PHRASAL VERB 句動詞 When you **strike up** a conversation or friendship with someone, you begin one. 仲よくなる [WRITTEN 書き言葉] ❑ *I trailed her into Penney's and struck up a conversation.* 私はペニーのうちで彼女の後をつけ，話しかけた．

strik|er /straɪkər/ (strikers) ¹ N-COUNT 可算名詞 In soccer and some other team sports, a **striker** is a player who mainly attacks and scores goals, rather than defends. ストライカー ❑ *...and the striker scored his sixth goal of the season.* そしてストライカーがシーズン6度目のゴールを決めて ² → see also **strike ❷ 1**

strik|ing /straɪkɪŋ/ ¹ ADJ 形容詞 Something that is **striking**

is very noticeable or unusual. 顕著な，目立つ ❑ *The most striking feature of those statistics is the high proportion of suicides.* それらの統計で最も顕著な特徴は自殺の割合が高いことだ． ❑ *He bears a striking resemblance to Lenin.* 彼はレーニンに驚くほどよく似ている． ● **strik|ing|ly** ADV 副詞 著しく ❑ *In one respect, however, the men really were strikingly similar.* しかしながら，ある意味で彼らの男性たちは本当に非常によく似ていた． ❑ *...a strikingly handsome man.* はっとするほどハンサムな男性 ² ADJ 形容詞 Someone who is **striking** is very attractive, in a noticeable way. はっとするほど魅力的な ❑ *She was a striking woman with long blonde hair.* 彼女は長いブロンド髪のはっとするほど魅力的な女性でした．

string /strɪŋ/ (strings, stringing, strung) ¹ N-VAR 可変性名詞 **String** is thin rope made of twisted threads, used for tying things together or tying up packages. ひも ❑ *He held out a small bag tied with string.* 彼はひもで結んだ小さな袋を差し出した． ² N-COUNT 可算名詞 A **string of** things is a number of them on a piece of string, thread, or wire. ひもでつないだもの 一連 ❑ *She wore a string of pearls around her neck.* 彼女は真珠のネックレスをしていた． ³ N-COUNT 可算名詞 A **string of** places or objects is a number of them that form a line. 列，連なり ❑ *The landscape is broken only by a string of villages.* 風景が途切れているのは村々の続いているところだけだった． ⁴ N-COUNT 可算名詞 A **string of** similar events is a series of them that happen one after the other. 一連，立て続け ❑ *The incident was the latest in a string of attacks.* その事件は一連の襲撃では最後に起きた． ⁵ N-COUNT 可算名詞 The **strings** on a musical instrument such as a violin or guitar are the thin pieces of wire or nylon stretched across it that make sounds when the instrument is played. 弦 ❑ *He went off to change a guitar string.* 彼はギターの弦を変えるのに立ち去った． ⁶ N-PLURAL 複数名詞 The **strings** are the section of an orchestra which consists of stringed instruments played with a bow. 弦楽器，ストリングス ❑ *The strings provided a melodic background to the passages played by the soloist.* 弦楽器部は，独奏者によって奏でられる楽節に美しい響きの背景音を出した． ⁷ PHRASE 句 If something is offered to you with **no strings attached** or with **no strings**, it is offered without any special conditions. 付帯条件のないこと ❑ *Aid should be given to developing countries with no strings attached.* 開発国への救済は付帯条件なしで行われるべきだ． ⁸ PHRASE 句 If you **pull strings**, you use your influence with other people in order to get something done, often unfairly. 裏工作をする ❑ *Tony is sure he can pull a few strings and get you in.* トニーは，裏工作をしてあなたを入学させられることに確信を持っている．

→ see Picture Dictionary: **strings**
→ see **orchestra**

▶ **string together** PHRASAL VERB 句動詞 If you **string** things **together**, you form something from them by adding them to each other, one at a time. つなぎ合わせる ❑ *As speech develops, the child starts to string more words together.* 言語能力が成長するにしたがって，子供のつなぎ合わせる言葉の数が増え始める．

Thesaurus		string また次を参照：
N.	cord, fiber, rope, twine ¹	
	chain, file, line, row, sequence, series ³ ⁴	

Word Partnership		string は次の語句と使われる：
N.	piece of string ¹	
	string of pearls ²	
	string of attacks, string of bombings, string of losses, string of scandals ⁴	
	banjo string, guitar string ⁵	
ADJ.	long string ¹–⁴	
	latest string of *something*, recent string of *something* ⁴	

strin|gent /strɪndʒ³nt/ ADJ 形容詞 **Stringent** laws, rules, or conditions are very severe or are strictly controlled. 厳しい，厳重な [FORMAL 形式ばった] ❑ *He announced that there would be more stringent controls on the possession of weapons.* 彼は，武器所持の管理がさらに厳重になることを発表した．

strip /strɪp/ (strips, stripping, stripped) ¹ N-COUNT 可算名詞 A **strip** of something such as paper, cloth, or food is a long, narrow piece of it. 細長い切れ ❑ *...a new kind of manufactured wood made by pressing strips of wood together and baking them.* 細長い木片を圧縮し焼き固めて製造される新しい種類の加工材 ❑ *The simplest rag-rugs are made with strips of fabric braided together.* 最も単純なラグラグは細長い布を編んでまとめて作られている． ² N-COUNT 可算名詞 A **strip** of land or water is a long narrow area of it. 細長い場所 ❑ *The coastal cities of Liguria sit on narrow strips of land lying under steep mountains.* リグリアの湾岸都市は険しい山々のふもとの細長い土地にある． ³ N-COUNT 可算名詞 A **strip** is a long street in a city or town, where there are a lot of stores, restaurants, and hotels. 大通り [AM 米国英語] ❑ *...Goff's Charcoal Hamburgers on Lover's Lane, a busy commercial strip in North Dallas.* にぎやかなノース・ダラスの商業地のラバーズ通りにあるゴフの炭焼きバーガー ⁴ V-I 自動詞 If you

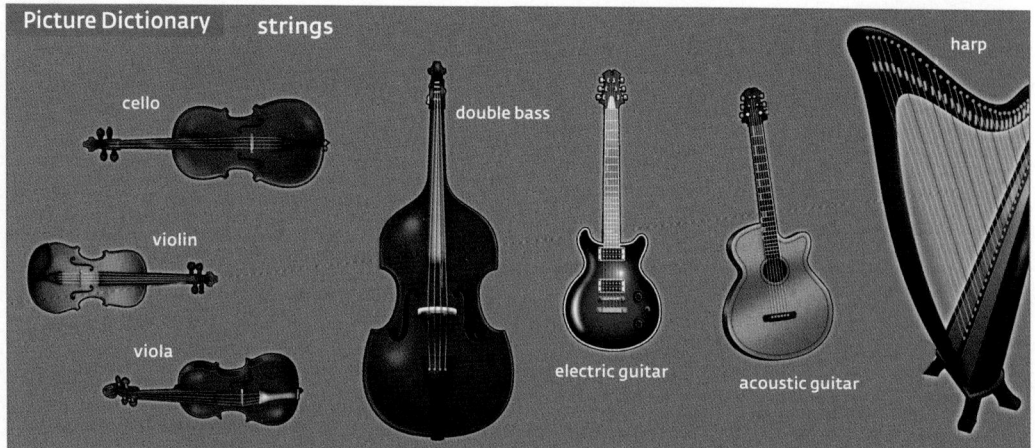

Picture Dictionary   strings

cello

violin

viola

double bass

electric guitar

acoustic guitar

harp

strip, you take off your clothes. 服を脱ぐ □*They stripped completely, and lay and turned in the damp grass.* 彼はすっかり脱ぎ、湿った草の上に寝転がった. ● PHRASAL VERB 句動詞 **Strip off** means the same as **strip.** 服を脱ぐ □*The children were brazenly stripping off and leaping into the sea.* 子供たちは平然と服を脱ぎ、海に飛び込んだ. ⑤ V-T 他動詞 If someone **is stripped**, their clothes are taken off by another person, for example in order to search for hidden or illegal things. 服を脱がせる [usu passive] □*One prisoner claimed he'd been dragged to a cell, stripped, and beaten.* ある囚人は、独房に引きずられ、服をはぎ取られてたたかれたと言い張った. ⑥ V-T 他動詞 To **strip** something means to remove everything that covers it. (覆いなどを) はがす □*After Mike left for work I stripped the beds and vacuumed the carpets.* マイクが仕事に出かけた後で私はベッドカバーをはがしてカーペットに掃除機をかけた. ⑦ V-T 他動詞 If you **strip** an engine or a piece of equipment, you take it to pieces so that it can be cleaned or repaired. 分解する □*Volvo's three-man team stripped the car and treated it to a restoration.* ボルボ車の3人チームはその車を分解して元に戻した. ● PHRASAL VERB 句動詞 **Strip down** means the same as **strip.** 分解する □*In five years I had to strip the water pump down four times.* 5年間の間に送水ポンプを4回分解しなければならなかった. ⑧ V-T 他動詞 To **strip** someone **of** their property, rights, or titles means to take those things away from them. 奪う, 剥奪 (はくだつ) する □*The soldiers have stripped the civilians of their passports, and every other type of document.* 兵士は市民からパスポートやその他すべての種類の書類を剥奪 (はくだつ) した. ⑨ N-COUNT 可算名詞 In a newspaper or magazine, a **strip** is a series of drawings which tell a story. The words spoken by the characters are often written on the drawings. コマ割り漫画 □*...the Doonesbury strip.* ドゥーンズベリーのコマ割り漫画.

▶ **strip away** PHRASAL VERB 句動詞 To **strip away** something, especially something that hides the true nature of a thing, means to remove it completely. はがす, 取り除く □*Altman strips away the pretense and mythology to expose the film industry as a business like any other.* アルトマンは映画産業が他のビジネスと変わらないことを暴くために見せかけや神話をはぎ取った.

▶ **strip off** ⓵ PHRASAL VERB 句動詞 If you **strip off** your clothes, you take them off. 脱ぐ □*He stripped off his wet clothes and stepped into the shower.* 彼は濡れた服を脱いでシャワーに入った. ② → see also **strip 4**

Word Partnership	*strip* は次の語句と使われる:
ADJ.	long strip, narrow strip ⓵ ②
	commercial strip ⓷
	strip *(someone)* naked ④ ⑤

stripe /straɪp/ (**stripes**) N-COUNT 可算名詞 A **stripe** is a long line which is a different color from the areas next to it. ストライプ, しま □*She wore a bright green jogging suit with a white stripe down the sides.* 彼女はサイドに白い線が入った鮮やかな緑のジョギングウェアを着ていた.

striped /straɪpt/ ADJ 形容詞 Something that is **striped** has stripes on it. ストライプの, しま模様の □*...a bottle green and maroon striped tie.* 深緑とくり色のしま模様のネクタイ.

strip|per /strɪpər/ (**strippers**) N-COUNT 可算名詞 A **stripper** is a person who earns money by stripping their clothes off. ストリッパー □*She worked as a stripper and did some acting.* 彼女はストリッパーとして働き、少し芝居にも出ていた.

strive /straɪv/ (**strives, striving**)

> The past tense is either **strove** or **strived**, and the past participle is either **striven** or **strived**.
>
> 過去時制は **strove** かまたは **strived** で, 過去分詞は **striven** かまたは **strived** である.

V-T/V-I 他動詞/自動詞 If you **strive to** do something or **strive for** something, you make a great effort to do it or get it. 努力する □*He strives hard to keep himself very fit.* 彼は、健康維持のためかなり努力をしている.

strode /stroʊd/ **Strode** is the past tense and past participle of **stride.** strideの過去形・過去分詞

stroke /stroʊk/ (**strokes, stroking, stroked**) ⓵ V-T 他動詞 If you **stroke** someone or something, you move your hand slowly and gently over them. なでる □*Carla, curled up on the sofa, was smoking a cigarette and stroking her cat.* カーラはソファーの上で丸くなって、たばこを吸いながらネコをなでていた. ② N-COUNT 可算名詞 If someone has a **stroke**, a blood vessel in their brain bursts or becomes blocked, which may kill them or make them unable to move one side of their body. 脳卒中 □*He had a minor stroke in 1987, which left him partly paralyzed.* 彼は1987年に軽度の脳卒中を起こし、部分麻痺になった. ③ N-COUNT 可算名詞 The **strokes** of a pen or brush are the movements or marks that you make with it when you are writing or painting. 筆跡, 線 □*Fill in gaps by using short, upward strokes of the pencil.* 空間を鉛筆で短く上向きに書いて埋めなさい. ④ N-COUNT 可算名詞 When you are swimming or rowing, your **strokes** are the repeated movements that you make with your arms or the oars. ストローク, ひとこぎ □*I turned and swam a few strokes further out to sea.* 向きを変えて海に向かってさらに少し泳いだ. ⑤ N-COUNT 可算名詞 A swimming **stroke** is a particular style or method of swimming. 泳法 □*She spent hours practicing the breast stroke.* 彼女は何時間も平泳ぎの練習をした. ⑥ N-COUNT 可算名詞 The **strokes** of a clock are the sounds that indicate each hour. (時計の) 鳴る音 □*On the stroke of 12, fireworks suddenly exploded into the night.* ちょうど12時に突然夜空に花火が上がった. ⑦ N-COUNT 可算名詞 In sports such as tennis, baseball, golf, and cricket, a **stroke** is the action of hitting the ball. ストローク, ショット □*Compton was swinging the ball here, there, and everywhere with each stroke.* コンプトンはショットごとにボールをあちこちあらゆる場所に飛ばしていた. ⑧ N-SING 単数名詞 A **stroke of** luck or good fortune is something lucky that happens. 思いがけないこと □*It didn't rain, which turned out to be a stroke of luck.* 雨が降らなかったのは、運がよかったですね. ⑨ N-SING 単数名詞 A **stroke of** genius or inspiration is a very good idea that someone suddenly has. ひらめき □*At the time, his appointment seemed a stroke of genius.* 当時は彼の任命が天才的なひらめきに思えた. ⑩ PHRASE 句 If someone does not **do a stroke of** work, they are very lazy and do no work at all. (否定形で) ちっとも仕事をしない [INFORMAL くだけた, EMPHASIS 強調] □*I never did a stroke of work in college.* 大学ではちっとも勉強しなかった.

Word Partnership	*stroke* は次の語句と使われる:
V.	die from a stroke, have a stroke, suffer a stroke ②
N.	risk of a stroke ②
	stroke of a pen ③

stroll /stroʊl/ (**strolls, strolling, strolled**) V-I 自動詞 If you **stroll** somewhere, you walk there in a slow, relaxed way. ぶらぶら歩く □*He collected some orange juice from the refrigerator and, glass in hand,*

strolled to the kitchen window. 彼は冷蔵庫からオレンジジュースを取って、コップを手に持ち、キッチンの窓のところまでぶらぶらと歩いた. ●N-COUNT 可算名詞 **Stroll** is also a noun. ぶらぶら歩き □*After dinner, I took a stroll round the city.* 夕食後、街中をぶらりと散歩に出かけた.

→ see **park**

stroll|er /stroʊlər/ (**strollers**) N-COUNT 可算名詞 A **stroller** is a small chair on wheels, in which a baby or small child can sit and be wheeled around. ベビーカー、ベビーバギー [AM 米国英語]

strong /strɔŋ/ (**stronger** /strɔŋgər/, **strongest** /strɔŋgɪst/) **1** ADJ 形容詞 Someone who is **strong** is healthy with good muscles and can move or carry heavy things, or do hard physical work. 力強い、たくましい □*I'm not strong enough to carry him.* 私は彼を抱えるほど力がない. **2** ADJ 形容詞 Someone who is **strong** is confident and determined, and is not easily influenced or worried by other people. 強い、しっかりした □*He is sharp and manipulative with a strong personality.* 彼は頭が切れてしっかりした性格で人を操るタイプだ. □*It's up to managers to be strong and do what they believe is right.* しっかりとして自分が正しいと思うことをするのはマネージャー次第だ. **3** ADJ 形容詞 **Strong** objects or materials are not easily broken and can support a lot of weight or resist a lot of strain. 丈夫な、頑丈な □*The vacuum flask has a strong casing, which won't crack or chip.* 真空フラスコのケーシングは丈夫で割れたりかけたりしない. □*Glue the mirror in with a strong adhesive.* 強力な接着剤で鏡を修理しなさい. ●**strong|ly** ADV 副詞 [ADV -ed] 丈夫に □*The fence was very strongly built, with very large posts.* 塀は非常に大きくないくいを使って非常に頑丈に建てられていた. **4** ADJ 形容詞 A **strong** wind, current, or other force has a lot of power or speed, and can cause heavy things to move. (風・流れ・力などが) 強い □*Strong winds and torrential rain combined to make conditions terrible for golfers in the Scottish Open.* 暴風と集中豪雨が重なってスコティッシュ・オープンは最悪の条件となった. □*A fairly strong current seemed to be moving the whole boat.* かなり強い水流がボート全体を動かしているようだった. ●**strong|ly** ADV 副詞 [ADV with v] 強く □*The metal is strongly attracted to the surface.* その金属はしっかりと表面に引きつけられていた. **5** ADJ 形容詞 A **strong** impression or influence has a great effect on someone. (影響が) 強い □*We're glad if our music makes a strong impression, even if it's a negative one.* 私たちの音楽が強い影響を与えられれば、たとえそれが否定的なものでもうれしく思う. □*There will be a strong incentive to enter into a process of negotiation.* 交渉を始める強い動機があるだろう. ●**strong|ly** ADV 副詞 [ADV with v] 強く □*He is strongly influenced by Spanish painters such as Goya and El Greco.* 彼はゴヤやエル・グレコのようなスペインの画家に強い影響を受けている. **6** ADJ 形容詞 If you have **strong** opinions on something or express them using **strong** words, you have extreme or very definite opinions which you are willing to express or defend. 強い、確固とした □*She is known to hold strong views on Cuba.* 彼女はキューバに関して強い見解を持っていることで知られている. □*I am a strong supporter of the president.* 私は大統領の強い支持者だ. ●**strong|ly** ADV 副詞 断固として □*Obviously you feel very strongly about this.* 明らかにこの件に関しては強い感情をお持ちですね. □*Republicans in the House were strongly opposed to lifting the ban.* 議会の共和党員は禁止解除をすることに断固反対していた. **7** ADJ 形容詞 If someone in authority takes **strong** action, they act firmly and severely. 断固として厳しい □*The American public deserves strong action from Congress.* アメリカ国民のために議会ははっきりとした行動をとるべきです. **8** ADJ 形容詞 If there is a **strong** case or argument for something, it is supported by a lot of evidence. 説得力がある □*The testimony presented offered a strong case for acquitting her on grounds of self-defense.* 公表された証言は彼女を自己防衛として無罪判決にするための揺るぎない証拠となった. ●**strong|ly** ADV 副詞 強弁に □*He argues strongly for retention of NATO as a guarantee of peace.* 彼は平和の保障のためにNATO軍を保持することを強く主張している. **9** ADJ 形容詞 If there is a **strong** possibility or chance that something is true or will happen, it is very likely to be true or to happen. 高い □*There is a strong possibility that the cat could be carrying the condition by eating contaminated pet food.* そのネコは汚染されたペットフードを食べたためにその病気にかかった可能性が高い. **10** ADJ 形容詞 [ADJ n] Your **strong** points are your best qualities or talents, or the things you are good at. 得意な □*Discretion is not Jeremy's strong point.* 口の堅さというのはジェレミーの得意とするところではない. □*Exports may be the only strong point in the economy over the next six to 12 months.* 向こう6～12か月の経済における強みは輸出だけかもしれません. **11** ADJ 形容詞 A **strong** competitor, candidate, or team is good or likely to succeed. 有力な、優秀な □*She was a strong contender for the Olympic team.* 彼女はオリンピックチームの有力な候補者だった. **12** ADJ 形容詞 If a relationship or link is **strong**, it is close and likely to last for a long time. (関係・きずなが) 強い □*He felt he had a relationship strong enough to talk frankly to Sarah.* 彼はサラに率直に話せるほど強いきずながあると思っていた. □*This has tested our marriage, and we have come through it stronger than ever.* これで私たちの結婚が試されたが、これまで以上に強いきずなで乗り越えた. **13** ADJ 形容詞 A **strong** currency, economy, or industry has a high value or is

very successful. 強い、好調な □*The U.S. dollar continued its strong performance in Tokyo today.* 米ドルは本日東京市場で引き続き好調でした. **14** ADJ 形容詞 If something is a **strong** element or part of something else, it is an important or large part of it. 有力な、重要な □*We are especially encouraged by the strong representation, this year, of women in information technology disciplines.* 特に情報技術部門において今年は有力な女性代表者がいることで心強く思っている. **15** ADJ 形容詞 You can use **strong** when you are saying how many people there are in a group. For example, if a group is twenty strong, there are twenty people in it. 人 [num ADJ] □*Ukraine indicated that it would establish its own army, 400,000 strong.* ウクライナは40万人の独自の軍隊を結成することを示唆しました. **16** ADJ 形容詞 A **strong** drink, chemical, or drug contains a lot of the particular substance which makes it effective. 強い、濃い □*Strong coffee or tea late at night may cause sleeplessness.* 夜遅く濃いコーヒーや紅茶を飲むと不眠になるかもしれない. **17** ADJ 形容詞 A **strong** color, flavor, smell, sound, or light is intense and easily noticed. 強い、きつい □*As she went past there was a gust of strong perfume.* 彼女が通り過ぎるとき、突然強い香水の香りがした. ●**strong|ly** ADV with v] 強く □*He leaned over her, smelling strongly of sweat.* 彼は彼女のほうに身をかがめたが、かなり汗臭かった. **18** ADJ 形容詞 If someone has a **strong** accent, they speak in a distinctive way that shows very clearly what country or region they come from. (なまりが) 強い □*"Good, Mr. Ryle," he said in English with a strong French accent.* 「よろしい、ライルさん」と彼は強いフランスなまりの英語で言った. **19** PHRASE 句 If someone or something is still **going strong**, they are still alive, in good condition, or popular after a long time. 活躍中の [INFORMAL くだけた] □*The old machinery was still going strong.* その古い機械はまだ活動していました.

> **Thesaurus**   **strong** また次を参照：
>
> ADJ.   mighty, powerful, tough; (ant.) weak **1**
>   confident, determined; (ant.) cowardly **2**
>   solid, sturdy **3**

strong|hold /strɔŋhoʊld/ (**strongholds**) N-COUNT 可算名詞 If you say that a place or region is a **stronghold** of a particular attitude or belief, you mean that most people there share this attitude or belief. 拠点、本拠地 □*Florida is a stronghold for pro-choice activists.* フロリダは中絶賛成活動家の本拠地だ.

strove /stroʊv/ **Strove** is a past tense of **strive**. striveの過去形

struck /strʌk/ **Struck** is the past tense and past participle of **strike**. strikeの過去形・過去分詞

struc|tur|al /strʌktʃərəl/ ADJ 形容詞 **Structural** means relating to or affecting the structure of something. 構造上の、構成上の □*The explosion caused little structural damage to the office towers themselves.* その爆発によりオフィスビルに構造的な損傷が少し生じました. ●**struc|tur|al|ly** ADV 副詞 構造上 □*When we bought the house, it was structurally sound, but I decided to redecorate throughout.* 私たちがその家を購入したとき、構造上には問題はなかったが、家全体を改装することにした.

struc|tur|al en|gi|neer (**structural engineers**) N-COUNT 可算名詞 A **structural engineer** is an engineer who works on large structures such as roads, bridges, and large buildings. 構造技術者

struc|ture /strʌktʃər/ (**structures, structuring, structured**) **1** N-VAR 可変性名詞 The **structure of** something is the way in which it is made, built, or organized. 構造 □*The typical family structure of Freud's patients involved two parents and two children.* フロイドの患者の典型的な家族構成は両親と子供が2人だった. **2** N-COUNT 可算名詞 A **structure** is something that consists of parts connected together in an ordered way. 構造 □*The feet are highly specialized structures made up of 26 small delicate bones.* 足は、26の小骨からできていて非常に特別な構造をしている. **3** N-COUNT 可算名詞 A **structure** is something that has been built. 建造物 □*About half of those funds has gone to repair public roads, structures, and bridges.* その資金の約半分が公道、建築物、橋などの修復に回されました. **4** V-T 他動詞 If you structure something, you arrange it in a careful, organized pattern or system. 組み立てる □*By structuring the course this way, we're forced to produce something the companies think is valuable.* コースをこのようにスケジュール化することで、企業が認めるものを実現せざるを得ない.

strug|gle /strʌgəl/ (**struggles, struggling, struggled**) **1** V-T/V-I 他動詞/自動詞 If you **struggle** to do something, you try hard to do it, even though other people or things may be making it difficult for you to succeed. 〜するのに奮闘する □*They had to struggle against all kinds of adversity.* 彼らはあらゆる困難と戦わねばならなかった. **2** N-VAR 可変性名詞 A **struggle** is a long and difficult attempt to achieve something such as freedom or political rights. 奮闘 □*Life became a struggle for survival.* 人生が生き残り闘争になった. □*...a young boy's struggle to support his poverty-stricken family.* 貧困に悩む家庭を援助するための少年の苦闘 **3** V-I 自動詞 If you **struggle** when you are being held, you twist, kick, and move violently in order to get free. もがく □*I struggled, but he was a tall man, well built.*

私はもがいたが，彼は背が高くて体格がよかった．**4** V-RECIP 相互動詞 If two people **struggle with** each other, they fight. 争う ❏She screamed at him to "stop it" as they struggled on the ground. 2人が地面で争っているとき，彼女は彼に「止めて」と叫んだ．●N-COUNT 可算名詞 **Struggle** is also a noun. 争い ❏He died in a struggle with prison officers less than two months after coming to Britain. 彼は英国に来て2か月もたたないうちに看守と争って死亡した．**5** V-T/V-I 他動詞/自動詞 If you **struggle to** move yourself or **to** move a heavy object, you try to do it, but it is difficult. 悪戦苦闘する ❏I could see the young boy struggling to free himself. 少年が自由になろうとして悪戦苦闘しているのが見えた．**6** V-T/V-I 他動詞/自動詞 If a person or organization **is struggling**, they are likely to fail in what they are doing, even though they might be trying very hard. 懸命に取り組んでいる，困っている [only cont] ❏The company is struggling to find buyers for its new product. その会社は新製品の買い手を見つけるのに困っている．❏One in five young adults was struggling with everyday mathematics. 5人に1人の若者は日常的な算数で困っていた．**7** N-SING 単数名詞 An action or activity that is a **struggle** is very difficult to do. 困難 ❏Losing weight was a terrible struggle. 減量するのは大変だった．

Word Partnership	*struggle* は次の語句と使われる:
ADJ.	**bitter** struggle, **internal** struggle, **long** struggle, **ongoing** struggle, **uphill** struggle **1** **2** **locked in a** struggle **1** **2** **political** struggle **2**
N.	struggle **for democracy**, struggle **for equality**, struggle **for freedom/independence**, **power** struggle, struggle **for survival** **2**

strum /strʌm/ (strums, strumming, strummed) V-T 他動詞 If you **strum** a stringed instrument such as a guitar, you play it by moving your fingers backward and forward across the strings. かき鳴らす ❏In the corner, one youth sat alone, softly strumming a guitar. 部屋の隅で若者が1人で座り，優しくギターをかき鳴らしていた．

strung /strʌŋ/ **Strung** is the past tense and past participle of **string**. stringの過去形・過去分詞

strut /strʌt/ (struts, strutting, strutted) **1** V-I 自動詞 Someone who **struts** walks in a proud way, with their head held high and their chest out, as if they are very important. 気取って歩く [DISAPPROVAL 不賛成] ❏He struts around town like he owns the place. 彼は町を我が物顔で気取って歩く．**2** N-COUNT 可算名詞 A **strut** is a piece of wood or metal which holds the weight of other pieces in a building or other structure. 支柱，筋交い ❏...the struts of a suspension bridge. つり橋の支柱

stub /stʌb/ (stubs, stubbing, stubbed) **1** N-COUNT 可算名詞 The **stub** of a cigarette or a pencil is the last short piece of it which remains when the rest has been used. (たばこの) 吸殻 (鉛筆の) 使い残り ❏He pulled the stub of a pencil from behind his ear. 彼は短くなった鉛筆を耳から抜いた．**2** N-COUNT 可算名詞 A ticket **stub** is the part that you keep when you go in to watch a performance. 半券 ❏Fans who still have their ticket stubs should contact the box office by July 3. チケットの半券をまだ持っているファンは7月3日までにチケット売り場に連絡するとよい．**3** N-COUNT 可算名詞 A check **stub** is the small part that you keep as a record of what you have paid. 控え ❏I have every check stub we've written since 1959. 1959年以降使った小切手の控えをすべて持っています．**4** V-T 他動詞 If you **stub** your **toe**, you hurt it by accidentally kicking something. つま先をぶつける ❏I stubbed my toes against a table leg. テーブルの脚につま先をぶつけた．

▶ **stub out** PHRASAL VERB 句動詞 When someone **stubs** out a cigarette, they put it out by pressing it against something hard. もみ消す ❏Signs across the entrances warn all visitors to stub out their cigarettes. 入り口周辺の標識には，訪問者はたばこの火を消すようにと書いてある．

stub|ble /stʌbᵊl/ **1** N-UNCOUNT 不可算名詞 **Stubble** is the short stalks which are left standing in fields after corn or wheat has been cut. 刈り株 ❏The stubble was burning in the fields. 刈り株が野原で燃えていた．**2** N-UNCOUNT 不可算名詞 The very short hairs on a man's face when he has not shaved recently are referred to as **stubble**. 無精ひげ ❏His face was covered with the stubble of several nights. 彼の顔は数日間生やしている無精ひげだらけだった．

stub|born /stʌbərn/ **1** ADJ 形容詞 Someone who is **stubborn** or who behaves in a **stubborn** way is determined to do what they want and is very unwilling to change their mind. 頑固な ❏He is a stubborn character used to getting his own way. 彼は自分の思い通りにすることに慣れている頑固な人だ．●**stub|born|ly** ADV 副詞 頑固に ❏He stubbornly refused to tell her how he had come to be in such a state. 彼は，どうしてそのような状態に陥ったのかを頑固にも彼女に話さなかった．●**stub|born|ness** N-UNCOUNT 不可算名詞 頑固さ ❏I couldn't tell if his refusal to talk was simple stubbornness. 彼が話そうとしないのは単に頑固なだけなのかどうか分からなかった．**2** ADJ 形容詞 A **stubborn** stain or problem is difficult to remove or to deal with. しつこい ❏This treatment removes the most stubborn stains. この方法

でかなりしつこい汚れも取れる．●**stub|born|ly** ADV 副詞 しつこく ❏Some interest rates have remained stubbornly high. いつまでたっても高金利を維持しているところもあります．

stuck /stʌk/ **1** **Stuck** is the past tense and past participle of **stick**. stickの過去形・過去分詞 **2** ADJ 形容詞 If something is **stuck** in a particular position, it is fixed tightly in this position and is unable to move. はまり込んで動かない [v-link ADJ] ❏He said his car had gotten stuck in the snow. 彼は車が雪で立ち往生したと言った．**3** ADJ 形容詞 If you are **stuck** in a place, you want to get away from it, but are unable to. 出られない [v-link ADJ prep/adv] ❏I was stuck at home with flu. インフルエンザで家にこもりきりだった．**4** ADJ 形容詞 If you are **stuck** in a boring or unpleasant situation, you are unable to change it or get away from it. 身動きが取れない，はまり込んでいる [v-link ADJ prep/adv] ❏I don't want to get stuck in another job like that. 似たような仕事にはまり込むのはいやです．**5** ADJ 形容詞 If something is **stuck** at a particular level or stage, it is not progressing or changing. 行き詰っている，とどまる [v-link ADJ prep/adv] ❏I think the economy is stuck on a plateau of slow growth. 経済は成長停滞期で行き詰まっていると思います．❏U.S. unemployment figures for March showed the jobless rate stuck at 7 percent. 米国の3月の失業者数は失業率が7%でとどまっているのを示していた．**6** ADJ 形容詞 If you are **stuck with** something that you do not want, you cannot get rid of it. しょい込んでいる [v-link ADJ "with" n] ❏Many people are now stuck with expensive fixed-rate mortgages. 近年多くの人々が固定金利の住宅ローンを抱えている．**7** ADJ 形容詞 If you get **stuck** when you are trying to do something, you are unable to continue doing it because it is too difficult. 行き詰る，お手上げ状態になる [v-link ADJ] ❏They will be there to help if you get stuck. 彼らはあなたが困ったときに助けるためにそこにいるでしょう．

stud /stʌd/ (studs) **1** N-COUNT 可算名詞 **Studs** are small pieces of metal which are attached to a surface for decoration. 飾りびょう ❏You see studs on lots of front doors. 多くの玄関で飾りびょうを見かける．**2** N-COUNT 可算名詞 **Studs** are small round objects attached to the bottom of boots, especially sports boots, so that the person wearing them does not slip. 滑り止め [BRIT 英国英語; AM cleats 米国英語 cleats] **3** N-UNCOUNT 不可算名詞 Horses or other animals that are kept for **stud** are kept to be used for breeding. 種付け ❏He was voted horse of the year and then was retired to stud. 彼は今年の馬に選ばれて，種馬になった．

stud|ded /stʌdɪd/ ADJ 形容詞 Something that is **studded** is decorated with studs or things that look like studs. 飾りびょうのついた ❏...studded leather jackets. 飾りをちりばめた革ジャン

stu|dent /studᵊnt/ (students) **1** N-COUNT 可算名詞 A **student** is a person who is studying at an elementary school, secondary school, college, or university. 生徒，学生 ❏Warren's eldest son is an art student. ウォレンの長男は美大生だ．**2** → see also **graduate student** **3** N-COUNT 可算名詞 Someone who is a **student of** a particular subject is interested in the subject and spends time learning about it. 研究家 ❏...a passionate student of history and an expert on nineteenth-century prime ministers. 歴史の情熱的な研究家で19世紀の首脳についての専門家

→ see **graduation**

stu|dio /studioʊ/ (studios) **1** N-COUNT 可算名詞 A **studio** is a room where a painter, photographer, or designer works. アトリエ，工房 ❏She was in her studio again, painting onto a large canvas. 彼女はまたアトリエで大きなキャンバスに絵を描いていた．**2** N-COUNT 可算名詞 A **studio** is a room where radio or television programs are recorded, CDs are produced, or movies are made. スタジオ ❏She's much happier performing live than in a recording studio. 彼女は録音スタジオよりもライブをするほうがずっと好きだ．**3** N-COUNT 可算名詞 You can also refer to film-making or recording companies as **studios**. 映画会社 ❏She wrote to Paramount Studios and asked if they would audition her. 彼女はパラマウント・スタジオに手紙を書き，オーディションの依頼をした．**4** N-COUNT 可算名詞 A **studio** or a **studio** apartment is a small apartment with one room for living and sleeping in, a kitchen, and a bathroom. You can also talk about a **studio apartment**. ワンルームマンション ❏Home for a couple of years was a studio apartment. 数年間はワンルームマンションだった．

→ see **art**

Word Partnership	*studio* は次の語句と使われる:
N.	studio **album**, studio **audience**, **music** studio, **recording** studio, **television/TV** studio **2** studio **executives**, **film/movie** studio **3**

study /stʌdi/ (studies, studying, studied) **1** V-T/V-I 他動詞/自動詞 If you **study**, you spend time learning about a particular subject or subjects. 勉強する ❏...a relaxed and happy atmosphere that will allow you to study to your full potential. 最大の可能性を生かして勉強できる和やかで楽しい雰囲気 ❏He studied History and Economics. 彼は歴史と経済学を勉強した．**2** N-UNCOUNT 不可算名詞 **Study** is

the activity of studying. 勉強 [also N in pl] ❑ ...*the use of maps and visual evidence in the study of local history*. 地元の歴史の勉強で地図や物的証拠を利用 ❸ N-COUNT 可算名詞 A **study** of a subject is a piece of research on it. 調査 ❑ *Recent studies suggest that as many as 5 in 1,000 new mothers are likely to have this problem*. 最近の調査によると新米ママの1000人中5人もがこの問題を抱えそうだ. ❹ N-PLURAL 複数名詞 You can refer to educational subjects or courses that contain several elements as **studies** of a particular kind. 一学, 一研究 ❑ ...*a center for Islamic studies*. イスラム研究のセンター ❺ V-T 他動詞 If you **study** something, you look at or watch it very carefully, in order to find something out. 注意深く見る ❑ *Debbie studied her friend's face for a moment*. デビーはしばらく友達の顔を注意深く見た. ❻ V-T 他動詞 If you **study** something, you consider it or observe it carefully in order to be able to understand it fully. 調べる, 研究する ❑ *I know that you've been studying chimpanzees for thirty years now*. あなたがこれまでの30年間チンパンジーの研究をしてきたことを知っている. ❼ N-COUNT 可算名詞 A **study** is a room in a house which is used for reading, writing, and studying. 書斎, 勉強部屋 ❑ *That evening we sat together in his study*. その晩, 私たちは彼の書斎で一緒に座った. ❽ → see also **case study**

→ see **laboratory**

stuff /stʌf/ (stuffs, stuffing, stuffed) ❶ N-UNCOUNT 不可算名詞 You can use **stuff** to refer to things such as a substance, a collection of things, events, or ideas, or the contents of something in a general way without mentioning the thing itself by name. (名前を言わずに漠然という場合に用いる) [INFORMAL くだけた] [usu with supp] ❑ *I'd like some coffee, and I don't object to the powdered stuff if it's all you've got*. コーヒーをお願いしたいのですが, インスタントしかなければそれで結構です. ❑ *He pointed to a duffle bag. "That's my stuff."* 彼はダッフルバッグを指して「それは僕のだ」と言った. ❷ V-T 他動詞 If you **stuff** something somewhere, you push it there quickly and roughly. 押し込む ❑ *I stuffed my hands in my pockets*. 私は手をポケットにさっと入れた. ❸ V-T 他動詞 If you **stuff** a container or space **with** something, you fill it with something or with a quantity of things until it is full. 詰め込む ❑ *He grabbed my purse, opened it and stuffed it full, then gave it back to me*. 彼は私のハンドバッグをひったくんで開けて, ものをいっぱいに詰め込んで私に返してきた. ❹ V-T 他動詞 If you **stuff yourself**, you eat a lot of food. おなかいっぱい食べる [INFORMAL くだけた] ❑ *I could stuff myself with ten chocolate bars and half an hour later eat a big meal*. 私はチョコバーを10本食べて, 半時間後に食事をしっかり取ることができる. ❺ V-T 他動詞 If you **stuff** a bird such as a chicken or a vegetable such as a pepper, you put a mixture of food inside it before cooking it. 詰め物をする ❑ *Will you stuff the turkey and shove it in the oven for me?* 七面鳥に詰め物をしてオーブンに放り込んでくれないか? ❻ V-T 他動詞 If a dead animal is **stuffed**, it is filled with a substance so that it can be preserved and displayed. 剥製(はくせい)にする [usu passive] ❑ ...*his collections of stamps and books and stuffed birds*. 切手, 本, 剥製(はくせい)の鳥のコレクション ❼ PHRASE 句 If you say that someone **knows** their **stuff**, you mean that they are good at doing something because they know a lot about it. お手のものである [INFORMAL くだけた, APPROVAL 賛成] ❑ *These guys know their stuff after seven years of war*. 7年間も戦争をしたからこいつらはよく分かっているんだ.

Thesaurus **stuff** また次を参照:

| N. | belongings, goods, material, substance ❶ |
| V. | crowd, fill, jam, squeeze ❷ ❸ |

stuff|ing /stʌfɪŋ/ (stuffings) ❶ N-MASS 質量名詞 **Stuffing** is a mixture of food that is put inside a bird such as a chicken, or a vegetable such as a pepper, before it is cooked. (料理に使う) 詰め物 ❑ *Chestnuts can be used at Christmastime, as a stuffing for turkey, guinea fowl, or chicken*. クリスマスの時期にはクリを七面鳥, ホロホロ鳥, ニワトリの詰め物として使うことができる. ❷ N-UNCOUNT 不可算名詞 **Stuffing** is material that is used to fill things such as cushions or toys in order to make them firm or solid. (ぬいぐるみやクッションに詰める) 詰め物 ❑ ...*a rag doll with all the stuffing coming out*. 中の詰め物が出ているぬいぐるみの人形

stuffy /stʌfi/ (stuffier, stuffiest) ADJ 形容詞 If it is **stuffy** in a place, it is unpleasantly warm and there is not enough fresh air. 息苦しい ❑ *It was hot and stuffy in the classroom even though two of the windows at the back had been opened*. 後ろの方の窓が2つ開いているにもかかわらず, 教室は暑く息苦しかった.

stum|ble /stʌmbᵊl/ (stumbles, stumbling, stumbled) V-I 自動詞 If you **stumble**, you put your foot down awkwardly while you are walking or running and nearly fall over. つまずく ❑ *He stumbled and almost fell*. 彼はつまずいてこけそうになった. ● N-COUNT 可算名詞 **Stumble** is also a noun. つまずき ❑ *I make it into the darkness with only one stumble*. ほんの少しよろめいただけで暗闇にたどり着く.

▸ **stumble across** or **stumble on** PHRASAL VERB 句動詞 If you **stumble across** something or **stumble on** it, you find it or discover it unexpectedly. 偶然見つける ❑ *I stumbled across an extremely simple*

but very exact method for understanding where my money went. 自分のお金をどこに使ったかが分かる簡単極まるがとても正確な方法をたまたま見つけた.

stum|bling block (stumbling blocks) N-COUNT 可算名詞 A **stumbling block** is a problem which stops you from achieving something. 障害 ❑ *The major stumbling block in the talks has been money*. 会談の主な障害は資金でした.

stump /stʌmp/ (stumps, stumping, stumped) ❶ N-COUNT 可算名詞 A **stump** is a small part of something that remains when the rest of it has been removed or broken off. 切り株 ❑ *If you have a tree stump, check it for fungus*. 切り株があれば, キノコがないか確認しなさい. ❷ V-T 他動詞 If you **are stumped** by a question or problem, you cannot think of any solution or answer to it. 返答に困らされる ❑ *John Diamond was stumped by an unexpected question*. ジョン・ダイアモンドは不意の質問で困惑した. ❸ V-I 自動詞 If politicians **stump for** a candidate, they travel around making campaign speeches before an election. 応援遊説をする [AM 米国英語] ❑ *Since September, the president has stumped for Republicans in 23 states*. 9月以来大統領は23州で共和党の応援遊説をした.

stun /stʌn/ (stuns, stunning, stunned) ❶ V-T 他動詞 If you **are stunned** by something, you are extremely shocked or surprised by it and are therefore unable to speak or do anything. ぼう然とさせる [他動詞] ❑ *He's stunned by today's resignation of his longtime ally*. 彼は長年の朋友(ほうゆう)が今日辞任したことでぼう然としています. [usu passive] ● **stunned** ADJ 形容詞 ぼう然とした ❑ *When they told me she was missing I was totally stunned*. 彼女が行方不明になっていると聞いて, 私は完全に動転した. ❷ V-T 他動詞 If something such as a blow on the head **stuns** you, it makes you unconscious or confused and unsteady. 気絶させる [他動詞] ❑ *Sam stood his ground and got a blow that stunned him*. サムは1歩も引かず1撃を食らって気絶した. ❸ → see also **stunning**

stung /stʌŋ/ **Stung** is the past tense and past participle of **sting**. stingの過去形・過去分詞

stunk /stʌŋk/ **Stunk** is the past participle of **stink**. stinkの過去分詞

stun|ning /stʌnɪŋ/ ❶ ADJ 形容詞 A **stunning** person or thing is extremely beautiful or impressive. はっとするほど美しい ❑ *She was 55 and still a stunning woman*. 彼女は55歳でなおはっとするほどきれいだった. ❷ ADJ 形容詞 A **stunning** event is extremely unusual or unexpected. 衝撃的な ❑ *He resigned last night after a stunning defeat in Sunday's vote*. 彼は, 日曜日の選挙で衝撃的な大敗をした昨夜辞任しました.

Word Partnership **stunning** は次の語句と使われる:

| N. | stunning **images**, stunning **views** ❶ |
| | stunning **blow**, stunning **defeat/loss**, stunning **success**, stunning **upset**, stunning **victory** ❷ |

stunt /stʌnt/ (stunts, stunting, stunted) ❶ N-COUNT 可算名詞 A **stunt** is something interesting that is done in order to attract attention and get publicity for the person or company responsible for it. 人目を引くための行為 ❑ *In a bold promotional stunt for the movie, he smashed his car into a passing truck*. 派手な映画プロモーションのために彼は車を通り過ぎるトラックにぶつけた. ❷ N-COUNT 可算名詞 A **stunt** is a dangerous and exciting piece of action in a movie. スタント ❑ *Sean Connery insisted on living dangerously for his new film by performing his own stunts*. ショーン・コネリーは新作映画のスタントを危険をかけて自分で演じると主張した. ❸ V-T 他動詞 If something **stunts** the growth or development of a person or thing, it prevents it from growing or developing as much as it should. 阻害する ❑ *The heart condition had stunted his growth a bit*. 心臓の病気のため彼の成長が少し妨げられました. ● **stunt|ed** ADJ 形容詞 不全の ❑ *Damage may result in stunted growth and sometimes death of the plant*. 被害のため生育不良になり, また場合によっては植物が枯れるかもしれません.

stu|pid /stuːpɪd/ (stupider, stupidest) ❶ ADJ 形容詞 If you say that someone or something is **stupid**, you mean that they show a lack of good judgment or intelligence and they are not at all sensible. ばかな, 頭が悪い ❑ *I'll never do anything so stupid again*. 二度とそんなばかなことをしない. ❑ *I made a stupid mistake*. ばかな間違いをしたんだ. ● **stu|pid|ly** ADV 副詞 愚かにも ❑ *We had stupidly been looking at the wrong column of figures*. 私たちは愚かにも誤った数字の列を見ていた. ● **stu|pid|ity** /stuːpɪdɪti/ N-VAR 可変性名詞 (stupidities) 愚かさ ❑ *I stared at him, astonished by his stupidity*. 私は彼の愚かさにすっかりあきれて彼をじっと見た. ❷ ADJ 形容詞 You say that something is **stupid** to indicate that you do not like it or that it annoys you. くだらない [DISAPPROVAL 不賛成] ❑ *I wouldn't call it art. It's just stupid and tasteless*. それを芸術とは呼ばない. ただのくだらない悪趣味だ.

stur|dy /stˈɜrdi/ (**sturdier, sturdiest**) ADJ 形容詞 Someone or
something that is **sturdy** looks strong and is unlikely to be easily
injured or damaged. 丈夫な, 頑丈な ❑ *She was a short, sturdy woman
in her early sixties.* 彼女は60代前半の背が低くてがっしりした女性だっ
た。 ● **stur|di|ly** ADV 副詞 頑丈に ❑ *It was a good table too, sturdily
constructed of elm.* それはニレの木を材料としてしっかり作られた良質
のテーブルでもあった。

stut|ter /stˈʌtər/ (**stutters, stuttering, stuttered**) 🔢 N-COUNT
可算名詞 If someone has a **stutter**, they find it difficult to say the
first sound of a word, and so they often hesitate or repeat it two
or three times. どもる, つまりながら話す [usu sing] ❑ *He spoke
with a pronounced stutter.* 彼の話し方はどもりが強かった。 🔢 V-I 自
動詞 If someone **stutters**, they have difficulty speaking because
they find it hard to say the first sound of a word. どもる, 滑らか
に話せない ❑ *I was trembling so hard, I thought I would stutter when I
spoke.* 私はあまりにも震えていて話そうとすればどもるだろうと思っ
た。 ● **stut|ter|ing** N-UNCOUNT 不可算名詞 どもり ❑ *He had to stop
talking because if he'd kept on, the stuttering would have started.* 彼が話
すのを止めなければならなかったのは, もし話し続けるとどもりが始ま
りそうだったからだ。

style /staɪl/ (**styles, styling, styled**) 🔢 N-COUNT 可算名詞
The **style** of something is the general way in which it is done
or presented, which often shows the attitudes of the people
involved. やり方, 形式 ❑ *Our children's different needs and learning
styles created many problems.* 子供たちの異なったニーズや学習法に
より多くの問題が生じた。 ❑ *Belmont Park is a broad sweeping track
which will suit the European style of running.* ベルモント・パークは
ヨーロッパ式の競走に適する広々とした幅の広い競技用トラック
だ。 🔢 N-UNCOUNT 不可算名詞 If people or places have **style**, they
are fashionable and elegant. おしゃれ, 上品 ❑ *Boston, you have
to admit, has style.* ボストンが上品な町だというのは認めざるを得な
い。 ❑ *Both love doing things in style.* 2人とも上品に物事をするのが大
好きだ。 🔢 N-VAR 可変性名詞 The **style** of a product is its design.
スタイル, デザイン ❑ *His 50 years of experience have given him strong
convictions about style.* 50年間の経験により彼はスタイルについて
強い確信を持つようになった。 🔢 N-COUNT 可算名詞 In the arts, a
particular **style** is characteristic of a particular period or group of
people. 様式 ❑ *...six scenes in the style of a classical Greek tragedy.* 古
典ギリシア悲劇様式の6つのシーン ❑ *...a mixture of musical styles.* い
ろいろな音楽様式 🔢 V-T 他動詞 If something such as a piece of
clothing, a vehicle, or someone's hair **is styled** in a particular way,
it is designed or shaped in that way. デザインする, 整える [usu
passive] ❑ *His thick blond hair had just been styled before his trip.* 彼
のふさふさしたブロンド髪は旅行前にちょうど整えられたところだっ
た。 🔢 → see also **self-styled**

styl|ish /stˈaɪlɪʃ/ ADJ 形容詞 Someone or something that is
stylish is elegant and fashionable. おしゃれな, かっこいい
❑ *...a very attractive and very stylish woman of 27.* 27歳のとても
魅力的でおしゃれな女性 ● **styl|ish|ly** ADV 副詞 おしゃれに
❑ *...stylishly dressed middle-aged women.* おしゃれな格好をした中年
女性

styl|is|tic /staɪlˈɪstɪk/ ADJ 形容詞 **Stylistic** describes things
relating to the methods and techniques used in creating a piece
of writing, music, or art. 文体の, 様式の ❑ *There are some stylistic
elements in the statue that just don't make sense.* 全くつじつまが合わな
いその銅像にはいくつかの様式的な要素があります。

styl|ized /stˈaɪlaɪzd/ ADJ 形容詞 Something that is **stylized** is
shown or done in a way that is not natural in order to create an
artistic effect. 様式化された ❑ *Some of it has to do with recent stage
musicals, which have been very, very stylized.* その一部は最近の舞台音楽
に関連していて, とてもとても様式化されている。

suave /swɑv/ (**suaver, suavest**) ADJ 形容詞 Someone who is
suave is charming, polite, and elegant, but may be insincere. い
んぎんな, 人当たりのよい ❑ *He is a suave, cool, and cultured man.* 彼は
いんぎんでかっこよくて教養のある人だ。

---

sub /sˈʌb/ (**subs**) 🔢 N-COUNT 可算名詞 A **sub** is the same as a
submarine sandwich. サブマリンサンド [mainly AM 主に米国英語]
🔢 N-COUNT 可算名詞 A **sub** is the same as a **substitute teacher**. 代
行教師 [AM 米国英語] 🔢 N-COUNT 可算名詞 In team games such as
football, a **sub** is a player who is brought into a game to replace
another player. 控え選手, サブ [INFORMAL くだけた] ❑ *We had a
few injuries and had to use youth team kids as subs.* 何人かが負傷し
たので代わりに若手チームのメンバーを起用しなければならなかっ
た。 🔢 N-COUNT 可算名詞 A **sub** is the same as a **submarine**. 潜水艦
[INFORMAL くだけた]

sub|com|mit|tee /sˈʌbkəmɪti/ (**subcommittees**) also **sub-
committee** N-COUNT-COLL 集合可算名詞 A **subcommittee** is a
small committee made up of members of a larger committee. 小
委員会, 分科会

sub|con|scious /sˈʌbkˈɒnʃəs/ 🔢 N-SING 単数名詞 Your
subconscious is the part of your mind that can influence you or
affect your behavior even though you are not aware of it. 潜在意識
❑ *...the hidden power of the subconscious.* 潜在意識の隠れた力 🔢 ADJ
形容詞 A **subconscious** feeling or action exists in or is influenced
by your subconscious. 潜在意識の, 意識下の ❑ *He caught her arm in
a subconscious attempt to detain her.* 彼は彼女を引き止めようとして
無意識に腕をつかまえた。 ● **sub|con|scious|ly** ADV 副詞 潜在意識
の中で, 意識下で ❑ *Subconsciously I had known that I would not be in
personal danger.* なんとなく私は個人的な危険にはさらされていないだ
ろうと分かっていた。
→ see **hypnosis**

sub|con|tract /sˈʌbkəntrˈækt/ (**subcontracts, subcontracting,
subcontracted**) V-T 他動詞 If one company **subcontracts** part of
its work to another company, it pays the other company to do
part of the work that it has been employed to do. 下請けに出す
[BUSINESS 実業] ❑ *The company is subcontracting production of most of
the parts.* その会社は部品生産のほとんどを下請けに出している。

sub|con|trac|tor /sˈʌbkˈɒntræktər/ (**subcontractors**) N-COUNT
可算名詞 A **subcontractor** is a person or company that has a
contract to do part of a job which another company is responsible
for. 下請け業者 [BUSINESS 実業] ❑ *The company was considered as a
possible subcontractor to build the airplane.* その会社は航空機を製造す
る下請け業者として有力な候補とみなされていた。

sub|cul|ture /sˈʌbkʌltʃər/ (**subcultures**) N-COUNT 可算名詞 A
subculture is the ideas, art, and way of life of a group of people
within a society, which are different from the ideas, art, and way
of life of the rest of the society. サブカルチャー, 分派 ❑ *...the latest
American subculture.* 最近のアメリカサブカルチャー
→ see **culture**

sub|di|vi|sion /sˈʌbdɪvɪʒ°n/ (**subdivisions**) 🔢 N-COUNT 可算名
詞 A **subdivision** is an area, part, or section of something which
is itself a part of something larger. 1区画, 1部門 ❑ *Months are a
conventional subdivision of the year.* 月は1年を慣習的に区切ったも
のだ。 🔢 N-COUNT 可算名詞 A **subdivision** is an area of land for
building houses on. 1区画, 1地区 [AM 米国英語] ❑ *Rammick lives
high on a ridge in a 400-home subdivision.* ラミックは400軒が立つ地区
の尾根の上の方に住んでいます。

sub|due /səbdˈu/ (**subdues, subduing, subdued**) 🔢 V-T 他動詞 If
soldiers or the police **subdue** a group of people, they defeat them
or bring them under control by using force. 鎮圧する ❑ *Senior
government officials admit they have not been able to subdue the rebels.*
政府高官は, 反逆者を鎮圧できていないことを認めている。 🔢 V-T 他
動詞 To **subdue** feelings means to make them less strong. 抑える,
鎮める ❑ *He forced himself to subdue and overcome his fears.* 彼は無理に
恐怖心を抑えて克服した。

sub|dued /səbdˈud/ 🔢 ADJ 形容詞 Someone who is **subdued**
is very quiet, often because they are sad or worried about
something. 沈んだ ❑ *He faced the press, initially, in a somewhat
subdued mood.* 彼は, 初めはいくらか沈んだ気分で報道陣に向かっ
た。 🔢 ADJ 形容詞 **Subdued** lights or colors are not very bright. 柔
らかな, おとなしい ❑ *The lighting was subdued.* 柔らかい照明だった。

sub|ject (**subjects, subjecting, subjected**)

The noun and adjective are pronounced /sˈʌbdʒɪkt/. The verb is
pronounced /səbdʒˈɛkt/.

名詞と形容詞は /sˈʌbdʒɪkt/ と発音される. 動詞は /səbdʒˈɛkt/ と発
音される.

🔢 N-COUNT 可算名詞 The **subject** of something such as a
conversation, letter, or book is the thing that is being discussed or
written about. 話題, テーマ ❑ *It was I who first raised the subject of
plastic surgery.* 整形手術の話題を最初に出したのは私だった。 ❑ *...the
president's own views on the subject.* その問題に関する大統領自身の
見解 🔢 N-COUNT 可算名詞 Someone or something that is the
subject of criticism, study, or an investigation is being criticized,
studied, or investigated. (批判・研究・調査の) 対象 ❑ *Over the*

past few years, some of the positions Mr. Meredith has adopted have made him the subject of criticism. 過去数年間において，メレディス氏がとった見解により彼が非難の対象となった． ❸ N-COUNT 可算名詞 A **subject** is an area of knowledge or study, especially one that you study in school, or college. 科目，教科 ❏ *Surprisingly, math was voted their favorite subject.* 意外にも，数学が好きな科目として選ばれた． ❹ N-COUNT 可算名詞 In an experiment or piece of research, the **subject** is the person or animal that is being tested or studied. 被験者，実験動物 [FORMAL 形式ばった] ❏ *"White noise" was played into the subject's ears through headphones.* 「ホワイト・ノイズ」がヘッドホンを通して被験者の耳に流された． ❺ N-COUNT 可算名詞 An artist's **subjects** are the people, animals, or objects that he or she paints, models, or photographs. 題材 ❏ *Sailboats and fish are popular subjects for local artists.* ヨットや魚は地元の芸術家にとって人気のある題材だ． ❻ N-COUNT 可算名詞 In grammar, the **subject** of a clause is the noun group that refers to the person or thing that is doing the action expressed by the verb. For example, in "My cat keeps catching birds," "my cat" is the subject. 主語，主部 ❼ ADJ 形容詞 To be **subject to** something means to be affected by it or to be likely to be affected by it. 〜の影響を受ける可能性がある [v-link ADJ "to" n] ❏ *Prices may be subject to alteration.* 価格は変動する可能性がある． ❽ ADJ 形容詞 If someone is **subject to** a particular set of rules or laws, they have to obey those rules or laws. 〜に従う ❏ [v-link ADJ "to" n] ❏ *The tribunal is unique because Mr. Jones is not subject to the normal police discipline code.* ジョーンズ氏は通常の警察行動規範に従わなくてよいという点でその裁判は他に類を見ない． ❾ V-T 他動詞 If you **subject** someone to something unpleasant, you make them experience it. 受けさせる [他動詞] ❏ *...the man who had subjected her to four years of beatings and abuse.* 彼女を4年間虐待した男性 ❿ N-COUNT 可算名詞 The people who live in or belong to a particular country, usually one ruled by a monarch, are the **subjects** of that monarch or country. 国民 ❏ *...his subjects regarded him as a great and wise monarch.* 彼を偉大で賢明な君主とみなしている国民 ⓫ PHRASE 句 When someone involved in a conversation **changes the subject**, they start talking about something else, often because the previous subject was embarrassing. 話題を変える，話をはぐらかす ❏ *He tried to change the subject, but she wasn't to be put off.* 彼は話をはぐらかそうとしたが，彼女は許さなかった． ⓬ PHRASE 句 If an event will take place **subject to** a condition, it will take place only if that thing happens. 〜を前提として ❏ *They denied a report that Egypt had agreed to a summit, subject to certain conditions.* 条件によってはエジプトが首脳会談することに合意したという報道は否定された．
→ see **hypnosis**

Word Partnership	*subject は次の語句と使われる:*
ADJ.	**controversial** subject, **favorite** subject, **touchy** subject ❶
N.	**knowledge of a** subject ❶ ❸ subject **of a debate**, subject **of an investigation** ❷ **research** subject ❹ subject **of a sentence**, subject **of a verb** ❻ subject **to approval**, subject **to availability**, subject **to laws**, subject **to scrutiny**, subject **to a tax** ❼
V.	**broach** a subject, **study** a subject ❶ ❸ **change the** subject ⓫

sub|jec|tive /səbdʒɛktɪv/ ADJ 形容詞 Something that is **subjective** is based on personal opinions and feelings rather than on facts. 主観的な ❏ *We know that taste in art is a subjective matter.* 芸術の好みは主観的な問題だと承知している． ● **sub|jec|tive|ly** ADV 副詞 主観的に ❏ *Our preliminary results suggest that people do subjectively find the speech clearer.* 仮集計の結果によると，人々は主観的にその話し方がより明瞭だと思っている． ● **sub|jec|tiv|ity** /sʌbdʒɛktɪvɪti/ N-UNCOUNT 不可算名詞 主観，主観的なこと ❏ *They accused her of flippancy and subjectivity in her reporting of events in their country.* 彼女のその国からの報道の仕方が軽率で主観的であると非難されている．

sub|ject mat|ter N-UNCOUNT 不可算名詞 The **subject matter** of something such as a book, lecture, movie, or painting is the thing that is being written about, discussed, or shown. テーマ，題材 ❏ *Then, attitudes changed and artists were given greater freedom in their choice of subject matter.* そして，考え方が変わり，芸術家は題材の選択においてさらに自由が与えられた．

sub|lime /səblaɪm/ ADJ 形容詞 If you describe something as **sublime**, you mean that it has a wonderful quality that affects you deeply. 崇高な，絶妙な [LITERARY 文語的, APPROVAL 賛成] ❏ *Sublime music floats on a scented summer breeze to the spot where you lie.* 崇高な音楽が夏のそよ風に乗って寝転がっているところにまで流れる． ● N-SING 単数名詞 You can refer to **sublime** things as **the sublime**. 崇高なもの，絶品 ❏ *She elevated every rare small success to the sublime.* 彼女はすべてのまれでささやかに成功した人を最高レベルに高めた． ● PHRASE 句 If you describe something as going **from the sublime to the ridiculous**, you mean that it involves a change from something very good or serious to something silly or

unimportant. 傑作から駄作まで，崇高なものからばかげたものまで

sub|limi|nal /sʌblɪmɪnᵊl/ ADJ 形容詞 **Subliminal** influences or messages affect your mind without you being aware of it. サブリミナルの，潜在意識に訴える ❏ *Color has a profound, though often subliminal, influence on our senses and moods.* 色には，潜在意識に訴えることがあり，感覚や気分に対して深い影響を与える．
→ see **advertising**

Word Link	*mar ≈ sea : marine, maritime, submarine*

Word Link	*sub ≈ below : subdivision, submarine, subtitle*

sub|ma|rine /sʌbmərin/ (**submarines**) N-COUNT 可算名詞 A **submarine** is a type of ship that can travel both above and below the surface of the sea. The abbreviation **sub** is also used. 潜水艦 ❏ *...a nuclear submarine.* 原子力潜水艦

Word Link	*merg ≈ sinking : emerge, merge, submerge*

sub|merge /səbmɜrdʒ/ (**submerges, submerging, submerged**) V-T/V-I 他動詞/自動詞 If something **submerges** or if you **submerge** it, it goes below the surface of some water or another liquid. 沈める [他動詞]，沈む [自動詞] ❏ *Hippos are unable to submerge in the few remaining water holes.* カバはいくらか残っている水たまりに潜水することができない．

sub|mis|sion /səbmɪʃᵊn/ N-UNCOUNT 不可算名詞 **Submission** is a state in which people can no longer do what they want to do because they have been brought under the control of someone else. 服従，降伏 ❏ *The army intends to take the city or simply starve it into submission.* 軍隊はその町を占領するか降伏するまで単に飢えさせるかを意図しています．

sub|mis|sive /səbmɪsɪv/ ADJ 形容詞 If you are **submissive**, you obey someone without arguing. 従順な ❏ *Most doctors want their patients to be submissive.* ほとんどの医者が患者が従順であることを望んでいる． ● **sub|mis|sive|ly** ADV 副詞 従順に ❏ *The troops submissively laid down their weapons.* 軍隊はおとなしく武器を下ろした．

sub|mit /səbmɪt/ (**submits, submitting, submitted**) ❶ V-I 自動詞 If you **submit to** something, you unwillingly allow something to be done to you, or you do what someone wants, for example because you are not powerful enough to resist. 服従する，応じる ❏ *In desperation, Mrs. Jones submitted to an operation on her right knee to relieve the pain.* せっぱ詰って，ジョーンズさんは痛みを鎮めるために右ひざの手術をすることに応じた． ❷ V-T 他動詞 If you **submit** a proposal, report, or request to someone, you formally send it to them so that they can consider it or decide about it. 提出する ❏ *They submitted their reports to the chancellor yesterday.* 昨日蔵相に報告書が提出されました．

sub|or|di|nate (**subordinates, subordinating, subordinated**)

> The noun and adjective are pronounced /səbɔrdᵊnɪt/. The verb is pronounced /səbɔrdᵊneɪt/.
>
> 名詞と形容詞は /səbɔrdᵊnɪt/ と発音される．動詞は /səbɔrdᵊneɪt/ と発音される．

❶ N-COUNT 可算名詞 If someone is your **subordinate**, they have a less important position than you in the organization that you both work for. 部下 ❏ *Haig tended not to seek guidance from subordinates.* ヘイグはふつう部下からは助言を求めなかった． ❷ ADJ 形容詞 Someone who is **subordinate to** you has a less important position than you and has to obey you. 部下の（立場の） ❏ *Sixty of his subordinate officers followed his example.* 彼の部下60人が彼の見本に従った． ❸ ADJ 形容詞 Something that is **subordinate to** something else is less important than the other thing. 副次的な，補足的な ❏ *It was an art in which words were subordinate to images.* 言葉が画像に対して補佐的な芸術だった． ❹ V-T 他動詞 If you **subordinate** something to another thing, you regard it or treat it as less important than the other thing. 軽視する，後回しにする ❏ *He was both willing and able to subordinate all else to this aim.* 彼はこの目標のためにすべてを喜んで後回しにし，またそれが可能だった． ● **sub|or|di|na|tion** /səbɔrdᵊneɪʃᵊn/ N-UNCOUNT 不可算名詞 服従，軽視 ❏ *...the social subordination of women.* 女性の社会的軽視

sub|poe|na /səpinə/ (**subpoenas, subpoenaing, subpoenaed**) ❶ N-COUNT 可算名詞 A **subpoena** is a legal document telling someone that they must attend a court of law and give evidence as a witness. 召喚状 ❏ *He has been served with a subpoena to answer the charges in court.* 彼には出廷して容疑に応えるよう召喚状が送付されました． ❷ V-T 他動詞 If someone **subpoenas** a person, they give them a legal document telling them to attend a court of law and give evidence. If someone **subpoenas** a piece of evidence, the evidence must be produced in a court of law. 召喚する ❏ *Select committees have the power to subpoena witnesses.* 特別委員会には目撃者を召喚する権力がある．

sub|scribe /səbskraɪb/ (**subscribes, subscribing, subscribed**) ❶ V-I 自動詞 If you **subscribe to** an opinion or belief, you are one

of a number of people who have this opinion or belief. 賛成する，支持する ❑ *I've personally never subscribed to the view that either sex is superior to the other.* どちらの性が優れているかもう一方よりという見解には個人的に賛成したことがない. ❷ V-I 自動詞 If you **subscribe to** a magazine or a newspaper, you pay to receive copies of it regularly. 定期購読する ❑ *My main reason for subscribing to New Scientist is to keep abreast of advances in science.* 『ニューサイエンティスト』誌を定期購読している主な理由は科学の進歩に遅れを取らないためだ. ❸ V-I 自動詞 If you **subscribe to** an online newsgroup or service, you send a message saying that you wish to receive it or belong to it. 加入する [COMPUTING コンピューティング] ❑ *Usenet is a collection of discussion groups, known as newsgroups, to which anybody can subscribe.* ユーズネットはニュースグループとして知られている討議グループの集まりで誰でも加入できる. ❹ V-I 自動詞 If you **subscribe for** shares in a company, you apply to buy shares in that company. 株式を購入申し込みをする [BUSINESS 実業] ❑ *Employees subscribed for far more shares than were available.* 従業員からの株式購入の申し込みは販売数をはるかに超えていた.

sub|scrib|er /səbskráɪbər/ (**subscribers**) ❶ N-COUNT 可算名詞 A magazine's or a newspaper's **subscribers** are the people who pay to receive copies of it regularly. 定期購読者 ❑ *I have been a subscriber to Newsweek for many years.* 長年，『ニューズウィーク』誌の定期購読をしている. ❷ N-COUNT 可算名詞 **Subscribers to** a service are the people who pay to receive the service. 加入者 ❑ *China has almost 15 million subscribers to satellite and cable television.* 中国には衛星テレビとケーブルテレビの加入者がほぼ1500万人いる.

sub|scrip|tion /səbskrɪpʃᵊn/ (**subscriptions**) ❶ N-COUNT 可算名詞 A **subscription** is an amount of money that you pay regularly in order to belong to an organization, to help a charity or campaign, or to receive copies of a magazine or newspaper. 定期購読料 ❑ *You can become a member by paying the yearly subscription.* 年間購読料を支払うことで入会できる. ❷ ADJ 形容詞 **Subscription** television is television that you can watch only if you pay a subscription. A **subscription** channel is a channel that you can watch only if you pay a subscription. 契約者専用の [ADJ n] ❑ *Premiere, a subscription channel which began in 1991, shows live football covering the top two divisions.* 1991年に開始した契約者専用のチャンネル，プレミアは生中継で上位2ディビジョンのサッカーの試合を放送する.

sub|se|quent /sʌbsɪkwənt/ ADJ 形容詞 You use **subsequent** to describe something that happened or existed after the time or event that has just been referred to. その後の，以降の [FORMAL 形式ばった] [ADJ n] ❑ *...the increase of population in subsequent years.* その後数年間の人口増加 ● **sub|se|quent|ly** ADV 副詞 その後 ❑ *He subsequently worked on Boeing's 747, 767 and 737 jetliner programs.* 彼はその後，ボーイング747，767，737のジェット旅客機プログラムに取り組んだ.

sub|ser|vi|ent /səbsɜ́rviənt/ ❶ ADJ 形容詞 If you are **subservient**, you do whatever someone wants you to do. 言いなりになる ❑ *Her willingness to be subservient to her children isolated her.* 彼女が進んで子供の言いなりになることで孤立してしまった. ● **sub|ser|vi|ence** /səbsɜ́rviəns/ N-UNCOUNT 不可算名詞 言いなり ❑ *...an austere regime stressing obedience and subservience to authority.* 権威への服従と従属を強調する厳しい政権 ❷ ADJ 形容詞 [v-link ADJ "to" n] If you treat one thing as **subservient to** another, you treat it as less important than the other thing. 副次的な ❑ *The woman's needs are seen as subservient to the group interest.* 女性の要求はその団体の関心事の二の次だとみなされている.

sub|side /səbsáɪd/ (**subsides, subsiding, subsided**) ❶ V-I 自動詞 If a feeling or noise **subsides**, it becomes less strong or loud. 静まる，和らぐ ❑ *The pain had subsided during the night.* 痛みが夜の間に和らいだ. ❷ V-I 自動詞 If fighting **subsides**, it becomes less intense or general. 収まる ❑ *Violence has subsided following two days of riots.* 2日間の暴動の後，事態が収まった. ❸ V-I 自動詞 If the ground or a building **is subsiding**, it is very slowly sinking to a lower level. 沈下する ❑ *Does that mean the whole house is subsiding?* それは，家全体が沈下しているということですか? ❹ V-I 自動詞 If a level of water, especially flood water, **subsides**, it goes down. 引く ❑ *Local officials say the flood waters have subsided.* 地方自治体職員によると，洪水は引いて通常レベルとなった.

sub|sidi|ary /səbsɪ́dieri/ (**subsidiaries**) ❶ N-COUNT 可算名詞 A **subsidiary** or a **subsidiary** company is a company which is part of a larger and more important company. 子会社 [BUSINESS 実業] ❑ *WM Financial Services is a subsidiary of Washington Mutual.* WM Financial Services 社は Washington Mutual 社の子会社である. ❷ ADJ 形容詞 If something is **subsidiary**, it is less important than something else with which it is connected. 補助の ❑ *The marketing department has always played a subsidiary role to the sales department.* マーケティング部は常に営業部の補助的な役割を務めてきた.

sub|si|dize /sʌ́bsɪdaɪz/ (**subsidizes, subsidizing, subsidized**) V-T 他動詞 If a government or other authority **subsidizes** something, they pay part of the cost of it. 助成金を支給する

❑ *Around the world, governments have subsidized the housing of middle- and upper-income groups.* 世界中の中高所得層は住宅に関して政府から優遇されてきた. ● **sub|si|dized** ADJ 形容詞 援助された ❑ *...heavily subsidized prices for housing, bread, and meat.* 住宅，パン，肉類の大幅に援助された価格

sub|si|dy /sʌ́bsɪdi/ (**subsidies**) N-COUNT 可算名詞 A **subsidy** is money that is paid by a government or other authority in order to help an industry or business, or to pay for a public service. 助成金 ❑ *European farmers are planning a massive demonstration against farm subsidy cuts.* ヨーロッパの農業経営者は農業助成金削減に反対する大規模なデモ行進を計画している.

sub|sist|ence /səbsɪ́stəns/ ❶ N-UNCOUNT 不可算名詞 **Subsistence** is the condition of just having enough food or money to stay alive. 最低生活 ❑ *...below the subsistence level.* 最低生活水準以下 ❷ ADJ 形容詞 In **subsistence** farming or **subsistence** agriculture, farmers produce food to eat themselves rather than to sell. 自給農業 [ADJ n] ❑ *Many Namibians are subsistence farmers who live in the arid borderlands.* ナミビア人の多くは不毛の奥地で零細農業に携わっている.

sub|stance /sʌ́bstəns/ (**substances**) ❶ N-COUNT 可算名詞 A **substance** is a solid, powder, liquid, or gas with particular properties. 物質 ❑ *There's absolutely no regulation of cigarettes to make sure that they don't include poisonous substances.* 有毒な物質がタバコに含まれないことを確実にするための規制は全くない. ❷ N-UNCOUNT 不可算名詞 **Substance** is the quality of being important or significant. 実質 [FORMAL 形式ばった] ❑ *It's questionable whether anything of substance has been achieved.* 実質のあるものが達成できたかどうかは疑わしい. ❸ N-SING 単数形 The **substance of** what someone says or writes is the main thing that they are trying to say. 内容 ❑ *The substance of his discussions doesn't really matter.* 彼の議論の内容は大して重要ではない. ❹ N-UNCOUNT 不可算名詞 If you say that something has no **substance**, you mean that it is not true. 実体 [FORMAL 形式ばった] ❑ *There is no substance in any of these allegations.* こうした申立てには実体がない.

<table>
<tr><td colspan="2">Word Partnership substance は次の語句と使われる:</td></tr>
<tr><td>ADJ.</td><td>banned substance, chemical substance, natural substance ❶</td></tr>
<tr><td>N.</td><td>lack of substance ❷</td></tr>
</table>

sub|stan|tial /səbstǽnʃᵊl/ ADJ 形容詞 **Substantial** means large in amount or degree. 相当な [FORMAL 形式ばった] ❑ *A substantial number of mothers with young children are deterred from undertaking paid work because they lack access to childcare.* 幼い子供のいる母親の多くは保育施設が利用できないため，職業を持つことができない.

<table>
<tr><td colspan="2">Word Partnership substantial は次の語句と使われる:</td></tr>
<tr><td>ADV.</td><td>fairly substantial, very substantial</td></tr>
<tr><td>N.</td><td>substantial amount, substantial changes, substantial difference, substantial evidence, substantial improvement, substantial increase, substantial loss, substantial number, substantial part, substantial progress, substantial savings, substantial support</td></tr>
</table>

sub|stan|tial|ly /səbstǽnʃəli/ ADV 副詞 If something changes **substantially** or is **substantially** different, it changes a lot or is very different. 相当に [FORMAL 形式ばった] ❑ *The percentage of girls in engineering has increased substantially.* 工学を学ぶ女子生徒の比率は大幅に増加した.

sub|stan|ti|ate /səbstǽnʃieɪt/ (**substantiates, substantiating, substantiated**) V-T 他動詞 To **substantiate** a statement or a story means to supply evidence which proves that it is true. 確証する [FORMAL 形式ばった] ❑ *There is little scientific evidence to substantiate the claims.* その主張を確証する科学的証拠はほとんどない.

sub|stan|tive /sʌ́bstəntɪv/ ADJ 形容詞 **Substantive** negotiations or issues deal with the most important and central aspects of a subject. 重要な [FORMAL 形式ばった] ❑ *They plan to meet again in Rome very soon to begin substantive negotiations.* 彼らは近い将来，ローマで再会し，重要な交渉を始める予定である.

sub|sti|tute /sʌ́bstɪtut/ (**substitutes, substituting, substituted**) ❶ V-T/V-I 他動詞/自動詞 If you **substitute** one thing **for** another, or if one thing **substitutes for** another, it takes the place or performs the function of the other thing. 代わりにする ❑ *They were substituting violence for dialogue.* 彼らは対話を行なう代わりに暴力に訴えていた. ❑ *He was substituting for the injured William Wales.* 彼は負傷したウィリアム・ウェールズの代わりを務めていた. ● **sub|sti|tu|tion** /sʌ̀bstɪtuʃᵊn/ N-VAR 可変性名詞 (**substitutions**) ❑ *In my experience a straight substitution of carob for chocolate doesn't work.* 私の経験ではチョコレートの代わりにイナゴマメを使うだけではうまく行かない. ❷ N-COUNT 可算名詞 A **substitute** is something that you have or use instead of something else. 代わりをするもの ❑ *She is seeking a substitute for*

the very man whose departure made her cry. 彼女はふられて泣かされた男の代わりを求めている。 ❸ N-COUNT 可算名詞 If you say that one thing is no **substitute for** another, you mean that it does not have certain desirable features that the other thing has, and is therefore unsatisfactory. If you say that there is no **substitute for** something, you mean that it is the only thing which is really satisfactory. 代用品 ❏ *The printed word is no substitute for personal discussion with a great thinker.* 活字は偉大な思想家とのじきじきの討論にはとても及ばない。 ❹ N-COUNT 可算名詞 In team games such as football, a **substitute** is a player who is brought into a game to replace another player. 補欠 ❏ *Jefferson entered as a substitute in the 6th minute.* ジェファーソンは60分目に補欠として入場した。

Word Partnership	substitute は次の語句と使われる:
ADJ.	**good** substitute ❷
	temporary substitute ❷ ❹
V.	**use** *someone/something* as a substitute ❷ ❹

sub|sti|tute teach|er (substitute teachers) N-COUNT 可算名詞 A **substitute teacher** is a teacher whose job is to take the place of other teachers at different schools when they are unable to be there. 臨時教員 [AM 米国英語]

Word Link	terr ≈ earth : subterranean, terrain, terrestrial

sub|ter|ra|nean /sʌbtərerniən/ ADJ 形容詞 A **subterranean** river or tunnel is under the ground. 地下の [FORMAL 形式ばった] ❏ *The city has 9 miles of such subterranean passages.* その町には9マイルの地下通路がある。

Word Link	sub ≈ below : subdivision, submarine, subtitle

sub|title /sʌbtaɪtəl/ (subtitles, subtitling, subtitled) ❶ N-COUNT 可算名詞 The **subtitle** of a piece of writing is a second title which is often longer and explains more than the main title. 副題 ❏ *"Kathleen" was, as its 1892 subtitle asserted, "An Irish Drama."* 「Kathleen」は1892年の副題にあるように「アイルランドの劇」である。 ❷ N-PLURAL 複数名詞 **Subtitles** are a printed translation of the words of a foreign film that are shown at the bottom of the picture. 字幕 ❏ *The dialogue is in Spanish, with English subtitles.* 会話はスペイン語だが英語の字幕入りである。 ❸ V-T 他動詞 If you say how a book or play is subtitled, you say what its subtitle is. 副題をつける ❏ *"Lorna Doone" is subtitled "a Romance of Exmoor."* 「Lorna Doone」には「エックスモアのロマンス」という副題がついている。

sub|ti|tled /sʌbtaɪtəld/ ADJ 形容詞 If a foreign film is **subtitled**, a printed translation of the words is shown at the bottom of the picture. 字幕がついている ❏ *Much of the film is subtitled.* その映画の大半は字幕つきである。

sub|tle /sʌtəl/ (subtler, subtlest) ❶ ADJ 形容詞 Something that is **subtle** is not immediately obvious or noticeable. 微妙な ❏ *...the slow and subtle changes that take place in all living things.* 全ての生物に徐々に起こる微妙な変化 ● **sub|tly** ADV 副詞 微妙に ❏ *The truth is subtly different.* 真実は微妙に違う。 ❷ ADJ 形容詞 A **subtle** person cleverly uses indirect methods to achieve something. 巧妙な ❏ *I even began to exploit him in subtle ways.* 私はそれどころか巧妙な方法で彼を利用し始めた。 ● **sub|tly** ADV 副詞 [ADV with v] 巧妙に ❏ *Nathan is subtly trying to turn her against Barry.* ネイサンは彼女がバリーに反感を持つよう巧妙に仕向けている。 ❸ ADJ 形容詞 **Subtle** smells, tastes, sounds, or colors are pleasantly complex and delicate. 微妙な ❏ *...subtle shades of brown.* 微妙なブラウンの色合い ● **sub|tly** ADV 副詞 微妙に ❏ *...a white sofa teamed with subtly colored rugs.* 微妙な色合いのラグと調和させた白いソファ

sub|tle|ty /sʌtəlti/ (subtleties) ❶ N-COUNT 可算名詞 **Subtleties** are very small details or differences which are not obvious. 微妙なもの ❏ *His fascination with the subtleties of human behavior makes him a good storyteller.* 彼が優れた物語作家なのは彼が人間の行動の微妙さに好奇心を持っているからである。 ❷ N-UNCOUNT 不可算名詞 **Subtlety** is the quality of being not immediately obvious or noticeable, and therefore difficult to describe. 名状しがたい特性 ❏ *African dance is vigorous, but full of subtlety, requiring great strength and control.* アフリカの踊りは精力的だが、大きな体力と制御力を要し、名状しがたい特性があふれている。 ❸ N-UNCOUNT 不可算名詞 **Subtlety** is the ability to notice and recognize things which are not obvious, especially small differences between things. 鋭い洞察力 ❏ *She analyzes herself with great subtlety.* 彼女は鋭い洞察力で自分自身を分析した。 ❹ N-UNCOUNT 不可算名詞 **Subtlety** is the ability to use indirect methods to achieve something, rather than doing something that is obvious. 巧妙さ ❏ *They had obviously been hoping to approach the topic with more subtlety.* 彼らは明らかにより巧妙にその話題にアプローチしたがっていた。

sub|to|tal /sʌbtoʊtəl/ (subtotals) N-COUNT 可算名詞 A **subtotal** is a figure that is the result of adding some numbers together but is not the final total. 小計 ❏ *...the subtotals for each category of investments.* 各投資部門の小計

Word Link	tract ≈ dragging, drawing : contract, subtract, tractor

sub|tract /səbtrækt/ (subtracts, subtracting, subtracted) V-T 他動詞 If you **subtract** one number **from** another, you do a calculation in which you take it away from the other number. For example, if you subtract 3 from 5, you get 2. 引く ❏ *Mandy subtracted the date of birth from the date of death.* マンディは死亡日から生年月日を引いた。 ● **sub|trac|tion** /səbtrækʃən/ N-VAR 可変性名詞 (subtractions) 引き算 ❏ *She's ready to learn simple addition and subtraction.* 彼女は簡単な足し算と引き算を学ぶ準備ができている。
→ see **mathematics**

sub|urb /sʌbɜrb/ (suburbs) ❶ N-COUNT 可算名詞 A **suburb** of a city or large town is a smaller area which is part of the city or large town but is outside its center. 郊外 ❏ *Anna was born in 1923 in a suburb of Philadelphia.* アンナは1923年にフィラデルフィアの郊外で生まれた。 ❷ N-PLURAL 複数名詞 If you live in **the suburbs**, you live in an area of houses outside the center of a city or large town. 郊外 ❏ *His family lived in the suburbs.* 彼の家族は郊外に住んでいた。
→ see **city, transportation**

sub|ur|ban /səbɜrbən/ ADJ 形容詞 **Suburban** means relating to a suburb. 郊外の [ADJ n] ❏ *...a comfortable suburban home.* 住みやすい郊外の住宅

sub|ur|bia /səbɜrbiə/ N-UNCOUNT 不可算名詞 Journalists often use **suburbia** to refer to the suburbs of cities and large towns considered as a whole. 郊外

Word Link	vers ≈ turning : subversion, versatile, version

sub|ver|sion /səbvɜrʒən/ N-UNCOUNT 不可算名詞 **Subversion** is the attempt to weaken or destroy a political system or a government. 転覆すること ❏ *He was arrested on charges of subversion for organizing the demonstration.* 彼はデモ行進を組織化したことに対して転覆の嫌疑で逮捕された。

sub|ver|sive /səbvɜrsɪv/ (subversives) ❶ ADJ 形容詞 Something that is **subversive** is intended to weaken or destroy a political system or government. 転覆させる ❏ *The play was promptly banned as subversive and possibly treasonous.* その演劇は破壊的でことによると反逆的という理由ですぐに禁止になった。 ❷ N-COUNT 可算名詞 **Subversives** are people who attempt to weaken or destroy a political system or government. 破壊活動分子 ❏ *Agents regularly rounded up suspected subversives.* 特務機関員は破壊活動分子と疑われる人物を定期的に検挙した。

Word Link	verg, vert ≈ turning : converge, diverge, subvert

sub|vert /səbvɜrt/ (subverts, subverting, subverted) V-T 他動詞 To **subvert** something means to destroy its power and influence. 転覆させる [FORMAL 形式ばった] ❏ *...an alleged plot to subvert the state.* 国家を倒す陰謀のうわさ

sub|way /sʌbweɪ/ (subways) ❶ N-COUNT 可算名詞 A **subway** is an underground railroad. 地下鉄 [mainly AM 主に米国英語] [oft N n, also "by" N] ❏ *I don't ride the subway late at night.* 私は夜遅く地下鉄に乗らない。 ❷ N-COUNT 可算名詞 A **subway** is the same as an **underpass**. 地下通路 [BRIT 英国英語]
→ see **transportation**

suc|ceed /səksid/ (succeeds, succeeding, succeeded) ❶ V-I 自動詞 If you **succeed** in doing something, you manage to do it. 成し遂げる ❏ *We have already succeeded in working out ground rules with the Department of Defense.* 我々は既に防衛庁と基本原則を案出するのに成功した。 ❷ V-I 自動詞 If something **succeeds**, it works in a satisfactory way or has the result that is intended. うまくいく ❏ *The talks can succeed if both sides are flexible and serious.* 話合いは両者が柔軟で真剣な場合にはうまくいく。 ❸ V-I 自動詞 Someone who **succeeds** gains a high position in what they do, for example in business or politics. 出世する ❏ *...the skills and qualities needed to succeed in small and medium-sized businesses.* 中小企業で出世するのに必要な技能と質 ❹ V-T 他動詞 If you **succeed** another person, you are the next person to have their job or position. 後任となる ❏ *David Rowland is almost certain to succeed him as chairman on January 1.* デイビッド・ローランドが1月1日に会長として彼の後任になることはほぼ確実だ。 ❺ V-T 他動詞 If one thing **is succeeded by** another thing, the other thing happens or comes after it. 続く [usu passive] ❏ *The presentation was succeeded by a roundtable discussion.* プレゼンテーションの後で円卓討論が行なわれた。

Thesaurus	succeed また次を参照:
V.	accomplish, conquer, master; (ant.) fail ❶
	displace, replace; (ant.) precede ❹

suc|cess /səksɛs/ (successes) ❶ N-UNCOUNT 不可算名詞 **Success** is the achievement of something that you have been trying to do. 成功 ❏ *It's important for the success of any diet that you vary your meals.* ダイエットが成功するためには食事に変化をつけることが重要だ。 ❷ N-UNCOUNT 不可算名詞 **Success** is the achievement of a high position in a particular field, for example in business or

politics. 出世 ❏ *We all believed that work was the key to success.* 私たちは皆努力が出世の鍵だと信じた. **3** N-UNCOUNT 不可算名詞 The **success** of something is the fact that it works in a satisfactory way or has the result that is intended. 上首尾 ❏ *We were amazed by the play's success.* 私達はその芝居の成功に驚いた. **4** N-COUNT 可算名詞 Someone or something that is a **success** achieves a high position, makes a lot of money, or is admired a great deal. 成功したもの ❏ *We hope it will be a commercial success.* 私達はそれが商業的に成功することを望んでいる.

Word Partnership   success は次の語句と使われる:

N.	success **of a business 1** **key to** success, success **or failure 1 2** **chance for/of** success, **lack of** success, **measure of** success **1 – 4**
V.	**achieve** success, success **depends on** *something*, **enjoy** success **1 – 4**
ADJ.	**great** success, **huge** success, **recent** success, **tremendous** success **1 – 4** **academic** success, **commercial** success **4**

suc|cess|ful /səksɛsfəl/ **1** ADJ 形容詞 Something that is **successful** achieves what it was intended to achieve. Someone who is **successful** achieves what they intended to achieve. 上出来の ❏ *How successful will this new treatment be?* この新しい治療はどの程度効き目があるでしょうか. ❏ *I am looking forward to a long and successful partnership with him.* 私は彼との共同事業が末永く成功するのを期待している. ● suc|cess|ful|ly ADV 副詞 [ADV with v] 首尾よく ❏ *The doctors have successfully concluded preliminary tests.* 医者は予備のテストをうまく完了した. **2** ADJ 形容詞 Something that is **successful** is popular or makes a lot of money. 大当たりの ❏ *...the hugely successful movie that brought Robert Redford an Oscar for his directing.* ロバート・レッドフォードがアカデミー監督賞を獲得した大ヒット映画. **3** ADJ 形容詞 Someone who is **successful** achieves a high position in what they do, for example in business or politics. 立身出世した ❏ *Women do not necessarily have to imitate men to be successful in business.* 女性は事業で成功するために必ずしも男性の真似をする必要はない.

suc|ces|sion /səksɛʃən/ (successions) **1** N-SING 単数名詞 A **succession of** things of the same kind is a number of them that exist or happen one after the other. 連続 [oft N "of" n, also "in" n] ❏ *Adams took a succession of jobs which have stood him in good stead.* アダムスは立て続けに職に就いたが, これは彼のためになった. **2** N-UNCOUNT 不可算名詞 **Succession** is the act or right of being the next person to have an important job or position. 継承順位 ❏ *She is now seventh in line of succession to the throne.* 彼女は現在王位への継承順位第7位である.

suc|ces|sive /səksɛsɪv/ ADJ 形容詞 **Successive** means happening or existing one after another without a break. 連続する ❏ *Jackson was the winner for a second successive year.* ジャクソンは2年続けて優勝した.

suc|ces|sor /səksɛsər/ (successors) N-COUNT 可算名詞 Someone's **successor** is the person who takes their job after they have left. 後任者 ❏ *He set out several principles that he hopes will guide his successors.* 彼は後任者のためにいくつかの原則を提示した.

suc|cinct /səksɪŋkt/ ADJ 形容詞 Something that is **succinct** expresses facts or ideas clearly and in few words. 簡明な [APPROVAL 賛成] ❏ *The book gives an admirably succinct account of the technology and its history.* その本はテクノロジーとその歴史を大変簡明に説明している. ● suc|cinct|ly ADV 副詞 簡明に ❏ *He succinctly summed up his manifesto as "Work hard, train hard and play hard."* 彼は「懸命に働き, 懸命に学び, 懸命に遊ぶこと」と彼の政綱を簡明に要約した.

suc|cu|lent /sʌkyələnt/ ADJ 形容詞 **Succulent** food, especially meat or vegetables, is juicy and good to eat. 汁気の多い [APPROVAL 賛成] ❏ *Cook pieces of succulent chicken with ample garlic and a little sherry.* 汁気の多い鳥肉の切り身をにんにくをたっぷり, シェリー酒を少量入れて調理しなさい.

suc|cumb /səkʌm/ (succumbs, succumbing, succumbed) V-I 自動詞 If you **succumb to** temptation or pressure, you do something that you want to do, or that other people want you to do, although you feel it might be wrong. 負ける [FORMAL 形式ばった] ❏ *Don't succumb to the temptation to have just one cigarette.* タバコを1本だけ吸うという誘惑に負けてはならない.

such /sʌtʃ/

When **such** is used as a predeterminer, it is followed by "a" and a count noun in the singular. When it is used as a determiner, it is followed by a count noun in the plural or by an uncountable noun.

such が前限定詞として使われるときには, a と単数の可算名詞が後続する. それが限定詞として使われるときには, 複数の可算名詞か不可算名詞が後続する.

1 DET 限定詞 You use **such** to refer back to the thing or person that you have just mentioned, or a thing or person like the one that you have just mentioned. You use **such as** and **such...as** to introduce a reference to the person or thing that has just been mentioned. そのような ❏ *There have been previous attempts at coups. We regard such methods as entirely unacceptable.* 以前にクーデターの試みがあった. 我々はそうした方法を全く容認できない. ● PREDET 前限定詞 **Such** is also a predeterminer. そのような [PREDET "a" n] ❏ *If your request is for information about a child, please contact the registrar to find out how to make such a request.* 要請がお子さんに関する情報の場合には, 登記係に要請方法をお問い合わせください. ❏ *She has told us that when she goes back to stay with her family, they make her pay rent. We could not believe such a thing.* 彼女は実家に帰ると家族から家賃を払わされるものと私達に告げた. 私達はそんなことは信じられなかった. ● PRON 代名詞 **Such** is also a pronoun used before **be.** そのようなもの ❏ *We are scared because we are being watched – such is the atmosphere in Pristina and other cities in Kosovo.* 私達は監視されているので怖い. プリシュテイナやコソボの他の町はそんな雰囲気だ. **2** DET 限定詞 You use **such...as** or **such as** to link something or someone with a clause in which you give a description of the kind of thing or person that you mean. のようなそんな ❏ *...incentive payments for such activities as planting hardwood trees.* 広葉樹の植林などの活動のための奨励金 ❏ *Children do not use inflections such as are used in mature adult speech.* 子供は大人が使うような抑揚である話し方をしない **3** DET 限定詞 You use **such...as** or **such as** to introduce one or more examples of the kind of thing or person that you have just mentioned. と同じような ❏ *...such careers as teaching, nursing, hairdressing and catering.* 教師, 看護婦, 美容師, 配膳業などの職業 ❏ *...serious offenses, such as assault on a police officer.* 警察官への暴行などの重罪 **4** DET 限定詞 You use **such** before noun groups to emphasize the extent of something or to emphasize that something is remarkable. それほど [EMPHASIS 強調] ❏ *I think most of us don't want to read what's in the newspaper anyway in such detail.* 大半の人はそれほど詳しく新聞記事を読みたくないと思う. ❏ *One will never be able to understand why these political issues can acquire such force.* こうした政治問題がそれほど影響力を得る理由は決して理解できないだろう. ● PREDET 前限定詞 **Such** is also a predeterminer. とても [PREDET "a" n] ❏ *It was such a pleasant surprise.* それは本当に思いがけない お祝いだった. **5** PREDET 前限定詞 You use **such...that** or **such that** in order to emphasize the degree of something by mentioning the result or consequence of it. 非常に…なので [EMPHASIS 強調] [PREDET "a" n that] ❏ *This is something where you can earn such a lot of money that there is not any risk that you will lose it.* それほど多額の金を稼げるものなので金を失う危険はない. ❏ *Though Vivaldi had earned a great deal in his lifetime, his extravagance was such that he died in poverty.* ビバルディは生涯多額の金を稼いだが, 浪費のあげく貧乏人で死んだ. ● DET 限定詞 **Such** is also a determiner. 非常に ❏ *She looked at him in such distress that he had to look away.* 彼女は非常に苦しそうに彼を見たので彼は思わず目をそむけた. **6** DET 限定詞 You use **such...that** or **such that** in order to say what the result or consequence of something that you have just mentioned is. そんな ❏ *The operation has uncovered such backstreet dealing in stolen property that police might now press for changes in the law.* 作戦の決死, そのような盗難品の不法取引が発見されたため, 警察は今や法の改正を要求する可能性がある. ❏ *Their cost structure is such that they just can't compete with the low-cost carriers.* 彼らはそのコスト構造により低コストの航空会社と張り合うことはできない. ● PREDET 前限定詞 **Such** is also a predeterminer. そのような [PREDET "a" n that/" as to"] ❏ *He could put an idea in such a way that Alan would believe it was his own.* 彼はそのような方法で発想できたのでアランはそれが彼自身のものと信じたものだった. **7** PHRASE 句 You use **such and such** to refer to a thing or person when you do not want to be exact or precise. これこれの [SPOKEN 口語, VAGUENESS あいまいさ] ❏ *I said, "Well, what time'll I get to Baltimore?" and he said such and such a time but I missed my connection.* 「それでは何時にバルティモアに到着する予定ですか」と私が聞くと, 彼はこれこれの時間と言ったが, 私は接続便に乗り遅れた. **8** PHRASE 句 You use **as such** with a negative to indicate that a word or expression is not a very accurate description of the actual situation. そのようなもの ❏ *I am not a learner as such – I used to ride a bike years ago.* 私は全く初心者という訳ではない. 自転車には昔よく乗っていた. **9** PHRASE 句 You use **as such** after a noun to indicate that you are considering that thing on its own, separately from other things or factors. それ自体 ❏ *Mr. Simon said he was not against taxes as such, "but I do object when taxation is justified on spurious or dishonest grounds," he says.* サイモン氏は「税金そのものに反対しているわけではないが偽りあるいは不正直な理由で徴税が正当化されることに反対だ」と述べた. **10** no such thing → see thing

S

Word Web   sugar

Sugar cane was discovered in prehistoric New Guinea*. As people migrated across the Pacific Islands and into India and China, they brought sugar cane with them. At first, people just chewed on the cane. They liked the **sweet taste**. When sugar cane reached the Middle East, people discovered how to **refine** it into **crystals**. Brown sugar is created by stopping the refining process earlier. This leaves some of the molasses syrup in the sugar. Today two-fifths of sugar comes from **beets**. Refined sugar is used in many **foods** and **beverages**. The overuse of sugar can cause many problems, such as **obesity** and **diabetes**.

New Guinea: a large island in the southern Pacific Ocean.

Such is followed by **a** when the noun is something that can be counted. ❏ …*such a pleasant surprise.* It is not followed by **a** when the noun is plural or something that cannot be counted. ❏ …*such beautiful girls. …such power.* You do not use **such** when you are talking about something that is present, or about the place where you are. You need to use the phrases **like that** or **like this**. For example, if you are admiring someone's watch, you do not say "I'd like such a watch." You say "**I'd like a watch like that.**" Similarly, you do not say about the town where you are living "There's not much to do in such a town." You say "**There's not much to do in a town like this.**" **Such** in other contexts is quite formal.

suck /sʌk/ (**sucks, sucking, sucked**) ◼ V-T/V-I 他動詞/自動詞 If you **suck** something, you hold it in your mouth and pull at it with the muscles in your cheeks and tongue, for example in order to get liquid out of it. 吸う ❏ *They waited in silence and sucked their sweets.* 彼らは黙ってお菓子をなめながら待った. ❏ *He sucked on his cigarette.* 彼はタバコを吸った. ◼ V-T 他動詞 If something **sucks** a liquid, gas, or object in a particular direction, it draws it there with a powerful force. 吸い上げる ❏ *The pollution-control team is at the scene and is due to start sucking up oil any time now.* 環境汚染管理チームは現場で今にも油を吸い上げ始める予定だ. ◼ V-T PASSIVE 受動態他動詞 If you **are sucked into** a bad situation, you are unable to prevent yourself from becoming involved in it. 巻き込まれる ❏ …*the extent to which they have been sucked into the cycle of violence.* 彼らが暴力の循環に巻き込まれた程度

sud|den /sʌdᵊn/ ◼ ADJ 形容詞 **Sudden** means happening quickly and unexpectedly. 突然の ❏ *He had been deeply affected by the sudden death of his father-in-law.* 彼は義父の突然の死に深く悲しんでいた. ❏ *It was all very sudden.* それは非常に突然だった. ●**sud|den|ness** N-UNCOUNT 不可算名詞 突然さ ❏ *The enemy seemed stunned by the suddenness of the attack.* 敵は攻撃の突然さに驚いたようだった. ◼ PHRASE 句 If something happens **all of a sudden**, it happens quickly and unexpectedly. 突然に ❏ *All of a sudden she didn't look sleepy any more.* 彼女は突然眠くなくなったようだった.

sud|den|ly /sʌdᵊnli/ ADV 副詞 If something happens **suddenly**, it happens quickly and unexpectedly. 突然に ❏ *Suddenly, she looked ten years older.* 彼女は突然10歳ふけて見えた. ❏ *Her expression suddenly altered.* 彼女の表情は突然変わった.

sue /su/ (**sues, suing, sued**) V-T/V-I 他動詞/自動詞 If you **sue** someone, you start a legal case against them, usually in order to claim money from them because they have harmed you in some way. 告訴する ❏ *Mr. Warren sued for libel over the remarks.* ワレン氏はその所見を文書誹毀(ひき)で訴えた. ❏ *The company could be sued for damages.* その企業は損害賠償請求で訴えられる可能性がある.

suede /sweɪd/ N-UNCOUNT 不可算名詞 **Suede** is leather with a soft, slightly rough surface. スエード革 ❏ *Albert wore a brown suede jacket and jeans.* アルバートは茶色のスエード革のジャケットとジーンズを着ていた.

suf|fer /sʌfər/ (**suffers, suffering, suffered**) ◼ V-T/V-I 他動詞/自動詞 If you **suffer** pain, you feel it in your body or in your mind. 苦しむ ❏ *Within a few days she had become seriously ill, suffering great pain and discomfort.* 数日のうちに彼女は重病になり、ひどい苦痛を味わった. ❏ *He suffered terribly the last few days.* 彼は過去数週間非常に苦しんだ. ◼ V-I 自動詞 If you **suffer from** an illness or from some other bad condition, you are badly affected by it. 病む ❏ *He was eventually diagnosed as suffering from terminal cancer.* 彼はついに末期の癌にかかっていると診断された. ◼ V-T 他動詞 If you **suffer** something bad, you are in a situation in which something painful, harmful, or very unpleasant happens to you. 受ける ❏ *The peace process has suffered a serious blow now.* 和平プロセスは今や深刻な打撃を受けた. ◼ V-I 自動詞 If you **suffer**, you are badly affected by an event or situation. 苦しむ ❏ *There are few who have not suffered.* 苦しまなかった者はほとんどいない. ◼ V-I 自動詞 If something **suffers**, it becomes worse because it has not been

given enough attention or is in a bad situation. 損害を受ける ❏ *I'm not surprised that your studies are suffering.* あなたの勉強がおろそかになっているのに私は驚かない.

suf|fer|ing /sʌfərɪŋ/ (**sufferings**) ◼ N-UNCOUNT 不可算名詞 **Suffering** is serious pain which someone feels in their body or their mind. 苦しみ [also N in pl] ❏ *They began to recover slowly from their nightmare of pain and suffering.* 彼らは痛みと苦しみの悪夢のような状態からゆっくりと回復し始めた. ❏ *It has caused terrible suffering to animals.* それは動物にひどい苦しみを与えた. ◼ → see also **long-suffering**

suf|fice /səfaɪs/ (**suffices, sufficing, sufficed**) ◼ V-I 自動詞 If you say that something will **suffice**, you mean it will be enough to achieve a purpose or to fulfill a need. 十分である [FORMAL 形式ばった] [no cont] ❏ *A cover letter should never exceed one page; often a far shorter letter will suffice.* 添え状は1ページを超えてはならない. もっと短い書簡で十分だ. ◼ PHRASE 句 **Suffice it to say** or **suffice to say** is used at the beginning of a statement to indicate that what you are saying is obvious, or that you will only give a short explanation. と言えば十分である ❏ *Suffice it to say that afterwards we never met again.* 私達はその後決して再会することはなかったと言うにとどめておこう.

suf|fi|cient /səfɪʃᵊnt/ ADJ 形容詞 If something is **sufficient for** a particular purpose, there is enough of it for the purpose. 十分な ❏ *One yard of fabric is sufficient to cover the exterior of an 18-in.-diameter hatbox.* 1ヤードの生地は直径18インチの帽子ケースを覆うのに十分である. ❏ *Lighting levels should be sufficient for photography without flash.* フラッシュなしで写真撮影に十分な照明であるべきだ. ●**suf|fi|cient|ly** ADV 副詞 十分に ❏ *She recovered sufficiently to accompany Chou on his tour of Africa in 1964.* 彼女は1964年のアフリカ旅行でChouに同伴できるほどに回復した.

Word Link   fix ≈ fastening : *af*fix, *pre*fix, *suf*fix

suf|fix /sʌfɪks/ (**suffixes**) N-COUNT 可算名詞 A **suffix** is a letter or group of letters, for example "-ly" or "-ness", which is added to the end of a word in order to form a different word, often of a different word class. For example, the suffix "-ly" is added to "quick" to form "quickly." Compare **affix** and **prefix**. 接尾辞

suf|fo|cate /sʌfəkeɪt/ (**suffocates, suffocating, suffocated**) ◼ V-T/V-I 他動詞/自動詞 If someone **suffocates** or **is suffocated**, they die because there is no air for them to breathe. 窒息死する ❏ *He either suffocated, or froze to death.* 彼は窒息死または凍死した. ●**suf|fo|ca|tion** /sʌfəkeɪʃᵊn/ N-UNCOUNT 不可算名詞 窒息 ❏ *Many of the victims died of suffocation.* 被害者の多くは窒息死した. ◼ V-T/V-I 他動詞/自動詞 If you say that you **are suffocating** or that something **is suffocating** you, you mean that you feel very uncomfortable because there is not enough fresh air and it is difficult to breathe. 息が詰まる ❏ *That's better. I was suffocating in that cell of a room.* その方がよい. 私はあの狭い部屋で息が詰まりそうだった.

sug|ar /ʃʊgər/ (**sugars**) ◼ N-UNCOUNT 不可算名詞 **Sugar** is a sweet substance that is used to make food and drinks sweet. It is usually in the form of small white or brown crystals. 砂糖 ❏ …*bags of sugar.* 1袋の砂糖. ◼ N-COUNT 可算名詞 If someone has one **sugar** in their tea or coffee, they have one small spoon of sugar or one sugar lump in it. 砂糖一さじ ❏ *How many sugars do you take?* 砂糖は何さじ入れますか. ◼ N-COUNT 可算名詞 **Sugars** are substances that occur naturally in food. When you eat them, the body converts them into energy. 糖 ❏ *Plants produce sugars and starch to provide themselves with energy.* 植物は活力を得るために糖分と澱粉くを生産する. (でんぷん) ◼ to **sugar the pill** → see **pill**
→ see Word Web: **sugar**
→ see **coffee, fruit**

sug|gest /səgdʒɛst/ (**suggests, suggesting, suggested**) ◼ V-T 他動詞 If you **suggest** something, you put forward a plan or idea for someone to think about. 提案する ❏ *He suggested a link between class size and test results of seven-year-olds.* 彼は7歳児クラスの人数と

テスト結果に関連性があると提案した. ❑ *I suggest you ask him some specific questions about his past.* 彼の過去について彼に特定の質問をすることを提案する. ❑ *No one has suggested how this might occur.* これがどのようにして起こるかを提案した者はいない. ② V-T 他動詞 If you **suggest** the name of a person or place, you recommend them to someone. 推薦する ❑ *Could you suggest someone to advise me how to do this?* これを行なう方法を教えてくれる人を私に推薦してくれませんか. ③ V-T 他動詞 If you **suggest that** something is the case, you say something which you believe to be true. 提案する ❑ *I'm not suggesting that is what is happening.* 私はそれが起こっていると言っている訳ではない. ❑ *It is wrong to suggest that there are easy alternatives.* 簡単な方法があると提案するのは間違っている. ④ V-T 他動詞 If one thing **suggests** another, it implies it or makes you think that it might be the case. 暗示する ❑ *Earlier reports suggested that a meeting would take place on Sunday.* 以前のレポートでは会合が日曜日に開かれると暗示されていた.

Note that **suggest** cannot usually be followed directly by a noun or pronoun referring to a person; you generally have to put the preposition **to** in front of it. You do not "suggest someone something," you "**suggest** something **to** someone." ❑ *John Caskey first suggested this idea to me.* Nor do you "suggest someone to do something." You "**suggest that** someone **do** something." ❑ *Beatrice suggested that he spend the summer at their place.* Do not confuse **suggest** and **advise**. If you **suggest** something, you mention it as an idea or plan for someone to think about. If you **advise** someone to do something, you tell them what you think they should do. ❑ *I advised him to leave as soon as possible.*

Word Partnership   *suggest* は次の語句と使われる:

N.   **analysts** suggest, **experts** suggest, **researchers** suggest ① – ③
     data suggest, **findings** suggest, **results** suggest, **studies** suggest, **surveys** suggest ④

sug|ges|tion /səgdʒˈɛstʃ^ən/ (suggestions) ① N-COUNT 可算名詞 If you make a **suggestion**, you put forward an idea or plan for someone to think about. 提案 ❑ *The dietitian was helpful, making suggestions as to how I could improve my diet.* 栄養士は役に立ち、食生活を改善する方法について提案してくれて役に立った. ❑ *Perhaps he'd followed her suggestion of a stroll to the river.* 多分彼は川まで歩くという彼女の提案に従ったのだと思う. ② N-COUNT 可算名詞 A **suggestion** is something that a person says which implies that something is the case. ほのめかし ❑ *We reject any suggestion that the law needs amending.* 我々は法律を改正する必要があるというほのめかしを拒否する. ③ N-SING 単数名詞 If there is no **suggestion that** something is the case, there is no reason to think that it is the case. 様子 ❑ *There is no suggestion whatsoever that the two sides are any closer to agreeing.* 両者が合意に近づいているという様子は全くない.

Word Partnership   *suggestion* は次の語句と使われる:

V.   **follow a** suggestion, **make a** suggestion ①
     reject a suggestion ① ②

sug|ges|tive /səgdʒˈɛstɪv/ ① ADJ 形容詞 Something that is **suggestive of** something else is quite like it or may be a sign of it. 示唆する [v-link ADJ "of" n] ❑ *The fingers were gnarled, lumpy, with long, curving nails suggestive of animal claws.* 指はごつごつしてこぶだらけで、長く曲がった爪が動物の爪を示唆していた. ② ADJ 形容詞 **Suggestive** remarks or looks cause people to think about sex, often in a way that makes them feel uncomfortable. 挑発的な ❑ *...another former employee who claims Thomas made suggestive remarks to her.* トマスが彼女に挑発的なことを言ったと主張する別の元社員

sui|cid|al /suːɪsˈaɪd^əl/ ADJ 形容詞 People who are **suicidal** want to kill themselves. 自殺の恐れのある ❑ *I was suicidal and just couldn't stop crying.* 私は自殺したくて現に涙が止まらなかった.

sui|cide /suːɪsaɪd/ (suicides) N-VAR 可変性名詞 People who commit **suicide** deliberately kill themselves because they do not want to continue living. 自殺 ❑ *She tried to commit suicide on several occasions.* 彼女は数回自殺しようとした. ❑ *...a case of attempted suicide.* 自殺未遂

Word Partnership   *suicide* は次の語句と使われる:

V.   **attempt** suicide, **commit** suicide
N.   suicide **bomber**, suicide **prevention**, suicide **rate**, **risk of** suicide

suit /suːt/ (suits, suiting, suited) ① N-COUNT 可算名詞 A man's **suit** consists of a jacket, pants, and sometimes a vest, all made from the same fabric. スーツ ❑ *...a dark pin-striped business suit.* 黒っぽいピンストライプの背広 ② N-COUNT 可算名詞 A woman's **suit** consists of a jacket and skirt, or sometimes pants, made from the

same fabric. スーツ ❑ *I was wearing my tweed suit.* 私はツイードのスーツを着ていた. ③ N-COUNT 可算名詞 A particular type of **suit** is a piece of clothing that you wear for a particular activity. 衣服 ❑ *The six survivors only lived through their ordeal because of the special rubber suits they were wearing.* 6名の生存者は特別なゴム製の衣服のおかげで恐ろしい試練をかろうじて切り抜けられた. ④ V-T 他動詞 If something **suits** you, it is convenient for you or is the best thing for you in the circumstances. 都合がよい [no cont] ❑ *They will only release information if it suits them.* 彼らはそれが彼らにとって好都合な場合にのみ情報を公開するだろう. ⑤ V-T 他動詞 If something **suits** you, you like it. 満足できる [no cont] ❑ *I don't think a sedentary life would altogether suit me.* 座ってばかりいて運動しない生活が私に合うとは思わない. ⑥ V-T 他動詞 If a piece of clothing or a particular style or color **suits** you, it makes you look attractive. 似合う [no cont] ❑ *Green suits you.* 緑色はあなたに似合う. ⑦ V-T 他動詞 If you **suit yourself**, you do something just because you want to do it, without bothering to consider other people. 好きなようにする ❑ *People have tended to suit themselves, not paying much heed to the reformers.* 人々は改革者にほとんど注意せず、好き勝手にしがちだった. ⑧ N-COUNT 可算名詞 In a court of law, a **suit** is a case in which someone tries to get a legal decision against a person or company, often so that the person or company will have to pay them money for having done something wrong to them. 訴訟 ❑ *Up to 2,000 former employees have filed personal injury suits against the company.* 最高2000名の元社員がその企業を相手取って人身傷害の訴訟を起こした. ● N-UNCOUNT 不可算名詞 You can also say that someone **files** or **brings suit against** another person. 訴訟を起こす ❑ *One insurance company has already filed suit against the city of Chicago.* ある保険会社は既にシカゴ市を相手取って訴訟を起こした. ⑨ → see also **pantsuit** ⑩ PHRASE 句 If people **follow suit**, they do the same thing that someone else has just done. 先例にならう ❑ *Efforts to persuade the remainder to follow suit have continued.* 残りの者を説得して後に続かせようとする努力が続いた.

→ see **clothing**

You do not use the verb **suit** if clothes are simply not the right size for you. The verb you need is **fit**. ❑ *The size 12 gown is gorgeous and fits perfectly... The gloves didn't fit.* You can say that something **suits** a person or place if it looks attractive on that person or in that place. ❑ *It is really feminine and pretty and it certainly suits you.* However, you cannot usually say that one color, pattern, or object **suits** another. The verb you need is **match**. ❑ *She wears a straw hat with a yellow ribbon to match her yellow cotton dress... His clothes don't quite match.*

---

suit|able /suːtəb^əl/ ADJ 形容詞 Someone or something that is **suitable for** a particular purpose or occasion is right or acceptable for it. 適している ❑ *Employers usually decide within five minutes whether someone is suitable for the job.* 雇用主は通常、ある人物が職に適しているかどうかを5分以内に決断する. ● suit|abil|ity /suːtəbɪlɪti/ N-UNCOUNT 不可算名詞 適していること ❑ *...information on the suitability of a product for use in the home.* 家庭での使用に適しているかについての製品情報

Word Partnership   *suitable* は次の語句と使われる:

V.   **find (a)** suitable *something*, **use (a)** suitable *something*

suit|ably /suːtəbli/ ADV 副詞 You use **suitably** to indicate that someone or something has the right qualities or things for a particular activity, purpose, or situation. 適切に [ADV adj/-ed] ❑ *There are problems in recruiting suitably qualified scientific officers for our laboratories.* 研究室向けの適切な資格を持つ科学の専門家の採用が難航している.

Word Link   cas = box, hold : *case, encase, suitcase*

suit|case /suːtkeɪs/ (suitcases) N-COUNT 可算名詞 A **suitcase** is a box or bag with a handle and a hard frame in which you carry your clothes when you are traveling. スーツケース ❑ *It did not take Andrew long to pack a suitcase.* アンドリューは短時間で荷造りした.

suite /swiːt/ (suites) ① N-COUNT 可算名詞 A **suite** is a set of rooms in a hotel or other building. 一続きの部屋 ❑ *They had a fabulous time during their week in a suite at the Paris Hilton.* 彼らはパリのヒルトンホテルの一続きの部屋に滞在し、楽しい時を過ごした. ② N-COUNT 可算名詞 A **suite** is a set of matching furniture. 家具の一揃い ❑ *...a three-piece suite.* 3点セット ③ N-COUNT 可算名詞 A bathroom **suite** is a matching bathtub, sink, and toilet. バスルームセット ❑ *...the horrible pink suite in the bathroom.* 悪趣味なピンクのバスルームセット
→ see **hotel**

suit|ed /suːtɪd/ ADJ 形容詞 If something is well **suited to** a particular purpose, it is right or appropriate for that purpose. If someone is well **suited to** a particular job, they are right or appropriate for that job. 適した [v-link ADJ] ❑ *The area is well suited to road cycling as well as off-road riding.* その地域は一般道路以外の場所で行なわれる乗馬だけでなく自転車のロードレースに適している.

Word Partnership suited は次の語句と使われる:

ADV. **ill** suited, **perfectly** suited, **uniquely** suited, **well** suited

PREP. suited **to** something

suit|or /sutər/ (**suitors**) **1** N-COUNT 可算名詞 A woman's **suitor** is a man who wants to marry her. 求婚者 [OLD-FASHIONED 古風な] ❑My mother had a suitor who adored her. 母には彼女をとても素晴らしいと思った求婚者がいた. **2** N-COUNT 可算名詞 A **suitor** is a company or organization that wants to buy another company. 会社を買収しようとする組織 [BUSINESS 実業] ❑The company was making little progress in trying to find a suitor. その企業が売却先を探す試みはほとんど進んでいなかった.

sul|fur /sʌlfər/ N-UNCOUNT 不可算名詞 **sulfur** is a yellow chemical which has a strong smell. 硫黄 ❑Burning sulfur creates poisonous fumes. 硫黄を燃やすと有害な煙が発生する.

→ see **firework**

sulk /sʌlk/ (**sulks, sulking, sulked**) V-I 自動詞 If you **sulk**, you are silent and bad-tempered for a while because you are annoyed about something. すねる ❑He turned his back and sulked. 彼は後ろを向き, ふてくされた. ● N-COUNT 可算名詞 **Sulk** is also a noun. すねること ❑He went off in a sulk. かれはすねて出て行った.

sul|len /sʌlən/ ADJ 形容詞 Someone who is **sullen** is bad-tempered and does not speak much. 不機嫌に黙り込んだ ❑The offenders lapsed into a sullen silence. 違反者は不機嫌に黙り込んだ.

sul|phur /sʌlfər/ → see **sulfur**

sul|tan /sʌltən/ (**sultans**) N-TITLE; N-COUNT 称号名詞, 可算名詞 A **sultan** is a ruler in some Muslim countries. スルタン ❑...during the reign of Sultan Abdul Hamid. アブドゥル・ハミド王の統治中

sul|try /sʌltri/ **1** ADJ 形容詞 **Sultry** weather is hot and damp. ひどく蒸し暑い [WRITTEN 書き言葉] ❑The climax came one sultry August evening. 最高潮はあるひどく蒸し暑い8月の夜に訪れた. **2** ADJ 形容詞 Someone who is **sultry** is attractive in a way that suggests hidden passion. なまめかしい [WRITTEN 書き言葉] ❑...a dark-haired sultry woman. 黒っぽい髪のなまめかしい女

sum /sʌm/ (**sums, summing, summed**) **1** N-COUNT 可算名詞 A **sum** of money is an amount of money. 金額 ❑Large sums of money were lost. 多額の金が失われた. **2** N-SING 単数名詞 In mathematics, the **sum** of two or more numbers is the number that is obtained when they are added together. 合計 ❑The sum of all the angles of a triangle is 180 degrees. 三角形の全ての角度を合計すると180度になる. **3** N-SING 単数名詞 The **sum** of something is all of it. You often use **sum** in this way to indicate that you are disappointed because the extent of something is rather small, or because it is not very good. 総量 ❑To date, the sum of my gardening experience had been futile efforts to rid the flower beds of grass. 今までのところ私の園芸の総決算は花壇の草むしりという無駄な努力であった. **4** N-COUNT 可算名詞 A **sum** is a simple calculation in arithmetic. 簡単な算数の計算 [BRIT 英国英語] **5** → see also **lump sum**

▶ **sum up** **1** PHRASAL VERB 句動詞 If you **sum** something **up**, you describe it as briefly as possible. 要約する ❑One voter in Brasilia summed up the mood – "Politicians have lost credibility," he complained. ブラジルのある有権者はムードを概説した. 「政治家は威信を失った」と彼は不満を言った. **2** PHRASAL VERB 句動詞 If something **sums** a person or situation up, it represents their most typical characteristics. すばやく把握する ❑"I love my wife, my horse and my dog," he said, and that summed him up. 「私は妻, 馬, 犬を愛している」と彼は言ったが, それは彼の人柄を示していた. **3** PHRASAL VERB 句動詞 If you **sum up** after a speech or at the end of a piece of writing, you briefly state the main points again. When a judge **sums up** after a trial, he reminds the jury of the evidence and the main arguments of the case they have heard. 要領を陳述する ❑When the judge summed up, it was clear he wanted a guilty verdict. 要領を陳述した際に判事が有罪の判決を望んでいることは明らかだった.

Word Partnership sum は次の語句と使われる:

ADJ. **equal** sum, **large** sum, **substantial** sum, **undisclosed** sum **1**

N. sum **of money 1**

sum|ma|rize /sʌməraɪz/ (**summarizes, summarizing, summarized**) V-T/V-I 他動詞/自動詞 If you **summarize** something, you give a summary of it. 要約する ❑Table 3.1 summarizes the information given above. 表3. 1は上記の情報を要約したものである. ❑Basically, the article can be summarized in three sentences. 要するにこの記事は3つのセンテンスに要約できる.

Word Link summ ≈ highest point : con**summ**ate, **summ**ary, **summ**it

sum|mary /sʌməri/ (**summaries**) **1** N-COUNT 可算名詞 A **summary** of something is a short account of it, which gives the main points but not the details. 要約 ❑What follows is a brief summary of the process. 次に述べるのはそのプロセスの簡単な要約である. ● PHRASE 句 You use **in summary** to indicate that what you are about to say is a summary of what has just been said. 要するに ❑In summary, it is my opinion that this complete treatment process was very successful. 要するにこの完全な治療過程が非常にうまく行ったというのが私の意見である. **2** ADJ 形容詞 **Summary** actions are done without delay, often when something else should have been done first or done instead. 即座の [FORMAL 形式ばった] [ADJ n] ❑It says torture and summary execution are common. それによると, 拷問と即座の死刑執行は一般的である.

sum|mer /sʌmər/ (**summers**) N-VAR 可変性名詞 **Summer** is the season between spring and fall. In the summer the weather is usually warm or hot. 夏 ❑I escaped the heatwave in Washington earlier this summer and flew to Maine. 私は今夏の初めにワシントンの猛暑を逃れ, メイン州に飛行機で行った. ❑It was a perfect summer's day. それは完璧な夏の日だった.

sum|mer camp (**summer camps**) N-COUNT 可算名詞 A **summer camp** is a place in the country where parents can pay to send their children during the school summer vacation. The children staying there can take part in many outdoor and social activities. サマーキャンプ

sum|mit /sʌmɪt/ (**summits**) **1** N-COUNT 可算名詞 A **summit** is a meeting at which the leaders of two or more countries discuss important matters. サミット ❑...next week's Washington summit. 来週のワシントンサミット **2** N-COUNT 可算名詞 The **summit** of a mountain is the top of it. 頂上 ❑...the first man to reach the summit of Mount Everest. エベレスト山の頂上に初めて登った男 → see **mountain**

sum|mon /sʌmən/ (**summons, summoning, summoned**) **1** V-T 他動詞 If you **summon** someone, you order them to come to you. 呼びつける ❑Howe summoned a doctor and hurried over. ハウは医者を呼び, 急いで行った. ❑Suddenly we were summoned to the interview room. 私達は突然面会室に呼び出された. **2** V-T 他動詞 If you **summon** a quality, you make a great effort to have it. For example, if you **summon** the courage or strength to do something, you make a great effort to be brave or strong, so that you will be able to do it. 奮い起こす ❑It took her a full month to summon the courage to tell her mother. 彼女が母親に告げる勇気を奮い起こすのにまる1ヶ月かかった. ● PHRASAL VERB 句動詞 **Summon up** means the same as **summon**. 奮い起こす ❑Painfully shy, he finally summoned up courage to ask her to a game. 彼は大変な shy にはかみやだったが, ようやく彼女を試合に誘う勇気を奮い起こした.

sum|mons /sʌmənz/ (**summonses**) **1** N-COUNT 可算名詞 A **summons** is an order to come and see someone. 呼び出しの命令 ❑I received a summons to the Warden's office. 私は学長の事務室に呼び出された. **2** N-COUNT 可算名詞 A **summons** is an official order to appear in court. 出廷命令 ❑She had received a summons to appear in court. 彼女は裁判所に出頭する命令を受け取った.

sump|tu|ous /sʌmptʃuəs/ ADJ 形容詞 Something that is **sumptuous** is grand and obviously very expensive. 豪華な ❑...a sumptuous feast. 豪奢な宴会

sun /sʌn/ **1** N-SING 単数名詞 The **sun** is the ball of fire in the sky that the Earth goes around, and that gives us heat and light. 太陽 ❑The sun was now high in the southern sky. 南国の空で太陽はもう高かった. ❑The sun came out, briefly. 日がしばらくさした. **2** N-UNCOUNT 不可算名詞 You refer to the light and heat that reach us from the sun as the **sun**. 日光 ❑Dena took them into the courtyard to sit in the sun. ディーナは日光浴するために彼らを中庭に案内した.

→ see Word Web: **sun**
→ see **astronomer, earth, eclipse, navigation, solar, solar system, star**

Sun. **Sun.** is a written abbreviation for **Sunday**. Sundayの縮約形 ❑The museum is open Mon.-Sun. 博物館は月〜金開館しています.

sun|bathe /sʌnbeɪð/ (**sunbathes, sunbathing, sunbathed**) V-I 自動詞 When people **sunbathe**, they sit or lie in a place where the sun shines on them, so that their skin becomes browner. 日光浴をする ❑Franklin swam and sunbathed at the pool every morning. フランクリンは毎朝プールで泳ぎ日光浴をした. ● **sun|bath|ing** N-UNCOUNT 不可算名詞 日光浴 ❑Nearby there is a stretch of white sand beach perfect for sunbathing. 近くには日光浴に最適の一筋の白砂の海岸がある.

sun|burn /sʌnbɜrn/ (**sunburns**) N-VAR 可変性名詞 If someone has **sunburn**, their skin is bright pink and sore because they have spent too much time in hot sunshine. 日焼け ❑The risk and severity of sunburn depend on the body's natural skin color. 日焼けのリスクと程度は生まれつきの皮膚の色による. → see **skin**

sun|burned /sʌnbɜrnd/ also **sunburnt** ADJ 形容詞 Someone who is **sunburned** has sore bright pink skin because they have spent too much time in hot sunshine. 日焼けした ❑A badly

Word Web sun

The **sun's** core contains **hydrogen** atoms. These atoms combine to form helium. This process is called **fusion**. It produces a core temperature of 15 million degrees Celsius. The **corona** is a layer of hot, glowing gases surrounding the sun. Large flames called solar flares also burn on the surface. Infrared and **ultraviolet** light are **invisible** parts of **sunlight**. Sometimes dark patches called **sunspots** appear on the sun. They occur in eleven-year cycles. Scientists believe that sunspots affect the growth of plant life on Earth. They also affect radio transmissions.

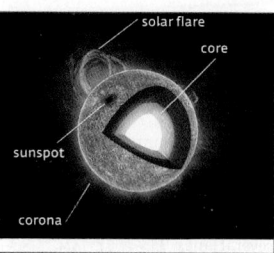

sunburned face or back is extremely painful. ひどく日焼けした顔や背中は非常に痛い.

Sun|day /sˈʌndeɪ, -di/ (Sundays) N-VAR 可変性名詞 **Sunday** is the day after Saturday and before Monday. 日曜日 ❑ I thought we might go for a drive on Sunday. 日曜日にドライブに行くのはどうでしょうか.

sun|dries /sˈʌndriz/ N-PLURAL 複数名詞 When someone is making a list of things, items that are not important enough to be listed separately are sometimes referred to together as **sundries**. 雑貨 [FORMAL 形式ばった] ❑ The inn gift shop stocks quality Indian crafts and sundries. その宿屋のギフトショップには良質のインド工芸品や雑貨が置いてある.

sun|dry /sˈʌndri/ ■ ADJ 形容詞 If someone refers to **sundry** people or things, they are referring to several people or things that are all different from each other. さまざまな [FORMAL 形式ばった] [ADJ n] ❑ Scientists, business people, and sundry others gathered on Monday for the official opening. 科学者, 会社で働く人, その他いろいろな人々が月曜の公式の開会式に集まった. ■ PHRASE 句 **All and sundry** means everyone. 誰も彼も ❑ I made tea for all and sundry at the office. 私はオフィスで全員にお茶を入れた.

sun|flower /sˈʌnflaʊər/ (sunflowers) N-COUNT 可算名詞 A **sunflower** is a very tall plant with large yellow flowers. Oil from sunflower seeds is used in cooking and to make margarine. ひまわり

sung /sˈʌŋ/ **Sung** is the past participle of **sing**. sing の過去・過去分詞形

sun|glasses /sˈʌnglæsɪz/ N-PLURAL 複数名詞 **Sunglasses** are glasses with dark lenses which you wear to protect your eyes from bright sunlight. サングラス [also "a pair of" N] ❑ She slipped on a pair of sunglasses. 彼女はサングラスをかけた.

sunk /sˈʌŋk/ **Sunk** is the past participle of **sink**. sink の過去・過去分詞形

sunk|en /sˈʌŋkən/ ■ ADJ 形容詞 **Sunken** ships have sunk to the bottom of a sea, ocean, or lake. 沈んだ [ADJ n] ❑ The sunken sail boat was a glimmer of white on the bottom. 沈没したセールボートは海底でちらちらと光る白い部分だった. ■ ADJ 形容詞 **Sunken** gardens, roads, or other features are below the level of their surrounding area. 一段下がった [ADJ n] ❑ Steps lead down to the sunken garden. 階段はサンクンガーデンに通じています. ■ ADJ 形容詞 **Sunken** eyes, cheeks, or other parts of the body curve inward and make you look thin and unwell. くぼんだ ❑ Her eyes were sunken and black-ringed. 彼女の目はくぼみ, 目の縁にくまが出ていた.

sun|light /sˈʌnlaɪt/ N-UNCOUNT 不可算名詞 **Sunlight** is the light that comes from the sun during the day. 太陽の光 ❑ I saw her sitting at a window table, bathed in sunlight. 私は彼女が日光を浴びながら窓テーブルに座っているのを見た.

→ see **rainbow, skin, sun**

sun|ny /sˈʌni/ (sunnier, sunniest) ■ ADJ 形容詞 When it is **sunny**, the sun is shining brightly. 日のよく照る ❑ The weather was surprisingly warm and sunny. 天気は驚くほど暖かく快晴だった. ■ ADJ 形容詞 **Sunny** places are brightly lit by the sun. 直射日光の当たる ❑ Most roses like a sunny position in a fairly fertile soil. 大半のバラはかなり肥沃な土と日の当たる場所を好む.

sun|rise /sˈʌnraɪz/ ■ N-UNCOUNT 不可算名詞 **Sunrise** is the time in the morning when the sun first appears in the sky. 日の出 ❑ The rain began before sunrise. 日の出前に雨が降り始めた. ■ N-COUNT 可算名詞 A **sunrise** is the colors and light that you see in the eastern part of the sky when the sun first appears. 朝焼け ❑ There was a spectacular sunrise yesterday. 昨日の朝焼けは素晴らしかった.

sun|roof /sˈʌnruːf/ (sunroofs) N-COUNT 可算名詞 A **sunroof** is a panel in the roof of a car that opens to let sunshine and air enter the car. サンルーフ ❑ ...extras like a sunroof, a CD player, or chrome wheels. サンルーフ, CDプレイヤー, またはクロム製車輪などの特別のもの

sun|screen /sˈʌnskriːn/ (sunscreens) N-MASS 質量名詞 A **sunscreen** is a cream that protects your skin from the sun's rays, especially in hot weather. 日焼け止め剤 ❑ Use a sunscreen suitable

for your skin type. 肌のタイプに合う日焼け止めを使いなさい.

→ see **skin**

sun|set /sˈʌnsɛt/ (sunsets) ■ N-UNCOUNT 不可算名詞 **Sunset** is the time in the evening when the sun disappears out of sight from the sky. 日暮れ時 ❑ The dance ends at sunset. 踊りは日暮れ時に終わる. ■ N-COUNT 可算名詞 A **sunset** is the colors and light that you see in the western part of the sky when the sun disappears in the evening. 夕焼け ❑ There was a red sunset over Paris. パリの空は夕焼けで赤かった.

sun|shine /sˈʌnʃaɪn/ N-UNCOUNT 不可算名詞 **Sunshine** is the light and heat that comes from the sun. 日光 ❑ In the marina yachts sparkle in the sunshine. マリーナのヨットが日差しを浴びて輝いた. ❑ She was sitting outside a cafe in bright sunshine. 彼女は明るい日光を浴びながらカフェの外に座っていた.

sun|stroke /sˈʌnstroʊk/ N-UNCOUNT 不可算名詞 **Sunstroke** is an illness caused by spending too much time in hot sunshine. 日射病 ❑ I was suffering from acute sunstroke, starvation and exhaustion. 私は急性の日射病, 飢餓状態, 極度の疲労にかかっていた.

sun|tan /sˈʌntæn/ (suntans) ■ N-COUNT 可算名詞 If you have a **suntan**, the sun has turned your skin an attractive brown color. 日焼け ❑ They want to go to the Bahamas and get a suntan. 彼らはバハマ諸島に行って日焼けすることを望んでいる. ■ ADJ 形容詞 **Suntan** lotion, oil, or cream protects your skin from the sun. 日焼け止めの [ADJ n] ❑ She playfully rubs suntan lotion on his neck. 彼女は日焼け止めローションをふざけて彼の首に塗る.

→ see **skin**

Word Link super ≈ above : super, superficial, supervise

su|per /sˈuːpər/ ■ ADV 副詞 **Super** is used before adjectives to indicate that something has a lot of a quality. とても [ADV adj] ❑ I'm going to Greece in the summer so I've got to be super slim. 私は夏にギリシャに行く予定なのでとてもスリムになる必要がある. ■ ADJ 形容詞 **Super** is used before nouns to indicate that something is larger, better, or more advanced than similar things. 最も強力な [ADJ n] ❑ Winners of each regional will advance to the super regionals. 地区大会の優勝者は最強地区大会に進む. ■ ADJ 形容詞 Some people use **super** to mean very nice or very good. 素晴らしい [INFORMAL, OLD-FASHIONED くだけた, 古風な] ❑ We had a super time. 私達は素晴らしい時を過ごした. ❑ That's a super idea. それは素晴らしい思いつきだ.

su|per|an|nua|tion /sˌuːpərænjuˈeɪʃən/ N-UNCOUNT 不可算名詞 **Superannuation** is the same as a **retirement fund**. 老齢者年金 [mainly BRIT 主に英国英語 BUSINESS 実業]

su|perb /sˈuːpɜːrb/ ■ ADJ 形容詞 If something is **superb**, its quality is very good indeed. 素晴らしく立派な ❑ There is a superb 18-hole golf course 6 miles away. 6マイル離れたところに18ホールの素晴らしいゴルフコースがある. ● **su|perb|ly** ADV 副詞 素晴らしく ❑ The orchestra played superbly. オーケストラの演奏は素晴らしかった. ■ ADJ 形容詞 If you say that someone has **superb** confidence, control, or skill, you mean that they have very great confidence, control, or skill. 優秀な ❑ With superb skill he managed to make a perfect landing. 優秀な技術を使い彼はどうにかして完璧な着陸をした. ● **su|perb|ly** ADV 副詞 素晴らしく ❑ ...his superbly disciplined opponent. 素晴らしく鍛錬された彼の相手

super|fi|cial /sˌuːpərfˈɪʃəl/ ■ ADJ 形容詞 If you describe someone as **superficial**, you disapprove of them because they do not think deeply, and have little understanding of anything serious or important. 皮相な [DISAPPROVAL 不賛成] ❑ This guy is a superficial yuppie with no intellect whatsoever. この男は知性のない皮相なヤッピーだ. ■ ADJ 形容詞 If you describe something such as an action, feeling, or relationship as **superficial**, you mean that it includes only the simplest and most obvious aspects of that thing, and not those aspects which require more effort to deal with or understand. 表面的な ❑ Their arguments do not withstand the most superficial scrutiny. 彼らの議論は最も表面的な吟味にも持ちこたえられない. ■ ADJ 形容詞 **Superficial** is used to describe the appearance of something or the impression that it gives, especially if its real nature is very different. 外見だけの ❑ Despite these superficial resemblances, this is a darker work than her earlier novels. 外見上は似

ているが、これは彼女のより以前の小説より暗い作品だ. **4** ADJ 形容詞 **Superficial** injuries are not very serious, and affect only the surface of the body. You can also describe damage to an object as **superficial**. 表面にある □ *The 69-year-old clergyman escaped with superficial wounds.* 69歳の牧師は外傷だけですんだ.

super|flu|ous /suːpɜːrfluəs/ ADJ 形容詞 Something that is **superfluous** is unnecessary or is no longer needed. 不必要な □ *My presence at the afternoon's proceedings was superfluous.* 午後の法廷審理に私が出席する必要はなかった.

super|high|way /suːpərhaɪweɪ/ (**superhighways**) **1** N-COUNT 可算名詞 A **superhighway** is a large, fast highway or freeway with several lanes. 超高速道路 [AM 米国英語] □ *He took off for the city on the eight-lane superhighway.* 8車線の超高速道路で彼はその町に向った. **2** N-COUNT 可算名詞 The information **superhighway** is the network of computer links that enables computer users all over the world to communicate with each other. スーパーハイウェー [COMPUTING コンピューティング] □ *...a superhighway using digital and fiber optic technology to provide new telecommunications links.* 新しい通信リンクのためにディジタルおよび光ファイバー技術を用いたスーパーハイウェー.

super|im|pose /suːpərɪmpoʊz/ (**superimposes, superimposing, superimposed**) **1** V-T 他動詞 If one image **is superimposed on** another, it is put on top of it so that you can see the second image through it. 重ね合わす [usu passive] □ *The image of a seemingly tiny dancer was superimposed on the image of the table.* 小さなダンサーのように見える画像がテーブルの画像の上に重ね焼きされた. **2** V-T 他動詞 If features or characteristics from one situation **are superimposed onto** or **on** another, they are transferred onto or used in the second situation, though they may not fit. 重ね合わす [usu passive] □ *Patterns of public administration and government are superimposed on traditional societies.* 官庁および政府の模範が伝統的な社会に重ね合わされた.

Word Link ent ≈ one who does, has : dependent, resident, superintendent

super|in|ten|dent /suːpərɪntɛndənt, suːprɪn-/ (**superintendents**) **1** N-COUNT 可算名詞 A **superintendent** is a person who is responsible for a particular thing or the work done in a particular department. 指導監督者 □ *He became superintendent of the bank's East African branches.* 彼は銀行の東アフリカ支店の管理者になった. **2** N-COUNT 可算名詞 A **superintendent** is a person whose job is to take care of a large building such as a school or an apartment building and deal with small repairs to it. 管理人 [AM 米国英語] □ *The superintendent, a bundle of keys hanging from his belt, was standing at the door.* ベルトに鍵の束をつるした管理人がドアのところに立っていた. **3** N-COUNT; N-TITLE 可算名詞, 称号名詞 A **superintendent** is the head of a police department. 警視 [BRIT 英国英語]

su|pe|ri|or /suːpɪəriər/ (**superiors**) **1** ADJ 形容詞 If one thing or person is **superior to** another, the first is better than the second. 勝る □ *We have a relationship infinitely superior to those of many of our friends.* 私達の間柄は友人のものよりはるかに勝っている. ●**su|peri|or|ity** N-UNCOUNT 不可算名詞 優越 □ *The technical superiority of laser discs over tape is well established.* レーザーディスクがテープに技術的に勝っていることは定評がある. **2** ADJ 形容詞 If you describe something as **superior**, you mean that it is good, and better than other things of the same kind. 質のよい □ *A few years ago it was virtually impossible to find superior quality coffee in local shops.* 数年前は地元の店で高級コーヒーを見つけるのはほとんど不可能だった. **3** ADJ 形容詞 A **superior** person or thing is more important than another person or thing in the same organization or system. 上級の □ *...negotiations between the mutineers and their superior officers.* 反逆者と彼らの上官との間の交渉. **4** N-COUNT 可算名詞 Your **superior** in an organization that you work for is a person who has a higher rank than you. 上官 □ *Other army units are completely surrounded and cut-off from communication with their superiors.* 他の軍隊は完全に包囲され, 上官と連絡することができない. **5** ADJ 形容詞 If you describe someone as **superior**, you disapprove of them because they behave as if they were better, more important, or more intelligent than other people. 人を見下すような [DISAPPROVAL 不賛成] □ *Finch gave a superior smile.* フィンチは人を見下すように微笑んだ. ●**su|peri|or|ity** N-UNCOUNT 不可算名詞 優越 □ *...a false sense of his superiority over mere journalists.* ただのジャーナリストに対して彼が感じている間違った優越感. **6** ADJ 形容詞 If one group of people has **superior** numbers to another group, the first has more people than the second, and therefore has an advantage over it. より多い [FORMAL 形式ばった] □ *The demonstrators fled when they saw the authorities' superior numbers.* デモ行進者は当局の人数が多いのを見て素早く逃げた.

Word Partnership superior は次の語句と使われる:

ADV.	**far** superior, **morally** superior, **vastly** superior **1**
N.	superior **performance**, superior **quality**, superior **service 2**

su|peri|or|ity /suːpɪəriɔːriti/ N-UNCOUNT 不可算名詞 If one side in a war or conflict has **superiority**, it has an advantage over its enemy, for example because it has more soldiers or better equipment. 優勢 [FORMAL 形式ばった] □ *We have air superiority.* 我々の空軍は優勢だ. **2** → see also **superior**

su|per|la|tive /suːpɜːrlətɪv/ (**superlatives**) **1** ADJ 形容詞 If you describe something as **superlative**, you mean that it is extremely good. 最高の □ *Some superlative wines are made in this region.* 一部の最高級ワインはこの地域で作られる. **2** N-COUNT 可算名詞 If someone uses **superlatives** to describe something, they use adjectives and expressions which indicate that it is extremely good. 最上級の賛辞 □ *...a spectacle which has critics world-wide reaching for superlatives.* 世界中の批評家がべた褒めする壮観. **3** ADJ 形容詞 In grammar, the **superlative** form of an adjective or adverb is the form that indicates that something has more of a quality than anything else in a group. For example, "biggest" is the superlative form of "big". Compare **comparative**. 最上級の [ADJ n] ●N-COUNT 可算名詞 **Superlative** is also a noun. 最上級の賛辞 □ *...his tendency toward superlatives and exaggeration.* 彼の誇張した表現を使うたち

super|mar|ket /suːpərmɑːrkɪt/ (**supermarkets**) N-COUNT 可算名詞 A **supermarket** is a large store which sells all kinds of food and some household goods. スーパーマーケット □ *Most of us do our food shopping in the supermarket.* 大半の人々はスーパーマーケットで食料品を買う.

super|model /suːpərmɒdəl/ (**supermodels**) N-COUNT 可算名詞 A **supermodel** is a very famous fashion model. スーパーモデル

super|natu|ral /suːpərnætʃərəl, -nætʃrəl/ ADJ 形容詞 **Supernatural** creatures, forces, and events are believed by some people to exist or happen, although they are impossible according to scientific laws. 超自然の □ *The Nakani were evil spirits who looked like humans and possessed supernatural powers.* ナカニは人間のように見え超自然的な力を持つ邪悪な魂だった. ●N-SING 単数名詞 **The supernatural** is things that are supernatural. 超自然的なもの □ *He writes short stories with a touch of the supernatural.* 彼は超自然的手法で短編を書いた.

super|pow|er /suːpərpaʊər/ (**superpowers**) N-COUNT 可算名詞 A **superpower** is a very powerful and influential country, usually one that is rich and has nuclear weapons. 超大国 □ *The United States could claim to be both a military and an economic superpower.* アメリカは軍事と経済の超大国と言えるだろう.

super|sede /suːpərsiːd/ (**supersedes, superseding, superseded**) V-T 他動詞 If something **is superseded by** something newer, it is replaced because it has become old-fashioned or unacceptable. 取って代わる [usu passive] □ *Hand tools are relics of the past that have now been superseded by the machine.* 手動式の道具は今や機械に取って代わられた過去の記念物だ.

Word Link son ≈ sound : resonate, sonata, supersonic

super|son|ic /suːpərsɒnɪk/ ADJ 形容詞 **Supersonic** aircraft travel faster than the speed of sound. 超音速機 [ADJ n] □ *There was a huge bang; it sounded like a supersonic jet.* 轟音 (ごうおん) がした. 超音速機のような音だった. → see **sound**

super|star /suːpərstɑːr/ (**superstars**) N-COUNT 可算名詞 A **superstar** is a very famous entertainer or athlete. スーパースター [INFORMAL くだけた] □ *He was more than a basketball superstar, he was a celebrity.* 彼はバスケットボールのスーパースター以上だった. 彼は有名人だった.

super|sti|tion /suːpərstɪʃən/ (**superstitions**) N-VAR 可変性名詞 **Superstition** is belief in things that are not real or possible, for example magic. 迷信 □ *Fortune-telling is a very much debased art surrounded by superstition.* 占いは迷信に取り囲まれた非常に劣った芸術である.

super|sti|tious /suːpərstɪʃəs/ **1** ADJ 形容詞 People who are **superstitious** believe in things that are not real or possible, for example magic. 迷信深い □ *Jean was extremely superstitious and believed the color green brought bad luck.* ジーンは非常に迷信深く, 緑色は不幸を招くと信じていた. **2** ADJ 形容詞 **Superstitious** fears or beliefs are irrational and not based on fact. 迷信的な [ADJ n] □ *A wave of superstitious fear spread among the townspeople.* 町民の間で迷信的な恐怖感の波が広がった.

super|store /suːpərstɔːr/ (**superstores**) N-COUNT 可算名詞 **Superstores** are very large supermarkets or stores selling household goods and equipment. Superstores are usually built outside cities and away from other stores. 大型小売店, 大型スーパーマーケット □ *...a Do-It-Yourself superstore.* ホームセンター

Word Link	super ≈ above : super, superficial, supervise

super|vise /súːpərvaɪz/ (**supervises, supervising, supervised**) V-T 他動詞 If you **supervise** an activity or a person, you make sure that the activity is done correctly or that the person is doing a task or behaving correctly. 監督する、指導する □ *A team was sent to supervise the elections in Nicaragua.* ニカラグアでの選挙を監督するめ一団が送り込まれた。

super|vi|sion /súːpərvɪʒ³n/ N-UNCOUNT 不可算名詞 **Supervision** is the supervising of people, activities, or places. 監督、監視 □ *A toddler requires close supervision and firm control at all times.* 幼児はいつも気をつけて見ていないといけないし、しっかり言い聞かせる必要がある。

super|vi|sor /súːpərvaɪzər/ (**supervisors**) N-COUNT 可算名詞 A **supervisor** is a person who supervises activities or people, especially workers or students. 監督者 □ *...a full-time job as a supervisor at a factory.* 工場で監督としての常勤職務

sup|per /sʌpər/ (**suppers**) ■ N-VAR 可変性名詞 Some people refer to the main meal eaten in the early part of the evening as **supper.** 夕食 □ *Some guests like to dress for supper.* 客の中には夕食のために正装するのが好きな人もいる。 ❷ N-VAR 可変性名詞 **Supper** is a simple meal eaten just before you go to bed at night. 寝る前の軽食 □ *She gives the children their supper, then puts them to bed.* 彼女は子供たちに軽食を与えてから彼らを寝かせる。

sup|ple /sʌp³l/ (**suppler, supplest**) ■ ADJ 形容詞 A **supple** object or material bends or changes shape easily without cracking or breaking. (物体や素材が) 柔軟な しなやかな □ *The leather is supple and sturdy enough to last for years.* その皮はしなやかな上に何年にもつほどしっかりしている。 ❷ ADJ 形容詞 A **supple** person can move and bend their body very easily. 体が柔らかい □ *Paul was incredibly supple and strong.* ポールはとても体が柔らかい上に頑丈だった。

sup|ple|ment /sʌplɪmənt/ (**supplements, supplementing, supplemented**) ■ V-T 他動詞 If you **supplement** something, you add something to it in order to improve it. 補足する、補う □ *...people doing extra jobs outside their regular jobs to supplement their incomes.* 収入を補うため、定職の他にも仕事をしている人たち ● N-COUNT 可算名詞 **Supplement** is also a noun. 補足 □ *Business sponsorship must be a supplement to, not a substitute for, public funding.* 企業への助成金は、公的資金の代用品ではなく補足でなければならない。 ❷ N-COUNT 可算名詞 A **supplement** is a pill that you take or a special kind of food that you eat in order to improve your health. 栄養補助食品、サプリメント □ *...a multiple vitamin and mineral supplement.* 総合ビタミンとミネラルのサプリメント ❸ N-COUNT 可算名詞 A **supplement** is a separate part of a magazine or newspaper, often dealing with a particular topic. (雑誌や新聞の) 特集版 別冊付録 □ *...a special supplement to a monthly financial magazine.* 月間経済誌の特集版 ❹ N-COUNT 可算名詞 A **supplement** to a book is an additional section, written some time after the main text and published either at the end of the book or separately. (本の) 補遺 別巻 □ *...the supplement to the Encyclopedia Britannica.* ブリタニカ百科事典補遺 ❺ N-COUNT 可算名詞 A **supplement** is an extra amount of money that you pay in order to obtain special facilities or services, for example when you are traveling or staying at a hotel. 追加料金 □ *If you are traveling alone, the single room supplement is $25 a night.* 一人旅の場合、シングルルームの追加料金は1泊25ドルです。

sup|ple|men|ta|ry /sʌplɪméntəri, -tri/ ADJ 形容詞 **Supplementary** things are added to something in order to improve it. 補助的な、補足の □ *...the question of whether or not we need to take supplementary vitamins.* 補助的にビタミンを取る必要があるかどうかという問題

sup|pli|er /səplaɪər/ (**suppliers**) N-COUNT 可算名詞 A **supplier** is a person, company, or organization that sells or supplies something such as goods or equipment to customers. 供給者、仕入先 [BUSINESS 実業] □ *...one of the country's biggest food suppliers.* 国内最大の食材メーカー

sup|ply /səplaɪ/ (**supplies, supplying, supplied**) ■ V-T 他動詞 If you **supply** someone with something that they want or need, you give them a quantity of it. 供給する □ *...an agreement not to produce or supply chemical weapons.* 化学兵器の生産または供給をしないという協定 □ *...a pipeline which will supply the major Greek cities with Russian natural gas.* ギリシャの主要都市にロシアの天然ガスを供給する予定のパイプライン ❷ N-PLURAL 複数名詞 You can use **supplies** to refer to food, equipment, and other essential things that people need, especially when these are provided in large quantities. 供給品、必需品 □ *What happens when food and gasoline supplies run low?* 食料とガソリンの供給が少なくなったらどうなる？ ❸ N-VAR 可変性名詞 A **supply of** something is an amount of it which someone has or which is available for them to use. 所持量、貯蔵量 □ *The brain requires a constant supply of oxygen.* 脳は常に酸素の供給を必要とする。 ❹ N-UNCOUNT 不可算名詞 **Supply** is the quantity of goods and services that can be made available for people to buy. 供給可能な量、在庫量 [BUSINESS 実業] □ *Prices change according to supply and demand.* 価格は在庫量と需要によって変わる。 ❺ PHRASE 句 If something is in **short supply,** there is very little of it available and it is difficult to find or obtain. 不足して □ *Food is in short supply all over the country.* 国中で食料が不足している。
→ see **economics**

Word Partnership	supply は次の語句と使われる:
N.	supply **electricity,** supply **equipment,** supply **information** ■
ADJ.	**abundant** supply, **large** supply, **limited** supply ❸

sup|port /səpɔ́rt/ (**supports, supporting, supported**) ■ V-T 他動詞 If you **support** someone or their ideas or aims, you agree with them, and perhaps help them because you want them to succeed. (考えや目標を) 支持する 後押しする □ *The vice president insisted that he supported the hard-working people of New York.* 副大統領はニューヨークの勤勉な市民を支持すると主張した。 ● N-UNCOUNT 不可算名詞 **Support** is also a noun. 支持、後押し □ *The president gave his full support to the reforms.* 大統領はその改革を全面的に後押しした。 ❷ N-UNCOUNT 不可算名詞 If you give **support** to someone during a difficult or unhappy time, you are kind to them and help them. 援助、支援 □ *It was hard to come to terms with her death after all the support she gave to me and the family.* 彼女があれほど私と家族を支えてくれた後だけに、彼女の死を受け入れるのは難しかった。 ❸ N-UNCOUNT 不可算名詞 Financial **support** is money provided to enable an organization to continue. 支援金、補助金 □ *State agencies continue to cut budgets and support to a number of organizations.* 州当局は引き続き多くの組織に対する予算と補助金を削減する。 ❹ V-I 他動詞 If you **support** someone, you provide them with money or the things that they need. (人を) 養う □ *I have children to support, money to be earned, and a home to be maintained.* 私は子供たちを養わねばならないし、お金を稼がなくちゃいけないし、家の手入れもしなければならないんだ。 ❺ V-T 他動詞 If a fact **supports** a statement or a theory, it helps to show that it is true or correct. (証言や理論を) 立証する □ *The Freudian theory about daughters falling in love with their father has little evidence to support it.* 娘が父親に恋をするというフロイトの説はそれを裏付ける証拠がほとんどない。 ● N-UNCOUNT 不可算名詞 **Support** is also a noun. 立証 □ *The two largest powers in any system must always be major rivals. History offers some support for this view.* どんな組織でも2大勢力というものは常に主要なライバル同士でなければならない。 ❻ V-T 他動詞 If something **supports** an object, it is underneath the object and holding it up. (物体を) 支える □ *...the thick wooden posts that supported the ceiling.* 天井を支えていた太い木の柱 ❼ N-COUNT 可算名詞 A **support** is a bar or other object that supports something. (物体を) 支える物 支柱 □ *Each slab was nailed to two straight wooden supports.* それぞれの厚板は2本のまっすぐな木の柱にくぎで打ち付けられていた。 ❽ V-T 他動詞 If you **support yourself,** you prevent yourself from falling by holding onto something or by leaning on something. (自分自身を倒れないように) 支える □ *He supported himself by means of a nearby post.* 彼は近くの柱で自分を支えた。 ● N-UNCOUNT 不可算名詞 **Support** is also a noun. 支え □ *Alice, very pale, was leaning against him as if for support.* アリスはとても顔色が悪く、自分を支えるかのように彼にもたれていた。 ❾ V-T 他動詞 If you **support** a sports team, you always want them to win and perhaps go regularly to their games. (チームを) 応援する □ *Tim, 17, supports the Knicks.* 17歳のティムはニックスを応援している。

	If you dislike something very much or get annoyed by it, you do not say "I can't support it." You say "**I can't bear it.**" or "**I can't stand it.**" □ *She can't bear the new Republican governor... I cannot stand going shopping.*

sup|port|er /səpɔ́rtər/ (**supporters**) N-COUNT 可算名詞 **Supporters** are people who support someone or something, for example a political leader or a sports team. 支持者、後援者、サポーター □ *Attacks against opposition supporters are continuing at levels higher than before the election.* 支持者に対する対抗勢力の攻撃は選挙前よりもひどい状態で今も続いている。

Word Partnership	supporter は次の語句と使われる:
ADJ.	**active** supporter, **big** supporter, **enthusiastic** supporter, **former** supporter, **longtime** supporter, **staunch** supporter, **strong** supporter

sup|port|ive /səpɔ́rtɪv/ ADJ 形容詞 If you are **supportive,** you are kind and helpful to someone at a difficult or unhappy time in their life. 協力的な、支えとなる □ *They were always supportive of each other.* 彼らはいつもお互いを支え合った。

sup|pose /səpóʊz/ (**supposes, supposing, supposed**) ■ V-T 他動詞 You can use **suppose** or **supposing** before mentioning a possible situation or action. You usually then go on to consider the effects that this situation or action might have. 仮定する □ *Suppose someone gave you an egg and asked you to describe exactly what was inside.* ある人があなたに卵をくれ、中に何が入っているかを

→ see **economics**

S

正確に説明するよう求めたとする。 **2** V-T 他動詞 If you **suppose that** something is true, you believe that it is probably true, because of other things that you know. (－だと) 思う ❑ *The policy is perfectly clear and I see no reason to suppose that it isn't working.* その方針は非常に明確なので，それが実際に機能していないと考える理由はまったくないと思う。 ❑ *I knew very well that the problem was more complex than he supposed.* その問題は彼が思うよりももっと複雑だということを私はよく知っていた。 **3** PHRASE 句 You can say "**I suppose**" when you want to express slight uncertainty. －だろうと思う [SPOKEN 口語, VAGUENESS あいまいさ] ❑ *I suppose I'd better do some homework.* 宿題をした方がいいんだろうな。 ❑ *"Is that the right way up?"—"Yeah, I suppose so."*「そっちが上で合ってるの？」「うん。そうだと思うよ。」 **4** PHRASE 句 You can say "**I suppose**" or "**I don't suppose**" before describing someone's probable thoughts or attitude, when you are impatient or slightly angry with them. (相手の言動に不快感を込めて) －んでしょう (－だと) [SPOKEN 口語, FEELINGS 感情] ❑ *I suppose you think you're funny.* 自分で自分のことを面白いと思ってるんだろう。 **5** PHRASE 句 You can say "**I don't suppose**" as a way of introducing a polite request. －していただけませんか (丁寧な要請) [SPOKEN 口語, POLITENESS 丁寧さ] ❑ *I don't suppose you could tell me where James Street is, could you?* ジェームズ・ストリートがどこにあるかを教えていただけないものでしょうか？ **6** PHRASE 句 You can use "**do you suppose**" to introduce a question when you want someone to give their opinion about something, although you know that they are unlikely to have any more knowledge or information about it than you. －だと思う？ (相手が答えを知らない可能性が高い時の聞き方) [SPOKEN 口語] ❑ *Do you suppose he was telling the truth?* 彼が本当のことを言っていたと思う？

Note that when you are using the verb **suppose** with a "that"-clause in order to state a negative opinion or belief, you normally make **suppose** negative, rather than the verb in the "that"-clause. For instance, it is more usual to say ❑ "*I don't suppose he ever saw it.*" than "I suppose he didn't ever see it." The same pattern applies to other verbs with a similar meaning, such as **believe, consider,** and **think.**

Word Partnership	*suppose* は次の語句と使われる:
V.	**let's** suppose **1**
ADV.	**now** suppose **1**

sup|posed

Pronounced /səpoʊzd/ or /səpoʊst/ for meanings **1** to **4**, and /səpoʊzɪd/ for meaning **5**.

/səpoʊzd/ から /səpoʊst/ の意味では **1** または **4** と発音され，/səpoʊzɪd/ の意味では **5** と発音される。

1 PHRASE 句 If you say that something **is supposed to** happen, you mean that it is planned or expected. Sometimes this use suggests that the thing does not really happen in this way. －することになっている，本当なら－するはずだ ❑ *He produced a hand-written list of nine men he was supposed to kill.* 彼は自分が殺すことになっている9人の男性のリストを手書きで作った。 **2** PHRASE 句 If something **was supposed to** happen, it was planned or intended to happen, but did not in fact happen. (実際には起こらなかったことに対して) －するはずだった ❑ *He was supposed to go back to Bergen on the last bus, but of course the accident prevented him.* 彼は最終バスでベルゲンに帰るはずだったが，当然その事故で帰れなくなった。 **3** PHRASE 句 If you say that something **is supposed to** be true, you mean that people say it is true but you do not know for certain that it is true. －だそうだ，－ということらしい ❑ *"The Whipping Block" has never been published, but it's supposed to be a really good poem.*「The Whipping Block」は一度も発表されなかったが，とても素晴らしい詩だそうだ。 **4** PHRASE 句 You can use "**be supposed to**" to express annoyance at someone's ideas, or because something is not happening in the right way. (相手の考え方にいら立ちを覚えて) －のはずだ [FEELINGS 感情] ❑ *You're supposed to be my friend!* あなたは私の友達でしょ！ **5** ADJ 形容詞 You can use **supposed** to suggest that something that people talk about or believe in may not in fact exist, happen, or be as it is described. 想定された，仮定の [ADJ n] ❑ *Not all developing countries are willing to accept the supposed benefits of free trade.* 発展途上国の中には自由貿易の想定利益を受け入れたがらない国もある。 ● **sup|pos|ed|ly** /səpoʊzɪdli/ ADV 副詞 恐らく，仮に ❑ *He was more of a victim than any of the women he supposedly offended.* 彼は，彼が不快な思いをさせたと言われるどの女性よりも犠牲者だった。

sup|press /səprɛs/ (**suppresses, suppressing, suppressed**) **1** V-T 他動詞 If someone in authority **suppresses** an activity, they prevent it from continuing, by using force or making it illegal. 抑圧する ❑ *...drug traffickers, who continue to flourish despite international attempts to suppress them.* 国際的な抑圧にもかかわらず幅を利かせる麻薬密輸業者 ● **sup|pres|sion** /səprɛʃⁿn/ N-UNCOUNT 不可算名詞 抑圧，制圧 ❑ *...people who were imprisoned after the violent*

suppression of the pro-democracy movement protests. 民主化要求運動に対する暴力的な抑圧の後に投獄された人々 **2** V-T 他動詞 If a natural function or reaction of your body **is suppressed**, it is stopped, for example by drugs or illness. (体の自然な機能や反応を) 抑える ❑ *The reproduction and growth of the cancerous cells can be suppressed by bombarding them with radiation.* 癌細胞の生殖作用と増殖は放射線を大量に浴びせることで抑えられる。 ● **sup|pres|sion** N-UNCOUNT 不可算名詞 抑制 ❑ *Eye problems can indicate an unhealthy lifestyle with subsequent suppression of the immune system.* 目の疾患は，将来的に免疫機能の低下を招く不健康な生活スタイルの現れであることがある。 **3** V-T 他動詞 If you **suppress** your feelings or reactions, you do not express them, even though you might want to. (感情や態度を) 抑制する ❑ *Liz thought of Barry and suppressed a smile.* リズはバリーのことを考え，笑いをかみ殺した。 ● **sup|pres|sion** N-UNCOUNT 不可算名詞 (感情の) 抑制 ❑ *A mother's suppression of her own feelings can cause problems.* 母親が自分の感情を抑えることで問題が起きることがある。 **4** V-T 他動詞 If someone **suppresses** a piece of information, they prevent other people from learning it. (情報などを) 隠す 差し止める ❑ *At no time did they try to persuade me to suppress the information.* 彼らが私に情報を隠すよう説得したことなど一度もない。 ● **sup|pres|sion** N-UNCOUNT 不可算名詞 (情報などを) 隠すこと 隠蔽 ❑ *The inspectors found no evidence which supported any allegation of suppression of official documents.* 検査官たちは公文書隠蔽の申し立てを立証する証拠を何も見つけられなかった。 **5** V-T 他動詞 If someone or something **suppresses** a process or activity, they stop it continuing or developing. (工程や活動を) 阻止する 食い止める ❑ *The government is suppressing inflation by increasing interest rates.* 政府は金利を上げることでインフレーションを食い止めている。

su|prema|cy /suprɛməsi/ **1** N-UNCOUNT 不可算名詞 If one group of people has **supremacy** over another group, they have more political or military power than the other group. 主導権，支配権 ❑ *The conservative old guard had re-established its political supremacy.* 筋金入りの保守派が再び政治の主導権を握った。 **2** N-UNCOUNT 不可算名詞 If someone or something has **supremacy** over another person or thing, they are better. 優位，優越 ❑ *In the United States Open final, Graf retained overall supremacy.* 全米オープン選手権の決勝で，グラフが全面的に優位を保った。

su|preme /suprim/ **1** ADJ 形容詞 **Supreme** is used in the title of a person or an official group to indicate that they are at the highest level in a particular organization or system. (称号や役職を表して) 最高の (称号や役職を表して) [ADJ n] (しばしばSは大文字) ❑ *MacArthur was Supreme Commander for the allied powers in the Pacific.* マッカーサーは太平洋沿岸の連合軍最高司令官だった。 ❑ *...the Supreme Court.* 最高裁判所 **2** ADJ 形容詞 You use **supreme** to emphasize that a quality or thing is very great. (質などが) 最高の この上ない [EMPHASIS 強調] ❑ *Her approval was of supreme importance.* 彼女の承認は最も重要だった。 ● **su|preme|ly** ADV 副詞 [ADV adj/adv] 最高に，この上なく ❑ *She does her job supremely well.* 彼女は仕事が非常によくできる。

Word Link	sur ≈ above : surcharge, surface, surveillance

sur|charge /sɜrtʃɑrdʒ/ (**surcharges**) N-COUNT 可算名詞 A **surcharge** is an extra payment of money in addition to the usual payment for something. It is added for a specific reason, for example by a company because costs have risen or by a government as a tax. 追加料金 ❑ *The government introduced a 15% surcharge on imports.* 政府は輸入品に15パーセントの追加税を導入した。

sure /ʃʊər/ (**surer, surest**) **1** ADJ 形容詞 If you are **sure** that something is true, you are certain that it is true. If you are not **sure** about something, you do not know for certain what the true situation is. (事実について) 確信がある [v-link ADJ] ❑ *He'd never been in a class before and he was not even sure that he should have been teaching.* 彼はそれまで一度も授業に出たことがなく，自分が教師をしていてもいいかさえ分からなかった。 ❑ *There had never been sure which direction he wanted to go in on this issue.* 大統領はこの問題に関して，どの方向に進むべきか全く確信がなかった。 **2** ADJ 形容詞 If someone is **sure of** getting something, they will definitely get it or they think they will definitely get it. (自分の能力に) 自信がある [v-link ADJ "of" -ing/n] ❑ *A lot of people think that it's better to pay for their education so that they can be sure of getting quality.* 多くの人が，確実に質の高い教育を受けるためにはお金を費やした方がよいと考えている。 **3** PHRASE 句 If you say that something **is sure to** happen, you are emphasizing your belief that it will happen. きっと (－が起こる) [EMPHASIS 強調] ❑ *With over 80 beaches to choose from, you are sure to find a place to lay your towel.* 80以上ものビーチから選べるので，きっとあなたのタオルを敷こうと思う場所が見つかるはず。 **4** ADJ 形容詞 **Sure** is used to emphasize that something such as a sign or ability is reliable or accurate. 信頼できる [EMPHASIS 強調] [ADJ n] ❑ *Sharpe's leg and shoulder began to ache, a sure sign of rain.* シャープの足と肩がうずき始めた。それは雨が降るという確かな前兆だった。 **5** ADJ 形容詞 If you tell someone to **be sure to** do something, you mean that they must not forget to do it. 必ず，(－する) 忘れずに [EMPHASIS 強調] [v-link ADJ]

❏ *Be sure to read about how mozzarella is made, on page 65.* 65ページのモッツァレラがどうやって作られるかというところを必ず読むように. **Sure** is an informal way of saying "yes" or "all right." (口語で) わかった 大丈夫 [FORMULAE 決まり文句] ❏ *"Do you know where she lives?"—"Sure."* 「彼女がどこに住んでるか知ってる?」「もちろん.」 **7** ADV 副詞 You can use **sure** in order to emphasize what you are saying. 確かに [INFORMAL くだけた, EMPHASIS 強調] [ADV before v] ❏ *"Has the whole world just gone crazy?"—"Sure looks that way, doesn't it."* 「全世界はほんとに狂ったのかい?」「まったくそんな感じだねえ.」 **8** PHRASE 句 You say **sure enough**, especially when telling a story, to confirm that something was really true or was actually happening. 案の定, やっぱり ❏ *We found the apple pie pudding too good to resist. Sure enough, it was delicious.* デザートのアップルパイがあまりにおいしそうだったので, 私たちはいちもおいしくいただいた, 案の定おいしかった. **9** PHRASE 句 If you say that something is **for sure** or that you know it **for sure**, you mean that it is definitely true. 間違いない, 絶対 ❏ *One thing's for sure, Manilow's vocal style hasn't changed much over the years.* 1つ確かなのは, マニロウの歌い方のスタイルが長い年月の間にあまり変わっていないということだ. **10** PHRASE 句 If you **make sure that** something is done, you take action so that it is done. 必ず~となるようにする ❏ *Make sure that you follow the instructions carefully.* 必ず注意深く指示に従ってください. **11** PHRASE 句 If you **make sure that** something is the way that you want or expect it to be, you check that it is that way. (~であることを) 確かめる ❏ *He looked in the bathroom to make sure that he was alone.* 彼は自分1人であることを確かめるため浴室の中をのぞいた. **12** PHRASE 句 If you are **sure of yourself**, you are very confident about your own abilities or opinions. 自分に自信がある ❏ *I'd never seen him like this, so sure of himself, so in command.* 自信に満ちあふれ, とても冷静なこんな彼を私はそれまで一度も見たことがなかった.

sure|fire /ʃʊərfaɪər/ also **sure-fire** ADJ 形容詞 A **surefire** thing is something that is certain to succeed or win. 必ずうまくいく, 成功間違いなしの [INFORMAL くだけた] [ADJ n] ❏ *These products are promoted as surefire cures for various diseases.* これらの製品はさまざま病気の確かな治療薬として推奨されている.

sure|ly /ʃʊərli/ **1** ADV 副詞 You use **surely** to emphasize that you think something should be true, and you would be surprised if it was not true. 間違いなく, 確かに [EMPHASIS 強調] [ADV with cl/group] ❏ *You're an intelligent woman; surely you realize by now that I'm helping you.* あなたは利口な女性だ. 私があなたを手助けしていることはきっともう分かっているでしょう. ❏ *You surely haven't forgotten Dr. Walters?* ウォルターズ先生のことをちゃんと覚えているでしょう? **2** ADV 副詞 If something will **surely** happen or is **surely** the case, it will definitely happen or is definitely the case. 必ず [FORMAL 形式ばった] ❏ *He knew that under the surgeon's knife he would surely die.* 彼はその外科医の執刀では必ず自分が死ぬことを分かっていた. **3** PHRASE 句 If you say that something is happening **slowly but surely**, you mean that it is happening gradually but it is definitely happening. ゆっくりだが確実に ❏ *Slowly but surely she started to fall in love with him.* ゆっくりだが確実に彼女は彼に恋し始めた.

You use **surely** to express disagreement or surprise. ❏ *Surely you care about what happens to her.* You use **certainly** to emphasize that what you say is definitely true. ❏ *His death was certainly not an accident.* Both British and American speakers use **certainly** to agree with requests and statements. ❏ *"It is still a difficult world for women."—"Oh, certainly."* Note that American speakers also use **surely** in this way.

Word Partnership *surely* は次の語句と使われる:

v.	surely **know** *something*, surely **think** *something* **1** surely **die** **2**

sure|ty /ʃʊəriti/ (sureties) N-VAR 可変性名詞 A **surety** is money or something valuable which you give to someone to show that you will do what you have promised. (履行を確約するための) 保証金 担保, 保証 ❏ *The insurance company will take warehouse stocks or treasury bonds as surety.* 保険会社は製品在庫か長期債券を担保に取るだろう.

surf /sɜrf/ (surfs, surfing, surfed) **1** N-UNCOUNT 不可算名詞 **Surf** is the mass of white bubbles that is formed by waves as they fall upon the shore. (打ち寄せる波によってできる) 白い泡 打ち寄せる白い波 ❏ *...surf rolling onto white sand beaches.* 白い砂浜にうねり来る白い波. **2** V-I 自動詞 If you **surf**, you ride on big waves in the sea on a special board. サーフィンをする, 波乗りをする ❏ *I'm going to buy a surfboard and learn to surf.* 僕はサーフボードを買って, サーフィンを習うつもりだ. ● **surf|er** N-COUNT 可算名詞 (surfers) サーファー, サーフィンをする人 ❏ *...this small fishing village, which continues to attract painters and surfers.* 画家やサーファーを引き付けてやまないこの小さな漁村. **3** V-T 他動詞 If you **surf** the Internet, you spend time finding and looking at things on the Internet. ネットサーフィンをする [COMPUTING コンピューティング] ❏ *No one knows how many people currently surf the Net.* 現在, どれだけの人がネットサーフィンをするかは誰にも分からない. ● **surf|er** N-COUNT 可算名詞 (surfers) ネットサーファー ❏ *Net surfers can use their credit cards to pay for anything from toys to train tickets.* ネットサーファーはおもちゃから電車の切符まですべての支払いにクレジットカードを使える. → see **beach**

Word Link sur ≈ above : surcharge, surface, surveillance

sur|face /sɜrfɪs/ (surfaces, surfacing, surfaced) **1** N-COUNT 可算名詞 The **surface** of something is the flat top part of it or the outside of it. (物体の) 表面 ❏ *Ozone forms a protective layer between 12 and 30 miles above the Earth's surface.* オゾンは地表の12から30マイル上空で保護層を形成している. ❏ *...tiny little waves on the surface of the water.* 水の表面の極めて小さな波 **2** N-COUNT 可算名詞 A work **surface** is a flat area, for example the top of a table, desk, or kitchen counter, on which you can work. (料理や作業に使う) 台 ❏ *It can simply be left on the work surface.* それはただ作業台の上に放置しておいてかまわない. **3** N-SING 単数名詞 When you refer to the **surface** of a situation, you are talking about what can be seen easily rather than what is hidden or not immediately obvious. 表面 (事態の) 外見 ❏ *Back home, things appear, on the surface, simpler.* うちでは, 一見すると状況はもう少し単純そうだ. **4** V-I 自動詞 If someone or something under water **surfaces**, they come up to the surface of the water. 水面に浮上する ❏ *He surfaced, gasping for air.* 彼はあえぎながら水面に浮かび上がった. **5** V-I 自動詞 When something such as a piece of news, a feeling, or a problem **surfaces**, it becomes known or becomes obvious. (問題などが) 明るみに出る 表ざたになる ❏ *The paper says the evidence, when it surfaces, is certain to cause uproar.* その証拠が表ざたになると間違いなく大騒動を起こすと新聞には書いてある.

Word Partnership *surface* は次の語句と使われる:

ADJ.	**flat** surface, **rough** surface, **smooth** surface **1**
N.	surface **area**, **Earth's** surface, surface **of the water** **1** surface **level** **1** **3**
V.	**break** the surface **1** **scratch** the surface **1** **3**

sur|face mail N-UNCOUNT 不可算名詞 **Surface mail** is the system of sending letters and packages by road, rail, or sea, not by air. (航空便に対し) 地上輸送郵便 船便 ❏ *Goods may be sent by surface mail or airmail.* 商品は船便か航空便で送られるかもしれない.

surf|ing /sɜrfɪŋ/ **1** N-UNCOUNT 不可算名詞 **Surfing** is the sport of riding on the top of a wave while standing or lying on a special board. サーフィン ❏ *...every type of watersport from jetskiing and surfing to sailing and fishing.* ジェットスキーやサーフィンからヨットや釣りまで, あらゆる種類の水上スポーツ **2** N-UNCOUNT 不可算名詞 **Surfing** is the activity of looking at different sites on the Internet, especially when you are not looking for anything in particular. ネットサーフィン [COMPUTING コンピューティング] ❏ *The simple fact is that, for most people, surfing is too expensive to do on a regular basis.* 実のところは, ほとんどの人にとって定期的にネットサーフィンをするのは高くつきすぎるというだけのことだ.

surge /sɜrdʒ/ (surges, surging, surged) **1** N-COUNT 可算名詞 A **surge** is a sudden large increase in something that has previously been steady, or has only increased or developed slowly. 急上昇, 急騰, 急増 ❏ *Specialists see various reasons for the recent surge in inflation.* 専門家は近年の急激なインフレーションのさまざまな要因を知っている. **2** V-I 自動詞 If something **surges**, it increases suddenly and greatly, after being steady or developing only slowly. 急増する, 急騰する ❏ *The Freedom Party's electoral support surged from just under 10 percent to nearly 17 percent.* 自由党の選挙支持率は10パーセント弱からほぼ17パーセントまで急上昇した. **3** V-I 自動詞 If a crowd of people **surge** forward, they suddenly move forward together. (群集が) 押し寄せる 殺到する ❏ *The photographers and cameramen surged forward.* 報道カメラマンたちが前に押し寄せた. **4** N-COUNT 可算名詞 A **surge** is a sudden powerful movement of a physical force such as wind or water. (風や水などが) 押し寄せること 急激な変化 ❏ *The whole car shuddered with an almost frightening surge of power.* 車全体が恐ろしいほどの急激な変化に, 車全体が激しく振動した. **5** V-I 自動詞 If a physical force such as wind or electricity **surges** through something, it moves through it suddenly and powerfully. (水や電気などが) どっと流れる 打ち寄せる ❏ *Thousands of volts surged through his car after he careered into a lamp post, ripping out live wires.* 彼が電柱に突っ込み送電線を引きちぎった時, 何千ボルトもの電流が彼の車を突き抜けた.

sur|geon /sɜrdʒ³n/ (surgeons) N-COUNT 可算名詞 A **surgeon** is a doctor who is specially trained to perform surgery. 外科医, 執刀医 ❏ *...a heart surgeon.* 心臓外科医

sur|gery /sɜrdʒəri/ (surgeries) **1** N-UNCOUNT 不可算名詞 **Surgery** is medical treatment in which someone's body is cut open so that a doctor can repair, remove, or replace a diseased or damaged part. 手術 ❏ *His father has just recovered from heart surgery.*

彼の父親はやっと心臓の手術から回復したばかりだ. **2** → see also **cosmetic surgery, plastic surgery** **3** N-COUNT 可算名詞 A **surgery** is the area in a hospital with operating rooms where surgeons operate on their patients. 手術室 [AM 米国英語] **4** N-COUNT 可算名詞 A **surgery** is the room or house where a doctor or dentist works. 診療所 [BRIT 英国英語; AM 米国英語 **doctor's office, dentist's office** 米国英語 **doctor's office, dentist's office**] **5** N-COUNT 可算名詞 A doctor's **surgery** is the period of time each day when a doctor sees patients at his or her surgery. 診察時間 [BRIT 英国英語; AM **office hours** 米国英語 **office hours**] → see **cancer, laser**

sur|gi|cal /sɜrdʒɪkəl/ **1** ADJ 形容詞 **Surgical** equipment and clothing is used in surgery. 外科用の ❏ ...*an array of surgical instruments.* ずらりと並んだ手術用の器具 **2** ADJ 形容詞 **Surgical** treatment involves surgery. 外科の [ADJ n] ❏ *A biopsy is usually a minor surgical procedure.* 生体組織検査はだいたい簡単な外科的措置だ. ● **sur|gi|cal|ly** ADV 副詞 [ADV with v] 外科的に ❏ *In very severe cases, bunions may be surgically removed.* 非常に重症な例では, 腱膜瘤 (けんまくりゅう) を手術で取り除くことがある.

sur|mise /sərmaɪz/ (**surmises, surmising, surmised**) **1** V-T 他動詞 If you **surmise** that something is true, you guess it from the available evidence, although you do not know for certain. 推測する [FORMAL 形式ばった] ❏ *There's so little to go on, we can only surmise what happened.* 手がかりがほとんどないので, 我々は何が起こったかを推測するしかない. **2** N-VAR 可変性名詞 If you say that a particular conclusion is **surmise**, you mean that it is a guess based on the available evidence and you do not know for certain that it is true. 推測 [FORMAL 形式ばった] ❏ *It is mere surmise that Bosch had Brant's poem in mind when doing this painting.* ボッシュがこの絵を描いている時にブラントの詩を念頭に置いていたというのは, 単なる推測にしか過ぎない.

sur|name /sɜrneɪm/ (**surnames**) N-COUNT 可算名詞 Your **surname** is the name that you share with other members of your family. In English-speaking countries and many other countries it is your last name. 姓, 名字 ❏ *She'd known his surname, only his first name.* 彼女は彼の名前を知っていたが, 名字はまったく知らなかった.

sur|pass /sərpæs/ (**surpasses, surpassing, surpassed**) **1** V-T 他動詞 If one person or thing **surpasses** another, the first is better than, or has more of a particular quality than, the second. (能力などが-より) 優れている 勝る ❏ *He was determined to surpass the achievements of his older brothers.* 彼は兄の業績を越えようと決心していた. **2** V-T 他動詞 If something **surpasses** expectations, it is much better than it was expected to be. (期待を) 上回る ❏ *Conrad Black gave an excellent party that surpassed expectations.* コンラッド・ブラックは期待を上回る素晴らしいパーティを開いた.

sur|plus /sɜrpləs, -pləs/ (**surpluses**) **1** N-VAR 可変性名詞 If there is a **surplus of** something, there is more than is needed. 余分, 余剰 ❏ ...*countries where there is a surplus of labor.* 労働力が余っている国々 **2** ADJ 形容詞 **Surplus** is used to describe something that is extra or that is more than is needed. 余分の, 過剰の ❏ *Few people have large sums of surplus cash.* 余分なお金をたくさん持っている人はほとんどいない. ❏ *I sell my surplus birds to a local pet shop.* 私は残りの鳥を地元のペットショップに売っている. **3** N-COUNT 可算名詞 If a country has a trade **surplus**, it exports more than it imports. (貿易の) 黒字 ❏ *Japan's annual trade surplus is in the region of 100 billion dollars.* 日本の年間貿易黒字は1千億ドルあたりだ. **4** N-COUNT 可算名詞 If a government runs a budget **surplus**, it has spent less than it received in taxes. (財政の) 黒字 ❏ *Norway's budget surplus has fallen from 5.9% in 1986 to an expected 0.1% this year.* ノルウェーの財政黒字は1986年の5.9パーセントから今年予想されている0.1パーセントまで減少した.

sur|prise /sərpraɪz/ (**surprises, surprising, surprised**) **1** N-COUNT 可算名詞 A **surprise** is an unexpected event, fact, or piece of news. 驚く事 ❏ *I have a surprise for you: we are moving to Switzerland!* ビックリすることがあるのよ, 私たちはスイスへ引っ越すの！ ❏ *It may come as a surprise to some that a normal, healthy child is born with many skills.* 普通の健康な赤ちゃんがさまざまな能力と共に生まれるというのは, ある人にとっては驚くべきことかもしれない. ● ADJ 形容詞 **Surprise** is also an adjective. 不意の, 突然の [ADJ n] ❏ *Baxter arrived here this afternoon, on a surprise visit.* バクスターは今日の午後, 不意にここへやって来た. **2** N-UNCOUNT 不可算名詞 **Surprise** is the feeling that you have when something unexpected happens. 驚き ❏ *The Pentagon has expressed surprise at these allegations.* 米国国防総省はこれらの申し立てに対する驚きを表明した. ❏ *"You mean he's going to vote against her?" Scobie asked in surprise.* 「彼が彼女に反対投票するだって？」とスコービーは驚いて聞いた. **3** V-T 他動詞 If something **surprises** you, it gives you a feeling of surprise. びっくりさせる, 驚かせる ❏ *We'll solve the case ourselves and surprise everyone.* 僕たちでこの事件を解決してみんなをビックリさせてやる. ❏ *It surprised me that a driver of Alain's experience should make those mistakes.* アランほどの経験を持った運転手がこうした失敗をするなんて, 驚いた. **4** V-T 他動詞 If you **surprise** someone, you give them, tell them, or do something pleasant

that they are not expecting. (内緒にしていた贈り物やパーティーなどで) 驚かせる ❏ *Surprise a new neighbor with one of your favorite home-made dishes.* あなたのお気に入りの手料理の1つで新しいご近所さんをビックリさせよう. **5** N-COUNT 可算名詞 If you describe someone or something as a **surprise**, you mean that they are very good or pleasant although you were not expecting this. 予期せぬ良いもの (誰もが予期していなかった好成績や素晴らしい選手など) ❏ ...*Senga MacFie, one of the surprises of the World Championships three months ago.* 3か月前の世界選手権で予想外に素晴らしかった選手の1人, センガ・マクフィー **6** V-T 他動詞 If you **surprise** someone, you attack, capture, or find them when they are not expecting it. 急襲する, 不意打ちにする ❏ *U.S. troops surprised eight enemy fighters in a cave complex.* 米国軍は洞窟地帯で8人の敵兵を不意打ちにした. **7** → see also **surprised, surprising** **8** PHRASE 句 If something **takes** you **by surprise**, it happens when you are not expecting it or when you are not prepared for it. -を驚かせる ❏ *His question took his two companions by surprise.* 彼の質問に2人の友人は驚いた.

sur|prised /sərpraɪzd/ **1** ADJ 形容詞 If you are **surprised** at something, you have a feeling of surprise, because it is unexpected or unusual. 驚いて ❏ *This lady was genuinely surprised at what happened to her pet.* この婦人は彼女のペットに起こったことに心から驚いた. **2** → see also **surprise**

sur|pris|ing /sərpraɪzɪŋ/ **1** ADJ 形容詞 Something that is **surprising** is unexpected or unusual and makes you feel surprised. 驚くべき, 予期しない ❏ *It is not surprising that children learn to read at different rates.* 子供たちがそれぞれ違う速さで読み方を覚えるというのは驚きに値しない. ● **sur|pris|ing|ly** ADV 副詞 驚くほど, 意外に ❏ *The party did surprisingly well in the South.* その政党は南部で意外に成功した. **2** → see also **surprise**

sur|re|al /sərɪəl/ ADJ 形容詞 If you describe something as **surreal**, you mean that the elements in it are combined in a strange way that you would not normally expect, like in a dream. 非現実的な, 超現実的な ❏ *"Performance" is one of the most surreal movies ever made.* 『パフォーマンス』はこれまで作られた中で最も超現実的な映画だ.

sur|ren|der /sərɛndər/ (**surrenders, surrendering, surrendered**) **1** V-I 自動詞 If you **surrender**, you stop fighting or resisting someone and agree that you have been beaten. 降伏する ❏ *General Martin Bonnet called on the rebels to surrender.* マーティン・ボンネット将軍は反逆者に降伏を呼びかけた. ● N-VAR 可変性名詞 **Surrender** is also a noun. 降伏 ❏ ...*the government's apparent surrender to demands made by the religious militants.* 宗教過激派の要求に対する政府の明らかな降伏 **2** V-T 他動詞 If you **surrender** something you would rather keep, you give it up or let someone else have it, for example after a struggle. (いやいや) 放棄する 引き渡す ❏ *Nadja had to fill out forms surrendering all rights to her property.* ナジャは彼女の財産に対するすべての権利を放棄し, 書類に記入しなければならなかった. ● N-UNCOUNT 不可算名詞 **Surrender** is also a noun. 放棄, 受け渡し ❏ ...*the sixteen-day deadline for the surrender of weapons and ammunition.* 武器や弾薬を放棄する16日間の期限 **3** V-T 他動詞 If you **surrender** something such as a ticket or your passport, you give it to someone in authority when they ask you to. (切符やパスポートを) 返上する 引き渡す [FORMAL 形式ばった] ❏ *They have been ordered to surrender their passports.* 彼らはパスポートの引き渡しを命じられた. → see **flag, war**

sur|ren|der val|ue (**surrender values**) N-COUNT 可算名詞 The **surrender value** of a life insurance policy is the amount of money you receive if you decide that you no longer wish to continue with the policy. (生命保険の) 解約払い戻し金 [BUSINESS 実業] ❏ *An ordinary life policy may have a cash surrender value of $50,000.* 普通の生命保険証券の解約払い戻し金は5万ドルになるかもしれない.

sur|ro|gate /sɜrəgeɪt, -gɪt/ (**surrogates**) **1** ADJ 形容詞 You use **surrogate** to describe a person or thing that is given a particular role because the person or thing that should have the role is not available. 代理の [ADJ n] ❏ *Martin had become Howard Cosell's surrogate son.* マーティンはハワード・コーセルの代理の息子になった. ● N-COUNT 可算名詞 **Surrogate** is also a noun. 代理人, 代用物 ❏ *Arms control should not be made into a surrogate for peace.* 軍備縮小が和平の代わりとなってはいけない.

sur|ro|gate moth|er (surrogate mothers) N-COUNT 可算名詞 A **surrogate mother** is a woman who has agreed to give birth to a baby on behalf of another woman. 代理母

sur|round /səraʊnd/ (surrounds, surrounding, surrounded) ■ V-T/V-I 他動詞/自動詞 If a person or thing **is surrounded** by something, that thing is situated all around them. (周辺を) 取り囲む ❑ The small churchyard was surrounded by a rusted wrought-iron fence. その小さな教会の墓地は、さびた錬鉄製の柵で囲まれていた。 ❑ The shell surrounding the egg has many important functions. 卵の周りの殻には多くの重要な役割がある。 ❑ ...Chicago and the surrounding area. シカゴとその周辺地域 ❷ V-T 他動詞 If you **are surrounded** by soldiers or police, they spread out so that they are in positions all the way around you. (軍隊や警察に) 包囲する ❑ When the car stopped in the town square it was surrounded by soldiers and militiamen. 車が町の広場に止まると、軍人や民兵に包囲された。 ❸ V-T 他動詞 The circumstances, feelings, or ideas which **surround** something are those that are closely associated with it. (状況や考えなどが〜を) 取り巻く ❑ The decision had been agreed in principle before today's meeting, but some controversy surrounded it. 今日の会議の前にその決議に対する基本的な同意は得られたが、いくつかの物議を醸していた。 ❹ V-T 他動詞 If you **surround yourself with** certain people or things, you make sure that you have a lot of them near you all the time. (〜で自分の) 周りを固める ❑ He had made it his business to surround himself with a hand-picked group of bright young officers. 彼はいつも生え抜きの利発な青年将校の一団を自分の周りにはべらせていた。

sur|round|ings /səraʊndɪŋz/ N-PLURAL 複数名詞 When you are describing the place where you are at the moment, or the place where you live, you can refer to it as your **surroundings**. 環境 ❑ Schumacher adapted effortlessly to his new surroundings. シューマッハは新しい環境に難なくなじんだ。

sur|tax /sɜːrtæks/ N-UNCOUNT 不可算名詞 **Surtax** is an additional tax on incomes higher than the level at which ordinary tax is paid. (高所得の人に課せられる) 付加税 [BUSINESS 実業] ❑ ...a 10% surtax for Americans earning more than $250,000 a year. 年収25万ドル以上の米国人に課される10パーセントの付加税

Word Link sur ≈ above : surcharge, surface, surveillance

sur|veil|lance /sərveɪləns/ N-UNCOUNT 不可算名詞 **Surveillance** is the careful watching of someone, especially by an organization such as the police or the army. 監視, 見張り ❑ He was arrested after being kept under constant surveillance. 彼は常に監視下に置かれた後、逮捕された。 ❑ Police swooped on the home after a two-week surveillance operation. 警察は2週間の監視の後、その家に踏み込んだ。

sur|vey (surveys, surveying, surveyed)

> The noun is pronounced /sɜːrveɪ/. The verb is pronounced /sərveɪ/, and can also be pronounced /sɜːrveɪ/ in meanings ❺ and ❻.
>
> 名詞は /sɜːrveɪ/ と発音される。動詞は /sərveɪ/ と発音され、/sɜːrveɪ/ と ❻ の意味では ❺ とも発音できる。

■ N-COUNT 可算名詞 If you carry out a **survey**, you try to find out detailed information about a lot of different people or things, usually by asking people a series of questions. 調査 (詳細な) アンケート ❑ The council conducted a survey of the uses to which farm buildings are put. 議会は農舎の用途についてのアンケートを行った。 ❷ V-T 他動詞 If you **survey** a number of people, companies, or organizations, you try to find out information about their opinions or behavior, usually by asking them a series of questions. アンケートを取る, 意見を調査する ❑ Business Development Advisers surveyed 211 companies for the report. 事業開発相談所はその報告書のために221社からアンケートを取った。 ❸ V-T 他動詞 If you **survey** something, you look at or consider the whole of it carefully. (全体を) 見回す ❑ He pushed himself to his feet and surveyed the room. 彼は自分を励まして立ち上がり、その部屋を見回した。 ❹ N-COUNT 可算名詞 If someone carries out a **survey** of an area of land, they examine it and measure it, usually in order to make a map of it. (土地の) 測量 ❑ ...the organizer of the geological survey of India. インドの地質調査のまとめ役 ❺ V-T 他動詞 If someone **surveys** an area of land, they examine it and measure it, usually in order to make a map of it. 測量する ❑ The city council commissioned geological experts earlier this year to survey the cliffs. 市議会は今年始め、地質学の専門家たちにそのがけの測量をするよう委託した。 ❻ N-COUNT 可算名詞 A **survey** is a careful examination of the condition and structure of a house, usually carried out in order to give information to a person who wants to buy it. (家などの) 検分査定 [mainly BRIT 主に英国英語] ❼ V-T 他動詞 If someone **surveys** a house, they examine it carefully and report on its structure, usually in order to give advice to a person who is thinking of buying it. 検分する, 査定する [mainly BRIT 主に英国英語] → see census

sur|vey|or /sərveɪər/ (surveyors) ■ N-COUNT 可算名詞 A **surveyor** is a person whose job is to survey land. 測量士 ❑ ...the surveyor's maps of the Queen Alexandra Range. 測量士のクイーン・アレクサンドラ山脈の地図 ❷ N-COUNT 可算名詞 A **surveyor** is a person whose job is to survey buildings. 建物の鑑定人, 建築工学技術者 [BRIT 英国英語; AM structural engineer 米国英語 structural engineer]

sur|viv|al /sərvaɪvəl/ ■ N-UNCOUNT 不可算名詞 If you refer to the **survival** of something or someone, you mean that they manage to continue or exist in spite of difficult circumstances. 存続 ❑ ...companies which have been struggling for survival in the advancing recession. 不況が進む中、存続のために苦労している会社 ❷ N-UNCOUNT 不可算名詞 If you refer to the **survival** of a person or living thing, you mean that they live through a dangerous situation in which it was possible that they might die. 生き残ること, 生き延びること ❑ If cancers are spotted early there's a high chance of survival. 癌が早期に発見されると生存の可能性は高い。

Word Link viv ≈ living : revival, survive, vivacious

sur|vive /sərvaɪv/ (survives, surviving, survived) ■ V-T/V-I 他動詞/自動詞 If a person or living thing **survives** in a dangerous situation such as an accident or an illness, they do not die. 生き残る, 生き延びる ❑ ...the sequence of events that left the eight pupils battling to survive in icy seas for over four hours. 8人の生徒が4時間以上も氷のような海で生き延びるために闘わされた一連の出来事 ❑ Those organisms that are most suited to the environment will be those that will survive. 自然環境に最も適したそれらの生物が生き残るものたちだろう。 ❑ He had survived heart bypass surgery. 彼は心臓のバイパス手術に耐えた。 ❷ V-T/V-I 他動詞/自動詞 If you **survive** in difficult circumstances, you manage to live or continue in spite of them and do not let them affect you very much. (困難な状況を) 切り抜ける [他動詞], うまく乗り越える [自動詞] ❑ On my first day here I thought, "Ooh, how will I survive?" ここでの初日に、私は「ああ、どうすればうまくやっていけるだろう?」と思った。 ❑ ...people who are struggling to survive without jobs. 仕事なしでなんとかやっていこうと苦労している人たち ❸ V-T/V-I 他動詞/自動詞 If something **survives**, it continues to exist even after being in a dangerous situation or existing for a long time. (危険な状況の) 後まで残る [他動詞], 存続する [自動詞] ❑ When the market economy is introduced, many factories will not survive. 市場経済が導入されると、多くの工場が生き残れないだろう。 ❑ No one survived the crash. その衝突で生き残った人は1人もいなかった。 ❹ V-T 他動詞 If you **survive** someone, you continue to live after they have died. (〜よりも) 長生きする ❑ Most women will survive their spouses. ほとんどの女性は夫よりも長生きする。

sur|vi|vor /sərvaɪvər/ (survivors) ■ N-COUNT 可算名詞 A **survivor of** a disaster, accident, or illness is someone who continues to live afterward in spite of coming close to death. (事故や病気の) 生存者 ❑ Officials said there were no survivors of the plane crash. 当局は、その飛行機墜落事故で全員が死亡したと発表した。 ❷ N-COUNT 可算名詞 A **survivor of** a very unpleasant experience is a person who has had such an experience, and who is still affected by it. (苦難を) 逃れた人 ❑ This book is written with survivors of child sexual abuse in mind. この本は子供の時に性的虐待を受けた被害者たちを念頭に置いて書かれている。 ❸ N-COUNT 可算名詞 A person's **survivors** are the members of their family who continue to live after they have died. 遺族 [AM 米国英語] ❑ The compensation bill offers the miners or their survivors as much as $100,000 apiece. その補償金に関する法案は、鉱山労働者もしくはその遺族に1人当たり10万ドルを提示している。

sus|cep|tible /səsɛptɪbəl/ ■ ADJ 形容詞 If you are **susceptible to** something or someone, you are very likely to be influenced by them. 影響を受けやすい, 多感な [v-link ADJ "to" n] ❑ Young people are the most susceptible to advertisements. 若者たちは最も広告の影響を受けやすい。 ❑ James was extremely susceptible to flattery. ジェームスはお世辞にとても弱かった。 ❷ ADJ 形容詞 If you are **susceptible to** a disease or injury, you are very likely to be affected by it. (病気などに) 感染しやすい (怪我を) しやすい ❑ Walking with weights makes the shoulders very susceptible to injury. 重いものを持って歩くととても肩を痛めやすい。

sus|pect (suspects, suspecting, suspected)

> The verb is pronounced /səspɛkt/. The noun and adjective are pronounced /sʌspɛkt/.
>
> 動詞は /səspɛkt/ と発音される。名詞と形容詞は /sʌspɛkt/ と発音される。

■ V-T 他動詞 You use **suspect** when you are stating something that you believe is probably true, in order to make it sound less strong or direct. 〜だろうと思う [VAGUENESS あいまいさ] ❑ I suspect they were right. 彼らは正しかったのだろう。 ❑ The complaints are, I suspect, just the tip of the iceberg. 上記の苦情は、恐らく氷山の一角にしか過ぎない。 ❷ V-T 他動詞 If you **suspect** that something dishonest or unpleasant has been done, you believe that it has probably been done. If you **suspect** someone **of** doing an action of

this kind, you believe that they probably did it. （人に）嫌疑をかける（人を~ではないかと）疑う □ *He suspected that the woman staying in the flat above was using heroin.* 彼は上のフラットに泊まっている女性がヘロインを使っているのではないかと疑った. □ *It was perfectly all right, he said, because the police had not suspected him of anything.* 彼は, 警察が彼のことをぜんぜん疑っていなかったのでまったく大丈夫だ, と言った. **3** N-COUNT 可算名詞 A **suspect** is a person who the police or authorities think may be guilty of a crime. 容疑者 □ *Police have arrested a suspect in a series of killings and sexual assaults in the city.* 警察はその街で起きた一連の殺人と性的暴行の容疑者を逮捕した. **4** ADJ 形容詞 **Suspect** things or people are ones that you think may be dangerous or may be less good or genuine than they appear. 疑わしい □ *Delegates evacuated the building when a suspect package was found.* 疑わしい荷物が見つかったので, 代表団はその建物から避難した.

sus|pend /səspɛnd/ (suspends, suspending, suspended) **1** V-T 他動詞 If you **suspend** something, you delay it or stop it from happening for a while or until a decision is made about it. 延期する, 保留にする □ *The union suspended strike action this week.* 労働組合は今週のストライキを延期した. **2** V-T 他動詞 If someone **is suspended**, they are prevented from holding a particular job or position for a fixed length of time or until a decision is made about them. （人を）停職にする 停学にする □ *Julie was suspended from her job shortly after the incident.* その事件の直後にジュリーは停職となった. **3** V-T 他動詞 If something **is suspended** from a high place, it is hanging from that place. （高い場所から）つるす ぶら下げる [usu passive] □ *...instruments that are suspended on cables.* ケーブル線の上につるされた機器

sus|pend|er /səspɛndər/ (suspenders) **1** N-PLURAL 複数名詞 **Suspenders** are a pair of straps that go over someone's shoulders and are fastened to their pants at the front and back to prevent the pants from falling down. サスペンダー, ズボンつり [AM 米国英語] [also "a" "pair" "of" N] □ *He also wore a pair of suspenders.* 彼はサスペンダーも着けていた. **2** → see **garter 1**

sus|pense /səspɛns/ **1** N-UNCOUNT 不可算名詞 **Suspense** is a state of excitement or anxiety about something that is going to happen very soon, for example about some news that you are waiting to hear. はらはらドキドキする気もち, 気がかり □ *The suspense over the two remaining hostages ended last night when the police discovered the bullet-ridden bodies.* 昨夜, 警察が無数の銃弾を打ち込まれた死体を発見した時, 残りの人質2人に対する懸念に終止符が打たれた. **2** PHRASE 句 If you **keep** or **leave** someone **in suspense**, you deliberately delay telling them something that they are very eager to know about. （人を）じらす, やきもきさせる, 気をもませる □ *Keppler kept all his men in suspense until that morning before announcing which two would be going.* ケップラーはどの2人が行くかを発表するその朝まで部下全員をやきもきさせた.

sus|pen|sion /səspɛnʃ°n/ (suspensions) **1** N-UNCOUNT 不可算名詞 The **suspension** of something is the act of delaying or stopping it for a while or until a decision is made about it. 保留, 一時差し止め □ *There's been a temporary suspension of flights out of LA.* ロサンゼルス発の航空便は一時的に運行を見合わせている. **2** N-VAR 可変性名詞 Someone's **suspension** is their removal from a job or position for a period of time or until a decision is made about them. 停職, （資格などの）一時的剥奪 （はくだつ） □ *The minister warned that any civil servant not at his desk faced immediate suspension.* 大臣は, 仕事をしていない公務員を今すぐ停職にすると警告した. **3** N-VAR 可変性名詞 A vehicle's **suspension** consists of the springs and other devices attached to the wheels, which give a smooth ride over uneven ground. （車の）サスペンション 懸架装置 □ *...the only small car with independent front suspension.* 前輪に独立したサスペンションが付いている唯一の小型車

→ see **bridge**

sus|pi|cion /səspɪʃ°n/ (suspicions) **1** N-VAR 可変性名詞 **Suspicion** or a **suspicion** is a belief or feeling that someone has committed a crime or done something wrong. （犯罪や不正の）容疑, 疑惑 □ *There was a suspicion that this runner attempted to avoid the procedures for drug testing.* この走者は薬物テストの手続きを逃れようとした疑いがある. □ *The police said their suspicions were aroused because Mr. Owens had other marks on his body.* 警察は, オウエン氏の体に他にもあざがあったため疑いを持ったと語った. **2** N-VAR 可変性名詞 If there is **suspicion of** someone or something, people do not trust them or consider them to be reliable. 不信感 □ *This tendency in his thought is deepened by his suspicion of all Utopian political programs.* 彼の考えのこうした傾向は, 現実不可能な政治計画すべてに対する不信感からますます強くなっている. **3** N-COUNT 可算名詞 A **suspicion** is a feeling that something is probably true or is likely to happen. （~だろうと）思うこと 予感 □ *I have a sneaking suspicion that they are going to succeed.* 私はひそかに, 彼らが成功するような気がする.

sus|pi|cious /səspɪʃəs/ **1** ADJ 形容詞 If you are **suspicious of** someone or something, you do not trust them, and are careful when dealing with them. 不信感を持った □ *He was rightly suspicious of meeting me until I reassured him I was not writing about him.* 彼は私が彼のことを記事にしないと再び保証するまで, 当然, 私に会うことを警戒していた. ● **sus|pi|cious|ly** ADV 形容詞 [ADV after v] うさんくさそうに, 疑わしげに □ *"What is it you want me to do?" Adams asked suspiciously.* 「君が僕にして欲しい事ってなんだい?」とアダムスはうさんくさそうに聞いた. **2** ADJ 形容詞 If you are **suspicious of** someone or something, you believe that they are probably involved in a crime or some dishonest activity. （~の犯罪や不正を）疑って □ *Two officers on patrol became suspicious of two men in a car.* パトロール中の2人の警官は, 車の中の2人の男に疑いを持った. **3** ADJ 形容詞 If you describe someone or something as **suspicious**, you mean that there is some aspect of them which makes you think that they are involved in a crime or a dishonest activity. 不審な, 疑わしい □ *He reported that two suspicious-looking characters had approached Callendar.* 彼は, 2人の不審な人物がカレンダーに近づいたと報告した. ● **sus|pi|cious|ly** ADV 副詞 挙動不審に, 不審な様子で □ *They'll question them as to whether anyone was seen acting suspiciously in the area over the last few days.* 彼らはその人たちに, ここ数日間にその地域で挙動不審な者を見かけなかったか質問するだろう.

Do not confuse **suspicious**, **doubtful**, and **dubious**. If you are **suspicious** of a person, you do not trust them and think they might be involved in something dishonest or illegal. □ *I am suspicious of his intentions. ...Miss Lenaut had grown suspicious.* If you describe something as **suspicious**, it suggests behavior that is dishonest, illegal, or dangerous. □ *He listened for any suspicious sounds. ...in suspicious circumstances.* If you feel **doubtful** about something, you are unsure about it or about whether it will happen or be successful. □ *Do you feel insecure and doubtful about your ability?... It was doubtful he would ever see her again.* If you are **dubious** about something, you are not sure whether it is the right thing to do. □ *Alison sounded very dubious. ...The men in charge were a bit dubious about taking him on.* If you describe something as **dubious**, you think it is not completely honest, safe, or reliable. □ *...his dubious abilities as a teacher.*

sus|pi|cious|ly /səspɪʃəsli/ **1** ADV 副詞 If you say that one thing looks or sounds **suspiciously** like another thing, you mean that it probably is that thing, or something very similar to it, although it may be intended to seem different. どうも~のように [ADV prep] □ *The tan-colored dog looks suspiciously like a pit bull terrier.* 黄褐色のその犬はどうもピットブルテリアのようだ. **2** ADV 副詞 You can use **suspiciously** when you are describing something that you think is slightly strange or not as it should be. 不気味なまでに [ADV adj/adv] □ *He lives alone in a suspiciously tidy apartment.* 彼は不気味なほどこぎれいなアパートに1人で住んでいる. **3** → see also **suspicious**

sus|tain /səsteɪn/ (sustains, sustaining, sustained) **1** V-T 他動詞 If you **sustain** something, you continue it or maintain it for a period of time. 持続する, 維持する □ *He has sustained his fierce social conscience from young adulthood through old age.* 彼は青年の頃から年をとってもその激しい社会的良心を持ち続けている. □ *Recovery can't be sustained unless more jobs are created.* さらに仕事が生み出されない限り, 景気回復は維持できない. **2** V-T 他動詞 If you **sustain** something such as a defeat, loss, or injury, it happens to you. （敗北を）喫する （損害などを）こうむる [FORMAL 形式ばった] □ *Every aircraft in there has sustained some damage.* そこにいたすべての飛行機が損傷を受けた. **3** V-T 他動詞 If something **sustains** you, it supports you by giving you help, strength, or encouragement. （援助や励ましで）支える 力づける [FORMAL 形式ばった] □ *The cash dividends they get from the cash crop would sustain them during the lean season.* 換金作物から得られた配当金が閑散期に彼らを支える.

sus|tain|able /səsteɪnəb°l/ **1** ADJ 形容詞 You use **sustainable** to describe the use of natural resources when this use is kept at a steady level that is not likely to damage the environment. 持続可能な, 環境を壊すことなく利用できる □ *...the management, conservation and sustainable development of forests.* 森林の管理, 保護, そして持続可能な開発 ● **sus|tain|abil|ity** /səsteɪnəbɪlɪti/ N-UNCOUNT 不可算名詞 持続可能性 □ *...the issue of long-term environmental sustainability.* 長期的な環境維持問題 **2** ADJ 形容詞 A **sustainable** plan, method, or system is designed to continue at the same rate or level of activity without any problems. （計画や制度などが）維持できる □ *The creation of an efficient and sustainable transport system is critical.* 効率的かつ継続可能な輸送システムの創設は非常に重要だ. ● **sus|tain|abil|ity** N-UNCOUNT 不可算名詞 （計画

や制度などの）継続可能性 ▢ ...unease about the sustainability of the American economic recovery. アメリカの景気回復の持続性に対する不安

SUV /ɛs yu vi/ (**SUVs**) N-COUNT 可算名詞 An **SUV** is a powerful vehicle with four-wheel drive that can be driven over rough ground. **SUV** is an abbreviation for **sport utility vehicle**. スポーツ用多目的車（sport utility vehicle）の略語
→ see **car**

swab /swɒb/ (**swabs**) N-COUNT 可算名詞 A **swab** is a small piece of cotton used by a doctor or nurse for cleaning a wound or putting a substance on it. 綿棒，消毒綿 ▢ "Okay," he replied and winced as she dabbed the cotton swab over the gash. 彼女が消毒綿で傷口を軽くたたくと，彼は「大丈夫」と答え，顔をしかめた.

swag|ger /swæɡər/ (**swaggers, swaggering, swaggered**) V-I 自動詞 If you **swagger**, you walk in a very proud, confident way, holding your body upright and swinging your hips. 偉そうに歩く ▢ A broad shouldered man wearing a dinner jacket swaggered confidently up to the bar. タキシードを着た肩幅の広い男が自信満々にバーの方へ歩いて行った. ●N-SING 単数名詞 **Swagger** is also a noun. 自信たっぷりな態度，威張った歩き方 ▢ He walked with something of a swagger. 彼はちょっと偉そうな態度で歩いた.

swal|low /swɒloʊ/ (**swallows, swallowing, swallowed**)
■ V-T/V-I 他動詞/自動詞 If you **swallow** something, you cause it to go from your mouth down into your stomach. 飲み込む，飲み下す ▢ You are asked to swallow a capsule containing vitamin B. ビタミンBの入ったカプセルを飲み込むよう求められる. ▢ Polly took a bite of the apple, chewed, and swallowed. ポリーはりんごをかじってかんだ後，飲み込んだ. ●N-COUNT 可算名詞 **Swallow** is also a noun. 飲み込むこと，飲み下すこと ▢ Jan lifted her glass and took a quick swallow. ジャンはグラスを持ち上げ，素早く飲み干した. ■ V-I 自動詞 If you **swallow**, you make a movement in your throat as if you are swallowing something, often because you are nervous or frightened. （緊張や恐怖から）つばを飲み込む ▢ Nancy swallowed hard and shook her head. ナンシーはゴクリとつばを飲み込み，頭を振った. ■ V-T 他動詞 If someone **swallows** a story or a statement, they believe it completely. （話を）信じ込む，うのみにする ▢ They cast doubt on his words when it suited their case, but swallowed them whole when it did not. 彼らはそれが彼らの問題に当てはまる時には彼の言葉を疑い，そうでない時には彼の言葉をうのみにした. ■ N-COUNT 可算名詞 A **swallow** is a kind of small bird with pointed wings and a forked tail. ツバメ ■ **a bitter pill to swallow** → see **pill**
▶ **swallow up** PHRASAL VERB 句動詞 ■ If one thing is **swallowed up** by another, it becomes part of the first thing and no longer has a separate identity of its own. （会社や組織を）吸収する ▢ During the 1980s monster publishing houses started to swallow up smaller companies. 1980年代に巨大出版社が小さな出版社を吸収し始めた. ■ PHRASAL VERB 句動詞 If something **swallows up** money or resources, it uses them entirely while giving very little in return. （金や資源を）使い尽くす ▢ A seven-day TV ad campaign could swallow up the best part of $100,000. 7日間のテレビ広告キャンペーンに10万ドルの大部分が使い果たされかねない.

swam /swæm/ **Swam** is the past tense of **swim**.

swamp /swɒmp/ (**swamps, swamping, swamped**) ■ N-VAR 可変性名詞 A **swamp** is an area of very wet land with wild plants growing in it. 沼地，湿地 ▢ I spent one whole night by a swamp behind the road listening to frogs. 私は道路の裏の沼地でかえるの声を聞きながら一晩中過ごした. ■ V-T 他動詞 If something **swamps** a place or object, it fills it with water. 水浸しにする ▢ Their electronic navigation failed and a rogue wave swamped the boat. 電子航行システムが故障し，異常な電波に導かれボートが水浸しになった. ■ V-T 他動詞 If you **are swamped** by things or people, you have more of them than you can deal with. 圧倒する，（仕事などに）忙殺される [usu passive] ▢ He is swamped with work. 彼は仕事に忙殺されている.
→ see **wetland**

swan /swɒn/ (**swans**) N-COUNT 可算名詞 A **swan** is a large bird with a very long neck. Swans live on rivers and lakes and are usually white. 白鳥

swap /swɒp/ (**swaps, swapping, swapped**) ■ V-RECIP 相互動詞 If you **swap** something with someone, you give it to them and receive a different thing in exchange. 交換する ▢ Next week they will swap places and will repeat the switch weekly. 彼らは次の週に立場を交替し，毎週その交替を繰り返していく. ▢ I know a sculptor who swaps her pieces for drawings by a well-known artist. 私は自分の作品を有名な画家のデッサンと交換する彫刻家を知っている. ●N-COUNT 可算名詞 **Swap** is also a noun. 交換 ▢ Over the long term, a swap of some kind is clearly in the public interest. 長期的に見ると，何らかの交換というのは明らかに人々の利益となる. ■ V-T 他動詞 If you **swap** one thing **for** another, you remove the first thing and replace it with the second, or you stop doing the first thing and start doing the second. 取り替える，交替する ▢ Despite the heat, he'd swapped his overalls for a suit and tie. その暑さにもかかわらず，彼はつなぎ服をスーツとネクタイに着替えていた. ▢ He has swapped his hectic rock star's lifestyle for that of a country gentleman. 彼はあわただしいロックスターの生き方を田舎紳士の生き方に替えた.

swarm /swɔrm/ (**swarms, swarming, swarmed**)
■ N-COUNT-COLL 集合可算名詞 A **swarm of** bees or other insects is a large group of them flying together. （虫の）群れ，大群 ▢ ...a swarm of locusts. ばったの大群 ■ V-I 自動詞 When bees or other insects **swarm**, they move or fly in a large group. （虫が）群れとなって動く ▢ A dark cloud of bees comes swarming out of the hive. はちの黒い大群が巣から群れをなして出てくる. ■ V-I 自動詞 When people **swarm** somewhere, they move there quickly in a large group. （人が場所に）群がり動く ▢ People swarmed to the stores, buying up everything in sight. 人々は店に群がり，目に付くもの全てを買い占めていた. ■ N-COUNT-COLL 集合可算名詞 A **swarm of** people is a large group of them moving about quickly. （動き回る人々の）大群，群集 ▢ A swarm of people encircled the hotel. 群集がホテルを取り囲んだ. ■ V-I 自動詞 If a place **is swarming with** people, it is full of people moving about in a busy way. （場所が一で）いっぱいになる，あふれ返る [usu cont] ▢ Within minutes the area was swarming with officers who began searching a nearby wood. 数分のうちにその区域は近くの森を捜査し始めた警官であふれ返った.

swat /swɒt/ (**swats, swatting, swatted**) V-T 他動詞 If you **swat** something such as an insect, you hit it with a quick, swinging movement, using your hand or a flat object. （虫などを）ピシャリとたたく ▢ Hundreds of flies buzz around us, and the workman keeps swatting them. 何百ものハエが私たちの周りをブンブン飛び回り，作業員がそれをピシャリとたたき続ける.

sway /sweɪ/ (**sways, swaying, swayed**) ■ V-I 自動詞 When people or things **sway**, they lean or swing slowly from one side to the other. ゆっくり揺れる ▢ The people swayed back and forth with arms linked. 人々は連結された腕木と共に前後に揺れた. ▢ The whole boat swayed and tipped. ボート全体が揺れてひっくり返った. ■ V-T 他動詞 If you **are swayed by** someone or something, you are influenced by them. 影響を与える ▢ Don't ever be swayed by fashion. 流行に決して左右されるな. ■ PHRASE 句 If someone or something **holds sway**, they have great power or influence over a particular place or activity. 大きな影響力を持つ ▢ Powerful traditional chiefs hold sway over more than 15 million people in rural areas. 力のある昔からの村長たちは地方で1千5百万人以上もの人に大きな影響力を持つ.

swear /swɛər/ (**swears, swearing, swore, sworn**) ■ V-I 自動詞 If someone **swears**, they use language that is considered to be vulgar or offensive, usually because they are angry. 悪態をつく，ののしる ▢ It's wrong to swear and shout. 悪態をついたりどなったりするのは間違っている. ■ V-T 他動詞 If you **swear to** do something, you promise in a serious way that you will do it. （ーすると）誓う ▢ Alan swore that he would do everything in his power to help us. アランは私たちを助けるため，彼の権限の中でできる限りのことをすると約束した. ▢ We have sworn to fight cruelty wherever we find it. 私たちはどこであろうと，残虐行為を見つけたらそれと闘うことを誓った. ■ V-T/V-I 他動詞/自動詞 If you say that you **swear** that something is true or that you can **swear** to it, you are saying very firmly that it is true. 断言する [EMPHASIS 強調] ▢ I swear I've told you all I know. 僕が知っていることは本当に全部あるよ. ▢ I swear on all I hold dear that I had nothing to do with this. 私はこれと何のかかわりもなかったことを，大切にしているすべてのものにかけて断言する. ■ V-T 他動詞 If someone **is sworn to** secrecy or **is sworn to** silence, they promise another person that they will not reveal a secret. （ーを固く守ることを）誓わせる [usu passive] ▢ She was bursting to announce the news but was sworn to secrecy. 彼女はその知らせを発表したくてうずうずしていたが，秘密を守ることを誓っていた. ■ → see also **sworn**
▶ **swear by** PHRASAL VERB 句動詞 If you **swear by** something, you believe that it can be relied on to have a particular effect. （ーの効果を）信じる [INFORMAL くだけた] ▢ Many people swear by vitamin C's ability to ward off colds. 多くの人がビタミンCには風邪を防ぐ効果があると信じている.
▶ **swear in** PHRASAL VERB 句動詞 When someone **is sworn in**, they formally promise to fulfill the duties of a new job or appointment. 宣誓就任させる ▢ Mary Robinson was formally sworn in as Ireland's first woman president. メアリー・ロビンソンはアイルランド初の女性大統領として正式に宣誓就任した.

sweat /swɛt/ (**sweats, sweating, sweated**) ■ N-UNCOUNT 不可算名詞 **Sweat** is the salty colorless liquid which comes through your skin when you are hot, sick, or afraid. 汗 ▢ Both horse and rider were dripping with sweat within five minutes. 5分もしないうちに馬も騎手も汗びっしょりになっていた. ■ V-I 自動詞 When you

Word Web   sweat

Vigorous physical activity and unpleasant emotions cause **sweat**. Scientists call it **perspiration**. Tiny **glands** under the skin produce sweat which exits through pores in the epidermis. This liquid then **evaporates** from the surface of the skin and cools the body off. A person living in a cool climate can produce only about a liter of sweat per hour. However, that total can rise to three liters if the person moves to a hot climate. Excess sweating causes **dehydration**. The body must maintain a balance of certain **salts** and water. Perspiration removes large quantities of both from the body.

sweat, sweat comes through your skin. 汗をかく ❑*Already they were sweating as the sun beat down upon them.* 太陽が照りつけ、彼らは既に汗をかいていた. ● **sweat|ing** N-UNCOUNT 不可算名詞 発汗 ❑*…symptoms such as sweating, irritability, anxiety, and depression.* 発汗、興奮、不安、鬱といった症状 ❸ N-COUNT 可算名詞 If someone is **in a sweat**, they are sweating a lot. 汗をかいていること ❑*Every morning I would break out in a sweat.* 毎朝、汗びっしょりになっていたものだ. ❑*Cool down very gradually after working up a sweat.* ひと汗かいた後はとってもゆっくり熱を冷ます. ❹ PHRASE 句 If someone is **in a cold sweat** or **in a sweat**, they feel frightened or embarrassed. 冷や汗をかいて ❑*The very thought brought me out in a cold sweat.* そう考えただけで冷や汗が吹き出た.
→ see Word Web: **sweat**

sweat|er /swɛtər/ (sweaters) N-COUNT 可算名詞 A **sweater** is a warm knitted piece of clothing which covers the upper part of your body and your arms. セーター
→ see **clothing**

sweat|shirt /swɛtʃɜrt/ (sweatshirts) also sweat shirt N-COUNT 可算名詞 A **sweatshirt** is a loose warm piece of casual clothing, usually made of thick stretchy cotton, which covers the upper part of your body and your arms. スウェットシャツ, トレーナー
→ see **clothing**

sweat|suit /swɛtsut/ (sweatsuits) also sweat suit N-COUNT 可算名詞 A **sweatsuit** is a loose, warm, stretchy suit consisting of long pants and a top which people wear to relax and do exercise. スウェットスーツ（スウェットシャツとパンツ一組）[AM 米国英語]
→ see **clothing**

sweaty /swɛti/ (sweatier, sweatiest) ❶ ADJ 形容詞 If parts of your body or your clothes are **sweaty**, they are soaked or covered with sweat. 汗びっしょりの, 汗にまみれた ❑*…sweaty hands.* 汗びっしょりの手 ❷ ADJ 形容詞 A **sweaty** place or activity makes you sweat because it is hot or tiring. (場所が) 蒸し暑い (活動が) 骨の折れる ❑*…a sweaty nightclub.* 蒸し暑いナイトクラブ

sweep /swip/ (sweeps, sweeping, swept) ❶ V-T/V-I 他動詞/自動詞 If you **sweep** an area of floor or ground, you push dirt or garbage off it using a brush with a long handle. (ほうきなどで) 掃く ❑*The owner of the store was sweeping his floor when I walked in.* 私が店に入ると、店主が床を掃いていた. ❑*She was in the kitchen sweeping crumbs into a dust pan.* 彼女は台所でパンくずをちりとりに掃き集めていた. ❷ V-T 他動詞 If you **sweep** things off something, you push them off with a quick smooth movement of your arm. (手で) 押しのける 払いのける ❑*I swept rainwater off the flat top of a gravestone.* 私は墓石の表面から雨水を払いのけた. ❑*With a gesture of frustration, she swept the cards from the table.* いらいらした身振りで彼女はテーブルからカードを払いのけた. ❸ V-T 他動詞 If someone with long hair **sweeps** their hair into a particular style, they put it into that style. (髪をある髪型に) する ❑*…stylish ways of sweeping your hair off your face.* 髪が顔にかからないようにするおしゃれな方法 ❹ V-T/V-I 他動詞/自動詞 If your arm or hand **sweeps** in a particular direction, or if you **sweep** it, it moves quickly and smoothly in that direction. (腕や手をある方向へ) さっと動かす[他動詞], (腕や手がある方向へ) さっと動く[自動詞] ❑*His arm swept around the room.* 彼の腕が部屋の中をぐるっと回転した. ❑*Daniels swept his arm over his friend's shoulder.* ダニエルズは友人の肩にさっと腕を回した. ● N-COUNT 可算名詞 **Sweep** is also a noun. (腕や手を) さっと ❑*With one sweep of her hand she threw back the sheets.* 彼女はさっと手を動かして, 書類を投げ返した. ❺ V-T 他動詞 If wind, a stormy sea, or another strong force **sweeps** someone or something along, it moves them quickly along. (強風や急流が人や物を) 吹き飛ばす, 押し流す ❑*…landslides that buried homes and swept cars into the sea.* 民家を飲み込み、車を海に押し流した地滑り ❻ V-T 他動詞 If you **are swept** somewhere, you are taken there very quickly. (ある場所へ) あっという間に運ぶ ❑*The visitors were swept past various monuments.* 訪問者はさまざまな記念碑の前を通り、あっという間に運ばれた. ❼ V-I 自動詞 If something **sweeps** from one place to another, it moves there extremely quickly. (ある場所から別の場所へ) さっと動く [WRITTEN 書き言葉] ❑*An icy wind swept through the streets.* 氷のように冷たい風が通りをさっと吹き抜けた. ❽ V-T/V-I 他動詞/自動詞 If

events, ideas, or beliefs **sweep** through a place or **sweep** a place, they spread quickly through it. (事象や考えが) あっという間に広がる ❑*A flu epidemic is sweeping through Moscow.* インフルエンザがモスクワ中で大流行している. ❾ V-T/V-I 他動詞/自動詞 If a person or group **sweeps** an election or **sweeps to** victory, they win the election easily. (選挙で) 圧勝する ❑*…a man who's promised to make radical changes to benefit the poor has swept the election.* 貧民層に利益をもたらすため大改革を公約した男性が選挙で圧勝した ❿ N-COUNT 可算名詞 If someone makes a **sweep of** a place, they search it, usually because they are looking for people who are hiding or for an illegal activity. (場所の) 捜査 ❑*Two of the soldiers swiftly began making a sweep of the premises.* 2人の兵士は素早く建物を捜査し始めた. ⓫ → see also **sweeping** ⓬ PHRASE 句 If someone **sweeps** something bad or wrong **under the carpet**, or if they **sweep** it **under the rug**, they try to prevent people from hearing about it. (不正などを) 知られないように隠す, 臭い物にふたをする ❑*For a long time this problem has been swept under the carpet.* 長い間この問題は隠されたままだった. ⓭ PHRASE 句 If you **make a clean sweep** of something such as a series of games or tournaments, you win them all. 全勝 ❑*…the first club to make a clean sweep of all three trophies.* 3つのトロフィーすべてを勝ち取る最初のクラブ ⓮ to **sweep the board** → see **board**
▸ **sweep up** PHRASAL VERB 句動詞 If you **sweep up** rubbish or dirt, you push it together with a brush and then remove it. 掃き集める ❑*Get a broom and sweep up that glass, will you?* ほうきを持ってきて、ガラスを掃き集めてくれる?

Word Partnership   **sweep** は次の語句と使われる:

ADV.   sweep *someone/something* away ❺ ❻
PREP.   sweep **into** *someplace* ❼
        sweep **through** *someplace* ❼ ❽

sweep|ing /swipɪŋ/ ❶ ADJ 形容詞 A **sweeping** curve is a long wide curve. ゆったりと湾曲した [ADJ n] ❑*…the long sweeping curve of Rio's Guanabara Bay.* リオのグアナバラ湾が描く長いゆるやかな曲線 ❷ ADJ 形容詞 If someone makes a **sweeping** statement or generalization, they make a statement which applies to all things of a particular kind, although they have not considered all the relevant facts carefully. 大ざっぱな [DISAPPROVAL 不賛成] ❑*It is far too early to make sweeping statements about gene therapy.* 遺伝子治療法について概括的な意見を述べるにはあまりにも早すぎる. ❸ ADJ 形容詞 **Sweeping** changes are large and very important or significant. 全面的な ❑*The new government has started to make sweeping changes in the economy.* 新政府は経済に関する全面的な変更を開始した. ❹ → see also **sweep**

sweet /swit/ (sweeter, sweetest, sweets) ❶ ADJ 形容詞 **Sweet** food and drink contains a lot of sugar. 甘い ❑*…a mug of sweet tea.* マグカップに入った甘い紅茶 ❑*If the sauce seems too sweet, add a dash of red wine vinegar.* もしソースが甘すぎるようであれば、赤ワイン酢を少々加えなさい. ● **sweet|ness** N-UNCOUNT 不可算名詞 甘味 ❑*Florida oranges have a natural sweetness.* フロリダ産のオレンジは自然の甘さがある. ❷ ADJ 形容詞 A **sweet** smell is a pleasant one, for example the smell of a flower. 芳香のある ❑*…the sweet smell of her shampoo.* 彼女のシャンプーの良いかおり ❸ ADJ 形容詞 A **sweet** sound is pleasant, smooth, and gentle. 耳に快い ❑*Her voice was as soft and sweet as a young girl's.* 彼女の声は少女の声のように柔らかくて快かった. ● **sweet|ly** ADV 副詞 良い声で ❑*He sang much more sweetly than he has before.* 彼は以前よりもさらに美しい声で歌った. ❹ ADJ 形容詞 If you describe something as **sweet**, you mean that it gives you great pleasure and satisfaction. 快い [WRITTEN 書き言葉] ❑*There are few things quite as sweet as revenge.* ふくしゅうほど気持ちよいものは他にない. ❺ ADJ 形容詞 If you describe someone as **sweet**, you mean that they are pleasant, kind, and gentle toward other people. 優しい ❑*He was a sweet man but when he drank he tended to quarrel.* 彼は親切な男であったが、酒を飲むとけんかしがちだった. ● **sweet|ly** ADV 副詞 優しく ❑*I just smiled sweetly and said no.* ちょっと優しくほほえんで、いいえと言った. ❻ ADJ 形容詞 If you describe a small person or thing as **sweet**, you mean that they are attractive in a simple or unsophisticated way. かわいらしい [INFORMAL くだけた] ❑*…a sweet little baby girl.*

かわいい小さな女の子の赤ちゃん **7** N-PLURAL 複数名詞 **Sweets** are foods that have a lot of sugar. 甘いもの [AM 米国英語] ❑ *To maintain her weight, she simply chooses fruits and vegetables over fats and sweets.* 体重を維持するために，彼女はただ単に脂肪分や甘い物より果物や野菜を選ぶ． **8** N-COUNT 可算名詞 **Sweets** are small sweet things such as chocolates and mints. キャンディー [BRIT 英国英語; AM **candy** 米国英語 **candy**] **9** N-VAR 可変性名詞 A **sweet** is the same as a **dessert**. 甘いデザート [BRIT 英国英語] **10** → see also **sweetness** **11** **a sweet tooth** → see **tooth**
→ see **fruit, sugar, taste**

sweet|corn /swíːtkɔːrn/ N-UNCOUNT 不可算名詞 **Sweetcorn** is a long rounded vegetable covered in small yellow seeds. It is part of the maize plant. The seeds themselves can also be referred to as **sweetcorn**. トウモロコシ

sweet|en /swíːtᵊn/ (**sweetens, sweetening, sweetened**) **1** V-T 他動詞 If you **sweeten** food or drink, you add sugar, honey, or another sweet substance to it. 甘くする ❑ *He liberally sweetened his coffee.* 彼はコーヒーをふんだんに甘くした． **2** V-T 他動詞 If you **sweeten** something such as an offer or a business deal, you try to make someone want it more by improving it or by increasing the amount you are willing to pay. 魅力的にする ❑ *Kalon Group has sweetened its takeover offer for Manders.* カーロングループ社は，買収の申し入れ条件をマンダーズにとって魅力的なようにした．

sweet|en|er /swíːtᵊnər/ (**sweeteners**) **1** N-MASS 質量名詞 **Sweetener** is an artificial substance that can be used in drinks instead of sugar. 人口甘味料 **2** N-COUNT 可算名詞 A **sweetener** is something that you give or offer someone in order to persuade them to accept an offer or business deal. 歓心を買うための贈り物 ❑ *A corporation can buy back its bonds by paying investors the face value (plus a sweetener).* 企業は，投資家に額面価格（に加えて贈り物）を払うことで，社債を買い戻すことができる．

sweet|heart /swíːthɑːrt/ (**sweethearts**) **1** N-VOC 呼格名詞 You call someone **sweetheart** if you are very fond of them. かわいい人 ❑ *Happy birthday, sweetheart.* いとしい人よ，お誕生日おめでとう． **2** N-COUNT 可算名詞 Your **sweetheart** is your boyfriend or your girlfriend. 恋人 [OLD-FASHIONED 古風な] ❑ *I married Shurla, my childhood sweetheart.* 幼なじみの恋人であるシューラと結婚した．

sweet|ness /swíːtnɪs/ **1** PHRASE 句 If you say that a relationship or situation is not **all sweetness and light**, you mean that it is not as pleasant as it appears to be. 快適で ❑ *It has not all been sweetness and light between him and the mayor.* 彼と市長の間は必ずしも常に快適とは言えない． **2** → see also **sweet**

swell /swél/ (**swells, swelling, swelled, swollen**)

The forms **swelled** and **swollen** are both used as the past participle.

swelled 形と **swollen** 形は両者ともに過去分詞として使われる

1 V-T/V-I 他動詞/自動詞 If the amount or size of something **swells** or if something **swells** it, it becomes larger than it was before. 増す ❑ *The human population swelled, at least temporarily, as migrants moved south.* 移民が南へ移動したので，人口は少なくとも一時的にふくれあがった． ❑ *His bank balance has swelled by $222,000 in the last three weeks.* 彼の口座残高は過去3週間で222,000ドル増加した． **2** V-I 自動詞 If something such as a part of your body **swells**, it becomes larger and rounder than normal. はれる ❑ *Do your ankles swell at night?* 夜は足首がはれるか？ ● PHRASAL VERB 句動詞 **Swell up** means the same as **swell**. はれる ❑ *When you develop a throat infection or catch a cold the glands in the neck swell up.* のどの感染や風邪にかかったりすると首にある腺がはれる． **3** → see also **swollen**

swell|ing /swélɪŋ/ (**swellings**) N-VAR 可変性名詞 A **swelling** is a raised, curved shape on the surface of your body which appears as a result of an injury or an illness. はれもの ❑ *His eye was partly closed, and there was a swelling over his lid.* 片目がつぶれかけていて，まぶたには，はれものがあった．

swel|ter|ing /swéltərɪŋ/ ADJ 形容詞 If you describe the weather as **sweltering**, you mean that it is extremely hot and makes you feel uncomfortable. うだるように暑い ❑ *...the sweltering heat of the St. Petersburg summer.* サンクトペテルブルグの夏のうだるような暑さ

swept /swépt/ **Swept** is the past tense and past participle of **sweep**.

swerve /swɜːrv/ (**swerves, swerving, swerved**) V-T/V-I 他動詞/自動詞 If a vehicle or other moving thing **swerves** or if you **swerve** it, it suddenly changes direction, often in order to avoid hitting something. 急に方向を変える ❑ *Drivers coming in the opposite direction swerved to avoid the bodies.* 反対側の方向から来ていた運転手達は，死体を避けるために急に方向を変えた． ❑ *Her car swerved off the road into a 6 ft high brick wall.* 彼女の車は道路から6フィートの高さのレンガの壁にぶつかった． ● N-COUNT 可算名詞 **Swerve** is also a noun. それること ❑ *He swung the car to the left and that swerve saved Malone's life.* 彼が車を左にぐるっと回してそれたので，マローンの命が助かった．

swift /swíft/ (**swifter, swiftest, swifts**) **1** ADJ 形容詞 A **swift** event or process happens very quickly or without delay. すばやい ❑ *Our task is to challenge the U.N. to make a swift decision.* 我々の課題は，迅速な判断をするように国連に挑戦することだ． ● **swift|ly** ADV 副詞 速やかに ❑ *Wall Street reacted swiftly to yesterday's verdict.* ウォールストリートは昨日の判定に速やかに反応した． **2** ADJ 形容詞 Something that is **swift** moves very quickly. 速い ❑ *With a swift movement, Matthew Jerrold sat upright.* マシュー・ジェロルドはさっと身を起こし，まっすぐ座った． ● **swift|ly** ADV 副詞 [ADV with v] 速く ❑ *Lenny moved swiftly and silently across the front lawn.* レニーは，前庭の芝をすばやく静かに横切っていった． **3** N-COUNT 可算名詞 A **swift** is a small bird with long curved wings. つばめ

swim /swím/ (**swims, swimming, swam, swum**) **1** V-T/V-I 他動詞/自動詞 When you **swim**, you move through water by making movements with your arms and legs. 泳ぐ ❑ *She learned to swim when she was really tiny.* ごく小さい時に泳ぐことを覚えた． ❑ *He was rescued only when an exhausted friend swam ashore.* 彼は，疲労こんぱいした友が岸に泳ぎついてからやっと救助された． ❑ *I swim a mile a day.* 1日あたり1マイル泳ぐ． ● N-SING 単数名詞 **Swim** is also a noun. 水泳 ❑ *When can we go for a swim?* いつ泳ぎに行けるの？ **2** V-T 他動詞 If you **swim** a race, you take part in a swimming race. 競泳に出場する ❑ *She swam the 400 meters medley.* 400メートルメドレー水泳に出場した． **3** V-T 他動詞 If you **swim** a stretch of water, you keep swimming until you have crossed it. 泳いで渡る ❑ *By the time we reached the other side, Maram vowed that he would never swim a river again.* 向こう岸に着くまでに，マラムはもう絶対に川を泳いで渡らないと誓った． **4** V-I 自動詞 When a fish **swims**, it moves through water by moving its body. 泳ぐ ❑ *The barriers are fatal to fish trying to swim upstream.* 上流に向かって泳ごうとしている魚にとっては障壁は致命的である． **5** V-I 自動詞 If your head **is swimming**, you feel unsteady and slightly ill. くらくらする ❑ *The musty aroma of incense made her head swim.* 香のかび臭いにおいで頭がくらくらした． **6** **sink or swim** → see **sink**

swim|mer /swímər/ (**swimmers**) N-COUNT 可算名詞 A **swimmer** is a person who swims, especially for sport or pleasure, or a person who is swimming. 泳ぎ手，泳いでいる人 ❑ *You don't have to worry about me. I'm a good swimmer.* 心配する必要はない．僕は泳ぎが得意だ．

swim|ming /swímɪŋ/ N-UNCOUNT 不可算名詞 **Swimming** is the activity of swimming, especially as a sport or for pleasure. 水泳 ❑ *Swimming is probably the best form of exercise you can get.* 水泳は，おそらく最も有益な運動だろう．

swim|ming pool (**swimming pools**) N-COUNT 可算名詞 A **swimming pool** is a large hole in the ground that has been made and filled with water so that people can swim in it. 水泳プール

swim|ming trunks N-PLURAL 複数名詞 **Swimming trunks** are the shorts that a man wears when he goes swimming. 水泳パンツ [also "a pair of" N]

swim|suit /swímsuːt/ (**swimsuits**) N-COUNT 可算名詞 A **swimsuit** is a piece of clothing that is worn for swimming, especially by women and girls. 水着 ❑ *...pictures of models in swimsuits.* 水着を着たモデルたちの絵

swin|dle /swíndᵊl/ (**swindles, swindling, swindled**) V-T 他動詞 If someone **swindles** a person or an organization, they deceive them in order to get something valuable from them, especially money. だまし取る ❑ *A businessman swindled investors out of millions of dollars.* ある実業家が，投資家たちから何百万ドルもだまし取った． ● N-COUNT 可算名詞 **Swindle** is also a noun. だますこと ❑ *He lied to Switzerland rather than face trial for a tax swindle.* 税金ごまかしの裁判に直面せずに，スイスへ逃げた．

swing /swíŋ/ (**swings, swinging, swung**) **1** V-T/V-I 他動詞/自動詞 If something **swings** or if you **swing** it, it moves repeatedly backward and forward or from side to side from a fixed point. 揺れる [自動詞]，振る [他動詞] ❑ *The sail of the little boat swung crazily from one side to the other.* 小さなボートの帆が，狂ったようにあちらへこちらへと振れ動いていた． ❑ *She was swinging a bottle of wine by its neck.* ワインの瓶の首をつかんで揺らしていた． ● N-COUNT 可算名詞 **Swing** is also a noun. 振ること ❑ *...a woman in a tight red dress, walking with a slight swing to her hips.* 軽く腰を振りながら歩いている，ぴったりした赤いドレスを着た女 **2** V-T/V-I 他動詞/自動詞 If something **swings** in a particular direction or if you **swing** it in that direction, it moves in that direction with a smooth, curving movement. ぐるっと回る [自動詞]，ぐるっと回す [他動詞] ❑ *The torchlight swung across the little beach and out over the water, searching.* 懐中電灯の光が小さな浜辺をぐるっと横切って伸びて行き，水の上を捜した． ❑ *The canoe found the current and swung around.* カヌーが水流に乗って，急にぐるっと向き直った． ● N-COUNT 可算名詞 **Swing** is also a noun. 振り ❑ *When he's not on the tennis court, you'll find him practicing his golf swing.* テニスコートにいなければ，ゴルフの振り方を練習しているだろうよ． **3** V-T/V-I 他動詞/自動詞 If a vehicle **swings** in a particular direction, or if the driver **swings** it in a particular direction, they turn suddenly in that direction. 回転する [自動詞]，回転させる [他動詞] ❑ *Joanna swung back on to*

S

the main approach and headed for the airport. ジョアンナはくるりと回って主要通路に戻り、空港をめざした. ❹ V-I 自動詞 If someone **swings around**, they turn around quickly, usually because they are surprised. 急に向き直る ❑ She swung around to him, spilling her tea without noticing it. 急に彼のほうに向き直り、紅茶がこぼれたのも気がつかなかった. ❺ V-I 自動詞 If you **swing at** a person or thing, you try to hit them with your arm or with something that you are holding. 大きく振って打つ ❑ Blanche swung at her but she moved her head back and Blanche missed. ブランチは彼女に向ってかかっていったが、彼女が後ろに頭をよけたので、打ちそこなった. ● N-COUNT 可算名詞 **Swing** is also a noun. 打つこと ❑ I often want to take a swing at someone to relieve my feelings. 気を晴らすために誰かを殴ってやりたいとよく思う. ❻ N-COUNT 可算名詞 A **swing** is a seat hanging by two ropes or chains from a metal frame or from the branch of a tree. You can sit on the seat and move forward and backward through the air. ぶらんこ ❑ Go to the neighborhood park. Run around, push the kids on the swings. 近くの公園に行って、走り回ったり、子どもたちをぶらんこに乗せたりしなさい. ❼ N-COUNT 可算名詞 A **swing** in people's opinions, attitudes, or feelings is a change in them, especially a sudden or big change. 急に変動すること ❑ Educational practice is liable to sudden swings and changes. 教育実践は突然方向が変わったり、変更されたりしがちである. ❑ Dieters suffer from violent mood swings. 減食をしている人たちは、激しい気分の変動に悩む. ❽ V-I 自動詞 If people's opinions, attitudes, or feelings **swing**, they change, especially in a sudden or extreme way. 急に変わる、大きく変わる ❑ In two years' time there is a presidential election, and the voters could swing again. あと2年すれば大統領選があり、投票者は大きく変わる可能性もある. ❾ PHRASE 句 If something is **in full swing**, it is operating fully and is no longer in its early stages. 最高潮である ❑ When we returned, the party was in full swing and the dance floor was crowded. 戻ってきた時にはパーティはまっ盛りであり、ダンス場は混雑していた. ❿ PHRASE 句 If you **get into the swing of** something, you become very involved in it and enjoy what you are doing. 調子が出てくる ❑ Everyone understood how hard it was to get back into the swing of things after such a long absence. 長い間やってなかったので、再度リズムに乗るのは大変であることは誰にも理解できた.

swipe /swaɪp/ (**swipes, swiping, swiped**) ❶ V-I 自動詞 If you **swipe at** a person or thing, you try to hit them with a stick or other object, making a swinging movement with your arm. ぶん殴る ❑ She swiped at Rusty as though he was a fly. ラスティがまるでハエでもあるみたいに横殴りにした. ● N-COUNT 可算名詞 **Swipe** is also a noun. 強打 ❑ He took a swipe at Andrew that deposited him on the floor. 彼はアンドリューが床にのびてしまうほどの一撃をくわせた. ❷ V-T 他動詞 If you **swipe** something, you steal it quickly. かっぱらう [INFORMAL くだけた] ❑ She was convicted of swiping more than $5,500 worth of goods from Saks Fifth Avenue. サックスフィフスアベニューから5,500ドル相当以上の物品を盗んだ件で有罪と宣告された. ❸ N-COUNT 可算名詞 If you take a **swipe at** a person or an organization, you criticize them, usually in an indirect way. 非難 ❑ Genesis recorded a song which took a swipe at greedy property developers who bought up and demolished people's homes. ジェネシスは、人々から家を買い上げて取り壊す、強欲な宅地造成業者を鋭く非難した歌を録音した. ❹ V-T 他動詞 If you **swipe** a credit card or swipe card through a machine, you pass it through a narrow space in the machine so that the machine can read information on the card's magnetic strip. カードを読取機に通す ❑ Swipe your card through the phone, then dial. 電話にカードを読ませてからダイアルしてください.

swipe card (**swipe cards**) also **swipecard** N-COUNT 可算名詞 A **swipe card** is a plastic card with a magnetic strip on it which contains information that can be read or transferred by passing the card through a special machine. 磁気データカード ❑ They use a swipe card to go in and out of their offices. 事務所の出入りには磁気データカードを使う.

swirl /swɜrl/ (**swirls, swirling, swirled**) V-T/V-I 他動詞/自動詞 If you **swirl** something liquid or flowing, or if it **swirls**, it moves around and around quickly. ぐるぐるかき混ぜる；渦を巻く ❑ She smiled, swirling the wine in her glass. グラスのワインを回しながら彼女はほほえんだ. ❑ The black water swirled around his legs, reaching almost to his knees. ほとんどひざまで届きそうな真っ黒な水が彼の足の周りで渦を巻いた. ● N-COUNT 可算名詞 **Swirl** is also a noun. 渦巻状の動き ❑ ...small swirls of chocolate cream. 渦巻き形の小さなチョコレートクリーム

swish /swɪʃ/ (**swishes, swishing, swished**) V-T/V-I 他動詞/自動詞 If something **swishes** or if you **swish** it, it moves quickly through the air, making a soft sound. ひゅうっと音を立てて動く [自動詞], ひゅうっと振り回す [他動詞] ❑ A car swished by, steady and fast, heading for the coast. 車が海岸に向かって着実に速いスピードでひゅうっと通り過ぎた. ❑ He swished his cape around his shoulders. マントを肩に回してシュッといわせた. ● N-COUNT 可算名詞 **Swish** is also a noun. ひゅうっと風を切る音 ❑ She turned with a swish of her skirt. スカートをシュッといわせて彼女は振り返った.

switch /swɪtʃ/ (**switches, switching, switched**) ❶ N-COUNT 可算名詞 A **switch** is a small control for an electrical device which you use to turn the device on or off. スイッチ ❑ Leona put some detergent into the dishwasher, shut the door, and pressed the switch. レオナは皿洗い機に洗剤をいくらか入れてドアを閉め、スイッチを押した. ❷ N-PLURAL 複数名詞 On a railroad track, the **switches** are the levers and rails at a place where two tracks join or separate. The **switches** enable a train to move from one track to another. 転てつ機 [AM 米国英語] ❑ ...a set of railroad tracks – including switches – and a model train. 転てつ機 - それに汽車の模型 - を含む線路一式 ❸ V-I 他動詞/自動詞 If you **switch to** something different, for example to a different system, task, or subject of conversation, you change to it from what you were doing or saying before. 転じる ❑ Estonia is switching to a market economy. エストニアは市場経済に転換中である. ❑ The law would encourage companies to switch from coal to cleaner fuels. その法律は、会社が石炭からよりきれいな燃料に切り換えることを奨励するだろう. ● N-COUNT 可算名詞 **Switch** is also a noun. 転換 [usu with supp] ❑ The spokesman implicitly condemned the United States policy switch. その代表者は、合衆国の方針転換を暗に責めた. ● PHRASAL VERB 句動詞 **Switch over** means the same as **switch**. 転換する ❑ Everywhere communists are tending to switch over to social democracy. いたるところで共産主義者が社会民主主義に転向する傾向がみられる. ❹ V-T/V-I 他動詞/自動詞 If you **switch** your attention from one thing **to** another or if your attention **switches**, you stop paying attention to the first thing and start paying attention to the second. 移す [他動詞], 移る [自動詞] ❑ My mother's interest had switched to my health. 母の関心は私の健康状態に移った. ❺ V-T 他動詞 If you **switch** two things, you replace one with the other. 交換する ❑ In half an hour, they'd switched the tags on every cable. 30分で全てのケーブルの札を交換した.
▶ **switch off** ❶ PHRASAL VERB 句動詞 If you **switch off** a light or other electrical device, you stop it working by operating a switch. スイッチを切る ❑ She switched off the coffee-machine. コーヒー沸かし器のスイッチを切った. ❷ PHRASAL VERB 句動詞 If you **switch off**, you stop paying attention or stop thinking or worrying about something. 興味を失う [INFORMAL くだけた] ❑ Thankfully, I've learned to switch off and let it go over my head. ありがたいことに、心配するのを止めて無視することを覚えた.
▶ **switch on** PHRASAL VERB 句動詞 If you **switch on** a light or other electrical device, you make it start working by operating a switch. スイッチを入れる ❑ She emptied both their mugs and switched on the electric kettle. 両方のマグカップを空にして、電気湯沸かし器のスイッチを入れた.

switch|board /swɪtʃbɔrd/ (**switchboards**) N-COUNT 可算名詞 A **switchboard** is a place in a large office or business where all the telephone calls are connected. 電話交換台 ❑ He asked to be connected to the central switchboard. 中央交換台に接続するように頼んだ.

swiv|el /swɪvəl/ (**swivels, swiveling** or **swivelling, swiveled** or **swivelled**) V-T/V-I 他動詞/自動詞 If something **swivels** or if you **swivel** it, it turns around a central point so that it is facing in a different direction. 回転する [自動詞], 回転させる [他動詞] ❑ She swiveled her chair and stared out the window. いすを回転させて窓の外を見つめた.

swol|len /swoʊlən/ ❶ ADJ 形容詞 If a part of your body is **swollen**, it is larger and rounder than normal, usually as a result of injury or illness. はれた ❑ My eyes were so swollen I could hardly see. 両眼がはれあがり、ほとんど何も見えなかった. ❷ ADJ 形容詞 A **swollen** river has more water in it and flows faster than normal, usually because of heavy rain. 増水した ❑ The river, brown and swollen with rain, was running fast. 雨で増水し茶色になった川は、流れが速かった. ❸ **Swollen** is the past participle of **swell**.

swoop /swup/ (**swoops, swooping, swooped**) ❶ V-I 自動詞 If police or soldiers **swoop on** a place, they go there suddenly and quickly, usually in order to arrest someone or to attack the place. 急襲する [JOURNALISM ジャーナリズム] ❑ The terror ended when armed police swooped on the car. 武装した警察が車を急襲して恐ろし

い出来事は終結した. ● N-COUNT 可算名詞 **Swoop** is also a noun. 急襲 ❑ *Police held 10 suspected illegal immigrants after a swoop on a Mexican truck.* 警察はメキシコのトラックを急襲し, 不法移民の疑いで10名を拘束した. **2** V-I 自動詞 When a bird or airplane **swoops**, it suddenly moves downwards through the air in a smooth curving movement. 急降下する ❑ *More than 20 helicopters began swooping in low over the ocean.* 20機以上のヘリコプターは海洋上で低く急降下し始めた. **3** PHRASE 句 If something is done **in one fell swoop**, it is done on a single occasion or by a single action. 一挙に ❑ *In one fell swoop the bank wiped away the tentative benefits of this policy.* 銀行は, この方針の暫定特典を一挙に拭い去った.

swop /swɒp/ → see **swap**

sword /sɔrd/ (**swords**) **1** N-COUNT 可算名詞 A **sword** is a weapon with a handle and a long sharp blade. 剣 **2** PHRASE 句 If you **cross swords with** someone, you disagree with them and argue with them about something. 論争する ❑ *...a candidate who's crossed swords with labor by supporting the free-trade pact.* 自由貿易協定を支持して労働者と論争した候補者 **3** PHRASE 句 If you say that something is a **double-edged sword**, you mean that it has negative effects as well as positive effects. 両刃の剣 ❑ *A person's looks are a double-edged sword. Sometimes it works in your favor, sometimes it works against you.* 人の容貌は両刃の剣だ. 得になることもあるし, 損することもある.

→ see **army**

swore /swɔr/ **Swore** is the past tense of **swear**.

sworn /swɔrn/ **1 Sworn** is the past participle of **swear**. **2** ADJ 形容詞 If you make a **sworn** statement or declaration, you swear that everything that you have said in it is true. 誓った [ADJ n] ❑ *The allegations against them were made in sworn evidence to the inquiry.* 彼らに対する申し立ては, 取調べ時の宣誓証言でなされた. **3** ADJ 形容詞 If two people or two groups of people are **sworn** enemies, they dislike each other very much. 断言した [ADJ n] ❑ *It somehow seems hardly surprising that Ms. Player is now his sworn enemy.* プレーヤーさんが今は彼の目の敵であることは特に驚くこともないように思える.

swum /swʌm/ **Swum** is the past participle of **swim**.

swung /swʌŋ/ **Swung** is the past tense and past participle of **swing**.

syl|la|ble /sɪləbəl/ (**syllables**) N-COUNT 可算名詞 A **syllable** is a part of a word that contains a single vowel sound and that is pronounced as a unit. So, for example, "book" has one syllable, and "reading" has two syllables. 音節 ❑ *We children called her Oma, accenting both syllables.* 私たち子どもは, 彼女を「オマ」と両方の音節にアクセントをおいて呼んだ.

syl|la|bus /sɪləbəs/ (**syllabuses**) **1** N-COUNT 可算名詞 A **syllabus** is an outline or summary of the subjects to be covered in a course. 教授摘要 [mainly AM 主に米国英語] ❑ *The course syllabus consisted mainly of novels by African-American authors, male and female.* 講義摘要は主に, 男女のアフリカ系アメリカ人作家による小説から成り立っていた. **2** N-COUNT 可算名詞 You can refer to the subjects that are studied in a particular course as the **syllabus**. 課程 [mainly BRIT 主に英国英語; AM usually **curriculum** 米国英語では通常 **curriculum**]

sym|bol /sɪmbəl/ (**symbols**) **1** N-COUNT 可算名詞 Something that is a **symbol of** a society or an aspect of life seems to represent it because it is very typical of it. 象徴 ❑ *To them, the monarchy is the special symbol of nationhood.* 彼らにとって, 王室は国家集団の特別な象徴である. **2** N-COUNT 可算名詞 A **symbol of** something such as an idea is a shape or design that is used to represent it. 象徴 ❑ *Later in this same passage Yeats resumes his argument for the Rose as an Irish symbol.* 同じ一節の後の方で, イェーツはバラがアイルランドの象徴であるこの議論を再開する. **3** N-COUNT 可算名詞 A **symbol for** an item in a calculation or scientific formula is a number, letter, or shape that represents that item. 符号 ❑ *What's the chemical symbol for mercury?* 水銀の化学記号は何ですか? **4** → see also **sex symbol**

→ see **flag, myth**

sym|bol|ic /sɪmbɒlɪk/ **1** ADJ 形容詞 If you describe an event, action, or procedure as **symbolic**, you mean that it represents an important change, although it has little practical effect. 象徴的な ❑ *A lot of Latin-American officials are stressing the symbolic importance of the trip.* ラテンアメリカ系の役員たちの多くが, その旅行の象徴的な重要性を強調している. ● **sym|bol|ical|ly** /sɪmbɒlɪkli/ ADV 副詞 ❑ *It was a simple enough gesture, but symbolically important.* 充分簡単な意思表示ではあるが, 象徴的に重要であった. **2** ADJ 形容詞 Something that is **symbolic of** a person or thing is regarded or used as a symbol of them. 象徴的な ❑ *Yellow clothes are symbolic of spring.* 黄色い服は春の象徴として着用される. ● **sym|boli|cal|ly** ADV 副詞 [ADV with v] ❑ *Each circle symbolically represents the whole of humanity.* 一つ一つの輪は人間性の全てを象徴的に表している. **3** ADJ 形容詞 **Symbolic** is used to describe things involving or relating to symbols. 符号の [ADJ n] ❑ *...symbolic representations of landscape.* 記号で表した地形

sym|bol|ism /sɪmbəlɪzəm/ **1** N-UNCOUNT 不可算名詞 **Symbolism** is the use of symbols in order to represent something. 象徴化 ❑ *The scene is so rich in symbolism that any explanation risks spoiling the effect.* その光景は豊かな象徴にあふれていて, 説明などすればかえってその効果が損なわれてしまう危険がある. **2** N-UNCOUNT 不可算名詞 You can refer to the **symbolism** of an event or action when it seems to show something important about a situation. 象徴的意味 ❑ *The symbolism of every gesture will be of vital importance during the short state visit.* 短い国家訪問中, 一つ一つの意思表示の象徴的意味はきわめて重要となるだろう.

sym|bol|ize /sɪmbəlaɪz/ (**symbolizes, symbolizing, symbolized**) V-T 他動詞 If one thing **symbolizes** another, it is used or regarded as a symbol of it. 象徴する ❑ *The fall of the Berlin Wall symbolized the end of the Cold War between East and West.* ベルリンの壁の崩壊は, 東西の冷戦の終結を象徴するものであった.

→ see **flag**

sym|met|ri|cal /sɪmɛtrɪkəl/ ADJ 形容詞 If something is **symmetrical**, it has two halves which are exactly the same, except that one half is the mirror image of the other. 対称の ❑ *...the neat rows of perfectly symmetrical windows.* 行儀よく並んだ, まったく対称的な窓の列 ● **sym|met|ri|cal|ly** /sɪmɛtrɪkli/ ADV 副詞 [ADV with v] 対称的に ❑ *The south garden was composed symmetrically.* 南側の庭は対称構成で造園された.

sym|me|try /sɪmɪtri/ (**symmetries**) **1** N-VAR 可変性名詞 Something that has **symmetry** is symmetrical in shape, design, or structure. 対称 ❑ *...the incredible beauty and symmetry of a snowflake.* 雪の結晶の信じられないほどの美と相称 **2** N-UNCOUNT 不可算名詞 **Symmetry** in a relationship or agreement is the fact of both sides giving and receiving an equal amount. つり合い ❑ *The superpowers pledged to maintain symmetry in their arms shipments.* 超強大国は, 武器の出荷についてはつり合いを維持することを誓約した.

sym|pa|thet|ic /sɪmpəθɛtɪk/ **1** ADJ 形容詞 If you are **sympathetic** to someone who is in a bad situation, you are kind to them and show that you understand their feelings. 思いやりのある ❑ *She was very sympathetic to the problems of adult students.* 社会人学生が感じる問題についてたいへん同情的であった. ● **sym|pa|theti|cal|ly** /sɪmpəθɛtɪkli/ ADV 副詞 [ADV with v] 同情的に ❑ *She nodded sympathetically.* 同情してうなずいた. **2** ADJ 形容詞 If you are **sympathetic to** a proposal or action, you approve of it and are willing to support it. 賛同した ❑ *Many of these early visitors were sympathetic to the Chinese socialist experiment.* このような初期の訪問客の多くは, 中国の社会主義者の試みに理解を示した. ● **sym|pa|theti|cal|ly** ADV 副詞 [ADV with v] 賛同して ❑ *After a year we will sympathetically consider an application for reinstatement.* 1年後に復帰申請を好意的に考慮しよう.

> Do not confuse **sympathetic** and **friendly**. If you have a problem and someone is **sympathetic** or shows a **sympathetic** attitude, they show that they care and would like to help you. ❑ *My boyfriend was very sympathetic.* A person who is **friendly** or has a **friendly** attitude is kind and pleasant and behaves the way a friend would. ❑ *...a friendly woman who offered me a coffee. ...a pleasant, friendly smile.* Note that people sometimes refer to characters in a play or novel who are easy to like as **sympathetic**. ❑ *There were no sympathetic characters in my book.* You usually say that real people are "nice" or "likable."

sym|pa|thize /sɪmpəθaɪz/ (**sympathizes, sympathizing, sympathized**) **1** V-I 自動詞 If you **sympathize** with someone who is in a bad situation, you show that you are sorry for them. 気の毒に思う ❑ *I must tell you how much I sympathize with you for your loss, Professor.* 教授, 御不幸をほんとうにお気の毒に思います. **2** V-I 自動詞 If you **sympathize with** someone's feelings, you understand them and are not critical of them. 同感である ❑ *Some Europeans sympathize with the Americans over the issue.* この件については欧州人の中にはアメリカ人と同感の人もいる. **3** V-I 自動詞 If you **sympathize with** a proposal or action, you approve of it and are willing to support it. 賛同する ❑ *Most of the people living there sympathized with the guerrillas.* そこに住んでいる人たちのほとんどはゲリラに賛同していた.

sym|pa|thiz|er /sɪmpəθaɪzər/ (**sympathizers**) N-COUNT 可算名詞 The **sympathizers** of an organization or cause are the people who approve of it and support it. 支持者 ❑ *Safta Hashmi was a well-known playwright and Communist sympathizer.* サフタ・ハシミは著名な劇作家であり, 共産主義者の支持者であった.

| Word Link | path ≈ feeling : apathy, empathy, sympathy |
| Word Link | sym ≈ together : sympathy, symphony, symposium |

sym|pa|thy /sɪmpəθi/ (**sympathies**) **1** N-UNCOUNT 不可算名詞 If you have **sympathy** for someone who is in a bad situation, you are sorry for them, and show this in the way you behave toward them. 同情 [also N in pl] ❑ *We expressed our sympathy for her loss.* 彼女に不幸のお悔やみを述べた. ❑ *I have had very little help from doctors*

and no sympathy whatsoever. 今までに医者からはほとんど何の援助も
なく、同情のひとかけらもなかった. **2** N-UNCOUNT 不可算名詞 If
you have **sympathy** with someone's ideas or opinions, you agree
with them. 賛成 [also N in pl, oft N "with/for" n] ❑ *I have
some sympathy with this point of view.* この見解にはある程度賛成する.
❑ *Lithuania still commands considerable international sympathy for its
cause.* リトアニアはいまだにその主義に対してかなりの国際的共感を
集めている. **3** N-UNCOUNT 不可算名詞 If you take some action **in
sympathy with** someone else, you do it in order to show that you
support them. 賛成して ❑ *Several hundred workers struck in sympathy
with their colleagues.* 同僚に共鳴して数百人がストをした.

Word Partnership   *sympathy* は次の語句と使われる:

ADJ.	deep sympathy, great sympathy, public sympathy **1**
V.	express sympathy, feel sympathy, gain sympathy, have sympathy **1** **2**

Word Link   *phon ≈ sound : microphone, symphony, telephone*

Word Link   *sym ≈ together : sympathy, symphony, symposium*

---

sym|pho|ny /sɪmfəni/ (**symphonies**) N-COUNT; N-IN-NAMES 可
算名詞, 名称中の名詞 A **symphony** is a piece of music written to be
played by an orchestra. Symphonies are usually made up of four
separate sections called movements. 交響曲 ❑ *...Beethoven's Ninth
Symphony.* ベートーベンの第九交響曲

→ see **music, orchestra**

sym|pho|ny or|ches|tra (**symphony orchestras**) N-COUNT;
N-IN-NAMES 可算名詞, 名称中の名詞 A **symphony orchestra** is a
large orchestra that plays classical music. 交響楽団

sym|po|sium /sɪmpoʊziəm/ (**symposia** /sɪmpoʊziə/ or
symposiums) N-COUNT 可算名詞 A **symposium** is a conference
in which experts or academics discuss a particular subject. 公
開討論会 ❑ *He had been taking part in an international symposium on
population.* 国際人口討論会に参加していた.

symp|tom /sɪmptəm/ (**symptoms**) **1** N-COUNT 可算名詞 A
symptom of an illness is something wrong with your body or
mind that is a sign of the illness. 症状 ❑ *One of the most common
symptoms of schizophrenia is hearing imaginary voices.* 精神分裂症の
最も一般的な症状には、実在しない声が聞こえてくる症状がある.
❑ *...patients with flu symptoms.* インフルエンザの症状のある患者
2 N-COUNT 可算名詞 A **symptom of** a bad situation is something
that happens which is considered to be a sign of this situation. き
ざし ❑ *Your problem with keeping boyfriends is just a symptom of a larger
problem: making and keeping friends.* 男友達が長続きしない君の問題
は、もっと大きな問題の一つの徴候にすぎない：友人を作り、うまく付
き合っていく問題だ.

→ see **diagnosis, illness**

symp|to|mat|ic /sɪmptəmætɪk/ ADJ 形容詞 If something is
symptomatic of something else, especially something bad, it is a
sign of it. 前兆である [FORMAL 形式ばった] [v-link ADJ] ❑ *The city's
problems are symptomatic of a crisis that is spreading throughout the
country.* 市の諸問題は、全国に広がりつつある危機の前兆である.

syna|gogue /sɪnəɡɒɡ/ (**synagogues**) N-COUNT; N-IN-NAMES
可算名詞, 名称中の名詞 A **synagogue** is a building where Jewish
people meet to worship or to study their religion. シナゴーグ (ユ
ダヤ教の礼拝堂や集会堂)

Word Link   *chron ≈ time : chronic, chronicle, synchronize*

Word Link   *syn ≈ together : synchronize, synergy, synopsis*

---

syn|chro|nize /sɪŋkrənaɪz/ (**synchronizes, synchronizing,
synchronized**) V-RECIP 相互動詞 If you **synchronize** two activities,
processes, or movements, or if you **synchronize** one activity,
process, or movement **with** another, you cause them to happen
at the same time and speed as each other. 同調させる ❑ *It was
virtually impossible to synchronize our lives so as to take vacations and
weekends together.* 休暇や週末を一緒に過ごすために生活の時間を合わ
せるのは、実質的に不可能であった. ❑ *Synchronize the score with the
film action.* 映画の動きと音楽を一致させてください.

syn|di|cate /sɪndɪkɪt/ (**syndicates, syndicating, syndicated**)
1 N-COUNT 可算名詞 A **syndicate** is an association of people or
organizations that is formed for business purposes or in order to
carry out a project. 組合、企業連合 ❑ *They formed a syndicate to buy
the car in which they competed in the race.* レースで競走する車を買うた
めにグループを結成した. ❑ *...a syndicate of 152 banks.* 152行加盟して
いる企業連合 **2** V-T 他動詞 When newspaper articles or television
programs **are syndicated**, they are sold to several different
newspapers or television stations, who then publish the articles
or broadcast the programs. 新聞雑誌連盟やテレビ局を通じて同時発
表する [usu passive] ❑ *Today his program is syndicated to 500 stations.*
今日では彼の番組は500局に同時発表される. **3** N-COUNT 可算名詞 A

press **syndicate** is a group of newspapers or magazines that are all
owned by the same person or company. 同一経営下の新聞雑誌出版

syn|drome /sɪndroʊm/ (**syndromes**) N-COUNT; N-IN-NAMES 可
算名詞, 名称中の名詞 A **syndrome** is a medical condition that is
characterized by a particular group of signs and symptoms. 症候
群 ❑ *Irritable bowel syndrome seems to affect more women than men.* 過
敏性腸症候群は、男性より女性がかかるように見える.

syn|er|gy /sɪnərdʒi/ (**synergies**) N-VAR 可変性名詞 If there
is **synergy** between two or more organizations or groups, they
are more successful when they work together than when they
work separately. 相乗作用 [BUSINESS 実業] ❑ *Of course, there's quite
obviously a lot of synergy between the two companies.* もちろん2社の間
に相当な相乗効果があるのは明らかだ.

Word Link   *onym ≈ name : acronym, anonymous, synonym*

---

syno|nym /sɪnənɪm/ (**synonyms**) N-COUNT 可算名詞 A
synonym is a word or expression which means the same
as another word or expression. 同義語 ❑ *The term "industrial
democracy" is often used as a synonym for worker participation.* 「産業民
主主義」という用語はほとんどの場合、従業員経営参加と同義語のよう
に使用されている.

syn|ony|mous /sɪnɒnɪməs/ ADJ 形容詞 If you say that one
thing is **synonymous** with another, you mean that the two things
are very closely associated with each other so that one suggests
the other or one cannot exist without the other. 同義の ❑ *Paris has
always been synonymous with elegance, luxury and style.* パリは常に優
雅、ぜいたく、気品を意味している.

syn|op|sis /sɪnɒpsɪs/ (**synopses** /sɪnɒpsiz/) N-COUNT 可算名詞
A **synopsis** is a summary of a longer piece of writing or work. 概
要 ❑ *For each title there is a brief synopsis of the book.* 本の題名ごとに短
い大意がある.

syn|the|sis /sɪnθɪsɪs/ (**syntheses** /sɪnθɪsiz/) **1** N-COUNT 可
算名詞 A **synthesis** of different ideas or styles is a mixture or
combination of these ideas or styles. 総合体 [FORMAL 形式ばった]
❑ *His novels are a rich synthesis of Balkan history and mythology.* 彼の小
説は、バルカン半島の歴史や神話が豊かに溶け合っている. **2** N-VAR
可変性名詞 The **synthesis** of a substance is the production of it by
means of chemical or biological reactions. 合成 [TECHNICAL 技術
的] ❑ *...the genes that regulate the synthesis of these compounds.* このよ
うな化合物の合成を調整する遺伝子

syn|the|size /sɪnθɪsaɪz/ (**synthesizes, synthesizing,
synthesized**) **1** V-T 他動詞 To **synthesize** a substance means to
produce it by means of chemical or biological reactions. 合成す
る [TECHNICAL 技術的] ❑ *After extensive research, Albert Hoffman first
succeeded in synthesizing the acid in 1938.* 広範囲に及ぶ研究の後、ア
ルバート・ホフマンは1938年に始めて酸の合成に成功した. **2** V-T
他動詞 If you **synthesize** different ideas, facts, or experiences,
you combine them to form a single idea or impression. 統合す
る [FORMAL 形式ばった] ❑ *The movement synthesized elements of
modern art that hadn't been brought together before, such as Cubism and
Surrealism.* その動きによって、それまでは別々であった立体派や超現
実主義などの近代美術要素が統合された.

syn|the|siz|er /sɪnθɪsaɪzər/ (**synthesizers**) N-COUNT 可
算名詞 A **synthesizer** is an electronic machine that produces
speech, music, or other sounds, usually by combining individual
syllables or sounds that have been previously recorded. シンセサ
イザー ❑ *Now he can only communicate through a voice synthesizer.* 今で
は彼は音声合成器でしか意思疎通ができない.

→ see **keyboard**

syn|thet|ic /sɪnθetɪk/ ADJ 形容詞 **Synthetic** products are made
from chemicals or artificial substances rather than from natural
ones. 合成の ❑ *Boots made from synthetic materials can usually be
washed in a machine.* 合成素材で作られているブーツは普通洗濯機で洗
うことができる.

sy|phon /saɪfᵊn/ → see **siphon**

sy|ringe /sɪrɪndʒ/ (**syringes**) N-COUNT 可算名詞 A **syringe** is
a small tube with a thin hollow needle at the end. Syringes are
used for putting liquids into things and for taking liquids out, for
example for injecting drugs or for taking blood from someone's
body. 注射器 ❑ *As he reached over, Azrak slid a hypodermic syringe into
his left arm.* 手を差し伸ばしてアズラックは左腕に皮下注射針を滑り
込ませた.

syr|up /sɪrəp, sɜr-/ (**syrups**) **1** N-MASS 質量名詞 **Syrup** is a
sweet liquid made by cooking sugar with water, and sometimes
with fruit juice as well. シロップ ❑ *...canned fruit with sugary
syrup.* 甘ったるいシロップ缶詰の果物 **2** N-MASS 質量名詞 **Syrup**
is a medicine in the form of a thick, sweet liquid. シロップ剤
❑ *...cough syrup.* 咳止めシロップ剤

sys|tem /sɪstəm/ (**systems**) **1** N-COUNT 可算名詞 A **system** is
a way of working, organizing, or doing something which follows
a fixed plan or set of rules. You can use **system** to refer to an
organization or institution that is organized in this way. 方法；組

織 ❏ *The present system of funding for higher education is unsatisfactory.* 高等教育の現財源体制は満足できるものではない。❏ *...a flexible and relatively efficient filing system.* 融通が利き，比較の効率の良い書類整理方法 **2** N-COUNT 可算名詞 **A system** is a set of devices powered by electricity, for example a computer or an alarm. 系統 ❏ *Viruses tend to be good at surviving when a computer system crashes.* コンピューター系統が故障してもウイルスはうまく生き残る傾向がある。**3** N-COUNT 可算名詞 **A system** is a set of equipment or parts such as water pipes or electrical wiring, which is used to supply water, heat, or electricity. 装置 ❏ *...a central heating system.* 中央暖房装置 **4** N-COUNT 可算名詞 **A system** is a network of things that are linked together so that people or things can travel from one place to another or communicate. 一網 ❏ *...Australia's road and rail system.* オーストラリアの道路網と鉄道網 **5** N-COUNT 可算名詞 Your **system** is your body's organs and other parts that together perform particular functions. 身体 ❏ *He had slept for over fourteen hours, and his system seemed to have recuperated admirably.* 彼は14時間以上も眠り，体は申し分なく回復したように思えた。**6** N-COUNT 可算名詞 **A system** is a particular set of rules, especially in mathematics or science, which is used to count or measure things. 方式 ❏ *...the decimal system of metric weights and measures.* 重量や計測のメートル法10進法 **7** N-SING 単数名詞 People sometimes refer to the government or administration of a country as **the system**. 現支配体制 ❏ *These feelings are likely to make people attempt to overthrow the system.* このような意識は国民が現支配体制を覆そうと試みる可能性につながる。**8** → see also **ecosystem, immune system, nervous system, solar system, sound system**

sys|tem|at|ic /sɪstəmætɪk/ ADJ 形容詞 Something that is done in a **systematic** way is done according to a fixed plan, in a thorough and efficient way. 系統だった ❏ *They went about their business in a systematic way.* 組織だった方法で仕事に精を出した。● **sys|tem|ati|cal|ly** /sɪstəmætɪkli/ ADV 副詞 系統的に ❏ *The army has systematically violated human rights.* 軍隊は計画的に人権を踏みにじっている。

sys|tem|ic /sɪstɛmɪk/ ADJ 形容詞 **Systemic** means affecting the whole of something. 全体的な [FORMAL 形式ばった] ❏ *The economy is locked in a systemic crisis.* 全面的な経済危機から抜け出せない。

sys|tems ana|lyst (**systems analysts**) N-COUNT 可算名詞 **A systems analyst** is someone whose job is to decide what computer equipment and software a company needs, and to provide it. システム分析者

S

Tt

T also **t** /tiː/ (**T's, t's**) **1** N-VAR 可変性名詞 T is the twentieth letter of the English alphabet. 英語アルファベットの第20字 **2** PHRASE 句 You can use **to a T** or **to a tee** to mean perfectly or exactly right. For example, if something suits you **to a T**, it suits you perfectly. If you have an activity or skill **down to a T**, you have succeeded in doing it exactly right. 完全に [INFORMAL くだけた] □ *A clerk had had to be rehearsed down to a T.* 何もかも完全に練習する必要があった. □ *The description fits us to a tee.* その描写は私たちにぴったり合っている.

tab /tæb/ (**tabs**) **1** N-COUNT 可算名詞 A **tab** is a small piece of cloth or paper that is attached to something, usually with information about that thing written on it. ラベル □ *A clerk had slipped the wrong tab on Tony's X-ray.* 病院実習生は間違ったラベルをトニーのレントゲンにつけた. **2** N-COUNT 可算名詞 A **tab** is the total cost of goods or services that you have to pay, or the bill or check for those goods or services. 値段 [mainly AM 主に米国英語] □ *At least one estimate puts the total tab at $7 million.* 総費用が7百万ドルの見積もりが少なくとも1つある. **3** PHRASE 句 If someone **keeps tabs on** you, they make sure that they always know where you are and what you are doing, often in order to control you. 注意を払う [INFORMAL くだけた] □ *It was obvious Hill had come over to keep tabs on Johnson and make sure he didn't do anything drastic.* ヒルはジョンソンが過激な行動を取らないよう監視するためにこちらに来たのは明らかだった. **4** PHRASE 句 If you **pick up the tab**, you pay a bill on behalf of a group of people or provide the money that is needed for something. 勘定を払う [INFORMAL くだけた] □ *Pollard picked up the tab for dinner that night.* ポラードはその晩, 食事の勘定を払った.

ta|ble /ˈteɪbəl/ (**tables, tabling, tabled**) **1** N-COUNT 可算名詞 A **table** is a piece of furniture with a flat top that you put things on or sit at. テーブル □ *She was sitting at the kitchen table eating a peach.* 彼女は台所用テーブルに座って桃を食べていた. **2** V-T 他動詞 If someone **tables** a proposal or plan which has been put forward, they decide to discuss it or deal with it at a later date, rather than right away. 棚上げにする [AM 米国英語] □ *We will table that for later.* 我々はそれを先送りする予定だ. **3** V-T 他動詞 If someone **tables** a proposal, they say formally that they want it to be discussed at a meeting. 審議に付す [BRIT 英国英語] □ *They've tabled a motion criticizing the government for doing nothing about the problem.* 彼らはその問題に何の対策も打っていないことに対して政府を批判する動議を提出した. **4** N-COUNT 可算名詞 A **table** is a written set of facts and figures arranged in columns and rows. 表 [also N num] □ *Consult the table on page 104.* 104ページの表を参照しなさい. **5** → see also **negotiating table**

table|cloth /ˈteɪbəlklɒθ/ (**tablecloths**) N-COUNT 可算名詞 A **tablecloth** is a cloth used to cover a table. テーブルクロス

table|spoon /ˈteɪbəlspuːn/ (**tablespoons**) N-COUNT 可算名詞 A **tablespoon** is a fairly large spoon used for serving food and in cooking. テーブルスプーン

tab|let /ˈtæblɪt/ (**tablets**) **1** N-COUNT 可算名詞 A **tablet** is a small solid mass of medicine which you swallow. 錠剤 □ *...half a tablet of aspirin.* アスピリンの錠剤半分 **2** N-COUNT 可算名詞 Clay **tablets** or stone **tablets** are the flat pieces of clay or stone which people used to write on before paper was invented. 書字板 **3** tablets of stone → see **stone**

tab|loid /ˈtæblɔɪd/ (**tabloids**) N-COUNT 可算名詞 A **tabloid** is a newspaper that has small pages, short articles, and a lot of photographs. Tabloids are usually considered to be less serious than other newspapers. Compare **broadsheet**. タブロイド紙 □ *The tabloids speculated as to whether she was having an affair, and with whom.* タブロイド紙は彼女が浮気やその相手についてあれこれ憶測する記事を掲載した.

ta|boo /təˈbuː/ (**taboos**) N-COUNT 可算名詞 A **taboo** against a subject or activity is a social custom to avoid doing that activity or talking about that subject, because people find them embarrassing or offensive. タブー □ *The topic of addiction remains something of a taboo in our family.* 常習癖の話題は我が家ではちょっとしたタブーとなっている. ● ADJ 形容詞 **Taboo** is also an adjective. 禁止された □ *Cancer is a taboo subject and people are frightened or embarrassed to talk openly about it.* 癌は触れてはいけない話題で人々はそれについて率直に話し合いたがらない.

tac|it /ˈtæsɪt/ ADJ 形容詞 If you refer to someone's **tacit** agreement or approval, you mean they are agreeing to something or approving it without actually having to admit to doing so. They are unwilling to admit to doing so. 暗黙のうちの □ *The question was a tacit admission that a mistake had indeed been made.* その質問は誤りが実際に発生したことを暗黙のうちに認めることに等しかった. ● **tac|it|ly** ADV 副詞 [ADV with v] 暗黙のうちに □ *He tacitly admitted that the government had breached regulations.* 彼は政府が規制違反を犯したことを暗黙のうちに認めた.

tack /tæk/ (**tacks, tacking, tacked**) **1** N-COUNT 可算名詞 A **tack** or a **thumbtack** is a short pin with a wide head that you can push with your thumb, especially for a bulletin board. 画鋲（びょう）□ *...a box of carpet tacks.* 1箱の敷物の留め鋲（びょう）**2** → see also **thumbtack** **3** N-COUNT 可算名詞 A **tack** is a short nail with a broad, flat head, especially one that is used for fastening carpets to the floor. 鋲（びょう）□ *...a box of carpet tacks.* 1箱の敷物の留め鋲（びょう）**4** → see also **thumbtack** **5** V-T 他動詞 If you **tack** something to a surface, you pin it there with tacks or thumbtacks. 鋲で留める □ *He had tacked this note to her door.* 彼はこのメモを彼女のドアに鋲で留めていた. **6** N-SING 単数名詞 If you change **tack** or try a different **tack**, you try a different method for dealing with a situation. 方針 [also no det] □ *Seeing the puzzled look on his face, she tried a different tack.* 彼の困惑した表情を見て彼女は別のやり方を試みた. **7** V-T 他動詞 If you **tack** pieces of material together, you sew them together with big, loose stitches in order to hold them firmly or check that they fit, before sewing them permanently. 仮に縫い付ける □ *Tack them together with a 1 cm seam.* 1cmの縫い目でそれらを縫い付けなさい.

▶ **tack on** PHRASAL VERB 句動詞 If you say that something **is tacked on** to something else, you think that it is added in a hurry and in an unsatisfactory manner. 追加する □ *The child-care bill is to be tacked on to the budget plan now being worked out in the Senate.* 保育法案は上院で現在検討中の予算案に追加されることになっている.

tack|le /ˈtækəl/ (**tackles, tackling, tackled**) **1** V-T 他動詞 If you **tackle** a difficult problem or task, you deal with it in a very determined or efficient way. 取り組む □ *The first reason to tackle these problems is to save children's lives.* こうした問題と取り組む第1の理由は子供の命を救うことだ. **2** V-T 他動詞 If you **tackle** someone in a game such as football or rugby, you knock them to the ground. If you **tackle** someone in soccer or hockey, you try to take the ball away from them. タックルする □ *Foley tackled the quarterback.* フォーリーはクォーターバックをタックルした. ● N-COUNT 可算名詞 **Tackle** is also a noun. タックル □ *...a tackle by fullback Brian Burrows.* ランニングバックのブライアン・バロウズによるタックル **3** V-T 他動詞 If you **tackle** someone about a particular matter, you speak to them honestly about it, usually in order to get it changed or done. 腹蔵なく話す □ *I tackled him about how anyone could live amidst so much poverty.* 私はあれほどひどい貧困生活をいかにできるかについて彼と話し合った. **4** V-T 他動詞 If you **tackle** someone, you attack them and fight them. 組み付ける □ *Two security guards tackled and apprehended a man suspected of robbing 17 banks.* 2人の警備員は17件の銀行強盗をしたと思われる男を組み伏せ, 逮捕（こういん）した. **5** N-UNCOUNT 不可算名詞 **Tackle** is the equipment that you need for a sport or activity, especially fishing. 道具 □ *...fishing tackle.* 釣り道具

tacky /ˈtæki/ (**tackier, tackiest**) **1** ADJ 形容詞 If you describe something as **tacky**, you dislike it because it is cheap and badly made or vulgar. やぼったい [INFORMAL くだけた, DISAPPROVAL 不賛成] □ *...a woman in a fake leopard-skin coat and tacky red sunglasses.* 偽のヒョウ革のコートとやぼったい赤のサングラス姿の女 **2** ADJ 形容詞 If something such as paint or glue is **tacky**, it is slightly sticky and not yet dry. べとべとする □ *Test to see if the finish is tacky, and if it is, leave it to harden.* 仕上げがべとべとしているかを調べ, べとべとしている場合には固くなるまでそのままにしなさい.

tact /tækt/ N-UNCOUNT 不可算名詞 **Tact** is the ability to avoid upsetting or offending people by being careful not to say or do things that would hurt their feelings. 如才なさ □ *Her tact and intuition never failed.* 彼女の臨機応変の才と直感が役に立たないことはなかった.

tact|ful /ˈtæktfəl/ ADJ 形容詞 If you describe a person or what they say as **tactful** you approve of them because they are careful not to offend or upset another person. 如才ない [APPROVAL 賛成] □ *He had been extremely tactful in dealing with the financial question.* 彼

は金銭的質問に非常にそつなく対処した. ● **tact|ful|ly** ADV 副詞 如才なく ❑ *Alex tactfully refrained from further comment.* アレックスはきかせていて以上言及を言うのを止めた.

tac|tic /tǽktɪk/ (**tactics**) N-COUNT 可算名詞 **Tactics** are the methods that you choose to use in order to achieve what you want in a particular situation. 術策 ❑ *The rebels would still be able to use guerrilla tactics to make the country ungovernable.* 反抗者はその国を統治できないようにするためにゲリラ戦術をまだ使うことができるだろう.

Word Partnership	*tactic* は次の語句と使われる:
ADJ.	**effective** tactic, **similar** tactic
N.	**scare** tactic

tac|ti|cal /tǽktɪkəl/ ■ ADJ 形容詞 You use **tactical** to describe an action or plan which is intended to help someone achieve what they want in a particular situation. 計算された ❑ *It's not yet clear whether his resignation offer is a serious one, or whether it's simply a tactical move.* 彼の辞職申出が真剣なものなのか, 単に計算された行動なのかはまだはっきりしない. ● **tac|ti|cal|ly** /tǽktɪkli/ ADV 副詞 戦術的に ❑ *The electorate is astute enough to vote tactically against the government.* 有権者には政府を不利にするために投票行動を変えるだけの抜け目なさがある. ❷ ADJ 形容詞 [ADJ n] **Tactical** weapons or forces are those which a military leader can decide for themselves to use in a battle, rather than waiting for a decision by a political leader. 戦術の ❑ *They have removed all tactical nuclear missiles that could strike Europe.* 彼らはヨーロッパを攻撃できる全ての戦術的な核ミサイルを取り除いた.

taf|fy /tǽfi/ N-UNCOUNT 不可算名詞 **Taffy** is a sticky candy that you chew. It is made by boiling sugar and butter together with water. タフィー [AM 米国英語]

tag /tǽg/ (**tags, tagging, tagged**) ■ N-COUNT 可算名詞 A **tag** is a small piece of card or cloth which is attached to an object or person and has information about that object or person on it. 名札 ❑ *Staff wore name tags and called inmates by their first names.* 職員は名札をつけ, 被収容者をファーストネームで呼んだ. ❷ → see also **price tag** ❸ N-COUNT 可算名詞 An electronic **tag** is a device that is firmly attached to someone or something and sets off an alarm if that person or thing moves away or is removed. タッグ ❑ *Ranchers are testing electronic tags on animals' ears to create a national cattle-tracking system.* 牧場主は全国家畜追跡システムを創設するために家畜の耳に電子タッグを試している. ❹ N-UNCOUNT 不可算名詞 **Tag** is a children's game where one child runs to touch or tag the others. 鬼ごっこ ❺ V-T 他動詞 If you **tag** something, you attach something to it or mark it so that it can be identified later. 識別する ❑ *Professor Orr has developed interesting ways of tagging chemical molecules using existing laboratory lasers.* オー教授は既存の実験用のレーザーを使って化学分子を識別する興味深い方法を開発した.

▸ **tag along** PHRASAL VERB 句動詞 If someone goes somewhere and you **tag along**, you go with them, especially when they have not asked you to. ついて行く ❑ *I let him tag along because he had not been too well recently.* 彼は最近体調が思わしくなかったため, 私は彼がついて来るのを許した.

tail /téɪl/ (**tails, tailing, tailed**) ■ N-COUNT 可算名詞 The **tail** of an animal, bird, or fish is the part extending beyond the end of its body. 尾 ❑ *...a black dog with a long tail.* 尻尾の長い黒犬 ❷ N-COUNT 可算名詞 You can use **tail** to refer to the end or back of something, especially something long and thin. 後部 ❑ *...the horizontal stabilizer bar on the plane's tail.* 飛行機の後部の水平のスタビライザーバー ❸ N-PLURAL 複数名詞 If a man is wearing **tails**, he is wearing a formal jacket which has two long pieces hanging down at the back. テールコート ❑ *...men in tails and women in party dresses.* テールコート姿の男性とパーティドレス姿の女性 ❹ V-T 他動詞 To **tail** someone means to follow close behind them and watch where they go and what they do. 尾行する [INFORMAL くだけた] ❑ *Officers had tailed the gang during a major undercover operation.* 警察官は大規模な秘密作戦中にギャングを尾行した. ❺ ADV 副詞 If you toss a coin and it comes down **tails**, you can see the side of it that does not have a picture of a head on it. 貨幣の裏面 [ADV after v] ❑ *"Heads or tails?"* 「表か裏か」 ❑ *The captain called heads as usual — and the coin came down tails.* キャプテンはいつものとおりに表と言ったが, 硬貨は裏だった. ❻ cannot **make head or tail of** something → see **head**

▸ **tail off** PHRASAL VERB 句動詞 When something **tails off**, it gradually becomes less in amount or value, often before coming to an end completely. しだいに消えていく ❑ *Last year, economic growth tailed off to below four percent.* 昨年経済成長率は4％以下に徐々に低下した.

tai|lor /téɪlər/ (**tailors, tailoring, tailored**) ■ N-COUNT 可算名詞 A **tailor** is a person whose job is to make men's clothes. テーラー ❷ V-T 他動詞 If you **tailor** something such as a plan or system to someone's needs, you make it suitable for a particular person or purpose by changing the details of it. 特殊な好みに適応させる

❑ *We can tailor the program to the patient's needs.* 私たちはその内容を患者さんのニーズに合わせることができます.

tailor-made ■ ADJ 形容詞 If something is **tailor-made**, it has been specially designed for a particular person or purpose. 特製の ❑ *Each client's portfolio is tailor-made.* 各ポートフォリオは顧客のニーズに合わせてあります. ❷ ADJ 形容詞 If you say that someone or something is **tailor-made for** a particular task, purpose, or need, you are emphasizing that they are perfectly suitable for it. ぴったりの [EMPHASIS 強調] ❑ *He was tailor-made, it was said, for the task ahead.* 彼は今後の作業にぴったりだと言われた. ❸ ADJ 形容詞 **Tailor-made** clothes have been specially made to fit a particular person. 注文仕立ての ❑ *He was wearing a suit that looked tailor-made.* 彼は注文仕立てに見える背広を着ていた.

tail|pipe /téɪlpaɪp/ (**tailpipes**) N-COUNT 可算名詞 A **tailpipe** is the end pipe of a car's exhaust system. テールパイプ [AM 米国英語] ❑ *a dramatic reduction in tailpipe emissions.* テールパイプ排出量の大幅な削減

taint /téɪnt/ (**taints, tainting, tainted**) ■ V-T 他動詞 If a person or thing **is tainted by** something bad or undesirable, their status or reputation is harmed because they are associated with it. 評判を失う ❑ *Opposition leaders said that the elections had been tainted by corruption.* 選挙は不正行為のために信用を失ったと反対党の指導者は述べた. ● **taint|ed** ADJ 形容詞 評判が傷つけられた ❑ *He came out only slightly tainted by telling millions of viewers he and his wife had had marital problems.* 彼は何百万もの視聴者に夫婦間の問題があったと告げたが, 彼の評判はほんのわずかしか傷つかなかった. ❷ N-COUNT 可算名詞 A **taint** is an undesirable quality which ruins the status or reputation of someone or something. 不名誉 ❑ *Her government never really shook off the taint of corruption.* 彼女の政府は不正行為の汚名を払い落とすことができなかった. ❸ V-T 他動詞 If an unpleasant substance **taints** food or medicine, the food or medicine is spoiled or damaged by it. 損なう ❑ *Rancid oil will taint the flavor.* 嫌なにおいのする油は風味を損なうだろう.

take

❶ USED WITH NOUNS DESCRIBING ACTIONS
❷ OTHER USES

❶ **take** /téɪk/ (**takes, taking, took, taken**)

Take is used in combination with a wide range of nouns, where the meaning of the combination is mostly given by the noun. Many of these combinations are common idiomatic expressions whose meanings can be found at the appropriate nouns. For example, the expression **take care** is explained at **care**.

Take は広範囲の名詞と結合して用いられ, その場合結合表現の意味は大部分がその名詞によって与えられる. これらの結合表現の多くは普通の慣用的表現で, その意味はそれらの適切な名詞のところで見つけることができる. 例えば, 表現 **take care** は **care** のところで説明されている.

■ V-T 他動詞 You can use **take** followed by a noun to talk about an action or event, when it would also be possible to use the verb that is related to that noun. For example, you can say "she took a shower" instead of "she showered." 浴する ❑ *She was too tired to take a shower.* 彼女は非常に疲れていたのでシャワーを浴びなかった. ❑ *Betty took a photograph of us.* ベティは私たちの写真を撮った. ❷ V-T 他動詞 In ordinary spoken or written English, people use **take** with a range of nouns instead of using a more specific verb. For example, people often say "he took control" or "she took a positive attitude" instead of "he assumed control" or "she adopted a positive attitude." とる ❑ *The Patriotic Front took power after a three-month civil war.* 3か月間続いた内戦の後, 愛国者戦線は権力を得た. ❑ *I felt it was important for women to join and take a leading role.* 私は女性が参加し指導的な役割を演じるのが大切だと感じた. → see **photography**

❷ **take** /téɪk/ (**takes, taking, took, taken**)
↪ Please look at category ❹❻ to see if the expression you are looking for is shown under another headword. ■ V-T 他動詞 If you **take** something, you reach out for it and hold it. 手に取る ❑ *Here, let me take your coat.* さあ, コートを取らせてください. ❑ *Colette took her by the shoulders and shook her.* コレットは彼女の肩をつかみ, 揺さぶった. ❷ V-T 他動詞 If you **take** something with you when you go somewhere, you carry it or have it with you. 運ぶ ❑ *Mark often took his books to Bess's house to study.* マークは勉強するためにしばしば教科書をベスの家に持って行った. ❑ *You should take your passport with you when changing money.* 両替する時にはパスポートを持っていく必要があります. ❸ V-T 他動詞 If a person, vehicle, or path **takes** someone somewhere, they transport or lead them there. 連れて行く ❑ *She took me to a Mexican restaurant.* 彼女は私をメキシコ料理のレストランに連れて行った. ❹ V-T 他動詞 If something such as a job or interest **takes** you to a place, it is the reason for

you going there. 到達させる ❏ *He was a poor student from Madras whose genius took him to Stanford.* 彼はその天賦の才のおかげでスタンフォード大学に入学したマドラス出身の貧しい学生だった. **5** V-T 他動詞 If you **take** something such as your problems or your business to someone, you go to that person when you have problems you want to discuss or things you want to buy. 持って行く ❏ *You need to take your problems to a trained counselor.* あなたは専門のカウンセラーに相談する必要がある. **6** V-T 他動詞 If one thing **takes** another **to** a particular level, condition, or state, it causes it to reach that level or condition. 到達させる ❏ *A combination of talent, hard work and good looks have taken her to the top.* 才能，努力そして美貌の組み合わせのおかげで彼女はトップに立った. **7** V-T 他動詞 If you **take** something from a place, you remove it from there. 取り出す ❏ *He took a handkerchief from his pocket and lightly wiped his mouth.* 彼はポケットからハンカチを取り出し，軽く口をぬぐった. **8** V-T 他動詞 If you **take** something from someone who owns it, you steal it or go away with it without their permission. 盗む ❏ *He has taken my money, and I have no chance of getting it back.* 私は彼に金を盗まれたが私がそれを取り戻す可能性はない. **9** V-T 他動詞 If an army or political party **takes** something or someone, they win them from their enemy or opponent. 占領する ❏ *A Serb army unit took the town.* セルビアの軍隊はその町を占領した. **10** V-T 他動詞 If you **take** one number or amount from another, you subtract it or deduct it. 引く ❏ *Take off the price of the house, that's another hundred thousand.* 家の値段，すなわちもう10万を引きなさい. **11** V-T 他動詞 If you cannot **take** something difficult, painful, or annoying, you cannot tolerate it without becoming upset, ill, or angry. 耐える [no passive, usu with brd-neg] ❏ *Don't ever ask me to look after those kids again. I just can't take it!.* あの子たちの世話を私に2度と頼まないで. ちょっと我慢できないのだ. **12** V-T 他動詞 If you **take** something such as damage or loss, you suffer it, especially in war or in a battle. 受ける ❏ *They have taken heavy casualties.* 多くの死傷者が出た. **13** V-T 他動詞 If something **takes** a certain amount of time, that amount of time is needed in order to do it. 必要とする [no passive] ❏ *Since the roads are very bad, the trip took us a long time.* 道路の状態が非常に悪いため，移動には時間がかかった. ❏ *I had heard an appeal could take years.* 私は上告には何年もかかると聞いていた. ❏ *The sauce takes 25 minutes to prepare and cook.* そのソースを作るには25分かかる. ❏ *It takes 15 minutes to convert the plane into a car by removing the wings and the tail.* 翼と尾部を取り除いて飛行機を自動車に変えるには15分かかる. **14** V-T 他動詞 If something **takes** a particular quality or thing, that quality or thing is needed in order to do it. 必要とする [no passive] ❏ *At one time, walking across the room took all her strength.* 一時は彼女は部屋を横切るのに全ての体力を必要とした. ❏ *It takes courage to say what you think.* 思っていることを言うのは勇気が必要だ. **15** V-T 他動詞 If you **take** something that is given or offered to you, you agree to accept it. 引き受ける ❏ *When I took the job I thought I could change the system, but it's hard.* その仕事を引き受けた時, 私はシステムを変えられると思ったが容易ではない. **16** V-T 他動詞 If you **take** a feeling such as pleasure, pride, or delight in a particular thing or activity, it gives you that feeling. 抱く ❏ *They take great pride in their heritage.* 彼らは彼らが受け継いだ伝統に大きな誇りを持っている. **17** V-T 他動詞 If you **take** a prize or medal, you win it. 獲得する ❏ *"Poison" took first prize at the 1991 Sundance Film Festival.* 1991年のサンダンス映画祭で「Poison」が一等賞を取った. **18** V-T 他動詞 If you **take** the blame, responsibility, or credit for something, you agree to accept it. 負う ❏ *His brother Raoul did it, but Leonel took the blame and kept his mouth shut.* 彼の兄弟のラウルがそれをしたが, レオネルは責めを負い, 何も言わなかった. **19** V T 他動詞 If you **take** patients or clients, you accept them as your patients or clients. 受け入れる ❏ *Some universities would be forced to take more students than they wanted.* 一部の大学は希望する学生数以上の学生を受け入れねばならないだろう. **20** V-T 他動詞 If you **take** a telephone call, you speak to someone who is telephoning you. 答える ❏ *Douglas telephoned Catherine at her office. She refused to take his calls.* ダグラスはキャサリンのオフィスに電話した. 彼女は電話に出るのを拒否した. **21** V-T 他動詞 If you **take** something in a particular way, you react in the way mentioned to a situation or to someone's beliefs or behavior. 受け取る ❏ *Unfortunately, no one took my opinion seriously.* 残念ながら私の意見を真面目に取った者はいなかった. **22** V-T 他動詞 You use **take** when you are discussing or explaining a particular question, in order to introduce an example or to say how the question is being considered. 取り上げる [usu imper] ❏ *There's confusion and resentment, and it's almost never expressed out in the open. Take this office, for example.* 混乱と憤慨があり, それが明るみに出たことはほとんどなかった. 例えば, このオフィスだ. **23** V-T 他動詞 If you **take** someone's meaning or point, you understand and accept what they are saying. 理解する ❏ *I had made it as plain as I could so that he could not fail to take my meaning.* 私は彼が私の言うことを必ず理解できるようにできるだけ簡単に説明した. **24** V-T 他動詞 If you **take** someone for something, you believe wrongly that they are that thing. 考える ❏ *She had taken him for a journalist.* 彼女は彼がジャーナリストだと思っていた. **25** V-T 他動詞 If you **take** a road or route, you choose to travel along it. 取って進む ❏ *From the community college take Old Mill Road to the outskirts of town.* コミュニティカレッジからオールド・ミル・ロードを通って町外れに進みなさい. **26** V-T 他動詞 If you **take** a car, train, bus, or plane, you use it to go from one place to another. 利用する ❏ *It's the other end of town so we should take the car.* それは街の反対側の外れにあるので車で行くべきだ. **27** V-T 他動詞 If you **take** a subject or course at school or college, you choose to study it. 専攻する ❏ *Students are allowed to take European history and American history.* 学生はヨーロッパ史とアメリカ史を専攻することが許されている. **28** V-T 他動詞 If you **take** a test or examination, you do it in order to show your knowledge or ability. 受ける ❏ *She took her driving test yesterday.* 彼女は昨日運転免許試験を受けた. **29** V-T 他動詞 If someone **takes** drugs, pills, or other medicines, they take them into their body, for example, by swallowing them. 飲む ❏ *She's been taking sleeping pills.* 彼女は睡眠薬を飲んでいる. **30** V-T 他動詞 If you **take** a note or a letter, you write down something you want to remember or the words that someone says. 取る ❏ *She sat expressionless, carefully taking notes.* 彼女は注意深くメモを取りながら無表情に座っていた. **31** V-T 他動詞 If you **take** a measurement, you find out what it is by measuring. 取る ❏ *By drilling, geologists can take measurements at various depths.* 地政学者は穿孔（せんこう）によって深度の異なる場所で測定することができる. **32** V-T 他動詞 If a place or container **takes** a particular amount or number, there is enough space for that amount or number. 収容する [no passive] ❏ *The place could just about take 2,000 people.* その場所は2000人の人々をどうにか収容できた. **33** V-T 他動詞 If you **take** a particular size in shoes or clothes, that size fits you. 合う ❏ *"What size do you take?"—"I take a size 7."* 「サイズは何ですか」「7号です」 **34** N-SING 単数名詞 You can use **take** to refer to the amount of money that a business such as a store or theater gets from selling its goods or tickets during a particular period. 売上高 [mainly AM 主に米国英語 BUSINESS 実業] ❏ *It added another $11.8 million to the take, for a grand total of $43 million.* それは売上高にもう1180万ドル加え, 総計4300万ドルとなった. **35** V-T 他動詞 If a store, restaurant, theater, or other business **takes** a certain amount of money, they get that amount from people buying goods or services. 稼ぐ [mainly BRIT 主に英国英語 BUSINESS 実業] [AM usually **take in** 米国英語では通常 **take in**] **36** V-T 他動詞 If you **are taken by** someone, you are cheated or deceived by them. だまされる [INFORMAL くだけた] ❏ *They got taken by a scam artist.* 彼らはペテン師にだまされた. **37** N-COUNT 可算名詞 A **take** is a short piece of action which is filmed in one continuous process for a movie. 1回分の撮影 ❏ *She couldn't get it right - she never knew the lines and we had to do several takes.* 彼女は正しく演じられなかった. 彼女はせりふを覚えておらず数回撮影を行なわねばならなかった. **38** N-SING 単数名詞 Someone's **take on** a particular situation or fact is their attitude to it or their interpretation of it. 見方 ❏ *What's your take on the new government? Do you think it can work?* 君は新政府をどう見ているか. うまくいくと思うか. **39** CONVENTION 慣習表現 If you say to someone "**take it or leave it**," you are telling them that they can accept something or not accept it, but that you are not prepared to discuss any other alternatives. 受けるかどうかは勝手である ❏ *A 72-hour week, 12 hours a day, six days a week, take it or leave it.* 1日12時間, 1週間に72時間, 週6日, 受けるかどうか決めてください. **40** PHRASE 句 If someone **takes** an insult or attack **lying down**, they accept it without protesting. 甘受する ❏ *The government is not taking such criticism lying down.* 政府はそのような批判を甘んじて受けてはいない. **41** PHRASE 句 If something **takes a lot out of** you or **takes it out of** you, it requires a lot of energy or effort and makes you feel very tired and weak afterward. 疲れさせる ❏ *He looked tired, as if the argument had taken a lot out of him.* その議論が彼を疲れさせたかのように彼は疲れて見えた. **42** PHRASE 句 If someone tells you to **take five** or to **take ten**, they are telling you to have a five or ten minute break from what you are doing. ちょっと5分ほど休憩する, ちょっと10分ほど休憩する [mainly AM 主に米国英語, INFORMAL くだけた] **43** PHRASE 句 Someone who is **on the take** is receiving illegal income such as bribes. 賄賂つかみ [INFORMAL くだけた] ❏ *I can also name cops who are on the take.* 賄賂を受けている警官を指名することもできる. **44** to be taken aback → see aback **45** to take up arms → see arm **46** to take the cake → see cake **47** to take your hat off to someone → see hat **48** to be taken for a ride → see ride **49** to take someone by surprise → see surprise **50** take my word for it → see word

→ see calorie

Take and **bring** are both used to talk about carrying something or accompanying someone somewhere, but **take** is used to suggest movement away from the speaker, and **bring** is used to suggest movement toward the speaker. *Anna took the book to school with her... Bring your calculator to every lesson.* In the first sentence, **took** suggests that Anna left the speaker when she went to school. In the second sentence, **bring** suggests that the person and the calculator should come to the place where the speaker is. You could also say "Anna brought the book to school with her" to suggest that Anna and the speaker were both at school, and "Take your calculator to every lesson" to suggest that the speaker will not be present at the lesson. The difference between **take** and **bring** is equivalent to that between **go** and **come**. **Fetch** suggests that someone goes away to get something and comes back with it. ❏ *O'Leary went to fetch tickets and was soon back.*

Thesaurus   *take* また次を参照：

v.	grab, grasp, hold ❷ 🔳
	drive, escort, transport ❷ 🔳
	steal ❷ 🔳
	capture, seize ❷ 🔳

▶ **take after** PHRASAL VERB 句動詞 If you **take after** a member of your family, you resemble them in your appearance, your behavior, or your character. 似る [no passive] ❏ *She was a smart, brave woman. You take after her.* 彼女は賢く勇敢な女性だった。君は彼女に似ている。

▶ **take apart** PHRASAL VERB 句動詞 If you **take** something **apart**, you separate it into the different parts that it is made of. 分解する ❏ *When the clock stopped, he took it apart, found what was wrong, and put the whole thing together again.* 時計が動かなくなった時、彼はそれを分解し、故障の原因を見つけ、再び組み立てた。

▶ **take away** 🔳 PHRASAL VERB 句動詞 If you **take** something **away from** someone, you remove it from them, so that they no longer possess it or have it with them. 奪い取る ❏ *They're going to take my citizenship away.* 彼らは私の市民権を奪い取ろうとしている。 ❏ *"Give me the toy," he said softly, "or I'll take it away from you."* 「僕におもちゃをくれ」と彼は優しく言った。「そうしないと君から奪い取るから」 🔳 PHRASAL VERB 句動詞 If you **take** one number or amount **away from** another, you subtract one number from the other. 引く ❏ *Add up the bills for each month. Take this away from the income.* 毎月の請求書を合計し、これを収入から引きなさい。 🔳 PHRASAL VERB 句動詞 To **take** someone **away** means to bring them from their home to an institution such as a prison or hospital. 連れ去る ❏ *Two men claiming to be police officers went to the pastor's house and took him away.* 警官と名乗る2人の男が牧師の家に行き、彼を連れ去った。 🔳 → see also **takeaway**

▶ **take back** 🔳 PHRASAL VERB 句動詞 If you **take** something **back**, you return it to the place where you bought it or where you borrowed it from, because it is unsuitable or broken, or because you have finished with it. 返す ❏ *If I buy something and it doesn't like it I'll take it back.* 何か買って彼がそれを気に入らない場合にはそれを返すつもりだ。 🔳 PHRASAL VERB 句動詞 If you **take** something **back**, you admit that something that you said or thought is wrong. 撤回する ❏ *Take back what you said about Jeremy!* ジェレミーについて言ったことを撤回しなさい。 🔳 PHRASAL VERB 句動詞 If you **take** someone **back**, you allow them to come home again, after they have gone away because of an argument or other problem. 再び迎え入れる ❏ *Why did she take him back?* 彼女はなぜ彼を再び受け入れたのか。 🔳 PHRASAL VERB 句動詞 If you say that something **takes** you **back**, you mean that it reminds you of a period of your past life and makes you think about it again. 思い出させる ❏ *I enjoyed experimenting with colors – it took me back to being five years old.* 私は色の実験を楽しんだ。それは私に5歳の頃を思い出させた。

▶ **take down** 🔳 PHRASAL VERB 句動詞 If you **take** something **down**, you reach up and get it from a high place such as a shelf. 降ろす ❏ *Alberto took the portrait down from the wall.* アルベルトは壁から肖像画を降ろした。 🔳 PHRASAL VERB 句動詞 If you **take down** a structure, you remove each piece of it. 取り壊す ❏ *The Canadian army took down the barricades erected by the Indians.* カナダ軍はインディアンが立てたバリケードを取り壊した。 🔳 PHRASAL VERB 句動詞 If you **take down** a piece of information or a statement, you write it down. 書き留める ❏ *We've been trying to get back to you, Tom, but we think we took your number down incorrectly.* トム、私たちはあなたに折り返し連絡しようとしていたがあなたの電話番号を間違って書き留めたようだ。

▶ **take in** 🔳 PHRASAL VERB 句動詞 If you **take** someone **in**, you allow them to stay in your house or your country, especially when they do not have anywhere to stay or are in trouble. 泊める ❏ *He persuaded Jo to take him in.* 彼はジョーに彼を泊めるよう説得した。 🔳 PHRASAL VERB 句動詞 If the police **take** someone **in**, they remove them from their home in order to question them. 警察へ連行する ❏ *The police have taken him in for questioning in connection with the murder of a girl.* 警察は少女殺害に関連する尋問のために彼を警察に連行した。 🔳 PHRASAL VERB 句動詞 If you **are taken in by** someone or something, you are deceived by them, so that you get a false impression of them. だまされる ❏ *I married in my late teens and was taken in by his charm – which soon vanished.* 私は10代後半で結婚し、まもなく消えてしまった彼の魅力にだまされた。 🔳 PHRASAL VERB 句動詞 If you **take** something **in**, you pay attention to it and understand it when you hear it or read it. 理解する ❏ *Lesley explains possible treatments but you can tell she's not taking it in.* レスリーは可能な治療方法について説明するが、彼女はそれを理解していないことが分かる。 🔳 PHRASAL VERB 句動詞 If you **take** something **in**, you see all of it. 観察する ❏ *The eyes behind the lenses were dark and quick-moving, taking in everything at a glance.* レンズの後ろの目は黒っぽく早く動き、一目で全てを観察していた。 🔳 PHRASAL VERB 句動詞 If people, animals, or plants **take in** air, drink, or food, they allow it to enter their body, usually by breathing or swallowing. 取り入れる ❏ *They will certainly need to take in plenty of liquid.* 彼らは確かに大量の水分を取る必要があるだろう。 🔳 PHRASAL VERB 句動詞 If a store, restaurant, theater, or other business **takes in** a certain amount of money, they get that amount from people buying goods or services. 売上がある [mainly AM 主に米国英語] ❏ *They plan to take in $1.6 billion.* 彼らは16億ドルの売上を見込んでいる。

▶ **take off** 🔳 PHRASAL VERB 句動詞 When an airplane **takes off**, it leaves the ground and starts flying. 離陸する ❏ *We eventually took off at 11 o'clock and arrived in Juneau at 1:30.* 我々は11時にやっと離陸し、ジューノーに1時半に到着した。 🔳 PHRASAL VERB 句動詞 If something such as a product, an activity, or someone's career **takes off**, it suddenly becomes very successful. うまく行き始める ❏ *In 1944, he met Edith Piaf, and his career took off.* 1944年に彼はエディットピアフに会い、彼のキャリアはうまく行き始めた。 🔳 PHRASAL VERB 句動詞 If you **take off** or **take yourself off**, you go away, often suddenly and unexpectedly. 急いで立ち去る ❏ *He took off at once and headed back to the motel.* 彼はただちに立ち去り、モーテルに引き返した。 🔳 PHRASAL VERB 句動詞 If you **take** a garment **off**, you remove it. 脱ぐ ❏ *He wouldn't take his hat off.* 彼は帽子を脱ごうとしない。 🔳 PHRASAL VERB 句動詞 If you **take** time **off**, you obtain permission not to go to work for a short period of time. 休む ❏ *Mitchel's schedule had not permitted him to take time off.* ミッチェルはスケジュールのおかげで休暇を取ることができなかった。

▶ **take on** 🔳 PHRASAL VERB 句動詞 If you **take on** a job or responsibility, especially a difficult one, you accept it. 引き受ける ❏ *No other organization was able or willing to take on the job.* その仕事を引き受ける能力あるいは心構えのある企業は他になかった。 🔳 PHRASAL VERB 句動詞 If something **takes on** a new appearance or quality, it develops that appearance or quality. 呈する [no passive] ❏ *Believing he had only a year to live, his writing took on a feverish intensity.* 彼は後1年しか余命がないと信じ、彼の執筆は熱っぽい激しさを帯びてきた。 🔳 PHRASAL VERB 句動詞 If a vehicle such as a bus or ship **takes on** passengers, goods, or fuel, it stops in order to allow them to get on or to be loaded on. 乗せる ❏ *This is a brief stop to take on passengers and water.* これは乗客と水を乗せるための短い停車だ。 🔳 PHRASAL VERB 句動詞 If you **take** someone **on**, you employ them to do a job. 雇う ❏ *He's spoken to a publishing company. They're going to take him on.* 彼は出版会社と話をした。彼らは彼を雇う予定だ。 🔳 PHRASAL VERB 句動詞 If you **take** someone **on**, you fight them or compete against them, especially when they are bigger or more powerful than you are. 争う [no passive] ❏ *Democrats were reluctant to take on a president whose popularity ratings were historically high.* 民主党は人気度が歴史的に高い大統領と競うことに消極的だった。 🔳 PHRASAL VERB 句動詞 If you **take** something **on** or **upon yourself**, you decide to do it without asking anyone for permission or approval. 引き受ける [no passive] ❏ *Knox had taken it on himself to choose the wine.* ノックスは自らワインを選ぶ役割を引き受けていた。 ❏ *He took upon himself the responsibility for protecting her.* 彼は自ら彼女を保護する責任を引き受けた。

▶ **take out** 🔳 PHRASAL VERB 句動詞 If you **take** something **out**, you remove it permanently from its place. 取り除く ❏ *I got an abscess so he took the tooth out.* 膿瘍（のうよう）ができたので彼は歯を抜いた。 🔳 PHRASAL VERB 句動詞 If you **take out** something such as a loan, a license, or an insurance policy, you obtain it by fulfilling the conditions and paying the money that is necessary. 取る ❏ *I'll have to stop by the bank and take out a loan.* 私は銀行に行ってローンを組む必要がある。 🔳 PHRASAL VERB 句動詞 If you **take** someone **out**, they go to something such as a restaurant or theater with you after you have invited them, and usually you pay for them. 連れ出す ❏ *Jessica's grandparents took her out for the day.* ジェシカの祖父母は彼女を1日中連れ出した。 ❏ *Sophia took me out to lunch.* ソフィアは私を昼食に連れ出した。

▶ **take over** 🔳 PHRASAL VERB 句動詞 If you **take over** a company, you get control of it, for example, by buying its shares. 買収する [BUSINESS 実業] ❏ *I'm going to take over the company one day.* 私はいつかその会社を買収するつもりだ。 🔳 PHRASAL VERB 句動詞 If someone **takes over** a country or building, they get control of it by force, for example, with the help of the army. 支配する ❏ *The Belgians took over Rwanda under a League of Nations mandate.* ベルギー人は国際連盟の委任統治の下でルワンダを支配した。 🔳 PHRASAL VERB 句動詞 If

you **take over** a job or role or if you **take over**, you become responsible for the job after someone else has stopped doing it. 引き継ぐ ❑ *His widow has taken over the running of his empire, including six theaters.* 彼の未亡人は6件の劇場を含む彼の財閥の経営を引き継いだ. ❑ *In 2001, I took over from him as governing mayor.* 2001年に私は運営市長として彼を引き継いだ. ❹ PHRASAL VERB 句動詞 If one thing **takes over** from something else, it becomes more important, successful, or powerful than the other thing, and eventually replaces it. 優勢になる ❑ *Cars gradually took over from horses.* 自動車は次第に馬より優勢になった. ❺ → see also **takeover**

▶ **take to** ❶ PHRASAL VERB 句動詞 If you **take to** someone or something, you like them, especially after knowing them or thinking about them for only a short time. 好きになる ❑ *Did the children take to him?* 子供たちは彼が好きになりましたか. ❷ PHRASAL VERB 句動詞 If you **take to** doing something, you begin to do it as a regular habit. 習慣がつく ❑ *They had taken to wandering through the streets arm-in-arm.* 彼らは腕を組んで通りをぶらぶらする習慣がついていた.

▶ **take up** ❶ PHRASAL VERB 句動詞 If you **take up** an activity or a subject, you become interested in it and spend time doing it, either as a hobby or as a career. やり始める ❑ *He did not particularly want to take up a competitive sport.* 彼は特に競技をやり始めたとは思わなかった. ❷ PHRASAL VERB 句動詞 If you **take up** a question, problem, or cause, you act on it or discuss how you are going to act on it. 取り上げる ❑ *If you have a problem with the law, take it up with your legislators.* 法律について問題がある場合には、法律制定者と話し合ってください. ❑ *She had taken up the cause of a generation of American youth.* 彼女はある世代のアメリカ人の若者の運動を支持していた. ❸ PHRASAL VERB 句動詞 If you **take up** a job, you begin to work at it. 就く ❑ *He will take up his post as the head of the civil courts at the end of next month.* 彼は来月末に民事法廷の責任者としての仕事に就くことになっている. ❹ PHRASAL VERB 句動詞 If you **take up** an offer or a challenge, you accept it. 取りかかる ❑ *Increasingly, more winemakers are taking up the challenge of growing Pinot Noir.* より多くのワイン醸造者がピノ・ノワールを栽培する課題と取り組みつつある. ❺ PHRASAL VERB 句動詞 If something **takes up** a particular amount of time, space, or effort, it uses that amount. とる ❑ *I know how busy you must be and naturally I wouldn't want to take up too much of your time.* 私はあなたがどんなに多忙か知っているので多くの時間を取りたくはありません. ❑ *A good deal of my time is taken up with driving the children to soccer games.* 私の余暇の多くは子供たちをサッカーの試合に車で連れて行くことに取られる.

▶ **take upon** → see **take on** 6

take|away /teɪkəweɪ/ (**takeaways**) ❶ N-COUNT 可算名詞 A **takeaway** is a store or restaurant which sells hot cooked food that you eat somewhere else. 持ち帰り料理を売る店 [BRIT 英国英語; AM **takeout** 米国英語] ❷ N-COUNT 可算名詞 A **takeaway** is hot cooked food that you buy from a store or restaurant and eat somewhere else. 持ち帰り料理 [BRIT 英国英語; AM **takeout** 米国英語]

take-home pay N-UNCOUNT 不可算名詞 Your **take-home pay** is the amount of your wages or salary that is left after income tax and other payments have been subtracted. 手取り賃金 [BUSINESS 実業] ❑ *Her monthly take-home pay is $1,500 after taxes.* 彼女の毎月の手取り賃金は税引き後1500ドルだ.

tak|en /teɪkən/ ❶ **Taken** is the past participle of **take**. take の過去分詞形 ❷ ADJ 形容詞 If you are **taken with** something or someone, you are very interested in them or attracted to them. 気に入る [INFORMAL くだけた] [v-link ADJ] ❑ *She seems very taken with the idea.* 彼女はその考えが大変気に入ったようだ.

take|off /teɪkɔf/ (**takeoffs**) also **take-off** N-VAR 可変性名詞 **Takeoff** is the beginning of a flight, when an aircraft leaves the ground. 離陸 ❑ *What time is takeoff?* 離陸は何時ですか.

take|out /teɪkaʊt/ (**takeouts**) ❶ N-COUNT 可算名詞 A **takeout** is a store or restaurant which sells hot cooked food that you eat somewhere else. 持ち帰り用の店 [AM 米国英語] ❑ *...a Chinese takeout restaurant.* 持ち帰り用中国料理店 ❷ N-UNCOUNT 不可算名詞 **Takeout** or **takeout** food is hot cooked food which you buy from a store or restaurant and eat somewhere else. 持ち帰り用の料理 [AM 米国英語] ❑ *...a takeout pizza.* 持ち帰り用のピザ → see **restaurant**

take|over /teɪkoʊvər/ (**takeovers**) ❶ N-COUNT 可算名詞 A **takeover** is the act of gaining control of a company by buying more of its shares than anyone else. 買収 [BUSINESS 実業] ❑ *He lost his job in a corporate takeover.* 彼は企業買収で職を失った. ❷ N-COUNT 可算名詞 A **takeover** is the act of taking control of a country, political party, or movement by force. 支配 ❑ *There's been a military takeover of some kind.* ある種の軍隊の支配があった.

tak|ings /teɪkɪŋz/ N-PLURAL 複数名詞 You can use **takings** to refer to the amount of money that a business such as a store or a movie theater gets from selling its goods or tickets during a particular period. 売上高 [BUSINESS 実業] ❑ *Their takings were fifteen to twenty thousand dollars a week.* 彼らの売上高は週1万5千～2万ドルだった.

tale /teɪl/ (**tales**) ❶ N-COUNT; N-IN-NAMES 可算名詞, 名称中の名詞 A **tale** is a story, often involving magic or exciting events. 物語 ❑ *...a collection of stories, poems and folk tales.* 物語、詩、伝説のコレクション ❷ N-COUNT 可算名詞 You can refer to an interesting, exciting, or dramatic account of a real event as a **tale**. 話 ❑ *The media have been filled with tales of horror and loss resulting from Monday's earthquake.* マスコミは月曜の地震による損害の話でもちきりだった. ❸ → see also **fairy tale**

tal|ent /tælənt/ (**talents**) N-VAR 可変性名詞 **Talent** is the natural ability to do something well. 才能 ❑ *She is proud that both her children have a talent for music.* 彼女は子供が2人とも音楽の才能を持っていることを誇りにしている. ❑ *He's got lots of talent.* 彼には多くの才能がある.

Thesaurus	*talent* また次を参照:
N.	ability, aptitude, gift

Word Partnership	*talent* は次の語句と使われる:
ADJ.	**great** talent, **musical** talent, **natural** talent
V.	**have (a)** talent, **have got** talent
N.	talent **pool**, talent **search**

tal|ent|ed /tæləntɪd/ ADJ 形容詞 Someone who is **talented** has a natural ability to do something well. 才能のある ❑ *Howard is a talented pianist.* ハワードは才能のあるピアニストだ.

talk /tɔk/ (**talks, talking, talked**) ❶ V-I 自動詞 When you **talk**, you use spoken language to express your thoughts, ideas, or feelings. 話す ❑ *He was too distressed to talk.* 彼は話すことが出来ないほど悲しんでいた. ❑ *The boys all began to talk at once.* 少年たちは全員が同時に話し始めた. ● N-UNCOUNT 不可算名詞 **Talk** is also a noun. 話 ❑ *That's not the kind of talk one usually hears from accountants.* それは普通会計士から聞くような話ではなかった. ❷ V-RECIP 相互動詞 If you **talk to** someone, you have a conversation with them. You can also say that two people **talk**. しゃべる ❑ *We talked and laughed a lot.* 私たちは大いにしゃべって大いに笑った. ❑ *I talked to him yesterday.* 私は昨日彼と話をした. ❑ *When she came back, they were talking about American food.* 彼女が戻ってきた時、彼らはアメリカの食べ物について話していた. ● N-COUNT 可算名詞 **Talk** is also a noun. 会話 ❑ *We had a long talk about her father, Tony, who was a friend of mine.* 私たちは私の友人で彼女のお父さんのトニーについて長い間話し合った. ❸ V-RECIP 相互動詞 If you **talk to** someone, you tell them about the things that are worrying you. You can also say that two people **talk**. 相談する ❑ *Your first step should be to talk to a teacher or school counselor.* あなたの最初の手段は教師や学校のカウンセラーに相談することです. ❑ *Do call if you want to talk about it.* それについて相談したい場合は是非お電話ください. ● N-COUNT 可算名詞 **Talk** is also a noun. 話し合い ❑ *I think it's time we had a talk.* そろそろ話し合いをする時だと思う. ❹ V-I 自動詞 If you **talk on** or **about** something, you make an informal speech telling people what you know or think about it. 話す ❑ *She will talk on the issues she cares passionately about including education and nursery care.* 彼女は教育や保育などの大きな関心のある問題について話すことになっている. ● N-COUNT 可算名詞 **Talk** is also a noun. 話 ❑ *A guide gives a brief talk on the history of the site.* ガイドがその場所の歴史に関して簡潔な話をする. ❺ N-PLURAL 複数名詞 **Talks** are formal discussions intended to produce an agreement, usually between different countries or between employers and employees. 会議 ❑ *...the next round of Middle East peace talks.* 次の中東和平会議 ❻ V-RECIP 相互動詞 If one group of people **talks to** another, or if two groups **talk**, they have formal discussions in order to do a deal or produce an agreement. 話し合う ❑ *We're talking to some people about opening an office in Boston.* 我々はボストンに事務所を開くことについて関係者と話し合いをしているところだ. ❑ *It triggered speculation that GM and Jaguar might be talking.* それはGMとジャガーが話し合いをしているという憶測を誘発した. ❼ V-RECIP 相互動詞 When different countries or different sides in a dispute **talk**, or **talk** to each other, they discuss their differences in order to try and settle the dispute. 協議する ❑ *They are collecting information in preparation for the day when the two sides sit down and talk.* 彼らは両者が協議をする日のために情報を収集中である. ❽ V-I 自動詞 If people **are talking about** another person or **are talking**, they are discussing that person. うわさ話をする ❑ *Everyone is talking about him.* 皆が彼についてうわさ話をする. ❑ *We'd better not be seen together. People will talk.* 一緒にいるところを見られない方がいい. 人がうわさ話をするから. ● N-UNCOUNT 不可算名詞 **Talk** is also a noun. うわさ話 ❑ *There has been a lot of talk about me getting married.* 私が結婚することについて沢山うわさ話があった. ❾ V-I 自動詞 If someone **talks** when they are being held by police or soldiers, they reveal important or secret information, usually unwillingly. もらす ❑ *They'll talk, they'll implicate me.* 彼らは口を割り、私を事件に巻き込むだろう. ❿ V-T/V-I 他動詞/自動詞 If you **talk** a particular language or **talk** with a particular accent, you use that language or have that accent when you speak. しゃべる [no passive] ❑ *You don't sound like a foreigner talking English.* あな

たは英語をしゃべる外国人には聞こえない. **11** V-T 他動詞 If you **talk** something such as politics or sports, you discuss it. 話し合う [no passive] ❑ *The guests were mostly middle-aged men talking business.* 客の大半は商談をする中年男だった. **12** V-T 他動詞 You can use **talk** to say what you think of the ideas that someone is expressing. For example, if you say that someone **is talking sense**, you mean that you think the opinions they are expressing are sensible. 話す ❑ *You must admit George, you're talking absolute nonsense.* ジョージ, あなたは全くばかなことを言っていると認めているはずだ. **13** V-T 他動詞 You can say that you **are talking** a particular thing to draw attention to your topic or to point out a characteristic of what you are discussing. ❑ *We're talking megabucks this time.* 我々は今回は大金について話している. **14** N-UNCOUNT 不可算名詞 If you say that something such as an idea or threat is just **talk**, or **all talk**, you mean that it does not mean or matter much, because people are exaggerating about it or do not really intend to do anything about it. 空言 ❑ *Has much of this actually been tried here? Or is it just talk?* このうちのどれくらいが実際にここで試されたのか. それともそれは単なる空言か. **15** PHRASE 句 You can say **talk about** before mentioning a particular expression or situation, when you mean that something is a very striking or clear example of that expression or situation. とんでもない [INFORMAL くだけた, EMPHASIS 強調] ❑ *Took us quite a while to get here, didn't it? Talk about fate moving in a mysterious way!* ここに着くのにかなりの時間がかかった. 運命が神秘的な方法で動いているとはとんでもないことだ. **16** PHRASE 句 You can use the expression **talking of** to introduce a new topic that you want to discuss, and to link it to something that has already been mentioned. と言えば ❑ *I'll give a prize to the best idea. Talking of good ideas, here's one to break the ice at a wedding reception.* 最良のアイデアに賞金を与えよう. 良いアイデアと言えばほらここに結婚披露宴で座を打ち解けさせるアイデアがある. **17** to **talk shop** → see **shop**

There are some differences in the way the verbs **speak** and **talk** are used. When you **speak**, you could, for example, be addressing someone or making a speech. **Talk** is more likely to be used when you are referring to a conversation or discussion. ❑ *I talked about it with my family at dinner… Sometimes we'd talk all night.* **Talk** can also be used to emphasize the activity of saying things, rather than the words that are spoken. ❑ *She thought I talked too much.*

▶ **talk back** PHRASAL VERB 句動詞 If you **talk back** to someone in authority such as a parent or teacher, you answer them in a rude way. 口答えする. ❑ *How dare you talk back to me!* おれに向かって口答えするのか.

▶ **talk down** **1** PHRASAL VERB 句動詞 To **talk down** someone who is flying an aircraft in an emergency means to give them instructions so that they can land safely. 無線で着陸誘導をする ❑ *The pilot began to talk him down by giving instructions over the radio.* パイロットは無線で指示を与えながら着陸誘導をし始めた. **2** PHRASAL VERB 句動詞 If someone **talks down** a particular thing, they make it less interesting, valuable, or likely than it originally seemed. 軽視する ❑ *They even blame the government for talking down the nation's fourth biggest industry.* 彼らはその国第4位の産業を軽視したことに対して政府を非難すらした. ❑ *Businessmen are tired of politicians talking the economy down.* 実業家は政治家が経済を軽視しているのにうんざりしている.

▶ **talk into** PHRASAL VERB 句動詞 If you **talk** a person **into** doing something they do not want to do, especially something wrong or stupid, you persuade them to do it. 説得して行動を起こさせる ❑ *He talked me into marrying him. He also talked me into having a baby.* 彼は私に彼との結婚を説得した. 彼はまた私が子供を生むことも説得した.

▶ **talk out of** PHRASAL VERB 句動詞 If you **talk** someone **out of** doing something they want or intend to do, you persuade them not to do it. 思いとどまらせる ❑ *My mother tried to talk me out of getting a divorce.* 私の母は私が離婚するのを思いとどまらせようとした.

▶ **talk over** PHRASAL VERB 句動詞 If you **talk** something **over**, you discuss it thoroughly and honestly. 相談する ❑ *He always talked things over with his friends.* 彼はいつも事柄について友人と相談した. ❑ *We should go somewhere quiet, and talk it over.* どこか静かな場所でそれについてじっくり話し合おう.

▶ **talk through** **1** PHRASAL VERB 句動詞 If you **talk** something **through** with someone, you discuss it with them thoroughly. 徹底的に話し合う ❑ *He and I have talked through this whole tricky problem.* 私は彼とこの扱いにくい問題についてじっくり話し合った. ❑ *Now her children are grown-up and she has talked through with them what happened.* 現在は彼女の子供たちも成人し, 彼女は起こったことについて彼らとじっくり話し合った. **2** PHRASAL VERB 句動詞 If someone **talks** you **through** something that you do not know, they explain it to you carefully. 説明する ❑ *Now she must talk her sister through the process a step at a time.* 今や彼女は1回に1段階でそのプロセスを説明しなければならない.

▶ **talk up** PHRASAL VERB 句動詞 If someone **talks up** a particular thing, they make it sound more interesting, valuable, or likely than it originally seemed. 興味を引くように話す ❑ *Politicians*

accuse the media of talking up the possibility of a riot. 政治家は報道関係者が暴動の可能性を熱心に話していると非難した. ❑ *He'll be talking up his plans for the economy.* 彼は彼の経済計画を興味を引くように話す予定だ.

Thesaurus	**talk** また次を参照:
v.	chat, discuss, gossip, say, share, speak, tell; *(ant.)* listen **2**
N.	argument, conversation, dialogue, discussion, interview, negotiation; *(ant.)* silence **2** chatter, chitchat, conversation, gossip, rumor **8**

talk|a|tive /tɔːkətɪv/ ADJ 形容詞 Someone who is **talkative** talks a lot. おしゃべりな ❑ *He suddenly became very talkative, his face slightly flushed, his eyes much brighter.* 彼は突然おしゃべりになり, 顔がやや紅潮し, 目が輝いていた.

talk show (**talk shows**) also **talk-show** N-COUNT 可算名詞 A **talk show** is a television or radio show in which people talk to a host in an informal way. トークショー

tall /tɔːl/ (**taller, tallest**) **1** ADJ 形容詞 Someone or something that is **tall** has a greater height than is normal or average. 背の高い ❑ *Being tall can make you feel incredibly self-confident.* 背が高いと大きな自信を持つことができる. **2** ADJ 形容詞 You use **tall** to ask or talk about the height of someone or something. 身長のある ❑ *How tall are you?* あなたの身長はどの位ですか. **3** PHRASE 句 If something is **a tall order**, it is very difficult. できない要求 ❑ *Financing your studies may seem like a tall order, but there is plenty of help available.* 学費の資金繰りはなかなかできないことのようだが利用できる援助は沢山ある. **4** PHRASE 句 If you say that someone **walks tall**, you mean that they behave in a way that shows that they have pride in themselves and in what they are doing. 非常に自信を持つ ❑ *They shouldn't be disappointed or let their heads fall, but walk tall.* 彼らは失望したり, 頭を垂れたりせずに自分に誇りを持つべきだ.

tal|ly /tæli/ (**tallies, tallying, tallied**) **1** N-COUNT 可算名詞 A **tally** is a record of amounts or numbers which you keep changing and adding to as the activity which affects it progresses. 勘定 ❑ *They do not keep a tally of visitors to the palace, but it is very popular.* 彼らは宮殿の訪問客数を記録していないがそれは大変人気がある. **2** V-RECIP 相互動詞 If one number or statement **tallies with** another, they agree with each other or are exactly the same. You can also say that two numbers or statements **tally**. 符合する ❑ *Its own estimate of three hundred tallies with that of another survey.* 独自の推定である300は他のアンケートの推定と符合している.

tame /teɪm/ (**tames, taming, tamed, tamer, tamest**) **1** ADJ 形容詞 A **tame** animal or bird is one that is not afraid of humans. 飼いならされた ❑ *They never became tame; they would run away if you approached them.* 彼らは決して人に慣れず, 近寄ると逃げた. **2** ADJ 形容詞 If you say that something or someone is **tame**, you are criticizing them for being weak and uninteresting, rather than forceful or shocking. たいしたことのない[DISAPPROVAL 不賛成] ❑ *These ideas may seem tame today, but they were inflammatory in his time.* こうした考えは今日たいしたことないように思えるが彼の時代には扇動的だった. **3** V-T 他動詞 If someone **tames** a wild animal or bird, they train it not to be afraid of humans and to do what they say. 飼いならす ❑ *The Amazons were believed to have been the first to tame horses.* アマゾン族は馬を初めて飼いならしたと言われている.

tam|per /tæmpər/ (**tampers, tampering, tampered**) V-I 自動詞 If someone **tampers** with something, they interfere with it or try to change it when they have no right to do so. いじくる ❑ *I don't want to be accused of tampering with the evidence.* 私は証拠をみだりに変更したと非難されたくない.

tam|pon /tæmpɒn/ (**tampons**) N-COUNT 可算名詞 A **tampon** is a tube made of cotton that a woman puts inside her vagina in order to absorb blood during menstruation. タンポン

tan /tæn/ (**tans, tanning, tanned**) **1** N-SING 単数名詞 If you have a **tan**, your skin has become darker than usual because you have been in the sun. 日焼け ❑ *She is tall and blonde, with a permanent tan.* 彼女は背が高く金髪でいつも日焼けしていた. **2** V-T/V-I 他動詞/自動詞 If a part of your body **tans** or if you **tan** it, your skin becomes darker than usual because you spend a lot of time in the sun. 日焼けする ❑ *I have very pale skin that never tans.* 私の肌は色白で決して日焼けしない. ● **tanned** ADJ 形容詞 日焼けした ❑ *Their skin was tanned and glowing from their weeks at the sea.* 彼らの肌は海で数週間過ごした後, 小麦色に輝いていた.

tan|dem /tændəm/ (**tandems**) **1** N-COUNT 可算名詞 A **tandem** is a bicycle designed for two riders, on which one rider sits behind the other. 二人乗り自転車 **2** PHRASE 句 If one thing happens or is done **in tandem with** another thing, the two things happen at the same time. 相伴して ❑ *…when literature is used in tandem with textbooks.* 文学が教科書と相伴して使われる時 → see **bicycle**

t

tan|gible /tˈændʒɪbəl/ ADJ 形容詞 If something is **tangible**, it is clear enough or definite enough to be easily seen, felt, or noticed. 触知できる ❏ *There should be some tangible evidence that the economy is starting to recover.* 経済が回復するという物証があるはずだ.

tan|gle /tˈæŋgəl/ (**tangles, tangling, tangled**) **1** N-COUNT 可算名詞 A **tangle of** something is a mass of it twisted together in a messy way. もつれたもの ❏ *A tangle of wires is all that remains of the computer and phone systems.* もつれた針金のみがコンピュータと電話システムの残存物だ. **2** V-T/V-I 他動詞/自動詞 If something **is tangled** or **tangles**, it becomes twisted together in a messy way. 絡まる ❏ *Animals get tangled in fishing nets and drown.* 動物はつり網に絡まり溺死する. ❏ *Her hair tends to tangle.* 彼女の髪はもつれやすい.

tank /tˈæŋk/ (**tanks, tanking, tanked**) **1** N-COUNT 可算名詞 A **tank** is a large container for holding liquid or gas. タンク ❏ *...an empty fuel tank.* 空の燃料タンク ❏ *Two water tanks provide a total capacity of 400 liters.* 2つの水槽の総容量は400リットルだ. **2** N-COUNT 可算名詞 A **tank** is a large military vehicle that is equipped with weapons and moves along on metal tracks that are fitted over the wheels. 戦車 **3** V-I 自動詞 If something such as a stock price or a movie **tanks**, it performs very badly, for example because it loses a lot of money. 悪くなる [AM 米国英語, INFORMAL くだけた] ❏ *Tech stocks have tanked.* ハイテク銘柄は落ち込んだ. ❏ *The movie, which cost $137 million, tanked, grossing only $32 million.* 1億3700万ドルもかかった映画はヒットせず, たったの3200万ドルしか総収益を上げなかった. ❏ *His career tanked after the show left the air.* 彼のキャリアはその番組が放送されなくなってから落ち込んだ.
→ see **scuba diving**

tank|er /tˈæŋkər/ (**tankers**) **1** N-COUNT 可算名詞 A **tanker** is a very large ship used for transporting large quantities of gas or liquid, especially oil. タンカー [oft supp N, also 'by' N] ❏ *A Greek oil tanker has run aground.* ギリシャの石油輸送船が浅瀬に乗り上げた. **2** N-COUNT 可算名詞 A **tanker** is a large truck, railroad vehicle, or aircraft used for transporting large quantities of a substance. タンクローリー [usu supp N, also 'by' N] ❏ *...aerial refueling tankers.* 空中給油機
→ see **oil, ship**

tan|ta|lize /tˈæntəlaɪz/ (**tantalizes, tantalizing, tantalized**) V-T 他動詞 If someone or something **tantalizes** you, they make you feel hopeful and excited about getting what you want, usually before disappointing you by not letting you have what they appeared to offer. じらす ❏ *...the dreams of democracy that have so tantalized them.* 彼らをあれほどじらした民主主義の夢 ● **tan|ta|liz|ing** ADJ 形容詞 人の期待をかきたてる ❏ *A tantalizing aroma of roast beef fills the air.* おいしそうなローストビーフの香りが漂う.

tan|ta|mount /tˈæntəmaʊnt/ ADJ 形容詞 If you say that one thing is **tantamount to** another, more serious thing, you are emphasizing how bad, unacceptable, or unfortunate the first thing is by comparing it to the second thing. 同等の [形式ばった, EMPHASIS 強調] [v-link ADJ 'to' n/-ing] ❏ *What Bracey is saying is tantamount to heresy.* ブレーシーが言っていることはうわさに等しい.

tan|trum /tˈæntrəm/ (**tantrums**) N-COUNT 可算名詞 If a child has a **tantrum**, they lose their temper in a noisy and uncontrolled way. If you say that an adult is throwing a **tantrum**, you are criticizing them for losing their temper and acting in a childish way. かんしゃく [DISAPPROVAL 不賛成] ❏ *He immediately threw a tantrum, screaming and stomping up and down like a child.* 彼はすぐにかんしゃくを起こし, 子供のように大声で叫び, 足を踏み鳴らした. ❏ *...a temper tantrum.* かんしゃく

tap /tˈæp/ (**taps, tapping, tapped**) **1** N-COUNT 可算名詞 A **tap** is a device that controls the flow of a liquid or gas from a pipe or container, for example, on a sink or on a cask or barrel. 蛇口 [mainly BRIT 主に英国英語; AM usually **faucet** 米国英語では通常 **faucet**] **2** V-T/V-I 他動詞/自動詞 If you **tap** something, you hit it with a quick light blow or a series of quick light blows. 軽くたたく ❏ *He tapped the table nervously with his fingers.* 彼は指でテーブルを神経質そうに軽くたたいた. ❏ *Grace tapped on the bedroom door and went in.* グレースは寝室のドアを軽くたたき, 中に入った. ● N-COUNT 可算名詞 **Tap** is also a noun. 軽くたたくこと ❏ *A tap on the door interrupted him and Sally Pierce came in.* ドアをたたく音が彼を中断し, サリー・ピアースが入ってきた. **3** V-T 他動詞 If you **tap** your fingers or feet, you make a regular pattern of sound by hitting a surface lightly and repeatedly with them, especially while you are listening to music. 軽く打ち付ける ❏ *The song's so catchy it makes you bounce around the living room or tap your feet.* その歌は覚えやすくて居間を飛び跳ねたり脚を軽く打ちつけたりしたくなる. **4** V-T 他動詞 If someone **taps** your telephone, they attach a special device to the line so that they can secretly listen to your conversations. 盗聴する ❏ *The government passed laws allowing the police to tap telephones.* 政府は警察が電話を盗聴することを認める法案を可決した. ● N-COUNT 可算名詞 **Tap** is also a noun. 盗聴 ❏ *He assured us that we not*

subjected to phone taps. 彼は私たちが電話盗聴を受けないことを私たちに保証した. **5** PHRASE 句 If drinks are **on tap**, they come from a tap rather than from a bottle. すぐ注いで出せるようになった [usu v-link PHR] ❏ *Filtered water is always on tap here.* ここにはフィルターで濾（こ）した水が常備されている.

tape /tˈeɪp/ (**tapes, taping, taped**) **1** N-UNCOUNT 不可算名詞 **Tape** is a sticky strip of plastic used for sticking things together. 粘着テープ ❏ *...strong adhesive tape.* 強い粘着テープ **2** N-UNCOUNT 不可算名詞 **Tape** is a narrow plastic strip covered with a magnetic substance. It is used to record sounds, pictures, and computer information. 磁気テープ ❏ *Tape is expensive and loses sound quality every time it is copied.* 磁気テープは高価で複製するたびに音質を失う. **3** N-COUNT 可算名詞 A **tape** is a cassette or spool with magnetic tape wound around it. テープ ❏ *...a new cassette tape.* 新しいカセットテープ **4** V-T/V-I 他動詞/自動詞 If you **tape** music, sounds, or television pictures, you record them using a tape recorder or a video recorder. テープに録音する ❏ *She has just taped an interview.* 彼女はちょうどインタビューを録音したところだ. ❏ *He shouldn't be taping without the singer's permission.* 彼は歌手の許可なしで録音すべきではない. **5** V-T 他動詞 If you **tape** one thing to another, you attach it using adhesive tape. 接着テープでくっつける ❏ *I taped the base of the feather onto the velvet.* 私は接着テープで羽の下部をベルベッドに付けた. **6** N-COUNT 可算名詞 A **tape** is a ribbon that is stretched across the finishing line of a race. テープ ❏ *...the finishing tape.* 仕上げ用のテープ **7** → see also **red tape, videotape**
→ see **office**

tape meas|ure (**tape measures**) N-COUNT 可算名詞 A **tape measure** is a strip of metal, plastic, or cloth which has numbers marked on it and is used for measuring. 巻き尺

ta|per /tˈeɪpər/ (**tapers, tapering, tapered**) **1** V-T/V-I 他動詞/自動詞 If something **tapers**, or if you **taper** it, it becomes gradually thinner at one end. しだいに細くなる ❏ *Unlike other trees, it doesn't taper very much. It stays fat all the way up.* その木は他の木と違って先細にはならない. それはずっと太いままだ. ● **ta|pered** ADJ 形容詞 先細になった ❏ *...the elegantly tapered legs of the dressing-table.* 品よく先細になった化粧台の脚 **2** N-COUNT 可算名詞 A **taper** is a long, thin candle or a thin wooden strip that is used for lighting fires. 細いろうそく, (点火用の) 細長い木 ❏ *Taking up a candlestick, he touched the wick to a lighted taper.* 彼はろうそくを取って, その灯心に点火用の棒で火をつけた.

tape re|cord|er (**tape recorders**) also **tape-recorder** N-COUNT 可算名詞 A **tape recorder** is a machine used for recording and playing music, speech, or other sounds. テープレコーダー

tap|es|try /tˈæpɪstri/ (**tapestries**) N-VAR 可変性名詞 A **tapestry** is a large piece of heavy cloth with a picture woven into it using colored threads. タペストリー ❏ *He stared in wonder at the tapestries on the walls.* 彼は壁にかかったタペストリーを驚嘆して見つめた.

tar /tˈɑr/ **1** N-UNCOUNT 不可算名詞 **Tar** is a thick black sticky substance that is used especially for making roads. タール ❏ *The oil has hardened to tar.* 油は固まってタールになりました. **2** N-UNCOUNT 不可算名詞 **Tar** is one of the poisonous substances contained in tobacco. やに ❏ *...strict guidelines as to the amount of tar contained in cigarettes.* タバコに含まれるやにの量に関する厳格な指導目標.

tar|get /tˈɑrgɪt/ (**targets, targeting** or **targetting, targeted** or **targetted**) **1** N-COUNT 可算名詞 A **target** is something at which someone is aiming a weapon or other object. 標的 ❏ *The village lies beside a main road, making it an easy target for bandits.* その村は主要道路のそばにあるため, 山賊の格好の標的になっています. **2** N-COUNT 可算名詞 A **target** is a result that you are trying to achieve. 達成目標 ❏ *She's won back her place too late to achieve her target of 20 goals this season.* 彼女は自分のポジションを取り戻したが, 今シーズン20ゴールという目標を達成するには遅すぎた. **3** V-T 他動詞 To **target** a particular person or thing means to decide to attack or criticize them. 攻撃目標にする [他動詞] ❏ *Republicans targeted her*

as vulnerable in her bid for reelection this year. 共和党員は，今年再選を目指し，攻撃されやすい彼女を標的にしました。● N-COUNT 可算名詞 **Target** is also a noun. 攻撃目標 [oft N 'of/for' n] ❑ *In the past they have been the target of racist abuse.* 過去，彼らは人種差別的虐待の標的になっていた。 4 V-T 他動詞 If you **target** a particular group of people, you try to appeal to those people or affect them. 対象にする [他動詞] ❑ *The campaign will target American insurance companies.* そのキャンペーンは米国の保険会社を対象にします。● N-COUNT 可算名詞 **Target** is also a noun. 対象 ❑ *Yuppies are a prime target group for marketing strategies.* ヤッピーは市場戦略の主要対象グループだ。 5 PHRASE 句 If someone or something is **on target**, they are making good progress and are likely to achieve the result that is wanted. 正しく目標に向かって ❑ *We were still right on target for our deadline.* 我々はまだ十分締め切りに間に合うところだった。

Word Partnership *target* は次の語句と使われる:

V. **attack a** target 1
hit a target, **miss a** target 1 2
ADJ. **easy** target, **moving** target 1
intended target, **likely** target, **possible** target, **prime** target 1 – 4
N. target **practice** 1
target **date** 2
target **of criticism**, target **of an investigation** 3
target **audience**, target **group**, target **population** 4

tar|iff /tærɪf/ (**tariffs**) N-COUNT 可算名詞 A **tariff** is a tax that a government collects on goods coming into a country. 関税 [BUSINESS 実業] ❑ *America wants to eliminate tariffs on items such as electronics.* 米国は電子機器などの品目に対する関税の排除を望んでいる。

tar|mac /tɑrmæk/ 1 N-UNCOUNT 不可算名詞 商標 **Tarmac** is a material used for making road surfaces, consisting of crushed stones mixed with tar. タールマク [BRIT 英国英語, TRADEMARK] [AM usually **blacktop** 米国英語では通常 **blacktop**] 2 N-SING 単数名詞 **The tarmac** is an area with a surface made of tarmac, especially the area from which planes take off at an airport. タールマカダム舗装の道路 ❑ *Standing on the tarmac were two American planes.* タールマカダム舗装の滑走路に待機しているのはアメリカの飛行機2機だ。

tar|nish /tɑrnɪʃ/ (**tarnishes, tarnishing, tarnished**) 1 V-T 他動詞 If you say that something **tarnishes** someone's reputation or image, you mean that it causes people to have a worse opinion of them than they would otherwise have had. （名誉などを）汚す [他動詞] ❑ *The affair could tarnish the reputation of the senator.* この事件は上院議員の評判を落としかねませんでした。● **tar|nished** ADJ 形容詞 汚された ❑ *He says he wants to improve the tarnished image of his country.* 彼は，国の汚されたイメージを高めたいと言っています。 2 V-T/V-I 他動詞/自動詞 If a metal **tarnishes** or if something **tarnishes** it, it becomes stained and loses its brightness. 曇らせる [他動詞] 曇る [自動詞] ❑ *It never rusts or tarnishes.* それは決してさびたり，色あせたりしない。

tart /tɑrt/ (**tarts**) 1 N-VAR 可変性名詞 A **tart** is a shallow pastry case with a filling of food, especially sweet food. タルト ❑ *...apple tarts.* アップルタルト。 2 ADJ 形容詞 If something such as fruit is **tart**, it has a sharp taste. ピリッとする ❑ *The blackberries were too tart on their own, so we stewed them gently with some apples.* 黒イチゴはそのままでは酸っぱ過ぎるので，私たちはリンゴと一緒にとろ火で煮た。 3 ADJ 形容詞 A **tart** remark or way of speaking is sharp and unpleasant, often in a way that is a little cruel. 辛らつな ❑ *The words were more tart than she had intended.* その言葉は彼女が意図したよりも辛らつだった。 4 N-COUNT 可算名詞 If someone refers to a woman or girl as a **tart**, they are criticizing her because they think she is sexually immoral or dresses in a way that makes her look sexually immoral. 身持ちの悪い女 [INFORMAL, OFFENSIVE くだけた，無礼な，DISAPPROVAL 不賛成] ❑ *You look like a tart.* 君は売女みたいだ。

tar|tan /tɑrtᵊn/ (**tartans**) N-VAR 可変性名詞 **Tartan** is a group of designs for cloth traditionally associated with Scotland. The design is made up of lines of different widths and colors crossing each other at right angles. **Tartan** is also used to refer to cloth which has this pattern. タータン ❑ *...traditional tartan kilts.* 伝統的なタータンキルト

task /tæsk/ (**tasks, tasking, tasked**) 1 N-COUNT 可算名詞 A **task** is an activity or piece of work which you have to do, usually as part of a larger project. 仕事 ❑ *Walker had the unenviable task of breaking the bad news to Mark.* ウォーカーは，マークに悪いニュースを伝えるという気の進まない役目を引き受けた。 2 V-T 他動詞 If you **are tasked with** doing a particular activity or piece of work, someone in authority asks you to do it. 仕事を課される [他動詞] ❑ *Jen was tasked with running a charity basketball tournament.* ジェンは慈善バスケットボールトーナメントを運営する仕事を課された。

Thesaurus *task* また次を参照:

N. assignment, job, responsibility 1

Word Partnership *task* は次の語句と使われる:

V. **accomplish a** task, **assign** *someone* **a** task, **complete a** task, **face a** task, **give** *someone* **a** task, **perform a** task 1
ADJ. **complex** task, **difficult** task, **easy** task, **enormous** task, **important** task, **impossible** task, **main** task, **simple** task 1

taste /teɪst/ (**tastes, tasting, tasted**) 1 N-UNCOUNT 不可算名詞 **Taste** is one of the five senses that people have. When you have food or drink in your mouth, your sense of taste makes it possible for you to recognize what it is. 味覚 ❑ *...a keen sense of taste.* 鋭い味覚。 2 N-COUNT 可算名詞 The **taste** of something is the individual quality that it has when you put it in your mouth and that distinguishes it from other things. For example, something may have a sweet, bitter, sour, or salty taste. 味 ❑ *I like the taste of wine and enjoy trying different kinds.* 私はワインの味が好きなので，様々な種類を試すのを楽しんでいる。 3 N-SING 単数名詞 If you have a **taste** of some food or drink, you try a small amount of it in order to see what the flavor is like. 少量 ❑ *Yves sometimes gives customers a taste of a wine before they order.* イブは顧客がワインを注文する前に試飲させることがある。 4 V-I 自動詞 If food or drink **tastes of** something, it has that particular flavor, which you notice when you eat or drink it. 味がする [no cont] [自動詞] ❑ *I drank a cup of tea that tasted of diesel.* 私はディーゼルオイルのような味のするお茶を飲んだ。 ❑ *It tastes like chocolate.* それはチョコレートの味がする。 5 V-T 他動詞 If you **taste** some food or drink, you eat or drink a small amount of it in order to try its flavor, for example, to see if you like it or not. 味をみる [他動詞] ❑ *I tasted the wine the waiter had produced.* 私はウェイターが出したワインの味をみた。 6 V-T 他動詞 If you can **taste** something that you are eating or drinking, you are aware of its flavor. 味わう [no passive] [他動詞] ❑ *You can taste the green chili in the dish but it is a little sweet.* この料理は青唐辛子の風味がするが，若干甘い。 7 N-SING 単数名詞 If you have a **taste of** a particular way of life or activity, you have a brief experience of it. 経験 ❑ *This voyage was his first taste of freedom.* この旅で彼は初めて自由を経験した。 8 V-T 他動詞 If you **taste** something such as a way of life or a pleasure, you experience it for a short period of time. 経験する [no passive] [他動詞] ❑ *Once you have tasted the outdoor life in southern California, it's hard to return to Montana in winter.* 南カリフォルニアでの野外生活を一度味わうと，冬のモンタナ州には帰りたくなりますよ。 9 N-SING 単数名詞 If you have a **taste for** something, you have a liking or preference for it. 好み ❑ *That gave me a taste for reading.* それが理由で私は読書が好きになった。 10 N-UNCOUNT 不可算名詞 A person's **taste** is their choice **in** the things that they like or buy, for example, their clothes, possessions, or music. If you say that someone has good **taste**, you mean that you approve of their choices. If you say that they have bad **taste**, you disapprove of their choices. 趣味 [also N in pl] ❑ *His taste in clothes is extremely good.* 彼の服の趣味は非常によい。 11 PHRASE 句 If you say that something that is said or done is **in bad taste** or **in poor taste**, you mean that it is offensive, often because it concerns death or sex and is inappropriate for the situation. If you say that something is **in good taste**, you mean that it is not offensive and that it is appropriate for the situation. 趣味がよい，趣味が悪い ❑ *He rejects the idea that his film is in bad taste.* 彼は彼の映画は下品だという意見を拒否しています。

→ see Word Web: **taste**
→ see **sugar**

Word Partnership *taste* は次の語句と使われる:

N. **sense of** taste 1
ADJ. **bitter/salty/sour/sweet** taste 2
taste **bitter/salty/sour/sweet**, taste **good** 4
acquired taste 9
bad/good/poor taste 10
in bad/good/poor taste 11
V. **like the** taste **of** *something* 2
get a taste **of** *something* 7

taste|ful /teɪstfəl/ ADJ 形容詞 If you say that something is **tasteful**, you consider it to be attractive, elegant, and in good taste. 審美眼のある ❑ *The decor is tasteful and restrained.* 飾り付けは趣きがあり落ち着いていた。● **taste|ful|ly** ADV 副詞 趣味豊かに ❑ *...a large and tastefully decorated home.* 風雅に装飾された大きな家

taste|less /teɪstlɪs/ 1 ADJ 形容詞 If you describe something such as furniture, clothing, or the way that a house is decorated as **tasteless**, you consider it to be vulgar and unattractive. 品のない ❑ *...a house crammed with tasteless furniture.* センスの悪い家具が所

Word Web   taste

What we think of as **taste** is mostly **odor**. The sense of **smell** accounts for about 80% of the experience. We actually taste only four **sensations: sweet, salty, sour,** and **bitter**. We experience sweetness and saltiness through taste buds near the tip of the **tongue**. We sense sourness at the sides and bitterness at the back of the tongue. Saltiness is felt all over the tongue. Some people have more taste buds than others. Scientists have discovered some "supertasters" with 425 taste buds per square centimeter. Most of us have about 184 and some "nontasters" have only about 96.

狭しと置かれた家。 **2** ADJ 形容詞 If you describe something such as a remark or joke as **tasteless**, you mean that it is offensive. 卑俗な ❑ *I think that is the most vulgar and tasteless remark I have ever heard in my life.* それは私がこれまでの人生で聞いた最も野卑で低俗な発言だと思う。 **3** ADJ 形容詞 If you describe food or drink as **tasteless**, you mean that it has very little or no flavor. 味のない ❑ *The fish was mushy and tasteless.* 魚は柔らかくて、無味乾燥だった。

tasty /téɪsti/ (**tastier, tastiest**) ADJ 形容詞 If you say that food is **tasty**, you mean that it has a fairly strong and pleasant flavor which makes it good to eat. うまい ❑ *Try this tasty dish for supper with a crispy salad.* このおいしい料理にシャキッとしたサラダを添えて夕食にお試しください。

tat|tered /tǽtərd/ ADJ 形容詞 If something such as clothing or a book is **tattered**, it is damaged or torn, especially because it has been used a lot over a long period of time. ぼろぼろの ❑ *He fled wearing only a sarong and a tattered shirt.* 彼はサロンとぼろぼろのシャツのみを着て逃げました。

tat|ters /tǽtərz/ **1** N-PLURAL 複数名詞 Clothes that are **in tatters** are badly torn in several places, so that pieces can easily come off. ぼろぼろになって ❑ *His jeans were left in tatters.* 彼のジーンズはぼろぼろになって放置されていた。 **2** N-PLURAL 複数名詞 If you say that something such as a plan or a person's state of mind is **in tatters**, you are emphasizing that it is weak, has suffered a lot of damage, and is likely to fail completely. こなごなになった [EMPHASIS 強調] ❑ *The economy is in tatters.* 経済はずたずたです。

tat|too /tætú/ (**tattoos, tattooing, tattooed**) **1** N-COUNT 可算名詞 A **tattoo** is a design that is drawn on someone's skin using needles to make little holes and filling them with colored dye. 入れ墨 ❑ *On the back of his neck he has a tattoo of a cross.* 彼は首の後ろに十字架の入れ墨をしている。 **2** V-T 他動詞 If someone **tattoos** you, they give you a tattoo. 入れ墨をする ❑ *In the old days, they would paint and tattoo their bodies for ceremonies.* 昔は、彼らは儀式のために身体にボディーペインティングを施し、入れ墨をした。

taught /tɔ́t/ **Taught** is the past tense and past participle of **teach**. teachの過去・過去分詞

taunt /tɔ́nt/ (**taunts, taunting, taunted**) V-T 他動詞 If someone **taunts** you, they say unkind or insulting things to you, especially about your weaknesses or failures. あざける [他動詞] ❑ *A gang taunted a disabled man.* 暴力団は体の不自由な男をなじった。 ● N-COUNT 可算名詞 **Taunt** is also a noun. あざけり ❑ *For years they suffered racist taunts.* 彼らは何年も人種差別的な嘲罵（ちょうば）に苦しんだ。

taut /tɔ́t/ (**tauter, tautest**) **1** ADJ 形容詞 Something that is **taut** is stretched very tight. ピンと張られた ❑ *The clothes line is pulled taut and secured.* 物干し用ロープはピンとしっかり張られている。 **2** ADJ 形容詞 If someone has a **taut** expression, they look very worried and tense. 緊張した ❑ *Ben sat up quickly, his face taut and terrified.* ベンは緊張しおびえた表情で、さっと立ち上がった。

tax /tǽks/ (**taxes, taxing, taxed**) **1** N-VAR 可変性名詞 **Tax** is an amount of money that you have to pay to the government so that it can pay for public services such as road and schools. 税金 [BUSINESS 実業] ❑ *No-one enjoys paying tax.* 税金は喜んで払いたくはないものだ。 ❑ *...a pledge not to raise taxes on people below a certain income.* 特定所得以下の人々の税金は上げないという誓約 **2** V-T 他動詞 When a person or company **is taxed**, they have to pay a part of their income or profits to the government. When goods **are taxed**, a percentage of their price has to be paid to the government. 課税される [BUSINESS 実業] [他動詞] ❑ *Husband and wife may be taxed separately on their incomes.* 夫婦は各々の所得に対し別々に課税されることもある。 **3** → see also **taxing, income tax**

tax|able /tǽksəbᵊl/ ADJ 形容詞 **Taxable** income is income on which you have to pay tax. 課税できる [BUSINESS 実業] ❑ *It is worth consulting the guide to see whether your income is taxable.* あなたの所得が課税対象かどうかパンフレットを調べてみる価値はある。

taxa|tion /tækséɪʃᵊn/ **1** N-UNCOUNT 不可算名詞 **Taxation** is the system by which a government takes money from people and spends it on things such as education, health, and defense. 税制 [BUSINESS 実業] ❑ *...the proposed reforms to taxation.* 提案された税制改革 **2** N-UNCOUNT 不可算名詞 **Taxation** is the amount of money that people have to pay in taxes. 課税 [BUSINESS 実業] ❑ *The result will be higher taxation.* その結果、課税額は高くなる。

tax break (**tax breaks**) N-COUNT 可算名詞 If the government gives a **tax break** to a particular group of people or type of organisation, it reduces the amount of tax they have to pay or changes the tax system in a way that benefits them. 税制上の優遇措置 [mainly AM 主に米国英語 BUSINESS 実業] ❑ *Today they'll consider tax breaks for businesses that create jobs in inner cities.* 今日では、彼らは大都市中心部で雇用を創出する企業を対象に税制上の優遇措置を考慮します。

tax cred|it (**tax credits**) N-COUNT 可算名詞 A **tax credit** is an amount of money on which you do not have to pay tax. 税額控除 [BUSINESS 実業] ❑ *The president proposed tax credits for buying environmentally-friendly cars.* 大統領は、環境に優しい車の購入を対象とした税金の控除を提案した。

tax-deductible /tǽks dɪdʌ́ktɪbᵊl/ ADJ 形容詞 If an expense is **tax-deductible**, it can be paid out of the part of your income on which you do not pay tax, so that the amount of tax you pay is reduced. 所得税計算過程で控除できる [BUSINESS 実業] ❑ *The cost of private childcare should be made tax-deductible.* 個人保育費用は課税控除の対象とすべきだ。

tax eva|sion N-UNCOUNT 不可算名詞 **Tax evasion** is the crime of not paying the full amount of tax that you should pay. 脱税 [BUSINESS 実業] ❑ *Mr. Kozlowski was charged with tax evasion.* コズラウスキー氏は脱税の罪で告発された。

Word Link   free ≈ without : care*free*, duty-*free*, tax-*free*

tax-free ADJ 形容詞 **Tax-free** is used to describe income on which you do not have to pay tax. 免税の [BUSINESS 実業] ❑ *...a tax-free investment plan.* 無税の投資計画。

tax ha|ven (**tax havens**) N-COUNT 可算名詞 A **tax haven** is a country or place which has a low rate of tax so that people choose to live there or register companies there in order to avoid paying higher tax in their own countries. タックスヘイブン [BUSINESS 実業] ❑ *The Caribbean has become an important location for international banking because it is a tax haven.* カリビアンはタックスヘイブンであるため、国際銀行業の中心地となった。

taxi /tǽksi/ (**taxis, taxiing, taxied**) **1** N-COUNT 可算名詞 A **taxi** is a car driven by a person whose job is to take people where they want to go in return for money. タクシー [also 'by' N] ❑ *The taxi drew up in front of the Riviera Club.* タクシーはリビエラクラブの正面に止まった。 **2** V-T 他動詞/自動詞 When an aircraft **taxis** a plane somewhere, or when a pilot **taxis** a plane somewhere, it moves slowly along the ground. 飛行機が地上で自らの動力によって移動する [自動詞] 地上でみずからの動力によって移動させる [他動詞] ❑ *She gave permission to the plane to taxi into position and hold for takeoff.* 彼女は飛行機に滑走開始地点までゆっくり進み、離陸を待機する許可を与えた。

tax|ing /tǽksɪŋ/ ADJ 形容詞 A **taxing** task or problem is one that requires a lot of mental or physical effort. 苦労の多い ❑ *It's unlikely that you'll be asked to do anything too taxing.* 君があまりに面倒なことをするよう頼まれることはないだろう。

taxi stand (**taxi stands**) N-COUNT 可算名詞 A **taxi stand** is a place where taxis wait for passengers, for example, at an airport or outside a station. タクシー乗り場 [mainly AM 主に米国英語]

tax|payer /tǽkspeɪər/ (**taxpayers**) N-COUNT 可算名詞 **Taxpayers** are people who pay a percentage of their income to the government as tax. 納税者 [BUSINESS 実業] ❑ *This is not going to cost the taxpayer anything. The company will bear the costs for the delay.* これは納税者には負担をかけない。会社が遅延の費用を負担する。

tax re|lief N-UNCOUNT 不可算名詞 **Tax relief** is a reduction in the amount of tax that a person or company has to pay, for example, because of expenses associated with their business or property.

Word Web tea

If you want to **brew** a good cup of **tea**, don't use a tea bag. For the best taste, try using fresh **tea leaves**. Begin by bringing a **teakettle** of water to a full boil. Use some of the water to warm the inside of a china **teapot**. Then empty the pot and add the tea leaves. Pour in more boiling water and let the tea steep for at least five minutes. Cover the pot with a tea cozy to keep it hot. Serve the tea in thin china teacups. Add milk and sugar if you wish.

税金免除 [BUSINESS 実業] ❏ …*mortgage interest tax relief.* 住宅ローンの金利の控除

tax re|turn (**tax returns**) N-COUNT 可算名詞 A **tax return** is an official form that you fill in with details about your income and personal situation, so that the tax you owe can be calculated. 所得申告 [BUSINESS 実業]

tax year (**tax years**) N-COUNT 可算名詞 A **tax year** is a particular period of twelve months which is used by the government as a basis for calculating taxes and for organizing its finances and accounts. 会計年度 [BUSINESS 実業]

TB /ti bi/ N-UNCOUNT 不可算名詞 **TB** is an extremely serious infectious disease that affects someone's lungs and other parts of their body. **TB** is an abbreviation for **tuberculosis.** 結核

TBA also **tba** **TBA** is sometimes written in announcements to indicate that something such as the place where something will happen or the people who will take part is not yet known and will be announced at a later date. **TBA** is an abbreviation for "to be announced." to be announced ❏ *When a manufacturer could not supply requested information, we have shown TBA.* メーカーが要求された情報を提供できなかった場合、我々はTBAを表示した.

tbc also **TBC** **Tbc** is sometimes written in announcements about future events to indicate that details of the event are not yet certain and will be confirmed later. **Tbc** is an abbreviation for "to be confirmed." to be confirmed [BRIT 英国英語]

tea /ti/ (**teas**) ■ N-MASS 質量名詞 **Tea** is a drink made by adding boiling water to tea leaves or tea bags. Tea usually refers to black tea from India or China. Herbal tea is made from various plants. 茶 ❏ …*a cup of tea.* お茶一杯 ❏ *Would you like some tea?* お茶はいかがですか. ❏ …*chamomile tea.* カモミール茶 ② N-MASS 質量名詞 The chopped dried leaves of the plant that tea is made from is referred to as **tea**. 茶の葉 ❏ …*a box of tea.* 茶箱
→ see Word Web: **tea**

teach /titʃ/ (**teaches, teaching, taught**) ■ V-T 他動詞 If you **teach** someone something, you give them instructions so that they know about it or how to do it. 教える [他動詞] ❏ *She taught me fractions and counting.* 彼女は私に分数と計算を教えてくれました. ❏ *George had taught him how to ride a horse.* ジョージは彼に乗馬を教えた. ② V-T 他動詞 To **teach** someone something means to make them think, feel, or act in a new or different way. 悟らせる [他動詞] ❏ *Their daughter's death had taught him humility.* 娘の死で彼は謙遜が大事だと悟った. ❏ *He taught his followers that they could all be members of the kingdom of God.* 彼は信奉者に誰もが天国に行けると教え込んだ. ③ V-T/V-I 他動詞/自動詞 If you **teach** or **teach** a subject, you help students to learn about it by explaining it or showing them how to do it, usually as a job at a school or college. 教授する [他動詞・自動詞] ❏ *Ingrid is currently teaching mathematics at the high school.* イングリッドは現在、高校で数学を教えている. ❏ *She taught English to Japanese business people.* 彼女は日本の実業家に英語を教えた. ❏ *She has taught for 34 years.* 彼女は34年間教職に就いていた. ④ → see also **teaching** ⑤ to **teach** someone **a lesson** → see **lesson**

Thesaurus teach また次を参照：
V.   educate, school, train ■ – ③

Word Partnership teach は次の語句と使われる：
ADV. teach *someone* how ■
N.   teach *someone* a skill, teach students ■
      teach children ■ – ③
      teach *someone* a lesson ②
      teach classes, teach courses, teach English/history/ reading/science, teach school ③
V.   try to teach ■ – ③

teach|er /titʃər/ (**teachers**) N-COUNT 可算名詞 A **teacher** is a person who teaches, usually as a job at a school or similar institution. 教師 ❏ *I'm a teacher with 21 years' experience.* 私は21年の経験を持つ教師だ.

Thesaurus teacher また次を参照：
N.   educator, instructor, professor, trainer

teach|ing /titʃɪŋ/ (**teachings**) ■ N-UNCOUNT 不可算名詞 **Teaching** is the work that a teacher does in helping students to learn. 教授 ❏ *The quality of teaching in the school is excellent.* その学校の授業の質は卓越している. ② N-COUNT 可算名詞 The **teachings** of a particular person, school of thought, or religion are all the ideas and principles that they teach. 教え ❏ …*the teachings of Jesus.* キリストの教え

teak /tik/ N-UNCOUNT 不可算名詞 **Teak** is the wood of a tall tree with very hard, light-colored wood which grows in Southeast Asia. チークの木 ❏ *The door is beautifully made in solid teak.* ドアは硬いチーク材で美しく作られていた.

tea|kettle /tiketəl/ (**teakettles**) also **tea kettle** N-COUNT 可算名詞 A **teakettle** is a kettle that is used for boiling water to make tea. やかん [mainly AM 主に米国英語]
→ see **tea**

team /tim/ (**teams, teaming, teamed**) ■ N-COUNT-COLL 集合可算名詞 A **team** is a group of people who play a particular sport or game together against other similar groups of people. チーム ❏ …*a soccer team.* サッカーチーム ❏ …*the swim team.* 水泳チーム ② N-COUNT-COLL 集合可算名詞 You can refer to any group of people who work together as a **team**. グループ ❏ *Each specialist has a team of doctors under him or her.* 各専門家は直属の医師団を抱えている.
▶ **team up** PHRASAL VERB 句動詞 If you **team up with** someone, you join them in order to work together for a particular purpose. You can also say that two people or groups **team up**. 協力する ❏ *Elton teamed up with Eric Clapton to wow thousands at the rock concert.* エルトンはエリック・クラプトンと競演し、ロックコンサートで何千人ものファンを熱狂させた.

team|mate /timmeɪt/ (**teammates**) also **team-mate** N-COUNT 可算名詞 In a game or sport, your **teammates** are the other members of your team. チームメート ❏ *He was always a solid player, a hard worker, a great example to his teammates.* 彼はいつも信頼できる選手であり、努力家であり、チームメートのよき模範だった.

team|work /timwɜrk/ N-UNCOUNT 不可算名詞 **Teamwork** is the ability a group of people have to work well together. チームワーク ❏ *Today's complex buildings require close teamwork between the architect and the builders.* 今日の複雑な建物は、建築家と建設業者間の密接なチームワークを必要とする.

tea|pot /tipɒt/ (**teapots**) also **tea pot** ■ N-COUNT 可算名詞 A **teapot** is a container with a lid, a handle, and a spout, used for making and serving tea. ティーポット ② PHRASE 句 If you describe a situation as a **tempest in a teapot**, you think that a lot of fuss is being made about something that is not important. 内輪もめ [AM 米国英語] [PHR after v, v-link PHR] ❏ *For some, it may seem silly, a tempest in a teapot.* 何人かの人にとってはばかばかしい空騒ぎに見えるかもしれない.
→ see **tea**

---

tear
❶ CRYING
❷ DAMAGING OR MOVING

❶ **tear** /tɪər/ (**tears**) ■ N-COUNT 可算名詞 **Tears** are the drops of salty liquid that come out of your eyes when you are crying. 涙 ❏ *Her eyes filled with tears.* 彼女の目は涙で一杯だった. ❏ *I just broke down and wept with tears of joy.* 私は喜びの涙に泣き崩れました. ② N-PLURAL 複数名詞 You can use **tears** in expressions such as **in tears, burst into tears,** and **close to tears** to indicate that someone is crying or is almost crying. 涙 ❏ *He was in floods of tears on the phone.* 彼は電話で大泣きに泣いていた. ❏ *She burst into tears and ran from the kitchen.* 彼女はワッと泣き出して、台所から出ていった.
→ see **cut, cry**

❷ **tear** /tɛər/ (**tears, tearing, tore, torn**)
⇨ Please look at category ⑧ to see if the expression you are looking for is shown under another headword. ■ V-T/V-I 他動詞/自動詞 If you **tear** paper, cloth, or another material, or if it **tears**, you pull it into two pieces or you pull it so that a hole appears in it. 裂く [他動詞] 裂ける [自動詞] ❏ *I tore my coat on a nail.* 私は釘で自分のコートを引き裂いてしまった. ● PHRASAL VERB 句動詞 **Tear up** means the same as **tear**. 引き裂く ❏ *She tore the letter up.* 彼女は手紙をビリビリに破った. ❏ *Don't you dare tear up her ticket.* 彼女のチケットをビリビリにしようなんて考えないでね. ② N-COUNT 可算名

詞 A **tear** in paper, cloth, or another material is a hole that has been made in it. 破れ目 ❑ *I peered through a tear in the van's curtains.* 私はライトバンのカーテンの裂け目からのぞき込んだ。 **3** V-T/V-I 他動詞/自動詞 If you **tear** one of your muscles or ligaments, or if it **tears**, you injure it by accidentally moving it in the wrong way. 裂ける [自動詞] 裂く [他動詞] ❑ *He tore a muscle in his right thigh.* 彼は右脚の筋肉に裂傷を負った。 ❑ *If the muscle is stretched again it could even tear.* その筋肉をもう一回無理に使ったら、肉離れすることもありうる。 **4** V-T 他動詞 To **tear** something from somewhere means to remove it roughly and violently. 引きはがす [他動詞] ❑ *She tore the windscreen wipers from his car.* 彼女は彼の車のフロントガラスからワイパーを引きちぎった。 **5** V-I 自動詞 If a person or animal **tears at** something, they pull it violently and try to break it into pieces. 引き裂こうとする [自動詞] ❑ *Female fans fought their way past bodyguards and tore at his clothes.* 女性ファンはどうにかこうにかボディーガードを通り抜け、彼の服を引き裂こうとした。 **6** V-I 自動詞 If you **tear** somewhere, you run, drive, or move there very quickly. 猛烈な勢いで行動する [自動詞] ❑ *The door flew open and Miranda tore into the room.* ドアがバッと開き、ミランダが荒々しく部屋に入ってきた。 **7** V-T PASSIVE 受動態他動詞 If you say that a place **is torn by** particular events, you mean that unpleasant events which cause suffering and division among people are happening there. 分裂させる、悩まされる [他動詞] ❑ *...a country that has been torn by civil war and foreign invasion since its independence.* 独立以来、市民戦争と外敵の襲来に悩まされてきた国 **8** → see also **torn, wear and tear**

▶ **tear apart** **1** PHRASAL VERB 句動詞 If something **tears** people **apart**, it causes them to argue or to leave each other. 分裂させる ❑ *Her pregnancy was tearing the family apart.* 彼女の妊娠は家族をバラバラにしていた。 **2** PHRASAL VERB 句動詞 If something **tears** you **apart**, it makes you feel very upset, worried, and unhappy. 心をかき乱す ❑ *Don't think it hasn't torn me apart to be away from you.* あなたから離れて私が平気だとでも思うの。

▶ **tear away** PHRASAL VERB 句動詞 If you **tear** someone **away from** a place or activity, you force them to leave the place or doing the activity, even though they want to remain there or carry on. 無理に引き離す ❑ *He finally tore himself away from the table long enough to pour me a drink.* 彼はやっとテーブルから離れて私のグラスに飲み物を注ぎにきてくれた。

▶ **tear down** PHRASAL VERB 句動詞 If you **tear** something **down**, you destroy it or remove it completely. 破壊する ❑ *Angry Russians may have torn down the statue of Felix Dzerzhinsky.* 憤慨したロシア人たちがフェリックス・ジェルジンスキーの銅像を破壊したのかもしれません。

▶ **tear off** PHRASAL VERB 句動詞 If you **tear off** your clothes, you take them off in a rough and violent way. 衣服を大急ぎで脱ぐ ❑ *Totally exhausted, he tore his clothes off and fell into bed.* すっかり疲れ果てて、彼は衣服を大急ぎで脱いで、ベッドに倒れ込んだ。

▶ **tear up** PHRASAL VERB 句動詞 If something such as a road, railroad, or area of land **is torn up**, it is completely removed or destroyed. 引き剥がす ❑ *Dozens of miles of railroad track have been torn up.* 何マイルもの鉄道線路が引きはがされた。 **2** → see **tear ❷ 1**

tear|ful /tɪərfəl/ ADJ 形容詞 If someone is **tearful**, their face or voice shows signs that they have been crying or that they want to cry. 涙ぐんだ ❑ *She became very tearful when pressed to talk about it.* それについて話すよう問い詰められると彼女はやたらと泣き出した。

tear gas /tɪər ɡæs/ N-UNCOUNT 不可算名詞 **Tear gas** is a gas that causes your eyes to sting and fill with tears so that you cannot see. It is sometimes used by the police or army to control crowds. 催涙ガス ❑ *Police used tear gas to disperse the demonstrators.* 警察は催涙ガスを使ってデモ参加者を散り散りにしました。

tease /tiz/ (**teases, teasing, teased**) **1** V-T 他動詞 To **tease** someone means to laugh at them or make jokes about them in order to embarrass, annoy, or upset them. いじめる [他動詞] ❑ *He told her how the boys had set on him, teasing him.* 彼は、少年たちが彼をどう攻撃し、いじめたかを彼女に話した。 ❑ *He teased me mercilessly about going Hollywood.* 彼は私のハリウッド行きを情け容赦なくからかった。 ● N-COUNT 可算名詞 **Tease** is also a noun. いじめること ❑ *Calling her by her real name had always been one of his teases.* 彼女を本当の名前で呼ぶことは彼の定番のからかいの1つだった。 **2** N-COUNT 可算名詞 If you refer to someone as a **tease**, you mean that they like laughing at people or making jokes about them. からかう人 ❑ *My brother's such a tease.* 私の弟はかなりのいじめっ子だ。 **3** V-T 他動詞 If someone **teases** their hair, they separate the individual strands from each other, for example by combing it. すく [他動詞] ❑ *Her hair was teased until it stood out and around her face.* 彼女の髪は顔の周り全体に逆毛を立てて膨んでいた。 ❑ *...two women in party dresses and teased hair.* パーティー向けドレスを着て、逆毛を立てた2人の女性

Thesaurus   *tease* また次を参照:

V.   aggravate, bother, provoke **1**

tea|spoon /tispun/ (**teaspoons**) N-COUNT 可算名詞 A **teaspoon** is a small spoon used for putting sugar into tea or

coffee, and in cooking. 茶さじ ❑ *Drop the dough onto a baking sheet with a teaspoon.* 茶さじで生地をベーキングシートの上に落とす。

Word Link   techn ≈ art, skill : bio**techn**ology, **techn**ical, **techn**ician

tech|ni|cal /tɛknɪkəl/ **1** ADJ 形容詞 **Technical** means involving the sorts of machines, processes, and materials that are used in industry, transportation, and communications. 技術的な ❑ *In order to reach this limit a number of technical problems will have to be solved.* この限界に達するには、多くの技術的問題を解決しなければならない。 ● **tech|ni|cal|ly** /tɛknɪkli/ ADV 副詞 [ADV adj] 技術的に ❑ *...the largest and most technically advanced furnace company in the world.* 世界で最大で、最も技術的に進歩した加熱炉会社 **2** ADJ 形容詞 You use **technical** to describe the practical skills and methods used to do an activity such as an art, a craft, or a sport. 手法の ❑ *Their technical ability is excellent.* 彼らの手法的な能力は卓越している ● **tech|ni|cal|ly** ADV 副詞 [ADV adj] 理屈の上では ❑ *While Sade's voice isn't technically brilliant it has a quality which is unmistakable.* セイドの声は厳密にはすばらしいとはいえないが、疑う余地のない特質がある。 **3** ADJ 形容詞 **Technical** language involves using special words to describe the details of a specialized activity. 専門の ❑ *The technical term for sunburn is erythema.* 日焼けの専門用語は紅斑（はん）です。 **4** → see also **technically**

Word Partnership   *technical* は次の語句と使われる:

N.	technical **knowledge 1**
	technical **assistance**, technical **difficulties**, technical **expertise**, technical **experts**, technical **information**, technical **issues**, technical **problems**, technical **services**, technical **skills**, technical **support**, technical **training 2**
ADV.	**highly** technical **1 2**

tech|ni|cal|ity /tɛknɪkælɪti/ (**technicalities**) **1** N-PLURAL 複数名詞 The **technicalities** of a process or activity are the detailed methods used to do it or to carry it out. 専門的方法 ❑ *...the technicalities of classroom teaching.* 教室での授業の専門的方法 **2** N-COUNT 可算名詞 A **technicality** is a point, especially a legal one, that is based on a strict interpretation of the law or of a set of rules but that may seem unimportant compared to a larger issue. 専門的事 ❑ *The earlier verdict was overturned on a legal technicality.* 細かい法的専門事項により、前回の判決は覆されました。

tech|ni|cal|ly /tɛknɪkli/ **1** ADV 副詞 If something is **technically** the case, it is the case according to a strict interpretation of facts, laws, or rules, but may not be important or relevant in a particular situation. 厳密には ❑ *More than a third of workers said they called into the office while technically on vacation.* 労働者の3分の1以上が、厳密には休暇中に事務所に立ち寄ったと言った。 **2** → see also **technical**

tech|ni|cal sup|port N-UNCOUNT 不可算名詞 **Technical support** is a repair and advice service that some companies such as computer companies provide for their customers, usually by telephone, fax, or e-mail. 技術サポート ❑ *...technical support for America Online users.* アメリカ・オンラインのユーザのための技術サポート

tech|ni|cian /tɛknɪʃən/ (**technicians**) **1** N-COUNT 可算名詞 A **technician** is someone whose job involves skilled practical work with scientific equipment, for example, in a laboratory. 専門家 ❑ *...a laboratory technician.* 検査技師 **2** N-COUNT 可算名詞 A **technician** is someone who is very good at the detailed technical aspects of an activity. 技術者 ❑ *...a versatile, veteran player, a superb technician.* 多芸多才でベテランの選手、優れた技術者

tech|nique /tɛknik/ (**techniques**) **1** N-COUNT 可算名詞 A **technique** is a particular method of doing an activity, usually a method that involves practical skills. 技術 ❑ *...tests performed using a new technique.* 新しい技術を使用して行われるテスト **2** N-UNCOUNT 不可算名詞 **Technique** is skill and ability in an artistic, sporting, or other practical activity that you develop through training and practice. 技巧 ❑ *He went off to the Amsterdam Academy to improve his technique.* 彼は自分の手法を改善するためにアムステルダム・アカデミーに出発した。

tech|no|logi|cal /tɛknəlɒdʒɪkəl/ ADJ 形容詞 **Technological** means relating to or associated with technology. 技術的な [ADJ n] ❑ *...an era of very rapid technological change.* 非常に迅速な技術進歩の時代。 ● **tech|no|logi|cal|ly** /tɛknəlɒdʒɪkli/ ADV 副詞 技術的に ❑ *...technologically advanced aircraft.* 技術的に進んだ飛行機

tech|nol|ogy /tɛknɒlədʒi/ (**technologies**) N-VAR 可変性名詞 **Technology** refers to methods, systems, and devices which are the result of scientific knowledge being used for practical purposes. 科学技術 ❑ *Technology is changing fast.* 科学技術は迅速に変化している。 ❑ *They should be allowed to wait for cheaper technologies to be developed.* 彼らはより安価な生産技術が開発されるのを待つことを許可されるべきだ。

→ see Word Web: **technology**

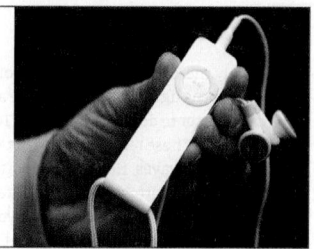

Innovative technologies affect every aspect of our lives. **State-of-the-art** computer systems coordinate heating, lighting, communication, and entertainment systems in new homes. **Gadgets** such as **digital** music players the size of a pack of gum are common. The high-tech trend also has a more serious side. **Biotechnology** may help us find cures for diseases, but it also raises many ethical questions. **Cutting-edge** biometric technology is replacing old-fashioned security systems. Soon your ATM will check your identity by scanning the iris of your eye and your laptop will scan your fingerprint.

Word Partnership   technology は次の語句と使われる:

ADJ. **advanced** technology, **available** technology, **educational** technology, **high** technology, **latest** technology, **medical** technology, **modern** technology, **new** technology, **sophisticated** technology, **wireless** technology

N. **computer** technology, **information** technology, **science and** technology

te|di|ous /tiːdiəs/ ADJ 形容詞 If you describe something such as a job, task, or situation as **tedious**, you mean it is boring and frustrating. 単調で退屈な ❑ *Such lists are long and tedious to read.* そんなリストは長くて読むのが退屈だ. ●**te|di|ous|ly** ADV 副詞 退屈するような ❑ *...the most tediously boring aspects of international relations.* 最もうんざりするほど退屈な国際関係の局面

teem /tiːm/ (teems, teeming, teemed) V-I 自動詞 If you say that a place **is teeming with** people or animals, you mean that it is crowded and the people and animals are moving around a lot. 充満している [usu cont] [自動詞] ❑ *For most of the year, the area is teeming with tourists.* 一年の大半, その地域は旅行客であふれている.

teen /tiːn/ (teens) ◼ N-PLURAL 複数名詞 If you are a **teen** in your **teens**, you are between thirteen and nineteen years old. Teen is informal for teenager. ティーンエージャー ❑ *Most people who smoke began smoking in their teens.* 喫煙者のほとんどはティーンエージャーの時に喫煙を開始している. ◻ ADJ 形容詞 **Teen** is used to describe things such as movies, magazines, bands, or activities that are aimed at or are done by people who are in their teens. ティーンエージャーの [ADJ n] ❑ *...a new teen center.* 新しいティーンエージャーセンター.

teen|age /tiːneɪdʒ/ ◼ ADJ 形容詞 **Teenage** children are aged between thirteen and nineteen years old. 13－19歳の [ADJ n] ❑ *She looked like any other teenage girl.* 彼女は典型的なティーンエージの少女のようだった. ◻ ADJ 形容詞 **Teenage** is used to describe things such as movies, magazines, bands, or activities that are aimed at or are done by teenage children. ティーンエージの [ADJ n] ❑ *"...Smash Hits," a teenage magazine.* ティーンエージマガジンの『スマッシュ・ヒッツ』

Word Link   teen ≈ plus ten, from 13-19 : eigh**teen**, seven**teen**, **teen**ager

teen|ager /tiːneɪdʒər/ (teenagers) N-COUNT 可算名詞 A **teenager** is someone who is between thirteen and nineteen years old. 13－19歳の人 ❑ *As a teenager he attended Tulse Hill Senior High School.* 彼はティーンエージャーの時, タルサヒル高等学校に通った.
→ see **age, child**

tee|ter /tiːtər/ (teeters, teetering, teetered) ◼ V-I 自動詞 **Teeter** is used in expressions such as **teeter on the brink** and **teeter on the edge** to emphasize that something seems to be in a very unstable situation or position. 動揺する [EMPHASIS 強調] [自動詞] ❑ *The hotel is teetering on the brink of bankruptcy.* そのホテルは倒産寸前にある. ◻ V-I 自動詞 If someone or something **teeters**, they shake in an unsteady way, and seem to be about to lose their balance and fall over. ぐらつく [他動詞] ❑ *Hyde shifted his weight and*

felt himself teeter forward, beginning to overbalance. ハイドは体重を移動し, バランスを失い始めて前にぐらつくのを感じた.

teeth /tiːθ/ **Teeth** is the plural of **tooth**. tooth の複数形
→ see Word Web: **teeth**
→ see **face**

tele|com|mu|ni|ca|tions /tɛlɪkəmjuːnɪkeɪʃ(ə)nz/

> The form **telecommunication** is used as a modifier.
>
> **telecommunication** 形は修飾語として使われる.

N-UNCOUNT 不可算名詞 **Telecommunications** is the technology of sending signals and messages over long distances using electronic equipment, for example, by radio and telephone. 遠距離通信 ❑ *...the telecommunications industry.* 電気通信産業

tele|com|mut|ing /tɛlɪkəmjuːtɪŋ/ N-UNCOUNT 不可算名詞 **Telecommuting** is working from home using equipment such as telephones, fax machines, and modems to contact people. テレコミューティング [BUSINESS 実業] ❑ *There is also the potential to develop telecommuting and other more flexible working practices.* テレコミューティングやそのほかの柔軟な業務慣例を展開する可能性もある.

tele|con|fer|ence /tɛlɪkɒnfərəns, -frəns/ (teleconferences) N-COUNT 可算名詞 A **teleconference** is a meeting involving people in various places around the world who use telephones or video links to communicate with each other. テレビ会議 [BUSINESS 実業] ❑ *Managers at their factory hold a two-hour teleconference with head office every day.* 工場のマネージャは毎日本店と2時間のテレビ会議を行う. ●**tele|con|fer|enc|ing** N-UNCOUNT 不可算名詞 テレビ会議 ❑ *...teleconferencing facilities.* テレビ会議設備

Word Link   gram ≈ writing : dia**gram**, pro**gram**, **tele**gram

Word Link   tele ≈ distance : **tele**gram, **tele**pathy, **tele**phone

tele|gram /tɛlɪgræm/ (telegrams) N-COUNT 可算名詞 A **telegram** is a message that is sent by telegraph and then printed and delivered to someone's home or office. 電報 [also 'by' N] ❑ *The president received a briefing by telegram.* 大統領は概況報告を電報で受け取った.

tele|mar|ket|er /tɛlɪmɑːrkɪtər/ (telemarketers) N-COUNT 可算名詞 **Telemarketers** are salespeople who are employed by a company to telephone people to persuade them to buy the company's products or services. テレマーケティングをする人 ❑ *They found that 18 million people a day were being called by telemarketers.* 彼らは1日当たり1800万人の人々が電話による販売勧誘を受けていることを発見した.

tele|mar|ket|ing /tɛlɪmɑːrkɪtɪŋ/ N-UNCOUNT 不可算名詞 **Telemarketing** is a method of selling in which someone employed by a company telephones people to try and persuade them to buy the company's products or services. テレマーケティング [BUSINESS 実業] ❑ *As postal rates go up, many businesses have been turning to telemarketing as a way of contacting new customers.* 郵便料金の値上がりに伴い, 多くの企業が新規顧客への接触方法としてテレマーケティングを利用し始めた.

tele|path|ic /tɛlɪpæθɪk/ ADJ 形容詞 If you believe that someone is **telepathic**, you believe that they have mental powers

---

Dentists suggest **brushing** and flossing every day to help prevent **cavities**. Brushing removes food from the surface of the **teeth**. Flossing helps remove the **plaque** that forms between teeth and **gums**. In many places, the water supply contains **fluoride** which also helps keep teeth healthy. If **tooth decay** does develop, a dentist can use a metal or plastic **filling** to repair the tooth. A badly damaged or broken tooth may require a **crown**. Orthodontists use **braces** to straighten uneven rows of teeth. Occasionally, a dentist must remove all of a patient's teeth. Then **dentures** take the place of natural teeth.

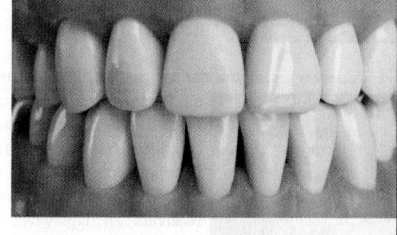

Word Web   telescope

Originally there were only two types of **telescopes**. Refracting telescopes used lenses to **focus light rays** and produce a clear **image**. **Reflecting** telescopes used a concave **mirror** to do the same thing. Today scientists use **radio telescopes** to study the **universe**. These telescopes can detect **X-rays**, gamma rays, and other types of invisible light **waves**. However, important discoveries don't always require fancy instruments. Robert Evans is an amateur **astronomer** in Australia. He has discovered more supernovas than anyone else in the world. And he uses a very simple 16-inch reflecting telescope set up in his backyard.

which cannot be explained by science, such as being able to communicate with other people's minds, and know what other people are thinking. テレパシーの ❑ *About half the subjects considered themselves to be telepathic.* 約半数の対象が自分にはテレパシーがあると考えていた.

Word Link   tele ≈ distance : telegram, telepathy, telephone

te|lep|a|thy /tɪlɛpəθi/ N-UNCOUNT 不可算名詞 If you refer to **telepathy**, you mean the direct communication of thoughts and feelings between people's minds, without the need to use speech, writing, or any other normal signals. テレパシー ❑ *You never tell me what you're thinking. Am I supposed to use telepathy?* 私は何を考えているか私に教えてくれたことがない. 私にテレパシーを使えとでもいうのか.

Word Link   phon ≈ sound : microphone, symphony, telephone

tele|phone /tɛlɪfoʊn/ (telephones, telephoning, telephoned) ■ N-UNCOUNT 不可算名詞 The **telephone** is the electrical system of communication that you use to talk directly to someone else in a different place. You use the telephone by dialing a number on a piece of equipment and speaking into it. 電話 ❑ *It's easier to reach her by telephone than by mail or email.* 彼女をつかまえるには郵便や電子メールよりも, 電話を使うほうが容易だ. ❑ *I hate to think what our telephone bill is going to be.* 電話代がいくらか考えたくない. ❷ N-COUNT 可算名詞 A **telephone** is the piece of equipment that you use when you talk to someone by telephone. 電話機 ❑ *He got up and answered the telephone.* 彼は起き上がって電話に出た. ❸ V-T/V-I 他動詞/自動詞 If you **telephone** someone, you dial their telephone number and speak to them by telephone. 電話をかける [他動詞・自動詞] ❑ *I felt so badly I had to telephone Owen to say I was sorry.* オーウェンに電話をかけて詫びなければならないのを私はとても不愉快に思った. ❑ *They usually telephone first to see if she's home.* 彼らはいつもはまず電話をかけて彼女が家にいるか確かめる. ❹ PHRASE 句 If you are **on the telephone**, you are speaking to someone by telephone. 電話口に出て ❑ *Linda remained on the telephone to the police for three hours.* リンダは3時間, 警察と話し続けた.

tele|sales /tɛlɪseɪlz/ N-UNCOUNT 不可算名詞 **Telesales** is the selling of a company's products or services by telephone, either by phoning possible customers or by answering calls from customers. 電話セールス [BUSINESS 実業] ❑ *Many people start their careers in telesales.* 多くの人が電話セールスからキャリアを始める.

Word Link   scope ≈ looking : horoscope, microscope, telescope

tele|scope /tɛlɪskoʊp/ (telescopes) N-COUNT 可算名詞 A **telescope** is a long instrument shaped like a tube. It has lenses inside it that make distant things seem larger and nearer when you look through it. 望遠鏡 ❑ *It's hoped that the telescope will enable scientists to see deeper into the universe than ever before.* 望遠鏡により, 科学者が従来にも増して宇宙のかなたを見ることができるようになることが望まれる.
→ see Word Web: **telescope**

tele|vise /tɛlɪvaɪz/ (televises, televising, televised) V-T 他動詞 If an event or program is **televised**, it is broadcast so that it can be seen on television. テレビで放映される [usu passive] ❑ *His comeback fight will be televised on network TV.* 彼のカムバックの試合はネットワークテレビで放映される.

tele|vi|sion /tɛlɪvɪʒ³n, -vɪʒ-/ (televisions) ■ N-COUNT 可算名詞 A **television** or **television set** is a piece of electrical equipment consisting of a box with a glass screen on it on which you can watch programs with pictures and sounds. テレビ受像機 ❑ *She turned the television on and flicked around between news programs.* 彼女はテレビをつけて, ニュース番組のチャンネルをカチャカチャ変えた. ❷ N-UNCOUNT 不可算名詞 **Television** is the system of sending pictures and sounds by electrical signals over a distance so that people can receive them on a television in their home. テレビジョン ❑ *Toy manufacturers began promoting some of their products on television.* 玩具メーカーは製品のいくつかをテレビで宣伝し始めた. ❸ N-UNCOUNT 不可算名詞 **Television** refers to all the programs that you can watch. テレビ番組 ❑ *I don't have much time to watch very much television.* 私にはテレビを見る時間があまりありません. ❹ N-UNCOUNT 不可算名詞 **Television** is the business or industry concerned with making programs and broadcasting them on television. テレビ放送 ❑ *I'd like a job in television.* 私はテレビ関係の仕事をしたい.
→ see Word Web: **television**
→ see **advertising**

tele|work|ing /tɛliwɜrkɪŋ/ N-UNCOUNT 不可算名詞 **Teleworking** is the same as **telecommuting**. 在宅勤務

tell /tɛl/ (tells, telling, told) ■ V-T 他動詞 If you **tell** someone something, you give them information. 告げる [他動詞] ❑ *In the evening I returned to tell Phyllis I got the job.* 私は夕方に戻り, フィリップに仕事をもらったと告げました. ❑ *I called Andie to tell her how spectacular the stuff looked.* 私はそれがどれほどすばらしく見えたかを伝えるためにアンディーに電話した. ❑ *Claire had made me promise to tell her the truth.* クレアは真実を述べることを私に約束させた. ❷ V-T 他動詞 If you **tell** something such as a joke, a story, or your personal experiences, you communicate it to other people using speech. 話す [他動詞] ❑ *His friends say he was always quick to tell a joke.* 彼の友人は, 彼はいつもすぐにジョークを言うと言っています. ❑ *He told his story to The L.A. Times and produced photographs.* 彼はその話を『L.A.タイムズ』に話し, 写真を提出した. ❸ V-T 他動詞 If you **tell** someone to do something, you order or advise them to do it. 忠告する [他動詞] ❑ *He said officers told him to get out of his car and lean against it.* 彼は, 車から出て, 車にもたれるよう警察官に命令されたと言った. ❹ V-T 他動詞 If you **tell yourself** something, you put it into words in your own mind because you want to encourage or persuade yourself about something. 言ってきかせる [他動詞] ❑ *"Come on," she told herself.* 「しっかりしろ」彼女は自分に言い聞かせた. ❺ V-T 他動詞 If you can **tell** what is happening or what is true, you are able to judge correctly what is happening or what is true. 見定める [no cont, oft with brd-neg] [他動詞] ❑ *It was already impossible to tell where the bullet had entered.* どこから銃弾が入ってきたのか今となっては知ることはできなかった. ❻ V-T 他動詞 If you can **tell** one thing **from** another, you are able to recognize the difference between it and other similar things. 識別する [no cont, oft with brd-neg] [他動詞] ❑ *I can't really tell the difference between their policies and ours.* 彼らの方針と我々の方針の違いはほとんど見分けがつかない. ❑ *How do you tell one from another?* それらをどう見分けるのですか. ❼ V-I 自動詞 If you **tell**, you reveal or give away a secret. 告げ口をする [INFORMAL くだけた] [自動詞] ❑ *Many of the*

Word Web   television

For many years, all **televisions** used cathode ray tubes to produce a picture. In the tube, a stream of **electrons** from one end strikes a **screen** at the other end. This creates tiny lighted areas called **pixels**. The average cathode ray TV screen has about 200,000 pixels. Recently, however, **high definition** TV has become very popular. Ground **stations**, **satellites**, and **cables** still supply the TV **signal**. However, high definition television creates its picture using **digital** information on a flat screen. Digital **receivers** can display two million pixels per square inch. This produces an extraordinarily clear **image**.

children know who they are but are not telling. 子供たちの多くは彼らが誰だか知っているが、教えてくれない。 **8** V-T 他動詞 If facts or events **tell** you something, they reveal certain information to you through ways other than speech. 示す [他動詞] □ *The facts tell us that this is not true.* その事実は、これが真実ではないことを私たちに物語っていた。 □ *I don't think the unemployment rate ever tells us much about the future.* 失業率が将来について多くを物語ることはないと思います。 **9** V-I 自動詞 If an unpleasant or tiring experience begins to **tell**, it begins to have a serious effect. こたえる [自動詞] □ *It wasn't long before the strain began to tell on our relationship.* 重圧が私たちの関係にものを言い出すには長くはかからなかった。 **10** → see also **telling** **11** PHRASE 句 You use **as far as I can tell** or **so far as I could tell** to indicate that what you are saying is based on the information you have, but that there may be things you do not know. いえる限りでは [VAGUENESS あいまいさ] □ *As far as I can tell, Jason is basically a nice guy.* 私が知っている限り、ジェイソンは基本的によいやつだ。 **12** CONVENTION 慣習表現 You can say "**I tell you**," "**I can tell you**," or "**I can't tell you**" to add emphasis to what you are saying. ほんとうに [INFORMAL くだけた, EMPHASIS 強調] □ *I tell you this, I will not rest until that day has come.* いいか、僕はその日が来るまで休まないぞ。 **13** CONVENTION 慣習表現 If someone disagrees with you or refuses to do what you suggest and you are eventually proved to be right, you can say "**I told you so**." それごらん [INFORMAL くだけた] □ *Her parents did not approve of her decision and, if she failed, her mother would say, "I told you so."* 彼女の両親は彼女の決断を認めなかった。もし彼女が失敗したら、母親は「それごらん」というだろう。 **14** CONVENTION 慣習表現 You use **I'll tell you what** or **I tell you what** to introduce a suggestion or a new topic of conversation. いい話があるからまあ聞け [SPOKEN 口語] □ *I tell you what, I'll bring the beer over to your house.* いいか、君の家にビールを持っていくぞ。 **15** to **tell the time** → see **time** **16** **time will tell** → see **time**

Note that the verb **tell** is usually followed by a direct object indicating the person who is being addressed. □ *He told Alison he was suffering from leukemia…What did you tell you?* is wrong. With the verb **say**, however, if you want to mention the person who is being addressed, you should use the preposition **to**. "What did she say you?" is wrong. "**What did she say to you?**" is correct. **Tell** is used to report information that is given to someone. □ *The manufacturer told me that the product did not contain corn.* **Tell** can also be used with a "to" infinitive to report an order or instruction. □ *My mother told me to shut up and eat my dinner.* **Say** is the most general verb for reporting the words that someone speaks.

▶ **tell apart** PHRASAL VERB 句動詞 If you can **tell** people or things **apart**, you are able to recognize the differences between them and can therefore identify each of them. 個々の区別をつける □ *It's easy to tell my pills apart because they're all different colors.* 私の薬は全部違う色なので容易に区別できる。

▶ **tell off** PHRASAL VERB 句動詞 If you **tell** someone **off**, you speak to them angrily or seriously because they have done something wrong. しかりつける □ *He never listened to us when we told him off.* 彼は私たちの小言をちゃんと聞いたことはなかった。 □ *I'm always being told off for being so awkward.* 私は非常に間が悪いという理由でいつもしかられる。

Thesaurus tell また次を参照:
V.	communicate, disclose, state **1** **2** advise, declare, order **3**

tell|er /tɛlər/ (**tellers**) N-COUNT 可算名詞 A **teller** is someone who works in a bank and who customers pay money to or get money from. 銀行の金銭出納係 [mainly AM OR SCOTTISH 主に米国英語、またはスコットランド方言] □ *Every bank pays close attention to the speed and accuracy of its tellers.* どの銀行も雇用している金銭出納係の速さと正確さに細心の注意を払っている。 □ *...a bank teller.* 銀行の出納係

tell|ing /tɛlɪŋ/ (**tellings**) **1** N-VAR 可変性名詞 The **telling** of a story or of something that has happened is the reporting of it to other people. 話すこと □ *Juan sat quietly through the telling of this saga.* ホアンは静かに座ってその英雄物語の語りを聞いた。 **2** ADJ 形容詞 If something is **telling**, it shows the true nature of a person or situation. □ *How a man shaves may be a telling clue to his age.* 男のひげのそり方は、年齢を明らかにする鍵となることがある。 ● **tell|ing|ly** ADV 副詞 明らかに □ *Most tellingly, perhaps, chimpanzees do not draw as much information from the world around them as we do.* 最も明らかなのは、おそらくチンパンジーは私たちほど周囲から情報を収集しないことだ。

tel|ly /tɛli/ (**tellies**) N-VAR 可変性名詞 A **telly** is a television. テレビ [BRIT 英国英語, INFORMAL くだけた] [AM TV 米国英語 TV]

temp /tɛmp/ (**temps, temping, temped**) **1** N-COUNT 可算名詞 A **temp** is a person who is employed by an agency that sends them to work in different offices for short periods of time, for example, to replace someone who is ill or on vacation. 臨時職員

[BUSINESS 実業] □ *She began working for the company as a temp.* 彼女はその企業で臨時職員として働き始めた。 **2** V-I 自動詞 If someone is **temping**, they are working as a temp. 臨時職員として働く [BUSINESS 実業] [only cont] [自動詞] □ *Like so many aspiring actresses, she ended up waiting tables and temping in office jobs.* 多くの野心ある女優と同じように、彼女も最後にはウェイトレスと臨時事務職員をすることになりました。

tem|per /tɛmpər/ (**tempers**) **1** N-VAR 可変性名詞 If you refer to someone's **temper** or say that they have a **temper**, you mean that they become angry very easily. 短気 □ *He had a temper and could be nasty.* 彼は怒りっぽくて、意地悪になることがあった。 □ *His short temper had become notorious.* 彼の短気は周知となった。 **2** N-VAR 可変性名詞 Your **temper** is the way you are feeling at a particular time. If you are in a good **temper**, you feel cheerful. If you are in a bad **temper**, you feel angry and impatient. 気分 □ *I was in a bad temper last night.* 私は昨夜不機嫌だった。 **3** PHRASE 句 If someone is in **a temper** or gets **into a temper**, the way that they are behaving shows that they are feeling angry and impatient. 腹を立てている □ *She was still in a temper when Colin arrived.* コリンが到着したとき、彼女はまだ腹を立てていた。 **4** PHRASE 句 If you **lose your temper**, you become so angry that you shout at someone or show in some other way that you are no longer in control of yourself. かんしゃくを起こす □ *I've never seen him get mad or lose his temper.* 彼が切れてかんしゃくを起こすのを私は見たことがない。

Word Partnership temper は次の語句と使われる:
ADJ.	**bad** temper, **explosive** temper, **quick** temper, **short** temper, **violent** temper **1**
N.	temper **tantrum 1**
V.	**control your** temper, **have a** temper **1** **lose your** temper **4**

tem|pera|ment /tɛmprəmənt/ (**temperaments**) **1** N-VAR 可変性名詞 Your **temperament** is your basic nature, especially as it is shown in the way that you react to situations or to other people. 気質 □ *His impulsive temperament regularly got him into difficulties.* 彼はその衝動的な気質で常にもめごとを起こした。 **2** N-UNCOUNT 不可算名詞 **Temperament** is the tendency to behave in an uncontrolled, bad-tempered, or unreasonable way. かんしゃく □ *Some of the models were given to fits of temperament.* モデルの何人かはややもすればかんしゃくの発作を起こした。

tem|pera|men|tal /tɛmprəmɛntˀl/ **1** ADJ 形容詞 If you say that someone is **temperamental**, you are criticizing them for not being calm or quiet by nature, but having moods that change often and suddenly. 気まぐれな [DISAPPROVAL 不賛成] □ *He is very temperamental and critical.* 彼は非常に神経質で、批判的だ。 **2** ADJ 形容詞 If you describe something such as a machine or car as **temperamental**, you mean that it often does not work well. 気分屋の □ *The boys couldn't start the temperamental motor.* 少年たちは気分屋のモーターを起動させることができなかった。

tem|per|ate /tɛmpərɪt, -prɪt/ ADJ 形容詞 **Temperate** is used to describe a climate or a place which is never extremely hot or extremely cold. 温和な □ *The Nile Valley keeps a temperate climate throughout the year.* ナイルバレーは一年を通して温和な気候が続く。

tem|pera|ture /tɛmprətʃər, -tʃuər/ (**temperatures**) **1** N-VAR 可変性名詞 The **temperature** of something is a measure of how hot or cold it is. 温度 □ *Winter closes in and the temperature drops below freezing.* 冬が近づくと、温度は氷点下に落ちる。 **2** N-UNCOUNT 不可算名詞 Your **temperature** is the temperature of your body. A normal temperature is about 98.6°Fahrenheit. 体温 □ *His temperature continued to rise and the cough worsened until Tania finally persuaded him to see a doctor.* 彼の体温は上がり続け、咳もひどくなったので、タニアはとうとう医者に行くよう彼を説得した。 **3** N-COUNT 可算名詞 You can use **temperature** to talk about the feelings and emotions that people have in particular situations. 心情、熱度 □ *There's also been a noticeable rise in the political temperature.* 政治熱もかなり上昇しました。 **4** PHRASE 句 If you **are running a temperature** or if you **have a temperature**, your temperature is higher than it should be. 熱を出す □ *He began to run an extremely high temperature.* 彼は非常な高熱を出し始めた。 **5** → see also **fever** **6** PHRASE 句 If you **take** someone's **temperature** you use an instrument called a thermometer to measure the temperature of their body in order to see if they are ill. 体温を計る □ *He will probably take your child's temperature too.* おそらく彼は君の子供の体温も計るだろう。

→ see **calorie, climate, cooking, forecast, greenhouse effect, refrigerator, wind**

t

In the United States, two different scales are commonly used for measuring temperature. On the **Celsius** (formerly **Centigrade**) scale, used for scientific purposes, water freezes at zero degrees and boils at 100 degrees. On the **Fahrenheit** scale, used for everyday subjects such as the weather and cooking, water freezes at 32 degrees and boils at 212 degrees. In Britain, the Celsius scale is used for most things, including the weather, but some people use the Fahrenheit scale informally.

Word Partnership   temperature は次の語句と使われる：

ADJ.	**average** temperature, **high/low** temperature, **normal** temperature 1
V.	**reach a** temperature 1
N.	**changes in/of** temperature, temperature **increase**, **ocean** temperature, **rise in** temperature, **room** temperature, **surface** temperature, **water** temperature 1 **body** temperature 2

tem|plate /tɛmplɪt/ (**templates**) 1 N-COUNT 可算名詞 A **template** is a thin piece of metal or plastic which is cut into a particular shape. It is used to help you cut wood, paper, metal, or other materials accurately, or to reproduce the same shape many times. 型板 □ *Trace around your template and transfer the design onto a sheet of card.* テンプレートの周りをなぞって、デザインをカードの上に転写しなさい。 2 N-COUNT 可算名詞 A **template** is a model of a document that you can use as a guide when creating a document of your own. テンプレート [COMPUTING コンピューティング] □ *Open any of the layout templates, insert your text, make any other changes, and print.* レイアウトテンプレートのいずれかを開き、テキストを挿入し、そのほかの変更があれば加えて印刷する。 3 N-COUNT 可算名詞 If one thing is a **template for** something else, the second thing is based on the first thing. モデル □ *The template for Adair's novel is not somebody else's fiction, but fact.* アデアの小説のモデルは誰か他の人の作り話ではなく事実だ。

tem|ple /tɛmpəl/ (**temples**) 1 N-COUNT; N-IN-NAMES 可算名詞、名称中の名詞 A **temple** is a building used for the worship of a god or gods, especially in the Buddhist, Jewish, Mormon, and Hindu religions, and in ancient Greek and Roman times. 寺院 □ *...a small Hindu temple.* 小さなヒンドゥー教寺院 □ *We go to temple on Saturdays.* 私たちは土曜日には寺院を参拝します。 2 N-COUNT 可算名詞 Your **temples** are the flat parts on each side of the front part of your head, near your forehead. こめかみ □ *Threads of silver ran through his beard and the hair at his temples.* 彼のあごひげとこめかみには白髪が何筋かあった。

tem|po /tɛmpoʊ/ (**tempos**)

Tempi can also be used as the plural form.

Tempi は複数形としても使える。

1 N-SING 単数名詞 The **tempo** of an event is the speed at which it happens. 速さ □ *...owing to the slow tempo of change in an overwhelmingly rural country.* 圧倒的な田舎における変化の速度が低いために 2 N-VAR 可変性名詞 The **tempo** of a piece of music is the speed at which it is played. テンポ □ *In a new recording, the Boston Philharmonic tried the original tempo.* 新しいレコーディングでは、ボストン・フィルハーモニックは独自のテンポを試みました。

Word Link   tempo ≈ time : contemporary, temporal, temporary

tem|po|ral /tɛmpərəl/ 1 ADJ 形容詞 **Temporal** powers or matters relate to ordinary institutions and activities rather than to religious or spiritual ones. 現世の [FORMAL 形式ばった] [ADJ n] □ *...the spiritual and temporal leader of the Tibetan people.* チベットの人々の精神的および俗事上の指導者 2 ADJ 形容詞 **Temporal** means relating to time. 時間の [FORMAL 形式ばった] [ADJ n] □ *One is also able to see how specific acts are related to a temporal and spatial context.* 特定の行動がどう時間的および空間的状況に関連しているかを理解することも可能だ。

tem|po|rary /tɛmpəreri/ ADJ 形容詞 Something that is **temporary** lasts for only a limited time. 一時の □ *His job here is only temporary.* ここでの彼の仕事は臨時のものに過ぎない。 □ *Most adolescent problems are temporary.* 青年期の問題のほとんどは一時的なものだ。 ● **tem|po|rar|i|ly** /tɛmpərɛrɪli/ ADV 副詞 一時的に □ *The peace agreement has at least temporarily halted the civil war.* 和平合意は少なくとも一時的に市民戦争を中止させました。

tempt /tɛmpt/ (**tempts, tempting, tempted**) 1 V-T 他動詞 Something that **tempts** you attracts you and makes you want it, even though it may be wrong or harmful. 誘惑する [他動詞] □ *Cars like that may tempt drivers to speed.* そのような車に乗るとドライバーはスピードを出したくなる。 □ *It is the fresh fruit that tempts me at this time of year.* この季節には新鮮な果物が私の食欲をそそる。 2 V-T 他動詞 If you **tempt** someone, you offer them something they want in order to encourage them to do what you want them to do. する

気にならせる [他動詞] □ *...a million dollar marketing campaign to tempt American tourists back to Britain.* アメリカ人観光客にイギリスを再度訪れる気にさせる百万ドルのマーケティングキャンペーン □ *Don't let credit tempt you to buy something you can't afford.* クレジットにつられて買う余裕のないものを買わせられるな。 3 → see also **tempted**

Word Link   tempt ≈ trying : attempt, temptation, tempted

temp|ta|tion /tɛmpteɪʃ°n/ (**temptations**) N-VAR 可変性名詞 If you feel you **want to** do something or have something, even though you know you really should avoid it, you can refer to this feeling as **temptation**. You can also refer to the thing you want to do or have as a **temptation**. 誘惑 □ *Will they be able to resist the temptation to buy?* 彼らは買うことの誘惑に抵抗できるでしょうか。

tempt|ed /tɛmptɪd/ ADJ 形容詞 If you say that you are **tempted to** do something, you mean that you would like to do it. したい [v-link ADJ] □ *I'm very tempted to sell my house.* 私は自分の家をどうしても売りたくなっている。

tempt|ing /tɛmptɪŋ/ ADJ 形容詞 If something is **tempting**, it makes you want to do it or have it. 誘惑する □ *In the end, I turned down Raoul's tempting offer of the Palm Beach trip.* 最終的に、私はラウルからの、誘惑的なパームビーチ旅行の提案を断った。 ● **tempt|ing|ly** ADV 副詞 誘惑的に □ *The good news is that prices are still temptingly low.* よかったのは価格はまだ誘惑的なほど低い。

ten /tɛn/ (**tens**) NUM 数詞 Ten is the number 10. 10 □ *Over the past ten years things have changed.* ここ10年で物事は変化した。

te|na|cious /tɪneɪʃəs/ ADJ 形容詞 If you are **tenacious**, you are very determined and do not give up easily. 粘り強い □ *He is regarded as a tenacious and persistent interviewer.* 彼は執拗で粘り強い面接官とみなされている。 ● **te|na|cious|ly** ADV 副詞 粘り強く □ *In spite of his illness, he clung tenaciously to his job.* 彼は病気にもかかわらず、いつまでも仕事にしがみついた。

te|nac|ity /tɪnæsɪti/ N-UNCOUNT 不可算名詞 If you have **tenacity**, you are very determined and do not give up easily. 粘り強さ □ *Talent, hard work and sheer tenacity are all crucial to career success.* 素質、努力、純然たる粘り強さすべてがキャリア上の成功の鍵を握っている。

ten|an|cy /tɛnənsi/ (**tenancies**) N-VAR 可変性名詞 **Tenancy** is the use that you have of land or property belonging to someone else, for which you pay rent. 借用 □ *His father took over the tenancy of the farm 40 years ago.* 彼の父は農場の賃借権を40年前に受け継いだ。

ten|ant /tɛnənt/ (**tenants**) N-COUNT 可算名詞 A **tenant** is someone who pays rent for the place they live in, or for land or buildings that they use. （土地や家屋などの）賃借人 □ *Regulations placed clear obligations on the landlord for the benefit of the tenant.* 規制により、賃借人の利益を守るため、地主に明確な義務が課された。

tend /tɛnd/ (**tends, tending, tended**) 1 V-T 他動詞 If something **tends to** happen, it usually happens or it often happens. しがちである [他動詞] □ *A problem for manufacturers is that lighter cars tend to be noisy.* メーカーの問題は軽量車は騒音が多い傾向にあることです。 2 V-I 自動詞 If you **tend toward** a particular characteristic, you often display that characteristic. しがちである [自動詞] □ *Artistic and intellectual people tend toward left-wing views.* 芸術家や知識人は左派の物の見方をしがちです。 3 V-T 他動詞 You can say that you **tend to** think something when you want to give your opinion, but do not want it to seem too forceful or definite. 思われる [VAGUENESS あいまいさ] [他動詞] □ *I tend to think that our Representatives by and large do a good job.* 我々の代表は概してよくやっていると思われる。

Word Partnership   tend は次の語句と使われる：

V.	tend **to avoid**, tend **to become**, tend **to develop**, tend **to forget**, tend **to happen**, tend **to lose**, tend **to stay** 1 tend **to agree**, tend **to blame**, tend **to feel**, tend **to think** 1 3
N.	**Americans** tend, **children/men/women** tend, **people** tend 1 2

ten|den|cy /tɛndənsi/ (**tendencies**) 1 N-COUNT 可算名詞 A **tendency** is a worrying or unpleasant habit or action that keeps occurring. 傾向 □ *...the government's tendency to secrecy in recent years.* 近年における政府の機密主義の傾向 2 N-COUNT 可算名詞 A **tendency** is a part of your character that makes you often behave in an unpleasant or worrying way. 性癖 □ *He is spoiled, arrogant and has a tendency toward snobbery.* 彼は甘やかされて育ち、ごうまんで、上にへつらい下に威張る性向がある。

Thesaurus   tendency また次を参照：

N.	habit, inclination, predisposition, weakness 1 2

tender

❶ ADJECTIVE USES
❷ NOUN AND VERB USES

❶ ten|der /tɛndər/ (tenderer, tenderest) **1** ADJ 形容詞 Someone or something that is **tender** expresses gentle and caring feelings. 優しい □*Her voice was tender, full of pity.* 彼女の声は優しく，哀れみにあふれていた. ●**ten|der|ly** ADV 副詞 [ADV with v] 優しく □*Mr. White tenderly embraced his wife.* ホワイト氏は妻を優しく抱きしめた. ●**ten|der|ness** N-UNCOUNT 不可算名詞 優しさ □*She smiled, politely rather than with tenderness.* 彼女は愛情を込めてというより，礼儀でほほえんだ. **2** ADJ 形容詞 [ADJ n] If you say that someone does something at a **tender** age, you mean that they do it when they are still young and have not had much experience. 若い □*He took up the game at the tender age of seven.* 彼は7歳という若さでそのゲームを始めた. **3** ADJ 形容詞 Meat or other food that is **tender** is easy to cut or chew. 柔らかい □*Cook for a minimum of 2 hours, or until the meat is tender.* 少なくとも2時間，あるいは肉が柔らかくなるまで煮る. **4** ADJ 形容詞 If part of your body is **tender**, it is sensitive and painful when it is touched. さわると痛い □*My tummy felt very tender.* 私はお腹がとても痛かった. ●**ten|der|ness** N-UNCOUNT 不可算名詞 か弱さ □*There is still some tenderness in her ankle.* 彼女の足首はさわるとまだ少し痛い.
→ see **cooking**

❷ ten|der /tɛndər/ (tenders, tendering, tendered) **1** N-VAR 可変性名詞 A **tender** is a formal offer to supply goods or to do a particular job, and a statement of the price that you or your company will charge. If a contract is **put out to tender**, formal offers are invited. If a company **wins a tender**, their offer is accepted. 入札 □*Builders will then be sent the specifications and asked to submit a tender for the work.* そして，建築業者に仕様書が送付され，その仕事に入札するよう依頼される. **2** V-I 自動詞 If a company **tenders for** something, it makes a formal offer to supply goods or do a job for a particular price. 入札する [BUSINESS 実業] [自動詞] □*The staff are forbidden to tender for private-sector work.* 職員が民間企業への仕事に入札することは禁止されている. **3** → see also **legal tender**

ten|don /tɛndən/ (tendons) N-COUNT 可算名詞 A **tendon** is a strong cord in a person's or animal's body which joins a muscle to a bone. 腱（けん）

ten|ement /tɛnəmənt/ (tenements) **1** N-COUNT 可算名詞 A **tenement** is a large, old building which is divided into a number of individual apartments. 棟割（むねわり） 長屋 **2** N-COUNT 可算名詞 A **tenement** is one of the apartments in a tenement. アパートの一区画 □*He struggled to pay the rent on his $88 a month tenement.* 彼は月88ドルの安アパートの家賃の支払いに苦労した.

ten|et /tɛnɪt/ (tenets) N-COUNT 可算名詞 The **tenets** of a theory or belief are the main principles on which it is based. 主義 [FORMAL 形式ばった] □*Non-violence and patience are the central tenets of their faith.* 非暴力と忍耐が彼らの信仰の中心的信条である.

ten|nis /tɛnɪs/ N-UNCOUNT 不可算名詞 **Tennis** is a game played by two or four players on a rectangular court. The players use an oval racket with strings across it to hit a ball over a net across the middle of the court. テニス
→ see **Picture Dictionary: tennis**
→ see **park**

ten|or /tɛnər/ (tenors) **1** N-COUNT 可算名詞 A **tenor** is a male singer whose voice is fairly high. テノール歌手 □*...a free, open-air concert given by the Italian tenor, Luciano Pavarotti.* イタリアのテノール歌手，ルチアーノ・パヴァロッティによる無料の野外コンサート **2** ADJ 形容詞 A **tenor** saxophone or other musical instrument has a range of notes that are of a fairly low pitch. テノールの □*...one of the best tenor sax players ever.* 史上最高のテナーサックス奏者の1人

tense /tɛns/ (tenser, tensest, tenses, tensing, tensed) **1** ADJ 形容詞 A **tense** situation or period of time is one that makes people anxious, because they do not know what is going to happen next. 緊張した □*This gesture of goodwill did little to improve the tense atmosphere at the talks.* この善意の印でも，会談の張り詰めた空気はほとんど和ぎませんでした. **2** ADJ 形容詞 If you are **tense**, you are anxious and nervous and cannot relax. 緊張した □*Mark, who had at first been very tense, at last relaxed.* マークは最初非常に緊張していたが，やっとくつろいだ. **3** ADJ 形容詞 If your body is **tense**, your muscles are tight and not relaxed. ピンと張った □*A bath can relax tense muscles.* お風呂はこった筋肉をほぐすことができる. **4** V-T/V-I 他動詞/自動詞 If your muscles **tense**, if you **tense**, or if you **tense** your muscles, your muscles become tight and stiff, often because you are anxious or frightened. 緊張させる [他動詞・自動詞] □*Newman's stomach muscles tensed.* ニュートンの腹筋は緊張する □*When we are under stress our bodies tend to tense up.* 我々はストレスがあるとき，体は緊張する傾向がある. **5** N-COUNT 可算名詞 The **tense** of a verb group is its form, which usually shows whether you are referring to past, present, or future time. 時制 □*It was as though Corinne was already dead: they were speaking of her in the past tense.* コリンが死んだかのように，彼らは彼女のことを過去形で話していた.

Word Partnership   *tense* は次の語句と使われる:

N.	tense **atmosphere**, tense **moment**, tense **situation** **1**
	tense **mood** **2**
	muscles tense **4**
	future/past/perfect/present tense **5**
ADV.	**very** tense **1** – **3**
V.	**feel** tense **2 3**

ten|sion /tɛnʃ°n/ (tensions) **1** N-UNCOUNT 不可算名詞 **Tension** is a feeling of worry and anxiety which makes it difficult for you to relax. 緊張 [also N in pl] □*Smiling and laughing has actually been shown to relieve tension and stress.* 笑いは緊張とストレスを和らげることが実証済みである. **2** N-UNCOUNT 不可算名詞 **Tension** is the feeling that is produced in a situation when people are anxious and do not trust each other, and when there is a possibility of sudden violence or conflict. 緊張関係 [also N in pl] □*The tension between the two countries is likely to remain.* 両国間の緊張関係は続きそうである. **3** N-VAR 可変性名詞 If there is a **tension** between forces, arguments, or influences, there are differences between them that cause difficulties. 葛藤（かっとう） □*The film explored the tension between public duty and personal affections.* その映画は社会に対する義務と個人的な愛情の間の葛藤を探求した. **4** N-UNCOUNT 不可算名詞 The **tension** in something such as a rope or wire is the extent to which it is stretched tight. 張力 □*As the cable wraps itself around the wheel, there is provision for adjusting the tension*

Picture Dictionary   tennis

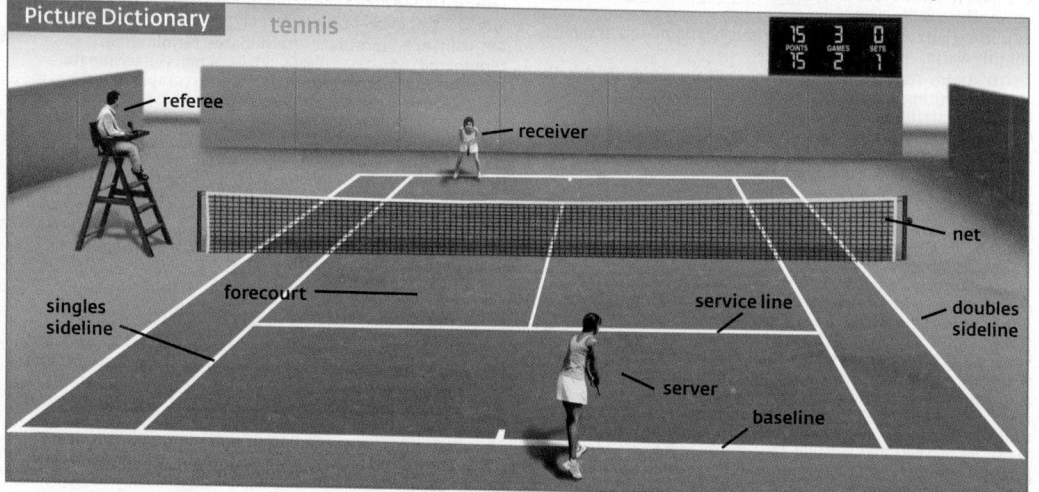

referee, receiver, net, singles sideline, forecourt, service line, doubles sideline, server, baseline

of the cable. 太綱が車輪を覆う際に太綱の張力を調整するための備えがある.

→ see **anger**

tent /tɛnt/ (**tents**) N-COUNT 可算名詞 A **tent** is a shelter made of canvas or nylon which is held up by poles and ropes, and is used mainly by people who are camping. テント

ten|ta|cle /tɛntək°l/ (**tentacles**) ❶ N-COUNT 可算名詞 The **tentacles** of an animal such as an octopus are the long thin parts that are used for feeling and holding things, for getting food, and for moving. 触手 ❷ N-COUNT 可算名詞 If you talk about the **tentacles** of a political, commercial, or social organisation, you are referring to the power and influence that it has in the outside community. 触手 [DISAPPROVAL 不賛成] ❏ *Free speech is being gradually eroded year after year by new tentacles of government control.* 発言の自由は政府支配の新しい触手によって年々むしばまれつつある.

ten|ta|tive /tɛntətɪv/ ❶ ADJ 形容詞 **Tentative** agreements, plans, or arrangements are not definite or certain, but have been made as a first step. 仮の ❏ *Political leaders have reached a tentative agreement to hold a preparatory conference next month.* 政界の指導者たちは来月準備会議を開く仮の合意に達した. ● **ten|ta|tive|ly** ADV 副詞 [ADV with v] 仮に, 暫定的に ❏ *The next round of talks is tentatively scheduled to begin October 21st in Washington.* 次の会議は10月21日にワシントンで始まることが暫定的に予定されている. ❷ ADJ 形容詞 If someone is **tentative**, they are cautious and not very confident because they are uncertain or afraid. ためらいがちな ❏ *My first attempts at complaining were kind of tentative.* 私はややためらいがちに初めて苦情を言った. ● **ten|ta|tive|ly** ADV 副詞 [ADV with v] ためらいがちに ❏ *Perhaps, he suggested tentatively, they should send for Dr. Esteves.* エスティーヴス先生を呼ぶべきだと思うと彼はためらいがちに言った.

tenth /tɛnθ/ (**tenths**) ❶ ORD 序数詞 The **tenth** item in a series is the one that you count as number ten. 10番目の ❏ *...her tenth birthday.* 彼女の10歳の誕生日 ❷ FRACTION 端数 A **tenth** is one of ten equal parts of something. 10分の1 ❏ *He finished three-tenths of a second behind Prost.* 彼はプロストに0.3秒遅れて競技を終えた.

tenu|ous /tɛnyuəs/ ADJ 形容詞 If you describe something such as a connection, a reason, or someone's position as **tenuous**, you mean that it is very uncertain or weak. 不確かな ❏ *He did not speculate on the future of his tenuous career.* 彼は不明確な彼の職業の将来について深く考えなかった.

ten|ure /tɛnyər/ ❶ N-UNCOUNT 不可算名詞 **Tenure** is the legal right to live in a particular building or to use a particular piece of land during a fixed period of time. 不動産の保有期間 ❏ *Lack of security of tenure was a reason for many families becoming homeless.* 不動産の保有期間の保証がないことが多くの家族がホームレスになる理由だった. ❷ N-UNCOUNT 不可算名詞 **Tenure** is the period of time during which someone holds an important job. 地位の保有 ❏ *...the challenges he faced during his tenure as chief executive officer.* CEOとして在職中に彼が直面した課題 ❸ N-UNCOUNT 不可算名詞 If you have **tenure** in your job, you have the right to keep it until you retire. 終身在職権

tep|id /tɛpɪd/ ADJ 形容詞 Water or another liquid that is **tepid** is slightly warm. 生ぬるい

term /tɜrm/ (**terms, terming, termed**) ❶ PHRASE 句 If you talk about something **in terms of** something or **in** particular **terms**, you are specifying which aspect of it you are discussing or from what point of view you are considering it. の点から ❏ *Our goods compete in terms of product quality, reliability and above all variety.* 当社の製品は製品の品質, 信頼性そして何よりもバラエティの点から競い合う. ❷ PHRASE 句 If you say something **in** particular **terms,** you say it using a particular type or level of language or using language which clearly shows your attitude. 言い方で ❏ *The video explains in simple terms how the new tax works.* そのビデオは新しい課税制度を分かりやすい言い方で説明している. ❸ N-COUNT 可算名詞 A **term** is a word or expression with a specific meaning, especially one which is used in relation to a particular subject. 用語 ❏ *Myocardial infarction is the medical term for a heart attack.* 心筋梗塞(こうそく)は心臓発作の医学用語である. ❹ V-T 他動詞 If you say that something **is termed** a particular thing, you mean that that is what people call it or that is their opinion of it. 呼ばれる ❏ *He had been termed a temporary employee.* 彼は臨時社員と呼ばれていた. ❺ N-VAR 可変性名詞 A **term** is one of the periods of time that a school, college, or university divides the year into. 学期 ❏ *...the summer term.* 夏季学期 ❻ N-COUNT 可算名詞 A **term** is a period of time between two elections during which a particular party or government is in power. 任期 ❏ *Nixon never completed his*

term of office. ニクソンは任期をやり遂げなかった. ❼ N-COUNT 可算名詞 A **term** is a period of time that someone spends doing a particular job or in a particular place. 勤務期間 ❏ *...a 12 month term of service.* 12か月の勤務期間 ❽ N-COUNT 可算名詞 A **term** is the period for which a legal contract or insurance policy is valid. 約定期間 ❏ *Premiums are guaranteed throughout the term of the policy.* 保険の約定期間中は保険料が保証される. ❾ N-UNCOUNT 不可算名詞 The **term** of a woman's pregnancy is the nine month period that it lasts. **Term** is also used to refer to the end of the nine month period. 出産予定日, 妊娠期間 ❏ *That makes her the first TV presenter to work the full term of her pregnancy.* それは彼女を妊娠期間中に産休を取らない最初のキャスターにする. ❿ N-PLURAL 複数名詞 The **terms** of an agreement, treaty, or other arrangement are the conditions that must be accepted by the people involved in it. 条件 ❏ *...the terms of the Helsinki agreement.* ヘルシンキ条約の条項 ⓫ PHRASE 句 If you **come to terms** with something difficult or unpleasant, you learn to accept and deal with it. 甘受する ❏ *She had come to terms with the fact that her husband would always be crippled.* 彼女は夫が一生身体障害者であるという事実を受け入れた. ⓬ PHRASE 句 If two people or groups compete **on equal terms** or **on the same terms,** neither of them has an advantage over the other. 平等な条件で ❏ *I had at last found a sport where I could compete on equal terms with able-bodied people.* 私はやっと身体的に健全な人々と平等な条件で競い合えるスポーツを見つけた. ⓭ PHRASE 句 If two people are **on good terms** or **on friendly terms,** they are friendly with each other. ～と仲の良い ❏ *Madeleine is on good terms with Sarah.* マドレーヌはセイラと仲がよい. ⓮ PHRASE 句 You use the expressions **in the long term, in the short term,** and **in the medium term** to talk about what will happen over a long period of time, over a short period of time, and over a medium period of time. 長期 (短期・中期) 的に見て ❏ *Organic fertilizers will have very positive results in the long term.* 有機肥料は長期的に見て非常に好ましい決果をもたらすだろう. ⓯ PHRASE 句 If you do something **on your terms,** you do it under conditions that you decide because you are in a position of power. 自分の思いのままに ❏ *They will sign the union treaty only on their terms.* 彼らは連合の条約を自分たちの思いのままに署名するだろう. ⓰ PHRASE 句 If you say that you **are thinking in terms of** doing a particular thing, you mean that you are considering it. ～に関して ❏ *You should be thinking in terms of graduating next year.* あなたは来年卒業することを考えて行動するべきだ. ⓱ **in no uncertain terms** → see **uncertain** ⓲ **in real terms** → see **real**

ter|mi|nal /tɜrmɪn°l/ (**terminals**) ❶ ADJ 形容詞 A **terminal** illness or disease causes death, often slowly, and cannot be cured. 不治の ❏ *...terminal cancer.* 末期的な癌(がん) ● **ter|mi|nal|ly** ADV 副詞 [ADV adj] 末期的に ❏ *The patient is terminally ill.* その患者は不治の病にかかっている. ❷ N-COUNT 可算名詞 A **terminal** is a place where vehicles, passengers, or goods begin or end a journey. ターミナル [USU supp N] ❏ *Plans are underway for a new terminal at Dulles airport.* ダラス空港で新しいターミナルを建設する案が進行中である. ❸ N-COUNT 可算名詞 A computer **terminal** is a piece of equipment consisting of a keyboard and a screen that is used for putting information into a computer or getting information from it. 端末 [COMPUTING コンピューティング] ❏ *Carl sits at a computer terminal 40 hours a week.* カールは1週間に40時間コンピュータの端末にかじりついている. ❹ N-COUNT 可算名詞 On a piece of electrical equipment, a **terminal** is one of the points where electricity enters or leaves it. 電極 ❏ *...the positive terminal of the battery.* 電池の陽極

ter|mi|nate /tɜrmɪneɪt/ (**terminates, terminating, terminated**) ❶ V-T/V-I 他動詞/自動詞 When you **terminate** something or when it **terminates**, it ends completely. 終わらせる, 終わる [FORMAL 形式ばった] ❏ *Her next remark abruptly terminated the conversation.* 彼女の次の意見はその会話を不意に終わらせた. ● **ter|mi|na|tion** /tɜrmɪneɪʃ°n/ N-UNCOUNT 不可算名詞 終結 ❏ *...a dispute which led to the abrupt termination of trade.* 貿易の突然の終結につながった紛争 ❷ V-T 他動詞 To **terminate** a pregnancy means to end it. 中絶する [MEDICAL 医学の] ❏ *After a lot of agonizing she decided to terminate the pregnancy.* 長いこと悩んだ後, 彼女は妊娠中絶することに決めた. ● **ter|mi|na|tion** (**terminations**) N-VAR 可変性名詞 妊娠中絶 ❏ *You should also have a medical check-up after the termination of a pregnancy.* あなたは妊娠中絶後に健康診断も受けるべきです. ❸ V-I 自動詞 When a train or bus **terminates** somewhere, it ends its journey there. 終点となる [FORMAL 形式ばった] ❏ *This train will terminate at Lamy.* この電車はラミーで終点となります.

ter|mi|nol|ogy /tɜrmɪnɒlədʒi/ (**terminologies**) N-VAR 可変性名詞 The **terminology** of a subject is the set of special words and expressions used in connection with it. 専門用語 ❏ *...gastritis, which in medical terminology means an inflammation of the stomach.* 医学用語の胃炎は胃の炎症を意味する.

ter|race /tɛrɪs/ (**terraces**) ❶ N-COUNT 可算名詞 A **terrace** is a flat area of stone or grass next to a building where people can sit. テラス ❏ *Some guests recline in deck chairs on the sea-facing terrace.*

一部の泊り客は海に面したテラスでデッキチェアに体を横たえる. **2** N-COUNT 可算名詞 **Terraces** are a series of flat areas built like steps on the side of a hill so that crops can be grown there. 段丘 ❏...massive terraces of corn and millet carved into the mountainside like giant steps. 巨大な階段のように山腹に刻みだされたとうもろこしとアワの巨大な段丘

ter|raced house /tɛrɪst haʊs/ (**terraced houses**) N-COUNT 可算名詞 A **terraced house** or a **terrace house** is one of a row of similar houses joined together by their side walls. テラスハウス [BRIT 英国英語]; AM **row house** 米国英語 **row house**)

terra|cotta /tɛrəkɒtə/ also **terra cotta** N-UNCOUNT 不可算名詞 **Terracotta** is a brownish-red clay that has been baked and is used for making things such as flower pots, small statues, and tiles. テラコッタ ❏...plants in terracotta pots. テラコッタの鉢の植物

| Word Link | terr ≈ earth : sub**terr**anean, **terr**ain, **terr**estrial |

ter|rain /təreɪn/ (**terrains**) N-VAR 可変性名詞 **Terrain** is used to refer to an area of land or a type of land when you are considering its physical features. 一帯の土地 ❏ The terrain changed quickly from arable land to desert. 地勢は耕地から砂漠にすばやく変化した.

ter|res|trial /tɪrɛstriəl/ **1** ADJ 形容詞 **Terrestrial** means relating to the planet Earth rather than to some other part of the universe. 地球の ❏...terrestrial life forms. 地球上の生物 **2** → see also **extraterrestrial**

ter|ri|ble /tɛrɪbəl/ **1** ADJ 形容詞 A **terrible** experience or situation is very bad or very unpleasant. ひどい ❏ Tens of thousands more suffered terrible injuries in the world's worst industrial disaster. さらに数万人の人々が世界最悪の産業大惨事でひどい負傷を負った. ❏ I often have terrible nightmares. 私はしばしばひどい悪夢を見る. ●**ter|ri|bly** ADV 副詞 [ADV after v] ひどく ❏ My son has suffered terribly. He has lost his best friend. 私の息子はひどく苦しんだ. 彼は親友を失った. **2** ADJ 形容詞 If something is **terrible**, it is very bad or of very poor quality. ひどく下手な ❏ She admits her French is terrible. 彼女はフランス語がひどく下手なことを認めている. **3** ADJ 形容詞 You use **terrible** to emphasize the great extent or degree of something. ひどい [EMPHASIS 強調] [ADJ n] ❏ I was a terrible fool, you know. 私はひどいばか者だった. ●**ter|ri|bly** ADV 副詞 ひどく ❏ I'm terribly sorry to bother you at this hour. こんな時間にお邪魔して大変ですみません.

ter|rif|ic /tərɪfɪk/ **1** ADJ 形容詞 If you describe something or someone as **terrific**, you are very pleased with them or very impressed by them. 素晴らしい [INFORMAL くだけた] ❏ What a terrific idea! 何て素晴らしいアイデアなんでしょう. **2** ADJ 形容詞 **Terrific** means very great in amount, degree, or intensity. 猛烈な [EMPHASIS 強調] [ADJ n] ❏ All of a sudden there was a terrific bang and a flash of smoke. 突然大きなドカンという音がし、煙がぱっと出た.

ter|ri|fy /tɛrɪfaɪ/ (**terrifies, terrifying, terrified**) **1** V-T 他動詞 If something **terrifies** you, it makes you feel extremely frightened. 恐れさせる ❏ Flying terrifies him. 彼は飛行機に乗るのを恐れている. ●**ter|ri|fied** ADJ 形容詞 怖がる ❏ He was terrified of heights. 彼は高所恐怖症だった. **2** → see also **terror**

ter|ri|fy|ing /tɛrɪfaɪɪŋ/ ADJ 形容詞 If something is **terrifying**, it makes you very frightened. 恐れさせる ❏ I still find it terrifying to find myself surrounded by large numbers of horses. 私は沢山の馬に取り囲まれるのがまだ怖い.

ter|ri|to|rial /tɛrɪtɔriəl/ **1** ADJ 形容詞 **Territorial** means concerned with the ownership of a particular area of land or water. 土地の ❏ It is the only republic which has no territorial disputes with the others. それは他の共和国と土地に関する紛争に巻き込まれていない唯一の共和国である. **2** ADJ 形容詞 If you describe an animal or its behavior as **territorial**, you mean that it has an area which it regards as its own, and which it defends when other animals try to enter it. 縄張り的習性を持つ ❏ Two cats or more in one house will also exhibit territorial behavior. 1軒に2匹以上の猫を飼うと縄張り的習性が見られるものである.

ter|ri|to|ry /tɛrɪtɔri/ (**territories**) **1** N-VAR 可変性名詞 **Territory** is land which is controlled by a particular country or ruler. 領土 ❏ The government denies that any of its territory is under rebel control. 政府は領土が反逆者の支配下にあることを否定している. ❏...the view that the US should use military force only when our borders or US territories are attacked. 米国は我が国の国境あるいは米国の領土が攻撃を受けた時のみ軍事力を使用すべきだという見方である. **2** N-COUNT 可算名詞 A **territory** is a country or region that is controlled by another country. 統治領 ❏ He toured some of the disputed territories now under UN control. 彼は現在国連の管理下にあり、論争の的になっている統治領の一部を視察した. **3** N-UNCOUNT 不可算名詞 You can use **territory** to refer to an area of knowledge or experience. 分野 [with supp] ❏ Following the futuristic "The Handmaid's Tale," Margaret Atwood's seventh novel, "Cat's Eye," returns to more familiar territory. 超現代的な「侍女の物語」に続き、マーガレット・アトウッドの7作目の「Cat's Eye」はおなじみの分野に戻る. ● **virgin territory** → see **virgin** **5** N-VAR 可変性名詞 An animal's **territory** is an area which it regards as its own and which it defends when other animals

try to enter it. 縄張り ❏ The territory of a cat only remains fixed for as long as the cat dominates the area. 猫の縄張りは猫がその場所を支配している間動かない. **6** N-UNCOUNT 不可算名詞 **Territory** is land with a particular character. 地方 ❏...mountainous territory. 山岳地方

Word Partnership	territory は次の語句と使われる:
N.	enemy territory, **part of** a territory **1** **2**
ADJ.	**vast** territory **1** – **4**
	controlled territory, **disputed** territory **2**
	familiar territory, **uncharted** territory **3**

ter|ror /tɛrər/ (**terrors**) **1** N-UNCOUNT 不可算名詞 **Terror** is very great fear. 恐怖 ❏ I shook with terror whenever I was about to fly in a plane. 私は飛行機に乗るたびに恐ろしさで震えた. **2** N-UNCOUNT 不可算名詞 **Terror** is violence or the threat of violence, especially when it is used for political reasons. テロ ❏...the war on terror. テロとの闘い ❏ The bomb attack on the capital could signal the start of a pre-election terror campaign. 首都の爆弾攻撃は選挙前のテロ活動の始まりを示している可能性がある. **3** N-COUNT 可算名詞 A **terror** is something that makes you very frightened. 恐怖を起こさせるもの ❏ As a boy, he had a real terror of facing people. 彼は少年の頃、人と会うのを非常に恐れていた.

Word Partnership	terror は次の語句と使われる:
N.	**acts of** terror, terror **alert**, terror **attack**, terror **campaign**, **fight against** terror, **reign of** terror, terror **suspects** **2**

ter|ror|ism /tɛrərɪzəm/ N-UNCOUNT 不可算名詞 **Terrorism** is the use of violence, especially murder and bombing, in order to achieve political goals or to force a government to do something. テロリズム [DISAPPROVAL 不賛成] ❏...the threat of global terrorism. グローバルテロリズムの脅威

ter|ror|ist /tɛrərɪst/ (**terrorists**) N-COUNT 可算名詞 A **terrorist** is a person who uses violence, especially murder and bombing, in order to achieve political aims. テロリスト [DISAPPROVAL 不賛成] ❏ One American was killed and three were wounded in terrorist attacks. テロリストの攻撃で1人のアメリカ人が死亡し、3名が負傷した.

ter|ror|ize /tɛrəraɪz/ (**terrorizes, terrorizing, terrorized**) V-T 他動詞 If someone **terrorizes** you, they keep you in a state of fear by making it seem likely that they will attack you. 恐れさせる ❏ Bands of gunmen have hijacked food shipments and terrorized relief workers. 銃を持つ一団が食料の船荷をハイジャックし、救援隊を恐怖に陥れた.

terse /tɜrs/ (**terser, tersest**) ADJ 形容詞 A **terse** statement or comment is brief and unfriendly. そっけない ❏ He issued a terse statement, saying he is discussing his future with colleagues before announcing his decision on Monday. 彼は月曜に決定事項を発表する前に同僚と将来について話し合うという手短な声明を発表した. ●**terse|ly** ADV 副詞 [ADV with v] そっけなく ❏ "It's too late," he said tersely. 「もう遅すぎる」と彼はそっけなく言った.

ter|tiary /tɜrʃiɛri/ **1** ADJ 形容詞 **Tertiary** means third in order, third in importance, or at a third stage of development. 第3の [FORMAL 形式ばった] ❏ He must have come to know those philosophers through secondary or tertiary sources. 彼は第2または第3の人たちを通してそうした哲学者を知るようになったに違いない. **2** ADJ 形容詞 **Tertiary education** is education at the university or college level. 第三次教育 [mainly BRIT 主に英国英語] [ADJ n] [AM usually **higher education** 米国英語では通常 **higher education**] → see **primary, secondary**

test /tɛst/ (**tests, testing, tested**) **1** V-T 他動詞 When you **test** something, you try it, for example, by touching it or using it for a short time, in order to find out what it is, what condition it is in, or how well it works. 試験する ❏ Either measure the temperature with a thermometer or test the water with your wrist. 温度計で水温を測るか、手首を水に入れて試してみなさい. **2** N-COUNT 可算名詞 A **test** is a deliberate action or experiment to find out how well something works. 実験 ❏...the banning of nuclear tests. 核実験の禁止 **3** V-T 他動詞 If you **test** someone, you ask them questions or tell them to perform certain actions in order to find out how much they know about a subject or how well they are able to do something. 人に試験をする ❏ There was a time when each teacher spent an hour, one day a week, testing students in every subject. 教師が1週間に1日、1時間かけて全科目で生徒を試験した時代があった. **4** N-COUNT 可算名詞 A **test** is a series of questions that you must answer or actions that you must perform in order to show how much you know about a subject or how well you are able to do something. 試験 ❏ Out of a total of 25 students only 15 passed the test. 25名の生徒のうち試験に受かったのはたった15人だった. **5** → see also **quiz** **6** V-T 他動詞 If you **test** someone, you deliberately make things difficult for them in order to see how they react. 試す ❏ From the first day, Rudolf was testing me, seeing if I would make him tea, bring him a Coke.

ルドルフは初日から私がお茶を入れ, コカ・コーラを持ってくるかどうかを知るために私を試していた. **7** N-COUNT 可算名詞 If an event or situation is a **test of** a person or thing, it reveals their qualities or effectiveness. 試金石 □ It is a fact that holidays a major test of any relationship. 休暇は人間関係の大きな試金石であることは事実だ. **8** V-T 他動詞 If you **are tested for** a particular disease or medical condition, you are examined or go through various procedures in order to find out whether you have that disease or condition. 検査を受ける [usu passive] □ My doctor wants me to be tested for diabetes. 医者は私に糖尿病の検査を受けることを勧める. **9** N-COUNT 可算名詞 A medical **test** is an examination of a part of your body in order to check that you are healthy or to find out what is wrong with you. 健康診断 □ If necessary, X-rays and blood tests will also be used to aid diagnosis. 必要であればレントゲンと血液検査も診断に使われるだろう. □ ...a pregnancy test. 妊娠テスト **10** PHRASE 句 If you **put** something **to the test**, you find out how useful or effective it is by using it. 試験する □ The team are now putting their theory to the test. そのチームは現在彼らの理論を試験中である. **11** PHRASE 句 If new circumstances or events **put** something or someone **to the test**, they put a strain on it and indicate how strong or stable it really is. 試練を与える □ Multiple hijackings are putting air traffic controllers to the test. 複数のハイジャックは航空交通管制官たちの試練となっている. **12** PHRASE 句 If you say that something **will stand the test of time**, you mean that it is strong or effective enough to last for a very long time. 時の試練に耐える □ It says a lot for her cooking skills that so many of her recipes have stood the test of time. 彼女のレシピのそれ程多くが年月が経っても好まれているのは彼女の料理技がいかに優れているかを示している. **13** to **test the waters** → see **water**

Student knowledge or skill can be measured by a **test**. If the test is not long or a significant share of the total grade, it may be called a **quiz**. An **examination** is a comprehensive test that contributes either all or a major portion of the final grade.

Word Partnership test は次の語句と使われる:

N.	test a drug, test a hypothesis **1**
	crash test, flight test, strength test, stress test **2** achievement test, aptitude test, test data/results, intelligence test, test items, math/reading test, test preparation, test scores, standardized test, test takers **4**
	blood test, drug test, HIV test, pregnancy test **7**
ADJ.	nuclear test **2**
	diagnostic test **4 8**
	test negative/positive **7**
V.	administer a test, test drive, fail a test, give someone a test, pass a test, study for a test, take a test **4**

tes|ta|ment /tɛstəmənt/ (testaments) **1** N-VAR 可変性名詞 If one thing is a **testament to** another, it shows that the other thing exists or is true. 立証 [FORMAL 形式ばった] □ For him to win the game like that is a testament to his perseverance. 彼があのように試合に勝つことは彼の粘り強さの証 (あかし) である. **2** PHRASE 句 Someone's **last will and testament** is the most recent will that they have made, especially the last will that they make before they die. 遺言書 [LEGAL 法律的]

test case (test cases) N-COUNT 可算名詞 A **test case** is a legal case which becomes an example for deciding other similar cases. テストケース □ It is considered an important test case by both advocates and opponents of gun control. それは銃砲規制の支持者と反対者の両方に重要なテストケースと考えられている.

tes|ti|cle /tɛstɪkəl/ (testicles) N-COUNT 可算名詞 A man's **testicles** are the two reproductive glands that produce sperm and are contained in the scrotum. 精巣

tes|ti|fy /tɛstɪfaɪ/ (testifies, testifying, testified) V-T/V-I 他動詞/自動詞 When someone **testifies** in a court of law, they give a statement of what they saw someone do or what they know of a situation, after having promised to tell the truth. 証言する □ Several eyewitnesses testified that they saw the officers hit Miller in the face. 数人の目撃者が警察官がミラーの顔を殴るのを見たと証言した. □ Eva testified to having seen Herndon with his gun on the stairs. エヴァはハーンドンがピストルを持っているのを階段で見たと証言した.

tes|ti|mo|nial /tɛstɪmoʊniəl/ (testimonials) **1** N-COUNT 可算名詞 A **testimonial** is a written statement about a person's character and abilities, often written by their employer. 証明書 □ She could hardly expect her employer to provide her with testimonials to her character and ability. 彼女は人格と能力の推薦状を雇用主に期待するのはまず無理だと思う. **2** N-COUNT 可算名詞 A **testimonial** is an event which is held to honor someone for their services or achievements. 感謝を表す行事 □ ...a testimonial dinner held in New York. ニューヨークで開かれる感謝ディナー

Word Link mony ≈ resulting state : cere**mony**, har**mony**, testi**mony**

tes|ti|mo|ny /tɛstɪmoʊni/ (testimonies) **1** N-VAR 可変性名詞 In a court of law, someone's **testimony** is a formal statement that they make about what they saw someone do or what they know of a situation, after having promised to tell the truth. 宣誓証言 □ His testimony was an important element of the prosecution's case. 彼の宣誓証言は検察官の申し立ての重要な要素だった. **2** N-UNCOUNT 不可算名詞 If you say that one thing is **testimony** to another, you mean that it shows clearly that the second thing has a particular quality. 証拠 [also 'a' N, usu N 'to' n] □ The environmental movement is testimony to the widespread feelings of support for nature's importance. 環境保護運動は自然の重要性が幅広く支持されていることの証拠である. → see **trial**

test|ing /tɛstɪŋ/ **1** ADJ 形容詞 A **testing** problem or situation is very difficult to deal with and shows a lot about the character of the person who is dealing with it. 最大限の努力が必要とされる □ The most testing time is undoubtedly in the early months of your return to work. 最もつらい時は確かに職場復帰後の数か月である. **2** N-UNCOUNT 不可算名詞 **Testing** is the activity of testing something or someone in order to find out information. 試験すること □ ...product testing and labelling. 製品検査とラベル張り → see **experiment**

tes|tos|ter|one /tɛstɒstəroʊn/ N-UNCOUNT 不可算名詞 **Testosterone** is a hormone found in men and male animals, which can also be produced artificially. It is thought to be responsible for the male sexual instinct and other male characteristics. テストステロン

teth|er /tɛðər/ (tethers, tethering, tethered) **1** PHRASE 句 If you say that you are **at the end of** your **tether**, you mean that you are so worried, tired, and unhappy because of your problems that you feel you cannot cope. 困り果てて □ She was jealous, humiliated, and emotionally at the end of her tether. 彼女はやきもちを焼き, 恥をかき, 感情的に我慢できない状態だった. **2** N-COUNT 可算名詞 A **tether** is a rope or chain which is used to tie an animal to a post or fence so that it can only move around within a small area. つなぎ綱 □ ...a dog that choked to death on its tether. つなぎ綱で窒息死した犬 **3** V-T 他動詞 If you **tether** an animal or object **to** something, you attach it there with a rope or chain so that it cannot move very far. つなぐ □ The officer dismounted, tethering his horse to a tree. 警官は馬から降り, 馬を木につないだ.

text /tɛkst/ (texts, texting, texted) **1** N-SING 単数名詞 The **text** of a book is the main part of it, rather than the introduction, pictures, or notes. 本文 □ The text was informative and well written. 本文は有益でうまく書かれていた. **2** N-UNCOUNT 不可算名詞 **Text** is any written material. 文章 □ The machine can recognize handwritten characters and turn them into printed text. 機械は手書きの文字を認識し, それらを印刷文章に変えることができる. **3** N-COUNT 可算名詞 The **text** of a speech, broadcast, or recording is the written version of it. 原文 □ The text of his recent speech was circulated among leading republicans. 彼の最近のスピーチの原文は主要な共和党員の間で回覧されていた. **4** N-COUNT 可算名詞 A **text** is a book or other piece of writing, especially one connected with science or learning. 原本 □ Her text is believed to be the oldest surviving manuscript by a female physician. 彼女の原本は女医による手稿の最古のものだと言われている. **5** N-COUNT 可算名詞 A **text** is the same as a **text message**. テキストメッセージ □ The new system can send a text to a cellphone, or to another landline phone. 新しいシステムでは携帯電話または固定電話にテキストメッセージを送ることができる. **6** V-T 他動詞 If you **text** someone, you send them a text message on a cellphone. テキストメッセージを送る □ Mary texted me when she got home. メアリーは帰宅してから私にテキストメッセージを送った. → see **diary**

text|book /tɛkstbʊk/ (textbooks) also text book **1** N-COUNT 可算名詞 A **textbook** is a book containing facts about a particular subject that is used by people studying that subject. 教科書 □ She wrote a textbook on international law. 彼女は国際法の教科書を書いた. **2** ADJ 形容詞 If you say that something is a **textbook** case or example, you are emphasizing that it provides a clear example of a type of situation or event. 典型的な [EMPHASIS 強調] [ADJ n] □ The house is a textbook example of medieval domestic architecture. その家は中世の住宅建築の典型的な例である.

tex|tile /tɛkstaɪl/ (textiles) **1** N-COUNT 可算名詞 **Textiles** are types of cloth or fabric, especially ones that have been woven. 織物 □ ...decorative textiles for the home. 家庭用の装飾的な織物 **2** N-PLURAL 複数名詞 **Textiles** are the industries concerned with the manufacture of cloth. 織物業界 [no det] □ Another 75,000 jobs will be lost in textiles and clothing. 織物・衣料業界でもう75000の職が失われるだろう. → see **cotton, industry, quilt**

text|ing /tɛkstɪŋ/ N-UNCOUNT 不可算名詞 **Texting** is the same as **text messaging**. テキストメッセージを送ること

text mes|sage (text messages) N-COUNT 可算名詞 A **text message** is a message that you send using a cellphone. テキストメッセージ □ *She has sent text messages to her family telling them not to worry.* 彼女は家族に心配しないよう告げるためにテキストメッセージを送った.

text mes|sag|ing N-UNCOUNT 不可算名詞 **Text messaging** is the sending of written messages using a cellphone. テキストメッセージを送ること □ *...the popularity of text messaging.* テキストメッセージの人気の高さ

tex|ture /tɛkstʃər/ (textures) **1** N-VAR 可変性名詞 The **texture** of something is the way that it feels when you touch it, for example, how smooth or rough it is. きめ □ *It is used in moisturizers to give them a wonderfully silky texture.* それはすべすべした肌触りを出すためにモイスチャーライザーに使われている. **2** N-VAR 可変性名詞 The **texture** of something, especially food or soil, is its structure, for example, whether it is light with lots of holes, or very heavy and solid. 組織 □ *Matured over 18 months, this cheese has an open, crumbly texture with a strong flavor.* 18か月かけて熟成したこのチーズは粗く崩れやすく強い香りがする.

than /ðən, STRONG ðæn/ **1** PREP 前置詞 You use **than** after a comparative adjective or adverb in order to link two parts of a comparison. よりも [compar PREP group] □ *Children learn faster than adults.* 子供は大人よりも物覚えが速い. □ *The radio only weighs a few ounces and is smaller than a pack of cigarettes.* そのラジオはたったの数オンスの重さでタバコの箱よりも小さい. ● CONJ 接続詞 **Than** is also a conjunction. よりも □ *He wished he could have helped her more than he did.* 彼はもっと彼女を助けてあげるべきだったと思った. **2** PREP 前置詞 You use **than** when you are stating a number, quantity, or value approximately by saying that it is above or below another number, quantity, or value. よりも ['more/less' PREP n] □ *They talked on the phone for more than an hour.* 彼らは1時間以上電話で話した. **3** CONJ 接続詞 You use **than** in to link two parts of a contrast, for example, in order to state a preference. よりも □ *The arrangement was more a formality than a genuine partnership of two nations.* その取り決めは2か国間の真の協力というよりも形式的なものだった. **4** less than → see **less 5** more than → see **more 6** more often than not → see **often 7** other than → see **other 8** rather than → see **rather**

thank /θæŋk/ (thanks, thanking, thanked) **1** CONVENTION 慣習表現 You use **thank you** or, in more informal English, **thanks** to express your gratitude when someone does something for you or gives you what you want. ありがとう [FORMULAE 決まり文句] □ *Thank you very much for your call.* お電話ありがとうございます. □ *Thanks for the information.* 情報をありがとう. **2** CONVENTION 慣習表現 You use **thank you** or, in more informal English, **thanks** to politely accept something that has just been offered to you. お願いする [FORMULAE 決まり文句] □ *"Would you like a cup of coffee?" — "Thank you, I'd love one."* 「コーヒーはいかがですか」「お願いします」 **3** CONVENTION 慣習表現 You use **no thank you** or, in more informal English, **no thanks** to politely refuse something that has just been offered to you. 結構です [FORMULAE 決まり文句] □ *"Would you like a cigarette?" — "No thank you."* 「タバコはいかがですか」「いいえ、結構です」 **4** CONVENTION 慣習表現 You use **thank you** or, in more informal English, **thanks** to politely acknowledge what someone has said to you, especially when they have answered your question or said something nice to you. ありがとう [FORMULAE 決まり文句] □ *"You look very nice indeed." — "Thank you."* 「とてもすてき」「ありがとう」 **5** CONVENTION 慣習表現 You use **thank you** or **thank you very much** in order to say firmly that you do not want someone's help or to tell them that you do not like the way that they are behaving toward you. もう結構です [EMPHASIS 強調] □ *I can find my own way home, thank you.* 自分で帰れますので結構です. **6** V-T 他動詞 When you **thank** someone for something, you express your gratitude to them for it. 謝意を表す □ *I thanked them for their long and loyal service.* 私は彼らの長期間にわたる忠実な奉仕に対して謝意を表した. **7** N-PLURAL 複数名詞 When you express your **thanks** to someone, you express your gratitude to them for something. 感謝 □ *They accepted their certificates with words of thanks.* 彼らはお礼を言いながら証書を受け取った. **8** PHRASE 句 You say "**Thank God**," "**Thank Goodness**," or "**Thank heavens**" when you are very relieved about something. ありがたい [FEELINGS 感情] □ *I was wrong, thank God.* ありがたい、私は間違っていた. **9** PHRASE 句 If you say that you **have** someone **to thank for** something, you mean that they caused it to happen. のおかげだ □ *I have her to thank for my life.* 私は彼女のおかげで命拾いした. □ *You have only yourself to thank for this mess.* この窮地に陥ったのはあなた1人の責任である. **10** PHRASE 句 If you say that something happens **thanks to** a particular person or thing, you mean that they are responsible for it happening or caused it to happen. のおかげで □ *It is thanks to this committee that many new sponsors have come forward.* 多くの新しい後援者が名乗りを上げたのはこの委員会のおかげだ.

thank|ful /θæŋkfəl/ ADJ 形容詞 When you are **thankful**, you are very happy and relieved to have something, or that something

has happened. 感謝している □ *Most of the time I'm just thankful that I've got a job.* ほとんどいつも私は職があることだけでありがたいと思っている.

thank|ful|ly /θæŋkfəli/ ADV 副詞 You use **thankfully** in order to express approval or happiness about a statement that you are making. ありがたいことに [ADV with cl/group] □ *Thankfully, she was not injured.* ありがたいことには彼女は無傷だった.

Thanks|giv|ing (Thanksgivings) **1** N-VAR 可変性名詞 In the United States, **Thanksgiving** or **Thanksgiving Day** is a public holiday on the fourth Thursday in November. On this day, people remember the first American thanksgiving, when the first European settlers had been taught how to grow food by the Native Americans, and they celebrated the successful harvest together. 感謝祭 □ *No matter where his business took him, he always managed to be home for Thanksgiving.* 彼は仕事でどこに出張しようとも感謝祭にはどうにかしていつも家で過ごすようにした. **2** N-VAR 可変性名詞 In Canada, **Thanksgiving** or **Thanksgiving Day** is a public holiday on the second Monday in October. On this day, people celebrate a successful harvest. 感謝祭

> A national holiday in the US and a big family occasion, **Thanksgiving** falls on the fourth Thursday in November. It commemorates the first harvest reaped by the **Pilgrims**, the first English settlers, in 1621, for which they gave thanks to God – hence the name of the festival. The traditional meal centers around a roast turkey, followed by "pumpkin pie" for dessert.

---

that

❶ DEMONSTRATIVE USES
❷ CONJUNCTION AND RELATIVE PRONOUN USES

---

❶ that /ðæt/

↻ **Please look at categories 19 – 21 to see if the expression you are looking for is shown under another headword. 1** PRON 代名詞 You use **that** to refer back to an idea or situation expressed in a previous sentence or sentences. それ □ *They said you particularly wanted to talk to me. Why was that?* あなたが特に私と話がしたがっていると彼らから聞きました. それはなぜですか. □ *"There's a party tonight." — "Is that why you're phoning?"* 「今晩パーティがあります」「あなたが電話したのはそのためですか」 **That** is also a determiner. その □ *She's away; for that reason I'm cooking tonight.* 彼女が留守なので私は今夜料理を作っている. **2** DET 限定詞 You use **that** to refer to someone or something already mentioned. その □ *The salesperson get between $50,000 and $60,000 a year but that amount can double with commission.* 営業社員は年に5万から6万の給料を受け取るがその金額は手数料を入れると倍増することがある. **3** DET 限定詞 When you have been talking about a particular period of time, you use **that** to indicate that you are still referring to the same period. You use expressions such as **that morning** or **that afternoon** to indicate that you are referring to an earlier period of the same day. その □ *The story was published in a Sunday newspaper later that week.* それはその週の後に新聞の日曜版に発表された. **4** PRON 代名詞 You use **that** in expressions such as **that of** and **that which** to introduce more information about something already mentioned, instead of repeating the noun which refers to it. それ [FORMAL 形式ばった] □ *A recession like that of 1973-74 could put one in ten American companies into bankruptcy.* 1973-74年のような景気後退は10社のアメリカ企業を破産に追い込むことがある. **5** PRON 代名詞 You use **that** in front of words or expressions which express agreement, responses, or reactions to what has just been said. それ □ *"She said she'd met you in England."* — *"That's true."* 「彼女はあなたとイギリスで会ったと言っていました」「それは本当だ」 **6** DET 限定詞 You use **that** when you are referring to someone or something which is a distance away from you in position or time, especially when you indicate or point to them. When there are two or more things near you, **that** refers to the more distant one. あの □ *Look at that guy. He's got red socks.* あの男を見てみなさい. 赤いソックスをはいている. ● PRON 代名詞 **That** is also a pronoun. もの □ *Leo, what's that you're writing?* レオ, あなたが書いているのは何ですか. **7** PRON 代名詞 You use **that** when you are identifying someone or asking about their identity. 人 □ *That's my wife you were talking to.* 君が話していたのは私の妻だ. □ *"Who's that with you?" — "A friend of mine."* 「あなたと一緒にいる人は誰ですか」「友人です」 **8** DET 限定詞 You can use **that** when you expect the person you are talking to to know what or who you are referring to, without needing to identify the particular person or thing fully. あの [SPOKEN 口語] □ *I really thought I was something when I wore that hat and my patent leather shoes.* あの帽子をかぶってエナメル革の靴を履いた時, 私は重要な人だと本当に思った. ● PRON 代名詞 **That** is also a pronoun. それ □ *That was a terrible case of blackmail in the paper today.* それは今日の新聞に載っていたひどいゆすりの事件だった. **9** ADV 副詞 If something is **not that** bad, funny, or expensive for example, it is not as bad, funny, or expensive as it

might be or as has been suggested. それほど [with brd-neg, ADV adj/adv] ❑ *Not even Gary, he said, was that stupid.* ギャリーですら、あんなに馬鹿ではないと彼は言った. **10** ADV 副詞 You can use **that** to emphasize the degree of a feeling or quality. それほど [INFORMAL くだけた, EMPHASIS 強調] [ADV adj/adv] ❑ *I would have walked out, I was that angry.* 私は立ち去ることもできた. 私はそれほど怒っていた. **11** → see also **those** **12** PHRASE 句 You use **and all that** or **and that** to refer generally to everything else which is associated with what you have just mentioned. など [INFORMAL くだけた, VAGUENESS あいまいさ] ❑ *I'm not a cook myself but I am interested in nutrition and all that.* 私自身は料理を作らないが栄養などについて興味がある. **13** PHRASE 句 You use **at that** after a statement which modifies or emphasizes what you have just said. 付け加えると [EMPHASIS 強調] ❑ *Success never seems to come but through hard work, often physically demanding work at that.* きつい仕事、そしてしばしば肉体的にきつい仕事を通じてしか成功は訪れないようだ. **14** PHRASE 句 You use **that is** or **that is to say** to indicate that you are about to express the same idea more clearly or precisely. すなわち ❑ *I am a disappointing, though generally dutiful, student. That is, I do as I'm told.* 私は概して従順だが失望させるような学生だ. 言い換えると、私は言われた通りにする. **15** PHRASE 句 You use **that's it** to indicate that nothing more needs to be done or that the end has been reached. これでおしまい ❑ *When he left the office, that was it, the workday was over.* 彼が事務所を出た時に就業時間は終わった. **16** CONVENTION 慣習表現 You use **that's it** to express agreement with or approval of what has just been said or done. まさにそのとおりだ [FORMULAE 決まり文句] ❑ *"You got married, right?" — "Yeah, that's it."* 「あなたは結婚しましたね」「はい、そのとおりです」 **17** PHRASE 句 You use **just like that** to emphasize that something happens or is done immediately or in a very simple way, often without much thought or discussion. いとも簡単に [INFORMAL くだけた, EMPHASIS 強調] ❑ *Just like that, I was in love.* いとも簡単に私は恋愛していた. **18** PHRASE 句 You use **that's that** to say there is nothing more you can do or say about a particular matter. それでおしまいだ [SPOKEN 口語] ❑ *"Well, if that's the way you want it," he replied, tears in his eyes, "I guess that's that."* 「でも君がそうしたいのならばそれでおしまいだ」と彼は目に涙を浮かべながら言った. **19** like that → see like **20** this and that → see this **21** this, that and the other → see this

❷ that /ðət, STRONG ðæt/ **1** CONJ 接続詞 You can use **that** after many verbs, adjectives, nouns, and expressions to introduce a clause in which you report what someone has said, or what they think or feel. ということ ❑ *He called her up one day and said that he and his wife were coming to New York.* 彼はある日彼女に電話し、彼は妻とニューヨークに来る予定だと告げた. **2** CONJ 接続詞 You use **that** after "it" and a linking verb and an adjective to comment on a situation or fact. ということ ❑ *It's interesting that you like him.* あなたが彼を気に入ったとは面白い. **3** PRON-REL 関係代名詞 You use **that** to introduce a clause which gives more information to help identify the person or thing you are talking about. する ❑ *...pills that will make the problem disappear.* 問題を取り除く薬 **4** CONJ 接続詞 You use **that** after expressions with "so" and "such" in order to introduce the result or effect of something. なので ❑ *She became so nervous that she shook violently.* 彼女は緊張のあまり激しく震えた.

thatched /θætʃt/ ADJ 形容詞 A **thatched** house or a house with a **thatched** roof has a roof made of straw or reeds. 草ぶき屋根の ❑ *...a 400-year-old thatched cottage.* 築400年の草ぶき屋根の田舎家

that's /ðæts/ **That's** is a spoken form of "that is." that is の縮約形

thaw /θɔ/ (thaws, thawing, thawed) **1** V-I 自動詞 When ice, snow, or something else that is frozen **thaws**, it melts. 解ける ❑ *It's so cold the snow doesn't get a chance to thaw.* 非常に寒いので雪が解ける可能性はない. **2** N-COUNT 可算名詞 A **thaw** is a period of warmer weather when snow and ice melt, usually at the end of winter. 雪解けの季節 ❑ *We slogged through the mud of an early spring thaw.* 我々は早春の雪解けの泥道を苦労して歩いた. **3** V-T/V-I 他動詞/自動詞 When you **thaw** frozen food or when it **thaws**, you leave it in a place where it can reach room temperature so that it is ready for use. 解凍する ❑ *Always thaw pastry thoroughly.* ペーストリーはいつも完全に解凍しなさい. ● PHRASAL VERB 句動詞 **Thaw out** means the same as **thaw.** 解凍する ❑ *Thaw it out completely before reheating in a saucepan.* 鍋で再び加熱する前に完全に解凍しなさい.

the

> **The** is the definite article. It is used at the beginning of noun groups. **The** is usually pronounced /ðə/ before a consonant and /ði/ before a vowel, but pronounced /ðiː/ when you are emphasizing it.

> **The** は定冠詞であり、名詞群のはじめに用いられる. **The** は通常子音の前では /ðə/ と、母音の前では /ði/ と発音されるが、強調しているときは /ðiː/ と発音される.

1 DET 限定詞 You use **the** at the beginning of noun groups to refer to someone or something that you have already mentioned or identified. その ❑ *Six of the 38 people were U.S. citizens.* 38名のうち6名はアメリカ人だった. **2** DET 限定詞 You use **the** at the

beginning of a noun group when the first noun is followed by an "of" phrase or a clause which identifies the person or thing. その ❑ *There has been a slight increase in the consumption of meat.* 肉の消費がやや増加した. **3** DET 限定詞 You use **the** in front of some nouns that refer to something in our general experience of the world. というもの ❑ *It's always hard to speculate about the future.* 将来というものを予測するのはいつも難しい. **4** DET 限定詞 You use **the** in front of nouns that refer to people, things, services, or institutions that are associated with everyday life. 集合名詞 ❑ *The doctor's on his way.* 医者はこちらに向かっている. **5** DET 限定詞 You use **the** instead of a possessive determiner, especially when you are talking about a part of someone's body or a member of their family. 体の ❑ *"How's the family?" — "Just fine, thank you."* 「ご家族はお元気ですか」「はい元気です」 **6** DET 限定詞 You use **the** in front of a singular noun when you want to make a general statement about things or people of that type. なるもの ❑ *An area in which the computer has made considerable strides in recent years is in playing chess.* 近年コンピュータが大幅な進歩をした分野はチェスだ. **7** DET 限定詞 You use **the** with the name of a musical instrument when you are talking about someone's ability to play the instrument. というもの ❑ *Did you play the piano as a child?* あなたは子供の時ピアノを弾きましたか. **8** DET 限定詞 You use **the** with nationality adjectives and nouns to talk about the people who live in a country. 集合名詞 ❑ *The Japanese, Americans, and even the French and Germans, judge economic policies by results.* 日本人、アメリカ人そしてフランス人やドイツ人すら経済政策を決果で評価する. **9** DET 限定詞 You use **the** with words such as "rich," "poor," "old," or "unemployed" to refer to all people of a particular type. 総称 ❑ *Conditions for the poor in Los Angeles have not improved.* ロサンジェルスの貧困者の状況は改善していない. **10** DET 限定詞 If you want to refer to a whole family or to a married couple, you can make their surname into a plural and use **the** in front of it. 家の人々 ❑ *The Taylors decided that they would employ an architect to do the work.* テイラー一家は建築士を雇うことに決めた. **11** DET 限定詞 You use **the** in front of an adjective when you are referring to a particular thing that is described by that adjective. 総称 ❑ *He knows he's wishing for the impossible.* 彼は不可能なことを望んでいることを知っている. **12** DET 限定詞 You use **the** to indicate whether or not you have enough of the thing mentioned for a particular purpose. に十分な ❑ *She may not have the money to maintain or restore her property.* 彼女は家を維持・修復する金を持っていないかもしれない. **13** DET 限定詞 You use **the** with some titles, place names, and other names. 固有名詞 ❑ *...the Seattle Times.* シアトルタイムズ ❑ *...the White House.* ホワイトハウス ❑ *...The Great Gatsby.* グレートギャッツビー **14** DET 限定詞 You use **the** in front of numbers such as first, second, and third. 日付 ❑ *The meeting should take place on the fifth of May.* 会合は5月5日に開かれるはずである. **15** DET 限定詞 You use **the** in front of numbers when they refer to decades. 10年をまとめて指す時 ❑ *It's sometimes hard to imagine how bad things were in the thirties.* 30年代に状況はどれほど悪かったかを想像するのは難しい. **16** DET 限定詞 You use **the** in front of superlative adjectives and adverbs. 形容詞の最上級 ❑ *Brisk daily walks are still the best exercise for young and old alike.* 年齢にかかわらず毎日きびきび歩くことはまだ最良の運動だ. **17** DET 限定詞 You use **the** in front of each of two comparative adjectives or adverbs when you are describing how one amount or quality changes in relation to another. すればするほどますます ❑ *The longer the therapy goes on, the more successful it will be.* 治療が長く続けば続くほどそれは成功するだろう. **18** DET 限定詞 When you express rates, prices, and measurements, you can use **the** to say how many units apply to each of the items being measured. 〜につき ❑ *...cars that get more miles to the gallon.* 1ガロンにつきより長い距離走れる自動車 **19** DET 限定詞 You use **the** to indicate that something or someone is the most famous, important, or best thing of its kind. In spoken English, you put more stress on it, and in written English, you often underline it or write it in capitals or italics. 理想の ❑ *The circus is the place to be this Saturday or Sunday.* 今週の土曜日または日曜日はサーカスがいちばんだ.

theater /θiətər/ (theaters) also **theatre** **1** N-COUNT; N-IN-NAMES 可算名詞, 名称中の名詞 A **theater** is a building with a stage in it, on which plays, shows, and other performances take place. 劇場 ❑ *They brought her to the theater where their new musical was in production.* 彼らは新しいミュージカルを上演中の劇場に彼女を連れて行った. **2** N-SING 単数名詞 You can refer to work in the theater such as acting or writing plays as the **theater**. 演劇界 ❑ *The story of her career in the theater is told in a new biography.* 演劇界における彼女の職歴の話は新しい自伝に書かれている. **3** N-COUNT 可算名詞 A **theater** or a **movie theater** is a place where people go to watch movies for entertainment. 映画館 [AM 米国英語] ❑ *A movie theater and roller rink attracted customers and profit.* 映画館とローラーリンクは大繁盛し、利益になった. **4** N-UNCOUNT 不可算名詞 **Theater** is entertainment that involves the performance of plays. 劇団 ❑ *...American musical theater.* アメリカのミュージカルシアター

→ see Word Web: **theater**

→ see **city**

Word Web

theater

Plays in ancient Greece were very different from those of today. **Performances** happened outdoors in open air **theaters**. Two or three male **actors** played all of the **roles** in the **production**. Women could not appear onstage. The actors would go **backstage**, change their **masks** and **costumes**, and re-emerge as new **characters**. A group of people, called the chorus, explained what was happening to the **audience**. Traditional Greek **tragedies** came from stories of the distant past. **Comedies** often made fun of contemporary public figures. Several **plays** appeared together as a contest. The **audience** voted for their favorite **show**.

the|at|ri|cal /θiǽtrɪk³l/ ■ ADJ 形容詞 **Theatrical** means relating to the theater. 演劇の [ADJ n] ❏ ...the most outstanding theatrical performances of the year. その年に最も高い評価を受けた演劇 ● **the|at|ri|cal|ly** /θiǽtrɪkli/ ADV 副詞 演劇的に ❏ Shaffer's great gift lies in his ability to animate ideas theatrically. シェファーの偉大なオ能は概念を舞台向きに脚色することにある. ② ADJ 形容詞 **Theatrical** behavior is exaggerated and unnatural, and intended to create an effect. 大げさな ❏ In a theatrical gesture Jim clamped his hand over his eyes. ジムは大げさなジェスチャーで手を目を覆った. ● **the|at|ri|cal|ly** ADV 副詞 大げさに ❏ He looked theatrically at his watch. 彼は大げさに時計を見た.

theft /θɛft/ (**thefts**) N-VAR 可変性名詞 **Theft** is the crime of stealing. 盗み ❏ Over the last decade, auto theft has increased by over 56 percent. 過去10年間に自動車泥棒は56%以上増えた.

their /ðɛər/

> **Their** is the third person plural possessive determiner.
> **Their** は3人称複数所有限定詞である.

■ DET 限定詞 You use **their** to indicate that something belongs or relates to the group of people, animals, or things that you are talking about. 彼らの ❏ Janis and Kurt have announced their engagement. ジャニスとカートは婚約を発表した. ② DET 限定詞 You use **their** instead of "his or her" to indicate that something belongs or relates to a person without saying whether that person is a man or a woman. Some people think this use is incorrect. その人の ❏ Each student determines their own pace in the yoga class. 学生はヨガ教室で自分のペースを決める.

theirs /ðɛərz/

> **Theirs** is the third person plural possessive pronoun.
> **Theirs** は3人称複数所有代名詞である.

■ PRON-POSS 所有代名詞 You use **theirs** to indicate that something belongs or relates to the group of people, animals, or things that you are talking about. 彼らのもの ❏ There was a big group of a dozen people at the table next to theirs. 彼らの隣のテーブルには10人余りの大きなグループがいた. ② PRON-POSS 所有代名詞 You use **theirs** instead of "his or hers" to indicate that something belongs or relates to a person without saying whether that person is a man or a woman. Some people think this use is incorrect. その人のもの ❏ He would leave the trailer unlocked. If there was something inside that someone wanted, it would be theirs for the taking. 彼はトレーラーに錠を下ろさずによく出かけた. 欲しいものがあれば誰でも自由に取ることができた.

them /ðəm, STRONG ðɛm/

> **Them** is a third person plural pronoun. **Them** is used as the object of a verb or preposition.
> **Them** は3人称複数の代名詞である. **Them** は動詞または前置詞の目的語として用いられる.

■ PRON-PLURAL 複数代名詞 You use **them** to refer to a group of people, animals, or things. 彼ら [V PRON, prep PRON] ❏ The Beatles – I never get tired of listening to them. ビートルズ, 彼らの音楽は何度聴いても飽きない. ❏ Kids these days have no one to tell them what's right and wrong. 最近の子供には物事の正邪を教えてくれる人がいない. ② PRON-PLURAL 複数代名詞 You use **them** instead of "him or her" to refer to a person without saying whether that person is a man or a woman. Some people think this use is incorrect. その人 [V PRON, prep PRON] ❏ It takes great courage to face your child and tell them the truth. 子供に面と向かって真実を告げるには大きな勇気が必要だ.

theme /θiːm/ (**themes**) ■ N-COUNT 可算名詞 A **theme** in a piece of writing, a talk, or a discussion is an important idea or subject that runs through it. 話題 ❏ The theme of the conference is renaissance Europe. 会議の話題はルネッサンス時代のヨーロッパである. ② N-COUNT 可算名詞 A **theme** in an artist's work or in a work of literature is an idea in it that the artist or writer develops or repeats. 主題 ❏ The novel's central theme is the ongoing conflict between men and women. その小説の主な主題は男女間の食い違いである. ❸ N-COUNT 可算名詞 A **theme** is a short simple tune on which a piece of music is based. 主旋律 ❏ ...variations on themes from Mozart's The Magic Flute. モーツァルトの『魔笛』の主旋律の変奏曲 ❹ N-COUNT 可算名詞 **Theme** music or a **theme** song is a piece of music that is played at the beginning and end of a movie or of a television or radio program. テーマ音楽 ❏ ...the theme from Dr. Zhivago. ドクトル・ジバゴのテーマ音楽
→ see myth

them|selves /ðəmsɛlvz/

> **Themselves** is the third person plural reflexive pronoun.
> **Themselves** は3人称複数再帰代名詞である.

■ PRON-REFL 再帰代名詞 You use **themselves** to refer to people, animals, or things when the object of a verb or preposition refers to the same people or things as the subject of the verb. 彼ら自身 [V PRON, prep PRON] ❏ They all seemed to be enjoying themselves. 彼らは皆楽しんでいるようだった. ② PRON-REFL-EMPH 強調的な再帰代名詞 You use **themselves** to emphasize the people or things that you are referring to. **Themselves** is also sometimes used instead of "them" as the object of a verb or preposition. 彼ら自身 [EMPHASIS 強調] ❏ Many mentally ill people are themselves unhappy about the idea of community care. 精神的に病んでいる人々の多くは彼ら自身コミュニティーケアの概念に不満である. ❸ PRON-REFL 再帰代名詞 You use **themselves** instead of "himself or herself" to refer back to the person who is the subject of sentence without saying whether it is a man or a woman. Some people think this use is incorrect. その人自身 [V PRON, prep PRON] ❏ What can a patient with emphysema do to help themselves? 肺気腫の患者が他人に頼らず自力でできることはあるか. ❹ PRON-REFL-EMPH 強調的な再帰代名詞 You use **themselves** instead of "himself or herself" to emphasize the person you are referring to without saying whether it is a man or a woman. **Themselves** is also sometimes used as the object of a verb or preposition. Some people think this use is incorrect. その人自身 [EMPHASIS 強調] ❏ Each student makes only one item themselves. 各々の学生は自分たちのために1つだけ品物を作成する. ❺ → see also ourselves

then /ðɛn/ ■ ADV 副詞 **Then** means at a particular time in the past or in the future. その時 ❏ He wanted to have a source of income after his retirement; until then, he wouldn't require additional money. 彼は定年退職後の収入源がほしかった. その時まで彼は追加の金を必要としないだろう. ❏ Executives pledged to get the company back on track. Since then, though, shares have fallen 30 per cent. 経営陣は会社を軌道に乗せることを誓った. だがそれ以来, 株価は30%下落した. ② ADJ 形容詞 **Then** is used when you refer to something which was true at a particular time in the past but is not true now. その時 [ADJ n] ❏ ...a tour of the then new airport. その時は新しかった空港のツアー ● ADV 副詞 **Then** is also an adverb. あの時 [ADV group] ❏ Richard Strauss, then 76 years old, suffered through the war years in silence. あの時76歳だったリチャード・ストラウスは無言で戦争の時代に耐えた. ❸ ADV 副詞 You use **then** to say that one thing happens after another, or is after another on a list. その後で ❏ Add the oil and then the scallops to the pan, leaving a little space for the garlic. 油, それからホタテを鍋に入れ, にんにくを入れる空間を残します. ❹ ADV 副詞 You use **then** in conversation to indicate that what you are

about to say follows logically in some way from what has just been said or implied. それでは [cl/group ADV] ❑*"I wasn't a very good scholar in school."* — *"Then why did you become a teacher?"* 「私は余り優秀な生徒ではなかった」「それではなぜ教師になったのですか」* ⑤ ADV 副詞 You use **then** to signal the end of a topic or the end of a conversation. それなら [cl/group ADV] ❑*I'll talk to you on Friday anyway."* — *"Yep. Okay then."* 「いずれにしても金曜日にあなたに話します」「それでオーケーです」* ⑥ ADV 副詞 You use **then** with words like "now," "well," and "okay," to introduce a new topic or a new point of view. さて [adv ADV] ❑*Now then, I'm going to explain everything to you before we do it.* さて私はそれをする前にあなたに全てを説明します. ⑦ ADV 副詞 You use **then** to introduce the second part of a sentence which begins with "if." The first part of the sentence describes a possible situation, and **then** introduces the result of the situation. その場合には [ADV cl] ❑*If the answer is "yes," then we need to leave now.* 回答が「はい」の場合には我々はすぐに立ち去らなければならない. ⑧ ADV 副詞 You use **then** at the beginning of a sentence or after "and" or "but" to introduce a comment or an extra piece of information to what you have already said. しかしまた一方では [ADV cl] ❑*He sounded sincere, but then, he always did.* 彼は誠実なように聞こえたが彼はいつもそうだった. ⑨ **now and then** → see **now** ⑩ **there and then** → see **there**

the|ol|ogy /θiɒlədʒi/ N-UNCOUNT 不可算名詞 **Theology** is the study of the nature of God and of religion and religious beliefs. 神学 ❑*...questions of theology.* 神学の問い● **theo|logi|cal** /θiəlɒdʒɪkəl/ ADJ 形容詞 神学の ❑*...theological books.* 神学の本

theo|reti|cal /θiərɛtɪkəl/ ❶ ADJ 形容詞 A **theoretical** study or explanation is based on or uses the ideas and abstract principles that relate to a particular subject, rather than the practical aspects or uses of it. 理論上の ❑*...theoretical physics.* 理論物理学 ❷ ADJ 形容詞 If you describe a situation as a **theoretical** one, you mean that although it is supposed to be true or to exist in the way stated, it may not in fact be true or exist in that way. 理論としてのみ存在する ❑*This is certainly a theoretical risk but in practice there is seldom a problem.* これは確かに理論的に存在するリスクだが実際に問題となることはほとんどない.

theo|reti|cal|ly /θiərɛtɪkli/ ADV 副詞 You use **theoretically** to say that although something is supposed to be true or to happen in the way stated, it may not in fact be true or happen in that way. 理論的に [ADV with cl/group] ❑*Theoretically, the price is supposed to be marked on the shelf.* 理論的には定価は棚についていることになっている.

theo|rist /θiərɪst/ (**theorists**) N-COUNT 可算名詞 A **theorist** is someone who develops an abstract idea or set of ideas about a particular subject in order to explain it. 理論家 ❑*...theorists unaligned with any particular doctrine.* 特定の主義と提携していない理論家

theo|ry /θiəri/ (**theories**) ❶ N-VAR 可変性名詞 A **theory** is a formal idea or set of ideas that is intended to explain something. 理論 ❑*Marx produced a new theory about historical change based upon conflict between competing groups.* マルクスは競い合うグループ間の紛争に基づく歴史的変化について新しい理論を打ち立てた. ❷ N-COUNT 可算名詞 If you have a **theory** about something, you have your own opinion about it which you cannot prove but which you think is true. 意見 ❑*There was a theory that he wanted to marry her.* 彼が彼女と結婚したがっているという見方があった. ❸ N-UNCOUNT 不可算名詞 The **theory** of a practical subject or skill is the set of rules and principles that form the basis of it. 理論 ❑*He taught us music theory.* 彼は私たちに音楽理論を教えた. ❹ PHRASE 句 You use **in theory** to say that although something is supposed to be true or to happen in the way stated, it may not in fact be true or happen in that way. 理論的に ❑*Achieving these goals is relatively easy in theory, yet quite difficult in practice.* こうした目標を達成するのは理論的には比較的簡単だが、実際はかなり難しい.
→ see **experiment, science**

Word Partnership	*theory* は次の語句と使われる:
N.	theory **and practice** ❶
	evidence for a theory, **support for a** theory ❶ ❸
	conspiracy theory ❷
	learning theory ❸
ADJ.	**scientific** theory ❶
	economic theory, **literary** theory ❸
V.	**advance a** theory, **propose a** theory ❶ – ❸
	develop a theory, **test a** theory ❶ ❸

thera|peu|tic /θɛrəpyutɪk/ ADJ 形容詞 If something is **therapeutic**, it helps you to relax or to feel better about things, especially about a situation that made you unhappy. 健康維持に役立つ ❑*Having a garden is therapeutic.* 庭があることは健康維持に役立つ.

thera|pist /θɛrəpɪst/ (**therapists**) N-COUNT 可算名詞 A **therapist** is a person who is skilled in a particular type of therapy,

especially psychotherapy. セラピスト ❑*My therapist helped me to deal with my anger.* 私のセラピストは怒りをうまく対処するのを助けた.

thera|py /θɛrəpi/ (**therapies**) ❶ N-UNCOUNT 不可算名詞 **Therapy** is the process or talking to a trained counselor about your emotional and mental problems and your relationships in order to understand and improve the way you feel and behave. 精神療法 ❑*Children may need therapy to help them deal with grief and death.* 子供たちは悲しみと死と取り組むために精神療法が必要かもしれない. ❑*Since I've been in therapy, I've grown to be a better husband and father.* 精神療法を受けて、よりよき夫そして父親になった. ❷ N-VAR 可変性名詞 **Therapy** or a **therapy** is a treatment for a particular illness or condition. 治療 [MEDICAL 医学の] ❑*...hormonal therapies.* ホルモン療法
→ see **cancer, illness**

there

Pronounced /ðər/, STRONG ðɛr/ for meanings ❶ and ❷, and / ðɛər/ for meanings ❸ to ❶⑨.

❶ と ❷ の意味では /ðər/, STRONG ðɛr/ と発音され、❸ から ❶⑨ の意味では /ðɛər/ と発音される.

❶ PRON 代名詞 **There** is used as the subject of the verb "be" to say that something exists or does not exist, or to draw attention to it. ～がある [PRON 'be' n] ❑*There are temporary traffic lights now at the school.* 学校には現在臨時の信号がある. ❑*Are there any cookies left?* クッキーは残っていますか.

There is normally followed by a plural form of the verb **be** when it is used to introduce a count noun in the plural. ❑*There were policemen everywhere.* However, when it introduces a series of nouns in the singular, linked by **and**, a singular form of the verb **be** is normally used. ❑*There is a time and a place for everything... There was a street fair and an old-fashioned brass band.* Take care not to confuse **there** and **their**.

❷ PRON 代名詞 You use **there** in front of certain verbs when you are saying that something exists, develops, or can be seen. Whether the verb is singular or plural depends on the noun which follows the verb. 形式的な主語 [PRON v n] ❑*There remains considerable doubt over when the road will be completed.* 道路工事がいつ完了するかについて大きな疑いが残されている. ❸ CONVENTION 慣習表現 **There** is used after "hello" or "hi" when you are greeting someone. やあ [INFORMAL くだけた] ❑*"Hello there,"* said the woman, smiling at them. — *"Hi!"* they chorused. 「やあ、こんにちは」とその女性は彼らにほほえみながら言った. 「こんにちわ」と彼らは口をそろえて言った. ❹ ADV 副詞 If something is **there**, it exists or is available. そこに ❑*The group of old buildings is still there today.* 一連の古い建物は今でもまだそこにある. ❺ ADV 副詞 You use **there** to refer to a place which has already been mentioned. そこに ❑*The next day we drove 33 miles to Siena (the Villa Arceno is a great place to stay while you are there).* 翌日、我々はシエナまで33マイル車を走らせた（Villa Arcenoはその場所の素晴らしい宿泊施設）. ❑*"Come on over, if you want." — "How do I get there?"* 「もしよかったら家に来ませんか」「そこに行く方法を教えてください」 ❻ ADV 副詞 You use **there** to indicate a place that you are pointing to or looking at, in order to draw someone's attention to it. ほら ❑*There it is, on the corner over there.* ほら、その角にある. ❑*There she is on the left up there.* ほら、彼女はその上の左側にいる. ❼ ADV 副詞 You use **there** in expressions such as **"there he was"** or **"there we were"** to sum up part of a story or to slow a story down for dramatic effect. 感嘆詞的 [SPOKEN 口語] [ADV cl] ❑*So there he was all covered in mud, and still in a good mood.* 彼は泥まみれだったがまだ機嫌がよかった. ❽ ADV 副詞 You use **there** when speaking on the telephone to ask if someone is available to speak to you. そこに [ADV with 'be'] ❑*Hello, is Gordon there please?* もしもし、ゴードンはいますか. ❾ ADV 副詞 You use **there** to refer to a point that someone has made in a conversation. その点で [ADV after v] ❑*I think you're right there John.* ジョン、君はその点で正しいと思う. ❶⓪ ADV 副詞 You use **there** to refer to a stage that has been reached in an activity or process. その状態 ❑*We are making further investigations and will take the matter from there.* 我々は追加の調査を行なっており、そこから事件と取り組む予定だ. ❶① ADV 副詞 You use **there** to indicate that something has reached a point or level which is completely successful. そこに ❑*We had hoped to fill the back page with extra news; we're not quite there yet.* 裏ページを追加のニュースで埋めたかったのだが、まだそこまで達していない. ❶② ADV 副詞 You can use **there** in expressions such as **there you go** or **there we are** when accepting that an unsatisfactory situation cannot be changed. しかたがない [SPOKEN 口語] [ADV cl] ❑*This is a little cruel, but there you go.* これはちょっと残酷だがしかたがない. ❶③ ADV 副詞 You can use **there** in expressions such as **there you go** and **there we are** when emphasizing that something proves that you were right. ほらね [SPOKEN 口語, EMPHASIS 強調] [ADV cl] ❑*You see? There you go. That's why I didn't mention it earlier. I knew you'd take it the wrong way.* ほらね、だから私はそれをもっと早く言わなかったんだ. 君がそれを誤解することは分かっていた. ❶④ PHRASE 句 Phrases such

as **there** you **go again** are used to show anger at someone who is repeating something that has annoyed you in the past. ほらまたやっている [SPOKEN 口語] ❑ *"There you go again, upsetting the child!" said Shirley.* 「ほらまたじゃくした。子供を動揺させないで」とシャーリーは言った. ᴵᴱ PHRASE 句 You can add **"so there"** to what you are saying to show that you have won an argument, or that you will not change your mind about a decision you have made, even though the person you are talking to disagrees with you. This is usually said by children or to be funny. そら見ろ [INFORMAL くだけた] ❑ *I think that's sweet, so there.* それは甘いと思う. そら見ろ. ❑ *You see? Mom said I could - so there!* ほら、お母さんは私にしていいと言った. そら見ろ. ᴵᴱ PHRASE 句 If something happens **there and then** or **then and there**, it happens immediately. すぐさま ❑ *Many felt that he should have resigned there and then.* 多くの人々は彼がすぐその場で辞任すべきだと思った. ᴵᴿ CONVENTION 慣習表現 You say **"there there"** to someone who is very upset, especially a small child, in order to comfort them. よしよし [SPOKEN 口語] ❑ *"There, there," said Mommy. "You've been having a bad dream."* 「よしよし、悪い夢を見ていただけですよ」とお母さんは言った. ᴵᴮ CONVENTION 慣習表現 You say **"there you are"** or **"there you go"** when you are offering something to someone. さあどうぞ [SPOKEN 口語, FORMULAE 決まり文句] ❑ *"There you go, Mr. Walters," she said, giving him his documents.* 「ウォルターさん、さあどうぞ」と彼女は言い、書類を彼に渡した. ᴵᴼ PHRASE 句 If someone **is there for** you, they help and support you, especially when you have problems. 頼りになる [INFORMAL くだけた] ❑ *Despite what happened in the past I want her to know I am there for him.* 過去の出来事にもかかわらず必要な時にはいつも頼りになることを私は彼女に知ってほしい.

there|after /ðɛəræftər/ ADV 副詞 **Thereafter** means after the event or date mentioned. その後は [FORMAL 形式ばった] [ADV with cl] ❑ *The plan will help you lose 3-4 pounds the first week, and 1-2 pounds the weeks thereafter.* このプログラムに従えば、1週目に3、4ポンド、それ以降は数週に1、2ポンドの減量ができるでしょう.

there|by /ðɛərbaɪ/ ADV 副詞 You use **thereby** to introduce an important result or consequence of the event or action you have just mentioned. それによって [FORMAL 形式ばった] [ADV with cl] ❑ *Our bodies can sweat, thereby losing heat by evaporation.* 私たちの体には発汗作用があり、その結果、汗が蒸発して体温が下がる.

there|fore /ðɛərfɔr/ ADV 副詞 You use **therefore** to introduce a logical result or conclusion. したがって [ADV with cl/group] ❑ *Muscle cells need lots of fuel and therefore burn lots of calories.* 筋肉細胞は多量のエネルギー源を必要とするため、多くのカロリーを消費する.

there|in /ðɛərɪn/ ❶ ADV 副詞 **Therein** means contained in the place that has been mentioned. そこに [LITERARY 文語的] [n ADV] ❑ *By burning tree branches, pine needles, and pine cones, many not only warm their houses but improve the smell therein.* 多くの人が木の枝、松葉、松かさなどを燃やすのは、屋内を暖めるためだけではなく、そこでの臭い対策も兼ねてのことだ. ❷ ADV 副詞 **Therein** means relating to something that has just been mentioned. それに関して [FORMAL 形式ばった] [n ADV] ❑ *Afternoon groups relate to the specific addictions and problems therein.* 午後の組は、特定の依存症とそれにかかわる問題をテーマにします.

ther|mal /θɜrmᵊl/ (thermals) ❶ ADJ 形容詞 **Thermal** means relating to or caused by heat or by changes in temperature. 熱による [ADJ n] ❑ *...thermal power stations.* 火力発電所 ❷ ADJ 形容詞 **Thermal** streams or baths contain water which is naturally hot or warm. 温泉の [ADJ n] ❑ *Volcanic activity has created thermal springs and boiling mud pools.* 火山活動によって温泉や沸き立つ泥泉が生まれた. ❸ ADJ 形容詞 **Thermal** clothes are specially designed to keep you warm in cold weather. 保温性のよい [ADJ n] ❑ *...thermal underwear.* 防寒下着 ❑ *My feet were like blocks of ice despite the thermal socks.* 防寒靴下を履いていたが、私の足は氷のようだった. ● N-PLURAL 複数名詞 **Thermals** are thermal clothes. 防寒下着 ❑ *Have you got your thermals on?* 防寒下着を着けてきたかい? ❹ N-COUNT 可算名詞 A **thermal** is a movement of rising warm air. 上昇気流 ❑ *Birds use thermals to lift them through the air.* 鳥は上昇気流を利用して飛ぶ.

→ see **solar system**

ther|mom|eter /θərmɒmɪtər/ (thermometers) N-COUNT 可算名詞 A **thermometer** is an instrument for measuring temperature. It usually consists of a narrow glass tube containing a thin column of a liquid which rises and falls as the temperature rises and falls. 温度計

the|sau|rus /θɪsɔrəs/ (thesauruses) N-COUNT 可算名詞 A **thesaurus** is a reference book in which words with similar meanings are grouped together. 類語辞典

these

The determiner is pronounced /ðiz/. The pronoun is pronounced /ðiz/.
限定詞は /ðiz/ と発音される. 代名詞は /ðiz/ と発音される.

❶ DET 限定詞 You use **these** at the beginning of noun groups to refer to someone or something that you have already mentioned or identified. これらの ❑ *A committee has been formed. These people can make decisions in ten minutes which would take us months.* 委員会が結成された. この委員たちは、我々なら数カ月かかりそうな意思決定を10分で行うことができる. ● PRON 代名詞 **These** is also a pronoun. これらのもの、これらの人々 ❑ *"I have faith in these guys," the coach said. "These are good players."* 「この選手たちは頼りになるよ. 彼らはいい選手だ」とコーチは言った. ❷ DET 限定詞 You use **these** to introduce people or things that you are going to talk about. 次に述べる ❑ *Your camcorder should have these basic features: autofocus, playback facility, zoom lens.* 今から言うような基本機能がついたビデオカメラにするべきだよ. オートフォーカス、再生装置、ズームレンズなどさ. ● PRON 代名詞 **These** is also a pronoun. 次に述べること ❑ *Take care of yourself while you are pregnant. These are some of the things you can do for yourself.* 妊娠中は健康管理が大切です. 次から自己管理の方法をいくつかお伝えします. ❸ DET 限定詞 In spoken English, people use **these** to introduce people or things into a story. とある— ❑ *I was by myself and these guys suddenly came towards me.* 一人で過ごしていたら、突然ある男たちが私の方にやって来たんだ. ❹ PRON 代名詞 You use **these** when you are identifying a group or asking about their identity. ここにいる人たち ❑ *These are my children.* これは私の子供たちです. ❺ DET 限定詞 You use **these** to refer to people or things that are near you, especially when you touch them or point to them. ここにいる、ここにある ❑ *These scissors are awfully heavy.* このはさみはとても重い. ● PRON 代名詞 **These** is also a pronoun. ここにいる人、ここにいるもの ❑ *These are the people who are helping us.* こちらは私たちを手伝ってくれる人たちです. ❻ DET 限定詞 You use **these** when you refer to something which you expect the person you are talking to to know about, or when you are checking that you are both thinking of the same person or thing. 例の— ❑ *You know these last few months when we've been expecting it to warm up a little bit?* ここ数カ月はもう少し温かくなりそうだって期待してたんだよね. ❼ DET 限定詞 You use **these** in the expression **these days** to mean "at the present time." 今は ❑ *These days, people appreciate a chance to relax.* 今は、人々はリラックスできる機会をありがたいと思っている.

the|sis /θisɪs/ (theses) /θisiz/ ❶ N-COUNT 可算名詞 A **thesis** is an idea or theory that is expressed as a statement and is discussed in a logical way. 主張 ❑ *This thesis does not stand up to close inspection.* 厳密に検討すればこの主張はくずれる. ❷ N-COUNT 可算名詞 A **thesis** is a long piece of writing based on your own ideas and research that you do as part of a college degree, especially a higher degree such as a Ph.D. 論文

→ see **graduation**

they /ðeɪ/

They is a third person plural pronoun. **They** is used as the subject of a verb.
They は3人称複数の代名詞である. **They** は動詞の主語として用いられる.

❶ PRON-PLURAL 複数代名詞 You use **they** to refer to a group of people, animals, or things. 彼ら、それら ❑ *Feed the dogs because they haven't eaten.* 犬たちはまだ何も食べていないから、えさをあげてね. ❑ *The two men were far more alike than they would ever admit.* 彼らが認める以上にその二人の男はそっくりだった. ❑ *People matter because of what they are, not what they have.* 人々の価値を決めるのは、彼らのあり方であって、彼らが所有するものではない. ❷ PRON-PLURAL 複数代名詞 You use **they** instead of "he or she" to refer to a person without saying whether that person is a man or a woman. Some people think this use is incorrect. 性を区別しない3人称単数形の代名詞として使用する ❑ *The teacher is not responsible for the student's success or failure. They are only there to help the student learn.* 教師は生徒の成績の良し悪しを左右する存在ではない. 教師の存在価値は、生徒の学習を支援することにある. ❸ PRON-PLURAL 複数代名詞 You use **they** in expressions such as "they say" or "they call it" to refer to people in general when you are making general statements about what people say, think, or do. ーだそうだ [VAGUENESS あいまいさ] ❑ *They say there's plenty of opportunities out there, you just have to look carefully and you'll find them.* そこにはチャンスがふんだんにあるそうだ. 慎重を期してればチャンスは来るさ.

they'd /ðeɪd/ ❶ **They'd** is a spoken form of "they had," especially when "had" is an auxiliary verb. they had の省略形. 口語で用いられ、特にhadが助動詞の場合にこの形をとる. ❑ *They'd both lived on this road all their lives.* 彼ら2人は生涯この道路沿いに住んでいた. ❷ **They'd** is a spoken form of "they would." they would の省略形. 口語で用いられる. ❑ *He agreed that they'd visit her after they stopped at Jan's for coffee.* 彼が同意したのは、彼らがジャンの店でコーヒーを飲んでから彼女を訪問する、という点だった.

they'll /ðeɪl/ **They'll** is the usual spoken form of "they will." they will の省略形. 口語で用いられる. ❑ *They'll probably be here Monday and Tuesday.* 彼らは月曜と火曜はここにいるだろう.

t

they're /ðɛər/ **They're** is the usual spoken form of "they are." they are の省略形. 口語で一般に用いられる. □*People eat when they're depressed.* 人は落ち込むと食べるものです.

they've /ðeɪv/ **They've** is the usual spoken form of "they have," especially when "have" is an auxiliary verb. they have の省略形. 口語で用いられ, 特にhaveが助動詞の場合にこの形をとる. □*The worst thing is when you call friends and they've gone out.* 最悪なのは, 友人を訪ねてから彼らが不在だと判断することだ.

thick /θɪk/ (**thicker, thickest**) **1** ADJ 形容詞 Something that is **thick** has a large distance between its two opposite sides. 厚い □*For breakfast I had a thick slice of bread and butter.* 朝食には, バターを塗った厚切りのトーストを1枚食べました. □*He wore thick glasses.* 彼は分厚い眼鏡をかけている. ●**thick|ly** ADV 副詞 [ADV with v] 厚く □*Slice the meat thickly.* 肉は厚くカットしてください. **2** ADJ 形容詞 You can use **thick** to talk or ask about how wide or deep something is. 厚さが～の □*The folder was two inches thick.* そのファイルは厚さ2インチだった. ●**Thick** is also a combining form. 厚さ～の [ADJ n] □*His life was saved by a quarter-inch-thick bullet-proof vest.* 彼は厚さ4分の1インチの防弾チョッキを着ていて命拾いした. ●**thick|ness** (**thicknesses**) N-VAR 可変性名詞 厚さ □*The size of the fish will determine the thickness of the steaks.* 魚の大きさで切り身の厚さが決まるだろう. **3** ADJ 形容詞 If something that consists of several things is **thick**, it has a large number of them very close together. 密な □*She inherited our father's thick, wavy hair.* 彼女は, 私たちの父の濃くて, くせのある髪質を受け継いだ. ●**thick|ly** ADV 副詞 密に □*I rounded a bend where the trees and brush grew thickly.* 木とやぶが生い茂った角を曲がった. **4** ADJ 形容詞 [v-link ADJ 'with' n] If something is **thick with** another thing, the first thing is full of or covered with the second. ～でいっぱいの □*The air is thick with acrid smoke from the fires.* その火事で鼻を突く異臭が立ち込めています. **5** ADJ 形容詞 **Thick** clothes are made from heavy cloth, so that they will keep you warm in cold weather. 厚地の □*In the winter she wears thick socks, boots and gloves.* 彼女は, 冬は厚手のソックス, ブーツ, 手袋を着用する. **6** ADJ 形容詞 **Thick** smoke, fog, or cloud is difficult to see through. 濃い □*The smoke was bluish-black and thick.* 青みがかった濃い煙だった. **7** ADJ 形容詞 **Thick** liquids are fairly stiff and solid and do not flow easily. (濃度が) 濃い □*It had rained last night, so the garden was thick mud.* 昨夜雨が降り, 庭はドロドロだった.

Word Partnership thick は次の語句と使われる:

N.	thick **glass**, thick **ice**, thick **layer**, thick **lips**, thick **neck**, thick **slice**, thick **wall** **1**
	thick **carpet**, **feet/inches** thick **2**
	thick **beard**, thick **fur**, thick **grass**, thick **hair** **3**
	thick **with smoke** **4**
	thick **air**, thick **clouds**, thick **fog**, thick **smoke** **6**
ADV.	so thick, too thick, very thick **1** – **7**

thick|en /θɪkən/ (**thickens, thickening, thickened**) **1** V-T/V-I 他動詞/自動詞 When you **thicken** a liquid or when it **thickens**, it becomes stiffer and more solid. 濃くなる □*Thicken the broth with the mashed potato.* つぶしたじゃがいもでスープにとろみをつけてください. **2** V-I 自動詞 If something **thickens**, it becomes more closely grouped together or more solid than it was before. 厚くなる □*The dust behind us grew closer and thickened into a cloud.* 背後で立ち昇った砂塵が近づいてきて, もうもうとして一固まりになった.

thief /θif/ (**thieves**) /θivz/ N-COUNT 可算名詞 A **thief** is a person who steals something from another person. どろぼう □*The thieves snatched the camera.* 窃盗団がカメラを強奪した.

Anyone who steals can be called a **thief**. A **robber** often uses violence or the threat of violence to steal things from places such as banks or businesses. A **burglar** breaks into houses or other buildings and steals things.

thigh /θaɪ/ (**thighs**) N-COUNT 可算名詞 Your **thighs** are the top parts of your legs, between your knees and your hips. 太もも □*The shorts are so small I can't fit my thighs into any of them.* そのパンツはサイズが小さくて, 両側とも太ももが全然入らないわ.

→ see **body**

thin /θɪn/ (**thinner, thinnest, thins, thinning, thinned**) **1** ADJ 形容詞 Something that is **thin** is much narrower than it is long. 細い □*A thin cable carries the signal to a computer.* 細いケーブルを通してコンピュータに信号が送られる. **2** ADJ 形容詞 A person or animal that is **thin** has no extra fat on their body. やせた □*He was a tall, thin man with grey hair that fell in a wild tangle to his shoulders.* 彼は背が高く, やせていて, 白髪が肩のあたりででらしなくもつれていた. **3** ADJ 形容詞 Something such as paper or cloth that is **thin** is flat and has only a very small distance between its two opposite surfaces. 薄い □*...a small, blue-bound book printed in fine type on thin paper.* 薄い紙に細かい字が印字された, 青で装丁された, 小さな本. ●**thin|ly** ADV 副詞 [ADV with v] 薄く □*Peel and thinly slice the*

onion. たまねぎの皮をむき, 薄くスライスしてください. **4** ADJ 形容詞 Liquids that are **thin** are weak and watery. 薄い □*The soup was thin and clear, yet mysteriously rich.* スープは薄くて透明だったが, 不思議に味わい深かった. **5** ADJ 形容詞 A crowd or audience that is **thin** does not have many people in it. まばらな □*The crowd, which had been thin for the first half of the race, had now grown considerably.* レースの前半はまばらだった観客が, 相当な人数に膨れ上がった. ●**thin|ly** ADV 副詞 まばらに □*The island is thinly populated.* その島の人口は少ない. **6** ADJ 形容詞 **Thin** clothes are made from light cloth and are not warm to wear. 薄手の □*Her gown was thin, and she shivered, partly from cold.* 薄手のガウンを着た彼女は, 寒さのせいもあって震えていた. **7** ADJ 形容詞 If you describe an argument, an explanation, or evidence as **thin**, you mean that it is weak and difficult to believe. (論拠が) 希薄な □*The DA was certain she had the right man, but the evidence was thin.* その地方検事は彼女が適切な人選を行ったと確信していたが, 根拠に乏しかった. ●**thin|ly** ADV 副詞 希薄に □*Much of the speech was a thinly disguised attack on environmentalists.* スピーチの大部分は環境保護主義者に対する見え見えの攻撃だった. **8** ADJ 形容詞 If someone's hair is described as **thin**, they do not have a lot of hair. (髪が) 薄い □*She had pale thin yellow hair she pulled back into a bun.* 彼女はボリュームのない淡い黄色の髪を後ろでおだんごに結っていた. **9** V-T/V-I 他動詞/自動詞 When you **thin** something or when it **thins**, it becomes less crowded because people or things have been removed from it. まばらにする, まばらになる □*It would have been better to have thinned the trees over several winters rather than all at one time.* その木立の間引きは一度に行ってしまわず, 幾冬かに分けて行ったほうがよかっただろう. ●PHRASAL VERB 句動詞 **Thin out** means the same as **thin**. 少なくする □*NATO will continue to thin out its forces.* NATOは引き続き軍縮を行うだろう. **10** PHRASE 句 If someone's patience, for example, **is wearing thin**, they are beginning to become impatient or angry with someone. 我慢の限界に近づく □*War has achieved little, and public patience is wearing thin.* 戦果はほとんどなく, 民衆の我慢は限界に近づきつつあります. **11** on thin ice → see **ice** **12** thin air → see **air**

Thesaurus thin また次を参照:

ADJ.	flimsy, transparent, wispy; (ant.) dense, solid, thick **1**
	lean, skinny, slender, slim, underweight; (ant.) fat, heavy **2**
	watery, weak; (ant.) thick **4**

Word Partnership thin は次の語句と使われる:

N.	thin **face**, thin **fingers**, thin **legs**, thin **line**, thin **lips**, thin **mouth**, thin **smile**, thin **strips** **1**
	thin **body**, thin **man/woman** **2**
	thin **film**, thin **ice**, thin **layer**, razor thin, thin **slice** **3**
ADJ.	long and thin **1**
	tall and thin **2**
ADV.	extremely thin, too thin, very thin **1** – **8**

thing

1 NOUN USES
2 PHRASES

1 thing /θɪŋ/ (**things**) **1** N-COUNT 可算名詞 You can use **thing** to refer to any object, feature, or event when you cannot, need not, or do not want to refer to it more precisely. 物 □*"What's that thing in the middle of the fountain?" —"Some kind of statue, I guess."* 噴水の真ん中にあるのは何だろう？」「何かの像だろうな」 □*She was in the middle of clearing the breakfast things.* 彼女は朝食の後片付けの真っただ中だった. **2** N-COUNT 可算名詞 **Thing** is used in lists and descriptions to give examples or to increase the range of what you are referring to. 事項 □*They spend their money on things like rent and groceries.* 彼らは賃料や日用品などの項目に支出した. **3** N-COUNT 可算名詞 **Thing** is often used after an adjective, where it would also be possible just to use the adjective. For example, you can say **it's a different thing** instead of **it's different.** ～なもの □*Of course, literacy isn't the same thing as intelligence.* もちろん, 識字能力と知能は同じものではありません. **4** N-SING 単数名詞 **Thing** is often used instead of the pronouns "anything," or "everything" in order to emphasize what you are saying. 何か [EMPHASIS 強調] □*I haven't done a thing all day.* 私は一日何もしないで過ごした. □*It isn't going to solve a single thing.* それはなにも解決しないよ. **5** N-COUNT 可算名詞 **Thing** is used in expressions such as **such a thing** or **a thing like that**, especially in negative statements, in order to emphasize the bad or different situation you are referring back to. そのようなこと [EMPHASIS 強調] □*I don't believe he would tell Leo such a thing.* 彼がレオにそんなことを言ったなんて信じられないな. **6** N-COUNT 可算名詞 You can use **thing** to refer in a vague way to a situation, activity, or idea, especially when you want to suggest that it is

not very important. 一関連のこと [INFORMAL くだけた, VAGUENESS あいまいさ] ❑ *I'm a bit unsettled tonight. This war thing's upsetting me.* 今夜は気持ちが少し落ち着かないわ。戦争ものはきっと気分が悪くなるわ。 **7** N-COUNT 可算名詞 You often use **thing** to indicate to the person you are addressing that you are about to mention something important, or something that you particularly want them to know. こと ❑ *One thing I am sure of was that she was scared.* 一つ確かなのは, 彼女が怖がっていたということです。 **8** N-COUNT 可算名詞 A **thing** is often used to refer back to something that has just been mentioned, either to emphasize it or to give more information about it. 一なこと ❑ *Getting drunk is a thing all young men do.* 若い男性ならだれでも酔っ払うものだ。 **9** N-COUNT 可算名詞 A **thing** is a physical object that is considered as having no life of its own. 物 ❑ *It's not a thing. It's a human being!* それではない。人間なんだ! **10** N-COUNT 可算名詞 **Thing** is used to refer to something, especially a physical object, when you want to express contempt or anger toward it. 軽蔑や怒りの対象となるもの ❑ *Turn that thing off!* そんなものは消してくれ! [SPOKEN 口語, DISAPPROVAL 不賛成] **11** N-COUNT 可算名詞 You can call a person or an animal a particular **thing** when you want to mention a particular quality that they have and express your feelings toward them, usually affectionate feelings. 一な人, 一なもの [INFORMAL くだけた] ❑ *She is such a cute little thing.* 彼女はとてもかわいいんだよ。 **12** N-PLURAL 複数名詞 Your **things** are your clothes or possessions. 所有物 ❑ *Sara told him to take all his things and not to return.* サラは彼に, 自分の荷物は全部持って行き, 帰ってこないように告げた。 **13** N-PLURAL 複数名詞 **Things** can refer to the situation or life in general and the way it is changing or affecting you. 状況 ❑ *Everyone agrees things are getting better.* 誰もが, 状況が好転し始めていることを認めています。

Thesaurus *thing* また次を参照:

N. device, figure, gadget, item, object, tool **❶** **1** **9**

---

❷ thing /θɪŋ/ (things) **1** PHRASE 句 If, for example, you **do the right thing** or **do the decent thing** in a situation, you do something which is considered correct or socially acceptable in that situation. 一なことをする ❑ *People want to do the right thing and buy "green."* 人々は正しいことをしたくて『環境にやさしい製品』を購入する。 **2** PHRASE 句 If you do something **first thing**, you do it at the beginning of the day, before you do anything else. If you do it **last thing**, you do it at the end of the day, before you go to bed or go to sleep. (その日の) 最初に (その日の) 最後に ❑ *I'll go see her, first thing.* 真っ先に彼女に会いにいくよ。 **3** PHRASE 句 You say **it is a good thing** to do something to introduce a piece of advice or a comment on a situation or activity. 一するのはよいことだ ❑ *Can you tell me whether it is a good thing to prune an apple tree?* りんごの木は枝を落としたほうがいいのか, 教えてもらえますか。 **4** PHRASE 句 You can say that the first of two ideas, actions, or situations **is one thing** when you want to contrast it with a second idea, action, or situation and emphasize that the second one is much more difficult, important, or extreme. 一は別のことだ [EMPHASIS 強調] ❑ *It was one thing to talk about leaving; it was another to physically walk out the door.* 出て行くと言うのと, 実際にドアから出て行くのは別のことだ。 **5** PHRASE 句 You can say **for one thing** when you are explaining a statement or answering a question, to suggest that you are not giving the whole explanation or answer, and that there are other points that you could add to it. 一例を挙げると ❑ *She was a monster. For one thing, she really enjoyed cruelty.* 彼女は恐ろしく残忍だった。例えば, 残酷な行為を楽しむんだ。 **6** PHRASE 句 You can use the expression **"one thing and another"** to suggest that there are several reasons for something or several items on a list, but you are not going to explain or mention them all. あれやこれやで [SPOKEN 口語] ❑ *What with one thing and another, it was fairly late in the day when we got home.* あれやこれやで, その日の家に着いたのはかなり遅い時間だった。 **7** PHRASE 句 If you say **it is just one of those things** you mean that you cannot explain something because it seems to happen by chance. どうにもならないことだ ❑ *"I wonder why." Mr. Dambar shrugged. "It must be just one of those things, I guess."* 「どうしてだろう」とダンバー氏は肩をすくめた。「きっとどうしようもないことにちがいないのさ」 **8** PHRASE 句 If you say that someone **is seeing** or **hearing things**, you mean that they believe they are seeing or hearing something, but it is not really there. 幻を見る, 空耳である ❑ *Dr. Payne led Lana back into the examination room and told her she was seeing things.* ペイン医師はラナを診察室に戻し, 君は幻を見ているんだ, と彼女に言った。 **9** PHRASE 句 You can say there is **no such thing as** something to emphasize that it does not exist or is not possible. 一はありえない [EMPHASIS 強調] ❑ *There really is no such thing as a totally risk-free industry.* まったくリスクがない業界というのは実際にありえないのです。 **10** PHRASE 句 You say **the thing is** to introduce an explanation, comment, or opinion, that relates to something that has just been said. **The thing is** is often used to identify a problem relating to what has just been said. 実は [SPOKEN 口語] ❑ *"What does your market research consist of?"—"Well, the thing is, it depends on our target age group."* 「あなたの

市場調査は何に基づくものですか」「実は, ターゲットにしている年齢層を対象にしたものです」 **11** **other things being equal** → see **equal**

---

think

❶ VERB AND NOUN USES
❷ PHRASES
❸ PHRASAL VERB

---

❶ think /θɪŋk/ (thinks, thinking, thought) **1** V-T/V-I 他動詞/自動詞 If you **think** that something is the case, you believe that it is the case. 考える [no cont] ❑ *I certainly think there should be a ban on tobacco advertising.* たばこの広告は禁止にするべきだ, と本当に思うよ。 ❑ *A generation ago, it was thought that babies born this small could not survive.* 一世代前は, こんなに小さく生まれた赤ちゃんは助からないと考えられていた。 ❑ *Tell me, what do you think of my theory?* 僕の理論をどう思うか聞かせてくれないか。 **2** V-T 他動詞 If you say that you **think** that something is true or will happen, you mean that you have the impression that it is true or will happen, although you are not certain of the facts. 思う [no cont] ❑ *Nora thought he was seventeen years old.* ノーラは彼が17歳だと思った。 ❑ *The storm is thought to be responsible for as many as four deaths.* その嵐で, 4人もの方が亡くなったと思われます。 **3** V-T/V-I 他動詞/自動詞 If you **think** in a particular way, you have those general opinions or attitudes. 考え方をする [no cont, no passive] ❑ *You were probably brought up to think like that.* 恐らくあなたはそんなふうに考えるよう育てられたのよ。 ❑ *If you think as I do, vote as I do.* 考え方が私と同じなら, 私が選ぶ人に投票してください。 ❑ *I don't blame you for thinking that way.* 君がそんな考え方をするからといって非難はしないよ。 **4** V-I 自動詞 When you **think** about ideas or problems, you make a mental effort to consider them. 思いめぐらす ❑ *She closed her eyes for a moment, trying to think.* 彼女はじっくり考えようとして, 少しの間目を閉じた。 ❑ *I have often thought about this problem.* この問題についてはよく思案してきました。 N-SING 単数名詞 ●**Think** is also a noun. 思案 [mainly BRIT 主に英国英語] ['a' N] ❑ *I'll have a think about that.* じっくり検討しておきましょう。 **5** V-T/V-I 他動詞/自動詞 If you **think** in a particular way, you consider things, solve problems, or make decisions in this way, for example, because of your job or your background. 考える [no passive] ❑ *To make the computer work at full capacity, the programmer has to think like the machine.* コンピュータの性能をフルに活用するには, プログラマーはコンピュータのように思考しなければならない。 ❑ *Why do they think the way they do?* 彼らはどうしてあのような考え方をするのだろう? **6** V-T/V-I 他動詞/自動詞 If you **think of** something, it comes into your mind or you remember it. 思う [no cont] ❑ *Nobody could think of anything to say.* 誰もが何も言うべきことを思いつかなかった。 ❑ *I was trying to think what else we had to do.* 私は, 他に自分たちが何をすべきだったかを思い出そうとしていた。 **7** V-I 自動詞 If you **think of** an idea, you make a mental effort and use your imagination and intelligence to create it or develop it. 考えつく ❑ *He thought of another way of making electricity.* 彼は電気を起こす方法をもう一つ考えついた。 **8** V-T 他動詞 If you **are thinking** something at a particular moment, you have words or ideas in your mind without saying them out loud. 思う [no passive] ❑ *She must be sick, Tatiana thought.* 彼女はきっと病気だわ, とタチアナは思った。 ❑ *I remember thinking how lovely he looked.* 彼はなんてすてきなんでしょう, って思ったことを覚えているわ。 **9** V-T/V-I 他動詞/自動詞 If you **think of** someone or something **as** having a particular quality or purpose, you regard them as having this quality or purpose. 一だと思う [no cont] ❑ *We all thought of him as a father.* 私たちは皆, 彼が父親だと思っていた。 ❑ *He thinks of it as his home.* 彼はそこを自分の家だと思っている。 ❑ *I wouldn't have thought him capable of it.* 私なら彼がそれをできるとは思わなかっただろうに。 **10** V-T/V-I 他動詞/自動詞 If you **think a lot of** someone or something, you admire them very much or think they are very good. 一を高く評価する [no cont] ❑ *To tell the truth, I don't think much of psychiatrists.* 正直言って, 精神科医なんて大したことはないと思ってるんだ。 ❑ *Everyone in my family thought very highly of him.* 私の家族は皆, 彼を高く評価していた。 **11** V-I 自動詞 If you **think of** someone or **about** someone, you show consideration for them and pay attention to their needs. 思いやる ❑ *I'm only thinking of you.* 私はあなたのことばかり考えているのよ。 **12** V-I 自動詞 If you **are thinking of** or **are thinking about** taking a particular course of action, you are considering it as a possible course of action. 一しようと考えている ❑ *Martin was thinking of taking legal action against Zuckerman.* マーチンはザッカーマンに訴訟を起こそうと考えていた。 **13** V-I 自動詞 You can say that you **are thinking of** a particular aspect or subject, in order to introduce an example or explain more exactly what you are talking about. 考えているのは一だ [usu cont] ❑ *The parts of the enterprise which are scientifically the most exciting are unlikely to be militarily useful. I am thinking here of the development of new kinds of lasers.* その事業はある部分で科学的に世間をとてもにぎわせています。しかし, その技術は軍用に使える見込みはなさそうです。そこで私が考えているのは, 新種のレーザーの開発なのです。 **14** V-I 自動詞 You use **think** in questions where you are expressing your

anger or shock at someone's behavior. (いったい何を) 考えているのか [DISAPPROVAL 不賛成] [only interrog] ❑ *What were you thinking of? You shouldn't steal.* いったい何を考えていたんだ? 盗みは許されないんだぞ. **15** V-T/V-I 他動詞/自動詞 You use **think** when you are commenting on something which you did or experienced in the past and which now seems surprising, foolish, or shocking to you. ~だったとは (驚きだ) [no cont, no passive] ❑ *To think I left you alone in a strange place.* 見知らぬところであなたを一人にしてしまったなんて. ❑ *When I think of how you've behaved and the trouble you've caused!* あなたがあんなにふるまって, 迷惑をかけたなんて! **16** → see also **thinking, thought**

Thesaurus	*think* また次を参照:
v.	believe, consider, feel, judge, understand **❶ 1**
	analyze, evaluate, meditate, reflect, study **❶ 4**
	recall, remember; (ant.) forget **❶ 6**

❷ think /θ**ɪŋk**/ (**thinks, thinking, thought**) **1** PHRASE 句 You use expressions such as **come to think of it, when you think about it,** or **thinking about it,** when you mention something that you have just suddenly remembered or realized. そういえば ❑ *He was her distant relative, as was everyone else on the island, come to think of it.* 彼は, そういえば, この島のみんなと同様, 彼女の遠い親戚だったな. **2** PHRASE 句 You use **"I think"** as a way of being polite when you are explaining or suggesting to someone what you want to do, or when you are accepting or refusing an offer. ~させてもらう [POLITENESS 丁寧さ] ❑ *I think I'll go home and have a shower.* おいとまして, 家でシャワーをあびさせていただく. **3** PHRASE 句 You use **"I think"** in conversations or speeches to make your statements and opinions sound less forceful, rude, or direct. 語調を弱めたり挿入句にするための挿入句 ❑ *Thanks, but I think I can handle it.* ありがたいのですが, 自分でも対処できるかと思います. [VAGUENESS あいまいさ] **4** PHRASE 句 You say **just think** when you feel excited, fascinated, or shocked by something, and you want the listener to feel the same. 考えてみなさい ❑ *Just think; tomorrow we shall walk out of this place and leave it all behind us forever.* 考えてみてよ. 私たちは明日ここを出たら二度と帰ってこないのよ. **5** PHRASE 句 If you **think again about** an action or decision, you consider it very carefully, often with the result that you change your mind and decide to do things differently. 考え直す ❑ *It has forced politicians to think again about the wisdom of trying to evacuate refugees.* そのことがきっかけで, 政治家たちは難民救済の知恵を再検討した. **6** PHRASE 句 If you **think nothing of** doing something that other people might consider difficult, strange, or wrong, you consider it to be easy or normal. ~をものともしない ❑ *I thought nothing of betting $1,000 on a horse.* 馬券に千ドル使うことなんて俺には何でもないことさ. **7** PHRASE 句 If something happens and you **think nothing of it,** you do not pay much attention to it or think of it as strange or important, although later you may realise that it is. 何とも思わない ❑ *When she went off to see her parents for the weekend I thought nothing of it.* その週末に彼女は両親に会いに出かけたが, 私はそれを何とも思わなかった. **8** you **can't hear** yourself **think** → see **hear** **9** to **think better of it** → see **better** **10** to **think big** → see **big** **11** to **think twice** → see **twice**

Note that when you are using the verb **think** with a "that" -clause in order to state a negative opinion or belief, you normally make **think** negative, rather than the verb in the "that" -clause. For instance, it is more usual to say **"I don't think he saw me"** than "I think he didn't see me." The same pattern applies to other verbs with a similar meaning, such as **believe, consider,** and **suppose.**

❸ think /θ**ɪŋk**/ (**thinks, thinking, thought**)
▸ **think back** PHRASAL VERB 句動詞 If you **think back,** you make an effort to remember things that happened to you in the past. 回想する ❑ *I thought back to the time in 1995 when my son was desperately ill.* 私は, 1995年に息子が重病だったときのことを思い出していた.
▸ **think over** PHRASAL VERB 句動詞 If you **think** something **over,** you consider it carefully before making a decision. よく考える ❑ *She said she needs time to think it over.* 彼女はじっくり考えさせてほしいと言った.
▸ **think through** PHRASAL VERB 句動詞 If you **think** a situation **through,** you consider it thoroughly, together with all its possible effects or consequences. とことん考える ❑ *I didn't think through the consequences of promotion.* 私は昇進の影響について深く考えていなかった. ❑ *The administration has not really thought through what it plans to do once the fighting stops.* 政府は停戦の場合の行動計画についてよく検討していませんでした.
▸ **think up** PHRASAL VERB 句動詞 If you **think** something **up,** for example, an idea or plan, you invent it using mental effort. 考え出す ❑ *Julian has been thinking up new ways of raising money.* ジュリアンは資金調達の新しい手法を考え出してきた.

think|er /θ**ɪŋ**kər/ (**thinkers**) N-COUNT 可算名詞 A **thinker** is a person who spends a lot of time thinking deeply about important

things, especially someone who is famous for thinking of new or interesting ideas. 思想家 ❑ *...some of the world's greatest thinkers.* 世界で最も偉大な思想家たち

think|ing /θ**ɪŋ**kɪŋ/ **1** N-UNCOUNT 不可算名詞 **Thinking** is the activity of using your brain by considering a problem or possibility or creating an idea. 思考 ❑ *This is a time of decisive action and quick thinking.* 断固として行動し, 敏速に決断すべきときだ. **2** N-UNCOUNT 不可算名詞 The general ideas or opinions of a person or group can be referred to as their **thinking.** 考え ❑ *There was undeniably a strong theoretical dimension to his thinking.* まぎれもなく, 彼の考えには強い理論的側面がある. **3** → see also **wishful thinking** **4** to my **way of thinking** → see **way**

third /θ**ɜrd**/ (**thirds**) **1** ORD 序数詞 The **third** item in a series is the one that you count as number three. 3番目の ❑ *I sleep on the third floor.* 私は3階で寝ている. **2** FRACTION 端数 A **third** is one of three equal parts of something. 3分の1 ❑ *A third of the cost went into technology and services.* 経費の3分の1は技術料やサービス料だった. **3** ADV 副詞 You say **third** when you want to make a third point or give a third reason for something. 第三に ❑ *First, interest rates may take longer to fall than is hoped. Second, lending may fall. Third, bad loans could wipe out much of any improvement.* 第一に, 金利の低下は予想よりも遅くなるでしょう. 第二に, 貸付は縮小するでしょう. 第三に, いかなる改善のきざしも不良債権によって帳消しになるでしょう. **4** N-COUNT 可算名詞 A **third** is the lowest honors degree that can be obtained from a British university. (成績が優, 良, 可の) 可 ❑ *...Ms. Hodge, who graduated in 2002 with a third in economics.* ホッジ女史は2002年の卒業だが, 経済学の成績は可だった.

third|ly /θ**ɜr**dli/ ADV 副詞 You use **thirdly** when you want to make a third point or give a third reason for something. 第三に ❑ *First of all, there are not many of them, and secondly, they have little money and, thirdly, they're hungry.* 第一に, 彼らは少数で, 第二に, 所持金もほとんどなく, 第三に, 空腹なのです.

Third World N-PROPER 固有名詞 The countries of Africa, Asia, and South and Central America are sometimes referred to all together as **the Third World,** especially those parts that are poor, do not have much power, and are not considered to be highly developed. 第三世界 ❑ *...development in the Third World.* 第三世界における開発

thirst /θ**ɜrst**/ (**thirsts**) **1** N-VAR 可変性名詞 **Thirst** is the feeling of wanting to drink something. のどの渇き ❑ *Instead of tea or coffee, drink water to quench your thirst.* 渇きをいやすには, お茶やコーヒーではなく, お水を飲みましょう. **2** N-UNCOUNT 不可算名詞 **Thirst** is the condition of not having enough to drink. 脱水状態 ❑ *They died of thirst on the voyage.* 彼らは航海中に脱水症で亡くなった.

thirsty /θ**ɜr**sti/ (**thirstier, thirstiest**) ADJ 形容詞 If you are **thirsty,** you feel a need to drink something. のどが渇いて ❑ *Drink whenever you feel thirsty during exercise.* 運動中にのどが渇いたらいつでも水分を取りましょう.

thir|teen /θ**ɜr**t**i**n/ (**thirteens**) NUM 数詞 **Thirteen** is the number 13. 13

thir|teenth /θ**ɜr**t**i**nθ/ ORD 序数詞 The **thirteenth** item in a series is the one that you count as number thirteen. 13番目の ❑ *...his thirteenth birthday.* 彼の13歳の誕生日

thir|ti|eth /θ**ɜr**tiəθ/ ORD 序数詞 The **thirtieth** item in a series is the one that you count as number thirty. 30番目の ❑ *...the thirtieth anniversary of my parents' wedding.* 両親の30回目の結婚記念日

thir|ty /θ**ɜr**ti/ (**thirties**) **1** NUM 数詞 **Thirty** is the number 30. 30 **2** N-PLURAL 複数名詞 When you talk about the **thirties,** you are referring to numbers between 30 and 39. For example, if you are **in** your **thirties,** you are aged between 30 and 39. If the temperature is **in** the **thirties,** the temperature is between 30 and 39 degrees. 30代 ❑ *Mozart clearly enjoyed good health throughout his twenties and early thirties.* 20代から30代前半, モーツアルトの健康状態は明らかによかった. **3** N-PLURAL 複数名詞 The **thirties** is the decade between 1930 and 1939. 1930年代 ❑ *She became quite a notable director in the thirties and forties.* 彼女は1930年代から40年代に監督として大いに注目されるようになりました.

this

The determiner is pronounced /ð**ɪs**/. In other cases, **this** is pronounced /ð**ɪs**/.

限定詞は /ð**ɪs**/と発音される. 他の場合は, **this** は /ð**ɪs**/と発音される.

1 DET 限定詞 You use **this** to refer back to a particular person or thing that has been mentioned or implied. この ❑ *The entire portfolio is worth $160,312. Of this amount, my investment is worth only $7,748.* ポートフォリオ全体の時価総額は16万312ドルで, 私の出資金はわずか7千748ドルにすぎません. ● PRON 代名詞 **This** is also a pronoun. これ ❑ *I don't know how bad the injury is, because I have never had one like this before.* 傷がどれくらい深刻なのか判断できません. このようなけがは経験がないからです. **2** PRON 代名

詞 You use **this** to introduce someone or something that you are going to talk about. 次のこと ❑ *This is what I will do. I will telephone Anna and explain.* 次にやろうと思ってるのは、アンナに電話をして訳を話すことなの。 ● DET 限定詞 **This** is also a determiner. 次の ❑ *This report is from our Science Unit.* 次の報告は当社の科学部門によるものです。 **3** PRON 代名詞 You use **this** to refer back to an idea or situation expressed in a previous sentence or sentences. それ ❑ *You feel that it's uneconomical. Why is this?* それは不経済だと思われるのですね。 その理由は何ですか。 ● DET 限定詞 **This** is also a determiner. その ❑ *There have been continual demands to put an end to this situation.* その状態に終止符を打つべきだという要求が次々と上がっています。 **4** DET 限定詞 In spoken English, people use **this** to introduce a person or thing into a story. とある ❑ *I came here by chance and was just watching what was going on, when this girl came up to me.* 私はたまたまここを通りがかり、事の成り行きを見ているだけだったのですが、ある少女が近づいてきたのです。 **5** PRON 代名詞 You use **this** to refer to a person or thing that is near you, especially when you touch them or point to them. When there are two or more people or things near you, **this** refers to the nearest one. この ❑ *I like this coat better than that one.* 私はあれよりこのコートの方が好きだ。 ❑ *"If you'd prefer something else I'll gladly have it changed for you." — "No, this is great."* 「もし他のものがよろしければ、よろこんでお取り替えいたしますよ」「いえ、これで結構です」● DET 限定詞 **This** is also a determiner. この ❑ *This church was built by the Emperor Constantine Monomarchus in the eleventh century.* この教会は11世紀にコンスタンティノス・モノマコス帝によって建てられた。 **6** PRON 代名詞 You use **this** when you refer to a general situation, activity, or event which is happening or has just happened and which you feel involved in. これが [PRON with 'be'] ❑ *I thought, this is why I've traveled thousands of miles.* 思うに、これが私が何千マイルも旅をしてきた理由なのです。 **7** DET 限定詞 You use **this** when you refer to the place you are in now or to the present time. この ❑ *This country is weird.* この国は不気味だ。 ❑ *This place is run like a hotel ought to be run.* ここの経営は、ホテルの経営状態のお手本のようだ。 ● PRON 代名詞 **This** is also a pronoun. ここ ❑ *This is the worst place I've come across.* ここは、たまたま立ち寄った中で最悪の店だ。 **8** DET 限定詞 You use **this** to refer to the next occurrence in the future of a particular day, month, season, or festival. この ❑ *...this Sunday's 7:45 performance.* この日曜の7時45分の上演 **9** ADV 副詞 You use **this** when you are indicating the size or shape of something with your hands. これくらいに [ADV adj] ❑ *"They'd said the wound was only about this big," and he showed me with his fingers.* 「彼らが言うには傷の大きさはだいたいこれくらいだったらしいよ」と彼は指で大きさを示してくれた。 **10** ADV 副詞 You use **this** when you are going to specify how much you know or how much you can tell someone. これくらいは [ADV adv] ❑ *I don't know if it's the best team I've ever had, but I can tell you this much, they're incredible people to be around.* このチームがこれまで担当した中でベストかどうかは分かりませんが、これくらいは言えます。 彼らは一緒にいて本当に素晴らしい人たちだということです。 **11** CONVENTION 慣習表現 If you say **this is it**, you are agreeing with what someone else has just said. そのとおりだ [BRIT 英国英語, FORMULAE 決まり文句] ❑ *"You know, people conveniently forget the things they say." — "Well this is it."* 「人は自分の言ったことを都合よく忘れるのさ」「ああ、まったくだ」 **12** PRON 代名詞 You use **this** in order to say who you are or what organisation you are representing, when you are speaking on the telephone, radio, or television. 私は一です、こちらは一です [this is] ❑ *Hello, this is John Thompson.* こんにちは、ジョン・トンプソンです。 **13** DET 限定詞 You use **this** to refer to the medium of communication that you are using at the time of speaking or writing. この ❑ *What I'm going to do in this lecture is focus on something very specific.* この講義では、ある具体的な事項に焦点を当ててお話しします。 **14** → see also **these** **15** PHRASE 句 If you say that you are doing or talking about **this and that**, or **this, that, and the other** you mean that you are doing or talking about a variety of things that you do not want to specify. あれこれ ❑ *"And what are you doing now?" — "Oh, this and that."* 「で、今何してるんだい？」「まあ、あれこれとね」

thorn /θɔrn/ (**thorns**) **1** N-COUNT 可算名詞 **Thorns** are the sharp points on some plants and trees, for example, on a rose bush. とげ ❑ *Roses will always have thorns but with care they can be avoided.* バラにはとげがつきものだが、注意すれば刺さらなくて済む。 **2** N-VAR 可変名詞 A **thorn** or a **thorn bush** or a **thorn tree** is a bush or tree which has a lot of thorns on it. とげのある ❑ *...the shade of a thorn bush.* とげのある低木の陰

thorny /θɔrni/ (**thornier, thorniest**) **1** ADJ 形容詞 A **thorny** plant or tree is covered with thorns. とげのある ❑ *...thorny hawthorn trees.* とげのあるサンザシの木 **2** ADJ 形容詞 If you describe a problem as **thorny**, you mean that it is very complicated and difficult to solve, and that people are often unwilling to discuss it. 悩ましい ❑ *...the thorny issue of immigration policy.* 移民政策の頭の痛い問題

thorough /θɜroʊ/ **1** ADJ 形容詞 A **thorough** action or activity is one that is done very carefully and in a detailed way so that nothing is forgotten. 徹底的な ❑ *We are making a thorough investigation.* 我々は徹底的に調べていきます。 ❑ *This very thorough survey goes back to 1784.* この綿密な調査は1784年から続いている。 ● **thor|ough|ly** ADV 副詞 [ADV with v] 徹底的に ❑ *Food that is being offered hot must be reheated thoroughly.* 熱くして出す料理は、しっかりと再加熱しなければなりません。 ● **thor|ough|ness** N-UNCOUNT 不可算名詞 徹底 ❑ *The thoroughness of the evaluation process we went through was impressive.* 我々が行ってきた評価プロセスの徹底は見事なものだった。 **2** ADJ 形容詞 Someone who is **thorough** is always very careful in their work, so that nothing is forgotten. きちょうめんな ❑ *Martin would be a good judge, I thought. He was calm and thorough.* マーチンは良い裁判官になると思った。 落ち着いていたし、きちょうめんだったからね。 ● **thor|ough|ness** N-UNCOUNT 不可算名詞 きちょうめんさ ❑ *His thoroughness and attention to detail is legendary.* 彼のきちょうめんさと細部へのこだわりは語りぐさになっている。 **3** ADJ 形容詞 [det ADJ] **Thorough** is used to emphasize the large degree or extent of something. 全くの [EMPHASIS 強調] ❑ *To me, this seemed like a thorough waste of time.* 自分にとって、これは全く時間の無駄に思えた。 ● **thor|ough|ly** ADV 副詞 すっかり ❑ *I thoroughly enjoy your program.* あなたのプログラムを大いに楽しませてもらいましたよ。

those

The determiner is pronounced /ðoʊz/. The pronoun is pronounced /ðoʊz/.

限定詞は /ðoʊz/ と発音される。 代名詞は /ðoʊz/ と発音される。

1 DET 限定詞 You use **those** to refer to people or things which have already been mentioned. それらの ❑ *Witnesses said that two people were killed, but those accounts could not be confirmed.* 複数の証人が殺されたのは2人だと言いましたが、それらの証言の立証は不可能でしょう。 ● PRON 代名詞 **Those** is also a pronoun. それら ❑ *I understand that there are a number of projects going on. Could you tell us a little bit about those?* いくつかのプロジェクトが進行中だそうですが、それについて少しお話ししていただけますか。 **2** DET 限定詞 You use **those** when you are referring to people or things that are a distance away from you in position or time, especially when you indicate or point to them. あれらの ❑ *What are those buildings?* あれらの建物は何ですか。 ● PRON 代名詞 **Those** is also a pronoun. あれら ❑ *I like these but not those.* これらは気に入りましたが、あそこのはもうひとつです。 ❑ *Those are nice shoes. Where'd you get them?* それはいい靴だね。 どこで買ったんだい？ **3** DET 限定詞 You use **those** to refer to someone or something when you are going to give details or information about them. それらの [FORMAL 形式ばった] ❑ *Those people who took up weapons to defend themselves are political prisoners.* 自らを守ろうと武器を手にしたその人々は、政治犯として収監されている。 **4** PRON 代名詞 You use **those** to introduce more information about something already mentioned, instead of repeating the noun which refers to it. 前に出た複数名詞を繰り返す代わりに用いる代名詞 ❑ *The interests he is most likely to enjoy will be those which enable him to show off himself or his talents.* 彼が最も楽しんでると思われる趣味は、自分自身や自分の才能を誇示できるようなものだろう。 [FORMAL 形式ばった] **5** PRON 代名詞 You use **those** to mean "people." 人々 ❑ *A little selfish behavior is unlikely to cause real damage to those around us.* 少し自己中心的な行動をしたからといって、我々に近い人々にはたいした影響はないだろう。 **6** DET 限定詞 You use **those** when you refer to things that you expect the person you are talking to to know about or when you are checking that you are both thinking of the same people or things. 例の ❑ *He did buy me those daffodils a week or so ago.* 彼は例の水仙をたしか1週間くらい前に買ってくれたのよ。

though /ðoʊ/ **1** CONJ 接続詞 You use **though** to introduce a statement in a subordinate clause which contrasts with the statement in the main clause. You often use **though** to introduce a fact which you regard as less important than the fact in the main clause. 一だけれども ❑ *Everything I told them was correct, though I forgot a few things.* 彼らに伝えたことは、いくつか言い忘れたけど、全部正しかったよ。 ❑ *I like him. Though he makes me angry sometimes.* 彼が好きよ。時々私を怒らせるけどね。 **2** CONJ 接続詞 You use **though** to introduce a subordinate clause which gives some information that is relevant to the main clause and weakens the force of what it is saying. とはいえ ❑ *He did reply, though not immediately.* すぐにではなかったが、彼は確かに返事をよこした。 **3** as **though** → see **as** **4** even **though** → see **even**

thought /θɔt/ (**thoughts**) **1** **Thought** is the past tense and past participle of **think**. think の過去・過去分詞 **2** N-COUNT 可算名詞 A **thought** is an idea that you have in your mind. 考え ❑ *The thought of Nick made her throat tighten.* ニックのことを考えると彼女は息が苦しくなった。 ❑ *I've just had a thought.* ちょっと考えごとをしていただけさ。 **3** N-PLURAL 複数名詞 A person's **thoughts** are their mind, or all the ideas in their mind when they are concentrating on one particular thing. 心 ❑ *I jumped to my feet so my thoughts wouldn't start to wander.* 私は心が揺れ動かないように、ぱっと立ち上がった。 ❑ *Usually at this time our thoughts are on Christmas.* この時期はいつも、私たちの心はクリスマスにある。 **4** N-PLURAL 複数名

t

詞 A person's **thoughts** are their opinions on a particular subject. 意見 ❑ *Many of you have written to us to express your thoughts on the conflict.* 多くのみなさんから、その紛争についての意見書が寄せられました. ⑤ N-UNCOUNT 不可算名詞 **Thought** is the activity of thinking, especially deeply, carefully, or logically. 思考 ❑ *Alice had been so deep in thought that she had walked past her car without even seeing it.* アリスはあまりに深く考えごとをしていたため、自分の車に目が止まることなく通り過ぎてしまった. ❑ *He had given some thought to what she had told him.* 彼は、彼女が自分に言ったことをしばらく考えていた. ⑥ N-COUNT 可算名詞 A **thought** is an intention, hope, or reason for doing something. 意図 ❑ *Sarah's first thought was to run back and get Max.* サラが最初に意図したのは、走って戻り、マックスをつかまえることだった. ⑦ N-UNCOUNT 不可算名詞 **Thought** is the group of ideas and beliefs which belongs, for example, to a particular religion, philosophy, science, or political party. 思想 ❑ *Aristotle's scientific theories dominated Western thought for fifteen hundred years.* アリストテレスの科学理論は西洋人の思想を1500年間支配した. ⑧ → see also **second thought**

thought|ful /θɔtfəl/ ❶ ADJ 形容詞 If you are **thoughtful**, you are quiet and serious because you are thinking about something. 物思いにふけった ❑ *Nancy, who had been thoughtful for some time, suddenly spoke.* ナンシーは、しばらく物思いにふけっていたが、突然言葉を発した. ● **thought|ful|ly** ADV 副詞 [ADV with v] 物思いにふけって ❑ *Daniel nodded thoughtfully.* ダニエルは考え込みながらうなずいた. ❷ ADJ 形容詞 If you describe someone as **thoughtful**, you approve of them because they remember what other people want, need, or feel, and try not to upset them. 思いやりが深い [APPROVAL 賛成] ● *a thoughtful and caring man.* 思いやりが深い配慮のある男性 ● **thought|ful|ly** ADV 副詞 [ADV with v] 親切に ❑ *...the bottle of wine he had thoughtfully purchased for the celebrations.* お祝い事のために彼が親切にも購入してくれたワインのボトル ❸ ADJ 形容詞 If you describe something such as a book, film, or speech as **thoughtful**, you mean that it is serious and well thought out. 考え抜かれた ❑ *...a thoughtful and scholarly book.* 綿密な学術本 ● **thought|ful|ly** ADV 副詞 [ADV with v] 綿密に ❑ *...these thoughtfully designed machines.* これらの綿密に設計された機械

thought|less /θɔtlɪs/ ADJ 形容詞 If you describe someone as **thoughtless**, you are critical of them because they forget or ignore other people's wants, needs, or feelings. 思いやりのない [DISAPPROVAL 不賛成] ❑ *...a small minority of thoughtless and inconsiderate people.* ごく一部の思いやりも分別もない人々 ● **thought|less|ly** ADV 副詞 [ADV with v] 思いやりがなく ❑ *They thoughtlessly planned a picnic without him.* 彼らは思いやりのないことに、彼抜きでピクニックをしようと計画した.

thou|sand /θaʊzᵊnd/ (thousands)

> The plural form is **thousand** after a number, or after a word or expression referring to a number, such as "several" or "a few."
>
> 複数形は数の後、あるいは **several** や **a few** のような数を指す単語や表現の後では **thousand** である.

❶ NUM 数詞 A **thousand** or **one thousand** is the number 1,000. 千 ❑ *...five thousand acres.* 5千エーカー ❷ QUANT 数量詞 If you refer to **thousands of** things or people, you are emphasizing that there are very many of them. とても多くの [EMPHASIS 強調] [QUANT 'of' pl-n] ❑ *Thousands of refugees are packed into overcrowded towns and villages.* 多数の難民が、人であふれた町や村に収容される. ● PRON 代名詞 You can also use **thousands** as a pronoun. 千個、千人 ❑ *Hundreds have been killed in the fighting and thousands made homeless.* その戦闘で数百人が殺され、数千人が家を失いました. ❸ **a thousand and one** → see **one**

thou|sandth /θaʊzᵊnθ/ (thousandths) ❶ ORD 序数詞 The **thousandth** item in a series is the one that you count as number one thousand. 千番目の ❑ *The magazine has just published its six thousandth edition.* その雑誌の創刊6千号が発売されたところです. ❷ ORD 序数詞 If you say that something has happened for the **thousandth** time, you are emphasizing that it has happened again and that it has already happened a large number of times. 何回も [EMPHASIS 強調] ❑ *The phone rings for the thousandth time.* 電話が何度も鳴った. ❸ FRACTION 端数 A **thousandth** is one of a thousand equal parts of something. 千分の1 ❑ *...a dust particle weighing only a thousandth of a gram.* 重さがわずか千分の1グラムのほこりの粒子

thrash /θræʃ/ (thrashes, thrashing, thrashed) ❶ V-T 他動詞 If one player or team **thrashes** another in a game or contest, they defeat them easily or by a large score. 打ち負かす [INFORMAL くだけた] ❑ *The Kings were thrashed by the Knicks last night.* 昨夜、キングスはニックスに大敗を喫しました. ❷ V-T 他動詞 If you **thrash** someone, you hit them several times as a punishment. 打ちすえる ❑ *"Liar!" Sarah screamed, as she thrashed the child. "You stole it."* サラはこどもをたたきながら「うそつき!」と叫んだ.「あなたが盗んだんでしょ」 ❸ V-T/V-I 他動詞/自動詞 If someone **thrashes around** or **thrashes** their arms or legs **around**, they move in a wild or violent way, often hitting against something. You can

also say that someone's arms or legs **thrash around**.（手足を）ばたつかせる ❑ *She would thrash around in her hospital bed and remove her intravenous line.* 彼女はよく入院先のベッドでばたばた動いて、点滴の管を抜いたものだった. ❑ *Many of the crew died a terrible death as they thrashed about in shark-infested waters.* 乗員の多くがサメの多い海域で手足をばたつかせたため、むごい死に方をした. ❹ V-T/V-I 他動詞/自動詞 If a person or thing **thrashes** something, or **thrashes at** something, they hit it continually in a violent or noisy way. たたく ❑ *...a magnificent paddle-steamer on the mighty Mississippi, her huge wheel thrashing the muddy water.* 洋々たるミシシッピー川に浮かぶ大きな蒸気船. その巨大な外輪が濁った水を打っている. ⑤ → see also **thrashing**

▶ **thrash out** ❶ PHRASAL VERB 句動詞 If people **thrash out** something such as a plan or an agreement, they decide on it after a lot of discussion. 議論の末に~に至る ❑ *John and Monica have thrashed out a divorce agreement.* ジョンとモニカは徹底した話し合いの結果、離婚の合意に至った. ❷ PHRASAL VERB 句動詞 If people **thrash out** a problem or a dispute, they discuss it thoroughly until they reach an agreement. 徹底的に議論して片付ける ❑ *...a sincere effort by two people to thrash out differences about which they have strong feelings.* 彼らが強い感情を持つ相違点について、議論を重ねて解決しようという二人の真摯な努力

thrash|ing /θræʃɪŋ/ (thrashings) ❶ N-COUNT 可算名詞 If one player or team beats another one a **thrashing**, they defeat them easily or by a large score. 打ち負かすこと [INFORMAL くだけた] ❑ *She dropped only eight points in the 43-minute thrashing of the former champion.* 彼女はチャンピオンに43分で圧勝し、その間の失点はわずか8点だった. ❷ N-COUNT 可算名詞 If someone gives someone else a **thrashing**, they hit them several times as a punishment. たたくこと ❑ *If Sarah caught her, she would get a terrible thrashing.* もしサラにつかまったら、彼女はひどくぶたれるだろう. ❸ → see also **thrash**

thread /θrɛd/ (threads, threading, threaded) ❶ N-VAR 可変性名詞 **Thread** or a **thread** is a long very thin piece of a material such as cotton, nylon, or silk, especially one that is used in sewing. 糸 ❑ *This time I'll do it right with a spool of thread.* 今度は、糸一巻きでうまくやれるでしょう. ❷ V-T 他動詞 When you **thread** a needle, you put a piece of thread through the hole in the top of the needle in order to sew with it. 糸を通す ❑ *I sit down, thread a needle, snip off an old button.* 私は座って、針に糸を通し、古いボタンを切り取った. ❸ N-COUNT 可算名詞 The **thread** of an argument, a story, or a situation is an aspect of it that connects all the different parts together. 脈絡 ❑ *The thread running through many of these proposals was the theme of individual power and opportunity.* これらの提案の多くに共通するのは、一人一人の力と機会という主題です. ❹ N-COUNT 可算名詞 A **thread of** something such as liquid, light, or color is a long thin line or piece of it. 一筋 ❑ *A thin, glistening thread of moisture ran along the rough concrete sill.* コンクリートの土台の上に、薄く、ぎらぎらとした水分が筋状についていた. ⑤ N-COUNT 可算名詞 The **thread** on a screw, or on something such as a lid or a pipe, is the raised spiral line of metal or plastic around it which allows it to be fixed in place by twisting. ねじ山 ❑ *The screw threads will be able to get a good grip.* そのねじ山でしっかりと固定できるでしょう. ❻ V-T/V-I 他動詞/自動詞 If you **thread** your **way** through a group of people or things, or **thread through** it, you move through it carefully or slowly, changing direction frequently as you move. 縫って進む ❑ *Slowly she threaded her way back through the moving mass of bodies.* 彼女はゆっくりと死体の山を縫って戻って行った. ❼ V-T 他動詞 If you **thread** a long thin object **through** something, you pass it through one or more holes or narrow spaces. 通す ❑ *...threading the laces through the eyelets of his shoes.* 彼の靴にひもを通して ❽ V-T 他動詞 If you **thread** small objects such as beads onto a string or thread, you join them together by pushing the string through them. 糸でつなぐ ❑ *Wipe the mushrooms clean and thread them on a string.* マッシュルームをきれいにぬぐって、糸でつないでください. ❾ N-COUNT 可算名詞 On websites such as newsgroups, a **thread** is one of the subjects that is being written about. スレッド [COMPUTING コンピューティング] ❑ *The dialogues are organized by month so you can go back to previous threads and read them.* 対話は月単位で整理されていますので、過去のスレッドに戻りその内容を確認することができます.

→ see **rope**

threat /θrɛt/ (threats) ❶ N-VAR 可変性名詞 A **threat** to a person or thing is a danger that something bad might happen to them. A **threat** is also the cause of this danger. 脅威 ❑ *Some couples see single women as a threat to their relationships.* 独身女性が自分たちの関係を脅かす存在だとするカップルもいる. ❷ N-COUNT 可算名詞 A **threat** is a statement by someone that they will hurt you in some way, especially if you do not do what they want. 脅し ❑ *He may be forced to carry out his threat to resign.* 彼が辞職を口にし、実行に移したのは強要されたからでしょう. ❸ PHRASE 句 If a person or thing is **under threat**, there is a danger that something bad might be done to them, or that they might cease to exist. 危ぶまれて ❑ *His position as leader is under threat.* 彼のリーダーとしての地位は危ぶまれている.

Word Partnership   threat は次の語句と使われる:

ADJ.	**biggest** threat, **greatest** threat, **major** threat 🔢 **credible** threat, **potential** threat, **real** threat, **serious** threat, **significant** threat 🔢 🔢
N.	threat **to** someone's **health** 🔢 threat **of attack**, **death** threat, threat **to peace**, threat **to stability**, threat **of a strike**, **terrorist** threat, threat **of violence**, threat **of war** 🔢 🔢

threat|en /θrɛtᵊn/ (threatens, threatening, threatened) 🔢 V-T 他動詞 If a person **threatens to** do something bad to you, or if they **threaten** you, they say or imply that they will hurt you in some way, especially if you do not do what they want. 一すると脅す ❑ He said army officers had threatened to destroy the town. 陸軍将校たちがその町を破壊すると脅した，と彼は言った．❑ He tied him up and threatened her with a six-inch knife. 彼は彼女を縛り上げ，6インチのナイフで脅した．🔢 V-T 他動詞 If something or someone **threatens** a person or thing, they are likely to harm that person or thing. 脅かす ❑ The newcomers directly threaten the livelihood of the established workers. 新しくやって来た人たちが，直接地元の労働者の生計を脅かした．🔢 V-T 他動詞 If something bad **threatens to** happen, it seems likely to happen. 一する恐れがある ❑ It's threatening to rain. 雨が降りそうだ．❑ The fighting is threatening to turn into full-scale war. その戦闘は全面戦争に発展する恐れが出てきています．🔢 → see also **threatening**

Word Partnership   threaten は次の語句と使われる:

N.	threaten **safety**, threaten **security**, threaten **stability**, threaten **survival** 🔢

threat|en|ing /θrɛtᵊnɪŋ/ 🔢 ADJ 形容詞 You can describe someone's behavior as **threatening** when you think that they are trying to harm you. 脅迫的な ❑ People who engage in threatening behavior should expect to be arrested. 脅迫行為に加担した人たちの逮捕が見込まれてしかるべきです．🔢 → see also **threaten**

three /θriː/ (threes) NUM 数詞 Three is the number 3. 3 ❑ We waited three months before going back to see the specialist. 私たちは次にその専門医に見てもらうまで3カ月待った．

three-dimensional 🔢 ADJ 形容詞 A **three-dimensional** object is solid rather than flat, because it can be measured in three different directions, usually the height, length, and width. The abbreviation **3-D** can also be used. 立体の ❑ ...a three-dimensional model. 立体モデル 🔢 ADJ 形容詞 A **three-dimensional** picture, image, or movie looks as though it is deep or solid rather than flat. The abbreviation **3-D** can also be used. 3次元の ❑ The software generates both two-dimensional drawings and three-dimensional images. そのソフトは2次元図と3次元像の両方を生成する．

three-quarters QUANT 数量詞 **Three-quarters** is an amount that is three out of four equal parts of something. 4分の3 [QUANT 'of' n] ❑ Three-quarters of the students are African American. 生徒の4分の3はアフリカ系アメリカ人です．● PRON 代名詞 **Three-quarters** is also a pronoun. 4分の3 ❑ Applications have increased by three-quarters. 申し込みが4分の3増加した．● ADV 副詞 **Three-quarters** is also an adverb. 4分の3 [ADV adj/-ed] ❑ We were left with an open bottle of champagne three-quarters full. 我々に残されたのは，栓が開いて中身が4分の3になったシャンパンだけだった．

thresh|old /θrɛʃhoʊld/ (thresholds) 🔢 N-COUNT 可算名詞 The **threshold** of a building or room is the floor in the doorway, or the doorway itself. 戸口 ❑ He stopped at the threshold of the bedroom. 彼は寝室の入り口で立ち止まった．🔢 N-COUNT 可算名詞 A **threshold** is an amount, level, or limit on a scale. When the **threshold** is reached, something else happens or changes. 限界 ❑ Moss has a high threshold for pain and a history of fast healing. モスは痛みに耐える限界点が高く，とても順調な経過をたどっている．🔢 PHRASE 句 If you are **on the threshold of** something exciting or new, you are about to experience it. まさに一しようとして ❑ We are on the threshold of a new era in astronomy. 我々は天文学の新たな時代に立とうとしています．

threw /θruː/ Threw is the past tense of **throw**. throwの過去形

thrift /θrɪft/ (thrifts) 🔢 N-UNCOUNT 不可算名詞 **Thrift** is the quality and practice of being careful with money and not wasting things. 倹約 [APPROVAL 賛成] ❑ They were rightly praised for their thrift and enterprise. 彼らが倹約的であり，かつ積極的なことは正当に評価された．🔢 N-COUNT 可算名詞 A **thrift** or a **thrift institution** is a kind of savings bank. 貯蓄金融機関 [AM 米国英語 BUSINESS 実業]

Thrift stores (or **charity shops** in the UK) are a great source of pleasure for the bargain-hunter. When people no longer need clothes, books, toys and other items, they may take them along to these shops, which rely on this type of donation. The proceeds all go to a particular charity.

thrill /θrɪl/ (thrills, thrilling, thrilled) 🔢 N-COUNT 可算名詞 If something gives you a **thrill**, it gives you a sudden feeling of great excitement, pleasure, or fear. スリル ❑ I can remember the thrill of not knowing what I would get on Christmas morning. クリスマスの朝にもらえるプレゼントが何なのかが分からず，どきどきしたのを覚えてるわ．🔢 V-T/V-I 他動詞/自動詞 If something **thrills** you, or if you **thrill at** it, it gives you a feeling of great pleasure and excitement. どきどきさせる，どきどきする ❑ The electric atmosphere both terrified and thrilled him. 熱狂的な雰囲気に彼はぞくっとしたり，どきどきしたりした．🔢 → see also **thrilling**, **thrilling**

thrilled /θrɪld/ 🔢 ADJ 形容詞 If someone is **thrilled**, they are extremely happy and excited about something. わくわくした [v-link ADJ] ❑ I was so thrilled to get a good grade from him. 彼の科目で良い評価が取れてとても感激したわ．🔢 → see also **thrill**

thrill|er /θrɪlər/ (thrillers) N-COUNT 可算名詞 A **thriller** is a book, movie, or play that tells an exciting fictional story about something such as criminal activities or spying. スリラー ❑ ...a tense psychological thriller. 手に汗にぎるサイコスリラー

thrill|ing /θrɪlɪŋ/ 🔢 ADJ 形容詞 Something that is **thrilling** is very exciting and enjoyable. 感動的な ❑ Our wildlife trips offer a thrilling encounter with wildlife in its natural state. 当社の野生観察旅行では，自然のままの野生生物との感動的な出会いをお楽しみいただけます．🔢 → see also **thrill**

thrive /θraɪv/ (thrives, thriving, thrived) 🔢 V-I 自動詞 If someone or something **thrives**, they do well and are successful, healthy, or strong. 良い状態にある ❑ He appears to be thriving. 彼は盛況なようだ．❑ Today her company continues to thrive. 今日も彼女の会社は活況です．🔢 V-I 自動詞 If you say that someone **thrives on** a particular situation, you mean that they enjoy it or that they can deal with it very well, especially when other people find it unpleasant or difficult. (逆境などを) 生きがいにする ❑ Many people thrive on a stressful lifestyle. 多くの人はストレスの多い暮らしに生きがいを感じている．

throat /θroʊt/ (throats) 🔢 N-COUNT 可算名詞 Your **throat** is the back of your mouth and the top part of the tubes that go down into your stomach and your lungs. 咽喉 (いんこう) ❑ She had a sore throat. 彼女はのどが痛かった．🔢 N-COUNT 可算名詞 Your **throat** is the front part of your neck. のど ❑ His striped tie was loosened at his throat. 彼のしま模様のネクタイはのどのところで緩められていた．🔢 PHRASE 句 If you **clear** your **throat**, you cough once either to make it easier to speak or to attract people's attention. せき払いをする ❑ Cross cleared his throat and spoke in low, polite tones. クロスはせき払いをして，低い声で丁重に話した．🔢 PHRASE 句 If you **ram** something **down** someone's **throat** or **force** it **down** their **throat**, you keep mentioning a situation or idea in order to make them accept it or believe it. 無理強いをする ❑ I've always been close to my dad but he's never rammed his career down my throat. 私はいつも父の間近にいたが，父は決して自分のキャリアを私に押し付けることはなかった．🔢 PHRASE 句 If two people or groups are **at each other's throats**, they are arguing or fighting violently with each other. 争って ❑ The idea that we are at each other's throats couldn't be further from the truth. 我々が対立させている考えは，現実とはまるで懸け離れたものだ．🔢 a **lump in** your **throat** → see **lump**

throb /θrɒb/ (throbs, throbbing, throbbed) 🔢 V-I 自動詞 If part of your body **throbs**, you feel a series of strong and usually painful beats there. ずきずきする，うずく ❑ His head throbbed. 彼の頭がずきずきと痛んだ．🔢 V-I 自動詞 If something **throbs**, it vibrates and makes a steady noise. 鼓動する，振動する [LITERARY 文語的] ❑ The engines throbbed. エンジンが鳴り響いた．

throne /θroʊn/ (thrones) 🔢 N-COUNT 可算名詞 A **throne** is a decorative chair used by a king, queen, or emperor on important official occasions. 王座 🔢 N-SING 単数名詞 You can talk about **the throne** as a way of referring to the position of being king, queen, or emperor. 王位 ❑ ...the queen's 40th anniversary on the throne. 女王の即位40周年

throng /θrɔŋ/ (throngs, thronging, thronged) 🔢 N-COUNT 可算名詞 A **throng** is a large crowd of people. 人だかり，群衆 [LITERARY 文語的] ❑ An official pushed through the throng. 関係者は人込みをかき分けて進んだ．🔢 V-I 自動詞 When people **throng** somewhere, they go there in great numbers. 群がる，押し寄せる [LITERARY 文語的] ❑ The crowds thronged into the stadium. 群衆が競技場に押しかけた．

throt|tle /θrɒtᵊl/ (throttles, throttling, throttled) 🔢 V-T 他動詞 To **throttle** someone means to kill or injure them by squeezing their throat or tightening something around it and preventing them from breathing. 絞め殺す，のどを絞める ❑ The attacker then tried to throttle her with wire. その後襲撃者は彼女を針金で絞め殺そう

とした. **2** N-COUNT 可算名詞 The **throttle** of a motor vehicle or aircraft is the device, lever, or pedal that controls the quantity of fuel entering the engine and is used to control the vehicle's speed. 絞り弁, スロットル □ *He gently opened the throttle, and the ship began to ease forward.* 彼が徐々に絞り弁を開けると, 船がそっと前に動き始めた.

through

❶ ADVERBS AND PREPOSITIONS: PHYSICAL MOVEMENTS AND POSITIONS
❷ ADVERBS AND PREPOSITIONS, ABSTRACT USES: TIMES, EXPERIENCES, CAUSES
❸ ADJECTIVES

❶ **through** **1** PREP 前置詞 To move **through** something such as a hole, opening, or pipe means to move directly from one side or end of it to the other. 〜を通って □ *The theater was evacuated when rain poured through the roof.* 雨が屋根を突き抜けて降り注いだとき, 人々は劇場から避難した. □ *Go straight through that door under the EXIT sign.* まっすぐに「出口」の標識の下のドアを通って行きなさい. ●ADV 副詞 **Through** is also an adverb. 通って [ADV after v] □ *There was a hole in the wall and water was seeping through.* 壁に穴があり, 水がしみ出ていた. **2** PREP 前置詞 To cut **through** something means to cut it in two pieces or to make a hole in it. 貫いて □ *Use a genuine fish knife and fork if possible as they are designed to cut through the flesh but not the bones.* できればちゃんとした魚肉用ナイフとフォークを使いなさい. なぜなら, 骨ではなくて魚肉を切るように作られているから. ●ADV 副詞 **Through** is also an adverb. 貫いて [ADV after v] □ *Score lightly at first and then repeat, scoring deeper each time until the board is cut through.* まずは軽く切れ目を入れて, 板を貫くまでだんだん深く切り込みを入れるのを繰り返しなさい. **3** PREP 前置詞 To go **through** a town, area, or country means to travel across it or in it. 通り抜けて □ *Go through North Carolina and into Virginia.* ノースキャロライナ州を通り抜けてバージニア州へ行きなさい. ●ADV 副詞 **Through** is also an adverb. 通り抜けて [ADV after v] □ *Few know that the tribe was just passing through.* その部族がただ通り過ぎるだけであることを知っているものはほとんどいなかった. **4** PREP 前置詞 If you move **through** a group of things or a mass of something, it is on either side of you or all around you. 〜の間を通り抜けて □ *We made our way through the crowd to the river.* 私たちは人込みの間を通り抜けて川にたどり着いた. ●ADV 副詞 **Through** is also an adverb. 間を通り抜けて [ADV after v] □ *He pushed his way through to the edge of the crowd where he waited.* 彼は人込みの中を端まで押し分けて進み, そこで待った. **5** PREP 前置詞 To get **through** a barrier or obstacle means to get from one side of it to the other. 通過して □ *Allow twenty-five minutes to get through passport control and customs.* 入国審査と税関を通過するのに25分考慮に入れなさい. ●ADV 副詞 **Through** is also an adverb. 通過して [ADV after v] □ *...a maze of concrete and steel barriers, designed to prevent vehicles driving straight through.* 車両が直進できないように設計されたコンクリートと鉄の柵の迷路 **6** PREP 前置詞 If a driver goes **through** a red light, they keep driving even though they should stop. 無視して □ *He was killed at an intersection by a driver who went through a red light.* 赤信号を無視して突っ切ったドライバーのせいで, 彼は交差点で死亡した. **7** PREP 前置詞 If something goes into an object and comes out of the other side, you can say that it passes **through** the object. 貫いて □ *The ends of the net pass through a wooden bar at each end.* 網の両端に木のさおを通している. ●ADV 副詞 **Through** is also an adverb. 貫通して [ADV after v] □ *I bored a hole so that the bolt would pass through.* ボルトが貫通するように穴を開けた. **8** PREP 前置詞 To go **through** a system means to move around it or to pass from one end of it to the other. 〜を経て □ *...electric currents traveling through copper wires.* 銅線を通って流れる電流 ●ADV 副詞 **Through** is also an adverb. 〜を経て [ADV after v] □ *Food should be allowed to go through immediately with fewer restrictions.* 食料は, ほとんど制限なしにただちに配送されるべきだ. **9** PREP 前置詞 If you see, hear, or feel something **through** a particular thing, that thing is between you and the thing you can see, hear, or feel. 〜越しに □ *Alice gazed pensively through the wet glass.* アリスは物思いに沈んで濡れたガラスの向こうを見た. **10** PREP 前置詞 If something such as a feeling, attitude, or quality happens **through** an area, organisation, or a person's body, it happens everywhere in it or affects all of it. 〜じゅうで, 〜の至る所に □ *An atmosphere of anticipation vibrated through the crowd.* 期待ムードが群衆全体に広がった.

❷ **through** **1** PREP 前置詞 If something happens or exists **through** a period of time, it happens or exists from the beginning until the end. 〜の間ずっと □ *She kept quiet all through breakfast.* 彼女は朝食中ずっと黙ったままだった. ●ADV 副詞 **Through** is also an adverb. ずっと [ADV after v] □ *We'll be working right through to the summer.* 夏までずっと働き続けます. **2** PREP 前置詞 If something happens from a particular period of time **through** another, it starts at the first period and continues until the end of the second

period. 〜まで [AM 米国英語] □ *...open Monday through Friday from 9 to 5.* 月曜から金曜の午前9時から午後5時まで営業 **3** PREP 前置詞 If you go **through** a particular experience or event, you experience it, and if you behave in a particular way **through** it, you behave in that way while it is happening. 経験して □ *Men go through a change of life emotionally just like women.* 男性は女性と同様に更年期を感情的に経験する. **4** PREP 前置詞 You use **through** in expressions such as **half-way through** and **all the way through** to indicate to what extent an action or task is completed. 〜のところで [n PREP n] □ *A thirty-nine-year-old competitor collapsed half-way through the marathon.* 39歳の走者がマラソンの半分のところで倒れた. ●ADV 副詞 **Through** is also an adverb. 〜のところで [n ADV] □ *Stir the pork until it turns white all the way through.* 豚肉が全体的に白くなるまでかき混ぜなさい. **5** PREP 前置詞 If something happens because of something else, you can say that it happens **through** it. 〜のために □ *I only succeeded through hard work.* 私は努力の結果成功したにすぎない. **6** PREP 前置詞 You use **through** when stating the means by which a particular thing is achieved. 〜によって □ *Those who seek to grab power through violence deserve punishment.* 暴力によって権力を得ようとする人々は懲罰に値する. **7** PREP 前置詞 If you do something **through** someone else, they take the necessary action for you. 〜を通して □ *Do I need to go through my doctor to get an appointment?* 担当医を通して予約を取らなければなりませんか? ●ADV 副詞 **Through** is also an adverb. 〜を通して [ADV after v] **8** PREP 前置詞 If something such as a proposal or idea goes **through**, it is accepted by people in authority and is made legal or official. 承認されて [ADV after v] □ *We're waiting for the building permit to go through.* 建築許可が承認されるのを待っている. ●PREP 前置詞 **Through** is also a preposition. 〜で承認されて □ *They want to get the plan through Congress as quickly as possible.* 彼らはできるだけ早く議会が計画を承認することを望んでいます. **9** PREP 前置詞 If someone gets **through** an examination or a round of a competition, they succeed or win. 〜を突破して □ *She was bright, learned languages quickly, and sailed through her exams.* 彼女は頭がよく, 言語を早急に学び, 試験を楽々と合格した. ●ADV 副詞 **Through** is also an adverb. 突破して [ADV after v] □ *Only the top four teams go through.* 上位4チームだけが次に進む. **10** ADV 副詞 When you get **through** while making a telephone call, the call is connected and you can speak to the person you are phoning. つながって [ADV after v] □ *Telephones are down so he can't get through.* 電話回線に問題があり, 彼につながらなかった. **11** PREP 前置詞 If you look or go **through** a lot of things, you look at them or deal with them one after the other. 〜のすみずみまで □ *Let's go through the numbers together and see if a workable deal is possible.* 一緒に数字を検討し取引が可能か考えてみよう. **12** PREP 前置詞 If you read **through** something, you read it from beginning to end. 〜の初めから終わりまで □ *She read through pages and pages of the music I had brought her.* 彼女は, 私が買ってあげた楽譜を初めから終わりまで何ページも読んだ. ●ADV 副詞 **Through** is also an adverb. 初めから終わりまで [ADV after v] □ *The article had been authored by Raymond Kennedy. He read it right through, looking for any scrap of information that might have passed him by.* その論文はレイモンド・ケネディによって執筆された. 彼は, 自分の知らない情報を少しでも見落とさないように初めから終わりまで読んだ. **13** ADV 副詞 If you say that someone or something is wet **through**, you are emphasizing how wet they are. すっかり [EMPHASIS 強調] [adj ADV] □ *I returned to the inn cold and wet, soaked through by the drizzling rain.* 私は, しとしと降る雨ですっかりずぶぬれになって, 凍えながら宿屋に戻った.

❸ **through** **1** ADJ 形容詞 If you are **through** with something or if it is **through**, you have finished doing it. 終えて [v-link ADJ] □ *We're through with dinner.* 私たちは夕食を食べ終えた. □ *Are you through with this?* これは終わったの? **2** ADJ 形容詞 If you are **through** with someone, you do not want to have anything to do with them again. 手を切った [v-link ADJ] □ *I'm through with her; she's bad news!* 彼女とは手を切ったよ. いやな女だよ!

The preposition is pronounced /θru/. In other cases, **through** is pronounced /θru/.

In addition to the uses shown here, **through** is used in phrasal verbs such as "follow through," "see through," and "think through."

through|out /θruaut/ **1** PREP 前置詞 If you say that something happens **throughout** a particular period of time, you mean that it happens during the whole of that period. 〜の間ずっと □ *The national tragedy of rival groups killing each other continued throughout 1990.* 対抗グループが殺し合いをする国家的悲劇は1990年の間中ずっと続いた. □ *Movie music can be made memorable because its themes are repeated throughout the film.* テーマ音楽が映画の上映中ずっと繰り返されるので, 映画音楽は覚えやすい. ●ADV 副詞 **Throughout** is also an adverb. 終始, 初めから終わりまで [ADV with cl] □ *The first song, "Blue Moon," didn't go too badly except that everyone talked throughout.* 最初の歌「ブルー・ムーン」はまあまあよかったが, だれもが終始おしゃべりをしていた. **2** PREP 前置詞 If you say that something happens or exists **throughout** a place, you mean that it happens or exists in all parts of that place. 〜の至るところ

に □"Sight Savers," founded in 1950, now runs projects throughout Africa, the Caribbean and Southeast Asia. 1950年に設立された「サイト・セーバー」は、現在ではアフリカ、カリブ、東南アジアのところで事業を行っている. ● ADV 副詞 **Throughout** is also an adverb. 至るところで [ADV with cl] □ The route is well sign-posted throughout. その道筋は分かりやすく標識が至るところに出ている.

throw /θroʊ/ (throws, throwing, threw, thrown) **1** V-T 他動詞 When you **throw** an object that you are holding, you move your hand or arm quickly and let go of the object, so that it moves through the air. 投げる □ He spent hours throwing a tennis ball against a wall. 彼は壁にテニスボールを投げながら何時間も過ごした. □ The crowd began throwing stones. 群衆は石を投げ始めた. ● N-COUNT 可算名詞 **Throw** is also a noun. 投げ, 投げること □ That was a good throw. 今の投げよかったよ. □ A throw of the dice allows a player to move himself forward. さいころを1度投げるとプレーヤーは前に進める. **2** V-T 他動詞 If you **throw** your body or part of your body into a particular position or place, you move it there suddenly and with a lot of force. 身を投げ出す □ She threw her arms around his shoulders. 彼女はさっと彼の肩に抱きついた. □ She threatened to throw herself in front of a train. 彼女は電車の前に飛び込むと脅した. **3** V-T 他動詞 If you **throw** something into a particular place or position, you put it there in a quick and careless way. ほうり投げる □ He struggled out of his bulky jacket and threw it on to the back seat. 彼は, ゴワゴワしたジャケットを何とか脱いで, 後部席にほうり投げた. **4** V-T 他動詞 To **throw** someone into a particular place or position means to force them roughly into that place or position. 投げ飛ばす □ He threw me to the ground. 彼は私を地面に投げ飛ばした. **5** V-T 他動詞 If you say that someone **is thrown into** prison, you mean that they are put there by the authorities. 入所させる [他動詞] □ Those two should have been thrown in jail. その2人は投獄されるべきだった. **6** V-T 他動詞 If a horse **throws** its rider, it makes him or her fall off, by suddenly jumping or moving violently. 振り落とす □ The horse reared, throwing its rider and knocking down a youth standing beside it. 馬が後ろ足立ちをし, 騎手を振り落とし, 横に立っていた若者を倒した. **7** V-T 他動詞 If a person or thing **is thrown into** a bad situation or state, something causes them to be in that situation or state. 陥らせる □ Abidjan was thrown into turmoil because of a protest by taxi drivers. アビジャンは, タクシー運転手による抗議のために混乱に陥った. **8** V-T 他動詞 If something **throws** light or a shadow **on** a surface, it causes that surface to have light or a shadow on it. 投じる □ The sunlight is white and blinding, throwing hard-edged shadows on the ground. 太陽の光がぎらぎらと輝き, 輪郭のはっきりした影を地面に投じている. **9** V-T 他動詞 If something **throws** doubt **on** a person or thing, it causes people to doubt or suspect them. (疑いを) かける □ This new information does throw doubt on their choice. この新情報は彼らの選択に疑問を投げかける. **10** V-T 他動詞 If you **throw** a look or smile at someone or something, you look or smile at them quickly and suddenly. (まなざし・ほほえみなどを) 投げかける [no cont] □ Emily turned and threw her a suggestive grin. エミリーは振り返って, 彼女に思わせぶりな笑いを投げかけた. **11** V-T 他動詞 If you **throw** yourself, your energy, or your money into a particular job or activity, you become involved in it very actively or enthusiastically. 打ち込む □ She threw herself into a modeling career. 彼女はモデルとしてのキャリアに打ち込んだ. **12** V-T 他動詞 If you **throw** a fit or a tantrum, you suddenly start to behave in an uncontrolled way. かんしゃくを起こす □ I used to get very upset and scream and swear, throwing tantrums all over the place. 私は以前は, あちこちに八つ当たりをしながら, 取り乱して大声を出したり, ののしりしたものだった. **13** V-T 他動詞 If something such as a remark or an experience **throws** you, it surprises you or confuses you because it is unexpected. 困惑させる [他動詞] □ Her sudden change in attitude threw me. 彼女の態度が突然変わったので私は困惑した. □ This new confession threw me for a loop. この新たな告白に私はあわてた. **14** V-T 他動詞 If you **throw** a punch, you punch someone. (パンチを) 食らわす □ Everything was fine until someone threw a punch. だれかがパンチを食らわすまですべては順調だった. **15** V-T 他動詞 When someone **throws** a party, they organize one, usually in their own home. (パーティを) 開く [INFORMAL くだけた] □ Why not throw a party for your friends? 友達のためにパーティを開いたら? **16** to **throw** someone **in at the deep end** → see **end** **17** to **throw down the gauntlet** → see **gauntlet** **18** to **throw light on** something → see **light** **19** to **throw money at** something → see **money** **20** to **throw in the towel** → see **towel** **21** to **throw your weight around** → see **weight**

▶ **throw away** or **throw out** **1** PHRASAL VERB 句動詞 When you **throw away** or **throw out** something that you do not want, you get rid of it, for example, by putting it in the trash. 捨てる □ I never throw anything away. 私は決して物を捨てない. **2** PHRASAL VERB 句動詞 If you **throw away** an opportunity, advantage, or benefit, you waste it, rather than using it sensibly. (チャンスなどを) 棒に振る ふいにする □ Failing to tackle the deficit would be throwing away an opportunity we haven't had for a generation. 赤字対策に失敗することはやっと恵まれた機会を無駄にすることだ.

▶ **throw out** **1** → see **throw away** 1 **2** PHRASAL VERB 句動詞 If

a judge **throws out** a case, he or she rejects it and the accused person does not have to stand trial. 却下する, 否決する □ The defense wants the district Judge to throw out the case. 被告側は地方裁判所判事が棄却することを望んでいます. **3** PHRASAL VERB 句動詞 If you **throw** someone **out**, you force them to leave a place or group. 追い出す, 追放する □ He was thrown out of the Olympic team after testing positive for drugs. 彼は, 麻薬検査で陽性が出たあとオリンピックチームから追放された. □ I wanted to kill him, but instead I just threw him out of the house. 彼を殺したかったが, その代わりに単に家から追い出した.

▶ **throw up** **1** PHRASAL VERB 句動詞 When someone **throws up**, they vomit. 吐く, もどす □ She said she had thrown up after reading reports of the trial. 彼女は裁判の報告書を読んだあと吐いたと述べた. **2** PHRASAL VERB 句動詞 If something **throws up** dust, stones, or water, when it moves or hits the ground, it causes them to rise up into the air. 舞い上げる, はね上げる □ If it had hit the Earth, it would have made a crater 100 miles across and thrown up an immense cloud of dust. もし地球にぶつかっていたら, 直径100マイルのクレーターができて, 巨大な砂ぼこりが舞い上がったことだろう.

thrown /θroʊn/ **Thrown** is the past participle of **throw**. throw の過去分詞

thrush /θrʌʃ/ (thrushes) **1** N-COUNT 可算名詞 A **thrush** is a fairly small bird with a brown back and sometimes a spotted breast. There are several different kinds of **thrush**. ツグミ **2** N-UNCOUNT 不可算名詞 **Thrush** is a medical condition caused by a fungus called Candida. It most often occurs in a baby's mouth or in a woman's vagina. がこうそう, 膣 (ちつ) カンジダ症 □ ...a medicine that's used to prevent and treat thrush and other fungal infections. がこうそうやその他の真菌感染症を予防し治療するのに使われた薬品

thrust /θrʌst/ (thrusts, thrusting, thrust) **1** V-T 他動詞 If you **thrust** something or someone somewhere, you push or move them there quickly with a lot of force. 押しのける, 突く □ They thrust him into the back of a jeep. 彼らは彼をジープの後ろに押し込んだ. ● N-COUNT 可算名詞 **Thrust** is also a noun. 突き □ Two of the knife thrusts were fatal. ナイフで2度突いたのは致命的だった. **2** V-T 他動詞 If you **thrust** your **way** somewhere, you move there, pushing between people or things which are in your way. 押し分けて進む □ She thrust her way into the crowd. 彼女は人込みをを押し分けて進んだ. **3** V-I 自動詞 If something **thrusts** up or out of something else, it sticks up or sticks out in a noticeable way. 突き出す [LITERARY 文語的] □ ...a seedling ready to thrust up into any available light. 差し込む光に向かって今にも突き出そうな苗 **4** N-UNCOUNT 不可算名詞 **Thrust** is the power or force that is required to make a vehicle move in a particular direction. 推進力 □ It provides the thrust that makes the craft move forward. それは飛行機を前進させる推進力をもたらす.
→ see **flight**

thud /θʌd/ (thuds, thudding, thudded) **1** N-COUNT 可算名詞 A **thud** is a dull sound, such as that which a heavy object makes when it hits something soft. ドスンという音 □ She tripped and fell with a sickening thud. 彼女はつまずいてドスンといういやな音を立てて転んだ. **2** V-I 自動詞 If something **thuds** somewhere, it makes a dull sound, usually when it falls onto or hits something else. ドサッとと落ちる, ドスンとぶつかる □ She ran up the stairs, her bare feet thudding on the wood. 彼女は, はだしで木製の階段をドスンドスンといわせながら駆け上がった. **3** V-I 自動詞 When your heart **thuds**, it beats strongly and somewhat quickly, for example, because you are very frightened or very happy. 高鳴る, ドッキンドッキンする □ My heart had started to thud, and my mouth was dry. 心臓がドキンドキンし始め, 口がカラカラになった.

thug /θʌg/ (thugs) N-COUNT 可算名詞 You can refer to a violent person or criminal as a **thug**. 暴漢, やくざ [DISAPPROVAL 不賛成] □ ...the cowardly thugs who mug old people. 高齢者を襲うひきょうな暴漢

thumb /θʌm/ (thumbs, thumbing, thumbed) **1** N-COUNT 可算名詞 Your hand has four fingers and one **thumb**. 親指 □ She bit the tip of her left thumb, not looking at me. 彼女は, 私の方を見ないで左の親指の先を噛んだ. **2** V-T 他動詞 If you **thumb** a lift or **thumb** a ride, you stand by the side of the road holding out your thumb until a driver stops and gives you a lift. ヒッチハイクをする □ It may interest you to know that a boy answering Rory's description

thumbed a ride to San Antonio. ロリーの描写どおりの男の子がヒッチハイクをしてサン・アントニオに行ったという情報があるんですよ. **3** PHRASE 句 If you are **under** someone's **thumb**, you are under their control, or very heavily influenced by them. 〜の言いなりで □ *I cannot tell you what pain I feel when I see how much my mother is under my father's thumb.* あまりにも母が父の言いなりになっているかを見て, どのくらいつらく感じるかは言葉では言い表せない. **4** green thumb → see green **5** rule of thumb → see rule → see hand

thumb|tack /θ∧mtæk/ (**thumbtacks**) N-COUNT 可算名詞 A **thumbtack** is a short pin with a broad flat top which is used for fastening papers or pictures to a board, wall, or other surface. 画鋲 (びょう) [AM 米国英語] → see office

thump /θ∧mp/ (**thumps, thumping, thumped**) **1** V-T/V-I 他動詞/自動詞 If you **thump** something, you hit it hard, usually with your fist. ドンドンと打つ □ *He thumped my shoulder affectionately, nearly knocking me over.* 彼は親しみを込めて私の方をドンと叩いたが, もう少しでひっくり返るところだった. □ *I heard you thumping on the door.* ドアをドンドン叩く音が聞こえた. ● N-COUNT 可算名詞 **Thump** is also a noun. ドンドンという音 □ *He felt a thump on his shoulder.* 彼は肩にドシンと感じた. **2** V-T 他動詞 If you **thump** someone, you attack them and hit them with your fist. (げんこつで) 殴る [INFORMAL くだけた] □ *Don't say it serves me right or I'll thump you.* ざまあみろなんて言ったら, 殴るぞ. **3** V-T/V-I 他動詞/自動詞 If you **thump** something somewhere or if it **thumps** there, it makes a loud, dull sound by hitting something else. ドサッと置く □ *Their teacher thumped her pen on her book.* 教師は彼女のペンを本の上にドンと置いた. ● N-COUNT 可算名詞 **Thump** is also a noun. ドサッという音 □ *There was a loud thump as the horse crashed into the van.* 馬がバンに激突したときドッスンという大きな音がした. **4** V-I 自動詞 When your heart **thumps**, it beats strongly and quickly, usually because you are afraid or excited. 高鳴る, ドキンドキンする □ *My heart was thumping wildly but I didn't let my face show any emotion.* 心臓がドンドンと高鳴っていたが, 感情を表情には出さなかった.

thun|der /θ∧ndər/ (**thunders, thundering, thundered**) **1** N-UNCOUNT 不可算名詞 **Thunder** is the loud noise that you hear from the sky after a flash of lightning, especially during a storm. 雷の音, 雷鳴 □ *There was thunder and lightning, and torrential rain.* 雷鳴と稲妻, そして集中豪雨があった. **2** V-I 自動詞 When it **thunders**, a loud noise comes from the sky after a flash of lightning. 雷が鳴る □ *The day was heavy and still. It would probably thunder later.* どんよりとして風がない日だった. おそらく後ほど雷が鳴るだろう. **3** N-UNCOUNT 不可算名詞 The **thunder** of something that is moving or making a sound is the loud deep noise it makes. とどろく □ *The thunder of the sea on the rocks seemed to blank out other thoughts.* 岩に打ち当たる波のとどろきで他の考えが打ち消されるようだった. **4** V-I 自動詞 If something or someone **thunders** somewhere, they move there quickly and with a lot of noise. ごう音を立てて走る □ *The horses thundered across the valley floor.* 馬が谷底をごう音を立てながら走った.

thun|der|ous /θ∧ndərəs/ ADJ 形容詞 If you describe a noise as **thunderous**, you mean that it is very loud and deep. とどろきわたる □ *The audience responded with thunderous applause.* 聴衆は万雷の拍手で応じた.

thun|der|storm /θ∧ndərstɔrm/ (**thunderstorms**) N-COUNT 可算名詞 A **thunderstorm** is a storm with thunder and lightning and a lot of heavy rain. 雷雨 → see erosion

Thurs.

The spelling **Thur.** is also used.

つづりの **Thur.** も使われる.

Thurs. is a written abbreviation for **Thursday**. 木曜日 [mainly BRIT 主に英国英語]

Thurs|day /θ3rzdeɪ, -di/ (**Thursdays**) N-VAR 可変性名詞 **Thursday** is the day after Wednesday and before Friday. 木曜日 □ *On Thursday Barrett invited me for a drink.* 木曜日にバレットは私を飲みに誘った. □ *We go and do the weekly shopping every Thursday morning.* 私たちは毎週木曜日の朝に1週間分の買い物をしに行く.

thus /ð∧s/ **1** ADV 副詞 You use **thus** to show that what you are about to mention is the result of something else that you have just mentioned. したがって [FORMAL 形式ばった] [ADV with cl/group] □ *Neither of them thought of turning on the news. Thus Caroline didn't hear of John's death until Peter telephoned.* 2人ともニュースをつけることを思いつかなかった. したがって, ピータが電話するまでキャロラインはジョンの死について知らなかった. **2** ADV 副詞 If you say that something is **thus** or happens **thus** you mean that it is, or happens, as you have just described or as you are just about to describe. このようにして [FORMAL 形式ばった] □ *Joanna was pouring the wine. While she was thus engaged, Charles sat on one of the bar-stools.* ジョアンナはワインを注いでいた. そうしている間に, チャ

ールズはバーのスツールに座った.

thwart /θwɔrt/ (**thwarts, thwarting, thwarted**) V-T 他動詞 If you **thwart** someone or **thwart** their plans, you prevent them from doing or getting what they want. 妨害する □ *The security forces were doing all they could to thwart terrorists.* 保安部隊はテロ活動を阻止するために全力を挙げていた.

thyme /taɪm/ N-UNCOUNT 不可算名詞 **Thyme** is a type of herb used in cooking. タイム

tick /tɪk/ (**ticks, ticking, ticked**) **1** V-I 自動詞 When a clock or watch **ticks**, it makes a regular series of short sounds as it works. カチカチ/チクタクと音を立てる □ *A wind-up clock ticked busily from the kitchen counter.* ネジ巻き時計が調理台でせわしくチクタクと音を立てていた. ● PHRASAL VERB 句動詞 **Tick away** means the same as **tick**. カチカチと音を立てる □ *A grandfather clock ticked away in a corner.* 隅で大時計がカチカチと音を刻んでいた. ● tick|ing N-UNCOUNT 不可算名詞 カチカチと鳴ること □ *...the endless ticking of clocks.* いつまでもカチカチと時計が刻む音 **2** N-COUNT 可算名詞 The **tick** of a clock or watch is the series of short sounds it makes when it is working, or one of those sounds. カチカチという音 □ *He sat listening to the tick of the grandfather clock.* 彼は座って, 大時計がカチカチという音を聞いていた. **3** N-COUNT 可算名詞 A **tick** is a written mark like a ✓. It is used to show that something is correct or has been selected or dealt with. チェックマーク, レ点 [BRIT 英国英語; AM check, checkmark 米国英語 check, checkmark] **4** N-COUNT 可算名詞 A **tick** is a small creature which lives on the bodies of people or animals and uses their blood as food. マダニ □ *The company produces chemicals that destroy ticks and mites.* その会社はダニ類を退治する薬品を製造している. **5** V-T 他動詞 If you **tick** something that is written on a piece of paper, you put a tick next to it. チェックをつける [BRIT 英国英語; AM check 米国英語 check] ▶ **tick off** PHRASAL VERB 句動詞 If you **tick off** items on a list, you write a tick or other mark next to them, in order to show that they have been dealt with. 済みの印を入れる, チェックマークをつける [BRIT 英国英語; AM usually check off 米国英語では通常 check off] PHRASAL VERB 句動詞 If you say that someone or something **ticks** you **off**, you mean that they annoy you. いらつかせる [AM 米国英語, INFORMAL くだけた] □ *I can't lay blame anywhere and that ticks me off.* 誰のせいにもできなくて, それで余計にむかつく.

tick|et /tɪkɪt/ (**tickets**) **1** N-COUNT 可算名詞 A **ticket** is a small, official piece of paper or card which shows that you have paid to enter a place such as a theater or a sports stadium, or shows that you have paid for a trip. 切符, チケット [also 'by' n] □ *He had a ticket for a flight on Friday.* 彼は金曜日のフライトのチケットを持っていた. □ *...two tickets for the game.* その試合のチケット2枚 **2** N-COUNT 可算名詞 A **ticket** is an official piece of paper which orders you to pay a fine or to appear in court because you have committed a driving or parking offense. 違反切符 □ *Slow down or you'll get a ticket.* スピードを落とさないと違反切符を切られますよ. **3** N-COUNT 可算名詞 A **ticket** for a game of chance such as a raffle or a lottery is a piece of paper with a number on it. If the number on your ticket matches the number chosen, you win a prize. 券, くじ □ *She bought a lottery ticket and won more than $33 million.* 彼女は宝くじを買って, 3300万ドル以上の賞金を得た. **4** → see also season ticket

	Word Partnership	*ticket* は次の語句と使われる:
N.	ticket **agent**, ticket **booth**, ticket **counter**, ticket **holder**, **plane** ticket, ticket **price** **1** **parking** ticket, **speeding** ticket **2** **lottery** ticket **3**	
ADJ.	**free** ticket **1** **winning** ticket **3**	
V.	**get** a ticket **1** **2** **buy/pay** for a ticket **1** **3**	

tick|le /tɪkəl/ (**tickles, tickling, tickled**) **1** V-T 他動詞 When you **tickle** someone, you move your fingers lightly over a sensitive part of their body, often in order to make them laugh. くすぐる □ *I was tickling him, and he was laughing and giggling.* 彼をくすぐると, くすくすグラグラ大笑いした. **2** V-T/V-I 他動詞/自動詞 If something **tickles** you or **tickles**, it causes an irritating feeling by lightly touching a part of your body. ちくちくする □ *...a yellow hat with a great feather that tickled her ear.* 彼女の耳にちくちくと当たった大きな羽根のついた黄色い帽子

tid|al /taɪdəl/ ADJ 形容詞 **Tidal** means relating to or produced by tides. 潮の □ *The tidal stream or current gradually decreases in the shallows.* 潮流が浅瀬で徐々に弱まっている. → see wetland

tid|al wave (**tidal waves**) N-COUNT 可算名詞 A **tidal wave** is a very large wave, often caused by an earthquake, that flows onto the land and destroys things. 高波, 津波 □ *...a massive tidal wave swept the ship up and away.* その船を洗い流した巨大な高波

tide /taɪd/ (**tides**) **1** N-COUNT 可算名詞 The **tide** is the regular

Word Web tide

The **gravitational** pull of the **moon** on the earth's **oceans** causes **tides**. **High tides** occur twice a day at any given point on the earth's surface. During the next six hours, the water gradually **ebbs** away, producing a **low tide**. In some places tidal energy powers hydroelectric **plants**. Riptides are responsible for the deaths of hundreds of swimmers each year. However, a riptide is not really a tide. It is a strong ocean **current**.

change in the level of the ocean on the beach. You say the tide is in when water reaches a high point on the land or out when the water leaves the land. 潮（の満ち引き） ❑ *The tide was at its highest.* 満潮だった. ❑ *The tide was going out, and the sand was smooth and glittering.* 潮が引いているところで, 砂が滑らかでキラキラしていた. **2** N-COUNT 可算名詞 A **tide** is a current in the sea that is caused by the regular and continuous movement of large areas of water toward and away from the shore. 潮（の流れ） ❑ *Roman vessels used to sail with the tide from Boulogne to Richborough.* ローマ船はボローニャからリッチバローにかけて潮流に乗って航海したものだった. **3** N-SING 単数名詞 The **tide** of opinion, for example, is what the majority of people think at a particular time. 風潮 ❑ *The tide of opinion seems overwhelmingly in his favor.* 世論は圧倒的に彼に有利なようだ.

→ see Word Web: **tide**

→ see **ocean**

tidy /ˈtaɪdi/ (tidier, tidiest, tidies, tidying, tidied) **1** ADJ 形容詞 Someone who is **tidy** likes everything to be neat and arranged in an organized way. きれい好きな [mainly BRIT 主に英国英語; AM **neat** 米国英語 neat] ●**tidi|ness** N-UNCOUNT 不可算名詞 きれい好きであること ❑ *I'm very impressed by your tidiness and order.* あなたがきれい好きなことにとても感心だ. **2** ADJ 形容詞 Something that is **tidy** is neat and is arranged in an organized way. せいとんしてある, きれいに片付いた [mainly BRIT 主に英国英語; AM **neat** 米国英語 neat] ●**tidi|ly** /ˈtaɪdɪli/ ADV 副詞 きちんと整理されて ❑ *...books and magazines stacked tidily on shelves.* 棚にきちんと並べられた本や雑誌 ●**tidi|ness** N-UNCOUNT 不可算名詞 せいとんされていること ❑ *Employees are expected to maintain a high standard of tidiness in their dress and appearance.* 従業員は, きちんと身だしなみを整え, 高水準を維持するよう求められている. **3** V-T 他動詞 When you **tidy** a place such as a room or closet, you make it neat by putting things in their proper places. 片付ける, 整理する [mainly BRIT 主に英国英語; AM **clean, neaten** 米国英語 clean, neaten]

▶ **tidy away** PHRASAL VERB 句動詞 When you **tidy** something **away**, you put it in something else so that it is not in the way. 片付ける, しまう [mainly BRIT 主に英国英語; AM **put away** 米国英語 put away]

▶ **tidy up** PHRASAL VERB 句動詞 When you **tidy up** or **tidy** a place **up**, you put things back in their proper places so that everything is neat. 片付ける, きちんとする [mainly BRIT 主に英国英語; AM **clean up, neaten up** 米国英語 clean up, neaten up]

tie /taɪ/ (ties, tying, tied) **1** V-T 他動詞 If you **tie** two things **together** or **tie** them, you fasten them together with a knot. 結びつける ❑ *He tied the ends of the plastic bag together.* 彼はナイロン袋の端をくくりつけた. **2** V-T 他動詞 If you **tie** something or someone in a particular place or position, you put them there and fasten them using rope or string. 縛りつける ❑ *He had tied the dog to one of the trees near the canal.* 彼は, そのイヌを運河の近くの木に縛りつけた. **3** V-T 他動詞 If you **tie** a piece of string or cloth around something or **tie** something **with** a piece of string or cloth, you put the piece of string or cloth around it and fasten the ends together. （ぐるっと回して）結ぶ, 縛る ❑ *She tied her scarf over her head.* 彼女は頭にスカーフをかぶっていた. ❑ *Roll the meat and tie it with string.* 肉を丸めて, ひもで縛りなさい. **4** V-T 他動詞 If you **tie** a knot or bow in something or **tie** something in a knot or bow, you fasten the ends together. 結び目にする ❑ *He took a short length of rope and swiftly tied a slip knot.* 彼は短いロープを取って, 素早く引き結びにした. ❑ *She tied a knot in a cherry stem.* 彼女はサクランボの茎で結び目を作った. **5** V-T/V-I 他動詞/自動詞 When you **tie** something or when something **ties**, you close or fasten it using a bow or knot. （先を）結ぶ, 縛る ❑ *He pulled on his heavy suede shoes and tied the laces.* 彼はがっしりとしたスエードの靴をはいて, 靴ひもを結んだ. ❑ *...a long white thing around his neck that tied in front in a floppy bow.* 首の回りにかけて前でだらりとちょう結びにしている白くて長いもの **6** N-COUNT 可算名詞 A **tie** is a long narrow piece of cloth that is worn around the neck under a shirt collar and tied in a knot at the front. Ties are worn mainly by men. ネクタイ ❑ *Jason had taken off his jacket and loosened his tie.* ジェイソンは上着を脱いでネクタイを緩めた. **7** V-T 他動詞 If one thing **is tied to** another or two things **are tied**, the two things have a close connection or link. 関連づける [usu passive] ❑ *Their cancers are not*

so clearly tied to radiation exposure. 彼らの癌ははっきりとは被ばくと関連がありません. **8** V-T 他動詞 If you **are tied to** a particular place or situation, you are forced to accept it and cannot change it. 拘束する [usu passive] ❑ *They had children and were consequently tied to the school vacations.* 彼女たちは子供がいて, そのため学校の休暇に拘束されていた. **9** N-COUNT 可算名詞 **Ties** are the connections you have with people or a place. 関連 [usu pl, oft N prep] ❑ *Quebec has always had particularly close ties to France.* クベック州は常にフランスと密接な関係を持ってきた. **10** V-RECIP 相互動詞 If two people **tie** in a competition or game or if they **tie with** each other, they have the same number of points or the same degree of success. 引き分ける, 同点になる ❑ *Ronan Rafferty had tied with Frank Nobilo.* ローナン・ラファーティはフランク・ニビロと同点に並んだ. ●N-COUNT 可算名詞 **Tie** is also a noun. 引き分け ❑ *The first game ended in a tie.* 最初の試合は引き分けに終わった. **11** N-COUNT 可算名詞 In sports, a **tie** is a match that is part of a competition. The losers leave the competition and the winners go on to the next round. 1試合 [BRIT 英国英語] ❑ *They'll meet the winners of the first round tie.* 彼らは第1試合の勝者と対戦する. **12** your **hands are tied** → see **hand**

→ see **clothing**

▶ **tie down** PHRASAL VERB 句動詞 A person or thing that **ties** you **down** restricts your freedom in some way. 束縛する ❑ *We'd agreed from the beginning not to tie each other down.* 私たちは初めからお互いを束縛しないと約束した. ❑ *He didn't want a family because he didn't want to be tied down.* 彼は束縛されたくなかったので, 家族を持ちたくなかった.

▶ **tie up** **1** PHRASAL VERB 句動詞 When you **tie** something **up**, you fasten string or rope around it so that it is firm or secure. 縛る ❑ *He tied up the bag and took it outside.* 彼は袋を縛って外に出した. **2** PHRASAL VERB 句動詞 If someone **ties** another person **up**, they fasten ropes around them so that they cannot move or escape. 縛りつける ❑ *Masked robbers broke in, tied him up, and made off with $8,000.* 覆面強盗が乱入し, 彼を縛りつけ, 8000ドルを奪って逃げた. **3** PHRASAL VERB 句動詞 If you **tie** an animal **up**, you fasten it to a fixed object with a piece of rope so that it cannot run away. つなぐ ❑ *Would you go and tie your horse up please?* 馬をつなぎに行ってくれませんか?

tier /tɪər/ (tiers) **1** N-COUNT 可算名詞 A **tier** is a row or layer of something that has other layers above or below it. 列, 段 ❑ *...the auditorium with the tiers of seats around and above it.* 階段式の座席がぐるりと, またその上段にも設置されている聴衆席 ●COMB IN ADJ 形容詞の複合 **Tier** is also a combining form. 一段の ❑ *...a three-tier wedding cake.* 3段重ねのウェディングケーキ **2** N-COUNT 可算名詞 A **tier** is a level in an organisation or system. 階層 ❑ *Islanders have campaigned for the abolition of one of the three tiers of municipal power on the island.* 島の住人は, 島の市政の3階層のうちのひとつを廃止するための運動を起こした. ●COMB IN ADJ 形容詞の複合 **Tier** is also a combining form. 一階層の ❑ *...the possibility of a two-tier system of universities.* 大学が2層構造になる可能性

ti|ger /ˈtaɪɡər/ (tigers) N-COUNT 可算名詞 A **tiger** is a large fierce animal belonging to the cat family. Tigers are orange with black stripes. トラ

tight /taɪt/ (tighter, tightest) **1** ADJ 形容詞 **Tight** clothes or shoes are small and fit closely to your body. きつい, ぴったりとした ❑ *She walked off the plane in a miniskirt and tight top.* 彼女はミニスカートにタイトなトップを着て飛行機から降りた. ●**tight|ly** ADV 副詞 [ADV with v] きつく ❑ *He buttoned his collar tightly round his thick neck.* 彼は太い首の周りの襟をきつくボタンで留めた. **2** ADJ 形容詞 If you hold someone or something **tight**, you hold them firmly and securely. しっかりと [ADV after v] ❑ *She just fell into my arms, clutching me tight for a moment.* 彼女は僕の腕に倒れ込み, しばらく僕をしっかりとつかんだ. ❑ *Just hold tight to my hand and follow along.* 私の手をしっかりと握って, 後をついて来なさい. ●ADJ 形容詞 **Tight** is also an adjective. しっかりって ❑ *As he and Hannah passed through the gate he kept a tight hold of her arm.* 彼とハナが門を通り過ぎるとき, 彼は彼女の腕をしっかりと握り続けた. ●**tight|ly** ADV 副詞 [ADV after v] しっかりと ❑ *She climbed back into bed and wrapped her arms tightly around her body.* 彼女はまたベッドにもぐりこんでしっかりと自分の体を抱き締めた. **3** ADJ 形容詞 **Tight** controls or rules are very strict. 厳しい ❑ *The measures include tight control of media coverage.* 法案にはマスコミ報道の厳しい管理が含まれている.

❑ *The government was prepared to keep a tight hold on public sector pay rises.* 政府は公共部門の昇給に関して厳しく管理をする覚悟だった. ● **tight|ly** ADV 副詞 厳しく ❑ *The internal media was tightly controlled by the government during the war.* 国内のマスコミは戦時中政府により厳しく管理されていた. ◻4 ADV 副詞 Something that is shut **tight** is shut very firmly. 固く, しっかりと ❑ *The baby lay on his back with his eyes closed tight.* 赤ちゃんはしっかりと目を閉じ, あおむけに寝ていた. ❑ *I keep the flour and sugar in individual jars, sealed tight with their glass lids.* 小麦粉と砂糖をそれぞれの瓶に, ガラスのふたで密封して保管している. ● **tight|ly** ADV 副詞 しっかりと ❑ *Pemberton frowned and closed his eyes tightly.* ペンバートンはしかめ面をして目を固く閉じた. ◻5 ADJ 形容詞 Skin, cloth, or string that is **tight** is stretched or pulled so that it is smooth or straight. ぴんと張った, つっぱる ❑ *My skin feels tight and lacking in moisture.* 私の肌はつっぱって水分に欠けている感じだ. ● **tight|ly** ADV [ADV with v] ぴんと張って, つっぱって ❑ *Her sallow skin was drawn tightly across the bones of her face.* 彼女の土色の肌がほお骨が露わになってやつれていた. ◻6 ADJ 形容詞 **Tight** is used to describe a group of things or an amount of something that is closely packed together. ぎゅっとくっついた ❑ *She curled up in a tight ball, with her knees tucked up at her chin.* 彼女は, ひざをあごまで引き寄せてぎゅっと小さく丸まっていた. ● ADV 副詞 **Tight** is also an adverb. ぎゅっとくっついて ❑ *The people sleep on army cots packed tight, end to end.* 人々は端から端までぎゅうぎゅう詰めになった軍用簡易ベッドで寝ている. ● **tight|ly** ADV 副詞 ぎゅうぎゅうになって ❑ *Many animals travel in tightly packed trucks and are deprived of food, water and rest.* トラックでぎゅうぎゅう詰めになって, えさ・水・休憩も与えられずに移動する動物が多い. ◻7 ADJ 形容詞 If a part of your body is **tight**, it feels uncomfortable and painful, for example, because you are sick, anxious, or angry. こわばった, 張りつめた ❑ *It is better to stretch the tight muscles first.* 張りつめた筋肉をまず伸ばすとよい. ◻8 ADJ 形容詞 A **tight** group of people is one whose members are closely linked by beliefs, feelings, or interests. 密接な関係の, 結びつきの強い ❑ *We're a tight group, so we do keep in touch.* 私たちは結束の固い団体なので, 連絡を取り続ける. ◻9 ADJ 形容詞 A **tight** bend or corner is one that changes direction very quickly so that you cannot see very far around it. 急な ❑ *They collided on a tight bend and both cars were extensively damaged.* 彼らは急カーブで衝突し, 双方の車が大きな損傷を受けた. ◻10 ADJ 形容詞 A **tight** schedule or budget allows very little time or money for unexpected events or expenses. 切迫した, きつい ❑ *It's difficult to cram everything into a tight schedule.* きついスケジュールにすべてを詰め込むのは難しい. ❑ *Emma is on a tight budget for clothes.* エマは衣類に割り当てる予算がほとんどない. ◻11 → see also **airtight** ◻12 to **keep a tight rein on** → see **rein** ◻13 to **sit tight** → see **sit**

Word Partnership   *tight* は次の語句と使われる:

N.	tight **dress/jeans/pants** ◻1
	tight **fit** ◻1 ◻5
	tight **grip**, tight **hold** ◻2
	tight **control**, tight **security** ◻3
	tight **squeeze** ◻6
	tight **lips**, tight **muscles**, tight **smile** ◻7
ADV.	**extremely** tight, **a little** tight, **so** tight, **too** tight, **very** tight ◻1 – ◻10
ADJ.	**closed** tight, **locked** tight, **shut** tight ◻4
	tight **knit** ◻8

tight|en /taɪtᵊn/ (**tightens, tightening, tightened**) ◻1 V-T/V-I 他動詞/自動詞 If you **tighten** your grip on something, or if your grip **tightens**, you hold the thing more firmly or securely. しっかり握る ❑ *Luke answered by tightening his grip on her shoulder.* ルークは, 彼女の肩に置いた手に力を込めることで応えた. ❑ *Her arms tightened about his neck in gratitude.* 彼女は感謝の気持ちを込めて彼の首の周りに腕を回してぎゅっと力を込めた. ◻2 V-T/V-I 他動詞/自動詞 If you **tighten** a rope or chain, or if it **tightens**, it is stretched or pulled hard until it is straight. ぴんと張る ❑ *The anchorman flung his whole weight back, tightening the rope.* アナウンサーは, 全体重をかけて後ろに反り, ロープがぴんと張った. ◻3 V-T/V-I 他動詞/自動詞 If a government or organization **tightens** its grip on a group of people or an activity, or if its grip **tightens**, it begins to have more control over it. 管理を強化する ❑ *He knows he has considerable support for his plans to tighten his grip on the machinery of central government.* 彼は, 中央政府の機構の管理を強化する計画にかなりの支持があることを知っている. ◻4 V-T 他動詞 When you **tighten** a screw, nut, or other device, you turn it or move it so that it is more firmly in place or holds something more firmly. きつく締める ❑ *I used my thumbnail to tighten the screw on my lamp.* スタンドのねじを締めるのに親指のつめを使った. ● PHRASAL VERB 句動詞 **Tighten up** means the same as **tighten**. きつく締める ❑ *It's important to tighten up the wheels properly, otherwise they vibrate loose and fall off.* 車輪をきっちりと締めておくことが大切だ. そうしないと, 振動で緩くなって, 外れる. ◻5 V-I 自動詞 If a part of your body **tightens**, the muscles in it become tense and stiff, for example, because you are angry

or afraid. こわばる, 引きつる ❑ *Sofia's throat had tightened and she couldn't speak.* ソフィアののどがこわばって, 話せなかった. ◻6 V-T 他動詞 If someone in authority **tightens** a rule, a policy, or a system, they make it stricter or more efficient. 強化する, 厳しくする ❑ *The United States plans to tighten the economic sanctions currently in place.* 米国は, 現在実施中の経済制裁を強化する計画をしています. ● PHRASAL VERB 句動詞 **Tighten up** means the same as **tighten**. 強化する, 厳しくする ❑ *Until this week, every attempt to tighten up the law had failed.* 今週に至るまで, その法律を強化する試みはすべて失敗していた. ◻7 to **tighten** your **belt** → see **belt**

tights /taɪts/ ◻1 N-PLURAL 複数名詞 **Tights** are a piece of clothing, worn by women and girls. They are usually made of nylon and cover the hips, legs, and feet. パンスト, タイツ [mainly BRIT 主に英国英語] [also 'a pair of' N] [AM also **pantyhose** 米国英語, また **pantyhose**] ◻2 N-PLURAL 複数名詞 **Tights** are a piece of tight clothing, usually worn by dancers, acrobats, or people in exercise classes, and covering the hips and each leg. スパッツ [also 'a pair of' N]

tile /taɪl/ (**tiles**) ◻1 N-VAR 可変性名詞 **Tiles** are flat, square pieces of baked clay, carpet, cork, or other substance, which are fixed as a covering onto a floor or wall. タイル ❑ *Amy's shoes squeaked on the tiles as she walked down the corridor.* エイミーが廊下を歩くとタイル床で靴がキューキューと鳴った. ◻2 N-VAR 可変性名詞 **Tiles** are flat pieces of baked clay which are used for covering roofs. かわら ❑ *...a fine building, with a neat little porch and ornamental tiles on the roof.* こぎれいなポーチと屋根には化粧れんががある素敵な建物

till /tɪl/ (**tills**) ◻1 PREP 前置詞 In spoken English and informal written English, **till** is often used instead of **until**. ～まで ❑ *They had to wait till Monday to phone the bank.* 彼らは, 銀行に電話するのに月曜日まで待たなければならなかった. ● CONJ 接続詞 **Till** is also a conjunction. ～するまで ❑ *I hadn't left home till I was nineteen.* 19歳になって, やっと家を出した. ◻2 N-COUNT 可算名詞 A **till** is the drawer of a cash register, where the money is kept. 現金入れ [AM 米国英語] ❑ *He checked the register. There was money in the till.* レジをチェックした. 現金入れにはお金があった. ◻3 N-COUNT 可算名詞 In a store or other place of business, a **till** is a counter or cash register where money is kept, and where customers pay for what they have bought. レジ [BRIT 英国英語; AM **cash register** 米国英語 **cash register**]

> Note that you only use **until** or **till** when you are talking about time. You do not use these words to talk about place or position. Instead, you should use **as far as** or **up to**. ❑ *Then you'll be riding with us as far as the village?...We walked up to where his bicycle was.*

tilt /tɪlt/ (**tilts, tilting, tilted**) ◻1 V-T/V-I 他動詞/自動詞 If you **tilt** an object or if it **tilts**, it moves into a sloping position with one end or side higher than the other. 傾ける [他動詞], 傾く [自動詞] ❑ *She tilted the mirror and began to comb her hair.* 彼女は鏡を傾けて髪をくしでとかし始めた. ❑ *Leonard tilted his chair back on two legs and stretched his long body.* レオナルドは, いすを後ろ脚2本の方に傾けて長い体を伸ばした. ◻2 V-T 他動詞 If you **tilt** part of your body, usually your head, you move it slightly upward or to one side. かしげる, 傾ける ❑ *Mari tilted her head back so that she could look at him.* マリは, 彼の顔を見るためにあごを上げた. ● N-COUNT 可算名詞 **Tilt** is also a noun. 傾けること ❑ *He opened the rear door for me with an apologetic tilt of his head.* 彼は, 申し訳なさそうに首をかしげながら私のために後部ドアを開けた. ◻3 N-COUNT 可算名詞 The **tilt** of something is the fact that it tilts or slopes, or the angle at which it tilts or slopes. 傾斜, 傾き ❑ *...calculations based on our understanding of the tilt of the Earth's axis.* 地軸の傾きへの理解に基づいた計算 ◻4 V-I 自動詞 If a person or thing **tilts toward** a particular opinion or if something **tilts** them **toward** it, they change slightly so that they become more in agreement with that opinion or position. 一寄りになる, 傾く ❑ *Political will might finally tilt toward some sort of national health plan.* 政治的な意志はついに国民医療計画のようなものに傾くかもしれない.

tim|ber /tɪmbər/ N-UNCOUNT 不可算名詞 **Timber** is wood that is used for building houses and making furniture. You can also refer to trees that are grown for this purpose as **timber**. 木材, 材木 ❑ *These Michigan woods have been exploited for timber since the Great Fire of Chicago.* シカゴ大火災以降, このミシガンの森は木材用に開発されてきた.
→ see **forest**

time

❶	NOUN USES
❷	VERB USES
❸	PHRASES: GROUP 1
❹	PHRASES: GROUP 2
❺	PHRASES: GROUP 3

❶ time /taɪm/ (**times**) ◻1 N-UNCOUNT 不可算名詞 **Time** is what we measure in minutes, hours, days, and years. 時間 ❑ *...a two-*

week period of time. 2週間という期間 □ *Time passed, and still Ma did not appear.* 時が過ぎたが，それでもマーは現れなかった． **2** N-SING 単数名詞 You use **time** to ask or talk about a specific point in the day, which can be stated in hours and minutes and is shown on clocks. 時刻 □ *"What time is it?"—"Eight o'clock."* 「何時ですか?」「8時です」 □ *He asked me the time.* 彼は私に時刻を尋ねた． **3** N-COUNT 可算名詞 The **time** when something happens is the point in the day when it happens or is supposed to happen. ～をする予定の時刻 □ *Departure times are 08:15 from Baltimore, and 10:15 from Newark.* 出発時刻はバルチモア発が8時15分でニューワーク発が10時15分だ． **4** N-UNCOUNT 不可算名詞 You use **time** to refer to the system of expressing time and counting hours that is used in a particular part of the world. ～時間 □ *The incident happened just after ten o'clock local time.* その事件は現地時間で10時をちょうど過ぎたときに起きた． **5** N-UNCOUNT 不可算名詞 You use **time** to refer to the period that you spend doing something or when something has been happening. (～する) 時間 [also 'a' N] □ *Adam spent a lot of time in his grandfather's office.* アダムは祖父のオフィスでかなりの時間を過ごした． □ *He wouldn't have the time or money to take care of me.* 彼は，私の世話をする時間もお金もないだろう． □ *Listen to me, I haven't got much time.* 聞いて，私には余り時間がないの． □ *It's obvious that you need more time to think.* 君にはもう少し考える時間が必要なのが明らかだ． **6** N-SING 単数名詞 If you say that something has been happening for **a time**, you mean that it has been happening for a fairly long period of time. 一時期 □ *He was also for a time an art critic.* 彼は一時期は芸術評論家だった． □ *He stayed for quite a time.* 彼はしばらくの間滞在した． **7** N-COUNT 可算名詞 You use **time** to refer to a period of time or a point in time, when you are describing what is happening then. For example, if something happened **at a particular time**, that is when it happened. If it happens **at all times**, it always happens. ～の頃，～のとき □ *We were in the same college, which was male-only at that time.* 私たちは同じ大学にいたのですが，その頃は男子学生専用でした． □ *By this time he was thirty.* この頃までには彼は30歳だった． □ *It was a time of terrible uncertainty.* ひどく不安定な時代だった． **8** N-COUNT 可算名詞 You use **time** or **times** to talk about a particular period in history or in your life. 時代，時期 □ *They were hard times and his parents had been struggling to raise their family.* そのころは大変な時代で，彼の両親は家族を養うのに苦労していた． □ *We'll be alone together, just like old times.* 2人きりになるわ，ちょうど昔のようにね． **9** N-PLURAL 複数名詞 You can use **the times** to refer to the present time and to modern fashions, tastes, and developments. For example, if you say that someone **keeps up with the times**, you mean they are fashionable or aware of modern developments. If you say they are **behind the times**, you mean they are unfashionable or not aware of them. 時代の流れ □ *This approach is now seriously out of step with the times.* この方法は，今ではかなり時代遅れだ． **10** N-COUNT 可算名詞 When you describe the **time** that you had on a particular occasion or during a particular part of your life, you are describing the sort of experience that you had then. ひととき □ *Sarah and I had a great time while the kids were away.* サラと僕は子供がいない間，楽しいひとときを過ごした． **11** N-SING 単数名詞 Your **time** is the amount of time that you have to live, or to do a particular thing. 時間，暇 □ *Now that Martin has begun to suffer the effects of AIDS, he says his time is running out.* 今やマーティンはエイズの影響で苦しみ始めたので，彼は「時間がないんだ」と言っています． **12** N-UNCOUNT 不可算名詞 If you say it is **time for** something, **time to** do something, or **time** you did something, you mean that this thing ought to happen or be done now. ～の時間，～の時 □ *Opinion polls indicated a feeling among the public that it was time for a change.* 世論調査によると，一般人は変革の時だと感じているようだ． □ *It was time for him to go to work.* 彼が出勤する時間だった． **13** N-COUNT 可算名詞 When you talk about a **time** when something happens, you are referring to a specific occasion when it happens. 特定の時を差して用いられる □ *Every time she travels on the bus it's delayed by at least three hours.* 彼女がバスに乗るたびに，最低3時間は遅れる． **14** N-COUNT 可算名詞 You use **time** after

numbers to say how often something happens. 一回 □ *It was her job to make tea three times a day.* 1日に3回紅茶を入れるのが彼女の仕事だった． **15** N-PLURAL 複数名詞 You use **times** after numbers when comparing one thing to another and saying, for example, how much bigger, smaller, better, or worse it is. ～倍 □ *Its profits are rising four times faster than the average company.* その会社の利潤は平均の4倍の速さで伸びている． **16** CONJ 接続詞 You use **times** to show multiplication. Three times five is 3x5. ～掛ける □ *Four times six is 24.* 4掛ける6は24． **17** N-COUNT 可算名詞 Someone's **time** in a race is the amount of time it takes them to finish the race. 記録タイム □ *He was over a second faster than his previous best time.* 彼は，自己最高記録より1秒以上速かった．

→ see Word Web: **time**

❷ time /taɪm/ (**times, timing, timed**) **1** V-T 他動詞 If you **time** something for a particular hour, day, or period, you plan or decide to do it or cause it to happen at this time. ～するように合わせる □ *He timed the election to coincide with new measures to boost the economy.* 彼は選挙に合わせて新しい景気対策を計画した． □ *I timed our visit for March 7.* 私たちの訪問を3月7日になるように手配した． **2** V-T 他動詞 If you **time** an action or activity, you measure how long someone takes to do it or how long it lasts. 時間を測る □ *A radar gun timed the speed of the baseball.* レーダーガンが野球ボールのスピードを測定した． **3** → see also **timing**

❸ time /taɪm/ (**times**) **1** PHRASE 句 If you say it is **about time** that something was done, you are saying in an emphatic way that it should happen or be done now, and really should have happened or been done sooner. そろそろ～するころ [EMPHASIS 強調] □ *It's about time a few movie makers with original ideas were given a chance.* そろそろ独自の考えを持った映画制作者がチャンスをもらってもいいころだ． **2** PHRASE 句 If you do something **ahead of time**, you do it before a particular event or before you need to, in order to be well prepared. 前もって □ *Find out ahead of time what regulations apply to your situation.* 前もって自分の事情に当てはまる規定を確認しなさい． **3** PHRASE 句 If someone is **ahead of** their **time** or **before** their **time**, they have new ideas a long time before other people start to think in the same way. 先駆けである □ *He was indeed ahead of his time in employing women, ex-convicts, and the handicapped.* 彼は，女性，前科者，身障者を雇うことで確かに時代の先駆けをしていた． **4** PHRASE 句 If something happens or is done **all the time**, it happens or is done continually. ～しどおし □ *We can't be together all the time.* 私たちはずっと一緒にいるわけにはいかないの． **5** PHRASE 句 You say **at a time** after an amount to say how many things or how much of something is involved in one action, place, or group. 一度に □ *Beat in the eggs, one at a time.* 卵を1つずつかき混ぜなさい． **6** PHRASE 句 If something could happen **at any time**, it is possible that it will happen very soon, though nobody can predict exactly when. すぐにでも □ *Conditions are still very tense and the fighting could escalate at any time.* 状況はなお非常に緊迫しており，戦闘がいつ悪化するか分かりません． **7** PHRASE 句 If you say that something was the case **at one time**, you mean that it was the case during a particular period in the past. かつて □ *At one time 400 men, women and children lived in the village.* かつては，400人の男性，女性，子供がその村に住んでいました． **8** PHRASE 句 If two or more things exist, happen, or are true **at the same time**, they exist, happen, or are true together although they seem to contradict each other. 同時に □ *I was afraid of her, but at the same time I really liked her.* 私は彼女のことを恐れていましたが，同時にとても好きでした． **9** PHRASE 句 **At the same time** is used to introduce a statement that slightly changes or contradicts the previous statement. その反面，一方で □ *I don't think I set out to come up with a different sound for each CD. At the same time, I do have a sense of what is right for the moment.* CDごとに違った音を出そうとはしていないが，その反面，差し当たりピンと来るものはある． **10** PHRASE 句 You use **at times** to say that something happens or is true on some occasions or at some moments. 時々 □ *The debate was highly emotional at times.* 議論は時によっては非常に感情的でした． **11** PHRASE 句 If you

t

Word Web   time

Before railroads began to move people rapidly over long distances, **time zones** were not an issue. The government of each community (or sometimes a local clockmaker) would set the "official" **time** and the citizens would adjust their **clocks** and **watches** accordingly. However, as long-distance railroad travel became more common in the 1800s, these disparate times created havoc with railroad schedules. In the 1840s, England, Scotland, and Wales adopted a "railway standard time," replacing several "local time" systems. In 1878, Sir Sanford Fleming, a Canadian railroad official, proposed the system of worldwide time zones that is still in use today.

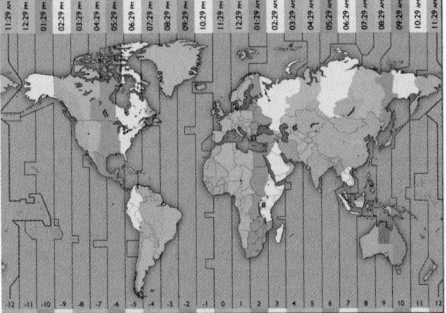

say that something will be the case **for all time**, you mean that it will always be the case. いつまでも ❏ *He promised to love her for all time.* 彼はいつまでも彼女を愛し続けると約束した. 12 PHRASE 句 If something is the case or will happen **for the time being**, it is the case or will happen now, but only until something else becomes possible or happens. 当分の間 ❏ *For the time being, however, immunotherapy is still in its experimental stages.* しかしながら当分の間は，免疫療法は依然として実験段階にある. 13 PHRASE 句 If you do something **from time to time**, you do it occasionally but not regularly. 時折 ❏ *Her daughters visited him from time to time when he was bedridden.* 彼女の娘は，彼が寝たきりのときに時々彼を訪ねた

❹ **time** /taɪm/ (times) 1 PHRASE 句 If you say that something is the case **half the time** you mean that it often is the case. しょっちゅう [INFORMAL くだけた] ❏ *Half the time, I don't have the slightest idea what he's talking about.* だいたいは，私は彼の言っていることが全く分からない. 2 PHRASE 句 If you are **in time for** a particular event, you are not too late for it. 間に合って ❏ *I arrived just in time for my flight to Hawaii.* ハワイ行きのフライトにぎりぎり間に合って到着した. 3 PHRASE 句 If you say that something will happen **in time** or **given time**, you mean that it will happen eventually, when a lot of time has passed. いずれ ❏ *He would sort out his own problems, in time.* 彼はいずれ自分の問題を解決するだろう. 4 PHRASE 句 If you are playing, singing, or dancing **in time** with a piece of music, you are following the rhythm and speed of the music correctly. If you are **out of time** with it, you are not following the rhythm and speed of the music correctly. 調子を合わせて/拍子が外れて ❏ *Her body swayed in time with the music.* 彼女の体は音楽に合わせて揺れた. 5 PHRASE 句 If you say that something will happen, for example, **in a week's time** or **in two years' time**, you mean that it will happen a week from now or two years from now. 一後に ❏ *Presidential elections are due to be held in ten days' time.* 大統領選挙は10日後に行われる予定だ. 6 PHRASE 句 If you arrive somewhere **in good time**, you arrive early so that there is time to spare before a particular event. 早めに ❏ *We got there in good time for the opening ceremony.* 私たちは開会式のために早めにそこに着いた. 7 PHRASE 句 If something happens **in no time** or **in next to no time**, it happens almost immediately or very quickly. 直ちに ❏ *He's going to be just fine. At his age he'll heal in no time.* 彼はちゃんと回復します. 彼の年齢ではすぐに治ります. 8 PHRASE 句 If you **keep time** when playing or singing music, you follow or play the beat, without going too fast or too slowly. 調子を合わせる ❏ *As he sang he kept time on a small drum.* 彼は歌いながら，小さなドラムでリズムを取った. 9 PHRASE 句 When you talk about how well a watch or clock **keeps time**, you are talking about how accurately it measures time. (時計が) 正確である ❏ *Some pulsars keep time better than the Earth's most accurate clocks.* 地球の最も正確な時計よりも正確に時を刻むパルサーがある. 10 PHRASE 句 If you **make time for** a particular activity or person, you arrange to have some free time so that you can do the activity or spend time with the person. 時間を割く ❏ *Before leaving the city, be sure to make time for a shopping trip.* その町を立つ前に，必ず買い物のために時間を割きなさい. 11 PHRASE 句 If you say that you **made good time** on a trip, you mean it did not take you very long compared to the length of time you expected it to take. 順調に進む ❏ *They had left early in the morning, on quiet roads, and made good time.* 彼は早朝に出発し，車がすいていたので順調に進んだ. 12 PHRASE 句 If someone **is making up for lost time**, they are doing something actively and with enthusiasm because they have not had the opportunity to do it before or when they were younger. 無駄にした時間を埋め合わす ❏ *Five years older than the majority of officers of his same rank, he was determined to make up for lost time.* 同じ地位の役員の大部分より5歳年上なので，彼は遅れを取り戻そうと心に決めていた. 13 PHRASE 句 If you say that something happens or is the case **nine times out of ten** or **ninety-nine times out of a hundred**, you mean that it happens on nearly every occasion or is almost always the case. 十中八九 ❏ *When they want something, nine times out of ten they get it.* 彼らは何かが欲しい時にはたいていは手に入れる.

❺ **time** /taɪm/ (times) 1 PHRASE 句 If you say that someone or something is, for example, the best writer **of all time**, or the most successful movie **of all time**, you mean that they are the best or most successful that there has ever been. 空前の ❏ *"Monopoly" is one of the best-selling games of all time.* 「モノポリー」は過去最高売上を出したゲームの1つだ. 2 PHRASE 句 If you are **on time**, you are not late. 時間どおりに ❏ *Don't worry, she'll be on time.* 心配しないで, 彼女は時間通りに来ます. 3 PHRASE 句 If you say that it is **only a matter of time** or **only a question of time** before something happens, you mean that it cannot be avoided and will definitely happen at some future date. 単なる時間の問題 ❏ *It now seems only a matter of time before they resign.* 今や彼らが辞任するのは単に時間の問題のようだ. 4 PHRASE 句 If you do something to **pass the time** you do it because you have some time available and not because you really want to do it. 時間をつぶす ❏ *Without particular interest and just to pass the time, I read a story.* 特に興味があるのではなくただ時間をつぶすために物語を読んだ. 5 PHRASE 句 If you

say that something will **take time**, you mean that it will take a long time. 時間がかかる ❏ *Change will come, but it will take time.* 変化は起こるだろうが，時間がかかる. 6 PHRASE 句 If you **take your time** doing something, you do it slowly and do not hurry. 時間をかける ❏ *"Take your time," Ted told him. "I'm in no hurry."* 「ゆっくりやって」とテッドは彼に言った. 「僕は，急いでいないから」 7 PHRASE 句 If a child can **tell the time**, they are able to find out what the time is by looking at a clock or watch. 時計を読む ❏ *My four-year-old daughter cannot quite tell the time.* 私の4歳の娘はうまく時計を読めない. 8 PHRASE 句 If something happens **time after time**, it happens in a similar way on many occasions. 何度も何度も ❏ *Burns had escaped from jail time after time.* バーンズは何度も脱獄した. 9 PHRASE 句 If you say that **time flies**, you mean that it seems to pass very quickly. あっという間に過ぎる ❏ *Time flies when you're having fun.* 楽しい時はあっという間に過ぎる. 10 PHRASE 句 If you say there is **no time to lose** or **no time to be lost**, you mean you must hurry as fast as you can to do something. 一刻の猶予もない ❏ *He rushed home, realizing there was no time to lose.* 彼は，一刻の猶予もないと気付いて急いで帰宅した. 11 PHRASE 句 If you say that **time will tell** whether something is true or correct, you mean that it will not be known until some time in the future whether it is true or correct. 時間がたてば明らかになる ❏ *Only time will tell whether Broughton's optimism is justified.* ブロートンの楽観主義が正当か否かは時間がたたなければ分からない. 12 PHRASE 句 If you **waste no time** in doing something, you take the opportunity to do it immediately or quickly. すぐに～する ❏ *Tom wasted no time in telling me why he had come.* トムは，すぐに彼が来た理由を私に話した. 13 **time and again** → see **again**

You do not say "one time a year" or "two times a year"; you say **once a year** or **twice a year**. You also do not say "two times as much"; you say **twice as much**.

---

time-consuming also **time consuming** ADJ 形容詞 If something is **time-consuming**, it takes a lot of time. 時間のかかる ❏ *It's just very time consuming to get such a large quantity of data.* ただそれほど膨大なデータを受け取るのはとても時間がかかるんです.

time|less /taɪmlɪs/ ADJ 形容詞 If you describe something as **timeless**, you mean that it is so good or beautiful that it cannot be affected by changes in society or fashion. 時代を超えた，不朽の ❏ *There is a timeless quality to his best work.* 彼の名作には時代を超えた素晴らしさがある.

time|line /taɪmlaɪn/ (timelines) also **time line** 1 N-COUNT 可算名詞 A **timeline** is a visual representation of a sequence of events, especially historical events. 年表 ❏ *The timeline shows important events from the Earth's creation to the present day.* 年表は，地球の創造から現在までの重要な出来事を示している. 2 N-COUNT 可算名詞 A **timeline** is the length of time that a project is expected to take. 日程，予定 [BUSINESS 実業] ❏ *Use your deadlines to establish the timeline for your research plan.* 締め切りを頭に入れて調査計画の日程を組みなさい.

→ see **history**

time|ly /taɪmli/ ADJ 形容詞 If you describe an event as **timely**, it happens exactly at the moment when it is most useful, effective, or relevant. ちょうどよいタイミングの [APPROVAL 賛成] ❏ *The recent outbreaks of cholera are a timely reminder that this disease is still a serious health hazard.* 最近のコレラの勃発は，この病気が依然として深刻な健康への危険要素であることを折りよく思いださせてくれた.

time out (time outs) also **time-out** 1 N-VAR 可変性名詞 In basketball, football, ice hockey, and some other sports, when a team calls a **time out**, they call a stop to the game for a few minutes in order to rest and discuss how they are going to play. タイム，タイムアウト ❏ *With 22.2 seconds to go before halftime, Brown wanted to call a time-out.* ハーフタイムまであと22.2秒というときに，ブラウンはタイムの要求を希望した. 2 N-UNCOUNT 不可算名詞 If you take **time out from** a job or activity, you have a break from it and do something different instead. 中断，休憩 [oft N 'from' n, N to-inf] ❏ *He took time out from campaigning to accompany his mother to dinner.* 彼は母親と食事に行くために活動を小休止した.

time|scale /taɪmskeɪl/ (timescales) also **time scale** N-COUNT 可算名詞 The **timescale** of an event is the length of time during which it happens or develops. 期間，タイムスケール ❏ *The likelihood is that these companies now will show excellent profits on a two-year timescale.* これらの会社が2年間の間に素晴らしい利益を上げる見込みはある.

time-share (time-shares) also **time share** N-VAR 可変性名詞 If you have a **time-share**, you have the right to use a particular property as vacation accommodations for a specific amount of time each year. タイムシェア ❏ *Other prizes include hotel discounts and a time-share at a resort in Palm Springs.* ほかにはホテルの割引券やパームスプリングズのリゾート地でのタイムシェアなどの賞品があります.

time|table /taɪmteɪbˀl/ (timetables) 1 N-COUNT 可算名詞 A **timetable** is a plan of the times when particular events

will take place. 日程，スケジュール ❑ *The timetable was hopelessly optimistic.* その日程はあきれるほど楽観的だ. ◻ N-COUNT 可算名詞 A **timetable** is a list of the times when trains, boats, buses, or airplanes are supposed to arrive at or leave from a particular place. 時刻表 [mainly BRIT 主に英国英語; AM usually **schedule** 米国英語では通常 **schedule**] ◻ N-COUNT 可算名詞 In a school or college, a **timetable** is a list that shows the times in the week at which particular subjects are taught. You can also refer to the range of subjects that a student learns or the classes that a teacher teaches as their **timetable**. 時間割 [BRIT 英国英語; AM usually **class schedule** 米国英語では通常 **class schedule**]

tim|id /tɪmɪd/ ADJ 形容詞 **Timid** people are shy, nervous, and lack courage or confidence in themselves. おどおどした，内気な ❑ *A timid child, Isabella had learned obedience at an early age.* 内気な子供のイザベラは小さい頃に従順にすることを学んだ. ● **ti|mid|ity** /tɪmɪdɪti/ N-UNCOUNT 不可算名詞 内気さ ❑ *She doesn't ridicule my timidity.* 彼女は私の内気さをばかにする. ● **tim|id|ly** ADV 副詞 おどおどしながら ❑ *The timid boy stepped forward timidly and shook Leo's hand.* その少年はおどおどしながら前に出て，レオの手を振った.

tim|ing /tɑɪmɪŋ/ ◻ N-UNCOUNT 不可算名詞 **Timing** is the skill or action of judging the right moment in a situation or activity at which to do something. 間の取り方，タイミング ❑ *His photo is a wonderful happy moment caught with perfect timing.* 彼の写真は完璧なタイミングでとても楽しい瞬間をとらえている. ◻ N-UNCOUNT 不可算名詞 **Timing** is used to refer to the time at which something happens or is planned to happen, or to the length of time that something takes. 時期，タイミング ❑ *They had concerns about the timing of the report.* 報告書のタイミングに関して懸念があった. ◻ → see also **time**

tin /tɪn/ (tins) ◻ N-UNCOUNT 不可算名詞 **Tin** is a soft silvery-white metal. ブリキ ❑ *...a factory that turns scrap metal into tin cans.* くず鉄をブリキ缶に作り変える工場 ◻ N-COUNT 可算名詞 A **tin** is a metal container with a lid in which things such as cookies, cakes, or tobacco can be kept. (クッキー・ケーキ・たばこなどを入れる) 缶 ❑ *Store the cookies in an airtight tin.* クッキーを密封缶に入れて保管しなさい. ◻ N-COUNT 可算名詞 You can use **tin** to refer to a tin and its contents, or to the contents only. 缶の（中身） ❑ *...a tin of paint.* ペンキの缶 ◻ N-COUNT 可算名詞 A **tin** is a metal container which is filled with food and sealed in order to preserve the food for long periods of time. (缶詰の) 缶 [mainly BRIT 主に英国英語] ◻ N-COUNT 可算名詞 You can use **tin** to refer to a tin and its contents, or to the contents only. 缶詰（の中身） [mainly BRIT 主に英国英語; AM usually **can** 米国英語では通常 **can**] ◻ N-COUNT 可算名詞 A baking **tin** is a metal container used for baking things such as cakes and bread in an oven. オーブン用のトレー [BRIT 英国英語; AM **pan** 米国英語 **pan**] ◻ **to have a tin ear** → see **ear** → see **can, pan**

tinge /tɪndʒ/ (tinges) N-COUNT 可算名詞 A **tinge** of a color, feeling, or quality is a small amount of it. かすかな色合い，気配 ❑ *His skin had an unhealthy greyish tinge.* 彼の肌は不健康そうに灰色がかっていた.

tinged /tɪndʒd/ ◻ ADJ 形容詞 If something is **tinged with** a particular color, it has a small amount of that color in it. ～がかった ❑ *His dark hair was just tinged with grey.* 彼の黒髪はほんの少し灰色がかっていた. ◻ ADJ 形容詞 If something is **tinged with** a particular feeling or quality, it has or shows a small amount of that feeling or quality. ～ぎみの，～を帯びた ❑ *Her homecoming was tinged with sadness.* 彼女の帰省は悲しみを帯びていた.

tin|gle /tɪŋgǝl/ (tingles, tingling, tingled) ◻ V-I 自動詞 When a part of your body **tingles**, you have a slight stinging feeling there. ひりひりする ❑ *The backs of his thighs tingled.* ももの裏側がひりひりした. ● **tin|gling** N-UNCOUNT 不可算名詞 ひりひりすること ❑ *Its effects on the nervous system include weakness, paralysis, and tingling in the hands and feet.* 神経系への影響には衰弱，まひ，手足がひりひりすることなどが含まれる. ◻ V-I 自動詞 If you **tingle with** a feeling such as excitement, you feel it very strongly. ぞくぞくする ❑ *She tingled with excitement.* 彼女はぞくぞくする興奮を感じていた. ● N-COUNT 可算名詞 **Tingle** is also a noun. ぞくぞくする気持ち ❑ *I felt a sudden tingle of excitement.* 突然ぞくぞくと興奮した.

tink|er /tɪŋkǝr/ (tinkers, tinkering, tinkered) V-I 自動詞 If you **tinker with** something, you make some small changes to it, in an attempt to improve it or repair it. いじる ❑ *Instead of the country admitting its error, it just tinkered with the problem.* その国は誤りを認めるのないわりに，ただ問題をいじっただけた.

tinned /tɪnd/ ADJ 形容詞 **Tinned** food is food that has been preserved by being sealed in a tin. 缶詰の [mainly BRIT 主に英国英語; AM usually **canned** 米国英語では通常 **canned**]

tint /tɪnt/ (tints, tinting, tinted) ◻ N-COUNT 可算名詞 A **tint** is a small amount of color. 色合い，ほのかな色 ❑ *Its large leaves often show a delicate purple tint.* その木の大きな葉にはよくほのかに紫がかっている. ◻ V-T 他動詞 If something is **tinted**, it has a small amount of a particular color or dye in it. 淡い色合いをつける [usu passive] ❑ *Eyebrows can be tinted with the same dye.* まゆは同じ染料で

薄く染めてもよい.

tiny /tɑɪni/ (tinier, tiniest) ADJ 形容詞 Something or someone that is **tiny** is extremely small. とても小さい ❑ *The living room is tiny.* 居間はとても小さい. ❑ *Though she was tiny, she had a very loud voice.* 彼女はとても小さいけれども，とても声が大きい.

tip /tɪp/ (tips, tipping, tipped) ◻ N-COUNT 可算名詞 The **tip** of something long and narrow is the end of it. 先 ❑ *The sleeves covered his hands to the tips of his fingers.* そでが指の先まで手を覆っている. ◻ V-T/V-I 他動詞/自動詞 If you **tip** an object or part of your body or if it **tips**, it moves into a sloping position with one end or side higher than the other. 傾ける [他動詞]，傾く [自動詞] ❑ *He leaned away from her, and she had to tip her head back to see him.* 彼は彼女から体を遠ざけたので，彼女は彼を見るのに頭を後ろに傾けなければならなかった. ◻ V-T 他動詞 If you **tip** something somewhere, you pour it there. 空ける，移し変える ❑ *Tip the vegetables into a bowl.* 野菜をボールに空けなさい. ◻ V-T 他動詞 If you **tip** someone such as a waiter in a restaurant, you give them some money in order to thank them for their services. チップを渡す ❑ *We usually tip 18-20%.* ふつう18から20%のチップを渡す. ◻ N-COUNT 可算名詞 If you give a **tip** to someone such as a waiter in a restaurant, you give some money to thank them for their services. チップ ❑ *I gave the barber a tip.* 床屋さんにチップをあげました. ◻ N-COUNT 可算名詞 A **tip** is a useful piece of advice. ヒント，助言 ❑ *It shows how to prepare a resume, and gives tips on applying for jobs.* それには履歴書の書き方が載っていて，仕事の応募についてのアドバイスもある. ◻ N-COUNT 可算名詞 A **tip** is the same as a **dump** or a **garbage dump**. ゴミ捨て場 [BRIT 英国英語] ◻ PHRASE 句 If you say that a problem is **the tip of the iceberg**, you mean that it is one small part of a much larger problem. 氷山の一角 ❑ *Unless we're all a lot more careful, the people who have died so far will be just the tip of the iceberg.* 我々みんながもっと気をつけないと，これまでに死亡した人々というのは氷山の一角に過ぎないだろう. ◻ PHRASE 句 If something **tips the scales** or **tips the balance**, it gives someone a slight advantage. 有利にする ❑ *Today's slightly shorter race could well help to tip the scales in her favor.* 今日のわずかに短いレースは彼女にきっと有利になるだろう. → see **restaurant**

▶ **tip off** PHRASAL VERB 句動詞 If someone **tips** you **off**, they give you information about something that has happened or is going to happen. 情報を漏らす，知らせる ❑ *Greg tipped police off about a drunk driver.* グレッグは飲酒運転者のことを警察に通報した.

▶ **tip over** PHRASAL VERB 句動詞 If you **tip** something **over** or if it **tips over**, it falls over or turns over. 引っ繰り返る ❑ *He tipped the table over in front of him.* 彼は目の前のテーブルを引っ繰り返した. ❑ *Don't tip over that glass.* そのコップを引っ繰り返さないで.

Word Partnership	tip は次の語句と使われる:
N.	**tip** of your finger/nose ◻ **tip** your hat ◻
ADJ.	northern/southern **tip** of an island ◻ anonymous **tip** ◻

tip-off (tip-offs) N-COUNT 可算名詞 A **tip-off** is a piece of information or a warning that you give to someone, often privately or secretly. 内報，密告 ❑ *The man was arrested at his home after a tip-off to police from a member of the public.* 一般人からの警察への内報のあと，彼は自宅で逮捕された.

tip|toe /tɪptoʊ/ (tiptoes, tiptoeing, tiptoed) ◻ V-I 自動詞 If you **tiptoe** somewhere, you walk there very quietly without putting your heels on the floor when you walk. つま先で歩く，忍び足で歩く ❑ *She slipped out of bed and tiptoed to the window.* 彼女はそっとベッドから出て，忍び足で窓まで歩いた. ◻ PHRASE 句 If you do something **on tiptoe** or **on tiptoes**, you do it standing or walking on the front part of your foot, without putting your heels on the ground. つま先立ちで ❑ *She leaned her bike against the stone wall and stood on tiptoe to peer over it.* 彼女は石壁に自転車を立てかけて，壁の向こうをのぞき見するためにつま先立ちをした.

ti|rade /tɑɪreɪd/ (tirades) N-COUNT 可算名詞 A **tirade** is a long angry speech in which someone criticizes a person or thing. 長い非難演説 ❑ *She launched into a tirade against the policies that ruined her business.* 彼女は，彼女のビジネスを倒産させた政策に対して長々と続く非難演説を開始した.

tire /tɑɪǝr/ (tires, tiring, tired) ◻ V-T/V-I 他動詞/自動詞 If something **tires** you or you **tire**, you feel that you have used a lot of energy and you want to rest or sleep. 疲れさせる [他動詞]，疲れる [自動詞] ❑ *If driving tires you, take the train.* 車の運転で疲れるなら電車で行きなさい. ◻ V-I 自動詞 If you **tire of** something, you no longer wish to do it, because you have become bored of it or unhappy with it. 飽きる，うんざりする [no passive] ❑ *He felt he would never tire of listening to her stories.* 彼は，決して彼女の話を聞くことにうんざりすることはないと感じた. ◻ N-COUNT 可算名詞 A **tire** is a thick piece of rubber which is fitted onto the wheels of vehicles such as cars, buses, and bicycles. タイヤ → see **bicycle**

tired /taɪərd/ **1** ADJ 形容詞 If you are **tired**, you feel that you want to rest or sleep. (体全体がが) 疲れた □ Michael is tired and he has to rest after his long trip. マイケルは疲れていて長旅の後の休養が必要だ. ● **tired|ness** N-UNCOUNT 不可算名詞 疲労 □ He had to cancel some engagements because of tiredness. 彼は疲労のためいくつかの約束をキャンセルしなければならなかった. **2** ADJ 形容詞 You can describe a part of your body as **tired** if it looks or feels as if you need to rest it or to sleep. (体の一部が) 疲れた □ Cucumber is good for soothing tired eyes. 疲れた目をいやすのにキュウリが効果的だ. **3** ADJ 形容詞 [v-link ADJ 'of' n/-ing] If you are **tired of** something, you do not want it to continue because you are bored of it or unhappy with it. うんざりした, 飽きた □ I am tired of all the speculation. いろいろな憶測にうんざりしている.
→ see **sleep**

Word Partnership   *tired* は次の語句と使われる:

V.	**look** tired **1**
	feel tired **1 2**
	be tired, **get** tired, **grow** tired **1** – **3**
ADJ.	tired **and hungry 1**
	sick and tired **of** *something* **3**
ADV.	**a little** tired, **(just) too** tired, **very** tired **1** – **3**

tire|less /taɪərlɪs/ ADJ 形容詞 If you describe someone or their efforts as **tireless**, you approve of the fact that they put a lot of hard work into something, and refuse to give up or take a rest. 疲れを知らない, 精力的な [APPROVAL 賛成] □ ...Mother Teresa's tireless efforts to help the poor. 貧しい人々を助けるためのマザー・テレサの不断の努力 ● **tire|less|ly** ADV 副詞 [ADV with v] 精力的に □ He worked tirelessly for the cause of health and safety. 彼は安全衛生運動のために精力的に働いた.

tire|some /taɪərsəm/ ADJ 形容詞 If you describe someone or something as **tiresome**, you mean that you find them irritating or boring. うんざりする, いらだたしい □ ...the tiresome old lady next door. 隣に住むいらだたしい老婦人

tir|ing /taɪərɪŋ/ ADJ 形容詞 If you describe something as **tiring**, you mean that it makes you tired so that you want to rest or sleep. 疲れる □ It had been a long and tiring day. 長くて疲れる1日だった.

tis|sue /tɪʃu/ (tissues) **1** N-UNCOUNT 不可算名詞 In animals and plants, **tissue** consists of cells that are similar to each other in appearance and that have the same function. 組織 [also n in pl] □ As we age we lose muscle tissue. 加齢に伴って筋肉組織を失う. **2** N-UNCOUNT 不可算名詞 **Tissue paper** is thin paper that is used for wrapping things that are easily damaged, such as objects of glass or china. 薄葉紙, インナーペーパー □ ...a small package wrapped in tissue paper. 薄葉紙に包まれた小さな小包 **3** N-COUNT 可算名詞 A **tissue** is a piece of thin soft paper that you use to blow your nose. ティッシュ (ペーパー) ちり紙 □ ...a box of tissues. ティッシュ1箱
→ see **cancer**

tit|il|late /tɪtɪleɪt/ (titillates, titillating, titillated) V-T 他動詞 If something **titillates** someone, it pleases and excites them, especially in a sexual way. 性的に刺激する □ The pictures were not meant to titillate audiences. その映画は観客を興奮させることを意図して作成されたのではありません. ● **tit|il|lat|ing** ADJ 形容詞 刺激的な □ ...deliberately titillating lyrics. 故意に刺激的な歌詞

ti|tle /taɪtəl/ (titles, titling, titled) **1** N-COUNT 可算名詞 The **title** of a book, play, movie, or piece of music is its name. 書名, 題名, タイトル □ "Patience and Sarah" was first published in 1969 under the title "A Place for Us." 『Patience and Sarah』は1969年に『A Place for Us』という書名で出版された. **2** V-T 他動詞 When a writer, composer, or artist **titles** a work, they give it a name. 題名をつける □ Pirandello titled his play "Six Characters in Search of an Author." ピランデロは彼の劇に『Six Characters in Search of an Author』という題をつけた. □ The single is titled "White Love." そのシングルには『White Love』というタイトルがついている. **3** N-COUNT 可算名詞 Publishers and booksellers often refer to books or magazines as **titles**. 出版社や書店が発売されている本や雑誌を差して用いる □ The magazine has become the biggest publisher of new poetry, with 50 new titles a year. その雑誌は年間に新刊50冊を発行し, 新しい詩歌の最大の出版社となった. **4** N-COUNT 可算名詞 Someone's **title** is a word such as "Mr", "Mrs", or "Doctor," that is used before their own name in order to show their status or profession. (地位や職業を示すのに用いられる) 称号, 敬称 □ Please fill in your name and title. 名前と称号を記入してください. **5** N-COUNT 可算名詞 Someone's **title** is a name that describes their job or status in an organization. 肩書き □ He was given the title of assistant manager. 彼はアシスタント・マネージャーという肩書きをもらった. **6** N-COUNT 可算名詞 If a person or team wins a particular **title**, they win a sports competition that is held regularly. Usually a person keeps a title until someone else defeats them. 選手権, タイトル □ He became Jamaica's first Olympic gold medalist when he won the 400 meter title in 1948. 彼は1948年の400メートル走でタイトルを獲得したとき

ジャマイカ最初のオリンピック金メダリストになった. **7** N-COUNT 可算名詞 In Britain, and some other countries, a person's **title** is a word such as "Sir," "Lord," or "Lady" that is used in front of their name, or a phrase that is used instead of their name, and indicates that they have a high rank in society. (英国で用いられる) 称号, 敬称 □ Her husband was also honored with his title "Sir Denis." 彼女の夫も「サー・デニス」という称号を授与された.
→ see **graph**

to

❶ PREPOSITION AND ADVERB USES
❷ USED BEFORE THE BASE FORM OF A VERB

❶ to

Usually pronounced /tə/ before a consonant and /tu/ before a vowel, but pronounced /tu/ when you are emphasizing it.

通常子音の前で /tə/, 母音の前で /tu/ と発音される. しかしそれが強調されている時は /tu/ と発音される.

In addition to the uses shown below, **to** is used in phrasal verbs such as "see to" and "come to." It is also used with some verbs that have two objects in order to introduce the second object.

下記の用法に加えて, **to** は **see to** や **come to** のような句動詞に使われる. また2つの目的語をもういくつかの動詞と共に用いられ, 第2の目的語を導く.

1 PREP 前置詞 You use **to** when indicating the place that someone or something visits, moves toward, or points at. (行き先を示して) ーへ, ーに □ Two friends and I drove to Florida during spring break. 2人の友人と私は春休みの期間中にフロリダへ車で行った. □ She went to the window and looked out. 彼女は窓際に行き外を見た. **2** PREP 前置詞 If you go to an event, you go where it is taking place. (行事などに) □ We went to a party at the Kurt's house. 私たちはカートの家で行われるパーティに行った. □ He came to dinner. 彼は夕食に来た. **3** PREP 前置詞 If something is attached to something larger or fixed **to** it, the two things are joined together. ーに (結合・接続先などを示して) □ There was a piece of cloth tied to the dog's collar. そのイヌの首輪に布が1枚結んであった. **4** PREP 前置詞 You use **to** when indicating the position of something. For example, if something is **to** your left, it is nearer your left side than your right side. (位置する方向を示して) ーの方に □ Hemingway's studio is to the right. ヘミングウェイのスタジオは右側にある. **5** PREP 前置詞 When you give something **to** someone, they receive it. (譲渡の対象となる人を示して) ーへ, ーに [v n PREP n] □ He picked up the knife and gave it to me. 彼はナイフを拾って私に渡してくれた. **6** PREP 前置詞 You use **to** to indicate who or what an action or a feeling is directed toward. ーへ, ーに [adj/n PREP n] □ Marcus has been really mean to me today. マーカスは今日私に本当に意地悪だった. □ ...troops loyal to the government. 政府に忠実な軍隊 **7** PREP 前置詞 **To** can show how is affected by something. ーに対して, ーにとって [adj/n PREP n] □ He is a witty man, and an inspiration to all of us. 彼は機知に富む人で私たち全員にとって刺激になる. **8** PREP 前置詞 If you say something **to** someone, you want that person to listen and understand what you are saying. ーに (言う) □ I will explain to them that I can't pay them. 彼らに支払いはできないと説明します. **9** PREP 前置詞 You use **to** when showing someone's reaction to something or their feelings about a situation or event. For example, if you say that something happens **to** someone's surprise you mean that they are surprised when it happens. ーしたことに □ To his surprise, the bedroom door was locked. 彼が驚いたことに, 寝室のドアは鍵がかかっていた. **10** PREP 前置詞 **To** can show whose opinion is being stated. ーにとって, ーには □ It was clear to me that he respected his boss. 彼が上司を尊敬していることは私には明らかだった. **11** PREP 前置詞 You use **to** when indicating what something or someone is becoming, or the state or situation that they are progressing toward. (変化を示して) ーへ, ーに □ The shouts changed to laughter. 叫び声が笑い声に変わった. □ ...an old ranch house that has been converted to a nature center. 自然センターに改造された古い牧場経営者の家 **12** PREP 前置詞 **To** can be used as a way of introducing the person or organisation you are employed by. (雇用関係を示して) ーの下で [n PREP n] □ Rickman worked as a dresser to Nigel Hawthorne. リックマンは衣裳係としてナイジェル・ホーソンの下で働いた. **13** PREP 前置詞 **To** can show a span of time. (期間を示して) ーまで □ From 1977 to 1985 the United States gross national product grew 21 percent. 1977年から1985年の期間に米国の国民総生産は21%成長した. **14** PREP 前置詞 You use **to** to show two extreme examples of something. ーに至るまで (限界・限度を示して) ['from' n PREP n] □ I read everything from fiction to history. 私は小説から歴史書に至るまで何でも読む. **15** PREP 前置詞 If someone goes from place **to** place or from job **to** job, they go to several places, or work in several jobs, and spend only a short time in each one. ーからーで

(fromを伴って)['from' n PREP n] ❑ *Larry and Andy had drifted from place to place, working at this and that.* ラリーとアンディはあちらこちらであれこれして働きながら漂流した. **16** PHRASE 句 If someone moves **to and fro**, they move repeatedly from one place to another and back again, or from side to side. 行ったり来たり, 左右に ❑ *She stood up and began to pace to and fro.* 彼女は立ち上がってあちこち歩き回り始めた. **17** PREP 前置詞 You use **to** when you are stating a time less than thirty minutes before an hour. For example, if it is "five to eight," it is five minutes before eight o'clock. 「一時…分前」という時刻を示して ❑ *At twenty to six I was waiting by the entrance to the station.* 6時20分前に, 私は駅の入り口で待っていた. [num/n PREP num] You use **to** when giving ratios and rates. 一につき(対比を示して) ❑ *...engines that can run at 60 miles to the gallon.* 1ガロンで60マイル走ることができるエンジン **19** PREP 前置詞 You use **to** when indicating that two things happen at the same time. For example, if something is done **to** music, it is done at the same time as music is being played. (音楽などに)合わせて ❑ *Romeo left the stage, to enthusiastic applause.* ロメオは熱烈なかっさいに合わせてステージを去った. **20** CONVENTION 慣習表現 If you say "There's nothing to it," "There's not much to it," or "That's all there is to it," you are emphasizing how simple you think something is. 簡単なことだ, なんてことはない [EMPHASIS 強調] ❑ *"There is nothing to it," those I asked about it told me.* 私がそのことについて尋ねた相手は「どうってことないよ」と答えた. **21** → see also **according to** **22** → see also **too**

❷ **to**

Pronounced /tə/ before a consonant and /tu/ before a vowel.

子音の前では /tə/と, 母音の前では /tu/と発音される.

1 PREP 前置詞 You use **to** before the base form of a verb to form the to-infinitive. You use the to-infinitive after certain verbs, nouns, and adjectives, and after words such as "how," "which," and "where." 一することを, 一するための ❑ *The management wanted to know what is was doing there.* 経営者は私がそこで何をしていたのかを知りたがっていた. ❑ *She told the family of her decision to resign.* 彼女は家族に辞職の決心について話した. **2** PREP 前置詞 You use **to** before the base form of a verb to indicate the purpose or intention of an action. 一するために ❑ *...using the experience of big companies to help small businesses.* 小規模企業を助けるために大手企業の経験を使うこと **3** PREP 前置詞 You use **to** before the base form of a verb when you are commenting on a statement that you are making, for example, when saying that you are being honest or brief, or that you are summing up or giving an example. 一すると ❑ *I'm disappointed, to be honest.* 正直に言うと, がっかりしている. **4** PREP 前置詞 You use **to** before the base form of a verb when indicating what situation follows a particular action. 次に起きる状況を示して ❑ *From the garden you walk down to discover a large and beautiful lake.* 庭から歩いて行くと, 大きくて美しい湖があるのに気付くだろう. **5** You use **to** with "too" and "enough" in expressions like **too much** or **old enough to**; see **too** and **enough**. 一するには

toad /toʊd/ (toads) N-COUNT 可算名詞 A **toad** is a creature which is similar to a frog but which has a drier skin and spends less time in water. ヒキガエル

toast /toʊst/ (toasts, toasting, toasted) **1** N-UNCOUNT 不可算名詞 **Toast** is bread which has been cut into slices and made brown and crisp by cooking at a high temperature. トースト ❑ *...a piece of toast.* トースト1枚 **2** V-T 他動詞 When you **toast** something such as bread, you cook it at a high temperature so that it becomes brown and crisp. トーストする, こんがり焼く ❑ *Toast the bread lightly on both sides.* パンの両面を軽く焼きなさい. **3** N-COUNT 可算名詞 When you drink a **toast to** someone or something, you drink some wine or another alcoholic drink as a symbolic gesture, in order to show your appreciation of them or to wish them success. 乾杯 ❑ *Eleanor and I drank a toast to the bride and groom.* エレノアと私は新郎新婦のために祝杯をあげた. **4** V-T 他動詞 When you **toast** someone or something, you drink a toast to them. 一のために乾杯する ❑ *We all toasted his health.* 我々一同彼の健康を願って乾杯した.

→ see **cook**

toast|er /toʊstər/ (toasters) N-COUNT 可算名詞 A **toaster** is a piece of electric equipment used to toast bread. トースター

to|bac|co /təbækoʊ/ (tobaccos) **1** N-MASS 質量名詞 **Tobacco** is dried leaves which people smoke in pipes, cigars, and cigarettes. You can also refer to pipes, cigars, and cigarettes as a whole as **tobacco**. たばこ ❑ *Try to do without tobacco and alcohol.* 禁煙禁酒をやってみなさい. **2** N-UNCOUNT 不可算名詞 **Tobacco** is the plant from which tobacco is obtained. タバコ ❑ *...Cuba's tobacco crop.* キューバのタバコの収穫量

to|day /tədeɪ/ **1** ADV 副詞 You use **today** to refer to this day on which you are speaking or writing. 今日は, 本日は [ADV with cl] ❑ *How are you feeling today?* 今日はご機嫌いかがですか? ● N-UNCOUNT 不可算名詞 **Today** is also a noun. 今日 ❑ *Today is Friday, September 14th.* 本日は9月14日金曜日です. **2** → see also **yesterday, tomorrow**

3 ADV 副詞 You can refer to the present period of history as **today**. 現在では, 今では ❑ *The United States is in a serious recession today.* 現在米国は深刻な不況下にある. ● N-UNCOUNT 不可算名詞 **Today** is also a noun. 現代 ❑ *In today's America, health care is one of the very biggest businesses.* 現代のアメリカでは医療がまさに最大のビジネスの1つだ.

tod|dler /tɒdlər/ (toddlers) N-COUNT 可算名詞 A **toddler** is a young child who has only just learned to walk or who still walks unsteadily with small, quick steps. よちよち歩きの子供, 幼児 ❑ *I had a toddler at home and two other children at school.* 私には小さい子が家にいて学校に上がった子供が他に2人いた.

→ see **age, child**

toe /toʊ/ (toes) **1** N-COUNT 可算名詞 Your **toes** are the five movable parts at the end of each foot. 足の指 ❑ *She wiggled her toes against the packed sand.* 彼女は固まった砂の上で足の指をぴくぴく動かした. **2** PHRASE 句 If you say that someone or something **keeps you on your toes**, you mean that they cause you to remain alert and ready for anything that might happen. 一の気を引き締める ❑ *His fiery campaign rhetoric has kept opposition parties on their toes for months.* 彼の熱烈な選挙演説のために反対党は何か月も気を緩めることがなかった.

→ see **foot**

toe|nail /toʊneɪl/ (toenails) N-COUNT 可算名詞 Your **toenails** are the thin hard areas at the end of each of your toes. 足のつめ

→ see **foot**

tof|fee /tɒfi/ (toffees) **1** N-VAR 可変性名詞 **Toffee** or **English toffee** is a hard brown candy made with butter and sugar. タフィー, バタースカッチ **2** N-VAR 可変性名詞 **Toffee** is a sticky candy that is very chewy. It is made by boiling sugar and butter together with water. タフィー, キャラメル [BRIT 英国英語; AM 米国英語 **taffy**]

to|geth|er /təgɛðər/

In addition to the uses shown below, **together** is used in phrasal verbs such as "piece together," "pull together," and "sleep together."

下記の用法に加えて, **together** は **piece together, pull together, sleep together** のような句動詞に使われる.

1 ADV 副詞 If people do something **together**, they do it with each other. 一緒に, 共に ❑ *We went on long bicycle rides together.* 私たちは一緒に長距離のサイクリングに出かけた. ❑ *He and I worked together on a book.* 彼と私はある本のプロジェクトで一緒に働きました. **2** ADV 副詞 If things are joined **together**, they are joined with each other so that they touch or form one whole. 一緒にて, 合わせて [ADV after v] ❑ *Mix the ingredients together thoroughly.* 材料を合わせてすっかり混ぜ合わせなさい. **3** ADV 副詞 If things or people are situated **together**, they are in the same place and very near to each other. 同じ場所で, とても近くに [ADV after v] ❑ *The trees grew close together.* その木々は密集して生育した. ❑ *Ginette and I gathered our things together.* ジネットと私は自分たちのものを1か所に寄せ集めた. **4** ADV 副詞 If a group of people are held or kept **together**, they are united with each other in some way. 結びつけて [ADV after v] ❑ *He has done a lot to keep the family together.* 彼は家族をまとめるのにかなり貢献した. ● ADJ 形容詞 **Together** is also an adjective. 結びついた [v-link ADJ] ❑ *We are together in the way we're looking at this situation.* 我々は状況の見方において合意している. **5** ADJ 形容詞 If two people are **together**, they are married or having a sexual relationship with each other. 結婚して, 交際して ❑ *We were together for five years.* 私たちは5年間一緒だった. **6** ADV 副詞 If two things happen or are done **together**, they happen or are done at the same time. 同時に [ADV after v] ❑ *Three horses crossed the finish line together.* 3頭の馬が同時にゴールした. **7** ADV 副詞 You use **together** when you are adding two or more amounts or things to each other in order to consider a total amount or effect. 合計して ❑ *Together we earn $60,000 per year.* 合計すると年間6万ドル稼いでいる. **8** PHRASE 句 If you say that two things **go together**, or that one thing **goes together with** another, you mean that they go well with each other or cannot be separated from each other. 合う, 釣り合っている ❑ *I can see that some colors go together and some don't.* 釣り合いの取れる色とそうでないのがあるのが分かる. **9** PHRASE 句 You use **together with** to mention someone or something else that is also involved in an action or situation. 一とともに ❑ *Every month we'll deliver the very best articles, together with the latest fashion and beauty news.* 毎月, 最新のファッションと美容のニュースとともに最高の記事をお届けします. **10** to **get your act together** → see **act** **11** to **put your heads together** → see **head** **12** **put together** → see **put**

Word Partnership　*together* は次の語句と使われる:

V.	**live** together, **play** together, **spend time** together, **work** together ❶
	come together ❶ – ❹
	get together ❶ ❺
	act together, **go** together ❶ ❽
	fit together, **glue** together, **join** together, **lump** together, **mix** together, **string** together, **stuck** together, **tied** together ❷
	bring together, **keep** together, **stay** together ❷ ❹ ❺
	gather together, **sit** together, **stand** together ❸
	hold together ❹
	stick together ❹ ❺
ADJ.	**bound** together ❷
	close together ❸

toil /tɔɪl/ (**toils, toiling, toiled**) V-T/V-I 他動詞/自動詞 When people **toil**, they work very hard doing unpleasant or tiring tasks. 骨を折って働く，あくせく働く [LITERARY 文語的] ❏ *People who toiled in dim, dank factories were too exhausted to enjoy their family life.* 暗くてじめじめした工場であくせく働いていた人々はあまりにも疲れていて家庭生活を楽しめなかった．❏ *Workers toiled long hours.* 労働者は長時間せっせと働いた．● PHRASAL VERB 句動詞 **Toil away** means the same as **toil**. あくせく働く ❏ *He doesn't spend every minute toiling away at his desk.* 彼はいつも机に向かってあくせく働いているわけではない．

toi|let /tɔɪlɪt/ (**toilets**) ❶ N-COUNT 可算名詞 A **toilet** is a large bowl with a seat, or a platform with a hole, which is connected to a water system and which you use when you want to get rid of urine or feces from your body. 便器 ❏ *She made Tina flush the pills down the toilet.* 彼女はティナに錠剤をトイレに流させた．❷ N-COUNT 可算名詞 A **toilet** is a room in a house or public building that contains a toilet. トイレ，お手洗い [mainly BRIT 主に英国英語; AM usually **bathroom, rest room** 米国英語では通常 **bathroom, rest room**] ❸ PHRASE 句 You can say that someone **goes to the toilet** to mean that they get rid of waste substances from their body, especially when you want to avoid using words that you think may offend people. トイレに行く [mainly BRIT 主に英国英語; AM usually **go to the bathroom** 米国英語では通常 **go to the bathroom**] → see **plumbing**

toi|let|ries /tɔɪlətriz/ N-PLURAL 複数名詞 **Toiletries** are things that you use when washing or taking care of your body, for example, soap and toothpaste. 洗面用具

to|ken /toʊkən/ (**tokens**) ❶ ADJ 形容詞 You use **token** to describe things or actions which are small or unimportant but are meant to show particular intentions or feelings which may not be sincere. 気持ちを示した，形だけの [ADJ n] ❏ *The announcement was welcomed as a step in the right direction, but was widely seen as a token gesture.* その発表は正しい方向へのステップとして歓迎されたが，一般には形だけのものだと見られている．❷ N-COUNT 可算名詞 A **token** is a round flat piece of metal or plastic that is sometimes used instead of money. トークン，コイン ❏ *...slot-machine tokens.* スロットマシン用コイン ❸ N-COUNT 可算名詞 A **token** is a piece of paper or card that can be exchanged for goods, either in a particular store or as part of a special offer. 商品券，割引券 [BRIT 英国英語; AM **coupon** 米国英語 **coupon**] ❹ PHRASE 句 You use **by the same token** to introduce a statement that you think is true for the same reasons that were given for a previous statement. 同時に，とはいえ ❏ *If you give up exercise, your muscles shrink and fat increases. By the same token, if you expend more energy you will lose fat.* 運動をやめると筋肉が減少し脂肪が増加する．同様にカロリー消費量を増やせば，脂肪が減るだろう．

told /toʊld/ ❶ **Told** is the past tense and past participle of **tell**. tell①の過去形・過去分詞 ❷ PHRASE 句 You can use **all told** to introduce or follow a summary, general statement, or total. 全部で ❏ *All told there were 104 people on the payroll.* 総計で従業員は104名だった．

tol|er|able /tɒlərəbᵊl/ ADJ 形容詞 If you describe something as **tolerable**, you mean that you can bear it, even though it is unpleasant or painful. 我慢できる，耐えられる ❏ *Our living conditions are tolerable, but I can't wait to leave.* 生活状況には我慢できるが，出発が待ちきれない．● **tol|er|ably** /tɒlərəbli/ ADV 副詞 我慢できるほどに ❏ *Their captors treated them tolerably well.* 監禁者は彼らを耐えられる程度に接した．

tol|er|ance /tɒlərəns/ (**tolerances**) ❶ N-UNCOUNT 不可算名詞 **Tolerance** is the quality of allowing other people to say and do what they like, even if you do not agree with or approve of it. 寛容，寛大さ [APPROVAL 賛成] ❏ *...his tolerance and understanding of diverse human nature.* さまざまな人間際に対する彼の理解と寛容さ ❷ N-UNCOUNT 不可算名詞 **Tolerance** is the ability to bear something painful or unpleasant. 耐性，抵抗力 ❏ *There is lowered pain tolerance, lowered resistance to infection.* 疼痛（とうつう）耐性が低下し，感染に対する抵抗力が低下する．

tol|er|ant /tɒlərənt/ ❶ ADJ 形容詞 If you describe someone as **tolerant**, you approve of the fact that they allow other people to say and do as they like and that they are willing to accept different races, religions, and lifestyles. 寛容な，寛大な [APPROVAL 賛成] ❏ *They need to be tolerant of different points of view.* 異なった考え方に対して寛容になる必要がある．❷ ADJ 形容詞 If a plant, animal, or machine is **tolerant of** particular conditions or types of treatment, it is able to bear them without being damaged or hurt. 耐性のある [v-link ADJ 'of' n] ❏ *...plants which are more tolerant of dry conditions.* 乾燥状態への耐性が高い植物

tol|er|ate /tɒləreɪt/ (**tolerates, tolerating, tolerated**) ❶ V-T 他動詞 If you **tolerate** a situation or person, you accept although you do not particularly like them. 許す，我慢する ❏ *She can no longer tolerate the position that she's in.* 彼女は自分の立場にこれ以上我慢できない．❷ V-T 他動詞 If you can **tolerate** something bad or painful, you are able to bear it. 耐える ❏ *The ability to tolerate pain varies from person to person.* 痛みを耐える能力は人によって異なる．

toll /toʊl/ (**tolls, tolling, tolled**) ❶ V-T/V-I 他動詞/自動詞 When a bell **tolls** or when someone **tolls** it, it rings slowly and repeatedly, often as a sign that someone has died. ゆっくりと鳴らす [他動詞]，ゆっくりと鳴る [自動詞] ❏ *Church bells tolled and black flags fluttered.* 教会の鐘がゆっくりと鳴り，黒旗がはためいていた．❷ N-COUNT 可算名詞 A **toll** is a sum of money that you have to pay in order to use a particular bridge or road. 通行料 ❏ *You can pay a toll to drive on Pike's Peak Highway or relax and take the Pike's Peak Cog Railway.* 通行料を支払ってパイクスピーク高速道路を使うか，あるいはのんびりとパイクスピーク・コグ鉄道で行ってもいい．❸ N-COUNT 可算名詞 A **toll road** or **toll bridge** is a road or bridge that you have to pay to use. 有料 [N n] ❏ *Most people who drive the toll roads don't use them every day.* 有料道路を使う人々のほとんどは毎日使用しない．❹ N-COUNT 可算名詞 A **toll** is a total number of deaths, accidents, or disasters that occur in a particular period of time. 総数 [JOURNALISM ジャーナリズム] ❏ *There are fears that the casualty toll may be higher.* 死傷者数はもっと高い恐れがある．❺ → see also **death toll** ❻ PHRASE 句 If you say that something **takes** its **toll** or **takes a heavy toll**, you mean that it has a bad effect or causes a lot of suffering. 悪影響をもたらす，大被害をもたらす ❏ *Winter takes its toll on your health.* 冬は健康に悪影響をもたらす．

to|ma|to /təmeɪtoʊ/ (**tomatoes**) N-VAR 可変性名詞 **Tomatoes** are soft, red fruit that you can eat raw in salads or cooked as a vegetable. トマト

tomb /tuːm/ (**tombs**) N-COUNT 可算名詞 A **tomb** is a grave, especially one that is above ground and that usually has a sculpture or other decoration on it. 墓 ❏ *...the continuing excavation of the emperor's tomb.* 引き続いて行われている天皇の墓の発掘

to|mor|row /təmɒroʊ/ ❶ ADV 副詞 You use **tomorrow** to refer to the day after today. 明日は，あしたは [ADV with cl] ❏ *Bye, see you tomorrow.* じゃあまたあした．● N-UNCOUNT 不可算名詞 **Tomorrow** is also a noun. 明日 ❏ *What's your agenda for tomorrow?* 明日の予定は何ですか？ ❷ ADV 副詞 You can refer to the future, especially the near future, as **tomorrow**. (近い) 将来に [ADV with cl] ❏ *What is education going to look like tomorrow?* 将来の教育はどうなるでしょうか？ ● N-UNCOUNT 不可算名詞 **Tomorrow** is also a noun. (近い) 将来 [also N in pl] ❏ *...tomorrow's computer industry.* 未来のコンピュータ産業

ton /tʌn/ (**tons**) ❶ N-COUNT 可算名詞 A **ton** is a unit of weight that is equal to 2,000 pounds. (伝統単位) トン ❏ *Hundreds of tons of oil spilled into the ocean.* 何百トンもの原油が海上に流出した．❷ N-COUNT 可算名詞 A **ton** is the same as a **tonne** or **metric ton**, which is 1,000 kilograms. (メートル法での) トン [BRIT 英国英語]

tone /toʊn/ (**tones, toning, toned**) ❶ N-COUNT 可算名詞 The **tone** of a sound is its particular quality. 口調 ❏ *Cross could hear him speaking in low tones to Sarah.* クロスは彼が低い口調でサラに話しているのが聞こえた．❷ N-COUNT 可算名詞 Someone's **tone** is a quality in their voice which shows what they are feeling or thinking. 声の調子，口のきき方 ❏ *I still didn't like his tone of voice; he sounded angry and accusing.* やっぱり彼の口のきき方が気に入らなかった．責めているように聞こえた．❸ N-SING 単数名詞 The **tone** of a speech or piece of writing is its style and the opinions are expressed in it. 調子，文体 [also 'in' N] ❏ *The tone of the letter was very friendly.* その手紙の文体はとても友好的でした．❹ N-SING 単数名詞 The **tone** of a place or an event is its general atmosphere. 雰囲気 ❏ *There were no stores that would lower the tone of the area.* その地域の雰囲気を下げるような店はなかった．❺ N-UNCOUNT 不可算名詞 The **tone** of someone's body, especially their muscles, is its degree of firmness and strength. 緊張 ❏ *...stretch exercises that improve muscle tone.* 筋肉の緊張力をよくするためのストレッチ運動 ❻ V-T/V-I 他動詞/自動詞 Something that **tones** your body makes it firm and strong. 引き締める，鍛える ❏ *This movement lengthens your spine and tones the spinal nerves.* この動きはせき髄を伸ばしせき髄神経の調子を整える．❏ *Try these toning exercises before you start the day.* 1日の初

めにこれらの筋力運動を試しなさい. ● PHRASAL VERB 句動詞 **Tone up** means the same as **tone**. 引き締める, 鍛える ❏ *Exercise tones up your body.* 運動によって体が鍛えられる. **7** N-VAR 可変性名詞 A **tone** is one of the lighter, darker, or brighter shades of the same color. 色調 ❏ *Each brick also varies slightly in tone, texture and size.* れんがはそれぞれ色調, 質感, 大きさが少しずつ異なる. **8** N-SING 単数名詞 A **tone** is one of the sounds that you hear when you are using a telephone, for example, the sound that tells you that a number is busy, or no longer exists. 電話で話し中の音や使われていない番号をかけたとき聞こえる音など, 受話器から聞こえてくる音 ❏ *I can't get a dial tone on this phone.* この電話で発信音が聞こえない.
▶ **tone down** ■ PHRASAL VERB 句動詞 If you **tone down** something that you have written or said, you make it less forceful, severe, or offensive. 調子を和らげる ❏ *The fiery right-wing leader toned down his militant statements after the meeting.* 過激な右派の指導者は会議のあと, 軍事声明の調子を和らげた. **2** PHRASAL VERB 句動詞 If you **tone down** a color or a flavor, you make it less bright or strong. (色調や風味を) 和らげる ❏ *He was asked to tone down the spices and garlic in his recipes.* 彼は料理に使う香辛料とニンニクを少し減らすように頼まれた.
→ see **drum**

Word Partnership   *tone* は次の語句と使われる:

ADJ.	**clear** tone, **low** tone ■
	different tone ❷
	serious tone ❷ ❸
V.	**change your** tone ❷
	set a tone ❹
N.	tone **of voice** ❷
	muscle tone ❺
	skin tone ❼

tongue /tʌŋ/ (**tongues**) ■ N-COUNT 可算名詞 Your **tongue** is the soft movable part inside your mouth which you use for tasting, eating, and speaking. 舌 ❏ *I walked over to the mirror and stuck my tongue out.* 鏡のところまで歩いていって, 舌を出した. **2** N-COUNT 可算名詞 You can use **tongue** to refer to the kind of things that a person says. 話し方, 弁舌 ❏ *She had a nasty tongue.* 彼女は口が悪い. **3** N-COUNT 可算名詞 A **tongue** is a language. 言語 [LITERARY 文語的] ❏ *The French feel passionately about their native tongue.* フランス人は母国語に対して情熱的に感じている. **4** PHRASE 句 A **tongue-in-cheek** remark or attitude is not serious, although it may seem to be. 冗談の, ふざけて ❏ *...a lighthearted, tongue-in-cheek approach.* 屈託のない冗談めいた取り組み方 **5** to **bite** your **tongue** → see **bite**
→ see **diagnosis, face, taste**

Word Partnership   *tongue* は次の語句と使われる:

V.	**bite your** tongue, **stick out your** tongue ■
ADJ.	**pink** tongue ■
	sharp tongue ❷
N.	**native** tongue ❸

ton|ic /tɒnɪk/ (**tonics**) ■ N-MASS 質量名詞 **Tonic** or **tonic water** is a colorless carbonated drink that has a slightly bitter flavor and is often mixed with alcoholic drinks, especially gin. トニック ❏ *Keeler sipped at his gin and tonic.* キーラーはジントニックを一口飲んだ. **2** N-MASS 質量名詞 A **tonic** is a medicine that makes you feel stronger, healthier, and less tired. 強壮剤 ❏ *People are spending twice as much on health tonics as they were five years ago.* 消費者は5年前と比べて滋養強壮剤に2倍のお金を使っている.

to|night /tənaɪt/ ADV 副詞 **Tonight** is used to refer to the evening of today or the night that follows today. 今夜は ❏ *I'm at home tonight.* 今夜は家にいる. ❏ *Tonight he proved what a great player he was.* 今夜, 彼はいかに素晴らしい選手であるかを証明しました. ● N-UNCOUNT 不可算名詞 **Tonight** is also a noun. 今夜 ❏ *Tonight is the opening night of the opera.* 今夜がそのオペラの初演だ.

tonne /tʌn/ (**tonnes**) ■ N-COUNT 可算名詞 A **tonne** is a metric unit of weight that is equal to 1,000 kilograms. (メートル法の) トン [BRIT 英国英語; AM **metric ton** 米国英語 **metric ton**] **2** → see also **ton**

<hr>

too
❶	ADDING SOMETHING OR RESPONDING
❷	INDICATING EXCESS

<hr>

❶ too /tuː/ ■ ADV 副詞 You use **too** after mentioning another person, thing, or aspect that a previous statement applies to or includes. ーもまた [cl/group ADV] ❏ *"Nice to talk to you."* —*"Nice to talk to you too."* 「お話できてよかったわ」「こちらこそ」 ❏ *"I've got a great feeling about it."* —*"Me too."* 「なんだかうまくいきそうに思う」「私も」 **2** ADV 副詞 You use **too** after adding a piece of

information or a comment to a statement, in order to emphasize that it is surprising or important. しかも [EMPHASIS 強調] [cl/group ADV] ❏ *We did learn to read, and quickly too.* 読み方を習ったんだ, しかも速読だよ.

❷ too /tuː/
⇨ Please look at category **4** to see if the expression you are looking for is shown under another headword. ■ ADV 副詞 You use **too** in order to indicate that there is a greater amount or degree of something than is desirable, necessary, or acceptable. ーすぎる, あまりにもーだ ❏ *Leather jeans that are too big will make you look larger.* ぶかぶかの皮のジーンズをはくと体が大きく見える. ❏ *I'm turning up the heat, it's too cold.* 暖房を強くします. 寒すぎるから. **2** ADV 副詞 You use **too** with a negative to make what you are saying sound less forceful or more polite or cautious. あまりーない [VAGUENESS あいまいさ] [with brd-neg, ADV adj] ❏ *I wasn't too happy with what I'd written so far.* それまでのところ自分が書いたものに今ひとつ満足していなかった. **3** PHRASE 句 You use **all too** or **only too** to emphasize that something happens to a greater extent or degree than is good or desirable. あまりにもー [EMPHASIS 強調] ❏ *She remembered it all too well.* 彼女はそのことを残念ながらよく覚えている. **4** none too → see **none**

> **Too** can be used to intensify the meaning of an adjective, an adverb, or a word like **much** or **many**. **Too**, however, also suggests an excessive or undesirable amount, often so much that a particular result does not or cannot happen. ❏ *She does wear too much makeup at times... He was too late to save her.* **Too** is not generally used to modify an adjective inside a noun group. For instance, you cannot say "the too heavy boxes" or "too expensive jewelry." There is one exception to this rule, which is when the noun group begins with **a** or **an**. Notice the word order in the following examples. ❏ *...if the products have been stored at too high a temperature... He found it too good an opportunity to miss... It was too long a drive for one day.*

took /tʊk/ **Took** is the past tense of **take**. take の過去形

tool /tuːl/ (**tools**) ■ N-COUNT 可算名詞 A **tool** is any instrument or simple piece of equipment that you hold in your hands and use to do a particular kind of work. For example, spades, hammers, and knives are all tools. 道具 ❏ *I find the best tool for the purpose is a pair of shears.* その目的にぴったりの道具は植木ばさみだと思う. **2** N-COUNT 可算名詞 You can refer to anything that you use for a particular purpose as a particular type of **tool**. 手段, ツール ❏ *Writing is a good tool for expressing feelings.* 書くことは感情を表すためのよい手段だ.
→ see **Picture Dictionary: tools**

Thesaurus   *tool* また次を参照:

N.	appliance, device, instrument ■ ❷

Word Partnership   *tool* は次の語句と使われる:

N.	tool **belt** ■
	communication tool, **learning** tool, **management** tool, **marketing** tool, **teaching** tool ❷
V.	**use a** tool ■ ❷
ADJ.	**effective** tool, **important** tool, **valuable** tool ■ ❷
	powerful tool ❷

tool|bar /tuːlbɑːr/ (**toolbars**) N-COUNT 可算名詞 A **toolbar** is a narrow strip across a computer screen containing pictures, called icons, which represent different computer functions. When you want to use a particular function, you move the cursor onto its icon using a mouse and click. ツールバー [COMPUTING コンピューティング]

tooth /tuːθ/ (**teeth**) ■ N-COUNT 可算名詞 Your **teeth** are the hard white objects in your mouth, which you use for biting and chewing. 歯 ❏ *She had very pretty straight teeth.* 彼女の歯はとてもきれいで歯並びがよかった. **2** N-PLURAL 複数名詞 The **teeth** of something such as a comb, saw, cog, or zipper are the parts that stick out in a row on its edge. (くし・のこぎり・歯車・ファスナーなどの) 歯 ❏ *The front cog has 44 teeth.* 前の歯車には44本の歯がある. **3** PHRASE 句 If you have **a sweet tooth**, you like sweet food very much. 甘党 ❏ *Add more honey if you have a sweet tooth.* 甘いものが好きならはちみつを追加しなさい. **4** to **grit** your **teeth** → see **grit** **5** a **kick in the teeth** → see **kick**

Word Partnership   *tooth* は次の語句と使われる:

N.	tooth **decay**, tooth **enamel** ■
V.	**lose a** tooth, **pull a** tooth ■

tooth|brush /tuːθbrʌʃ/ (**toothbrushes**) N-COUNT 可算名詞 A **toothbrush** is a small brush that you use for cleaning your teeth. 歯ブラシ

t

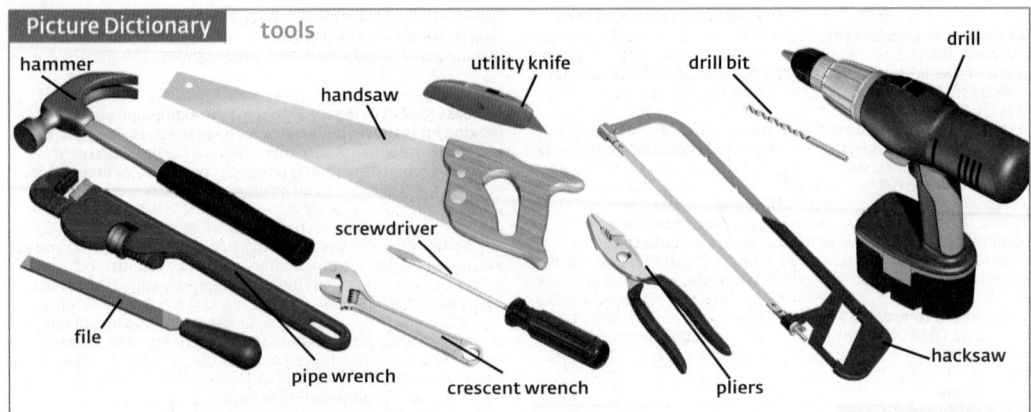

Picture Dictionary   tools

hammer — utility knife — drill bit — drill

handsaw

screwdriver

file — pipe wrench — crescent wrench — pliers — hacksaw

---

tooth|paste /tuːθpeɪst/ (**toothpastes**) N-MASS 質量名
詞 **Toothpaste** is a thick substance which you put on your
toothbrush and use to clean your teeth. 練り歯磨き □*Shaving
supplies, toothpaste, and soap were found inside.* ひげそり用具、練り歯
磨き、せっけんが中にあった。

---

top

❶ NOUN AND ADJECTIVE USES
❷ VERB AND PHRASAL VERB
❸ PHRASES

---

❶ **top** /tɒp/ (**tops**) **1** N-COUNT 可算名詞 The **top** of something is
its highest point or part. 最上部 □*I waited at the top of the stairs.* 階
段の最上段で待った. □*...the picture at the top of the page.* ページの最
上部にある絵 ● ADJ 形容詞 **Top** is also an adjective. 最上部の [ADJ n]
□*...the top corner of the newspaper.* 新聞の最上段の隅 **2** ADJ 形容詞
The **top** thing or layer in a series of things or layers is the highest
one. いちばん上の [ADJ n] □*I can't reach the top shelf.* いちばん上の
棚に手が届きません. **3** N-COUNT 可算名詞 The **top** of something
such as a bottle, jar, or tube is a cap, lid, or other device that fits
or screws onto one end of it. 栓、ふた □*...the plastic tops from soda
bottles.* 炭酸飲料のボトルのプラスチックのふた **4** N-SING 単数名
詞 The **top** of a street, garden, bed, or table is the end of it that is
farthest away from where you usually enter it or from where you
are. 突き当たり、向こう側 [BRIT 英国英語; AM end 米国英語 end]
5 N-COUNT 可算名詞 A **top** is a piece of clothing that you wear
on the upper half of your body, for example, a blouse or shirt. ト
ップ [INFORMAL くだけた] □*Look at my new top.* 新しいトップを見
て. **6** ADJ 形容詞 You can use **top** to indicate that something or
someone is at the highest level of a scale or measurement. 最
高の [ADJ n] □*The vehicles have a top speed of 80 miles per hour.* その
車両の最高時速は80マイルだ. **7** N-SING 単数名詞 The **top** of an
organization or career structure is the highest level in it. トップ、
幹部 □*We started from the bottom and we had to work our way up to the
top.* 私たちは底辺からスタートして努力してトップまで上り詰めなけ
ればならなかったんです. □*...his dramatic rise to the top of the military
hierarchy.* 彼の軍隊の階級組織トップへの目覚しい出世 ● ADJ 形容詞
Top is also an adjective. トップの、最高幹部の [ADJ n] □*I need to
have the top people in this company pull together.* 当社の最高幹部に協
力してもらう必要がある. **8** ADJ 形容詞 You can use **top** to describe
the most important or famous people or things in a particular
area of work or activity. 一流の、トップの [ADJ n] □*So you want to
be a top model.* じゃあ、トップモデルになりたいんだね. **9** N-SING 単
数名詞 If someone is **at the top of**, for example, a table or league
or is **the top of** the table or league, their performance is better
than that of all the other people involved. 首位 □*...the golfer at
the top of the leaderboard.* リーダーボードで首位のゴルファー ● ADJ
形容詞 **Top** is also an adjective. 首位の □*He was the top student in
physics.* 彼は物理でトップの学生でした. **10** ADJ 形容詞 You can use
top to indicate that something is the first thing you are going to
do, because you consider it to be the most important. 最優先の
□*Cleaning up the water supply is their top priority.* 上水道の清掃が最優
先事項だ. **11** ADJ 形容詞 You can use **top** to indicate that someone
does a particular thing more times than anyone else or that
something is chosen more times than anything else. 最優秀の、
第1位の [ADJ n] □*Jamillah Lang was Colorado's top scorer.* ジャミーラ・
ラングはコロラド州の得点王だった.

Thesaurus   top また次を参照：

N.   peak, summit, zenith; (ant.) base, bottom ❶ **1**
ADJ.   best, finest, first-rate ❶ **8**

❷ **top** /tɒp/ (**tops, topping, topped**) V-T 他動詞 To **top** a list
means to be mentioned or chosen more times than anyone or
anything else. 〜の第1位である [JOURNALISM ジャーナリズム] □*It
was the first time in years that a Japanese manufacturer had not topped
the list for imported vehicles.* 日本のメーカーが輸入車の第1位でないの
は数年ぶりだ.
▶ **top out** PHRASAL VERB 句動詞 If something such as a price **tops
out at** a particular amount, that is the highest amount that it
reaches.' 最高に達する [AM 米国英語] □*The stock topped out at more
than $25.* 株価の最高額は25ドル以上に達した. □*Last Friday was a
warm day, topping out at 85 degrees.* 先週の金曜日は暖かくて、最高気
温が85度に達した.
▶ **top up** PHRASAL VERB 句動詞 If you **top** something **up**, you
make it full again when part of it has been used. 補給する、つぎ足
す [mainly BRIT 主に英国英語] □*We topped up the water tanks.* 私た
ちは貯水槽に水を補給した.

❸ **top** /tɒp/ (**tops**) **1** PHRASE 句 If you say that you clean or
examine something **from top to bottom**, you are emphasizing
that you do it completely and thoroughly. 徹底的に [EMPHASIS 強
調] □*She would clean the house from top to bottom.* 彼女は徹底的に家
を掃除するだろう. **2** PHRASE 句 You can use **from top to toe** to
emphasize that the whole of someone's body is covered or dressed
in a particular thing or type of clothing. 頭のてっぺんからつま
先まで [mainly BRIT 主に英国英語, EMPHASIS 強調] □*They
were sensibly dressed from top to toe in rain gear.* 彼らは賢明にも雨具で
完全防備をしていた. **3** PHRASE 句 When something **gets on top
of** you, it makes you feel unhappy or depressed because it is very
difficult or worrying, or because it involves more work than you
can manage. 手に負えなくなる □*Things have been getting on top of
me lately.* 最近、いろいろと手に負えなくなってきている. **4** PHRASE
句 If you **are on top of** or **get on top of** something that you are
doing, you are dealing with it successfully. うまく処理している
□*...the government's inability to get on top of the situation.* 政府が状況
をうまく処理できないこと **5** PHRASE 句 If you say something **off
the top of** your head, you say it without thinking about it much
before you speak, especially because you do not have enough
time. 思いつきで、即興で □*It was the best I could think of off the
top of my head.* それは、思いつきでは最高の考えだった. **6** PHRASE
句 If one thing is **on top of** another, it is placed over it or on its
highest part. 〜の上で □*He was sound asleep on top of the covers.* 彼
は掛け布団の上で熟睡していました. **7** PHRASE 句 You can use **on
top** or **on top of** to indicate that a particular problem exists in
addition to a number of other problems. 〜に加えて □*A stepfamily
faces all the problems that a normal family has, with a set of additional
problems on top.* 再婚家族は、普通の家族と同じ問題に直面するが、
それに加えて一連の別の問題がある. **8** PHRASE 句 You say that
someone is **on top** when they have reached the most important
position in an organisation or business. トップの座で □*In such a
fast-changing business, it's hard to stay on top.* そのような急速に変化
のある会社でトップの座にとどまるのは難しい. **9** PHRASE 句 If you
say that you feel **on top of the world**, you are emphasizing that
you feel extremely happy and healthy. 天にも昇るような気持ちで
[EMPHASIS 強調] □*Two months before she gave birth to Jason she left
work feeling on top of the world.* ジェイソンを出産する2か月前に、彼女
は天にも上るような気持ちで仕事を辞めた. **10** PHRASE 句 If someone
pays **top dollar** for something, they pay the highest possible

price for it. 最高額 [INFORMAL くだけた] [V PHR, PHR n] ❑ People will always pay top dollar for something exclusive. 人々は，他で手に入らないものには常に最高額を出すだろう． **11** PHRASE 句 If one thing is **over the top** of another, it is placed over it so that it is completely covering it. すっかり覆って ❑ I placed a sheet of plastic over the top of the container. その容器の上をビニールシートですっかり覆った． **12** PHRASE 句 You describe something as **over the top** when you think that it is exaggerated, and therefore unacceptable. 大げさな，やり過ぎの [mainly BRIT 主に英国英語, INFORMAL くだけた] ❑ The special effects are a bit over the top but I enjoyed it. 特殊効果はちょっと大げさだったけど，楽しかった． **13** PHRASE 句 If you say something **at the top of** your voice, you say it very loudly. 声を張り上げて ❑ "Stephen, come back!" shouted Marcia at the top of her voice. 「スティーブン，戻って来て！」とマーシアは声を限りに叫んだ．

top-end /ˈtɒpˈɛnd/ ADJ 形容詞 **Top-end** products are expensive and of extremely high quality. 最高級の [BUSINESS 実業] ❑ …top-end camcorders. 最高級のビデオカメラ

top|ic /ˈtɒpɪk/ (topics) N-COUNT 可算名詞 A **topic** is a particular subject that you discuss, study, or write about. 話題，テーマ ❑ The weather is a constant topic of conversation in Alaska. アラスカでは常に天気が話題になる．

top|i|cal /ˈtɒpɪkˀl/ ADJ 形容詞 **Topical** is used to describe something that concerns or relates to events that are happening at the present time. 話題になっている，時事の ❑ The newscast covers topical events and entertainment. ニュース放送では話題の出来事や娯楽について報道する．

top|less /ˈtɒpləs/ ADJ 形容詞 If a woman is **topless**, she does not wear anything to cover her breasts. トップレスの，上半身裸の ❑ I wouldn't sunbathe topless if I thought I might offend anyone. 誰かの気分を害するかもしれないと思ったらトップレスで日光浴なんてしない．

top|ple /ˈtɒpˀl/ (topples, toppling, toppled) **11** V-T/V-I 他動詞/自動詞 If someone or something **topples** somewhere or if you **topple** them, they become unsteady or unstable and fall over. 倒す，ぐらつかせる [他動詞]，倒れる，ぐらつく [自動詞] ❑ He just released his hold and toppled slowly backwards. 彼はちょうど手を緩め，ぐらつきながらゆっくりと後ろに倒れた． ● PHRASAL VERB 句動詞 **Topple over** means the same as **topple**. 倒す [他動詞]，倒れる [自動詞] ❑ The tree is so badly damaged they are worried it might topple over. その木はあまりにも損傷していたので，倒れるかもしれないと心配している． **2** V-T 他動詞 To **topple** a government or leader, especially one that is not elected by the people, means to cause them to lose power. 転覆させる，失脚させる [他動詞] ❑ …the revolution which toppled the regime. その政権を倒した革命 [JOURNALISM ジャーナリズム]

top se|cret ADJ 形容詞 **Top secret** information or activity is intended to be kept completely secret, for example, in order to prevent a country's enemies from finding out about it. 最高機密の，極秘の ❑ The top secret documents had to do with the most advanced military equipment. 極秘書類は最高機能軍事機器と関連があった．

torch /ˈtɔːtʃ/ (torches) **11** N-COUNT 可算名詞 A **torch** is a long stick with burning material at one end, used to provide light or to set things on fire. たいまつ，火を点ける棒 ❑ The shepherd followed, carrying a torch to light his way. 羊飼いはたいまつで行き先を照らしながら後に続いた． **2** N-COUNT 可算名詞 A **torch** is a device that produces a hot flame and is used for tasks such as cutting or joining pieces of metal. バーナー ❑ The gang worked for up to ten hours with acetylene torches to open the vault. その一団は金庫を開けるのにアセチレン灯を使って10時間まで取り組んだ． **3** N-COUNT 可算名詞 A **torch** is a small electric light which is powered by batteries and which you can carry in your hand. 懐中電灯 [BRIT 英国英語; AM **flashlight** 米国英語 **flashlight**]

tore /ˈtɔːr/ **Tore** is the past tense of **tear**. tearの過去形

tor|ment (torments, tormenting, tormented)

The noun is pronounced /ˈtɔːmɛnt/. The verb is pronounced /tɔːˈmɛnt/.

名詞は /ˈtɔːmɛnt/ と発音される．動詞は /tɔːˈmɛnt/ と発音される．

11 N-UNCOUNT 不可算名詞 **Torment** is extreme suffering, usually mental suffering. 苦悩 ❑ After years of turmoil and torment, she is finally at peace. 何年間も続いた混乱と苦悩が終わり，彼女はやっと落ち着いた． **2** N-COUNT 可算名詞 A **torment** is something that causes extreme suffering, usually mental suffering. 苦悩の種 ❑ Sooner or later most writers end up making books about the torments of being a writer. 早かれ遅かれほとんどの作家は最終的には作家であることの苦しみについての本を書く． **3** V-T 他動詞 If something **torments** you, it causes you extreme mental suffering. 苦しめる [他動詞] ❑ At times the memories returned to torment her. 時折記憶がよみがえり彼女を苦しめた．

torn /ˈtɔːrn/ **11** **Torn** is the past participle of **tear**. tearの過去分詞 **2** ADJ 形容詞 If you are **torn between** two or more things, you cannot decide which to choose, and so you feel anxious or troubled. 迷った ❑ Robb is torn between becoming a doctor and a career in athletics. ロブは医者になるか運動選手になるか迷っている．

tor|na|do /tɔːrˈneɪdoʊ/ (tornadoes or tornados) N-COUNT 可算名詞 A **tornado** is a violent wind storm consisting of a tall column of air which spins around very fast and causes a lot of damage. 竜巻

tor|pe|do /tɔːrˈpiːdoʊ/ (torpedoes, torpedoing, torpedoed) **11** N-COUNT 可算名詞 A **torpedo** is a bomb that is shaped like a tube and that travels under water. 水雷，魚雷 **2** V-T 他動詞 If a ship **is torpedoed**, it is hit, and usually sunk, by a torpedo or torpedoes. 水雷で攻撃する [usu passive] ❑ More than a thousand people died when the Lusitania was torpedoed. ルシタニア号が水雷で撃沈されたとき1000人以上が死亡した．

tor|rent /ˈtɔːrənt/ (torrents) **11** N-COUNT 可算名詞 A **torrent** is a lot of water falling or flowing rapidly or violently. 激流，どしゃ降り ❑ Torrents of water gushed into the reservoir. 滝のような水がごうごうと貯水池に流れた． **2** N-COUNT 可算名詞 A **torrent of** abuse or questions is a lot of abuse or questions directed continuously at someone. あらし ❑ He turned around and directed a torrent of abuse at me. 彼は振り返って私に非難のあらしを浴びせた．

tor|ren|tial /tɔːˈrɛnʃl/ ADJ 形容詞 **Torrential** rain pours down very rapidly and in great quantities. どしゃ降りの ❑ The storms and torrential rain caused traffic chaos across the country. あらしと集中豪雨により全国で交通混乱が起きた．

tor|so /ˈtɔːrsoʊ/ (torsos) N-COUNT 可算名詞 Your **torso** is the main part of your body, and does not include your head, arms, and legs. 胴 [FORMAL 形式ばった] ❑ The man had the bulky upper torso of a weightlifter. その男性は重量挙げ選手らしいがっしりとした上半身をしていた．

tor|toise /ˈtɔːrtəs/ (tortoises) N-COUNT 可算名詞 A **tortoise** is a slow-moving animal with a shell into which it can pull its head and legs for protection. カメ

tor|tu|ous /ˈtɔːrtʃuəs/ **11** ADJ 形容詞 A **tortuous** road is full of bends and twists. 曲がりくねった ❑ The only road access is a tortuous mountain route. 唯一の道からのアクセスは曲がりくねった峠道だった． **2** ADJ 形容詞 A **tortuous** process or piece of writing is very long and complicated. ややこしい ❑ …these long and tortuous negotiations aimed at ending the conflict. 紛争を終えることを目的とした長くて複雑な交渉

tor|ture /ˈtɔːrtʃər/ (tortures, torturing, tortured) **11** V-T 他動詞 If someone **is tortured**, another person deliberately causes them terrible pain over a period of time, in order to punish them or to make them reveal information. 拷問にかける [他動詞] ❑ Despite being tortured she proclaimed her innocence. 拷問を受けたにもかかわらず，彼女は公の場で自分の無実を主張した． ● N-VAR 可変性名詞 **Torture** is also a noun. 拷問 ❑ …alleged cases of torture and murder by the security forces. 治安部隊による拷問と殺人の申し立て **2** V-T 他動詞 To **torture** someone means to cause them to suffer mental pain or anxiety. 苦しめる [他動詞] ❑ He would not torture her further by trying to argue with her. 彼は，彼女と口論としようとしてこれ以上苦しめたりはしないだろう．

toss /ˈtɒs/ (tosses, tossing, tossed) **11** V-T 他動詞 If you **toss** something somewhere, you throw it there lightly, often in a careless way. ぽんと投げる ❑ Just toss it in the trash. ただごみ箱に捨てなさい． **2** V-T 他動詞 If you **toss** your head or **toss** your hair, you move your head backward, quickly and suddenly, often as a way of expressing an emotion such as anger or contempt. (髪・頭を）振り上げる ❑ "I'm sure I don't know." Deb tossed her head. 「確かに知らないわ」デブは頭を振り上げた． ● N-COUNT 可算名詞 **Toss** is also a noun. (髪・頭を）振り上げること ❑ With a toss of his head and a few hard gulps, Bob finished the last of his beer. 頭を振り上げ何度かごくごく飲んで，ボブはビールの最後の1杯を飲み終えた． **3** V-T 他動詞 In sports and some informal situations, if you decide something by **tossing** a coin, you spin a coin into the air and guess which side of the coin will face upward when it lands. コイントスをする ❑ We tossed a coin to decide who would go out and buy the bagels. 私たちは，ベーグルを買いに行く人をコイントスして決めた． ● N-COUNT 可算名詞 **Toss** is also a noun. コイントス ❑ It would be better to decide it on the toss of a coin. コイントスして決めた方がいい． **4** PHRASE 句 If you **toss and turn**, you keep moving around in bed and cannot sleep, for example, because you are sick or worried. 何度も寝返りを打つ ❑ I try to go back to sleep and toss and turn for a while. また眠りにつこうとしてしばらく何度も寝返りを打つ．

→ see **sleep**

to|tal /ˈtoʊtˀl/ (totals, totaling or totalling, totaled or totalled) **11** N-COUNT 可算名詞 A **total** is the number that you get when you add several numbers together or when you count how many things there are in a group. 総計 ❑ The companies have a total of 1,776 employees. その会社には総計1776人の従業員がいる． **2** ADJ 形容詞 The **total** number or cost of something is the number or cost that you get when you add together or count all the parts in it. 総計の [ADJ n] ❑ They said that the total number of cows dying from BSE would be twenty thousand. 彼らは狂牛病で死ぬ牛の総数は2万人だと言った． **3** PHRASE 句 If there are a number of things **in total**, there are that number when you count or add them all together. 総計

で □ *I was with my husband for eight years in total.* 私は合計8年を主人と過ごした. ◆ V-T 他動詞 If several numbers or things **total** a certain figure, that figure is the total of all the numbers or all the things. 総計…になる [他動詞] □ *The unit's exports will total $85 million this year.* そのユニットの今年の輸出高は総計8500万ドルになる. ◆ V-T 他動詞 If someone **totals** a vehicle, they are in a serious accident and the vehicle is so badly damaged that it is not worth repairing. (事故などで車を) 完全に破壊する [AM 米国英語, INFORMAL くだけた] [他動詞] □ *Buddy totaled his car.* バディは彼の車を完全に破壊した. ◆ ADJ 形容詞 You can use **total** to emphasize that something is as great in extent, degree, or amount as it possibly can be. 全くの [EMPHASIS 強調] □ *You were a total failure if you hadn't married by the time you were about twenty-three.* 23歳ごろまでに結婚できなかったら君は大失敗者だ. ●**to|tal|ly** ADV 副詞 全く □ *Young people want something totally different from the old ways.* 若者は古いものとはまったく違うものを欲しがる.

to|tali|tar|ian /toʊtælɪtɛəriən/ ADJ 形容詞 A **totalitarian** political system is one in which there is only one political party which controls everything and does not allow any opposition parties. 一国一党主義の [DISAPPROVAL 不賛成] □ *...a brutal totalitarian regime.* 残忍な一党独裁政権

tot|ter /tɒtər/ (**totters, tottering, tottered**) V-I 自動詞 If someone **totters** somewhere, they walk there in an unsteady way, for example, because they are drunk. よろめく [自動詞] □ *She came tottering in in her mother's high heels.* 彼女は母親のハイヒールをはいてよろめきながらやってきた.

touch

❶ VERB AND NOUN USES
❷ PHRASES AND PHRASAL VERBS

❶ **touch** /tʌtʃ/ (**touches, touching, touched**) ◆ V-T/V-I 他動詞/自動詞 If you **touch** something, you put your hand onto it in order to feel it or to make contact with it. 触れる [他動詞] さわる [他動詞] □ *Her tiny hands gently touched my face.* 彼女の小さな手が優しく私の顔に触れた. □ *Don't touch!* 触らないで. ●N-COUNT 可算名詞 **Touch** is also a noun. 触れること □ *Sometimes even a light touch on the face is enough to trigger off this pain.* 時には, 顔にそっと触れるだけでも痛みが和らげられた. ◆ V-RECIP 相互動詞 If two things **are touching**, or if one thing **touches** another, or if you touch two things, their surfaces come into contact with each other. 接触している □ *Their knees were touching.* 彼らはお互いのひざを接触させていた. □ *A cyclist crashed when he touched wheels with another rider.* サイクリストは車輪が別のライダーのものと接触して衝突した. ◆ N-UNCOUNT 不可算名詞 Your sense of **touch** is your ability to tell what something is like when you feel it with your hands. 触覚 □ *The evidence suggests that our sense of touch is programmed to diminish with age.* その証拠は私たちの触覚は加齢とともに低下することを示している. ◆ V-T 他動詞 To **touch** something means to strike it, usually quite gently. 軽く力を加える [他動詞] □ *He scored the first time he touched the ball.* 彼はボールに初めて触れたときに得点した. ◆ V-T 他動詞 If something has **not been touched**, nobody has dealt with it or taken care of it. 手を出していない [usu passive, with brd-neg] [他動詞] □ *When John began to restore the house in the 1960s, nothing had been touched for 40 years.* その家はジョンが1960年代に修復を始めた際, 40年間何も手を付けられていなかった. ◆ V-T 他動詞 If you say that you did not **touch** someone or something, you are emphasizing that you did not attack, harm or destroy them, especially when you have been accused of doing so. 手をつけていない [EMPHASIS 強調] [with brd-neg] [他動詞] □ *Pearce remained adamant, saying "I didn't touch him."* ピアスは断固として「私は彼には手をつけていない」と言った. ◆ V-T 他動詞 You say that you never **touch** something or that you have not **touched** something for a long time to emphasize that you never use it, or you have not used it for a long time. 手を出していない [EMPHASIS 強調] [no passive, with brd-neg] [他動詞] □ *He doesn't drink much and doesn't touch drugs.* 彼はあまり飲まないし, 薬にも手を出していない. ◆ V-I 自動詞 If you **touch on** a particular subject or problem, you mention it or write briefly about it. 言及する [自動詞] □ *The film touches on these issues, but only superficially.* その映画はこれらの問題に言及してはいますが, 表面的にのみです. ◆ V-T 他動詞 If something **touches** you, it affects you in some way for a short time. 干渉する [他動詞] □ *...a guilt that in some sense touches everyone.* ある意味で誰にもある罪の意識 ◆ V-T 他動詞 If something that someone says or does **touches** you, it affects you emotionally, often because you see that they are suffering a lot or that they are being very kind. 影響を与える [他動詞] □ *It has touched me deeply to see how these people live.* これらの人たちの生き方を知って私は深く

感動しました. ●**touched** ADJ 形容詞 [v-link ADJ] 感動した □ *I was touched to find that he regards me as engaging.* 私は彼が私を魅力的だと思ってくれていることにほろりとさせられた. ⓫ N-COUNT 可算名詞 A **touch** is a detail which is added to something to improve it. 仕上げ [supp N] □ *They called the event "a tribute to heroes," which was a nice touch.* 彼らはそのイベントを「ヒーローに捧げる賛辞」と呼びましたが, それは素敵な脚色でした. ⓬ N-SING 単数名詞 If someone has a particular kind of **touch**, they have a particular way of doing something. やり口 □ *The dishes he produces all have a personal touch.* 彼の作る皿すべてに彼独自の特徴が現れている. ⓭ QUANT 数量詞 A **touch of** something is a very small amount of it. ちょっと [QUANT 'of' n-uncount] □ *She thought she just had a touch of the flu.* 彼女は風邪気味だと思った. ⓮ → see also **touching**

❷ **touch** /tʌtʃ/ (**touches, touching, touched**) ◆ PHRASE 句 You use **at the touch of** in expressions such as **at the touch of a button** and **at the touch of a key** to indicate that something is possible by simply touching a switch or one of the keys of a keyboard. タッチするだけで □ *Staff will be able to trace calls at the touch of a button.* 職員はボタンに触れるだけで電話を追跡することができるようになる. ◆ PHRASE 句 If you get **in touch** with someone, you contact them by writing to them or telephoning them. If you are, keep, or stay **in touch** with them, you write, phone, or visit each other regularly. 連絡をとる □ *I will get in touch with my lawyer about this.* これについて私は弁護士に連絡をとる. ◆ PHRASE 句 If you are **in touch** with a subject or situation, or if someone keeps you **in touch** with it, you know the latest news or information about it. If you are **out of touch** with it, you do not know the latest news or information about it. 接触して, 遠ざかって □ *...keeping the unemployed in touch with the job market.* 失業者に求人市場情報を常に提供すること ◆ PHRASE 句 If you **lose touch** with someone, you gradually stop writing, telephoning, or visiting them. 接触を失う □ *In my job one tends to lose touch with friends.* 私の職業では, 友人との連絡が途絶える傾向がある. ◆ PHRASE 句 If you **lose touch** with something, you no longer have the latest news or information about it. 連絡を失う □ *Their leaders have lost touch with what is happening in the country.* 彼らの指導者は国で何が起こっているのか分からなくなりました. ◆ **the finishing touch** → see **finish** ◆ **touch wood** → see **wood**

▶ **touch down** PHRASAL VERB 句動詞 When an aircraft **touches down**, it lands. 着地する □ *The space shuttle touched down yesterday.* スペースシャトルは昨日着地した.
▶ **touch off** PHRASAL VERB 句動詞 If something **touches off** a situation or series of events, it causes it to start happening. 誘発させる □ *The lightning could touch off wildfires in Eastern Washington.* ワシントン州東部では稲妻が森林火災を誘発することがある.
▶ **touch up** PHRASAL VERB 句動詞 If you **touch** something **up**, you improve its appearance by covering up small marks with paint or another substance. 修正する □ *...editing tools to help people touch up photos.* 写真の修正を可能にする編集ツール □ *The painting has yellowed but the gallery has resisted pressure to touch it up.* 絵画は黄ばんでいたが, 画廊はそれを修正する圧力に抵抗した.

touch|ing /tʌtʃɪŋ/ ◆ ADJ 形容詞 If something is **touching**, it causes feelings of sadness or sympathy. 人を感動させる □ *Her story is the touching tale of a wife who stood by the husband she loved.* 彼女の話は, 愛する夫を援助した妻の感動の物語である. ◆ → see also **touch**

touch|screen /tʌtʃskrin/ (**touchscreens**) also **touch-screen** N-COUNT 可算名詞 A **touchscreen** is a computer screen that allows the user to give commands to the computer by touching parts of the screen rather than by using a keyboard or mouse. タッチスクリーン [COMPUTING コンピューティング] □ *...touchscreen voting machines.* タッチスクリーン付き自動投票集計機

touch-tone ADJ 形容詞 A **touch-tone** telephone has numbered buttons that make different sounds when you press them. Some automatic telephone services can only be used with this kind of telephone. 押しボタン式の [ADJ N]

touchy /tʌtʃi/ (**touchier, touchiest**) ADJ 形容詞 If you describe someone as **touchy**, you mean that they are easily upset, offended, or irritated. 怒りっぽい [DISAPPROVAL 不賛成] □ *She is very touchy about her past.* 彼女は過去に関しては神経質だ.

tough /tʌf/ (**tougher, toughest**) ◆ ADJ 形容詞 A **tough** person is strong and determined, and can tolerate difficulty or suffering. 断固とした □ *He built up a reputation as a tough businessman.* 彼は手ごわい実業家としての名声を築き上げた. ●**tough|ness** N-UNCOUNT 不可算名詞 頑固さ □ *Ms. Potter has won a reputation for toughness and determination on her way to the top.* ポッター婦人は頑固さとトップへのし上がるという決意の固さで名声を博しました. ◆ ADJ 形容詞 If

you describe someone as **tough**, you mean that they are rough and violent. 乱暴な ❏ *He had shot three people dead earning himself a reputation as a tough guy.* 彼は3人を撃ち殺し、無法者の評判を得た. ❸ ADJ 形容詞 A **tough** place or area is considered to have a lot of crime and violence. 無法の ❏ *She doesn't seem cut out for this tough neighborhood.* 彼女はこの無法者の多い界隈には向いていなさそうだ. ❹ ADJ 形容詞 A **tough** way of life or period of time is difficult or full of suffering. 骨の折れる ❏ *She had a pretty tough childhood.* 彼女はかなり苦労の多い子供時代を送った. ❺ ADJ 形容詞 A **tough** task or problem is difficult to do or solve. 困難な ❏ *It was a very tough decision but we feel we made the right one.* それは非常に困難な決断だったが、正しい決断をしたと私たちは感じている. ❻ ADJ 形容詞 **Tough** policies or actions are strict and firm. きびしい ❏ *He is known for taking a tough line on security.* 彼は安全確保に対して強硬政策をとることで有名です. ❼ ADJ 形容詞 A **tough** substance is strong, and difficult to break, cut, or tear. 強靭（きょうじん）な ❏ *In industry, diamond can form a tough, non-corrosive coating for tools.* 産業界では、ダイアモンドで強靭で非腐食性のツールコーティングを形成可能である. ❽ ADJ 形容詞 **Tough** meat is difficult to cut and chew. なかなかかみ切れない ❏ *The steak was tough and the peas were like bullets.* ステーキはゴムのようで、豆は弾丸のようだった.

Word Partnership	*tough* は次の語句と使われる:
N.	tough **guy** ❷
	tough **conditions**, tough **going**, tough **luck**, tough **situation**, tough **time** ❹
	tough **choices**, tough **competition**, tough **decision**, tough **fight**, tough **job**, tough **question**, tough **sell** ❺
	tough **laws**, tough **policy**, tough **talk** ❻
V.	get tough ❷ ❹
	make the tough **decisions** ❺
	talk tough ❻

tough|en /tʌfˀn/ (toughens, toughening, toughened) ❶ V-T 他動詞 If you **toughen** something or if it **toughens**, you make it stronger so that it will not break easily. 強健にする [他動詞] ❏ *Months of walking barefoot had toughened his feet.* 何か月もはだしで歩いたため彼の足は強くなった. ❷ V-T 他動詞 If a person, institution, or law **toughens** its policies, regulations, or punishments, it makes them firmer or stricter. 厳しくする [他動詞] ❏ *Talks are under way to toughen trade restrictions.* 貿易制限を厳しくする交渉が行われている. ● PHRASAL VERB 句動詞 **Toughen up** means the same as **toughen**. 厳しくする ❏ *The new law toughens up penalties for those that misuse guns.* 新しい法律により銃を悪用した人に対する罰則が強化されます. ❸ V-T 他動詞 If an experience **toughens** you, it makes you stronger and more independent in character. 精神的に強くする [他動詞] ❏ *They believe that participating in fights toughens boys and shows them how to be men.* けんかに加わることで男の子は強くなり、大人の男になる方法を学ぶと彼らは考えている. ● PHRASAL VERB 句動詞 **Toughen up** means the same as **toughen**. 強くする ❏ *He thinks boxing is good for kids, that it toughens them up.* ボクシングは子供を丈夫にするので彼らにとってよいと彼は思っている.

tour /tʊər/ (tours, touring, toured) ❶ N-COUNT 可算名詞 A **tour** is an organized trip that people such as musicians, politicians, or theater companies go on to several different places, stopping to meet people or perform. 巡業 ❏ *The band is currently on a two-month tour of Europe.* バンドは現在ヨーロッパの2か月ツアーに出ている. ● PHRASE 句 When people are traveling on a tour, you can say that they are **on tour**. 巡業中 ❏ *The band will be going on tour.* バンドは巡業に出る. ❷ V-T/V-I 他動詞/自動詞 When people such as musicians, politicians, or theater companies **tour**, they go on a tour, for example, in order to perform or to meet people. 巡回公演を行う [他動詞] ❏ *A few years ago they toured the country with a roadshow.* 数年前、彼らはロードショーで国を旅行した. ❸ N-COUNT 可算名詞 A **tour** is a trip during which you visit several places that interest you. 旅行 ❏ *It was week five of my tour of the major cities of Europe.* それはヨーロッパの主要都市を巡る、私の旅行の5週目でした. ❹ N-COUNT 可算名詞 A **tour** is a short trip that you make around a place, for example, around a historical building, so that you can look at it. 見学 ❏ *...a guided tour.* ガイド付きツアー. ❺ V-T 他動詞 If you **tour** a place, you go on a trip or journey around it. 歩き回る [他動詞] ❏ *You can also tour the site on bicycle.* 遺跡は自転車で見て回ることもできます.

Word Partnership	*tour* は次の語句と使われる:
N.	concert tour, farewell tour ❶
	world tour ❸
	tour bus, tour guide, walking tour ❸ ❹
	museum tour ❹
V.	begin a tour, finish a tour ❶ ❸ ❹
	take a tour ❸ ❹

tour|ism /tʊərɪzəm/ N-UNCOUNT 不可算名詞 **Tourism** is

the business of providing services for people on vacation, for example, hotels, restaurants, and trips. 観光事業 ❏ *Tourism is vital for the economy.* 観光事業は経済にとって極めて重要だ.
→ see **industry**

tour|ist /tʊərɪst/ (tourists) N-COUNT 可算名詞 A **tourist** is a person who is visiting a place for pleasure and interest, especially when they are on vacation. 観光旅行者 ❏ *...a tourist attraction.* 観光名所
→ see **city**

tour|na|ment /tʊərnəmənt, tɜr-/ (tournaments) N-COUNT 可算名詞 A **tournament** is a sports competition in which players who win a match continue to play further matches in the competition until just one person or team is left. トーナメント ❏ *...the biggest golf tournament to be held in Australia.* オーストラリアで開催される、最大のゴルフトーナメント

tout /taʊt/ (touts, touting, touted) ❶ V-T 他動詞 If someone **touts** something, they try to sell it or convince people that it is good. うまく売り付ける [DISAPPROVAL 不賛成] [他動詞] ❏ *...slick television ads touting the candidates.* 候補者をうるさく宣伝する口のうまいテレビコマーシャル ❷ V-T 他動詞 If someone **touts** tickets, they sell them outside a sports stadium or theater, usually for more than their original value. 高く転売する [BRIT 英国英語] [他動詞] [AM **scalp** 米国英語 **scalp**] ❸ N-COUNT 可算名詞 A **tout** is someone who sells things such as tickets unofficially, usually at prices which are higher than the official ones. ダフ屋 [BRIT 英国英語; AM **scalper** 米国英語 **scalper**]

tow /toʊ/ (tows, towing, towed) V-T 他動詞 If one vehicle **tows** another, it pulls it along behind it. 牽引する ❏ *He had been using the vehicle to tow his work trailer..* 彼は車で仕事用トレーラーを牽引していた. ❏ *They threatened to tow away my car.* 彼らは私の車をレッカー移動させると脅した.

to|ward /tɔrd/ also **towards**

In addition to the uses shown below, **toward** is used in phrasal verbs such as "count toward" and "lean toward."

下記の用法に加えて、**toward** は **count toward** や **lean toward** のような句動詞に使われる.

❶ PREP 前置詞 If you move, look, or point **toward** something or someone, you move, look, or point in their direction. 方へ ❏ *They were all moving toward him down the stairs.* 彼らはみな、階段下の彼の方に移動していた. ❏ *When he looked toward me, I smiled and waved.* 彼が私の方を見たので、私はほほえんで手を振った. ❷ PREP 前置詞 If things develop **toward** a particular situation, that situation becomes nearer in time or more likely to happen. 向かって [PREP n/-ing] ❏ *The agreement is a major step toward peace.* 協定は和平への大きなステップである. ❸ PREP 前置詞 If you have a particular attitude **toward** something or someone, you have that attitude when you think about them or deal with them. 対して ❏ *My attitude toward religion has been shaped by this man.* 私の宗教に対する態度はこの男によって形成された. ❹ PREP 前置詞 If something happens **toward** a particular time, it happens just before that time. 近く ❏ *There was a forecast of cooler weather toward the end of the week.* 週末にかけて、涼しい天気が予想された. ❺ PREP 前置詞 If something is **toward** part of a place or thing, it is near that part. 近くに ❏ *Gulls are nesting on a small island toward the eastern shore.* カモメは東海岸近くの小さな島に巣を作っている. ❻ PREP 前置詞 If you give money **toward** something, you give it to help pay for that thing. ために ❏ *Taxes only get part of the way toward a $50 billion deficit.* 税金は500億ドルの赤字を支払う手段の一部に過ぎない.

tow|el /taʊəl/ (towels, toweling or towelling, toweled or towelled) ❶ N-COUNT 可算名詞 A **towel** is a piece of thick soft cloth that you use to dry yourself. タオル ❏ *...a bath towel.* バスタオル ❏ *...a hand towel.* ハンドタオル ❏ *...a beach towel.* ビーチタオル ❷ V-T 他動詞 If you **towel** something or **towel** it dry, you dry it with a towel. タオルで乾かす [他動詞] ❏ *James came out of his bedroom, toweling his wet hair.* ジェームスはタオルで濡れた髪を乾かしながら寝室から出てきた. ❏ *I toweled myself dry.* 私はタオルで体を拭いた. ❸ PHRASE 句 If you **throw in the towel**, you stop trying to do something because you realize that you cannot succeed. 敗北を認める [INFORMAL くだけた] ❏ *It seemed as if the police had thrown in the towel and were abandoning the investigation.* 警察は敗北を認め、捜査を打ち切ったかのようだった.

tow|er /taʊər/ (towers, towering, towered) ❶ N-COUNT; N-IN-NAMES 可算名詞, 名称中の名詞 A **tower** is a tall, narrow building, that either stands alone or forms part of another building such as a church or castle. 塔 ❏ *...an eleventh century castle with 120-foot high towers.* 高さ120フィートの塔のある11世紀の城 ❷ V-I 自動詞 Someone or something that **towers over** surrounding people or things is a lot taller than they are. そびえる [自動詞] ❏ *He stood up and towered over her.* 彼が立ち上がると、彼女よりもはるかに高かった. ❸ N-COUNT 可算名詞 A **tower** is a tall structure that is used for sending radio or television signals. 無線塔 ❏ *Troops are still in control of the television and radio tower.* 軍隊はい

まだにテレビやラジオ放送塔を掌握しています. ◪ N-COUNT 可算名詞 A **tower** is a tall box that contains the main parts of a computer, such as the hard disk and the drives. タワー [COMPUTING コンピューティング]

tow|er|ing /ˈtaʊərɪŋ/ ◨ ADJ 形容詞 If you describe something such as a mountain or cliff as **towering**, you mean that it is very tall and therefore impressive. 高くそびえる [LITERARY 文語的] [ADJ n] ❏...towering cliffs of black granite which rise straight out of the sea. 海からまっすぐそびえ立つ黒い花崗岩の崖 ◪ ADJ 形容詞 If you describe someone or something as **towering**, you are emphasizing that they are impressive because of their importance, skill, or intensity. 高大な [LITERARY 文語的, EMPHASIS 強調] [ADJ n] ❏ He remains a towering figure in rock and roll. 彼はロックンロール界で非凡な大人物であり続けます.

town /taʊn/ (towns) ◨ N-COUNT 可算名詞 A **town** is a place with streets and buildings, where people live and work. Towns are larger than neighborhoods and smaller than cities. In informal English, cities are sometimes called towns. 町 ❏...the northern California town of Albany. カリフォルニア州北部の町, アルバニー ● N-COUNT 可算名詞 You can use **the town** to refer to the people of a town. 町民たち ❏ The town takes immense pride in recent achievements. 町民たちは最近の成果を非常な誇りとしている. ◪ N-UNCOUNT 不可算名詞 You use **town** in order to refer to the town where you live. 住んでいる町 ❏ He admits he doesn't even know when his brother is in town. 彼は自分の兄がいつ町に来るかさえ知らないことを認めている. ◩ N-UNCOUNT 不可算名詞 You use **town** in order to refer to the central area of a town where most of the stores and offices are. 中心都市 ❏ I walked into town. 私は歩いて繁華街に入った. ◪ → see also **downtown, uptown**

town hall (town halls) also **Town Hall** N-COUNT 可算名詞 A **town hall** is a building or hall used for local government business, usually a building which is the main office of a town council. 町政庁舎

tox|ic /ˈtɒksɪk/ ADJ 形容詞 A **toxic** substance is poisonous. 有毒な ❏...the cost of cleaning up toxic waste. 有毒廃棄物の清浄費用 → see **cancer**

toy /tɔɪ/ (toys, toying, toyed) N-COUNT 可算名詞 A **toy** is an object that children play with, for example, a doll or a model car. おもちゃ ❏ He was really too old for children's toys. 彼は子供用のおもちゃで遊ぶには本当に大きすぎた.
▶ **toy with** ◨ PHRASAL VERB 句動詞 If you **toy with** an idea, you consider it casually without making any decisions about it. 空想などで遊ぶ ❏ He toyed with the idea of going to China. 彼は中国に行ってみようかと漠然と考えた. ◪ PHRASAL VERB 句動詞 If you **toy with** food or drink, you do not eat or drink it with any enthusiasm, but only take a bite or a little drink from time to time. いいかげんに扱う ❏ She had no appetite, and merely toyed with the bread and cheese. 彼女は食欲がなく, パンとチーズをつっついただけだった.

trace /treɪs/ (traces, tracing, traced) ◨ V-T 他動詞 If you **trace** the origin or development of something, you find out or describe how it started or developed. 跡をたどる [他動詞] ❏ The exhibition traces the history of graphic design in America from the 19th century to the present. その展覧会は19世紀から現在までの, アメリカにおけるグラフィックデザインの歴史をたどっている. ● PHRASAL VERB 句動詞 **Trace back** means the same as **trace**. さかのぼる ❏...Bronx residents who trace their families back to Dutch settlers. 家族歴がオランダの入植者に由来するブロンクスの住民 ◪ V-T 他動詞 If you **trace** someone or something, you find them after looking for them. 突きとめる [他動詞] ❏ Police are anxious to trace two men seen leaving the house just before 8am. 警察は午前8時直前にその家を去った2人の男を探し出そうと躍起になっている. ◩ V-T 他動詞 If you **trace** something such as a pattern or a shape, for example, with your finger or toe, you mark its outline on a surface. なぞる [他動詞] ❏ I traced the course of the river on the map spread out on my briefcase. 私はブリーフケースの上に地図を広げて河の流路をなぞった. ◪ V-T 他動詞 If you **trace** a picture, you copy it by covering it with a piece of transparent paper and drawing over the lines underneath. 透写する [他動詞] ❏ She learned to draw by tracing pictures out of old storybooks. 彼女は古い童話の本から絵を敷き写しして絵の描き方を学びました. ◫ N-COUNT 可算名詞 A **trace** of something is a very small amount of it. 微量 ❏ Wash them in cold water to remove all traces of sand. こびりついた砂をすべて冷水で洗い流しなさい. ◬ PHRASE 句 If you say that someone or something **disappears without a trace**, you mean that they stop existing or stop being successful very suddenly and completely. 跡形もなく消える ❏ One day he left, disappeared without a trace. ある日, 彼は跡形も残さず消え去った. → see **fossil**

track /træk/ (tracks, tracking, tracked) ◨ N-COUNT 可算名詞 A **track** is a rough, unpaved road or path. 踏みならした道 ❏ We set off once more, over a rough mountain track. 私たちはでこぼこの山道でもう一度作動させた. ◪ N-COUNT 可算名詞 A **track** is a piece of ground, often oval-shaped, that is used for races involving running, cars, bicycles, horses, or dogs called greyhounds. 競争路 ❏...the athletics track. 陸上競技場 ◩ N-COUNT 可算名詞 Railroad **tracks** are the rails that a train travels along. 鉄道線路 ❏ A cow stood on the tracks. ウシが線路に立っていた. ◪ N-COUNT 可算名詞 A **track** is one of the songs or pieces of music on a CD, record, or tape. トラック ❏ I only like two of the ten tracks on this CD. このCDに含まれる10曲の内, 私が好きなのは2つだけだ. ◫ N-PLURAL 複数名詞 **Tracks** are marks left in the ground by the feet of animals or people. 足跡 ❏ The only evidence of pandas was their tracks in the snow. パンダの唯一の痕跡はパンダが雪に残した足跡だった. ◬ V-T 他動詞 If you **track** animals or people, you try to follow them by looking for the signs that they have left behind, for example, the marks left by their feet. 跡を追う [他動詞] ❏ He thought he had better track this wolf and see where it lived. 彼は, このオオカミの跡をつけてどこに住んでいるのかを突きとめるべきだと思った. ◭ V-T 他動詞 To **track** someone or something means to follow their movements by means of a special device, such as a satellite or radar. 探知する [他動詞] ❏ Our radar began tracking the jets. 我々のレーダーはジェット機の探知を開始した. ◮ → see also **fast track, racetrack, soundtrack** ◯ PHRASE 句 If you **keep track** of a situation or a person, you make sure that you have the newest and most accurate information about them all the time. 消息を失わないようにする ❏ With eleven thousand employees, it's very difficult to keep track of them all. 従業員が11000人もいるので, 全員を覚えているのは大変むずかしい. ◉ PHRASE 句 If you **lose track** of someone or something, you no longer know where they are or what is happening. 消息を失う ❏ You become so deeply absorbed in an activity that you lose track of time. 君はあまりに活動に没頭するあまり時間を忘れる. ◗ PHRASE 句 If someone or something is **on track**, they are acting or progressing in a way that is likely to result in success. 軌道に乗って ❏ It may take some time to get the economy back on track. 経済を再度軌道に乗せるには多少時間がかかるかもしれません. ◘ PHRASE 句 If you are **on the right track**, you are acting or progressing in a way that is likely to result in success. If you are **on the wrong track**, you are acting or progressing in a way that is likely to result in failure. 妥当で/誤って ❏ Guests are returning in increasing numbers – a sure sign that we are on the right track. 常連客が増えているということは私たちが正しい方向に向かっているという確かな証拠だ. ◙ PHRASE 句 If someone or something **stops** you **in** your **tracks**, or if you **stop dead in** your **tracks**, you suddenly stop moving because you are very surprised, impressed, or frightened. その場で急に立ち止まる ❏ This magnificent church cannot fail to stop you in your tracks. この壮大な教会を見たらあなたはきっと驚いて立ち尽くすでしょう. ◚ PHRASE 句 If someone or something **stops** a process or activity **in its tracks**, or if it **stops dead in its tracks**, they prevent the process or activity from continuing. 急に止まらせる ❏ Francis felt he would like to stop this conversation in its tracks. 彼はこの会話をすぐに終わらせたがっているとフランシスは感じた. ◛ **off the beaten track** → see **beaten**
→ see **fossil, transportation**
▶ **track down** PHRASAL VERB 句動詞 If you **track down** someone or something, you find them, or find information about them, after a difficult or long search. (追跡などによって) 見つける ❏ She had spent years trying to track down her parents. 彼女は両親を見つけるのに何年をも費やした.

track and field N-UNCOUNT 不可算名詞 **Track and field** refers to sports that are played or performed on a racetrack and a nearby field, such as running, the high jump, and the javelin. トラックおよびフィールド種目 ❏...events that range from track and field to soccer, rugby and hockey. 陸上競技からサッカー, ラグビー, ホッケーなど多岐にわたるイベント

track rec|ord (track records) N-COUNT 可算名詞 If you talk about the **track record** of a person, company, or product, you are referring to their past performance, achievements, or failures in it. 実績 ❏ The job needs someone with a good track record in investment. その仕事は, 投資でよい実績を持つ人を必要としている.

track|suit /ˈtræksuːt/ (tracksuits) also **track suit** N-COUNT 可算名詞 A **tracksuit** is a loose, warm suit consisting of pants and a top which people wear to relax and to do exercise. トラックスーツ

trac|tor /ˈtræktər/ (tractors) ◨ N-COUNT 可算名詞 A **tractor** is a farm vehicle that is used to pull farm machinery. トラクター

2 N-COUNT 可算名詞 A **tractor** is a short vehicle with a powerful engine and a driver's cab. It is used to pull a trailer, such as in a tractor-trailer. トレーラー牽引用トラック ❑ *The truck was an 18-wheeler with a white tractor.* そのトラックは白いトラクター付きの18ホイーラーだった。
→ see **barn**

tractor-trailer (tractor-trailers) N-COUNT 可算名詞 A **tractor-trailer** is a large truck that is made in two separate sections, a tractor and a trailer, which are joined together by metal bars. トレーラートラック [AM 米国英語] ❑ *Driving a tractor-trailer is not an easy job.* トレーラートラックの運転は簡単な仕事ではない。

trade /treɪd/ (trades, trading, traded) **1** V-RECIP 相互動詞 If someone **trades** one thing **for** another or if two people **trade** things, they agree to exchange one thing for the other thing. 交換する [mainly AM 主に米国英語] ❑ *They traded land for goods and money.* 彼らは土地を売って物品と金を得た。 ❑ *Kids used to trade baseball cards.* 子供たちはベースボールカードを交換しあったものだった。 ● N-COUNT 可算名詞 **Trade** is also a noun. 交換 ❑ *I am willing to make a trade with you.* 私はよろこんであなたと交換します。 **2** V-RECIP 相互動詞 If you **trade** places **with** someone or if the two of you **trade** places, you move into the other person's position or situation, and they move into yours. 入れ替わる [mainly AM 主に米国英語] ❑ *Mike asked George to trade places with him so he could ride with Tomas.* マイクは、自分がトマスと一緒に乗れるように席を替わってくれないかとジョージに頼んだ。 **3** V-RECIP 相互動詞 If two people or groups **trade** something such as blows, insults, or jokes, they hit each other, insult each other, or tell each other jokes. 交換し合う [mainly AM 主に米国英語] ❑ *Children would settle disputes by trading punches or insults in the schoolyard.* 子供たちは校庭で殴りあい、悪口を言い合ってけんかを両成敗にするだろう。 **4** N-UNCOUNT 不可算名詞 **Trade** is the activity of buying, selling, or exchanging goods or services between people, companies, or countries. 取引 [BUSINESS 実業] ❑ *Texas has a long history of trade with Mexico.* テキサス州はメキシコとの長い貿易の歴史を持つ。 ❑ *...negotiations on a new international trade agreement.* 新しい国際通商協定に関する交渉 **5** V-I 自動詞 When people, companies, or countries **trade**, they buy, sell, or exchange goods or services between themselves. 交易する [BUSINESS 実業] ❑ *They may refuse to trade, even when offered attractive prices.* 彼らは魅力的な価格を提供されても、取引を拒否するかもしれない。 ❑ *They had years of experience of trading with the West.* 彼らは西欧諸国との貿易で長い経験をしてきた。 ● **trading** N-UNCOUNT 不可算名詞 商取引 ❑ *Trading on the stock exchange may be suspended.* 株式市場での取引は一時中止されるかもしれない。 **6** N-COUNT 可算名詞 A **trade** is a particular area of business or industry. 業界 [BUSINESS 実業] ❑ *They've ruined the tourist trade for the next few years.* 彼らは観光業の将来数年間をぶち壊した。 **7** N-COUNT 可算名詞 Someone's **trade** is the kind of work that they do, especially when they have been trained to do it over a period of time. 職業 [BUSINESS 実業] ❑ *He learned his trade as a diver in the North Sea.* 彼はドライバーとしての仕事を北海で学んだ。 ❑ *Alicia was a jeweler by trade.* アリシアの職業は宝石商だ。
→ see **company, stock market**

▶ **trade down** PHRASAL VERB 句動詞 If someone **trades down**, they sell something such as their car or house and buy a less expensive one. より安い商品を買う ❑ *They are selling their five-bedroom house and trading down to a two-bedroom apartment.* 彼らは5部屋の家を売って、2部屋のアパートを買おうとしている。

▶ **trade up** PHRASAL VERB 句動詞 If someone **trades up**, they sell something such as their car or their house and buy a more expensive one. より高価な商品を買う ❑ *Gas prices are discouraging small car owners from trading up to SUV's.* ガソリン価格が高いために、小型車所有者はSUVへの買い替えをためらっている。

trade fair (trade fairs) N-COUNT 可算名詞 A **trade fair** is the same as a **trade show**. 貿易見本市

trade gap (trade gaps) N-COUNT 可算名詞 A **trade gap** is the same as a **trade deficit**. 貿易欠損 [BUSINESS 実業] [usu sing] ❑ *The trade gap surprised most analysts by shrinking, rather than growing.* 貿易収支の赤字は増加せず、むしろ減少し、ほとんどのアナリストを驚かせた。

trade-in (trade-ins) N-COUNT 可算名詞 A **trade-in** is an arrangement in which someone buys a new car at a reduced price by giving their old one, as well as money, in payment. 下取り [BUSINESS 実業] ❑ *...the trade-in value of the car.* 車の下取り評価額

trade|mark /treɪdmɑrk/ (trademarks) also **trade mark**

1 N-COUNT 可算名詞 A **trademark** is a name or symbol that a company uses on its products and that cannot legally be used by another company. 商標 [BUSINESS 実業] ❑ *She has registered a trademark for a new range of perfumes.* 彼女は新しい香水シリーズの商標を登録した。 **2** N-COUNT 可算名詞 If you say that something is the **trademark** of a particular person or place, you mean that it is characteristic of them or typically associated with them. 人を象徴する特徴 ❑ *...the spiky punk hairdo that became his trademark.* 彼のトレードマークになったつんつん髪のパンク風ヘアスタイル

trade name (trade names) N-COUNT 可算名詞 A **trade name** is the name which manufacturers give to a product or to a range of products. 商標名 [BUSINESS 実業] ❑ *It's marketed under the trade name "Mirage."* それは「ミラージュ」という商品名で市販されている。

trad|er /treɪdər/ (traders) N-COUNT 可算名詞 A **trader** is a person whose job is to trade in goods or stocks. 商人 [BUSINESS 実業] ❑ *Market traders display an exotic selection of the island's produce.* 市場の商人はその島のエキゾチックな農産物を選りすぐって陳列している。

trade se|cret (trade secrets) N-COUNT 可算名詞 A **trade secret** is information that is known, used, and kept secret by a particular company, for example, about a method of production or a chemical process. 企業秘密 [BUSINESS 実業] ❑ *The nature of the polymer is currently a trade secret.* そのポリマーの性質は現在企業秘密です。

trades|man /treɪdzmən/ (tradesmen) N-COUNT 可算名詞 A **tradesman** is a person, usually a man, who is a skilled worker. 熟練工 [BUSINESS 実業] ❑ *...tradesmen such as electricians or plumbers.* 電気技師や配管工などの熟練工

trade sur|plus (trade surpluses) N-COUNT 可算名詞 If a country has a **trade surplus**, it exports more than it imports. 貿易収支の黒字 [BUSINESS 実業] ❑ *The country's trade surplus widened to 16.5 billion dollars.* その国の貿易収支の黒字は165億ドルまで拡大した。

trade un|ion → see **union, labor union**

tra|di|tion /trədɪʃ°n/ (traditions) N-VAR 可変性名詞 A **tradition** is a custom or belief that has existed for a long time. 伝統 ❑ *...the rich traditions of Afro-Cuban music and dance.* アフロキューバン音楽とダンスの豊かな伝統

tra|di|tion|al /trədɪʃən°l/ **1** ADJ 形容詞 **Traditional** customs, beliefs, or methods are ones that have existed for a long time without changing. 伝統的な ❑ *Traditional teaching methods sometimes only succeeded in putting students off learning.* ありきたりの授業方法は生徒に学習意欲をなくさせるだけのこともあった。 ● **tra|di|tion|al|ly** ADV 副詞 [ADV with cl/group] 伝統的に ❑ *Married women have traditionally been treated as dependent on their husbands.* 既婚の女性は従来夫の扶養者とみなされていた。 **2** ADJ 形容詞 A **traditional** organization or person prefers older methods and ideas to modern ones. 因襲的な ❑ *We're still a traditional school in a lot of ways.* 私たちの学校は多くの意味でまだ因襲的です。 ● **tra|di|tion|al|ly** ADV 副詞 因襲的に ❑ *He is loathed by some of the more traditionally minded officers.* 彼はより因襲的な役員の何人かにひどく嫌われている。

traf|fic /træfɪk/ (traffics, trafficking, trafficked) **1** N-UNCOUNT 不可算名詞 **Traffic** refers to all the vehicles that are moving along the roads in a particular area. 交通 [also 'the' N] ❑ *There was heavy traffic on the roads.* 道路の交通は激しかったです。 ❑ *Traffic was unusually light for that time of day.* この時間帯にしてはめずらしく交通があまりなかった。 **2** N-UNCOUNT 不可算名詞 **Traffic** refers to the movement of ships, trains, or aircraft between one place and another. **Traffic** also refers to the people and goods that are being transported. 交通運輸 ❑ *Air traffic had returned to normal.* 空の交通は通常に戻りました。 **3** N-UNCOUNT 不可算名詞 **Traffic in** something such as drugs or stolen goods is an illegal trade in them. 密輸 ❑ *...the widespread traffic in stolen cultural artifacts.* 盗難文化遺物の密輸の蔓延 **4** V-I 自動詞 Someone who **traffics in** something such as drugs or stolen goods buys and sells them even though it is illegal to do so. 取り引きする [自動詞] ❑ *The president said illegal drugs are hurting the entire world and anyone who traffics in them should be brought to justice.* 大統領は、違法薬物は全世界を苦しめており、それらを売買する者すべて法に基づいて裁かれるべきだと言いました。 ● **traf|fick|ing** N-UNCOUNT 不可算名詞 密輸 ❑ *He was sentenced to ten years in prison on charges of drug trafficking.* 彼は麻薬密売の罪で禁固2年を宣告された。

→ see Word Web: **traffic**

t

Word Web   traffic

Boston's Southeast Expressway was built to handle 75,000 **vehicles** a day. But from the day it opened in 1959, **commuter traffic** crawled. Sometimes it **stalled** completely. The 27 entrance **ramps** and lack of **breakdown lanes** caused frequent **gridlock**. By the 1990s, **traffic congestion** was even worse. Nearly 200,000 cars a day were using the **highway** and there were constant **traffic jams**. In 1994, a ten-year **road** construction project called the Big Dig began. The project built underground roadways, six-**lane** bridges, and improved **tunnels**. As a result of the project traffic **flows** more smoothly through the city.

Word Partnership   traffic は次の語句と使われる：

ADJ.	**heavy** traffic, **light** traffic, **oncoming** traffic, **stuck in** traffic 🔟
N.	traffic **accident**, **city** traffic, traffic **congestion**, traffic **flow**, traffic **pollution**, traffic **problems**, **rush hour** traffic, traffic **safety**, traffic **signals**, traffic **violation** 🔟
	air traffic, **Internet** traffic, **network** traffic 🔢
	drug traffic 🔢

traf|fic cir|cle (**traffic circles**) N-COUNT 可算名詞 A **traffic circle** is a circular structure in the road at a place where several roads meet. You drive around it until you come to the road that you want. 環状交差路 [AM 米国英語]

traf|fick|er /tráefɪkər/ (**traffickers**) N-COUNT 可算名詞 A **trafficker** in particular goods, especially drugs, is a person who illegally buys or sells these goods. 不正取引商人 ❏ They have been arrested as suspected drug traffickers. 彼らは麻薬密輸容疑者として逮捕されました.

traf|fic light (**traffic lights**) N-COUNT 可算名詞 **Traffic lights** are sets of red, yellow, and green lights at the places where roads meet. They control the traffic by signaling red when vehicles have to stop and green when they can go. 交通信号

trag|edy /tráedʒɪdi/ (**tragedies**) 🔟 N-VAR 可変性名詞 A **tragedy** is an extremely sad event or situation. 惨事 ❏ They have suffered an enormous personal tragedy. 彼らは最悪の個人的悲劇を被った. 🔢 N-VAR 可変性名詞 **Tragedy** is a type of literature, especially drama, that is serious and sad, and often ends with the death of the main character. 悲劇 ❏ The story has elements of tragedy and farce. その話には悲劇と笑劇の要素がある.

→ see **theater**

trag|ic /tráedʒɪk/ 🔟 ADJ 形容詞 A **tragic** event or situation is extremely sad, usually because it involves death or suffering. 悲惨な ❏ It was just a tragic accident. それはただ悲惨な事故だった. ❏ ...the tragic loss of so many lives. 多くの人々のいたましい死. ●**tragi|cal|ly** /tráedʒɪkli/ ADV 副詞 悲惨に ❏ Tragically, she never saw the completed building because she died before it was finished. 悲しいことに, 彼女は完成した建物を見ることはなかった. 🔢 ADJ 形容詞 [ADJ n] **Tragic** is used to refer to tragedy as a type of literature. 悲劇の ❏ ...Shakespeare's tragic hero, Hamlet. シェークスピアの悲劇の主人公, ハムレット

trail /treɪl/ (**trails**, **trailing**, **trailed**) 🔟 N-COUNT 可算名詞 A **trail** is a rough path across open country or through forests. 踏み分け道 ❏ He was following a trail through the trees. 彼は木の間を通り抜けて行く道をたどっていた. 🔢 N-COUNT 可算名詞 A **trail** is a route along a series of paths or roads, often one that has been planned and marked out for a particular purpose. コース ❏ ...a large area of woodland with hiking and walking trails. ハイキングやウォーキングコースのある広大な森林地帯 🔢 N-COUNT 可算名詞 A **trail** is a series of marks or other signs of movement or other activities left by someone or something. 痕跡 ❏ Everywhere in the house was a sticky trail of orange juice. この家のあらゆるところにオレンジジュースのべとついた痕があった. 🔢 V-T 他動詞 If you **trail** someone or something, you follow them secretly, often by finding the marks or signs that they have left. 追跡する [他動詞] ❏ Two detectives were trailing him. 刑事2人が彼を追跡していた. 🔢 N-COUNT 可算名詞 You can refer to all the places that a politician visits in the period before an election as their campaign **trail**. 選挙遊説地 ❏ During a recent speech on the campaign trail, he was interrupted by hecklers. 最近の選挙戦の一環として行われた演説で, 彼は妨害者に話を中断されました. 🔢 V-T/V-I 他動詞/自動詞 If you **trail** something or it **trails**, it hangs down loosely behind you as you move along. ひきずる [他動詞・自動詞] ❏ She came down the stairs slowly, trailing the coat behind her. 彼女は後ろにコートをひきずりながら階段をゆっくり降りてきた. 🔢 PHRASE 句 If you are **on the trail of** a person or thing, you are trying hard to find them or find out about them. 跡を追って ❏ The police were hot on his trail. 警察は彼を追い詰めていた.

Word Partnership   trail は次の語句と使われる：

V.	**follow a** trail 🔟 – 🔢
	leave a trail, **pick up a** trail 🔢
N.	**hiking** trail 🔢
	campaign trail 🔢

trail|er /treɪlər/ (**trailers**) 🔟 N-COUNT 可算名詞 A **trailer** is a long narrow house made to be delivered to a home site, where it becomes a permanent home. トレーラーハウス 🔢 N-COUNT 可算名詞 A **trailer** is a temporary vacation home that is pulled by a car to each vacation spot. 移動住宅 🔢 N-COUNT 可算名詞 A **trailer** is a container on wheels which is pulled by a car or other vehicle and which is used for transporting large or heavy items. トレーラー 🔢 N-COUNT 可算名詞 A **trailer** for a movie or television program is a set of short extracts which are shown to advertise it. 予告編 ❏ ...a misleadingly violent trailer for the movie. 誤解を招くほど暴力的な映画の予告編

trail|er park (**trailer parks**) N-COUNT 可算名詞 A **trailer park** is an area where people can pay to park their trailers and live in them. トレーラーキャンプ [AM 米国英語]

---

train

❶ NOUN USES
❷ VERB USES

---

❶ train /treɪn/ (**trains**) 🔟 N-COUNT 可算名詞 A **train** is a number of containers on wheels which are all connected together and which are pulled by an engine along a railroad. Trains carry people and goods from one place to another. 列車 [also 'by' N] ❏ The train pulled into a station. その列車が駅に入った. ❏ We can catch the early morning train. 私たちは早朝の列車に間に合う. 🔢 N-COUNT 可算名詞 A **train of** vehicles, people, or animals is a long line of them traveling slowly in the same direction. 一列に続くもの ❏ In the old days this used to be done with a baggage train of camels. これはかつて荷物を運ぶラクダの一行を使って行われていたものだった. 🔢 N-COUNT 可算名詞 A **train of** thought or a **train of** events is a connected sequence, in which each thought or event seems to occur naturally or logically as a result of the previous one. (思考などの) 連続 ❏ He lost his train of thought for a moment, then recovered it. 彼は思考の脈絡を一瞬なくしたが, すぐに取り戻した.

→ see Word Web: **train**
→ see **transportation**

❷ train /treɪn/ (**trains**, **training**, **trained**) 🔟 V-T/V-I 他動詞/自動詞 If someone **trains** you **to** do something, they teach you the skills that you need in order to do it. If you **train to** do something, you learn the skills that you need in order to do it. 訓練する [他動詞] トレーニングする [自動詞] ❏ He was training us to be soldiers. 彼は僕たちを兵士に育てようと訓練していました. ●**-trained** COMB IN ADJ 形容詞の複合 訓練された ❏ Michael is a professionally-trained chef. マイケルは専門的に訓練されたシェフです. ●**train|er** (**trainers**) N-COUNT 可算名詞 訓練者 ❏ ...a book for both teachers and teacher trainers. 教員と教員養成者両方を対象とした本 🔢 V-T 他動詞 To **train** a natural quality or talent that someone has, for example, their voice or musical ability, means to help them to develop it. 鍛える [他動詞] ❏ I see my degree as something which will train my mind and improve my chances of getting a job. 学位は精神を鍛え, 就職のチャンスを増やすものと私は考えている. 🔢 V-T/V-I 他動詞/自動詞 If you **train for** a physical activity such as a race or if someone **trains** you **for** it, you prepare for it by doing particular physical exercises. 練習する [自動詞] 調整する [他動詞] ❏ Strachan is training for the new season. ストラッチャンは新しいシーズンに向けて練習している. ●**train|er** N-COUNT 可算名詞 トレーナー ❏ She went to the gym with her personal trainer. 彼女はパーソナルトレーナーとジムへ行った. 🔢 V-T 他動詞 If an animal or bird **is trained to** do particular things, it is taught to do them, for example, in order to be able to work for someone or to be a good pet. 調教される [他動詞] ❏ Sniffer dogs could be trained to track them down. 麻薬犬は麻薬を見つけ出す

Word Web   train

In sixteenth-century Germany, a **railway** was a **horse-drawn wagon** traveling along wooden **rails**. By the 19th century, **steam locomotives** and **steel rails** had replaced the older system. At first, railroads operated only **freight lines**. Later, they began to run **passenger** trains. And soon Pullman cars were added to make overnight trips more comfortable. Today, Japan's bullet trains carry people at speeds up to 300 miles per hour. This type of train doesn't have an engine or use tracks. Instead, an electromagnetic field allows the **cars** to float just above the ground. This electromagnetic field also propels them ahead.

A Japanese Bullet Train

ように仕込むことができる. ●**train|er** N-COUNT 可算名詞 調教師 ❑ *The horse made a winning start for his new trainer.* その馬は新しい調教師のおかげで初戦に勝利した. **5** → see also **training**

Thesaurus   *train* また次を参照:

N.	caravan, procession, series ❶ ❷
V.	coach, educate, guide, prepare ❷ ❶

trainee /treɪniː/ (**trainees**) N-COUNT 可算名詞 A **trainee** is someone who is employed at a low level in a particular job in order to learn the skills needed for that job. 練習生 [BUSINESS 実業] [oft N n] ❑ *He is a 24-year-old trainee reporter.* 彼は24歳のレポーター見習いで.

train|er /treɪnər/ (**trainers**) ❶ N-COUNT 可算名詞 **Trainers** are shoes that people wear, especially for running and other sports. スニーカー [BRIT 英国英語; AM sneakers, running shoes, tennis shoes 米国英語 sneakers, running shoes, tennis shoes] ❷ → see also **train**

train|ing /treɪnɪŋ/ ❶ N-UNCOUNT 不可算名詞 **Training** is the process of learning the skills that you need for a particular job or activity. 訓練 [BUSINESS 実業] ❑ *He called for much higher spending on education and training.* 彼は教育と訓練にかなり高い経費を要求しました. ❑ *Kennedy had no formal training as a decorator.* ケネディーは装飾者として正式な訓練は受けていなかった. ❷ N-UNCOUNT 不可算名詞 **Training** is physical exercise that you do regularly in order to keep fit or to prepare for an activity such as a race. トレーニング ❑ *The emphasis is on developing fitness through exercises and training.* エクササイズとトレーニングによる健康維持が強調されている.

trait /treɪt/ (**traits**) N-COUNT 可算名詞 A **trait** is a particular characteristic, quality, or tendency that someone or something has. 特性 ❑ *The study found that some alcoholics had clear personality traits showing up early in childhood.* アルコール依存症者には発生の初期段階で明らかな人格特性を示す者がいたことがその研究により分かりました.
→ see **culture, gene**

trai|tor /treɪtər/ (**traitors**) ❶ N-COUNT 可算名詞 If you call someone a **traitor**, you mean that they have betrayed beliefs that they used to hold, or that their friends hold, by their words or actions. 裏切り者 [DISAPPROVAL 不賛成] ❑ *Some say he's a traitor to the peace movement.* 彼は平和運動の反逆者だという人もいる. ❷ N-COUNT 可算名詞 If someone is a **traitor**, they betray their country, friends, or a group of which they are a member by helping its enemies, especially during time of war. 売国奴 ❑ *...rumors that there were traitors among us who were sending messages to the enemy.* 敵にメッセージを送った売国奴が我々の中にいたという噂.

tram /træm/ (**trams**) ❶ N-COUNT 可算名詞 A **tram** is a public transportation vehicle, usually powered by electricity from wires above it, which travels along rails laid in the surface of a street. 路面電車 [also 'by' n] ❑ *You can get to the beach easily from the center of town by tram.* その海岸へは町の中心部から路面電車で簡単に行ける. ❷ N-COUNT 可算名詞 A **tram** is the same as a **cable car**. ケーブルカー [AM 米国英語]
→ see **transportation**

tramp /træmp/ (**tramps, tramping, tramped**) ❶ N-COUNT 可算名詞 A **tramp** is a person who has no home or job, and very little money. Tramps go from place to place, and get food or money by asking people or by doing casual work. 浮浪者 ❑ *Hypothermia is common among tramps sleeping outdoors.* 低体温症は野宿する浮浪者によくある病気である. ❷ V-T/V-I 他動詞/自動詞 If you **tramp** somewhere, you walk there slowly and with regular, heavy steps, for a long time. 足取り重く歩く [他動詞・自動詞] ❑ *They put on their coats and tramped through the falling snow.* 彼らはコートを着て, 降り続ける雪の中を足取り重く歩いた. ❸ N-UNCOUNT 不可算名詞 The **tramp** of people is the sound of their heavy, regular walking. ドシンドシンと歩く音 ❑ *He heard the slow, heavy tramp of feet on the stairs.* 彼は階段をゆっくり踏みつける重い足音を聞いた. ❹ N-COUNT 可算名詞 If someone refers to a woman as a **tramp**, they are insulting

her, because they think that she is immoral in her sexual behavior. 売春婦 [mainly AM 主に米国英語, OFFENSIVE 無礼な, DISAPPROVAL 不賛成] ❑ *He'd think I was a tramp, a cheap slut, and he'd lose all respect for me.* 彼は私が売春婦, だらしのない尻軽女だと思って, 私に対する敬意を全く失ってしまうだろう.

tram|ple /træmpᵊl/ (**tramples, trampling, trampled**) ❶ V-T/V-I 他動詞/自動詞 To **trample on** someone's rights or values or to **trample** them means to deliberately ignore them. 無視する [他動詞・自動詞] ❑ *They say loggers are destroying rain forests and trampling on the rights of natives.* 彼らは, 伐採者は熱帯雨林を破壊し, 先住民の権利を無視していると言っている. ❷ V-T 他動詞 If someone **is trampled**, they are injured or killed by being stepped on by animals or by other people. 踏み殺される [usu passive] [他動詞] ❑ *Many people were trampled in the panic that followed.* その後に起こったパニックの中, 多くの人が踏み殺されました. ❸ V-T/V-I 他動詞/自動詞 If someone **tramples** something or **tramples on** it, they step heavily and carelessly on it and damage it. 踏みつける [他動詞] ❑ *They don't want people trampling the grass, pitching tents or building fires.* 彼らは人々に芝生を踏みつけられたり, テントを張られたり, キャンプファイアをしてもらいたくありません.

trance /træns/ (**trances**) N-COUNT 可算名詞 A **trance** is a state of mind in which someone seems to be asleep and to have no conscious control over their thoughts or actions, but in which they can see and hear things and respond to commands given by other people. 恍惚 ❑ *Like a man in a trance, Blake found his way back to his rooms.* あたかも恍惚状態の人のように, ブレークは自分の部屋にたどりついた.
→ see **hypnosis**

tranche /trɑːnʃ/ (**tranches**) ❶ N-COUNT 可算名詞 In economics, a **tranche** of shares in a company, or a **tranche** of a company, is a number of shares in that company. 株式 [BUSINESS 実業] [usu N 'of' n] ❑ *On February 12th he put up for sale a second tranche of 32 state-owned companies.* 2月12日, 彼は国営32社の株式を売りに出した. ❷ N-COUNT 可算名詞 A **tranche** of something is a piece, section, or part of it. A **tranche** of something is a group of them. 一部分 [FORMAL 形式ばった] [usu N 'of' n] ❑ *They risk losing the next tranche of funding.* 彼らは次の財政的支援を失うリスクを犯す.

tran|quil /træŋkwɪl/ ADJ 形容詞 Something that is **tranquil** is calm and peaceful. 平穏な ❑ *The tranquil atmosphere of the inn allows guests to feel totally at home.* その宿屋の平穏な雰囲気は客をすっかりくつろいだ気持ちにさせる. ●**tran|quil|lity** /træŋkwɪlɪti/ N-UNCOUNT 不可算名詞 静穏 ❑ *The hotel is a haven of peace and tranquillity.* そのホテルは平和と静穏の安息所だ.

tran|quil|ize /træŋkwɪlaɪz/ (**tranquilizes, tranquilizing, tranquilized**) V-T 他動詞 To **tranquilize** a person or an animal means to make them become calm, sleepy, or unconscious by means of a drug. 落ち着かせる [他動詞] ❑ *This powerful drug is used to tranquilize patients undergoing surgery.* この強い薬は手術を受ける患者を落ち着かせるために使用されます.

tran|quil|iz|er /træŋkwɪlaɪzər/ (**tranquilizers**) N-COUNT 可算名詞 A **tranquilizer** is a drug that makes people feel calmer or less anxious. Tranquilizers are sometimes used to make people or animals become sleepy or unconscious. 精神安定薬 ❑ *If a tranquilizer is prescribed, be sure your physician informs you of its possible side effects, such as addiction.* 精神安定薬を処方される場合, 依存症など考えうる副作用について医師から必ず説明を受けてください.

trans|ac|tion /trænzækʃᵊn/ (**transactions**) N-COUNT 可算名詞 A **transaction** is a piece of business, for example, an act of buying or selling something. 商取引 [FORMAL 形式ばった BUSINESS 実業] ❑ *The transaction is completed by payment of the fee.* 取引は料金の支払いで完了する.
→ see **bank**

Word Partnership   *transaction* は次の語句と使われる:

N.	**cash** transaction, transaction **costs**, transaction **fee**
V.	**complete a** transaction

trans|at|lan|tic /trænzətlæntɪk/ ADJ 形容詞 Transatlantic flights or signals go across the Atlantic Ocean, usually between the United States and Britain. 大西洋横断の [ADJ n] □*Many transatlantic flights land there.* そこには多くの大西洋横断のフライトが着陸する.

trans|cend /trænsɛnd/ (transcends, transcending, transcended) V-T 他動詞 Something that transcends normal limits or boundaries goes beyond them, because it is more significant than them. 限界を超える □*...issues like disaster relief that transcend party loyalty.* 災害救済など, 愛党心を超越した問題

Word Link | *scrib ≈ writing : inscribe, scribble, transcribe*

tran|scribe /trænskraɪb/ (transcribes, transcribing, transcribed) V-T 他動詞 If you transcribe a speech or text, you write or type it out, for example, from notes or from a tape recording. 文字に置き換える [他動詞] □*She is transcribing, from his dictation, the diaries of Simon Forman.* 彼女は彼の口述からサイモン・フォルマンの日記を書き起こしている.

Word Link | *script ≈ writing : manuscript, scripture, transcript*

tran|script /trænskrɪpt/ (transcripts) N-COUNT 可算名詞 A transcript of a conversation or speech is a written text of it, based on a recording or notes. 書き起こし原稿 □*A transcript of this PBS program is available through our website, pbs.com.* このPBSの番組の書き起こし原稿は, 私どものウェブサイトpbs.comで入手可能です.

Word Link | *trans ≈ across : transfer, transition, translate*

trans|fer (transfers, transferring, transferred)

The verb is pronounced /trænsf3r/. The noun is pronounced /trænsf3r/.

動詞は /trænsf3r/ と発音される. 名詞は /trænsf3r/ と発音される.

◼ V-T/V-I 他動詞/自動詞 If you transfer something or someone from one place to another, or they transfer from one place to another, they go from the first place to the second. 移る [他動詞・自動詞] □*Transfer the meat to a platter and leave in a warm place.* 肉を皿に移して温かい場所に放置しなさい. ●N-VAR 可変性名詞 Transfer is also a noun. 移動 [oft N 'of' n] □*Arrange for the transfer of medical records to your new doctor.* あなたの新しい担当医にカルテを転送するよう手配しなさい. ◼ V-T/V-I 他動詞/自動詞 If something is transferred, or transfers, from one person or group of people to another, the second person or group gets it instead of the first. 移転する □*The decision to transfer the investigation from the police to the district attorney's office is a mutual one.* 捜査を警察から地方弁護士事務所に移転する決断は合意の上による. ●N-VAR 可変性名詞 Transfer is also a noun. 移転 □*...the transfer of power from the old to the new regimes.* 古い政体から新体制への権力の移転 ◼ V-T/V-I 他動詞/自動詞 If you are transferred, or if you transfer, to a different job or place, the company moves you to a different job or you start working in a different part of the same company or organization. 転任させられる [他動詞] □*I was transferred to the book department.* 私は書籍部門に異動になった. □*I suspect that she is going to be transferred to Fort Meyer.* 彼女はフォート・メイヤーに転任させられるのではないかと私はうすうす感じています. ●N-VAR 可変性名詞 Transfer is also a noun. 転任 [oft N 'to' n] □*They will be offered transfers to other locations.* 彼らにはその他の場所への転任も提示される. ◼ V-T 他動詞 When information is transferred onto a different medium, it is copied from one medium to another. 転送する [他動詞] □*Such information is easily transferred onto microfilm.* こういった情報はマイクロフィルムに簡単に転送できる. ●N-UNCOUNT 不可算名詞 Transfer is also a noun. 転送 □*It can be connected to a PC for the transfer of information.* それは情報転送目的でPCに接続できる

Word Partnership | *transfer* は次の語句と使われる:

N.	balance transfer, transfer funds, transfer money ◼
	transfer ownership, transfer of power ◼
	transfer schools, students transfer ◼
	transfer data, transfer information ◼

trans|fer|able /trænsf3rəb°l/ ADJ 形容詞 If something is transferable, it can be passed or moved from one person or organisation to another and used by them. 移すことができる □*Use the transferable skills acquired from your previous working background.* 君の過去の職業経験から得たスキルで移転可能なものを利用しなさい.

trans|form /trænsf3rm/ (transforms, transforming, transformed) ◼ V-T 他動詞 To transform something into something else means to change or convert it into that thing. 変える [他動詞] □*Your metabolic rate is the speed at which your body transforms food into energy.* 代謝速度はあなたの体が食べ物をエネルギーに変える速度のことです. ●**trans|for|ma|tion** /trænsf3rmeɪʃ°n/

(transformations) N-VAR 可変性名詞 変形 □*Norah made plans for the transformation of an attic room into a study.* ノラは屋根裏部屋を書斎に変える計画を立てた. ◼ V-T 他動詞 To transform something or someone means to change them completely and suddenly so that they are much better or more attractive. 変革させる [他動詞] □*Industrialization transformed the world.* 工業化は世界に変革をもたらした. ●**trans|for|ma|tion** N-VAR 可変性名詞 変革 □*In the last five years he's undergone a personal transformation.* 過去5年間, 彼は自分自身を変え, 向上させてきました.

Thesaurus | *transform* また次を参照:

| v. | alter, change, convert ◼ ◼ |

trans|fu|sion /trænsfyuʒ°n/ (transfusions) N-VAR 可変性名詞 A transfusion is the same as a blood transfusion. 輸血

trans|ient /trænʃ°nt/ ◼ ADJ 形容詞 Transient is used to describe a situation that lasts only a short time or is constantly changing. 瞬間的な [FORMAL 形式ばった] □*...the transient nature of high fashion.* 最新ファッションの変わりやすい特質 ◼ N-COUNT 可算名詞 Transients are people who stay in a place for only a short time and then move somewhere else. 短期滞在客 [FORMAL 形式ばった] [usu pl] □*...a dormitory for transients.* 短期滞在客用の寮

trans|it /trænzɪt/ ◼ N-UNCOUNT 不可算名詞 Transit is the carrying of goods or people by vehicle from one place to another. 運搬 □*During their talks, the two presidents discussed the transit of goods between the two countries.* 対談の間, 大統領2人は2国間の物資輸送について話し合った. □*...a transit time of about 42 minutes.* 約42分の輸送時間 ●PHRASE 句 If people or things are in transit, they are travelling or being taken from one place to another. 輸送中で ◼ ADJ 形容詞 A transit area is an area where people wait or where goods are kept between different stages of a journey. 通過場所 [ADJ n] □*...refugees arriving at the two transit camps.* 2つの一時滞在キャンプに到着する難民たち ◼ N-UNCOUNT 不可算名詞 A transit system is a system for moving people or goods from one place to another, for example, using buses or trains. 輸送 [AM 米国英語] □*The president wants to improve the nation's highways and mass transit systems.* 大統領は国の高速道路と公共交通機関の改善を欲しています.

→ see transportation

trans|si|tion /trænzɪʃ°n/ (transitions, transitioning, transitioned) ◼ N-VAR 可変性名詞 Transition is the process in which something changes from one state to another. 移行 □*The transition from a dictatorship to a multi-party democracy is proving to be difficult.* 独裁体制から多党民主主義への移行は困難であることが判明しつつあります. ◼ V-I 自動詞 If someone transitions from one state or activity to another, they move gradually from one to the other. 移り変わる [BUSINESS 実業] [自動詞] □*Most of the discussion was on what needed to be done now as we transitioned from the security issues to the challenging economic issues.* 我々は安全保障問題から, 難しい経済問題に話題を移しながら, 現在すべきことを主に話し合った.

trans|si|tion|al /trænzɪʃ°n°l/ ◼ ADJ 形容詞 A transitional period is one in which things are changing from one state to another. 変わり目の [ADJ n] □*...a transitional period following more than a decade of civil war.* 10年以上にわたる市民戦争後の過渡期 ◼ ADJ 形容詞 Transitional is used to describe something that happens or exists during a transitional period. 過渡的な [ADJ n] □*The main rebel groups have agreed to join in a meeting to set up a transitional government.* 主要な反乱軍は暫定政権を設立する会議への参加に同意しました.

trans|i|tive /trænzɪtɪv/ ADJ 形容詞 A transitive verb has a direct object. 他動詞

trans|late /trænzleɪt/ (translates, translating, translated) ◼ V-T/V-I 他動詞/自動詞 If something said or written is translated from one language into another, it is said or written again in the second language. 翻訳する [他動詞・自動詞] □*Only a small number of Kadare's books have been translated into English.* 英語に翻訳されたカダレの本はほんの少数だ. □*The Spanish word "acequia" is translated as "irrigation ditch."* スペイン語の「acequia」は「用水路」と翻訳される. □*The girls waited for Mr. Esch to translate.* 少女たちはエシュ氏の翻訳を待った. ●**trans|la|tion** N-UNCOUNT 不可算名詞 翻訳 □*The papers have been sent to Saudi Arabia for translation.* 論文は翻訳目的でサウジアラビアに送られた. ◼ V-I 自動詞 If a name, a word, or an expression translates as something in a different language, that is what it means in that language. 訳せる [自動詞] □*His family's Cantonese nickname for him translates as Never Sits Still.* 彼の家族が彼に与えた広東語のニックネームは「少しもじっとしていない」と訳せる. ◼ V-T/V-I 他動詞/自動詞 If one thing translates or is translated into another, the second happens or is done as a result of the first. (結果として)なる [他動詞・自動詞] □*Reforming the stagnant economy requires harsh measures that would translate into job losses.* 停滞経済の改革は, 雇用の損失を引き起こす可能性のある過酷な手段を必要とする.

Thesaurus   *translate* また次を参照：

v.   alter, change, transform 🔢

trans|la|tion /trænzleɪʃ⁰n/ (**translations**) 🔢 N-COUNT 可算名詞 A **translation** is a piece of writing or speech that has been put into a different language. 翻訳 [also 'in' N] ❏ ...*a translation of the Iliad.* イリアッドの翻訳 🔢 → see also **translate**

trans|la|tor /trænzleɪtər/ (**translators**) N-COUNT 可算名詞 A **translator** is a person whose job is translating writing or speech from one language to another. 翻訳者

Word Link   *luc ≈ light : hallucinate, lucid, translucent*

trans|lu|cent /trænzluːs⁰nt/ ADJ 形容詞 If a material is **translucent**, some light can pass through it. 半透明の ❏ *The building is roofed entirely with translucent corrugated plastic.* その建物の屋根は、全体が半透明のプラスチック波板である.
→ see **pottery**

trans|mis|sion /trænzmɪʃ⁰n/ (**transmissions**) 🔢 N-UNCOUNT 不可算名詞 The **transmission** of something is the passing or sending of it to a different person or place. 伝達 ❏ *Heterosexual contact is responsible for the bulk of HIV transmission.* HIV感染の大部分は異性との性交が原因である. 🔢 N-UNCOUNT 不可算名詞 The **transmission** of television or radio programs is the broadcasting of them. 放送番組 ❏ *The transmission of the program was brought forward due to its unexpected topicality.* その番組は予期しない話題を呼んだために、放送されることになった. 🔢 N-COUNT 可算名詞 A **transmission** is a broadcast. 放送 ❏ ...*foreign television transmissions.* 外国テレビ番組の放送

trans|mit /trænzmɪt/ (**transmits, transmitting, transmitted**) 🔢 V-T/V-I 他動詞／自動詞 When radio and television programs, computer data, or other electronic messages are **transmitted**, they are sent from one place to another, using wires, radio waves, or satellites. 送信される [他動詞・自動詞] ❏ *The game was transmitted live.* その試合は生中継された. ❏ *This is currently the most efficient way to transmit certain types of data like electronic mail.* これは、現在最も効果的な、電子メールといった特定タイプのデータの送信方法です. 🔢 V-T 他動詞 If one person or animal **transmits** a disease to another, they have the disease and cause the other person or animal to have it. 伝染させる [FORMAL 形式ばった] [他動詞] ❏ ...*mosquitoes that transmit disease to humans.* 人間に病気をうつすカ 🔢 V-T 他動詞 If an object or substance **transmits** something such as sound or electrical signals, the sound or signals are able to pass through it. 通す [他動詞] ❏ *These thin crystals transmit much of the power.* これらの薄い水晶は力のほとんどを通す

trans|mit|ter /trænzmɪtər/ (**transmitters**) N-COUNT 可算名詞 A **transmitter** is a piece of equipment that is used for broadcasting television or radio programs. 送信機 ❏ ...*a homemade radio transmitter.* 自家製無線送信機
→ see **cellphone, radio**

trans|par|en|cy /trænspɛərənsi, -pær-/ (**transparencies**) 🔢 N-COUNT 可算名詞 A **transparency** is a small piece of photographic film with a frame around it which can be projected onto a screen so that you can see the picture. スライド ❏ ...*transparencies of masterpieces from Lizzie's art collection.* リジーの芸術収集からの名作のスライド 🔢 N-UNCOUNT 不可算名詞 **Transparency** is the quality that an object or substance has when you can see through it. 透明性 ❏ *Cataracts affect the transparency of the eye's lenses.* 白内障は目のレンズの透明性に影響を与える.

trans|par|ent /trænspɛərənt, -pær-/ 🔢 ADJ 形容詞 If an object or substance is **transparent**, you can see through it. 透明な ❏ ...*a sheet of transparent colored plastic.* 透明な着色プラスチックシート 🔢 ADJ 形容詞 If a situation, system, or activity is **transparent**, it is easily understood or recognized. 分かりやすい ❏ *The company has to make its accounts and operations as transparent as possible.* その企業は会計と営業をできる限り透明にしなくてはならない. 🔢 ADJ 形容詞 You use **transparent** to describe a statement or action that is obviously dishonest or wrong, and that you think will

not deceive people. If a person is **transparent**, you can see their true bad motives. 見え透いた ❏ *He thought he could fool people with transparent deceptions.* 彼は見え透いたうそで人をだますことができると思っていた. ❏ *He's so transparent.* 彼は感情がすぐ顔に出る.
→ see **glass**

tran|spire /trænspaɪər/ (**transpires, transpiring, transpired**) 🔢 V-I 他動詞 When **it transpires that** something is the case, people discover that it is the case. 明らかになる [FORMAL 形式ばった] [他動詞] ❏ *It transpired that Kareem had left his driver's license at home.* カリームが家に運転免許証を忘れたことが分かった. 🔢 V-I 自動詞 When something **transpires**, it happens. 起こる [自動詞] ❏ *Nothing is known as yet about what transpired at the meeting.* 会議で何が起こったのかについてはまだ何も分かっていません.

trans|plant (**transplants, transplanting, transplanted**)

> The noun is pronounced /trænsplænt/. The verb is pronounced /trænsplænt/.
>
> 名詞は /trænsplænt/ と発音される. 動詞は /trænsplænt/ と発音される.

🔢 N-VAR 可変性名詞 A **transplant** is a medical operation in which a part of a person's body is replaced because it is diseased. 臓器移植 ❏ *He was recovering from a heart transplant operation.* 心臓移植手術から回復中であった. 🔢 V-T 他動詞 If doctors **transplant** an organ such as a heart or a kidney, they use it to replace a patient's diseased organ. 臓器移植をする ❏ *The operation to transplant a kidney is now fairly routine.* 腎臓移植手術は現在ではかなり日常のことである. 🔢 V-T 他動詞 To **transplant** a plant, person, or thing means to move them to a different place. 移す；移住させる ❏ *I have to transplant the begonias.* ベゴニアを移し植えなければならない.
→ see **donor, hospital**

trans|port (**transports, transporting, transported**)

> The verb is pronounced /trænspɔrt/. The noun is pronounced /trænspɔrt/.
>
> 動詞は /trænspɔrt/ と発音される. 名詞は /trænspɔrt/ と発音される.

🔢 V-T 他動詞 To **transport** people or goods somewhere is to take them from one place to another in a vehicle. 運送する ❏ *They are banned from launching any flights except to transport people.* 人を輸送する以外は飛行することを禁止される. 🔢 N-UNCOUNT 不可算名詞 **Transport** refers to any vehicle that you can travel in or carry goods in. 乗り物 [mainly BRIT 主に英国英語; AM usually **transportation** 米国英語では通常 **transportation**] 🔢 N-UNCOUNT 不可算名詞 **Transport** is a system for taking people or goods from one place to another, for example, using buses or trains. 輸送機関 [mainly BRIT 主に英国英語; AM usually **transportation** 米国英語では通常 **transportation**] 🔢 N-UNCOUNT 不可算名詞 **Transport** is the activity of taking goods or people from one place to another in a vehicle. 輸送 [mainly BRIT 主に英国英語; AM usually **transportation** 米国英語では通常 **transportation**]

trans|por|ta|tion /trænspɔrteɪʃ⁰n/ 🔢 N-UNCOUNT 不可算名詞 **Transportation** refers to any type of vehicle that you can travel in or carry goods in. 乗り物 [mainly AM 主に米国英語] ❏ *The company will provide transportation.* 会社が輸送手段を用意する. 🔢 N-UNCOUNT 不可算名詞 **Transportation** is a system for taking people or goods from one place to another, for example, using buses or trains. 輸送機関 [mainly AM 主に米国英語] ❏ *Campuses are usually accessible by public transportation.* 学園へはふつう一般の交通機関で行くことができる. 🔢 N-UNCOUNT 不可算名詞 **Transportation** is the activity of taking goods or people from one place to another in a vehicle. 輸送 [mainly AM 主に米国英語] ❏ *The baggage was being rapidly stowed away for transportation.* 荷物は輸送のために手早く詰め込まれていた.
→ see Word Web: **transportation**

trap /træp/ (**traps, trapping, trapped**) 🔢 N-COUNT 可算名詞 A **trap** is a device which is placed somewhere or a hole which is dug somewhere in order to catch animals or birds. わな ❏ *Nathan's dog got caught in a trap.* ナサンの犬はわなにかかってしまった. 🔢 V-T 他

Word Web   transportation

Urban **mass transportation** began more than 200 years ago. By 1830, there were **horse-drawn streetcars** in New York City and New Orleans. They ran on **rails** built into the right of way of city streets. The first electric **tram** opened in Berlin in 1881. Later on, **buses** became more popular because they didn't require **tracks**. Today, **commuter trains** link **suburbs** to cities everywhere. Many large cities also have an underground train system. It's called the **subway, metro,** or **tube** depending on where you live. In cities with steep hills, cable cars are a popular form of mass **transit**.

t

動詞 If a person **traps** animals or birds, he or she catches them using traps. わなで捕らえる □ *The locals were encouraged to trap and kill mice to stop the spread of the virus.* 地元の人々は、ウィルスのまんえんを阻止するためにネズミをわなで捕らえて殺すように奨励された. ③ N-COUNT 可算名詞 A **trap** is a trick that is intended to catch or deceive someone. 計略 □ *He failed to keep a rendezvous after sensing a police trap.* 警察の策略に気づいて、待ち合わせを守らなかった. ④ V-T 他動詞 If you **trap** someone **into** doing or saying something, you trick them so that they do or say it, although they did not want to. 計略にかける □ *Were you just trying to trap her into making some admission?* 彼女をだましてちょっと何か認めさせようとしていたのか？ ⑤ V-T 他動詞 To **trap** someone, especially a criminal, means to capture them. 策略で捕まえる □ *The police knew they had to trap the killer.* 警察は、殺人者を策略で捕えなければならないと分かっていた. ⑥ N-COUNT 可算名詞 A **trap** is an unpleasant situation that you cannot easily escape from. 困難な状況 □ *The government has found that it's caught in a trap of its own making.* 政府は、自らが仕掛けたわなにかかってしまったことに気づいた. ⑦ V-T 他動詞 If you **are trapped** somewhere, something falls onto you or blocks your way and prevents you from moving or escaping. 閉じ込められる □ *The train was trapped underground by a fire.* 電車は火事のために地下に閉じ込められた. □ *The light aircraft then cartwheeled, trapping both men.* それから、2人の男を閉じ込めたまま軽飛行機は回転した. ⑧ V-T 他動詞 When something **traps** gas, water, or energy, it prevents it from escaping. 流れを止める □ *Wool traps your body heat, keeping the chill at bay.* 毛糸は体温を外に出さず、寒さを寄せつけない. ⑨ → see also **deathtrap, trapped**
→ see **golf**

V.   **avoid a** trap, **caught in a** trap, **fall into a** trap, **set a** trap ① ③ ⑥

trapped /træpt/ ① ADJ 形容詞 If you feel **trapped**, you are in an unpleasant situation in which you lack freedom, and you feel you cannot escape from it. 捕われの □ *...people who think of themselves as trapped in mundane jobs.* つまらない仕事で身動きが取れないと考えている人たち ② → see also **trap**

trap|pings /træpɪŋz/ N-PLURAL 複数名詞 The **trappings** of power, wealth, or a particular job are the extra things, such as decorations and luxury items, that go with it. 装飾 [DISAPPROVAL 不賛成] □ *The family ruled for several generations and evidently loved the trappings of power.* その家系は数世代にわたり統治し、明らかに権力に伴う虚飾を好んだ.

trash /træʃ/ ① N-UNCOUNT 不可算名詞 **Trash** consists of unwanted things or waste material such as used paper, empty containers and bottles, and waste food. ごみ [AM 米国英語] [also 'the' N] □ *The yards are overgrown and cluttered with trash.* 裏庭は雑草が生い茂り、ごみが散乱している. □ *Would you take out the trash?* ごみを外に出してくれませんか？ ② N-UNCOUNT 不可算名詞 If you say that something such as a book, painting, or movie is **trash**, you mean that it is of very bad quality. つまらないもの [INFORMAL くだけた] □ *Pop music doesn't have to be trash; it can be art.* 流行歌はつまらないものである必要はなく、芸術であり得る. ③ N-SING 単数名詞 **The trash** means the trash can. ごみ箱 □ *I threw it in the trash.* ごみ箱に投げ捨てた.

N.   debris, garbage, junk, litter ①

In American English, the words **trash** and **garbage** are most commonly used to refer to waste material that is thrown away. □ *...the smell of rotting garbage... She threw the bottle into the trash.* In British English, **rubbish** is the usual word. **Trash** and **garbage** are and are sometimes used in British English, but only informally and metaphorically. □ *I don't have to listen to this garbage... The book was trash.*

trash can (**trash cans**) N-COUNT 可算名詞 A **trash can** is a large round container where people put their trash. 大型ごみ入れ容器 [AM 米国英語]

trashed /træʃt/ ADJ 形容詞 If someone is **trashed**, they are very drunk. 酔っ払って □ *They get trashed and act totally out of character, shouting and swearing.* 酔っ払って叫んだり、悪口を言ったり、まったくその人たちらしくない行動をとる.

trau|ma /trɔːmə/ (**traumas**) N-VAR 可変性名詞 **Trauma** is a very severe shock or very upsetting experience, which may cause psychological damage. 精神的衝撃 □ *I'd been through the trauma of losing a house.* 家を失うという精神的打撃を経てきた.

trau|mat|ic /trɔːmætɪk/ ADJ 形容詞 A **traumatic** experience is very shocking and upsetting, and may cause psychological damage. 精神的外傷となるような □ *I suffered a nervous breakdown.*

It was a traumatic experience. 神経衰弱に苦しみ、心の傷となる経験であった.

trau|ma|tize /trɔːmətaɪz, trɔː-/ (**traumatizes, traumatizing, traumatized**) V-T 他動詞 If someone **is traumatized** by an event or situation, it shocks or upsets them very much, and may cause them psychological damage. 精神的外傷を与える □ *My wife was traumatized by the experience.* 妻はその経験で精神的な外傷を負った. ● **trau|ma|tized** ADJ 形容詞 精神的外傷を負った □ *He left her in the middle of the road, shaking and deeply traumatized.* 深く心に傷を負って震えている彼女を道の真ん中に置き去りにした.

trav|el /trævəl/ (**travels, traveling** or **travelling, traveled** or **travelled**) ① V-T/V-I 他動詞/自動詞 If you **travel**, you go from one place to another, often to a place that is far away. 旅行する □ *You had better travel to Nova Scotia tomorrow.* 明日ノバスコシアに旅行する方がいい. □ *I've been traveling all day.* 今日は一日中旅をしている. □ *Students often travel hundreds of miles to get here.* よく学生はここに到達するのに何百マイルもの旅をする. ② N-UNCOUNT 不可算名詞 **Travel** is the activity of traveling. 旅行 □ *Information on travel in New Zealand is available at the hotel.* ニュージーランド国内での旅行情報はそのホテルから得られる. □ *He detested air travel.* 飛行機の旅が大嫌いであった. ③ V-T 他動詞 If you **travel** the world, the country, or the area, you go to many different places in the world or in a particular country or area. 旅行する □ *He was a very wealthy man who had traveled the world.* 彼は世界を旅行した非常に裕福な男であった. ④ V-I 自動詞 When light or sound from one place reaches another, you say that it **travels** to the other place. 伝わる □ *When sound travels through water, strange things can happen.* 音が水中を伝わるとき、不思議なことが起きることがある. ⑤ V-I 自動詞 When news becomes known by people in different places, you can say that it **travels** to them. 伝わる □ *News of his work traveled all the way to Asia.* 彼の仕事のニュースははるばるアジアまで伝わっていった. ⑥ N-PLURAL 複数名詞 Someone's **travels** are the trips that they make to places a long way from their home. 旅行 □ *He also collects things for the house on his travels abroad.* 外国旅行するときは、家のためにいろいろなものも集める. ⑦ PHRASE 句 If you **travel light**, you travel without taking much luggage. 身軽に旅する □ *It would be good to be able to travel light, but I end up taking too many clothes.* 身軽に旅ができればいいのだが、最後には衣類を持って行きすぎるはめになる.

The noun **travel** is used to talk about the general activity of traveling. It is either uncount or plural. You cannot say "a travel," you would use the word **trip** or **journey** instead. □ *First-class rail travel to Paris or Brussels is included... We were going to go on a trip to Florida together.*

V.   explore, trek, visit ① ③
N.   expedition, journey, trip ②

ADV.   travel **abroad** ① – ③
N.   **air** travel, travel **arrangements**, travel **books, car** travel, travel **delays**, travel **expenses**, travel **guide**, travel **industry**, travel **insurance**, travel **plans**, travel **reports**, travel **reservations** ②, travel **the world**

trav|el agent (**travel agents**) ① N-COUNT 可算名詞 A **travel agent** or **travel agent's** is a store or office where you can go to arrange a vacation or trip. 旅行代理店 □ *He worked in a travel agent's.* 旅行代理店で働いた. ② N-COUNT 可算名詞 A **travel agent** is a person or business that arranges people's vacations and trips. 旅行案内業者

trav|el|er /trævələr/ (**travelers**) also **traveller** N-COUNT 可算名詞 A **traveler** is a person who is on a trip or a person who travels a lot. 旅行者 □ *Airline travelers need to be confident that their bookings will be honored.* 飛行機で旅行する人は、自分の予約は守られると自信を持つ必要がある.

trav|el|er's check (**traveler's checks**) N-COUNT 可算名詞 **Traveler's checks** are checks that you buy at a bank and take with you when you travel, for example, so that you can exchange them for the currency of the country that you are in. 旅行者用小切手

trav|es|ty /trævɪsti/ (**travesties**) N-COUNT 可算名詞 If you describe something as a **travesty of** another thing, you mean that it is a very bad representation of that other thing. へたなまね □ *Her research suggests that Smith's reputation today is a travesty of what he really stood for.* 彼女の調査では、スミスの今日の評判は、彼が

本当に支持したものを曲解したものであることが提示されている.

trawl /trɔl/ (trawls, trawling, trawled) **1** V-T/V-I 他動詞/自動詞 If you **trawl through** a large number of similar things, you search through them looking for something that you want or something that is suitable for a particular purpose. 徹底的に探す ❏ A team of officers is trawling through the records of thousands of petty thieves. 警官のチームが, 何千と言うこそどろの記録を徹底調査中である. ❏ Petra trawled the aisles of the Europa supermarket. ペトラはヨーロッパスーパー店の各通路を徹底的に探した. **2** V-T/V-I 他動詞/自動詞 When fishermen **trawl for** fish, they pull a wide net behind their ship in order to catch fish. トロール漁業をする [自動詞], トロール網で取る [他動詞] ❏ They had seen him trawling and therefore knew that there were fish. 彼がトロール網で取っていたのを見たので, 魚がいることが分かった. ❏ She would walk on to the beach and watch the night fishermen trawl the shallow waters. 砂浜に歩いていって, 漁師たちが夜間浅瀬でトロール漁業をしているのをよく眺めたものだった.
→ see **fish**

trawl|er /trɔlər/ (trawlers) N-COUNT 可算名詞 A **trawler** is a fishing boat that is used for trawling. トロール船
→ see **fish**

tray /treɪ/ (trays) N-COUNT 可算名詞 A **tray** is a flat piece of wood, plastic, or metal, which usually has raised edges and which is used for carrying things, especially food and drinks. 盆

treach|er|ous /trɛtʃərəs/ **1** ADJ 形容詞 If you describe someone as **treacherous**, you mean that they are likely to betray you and cannot be trusted. [DISAPPROVAL 不賛成] ❏ He publicly left the party and denounced its treacherous leaders. 公衆の面前で脱党して, 不誠実な党首を公然と非難した. **2** ADJ 形容詞 If you say that something is **treacherous**, you mean that it is very dangerous and unpredictable. 危険をはらんでいる ❏ The current of the river is fast flowing and treacherous. 川の流れは速く, 油断できない.

treach|ery /trɛtʃəri/ (treacheries) N-UNCOUNT 不可算名詞 **Treachery** is behavior or an action in which someone betrays their country or betrays a person who trusts them. 裏切り ❏ He was deeply wounded by the treachery of close aides and old friends. 身近な側近や古い友達の裏切りに深く傷ついた.

tread /trɛd/ (treads, treading, trod, trodden) **1** N-VAR 可変性名詞 The **tread** of a tire or shoe is the pattern of thin lines cut into its surface that stops it from slipping. 溝形模様 ❏ The fat, broad tires had a good depth of tread. 幅広いずんぐりしたタイヤの溝は十分な深さがあった. **2** V-I 自動詞 If you **tread** in a particular way, you walk that way. 歩く [LITERARY 文語的] ❏ She trod casually, enjoying the touch of the damp grass on her feet. 足に触れる湿った草の感触を楽しみながら気楽に歩いた. **3** V-I 自動詞 If you **tread** carefully, you behave in a careful or cautious way. 慎重に進む ❏ If you are hoping to form a new relationship tread carefully and slowly to begin with. もし新しく関係を築きたいと望んでいるのなら, 最初はゆっくりと注意しながら慎重に扱うこと. **4** V-I 自動詞 If you **tread on** something, you put your foot on it when you are walking or standing. 踏む [mainly BRIT 主に英国英語; AM usually **step** 米国英語では通常 **step**] **5** PHRASE 句 If you **tread** a particular **path**, you take a particular course of action or do something in a particular way. 道を行く ❏ He continues to tread an unconventional path. 型破りの道を進み続けている.

tread|mill /trɛdmɪl/ (treadmills) **1** N-COUNT 可算名詞 You can refer to a task or a job as a **treadmill** when you have to keep doing it although it is unpleasant and exhausting. 単調で疲れる仕事 ❏ He exhausted himself on an endless treadmill to pay for rent and food. 家賃と食費を払うための終わりのない単調な仕事に疲労困ぱいした. **2** N-COUNT 可算名詞 A **treadmill** is a piece of equipment, for example, an exercise machine, consisting of a wheel with steps around its edge or a continuous moving belt. The weight of a person or animal walking on it causes the wheel or belt to turn. ランニングマシン

trea|son /trizⁿn/ N-UNCOUNT 不可算名詞 **Treason** is the crime of betraying your country, for example, by helping its enemies or by trying to remove its government using violence. 謀反 ❏ They were tried and found guilty of treason. 裁判にかけられ, 反逆罪で有罪となった.

treas|ure /trɛʒər/ (treasures, treasuring, treasured) **1** N-UNCOUNT 不可算名詞 **Treasure** is a collection of valuable old objects such as gold coins and jewels that has been hidden or lost. 宝物 [LITERARY 文語的] ❏ It was here, the buried treasure, she knew it was. ここだ, 埋められた宝物だ, 彼女は確信があった. **2** N-COUNT 可算名詞 **Treasures** are valuable objects, especially works of art and items of historical value. 貴重品 ❏ The house was large and full of art treasures. 家は大きく, 貴重な美術品でいっぱいであった. **3** V-T 他動詞 If you **treasure** something that you have, you keep it or care for it carefully because it gives you great pleasure and you think it is very special. 大切にする ❏ She treasures her memories of those joyous days. 喜びに満ちた日々の思い出を大切にしている. ● N-COUNT 可算名詞 **Treasure** is also a noun. 大切なもの ❏ His

greatest treasure is his collection of rock records. 彼が一番大切にしているものはロックの収集レコードである. ● **treas|ured** ADJ 形容詞 [ADJ n] 貴重な ❏ These books are still among my most treasured possessions. このような本は, 依然として私の最も貴重な所有品の中に入る.

treas|ur|er /trɛʒərər/ (treasurers) N-COUNT 可算名詞 The **treasurer** of a society or organization is the person who is in charge of its finances and keeps its accounts. 会計係

treas|ury /trɛʒəri/ (treasuries) **1** N-COUNT-COLL 集合可算名詞 In the United States and some other countries, **the Treasury** is the government department that deals with the country's finances. 財務省 ❏ a senior official at the Treasury. 財務省の高官 **2** N-PLURAL 複数名詞 **Treasuries** are financial bonds that are issued by the United States government in order to raise money. 財務省債券 [AM 米国英語] ❏ people who invest in 10- and 20- and 30-year Treasuries. 10年債券, 20年債券, 30年債券に投資する

treat /trit/ (treats, treating, treated) **1** V-T 他動詞 If you **treat** someone or something in a particular way, you behave toward them or deal with them in that way. 取り扱う ❏ Artie treated most women with indifference. アーティはほとんどの女に冷淡であった. ❏ Police say they're treating it as a case of attempted murder. 警察は, 殺人未遂事件として扱っていると述べている. **2** V-T 他動詞 When a doctor or nurse **treats** a patient or an illness, he or she tries to make the patient well again. 治療する ❏ Doctors treated her with aspirin. 医者は彼女をアスピリンで治療した. ❏ The boy was treated for a minor head wound. 少年は軽い頭部負傷に対する治療を受けた. **3** V-T 他動詞 If something **is treated with** a particular substance, the substance is put onto or into it in order to clean it, to protect it, or to give it special properties. 処理する ❏ About 70% of the cocoa acreage is treated with insecticide. ココアを植えている面積の約70%が殺虫剤で処理されている. **4** V-T 他動詞 If you **treat** someone **to** something special which they will enjoy, you buy it or arrange it for them. おごる ❏ She was always treating him to ice cream. いつも彼にアイスクリームをごちそうしていた. ❏ Tomorrow I'll treat myself to a day's gardening. 明日は一日庭仕事を楽しもう. **5** N-COUNT 可算名詞 If you give someone a **treat**, you buy or arrange something special for them which they will enjoy. おごり ❏ Lettie had never yet failed to return from town without some special treat for him. レティーが町から戻ってきたときに, 何か特別ないいものを彼のために持ってこなかったことはいまだなかった.

Word Partnership   treat は次の語句と使われる:

ADV.	treat **differently**, treat **equally**, treat **fairly**, treat **well** **1**
N.	treat **with contempt/dignity/respect** **1** treat **people**, treat **women** **1** **2** treat **AIDS**, treat **cancer**, treat **a disease**, **doctors** treat **2**

---

treat|ment /tritmənt/ (treatments) **1** N-VAR 可変性名詞 **Treatment** is medical attention given to a sick or injured person or animal. 治療 ❏ Many patients are not getting the medical treatment they need. 患者の多くは, 必要とする医療を受けていない. ❏ a veterinary surgeon who specializes in the treatment of caged birds. 鳥かごの鳥を専門に治療する獣医 **2** N-UNCOUNT 不可算名詞 Your **treatment** of someone is the way you behave toward them or deal with them. 取り扱い ❏ We don't want any special treatment. 特別な待遇はいらない. **3** N-VAR 可変性名詞 **Treatment** of something involves putting a particular substance onto or into it, in order to clean it, to protect it, or to give it special properties. 処理 ❏ There should be greater treatment of sewage before it is discharged. 下水道を排出する前にさらなる処理があるべきである.
→ see **cancer**, **illness**

Word Partnership   treatment は次の語句と使われる:

V.	**get/receive** treatment, **give** treatment, **undergo** treatment **1**
ADJ.	**effective** treatment, **medical** treatment **1** **better** treatment, **equal/unequal** treatment, **fair** treatment, **humane** treatment **2** **special** treatment **2** **3**
N.	treatment **of addiction**, **AIDS** treatment, **cancer** treatment, **treatment center**, **treatment of an illness** **1** treatment **of prisoners** **2** treatment **plant**, **water** treatment **3**

---

trea|ty /triti/ (treaties) N-COUNT 可算名詞 A **treaty** is a written agreement between countries in which they agree to do a particular thing or to help each other. 条約 ❏ negotiations over a treaty on global warming. 地球温暖化の協定に関する交渉

tre|ble /trɛbⁿl/ (trebles, trebling, trebled) **1** N-COUNT 可算名詞 On a stereo system or radio, the **treble** is the ability to reproduce the higher musical notes. The **treble** is also the knob which controls this. 高音にすること; 高音用のつまみ **2** V-T/V-I 他動詞/

Word Web   tree

Trees are one of the oldest living things. They are also the largest **plant**. Some scientists believe that the largest living thing on Earth is a coniferous giant redwood tree named General Grant. Other scientists point to a huge grove of deciduous aspen trees known as Pando. This grove is a single plant because all of the trees grow from the root system of just one tree. Pando covers more than 106 acres. Some aspen trees **germinate** from seeds, but most result from natural cloning. In this process the parent tree sends up new **sprouts** from its root system. Fossil records show tree clones may live up to a million years.

自動詞 If something **trebles** or if you **treble** it, it becomes three times greater in number or amount than it was. 3倍になる [自動詞]、3倍にする [他動詞] [AM **triple** 米国英語 **triple**] ❑ *They will have to pay much more when rents treble in January.* 1月に家賃が3倍になると、さらに高額を支払わなければならないだろう。 [mainly BRIT 主に英国英語] ❸ PREDET 前限定詞 If one thing is **treble** the size or amount of another thing, it is three times greater in size or amount. 3倍の [mainly BRIT 主に英国英語, FORMAL 形式ばった] [AM **triple** 米国英語 **triple**]

tree /triː/ (**trees**) N-COUNT 可算名詞 A **tree** is a tall plant that has a hard trunk, branches, and leaves. 木 ❑ *I planted those apple trees.* これらのりんごの木を植えた。
→ see Word Web: **tree**
→ see **forest**, **mountain**, **plant**

trek /trɛk/ (**treks**, **trekking**, **trekked**) ❶ V-I 自動詞 If you **trek** somewhere, you go on a journey across difficult country, usually on foot. 骨の折れる徒歩旅行をする ❑ *...trekking through the jungles.* ジャングルを歩いて苦労の徒歩旅行 ● N-COUNT 可算名詞 **Trek** is also a noun. 骨の折れる徒歩旅行 ❑ *He is on a trek through the South Gobi desert.* 南ゴビ砂漠を通る徒歩旅行中である。 ❷ V-I 自動詞 If you **trek** somewhere, you go there heavily and unwillingly, usually because you are tired. のろのろと前進する ❑ *They trekked from shop to shop in search of white knee-high socks.* ひざまでの白いソックスを求めて店から店へのろのろと歩いて回った。

Word Link   trem ≈ shaking : tremble, tremendous, tremor

trem|ble /trɛmbᵊl/ (**trembles**, **trembling**, **trembled**) ❶ V-I 自動詞 If you **tremble**, you shake slightly because you are frightened or cold. 小刻みに震える ❑ *His mouth became dry, his eyes widened, and he began to tremble all over.* 彼の口は渇き、目は大きくなり、体全体が震えた始めた。 ❑ *Lisa was white and trembling with anger.* リサは怒りで震え、蒼白 (そうはく) だった。● N-SING 単数名詞 **Tremble** is also a noun. 震え ❑ *I will never forget the look on the patient's face, the tremble in his hand.* 患者の手の表情、手の震えを絶対に忘れることはできない。 ❷ V-I 自動詞 If something **trembles**, it shakes slightly. 揺れる [LITERARY 文語的] ❑ *He felt the earth tremble under him.* 足の下で地面が震動するのを感じた。 ❸ V-I 自動詞 If your voice **trembles**, it sounds unsteady and uncertain, usually because you are upset or nervous. 震える [LITERARY 文語的] ❑ *His voice trembled, on the verge of tears.* いまにも涙が流れ出そうに声が震えた。● N-SING 単数名詞 **Tremble** is also a noun. 震え ❑ *"Please understand this," she began, a tremble in her voice.* 「このことを理解してください」と震える声で彼女は始めた。

tre|men|dous /trɪmɛndəs/ ❶ ADJ 形容詞 You use **tremendous** to emphasize how strong a feeling or quality is, or how large an amount is. 途方もない [EMPHASIS 強調] ❑ *I felt a tremendous pressure on my chest.* 胸にものすごい圧力を感じた。 ● **tre|men|dous|ly** ADV 副詞 途方もなく ❑ *I thought they played tremendously well, didn't you?* 非常にいいプレーだったと思ったが、君はそう思わなかったかい? ❷ ADJ 形容詞 You can describe someone or something as **tremendous** when you think they are very good or very impressive. すばらしい ❑ *I thought it was absolutely tremendous.* まったくすばらしいと思った。

trem|or /trɛmər/ (**tremors**) ❶ N-COUNT 可算名詞 A **tremor** is a small earthquake. 微震 ❑ *The earthquake sent tremors through the region.* その地震で地域全体が震動した。 ❷ N-COUNT 可算名詞 If an event causes a **tremor** in a group or organisation, it threatens to make the group or organisation less strong or stable. 揺さぶること ❑ *News of 160 lay-offs had sent tremors through the community.* 160人解雇のニュースで地域社会は揺さぶられた。 ❸ N-COUNT 可算名詞 A **tremor** is a shaking of your body or voice that you cannot control. 震え ❑ *The old man has a tremor in his hands.* じいさんは両手が震える。

trench /trɛntʃ/ (**trenches**) ❶ N-COUNT 可算名詞 A **trench** is a long narrow channel that is cut into the ground, for example, in order to lay pipes or get rid of water. 深い溝、堀 ❷ N-COUNT 可算名詞 A **trench** is a long narrow channel in the ground used

by soldiers in order to protect themselves from the enemy. People often refer to the battlegrounds of the First World War in Northern France and Belgium as **the trenches**. ざんごう、防御陣地 ❑ *We fought with them in the trenches.* ざんごうの中で彼らと戦った。

trend /trɛnd/ (**trends**) ❶ N-COUNT 可算名詞 A **trend** is a change or development toward something new or different. 傾向 ❑ *This is a growing trend.* この傾向が増加している。 ❷ N-COUNT 可算名詞 To set a **trend** means to do something that becomes accepted or fashionable, and that a lot of other people copy. 流行を生むこと ❑ *The latest trend is gardening.* 最新の流行は庭仕事だ。
→ see **population**

Thesaurus   trend また次を参照 :

N.	craze, fad, style ❷

Word Partnership   trend は次の語句と使われる :

ADJ.	**overall** trend, **upward** trend, **warming** trend ❶ **current** trend, **disturbing** trend, **growing** trend, **latest** trend, **new** trend, **recent** trend ❶ ❷
V.	**continue** a trend, **reverse** a trend, **start** a trend ❶ ❷

trendy /trɛndi/ (**trendier**, **trendiest**) ADJ 形容詞 If you say that something or someone is **trendy**, you mean that they are very fashionable and modern. 流行の先端を行く [INFORMAL くだけた] ❑ *...a trendy Seattle night club.* シアトルのいきなナイトクラブ

trepi|da|tion /trɛpɪdeɪʃᵊn/ N-UNCOUNT 不可算名詞 **Trepidation** is fear or anxiety about something that you are going to do or experience. おののき [FORMAL 形式ばった] ❑ *It was with some trepidation that I viewed the prospect of cycling across Uganda.* ある不安を抱いてウガンダを自転車で横切る見込みに思いを巡らした。

tres|pass /trɛspəs, -pæs/ (**trespasses**, **trespassing**, **trespassed**) V-I 自動詞 If someone **trespasses**, they go onto someone else's land without their permission. 不法侵入する ❑ *They were trespassing on private property.* 個人所有の土地に不法侵入していた。 N-VAR 可変性名詞 ● **Trespass** is the act of trespassing. 不法侵入 [LEGAL 法律的] ❑ *You could be prosecuted for trespass.* 不法侵入で起訴されるかもしれない。

tri|al /traɪəl/ (**trials**) ❶ N-VAR 可変性名詞 A **trial** is a formal meeting in a law court, at which a judge and jury listen to evidence and decide whether a person is guilty of a crime. 裁判 ❑ *New evidence showed the police lied at the trial.* 警察が裁判でうそを言ったことが新しい証拠で分かった。 ❑ *I have the right to a trial with a jury of my peers.* 同輩の陪審員と一緒に審理を受ける権利がある。 ❷ N-VAR 可変性名詞 A **trial** is an experiment in which you test someone or something by using it or doing it for a period of time to see how well it works. If something is **on trial**, it is being tested in this way. 試験; 試験中で ❑ *They have been treated with this drug in clinical trials.* 臨床試験でこの薬を使った処置を受けた。 ❑ *I took the car out for a trial on the roads.* 路上試運転のために車を持ち出した。 ❸ N-COUNT 可算名詞 If you refer to the **trials** of a situation, you mean the unpleasant things that you experience in it. 試練 ❑ *...the trials of adolescence.* 思春期の試練 ❹ PHRASE 句 If you do something **by trial and error**, you try several different methods of doing it until you find the method that works best. 試行錯誤 ❑ *Many drugs were found by trial and error.* 薬の多くは試行錯誤で発見された。 ❺ PHRASE 句 If someone is **on trial**, they are being tried in a court of law. 公判中で ❑ *He is currently on trial for drunk driving.* 飲酒運転で現在裁判にかけられている。 ❻ PHRASE 句 If you say that someone or something is **on trial**, you mean that they are in a situation where people are observing them to see whether they succeed or fail. 試験中で ❑ *The president will be drawn into a damaging battle in which his credentials will be on trial.* 大統領の信用が試される、不利な闘争に引き込まれるであろう。 ❼ PHRASE 句 If someone **stands trial**, they are tried in court for a crime they are accused of. 裁判を受ける ❑ *He was found to be mentally unfit to stand trial.* 裁判を受けるには精神的に健全でないことが分かった。
→ see Word Web: **trial**

Many countries guarantee the right to a **trial** by jury. The **judge** begins by explaining the **charges** against the **defendant**. Next the defendant **pleads guilty** or not guilty. Then the **lawyers** for the **plaintiff** and the defendant present **evidence**. Both **attorneys** interview **witnesses**. They can also question each other's **clients**. Sometimes the lawyers go back and **cross-examine** witnesses about **testimony** they gave earlier. When they finish, the **jury** meets to **deliberate**. They deliver their **verdict** and the judge **pronounces** the **sentence**. At this point, the defendant may be able to **appeal** the verdict and request a new trial.

Word Partnership *trial* は次の語句と使われる:

ADJ.	**civil** trial, **fair** trial, **federal** trial, **speedy** trial, **upcoming** trial ① **clinical** trial ②
N.	trial **date**, **jury** trial, **murder** trial, **outcome of a** trial ① trial **and error** ④
V.	**await** trial, **bring** *someone* to trial, **face** trial, **go on** trial, **put on** trial ⑤

Word Link tri ≈ three : triangle, trilogy, triplet

tri|an|gle /traɪˈæŋgəl/ (triangles) ① N-COUNT 可算名詞 A **triangle** is an object, arrangement, or flat shape with three straight sides and three angles. 三角形 □ *This design is in pastel colors with three rectangles and three triangles.* 三角形が3つずつ2組ある柔らかく淡い色調のデザインである。 □ *Its outline roughly forms an equilateral triangle.* その輪郭はおおよそ正三角形の形になる。 ② N-COUNT 可算名詞 The **triangle** is a musical instrument that consists of a piece of metal shaped like a triangle. You play it by hitting it with a short metal bar. トライアングル □ *My musical career consisted of playing the triangle in kindergarten.* 音楽の経歴は、幼稚園でトライアングルを鳴らしたことであった。 → see **circle, shape**

tri|an|gu|lar /traɪˈæŋgyələr/ ADJ 形容詞 Something that is **triangular** is in the shape of a triangle. 三角形の □ *...a triangular roof.* 三角形の屋根

trib|al /ˈtraɪbəl/ ADJ 形容詞 **Tribal** is used to describe things relating to or belonging to tribes and the way that they are organized. 部族の □ *...tribal warfare.* 部族間の交戦 □ *...the Navajo Tribal Council.* ナバホ族評議会

tribe /traɪb/ (tribes) N-COUNT-COLL 集合可算名詞 **Tribe** is sometimes used to refer to a group of people of the same race, language, and customs, especially in a developing country. Some people disapprove of this use. 部族 □ *...three-hundred members of the Xhosa tribe.* コーサ族に属する300人 → see **society**

tribu|la|tion /ˌtrɪbyəˈleɪʃən/ (tribulations) N-VAR 可変性名詞 You can refer to the suffering or difficulty that you experience in a particular situation as **tribulations**. 苦難 [FORMAL 形式ばった] □ *...the trials and tribulations of everyday life.* 日常生活の試練と苦難

tri|bu|nal /traɪˈbyuːnəl/ (tribunals) N-COUNT-COLL 集合可算名詞 A **tribunal** is a special court or committee that is appointed to deal with particular problems. 裁判の場 □ *His case comes before an industrial tribunal in March.* 彼の件は3月に労働審判所で審理される。

trib|ute /ˈtrɪbyuːt/ (tributes) ① N-VAR 可変性名詞 A **tribute** is something that you say, do, or make to show your admiration and respect for someone. 賛辞 □ *The song is a tribute to Roy Orbison.* それはロイ・オービソンをたたえる歌だ。 ② N-SING 単数名詞 If one thing is a **tribute to** another, the first thing is the result of the second and shows how good it is. あかし □ *His success has been a tribute to hard work, to professionalism.* 彼の成功は勤勉や専門家かたぎの表れである。

trick /trɪk/ (tricks, tricking, tricked) ① N-COUNT 可算名詞 A **trick** is an action that is intended to fool or deceive someone. いたずら □ *We are playing a trick on a man who keeps bothering me.* いつも僕にうるさく言う人の人にいたずらをしている最中です。 ② V-T 他動詞 If someone **tricks** you, they deceive you, often in order to make you do something. だましてーさせる □ *Stephen is going to be pretty upset when he finds out how you tricked him.* 君がスティーブンをいかにだましたかがばれたら、彼は相当腹を立てるぜ。 □ *His family tricked him into going to Pakistan, and once he was there, they took away his passport.* 彼の家族は彼をだましてパキスタンに行かせ、着くやいなやパスポートを取り上げた。 ③ N-COUNT 可算名詞 A **trick** is a clever or skillful action that someone does in order to entertain people. 手品 □ *...magic tricks.* 魔法の手品 □ *He shows me card tricks.* トランプの手品を見せてくれる。 ④ N-COUNT 可算名詞 A **trick** is a clever

way of doing something. こつ □ *Everything I cooked was a trick of my mother's.* 私が料理したこつは全て母のものだった。 ⑤ → see also **hat trick** ⑥ PHRASE 句 If something **does the trick**, it achieves what you wanted. うまくいく [INFORMAL くだけた] □ *Sometimes a few choice words will do the trick.* ときどき言葉を適切に選べばうまくいくことがある。 ⑦ PHRASE 句 If someone tries **every trick in the book**, they try every possible thing that they can think of in order to achieve something. ありとあらゆる手 [INFORMAL くだけた] □ *Companies are using every trick in the book to stay one step in front of their competitors.* 会社は競合先の一歩先手を行くために、ありとあらゆる手段を使っている。 ⑧ PHRASE 句 The **tricks of the trade** are the quick and clever ways of doing something that are known by people who regularly do a particular activity. 商売の秘訣 □ *To get you started, we have asked five successful writers to reveal some of the tricks of the trade.* 手始めとして、成功している作家5人に商売の秘訣を少し明かしてもらうことをお願いしました。

Word Partnership *trick* は次の語句と使われる:

ADJ.	**cheap** trick ① **old** trick ① ③ **clever** trick, **neat** trick ① ③ ④
V.	**play a** trick, **pull a** trick ① **try to** trick *someone* ② **do the** trick ⑥
N.	**card** trick ③ **every** trick **in the book** ⑦

trick|le /ˈtrɪkəl/ (trickles, trickling, trickled) ① V-T/V-I 他動詞/自動詞 When a liquid **trickles**, or when you **trickle** it, it flows slowly in a thin stream. ちょろちょろ流れる [自動詞]、少しずつ流す [他動詞] □ *A tear trickled down the old man's cheek.* 涙がじいさんのほおを流れて落ちた。 ● N-COUNT 可算名詞 **Trickle** is also a noun. 細い流れ □ *There was not so much as a trickle of water.* わずかな水の流れさえもなかった。 ② V-I 自動詞 When people or things **trickle** in a particular direction, they move there slowly in small groups or amounts, rather than all together. 少しずつ行く □ *Some donations are already trickling in.* 寄付はすでに少しずつ入ってきている。 ● N-COUNT 可算名詞 **Trickle** is also a noun. ゆっくりと動くこと □ *The flood of cars has now slowed to a trickle.* 車の殺到は現在軽減し、ぽつぽつと流れている。

▶ **trickle down** PHRASAL VERB 句動詞 If benefits given to people at the top of a society or system **trickle down**, they are eventually passed on to people lower down the society or system. 徐々に伝わる □ *...the failure of the prosperity of Las Vegas' casinos to trickle down to poor neighborhoods.* ラスベガスのカジノの繁栄が貧しい近隣に流れていかない不首尾

tricky /ˈtrɪki/ (trickier, trickiest) ADJ 形容詞 If you describe a task or problem as **tricky**, you mean that it is difficult to do or deal with. 扱いにくい □ *Parking can be tricky downtown.* 下町では駐車が難しいこともある。

tried /traɪd/ ① ADJ 形容詞 **Tried** is used in the expressions **tried and tested**, **tried and trusted**, and **tried and true**, which describe a product or method that has already been used and has been found to be successful. 試験済みの [ADJ 'and' adj] □ *...over 1,000 tried-and-tested recipes.* 1,000種類以上の絶対おいしいレシピ ② → see also **try**

tri|fle /ˈtraɪfəl/ (trifles) ① PHRASE 句 You can use a **trifle** to mean slightly or to a small extent, especially in order to make something you say seem less extreme. 少し [OLD-FASHIONED 古風な, VAGUENESS あいまいさ] □ *As a photographer, he'd found both locations just a trifle disappointing.* 写真家として、両方の場所ともやや失望を感じた。 ② N-COUNT 可算名詞 A **trifle** is something that is considered to have little importance, value, or significance. つまらない物 □ *He had no money to spare on trifles.* くだらない物に割く金はなかった。 ③ N-VAR 可変性名詞 **Trifle** is a cold dessert made of layers of sponge cake, fruit gelatin, fruit, and custard, and usually covered with cream. トライフル □ *...a bowl of trifle.* ボウルに入ったトライフル

trig|ger /trɪgər/ (triggers, triggering, triggered) **1** N-COUNT 可算名詞 The **trigger** of a gun is a small lever which you pull to fire it. 引き金 □*A man pointed a gun at them and pulled the trigger.* 男は彼らに銃を向け、そして引き金を引いた. **2** N-COUNT 可算名詞 The **trigger** of a bomb is the device which causes it to explode. 起爆装置 □*...trigger devices for nuclear weapons.* 核兵器の起爆装置 **3** V-T 他動詞 To **trigger** a bomb or system means to cause it to work. 起動させる □*The thieves must have deliberately triggered the alarm and hidden inside the house.* 泥棒たちは警報をわざと起動させて家の中に隠れていたに違いない. **4** V-T 他動詞 If something **triggers** an event or situation, it causes it to happen or exist. きっかけとなる □*...the incident which triggered the outbreak of the First World War.* 世界第一次大戦の勃発（ぼっぱつ）のきっかけとなった事件 ●PHRASAL VERB 句動詞 **Trigger off** means the same as **trigger**. きっかけとなる □*It is still not clear what events triggered off the demonstrations.* どんな出来事がデモのきっかけとなったのか、いまだ明らかでない. **5** N-COUNT 可算名詞 If something acts as a **trigger for** another thing such as an illness, event, or situation, the first thing causes the second thing to begin to happen or exist. 誘発 □*Stress may act as a trigger for these illnesses.* ストレスがこのような疾病を誘発する可能性もある.

tril|lion /trɪlyən/ (trillions)

> The plural form is **trillion** after a number, or after a word or expression referring to a number, such as "several" or "a few."
>
> 複数形は数の後、あるいは **several** や **a few** のような数を指す単語や表現の後では **trillion** である.

1 NUM 数詞 A **trillion** is 1,000,000,000,000. 兆 [AM 米国英語] □*...a 4 trillion dollar debt.* 4兆ドルの負債 **2** NUM 数詞 A **trillion** is 1,000,000,000,000,000,000. 百京 [BRIT 英国英語; AM **quintillion** 米国英語 **quintillion**]

tril|ogy /trɪlədʒi/ (trilogies) N-COUNT 可算名詞 A **trilogy** is a series of three books, plays, or movies that have the same subject or the same characters. 三部作 □*...Tolkien's trilogy, The Lord of the Rings.* トルキンの三部作『指輪物語』

trim /trɪm/ (trimmer, trimmest, trims, trimming, trimmed) **1** ADJ 形容詞 Something that is **trim** is neat, and attractive. きちんとした □*The neighbors' gardens were trim and neat.* 近所の庭はきちんとよく手入れされていた. **2** ADJ 形容詞 If you describe someone's figure as **trim**, you mean that it is attractive because there is no extra fat on their body. ほっそりした [APPROVAL 賛成] □*The driver was a trim young woman of perhaps thirty.* 運転手は多分30くらいのほっそりした若い女であった. **3** V-T 他動詞 If you **trim** something, for example, someone's hair, you cut off small amounts of it, in order to make it look neater. 刈り込む □*My friend trims my hair every eight weeks.* 8週間ごとに髪の毛を友達に切ってもらう. ●N-SING 単数名詞 **Trim** is also a noun. 散髪 □*His hair needed a trim.* 散髪が必要だった. **4** V-T 他動詞 If a government or other organization **trims** something such as a plan, policy, or amount, they reduce it slightly in extent or size. 削減する □*American companies looked at ways they could trim these costs.* アメリカの企業はこのようなコストを削減できる方法を調べてみた. **5** V-T 他動詞 If something such as a piece of clothing **is trimmed with** a type of material or design, it is decorated with it, usually along its edges. 縁飾りをつける [usu passive] □*...jackets, which are then trimmed with crocheted flowers.* その後にかぎ針編みの花を縁飾りした上着 **6** N-VAR 可変性名詞 The **trim** on something such as a piece of clothing is a decoration, for example, along its edges, that is in a different color or material. 縁飾り □*...a white satin scarf with black trim.* 黒の縁飾りのある白しゅすのスカーフ

trim|ming /trɪmɪŋ/ (trimmings) **1** N-VAR 可変性名詞 The **trimming** on something such as a piece of clothing is the decoration, for example, along its edges, that is in a different color or material. 縁飾り □*...the lace trimming on her satin nightgown.* 彼女のしゅすのネグリジェのレース縁飾り **2** N-PLURAL 複数名詞 **Trimmings** are pieces of something, usually food, which are left over after you have cut what you need. 切りくず □*Use the pastry trimmings to decorate the pie.* パイの装飾にはパイ皮の切り残りを使ってください.

trio /triou/ (trios) N-COUNT-COLL 集合可算名詞 A **trio** is a group of three people together, especially musicians or singers, or a group of three things that have something in common. 三重奏（唱）者; 三つ組 □*...classy American songs from a Texas trio.* テキサス三重唱者によるセンスのいいアメリカの歌

trip /trɪp/ (trips, tripping, tripped) **1** N-COUNT 可算名詞 A **trip** is a journey that you make to a particular place. 旅行 □*We're taking a trip to Montana.* モンタナに旅行に行くつもりだ. □*On Thursday we went out on a day trip.* 木曜日に日帰り旅行に行った. **2** → see also **round trip 3** V-I 自動詞 If you **trip** when you are walking, you knock your foot against something and fall or nearly fall. つまずいて倒れる（倒れそうになる） □*She tripped and*

fell last night and broke her hip. 昨夜つまずいて転び腰の骨を折った. ●PHRASAL VERB 句動詞 **Trip up** means the same as **trip**. つまずいて倒れる（倒れそうになる） □*I tripped up and hurt my foot.* つまずいて片足を痛めた. **4** V-T 他動詞 If you **trip** someone who is walking or running, you put your foot or something else in front of them, so that they knock their own foot against it and fall or nearly fall. つまずかせて転ばせる（よろめかせる） □*One guy stuck his foot out and tried to trip me.* ある野郎が足を出して僕をつまずかせようとした. ●PHRASAL VERB 句動詞 **Trip up** means the same as **trip**. つまずかせて転ばせる（よろめかせる） □*He made a sudden dive for Uncle Jim's legs to try to trip him up.* ジムおじさんの足に急に飛びつき、つまずかせようとした.

trip

> The noun **travel** is used to talk about the general activity of traveling. It is either uncount or plural. You cannot say "a travel," you would use the word **trip** or **journey** instead. □*First-class rail travel to Paris or Brussels is included...We were going to go on a trip to Florida together.*

tri|ple /trɪpª l/ (triples, tripling, tripled) **1** ADJ 形容詞 **Triple** means consisting of three things or parts. 3成分からなる [ADJ n] □*...a triple somersault.* 連続3回の宙返り **2** V-T/V-I 他動詞/自動詞 If something **triples** or if you **triple** it, it becomes three times as large in size or number. 3倍になる [自動詞], 3倍にする [他動詞] □*I got a fantastic new job and my salary tripled.* すばらしい仕事を新しく得て、給料が3倍になった. □*The exhibition has tripled in size from last year.* 展示は去年の3倍の大きさになった. **3** PREDET 前限定詞 If something is **triple** the amount or size of another thing, it is three times as large. 3倍の [PREDET 'the' n] □*The mine reportedly had an accident rate triple the national average.* 伝えられるところによると、その鉱山は全国平均の3倍の事故率があった.

tri|plet /trɪplɪt/ (triplets) N-COUNT 可算名詞 **Triplets** are three children born at the same time to the same mother. 三つ子 □*"Guess what? Katinka had triplets – all healthy."* 「びっくりだけど、カティンカが三つ子を産んだよ – みな元気だ.」

tri|pod /traɪpɒd/ (tripods) N-COUNT 可算名詞 A **tripod** is a stand with three legs that is used to support something such as a camera or a telescope. 三脚台

tri|umph /traɪʌmf/ (triumphs, triumphing, triumphed) **1** N-VAR 変性名詞 A **triumph** is a great success or achievement, often one that has been gained with a lot of skill or effort. 大勝利 □*The championships proved to be a personal triumph for the coach, Dave Donovan.* 選手権は、指導員のディブ・ドナバンにとって個人的な大勝利となった **2** N-UNCOUNT 不可算名詞 **Triumph** is a feeling of great satisfaction and pride resulting from a success or victory. 勝利感 □*Her sense of triumph was short-lived.* 勝利感は長続きしなかった. **3** V-I 自動詞 If someone or something **triumphs**, they gain complete success, control, or victory, often after a long or difficult struggle. 勝利を収める □*All her life, Kelly had stuck with difficult tasks and challenges, and triumphed.* ケリーは生まれてこのかた難しい仕事や挑戦に負けずについていき、勝利を収めた.

tri|um|phant /traɪʌmfənt/ ADJ 形容詞 Someone who is **triumphant** has gained a victory or succeeded in something and feels very happy about it. 勝ち誇った □*The captain's voice was triumphant.* キャプテンの声は意気揚々としていた. ●**tri|um|phant|ly** ADV 副詞 勝ち誇って □*They marched triumphantly into the capital.* 意気揚々と首都へ行進して行った.

trivia /trɪviə/ N-UNCOUNT 不可算名詞 **Trivia** is unimportant facts or details that are considered to be interesting rather than serious or useful. ささいなこと □*The two men chatted about such trivia as their favorite kinds of fast food.* 二人の男が、好きな種類の簡易食品などのつまらないことをしゃべっていた.

triv|ial /trɪviəl/ ADJ 形容詞 If you describe something as **trivial**, you think that it is unimportant and not serious. ささいな □*The director tried to wave aside these issues as trivial details that could be settled later.* 重役は、このような件を後で決着できるささいなこととして退けようとした.

trivi|al|ize /trɪviəlaɪz/ (trivializes, trivializing, trivialized) V-T 他動詞 If you say that someone **trivializes** something important, you disapprove of them because they make it seem less important, serious, and complex than it is. 平凡にする [DISAPPROVAL 不賛成] ❑ It never ceases to amaze me how the business world continues to trivialize the world's environmental problems. 実業界がいかに世界の環境問題を取るに足らないものとみなし続けているかについては驚くばかりだ.

trod /trɒd/ **Trod** is the past tense of **tread**. tread の過去形

trod|den /trɒdªn/ **Trodden** is the past participle of **tread**. tread の過去分詞

trol|ley /trɒli/ (trolleys) ■ N-COUNT 可算名詞 A **trolley** or **trolley car** is an electric vehicle for carrying people which travels on rails in the streets of a city or town. 路面電車 [AM 米国英語] ❑ He took a northbound trolley on State Street. ステート通りで北方面行きの路面電車に乗った. ☑ N-COUNT 可算名詞 A **trolley** is an object with wheels that you use to transport heavy things such as shopping or luggage. 手押し車 [BRIT 英国英語; AM **cart** 米国英語 **cart**] ☒ N-COUNT 可算名詞 A **trolley** is a small table on wheels which is used for serving drinks or food. ワゴン車 [BRIT 英国英語; AM **cart** 米国英語 **cart**] ☓ N-COUNT 可算名詞 A **trolley** is a bed on wheels for moving patients in a hospital. 担送車 [BRIT 英国英語; AM **gurney** 米国英語 **gurney**]

trom|bone /trɒmboʊn/ (trombones) N-VAR 可変性名詞 A **trombone** is a large musical instrument of the brass family. It consists of two long oval tubes, one of which can be pushed backward and forward to play different notes. トロンボーン [oft 'the' N] ❑ Her husband had played the trombone in the band for a decade. 彼女の夫は10年間楽団でトロンボーンを演奏した.

→ see **orchestra**

troop /truːp/ (troops, trooping, trooped) ■ N-PLURAL 複数名詞 **Troops** are soldiers, especially when they are in a large organized group doing a particular task. 軍隊 ❑ The next phase of the operation will involve the deployment of more than 35,000 troops from a dozen countries. 次段階の軍事行動では、10余か国から35,000人以上の軍隊を動員することが含まれる. ☑ N-COUNT 可算名詞 A **troop** is a group of soldiers. 隊 ❑ ...a troop of American Marines. アメリカ海軍隊. ☒ N-COUNT-COLL 集合可算名詞 A **troop** of people or animals is a group of them. 集まり ❑ The whole troop of men and women wore their hair fairly short. その一団の男女は全員髪をかなり短くしていた. ☓ V-I 自動詞 If people **troop** somewhere, they walk there in a group, often in a sad or tired way. ぞろぞろ群がって動く [INFORMAL くだけた] ❑ They all trooped back to the house for a rest. 休むために全員ぞろぞろと家に戻っていった.

→ see **army**

troop|er /truːpər/ (troopers) ■ N-COUNT 可算名詞 In the United States, a **trooper** is a police officer in a state police force. 州警察の警官 ❑ Once long ago he had considered becoming a state trooper. ずっと昔、州の警官になろうと考えたことがあった. ☑ N-COUNT; N-TITLE 可算名詞, 称号名詞 A **trooper** is a soldier of low rank in the cavalry or in an armored regiment in the army. 騎兵 ❑ ...a trooper from the 7th Cavalry. 第7騎兵隊の騎兵

tro|phy /troʊfi/ (trophies) ■ N-COUNT 可算名詞 A **trophy** is a prize, for example, a silver cup, that is given to the winner of a competition or race. 優勝記念品 ❑ The special trophy for the best rider went to Chris Read. 最優秀騎手特別賞トロフィーはクリス・リードに授与された. ☑ N-COUNT 可算名詞 A **trophy** is something that you keep in order to show that you have done something very difficult. 戦勝記念物 ❑ His office was lined with animal heads, trophies of his hunting hobby. 事務所には趣味の狩りの戦勝品である動物の頭が並んでいた.

tropi|cal /trɒpɪkªl/ ■ ADJ 形容詞 **Tropical** means belonging to or typical of the tropics. 熱帯の [ADJ n] ❑ ...tropical diseases. 熱帯病 ☑ ADJ 形容詞 **Tropical** weather is hot and damp weather typical of the tropics. 酷暑の ❑ The cool, sweet milk is just what you need in the tropical heat. 熱帯の酷熱では、冷たくて甘い牛乳こそまさに必要なものだ.

→ see **disaster**, **hurricane**

trop|ics /trɒpɪks/ N-PLURAL 複数名詞 The **tropics** are the parts of the world that lie between two lines of latitude, the tropic of Cancer, 23½° north of the equator, and the tropic of Capricorn, 23½° south of the equator. 熱帯地方 ❑ Being in the tropics meant that insects formed a large part of our life. 熱帯地方にいれば、昆虫は生活の大きな部分であった.

→ see **globe**

trot /trɒt/ (trots, trotting, trotted) ■ V-I 自動詞 If you **trot** somewhere, you move fairly fast at a speed between walking and running, taking small quick steps. 小走りで行く ❑ I trotted down the steps and out to the shed. 小走りで階段を駆け降りて外に出て、納屋に行った. ● N-SING 単数名詞 **Trot** is also a noun. 小走り ❑ He walked briskly, but without breaking into a trot. 小走りにはならない程度にさっさと歩いた. ☑ V-I 自動詞 When an animal such as a horse **trots**, it moves fairly fast, taking quick steps. You can also

say that the rider of the animal **is trotting**. だく足で進む ❑ Alan took the reins and the small horse started trotting. アランが手綱を取ると、小さい馬はだく足で進み始めた. ● N-SING 単数名詞 **Trot** is also a noun. だく足 ❑ As they started up again, the horse broke into a brisk trot. 再度動き始めると、急に馬はきびきびしただく足になった.

trou|ble /trʌbªl/ (troubles, troubling, troubled) ■ N-UNCOUNT 不可算名詞 You can refer to problems or difficulties as **trouble**. 困難 [oft 'in' N, also N in pl] ❑ I had trouble parking. 駐車が困難だった. ❑ You've caused us a lot of trouble. お前にはずいぶんと苦労させられている. ☑ N-SING 単数名詞 If you say that one aspect of a situation is **the trouble**, you mean that it is the aspect which is causing problems or making the situation unsatisfactory. やっかいな点 ❑ The trouble is that these restrictions have remained while other things have changed. 問題は、他のものは変わっているのにこのような制限がまだ残っていることだ. ☒ N-PLURAL 複数名詞 Your **troubles** are the things that you are worried about. 心配事 ❑ She tells me her troubles. I tell her mine. 彼女は私に悩み事を話し、私は彼女に私の悩み事を話す. ☓ N-UNCOUNT 不可算名詞 If you have kidney **trouble** or back **trouble**, for example, there is something wrong with your kidneys or your back. 病気 ❑ An old bed is the most likely cause of back trouble. 腰の病気はベッドが古いことが原因であることが多い. ❑ Her husband had never before had any heart trouble. 彼女の夫はこれまで心臓の病気になったことがなかった. ☖ N-UNCOUNT 不可算名詞 If there is **trouble** somewhere, especially in a public place, there is fighting or rioting there. 紛争 [also N in pl] ❑ Riot police are being deployed throughout the city to prevent any trouble. 暴動防止のために市全体に警察機動隊を動員中である. ❑ Fans who make trouble during the World Cup will be arrested. ワールドカップで騒ぎを起こすファンは逮捕されるだろう. ☗ N-UNCOUNT 不可算名詞 If you tell someone that it is **no trouble** to do something for them, you are saying politely that you can or will do it, because it is easy or convenient for you. 骨折りでない [POLITENESS 丁寧さ] ❑ It's no trouble at all; on the contrary, it will be a great pleasure to help you. お安いご用ですよ. それどころか、お手伝いできるのをうれしく思います. ☘ N-UNCOUNT 不可算名詞 If you say that a person or animal is **no trouble**, you mean that they are very easy to look after. 手数がかからない ❑ My little grandson is no trouble at all, but his 6-year-old sister is a handful. 孫の小さい男の子はぜんぜん手数がかからないが、6歳になる姉は手に余る. ☙ V-T 他動詞 If something **troubles** you, it makes you feel worried. 悩ます ❑ Is anything troubling you? 何か心配ですか? ● **trou|bling** ADJ 形容詞 悩み ❑ But most troubling of all was the simple fact that nobody knew what was going on. 一番の心配事は、誰も何が起こっているのか分からないという単純な事実であった. ❿ V-T 他動詞 If a part of your body **troubles** you, it causes you physical pain or discomfort. 苦しめる ❑ The ulcer had been troubling her for several years. 彼女は数年間かいようで苦しんでいた. ⓫ V-T 他動詞 If you say that someone does **not trouble** to do something, you are critical of them because they do not do something that they should, and you think that this would require very little effort. 一しようともしない [DISAPPROVAL 不賛成] ❑ He burps, not troubling to cover his mouth. 口を覆うともせずに公然とげっぷをする. ⓬ V-T 他動詞 You use **trouble** in expressions such as **I'm sorry to trouble you** when you are apologizing to someone for disturbing them in order to ask them something. 迷惑をかける [FORMULAE 決まり文句] ❑ I'm sorry to trouble you, but I wondered if by any chance you know where he is. ご迷惑をおかけしますが、もしかして彼がどこにいるかご存知でしょうか. ⓭ PHRASE 句 If someone is **in trouble**, they are in a situation in which a person in authority is angry with them or is likely to punish them because they have done something wrong. 問題を起こしている ❑ He was in trouble with his teachers. 先生たちとごたごたを起こしていた. ⓮ PHRASE 句 If you **take the trouble to** do something, you do something which requires a small amount of additional effort. わざわざーする ❑ He did not take the trouble to see the movie before he attacked it. 映画を非難する前に、それを見る手間をかけなかった.

Word Partnership		trouble は次の語句と使われる:
V.	**run into** trouble ■	
	have trouble ■ ☓	
	cause trouble, **make** trouble, **spell** trouble, **start** trouble ■ ☖	
	get in/into trouble, **get out of** trouble, **stay out of** trouble ⓭	
N.	**engine** trouble ■	
	sign of trouble ■ ☓ ☖	
ADJ.	**financial** trouble ■	
	big trouble, **deep** trouble, **real** trouble, **serious** trouble ■ ☖	
	heart trouble ☓	
PREP.	trouble **with** ■ ☓ ☖	
	in trouble ⓭	
ADV.	trouble **ahead** ■ ☖	

trou|bled /trʌbᵊld/ ■ ADJ 形容詞 Someone who is **troubled** is worried because they have problems. 心の安まらない ❑ *Rose sounded deeply troubled.* ローズがひどく困っているように思えた. ■ ADJ 形容詞 A **troubled** place, situation, organization, or time has many problems or conflicts. 問題の多い ❑ *There is so much we can do to help this troubled country.* この問題の多い国を助けるために, 私たちにできることがたくさんある.

trouble|maker /trʌbᵊlmeɪkər/ (**troublemakers**) N-COUNT 可算名詞 If you refer to someone as a **troublemaker**, you mean that they cause unpleasantness, quarrels, or fights, especially by encouraging people to oppose authority. いざこざを起こす人 [DISAPPROVAL 不賛成] ❑ *The fair coordinator has been given powers to expel suspected troublemakers.* 美人のまとめ役は, もんちゃくを起こすと疑われている人々を除名する権限が与えられている.

trouble|shooter /trʌbᵊlʃuːtər/ (**troubleshooters**) also **trouble-shooter** N-COUNT 可算名詞 A **troubleshooter** is a person whose job is to solve major problems or difficulties that occur in a company or government. 問題解決者 ❑ *The United Nations dispatched a team of troubleshooters to Somalia today.* 国連は本日ソマリアに調停者チームを派遣した.

Word Link some ≈ causing : awesome, fearsome, troublesome

trou|ble|some /trʌbᵊlsəm/ ADJ 形容詞 You use **troublesome** to describe something or someone that causes annoying problems or difficulties. 迷惑な ❑ *He needed surgery to cure a troublesome back injury.* やっかいな腰の負傷を治すために外科手術が必要であった.

trough /trɔf/ (**troughs**) ■ N-COUNT 可算名詞 A **trough** is a long narrow container from which farm animals drink or eat. 水, 飼葉 (かいば) おけ ❑ *The old stone cattle trough still sits by the main entrance.* 表玄関には, 古い石の家畜用水おけがまだ置かれている. ■ N-COUNT 可算名詞 A **trough** is a low area between two big waves on the sea. 波間のくぼみ ❑ *The boat rolled heavily in the troughs between the waves.* 船は大波と大波の底で激しく横揺れした. ■ N-COUNT 可算名詞 A **trough** is a low point in a process that has regular high and low points, for example, a period in business when people do not produce as much as usual. 谷 ❑ *...recovery from the industry's worst-ever trough in 2001 and 2002.* 2001年および2002年の産業史上最悪の谷間からの回復 ■ N-COUNT 可算名詞 A **trough** of low pressure is a long narrow area of low air pressure between two areas of higher pressure. 気圧の谷 [TECHNICAL 技術的] ❑ *The trough of low pressure extends over 1,000 miles.* 低気圧の谷は1,000マイル以上にも及んでいる.
→ see sound

troupe /truːp/ (**troupes**) N-COUNT-COLL 集合可算名詞 A **troupe** is a group of actors, singers, or dancers who work together and often travel around together, performing in different places. 巡業一座 ❑ *...troupes of traveling actors.* 巡業俳優一座

trou|sers /traʊzərz/

The form **trouser** is used as a modifier.

trouser 形は修飾語として使われる.

N-PLURAL 複数名詞 **Trousers** are a piece of men's clothing that cover the body from the waist downward, and that cover each leg separately. ズボン [FORMAL 形式ばった] [also 'a pair of' N] ❑ *He was dressed in a shirt, dark trousers and boots.* シャツを着て, 黒っぽいズボンとブーツをはいていた.

trou|ser suit (**trouser suits**) N-COUNT 可算名詞 A **trouser suit** is women's clothing consisting of a pair of trousers and a jacket which are made from the same material. ズボンと上着のスーツ [BRIT 英国英語; AM 米国英語 **pantsuit**, **pants suit**]

trout /traʊt/ (**trout** or **trouts**)

The plural can be either **trout** or **trouts**.

複数は **trout** か **trouts** のいずれかである.

N-VAR 可変性名詞 A **trout** is a fairly large fish that lives in rivers and streams. マス ● N-UNCOUNT 不可算名詞 **Trout** is this fish eaten as food. マスの肉 ❑ *Grilled trout needs only a squeeze of lemon.* 焼いたマスは, レモンのひとしぼりさえあればよい.

tru|ant /truːənt/ (**truants**) ■ N-COUNT 可算名詞 A **truant** is a student who stays away from school without permission. 無断欠席する生徒 ❑ *The parents of persistent truants can be put in jail.* しつこくずる休みする子の両親は刑務所に入れられることもある. ■ PHRASE 句 If a student **plays truant**, he or she stays away from school without permission. 無断欠席する [BRIT 英国英語] ❑ *She was getting into trouble over playing truant from school.* 学校をずる休みしてまずい事になりかかっていた.

truce /truːs/ (**truces**) N-COUNT 可算名詞 A **truce** is an agreement between two people or groups of people to stop fighting or arguing for a short time. 休戦 ❑ *The fighting of recent days has given way to an uneasy truce between the two sides.* 最近の戦いは, 両者間のぎこちない休戦に取って代わった.

truck /trʌk/ (**trucks, trucking, trucked**) ■ N-COUNT 可算名詞 A **truck** is a large vehicle that is used to transport goods by road. トラック [mainly AM 主に米国英語] ❑ *Now and then they heard the roar of a heavy truck.* ときどき大型トラックのごう音が聞こえた. ❑ *My dad is a truck driver.* とうさんはトラックの運転手だ. ■ N-COUNT 可算名詞 A **truck** is a vehicle with a large area in the back for carrying things with low sides to make it easy to load and unload. A **truck** is the same as a **pickup**. 小型無蓋 (むがい) トラック [mainly AM 主に米国英語] ❑ *We can only seat two in the truck.* トラックには二人しか座れない. ❑ *Throw the dogs in the back of the truck.* 犬どもをトラックの後ろに放り込め. ■ N-COUNT 可算名詞 A **truck** is an open vehicle used for carrying goods on a railroad. 無蓋貨車 [BRIT 英国英語; AM **freight car** 米国英語 **freight car**] ■ V-T 他動詞 When something or someone **is trucked** somewhere, they are driven there in a truck. トラックで運ぶ [mainly AM 主に米国英語] [usu passive] ❑ *The liquor was sold legally and trucked out of the state.* 蒸留酒は合法的に売られ, トラックで州外に運ばれた.

truck|er /trʌkər/ (**truckers**) N-COUNT 可算名詞 A **trucker** is someone who drives a truck as their job. トラック運転手 [mainly AM 主に米国英語] ❑ *...the type of place where truckers and farmers stopped for coffee and pie.* トラックの運転手や農夫がコーヒーやパイのために一休みした場所のタイプ

trudge /trʌdʒ/ (**trudges, trudging, trudged**) V-I 自動詞 If you **trudge** somewhere, you walk there slowly and with heavy steps, especially because you are tired or unhappy. 駅までの道を重い足取りで戻って行かなければならなかった. ● N-SING 単数名詞 **Trudge** is also a noun. 重い足取り ❑ *We were reluctant to start the long trudge home.* 家までの長い道のりを歩き始めたくなかった.

true /truː/ (**truer, truest**) ■ ADJ 形容詞 If something is **true**, it is based on facts rather than being invented or imagined, and is accurate and reliable. 事実の ❑ *Everything I had heard about him was true.* 彼のことで聞いたことは全部事実だった. ❑ *He said it was true that a collision had happened.* 衝突が起こったことは事実だと彼は言った. ■ ADJ 形容詞 You use **true** to emphasize that a person or thing is sincere or genuine, often in contrast to something that is pretended or hidden. 本当の [EMPHASIS 強調] [ADJ n] ❑ *I allowed myself to acknowledge my true feelings.* 自分の本当の感情を思い切って認めた. ■ ADJ 形容詞 If you use **true** to describe something or someone, you approve of them because they have all the characteristics or qualities that such a person or thing typically has. 正真正銘の [APPROVAL 賛成] [ADJ n] ❑ *This country professes to be a true democracy.* この国は正真正銘の民主制であることを断言している. ❑ *Maybe one day you'll find true love.* いつかは真実の愛を見つけるだろう. ■ ADJ 形容詞 If you say that a fact is **true of** a particular person or situation, you mean that it is valid or relevant for them. 妥当な [v-link ADJ 'of/for' n] ❑ *I accept that the romance may have gone out of the marriage, but surely this is true of many couples.* 結婚生活ではロマンスが消えてしまったかもしれないことは認めるが, これは多くのカップルに当てはまるに違いない. ■ ADJ 形容詞 If you are **true** to someone, you remain committed and loyal to them. If you are **true** to an idea or promise, you remain committed to it and continue to act according to it. 忠実な [v-link ADJ 'to' n] ❑ *David was true to his wife.* ディビットは妻に対して節操を守った. ❑ *India has remained true to democracy.* インディアはずっと民主主義に忠実である. ■ PHRASE 句 If a dream, wish, or prediction **comes true**, it actually happens. 実現する ❑ *Many of his predictions are coming true.* 彼の予言の多くが実現してきている. ■ PHRASE 句 If a general statement **holds true** in particular circumstances, or if your previous statement **holds true** in different circumstances, it is true or valid in those circumstances. 当てはまる [FORMAL 形式ばった] ❑ *This law is known to hold true for galaxies at a distance of at least several billion light years.* この法則は少なくとも数十億光年の距離にある星雲にも当てはまることが知られている. ■ PHRASE 句 If you say that something seems **too good to be true**, you are suspicious of it because it seems better than you had expected, and you think there may be something wrong with it that you have not noticed. うますぎるすぎる ❑ *On the whole the celebrations were remarkably good-humored and peaceful. It seemed almost too good to be true.* 全般的に式典は以外にも陽気で穏やかであり, ほとんどまゆつばものように思えた. ■ **to ring true** → see ring ■ **tried and true** → see tried

tru|ly /truːli/ ■ ADV 詞 You use **truly** to emphasize that something has all the features or qualities of a particular thing, or is the case to the fullest possible extent. 偽りなく [EMPHASIS 強調] ❑ *...a truly democratic system.* 真の民主主義制度 ❑ *Not all doctors truly understand the reproductive cycle.* 生殖サイクルは, 医者の全てが正確に理解しているわけではない. ■ ADV 副詞 You can use **truly** in order to emphasize your description of something. 実に [EMPHASIS 強調] [ADV adj] ❑ *...a truly splendid man.* 全くすばらしい男性 ■ ADV 副詞 You use **truly** to emphasize that feelings are genuine and sincere. 心から [EMPHASIS 強調] ❑ *Believe me, Susan, I am truly sorry.* 信じてくれスーザン, 心からすまないと思っている. ■ **well and truly** → see well ■ CONVENTION 慣習表現 You write **Yours truly** at the end of a formal letter, and before

signing your name, to someone you do not know very well. 敬具 [OLD-FASHIONED 古風な] ❑ *Yours truly, Phil Turner.* 敬具。フィル・ターナー。

trump /trʌmp/ (trumps, trumping, trumped) **1** N-UNCOUNT-COLL 集合的不可算名詞 In a game of cards, **trumps** is the suit which is chosen to have the highest value in one particular game. 切り札の組 ❑ *Hearts are trumps.* ハートが切り札の組だ。 **2** N-COUNT 可算名詞 In a game of cards, a **trump** is a playing card which belongs to the suit which has been chosen as trumps. 切り札 ❑ *He played a trump.* 切り札を出した。 **3** V-T 他動詞 If you **trump** what someone has said or done, you beat it by saying or doing something else that seems better. 打ち負かす ❑ *The Republicans tried to trump this with their slogan.* 共和党はこれをスローガンで負かそうとした。 **4** PHRASE 句 Your **trump card** is something powerful that you can use or do, which gives you an advantage over someone. 切り札 ❑ *The administration knows that's their trump card and will keep playing it as long as they can.* 行政部はそれが切り札であることを知っており、使える限り長く使い続けるだろう。

trum|pet /trʌmpɪt/ (trumpets) N-VAR 可変性名詞 A **trumpet** is a musical instrument of the brass family which plays comparatively high notes. トランペット [oft 'the' N] ❑ *I played the trumpet in the school orchestra.* 学校のオーケストラでトランペットを演奏した。
→ see **orchestra**

trun|dle /trʌndəl/ (trundles, trundling, trundled) **1** V-I 自動詞 If a vehicle **trundles** somewhere, it moves there slowly, often with difficulty or an irregular movement. がたごと走る ❑ *The truck was trundling along the escarpment of the Zambesi valley.* トラックはザンベジ谷の急斜面に沿ってがたごと走っていた。 **2** V-T 他動詞 If you **trundle** something somewhere, especially a small, heavy object with wheels, you move or roll it along slowly. ゴロゴロ転がす ❑ *The old man lifted the wheelbarrow and trundled it away.* じいさんは手押し車を持ち上げて、ゴロゴロと押して行った。

trunk /trʌŋk/ (trunks) **1** N-COUNT 可算名詞 The **trunk** of a tree is the large main stem from which the branches grow. 幹 ❑ *...the gnarled trunk of a birch tree.* カバノキの曲がりくねった幹。 **2** N-COUNT 可算名詞 A **trunk** is a large, strong case or box used for storing things or for taking on a trip. 大型旅行ケース ❑ *Maloney unlocked his trunk and took out some coveralls.* マローニは大きな旅行ケースの鍵を開け作業服を取り出した。 **3** N-COUNT 可算名詞 An elephant's **trunk** is its very long nose that it uses to lift food and water to its mouth. 鼻 ❑ *Manfred the elephant reached out with his trunk and gently scooped up the baby.* 象のマンフレッドは鼻を伸ばして赤ん坊をやさしくすくい上げた。 **4** N-COUNT 可算名詞 The **trunk** of a car is a covered space at the back or front in which you put luggage or other things. トランク [AM 米国英語] ❑ *She opened the trunk of the car and started to take out a bag of groceries.* 彼女は車のトランクを開けて食料品の入った袋を取り出したところだった。 **5** N-PLURAL 複数名詞 **Trunks** are shorts that a man wears when he goes swimming. トランクス水着 **6** N-COUNT 可算名詞 Your **trunk** is the central part of your body, from your neck to your waist. 胴体 [FORMAL 形式ばった] [usu sing] ❑ *The leg to be stretched should be positioned behind your trunk with your knee bent.* 足のひざを曲げて、ストレッチする足が胴体の後ろに来るようにすること。

trust /trʌst/ (trusts, trusting, trusted) **1** V-T 他動詞 If you **trust** someone, you believe that they are honest and sincere and will not deliberately do anything to harm you. 信用する ❑ *"I trust you completely,"he said.* 「きみのことを完全に信用しているよ」と彼は言った。 **2** N-UNCOUNT 不可算名詞 Your **trust** in someone is your belief that they are honest and sincere and will not deliberately do anything to harm you. 信用 ❑ *He destroyed me and my trust in men.* 彼から壊滅的な打撃を受け、すっかり人を信じられなくなった。 ❑ *You've betrayed their trust.* あなたは彼らの信用を裏切った。 **3** V-T 他動詞 If you **trust** someone **to** do something, you believe that they will do it. 当てにする ❑ *That's why I trust you to keep this secret.* だから私はあなたがこの秘密を守ることを当てにせざるを得ない。 **4** V-T 他動詞 If you **trust** someone **with** something important or valuable, you allow them to look after it or deal with it. 任せる ❑ *This could make your superiors hesitate to trust you with major responsibilities.* これによりあなたの上司はあなたに大きな仕事を任せるのをためらうようになるかもしれない。 ● N-UNCOUNT 不可算名詞 **Trust** is also a noun. 信頼 [also 'a' N] ❑ *She was organizing and running a large household, a position of trust which was generously paid.* 彼女は自分の所に取り仕切っていて、たっぷり給料をもらえる信用される立場にいた。 **5** V-T 他動詞 If you do not **trust** something, you feel that it is not safe or reliable. 頼る ❑ *She nodded, not trusting her own voice.* 彼女は自分の声には頼らないで、首を縦に振った合図した。 ❑ *For one thing, he didn't trust his legs to hold him up.* ひとつには、彼は自分の足で立つ自信がなかった。 **6** V-T 他動詞 If you **trust** someone's judgment or advice, you believe that it is good or right. 信頼する ❑ *Jake has raised two incredible kids and I trust his judgement.* ジェークは二人のとてもすばらしい子供を育て上げたので、私は彼の判断を信じるわ。 **7** V-T 他動詞 If you say you **trust that** something is true, you mean you hope and expect that it is true. 期待する

[FORMAL 形式ばった] ❑ *I trust you will take the earliest opportunity to make a full apology.* あなたができるだけ早い機会に完全に謝罪することを私は期待している。 **8** V-I 自動詞 If you **trust in** someone or something, you believe strongly in them, and do not doubt their powers or their good intentions. 信じる [FORMAL 形式ばった] ❑ *For a believer, replies to all the questions about life and work are far different because he trusts in God.* 彼は神を信じているので、生命と仕事に関するすべての質問に対する一信者としての答えはかなり趣を異にしている。 **9** N-COUNT 可算名詞 A **trust** is a financial arrangement in which a group of people or an organization keeps and invests money for someone. 信託 [BUSINESS 実業] [also 'in' N] ❑ *You could also set up a trust so the children can't spend any inheritance until they are a certain age.* 子供達がある年齢に達するまで遺産を使えないように信託を設定することもできる。 **10** N-COUNT 可算名詞 A **trust** is a group of people or an organization that has control of an amount of money or property and invests it on behalf of other people or as a charity. トラスト, 信託 [BUSINESS 実業] ❑ *He had set up two charitable trusts.* 彼は二つの公益信託を設定した。 **11** → see also **unit trust** **12** **tried and trusted** → see **tried**

<table>
<tr><td colspan="2">**Word Partnership** trustは次の語句と使われる:</td></tr>
<tr><td>V.</td><td>**build** trust, **create** trust, **place** trust in *someone* **2**
learn to trust **1**</td></tr>
<tr><td>ADJ.</td><td>**mutual** trust **2**
charitable trust **10**</td></tr>
<tr><td>N.</td><td>trust *your* **instincts**, trust *someone's* **judgment 6**
investment trust **9**</td></tr>
</table>

trus|tee /trʌstiː/ (trustees) N-COUNT 可算名詞 A **trustee** is someone with legal control of money or property that is kept or invested for another person, company, or organization. 受託者 [BUSINESS 実業] ❑ *The trustees of your pension fund decide which fund manager will invest some or all of your future income.* あなたの年金基金の受託者がどのファンド・マネージャーにあなたの今後の所得の一部あるいは全部を投資させるのかを決める。

trust fund (trust funds) N-COUNT 可算名詞 A **trust fund** is an amount of money or property that someone owns, usually after inheriting it, but which is kept and invested for them. 信託資金 [BUSINESS 実業] ❑ *The money will be placed in a trust fund for her daughter.* 彼女の娘の信託資金にその金は置かれるであろう。

<table>
<tr><td>**Word Link**</td><td>**worthy** ≈ *deserving, suitable* : **credit**worthy, **trust**worthy, **un**worthy</td></tr>
</table>

trust|worthy /trʌstwɜːði/ ADJ 形容詞 A **trustworthy** person is reliable, responsible, and can be trusted completely. 信頼できる ❑ *He is a trustworthy and level-headed leader.* 彼は信頼のおける穏健な指導者です。

truth /truːθ/ (truths) **1** N-UNCOUNT 不可算名詞 The **truth** about something is all the facts about it, rather than things that are imagined or invented. 事実, 真実 ❑ *Is it possible to separate truth from fiction?* 作り話と事実を区別するのは可能か? ❑ *I must tell you the truth about this business.* この件について、私はあなたに真実を伝えなければならない。 **2** N-UNCOUNT 不可算名詞 If you say that there is some **truth in** a statement or story, you mean that it is true, or at least partly true. 真実性 ❑ *There is no truth in this story.* この話には全く真実性がない。 ❑ *Is there any truth to the rumors?* そのうわさには少しでも本当のことが含まれているの? **3** N-COUNT 可算名詞 A **truth** is something that is believed to be true. 真理 ❑ *It is an almost universal truth that the more we are promoted in a job, the less we actually exercise the skills we initially used to perform it.* 仕事で昇進すればするほど、当初使っていた技量を実際に使わなくなるというのはほぼ普遍的な事実である。 **4** PHRASE 句 You say **to tell you the truth** or **truth to tell** in order to indicate that you are telling someone something in an open and honest way, without trying to hide anything. 実は ❑ *To tell you the truth, I was afraid to see him.* 本当のところ私は彼に会うのが怖かった。

<table>
<tr><td colspan="2">**Word Partnership** truthは次の語句と使われる:</td></tr>
<tr><td>N.</td><td>a grain of truth, the truth of the matter **1**</td></tr>
<tr><td>ADJ.</td><td>the awful truth, the plain truth, the sad truth, the simple truth, the whole truth **1**
absolute truth **1 3**</td></tr>
<tr><td>V.</td><td>accept the truth, find the truth, know the truth, learn the truth, search for the truth, tell the truth **1**
to tell you the truth **4**</td></tr>
</table>

truth|ful /truːθfəl/ ADJ 形容詞 If a person or their comments are **truthful**, they are honest and do not tell any lies. うそを言わない ❑ *Most religions teach you to be truthful.* ほとんどの宗教にはうそをつかないようにとの教えがある。 ❑ *We've all learned to be fairly truthful about our personal lives.* 私たちはみんな私生活に関してそれなりに正直に話すようになった。 ● **truth|ful|ly** ADV 副詞 [ADV with v]

正直に，誠実に ❏ *I answered all their questions truthfully.* 私は質問全部に正直に答えた．● **truth|ful|ness** N-UNCOUNT 不可算名詞 真実性 ❏ *I can say, with absolute truthfulness, that I did my best.* 私は最善を尽くした，と全く偽ることなく言える．

try /traɪ/ (**tries, trying, tried**) **1** V-T/V-I 他動詞/自動詞 If you **try** to do something, you want to do it, and you take action which you hope will help you to do it. 努める，しようとする，努力する ❏ *He secretly tried to help her at work.* 彼は内緒で彼女の仕事を援助しようとした．❏ *Does it annoy you if others don't seem to try hard enough?* 人が精一杯やっていない様子だと気に障るか．● N-COUNT 可算名詞 **Try** is also a noun. やってみること ❏ *It wasn't that she'd really expected to get any money out of him; it had just seemed worth a try.* 彼女は実際に彼から少しでも金をもらえるだろうとは思ってはいなかった．単にやってみる価値があるような気がしただけだった．**2** V-T 他動詞 To **try and** do something means to try to do it. しようとする [INFORMAL くだけた] ❏ *I must try and see him.* 彼に会ってみなければ．**3** V-I 自動詞 If you **try for** something, you make an effort to get it or achieve it. 得ようとする ❏ *My partner and I have been trying for a baby for two years.* パートナーと私はこの2年間子供を作ろうとしている．**4** V-T 他動詞 If you **try** something new or different, you use it, do it, or experience it in order to discover its qualities or effects. 試す ❏ *It's best not to try a new recipe for the first time on such an important occasion.* このように重要な時で新しいレシピを初めて試すのは止めた方がいい．● N-COUNT 可算名詞 **Try** is also a noun. 試み ❏ *If you're still skeptical about exercising, we can only ask you to trust us and give it a try.* まだ運動することに疑いを感じているなら，とにかく私たちを信じて試してみて下さいとしか言いようがない．**5** V-T 他動詞 If you **try** a particular place or person, you go to that place or person because you think that they may be able to provide you with what you want. 当たってみる ❏ *Have you tried the local music shops?* その近所の音楽の店を当たってみたか．**6** V-T 他動詞 If you **try** a door or window, you try to open it. 試す ❏ *Bob tried the door. To his surprise it opened.* ボブがドアを試すと，意外にもドアは開いた．**7** V-T 他動詞 When a person **is tried**, he or she has to appear in a law court and is found innocent or guilty after the judge and jury have heard the evidence. When a legal case **is tried**, it is considered in a court of law. 裁く ❏ *He suggested that those responsible should be tried for crimes against humanity.* これに責任がある者たちは人類に対する犯罪で裁かれるべきだと彼は提案しました．❏ *Whether he is innocent or guilty is a decision that will be made when the case is tried in court.* 彼が果たして有罪か無罪なのかは法廷でこの件を審理した上で決まるものだ．**8** N-COUNT 可算名詞 In the game of rugby, a **try** is the action of scoring by putting the ball down behind the goal line of the opposing team. トライ ❏ *The French, who led 21-3 at half time, scored eight tries.* ハーフタイムの段階で21対3で優勢だったフランスは8つトライを決めた．**9** → see also **tried, trying 10** to **try** your **best** → see **best 11** to **try** your **hand** → see **hand 12** to **try** someone's **patience** → see **patience**

Try and is often used instead of **try to** in spoken English, but you should avoid it in writing. ❏ *Just try and stop me!* Notice also the difference between **try to** and **try** with the "-ing" form of the verb, which often suggests doing something. ❏ *I'm going to try to open a jammed door… Try opening the windows to freshen the air.*

▶ **try on** PHRASAL VERB 句動詞 If you **try on** a piece of clothing, you put it on to see if it fits you or if it looks nice. 試着する ❏ *Try on clothing and shoes to make sure they fit.* 服や靴は合うかどうか試着してみること．

▶ **try out** PHRASAL VERB 句動詞 If you **try** something **out**, you test it in order to find out how useful or effective it is or what it is like. 試してみる ❏ *I wanted to try the boat out next weekend.* この週末にボートを試してみたい．❏ *Some owners wish they could try out the car in a race track.* 自分の車をレースコースで試してみたいと思っている人もいる．

Thesaurus   *try* また次を参照:

V.	attempt, endeavor, risk, venture **1 3 4**
N.	attempt, effort, shot **1 4**

---

try|ing /traɪɪŋ/ **1** ADJ 形容詞 If you describe something or someone as **trying**, you mean that they are difficult to deal with and make you feel impatient or annoyed. つらい ❏ *Support from those closest to you is vital in these trying times.* このようにつらい時期には最も親しい人たちのサポートが重要です．**2** → see also **try**

T-shirt (**T-shirts**) also **tee-shirt** N-COUNT 可算名詞 A **T-shirt** is a cotton shirt with no collar or buttons. T-shirts usually have short sleeves. ティーシャツ → see **clothing**

tub /tʌb/ (**tubs**) **1** N-COUNT 可算名詞 A **tub** is the same as a **bathtub**. 浴槽 [AM 米国英語] ❏ *She lay back in the tub.* 彼女は浴槽に横になった．**2** N-COUNT 可算名詞 A **tub** is a deep container of any size. 深い容器 ❏ *He peeled the paper top off a little white tub and poured the cream into his coffee.* 彼は小さな白い容器のふたのシールをはがしてクリームをコーヒーに入れた．**3** N-COUNT 可算名詞 You can use

tub to refer to a tub and its contents, or to the contents only. 容器に入った ❏ *She would eat four tubs of ice cream in one sitting.* 彼女は一度にアイスクリームを4箱食べちゃうだろう． → see **soap**

tube /tub/ (**tubes**) **1** N-COUNT 可算名詞 A **tube** is a long hollow object that is usually round, like a pipe. 管 ❏ *He is fed by a tube that enters his nose.* 彼は鼻から通した管で栄養補給を受けている．**2** N-COUNT 可算名詞 A **tube of** something such as paste is a long, thin container which you squeeze in order to force the paste out. チューブ ❏ *I went out today and bought a tube of toothpaste.* 今日は出かけてチューブ入り歯磨きを買った．**3** N-COUNT 可算名詞 Some long, thin, hollow parts in your body are referred to as **tubes**. 管 ❏ *The lungs are in fact constructed of thousands of tiny tubes.* 実際に肺は何千もの小さな管でできている．**4** N-COUNT 可算名詞 You can refer to the television as **the tube**. テレビ [AM 米国英語, INFORMAL くだけた] ❏ *The only baseball he saw was on the tube.* 彼はテレビでしか野球を見たことがない．**5** N-SING 単数名詞 **The tube** is the underground railway system in London. 地下鉄 [BRIT 英国英語] → see **transportation**

tu|ber|cu|lo|sis /tʊbɜrkyəloʊsɪs/ N-UNCOUNT 不可算名詞 **Tuberculosis** is a serious infectious disease that affects someone's lungs and other parts of their body. The abbreviation **TB** is also used. 結核

tub|ing /tubɪŋ/ N-UNCOUNT 不可算名詞 **Tubing** is plastic, rubber, or another material in the shape of a tube. 管 ❏ *…metres of plastic tubing.* 数メーターにわたるプラスチックの配管

tuck /tʌk/ (**tucks, tucking, tucked**) **1** V-T 他動詞 If you **tuck** something somewhere, you put it there so that it is safe, comfortable, or neat. しまい込む ❏ *He tried to tuck his flapping shirt inside his trousers.* 彼はひらひらするシャツのすそをズボンの中に押し込もうとした．**2** N-COUNT 可算名詞 You can use **tuck** to refer to a form of plastic surgery which involves reducing the size of a part of someone's body. 形成術 ❏ *She'd undergone 13 operations, including a tummy tuck.* 彼女は腹部形成を含む手術を13回受けている．

▶ **tuck away 1** PHRASAL VERB 句動詞 If you **tuck away** something such as money, you store it in a safe place. 貯め込む ❏ *The extra income has meant Phillippa can tuck away the rent.* この臨時収入があったのでフィリッパは賃貸料を貯め込むことができた．**2** PHRASAL VERB 句動詞 If someone or something **is tucked away**, they are well hidden in a quiet place where very few people go. しまい込む，隠す ❏ *We were tucked away in a secluded corner of the room.* 私たちはその部屋の人目に付かない片隅に隠されていた．

▶ **tuck in 1** PHRASAL VERB 句動詞 If you **tuck in** a piece of material, you keep it in position by placing one edge or end of it behind or under something else. For example, if you **tuck in** your shirt, you place the bottom part of it inside your pants or skirt. 押し込む，はさみ込む，折り込む **2** PHRASAL VERB 句動詞 If you **tuck** a child **in** bed or **tuck** them **in**, you make them comfortable by straightening the sheets and blankets and pushing the loose ends under the mattress. 寝具にくるむ ❏ *I read Lili a story and tucked her in.* 私はリリーに物語を読んで聞かせて，布団にくるんで寝かせた．

Tues.

The spelling **Tue.** is also used.

つづりの **Tue.** も使われる．

Tues. is a written abbreviation for **Tuesday**. 火曜

Tues|day /tuzdeɪ, -di/ (**Tuesdays**) N-VAR 可変性名詞 **Tuesday** is the day after Monday and before Wednesday. 火曜日 ❏ *He phoned on Tuesday, just before you came.* 彼は火曜に君が来る直前に電話した．❏ *Talks are likely to start next Tuesday.* 話し合いは来週の火曜に始まると思われます．

tug /tʌg/ (**tugs, tugging, tugged**) **1** V-T/V-I 他動詞/自動詞 If you **tug** something or **tug at** it, you give it a quick and usually strong pull. 強く引く，ぐいと引っ張る，引っ張る ❏ *A little boy came running up and tugged at his sleeve excitedly.* 小さな男の子が走りよって興奮した様子で彼のそでを引っ張った．● N-COUNT 可算名詞 **Tug** is also a noun. ぐいと引くこと ❏ *I felt a tug at my sleeve.* 私はそでを引っ張られるのを感じた．**2** N-COUNT 可算名詞 A **tug** or a **tug boat** is a small powerful boat which pulls large ships, usually when they come into a port. タグボート ❏ *…a 76,000-ton barge pulled by five tug boats.* 5そうのタグボートに引かれた7万6千トンの船

Word Link   *tu ≈ watching over : tuition, tutor, tutorial*

---

tui|tion /tuɪʃⁿn/ **1** N-UNCOUNT 不可算名詞 You can use **tuition** to refer to the amount of money that you have to pay for being taught in a university, college, or private school. 授業料 ❏ *Angela's $7,000 tuition at university this year will be paid for with scholarships.* 今年のアンジェラの大学の授業料の7千ドルは奨学金で支払われるでしょう．**2** N-UNCOUNT 不可算名詞 If you are given **tuition** in a particular subject, you are taught about that subject. 授業 [mainly BRIT 主に英国英語; AM usually **instruction** 米国英語では通常 **instruction**]

tu|lip /tˈuːlɪp/ (tulips) N-COUNT 可算名詞 **Tulips** are flowers that grow in the spring from bulbs, and have oval or pointed petals packed closely together. チューリップ

tum|ble /tˈʌmbəl/ (tumbles, tumbling, tumbled) **1** V-I 自動詞 If someone or something **tumbles** somewhere, they fall there with a rolling or bouncing movement. 転げ落ちる □ *A small boy tumbled off the porch.* 小さな男の子がベランダから転げ落ちました。 ● N-COUNT 可算名詞 **Tumble** is also a noun. 転げ落ちること [usu sing] □ *He injured his ribs in a tumble from his horse.* 彼は馬から転げ落ちてあばら骨を痛めた。 **2** V-I 自動詞 If prices or levels of something **are tumbling**, they are decreasing rapidly. 急降下する, 暴落する [JOURNALISM ジャーナリズム] □ *Profit after taxes tumbled by half to $15.8 million.* 税引き後利益は半減して1580万ドルに急降下しました。 □ *Share prices continued to tumble today on the Tokyo stock market.* 東京株式市場では今日も株価の暴落が続きました。 ● N-COUNT 可算名詞 **Tumble** is also a noun. 暴落 □ *Oil prices took a tumble yesterday.* 昨日原油価格が暴落しました。 **3** V-I 自動詞 If water **tumbles**, it flows quickly over an uneven surface. しぶきを上げながら流れる □ *Waterfalls crash and tumble over rocks.* 滝は岩にぶつかってしぶきを上げながら流れ落ちた。

tum|ble dry|er (tumble dryers) also **tumble drier** N-COUNT 可算名詞 A **tumble dryer** is an electric machine which dries washing by turning it over and over and blowing warm air onto it. 回転式乾燥機 [mainly BRIT 主に英国英語; AM **dryer** 米国英語 **dryer**]

tum|my /tˈʌmi/ (tummies) **1** N-COUNT 可算名詞 Your **tummy** is the part of the front of your body below your waist. **Tummy** is often used by children or by adults talking to children. おなか □ *Your baby's tummy should feel warm, but not hot.* 赤ちゃんのおなかは温かいはずですが、熱くてはいけません。 **2** N-COUNT 可算名詞 You can use **tummy** to refer to the parts inside your body where food is digested. **Tummy** is often used by children or by adults talking to children. おなか □ *I've got a sore tummy.* おなかが痛い。 □ *...a tummy ache.* 腹痛

tu|mor /tˈuːmər/ (tumors) N-COUNT 可算名詞 A **tumor** is a mass of diseased or abnormal cells that has grown in a person's or animal's body. しゅよう □ *...a malignant brain tumor.* 悪性脳しゅよう

tu|mul|tu|ous /tʊmˈʌltʃuəs/ **1** ADJ 形容詞 A **tumultuous** event or period of time involves many exciting and confusing events or feelings. 激動 □ *...the tumultuous changes in Eastern Europe.* 東欧の激変 **2** ADJ 形容詞 A **tumultuous** reaction to something is very noisy, because the people involved are very happy or excited. 騒々しい □ *A tumultuous welcome from a 2,000 strong crowd greeted the champion.* 2千人もの群集が騒がしくチャンピオンを歓迎した。

tu|na /tˈuːnə/ (tuna or tunas)

The plural can be either **tuna** or **tunas**.

複数は **tuna** か **tunas** のいずれかである。

N-VAR 可変性名詞 **Tuna** or **tuna fish** are large fish that live in warm seas and are caught for food. マグロ □ *...a shoal of tuna.* マグロの群れ ● N-UNCOUNT 不可算名詞 **Tuna** or **tuna fish** is this fish eaten as food. マグロ, ツナ □ *She began opening a can of tuna.* 彼女はツナの缶詰を開け始めた。

tune /tˈuːn/ (tunes, tuning, tuned) **1** N-COUNT 可算名詞 A **tune** is a series of musical notes that is pleasant and easy to remember. メロディー □ *She was humming a merry little tune.* 彼女は陽気な短いメロディーを鼻歌で歌っていた。 **2** N-COUNT 可算名詞 You can refer to a song or a short piece of music as a **tune**. □ *She'll also be playing your favorite pop tunes.* 彼女はあなたのお気に入りの流行曲も演奏するでしょう。 **3** V-T 他動詞 When someone **tunes** a musical instrument, they adjust it so that it produces the right notes. 調

律する □ *"We do tune our guitars before we go on," he insisted.* 「ぼくたちは演奏の前にギターの調律、本当にしてますよ」と彼は主張した。 ● PHRASAL VERB 句動詞 **Tune up** means the same as **tune**. 調律する □ *Others were quietly tuning up their instruments.* 他の人たちは静かに楽器を調律していた。 **4** V-T 他動詞 When an engine or machine **is tuned**, it is adjusted so that it works well. 調節する, 調整する [usu passive] □ *Drivers are urged to make sure that car engines are properly tuned.* 運転手たちは車のエンジンがきちんと調整されていることを確認するように強く勧められています。 ● PHRASAL VERB 句動詞 **Tune up** means the same as **tune**. チューンする □ *The shop charges up to $500 to tune up a Porsche.* その工場はポルシェの調整には最高500ドル請求します。 **5** V-T 他動詞 If your radio or television **is tuned to** a particular channel or broadcasting station, you are listening to or watching the programs being broadcast by that station. 合わせる, 選局する [usu passive] □ *A small color television was tuned to an afternoon soap opera.* 小さなカラーテレビには午後の連続ドラマが映っていた。 **6** → see also **fine-tune** **7** PHRASE 句 If you say that a person or organisation **is calling the tune**, you mean that they are in a position of power or control in a particular situation. 主導権を握る, 牛耳る □ *It is Coulthard who is calling the tune so far this season.* 今シーズンは今のところクルサードが主導権を握っています。 **8** PHRASE 句 If you say that someone **has changed** their **tune**, you are criticizing them because they have changed their opinion or way of doing things. 調子を変える [DISAPPROVAL 不賛成] □ *You've changed your tune since this morning, haven't you?* あなたは今朝と調子を変えましたね？ **9** PHRASE 句 A person or musical instrument that is **in tune** produces exactly the right notes. A person or musical instrument that is **out of tune** does not produce exactly the right notes. 正しい旋律で・正しくない旋律で □ *It was just an ordinary voice, but he sang in tune.* 声はごくありふれていたが彼は音を外さずに歌った。

▶ **tune in** **1** PHRASAL VERB 句動詞 If you **tune in** to a particular television or radio station or program, you watch or listen to it. 見る, 聞く □ *All over the country, youngsters tune in to Sesame Street every day.* 全国の子供たちは毎日セサミストリートを見ています。 **2** PHRASAL VERB 句動詞 If you **tune in to** something such as your own or other people's feelings, you become aware of them. 理解を示す □ *You can start now to tune in to your own physical, social and spiritual needs.* あなたはこれで今後自分が肉体的、社会的、精神的に何を欲求しているのかが理解できるようになる。

▶ **tune out** PHRASAL VERB 句動詞 If you **tune out**, you stop listening or paying attention to what is being said. 関心を失う, 無視する □ *Children rapidly tune out if you go beyond them.* あなたが子供たちに分からないことを言い出すと子供たちは即座に関心を失う。 □ *Rose heard the familiar voice, but tuned out the words.* ローズにはなじみのある声が聞こえたが、何を言っているのかは無視した。

tu|nic /tˈuːnɪk/ (tunics) N-COUNT 可算名詞 A **tunic** is a long sleeveless garment that is worn on the top part of your body. チュニック □ *...a cotton tunic.* 綿のチュニック

tun|nel /tˈʌnəl/ (tunnels, tunneling, tunneled) **1** N-COUNT 可算名詞 A **tunnel** is a long passage which has been made under the ground, usually through a hill or under the sea. トンネル □ *Boston drivers love the tunnel.* ボストンで車を運転する人たちはそのトンネルが大好きです。 **2** V-I 自動詞 To **tunnel** somewhere means to make a tunnel there. トンネルを掘る □ *The thieves tunneled under all the security devices.* 泥棒たちはすべての防犯設備の下にトンネルを掘った…。

→ see Word Web: **tunnel**

→ see **traffic**

tur|bine /tˈɜːrbaɪn, -baɪn/ (turbines) N-COUNT 可算名詞 A **turbine** is a machine or engine which uses a stream of air, gas, water, or steam to turn a wheel and produce power. タービン □ *The new ship will be powered by two gas turbines and four diesel engines.* その新しい船

Word Web   tunnel

The Egyptians built the first **tunnels** as entrances to tombs. Later the Babylonians* built a tunnel under the Euphrates River*. It linked the royal palace with the Temple of Jupiter*. The Romans **dug** tunnels when **mining** for gold. By the late 1600s, **explosives** had replaced **digging**. Gunpowder was used to build the **underground** section of a canal in France in 1679. Nitroglycerin explosions helped create a railroad tunnel in Massachusetts in 1867. The longest continuous tunnel in the world is the Delaware Aqueduct. It carries water from the Catskill Mountains* to New York City and is 105 miles long.

Babylonians: people who lived in the ancient city of Babylon.
Euphrates River: a large river in the Middle East.
Temple of Jupiter: a religious building.
Catskill Mountains: a mountain range in the northeastern U.S.

t

はガスタービン2台とディーゼルエンジン4台で駆動される予定だ.
→ see **electricity, wheel**

tur|bu|lence /t3rbyələns/ **1** N-UNCOUNT 不可算名詞
Turbulence is a state of confusion and disorganized change. 動乱
❑ *The 1960s and early 1970s were a time of change and turbulence.* 1960
年代と1970年代前半は変化と動乱の時代だった. **2** N-UNCOUNT 不
可算名詞 **Turbulence** is violent and uneven movement within
a particular area of air, liquid, or gas. 流れの乱れ ❑ *The plane
encountered severe turbulence and winds of nearly two-hundred miles an
hour.* 飛行機は激しい気流の乱れと時速200マイル近くある風に遭遇し
た.

tur|bu|lent /t3rbyələnt/ **1** ADJ 形容詞 A **turbulent** time, place,
or relationship is one in which there is a lot of change, confusion,
and disorder. 騒然とした, 動乱の ❑ *They had been together for five
or six turbulent years of break-ups and reconciliations.* 彼らは別れては
仲直りを繰り返し, もめながら5、6年付き合っていた. **2** ADJ 形容
詞 **Turbulent** water or air contains strong currents which change
direction suddenly. 荒れた ❑ *I had to have a boat that could handle
turbulent seas.* 荒れた海に耐えられるボートが私には必要だった.

turf /t3rf/ **1** N-UNCOUNT 不可算名詞 **Turf** is short, thick, even
grass. 芝生 [also 'the' N] ❑ *They shuffled slowly down the turf toward
the cliff's edge.* 彼らは芝生の上をがけっぷちに向かってゆっくり足を引
きずりながら下りて行った. **2** N-UNCOUNT 不可算名詞 Someone's
turf is the area which is most familiar to them or where they feel
most confident. 縄張り ❑ *Their turf was St.Louis: its streets, theaters,
homes, and parks.* 彼らの縄張りは, セントルシアの通り, 映画館, 家
と公園だった.

tur|key /t3rki/ **(turkeys)** N-COUNT 可算名詞 A **turkey** is a large
bird that is kept on a farm for its meat. 七面鳥 ● N-UNCOUNT 不可
算名詞 **Turkey** is the meat of this bird eaten as food. 七面鳥 ❑ *They
will sit down to a traditional turkey dinner early this afternoon.* 彼らは今
日の昼過ぎに伝統的な七面鳥のディナーのテーブルにつくだろう.

tur|moil /t3rmɔɪl/ **(turmoils)** N-VAR 可変性名詞 **Turmoil** is a
state of confusion, disorder, uncertainty, or great anxiety. 混迷
❑ *...the political turmoil of 1989.* 1989年の政治の混迷.

---

turn

❶ VERB AND NOUN USES
❷ PHRASES
❸ PHRASAL VERBS

---

❶ turn /t3rn/ **(turns, turning, turned)** **1** V-T/V-I 他動詞/自動
詞 When you **turn** or when you **turn** part of your body, you move
your body or part of your body so that it is facing in a different or
opposite direction. 向きを変える, 向ける, 向く ❑ *He turned abruptly
and walked away.* 彼は急に向きを変えて歩き去った. ❑ *He sighed,
turning away and surveying the sea.* ため息をついて海を眺めながら,
ため息をついた. ● PHRASAL VERB 句動詞 **Turn around** means the
same as **turn**. 振り向く ❑ *I felt a tapping on my shoulder and I turned
around.* 私は肩を叩かれたので振り向きました. **2** V-T 他動詞 When
you **turn** something, you move it so that it is facing in a different
or opposite direction, or is in a very different position. 向ける, 向
きを変える ❑ *They turned their telescopes toward other nearby galaxies.*
彼らは望遠鏡をほかの近くの銀河に向けた. ❑ *She had turned the
bedside chair to face the door.* 彼女は枕もとの椅子がドアに面するように
向きを変えた. **3** V-T/V-I 他動詞/自動詞 When something such as
a wheel **turns**, or when you **turn** it, it continually moves around
in a particular direction. 回転する, 回転させる ❑ *As the wheel
turned, the potter shaped the clay.* ろくろが回ると, その陶芸家は粘土
を形にした. **4** V-T/V-I 他動詞/自動詞 When you **turn** something
such as a key, knob, or switch, or when it **turns**, you hold it and
twist your hand, in order to open something or make it start
working. 回す ❑ *Turn the key three times to the right.* 鍵を右に3回回す
こと. ❑ *Turn the heat to very low and cook for 20 minutes.* 火を落とし
て20分間加熱すること. **5** V-T/V-I 他動詞/自動詞 When you **turn** in
a particular direction or **turn** a corner, you change the direction
in which you are moving or traveling. 曲がる, 入る ❑ *He turned
into the narrow street where he lived.* 彼は彼が住んでいる細い通りに入
った. ❑ *Now turn right to follow West Ferry Road.* 今度はウェスト・
フェリー・ロードに沿って右に曲がる. ● N-COUNT 可算名詞 **Turn**
is also a noun. 曲がること ❑ *You can't do a right-hand turn here.* こ
こでは右折できない. **6** V-I 自動詞 The point where a road, path,
or river **turns** is the point where it has a bend or curve in it. 曲が
る ❑ *...the corner where Tenterfield Road turned into the main road.* テ
ンターフィールド・ロードが幹線道路と合流する角 ● N-COUNT 可算
名詞 **Turn** is also a noun. 曲がっているところ ❑ *...a sharp turn in the
road.* 道路の急カーブ **7** V-I 自動詞 When the tide **turns**, it starts
coming in or going out. 変わる ❑ *There was not much time before
the tide turned.* 潮の変わり目までにあまり時間がなかった. **8** V-T 他
動詞 When you **turn** a page of a book or magazine, you move it
so that it is flat against the previous page, and you can read the
next page. めくる ❑ *He turned the pages of a file in front of him.* 彼
は目の前のファイルのページをめくった. **9** V-T 他動詞 If you **turn**
a weapon or an aggressive feeling **on** someone, you point it at
them or direct it at them. 向ける ❑ *He tried to turn the gun on me.*
彼は私に銃を向けようとした. **10** V-I 自動詞 If you **turn to** a
particular page in a book or magazine, you open it at that page.
開ける ❑ *To order, turn to page 236.* 注文するためには, 236ページを開
けてください. **11** V-T/V-I 他動詞/自動詞 If you **turn** your attention
or thoughts to a particular subject or if you **turn to** it, you start
thinking about it or discussing it. 着目する, 目を向ける, 取りかか
る ❑ *We turned our attention to the practical matters relating to forming
a company.* 私たちは会社を設立することに関する実践的な事項につい
て目を向けた. ❑ *We turn now to our primary question.* ここで最初の
質問について考えてみよう. **12** V-I 自動詞 If you **turn to** someone,
you ask for their help or advice. 頼りとする ❑ *For assistance, they
turned to one of the city's most innovative museums.* 彼らはその都市で
最も革新的な美術館に援助を求めました. **13** V-I 自動詞 If you **turn
to** a particular activity, job, or way of doing something, you start
doing or using it. 取りかかる ❑ *These communities are now turning to
recycling as a cheaper alternative to landfills.* これらの地域では今はごみ
の埋め立てより安い方法としてリサイクルを始めています. **14** V-T/V-I
他動詞/自動詞 To **turn** or **be turned into** something means to
become that thing. 変わる, なる, 変える ❑ *A prince turns into a frog
in this cartoon fairytale.* このマンガのおとぎ話では王子様がカエルに
なります. **15** V-LINK 連結動詞 You can use **turn** before an adjective
to indicate that something or someone changes by acquiring the
quality described by the adjective. なる ❑ *If the bailiff thinks that
things could turn nasty he will enlist the help of the police.* 執行吏が状況
が悪化しそうだと判断した場合には警察の協力を求める. **16** V-LINK
連結動詞 If something **turns** a particular color or if something
turns it a particular color, it becomes that color. なる ❑ *The sea
would turn pale pink and the sky blood red.* 海は薄桃色に, 空は血のよう
に赤くなる. **17** V-LINK 連結動詞 You can use **turn** to indicate that
there is a change to a particular kind of weather. For example, if
it **turns** cold, the weather starts being cold. なる ❑ *If it turns cold,
cover the plants.* 寒くなったら植物に覆いをかけること. **18** N-COUNT
可算名詞 If a situation or trend takes a particular kind of **turn**,
it changes so that it starts developing in a different or opposite
way. 展開する ❑ *The scandal took a new turn over the weekend.* 週末
の間にそのスキャンダルは新局面を展開した. **19** V-T 他動詞 If a
business **turns** a profit, it earns more money than it spends. あ
げる [BUSINESS 実業] [no passive] ❑ *The firm will be able to pay off its
debts and still turn a modest profit.* その会社は借金を払い戻してその上
ささやかな収益を上げることができるでしょう. **20** V-T 他動詞 When
someone **turns** a particular age, they pass that age. When it **turns**
a particular time, it passes that time. なる ❑ *It was his ambition to
accumulate a million dollars before he turned thirty.* 彼が30歳になる前
に100万ドル貯めるのが彼の野心だった. **21** N-SING 単数名詞 **Turn** is
used in expressions such as **the turn of the century** and **the turn
of the year** to refer to a period of time when one century or year
is ending and the next one is beginning. 変わり目 ❑ *They fled to
South America around the turn of the century.* その世紀の初めあたりに
彼らは南米に逃げた. **22** N-COUNT 可算名詞 If it is your **turn to** do
something, you now have the duty, chance, or right to do it, when
other people have done it before you or will do it after you. 順番
❑ *Tonight it's my turn to cook.* 今夜は私が料理する番だ. **23** → see also
turning

Thesaurus	turn また次を参照:
v.	bend, pivot, revolve, rotate, spin, twist **❶ 1 – 4** become **❶ 15 – 17**
N.	chance, opportunity **❶ 21**

❷ turn /t3rn/ **(turns)** **1** PHRASE 句 If there is a particular **turn
of events**, a particular series of things happen. 事の成り行き
❑ *They were horrified at this unexpected turn of events.* 彼らはこの予想
すらしなかった事の成り行きにぞっとした. **2** PHRASE 句 If you say
that something happens **at every turn**, you are emphasizing that
it happens frequently or all the time, usually so that it prevents
you from achieving what you want. いつも [EMPHASIS 強調]
❑ *Its operations were hampered at every turn by inadequate numbers
of trained staff.* 訓練を受けた従業員が不足していたための運用には
いつも難航した. **3** PHRASE 句 If you do someone **a good turn**,
you do something that helps or benefits them. いい結果 ❑ *He did
you a good turn by resigning.* 彼が辞任して君に良い結果をもたらし
た. **4** PHRASE 句 You use **in turn** to refer to actions or events that
are in a sequence one after the other, for example, because one
causes the other. 今度は ❑ *One of the members of the surgical team
leaked the story to a fellow physician who, in turn, confided in a reporter.*
その外科チームのメンバーの一人が同僚の医者にその話を漏らして,
今度はその医者が記者にその話を打ち明けた. **5** PHRASE 句 If each
person in a group does something **in turn**, they do it one after the
other in a fixed or agreed order. 順番に, 次々に ❑ *There were
cheers for each of the women as they spoke in turn.* 女性たちが順番に
話すとそのたびに喝采が送られた. **6** PHRASE 句 If two or more people
take turns to do something, they do it one after the other several
times, rather than doing it together. 交代する ❑ *We took turns*

driving. 私たちは交代で運転した. **7** PHRASE 句 If a situation **takes a turn for the worse**, it suddenly becomes worse. If a situation **takes a turn for the better**, it suddenly becomes better. 悪化する, 好転する □ *Her condition took a sharp turn for the worse.* 彼女の病状は急に悪化した.

❸ turn /tɜrn/ (turns, turning, turned)

▶ **turn against** PHRASAL VERB 句動詞 If you **turn against** someone or something, or if you **are turned against** them, you stop supporting them, trusting them, or liking them, and sometimes you work against them. 反感を買う, 反感を抱かせる □ *A kid I used to be friends with turned against me after being told that I'd been insulting him.* 前に親しくしていた子がぼくがその子の悪口を言ってたと聞いて, ぼくに敵意を抱くようになった.

▶ **turn around 1** → see **turn ❶ 1 2** PHRASAL VERB 句動詞 If you **turn** something **around**, or if it **turns around**, it is moved so that it faces the opposite direction. 向きを変える, 回す □ *Bud turned the truck around, and started back for Dalton Pond.* バッドはトラックの向きを変えてドルトン池に向けて戻り始めた. □ *He had reached over to turn around a bottle of champagne so that the label didn't show.* 彼はシャンパンの瓶に手を伸ばしラベルが見えないように向きを変えた. **3** PHRASAL VERB 句動詞 If something such as a business or economy **turns around**, or if someone **turns** it **around**, it becomes successful, after being unsuccessful for a period of time. 好転する, 好転させる [BUSINESS 実業] □ *Turning the company around won't be easy.* 会社を好転させるのはたやすいことではない. □ *In his long career, Horton turned around two entire divisions.* 長い職歴の中で, ホートンは2つの部門全体を好転させた.

▶ **turn away 1** PHRASAL VERB 句動詞 If you **turn** someone **away**, you do not allow them to enter your country, home, or other place. 追い払う, 追い返す □ *Turning Cuban boat people away would be an inhumane action.* キューバの漂流難民を追い返すのは非人間的な行為といえるでしょう. **2** PHRASAL VERB 句動詞 To **turn away from** something such as a method or an idea means to stop using it or to become different from it. 遠ざかる, 注意をそむける □ *Japanese companies have been turning away from production and have moved into real estate.* 日本の企業は生産から遠ざかりだして, 不動産に進出した.

▶ **turn back 1** PHRASAL VERB 句動詞 If you **turn back** or if someone **turns** you **back** when you are going somewhere, you change direction and go toward where you started from. 引き返す, 引き返させる □ *She turned back toward home.* 彼女は家に引き返した. □ *Police attempted to turn back.* 警察は引き返そうとしました. **2** PHRASAL VERB 句動詞 If you **cannot turn back**, you cannot change your plans and decide not to do something, because the action you have already taken makes it impossible. 戻る [with brd-neg] □ *The Senate has now endorsed the bill and can't turn back.* 上院が議案をもう承認してしまったので, 引き戻せません.

▶ **turn down 1** PHRASAL VERB 句動詞 If you **turn down** a person or their request or offer, you refuse their request or offer. 断る □ *I thanked him for the offer but turned it down.* 私は彼の申し出に感謝したが断った. **2** PHRASAL VERB 句動詞 When you **turn down** a radio, heater, or other piece of equipment, you reduce the amount of sound or heat being produced, by adjusting the controls. 下げる □ *He kept turning the central heating down.* 彼はセントラルヒーティングの温度を下げたままだった.

▶ **turn off 1** PHRASAL VERB 句動詞 If you **turn off** the road or path you are going along, you start going along a different road or path which leads away from it. わき道に入る □ *The truck turned off the main road, and went along the gravelly track which led to the farm.* トラックは幹線道路からわき道に入り, 農場へと続く砂利道を進んだ. **2** PHRASAL VERB 句動詞 When you **turn off** a piece of equipment or a supply of something, you stop heat, sound, or water from being produced by adjusting the controls. 消す, 止める □ *The light's a bit too harsh. You can turn it off.* 明かりがちょっときつすぎる. 消してくれ. **3** PHRASAL VERB 句動詞 If something **turns** you **off** a particular subject or activity, it makes you have no interest in it. うんざりさせる □ *What turns teenagers off science?* 若者の科学への関心を失わせているのは何か. □ *Greed on the part of owners and athletes turns fans off completely.* オーナーと選手の欲がファンを完全にしらけさせています.

▶ **turn on 1** PHRASAL VERB 句動詞 When you **turn on** a piece of equipment or a supply of something, you cause heat, sound, or water to be produced by adjusting the controls. つける, 出す □ *I want to turn on the television.* 私はテレビをつけようとした. **2** PHRASAL VERB 句動詞 If someone or something **turns** you **on**, they attract you and make you feel sexually excited. その気にさせる [INFORMAL くだけた] □ *The body that turns men on doesn't have to be perfect.* 男性をその気にさせる体というものは完璧である必要はない. **3** PHRASAL VERB 句動詞 If someone **turns on** you, they suddenly attack you or speak angrily to you. 突然攻撃する, 食ってかかる □ *Demonstrators turned on police, overturning vehicles and setting fire to them.* デモに参加している人たちは車をひっくり返して火をつけ, 突然警察を攻撃した.

▶ **turn out 1** PHRASAL VERB 句動詞 If something **turns out** a

particular way, it happens in that way or has the result or degree of success indicated. なる, 展開する □ *If I had known my life was going to turn out like this, I would have let them kill me.* もし私の人生がこんな風になるって分かっていたら, 私は彼らに殺されるままになっていたと思います. □ *I was positive things were going to turn out fine.* 私は事がうまく運ぶことを確信していた. **2** PHRASAL VERB 句動詞 If something **turns out to** be a particular thing, it is discovered to be that thing. 分かる □ *Cosgrave's forecast turned out to be completely wrong.* コスグレーブの森は結局全く間違っていたことが分かった. **3** PHRASAL VERB 句動詞 When you **turn out** something such as a light, you move the switch or knob that controls it so that it stops giving out light or heat. 消す □ *The janitor comes around to turn the lights out.* 管理人が電気を消しに巡回する. **4** → see also **turnout**

▶ **turn over 1** PHRASAL VERB 句動詞 If you **turn** something **over**, or if it **turns over**, it is moved so that the top part is now facing downward. ひっくり返す, ひっくり返る □ *Liz picked up the blue envelope and turned it over curiously.* リズは青い封筒を拾い上げて, もの珍しそうに裏返した. □ *The buggy turned over and Nancy was thrown out.* 乳母車がひっくり返り, ナンシーは放り出された. **2** PHRASAL VERB 句動詞 If you **turn over**, for example, when you are lying in bed, you move your body so that you are lying in a different position. 向きを変える □ *Ann turned over in her bed once more.* アンはもう一度寝返りを打った. **3** PHRASAL VERB 句動詞 If you **turn** something **over in** your mind, you think carefully about it. 考えめぐらす □ *Even when she didn't say anything you could see her turning things over in her mind.* 彼女は何も言わなくても頭の中でいろいろあれこれ考えていたのが分かった. **4** PHRASAL VERB 句動詞 If you **turn** something **over to** someone, you give it to them when they ask for it, because they have a right to it. 引き渡す □ *I would have to turn the evidence over to the police.* 私は証拠を警察に引き渡さなくてはならないだろう. **5** → see also **turnover**

▶ **turn round** → see **turn around**

▶ **turn up 1** PHRASAL VERB 句動詞 If you say that someone or something **turns up**, you mean that they arrive unexpectedly or after you have been waiting a long time. 現れる, ひょっこりやって来る [BRIT 英国英語] □ *They finally turned up at nearly midnight.* 真夜中近くなって彼らはついに現れた. □ *Richard had turned up on Christmas Eve with Tony.* リチャードはトニーを連れてクリスマスイブにひょっこりやって来た. **2** PHRASAL VERB 句動詞 If you **turn** something **up** or if it **turns up**, you find, discover, or notice it. 見つける, 見つかる □ *Investigations have never turned up any evidence.* 捜査の結果全く何も証拠が見つかりませんでした. **3** PHRASAL VERB 句動詞 When you **turn up** a radio, heater, or other piece of equipment, you increase the amount of sound, heat, or power being produced, by adjusting the controls. ボリュームを上げる, 出力を上げる □ *Can you turn up the TV?* テレビのボリューム上げてくれる? □ *I turned the volume up.* 私はボリュームを上げた.

> **Turn** is used in a large number of other expressions which are explained under other words in the dictionary. For example, the expression "turn over a new leaf" is explained at **leaf**.

turn|ing /tɜrnɪŋ/ (turnings) N-COUNT 可算名詞 If you take a particular **turning**, you go along a road which leads away from the side of another road. 曲がり角 [mainly BRIT 主に英国英語; AM usually **turn** 米国英語では通常 **turn**]

turn|ing point (turning points) N-COUNT 可算名詞 A **turning point** is a time at which an important change takes place which affects the future of a person or thing. 曲がり角, 転機 □ *The vote yesterday appears to mark a turning point in the war.* 昨日の投票で戦争の転機が示されたようです.

tur|nip /tɜrnɪp/ (turnips) N-VAR 可変性名詞 A **turnip** is a round root vegetable with a cream-colored skin. カブ

turn|out /tɜrnaʊt/ (turnouts) N-COUNT 可算名詞 The **turnout** at an event is the number of people who go to it or take part in it. 人出 □ *On the big night there was a massive turnout.* その重要な夜には大勢の人が出向いた.

turn|over /tɜrnoʊvər/ (turnovers) **1** N-VAR 可変性名詞 The **turnover** of a company is the value of the goods or services sold during a particular period of time. 総売り上げ高, 出来高 [BUSINESS 実業] □ *The company had a turnover of $3.8 million.* その会社の出来高は380万ドルだった. **2** N-VAR 可変性名詞 The **turnover** of people in an organization or place is the rate at which people leave and are replaced. 回転率 [BUSINESS 実業] □ *Short-term contracts increase staff turnover.* 短期契約は社員の回転率を上げる.

turn sig|nal (turn signals) N-COUNT 可算名詞 A car's **turn signals** are the flashing lights that tell you it is going to turn left or right. 方向指示器 [AM 米国英語] □ *He flipped his turn signal, and took a left.* 彼は方向指示器を出して, 左折した.

tur|quoise /tɜrkwɔɪz/ (turquoises) **1** COLOR 色彩語 **Turquoise** or **turquoise blue** is used to describe things that are of a light greenish-blue color. 明るい青緑色 □ *...a clear turquoise sea.* 澄んだ青緑の海 □ **2** N-VAR 可変性名詞 **Turquoise** is a bright blue stone that is often used in jewelry. トルコ石 [oft N N] □ *...beautiful silver and*

turquoise jewelry. 美しい銀とトルコ石の装身具

tur|tle /tɜrtəl/ (**turtles**) N-COUNT 可算名詞 A **turtle** is any reptile that has a thick shell around its body, for example a tortoise or terrapin, and can pull its whole body into its shell. カメ [AM 米国英語] □...*a pet turtle.* ペットのカメ □...*the giant sea turtle.* 巨大なウミガメ

tusk /tʌsk/ (**tusks**) N-COUNT 可算名詞 The **tusks** of an elephant, wild boar, or walrus are its two very long, curved, pointed teeth. きば

tus|sle /tʌsəl/ (**tussles, tussling, tussled**) V-RECIP 相互動詞 If one person **tussles with** another, or if they **tussle**, they get hold of each other and struggle or fight. 取っ組み合いをする □ They ended up ripping down perimeter fencing and tussling with the security staff. 結局かれらは囲いの柵を引き倒して警備員と取っ組み合いをするはめになった。□ He grabbed my microphone and we tussled over that. 彼は私のマイクをひっつかんで、それで私たちは取っ組み合いのいさかいをした。 • N-COUNT 可算名詞 **Tussle** is also a noun. 取っ組み合い □ Two players were ejected after a tussle on the field. 球場で乱闘の末、選手二人が退場となった。

Word Link tu ≈ watching over : tuition, tutor, tutorial

tu|tor /tutər/ (**tutors**) ■ N-COUNT 可算名詞 A **tutor** is someone who gives private lessons to one student or a very small group of students. 家庭教師, 指導教員 □...*a Spanish tutor.* スペイン語の家庭教師 ■ N-COUNT 可算名詞 In some American universities or colleges, a **tutor** is a teacher of the lowest rank. 助手

tu|to|rial /tutɔriəl/ (**tutorials**) ■ N-COUNT 可算名詞 In a university or college, a **tutorial** is a regular meeting between a tutor or professor and one or several students, for discussion of a subject that is being studied. 個人指導 □ The methods of study include lectures, tutorials, case studies and practical sessions. 勉強のしかたには、授業、個人指導、実例研究、実習がある。 ■ N-COUNT 可算名詞 A **tutorial** is part of a book or a computer program which helps you learn something step-by-step without a teacher. チュートリアル □ There is an excellent tutorial section, which carefully walks you through how to play. 使い方を丁寧に解説してくれるすばらしいチュートリアルの部があります。 ■ ADJ 形容詞 **Tutorial** means relating to a tutor or tutors, especially one at a university or college. 教員の [ADJ n] □ Students may decide to seek tutorial guidance. 学生は教員の指導を受けることもできる。

tux|edo /tʌksidoʊ/ (**tuxedos**) ■ N-COUNT 可算名詞 A **tuxedo** is a suit, usually black, that is worn by men for formal social events. タキシード一式 [mainly AM 主に米国英語] ■ N-COUNT 可算名詞 A **tuxedo** is a jacket, usually black or white, that is worn by men for formal social events. タキシードジャケット [mainly AM 主に米国英語]

TV /ti vi/ (**TVs**) N-VAR 可変性名詞 **TV** means the same as television. テレビ □ The TV was on. テレビがついていた。 □ What's on TV? テレビでなにやってる？ □ They watch too much TV. かれらはテレビを見すぎる。

tweed /twid/ (**tweeds**) N-MASS 質量名詞 **Tweed** is a thick woolen cloth, often woven from different colored threads. ツイード □...*a tweed jacket.* ツイードの上着

twelfth /twelfθ/ (**twelfths**) ■ ORD 序数詞 The **twelfth** item in a series is the one that you count as number twelve. 12番目の □...*the twelfth anniversary of the April revolution.* 4月革命の12周年 ■ FRACTION 端数 A **twelfth** is one of twelve equal parts of something. 12分の1 □ She is entitled to a twelfth of the cash 彼女はその現金の12分の1をもらう権利がある。

twelve /twelv/ (**twelves**) NUM 数詞 **Twelve** is the number 12. 12

twen|ti|eth /twentiəθ/ (**twentieths**) ■ ORD 序数詞 The **twentieth** item in a series is the one that you count as number twenty. 20番目の □...*the twentieth century.* 20世紀 ■ FRACTION 端数 A **twentieth** is one of twenty equal parts of something. 20分の1 □ A few twentieths of a gram could be critical. ほんの20分の1グラムが決定的なこともある。

twen|ty /twenti/ (**twenties**) ■ NUM 数詞 **Twenty** is the number 20. 20 ■ N-PLURAL 複数名詞 When you talk about the **twenties**, you are referring to numbers between 20 and 29. For example, if you are in your **twenties**, you are aged between 20 and 29. If the temperature is **in the twenties**, the temperature is between 20 and 29 degrees. 20代 □ They're both in their twenties and both married with children of their own. 彼らはどちらも20代で、二人とも結婚していて、それぞれ子供もいる。 ■ N-PLURAL 複数名詞 The **twenties** is the decade between 1920 and 1929. 20年代 □ It was written in the Twenties, but it still really stands out. これは20年代に書かれたものだが、今でも本当に際立っている。

24-7 /twentiforsevən/ also **twenty-four seven** ADV 副詞 If something happens **24-7**, it happens all the time without ever stopping. **24-7** means twenty-four hours a day, seven days a week. いつもいつも [mainly AM 主に米国英語, INFORMAL くだけた] [ADV after v] □ I feel like sleeping 24-7. 年がら年中眠くってしかたない。 • ADJ 形容詞 **24-7** is also an adjective. 年中無休終日営業の [ADJ n] □ Now it is a 24-7 radio station that generates $30 million a year in advertising revenue. 今では年中無休終日営業のラジオ局となり、広告活動で年間3千万ドルの売り上げがある。

Word Link twi ≈ two : twice, twilight, twin

twice /twaɪs/ ■ ADV 副詞 If something happens **twice**, it happens two times, or there are two actions or events of the same kind. 2度 □ He visited me twice that fall and called me on the telephone often. 彼はその年の秋2度私を訪ねてきて、電話もよくしてきた。 □ The government has twice declined to back the scheme. 政府は2度その計画を援助することを辞退しました。 ■ ADV 副詞 You use **twice** in expressions such as **twice a day** and **twice a week** to indicate that something happens two times in each day or week. 2回 [ADV 'a' n] □ I phoned twice a day, leaving messages with his wife. 私は1日に2回電話して彼の妻に言づてを頼んだ。 ■ ADV 副詞 If one thing is, for example, **twice as** big or old **as** another, the first thing is double the size or age of the second. People sometimes say that one thing is **twice as** good or hard **as** another when they want to emphasize that the first thing is much better or harder than the second. 2倍の [ADV 'as' adj/adv] □ The figure of seventy-million dollars was twice as big as expected. 7千万ドルという値は予想の2倍でした。 • PREDET 前限定詞 **Twice** is also a predeterminer. 2倍 [PREDET 'the' n] □ Unemployment here is twice the national average. ここの失業率は全国平均の2倍です。 ■ PHRASE 句 If you **think twice** about doing something, you consider it again and decide not to do it, or decide to do it differently. よく考えてみる □ From now on, think twice before saying stupid things. 今後は、馬鹿な発言をする前にもう一度よく考えてみること。 ■ **once or twice** → see **once** ■ **twice over** → see **over**

twig /twɪg/ (**twigs**) N-COUNT 可算名詞 A **twig** is a very small thin branch that grows out from a main branch of a tree or bush. 小枝 □ There is the bird, sitting on a twig halfway up the tree. 小鳥が木の中ほどの小枝に止まっている。

twi|light /twaɪlaɪt/ N-UNCOUNT 不可算名詞 **Twilight** is the time just before night when the daylight has almost gone but when it is not completely dark. たそがれ時 □ They returned at twilight. 彼らが戻ったのはたそがれ時だった。

twin /twɪn/ (**twins**) ■ N-COUNT 可算名詞 **Twins** are two people who were born at the same time from the same mother. 双子 □ Sarah was looking after the twins. サラは双子の面倒を見ていた。 □ I think there are many positive aspects to being a twin. 双子であることにはたくさんの利点があると思う。 ■ ADJ 形容詞 **Twin** is used to describe a pair of things that look the same and are close together. 対の [ADJ n] □...*the twin spires of the cathedral.* 大聖堂の一対の尖塔 ■ ADJ 形容詞 **Twin** is used to describe two things or ideas that are similar or connected in some way. 対をなす [ADJ n] □...*the twin concepts of liberty and equality.* 自由と平等という一対の概念 → see **clone**

twin|kle /twɪŋkəl/ (**twinkles, twinkling, twinkled**) ■ V-I 自動詞 If a star or a light **twinkles**, it shines with an unsteady light which rapidly and constantly changes from bright to faint. きらきら光る □ At night, lights twinkle in distant cabins across the valleys. 夜には、谷の反対側の遠く離れた山小屋の明かりがきらきら光る。 ■ V-I 自動詞 If you say that someone's eyes **twinkle**, you mean that their eyes express good humor or amusement. 輝く □ She saw her mother's eyes twinkle with amusement. 彼女は彼女の母親の目が愉快そうにきらめくのに気付いた。 • N-SING 単数名詞 **Twinkle** is also a noun. 輝き □ A kindly twinkle came into her eyes. 彼女の目が優しく輝いた。

twirl /twɜrl/ (**twirls, twirling, twirled**) ■ V-T/V-I 他動詞/自動詞 If you **twirl** something or if it **twirls**, it turns around and around with a smooth, fast movement. くるくる回す, くるくる回る □ Bonnie twirled her empty glass in her fingers. ボニーは空っぽのグラスを指でくるくる回した。 ■ V-I 自動詞 If you **twirl**, you turn around and around quickly, for example, when you are dancing. 回る □ Several hundred people twirl around the ballroom dance floor. 数百人の人たちがダンスホールでクルクル回った。

twist /twɪst/ (**twists, twisting, twisted**) ■ V-T 他動詞 If you **twist** something, you turn it to make a spiral shape, for example, by turning the two ends of it in opposite directions. ねじる □ Her hands began to twist the handles of the bag she carried. 彼女は持っていたかばんの取っ手を両手でねじり始めた。 ■ V-T/V-I 他動詞/自動詞 If you **twist** something, especially a part of your body, or if it **twists**, it moves into an unusual, uncomfortable, or bent position, for example, because of being hit or pushed, or because you are upset. よじる、ねじる、よじれる □ He twisted her arms behind her back and clipped a pair of handcuffs on her wrists. 彼は彼女の腕を彼女の背中でねじり彼女の手首に手錠をかけた。 □ Sophia's face twisted in perplexity. ソフィアはまごついて顔をゆがめた。 ■ V-T/V-I 他動詞/自動詞 If you **twist** part of your body such as your head or your shoulders, you turn that part while keeping the rest of

your body still. ひねる，よじる ❑ *She twisted her head sideways and looked toward the door.* 彼女は横を振り向いてドアを見た． ❑ *Susan twisted round in her seat until she could see Graham behind her.* スーザンは椅子に座ったまま後ろにいるグラハムが見えるまで身をよじった． ◾ V-T 他動詞 If you **twist** a part of your body such as your ankle or wrist, you injure it by turning it too sharply, or in an unusual direction. くじく ❑ *He fell and twisted his ankle.* 彼は転んで足首をくじいた． ◾ V-T 他動詞 If you **twist** something, you turn it so that it moves around in a circular direction. 回転させる ❑ *She was staring down at her hands, twisting the ring on her finger.* 彼女は下を向いて手を見つめながら，指にしている指輪を回していた． ●N-COUNT 可算名詞 **Twist** is also a noun. ひねること ❑ *Just a twist of the handle is all it takes to wring out the mop.* 取っ手をひねるだけでモップが絞れる． ◾ V-I 自動詞 If a road or river **twists**, it has a lot of sudden changes of direction in it. 曲がりくねる ❑ *The roads twist around hairpin bends.* 道がヘアピンカーブを縫うようにして走る． ●N-COUNT 可算名詞 **Twist** is also a noun. 曲がること [usu pl] ❑ *It allows the train to maintain a constant speed through the twists and turns of existing track.* これにより列車は今ある曲がりくねった線路を一定の速度を保ちながら通過することが可能です． ◾ V-T 他動詞 If you say that someone **has twisted** something that you have said, you disapprove of them because they have repeated it in a way that changes its meaning, in order to harm you or benefit themselves. こじつける [DISAPPROVAL 不賛成] ❑ *It's a shame the way the media can twist your words and misrepresent you.* メディアがああやってあなたの言葉をゆがめて不正確に報道できるというのはあんまりだ． ◾ N-COUNT 可算名詞 A **twist** in something is an unexpected and significant development. 意外な展開 ❑ *The battle of the sexes also took a new twist.* 男女の戦いにも新しく意外な展開があった． ◾ to **twist** someone's **arm** → see arm ◾ to **twist the knife** → see knife

Word Partnership　twistは次の語句と使われる：

ADV.	twist **around** ◾ ◾
V.	twist **and turn** ◾
	plot twist, **story** twist ◾
ADJ.	**added** twist, **bizarre** twist, **interesting** twist, **latest** twist, **new** twist, **unexpected** twist ◾

twist|er /twɪstər/ (twisters) N-COUNT 可算名詞 A **twister** is the same as a **tornado**. 竜巻 [AM 米国英語, INFORMAL くだけた]

twitch /twɪtʃ/ (twitches, twitching, twitched) V-T/V-I 他動詞／自動詞 If something, especially a part of your body, **twitches** or if you **twitch** it, it makes a little jumping movement. ぴくぴく動かす，ぴくぴくする ❑ *When I stood up to her, her right cheek would begin to twitch.* 私が彼女に立ち向かうと，彼女の右のほおがピクピク動き始めたものだった． ●N-COUNT 可算名詞 **Twitch** is also a noun. ひきつり ❑ *He developed a nervous twitch and began to blink constantly.* 彼は神経性けいれんをおこし，絶え間なく目をしばたたき始めた．

two /tu/ (twos) ◾ NUM 数詞 **Two** is the number 2. 2 ◾ PHRASE 句 If you say **it takes two** or **it takes two to tango**, you mean that a situation or argument involves two people and they are both therefore responsible for it. ひとりだけではできない，どちらにも責任がある ❑ *Divorce is never the fault of one partner; it takes two.* 離婚では非が一方にしかないということは決してない．どちらにも非があるものだ． ◾ PHRASE 句 If you **put two and two together**, you work out the truth about something for yourself, by using the information that is available to you. あれこれ考え合わせる ❑ *Putting two and two together, I assume that this was the car he used.* あれこれ考え合わせると，彼が使ったのはこの車だと想定される． ◾ to **kill two birds with one stone** → see bird

two-faced ADJ 形容詞 If you describe someone as **two-faced**, you are critical of them because they say they do or believe one thing when their behavior or words show that they do not do it or do not believe it. 裏表がある，偽善的な [DISAPPROVAL 不賛成] ❑ *The scientists saw the public as being particularly two-faced about animal welfare in view of the way domestic animals are treated.* 科学者たちは家畜がどのように取り扱われているかを考えると一般の人たちは動物愛護について特に偽善的であるという印象を持っていた．

two|fold /tufoʊld/ also **two-fold** ADJ 形容詞 You can use **twofold** to introduce a topic that has two equally important parts. 2重の [FORMAL 形式ばった] ❑ *The reason for the interview is twofold: we want to find out what he can tell us, plus we also want to find out what condition he is in.* インタビューをする理由が2重にある．彼の話を聞きたいし，さらに彼が置かれている状況がどのようなものかも知りたい．

two-way ◾ ADJ 形容詞 **Two-way** means moving or working in two opposite directions or allowing something to move or work in two opposite directions. 2方向の ❑ *The bridge is now open to two-way traffic.* この橋は今は両面通行できる． ◾ ADJ 形容詞 A **two-way** radio can send and receive signals. 送受信兼用の [ADJ n] ❑ *Each squad has a two-way radio to stay in touch.* 絶えず連絡を取り合うために各分隊が送受信兼用の無線機を持っている．

ty|coon /taɪkun/ (tycoons) N-COUNT 可算名詞 A **tycoon** is a person who is successful in business and so has become rich and powerful. 大物 ❑ *...a self-made Irish-American property tycoon.* アイルランド系アメリカ人の不動産界でたたき上げた大物

type

❶ SORT OR KIND
❷ WRITING AND PRINTING

❶ **type** /taɪp/ (types) ◾ N-COUNT 可算名詞 A **type** of something is a group of those things that have particular features in common. 型式，タイプ ❑ *...several types of lettuce.* さまざまなタイプのレタス ❑ *There are various types of the disease.* その疾患には様々なタイプがある． ◾ N-COUNT 可算名詞 If you refer to a particular thing or person as a **type of** something more general, you are considering that thing or person as an example of that more general group. タイプ，種類 ❑ *Have you done this type of work before?* この種の仕事をしたことがありますか． ❑ *Rates of interest for this type of borrowing can be high.* この手の借金は金利が高いことがある． ◾ N-COUNT 可算名詞 If you refer to a person as a particular **type**, you mean that they have that particular appearance, character, or type of behavior. タイプの人 ❑ *It's the first time I, a fair-skinned, freckly type, have sailed in the sun without burning.* 色白でそばかすだらけの日焼けしやすいタイプであるこの私が日に当たりながらもひどい日焼けをしないで航海したのはこれが初めてだ．

The **brand** of a product such as jeans, tea, or soap is its name, which can also be the name of the company that makes or sells it. The **make** of a car or electrical appliance such as a radio or washing machine is the name of the company that produces it. If you talk about what **type** of product or service you want, you are talking about its quality and what features it should have. You can also talk about **types** of people or of abstract things. ❑ *...which type of coffeemaker to choose. ...a new type of bank account. ...looking for a certain type of actor.* A **model** of car or of some other devices is a name that is given to a particular **type**, for example, a Ford Escort. Note that **type** can also be used informally to mean either **make** or **model**. For example, if someone asks what **type** of car you have got, you could reply "an SUV," "a Ford," or perhaps "an Escort."

❷ **type** /taɪp/ (types, typing, typed) ◾ V-T/V-I 他動詞／自動詞 If you **type** something, you use a typewriter or computer keyboard to write it. タイプする，タイプライターを打つ ❑ *I can type your essays for you.* あなたのエッセイを私がタイプしてあげることもできる． ❑ *I had never really learned to type properly.* 私は実際にタイプの仕方をちゃんと習ったことはない． ◾ N-UNCOUNT 不可算名詞 **Type** is printed text as it appears in a book or newspaper, or the small pieces of metal that are used to create this. 活字，印字体 ❑ *The correction had already been set in type.* 訂正はもう既に活字に組まれていた． ❑ *I can't read this small type.* この小さな活字が私には読めない． ◾ → see also **typing** → see **printing**

Thesaurus　typeまた次を参照：

N.	class, kind, sort ❶ ◾ – ◾
	print ❷ ◾
V.	transcribe, write ❷ ◾

▶ **type in** or **type into** PHRASAL VERB 句動詞 If you **type** information **into** a computer or **type it in**, you press keys on the keyboard so that the computer stores or processes the information. 打ち込む ❑ *Officials type each passport number into a computer.* 担当官は各旅券番号をコンピューターに打ち込む． ❑ *You have to type in commands, such as "help" and "print."* コマンドを「ヘルプ」とか「印刷」とか打ち込まなければならない．
▶ **type up** PHRASAL VERB 句動詞 If you **type up** a text that has been written by hand, you produce a typed copy of it. タイプして清書する ❑ *When the first draft was completed, Nichols typed it up.* 最初の下書きが完成したとき，ニコラスはそれをタイプして清書した．

type|face /taɪpfeɪs/ (typefaces) N-COUNT 可算名詞 In printing, a **typeface** is a set of alphabetical characters, numbers, and other characters that all have the same design. There are many different typefaces. 活字書体 ❑ *...the ubiquitous Times New Roman typeface.* 偏在的な活字書体であるタイムズニューローマン

type|writ|er /taɪpraɪtər/ (typewriters) N-COUNT 可算名詞 A **typewriter** is a machine with keys which are pressed in order to print letters, numbers, or other characters onto paper. タイプライター

ty|phoon /taɪfun/ (typhoons) N-COUNT 可算名詞 A **typhoon** is a very violent tropical storm. 台風
→ see **disaster, hurricane**

typi|cal /tɪpɪkᵊl/ ◾ ADJ 形容詞 You use **typical** to describe someone or something that shows the most usual characteristics of a particular type of person or thing, and is therefore a good

example of that type. 典型的な ❏ *Cheney is everyone's image of a typical cop: a big white guy, six feet, 220 pounds.* チェイネーは誰もが描く典型的な警官のイメージがあります。背が6フィートで体重が220ポンドある、大きな白人の男性です。 **2** ADJ 形容詞 If a particular action or feature is **typical of** someone or something, it shows their usual qualities or characteristics. よくある ❏ *This reluctance to move toward a democratic state is typical of totalitarian regimes.* このように国を民主化する動きをためらうのは全体主義体制にはよく見られることです。 **3** ADJ 形容詞 If you say that something is **typical of** a person, situation, or thing, you are criticizing them or complaining about them and saying that they are just as bad or disappointing as you expected them to be. らしい [FEELINGS 感情] ❏ *She threw her hands into the air. "That is just typical of you, isn't it?"* 彼女はあきれかえった様子で両手をふりあげた。「まったく、いかにもあなたらしいわね！」

typi|cal|ly /tɪpɪkli/ **1** ADV 副詞 You use **typically** to say that something usually happens in the way that you are describing. 一般的には [ADV with cl/group] ❏ *It typically takes a day or two, depending on size.* 大きさによりますが、通常1日か2日、かかります。 **2** ADV 副詞 You use **typically** to say that something shows all the most usual characteristics of a particular type of person or thing. 典型的に [ADV adj] ❏ *Philip paced the floor, a typically nervous expectant father.* 出産を目前に控えた典型的な父親であるフィリップは落ち着かなさそうに歩き回った。 **3** ADV 副詞 You use **typically** to indicate that someone has behaved in the way that they normally do. 大抵 ❏ *Typically, the Norwegians were on the mountain two hours before anyone else.* 大抵、ノルウェー人は他の人たちより2時間早く山に出た。

typi|fy /tɪpɪfaɪ/ (**typifies, typifying, typified**) V-T 他動詞 If something or someone **typifies** a situation or type of thing or person, they have all the usual characteristics of it and are a typical example of it. 象徴する、典型である ❏ *These two buildings typify the rich extremes of local architecture.* これらの2つの建物は極めてぜいたくな地方建築物の典型である。

typ|ing /taɪpɪŋ/ **1** N-UNCOUNT 不可算名詞 **Typing** is the work or activity of typing something by means of a typewriter or computer keyboard. タイピング ❏ *I'm taking a typing class.* 私はタイピングの授業を受けている。 **2** N-UNCOUNT 不可算名詞 **Typing** is the skill of using a typewriter or keyboard quickly and accurately. タイピング技術 ❏ *My typing is hideous.* 私はタイピングがひどく下手だ。

typ|ist /taɪpɪst/ (**typists**) N-COUNT 可算名詞 A **typist** is someone who works in an office typing letters and other documents. タイピスト

tyr|an|ny /tɪrəni/ (**tyrannies**) **1** N-VAR 可変性名詞 A **tyranny** is a cruel, harsh, and unfair government in which a person or small group of people have power over everyone else. 暴政 ❏ *Self-expression and individuality are the greatest weapons against tyranny.* 暴政に対する最も強力な対抗手段は自己表現と個性である。 **2** N-UNCOUNT 不可算名詞 If you describe someone's behavior and treatment of others that they have authority over as **tyranny**, you mean that they are severe with them or unfair to them. 虐待 ❏ *I'm the sole victim of Mother's tyranny.* 母から虐待を受けた唯一の被害者は私だ。

tyr|ant /taɪrənt/ (**tyrants**) N-COUNT 可算名詞 You can use **tyrant** to refer to someone who treats the people they have authority over in a cruel and unfair way. 暴君 ❏ *...households where the father was a tyrant.* 父親が暴君だった家庭

tyre /taɪər/ → see **tire**

Uu

U also **u** (**U's, u's**) /yu/ N-VAR 可変性名詞 **U** is the twenty-first letter of the English alphabet. 英語アルファベットの第21字

ubiqui|tous /yubɪkwɪtəs/ ADJ 形容詞 If you describe something or someone as **ubiquitous**, you mean that they seem to be everywhere. 至る所に存在する [FORMAL 形式ばった] □ *Sugar is ubiquitous in the diet.* 砂糖は様々な食事に含まれている.

ugly /ʌgli/ (**uglier, ugliest**) **1** ADJ 形容詞 If you say that someone or something is **ugly**, you mean that they are very unattractive and unpleasant to look at. 醜い □ ...*an ugly little hat.* 不恰好な小さな帽子 ● **ug|li|ness** N-UNCOUNT 不可算名詞 醜さ □ *Dekkeret found the landscape startling in its ugliness.* デクレットは その風景が驚くほど醜いと思った. **2** ADJ 形容詞 If you refer to an event or situation as **ugly**, you mean that it is very unpleasant, usually because it involves violent or aggressive behavior. 不快な □ *There have been some ugly scenes.* ある不快な出来事があった. □ *The confrontation turned ugly.* 対決は険悪になった. ● **ug|li|ness** N-UNCOUNT 不可算名詞 不快さ □ ...*the ugliness of sexual harassment.* セクハラの不快さ **3** to **rear** its **ugly head** → see **head**

U.K. /yu keɪ/ also **UK** N-PROPER 固有名詞 The **U.K.** is England, Wales, Scotland, and Northern Ireland. **U.K.** is an abbreviation for **United Kingdom**. United Kingdomの縮約形 ['the' N]

ul|cer /ʌlsər/ (**ulcers**) N-COUNT 可算名詞 An **ulcer** is a sore area on the outside or inside of your body which is very painful and may bleed or produce a poisonous substance. 潰瘍（かいよう）□ *In addition to headaches, you may develop stomach ulcers as well.* 頭痛の他に胃潰瘍になる可能性もある.

ul|te|ri|or /ʌltɪəriər/ ADJ 形容詞 If you say that someone has an **ulterior** motive for doing something, you believe that they have a hidden reason for doing it. 隠された [ADJ n] □ *Sheila had an ulterior motive for trying to help Stan.* シーラがスタンを援助しようとすることには秘めた動機があった.

Word Link ultim ≈ end, last : penultimate, ultimate, ultimatum

ul|ti|mate /ʌltɪmɪt/ **1** ADJ 形容詞 You use **ultimate** to describe the final result or aim of a long series of events. 最終的な [ADJ n] □ *He said it is still not possible to predict the ultimate outcome.* 彼は最終的な結果を予想することはまだできないと言った. **2** ADJ 形容詞 You use **ultimate** to describe the original source or cause of something. 根本的な [ADJ n] □ *Plants are the ultimate source of all foodstuffs.* 植物は全ての食料の根源である. **3** ADJ 形容詞 You use **ultimate** to describe the most important or powerful thing of a particular kind. 最大の [ADJ n] □ *My experience as player, coach and manager has prepared me for this ultimate challenge.* 選手、コーチ、マネージャーとしての経験を通じて私はこの最大の課題と取り組む準備ができた. **4** ADJ 形容詞 You use **ultimate** to describe the most extreme and unpleasant example of a particular thing. 最悪の [ADJ n] □ *Bringing back the death penalty would be the ultimate abuse of human rights.* 死刑の復活は人権の最大の悪用となるだろう. □ *Treachery was the ultimate sin.* 背信行為は最悪の罪だった. **5** ADJ 形容詞 You use **ultimate** to describe the best possible example of a particular thing. 究極の [ADJ n] □ *Experience the ultimate adventure!* 最高の冒険を体験しませんか. **6** PHRASE 句 **The ultimate in** something is the best or most advanced example of it. 最も優れたもの □ *Ballet is the ultimate in human movement.* バレエは最も素晴らしい人間の動きだ. □ *This hotel is the ultimate in luxury.* そのホテルはぜいたくさでは極め付けだ.

ul|ti|mate|ly /ʌltɪmɪtli/ **1** ADV 副詞 **Ultimately** means finally, after a long and often complicated series of events. つ いに □ *Whatever the scientists ultimately conclude, all of their data*

---

will immediately be disputed. 科学者が最後にどんな結論を下そうと彼らのデータは全て直ちに反論されるだろう. **2** ADV 副詞 You use **ultimately** to indicate that what you are saying is the most important point in a discussion. 結局 [ADV with cl] □ *Ultimately, Judge Lewin has the final say.* 結局ルウィン判事が最終的な決定権を持つ.

ul|ti|ma|tum /ʌltɪmeɪtəm/ (**ultimatums**) N-COUNT 可算名詞 An **ultimatum** is a warning to someone that unless they act in a particular way, action will be taken against them. 最後通告 □ *They issued an ultimatum to the police to rid the area of racist attackers, or they will take the law into their own hands.* 彼らはその地区から人種差別主義の攻撃者を排除しない場合には自分勝手に制裁すると警察に最後通告を出した.

ultra|sound /ʌltrəsaʊnd/ N-UNCOUNT 不可算名詞 **Ultrasound** is sound waves which travel at such a high frequency that they cannot be heard by humans. Ultrasound is used in medicine to get pictures of the inside of people's bodies. 超音波 □ *I had an ultrasound scan to see how the pregnancy was progressing.* 私は妊娠の経過を知るために超音波スキャンを受けた.

ultra|vio|let /ʌltrəvaɪəlɪt/ ADJ 形容詞 **Ultraviolet** light or radiation is what causes your skin to become darker in color after you have been in sunlight. In large amounts ultraviolet light is harmful. 紫外の □ *The sun's ultraviolet rays are responsible for both tanning and burning.* 太陽の紫外線は小麦色の日焼けと炎症を伴う日焼けの原因である.

→ see **skin, sun, wave**

um|brel|la /ʌmbrelə/ (**umbrellas**) **1** N-COUNT 可算名詞 An **umbrella** is an object which you use to protect yourself from the rain or hot sun. It consists of a long stick with a folding frame covered in cloth. 傘 □ *Harry held an umbrella over Denise.* ハリーはデニースに傘をさしかけた. **2** N-SING 単数名詞 **Umbrella** is used to refer to a single group or description that includes a lot of different organizations or ideas. 組織 □ *The country's blood banks are under the umbrella of the American Red Cross.* その国の血液銀行はアメリカ赤十字の傘下にある.

um|pire /ʌmpaɪr/ (**umpires, umpiring, umpired**) **1** N-COUNT 可算名詞 An **umpire** is a person whose job is to make sure that a sports contest or game is played fairly and that the rules are not broken. 審判員 □ *The umpire's decision is final.* 審判員の決定はくつがえせない. **2** V-T/V-I 他動詞/自動詞 To **umpire** means to be the umpire in a sports contest or game. 審判をする □ *He umpired baseball games.* 彼はベースボールの審判をした.

U.N. /yu ɛn/ also **UN** N-PROPER 固有名詞 The **U.N.** is the same as the **United Nations**. United Nationsの縮約形 □ ...*a U.N. peacekeeping mission.* 国連の平和維持活動

un|able /ʌneɪbəl/ ADJ 形容詞 If you are **unable to** do something, it is impossible for you to do it, for example because you do not have the necessary skill or knowledge, or because you do not have enough time or money. できない [v-link ADJ to-inf] □ *The military may feel unable to hand over power to a civilian president next year.* 軍隊は来年一般人の大統領に権力を譲り渡すことはできないと感じるかもしれない.

un|ac|cep|table /ʌnəksɛptəbəl/ ADJ 形容詞 If you describe something as **unacceptable**, you strongly disapprove of it or object to it and feel that it should not be allowed to continue. 受け入れられない □ *It is totally unacceptable for children to swear.* 子供が毒づくのは絶対に容認できない.

Word Partnership   *unacceptable* は次の語句と使われる:

ADV.   **absolutely** unacceptable, **completely** unacceptable, **simply** unacceptable, **socially** unacceptable, **totally** unacceptable

N.   unacceptable **behavior**, unacceptable **conditions**

un|af|fect|ed /ʌnəfɛktɪd/ **1** ADJ 形容詞 If someone or something is **unaffected by** an event or occurrence, they are not changed by it in any way. 影響されない [v-link ADJ] ❑ *She seemed totally unaffected by what she'd drunk.* 彼女は何を飲んでも全く変らないようだった. **2** ADJ 形容詞 If you describe someone as **unaffected**, you mean that they are natural and genuine in their behavior, and do not act as though they are more important than other people. 見せかけでない [APPROVAL 賛成] ❑ *...this unaffected, charming couple.* この気取らない魅力的なカップル

Thesaurus   *unaffected* また次を参照:

ADJ.   unaltered, unchanged **1**   genuine, honest, natural **2**

una|nim|ity /yunənɪmɪti/ N-UNCOUNT 不可算名詞 When there is **unanimity** among a group of people, they all agree about something or all vote for the same thing. 満場一致 ❑ *All decisions would require unanimity.* 全ての決定は全員の合意を必要とする.

Word Link   anim ≈ alive, mind : animal, animated, unanimous

unani|mous /yunænɪməs/ **1** ADJ 形容詞 When a group of people are **unanimous**, they all agree about something or all vote for the same thing. 同意見の ❑ *Editors were unanimous in their condemnation of the proposals.* 編集者はその提案をこぞって非難した. ● **unani|mous|ly** ADV 副詞 [ADV with v] 満場一致で ❑ *The board unanimously approved the project last week.* 取締役会は先週満場一致でそのプロジェクトを承認した. **2** ADJ 形容詞 A **unanimous** vote, decision, or agreement is one in which all the people involved agree. 満場一致の ❑ *Their decision was unanimous.* 彼らの決定は満場一致だった.

un|an|nounced /ʌnənaʊnst/ ADJ 形容詞 If someone arrives or does something **unannounced**, they do it unexpectedly and without anyone having been told about it beforehand. 公表されていない ❑ *He had just arrived unannounced from South America.* 彼は南米から前触れなく到着したばかりだった.

un|an|swered /ʌnænsərd/ ADJ 形容詞 Something such as a question or letter that is **unanswered** has not been answered. 返事のない ❑ *Some of the most important questions remain unanswered.* 最も重要な質問の一部は未回答のままである. ❑ *The report of the judges leaves a lot of unanswered questions.* 判事のリポートには未回答の質問が沢山残っている.

un|ap|pe|tiz|ing /ʌnæpɪtaɪzɪŋ/ ADJ 形容詞 If you describe food as **unappetizing**, you think it will be unpleasant to eat because of its appearance. 食欲をそそらない ❑ *...cold and unappetizing chicken.* 冷たくてまずそうなチキン

un|armed /ʌnɑrmd/ ADJ 形容詞 If a person or vehicle is **unarmed**, they are not carrying any weapons. 武装していない ❑ *The soldiers concerned were unarmed at the time.* 関与した兵士は当時武装していなかった. ● ADV 副詞 **Unarmed** is also an adverb. 武装していない [ADV after v] ❑ *He says he walks inside the prison without guards, unarmed.* 彼は看守なし、武装なしで刑務所の中を歩くと言っている.

un|ashamed /ʌnəʃeɪmd/ ADJ 形容詞 If you describe someone's behavior or attitude as **unashamed**, you mean that they are open and honest about things that other people might find embarrassing or shocking. あからさまの ❑ *I grinned at him in unashamed delight.* 私は喜びを隠さずに彼に微笑みかけた. ● **un|asham|ed|ly** /ʌnəʃeɪmɪdli/ ADV 副詞 あからさまに ❑ *Drugs are sold unashamedly in broad daylight.* 麻薬は真昼間にあからさまに売られている.

un|at|tend|ed /ʌnətɛndɪd/ ADJ 形容詞 When people or things are left **unattended**, they are not being watched or taken care of. 世話されていない ❑ *Never leave young children unattended near any pool or water tank.* 幼い子供をプールや水槽の近くにほったらかしにしてはならない. ❑ *An unattended backpack was found in a garbage pail.* うっちゃらかしになったバックパックがゴミ箱に見つかった.

un|at|trac|tive /ʌnətræktɪv/ **1** ADJ 形容詞 **Unattractive** people and things are unpleasant in appearance. 魅力のない ❑ *I felt lonely and unattractive.* 私は寂しくて魅力がないと感じた. ❑ *...an unattractive shade of orange.* 変な色合いのオレンジ色 **2** ADJ 形容詞 If you describe something as **unattractive**, you mean that people do not like it and do not want to be involved with it. 魅力のない ❑ *The market is still unattractive to many insurers.* 市場は多くの保険会社にとっても魅力がない.

un|author|ized /ʌnɔθəraɪzd/ ADJ 形容詞 If something is

unauthorized, it has been produced or is happening without official permission. 許可されていない ❑ *...a new unauthorized biography of the Russian president.* 無許可のロシア大統領に関する新しい伝記 ❑ *It has also been quite clear that the trip was unauthorized.* その旅行が許可されていないこともかなり明確にされた.

un|avail|able /ʌnəveɪləbəl/ 形容詞 When things or people are **unavailable**, you cannot obtain them, meet them, or talk to them. 入手できない ❑ *Mr. Hicks is out of the country and so unavailable for comment.* ヒックス氏は国外にいるため意見を聞くことはできない.

Word Link   able ≈ able to be : incurable, portable, unavoiable

un|avoid|able /ʌnəvɔɪdəbəl/ ADJ 形容詞 If something is **unavoidable**, it cannot be avoided or prevented. 避けられない ❑ *Managers said the job losses were unavoidable.* マネージャーは職員の削減は避けられないと言った.

Word Link   un ≈ not : unaware, uncommon, undecided

un|aware /ʌnəwɛər/ ADJ 形容詞 If you are **unaware of** something, you do not know about it. 気づかない [v-link ADJ] ❑ *Many people are unaware of just how much food and drink they consume.* 多くの人はどの位の食料と飲料を消費しているのか知らない.

Word Partnership   *unaware* は次の語句と使われる:

ADV.   **apparently** unaware, **blissfully** unaware, **completely** unaware, **totally** unaware

un|bal|anced /ʌnbælənst/ **1** ADJ 形容詞 If you describe someone as **unbalanced**, you mean that they appear disturbed and upset or they seem to be slightly crazy. 取り乱した ❑ *I knew how unbalanced Paula had been since my uncle Peter died.* 私はピーターおじさんが死んでからどれ程ポーラが精神的に不安定だったかを知っていた. **2** ADJ 形容詞 If you describe something such as a report or argument as **unbalanced**, you think that it is unfair or inaccurate because it emphasizes some things and ignores others. 偏った ❑ *UN officials argued that the report was unbalanced.* 国連当局者はそのリポートが偏っていると主張した.

un|bear|able /ʌnbɛərəbəl/ ADJ 形容詞 If you describe something as **unbearable**, you mean that it is so unpleasant, painful, or upsetting that you feel unable to accept it or deal with it. 耐えられない ❑ *War has made life almost unbearable for the civilians remaining in the capital.* 戦争は首都に残っている民間人の生活を耐えられないものにした. ● **un|bear|ably** /ʌnbɛərəbli/ 副詞 耐えられないほど ❑ *By the evening it had become unbearably hot.* 夕方までには耐えられないほど暑くなっていた.

un|beat|able /ʌnbitəbəl/ **1** ADJ 形容詞 If you describe something as **unbeatable**, you mean that it is the best thing of its kind. 卓越した [EMPHASIS 強調] ❑ *These resorts remain unbeatable in terms of price.* こうしたリゾートは価格の点でまだ他のリゾートをしのいでいる. **2** ADJ 形容詞 In a game or competition, if you describe a person or team as **unbeatable**, you mean that they win so often, or perform so well that they are unlikely to be beaten by anyone. 負かすことのできない ❑ *With two more days of competition to go China is in an unbeatable position.* 競技は残すところ後2日だが中国は無敵の立場にある.

un|beat|en /ʌnbitən/ ADJ 形容詞 In sports, if a person or their performance is **unbeaten**, nobody else has performed well enough to beat them. 負けない ❑ *He's unbeaten in 20 fights.* 彼は20回の試合で負けたことがない.

un|be|liev|able /ʌnbɪlivəbəl/ **1** ADJ 形容詞 If you say that something is **unbelievable**, you are emphasizing that it is very good, impressive, intense, or extreme. 信じられない [EMPHASIS 強調] ❑ *His guitar solos are just unbelievable.* 彼のギターのソロ演奏は全く信じられないほど素晴らしい. ❑ *The pressure they put us under was unbelievable.* 彼らが我々に与えた重圧は信じられないほど大きかった. ● **un|be|liev|ably** /ʌnbɪlivəbli/ 副詞 [ADV with cl/group] 信じられないほど ❑ *It was unbelievably dramatic as lightning crackled all around the van.* 稲妻が小型トラックの周りをパチパチ音を立て、それは信じられないほど劇的だった. ❑ *Our car was still going unbelievably well.* 我々の車はまだ信じられないほど調子が良かった. **2** ADJ 形容詞 You can use **unbelievable** to emphasize that you think something is very bad or shocking. 信じられない [EMPHASIS 強調] ❑ *I find it unbelievable that people can accept this sort of behavior.* 私は人々がこのような言動を受け入れることを信じられないことだと思う. ● **un|be|liev|ably** ADV 副詞 [ADV with cl/group] 信じられないほどに ❑ *What you did was unbelievably stupid.* あなたのしたことは信じられないほど愚かなことだ. **3** ADJ 形容詞 If an idea or statement is **unbelievable**, it seems so unlikely to be true that you cannot believe it. 信じられない ❑ *I still find this story both fascinating and unbelievable.* 私はまだこの物語が魅惑的であると同時に信じられないと思う. ● **un|be|liev|ably** ADV 副詞 [ADV with cl/group] 信じられないことに ❑ *Lainey was, unbelievably, pregnant again.* レイニーは信じられないことにまた妊娠していた.

| Thesaurus | *unbelievable* また次を参照: |

ADJ. astounding, incredible, remarkable **1** inconceivable, preposterous, unimaginable **3**

un|born /ʌnbɔrn/ ADJ 形容詞 An **unborn** child has not yet been born and is still inside its mother's uterus. やがて生まれる ❑ *...her unborn baby.* 胎児 ● N-PLURAL 複数名詞 **The unborn** are children who are not born yet. 胎児 ❑ *a law that protects the lives of pregnant women and the unborn.* 妊娠した女性と胎児の生活を守る法律

un|bro|ken /ʌnbroʊkən/ ADJ 形容詞 If something is **unbroken**, it is continuous or complete and has not been interrupted or broken. 中断されていない ❑ *...an unbroken string of victories.* 連続的な勝利 ❑ *We've had ten days of almost unbroken sunshine.* 10日間ほとんど毎日晴天の日だった.

un|can|ny /ʌnkæni/ ADJ 形容詞 If you describe something as **uncanny**, you mean that it is strange and difficult to explain. 異常な ❑ *The hero, Danny, bears an uncanny resemblance to Kirk Douglas.* 主人公のダニーはカーク・ダグラスに不気味なほど似ている. ● **un|can|ni|ly** /ʌnkænɪli/ ADV 副詞 気味が悪くなるほど ❑ *They have uncannily similar voices.* 彼らの声は不気味なほど似ている.

un|cer|tain /ʌnsɜrtən/ **1** ADJ 形容詞 If you are **uncertain about** something, you do not know what you should do, what is going to happen, or what the truth is about something. はっきり知らない ❑ *He was uncertain about his brother's intentions.* 彼は兄弟の意向をよく知らなかった. ❑ *They were uncertain of the total value of the transaction.* 彼らは取引の総額をはっきり知らなかった. ● **un|cer|tain|ly** ADV 副詞 確信なく ❑ *He entered the hallway and stood uncertainly.* 彼は玄関に入り, 自信なさそうに立っていた. **2** ADJ 形容詞 If something is **uncertain**, it is not known or definite. 不明確な ❑ *How much practical help they can give us is uncertain.* 彼らが我々にどの程度の実用的な援助をしてくれるかは不明確だ. ❑ *It's uncertain whether they will accept the plan.* 彼らがその計画を受け入れるかどうかは不確かだ. **3** PHRASE 句 If you say that someone tells a person something **in no uncertain terms**, you are emphasizing that they say it strongly and clearly so that there is no doubt about what they mean. きっぱりと [EMPHASIS 強調] ❑ *She told him in no uncertain terms to go away.* 彼女は彼にあっちへ行けときっぱりと言った.

| Word Partnership | *uncertain* は次の語句と使われる: |

PREP. uncertain **about** *something* **1**
V. be uncertain, **remain** uncertain **1** **2**
ADV. **highly** uncertain, **still** uncertain **1** **2**

un|cer|tain|ty /ʌnsɜrtənti/ (**uncertainties**) N-VAR 可変性名詞 **Uncertainty** is a state of doubt about the future or about what is the right thing to do. 不確実なこと ❑ *...a period of political uncertainty.* 政治的な不安定

| Word Partnership | *uncertainty* は次の語句と使われる: |

ADJ. **economic** uncertainty, **great** uncertainty, **political** uncertainty

un|chal|lenged /ʌntʃælɪndʒd/ **1** ADJ 形容詞 When something goes **unchallenged** or is **unchallenged**, people accept it without asking questions about whether it is right or wrong. 挑戦されていない ❑ *These views have not gone unchallenged.* こうした見解は論議されたことがなかったわけではない. ❑ *His integrity was unchallenged.* 彼の高潔さはゆるぎないものだった. **2** ADJ 形容詞 If you say that someone's position of authority is **unchallenged**, you mean that it is strong and no one tries to replace them. 確固たる ❑ *He is the unchallenged leader of the chess club.* 彼はチェスクラブの確固たるリーダーである.

un|changed /ʌntʃeɪndʒd/ ADJ 形容詞 If something is **unchanged**, it has stayed the same for a particular period of time. 不変の ❑ *For many years prices have remained virtually unchanged.* 価格は何年間も実質的に変わっていない.

un|char|ac|ter|is|tic /ʌnkærɪktərɪstɪk/ ADJ 形容詞 If you describe something as **uncharacteristic of** someone, you mean that it is not typical of them. 特徴を示していない ❑ *It was uncharacteristic of her father to disappear like this.* こんな風に姿を消すのは彼女のお父さんらしくなかった. ● **un|char|ac|ter|is|ti|cal|ly** /ʌnkærɪktərɪstɪkli/ ADV 副詞 珍しく ❑ *Owen has been uncharacteristically silent.* オーウェンは珍しく默っていた.

un|checked /ʌntʃɛkt/ ADJ 形容詞 If something harmful or undesirable is left **unchecked**, nobody controls it or prevents it from growing or developing. 抑制されない ❑ *If left unchecked, weeds will flourish.* そのままにしておくと雑草は繁茂するものである. ❑ *...a world in which brutality and lawlessness are allowed to go unchecked.* 残虐行為と不法行為が抑制されない世界

un|civi|lized /ʌnsɪvɪlaɪzd/ ADJ 形容詞 If you describe someone's behavior as **uncivilized**, you find it unacceptable, for example because it is very cruel or very rude. 野蛮な [DISAPPROVAL 不賛成] ❑ *I think any sport involving harm to animals is barbaric and uncivilized.* 私は動物に害を与えるスポーツは全て原始的で野蛮だと思う.

un|cle /ʌŋkəl/ (**uncles**) N-FAMILY; N-TITLE 家族名詞, 称号名詞 Someone's **uncle** is the brother of their mother or father, or the husband of their aunt. おじ ❑ *My uncle was the mayor of Memphis.* 私のおじはメンフィスの市長だった. ❑ *An e-mail from Uncle Fred arrived.* フレッドおじさんからのEメールが届いた.
→ see **family**

un|clear /ʌnklɪər/ **1** ADJ 形容詞 If something is **unclear**, it is not known or not certain. はっきりしない ❑ *It is unclear how much popular support they have among the island's population.* その島の住民の間で彼らがどの程度支持されているのか不確かだ. ❑ *Just what the soldier was doing there is unclear.* そこで兵士がいったい何をしていたかは分からない. **2** ADJ 形容詞 If you are **unclear** about something, you do not understand it well or are not sure about it. はっきりとは分からない [v-link ADJ] ❑ *He is still unclear about his own future.* 彼は自分の将来がどうなるかはまだはっきり分からない.

un|com|fort|able /ʌnkʌmftəbəl, -kʌmfərtə-/ **1** ADJ 形容詞 If you are **uncomfortable**, you are slightly worried or embarrassed, and not relaxed and confident. 困った ❑ *The request for money made them feel uncomfortable.* 金の要求は彼らに気まずい思いをさせた. ❑ *If you are uncomfortable with your therapist, you must discuss it.* セラピストが気に入らない場合はそれについて話し合わなければならない. ● **un|com|fort|ably** /ʌnkʌmftəbli, -kʌmfərtə-/ 副詞 心地悪く ❑ *Sandy leaned across the table, his face uncomfortably close to Brad's.* サンディはテーブル越しに身を乗り出し, 顔をブラッドの顔に心地悪いほど近づけた. ❑ *I became uncomfortably aware that the people at the next table were watching me.* 私は隣のテーブルの人々が私をじっと見ているのを心地悪いほど気づいた. **2** ADJ 形容詞 Something that is **uncomfortable** makes you feel slight pain or physical discomfort when you experience it or use it. 心地よくない ❑ *Wigs are hot and uncomfortable to wear constantly.* かつらはいつも被るには暑くて心地よくない. ❑ *The ride back to the center of the town was hot and uncomfortable.* 街の中心部に車で戻ったが車の中は暑くて不快だった. ● **un|com|fort|ably** ADV 副詞 [ADV adj] 心地よくないほど ❑ *The water was uncomfortably cold.* 水はひどく冷たかった. **3** ADJ 形容詞 If you are **uncomfortable**, you are not physically content and relaxed, and feel slight pain or discomfort. 不快感を抱く ❑ *I sometimes feel uncomfortable after eating in the evening.* 私は夕食後気持ちが悪くなることがある. ● **un|com|fort|ably** ADV 副詞 不快感を抱くほど ❑ *He felt uncomfortably hot.* 彼は気持ちが悪くなるほど暑かった.

| Thesaurus | *uncomfortable* また次を参照: |

ADJ. awkward, embarrassed, troubled; (*ant.*) comfortable **1** irritating, painful **2** **3**

| Word Link | un ≈ not : unaware, uncommon, undecided |

un|com|mon /ʌnkɒmən/ ADJ 形容詞 If you describe something as **uncommon**, you mean that it does not happen often or is not often seen. 珍しい ❑ *Fortunately, cancer of the breast in young women is uncommon.* 幸い若い女性の乳がんはまれである.

un|com|pli|cat|ed /ʌnkɒmplɪkeɪtɪd/ ADJ 形容詞 If you describe someone or something as **uncomplicated**, you approve of them because they are easy to deal with or understand. 複雑でない [APPROVAL 賛成] ❑ *She is a beautiful, uncomplicated girl.* 彼女は美しく純真な少女だ.

un|com|pro|mis|ing /ʌnkɒmprəmaɪzɪŋ/ **1** ADJ 形容詞 If you describe someone as **uncompromising**, you mean that they are determined not to change their opinions or aims in any way. 妥協しない ❑ *Voters have elected an uncompromising nationalist as their new president.* 有権者は信念の固い愛国主義者を新しい大統領に選んだ. **2** ADJ 形容詞 If you describe something as **uncompromising**, you mean that it does not attempt to make something that is shocking or unpleasant any more acceptable to people. 徹底的な ❑ *...a movie of uncompromising brutality.* 徹底的に残虐な映画

un|con|cerned /ʌnkənsɜrnd/ ADJ 形容詞 If a person is **unconcerned about** something, usually something that most people would care about, they are not interested in it or worried about it. 関心を持たない ❑ *Paul was unconcerned about what he had done.* ポールは自分のしたことを気にしていなかった.

un|con|di|tion|al /ʌnkəndɪʃənəl/ ADJ 形容詞 If you describe something as **unconditional**, you mean that the person doing or giving it does not require anything to be done by other people in exchange. 無条件の ❑ *Children need unconditional love from their parents.* 子供には両親の無条件の愛情が必要だ. ● **un|con|di|tion|al|ly** ADV 副詞 [ADV with v] 無条件で ❑ *The hostages were released unconditionally.* 捕虜は無条件で解放された.

un|con|firmed /ʌnkənfɜrmd/ ADJ 形容詞 If a report or a rumor is **unconfirmed**, there is no definite proof as to whether it is true

or not. 確認されていない ❑ *There are unconfirmed reports of several small villages buried by mudslides.* いくつかの村落が泥流で埋められたという未確認の報告がある.

un|con|nect|ed /ʌnkənɛktɪd/ ADJ 形容詞 If one thing is **unconnected with** another or the two things are **unconnected**, the things are not related to each other in any way. 関係のない ❑ *She had personal problems unconnected with her marriage.* 彼女は結婚とは無関係の個人的な問題を抱えていた.

Word Link	*sci ≈ knowing : conscience, science, unconscious*

un|con|scious /ʌnkɒnʃəs/ ■ ADJ 形容詞 Someone who is **unconscious** is in a state similar to sleep, usually as the result of a serious injury or a lack of oxygen. 意識不明の ❑ *By the time the ambulance arrived he was unconscious.* 救急車が到着した時には彼は意識不明だった. ● **un|con|scious|ness** N-UNCOUNT 不可算名詞 意識不明 ❑ *He knew that he might soon lapse into unconsciousness.* 彼はまもなく意識を失うかもしれないことを知っていた. ② ADJ 形容詞 [v-link ADJ 'of' n] If you are **unconscious of** something, you are unaware of it. 気づかない ❑ *He himself seemed totally unconscious of his failure.* 彼自身が自分の失敗についてまったく気づいていないようだった. ● **un|con|scious|ly** ADV 副詞 無意識に ❑ *"I was very unsure of myself after the divorce," she says, unconsciously sweeping back the curls from her forehead.* 「私は離婚の後, 自信が全くありませんでした」と彼女は額から巻き毛を無意識に払いのけながら言った. ❸ ADJ 形容詞 If feelings or attitudes are **unconscious**, you are not aware that you have them, but they show in the way that you behave. 気づいていない ❑ *...my unconscious ambivalence about becoming a mother.* 母親になることについての無意識なためらい ● **un|con|scious|ly** ADV 副詞 無意識に ❑ *Many women whose fathers left home unconsciously expect to be betrayed by their own mates.* 父親に見捨てられた女性の多くは無意識に自らの友人に裏切られると思っている.
→ see **dream**

Thesaurus	*unconscious* また次を参照:
ADJ.	comatose; (*ant.*) conscious ■
	subconscious, subliminal; (*ant.*) conscious ❸

un|con|sti|tu|tion|al /ʌnkɒnstɪtjuʃənəl/ ADJ 形容詞 If something is **unconstitutional**, it breaks the rules of a constitution. 憲法違反の ❑ *Lincoln decided that seceding from the Union was unconstitutional.* リンカーンは連邦軍から脱退することは憲法違反だと判断した. ● **un|con|sti|tu|tion|al|ly** ADV 副詞 [ADV with v] 憲法に違反して ❑ *They claimed that he acted unconstitutionally when he banned their party.* 彼らは彼に政党を禁止された時, 憲法違反だと主張した. ● **un|con|sti|tu|tion|al|ity** /ʌnkɒnstɪtjuʃənæliti/ N-UNCOUNT 不可算名詞 憲法に違反すること ❑ *...the unconstitutionality of such legislation.* そうした規制が憲法違反を犯していること

un|con|trol|la|ble /ʌnkəntroʊləbl/ ■ ADJ 形容詞 If you describe a feeling or physical action as **uncontrollable**, you mean that you cannot control it or prevent yourself from feeling or doing it. 抑制できない ❑ *It had been a time of almost uncontrollable excitement.* 抑制できないほど興奮した時代だった. ❑ *William was seized with uncontrollable rage.* ウィリアムは抑えきれない怒りに襲われた. ● **un|con|trol|la|bly** /ʌnkəntroʊləbli/ ADV 副詞 抑えきれずに ❑ *I started shaking uncontrollably and began to cry.* 私は抑えきれずに震え始め, 泣き出した. ② ADJ 形容詞 If you describe a person as **uncontrollable**, you mean that their behavior is bad and that nobody can make them behave more sensibly. 手に負えない ❑ *Mark was withdrawn and uncontrollable.* マークは内気で手に負えなかった. ❸ ADJ 形容詞 If you describe a situation or series of events as **uncontrollable**, you believe that nothing can be done to control them or to prevent things from getting worse. 制御できない ❑ *If political problems are not resolved, the situation may become uncontrollable.* 政治問題が解決されない場合には状況は制御できなくなるかもしれない.

un|con|trolled /ʌnkəntroʊld/ ■ ADJ 形容詞 If you describe someone's behavior as **uncontrolled**, you mean they appear unable to stop it or to make it less extreme. 制御されていない ❑ *His uncontrolled behavior disturbed the entire class.* 彼の手に負えない態度はクラス全体の邪魔になった. ② ADJ 形容詞 If a situation or activity is **uncontrolled**, no one is controlling it or preventing it from continuing or growing. 制御されていない ❑ *The capital, Nairobi, is choking on uncontrolled immigration.* 首都のナイロビは制御されていない移民で1杯である.

un|con|ven|tion|al /ʌnkənvɛnʃənəl/ ■ ADJ 形容詞 If you describe a person or their attitude or behavior as **unconventional**, you mean that they do not behave in the same way as most other people in their society. 型にはまらない ❑ *Linus Pauling is an unconventional genius.* ライナス・ポーリングは型破りの天才だ. ❑ *He was known for his unconventional behavior.* 彼は型にはまらない言動で知られている. ② ADJ 形容詞 An **unconventional** way of doing something is not the usual way of doing it, and may be

surprising. 型にはまらない ❑ *The vaccine had been produced by an unconventional technique.* ワクチンは型破りな技術で生産されていた. ❑ *Despite his unconventional methods, he has inspired students more than anyone else.* 彼はその型破りの方法にもかかわらず誰よりも学生にインスピレーションを与えた.

un|con|vinc|ing /ʌnkənvɪnsɪŋ/ ■ ADJ 形容詞 If you describe something such as an argument or explanation as **unconvincing**, you find it difficult to believe because it does not seem real. 説得力のない ❑ *Mr. Patel phoned the university for an explanation, and he was given the usual unconvincing excuses.* パテル氏は説明を聞くために大学に電話したがいつもの納得できない言い訳を与えられた. ● **un|con|vinc|ing|ly** ADV 副詞 [ADV with v] 説得力なく ❑ *"It's not that I don't believe you, Meg," Jack said, unconvincingly.* 「メグ, 君を信じないわけではないが」とジャックは説得力なく言った. ② ADJ 形容詞 If you describe a story or a character in a story as **unconvincing**, you think they do not seem likely or real. 非現実的な ❑ *...an unconvincing love story.* 非現実的な恋愛物語

un|count|able noun /ʌnkaʊntəbl naʊn/ (**uncountable nouns**) N-COUNT 可算名詞 An **uncountable noun** is a noun such as "gold," "information," or "furniture" which has only one form and can be used without a determiner. 不可算名詞

un|count noun /ʌnkaʊnt naʊn/ (**uncount nouns**) N-COUNT 可算名詞 An **uncount noun** is the same as an **uncountable noun**. uncountable nounの縮約形

un|cov|er /ʌnkʌvər/ (**uncovers, uncovering, uncovered**) ■ V-T 他動詞 If you **uncover** something, especially something that has been kept secret, you discover or find out about it. 発見する ❑ *Auditors said they had uncovered evidence of fraud.* 会計検査官は詐欺の証拠を発見したと述べた. ② V-T 他動詞 To **uncover** something means to remove something that is covering it. おおいを取る ❑ *When the seedlings sprout, uncover the tray.* 芽が出たらトレーのおおいを取りなさい.

Word Partnership	*uncover*は次の語句と使われる:
N.	uncover **evidence**, uncover **a plot**, uncover **the truth** ■
V.	**help** uncover *something* ■ ②

un|daunt|ed /ʌndɔntɪd/ ADJ 形容詞 If you are **undaunted**, you are not at all afraid or worried about dealing with something, especially something that would frighten or worry most people. 恐れない ❑ *Undaunted by the scale of the job, Lesley set about planning how each room should look.* レスリーは作業の規模に臆（おく）せずに部屋のデザインを計画し始めた.

Word Link	*un ≈ not : unaware, uncommon, undecided*

un|decid|ed /ʌndɪsaɪdɪd/ ADJ 形容詞 If someone is **undecided**, they cannot decide about something or have not yet decided about it. 未決定の ❑ *After college she was still undecided as to what career she wanted to pursue.* 大学卒業後, 彼女はどんな仕事がしたいかについてまだ決めかねていた.

Word Link	*demo ≈ people : democracy, demographic, undemocratic*

un|demo|crat|ic /ʌndɛməkrætɪk/ ADJ 形容詞 A system, process, or decision that is **undemocratic** is one that is controlled or made by one person or a small number of people, rather than by all the people involved. 非民主的な ❑ *...the undemocratic rule of the former political establishment.* 旧政治態勢の非民主的な規則 ❑ *Opponents denounced the law as undemocratic and unconstitutional.* 反対者はこの法律を非民主的で憲法違反だと非難した.

un|deni|able /ʌndɪnaɪəbl/ ADJ 形容詞 If you say that something is **undeniable**, you mean that it is definitely true. 否定できない ❑ *Her charm is undeniable.* 彼女の魅力は明白だ. ● **un|deni|ably** /ʌndɪnaɪəbli/ ADV 副詞 否定できないほど ❑ *Bringing up a baby is undeniably hard work.* 育児は明らかに重労働だ.

un|der /ʌndər/

In addition to the uses shown below, **under** is also used in phrasal verbs such as "go under" and "knuckle under."

下に示された用法に加えて, **under**は **go under** や **knuckle under** のような句動詞にも使われる.

■ PREP 前置詞 If a person or thing is **under** something, they are at a lower level than that thing, and may be covered or hidden by it. 下に ❑ *They found a labyrinth of tunnels under the ground.* 彼らは地下に入り組んだトンネルを見つけた. ❑ *...swimming in the pool or lying under an umbrella.* プールで泳いだり傘の下で横たわること ❑ *A path runs under the trees.* 小道は木の下を走っている. ② PREP 前置詞 In a place such as an ocean, river, or swimming pool, if someone or something is **under** the water, they are fully in the water and covered by it. 下に ❑ *She held her breath for three minutes under the water.* 彼女は水面下で3分間息を止めた. ● ADV 副詞 **Under** is also an

adverb. 水面下に [ADV after v] ❏ *He took a deep breath before he went under.* 彼は飛び込む前に深呼吸した. ❸ PREP 前置詞 If you go **under** something, you move from one side to the other of something that is at a higher level than you. 下に ❏ *He went under a brick arch.* 彼はレンガのアーチの下をくぐった. ❹ PREP 前置詞 Something that is **under** a layer of something, especially clothing, is covered by that layer. 内側に ❏ *I was wearing two sweaters under the green army jacket.* 私は緑色の軍隊のジャケットの下にセーターを2枚着ていた. ❏ *a faded striped shirt under a knit sweater.* ニットのセーターの下の色あせたストライプのシャツ ❺ PREP 前置詞 You can use **under** before a noun to indicate that a person or thing is being affected by something or is going through a particular process. 受けて ❏ *...fishermen whose livelihoods are under threat.* 生活が脅かされる漁民 ❏ *Firemen said they had the blaze under control.* 消防士は火が燃え広がるのを抑えたと述べた. ❻ PREP 前置詞 If something happens **under** particular circumstances or conditions, it happens when those circumstances or conditions exist. もとで ❏ *His best friend died under questionable circumstances.* 彼の親友は不審な状況のもとで死んだ. ❏ *Under normal conditions, only about 20 to 40 percent of vitamin E is absorbed.* 通常はビタミンEの約20-40%のみが吸収される. ❼ PREP 前置詞 If something happens **under** a law, agreement, or system, it happens because that law, agreement, or system says that it should happen. もとで ❏ *Under law, your employer has the right to hire a temporary worker to replace you.* 法律のもとであなたの雇用主はあなたの代わりに臨時職員を雇う権利を持っている. ❏ *Under the new regulations, one in five cars may need repairs costing as much as $120.* 新しい規制のもとで2割の車は最高120ドルの修理が必要になるかもしれない. ❽ PREP 前置詞 If something happens **under** a particular person or government, it happens when that person or government is in power. もとで ❏ *There would be no new taxes under his leadership.* 彼の指導のもとでは新しい税金が導入されることはないと思う. ❏ *...the realities of life under a brutal dictatorship.* 残忍な独裁政権下の生活の現実 ❾ PREP 前置詞 If you study or work **under** a particular person, that person teaches you or tells you what to do. もとに ❏ *Kiefer was just one of the artists who had studied under Beuys in the early Sixties.* キーファーは60年代初期にボイスのもとに学んだアーティストの1人にすぎなかった. ❏ *General Lewis Hyde had served under General Mitchell.* ルイス・ハイド大将はミッチェル大将に仕えた. ❿ PREP 前置詞 If you do something **under** a particular name, you use that name instead of your real name. という名で ❏ *Were any of your books published under the name Amanda Fairchild?* あなたの本にはアマンダ・フェアチャイルドという名で出版された本がありますか. ⓫ PREP 前置詞 You use **under** to say which section of a list, book, or system something is in. 中に ❏ *The "General Diseases of the Eye" study is filed under E.* 「一般的な眼病」研究はEの下にファイルされている. ⓬ PREP 前置詞 If something or someone is **under** a particular age or amount, they are less than that age or amount. 未満の [PREP amount] ❏ *...jobs for those under 65.* 65歳未満の人向けの仕事 ❏ *Nearly half of mothers with children under five have a job.* 5歳以下の子供を持つ母親の半分近くが仕事を持っている. ● ADV 副詞 **Under** is also an adverb. 以下で [amount 'and' v] ❏ *...free or subsidized health insurance for children 13 and under.* 13歳以下の子供のための無料または助成金の支給された健康保険 ⓭ **under wraps** → see **wrap**

under|brush /ʌndərbrʌʃ/ N-UNCOUNT 不可算名詞 **Underbrush** consists of bushes and plants growing close together under the trees in a forest. 下草 [AM 米国英語] ❏ *...the cool underbrush of the rainforest.* 多雨林の冷たい下草

under|cov|er /ʌndərkʌvər/ ADJ 形容詞 **Undercover** work involves secretly obtaining information for the government or the police. 秘密の ❏ *...an undercover operation designed to catch drug smugglers.* 麻薬密輸者を捕らえるための秘密活動 ❏ *undercover FBI agents.* FBIの覆面捜査官 ● ADV 副詞 **Undercover** is also an adverb. 秘密で [ADV after v] ❏ *Swanson persuaded Hubley to work undercover to capture the killer.* スワンソンはハブリーに殺人犯を捕まえるために秘密捜査員となることを説得した.

under|cur|rent /ʌndərkɜrənt/ (**undercurrents**) ❶ N-COUNT 可算名詞 If there is an **undercurrent of** a feeling, you are hardly aware of the feeling, but it influences the way you think or behave. 低意 ❏ *...the strong undercurrent of pro-business sentiment in Congress.* 国会における企業志向の強い低意 ❷ N-COUNT 可算名詞 An **undercurrent** is a strong current of water that is moving below the surface current and in a different direction to it. 底流 ❏ *Karen tried to swim after him but the strong undercurrent swept them apart.* カレンは彼の後に続こうとしたが強い底流が彼らを引き離した.

under|cut /ʌndərkʌt/ (**undercuts, undercutting**)

The form **undercut** is used in the present tense and is also the past tense and past participle.

undercut 形は現在時制に使われ、過去時制と過去分詞でもある.

V-T 他動詞 If you **undercut** someone or **undercut** their prices, you sell a product more cheaply than they do. 安く売る [BUSINESS 実業] ❏ *Subsidies allow growers to undercut competitors and depress world prices.* 助成金は栽培者が競争者の価格より安く販売し、世界価格を抑え

ることを可能にする. ❏ *...promises to undercut air fares on some routes by 40 percent.* 一部のルートの航空運賃を40%安く売る約束

under|de|vel|oped /ʌndərdɪvɛləpt/ ADJ 形容詞 An **underdeveloped** country or region does not have modern industries and usually has a low standard of living. Some people dislike this term and prefer to use **developing**. 低開発の ❏ *Underdeveloped countries should be assisted by allowing them access to modern technology.* 低開発国は近代的技術の利用という形で援助を受けるべきである.

under|dog /ʌndərdɔg/ (**underdogs**) N-COUNT 可算名詞 The **underdog** in a competition or situation is the person who seems least likely to succeed or win. 勝てそうもない人 ❏ *Most of the crowd were cheering for the underdog to win just this one time.* 大半の群衆は今回だけは勝ち目の薄い人が勝つよう応援した.

under|esti|mate /ʌndərɛstɪmeɪt/ (**underestimates, underestimating, underestimated**) ❶ V-T 他動詞 If you **underestimate** something, you do not realize how large or great it is or will be. 過小評価する ❏ *None of us should ever underestimate the degree of difficulty women face in career advancement.* 女性がキャリアアップを試みる際に直面する問題の規模を過小評価してはならない. ❷ V-T 他動詞 If you **underestimate** someone, you do not realize what they are capable of doing. 見くびる ❏ *I think a lot of people still underestimate him.* 多くの人々はまだ彼を過小評価していると私は思う.

under|fund|ed /ʌndərfʌndɪd/ ADJ 形容詞 An organization or institution that is **underfunded** does not have enough money to spend, and so it cannot function properly. 資金不足の ❏ *For years we have argued that the FDA is underfunded.* 我々は長いことFDAが資金不足だと主張してきた.

under|go /ʌndərgoʊ/ (**undergoes, undergoing, underwent, undergone**) V-T 他動詞 If you **undergo** something necessary or unpleasant, it happens to you. 経験する ❏ *New recruits have been undergoing training in recent weeks.* 新入社員はここ数週間、研修を受けている.

under|gradu|ate /ʌndərgrædʒuɪt/ (**undergraduates**) N-COUNT 可算名詞 An **undergraduate** is a student at a university or college who is studying for a bachelor's or associate's degree. 大学生 ❏ *Economics undergraduates are probably the brightest in the university.* 経済学部の学生はおそらく大学で最も優秀な学生だろう.

under|ground

The adverb is pronounced /ʌndərgraʊnd/. The noun and adjective are pronounced /ʌndərgraʊnd/.

副詞は /ʌndərgraʊnd/ と発音される. 名詞と形容詞は /ʌndərgraʊnd/ と発音される.

❶ ADV 副詞 Something that is **underground** is below the surface of the ground. 地下に [ADV after v] ❏ *Solid low-level waste will be disposed of deep underground.* 固体の低水準廃棄物は地下深くに処分されることになっている. ● ADJ 形容詞 **Underground** is also an adjective. 地下の [ADJ n] ❏ *...an underground parking garage for 2,100 vehicles.* 2100台を収容できる地下の駐車場 ❷ N-SING 単数名詞 The **underground** in a city is the railroad system in which electric trains travel below the ground in tunnels. 地下鉄 [BRIT 英国英語] ['the' N, also 'by' N] [AM **subway** 米国英語 **subway**] ❸ ADJ 形容詞 **Underground** groups and activities are secret because their purpose is to oppose the government and they are illegal. 秘密の [ADJ n] ❏ *...the underground Kashmir Liberation Front.* 秘密カシミア解放運動 ❹ ADV 副詞 If you go **underground**, you hide from the authorities or the police because your political ideas or activities are illegal. ひそかに [ADV after v] ❏ *After the violent clashes of 1981 they either went underground or left the country.* 1981年の激しい衝突の後、彼らは秘密の活動をするか国を去った.

→ see **tunnel**

under|growth /ʌndərgroʊθ/ also **underbrush** N-UNCOUNT 不可算名詞 **Undergrowth** consists of bushes and plants growing together under the trees in a forest. 下草 ❏ *...plunging through the undergrowth.* 下草を突っ込むようにして進むこと

under|hand /ʌndərhænd/ also **underhanded** ❶ ADJ 形容詞 If an action is **underhand** or if it is done in an **underhand** way, it is done secretly and dishonestly. 公明正大でない [DISAPPROVAL 不賛成] [usu ADJ n] ❏ *...underhand financial deals.* 秘密の金融取引 ❏ *a list of the underhanded ways in which their influence operates in the United States.* 米国で影響を及ぼす秘密手段のリスト ❷ ADJ 形容詞 You use **underhand** or **underhanded** to describe actions, such as throwing a ball, in which you do not raise your arm above your shoulder. 下手投げの [AM 米国英語] [ADJ n] ❏ *...an underhand pitch.* 下手投げの投球 ❸ ● ADV 副詞 **Underhand** is also an adverb. 下手投げで [ADV after v] ❏ *In softball, pitches are tossed underhand.* ソフトボールではボールを下手投げでトスする.

under|lie /ʌndərlaɪ/ (**underlies, underlying, underlay, underlain**) ❶ V-T 他動詞 If something **underlies** a feeling or situation, it is the cause or basis of it. 根底にある ❏ *Try to figure out*

what feeling underlies your anger. あなたの怒りの根底にどんな感情があるかを理解しなさい. **2 → see also underlying**

under|line /ʌndərlaɪn/ (underlines, underlining, underlined)
1 V-T 他動詞 If one thing, for example an action or an event, **underlines** another, it draws attention to it and emphasizes its importance. 強調する □ *The report underlined his concern that standards were at risk.* そのリポートは基準が危険にさらされているという彼の懸念を強調した. □ *This incident underlines the danger of traveling in the border area.* この事件は国境地域を旅行することの危険性を強調している. **2** V-T 他動詞 If you **underline** something such as a word or a sentence, you draw a line underneath it in order to make people notice it or to give it extra importance. 下線を施す □ *Underline the following that apply to you.* 次の該当するものに下線を引きなさい.

Word Partnership *underline* は次の語句と使われる:
N. underline **the need for** *something* **1**
  underline **passages**, underline **text**, underline **titles**, underline **words 2**

un|der|ly|ing /ʌndərlaɪɪŋ/ **1** ADJ 形容詞 The **underlying** features of an object, event, or situation are important, and it may be difficult to discover or reveal them. 根本的な [ADJ n] □ *To stop a problem you have to understand its underlying causes.* 問題を防止するためには根本的な原因を理解する必要がある. **2** ADJ 形容詞 You describe something as **underlying** when it is below the surface of something else. 下にある [ADJ n] □ *...hills with the hard underlying rock poking through the turf.* 下にある固い岩が芝生から突き出ている丘陵 **3 → see also underlie**

under|mine /ʌndərmaɪn/ (undermines, undermining, undermined) **1** V-T 他動詞 If you **undermine** something such as a feeling or a system, you make it less strong or less secure than it was before, often by a gradual process or by repeated efforts. 傷つける □ *Offering advice on each and every problem will undermine her feeling of being adult.* あらゆる問題に助言を提供すると彼女の大人であるという意識が傷つくものである. **2** V-T 他動詞 If you **undermine** someone or **undermine** their position or authority, you make their authority or position less secure, often by indirect methods. ひそかに傷つける □ *She undermined him and destroyed his confidence in his own talent.* 彼女は彼を傷つけ, 自分の才能に対する自信を失わせた. **3** V-T 他動詞 If you **undermine** someone's efforts or **undermine** their chances of achieving something, you behave in a way that makes them less likely to succeed. 害する □ *The continued fighting threatens to undermine efforts to negotiate an agreement.* 継続的な戦闘は合意に達しようとする試みを害する恐れがある.

Word Partnership *undermine* は次の語句と使われる:
N. undermine **government**, undermine **peace**,
  undermine **security 1**
  undermine **authority 1 2**
  undermine **confidence 2**
V. **threaten to** undermine, **try to** undermine **1 – 3**

under|neath /ʌndərniːθ/ **1** PREP 前置詞 If one thing is **underneath** another, it is directly under it, and may be covered or hidden by it. 真下に □ *The device exploded underneath a van.* その機器は小型トラックの真下で爆発した. □ *...using dogs to locate people trapped underneath collapsed buildings.* 犬を使って崩壊した建物の下に閉じ込められた人々を探し出すこと ● ADV 副詞 **Underneath** is also an adverb. 下に □ *He has on his jeans and a long-sleeved blue denim shirt with a white T-shirt underneath.* 彼はジーンズをはき, 長袖のブルーのデニムのシャツの下に白いTシャツの上を着ている. □ *The shooting-range is lit from underneath by rows of ruby-red light fixtures.* 射撃練習場は数列の真紅の照明装置を使って下から照明されている. **2** ADV 副詞 The part of something which is **underneath** is the part which normally touches the ground or faces toward the ground. 下面に □ *Check the actual construction of the chair by looking underneath.* 下面を見て椅子の実際の構造を調べなさい. □ *The sand martin is a brown bird with white underneath.* ショウドウツバメは下部が白い茶色の鳥である. ● N-SING 単数名詞 **Underneath** is also a noun. 底 □ *Now I know what the underneath of a car looks like.* これで車の下側がどんなものかが分かった. **3** ADV 副詞 You use **underneath** when talking about feelings and emotions that people do not show in their behavior. 心の底では [ADV with cl] □ *He was as violent as Nick underneath.* 彼は根っこはニックと同じくらい凶暴だった. ● PREP 前置詞 **Underneath** is also a preposition. 見せかけて □ *Underneath his outgoing behavior Luke was shy.* ルークは社交的に見えるが本当は内気だった.

under|paid /ʌndərpeɪd/ ADJ 形容詞 People who are **underpaid** are not paid enough money for the job that they do. 十分な賃金を支払われていない □ *Women are frequently underpaid for the work that they do.* 女性はしばしば仕事に対して十分な賃金を受け取っていない.

under|pants /ʌndərpænts/ N-PLURAL 複数名詞 **Underpants**

are a piece of underwear which have two holes to put your legs through and elastic around the top to hold them up around your waist or hips. パンツ [also 'a pair of' N] □ *Half of men admit that their underpants are their oldest item of clothing.* 男性の半分はパンツが最も古い衣料品目だということを認めている.

under|pass /ʌndərpæs/ (underpasses) N-COUNT 可算名詞 An **underpass** is a road or path that goes underneath a railroad or another road. 地下道 □ *The underpass was closed through flooding.* 地下道は洪水のため閉鎖されていた.

under|rate /ʌndəreɪt/ (underrates, underrating, underrated) V-T 他動詞 If you **underrate** someone or something, you do not recognize how intelligent, important, or significant they are. 過小評価する □ *We women have a lot of good business skills, although we tend to underrate ourselves.* 私達女性は自分自身を過小評価しがちだが, 多くのビジネス技能を備えている. ● **under|rat|ed** ADJ 形容詞 過小評価された □ *He is a very underrated poet.* 彼は非常に過小評価された詩人である.

under|score /ʌndərskɔr/ (underscores, underscoring, underscored) **1** V-T 他動詞 If something such as an action or an event **underscores** another, it draws attention to the other thing and emphasizes its importance. 強調する [mainly AM 主に米国英語] □ *The Labor Department figures underscore the shaky state of the economic recovery.* 労働省のデータは経済回復の不安定な状態を強調している. **2** V-T 他動詞 If you **underscore** something such as a word or a sentence, you draw a line underneath it in order to make people notice it or give it extra importance. 下線を施す [mainly AM 主に米国英語] □ *He heavily underscored his note to Shelley.* 彼はシェリーへのメモに大量に下線を引いた.

under|shirt /ʌndərʃɜrt/ (undershirts) N-COUNT 可算名詞 An **undershirt** is a piece of clothing that you wear on the top half of your body next to your skin and under your regular shirt, in order to keep warm. アンダーシャツ [AM 米国英語] □ *He put on a pair of boxer shorts and an undershirt.* 彼はボクサーショーツとアンダーシャツを身につけた.

under|side /ʌndərsaɪd/ (undersides) N-COUNT 可算名詞 The **underside** of something is the part of it which normally faces towards the ground. 下側 □ *...the underside of the car.* 車の下側

under|spend /ʌndərspɛnd/ (underspends, underspending, underspent) V-T/V-I 他動詞/自動詞 If an organization or country **underspends**, it spends less money than it plans to or less money than it can afford. 少ない金を使う [BUSINESS 実業] □ *...a country that underspends on health and overspends on statisticians.* 医療に十分な金を使わず, 統計家に金を使いすぎる国 ● N-COUNT 可算名詞 **Underspend** is also a noun. 少なく金を使うこと □ *There has been an underspend in the department's budget.* その省の予算には使い切れなかった部分もあった.

under|stand /ʌndərstænd/ (understands, understanding, understood) **1** V-T 他動詞 If you **understand** someone or **understand** what they are saying, you know what they mean. 理解する [no cont] □ *I think you heard and also understand me.* 私の言うことを聞き, 理解したと思う. □ *I don't understand what you are talking about.* あなたが何を話しているのか理解できない. **2** V-T 他動詞 If you **understand** a language, you know what someone is saying when they are speaking that language. 分かる [no cont] □ *I couldn't read or understand a word of Yiddish, so I asked him to translate.* イディッシュは全然分からないので彼に翻訳するよう頼んだ. **3** V-T 他動詞 To **understand** someone means to know how they feel and why they behave in the way that they do. 理解する [no cont] □ *It would be nice to have someone who really understood me, a friend.* 私のことを本当に理解してくれる人, 友人がいたらいいのに. □ *Trish had not exactly understood his feelings.* トリッシュは彼の気持ちを完全には理解できていなかった. **4** V-T 他動詞 You say that you **understand** something when you know why or how it happens. 理解する [no cont] □ *They are too young to understand what is going on.* 彼らは何が起きているかを理解するには若すぎる. □ *She didn't understand why the TV was kept out of reach of the patients.* 彼女は何故テレビが患者の手の届かない場所に置いてあったのか理解できなかった. **5** V-T 他動詞 If you **understand** that something is the case, you think it is true because you have heard or read that it is. You can say that something is **understood** to be the case to mean that people generally think it is true. 知る [no cont] □ *We understand that she's in the studio recording her second album.* 彼女はスタジオで2番目のアルバムを録音中だと聞いている. □ *As I understand it, she has a house in the city.* 彼女はその町に家を持っているらしい.
→ see philosophy

Thesaurus *understand* また次を参照:
V. catch on, comprehend, get, grasp;
  (ant.) misunderstand **1**

under|stand|able /ʌndərstændəbəl/ **1** ADJ 形容詞 If you describe someone's behavior or feelings as **understandable**, you think that they have reacted to a situation in a natural way or

U

in the way you would expect. よく分かる ❑ *His unhappiness was understandable.* 彼の不幸はよく分かった. ● **under|stand|ably** /ˌʌndərstǽndəbli/ ADV 副詞 もちろん ❑ *Officials are understandably nervous about the tense situation in the neighborhood.* 警官はこの付近の緊張した状況について当然神経質になっていた. **2** ADJ 形容詞 If you say that something such as a statement or theory is **understandable**, you mean that people can easily understand it. 分かりやすい ❑ *Roger Neuberg writes in a simple and understandable way.* ロジャー・ニューバーグの作品はシンプルで分かりやすい.

under|stand|ing /ˌʌndərstǽndɪŋ/ (**understandings**) **1** N-VAR 可変性名詞 If you have an **understanding of** something, you know how it works or know what it means. 知識 ❑ *They have to have a basic understanding of computers in order to use the advanced technology.* 高度な技術を使うためにはコンピュータの基礎知識が必要だ. **2** ADJ 形容詞 If you are **understanding** toward someone, you are kind and forgiving. 物分かりがよい ❑ *Her boss, who was very understanding, gave her time off.* 彼女の上司は大変物分かりがよく, 彼女に休暇を与えた. **3** N-UNCOUNT 不可算名詞 If you show **understanding**, you show that you realize how someone feels or why they did something, and are not hostile toward them. 思慮 ❑ *We would like to thank them for their patience and understanding.* 我々はその忍耐力と思いやりに対して彼らに感謝したい. **4** N-UNCOUNT 不可算名詞 If there is **understanding between** people, they are friendly toward each other and trust each other. 意思疎通 ❑ *There was complete understanding between Wilson and myself.* ウィルソンと私の間では完全な意思疎通があった. **5** N-COUNT 可算名詞 An **understanding** is an informal agreement about something. 合意 ❑ *We had not set a date for marriage but there was an understanding between us.* 私達は結婚式の日取りを決めていなかったが, 合意があった. **6** N-SING 単数名詞 If you say that it is your **understanding that** something is the case, you mean that you believe it to be the case because you have heard or read that it is. 聞き知ること ❑ *It is my understanding that the meeting is Thursday.* 会合は木曜日だと私は聞いている. **7** PHRASE 句 If you agree to do something **on the understanding that** something else will be done, you do it because you have been told that the other thing will definitely be done. という条件で ❑ *Poverty forced her to surrender him to foster families, but only on the understanding that she could eventually regain custody.* 貧困のために彼を里子に出さざるを得なかった. だがそれはやがては養育権を取り戻すという条件付だった.

under|state /ˌʌndərstéɪt/ (**understates, understating, understated**) V-T 他動詞 If you **understate** something, you describe it in a way that suggests that it is less important or serious than it really is. 少なく言う ❑ *The government chooses deliberately to understate the increase in prices.* 政府は意図的に価格の上昇を控えめに述べることを選んだ.

under|stat|ed /ˌʌndərstéɪtɪd/ ADJ 形容詞 If you describe a style, color, or effect as **understated**, you mean that it is simple and plain, and does not attract attention to itself. 派手さを抑えた [ADJ n] ❑ *I have always liked understated clothes.* 私はいつも派手さを抑えた洋服が好きだった.

under|state|ment /ˌʌndərstéɪtmənt/ (**understatements**) **1** N-COUNT 可算名詞 If you say that a statement is an **understatement**, you mean that it does not fully express the extent to which something is true. 控えめに言うこと ❑ *To say I'm disappointed is an understatement.* 私は失望したと言うのは控えめな表現だ. **2** N-UNCOUNT 不可算名詞 **Understatement** is the practice of suggesting that things have much less of a particular quality than they really have. 控えめな表現 ❑ *...typical British understatement.* 典型的な英国人の控えめな表現

un|der|stood /ˌʌndərstʊd/ **Understood** is the past tense and past participle of **understand**. understandの過去・過去分詞形

under|take /ˌʌndərtéɪk/ (**undertakes, undertaking, undertook, undertaken**) **1** V-T 他動詞 When you **undertake** a task or job, you start doing it and accept responsibility for it. 引き受ける ❑ *She undertook the task of monitoring the elections.* 選挙を監視する作業を引き受けた. **2** V-T 他動詞 If you **undertake to** do something, you promise that you will do it. 約束する ❑ *He undertook to edit the text himself.* 彼は自分自身で本文を編集することに同意した.

under|tak|er /ˈʌndərteɪkər/ (**undertakers**) N-COUNT 可算名詞 An **undertaker** is a person whose job is to deal with the bodies of people who have died and to arrange funerals. 葬儀屋 ❑ *An undertaker had already taken the body to be embalmed.* 葬儀屋は防腐処置のために既に死体を連れ去った.

under|tak|ing /ˈʌndərteɪkɪŋ/ (**undertakings**) N-COUNT 可算名詞 An **undertaking** is a task or job, especially a large or difficult one. 引き受けた仕事 ❑ *Organizing the show has been a massive undertaking.* ショーを企画することは大変な仕事だった.

un|der|took /ˌʌndərtʊk/ **Undertook** is the past tense of **undertake**. undertakeの過去形

under|value /ˌʌndərvǽlyu/ (**undervalues, undervaluing, undervalued**) V-T 他動詞 If you **undervalue** something or someone, you fail to recognize how valuable or important they are. 過小評価する ❑ *We must never undervalue freedom.* 自由を決して軽視してはならない.

under|wa|ter /ˌʌndərwɔ́tər/ **1** ADV 副詞 Something that exists or happens **underwater** exists or happens below the surface of the ocean, a river, or a lake. 水中で ❑ *...giant submarines able to travel at high speeds underwater.* 水中を高速で行くことのできる巨大な潜水艦 ❑ *Some stretches of beach are completely underwater at high tide.* 海岸の一部は高潮で完全に水面下にある. ● ADJ 形容詞 **Underwater** is also an adjective. 水中の [ADJ n] ❑ *...underwater exploration.* 水中探検 ❑ *...underwater fishing with harpoons.* 銛(もり)を使った水中漁業 **2** ADJ 形容詞 **Underwater** devices are specially made so that they can work in water. 水中で使える [ADJ n] ❑ *...underwater camera equipment.* 水中カメラ機器

under|way /ˌʌndərwéɪ/ ADJ 形容詞 If an activity is **underway**, it has already started. If an activity gets **underway**, it starts. 進行中の [v-link ADJ] ❑ *An investigation is underway to find out how the disaster happened.* 惨事がどのように起こったかを知るための調査が進行中である. ❑ *It was a cold evening, winter well underway.* それは寒い晩だった. 冬がかなり進んでいた.

under|wear /ˈʌndərweər/ N-UNCOUNT 不可算名詞 **Underwear** is items of clothing that you wear next to your skin and under your other clothes. 下着 ❑ *For Christmas my brother and I got new underwear, one toy and one book.* 私と兄弟はクリスマスに新しい下着, おもちゃ1個, 本1冊をもらった.

un|der|went /ˌʌndərwént/ **Underwent** is the past tense of **undergo**. undergoの過去形

under|world /ˈʌndərwɜrld/ N-SING 単数名詞 The **underworld** in a city is the organized crime there and the people who are involved in it. 悪の世界 ❑ *...a Spanish Harlem underworld of gangs, drugs and violence.* ギャング, 麻薬, 暴力のスパニッシュハーレムの世界 ❑ *Some claim that she still has connections to the criminal underworld.* 彼女はまだ犯罪社会とかかわっていると言う人もいる.

under|write /ˌʌndərráɪt/ (**underwrites, underwriting, underwrote, underwritten**) V-T 他動詞 If an institution or company **underwrites** an activity or **underwrites** the cost of it, they agree to provide any money that is needed to cover losses or buy special equipment, often for an agreed-upon fee. 費用負担を同意する [BUSINESS 実業] ❑ *The government will have to create a special agency to underwrite small business loans.* 政府は小規模の企業貸付の費用負担を同意する特別庁を設立しなければならないだろう.

under|writ|er /ˈʌndərraɪtər/ (**underwriters**) **1** N-COUNT 可算名詞 An **underwriter** is someone whose job involves agreeing to provide money for a particular activity or to pay for any losses. 証券引受業者 [BUSINESS 実業] ❑ *If the market will not buy the shares, the underwriter buys them.* 市場がどうしても株式を買わない場合には証券引受業者が買う. **2** N-COUNT 可算名詞 An **underwriter** is someone whose job is to judge the risks involved in certain activities and decide how much to charge for insurance. 保険業者 [BUSINESS 実業] ❑ *AIG is an organization of insurance underwriters.* AIGは保険業者の組織である.

un|de|sir|able /ˌʌndɪzáɪərəbəl/ ADJ 形容詞 If you describe something or someone as **undesirable**, you think they will have harmful effects. 望ましくない ❑ *Inflation is considered to be undesirable because of its adverse effects on income distribution.* インフレはその悪い影響のため望ましくないと見なされている.

un|did /ˌʌndɪd/ **Undid** is the past tense of **undo**. undoの過去形

un|dis|closed /ˌʌndɪsklóʊzd/ ADJ 形容詞 **Undisclosed** information is not revealed to the public. 明らかにされていない ❑ *The company has been sold for an undisclosed amount.* その会社は未公開の金額で売却された.

un|dis|put|ed /ˌʌndɪspyútɪd/ **1** ADJ 形容詞 If you describe a fact or opinion as **undisputed**, you are trying to persuade

someone that it is generally accepted as true or correct. 議論の
余地のない ❑...an undisputed fact. 明白な事実 ❑...his undisputed
genius. 議論の余地のない彼の才能 **2** ADJ 形容詞 If you describe
someone as the **undisputed** leader or champion, you mean that
everyone accepts their position as leader or champion. 異議なしの
❑ Seles won 10 tournaments, and was the undisputed world champion. セ
レスは10試合勝ち、異議なしの世界チャンピオンだった。 ❑ At 78 years of
age, he's still undisputed leader of his country. 78歳で彼はまだその国の
異議なしの指導者である。

un|dis|turbed /ˌʌndɪstɜ́rbd/ **1** ADJ 形容詞 Something that
remains **undisturbed** is not touched, moved, or used by anyone.
乱されない ❑ The desk looked undisturbed. その机は乱されていないよ
うに見えた。 **2** ADJ 形容詞 A place that is **undisturbed** is peaceful
and has not been affected by changes that have happened in
other places. 平穏な ❑ It was one of the most peaceful and undisturbed
places she had found. それは彼女が見つけた場所で最も平和で平穏な場
所の1つだった。 **3** ADJ 形容詞 If you are **undisturbed** in something
that you are doing, you are able to continue doing it and are not
affected by something that is happening. 邪魔されない ❑ I can
spend the whole day undisturbed at the warehouse. 私は倉庫で邪魔
されずに1日中費やすことができる。 ❑ There was a small restaurant
on Sullivan Street where we could talk undisturbed. 邪魔されずに話が
できる小さなレストランがサリバン通りにあった。 **4** ADJ 形容詞 If
someone is **undisturbed by** something, it does not affect, bother,
or upset them. 悩まされない ❑ Victoria was strangely undisturbed by
this symptom, even though her husband and family were frightened. ヴィ
クトリアは夫と家族が怖がったにもかかわらず不思議とこの症状に悩
まされなかった。

undo /ʌndúː/ (**undoes, undoing, undid, undone**) **1** V-T 他動
詞 If you **undo** something that is closed, tied, or held together, or
if you **undo** the thing holding it, you loosen or remove the thing
holding it. (チャックやひも、ボタンなどを) 下ろす はずす、ほどく
❑ I managed secretly to undo a corner of the parcel. 私はなんとか小包の
すみをこっそり開けた。 ❑ I undid the bottom two buttons of my yellow
and gray shirt. 私は黄色とグレーのシャツの下のボタンを2つはずし
た。 **2** V-T 他動詞 To **undo** something that has been done means
to reverse its effect. 元に戻す、取り消す ❑ A heavy-handed approach
from the police could undo that good impression. 警察の荒いやり方は
好印象を壊しかねない。 ❑ She knew it would be difficult to undo the
damage that had been done. 彼女は与えられた損害を元に戻すのは難し
いだろうことを知っていた。 **3** → see also **undoing**

un|do|ing /ʌndúːɪŋ/ N-SING 単数名詞 If something is someone's
undoing, it is the cause of their failure. 失敗の原因 ❑ His lack of
experience may prove to be his undoing. 経験不足が彼の失敗の原因とな
るかもしれない。

un|doubt|ed /ʌndáʊtɪd/ ADJ 形容詞 You can use **undoubted** to
emphasize that something exists or is true. 疑う余地のない、確か
な [EMPHASIS 強調] ❑ The event was an undoubted success. そのイベン
トは間違いなく成功だった。 ❑...a man of your undoubted ability. 明ら
かに能力のある男性 ● **un|doubt|ed|ly** ADV 副詞 間違いなく、確かに
❑ Undoubtedly, political and economic factors have played their part. 明
らかに政治的また経済的要因が絡んでいる。

un|dress /ʌndrés/ (**undresses, undressing, undressed**) V-T/V-I
他動詞/自動詞 When you **undress** or **undress** someone, you take
off your clothes or someone else's clothes. (人の) 服を脱がせる [他
動詞]、服を脱ぐ [自動詞] ❑ She went out, leaving Rachel to undress and
take a shower. 彼女はレイチェルが服を脱いでシャワーを浴びるように
外へ出た。

un|dressed /ʌndrést/ ADJ 形容詞 If you are **undressed**, you
are wearing no clothes or your underwear or pajamas. If you get
undressed, you take off your clothes. 裸の、服を脱いだ ❑ Fifteen
minutes later he was undressed and in bed. 15分後に彼は服を脱いでベッ
ドに入っていた。

un|due /ʌndúː/ ADJ 形容詞 If you describe something bad as
undue, you mean that it is greater or more extreme than you
think is reasonable or appropriate. 過度の、必要以上の [ADJ n]
❑ This would help the families to survive the drought without undue
suffering. これはその家族が過度の苦しみにさらされず日照りを切り
抜けるのに役立つだろう。 ❑ It is unrealistic to put undue pressure on
ourselves by saying we are the best. 自分が一番だと言って、必要以上の
プレッシャーを自分にかけるのは実際的でない。

Word Partnership undue は次の語句と使われる:

N. undue **attention**, undue **burden**, undue **delay**, undue
emphasis, undue **hardship**, undue **influence**, undue
interference, undue **pressure**, undue **risk**

un|du|ly /ʌndúːli/ ADV 副詞 If you say that something does not
happen or is not done **unduly**, you mean that it does not happen
or is not done to an excessive or unnecessary extent. 過度の、必要
以上に ❑ "But you're not unduly worried about doing this report?"—"No."
「でもあなたはこれを報告することをそんなに心配していないんでし
ょう?」「うん。」 ❑ This will achieve greater security without unduly

burdening the consumers or the economy. これで顧客や経済に必要以上
の負担をかけることなく警備をさらに強化できるだろう。

un|earned in|come /ʌnɜ́rnd ɪ́nkʌm/ N-UNCOUNT 不可算名
詞 **Unearned income** is money that people gain from interest or
profit from property or investment, rather than money that they
earn from a job. 不労所得 [BUSINESS 実業] ❑ Your IRA deduction
cannot be taken from unearned income. 個人退職年金の控除は不労所得
からは引かれない。

un|earth /ʌnɜ́rθ/ (**unearths, unearthing, unearthed**) **1** V-T 他
動詞 If someone **unearths** facts or evidence, they discover them
with difficulty. (事実や証拠を苦労して) 発見する ❑ Researchers
have unearthed documents from the 1600s. 研究者たちは1600年代からの
書類を発見した。 ❑ Other financial scandals are out there waiting to be
unearthed. 他の金融不祥事も暴かれるのを待つばかりだ。 **2** V-T 他動
詞 If someone **unearths** something that is buried, they find it by
digging in the ground. (土の中から) 掘り起こす 発掘する ❑ Fossil
hunters have unearthed the bones of an elephant believed to be 500,000
years old. 化石ハンターたちは50万年前のものと思われる象の骨を掘り
起こした。 ❑ More human remains have been unearthed in the north. さ
らに多くの人の遺骨が北の方で発掘された。 **3** V-T 他動詞 If you say
that someone **has unearthed** something, you mean that they
have found it after it had been hidden or lost for some time. (隠さ
れていた物や遺物を) 探し出す ❑ From somewhere, he had unearthed
a black silk suit. どこからか彼は黒いシルクのスーツを見つけ出した。
❑ Today I unearthed a copy of "90 Minutes" and had a chuckle at your
article. 今日『90 Minutes』を一冊見つけ出し、きみの記事を読んでク
スクス笑った。

un|ease /ʌníːz/ **1** N-UNCOUNT 不可算名詞 If you have a feeling
of **unease**, you feel anxious or afraid, because you think that
something is wrong. 心配、不安 ❑ Sensing my unease about the
afternoon ahead, he told me, "These men are pretty easy to talk to." この
午後に対するわたしの不安を察知して、彼がわたしに言った。「彼ら
はとても話しやすい人だよ。」 ❑ We left with a deep sense of unease,
because we knew something was being hidden from us. 何かが隠され
ていると分かっていたため、わたしたちはとても不安な気持ちで退出
した。 **2** N-UNCOUNT 不可算名詞 If you say that there is **unease**
in a situation, you mean that people are dissatisfied or angry,
but have not yet started to take any action. 不満、怒り ❑ He faces
growing unease among the Democrats about the likelihood of war. 戦争の
可能性に対し民主党員内で高まりつつある不満に彼は直面している。
❑...the depth of public unease about the economy. 景気に対する国民の
不満の深刻さ

un|easy /ʌníːzi/ **1** ADJ 形容詞 If you are **uneasy**, you feel
anxious, afraid, or embarrassed, because you think that
something is wrong or that there is danger. 不安な、心配な ❑ He
said nothing but gave me a sly grin that made me feel terribly uneasy.
彼は何も言わず、ただずるそうにわたしにやって笑った。それがわたしを
恐ろしく不安にさせた。 ❑ He looked uneasy and refused to answer
questions. 彼は不安そうな様子で、質問に答えるのを拒否した。
● **un|eas|i|ly** /ʌníːzɪli/ ADV 副詞 不安そうに、心配そうに ❑ Meg
shifted uneasily on her chair. メグはいすの上で不安そうに体を動かし
た。 ● **un|eas|i|ness** N-UNCOUNT 不可算名詞 不安、心配 ❑ With a
small degree of uneasiness, he pulled it open and stuck his head inside. 彼
はちょっと不安そうにそれを押し開け、頭を中に突っ込んだ。 **2** ADJ
形容詞 If you are **uneasy about** doing something, you are not
sure that it is correct or wise. 確信のない、心もとない ❑ Richard
was uneasy about how best to approach his elderly mother. リチャード
は彼の年老いた母にどう話を持ちかけるのが一番いいのか心もとなか
った。 ● **un|eas|i|ness** N-UNCOUNT 不可算名詞 確信のなさ ❑ I felt
a certain uneasiness about meeting her again. 私は彼女にまた会うべき
かどうか確信がなかった。 **3** ADJ 形容詞 If you describe a situation
or relationship as **uneasy**, you mean that the situation is not
settled and may not last. (状況や関係が) 不安定な [JOURNALISM ジ
ャーナリズム] ❑ An uneasy calm has settled over Los Angeles. 不穏な静
けさがロサンゼルスを覆っていた。 ❑...there is an uneasy relationship
between us and the politicians. 我々と政治家の関係には不安定さがあ
る。 ● **un|eas|i|ly** ADV 副詞 不安定に ❑...a country whose component
parts fit uneasily together. 国家を構成する要素が不安定に組み合わさ
っている国

un|em|ployed /ʌnɪmplɔ́ɪd/ ADJ 形容詞 Someone who is
unemployed does not have a job. 仕事のない、失業している ❑ The
problem is millions of people are unemployed. 問題は何百万もの人が失業
していることだ。 ❑ This workshop helps young unemployed people. こ
のセミナーは仕事のない若者を支援する。 ● N-PLURAL 複数名詞 The
unemployed are people who are unemployed. 失業者 ❑ We want to
create jobs for the unemployed. 我々は失業者への仕事を作り出したい。

un|em|ploy|ment /ʌnɪmplɔ́ɪmənt/ **1** N-UNCOUNT 不可算名
詞 **Unemployment** is the fact that people who want jobs cannot
get them. 失業 ❑ The state's unemployment rate rose slightly to 7.1
percent last month.. 先月、その国の失業率は7.1パーセントへわずかに
上昇した。 **2** N-UNCOUNT 不可算名詞 **Unemployment** is the same
as **unemployment compensation**. 失業手当 [AM 米国英語] ❑ He
worked most of the year. Now he's getting unemployment. 彼は1年のほと

んど仕事をしていた．今は失業手当を受けている．

un|employ|ment com|pen|sa|tion N-UNCOUNT 不可算名詞 **Unemployment compensation** is money that some people receive from the state, usually for a limited time after losing a job, when they do not have a job and are unable to find one. 失業手当 [AM 米国英語] □ *He has to get by on unemployment compensation.* 彼は失業手当でなんとか生活しなければならない．

un|equivo|cal /ʌnɪkwɪvək⁰l/ ADJ 形容詞 If you describe someone's attitude as **unequivocal**, you mean that it is completely clear and very firm. 明確な，はっきりとした [FORMAL 形式ばった] □ *...Richardson's unequivocal commitment to fair play.* リチャードソンのフェアプレーをするというはっきりとした意思 ● **un|equivo|cal|ly** /ʌnɪkwɪvəkli/ ADV 副詞 明確に，はっきりと □ *He stated unequivocally that the forces were ready to go to war.* 彼はいつでも軍隊は戦争に行く構えであると明言した．

un|ethi|cal /ʌnɛθɪk⁰l/ ADJ 形容詞 Behavior that is **unethical** is wrong and unacceptable according to rules or beliefs about morality. 倫理に反する，道徳に反する □ *It's simply unethical to promote and advertise such a dangerous product.* そんな危険な製品を推薦したり宣伝するのはまったく倫理に反している． □ *I thought it was unethical for doctors to operate upon their families.* 私は，医師が彼らの家族に手術を施すのは倫理的でないと思った．

un|even /ʌniv⁰n/ **1** ADJ 形容詞 An **uneven** surface or edge is not smooth, flat, or straight. 平らでない，でこぼこした □ *He staggered on the uneven surface.* 彼はでこぼこした表面の上でよろめいた． □ *The pathways were uneven, broken, and dangerous.* その歩道はでこぼこの上に割れていて危険だった． **2** ADJ 形容詞 Something that is **uneven** is not regular or consistent. 不規則な，むらのある □ *He could hear that her breathing was uneven.* 彼には彼女の呼吸が不規則なのが聞きとれた． **3** ADJ 形容詞 An **uneven** system or situation is unfairly arranged or organized. (制度などが) 不公平な 不均衡な □ *Some of the victims are complaining loudly about the uneven distribution of emergency aid.* 被災者の何人かは，緊急援助の不公平な配り方に大声で文句を言っている．

Thesaurus   uneven また次を参照：

| ADJ. | jagged, rough; (ant.) even **1** |
| | inconsistent, irregular **2** |

---

un|event|ful /ʌnɪvɛntfəl/ ADJ 形容詞 If you describe a period of time as **uneventful**, you mean that nothing interesting, exciting, or important happened during it. 平穏な，特に面白いこともない □ *The return trip was uneventful, the car running perfectly.* 帰りの道は，車も申し分なく走り，平穏なものだった．

un|ex|pec|ted /ʌnɪkspɛktɪd/ ADJ 形容詞 If an event or someone's behavior is **unexpected**, it surprises you because you did not think that it was likely to happen. 予期しない，意外な □ *His death was totally unexpected.* 彼の死はまったく予期しないものだった． □ *He made a brief, unexpected appearance at the office.* 彼は突然ちらっと職場に顔を出した． ● **un|ex|pec|ted|ly** ADV 副詞 思いがけなく，突然 □ *Moss had clamped an unexpectedly strong grip on his arm.* モスはいきなり彼の腕をぎゅっとつかんだ．

Thesaurus   unexpected また次を参照：

| ADJ. | startling, surprising |

---

un|ex|plained /ʌnɪkspleɪnd/ ADJ 形容詞 If you describe something as **unexplained**, you mean that the reason for it or cause of it is unclear or is not known. 説明できない，原因不明の □ *An unexplained death is difficult to come to terms with.* 原因不明の死というものは受け入れるのが難しい． □ *The city's water supply has been cut for unexplained reasons.* 街の給水がなぜか止まってしまった．

un|fair /ʌnfɛər/ ADJ 形容詞 An **unfair** action or situation is not right or fair. 不当な，不公平な □ *She was awarded $5,000 in compensation for unfair dismissal.* 彼女は不当解雇に対する償いとして5千ドルを受け取った． □ *It was unfair that he should suffer so much.* 彼があんなに苦しまなくてはならないのは不公平だった． ● **un|fair|ly** ADV 副詞 不当に，不公平に □ *He unfairly blamed Frances for the failure.* 彼はその失敗のことで不当にフランシスを責めた．

Thesaurus   unfair また次を参照：

| ADJ. | unjust, unreasonable, unwarranted; (ant.) fair |

---

un|faith|ful /ʌnfeɪθəl/ ADJ 形容詞 If someone is **unfaithful to** their lover or to the person they are married to, they have a sexual relationship with someone else. 不誠実な，浮気をして □ *James had been unfaithful to Christine for the entire four years they'd been together.* ジェイムズは彼らが一緒だった4年間，ずっとクリスティンに対し浮気をしていた．

un|fa|mil|iar /ʌnfəmɪlyər/ **1** ADJ 形容詞 If something is **unfamiliar to** you, you know nothing or very little about it, because you have not seen or experienced it before. (一が人に) なじみのない □ *She grew many wonderful plants that were unfamiliar to*

me. 彼女はわたしにはなじみのない，たくさんの素晴らしい植物を育てていた． **2** ADJ 形容詞 If you are **unfamiliar with** something, you know nothing or very little about it. (人が一を) よく知らない [V-LINK ADJ 'with' n] □ *She speaks no Japanese and is unfamiliar with Japanese culture.* 彼女は日本語を話さないし，日本の文化をよく知らない．

un|fash|ion|able /ʌnfæʃənəb⁰l/ ADJ 形容詞 If something is **unfashionable**, it is not approved of or done by most people because it is out of style. 流行遅れの □ *Wearing fur has become unfashionable.* 毛皮を着るのは流行遅れとなった．

un|fa|vor|able /ʌnfeɪvərəb⁰l/ **1** ADJ 形容詞 **Unfavorable** conditions or circumstances cause problems for you and reduce your chances of success. 不利な，都合が悪い □ *The decision to delay the launch stems from unfavorable weather conditions.* 打ち上げ遅延の決定は悪天候に起因している． □ *The whole international economic situation is very unfavorable for the countries in the south.* 全世界の経済情勢は南の国々にとても不利だ． **2** ADJ 形容詞 If you have an **unfavorable** reaction to something, you do not like it. 批判的な □ *The president is drawing unfavorable comments on his new forest policy.* 大統領の新しい森林政策は批判的な意見を呼んでいる． □ *...views unfavorable to the capitalist system.* 資本主義制度に批判的な見方 ● **un|fa|vor|ably** /ʌnfeɪvərəbli/ ADV 副詞 [ADV after v] 批判的に，望ましくない形で □ *Other medications or foods may react unfavorably with it.* 他の薬や食べ物は悪い形でそれに反応するかもしれない． **3** ADJ 形容詞 If you make an **unfavorable** comparison between two things, you say that one thing seems worse than the other. (一と比較し) 劣っている [ADJ n] □ *I didn't expect unfavorable comparisons between my sons and their friends.* 私の息子たちとその友達を比べて劣っていると言われるとは思いもしなかった． ● **un|fa|vor|ably** ADV 副詞 [ADV with v] 劣っていて □ *Tax rates compare unfavorably with the less heavy-handed North American agreement.* 税率は比較的穏やかな北米の取り決めに比べると劣っている．

un|fin|ished /ʌnfɪnɪʃt/ ADJ 形容詞 If you describe something such as a work of art or a piece of work as **unfinished**, you mean that it is not complete, for example because it was abandoned or there was no time to complete it. 未完成の □ *...Jane Austen's unfinished novel.* ジェーン・オースティンの未完の小説 □ *The cathedral was eventually completed in 1490, though the Gothic facade remains unfinished.* ゴシック調の正面はまだ終わっていないが，大聖堂は1490年にようやく完成した．

un|fit /ʌnfɪt/ **1** ADJ 形容詞 If you are **unfit**, your body is not in good condition because you have not been getting regular exercise. (運動不足から) 体力不足の □ *Many children are so unfit they are unable to do even basic exercises.* 多くの子供たちがひどい体力不足で，基本的な運動さえできない． **2** ADJ 形容詞 If someone is **unfit** for something, he or she is unable to do it because of injury or illness. (けがや病気のため) 体調が不十分な □ *He had a third examination and was declared unfit for duty.* 彼は3度目の診察を受け，その任務には耐えられないと言い渡された． **3** ADJ 形容詞 If you say that someone or something is **unfit** for a particular purpose or job, you are criticizing them because they are not good enough for that purpose or job. (目的や仕事に) 不向きな 不適当な [DISAPPROVAL 不賛成] □ *Existing houses are becoming totally unfit for human habitation.* 現存する家々は人間が住むにはまったく向かなくなりつつある． □ *They were utterly unfit to govern.* 彼らは統治するにはまったく向いていなかった．

un|fold /ʌnfoʊld/ (**unfolds, unfolding, unfolded**) **1** V-I 自動詞 If a situation **unfolds**, it develops and becomes known or understood. (状況が) 明らかになる □ *The outcome depends on conditions as well as how events unfold.* 結果は，事の展開だけでなく条件によっても決まる． **2** V-T/V-I 他動詞/自動詞 If a story **unfolds** or if someone **unfolds** it, it is told to someone. (話を) 展開する [他動詞]，(話が) 展開する [自動詞] □ *Don's story unfolded as the cruise got under way.* 航海が始まり，ドンの物語が始まった． **3** V-T/V-I 他動詞/自動詞 If someone **unfolds** something which has been folded or if it **unfolds**, it is opened out and becomes flat. (折りたたまれていた物を) 広げる，開く [他動詞]，(折りたたまれていた物が) 広がる，開く [自動詞] □ *He quickly unfolded the blankets and spread them on the mattress.* 彼は手早く毛布を広げ，マットレスの上に広げた．

un|fore|seen /ʌnfɔrsin/ ADJ 形容詞 If something that has happened was **unforeseen**, it was not expected to happen or known about beforehand. 予期しない，思いがけない □ *Radiation may damage cells in a way that was previously unforeseen.* 放射線は，以前なら予測できなかった方法で細胞を破壊する可能性がある． □ *Unfortunately, due to unforeseen circumstances, this year's show has been canceled.* 残念ながら，予期せぬ事情により今年の公演はキャンセルされた．

un|for|get|table /ʌnfərgɛtəb⁰l/ ADJ 形容詞 If you describe something as **unforgettable**, you mean that it is, for example, extremely beautiful, enjoyable, or unusual, so that you remember it for a long time. You can also refer to extremely unpleasant things as **unforgettable**. 忘れられない □ *A visit to the*

u

museum is an unforgettable experience. その博物館への訪問は忘れられない経験だ。 ❑ *...the outdoor activities that will make your vacation unforgettable.* あなたの休暇をいつまでも記憶に残るものにするアウトドア活動

un|for|tu|nate /ʌnfɔ́rtʃənɪt/ (**unfortunates**) **1** ADJ 形容詞 If you describe someone as **unfortunate**, you mean that something unpleasant or unlucky has happened to them. You can also describe the unpleasant things that happen to them as **unfortunate**. 不幸な, 不運な ❑ *Some unfortunate person passing below could all too easily be seriously injured.* その下を通った不運な人たちはみな, あっけなく重傷を負うだろう。 ❑ *Apparently he had been unfortunate enough to fall victim to a gang of thugs.* どうも彼は本当に運悪く暴力団の被害に遭ったらしい。 **2** ADJ 形容詞 If you describe something that has happened as **unfortunate**, you think that it is inappropriate, embarrassing, awkward, or undesirable. 不適切な, 間が悪い ❑ *...the unfortunate incident of the upside-down Canadian flag.* カナダの国旗が上下逆さになっていた残念な出来事 **3** ADJ 形容詞 You can describe someone as **unfortunate** when they are poor or have a difficult life. 貧しい, 不幸な境遇の ❑ *Every year we have fundraisers to raise money for unfortunate people.* 毎年, わたしたちは不幸な境遇の人たちのために募金活動をする。 ● N-COUNT 可算名詞 An **unfortunate** is someone who is unfortunate. 貧しい人, 不幸な境遇の人 ❑ *Dorothy was another of life's unfortunates.* ドロシーは人生の不運に見舞われたもう一人だった。

un|for|tu|nate|ly /ʌnfɔ́rtʃənɪtli/ ADV 副詞 You can use **unfortunately** to introduce or refer to a statement when you consider that it is sad or disappointing, or when you want to express regret. 残念なことに, あいにく [FEELINGS 感情] ❑ *Unfortunately, my time is limited.* 残念だが, わたしには時間がないんだ。 ❑ *Unfortunately for him, his title brought obligations as well as privileges.* あいにく, 彼の肩書きは彼に特権と共に義務ももたらした。

un|found|ed /ʌnfaʊndɪd/ ADJ 形容詞 If you describe a rumor, belief, or feeling as **unfounded**, you mean that it is wrong and is not based on facts or evidence. 根拠のない, 事実無根の ❑ *Unfounded rumors of accounting problems hit stocks of other companies.* 会計問題の根も葉もないうわさが他の会社の株価に打撃を与えた。 ❑ *The allegations were totally unfounded.* その申し立てはまったく事実無根だった。

un|friend|ly /ʌnfréndli/ ADJ 形容詞 If you describe a person, organization, or their behavior as **unfriendly**, you mean that they behave toward you in an unkind or slightly hostile way. 無愛想な, 不親切な ❑ *Some people were unfriendly to the new recruit.* ある人たちは新入社員に冷たかった。 ❑ *People always complain that the big banks and big companies are unfriendly and unhelpful.* 人々はいつも大銀行や大会社は不親切で助けにならないと文句を言う。

Thesaurus *unfriendly* また次を参照:

ADJ. cold, unkind, unsociable; (ant.) friendly

un|ful|filled /ʌnfʊlfɪld/ **1** ADJ 形容詞 If you use **unfulfilled** to describe something such as a promise, ambition, or need, you mean that what was promised, hoped for, or needed has not happened. (約束が) 果たされていない (必要が) 満たされていない ❑ *Do you have any unfulfilled ambitions?* あなたには満たされていない野望がありますか ❑ *...angry at unfulfilled promises of jobs and decent housing.* 仕事やまともな家への実行されない約束に対する怒り **2** ADJ 形容詞 If you describe someone as **unfulfilled**, you mean that they feel dissatisfied with life or with what they have done. (人生や業績に) 不満のある ❑ *You must let go of the idea that to be single is to be unhappy and unfulfilled.* あなたは, 独身だと不幸で満たされていないという考えを捨てないといけない。

un|furl /ʌnfɜ́rl/ (**unfurls, unfurling, unfurled**) **1** V-T/V-I 他動詞/自動詞 If you **unfurl** something rolled or folded such as an umbrella, sail, or flag, you open it, so that it is spread out. You can also say that it **unfurls**. (巻かれた物などを) 広げる [他動詞], (巻かれた物などが) 広がる [自動詞] ❑ *Once outside the inner breakwater, we began to unfurl all the sails.* 防波堤の内側から外に出るとすぐに, わたしたちはすべての帆を広げ始めた。 **2** V-I 自動詞 If you say that events, stories, or scenes **unfurl** before you, you mean that you are aware of them or can see them as they happen or develop. (出来事や場面などが) 目の前で) 広がる, 展開する ❑ *The dramatic changes in Europe continue to unfurl.* ヨーロッパで大きな変化が起こり続けている。

un|grate|ful /ʌngréɪtfəl/ ADJ 形容詞 If you describe someone as **ungrateful**, you are criticizing them for not showing thanks or for being unkind to someone who has helped them or done them a favor. 感謝の気持ちがない, 恩知らずな [DISAPPROVAL 不賛成] ❑ *I thought it was ungrateful of her.* 私は彼女が恩知らずだと思った。

un|hap|pi|ly /ʌnhǽpɪli/ ADV 副詞 You use **unhappily** to introduce or refer to a statement when you consider it to be sad and wish that it were different. 悲しいことに, 不幸にも [ADV with cl]

❑ *On May 23rd, unhappily, the little boy died.* 悲しいことにその少年は5月23日に亡くなった。 ❑ *Unhappily the facts do not wholly bear out the theory.* あいにく, それらの事実はその理論を完全に裏付けるものではない。

un|hap|py /ʌnhǽpi/ (**unhappier, unhappiest**) **1** ADJ 形容詞 If you are **unhappy**, you are sad and depressed. 悲しい, 惨めな, 不運な ❑ *Her marriage is in trouble and she is desperately unhappy.* 彼女の結婚生活は問題を抱えていて, 彼女はひどく惨めだ。 ❑ *He was a shy, sometimes unhappy man.* 彼は恥ずかしがり屋で, 時に不幸な男性だった。 ● **un|hap|pi|ly** ADV 副詞 悲しそうに, 惨めに ❑ *"I don't have your imagination,"Kevin said unhappily.*「ぼくにはきみみたいに想像力がないんだ」とケビンは悲しそうに言った。 ● **un|hap|pi|ness** N-UNCOUNT 不可算名詞 ❑ *There was a lot of unhappiness in my adolescence.* 私の思春期には不幸な出来事が多かった。 **2** ADJ 形容詞 [v-link ADJ] If you are **unhappy about** something, you are not pleased about it or not satisfied with it. (人が) 満足していない 不満のある ❑ *He has been unhappy with his son's political leanings.* 彼は息子の政治傾向に不満だった。 ❑ *College students are unhappy with their school bookstores.* 大学の学生たちは学校の本屋に不満がある。 ● **un|hap|pi|ness** N-UNCOUNT 不可算名詞 不満, 不服 ❑ *He has, by submitting his resignation, signaled his unhappiness with the government's decision.* 彼は辞表を提出することで, 政府の決定に対する不服を示した。 **3** ADJ 形容詞 [ADJ n] An **unhappy** situation or choice is not satisfactory or desirable. (状況や選択が) 残念な 不適切な ❑ *It is our hope that this unhappy chapter in the history of relations between our two countries will soon be closed.* 我々二国間関係の歴史の不幸な一節に早く終止符が打たれるよう望んでいる。 ❑ *The legislation represents in itself an unhappy compromise.* その法律はそれ自体が不適切な妥協を表している。

Thesaurus *unhappy* また次を参照:

ADJ. depressed, miserable, sad; (ant.) happy **1**

un|harmed /ʌnhɑ́rmd/ ADJ 形容詞 If someone or something is **unharmed** after an accident or violent incident, they are not hurt or damaged in any way. 無傷の [ADJ after v, v-link ADJ] ❑ *They both escaped unharmed.* 彼らは2人とも無傷で逃れた。

un|healthy /ʌnhélθi/ (**unhealthier, unhealthiest**) **1** ADJ 形容詞 Something that is **unhealthy** is likely to cause illness or bad health. 体によくない, 健康を害する ❑ *Avoid unhealthy foods such as hamburgers and fries.* ハンバーガーやフライドポテトなどの体によくない食べ物を避ける。 **2** ADJ 形容詞 If you are **unhealthy**, you are sick or not in good physical condition. 病気の, 健康でない ❑ *...a pale, unhealthy looking man.* 青白い不健康そうな男 **3** ADJ 形容詞 An **unhealthy** economy or company is financially weak and unsuccessful. (経済や経営が) 不振の ❑ *If you have an unhealthy economy, the poor will get hurt worst because they are the weakest.* 経済不振の場合, 貧民層が最も弱い立場にあるので一番被害を受ける。 **4** ADJ 形容詞 If you describe someone's behavior or interests as **unhealthy**, you do not consider them to be normal and think they may involve mental problems. (行動や興味の対象が) 不健全な 病的な ❑ *Frank has developed an unhealthy relationship with these people.* フランクはこの人たちと不健全な関係を築いていた。

un|heard of /ʌnhɜ́rd ʌv/ ADJ 形容詞 An event or situation that is **unheard of** never happens. 聞いたことがない, 前代未聞の [v-link ADJ] ❑ *Riots are almost unheard of in Japan.* 日本で暴動なんてほとんど聞いたことがない。

un|help|ful /ʌnhélpfəl/ ADJ 形容詞 If you say that someone or something is **unhelpful**, you mean that they do not help you or improve a situation, and may even make things worse. 役に立たない, 手を貸そうとしない ❑ *The criticism is both unfair and unhelpful.* その批判は不当な上に何の助けにもならない。

un|hurt /ʌnhɜ́rt/ ADJ 形容詞 If someone who has been attacked, or involved in an accident, is **unhurt**, they are not injured. 無傷の [ADJ after v, v-link ADJ] ❑ *The driver escaped unhurt, but a pedestrian was injured.* 運転手は無傷で逃れたが, 歩行者が1人けがをした。

Word Link *ident = same : identical, identification, unidentified*

un|iden|ti|fied /ʌnaɪdéntɪfaɪd/ **1** ADJ 形容詞 If you describe someone or something as **unidentified**, you mean that nobody knows who or what they are. 身元不明の ❑ *He was shot this morning by unidentified intruders at his house.* 彼は今朝方, 身元不明の侵入者によって自宅で狙撃された。 **2** ADJ 形容詞 If you use **unidentified** to describe people, groups, and organizations, you do not want to give their names. 匿名の [JOURNALISM ジャーナリズム] ❑ *His claims were based on the comments of anonymous and unidentified sources.* 彼の主張は, 匿名で出所不明の情報筋の意見を基にしていた。

uni|fi|ca|tion /yúnɪfɪkéɪʃən/ N-UNCOUNT 不可算名詞 **Unification** is the process by which two or more countries join together and become one country. 統一, 統合 ❑ *...the process of European unification.* ヨーロッパ統一の過程

union

Word Link	uni ≈ one : uniform, unilateral, union

uni|form /yúnɪfɔ̀rm/ (uniforms) **1** N-VAR 可変性名詞 A **uniform** is a special set of clothes which some people, for example soldiers or the police, wear to work in and which some children wear in school. 制服 ❑ *The police wear dark blue uniforms.* 警察官は紺色の制服を着ている. ❑ *Felipe was in uniform for the parade.* フェリペはパレード用の制服を着ていた. **2** ADJ 形容詞 If something is **uniform**, it does not vary, but is even and regular throughout. 一定の, 均一の ❑ *Cut down between the bones so that all the chops are of uniform size.* すべてのリブ付きチョップが同じサイズになるように骨の間で切る. ❑ *All flowing water, though it appears to be uniform, is actually divided into extensive inner surfaces, or layers, moving against one another.* 流水はすべて同じように見えるが, 実は多くの内側の面や層に分けられ, お互いに逆の方向へ動いている. ● **uni|form|ity** /yùnɪfɔ́rmiti/ N-UNCOUNT 不可算名詞 均一, 一貫性 ❑ *...the caramel that was used to maintain uniformity of color in the brandy.* ブランデーの色を均等に保つために使われたカラメル ● **uni|form|ly** ADV 副詞 均一に, 一貫して ❑ *Beyond the windows, a November midday was uniformly gray.* 窓の向こう側では, 11月の正午は一様に灰色だった. **3** ADJ 形容詞 If you describe a number of things as **uniform**, you mean that they are all the same. (複数の物が) 一様な そろいの ❑ *Along each wall stretched uniform green metal filing cabinets.* それぞれの壁に沿って, 金属でできた同じ形の緑の書類整理棚がズラッと並んでいた. ● **uni|form|ity** N-UNCOUNT 不可算名詞 同一性, 画一性 ❑ *...the dull uniformity of the houses.* 家々の味気ないまでの画一性 ● **uni|form|ly** ADV 副詞 一様に ❑ *They are all about twenty years old, serious, smart, a bit conventional perhaps, but uniformly pleasant.* 彼らはみな20歳といったところ. まじめで頭が切れ, ちょっと型にはまっているかもしれないが, 一様に愛想がよい.
→ see **football, soccer**

uni|formed /yúnɪfɔ̀rmd/ ADJ 形容詞 If you use **uniformed** to describe someone who does a particular job, you mean that they are wearing a uniform. 制服を着た ❑ *...uniformed policemen.* 制服を着た警察官

uni|form|ity /yùnɪfɔ́rmiti/ **1** N-UNCOUNT 不可算名詞 If there is **uniformity** in something such as a system, organization, or group of countries, the same rules, ideas, or methods are applied in all parts of it. (規則や考えなどの) 一貫性 統一 ❑ *He argues that we need statewide uniformity.* 我々には州全体の統一性が必要なのだと彼は主張する. **2** → see also **uniform**

uni|fy /yúnɪfàɪ/ (unifies, unifying, unified) V-T/V-I 他動詞/自動詞 If someone **unifies** different things or parts, or if the things or parts **unify**, they are brought together to form one thing. 一つにまとめる, 統一する [他動詞], 一つになる, 一体化する [自動詞] ❑ *He pledged to unify the city's political factions.* 彼は市の政治的派閥を統一することを約束した. ● **unified** ADJ 形容詞 統一された, 統合された ❑ *...a unified system of taxation.* 統一された税制

uni|lat|er|al /yùnɪlǽtərəl/ ADJ 形容詞 A **unilateral** decision is made by only one of the groups, organizations, or countries that are involved in a particular situation, without the agreement of the others. 一方的な, 単独の ❑ *...unilateral nuclear disarmament.* 一方的な核軍縮

un|im|agi|nable /ʌ̀nɪmǽdʒɪnəbəl/ ADJ 形容詞 If you describe something as **unimaginable**, you are emphasizing that it is difficult to imagine or understand well, because it is not part of people's normal experience. 想像できない, 想像を絶する [EMPHASIS 強調] ❑ *The scale of the fighting is almost unimaginable.* その戦いの規模はほとんど想像を絶する. ● **un|im|agi|nably** /ʌ̀nɪmǽdʒɪnəbli/ ADV 副詞 [ADV adj] 想像を絶するほど ❑ *Conditions in prisons out there are unimaginably bad.* 世の中の刑務所の状態というのは想像を絶するほどひどい.

un|im|por|tant /ʌ̀nɪmpɔ́rtənt/ ADJ 形容詞 If you describe something or someone as **unimportant**, you mean that they do not have much influence, effect, or value, and are therefore not worth serious consideration. 重要ではない, 取るに足りない ❑ *When they had married, six years before, the difference in their ages had* seemed unimportant. 6年前に彼らが結婚した時, 2人の年の差は取るに足りないことに思えた.

Thesaurus	unimportant また次を参照:

ADJ. frivolous, insignificant, trivial; (ant.) important

un|im|pressed /ʌ̀nɪmprést/ ADJ 形容詞 If you are **unimpressed** by something or someone, you do not think they are very good, intelligent, or useful. 感銘を受けない, 感動しない [v-link ADJ] ❑ *He was also very unimpressed by his teachers.* 彼もまた先生たちから何の感銘を受けなかった.

un|in|hib|it|ed /ʌ̀nɪnhíbɪtɪd/ ADJ 形容詞 If you describe a person or their behavior as **uninhibited**, you mean that they express their opinions and feelings openly, and behave as they want to, without worrying what other people think. (言動が) 抑制されていない 非常に自由な, 遠慮のない ❑ *...a bold and uninhibited entertainer.* 大胆で遠慮のない芸人 ❑ *The dancing is uninhibited and as frenzied as an aerobics class.* その踊りは非常に自由で, エアロビクスクラスのように熱狂的だった.

un|in|stall /ʌ̀nɪnstɔ́l/ (uninstalls, uninstalling, uninstalled) V-T 他動詞 If you **uninstall** a computer program, you remove it permanently from your computer. (コンピュータ・プログラムを) 削除する, アンインストールする [COMPUTING コンピューティング] ❑ *If you don't like the program, just uninstall it and forget it.* もしそのプログラムを好きじゃないなら, アンインストールして忘れてしまえばいいだけさ.

un|in|tel|li|gible /ʌ̀nɪntélɪdʒɪbəl/ ADJ 形容詞 **Unintelligible** language is impossible to understand, for example because it is not written or pronounced clearly, or because its meaning is confused or complicated. 理解できない, 不めいりょうな, あいまいな ❑ *He muttered something unintelligible.* 彼は何かよく分からないことをつぶやいた.

un|in|ten|tion|al /ʌ̀nɪnténʃənəl/ ADJ 形容詞 Something that is **unintentional** is not done deliberately, but happens by accident. 故意でない, 意図しない ❑ *Perhaps he had slightly misled them, but it was quite unintentional.* 彼は彼らを少し間違った方向に導いてしまったかもしれないが, それは意図的ではなかった. ● **un|in|ten|tion|al|ly** ADV 副詞 意図せずに, うかつに ❑ *...an overblown and unintentionally funny adaptation of "Dracula."* オーバーで, 意図せずおかしい『吸血鬼ドラキュラ』の脚色

un|in|ter|rupt|ed /ʌ̀nɪntərʌ́ptɪd/ **1** ADJ 形容詞 If something is **uninterrupted**, it is continuous and has no breaks or interruptions in it. 途切れない, 絶え間ない ❑ *This enables the healing process to continue uninterrupted.* これで休みなく回復が続くようになる. ❑ *His hearing remained good, so that his contact with the world was uninterrupted.* 彼の聴力はずっとよいままだったので, 彼は世の中とのつながりを失うことがなかった. **2** ADJ 形容詞 An **uninterrupted** view of something is a clear view of it, without any obstacles in the way. (眺めが) さえぎられない ❑ *Diners can enjoy an uninterrupted view of the gardens.* 食事客はさえぎるもののない庭の眺めを楽しめる.

un|ion /yúnyən/ (unions) **1** N-COUNT 可算名詞 A **union** is a workers' organization which represents its members and which tries to improve things such as their working conditions and pay. 労働組合 ❑ *Do all teachers have a right to join a union?* すべての教師は労働組合に入る権利が持つか? **2** N-UNCOUNT 不可算名詞 When the **union** of two or more things occurs, they are joined together and become one thing. (2つ以上の物の) 結合 融合 ❑ *In 1918 the Romanian majority in this former czarist province voted for union with Romania.* 1918年, この旧ロシア帝政地方の大多数のルーマニア人がルーマニアとの統合に賛成票を投じた. **3** N-SING 単数名詞 When two or more things, for example countries or organizations, have been joined together to form one thing, you can refer to them as a **union**. (国や組織などの) 連合 同盟 ❑ *Tanzania is a union of the states of Tanganyika and Zanzibar.* タンザニアはタンガニーカとザンジバルの連合共和国だ.
→ see Word Web: **union**
→ see **empire, factory**

Word Web	union

In some places, **laborers** work long hours with little chance for a **raise** in **wages**. **Workdays** of 10 to 12 hours are not uncommon. Some people even work seven days a week. Conditions like this lead to unrest among **workers**. At that point, **organizers** can sometimes get them to join a **union**. Union leaders engage in **collective bargaining** with business owners. They try to win a shorter workday or better working conditions for workers. If the **employees** are not satisfied with the results, they may **strike**. In Sweden, 85% of laborers and 75% of **white-collar** employees belong to unions.

u

unique /yuniːk/ **1** ADJ 形容詞 Something that is **unique** is the only one of its kind. 唯一の、1つしかない ❑ *Each person's signature is unique.* どの人の署名もただ1つしかない. ●**unique|ly** ADV 副詞 独自に ❑ *Because of the extreme cold, the Antarctic is a uniquely fragile environment.* 南極地域は、その非常な寒さのために、他に類を見ないほど壊れやすい環境となっている. ●**unique|ness** N-UNCOUNT 不可算名詞 唯一無二 ❑ *...the uniqueness of China's own experience.* 中国独自の経験の特異性 **2** ADJ 形容詞 You can use **unique** to describe things that you admire because they are very unusual and special. たぐいまれな、比類なき [APPROVAL 賛成] ❑ *She was a woman of unique talent and determination.* 彼女はたぐいまれな才能と決意に満ちた女性だった. ●**unique|ly** ADV 副詞 極めてまれに、比類なく ❑ *There'll never be a shortage of people who consider themselves uniquely qualified to be president of the United States.* 自分は米国大統領になる比類なき資質を備えていると考える人たちが不足することは決してないだろう. **3** ADJ 形容詞 [v-link ADJ 'to' n] If something is **unique to** one thing, person, group, or place, it concerns or belongs only to that thing, person, group, or place. (一に) 特有の ❑ *No one knows for sure why adolescence is unique to humans.* なぜ青年期が人類特有のものであるかは誰にもはっきりとは分からない. ●**unique|ly** ADV 副詞 [ADV adj] 特有に ❑ *The problem isn't uniquely American.* その問題はアメリカ特有のものではない.

uni|sex /yuːnɪsɛks/ ADJ 形容詞 **Unisex** is used to describe things, usually clothes or places, which are designed for use by both men and women rather than by only one sex. 男女両用の、ユニセックスの ❑ *...the classic unisex hair salon.* 昔ながらの男女両用の美容院

uni|son /yuːnɪsən, -zən/ **1** PHRASE 句 If two or more people do something **in unison**, they do it together at the same time. 同時に、いっせいに ❑ *Every morning the kids say the Pledge of Allegiance in unison.* 毎朝、子供たちは「忠誠の近い」を斉唱する. **2** PHRASE 句 If people or organizations act **in unison**, they act the same way because they agree with each other or because they want to achieve the same goals. 一致協力して ❑ *The international community is ready to work in unison against him.* 国際社会は一致協力して彼に対抗する構えだ.

unit /yuːnɪt/ (**units**) **1** N-COUNT 可算名詞 If you consider something as a **unit**, you consider it as a single, complete thing. 一個、一群、単体 ❑ *Agriculture was based in the past on the family as a unit.* 農業は昔は家族単位で行われていた. **2** N-COUNT 可算名詞 A **unit** is a group of people who work together at a specific job, often in a particular place. (仕事の) 部署、課 ❑ *...the environmental research unit.* 環境調査課 **3** N-COUNT 可算名詞 A **unit** is a group within an armed force or police force, whose members fight or work together or carry out a particular task. (軍の) 部隊 ❑ *...a firefighting unit.* 戦闘部隊 **4** N-COUNT 可算名詞 A **unit** is a small machine which has a particular function, often part of a larger machine. (機械の) 装置 ❑ *The unit plugs into any TV set.* この装置はどのテレビにもつながる. **5** N-COUNT 可算名詞 A **unit** of measurement is a fixed standard quantity, amount, or weight that is used for measuring things. The quart, the inch, and the ounce are all units. (計測の) 単位 **6** N-COUNT 可算名詞 A **unit** is one of the parts that a textbook is divided into. (教科書の) 単元 ❑ *Unit V of this book explains those errors in detail and shows you ways to correct them.* この本の単元Vに、それらの間違いが詳細に説明されており、その修正方法も載っている.

→ see **graph**

unit cost (**unit costs**) N-COUNT 可算名詞 **Unit cost** is the amount of money that it costs a company to produce one article. 単位原価、単価 [BUSINESS 実業] ❑ *They hope to reduce unit costs through extra sales.* 彼らは追加販売を通して単位原価を下げたいと思っている.

unite /yuːnaɪt/ (**unites, uniting, united**) V-T/V-I 他動詞/自動詞 If a group of people or things **unite** or if something **unites** them, they join together and act as a group. 団結させる、結合させる [他動詞]、団結する、結合する [自動詞] ❑ *We need to unite against terrorism.* 我々はテロ行為に対抗し団結する必要がある.

unit|ed /yuːnaɪtɪd/ **1** ADJ 形容詞 When people are **united** about something, they agree about it and act together. 団結した、結束した ❑ *The entire Brazilian people are united by their love of soccer.* ブラジル国民全員がサッカーへの愛で結ばれている. **2** ADJ 形容詞 **United** is used to describe a country which has been formed from two or more states or countries. (国が) 統一された ❑ *...the first elections to be held in a united Germany for fifty eight years.* 58年間で初めて統一ドイツで開かれる選挙

Unit|ed Na|tions N-PROPER 固有名詞 The **United Nations** is an organization which most countries belong to. Its role is to encourage international peace, cooperation, and friendship. 国際連合

unit sales N-PLURAL 複数名詞 **Unit sales** refers to the number of individual items that a company sells. 売上数量 [BUSINESS 実業] ❑ *Unit sales of T-shirts increased 6%.* Tシャツの売上数量が6パーセント増えた.

unit trust (**unit trusts**) N-COUNT 可算名詞 A **unit trust** the same as a **mutual fund**. 契約型投資信託会社 [BRIT 英国英語 BUSINESS 実業]

unity /yuːnɪti/ **1** N-UNCOUNT 不可算名詞 **Unity** is the state of different areas or groups being joined together to form a single country or organization. (国や組織の) 統一 ❑ *We have to act to preserve the unity of this nation.* 我々はこの国の統一を維持するために行動しなくてはならない. **2** N-UNCOUNT 不可算名詞 When there is **unity**, people are in agreement and act together for a particular purpose. 結束、団結 ❑ *...a renewed unity of purpose.* 目的のための新たな団結 ❑ *Speakers at the rally expressed sentiments of unity.* 集会の演説者は団結の気持ちを表した.

uni|ver|sal /yuːnɪvɜrsəl/ **1** ADJ 形容詞 Something that is **universal** relates to everyone in the world or everyone in a particular group or society. 世界共通の、(人々の間で) みなに共通する ❑ *The insurance industry has produced its own proposals for universal health care.* 保険業は万人の健康管理に対する独自の提案を行った. ❑ *The desire to look attractive is universal.* 魅力的に見られたいという願望は世界共通だ. **2** ADJ 形容詞 Something that is **universal** affects or relates to every part of the world or the universe. 全世界の、宇宙の ❑ *...universal diseases.* 世界的な病気

uni|ver|sal bank (**universal banks**) N-COUNT 可算名詞 A **universal bank** is a bank that offers both banking and stockbroking services to its clients. 総合銀行 (銀行業と株式仲買業の両方を行う) [BUSINESS 実業] ❑ *...universal banks offering a wide range of services.* 幅広いサービスを提供する総合銀行

uni|ver|sal|ly /yuːnɪvɜrsəli/ **1** ADV 副詞 If something is **universally** believed or accepted, it is believed or accepted by everyone with no disagreement. 万人に、広く ❑ *...a universally accepted point of view.* 一般に受け入れられている考え方 **2** ADV 副詞 If something is **universally** true, it is true everywhere in the world or in all situations. 普遍的に、世界的に ❑ *The disadvantage is that it is not universally available.* 不利な点は、それが世界のどこでも入手可能ではないことだ.

uni|verse /yuːnɪvɜrs/ (**universes**) **1** N-COUNT 可算名詞 The **universe** is the whole of space and all the stars, planets, and other forms of matter and energy in it. 宇宙 ❑ *Einstein's equations showed the universe to be expanding.* アインシュタイン方程式は宇宙が膨張していることを証明した. **2** N-COUNT 可算名詞 If you talk about someone's **universe**, you are referring to the whole of their experience or an important part of it. (個人の) 世界 ❑ *Good writers suck in what they see of the world, re-creating their own universe on the page.* 優れた作家は彼らが見た世界を吸収し、紙の上に独自の世界を再び作り上げる.

→ see **galaxy, telescope**

uni|ver|sity /yuːnɪvɜrsɪti/ (**universities**) N-VAR; N-IN-NAMES 可変性名詞、名称中の名詞 A **university** is an institution where students study for degrees and where academic research is done. 大学 ❑ *Offenbacker earned an education degree at the University of Washington and taught elementary school.* オッフェンバッカーはワシントン大学で教育の学位を取得し、小学校で教えた. ❑ *She goes to Duke University.* 彼女はデューク大学に通っている.

un|just /ʌndʒʌst/ ADJ 形容詞 If you describe an action, system, or law as **unjust**, you think that it treats a person or group badly in a way that they do not deserve. 不公平な、不当な ❑ *The attack on Charles was unjust.* チャールズへの攻撃は不当なものだった. ●**un|just|ly** ADV 副詞 不公平に、不当に ❑ *She was unjustly accused of stealing money, and then fired.* 彼女はお金を盗んだと不当に訴えられ、その後、解雇された.

un|jus|ti|fied /ʌndʒʌstɪfaɪd/ ADJ 形容詞 If you describe a belief or action as **unjustified**, you think that there is no good reason for having it or doing it. 不当な、理由のない ❑ *Your report last week was unfair. It was based upon wholly unfounded and totally unjustified allegations.* あなたの先週の記事は公平さに欠ける. あれはまったく根拠のない、完全に不当な申し立てを基にしている.

un|kind /ʌnkaɪnd/ (**unkinder, unkindest**) **1** ADJ 形容詞 If someone is **unkind**, they behave in an unpleasant, unfriendly,

or slightly cruel way. You can also describe someone's words or actions as **unkind**. 不親切な，冷酷な □*All last summer he'd been unkind to her.* 彼は去年の夏中ずっと彼女に冷たかった．□*No one has an unkind word to say about him.* 彼のことを悪く言う人は誰もいない．●**un|kind|ly** ADV 副詞 不親切に，意地悪く □*Several viewers commented unkindly on her costumes.* 何人もの視聴者が彼女の衣装を意地悪く批評した．●**un|kind|ness** N-UNCOUNT 不可算名詞 不親切，意地悪さ □*He realized the unkindness of the remark and immediately regretted having hurt her with it.* 彼はその言葉の冷たさに気づき，彼女を傷つけたことをすぐに後悔した．**2** ADJ 形容詞 If you describe something bad that happens to someone as **unkind**, you mean that they do not deserve it. (天気など) 悪い，厳しい [WRITTEN 書き言葉] □*The weather was unkind to those pipers who played in the morning.* 今朝，笛を演奏した人たちには残念な天気だった．

Thesaurus　unkind また次を参照：

ADJ.　harsh, mean, unfriendly; (ant.) kind **1**

un|known /ʌnnoʊn/ (unknowns) **1** ADJ 形容詞 If something is **unknown** to you, you have no knowledge of it. 知られていない □*An unknown number of demonstrators were arrested.* 数知れないほどのデモの参加者が逮捕された．□*The motive for the killing is unknown.* 殺害の動機は分からない．●N-COUNT 可算名詞 An **unknown** is something that is unknown. 知られていないもの □*The length of the war is one of the biggest unknowns.* 戦争期間は最も不明な要素の1つだ．**2** ADJ 形容詞 An **unknown** person is someone whose name you do not know or whose character you do not know anything about. 名前も知らない，名も無い □*...the tomb of the unknown soldier.* 名も無い兵士の墓 **3** ADJ 形容詞 An **unknown** person is not famous or publicly recognized. 無名の □*He was an unknown writer.* 彼は無名の作家だった．●N-COUNT 可算名詞 An **unknown** is a person who is unknown. 無名の人 □*Within a short space of time a group of complete unknowns had established a wholly original form of humor.* 短期間のうちに，まったく無名だったグループが，とても独創的なユーモアの形を築き上げた．**4** ADJ 形容詞 If you say that a particular problem or situation is **unknown**, you mean that it never occurs. 未知の □*A hundred years ago coronary heart disease was virtually unknown in America.* 100年前に冠状動脈性心臓病はアメリカでほとんど知られていなかった．**5** N-SING 単数名詞 The **unknown** refers generally to things or places that people do not know about or understand. 未知のもの，未知の場所 □*Ignorance of people brings fear, fear of the unknown.* 人々の無知は恐怖をもたらす．未知のものへの恐怖だ．

un|law|ful /ʌnlɔːfəl/ ADJ 形容詞 If something is **unlawful**, the law does not allow you to do it. 違法の，非合法の [FORMAL 形式ばった] □*...employees who believe their dismissal was unlawful.* 彼らを解雇したのは違法だと確信している従業員 ●**un|law|ful|ly** ADV 副詞 [ADV with v] 違法に，非合法的に □*The government acted unlawfully in imposing the restrictions.* 政府はそれらの制限を加えるという違法な行動に出た．

un|lead|ed /ʌnlɛdɪd/ ADJ 形容詞 **Unleaded** fuel contains a smaller amount of lead than most fuels so that it produces less harmful substances when it is burned. 無鉛の □*He filled up his Toyota with regular unleaded gas.* 彼は自分のトヨタ車をレギュラーの無鉛ガソリンで満タンにした．●N-UNCOUNT 不可算名詞 **Unleaded** is also a noun. 無鉛ガソリン □*All its V8 engines will run happily on unleaded.* その車のV8エンジンはすべて，無鉛ガソリンでちゃんと走るだろう．

un|leash /ʌnliːʃ/ (unleashes, unleashing, unleashed) V-T 他動詞 If you say that someone or something **unleashes** a powerful force, feeling, activity, or group, you mean that they suddenly start it or send it somewhere. (エネルギーや感情などを) 解き放つ，引き起こす □*The announcement unleashed a storm of protest from the public.* その発表は国民からの抗議の嵐を巻き起こした．□*The officers were still reluctant to unleash their troops in pursuit of a defeated enemy.* 将校たちは敗れた敵の追跡に彼らの部隊を放つことをまだためらっていた．

un|less /ʌnlɛs/ CONJ 接続詞 You use **unless** to introduce the only circumstances in which an event you are mentioning will not take place or in which a statement you are making is not true. —でない限り，—でないならば □*Unless you are trying to lose weight to please yourself, it's going to be tough to keep your motivation level high.* 自分を喜ばせるために減量しようとしているのでなければ，やる気を高く持ち続けることは難しいだろう．□*We cannot understand disease unless we understand the person who has the disease.* 病気になっている人を理解しない限り，その病気を理解することはできない．

Do not confuse **unless, except, except for,** and **besides. Unless** is used to introduce the only situation in which something will take place or be true. □*In the 1940s, unless she wore gloves a woman was not properly dressed...You must not give compliments unless you mean them.* You use **except** to introduce the only things, situations, people, or ideas that a statement does not apply to. □*All of his body relaxed except his right hand...Traveling was impossible, except in the cool of the morning.* You use **except for** before something that prevents a statement from being completely true. □*The classrooms were silent, except for the scratching of pens on paper... I had absolutely no friends except for Tom.* You use **besides** to introduce extra things in addition to the ones you are mentioning already. □*Fruit will give you, besides enjoyment, a source of vitamins.* However, note that if you talk about "the only thing" or "the only person **besides**" a particular person or thing, **besides** means the same as "apart from." □*He was the only person besides Gertrude who talked to Guy.*

un|like /ʌnlaɪk/ **1** PREP 前置詞 If one thing is **unlike** another thing, the two things have different qualities or characteristics from each other. (質や特徴などが) —とは違って —とは似ていない □*This was a foreign country, so unlike San Jose.* これはサンノゼとはまったく違う外国だった．**2** PREP 前置詞 You can use **unlike** to contrast two people, things, or situations, and show how they are different. (2人の人や2つのものを比較し) —とは違って —とは対照的に □*Unlike aerobics, walking entails no expensive fees for classes or clubs.* エアロビクスとは違い，ウォーキングには高いレッスン料やクラブ費がかからない．**3** PREP 前置詞 If you describe something that a particular person has done as being **unlike** them, you mean that you are surprised by it because it is not typical of their character or normal behavior. —らしくない □*It was so unlike him to say something like that, with such intensity, that I was astonished.* 彼がそんなことを，しかもわたしがビックリするような激しさで言うなんて，まったく彼らしくなかった．

un|like|ly /ʌnlaɪkli/ (unlikelier, unlikeliest) ADJ 形容詞 If you say that something is **unlikely to** happen or **unlikely to** be true, you believe that it will not happen or that it is not true, although you are not completely sure. ありそうもない，起こりそうにない □*A military coup seems unlikely.* 軍事クーデターはありそうにない．□*As with many technological revolutions, you are unlikely to be aware of it.* 多くの技術革命と同じで，あなたがそれに気づいている可能性はないだろう．

Word Partnership　unlikely は次の語句と使われる：

ADV.	**extremely** unlikely, **highly** unlikely, **most** unlikely, **very** unlikely
N.	unlikely **event**
V.	unlikely **to change,** unlikely **to happen, seem** unlikely

un|lim|it|ed /ʌnlɪmɪtɪd/ ADJ 形容詞 If there is an **unlimited** quantity of something, you can have as much or as many of that thing as you want. 無制限の，無限の □*An unlimited number of copies can still be made from the original.* 原型からまだ数限りないコピーを作ることができる．□*You'll also have unlimited access to the swimming pool.* またスイミングプールを無制限に使うことができます．

un|list|ed /ʌnlɪstɪd/ **1** ADJ 形容詞 If a person or their telephone number is **unlisted**, the number is not listed in the telephone book, and the telephone company will refuse to give it to people who ask for it. 電話帳に載っていない [mainly AM 主に米国英語] □*Mr. Marra, whose New York telephone number is unlisted, could not be contacted yesterday.* ニューヨークの電話番号が電話帳に載っていないマラ氏とは昨日，連絡が取れなかった．**2** ADJ 形容詞 An **unlisted** company or **unlisted** stock is not listed officially on a stock exchange. 非上場の，非公開の [BUSINESS 実業] □*Its shares are traded on the Unlisted Securities Market.* その株は非上場証券市場で取引されている．

un|load /ʌnloʊd/ (unloads, unloading, unloaded) V-T 他動詞 If you **unload** goods from a vehicle, or you **unload** a vehicle, you remove the goods from the vehicle, usually after they have been transported from one place to another. (荷を) 降ろす □*Unload everything from the boat and clean it thoroughly.* 船から何もかも降ろし，船を丁寧に洗う．

un|lock /ʌnlɒk/ (unlocks, unlocking, unlocked) **1** V-T 他動詞 If you **unlock** something such as a door, a room, or a container that has a lock, you open it using a key. (ドアや部屋の) かぎを開ける □*He unlocked the car and threw the coat on to the back seat.* 彼は車のかぎを開け，コートを後ろの座席に放り投げた．**2** V-T 他動詞 If you **unlock** the potential or the secrets of something or someone, you release them. (才能を) 解き放つ (秘密を) 明かす □*The point of the competition is to encourage all people to unlock their hidden potential.* そのコンテストの趣旨は，みんなの隠された才能を解き放つよう促すことだ．

un|lucky /ʌnlʌki/ (**unluckier, unluckiest**) **1** ADJ 形容詞 If someone is **unlucky**, they have bad luck. (人が) 運の悪い □*You certainly were unlucky to get that horrible illness.* あのひどい病気をもらうなんて、きみは確かに運が悪かったよ. **2** ADJ 形容詞 You can use **unlucky** to describe unpleasant things which happen to someone, especially when you feel that the person does not deserve them. (物事が) 残念な あいにくの □*...Argentina's unlucky defeat by Ireland.* アルゼンチンのアイルランドに対する不運な敗北 **3** ADJ 形容詞 **Unlucky** is used to describe something that is thought to cause bad luck. 縁起の悪い、不吉な □*Some people think it is unlucky to walk under a ladder.* ある人たちははしごの下を歩くのは縁起が悪いと思っている.

un|marked /ʌnmɑːrkt/ **1** ADJ 形容詞 Something that is **unmarked** has no marks on it. しみが付いていない □*Her shoes are still white and unmarked.* 彼女の靴はまだ真っ白でしみが付いていない. **2** ADJ 形容詞 Something that is **unmarked** has no marking on it which identifies what it is or whose it is. 標示のない □*He had seen them come out and get into the unmarked police car.* 彼は、彼らが出てきて覆面パトカーに乗り込むのを見た.

un|me|tered /ʌnmiːtərd/ ADJ 形容詞 An **unmetered** service for something such as water supply is one that allows you to use as much as you want for a basic cost, instead of paying for the amount you use. 定額制の、メーター制でない □*Clients are not charged by the minute but given unmetered access to the Internet for a fixed fee.* 顧客は分刻みで課金されず、固定料金でインターネットにアクセスし放題だ.

un|mis|tak|able /ʌnmɪsteɪkəbəl/ also **unmistakeable** ADJ 形容詞 If you describe something as **unmistakable**, you mean that it is so obvious that it cannot be mistaken for anything else. 間違えようのない、紛れもない □*He didn't give his name, but the voice was unmistakable.* 彼は名前を名乗らなかったが、その声は聞き違えようがなかった. ●**un|mis|tak|ably** /ʌnmɪsteɪkəbli/ ADV 副詞 紛れもなく □*It's still unmistakably a Minnelli movie.* それはまだ紛れもなくミネリの映画だ.

un|miti|gat|ed /ʌnmɪtɪgeɪtɪd/ ADJ 形容詞 You use **unmitigated** to emphasize that a bad situation or quality is totally bad. (悪いことを強調して) まったくの [EMPHASIS 強調] [ADJ n] □*Last year's cotton crop was an unmitigated disaster.* 昨年の綿の収穫はまったく悲惨だった.

Word Link mov ≈ moving : movement, movie, unmoved

un|moved /ʌnmuːvd/ ADJ 形容詞 If you are **unmoved** by something, you are not emotionally affected by it. 心を動かされない、動じない [v-link ADJ] □*Mr. Bird remained unmoved by the corruption allegations.* バード氏は汚職疑惑に動じなかった.

un|named /ʌnneɪmd/ **1** ADJ 形容詞 **Unnamed** people or things are talked about but their names are not mentioned. 名前を伏せた □*Perot accused unnamed U.S. officials of covering up the facts.* ペローは、名前を伏せた米国担当官が事実を隠蔽したとして告発した. **2** ADJ 形容詞 **Unnamed** things have not been given a name. 名前のない □*...unnamed comets and asteroids.* 名も無いすい星や小惑星

un|natu|ral /ʌnnætʃərəl/ **1** ADJ 形容詞 If you describe something as **unnatural**, you mean that it is strange and often frightening, because it is different from what you normally expect. (物事が) 異常な 異様な □*The aircraft rose with unnatural speed on takeoff.* 飛行機は離陸時に異常なスピードで上昇した. ●**un|natu|ral|ly** ADV 副詞 [ADV adj] 異常に、異様に □*The house was unnaturally silent.* その家は異様に静かだった. **2** ADJ 形容詞 Behavior that is **unnatural** seems artificial and not normal or genuine. (行動が) 不自然な わざとらしい □*She gave him a bright, determined smile which seemed unnatural.* 彼女は彼に、にこやかに決然とほほえんだが、そのほほえみは不自然に見えた. ●**un|natu|ral|ly** ADV 副詞 [ADV with v] わざとらしく □*Try to avoid shouting or speaking unnaturally.* どなったりわざとらしい話し方をしないよう心がける.

un|natu|ral|ly /ʌnnætʃərəli/ **1** PHRASE 句 You can use **not unnaturally** to indicate that the situation you are describing is exactly as you would expect in the circumstances. 案の定、思ったとおり □*The result, not unnaturally, was that he became more tense and increasingly frustrated.* その結果、思ったとおり彼はさらにピリピリし、ますますいら立ってきた. **2** → see also **unnatural**

un|nec|es|sary /ʌnnɛsəseri/ ADJ 形容詞 If you describe something as **unnecessary**, you mean that it is not needed or does not have to be done. 必要ない、不要な □*The slaughter of whales is unnecessary and inhuman.* 鯨の大量殺戮は不要にも残酷だ. ●**un|nec|es|sari|ly** /ʌnnɛsəsɛrɪli/ ADV 副詞 不必要に、いたずらに □*I didn't want to upset my husband or my daughter unnecessarily.* わたしは夫や娘をいたずらに動揺させたくなかった.

Thesaurus *unnecessary* また次を参照 :

ADJ. dispensable, superfluous, useless; (*ant.*) necessary

un|nerve /ʌnnɜːrv/ (**unnerves, unnerving, unnerved**) V-T 他動詞 If you say that something **unnerves** you, you mean that it worries or troubles you. はらはらさせる、ろうばいさせる □*The news about Dermot had unnerved me.* ダーモットのそのニュースにわたしはギョッとした.

un|nerv|ing /ʌnnɜːrvɪŋ/ ADJ 形容詞 If you describe something as **unnerving**, you mean that it makes you feel worried or uncomfortable. はらはらするような、うろたえるような □*It is very unnerving to find out that someone you see every day is carrying a potentially deadly virus.* 毎日会う人が、致死の可能性があるウィルス保持者だと発見するのは、とてもろうばいする.

un|no|ticed /ʌnnoʊtɪst/ ADJ 形容詞 If something happens or passes **unnoticed**, it is not seen or noticed by anyone. 見られない、気付かれない □*I tried to slip up the stairs unnoticed.* わたしは気づかれないように2階へこっそり上がろうとした.

un|ob|tru|sive /ʌnəbtruːsɪv/ ADJ 形容詞 If you describe something or someone as **unobtrusive**, you mean that they are not easily noticed or do not draw attention to themselves. 目立たない、控えめな [FORMAL 形式ばった] □*The coffee table is glass, to be as unobtrusive as possible.* コーヒーテーブルはできるだけ目立たないようガラス製だ. ●**un|ob|tru|sive|ly** ADV 副詞 目立たず □*They slipped away unobtrusively.* 彼らは目立たないよう席を外した.

un|of|fi|cial /ʌnəfɪʃəl/ ADJ 形容詞 An **unofficial** action or statement is not organized or approved by a person or group in authority. 非公式の □*Staff voted to continue an unofficial strike in support of seven colleagues who were dismissed last week.* 先週、解雇された7人の同僚を支援して、スタッフは非公式のストライキの続行を投票決定した. ●**un|of|fi|cial|ly** ADV 副詞 非公式に □*Some workers are legally employed, but the majority work unofficially with neither health insurance nor wage security.* 労働者の数名は合法的に雇われているが、大半が非公式に健康保険も賃金保証もなく働いている.

Word Link dox ≈ opinion : orthodoxy, paradox, unorthodox

un|ortho|dox /ʌnɔːrθədɒks/ ADJ 形容詞 If you describe someone's behavior, beliefs, or customs as **unorthodox**, you mean that they are different from what is generally accepted. 正統的でない、型破りな □*The reality-based show followed the unorthodox lives of Ozzy, his wife Sharon, daughter Kelly, and son, Jack.* オジーとその妻シャロン、娘ケリーと息子ジャックの型破りなライブの後にリアリティ・ショーが続いた.

un|pack /ʌnpæk/ (**unpacks, unpacking, unpacked**) V-T/V-I 他動詞/自動詞 When you **unpack** a suitcase, box, or similar container, or you **unpack** the things inside it, you take the things out of the container. (荷物などを) 開ける 中身を取り出す [他動詞]、荷をほどく [自動詞] □*He unpacked his bag.* 彼はバッグを開けた.

un|paid /ʌnpeɪd/ **1** ADJ 形容詞 If you do **unpaid** work or are an **unpaid** worker, you do a job without receiving any money for it. 無給の [ADJ n] □*Even unpaid work for charity is better than nothing.* チャリティーのための無給労働でさえ何もないよりはまし. **2** ADJ 形容詞 **Unpaid** taxes or bills, for example, are taxes or bills which have not been paid yet. 未払いの □*...millions of dollars in unpaid taxes.* 未払い税金の何百万ドル

un|pal|at|able /ʌnpælɪtəbəl/ **1** ADJ 形容詞 If you describe an idea as **unpalatable**, you mean that you find it unpleasant and difficult to accept. (考えなどが) 不快で 受け入れがたい □*It was only then that I began to learn the unpalatable truth about John.* その時になって初めて、わたしはジョンの受け入れがたい事実を知り始めた. **2** ADJ 形容詞 If you describe food as **unpalatable**, you mean that it is so unpleasant that you can hardly eat it. (食べ物が) まずい とても食べられない □*...a lump of dry, unpalatable cheese.* 乾いたまずいチーズの塊

un|par|al|leled /ʌnpærəleld/ ADJ 形容詞 If you describe something as **unparalleled**, you are emphasizing that it is, for example, bigger, better, or worse than anything else of its kind, or anything that has happened before. 並ぶもののない、空前の [EMPHASIS 強調] □*...a period of unparalleled economic growth.* 比類のない経済成長期

un|pleas|ant /ʌnplɛzənt/ **1** ADJ 形容詞 If something is **unpleasant**, it gives you bad feelings, for example by making you feel upset or uncomfortable. 不愉快な、不快な □*The symptoms can be uncomfortable, unpleasant, and serious.* 症状は気持ち悪く、不快で深刻なことがある. □*The vacuum has an unpleasant smell.* その掃除機は嫌なにおいがする. ●**un|pleas|ant|ly** ADV 副詞 気持ち悪くなるくらい □*The water moved around the body, unpleasantly thick and brown.* 気持ち悪いくらいどろどろした茶色い水がその体の周りを動いていた. □*The smell was unpleasantly strong.* そのにおいは気持ち悪いくらい強烈だった. **2** ADJ 形容詞 An **unpleasant** person is very unfriendly and rude. 不親切な、失礼な □*She thought he was an unpleasant man.* 彼女は彼のことを失礼な人だと思った. ●**un|pleas|ant|ly** ADV 副詞 不親切に、無礼に □*Melissa laughed unpleasantly.* メリッサは失礼にも笑った.

Thesaurus   *unpleasant* また次を参照：

ADJ. irksome, troublesome; (ant.) pleasant 1
      mean, rude, unkind 2

un|plug /ʌnplʌg/ (unplugs, unplugging, unplugged) V-T 他動詞
If you **unplug** an electrical device or telephone, you pull a wire out
of an outlet so that it stops working. (電気製品などの) コンセント
を抜く □*Whenever there's a storm, I unplug my computer.* 嵐の時はいつ
でも私はコンピュータのコンセントを抜く.

un|pop|ular /ʌnpɒpyʊlər/ ADJ 形容詞 If something or
someone is **unpopular**, most people do not like them. 人気がない,
不評の □*It was a painful and unpopular decision.* それはつらくて不評の
決断だった. □*In high school, I was very unpopular, and I did encounter
a little prejudice.* 高校でわたしは人気がなく, ちょっとした偏見にあっ
た. ● **un|pop|ular|ity** /ʌnpɒpyʊlærɪti/ N-UNCOUNT 不可算名詞
人気のないこと, 不評 □*...his unpopularity among his colleagues.* 同僚
の間で彼の評判が悪いこと

un|prec|edent|ed /ʌnprɛsɪdəntɪd/ 1 ADJ 形容詞 If something
is **unprecedented**, it has never happened before. 前代未聞の, 今
までにない □*Such a move is rare, but not unprecedented.* そんな映画は
珍しいが, 前代未聞ってわけではない. 2 ADJ 形容詞 If you describe
something as **unprecedented**, you are emphasizing that it is very
great in quality, amount, or scale. (質やスケールが) かつてない
[EMPHASIS 強調] □*The mission has been hailed as an unprecedented
success.* その任務はかつてない成功として称讃されている.

un|pre|dict|able /ʌnprɪdɪktəbəl/ ADJ 形容詞 If you describe
someone or something as **unpredictable**, you mean that you
cannot tell what they are going to do or how they are going to
behave. 予測できない, 気まぐれな □*He is utterly unpredictable.* 彼
は本当に気まぐれだ. ● **un|pre|dict|abil|ity** /ʌnprɪdɪktəbɪlɪti/
N-UNCOUNT 不可算名詞 [oft with poss] 予測不可能であること
□*...the unpredictability of the weather.* 天気の予測がつかないこと

un|pre|pared /ʌnprɪpɛərd/ 1 ADJ 形容詞 If you are
unprepared for something, you are not ready for it, and you
are therefore surprised or at a disadvantage when it happens.
(～に対する) 準備ができていない □*I was totally unprepared for the
announcement on the next day.* わたしは翌日の発表の準備がまったく
できていなかった. □*Faculty members complain that their students are
unprepared to do college-level work.* 教授らは, 学生が大学レベルの
勉強をする準備ができていないとこぼしている. 2 ADJ 形容詞 If you
are **unprepared to** do something, you are not willing to do it. (～
することに) 乗り気でない [v-link ADJ to-inf] □*They are unprepared to
accept the real reasons for their domestic and foreign situation.* 彼らは国
内外の問題の本当の理由を受け入れたがらない.

un|pro|duc|tive /ʌnprədʌktɪv/ ADJ 形容詞 Something that is
unproductive does not produce any good results. 非生産的な, 効
果のない □*Research workers are well aware that much of their time and
effort is unproductive.* 研究者たちは彼らの時間と労力の大半が無益であ
ることをよく知っている.

un|pro|fes|sion|al /ʌnprəfɛʃənəl/ ADJ 形容詞 If you use
unprofessional to describe someone's behavior at work, you are
criticizing them for not behaving according to the standards
that are expected of a person in their profession. プロとは思えな
い, プロとしてふさわしくない [DISAPPROVAL 不賛成] □*He was fired
for unprofessional conduct.* 彼はプロとしてふさわしくない行動のため
に解雇された.

un|prof|it|able /ʌnprɒfɪtəbəl/ 1 ADJ 形容詞 An industry,
company, or product that is **unprofitable** does not make any
profit or does not make enough profit. 採算の取れな
い [BUSINESS 実業] □*...unprofitable, badly-run industries.* 採算性が
なく, 経営のひどい産業 2 ADJ 形容詞 **Unprofitable** activities or
efforts do not produce any useful or helpful results. (努力などが)
無駄な □*...an endless, unprofitable argument.* きりのない無駄な議論

un|pro|tect|ed /ʌnprətɛktɪd/ 1 ADJ 形容詞 An **unprotected**
person or place is not watched over or defended, and so they may
be harmed or attacked. 保護のない □*The landing beaches would be
unprotected.* 上陸浜は無装甲だと思う. 2 ADJ 形容詞 If something
is **unprotected**, it is not covered or treated with anything, and so
it may easily be damaged. 無防備な □*Exposure of unprotected skin
to the sun carries the risk of developing skin cancer.* 日焼け止めなしの
日光浴には皮膚癌の危険が伴う. 3 ADJ 形容詞 If two people have
unprotected sex, they do not use a condom to protect against
sexually-transmitted diseases and pregnancy. 無防備の [ADJ n]
□*...the dangers of unprotected sex.* 無防備の性行為の危険性

un|pub|lished /ʌnpʌblɪʃt/ ADJ 形容詞 An **unpublished** book,
letter, or report has never been published. An **unpublished** writer
has never had his or her work published. 未発表の □*Much of his
writing remains unpublished.* 彼の作品の多くは未発表のままである.

un|quali|fied /ʌnkwɒlɪfaɪd/ 1 ADJ 形容詞 If you are
unqualified, you do not have any qualifications, or you do not
have the right qualifications for a particular job. 資格のない □*She
was unqualified for the job.* 彼女はその仕事には不適任だった. 2 ADJ

形容詞 **Unqualified** means total or unlimited. 完全な [EMPHASIS
強調] □*The event was an unqualified success.* その行事は文句なしの成
功だった.

un|ques|tion|able /ʌnkwɛstʃənəbəl/ 形容詞 If you
describe something as **unquestionable**, you are emphasizing
that it is so obviously true or real that nobody can doubt it. 疑い
のない [EMPHASIS 強調] □*He inspires affection and respect as a man of
unquestionable integrity.* 彼は誠実そのものの人として人々に愛情と尊
敬の気持ちを抱かせる. ● **un|ques|tion|ably** /ʌnkwɛstʃənəbli/ ADV
副詞 [ADV with cl/group] □*They have seen the change as
unquestionably beneficial to the country.* 彼らは変化がその国に確かに
有益であることを見てきた.

un|rav|el /ʌnrævəl/ (unravels, unraveling, unraveled)
1 V-T/V-I 他動詞/自動詞 If you **unravel** something that is knotted,
woven, or knitted, or if it **unravels**, it becomes one straight piece
again or separates into its different threads. 解く □*He could
unravel a knot that others wouldn't even attempt.* 彼は他の人がやってみ
ようとすらしない結び目を解くことができた. 2 V-T/V-I 他動詞/自動
詞 If you **unravel** a mystery or puzzle, or it **unravels**, it gradually
becomes clearer until you can work out the answer to it. 解明す
る □*A young mother has flown to Iceland to unravel the mystery of her
husband's disappearance.* 若い母親は夫の失踪 (そう) のなぞを解明する
ためにアイスランドに飛行機で行った.
→ see **rope**

un|real /ʌnriːl/ 1 ADJ 形容詞 If you say that a situation is
unreal, you mean that it is so strange that you find it difficult to
believe it is happening. 非現実的な [v-link ADJ] □*Then we won our
next 10 games, which remains a record. It was unreal* それから私達は次
の10試合に勝ち, それは今でも最高記録だ. 信じられないことだった.
● **un|real|ity** /ʌnriːæliti/ N-UNCOUNT 不可算名詞 非現実性 □*To
his surprise he didn't feel too weak. Light-headed certainly, and with a
sense of unreality, but able to walk.* 驚いたことに彼はそれほど衰弱し
ていなかった. 確かにめまいがして, 非現実的な感じがしたが歩くこと
はできた. 2 ADJ 形容詞 If you use **unreal** to describe something,
you are critical of it because you think that it is not like, or not
related to, things you expect to find in the real world. 実在しない
[DISAPPROVAL 不賛成] □*Almost all fictional detectives are unreal.* 小説
に出てくる探偵の大半はありえないようだらしい.

un|re|al|is|tic /ʌnriːəlɪstɪk/ ADJ 形容詞 If you say that someone
is being **unrealistic**, you mean that they do not recognize the
truth about a situation, especially about the difficulties involved
in something they want to achieve. 非現実的な □*There are
many who feel that the players are being completely unrealistic in their
demands.* 選手はひどく非現実的な要求をしていると多くの人々が感
じている. □*It would be unrealistic to expect such a process ever to be
completed.* そもそもそうしたプロセスが完了するのを期待するのは非
現実的だと思う.

un|rea|son|able /ʌnriːzənəbəl/ 1 ADJ 形容詞 If you say
that someone is being **unreasonable**, you mean that they are
behaving in a way that is not fair or sensible. 不当な □*The
strikers were being unreasonable in their demands, having rejected the
deal two weeks ago.* 示談を2週間前に拒否したストライキ参加者は不
当な要求をしていた. □*It was her unreasonable behavior with a Texan
playboy which broke up her marriage.* 彼女の結婚が破綻 (たん) した
原因はテキサス出身のプレーボーイに対する彼女の無分別な態度だ
った. ● **un|rea|son|ably** /ʌnriːzənəbli/ ADV 副詞 不当に □*We
unreasonably expect near perfect behavior from our children.* 私達は現
実を無視して完ぺきに近い言動を子供に期待する. 2 ADJ 形容詞 An
unreasonable decision, action, price, or amount seems unfair
and difficult to justify. 不当な □*...unreasonable increases in the price
of gas.* 法外なガス料金値上げ ● **un|rea|son|ably** ADV 副詞 法外に
□*The banks' charges are unreasonably high.* 銀行の手数料は法外に高い.

un|rec|og|niz|able /ʌnrɛkəgnaɪzəbl, -naɪz-/ ADJ 形容詞 If
someone or something is **unrecognizable**, they have become
impossible to recognize or identify, for example because they
have been greatly changed or damaged. 見分けのつかない [oft ADJ
'to' n] □*Today that same hotel is almost unrecognizable.* 今日あの同じ
ホテルはほとんど見分けがつかない.

un|re|lat|ed /ʌnrɪleɪtɪd/ 1 ADJ 形容詞 If one thing is **unrelated**
to another, there is no connection between them. You can also
say that two things are **unrelated**. 関係のない □*My line of work is
entirely unrelated to politics.* 私のしている仕事は政治とは全く関係な
い. 2 ADJ 形容詞 If one person is **unrelated to** another, they are
not members of the same family. You can also say that two people
are **unrelated**. 親族でない [WRITTEN 書き言葉] □*Jimmy is adopted
and thus unrelated to Beth by blood.* ジミーは養子なのでベスと血のつ
ながりはない.

un|re|lent|ing /ʌnrɪlɛntɪŋ/ 1 ADJ 形容詞 If you describe
someone's behavior as **unrelenting**, you mean that they are
continuing to do something in a very determined way, often
without caring whether they hurt or embarrass other people.

u

確固不動の ❏ *She established her authority with unrelenting thoroughness.* 彼女は確固不動の徹底さで権威を築き上げた. **2** ADJ 形容詞 If you describe something unpleasant as **unrelenting**, you mean that it continues without stopping. たゆまない ❏ *…an unrelenting downpour of rain.* なかなかやみそうにない大降りの雨

un|re|li|able /ʌnrɪlaɪəbᵊl/ ADJ 形容詞 If you describe a person, machine, or method as **unreliable**, you mean that you cannot trust them. 当てにならない ❏ *Diplomats can be a notoriously unreliable and misleading source of information.* 外交官は信頼できず誤解を招く情報を流すことで有名だ. ❏ *His judgment was unreliable.* 彼の判断は当てにならなかった.

un|re|mark|able /ʌnrɪmɑrkəbᵊl/ ADJ 形容詞 If you describe someone or something as **unremarkable**, you mean that they are very ordinary, without many exciting, original, or attractive qualities. 目立たない ❏ *…a tall, lean man, with an unremarkable face.* 目立たない痩せた背の高く痩せた男

un|re|pent|ant /ʌnrɪpɛntənt/ ADJ 形容詞 If you are **unrepentant**, you are not ashamed of your beliefs or actions. 恥じていない ❏ *Pamela was unrepentant about her strong language and abrasive remarks.* パメラは極端な表現と鋭い意見について弁解がましくなかった.

un|re|solved /ʌnrɪzɒlvd/ ADJ 形容詞 If a problem or difficulty is **unresolved**, no satisfactory solution has been found to it. 未解決の ❏ *The murder remains unresolved.* 殺人は未解決のままである.

un|rest /ʌnrɛst/ N-UNCOUNT 不可算名詞 If there is **unrest** in a particular place or society, people are expressing anger and dissatisfaction about something, often by demonstrating or rioting. 不安 [JOURNALISM ジャーナリズム] ❏ *The real danger is civil unrest in the east of the country.* 本当の危険はその国の東部における一般人の不穏状態である.

un|re|strict|ed /ʌnrɪstrɪktɪd/ **1** ADJ 形容詞 If an activity is **unrestricted**, you are free to do it in the way that you want, without being limited by any rules. 制限されない ❏ *Freedom to pursue extracurricular activities is totally unrestricted.* 課外活動を続けることは全く自由である. **2** ADJ 形容詞 If you have an **unrestricted** view of something, you can see it fully and clearly, because there is nothing in the way. 制限されない ❏ *Nearly all seats have an unrestricted view.* ほぼ全席が視界に制限がない.

un|ri|valed /ʌnraɪvᵊld/ ADJ 形容詞 If you describe something as **unrivaled**, you are emphasizing that it is better than anything else of the same kind. 無比の [EMPHASIS 強調] ❏ *He acquired unrivaled knowledge of party affairs.* 彼は党の業務について無比の知識を取得した.

un|ru|ly /ʌnruli/ **1** ADJ 形容詞 If you describe people, especially children, as **unruly**, you mean that they behave badly and are difficult to control. 始末に負えない ❏ *…unruly behavior.* 手に負えない言動 **2** ADJ 形容詞 **Unruly** hair is difficult to keep tidy. 乱れがちの ❏ *The man had remarkably black, unruly hair.* その男の髪は真っ黒で乱れていた.

un|safe /ʌnseɪf/ **1** ADJ 形容詞 If a building, machine, activity, or area is **unsafe**, it is dangerous. 安全でない ❏ *Critics claim the trucks are unsafe.* 批評家はトラックが安全でないと主張する. **2** ADJ 形容詞 If you are **unsafe**, you are in danger of being harmed. 危険な [v-link ADJ] ❏ *In the larger neighborhood, I felt very unsafe.* より大きな地域では私は非常に不安に感じた.

un|sat|is|fac|tory /ʌnsætɪsfæktəri/ ADJ 形容詞 If you describe something as **unsatisfactory**, you mean that it is not as good as it should be, and cannot be considered acceptable. 不満足な ❏ *He asked a few more questions, to which he received unsatisfactory answers.* 彼はもう少し質問をしたが, その回答は不満足だった.

Thesaurus

unsatisfactory また次を参照:

ADJ. inadequate, insufficient, unacceptable; (ant.) satisfactory

---

un|sa|vory /ʌnseɪvəri/ ADJ 形容詞 If you describe a person, place, or thing as **unsavory**, you mean that you find them unpleasant or morally unacceptable. 好ましくない [DISAPPROVAL 不賛成] ❏ *Police officers meet more unsavory characters in a week than most of us do in a lifetime.* 警察官は1週間に私達が一生会うより多くの好ましくない人物に会う.

un|scathed /ʌnskeɪðd/ ADJ 形容詞 If you are **unscathed** after a dangerous experience, you have not been injured or harmed by it. 無傷の [ADJ after v, v-link ADJ] ❏ *Tony emerged unscathed apart from a severely bruised finger.* トニーは指にひどくあざができたことを除いて無傷だった. ❏ *East Los Angeles was left relatively unscathed by the riots.* ロサンジェルスの東部は暴動の影響をそれほど受けなかった.

un|scru|pu|lous /ʌnskrupyələs/ ADJ 形容詞 If you describe a person as **unscrupulous**, you are critical of the fact that they are prepared to act in a dishonest or immoral way in order to get what they want. 非良心的な [DISAPPROVAL 不賛成] ❏ *These kids are*

being exploited by very unscrupulous people. こうした子供達は非常に不道徳な人々に利用されている.

un|secured /ʌnsɪkyʊərd/ ADJ 形容詞 **Unsecured** is used to describe loans or debts that are not guaranteed by a particular asset such as a person's home. 無担保の [BUSINESS 実業] ❏ *Sam received an unsecured loan of $282,000.* サムは28万2000ドルの無担保ローンを受けた.

un|seen /ʌnsin/ **1** ADJ 形容詞 If you describe something as **unseen**, you mean that it has not been seen for a long time. 見られていない ❏ *…a spectacular ballroom, unseen by the public for over 30 years.* 30年以上一般公開されていない豪華な舞踏場 **2** ADJ 形容詞 You can use **unseen** to describe things which people cannot see. 目に見えない [ADJ n, after v] ❏ *For me, a performance is in front of a microphone, over the radio, to an unseen audience.* 私の仕事はマイクの前でラジオ聴取者のために放送することだ.

un|set|tled /ʌnsɛtᵊld/ **1** ADJ 形容詞 In an **unsettled** situation, there is a lot of uncertainty about what will happen. 不安定な ❏ *The developments leave the airline with several problems, including an unsettled labor situation.* その発展の決果, 航空会社は不安定な労使問題などの問題を抱えたままである. **2** ADJ 形容詞 If you are **unsettled**, you cannot concentrate on anything because you are worried. 動揺した [v-link ADJ] ❏ *To tell the truth, I'm a bit unsettled tonight.* 実は私は今夜ちょっと動揺している. **3** ADJ 形容詞 An **unsettled** argument or dispute has not yet been resolved. 未解決の ❏ *They were in the process of resolving all the unsettled issues.* 彼らは全ての未解決の問題を解決している最中だった. **4** ADJ 形容詞 **Unsettled** weather is unpredictable and changes a lot. 変わりやすい ❏ *Despite the unsettled weather, we had a marvelous weekend.* 変わりやすい天候にもかかわらず, 私達は素晴らしい週末を過ごした.

un|set|tling /ʌnsɛtlɪŋ/ ADJ 形容詞 If you describe something as **unsettling**, you mean that it makes you feel worried or uncertain. 動揺させる ❏ *Phil had several unsettling dreams every night.* フィルは毎晩心を騒がせる夢をいくつか見た.

un|sight|ly /ʌnsaɪtli/ ADJ 形容詞 If you describe something as **unsightly**, you mean that it is ugly. みっともない ❏ *…an unsightly pile of garbage right in front of the restaurant.* レストランのまん前の見苦しいゴミの山

un|skilled /ʌnskɪld/ **1** ADJ 形容詞 People who are **unskilled** do not have any special training for a job. 技術訓練を受けていない ❏ *He worked as an unskilled laborer.* 彼は未熟練労働者として働いた. **2** ADJ 形容詞 **Unskilled** work does not require any special training. 特別の訓練を要しない ❏ *In the U.S., minorities and immigrants have generally gone into low-paid, unskilled jobs.* 米国では少数民族と移民は概して低賃金で特別の訓練を要しない職に就いている.

un|so|lic|it|ed /ʌnsəlɪsɪtɪd/ ADJ 形容詞 Something that is **unsolicited** has been given without being asked for and may not have been wanted. 要求しないのに与えられた ❏ *She's always full of unsolicited advice.* 彼女はいつも頼まれもせずに助言ばかりする.

un|solved /ʌnsɒlvd/ ADJ 形容詞 An **unsolved** mystery or problem has never been solved. 未解決の ❏ *…America's unsolved problems of poverty and racism.* 貧困と人種差別というアメリカの未解決の問題

un|speak|able /ʌnspikəbᵊl/ ADJ 形容詞 If you describe something as **unspeakable**, you are emphasizing that it is extremely unpleasant. 言いようのないほど悪い [EMPHASIS 強調] ❏ *…the unspeakable horrors of chemical weapons.* 化学兵器の言いようのないほどの惨事 ❏ *The pain is unspeakable.* 痛みは言いようのないほどひどい. ● **un|speak|ably** /ʌnspikəbli/ ADV 副詞 言いようのないほど ❏ *The novel was unspeakably boring.* その小説は言いようのないほど退屈だった.

un|speci|fied /ʌnspɛsɪfaɪd/ ADJ 形容詞 You say that something is **unspecified** when you are not told exactly what it is. 明示してない ❏ *The company said that an unspecified number of people were offered jobs.* その企業は不特定数の人々が採用されたと述べた.

un|spoiled /ʌnspɔɪld/ ADJ 形容詞 If you describe a place as **unspoiled**, you think it is beautiful because it has not been changed or built on for a long time. 害されていない ❏ *The port is quiet and unspoiled.* その港は静かで損なわれていない.

un|spo|ken /ʌnspoʊkən/ **1** ADJ 形容詞 If your thoughts, wishes, or feelings are **unspoken**, you do not speak about them. 口に出さない ❏ *His face was expressionless, but Alex felt the unspoken criticism.* 彼の顔は無表情だったが, アレックスは無言の批判を感じた. **2** ADJ 形容詞 When there is an **unspoken** agreement or understanding between people, their behavior shows that they agree about something or understand it, even though they have never spoken about it. 暗黙の [ADJ n] ❏ *There was an unspoken agreement that he and Viv would look after the frail old couple.* 彼とヴィブは虚弱な老人の世話をするという暗黙の合意があった.

un|sta|ble /ʌnsteɪbᵊl/ **1** ADJ 形容詞 You can describe something as **unstable** if it is likely to change suddenly, especially if this creates difficulty or danger. 不安定な ❏ *The situation is unstable and potentially dangerous.* 状況は不安定で潜在的に危険である. **2** ADJ 形容詞 **Unstable** objects are likely to move or

fall. 不安定な ☐ Both clay and sandstone are unstable rock formations. 粘土と砂岩は共に不安定な岩片の堆積（たいせき）作用である. **3** ADJ 形容詞 If people are **unstable**, their emotions and behavior keep changing because their minds are disturbed or upset. 情緒不安定な ☐ He was emotionally unstable. 彼は情緒不安定だった.

un|steady /ʌnstédi/ **1** ADJ 形容詞 If you are **unsteady**, you have difficulty doing something, for example walking, because you cannot completely control your legs or your body. ふらふらする ☐ The boy was very unsteady and had staggered around when he got up. その少年は足がふらつき, 立ち上がったときによろめいた. ● **un|steadi|ly** /ʌnstédⁱli/ ADV 副詞 [ADV with v] ふらついて ☐ She pulled herself unsteadily from the bed to the dresser. 彼女はふらつく足で自力で何とかベッドから化粧台に移動した. **2** ADJ 形容詞 If you describe something as **unsteady**, you mean that it is not regular or stable, but unreliable or unpredictable. 弱い ☐ His voice was unsteady and only just audible. 彼の声は低くやっと聞き取れた. **3** ADJ 形容詞 **Unsteady** objects are not held, attached, or balanced securely. 据わりの悪い ☐ ...a slightly unsteady table. 少しぐらつくテーブル.

un|sub|scribe /ʌnsəbskráɪb/ (unsubscribes, unsubscribing, unsubscribed) V-I 自動詞 If you **unsubscribe** from an online service, you send a message saying that you no longer wish to receive that service. 予約購読をキャンセルする [COMPUTING コンピューティング] ☐ Go to the website today and you can unsubscribe online. 今日ウェブサイトにアクセスすればインターネットで予約購読をキャンセルできる.

un|sub|stan|ti|at|ed /ʌnsəbstǽnʃieɪtɪd/ ADJ 形容詞 A claim, accusation, or story that is **unsubstantiated** has not been proven to be valid or true. 確証のない ☐ I do object to their claim, which I find totally unsubstantiated. 私は全く確証のないと思われる彼らの申し立てに反対だ.

un|suc|cess|ful /ʌnsəksésfəl/ **1** ADJ 形容詞 Something that is **unsuccessful** does not achieve what it was intended to achieve. 不成功の ☐ His efforts were unsuccessful. 彼の努力は不成功に終わった. ☐ ...a second unsuccessful operation on his knee. 彼の膝の2度目の不成功な手術 ● **un|suc|cess|ful|ly** ADV 副詞 [ADV with v] 不成功に ☐ He has been trying unsuccessfully to sell the business in one piece since early last year. 彼は昨年初頭からその事業をすべて売却しようとしていたがまだ成功していない. **2** ADJ 形容詞 Someone who is **unsuccessful** does not achieve what they intended to achieve, especially in their career. 失敗した ☐ The difference between successful and unsuccessful people is that successful people put into practice the things they learn. 成功した人と失敗した人の間の違いは成功した人々は学んだことを実行に移すことである.

un|suit|able /ʌnsútəbⁱl/ ADJ 形容詞 Someone or something that is **unsuitable for** a particular purpose or situation does not have the right qualities for it. 不適切な ☐ Amy's shoes were unsuitable for walking any distance. エイミーの靴は長距離を歩くには不適切だった.

un|sure /ʌnʃʊər/ **1** ADJ 形容詞 If you are **unsure of yourself**, you lack confidence. 自信のない ☐ The evening show was terrible, with hesitant unsure performances from all. 夕方のショーは全員のパフォーマンスがためらいがちで不確かでひどかった. **2** ADJ 形容詞 If you are **unsure about** something, you feel uncertain about it. 確信がない [v-link ADJ] ☐ Fifty-two percent were unsure about the idea. 52%はそのアイデアに確信を持てなかった.

un|sus|pect|ing /ʌnsəspéktɪŋ/ ADJ 形容詞 You can use **unsuspecting** to describe someone who is not at all aware of something that is happening or going to happen. 怪しまない ☐ She threw a surprise party for her unsuspecting husband. 彼女は夫に怪しまれずにびっくりパーティを開いた.

un|sym|pa|thet|ic /ʌnsɪmpəθétɪk/ **1** ADJ 形容詞 If someone is **unsympathetic**, they are not kind or helpful to a person in difficulties. 冷淡な ☐ Her husband was unsympathetic and she felt she had no one to turn to. 彼女の夫は冷淡で彼女には援助を求める人がいなかった. **2** ADJ 形容詞 An **unsympathetic** person is unpleasant and difficult to like. 思いやりがない ☐ ...a very unsympathetic main character. 全く思いやりのない主人公 **3** ADJ 形容詞 If you are **unsympathetic to** a particular idea or aim, you are not willing to support it. 共鳴しない [v-link ADJ 'to' n] ☐ I'm highly unsympathetic to what you are trying to achieve. 私はあなたが達成しようとしていることに全然共鳴できない.

un|ten|able /ʌnténəbⁱl/ ADJ 形容詞 An argument, theory, or position that is **untenable** cannot be defended successfully against criticism or attack. 支持できない ☐ This argument is untenable on an intellectual, moral, and practical standpoint. この議論は知的, 道徳的そして実用的な観点から支持できない.

un|think|able /ʌnθɪŋkəbⁱl/ **1** ADJ 形容詞 If you say that something is **unthinkable**, you are emphasizing that it cannot possibly be accepted or imagined as a possibility. 考えられない [EMPHASIS 強調] ☐ Her strong Catholic beliefs made abortion unthinkable. 敬けんなカソリック教徒である彼女には妊娠中絶は考えられなかった. ● N-SING 単数名詞 **The unthinkable** is something that

is unthinkable. 考えられないこと ['the' N] ☐ Teresa Zapata told her family the unthinkable; she was going to work in the United States. テレサ・ザパタは彼女の家族に考えられないことを告げた. 彼女はアメリカで働くつもりだった.

un|ti|dy /ʌntáɪdi/ → see **messy**

| Word Link | un = reversal : untie, unusual, unwrap |

un|tie /ʌntáɪ/ (unties, untying, untied) **1** V-T 他動詞 If you **untie** something that is tied to another thing or if you **untie** two things that are tied together, you remove the string or rope that holds them or that has been tied around them. 解き放す ☐ Nicholas untied the boat from her mooring. ニコラスは係船から船を解き放した. ☐ Just untie my hands. とにかく私の手を解放してください. **2** V-T 他動詞 If you **untie** something such as string or rope, you undo it so that there is no knot or so that it is no longer tying something. ほどく ☐ She hurriedly untied the ropes binding her ankles. 彼女は急いで足首に縛りつけられたロープをほどいた. **3** V-T 他動詞 When you **untie** your shoelaces or your shoes, you loosen or undo the laces of your shoes. ほどく ☐ She untied the laces on one of her sneakers. 彼女は片方のスニーカーのひもをほどいた.

un|til /ʌntɪl/ **1** PREP 前置詞 If something happens **until** a particular time, it happens during the period before that time and stops at that time. まで [PREP n/-ing] ☐ Until 2004 she lived in Canada. 2004年まで彼女はカナダに住んでいた. ● CONJ 接続詞 **Until** is also a conjunction. まで ☐ I waited until it got dark. 私は暗くなるまで待っていた. **2** PREP 前置詞 You use **until** with a negative to emphasize the moment in time after which the rest of your statement becomes true, or the condition which would make it true. まで [PREP after neg] ☐ The traffic laws don't take effect until the end of the year. 交通法は年末までは効力を発揮しない. ● CONJ 接続詞 **Until** is also a conjunction. まで ☐ The government said that it has suspended all aid to Haiti until that country's legitimate government is restored. 政府は合法的な政府が復活するまではハイチへの援助を全て一時停止すると述べた. **3** **up until** → see **up ❷**

Note that you only use **until** or **till** when you are talking about time. You do not use these words to talk about place or position. Instead, you should use **as far as** or **up to**. ☐ Then you'll be riding with us as far as the village?...We walked up to where his bicycle was.

un|told /ʌntóʊld/ **1** ADJ 形容詞 You can use **untold** to emphasize how bad or unpleasant something is. 口で言い表せない [EMPHASIS 強調] [ADJ n] ☐ Landmines have caused untold misery to thousands of innocent people. 地雷は何千人もの無実な人々を言うに言われぬほど不幸にした. **2** ADJ 形容詞 You can use **untold** to emphasize that an amount or quantity is very large, especially when you are not sure how large it is. 数えられない [EMPHASIS 強調] [ADJ n] ☐ ...the nation's untold millions of anglers. その国の数百万もの釣り師

un|touched /ʌntátʃt/ **1** ADJ 形容詞 Something that is **untouched by** something else is not affected by it. 影響されていない [v-link ADJ, ADJ after v] ☐ Asian airlines remain untouched by the deregulation that has swept the U.S. アジア大の航空会社は米国を襲った規制緩和の影響を受けていないままである. **2** ADJ 形容詞 If something is **untouched**, it is not damaged in any way, although it has been in a situation where it could easily have been damaged. 損害をこうむっていない [v-link ADJ, ADJ after v] ☐ Michael pointed out to me that in all the rubble, there was one building that remained untouched. マイケルはがれきの中に無傷の建物が1つ残っていることを私に指摘した. **3** ADJ 形容詞 An **untouched** area or place is thought to be beautiful because it is still in its original state and has not been changed or damaged in any way. 未開発の ☐ Ducie is one of the world's last untouched islands. デュシー島は世界最後の未踏査の島の1つである. **4** ADJ 形容詞 If food or drink is **untouched**, none of it has been eaten or drunk. 口をつけていない ☐ The coffee was untouched, the toast was cold. コーヒーは手をつけないままで, トーストは冷たくなっていた.

un|trained /ʌntréɪnd/ ADJ 形容詞 Someone who is **untrained** has not been taught the skills that they need for a particular job, activity, or situation. 訓練を受けていない ☐ It is nonsense to say we have untrained staff dealing with emergencies. 訓練を受けていない職員が緊急事態を処理していると言うのはナンセンスだ.

un|treat|ed /ʌntrítɪd/ **1** ADJ 形容詞 If an injury or illness is left **untreated**, it is not given medical treatment. 治療をまだ受けていない ☐ If left untreated, the condition may become chronic. 治療を受けないままだと病気は慢性化するかもしれない. **2** ADJ 形容詞 **Untreated** materials, water, or chemicals are harmful and have not been made safe. 未処理の ☐ ...the dumping of nuclear waste and untreated sewage. 核廃棄物の投げ捨てと未処理の下水 **3** ADJ 形容詞 **Untreated** materials are in their natural or original state, often before being prepared for use in a particular process. 未処理の ☐ All the bedding is made of simple, untreated cotton. 全ての寝具はシンプルで未処理の木綿でできている.

un|true /ʌntrú/ ADJ 形容詞 If a statement or idea is **untrue**, it

u

is false and not based on facts. 真実でない ❑ *The allegations were completely untrue.* 申立ては全く真実ではなかった. ❑ *It was untrue to say that all political prisoners have been released.* 全ての政治犯が解放されたと言うのは真実ではなかった.

un|used

> Pronounced /ʌnyuːzd/ for meaning ■, and /ʌnyuːst/ for meaning ②.
>
> /ʌnyuːzd/の意味では■と, /ʌnyuːst/の意味では②と発音される.

■ ADJ 形容詞 Something that is **unused** has not been used or is not being used at the moment. 使用しない ❑ *...unused containers of food.* 未使用の食べ物容器 ② ADJ 形容詞 If you are **unused to** something, you have not often done it or experienced it before, so it feels unusual and unfamiliar to you. 慣れていない [v-link ADJ 'to' n] ❑ *My mother was entirely unused to such hard work.* 私の母はそのような重労働に全く慣れていなかった.

> **Word Link** un ≈ reversal : untie, unusual, unwrap

un|usu|al /ʌnyuːʒuəl/ ■ ADJ 形容詞 If something is **unusual**, it does not happen very often or you do not see it or hear it very often. 珍しい ❑ *They have replanted many areas with rare and unusual plants.* 彼らは多くの場所に珍しい植物を植えなおした. ② ADJ 形容詞 If you describe someone as **unusual**, you think that they are interesting and different from other people. 一風変った ❑ *He was an unusual man with great business talents.* 彼は偉大な商才を持つ一風変った男だった.

> **Thesaurus** unusual また次を参照:
>
> ADJ. abnormal, strange, uncommon; (ant.) usual ■
> different, interesting, unconventional ②

un|usu|al|ly /ʌnyuːʒuəli/ ■ ADV 副詞 You use **unusually** to emphasize that someone or something has more of a particular quality than is usual. ひどく [EMPHASIS 強調] [ADV adj] ❑ *He was an unusually complex man.* 彼はひどく複雑な男だった. ② ADV 副詞 You can use **unusually** to suggest that something is not what normally happens. 珍しく ❑ *Unusually, for a Japanese politician, he's a fluent English speaker.* 日本人の政治家には珍しく彼は達者な英語を話した.

un|veil /ʌnveɪl/ (unveils, unveiling, unveiled) ■ V-T 他動詞 If someone formally **unveils** something such as a new statue or painting, they draw back the curtain which is covering it. 初公開する ❑ *...a ceremony to unveil a monument to the victims.* 犠牲者の記念碑を初公開する式典 ② V-T 他動詞 If you **unveil** a plan, new product, or some other thing that has been kept secret, you introduce it to the public. 公表する ❑ *Mr. Werner unveiled his new strategy this week.* ワーナー氏は今週新しい戦略を公表した.

un|want|ed /ʌnwɒntɪd/ ADJ 形容詞 If you say that something or someone is **unwanted**, you mean that you do not want them, or that nobody wants them. 望まれていない ❑ *...the misery of unwanted pregnancies.* 望まない妊娠の不幸 ❑ *She felt unwanted.* 彼女は望まれていないと感じた.

un|war|rant|ed /ʌnwɔːrəntɪd/ ADJ 形容詞 If you describe something as **unwarranted**, you are critical of it because there is no need or reason for it. 正当とされない [FORMAL 形式ばった, DISAPPROVAL 不賛成] ❑ *Any attempt to discuss the issue of human rights was rejected as an unwarranted interference in the country's internal affairs.* 人権問題を議論する試みは全てその国の内務への不当な干渉として拒否された.

un|wel|come /ʌnwelkəm/ ■ ADJ 形容詞 An **unwelcome** experience is one that you do not like and did not want. 歓迎されない ❑ *The mayor delivered the unwelcome news that city employees may have to take unpaid time off.* 市長は市の職員は無給の休暇を取らねばならないかもしれないという嫌な知らせを届けた. ② ADJ 形容詞 If you say that a visitor is **unwelcome**, you mean that you did not want them to come. 嫌がられる ❑ *...an unwelcome guest.* 嫌がられる客

un|well /ʌnwel/ ADJ 形容詞 If you are **unwell**, you are sick. 体の具合が悪い [v-link ADJ] ❑ *Their grandmother was feeling unwell and had to stay at home.* 彼らの祖母は体調が悪く外出できなかった.

un|wieldy /ʌnwiːldi/ ■ ADJ 形容詞 If you describe an object as **unwieldy**, you mean that it is difficult to move or carry because it is so big or heavy. 動かしにくい ❑ *They came panting up to his door with their unwieldy baggage.* 彼らは扱いにくい荷物を持って彼のドアまでハアハア言いながら上ってきた. ② ADJ 形容詞 If you describe a system as **unwieldy**, you mean that it does not work very well as a result of it being too large or badly organized. 扱いにくい ❑ *His company has to deal with unwieldy Russian bureaucracy.* 彼の会社は扱いにくいロシアの官僚主義と対応しなければならなかった.

un|will|ing /ʌnwɪlɪŋ/ ■ ADJ 形容詞 If you are **unwilling** to do something, you do not want to do it and will not agree to do it. 気が進まない ❑ *Initially the government was unwilling to accept the defeat.* 最初政府は敗北を認めたがらなかった. ● **un|will|ing|ness**

N-UNCOUNT 不可算名詞 欲しないこと ❑ *...their unwillingness to accept responsibility for mistakes.* 彼らが過ちの責任を認めたがらないこと ② ADJ 形容詞 You can use **unwilling** to describe someone who does not really want to do the thing they are doing. 不承不承 ❑ *A youthful teacher, he finds himself an unwilling participant in school politics.* 若い教師, 彼は学校の駆け引きに不本意ながら参加していることに気づいた. ● **un|will|ing|ly** ADV 副詞 不承不承 ❑ *He accepted his orders very unwillingly.* 彼は命令を不承不承受け入れた.

un|wind /ʌnwaɪnd/ (unwinds, unwinding, unwound) ■ V-I 自動詞 When you **unwind**, you relax after you have done something that makes you tense or tired. くつろぐ ❑ *It helps them to unwind after a busy day at work.* 1日中せっせと仕事した後にくつろぐのは彼らのためになる. ② V-T/V-I 他動詞/自動詞 If you **unwind** a length of something that is wrapped around something else or around itself, you loosen it and make it straight. You can also say that it **unwinds**. 解く ❑ *One of them unwound a length of rope from around his waist.* 彼らの1人が彼の腰に巻かれたロープを端から端まで解いた.

un|wise /ʌnwaɪz/ ADJ 形容詞 If you describe something as **unwise**, you think that it is foolish and likely to lead to a bad result. 賢明でない ❑ *It would be unwise to expect too much.* 多くを期待しすぎるのは賢明ではないと思う. ❑ *I think this is extremely unwise.* これは非常に愚かだと私は思う. ● **un|wise|ly** ADV 副詞 無分別に ❑ *She accepted that she had acted unwisely.* 彼女は無分別に行動したことを認めた.

un|wit|ting /ʌnwɪtɪŋ/ ADJ 形容詞 If you describe a person or their actions as **unwitting**, you mean that the person does something or is involved in something without realizing it. 故意でない ❑ *We were unwitting collaborators in his plan.* 我々は彼の計画の偶然の協力者だった. ● **un|wit|ting|ly** ADV 副詞 偶然に ❑ *He was unwittingly caught up in the confrontation.* 彼は対立に偶然巻き込まれた.

un|work|able /ʌnwɜːrkəbəl/ ADJ 形容詞 If a plan, law, or system is **unworkable**, it cannot be successful. 実行不可能な ❑ *There is the strong possibility that such cooperation will prove unworkable.* そうした協力は実行不可能であると分かる可能性が大きい.

> **Word Link** worthy ≈ deserving, suitable : creditworthy, trustworthy, unworthy

un|wor|thy /ʌnwɜːrði/ ADJ 形容詞 If a person or thing is **unworthy of** something good, they do not deserve it. 値しない ❑ *You may feel unworthy of the attention and help people offer you.* あなたは人々の注目と援助に値しないと感じるかもしれない.

un|wound /ʌnwaʊnd/ **Unwound** is the past tense and past participle of **unwind**. unwindの過去・過去分詞形

un|wrap /ʌnræp/ (unwraps, unwrapping, unwrapped) V-T 他動詞 When you **unwrap** something, you take off the paper, plastic, or other covering that is around it. 包装を解く ❑ *I untied the bow and unwrapped the small box.* 私はリボンをほどき, 小さな箱の包装を解いた.

un|writ|ten /ʌnrɪtən/ ■ ADJ 形容詞 Something such as a book that is **unwritten** has not been printed or written down. 書いていない ❑ *Universal has agreed to pay $5 million for Grisham's next, as yet unwritten, novel.* ユニバーサルはグリシャムがこれから書く小説に5百万ドル支払うことに合意した. ② ADJ 形容詞 An **unwritten** rule, law, or agreement is one that is understood and accepted by everyone, although it may not have been formally or officially established. 成文化していない ❑ *They obey the one unwritten rule that binds them all – no talking.* 彼らは彼ら全員を結ぶ1つの成文化していない規則に従う一話すべからず

un|zip /ʌnzɪp/ (unzips, unzipping, unzipped) ■ V-T/V-I 他動詞/自動詞 When you **unzip** something which is fastened by a zipper or when it **unzips**, you open it by pulling open the zipper. ジッパーを開ける ❑ *James unzipped his bag.* ジェームスは彼のバッグのジッパーを開けた. ② V-T 他動詞 To **unzip** a computer file means to open a file that has been compressed. 圧縮情報を表示する [COMPUTING コンピューティング] ❑ *Unzip the icons into a subdirectory.* アイコンの圧縮情報をサブディレクトリに表示しなさい.

> **up**
>
> ❶ PREPOSITION, ADVERB, AND ADJECTIVE USES
> ❷ USED IN COMBINATION AS A PREPOSITION
> ❸ VERB USES

❶ up

> The preposition is pronounced /ʌp/. The adverb and adjective are pronounced /ʌp/.
>
> 前置詞は /ʌp/と発音される. 副詞と形容詞は /ʌp/と発音される.

U

Up is often used with verbs of movement such as "jump" and "pull," and also in phrasal verbs such as "give up" and "wash up."

Upはしばしば jump や pull のような移動の動詞と共に用いられ，また give up や wash up のような句動詞にも用いられる.

⇨ Please look at meaning 16 to see if the expression you are looking for is shown under another headword. **1** PREP 前置詞 If a person or thing goes **up** something such as a slope, ladder, or chimney, they move away from the ground or to a higher position. 上に □ They were climbing up a narrow mountain road. 彼らは細い山道を登っていた. □ I ran up the stairs and saw Alison lying at the top. 私は階段を駆け上りアリソンが1階に横たわっているのを見た. ● ADV 副詞 **Up** is also an adverb. 上方へ □ Finally, after an hour, I went up to Jeremy's room. 結局1時間後に私はジェレミーの部屋に上がって行った. □ Intense balls of flame rose up into the sky. 猛烈な火の玉が空に舞い上がった. **2** PREP 前置詞 If a person or thing is **up** something such as a ladder or a mountain, they are near the top of it. 上がって □ He was up a ladder sawing off the tops of his apple trees. 彼ははしごに上がってリンゴの木の上部を切り取っていた. ● ADV 副詞 **Up** is also an adverb. 上へ [ADV after v] □ ...a research station perched 4,000 meters up on the lip of the crater. 火口の縁の4000メートル上部にある研究所 **3** ADV 副詞 You use **up** to indicate that you are looking or facing in a direction that is away from the ground or toward a higher level. 上方へ [ADV after v] □ Keep your head up, and look around you from time to time. 頭をもたげ時々見回しなさい. **4** ADV 副詞 If someone stands **up**, they move so that they are standing. 高い姿勢に [ADV after v] □ He stood up and went to the window. 彼は立ち上がり窓の方に行った. **5** PREP 前置詞 If you go or look **up** something such as a road or river, you go or look along it. If you are **up** a road or river, you are somewhere along it. 上方へ [v PREP n] □ A line of tanks came up the road from the city. 一列に並んだ戦車が町から道路を上ってきた. □ We leaned on the wooden rail of the bridge and looked up the river. 私達は橋の木のレールにもたれ，川を見上げた. **6** ADV 副詞 If you are traveling to a particular place, you can say that you are going **up** to that place, especially if you are going toward the north or to a higher level of land. If you are already in such a place, you can say that you are **up** there. 高い位置へ [mainly SPOKEN 主に口語] □ I'll be up to see you tomorrow. 私は明日あなたに会いに来る予定だ. □ He was living up North. 彼は北部に住んでいた. **7** ADV 副詞 If you go **up** to something or someone, you move to the place where they are and stop there. 方へ □ The girl ran the rest of the way across the street and up to the car. その少女は通りを横切り車のところまで走った. □ On the way out a boy of about ten came up on roller skates. 出る途中で10歳位の少年がローラースケートでやってきた. **8** ADV 副詞 If an amount of something goes **up**, it increases. If an amount of something is **up**, it has increased and is at a higher level than it was. 上向きで □ The total budget went up almost $300 million. 予算の総額は3億ドル近く増えた. □ Tourism is up, jobs are up, individual income is up. 観光客は増え，職は増え，個人の所得も増えている. **9** ADJ 形容詞 If you are **up**, you are not in bed. 起きて [v-link ADJ] □ Are you sure you should be up? 起きていて本当に大丈夫ですか. □ These days they were up at the crack of dawn. 最近彼らは夜明けに起きていた. **10** ADJ 形容詞 If a period of time is **up**, it has come to an end. 終わって [v-link ADJ] □ The moment the half-hour was up, Brooks rose. 半時間が終わった瞬間にブルックスは立ち上がった. **11** ADJ 形容詞 If a computer or computer system is **up**, it is working. Compare **down**. 稼動中で [v-link ADJ] □ The new system is up and ready to run. 新しいシステムは稼動中で，すぐに操作できる. **12** PHRASE 句 If someone who has been in bed for some time, for example because they have been sick, is **up and about**, they are now out of bed and living their normal life. 動けるようになって □ How are you Lennox? Good to see you up and about. レノックス, 元気かい. 動けるようになってよかったね. **13** PHRASE 句 If you say that **something is up**, you mean that something is wrong or that something worrying is happening. 奇妙なことが起きている [INFORMAL くだけた] □ What is it then? Something's up, isn't it? どうかしたのか. 何か変なことが起きているんじゃないか. **14** PHRASE 句 If you say to someone "**What's up?**" or if you tell them **what's up**, you are asking them or telling them what is wrong or what is worrying them. どうしたのか [INFORMAL くだけた] □ "What's up?" I said to him. — "Just tired," he answered. 「どうしたのか」と私は彼に言った. 「ちょっと疲れただけだ」と彼は答えた. **15** PHRASE 句 If you move **up and down** somewhere, you move there repeatedly in one direction and then in the opposite direction. 上がったり下がったり □ I used to jump up and down to keep warm. 私は温まるためによくひょいひょい飛び跳ねたものだった. □ I strolled up and down thoughtfully before calling a taxi. 私はタクシーを呼ぶ前に物思いに沈みながら行ったり来たりした. **16 up in arms** → see **arm**

❷ up /ʌp/
⇨ Please look at meaning 9 to see if the expression you are looking for is shown under another headword. **1** PHRASE 句 If you feel **up to** doing something, you are well enough to do it. 能力がある □ Those patients who were up to it could move to the adjacent pool. それに耐えられる患者は近接するプールに移動することができた. □ His fellow directors were not up to running the business without him. 彼の同僚の取締役には彼なしでは事業を経営する能力はなかった. **2** PHRASE 句 To be **up** to something means to be secretly doing something that you should not be doing. たくらんで [INFORMAL くだけた] □ Why did you need a room unless you were up to something? あなたは何かを企んでいなければ何故部屋が必要だったのか. □ They must have known what their father was up to. 彼らは父親が何を企んでいたのか知っていたはずだ. **3** PHRASE 句 If you say that it is **up** to someone to do something, you mean that it is their responsibility to do it. 次第で □ It was up to him to make it right, no matter how long it took. どんなに長くかかろうもそれを正すのは彼次第だった. □ I'm sure I'd have spotted him if it had been up to me. それが私次第ならば私は彼を見つけ出していただろう. **4** PHRASE 句 **Up until** or **up to** are used to indicate the latest time at which something can happen, or the end of the period of time that you are referring to. までに □ Please feel free to call me any time up until 9:30 at night. 夜の9時半まででだったらお電話ください. **5** PHRASE 句 You use **up to** to say how large something can be or what level it has reached. に至るまで □ Up to twenty thousand students paid between five and six thousand dollars. 2千人までの学生が5000〜6000ドル支払った. **6** PHRASE 句 If someone or something is **up for** election, review, or discussion, they are about to be considered. 出されて □ A third of the Senate and the entire House are up for re-election. 上院の3分の1と下院の全ては再選挙に立候補している. **7** PHRASE 句 If you are **up for** something, you are willing or eager to do it. 気乗りがしている [INFORMAL くだけた] □ I'm starved. Who's up for pizza? お腹がぺこぺこだ. ピザを食べたい人はいるか. **8** PHRASE 句 If you are **up against** something, you have a very difficult situation or problem to deal with. 直面して □ The chairwoman is up against the greatest challenge to her position. 女性議長は彼女の立場への最大の挑戦に直面している. **9 up to par** → see **par**

❸ up /ʌp/ (**ups, upping, upped**) **1** V-T 他動詞 If you **up** something such as the amount of money you are offering for something, you increase it. 引き上げる □ He upped his offer for the company. 彼はその企業の指し値を引き上げた. □ Drug stores upped sales by 63 percent. 薬局は販売高を63%増大した. **2** V-I 自動詞 If you **up** and leave a place, you go away from it, often suddenly or unexpectedly. 急に…しだす □ One day he just upped and left. ある日彼は突然立ち去った.

up-and-coming ADJ 形容詞 **Up-and-coming** people are likely to be successful in the future. 成功しそうな [ADJ n] □ ...his readiness to share the limelight with young, up-and-coming stars. 若くて有望なスターと快くスポットライトを分かち合う彼の気持ち

up|beat /ʌpbiːt/ ADJ 形容詞 If people or their opinions are **upbeat**, they are cheerful and hopeful about a situation. 楽天的な [INFORMAL くだけた] □ The Defense Secretary gave an upbeat assessment of the war so far. 国防長官は今までのところ戦争に楽天的な評価をした. □ Neil's colleagues said he was actually in a joking, upbeat mood in spite of the bad news. ニールの同僚は彼は悪い知らせにもかかわらず, 冗談を言い予測に反して陽気なムードだと述べた.

up|bring|ing /ʌpbrɪŋɪŋ/ N-UNCOUNT 不可算名詞 Your **upbringing** is the way that your parents treat you and the things that they teach you when you are growing up. しつけ □ Martin's upbringing shaped his whole life. マーティンの教育は彼の全人生を形成した.

up|com|ing /ʌpkʌmɪŋ/ ADJ 形容詞 **Upcoming** events will happen in the near future. やがて起こる [ADJ n] □ We'll face a tough fight in the upcoming election. 我々は来るべき選挙で厳しい戦いに直面するだろう.

up|date /ʌpdeɪt/ (**updates, updating, updated**)

The verb is pronounced /ʌpdeɪt/. The noun is pronounced /ʌpdeɪt/.

動詞は /ʌpdeɪt/ と発音される. 名詞は /ʌpdeɪt/ と発音される.

1 V-T/V-I 他動詞/自動詞 If you **update** something, you make it more modern, usually by adding new parts to it or giving new information. 更新する □ He was back in the office, updating the work schedule on the computer. 彼は事務所に戻りコンピュータの業務予定表を更新した. □ Airlines would prefer to update rather than retrain crews. 航空会社は乗務員を再訓練するよりも改訂することを好むと思う. **2** N-COUNT 可算名詞 An **update** is a news item containing the latest information about a particular situation. 最新情報 □ She had heard the newsflash on a TV channel's news update. 彼女はテレビ番組のニュースの最新情報についてニュース速報を聞いていた. □ ...a weather update. 天気予報の最新情報 **3** V-T 他動詞 If you **update** someone **on** a situation, you tell them the latest developments in that situation. 最新情報を与える □ We'll update you on the day's top news stories. 我々はその日のトップニュースについてあなたに最新情報を与えるつもりだ.

up front also **up-front 1** ADJ 形容詞 If you are **up front** about something, you act openly or publicly so that people know what you are doing or what you believe. 率直な [INFORMAL くだけた]

❑ *You can't help being biased so you may as well be up front about it.* 偏見を持たずにはいられないからそれについて正直である方がよい. **2** ADV 副詞 If a payment is made **up front**, it is made in advance and openly, so that the person being paid can see that the money is there. 前金で [ADV after v] ❑ *Some companies charge a fee up front, but we don't think that's right.* 一部の企業は先払い手数料を請求するが, 我々はそれが正しいと思わない. ● ADJ 形容詞 **Up front** is also an adjective. 前もっての [ADJ n] ❑ *The eleven percent loan has no up-front costs.* 11%のローンには先払いの費用はない.

up|grade /ʌpgreɪd, -greɪd/ (**upgrades, upgrading, upgraded**) **1** V-T 他動詞 If equipment or services **are upgraded**, they are improved or made more efficient. 改善された [usu passive] ❑ *Helicopters have been upgraded and modernized.* ヘリコプターは改善され, 近代化された. ❑ *Medical facilities are being reorganized and upgraded.* 医療施設は再編成され, 改善されつつある. ● N-COUNT 可算名詞 **Upgrade** is also a noun. 向上 ❑ *...equipment which needs expensive upgrades.* 高価な品質向上を必要とする機器 **2** V-T 他動詞 If someone **is upgraded**, their job or status is changed so that they become more important or receive more money. 昇格する [usu passive] ❑ *He was upgraded to security guard.* 彼はガードマンに昇格した. **3** V-T/V-I 他動詞/自動詞 If you **upgrade** or **are upgraded**, you change something such as your plane ticket or your hotel room to one that is more expensive. グレードアップする, グレードアップされる ❑ *His family was upgraded from economy to business class.* 彼の家族はエコノミーからビジネスクラスに格上げされた.

→ see hotel

up|heav|al /ʌphiv²l/ (**upheavals**) N-COUNT 可算名詞 An **upheaval** is a big change which causes a lot of trouble, confusion, and worry. 大変動 ❑ *Algeria has been going through political upheaval for the past two months.* アルジェリアでは過去2ヶ月間政治の大変革が起こっている.

up|held /ʌpheld/ **Upheld** is the past tense and past participle of **uphold**. upholdの過去・過去分詞形

up|hill /ʌphɪl/ **1** ADV 副詞 If something or someone is **uphill** or is moving **uphill**, they are near the top of a hill or are going up a slope. 坂を上って ❑ *He had been running uphill a long way.* 彼は長い距離上り坂を走っていた. ❑ *The man was no more than ten yards away and slightly uphill.* その男は10ヤードも離れていない, 少し坂を上ったところにいた. ● ADJ 形容詞 **Uphill** is also an adjective. 上り坂の ❑ *...a long, uphill journey.* 長い上り坂の旅 **2** ADJ 形容詞 If you refer to something as an **uphill** battle or an **uphill** struggle, you mean that it requires a lot of effort and determination, but it should be possible to achieve it. 骨の折れる [ADJ n] ❑ *It had been an uphill battle to achieve what she had wanted.* 彼女が欲することを達成するのは困難な闘いであった.

up|hold /ʌphoʊld/ (**upholds, upholding, upheld**) **1** V-T 他動詞 If you **uphold** something such as a law, a principle, or a decision, you support and maintain it. 支持する ❑ *Our policy has been to uphold the law.* 我々の政策は法律を守ることであった. ❑ *It is the responsibility of every government to uphold certain basic principles.* 特定の基礎的道徳基準を守るのは全ての政府の責任である. **2** V-T 他動詞 If a court of law **upholds** a legal decision that has already been made, it decides that it was the correct decision. 支持する ❑ *The State Supreme Court upheld the Superior Court judge's decision.* 州最高裁判所は上級司法裁判所の判決を支持する.

up|hol|stery /ʌphoʊlstəri, əpoʊl-/ N-UNCOUNT 不可算名詞 **Upholstery** is the soft covering on chairs and seats that makes them more comfortable to sit on. 椅子張り ❑ *...white leather upholstery.* 白い革の椅子張り

up|keep /ʌpkip/ **1** N-UNCOUNT 不可算名詞 The **upkeep** of a building or place is the work of keeping it in good condition. 維持 ❑ *The money will be used for the upkeep of the park.* その金は公園の維持に使われる予定である. **2** N-UNCOUNT 不可算名詞 The **upkeep** of a group of people or services is the process of providing them with the things that they need. 扶養 ❑ *He offered to pay $250 a month toward his son's upkeep.* 彼は息子の扶養費として月々250ドル支払うことを申し出た.

up|lift|ing /ʌpliftɪŋ/ ADJ 形容詞 You describe something as **uplifting** when it makes you feel very cheerful and happy. 励みとなる ❑ *...a charming and uplifting love story.* 魅力的で希望を与える恋愛物語

up|load /ʌploʊd/ (**uploads, uploading, uploaded**) V-T 他動詞 If you **upload** data, you transfer it from a disk to your computer or from your computer to another computer. 転送する [COMPUTING コンピューティング] ❑ *All you need to do is upload the files on to your web space.* 必要なのはあなたのウェブ空間にファイルを転送することだけだ.

up|market /ʌpmɑrkɪt/ also **up-market** ADJ 形容詞 **Upmarket** products or services are expensive, of good quality, and intended to appeal to people with money and education. 高所得層向けの [mainly BRIT 主に英国英語; AM usually **upscale** 米国英語では通常 **upscale**]

upon /əpɒn/

In addition to the uses shown below, **upon** is used in phrasal verbs such as "come upon" and "look upon," and after some other verbs such as "decide" and "depend."

下記の用法に加えて, **upon** は **come upon** や **look upon** のような句動詞に使われ, また **decide** や **depend** のようないくつかの他の動詞の後で使われる.

1 PREP 前置詞 If one thing is **upon** another, it is on it. 上に [LITERARY 文語的] ❑ *He set the tray upon the table.* 彼はテーブルの上にトレーを置いた. ❑ *He bent forward and laid a kiss softly upon her forehead.* 彼はかがんで彼女の額にそっとキスした. **2** PREP 前置詞 You use **upon** when mentioning an event that is followed immediately by another event. するとすぐに [FORMAL 形式ばった] [PREP -ing/n] ❑ *The door on the left, upon entering the church, leads to the Crypt of St. Issac.* 教会に入ってすぐの左側のドアはSt. Issacの地下室に通じている. **3** PREP 前置詞 You use **upon** between two occurrences of the same noun in order to say that there are large numbers of the thing mentioned. 累積の意を表わす [n PREP n] ❑ *Row upon row of women surged forward.* 何列もの大勢の女性が前方に押し寄せた. **4** PREP 前置詞 If an event is **upon** you, it is just about to happen. めがけて [LITERARY 文語的] [PREP pron] ❑ *The long-threatened storm was upon us.* 長い間起こりそうだった嵐がやってきた. ❑ *The wedding season is upon us.* 結婚の季節がやってきた.

up|per /ʌpər/ **1** ADJ 形容詞 You use **upper** to describe something that is above something else. さらに上の [ADJ n, 'the' ADJ] ❑ *There is a good restaurant on the upper floor.* 上階には良いレストランがある. **2** ADJ 形容詞 You use **upper** to describe the higher part of something. 上の方の ❑ *...the upper part of the foot.* 足の上の方の部分 ❑ *...the muscles of the upper back and chest.* 背中と胸の上のほうの筋肉 **3** PHRASE 句 If you have **the upper hand** in a situation, you have an advantage over other people involved, for example because you have more power or success. 優勢 ❑ *The home team was beginning to gain the upper hand.* 本国のチームは優勢になりつつあった.

upper|case /ʌpərkeɪs/ also **upper case** ADJ 形容詞 **Uppercase** letters are capital letters. 大文字の ❑ *Most schools teach children lowercase letters first, and uppercase letters later.* 大半の学校は子供に最初に小文字を教え, その後で大文字を教える. ● N-UNCOUNT 不可算名詞 **Uppercase** is also a noun. 大文字 ❑ *They should use uppercase.* 彼らは大文字を使うべきである.

up|per class (**upper classes**) also **upper-class** N-COUNT-COLL 集合可算名詞 The **upper class** or the **upper classes** are the group of people in a society who own the most property and have the highest social status, and who may not need to work for money. 上流階級 ❑ *...goods specifically designed to appeal to the tastes of the upper class.* 上流階級の好みに合うように作られた商品 ● ADJ 形容詞 **Upper class** is also an adjective. 上流階級の ❑ *All of them came from wealthy, upper class families.* 彼らは全員裕福な上流階級の出身だった.

up|right /ʌpraɪt/ (**uprights**) **1** ADJ 形容詞 If you are sitting or standing **upright**, you are sitting or standing with your back straight, rather than bending or lying down. まっすぐな ❑ *Helen sat upright in her chair.* ヘレンは椅子にまっすぐな姿勢で座った. ❑ *He moved into an upright position.* 彼はまっすぐな姿勢になった. **2** ADJ 形容詞 An **upright** vacuum cleaner or freezer is tall rather than wide. 縦長の [ADJ n] **3** ADJ 形容詞 An **upright** chair has a straight back and no arms. 縦長の ❑ *He was sitting on an upright chair beside his bed, reading.* 彼はベッドの脇にある縦長の椅子に座り読書していた. **4** N-COUNT 可算名詞 You can refer to vertical posts or the vertical parts of an object as **uprights**. まっすぐなもの ❑ *...the uprights of a canopy bed.* 天蓋（てんがい）ベッドの直立柱 **5** ADJ 形容詞 You can describe people as **upright** when they are careful to follow acceptable rules of behavior and behave in a moral way. 高潔な ❑ *...a very upright, trustworthy man.* 非常に正直で信頼できる男性

up|ris|ing /ʌpraɪzɪŋ/ (**uprisings**) N-COUNT 可算名詞 When there is an **uprising**, a group of people start fighting against the people who are in power in their country, because they want to bring about a political change. 反乱 ❑ *...an uprising against the government.* 政府に対する反乱

up|roar /ʌprɔr/ **1** N-UNCOUNT 不可算名詞 If there is **uproar**, there is a lot of shouting and noise because people are very angry or upset about something. わめき叫ぶ声 [also 'an' N, oft 'in' N] ❑ *The announcement caused an uproar in the crowd.* その発表で群衆からわめき声が起こった. **2** N-UNCOUNT 不可算名詞 You can also use **uproar** to refer to a lot of public criticism and debate about something that has made people angry. 大騒ぎ [also 'an' N] ❑ *The town is in an uproar over the dispute.* その町はその論争について大騒ぎだ.

up|root /ʌprut/ (**uproots, uprooting, uprooted**) **1** V-T 他動詞 If you **uproot yourself** or if you **are uprooted**, you leave, or are made to leave, a place where you have lived for a long time. 立ち退かせる ❑ *...the trauma of uprooting themselves from their homes.* 家から

立ち退く精神的衝撃 ❑*He had no wish to uproot Dena from her present home.* 彼はディーナを今の家から立ち退かせたいとは思っていなかった. ❷ V-T 他動詞 If someone **uproots** a tree or plant, or if the wind **uproots** it, it is pulled out of the ground. 引っこ抜く ❑*They had been forced to uproot their vines and plant wheat.* 彼らはブドウの木を引っこ抜き、麦を植えることを強要されていた. ●❑*...fallen trees which have been uprooted by the storm.* 嵐で倒れた木々

up|scale /ʌpskeɪl/ ADJ 形容詞 **Upscale** is used to describe products or services that are expensive, of good quality, and intended to appeal to people with a lot of money and education. 高級な [AM 米国英語] [usu ADJ n] ❑*...upscale department-store chains such as Bloomingdale's and Saks Fifth Avenue.* ブルーミングデールズやサックス・フィフス・アヴェニューなどの高級デパート ● ADV 副詞 **Upscale** is also an adverb. より上級に [ADV after v] ❑*T-shirts, the epitome of American casualness, have moved upscale.* アメリカのカジュアルな服の象徴であるTシャツは、高級化している.

up|set (upsets, upsetting, upset)

> The verb and adjective are pronounced /ʌpsɛt/. The noun is pronounced /ʌpsɛt/.

> 動詞と形容詞は /ʌpsɛt/ と発音される. 名詞は /ʌpsɛt/ と発音される.

❶ ADJ 形容詞 If you are **upset**, you are unhappy or disappointed because something bad has happened to you. 気が転倒した ❑*After she died I felt very, very upset.* 彼女の死後、私はとても気が乱れた. ❑*Marta looked upset.* マータは気が動転しているようだった. ● N-COUNT 可算名詞 **Upset** is also a noun. 気の転倒 ❑*...stress and other emotional upsets.* ストレスやその他の感情的乱れ ❷ V-T 他動詞 If something **upsets** you, it makes you feel worried or unhappy. 気を転倒させる ❑*The whole incident had upset me and my fiancee terribly.* その事件全体が私と私のフィアンセをひどく動揺させた. ❑*She warned me not to say anything to upset him.* 彼女は彼を動揺させるようなことを言わないよう私に警告した. ● **up|set|ting** ADJ 形容詞 動揺させるような ❑*Childhood sickness can be upsetting for children and parents alike.* 子供の病気には子供も親も同じように気が動転することがある. ❸ V-T 他動詞 If events **upset** something such as a procedure or a state of affairs, they cause it to go wrong. 完全に混乱させる ❑*Political problems could upset agreements between Moscow and Kabul.* 政治問題はモスクワとカブール間の合意を駄目にする可能性がある. ● N-COUNT 可算名詞 **Upset** is also a noun. 混乱 ❑*Markets are very sensitive to any upsets in the Japanese economic machine.* 市場は日本経済の混乱に非常に影響を受けやすい. ❹ V-T 他動詞 If you **upset** an object, you accidentally knock or push it over so that it scatters over a large area. ひっくり返す ❑*Don't upset the piles of sheets under the box.* 箱の下の書類の山をひっくり返さないでください. ❺ N-COUNT 可算名詞 A stomach **upset** is a slight sickness in your stomach caused by an infection or by something that you have eaten. 異常 ❑*Paul was unwell last night with a stomach upset.* ポールは昨夜胃の具合が悪かった. ● ADJ 形容詞 [ADJ n] **Upset** is also an adjective. 異常な ❑*Larry has an upset stomach.* ラリーは胃を悪くした. ❻ to **upset the applecart** → see applecart
→ see anger

Thesaurus   *upset* また次を参照:

ADJ.	disappointed, hurt, unhappy; (*ant.*) happy ❶
	ill, sick, unsettled ❺
V.	overturn, spill, topple ❹

Word Partnership   *upset* は次の語句と使われる:

PREP.	upset **about/by/over** something ❶
ADV.	**visibly** upset, **so** upset, **very** upset ❶
	really upset ❶ ❷
V.	**become** upset, **feel** upset, **get** upset ❶ ❺
N.	**stomach** upset (*or* upset **stomach**) ❺

up|shot /ʌpʃɒt/ N-SING 単数名詞 The **upshot** of a series of events or discussions is the final result of them, usually a surprising result. 結末 ❑*The upshot is that we have lots of good but not very happy employees.* 結局のところ当社には優秀だがあまり満足していない従業員が沢山いるということだ.

up|side down /ʌpsaɪd daʊn/ also **upside-down** ADV 副詞 If something is or has been turned **upside down**, it has been turned around so that the part that is usually lowest is above the part that is usually highest. 逆さまに ❑*The painting was hung upside down.* その絵は逆さまにかかっていた. ● ADJ 形容詞 **Upside down** is also an adjective. 逆さまの ❑*...chandeliers that resemble upside-down wedding cakes.* 逆さまになったウエディングケーキのようなシャンデリア

up|stage /ʌpsteɪdʒ/ (upstages, upstaging, upstaged) V-T 他動詞 If someone **upstages** you, they draw attention away from you by being more attractive or interesting. 人の関心をそらす自分に向けさせる ❑*He had a younger brother who always publicly upstaged him.*

彼にはいつも人前で人の関心を自分に向けさせる弟がいた.

up|stairs /ʌpstɛərz/ ❶ ADV 副詞 If you go **upstairs** in a building, you go up a staircase toward a higher floor. 上階へ [ADV after v] ❑*He went upstairs and changed into clean clothes.* 彼は2階に上り洗濯したての洋服に着替えた. ❷ ADV 副詞 If something or someone is **upstairs** in a building, they are on a floor that is higher than the ground floor. 上階に ❑*The restaurant is upstairs and consists of a large, open room.* レストランは上階にあり広々とした開放型の部屋である. ❸ ADJ 形容詞 An **upstairs** room or object is situated on a floor of a building that is higher than the ground floor. 上階の [ADJ n] ❑*Marsani moved into the upstairs apartment.* マーサーニーは上階のアパートに引っ越した. ❹ N-SING 単数名詞 The **upstairs** of a building is the floor or floors that are higher than the ground floor. 上階 ❑*Together we went through the upstairs.* 私達は一緒に上階を注意深く調べた.

up|start /ʌpstɑrt/ (upstarts) N-COUNT 可算名詞 You can refer to someone as an **upstart** when they behave as if they are important, but you think that they are too new in a place or job to be treated as important. 成り上がり者 [DISAPPROVAL 不賛成] ❑*Many prefer a familiar authority figure to a young upstart.* 多くの人々は若い成り上がり者よりも顔見知りの権威のある人物を好む.

up|stream /ʌpstrim/ ADV 副詞 Something that is moving **upstream** is moving toward the source of a river against the current, from a point further down the river. Something that is **upstream** is toward the source of a river. 上流へ ❑*Salmon manage to swim upstream to lay their eggs.* サケは産卵のために遡上（そじょう）する. ❑*...the river police, whose headquarters are just upstream of the Ile St. Louis.* 本部がサンルイ島の上流にある河川警察 ● ADJ 形容詞 **Upstream** is also an adjective. 上流にある [ADJ n] ❑*We'll go to the upstream side of that big rock.* 私達はあの大きな岩の上流側に行く予定だ.

up|surge /ʌpsɜrdʒ/ N-SING 単数名詞 If there is an **upsurge** in something, there is a sudden, large increase in it. 高まり ❑*...the upsurge in oil prices.* 石油価格の急騰

up|tight /ʌptaɪt/ ADJ 形容詞 Someone who is **uptight** is tense, nervous, or annoyed about something and so is difficult to be with. 緊張した [INFORMAL くだけた] ❑*Penny never got uptight about exams.* ペニーは試験のことで神経をぴりぴりさせたことはなかった.

up-to-date also **up to date** ❶ ADJ 形容詞 If something is **up-to-date**, it is the newest thing of its kind. 最新の ❑*...the most up-to-date information available on foods today.* 現在手に入る食品についての最新情報 ❑*Web services are always up-to-date and available.* ウェブサービスは常に最新情報を提供し、利用可能だ. ❷ ADJ 形容詞 If you are **up-to-date** about something, you have the latest information about it. 最新の情報を持っている ❑*We'll keep you up to date with any news.* 新しい情報が入り次第あなたにお知らせするつもりだ.

up|town /ʌptaʊn/ ADV 副詞 If you go **uptown**, or go to a place **uptown**, you go away from the center of a city or town toward the edge. **Uptown** sometimes refers to a part of the city other than the main business district. 住宅地区へ [mainly AM 主に米国英語] [ADV after v] ❑*He rode uptown and made his way to Bob's apartment.* 彼は乗り物で住宅地区に出かけボブのアパートに向った. ❑*Susan continued to live uptown.* スーザンは住宅地区に住み続けた. ● ADJ 形容詞 **Uptown** is also an adjective. 住宅地区の [ADJ n] ❑*...uptown clubs.* 住宅地区のクラブ ❑*...a small uptown radio station.* 住宅地区にある小さなラジオ局

up|trend /ʌptrɛnd/ N-SING 単数名詞 An **uptrend** is a general improvement in something such as a market or the economy. 上昇傾向 ❑*Racal Electronics shares have been in a strong uptrend.* ラカルエレクトロニクス社株は、強い上昇傾向が続いている.

up|turn /ʌptɜrn/ (upturns) N-COUNT 可算名詞 If there is an **upturn** in the economy or in a company or industry, it improves or becomes more successful. 好転 [BUSINESS 実業] ❑*They do not expect an upturn in the economy until the end of the year.* 年末まで景気の好転は期待していない.

up|ward /ʌpwərd/

> The form **upwards** is also used for the adverb.

> **upwards**形は副詞にも使われる.

❶ ADJ 形容詞 An **upward** movement or look is directed towards a higher place or a higher level. 上方への [ADJ n] ❑*She started once again on the steep upward climb.* 再び急な登りを始めた. ❑*She gave him a quick, upward look, then lowered her eyes.* 彼をさっと見上げてから、視線を落とした. ❷ ADJ 形容詞 If you refer to an **upward** trend or an **upward** spiral, you mean that something is increasing in quantity or price. 上向きの [ADJ n] ❑*...the army's concern that the upward trend in the numbers avoiding military service may continue.* 兵役を避ける数の上向き傾向が続くかもしれないことに対する陸軍の懸念 ❸ ADV 副詞 If someone moves or looks **upward**, they move or look up toward a higher place. 上の方へ ❑*They climbed upward along the steep cliffs surrounding the village.* 村を取り巻いている急ながけに沿って上の方へ登って行った. ❑*"There," said Jack, pointing upwards.* 「あ

そこ」と，上方を指差しながらジャックが言った．**4** ADV 副詞 If an amount or rate moves **upward**, it increases. 上昇して [ADV after v] □ *...with prices soon heading upward in stores.* 商店でまもなく上向きになる価格 □ *Unemployment will continue upward for much of this year.* 今年はほぼずっと失業率が上昇していくだろう．**5** PHRASE 句 A quantity that is **upwards of** a particular number is more than that number. 越える □ *It costs upwards of $40,000 a year to keep some prisoners in prison.* ある種の囚人たちは，刑務所に入れておくのに年間40,000ドルを越える費用がかかる．

up|wards /ʌpwərdz/ → see **upward**

ura|nium /yʊreɪniəm/ N-UNCOUNT 不可算名詞 **Uranium** is a naturally occurring radioactive metal that is used to produce nuclear energy and weapons. ウラニウム

ur|ban /ɜrbən/ ADJ 形容詞 **Urban** means belonging to, or relating to, a city or town. 都市の □ *For a small state it has a large urban population.* 小さな州にしては都市人口が高い． □ *Most urban areas are close to a park.* ほとんどの都市地区は公園に近い． → see **city**

urge /ɜrdʒ/ (urges, urging, urged) **1** V-T 他動詞 If you **urge** someone to do something, you try hard to persuade them to do it. しきりに勧める □ *They urged Congress to approve plans for their reform program.* 改革企画のための諸計画の承認を国会に迫った．**2** V-T 他動詞 If you **urge** someone somewhere, you make them go there by touching them or talking to them. せきたてる □ *He slipped his arm around her waist and urged her away from the window.* 彼は腕を彼女の腰に回して，窓から離れるように促した．**3** V-T 他動詞 If you **urge** a course of action, you strongly advise that it should be taken. 力説する □ *He urged restraint on the security forces.* 防衛軍の抑制を強く唱えた．**4** N-COUNT 可算名詞 If you have an **urge** to do or have something, you have a strong wish to do or have it. 強い衝動 □ *He had an urge to open a shop of his own.* 自分の店を開きたい気持ちにかられた．

Word Partnership	*urge* は次の語句と使われる:
N.	urge **people**, urge **voters** **1**
	leaders/officials urge **1 3**
	urge **action**, urge **caution**, urge **restraint**, urge **support 3**
ADV.	**strongly** urge **1 3**
V.	**feel an** urge, **fight an** urge, **get an** urge, **resist an** urge **4**

ur|gent /ɜrdʒ°nt/ **1** ADJ 形容詞 If something is **urgent**, it needs to be dealt with as soon as possible. 緊急の □ *There is an urgent need for food and water.* 食べ物と水が緊急に必要だ． ● **ur|gen|cy** N-UNCOUNT 不可算名詞 緊急 □ *The urgency of finding a cure attracted some of the best minds in medical science.* 治療を緊急に見つける必要性が，医学界の優秀な人たちを引きつけた． ● **ur|gent|ly** ADV 副詞 [ADV with v] □ *Red Cross officials said they urgently needed bread and water.* 赤十字の職員たちは，パンと水が緊急に必要だといった．**2** ADJ 形容詞 If you speak in an **urgent** way, you show that you are anxious to be noticed or to do something. 切迫した □ *His voice was low and urgent.* 彼の声は低く差し迫っていた． ● **ur|gen|cy** N-UNCOUNT 不可算名詞 切迫 □ *She was surprised at the urgency in his voice.* 差し迫った彼の声にびっくりした． ● **ur|gent|ly** ADV 副詞 [ADV with v] 切迫して □ *They hastened to greet him and asked urgently, "Did you find it?"* 彼を迎えるために急いで行き，「見つかったか？」と差し迫って尋ねた．

Word Partnership	*urgent* は次の語句と使われる:
N.	urgent **action**, urgent **business**, urgent **care**, urgent **matter**, urgent **meeting**, urgent **mission**, urgent **need**, urgent **problem 2**
	urgent **appeal**, urgent **message 2**

uri|nate /yʊərɪneɪt/ (urinates, urinating, urinated) V-I 自動詞 When someone **urinates**, they get rid of urine from their body. 排尿する

urine /yʊərɪn/ N-UNCOUNT 不可算名詞 **Urine** is the liquid that you get rid of from your body when you go to the toilet. 尿 □ *The doctor took a urine sample and a blood sample.* 医者は尿検体と血液検体を採った．

URL /yu ɑr ɛl/ (URLs) N-COUNT 可算名詞 A **URL** is an address that shows where a particular page can be found on the World Wide Web. **URL** is an abbreviation for "Uniform Resource Locator." URL [COMPUTING コンピューティング] □ *The URL for the Lonely Planet travel center is http://www.lonelyplanet.com.* ロンリープラネット旅行センターのURLはhttp://www.lonelyplanet.comだ．

urn /ɜrn/ (urns) **1** N-COUNT 可算名詞 An **urn** is a container in which a dead person's ashes are kept. 骨つぼ □ *...a funeral urn.* 葬式用骨つぼ **2** N-COUNT 可算名詞 An **urn** is a metal container used for making a large quantity of tea or coffee and keeping it hot.

紅茶（コーヒー）沸かし □ *...the ten gallon coffee urn.* 10ガロン入りのコーヒー沸かし

us /əs, STRONG ʌs/

Us is the first person plural pronoun. **Us** is used as the object of a verb or a preposition.

Us は1人称複数代名詞である．**Us** は動詞または前置詞の目的語として使われる．

1 PRON-PLURAL 複数代名詞 A speaker or writer uses **us** to refer both to himself or herself and to one or more other people. You can use **us** before a noun to make it clear which group of people you are referring to. わたしたちに（を）[V PRON, prep PRON] □ *Neither of us forgot about it.* 私たちのどちらもそれを忘れなかった． □ *Heather went to the kitchen to get drinks for us.* ヘザーは私たちのために飲み物を取りにキッチンに行った． □ *They don't like us much.* 私たちにあまり好感を持っていない．**2** PRON-PLURAL 複数代名詞 **Us** is sometimes used to refer to people in general. 人に（を）[V PRON, prep PRON] □ *All of us will struggle fairly hard to survive if we are in danger.* 危険に面していれば，誰もが生き残るために本当に一生懸命戦う．**3** PRON-PLURAL A speaker or writer may use **us** instead of "me" in order to include the audience or reader in what they are saying. わたしたちに（を）[mainly FORMAL 主に形式ばった] [V PRON, prep PRON] □ *This brings us to the second question I asked.* これは私が尋ねた2つ目の質問に続きます．

U.S. /yu ɛs/ also **US** N-PROPER 固有名詞 The **U.S.** is an abbreviation for **the United States**. 合衆国の略語 ['the' N, N n] □ *The first time I saw TV was when I arrived in the U.S. in 1956.* 最初にテレビを見たのは，1956年に合衆国に着いた時であった． □ *He inherited 10,000 U.S. dollars.* 彼は10,000ドルを相続した．

U.S.A. /yu ɛs eɪ/ also **USA** N-PROPER 固有名詞 The **U.S.A.** is an abbreviation for **the United States of America**. アメリカ合衆国の略語 ['the' N]

us|able /yuzəb°l/ ADJ 形容詞 If something is **usable**, it is in a good enough state or condition to be used. 使用可能の □ *It's been reported that no usable fingerprints were found at the scene.* 現場では使用に適した指紋は見つからなかった，と報告されている．

us|age /yusɪdʒ/ (usages) **1** N-UNCOUNT 不可算名詞 **Usage** is the way in which words are actually used in particular contexts, especially with regard to their meanings. 語法 □ *He was a stickler for the correct usage of English.* 英語の正しい語法にうるさい人であった．**2** N-COUNT 可算名詞 A **usage** is a meaning that a word has or a way in which it can be used. 用法 □ *It's very definitely a usage which has come over to Britain from America.* これは確かにアメリカからイギリスに渡ってきた用法である．**3** N-UNCOUNT 不可算名詞 **Usage** is the degree to which something is used or the way in which it is used. 取り扱い方 □ *Parts of the motor wore out because of constant usage.* 常に使用しているのでモーターの部品が摩耗した．

USB /yu ɛs bi/ (USBs) N-COUNT 可算名詞 A **USB** or **USB port** on a computer is a place where you can attach another piece of equipment, for example a printer. **USB** is an abbreviation for "Universal Serial Bus." USB, USBポート [COMPUTING コンピューティング] □ *The device plugs into one of the laptop's USB ports.* この装置は，ノート型パソコンのUSBポートに接続する．

use

❶ VERB USES
❷ NOUN USES

❶ use /yuz/ (uses, using, used) **1** V-T 他動詞 If you **use** something, you do something with it in order to do a job or to achieve a particular result or effect. 使う □ *Trim off the excess pastry using a sharp knife.* よく切れるナイフを使って余分なパイ皮を切り取ってください． □ *The U.S. has used ships to bring most of its heavy material, like tanks, to the region.* 合衆国は船を使って，その地域に戦車などの重い機材の大多数を運んだ．**2** V-T 他動詞 If you **use** a supply of something, you finish it so that none of it is left. 消耗する □ *You used all the ice cubes and didn't put the ice trays back.* 氷を全部使ってしまったのに，製氷皿を元に戻しておかなかった． ● **PHRASAL VERB** 句動詞 **Use up** means the same as **use**. 使い尽くす □ *It isn't animals who use up the world's resources.* 世界の資源を使い尽くしているのは動物ではない．**3** V-T 他動詞 If someone **uses** drugs, they take drugs regularly, especially illegal ones. 常用する □ *He denied he had used drugs.* 麻薬を常用したことを否定した．**4** V-T 他動詞 You can say that someone **uses** the toilet or bathroom as a polite way of saying that they go to the toilet. トイレを使う [POLITENESS 丁寧さ] □ *Wash your hands after using the bathroom.* トイレを使ったら手を洗いなさい．**5** V-T 他動詞 If you **use** a particular word or expression, you say or write it, because it has the meaning that you want to express. 言葉を使う □ *The judge liked using the word "wicked" of people he had sent to jail.* その裁判官は，拘留刑にした人たちについて「悪者」という言葉を使うのを好んだ．**6** V-T 他動詞 If you **use** a particular name, you call yourself by that name, especially when it is not the name that you usually call yourself. 名前を使う □ *Now*

I use a false name if I'm meeting people for the first time. はじめて人と会うときは、今は偽名を使う。 **7** V-T 他動詞 If you say that someone **uses** people, you disapprove of them because they make others do things for them in order to benefit or gain some advantage from it, and not because they care about the other people. 利用する [DISAPPROVAL 不賛成] □ *Why do I have the feeling I'm being used again?* また利用されてると感じるのはなぜだろうか。 **8** → see also **used**

❷ use /yus/ (uses) **1** N-UNCOUNT 不可算名詞 Your **use** of something is the action or fact of your using it. 使用 [also 'a' N, usu N 'of' n] □ *The treatment does not involve the use of any artificial drugs.* この治療は合成薬を少しも使わない。 □ *...research related to microcomputers and their use in classrooms.* 超小型コンピューターおよび教室でのその使用に関する調査。 **2** N-SING 単数名詞 If you have **a use for** something, you need it or can find something to do with it. 必要 □ *You will no longer have a use for the magazines.* 雑誌の必要はもはやないでしょう。 **3** N-VAR 可変名詞 If something has a particular **use**, it is intended for a particular purpose. 用途 □ *Infrared detectors have many uses.* 赤外線感知器の用途は多い。 □ *It's an interesting scientific phenomenon, but of no practical use whatever.* 科学的には興味ある現象であるが、実際的にはまったく何の用途もない。 □ *The report outlined possible uses for the new weapon.* 報告書は、新武器に対する用途の可能性の概要が述べられていた。 **4** N-UNCOUNT 不可算名詞 If you have the **use of** something, you have the permission or ability to use it. 使用の自由 [also 'the' N, usu N 'of' n] □ *She will have the use of the car one night a week.* 一週間に一晩車を使えるだろう。 □ *...young people who at some point in the past have lost the use of their limbs.* 過去のある時点で四肢が使えなくなった若者。 **5** N-COUNT 可算名詞 A **use** of a word is a particular meaning that it has or a particular way in which it can be used. 慣用 □ *There are new uses of words coming in and old uses dying out.* 言葉の新しい使い方が入ってきて、古い使い方は消えていっている。 **6** N-UNCOUNT 不可算名詞 Your **use of** a particular name is the fact of your calling yourself by it. 名前の使用 □ *Police have been hampered by Mr. Urquhart's use of bogus names.* アーカート氏のうその名前が警察の調査を妨げている。 **7** PHRASE 句 If something is **for the use of** a particular person or group of people, it is for that person or group to use. 使用するための □ *The facilities are there for the use of guests.* 施設は客が利用するためのものだ。 **8** PHRASE 句 If you say that being something or knowing someone **has its uses**, you mean that it makes it possible for you to do what you otherwise would not be able to do. 役に立つ [INFORMAL くだけた] □ *It wasn't a life she particularly enjoyed, but it had its uses.* 彼女にとって特に楽しいという生活ではなかったが、役に立った。 **9** PHRASE 句 If something such as a technique, building, or machine is **in use**, it is used regularly by people. If it has gone **out of use**, it is no longer used regularly by people. 用いられて；使用されなくなって □ *...the methods of making champagne which are still in use today.* 今日でもまだ使われているシャンペンの作り方。 **10** PHRASE 句 If you **make use of** something, you do something with it in order to do a job or achieve a particular result or effect. 利用する [WRITTEN 書き言葉] □ *Few found jobs in which they could make use of their new skills.* 新しい技能を利用できる仕事を見つけた人はほとんどいなかった。 **11** PHRASE 句 If you say that **it's no use**, you mean that you have failed to do something and realize that it is useless to continue trying because it is impossible. ―してもむだである □ *It's no use. Let's hang up and try for a better line.* だめだ。電話を切ってよくなるか試してみよう。 **12** PHRASE 句 If something or someone is **of use**, they are useful. If they are **no use**, they are not at all useful. 役に立って；役に立たない □ *The contents of this booklet should be of use to all students.* この小冊子の内容は学生全員の役に立つだろう。

Thesaurus   *use* また次を参照：

V.	utilize ❶ **1**
N.	application, function ❷ **1**

---

used

❶ MODAL USES AND PHRASES
❷ ADJECTIVE USES

❶ used /yust/ **1** PHRASE 句 If something **used to** be done or **used to** be the case, it was done regularly in the past or was the case in the past. ―する習慣だった；以前は―だった □ *People used to come and visit him every day.* 毎日誰かが彼に会いに来ていたものだった。 □ *He used to be one of my professors.* かつてはわたしの教授の一人であった。 **2** PHRASE 句 If something **did not use to** be done, **used to not** be done or **used not to** be done, it was not done in the past. 以前は―でなかった □ *Borrowing used to not be recommended.* 借りることは以前は推奨されていなかった。 □ *At some point kids start doing things they didn't use to do. They get more independent.* ある時点で子供たちは以前はしてなかったことをし始める。だんだん一人立ちしていく。 **3** PHRASE 句 If you **are used to** something, you are familiar with it because you have done it or experienced it many times before. 慣れている □ *I'm used to having my sleep interrupted.*

睡眠の邪魔をされるのは慣れている。 **4** PHRASE 句 If you **get used to** something or someone, you become familiar with it or get to know them, so that you no longer feel that the thing or person is unusual or surprising. 慣れる □ *This is how we do things here. You'll soon get used to it.* ここではこういうふうにやるんだ。すぐに慣れるよ。 □ *You quickly get used to using the brakes.* ブレーキを使うことにすぐに慣れる。

❷ used /yuzd/ **1** ADJ 形容詞 A **used** object is dirty or spoiled because it has been used, and usually needs to be thrown away or washed. 使用された □ *...a used cotton ball stained with makeup.* 化粧でしみになった使用済みの脱脂綿棒。 **2** ADJ 形容詞 A **used** car has already had one or more owners. 中古の □ *Would you buy a used car from this man?* この男から中古車を買いますか？

use|ful /yusfəl/ **1** ADJ 形容詞 If something is **useful**, you can use it to do something or to help you in some way. 役に立つ □ *The pressure cooker is very useful for people who go out all day.* 一日中外に出る人にとって圧力鍋はたいへん役に立つ。 □ *Hypnotherapy can be useful in helping you give up smoking.* 喫煙を止めるために催眠療法が役に立つこともある。 ● **use|ful|ly** ADV 副詞 [ADV with v] 役に立つように □ *...the problems to which computers could be usefully applied.* コンピューターを有効に適用できるかもしれない問題。 ● **use|ful|ness** N-UNCOUNT 不可算名詞 役に立つこと □ *His interest lay in the usefulness of his work, rather than in any personal credit.* 彼の関心は、個人的な名声ではなく、自分の仕事が役に立つことにある。 **2** PHRASE 句 If an object or skill **comes in useful**, it can help you achieve something in a particular situation. 必要時に役に立つ □ *Extra blank paper will probably come in useful.* 余計な白紙は多分役に立つだろう。

Word Partnership	*useful* は次の語句と使われる：

ADV.	**also** useful, **especially** useful, **extremely** useful, **less/more** useful, **particularly** useful, **very** useful **1**
N.	useful **information**, useful **knowledge**, useful **life**, useful **purpose**, useful **strategy**, useful **tool** **1**

---

use|less /yuslɪs/ **1** ADJ 形容詞 If something is **useless**, you cannot use it. 役に立たない □ *He realized that their money was useless in this country.* 彼らのお金はこの国では使いものにならないことがよく分かった。 **2** ADJ 形容詞 If something is **useless**, it does not achieve anything helpful or good. 無益な □ *She knew it was useless to protest.* 抗議してもむだだと分かっていた。 **3** ADJ 形容詞 If you say that someone or something is **useless**, you mean that they are no good at all. 無能な □ *Their education system is useless.* 彼らの教育体制は役立たずだ。 **4** ADJ 形容詞 If someone feels **useless**, they feel bad because they are unable to help someone or achieve anything. 何もできない □ *She sits at home all day, watching TV and feeling useless.* 一日中家に座ってテレビを見ながら、自分の無能さを思っている。

user /yuzər/ (users) N-COUNT 可算名詞 A **user** is a person or thing that uses something such as a place, facility, product, or machine. 利用者 □ *Beach users have complained that the bikes are noisy.* 砂浜を使う人たちは、オートバイがうるさいと文句を言っている。 □ *...a regular user of the subway.* 地下鉄をいつも利用する人 → see **Internet**

user-friendly ADJ 形容詞 If you describe something such as a machine or system as **user-friendly**, you mean that it is well designed and easy to use. 使いやすい □ *This is an entirely computer-operated system which is very user-friendly.* 全てコンピューターで操作されている、たいへん使いやすい体制である。

ush|er /ʌʃər/ (ushers, ushering, ushered) **1** V-T 他動詞 If you **usher** someone somewhere, you show them where they should go by going with them. 案内する [FORMAL 形式ばった] □ *I ushered him into the office.* 彼を事務所に案内した。 **2** N-COUNT 可算名詞 An **usher** is a person who shows people where to sit, for example at a wedding or at a concert. 案内係 □ *He did part-time work as an usher in a theater.* 劇場の案内係として短時間勤務をした。

USP /yu ɛs pi/ (USPs) N-COUNT 可算名詞 The **USP** of a product or service is a particular feature of it which can be used in advertising to show how it is different from, and better than, other similar products or services. **USP** is an abbreviation for "Unique Selling Point." 独自のセールスポイント [BUSINESS 実業] □ *With Volvo, safety was always the USP.* ボルボでは常に安全性が独自のセールスポイントである。

usu|al /yuʒuəl/ **1** ADJ 形容詞 **Usual** is used to describe what happens or what is done most often in a particular situation. いつもの □ *It is a neighborhood beset by all the usual inner-city problems.* 通常のありとあらゆるスラム問題につきまとわれている場所である。 □ *After lunch there was a little more clearing up to do than usual.* 昼食後、普段よりも片づけものが少し多かった。 ● N-SING 単数名詞 **Usual** is also a noun. □ *The stout barman in a bow tie presented himself to take their order. "Good morning, sir. The usual?"* 蝶ネクタイの太ったバーテンが注文を取りに来た。「おはようございます。いつものものでございますか？」 **2** PHRASE 句 You use **as usual** to indicate

that you are describing something that normally happens or that is normally the case. いつものとおりに ❏ *As usual there will be the local and regional elections on June the twelfth.* いつものように、6月12日には地方選挙があろう。 ❸ PHRASE 句 If something happens **as usual**, it happens in the way that it normally does, especially when other things have changed. いつものように ❏ *Surgery was scheduled, but life went on as usual.* 外科手術は予定されたが、人生はいつものように過ぎていった。 ❹ **business as usual → see business**

usu|al|ly /yúʒuəli/ ❶ ADV 副詞 If something **usually** happens, it is the thing that most often happens in a particular situation. 普通は ❏ *The best information about hotels usually comes from friends and acquaintances who have been there.* ホテルに関する一番いい情報源は、たいていはそこに泊まったことのある友人や知人である。 ❏ *Usually, the work is boring.* 普通はその仕事は退屈だ。 ❷ PHRASE 句 You use **more than usually** to show that something shows even more of a particular quality than it normally does. 異常に ❏ *She felt more than usually hungry after her excursion.* 小旅行後は異常に空腹を感じた。

usurp /yusɜ́rp, -zɜ́rp/ (usurps, usurping, usurped) V-T 他動詞 If you say that someone **usurps** a job, role, title, or position, they take it from someone when they have no right to do this. 奪う [FORMAL 形式ばった] ❏ *Did she usurp his place in his mother's heart?* 彼の母親の心に占める彼の場所を彼女は奪ったのか？

uten|sil /yutɛ́nsɪl/ (utensils) N-COUNT 可算名詞 **Utensils** are tools or objects that you use in order to help you to cook, serve food, or eat. 台所用具 ❏ *...utensils such as bowls, steamers and frying pans.* ボウル、蒸し器、フライパンなどの台所用具

uter|us /yútərəs/ (uteruses) N-COUNT 可算名詞 The **uterus** of a woman or female mammal is the part of her body where babies develop. 子宮 [MEDICAL 医学の] ❏ *...an ultrasound scan of the uterus.* 子宮の超音波スキャン

uti|lise /yútɪlaɪz/ → see **utilize**

utili|tar|ian /yutɪlɪtɛ́əriən/ (utilitarians) ❶ ADJ 形容詞 **Utilitarian** objects and buildings are designed to be useful rather than attractive. 実用的な ❏ *Bruce's office is utilitarian and unglamorous.* ブルースの事務所は実用的で何の魅力もない。 ❷ ADJ 形容詞 **Utilitarian** means based on the idea that the morally correct course of action is the one that produces benefit for the greatest number of people. 功利主義の [TECHNICAL 技術的] ❏ *It was James Mill who was the best publicist for utilitarian ideas on government.* 政治功利主義思想を一番広めたのはジェームズ・ミルであった。 ● N-COUNT 可算名詞 A **utilitarian** is someone with utilitarian views. 功利主義者 ❏ *One of the greatest utilitarians was Claude Helvetius.* 最も偉大な功利主義者の一人としてクロード・エルベシウスがいた。

util|ity /yutɪ́lɪti/ (utilities) N-COUNT 可算名詞 A **utility** is an important service such as water, electricity, or gas that is provided for everyone, and that everyone pays for. 公共施設 ❏ *...public utilities such as gas, electricity and phones.* ガス、電気、電話などの公共設備

uti|lize /yútɪlaɪz/ (utilizes, utilizing, utilized) V-T 他動詞 If you **utilize** something, you use it. 利用する [FORMAL 形式ばった] ❏ *Sound engineers utilize a range of techniques to enhance the quality of the recordings.* 音響技師は録音の質を高くするためにさまざまな専門技術を活用する。 ● uti|li|za|tion /yutɪlɪzéɪʃən/ N-UNCOUNT 不可算名詞 利用 ❏ *...the utilization of human resources.* 人材の活用

ut|most /ʌ́tmoust/ ❶ ADJ 形容詞 You can use **utmost** to emphasize the importance or seriousness of something or to emphasize the way that it is done. 最大の [EMPHASIS 強調] [ADJ n] ❏ *It is a matter of the utmost urgency to find out what has happened to these people.* このような人々がどうなったのかを調べるのは、たいへん緊急を要する問題である。 ❏ *Security matters are treated with the utmost seriousness.* 警備問題は最大限真剣に扱われている。 ❷ N-SING 単数名詞 If you say that you are doing your **utmost** to do something, you are emphasizing that you are trying as hard as you can to do it. 最高の [EMPHASIS 強調] ❏ *He would have done his utmost to help her.* 彼女を助けるために全力を尽くしただろうに。

uto|pia /yutóupiə/ (utopias) N-VAR 可変性名詞 If you refer to an imaginary situation as a **utopia**, you mean that it is one in which society is perfect and everyone is happy. 理想郷 ❏ *We weren't out to design a contemporary utopia.* 近代的な理想郷を設計しようとやっきになっていたのではなかった。

uto|pian /yutóupiən/ ❶ ADJ 形容詞 If you describe a plan or idea as **utopian**, you are criticizing it because it is unrealistic and shows a belief that things can be improved much more than is possible. 夢想的な [DISAPPROVAL 不賛成] ❏ *He was pursuing a utopian dream of world prosperity.* 世界繁栄の理想郷の夢を追いかけていた。 ❷ ADJ 形容詞 **Utopian** is used to describe political or religious philosophies which claim that it is possible to build a new and perfect society in which everyone is happy. 理想郷の [FORMAL 形式ばった] ❏ *His was a utopian vision of nature in its purest form.* 彼の展望は、全く純粋な理想郷の自然であった。

ut|ter /ʌ́tər/ (utters, uttering, uttered) ❶ V-T 他動詞 If someone **utters** sounds or words, they say them. 発する [LITERARY 文語的] ❏ *He uttered a snorting laugh.* 鼻を鳴らして笑った。 ❷ ADJ 形容詞 You use **utter** to emphasize that something is great in extent, degree, or amount. 全くの [EMPHASIS 強調] [ADJ n] ❏ *This, of course, is utter nonsense.* これはもちろん全くばかげたことだ。 ❏ *...this utter lack of responsibility.* 完全な責任の欠落

ut|ter|ance /ʌ́tərəns/ (utterances) N-COUNT 可算名詞 Someone's **utterances** are the things that they say. 発言 [FORMAL 形式ばった] ❏ *These two utterances communicate the same message.* この二つの言葉は同じ内容の伝達である。

ut|ter|ly /ʌ́tərli/ ADV 副詞 You use **utterly** to emphasize that something is very great in extent, degree, or amount. 全く [EMPHASIS 強調] ❏ *China is utterly different.* 中国は全く違う。 ❏ *The new laws coming in are utterly ridiculous.* 導入予定の新しい法律はまったくばかげている。

U-turn (U-turns) ❶ N-COUNT 可算名詞 If you make a **U-turn** when you are driving or riding a bicycle, you turn in a half circle in one movement, so that you are then going in the opposite direction. Uターン ❏ *Dave made a U-turn on North Main and drove back to Depot Street.* ディブはノースメイン通りでUターンして、運転しながらデポー通りに戻っていった。 ❷ N-COUNT 可算名詞 If you describe a change in a someone's policy, plans, or actions as a **U-turn**, you mean that it is a complete change. 方向転換 [DISAPPROVAL 不賛成] ❏ *He's doing a U-turn and forecasting 1% growth this year after earlier predicting a 2% drop.* 以前の2%後退予想を方向転換して、今年の成長率は1%と予想した。

U

Vv

V also v /viː/ (V's, v's) N-VAR 可変性名詞 V is the twenty-second letter of the English alphabet. 英語のアルファベットの第22字

va|can|cy /veɪkənsi/ (vacancies) **1** N-COUNT 可算名詞 A **vacancy** is a job or position that has not been filled. 欠員 ❑ *Most vacancies are at the senior level, requiring appropriate qualifications.* ほとんどの欠員は，しかるべき能力を必要とする上級レベルだ. **2** N-COUNT 可算名詞 If there are **vacancies** at a building such as a hotel, some of the rooms are available to rent. 空き部屋 ❑ *This year hotels that usually are jammed had vacancies all summer.* 今年は，たいていは満室になるホテルに夏中空き部屋があった.

Word Link	vac ≈ empty : *evacuate*, *vacant*, *vacate*

va|cant /veɪkənt/ **1** ADJ 形容詞 If something is **vacant**, it is not being used by anyone. 使われていない ❑ *Halfway down the bus was a vacant seat.* バスの真ん中あたりに空席があった. **2** ADJ 形容詞 If a job or position is **vacant**, no one is doing it or in it at present, and people can apply for it. 欠員の ❑ *The position of chairman has been vacant for some time.* 会長の職がしばらく空席になっている. **3** ADJ 形容詞 A **vacant** look or expression is one that suggests that someone does not understand something or that they are not thinking about anything in particular. うつろな，放心したような ❑ *She had a kind of vacant look on her face.* 彼女はうつろな表情をしていた. ● va|cant|ly ADV 副詞 [ADV after v] ぼんやりと ❑ *He looked vacantly out of the window.* 彼はぼんやりと窓の外を見ていた.

va|cate /veɪkeɪt/ (vacates, vacating, vacated) V-T 他動詞 If you **vacate** a place or a job, you leave it or give it up, making it available for other people. 空ける，ゆずる [他動詞] ❑ *He quickly vacated the gym after the workout.* 彼は，トレーニングのあと急いでジムを出た. [FORMAL 形式ばった]

va|ca|tion /veɪkeɪʃ^ən/ (vacations, vacationing, vacationed) **1** N-COUNT 可算名詞 A **vacation** is a period of time during which you relax and enjoy yourself away from home. バカンス，休暇 [AM 米国英語] [also 'on/from' N] ❑ *They planned a late summer vacation in Europe.* 彼らは夏の終わりにヨーロッパでの休暇を計画していました.

> American workers generally get 2 weeks a year of paid vacation. Most people take their vacation time in the summer when their children are not in school. In the UK, workers usually get 4-5 weeks of paid vacation per year.

2 N-COUNT 可算名詞 A **vacation** is a period of the year when schools, universities, and colleges are officially closed. (学校・大学の) 休み ❑ *During his summer vacation he visited Russia.* 夏休み中に彼はロシアを訪ねた. **3** N-UNCOUNT 不可算名詞 If you have a particular number of days' or weeks' **vacation**, you do not have to go to work for that number of days or weeks. (仕事の) 休暇 [AM 米国英語] ❑ *The French get five to six weeks' vacation a year.* フランス人には年間5週間から6週間の休暇がある. **4** V-I 自動詞 If you **are vacationing** in a place away from home, you are on vacation there. 休暇を過ごす [AM 米国英語] ❑ *Myles vacationed in Jamaica.* マイルズはジャマイカで休暇を過ごした.

va|ca|tion|er /veɪkeɪʃənər/ (vacationers) N-COUNT 可算名詞 **Vacationers** are people who are on vacation in a particular place. 旅行客，バカンス客 [mainly AM 主に米国英語] [usu pl] ❑ *Camping, biking, hiking and swimming are all available for the vacationer.* バカンス客は，キャンプ，サイクリング，ハイキング，水泳のどれでも楽しむことができる.

vac|ci|nate /væksɪneɪt/ (vaccinates, vaccinating, vaccinated) V-T 他動詞 If a person or animal **is vaccinated**, they are given a vaccine, usually by injection, to prevent them from getting a disease. 予防接種をする [usu passive] ❑ *Dogs must be vaccinated against distemper.* イヌはジステンパーの予防接種を受けなければならない. ❑ *Have you had your child vaccinated against whooping cough?* お子さんは，百日ぜきの予防接種を受けましたか? ● vac|ci|na|tion /væksɪneɪʃ^ən/ (vaccinations) N-VAR 可変性名詞 予防接種 ❑ *Anyone who wants to avoid the flu should consider getting a vaccination.* インフルエンザを避けたい人は予防接種を考慮するべきです.

vac|cine /væksiːn/ (vaccines) N-MASS 質量名詞 A **vaccine** is a substance containing a harmless form of the germs that cause a particular disease. It is given to people, usually by injection, to prevent them from getting that disease. ワクチン ❑ *Anti-malarial*

vaccines are now undergoing trials. 現在，抗マラリアワクチンが試験段階にある.

→ see **hospital**

vacu|um /vækyum, -yuəm/ (vacuums, vacuuming, vacuumed) **1** N-COUNT 可算名詞 If someone or something creates a **vacuum**, they leave a place or position that then needs to be filled by another person or thing. 空白 ❑ *His presence should fill the power vacuum that has been developing over the past few days.* 彼の存在が過去数日間でできた権力の空白を埋めるでしょう. **2** PHRASE 句 If something is done **in a vacuum**, it is not affected by any outside influences or information. 孤立して ❑ *Moral values cannot be taught in a vacuum.* 倫理的価値は孤立して教わることはできない. **3** N-COUNT 可算名詞 A **vacuum** is a space that contains no air or other gas. 真空 ❑ *Wind is a current of air caused by a vacuum caused by hot air rising.* 風は，熱気の上昇によって生じる真空が原因で起こる空気の流れだ. **4** N-COUNT 可算名詞 A **vacuum** is the same as a **vacuum cleaner**. 掃除機 **5** V-T/V-I 他動詞/自動詞 If you **vacuum** something, you clean it using a vacuum cleaner. 掃除機をかける ❑ *I vacuumed the carpets today.* 今日はカーペットに掃除機をかけた. ❑ *It's important to vacuum regularly.* 定期的に掃除機をかけるのは大切だ.

vacu|um clean|er (vacuum cleaners) N-COUNT 可算名詞 A **vacuum cleaner** or a **vacuum** is an electric machine that sucks up dust and dirt from carpets. 掃除機

va|gi|na /vədʒaɪnə/ (vaginas) N-COUNT 可算名詞 A woman's **vagina** is the passage connecting her outer sex organs to her uterus. 膣(ちつ)

vagi|nal /vædʒɪn^əl/ ADJ 形容詞 **Vaginal** means relating to or involving the vagina. 膣(ちつ)の [ADJ n] ❑ *The creams have been used to reduce vaginal infections.* 膣(ちつ)感染を減らすためにクリームが使用されてきた.

vague /veɪg/ (vaguer, vaguest) **1** ADJ 形容詞 If something written or spoken is **vague**, it does not explain or express things clearly. あいまいな ❑ *A lot of the talk was apparently vague and general.* 話し合いの多くは明らかにあいまいで一般的でした. ❑ *The description was pretty vague.* その記述はとてもあいまいだった. ● vague|ly ADV 副詞 あいまいに ❑ *"I'm not sure," Liz said vaguely.* 「よく分からないわ」とリズはあいまいに言った. **2** ADJ 形容詞 If you have a **vague** memory or idea of something, the memory or idea is not clear. 漠然とした ❑ *They have only a vague idea of the amount of water available.* 利用可能な水の量に関して漠然とした考えしかなかった. ● vague|ly ADV 副詞 [ADV with v] 漠然と ❑ *Judith could vaguely remember her mother lying on the sofa.* ジュディスは，母親がソファーで横たわっていたのを漠然と思い出すことができた. **3** ADJ 形容詞 If you are **vague** about something, you deliberately do not tell people much about it. 明言しない ❑ *He was vague, however, about just what U.S. forces might actually do.* しかしながら，彼は米軍が実際にとる可能性のある行動について明言しませんでした. **4** ADJ 形容詞 If something such as a feeling is **vague**, you experience it only slightly. かすかな ❑ *He was conscious of that vague feeling of irritation again.* 彼はまた少しいらいらを感じていることに気づいた. **5** ADJ 形容詞 A **vague** shape or outline is not clear and is therefore not easy to see. ぼんやりとした ❑ *The bus was a vague shape in the distance.* バスは遠くでぼんやりと見えた.

vague|ly /veɪgli/ **1** ADV 副詞 **Vaguely** means to some degree but not to a very large degree. ある程度 [ADV adj] ❑ *The voice on the line was vaguely familiar, but Crook couldn't place it at first.* 電話の声はなんとなく聞いたことがあったが，クルックは初めのうちは分からなかった. **2** → see also **vague**

vain /veɪn/ (vainer, vainest) **1** ADJ 形容詞 A **vain** attempt or action is one that fails to achieve what was intended. 無駄な [ADJ n] ❑ *The drafting committee worked through the night in a vain attempt*

to finish on schedule. 起草委員会は予定通り終えようと夜通し働いたが、無駄だった。 ● **vain|ly** ADV 副詞 [ADV with v] 無駄に ❑He hunted vainly through his pockets for a piece of paper. 彼はポケットの中の紙を探したが、見つからなかった。 **2** ADJ 形容詞 If you describe a hope that something will happen as a **vain** hope, you mean that there is no chance of it happening. むなしい [ADJ n] ❑He married his fourth wife, Susan, in the vain hope that she would improve his health. 彼は健康改善できるかもしれないというはかない期待を抱いて、4人目の妻、スーザンと結婚した。 ● **vain|ly** ADV 副詞 [ADV with v] はかなく ❑He then set out for Virginia for what he vainly hoped would be a peaceful retirement. そして彼は、のどかな退職後の生活をはかなくも期待してバージニア州に向けて出発した。 **3** ADJ 形容詞 If you describe someone as **vain**, you are critical of their extreme pride in their own beauty, intelligence, or other good qualities. うぬぼれの強い [DISAPPROVAL 不賛成] ❑He wasn't so vain as to think he was smarter than his boss. 彼は上司よりも自分の方が頭がいいと思うほどうぬぼれが強くはなかった。 **4** PHRASE 句 If you do something **in vain**, you do not succeed in achieving what you intend. むなしく ❑He stopped at the door, waiting in vain for her to acknowledge his presence. 彼はむなしくも彼女が彼の存在を気付くのを待って、戸口で立ち止まった。 **5** PHRASE 句 If you say that something such as someone's death, suffering, or effort was **in vain**, you mean that it was useless it did not achieve anything. 無駄に ❑He wants the world to know his son did not die in vain. 彼は、息子が無駄死にをしなかったことを世界中に分かってもらいたいと思っています。

val|iant /vǽlyənt/ ADJ 形容詞 A **valiant** action is very brave and determined, though it may lead to failure or defeat. 勇敢な ❑Despite valiant efforts by the finance minister, inflation rose to 36%. 財務大臣の果敢な努力にもかかわらず、インフレ率は36%に上昇した。 ● **val|iant|ly** ADV 副詞 [ADV with v] 勇敢に ❑He suffered further heart attacks and strokes, all of which he fought valiantly. 彼はさらに心臓まひや脳卒中を患ったが、そのすべてと勇敢に戦った。

val|id /vǽlɪd/ **1** ADJ 形容詞 A **valid** argument, comment, or idea is based on sensible reasoning. もっともな、妥当な ❑They put forward many valid reasons for not exporting. 彼らは輸出反対の正当な理由をたくさん提案した。 ● **va|lid|ity** /vəlɪ́dɪti/ N-UNCOUNT 不可算名詞 妥当性 ❑The editorial says this argument has lost much of its validity. 社説には、この議論は妥当性をほとんど失ったと述べている。 **2** ADJ 形容詞 Something that is **valid** is important or serious enough to make it worth saying or doing. 正当な ❑Most designers share the unspoken belief that fashion is a valid form of visual art. ほとんどのデザイナーは、ファッションは視覚的芸術の正当な一形式だという暗黙の信頼を分かち合っている。 ● **va|lid|ity** N-UNCOUNT 不可算名詞 正当性 ❑...the validity of making children wear bicycle helmets. 子供に自転車用ヘルメット着用を強制する正当性。 **3** ADJ 形容詞 If a ticket or other document is **valid**, it can be used and will be accepted by people in authority. 有効な ❑All tickets are valid for two months. すべての切符は2か月間有効だ。 **4** → see also **validity**

val|i|date /vǽlɪdeɪt/ (**validates, validating, validated**) **1** V-T 他動詞 To **validate** something such as a claim or statement means to prove or confirm that it is true or correct. 証明する [FORMAL 形式ばった] ❑This discovery seems to validate the claims of popular astrology. この発見は、一般に人気の占星術を証明するものと思われる。 ● **vali|da|tion** /vǽlɪdeɪʃᵊn/ (**validations**) N-VAR 可変性名詞 証明 ❑When we want validation for our decisions we often turn to friends for advice and approval. 自分の決心が正しいと証明したいとき、しばしば友人に助言や承認を求める。 **2** V-T 他動詞 To **validate** a person, state, or system means to prove or confirm that they are valuable or worthwhile. 認める、認証する ❑The Academy Awards appear to validate his career. アカデミー賞によって彼のキャリアが認められるようだ。 ● **vali|da|tion** N-VAR 可変性名詞 認めること ❑I think the film is a validation of our lifestyle. その映画は私たちのライフスタイルを認めるものだと思います。

va|lid|ity /vəlɪ́dɪti/ **1** N-UNCOUNT 不可算名詞 The **validity** of something such as a result or a piece of information is whether it can be trusted or believed. 正当性、有効性 ❑Shocked by the results of the elections, they now want to challenge the validity of the vote. 選挙結果にショックを受けて、今度は投票の正当性に異議を唱えようとしている。 **2** Some people, of course, denied the validity of any such claim. もちろんそのような主張の正当性を否定した人々もいる。 **3** → see also **valid**

Va|lium /vǽliəm/ (**Valium**)

Valium is both the singular and the plural form.

Valium は単数形でも複数形でもある。

N-VAR 可変性名詞 商標 **Valium** is a drug given to people to calm their nerves when they are very depressed or upset. バリアム [TRADEMARK 商標] ❑Do you have any Valium? バリアムはありますか?

val|ley /vǽli/ (**valleys**) N-COUNT; N-IN-NAMES 可算名詞、名称中の名詞 A **valley** is a low stretch of land between hills, especially one that has a river flowing through it. 谷 ❑...a wooded valley set against the backdrop of Monte Rosa. モンテローザ山が背景にある樹木が茂った谷
→ see **river**

valu|able /vǽlyuəbᵊl/ **1** ADJ 形容詞 If you describe something or someone as **valuable**, you mean that they are very useful and helpful. 有益な ❑Many of our teachers also have valuable academic links with Heidelberg University. ハイデルベルグ大学と有益な学術的リンクを持っている教師も多い。 **2** ADJ 形容詞 **Valuable** objects are objects that are worth a lot of money. 貴重な、高価な ❑Just because a camera is old does not mean it is valuable. カメラが古いからといって高価だとは限らない。

Thesaurus valuable また次を参照:

ADJ.	helpful, important, useful; (ant.) useless **1**
	costly, expensive, priceless; (ant.) worthless **2**

Word Partnership valuable は次の語句と使われる:

V.	learn a valuable **lesson 1**
N.	valuable **experience**, valuable **information**, valuable **lesson**, **time** is valuable **1** valuable **asset**, valuable **resource 1 2** valuable **property 2**
ADV.	**extremely** valuable, **less** valuable, **very** valuable **1 2**

valu|ables /vǽlyuəbᵊlz/ N-PLURAL 複数名詞 **Valuables** are things that you own that are worth a lot of money, especially small objects such as jewelry. 貴重品 ❑Leave your valuables in the hotel safe behind the reception desk. 貴重品は受付でホテルの金庫に預けなさい。

valu|a|tion /vǽlyueɪʃᵊn/ (**valuations**) N-VAR 可変性名詞 A **valuation** is a judgment that someone makes about how much money something is worth. 査定 ❑Valuation lies at the heart of all takeovers. 査定はすべての買収の核心となる。

value /vǽlyu/ (**values, valuing, valued**) **1** N-UNCOUNT 不可算名詞 The **value** of something such as a quality, attitude, or method is its importance or usefulness. If you place a particular **value** on something, that is the importance or usefulness you think it has. 価値、重要性 [also 'a' N] ❑The value of this work experience should not be underestimated. この実務経験の価値は少なく見積もるべきではない。 ● PHRASE 句 If something is **of value**, it is useful or important. If it is **of no value**, it has no usefulness or importance. 有益な、重要な ❑This weekend course will be of value to everyone interested in the Pilgrim Route. この週末のコースはピルグリム・ルートに関心のある人には誰にでも有益だろう。 **2** V-T 他動詞 If you **value** something or someone, you think that they are important and you appreciate them. 評価する、価値を認める ❑I value the opinion of my husband and we agree on most things. 夫の意見を評価しほとんどのことには合意する。 **3** N-VAR 可変性名詞 The **value** of something is how much money it is worth. 金銭的価値 ❑The value of his investment has risen by more than $50,000. 彼の投資の金銭的価値は5万ドル以上も上昇した。 ● PHRASE 句 If something is **of value**, it is worth a lot of money. If it is **of no value**, it is worth very little money. 高価な/価値がない ❑...a brooch that is really of no value. 実際には価値がないブローチ。 **4** V-T 他動詞 When experts **value** something, they decide how much money it is worth. 査定する ❑The school board valued the property at $130,000. 教育委員会はその不動産は13万ドルの価値があると査定した。 ❑I asked him to have my jewelry valued. 彼に私の宝石の価格を査定するように依頼した。 **5** N-UNCOUNT 不可算名詞 You use **value** in certain expressions to say whether something is worth the money that it costs. For example, if something is **good value**, or if you get **good value** for your money when you buy something, then it is worth the money that it costs. 買い得 ❑We believe that is good value for money for our customers. 当店の客にとってお買い得であると思う。 **6** N-PLURAL 複数名詞 The **values** of a person or group are the moral principles and beliefs that they think are important. 価値観 ❑The countries of South Asia also share many common values. 南アジアの国々もまた多くの価値観を分かち合う。 **7** N-UNCOUNT 不可算名詞 **Value** is used after another noun when mentioning an important or noticeable feature about something. 重要あるいは際立った特徴を述べるときに使われる ❑The script has lost all of its shock value over the intervening 24 years. その脚本は24年間の月日が流れ、衝撃度をすっかり失った。

Thesaurus value また次を参照:

N.	importance, merit, usefulness **1**
	cost, price, worth **3**
V.	admire, honor, respect **2**
	appraise, estimate, price **4**

Word Partnership

value は次の語句と使われる:

ADJ.	**artistic** value 1
	actual value, **equal** value, **great** value 1 3
	estimated value 3
V.	**decline in** value, **increase in** value, **lose** value 1 3
N.	**cash** value, **dollar** value, value **of an investment**, **market** value 3

valve /vǽlv/ (valves) N-COUNT 可算名詞 A **valve** is a device attached to a pipe or a tube that controls the flow of air or liquid through the pipe or tube. 弁, バルブ
→ see **engine**

vam|pire /vǽmpaɪər/ (vampires) N-COUNT 可算名詞 A **vampire** is a creature in legends and horror stories. Vampires are said to come out of graves at night and suck the blood of living people. 吸血鬼
→ see **bat**

van /vǽn/ (vans) N-COUNT 可算名詞 A **van** is a small or medium-sized road vehicle with one row of seats at the front and a space for carrying goods behind. 小型トラック, バン
→ see **car**

van|dal /vǽndəl/ (vandals) N-COUNT 可算名詞 A **vandal** is someone who deliberately damages things, especially public property. 公共物などを破壊する者 □ *The street lights were out, smashed by vandals.* 街頭は破壊されて消えていた.

van|dal|ism /vǽndəlɪzəm/ N-UNCOUNT 不可算名詞 **Vandalism** is the deliberate damaging of things, especially public property. 公共物の破壊活動, ヴァンダリズム □ *...a 13-year-old boy whose crime file includes violence, theft, vandalism, and bullying.* 暴力行為, 窃盗, 公共物破壊, いじめなどの犯罪を犯した13歳の少年

van|dal|ize /vǽndəlaɪz/ (vandalizes, vandalizing, vandalized) V-T 他動詞 If something such as a building or part of a building **is vandalized** by someone, it is damaged on purpose. 故意に破壊する □ *The walls had been horribly vandalized with spray paint.* 壁はスプレー式塗料でひどく落書きされていた.

van|guard /vǽngɑrd/ N-SING 単数名詞 If someone is **in the vanguard of** something such as a revolution or an area of research, they are involved in the most advanced part of it. You can also refer to the people themselves as **the vanguard**. 先頭, 先駆け, 先駆者 □ *Students and intellectuals have been in the vanguard of revolutionary change in China.* 学生や知識人たちが中国での画期的な変化の先駆けとなってきた.

va|nil|la /vənɪ́lə/ N-UNCOUNT 不可算名詞 **Vanilla** is a flavoring used in ice cream and other sweet food. バニラエッセンス □ *I added a dollop of vanilla ice cream to the pie.* パイにバニラアイスクリームを少し加えた.

van|ish /vǽnɪʃ/ (vanishes, vanishing, vanished) 1 V-I 自動詞 If someone or something **vanishes**, they disappear suddenly or in a way that cannot be explained. こつ然と消える □ *He just vanished and was never seen again.* 彼はただ突然いなくなって, 再び現れることはなかった. □ *Anne vanished from outside her home last Wednesday.* アンは先週の水曜日に自宅の外から姿を消した. 2 V-I 自動詞 If something such as a species of animal or a tradition **vanishes**, it stops existing. 消滅する □ *Many of these species have vanished or are facing extinction.* この種の多くは消滅したか, 絶滅の危機にひんしている.

van|ity /vǽnɪti/ N-UNCOUNT 不可算名詞 If you refer to someone's **vanity**, you are critical of them because they take great pride in their appearance or abilities. うぬぼれ, 虚栄心 [DISAPPROVAL 不賛成] □ *Men who use steroids are motivated by sheer vanity.* ステロイドを使う男性は純然たる虚栄心に動機づけられている.

van|tage point /vǽntɪdʒpɔɪnt/ (vantage points) 1 N-COUNT 可算名詞 A **vantage point** is a place from which you can see a lot of things. 見晴らしのよい場所 □ *From a concealed vantage point, he saw a car arrive.* 見晴らしがよく隠れた場所から彼は自動車が到着するのを見た. 2 N-COUNT 可算名詞 If you view a situation **from a** particular **vantage point**, you have a clear understanding of it because of the particular period of time you are in. 観点 □ *From today's vantage point, the 1987 crash seems just a blip in the upward progress of the market.* 今日の観点からみると, 1987年の暴落は市場の上昇過程における一時的な急下落にすぎないようだ.

va|por /véɪpər/ (vapors) N-VAR 可変性名詞 **Vapor** consists of tiny drops of water or other liquids in the air, that appear as mist. 蒸気 □ *...water vapor.* 水蒸気
→ see **greenhouse effect**, **water**

vari|able /vɛ́əriəbəl/ (variables) 1 ADJ 形容詞 Something that is **variable** changes quite often, and there usually seems to be no fixed pattern to these changes. 変わりやすい □ *The potassium content of foodstuffs is very variable.* 食品のカリウム含有量はさまざまだ. ● **vari|abil|ity** /vɛ̀əriəbɪ́lɪti/ N-UNCOUNT 不可算名詞 多様性

□ *There's a great deal of variability between individuals.* 個人によってかなりの多様性がある. 2 N-COUNT 可算名詞 A **variable** is a factor that can change in quality, quantity, or size, that you have to take into account in a situation. 要因 □ *Decisions could be made on the basis of price, delivery dates, after-sales service or any other variable.* 値段, 配達日, アフターサービス, そして他の要素に基づいて決定が下されるだろう.
→ see **experiment**

vari|ance /vɛ́əriəns/ PHRASE 句 If one thing is **at variance with** another, the two things seem to contradict each other. 矛盾して, 食い違って [FORMAL 形式ばった] □ *Many of his statements were at variance with the facts.* 彼の発言の多くは事実と食い違っていた.

vari|ant /vɛ́əriənt/ (variants) N-COUNT 可算名詞 A **variant** of a particular thing is something that has a different form from that thing, although it is related to it. バリエーション, 変異形 □ *The quagga was a strikingly beautiful variant of the zebra.* グアッガはシマウマのひときわ美しい変異体だった.

vari|ation /vɛ̀əriéɪʃən/ (variations) 1 N-COUNT 可算名詞 A **variation on** something is the same thing presented in a slightly different form. 変形, バリエーション □ *This delicious variation on an omelette is quick and easy to prepare.* このおいしいオムレツのバリエーションは手早く簡単に調理できる. 2 N-VAR 可変性名詞 A **variation** is a change or slight difference in a level, amount, or quantity. 変化, 差異 □ *The survey found a wide variation in the prices charged for canteen food.* 調査により, 会社や学校などの食堂で請求される値段にかなりの差があることが分かった.

var|ied /vɛ́ərid/ 1 ADJ 形容詞 Something that is **varied** consists of things of different types, sizes, or qualities. 変化に富む, さまざまな □ *It is essential that your diet is varied and balanced.* 食生活は変化に富みバランスが取れていることが必要だ. 2 → see also **vary**

va|ri|ety /vəráɪɪti/ (varieties) 1 N-UNCOUNT 不可算名詞 If something has **variety**, it consists of things that are different from each other. 変化に富んでいること □ *Susan's idea of freedom was to have variety in her life style.* スーザンの自由についての考え方は, ライフスタイルが変化に富んでいることだった. 2 N-SING 単数名詞 A **variety of** things is a number of different kinds or examples of the same thing. さまざまな種類 □ *West Hampstead has a variety of good stores and supermarkets.* ウェスト・ハムステッドにはさまざまない店やスーパーがある. □ *The island offers such a wide variety of scenery and wildlife.* その島ではいろいろな景色や野生生物を楽しめる. 3 N-COUNT 可算名詞 A **variety** of something is a type of it. 種類 □ *I'm always pleased to try out a new variety.* いつでも喜んで新しい種類を試します.

Thesaurus

variety また次を参照:

N.	diversity, variation; *(ant.)* uniformity 1
	assortment 2
	breed, sort, type 3

Word Partnership

variety は次の語句と使われる:

N.	variety **of activities**, variety **of colors**, variety **of foods**, variety **of issues**, variety **of problems**, variety **of products**, variety **of reasons**, variety **of sizes**, variety **of styles**, variety **of ways** 2
V.	**choose** a variety, **offer** a variety, **provide** a variety 2

vari|ous /vɛ́əriəs/ 1 ADJ 形容詞 If you say that **various** things, you mean there are several different things of the type mentioned. さまざまな, いろいろな □ *His plan is to spread the capital between various building society accounts.* 彼の計画は資本をいくつかの住宅金融組合の口座に分けることだ. 2 ADJ 形容詞 If a number of things are described **as various**, they are very different from one another. 異なった □ *The methods are many and various.* 方法は種種雑多だ.

vari|ous|ly /vɛ́əriəsli/ ADV 副詞 You can use **variously** to introduce a number of different ways that something can be described. さまざまに □ *...the crowds, which were variously estimated at two to several thousand.* 2千かそこらと見積もられる群集

var|nish /vɑ́rnɪʃ/ (varnishes, varnishing, varnished) 1 N-MASS 質量名詞 **Varnish** is an oily liquid that is painted onto wood or other material to give it a hard, clear, shiny surface. ニス □ *The varnish comes in six natural wood shades.* ニスは6段階の天然材の色合いで販売されている. 2 V-T 他動詞 If you **varnish** something, you paint it with varnish. ニスを塗る □ *Varnish the table with two or three coats of water-based varnish.* テーブルを水性のニスで2, 3回塗りなさい.

vary /vɛ́əri/ (varies, varying, varied) 1 V-I 自動詞 If things **vary**, they are different from each other in size, amount, or degree. 異なる □ *As they are handmade, each one varies slightly.* 手製なので一つ一つが少しずつ異なる. □ *The text varies from the earlier versions.* その文章は前版とは異なる. 2 V-T/V-I 他動詞/自動

Word Web vegetables

Fresh vegetables are good for you! They're low in fat and calories so they may help you lose weight. **Broccoli** contains vitamin C. It can help you avoid colds and other infections. **Carrots** are a good source of vitamin A, which is good for the eyes. Because they grow in soil, vegetables also contain minerals such as calcium and iron. These substances help keep bones, teeth, and hair healthy. **Leafy** green vegetables like **cabbage** contain antioxidants. These natural chemicals may help prevent cancer. Vegetables also contain **fiber**. This aids digestion and helps carry toxins out of the body quickly.

詞 If something **varies** or if you **vary** it, it becomes different or changed. 変化をつける [他動詞]，変化する [自動詞] ❑ *The cost of the alcohol duty varies according to the amount of wine in the bottle.* 酒税額はボトル内の酒の量によって異なる. ❸ → see also **varied**

Word Partnership *vary* は次の語句と使われる:

N.	prices vary, rates vary, styles vary **1** vary **by location**, vary **by size**, vary **by state**, vary **by store 1 2**
ADV.	vary **considerably**, vary **greatly**, vary **slightly**, vary **widely 1 2**

vase /veɪs, vɑz/ (**vases**) N-COUNT 可算名詞 A **vase** is a jar, usually made of glass or pottery, used for holding cut flowers or as an ornament. 花瓶 ❑ *...a vase of red roses.* 赤いバラを生けた花瓶 → see **glass**

vast /væst/ (**vaster, vastest**) ADJ 形容詞 Something that is **vast** is extremely large. 広大な，膨大な ❑ *...Afrikaner farmers who own vast stretches of land.* 広大な土地を所有するアフリカーナ人の農業経営者

Thesaurus *vast* また次を参照:

ADJ.	broad, endless, massive; (*ant.*) limited

Word Partnership *vast* は次の語句と使われる:

N.	vast **amounts**, vast **distance**, vast **expanse**, vast **knowledge**, vast **majority**, vast **quantities**

vast|ly /væstli/ ADV 副詞 **Vastly** means to an extremely great degree or extent. 非常に，大いに ❑ *The jury has heard two vastly different accounts.* 陪審員は2つの大いに異なる答弁を聞いた.

Vati|can /vætɪkən/ N-PROPER 固有名詞 The **Vatican** is the city state in Rome ruled by the pope that is the center of the Roman Catholic Church. You can also use **the Vatican** to refer to the pope or his officials. バチカン市国，ローマ法王，バチカン当局 ❑ *The president had an audience with the pope in the Vatican.* 大統領はローマ法王とバチカン市国で接見した.

vault /vɔlt/ (**vaults, vaulting, vaulted**) **1** N-COUNT 可算名詞 A **vault** is a secure room where money and other valuable things can be kept safely. 金庫室 ❑ *Most of the money was in storage in bank vaults.* お金のほとんどは銀行の金庫室に保管されていました. **2** N-COUNT 可算名詞 A **vault** is a room underneath a church or in a cemetery where people are buried, usually the members of a single family. 地下納骨所，墓地 ❑ *He ordered that Matilda's body should be buried in the family vault.* 彼は，マチルダの遺体を家族用の墓地に埋葬するべきだと命じた. **3** V-T/V-I 他動詞/自動詞 If you **vault** something or **vault over** it, you jump quickly onto or over it, especially by putting a hand on top of it to help you balance while you jump. (手で支えて) 飛び越える ❑ *He could easily vault the wall.* 彼ならたやすくその壁を乗り越えられるだろう.

VCR /vi si ɑr/ (**VCRs**) N-COUNT 可算名詞 A **VCR** is a machine that can be used to record television programs or movies onto videotapes, so that people can play them back and watch them later on a television set. **VCR** is an abbreviation for "video cassette recorder." ビデオデッキ ❑ *Panasonic's Program Director lets you program your VCR so easily!* パナソニックのプログラム・ディレクターを使うと，とっても簡単にビデオデッキをセットできます!

veal /vil/ N-UNCOUNT 不可算名詞 **Veal** is meat from a calf. 仔牛の肉 ❑ *...a veal cutlet.* 小牛肉のカツレツ

veer /vɪər/ (**veers, veering, veered**) **1** V-I 自動詞 If something **veers** in a certain direction, it suddenly moves in that direction. 急に向きを変える ❑ *The plane veered off the runway and crashed through the perimeter fence.* 飛行機は急に滑走路からそれて外周フェンスに衝突した. **2** V-I 自動詞 If someone or something **veers** in a certain direction, they change their position or direction in a particular situation. (意見などが) 変わる ❑ *He is unlikely to veer from his boss's strongly held views.* 彼は，上司の強い意見から大きくずれることはないだろう.

ve|gan /vigən/ (**vegans**) ADJ 形容詞 Someone who is **vegan** never eats meat or any animal products such as milk, butter, or cheese. 完全菜食主義の ❑ *The menu changes weekly and usually includes a vegan option.* メニューは週替わりでたいていは完全菜食主義の料理も含まれている. ● N-COUNT 可算名詞 A **vegan** is someone who is vegan. 完全菜食主義者 ❑ *...vegetarians and vegans.* 菜食主義者と完全菜食主義者 → see **vegetarian**

veg|eta|ble /vɛdʒtəbəl, vɛdʒɪ-/ (**vegetables**) **1** N-COUNT 可算名詞 **Vegetables** are plants such as cabbages, potatoes, and onions that you can cook and eat. 野菜 ❑ *A good general diet should include plenty of fresh vegetables.* ふだんの健康的な食生活にはたくさんの新鮮な野菜を含めるべきだ. **2** ADJ 形容詞 **Vegetable** matter comes from plants. 植物の [FORMAL 形式ばった] ❑ *...compounds of animal, vegetable or mineral origin.* 動物，植物，あるいは鉱物が由来の化合物 **3** N-COUNT 可算名詞 If someone refers to a brain-damaged person as a **vegetable**, they mean that the person cannot move, think, or speak. 植物人間 [INFORMAL, OFFENSIVE くだけた，無礼な] [usu sing] → see Word Web: **vegetables** → see **vegetarian**

Word Link *arian* ≈ believing in, having : authori*tarian*, humani*tarian*, veget*arian*

veg|etar|ian /vɛdʒɪtɛəriən/ (**vegetarians**) **1** ADJ 形容詞 Someone who is **vegetarian** never eats meat or fish. 菜食主義の，ベジタリアンの ❑ *Yasmin sticks to a strict vegetarian diet.* ヤスミンは厳格な菜食料理にこだわっている. ● N-COUNT 可算名詞 A **vegetarian** is someone who is vegetarian. 菜食主義者，ベジタリアン ❑ *...a special menu for vegetarians.* 菜食主義者用の特別メニュー **2** ADJ 形容詞 **Vegetarian** food does not contain any meat or fish. 菜食の，ベジタリアンの ❑ *...vegetarian lasagnes.* ベジタリアン・ラザニア → see Word Web: **vegetarian**

veg|eta|tion /vɛdʒɪteɪʃⁿn/ N-UNCOUNT 不可算名詞 Plants, trees, and flowers can be referred to as **vegetation**. 植物 [FORMAL 形式ばった] ❑ *The inn has a garden of semi-tropical vegetation.* その旅館には亜熱帯植物の庭園がある. → see **erosion**

ve|he|ment /viəmənt/ ADJ 形容詞 If a person or their actions or comments are **vehement**, the person has very strong feelings

Word Web vegetarian

The Greek philosopher Pythagoras was a **vegetarian**. He believed that as long as humans kept killing animals, they would keep killing each other. He decided not to eat **meat**. Vegetarians eat more than just **vegetables**. They also eat fruits, grains, oils, fats, and sugar. **Vegans** are vegetarians who don't eat eggs or dairy products. Some people choose this **diet** for health reasons. A well-balanced veggie diet can be healthy. Some people choose this diet for religious reasons. Others want to make the world's **food** supply go further. It takes fifteen pounds of grain to produce one pound of meat.

or opinions and expresses them forcefully. 猛烈な，断固とした □*She suddenly became very vehement and agitated, jumping around and shouting.* 突然彼女は感情が高まっていらつき，飛び回って大声で叫び出した. ●**ve|he|mence** N-UNCOUNT 不可算名詞 激しさ □*He spoke more loudly and with more vehemence than he had intended.* 彼は意図していたよりも大声で断固として話した. ●**ve|he|ment|ly** ADV 副詞 猛烈に □*Krabbe has always vehemently denied using drugs.* クラッベはいつも猛烈に麻薬の使用を否定してきた.

ve|hi|cle /víːkəl/ (**vehicles**) **1** N-COUNT 可算名詞 A **vehicle** is a machine with an engine, such as a bus, car, or truck, that carries people or things from place to place. 乗り物，車両 □*...a vehicle that was somewhere between a tractor and a truck.* トラクターとトラックを足して2で割ったような乗り物 **2** N-COUNT 可算名詞 You can use **vehicle** to refer to something that you use in order to achieve a particular purpose. 手段，媒体 □*Her art became a vehicle for her political beliefs.* 彼女の芸術は政治理念を表す媒体となった.
→ see **car, traffic**

veil /véɪl/ (**veils**) **1** N-COUNT 可算名詞 A **veil** is a piece of thin soft cloth that women sometimes wear over their heads and that can also cover their face. （女性の頭や顔を覆う）ベール □*She's got long hair but she's got a veil over it.* 彼女は長い金髪だがベールで覆い隠している. **2** N-COUNT 可算名詞 You can refer to something that hides or partly hides a situation or activity as a **veil**. 覆い隠すもの，ベール □*The country is ridding itself of its disgraced prime minister in a veil of secrecy.* その国は秘密のベールの下で不祥事を起こした首相を辞任させようとしています. **3** N-COUNT 可算名詞 You can refer to something that you can partly see through, such as a mist, as a **veil**. かすみ [LITERARY 文語的] □*The eruption has left a thin veil of dust in the upper atmosphere.* 噴火により大気圏上層部に薄いほこりのもやができた.

veiled /véɪld/ **1** ADJ 形容詞 A **veiled** comment is expressed in a disguised form rather than directly and openly. 遠回しの [ADJ n] □*He made only a veiled reference to international concerns over human rights issues.* 彼は人権問題に関する国際的な懸念について遠回しに言及しただけだった. **2** ADJ 形容詞 A woman or girl who is **veiled** is wearing a veil. ベールをかぶった □*A veiled woman gave me a kindly smile.* ベールをかぶった女性が私に優しくほほえんだ.

vein /véɪn/ (**veins**) **1** N-COUNT 可算名詞 Your **veins** are the thin tubes in your body through which your blood flows toward your heart. Compare **artery**. 静脈 □*Many veins are found just under the skin.* 静脈の多くは皮膚の真下にある. **2** N-COUNT 可算名詞 Something that is written or spoken **in** a particular **vein** is written or spoken in that style or mood. 調子 □*It is one of his finest works in a lighter vein.* それは軽やかなスタイルの彼の最高作品の1つだ. **3** N-COUNT 可算名詞 A **vein of** a particular quality is evidence of that quality that someone often shows in their behavior or work. 特性があること □*A rich vein of humor runs through the book.* その本を通してユーモアがあふれている. **4** N-COUNT 可算名詞 The **veins** on a leaf are the thin lines on it. 葉脈 □*...the serrated edges and veins of the feathery leaves.* 柔らかい葉のギザギザの端と葉脈.

ve|loc|ity /vəlɒsɪti/ (**velocities**) N-VAR 可変性名詞 **Velocity** is the speed at which something moves in a particular direction. 速度 [TECHNICAL 技術的] □*...the velocities at which the stars orbit.* 星が軌道を回る速度.

vel|vet /vélvɪt/ (**velvets**) N-MASS 質量名詞 **Velvet** is soft material made from cotton, silk, or nylon, that has a thick layer of short cut threads on one side. ベルベット，ビロード □*...a charcoal-gray overcoat with a velvet collar.* ビロードの襟がついたダークグレーのオーバー.

ven|det|ta /vɛndétə/ (**vendettas**) N-VAR 可変性名詞 If one person has a **vendetta against** another, the first person wants revenge for something the second person did to them in the past. 恨み，ふくしゅうの念 □*The vice president said the cartoonist has a personal vendetta against him.* その漫画家は彼に個人的な恨みがあると副大統領は述べた.

vend|ing ma|chine /véndɪŋ məʃiːn/ (**vending machines**) N-COUNT 可算名詞 A **vending machine** is a machine from which you can get things such as cigarettes, chocolate, or coffee by putting in money and pressing a button. 自動販売機.

ven|dor /véndər/ (**vendors**) **1** N-COUNT 可算名詞 A **vendor** is someone who sells things such as newspapers, cigarettes, or food from a small stall or cart. 物売り，行商人 □*...ice cream vendors.* アイスクリーム売り **2** N-COUNT 可算名詞 A **vendor** is a company or person that sells a product or service, especially one who sells to other companies that sell to the public. 販売業者 [LEGAL 法律的] □*Tour America acts as an agent for other vendors and cannot be held responsible for any delays.* ツアー・アメリカは他の販売業者の代行をしていて遅延に対する責任を負わない.

ve|neer /vɪníər/ (**veneers**) **1** N-SING 単数名詞 If you refer to the pleasant way that someone or something appears as a **veneer**, you are critical of them because you believe that their true, hidden nature is not good. うわべ [DISAPPROVAL 不賛成] □*He was able to fool the world with his veneer of education.* 彼はうわべだけの知識

で世界中を欺くことができた. **2** N-VAR 可変性名詞 **Veneer** is a thin layer of wood or plastic that is used to improve the appearance of something. ベニヤ板，化粧板 □*The wood was cut into large sheets of veneer.* その木材は大きいベニヤ板に切り分けられた.

ven|er|able /vénərəbəl/ **1** ADJ 形容詞 A **venerable** person deserves respect because they are old and wise. 尊い，立派な □*Her Chinese friends referred to the empress as their venerable ancestor.* 彼女の中国人の友達はその女帝を立派な祖先だと言った. **2** ADJ 形容詞 Something that is **venerable** is impressive because it is old or important historically. 由緒のある □*May Day has become a venerable institution.* メーデーは伝統を誇る慣例となった.

venge|ance /véndʒəns/ **1** N-UNCOUNT 不可算名詞 **Vengeance** is the act of killing, injuring, or harming someone because they have harmed you. ふくしゅう，報復 □*He swore vengeance on everyone involved in the murder.* 彼はその殺人に関係した者全員にふくしゅうを誓った. **2** PHRASE 句 If you say that something happens **with a vengeance**, you are emphasizing that it happens to a much greater extent than was expected. 猛烈な勢いで [EMPHASIS 強調] □*It began to rain again with a vengeance.* 激しい雨が降り出した.

veni|son /vénɪsən, -zən/ N-UNCOUNT 不可算名詞 **Venison** is the meat of a deer. シカ肉 □*They had a wonderful lunch of salmon salad and roast venison.* 彼らはサーモンサラダとシカ肉ローストの素晴らしい昼食をとった.

ven|om /vénəm/ (**venoms**) **1** N-UNCOUNT 不可算名詞 You can use **venom** to refer to someone's feelings of great bitterness and anger toward someone. 悪意，憎悪 □*He reserved particular venom for critics of his foreign policy.* 彼は外交政策の～批判者に対し特別な恨みを持っていた. **2** N-MASS 質量名詞 The **venom** of a creature such as a snake or spider is the poison that it puts into your body when it bites or stings you. 毒 □*...snake handlers who grow immune to snake venom.* ヘビ毒に免疫ができたヘビ使い.

ven|om|ous /vénəməs/ **1** ADJ 形容詞 If you describe a person or their behavior as **venomous**, you mean that they show great bitterness and anger toward someone. 悪意に満ちた □*...his terrifying and venomous Aunt Bridget.* 彼の恐ろしくて悪意に満ちたブリジットおばさん **2** ADJ 形容詞 A **venomous** snake, spider, or other creature uses poison to attack other creatures. 毒を持った □*He had been bitten by a venomous snake.* 彼は毒ヘビにかまれた.

vent /vént/ (**vents, venting, vented**) **1** N-COUNT 可算名詞 A **vent** is a hole in something through which air can come in and smoke, gas, or smells can go out. 排気口 □*A lot of steam escaped from the vent at the front of the machine.* たくさんの蒸気が機械の前の排気口から出た. **2** V-T 他動詞 If you **vent** your feelings, you express your feelings forcefully. 発散する，ぶちまける □*She telephoned her best friend to vent her frustration.* 彼女は親友に電話をして不満をぶちまけた. **3** PHRASE 句 If you **give vent to** your feelings, you express them forcefully. 吐き出す [FORMAL 形式ばった] □*She gave vent to her anger and jealousy.* 彼女は怒りとしっと心を吐き出した.

ven|ti|late /véntəleɪt/ (**ventilates, ventilating, ventilated**) V-T 他動詞 If you **ventilate** a room or building, you allow fresh air to get into it. 換気する □*Ventilate the room properly when stripping paint.* ペンキをはがすときはきちんと部屋を換気しなさい. ●**ven|ti|la|tion** /ventəléɪʃən/ N-UNCOUNT 不可算名詞 換気 □*The only ventilation comes from tiny sliding windows.* 小さな引き窓からしか換気できない.

ven|ture /véntʃər/ (**ventures, venturing, ventured**) **1** N-COUNT 可算名詞 A **venture** is a project or activity that is new, exciting, and difficult because it involves the risk of failure. ベンチャー，冒険的事業 □*...a Russian-American joint venture.* ロシアとアメリカのジョイントベンチャー **2** V-I 自動詞 If you **venture** somewhere, you go somewhere that might be dangerous. 危険を冒して～する [LITERARY 文語的] □*People are afraid to venture out for fear of sniper attacks.* 人々は狙撃（そげき）攻撃を恐れてあえて出かけることをためらっています. **3** V-T 他動詞 If you **venture** a question or statement, you say it in an uncertain way because you are afraid it might be stupid or wrong. 思い切って言う／尋ねる [WRITTEN 書き言葉] □*"So you're Leo's girlfriend?" he ventured.* 「それで，君はレオの彼女なの？」と彼は思い切って尋ねた. □*He ventured that plants draw part of their nourishment from the air.* 植物は栄養の一部を大気から吸収すると彼は思い切って述べた. **4** V-T 他動詞 If you **venture to** do something that requires courage or is risky, you do it. あえて～する □*"Don't ask," he said, whenever Ginny ventured to raise the subject.* ジニーがあえてその話題を出すたびに彼は「聞かないでくれ」と言った. **5** V-I 自動詞 If you **venture into** an activity, you do something that involves the risk of failure because it is new and different. （リスクを覚悟で）乗り出す 挑戦する □*He enjoyed little success when he ventured into business.* 彼は事業に乗り出したが，あまりうまくいきませんでした.

ven|ture capi|tal N-UNCOUNT 不可算名詞 **Venture capital** is capital that is invested in projects that have a high risk of failure, but that will bring large profits if they are successful. ベンチャーキャピタル [BUSINESS 実業] □*Successful venture capital investment is a lot harder than it sometimes looks.* ベンチャーキャピタルへの投資に成功することは予想以上に難しい.

ven|ture capi|tal|ist (venture capitalists) N-COUNT 可算名詞 A **venture capitalist** is someone who makes money by investing in high risk projects. ベンチャーキャピタリスト, 新規事業への投資家 [BUSINESS 実業] ❑ *The International Convention Centre is the venue for a three-day arts festival.* 国際会議センターが3日間開催される芸術祭の会場となっている.

venue /vɛnyu/ (venues) N-COUNT 可算名詞 The **venue** for an event or activity is the place where it will happen. 会場, 開催地 ❑ *The International Convention Centre is the venue for a three-day arts festival.* 国際会議センターが3日間開催される芸術祭の会場となっている.

→ see **concert**

ve|ran|da /vərændə/ (verandas) also verandah N-COUNT 可算名詞 A **veranda** is a roofed platform along the outside of a house. ベランダ ❑ *They had their coffee and tea on the veranda.* 彼らはベランダでコーヒーや紅茶を飲んだ.

verb /vɜrb/ (verbs) ■ N-COUNT 可算名詞 A **verb** is a word such as "sing," "feel," or "die" that is used with a subject to say what someone or something does or what happens to them, or to give information about them. 動詞 ■ → see also **phrasal verb**

Word Link verb ≈ word : proverb, verbal, verbatim

ver|bal /vɜrbᵊl/ ■ ADJ 形容詞 You use **verbal** to indicate that something is expressed in speech rather than in writing or action. 口頭の ❑ *They were jostled and subjected to a torrent of verbal abuse.* 彼らは押しのけあって激しい悪口雑言にさらされた. ● **ver|bal|ly** ADV 副詞 口頭で ❑ *Dave drank heavily and became verbally abusive.* デイブはかなり飲んで暴言を吐き始めた. ② ADJ 形容詞 [ADJ n] You use **verbal** to indicate that something is connected with words and the use of words. 言葉に関する, 言語の ❑ *The test has scores for verbal skills, mathematical skills, and abstract reasoning skills.* そのテストは語学力, 数学能力, 論理的思考能力を試験する. ③ ADJ 形容詞 In grammar, **verbal** means relating to a verb. 動詞の ❑ *...a verbal noun.* 動名詞

Word Link ver ≈ truth : verbatim, verdict, verify

ver|ba|tim /vərbeɪtɪm/ ADV 副詞 If you repeat something **verbatim**, you use exactly the same words as were used originally. 一語一語, 逐語的に [ADV after v] ❑ *The president's speeches are regularly reproduced verbatim in the state-run newspapers.* 大統領の演説は州が発行している新聞で定期的に一語一句再現された. ● ADJ 形容詞 **Verbatim** is also an adjective. 言葉どおりの [ADJ n] ❑ *I was treated to a verbatim report of every conversation she's taken part in over the past week.* 彼女が先週参加したおしゃべりの一語一語の報告を聞かせてもらった.

ver|dict /vɜrdɪkt/ (verdicts) ■ N-COUNT 可算名詞 In a court of law, the **verdict** is the decision that is given by the jury or judge at the end of a trial. 評決 ❑ *The jury returned a unanimous guilty verdict.* 陪審団は全員一致で有罪判決を下した. ② N-COUNT 可算名詞 Someone's **verdict** on something is their opinion of it, after thinking about it or investigating it. 判断, 意見 ❑ *The doctor's verdict was that he was entirely healthy.* 医者は, 彼が全く健康だという判断を下した.

→ see **trial**

verge /vɜrdʒ/ (verges, verging, verged) ■ PHRASE 句 If you are **on the verge of** something, you are going to do it very soon or it is likely to happen or begin very soon. 〜する寸前である ❑ *The country was on the verge of becoming prosperous and successful.* その国は今にも繁栄し成功しそうだった. ② N-COUNT 可算名詞 The **verge** of a road is a narrow piece of ground by the side of a road, which is usually covered with grass or flowers. 路肩 [BRIT 英国英語; AM shoulder 米国英語 **shoulder**]

▶ **verge on** PHRASAL VERB 句動詞 If someone or something **verges on** a particular state or quality, they are almost the same as that state or quality. ほぼ〜という状態である ❑ *...a fury that verged on madness.* 狂気に近い激怒

veri|fy /vɛrɪfaɪ/ (verifies, verifying, verified) ■ V-T 他動詞 If you **verify** something, you check that it is true by careful examination or investigation. 検証する ❑ *I verified the source from which I had that information.* その情報を得た情報源を検証した. ● **veri|fi|ca|tion** /vɛrɪfɪkeɪʃᵊn/ N-UNCOUNT 不可算名詞 検証 ❑ *All charges against her are dropped pending the verification of her story.* 彼女に対する告訴はすべて彼女の言い分が立証されるまで取り下げられた. ② V-T 他動詞 If you **verify** something, you state or confirm that it is true. [no cont] 真実であると証明する ❑ *The government has not verified any of those reports.* 政府はこれらの報告書が真実であるという証明をしていない.

veri|table /vɛrɪtəbᵊl/ ADJ 形容詞 You can use **veritable** to emphasize the size, amount, or nature of something. 正真正銘の, 紛れもない [EMPHASIS 強調] ❑ *...a veritable feast of pre-game entertainment.* 試合前のエンターテイメントとしての真の祭典

ver|nacu|lar /vərnækyələr/ (vernaculars) N-COUNT 可算名詞 The **vernacular** is the language or dialect that is most widely spoken by ordinary people in a region or country. その土地特有の ❑ *...books or plays written in the vernacular.* 方言で書かれた本や芝居

Word Link vers ≈ turning : subversion, versatile, version

ver|sa|tile /vɜrsətᵊl/ ■ ADJ 形容詞 If you say that a person is **versatile**, you approve of them because they have many different skills. 多才な [APPROVAL 賛成] ❑ *He had been one of the game's most versatile athletes.* 彼はその試合で最も多才な選手の1人だった. ● **ver|sa|til|ity** /vɜrsətɪlɪti/ N-UNCOUNT 不可算名詞 ❑ *Aileen stands out for her incredible versatility as an actress.* エイリーンは俳優として信じられないほど多才で卓越している. ② ADJ 形容詞 A **tool**, machine, or material that is **versatile** can be used for many different purposes. 使いみちが多い, 用途が広い ❑ *Never before has computing been so versatile.* 今までコンピュータがこれほど多目的に使われたことがない. ● **ver|sa|til|ity** N-UNCOUNT 不可算名詞 用途の広さ ❑ *Velvet as a fabric is not known for its versatility.* 布地としてのビロードは多様性に欠ける.

verse /vɜrs/ (verses) ■ N-UNCOUNT 不可算名詞 **Verse** is writing arranged in lines that have rhythm and that often rhyme at the end. 韻文 ❑ *I have been moved to write a few lines of verse.* 韻文を一筆書く気にさせられた. ② N-COUNT 可算名詞 A **verse** is one of the parts into which a poem, a song, or a chapter of the Bible or the Koran is divided. 節, 連 ❑ *This verse describes three signs of spring.* この節では3つの春の兆しを描写している.

ver|sion /vɜrʒᵊn/ (versions) ■ N-COUNT 可算名詞 A **version** of something is a particular form of it in which some details are different from earlier or later forms. 一版, バージョン ❑ *...an updated version of his bestselling book.* 彼のベストセラー本の改訂版 ❑ *Ludo is a version of an ancient Indian racing game.* ルドーは古代インドのレースゲームの1つだ. ② N-COUNT 可算名詞 Someone's **version of** an event is their own description of it, especially when it is different from other people's. 説明, 見解 ❑ *Some former hostages contradicted the official version of events.* 元人質の一部は, その事件の公式見解に反論した.

ver|sus /vɜrsəs/ ■ PREP 前置詞 You use **versus** to indicate that two figures, ideas, or choices are opposed. 〜に対して ❑ *Only 18.8% of the class of 1982 had some kind of diploma four years after high school, versus 45% of the class of 1972.* 1972年のクラスの45%が高校卒業4年後に何らかの学位をとったのに対し, 1982年のクラスは18.8%にすぎない. ② PREP 前置詞 **Versus** is used to indicate that two teams or people are competing against each other in a sports event. (競技における) 一対一 ❑ *Italy versus Japan is turning out to be a surprisingly well matched competition.* イタリア対日本は意外にも互角の勝負となりつつある. ③ PREP 前置詞 **Versus** is used in a court of law to indicate that two people or organizations are involved in a law suit. The abbreviation **v** is also used. (訴訟における) 一対一 ❑ *That case became known as Healey versus Jones.* その訴訟は「ヒーリー対ジョーンズ」として知られるようになった.

ver|te|bra /vɜrtɪbrə/ (vertebrae /vɜrtɪbreɪ, -bri/) N-COUNT 可算名詞 **Vertebrae** are the small circular bones that form the spine of a human being or animal. つい骨

ver|ti|cal /vɜrtɪkᵊl/ ADJ 形容詞 Something that is **vertical** stands or points straight up. 縦の, 垂直の ❑ *The climber inched up a vertical wall of rock.* その登山家は垂直壁をじりじりと登った. ● **ver|ti|cal|ly** ADV 副詞 [ADV after v] 垂直に, 縦に ❑ *Cut each bulb in half vertically.* それぞれの球根を縦に半分に切りなさい.

→ see **graph**

very /vɛri/ ■ ADV 副詞 **Very** is used to give emphasis to an adjective or adverb. とても, 非常に [EMPHASIS 強調] [ADV adj/adv] ❑ *The problem and the answer are very simple.* その問題と答えはとても簡単だ. ❑ *I'm very sorry.* 本当にごめんなさい. ❑ *They are getting the hang of it very quickly.* 彼らはあっという間にコツをつかんでいる. ② PHRASE 句 **Not very** is used with an adjective or adverb to say that something is not at all true, or that it is true only to a small degree. あまり〜でない ❑ *She's not very impressed with them.* 彼女は彼らからあまり好印象を受けていません. ❑ *"How well do you know her?"—"Not very."* 「彼女のことがどのくらい知っているの?」「あまり知らないよ」 ③ ADV 副詞 You use **very** to give emphasis to a superlative adjective or adverb. For example, if you say that something is **the very best**, you are emphasizing that it is the best. まさに [EMPHASIS 強調] [ADV superl] ❑ *They will be helped by the very latest in navigation aids.* 超最新式の航行補助装置が彼らの役に立つだろう. ❑ *I am feeling in the very best of spirits.* 気分は最高だ. ④ ADJ 形容詞 You use **very** with certain nouns in order to specify an extreme position or extreme point in time. 最も, いちばん [EMPHASIS 強調] [ADJ n] ❑ *At the very back of the yard was a wooden shack.* その庭のいちばん奥に木の小屋があった. ❑ *I turned to the very end of the book, to read the final words.* 最後の文章を読むために本のいちばん最後のページを開けた. ⑤ ADJ 形容詞 You use **very** with nouns to emphasize that something is exactly the right one or exactly the same one. まさにその [EMPHASIS 強調] [ADJ n] ❑ *Everybody says he is the very man for the case.* 彼がこの件の適任者だとみんなが言う. ⑥ ADJ 形容詞 You use **very** with

nouns to emphasize the importance or seriousness of what you are saying. ~そのもの [EMPHASIS 強調] [ADJ n] ❏ At one stage his very life was in danger. あるときは彼の命そのものが危険状態にあった. ❏ History is taking place before your very eyes. 歴史はまさに目の前で起きている. **7** PHRASE 句 The expression **very much so** is an emphatic way of answering "yes" to something or saying that it is true or correct. まったくそのとおりです [EMPHASIS 強調] ❏ "Are you enjoying your vacation?" — "Very much so." 「休暇を楽しんでいますか?」「ええ、とても」 **8** CONVENTION 慣習表現 **Very well** is used to say that you agree to do something or you accept someone's answer, even though you might not be completely satisfied with it. よろしい [FORMULAE 決まり文句] ❏ "We need proof, sir." Another pause. Then, "Very well." 「証拠が必要です」再び沈黙があり、そして「よろしい」. **9** PHRASE 句 If you say that you **cannot very well** do something, you mean that it would not be right or possible to do it. ~するのは無理である ❏ I said yes. I can't very well say no under the circumstances. 私は承諾した. その状況下ではとても断れない.

Very, **so**, and **too** can all be used to intensify the meaning of an adjective, an adverb, or a word like **much** or **many**. However, they are not used in the same way. **Very** is the simplest intensifier. It has no other meaning beyond that. **So** can suggest an emotional reaction on the part of the speaker, such as pleasure, surprise, or disappointment. ❏ John makes me so angry!... Oh thank you so much! **So** can also refer forward to a result clause introduced by **that**. ❏ The procession was forced to move so slowly that it arrived three hours late. **Too** suggests an excessive or undesirable amount, often so much that a particular result does not or cannot happen. ❏ She does wear too much makeup at times... He was too late to save her.

Thesaurus   *very* また次を参照:

ADV.   absolutely, extremely, greatly, highly **1**

ves|sel /vɛsᵊl/ (vessels) **1** N-COUNT 可算名詞 A **vessel** is a ship or large boat. 船 [FORMAL 形式ばった] ❏ ...a New Zealand navy vessel. ニュージーランドの軍艦 **2** → see also **blood vessel**
→ see **ship**

vest /vɛst/ (vests) **1** N-COUNT 可算名詞 A **vest** is a sleeveless piece of clothing with buttons that people usually wear over a shirt. ベスト、チョッキ [AM 米国英語] **2** N-COUNT 可算名詞 A **vest** is a piece of underwear that you can wear on the top half of your body in order to keep warm. 肌着 [BRIT 英国英語; AM **undershirt** 米国英語]

vest|ed in|ter|est (vested interests) N-VAR 可変性名詞 If you have a **vested interest** in something, you have a very strong reason for acting in a particular way, for example, to protect your money, power, or reputation. 確定権利、既得権 ❏ The administration has no vested interest in proving public schools good or bad. 運営陣には公立学校がよいか悪いかを検証することに既得権益がない

ves|tige /vɛstɪdʒ/ (vestiges) N-COUNT 可算名詞 A **vestige of** something is a very small part that still remains of something that was once much larger or more important. 痕跡 (こんせき) [FORMAL 形式ばった] ❏ We represent the last vestige of what made this nation great – hard work. 我々がこの国を偉大にした最後の名残です. 大変な努力をしました.

vet /vɛt/ (vets, vetting, vetted) **1** N-COUNT 可算名詞 A **vet** is someone who is qualified to treat sick or injured animals. **Vet** is an abbreviation for **veterinarian**. 獣医 ❏ She's at the vet, with her dog, right now. ただ今彼女は愛犬と獣医のところにいる. **2** N-COUNT 可算名詞 A **vet** is someone who has served in the armed forces of their country, especially during a war. **Vet** is an abbreviation for **veteran**. 退役軍人 [AM 米国英語, INFORMAL くだけた] ❏ The New England Shelter in Boston will serve Christmas dinner for 200 vets. ボストンのニューイングランドシェルターではクリスマスディナーを200年の退役軍人に出します. **3** V-T 他動詞 If someone **is vetted**, they are investigated fully before being given a particular job, role, or position, especially one that involves military or political secrets. 身元を調査する [mainly BRIT 主に英国英語] [usu passive] ❏ She was secretly vetted before she ever undertook any work for me. 彼女が私の元で働き始める前にこっそり身元調査をした. ● **vet|ting** N-UNCOUNT 不可算名詞 ❏ The government is to make major changes to the procedure for carrying out security vetting. 政府は身元調査を行う手続きを大幅に変更する予定だ.

vet|er|an /vɛtərən/ (veterans) **1** N-COUNT 可算名詞 A **veteran** is someone who has served in the armed forces of their country, especially during a war. 退役軍人 ❏ They approved a $1.1 billion package of pay increases for the veterans of the Persian Gulf War. ペルシア湾岸戦争で戦った退役軍人に11億ドル増しの総合対策費が認められた. **2** N-COUNT 可算名詞 You use **veteran** to refer to someone who has been involved in a particular activity for a long time. ベテラン、老練者 ❏ ...Annette Michelson, the veteran critic and professor

of cinema studies at New York University. ベテラン評論家であり、ニューヨーク大学の映画研究教授であるアネット・マイケルソン

vet|eri|nar|ian /vɛtərɪnɛəriən/ (veterinarians) N-COUNT 可算名詞 A **veterinarian** is a person who is qualified to treat sick or injured animals. 獣医 [mainly AM 主に米国英語]

vet|eri|nary /vɛtərəneri/ ADJ 形容詞 **Veterinary** is used to describe the work of a person whose job is to treat sick or injured animals, or to describe the medical treatment of animals. 獣医の [ADJ n] ❏ It was decided that our veterinary screening of horses at events should be continued. イベントでの獣医によるウマの検診は続けられるべきだと決定した.

veto /vitoʊ/ (vetoes, vetoing, vetoed) **1** V-T 他動詞 If someone in authority **vetoes** something, they forbid it, or stop it from being put into action. 拒否権を発動する ❏ The president vetoed the economic package passed by Congress. 大統領は議会を通過した経済対策に拒否権を行使した. ● N-COUNT 可算名詞 **Veto** is also a noun. 拒否権の行使 ❏ They need 12 votes to override his veto. 彼が発動した拒否権を無効にするには12票が必要だ. **2** N-UNCOUNT 不可算名詞 **Veto** is the right that someone in authority has to forbid something. 拒否権 ❏ ...the president's power of veto. 大統領の拒否権

vex /vɛks/ (vexes, vexing, vexed) **1** V-T 他動詞 If someone or something **vexes** you, they make you feel annoyed, puzzled, and frustrated. いらだたせる、悩ませる ❏ It vexed me to think of others gossiping behind my back. 私のいないところでほかの人がうわさ話をしていると思うとむかついた. ● **vexed** ADJ 形容詞 ❏ Exporters, farmers and industrialists alike are vexed and blame the government. 輸出業者、農業経営者、実業家は一様にいらだって、政府を非難した. ● **vex|ing** ADJ 形容詞 いらだたせる ❏ There remains, however, another and more vexing problem. しかしながら、まだまだ困った問題が残っている. **2** → see also **vexed**

vexed /vɛkst/ **1** ADJ 形容詞 A **vexed** problem or question is very difficult and causes people a lot of trouble. 厄介な ❏ Ministers have begun work on the vexed issue of economic union. 大臣は経済同盟の難問に取り組み始めた. **2** → see also **vex**

via /vaɪə, viːə/ **1** PREP 前置詞 If you go somewhere **via** a particular place, you go through that place on the way to your destination. ~経由で ❏ We drove via Lovech to the old Danube town of Ruse. 私たちはロベチ経由でルセにある古い町ダニューブに車で行った. **2** PREP 前置詞 If you do something **via** a particular means or person, you do it by making use of that means or person. ~を介して ❏ The technology to allow relief workers to contact the outside world via satellite already exists. 難民救済ワーカーが人工衛星を介して外部の世界に連絡を取る技術はすでに存在する.

vi|able /vaɪəbᵊl/ ADJ 形容詞 Something that is **viable** is capable of doing what it is intended to do. 実行可能な ❏ Cash alone will not make Eastern Europe's banks viable. 現金だけでは東ヨーロッパの銀行の経営を成功させることはできないだろう. ● **vi|abil|ity** /vaɪəbɪliti/ N-UNCOUNT 不可算名詞 実現可能性 ❏ ...the shaky financial viability of the nuclear industry. 原子力産業の不安定な財政的実行可能性

vibe /vaɪb/ (vibes) N-COUNT 可算名詞 **Vibes** are the good or bad atmosphere that you sense with in a person or a place. 雰囲気、感じ [INFORMAL くだけた] ❏ Sorry, Chris, but I have bad vibes about this guy. クリス、悪いけどこの男とはうまが合わない気がするの.

vi|brant /vaɪbrənt/ **1** ADJ 形容詞 Someone or something that is **vibrant** is full of life, energy, and enthusiasm. 生き生きした、活発的な ❏ Tom felt himself being drawn toward her vibrant personality. トムは、彼女の活発な性格に引かれていくのを感じた. ❏ ...Shakespeare's vibrant language. シェークスピアの生き生きとした言葉遣い ● **vi|bran|cy** /vaɪbrənsi/ N-UNCOUNT 不可算名詞 精力的なこと、活気 ❏ She was a woman with extraordinary vibrancy and extraordinary knowledge. 彼女は並外れて活発で並外れた知識を持った女性でした. **2** ADJ 形容詞 **Vibrant** colors are very bright and clear. 鮮やかな ❏ Horizon blue, corn yellow and pistachio green are just three of the vibrant colors in this range. この部屋で色鮮やかなのは、ホライゾンブルー、コーンイエロー、ピスタチオグリーンの3色だけだ. ● **vi|brant|ly** ADV 副詞 [ADV adj] 色鮮やかに ❏ ...a selection of vibrantly colored French cast-iron saucepans. 色鮮やかなフランス製鋳鉄ソースパンの品ぞろえ

vi|brate /vaɪbreɪt/ (vibrates, vibrating, vibrated) V-T/V-I 他動詞/自動詞 If something **vibrates** or if you **vibrate** it, it shakes with repeated small, quick movements. 振動させる、揺らす [他動詞]、振動する、揺れる [自動詞] ❏ The ground shook and the cliffs seemed to vibrate. 地面が揺れ、崖が振動しているようだった. ● **vi|bra|tion** /vaɪbreɪʃᵊn/ N-VAR 可変性名詞 振動 ❏ The vibrations of the vehicles rattled the store windows. 車両の振動でショーウィンドーがガタガタと音を立てた.
→ see **ear**, **sound**

vic|ar /vɪkər/ (vicars) N-COUNT; N-VOC 可算名詞、呼格名詞 A **vicar** is a priest who is in charge of a chapel that is associated with a parish church in the Episcopal Church in the United States. 会堂牧師 [AM 米国英語]

vice /vaɪs/ (vices) **1** N-COUNT 可算名詞 A **vice** is a habit that is

regarded as a weakness in someone's character, but not usually as a serious fault. 欠点 ❑*His only vice is to get drunk on champagne after concluding a successful piece of business.* 彼の唯一の欠点は，事業を成功させた後のシャンパンで酔っ払うことだ. **2** N-UNCOUNT 不可算名詞 **Vice** refers to criminal activities, especially those connected with pornography or prostitution. 風俗犯罪 ❑*He said those responsible for offences connected with vice, gaming, and drugs should be deported on conviction.* 風俗，とばく，麻薬に関連した犯罪の責任者には有罪判決後に強制送還されるべきだと彼は述べた. **3** N-COUNT 可算名詞 A **vice** is a tool with a pair of parts that hold an object tightly while you do work on it. 万力 [BRIT 英国英語; AM vise 米国英語 vise]

vice ver|sa /ˌvaɪsəˈvɜːrsə, vaɪs/ PHRASE 句 **Vice versa** is used to indicate that the reverse of what you have said is true. For example, "women may bring their husbands with them, and vice versa" means that men may also bring their wives with them. 逆もまた同様 ❑*They want to send students from low-income homes into more affluent neighborhoods and vice versa.* 低所得家庭出身の学生をもっと裕福な地域に送り，またその逆も同様に希望している.

vi|cin|ity /vɪˈsɪnɪti/ N-SING 単数名詞 If something is **in the vicinity** of a particular place, it is near it. 付近 [FORMAL 形式ばった] ❑*There were a hundred or so hotels in the vicinity of the station.* その駅の近辺には100軒ほどのホテルがあった.

vi|cious /ˈvɪʃəs/ **1** ADJ 形容詞 A **vicious** person or a **vicious** blow is violent and cruel. 凶暴な ❑*He was a cruel and vicious man.* 彼は残酷で凶暴だった. ❑*He suffered a vicious attack by a gang of white youths.* 彼は白人の若者の一団に容赦ない攻撃を受けた. ● **vi|cious|ly** ADV 副詞 容赦なく，凶暴に ❑*She had been viciously attacked with a hammer.* 彼女はハンマーで容赦なく攻撃された. ● **vi|cious|ness** N-UNCOUNT 不可算名詞 凶暴さ ❑*...the intensity and viciousness of these attacks.* ...これらの攻撃の激しさと凶暴さ. **2** ADJ 形容詞 A **vicious** remark is cruel and intended to upset someone. 悪意のある ❑*It is a deliberate, nasty and vicious attack on a young man's character.* それは若者の性格に対する故意で意地悪で悪意に満ちた攻撃だ. ● **vi|cious|ly** ADV 副詞 [ADV with v] 意地悪く ❑*"He deserved to die," said Penelope viciously.* 「彼は死んで当然だったよ」とペネロピは意地悪く言った.

Thesaurus   *vicious* また次を参照:

ADJ.   brutal, cruel, violent; (ant.) nice **1 2**

vi|cious cir|cle (vicious circles) also **vicious cycle** N-COUNT 可算名詞 A **vicious circle** is a problem or difficult situation that has the effect of creating new problems that then cause the original problem or situation to occur again. 悪循環 ❑*The more pesticides are used, the more resistant the insects become so the more pesticides have to be used. It's a vicious circle.* 殺虫剤を使えば使うほど，昆虫の抵抗性が発達し，そのため殺虫剤の使用量を増やさなければならない. 悪循環だ.

vic|tim /ˈvɪktəm/ (victims) **1** N-COUNT 可算名詞 A **victim** is someone who has been hurt or killed. (死傷を負う) 被害者 犠牲者 ❑*Statistically our chances of being the victims of violent crime are remote.* 統計上は，暴力犯罪の被害者になる確率はとても低い. **2** N-COUNT 可算名詞 A **victim** is someone who has suffered as a result of someone else's actions or beliefs, or as a result of unpleasant circumstances. (他人の行為・悪状況などの) 被害者 犠牲者 ❑*He was a victim of racial prejudice.* 彼は人種差別の犠牲者だった. ❑*He described himself and Altman as victims rather than participants in the scandal.* 彼は自分自身とアルトマンをスキャンダルの参加者というよりは被害者であると説明した.

vic|tim|ize /ˈvɪktəmaɪz/ (victimizes, victimizing, victimized) V-T 他動詞 If someone **is victimized**, they are deliberately treated unfairly. 不当に扱う ❑*He felt the students had been victimized because they'd voiced opposition to the government.* 彼は，学生が政府への反対を表明したために不当に扱われたと感じた. ● **vic|timi|za|tion** /ˌvɪktəmɪˈzeɪʃən/ N-UNCOUNT 不可算名詞 不当に扱うこと ❑*...society's cruel victimization of women.* 社会が女性をひどく不当に扱うこと

vic|tor /ˈvɪktər/ (victors) N-COUNT 可算名詞 The **victor** in a battle or contest is the person who wins. 勝利者 [LITERARY 文語的] ❑*Oliver Townsend and co-driver Kirk Lee eventually emerged as victors after five different cars had led the event.* 5台の異なる車がレースから降りた後，最終的にオリバー・タウンゼントと交代運転手のカーク・リーが勝者として浮上した.

Vic|to|rian /vɪkˈtɔːriən/ (Victorians) **1** ADJ 形容詞 **Victorian** means belonging to, connected with, or typical of Britain in the middle and last parts of the 19th century, when Victoria was Queen. ビクトリア女王時代の ❑*We have a lovely old Victorian house.* 私たちはビクトリア風の古い美しい家を持っています. ❑*...a Victorian-style family portrait.* ...ビクトリア朝スタイルの家族肖像画. **2** ADJ 形容詞 You can use **Victorian** to describe people who have old-fashioned attitudes, especially about good behavior and morals. 旧式な ❑*Victorian values are much misunderstood.* 旧式な

価値観の真価はあまり認められていない. **3** N-COUNT 可算名詞 The **Victorians** were the British people who lived in the time of Queen Victoria. ビクトリア女王時代の人 ❑*The Victorians were the last people to invest properly in the railways.* 鉄道路線に適切な投資を行ったのはビクトリア女王時代の人が最後である.

vic|to|ri|ous /vɪkˈtɔːriəs/ ADJ 形容詞 You use **victorious** to describe someone who has won a victory in a struggle, war, or competition. 勝利を得た ❑*In 1978 he played for the victorious Argentinian side in the World Cup.* 1978年，彼はワールドカップで勝利を得たアルゼンチン代表としてプレイしました.

vic|to|ry /ˈvɪktəri, ˈvɪktri/ (victories) **1** N-VAR 可変性名詞 A **victory** is a success in a struggle, war, or competition. 勝利 ❑*Union leaders are heading for victory in their battle over workplace rights.* 労働組合の幹部は職場における権利をかけた戦いに勝利しつつある. **2** PHRASE 句 If you say that someone has won a **moral victory**, you mean that although they have officially lost a contest or dispute, they have succeeded in showing they are right about something. 事実上の勝利 ❑*She said her party had won a moral victory.* 彼女は党は事実上勝利したと言いました.

Thesaurus   *victory* また次を参照:

N.   conquest, success, win; (ant.) defeat **1**

video /ˈvɪdioʊ/ (videos, videoing, videoed) **1** N-COUNT 可算名詞 A **video** is a movie or television program recorded on tape for people to watch on a television set. ビデオ ❑*...sports and exercise videos.* スポーツおよびエクササイズのビデオ. **2** N-UNCOUNT 不可算名詞 **Video** is the system of recording movies and events on tape so that people can watch them on a television set. ビデオ装置 ❑*She has watched the race on video.* 彼女はレースをビデオで見た. ❑*...manufacturers of audio and video equipment.* ...オーディオおよびビデオ装置の製造業者. **3** N-COUNT 可算名詞 A **video** is a machine that you can use to record television programs and play videotapes on a television set. ビデオカセットレコーダー [mainly BRIT 主に英国英語; AM usually **VCR** 米国英語では通常 **VCR**] **4** V-T 他動詞 If you **video** a television program or event, you record it on tape using a VCR or video camera, so that you can watch it later. ビデオテープに録画する [mainly BRIT 主に英国英語] [他動詞] [AM usually **tape**, **videotape** 米国英語では通常 **tape**, **videotape**] → see **DVD**

video cas|sette (video cassettes) also **videocassette** N-COUNT 可算名詞 A **video cassette** is a cassette containing videotape, on which you can record or watch moving pictures and sounds. ビデオカセット

video-conference (video-conferences) also **videoconference** N-COUNT 可算名詞 A **video-conference** is a meeting that takes place using video conferencing. テレビ会議 [BUSINESS 実業] ❑*It is now possible to hold a video conference in real time on a cellphone.* 今では，携帯電話でリアルタイムにテレビ会議を催すことができるようになった.

video con|fer|enc|ing /ˈvɪdioʊ ˌkɒnfərənsɪŋ/ also **video-conferencing** or **videoconferencing** N-UNCOUNT 不可算名詞 **Video conferencing** is a system that enables people in various places around the world to have a meeting by seeing and hearing each other on a screen. テレビ会議 [BUSINESS 実業] ❑*We also hope to use video conferencing to train and supervise staff.* 我々は職員の訓練および指導目的でもテレビ会議を使いたいと願っている.

video game (video games) N-COUNT 可算名詞 A **video game** is an electronic or computerized game that you play on your television or on a computer screen. ビデオゲーム

video|phone /ˈvɪdioʊfoʊn/ (videophones) also **video phone** N-COUNT 可算名詞 A **videophone** is a telephone that has a camera and screen so that people who are using the phone can see and hear each other. テレビ電話

video re|cord|er (video recorders) N-COUNT 可算名詞 A **video recorder** or a **video cassette recorder** is the same as a **VCR**. ビデオカセットレコーダー

Word Link   vid, vis ≈ seeing : audiovisual, videotape, visible

video|tape /ˈvɪdioʊteɪp/ (videotapes, videotaping, videotaped) also **video tape** **1** N-UNCOUNT 不可算名詞 **Videotape** is magnetic tape that is used to record moving pictures and sounds to be shown on television. ビデオテープ ❑*...the use of videotape in criminal court rooms.* 刑事法廷における videoテープの使用. **2** N-COUNT 可算名詞 A **videotape** is the same as a **video cassette**. ビデオカセット **3** V-T 他動詞 If you **videotape** a television program or event, you record it on tape using a video recorder or video camera, so that you can watch it later. ビデオテープに録画する [mainly AM 主に米国英語] [他動詞] ❑*She videotaped the entire trip.* 彼女は旅の一部始終をビデオテープに録画した.

vie /vaɪ/ (vies, vying, vied) V-RECIP 相互動詞 If one person or thing is **vying with** another for something, the people or

V

things are competing for it. 争っている [FORMAL 形式ばった] □ California is vying with other states to capture a piece of the growing communications market. カリフォルニア州は成長し続ける通信市場のシェアを得ようと他州と争っています。 □ The two are vying for the support of New York voters. 2人はニューヨーク州の有権者の支持を得ようと張り合っている。

view /vyuː/ (**views, viewing, viewed**) **1** N-COUNT 可算名詞 Your **views** on something are the beliefs or opinions that you have about it, for example, whether you think it is good, bad, right, or wrong. 意見 □ Washington and Moscow are believed to have similar views on Kashmir. ワシントンとモスクワはカシミール問題について同様な見解を持っていると考えられている。 □ You should also make your views known to your congressperson. あなたも国会議員に自分の見解を知ってもらうべきだ。 **2** N-SING 単数名詞 Your **view of** a particular subject is the way that you understand and think about it. 考え □ The whole point was to get away from a Christian-centered view of religion. 一番大切なことはキリスト教中心の宗教的な物の見方から逃れることだった。 **3** V-T 他動詞 If you **view** something in a particular way, you think of it in that way. ある見方でみる [他動詞] □ First-generation Americans view the United States as a land of golden opportunity. 一世のアメリカ人は米国を千載一遇の好機を提供する国だと考えている。 □ Abigail's mother Linda views her daughter's talent with a mixture of pride and worry. アビゲイルの母リンダは彼女の才能を誇りと心配の混じった目で見ている。 **4** N-COUNT 可算名詞 The **view** from a window or high place is everything that can be seen from that place, especially when it is considered to be beautiful. 眺め □ The view from our window was one of beautiful green countryside. 我々の窓からは、美しい緑の田園風景が眺められた。 **5** N-SING 単数名詞 If you have a **view of** something, you can see it. 見えるという状態 □ He stood up to get a better view of the blackboard. 黒板がよく見えるよう彼は立ち上がった。 **6** N-UNCOUNT 不可算名詞 You use **view** in expressions to do with being able to see something. For example, if something is **in view**, you can see it. If something is **in full view of everyone**, everyone can see it. 見える所に □ She was lying there in full view of anyone who walked by. そこに横たわった彼女の様子は通りかかる人誰もに丸見えになっていた。 **7** V-T 他動詞 If you **view** something, you look at it for a particular purpose. 調べる [FORMAL 形式ばった] [他動詞] □ They came back to view the house again. 彼らは家をもう1度調べるために戻ってきた。 **8** V-T 他動詞 If you **view** a television program, video, or movie, you watch it. 見る [FORMAL 形式ばった] [他動詞] □ We have viewed the video recording of the incident. 私たちは事件のビデオ撮影を見た。 **9** N-SING 単数名詞 **View** refers to the way in which a piece of text or graphics is displayed on a computer screen. 表示 [COMPUTING コンピューティング] □ To see the current document in full-page view, click the Page Zoom Full button. 現在の文書のページ全体を表示するには全ページズームボタンをクリックします。 **10** PHRASE 句 You use **in my view** when you want to indicate that you are stating a personal opinion, that other people might not agree with. 私の意見では □ In my view things won't change. 私の意見では物事は変化しない。 **11** PHRASE 句 You use **in view of** when you are taking into consideration facts that have just been mentioned or are just about to be mentioned. 考慮して □ In view of the fact that Hobson was not a trained economist his achievements were remarkable. ホブソンは訓練を受けた経済学者ではなかった事実を考慮すると、彼の実績は注目に値するものだった。 **12** PHRASE 句 If something such as a work of art is **on view**, it is shown in public for people to look at. 展示されて □ A significant exhibition of contemporary sculpture will be on view at the Portland Gallery. 現在彫刻の意義深い展覧会がポートランドギャラリーで展示される。 **13** PHRASE 句 If you do something **with a view to** doing something else, you do it because you hope it will result in that other thing being done. する目的で □ He has called a meeting of all parties tomorrow, with a view to forming a national reconciliation government. 彼は、国家和解政府を組織する目的で明日の超党派会議を召集しました。

view|er /vyuːər/ (**viewers**) **1** N-COUNT 可算名詞 **Viewers** are people who watch television, or who are watching a particular program on television. テレビ視聴者 □ These programs are each watched by around 19 million viewers every week. これらの番組はそれぞれ、毎週およそ1900万の視聴者が見ている。 **2** N-COUNT 可算名詞 A **viewer** is someone who is looking carefully at a picture or other interesting object. 見る人 □ ...the relationship between the art object and the viewer. 芸術品とそれを見る人との関係。

view|point /vyuːpɔɪnt/ (**viewpoints**) **1** N-COUNT 可算名詞 Someone's **viewpoint** is the way that they think about things in general, or the way they think about a particular thing. 観点 □ The novel is shown from the girl's viewpoint. その小説は少女の観点から書かれている。 **2** N-COUNT 可算名詞 A **viewpoint** is a place from which you can get a good view of something. 見える地点 □ You have to know where to stand for a good viewpoint. 君はどこに立てばよく見えるかを知る必要がある。

vig|il /vɪdʒɪl/ (**vigils**) N-COUNT 可算名詞 A **vigil** is a period of

time when people remain quietly in a place, especially at night, for example, because they are praying or are making a political protest. 徹夜 □ Protesters are holding a twenty-four hour vigil outside the socialist party headquarters. 抗議者は社会党本部の外で24時間の不寝番をしています。 ● PHRASE 句 If someone **keeps a vigil** or **keeps vigil** somewhere, they remain there quietly for a period of time, especially at night, for example, because they are praying or are making a political protest. 寝ずの番をする

vigi|lant /vɪdʒɪlənt/ ADJ 形容詞 Someone who is **vigilant** gives careful attention to a particular problem or situation and concentrates on noticing any danger or trouble that there might be. 油断のない □ He warned the public to be vigilant and report anything suspicious. 彼は絶えず警戒を怠らず、疑わしいものがあれば報告するよう一般市民に警告した。 ● **vigi|lance** N-UNCOUNT 不可算名詞 警戒 □ Constant vigilance is needed to combat this evil. この害悪と戦うためには不断の警戒が必要である。

vigi|lan|te /vɪdʒɪlænti/ (**vigilantes**) N-COUNT 可算名詞 **Vigilantes** are people who organize themselves into an unofficial group to protect their community and to catch and punish criminals. 自警団 □ The vigilantes dragged the men out. 自警団はその男どもを引っ張り出しました。

vig|or /vɪgər/ N-UNCOUNT 不可算名詞 **Vigor** is physical or mental energy and enthusiasm. 精力 □ He has approached his job with renewed vigor. 彼は新たな気力を持って仕事に取り組んだ。

vig|or|ous /vɪgərəs/ **1** ADJ 形容詞 **Vigorous** physical activities involve using a lot of energy, usually to do short and repeated actions. 激しい □ Very vigorous exercise can increase the risk of heart attacks. 非常に激しい運動は心臓発作の危険性を高める。 ● **vig|or|ous|ly** ADV 副詞 [ADV after v] 激しく □ He shook his head vigorously. 彼は頭を激しく振った。 **2** ADJ 形容詞 A **vigorous** person does things with great energy and enthusiasm. A **vigorous** campaign or activity is done with great energy and enthusiasm. 活発な □ Theodore Roosevelt was a strong and vigorous politician. セオドア・ルーズベルトは強力で精力的な政治家だった。 ● **vig|or|ous|ly** ADV 副詞 [ADV with v] 活発に □ The police vigorously denied that excessive force had been used. 警察は必要以上の武力が使用されたことを強く否定しました。

vig|our /vɪgər/ → see **vigor**

vile /vaɪl/ (**viler, vilest**) ADJ 形容詞 If you say that someone or something is **vile**, you mean that they are very unpleasant. 嫌な □ The weather was consistently vile. 天気はいつも悪かった。

vil|la /vɪlə/ (**villas**) N-COUNT 可算名詞 A **villa** is a fairly large house, especially one in a hot country or a resort. 別荘 □ He lives in a secluded five-bedroom luxury villa. 彼は人里離れた、豪華な5部屋の別荘に住んでいる。

vil|lage /vɪlɪdʒ/ (**villages**) N-COUNT 可算名詞 A **village** consists of a group of houses, together with other buildings such as a church and a school, in a country area. 村落 □ He lives quietly in the country in a village near Lahti. 彼はラハティ近郊にある村の田舎で静かに暮らしている。

vil|lain /vɪlən/ (**villains**) **1** N-COUNT 可算名詞 A **villain** is someone who deliberately harms other people or breaks the law in order to get what he or she wants. 悪党 □ I left the room, feeling like a villain and a murderer. 私はまるで自分が悪党か殺人者のように感じながら部屋を出た。 **2** N-COUNT 可算名詞 The **villain** in a novel, movie, or play is the main bad character. 悪役 □ He also played a villain opposite Sylvester Stallone in Demolition Man (1992). 彼は1992年の『デモリションマン』でシルベスター・スタローンの敵役も演じた。

vin|di|cate /vɪndɪkeɪt/ (**vindicates, vindicating, vindicated**) V-T 他動詞 If a person or their decisions, actions, or ideas **are vindicated**, they are proved to be correct, after people have said that they were wrong. 正しさを証明される [FORMAL 形式ばった] [他動詞] □ The director said he had been vindicated by the experts' report. 理事長は専門家の報告書により正当性を立証されたと言いました。 ● **vin|di|ca|tion** /vɪndɪkeɪʃən/ N-UNCOUNT 不可算名詞 [also 'a' N, usu N 'of' n] 正当化 □ He called the success a vindication of his party's free-market economic policy. 彼は自党の自由市場経済政策の擁護を成功と呼んだ。

vin|dic|tive /vɪndɪktɪv/ ADJ 形容詞 If you say that someone is **vindictive**, you are critical of them because they deliberately try to upset or cause trouble for someone who they think has done them harm. 報復的な [DISAPPROVAL 不賛成] □ ...a vindictive woman desperate for revenge against the man who loved and left her. 自分を愛し、去った男への復讐に必死の執念深い女。 ● **vin|dic|tive|ness** N-UNCOUNT 不可算名詞 執念深さ □ ...a dishonest person who is operating completely out of vindictiveness. 報復心のみに基づいて行動している不正直な人。

vine /vaɪn/ (**vines**) N-VAR 可変性名詞 A **vine** is a plant that grows up or over things, especially one that produces grapes. ブドウのつる □ Every square meter of soil was used, mainly for olives, vines, and almonds. 土壌のすべてが使用され、主にオリーブ、ブドウの木、アーモンドが育てられていた。

vin|egar /vɪnɪgər/ (**vinegars**) N-MASS 質量名詞 **Vinegar** is a sharp-tasting liquid, usually made from sour wine or malt, that is used in cooking to make things such as salad dressing. 食酢

vine|yard /vɪnyərd/ (**vineyards**) N-COUNT 可算名詞 A **vineyard** is an area of land where grape vines are grown in order to produce wine. You can also use **vineyard** to refer to the set of buildings in which the wine is produced. ブドウ園

vin|tage /vɪntɪdʒ/ (**vintages**) **1** N-COUNT 可算名詞 The **vintage** of a good quality wine is the year and place that it was made before being stored to improve it. You can also use **vintage** to refer to the wine that was made in a certain year. 特定地・年度・銘柄の優良ブドウ酒, 当たり年のブドウ酒 □ This wine is from one of the two best vintages of the decade in this region. このワインはここ10年間における当地域の最良ブドウ酒2種の内1つだ. **2** ADJ 形容詞 **Vintage** wine is good quality wine that has been stored for several years in order to improve its quality. 時代ものの [ADJ n] □ If you can buy only one case at auction, it should be vintage port. オークションで1箱しか購入できないなら時代もののポートワインに違いない. **3** ADJ 形容詞 **Vintage** cars or airplanes are old but are admired because they are considered to be the best of their kind. 最高級の歴史的名車 [ADJ n] □ The museum will have a permanent exhibition of 60 vintage and racing cars. その美術館は60台のクラシックカーとレーシングカーを常設展示する. **4** ADJ 形容詞 **Vintage** clothing and furniture is old or secondhand, but usually of good quality. 古くて価値のある □ ...collectors of vintage clothing. 年代物の服の収集家.

vi|nyl /vaɪnl/ (**vinyls**) **1** N-MASS 質量名詞 **Vinyl** is a strong plastic used for making things such as floor coverings and furniture. ビニル, ビニール □ ...a modern vinyl floor covering. 現代的なビニルの床仕上げ材. **2** N-UNCOUNT 不可算名詞 You can use **vinyl** to refer to records, especially in contrast to cassettes or compact discs. レコード盤 □ This compilation was first issued on vinyl in 1984. このコンピレーションアルバムは最初に1984年にレコード盤で発表された.

vio|la /viovlə/ (**violas**) N-VAR 可変性名詞 A **viola** is a musical instrument with four strings that is played with a bow. It is like a violin, but is slightly larger and can play lower notes. ヴィオラ □ She also played the viola in some amateur orchestras. 彼女はいくつかのアマチュア交響楽団でヴィオラも演奏した.
→ see **orchestra, string**

vio|late /vaɪəleɪt/ (**violates, violating, violated**) **1** V-T 他動詞 If someone **violates** an agreement, law, or promise, they break it. 破る [FORMAL 形式ばった] [他動詞] □ They went to prison because they violated the law. 彼らは法律に違反したために刑務所に収容されました. ● **vio|la|tion** /vaɪəleɪʃn/ (**violations**) N-VAR 可変性名詞 違反 □ To deprive the boy of his education is a violation of state law. その少年に教育を受けさせないことは国法違反です. **2** V-T 他動詞 If you **violate** someone's privacy or peace, you disturb it. 妨害する [FORMAL 形式ばった] [他動詞] □ These men were violating my family's privacy. これらの男たちは彼女の家族のプライバシーを侵害していた. **3** V-T 他動詞 If someone **violates** a special place such as a grave, they damage it or treat it with disrespect. 神聖を汚す [他動詞] □ Detectives are still searching for those who violated the graveyard. 刑事は墓地を侵害した者を今も探しています. ● **vio|la|tion** N-UNCOUNT 不可算名詞 冒涜 □ The violation of the graves is not the first such incident. 墓の冒涜はこれが最初ではありませんでした.

Word Partnership violate は次の語句と使われる:

N.   violate **an agreement**, violate **the Constitution**, violate **the law**, violate **rights**, violate **rules** **1**
violate **someone's privacy** **2**

vio|lence /vaɪələns/ **1** N-UNCOUNT 不可算名詞 **Violence** is behavior that is intended to hurt, injure, or kill people. 暴力 □ Twenty people were killed in the violence. その暴行で20人が殺されました. □ ...domestic violence between husband and wife. 夫婦間の家庭内暴力. **2** N-UNCOUNT 不可算名詞 If you do or say something with **violence**, you use a lot of force and energy in doing or saying it, often because you are angry. 猛烈さ [LITERARY 文語の] □ The violence in her tone gave Tyler a shock. 彼女の声のすさまじさはタイラーにショックを与えた.

Word Partnership violence は次の語句と使われる:

N.   **acts of** violence, **outbreak of** violence, **victims of** violence, violence **against women** **1**
V.   **condemn** violence, violence **erupts**, **prevent** violence, **resort to** violence, **stop** violence **1**
ADJ.   **ethnic** violence, **increasing** violence, **physical** violence, **racial** violence, **widespread** violence **1**

vio|lent /vaɪələnt/ **1** ADJ 形容詞 If someone is **violent**, or if they do something that is **violent**, they use physical force or weapons to hurt, injure, or kill other people. 暴力的な □ A quarter of current inmates have committed violent crimes. 現在の囚人の4分の1が暴力犯罪を犯している. □ ...violent anti-government demonstrations. 暴力的な反政府デモ. ● **vio|lent|ly** ADV 副詞 [ADV with v] 乱暴に □ Some opposition activists have been violently attacked. 一部の反対派勢力が激しく攻撃されました. **2** ADJ 形容詞 A **violent** event happens suddenly and with great force. 強烈な □ A violent impact hurtled her forward. 強烈な衝撃で彼女は前に突進した. ● **vio|lent|ly** ADV 副詞 [ADV with v] □ A nearby volcano erupted violently, sending out a hail of molten rock and boiling mud. 付近の火山が猛烈に噴火し, 溶岩と高温の泥が雨あられと流れ出しました. **3** ADJ 形容詞 If you describe something as **violent**, you mean that it is said, done, or felt very strongly. 激しい □ Violent opposition to the plan continues. 計画に対する激しい抵抗が続いています. □ He had violent stomach pains. 彼は激しい腹痛を起こした. ● **vio|lent|ly** ADV 副詞 激しく □ He was violently scolded. 彼は猛烈にしかられた. **4** ADJ 形容詞 A **violent** death is painful and unexpected, usually because the person who dies has been murdered. 非業の □ ...an innocent man who had met a violent death. 非業の死を迎えた無実の男. ● **vio|lent|ly** ADV 副詞 [ADV with v] 乱暴に □ ...a girl who had died violently nine years earlier. 9年前に変死した少女. **5** ADJ 形容詞 A **violent** movie or television program contains a lot of scenes that show violence. 暴力的な □ It was the most violent movie that I have ever seen. それは私が見たもののなかで最も暴力的な映画だった.

Word Partnership violent は次の語句と使われる:

N.   violent **acts**, violent **attacks**, violent **behavior**, violent **clash**, violent **conflict**, violent **confrontations**, violent **crime**, violent **criminals**, violent **demonstrations**, violent **incidents**, violent **offenders** **1**
violent **protests**, violent **reaction** **1** **3**
violent **death** **4**
violent **films/movies** **5**
ADV.   **extremely** violent, **increasingly** violent **1** **3**

vio|let /vaɪəlɪt/ (**violets**) **1** N-COUNT 可算名詞 A **violet** is a small plant that has purple or white flowers in the spring. スミレ **2** COLOR 色彩語 Something that is **violet** is a bluish-purple color. すみれ色 □ The light was beginning to drain from a violet sky. すみれ色の空から光が消え始めていた. **3** PHRASE 句 If you say that someone is no **shrinking violet**, you mean that they are not at all shy. 引っ込みがちな人 □ When it comes to expressing himself he is no shrinking violet. 自分を表現することになると, 彼は引っ込み思案ではなくなる.
→ see **color, rainbow**

vio|lin /vaɪəlɪn/ (**violins**) N-VAR 可変性名詞 A **violin** is a musical instrument. Violins are made of wood and have four strings. You play the violin by holding it under your chin and moving a bow across the strings. ヴァイオリン □ Lizzie used to play the violin. リジーは以前ヴァイオリンを弾いていた.
→ see **orchestra, string**

vio|lin|ist /vaɪəlɪnɪst/ (**violinists**) N-COUNT 可算名詞 A **violinist** is someone who plays the violin. ヴァイオリン奏者 □ Rose's father was a talented violinist. ローズの父は才能あるヴァイオリン奏者だった.

VIP /vi aɪ pi/ (**VIPs**) N-COUNT 可算名詞 A **VIP** is someone who is given better treatment than ordinary people because they are famous, influential, or important. **VIP** is an abbreviation for "very important person." 要人 □ ...such VIPs as Prince Charles and Bill Clinton. チャールズ皇太子やリチャード・ニクソンらの貴賓.

Word Link vir ≈ poison : viral, virulent, virus

vi|ral /vaɪrəl/ ADJ 形容詞 A **viral** disease or infection is caused by a virus. ウィルスの □ ...a 65-year-old patient suffering from severe viral pneumonia. 重症のウィルス性肺炎を患う65歳の患者.

vir|gin /vɜrdʒɪn/ (**virgins**) **1** N-COUNT 可算名詞 A **virgin** is someone, especially a woman or girl, who has never had sex. 処女 □ I was a virgin until I was thirty years old. 私は30歳になるまで処女だった. **2** ADJ 形容詞 You use **virgin** to describe something such as land that has never been used or spoiled. 未開拓の □ Within 40 years there will be no virgin forest left. 原始林は40年の内になくなってしまうだろう. **3** PHRASE 句 If you say that a situation is **virgin territory**, you mean that you have no experience of it and it is completely new for you. 未経験の分野 □ The World Cup is virgin territory for Ecuador. ワールドカップはエクアドルにとって未経験である. **4** N-COUNT 可算名詞 You can use **virgin** to describe someone who has never used or done a particular thing before. 未経験者 □ Until he appeared in "In the Line of Fire" Malkovich had been an action-movie virgin. 『ザ・シークレット・サービス』に出演するまでマルコビッチはアクション映画に出たことがなかった.

vir|ile /vɪrl/ ADJ 形容詞 If you describe a man as **virile**, you mean that he has the qualities that a man is traditionally expected to have, such as strength and sexual power. 成年男子の □ He wanted his sons to become strong, virile, and athletic like himself. 彼は息子たちに自分のように強く, 男らしく強健に育って欲しい. ● **vi|ril|ity** /vɪrɪliti/ N-UNCOUNT 不可算名詞 男らしさ □ Children are

also considered proof of a man's virility. 子供たちも男らしさの証明と考えられています.

vir|tual /vˈɜːtʃuəl/ ■ ADJ 形容詞 You can use **virtual** to indicate that something is so nearly true that for most purposes it can be regarded as true. 事実上の [ADJ n] ▫ Argentina came to a virtual standstill while the game was being played. アルゼンチンは試合が行われている間, 実質的な停止状態に陥りました. ■ ADJ 形容詞 **Virtual** objects and activities are generated by a computer to simulate real objects and activities. 仮想の [COMPUTING コンピューティング] [ADJ n] ▫ Up to four players can compete in a virtual world of role playing. 仮想ロールプレイングの世界では選手4人までが競争できる. ● **vir|tu|al|ity** N-UNCOUNT 不可算名詞 実質 ▫ People speculate about virtuality systems, but we're already working on it. 人々は仮想システムを思索しているが, 私たちはすでに研究に取り掛かっている.

vir|tu|al|ly /vˈɜːtʃuəli/ ADV 副詞 You can use **virtually** to indicate that something is so nearly true that for most purposes it can be regarded as true. 実質的に [ADV with group] ▫ Virtually all cooking was done over coal-fired ranges. 実質的には料理はすべて石炭レンジで行われた.

vir|tual memo|ry N-UNCOUNT 不可算名詞 **Virtual memory** is a computing technique in which you increase the size of a computer's memory by arranging or storing the data in it in a different way. 仮想記憶 [COMPUTING コンピューティング] ▫ ...with 512mb RAM and 768mb virtual memory. 512MBのRAMと768MBの仮想記録.

vir|tual re|al|ity N-UNCOUNT 不可算名詞 **Virtual reality** is an environment that is produced by a computer and seems very like reality to the person experiencing it. 仮想現実 [COMPUTING コンピューティング] ▫ One day virtual reality will revolutionize the entertainment industry. いつの日か仮想現実が娯楽産業に革命をもたらすだろう.

vir|tual stor|age N-UNCOUNT 不可算名詞 **Virtual storage** is the same as **virtual memory**. 仮想記憶装置 [COMPUTING コンピューティング]

vir|tue /vˈɜːtʃuː/ (virtues) ■ N-UNCOUNT 不可算名詞 **Virtue** is thinking and doing what is right and avoiding what is wrong. 善行 ▫ Virtue is not confined to the Christian world. 善行はキリスト教の世界に限られたことではない. ■ N-COUNT 可算名詞 A **virtue** is a good quality or way of behaving. 美徳 ▫ His virtue is patience. 彼の美徳は辛抱強さだ. ■ N-COUNT 可算名詞 The **virtue** of something is an advantage or benefit that it has, especially in comparison with something else. 美点 ▫ There was no virtue in returning to Calvi the way I had come. 私が来たようにカルビに帰る利点はなかった. ■ PHRASE 句 You use **by virtue of** to explain why something happens or is true. 理由で [FORMAL 形式ばった] ▫ The article stuck in my mind by virtue of one detail. ある詳細が理由でその記事は私の頭に残っている.

vir|tuo|so /vˈɜːtʃuˈəʊsəʊ/ (virtuosos or virtuosi /vˈɜːtʃuˈəʊsiː/) ■ N-COUNT 可算名詞 A **virtuoso** is someone who is extremely good at something, especially at playing a musical instrument. 名人 ▫ ...one of the nation's leading violin virtuosos. わが国で第1級のヴァイオリン演奏家の1人. ■ ADJ 形容詞 A **virtuoso** performance or display shows great skill. 大家の [ADJ n] ▫ The game was a triumph; the team gave a virtuoso performance. その試合は大勝利で, チームは名人芸を見せました.

vir|tu|ous /vˈɜːtʃuəs/ ■ ADJ 形容詞 A **virtuous** person behaves in a moral and correct way. 高潔な ▫ Louis was shown as an intelligent, courageous and virtuous family man. ルイスは知的で, 勇気ある高徳のマイホーム主義者として表現されました. ■ ADJ 形容詞 If you describe someone as **virtuous**, you mean that they have done what they ought to and feel very pleased with themselves, perhaps too pleased. 自己満足している ▫ I cleaned the apartment, which left me feeling virtuous. 私はアパートの掃除をして, 鼻高々になった. ● **vir|tu|ous|ly** ADV 副詞 鼻高々に ▫ "I've already done that," said Ronnie virtuously. 「それ, 僕はもうやったよ」ロニーは鼻高々に言った.

Word Link ulent ≈ full of : fraudulent, opulent, virulent

Word Link vir ≈ poison : viral, virulent, virus

viru|lent /vˈɪrʊlənt/ ■ ADJ 形容詞 **Virulent** feelings or actions are extremely bitter and hostile. 悪意に満ちた [FORMAL 形式ばった] ▫ Now he faces virulent attacks from the Italian media. 今後はイタリアのマスコミからの悪意に満ちた攻撃に直面している. ● **viru|lent|ly** ADV 副詞 悪意に満ちて ▫ The talk was virulently hostile to the leadership. その会談は指導者に対する激しい敵意に満ちていた. ■ ADJ 形容詞 A **virulent** disease or poison is extremely powerful and dangerous. 悪性の ▫ A very virulent form of the disease appeared in Belgium. ベルギーで発生した疾病の非常に悪性の病原型.

vi|rus /vˈaɪrəs/ (viruses) ■ N-COUNT 可算名詞 A **virus** is a kind of germ that can cause disease. ウイルス ▫ There are many different strains of flu virus. インフルエンザウイルスには様々に異なる菌体がある. ■ N-COUNT 可算名詞 In computer technology, a

virus is a program that introduces itself into a system, altering or destroying the information stored in the system. ウイルス [COMPUTING コンピューティング] ▫ Hackers are said to have started a computer virus. コンピュータウイルスを発生させたのはハッカーだとされています.
→ see **illness**

visa /vˈiːzə/ (visas) N-COUNT 可算名詞 A **visa** is an official document, or a stamp put in your passport, that allows you to enter or leave a particular country. ビザ ▫ His visitor's visa expired. 彼の観光ビザは期限切れです. ▫ ...an exit visa. 出国ビザ.

vise /vˈaɪs/ (vises) N-COUNT 可算名詞 A **vise** is a tool with a pair of parts that hold an object tightly while you do work on it. 万力 [AM 米国英語]

vis|ibil|ity /vˌɪzɪbˈɪlɪti/ ■ N-UNCOUNT 不可算名詞 **Visibility** means how far or how clearly you can see in particular weather conditions. 可視性 ▫ Visibility was poor. 視界は悪かった. ■ N-UNCOUNT 不可算名詞 If you refer to the **visibility** of something such as a situation or problem, you mean how much it is seen or noticed by other people. 認知度 ▫ The plight of the Kurds gained global visibility. クルド人の窮状は世界的に認知されるようになりました.

Word Link vid, vis ≈ seeing : audiovisual, videotape, visible

vis|ible /vˈɪzɪbəl/ ■ ADJ 形容詞 If something is **visible**, it can be seen. 見える ▫ The warning lights were clearly visible. 警告灯ははっきりと見えた. ■ ADJ 形容詞 You use **visible** to describe something or someone that people notice or recognize. 認識できる ▫ The most visible sign of the intensity of the crisis is unemployment. 恐慌の激しさを最も明らかに示す兆候は失業だ. ● **vis|ibly** /vˈɪzɪbli/ ADV 副詞 明らかに ▫ The Russians were visibly wavering. ロシア人らはかなりためらっていた.
→ see **wave**

Word Partnership visible は次の語句と使われる:

N.	visible **to the naked eye** ■
ADV.	**barely** visible, **clearly** visible, **highly** visible, **less** visible, **more** visible, **still** visible, **very** visible ■ ■
V.	**become** visible ■ ■

vi|sion /vˈɪʒən/ (visions) ■ N-COUNT 可算名詞 Your **vision** of a future situation or society is what you imagine or hope it would be like, if things were very different from the way they are now. 空想 ▫ I have a vision of a society that is free of exploitation and injustice. 私は搾取や不正行為のない社会という幻想を抱いている. ▫ That's my vision of how the world could be. それが私が空想する世界の姿だ. ■ N-COUNT 可算名詞 If you have a **vision of** someone in a particular situation, you imagine them in that situation, for example because you are worried that it might happen, or hope that it will happen. 想像 ▫ He had a vision of Cheryl, slumped on a plastic chair in the waiting room. 彼はシェリルが待合室のプラスチック製いすにぐったり座っているのを想像した. ■ N-COUNT 可算名詞 A **vision** is the experience of seeing something that other people cannot see, for example in a religious experience or as a result of madness or taking drugs. 幻覚 ▫ It was on June 24, 1981 that young villagers first reported seeing the Virgin Mary in a vision. 若い村民が幻覚で聖母マリアを見たと最初に報告したのは1981年6月24日でした. ■ N-UNCOUNT 不可算名詞 Your **vision** is your ability to see clearly with your eyes. 視力 ▫ It causes blindness or serious loss of vision. それは失明または深刻な視力損失の原因となります. ■ N-UNCOUNT 不可算名詞 Your **vision** is everything that you can see from a particular place or position. 視野 ▫ Jane blocked Craig's vision and he could see nothing. ジェーンがクレイグの視界を遮ったので, 彼は何も見えなかった.

Word Partnership vision は次の語句と使われる:

V.	**share a** vision ■
	have a vision ■ – ■
	see a vision ■
N.	vision **of the future**, vision **of peace**, vision **of reality** ■
	color vision ■
	field of vision ■
ADJ.	**clear** vision ■ ■
	blurred vision ■

vi|sion|ary /vˈɪʒənɛri/ (visionaries) ■ N-COUNT 可算名詞 If you refer to someone as a **visionary**, you mean that they have strong, original ideas about how things might be different in the future, especially about how things might be improved. 洞察力のある人 ▫ An entrepreneur is more than just a risk taker. He is a visionary. 起業家は単に危険を冒す人ではなく, 先見の明のある人である. ■ ADJ 形容詞 You use **visionary** to describe the strong, original ideas of a visionary. 洞察力のある ▫ ...the visionary architecture of Etienne

Boulle. エンヌ・ブーレーの幻想的な建築

vis|it /vɪzɪt/ (**visits, visiting, visited**) ◼1 V-T/V-I 他動詞/自動詞 If you **visit** someone, you go to see them and spend time with them. 訪問する [他動詞・自動詞] ◻ *He wanted to visit his brother in Worcester.* 彼はウースターにいる兄を訪問したがっていた. ◻ *In the evenings, friends would visit.* 夕方になると友人たちが遊びにくる. ● N-COUNT 可算名詞 **Visit** is also a noun. 訪問 ◻ *Helen had recently paid him a visit.* ヘレンは最近彼を訪問した. ◼2 V-T/V-I 他動詞/自動詞 If you **visit** a place, you go there for a short time. 訪問する [他動詞・自動詞] ◻ *He'll be visiting four cities including Cagliari in Sardinia.* 彼はサルジニア島のカリアリをはじめ4都市を訪問します. ◻ *a visiting family from Texas.* テキサス州から来訪中の家族. ● N-COUNT 可算名詞 **Visit** is also a noun. 訪問 ◻ *...the pope's visit to Canada.* ローマ法王のカナダ訪問. ◼3 V-T 他動詞 If you **visit** a website, you look at it. 見る [COMPUTING コンピューティング] [他動詞] ◻ *For details visit our website at www.harpercollins.com.* 詳細は当社のウェブサイトharpercollins.comをご覧ください. ◼4 V-T 他動詞 If you **visit** a professional person such as a doctor or lawyer, you go and see them in order to get professional advice. If they **visit** you, they come to see you in order to give you professional advice. 会いに行く，往診する [他動詞] ◻ *If necessary the patient can then visit his doctor for further advice.* 必要であれば，医師に会ってさらなる忠告を受けられる. ● N-COUNT 可算名詞 **Visit** is also a noun. 往診 ◻ *You may have regular home visits from a neonatal nurse.* 新生児看護師に定期的に往診してもらうことが可能です.

▶ **visit with** PHRASAL VERB 句動詞 If you **visit with** someone, you go to see them and spend time talking with them. 話をしに立ち寄る [AM 米国英語] ◻ *I visited with him in San Francisco.* 私はサンフランシスコにいる彼に会いにいった.

Thesaurus	*visit* また次を参照:
V.	call on, go, see, stop by ◼1

Word Partnership	*visit* は次の語句と使われる:
N.	visit **family/relatives**, visit **friends**, visit **your mother** ◼1 **weekend** visit ◼1 ◼2 visit **a museum**, visit **a restaurant** ◼2 visit **a website** ◼3 visit **a doctor** ◼4
V.	**come** to visit, **go** to visit, **invite** *someone* to visit, **plan** to visit ◼1 ◼2
ADJ.	**brief** visit, **last** visit, **next** visit, **recent** visit, **short** visit, **surprise** visit ◼1 ◼2 **foreign** visit, **official** visit ◼2

visi|tor /vɪzɪtər/ (**visitors**) N-COUNT 可算名詞 A **visitor** is someone who is visiting a person or place. 訪問者 ◻ *The other day we had some visitors from Switzerland.* この間，私たちにはスイスから来客があった.

vis|ta /vɪstə/ (**vistas**) N-COUNT 可算名詞 A **vista** is a view from a particular place, especially a beautiful view from a high place. 見通しの眺め [WRITTEN 書き言葉] ◻ *From my bedroom window I looked out on a crowded vista of hills and rooftops.* 私は寝室の窓から丘と屋上の混雑した景色を眺めた.

vis|ual /vɪʒuəl/ (**visuals**) ◼1 ADJ 形容詞 **Visual** means relating to sight, or to things that you can see. 視覚の ◻ *...the graphic visual depiction of violence.* グラフィックによる視覚的な暴力描写 ● **vis|ual|ly** ADV 副詞 視覚的に ◻ *...visually handicapped boys and girls.* 目の不自由な少年少女. ◼2 N-COUNT 可算名詞 A **visual** is something such as a picture, diagram, or piece of film that is used to show or explain something. 視覚に訴える表現 ◻ *Remember you want your visuals to reinforce your message, not detract from what you are saying.* 映像はメッセージを補強するもので，言いたいことから注意をそらすものではないことを覚えておきなさい.

Word Partnership	*visual* は次の語句と使われる:
N.	visual **arts**, visual **effects**, visual **information**, visual **memory**, visual **perception** ◼1

vis|ual aid (**visual aids**) N-COUNT 可算名詞 **Visual aids** are things that you can look at, such as a film, model, map, or slides, to help you understand something or to remember information. 視覚教材

visu|al|ize /vɪʒuəlaɪz/ (**visualizes, visualizing, visualized**) V-T 他動詞 If you **visualize** something, you imagine what it is like by forming a mental picture of it. 思い浮かべる [他動詞] ◻ *Susan visualized her wedding day and saw herself walking down the aisle on her father's arm.* スーザンは婚礼の日に父の腕を取って通路を歩く自分の姿を思い浮かべた. ◻ *He could not visualize her as old.* 彼は，彼女が年老いた姿を思い浮かべることができなかった.

Word Link	*vita ≈ life : re**vita**lize, **vita**l, **vita**lity*

vi|tal /vaɪtᵊl/ ADJ 形容詞 If you say that something is **vital**, you mean that it is necessary or very important. 極めて重要な ◻ *The port is vital to supply relief to millions of drought victims.* その港は何百万人もの干ばつ被災者への供給救助手段に非常に重要です. ◻ *It is vital that parents give children clear and consistent messages about drugs.* 親が子供に対し薬物に関する明確かつ一貫した警告を与えることは極めて重要です. ● **vi|tal|ly** ADV 副詞 極めて重要で ◻ *Lesley's career in the church is vitally important to her.* 教会におけるレスリーの職業は彼女にとって極めて重要である.

Thesaurus	*vital* また次を参照:
ADJ.	crucial, essential, necessary; (*ant.*) unimportant

Word Partnership	*vital* は次の語句と使われる:
N.	vital **importance**, vital **information**, vital **interests**, vital **link**, vital **organs**, vital **part**, vital **role**

vi|tal|ity /vaɪtælɪti/ N-UNCOUNT 不可算名詞 If you say that someone or something has **vitality**, you mean that they have great energy and liveliness. 活力 ◻ *Without continued learning, graduates will lose their intellectual vitality.* 継続的に学習し続けなければ，卒業生の知的判断力は低下する.

vita|min /vaɪtəmɪn/ (**vitamins**) N-COUNT 可算名詞 **Vitamins** are substances that you need in order to remain healthy, which are found in food or can be eaten in the form of pills. ビタミン ◻ *Lack of vitamin D is another factor to consider.* ビタミンDの不足も考慮すべきもう1つの要因である.

Word Link	*viv ≈ living : re**viv**al, sur**viv**e, **viv**acious*

vi|va|cious /vɪveɪʃəs/ ADJ 形容詞 If you describe someone, usually a woman, as **vivacious**, you mean that they are lively, exciting, and attractive. 活発な [WRITTEN 書き言葉, APPROVAL 賛成] ◻ *She's beautiful, vivacious, and charming.* 彼女は美しく，活発でチャーミングだ.

viv|id /vɪvɪd/ ◼1 ADJ 形容詞 If you describe memories and descriptions as **vivid**, you mean that they are very clear and detailed. 鮮明な ◻ *People of my generation who lived through World War II have vivid memories of confusion and incompetence.* 第2次世界大戦を生き抜いた私と同世代の人々には混乱と無能の鮮明な記憶がある. ● **viv|id|ly** ADV 副詞 ありありと ◻ *I can vividly remember the feeling of panic.* 私はパニックになった感じをありありと思い出すことができる. ◼2 ADJ 形容詞 Something that is **vivid** is very bright in color. 鮮やかな ◻ *...a vivid blue sky.* 鮮やかな青い空. ● **viv|id|ly** ADV 副詞 [ADV -ed/adj] 鮮やかに ◻ *...vividly colored birds.* 鮮やかな色をした鳥たち.

vivi|sec|tion /vɪvɪsekʃᵊn/ N-UNCOUNT 不可算名詞 **Vivisection** is the practice of using live animals for scientific experiments. 生体解剖 ◻ *...a fierce opponent of vivisection.* 生体解剖に激しく反対する人.

viz. **viz.** is used in written English to introduce a list of specific items or examples. すなわち ◻ *The school offers two modules in Teaching English as a Foreign Language, viz. Principles and Methods of Language Teaching and Applied Linguistics.* その学校はTESOLで2つのモジュール，すなわち語学教育の原理・方法及び応用言語学を提供している.

Word Link	*voc ≈ speaking : ad**voc**ate, **voc**abulary, **voc**al*

vo|cabu|lary /voʊkæbyəleri/ (**vocabularies**) ◼1 N-VAR 可変性名詞 Your **vocabulary** is the total number of words you know in a particular language. 語彙 ◻ *His speech is immature, his vocabulary limited.* 彼の話し方は未熟で，語彙も限られている. ◼2 N-SING 単数名詞 The **vocabulary** of a language is all the words in it. 一言語中の語の総体 ◻ *a new word in the German vocabulary.* ドイツ語の総体における新語. ◼3 N-VAR 可変性名詞 The **vocabulary** of a subject is the group of words that are typically used when discussing it. 用語 ◻ *the vocabulary of natural science.* 自然科学の用語集. → see English

Word Partnership	*vocabulary* は次の語句と使われる:
N.	**part of** *someone's* vocabulary ◼1 ◼2 vocabulary **development** ◼1 ◼2
V.	**learn** vocabulary ◼2 ◼3
ADJ.	**specialized** vocabulary, **technical** vocabulary ◼3

vo|cal /voʊkᵊl/ ◼1 ADJ 形容詞 You say that people are **vocal** when they speak forcefully about something that they feel strongly about. ずけずけ意見を述べる ◻ *He has been very vocal in his displeasure over the results.* 結果に対する不満を彼は非常にずけずけけと言った. ◼2 ADJ 形容詞 **Vocal** means involving the use of the human voice, especially in singing. 声の [ADJ n] ◻ *...a wider range*

of vocal styles. より広い範囲の声種

vo|cal|ist /voʊkəlɪst/ (**vocalists**) N-COUNT 可算名詞 A **vocalist** is a singer who sings with a group. ヴォーカリスト □ He and Carla Torgerson take turns as the band's lead vocalist. 彼とカルラ・トガーソンは代わり交代にバンドのリードヴォーカルを務めます.

vo|cals /voʊkəlz/ N-PLURAL 複数名詞 In a pop song, the **vocals** are the singing, in contrast to the playing of instruments. ヴォーカル □ Johnson now sings backing vocals for Mica Paris. ジョンソンは今、ミーシャ・パリスのバックヴォーカルをしている.

vo|ca|tion /voʊkeɪʃⁿn/ (**vocations**) ■ N-VAR 可変性名詞 If you have a **vocation**, you have a strong feeling that you are especially suited to do a particular job or to fulfill a particular role in life, especially one that involves helping other people. 使命感 □ It could well be that he has a real vocation. 彼は本当の使命感を持っているからかもしれない. ■ N-VAR 可変性名詞 If you refer to your job or profession as your **vocation**, you feel that you are particularly suited to it. 天職 □ Her vocation is her work as an actress. 彼女の天職は女優としての仕事だ.

vo|ca|tion|al /voʊkeɪʃⁿl/ ADJ 形容詞 **Vocational** training and skills are the training and skills needed for a particular job or profession. 職業上の □ ...a course designed to provide vocational training in engineering. エンジニアリングの職業訓練を提供するようにデザインされたコース.

vo|cif|er|ous /voʊsɪfərəs/ ADJ 形容詞 If you describe someone as **vociferous**, you mean that they speak with great energy and determination, because they want their views to be heard. 大声でどなる □ He was a vociferous opponent of Conservatism. 彼は保守主義に執拗に反対していました. ● **vo|cif|er|ous|ly** ADV 副詞 やかましく □ He vociferously opposed the state of emergency imposed by the government. 彼は政府により課された非常事態にやかましく反対した.

vod|ka /vɒdkə/ (**vodkas**) N-MASS 質量名詞 **Vodka** is a strong, clear, alcoholic drink. ウォッカ

vogue /voʊg/ ■ N-SING 単数名詞 If there is a **vogue** for something, it is very popular and fashionable. 流行 □ Despite the vogue for so-called health teas, there is no evidence that they are any healthier. 健康茶と呼ばれるものが流行していたにもかかわらず、彼らが以前よりも健康だという証拠はない. ■ PHRASE 句 If something is **in vogue**, it is very popular and fashionable. If it comes **into vogue**, it becomes very popular and fashionable. 流行して □ Pale colors are much more in vogue than autumnal bronzes and coppers. 浅い色は、秋を思わせるブロンズや銅といった色よりもずっと流行している.

voice /vɔɪs/ (**voices, voicing, voiced**) ■ N-COUNT 可算名詞 When someone speaks or sings, you hear their **voice**. 声 □ Miriam's voice was strangely calm. ミリアムの声は異様に落ち着いていた. □ "The police are here," she said in a low voice. 「警察が来ているの」彼女は低い声で言った. ■ N-COUNT 可算名詞 Someone's **voice** is their opinion on a particular topic and what they say about it. 意見 □ What does one do when a government simply refuses to listen to the voice of the opposition? 政府が反対派の意見を聞くのを断固拒否したらどうすべきでしょうか. ■ V-T 他動詞 If you **voice** something such as an opinion or an emotion, you say what you think or feel. 声に出す [他動詞] □ Some scientists have voiced concern that the disease could be passed on to humans. その疾病は人間にも移るという懸念を表明する科学者もいました. ■ PHRASE 句 If you **give voice to** an opinion, a need, or a desire, you express it aloud. 口に出す □ ...a community radio run by the Catholic Church that gave voice to the protests of the slum-dwellers. 貧民街居住者の抗議に声を与える、カトリック教会の運営する地域社会ラジオ放送. ■ PHRASE 句 If someone tells you to **keep** your **voice down**, they are asking you to speak more quietly. 声を抑える □ Keep your voice down, for goodness' sake. お願いだから声を抑えてください. ■ PHRASE 句 If you **lose** your **voice**, you cannot speak for a while because of an illness. 声がつぶれる □ I had to be careful not to get a sore throat and lose my voice. 咽頭炎になって声をつぶさないように注意しなくてはならない. ■ PHRASE

句 If you **raise** your **voice**, you speak more loudly. If you **lower** your **voice**, you speak more quietly. 声を大きくする、声を小さくする □ He raised his voice for the benefit of the other two women. 彼は他の2人の女性への当てつけに声を大きくした. ■ PHRASE 句 If you say something **at the top of** your **voice**, you say it as loudly as possible. 声を限りに [EMPHASIS 強調] □ "Damn!" he yelled at the top of his voice. 「しまった」彼は声を限りに叫んだ.

voice mail N-UNCOUNT 不可算名詞 **Voice mail** is a system of sending messages over the telephone. Calls are answered by a machine that connects you to the person you want to leave a message for, and they can listen to their messages later. ボイスメール □ He was on a call, so I left a message on his voice mail. 彼は通話中だったので、私はボイスメールにメッセージを残した.

voice-over (**voice-overs**) also **voiceover** N-COUNT 可算名詞 The **voice-over** of a film, television program, or advertisement consists of words spoken by someone who is not seen. 画面に現れないナレーターの声 □ 89% of advertisements had a male voice-over. 宣伝の89%は男性のナレーターを使用している.

void /vɔɪd/ (**voids, voiding, voided**) ■ N-COUNT 可算名詞 If you describe a situation or a feeling as a **void**, you mean that it seems empty because there is nothing interesting or worthwhile about it. 空虚 □ His death has left a void in the entertainment world that can never be filled. 彼の死は埋められることのない空虚を芸能界に残した. ■ N-COUNT 可算名詞 You can describe a large or frightening space as a **void**. 空間 □ He stared into the dark void where the battle had been fought. 彼は、戦いが繰り広げられた暗黒の虚空を見つめた. ■ ADJ 形容詞 Something that is **void** or **null and void** is officially considered to have no value or authority. 無効の [v-link ADJ] □ The original elections were declared void by the former military ruler. 元々の選挙は前軍事支配者により無効と宣言された. ■ ADJ 形容詞 If you are **void of** something, you do not have any of it. 無い [FORMAL 形式ばった] [v-link ADJ 'of' n] □ He rose, his face void of emotion as he walked toward the door. 彼は立ち上がり、無表情でドアのほうに歩いた. ■ V-T 他動詞 To **void** something means to officially say that it is not valid. 無効にする [FORMAL 形式ばった] [他動詞] □ The Supreme Court threw out the confession and voided his conviction for murder. 最高裁判所は彼の自白を却下し、殺人の有罪判決を取り消しました.

vol. (**vols.**) Vol. is used as a written abbreviation for **volume** when you are referring to one or more books in a series of books. volumeの略

vola|tile /vɒlətⁿl/ ■ ADJ 形容詞 A situation that is **volatile** is likely to change suddenly and unexpectedly. 不安定な □ There have been riots before and the situation is volatile. 暴動は以前に起こっており、状況は不安定である. ■ ADJ 形容詞 If someone is **volatile**, their mood often changes quickly. 気まぐれな □ He accompanied the volatile actress to Hollywood the following year. 彼は翌年、移り気な女優に同伴してハリウッドに行った. ■ ADJ 形容詞 A **volatile** liquid or substance is one that will quickly change into a gas. 揮発性の [TECHNICAL 技術的] □ The blast occurred when volatile chemicals exploded. 揮発性の化学薬品が爆発した際、爆風が起こった.

vol|can|ic /vɒlkænɪk/ ADJ 形容詞 **Volcanic** means coming from or created by volcanoes. 火山の □ Over 200 people have been killed by volcanic eruptions. 火山の爆発で200人以上が亡くなりました.

vol|ca|no /vɒlkeɪnoʊ/ (**volcanoes**) N-COUNT 可算名詞 A **volcano** is a mountain from which hot melted rock, gas, steam, and ash from inside the earth sometimes burst. 火山 □ The volcano erupted last year killing about 600 people. その火山は昨年爆発し、約600名の死者を出しました.

→ see Word Web: volcano
→ see rock

vol|ley /vɒli/ (**volleys, volleying, volleyed**) ■ V-T/V-I 他動詞/自動詞 In sports, if someone **volleys** the ball or if they **volley**, they hit the ball before it touches the ground. ボレーをする [他動詞・自動詞] □ He volleyed the ball spectacularly into the far corner of the net. 彼

Word Web　　volcano

The most famous **volcano** in the world is Mount Vesuvius, near Naples, Italy. This mountain sits in the middle of the much older **volcanic cone** of Mount Somma. In 79 AD the sleeping volcano **erupted** and magma surged to the surface. The people of the nearby city of Pompeii were terrified. Soon huge black clouds of **ash** and pumice came rushing toward them. The clouds blocked out the sun and smothered thousands of people. Pompeii was buried under hot ash and **molten lava**. Centuries later the remains of the people and town were exposed. The discovery made this active volcano world famous.

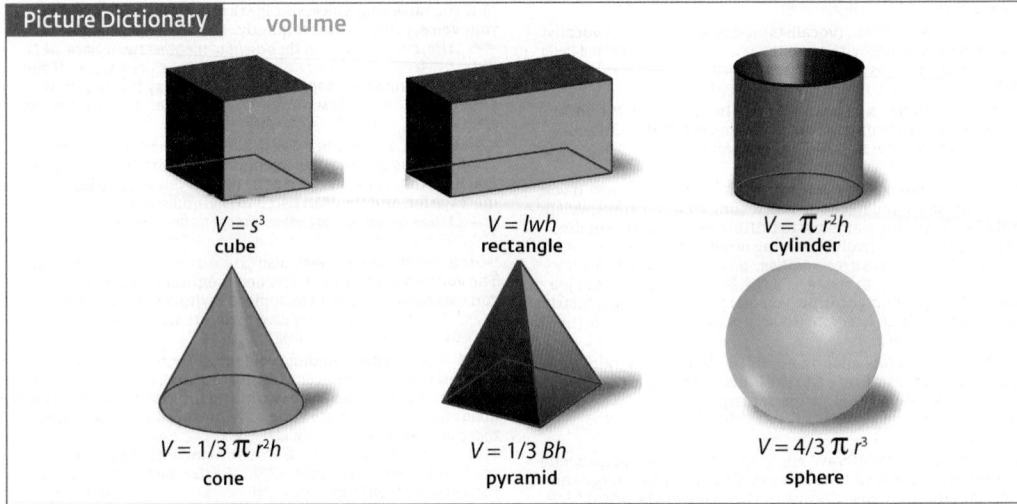

Picture Dictionary — volume

$V = s^3$
cube

$V = lwh$
rectangle

$V = \pi r^2 h$
cylinder

$V = 1/3\,\pi\, r^2 h$
cone

$V = 1/3\,Bh$
pyramid

$V = 4/3\,\pi\, r^3$
sphere

はネットの遠い角にボールをボレーで見事に打ち返した．●N-COUNT
可算名詞 **Volley** is also a noun. ボレー ❑ *She hit most of the winning volleys.* 彼女は勝利のボレーのほとんどを打ち出した． **2** N-COUNT 可算名詞 A **volley of** gunfire is a lot of bullets that travel through the air at the same time. 一斉射撃 ❑ *It's still not known how many died in the volleys of gunfire.* 砲火の一斉射撃で何名が死亡したかいまだにわかっていません．

volley|ball /vɒlibɔl/ N-UNCOUNT 不可算名詞 **Volleyball** is a game in which two teams hit a large ball with their hands back and forth over a high net. If you allow the ball to touch the ground, the other team wins a point. バレーボール

volt /voʊlt/ (**volts**) N-COUNT 可算名詞 A **volt** is a unit used to measure the force of an electric current. ボルト

volt|age /voʊltɪdʒ/ (**voltages**) N-VAR 可変性名詞 The **voltage** of an electrical current is its force measured in volts. ボルト数 ❑ *The systems are getting smaller and using lower voltages.* システムはますます小型化し，使用電圧も下がっている．

vol|ume /vɒlyum/ (**volumes**) **1** N-COUNT 可算名詞 The **volume of** something is the amount of it that there is. 量 ❑ *Senior officials will be discussing how the volume of sales might be reduced.* 上級職員は販売量の削減方法を議論することになります． **2** N-COUNT 可算名詞 The **volume** of an object is the amount of space that it contains or occupies. 体積 ❑ *When egg whites are beaten they can rise to seven or eight times their original volume.* 卵白をかき混ぜて泡立てると，体積が元の7倍から8倍に増える． **3** N-COUNT 可算名詞 A **volume** is one book in a series of books. 巻 ❑ *...the first volume of his autobiography.* 彼の自叙伝の第1巻と． **4** N-COUNT 可算名詞 A **volume** is a collection of several issues of a magazine, for example, all the issues for one year. 定期刊行物の一期分 ❑ *...bound volumes of the magazine.* 製本済み雑誌 **5** N-UNCOUNT 不可算名詞 The **volume** of a radio, television, or sound system is the loudness of the sound it produces. 音量 ❑ *He turned down the volume.* 彼は音量を絞った． **6** PHRASE 句 If something such as an action **speaks volumes about** a person or thing, it gives you a lot of information about them. 多くのことを語る ❑ *What you wear speaks volumes about you.* 君が着ているものは君について多くのことを語っている．
→ see Picture Dictionary: volume

vol|un|tary /vɒlənteri/ **1** ADJ 形容詞 **Voluntary** actions or activities are done because someone chooses to do them and not because they have been forced to do them. 自発的な ❑ *Attention is drawn to a special voluntary course in Commercial French.* ビジネスフランス語の特別自主コースが注目されている． ●**vol|un|tar|ily** /vɒləntɛərɪli/ ADV 副詞 [ADV with v] ❑ *I would never leave here voluntarily.* 私がここを自発的に去ることはない． **2** ADJ 形容詞 **Voluntary** work is done by people who are not paid for it, but who do it because they want to do it. 自由意志で（ある役を）務める ❑ *In her spare time she does voluntary work.* 彼女は余暇に奉仕活動を行っています． **3** ADJ 形容詞 A **voluntary** organization is controlled and organized by the people who have chosen to work for it, often without being paid, rather than receiving help or money from the government. 任意の [ADJ n] ❑ *Some voluntary organizations run workshops for disabled people.* 任意団体には体の不自由な人向けのワークショップを開いているものもある．
→ see **muscle**

Word Partnership *voluntary* は次の語句と使われる:

N.   voluntary **action**, voluntary **basis**, voluntary **compliance**, voluntary **contributions**, voluntary **program**, voluntary **retirement**, voluntary **test** **1** voluntary **organizations** **3**

Word Link *eer ≈ one who does* : auction*eer*, mountain*eer*, volunt*eer*

Word Link *vol ≈ will* : bene*vol*ent, in*vol*untary, *vol*unteer

vol|un|teer /vɒləntɪər/ (**volunteers, volunteering, volunteered**) **1** N-COUNT 可算名詞 A **volunteer** is someone who does work without being paid for it, because they want to do it. ボランティア ❑ *She now helps in a local school as a volunteer three days a week.* 彼女は現在週に3日ボランティアとして地元の学校の手伝いをしている． **2** N-COUNT 可算名詞 A **volunteer** is someone who offers to do a particular task or job without being forced to do it. 志願者 ❑ *Right. What I want now is two volunteers to come down to the front.* そうだ．今志願者2人に前に出てきて欲しいのだ． **3** V-I 自動詞 If you **volunteer** to do something, you offer to do it without being forced to do it. 志願する [自動詞] ❑ *Aunt Mary volunteered to clean up the kitchen.* メリーおばさんは台所を掃除すると申し出た． ❑ *He volunteered for the army in 1939.* 彼は1939年に志願兵になった． **4** V-T 他動詞 If you **volunteer** information, you tell someone something without being asked. 自発的に提供する [FORMAL 形式ばった] [他動詞] ❑ *The room was quiet; no one volunteered any further information.* その部屋は静かで，それ以上の情報を進んで提供するものはいなかった． ❑ *"They were both great supporters of Franco," Ryle volunteered.*「彼らは2人ともフランコをとてもよく助けてくれている」とライルはよろこんで言った． **5** N-COUNT 可算名詞 A **volunteer** is someone who chooses to join the armed forces, especially during a war, as opposed to someone who is forced to join by law. 志願兵 ❑ *They fought as volunteers with the Afghan guerrillas.* 彼らは志願兵としてアフガニスタンのゲリラと戦いました．

Word Partnership *volunteer* は次の語句と使われる:

N.   **community** volunteer, **Red Cross** volunteer **1** volunteer **organization**, volunteer **program**, volunteer **work** **1** **2** volunteer **for service**, volunteer **for the army** **3** volunteer **information** **4**
V.   **need a** volunteer **1** **2** **5** volunteer **to help**, volunteer **to work** **3**

vom|it /vɒmɪt/ (**vomits, vomiting, vomited**) **1** V-T/V-I 他動詞/自動詞 If you **vomit**, food and drink comes back up from your stomach and out through your mouth. 吐く [他動詞・自動詞] ❑ *Any product made from cow's milk made him vomit.* 牛乳が原料の食品を食べると彼は必ず嘔吐した． ❑ *She began to vomit blood a few days before she died.* 彼女は死の数日前から喀血し始めた． **2** N-UNCOUNT 不可算名詞 **Vomit** is partly digested food and drink that has come back up from someone's stomach and out through their mouth. 吐物 ❑ *Zimmer slipped and nearly fell on a pool of vomit.* ジマーは滑って吐物の上に倒れそうになった．

V

Word Link	vor ≈ eating : herbivorous, savory, voracious

vo|ra|cious /vəreɪʃəs/ ADJ 形容詞 If you describe a person, or their appetite for something, as **voracious**, you mean that they want a lot of something. 貪欲な [LITERARY 文語的] □ *Joseph Smith was a voracious book collector.* ジョゼフ・スミスは飽くことを知らない本の収集家だった。□ *All otters have a voracious appetite.* カワウソはすべて貪欲である。

vote /voʊt/ (votes, voting, voted) **1** N-COUNT 可算名詞 A **vote** is a choice made by a particular person or group in a meeting or an election. 投票 □ *He walked to the local polling place to cast his vote.* 彼は地元の投票所に行って一票を投じました。□ *Mr. Reynolds was re-elected by 102 votes to 60.* レイノルズ氏は102対60で再選された。**2** N-COUNT 可算名詞 A **vote** is an occasion when a group of people make a decision by each person indicating his or her choice. The choice that most people support is accepted by the group. 票決 □ *Why do you think we should have a vote on that?* それについて票決すべきだと君が考えるのはどうしてだ。**3** N-SING 単数名詞 The **vote** is the total number of votes or voters in an election, or the number of votes received or cast by a particular group. 投票総数, 得票数 □ *Opposition parties won about fifty-five percent of the vote.* 野党は投票総数の約半数を得ました。**4** N-SING 単数名詞 If you have **the vote** in an election, or have **a vote** in a meeting, you have the legal right to indicate your choice. 投票権 □ *Before that, women did not have a vote at all.* それ以前, 女性には投票権が全くなかった。**5** V-T/V-I 他動詞/自動詞 When you **vote**, you indicate your choice officially at a meeting or in an election, for example, by raising your hand or writing on a piece of paper. 投票する [他動詞・自動詞] □ *Two-thirds of the national electorate had the chance to vote in these elections.* その国の有権者の3分の2がこれらの選挙で投票する機会を得ました。□ *Nearly two-thirds of this group voted for Buchanan.* このグループの3分の2近くがブキャナンに投票した。□ *The residents of Leningrad voted to restore the city's original name of St. Petersburg.* レニングラードの住民は都市の元の名前であるセントピーターズバーグの復活に賛成投票しました。● **vot|ing** N-UNCOUNT 不可算名詞 投票 □ *Voting began about two hours ago.* 投票は約2時間前に始めました。**6** V-T 他動詞 If you **vote** a particular political party or leader, or **vote yes** or **no**, you make that choice with the vote that you have. 投票して選ぶ [他動詞] □ *52.5% of those questioned said they'd vote Republican.* 質問された人々の52.5%が共和党に投票すると言いました。**7** V-T 他動詞 If people **vote** someone a particular title, they choose that person to have that title. 選出する [他動詞] □ *His class voted him the man "who had done the most for Yale."* そのクラスは彼を「エールに最も貢献した」男に選んだ。**8** PHRASE 句 If you **vote with** your **feet**, you show that you do not support something by leaving the place where it is happening or leaving the organization that is supporting it. 逃亡することによって異議申し立ての意思表示をする □ *Thousands of citizens are already voting with their feet, and leaving the country.* 何千もの市民がすでに国を退去して反対の意思表示をしました。**9** PHRASE 句 If you say, for example, "**I vote that** we go" or "**I vote** we stay," you are suggesting that you should go or stay. 提案する [INFORMAL くだけた] □ *I vote that we all go to Houston immediately.* 私は全員がヒューストンに今すぐ行くことを提案する。**10** PHRASE 句 **One man one vote** or **one person one vote** is a system of voting in which every person in a group or country has the right to cast their vote, and in which each individual's vote is counted and has equal value. 一人一票原則 □ *Mr. Gould called for a move toward "one man one vote."* グールド氏は「一人一票原則」への移行を要求した。
→ see Word Web: **vote**
→ see **election**

vote of thanks (votes of thanks) N-COUNT 可算名詞 A **vote of thanks** is an official speech in which the speaker formally thanks a person for doing something. 感謝の決議 □ *I would like to propose a vote of thanks to our host.* 主催者に対する感謝を込めて乾杯の音頭を取らせていただきます。

vot|er /voʊtər/ (voters) N-COUNT 可算名詞 **Voters** are people who have the legal right to vote in elections, or people who are voting in a particular election. 有権者 □ *The turnout was at least* 62 percent of registered voters. 投票率は少なくとも登録有権者の62%でした。
→ see **election**

vouch /vaʊtʃ/ (vouches, vouching, vouched)
▶ **vouch for** **1** PHRASAL VERB 句動詞 If you say that you can or will **vouch for** someone, you mean that you can guarantee their good behavior. 保証する □ *Kim's mother agreed to vouch for Maria and get her a job.* キムの母親はマリアが仕事を得る際の保証人となることに同意した。**2** PHRASAL VERB 句動詞 If you say that you can **vouch for** something, you mean that you have evidence from your own personal experience that it is true or correct. 断言する □ *He cannot vouch for the accuracy of the story.* 彼はその話がどの位正確かについて請け合うことはできない。

vouch|er /vaʊtʃər/ (vouchers) N-COUNT 可算名詞 A **voucher** is a ticket or piece of paper that can be used instead of money to pay for something. 引換券 □ *The winners will each receive a voucher for a pair of movie tickets.* 勝者それぞれは映画招待券2枚の引換券を受け取る。

vow /vaʊ/ (vows, vowing, vowed) **1** V-T 他動詞 If you **vow** to do something, you make a serious promise or decision that you will do it. 誓う [他動詞] □ *While many models vow to go back to college, few do.* 多くのモデルが大学に戻ると断言するが, 戻るのは少数である。□ *I solemnly vowed that someday I would return to live in Europe.* 私はいつかヨーロッパに戻って住むことを厳粛に誓約する。**2** N-COUNT 可算名詞 A **vow** is a serious promise or decision to do a particular thing. 誓い □ *I made a silent vow to be more careful in the future.* 私は今後はもっと気をつけようとひそかに誓った。**3** N-COUNT 可算名詞 **Vows** are a particular set of serious promises, such as the promises two people make when they are getting married. 誓約 □ *I took my marriage vows and kept them.* 私は結婚時の貞節の誓いを守った。

vow|el /vaʊəl/ (vowels) N-COUNT 可算名詞 A **vowel** is a sound such as the ones represented in writing by the letters **a**, **e**, **i**, **o** and **u**, that you pronounce with your mouth open, allowing the air to flow through it. Compare **consonant**. 母音 □ *The vowel in words like "my" and "thigh" is not very difficult.* 「my」や「thigh」といった単語の母音はあまり難しくない。

voy|age /vɔɪdʒ/ (voyages) N-COUNT 可算名詞 A **voyage** is a long journey on a ship or in a spacecraft. 旅 □ *We were to follow Columbus's voyage to the West Indies.* 彼の目的はコロンブスの西インド諸島への旅を追跡することである。

vs. **vs.** is a written abbreviation for **versus**. versusの略 □ *We were watching the Yankees vs. the Red Sox.* 私たちはヤンキー対レッドソックスの試合を見ていた。

vul|gar /vʌlɡər/ **1** ADJ 形容詞 If you describe something as **vulgar**, you think it is in bad taste or of poor artistic quality. 低俗な [DISAPPROVAL 不賛成] □ *I think it's a very vulgar house.* それは非常に悪趣味な家だと思う。● **vul|gar|ity** /vʌlɡærɪti/ N-UNCOUNT 不可算名詞 野卑なこと □ *I hate the vulgarity of the bright colors in this room.* 私はこの部屋の鮮やかな色の下品さが嫌いだ。**2** ADJ 形容詞 If you describe pictures, gestures, or remarks as **vulgar**, you dislike them because they refer to sex or parts of the body in an offensive way that you find unpleasant. ひわいな [DISAPPROVAL 不賛成] □ *The women laughed coarsely at the comedian's vulgar jokes.* コメディアンのひわいなジョークに女たちは下品な声を立てて笑った。● **vul|gar|ity** N-UNCOUNT 不可算名詞 下品なこと □ *Charles was a complete gentleman, incapable of rudeness or vulgarity.* チャールズは正真正銘の紳士で, 無礼や俗悪さのかけらは1つもなかった。**3** ADJ 形容詞 If you describe a person or their behavior as **vulgar**, you mean that they lack taste or behave offensively. 下品な [DISAPPROVAL 不賛成] □ *He was a vulgar old man, but he never swore in front of a woman.* 彼は鼻持ちならない老人だが, 女性の前で悪態をついたことはない。● **vul|gar|ity** N-UNCOUNT 不可算名詞 野卑なこと □ *It's his vulgarity that I can't take.* 私が我慢ならないのは彼の無作法な態度だ。

vul|ner|able /vʌlnərəbəl/ **1** ADJ 形容詞 Someone who is **vulnerable** is weak and without protection, with the result that they are easily hurt physically or emotionally. 脆弱な □ *Old*

Word Web	vote

Today in almost all **democracies** any adult can **vote** for the **candidate** of his or her choice. However, this hasn't always been true. Until the suffrage movement revolutionized voting rights, women had been **disenfranchised**. In 1893, New Zealand became the first country to give women full voting rights. Women could finally enter a **polling place** and **cast** a **ballot**. Countries such as Canada, Finland, Germany, Sweden, and the U.S. soon followed. However, China, France, India, Italy, and Japan didn't grant suffrage until the mid-1900s.

people are particularly vulnerable members of our society. 老人は特に脆弱な社会の構成員である. ● **vul|ner|abil|ity** /vʌlnərəbɪlɪti/ (**vulnerabilities**) N-VAR 可変性名詞 脆弱さ ❏ David accepts his own vulnerability. デイビッドは自分自身の脆弱さを受け入れている. **2** ADJ 形容詞 If a person, animal, or plant is **vulnerable to** a disease, they are more likely to get it than other people, animals, or plants. (病気に) かかりやすい ❏ People with high blood pressure are especially vulnerable to diabetes. 高血圧症の人は特に糖尿病になりやすい. ● **vul|ner|abil|ity** N-UNCOUNT 不可算名詞 弱さ ❏ Taking long-term courses of certain medicines may increase vulnerability to infection. 特定の薬剤を長期間服用し続けると, 感染にかかりやすくなる. **3** ADJ 形容詞 Something that is **vulnerable** can be easily harmed or affected by something bad. 傷つきやすい ❏ Their tanks would be vulnerable to attack from the air. 彼らのタンク車は空から攻撃されやすいだろう. ● **vul|ner|abil|ity** N-UNCOUNT 不可算名詞 傷つきやすいこと ❏ ...anxieties about the country's vulnerability to invasion. 国が侵略されやすいことに関する懸念.

Word Partnership	vulnerable は次の語句と使われる:
N.	vulnerable **children/people/women** **1** **2** vulnerable **to attack** **3**
ADV.	**especially** vulnerable, **extremely** vulnerable, **highly** vulnerable, **particularly** vulnerable, **so** vulnerable, **too** vulnerable, **very** vulnerable **1** – **3**
V.	**become** vulnerable, **remain** vulnerable **1** – **3** **feel** vulnerable **1** **3**

vul|ture /vʌltʃər/ (**vultures**) **1** N-COUNT 可算名詞 A **vulture** is a large bird that eats the flesh of dead animals. ハゲタカ, ハゲワシ **2** N-COUNT 可算名詞 If you describe a person as a **vulture**, you disapprove of them because you think they are trying to gain from another person's troubles. 弱者を食い物にする人 [JOURNALISM ジャーナリズム, DISAPPROVAL 不賛成] ❏ With no buyer in sight for the company as a whole, the vultures started to circle. そのまま会社には買い手がつかなさそうなのを見て, 弱者を食い物にするハゲタカたちが上空を旋回し始めた.

vy|ing /vaɪɪŋ/ **Vying** is the present participle of **vie**. vie の現在分詞

V

Ww

W also **w** /dʌbəlyu/ (**W's, w's**) N-VAR 可変性名詞 **W** is the twenty-third letter of the English alphabet. 英語アルファベットの第23字

wacky /wǽki/ (**wackier, wackiest**) also **whacky** ADJ 形容詞 If you describe something or someone as **wacky**, you mean that they are eccentric, unusual, and often funny. 風変わりな [INFORMAL くだけた] □ ...a wacky new television comedy series. テレビの一風変わった新しいコメディ番組

wad /wɒd/ (**wads**) N-COUNT 可算名詞 A **wad of** something such as paper or cloth is a tight bundle or ball of it. 束 □ ...a wad of banknotes. 札束

wade /weɪd/ (**wades, wading, waded**) **1** V-I 自動詞 If you **wade** through something that makes it difficult to walk, usually water or mud, you walk through it. 骨折って通る □ Her mother came to find them, wading across a river to reach them. 彼女の母親は川を歩いて渡り、彼らを見つけに来た. **2** V-I 自動詞 To **wade through** a lot of documents or pieces of information means to spend a lot of time and effort reading them or dealing with them. 苦労して進む □ It has taken a long time to wade through the "incredible volume" of evidence. 「信じられない量の証拠」をやっと読み終えるまで長いことかかった.
▶ **wade in** or **wade into** PHRASAL VERB 句動詞 If someone **wades in** or **wades into** something, they get involved in a very determined and forceful way, often without thinking enough about the consequences of their actions. 議論に加わる □ They don't just listen sympathetically, they wade in with remarks like, "If I were you…" 彼らは同情して聞くだけでなく、「もし私があなただったら」などの意見を述べて議論に加わる.

wafer /weɪfər/ (**wafers**) N-COUNT 可算名詞 A **wafer** is a thin crisp cookie that is usually eaten with ice cream. ウエハース

waffle /wɒfəl/ (**waffles, waffling, waffled**) V-I 自動詞 If someone **waffles** on an issue or question, they cannot decide what to do or what their opinion is about it. 言葉を濁す [AM 米国英語] □ He has waffled on abortion and gay rights. 彼は妊娠中絶と同性愛者の権利について煮え切らない態度を取ってきた.

waft /wɒft, wæft/ (**wafts, wafting, wafted**) V-T/V-I 他動詞/自動詞 If sounds or smells **waft** through the air, or if something such as a light wind **wafts** them, they move gently through the air. 漂わせる, 漂う □ The scent of climbing roses wafts through the window. 窓越しにツルバラのにおいがする.

wag /wæg/ (**wags, wagging, wagged**) **1** V-T 他動詞 When a dog **wags** its tail, it repeatedly waves its tail from side to side. 振る □ The dog was biting, growling and wagging its tail. その犬はかみ, うなり, しっぽを振っていた. **2** V-T 他動詞 If you **wag** your finger, you shake it repeatedly and quickly from side to side, usually because you are annoyed with someone. 振る □ He wagged a disapproving finger. 彼は指を振って非難した.

wage /weɪdʒ/ (**wages, waging, waged**) **1** N-COUNT 可算名詞 Someone's **wages** are the amount of money that is regularly paid to them for the work that they do. 賃金 □ His wages have gone up. 彼の給料は上がった. **2** V-T 他動詞 If a person, group, or country **wages** a campaign or a war, they start it and continue it over a period of time. 行なう □ The government, along with the three factions that had been waging a civil war, signed a peace agreement. 政府は市民戦争を行なってきた3派閥と共に和平協定に署名した.
→ see **factory, union**

When used as a noun, **pay** is a general word which you can use to refer to the money you get from your employer for doing your job. Manual workers are paid **wages**, or a **wage**. The plural is more common than the singular, especially when you are talking about the actual cash that someone receives. □ Every week he handed all his wages in cash to his wife. Wages are usually paid, and quoted, as a weekly sum. □ ...a starting wage of five dollars an hour. Professional people and office workers receive a **salary**, which is paid monthly. However, when talking about someone's salary, you usually give the annual figure. □ I'm paid a salary of $29,000 a year. Your **income** consists of all the money you receive from all sources, including your pay.

Thesaurus
wage また次を参照:

N.　earnings, pay, salary **1**

Word Partnership
wage は次の語句と使われる:

ADJ.	**average** wage, **high/higher** wage, **hourly** wage, **low/lower** wage **1**
V.	**offer** a wage, **pay** a wage, **raise** a wage **1**
N.	wage **cuts**, wage **earners**, wage **increases**, wage **rates** **1** wage a **campaign**, wage **war** **2**

wage pack|et (**wage packets**) N-COUNT 可算名詞 People's wages can be referred to as their **wage packet**. 給料袋 [mainly BRIT 主に英国英語; AM usually **paycheck** 米国英語では通常 **paycheck**]

wa|ger /weɪdʒər/ (**wagers, wagering, wagered**) V-T/V-I 他動詞/自動詞 If you **wager on** the result of a horse race, baseball game, or other event, you give someone a sum of money which they give you back with extra money if the result is what you predicted, or which they keep if it is not. 賭(か)ける [JOURNALISM ジャーナリズム] □ Just because people wagered on the Yankees did not mean that they liked them. ヤンキースに賭けたからと言って人々は彼らが好きだとは限らなかった. □ They wagered a lot of money on the race. 彼らはそのレースに大金を賭けた. ● N-COUNT 可算名詞 **Wager** is also a noun. 賭け □ There have been various wagers on certain candidates since the senator announced his retirement. 議員が引退を発表してから特定の候補者が様々な賭けの対象となってきた.

wag|on /wǽgən/ (**wagons**) **1** N-COUNT 可算名詞 A **wagon** is a strong vehicle with four wheels, usually pulled by horses or oxen and used for carrying heavy loads. 四輪車 **2** N-COUNT 可算名詞 A **wagon** is a large container on wheels which is pulled by a train. 貨車 [BRIT 英国英語; AM **freight car** 米国英語 **freight car**]
→ see **train**

wail /weɪl/ (**wails, wailing, wailed**) **1** V-I 自動詞 If someone **wails**, they make long, loud, high-pitched cries which express sorrow or pain. 長く悲しげに叫ぶ □ The women began to wail in mourning. 女達は死者を悼み, 悲しげに泣き始めた. ● N-COUNT 可算名詞 **Wail** is also a noun. 泣き叫ぶこと □ Wails of grief were heard as visitors filed past the site of the disaster. 訪問者が大惨事の現場を列を作って通り過ぎた時に悲しげな叫び声が聞こえた. **2** V-T 他動詞 If you **wail** something, you say it in a loud, high-pitched voice that shows that you are unhappy or in pain. 泣き叫ぶ □ "Now look what you've done!" Shirley wailed. 「まあなんてことしてくれたの」とシャーリーは泣き叫んだ. **3** V-I 自動詞 If something such as a siren or an alarm **wails**, it makes a long, loud, high-pitched sound. 高い音を上げる □ Police cars, their sirens wailing, accompanied the trucks. 警察の車はサイレンの音をあげながらトラックに同行した. ● N-UNCOUNT 不可算名詞 **Wail** is also a noun. 高い音 □ The wail of the bagpipe could be heard in the distance. バグパイプの高い音は遠くまで聞こえた.

waist /weɪst/ (**waists**) **1** N-COUNT 可算名詞 Your **waist** is the middle part of your body where it narrows slightly above your hips. 腰 □ Ricky kept his arm around her waist. リッキーは腕を彼女の腰の回りに置いたままだった. **2** N-COUNT 可算名詞 The **waist** of a garment such as a dress, coat, or pair of pants is the part of it which covers the middle part of your body. ウエスト □ She tucked her thumbs into the waist of her trousers. 彼女はズボンのウエストに親指を押し込んだ.
→ see **body**

waist|coat /weɪstkoʊt, wɛskət/ (**waistcoats**) N-COUNT 可算名詞 A **waistcoat** is a sleeveless piece of clothing with buttons that people usually wear over a shirt. ベスト [BRIT 英国英語; AM **vest** 米国英語 **vest**]

wait /weɪt/ (**waits, waiting, waited**) **1** V-T/V-I 他動詞/自動詞 When you **wait** for something or someone, you spend some time doing very little, because you cannot act until that thing happens or that person arrives. 待つ [no passive] □ I walk to a street corner and wait for the school bus. 私は通りの角まで歩いてスクールバスを待つ. □ I waited to see how she responded. 私は彼女の対応を待った. □ We had to wait a week before we got the results. 私達は結果が出るまで1週間待たねばならなかった. ● **wait|ing** N-UNCOUNT 不可算名詞 待つこと □ The waiting became almost unbearable. 待つことはほとんど耐えられなくなった. **2** N-COUNT 可算名詞 A **wait** is a period of time in which you do very little, before something happens

or before you can do something. 待ち時間 ❑ ...*the four-hour wait for the organizers to declare the result.* 主催者が結果を発表するまで4時間の待ち時間 ❑ V-T/V-I 他動詞/自動詞 If something is **waiting for** you, it is ready for you to use, have, or do. 用意されている ❑ *There'll be a car waiting for you.* あなたのために車が待機しているでしょう。❑ *When we came home we had a meal waiting for us.* 私達が帰宅した時、食事の支度ができていた。❹ V-I 自動詞 If you say that something can **wait**, you mean that it is not important or urgent and so you will deal with it or do it later. 急を要しない [no cont] ❑ *I want to talk to you, but it can wait.* あなたと話がしたいが、後でよい。❺ V-I 自動詞 You can use **wait** when you are trying to make someone feel excited, or to encourage or threaten them. 待つ [only imper] ❑ *If you think this all sounds very exciting, just wait until you read the book.* このすべてがとてもわくわくすると思うのならちょっとその本を読んでみなさい。❻ V-T 他動詞 **Wait** is used in expressions such as **wait a minute, wait a second,** and **wait a moment** to interrupt someone when they are speaking, for example, because you object to what they are saying or because you want them to repeat something. 待つ [SPOKEN 口語] [only imper] ❑ *"Wait a minute!" he broke in. "This is not giving her a fair hearing!"* 「ちょっと待って」と彼が突然口を差し挟んだ。「これは彼女に公正に発言の機会を与えていない」❼ V-I 自動詞 If an employee **waits on** you, for example, in a restaurant or hotel, they take orders from you and bring you what you want. 仕える ❑ *There were plenty of servants to wait on her.* 彼女に仕える使用人はたくさんいた。❽ PHRASE 句 If you say that you **can't wait** to do something or **can hardly wait** to do it, you are emphasizing that you are very excited about it and eager to do it. 待ち遠しくてたまらない [SPOKEN 口語, EMPHASIS 強調] ❑ *We can't wait to get started.* 私たちは始めるのが待ち遠しくてたまらない。❾ PHRASE 句 If you tell someone to **wait and see**, you tell them that they must be patient or that they must not worry about what is going to happen in the future because they have no control over it. 成り行きを見守る ❑ *We'll have to wait and see what happens.* 我々は何が起こるか静観しなければならないだろう。

Do not confuse **wait for, expect,** and **look forward to.** When you **wait for** someone or something, you stay in the same place until the person arrives or the thing happens. ❑ *Soft drinks were served while we waited for him...We got off the plane and waited for our luggage.* When you are **expecting** someone or something, you think that the person or thing is going to arrive or that the thing is going to happen. ❑ *I sent a postcard, so they were expecting me...We are expecting rain.* When you **look forward to** something that is going to happen, you feel happy because you think you will enjoy it. ❑ *I'll bet you're looking forward to your holidays... I always looked forward to seeing her.*

▶ **wait around** PHRASE VERB 句動詞 If you **wait around**, you stay in the same place, usually doing very little, because you cannot act before something happens or before someone arrives. ぶらぶらして待つ ❑ *The attacker may have been waiting around for an opportunity to strike.* 攻撃者はぶらぶらしながら襲う機会を待っていた可能性がある。❑ *I waited around to speak to the doctor.* 私は医者と話すためぶらぶら待っていた。

▶ **wait up** PHRASE VERB 句動詞 If you **wait up**, you deliberately do not go to bed, especially because you are expecting someone to return home late at night. 寝ずに待つ ❑ *I hope he doesn't expect you to wait up for him.* 彼はあなたが寝ずに待っていることを期待しないといいのだが。

Thesaurus   *wait* また次を参照：

V.	anticipate, expect, hold on, stand by; (*ant.*) carry out, go ahead ❶
N.	delay, halt, hold-up, pause ❷

Word Partnership   *wait* は次の語句と使われる：

V.	(can't) afford to wait ❶ can/can't/couldn't wait, have to wait, will/won't/wouldn't wait ❶ ❹ wait to hear, wait to say ❶ ❹ ❽ can't wait, can hardly wait ❽ wait and see ❾
N.	wait for an answer, wait days/hours, wait a long time, wait your turn ❶ wait a minute, wait until tomorrow ❶ ❹ ❻
ADV.	wait forever, wait here, wait outside, wait patiently ❶ just wait ❶ ❺
ADJ.	worth the wait ❷

wait|er /weɪtər/ (**waiters**) N-COUNT 可算名詞 A **waiter** is a man who works in a restaurant, serving people food and drink. ウエーター
→ see **restaurant**

Waiter and **waitress** are used less often in the U.S. these days, although they are still the usual terms in the U.K.. Restaurant staff, especially in the U.S., can be called **servers** or **waitpersons,** and these terms are used to refer to both men and women.

wait|ing list (**waiting lists**) N-COUNT 可算名詞 A **waiting list** is a list of people who have asked for something that cannot be given to them immediately, such as medical treatment, housing, or training, and who must therefore wait until it is available. ウエーティングリスト ❑ *There were 20,000 people on the waiting list for a home.* 2万人の人々が住宅の順番を待っていた。

wait|ress /weɪtrɪs/ (**waitresses**) N-COUNT 可算名詞 A **waitress** is a woman who works in a restaurant, serving people food and drink. ウエートレス
→ see **restaurant**

waive /weɪv/ (**waives, waiving, waived**) ❶ V-T 他動詞 If you **waive** your right to something, such as legal representation, you choose not to have it or do it. 放棄する ❑ *He pleaded guilty to the murders of three boys and waived his right to appeal.* 彼は3人の少年の殺人罪を認め、上訴の権利を放棄した。❷ V-T 他動詞 If someone **waives** a rule, they say that people do not have to obey it in a particular situation. 要求をやめる ❑ *The art gallery waives admission charges on Sundays.* アートギャラリーは日曜日は入場料を取らない。

waiv|er /weɪvər/ (**waivers**) N-COUNT 可算名詞 A **waiver** is when a person, government, or organization agrees to give up a right or says that people do not have to obey a particular rule or law. 権利放棄 ❑ ...*a waiver of constitutional rights.* 憲法上の権利の放棄

Word Link   *wak* ≈ *being awake : a*wake*, a*wak*ening, *wake

wake /weɪk/ (**wakes, waking, woke, woken** or **waked**) ❶ V-T/V-I 他動詞/自動詞 When you **wake** or when someone or something **wakes** you, you become conscious again after being asleep. 起きる、起こす ❑ *It was cold and dark when I woke at 6:30.* 私が6時半に起きた時は寒くて暗かった。❑ *She went upstairs to wake Milton.* 彼女はミルトンを起こすために2階に上がった。● PHRASAL VERB 句動詞 **Wake up** means the same as **wake.** 起きる ❑ *One morning I woke up and felt something was wrong.* ある朝私は目が覚めて何かがおかしいと感じた。❷ N-COUNT 可算名詞 The **wake** of a boat or other object moving in the water is the track of waves it makes behind it as it moves through the water. 波の跡 [usu sing, with poss] ❑ *Dolphins sometimes play in the wake of the boats.* イルカは時々船の航跡で遊ぶ。❸ N-COUNT 可算名詞 A **wake** is a gathering or social event that is held before or after someone's funeral. 通夜 ❑ *A funeral wake was in progress.* 通夜が行なわれている最中だった。❹ PHRASE 句 If one thing follows **in the wake of** another, it happens after the other thing is over, often as a result of it. 〜の決果 ❑ *The governor has enjoyed a huge surge in the polls in the wake of last week's convention.* 州知事は先週の集会の決果、世論調査で人気が急に高まった。
→ see **funeral**

▶ **wake up** PHRASAL VERB 句動詞 If something such as an activity **wakes** you **up,** it makes you more alert and ready to do things after you have been lazy or inactive. 目覚める ❑ *A cool shower wakes up the body and boosts circulation.* 冷たいシャワーは体を活気づけ、血液の循環をよくする。→ see also **wake 1**

Word Partnership   *wake* は次の語句と使われる：

ADV.	wake (*someone*) up ❶
PREP-P.	wake up during the night, wake up in the middle of the night, wake up in the morning ❶

wake-up call (**wake-up calls**) ❶ N-COUNT 可算名詞 A **wake-up call** is a telephone call that you can arrange through an operator or at a hotel to make sure that you wake up at a particular time. モーニングコール ❑ *I book a wake-up call for 4:45 a.m.* 私は午前4時45分のモーニングコールを予約する。❷ N-COUNT 可算名詞 If you describe something bad that happens as a **wake-up call,** you mean that it acts as a warning that action needs to be taken to prevent something even worse from happening. ❑ *He urged her to treat the arrest as a wake-up call.* 彼は彼女に逮捕を警告として扱うよう説得した。

walk /wɔk/ (**walks, walking, walked**) ❶ V-T/V-I 他動詞/自動詞 When you **walk**, you move forward by putting one foot in front of the other in a regular way. 歩く ❑ *Rosanna and Forbes walked in silence.* ロザンナとフォーブスは無言で歩いた。❑ *We walked into the foyer.* 我々はロビーに入った。❑ *I walked a few steps toward the fence.* 私は柵の方向に数歩歩いた。❷ N-COUNT 可算名詞 A **walk** is a trip that you make by walking, usually for pleasure. 散歩 ❑ *I went for a walk.* 私は散歩に行った。❸ N-SING 単数名詞 A **walk** of a particular distance is the distance that a person has to walk to get somewhere. 歩行距離 ❑ *It was only a three-mile walk to Kabul*

from there. そこからカブールまでは歩いてたったの3マイルだった. **4** N-COUNT 可算名詞 A **walk** is a route suitable for walking along for pleasure. 散歩道 □ *...a 2-mile coastal walk.* 2マイルの海岸沿いの遊歩道 **5** N-SING 単数名詞 A **walk** is a paved pathway. 歩道 □ *She started up the walk toward the front door.* 彼女は歩道を玄関の方向に歩き出した. **6** N-SING 単数名詞 A **walk** is the action of walking rather than running. 並足 □ *She slowed to a steady walk.* 彼女は速度を規則的な並足まで落とした. **7** N-SING 単数名詞 Someone's **walk** is the way that they walk. 歩き方 □ *George, despite his great height and gangling walk, was a great dancer.* ジョージは背が高くひょろひょろした歩き方をするが, 踊りが大変上手だった. **8** V-T 他動詞 If you **walk** someone somewhere, you walk there with them in order to show politeness or to make sure that they get there safely. 歩いて案内する □ *She walked me to my car.* 彼女は私の車まで私と一緒に歩いた. **9** to **walk tall** → see **tall**

▶ **walk away** PHRASAL VERB 句動詞 If you **walk away** from a problem or a difficult situation, you do nothing about it or do not face any bad consequences from it. 顔をそむける □ *The most appropriate strategy may simply be to walk away from the problem.* 最も適切な戦略は問題に巻き込まれないようにすることかもしれない.

▶ **walk away with** PHRASAL VERB 句動詞 If you **walk away with** something such as a prize, you win it or get it very easily. 楽々と取る [JOURNALISM ジャーナリズム] □ *Enter our competition and you could walk away with $10,000.* 競争に参加すれば1万ドルを獲得することができます.

▶ **walk into** PHRASAL VERB 句動詞 If you **walk into** an unpleasant situation, you become involved in it without expecting to, especially because you have been careless. ぶつかる □ *He's walking into a situation that he absolutely can't control.* 彼は彼が絶対に制御できない状況にぶつかっている.

▶ **walk off with** PHRASAL VERB 句動詞 If you **walk off with** something such as a prize, you win it or get it very easily. 楽勝する [JOURNALISM ジャーナリズム] □ *We'd like nothing better than to see him walk off with the big prize.* 彼に大きな賞金をさらってもらうことほど望ましいことはない.

▶ **walk out** **1** PHRASAL VERB 句動詞 If you **walk out of** a meeting, a performance, or an unpleasant situation, you leave it suddenly, usually in order to show that you are angry or bored. 突然退場する □ *Several dozen councillors walked out of the meeting in protest.* 数十名の評議員が抗議して会合を退席した. **2** PHRASAL VERB 句動詞 If someone **walks out on** their family or their partner, they leave them suddenly and go to live somewhere else. 捨てる □ *Her husband walked out on her.* 彼女の夫は彼女を捨てた. **3** PHRASAL VERB 句動詞 If workers **walk out**, they stop doing their work for a period of time, usually in order to try to get better pay or conditions for themselves. ストライキをする □ *The miners were furious and threatened to walk out.* 炭鉱労働者は立腹しストライキをすると脅した.

Thesaurus *walk* また次を参照:

V.	amble, hike, stroll **1**
N.	hike, jaunt, march, parade, stroll **1** **2**

Word Partnership *walk* は次の語句と使われる:

ADV.	walk **alone**, walk **away**, walk **back**, walk **home**, walk **slowly** **1**
V.	**begin to** walk, **start to** walk **1**
	go for a walk, **take a** walk **2** **3**
ADJ.	**(un)able to** walk **1**
	brisk walk, **long** walk, **short** walk **2** – **4**

walk|ing /wɔkɪŋ/ N-UNCOUNT 不可算名詞 **Walking** is the activity of taking walks for exercise or pleasure, especially in the country. 散歩 □ *Recently I've started to do a lot of walking and cycling.* 最近私は散歩とサイクリングし始めた.

Walk|man /wɔkmən/ (**Walkmans**) N-COUNT 可算名詞 商標 A **Walkman** is a small cassette player with headphones which people carry around so that they can listen to music, for example, while they are traveling. ウォークマン [TRADEMARK]

walk of life (**walks of life**) N-COUNT 可算名詞 The **walk of life** that you come from is the type of situation you have in society and the kind of job you have. 社会的地位 □ *One of the greatest pleasures of this job is meeting people from all walks of life.* この仕事の最大の楽しみの1つはあらゆる階層の人々と会うことだ.

walk|out /wɔkaʊt/ (**walkouts**) **1** N-COUNT 可算名詞 A **walkout** is a strike. ストライキ □ *But union leaders are holding off on calling the walkout while talks are showing progress.* しかし組合の指導者は話合いが進展している間, ストライキを呼びかけることをためらっている. **2** N-COUNT 可算名詞 If there is a **walkout** during a meeting, some or all of the people attending it leave in order to show their disapproval of something that has happened at the meeting. 退場 □ *The commission's proceedings have been wrecked by tantrums and*

walkouts. 委員会の進行は立腹し退場する人物がいたため台無しになった.

walk|way /wɔkweɪ/ (**walkways**) N-COUNT 可算名詞 A **walkway** is a passage or path for people to walk along. Walkways are often raised above the ground. 歩行路 □ *...a new concrete walkway between two rows of apartment blocks.* 2棟のアパート間の新しいコンクリートの歩行路

wall /wɔl/ (**walls**) **1** N-COUNT 可算名詞 A **wall** is one of the vertical sides of a building or room. 壁 □ *Kathryn leaned against the wall of the church.* キャサリンは教会の壁に寄りかかった. □ *The bedroom walls would be papered with chintz.* 寝室の壁はチンツの壁紙を張る予定だ. **2** N-COUNT 可算名詞 A **wall** is a long narrow vertical structure made of stone or brick that surrounds or divides an area of land. 塀 □ *He sat on the wall in the sun.* 彼は日の当たる塀に腰を下ろした. **3** N-COUNT 可算名詞 The **wall** of something that is hollow is its side. 側面 □ *He ran his fingers along the inside walls of the box.* 彼は箱の内側に指を走らせた. **4** → see also **off-the-wall** **5** PHRASE 句 If you say that something or someone **is driving** you **up the wall**, you are emphasizing that they annoy and irritate you. 悩ます [INFORMAL くだけた, EMPHASIS 強調] □ *The heat is driving me up the wall.* 暑さで私はすっかりまいっている.

Word Partnership *wall* は次の語句と使われる:

PREP.	**against a** wall, **along a** wall, **behind a** wall, **near a** wall, **on a** wall **1** **2**
N.	**back to the** wall, **brick** wall, **concrete** wall, **glass** wall, **stone** wall **1** **2**
V.	**lean against/on a** wall, **build a** wall, **climb a** wall **1** **2**

walled /wɔld/ ADJ 形容詞 If an area of land or a city is **walled**, it is surrounded or enclosed by a wall. 壁を巡らした □ *The city was walled and built upon a rock.* その町は壁で囲まれ岩の上に建てられていた.

wal|let /wɒlɪt/ (**wallets**) N-COUNT 可算名詞 A **wallet** is a small flat folded case, usually made of leather or plastic, in which you can keep money and credit cards. 札入れ

wal|low /wɒloʊ/ (**wallows, wallowing, wallowed**) **1** V-I 自動詞 If you say that someone **is wallowing in** an unpleasant situation, you are criticizing them for being deliberately unhappy. おぼれる [DISAPPROVAL 不賛成] □ *His tired mind continued to wallow in self-pity.* 彼の疲れきった心は自己憐憫 (れんびん) におぼれ続けた. **2** V-I 自動詞 If a person or animal **wallows in** water or mud, they lie or roll about in it slowly for pleasure. ごろごろする □ *Never have I had such a good excuse for wallowing in deep warm baths.* それは深い暖かい浴場でごろごろするための最高の言い訳だった.

wall|paper /wɔlpeɪpər/ (**wallpapers, wallpapering, wallpapered**) **1** N-MASS 質量名詞 **Wallpaper** is thick colored or patterned paper that is used for covering and decorating the walls of rooms. 寝室の壁紙 **2** V-T 他動詞 If someone **wallpapers** a room, they cover the walls with wallpaper. 壁紙を張る □ *We were going to wallpaper that room anyway.* 我々はいずれにしても別の部屋に壁紙を張るつもりだった. **3** N-UNCOUNT 不可算名詞 **Wallpaper** is the background on a computer screen. デスクトップ壁紙 [COMPUTING コンピューティング] □ *...preinstalled wallpaper images.* インストール済みのデスクトップ壁紙の画像

Wall Street N-PROPER 固有名詞 **Wall Street** is a street in New York where the Stock Exchange and financial businesses are located. **Wall Street** is often used to refer to the financial business carried out there and to the people who work there. ウォール街 [BUSINESS 実業] □ *On Wall Street, stocks closed at their second highest level today.* ウォール街では株価は本日2番目に高い水準で取引を終えた.

wal|nut /wɔlnʌt, -nət/ (**walnuts**) N-VAR 可変性名詞 **Walnuts** are edible nuts that have a wrinkled shape and a hard round shell that is light brown in color. クルミ □ *...chopped walnuts.* 切り刻んだクルミ

waltz /wɔlts, wɒls/ (**waltzes, waltzing, waltzed**) **1** N-COUNT; N-IN-NAMES 可算名詞, 名称中の名詞 A **waltz** is a piece of music with a rhythm of three beats in each bar, which people can dance to. ワルツ □ *...Tchaikovsky's "Waltz of the Flowers."* チャイコフスキーの「花のワルツ」 **2** N-COUNT 可算名詞 A **waltz** is a dance in which two people hold each other and move around the floor doing special steps in time to waltz music. ワルツ □ *Arthur Murray taught the foxtrot, the tango and the waltz.* アーサー・マレーはフォックストロット, タンゴ, ワルツを教えた. **3** V-RECIP 相互動詞 If you **waltz with** someone, you dance a waltz with them. ワルツを踊る □ *"Waltz with me," he said, taking her hand.* 「私とワルツを踊ってください」と彼は彼女の手を取りながら言った.

wan|der /wɒndər/ (**wanders, wandering, wandered**) **1** V-T/V-I 他動詞/自動詞 If you **wander** in a place, you walk around there in a casual way, often without intending to go in any particular direction. 歩き回る □ *When he got bored he wandered around the*

Word Web war

The Hague Conventions* and the Geneva Convention* attempt to provide humane guidelines for **war**. First of all, they advise avoiding **armed conflict**. The regulations suggest using a **neutral mediator** or setting up a 30-day "time out." Before **combat** can begin, a country must formally **declare** war. Sneak **attacks** are prohibited. The rules governing the use of **firearms** are quite simple. One regulation states it is illegal to **kill** or **injure a person** who has **surrendered**. **Wounded soldiers, prisoners**, and **civilians** must receive immediate medical care. The rules also prohibit the use of **biological** and **chemical weapons**.

Hague Conventions: agreements between many nations on rules to limit warfare and weapons.
Geneva Convention: an agreement between most nations on treatment of prisoners of war and the sick, injured, or dead.

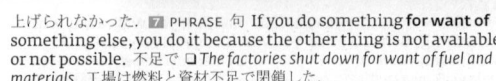

fair. 彼は退屈すると遊園地を歩き回った。❑ *They wandered off in the direction of the nearest store.* 彼らは近くの店の方向にそれた。❑ *People wandered the streets aimlessly.* 人々は当てもなく通りをさまよった。
● N-SING 単数名詞 **Wander** is also a noun. 歩き回ったこと ❑ *A wander around any market will reveal stalls piled high with vegetables.* 市場を歩き回ると野菜が高く積まれた屋台が見える。❷ V-I 自動詞 If a person or animal **wanders** from a place where they are supposed to stay, they move away from the place without going in a particular direction. さまよう ❑ *Because Mother is afraid we'll get lost, we aren't allowed to wander far.* 母は私たちが道に迷うのを心配しているので遠くをさまようことはできない。❸ V-I 自動詞 If your mind **wanders** or your thoughts **wander**, you stop concentrating on something and start thinking about other things. 取り留めがなくなる ❑ *His mind would wander, and he would lose track of what he was doing.* 彼の心はよく取り留めがなくなり、何をしていたのか忘れるものだった。❹ V-I 自動詞 If your eyes **wander**, you stop looking at one thing and start looking around at other things. きょろきょろ見回す ❑ *His eyes wandered restlessly around the room.* 彼は部屋をきょろきょろ見回した。

wane /weɪn/ (**wanes, waning, waned**) V-I 自動詞 If something **wanes**, it becomes gradually weaker or less, often so that it eventually disappears. 徐々に弱くなる ❑ *While his interest in these sports began to wane, a passion for lacrosse developed.* 彼はこうしたスポーツへの関心を失う一方で、ラクロスに興味を持つようになった。

want /wɒnt/ (**wants, wanting, wanted**) ❶ V-T 他動詞 If you **want** something, you feel a desire or a need for it. 欲する [no cont, no passive] ❑ *I want a drink.* 飲み物をくれ。❑ *People wanted to know who this talented designer was.* 人々はこの才能豊かなデザイナーが誰なのか知りたがった。❑ *They began to want their father to be the same as other daddies.* 彼らは他の父親と同じ父親をほしがり始めた。❑ *They didn't want people staring at them as they sat on the lawn, so they put up high walls.* 彼らは芝生に座っている時に人にじろじろ見られたくなかったので高い壁を取り付けた。

Note that **want** and **wish** have similar meanings, but are used differently. If you **want** something, you feel a need for it or a desire to have it. You can say that you **want** to do something, that you **want** someone to do something, or that you **want** something to happen. If you use **wish** with a "to" infinitive, this has the same meaning as **want** but is more formal. ❑ *I want to get out of here... She wished to consult him about her future.*

❷ V-T 他動詞 You can say that you **want to** say something to indicate that you are about to say it. 望む [no cont, no passive] ❑ *I want to say how delighted I am that you're having a baby.* 妊娠おめでとう。❸ V-T 他動詞 If you say to someone that you **want** something, or ask them if they **want** to do it, you are firmly telling them what you want or what you want them to do. 欲する [no cont, no passive] ❑ *I want an explanation from you, Jeremy.* ジェレミー、きみから説明してほしい。❑ *Do you want to tell me what all this is about?* これが何のことか私に説明してくれないか。❹ V-T 他動詞 If you tell someone that they **want** to do a particular thing, you are advising them to do it. すべきである [INFORMAL くだけた] [no cont, no passive] ❑ *You want to be very careful not to have a man like Crevecoeur for an enemy.* クレーヴクールのような男を敵に回さないように注意したほうがよい。*... She wished to consult him about her future.* ❺ V-T 他動詞 If someone **is wanted** by the police, the police are searching for them because they are thought to have committed a crime. 指名手配されている [usu passive] ❑ *He was wanted for the murder of a judge.* 彼は判事殺人の罪で指名手配されていた。●**want|ed** ADJ 形容詞 [ADJ n] 指名手配中の ❑ *He is one of the most wanted criminals in Europe.* 彼はヨーロッパ一の指名手配者の1人だ。❻ N-PLURAL 複数名詞 Your **wants** are the things that you want. 必要物 ❑ *She couldn't lift a spoon without a servant anticipating her wants and getting it for her.* 彼女は使用人が彼女の必要なものを予期し、それを彼女のために取って来ることなしにはスプーン1つ持ち

上げられなかった。❼ PHRASE 句 If you do something **for want of** something else, you do it because the other thing is not available or not possible. 不足で ❑ *The factories shut down for want of fuel and materials.* 工場は燃料と資材不足で閉鎖した。

Thesaurus		want また次を参照：
v.	covet, desire, long, need, require, wish ❶	

want|ing /wɒntɪŋ/ ADJ 形容詞 If you find something or someone **wanting**, they are not of as high a standard as you think they should be. ふさわしい力を発揮していない [v-link ADJ] ❑ *He analyzed his game and found it wanting.* 彼は試合を分析し、ふさわしい力を発揮していないことに気づいた。

WAP /wæp/ N-UNCOUNT 不可算名詞 **WAP** is a system that allows devices such as cellphones to connect to the Internet. **WAP** is an abbreviation for **Wireless Application Protocol**. WAP ❑ *...a WAP phone.* WAP対応携帯電話

war /wɔr/ (**wars**) ❶ N-VAR 可変性名詞 A **war** is a period of fighting or conflict between countries or states. 戦争 ❑ *He spent part of the war in the National Guard.* 彼は戦争中に州兵を務めたことがあった。❑ *...matters of war and peace.* 戦争と平和の問題 ❷ N-VAR 可変性名詞 **War** is intense economic competition between countries or organizations. 競争 ❑ *The most important thing is to reach an agreement and to avoid a trade war.* 最も大切なことは合意に達し、貿易競争を回避することだ。❸ N-VAR 可変性名詞 If you make **war on** someone or something that you are opposed to, you do things to stop them from succeeding. 戦い ❑ *She has been involved in the war against organized crime.* 彼女は組織犯罪をなくす戦いに関与してきた。❹ → see also civil war, warring ❺ PHRASE 句 If a country **goes to war**, it starts fighting a war. 戦いを始める ❑ *Do you think this crisis can be settled without going to war?* この危機は戦いを始めずに解決できると思うか。

→ see Word Web: war
→ see army, history

war|ble /wɔrbəl/ (**warbles, warbling, warbled**) ❶ V-T/V-I 他動詞/自動詞 When a bird **warbles**, it sings pleasantly. さえずる ❑ *The bird continued to warble.* 鳥はさえずり続けた。❑ *...birds warbling a morning chorus.* 朝聞こえてくる鳥のさえずり ❷ V-T/V-I 他動詞/自動詞 If someone **warbles**, they sing in a high-pitched, rather unsteady voice. 声を震わせて歌う ❑ *She warbled as she worked.* 彼女は仕事をしながら声を震わせて歌った。❑ *...singers warbling "Over the Rainbow."* 「オーヴァー・ザ・レインボー」を声を震わせて歌う歌手

ward /wɔrd/ (**wards, warding, warded**) N-COUNT 可算名詞 A **ward** is a room in a hospital which has beds for many people, often people who need similar treatment. 病棟 ❑ *They transferred her to the psychiatric ward.* 彼女は精神科の病棟に移された。

→ see hospital

▶ **ward off** PHRASAL VERB 句動詞 To **ward off** a danger or illness means to prevent it from affecting you or harming you. 寄せつけない ❑ *She may have put up a fight to try to ward off her assailant.* 彼女は攻撃者を撃退しようとして闘ったのかもしれない。

war|den /wɔrdən/ (**wardens**) ❶ N-COUNT 可算名詞 A **warden** is a person who is responsible for a particular place or thing, and for making sure that the laws or regulations that relate to it are obeyed. 監視人 ❑ *He was a warden at the local parish church.* 彼は地元の教区教会の管理人だった。❷ N-COUNT 可算名詞 The **warden** of a prison is the person in charge of it. 刑務所長 [AM 米国英語] ❑ *A new warden took over the prison.* 新しい刑務所長が刑務所を引き継いだ。

war|der /wɔrdər/ (**warders**) N-COUNT 可算名詞 A **warder** is someone who works in a prison supervising the prisoners. 看守 [BRIT 英国英語; AM **guard** 米国英語 **guard**]

ward|robe /wɔrdroʊb/ (**wardrobes**) **1** N-COUNT 可算名詞 Someone's **wardrobe** is the total collection of clothes that they have. 持ち衣装 □ *Her wardrobe consists primarily of huge cashmere sweaters and tiny Italian sandals.* 彼女の衣装は主に大きなカシミアのセーターと小さなイタリア製のサンダルから成る. **2** N-COUNT 可算名詞 A **wardrobe** is a tall closet or cabinet in which you can hang your clothes. 洋服ダンス

ware|house /wɛərhaʊs/ (**warehouses**) N-COUNT 可算名詞 A **warehouse** is a large building where raw materials or manufactured goods are stored until they are exported to other countries or distributed to stores to be sold. 倉庫

war|fare /wɔrfɛər/ **1** N-UNCOUNT 不可算名詞 **Warfare** is the activity of fighting a war. 戦争行為 □ *...the threat of chemical warfare.* 化学戦争の脅威 **2** N-UNCOUNT 不可算名詞 **Warfare** is sometimes used to refer to any violent struggle or conflict. 闘争 □ *Much of the violence is related to drugs and gang warfare.* 暴力の大半は麻薬とギャングの争いに関連している.

war|head /wɔrhɛd/ (**warheads**) N-COUNT 可算名詞 A **warhead** is the front part of a bomb or missile where the explosives are carried. 弾頭 □ *...nuclear warheads.* 核弾頭

warm /wɔrm/ (**warmer, warmest, warms, warming, warmed**) **1** ADJ 形容詞 Something that is **warm** has some heat but not enough to be hot. 暖かい □ *Wheat is grown in places which have cold winters and warm, dry summers.* 麦は冬寒く, 夏は暖かく雨が少ない地域で栽培される. □ *Because it was warm, David wore only a white cotton shirt.* 暖かったためデイビッドが着ていたのは白い木綿のシャツだけだった.

> In informal English, if you want to emphasize how hot the weather is, you can say that it is **boiling** or **scorching**. In winter, if the temperature is above average, you can say that it is **mild**. In general, **hot** suggests a higher temperature than **warm**, and **warm** things are usually pleasant. □ *...a warm evening.*

2 ADJ 形容詞 **Warm** clothes and blankets are made of a material such as wool that protects you from the cold. 温かい □ *They have been forced to sleep in the open without food or warm clothing.* 彼らは食料や温かい衣服なしで野外で眠ることを余儀なくされた. ● **warm|ly** ADV 副詞 □ *Remember to wrap up warmly on cold days.* 寒い日には温かい服装をするのですよ. **3** ADJ 形容詞 **Warm** colors have red or yellow in them rather than blue or green, and make you feel comfortable and relaxed. 暖色の □ *The basement hallway is painted a warm yellow.* 地下の入口は暖かさを感じさせる黄色のペンキが塗られていた. **4** ADJ 形容詞 A **warm** person is friendly and shows a lot of affection or enthusiasm in their behavior. 心の温かい □ *She was a warm and loving mother.* 彼女は心が温かく, 愛情深い母親だった. ● **warm|ly** ADV 副詞 [ADV with v] 温かく □ *New members are warmly welcomed.* 新しい会員は温かく歓迎される. **5** V-T 他動詞 If you **warm** a part of your body or if something hot **warms** it, it stops feeling cold and starts to feel hotter. 暖める □ *The sun had come out to warm his back.* 日差しが彼の背中を暖めた. **6** V-I 自動詞 If you **warm to** a person or an idea, you become fonder of the person or more interested in the idea. 心引かれる □ *Those who got to know him better warmed to his openness and honesty.* 彼をよく知るようになった人々は彼の率直さと正直さに引かれた.

▶ **warm up** **1** PHRASAL VERB 句動詞 If you **warm** something **up** or if it **warms up**, it gets hotter. 暖める □ *He blew on his hands to warm them up.* 彼は手を温めるために息を吹きかけた. □ *All that she would have to do was warm up the pudding.* 彼女がしなければならないことはプディングを温めることだけだった. **2** PHRASAL VERB 句動詞 If you **warm up** for an event such as a race, you prepare yourself for it by doing exercises or by practicing just before it starts. ウォーミングアップする □ *In an hour the drivers will be warming up for the main event.* 1時間後にドライバーはメインイベントのためのウォーミングアップをする予定だ. **3** PHRASAL VERB 句動詞 When a machine or engine **warms up** or someone **warms** it **up**, it becomes ready for use a little while after being switched on or started. 暖める, 暖まる □ *He waited for his car to warm up.* 彼は車が暖まるまで待った.
→ see **greenhouse effect**

<table>
<tr><td colspan="2">**Word Partnership** warm は次の語句と使われる:</td></tr>
<tr><td>ADJ.</td><td>warm **and sunny** **1**
warm **and cozy**, warm **and dry** **1** **2**
soft and warm **2**
warm **and friendly** **4**</td></tr>
<tr><td>N.</td><td>warm **air**, warm **bath**, warm **breeze**, warm **hands**, warm **water**, warm **weather** **1**
warm **clothes** **2**
warm **smile**, warm **welcome** **4**</td></tr>
</table>

warmth /wɔrmθ/ **1** N-UNCOUNT 不可算名詞 The **warmth** of something is the heat that it has or produces. 暖かさ □ *She went further into the room, drawn by the warmth of the fire.* 彼女は炉火の暖かさに引かれて部屋の中に入った. **2** N-UNCOUNT 不可算名詞 The **warmth** of something such as a garment or blanket is the

protection that it gives you against the cold. 温暖 □ *The blanket will provide additional warmth and comfort in bed.* 毛布は寝る時に追加の暖かさと心地よさを提供する.

warm-up (**warm-ups**) N-COUNT 可算名詞 A **warm-up** is something that prepares you for an activity or event, usually because it is a short practice or example of what the activity or event will involve. ウォーミングアップ □ *The exercises can be fun and a good warm-up for the latter part of the program.* その運動は楽しく, プログラムの後半のためのよいウォーミングアップとなりうる.

warn /wɔrn/ (**warns, warning, warned**) **1** V-T/V-I 他動詞/自動詞 If you **warn** someone about something such as a possible danger or problem, you tell them about it so that they are aware of it. 警告をする □ *When I had my first baby friends warned me that children were expensive.* 初産をした時, 私は子供は費用がかかると友人に警告された. □ *They warned him of the dangers of sailing alone.* 彼らは彼に1人で船旅をすることの危険について警告をした. □ *He warned of a possibility of a new terrorist attack.* 彼は新しいテロリストの攻撃の可能性について警告をした. **2** V-T/V-I 他動詞/自動詞 If you **warn** someone not to do something, you advise them not to do it so that they can avoid possible danger or punishment. 注意するように言う □ *Mrs. Blount warned me not to interfere.* ブラウント夫人は干渉しないように私に注意した. □ *"Don't do anything yet," he warned. "Too risky."* 「まだ何もしてはいけない. 危険すぎる」と彼は注意するように言った.

<table>
<tr><td colspan="2">**Thesaurus** warn また次を参照:</td></tr>
<tr><td>v.</td><td>alert, caution, notify **1** **2**</td></tr>
</table>

warn|ing /wɔrnɪŋ/ (**warnings**) **1** N-COUNT 可算名詞 A **warning** is something said or written to tell people of a possible danger, problem, or other unpleasant thing that might happen. 警告 □ *The minister gave a warning that if war broke out, it would be catastrophic.* 大臣はもし戦争が起きた場合は大惨事となるだろうと警告した. □ *He was killed because he ignored a warning to put stronger cords on his parachute.* 彼はパラシュートにもっと頑丈なひもを取り付けるべきだという警告を無視したため, 死亡した. **2** N-VAR 可変性名詞 A **warning** is an advance notice of something that will happen, often something unpleasant or dangerous. 警告 □ *The soldiers opened fire without warning.* 兵隊は警告なしに射撃を始めた. **3** ADJ 形容詞 **Warning** actions or signs give a warning. 注意を促す [ADJ n] □ *She ignored the warning signals and did not check the patient's medical notes.* 彼女は警報を無視し患者のカルテをチェックしなかった.

<table>
<tr><td colspan="2">**Word Partnership** warning は次の語句と使われる:</td></tr>
<tr><td>ADJ.</td><td>**stern** warning **1**
advance warning, **early** warning **1** **2**</td></tr>
<tr><td>N.</td><td>warning **of danger**, **hurricane** warning, **storm** warning **1**
warning **labels**, warning **signs** **3**</td></tr>
<tr><td>V.</td><td>**give (a)** warning, **ignore a** warning, **receive (a)** warning, **send a** warning **1** **2**</td></tr>
</table>

warp /wɔrp/ (**warps, warping, warped**) V-T/V-I 他動詞/自動詞 If something **warps** or **is warped**, it becomes damaged by bending or curving, often because of the effect of heat or water. 曲がる □ *Left out in the heat of the sun, tapes easily warp or get stuck in their cases.* 日の当たる場所に置いたままにしておくとテープは簡単に曲がったり, 容器に張り付く.

war|rant /wɔrənt/ (**warrants, warranting, warranted**) **1** V-T 他動詞 If something **warrants** a particular action, it makes the action seem necessary or appropriate for the circumstances. 正当な根拠となる □ *The allegations are serious enough to warrant an investigation.* その申し立ては調査する価値があるほど深刻である. **2** N-COUNT 可算名詞 A **warrant** is a legal document that allows someone to do something, especially one that is signed by a judge or magistrate and gives the police permission to arrest someone or search their house. 令状 [oft N 'for' n, also 'by' n] □ *Police confirmed that they had issued a warrant for his arrest.* 警察は彼に逮捕状が出たことを確認した.

war|ran|ty /wɔrənti/ (**warranties**) N-COUNT 可算名詞 A **warranty** is a written promise by a company that, if you find a fault in something they have sold you within a certain time, they will repair it or replace it free of charge. 保証書 [also 'under' N] □ *...a twelve-month warranty.* 12ヶ月間の保証書

war|ring /wɔrɪŋ/ ADJ 形容詞 **Warring** is used to describe groups of people who are involved in a conflict or quarrel with each other. 交戦中の [ADJ n] □ *An official said the warring factions have not yet turned in all their heavy weapons.* 政府筋は争争中の両党派はまだ重火器をすべて引き渡していないと言った.

war|ri|or /wɔriər/ (**warriors**) N-COUNT 可算名詞 A **warrior** is a fighter or soldier, especially one in former times who was very brave and experienced in fighting. 戦士 □ *...the tale of Bima, the great warrior of Indonesian folklore.* インドネシアの伝説の偉大な戦士, ビーマの物語

w

war|ship /wɔːrʃɪp/ (**warships**) N-COUNT 可算名詞 A **warship** is a ship with guns that is used for fighting in wars. 軍艦
→ see **ship**

wart /wɔːrt/ (**warts**) N-COUNT 可算名詞 A **wart** is a small lump that grows on your skin. いぼ

war|time /wɔːrtaɪm/ N-UNCOUNT 不可算名詞 **Wartime** is a period of time when a war is being fought. 戦時中 ❑ The government will commandeer ships only in wartime. 政府は戦時中のみに船を徴発する。

| Word Link | war ≈ watchful : aware, beware, wary |

wary /wɛəri/ (**warier, wariest**) ADJ 形容詞 If you are **wary of** something or someone, you are cautious because you do not know much about them and you believe they may be dangerous or cause problems. 警戒している ❑ People did not teach their children to be wary of strangers. 人々は見知らぬ人に用心することを子供に教えなかった。 ● **warily** /wɛərɪli/ ADV 副詞 用心深く ❑ She studied me warily, as if I might turn violent. 彼女は私がまるで暴力的になるかのように私を注意深く観察した。

was /wəz, STRONG wʌz, wɒz/ **Was** is the first and third person singular of the past tense of **be**. be の一人称および三人称単数過去形

wash /wɒʃ/ (**washes, washing, washed**) 1 V-T 他動詞 If you **wash** something, you clean it using water and usually a substance such as soap or detergent. 洗う ❑ We did odd jobs like farm work and washing dishes. 我々は農場の作業や皿洗いなどの片手間仕事をした。 ❑ It took a long time to wash the mud out of his hair. 彼の髪の毛から泥を洗い流すのに長いことかかった。 2 V-T/V-I 他動詞/自動詞 If you **wash** or if you **wash** part of your body, especially your hands and face, you clean part of your body using soap and water. 洗う ❑ They looked as if they hadn't washed in days. 彼らは何日も体をお風呂に入っていないように見えた。 ❑ She washed her face with cold water. 彼女は冷たい水で顔を洗った。 3 V-T/V-I 他動詞/自動詞 If a sea or river **washes** somewhere, it flows there gently. You can also say that something carried by a sea or river **washes** or **is washed** somewhere. 打ち寄せる ❑ The sea washed against the shore. 海は浜辺に打ち寄せた。 4 V-I 自動詞 If a feeling **washes over** you, you suddenly feel it very strongly and cannot control it. 心をよぎる [WRITTEN 書き言葉] ❑ A wave of self-consciousness can wash over her when someone new enters the room. 彼女は誰か新しい人が部屋に入ってくると自意識過剰の感情がこみ上げることがある。 5 → see also **washing** 6 PHRASE 句 If you say that something such as an item of clothing **is in the wash**, you mean that it is being washed, is waiting to be washed, or has just been washed and should therefore not be worn or used. 洗濯に出してある [INFORMAL くだけた] ❑ Your jeans are in the wash. あなたのジーンズは洗濯に出してある。 7 to **wash** your **hands** of something → see **hand**

▸ **wash away** PHRASAL VERB 句動詞 If rain or floods **wash away** something, they destroy it and carry it away. 洗い流す ❑ Flood waters washed away one of the main bridges in Pusan. 洪水は釜山（プサン）の主な橋の1つを押し流した。

▸ **wash down** 1 PHRASAL VERB 句動詞 If you **wash** something, especially food, **down** with a drink, you drink the drink after eating the food, especially to make the food easier to swallow or digest. 流し込む ❑ He took two aspirin immediately and washed them down with three cups of water. 彼は即座にアスピリンを2錠手に取り、コップ3杯の水で飲み込んだ。 2 PHRASAL VERB 句動詞 If you **wash down** an object, you wash it all, from top to bottom. 隅々まで洗い流す ❑ The prisoner started to wash down the walls of his cell. その囚人は独房の壁を隅から隅まで洗い流し始めた。

▸ **wash up** 1 PHRASAL VERB 句動詞 If you **wash up**, you clean part of your body with soap and water, especially your hands and face. 顔や手を洗う [AM 米国英語] ❑ He headed to the bathroom to wash up. 彼は洗面するためにバスルームに向かった。 2 PHRASAL VERB 句動詞 If something **is washed up on** a piece of land, it is carried by a river or sea and left there. 打ち上げられる ❑ Thousands of herring and crab are washed up on the beaches during every storm. 何千というニシンとカニが嵐が起きる毎に海岸に打ち上げられる。 3 PHRASAL VERB 句動詞 If you **wash up**, you wash the plates, cups, flatware, and pans that have been used for cooking and eating a meal. 食器類を洗う [BRIT 英国英語; AM **wash the dishes** 米国英語 **wash the dishes**]
→ see **dry-cleaning, soap**

Thesaurus	wash また次を参照 :
V.	clean, rinse, scrub
	clean, bathe, soap 2

Word Partnership	wash は次の語句と使われる :
N.	wash **a car**, wash **clothes**, wash **dishes** 1
	wash **your face/hair/hands** 2

wash|able /wɒʃəbəl/ ADJ 形容詞 **Washable** clothes or materials can be washed in water without being damaged. 洗える ❑ Choose

washable curtains. 洗えるカーテンを選びなさい。

wash|cloth /wɒʃklɔːθ/ (**washcloths**) N-COUNT 可算名詞 A **washcloth** is a small cloth that you use for washing yourself. 洗面タオル [AM 米国英語]

wash|er /wɒʃər/ (**washers**) 1 N-COUNT 可算名詞 A **washer** is a thin flat ring of metal or rubber that is placed over a bolt before the nut is screwed on. ワッシャー 2 N-COUNT 可算名詞 A **washer** is the same as a **washing machine**. 洗濯機 [INFORMAL くだけた]

wash|ing /wɒʃɪŋ/ N-UNCOUNT 不可算名詞 **Washing** is a collection of clothes, sheets, and other things that are waiting to be washed, are being washed, or have just been washed. 洗濯物 ❑ ...plastic bags full of dirty washing. 汚れた洗濯物でいっぱいのプラスチックの袋

wash|ing ma|chine (**washing machines**) N-COUNT 可算名詞 A **washing machine** is a machine that you use to wash clothes in. 洗濯機

wasn't /wʌzənt, wɒz-/ **Wasn't** is the usual spoken form of "was not." 口語で用いられる。 was not の短縮形

wasp /wɒsp/ (**wasps**) N-COUNT 可算名詞 A **wasp** is an insect with wings and yellow and black stripes across its body. Wasps have a painful sting like a bee but do not produce honey. ハチ

wast|age /weɪstɪdʒ/ N-UNCOUNT 不可算名詞 **Wastage** of something is the act of wasting it or the amount of it that is wasted. 浪費 ❑ There was a lot of wastage and many wrong decisions were hastily taken. 多くの浪費が発生し、多くの誤った決定が性急にされた。

waste /weɪst/ (**wastes, wasting, wasted**) 1 V-T 他動詞 If you **waste** something such as time, money, or energy, you use too much of it doing something that is not important or necessary, or is unlikely to succeed. 無駄にする ❑ There could be many reasons and he was not going to waste time speculating on them. 数多くの理由があったかもしれないが彼はそれらを推測することに時間を浪費するつもりはなかった。 ❑ I resolved not to waste money on a hotel. 私はホテル代に金を無駄遣いしないことに決めた。 ● N-SING 単数名詞 **Waste** is also a noun. 浪費 ❑ It is a waste of time going to the doctor with most mild complaints. ひどく軽い症状で医者に行くのは時間の無駄遣いだ。 2 N-UNCOUNT 不可算名詞 **Waste** is the use of money or other resources on things that do not need it. 無駄な消費 ❑ The packets are measured to reduce waste. パケットは無駄な消費を削減するよう測定されている。 3 N-UNCOUNT 不可算名詞 **Waste** is material that has been used and is no longer wanted, for example, because the valuable or useful part of it has been taken out. 廃棄物 [also N in pl] ❑ Congress passed a law that regulates the disposal of waste. 議会は廃棄物処分を規制する法律を可決した。 ❑ ...the dangers posed by toxic waste. 有毒廃棄物の危険 4 V-T 他動詞 If you **waste** an opportunity to do something, you do not take advantage of it when it is available. 利用しそこなう ❑ Let's not waste an opportunity to see the children. 子供たちに会う機会を逃さないようにしよう。 5 ADJ 形容詞 **Waste** land is land, especially in or near a city, that is not used or taken care of by anyone, and so is covered by wild plants and garbage. 空き地 [BRIT 英国英語; AM **vacant land** 米国英語 **vacant land**] 6 PHRASE 句 If something **goes to waste**, it remains unused or has to be thrown away. 無駄になる ❑ So much of his enormous effort and talent will go to waste if we are forced to drop one hour of the film. 我々がその映画フィルムの1時間分をカットしたら彼の努力と才能の多くは無駄になるだろう。 7 to **waste no time** → see **time**
→ see **dump**

▸ **waste away** PHRASAL VERB 句動詞 If someone **wastes away**, they become extremely thin or weak because they are ill or worried and they are not eating properly. やせ衰える ❑ Persons dying from cancer grow thin and visibly waste away. 末期がんの患者はやせ細り、目に見えて衰弱してくる。

Thesaurus	waste また次を参照 :
V.	misuse, squander 1
N.	garbage, junk, trash 3

Word Partnership	waste は次の語句と使われる :
N.	waste **energy**, waste **money**, waste **time**, waste **water** 1
V.	**reduce** waste 2
	recycle waste 3
ADJ.	**hazardous** waste, **human** waste, **industrial** waste, **nuclear** waste, **toxic** waste 3

waste|ful /weɪstfəl/ ADJ 形容詞 Action that is **wasteful** uses too much of something valuable such as time, money, or energy. 無駄の多い ❑ This kind of training is ineffective, and wasteful of scarce resources. こうした類の訓練は効果がなく、乏しい資源の無駄になる。

waste|land /weɪstlænd/ (**wastelands**) 1 N-VAR 可変性名詞 A **wasteland** is an area of land on which not much can grow

or which has been spoiled in some way. 荒れ地 ❑ *The pollution has already turned vast areas into a wasteland.* 環境汚染は既に莫大な地域を荒れ地にした. **2** N-COUNT 可算名詞 If you refer to a place, situation, or period in time as a **wasteland**, you are criticizing it because you think there is nothing interesting or exciting in it. 不毛の時代 [DISAPPROVAL 不賛成] ❑ *...the cultural wasteland of Franco's repressive rule.* フランコの抑圧的な支配の文化的不毛の時代

---

watch

❶ LOOKING AND PAYING ATTENTION
❷ INSTRUMENT THAT TELLS THE TIME

---

❶ watch /wɒtʃ/ (**watches, watching, watched**)
↪ Please look at meaning **11** to see if the expression you are looking for is shown under another headword. **1** V-T/V-I 他動詞/自動詞 If you **watch** someone or something, you look at them, usually for a period of time, and pay attention to what is happening. じっと見る ❑ *The man was standing in his doorway watching him.* その男は出入り口に立ち, 彼をじっと見ていた. ❑ *He seems to enjoy watching me work.* 彼は私が作業しているのを見て楽しんでいるようだ. ❑ *Here, now watch how I cut this, OK?* さあ, 私がこれを切る方法をよく見なさい. ❑ *He watched as the Yankees rallied for a second comeback victory.* 彼はヤンキースが2度目の返り咲き勝利のために奮起するのを見ていた. **2** V-T 他動詞 If you **watch** something on television or an event such as a sports contest, you spend time looking at it, especially when you see it from the beginning to the end. 見る ❑ *I'd stayed up late to watch the movie.* 私はよく遅くまで起きて映画を見た. **3** V-T/V-I 他動詞/自動詞 If you **watch a** situation or event, you pay attention to it or you are aware of it, but you do not influence it. 観察する ❑ *Human rights groups have been closely watching the case.* 人権団体は事件を綿密に観察してきた. ❑ *He watched as nine people were swept into the crevasse.* 彼は9人の人々がクレバスに押し流されるのを見ていた. **4** V-T 他動詞 If you **watch** people, especially children or animals, you are responsible for them, and make sure that they are not in danger. 監視する ❑ *Parents can't be expected to watch their children 24 hours a day.* 両親には子供を1日24時間監視する義務はない. **5** V-T 他動詞 If you tell someone to **watch** a particular person or thing, you are warning them to be careful that the person or thing does not get out of control or do something unpleasant. 気をつける ❑ *You really ought to watch these quiet types.* こうした物静かなタイプには本当に気をつけなければならない. **6** PHRASE 句 If someone **keeps watch**, they look and listen all the time, while other people are asleep or doing something else, so that they can warn them of danger or an attack. 見張る ❑ *Jose, as usual, had climbed a tree to keep watch.* ホセはいつものとおりに見張りのために木に登った. **7** PHRASE 句 If you **keep watch** on events or a situation, you pay attention to what is happening, so that you can take action at the right moment. 監視する ❑ *U.S. officials have been keeping close watch on the situation.* 米国政府筋はその状況を綿密に監視してきた. **8** PHRASE 句 You say "**watch it**" in order to warn someone to be careful, especially when you want to threaten them about what will happen if they are not careful. 気をつけろ ❑ *"Now watch it, Patsy," the sergeant told her.* 「これ, 気をつけろ, パッツィ」と軍曹は彼女に言った. **9** PHRASE 句 If someone is being watched **under watch**, they are being guarded or observed all the time. 監視されて ❑ *Doctors confirmed how serious Josephine's condition was, and she is still being kept under watch.* 医者はジョセフィーンの状態がとても深刻であることを確認した. 彼女は今も看視下に置かれている. **10** PHRASE 句 You say to someone "**you watch**" or "**just watch**" when you are predicting that something will happen, and you are very confident that it will happen as you say. 今に見ていなさい ❑ *You watch. Things will get worse before they get better.* 今に見ていなさい. 状況は改善する前に悪化するだろう. **11** to **watch** your **step** → see **step**

▸ **watch for** or **watch out for** PHRASAL VERB 句動詞 If you **watch for** something or **watch out for** it, you pay attention so that you notice it, either because you do not want to miss it or because you want to avoid it. 見守る ❑ *We'll be watching for any developments.* 私たちは進展を見守るつもりだ.

▸ **watch out** PHRASAL VERB 句動詞 If you tell someone to **watch out**, you are warning them to be careful, because something unpleasant might happen to them or they might get into difficulties. 注意する ❑ *You have to watch out because there are land mines all over the place.* 至る所に地雷があるため注意する必要がある.

▸ **watch out for** → see **watch for**

If you want to say that someone is paying attention to something they can see, you say that they **are watching** or **looking at** it. In general, you **watch** something that is moving or changing, and you **look at** something that is not moving. ❑ *I asked him to look at the picture above his bed... He watched Blake run down the stairs.* You use **see** to talk about things that you are aware of because a visual impression reaches your eyes. You often use **can** in this case. ❑ *I can see the fax here on the desk.*

❷ watch /wɒtʃ/ (**watches**) N-COUNT 可算名詞 A **watch** is a small clock that you wear on a strap on your wrist, or on a chain. 時計
→ see **jewelry**, **time**

Word Partnership   watch は次の語句と使われる:

ADV.	watch **carefully**, watch **closely** ❶ **1 3 5**
N.	watch **a DVD**, watch **a film/movie**, watch **fireworks**, watch **a game**, watch **the news**, watch **people**, watch **television/TV**, watch **a video** ❶ **2**
	watch **children** ❶ **4**
V.	check **your** watch, glance at **your** watch, look at **your** watch ❷ **1**

watch|dog /wɒtʃdɒg/ (**watchdogs**) **1** N-COUNT 可算名詞 A **watchdog** is a person or committee whose job is to make sure that companies do not act illegally or irresponsibly. 監視人 ❑ *...an anticrime watchdog group funded by New York businesses.* ニューヨークの企業が資金提供した犯罪と戦う監視人グループ **2** N-COUNT 可算名詞 A **watchdog** is a fierce dog that has been specially trained to protect a particular place. 番犬 [mainly AM 主に米国英語]

watch|ful /wɒtʃfəl/ ADJ 形容詞 Someone who is **watchful** notices everything that is happening. 油断のない ❑ *The best thing is to be watchful and see the family doctor for any change in your normal health.* いちばんいいことは油断せずに体調に変化があったら家庭医に診てもらうことだ.

watch|word /wɒtʃwɜrd/ (**watchwords**) N-COUNT 可算名詞 Someone's **watchword** is a word or phrase that sums up their attitude or approach to a particular subject or to things in general. モットー ❑ *Caution has been one of Mr. Allan's watchwords.* 用心はアラン氏のモットーの1つだった.

wa|ter /wɔtər/ (**waters, watering, watered**) **1** N-UNCOUNT 不可算名詞 **Water** is a clear thin liquid that has no color or taste when it is pure. It falls from clouds as rain and enters rivers and seas. All animals and people need water in order to live. 水 ❑ *Get me a glass of water.* グラス1杯の水をください. ❑ *...the sound of water hammering on the metal roof.* 金属製の屋根に水が打ちつける音 **2** N-PLURAL 複数名詞 You use **waters** to refer to a large area of sea, especially the area of sea that is near to a country and that is regarded as belonging to it. 水域 ❑ *The ship will remain outside Chinese territorial waters.* 船は中国の水域の外にとどまる予定だ. **3** V-T 他動詞 If you **water** plants, you pour water over them in order to help them to grow. 水をやる ❑ *He went out to water the plants.* 彼は植物に水をやるため外に出た. **4** V-I 自動詞 If your eyes **water**, tears build up in them because they are hurting or because you are upset. 涙が出る ❑ *His eyes watered from cigarette smoke.* 彼はタバコの煙で涙が出た. **5** V-I 自動詞 If you say that your mouth **is watering**, you mean that you can smell or see some nice food that makes you want to eat it. よだれが出る ❑ *...cookies to make your mouth water.* よだれが出そうなクッキー **6** PHRASE 句 If you say that an event or incident is **water under the bridge**, you mean that it has happened and cannot now be changed, so there is no point in worrying about it anymore. 過ぎてしまったこと ❑ *He was relieved his time in jail was over and regarded it as water under the bridge.* 彼は服役を終えてほっとし, それを過ぎてしまったことと考えた. **7** PHRASE 句 If you are **in deep water**, you are in a difficult or awkward situation. 非常に困って ❑ *You certainly seem to be in deep water.* あなたは確かに苦境に陥っているようだ. **8** PHRASE 句 If an argument or theory does not **hold water**, it does not seem to be reasonable or be in accordance with the facts. 筋道が通る ❑ *This argument simply cannot hold water in Europe.* この議論はヨーロッパでは通用しない. **9** PHRASE 句 If you are **in hot water**, you are in trouble. 苦境にある [INFORMAL くだけた] ❑ *The company has already been in hot water over high prices this year.* その企業は今年, 高価格をめぐって既に苦境に陥っている. **10** PHRASE 句 If you **pour cold water on** an idea or suggestion, you show that you have a low opinion of it. 水を差す ❑ *University economists pour cold water on the idea that the economic recovery has begun.* 大学の経済学者は経済回復が始まったという考えに水を差す. **11** PHRASE 句 If you **test the water** or **test the waters**, you try to find out what reaction an action or idea will get before you do it or tell it to people. 成り行きを見る ❑ *You should be cautious when getting involved and test the water before committing yourself.* 係わり合いになる時には用心し, 約束する前に様子を見るべきだ. **12** **like water off a duck's back** → see **duck** **13** to **take**

w

Word Web　water

Water changes its form in the **hydrologic cycle**. The sun warms oceans, lakes, and rivers. This causes some water to **evaporate**. Evaporation creates a gas called **water vapor**. Plants also give off water vapor through transpiration. Water vapor rises into the **atmosphere**. When it hits cooler air, it **condenses** into drops of water and forms **clouds**. When these drops get heavy enough, they begin to fall. They form different types of precipitation. Rain forms in warm air. Cold air creates **freezing rain**, **sleet**, and **snow**.

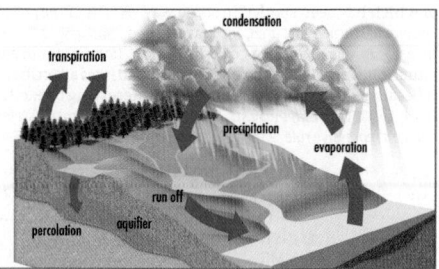

to something **like a duck to water** → see **duck** 14 to keep your **head above water** → see **head**

→ see Word Web: **water**

→ see **erosion, glacier, greenhouse effect, lake, ocean, plumbing**

▶ **water down** 1 PHRASAL VERB 句動詞 If you **water down** a substance, such as food or drink, you add water to it to make it weaker. 水で薄める ❏ *You can water down a glass of wine and make it last twice as long.* グラス1杯のワインを水で薄め、倍の時間をもつようにできる. 2 PHRASAL VERB 句動詞 If something such as a proposal, speech, or statement **is watered down**, it is made much weaker and less forceful, or less likely to make people angry. 弱める ❏ *Proposed legislation affecting bird-keepers has been watered down.* 鳥飼育者に影響する法律案は和らげられた.

water|color /wɔ́tərkʌlər/ (**watercolors**) 1 N-VAR 可変性名詞 **Watercolors** are colored paints, used for painting pictures, which you apply with a wet brush or dissolve in water first. 水彩絵の具 ❏ *Oil paints can be replaced with watercolors.* 油絵の具は水彩絵の具と取り替えることができる. 2 N-COUNT 可算名詞 A **watercolor** is a picture that has been painted with watercolors. 水彩画 ❏ *...a lovely watercolor by J. M. W. Turner.* ターナーの美しい水彩画

water|fall /wɔ́tərfɔl/ (**waterfalls**) N-COUNT 可算名詞 A **waterfall** is a place where water flows over the edge of a steep, high cliff in hills or mountains, and falls into a pool below. 滝 ❏ *...Angel Falls, the world's highest waterfall.* 世界で最も高いエンジェル滝

water|front /wɔ́tərfrʌnt/ (**waterfronts**) N-COUNT 可算名詞 A **waterfront** is a street or piece of land next to an area of water, such as a harbor or the sea. 海岸通り ❏ *They went for a stroll along the waterfront.* 彼らは海岸通り沿いに散歩に行った.

water|proof /wɔ́tərpruf/ ADJ 形容詞 Something that is **waterproof** does not let water pass through it. 防水の ❏ *Take waterproof clothing – Oregon weather is unpredictable.* 防水服を持って行きなさい. オレゴンの天気は変りやすいので.

water|shed /wɔ́tərʃɛd/ (**watersheds**) N-COUNT 可算名詞 If something such as an event is a **watershed** in the history or development of something, it is very important because it represents the beginning of a new stage in it. 決定的な分かれ目 ❏ *The election of Mary Robinson in 1990 was a watershed in Irish politics.* 1990年にメアリー・ロビンソンが選ばれたことはアイルランド政治の重大な分岐点だった.

water|tight /wɔ́tərtaɪt/ also **water-tight** 1 ADJ 形容詞 Something that is **watertight** does not allow water to pass through it, for example, because it is tightly sealed. 水の漏らない ❏ *The flask is completely watertight, even when laid on its side.* その魔法瓶は横にしても全く水漏れがしない. 2 ADJ 形容詞 A **watertight** case, argument, or agreement is one that has been so carefully put together that nobody will be able to find a fault in it. 手抜かりのない [mainly BRIT 主に英国英語; AM usually **airtight** 米国英語では通常 **airtight**]

water|way /wɔ́tərweɪ/ (**waterways**) N-COUNT 可算名詞 A **waterway** is a canal, river, or narrow channel of sea which ships or boats can sail along. 水路 ❏ *There are more than 400 miles of waterways to explore in the area.* その地域には40マイル以上の水路がある.

wa|tery /wɔ́təri/ 1 ADJ 形容詞 Something that is **watery** is weak or pale. 水のような ❏ *A watery light began to show through the branches.* 水のように薄い光が枝の間から見え始めた. 2 ADJ 形容詞 If you describe food or drink as **watery**, you dislike it because it contains too much water, or has no flavor. 水っぽい [DISAPPROVAL 不賛成] ❏ *...a bowl of watery soup.* 深皿1杯の水っぽいスープ 3 ADJ 形容詞 Something that is **watery** contains, resembles, or consists of water. 水のような ❏ *There was a watery discharge from her ear.* 彼女の耳から水のような耳垂れが出てきた.

watt /wɒt/ (**watts**) N-COUNT 可算名詞 A **watt** is a unit of measurement of electrical power. ワット ❏ *Use a 3 amp fuse for equipment up to 720 watts.* 720ワットまでの機器には3アンペアのヒューズを使いなさい.

wave /weɪv/ (**waves, waving, waved**) 1 V-T/V-I 他動詞/自動

詞 If you **wave** or **wave** your hand, you move your hand from side to side in the air, usually in order to say hello or goodbye to someone. 手を振る ❏ *He grinned, waved, and said, "Hi!"* 彼はにっこり笑い, 手を振り, 「こんにちは」と言った. ● N-COUNT 可算名詞 **Wave** is also a noun. 手を振ること ❏ *Steve stopped him with a wave of the hand.* スティーブは手を振って彼を止めた. 2 V-T 他動詞 If you **wave** someone away or **wave** them on, you make a movement with your hand to indicate that they should move in a particular direction. 手に振って合図する ❏ *Leshka waved him away with a show of irritation.* レシュカはいらだちを示して彼を向こうへ行けと合図した. ❏ *He waited for a policeman to stop the traffic and wave the people on.* 彼は警官が交通を止め, 人々に進むよう指示するのを待った. 3 V-T 他動詞 If you **wave** something, you hold it up and move it rapidly from side to side. 振る ❏ *Hospital staff were outside to welcome him, waving flags and applauding.* 病院の職員は旗を振り拍手をしながら外で彼を歓迎した. 4 V-I 自動詞 If something **waves**, it moves gently from side to side or up and down. 揺れ動く ❏ *...grass and flowers waving in the wind.* 風に揺れる草花 5 N-COUNT 可算名詞 A **wave** is a raised mass of water on the surface of water, especially the sea, which is caused by the wind or by tides making the surface of the water rise and fall. 波 ❏ *...the sound of the waves breaking on the shore.* 岸辺に打ち寄せる波の音 6 N-COUNT 可算名詞 If someone's hair has **waves**, it curves slightly instead of being straight. ウエーブ ❏ *Her blue eyes shone and caught the light, and so did the platinum waves in her hair.* 彼女の青い目は光を浴びて輝き, 彼女の髪のプラチナ色のウエーブも光を浴びて輝いた. 7 N-COUNT 可算名詞 A **wave** is a sudden increase in heat or energy that spreads out from an earthquake or explosion. 波 ❏ *The shock waves of the earthquake were felt in Teheran.* 地震の余波はテヘランで感じられた. 8 N-COUNT 可算名詞 **Waves** are the form in which things such as sound, light, and radio signals travel. 波動 ❏ *Regular repeating actions such as sound waves, light waves, or radio waves have a certain frequency, or number of waves per second.* 音波, 光波, 電波などの規則的な反復活動には特定の周波数あるいは毎秒サイクル数がある. 9 N-COUNT 可算名詞 If you refer to a **wave of** a particular feeling, you mean that it increases quickly and becomes very intense, and then often decreases again. 押し寄せ ❏ *She felt a wave of panic, but forced herself to leave the room calmly.* 彼女はパニックが襲ってくるのを感じたが平静を装って部屋を出た. 10 N-COUNT 可算名詞 A **wave** is a sudden increase in a particular activity or type of behavior, especially an undesirable or unpleasant one. 動向 ❏ *...the current wave of violence.* 現在の暴力の波 11 → see also **new wave, tidal wave**

→ see Word Web: **wave**

→ see **beach, ear, earthquake, echo, ocean, radio, sound, telescope, weather**

Word Partnership　*wave* は次の語句と使われる:

N.	**wave your hand** 1
	wave a flag 3
	crest of a wave 5
	radio wave 8
	wave of attacks/bombings, wave of violence 10
V.	**smile and wave** 1
	ride a wave 5 9

wave|length /wéɪvlɛŋθ/ (**wavelengths**) 1 N-COUNT 可算名詞 A **wavelength** is the distance between a part of a wave of energy such as light or sound and the next similar part. 波長 ❏ *Sunlight consists of different wavelengths of radiation.* 日光は異なる波長の放射線で構成される. 2 N-COUNT 可算名詞 A **wavelength** is the size of radio wave that a particular radio station uses to broadcast its programs. 波長 ❏ *She found the wavelength of their broadcasts, and left the radio tuned to their station.* 彼女は彼らの放送番組の波長を見つけ, ラジオをその局に合わせたままにしておいた. 3 PHRASE 句 If two people are **on the same wavelength**, they find it easy to understand each other and they tend to agree, because they share similar interests or opinions. 一と波長が合って ❏ *We could complete each other's sentences because we were on the same wavelength.* 私たちはウマが合うのでお互いの会話のセンテンスを締めくくることができた.

W

Word Web   wave

As **wind** blows across water, it creates **waves**. It does this by transferring energy to the water. If the waves encounter an object, they bounce off it. Light also travels in waves and behaves the same way. We are able to see an object only if light waves bounce off it. Light waves can be categorized by their **frequency**. Wave frequency is usually the measure of the number of waves per second. **Radio waves** and **microwaves** are examples of low-frequency light waves. **Visible light** consists of medium-frequency light waves. **Ultraviolet radiation** and **X-rays** are high-frequency light waves.

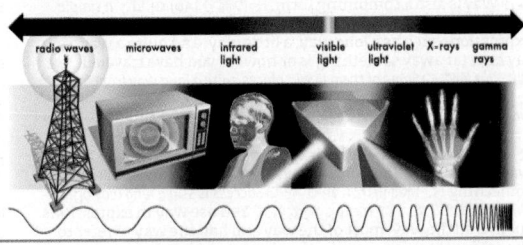

THE ELECTROMAGNETIC SPECTRUM

radio waves   microwaves   infrared light   visible light   ultraviolet light   X-rays   gamma rays

wa|ver /ˈweɪvər/ (**wavers, wavering, wavered**) **1** V-I 自動詞 If you **waver**, you cannot decide about something or you consider changing your mind about something. 迷う □ *Some military commanders wavered over whether to support the coup.* 一部の軍の指揮官はクーデターを支持すべきかどうか迷った. **2** V-I 自動詞 If something **wavers**, it shakes with very slight movements or changes. 揺れ動く □ *The shadows of the dancers wavered continually.* ダンサーの影が断続的に揺れ動いた.

wav|y /ˈweɪvi/ (**wavier, waviest**) **1** ADJ 形容詞 **Wavy** hair is not straight or curly, but curves slightly. ウェーブした □ *She had short, wavy brown hair.* 彼女はウエーブした短い茶色の髪をしていた. **2** ADJ 形容詞 A **wavy** line has a series of regular curves along it. 波のような □ *The boxes were decorated with a wavy gold line.* 箱には波状の金の線の装飾が施されていた.

wax /wæks/ (**waxes, waxing, waxed**) **1** N-MASS 質量名詞 **Wax** is a solid, slightly shiny substance made of fat or oil that is used to make candles and polish. It melts when it is heated. ロウ □ *There were colored candles which had spread pools of wax on the furniture.* 色のついたキャンドルのロウの海が家具の上に広がっていた. **2** → see also **beeswax** **3** V-T 他動詞 If you **wax** a surface, you put a thin layer of wax onto it, especially in order to polish it. ワックスで磨く □ *We'd have long talks while she helped me wax the floor.* 私達は彼女に床をワックスで磨くのを手伝ってもらいながら長話をした. **4** N-UNCOUNT 不可算名詞 **Wax** is the sticky yellow substance found in your ears. 耳あか □ *Use a Q-Tip to remove the wax from your ears.* 綿棒で耳あかを取りなさい. **5** V-T 他動詞 If you have a part of your body **waxed**, for example your legs, you have the hair removed from the area by having wax put on it and then pulled off quickly. ロウで固めてむだ毛を抜く □ *She has just had her legs waxed at the local beauty parlor.* 彼女は近くの美容院で足のむだ毛を抜いてもらったばかりだ.

way

❶ NOUN AND ADVERB USES
❷ PHRASES: GROUP 1
❸ PHRASES: GROUP 2
❹ PHRASES: GROUP 3
❺ PHRASES: GROUP 4

❶ **way** /weɪ/ (**ways**) **1** N-COUNT 可算名詞 If you refer to a **way** of doing something, you are referring to how you can do it, for example, the action you can take or the method you can use to achieve it. (〜する) やり方 方法 □ *Freezing isn't a bad way of preserving food.* 冷凍は食料の保存方法としては悪くない. □ *I worked myself into a frenzy plotting ways to make him jealous.* 私は彼にしっとさせる方法をたくらむことに躍起になった. □ *There just might be a way.* 何か方法があるかもしれない. **2** N-COUNT 可算名詞 If you talk about the **way** someone does something, you are talking about the qualities their action has. (何かをする時の) 特徴 姿勢 □ *She smiled in a friendly way.* 彼女はにこやかにほほえんだ. □ *He had a strange way of talking.* 彼の話し方は変だった. **3** N-COUNT 可算名詞 If a general statement or description is true in a particular **way**, this is the form of it that is true in a particular case. (〜という) 点 □ *Computerized reservation systems help airline profits in several ways.* コンピュータ化された予約システムはさまざまな点で航空会社の利益に貢献する. □ *She was afraid in a way that was quite new to her.* 彼女はこれまでにないような恐怖を感じた. **4** N-COUNT 可算名詞 You use **way** in expressions such as **in some ways**, **in many ways**, and **in every way** to indicate the degree or extent to which a statement is true. (ある) 意味 □ *In some ways, the official opening is a formality.* ある意味, 公式なオープニングというのは形式的なものだ. **5** N-PLURAL 複数名詞 The **ways** of a particular person or group of people are their customs or their usual behavior. 習慣, 癖 □ *He denounces people who urge him to alter his ways.* 彼は, 彼のやり方を変えようと迫る人を非難する. □ *She began to study the ways of the Native Americans.* 彼女はアメリカ先住民の習慣を調べ始

めた. **6** N-SING 単数名詞 If you refer to someone's **way**, you are referring to their usual or preferred type of behavior. (個人の決まった) やり方 □ *She is now divorced and, in her usual resourceful way, has started her own business.* 今, 彼女は離婚しており, 彼女らしい機知に富んだやり方で, 自分の事業を始めた. **7** N-COUNT 可算名詞 You use **way** to refer to one particular opinion or interpretation of something, when others are possible. (解釈などの) しかた □ *I suppose that's one way of looking at it.* それも1つの見方だと思うよ. □ *With most of Dylan's lyrics, however, there are other ways of interpreting the words.* しかし, ディランの歌詞のほとんどは, 他にも解釈の仕方がある. **8** N-COUNT 可算名詞 You use **way** when mentioning one of a number of possible, alternative results or decisions. (可能性や決定の) 選択肢 方向性 □ *There is no indication which way the vote could go.* その票がどちらに行くかはまったく予測がつかない. **9** N-SING 単数名詞 The **way** you feel about something is your attitude to it or your opinion about it. (物事に対する) 感じ方 考え方 □ *I'm so sorry – I had no idea you felt that way.* 本当にごめんなさい. あなたがそんなふうに感じていたなんて思ってもみなかったわ. **10** N-SING 単数名詞 If you mention **the way** that something happens, you are mentioning the fact that it happens. 〜すること □ *I hate the way he manipulates people.* 私は彼が人を巧みに操るのが嫌いだ. **11** N-SING 単数名詞 You use **way** in expressions such as **push your way**, **work your way**, or **eat your way**, followed by a prepositional phrase or adverb, in order to indicate movement, progress, or force as well as the action described by the verb. 前置詞句や副詞を後ろに伴い, 前の動詞の動きを意味する. □ *She thrust her way into the crowd.* 彼女は群衆の中に分け入った. **12** N-COUNT 可算名詞 The **way** somewhere consists of the different places that you go through or the route that you take in order to get there. 行き, 道順 □ *Does anybody know the way to the bathroom?* 化粧室への行き方を誰か知ってる? □ *I'm afraid I can't remember the way.* 悪いけど, 道を思い出せないんだ. **13** N-SING 単数名詞 If you go or look a particular **way**, you go or look in that direction. 方向, 方角 □ *As he strode into the kitchen, he passed Pop coming the other way.* 彼は大またで台所に入って行く時, 向こうから来るポップとすれ違った. □ *They paused at the top of the stairs, doubtful as to which way to go next.* 彼らは, 次にどこへ行くかが分からず階段の上で立ち止まった. **14** N-SING 単数名詞 You can refer to the direction you are traveling in as your **way**. (人が) 行く方向 [SPOKEN 口語] □ *She would say she was going my way and offer me a lift.* 彼女なら, 同じ方向に行くからと言って私を送ってくれるだろう. **15** N-SING 単数名詞 If you lose your **way**, you take a wrong or unfamiliar route, so that you do not know how to get to the place that you want to go to. If you find your **way**, you manage to get to the place that you want to go to. (場所への) 行き方 □ *The men lost their way in a sandstorm and crossed the border by mistake.* 男たちは砂嵐の中で道に迷い, 誤って国境を越えた. **16** N-COUNT 可算名詞 You talk about people going their different **ways** in order to say that their lives develop differently and they have less contact with each other. (別々の) 生き方 道 □ *It wasn't until we each went our separate ways that I began to learn how to do things for myself.* 私が物事を自分でするということを学び始めたのは, 私たちがそれぞれの道を歩み始めてからだった. **17** N-SING 単数名詞 If something comes your **way**, you get it or receive it. (人の) ところ 下 (もと) □ *Take advantage of the opportunities coming your way in a couple of months.* 2か月後にあなたの下に来るチャンスを生かそう. **18** N-SING 単数名詞 You use **way** in expressions such as **the right way up** and **the other way around** to refer to one of two or more possible positions or arrangements that something can have. 配置, 配列 □ *Books have a right and a wrong way up.* 本には正しい向きがある. **19** ADV 副詞 You can use **way** to emphasize, for example, that something is a great distance away or is very much below or above a particular level or amount. (場所やレベルなどが) はるかに ずっと [EMPHASIS 強調] [ADV adv/prep] □ *Way down in the valley to the west is the town of Freiburg.* 谷を西へずっと下ったところにフライブルグの町がある. □ *You've waited way too long.* きみは長く待ちすぎたんだよ. **20** N-PLURAL 複数名詞 If you split something a number of **ways**, you divide it into a number of different parts or quantities,

W

usually fairly equal in size. （分割された）部分 ❑ *The region was split three ways, between Greece, Serbia and Bulgaria.* その地方はギリシャとセルビアとブルガリアの間で3分割された. ● **COMB IN ADJ** 形容詞の複合 **Way** is also a combining form. 一の部分 [ADJ n] ❑ *...a simple three-way division.* 単純な3分割 ㉑ **N-SING** 単数名詞 **Way** is used in expressions such as **a long way, a little way,** and **quite a way,** to say how far away something is or how far you have traveled. （地理的な）距離 ❑ *Some of them live in places quite a long way from here.* 彼らのうちの何人かはここからかなり離れた所に住んでいる. ❑ *A little way further down the lane we passed the driveway to a house.* その通りをもう少し下ったところで, 私たちは家につながる私有車道を通り過ぎた. ㉒ **N-SING** 単数名詞 **Way** is used in expressions such as **a long way, a little way,** and **quite a way,** to say how far away in time something is. （時間的な）距離 先 ❑ *Success is still a long way off.* 成功はまだまだ先だ. ㉓ **N-SING** 単数名詞 **way** in expressions such as **all the way, most of the way** and **half the way** to refer to the extent to which an action has been completed. （これまでの）地点 ❑ *He had unscrewed the caps most of the way.* 彼はほとんどのふたを外していた.

Thesaurus

way また次を参照:

N.	method, practice, style, technique ❶ ① ② ⑤ ⑥
	behavior, characteristic, habit, personality ❶ ②

---

❷ **way** /weɪ/ (ways) ① **PHRASE** 句 You use **all the way** to emphasize how long a distance is. （遠い所）はるばる [EMPHASIS 強調] ❑ *He had to walk all the way home.* 彼は家までずっと歩いて帰らなくてはならなかった. ② **PHRASE** 句 You can use **all the way** to emphasize that your remark applies to every part of a situation, activity, or period of time. 最後まで [EMPHASIS 強調] ❑ *Having started a revolution we must go all the way.* 革命を起こしたのだから, 行き着くところまで行かなくてはならない. ③ **PHRASE** 句 If someone says that you **can't have it both ways,** they are telling you that you have to choose between two things and cannot do or have them both. 両方は取れない ❑ *Countries cannot have it both ways: the cost of a cleaner environment may sometimes be fewer jobs in dirty industries.* 国は両方を取ることはできない. より汚染の少ない環境の代償は結果として公害産業の仕事の減少となる. ④ **PHRASE** 句 You say **by the way** when you add something to what you are saying, especially something that you have just thought of. ところで [SPOKEN 口語] ❑ *The name Latifah, by the way, means "delicate."* ところで, ラティファという名前は「繊細な」という意味だ. ⑤ **PHRASE** 句 If you **clear the way, open the way,** or **prepare the way** for something, you create an opportunity for it to happen. 道を開く ❑ *The talks are meant to clear the way for formal negotiations on a new constitution.* その話し合いは新しい憲法への正式な交渉の道を開くためにある. ⑥ **PHRASE** 句 If you say that someone takes **the easy way out,** you disapprove of them because they do what is easiest for them in a difficult situation, rather than dealing with it properly. 安易な解決策, お茶を濁すこと [DISAPPROVAL 不賛成] ❑ *As soon as things got difficult he took the easy way out.* 事態が難しくなるや否や, 彼は安易な解決策をとった. ⑦ **PHRASE** 句 You use **either way** in order to introduce a statement that is true in each of the two possible or alternative cases that you have just mentioned. どちらにしても ❑ *The sea may rise or the land may fall; either way the sand dunes will be gone in a short time.* 海面が高くなるか地面が沈下するか. どちらにしても砂丘は短時間で消え去るだろう. ⑧ **PHRASE** 句 If you say that a particular type of action or development is **the way forward,** you approve of it because it is likely to lead to success. 前進, 解決策 [APPROVAL 賛成] ❑ *...people who genuinely believe that anarchy is the way forward.* 無政府状態が前進につながると心から信じる人たち ⑨ **PHRASE** 句 If someone **gets** their way or **has** their way, nobody stops them from doing what they want to do. You can also say that someone **gets** their own way or **has** their own way. やりたいようにする, 好き勝手にする ❑ *She is very good at using her charm to get her way.* 彼女は自分の魅力を使って思い通りにするのがとてもうまい. ⑩ **PHRASE** 句 If one thing **gives way to** another, the first thing is replaced by the second. 一に取って代わられる, 一に譲る ❑ *First he had been numb. Then the numbness gave way to anger.* 最初, 彼はぼう然とした. 次にそれは怒りに変わって代わられた. ⑪ **PHRASE** 句 If an object that is supporting something **gives way,** it breaks or collapses, so that it can no longer support that thing. （物体が）壊れる 崩壊する ❑ *The hook in the ceiling had given way and the lamp had fallen blazing on to the table.* 天井の留め金が壊れ, ランプが赤々と燃えながらテーブルの上に落ちた.

❸ **way** /weɪ/ (ways) ① **PHRASE** 句 You use **in no way** or **not in any way** to emphasize that a statement is not at all true. まったく一ない [EMPHASIS 強調] ❑ *In no way am I going to adopt any of his methods.* 彼のやり方なんて取り入れるつもりはまったくない. ② **PHRASE** 句 If you say that something is true **in a way,** you mean that although it is not completely true, it is true to a limited extent or in certain respects. You use **in a way** to reduce the force of a statement. ある意味で, ある点で [VAGUENESS あいまいさ] ❑ *In a way, I suppose I'm frightened of failing.* ある意味, 私は失敗するのを恐れているんだと思う. ③ **PHRASE** 句 If you say

that someone **gets in the way** or **is in the way,** you are annoyed because their presence or their actions stop you from doing something properly. 邪魔になって ❑ *"We wouldn't get in the way,"* Suzanne promised. "We'd just stand quietly in a corner." 「私たちは邪魔したりしないわ」とスザンヌは約束した. 「隅っこに静かに立ってるだけよ. 」 ④ **PHRASE** 句 To **get in the way of** something means to make it difficult for it to happen, continue, or be appreciated properly. （一の）邪魔になる 足を引っ張る ❑ *She had a job which never got in the way of her leisure interests.* 彼女は余暇の趣味に支障をきたさない仕事をしていた. ⑤ **PHRASE** 句 If you **know** your **way around** a particular subject, system, or job, you know all the procedures and facts about it. （科目や制度などに）精通している 熟知している ❑ *He knows his way around the intricate maze of patent law.* 彼は迷路のように複雑な特許法を熟知している. ⑥ **PHRASE** 句 If you **lead the way** along a particular route, you go along it in front of someone in order to show them where to go. 案内する ❑ *She grabbed his suitcase and led the way.* 彼女は彼のスーツケースをつかんで案内した. ⑦ **PHRASE** 句 If a person or group **leads the way** in a particular activity, they are the first person or group to do it or they make the most new developments in it. （活動や開発の）先頭を行く ❑ *Sony has also led the way in shrinking the size of compact-disc players.* ソニーもまたCDプレーヤーのサイズ縮小の先駆けとなった. ⑧ **PHRASE** 句 If you say that someone or something **has come a long way,** you mean that they have developed, progressed, or become very successful. 大きな進歩を遂げる, 大きな成功を収める ❑ *He has come a long way since the days he could only afford one meal a day.* 彼は1日1食分のお金しかない日々から大きな成功を収めた. ⑨ **PHRASE** 句 If you say that something is **a long way from** being true, you are emphasizing that it is definitely not true. （真実から）程遠い [EMPHASIS 強調] ❑ *She is a long way from being the richest person in Florida.* 彼女はフロリダで一番のお金持ちというには程遠い. ⑩ **PHRASE** 句 If you say that something **goes a long way toward** doing a particular thing, you mean that it is an important factor in achieving that thing. 大きな役割を果たす ❑ *Being respectful and courteous goes a long way toward building a relationship.* 尊敬の念を持つことと礼儀正しくあることは, 人間関係を築く上で大いに役立つ.

❹ **way** /weɪ/ (ways) ① **PHRASE** 句 If you say that someone has **lost** their **way,** you are criticizing them because they do not have any good ideas anymore, or seem to have become unsure about what to do. 良い考えが浮かばない, 途方にくれる [DISAPPROVAL 不賛成] ❑ *Why has the White House lost its way on tax and budget policy?* ホワイトハウスはなぜ税務政策と予算政策に関する方向性を見失ってしまったのか? ② **PHRASE** 句 When you **make** your **way** somewhere, you walk or travel there. 歩いて行く, 移動する ❑ *He made his way to the marketplace.* 彼は市場まで歩いて行った. ③ **PHRASE** 句 If one person or thing **makes way for** another, the first is replaced by the second. （一に）譲る 取って代わられる ❑ *He said he was prepared to make way for younger people in the party.* 彼は若者に道を譲る用意があることをパーティーで述べた. ④ **PHRASE** 句 If you say **there's no way** that something will happen, you are emphasizing that you think it will definitely not happen. 決して一ない [EMPHASIS 強調] ❑ *There was absolutely no way that we were going to be able to retrieve it.* 私たちがそれを取り戻せる可能性はまったくなかった. ⑤ **PHRASE** 句 You can say **no way** as an emphatic way of saying no. 絶対だめ [INFORMAL くだけた, EMPHASIS 強調] ❑ *Mike, no way am I playing cards with you for money.* マイク, お金のためにきみとトランプでかけをするなんて絶対いやだよ. ⑥ **PHRASE** 句 If you **are on** your **way,** you have started your trip somewhere. （一に）向かっている最中である （一の）途中にいる ❑ *He has been allowed to leave the country and is on his way to Hawaii.* 彼は国を離れることを許され, ハワイに向かっているところだ. ⑦ **PHRASE** 句 If something happens **on the way** or **along the way,** it happens during the course of a particular event or process. （出来事や工程の）途中で ❑ *You may have to learn a few new skills along the way.* あなたはその過程で新しい技術をいくつか習わないといけないかもしれない. ⑧ **PHRASE** 句 If you are **on your way** or **well on your way** to something, you have made so much progress that you are almost certain to achieve that thing. （目的などに）向かっている 近づいている ❑ *I am now out of the hospital and well on the way to recovery.* 私はもう退院して, 回復に向かっている. ⑨ **PHRASE** 句 If something is **on the way,** it will arrive soon. 間もなく到着する ❑ *The forecasters say more snow is on the way.* 気象予報士によると間もなくまた雪が降る. ⑩ **PHRASE** 句 You can use **one way or another** or **one way or the other** when you want to say that something definitely happens, but without giving any details about how it happens. どうにかして, 何らかの方法で [VAGUENESS あいまいさ] ❑ *You know pretty well everyone here, one way or the other.* どういう訳か, きみはここの人たちみんなをよく知っている. ⑪ **PHRASE** 句 You use **one way or the other** or **one way or another** to refer to two possible decisions or conclusions that have previously been mentioned, without stating which one is reached or preferred. どちらにしても, いずれにせよ ❑ *We've got to make our decision one way or the other.* どちらにしても, それを決めないといけない.

❺ way /weɪ/ (**ways**) **1** PHRASE 句 You use **the other way around** to refer to the opposite of what you have just said. 逆に，反対に □ *You'd think you were the one who did me the favor, and not the other way around.* きみは，私に手を貸したのであって，その逆ではないと思っているだろう。 **2** PHRASE 句 If something or someone is **on the way out** or on their **way out**, they are likely to disappear or to be replaced very soon. 消滅しかけている，取って代わられつつある □ *There are encouraging signs that cold war attitudes are on the way out.* 冷戦の構えが消えつつあるという明るい兆しがある。 **3** PHRASE 句 If you **go out of** your **way to** do something, for example, to help someone, you make a special effort to do it. 特別に努力する，わざわざ〜する □ *He was very kind to me and seemed to go out of his way to help me.* 彼は私にとても親切にしてくれ，わざわざ手伝ってくれた。 **4** PHRASE 句 If you **keep out of** someone's **way** or **stay out of** their **way**, you avoid them or do not get involved with them. 〜を避ける，〜に巻き込まれない □ *I'd kept out of his way as much as I could.* 私はできるだけ彼を避けていた。 **5** PHRASE 句 When something is **out of the way**, it has finished or you have dealt with it, so that it is no longer a problem or needs no more time spent on it. （問題などが）処理されて片付いて □ *The plan has to remain confidential at least until the local elections are out of the way.* 少なくとも地方選挙が終わるまではその計画を伏せておかなくてはならない。 **6** PHRASE 句 If you **go your own way**, you do what you want rather than what everyone else does or expects. 自分のやりたいことをする，わが道を行く □ *In school I was a loner. I went my own way.* おれは学校では一匹おおかみだった。自分のやりたいことをしていた。 **7** PHRASE 句 You use **in the same way** to introduce a situation that you are comparing with one that you have just mentioned, because there is a strong similarity between them. 同様に □ *There is no reason why an aircraft designer should also be a good pilot. In the same way, a good pilot can be a bad driver.* 飛行機の設計技師は優秀なパイロットでもあるべきという道理はない。同様に，優秀なパイロットが車の運転は下手ということだってあり得る。 **8** PHRASE 句 You can use **that way** and **this way** to refer to a statement or comment that you have just made. そのように/このように □ *We have a beautiful city and we pray it stays that way.* 私たちには美しい都市がある。そしてそれがそのまま続くことを祈る。 **9** PHRASE 句 You can use **that way** or **this way** to refer to an action or situation that you have just mentioned, when you go on to mention the likely consequence or effect of it. そうすると／こうすると □ *Keep the soil moist. That way, the seedling will flourish.* 土を湿った状態に保つ。そうすることで，苗がすくすく育つ。 **10** → see also **underway**

way of life (**ways of life**) **1** N-COUNT 可算名詞 A **way of life** is the behavior and habits that are typical of a particular person or group, or that are chosen by them. （人の）生き方 生活様式 □ *Mining activities have totally disrupted the traditional way of life of the Yanomami Indians.* 採鉱活動はヤノマミ・インディアンの伝統的な生活様式を完全に破壊した。 **2** N-COUNT 可算名詞 If you describe a particular activity as a **way of life** for someone, you mean that it has become a very important and regular thing in their life, rather than something they do or experience occasionally. 生きがい □ *She likes traveling so much it's become a way of life for her.* 彼女は旅行が大好きで，それが生きがいになっている。

way|ward /weɪwərd/ ADJ 形容詞 If you describe a person or their behavior as **wayward**, you mean that they behave in a selfish, bad, or unpredictable way, and are difficult to control. わがままな，気まぐれな □ *...wayward children with a history of severe emotional problems.* 深刻な情緒問題の経歴があるわがままな子供たち

we /wɪ, STRONG wiː/

We is the first person plural pronoun. **We** is used as the subject of a verb.

We は1人称複数代名詞である。 **We** は動詞の主語として使われる。

1 PRON-PLURAL 複数代名詞 A speaker or writer uses **we** to refer both to himself or herself and to one or more other people as a group. You can use **we** before a noun to make it clear which group of people you are referring to. （Iの複数形）私たち 我々 □ *We both swore we'd be friends ever after.* 私たち2人はずっと友達でいることを誓った。 □ *We ordered another bottle of champagne.* 私たちはシャンパンをもう1本注文した。 **2** PRON-PLURAL 複数代名詞 **We** is sometimes used to refer to people in general. 私たち（世間一般の人々を指す） □ *We need to take care of our bodies.* 私たちはみな自分の体を大事にする必要がある。 **3** PRON-PLURAL 複数代名詞 A speaker or writer may use **we** instead of "I" in order to include the audience or reader in what they are saying, especially when discussing how a talk or book is organized. 私たち（話し手や作家が聴衆や読者を引き込むために使う）[FORMAL 形式ばった] □ *We will now consider the raw materials from which the body derives energy.* 私たちはこれから体のエネルギー源となる原料について検討します。

weak /wiːk/ (**weaker, weakest**) **1** ADJ 形容詞 If someone is **weak**, they are not healthy or do not have good muscles, so that they cannot move quickly or carry heavy things. （体が）弱い 虚弱な □ *I was too weak to move or think or speak.* 私はあまりにも弱りすぎ

て，動くことも考えることもしゃべることもできなかった。 ●**weak|ly** ADV 副詞 [ADV with v] 弱々しく □ *"I'm all right," Max said weakly, but his breathing came in jagged gasps.* 「大丈夫だよ」とマックスは弱々しく言ったが，彼の呼吸はゼエゼエと息切れしていた。 ●**weak|ness** N-UNCOUNT 不可算名詞 虚弱，体力のなさ □ *Symptoms of anemia include weakness, fatigue and iron deficiency.* 貧血の症状には虚弱，倦怠（けんたい）感，鉄分の欠乏がある。 **2** ADJ 形容詞 If someone has an organ or sense that is **weak**, it is not very effective or powerful, or is likely to fail. （臓器や感覚が）弱い 鈍い □ *She tired easily and had a weak heart.* 彼女は疲れやすく，心臓が弱かった。 **3** ADJ 形容詞 If you describe someone as **weak**, you mean that they are not very confident or determined, so that they are often frightened or worried, or easily influenced by other people. 自信のない，意志の弱い □ *He was a nice doctor, but a weak man who wasn't going to stick his neck out.* 彼は親切な医者だったが，あえて危険を冒したりしない気の弱い人だった。 ●**weak|ness** N-UNCOUNT 不可算名詞 自信のなさ，意志薄弱 □ *Many people felt that admitting to stress was a sign of weakness.* 多くの人が緊張を認めることは自信のなさの表れだと感じた。 **4** ADJ 形容詞 If you describe someone's voice or smile as **weak**, you mean that it not very loud or big, suggesting that the person lacks confidence, enthusiasm, or physical strength. （声が）か細い（笑みが）弱々しい □ *His weak voice was almost inaudible.* 彼のか細い声はほとんど聞き取れなかった。 ●**weak|ly** ADV 副詞 [ADV after v] か細く，弱々しく □ *He smiled weakly at reporters.* 彼は記者たちに弱々しくほほえみかけた。 **5** ADJ 形容詞 If an object or surface is **weak**, it breaks easily and cannot support a lot of weight or resist a lot of strain. （物や表面が）もろい 弱い □ *The owner said the bird may have escaped through a weak spot in the aviary.* 持ち主は，その鳥が鳥小屋のもろい部分を通って逃げたのかもしれないと言った。 **6** ADJ 副詞 A **weak** physical force does not have much power or intensity. （物理的な力が）弱い かすかな □ *The molecules in regular liquids are held together by relatively weak bonds.* 通常の液体の分子は比較的弱い結合力でお互いにつながっている。 ●**weak|ly** ADV 副詞 弱く，かすかに □ *The mineral is weakly magnetic.* そのミネラルはかすかに磁気を帯びている。 **7** ADJ 形容詞 If individuals or groups are **weak**, they do not have any power or influence. 無力な，影響力のない □ *The council was too weak to do anything about it.* 議会はそれをどうにかする力に欠けていた。 ●**N-PLURAL** 複数名詞 **The weak** are people who are weak. 無力な人々，弱い立場の人たち □ *He voiced his solidarity with the weak and defenseless.* 彼は無力で無防備な人々との団結を表明した。 ●**weak|ness** N-UNCOUNT 不可算名詞 （人や組織の）無力さ □ *It made me feel patronized, in a position of weakness.* 弱い立場にある私は，それによって見下されたような気持ちになった。 **8** ADJ 形容詞 A **weak** government or leader does not have much control, and is not prepared or able to act firmly or severely. （政府や指導者が）指導力に欠ける 支配力のない □ *The changes come after mounting criticism that the government is weak and indecisive.* 変化は，政府が指導力と決断力に欠けるという批判が高まった後にやって来る。 ●**weak|ly** ADV 副詞 …*the weakly-led movement for reform.* 改革への率先力に欠ける動き ●**weak|ness** N-UNCOUNT 不可算名詞 指導力のなさ，支配力の欠如 □ *Officials fear that he might interpret the emphasis on diplomacy as a sign of weakness.* 担当官たちは，彼が外交重視を指導力のなさの表れだと解釈しないか恐れている。 **9** ADJ 形容詞 If you describe something such as a country's currency, economy, industry, or government as **weak**, you mean that it is not successful, and may be likely to fail or collapse. （通貨が）弱い 安い，（経済が）低迷している □ *The weak dollar means American goods are relative bargains for foreigners.* ドル安は外国人にとってアメリカ製品が比較的安いことを意味する。 ●**weak|ness** N-UNCOUNT 不可算名詞 低迷，弱体化 □ *The weakness of his regime is showing more and more.* 彼の政権が弱体化していることはますます明らかになりつつある。 **10** ADJ 形容詞 If something such as an argument or case is **weak**, it is not convincing or there is little evidence to support it. （議論や訴訟が）説得力に欠ける 証拠に欠ける □ *Do you think the prosecution made any particular errors, or did they just have a weak case?* あなたは，検察側が何か際立ったミスをしたと思いますか？それとも彼らの訴訟自体が証拠に欠けるものだったのでしょうか？ ●**weak|ly** ADV 副詞 [ADV before v] 説得力に欠ける方法で □ *Bush listened to that statement and responded rather weakly.* ブッシュはその発言に耳を傾け，かなり説得力に欠ける応答をした。 ●**weak|ness** (**weaknesses**) N-VAR 可変性名詞 説得力に欠ける部分，証拠に欠ける部分 □ *Critical thinking requires that you examine the weaknesses of any argument.* 批判的思考法には，すべての議論の説得力に欠ける部分を自分で分析することが必要となる。 **11** ADJ 形容詞 A **weak** drink, chemical, or drug contains very little of a particular substance, for example, because a lot of water has been added to it. （飲み物や薬剤などが）薄い 水っぽい □ *Grace poured a cup of weak tea.* グレースは薄い紅茶をカップに注いだ。 **12** ADJ 形容詞 Your **weak** points are the qualities or talents you do not possess, or the things you are not very good at. 苦手な，不得手な □ *Geography was my weak subject.* 地理は私の苦手な科目だった。 ●**weak|ness** N-VAR 可変性名詞 弱点，欠点 □ *His only weakness is his temperament.* 彼の唯一の欠点は気性の激しさだ。 **13** → see also **weakness**
→ see **muscle**

W

Thesaurus

weak また次を参照:

| ADJ. | feeble, frail, puny; (*ant.*) strong **1**
cowardly, insecure, wimpy; (*ant.*) strong **3** |

Word Partnership

weak は次の語句と使われる:

| ADV. | **relatively** weak, **still** weak, **too** weak, **very** weak **1** – **12** |
| N. | weak **dollar**, weak **economy**, weak **sales**, weak **spending** **9** |

weak|en /wíkən/ (**weakens, weakening, weakened**) **1** V-T/V-I 他動詞/自動詞 If you **weaken** something or if it **weakens**, it becomes less strong or less powerful. 弱める、弱体化させる [他動詞]、弱くなる、弱体化する [自動詞] ❑ *The recession has weakened so many businesses that many can no longer survive.* 景気の後退で非常にたくさんの事業が弱体化しており、その多くはもや存続不能となっている。❑ *Family structures are weakening and breaking up.* 家族のきずなは弱くなり断ち切られつつある。**2** V-T/V-I 他動詞/自動詞 If your resolve **weakens** or if something **weakens** it, you become less determined or less certain about taking a particular course of action that you had previously decided to take. (決心を) 鈍らせる 心もとなくさせる [他動詞]、鈍る、心もとなくなる [自動詞] ❑ *I looked at the list and felt my resolve weakening.* 私はそのリストを見て、決心が鈍るのを感じた。❑ *Jennie weakened, and finally relented.* ジェニーは弱気になり、とうとう折れた。**3** V-T 他動詞 If something **weakens** you, it causes you to lose some of your physical strength. (体力を) 弱らせる ❑ *Malnutrition obviously weakens the patient.* 栄養失調は明らかに患者を衰弱させる。**4** V-T 他動詞 If something **weakens** an object, it does something to it that causes it to become less firm and more likely to break. (物体を) もろくする ❑ *A bomb blast had weakened an area of brick on the back wall.* 爆風により、後ろの壁のレンガの部分がもろくなっていた。

Word Partnership

weaken は次の語句と使われる:

| N. | weaken **the economy** **1**
weaken *someone's* **ability**, weaken *someone's* **resolve** **2** |

weak|ling /wíklɪŋ/ (**weaklings**) N-COUNT 可算名詞 If you describe a person or an animal as a **weakling**, you mean that they are physically weak. 体の弱い人・動物 [DISAPPROVAL 非難] ❑ *You were never a ninety-eight pound weakling.* あなたは98ポンドのひ弱な人間では決してなかったのよ。

weak|ness /wíknɪs/ (**weaknesses**) **1** N-COUNT 可算名詞 If you have a **weakness** for something, you like it very much, although this is perhaps surprising or undesirable. (一に) 目がないこと 偏愛 ❑ *Stephen himself had a weakness for cats.* ステファン自身は猫に目がなかった。**2** → see also **weak**

wealth /wélθ/ **1** N-UNCOUNT 不可算名詞 **Wealth** is the possession of a large amount of money, property, or other valuable things. You can also refer to a particular person's money or property as their **wealth**. 財産、富 ❑ *Economic reform has brought relative wealth to peasant farmers.* 経済改革は貧しい小作民にそれなりの富をもたらした。**2** N-SING 単数名詞 If you say that someone or something has **a wealth of** good qualities or things, you are emphasizing that they have a very large number or amount of them. 豊富 [FORMAL 形式ばった, EMPHASIS 強調] ['a' N 'of' n] ❑ *Their websites contain a wealth of information on the topic.* 彼らのウェブサイトにはその話題に関する情報がたくさん載っている。❑ *The city boasts a wealth of beautiful churches.* その市にはたくさんの美しい教会がある。

→ see **economics**

Thesaurus

wealth また次を参照:

| N. | affluence, funds, money; (*ant.*) poverty **1** |

wealthy /wélθi/ (**wealthier, wealthiest**) ADJ 形容詞 Someone who is **wealthy** has a large amount of money, property, or valuable possessions. 裕福な、お金持ちの ❑ *...a wealthy international businessman.* 裕福で国際的な実業家 ● N-PLURAL 複数名詞 **The wealthy** are people who are wealthy. 裕福な人々 ❑ *The best education should not be available only to the wealthy.* 最高の教育が富裕層だけに開かれているようではいけない。

wean /wín/ (**weans, weaning, weaned**) **1** V-T 他動詞 When a baby or young animal **is weaned**, its mother stops feeding it milk and starts giving it other food, especially solid food. (人間や動物の赤ちゃんを) 離乳させる ❑ *When would be the best time to start weaning my baby?* うちの子供の離乳を始めるのに一番よい時期はいつですか？ **2** V-T 他動詞 If you **wean** someone off a habit or something they like, you gradually make them stop doing it or liking it, especially when you think is bad for them. (人に一を) 徐々にやめさせる ❑ *You are given capsules or pills with small quantities of nicotine to wean you from the habit.* あなたがその習慣を徐々にやめる

よう、少量のニコチンを含むカプセルか錠剤が出される。

weap|on /wépən/ (**weapons**) N-COUNT 可算名詞 A **weapon** is an object such as a gun, a knife, or a missile, which is used to kill or hurt people in a fight or a war. 武器、凶器 ❑ *...nuclear weapons.* 核兵器

→ see **army, war**

weap|on|ry /wépənri/ N-UNCOUNT 不可算名詞 **Weaponry** is all weapons that a group or country has or that are available to it. (集団や国が持つ) すべての兵器 ❑ *...rich nations, armed with superior weaponry.* 優れた兵器を装備している富裕国

wear /wéər/ (**wears, wearing, wore, worn**) **1** V-T 他動詞 When you **wear** something such as clothes, shoes, or jewelry, you have them on your body or on part of your body. (着物や装飾品を) 身につける 着る ❑ *He was wearing a brown uniform.* 彼は茶色の制服を着ていた。❑ *I sometimes wear contact lenses.* 私は時々コンタクトレンズをつける。

After you get up in the morning, you **get dressed**, or you **dress**, by **putting on** your clothes. ❑ *He put on his shoes and socks.* Small children and sick people may be unable to **dress themselves**, so someone else has to **dress** them. When you **are wearing** your clothes, or you **have** them **on**. ❑ *Edith had her hat on... They ought to stop walking around the house with nothing on.* During the day you might want to **get changed**, or to **change** your clothes. ❑ *She returned having changed from pants into a skirt... Adams changed his shirt a couple of times a day.* Before you go to bed, you **get undressed**, or you **undress**, by **taking off** your clothes. ❑ *He won't take his clothes off in front of me.* See also note at **clothes**.

2 V-T 他動詞 If you **wear** your hair or beard in a particular way, you have it cut or styled in that way. (髪やひげを一の) スタイルにする ❑ *She wore her hair in a long braid.* 彼女は髪を三つ編みにしていた。**3** N-UNCOUNT 不可算名詞 You use **wear** to refer to clothes that are suitable for a certain time or place. For example, **evening wear** is clothes suitable for the evening. (それぞれの機会にふさわしい) 服 ❑ *The shop stocks an extensive range of beach wear.* その店は豊富な品ぞろえのビーチウェアを置いている。**4** N-UNCOUNT 不可算名詞 **Wear** is the amount or type of use that something has over a period of time. 使用度、使用の機会 ❑ *You'll get more wear out of a hat if you choose one in a neutral color.* 中間色の帽子を選ぶともっとかぶる機会が増えるだろう。**5** N-UNCOUNT 不可算名詞 **Wear** is the damage or change that is caused by something being used a lot or for a long time. 磨耗 ❑ *...a large, well-upholstered armchair which showed signs of wear.* すり切れの兆しが見える、詰め物がいっぱい入った大きなひじ掛けいす ❑ V-I 自動詞 If something **wears**, it becomes thinner or weaker because it is constantly being used over a long period of time. 磨耗する、すり減る ❑ *The stone steps, dating back to 1855, are beginning to wear.* 1855年までさかのぼる石段はすり減りかけている。**7** V-I 自動詞 You can use **wear** to talk about how well something lasts over a period of time. For example, if something **wears well**, it still seems quite new or useful after a long time or a lot of use. 長持ちする ❑ *Ten years on, the original concept was wearing well.* 10年たった今でも、元々の概念は脈々と流れていた。

▶ **wear away** PHRASAL VERB 句動詞 If you **wear** something **away** or if it **wears away**, it becomes thin and eventually disappears because it is used a lot or rubbed a lot. すり減らす、摩滅させる [他動詞]、すり切れる、摩滅する [自動詞] ❑ *It had a saddle with springs sticking out, which wore away the seat of my pants.* それにはばねが飛び出ているサドルが付いており、私のズボンのおしりの部分はそこにこすれて薄くなっていた。

▶ **wear down** **1** PHRASAL VERB 句動詞 If you **wear** something **down** or if it **wears down**, it becomes flatter or smoother as a result of constantly rubbing against something else. 摩擦で平らにする [他動詞]、すり切れて平らになる [自動詞] ❑ *Pipe smokers sometimes wear down the tips of their teeth where they grip their pipes.* パイプの喫煙者は時おり、パイプをくわえる歯がすり切れていることがある。❑ *The heels on his shoes had worn down.* 彼の靴のかかとはすり減っていた。**2** PHRASAL VERB 句動詞 If you **wear** someone **down**, you make them gradually weaker or less determined until they eventually do what you want. (人の決意などを) 次第に弱める ❑ *None can match your sheer will-power and persistence in wearing down the opposition.* 対戦相手を弱らせようとするあなたの強い意志と粘り強さに匹敵するものは何もない。❑ *They hoped the waiting and the uncertainty would wear down my resistance.* 彼らは私の抵抗が待ち時間と不安によって弱まることを願っていた。

▶ **wear off** PHRASAL VERB 句動詞 If a drug, sensation, or feeling **wears off**, it disappears slowly until it no longer exists or has any effect. (薬の効果や感情が) 徐々に消える ❑ *For many the philosophy was merely a fashion, and the novelty soon wore off.* 多くの人にとってその考え方は単なるはやりでしかなく、その目新しさはすぐに消えてしまった。

▶ **wear out** **1** PHRASAL VERB 句動詞 When something **wears out** or when you **wear** it **out**, it is used so much that it becomes thin or weak and unable to be used anymore. 使い古す、使い切る ❑ *Every time she consulted her watch, she wondered if the batteries were*

W

wearing out. 腕時計を見るたび彼女は電池が切れかけているのではないかと思った. ❑ *Horses used for long-distance riding tend to wear their shoes out more quickly.* 長距離の乗馬に使われる馬は, 蹄鉄（ていてつ）がより早くすり切れがちだ. **2** PHRASAL VERB 句動詞 If something **wears** you **out**, it makes you feel extremely tired. （人を）疲れ果てさせる [INFORMAL くだけた] ❑ *The past few days had really worn him out.* この3日間で彼は疲労こんぱいしてしまった. ❑ *The young people run around kicking a ball, wearing themselves out.* 若者たちはボールを蹴って走り回り, へとへとになっていた. **3** → see also **worn out**
→ see **makeup**

N.	wear **black/red/white**, wear **clothes**, wear **contact lenses**, wear **glasses**, wear **gloves**, wear **a hat/helmet**, wear **a jacket**, wear **jeans**, wear **makeup**, wear **a mask**, wear **a suit**, wear **a uniform** **1**
ADJ.	**casual** wear, **day** wear, **evening** wear **3**

wear and tear /wɛər ən tɛər/ N-UNCOUNT 不可算名詞 **Wear and tear** is the damage or change that is caused to something when it is being used normally. 損傷, 磨耗 ❑ *...the problem of wear and tear on the equipment in the harsh desert conditions.* 厳しい砂漠の環境で機材が傷む問題

wea|ry /wɪəri/ (**wearier, weariest**) **1** ADJ 形容詞 If you are **weary**, you are very tired. とても疲れた ❑ *Rachel looked pale and weary.* レイチェルは顔色がなく, 疲れて見えた. **2** ADJ 形容詞 If you are **weary of** something, you have become tired of it and have lost your enthusiasm for it. うんざりして [v-link ADJ 'of' n/-ing] ❑ *They're getting awfully weary of this silly war.* 彼らはこのばかげた戦争にひどくうんざりし始めている.

weath|er /wɛðər/ (**weathers, weathering, weathered**) **1** N-UNCOUNT 不可算名詞 The **weather** is the condition of the atmosphere in one area at a particular time, for example, if it is raining, hot, or windy. 天気, 気候 ❑ *The weather was bad.* 天気が悪かった. ❑ *I like cold weather.* 私は寒い気候が好きだ. **2** V-T/V-I 他動詞/自動詞 If something such as wood or rock **weathers** or **is weathered**, it changes color or shape as a result of the wind, sun, rain, or cold. 風化させる, 変色させる [他動詞], 風化する, 色あせる [自動詞] ❑ *Unpainted wooden furniture weathers to a gray color.* 塗装していない木製の家具は灰色に色あせる. **3** V-T 他動詞 If you **weather** a difficult time or a difficult situation, you survive it and are able to continue normally after it has passed or ended. （困難な時期や状況を）切り抜ける ❑ *The company has weathered the recession.* 会社は不況を切り抜けてきた. **4** PHRASE 句 If you say that you are **under the weather**, you mean that you feel slightly ill. 体調がよくない ❑ *I was still feeling a bit under the weather.* 私の体調はまだ今一つだった.
→ see Word Web: **weather**
→ see **forecast, storm**

ADJ.	**bad** weather, **clear** weather, **cold** weather, **cool** weather, **dry** weather, **fair** weather, **good** weather, **hot** weather, **inclement** weather, **mild** weather, **nice** weather, **rainy** weather, **rough** weather, **severe** weather, **stormy** weather, **sunny** weather, **warm** weather, **wet** weather **1**
N.	weather **conditions**, weather **prediction**, weather **report**, weather **service** **1**
V.	weather **permitting** **1**

weath|er fore|cast (**weather forecasts**) N-COUNT 可算名詞 A **weather forecast** is a statement saying what the weather will be

like the next day or for the next few days. 天気予報

weave /wiv/ (**weaves, weaving, wove, woven**)

The form **weaved** is used for the past tense and past participle for meaning **3**.

weaved 形は **3** を意味する過去形と過去分詞として使われる.

1 V-T/V-I 他動詞/自動詞 If you **weave** cloth or a carpet, you make it by crossing threads over and under each other using a frame or machine called a loom. （布やカーペットを）織る [他動詞], 機を織る [自動詞] ❑ *They would spin and weave cloth, cook and attend to the domestic side of life.* 彼女らは糸をつむいで布を織ったり, 料理や生活の家庭内のことをする. ❑ *She sat at her loom and continued to weave.* 彼女は織機に向かって座り, 機を織り続けた. ● **wo|ven** ADJ 形容詞 織って作った ❑ *...woven cotton fabrics.* 綿織物 ● **weav|ing** N-UNCOUNT 不可算名詞 機織り, 織物 ❑ *When I studied weaving, I became intrigued with natural dyes.* 私は織物の勉強をした時に天然の染料に興味を持った. **2** V-T 他動詞 If you **weave** something such as a basket, you make it by crossing long plant stems or fibers over and under each other. （かごなどを）編む ❑ *Jenny weaves baskets from willow she grows herself.* ジェニーは自分で育てた柳でバスケットを編む. ● **wo|ven** ADJ 形容詞 編んで作った ❑ *The floors are covered with woven straw mats.* 床にはわらで編んだ敷物が敷かれている. **3** V-T/V-I 他動詞/自動詞 If you **weave** your way somewhere, you move between and around things as you go there. （一の間を）縫うように進む ❑ *The cars then weaved in and out of traffic at top speed.* そしてそれらの車は全速力で他の車の間を縫うように走り抜けた. ❑ *He weaved around the tables to where she sat with Bob.* 彼は彼女がボブと座っているところまで, テーブルの間を縫って進んだ.
→ see **industry**

weav|er /wivər/ (**weavers**) N-COUNT 可算名詞 A **weaver** is a person who weaves cloth, carpets, or baskets. 織工, 機織り職人

web /wɛb/ (**webs**) **1** N-PROPER 固有名詞 The **Web** is a computer system that links documents and pictures into a database that is stored in computers in many different parts of the world and that people everywhere can use. It is also referred to as the **World Wide Web**. （インターネットの）ウェブ WWW（World Wide Web） も指す [COMPUTING コンピューティング] [oft N n] ❑ *The handbook is available on the Web.* 手引書はウェブ上で入手でき る. ❑ *She recommended the service on her Web journal after trying it out.* 彼女はそのサービスを試した後, 自分のウェブ上の日記で推薦した. **2** N-COUNT 可算名詞 A **web** is a complicated pattern of connections or relationships, sometimes considered as an obstacle or a danger. 複雑なつながり, 入り組んだ関係 ❑ *He's forced to untangle a complex web of financial dealings.* 彼は金融取引の複雑な問題を解決するよう迫られている. **3** N-COUNT 可算名詞 A **web** is the thin net made by a spider from a sticky substance that it produces in its body. クモの巣 ❑ *...the spider's web in the window.* 窓にかかるクモの巣
→ see **blog**

web|cam /wɛbkæm/ (**webcams**) also **Webcam** N-COUNT 可算名詞 A **webcam** is a video camera that takes pictures that can be viewed on a website. The pictures are often of something that is happening while you watch. ウェブカメラ [COMPUTING コンピューティング]

web|cast /wɛbkæst/ (**webcasts**) also **Webcast** N-COUNT 可算名詞 A **webcast** is an event such as a musical performance that you can listen to or watch on the Internet. ウェブ放送 [COMPUTING コンピューティング] ❑ *...a Webcast of the Saturday and Sunday concerts.* 土曜日と日曜日のコンサートのウェブ放送

web|master /wɛbmæstər/ (**webmasters**) N-COUNT 可算名詞 **webmaster** is someone who is in charge of a website, especially someone who does that as their job. ウェブマスター（ウェブサイト

W

Researchers believe the **weather** affects our bodies and minds. When **barometric pressure** drops before a **storm**, some people get migraine headaches. The difference in pressure may change the blood flow in the brain. **Damp, humid** weather leads to increased problems with arthritis. A sudden heat wave can produce heatstroke. Seasonal affective disorder or SAD occurs during the short, **gloomy** days of winter. As the word "sad" suggests, people with this condition feel depressed. The bitter cold of a **blizzard** can cause frostbite. The **hot, dry** Santa Ana winds* in southern California create confusion and depression in some people.

Santa Ana winds: strong, hot, dry winds that blow in southern California in fall and early spring.

の制作・管理をする責任者）[COMPUTING コンピューティング]
→ see **Internet**

web page (**web pages**) also **Web page** N-COUNT 可算名詞 A **web page** is a set of data or information that is designed to be viewed as part of a website. ウェブページ，ホームページ [COMPUTING コンピューティング] ❑ *The company also has a Web page for small businesses and a hotline.* またその会社は中小企業向けのホームページを持っており，電話相談サービスを行っている.
→ see **Internet**

web ring (**web rings**) also **Web ring** or **webring** N-COUNT 可算名詞 A **web ring** is a set of related websites that you can visit one after the other. ウェブリング（同じ趣向のホームページを収録したサイト）[COMPUTING コンピューティング] ❑ *Log on to the Hammer Web ring, with 12 more sites devoted to macabre movies.* 気持ち悪い映画をテーマにしたサイトが他に12も登録されているハマー・ウェブリングにログインする.

Word Link site, situ ≈ position, location : campsite, situation, website

---

web|site /wɛbsaɪt/ (**websites**) also **Web site** or **web site** N-COUNT 可算名詞 A **website** is a set of data and information about a particular subject that is available on the Internet. ウェブサイト，ホームページ [COMPUTING コンピューティング] ❑ *...a website devoted to hip-hop music.* ヒップホップ・ミュージックをテーマにしたウェブサイト
→ see **blog**, **Internet**

web|zine /wɛbzin/ (**webzines**) N-COUNT 可算名詞 A **webzine** is a website that contains the kind of articles, pictures, and advertisements that you would find in a magazine. ウェブジン（インターネット上の雑誌）オンライン・マガジン [COMPUTING コンピューティング] ❑ *The Dismal Scientist, a webzine dedicated to economic news, is fun.* 経済ニュースを扱うウェブジン，The Dismal Scientist は面白い.

wed /wɛd/ (**weds, wedded**)

> The form **wed** is used in the present tense and is the past tense. The past participle can be either **wed** or **wedded**.
>
> wed 形は現在時制に使われ，過去形でもある．過去分詞は wed か wedded のいずれかである.

V-RECIP 相互動詞 If one person **weds** another or if two people **wed** or **are wed**, they get married. (—と) 結婚する [OLD-FASHIONED 古風な JOURNALISM ジャーナリズム] [no cont] ❑ *In 1952 she wed film director Roger Vadim.* 1952年に彼女は映画監督のロジャー・バディムと結婚した.

Wed.

> The spelling **Weds.** is also used.
>
> つづりの **Weds.** も使われる.

Wed. is a written abbreviation for **Wednesday**. 水曜日（Wednesday）の略語

we'd /wid, STRONG wid/ ■ **We'd** is the usual spoken form of "we had," especially when "had" is an auxiliary verb. 口語で用いられる we had の短縮形 ❑ *Come on, George, we'd better get back now.* おいで，ジョージ，もう戻った方がよさそうだ. ■ **We'd** is the usual spoken form of "we would." 口語で用いられる we would の短縮形 ❑ *If we smoked, we'd light a cigarette and let her try it out.* もし私たちがたばこを吸うなら，たばこに火をつけて彼女に吸わせてみるだろう.

wed|ding /wɛdɪŋ/ (**weddings**) N-COUNT 可算名詞 A **wedding** is a marriage ceremony and the party or special meal that often takes place after the ceremony. 結婚式 ❑ *Most couples want a traditional wedding.* ほとんどのカップルは伝統的な結婚式を望んでいる. ❑ *...the couple's 22nd wedding anniversary.* 夫婦の結婚22周年の記念日
→ see Word Web: **wedding**

Do not confuse **wedding** and **marriage**. A **wedding** is a ceremony in which a man and woman get married. It usually includes a meal or other celebration that takes place after the ceremony itself. ❑ *It wasn't a formal wedding.* This ceremony can also be called a **marriage**. ❑ *...the day of my marriage.* **Marriage** can also be used to refer to the relationship between a husband and wife. ❑ *It has been a happy marriage*

wedge /wɛdʒ/ (**wedges, wedging, wedged**) ■ V-T 他動詞 If you **wedge** something, you force it to remain in a particular position by holding it there tightly or by sticking something next to it to prevent it from moving. くさびで留める，くさびで固定する ❑ *I shut the shed door and wedged it with a log of wood.* 私は納屋の戸を閉め，それを丸太で固定した. ■ V-T 他動詞 If you **wedge** something somewhere, you fit it there tightly. 固く固定する ❑ *Wedge the plug into the hole.* プラグを穴にしっかり差し込む. (—の) ■ N-COUNT 可算名詞 A **wedge** of something such as fruit or cheese is a piece of it that has a thick triangular shape. くさび状のもの ❑ *Serve with a wedge of lime.* くし切りにしたライムを添えて出す.

Wednes|day /wɛnzdeɪ, -di/ (**Wednesdays**) N-VAR 可変性名詞 **Wednesday** is the day after Tuesday and before Thursday. 水曜日 ❑ *Come and have supper with us on Wednesday, if you're free.* もしあなたの予定が空いていたら，水曜日にうちに来て私たちと食事をしようよ. ❑ *Did you happen to see her leave last Wednesday?* 先週の水曜日に彼女が出て行くのをたまたま見たの?

wee /wi/ ADJ 形容詞 **Wee** means small in size or extent. 小さい，ちょっとした [mainly SCOTTISH 主にスコットランド方言, INFORMAL くだけた] [ADJ n] ❑ *He just needs to calm down a wee bit.* 彼はただもうちょっと落ち着く必要があるだけだ.

weed /wid/ (**weeds, weeding, weeded**) ■ N-COUNT 可算名詞 A **weed** is a wild plant that grows in gardens or fields of crops and prevents the plants that you want from growing properly. 雑草 ❑ *With repeated applications of weedkiller, the weeds were overcome.* 除草剤を繰り返しまいたら，その雑草はなくなった. ■ V-T/V-I 他動詞/自動詞 If you **weed** an area, you remove the weeds from it. (—の) 草取りをする ❑ *Caspar was weeding the garden.* キャスパーは庭の草むしりをしていた. ❑ *Try not to walk on the flowerbeds while weeding.* 草取りをしている間は花壇の上を歩かないように気をつけて. ▶ **weed out** PHRASAL VERB 句動詞 If you **weed out** things or people that are useless or unwanted in a group, you find them and get rid of them. (不要物を) 除去する ❑ *He is eager to weed out the many applicants he believes may be frauds.* 彼は詐欺かもしれないと思える多くの応募者を除外したがっている.

week /wik/ (**weeks**) ■ N-COUNT 可算名詞 A **week** is a period of seven days. Some people consider that a week starts on Monday and ends on Sunday. 1週間 ❑ *I had a letter from my mother last week.* 私は先週，母から手紙を受け取った. ❑ *This has been on my mind all week.* この考えが1週間ずっと私の頭にあった. ■ N-COUNT 可算名詞 A **week** is a period of about seven days. 約一週間 ❑ *Her mother stayed for another two weeks.* 彼女の母はもう2週間ほど滞在した. ❑ *Only 12 weeks ago he underwent major heart transplant surgery.* ほんの12週間ほど前に，彼は大きな心臓移植手術を受けた. ■ N-COUNT 可算名詞 Your working **week** is the hours that you spend at work during a week. (1週間の) 就業時間 ❑ *It is not unusual for women to work a 40-hour week.* 女性が週に40時間働くのは珍しくない. ■ N-SING 単数名詞 **The week** is the part of the week that does not include Saturday and Sunday. 平日 ❑ *...the hard work of looking after the children during the week.* 平日にその子供たちの面倒を見る大変な仕事 ■ N-COUNT 可算名詞 You use **week** in expressions such as "a week last Monday," "a week ago this Tuesday," and "a week ago yesterday" to mean exactly one week before the day that you mention. 1週間前 ❑ *"That's the time you weren't well, wasn't it?" — "Yes, that's right, that was a week ago last Monday."* 「それってあなたの体調が悪かった時じゃない?」「ああ，そうだ．先週の月曜日だった.」
→ see **year**

week|day /wikdeɪ/ (**weekdays**) N-COUNT 可算名詞 A **weekday** is any of the days of the week except Saturday and Sunday. 平日（1週間のうち土日をのぞく日）❑ *If you want to avoid the crowds, it's*

Word Web wedding

Some **weddings** are fancy, like the one in this picture. Most ceremonies include a similar group of attendants. The maid of honor or matron of honor helps the **bride** get ready for the ceremony. She also signs the **marriage certificate** as a legal **witness**. The **bridesmaids** plan the bride's wedding **shower**. The best man arranges for the bachelor party the night before the wedding. He also helps the **groom** dress for the wedding. After the **ceremony**, the guests gather for a **reception**. When the party is over, many couples leave on a **honeymoon** trip.

W

best to come on a weekday. もし人ごみを避けたいなら，平日に来るのが一番だよ．

week|end /wiːkend/ (**weekends**) N-COUNT 可算名詞 A **weekend** is Saturday and Sunday. 週末 ❑ She had agreed to have dinner with him in town the following weekend. 彼女は次の週末に彼と街で食事をすることを承諾した．

week|ly /wiːkli/ (**weeklies**) **1** ADJ 形容詞 A **weekly** event or publication happens or appears once a week or every week. 週に一度の，毎週の [ADJ n] ❑ Each course comprises 10-12 informal weekly meetings. どのコースにも週に一度の非公式な会議が10から12，組み込まれている． ❑ We go and do the weekly shopping every Thursday. 私たちは毎週木曜日に週1回の買い物に出かける． ● ADV 副詞 **Weekly** is also an adverb. 週に1回，毎週 [ADV after v] ❑ The group meets weekly. そのグループは週に1回集まっている． **2** ADJ 形容詞 **Weekly** quantities or rates relate to a period of one week. 1週間の [ADJ n] ❑ Of course, in addition to my weekly pay, I got a lot of tips. もちろん週給に加え，私はたくさんのチップをもらった． **3** N-COUNT 可算名詞 A **weekly** is a newspaper or magazine that is published once a week. 週刊紙，週刊誌 ❑ Two of the four national daily papers are to become weeklies. 全国版の日刊紙4紙のうち2紙が週刊紙になる予定だ．

weep /wiːp/ (**weeps, weeping, wept**) V-T/V-I 他動詞/自動詞 If someone **weeps**, they cry. (~を) 嘆き悲しむ (~に) 涙を流す [LITERARY 文語的] [他動詞]，_marker_涙を流す，しくしく泣く [自動詞] ❑ She wanted to laugh and weep all at once. 彼女は笑いたい気持ちと泣きたい気持ちに同時になった． ❑ The weeping family hugged and comforted each other. 嘆き悲しむ家族はお互いを抱きしめ慰め合った． ❑ She wept tears of joy. 彼女は喜びの涙を流した．
→ see **cry**

weigh /weɪ/ (**weighs, weighing, weighed**) **1** V-T 他動詞 If someone or something **weighs** a particular amount, this amount is how heavy they are. (~の) 重さになる 重さが~だ [no cont] ❑ It weighs nearly 27 kilos (about 65 pounds). それは重さが27キロ (約65ポンド) だ． ❑ This little ball of gold weighs a quarter of an ounce. この小さな金の玉は重さが4分の1オンスある． **2** V-T 他動詞 If you **weigh** something or someone, you measure how heavy they are. 重さを量る ❑ The scales can be used to weigh other items such as parcels. それらのはかりは他にも小包のようなアイテムを量るのにも使える． **3** V-T 他動詞 If you **weigh** the facts about a situation, you consider them very carefully before you make a decision, especially by comparing the various facts involved. 熟考する，比較検討する ❑ She weighed her options. 彼女は選択肢を比較して熟考した． ❑ He is weighing the possibility of filing criminal charges against the doctor. 彼はその医師に対し刑事訴訟を起こす可能性を検討している．
▶ **weigh down** PHRASAL VERB 句動詞 If something that you are wearing or carrying **weighs** you **down**, it stops you moving easily by making you heavier. (重みで) 押さえつける 動きを妨げる ❑ He wrenched off his sneakers. If he had to swim, he didn't want anything weighing him down. 彼はスニーカーをもぎ取った．もし泳がなければならないなら，動きを妨げるものを全部外しておきたかったからだ．

Word Partnership		weigh は次の語句と使われる:
ADV.	weigh **less**, weigh **more 1**	
	weigh **carefully 2 3**	
N.	weigh **ten pounds 1**	
	weigh **alternatives**, weigh **benefits**, weigh **costs**,	
	weigh **the evidence**, weigh **risks 3**	

weight /weɪt/ (**weights, weighting, weighted**) **1** N-VAR 可変性名詞 The **weight** of a person or thing is how heavy they are, measured in units such as kilograms, pounds, or tons. 体重 ❑ What is your height and weight? あなたの身長と体重はいくらですか？ ● PHRASE 句 If someone **loses weight**, they become lighter. If they **gain weight** or **put on weight**, they become heavier. 体重を減らす，体重が増える ❑ I'm lucky really as I never put on weight. 私って太ることがないから，ほんとにラッキーだよ． ❑ The boy appeared anxious, had lost weight and was not sleeping well. その少年は悩んでいる様子で，体重も減り，よく眠っていなかった． **2** N-UNCOUNT 不可算名詞 A person's or thing's **weight** is the fact that they are very heavy. 体重が重いこと ❑ His weight was harming his health. 彼の重い体重は健康に害を与えていた． **3** N-SING 単数名詞 If you move your **weight**, you change position so that most of the pressure of your body is on a particular part of your body. (体重の) 重心 重圧 ❑ He shifted his weight from one foot to the other. 彼は重心を片方の足からもう片方へ移した． **4** N-COUNT 可算名詞 **Weights** are objects that weigh a known amount and that people lift as a form of exercise. (ウェイトトレーニングなどに使う) ウェイト ❑ I was in the gym lifting weights. 私はジムでウェイトを持ち上げていた． **5** N-COUNT 可算名詞 **Weights** are metal objects that weigh a known amount and that are used on a set of scales to weigh other things. (重さを量る) 重り **6** N-COUNT 可算名詞 You can refer to a heavy object as a **weight**, especially when you have to lift it. 重い物 ❑ Straining to lift heavy weights can lead to a rise in blood pressure. 無理して重いものを持ち上げるのは血圧上昇を招く可能性がある． **7** V-T 他動詞 If you **weight** something, you make it heavier by adding

something to it, for example, in order to stop it from moving easily. おもりをつける，おもしを加える ❑ It can be sewn into curtain hems to weight the curtain and so allow it to hang better. それをカーテンのすそにおもしとして縫い込み，カーテンがさらにいい感じに垂れ下がるようにできる． **8** N-VAR 可変性名詞 If something is given a particular **weight**, it is given a particular value according to how important or significant it is. (物事の) 価値 ❑ The scientists involved put different weight on the conclusions of different models. 参加した科学者たちは，異なるサンプルの結果にそれぞれ違う重点を置いた． **9** N-UNCOUNT 不可算名詞 If someone or something gives **weight** to what a person says, thinks, or does, they emphasize its significance. (意味や重大さを) 強調 ❑ The fact that he is gone has given more weight to fears that he may try to launch a civil war. 彼が行ってしまったという事実は，彼が内戦を起こそうとするかもしれないという不安をよりいっそうかき立てた． **10** N-UNCOUNT 不可算名詞 If you give something or someone **weight**, you consider them to be very important or influential in a particular situation. (人や物事の) 重要性 影響力 ❑ Consumers generally place more weight on negative information than on the positive when deciding what to buy. 通常，消費者は買う物を決める時に，前向きな情報よりも否定的な情報により重きを置く． **11** → see also **weighting** **12** PHRASE 句 If a person or their opinion **carries weight**, they are respected and are able to influence people. 重要である，影響力がある ❑ Senator Kerry carries considerable weight in Washington. ケリー上院議員はワシントンでかなりの影響力を持っている． **13** PHRASE 句 If you say that someone or something is **worth** their **weight in gold**, you are emphasizing that they are so useful, helpful, or valuable that you feel you could not manage without them. 非常に役立つ，とても貴重である [EMPHASIS 強調] ❑ Any successful manager is worth his weight in gold. やり手の支配人というものはみな，とても貴重な存在だ． **14** PHRASE 句 If you **pull your weight**, you work as hard as everyone else who is involved in the same task or activity. 自分の役割を精一杯果たす ❑ He accused the team of not pulling their weight. 彼はチームのみんながそれぞれの仕事を精一杯やっていないと非難した． **15 a weight off your mind** → see **mind**
→ see **diet**

Word Partnership		weight は次の語句と使われる:
V.	**add** weight, **gain/lose** weight, **put on** weight **1**	
N.	weight **gain/loss**, **height and** weight **1**	
	size and weight **1 2**	
	body weight **3**	
	weight **training 4**	
ADJ.	**excess** weight, **healthy** weight, **ideal** weight, **normal**	
	heavy weight, **light** weight **4 6**	

weight|ed /weɪtɪd/ ADJ 形容詞 A system that is **weighted** in favor of a particular person or group is organized so that this person or group has an advantage. (~に) 有利な ❑ The current electoral law is still heavily weighted in favor of the ruling party. 現行の選挙法はまだ与党にとても有利だ．

weight|ing /weɪtɪŋ/ (**weightings**) N-COUNT 可算名詞 A **weighting** is a value given to something according to how important or significant it is. 重要性，重み ❑ ...an index formed of equal weightings of three statistics. 同等に重要な3つの統計データから成る指数

weight|lift|ing /weɪtlɪftɪŋ/ N-UNCOUNT 不可算名詞 **Weightlifting** is a sport in which the competitor who can lift the heaviest weight wins. 重量挙げ

weight train|ing N-UNCOUNT 不可算名詞 **Weight training** is a kind of physical exercise in which people lift or push heavy weights with their arms and legs in order to strengthen their muscles. ウェイトトレーニング ❑ I used to do weight training years ago. 私は何年も前にウェイトトレーニングをしていた．

weighty /weɪti/ (**weightier, weightiest**) ADJ 形容詞 If you describe something such as an issue or a decision as **weighty**, you mean that it is serious or important. (問題などが) 深刻な 重要な [FORMAL 形式ばった] ❑ Surely such weighty matters merit a higher level of debate? きっとそんな重要な問題はもっと高いレベルでの議論に値するのではないか？

weir /wɪər/ (**weirs**) N-COUNT 可算名詞 A **weir** is a low barrier built across a river in order to control or direct the flow of water. (川の) せき

weird /wɪərd/ (**weirder, weirdest**) ADJ 形容詞 If you describe something or someone as **weird**, you mean that they are strange. 変わった，奇妙な [INFORMAL くだけた] ❑ That first day was weird. その1日目は奇妙だった． ❑ Drugs can make you do all kinds of weird things. 薬は人をさまざまな奇行に走らせることがある．

wel|come /welkəm/ (**welcomes, welcoming, welcomed**) **1** V-T 他動詞 If you **welcome** someone, you greet them in a friendly way when they arrive somewhere. (人の到着を) 歓迎する [他動詞]，歓迎の挨拶をする [自動詞] ❑ Several people came by to welcome me. 何人

かの人が私を歓迎するために来てくれた． ❑*She was there to welcome him home from war.* 彼女は戦争から戻って来た彼を家に迎えるためにそこにいた． ❑*...a welcoming speech.* 歓迎のスピーチ ● N-COUNT 可算名詞 **Welcome** is also a noun. 歓迎 ❑*There would be a fantastic welcome awaiting him back here.* ここに戻ってくる彼を素晴らしい歓迎が待っているだろう． **2** CONVENTION 慣習表現 You use **welcome** in expressions such as **welcome home**, **welcome to Boston**, and **welcome back** when you are greeting someone who has just arrived somewhere. ようこそ [FORMULAE 決まり文句] ❑*Welcome to Washington.* ようこそワシントンへ． **3** V-T 他動詞 If you **welcome** an action, decision, or situation, you approve of it and are pleased that it has occurred. (決定や状況などを) 喜んで認める ❑*She welcomed this move but said that overall the changes didn't go far enough.* 彼女はこの動きに賛成だったが、全体的に見ると変化はまだ十分でないと述べた． ● N-COUNT 可算名詞 **Welcome** is also a noun. 承認、受け入れ ❑*Environmental groups have given a guarded welcome to the prime minister's proposal.* 環境保護団体は首相の提案を用心深く受け入れた． **4** ADJ 形容詞 If you describe something as **welcome**, you mean that people wanted it and are happy that it has occurred. (状況が) 歓迎されて 求められて ❑*Any progress in reducing chemical weapons is welcome.* 化学兵器の縮小に向けた進展ならどのようなものでも歓迎される． **5** V-T 他動詞 If you say that you **welcome** certain people or actions, you are inviting and encouraging people to do something, for example, to come to a particular place. (人々や行動を) 募る ❑*We would welcome your views about the survey.* アンケートに関するあなたの意見をお待ちしています． **6** ADJ 形容詞 If you say that someone is **welcome** in a particular place, you are encouraging them to go there by telling them that they will be liked and accepted. (人が) 歓迎されて ❑*New members are always welcome.* 新しいメンバーはいつでも歓迎だ． **7** ADJ 形容詞 If you tell someone that they are **welcome** to do something, you are encouraging them to do it by telling them that they are allowed to do it. 自由にしてもよい [v-link ADJ] ❑*You are welcome to visit the hospital at any time.* あなたはいつ病院を訪れてもよい． **8** ADJ 形容詞 If you say that someone is **welcome to** something, you mean that you do not want it yourself because you do not like it and you are very willing for them to have it. (物を) 自由に取ってよい [v-link ADJ 'to' n] ❑*If women want to take on the business world they are welcome to it as far as I'm concerned.* 私に言わせれば、女性がビジネスの世界に挑みたいならご自由にどうぞといったところだ． **9** → see also **welcoming** **10** PHRASE 句 If you **make** someone **welcome** or **make** them **feel welcome**, you make them feel happy and accepted in a new place. (人を) 歓迎する 温かく迎える ❑*Here are six Mexican hotels where children are made to feel welcome.* 子供を歓迎するメキシコのホテル6軒は以下のとおりだ． **11** CONVENTION 慣習表現 You say "**You're welcome**" to someone who has thanked you for something in order to acknowledge their thanks in a polite way. どういたしまして (お礼の言葉に対する返答) [FORMULAE 決まり文句] ❑*"Thank you for the information." — "You're welcome."* 「情報をありがとう」 「どういたしまして． 」

wel|com|ing /wɛlkəmɪŋ/ ADJ 形容詞 If someone is **welcoming** or if they behave in a **welcoming** way, they are friendly to you when you arrive somewhere, so that you feel happy and accepted. 歓迎して ❑*When we arrived at her house Susan was very welcoming.* 私たちがスーザンの家に着いた時、彼女はとても歓迎してくれた．

weld /wɛld/ (**welds**, **welding**, **welded**) V-T/V-I 他動詞/自動詞 To **weld** one piece of metal to another means to join them by heating the edges and putting them together so that they cool and harden into one piece. 溶接する ❑*It's possible to weld stainless steel to ordinary steel.* ステンレス鋼は普通鋼に溶接できる． ❑*Where did you learn to weld?* あなたはどこで溶接を習ったの？

wel|fare /wɛlfɛər/ **1** N-UNCOUNT 不可算名詞 The **welfare** of a person or group is their health, comfort, and happiness. 健康、快適さ、幸せ ❑*I do not think he is considering Emma's welfare.* 私は、彼がエマの幸せを考えているとは思わない． **2** ADJ 形容詞 **Welfare** services are provided to help with people's living conditions and financial problems. 福祉の ❑*Child welfare services are well established and comprehensive.* 児童福祉事業はしっかり定着しており、広い範囲をカバーしている． **3** N-UNCOUNT 不可算名詞 **Welfare** is money that is paid by the government to people who are unemployed, poor, or sick. 生活保護 (手当) ❑*States such as Michigan are making deep cuts in welfare.* ミシガン州のような州では生活保護手当の大幅削減を行っている．

The American government has a variety of programs to help people who are poor. They may receive a monthly unemployment check, food stamps, subsidized housing, health care, and other services. This system is called **welfare** and is funded by taxes.

wel|fare state N-SING 単数名詞 In some countries, the **welfare state** is a system in which the government provides free social services such as health and education and gives money to people when they are unable to work, because they are old, unemployed, or sick. 社会保障制度 ❑*...the future of the welfare state.* 社会保障制度の将来

well

1	DISCOURSE USES
2	ADVERB USES
3	PHRASES
4	ADJECTIVE USE
5	NOUN USES
6	VERB USES

❶ well /wɛl/

Well is used mainly in spoken English.

Well は主に口語英語で使われる．

➪ Please look at meaning **9** to see if the expression you are looking for is shown under another headword. **1** ADV 副詞 You say **well** to indicate that you are about to say something. (何かを言う前に) さて [ADV cl] ❑*Well, it's a pleasure to meet you.* さて、お会いできてうれしいです． **2** ADV 副詞 You say **well** just before or after you pause, especially to give yourself time to think about what you are going to say. (次の言葉を考える間を取る) えーっと えー [ADV cl] ❑*Look, I'm really sorry I woke you, and, well, I just wanted to tell you I was all right.* ねえ、起こして本当にごめんよ． それから、えーっと、ぼくは大丈夫だって言いたかっただけなんだ． **3** ADV 副詞 You say **well** when you are correcting something that you have just said. (今言った言葉を訂正して) というか まあ [ADV cl/group] ❑*The comet is going to come back in 2061 and we are all going to be able to see it. Well, our offspring are, anyway.* そのすい星は2061年に戻ってくるはずで、私たちはみんなそれを見ることができるでしょう． というか、私たちの子供たちはとにかく見られるでしょう． **4** ADV 副詞 You say **well** to express your doubt about something that someone has said. (相手の言葉を疑って) そうかなあ うーん [FEELINGS 感情] [ADV cl] ❑*"But finance is far more serious." — "Well I don't know really."* 「でも経営状態ははるかに深刻だよ」 「そうかなあ、よく分からないよ． 」 **5** EXCLAM 感嘆詞 You say **well** to express your surprise or anger at something that someone has just said or done. (驚きや怒りを表して) まあ もう [FEELINGS 感情] ❑*She beamed at Patty. "Well! That was a bit of unexpected excitement."* 彼女はパティに大きな笑顔を見せた． 「まあ！ちょっと思わず興奮したわ． 」 **6** CONVENTION 慣習表現 You say **well** to indicate that you are waiting for someone to say something and often to express your irritation with them. (相手の言葉を促して) それで [FEELINGS 感情] ❑*"Well?" asked Barry, "what does it tell us?"* 「それで？」とバリーが聞いた． 「なんて書いてあるの？」 ❑*"Well, why don't you ask me?" he said sharply.* 「それなら、ぼくに聞けば？」と彼はついに言った． **7** CONVENTION 慣習表現 You use **well** to indicate that you are amused by something you have heard or seen, and often to introduce a comment on it. (聞いたことや見たことを面白がって) ほぉー へぇー [FEELINGS 感情] ❑*Well, well, well. How quickly things change.* へぇーーーー． 物事は変わるもんだなんて早いんだ． **8** CONVENTION 慣習表現 You say **oh well** to indicate that you accept a situation or that someone else should accept it, even though you or they are not very happy about it, because it is not too bad and cannot be changed. (理想的ではないが状況を受け入れざるを得ない時) まあ [FEELINGS 感情] ❑*Oh well, it could be worse.* でもまあそれよりひどいことだってあるんだしね． ❑*"I called her and she said no." — "Oh well."* 「彼女に電話したけど、彼女、いやだってさ． 」 「まあ、しょうがないよ． 」 **9** very **well** → see very

❷ well /wɛl/ (**better**, **best**) **1** ADV 副詞 If you do something **well**, you do it to a high standard or to a great extent. 上手に、よく [ADV after v] ❑*It's important that we play well at home.* 家でよく遊ぶことは大切だ． ❑*He speaks English better than I do.* 彼は私よりも英語がうまい． **2** ADV 副詞 If you do something **well**, you do it

thoroughly and completely. 十分に、よく [ADV after v] ❑ *Mix all the ingredients well.* 材料を全部よく混ぜる。 **3** ADV 副詞 If you speak or think **well** of someone, you say or think favorable things about them. (人のことを) よく (言う、考える) [ADV after v] ❑ *"He speaks well of you."—"I'm glad to hear that."* 「彼がきみのことをよく言ってたよ。」「それは嬉しいね。」 **4** COMB IN ADJ 形容詞の複合 **Well** is used in front of past participles to indicate that something is done to a high standard or to a great extent. (後ろに過去分詞を伴い) 非常に [ADV after v] ❑ *Helen is a very well-known novelist in Australia.* ヘレンはオーストラリアでとても有名な作家だ。 ❑ *People live longer nowadays, and they are better educated.* 近年、人々の寿命は長くなっているし、教養も高くなっている。 **5** ADV 副詞 You use **well** to ask or talk about the extent or standard of something. (疑問形で) どれほどよく 素晴らしく ❑ *How well do you remember your mother, Franzi?* フランツィ、きみはどれだけお母さんのことを覚えている？ ❑ *He wasn't dressed any better than me.* 彼は私よりもきちんした服装をしていたわけではなかった。 **6** ADV 副詞 You use **well** in front of a prepositional phrase to emphasize it. For example, if you say that one thing happened **well before** another, you mean that it happened a long time before it. ～をはるかに越えて [EMPHASIS 強調] [ADV prep] ❑ *Franklin did not turn up until well after midnight.* フランクリンは真夜中をずいぶん過ぎるまで現れなかった。 ❑ *...a war in which well over a million people died.* 100万人をはるかに越える人々が亡くなった戦争 **7** ADV 副詞 You use **well** before certain adjectives to emphasize them. とても、はっきりと、十分に [EMPHASIS 強調] [ADV adj] ❑ *She has a close group of friends who are very well aware of what she has suffered.* 彼女には、彼女の苦しい経験をとてもよく分かってくれている親友のグループがいる。 **8** ADV 副詞 You use **well** after adverbs such as "perfectly," "jolly," or "damn" in order to emphasize an opinion or the truth of what you are saying. (前の副詞を強調して) よく 素晴らしく [EMPHASIS 強調] ❑ *You know perfectly well I can't be blamed for the failure of that mission.* あの任務の失敗が私のせいではないことをきみはよく知っているだろう。 **9** ADV 副詞 You use **well** after verbs such as "may" and "could" when you are saying what you think is likely to happen. (mayやcouldに続き) 多分～だろう ―の可能性が高い [EMPHASIS 強調] [modal ADV] ❑ *Ours could well be the last generation for which moviegoing has a sense of magic.* 恐らく私たちが映画見物を魔法のように感じる最後の世代だろう。

③ well /wɛl/
⇨ Please look at meanings **7** – **8** to see if the expression you are looking for is shown under another headword. **1** PHRASE 句 You use **as well** when mentioning something that happens in the same way as something else already mentioned, or that should be considered at the same time as that thing. また ❑ *It is most often diagnosed in women in their thirties and forties, although I've seen it in many younger women, as well.* 30代と40代の女性が最も頻繁にその診断を受ける。とはいうもののもっと若い女性の間でも多くの女性がその病気にかかっているのを見てきたが。 **2** PHRASE 句 You use **as well as** when you want to mention another item connected with the subject you are discussing. だけでなく ❑ *The movie will appeal to adults as well as children.* その映画は大人だけでなく子供にも受けるだろう。 **3** PHRASE 句 If you say that something has happened **is just as well**, you mean that it is fortunate that it happened in the way it did. かえって幸いな ❑ *Blue asbestos is far less common in buildings, which is just as well because it's more dangerous than white asbestos.* 青石綿が建物に使われることはずっと少ない。白石綿より有毒性が高いのでかえって幸いだ。 **4** PHRASE 句 If you say that something, usually something bad, **might as well** be true or **may as well** be true, you mean that the situation is the same or almost the same as if it were true. ❑ *The couple might as well have been strangers.* そのカップルは見知らぬ人と変わらなかった。 **5** PHRASE 句 If you say that you **might as well** do something, or that you **may as well** do it, you mean that you will do it although you do not have a strong desire to do it and may even feel slightly unwilling to do it. そうしてもいい ❑ *If I've got to go somewhere I may as well go to Tulsa.* どこかに行かなければならないのならタルサに行くことにするか。 ❑ *Anyway, you're here; you might as well stay.* とにかく、きみはここにいるのだから泊まっていきなさい。 **6** PHRASE 句 If you say that something is **well and truly** finished, gone, or done, you are emphasizing that it is completely finished or gone, or thoroughly done. 決定的に [mainly BRIT 主に英国英語、EMPHASIS 強調] ❑ *The war is well and truly over.* 戦争は完全に終わった。 **7** all **very well** → see all **8** to **know full well** → see full

④ well /wɛl/ ADJ 形容詞 If you are **well**, you are healthy and not ill. 健康な ❑ *I'm not very well today, I can't come in.* 今日は体の調子がよくないので来られません。

⑤ well /wɛl/ (**wells**) **1** N-COUNT 可算名詞 A **well** is a hole in the ground from which a supply of water is extracted. 井戸 ❑ *I had to fetch water from the well.* 私は井戸から水をくんでくる必要があった。 **2** N-COUNT 可算名詞 A **well** is an oil well. 油井 ❑ *About 650 wells are on fire.* 約650の油井が燃えている。
→ see oil

⑥ well /wɛl/ (**wells, welling, welled**) V-I 自動詞 If liquids **well**,

they come to the surface and form a pool. わき出る ❑ *Tears welled in her eyes.* 彼女の目に涙があふれた。 ● PHRASAL VERB 句動詞 **Well up** means the same as **well**. わき出る ❑ *Tears welled up in Anni's eyes.* アニーの目に涙があふれた。

we'll /wɪl, STRONG wil/ **We'll** is the usual spoken form of "we shall" or "we will." 口語で用いられる we shallまたはwe willの短縮形 ❑ *Whatever you want to chat about, we'll do it tonight.* きみがどんなことを話したいのかは分からないけど今晩話そう。

well-balanced 1 ADJ 形容詞 If you describe someone as **well-balanced**, you mean that they are sensible and do not have many emotional problems. 常識のある ❑ *...a fun-loving, well-balanced individual.* 楽しむのが好きで分別のある人物 **2** ADJ 形容詞 If you describe something that is made up of several parts as **well-balanced**, you mean that the way that the different parts are put together is good, because there is not too much or too little of any one part. バランスの取れた ❑ *...a well-balanced diet.* バランスの取れた食事

well-behaved ADJ 形容詞 If you describe someone, especially a child, as **well-behaved**, you mean that they behave in a way that adults generally like and think is correct. 行儀のいい ❑ *...well-behaved little boys.* 行儀のいい少年達

well-being N-UNCOUNT 不可算名詞 Someone's **well-being** is their health and happiness. 健康で幸福な状態 ❑ *Singing can create a sense of well-being.* 歌うことで幸せな気分になることができる。

well-built ADJ 形容詞 A **well-built** person, especially a man, has big and strong muscles. 体格がよい ❑ *Mitchell is well-built, of medium height, with a dark complexion.* ミッチェルは体格がよく、中背で浅黒い顔をしている。

well-connected ADJ 形容詞 Someone who is **well-connected** has important or influential relatives or friends. 有力な友人がいる ❑ *Mr. Guber and Mr. Peters aren't universally loved in Hollywood but they are well-connected.* グーバー氏とピータース氏はハリウッドであまねく好かれている訳ではないが有力な友人がいる。

well-defined ADJ 形容詞 Something that is **well-defined** is clear and precise and therefore easy to recognize or understand. 明確に定義された ❑ *Today's pawnbrokers operate within well-defined financial regulations.* 現代の質屋は明確に定義された金融規制の範囲内で事業を営む。

well done 1 CONVENTION 慣用表現 You say **Well done** to indicate that you are pleased that someone has done something good. お見事 [FEELINGS 感情] ❑ *"Daddy! I came second in history"—"Well done, sweetheart!"* 「お父さん、歴史で2位になったよ」「よくやったね」 **2** ADJ 形容詞 If something that you have cooked, especially meat, is **well done**, it has been cooked thoroughly. 十分に焼けた ❑ *Allow an extra 10-15 min if you prefer lamb well done.* よく焼けた子羊を好む場合には10―15分余分に焼きなさい。

well-dressed ADJ 形容詞 Someone who is **well-dressed** is wearing fashionable or elegant clothes. 身なりのよい ❑ *She's always well-dressed.* 彼女はいつもよく合った服を着ている。

well-established ADJ 形容詞 If you say that something is **well-established**, you mean that it has been in existence for a long time and is successful. 定評のある ❑ *The university has a well-established tradition of welcoming postgraduate students from overseas.* その大学は海外から大学院生を歓迎する伝統で定評がある。

well-informed (**better-informed**) ADJ 形容詞 If you say that someone is **well-informed**, you mean that they know a lot about many different subjects or about one particular subject. 情報に通じた ❑ *...a lending library to encourage members to become as well-informed as possible.* 会員ができるだけ博識になることを奨励する公共図書館の貸出部門

well-intentioned also **well intentioned** ADJ 形容詞 If you say that a person or their actions are **well-intentioned**, you mean that they intend to be helpful or kind but they are unsuccessful or cause problems. 善意の ❑ *He is well-intentioned but a poor administrator.* 彼は善意的だが管理能力に欠けている。

well-known 1 ADJ 形容詞 A **well-known** person or thing is known about by a lot of people and is therefore famous or familiar. If someone is **well-known** for a particular activity, a lot of people know about them because of their involvement with that activity. 有名な ❑ *Hubbard was well known for his work in the field of drug rehabilitation.* ハバードは麻薬リハビリテーションの分野の著作で有名だった。

A **famous** person or thing is known to more people than a **well-known** one. A **notorious** person or thing is famous because they are connected with something bad or undesirable. **Infamous** is not the opposite of **famous**. It has a similar meaning to **notorious**, but is a stronger word.

2 ADJ 形容詞 A **well-known** fact is a fact that is known by people in general. 周知の ❑ *It is well-known that bamboo shoots are a panda's staple diet.* 竹の子はパンダの主食であることは周知だ。

well-meaning ADJ 形容詞 If you say that a person or their actions are **well-meaning**, you mean that they intend to be helpful or kind but they are unsuccessful or cause problems. 善意の □He is a well-meaning but ineffectual leader. 彼は善意的だが無能な指導者だ.

well-off ADJ 形容詞 Someone who is **well-off** is rich enough to be able to do and buy most of the things that they want. 裕福な [INFORMAL くだけた] □My grandparents were quite well-off. 私の祖父母はかなり裕福だった.

well-paid ADJ 形容詞 If you say that a person or their job is **well-paid**, you mean that they receive a lot of money for the work that they do. よい給料をもらっている □Kate was well-paid and enjoyed her job. ケイトは高給取りで仕事が好きだった.

well-to-do ADJ 形容詞 A **well-to-do** person is rich enough to be able to do and buy most of the things that they want. 裕福な □...a well-to-do family of diamond cutters. ダイアモンド職人の裕福な家族

well-wisher (**well-wishers**) N-COUNT 可算名詞 **Well-wishers** are people who hope that a particular person or thing will be successful, and who show this by their behavior. 好意を寄せる人 □The main street was lined with well-wishers. 大通りには支持者がずらっと並んでいた.

went /wɛnt/ **Went** is the past tense of **go**. goの過去形

wept /wɛpt/ **Wept** is the past tense and past participle of **weep**. weepの過去分詞

were /wər, STRONG wɜːr/ **1** Were is the plural and the second person singular of the past tense of **be**. beの二人称単数および各人称複数の過去形 **2** Were is sometimes used instead of "was" in certain structures, for example, in conditional clauses or after the verb "wish." beの仮定法過去 [FORMAL 形式ばった] □He told a diplomat that he might withdraw if he were allowed to keep part of a disputed oil field. 彼は問題の油田の一部を維持できれば撤退するかもしれないと外交官に伝えた. **3** as it were → see **as**

we're /wɪər/ **We're** is the usual spoken form of "we are." 口語で用いられるwe areの短縮形 □I'm married, but we're separated. 私は結婚しているが別居中である.

weren't /wɜːrnt, wɜːrənt/ **Weren't** is the usual spoken form of "were not." 口語で用いられるwere notの短縮形

west /wɛst/ also **West** **1** N-UNCOUNT 不可算名詞 The **west** is the direction you look toward in the evening in order to see the sun set. 西 [also 'the' N] □I pushed on toward Flagstaff, a hundred miles to the west. 私は100マイル西方のフラッグスタッフに向けて前進した. **2** N-SING 単数名詞 The **west** of a place, country, or region is the part of it which is in the west. 西部 □Many of the buildings in the west of the city are on fire. その町の西部の建物の多くは燃えている. **3** ADV 副詞 If you go **west**, you travel toward the west. 西へ [ADV after v] □We are going west to California. 私たちは西のカリフォルニアに行く予定だ. **4** ADV 副詞 Something that is **west** of a place is positioned to the west of it. 西方に □Penryn is about 60 miles west of Philadelphia. ペンリンはフィラデルフィアの西方約60マイルのところにある. **5** ADJ 形容詞 The **west** part of a place, country, or region is the part which is toward the west. 西方の [ADJ n] □...a small island off the west coast of South Korea. 韓国の西海岸沖の小さな島 **6** ADJ 形容詞 **West** is used in the names of some countries, states, and regions in the west of a larger area. 西の [ADJ n] □Mark has been working in West Africa for about six months. マークは約6ヶ月間西アフリカで働いていた. □...his West Hollywood home. 西ハリウッドの彼の家 **7** ADJ 形容詞 A **west** wind blows from the west. 西から吹いてくる [ADJ n] □...the warm west wind. 暖かい西風 **8** N-SING 単数名詞 The **West** is used to refer to the United States, Canada, and the countries of Western, Northern, and Southern Europe. 欧米諸国 □...relations between Iran and the West. イランと欧米諸国間の関係

west|er|ly /wɛstərli/ **1** ADJ 形容詞 A **westerly** point, area, or direction is to the west or toward the west. 西方にある □...Finisterre, Spain's most westerly point. スペインの最西端の地点、フィニステラ **2** ADJ 形容詞 A **westerly** wind blows from the west. 西から吹いてくる □...a prevailing westerly wind. 優勢な西風

west|ern /wɛstərn/ (**westerns**) also **Western** **1** ADJ 形容詞 **Western** means in or from the west of a region, state, or country. 西の [ADJ n] □...hand-made rugs from Western and Central Asia. 西・中央アジア産の手製のじゅうたん **2** ADJ 形容詞 **Western** is used to describe things, people, ideas, or ways of life that come from or are associated with the United States, Canada, and the countries of Western, Northern, and Southern Europe. 欧米の □Mexico had the support of the big western governments. メキシコは欧米政府の大きな援助を受けた. **3** N-COUNT 可算名詞 A **western** is a book or movie about life in the western United States and territories in the nineteenth century, especially the lives of cowboys. 西部劇 □John Agar starred in westerns, war films and low-budget science fiction pictures. ジョン・アガーは西部劇、戦争映画、低予算のSF映画に主演した. → see **genre**

west|ern|er /wɛstərnər/ (**westerners**) also **Westerner** N-COUNT 可算名詞 A **westerner** is a person who was born in or lives in the United States, Canada, or Western, Northern, or Southern Europe. 欧米人 □It's the first time a Westerner has been convicted for a drug-related offense in recent years in China. 中国で最近欧米人が麻薬関連の犯罪で有罪となったのは初めてのことだ.

west|erni|za|tion /wɛstərnɪzeɪʃən/ N-UNCOUNT 不可算名詞 The **westernization** of a country, place, or person is the process of them adopting ideas and behavior that are typical of Europe and North America, rather than preserving the ideas and behavior traditional in their culture. 西洋化 □...fundamentalists unhappy with the westernization of Afghan culture. アフガニスタンの文化の西洋化に不満な原理主義者

west|ern|ized /wɛstərnaɪzd/ ADJ 形容詞 A **westernized** country, place, or person has adopted ideas and behavior typical of Europe and North America, rather than preserving the ideas and behavior that are traditional in their culture. 西洋化した □Rapid urbanization brings with it a more westernized and generally more sugary diet. 急速な都市化はより西洋化し、概してより多くの砂糖を含む食事をもたらす.

west|ward /wɛstwərd/

The form **westwards** is also used.

westwards 形も使われる.

ADV 副詞 **Westward** or **westwards** means toward the west. 西方に □He sailed westward from Palos de la Frontera. パロス・ドゥ・ラ・フロンテーラから西方に航行した. ● ADJ 形容詞 **Westward** is also an adjective. 西方への [ADJ n] □...the one-hour westward flight over the Andes to Lima. アンデス山脈を西に越えリマまで1時間の便

wet /wɛt/ (**wetter, wettest, wets, wetting, wet** or **wetted**) **1** ADJ 形容詞 If something is **wet**, it is covered in water, rain, sweat, tears, or another liquid. ぬれた □I lowered myself to the water's edge, getting my feet wet. 私は水辺にかがみ、足をぬらした. **2** V-T 他動詞 To **wet** something means to get water or some other liquid over it. ぬらす □When assembling the pie, wet the edges where the two crusts join. パイを形成する時は2枚の外皮がくっつく端の部分をぬらします. **3** ADJ 形容詞 If the weather is **wet**, it is raining. 雨の □If the weather is wet or cold choose an indoor activity. 雨の日や寒い日は屋内の活動を選びなさい. ● N-SING 単数名詞 The **wet** is used to mean wet weather. 雨天 □They had come in from the cold and the wet. 彼らは雨が降り寒い屋外から家に入ってきた. **4** ADJ 形容詞 If something such as paint, ink, or cement is **wet**, it is not yet dry or solid. まだ乾いていない □...leaves dipped in wet paint then pressed on white paper. 塗りたてのペンキに浸し、白い紙に押し付けられた葉 **5** V-T 他動詞 If people, especially children, **wet** their beds or clothes or **wet** themselves, they urinate in their beds or in their clothes because they cannot stop themselves. おねしょする □A quarter of 4-year-olds frequently wet the bed. 4歳児の25%は頻繁におねしょする.

Word Partnership *wet* は次の語句と使われる:

V.	get wet **1**
ADJ.	soaking wet **1**
	cold and wet **1** **3**
N.	wet **clothes**, wet **feet**, wet **grass**, wet **hair**, wet **sand** **1**
	wet **snow**, wet **weather** **3**
	wet **the bed** **5**

wet|land /wɛtlænd/ (**wetlands**) N-VAR 可変性名詞 A **wetland** is an area of very wet, muddy land with wild plants growing in it. You can also refer to an area like this as **wetlands**. 湿地帯 □...a plan that aims to protect the wilderness of the wetlands. 湿地帯の大自然保護を目指す計画 → see Word Web: **wetlands**

we've /wɪv, STRONG wiv/ **We've** is the usual spoken form of "we have," especially when "have" is an auxiliary verb. we haveの短縮形 □It's the first time we've been to the cinema together as a family. 私たちが家族で連れ立って映画を見に行ったのは初めてだった.

whack /wæk/ (**whacks, whacking, whacked**) **1** V-T 他動詞 If you **whack** someone or something, you hit them hard. 激しく打つ [INFORMAL くだけた] □You really have to whack the ball. 本当にボールを激しく打つ必要がある. ● N-COUNT; SOUND 可算名詞, 音声語 **Whack** is also a noun. 激しく打つこと □He gave the donkey a whack across the back with his stick. 彼はロバの背中を杖で激しく打った. **2** PHRASE 句 If something is **out of whack**, it is not working properly, often because its natural balance has been upset. 調子が狂って [mainly AM 主に米国英語, INFORMAL くだけた] [PHR after v, oft v-link PHR] □The ecosystem will be thrown out of whack. 生態系は調子が狂うだろう.

whacky /wæki/ → see **wacky**

whale /weɪl/ (**whales**) **1** N-COUNT 可算名詞 **Whales** are very

Word Web — wetlands

Saltwater **wetlands** protect beaches from erosion. These **tidal flats** also provide homes for shellfish and migrating birds. In some areas, mangrove **swamps** form along the shore. They shelter many species of fish and help filter groundwater before it reaches the ocean. Inland wetlands also form along rivers and streams. They become **marshes** and **freshwater** swamps. A **bog** is an unusual type of freshwater wetland. In a bog, a layer of **peat** forms on the surface of the water. This layer can support shrubs, trees, and small animals. In some places people dry peat and use it for cooking and heating.

large mammals that live in the sea. クジラ **2** PHRASE 句 If you say that someone **is having a whale of a time**, you mean that they are enjoying themselves very much. 素晴らしい時を過ごす [INFORMAL くだけた] ❑ I had a whale of a time in Fargo. 私はファーゴ で素晴らしい時を過ごした.
→ see Word Web: **whale**
→ see **Arctic**

whal|ing /ˈweɪlɪŋ/ N-UNCOUNT 不可算名詞 **Whaling** is the activity of hunting and killing whales. 捕鯨 ❑ ...a ban on commercial whaling. 商業捕鯨の禁止

wharf /wɔrf/ (**wharves** or **wharfs**) N-COUNT 可算名詞 A **wharf** is a platform by a river or the sea where ships can be tied up. 波止場

what /wʌt, wɒt/

Usually pronounced /wɒt/ for meanings **2**, **4** and **5**.

/wɒt/, **2**, **4**の意味には通常 **5** と発音される.

1 QUEST 疑問詞 You use **what** in questions when you ask for specific information about something that you do not know. 何 ❑ What do you want? 何が欲しいのか. ❑ What did she tell you, anyway? とにかく彼女はきみに何と言ったのか. ❑ "Has something happened?" — "It certainly has." — "What?" 「何かが起こったのか」「その通りだ」「何だ」 • DET 限定詞 **What** is also a determiner. 何の ❑ What time is it? 何時ですか. ❑ What crimes are the defendants being charged with? 被告は何の罪で起訴されているのか. ❑ "The heater works." — "What heater?" 「ヒーターは動いている」「どのヒーターか」 **2** CONJ 接続詞 You use **what** after certain verbs and adjectives, especially when you are referring to a situation that is unknown or has not been specified. もの ❑ You can imagine what it would be like driving a car into a brick wall at 30 miles an hour. 時速30マイルで車をレンガの塀にぶつけることがどんなものかは想像できる. ❑ I want to know what happened to Norman. 私はノーマンに何が起きたのかを知りたい. • DET 限定詞 **What** is also a determiner. どの ❑ I didn't know what college I wanted to go to. 私はどの大学に行きたいのか分からなかった. ❑ I didn't know what else to say. 私はそれ以外に何を言ってよいのか分からなかった. **3** CONJ 接続詞 You use **what** at the beginning of a clause in structures where you are changing the order of the information to give special emphasis to something. もの [EMPHASIS 強調] ❑ What precisely triggered off yesterday's riot is still unclear. 何が正確に昨日の暴動のきっかけになったのかはまだ分からない. ❑ What I wanted, more than anything, was a few days' rest. 私が最も欲しいものは数日間の静養だった. **4** CONJ 接続詞 You use **what** in expressions such as **what is called** and **what amounts to** when you are giving a description of something. もの ❑ She had been in what doctors described as an irreversible vegetative state for five years. 彼女は5年間医者が遷延性意識障害と呼ぶ状態だった. **5** CONJ 接続詞 You use **what** to indicate that you are talking about the whole of an amount that is available to you. もの ❑ He drinks what is left in his glass as if it were water. 彼をグラスに残されたものをまるで水であるかのように飲んだ. • DET 限定詞 **What** is also a determiner. 全部の ❑ They had used what money they had. 彼らは持っていた金はみな使った. **6** CONVENTION 慣習表現 You say "**What?**" to tell someone who has indicated that they want to speak to you that you have heard them and are inviting them to continue. なんだい [SPOKEN 口語, FORMULAE 決まり文句?] ❑ "Dad?" — "What?" — "Can I have the car tonight?" 「お父さん」「何だい」「今夜車を使っていい」 **7** CONVENTION 慣習表現 You say "**What?**" when you ask

someone to repeat the thing that they have just said because you did not hear or understand it properly. "What?" is more informal and less polite than expressions such as "Pardon?" and "Excuse me?" 何だって [SPOKEN 口語, FORMULAE 決まり文句] ❑ "They could paint this place," she said. "What?" he asked. 「彼らはこの家にペンキを塗ることができるのに」と彼女は言った.「何だって」と彼は聞いた. **8** CONVENTION 慣習表現 You say "**What**" to express surprise. 何だって [FEELINGS 感情] ❑ "Adolphus Kelling, I arrest you on a charge of trafficking in narcotics." — "What?" 「アドルファス・ケリング, 私はあなたを麻薬取引罪で逮捕する」「何だって」 **9** PREDET 前限定詞 You use **what** in exclamations to emphasize an opinion or reaction. 何と [EMPHASIS 強調] ❑ What a horrible thing to do. 何てひどいことをするんでしょう. • DET 限定詞 **What** is also a determiner. 何と ❑ What pretty hair she has, nice and thick. 彼女の髪は何てきれいなんでしょう. つやがあってふさふさしている. **10** ADV 副詞 You use **what** to indicate that you are making a guess about something such as an amount or value. まあ [ADV n] ❑ It's, what, eleven years or more since he's seen her. 彼は彼女と, まあ11年以上会っていない. **11** CONVENTION 慣習表現 You say **guess what** or **do you know what** to introduce a piece of information that is surprising, that is not generally known, or that you want to emphasize. あのね, 何だと思う ❑ Guess what? I'm going to dinner at Mrs. Chang's tonight. あのね, 今夜チャン夫人に夕食に呼ばれているんだ. **12** PHRASE 句 In conversation, you say **or what?** after a question as a way of stating an opinion forcefully and showing that you expect other people to agree. でないとでも言うのか [EMPHASIS 強調] ❑ Look at that moon. Is that beautiful or what? あの月を見てごらん. 美しいだろう. **13** CONVENTION 慣習表現 You say **so what?** or **what of it?** to indicate that the previous remark seems unimportant, uninteresting, or irrelevant to you. それがどうしたというのか [FEELINGS 感情] ❑ "What if there is no kerosene this winter?" said Al. — "So what?" she said. "We still have electricity." 「今冬灯油が切れたらどうする」とアルは言った.「だからどうしたって言うの, まだ電気があるわ」と彼女は言った. ❑ "You're talking to yourself." — "Well, what of it?" 「きみは独り言を言っている」「だからどうしたって言うんだ」 **14** PHRASE 句 You say "**Tell you what**" to introduce a suggestion or offer. いいかい ❑ Tell you what, let's stay here another day. いいか, もう1日ここに泊まろう. **15** PHRASE 句 You use **what about** at the beginning of a question when you make a suggestion, offer, or request. 一はどうかね ❑ What about going out with me tomorrow? 明日私と一緒に外出しないか. **16** PHRASE 句 You use **what about** or **what of** when you introduce a new topic or a point that seems relevant to a previous remark. についてはどう思うかね ❑ Now you've talked about work on daffodils, what about other commercially important flowers, like roses? さてあなたは水仙に関する作業について話したが, バラなどの商業的に重要な花についてはどう思うか. **17** PHRASE 句 You say **what about** a particular person or thing when you ask someone to explain why they have asked you about that person or thing. どうしたというのだ ❑ "This thing with the Corbett woman." — "Oh, yeah. What about her?" 「コーベットという女とのこの出来事」「ああ, 彼女がどうしたって言うんだ」 **18** PHRASE 句 You say **what if** at the beginning of a question when you ask about the consequences of something happening, especially something undesirable. 一としたらどうなるだろうか ❑ What if this doesn't work out? もしこれがうまく行かなかったらどうしようか. **19** **what's more** → see **more**

what|ev|er /wʌtˈɛvər, wɒt-/ **1** CONJ 接続詞 You use **whatever** to refer to anything or everything of a particular type. するもの

Word Web — whale

Whales are part of a group of animals called cetaceans. This group also includes **dolphins** and **porpoises**. Although whales live in the water, they are **mammals**. They breathe air and are warm-blooded. Whales have adapted to life in the open **ocean**. They have a 2-inch thick layer of blubber just under their skin. This insulates them from the cold ocean water. They sing beautiful songs that can be heard miles away. Blue whales are the largest animals in the world. They can become almost 100 feet long and weigh up to 145 tons.

は何でも ❏ *Franklin was free to do pretty much whatever he pleased.* フランクリンはほとんど何でも思いのままにすることができた。❏ *When you're older I think you're better equipped mentally to cope with whatever happens.* もっと年を取ったらきみは何が起ころうと精神的により上手に対処できるようになると思う。● DET 限定詞 **Whatever** is also a determiner. たとえ―でも ❏ *Whatever doubts he might have had about Ingrid were all over now.* 彼がイングリッドについてのどんな疑いを持っていたとしても今はすべて終わった。 **2** CONJ 接続詞 You use **whatever** to say that something is the case in all circumstances. いかに―でも ❏ *We shall love you whatever happens, Diana.* ダイアナ、どんなことが起ころうと私たちはあなたを愛し続ける。 **3** ADV 副詞 You use **whatever** after a noun group in order to emphasize a negative statement. 少しの―も [EMPHASIS 強調] [with brd-neg, n ADV] ❏ *There is no evidence whatever that competition in broadcasting has ever reduced costs.* 放送業界の競争が経費の削減につながったという証拠は少しもない。 **4** QUEST 疑問詞 You use **whatever** to ask in an emphatic way about something which you are very surprised about. 一体何が [EMPHASIS 強調] ❏ *Whatever can you mean?* 一体何のつもりかね。 **5** CONJ 接続詞 You use **whatever** when you are indicating that you do not know the precise identity, meaning, or value of the thing just mentioned. 何であろうと [VAGUENESS あいまいさ] ❏ *I thought that my upbringing was "normal," whatever that is.* 私はそれが何であれ私の育ちは「普通」だと思った。 **6** PHRASE 句 You say **or whatever** to refer generally to something else of the same kind as the thing or things that you have just mentioned. その他なんでも [INFORMAL くだけた] ❏ *They're always protesting about something or saving the trees or whatever.* 彼らはいつも何かについての抗議や樹木の保護などの活動をしているのでやっている。 **7** PHRASE 句 You say **whatever** you **do** when giving advice or warning someone about something. たとえ―でも [EMPHASIS 強調] ❏ *Whatever you do, don't ask for a pay increase.* たとえどんなことをしても昇給を求めてはならない。

what's /wʌts, wɒts/ **What's** is the usual spoken form of "what is" or "what has," especially when "has" is an auxiliary verb. 口語で用いられるwhat isまたはwhat hasの短縮形。

what·so·ev·er /wʌtsoʊ̯ɛvər, wɒt-/ ADV 副詞 You use **whatsoever** after a noun group in order to emphasize a negative statement. 全く [EMPHASIS 強調] ❏ *My school did nothing whatsoever in the way of athletics.* 私の学校は陸上競技の点では全く何もしなかった。

wheat /wiːt/ (wheats) N-MASS 質量名詞 **Wheat** is a cereal crop grown for food. **Wheat** is also used to refer to the grain of this crop, which is usually ground into flour and used to make bread. 小麦 ❏ *…farmers growing wheat, corn, or other crops.* 小麦、とうもろこし、あるいはその他の穀物を栽培する農場主
→ see **grain**

wheel /wiːl/ (wheels, wheeling, wheeled) **1** N-COUNT 可算名詞 The **wheels** of a vehicle are the circular objects that are attached underneath it and that enable it to move along the ground. 車輪 ❏ *The car wheels spun and slipped on some oil on the road.* 車の車輪は道路の油に空転し、滑った。 **2** N-COUNT 可算名詞 A **wheel** is a circular object that forms a part of a machine, usually a moving part. 回転盤 ❏ *The wheels are usually fairly large.* 回転盤は普通かなり大きい。 **3** N-COUNT 可算名詞 The **wheel** of a car or other vehicle is the circular object that is used to steer it. The **wheel** is used in expressions to talk about who is driving a vehicle. For example, if someone is **at the wheel** or **behind the wheel** of a car, they are driving it. ハンドル ❏ *My co-pilot suddenly grabbed the wheel.* 私の運転助手は突然ハンドルをつかんだ。 ❏ *Curtis got behind the wheel and they started back toward the cottage.* カーティスは運転席につき、別荘の方向にバックし始めた。 **4** V-T 他動詞 If you **wheel** an object that has wheels somewhere, you push it along. 押す ❏ *He wheeled his bike into the alley at the side of the house.* 彼は家の横の路地に自転車を押した。 **5** N-PLURAL 複数名詞 People talk about **the wheels of** an organization or system to mean the way in which it operates. 原動力 ❏ *He knows the wheels of administration turn slowly.* 彼は行政活動はゆっくりと進むことを知っている。 **6** → see also **steering wheel**
→ see Word Web: **wheel**
→ see **bicycle, color, skateboarding**

Word Partnership   *wheel* は次の語句と使われる：

| N. | **wheel of** a car/truck/vehicle **1** **3** |
| V. | **grip the** wheel, **slide behind the** wheel, **spin the** wheel, **turn the** wheel **3** |

wheel and deal (wheels and deals, wheeling and dealing, wheeled and dealed) V-I 自動詞 If you say that someone **wheels and deals**, you mean that they use a lot of different methods and contacts to achieve what they want in business or politics, often in a way which you consider dishonest. 敏腕をふるう ❏ *He still wheels and deals around the globe.* 彼はまだ世界中で敏腕をふるっている。● **wheel·ing and deal·ing** N-UNCOUNT 不可算名詞 抜け目なく策動すること ❏ *He hates the wheeling and dealing associated with conventional political life.* 彼は伝統的な政治生活に関連する策謀が嫌いである。

wheel·chair /wiːltʃɛər/ (wheelchairs) N-COUNT 可算名詞 A **wheelchair** is a chair with wheels that you use in order to move around in if you cannot walk properly, for example, because you are disabled or sick. 車椅子
→ see **disability**

wheeze /wiːz/ (wheezes, wheezing, wheezed) V-I 自動詞 If someone **wheezes**, they breathe with difficulty and make a whistling sound. ぜいぜいと息をする ❏ *He had serious problems with his chest and wheezed and coughed all the time.* 彼は肺に問題があり、四六時中ぜいぜいげいと息をし、咳をした。

when /wɛn/ **1** QUEST 疑問詞 You use **when** to ask questions about the time at which things happen. いつ ❏ *When are you going home?* いつ家に帰るのか。 ❏ *When did you get married?* いつ結婚したのか。 **2** CONJ 接続詞 If something happens **when** something else is happening, the two things are happening at the same time. ―のとき ❏ *When eating a whole cooked fish, you should never turn it over to get at the flesh on the other side.* 丸ごとの魚を食べる時はひっくり返して反対側の身を食べてはならない。 **3** CONJ 接続詞 You use **when** to introduce a clause in which you mention something that happens at some point during an activity, event, or situation. ―のとき ❏ *When I met the Gills, I had been gardening for nearly ten years.* 私がジル一家に会った時、私は10年間近くガーデニングをしていた。 **4** CONJ 接続詞 You use **when** to introduce a clause where you mention the circumstances under which the event in the main clause happened or will happen. ―すると ❏ *When he brought Imelda her drink she gave him a genuine, sweet smile of thanks.* 彼がイメルダに飲み物を持ってくると、彼女は心から感謝して彼にほほえみかけた。 **5** CONJ 接続詞 You use **when** after certain words, especially verbs and adjectives, to introduce a clause where you mention the time at which something happens. いつ ❏ *I asked him when he'd be back to pick me up.* 私は彼に私を迎えに戻ってくるか聞いた。 **6** PRON-REL 関係代名詞 You use **when** to introduce a clause that specifies or refers to the time at which something happens. ―する時 ❏ *He could remember a time when he had worked like that himself.* 彼は彼自身のように働いた時のことを思い出すことができた。 **7** CONJ 接続詞 You use **when** to introduce the reason for an opinion, comment, or question. ―なのに ❏ *How can I love myself when I look like this?* 私はこんな外見なのにどうして自分自身を愛せようか。 **8** CONJ 接続詞 You use **when** in order to introduce a fact or comment which makes the other part of the sentence rather surprising or unlikely. ―であるにもかかわらず ❏ *Our mothers sat us down to read and paint, when all we really wanted to do was to make a mess.* 私たちが本当にしたかったのは散らかすことだったのに、私たちの母親は私達を座らせ読書とお絵かきをさせた。

when·ev·er /wɛnɛvər/ **1** CONJ 接続詞 You use **whenever** to refer to any time or every time that something happens or is true. ―する時はいつも ❏ *Whenever I talked to him, he seemed like a pretty regular guy.* 私と話をした時はいつも彼は普通の男性のようだった。 ❏ *You can stay at my cottage in the country whenever you like.* 好きなときにいつでも田舎の別荘に泊まっていいですよ。 **2** CONJ 接続詞 You use **whenever** to refer to a time that you do not know or are not sure about. ―かあるいはそのころ ❏ *He married Miss Vancouver*

Word Web   wheel

The **wheel** was invented about 5000 BC in Mesopotamia, part of modern-day Iraq. That's when someone first **spun** a **potter's wheel** to make a clay jar. About 1500 years later, people put wheels on an **axle** and created the **chariot**. These first wheels were solid wood and were very heavy. However, in about 2000 BC the Egyptians introduced much lighter wheels with **spokes**. The wheel has driven the development of all kinds of modern technology. The **waterwheel, spinning wheel,** and **turbine** played an important part in the Industrial Revolution. Even the propeller and jet engine are descendants of the wheel.

in 1963, or whenever it was. 彼は1963年かあるいはそのころ, バンクーバー一嬢と結婚した.

where /wɛər/

> Usually pronounced /weər/ for meanings **2** and **3**.

> /wɛər/と **2** の意味には通常 **3** と発音される.

1 QUEST 疑問詞 You use **where** to ask questions about the place something is in, or is coming from or going to. どこ □ *Where did you meet him?* 彼とはどこで会ったのか. □ *Where's Anna?* アナはどこにいるか. **2** CONJ 接続詞 You use **where** after certain words, especially verbs and adjectives, to introduce a clause in which you mention the place in which something is situated or happens. どこ □ *People began looking across to see where the noise was coming from.* 人々はどこから騒音がするのかを知るために見渡し始めた. □ *He knew where Henry Carter had gone.* 彼はヘンリー・カーターがどこに行ったのか知っていた. ● PRON-REL 関係代名詞 **Where** is also a relative pronoun. する場所 □ *The area where the explosion occurred was closed off by police.* 爆発が起こった地区は警察によって閉鎖された. **3** QUEST 疑問詞 You use **where** to ask questions about a situation, a stage in something, or an aspect of something. どんな状態で □ *If they get their way, where will it stop?* 彼らの思いのままになった場合にはどこで止まるか. **4** CONJ 接続詞 You use **where** after certain words, especially verbs and adjectives, to introduce a clause in which you mention a situation, a stage in something, or an aspect of something. どこで □ *It's not hard to see where she got her feelings about herself.* 彼女がどこで自分自身についての意見を得たのかを知るのは難しくない. □ *She had a feeling she already knew where this conversation was going to lead.* 彼女はこの会話がどこに進むのかを既に知っているような気がした. ● PRON-REL 関係代名詞 **Where** is also a relative pronoun. する □ *The government is at a stage where it is willing to talk to almost anyone.* 政府はほとんどだれとでも進んで話し合いをする段階である.

where|abouts

> Pronounced /wɛərəbaʊts/ for meaning **1**, and /wɛərəbaʊts/ for meaning **2**.

> /wɛərəbaʊts/の意味では **1** と, /wɛərəbaʊts/の意味では **2** と発音される.

1 N-SING-COLL 集合的単数名詞 If you refer to the **whereabouts** of a particular person or thing, you mean the place where that person or thing may be found. 所在 □ *The police are anxious to hear from anyone who may know the whereabouts of the firearms.* 警察は武器のありかを知っている人物から連絡があることを切望している. **2** QUEST 疑問詞 You use **whereabouts** in questions when you are asking precisely where something is. どの辺に □ *"Whereabouts in France?" — "Normandy," I said.* 「フランスのどの辺に」「ノルマンディーだ」と私は言った. □ *Whereabouts are you living?* あなたはどの辺に住んでいるのか.

where|as /wɛəræz/ CONJ 接続詞 You use **whereas** to introduce a comment that contrasts with what is said in the main clause. であるのに反して □ *Benefits are linked to inflation, whereas they should be linked to the cost of living.* 諸手当はインフレに連動しているが, 生活費に連動すべきだ.

where|by /wɛərbaɪ/ PRON-REL 関係代名詞 A system or action whereby something happens is one that makes that thing happen. それによって—するところの [FORMAL 形式ばった] □ *The company operates an arrangement whereby employees may select any 8-hour period between 6 a.m. to 8 p.m. to go to work.* その企業はそれによって社員が午前6時から午後8時までの間の8時間を選べる取り決めを採用している.

where|upon /wɛərəpɒn/ CONJ 接続詞 You use **whereupon** to say that one thing happens immediately after another thing, and usually as a result of it. その決果 [FORMAL 形式ばった] □ *Mr. Jones refused to talk to them except in the company of his legal colleagues, whereupon the police officers departed.* ジョーンズ氏は弁護士の同僚がいる場所以外で彼らに話しをするのを拒否したため, 警察官は出発した.

wher|ever /wɛrɛvər/ **1** CONJ 接続詞 You use **wherever** to indicate that something happens or is true in any place or situation. どんな所でも □ *Some people enjoy themselves wherever they are.* どこにいても楽しい思いをする人々がいる. **2** CONJ 接続詞 You use **wherever** when you indicate that you do not know where a person or place is. どこでも □ *I'd like to leave as soon as possible and join my children, wherever they are.* 私はできるだけ早く出発し, どこにいようと子供達に同伴したい. **3** QUEST 疑問詞 You use **wherever** in questions as an emphatic form of "where," usually when you are surprised about something. いったいどこで [EMPHASIS 強調] □ *Wherever did you get that idea?* いったいどこでその着想を得たのか.

where|with|al /wɛrwɪðɔl, -wɪθ-/ N-SING 単数名詞 If you have the **wherewithal** for something, you have the means, especially the money, that you need for it. 資金 □ *Some of the companies illegally sent the wherewithal for making chemical weapons.* 一部の企業は化学兵器を作るための資金を不法に送金した.

wheth|er /wɛðər/

1 CONJ 接続詞 You use **whether** when you are talking about a choice or doubt between two or more alternatives. —かどうか □ *To this day, it's unclear whether he shot himself or was murdered.* 彼が銃で自殺したのか殺されたのかはいまだにはっきりしない. □ *Whether it turns out to be a good idea or a bad idea, we'll find out.* それが良い考えであるのか悪い考えであるのかは後で分かるだろう. **2** CONJ 接続詞 You use **whether** to say that something is true in any of the circumstances that you mention. —にせよ—にせよ □ *This happens whether the children are in two-parent or one-parent families.* これは子供が両親のそろった家庭であろうと片親の家庭であろうと起こるものだ. □ *Whether they say it aloud or not, most men expect their wives to be faithful.* 声に出して言おうと言うまいと, 大半の男は妻に貞淑を求める.

which /wɪtʃ/

> Usually pronounced /wɪtʃ/ for meanings **2**, **3** and **4**.

> /wɪtʃ/, **2**, **3** の意味には通常 **4** と発音される.

1 QUEST 疑問詞 You use **which** in questions when there are two or more possible answers or alternatives. どの □ *"You go down that passageway over there." — "Which one?"* 「あの通路を降りて行きなさい.」「どっちの」 □ *Which vitamin supplements are good for you?* どのビタミン剤が効くのか. **2** DET 限定詞 You use **which** to refer to a choice between two or more possible answers or alternatives. どちらの □ *I wanted to know which school it was you went to.* 私はあなたが通ったのはどの学校か知りたかった. □ *I can't remember which teachers I had.* 私はどの教師だったか思い出せない. ● CONJ 接続詞 **Which** is also a conjunction. どちら □ *In her panic she couldn't remember which was Mr. Grainger's cabin.* うろたえくいためた彼女はどちらがグレインジャー氏の部屋だったのか思い出せなかった. **3** PRON-REL 関係代名詞 You use **which** at the beginning of a relative clause when specifying the thing that you are talking about. In such clauses, which has the same meaning as **that**. するところの □ *Soldiers opened fire on a car which failed to stop at an army checkpoint.* 兵隊は軍の検問所で停車しなかった車に発砲した. **4** PRON-REL 関係代名詞 You use **which** to refer back to an idea or situation expressed in a previous sentence or sentences, especially when you want to give your opinion about it. そしてそれは □ *They ran out of drink. Which actually didn't bother me because I wasn't drinking.* 彼らは飲み物を切らした. だが私は飲んでいなかったのでそれは実は気にならなかった. ● DET 限定詞 **Which** is also a determiner. そしてその □ *The chances are you haven't fully decided what you want from your career at the moment, in which case you're definitely not cut out to be a boss yet!* たぶんきみはまだ今職業生活から何を欲するのか完全に決めていないだろう. その場合, きみは絶対にまだ上司になるには適していない. **5** PHRASE 句 If you cannot tell the difference between two things, you can say that you do not know **which is which**. どれがどれやら □ *They all look so alike to me that I'm never sure which is which.* それらはすべてひどく似ているのでどれがどれやら私にはさっぱり分からない.

which|ever /wɪtʃɛvər/ **1** DET 限定詞 You use **whichever** in order to indicate that it does not matter which of the possible alternatives happens or is chosen. どちらの—をするとしても □ *Whichever way you look at it, nuclear power is the energy of the future.* どのように考えても原子力は将来の燃料である. ● CONJ 接続詞 **Whichever** is also a conjunction. するどれでも □ *If you are unhappy with anything you have bought from us, we will gladly exchange your purchase, or refund your money, whichever you prefer.* 当店でお買い求めの商品にご不満がある場合には喜んで商品の交換あるいは払い戻しをします. **2** DET 限定詞 You use **whichever** to specify which of a number of possibilities is the right one or the one you mean. どちらの—でも □ *Learning to relax by whichever method suits you best is a positive way of contributing to your overall good health.* どちらの方法でもあなたに最も適した方法でリラックスすることはあなたの総合的な健康に役立つ. ● CONJ 接続詞 **Whichever** is also a conjunction. どちらが—しようとも □ *He has been extraordinarily fortunate or clever, whichever is the right word.* どちらが正しい言葉であろうとも彼は並外れて幸運だった, あるいは利口だった.

whiff /wɪf/ (**whiffs**) N-COUNT 可算名詞 If there is a **whiff** of a particular smell, you smell it only slightly or only for a brief period of time, for example, as you walk past someone or something. ほのかな香り □ *He caught a whiff of her perfume.* 彼には彼女の香水のほのかな香りがした.

while

> **❶** CONJUNCTION USES
> **❷** NOUN AND VERB USES

❶ while /waɪl/

> Usually pronounced /waɪl/ for meaning **4**.

> /waɪl/の意味には通常 **4** と発音される.

1 CONJ 接続詞 If something happens **while** something else is happening, the two things are happening at the same time. —す

w

る間に ❑ *They were grinning and watching while one man laughed and poured beer over the head of another.* 彼らは1人の男が笑いながらビールをもう1人の男の頭にかけるのをニヤニヤ見ていた. ❑ *I sat on the chair to unwrap the package while he stood behind me.* 私は彼が私の後ろに立っている間に椅子に座って小包をほどいた. **2** CONJ 接続詞 If something happens **while** something else happens, the first thing happens at some point during the time that the second thing is happening. ―するうちに ❑ *The two ministers have yet to meet, but may do so while in New York.* 2人の大臣はまだ面識がないがニューヨークにいる間に知り合いになるかもしれない. **3** CONJ 接続詞 You use **while** at the beginning of a clause to introduce information that contrasts with information in the main clause. なのに対して ❑ *Most digital camera owners are male, while women prefer film.* 大半のデジタルカメラの所有者は男性なのに対して女性はフィルムを好む. **4** CONJ 接続詞 You use **while**, before making a statement, in order to introduce information that partly conflicts with your statement. ―とはいえ ❑ *While the news, so far, has been good, there may be days ahead when it is bad.* 今までのニュースは好ましいものだったが今後悪いニュースがあるかもしれない.

❷ **while** /waɪl/ (whiles, whiling, whiled)
⇨ Please look at meanings **3** – **4** to see if the expression you are looking for is shown under another headword. **1** N-SING 単数名詞 A **while** is a period of time. 少しの時間 ❑ *They walked on in silence for a while.* 彼らは少しの間黙って歩いた. ❑ *He was married a little while ago.* 彼は少し前に結婚した. **2** PHRASE 句 You use **all the while** in order to say that something happens continually or that it happens throughout the time when something else is happening. ❑ *All the while the people at the next table watched me eat.* 隣のテーブルの人々はずっと私が食べるのを見ていた. **3** once in a while→ see once **4** worth your while→ see worth
▸ **while away** PHRASAL VERB 句動詞 If you **while away** the time in a particular way, you spend time in that way, because you are waiting for something else to happen, or because you have nothing else to do. 過ごす ❑ *Craig had been whiling away his spare time in our basement.* クレイグは我が家の地下室で退屈を紛らわしてきた.

whilst /waɪlst/ CONJ 接続詞 [mainly BRIT 主に英国英語] **Whilst** means the same as the conjunction **while**. なのに対して

whim /wɪm/ (whims) N-VAR 可変性名詞 A **whim** is a wish to do or have something that seems to have no serious reason or purpose behind it, and often occurs suddenly. 気まぐれ ❑ *We decided, more or less on a whim, to sail to Morocco.* 私たちはほとんど思いつきでモロッコに航行することに決めた.

whim|per /wɪmpər/ (whimpers, whimpering, whimpered) V-I 自動詞 If someone **whimpers**, they make quiet unhappy or frightened sounds, as if they are about to start crying. 弱々しい声で泣く ❑ *She lay at the bottom of the stairs, whimpering in pain.* 彼女は苦痛でしくしく泣きながら階段の下に横たわっていた. ● N-COUNT 可算名詞 **Whimper** is also a noun. めそめそした泣き声 ❑ *David's crying subsided to a whimper.* デイビットの泣き叫ぶ声はしくしくした泣き声に変わった.

whim|si|cal /wɪmzɪkəl/ ADJ 形容詞 A **whimsical** person or idea is unusual, playful, and unpredictable, rather than serious and practical. 気まぐれな ❑ *McGrath remembers his offbeat sense of humor, his whimsical side.* マクグレイスは彼の風変わりなユーモア心, 彼の気まぐれな性格を覚えている.

whine /waɪn/ (whines, whining, whined) **1** V-I 自動詞 If something or someone **whines**, they make a long, high-pitched noise, especially one that sounds sad or unpleasant. 哀訴するような声で泣く ❑ *He could hear her dog barking and whining in the background.* 彼は彼女の犬が吠え, 哀れっぽく鳴くのを聞いた. ● N-COUNT 可算名詞 **Whine** is also a noun. ヒューヒューいう音 ❑ *...the whine of air-raid sirens.* 空襲のサイレンのヒューという音. **2** V-T/V-I 他動詞/自動詞 If someone **whines**, they complain in an annoying way about something unimportant. 泣き言を言う [DISAPPROVAL 不賛成] ❑ *They come to me to whine about their troubles.* 彼らは彼らの問題について泣き言を言うために私のところに来た. ❑ *...children who whine that they are bored.* 退屈したと泣き言を言う子供たち.

whip /wɪp/ (whips, whipping, whipped) **1** N-COUNT 可算名詞 A **whip** is a long thin piece of material such as leather or rope, fastened to a stiff handle. It is used for hitting people or animals. むち **2** V-T 他動詞 If someone **whips** a person or animal, they beat them or hit them with a whip or something like a whip. むちで打つ ❑ *Eye-witnesses claimed Mr. Melton whipped the horse up to 16 times.* 目撃者はメルトン氏が最高16回馬をむちで打ったと述べた. ● **whip|ping** (whippings) N-COUNT 可算名詞 むち打ち ❑ *He threatened to give her a whipping.* 彼は彼女をむちで打つと脅かした. **3** V-T 他動詞 If someone **whips** something out or **whips** it off, they take it out or take it off very quickly and suddenly. さっと取り出す, ぱっと脱ぐ ❑ *Bob whipped out his notebook.* ボブはメモ帳をさっと取り出した. ❑ *Players were whipping their shirts off.* 選手達はシャツをぱっと脱いだ. **4** V-T 他動詞 When you **whip** something

liquid such as cream or an egg, you stir it very fast until it is thick or stiff. 泡立たせる ❑ *Whip the cream until thick.* クリームを角が立つまで泡立てる. ❑ *Whip the eggs, oils and honey together.* 卵, 油, はちみつを一緒に泡立てなさい. **5** V-T 他動詞 If you **whip** people **into** an emotional state, you deliberately cause and encourage them to be in that state. 急に動かす ❑ *He could whip a crowd into hysteria.* 彼は群衆をヒステリー状態にすることができた.
▸ **whip up** PHRASAL VERB 句動詞 If someone **whips up** an emotion, especially a dangerous one such as hatred, or if they **whip** people **up** into an emotional state, they deliberately cause and encourage people to feel that emotion. 誘発する ❑ *He accused politicians of whipping up antiforeign sentiments in order to win right-wing votes.* 彼は政治家が右翼の投票を勝ち取るために排外的な感情を誘っていると非難した.

whip|lash /wɪplæʃ/ N-UNCOUNT 不可算名詞 **Whiplash** is a neck injury caused by the head suddenly moving forward and then back again, for example, in a car accident. むち打ち症 ❑ *His wife suffered whiplash and shock.* 彼の妻はむち打ち症とショックにかかった.

whirl|wind /wɜrlwɪnd/ (whirlwinds) **1** N-COUNT 可算名詞 A **whirlwind** is a tall column of air that spins around and around very fast and moves across the land or sea. つむじ風. **2** N-COUNT 可算名詞 You can describe a situation in which a lot of things happen very quickly and are very difficult for someone to control as a **whirlwind**. あわただしい行動 ❑ *I had been running around southern California in a whirlwind of activity.* 私はあわただしくカリフォルニア南部をあちこち移動していた. **3** ADJ 形容詞 A **whirlwind** event or action happens or is done much more quickly than normal. 大急ぎの [ADJ n] ❑ *He got married after a whirlwind romance.* 彼は性急な恋愛の後で結婚した.

whisk /wɪsk/ (whisks, whisking, whisked) **1** V-T 他動詞 If you **whisk** someone or something somewhere, you take or move them there quickly. さっと動かす ❑ *He whisked her across the dance floor.* 彼はダンスフロアーで彼女をさっと動かした. **2** V-T 他動詞 If you **whisk** something such as eggs or cream, you stir it very fast, often with an electric device, so that it becomes full of small bubbles. 泡立てる ❑ *Just before serving, whisk the cream.* 出す直前にクリームを泡立てなさい. **3** N-COUNT 可算名詞 A **whisk** is a kitchen tool used for whisking eggs or cream. 泡立て器 ❑ *Using a whisk, mix the yolks and sugar to a smooth paste.* 泡立て器を使って卵黄と砂糖を混ぜ, よく練られたペーストにしなさい.

whisk|er /wɪskər/ (whiskers) **1** N-COUNT 可算名詞 The **whiskers** of an animal such as a cat or a mouse are the long stiff hairs that grow near its mouth. ひげ **2** N-PLURAL 複数名詞 You can refer to the hair on a man's face, especially on the sides of his face, as his **whiskers**. ひげ ❑ *...wild, savage-looking fellows, with large whiskers and dirty faces.* 汚れた顔に大きなひげを生やし, 野蛮で凶暴そうな男

whis|key /wɪski/ (whiskeys) N-MASS 質量名詞 **Whiskey** is a strong alcoholic drink made, especially in the United States and Ireland, from grain such as barley or rye. ウィスキー ❑ *...a tumbler with about an inch of whiskey in it.* 約1インチのウィスキーの入ったタンブラー. ● N-COUNT 可算名詞 A **whiskey** is a glass of whiskey. グラス1杯のウィスキー ❑ *Stark took two whiskeys from a tray.* スタークはトレーからウィスキーの入ったグラスを2つ取った.

whis|ky /wɪski/ (whiskies) N-MASS 質量名詞 **Whisky** is whiskey that is made especially in Scotland and Canada. ウィスキー ● N-COUNT 可算名詞 A **whisky** is a glass of whisky. グラス1杯のウィスキー

whis|per /wɪspər/ (whispers, whispering, whispered) V-T/V-I 他動詞/自動詞 When you **whisper**, you say something very quietly, using your breath rather than your throat, so that only one person can hear you. ささやく ❑ *"Keep your voice down," I whispered.* 「声を落としてくれ」と私は小声で言った. ❑ *She sat on Rossi's knee as he whispered in her ear.* 彼が彼女の耳にささやいた時彼女はロシーの膝に座っていた. ❑ *He whispered the message to David.* 彼はデイビッドに伝言をささやき声で伝えた. ● N-COUNT 可算名詞 **Whisper** is also a noun. ささやき声 ❑ *Men were talking in whispers in every office.* 男達はすべてのオフィスで小声で話していた.

whis|tle /wɪsəl/ (whistles, whistling, whistled) **1** V-T/V-I 他動詞/自動詞 When you **whistle** or when you **whistle** a tune, you make a series of musical notes by forcing your breath out between your lips, or your teeth. 口笛を吹く ❑ *He whistled and sang snatches of songs.* 彼は口笛を吹き, 歌の一部を歌った. ❑ *He was whistling softly to himself.* 彼はそっと口笛を吹いていた. **2** V-I 自動詞 When someone **whistles**, they make a sound by forcing their breath out between their lips or their teeth. People sometimes whistle when they are surprised, or to call a dog, to get someone's attention, or to show that they are impressed. 口笛音を発する ❑ *He whistled, surprised but not shocked.* 彼は驚きでヒューと口笛を鳴らしたが, ショックは受けていなかった. ❑ *Jenkins whistled through his teeth, impressed at last.* ジェンキンスはやっと感動し, ヒューと口笛を鳴らした. ● N-COUNT 可算名詞 **Whistle** is also a noun. ピュ

W

一という音 ❑ *Jackson gave a low whistle.* ジャクソンは低いピューという音を立てた. **3** V-I 自動詞 If something such as a train or a kettle **whistles**, it makes a loud, high sound. ピューという音を出す ❑ *Somewhere a train whistled.* どこかで電車がピューという音を立てた. **4** V-I 自動詞 If something such as the wind or a bullet **whistles** somewhere, it moves there, making a loud, high sound. 笛を鳴らす ❑ *The wind was whistling through the building.* 風が建物をピューっと吹き抜けていた. **5** N-COUNT 可算名詞 A **whistle** is a loud sound produced by air or steam being forced through a small opening, or by something moving quickly through the air. ピューという音 ❑ *...the whistle of the wind.* 風がヒューヒュー吹く音 ❑ *...a shrill whistle from the boiling kettle.* 沸騰したヤカンのけたたましいピューという音 **6** N-COUNT 可算名詞 A **whistle** is a small metal tube that you blow in order to produce a loud sound and attract someone's attention. 口笛 ❑ *On the platform, the guard blew his whistle.* プラットホームで車掌は口笛を吹いた. **7** PHRASE 句 If you **blow the whistle on** someone, or on something secret or illegal, you tell another person, especially a person in authority, what is happening. 内部告発する ❑ *Companies should protect employees who blow the whistle on dishonest workmates and work practices.* 企業は不正を働く同僚や業務慣行を内部告発する従業員を保護すべきだ. **8** PHRASE 句 If you describe something as **clean as a whistle**, you mean that it is completely clean. 汚れ1つなくきれいで ❑ *The kitchen was clean as a whistle.* キッチンはピカピカに掃除されていた.

whistle-blowing also **whistleblowing** N-UNCOUNT 不可算名詞 **Whistle-blowing** is the act of telling the authorities or the public that the organization you work for is doing something immoral or illegal. 内部告発をすること ❑ *It took internal whistle-blowing and investigative journalism to uncover the rot.* 腐敗を見つけるには内部告発と調査報道が必要だった.

white /waɪt/ (whiter, whitest, whites) **1** COLOR 色彩語 Something that is **white** is the color of snow or milk. 白い ❑ *He had nice square white teeth.* 彼は白くて四角い歯をしていた. ❑ *Issa's white beach hat gleamed in the harsh lights.* イッサの白いビーチ用帽子は強い日差しの中できらりと光った. **2** ADJ 形容詞 A **white** person has a pale skin and belongs to a race of European origin. 白色人種の ❑ *Working with white people hasn't been a problem for me or for them.* 白人と働くことは私にとっても彼らにとっても問題ではなかった. ●N-COUNT 可算名詞 **Whites** are white people. 白人 ❑ *It's a school that's brought blacks and whites and Hispanics together.* 黒人と白人とヒスパニックを知り合いにさせたのは学校だ. **3** ADJ 形容詞 **White** wine is pale yellow in color. 白い ❑ *Gregory poured another glass of white wine and went back to his bedroom.* グレゴリーはもう1杯白ワインを注ぎ, 寝室に戻った. **4** ADJ 形容詞 **White** blood cells are the cells in your blood your body uses to fight infection. 白い [ADJ n] ❑ *...an AIDS drug that helps restore a patient's white blood cells.* 患者の白血球を回復するのに役立つAIDSの薬 **5** N-VAR 可変性名詞 The **white** of an egg is the transparent liquid that surrounds the yellow part called the yolk. 白身 ❑ *As soon as the whites of the eggs have set, remove the cover.* 卵の白身が固まった後すぐに覆いをはずしなさい. **6** N-COUNT 可算名詞 The **white** of someone's eye is the white part that surrounds the colored part called the iris. 白い部分 ❑ *Susanne stared at me, the whites of her eyes gleaming in the streetlight.* スザンヌは私をじっと見つめ, 彼女の白目は街灯できらりと光った.
→ see **color**

white|board /waɪtbɔrd/ (whiteboards) N-COUNT 可算名詞 A **whiteboard** is a shiny white board on which people draw or write using special pens. Whiteboards are often used for teaching or giving talks. ホワイトボード

white-collar also **white collar** **1** ADJ 形容詞 **White-collar** workers work in offices rather than doing physical work such as making things in factories or building things. 頭脳労働の [ADJ n] ❑ *White-collar workers now work longer hours.* サラリーマンは今やより長時間働く. **2** ADJ 形容詞 **White-collar** crime is committed by people who work in offices, and involves stealing money secretly from companies or the government, or getting money in an illegal way. 知能犯の [ADJ n] ❑ *...a New York lawyer who specializes in white-collar crime.* 知能犯による犯罪を専門とするニューヨークの弁護士
→ see **union**

white goods N-PLURAL 複数名詞 People in business sometimes refer to refrigerators, washing machines, and other large pieces of electrical household equipment as **white goods**. 大型の家庭用品 ❑ *...the third largest manufacturer of white goods in the South.* 南部で3位の大型家庭用品メーカー

White House N-PROPER 固有名詞 The **White House** is the official home in Washington DC of the president of the United States. You can also use the **White House** to refer to the president of the United States and his or her officials. ホワイトハウス ❑ *He drove to the White House.* 彼はホワイトハウスに車で行った. ❑ *The White House has not participated in any talks.* 連邦政府の行政府は話合いには参加していない.

white knight (white knights) N-COUNT 可算名詞 A **white knight** is a person or an organization that rescues a company from difficulties such as financial problems or an unwelcome takeover bid. 企業買収の危機にある会社などを救済するために介入する第三の企業 [BUSINESS 実業] ❑ *...a white-knight bid.* 救済に現れた企業の入札

white|wash /waɪtwɒʃ/ (whitewashes, whitewashing, whitewashed) **1** N-UNCOUNT 不可算名詞 **Whitewash** is a mixture of lime or chalk and water that is used for painting walls white. 水しっくい ❑ *...v-T 他動詞 If a wall or building has been whitewashed*, it has been painted white with whitewash. 水しっくいが塗られた ❑ *The walls had been whitewashed.* 壁には水しっくいが塗られていた. **3** V-T 他動詞 If you say that people **whitewash** something, you are accusing them of hiding the unpleasant facts or truth about it in order to make it acceptable. かばい立てする [DISAPPROVAL 不賛成] ❑ *The administration is whitewashing the regime's actions.* 行政機関は政府の行動を取り繕おうとしている.

whit|tle /wɪtᵊl/ (whittles, whittling, whittled) V-T 他動詞 If you **whittle** something from a piece of wood, you carve it by cutting pieces off the wood with a knife. 木を削って作る ❑ *He whittled a new handle for his ax.* 彼は木を削って斧 (おの) の新しい取っ手を作った.
▸ **whittle away** PHRASAL VERB 句動詞 To **whittle away** something or **whittle away** at it means to gradually make it smaller, weaker, or less effective. だんだんと減らす ❑ *...the plight of monkeys and other primates as people whittle away their habitat.* 人間のおかげで生息環境を少しずつ失って行く猿などの霊長類の窮状

whiz /wɪz/ (whizzes, whizzing, whizzed) also **whizz** **1** V-I 自動詞 If something **whizzes** somewhere, it moves there very fast. ブーンと音を立てて動く [INFORMAL くだけた] ❑ *They heard bullets continue to whiz over their heads.* 彼らの頭上を弾丸がヒューっと音を立てて飛び続ける. **2** N-COUNT 可算名詞 If you are a **whiz** at something, you are very good at it. 達人 [INFORMAL くだけた] ❑ *Simon's a whiz at card games.* サイモンはトランプの名人だ. [oft 'a' N 'at/with/on' n]

who /hu/

> Usually pronounced /hu/ for meanings **2** and **3**.

> /hu/ と **2** の意味には通常 **3** と発音される.

> **Who** is used as the subject or object of a verb. See entries at **whom** and **whose**.

> **Who** は動詞の主語または目的語に使われる. **whom** と **whose** の見出し語を参照.

1 QUEST 疑問詞 You use **who** in questions when you ask about the name or identity of a person or group of people. だれ ❑ *Who's there?* そこにいるのはだれか. ❑ *Who is the least popular man around here?* ここで一番人気のない男はだれか. ❑ *"You reminded me of somebody." — "Who?"* 「あなたは私にだれかを思い出させる」「だれだ」 **2** CONJ 接続詞 You use **who** after certain words, especially verbs and adjectives, to introduce a clause where you talk about the identity of a person or a group of people. 〜する人 ❑ *Police have not been able to find out who was responsible for the forgeries.* 警察は偽造を行った人物を見つけることができていない. ❑ *I went over to start up a conversation, asking her who she knew at the party.* 私はパーティで知っている人がいるかと聞きながら彼女と会話を始めに行った. **3** PRON-REL 関係代名詞 You use **who** at the beginning of a relative clause when specifying the person or group of people you are talking about or when giving more information about them. 〜する ❑ *There are those who eat out for a special occasion, or treat themselves.* 特別な出来事のために外食する人もいれば自分自身にプレゼントを買う人もいる.

> **Who** is now commonly used where it used only to be considered to be correct to use **whom**. **Who**, however, cannot be used directly after a preposition, for example, you cannot say "...the woman to who I spoke." Instead you can say "...the woman to whom I spoke" or "...the woman I spoke to." There are some types of sentence in which **who** cannot be used, for example when you are talking about quantities. ❑ *...twenty masked prisoners, many of whom are armed with makeshift weapons.*

who'd /hud, hud/ **1** **Who'd** is the usual spoken form of "who had," especially when "had" is an auxiliary verb. 口語で用いられる who had の短縮形 **2** **Who'd** is a spoken form of "who would." 口語で用いられる who would の短縮形

who|ever /huɛvər/ **1** CONJ 接続詞 You use **whoever** to refer to someone when their identity is not yet known. 誰が〜でも ❑ *Whoever did this will sooner or later be caught and be punished.* これを行なった人物が誰であろうと遅かれ早かれ逮捕され, 処罰されるだろう. ❑ *Whoever wins the election is going to have a tough job getting the economy back on its feet.* 誰が選挙に勝っても経済を回復させるのは か

なり骨の折れる仕事になるだろう。 **2** CONJ 接続詞 You use **whoever** to indicate that the actual identity of the person who does something will not affect a situation. する人は誰でも ❑ *You can have whoever you like to visit you.* あなたは誰でも好きな人に訪問してもらえる。 **3** QUEST 疑問詞 You use **whoever** in questions as an emphatic way of saying "who," usually when you are surprised about something. いったい誰が [EMPHASIS 強調] ❑ *Whoever thought up that joke?* その冗談はいったい誰が考えついたのか。

whole /hoʊl/ (wholes) **1** QUANT 数量詞 If you refer to **the whole of** something, you mean all of it. 全体 [QUANT 'of' def-n] ❑ *He has said he will make an apology to the whole of Asia for his country's past behavior.* 彼は自国の過去の行動に対してアジア諸国全体に謝罪すると述べた。 ❑ *I was cold throughout the whole of my body.* 私は体全体が寒かった。 ● ADJ 形容詞 **Whole** is also an adjective. 全体の [ADJ n] ❑ *We spent the whole summer in Italy that year.* 私達はその年の夏中イタリアで過ごした。 **2** N-COUNT 可算名詞 A **whole** is a single thing that contains several different parts. 完全体 ❑ *An atom itself is a complete whole, with its electrons, protons and neutrons and other elements.* 原子自身はそのエレクトロン、プロトン、ニュートロンなどの要素を伴う完全体である。 **3** ADJ 形容詞 If something is **whole**, it is in one piece and is not broken or damaged. 損傷のない [v-link ADJ, v n ADJ] ❑ *I struck the glass with my fist with all my might; yet it remained whole.* 私は精一杯の力を出してガラスをげんこつで打ったがそれはもとのままだった。 **4** ADV 副詞 You use **whole** to emphasize what you are saying. 全く [INFORMAL くだけた, EMPHASIS 強調] [ADV adj] ❑ *It was like seeing a whole different side of somebody.* それはある人の全く異なる面を見るようなものだった。 ● ADJ 形容詞 **Whole** is also an adjective. 大きな [ADJ n] ❑ *That saved me a whole bunch of money.* そのおかげで私は大金を節約できた。 **5** PHRASE 句 If you refer to something **as a whole**, you are referring to it generally and as a single unit. 全体として ❑ *He described the move as a victory for the people of South Africa as a whole.* 彼はその動きを南アフリカの人々全体のための勝利と言い表した。 **6** PHRASE 句 You use **on the whole** to indicate that what you are saying is true in general but may not be true in every case, or that you are giving a general opinion or summary of something. 全体から見て ❑ *On the whole, people miss the opportunity to enjoy leisure.* 概して人々はレジャーを楽しむ機会を逃す。

Whole is often used to mean the same as **all** but when used in front of plurals, **whole** and **all** have different meanings. For example, if you say "**Whole buildings have been destroyed**", you mean that some buildings have been destroyed completely. If you say "**All the buildings have been destroyed**," you mean that every building has been destroyed.

---

whole|hearted /hoʊlhɑrtɪd/ ADJ 形容詞 If you support or agree to something in a **wholehearted** way, you support or agree to it enthusiastically and completely. 心からの、誠心誠意の [EMPHASIS 強調] ❑ *The governor deserves our wholehearted support for having taken a step in this direction.* 知事がこの方向に足を踏み入れたことに我々の心からの支持を送るべきだ。 ● **whole|heart|ed|ly** ADV 副詞 心から、全面的に ❑ *That's exactly right. I agree wholeheartedly with you.* まったくその通りです。心から同意します。

whole|sale /hoʊlseɪl/ **1** N-UNCOUNT 不可算名詞 **Wholesale** is the activity of buying and selling goods in large quantities and therefore at cheaper prices, usually to stores who then sell them to the public. Compare **retail**. 卸売り [BUSINESS 実業] ❑ *Warehouse clubs allow members to buy goods at wholesale prices.* ウェアハウス・クラブでは会員が卸売価格で買い物ができる。 **2** ADV 副詞 If something is sold **wholesale**, it is sold in large quantities and at cheaper prices, usually to stores. 卸売りで [BUSINESS 実業] [ADV after v] ❑ *The fabrics are sold wholesale to retailers, fashion houses, and other manufacturers.* その布地は卸売りで小売業者、ブティック、製造業者などに卸売りされる。 **3** ADJ 形容詞 You use **wholesale** to describe the destruction, removal, or changing of something when it affects a very large number of things or people. 大規模な [EMPHASIS 強調] [ADJ n] ❑ *They are only doing what is necessary to prevent wholesale destruction of vegetation.* 植物の大規模な破壊を防ぐために必要な処置をしているにすぎない。

whole|sal|er /hoʊlseɪlər/ (wholesalers) N-COUNT 可算名詞 A **wholesaler** is a person whose business is buying large quantities of goods and selling them in smaller amounts, for example, to stores. 卸売業者 [BUSINESS 実業] ❑ *Under state law, bar owners must buy their liquor from wholesalers.* 州法の下では、バーの経営者はアルコール類を卸売業者から購入しなければならない。

whole|sal|ing /hoʊlseɪlɪŋ/ N-UNCOUNT 不可算名詞 **Wholesaling** is the activity of buying or selling goods in large amounts, especially in order to sell them in stores or supermarkets. Compare **retailing**. 卸売り [BUSINESS 実業] ❑ *The business thrived and he turned to wholesaling.* 事業は成功し、彼は卸売りを始めた。

whole|some /hoʊlsəm/ **1** ADJ 形容詞 If you describe something as **wholesome**, you approve of it because you think

it is likely to have a positive influence on people's behavior or mental state, especially because it does not involve anything sexually immoral. 健全な [APPROVAL 賛成] ❑ *The Dove Foundation aims to promote wholesome family entertainment.* Dove Foundation は健全な家族で楽しめる娯楽の推進を目標としている。 **2** ADJ 形容詞 If you describe food as **wholesome**, you approve of it because you think it is good for your health. 健康によい [APPROVAL 賛成] ❑ *...fresh, wholesome ingredients.* 新鮮で健康的な原料

who'll /hul, hul/ **Who'll** is a spoken form of "who will" or "who shall." 口語で用いられるwho willあるいはwho shallの短縮形

Word Link hol ≈ whole : holistic, holocaust, wholly

---

whol|ly /hoʊlli/ ADV 副詞 You use **wholly** to emphasize the extent or degree to which something is the case. 全く [EMPHASIS 強調] ❑ *While the two are only days apart in age they seem to belong to wholly different generations.* その2人はほんの2日違いで生まれたが、全く異なる世代に属しているようだ。

wholly-owned sub|sidi|ary (wholly-owned subsidiaries) N-COUNT 可算名詞 A **wholly-owned subsidiary** is a company whose shares are all owned by another company. 100%子会社 [BUSINESS 実業] ❑ *The Boston-owned software company became a wholly-owned subsidiary of IBM.* ボストンのソフトウェア会社がIBMの100%子会社になった。

whom /hum/

Whom is used in formal or written English instead of "who" when it is the object of a verb or preposition.

whom は、形式ばった英語あるいは書き言葉では、動詞あるいは前置詞の目的語のときwhoの代わりに用いられる。

---

1 QUEST 疑問詞 You use **whom** in questions when you ask about the name or identity of a person or group of people. だれに ❑ *"I want to send a telegram." — "Fine, to whom?"* 「電報を送りたいのですが」「結構です。どちら様宛ですか?」 ❑ *Whom did he expect to answer his phone?* 彼はだれが電話に出ると思ったのか? **2** CONJ 接続詞 You use **whom** after certain words, especially verbs and adjectives, to introduce a clause where you talk about the name or identity of a person or a group of people. (動詞・形容詞などの目的語節を導いて) だれに ❑ *He asked whom I'd told about his having been away.* 彼は、私がだれに彼がしばらくいなかったことを話したかを尋ねた。 **3** PRON-REL 関係代名詞 You use **whom** at the beginning of a relative clause when specifying the person or group of people you are talking about or when giving more information about them. (関係代名詞で) その人たちに ❑ *One writer in whom I had taken an interest was Immanuel Velikovsky.* 私が興味を持った作家はイマニュエル・ベリコフスキーだった。

whoop /hup/ (whoops, whooping, whooped) V-I 自動詞 If you **whoop**, you shout loudly in a very happy or excited way. 歓声を上げる [WRITTEN 書き言葉] ❑ *She whoops with delight at a promise of money.* 彼女は入金の見込みを知って大喜びで歓声を上げた。 ● N-COUNT 可算名詞 **Whoop** is also a noun. 歓声 ❑ *Scattered groans and whoops broke out in the crowd.* 観衆の中からあちこちでうめき声や叫び声が発せられた。

who're /huər, huər/ **Who're** is a spoken form of "who are." 口語で用いられるwho areの短縮形 ❑ *I've got loads of friends who're unemployed.* 失業中の友達がたくさんいます。

who's /huz, huz/ **Who's** is the usual spoken form of "who is" or "who has," especially when "has" is an auxiliary verb. 口語で用いられるwho isあるいはwho hasの短縮形

whose /huz/

Usually pronounced /huz/ for meanings **2** and **3**.

/huz/と **2** **3** の意味には通常 **3** と発音される。

---

1 PRON-REL 関係代名詞 You use **whose** at the beginning of a relative clause where you mention something that belongs to or is associated with the person or thing mentioned in the previous clause. 〜の (関係代名詞で所属を表す) ❑ *I saw a man shouting at a driver whose car was blocking the street.* 男性が道をふさいでいる車の運転手にどなっているのを見た。 ❑ *...a speedboat, whose fifteen-strong crew claimed to belong to China's navy.* 総勢15人の乗組員が中国の海軍に属していると主張している高速モーターボート **2** QUEST 疑問詞 You use **whose** in questions to ask about the person or thing that something belongs to or is associated with. だれの ❑ *"Whose is this?" — "It's mine."* 「これはだれのですか?」「私のです」 ❑ *"It wasn't your fault, John." — "Whose, then?"* 「ジョン、あなたのせいじゃなかったよ」「じゃあ、だれなんだい?」 ❑ *Whose car were they in?* だれの車に乗っていたの? ❑ *Whose daughter is she?* 彼女はだれの娘なの? **3** DET 限定詞 You use **whose** after certain words, especially verbs and adjectives, to introduce a clause where you talk about the person or thing that something belongs to or is associated with. (間接疑問を導いて) だれの ❑ *I'm wondering whose mother she is then.* それじゃあ彼女はだれのお母さんなのかしら。 ❑ *I can't remember whose idea it was.* だれの考えだったのか思い出せない。 ● CONJ 接続

詞 **Whose** is also a conjunction. だれのもの □ *I wondered whose the coat was.* そのコートがだれのものなのかと思いました.

who've /huv, huv/ **Who've** is the usual spoken form of "who have," especially when "have" is an auxiliary verb. 口語で用いられる who have の短縮形

why /waɪ/

> The conjunction and the pronoun are usually pronounced /waɪ/.
>
> 接続詞と代名詞は通常 /waɪ/ と発音される.

1 QUEST 疑問詞 You use **why** in questions when you ask about the reasons for something. なぜ, どうして □ *Why hasn't he brought the whiskey?* どうして彼はウィスキーを買っていないの? □ *Why didn't he stop me?* どうして彼は私を止めなかったの? **2** CONJ 接続詞 You use **why** at the beginning of a clause in which you talk about the reasons for something. 〜する理由, どうして〜か □ *He still could not throw any further light on why the elevator could have been jammed.* やはり彼は, エレベーターが故障した理由をそれ以上解明することができなかった. □ *Experts wonder why the U.S. government is not taking similarly strong actions against AIDS in this country.* 専門家は, 米国政府が当国で同様にエイズ対策を取っていない理由を案じています. ● ADV 副詞 **Why** is also an adverb. どうしてか, 理由 □ *I don't know why.* 理由は明らかだ. □ *It's obvious why.* 理由は明らかだ. **3** PRON-REL 関係代名詞 You use **why** to introduce a relative clause after the word "reason." 先行詞 reason に続く関係詞 □ *There's a reason why women don't read this stuff; it's not funny.* 女性がこの類のものを読まない理由がある. 面白くないからだ. ● ADV 副詞 **Why** is also an adverb. 先行詞 reason に続く関係副詞 □ *He confirmed that the city had been closed to foreigners, but gave no reason why.* その町が外国人に閉鎖されていたことを確認したが, 理由は述べなかった. [n ADV] **4** QUEST 疑問詞 You use **why** with "not" in questions in order to introduce a suggestion. 〜したらどう □ *Why not give Charmaine a call?* シャーメインに電話をかけたらどう? **5** QUEST 疑問詞 You use **why** with "not" in questions in order to express your annoyance or anger. (いらだちを表して) どうして〜しないんだ [FEELINGS 感情] □ *Why don't you look where you're going?* どうして行く先を見ないの? **6** CONVENTION 慣習表現 You say **why not** in order to agree with what someone has suggested. (賛同を表して) もちろん [FORMULAE 決まり文句] □ *"Want to spend the afternoon with me?" — "Why not?"* 「今日の午後一緒に過ごさない?」「いいよ」 **7** EXCLAM 感嘆詞 People say **"Why!"** at the beginning of a sentence when they are surprised, shocked, or angry. あら, おや [mainly AM 主に米国英語, FEELINGS 感情] □ *Why hello, Tom.* あら, トムきみこんにちは.

wick|ed /wɪkɪd/ ADJ 形容詞 You use **wicked** to describe someone or something that is very bad and deliberately harmful to people. 意地悪な, 不道徳な □ *She described the shooting as a wicked attack.* 彼女はその銃撃は悪意のある攻撃だったと説明した.

wick|et /wɪkɪt/ (**wickets**) **1** N-COUNT 可算名詞 In cricket, a **wicket** is a set of three upright sticks with two small sticks on top of them at which the ball is bowled. ウィケット, 三柱門 **2** N-COUNT 可算名詞 In cricket, a **wicket** is the area of grass in between the two wickets on the field. ウィケット間, 投球バウンド地点 **3** N-COUNT 可算名詞 In cricket, when a **wicket** falls or is taken, a batsman is out. ウィケット, アウト □ *Matthew Hoggard took three wickets in six balls.* マシュー・ホガードは6投球で3アウトを取った.

wide /waɪd/ (**wider, widest**) **1** ADJ 形容詞 Something that is **wide** measures a large distance from one side or edge to the other. 幅が広い □ *All worktops should be wide enough to allow plenty of space for food preparation.* 調理台は食事の準備のためにたっぷりスペースがあるくらい幅が広いのが望ましい. **2** ADJ 形容詞 If you open or spread something **wide**, you open or spread it as far as possible or to the fullest extent. 大きく広げて □ *"It was huge," he announced, spreading his arms wide.* 「すっごく大きかったよ」彼は両手を大きく広げながら言った. **3** ADJ 形容詞 You use **wide** to talk or ask about how much something measures from one side or edge to the other. 幅が〜 □ *...a corridor of land four miles wide.* 幅4マイルの回廊地帯 □ *The road is only one lane wide.* その道路は1車線分の広さしかありません. **4** ADJ 形容詞 You use **wide** to describe something that includes a large number of different things or people. 豊富な □ *The brochure offers a wide choice of hotels, apartments and vacation homes.* そのパンフレットにはさまざまなホテル, アパート, 別荘などが載っている. ● **wide|ly** ADV 副詞 広く □ *He published widely in scientific journals.* 彼は科学雑誌で広く出版した. **5** ADJ 形容詞 You use **wide** to say that something is found, believed, known, or supported by many people or throughout a large area. 広範な □ *The case has attracted wide publicity.* その事件はかなり評判になった. ● **wide|ly** ADV 副詞 [ADV with v] 広範囲に □ *At present, no widely approved vaccine exists for malaria.* 現在のところ, マラリアに対して一般的に承認されたワクチンは存在しない. **6** ADJ 形容詞 A **wide** difference or gap between two things, ideas, or qualities is a large difference or gap. 大きな, 大幅な □ *Research shows a wide*

difference in tastes around the country. 調査は, 地方によって嗜好 (しこう) に大きな相違があることを示している. ● **wide|ly** ADV 副詞 大きく, 大幅に □ *The treatment regime may vary widely depending on the type of injury.* 治療法は, けがの種類によって大きく異なるかもしれない. **7** ADJ 形容詞 [ADJ n] **Wider** is used to describe something that relates to the most important or general parts of a situation, rather than to the smaller parts or to details. 大局的な □ *He emphasized the wider issue of superpower cooperation.* 彼は超大国の協力のより大局的な問題を強調した. **8** **wide awake** → see **awake** **9** **wide of the mark** → see **mark** **10** **wide open** → see **open** → see **ratio**

wid|en /waɪdᵊn/ (**widens, widening, widened**) **1** V-T/V-I 他動詞/自動詞 If you **widen** something or if it **widens**, it becomes greater in measurement from one side or edge to the other. 幅を広げる [他動詞], 幅が広くなる [自動詞] □ *He had an operation last year to widen a heart artery.* 彼は昨年大動脈を広げる手術を受けた. **2** V-T/V-I 他動詞/自動詞 If you **widen** something or if it **widens**, it becomes greater in range or it affects a larger number of people or things. 拡大する □ *U.S. prosecutors have widened a securities-fraud investigation.* 米国検察当局は証券詐欺の調査を拡大した. **3** V-T/V-I 他動詞/自動詞 If a difference or gap **widens** or if something **widens** it, it becomes greater. (差を) 広げる [他動詞], (差が) 広がる [自動詞] □ *Wage differences in the two areas are widening.* その2地域の賃金格差は広がっている.

wide-ranging ADJ 形容詞 If you describe something as **wide-ranging**, you mean it deals with or affects a great variety of different things. 多方面にわたる, 広範な □ *...a package of wide-ranging economic reforms.* 広範囲にわたる経済改革の総合計画

wide|screen /waɪdskrin/ ADJ 形容詞 A **widescreen** television has a screen that is wide in relation to its height. ワイドスクリーンの

wide|spread /waɪdspred/ ADJ 形容詞 Something that is **widespread** exists or happens over a large area, or to a great extent. 広範囲にわたる □ *There is widespread support for the new proposals.* 新案に対して幅広い支持がある.

wid|ow /wɪdoʊ/ (**widows**) N-COUNT 可算名詞 A **widow** is a woman whose husband has died and who has not married again. 未亡人 □ *She became a widow a year ago.* 彼女は1年前に未亡人になった.

wid|owed /wɪdoʊd/ V-T PASSIVE 受動態他動詞 If someone **is widowed**, their husband or wife dies. 夫/妻と死別する □ *More and more young men are widowed by cancer.* がんのために妻に先立たれる若者が増えている.

wid|ow|er /wɪdoʊər/ (**widowers**) N-COUNT 可算名詞 A **widower** is a man whose wife has died and who has not married again. 男やもめ □ *He is a widower and lives in Durango.* 彼は男やもめでドゥランゴに住んでいる.

width /wɪdθ, wɪtθ/ (**widths**) N-VAR 可変性名詞 The **width** of something is the distance it measures from one side or edge to the other. 幅 □ *Measure the full width of the window.* 窓の端から端までの長さを測りなさい. □ *The road was reduced to 18 ft in width by adding parking bays.* 駐車スペースを増設したためにその道路の幅は18フィートに狭まった. → see **ratio**

wield /wild/ (**wields, wielding, wielded**) **1** V-T 他動詞 If you **wield** a weapon, tool, or piece of equipment, you carry and use it. 手にする, 扱う □ *He was attacked by a man wielding a knife.* 彼はナイフを持った男に攻撃された. **2** V-T 他動詞 If someone **wields** power, they have it and are able to use it. 振るう, 握る □ *He remains chairman, but wields little power at the company.* 彼は会長として残るが, 会社での権力はほとんど握らない.

wife /waɪf/ (**wives**) N-COUNT 可算名詞 A man's **wife** is the woman he is married to. 妻 □ *He married his wife Jane 37 years ago.* 彼は妻のジェインと37年前に結婚した. → see **family, love**

wig /wɪg/ (**wigs**) N-COUNT 可算名詞 A **wig** is a covering of false hair that you wear on your head, for example, because you have little hair of your own or because you want to cover up your own

hair. かつら ❏ *Jo wore a long wig that made her look very sexy.* ジョーはとてもセクシーに見えるような髪の長いかつらをかぶっていた.

wig|gle /wɪɡ²l/ (**wiggles, wiggling, wiggled**) V-T/V-I 他動詞/自動詞 If you **wiggle** something or if it **wiggles**, it moves up and down or from side to side in small quick movements. ぴくぴく動かす [他動詞], ぴくぴく動く [自動詞] ❏ *She wiggled her finger.* 彼女は指をぴくぴく動かした. ● N-COUNT 可算名詞 **Wiggle** is also a noun. ぴくぴく動かすこと ❏ *...a wiggle of the hips.* 腰をくねくね揺らすこと

wild /waɪld/ (**wilds, wilder, wildest**) ▮ ADJ 形容詞 **Wild** animals or plants live or grow in natural surroundings and are not taken care of by people. 野生の ❏ *We saw two more wild cats creeping toward us in the darkness.* 私たちはさらに2匹の野生のネコが暗闇の中でゆっくりと近づいてくるのを見た. ▮ ADJ 形容詞 **Wild** land is natural and is not used by people. 自然のままの ❏ *...a wild area of woods and lakes.* 森や湖のある未開地 ▮ N-PLURAL 複数名詞 **The wilds** of a place are the natural areas that are far away from cities and towns. 未開地 ❏ *They went canoeing in the wilds of Canada.* 彼らはカナダの未開地にカヌーこぎに行った. ▮ ADJ 形容詞 **Wild** is used to describe the weather or the sea when it is stormy. 荒れた ❏ *The wild weather did not deter some people from taking an unseasonable dip in the sea.* 荒れた天気にもかかわらず, 季節外れの海で一泳ぎした人々がいた. ▮ ADJ 形容詞 **Wild** behavior is uncontrolled, excited, or energetic. 熱狂した ❏ *The children are wild with joy.* 子供たちは手放しで喜んでいる. ❏ *As George himself came on stage they went wild.* ジョージ自身がステージに登場したので彼らは熱狂した. ● **wild|ly** ADV 副詞 熱狂して ❏ *As she finished each song, the crowd clapped wildly.* 彼女が1曲終えるごとに観衆は熱狂して拍手した. ▮ ADJ 形容詞 If you describe someone or their behavior as **wild**, you mean that they behave in a very uncontrolled way. 手に負えない ❏ *The house is in a mess after a wild party.* その家はワイルドなパーティのあとで散らかっている. ● **wild|ly** ADV 副詞 [ADV with v] むやみやたらに ❏ *Five people were injured as Reynolds slashed out wildly with a kitchen knife.* レイノルズが包丁を狂ったように振り回し, 5人が負傷した. ▮ ADJ 形容詞 A **wild** idea is unusual or extreme. A **wild** guess is one that you make without much thought. 突拍子もない, とっぴな, いいかげんな [ADJ n] ❏ *Browning's prediction is no better than a wild guess.* ブラウニングの予想は当てずっぽうです. ● **wild|ly** ADV 副詞 とっぴに, いいかげんに ❏ *"Thirteen?" he guessed wildly.* 「13?」と彼は当てずっぽうで言った. ▮ → see also **wildly** ▮ PHRASE 句 Animals that live **in the wild** live in a free and natural state and are not taken care of by people. 野生状態で ❏ *Fewer than a thousand giant pandas still live in the wild.* 今なお野生状態で消息しているジャイアントパンダは1000頭に満たない. ▮ **beyond your wildest dreams** → see **dream** ▮ **in your wildest dreams** → see **dream** ▮ **to sow your wild oats** → see **oats**

Thesaurus		*wild* また次を参照:
ADJ.	feral, untamed ▮	
	desolate, natural, overgrown ▮	
	choppy, stormy, tempestuous ▮	
	excited, rowdy, uncontrolled ▮ ▮	

Word Partnership		*wild* は次の語句と使われる:
N.	wild **animal**, wild **beasts/creatures**, wild **game**, wild **horse**, wild **mushrooms** ▮	
	wild **pitch**, wild **swing** ▮	
ADJ.	wild-**eyed** ▮	
V.	**run** wild ▮ ▮	
	go wild ▮ ▮	

wild card (**wild cards**) also **wildcard** ▮ N-COUNT 可算名詞 If you refer to someone or something as a **wild card** in a particular situation, you mean that they cause uncertainty because you do not know how they will behave. 行動や予測がつかない人, 先が予測ができないもの ❏ *The wild card in the picture is eastern Europe.* この状況下で予測がつかないのは東ヨーロッパだ. ▮ N-COUNT 可算名詞 A **wildcard** is a symbol such as * or ? used in some computing commands or searches in order to represent any character or range of characters. ワイルドカード (コンピュータで任意の文字を代用する記号) [COMPUTING コンピューティング] ▮ N-COUNT 可算名詞 In card games, if a particular card is named as a **wild card**, the player who holds it may give it any value he chooses. ワイルドカード (トランプでどんな札としても使えるカード) ❏ *Look. I have a straight of 3, 4, 6, 7 and the wild card for the 5.* ほら, 続き番号で3, 4, 6, 7があって, 5の代わりにワイルドカードだよ.

wil|der|ness /wɪldərnɪs/ (**wildernesses**) N-COUNT 可算名詞 A **wilderness** is a desert or other area of natural land which is not used by people. 荒野, 原野 ❏ *...the icy Canadian wilderness.* 氷に覆われたカナダの荒野

wild|fire /waɪldfaɪər/ (**wildfires**) ▮ N-COUNT 可算名詞 A **wildfire** is a fire that starts, usually by itself, in a wild area such as a forest, and spreads rapidly, causing great damage. 山火事 ❏ *...a wildfire in Montana that's already burned thousands of acres of rich*

grassland. モンタナ州ですでに何千エーカーもの肥沃な草原を焼き払った山火事 ▮ PHRASE 句 If something, especially news or a rumor, **spreads like wildfire**, it spreads extremely quickly. 瞬く間に広がる ❏ *These stories are spreading like wildfire through the city.* これらの話は町中に瞬く間に広がった.

→ see **fire**

wild|life /waɪldlaɪf/ N-UNCOUNT 不可算名詞 You can use **wildlife** to refer to the animals and other living things that live in the wild. 野生生物 ❏ *People were concerned that pets or wildlife could be affected by the pesticides.* ペットや野生生物が殺虫剤の影響を受けるのではないかと人々は懸念していた.

→ see **zoo**

wild|ly /waɪldli/ ▮ ADV 副詞 You use **wildly** to emphasize the degree, amount, or intensity of something. 極めて, 非常に [EMPHASIS 強調] ❏ *Here again, the community and police have wildly different stories of what happened.* 今回もまた地域社会と警察側で事件について全く異なった説明をしています. ▮ → see also **wild**

	will	
❶	MODAL VERB USES	
❷	WANTING SOMETHING TO HAPPEN	

❶ **will** /wɪl/

Will is a modal verb. It is used with the base form of a verb. In spoken English and informal written English, the form **won't** is often used in negative statements.

Will は法動詞であり, 動詞の原形と共に用いられる. 口語英語とくだけた書き言葉では, **won't** 形はしばしば否定陳述文に使われる.

▮ MODAL 法動詞 You use **will** to indicate that you hope, think, or have evidence that something is going to happen or be the case in the future. 未来の出来事に対する希望・考えなどを表す ❏ *I'm sure we will find a wide variety of choices available in school cafeterias.* きっと学食にはさまざまなメニューを取りそろえていることが分かるでしょう. ❏ *Will you ever feel at home here?* いつかここでくつろげますか? ❏ *The ship will not be ready for a month.* その船は準備に1か月かかる. ▮ MODAL 法動詞 You use **will** in order to make statements about official arrangements in the future. 未来の予定を述べるのに用いる ❏ *The show will be open to the public at 2 pm; admission will be $5.* 展示会は午後2時から一般公開が開始される. 入場料は5ドル. ▮ MODAL 法動詞 You use **will** in order to make promises and threats about what is going to happen or be the case in the future. 約束・警告などを述べるのに用いる ❏ *I'll call you tonight.* 今晩電話する. ❏ *Price quotes on selected product categories will be sent on request.* 申し込みを受け付け次第, お選びの製品部門の見積価格をお送りします. ▮ MODAL 法動詞 You use **will** to indicate someone's intention to do something. (意志を込めて) ～するつもりである ❏ *I will say no more on these matters, important though they are.* これらの問題は重要ではあるが, これ以上は申し上げられません. ❏ *In this section we will describe common myths about cigarettes, alcohol, and marijuana.* この項ではタバコ, アルコール, マリファナについての間違った社会通念について説明します. ❏ *"Dinner's ready." — "Thanks, Carrie, but we'll have a drink first."* 「晩御飯ができましたよ」「ありがとう, キャリー. でもまず1杯飲ませていただきます.」 ❏ *Will you be remaining in the city?* 町に残るつもりなの? ▮ MODAL 法動詞 You use **will** in questions in order to make polite invitations or offers. ～しませんか [POLITENESS 丁寧さ] ❏ *Will you stay for supper?* 夕食までゆっくりしませんか? ❏ *Will you join me for a drink?* 一緒に飲みに行きませんか? ▮ MODAL 法動詞 You use **will** in questions in order to ask or tell someone to do something. ～してもらえませんか, ～しなさい ❏ *Will you drive me home?* 車で家まで送ってもらえませんか? ❏ *Will you listen again, Andrew?* アンドリュー, もう一度よく聞きなさい. ▮ MODAL 法動詞 You use **will** to say that someone is willing to do something. You use **will not** or **won't** to indicate that someone refuses to do something. (進んで) ～する ❏ *All right, I'll forgive you.* わかりました. あなたを許します. ▮ → see also **willing** ▮ MODAL 法動詞 You use **will** to say that a person or thing is able to do something in the future. ～できる ❏ *How the country will defend itself in the future has become increasingly important.* 国が将来どのように自衛するかということはますます重要になった. ▮ MODAL 法動詞 You use **will** to indicate that an action usually happens in the particular way mentioned. 習性・習慣を表す ❏ *The thicker the material, the less susceptible the garment will be to wet conditions.* 生地が厚くなればなるほど布地は湿潤状態に左右されなくなる. ▮ MODAL 法動詞 You use **will** in the main clause of some "if" and "unless" sentences to indicate something that you consider to be fairly likely to happen. ifやunlessを用いた文の主節で可能性が高い場合に用いる ❏ *If you overcook the meat it will be dry.* 肉を調理しすぎるとかさかさになります. ▮ MODAL 法動詞 You use **will** to say that someone insists on behaving or doing something in a particular way and you cannot change them. You emphasize **will** when you use it in this way. いつも～してばかりいる ❏ *He will leave his socks lying all*

over the place and it drives me crazy. 彼はいつもあちこちに靴下を脱ぎっぱなしにするので頭にくる. **13** MODAL 法動詞 You use **will have** with a past participle when you are saying that you are fairly certain that something will be true by a particular time in the future. 未来のある時点の推測を表す ❑ As many as ten-million children will have been infected with the virus by the end of the decade. 1000万人もの子供が10年以内にそのウィルスに感染するだろう. **14** MODAL 法動詞 You use **will have** with a past participle to indicate that you are fairly sure that something is the case. ～に違いない ❑ Jack will have been very upset by all this. ジャックはこのことできっとかなり動揺しているに違いない.

❷ **will** /wɪl/ (**wills, willing, willed**) **1** N-VAR 可変性名詞 **Will** is the determination to do something. 意志, 決意 ❑ He was said to have lost his will to live. 彼は生きる意志を失ったといわれていた. **2** → see also **free will** **3** N-SING 単数名詞 If something is **the will of** a person or group of people with authority, they want it to happen. 望み, 願望 ❑ He has submitted himself to the will of God. 彼は自ら神のおぼしめしに応じた. **4** V-T 他動詞 If you **will** something **to** happen, you try to make it happen by using mental effort rather than physical effort. (精神的な努力で) 実現させようとする ❑ I looked at the telephone, willing it to ring. 私は, ベルを鳴らそうとしながら電話を見た. **5** N-COUNT 可算名詞 A **will** is a document in which you declare what you want to happen to your money and property when you die. 遺言 ❑ Attached to his will was a letter he had written to his wife just days before his death. 彼の遺言には, 死のほんの数日前に妻宛に書いた手紙が添付されていた. **6** PHRASE 句 If something is done **against** your **will**, it is done even though you do not want it to be done. 意思に反して ❑ No doubt he was forced to leave his family against his will. きっと彼は意思に反して家族を置いていかざるをえなかったんだ.

will|ful /wɪlfəl/ **1** ADJ 形容詞 If you describe actions or attitudes as **willful**, you are critical of them because they are done or expressed deliberately, especially with the intention of causing someone harm. 故意の, 意図的な [ADJ n] ❑ The sergeant faces a lesser charge of willful neglect of duty. 軍曹は職務怠慢という軽罪で告訴されています. **2** ADJ 形容詞 If you describe someone as **willful**, you mean that they are determined to do what they want to do, even if it is not sensible. 強情な ❑ Molly was at times impatient and willful. モリーは時折せっかちで強情だった.

will|ing /wɪlɪŋ/ **1** ADJ 形容詞 If someone is **willing to** do something, they are fairly happy about doing it and will do it if they are asked or required to do it. ～する気がある, ～するのをいとわない [v-link ADJ to-inf] ❑ There are, of course, questions which she will not be willing to answer. 彼女が答える気のない質問も当然ある. **2** ADJ 形容詞 **Willing** is used to describe someone who does something fairly enthusiastically and because they want to do it rather than because they are forced to do it. 進んでする, 喜んでする ❑ Have the party on a Saturday, when you can get your partner and other willing adults to help. パートナーやほかの意欲的な大人に手伝ってもらえるように, 土曜日にパーティを開きなさい. **3** God **willing** → see **god**

wil|low /wɪloʊ/ (**willows**) N-COUNT 可算名詞 A **willow** or a **willow tree** is a type of tree with long branches and long narrow leaves that grows near water. 柳

will|power /wɪlpaʊər/ also **will-power** or **will power** N-UNCOUNT 不可算名詞 **Willpower** is a very strong determination to do something. 強い意志, 自制心 ❑ He came in for help after his attempts to stop smoking by willpower alone failed. 彼は, 意志の力だけで禁煙しようとして失敗したあと助けを求めてやってきた.

wilt /wɪlt/ (**wilts, wilting, wilted**) V-I 自動詞 If a plant **wilts**, it gradually bends downward and becomes weak because it needs more water or it is dying. しおれる ❑ The roses wilted the next day. そのバラは次の日にはしおれていました.

wily /waɪli/ (**wilier, wiliest**) ADJ 形容詞 If you describe someone or their behavior as **wily**, you mean that they are clever at achieving what they want, especially by tricking people. ずる賢い ❑ This is a wily politician. こちらは戦略に長けた政治家だ.

wimp /wɪmp/ (**wimps**) N-COUNT 可算名詞 If you call someone a **wimp**, you disapprove of them because they lack confidence or determination, or because they are often afraid of things. 弱虫, 意気地なし [INFORMAL くだけた, DISAPPROVAL 不賛成] ❑ I was a wimp, because I had spent my life being bullied by my Dad. 私は生涯を父親にいじめられて過ごしたので, 意気地なしだった.

win /wɪn/ (**wins, winning, won**) **1** V-T/V-I 他動詞/自動詞 If you **win** something such as a competition, battle, or argument, you defeat those people you are competing or fighting against, or you do better than everyone else involved. 勝つ ❑ He does not have any realistic chance of winning the election. 彼はこの選挙に勝つ現実的な可能性はありません. ❑ The top four teams all won. 上位4チームがすべて勝った. ● N-COUNT 可算名詞 **Win** is also a noun. 勝利 ❑ The voters gave a narrow win to Vargas Llosa. バルガス・リョサはぎりぎり当選した. **2** V-T 他動詞 If something **wins** you something such as an election, competition, battle, or argument, it causes you to defeat

the people competing with you or fighting you, or to do better than everyone else involved. 獲得させる [他動詞] ❑ The Democrats had found a message that could win them the White House. 民主党員は大統領選挙に勝つことにつながりそうなメッセージを見つけた. **3** V-T 他動詞 If you **win** something such as a prize or medal, you get it because you have defeated everyone else in something such as an election, competition, battle, or argument, or have done very well in it. 獲得する, 受賞する ❑ Trent Dimas won gold in the final men's gymnastic event. トレント・ディマスは男子体操競技の決勝戦で金メダルを獲得した. **4** V-T 他動詞 If you **win** something that you want or need, you succeed in getting it. 得る ❑ ...moves to win the support of the poor. 貧困層の支持を得るための運動 **5** → see also **winning** **6** to **win hands down** → see **hand**

▶ **win over** PHRASAL VERB 句動詞 If you **win** someone **over**, you persuade them to support you or agree with you. 説得して味方につける, 口説き落とす ❑ He has won over a significant number of the left-wing deputies. 彼はかなりの数の左派の代議員を説得した.

wince /wɪns/ (**winces, wincing, winced**) V-I 自動詞 If you **wince**, the muscles of your face tighten suddenly because you have felt a pain or because you have just seen, heard, or remembered something unpleasant. しかめる ❑ Every time he put any weight on his left leg he winced in pain. 彼は左足に力を入れるたびに, 痛みで顔をしかめた.

winch /wɪntʃ/ (**winches, winching, winched**) **1** N-COUNT 可算名詞 A **winch** is a machine that is used to lift heavy objects or people who need to be rescued. It consists of a cylinder around which a rope or chain is wound. ウィンチ, 巻き上げ機 **2** V-T 他動詞 If you **winch** an object or person somewhere, you lift or lower them using a winch. ウィンチで引き上げる ❑ He would attach a cable around the chassis of the car and winch it up on to the canal bank. 彼だったら車のシャーシーの周りにケーブルを取り付けウィンチで運河のほとりまで引き上げるだろう.

wind

| ❶ | AIR |
| ❷ | TURNING OR WRAPPING |

❶ **wind** /wɪnd/ (**winds, winding, winded**) **1** N-VAR 可変性名詞 A **wind** is a current of air that is moving across the earth's surface. 風 ❑ There was a strong wind blowing. 強い風が吹いていた. **2** N-COUNT 可算名詞 Journalists often refer to a trend or factor that influences events as a **wind of** a particular kind. 風潮 ❑ The winds of change are blowing across the country. 変革の風が国中で吹いています. **3** V-T 他動詞 If you **are winded** by something such as a blow, the air is suddenly knocked out of your lungs so that you have difficulty breathing for a short time. 息を詰まらせる ❑ He was winded and shaken. 彼は息を切らし動揺していた. **4** PHRASE 句 If someone **breaks wind**, they release gas from their intestines through their anus. おならをする ❑ If I break wind at dinner, should I say "Pardon," or pretend nothing has happened? 目下のところ, 一般人, 特に報道陣に聞きつけられないことを願っている. **5** PHRASE 句 If you **get wind of** something, you hear about it, especially when someone else did not want you to know about it. 聞きつける, かぎつける [INFORMAL くだけた] ❑ I don't want the public, and especially not the press, to get wind of it at this stage. 目下のところ, 一般人, 特に報道陣に聞きつけられないことを願っている.
→ see Word Web: **wind**
→ see **beach, electricity, erosion, storm, wave**

❷ **wind** /waɪnd/ (**winds, winding, wound**) **1** V-T/V-I 他動詞/自動詞 If a road, river, or line of people **winds** in a particular direction, it goes in that direction with a lot of bends or twists in it. 曲がりくねりながら行く ❑ Quiet mountain roads wind through groves of bamboo and cedar. 静かな山岳道路は竹林や杉林を通って曲がりくねっている. ❑ ...a narrow winding road. 狭くて曲がりくねった道 ❑ We wound our way southeast. 私たちは南東に向かって曲がりくねった道を進んだ. **2** V-T 他動詞 When you **wind** something flexible around something else, you wrap it around it several times. 巻きつける ❑ The horse jumped forward and around her, winding the rope

Word Web   wind

The earth's surface **temperature** isn't the same everywhere. This temperature difference causes **air** to flow from one area to another. We call this airflow **wind**. As warm air expands and rises, air pressure goes down. Then denser cool air **blows** in. The amount of difference in air pressure determines how strong the wind will be. It can be anything from a **breeze** to a **gale**. The earth's geography creates **prevailing winds**. For example, air in the warmer areas near the Equator is always rising, and cooler air from polar regions is always flowing in to take its place.

around her waist. 馬は前方や彼女の周りを跳びはねながら，ロープを彼女の腰に巻きつけた． ▣ V-T 他動詞 When you **wind** a mechanical device, for example, a watch or a clock, you turn a knob, key, or handle on it several times in order to make it operate. ねじを巻く ❏ I still hadn't wound my watch so I didn't know the time. まだ腕時計のねじを巻いていなかったので何時か分からなかった． ● PHRASAL VERB 句動詞 **Wind up** means the same as **wind**. ねじを巻く ❏ I wound up the watch and listened to it tick. 腕時計のねじを巻いてカチコチと鳴る音を聞きました． ▣ V-T 他動詞 To **wind** a tape or film **back** or **forward** means to make it move toward its starting or ending position. (テープ・フィルムを) 巻き戻す・早送りする ❏ The camcorder winds the tape back or forward at high speed. そのビデオカメラはテープの巻き戻しや早送りをする．

Thesaurus   wind また次を参照:

N.	air, current, gust ❶ ▣
V.	bend, loop, twist; (ant.) straighten ❷ ▣

▶ **wind down** ▣ PHRASAL VERB 句動詞 When you **wind down** something such as the window of a car, you make it move downwards by turning a handle. 下ろす，開ける ❏ Glass motioned to him to wind down the window. グラスは彼に窓を開けるように合図した． ▣ PHRASAL VERB 句動詞 If you **wind down**, you relax after doing something that has made you feel tired or tense. くつろぐ [INFORMAL くだけた] ❏ I regularly have a drink to wind down. くつろぐためにいつも決まって一杯引っかける． ▣ PHRASAL VERB 句動詞 If someone **winds down** a business or activity, they gradually reduce the amount of work that is done or the number of people that are involved, usually before closing or stopping it completely. 徐々に縮小する ❏ Aid workers have begun winding down their operation. 救援隊員は徐々に事業を縮小し始めた．

▶ **wind up** ▣ PHRASAL VERB 句動詞 When you **wind up** an activity, you finish it or stop doing it. 終わりにする ❏ The president is about to wind up his visit to Somalia. 大統領はソマリアへの訪問を締めくくるところだ． ▣ PHRASAL VERB 句動詞 When you **wind up** something such as the window of a car, you make it move upwards by turning a handle. 上げる，閉める ❏ He started winding the window up but I grabbed the door and opened it. 彼は窓を閉め始めたが，私はドアにさっと手を伸ばして開けた． ▣ → see also **wind** ❷ 3 → see also **wound up**

wind|fall /wɪndfɔl/ (windfalls) N-COUNT 可算名詞 A **windfall** is a sum of money that you receive unexpectedly or by luck, for example, if you win a lottery. 予想外の収入 ❏ ...the man who received a $250,000 windfall after a banking error. 銀行の手違いで予想外に25万ドルを受け取った男性

wind|mill /wɪndmɪl/ (windmills) N-COUNT 可算名詞 A **windmill** is a building with long pieces of wood on the outside that turn around as the wind blows and provide energy for a machine that crushes grain. A **windmill** is also a similar structure that uses the power of the wind to pump water or make electricity. 風車，風車小屋

win|dow /wɪndoʊ/ (windows) ▣ N-COUNT 可算名詞 A **window** is a space in the wall of a building or in the side of a vehicle, which has glass in it so that light can come in and you can see out. 窓 ❏ He stood at the window, moodily staring out. 彼は窓際に立って，むっつりと外を見ていた． ❏ The room felt very hot and she wondered why someone did not open a window. その部屋はとても暑くて，彼女はどうしてだれも窓を開けないのか不思議に思った． ▣ N-COUNT 可算名詞 A **window** is a glass-covered opening above a counter, for example, in a bank, post office, train station, or museum, which the person serving you sits behind. 窓口 ❏ The woman at the ticket window told me that the admission fee was $17.50. 切符売り場の女性が入場料は17.5ドルだと教えてくれた． ▣ N-COUNT 可算名詞 On a computer screen, a **window** is one of the work areas that the screen can be divided into. ウィンドウ [COMPUTING コンピューティング] ❏ Yahoo! Pager puts a small window on your screen containing a list of your "friends." Yahoo! ページャーで画面に「友人」リストを掲載した小さなウィンドウが表示される． ▣ PHRASE 句 If you say that something such as a plan or a particular way of thinking or behaving **has gone out of the window** or **is out the window**, you mean that it has disappeared completely. 消えてな

くなる ❏ By now all logic had gone out of the window. すでにすべての論理は消えうせてしまった． → see **glass**

Word Partnership   window は次の語句と使われる:

V.	close/open a window ▣ look in/out a window, peer in/into/out/through a window, watch through a window ▣ ▣
ADJ.	open window ▣ broken window, dark window, large/small window, narrow window ▣ ▣
N.	car window, window curtains, kitchen window, window screen, window treatment ▣ window display, shop window, store window ▣

wind|shield /wɪndʃild/ (windshields) N-COUNT 可算名詞 The **windshield** of a car or other vehicle is the glass window at the front through which the driver looks. フロントガラス [AM 米国英語]

wind|shield wip|er (windshield wipers) N-COUNT 可算名詞 A **windshield wiper** is a device that wipes rain from a vehicle's windshield. ワイパー [AM 米国英語]

wind|surf|ing /wɪndsɜrfɪŋ/ N-UNCOUNT 不可算名詞 **Windsurfing** is a sport in which you move along the surface of the sea or a lake on a long narrow board with a sail on it. ウィンドサーフィン

windy /wɪndi/ (windier, windiest) ADJ 形容詞 If it is **windy**, the wind is blowing a lot. 風の強い ❏ It was windy and Jake felt cold. 風が強くてジェイクは寒気を感じた．

wine /waɪn/ (wines) N-MASS 質量名詞 **Wine** is an alcoholic drink made from grapes. You can also refer to alcoholic drinks made from other fruits or vegetables as **wine**. ワイン，ぶどう酒，一酒 ❏ ...a bottle of white wine. 白ワイン1本

wine bar (wine bars) N-COUNT 可算名詞 A **wine bar** is a place where people can buy and drink wine, and sometimes eat food as well. ワインバー

wing /wɪŋ/ (wings) ▣ N-COUNT 可算名詞 The **wings** of a bird or insect are the two parts of its body that it uses for flying. 翼，羽 ❏ The bird flapped its wings furiously. その鳥は翼をバタバタさせた． ▣ N-COUNT 可算名詞 The **wings** of an airplane are the long flat parts sticking out of its side which support it while it is flying. (飛行機の) 翼 ❏ The plane made one pass, dipped its wings, then circled back. その飛行機は1回上空飛行して，翼を傾け，そして旋回して戻った． ▣ N-COUNT 可算名詞 A **wing** of a building is a part of it that sticks out from the main part. 翼，袖 ❏ We were given an office in the empty west wing. 使われていない西棟に事務所を与えられた． ▣ N-COUNT 可算名詞 A **wing** of an organization, especially a political organization, is a group within it which has a particular function or particular beliefs. 派，部門 ❏ ...the military wing of the African National Congress. アフリカ民族会議の軍事組織5 → see also **left-wing**, **right-wing** ▣ N-PLURAL 複数名詞 In a theater, the **wings** are the sides of the stage that are hidden from the audience by curtains or scenery. (舞台の) そで ❏ Most nights I watched the start of the play from the wings. ほとんどの夜，私は舞台のそでから芝居の始まりを見た． ▣ PHRASE 句 If you say that someone is waiting **in the wings**, you mean that they are ready and waiting for an opportunity to take action. 待機して ❏ There are now more than 20 big companies waiting in the wings to take over some of its business. その事業の一部を引き継ごうと待ち構えている大手企業が現在20社以上ある． ▣ PHRASE 句 If you **spread your wings**, you do something new and somewhat difficult or move to a new place, because you feel more confident in your abilities than you used to and you want to gain wider experience. 新しいことに乗り出す，活動の幅を広げる ❏ I led a very confined life in my village so I suppose that I wanted to spread my wings. 村で非常に閉ざされた生活を送っていたので，新しいことに乗り出してみたかったんだと思います． ▣ PHRASE 句 If you **take** someone **under your wing**, you look after them, help them, and protect them. かばう ❏ Her boss took her under his wing after fully realizing her potential. 彼女の上司は彼女の潜在能力に実感してから彼女の面倒を見るようになった． → see **bird**

winged /wɪŋd/ ADJ 形容詞 A **winged** insect or other creature has wings. 羽のある A **winged** insect or other creature has wings. 羽のある *Flycatchers feed primarily on winged insects.* ヒタキは主に羽の昆虫をえさにする.

wink /wɪŋk/ (winks, winking, winked) **1** V-I 自動詞 When you **wink at** someone, you look toward them and close one eye very briefly, usually as a signal that something is a joke or a secret. ウィンクする, 目くばせする *Brian winked at his bride-to-be.* ブライアンは彼のフィアンセにウィンクをした. ● N-COUNT 可算名詞 **Wink** is also a noun. ウィンク *I gave her a wink.* 彼女にウィンクをした. **2** PHRASE 句 If you say that you **did not sleep a wink** or **did not get a wink of sleep**, you mean that you tried to go to sleep but could not. 一睡もできない [INFORMAL くだけた] *I didn't get a wink of sleep on the flight.* 飛行機の中で一睡もできなかった.

win|ner /wɪnər/ (winners) N-COUNT 可算名詞 The **winner** of a prize, race, or competition is the person, animal, or thing that wins it. 当選者, 勝者, 優勝者 *She will present the trophies to the award winners.* 彼女は受賞者にトロフィーを授与します.
→ see **lottery**

win|ning /wɪnɪŋ/ **1** ADJ 形容詞 You can use **winning** to describe a person or thing that wins something such as a competition, game, or election. 受賞した, 勝利を得た [ADJ n] *...the winning lotto ticket.* 当選した宝くじ. **2** ADJ 形容詞 You can use **winning** to describe actions or qualities that please other people and make them feel friendly toward you. 人好きのする [ADJ n] *She gave him another of her winning smiles.* 彼女は彼に向かって再びあいきょうのあるほほえみを浮かべた. **3** → see also **win**
→ see **lottery**

win|nings /wɪnɪŋz/ N-PLURAL 複数名詞 You can use **winnings** to refer to the money that someone wins in a competition or by gambling. 賞金 *I have come to collect my winnings.* 賞金を受け取りに来た.
→ see **lottery**

win|ter /wɪntər/ (winters) N-VAR 可変性名詞 **Winter** is the season between fall and spring. In the winter the weather is usually cold. 冬 *In winter the nights are long and cold.* 冬の夜は長くて冷える. *...the late winter of 1941.* 1941年の晩冬

win-win ADJ 形容詞 A **win-win** situation is certain to bring good results, sometimes for two people or groups. だれもが得をする, 双方に有利な [ADJ n] *It is surprising that it has taken people so long to take advantage of what is a win-win opportunity.* 人々が双方に有利な機会を利用するのにあまりにも時間がかかったことは意外だ.

wipe /waɪp/ (wipes, wiping, wiped) **1** V-T 他動詞 If you **wipe** something, you rub its surface to remove dirt or liquid from it. ふく *I'll just wipe the table.* ちょっとテーブルをふきます. *When he had finished washing he began to wipe the basin clean.* 彼は洗い終えると, 洗面台をきれいにふき始めた. ● N-COUNT 可算名詞 **Wipe** is also a noun. ふくこと *Tomorrow I'm going to give the toys a good wipe as some seem a bit greasy.* おもちゃが少し汚れているようなので, 明日しっかりふくつもりだ. **2** V-T 他動詞 If you **wipe** dirt or liquid from something, you remove it by using a cloth or your hand. ふき取る, ぬぐう *Gleb wiped the sweat from his face.* グレブは顔の汗をぬぐった. **3** N-COUNT 可算名詞 A **wipe** is a small moist cloth for cleaning things and is designed to be used only once. ウェットティッシュ *...antiseptic wipes.* 除菌ウェットティッシュ
▶ **wipe out** PHRASAL VERB 句動詞 To **wipe out** something such as a place or a group of people or animals means to destroy them completely. 全滅させる, 絶滅させる *Experts say if the island is not protected, the spill could wipe out the gulf's turtle population.* その島が保護されなければ流出により湾のカメが絶滅するかもしれないと専門家は述べています.

wip|er /waɪpər/ (wipers) N-COUNT 可算名詞 A **wiper** is a device that wipes rain from a vehicle's windshield. ワイパー

wire /waɪər/ (wires, wiring, wired) **1** N-VAR 可変性名詞 A **wire** is a long thin piece of metal that is used to fasten things or to carry electric current. 針金 *...fine copper wire.* 細い銅線 **2** N-COUNT 可算名詞 A **wire** is a cable that carries power or signals from one place to another. 電線 *I ripped out the telephone wire that ran through to his office.* 私は彼のオフィスにつながっている電話線を引き抜いた. **3** V-T 他動詞 If you **wire** something such as a building or piece of equipment, you put wires inside it so that electricity or signals can pass into or through it. 配線工事をする *...learning to wire and plumb the house herself.* 自分で家の

配線工事や配管工事をできるようになること *Each of the homes has a security system and is wired for cable television.* 各家は防犯システムを設置していてケーブルテレビを引いている. ● PHRASAL VERB 句動詞 **Wire up** means the same as **wire**. 配線工事をする *Wire the thermometers up to trigger off an alarm bell if the temperature drops.* 温度が下がると警報が鳴るように温度計を配線しなさい. **4** PHRASE 句 If something goes **to the wire**, it continues until the last possible moment. 最後の最後まで [MAINLY JOURNALISM 主にジャーナリズム] *Negotiators again worked right down to the wire to reach an agreement.* 交渉人らは合意に達するまで再びとことん話し合った. **5** → see also **barbed wire**
→ see **metal**

wire|less /waɪərlɪs/ ADJ 形容詞 **Wireless** technology uses radio waves rather than electricity and therefore does not require any wires. ワイヤレス, 無線の *...the fast-growing wireless communication market.* 急成長している無線通信市場
→ see **cellphone**

wir|ing /waɪərɪŋ/ N-UNCOUNT 不可算名詞 The **wiring** in a building or machine is the system of wires that supply electricity to the different parts of it. 配線 *Faulty wiring is the major cause of house fires.* 誤配線が住宅火災の主な原因だ.

wiry /waɪəri/ **1** ADJ 形容詞 Someone who is **wiry** is somewhat thin but is also strong. 細身で筋肉質の *His body is wiry and athletic.* 彼の体は細身でたくましい. **2** ADJ 形容詞 Something such as hair or grass that is **wiry** is stiff and rough to touch. ごわごわした *Her wiry hair was pushed up on top of her head in an untidy bun.* 彼女のごわごわした髪が頭のてっぺんに押し上げられてだらしないシニョンになっていた.

wis|dom /wɪzdəm/ **1** N-UNCOUNT 不可算名詞 **Wisdom** is the ability to use your experience and knowledge in order to make sensible decisions or judgments. 知恵 *...the patience and wisdom that comes from old age.* 年をとることによってもたらされる忍耐力と知恵 **2** N-SING 単数名詞 If you talk about the **wisdom of** a particular decision or action, you are talking about how sensible it is. 賢明さ *Many Lithuanians have expressed doubts about the wisdom of the decision.* 多くのリトアニア人はその決定の賢明さに疑念を表した.

wise /waɪz/ (wiser, wisest) **1** ADJ 形容詞 A **wise** person is able to use their experience and knowledge in order to make sensible decisions and judgments. 賢い, 思慮深い *She has the air of a wise woman.* 彼女は賢しこそうな雰囲気を持っている. ● **wise|ly** ADV 副詞 [ADV with v] 賢く *The three of us stood around the machine nodding wisely.* 私たち3人は賢そうにうなずきながら機械の周りに立っていた. **2** ADJ 形容詞 A **wise** action or decision is sensible. 賢明な *It's never wise to withhold evidence.* 証拠を提供しないのは決して賢明ではない. *She had made a very wise decision.* 彼女はとても賢明な決断をした. ● **wise|ly** ADV 副詞 賢明に *They've invested their money wisely.* 彼らは賢明に投資をした.

wish /wɪʃ/ (wishes, wishing, wished) **1** N-COUNT 可算名詞 A **wish** is a desire or strong feeling that you want to have something or do something. 希望, 願い *She was sincere and genuine in her wish to make amends for the past.* 彼女は心の底から過去の償いをしたいと願っていた. *The decision was made against the wishes of the party leader.* 党首の希望に反してその決断が下された. **2** V-T/V-I 他動詞/自動詞 If you **wish** to do something or to have it done for you, you want to do it or have it done. 願う, 望む [FORMAL 形式ばった] *If you wish to go away for the weekend, our office will be delighted to make hotel reservations.* 週末旅行にご希望なら当代理店で宿泊手続きができます. *We can dress as we wish now.* 今では着たい服を着ることができる. **3** V-T 他動詞 If you **wish** something were true, you would like it to be true, even though you know that it is impossible or unlikely. ―だったらなあと思う. [no cont] *I wish I could do that.* それができたらなあと思う. *Pa, you wouldn't shout.* お父ちゃん, どならないでくれたらなあ. **4** V-I 自動詞 If you **wish for** something, you express the desire for that thing silently to yourself. In fairy tales, when a person wishes for something, the thing they wish for often happens by magic. 願い事をする, 祈る *Be careful what you wish for. You might get it!* 慎重に願い事をしなさい. 実現するかもしれないから! ● N-COUNT 可算名詞 **Wish** is also a noun. 願い事 *The custom is for people to try and eat 12 grapes as the clock strikes midnight. Those who are successful can make a wish.* 時計が深夜の12時を打ったら12個のブドウを食べようとするのが慣習だ. それができた人は願い事をすることができる. **5** V-T 他動詞 If you say that you would not **wish** a particular thing **on** someone, you mean that the thing is so unpleasant that you would not want them to be forced to experience it. (否定文で) 自分一人でたくさんだ [no cont, with brd-neg] *It's a horrid experience and I wouldn't wish it on my worst enemy.* こんな恐ろしい経験は自分一人でたくさんだ. **6** V-T 他動詞 If you **wish** someone something such as luck or happiness, you express the hope that they will be lucky or happy. 祈る *I wish you both a good trip.* 2人とも気をつけて行ってらっしゃい. **7** N-PLURAL 複数名詞 If you express your good **wishes** toward

someone, you are politely expressing your friendly feelings toward them and your hope that they will be successful or happy. 成功や多幸を願うあいさつで用いられる ❑ *I found George's story very sad. Please give him my best wishes.* ジョージの話を聞いてとても悲しく思う。どうか彼によろしくお伝えください。 [POLITENESS 丁寧さ]

Note that **wish** and **want** have similar meanings, but are used differently. If you **want** something, you feel a need for it or a desire to have it. You can say that you **want** to do something, that you **want** someone to do something, or that you **want** something to happen. If you use **wish** with a "to" infinitive, this has the same meaning as **want** but is more formal. ❑ *I want to get out of here... She wished to consult him about her future.* **Wish** is normally followed by a "that" -clause, although the word "that" is often omitted from the clause. If you **wish** that something was the case, you would like it to be the case, even though this is unlikely or impossible. ❑ *I wish I lived near Miami... He wished he had phoned for a cab.* Note the use of the tenses in the examples; when **wish** is in the present tense, the past tense is used in the clause, and when **wish** is in the past tense, the past perfect tense is used in the clause.

Word Partnership   *wish は次の語句と使われる:*

V.   **get your** wish, **grant a** wish, **have a** wish, **make a** wish **1** **4**
      I wish **I knew** **3**
      wish **come true** **4**
N.   wish *someone* **the best**, wish *someone* **luck** **6**

wish|ful think|ing N-UNCOUNT 不可算名詞 If you say that an idea, wish, or hope is **wishful thinking**, you mean that it has failed to come true or is unlikely to come true. 甘い考え、希望的観測 ❑ *It is wishful thinking to expect deeper change under his leadership.* 彼の指導の下でさらに奥深い変化を期待するのは希望的観測だ.

wist|ful /wɪstfəl/ ADJ 形容詞 Someone who is **wistful** is sad because they want something and know that they cannot have it. やるせない、未練のある ❑ *I can't help feeling slightly wistful about the perks I'm giving up.* 断念しかけている特典に関して少し未練を感じないわけにはいかない.

wit /wɪt/ ❶ N-UNCOUNT 不可算名詞 **Wit** is the ability to use words or ideas in an amusing, clever, and imaginative way. 機知、ウィット ❑ *Boulding was known for his biting wit.* ボールディングは痛烈な機知に富んでいることで知られている. ❷ N-SING 単数名詞 If you say that someone has **the wit to** do something, you mean that they have the intelligence and understanding to make the right decision or take the right action in a particular situation. 分別、知恵 ❑ *The information is there and waiting to be accessed by anyone with the wit to use it.* 資料は存在し、それを利用するくらいの分別がある人がアクセスするのを待っている. ❸ N-PLURAL 複数名詞 You can refer to your ability to think quickly and effectively in a difficult situation as your **wits**. 機転 ❑ *She has used her wits to progress to the position she holds today.* 彼女は機転を利かせて現在の地位まで進んだ. ❹ N-PLURAL 複数名詞 You can use **wits** in expressions such as **frighten** someone **out of their wits** and **scare the wits out of** someone to emphasize that a person or thing worries or frightens someone very much. 「正気を失って」「震え上がらせる」などの意の表現で使われる ❑ *You scared us out of our wits. We heard you had an accident.* びっくりして腰を抜かしたわ。あなたが事故に遭ったって聞いたから. [EMPHASIS 強調]

witch /wɪtʃ/ (**witches**) ❶ N-COUNT 可算名詞 In fairy tales, a **witch** is a woman, usually an old woman, who has evil magic powers. Witches often wear a pointed black hat. 魔女 ❷ N-COUNT 可算名詞 A **witch** is a man or woman who claims to have magic powers and to be able to use them for good or bad purposes. 魔法使い

witch|craft /wɪtʃkræft/ N-UNCOUNT 不可算名詞 **Witchcraft** is the use of magic powers, especially evil ones. 魔術、魔法 ❑ *This week Sabrina uses witchcraft to overcome her fear of giving a speech.* 今週サブリナはスピーチをする恐怖を克服するために魔術を使う.

witch-hunt (**witch-hunts**) N-COUNT 可算名詞 A **witch-hunt** is an attempt to find and punish a particular group of people who are being blamed for something, often simply because of their opinions and not because they have actually done anything wrong. 弾圧、魔女狩り [DISAPPROVAL 不賛成] ❑ *...Senator Joe McCarthy, who led the witch-hunt against alleged communists in the 1950s.* 1950年代に共産党員とされる人々に対する迫害を率いたジョー・マッカーシー上院議員

---

with

❶ IN THE SAME PLACE AT THE SAME TIME
❷ OTHER USES: METHODS, FEATURES, QUALITIES

❶ **with** /wɪð, wɪθ/ ❶ PREP 前置詞 If one person is **with** another, they are together in one place. 一と一緒に ❑ *With her were her son and daughter-in-law.* 彼女と一緒にいたのは息子と義理の娘だった. ❷ PREP 前置詞 If something is put **with** or is **with** something else, they are used at the same time. 一を添えて、一とともに ❑ *Serve hot, with pasta or rice and French beans.* パスタかライス、そしてサヤインゲンを添えて熱々のうちに出しなさい. ❸ PREP 前置詞 If you do something **with** someone else, you both do it together or are both involved in it. 一と ❑ *Parents will be given reports on their child's progress and the right to discuss it with a teacher.* 保護者は子供の成績についてのレポートを渡され、それについて教師と話し合う権利がある.

❷ **with** /wɪð, wɪθ/

Pronounced /wɪð/ for meanings **17** and **18**.

/wɪð/と **17** の意味では **18** と発音される.

❶ PREP 前置詞 If you fight, argue, or compete **with** someone, you oppose them. (争いの対象を示して) 一と ❑ *About a thousand students fought with riot police in the capital.* 約1000人の学生が首都で機動隊と衝突した. ❷ PREP 前置詞 If you do something **with** a particular tool, object, or substance, you do it using that tool, object, or substance. 一を使って ❑ *Remove the meat with a fork and divide it among four plates.* フォークを使って肉を取り、4枚の皿に分ける. ❑ *Pack the fruits and nuts into the jars and cover with brandy.* フルーツとナッツを瓶に詰めてブランディに浸しなさい. ❸ PREP 前置詞 If someone stands or goes somewhere **with** something, they are carrying it. 一を持ち運んで ❑ *A young woman came in with a cup of coffee.* 若い女性がコーヒーを持って入ってきた. ❹ PREP 前置詞 Someone or something **with** a particular feature or possession has that feature or possession. (性質・所有物などを示して) 一を持った ❑ *He was in his early forties, tall and blond with bright blue eyes.* 彼は40代前半で背が高く金髪で鮮やかな青い目をしていた. ❺ PREP 前置詞 Someone **with** an illness has that illness. (病気などを示して) 一で ❑ *I spent a week in bed with flu.* 私はインフルエンザで1週間寝込んでいた. ❻ PREP 前置詞 If something is filled or covered **with** a substance or **with** things, it has that substance or those things in it or on it. (満ちるもの・覆うものを示して) 一で ❑ *His legs were caked with dried mud.* 彼の足には乾いた泥がこびりついていた. ❼ PREP 前置詞 If you are, for example, pleased or annoyed **with** someone or something, you have that feeling toward them. (感情の対象を示して) 一に [adj/n PREP n] ❑ *He was still a little angry with her.* 彼はまだ彼女に少し怒っていた. ❽ PREP 前置詞 You use **with** to indicate what a state, quality, or action relates to, involves, or affects. (関連の対象を示して) 一と、一に関する ❑ *Our aim is to allow student teachers to become familiar with the classroom.* 目的は教育実習生が教室に慣れ親しんでもらうことだ. ❑ *He still has a serious problem with money.* 彼はまだお金に関する深刻な問題を抱えている. ❾ PREP 前置詞 You use **with** when indicating the way that something is done or the feeling that a person has when they do something. (やり方・感情などを示して) 一をもって ❑ *...teaching her to read music with skill and sensitivity.* 上手に思いやりながら彼女に楽譜を読むのを教えること ❿ PREP 前置詞 You use **with** when indicating a sound or gesture that is made when something is done, or an expression that a person has on their face when they do something. (音・動作などを示して) 一しながら ❑ *With a sigh, she leant back and closed her eyes.* 彼女はため息をついて後ろにもたれ、目を閉じた. ⓫ PREP 前置詞 You use **with** to indicate the feeling that makes someone have a particular appearance or type of behavior. (表情・行動などを示して) 一で ❑ *Gil was white and trembling with anger.* ジルは青ざめて怒りで震えていた. ⓬ PREP 前置詞 You use **with** when mentioning the position or appearance of a person or thing at the time that they do something, or what someone else is doing at that time. (位置・動作などを示して) 一しながら [PREP n prep/-ing] ❑ *Joanne stood with her hands on the sink, staring out the window.* ジョアンナは流し台に両手を置いて立ち、窓の外をじっと見ていた. ⓭ PREP 前置詞 You use **with** to introduce a current situation that is a factor affecting another situation. (ある状況によって生じる結果を示して) 一なので ❑ *With all the night school courses available, there is no excuse for not getting some sort of training.* あらゆる夜間コースが開催されているので何かしらの研修を受けられない理由はない. ⓮ PREP 前置詞 You use **with** when making a comparison or contrast between the situations of different people or things. (比較の対象を示して) 一と ❑ *We're not like them. It's different with us.* 彼らとは似ていない。私たちは違うんだ. ⓯ PREP 前置詞 If something increases or decreases **with** a particular factor, it changes as that factor changes. (変化に伴う要因を示して) 一につれて [V PREP n] ❑ *The risk of developing heart*

disease increases with the number of cigarettes smoked. 心臓病を患う可能性は喫煙量につれて高まる. **16** PREP 前置詞 If something moves **with** a wind or current, it moves in the same direction as the wind or current. (方向を示して) —とともに ❏ *...a piece of driftwood carried down with the current.* 流されてきた流木 **17** PREP 前置詞 If someone says that they are **with** you, they mean that they understand what you are saying. —の言うことが分かる [INFORMAL くだけた] [V-link PREP n] ❏ *Yes, I know who you mean. Yes, now I'm with you.* ああ, だれのことか分かったよ. うん, きみの言っていることが分かった. **18** PREP 前置詞 If someone says that they are **with** you, they mean that they support or approve of what you are doing. (支持・賛成を示して) —を支持して, —に賛成して [V-link PREP n] ❏ *"I'm with you all the way." — "Thank you."* 「最後まで応援します」「ありがとう」

> In addition to the uses shown here, **with** is used after some verbs, nouns and adjectives in order to introduce extra information. **With** is also used in most reciprocal verbs, such as "agree" or "fight," and in some phrasal verbs, such as "deal with" and "dispense with."

Word Link
with ≈ against, away : withdraw, withhold, withstand

with|draw /wɪðdrɔː, wɪθ-/ (**withdraws, withdrawing, withdrew, withdrawn**) **1** V-T 他動詞 If you **withdraw** something from a place, you remove it or take it away. 取り除く, 取り出す [FORMAL 形式ばった] ❏ *He reached into his pocket and withdrew a sheet of notepaper.* 彼はポケットに手を入れて便せんを取り出した. **2** V-T/V-I 他動詞/自動詞 When groups of people such as troops **withdraw** or when someone **withdraws** them, they leave the place where they are fighting or where they are based and return nearer home. 撤退させる [他動詞], 撤退する [自動詞] ❏ *He stated that all foreign forces would withdraw as soon as the crisis ended.* 危機が終わり次第, 外国部隊はすべて撤退すると彼は述べた. ❏ *The United States has announced it is to withdraw forty-thousand troops from Western Europe in the next year.* 米国は, 来年西ヨーロッパから4万人の軍隊を撤退させると発表した. **3** V-T 他動詞 If you **withdraw** money from a bank account, you take it out of that account. 引き出す ❏ *Open a savings account that does not charge ridiculous fees to withdraw money.* 預金の引き出しに法外な手数料をとらない普通口座を開設しよう. **4** V-I 自動詞 If you **withdraw from** an activity or organization, you stop taking part in it. 手を引く, 脱退する ❏ *The African National Congress threatened to withdraw from the talks.* アフリカ民族会議は交渉から手を引く恐れがありました.

Word Partnership
withdraw は次の語句と使われる:

N. withdraw **an offer**, withdraw **support** **1**
decision to withdraw **1** – **4**
deadline to withdraw, **forces/troops** withdraw **2**
withdraw **money** **3**

with|draw|al /wɪðdrɔːəl, wɪθ-/ (**withdrawals**) **1** N-VAR 可変性名詞 The **withdrawal** of something is the act or process of removing it, or ending it. 中止 [FORMAL 形式ばった] ❏ *If you experience any unusual symptoms after withdrawal of the treatment then contact your doctor.* 治療を中止したあとに異常がみられた場合は医者の診断を受けなさい. **2** N-UNCOUNT 不可算名詞 Someone's **withdrawal from** an activity or an organization is their decision to stop taking part in it. 離脱, 脱退 ❏ *...his withdrawal from government in 1946.* 1946年に彼が政治から引退したこと **3** N-COUNT 可算名詞 A **withdrawal** is an amount of money that you take from your bank account. 引き出し額 ❏ *I went to the machine to make the withdrawal and it told me to see someone inside the bank.* お金を下ろすためにATMに行ったら, 行内の職員に連絡をするようにという表示が出た. **4** N-UNCOUNT 不可算名詞 **Withdrawal** is the period during which someone feels ill after they have stopped taking a drug they were addicted to. 禁断症状の期間 ❏ *Withdrawal from heroin is actually like a severe attack of gastric flu.* ヘロインの禁断症状は実際には胃腸炎によるひどい発作に似ている.

with|drawn /wɪðdrɔːn, wɪθ-/ **1** Withdrawn is the past participle of **withdraw.** withdrawの過去分詞 **2** ADJ 形容詞 Someone who is **withdrawn** is very quiet, and does not want to talk to other people. 内気な [V-link ADJ] ❏ *Her husband had become withdrawn and moody.* 彼女の夫は内向的で不機嫌になっていた.
→ see bank

with|drew /wɪðdruː, wɪθ-/ Withdrew is the past tense of **withdraw.** withdrawの過去形

with|er /wɪðər/ (**withers, withering, withered**) **1** V-I 自動詞 If someone or something **withers**, they become very weak. 弱まる [自動詞] ❏ *When he went into retirement, he visibly withered.* 彼が退職したとき明らかに弱くなった. ● PHRASAL VERB 句動詞 **Wither away** means the same as **wither.** 弱まる ❏ *To see my body literally wither away before my eyes was exasperating.* 自分の体が本当に衰えていくのを目の当たりにするのは腹立たしかった. **2** V-I 自動詞 If a flower or

---

plant **withers**, it dries up and dies. しおれる, 枯れる ❏ *The flowers in Isabel's room had withered.* イザベルの部屋にある花は枯れてしまった.

with|ered /wɪðərd/ ADJ 形容詞 If you describe a person or a part of their body as **withered**, you mean that they are thin and their skin looks old. やせ衰えた ❏ *Diana grasped his face in her withered hands.* ダイアナは か細い手で両側から彼の顔をつかんだ.

with|hold /wɪðhoʊld, wɪθ-/ (**withholds, withholding, withheld**) /wɪðheld, wɪθ-/ V-T 他動詞 If you **withhold** something that someone wants, you do not let them have it. 保留する, 与えないでおく [FORMAL 形式ばった] ❏ *Police withheld the dead boy's name yesterday until relatives could be told.* 警察は昨日家族に連絡が取れるまで死亡した少年の名を公表しなかった.

with|hold|ing tax (**withholding taxes**) N-VAR 可変性名詞 A **withholding tax** is an amount of money that is taken in advance from someone's income, in order to pay some of the tax they will owe. 源泉徴収税 [mainly AM 主に米国英語 BUSINESS 実業]

with|in /wɪðɪn, wɪθ-/ **1** PREP 前置詞 If something is **within** a place, area, or object, it is inside it or surrounded by it. (場所・地域・物などについて) —の中で [FORMAL 形式ばった] ❏ *Clients are entertained within private dining rooms.* クライアントは個室で接待を受ける. ● ADV 副詞 Within is also an adverb. 中で, 内部で ❏ *A small voice called from within. "Yes, just coming."* 「はい, 今行きます」と内側から小さな声が聞こえてきた. **2** PREP 前置詞 Something that happens or exists **within** a society, organization, or system, happens or exists inside it. (社会・組織・制度などについて) —の中で, —の内部で ❏ *...the spirit of self-sacrifice within an army.* 軍隊の内部での犠牲的精神 ● ADV 副詞 Within is also an adverb. 内部で ❏ *The real danger is to these rebels came from within.* これらの反逆者への身に迫る危険は内部から発生した. **3** PREP 前置詞 If something is **within** a particular limit or set of rules, it does not go beyond it or is not more than what is allowed. (限度・規則などについて) —の範囲内で ❏ *Troops have agreed to stay within specific boundaries to avoid confrontations.* 軍隊は, 対立を回避するために特別境界線内にとどまることに合意した. **4** PREP 前置詞 If you are **within** a particular distance of a place, you are less than that distance from it. (距離的に) —以内で ❏ *The man was within a few feet of him.* その男は彼から数フィート以内のところにいた. **5** PREP 前置詞 **Within** a particular length of time means before that length of time has passed. (時間的に) —以内に [PREP amount] ❏ *About 40% of all students entering as freshmen graduate within 4 years.* 大学に1回生として入学する全生徒の約4割が4年以内に卒業する. **6** PREP 前置詞 If something is **within sight**, **within earshot**, or **within reach**, you can see it, hear it, or reach it. —の見える所に ❏ *His twenty-five-foot boat was moored within sight of his house.* 彼の25フィートのボートは自宅から見えるところに係留していた. **7** within reason → see reason

with|out /wɪðaʊt, wɪθ-/

> In addition to the uses shown below, **without** is used in the phrasal verbs "do without," "go without," and "reckon without."

下記の用法に加えて, **without** は do without, go without, reckon without の句動詞に使われる.

1 PREP 前置詞 You use **without** to indicate that someone or something does not have or use the thing mentioned. —なしに ❏ *I don't like myself without a beard.* 私はあごひげがないのは似合わない. ❏ *She wore a brown shirt pressed without a wrinkle.* 彼女はしわ1つないよくアイロンのかかった茶色のブラウスを着ていた. **2** PREP 前置詞 If one thing happens **without** another thing, or if you do something **without** doing something else, the second thing does not happen or occur. —せずに [PREP n/-ing] ❏ *He was offered a generous pension provided he left without a fuss.* 彼は大騒ぎせずに辞めることを条件に高額の年金を約束された. ❏ *They worked without a break until about eight in the evening.* 彼らは夜の8時ごろまで休まずに働いた. **3** PREP 前置詞 If you do something **without** a particular feeling, you do not have that feeling when you do it. —なしに ❏ *Janet Magnusson watched his approach without enthusiasm.* ジャネット・マグナソンは彼のアプローチを興味なさそうに見ていた. **4** PREP 前置詞 If you do something **without** someone else, they are not in the same place as you are or are not involved in the same action as you. —なしで ❏ *I told Franklin he would have to start dinner without me.* 私はフランクリンに私なしで食事を始めなければならないだろうと告げた.

with|stand /wɪðstænd, wɪθ-/ (**withstands, withstanding, withstood**) /wɪðstʊd, wɪθ-/) V-T 他動詞 If something or someone **withstands** a force or action, they survive it or do not give in to it. 持ちこたえる [FORMAL 形式ばった] ❏ *...armored vehicles designed to withstand chemical attack.* 化学攻撃に持ちこたえるよう設計された装甲車

wit|ness /wɪtnɪs/ (**witnesses, witnessing, witnessed**) **1** N-COUNT 可算名詞 A **witness** to an event such as an accident or crime is a person who saw it. 目撃者 ❏ *Witnesses to the crash say they saw an explosion just before the disaster.* 墜落の目撃者は大

W

災害が起こる直前に爆発を見たと言っている. **2** V-T 他動詞 If you **witness** something, you see it happen. 目撃する ❑ *Anyone who witnessed the attack should call the police.* 攻撃を目撃した者は警察に電話すべきである. **3** N-COUNT 可算名詞 A **witness** is someone who appears in a court of law to say what they know about a crime or other event. 証人 ❑ *In the next three or four days, eleven witnesses will be called to testify.* 今後3〜4日間に11人の証人が喚問されて証言することになっている. **4** N-COUNT 可算名詞 A **witness** is someone who writes their name on a document that you have signed, to confirm that it really is your signature. 連署人 ❑ *The codicil must first be signed and dated by you in the presence of two witnesses.* 遺言補足書は2名の連署人と面前でまずあなたが日付を記入し署名しなければならない. **5** V-T 他動詞 If someone **witnesses** your signature on a document, they write their name after it, to confirm that it really is your signature. 連署して保証する ❑ *Ask a friend, (not your spouse), to witness your signature.* （配偶者ではなく）友人にあなたの署名を連署して保証してもらいなさい. **6** V-T 他動詞 If you say that a place, period of time, or person **witnessed** a particular event or change, you mean that it happened in that place, during that period of time, or while that person was alive. 舞台となる ❑ *India has witnessed many political changes in recent years.* インドでは近年多くの政治改革が行なわれた.

→ see **trial, wedding**

Word Partnership	*witness* は次の語句と使われる:
V.	call a witness, witness tells, witness testifies **3**
N.	defense witness, key witness, material witness, prosecution witness, star witness **3**

wit|ty /wɪti/ ADJ 形容詞 Someone or something that is **witty** is amusing in a clever way. 機知のある ❑ *His plays were very good, very witty.* 彼の演劇は非常に優れ, 非常に機知に富んでいた.

wives /waɪvz/ **Wives** is the plural of **wife**. wifeの複数形

wiz|ard /wɪzərd/ (**wizards**) **1** N-COUNT 可算名詞 In legends and fairy tales, a **wizard** is a man who has magic powers. 魔法使い **2** N-COUNT 可算名詞 If you admire someone because they are very good at doing a particular thing, you can say that they are a **wizard**. 名人 [APPROVAL 賛成] ❑ *...a financial wizard.* 金もうけの名人 **3** N-COUNT 可算名詞 A **wizard** is a computer program that guides you through the stages of a particular task. ウィザード [COMPUTING コンピューティング] ❑ *Wizards and templates can help you create brochures, calendars, and Web pages.* ウィザードとテンプレートはパンフレット, カレンダー, ホームページの作成に役立つ.

→ see **fantasy**

wk (**wks**) **wk** is a written abbreviation for **week**. weekの短縮形

wob|ble /wɒbᵊl/ (**wobbles, wobbling, wobbled**) V-I 自動詞 If something or someone **wobbles**, they make small movements from side to side, for example, because they are unsteady. よろめく ❑ *Some of the tables wobble.* いくつかのテーブルはぐらぐらする. ● N-VAR 可変性名詞 **Wobble** is also a noun. ぐらつき ❑ *We might look for a tiny wobble in the position of a star.* 我々は星の位置に小さなぐらつきを探求するかもしれない.

wob|bly /wɒbli/ ADJ 形容詞 Something that is **wobbly** moves unsteadily from side to side. 不安定な ❑ *I was sitting on a wobbly plastic chair.* 私はぐらぐらするプラスチックの椅子に座っていた. ❑ *...a wobbly green dessert.* ブルブルした緑色のデザート

woe /woʊ/ N-UNCOUNT 不可算名詞 **Woe** is great sadness. 悲痛 [LITERARY 文語的] ❑ *He listened to my tale of woe.* 彼は私の悲しい身の上話に耳を傾けた.

woe|ful /woʊfəl/ **1** ADJ 形容詞 If someone or something is **woeful**, they are very sad. 悲しみに沈んだ ❑ *...a woeful ballad.* 哀調を帯びたバラード ● **woe|ful|ly** ADV 副詞 [ADV with v] 悲しげに ❑ *He said woefully: "I love my country, but it does not give a damn about me."* 彼は悲しげに言った「私は母国を愛しているが母国は私のことはどうでもいいんだ」 **2** ADJ 形容詞 You can use **woeful** to emphasize that something is very bad or undesirable. 情けない [JOURNALISM ジャーナリズム, EMPHASIS 強調] ❑ *...the woeful state of the economy.* 情けない経済状態 ● **woe|ful|ly** ADV 副詞 情けないほど ❑ *Public expenditure on the arts is woefully inadequate.* 芸術に対する公共支出は情けないほど不十分だ.

woke /woʊk/ **Woke** is the past tense of **wake**. wakeの過去形

wok|en /woʊkən/ **Woken** is the past participle of **wake**. wakeの過去分詞形

wolf /wʊlf/ (**wolves, wolfs, wolfing, wolfed**) **1** N-COUNT 可算名詞 A **wolf** is a wild animal that looks like a large dog. オオカミ **2** V-T 他動詞 If someone **wolfs** their food, they eat it all very quickly and greedily. がつがつ食う [INFORMAL くだけた] ❑ *Hotels were full of rich people wolfing expensive meals.* ホテルは高価な食事をがつがつ食べる人々で1杯だった. ● PHRASAL VERB 句動詞 **Wolf down** means the same as **wolf**. むさぼり食う ❑ *He wolfed down the rest of the biscuit and cheese.* 彼は残ったビスケットとチーズをむさぼり食った.

Word Link	man ≈ human being : fore**man**, hu**man**e, wo**man**

wom|an /wʊmən/ (**women**) **1** N-COUNT 可算名詞 A **woman** is an adult female human being. 女 ❑ *...a young Lithuanian woman named Dayva.* デイヴァという名のリトアニア人の若い女性 ❑ *...men and women over 75 years old.* 75歳以上の男女 **2** N-UNCOUNT 不可算名詞 You can refer to women in general as **woman**. 女性 ❑ *...the oppression of woman.* 女性の抑圧 **3** → see also **career woman**

→ see **age**

wom|an|hood /wʊmənhʊd/ **1** N-UNCOUNT 不可算名詞 **Womanhood** is the state of being a woman rather than a girl, or the period of a woman's adult life. 女であること ❑ *Pregnancy is a natural part of womanhood.* 妊娠は女であることの自然な要素である. **2** N-UNCOUNT 不可算名詞 You can refer to women in general or the women of a particular country or community as **womanhood**. 女 ❑ *She symbolized for me the best of Indian womanhood.* 彼女は私にとってインド人女性の最善のものを象徴した.

womb /wuːm/ (**wombs**) N-COUNT 可算名詞 A woman's **womb** is the part inside her body where a baby grows before it is born. 子宮 ❑ *...the development of the fetus in the womb.* 子宮での胎児の発育

wom|en /wɪmɪn/ **Women** is the plural of **woman**. womanの複数形

won /wʌn/ **Won** is the past tense and past participle of **win**. winの過去形

→ see **election**

won|der /wʌndər/ (**wonders, wondering, wondered**) **1** V-T/V-I 他動詞/自動詞 If you **wonder** about something, you think about it, either because it interests you and you want to know more about it, or because you are worried or suspicious about it. を不思議に思う ❑ *I wondered what that noise was.* あの騒音は何だろうと私は思った. ❑ *"He claims to be her father," said Max. "We've been wondering about him."* 「彼は彼女の父親だと言っている」とマックスは言った. 「私達は彼について知りたいと思っていた」 **2** V-T/V-I 他動詞/自動詞 If you **wonder at** something, you are very surprised about it or think about it in a very surprised way. 感嘆する ❑ *I could only wonder at how far this woman had come.* 私はこの女性の成功にただただ感嘆するばかりだった. ❑ *I wonder you don't feel it too.* あなたもそれを感じないのかと思う. **3** N-SING 単数名詞 If you say that it is a **wonder** that something happened, you mean that it is very surprising and unexpected. 驚き ❑ *It's a wonder that it took almost ten years.* それが10年近くかかったのは驚きだ. **4** N-UNCOUNT 不可算名詞 **Wonder** is a feeling of great surprise and pleasure that you have, for example, when you see something that is very beautiful, or when something happens that you thought was impossible. 感嘆の念 ❑ *"That's right!" Bobby exclaimed in wonder. "How did you remember that?"* 「その通りだ」とボビーは驚いて叫んだ. 「どうやって覚えていたんだ」 **5** N-COUNT 可算名詞 A **wonder** is something that causes people to feel great surprise or admiration. 驚異の念 ❑ *...a lecture on the wonders of space and space exploration.* 宇宙と宇宙探検の驚異についての講演 **6** ADJ 形容詞 If you refer, for example, to a young man as a **wonder** boy, or to a new product as a **wonder** drug, you mean that they are believed by many people to be very good or very effective. 驚くべき成功をする [ADJ n] ❑ *Mickelson was hailed as the wonder boy of American golf.* ミッケルソンはアメリカのゴルフ界の神童とたたえられた. **7** PHRASE 句 You can say "**I wonder**" if you want to be very polite when you are asking someone to do something, or when you are asking them for their opinion or for information. していただけませんか [POLITENESS 丁寧さ] ❑ *I was just wondering if you could help me.* 手を貸してくださいませんか. **8** PHRASE 句 If you say "**no wonder,**" "**little wonder,**" or "**small wonder,**" you mean that something is not surprising. それもそのはず ❑ *No wonder my brother wasn't feeling well.* 道理で私の兄弟は体調が良くなかった. **9** PHRASE 句 You can say "**No wonder**" when you find out the reason for something that has been puzzling you for some time. 道理で ❑ *Brad was Jane's brother! No wonder he reminded me so much of her!* ブラッドはジェインの兄弟だった. 道理で彼は私に彼女を思い出させた. **10** PHRASE 句 If you say that a person or thing **works wonders** or **does wonders**, you mean that they have a very good effect on something. 驚くほどよく効く ❑ *A few moments of relaxation can work wonders.* 少しの間リラックスすると驚くほど成果が上がる.

Word Partnership	*wonder* は次の語句と使われる:
V.	begin to wonder, wonder **what happened**, make *someone* wonder **1**
CONJ.	wonder **how**, wonder **what**, wonder **when**, wonder **where**, wonder **whether**, wonder **who**, wonder **why**, wonder **that** **3**

won|der|ful /wʌndərfəl/ ADJ 形容詞 If you describe something or someone as **wonderful**, you think they are extremely good. 素晴らしい ❑ *The cold, misty air felt wonderful on his face.* 霧の立ち込めたひんやりした空気は彼の顔に心地よかった. ❑ *It's wonderful to see*

you. きみに会えてうれしい. ● **won|der|ful|ly** ADV 副詞 素晴らしく ❑ *It's a system that works wonderfully well.* それは素晴らしくうまく行くシステムだ.

won't /woʊnt/ **Won't** is the usual spoken form of "will not." will notの短縮形 ❑ *The space shuttle won't lift off the launch pad until Sunday at the earliest.* スペース・シャトルは早くとも日曜日まで発射パッドから離昇しない予定だ.

woo /wu/ (**woos, wooing, wooed**) V-T 他動詞 If you **woo** people, you try to encourage them to help you, support you, or vote for you, for example, by promising them things which they would like. しつこく求める ❑ *They wooed customers by offering low interest rates.* 彼らは低金利を約束して顧客を獲得しようとした.
→ see **love**

wood /wʊd/ (**woods**) ◼ N-MASS 質量名詞 **Wood** is the material that forms the trunks and branches of trees. 木材 ❑ *Their dishes were made of wood.* 彼らの皿は木製だった. ❑ *There was a smell of damp wood and machine oil.* 湿った木と機械油の匂いがした. ◼ N-COUNT 可算名詞 A **wood** or **woods** is a fairly large area of trees growing near each other. 森林 ❑ *After dinner Alice slipped away for a walk in the woods with Artie.* 夕食後アリスはアーティと一緒にそっと森林の散歩に出かけた. ◼ PHRASE 句 If something or someone is **not out of the woods** yet, they are still having difficulties or problems. 困難を切り抜けていない [INFORMAL くだけた] ❑ *The nation's economy is not out of the woods yet.* その国の経済はまだ困難を切り抜けていない. ◼ CONVENTION 慣習表現 You can say "**knock on wood**" to indicate that you hope to have good luck in something you are doing, usually after saying that you have been lucky with it so far. おっと ❑ *I got it all taken care of, knock on wood.* 準備万端だ, おっと.
→ see **energy, fire, forest**

wood|ed /wʊdɪd/ ADJ 形容詞 A **wooded** area is covered in trees. 樹林の茂った ❑ *...a wooded valley.* 樹林の茂った峡谷

wood|en /wʊdᵊn/ ADJ 形容詞 **Wooden** objects are made of wood. 木でできた [ADJ n] ❑ *...the shop's bare brick walls and faded wooden floorboards.* その店のむき出しのレンガの壁と色あせた木でできた床板

wood|land /wʊdlənd/ (**woodlands**) N-VAR 可変性名詞 **Woodland** is land with a lot of trees. 森林地 ❑ *...an area of dense woodland.* 密林地区

wood|work /wʊdwɜrk/ ◼ N-UNCOUNT 不可算名詞 You can refer to the doors and other wooden parts of a house as the **woodwork**. 木工品 ❑ *I love the living room, with its dark woodwork, oriental rugs, and chunky furniture.* 私は黒っぽい木工品, オリエンタルカーペット, そして重厚な家具のある居間が大好きだ. ◼ N-UNCOUNT 不可算名詞 **Woodwork** is the activity or skill of making things out of wood. 木工技術 ❑ *I have done woodwork for many years.* 私は長年木細工師をやってきた.

wool /wʊl/ (**wools**) ◼ N-UNCOUNT 不可算名詞 **Wool** is the hair that grows on sheep and on some other animals. 羊毛 ❑ *A new invention means sheep do not have to be sheared – the wool just falls off.* 新発明の決果, 羊毛を刈り取る必要はなくなり, 羊毛は自然に抜けるようになった. ◼ N-MASS 質量名詞 **Wool** is a material made from animal's wool that is used to make things such as clothes, blankets, and carpets. ウール ❑ *...a wool overcoat.* ウールのオーバー

wool|en /wʊlən/ ADJ 形容詞 **Woolen** clothes or materials are made from wool or from a mixture of wool and artificial fibers. ウールの ❑ *...thick woolen socks.* 厚みのあるウールのソックス

wool|ly /wʊli/ also **wooly** ADJ 形容詞 Something that is **woolly** is made of wool or looks like wool. 羊毛の ❑ *She wore this woolly hat with pompoms.* 彼女は飾り玉房のついたウールの帽子をかぶっていた.

---

word

❶ NOUN AND VERB USES
❷ PHRASES

---

❶ word /wɜrd/ (**words, wording, worded**) ◼ N-COUNT 可算名詞 A **word** is a single unit of language that can be represented in writing or speech. In English, a word has a space on either side of it when it is written. 単語 ❑ *The words stood out clearly on the page.* その言葉はそのページの上ではっきりと目立った. ❑ *The word "ginseng" comes from the Chinese word "Shen-seng."* 「ginseng」という言葉の語源は「Shen-seng」という中国語である. ◼ N-PLURAL 複数名詞 Someone's **words** are what they say or write. 言葉 ❑ *I was devastated when her words came true.* 私は彼女の言葉が本当になった時, 途方に暮れた. ◼ N-PLURAL 複数名詞 **The words** of a song consist of the text that is sung, in contrast to the music that is played. 歌詞 ❑ *Can you hear the words on the album?* アルバムの歌詞が聞こえるか. ◼ N-SING 単数名詞 If you have a **word** with someone, you have a short conversation with them. 短い談話 [SPOKEN 口語] ❑ *I think it's time you had a word with him.* あなたは彼とちょっと話してもよいころだと私は思う. ◼ N-COUNT 可算名詞 If you offer someone **a word of** something such as warning, advice, or praise,

you warn, advise, or praise them. の言葉 ❑ *A word of warning. Don't stick too precisely to what it says in the book.* 警告の言葉. 本の内容に正確すぎないようにしなさい. ◼ N-SING 単数名詞 If you say that someone does **not** hear, understand, or say **a word**, you are emphasizing that they hear, understand, or say nothing at all. 一言 [EMPHASIS 強調] ❑ *I can't understand a word she says.* 私は彼女の言うことが一言も理解できない. ◼ N-UNCOUNT 不可算名詞 If there is **word** of something, people receive news or information about it. 知らせ ❑ *There is no word from the authorities on the reported attack.* 報道された攻撃について当局からは何の知らせもない. ◼ N-SING 単数名詞 If you give your **word**, you make a sincere promise to someone. 約束 ❑ *...an adult who gave his word the boy would be supervised.* その少年が監視されることを約束した大人 ◼ N-SING 単数名詞 If someone gives **the word** to do something, they give an order to do it. 命令 ❑ *I want nothing said about this until I give the word.* 私が命令を下すまではこれについて何も言ってほしくない. ◼ V-T 他動詞 To **word** something in a particular way means to choose or use particular words to express it. 言葉に表わす ❑ *If I had written the letter, I might have worded it differently.* 私が手紙を書いていたら異なる表現を使っていただろう. ● **-worded** COMB IN ADJ 形容詞の複合 言い表された ❑ *...a strongly-worded statement.* 強い表現の声明 ◼ → see also **wording**
→ see **English**

❷ word /wɜrd/ (**words**) ◼ PHRASE 句 If you say that people consider something to be a **dirty word**, you mean that they disapprove of it. けがらわしい言葉 ❑ *So many people think feminism is a dirty word.* 非常に多くの人々がフェミニズムをけがらわしい言葉だと考えている. ◼ PHRASE 句 If you do something **from the word go**, you do it from the very beginning of a period of time or situation. 始めから ❑ *It's essential you make the right decisions from the word go.* 最初から正しい決断を下すことが重要だ. ◼ PHRASE 句 You can use **in** their **words** or **in** their **own words** to indicate that you are reporting what someone said using the exact words that they used. 独自の言葉 ❑ *Even the Assistant Secretary of State had to admit that previous policy did not, in his words, produce results.* 国務次官ですら, 彼の言葉を借りて言うと, 以前の政策は成果をもたらさなかったと認めねばならなかった. ◼ PHRASE 句 If someone has **the last word** or **the final word** in a discussion, argument, or disagreement, they are the one who wins it or who makes the final decision. 最後の言葉 ❑ *She does like to have the last word in any discussion.* 本当に彼女はどんな話し合いでも最後の断を下すのが好きだ. ◼ PHRASE 句 If news or information passes **by word of mouth**, people tell it to each other rather than it being printed in written form. 口づて ❑ *The story has been passed down by word of mouth.* その話は口づてで広まった. ◼ PHRASE 句 You say **in other words** in order to introduce a different, and usually simpler, explanation or interpretation of something that has just been said. 言い換えれば ❑ *...coronary heart disease, in other words, heart attacks and strokes.* 冠状動脈性心臓病, すなわち心臓発作と脳卒中 ◼ PHRASE 句 If you say something **in** your **own words**, you express it in your own way, without copying or repeating someone else's description. 自分の言葉で ❑ *Now tell us in your own words about the events of Saturday.* さあ, あなた自身の言葉で土曜日の出来事を説明しなさい. ◼ PHRASE 句 If you say to someone "**take** my **word for it**," you mean that they should believe you because you are telling the truth. 私の言葉を信じる ❑ *You'll buy nothing but trouble if you buy that house, take my word for it.* あなたはあの家を買えば問題ばかり抱え込むことになるだろう, 私の言葉を信じてくれ. ◼ PHRASE 句 If you repeat something **word for word**, you repeat it exactly as it was originally said or written. 逐語的な ❑ *I don't try to memorize speeches word for word.* 私はスピーチを1語ずつ覚えようとはしない. ◼ **the operative word** → see **operative**

word|ing /wɜrdɪŋ/ N-UNCOUNT 不可算名詞 The **wording** of a piece of writing or a speech are the words used in it, especially when these are chosen to have a particular effect. 言い回し ❑ *The two sides failed to agree on the wording of a final report.* 両者は最終的なリポートの言い回しについて合意しなかった.

word pro|cess|ing also **word-processing** N-UNCOUNT 不可算名詞 **Word processing** is the work or skill of producing printed documents using a computer. ワードプロセッシング [COMPUTING コンピューティング] ❑ *Many temp agencies offer word processing courses to those with rusty office skills.* 多くの派遣会社は事務技能がさびついた人々にワードプロセッシングのコースを提供している.

word pro|ces|sor (**word processors**) N-COUNT 可算名詞 A **word processor** is a computer program or a computer which is used to produce printed documents. ワードプロセッサー [COMPUTING コンピューティング]

word wrap|ping N-UNCOUNT 不可算名詞 In computing, **word wrapping** is a process by which a word that comes at the end of a line is automatically moved onto a new line in order to keep the text within the margins. ワードラップ [COMPUTING コンピューティング]

W

wore /wɔːr/ **Wore** is the past tense of **wear**. wearの過去形

---

work

❶ VERB USES AND PHRASES
❷ NOUN USES AND PHRASES
❸ PHRASAL VERBS

---

❶ work /wɜːrk/ (works, working, worked) **1** V-I 自動詞 People who **work** have a job, usually one which they are paid to do. 働く □ I started working in a recording studio. 私は録音スタジオで働き始めた. □ He worked as a teacher for 50 years. 彼は50年間教師として働いた. □ I want to work, I don't want to be on welfare. 私は働きたい, 国からの金銭的援助に頼りたくない. **2** V-T/V-I 他動詞/自動詞 When you **work**, you do the things that you are paid or required to do in your job. 仕事をする □ I can't talk to you right now – I'm working. 今はきみと話せない. 仕事中だから. □ He was working at his desk. 彼は机で仕事をしていた. □ They work forty hours a week. 彼らは1週間に40時間働く. **3** V-I 自動詞 When you **work**, you spend time and effort doing a task that needs to be done or trying to achieve something. 仕事する □ Linda spends all her time working on the garden. リンダは四六時中庭仕事をしている. **4** V-I 自動詞 If someone **is working on** a particular subject or question, they are studying or researching it. 研究する □ Professor Bonnet has been working for many years on molecules of this type. ボネット教授はこの種類の微粒子について長年研究してきた. **5** V-I 自動詞 If you **work with** a person or a group of people, you spend time and effort trying to help them in some way. 奉仕する □ She spent a period of time working with people dying of cancer. 彼女は末期のガン患者のために奉仕した時期があった. **6** V-I 自動詞 If a machine or piece of equipment **works**, it operates and performs a particular function. 動く □ The pump doesn't work and we have no running water. ポンプが動かないので水道水は使えない. **7** V-I 自動詞 If an idea, system, or way of doing something **works**, it is successful, effective, or satisfactory. うまく行く □ 95 percent of these diets do not work. こうしたダイエットの95%は効果が出る. **8** V-I 自動詞 If a drug or medicine **works**, it produces a particular physical effect. 効き目がある □ I wake up at 6 a.m. as the sleeping pill doesn't work for more than nine hours. 睡眠薬は9時間経つと効き目がなくなるので私は午前6時に目が覚める. **9** V-I 自動詞 If your mind or brain **is working**, you are thinking about something or trying to solve a problem. 動揺する □ My mind was working frantically, running over the events of the evening. 私の心はその夜の出来事を思い出しながら激しく動揺していた. **10** V-I 自動詞 If you **work on** an assumption or idea, you act as if it were true or base other ideas on it, until you have more information. ～に基づいて行動する □ We are working on the assumption that it was a gas explosion. 我々はそれがガス爆発だったという仮定に基づいて行動している. **11** V-T 他動詞 If you **work** someone, you make them spend time and effort doing a particular activity or job. 働かせる □ They're working me too hard. I'm too old for this. 彼らは私をこき使っている. 私はこれには年を取りすぎている. **12** V-T 他動詞 When people **work** the land, they do all the tasks involved in growing crops. 耕作する □ Farmers worked the fertile valleys. 農夫は肥沃 (よく) な峡谷を耕作した. **13** V-T 他動詞 If you **work** a machine or piece of equipment, you use or control it. 操作する □ Many adults still depend on their children to work the video. 多くの大人はまだ子供に頼りながらビデオを操作している. **14** V-I 自動詞 If something **works** into a particular state or condition, it gradually moves so that it is in that state or condition. もたらす □ It's important to put a lock washer on that last nut, or it can work loose. 止め座金をあの最後のナットに取り付けるのが大切だ. そうしないと緩みが生じることがある. **15** → see also **working 16** PHRASE 句 If you **work** your **way** somewhere, you move or progress there slowly, and with a lot of effort or work. 苦心して進む □ Rescuers were still working their way toward the trapped men. 救助隊はまだ閉じ込められた男達の方向に苦心して進んでいた.
→ see **book, drawing, factory, gallery**

❷ work /wɜːrk/ (works) **1** N-UNCOUNT 不可算名詞 People who have **work** or who are **in work** have a job, usually one which they are paid to do. 仕事 □ Fewer and fewer people are in work. 定職について いる人は減少しつつある. **2** N-UNCOUNT 不可算名詞 Your **work** consists of the things you are paid or required to do in your job. 仕事 □ We're supposed to be running a business here. I've got work to do. 我々はここで事業を経営するよう期待されている. 私にはするべき仕事がある. □ I used to take work home, but I don't do it any more. 私はよく仕事を家に持ち帰っていたものだが, もうそうしない. **3** N-UNCOUNT 不可算名詞 **Work** is tasks that need to be done or things that need to be achieved. 作業 □ There was a lot of work to do on their house. 彼らの家には手入れする場所がたくさんあった. **4** N-UNCOUNT 不可算名詞 **Work** is the place where you do your job. 仕事場 □ Many people travel to work by car. 多くの人々は車で通勤する. **5** N-UNCOUNT 不可算名詞 **Work** is something that you produce as a result of an activity or as a result of doing your job. 成果 □ It can help to have an impartial third party look over your work. あなたの成果を偏見のない第三者に見てもらうことがためになる場合がある. **6** N-COUNT 可算名詞 A **work** is something such as a painting, book, or piece of

music produced by an artist, writer, or composer. 作品 □ In my opinion, this is Rembrandt's greatest work. 私の意見ではこれはレンブラントの最も優れた作品だ. **7** N-UNCOUNT 不可算名詞 Someone's **work** is the study or research that they have done on a particular subject or question. 研究 □ Their work shows that one-year-olds are much more likely to have allergies if either parent smokes. 彼らの研究によると, 両親のいずれかが喫煙する場合には1歳児がアレルギー体質になる可能性が高まる. **8** N-UNCOUNT 不可算名詞 **Work** with a particular person or a group of people is time and effort spent trying to help them in some way. 福祉事業 □ She became involved in social and relief work among the refugees. 彼女は避難民間の社会・救済福祉事業に関与するようになった. **9** N-COUNT-COLL 集合可算名詞 A **works** is a place where something is manufactured or where an industrial process is carried out. **Works** is used to refer to one or to more than one of these places. 工場 □ ...the steelworks in Gary, Indiana. インディアナ州, ギャリーの製鋼所 **10** N-PLURAL 複数名詞 **Works** are activities such as digging the ground or building on a large scale. 建設工事 □ ...six years of disruptive building works, road construction and urban development. 6年にわたる迷惑な建設工事, 道路建築および都市開発 **11** PHRASE 句 If someone is **at work** they are doing their job or are busy doing a particular activity. 働いている □ The salvage teams are already hard at work trying to deal with the spilled oil. 救助隊は既に漏出油と懸命に取り組んでいる. **12** PHRASE 句 If a force or process is **at work**, it is having a particular influence or effect. 働いている □ It is important to understand the powerful economic and social forces at work behind our own actions. 我々自身の行動の裏で働いている力強い経済・社会の影響力を理解することが大切だ. **13** PHRASE 句 If you **put** someone **to work** or **set** them **to work**, you give them a job or task to do. 仕事に就ける □ By stimulating the economy, we're going to put people to work. 経済を刺激することで我々は人々を仕事に就ける予定である. **14** PHRASE 句 If you **get to work**, or **set to work** on a job, task, or problem, you start doing it or dealing with it. 仕事を始める □ He promised to get to work on the state's massive deficit. 彼は州の膨大な赤字に取り掛かることを約束した.

The verb **work** has a different meaning in the continuous tenses than it does in the simple tenses. You use the continuous tenses, with the "-ing" form, to talk about a temporary job, but the simple tenses to talk about a permanent job. For example, if you say **"I'm working in Boston,"** this suggests that the situation is temporary and you may soon move to a different place. If you say **"I work in Boston"**, this suggests that Boston is your permanent place of work.

Thesaurus   work また次を参照:

V.	labor ❶ **1** – **3**
	function, go, operate, perform, run ❶ **6 7**
N.	business, craft, job, occupation, profession, trade, vocation; (ant.) entertainment, fun, pastime ❷ **1** – **3**

---

❸ work /wɜːrk/ (works, working, worked)
▶ **work off** PHRASAL VERB 句動詞 If you **work off** energy, stress, or anger, you get rid of it by doing something that requires a lot of physical effort. 晴らす □ Cleaning my kitchen really works off frustration if I've had a fight with somebody. だれかとけんかした時に台所の掃除をすると嫌な気分が消えて気分がすっかとなる.
▶ **work out 1** PHRASAL VERB 句動詞 If you **work out** a solution to a problem or mystery, you manage to find the solution by thinking or talking about it. 苦心して作り出す, 理解する □ Negotiators are due to meet later today to work out a compromise. 交渉人は今日, 妥協案を作り出すため後で会うことになっている. □ It took me some time to work out what was causing this. この原因が何かを理解するまでしばらくかかった. **2** PHRASAL VERB 句動詞 If you **work out** the answer to a mathematical problem, you calculate it. 計算する □ It is proving hard to work out the value of bankrupt companies' assets. 破綻 (はたん) 企業の資産価値を算出するのが難しくなっている. **3** PHRASAL VERB 句動詞 If something **works out** at a particular amount, it is calculated to be that amount after all the facts and figures have been considered. 算出される □ The price per pound works out at $3.20. 1ポンド当たりの価格は3.20ドルとなる. **4** PHRASAL VERB 句動詞 If a situation **works out** well or **works out**, it happens or progresses in a satisfactory way. うまくいく □ Things just didn't work out as planned. 事態は全く計画通りにはいかなかった. □ The deal just isn't working out the way we were promised. その取引は全く約束通りに進んでいない. **5** PHRASAL VERB 句動詞 If a process **works** itself **out**, it reaches a conclusion or satisfactory end. そのうちなんとかなる □ People involved in it think it's a nightmare, but I'm sure it will work itself out. それに関与した人々はそれが悪夢のような出来事だと思っているがそのうちなんとかなると思う. **6** PHRASAL VERB 句動詞 If you **work out**, you do physical exercises in order to make your body fit and strong. 運動をする □ Work out at a gym or swim twice a week. 週に2回ジムで運動をするか水泳をしなさい. **7** → see also **workout**
▶ **work up 1** PHRASAL VERB 句動詞 If you **work** yourself **up**, you make yourself feel very upset or angry about something. 興奮する

❏ *She worked herself up into a bit of a state.* 彼女は興奮してひどい状態になった. **2** → see also **worked up** **3** PHRASAL VERB 句動詞 If you **work up** the enthusiasm or courage to do something, you succeed in making yourself feel it. 扇動する ❏ *Your creative talents can also be put to good use, if you can work up the energy.* その気になればきみの創造の才能もうまく利用することができる. **4** PHRASAL VERB 句動詞 If you **work up** a sweat or an appetite, you make yourself sweaty or hungry by doing exercise or hard work. 運動して出す ❏ *Even if you are not prepared to work up a sweat three times a week, any activity is better than none.* たとえ週に3回運動して汗をかく覚悟はなくともどんな活動でもしないよりましだ.

work|able /wɜ́rkəbəl/ ADJ 形容詞 A **workable** idea or system is realistic and practical, and likely to be effective. 実行可能な ❏ *Investors can simply pay cash, but this isn't a workable solution in most cases.* 投資家はただ現金を支払うことができるが大半の場合, これは実現可能な解決策ではない.

worka|hol|ic /wɜ̀rkəhɔ́lɪk/ (**workaholics**) N-COUNT 可算名詞 A **workaholic** is a person who works most of the time and finds it difficult to stop working in order to do other things. 仕事の虫 [INFORMAL くだけた] ❏ *Eighteen percent of 30-year-olds claim they are workaholics.* 30歳の人々の18%は仕事の虫だと断言している.

work|book /wɜ́rkbʊk/ (**workbooks**) N-COUNT 可算名詞 A **workbook** is a book to help you learn a particular subject that has questions in it with spaces for the answers. 学習帳 ❏ *Just do one more exercise in this workbook.* この学習帳で実習をもう1つだけしなさい.

work|day /wɜ́rkdeɪ/ (**workdays**) also **work day** **1** N-COUNT 可算名詞 A **workday** is the amount of time during a day that you spend doing your job. 1日の労働時間 [mainly AM 主に米国英語] ❏ *His workday starts at 3.30 a.m. and lasts 12 hours.* 彼の勤務時間は午前3時半から12時間続く. **2** N-COUNT 可算名詞 A **workday** is a day on which people go to work. 平日 ❏ *What's he doing home on a workday?* 平日に彼は家で何をしているのか.

→ see **union**

worked up ADJ 形容詞 If someone is **worked up**, they are angry or upset. 気の立った [v-link ADJ] ❏ *Steve shouted at her. He was really worked up now.* スティーブは彼女に向かって怒鳴った. 彼は今, 本当に気が立っていた.

work|er /wɜ́rkər/ (**workers**) **1** N-COUNT 可算名詞 A particular kind of **worker** does the kind of work mentioned. を行なう人 ❏ *She ate her sandwich alongside several other office workers taking their break.* 彼女は休憩中の他の事務員と一緒にサンドイッチを食べた. **2** N-COUNT 可算名詞 **Workers** are people who are employed in industry or business and who are not managers. 従業員 ❏ *Wages have been frozen and workers laid off.* 賃金は凍結され, 従業員は解雇された. **3** N-COUNT 可算名詞 You can use **worker** to say how well or badly someone works. 働く人 ❏ *He is a hard worker and a skilled gardener.* 彼はよく働く, 熟練した庭師だ. **4** → see also **social worker**

→ see **factory**, **union**

Thesaurus	*worker* また次を参照:
N.	employee, help, laborer **2**

work|force /wɜ́rkfɔrs/ (**workforces**) **1** N-COUNT 可算名詞 The **workforce** is the total number of people in a country or region who are physically able to do a job and are available for work. 全労働人口 ❏ *...a country where half the workforce is unemployed.* 労働人口の半分が失業中の国 **2** N-COUNT 可算名詞 The **workforce** is the total number of people who are employed by a particular company. 全従業員 ❏ *...an employer of a very large workforce.* 多くの従業員を抱える雇用主

work|ing /wɜ́rkɪŋ/ (**workings**) **1** ADJ 形容詞 **Working** people have jobs that they are paid to do. 仕事を持った [ADJ n] ❏ *Like working women anywhere, Asian women are buying convenience foods.* 他の地域の仕事を持った女性と同様に, アジアの女性はインスタント食品を買っている. **2** ADJ 形容詞 **Working** people are ordinary people who do not have professional or very highly paid jobs. 賃金労働者 [ADJ n] ❏ *The needs and opinions of ordinary working people were ignored.* 普通の賃金労働者の要求と意見は無視された. **3** ADJ 形容詞 Your **working** life is the period of your life in which you have a job or are of a suitable age to have a job. 労働に従事する [ADJ n] ❏ *He started his working life as a truck driver.* 彼の最初の仕事はトラックの運転手だった. **4** ADJ 形容詞 The **working** population of an area consists of all the people in that area who have a job or who are of a suitable age to have a job. 現役の [ADJ n] ❏ *Almost 13 percent of the working population is already unemployed.* 労働人口の13%近くが既に失業中である. **5** ADJ 形容詞 **Working** conditions or practices are ones that you have in your job. 労働に関する [ADJ n] ❏ *The strikers are demanding higher pay and better working conditions.* ストライキを行なう人は賃金の引き上げと労働条件の改善を要求している. **6** ADJ 形容詞 A **working** farm or business exists to do normal work and make a profit, and not only for tourists or as someone's hobby. 活動中の [ADJ n] ❏ *...a vacation spent on a working farm.* 活動中の農

場で過ごした休暇 **7** ADJ 形容詞 The **working** parts of a machine are the parts that move and operate the machine, in contrast to the outer case or container in which they are enclosed. 運転中の [ADJ n] ❏ *The reel comes complete with a set of spares for all the working parts.* そのリールは全可動部分の部品セット付きで売っている. **8** ADJ 形容詞 A **working** knowledge or majority is not very great, but is enough to be useful. 日常に役立つ [ADJ n] ❏ *This book was designed in order to provide a working knowledge of finance and accounts.* この本は金融および会計の実用的な知識を提供するために書かれた. **9** N-PLURAL 複数名詞 The **workings** of a piece of equipment, an organization, or a system are the ways in which it operates and the processes which are involved in it. 働き ❏ *Neural networks are computer systems which mimic the workings of the brain.* ニューラルネットワークは脳の働きをシミュレーションするコンピュータのことである. **10** in working order → see **order**

work|ing capi|tal N-UNCOUNT 不可算名詞 **Working capital** is money available for use immediately, rather than money invested in land or equipment. 運転資金 [BUSINESS 実業] ❏ *He borrowed a further $1.5 m from conventional sources to provide working capital.* 彼は運転資金を提供するために更に150万ドルを一般的な貸出元から借りた.

work|ing class (**working classes**) N-COUNT-COLL 集合可算名詞 The **working class** or the **working classes** are the group of people in a society who do not own much property, who have low social status, and who do jobs that involve using physical skills rather than intellectual skills. 労働者階級 ❏ *A quarter of the working class voted for him.* 労働者階級の4分の1が彼に投票した. ● ADJ 形容詞 **Working class** is also an adjective. 労働者階級の ❏ *...a self-educated man from a working class background.* 労働者階級出身の独学の男

work|load /wɜ́rkloʊd/ (**workloads**) N-COUNT 可算名詞 The **workload** of a person or organization is the amount of work that has to be done by them. 仕事量 ❏ *You need someone to bounce ideas off and share your workload.* あなたには着想への反応をさぐり仕事量を分け合う人物が必要だ.

work|man /wɜ́rkmən/ (**workmen**) N-COUNT 可算名詞 A **workman** is a man who works with his hands, for example, building or repairing houses or roads. 職人 ❏ *In University Square workmen are building a steel fence.* 大学広場の職人は鉄の塀を建設中だ.

work|man|ship /wɜ́rkmənʃɪp/ N-UNCOUNT 不可算名詞 **Workmanship** is the skill with which something is made and which affects the appearance and quality of the finished object. 腕前 ❏ *The problem may be due to poor workmanship.* 問題は劣った技量によるものかもしれない.

work|mate /wɜ́rkmeɪt/ (**workmates**) N-COUNT 可算名詞 Your **workmates** are the people you work with. 職場の同僚 [mainly BRIT 主に英国英語, INFORMAL くだけた]

work of art (**works of art**) N-COUNT 可算名詞 A **work of art** is a painting or piece of sculpture of high quality. 芸術品 ❏ *...a collection of works of art of international significance.* 国際的に重要な芸術品のコレクション

work|out /wɜ́rkaʊt/ (**workouts**) N-COUNT 可算名詞 A **workout** is a period of physical exercise or training. 運動 ❏ *Give your upper body a workout by using handweights.* ハンドウェイトを使って上半身を訓練しなさい.

→ see **muscle**

work|place /wɜ́rkpleɪs/ (**workplaces**) also **work place** N-COUNT 可算名詞 Your **workplace** is the place where you work. 職場 ❏ *...the difficulties facing women in the workplace.* 職場で女性が直面する問題

work|sheet /wɜ́rkʃit/ (**worksheets**) N-COUNT 可算名詞 A **worksheet** is a specially prepared page of exercises designed to improve your knowledge or understanding of a particular subject. 問題プリント ❏ *Complete this worksheet before you decide on the model you want.* 希望するスタイルを決める前にこの問題プリントを完了しなさい.

work|shop /wɜ́rkʃɒp/ (**workshops**) **1** N-COUNT 可算名詞 A **workshop** is a period of discussion or practical work on a particular subject in which a group of people share their knowledge or experience. 講習会 ❏ *Trumpeter Marcus Belgrave ran a jazz workshop for young artists.* トランペット奏者のマーカス・ベルグレーブは若いアーティストのために講習会を開いた. **2** N-COUNT 可算名詞 A **workshop** is a building that contains tools or machinery for making or repairing things, especially using wood or metal. 作業場 ❏ *...a modestly equipped workshop.* 限定的な設備の作業場

work|station /wɜ́rksteɪʃən/ (**workstations**) also **work station** N-COUNT 可算名詞 A **workstation** is a screen and keyboard that are part of an office computer system. ワークステーション ❏ *Or you can set up databases on any number of servers and access them from particular workstations.* または, あらゆる数のサーバーにデータベースを設定し, 特定のワークステーションからアクセスすることができる.

W

work|week /wɜrkwik/ (workweeks) N-COUNT 可算名詞 A **workweek** is the amount of time during a normal week that you spend doing your job. 週労働日数 [mainly AM 主に米国英語] ❑ *The union has sought a wage increase, a shorter workweek.* 組合は賃金の引き上げと週労働日数の削減を要求していた.

world /wɜrld/ (worlds) ◼ N-SING 単数名詞 **The world** is the planet that we live on. 世界 ❑ *The satellite enables us to calculate their precise location anywhere in the world.* サテライトにより我々は世界中の正確な位置を算出することができる. ◻ N-SING 単数名詞 **The world** refers to all the people who live on this planet, and our societies, institutions, and ways of life. 世界の人々 ❑ *The world was, and remains, shocked.* 世界の人々はショックから回復していない. ◼ ADJ 形容詞 You can use **world** to describe someone or something that is one of the most important or significant of its kind on earth. 世界の [ADJ n] ❑ *China has once again emerged as a world power.* 中国は再び世界的な大国として立ち上がってきた. ◼ N-SING 単数名詞 You can use **world** in expressions such as **the Arab world**, **the Western world**, and **the ancient world** to refer to a particular group of countries or a particular period in history. 世界 ❑ *Athens had strong ties to the Arab world.* アテネはアラブ世界と強い結びつきを持っていた. ◼ N-COUNT 可算名詞 Someone's **world** is the life they lead, the people they have contact with, and the things they experience. 世界 ❑ *His world seemed so different from mine.* 彼の世界は私のそれとは非常に異なっているようだった. ◼ N-SING 単数名詞 You can use **world** to refer to a particular field of activity, and the people involved in it. 業界 ❑ *The publishing world had certainly never seen an event quite like this.* 出版界は確かにこのような行事を見たことがなかった. ◼ N-SING 単数名詞 You can use **world** to refer to a particular group of living things, for example, **the animal world**, **the plant world**, and **the insect world**. 界 ❑ *When it comes to dodging disaster, the champions of the insect world have to be cockroaches.* 災難から逃れることになると、昆虫界のチャンピオンはゴキブリに違いない. ◼ → see also **real world, Third World** ◼ PHRASE 句 If you say that someone has **the best of both worlds**, you mean that they have only the benefits of two things and none of the disadvantages. 両者のよい点を取る ❑ *Her living room provides the best of both worlds, with an office at one end and comfortable sofas at the other.* 彼女の居間は一角に仕事場があり、もう一角にソファーがあり、両手に花だ. ◼ PHRASE 句 If you say that something **has done** someone **a world of good**, you mean that it has made them feel better or improved their life. 大いに役立つ [INFORMAL くだけた] ❑ *Just sit for a while and relax. It will do you a world of good.* ちょっと座ってくつろぎなさい. きみに大いに役立つと思う. ◼ PHRASE 句 You can use **in the world** in expressions such as **what in the world** and **who in the world** to emphasize a question, especially when expressing surprise or anger. いったい全体 [EMPHASIS 強調] ❑ *What in the world is he doing?* いったい全体彼は何をしているのか. ◼ PHRASE 句 You can use **in an ideal world** or **in a perfect world** when you are talking about things that you would like to happen, although you realize that they are not likely to happen. 理想郷では ❑ *In an ideal world Karen Stevens says she would love to stay at home with her two-and-half-year-old son.* 理想郷は2歳半の息子と一緒に家にいることだとカレン・スティーブンスは言っている. ◼ PHRASE 句 You can use **the outside world** to refer to all the people who do not live in a particular place or who are not involved in a particular situation. 外の世界 ❑ *For many, the post office is the only link with the outside world.* 多くの人々にとって郵便局が外の世界との唯一のつながりである. ◼ **not be the end of the world** → see **end** ◼ **the world is your oyster** → see **oyster** ◼ **on top of the world** → see **top**

Word Partnership	*world* は次の語句と使われる:
PREP.	**all over the** world, **anywhere in the** world, **around the** world ◼
V.	**travel the** world ◼
N.	world **history**, world **peace**, world **premiere** ◼ world **of** *something* ◼ ◼ ◼ world **record** ◼

world-class ADJ 形容詞 A **world-class** athlete, performer, or organization is one of the best in the world. 世界で一流の [JOURNALISM ジャーナリズム] ❑ *He was determined to become a world-class player.* 彼は世界で一流の選手になることを固く決心していた.

world-famous ADJ 形容詞 Someone or something that is **world-famous** is known about by people all over the world. 世界的に有名な ❑ *...the world-famous Hollywood Bowl.* 世界的に有名なハリウッド・ボウル.

world|ly /wɜrldli/ ◼ ADJ 形容詞 Someone who is **worldly** is experienced and knows about the practical or social aspects of life. 世事に通じた ❑ *He was different from anyone I had known, very worldly, everything that Duane was not.* 彼は私が知っているどんな人物とも違っていた. とても世知にたけていて、デュアンとは正反対だった. ◼ ADJ 形容詞 You can refer to someone's possessions as their **worldly** goods or possessions. この世の [LITERARY 文語的] [ADJ n]

❑ *...a man who had given up all his worldly goods.* すべての世俗的な財産を捨てた男

world view (world views) also **world-view** N-COUNT 可算名詞 A person's **world view** is the way they see and understand the world, especially regarding issues such as politics, philosophy, and religion. 世界観 ❑ *...their Christian world view.* 彼らのキリスト教の世界観

world war (world wars) N-VAR 可変性名詞 A **world war** is a war that involves countries all over the world. 世界大戦 ❑ *Many senior citizens have been through two world wars.* 高齢者の多くは2つの世界大戦を体験してきた.

Word Link	*wide* ≈ *extending throughout : nationwide,* *widespread, worldwide*

world|wide /wɜrldwaɪd/ ADV 副詞 If something exists or happens **worldwide**, it exists or happens throughout the world. 世界中で ❑ *His books had sold more than 20 million copies worldwide.* 彼の本は世界中で2千万部以上も売れた. ● ADJ 形容詞 **Worldwide** is also an adjective. 世界中に及ぶ ❑ *Today, doctors are fearing a worldwide epidemic.* 今日、医者は世界的な流行を恐れている.

World-Wide Web N-PROPER 固有名詞 **The World Wide Web** is a computer system that links documents and pictures into a database that is stored in computers in many different parts of the world and that people everywhere can use. The abbreviations **WWW** and **the Web** are often used. ワールドワイドウェブ [COMPUTING コンピューティング] → see **Internet**

worm /wɜrm/ (worms, worming, wormed) ◼ N-COUNT 可算名詞 A **worm** is a small animal with a long thin body, no bones, and no legs. 虫 ◼ V-T 他動詞 If you say that someone is **worming** their **way** to success, or **is worming** their **way** into someone else's affection, you disapprove of the way that they are gradually making someone trust them or like them, often in order to deceive them or gain some advantage. 徐々に得る [DISAPPROVAL 不賛成] ❑ *She never misses a chance to worm her way into the public's hearts.* 彼女は巧妙に取り入って国民の人気を得る機会を逃すことはない. ◼ N-COUNT 可算名詞 A **worm** is a computer program that contains a virus which duplicates itself many times in a network. ワーム [COMPUTING コンピューティング] ❑ *...a new computer worm that disables security software.* セキュリティのソフトを不具合にする新しいコンピュータ・ワーム ◼ PHRASE 句 If you say that someone is **opening a can of worms**, you are warning them that they are planning to do or talk about something that is much more complicated, unpleasant, or difficult than they realize and that might be better left alone. 厄介な問題 ❑ *Introducing this legislation would be like opening a can of worms.* この規制を導入することは厄介な問題を明らかにするようなものだろう.

worn /wɔrn/ ◼ **Worn** is the past participle of **wear**. wearの過去分詞 ◼ ADJ 形容詞 **Worn** is used to describe something that is damaged or thin because it is old and has been used a lot. 使い古しの ❑ *Worn rugs increase the danger of tripping.* 擦り切れたじゅうたんはつまずく危険を高める. ◼ ADJ 形容詞 If someone looks **worn**, they look tired and old. 疲れきった [v-link ADJ] ❑ *She was looking very haggard and worn.* 彼女は非常にやつれて疲れきっているように見えた.

worn out also **worn-out** ◼ ADJ 形容詞 Something that is **worn out** is so old, damaged, or thin from use that it cannot be used anymore. 使い古した ❑ *Car buyers tend to replace worn-out tires with the same brand.* 車を買う人は使い古したタイヤを同じブランドのものと取替える傾向がある. ◼ ADJ 形容詞 Someone who is **worn out** is extremely tired after hard work or a difficult or unpleasant experience. 疲れきった ❑ *Before the race, he is fine. But afterwards he is worn out.* レース前の彼は元気だったが終わった後は疲れきっている.

wor|ried /wɜrid/ ADJ 形容詞 When you are **worried**, you are unhappy because you keep thinking about problems that you have or about unpleasant things that might happen in the future. 心配した ❑ *He seemed very worried.* 彼は大変心配しているようだった.

wor|ri|some /wɜrisəm/ ADJ 形容詞 Something that is **worrisome** causes people to worry. 困った [mainly AM 主に米国英語] ❑ *It's Houston's injury that is now the most worrisome.* 現在最も心配なのはヒューストンの負傷である.

wor|ry /wɜri/ (worries, worrying, worried) ◼ V-T/V-I 他動詞/自動詞 If you **worry**, you keep thinking about problems that you have or about unpleasant things that might happen. 心配する ❑ *Don't worry, your luggage will come on afterwards by taxi.* 心配するな、きみの荷物は後でタクシーで届く予定だ. ❑ *I worry about her constantly.* 私はいつも彼のことを心配している. ❑ *They worry that high interest rates are keeping the dollar too high.* 彼らは高金利のためにドル高が続いていることを心配している. ◼ V-T 他動詞 If someone or something **worries** you, they make you anxious because you keep thinking about problems or unpleasant things that might

be connected with them. 悩ませる ❑ *I'm still in the early days of my recovery and that worries me.* 私はまだ回復の初期のためいらいらしている. ❸ V-T 他動詞 If someone or something does not **worry** you, you do not dislike them or you are not annoyed by them. 悩ませる [SPOKEN 口語] [oft with neg] ❑ *The cold doesn't worry me.* 寒さは気にならない方だ. ❹ N-UNCOUNT 不可算名詞 **Worry** is the state or feeling of anxiety and unhappiness caused by the problems that you have or by thinking about unpleasant things that might happen. 心配 ❑ *Modern American life is full of worry: the job, the kids, money, the stock market.* 現代のアメリカ人の生活は仕事, 子供, お金, 株式市場と, 心配事でいっぱいだ. ❺ N-COUNT 可算名詞 A **worry** is a problem that you keep thinking about and that makes you unhappy. 悩みの種 ❑ *My main worry was that Madeleine Johnson would still be there.* 私の主な悩みはマドレーヌ・ジョンソンがまだそこにいるということだった.

Word Partnership   worry は次の語句と使われる:

N.	**analysts** worry, **experts** worry, **people** worry ❶ **no need to** worry ❶ ❷
V.	**begin to** worry, **don't** worry, **have things/nothing to** worry **about, not going to** worry ❶ ❷

wor|ry|ing /wɜːriɪŋ/ ADJ 形容詞 If something is **worrying**, it causes people to worry. 心配な [mainly BRIT 主に英国語; AM usually **worrisome** 米国英語では通常 **worrisome**]

worse /wɜːrs/ ❶ **Worse** is the comparative of **bad**. bad の比較級 ❷ **Worse** is the comparative of **badly**. badly の比較級 ❸ PHRASE 句 If a situation changes **for the worse**, it becomes more unpleasant or more difficult. さらに悪い方へ ❑ *The grandparents sigh and say how things have changed for the worse.* 祖父母はため息をつき, 事態がいかに悪化したかを語る.

wors|en /wɜːrsən/ (**worsens, worsening, worsened**) V-T/V-I 他動詞/自動詞 If a bad situation **worsens** or if something **worsens** it, it becomes more difficult, unpleasant, or unacceptable. より悪くなる ❑ *The security forces had to intervene to prevent the situation worsening.* 保安隊は状況が悪化するのを防ぐために介入しなければならなかった.

wor|ship /wɜːrʃɪp/ (**worships, worshiping, worshiped**) ❶ V-T/V-I 他動詞/自動詞 If you **worship** a god, you show your respect to the god, for example, by saying prayers. 崇拝する ❑ *..disputes over ways of life and ways of worshiping God.* 世の常と神を敬うしきたりについての論議 ❑ *He prefers to worship in his own home.* 彼は自宅で崇拝するほうが好きだ. ● N-UNCOUNT 不可算名詞 **Worship** is also a noun. 崇拝 ❑ *...the worship of the ancient Roman gods.* 古代ローマの神の崇拝 ● **wor|ship|er** (**worshipers**) N-COUNT 可算名詞 崇拝者 ❑ *She burst into tears and loud sobs that disturbed the other worshipers.* 彼女は突然泣き出し, 泣きじゃくる声は他の礼拝者のじゃまになった. ❷ V-T 他動詞 If you **worship** someone or something, you love them or admire them very much. 熱愛する ❑ *She had worshiped him for years.* 彼女は彼を長年熱愛してきた.

worst /wɜːrst/ ❶ **Worst** is the superlative of **bad**. bad の最上級 ❷ **Worst** is the superlative of **badly**. badly の最上級 ❸ N-SING 単数名詞 **The worst** is the most unpleasant or unfavorable thing that could happen or does happen. 最も悪いこと ❑ *Though mine safety has much improved, miners' families still fear the worst.* 炭鉱の安全性はかなり改善したが炭鉱夫の家族はまだ最悪の事態が起こるのを恐れている. ❹ **Worst** is used to form the superlative of compound adjectives beginning with "bad" and "badly." 最もひどく ❑ *The worst-affected areas were in Jefferson Parish.* 最もひどい影響を受けた地域はジェファーソン郡だった. ❺ PHRASE 句 You say **worst of all** to indicate that what you are about to mention is the most unpleasant or has the most disadvantages out of all the things you are mentioning. 何よりも悪いことに ❑ *The people most closely affected are the passengers who were injured and, worst of all, those who lost relatives.* 最もひどい影響を受けた人々は負傷した乗客と, 何よりも悪いことには親戚を失った人々である. ❻ PHRASE 句 You use **at worst** or **at the worst** to indicate that you are mentioning the worst thing that might happen in a situation. 最悪の場合には ❑ *At best Nella would be an invalid; at worst she would die.* ネラはよくても肢体不自由者となり, 最悪の場合には死亡するだろう. ❼ PHRASE 句 When someone is **at their worst**, they are as unpleasant, bad, or unsuccessful as it is possible for them to be. 最悪の状態で ❑ *This was their mother at her worst. Her voice was strident, she was ready to be angry at anyone.* これは彼女の母親が最悪の状態の時だった. かん高い声で話し, だれにでも腹を立てがちだった. ❽ PHRASE 句 You use **if worst comes to worst** or **if the worst comes to the worst** to say what you might do if a situation develops in the most unfavorable way possible. 最悪の場合には ❑ *If worst comes to worst, Europe could withstand a trade war.* 最悪の場合には, ヨーロッパは貿易戦争に抵抗することができるだろう.

worth /wɜːrθ/ ❶ V-T 他動詞 If something is **worth** a particular amount of money, it can be sold for that amount or is considered

to have that value. 一の値打ちがある [v-link 'worth' amount] ❑ *A local jeweler says the pearl is worth at least $500.* 地元の宝石屋はその真珠は少なくとも500ドルの値打ちがあると言っている. ❑ *His mother inherited a business worth 15,000 dollars a year.* 彼女の母親は年間利益が1万5千ドルの事業を相続した. ❷ COMB IN QUANT 数量詞の複合 **Worth** combines with amounts of money, so that when you talk about a particular amount of money's **worth** of something, you mean the quantity of it that you can buy for that amount of money. 相当の [QUANT 'of' n] ❑ *I went and bought about six dollars' worth of potato chips.* 私は約6ドル分のポテトチップスを買った. ● PRON 代名詞 **Worth** is also a pronoun. 価値 ❑ *Gold reserves had fallen to less than $3 billion worth.* 金の準備金は30億ドル以下に減少した. ❸ COMB IN QUANT 数量詞の複合 **Worth** combines with time expressions, so you can use **worth** when you are saying how long an amount of something will last. For example, a week's **worth** of food is the amount of food that will last you for a week. 分の [QUANT 'of' n] ❑ *You've got three years' worth of research money to do what you want with.* きみは3年分の研究費を自由に使える. ● PRON 代名詞 **Worth** is also a pronoun. 一分 ❑ *There's really not very much food down there. About two weeks' worth.* あそこにはあまり食料がない. 約2週間分かな. ❹ V-T 他動詞 If you say that something is **worth** having, you mean that it is pleasant or useful, and therefore a good thing to have. 価値がある [v-link 'worth' -ing] ❑ *He's decided to get a look at the house and see if it might be worth buying.* 彼は買う価値があるかどうかを調べるためにその家を見にいくことに決めた. ❑ *Most things worth having never come easy.* 持つ価値のある大半のものは簡単に手に入らない. ❺ V-T 他動詞 If something is **worth** a particular action, or if an action is **worth** doing, it is considered to be important enough for that action. 価値がある [v-link 'worth' n/-ing] ❑ *I am spending a lot of money and time on this boat, but it is worth it?* 私はこのボートに多くの金と手間をかけているがそれだけの価値があるか? ❑ *This restaurant is well worth a visit.* このレストランは行ってみる価値が大いにある. ❻ PHRASE 句 If an action or activity is **worth** someone's **while**, it will be helpful, useful, or enjoyable for them if they do it, even though it requires some effort. 骨折りがいがある ❑ *It might be worth your while to go to court and ask for the agreement to be changed.* 裁判所に出向き, 契約を変えてもらう価値があるかもしれない. ❼ **worth** your **weight in gold** → see **weight**

Word Partnership   worth は次の語句と使われる:

N.	worth **five dollars**, worth **a fortune**, worth **money**, worth **the price** ❶ worth **the effort**, worth **the risk**, worth **the trouble**, worth **a try** ❺
V.	worth **buying**, worth **having** ❹ worth **fighting for**, worth **remembering**, worth **saving**, worth **watching** ❺

Word Link   less ≈ without : aim**less**, harm**less**, worth**less**

worth|less /wɜːrθləs/ ❶ ADJ 形容詞 Something that is **worthless** is of no real value or use. 価値のない ❑ *The guarantee could be worthless if the store goes out of business.* 保証書はその店がつぶれた場合には役に立たないだろう. ❑ *Training is worthless unless there is proof that it works.* 研修は効果があるという証拠がない限り価値がない. ❷ ADJ 形容詞 Someone who is described as **worthless** is considered to have no good qualities or skills. 役立たずの ❑ *You feel you really are completely worthless and unlovable.* 人は本当に全くの役立たずで愛らしくないと感じる.

worth|while /wɜːrθwaɪl/ ADJ 形容詞 If something is **worthwhile**, it is enjoyable or useful, and worth the time, money, or effort that is spent on it. 時間を費やす価値のある ❑ *The president's recent trip to Washington this week seems to have been worthwhile.* 今週の大統領のワシントン旅行は行きがいがあったと思われる.

Thesaurus   worthwhile また次を参照:

ADJ.	beneficial, helpful, useful; (ant.) worthless

wor|thy /wɜːrði/ (**worthier, worthiest**) ADJ 形容詞 If a person or thing is **worthy** of something, they deserve it because they have the qualities or abilities required. ふさわしい [FORMAL 形式ばった] ❑ *The bank might think you're worthy of a loan.* 銀行はあなたがローンを受ける資格があると判断するかもしれない.

would /wəd, STRONG wʊd/

> **Would** is a modal verb. It is usually used with the base form of a verb. In spoken English, **would** is often abbreviated to **'d**.
>
> **Would** は法動詞であり, 通常動詞の原形と共に用いられる. 口語英語では **would** はしばしば **'d** に短縮される.

❶ MODAL 法動詞 You use **would** when you are saying what someone believed, hoped, or expected to happen or be the case. 一だろう ❑ *No one believed the soldiers stationed at the border would actually open fire.* 国境に駐屯する兵隊が実際に発砲するとは誰も考

えなかった. ❑*Would he always be like this?* 彼はいつもこんな調子でしょうか. **2** MODAL 法動詞 You use **would** when saying what someone intended to do. ―しよう ❑*The statement added that although there were a number of differing views, these would be discussed by both sides.* その声明は複数の異なる見解があったが、こうした見解は両当事者によって論議されるだろうと書き足した. **3** MODAL 法動詞 You use **would** when you are referring to the result or effect of a possible situation. ―でしょう ❑*Ordinarily it would be fun to be taken to fabulous restaurants.* 普通ステキなレストランに招待されるのは楽しいでしょう. ❑*It would be wrong to suggest that police officers were not annoyed by acts of indecency.* 警察官は猥褻(わいせつ)行為に腹を立てないと言うのは間違っているだろう. **4** MODAL 法動詞 You use **would**, or **would have** with a past participle, to indicate that you are assuming or guessing that something is true, because you have good reasons for thinking it. ―だろう ❑*You wouldn't know him.* きみは多分彼を知らないだろう. ❑*His fans would already be familiar with Caroline.* 彼のファンは既にキャロラインをよく知っているだろう. **5** MODAL 法動詞 You use **would** in the main clause of some "if" and "unless" sentences to indicate something you consider to be fairly unlikely to happen. ―だろう ❑*If only I could get some sleep, I would be able to cope.* 眠ることさえできれば私はうまく対応できるのに. **6** MODAL 法動詞 You use **would** to say that someone was willing to do something. You use **would not** to indicate that they refused to do something. ―しようとする ❑*They said they would give the police their full cooperation.* 彼らは警察に全面的に協力するつもりだと言った. ❑*He wouldn't say where he had picked up the information.* 彼はどこでその情報を得たかをどうしても言おうとしなかった. **7** MODAL 法動詞 You use **would not** to indicate that something did not happen, often in spite of a lot of effort. どうしても―しない ❑*He kicked, pushed, and hurled his shoulder at the door. It wouldn't open.* 彼はドアをけり、押し、肩をぶつけたが、それはどうしても開かなかった. **8** MODAL 法動詞 You use **would**, especially with "like," "love," and "wish," when saying that someone wants to do or have a particular thing or wants a particular thing to happen. ―したいと思う ❑*She asked me what I would like to do and mentioned a particular job.* 彼女は私に何がしたいかと聞き、特定の職について話した. ❑*Ideally, she would love to become pregnant again.* 理想的には彼女はまた妊娠したいと思っている. **9** **would rather** → see **rather** **10** MODAL 法動詞 You use **would** with "if" clauses in questions when you are asking for permission to do something. ―してよろしいですか ❑*Do you think it would be all right if I smoked?* タバコを吸ってよろしいでしょうか. **11** MODAL 法動詞 You use **would**, usually in questions with "like," when you are making a polite offer or invitation. ―しませんか[POLITENESS 丁寧さ] ❑*Would you like a drink?* お飲み物はいかがですか. ❑*Would you like to stay?* 泊まっていらっしゃいませんか. **12** MODAL 法動詞 You use **would**, usually in questions, when you are politely asking someone to do something. していただけませんか[POLITENESS 丁寧さ] ❑*Would you do me a favor and get rid of this letter I've just received?* お願いですが、たった今受け取った手紙を捨ててくださいませんか. ❑*Would you come in here a moment, please?* ちょっとここに来ていただけませんか. **13** MODAL 法動詞 You say that someone **would** do something when it is typical of them and you are critical of it. You emphasize the word **would** when you use it in this way. 決まって―する[DISAPPROVAL 不賛成] ❑*Well, you would say that: you're a man.* まああなたはそう言うに決まっている. 男だから. **14** MODAL 法動詞 You use **would**, or sometimes **would have** with a past participle, when you are expressing your opinion about something or seeing if people agree with you, especially when you are uncertain about what you are saying. ―だろう [VAGUENESS あいまいさ] ❑*I think you'd agree he's a very respected columnist.* 彼が大変立派なコラムニストであることにあなたは同意見だと思う. ❑*I would have thought he was too old to do that job.* 彼はその仕事をするには年を取りすぎていると思ったでしょう. **15** MODAL 法動詞 You use **I would** when you are giving someone advice in an informal way. ―だろう ❑*If I were you I would simply ring your friend's doorbell and ask for your bike back.* 私がきみだったら友達の玄関の呼び鈴を鳴らして自転車を返してくれるよう頼むのだ. **16** MODAL 法動詞 You use **you would** in negative sentences with verbs such as "guess" and "know" when you want to say that something is not obvious, especially something surprising. ―だろう ❑*Chris is so full of artistic temperament you'd never think she was the daughter of a banker.* クリスは全くの芸術家肌なので人はまさか銀行家の娘だとは思わないだろう. **17** MODAL 法動詞 You use **would have** with a past participle when you are saying what was likely to have happened by a particular time. ―しただろう ❑*Within ten weeks of the introduction, 34 million people would have been reached by our television commercials.* 発表してから10週間以内に3400万人の人々が当局のテレビのコマーシャルを見ただろう. **18** MODAL 法動詞 You use **would have** with a past participle when you are referring to the result or effect of a possible event in the past. ―しただろう ❑*My daughter would have been 17 this week if she had lived.* 私の娘はもし生きていたら今週17歳になっていたでしょう. **19** MODAL 法動詞 If you say that someone **would have** liked or preferred something, you mean that they wanted to do it or have it but were unable to. ―し

ただろう ❑*I would have liked a life in politics.* 私はできれば政治家になっていたかった.

would-be ADJ 形容詞 You can use **would-be** to describe someone who wants or attempts to do a particular thing. For example, a **would-be** writer is someone who wants to be a writer. 志望の [ADJ n] ❑*…a book that provides encouragement for would-be writers who cannot get their novel into print.* 小説を発行できない小説家志願者を励ます本

wouldn't /wʊdᵊnt/ **Wouldn't** is the usual spoken form of "would not." 口語で用いられるwould notの省略形 ❑*They wouldn't allow me to smoke.* 彼らは私の喫煙を許さないだろう.

would've /wʊdəv/ **Would've** is a spoken form of "would have," when "have" is an auxiliary verb. 口語で用いられるwould haveの省略形 ❑*I knew deep down that my mom would've loved one of us to go to college.* 僕らの誰か1人が大学に行くことを母は望んでいただろうことを私は内心知っていた.

---

wound

❶ VERB FORM OF "WIND"
❷ INJURY

---

❶ wound /waʊnd/ **Wound** is the past tense and past participle of **wind**. windの過去形および過去分詞 → see **wind ❷**
❷ wound /wuːnd/ **(wounds, wounding, wounded)** **1** N-COUNT 可算名詞 A **wound** is damage to part of your body, especially a cut or a hole in your flesh, which is caused by a gun, knife, or other weapon. 傷 ❑*The wound is healing nicely and the patient is healthy.* 傷は良好に治癒しており、患者も健康だ. **2** V-T 他動詞 If a weapon or something sharp **wounds** you, it damages your body. 傷つける [他動詞] ❑*A bomb exploded in a hotel, killing six people and wounding another five.* ホテル内で爆弾が炸裂し、6人が死亡し、5人が負傷しました. ● N-PLURAL 複数名詞 **The wounded** are people who are wounded. 負傷者 ❑*Hospitals said they could not cope with the wounded.* 病院側は負傷者に対応することができないと言いました. **3** V-T 他動詞 If you **are wounded** by what someone says or does, your feelings are deeply hurt. 傷つける ❑*He was deeply wounded by his son's comments.* 彼は息子のコメントに深く傷ついた. → see **war**

> Note that when someone is hurt accidentally, for example, in a car crash or when they are playing sports, you do not use the word **wound**. You use **injury** instead. ❑*A man and his baby were injured in the explosion… Many of the deaths that occur in cycling are due to head injuries.* In more formal English, **injury** can also be an uncount noun. ❑*Two teenagers escaped serious injury when their car rolled down an embankment.* **Wound** is normally restricted to soldiers who are injured in battle, or to deliberate acts of violence against a particular person. ❑*…stab wounds*

Word Partnership   *wound* は次の語句と使われる:

N.	**bullet** wound, **chest** wound, **gunshot** wound, **head** wound ❷ **1**
V.	**die from a** wound, wound **heals**, **inflict a** wound ❷ **1**
ADJ.	**fatal** wound, **open** wound ❷ **1**

wound up /waʊnd ʌp/ ADJ 形容詞 If someone is **wound up**, they are very tense and nervous or angry. 緊張した ❑*"My caddie got so wound up I had to calm him down," Lancaster said.* 「僕のキャディーは非常に緊張していたから落ち着かせなければならなかったんだ」とランカスターは言った.

wove /woʊv/ **Wove** is the past tense of **weave**. weaveの過去形

wo|ven /woʊvᵊn/ **Woven** is a past participle of **weave**. weaveの過去分詞

wow /waʊ/ EXCLAM 感嘆詞 You can say "**wow**" when you are very impressed, surprised, or pleased. ワァー [INFORMAL くだけた、FEELINGS 感情] ❑*I thought, "Wow, what a good idea."* 「すごい、なんていいアイデアなんだ」と私は思いました.

wran|gle /ræŋgᵊl/ **(wrangles, wrangling, wrangled)** V-RECIP 相互動詞 If you say that someone is **wrangling with** someone **over** a question or issue, you mean that they have been arguing angrily for a long time about it. 論争している ❑*The two sides have spent most of their time wrangling over procedural problems.* 双方とも手順上の問題についての討論でほとんどの時間を費やしました.

wrap /ræp/ **(wraps, wrapping, wrapped)** **1** V-T 他動詞 When you **wrap** something, you fold paper or cloth tightly around it to cover it completely, for example, in order to protect it or so that you can give it to someone as a present. 包む [他動詞] ❑*Harry had carefully bought and wrapped presents for Mark to give the children.* ハリーはマークが子供たちに与えるプレゼントを慎重に選んで購入し、包装した. ● PHRASAL VERB 句動詞 **Wrap up** means the same as **wrap**. 包む ❑*Diana is taking the opportunity to wrap up the family presents.* ダイアナは潮時を見て家族のプレゼントを包んでいる. **2** V-T 他動

詞 When you **wrap** something such as a piece of paper or cloth around another thing, you put it around it. 巻く □ *She wrapped a handkerchief around her bleeding palm in an effort to protect it.* 彼女は出血している手のひらにハンカチを巻いて保護しようとした. ⁵ → see also **wrapping** ⁴ PHRASE 句 If you keep something **under wraps**, you keep it secret, often until you are ready to announce it at some time in the future. 秘密にされた □ *The bids were submitted in May and were kept under wraps until October.* 入札は5月に提出され, 10月まで公表されなかった.

▶ **wrap up** ¹ PHRASAL VERB 句動詞 If you **wrap up**, you put warm clothes on. くるまる □ *She wrapped up in her mother's red shawl.* 彼女は母の赤いショールにくるまった. □ *Kids just love being able to romp around in the fresh air without having to wrap up warm.* 子供たちは厚着の服を着ずに新鮮な空気の中で遊び騒ぐことができるのがただ単に大好きだ. ² PHRASAL VERB 句動詞 If you **wrap up** something such as a job or an agreement, you complete it in a satisfactory way. 終える □ *NATO defense ministers wrap up their meeting in Brussels today.* NATO国防相らはブリュッセルでの会議を本日終了します. ³ → see also **wrap 1, wrapped up**

wrapped up ADJ 形容詞 If someone is **wrapped up** in a particular person or thing, they spend nearly all their time thinking about them, so that they forget about other things that may be important. 夢中になっている [v-link ADJ 'in/with' n] □ *He's too serious and dedicated, wrapped up in his career.* 彼はあまりにも真剣で献身的で, 仕事に心を奪われている.

wrap|per /ˈræpər/ (**wrappers**) N-COUNT 可算名詞 A **wrapper** is a piece of paper, plastic, or thin metal that covers and protects something that you buy, especially food. 包むもの □ *I emptied the candy wrappers from the ashtray.* 私は灰皿からキャンディーの包み紙を取り出した.

wrap|ping /ˈræpɪŋ/ (**wrappings**) N-VAR 可変性名詞 **Wrapping** is something such as paper or plastic that is used to cover and protect something. 包装材料 □ *Nick asked for the tile to be delivered in waterproof wrapping.* ニックは防水包装材料でタイルを梱包して配達するよう依頼しました.

wrath /ræθ/ N-UNCOUNT 不可算名詞 **Wrath** means the same as anger. 激怒 [LITERARY 文語的] □ *He incurred the wrath of the authorities in speaking out against government injustices.* 彼は政府の不当な処置を猛烈に非難したために関係官庁の怒りを買った.

wreak /riːk/ (**wreaks, wreaking, wreaked**)

> Some people use the form **wrought** as the past tense and past participle of **wreak**, but many people consider this to be wrong.
>
> **wrought** 形を **wreak** の過去形や過去分詞として使う人があるが, 多くの人たちはこれは間違いだと考えている.

V-T 他動詞 Something or someone that **wreaks** havoc or destruction causes a great amount of disorder or damage. (大惨事や破壊を) もたらす [LITERARY 文語的] JOURNALISM ジャーナリズム] [他動詞] □ *Violent storms wreaked havoc on the French Riviera, leaving three people dead and dozens injured.* 大嵐はフランス・リビエラに大惨事をもたらし, 死者3人と多数の負傷者を出した.

wreath /riːθ/ (**wreaths**) ¹ N-COUNT 可算名詞 A **wreath** is an arrangement of flowers and leaves in the shape of a circle, which you put on a grave or by a statue to show that you remember a person who has died or people who have died. 花輪 □ *The coffin lying before the altar was bare, except for a single wreath of white roses.* 祭壇の前に置かれたひつぎは白いバラの花輪が1つある以外何も飾りがなかった. ² N-COUNT 可算名詞 A **wreath** is a circle of leaves that some people hang somewhere in their house or on the front door as decoration. 飾り葉 □ *A Christmas wreath exclaiming PEACE ON EARTH hangs on the restaurant door.* 世界の平和を叫ぶクリスマスの花輪がレストランのドアにかかっている.

wreck /rɛk/ (**wrecks, wrecking, wrecked**) ¹ V-T 他動詞 To **wreck** something means to completely destroy or ruin it. 粉砕する □ *He wrecked the garden.* 彼は庭を破壊した. □ *His life has been wrecked by the tragedy.* 彼の人生はその悲劇で完全に破壊されました. ² N-COUNT 可算名詞 A **wreck** is something such as a ship, car, plane, or building that has been destroyed, usually in an accident. 難破物 □ *...the wreck of a sailing ship.* 難破帆船の残骸 (ざんがい) □ *The car was a total wreck.* その車は完全に破壊されていました. ³ N-COUNT 可算名詞 A **wreck** is an accident in which a moving vehicle hits something and is damaged or destroyed. 破壊 [mainly AM 主に米国英語] □ *He was killed in a car wreck.* 彼は自動車事故で亡くなりました. ⁴ N-COUNT 可算名詞 If you say that someone is a **wreck**, you mean that they are very exhausted or unhealthy. 健康をそこねた人 [INFORMAL くだけた] □ *You look a wreck.* きみは非常に参っているようだ.

wreck|age /ˈrɛkɪdʒ/ N-UNCOUNT 不可算名詞 When something such as a plane, car, or building has been destroyed, you can refer to what remains as **wreckage** or **the wreckage**. 残骸 [also 'the' N] □ *Mark was dragged from the burning wreckage of his car just before it exploded.* マークは燃え上がる自分の車の残骸が爆発する前に引っ張り出された.

wrench /rɛntʃ/ (**wrenches, wrenching, wrenched**) ¹ V-T 他動詞 If you **wrench** something that is fixed in a particular position, you pull or twist it violently, in order to move or remove it. ねじ取る □ *He felt two men wrench the suitcase from his hand.* 彼は2人の男が彼の手からスーツケースをもぎ取るのを感じた. ² V-T 他動詞 If you **wrench** yourself free from someone who is holding you, you get away from them by suddenly twisting the part of your body that is being held. ねじりながら引っ張る □ *She wrenched herself from his grasp.* 彼は彼女をつかんだが彼女は身を振り切って逃げた. □ *He wrenched his arm free.* 彼は腕をひねって離した. ³ N-COUNT 可算名詞 A **wrench** is an adjustable metal tool used for tightening or loosening metal nuts of different sizes. レンチ → see also **monkey wrench** ⁵ V-T 他動詞 If you **wrench** your neck, you hurt it by pulling or twisting it in an unusual way. 強くねじって違える □ *She was involved in a car accident and she wrenched her neck.* 彼女は自動車事故に巻き込まれてムチ打ちになった. ⁶ PHRASE 句 If someone **throws a wrench** or **throws a monkey wrench** into a process, they prevent something happening smoothly by deliberately causing a problem. 妨害する [AM 米国英語] □ *The decision will throw a monkey wrench into our efforts to develop a national broadband policy.* その決定は全国広帯域政策を立てる我々の取り組みに待ったをかけるだろう.

→ see **tool**

wres|tle /ˈrɛsəl/ (**wrestles, wrestling, wrestled**) ¹ V-I 自動詞 When you **wrestle with** a difficult problem, you try to deal with it. 取り組む □ *Delegates wrestled with the problems of violence and sanctions.* 代表者らは暴力と制裁措置の問題に取り組みました. ² V-I 自動詞 If you **wrestle** with someone, you fight them by forcing them into painful positions or throwing them to the ground, rather than by hitting them. Some people wrestle as a sport. 格闘する □ *They taught me to wrestle.* 彼らは私にレスリングを教えてくれた. ³ V-T 他動詞 If you **wrestle** a person or thing somewhere, you move them there using a lot of force, for example, by twisting a part of someone's body into a painful position. 組み敷く □ *We had to physically wrestle the child from the man's arms.* 私たちはその男の腕から物理的に子供をもぎ取らねばならなかった. ⁴ → see also **wrestling**

wres|tler /ˈrɛslər/ (**wrestlers**) N-COUNT 可算名詞 A **wrestler** is someone who wrestles as a sport. レスリング選手

wres|tling /ˈrɛslɪŋ/ N-UNCOUNT 不可算名詞 **Wrestling** is a sport in which two people wrestle and try to throw each other to the ground. レスリング □ *...a championship wrestling match.* レスリングの選手権試合

wretch|ed /ˈrɛtʃɪd/ ¹ ADJ 形容詞 You use **wretched** to describe someone or something that you dislike or feel angry with. 実に不快な [INFORMAL くだけた, FEELINGS 感情] [ADJ n] □ *Wretched woman, he thought, why the hell can't she wait?* 全くいやな女だ, いったいどうして待てないんだ, と彼は思った. ² ADJ 形容詞 Someone who feels **wretched** feels very unhappy. 不幸な [FORMAL 形式ばった] □ *I feel really confused and wretched.* 私は実に複雑で惨めな気分だ.

wrig|gle /ˈrɪɡəl/ (**wriggles, wriggling, wriggled**) V-T/V-I 他動詞/自動詞 If you **wriggle** or **wriggle** part of your body, you twist and turn with quick movements, for example, because you are uncomfortable. のたうつ □ *The babies are wriggling on their tummies.* 赤ちゃんたちはうつぶせでのたくっている.

▶ **wriggle out of** PHRASAL VERB 句動詞 If you say that someone has **wriggled out of** doing something, you disapprove of the fact that they have managed to avoid doing it, although they should have done it. すり抜ける [DISAPPROVAL 不賛成] □ *He's wriggled out of doing the dishes again.* 彼は皿洗いからのらりくらりと逃れた.

wring /rɪŋ/ (**wrings, wringing, wrung**) ¹ V-T 他動詞 If you **wring** something **out of** someone, you manage to make them give it to you even though they do not want to. 無理に得る □ *Buyers use different ruses to wring free credit out of their suppliers.* 買い手は様々な策略を使用してサプライヤから無条件信用を強引に得る. ² PHRASE 句 If someone **wrings** their **hands**, they hold them together and twist and turn them, usually because they are very worried or upset about something. You can also say that someone is **wringing** their **hands** when they are expressing sorrow that a situation is so bad but are saying that they are unable to change it. 悲痛のあまり自分の手をもみしぼる □ *We can't simply stand by wringing our hands. We have to do something.* 私たちは手をもみしぼってただ突っ立っているわけにはいかない. 何かしなければならない.

▶ **wring out** PHRASAL VERB 句動詞 When you **wring out** a wet cloth or a wet piece of clothing, you squeeze the water out of it by twisting it strongly. しぼり出す □ *He turned away to wring out the wet shirt.* 彼は横を向いてぬれたシャツを絞った.

wrin|kle /ˈrɪŋkəl/ (**wrinkles, wrinkling, wrinkled**) ¹ N-COUNT 可算名詞 **Wrinkles** are lines that form on someone's face as they grow old. しわ □ *His face was covered with wrinkles.* 彼の顔にはしわがいっぱいあった. ² V-T/V-I 他動詞/自動詞 When someone's skin **wrinkles** or when something **wrinkles** it, lines start to form in it because the skin is getting old or damaged. しわを寄せる [他動

詞] しわになる [自動詞] ❑ *The skin on her cheeks and around her eyes was beginning to wrinkle.* 彼女のほほと目の周りの皮膚にはしわが寄り始めていた. ●**wrin|kled** ADJ 形容詞 しわになった ❑ *I did indeed look older and more wrinkled than ever.* 私は確かに老けて見え, 前よりもしわが増えた. **3** N-COUNT 可算名詞 A **wrinkle** is a raised fold in a piece of cloth or paper that spoils its appearance. しわ ❑ *Ben brushed smooth a wrinkle in his pants.* ベンはズボンにブラシをかけしわをのばした. **4** V-T/V-I 他動詞/自動詞 If cloth **wrinkles**, or if someone or something **wrinkles** it, it gets folds or lines in it. しわになる ❑ *Her stockings wrinkled at the ankles.* 彼女のストッキングは足首にしわが寄っていた. ●**wrin|kled** ADJ 形容詞 しわの寄った ❑ *His suit was wrinkled and he looked very tired.* 彼のスーツはしわになり, 彼はとても疲れた顔をしていた. **5** V-T/V-I 他動詞/自動詞 When you **wrinkle** your nose or forehead, or when it **wrinkles**, you tighten the muscles in your face so that the skin folds. しわを寄らせる [他動詞] しわが寄る [自動詞] ❑ *Donna wrinkled her nose at her daughter.* ドナは娘に向かって鼻筋にしわを寄せた.
→ see **skin**

wrist /rɪst/ (**wrists**) N-COUNT 可算名詞 Your **wrist** is the part of your body between your hand and your arm that bends when you move your hand. 手首 ❑ *He broke his wrist climbing rocks for a cigarette ad.* 彼はタバコの広告のために岩を登って手首を骨折した.
→ see **body, hand**

writ /rɪt/ (**writs**) N-COUNT 可算名詞 A **writ** is a legal document that orders a person to do a particular thing. 令状 ❑ *He issued a writ against one of his accusers.* 彼は告訴人の1人に対して令状を発行した.

write /raɪt/ (**writes, writing, wrote, written**) **1** V-T/V-I 他動詞/自動詞 When you **write**, you use something such as a pen or pencil to produce words, letters, or numbers. 書く ❑ *Simply write your name and address on a postcard and send it to us.* ただ葉書に名前と住所を書いて私どもにお送りください. ❑ *They were still trying to teach her to read and write.* 彼らはいまだに彼女に読み書きを教えようとしていた. **2** V-T 他動詞 If you **write** something such as a book, a poem, or a piece of music, you create it and record it on paper or perhaps on a computer. 書く ❑ *I had written quite a lot of orchestral music in my student days.* 私は学生時代かなりたくさんの管弦楽曲を書いた. ❑ *Thereafter she wrote articles for papers and magazines in Paris.* その後, 彼女はパリの新聞や雑誌に原稿を寄稿した. **3** V-I 自動詞 Someone who **writes** creates books, stories, or articles, usually for publication. 著作する ❑ *Jay wanted to write.* ジェイは作家になりたかった. **4** V-T/V-I 他動詞/自動詞 When you **write** someone or **write** to someone or **write** them a letter, you give them information, ask them something, or express your feelings in a letter. 手紙を書く ❑ *Apparently she had written to her aunt in Holland asking for advice.* 明らかに, 彼女はオランダにいる叔母にアドバイスを求める手紙を書いた. ❑ *She had written him a note a couple of weeks earlier.* 彼女は2, 3週間前彼にメモを書き送った. ❑ *I wrote a letter to the car rental agency, explaining what had happened.* 私はレンタカー取扱店に手紙を書いて, 何が起こったのかを説明した. ❑ **nothing to write home about** → see **home 6** V-T 他動詞 When someone **writes** something such as a check, receipt, or prescription, they put the necessary information on it and usually sign it. 記入する ❑ *Snape wrote a receipt with a gold fountain pen.* スネイプは金色の万年筆で領収書を書いた. **7** V-I 自動詞 If you **write** to a computer or a disk, you record data on it. 書き込む [COMPUTING コンピューティング] ❑ *You should write-protect all disks that you do not usually need to write to.* 普段書き込む必要のないディスクすべてを書込禁止にすべきだ. **8** → see also **writing**

▶ **write back** PHRASAL VERB 句動詞 If you **write back** to someone who has sent you a letter, you write them a letter in reply. 返事を書く ❑ *Macmillan wrote back saying that he could certainly help.* マクミランはもちろん援助できると返事を書いた.

▶ **write down** PHRASAL VERB 句動詞 When you **write** something **down**, you record it on a piece of paper using a pen or pencil. 書き留める ❑ *On the morning before starting a diet, write down your starting weight.* 朝, ダイエットを開始する前に開始時の体重を記録しなさい.

▶ **write in** PHRASAL VERB 句動詞 If you **write in** to an organization, you send them a letter. 手紙を書き送る ❑ *What's the point in writing in when you only print half the letter anyway?* どうせ手紙の半分しか印刷しないのに送る意味があるのか.

▶ **write into** PHRASAL VERB 句動詞 If a rule or detail **is written into** a contract, law, or agreement, it is included in it when the contract, law, or agreement is made. 書き込まれる ❑ *They insisted that a guaranteed supply of Chinese food was written into their contracts.* 彼らは中国料理の供給保証が契約に書き込まれていると主張した.

▶ **write off 1** PHRASAL VERB 句動詞 If someone **writes off** a debt or an amount of money that has been spent on a project, they accept that they are never going to get the money back. 回収不可能とみなす [BUSINESS 実業] ❑ *It was the president who persuaded the West to write off Polish debts.* ポーランドの債務を切り捨てるよう西側諸国を説得したのは大統領だった. **2** PHRASAL VERB 句動詞 If you **write** someone or something **off**, you decide that they are unimportant or useless and that they are not worth further

serious attention. 無価値とみなす ❑ *He is fed up with people writing him off because of his age.* 年齢で彼を無用なものとみなす人々に彼は愛想を尽かしている. **3** PHRASAL VERB 句動詞 If critics **write off** a plan or project, you accept that it is not going to be successful and do not continue with it. ないものとする ❑ *We decided to write off the rest of the day and go shopping.* 我々はその日はもうあきらめて買い物にでかけることにした. **4** PHRASAL VERB 句動詞 If you **write off** something such as a living expense, you deduct it from your taxes. 控除の対象として記載する ❑ *Teachers are still entitled to write off business expenses.* 教師はいまだに必要経費を控除項目として記載する権利がある. **5** PHRASAL VERB 句動詞 If you **write off** to a company or organization, you send them a letter, usually asking for something. 郵便で請求する [BRIT 英国英語] **6** → see also **write-off**

▶ **write out 1** PHRASAL VERB 句動詞 When you **write out** something fairly long such as a report or a list, you write it on paper. すっかり書く ❑ *We had to write out a list of ten jobs we'd like to do.* 我々はやりたい仕事を10個リストアップしなければならなった. **2** PHRASAL VERB 句動詞 If a character in a drama series **is written out**, he or she is taken out of the series. 登場人物を消す ❑ *Terry's character has been written out of the show.* テリーの役柄は番組から消された.

▶ **write up** PHRASAL VERB 句動詞 If you **write up** something that has been done or said, you record it on paper in a neat and complete form, usually using notes that you have made. 書き改めてきちんとする ❑ *He wrote up his visit in a report of over 600 pages.* 彼は600ページを超える詳しい視察報告書を書いた.

Thesaurus		*write* また次を参照:
v.		jot down, note down, scribble **1** author, compose, draft **2**

write-off (**write-offs**) **1** N-SING 単数名詞 If you describe a plan or period of time as a **write-off**, you mean that it has been a failure and you have achieved nothing. 帳消しにしたもの [INFORMAL くだけた] ❑ *Today was really a write-off for me.* 今日は本当に大失敗の日だった. **2** N-COUNT 可算名詞 A **write-off** is something, such as a living expense, that can be deducted from your taxes. 控除 ❑ *She got a nice $20,000 tax write-off for 2004.* 彼女は2004年2万ドルもの控除を受けた.

Word Link	er, or ≈ one who does, that which does : astronomer, author, writer

writ|er /raɪtər/ (**writers**) **1** N-COUNT 可算名詞 A **writer** is a person who writes books, stories, or articles as a job. 著者 ❑ *Turner is a writer and critic.* ターナーは作家であり, 批評家だ. ❑ *...detective stories by American writers.* アメリカの作家による推理小説 **2** N-COUNT 可算名詞 The **writer** of a particular article, report, letter, or story is the person who wrote it. 執筆者 ❑ *No one is to see the document without the permission of the writer of the report.* 報告書の執筆者の許可を得ずして文書を見ることは許されない.

writhe /raɪð/ (**writhes, writhing, writhed**) V-I 自動詞 If you **writhe**, your body twists and turns violently backward and forward, usually because you are in great pain or discomfort. 身もだえする ❑ *He was writhing in agony.* 彼は心痛にもだえ苦しんだ.

writ|ing /raɪtɪŋ/ **1** N-UNCOUNT 不可算名詞 **Writing** is something that has been written or printed. 文書 ❑ *If you have a complaint about your vacation, please inform us in writing.* 休暇について不満がある場合は書面にて我々にお知らせください. **2** N-UNCOUNT 不可算名詞 You can refer to any piece of written work as **writing**, especially when you are considering the style of language used in it. 作品 ❑ *The writing is brutally tough and savagely humorous.* その作品は残忍なほどタフで猛烈にユーモアがある. **3** N-UNCOUNT 不可算名詞 **Writing** is the activity of writing, especially of writing books for money. 著述業 ❑ *She had begun to be a little bored with novel writing.* 彼女は小説執筆にすこし飽き始めていた. **4** N-UNCOUNT 不可算名詞 Your **writing** is the way that you write with a pen or pencil, which can usually be recognized as belonging to you. 筆跡 ❑ *It was a little difficult to read your writing.* きみの筆跡は少々読みにくかった.

writ|ten /rɪtˀn/ **1** Written is the past participle of **write**. write の過去分詞 **2** ADJ 形容詞 A **written** test or piece of work is one that involves writing rather than doing something practical or giving spoken answers. 筆記の ❑ *...knowledge that can be assessed in a short written test.* 短い筆記試験で評価できる知識 **3** ADJ 形容詞 A **written** agreement, rule, or law has been officially written down. 成文の [ADJ n] ❑ *The newspaper broke a written agreement not to sell certain photographs.* その新聞社は特定の写真を販売しないという成文の協定を侵害した.

wrong /rɔŋ/ (**wrongs**) **1** ADJ 形容詞 If you say there is something **wrong**, you mean there is something unsatisfactory about the situation, person, or thing you are talking about. 正し

くない [v-link ADJ] ❑ *Pain is the body's way of telling us that something is wrong.* 痛みは私たちの体が何かおかしいことを知らせる方法である。❑ *Nobody seemed to notice anything wrong.* 何かおかしいことにだれも気づかなかったようだ。❑ *What's wrong with him?* 彼はどうしたのだ。❷ ADJ 形容詞 If you choose the **wrong** thing, person, or method, you make a mistake and do not choose the one that you really want. 間違った ❑ *He went to the wrong house.* 彼は間違った家に行った。❑ *The wrong man had been punished.* 間違った男性が罰せられた。● ADV 副詞 **Wrong** is also an adverb. 間違った風に [ADV after v] ❑ *You've done it wrong.* きみはやり方を誤った。❸ ADJ 形容詞 If something such as a decision, choice, or action is **the wrong** one, it is not the best or most suitable one. 不適当な [ADJ n] ❑ *I really made the wrong decision there.* 私はそこで本当に不適当な決断をした。❑ *The wrong choice of job might limit your chances of success.* 仕事の選択を誤ると成功のチャンスが限られる可能性がある。❹ ADJ 形容詞 If something is **wrong**, it is incorrect and not in accordance with the facts. 誤った ❑ *How do you know that this explanation is wrong?* この説明が間違っていることがどうしてわかったのだ。❑ *...a clock which showed the wrong time.* 間違った時間を示す時計。● ADV 副詞 **Wrong** is also an adverb. 間違った風に [ADV after v] ❑ *I must have added it up wrong, then.* では私は足し算を間違ったに違いない。❑ *It looks like it's spelled wrong.* つづりが間違っているようだ。● **wrong|ly** ADV 副詞 [ADV with v] 間違って ❑ *A child was wrongly diagnosed as having a bone tumor.* 子供は間違って骨しゅようと診断された。❺ ADJ 形容詞 If something is **wrong** or goes **wrong with** a machine or piece of equipment, it stops working properly. 故障で [v-link ADJ] ❑ *We think there's something wrong with the computer.* 我々はコンピュータはどこか故障していると思う。❻ ADJ 形容詞 If you are **wrong** about something, what you say or think about it is not correct. 間違った [v-link ADJ] ❑ *I was wrong about it being a casual meeting.* それが偶然の出会いだったというのは私の間違いだった。❑ *I'm sure you've got it wrong. Kate isn't like that.* きみは間違った思い込みをしていると思う。ケイトはそんな人じゃない。❼ ADJ 形容詞 If you think that someone was **wrong to** do something, you think that they should not have done it because it was bad or immoral. 正しくない [ADJ to-inf] ❑ *She was wrong to leave her child alone.* 彼女が自分の子供を一人にしておくのは間違っていた。● N-UNCOUNT 不可算名詞 **Wrong** is also a noun. 不正 ❑ *...a man who believes that he has done no wrong.* 何も悪いことはしていないと信じている男。❽ ADJ 形容詞 **Wrong** is used to refer to activities or actions that are considered to be morally bad and unacceptable. 間違った [v-link ADJ] ❑ *Is it wrong to try to save the life of someone you love?* 愛している人の命を救おうとするのは間違っているか。❑ *They thought slavery was morally wrong.* 彼らは奴隷制は道徳的に間違っていると思った。● N-UNCOUNT 不可算名詞 **Wrong** is also a noun. 悪 ❑ *Johnson didn't seem to be able to tell the difference between right and wrong.* ジョンソンは善と悪の区別がつけられるようには見えなかった。❾ N-COUNT 可算名詞 A **wrong** is an unfair or immoral action. 罪 ❑ *No matter how difficult it might be, she had to right the terrible wrong she'd done to him.* 彼女はどれほど困難であろうとも、彼に行ったひどい不当行為を正す必要があった。❿ ADJ 形容詞 You use **wrong** to describe something that is not thought to be socially acceptable or desirable. ふさわしくない [ADJ n] ❑ *If you went to the wrong school, you won't get the job.* 悪い学校に行くと仕事が得られない。⓫ PHRASE 句 If a situation **goes wrong**, it stops progressing in the way that you expected or intended, and becomes much worse. うまくいかない ❑ *We should investigate what happened, what went wrong.* 何が起こったのか、何が失敗したのかを調べる必要がある。⓬ PHRASE 句 If someone who is involved in an argument or dispute has behaved in a way which is morally or legally wrong, you can say that they are **in the wrong**. 誤って ❑ *He*

didn't press charges because he was in the wrong.* 悪かったのは彼女なので、彼は告発しなかった。⓭ to get off on the wrong foot → see **foot** ⓮ to get hold of the wrong end of the stick → see **stick**

Thesaurus	wrong また次を参照:
ADJ.	incorrect; (*ant.*) right ❹
	corrupt, immoral, unjust ❽
N.	abuse, offense, sin ❾

wrong|doing /rɔ̃nduɪŋ/ (**wrongdoings**) N-VAR 可変性名詞 **Wrongdoing** is behavior that is illegal or immoral. 悪行 ❑ *The city attorney's office hasn't found any evidence of criminal wrongdoing.* 市の弁護士事務所は犯罪の証拠を何も見つけていない。

wrong|ful /rɔ̃nfəl/ ADJ 形容詞 A **wrongful** act is one that is illegal, immoral, or unjust. 悪い ❑ *He is on hunger strike in protest at what he claims is his wrongful conviction for murder.* 彼は殺人による有罪判決を受けたのは間違いだと主張し、抗議のハンストを行っている。● **wrong|ful|ly** ADV 副詞 [ADV with v] 不正に ❑ *The criminal justice system is in need of urgent reform to prevent more people being wrongfully imprisoned.* より多くの人たちが誤って投獄されるのを防ぐため、刑事司法制度の緊急改革が必要である。

wrote /rout/ **Wrote** is the past tense of **write**. write の過去形

wrought /rɔt/ V-T 他動詞 If something has **wrought** a change, it has made it happen. 引き起こす [LITERARY 文語的 JOURNALISM ジャーナリズム] [only past] [他動詞] ❑ *Nuclear weapons have wrought a revolution in international relations.* 核兵器は国際関係に革命を引き起こした。

wrung /rʌŋ/ **Wrung** is the past tense of **wring**. wring の過去形

wry /raɪ/ ❶ ADJ 形容詞 If someone has a **wry** expression, it shows that they find a bad situation or a change in a situation slightly amusing. 皮肉を込めた ❑ *Matthew allowed himself a wry smile.* マシューは苦笑いを浮かべた。❷ ADJ 形容詞 A **wry** remark or piece of writing refers to a bad situation or a change in a situation in an amusing way. 皮肉な笑いを誘う ❑ *There is a wry sense of humor in his work.* 彼の作品には皮肉な笑いを誘うユーモアのセンスがある。

WTO /dʌbªlyu ti ou/ N-PROPER 固有名詞 **WTO** is an abbreviation for "World Trade Organization." World Trade Organization の略、世界貿易機関 ❑ *The world desperately needs an effective WTO.* 世界は効率的な WTO を切実に欲している。

wuss /wʊs/ (**wusses**) N-COUNT 可算名詞 If you call someone a **wuss**, you are criticizing them for being afraid. 臆病者 [INFORMAL くだけた, DISAPPROVAL 不賛成] ❑ *"I confess to being a big wuss,"* she admitted. 「実は私はすごい怖がりなの」と彼女は認めた。

WWW /dʌbªlyu dʌbªlyu dʌbªlyu/ **WWW** is an abbreviation for **World-Wide Web**. It appears at the beginning of website addresses in the form www. World-Wide Web の略、ワールドワイドウェブ [COMPUTING コンピューティング] ❑ *Check our website at www.harpercollins.com.* 当社のウェブサイト www. harpercollins.com をご覧ください。

WYSIWYG /wɪziwɪg/ **WYSIWYG** is used to refer to a computer screen display that exactly matches the way that a document will appear when it is printed. **WYSIWYG** is an abbreviation for "what you see is what you get." what you see is what you get の略 [COMPUTING コンピューティング] ❑ *WYSIWYG editing makes your word processing smoother and more flexible.* WYSIWYG による編集は文書処理をより円滑かつ柔軟にする。

W

X also x /ɛks/ (**X's, x's**) N-VAR 可変性名詞 **X** is the twenty-fourth letter of the English alphabet. エックス　(アルファベットの第２４文字)

Word Link   *phob ≈ fear : homophobic, phobia, xenophobia*
---

xeno|pho|bia /zɛnəfoʊbiə/ N-UNCOUNT 不可算名詞 **Xenophobia** is strong and unreasonable dislike or fear of people from other countries. 外国人嫌い [FORMAL 形式ばった] ❑ ...*a just and tolerant society which rejects xenophobia and racism.* 外国人嫌いと人種差別を退ける、公正で寛容な社会.

xeno|pho|bic /zɛnəfoʊbɪk/ ADJ 形容詞 If you describe someone as **xenophobic**, you disapprove of them because they show strong dislike or fear of people from other countries. 外国人嫌いの [FORMAL 形式ばった, DISAPPROVAL 不賛成] ❑ *Service in the armed forces gave many Americans a less xenophobic view of the world.* 軍隊の兵役により、多くのアメリカ人がさほど外国人嫌いの世界の見方をしなくなった.

Xer|ox /zɪərɒks/ (**Xeroxes, Xeroxing, Xeroxed**) **1** N-COUNT 可算名詞 商標 A **Xerox** is a machine that can make copies of pieces of paper which have writing or other marks on them. コピー機 [TRADEMARK] ❑ *The rooms are crammed with humming Xerox machines.* 部屋の中はブンブン音を立てるコピー機でいっぱいです. **2** N-COUNT 可算名詞 A **Xerox** is a copy of something written or printed on a piece of paper, which has been made using a Xerox machine. コピー ❑ *I got a Xerox of the lyrics, handed them out, and then we had the rehearsals.* わたしは歌詞のコピーをとり、手渡して、リハーサルをした. **3** V-T 他動詞 If you **Xerox** a document, you make a copy of it using a Xerox machine. コピーする ❑ *I should have simply Xeroxed this sheet for you.* この書面を君にコピーしてあげさえすればよかったのに.

Xmas **Xmas** is used in informal written English to represent the word Christmas. クリスマス ❑ *It would be nice to have my Dad home for Xmas.* クリスマスにお父さんが家にいればいいなあ.

X-ray (**X-rays, X-raying, X-rayed**) also **x-ray** **1** N-COUNT 可算名詞 **X-rays** are a type of radiation that can pass through most solid materials. X-rays are used by doctors to examine the bones or organs inside your body and are also used at airports to see inside people's luggage. X線, レントゲン線 **2** N-COUNT 可算名詞 An **X-ray** is a picture made by sending X-rays through something, usually someone's body. X線写真, レントゲン検査 ❑ *She was advised to have an abdominal X-ray.* 彼女は腹部のレントゲン検査を受けるように勧められた. **3** V-T 他動詞 If someone or something **is X-rayed**, an X-ray picture is taken of them. X線写真を撮る, X線検査する ❑ *All hand baggage would be x-rayed.* すべての手荷物がX線検査を受けます.

→ see **telescope, wave**

Yy

Y also **y** /waɪ/ (**Y's, y's**) N-VAR 可変性名詞 Y is the twenty-fifth letter of the English alphabet. 英語アルファベットの第25番目の文字

yacht /yɒt/ (**yachts**) N-COUNT 可算名詞 A **yacht** is a large boat with sails or a motor, used for racing or pleasure trips. ヨット ❑ His 36 ft yacht sank suddenly last summer. 去年の夏, 彼の36フィートのヨットが突然沈んだ.

yacht|ing /yɒtɪŋ/ N-UNCOUNT 不可算名詞 **Yachting** is the sport or activity of sailing a yacht. ヨットの操縦 ❑ ...the joys of yachting. ヨットを操る喜び.

yank /yæŋk/ (**yanks, yanking, yanked**) V-T/V-I 他動詞/自動詞 If you **yank** someone or something somewhere, you pull them there suddenly and with a lot of force. 強く引っ張る ❑ She yanked open the drawer. 彼女は引き出しをぐいっと開けた. ❑ She couldn't open the door no matter how hard she yanked. 彼女がどんなに強く引っ張ってもそのドアは開かなかった. ● N-COUNT 可算名詞 **Yank** is also a noun. 強く引くこと ❑ Grabbing his ponytail, Shirley gave it a yank. シャーリーは彼のポニーテールを握り, ぐっと引っ張った.

yard /yɑrd/ (**yards**) **1** N-COUNT 可算名詞 A **yard** is a unit of length equal to thirty-six inches or approximately 91.4 centimeters. ヤード（長さの単位．1ヤードは約91.4cm，または36インチに等しい．）❑ The incident took place about 500 yards from where he was standing. 事件は彼が立っていたところから約500ヤードの所で起った. ❑ ...a long narrow strip of linen two or three yards long. 長さ2，3ヤードの細長い麻の布切れ. **2** N-COUNT 可算名詞 A **yard** is a flat area of concrete or stone that is next to a building and often has a wall around it. （舗装された）中庭 ❑ I saw him standing in the yard. 私は彼が中庭に立っているのを見た. **3** N-COUNT 可算名詞 You can refer to a large open area where a particular type of work is done as a **yard**. 作業場 ❑ ...a rail yard. 車両基地. **4** N-COUNT 可算名詞 A **yard** is a piece of land next to someone's house, with grass and plants growing in it. 庭 [AM 米国英語] ❑ He dug a hole in our yard on Edgerton Avenue to plant a maple tree when I was born. 私が生まれたとき, 彼はカエデの木を植えようとして, エジャートン通りに面した私たちの庭に穴を掘った.

→ see **barn**

> In the USA and Australia, when people need to clear out their cupboards, basements or attics (for example if they are moving house), they sometimes hold **yard sales** or **garage sales,** where they set up stalls in the yard or garage and sell unwanted items. In the UK, **car boot sales** are a very popular way of selling unwanted items. The organizers charge a small fee and in return, sellers come together, usually in a car park or a field to set out their goods in the open trunks of their cars.

yard|stick /yɑrdstɪk/ (**yardsticks**) N-COUNT 可算名詞 If you use someone or something as a **yardstick**, you use them as a standard for comparison when you are judging other people or things. 尺度 ❑ The book gives a yardstick for measuring assets. その本には資産の評価基準が掲載されている.

yarn /yɑrn/ (**yarns**) N-MASS 質量名詞 **Yarn** is thread used for knitting or making cloth. 糸 ❑ She still spins the yarn and knits sweaters for her family. 彼女は今でも糸を紡ぎ, 家族のためにセーターを編んでいる.

yawn /yɔn/ (**yawns, yawning, yawned**) V-I 自動詞 If you **yawn**, you open your mouth very wide and breathe in more air than usual, often when you are tired or when you are not interested in something. あくびをする ❑ She yawned, and stretched lazily. 彼女はあくびをし, けだるそうに伸びをした. ● N-COUNT 可算名詞 **Yawn** is also a noun. あくび ❑ Rosanna stifled a huge yawn. ロザーナは大きなあくびをかみ殺した.

→ see **sleep**

yd. (**yds.**) **yd.** is a written abbreviation for **yard.** ヤードの省略記号 ❑ The entrance is on the left 200 yds. further on up the road. 入り口はこの道路を200ヤード行ったところの左側にあります.

yeah /yɛə/ **1** CONVENTION 慣習表現 **Yeah** means yes. はい, うん [INFORMAL, SPOKEN くだけた, 口語] ❑ "Bring us something to drink." —"Yeah, yeah." 「何か飲み物を出してくれないか.」「はい, はい.」 **2** → see also **yes**

year /yɪər/ (**years**) **1** N-COUNT 可算名詞 A **year** is a period of twelve months or 365 or 366 days, beginning on the first of January and ending on the thirty-first of December. 年 ❑ The year was 1840. その年は1840年でした. ❑ We had an election last year. 昨年, 選挙がありました. **2** → see also **leap year** **3** N-COUNT 可算名詞 A **year** is any period of twelve months. 1年間 ❑ The museums attract more than two and a half million visitors a year. その博物館の年間入場者数は250万人以上にものぼります. ❑ She's done quite a bit of work this past year. 彼女はこの1年間でかなりの仕事をこなした. **4** N-COUNT 可算名詞 **Year** is used to refer to the age of a person. For example, if someone or something is twenty **years** old or twenty **years** of age, they have lived or existed for twenty years. 一歳 ❑ He's 58 years old. 彼は58歳です. ❑ I've been in trouble since I was eleven years of age. 私は11歳のときから問題を抱えてきました. **5** N-COUNT 可算名詞 A school **year** or academic **year** is the period of time in each twelve months when schools or colleges are open and students are studying there. The school year starts in August or September. 学年, 学年度 ❑ ...the 1990/91 academic year. 1990，91学年度 **6** N-COUNT 可算名詞 A financial or business **year** is an exact period of twelve months which businesses or institutions use as a basis for organizing their finances. 年度 [BUSINESS 実業] ❑ He announced big tax increases for the next two financial years. 彼は来る2会計年度で大幅な増税をすると発表した. **7** N-PLURAL 複数名詞 You can use **years** to emphasize that you are referring to a long time. 長期間 [EMPHASIS 強調] ❑ I haven't laughed so much in years. 長い間そんなに笑ったことはなかった. **8** → see also **calendar year, fiscal year** **9** PHRASE 句 If something happens **year after year**, it happens regularly every year. 年々 ❑ Regulars return year after year. 正規兵が毎年帰還してくる. **10** PHRASE 句 If something changes **year by year**, it changes gradually each year. 年を追うごとに ❑ This problem has increased year by year. この問題は年を追うごとに重大なものになってきた. **11** PHRASE 句 If you say something happens **all year round** or **all the year round**, it happens continually throughout the year. 一年中 ❑ Town gardens are ideal because they produce flowers nearly all year round. 町に公園があるのが理想的だ. そこではほぼ1年中花を楽しめるからだ.

→ see Word Web: **year**
→ see **season**

year|ly /yɪərli/ **1** ADJ 形容詞 A **yearly** event happens once a year or every year. 年一回の, 例年の ❑ The two sisters looked forward to their yearly meetings. その二人の姉妹は, 毎年会うのを楽しみにしていました. ● ADV 副詞 **Yearly** is also an adverb. 年に1度, 毎年 [ADV after v] ❑ Clients normally pay fees in advance, monthly, quarterly, or yearly. お客様は普通, 月, 四半期, もしくは年払いのいずれかで料金を前払いされます. **2** ADJ 形容詞 You use **yearly** to

A **year** is the time it takes the earth to orbit around the sun—about 365 **days**. The exact time is 365.242199 days. To adjust for this, every four years there is a **leap year** with 366 days. The **months** on a calendar were inspired by the phases of the moon. The Greeks had a 10-month calendar, but there were about 60 days left over. So the Romans added two months. The idea of seven-day **weeks** came from the Bible. The Romans named the days. We still use three of these names: Sunday (sun day), Monday (moon day), and Saturday (Saturn day).

December

January

describe something such as an amount that relates to a period of one year. 1年間の [ADJ n] □ *In Holland, the government sets a yearly budget for health care.* オランダでは，政府が年単位で保健医療の予算を組みます。 ● ADV 副詞 **Yearly** is also an adverb. 1 年間に [ADV after v] □ *Novello says college students will spend $4.2 billion yearly on alcoholic beverages.* ノベロは，大学生が1年間にアルコール飲料に支払う額は42億ドルに上るだろう，と述べている。

Thesaurus	*yearly* また次を参照：
ADJ.	annual ① ②

yearn /yɜrn/ (**yearns, yearning, yearned**) V-T/V-I 他動詞/自動詞 If someone **yearns for** something that they are unlikely to get, they want it very much. 切望する □ *He yearned for freedom.* 彼は自由を望んでいた。 □ *I yearned to be an actor.* 私は俳優になりたかった。

-year-old /-yɪər-oʊld/ (**-year-olds**) COMB IN ADJ 形容詞の複合 **-year-old** combines with numbers to describe the age of people or things. 一歳の，一年の [ADJ n] □ *She has a six-year-old daughter.* 彼女には6歳になる娘がいる。 ● COMB IN N-COUNT 可算名詞の複合 **-year-old** also combines to form nouns. 一歳の人 □ *Snow Puppies is a ski school for 3 to 6-year-olds.* スノー・パピーズは3から6歳児対象のスキー教室です。

yeast /yist/ (**yeasts**) N-MASS 質量名詞 **Yeast** is a kind of fungus which is used to make bread rise, and in making alcoholic drinks such as beer. イースト，酵母菌
→ see **fungus**

yell /yɛl/ (**yells, yelling, yelled**) ① V-T/V-I 他動詞/自動詞 If you **yell**, you shout loudly, usually because you are excited, angry, or in pain. 大声をあげる □ *"Eva!" he yelled.* 「エバ！」と彼は大声で呼んだ。 □ *I'm sorry I yelled at you last night.* 昨夜はどなってしまい，すみませんでした。 ● PHRASAL VERB 句動詞 **Yell out** means the same as **yell**. 大声を出す □ *"Are you coming or not?" they yelled out after him.* 彼らは「来るの？来ないの？」と彼の後ろから大声で叫んだ。 ② N-COUNT 可算名詞 A **yell** is a loud shout given by someone who is afraid or in pain. 叫び声 □ *Something brushed past Bob's face and he let out a yell.* 何かがボブの顔をかすめ，彼は叫び声を上げた。

Thesaurus	*yell* また次を参照：
V.	cry, scream, shout; (ant.) whisper ①

yel|low /yɛloʊ/ (**yellows**) COLOR 色彩語 Something that is **yellow** is the color of lemons, butter, or the middle part of an egg. 黄色 □ *The walls have been painted bright yellow.* 壁は明るい黄色に塗られていた。
→ see **color, rainbow**

yel|low card (**yellow cards**) N-COUNT 可算名詞 In soccer, if a player is shown the **yellow card**, the referee holds up a yellow card to indicate that the player has broken the rules, and that if they do so again, they will be ordered to leave the field. イエローカード □ *Sheringham was then shown a yellow card for dissent.* そしてシェリンガムは抗議でイエローカードを出された。

yen /yɛn/ (**yen**)

> Yen is both the singular and the plural form.

> Yen は単数形でも複数形でもある。

N-COUNT 可算名詞 The **yen** is the unit of currency used in Japan. 円 □ *She's got a part-time job for which she earns 2,000 yen a month.* 彼女は月に2千円もらえるパート職に就きました。 ● N-SING 単数名詞 The **yen** is also used to refer to the Japanese currency system. 円 □ *...sterling's devaluation against the dollar and the yen.* ドルと円に対するポンドの下落。

yep /yɛp/ CONVENTION 慣習表現 **Yep** means yes. うん [INFORMAL, SPOKEN くだけた，口語] □ *"Did you like it?" —"Yep."* 「それは気に入ったかい？」「うん。」

yes /yɛs/

> In informal English, **yes** is often pronounced in a casual way that is usually written as **yeah**.

> くだけた英語では **yes** はしばしば気さくに発音され，通常 yeah と書かれる。

① CONVENTION 慣習表現 You use **yes** to give a positive response to a question. はい □ *"Are you a friend of Nick's?" —"Yes."* 「あなたはニックの友人ですか。」「はい。」 □ *"You actually wrote it down, didn't you?" —"Yes."* 「あなたが実際にそれを書いたんですね？」「はい。」

> There are many other informal ways of expressing agreement. **Yeah** is common in everyday speech. People also say **Yep, Yup, Uh-huh,** and **Mm-hmm** in informal situations. Body language for agreement is a forward nod of the head. This gesture is different in other cultures.

② CONVENTION 慣習表現 You use **yes** to accept an offer or request, or to give permission. はい □ *"More wine?" —"Yes, please."* 「ワイン

のおかわりはいかがですか？」「はい，いただきます。」 □ *"Will you take me there?" —"Yes, I will."* 「そこに連れて行ってくださる？」「ええ，いいですよ。」 ③ CONVENTION 慣習表現 You use **yes** to tell someone that what they have said is correct. その通りだ □ *"Well I suppose it is based on the old lunar months, isn't it?" —"Yes, that's right."* 「もしかして，それは旧暦の太陰月に基づいていますよね。」「ええ，その通りです。」 ④ CONVENTION 慣習表現 You use **yes** to show that you are ready or willing to speak to the person who wants to speak to you, for example when you are answering a telephone or a knock at your door. はい？ □ *He pushed a button on the intercom. "Yes?" came a voice.* 彼はインターホンを押した。「はい？」と声がした。 ⑤ CONVENTION 慣習表現 You use **yes** to indicate that you agree with, accept, or understand what the previous speaker has said. その通りだ □ *"A lot of people find it very difficult indeed to give up smoking." —"Oh, yes. I used to smoke three packs a day."* 「多くの人が禁煙は本当に難しいと感じています。」「まったくです。私は1日に3箱吸っていましたから。」 ⑥ CONVENTION 慣習表現 You use **yes** to encourage someone to continue speaking. それで □ *"I remembered something funny today." —"Yes?"* 「今日は面白いことがあったんだ。」「それで？」 ⑦ CONVENTION 慣習表現 You use **yes**, usually followed by "but," as a polite way of introducing what you want to say when you disagree with something the previous speaker has just said. そうだが [POLITENESS 丁寧さ] □ *"She is entitled to her personal allowance which is three thousand dollars of income." —"Yes, but she doesn't earn any money."* 「彼女は3千ドルの個人手当を受けられるのよ。」「そうだけど，彼女は何の利益も上げていないわ。」 ⑧ CONVENTION 慣習表現 You use **yes** to say that a negative statement or question that the previous speaker has made is wrong or untrue. いいえ □ *"That is not possible," she said. —"Oh, yes, it is!" Mrs. Gruen insisted.* 「それは不可能だわ」と彼女は言った。「いいえ，可能です」とグルーエン夫人は言い張った。 ⑨ CONVENTION 慣習表現 You can use **yes** to suggest that you do not believe or agree with what the previous speaker has said, especially when you want to express your annoyance about it. そう？ [FEELINGS 感情] □ *"There was no way to stop it." —"Oh, yeah? Well, here's something else you won't be able to stop."* 「それをやめるすべはなかったのさ。」「ふーん？でも，そのほかにも君がやめられそうにないことがあるぞ。」 ⑩ CONVENTION 慣習表現 You use **yes** to indicate that you had forgotten something and have just remembered it. そうだ □ *What was I going to say. Oh, yeah, we've finally got our second computer.* 何を言おうとしてたんだろう。ああ，そうそう。僕たちはついに2台目のコンピュータを買ったんだ。 ⑪ CONVENTION 慣習表現 You use **yes** to emphasize and confirm a statement that you are making. なんと [EMPHASIS 強調] □ *He collected the $10,000 first prize. Yes, $10,000.* 彼は1万ドルの優勝賞金を受け取ったんだ。なんと，1万ドルだと。 ⑫ CONVENTION 慣習表現 You say **yes and no** in reply to a question when you cannot give a definite answer, because in some ways the answer is yes and in other ways the answer is no. どちらとも言えない [VAGUENESS あいまいさ] □ *"Was it strange for you, going back after such a long absence?" —"Yes and no."* 「ほんとに久しぶりに帰ってみると妙な感じがしたんじゃない？」「さあね。」

yes|ter|day /yɛstərdeɪ, -di/ (**yesterdays**) ① ADV 副詞 You use **yesterday** to refer to the day before today. 昨日 [ADV with cl] □ *She left yesterday.* 彼女は昨日出発した。 ● N-UNCOUNT 不可算名詞 **Yesterday** is also a noun. 昨日 □ *In yesterday's games, Switzerland beat the United States two to one.* 昨日の試合で，スイスはアメリカを2対1で破った。 ② N-UNCOUNT 不可算名詞 You can refer to the past, especially the recent past, as **yesterday**. 最近の [also N in pl] □ *The worker of today is different from the worker of yesterday.* 今の労働者は以前とは違う。

yet /yɛt/ ① ADV 副詞 You use **yet** in negative statements to indicate that something has not happened up to the present time, although it probably will happen. You can also use **yet** in questions to ask if something has happened up to the present time. まだ □ *They haven't finished yet.* 彼らはまだやり終えていない。 □ *No decision has yet been made.* まだ何の決定もされていない。 □ *She hasn't yet set a date for her marriage.* 彼女はまだ結婚式の日取りを決めていないのよ。 ② ADV 副詞 You use **yet** with a negative statement when you are talking about the past, to report something that was not the case then, although it became the case later. まだ □ *There was so much that Sam didn't know yet.* サムがまだ知らないことがそんなにもあった。

> In British English, **yet** and **already** are usually used with the present perfect tense. □ *Have they said sorry yet?... I have already started knitting baby clothes.* In American English, a past tense is commonly used. □ *I didn't get any sleep yet... She already told the neighbors not to come.*

③ ADV 副詞 If you say that something should not or cannot be done **yet**, you mean that it should not or cannot be done now, although it will have to be done at a later time. まだ [with brd-neg, ADV with v] □ *Don't get up yet.* まだ起き上がってはいけません。 □ *The hostages cannot go home just yet.* 人質はまだ帰国できま

せん。 **4** ADV 副詞 You use **yet** after a superlative to indicate, for example, that something is the worst or the best of its kind up to the present time. これまでで ❑ *This is the network's worst idea yet.* このネットワークの構想は過去最悪のものだ。 ❑ *Her latest novel is her best yet.* 彼女の最新の小説がこれまでで一番よい作品だ。 **5** ADV 副詞 You can use **yet** to say that there is still a possibility that something will happen. やがて [ADV before v] ❑ *Like the best stories, this one may yet have a happy ending.* 優れた物語と同様に、この話もやがてハッピーエンドを迎えるだろう。 **6** ADV 副詞 You can use **yet** after expressions that refer to a period of time, when you want to say how much longer a situation will continue for. まだ—の間は [n ADV] ❑ *Unemployment will go on rising for some time yet.* 失業率はまだしばらくは上昇を続けるだろう。 ❑ *Nothing will happen for a few years yet.* 数年間くらいはまだ何も起こらないだろう。 **7** ADV 副詞 If you say that you have **yet** to do something, you mean that you have never done it, especially when this is surprising or bad. まだ—ない [ADV to-inf] ❑ *She has yet to spend a Christmas with her husband.* 彼女はまだ夫とクリスマスを過ごしたことがありません。 **8** CONJ 接続詞 You can use **yet** to introduce a fact that is rather surprising after the previous fact you have just mentioned. それにもかかわらず ❑ *I don't eat much, yet I am a size 16.* 私はあまり食べないが、それでも服のサイズは16だ。 **9** ADV 副詞 You can use **yet** to emphasize a word, especially when you are saying that something is surprising because it is more extreme than previous things of its kind, or a further case of them. さらに [EMPHASIS 強調] ❑ *I saw yet another doctor.* 私はさらに別の医者に見てもらった。 ● *They would criticize me, or worse yet, pay me no attention.* 彼らは私を非難するか、さらに悪ければ、無視するでしょう。 **10** PHRASE 句 You use **as yet** with negative statements to describe a situation that has existed up until the present time. 今のところ [FORMAL 形式ばった] ❑ *As yet it is not known whether the crash was the result of an accident.* 今のところ、その衝突が事故だったのかは分かっていません。

yield /yiːld/ (**yields, yielding, yielded**) **1** V-I 自動詞 If you **yield to** someone or something, you stop resisting them. 屈する [FORMAL 形式ばった] ❑ *Carmen yielded to general pressure and grudgingly took the child to a specialist.* カルメンは様々な圧力に屈し、しぶしぶ子供を専門家に連れて行った。 **2** V-T 他動詞 If you **yield** something that you have control of or responsibility for, you allow someone else to have control or responsibility for it. 譲る [FORMAL 形式ばった] ❑ *He may yield control.* 彼は支配権を譲るでしょう。 **3** V-I 自動詞 If a moving person or a vehicle **yields**, they slow down in order to allow other people or vehicles to pass in front of them. 譲る [AM 米国英語] ❑ *When entering a trail or starting a descent, yield to other skiers.* ゲレンデに入るときや、すべり始めるときは、他のスキーヤーに道を譲ってください。 ❑ *...examples of common signs like No Smoking and Yield.* 禁煙、道を譲れ、などのような一般的な標識の例。 **4** V-I 自動詞 If something **yields**, it breaks or moves position because force or pressure has been put on it. 動く ❑ *He reached the massive door of the barn and pushed. It yielded.* 彼は倉庫に着くと、その重厚な扉を押した。すると扉は動いた。 **5** V-T 他動詞 If an area of land **yields** a particular amount of a crop, this is the amount that is produced. You can also say that a number of animals **yield** a particular amount of meat. 産出する ❑ *Last year 400,000 acres of land yielded a crop worth $1.75 billion.* 昨年は、40万エーカーの土地から10億7千5百万ドル相当の作物が取れました。 **6** N-COUNT 可算名詞 A **yield** is the amount of food produced on an area of land or by a number of animals. 収穫高 ❑ *...improving the yield of the crop.* その作物の収穫高を改善する。 **7** V-T 他動詞 If a tax or investment **yields** an amount of money or profit, this money or profit is obtained from it. 生ずる [BUSINESS 実業] ❑ *It yielded a profit of at least $36 million.* それにより、少なくとも3千6百万ドルの利益が生じた。 **8** N-COUNT 可算名詞 A **yield** is the amount of money or profit produced by an investment. 利回り [BUSINESS 実業] ❑ *...a yield of 4%.* 4パーセントの利回り。 ❑ *The high yields available on the dividend shares made them attractive to private investors.* それらは株主配当の利回りが高く、多くの個人投資家を引き付けた。 **9** V-T 他動詞 If something **yields** a result or piece of information, it produces it. もたらす ❑ *This research has been in progress since 1961 and has yielded a great number of positive results.* 当研究は1961年以来続けられており、多くの成果を上げてきた。

Thesaurus   yield また次を参照：

V.	give in, submit, succumb, surrender; (ant.) resist **1 2 4**
	bear, produce, supply **5**

Word Partnership   yield は次の語句と使われる：

N.	yield **to pressure**, yield **to temptation** **1**
	yield **a profit** **7 8**
	yield **information**, yield **results** **9**
V.	**refuse to** yield **1** – **4**
ADJ.	**annual** yield, **expected** yield, **high/higher** yield **6 8**

yoga /yóʊgə/ N-UNCOUNT 不可算名詞 **Yoga** is a type of exercise in which you move your body into various positions in order to become more fit or flexible, to improve your breathing, and to relax your mind. ヨガ ❑ *I do yoga twice a week.* 私は週に2回ヨガを行っている。

yogurt /yóʊgərt/ (**yogurts**) also **yoghurt** N-VAR 可変性名詞 **Yogurt** is a food in the form of a thick, slightly sour liquid that is made by adding bacteria to milk. A **yogurt** is a small container of yogurt. ヨーグルト

yolk /yóʊk/ (**yolks**) N-VAR 可変性名詞 The **yolk** of an egg is the yellow part in the middle. 黄身 ❑ *Only the yolk contains cholesterol.* コレステロールは黄身だけに含まれる。

you /yuː/

You is the second person pronoun. **You** can refer to one or more people and is used as the subject of a verb or the object of a verb or preposition.

You は2人称代名詞である。 **You** は1人またはそれ以上の人を指すことができ、動詞の主語として、あるいは動詞または前置詞の目的語として用いられる。

1 PRON 代名詞 A speaker or writer uses **you** to refer to the person or people that they are talking or writing to. It is possible to use **you** before a noun to make it clear which group of people you are talking to. あなた ❑ *When I saw you across the room I knew I'd met you before.* 部屋の反対側にあなたの姿を見かけたとき、以前会ったことがある人だと思った。 ● *You two seem very different to me.* あなたがた二人は私とはとても違っているようです。 **2** PRON 代名詞 In spoken English and informal written English, **you** is sometimes used to refer to people in general. （一般の）人 ❑ *Getting good results gives you confidence.* 良い結果が出ると人は自身を得ます。 ❑ *In those days you did what you were told.* その時代、人々は言われたとおりに行動していた。

you'd /yuːd/ **1** **You'd** is the usual spoken form of "you had," when "had" is an auxiliary verb. 口語におけるyou hadの省略形で、hadが助動詞の場合に用いられる。 ❑ *I think you'd better tell us why you're asking these questions.* なぜこんな質問をするのか、私たちに話してくれたほうがいいよ。 **2** **You'd** is the usual spoken form of "you would." 口語におけるyou wouldの省略形 ❑ *With your hair and your beautiful skin, you'd look good in red and other bright colors.* あなたの髪ときれいな肌には、赤や鮮やかな色が映えますよ。

you'll /yuːl/ **You'll** is the usual spoken form of "you will." 口語におけるyou willの省略形 ❑ *Promise you'll take very special care of yourself.* 体に十分気をつけるって私に約束してちょうだい。

young /yʌŋ/ (**younger** /yʌ́ŋgər/ (**youngest** /yʌ́ŋgɪst/) **1** ADJ 形容詞 A **young** person, animal, or plant has not lived or existed for very long and is not yet mature. 若い ❑ *...sex information written for young people.* 若者向けに書かれた性に関する情報。 ❑ *I crossed the hill, and found myself in a field of young barley.* 丘を渡ると、そこが青い麦畑だと気づいた。 ● N-PLURAL 複数名詞 **The young** are people who are young. 若者 ❑ *The association is advising pregnant women, the very young and the elderly to avoid such foods.* 協会は、妊婦、小さい子供達、お年寄りはそのような食品を取らないよう忠告している。 **2** ADJ 形容詞 You use **young** to describe a time when a person or thing was young. 若いころの [ADJ n] ❑ *In her younger days my mother had been a successful saleswoman.* 若いころ、母は優秀な営業員だった。 **3** ADJ 形容詞 Someone who is **young** in appearance or behavior looks or behaves as if they are young. 若々しい ❑ *I was twenty-three, I suppose, and young for my age.* 思えば、私は23歳で、年の割には若かった。 **4** N-PLURAL 複数名詞 The **young** of an animal are its babies. （動物の）子 ❑ *The hen may not be able to feed its young.* そのめんどりは自分のヒナに餌をやることはできないだろう。

→ see age, mammal

Thesaurus   young また次を参照：

ADJ.	childish, immature, youthful; (ant.) mature, old **1**
N.	family, litter **4**

Word Link   ster = one who does : barrister, gangster, youngster

youngster /yʌ́ŋstər/ (**youngsters**) N-COUNT 可算名詞 Young people, especially children, are sometimes referred to as **youngsters**. 子供 ❑ *Other youngsters are not so lucky.* そんなに幸運でない子供たちもいる。

your /yɔr, yʊər/

Your is the second person possessive determiner. Your can refer to one or more people.

Yourは2人称所有限定詞である. Yourは1人またはそれ以上の人を指すことができる.

■ DET 限定詞 A speaker or writer uses **your** to indicate that something belongs or relates to the person or people that they are talking or writing to. あなたの ❑ *Emma, I trust your opinion a great deal.* エマ, 私はあなたの意見をとても信頼しているのよ. ❑ *I left all of your messages on your desk.* 伝言は全てあなたの机の上に置いておきました. ② DET 限定詞 In spoken English and informal written English, **your** is sometimes used to indicate that something belongs to or relates to people in general. (一般の) 人の ❑ *Painkillers are very useful in small amounts to bring your temperature down.* 少量の鎮痛薬は解熱に非常に効果があります. ③ DET 限定詞 In spoken English, a speaker sometimes uses **your** before an adjective such as "typical" or "normal" to indicate that the thing referred to is a typical example of its type. いわゆる ❑ *This isn't your typical economics class.* これは, いわゆる普通の経済学のクラスではありません.

you're /yɔr, yʊər/ **You're** is the usual spoken form of "you are." 口語におけるyou areの省略形 ❑ *Go to him, tell him you're sorry.* 彼のところにいって, ごめんなさい, と言いなさい.

yours /yɔrz, yʊərz/

Yours is the second person possessive pronoun. Yours can refer to one or more people.

Yoursは2人称所有代名詞である. Yoursは1人またはそれ以上の人を指すことができる.

■ PRON-POSS 所有代名詞 A speaker or writer uses **yours** to refer to something that belongs or relates to the person or people that they are talking or writing to. あなたのもの ❑ *I'll take my coat upstairs. Shall I take yours, Roberta?* 2階にコートをとりに上がるわ, ロベルタ, あなたのもとってきてあげましょうか. ❑ *I believe Paul was a friend of yours.* きっとポールは君の友人だったのだろう. ② CONVENTION 慣習表現 People write **yours, yours sincerely, sincerely yours,** or **yours truly** at the end of a letter before they sign their name. 敬具 ❑ *With best regards, Yours, George.* 敬意をこめて. ジョージより.

your|self /yɔrsɛlf, yʊər-/ **(yourselves)**

Yourself is the second person reflexive pronoun.

Yourselfは2人称再帰代名詞である.

■ PRON-REFL 再帰代名詞 A speaker or writer uses **yourself** to refer to the person that they are talking or writing to. **Yourself** is used when the object of a verb or preposition refers to the same person as the subject of the verb. あなた自身 [V PRON, prep PRON] ❑ *Have the courage to be honest with yourself and about yourself.* あなた自身の気持ちに正直であり, またそれを伝える勇気を持ちなさい. ❑ *Your baby depends on you to look after yourself properly while you are pregnant.* 妊娠中, 胎児は, あなた自身が適切に体調を管理するかどうかに影響されます. ② PRON-REFL-EMPH 強調的再帰代名詞 You use **yourself** to emphasize the person that you are referring to. あなた自身 [EMPHASIS 強調] ❑ *You can't convince others if you yourself aren't convinced.* あなた自身が納得していなければ人を説得することなんかできません. ③ PRON-REFL-EMPH 強調的再帰代名詞 You use **yourself**

instead of "you" for emphasis or in order to be more polite when "you" is the object of a verb or preposition. youのていねいな表現 ❑ *A wealthy man like yourself is bound to make an enemy or two along the way.* あなたのような裕福な人には今後1人や2人の敵が現れるのはしかたがないことです. [POLITENESS 丁寧さ] [V PRON, prep PRON] ④ **by yourself →** see **by**

youth /yuθ/ **(youths)** /yuðz/ ■ N-UNCOUNT 不可算名詞 Someone's **youth** is the period of their life during which they are a child, before they are a fully mature adult. 青年時代 ❑ *In my youth my ambition had been to be an inventor.* 若いときは発明家になりたいと思っていた. ② N-UNCOUNT 不可算名詞 **Youth** is the quality or state of being young. 若さ ❑ *The team is now a good mixture of experience and youth.* チームでは今, 経験と若さが良い感じで調和している. ③ N-COUNT 可算名詞 Journalists often refer to young men as **youths**, especially when they are reporting that the young men have caused trouble. 青年 ❑ *A 17-year-old youth was arrested yesterday.* 17歳の青年が昨日逮捕された. ④ N-PLURAL 複数名詞 The **youth** are young people considered as a group. 若者たち ❑ *He represents the opinions of the youth of today.* 彼は今日の若者の意見を代弁する.

youth|ful /yuθfəl/ ADJ 形容詞 Someone who is **youthful** behaves as if they are young or younger than they really are. 若々しい ❑ *I'm a very youthful 50.* 私はとてもはつらつとした50歳です. ❑ *...youthful enthusiasm and high spirits.* 若い情熱と高い志.

youth hos|tel (youth hostels) N-COUNT 可算名詞 A **youth hostel** is a place where people can stay cheaply when they are traveling. ユースホステル

you've /yuv/ **You've** is the usual spoken form of "you have," when "have" is an auxiliary verb. 口語におけるyou haveの省略形で, haveが助動詞の場合に用いられる. ❑ *You've got to see it to believe it.* それは実際に見てみなければ信じられないでしょう.

yo-yo (yo-yos) N-COUNT 可算名詞 A **yo-yo** is a toy made of a round piece of wood or plastic attached to a piece of string. You play with the yo-yo by letting it rise and fall on the string. ヨーヨー ❑ *...a competition to find the boy or girl who could do the most tricks with a yo-yo.* ヨーヨーを最もうまく操れる少年少女を決める競技会.

yr. (yrs.) **yr.** is a written abbreviation for **year.** yearの省略形 ❑ *Their imaginations are quite something for 2 yr. olds.* 彼らの想像力は2歳児かそこらくらいのものだ.

yuan /yuɑn/ **(yuan)** ■ N-COUNT 可算名詞 The **yuan** is the unit of money used in the People's Republic of China. 元 ❑ *For most events, tickets cost one, two or three yuan.* イベントのチケット代金は, 大体が1元か2, 3元くらいです. ● N-SING 単数名詞 **The yuan** is also used to refer to the Chinese currency system. 元 ['the' N] ❑ *The yuan recovered a little; it now hovers around 8.2 to the dollar.* 元は少し盛り返りを見せ, 現在, 1ドル当たり8.2元前後だ.

yup|pie /yʌpi/ **(yuppies)** N-COUNT 可算名詞 A **yuppie** is a young person who has a well-paid job and likes to show that they have a lot of money by buying expensive things and living in an expensive way. ヤッピー (若手のエリート層) [DISAPPROVAL 不賛成] ❑ *The Porsche 911 reminds me of the worst parts of the yuppie era.* ポルシェ911はヤッピー時代の最悪の頃をほうふつさせる.

Zz

Z also **z** /ziː/ (**Z's, z's**) N-VAR 可変性名詞 Z is the twenty-sixth and last letter of the English alphabet. ゼット　アルファベットの第26文字)

zap /zæp/ (**zaps, zapping, zapped**) ◼ V-T 他動詞 To **zap** someone or something means to kill, destroy, or hit them, for example, with a gun or in a computer game. 撃つ、やっつける [INFORMAL くだけた] □A guard zapped him with the stun gun. 監視の人がスタンガンで彼を撃った. ◻ V-T 他動詞 To **zap** something such as a computer file or document means to delete it from the computer memory or to clear it from the screen. 消去する [INFORMAL くだけた COMPUTING コンピューティング] □"We zap millions and millions of spam mails a day from our servers," AOL spokesman Nicholas Graham said. 「サーバーから毎日何千万もの膨大な数のスパムメールを消去しています。」とAOL社の広報担当ニコラス・グラハムは語った.

zeal /ziːl/ N-UNCOUNT 不可算名詞 **Zeal** is great enthusiasm, especially in connection with work, religion, or politics. 熱意 □...his zeal for teaching. 彼の教育に対する情熱.

zeal|ous /zɛləs/ ADJ 形容詞 Someone who is **zealous** spends a lot of time and energy in supporting something that they believe in very strongly, especially a political or religious ideal. 熱心な □She was a zealous worker for charity. 彼女はチャリティーの仕事に熱心だった.

Thesaurus　　zealous また次を参照：

ADJ.　　eager, enthusiastic, gung-ho

zeb|ra /zɪbrə/ (**zebras** or **zebra**) N-COUNT 可算名詞 A **zebra** is an African wild horse that has black and white stripes. シマウマ

zen|ith /zɪniːθ/ N-SING 単数名詞 The **zenith** of something is the time when it is most successful or powerful. 頂点 □His career is now at its zenith. 彼のキャリアは今絶頂にあります.

zero /zɪərou/ (**zeros** or **zeroes**) ◼ NUM 数詞 **Zero** is the number 0. 0 □Visibility at the city's airport came down to zero, bringing air traffic to a standstill. その都市の空港の視界はゼロまで落ちていて、空の交通は途絶えていた. ◻ N-UNCOUNT 不可算名詞 **Zero** is a temperature of 0°. It is freezing point on the centigrade and Celsius scales, and 32° below freezing point on the Fahrenheit scale. 零度 □It's a sunny late winter day, just a few degrees above zero. 気温は零度よりほんの数度だけ上回る、冬も終わりに近い晴れた日です. ◼ ADJ 形容詞 You can use **zero** to say that there is none at all of the thing mentioned. ゼロの、皆無の □This new ministry was being created with zero assets and zero liabilities. この新しい省は資産ゼロ負債ゼロで設立された.
→ see Word Web: **zero**

Thesaurus　　zero また次を参照：

NUM.　　none, nothing, zilch ◼ ◼

As a number, **zero** is used mainly in scientific contexts, or when you want to be precise. In spoken American English, different informal words stand for **zero**, such as **zip**. □...from zip to 60 in a fraction of one second. However, when you stating a telephone number, you say **o** (/oʊ/). In some sports contexts, especially in football scores, **nothing** is used. □Dallas beat San Diego 18 to nothing. In tennis, **love** is the usual word. □...a two-games-to-love lead.

zero-sum game N-SING 単数名詞 If you refer to a situation as a **zero-sum game**, you mean that if one person gains an advantage from it, someone else involved must suffer an equivalent disadvantage. ゼロ和の試合 □They believe they're playing a zero-sum game, where both must compete for the same resources. 彼らは同じ資源をめぐって争いあわなければならないゼロ和の試合をしていると思っています.

zero tol|er|ance N-UNCOUNT 不可算名詞 If a government or organization has a policy of **zero tolerance** of a particular type of behavior or activity, they will not tolerate it at all. □They have a policy of zero tolerance for sexual harassment. 彼らはセクハラを全く許さない方針を取っています.

zest /zɛst/ (**zests**) ◼ N-UNCOUNT 不可算名詞 **Zest** is a feeling of pleasure and excitement. 情熱 □He has a zest for life and a quick intellect. 彼は人生に対する情熱と鋭い知性を持ち合わせています. ◻ N-UNCOUNT 不可算名詞 **Zest** is a quality in an activity or situation which you find exciting. 魅力 □Live interviews add zest and a touch of the unexpected to any piece of research. 生インタビューはどんな研究にも魅力とちょっとした意外な出来事を足します.

zig|zag /zɪgzæg/ (**zigzags, zigzagging, zigzagged**) also **zig-zag** ◼ N-COUNT 可算名詞 A **zigzag** is a line that has a series of angles in it like a continuous series of Ws. ジグザグの □They staggered in a zigzag across the road. 彼らは道路を千鳥足でよたよたと渡った. ◻ V-T/V-I 他動詞/自動詞 If you **zigzag**, you move forward by going at an angle first to one side then to the other. ジグザグに進む、ジグザグに進ませる □I zigzagged down a labyrinth of alleys. わたしは迷路のような路地をジグザグと下がっていった. □He zigzagged his way across the field. 彼は原っぱをジグザグに進んでいった.

zinc /zɪŋk/ N-UNCOUNT 不可算名詞 **Zinc** is a bluish-white metal which is used to make other metals such as brass, or to cover other metals such as iron to stop rust from forming. 亜鉛

zip /zɪp/ (**zips, zipping, zipped**) ◼ V-T 他動詞 When you **zip** something, you fasten it using a zipper. ファスナーで締める □She zipped her jeans. 彼女はジーンズのチャックを締めた. ◻ V-T 他動詞 To **zip** a computer file means to compress it so that it needs less space for storage on disk and can be transmitted more quickly. 圧縮する [COMPUTING コンピューティング] □If you zipped the files first, they did not become read-only when written to the CD. まず最初にファイルを圧縮したのなら、CDに書き込んだ時に読み取り専用にはならなかっただろう. ◼ N-COUNT 可算名詞 A **zip** or **zip fastener** is the same as a **zipper**. ファスナー、チャック [mainly BRIT 主に英国英語] □He pulled the zip of his leather jacket down slightly. 彼は革ジャケットのファスナーをゆっくりと開けた.

▶ **zip up** ◼ PHRASAL VERB 句動詞 If you **zip up** something such as a piece of clothing or if it **zips up**, you are able to fasten it using its zipper. ファスナーで締まる、ファスナーを上まで締める □He zipped up his jeans. 彼はジーンズのチャックをちゃんと締めた. ◻ PHRASAL VERB 句動詞 To **zip up** a computer file means to compress it so that it needs less space for storage on disk and can be transmitted more quickly. 圧縮する [COMPUTING コンピューティング] □These files have been zipped up so they take up less disk space so they take less time to download. これらのファイルはディスクの場所を取らないように圧縮してあるのでダウンロードするのにあまり時間がかからない.

zip code (**zip codes**) also **ZIP code** N-COUNT 可算名詞 Your **zip code** is a short sequence of letters and numbers at the end of your address, which helps the post office to sort the mail. 郵便番号 [AM

Word Web　　zero

The **number zero** developed after the other numbers. Ancient peoples first used numbers in concrete situations—to **count** two children or four sheep. It took a while to move from "four sheep" to "four things" to the abstract concept of "four." The use of a **place** holder like zero came from the Babylonians*. Originally, they wrote numbers like 23 and 203 the same way. The reader had to figure out the difference based on the context. The use of zero later came to include the concept of **null** value. It shows that there is no amount of something.

Babylonians: people who lived in the ancient city of Babylon.

z

Word Web   ZOO

Zoos are not just places where people enjoy looking at animals. They perform another very important function. As increasing numbers of **species** become extinct, zoos help preserve **biological diversity**. They do this through educational programs, **breeding** programs, and **research** studies. The Smithsonian National Zoological Park in Washington, DC, provides training for **wildlife** managers from 80 different countries. A breeding program at the Wolong Reserve in China has produced 38 **pandas** since 1991. And the Tama Zoo in Hino, Japan, is conducting research studies of **chimpanzee** behavior. Surprisingly, one chimp has learned to use a vending machine.

米国英語] ❏ *Type your street address and zip code.* 住所と郵便番号を入力してください.

zip disk (**zip disks**) N-COUNT 可算名詞 A **zip disk** is a removable computer disk that is capable of storing great amounts of data. Zipディスク [COMPUTING コンピューティング] ❏ *Zip disks could be used to store the equivalent of three music CDs.* Zipディスクには音楽CD3枚分に相当する情報を保管することができる.

zip drive (**zip drives**) N-COUNT 可算名詞 A **zip drive** is a piece of computer equipment that reads and writes to zip disks. Zipドライブ [COMPUTING コンピューティング] ❏ *Zip drives help people to organize their important information.* 重要な情報を整理するのにZipドライブが役立ちます.

zip file (**zip files**) N-COUNT 可算名詞 A **zip file** is a computer file containing data that has been compressed. ZIPファイル [COMPUTING コンピューティング] ❏ *When you download the font it may be in a compressed format, such as a zip file.* フォントをダウンロードする場合、ZIPファイルのような圧縮した形式になっていることがある.

zip|per /zɪpər/ (**zippers**) N-COUNT 可算名詞 A **zipper** is a device used to open and close parts of clothes and bags. It consists of two rows of metal or plastic teeth which separate or fasten together as you pull a small handle along them. ジッパー [mainly AM 主に米国英語] ❏ *...the metal zipper on his jacket.* 彼のジャケットの金属製ジッパー.

zo|di|ac /zoʊdiæk/ N-SING 単数名詞 The **zodiac** is a diagram used by astrologers to represent the positions of the planets and stars. It is divided into twelve sections, each of which has its own name and symbol. The zodiac is used to try to calculate the influence of the planets on people's lives. 黄道帯、十二宮 ❏ *...the twelve signs of the zodiac.* 横道12星座.

zone /zoʊn/ (**zones, zoning, zoned**) **1** N-COUNT 可算名詞 A **zone** is an area that has particular features or characteristics. 地域 ❏ *Many people have stayed behind in the potential war zone.* 交戦地帯となる可能性のある場所に多くの人が留まりました. ❏ *The area has been declared a disaster zone.* その地域は災害激甚地として指定されま

した. **2** V-T 他動詞 If an area of land **is zoned**, it is formally set aside for a particular purpose. 地域とする [usu passive] ❏ *The land was not zoned for commercial purposes.* その土地は商業地域とはされていなかった. ●**zon|ing** N-UNCOUNT 不可算名詞 地域を設定すること、土地利用規制 ❏ *...the use of zoning to preserve agricultural land.* 農業用地を保護するための土地利用規制の適用.
→ see **football, time**

Thesaurus   *zone* また次を参照：

| N. | area, region, section **1** |

zoo /zu/ (**zoos**) N-COUNT; N-IN-NAMES 可算名詞，名称中の名詞 A **zoo** is a park where live animals are kept so that people can look at them. 動物園 ❏ *He took his son Christopher to the zoo.* 彼は息子のクリストファーを公園に連れて行った.
→ see **Word Web: zoo**
→ see **park**

zo|ol|ogy /zoʊɒlədʒi/ N-UNCOUNT 不可算名詞 **Zoology** is the scientific study of animals. 動物学

zoom /zum/ (**zooms, zooming, zoomed**) V-I 自動詞 If you **zoom** somewhere, you go there very quickly. すばやく行く [INFORMAL くだけた] ❏ *We zoomed through the gallery.* 私たちは美術館を駆け足で見て回った.
▶ **zoom in** PHRASAL VERB 句動詞 If a camera **zooms in on** something that is being filmed or photographed, it gives a close-up picture of it. ズームインする ❏ *...a tracking system which can follow a burglar around a building and zoom in on his face.* 建物の中を泥棒について回りその顔にズームインすることのできる追跡装置.

Thesaurus   *zoom* また次を参照：

| v. | dart, rush, speed; (*ant.*) slow |

zuc|chi|ni /zukini/ (**zucchini** or **zucchinis**) N-VAR 可変性名詞 **Zucchini** are long thin vegetables with a dark green skin. ズッキーニ [mainly AM 主に米国英語]

Index

This is an alphabetical index of the translations found in this dictionary. English references in the text are given in alphabetical order following the Japanese word.

The order of the English words does not imply any order of importance and words with similar senses are not grouped together.

The index directs you to the relevant English entry in the dictionary through the medium of Japanese. The index is not a dictionary as such, although the English words to which you are referred can function as translations of the Japanese in many cases.

階, floor, level, story
～回, often, time
～界, domain
害, ill, risk
かい, paddle
害悪の, evil
買い入れ, acquisition
会員, member, membership
会員数, membership
会員であること, membership
海運業, shipping
開花, flowering
階下, downstairs
絵画, painting
外貨, foreign exchange
開会する, sit
階下に, downstairs
海外に投資・設立された, offshore
海外の, overseas
海外へ, abroad
改革, reform
改革者, reformer
改革する, reform
開花している, bloom
開花する, bloom
快活さ, buoyancy, spirit
快活な, bouncy, breezy, spirited
階下の, downstairs
絵画の, pictorial
買いかぶる, overestimate
貝殻, shell
会館, institute
海岸, coast, seashore
外観, exterior, guise, look, semblance
概観, overview, panorama
海岸線, coastline, shoreline
海岸通り, seafront, waterfront
外観を汚損する, deface
外観を損じる, disfigure
会期, session
懐疑, skepticism
会議, assembly, conference, consultation, council, talk
懐疑的な, skeptical
階級, grade, rank
階級差別のない, classless
階級制度, caste
海峡, strait
開業医, practitioner
開業している, practice
開業する, open
概況報告書, fact sheet
懐疑論者, skeptic
街区, block
海軍, navy
海軍大将, admiral
海軍中佐, commander
海軍の, naval
会計, accounting
会計係, treasurer
会計学, accountancy
会計監査役, controller
会計検査官, comptroller
会計士, accountant
会計事務, accountancy
会計年度, fiscal year, tax year
会計簿, account
解決, resolution
解決策, answer, fix, formula, way
解決する, clear, crack, cure, fix, resolve, settle, sort, straighten
解決できない, insoluble
解決法, antidote, cure
外見, appearance, surface
外見から判断すると, look
外見上の, seeming
外見だけの, superficial
外見の, outward
外見を取りつくろった, cosmetic
解雇, dismissal, layoff, sack, sacking

会合, function, meeting, rendezvous, session
外交, diplomacy
外交員, rep, representative
外交官, diplomat
会合する, convene
外交団, diplomatic corps
外向的な, extrovert, extroverted
外交に関する, diplomatic
会合場所, rendezvous
会合を開く, meet
介護休暇, compassionate leave
外国行きの, outward
外国からの, overseas
外国為替, foreign exchange
外国人, foreigner
外国人嫌い, xenophobia
外国人嫌いの, xenophobic
外国との交流, foreign exchange
外国の, foreign
解雇時の退職金, payoff
介護者, caregiver, carer
解雇する, dismiss, drop, fire, let
がい骨, skeleton
解雇手当, severance
回顧展, retrospective
買い込む, stock
解雇を強いられる, scrapheap
解雇を通告する, notice
開催される, convene, open
開催する, hold, mount, run
介在する, intervening
開催地, venue
改作, adaptation
害されていない, unspoiled
解散, dissolution
概算, estimation
解散させる, disperse, dissolve
海産食物, seafood
解散する, demobilize, disband, disperse, liquidate
改ざんする, doctor, falsify, massage
開始, commencement, initiation, kickoff, onset
解しがたい, obscure
開始して, stream
開始する, begin, commence, inaugurate, launch
概して, all, broadly, general, generally, rule
買い占める, buy
会社, company, corporation, enterprise, firm, house
会社からの貸与車, company car
解釈, interpretation, reading
解釈する, construe, gloss, interpret, read
会社の, corporate
会社を買収しようとする組織, suitor
改宗, conversion
回収, collection, repossession, retrieval
会衆, congregation
懐柔, appeasement
外周, circumference
改宗させる, convert
改宗者, convert, renegade
改宗する, convert
改修する, refit
回収する, recall, recover, retrieve
回収する人, collector
懐柔的な, conciliatory
回収不可能とみなす, write
回収不能金, bad debt
外出して, out
外出する, get, go
外出を禁止する, ground
解消, dissolution
回状, circular
会場, venue

解消する, break, dissolve
甲斐性なし, bum
解除する, lift
改心させる, reform
改心する, mend, reform
海図, chart
海水面, sea level
回数を記録する, score
害する, harm, prejudice, undermine
解説, commentary
解説者, commentator
開設する, open
解説する, commentate
～回戦, round
改善, advance, good, improvement
改善策, remedy
改善された, upgrade
改善されたもの, advance
改善して, mend
改善する, better, improve, remedy, strengthen
改善の, remedial
回線をパンクさせる, jam
回想, reminiscence
海草, seaweed
階層, bracket, echelon, layer, tier
改造, conversion
回想シーン, flashback
会葬者, mourner
改装する, refurbish, renovate
回想する, think
改造する, convert
階層性, hierarchy
階層性の, hierarchical
海賊, pirate
海賊行為, piracy
海賊版, pirate
解体, breakup, demolition
解体処理する, slaughter
解体する, dismantle
開拓者, pioneer, settler
開拓する, pioneer
外為, forex
階段, ladder, stair, staircase, stairway, step
害虫, pest
懐中電灯, flash, flashlight, torch
会長, chairman
快調な音を出す, purr
開通式を行なう, inaugurate
雇い続ける, keep
買い手, buyer
買い手/売り手市場, market
書いてある, go, read, say
改訂, revision
海底, seabed
改訂する, revise
開廷する, sit
書いていない, unwritten
欠けている, devoid
快適, comfort
快適さ, welfare
快適で, sweetness
快適な, comfortable, comfy, good, hospitable, smooth
かいてきれいにする, rake
かいでこぐ, paddle
買い手市場, buyer's market
回転, rotation, spin
回転させる, rotate, swing, swivel, turn, twist
回転式乾燥機, tumble dryer
回転式拳銃, revolver
回転式の, rotary
回転する, revolve, rotary, rotate, swing, swivel, turn
閉店する, open
回転盤, wheel
回転木馬, carousel, merry-go-round, roundabout

回転遊具, roundabout
回転率, turnover
回答, response
街頭, street
解凍する, thaw
解答, solution
会堂牧師, vicar
買い得, value
解読する, break, crack, decipher, decode
買い得な, economy
買い得品, buy
害毒を受ける, poison
買い取る, buy
～がいないのを寂しく思う, miss
飼いならされた, domestic, tame
飼いならす, tame
介入, intervention
介入する, intervene
解任する, discharge, relieve, remove
雇い主, master
概念, concept, notion
下位の, junior
害のない, innocuous
会派, caucus
かいば, fodder
外泊, sleepover
開発, development
海抜, altitude, elevation
開発銀行, development bank
開発事業者, developer
開発者, developer
開発する, develop, exploit
開発地, development
回避, evasion
回避行動をとる, evasive
回避する, sidestep, stall
回避的な, evasive
外部から調達する, outsource
回復, recovery
回復期, convalescence
回復して, mend
回復する, heal, improve, mend, pull, recover, recuperate, repair, restore
回復力のある, resilient
怪物, monster
怪物のような, monstrous
外部の, outside
海兵隊員, marine
回報, memorandum
会報, bulletin, newsletter
解放, release
解法, solution
解剖学, anatomy
解剖学上の, anatomical
解放される, rid
開廷する, open
解放する, emancipate, free, liberate, release, relieve
解剖する, dissect
開放的な, expansive, inclusive
海盆, basin
かいま見える, peep
垣間見させる経験Đまたは考え, glimpse
かいま見る, peek, peep
皆無の, zero
解明する, illuminate, unravel
壊滅, devastation
壊滅させる, crush
壊滅的な, catastrophic, disastrous
外面的な, outward
海面に流出した油, oil slick
買い戻し, buy-back
買い物, shopping
買い物をする, shop
解約払い戻し金, surrender value
回遊魚, migrant
回遊する, migrate

index

進行役, facilitator
信号を送る, signal
深刻さ, enormity
申告書, declaration
申告する, declare
深刻な, grave, grievous, real, serious, severe, weighty
深刻にする, deepen
深刻になる, deepen
真言, mantra
審査, audition
人材, manpower
審査委員会, jury
人材派遣会社, employment agency
審査員, judge
新作の, original
真作品リスト, canon
審査する, audition, judge, screen
審査員団, panel
診察, consultation, exam, examination
心雑音, murmur
診察時間, surgery
診察室, doctor's office, doctor's surgery
診察する, examine
診察の, exploratory
審査を受ける, audition
新参者, stranger
紳士, gent, gentleman
人事, HR
信じ難い, far-fetched
新事業を開始する際の, startup
信じ込ませる, delude
新事実, revelation
寝室, bedroom
真実, reality, truth
真実性, truth
真実だとわかる, hold
真実であると証明する, verify
真実でない, untrue
寝室に隣接する, en suite
真実味がある/むなしく響く, ring
紳士服, menswear
人事部門, human resources, personnel
信者, believer
神社, shrine
真珠, pearl
人種, race
人種関係, race relations
人種間の境界線, color line
人種差別がなくなる, integrate
人種差別主義, racism
人種差別的な, racist
人種差別を撤廃する, integrate
進出, foray
浸出する, bleed
進出する, move
進取的な, enterprising
真珠の, pearl
人種の, racial
進取の気性, enterprise
真珠のような, pearl
新手法, innovation
浸潤性の, invasive
心象, image
心情, heart
信条, creed, doctrine, persuasion, principle
重症の, massive
心情の熱度, temperature
浸食, erosion
浸食される, erode
浸食する, erode
侵食する, eat, encroach
信じられない, incredible, unbelievable
信じられないほど, ridiculously

信じられないほどの, belief
信じられる, believable, stand
信じる, believe, follow, swear, trust
信じること, belief
信じる人, believer
新人, newcomer, recruit
新進気鋭, new blood
新人選手, rookie
純真な, innocent
新進の, budding
信心深い, devout, religious
進水させる, launch
人生, life
神聖化する, consecrate
人生観, outlook
神聖さ, sanctity
申請する, put
人生相談回答者, advice columnist
神聖な, hallowed, holy, sacred
新生の, newborn
真正の, authentic
新製品, introduction
新勢力, blood, new blood
神聖を汚す, violate
シンセサイザー, synthesizer
親切な, accommodating, friendly, genial, nice
親切な行為, favor
親切な心, gold
親切な人, angel
親切にもてなす, hospitable
新鮮さを失った, stale
親善試合, friendly
新鮮でない, stale
新鮮な, fresh
新鮮な空気を吸うために, breath
親善のための, friendly
真相, truth
心像, picture
心臓, heart
腎臓, kidney
心臓の, cardiac, coronary
心臓病, heart failure
心臓発作, heart attack
真相を極める, bottom
真相を知る, score
親族, next of kin, relation, relative
親族でない, unrelated
親族の, related
心底嫌う, gut
心底は, heart
死んだ, dead
身体, body, person, system
寝台, berth, couch
靭帯, ligament
身体障害を引き起こす, crippling
身体の, personal, physical
信託, trust
信託資金, trust fund
死んだような, lifeless
診断, diagnosis
診断する, diagnose
診断の, diagnostic
新築の, new
真鍮, brass
身長, stature
慎重さ, delicacy, discretion
慎重な, cautious, conservative, deliberate, discreet, prudent
慎重に選び取る, cherry-pick
慎重に進む, tread
慎重にふるまう, step
身長のある, tall
慎重を要する, delicate, sensitive
進捗させる, progress
進捗する, headway
新陳代謝, metabolism
新陳代謝の, metabolic

心痛, heartache
陣痛, contraction
死んでいる, lifeless
進展, development, march, movement, progress, progression
進展する, get
進展する, come, get, move, progress
新天地を切り開く, ground
震盪, concussion
振動させる, vibrate
震動させる, shake
人道主義, humanism
人道主義者, humanism
人道主義の, humanitarian
浸透する, permeate
振動する, jar, throb, vibrate
震動する, shake
人道的な, humane
潜入させる, infiltrate
新入者, entrant
侵入者, intruder
潜入する, infiltrate, penetrate
侵入する, inroads, intrude
進入する, penetrate
信任, mandate
信任状, credentials
新年, New Year
信念, conviction, idea
信念の, ideological
信念を持った, principled
真の, real
心配, care, disquiet, unease, worry
心配事, concern, trouble
心配させる, bother, concern
心配した, worried
心配して, afraid, anxious
心配しないで, mind
心配性な, nervous
心配する, bother, care, fear, worry
心配そうな, strained
心配な, uneasy, worrying
新発見, revelation
新発見の, newfound
新盤, release
審判, ref, referee
審判員, umpire
審判をする, referee, umpire
神秘, mystery
審美眼のある, tasteful
神秘主義, mysticism
神秘主義者, mystic
神秘性, mystique
神秘的な, mystic, mystical
新品同様で, good
新品の, brand-new, new
深部, depth
新婦, bride
新風を吹き込むもの, breath
人物, character
人物証明書, credentials
人物像, figure
人物評, profile
～新聞, journal
新聞, gazette, newspaper, paper, press
～新聞, chronicle
新聞印刷用紙, newsprint
人文科学, art
人文学, humanity
人文系科学, science
新聞雑誌連盟やテレビ局を通じて同時発表する, syndicate
新聞紙, newspaper
新聞紙のインク, newsprint
新聞社, newspaper
新兵, recruit
進歩, march, progress, progression, stride

信望, status
信奉者, follower
信奉する, espouse
辛抱強い, long-suffering, patient
親睦会, reunion
進歩的な, progressive
新米, rookie
新米の, new
親密, intimacy
親密な, close, intimate
親密な関係, involvement, rapport
親密な関係になる, hook
親身になって悩みを聞いてくれる人, shoulder
人脈, network
人脈を築く, network
新芽, shoot
尋問, interrogation
審問する, hear
尋問する, interrogate
親友の, inseparable
信用, credence, faith, trust
陣容, lineup
信用格付け, credit rating
信用詐欺, scam
信用しない, distrust, mistrust
信用証明, credentials
信用する, trust
信用性, credibility
信用できない, doubt
信用できる, credible, creditworthy
信用を傷つける, discredit
信頼, confidence, goodwill
信頼関係, goodwill
信頼する, believe, depend, rely, trust
信頼できる, authentic, authoritative, reliable, solid, sure, trustworthy
信頼を失って, disrepute
信頼を寄せる, put
しんらつな, sharp
辛らつな, blistering, cutting, tart
辛辣な, cutting
心理, psychology
心理学, psychology
心理学者, psychologist
心理学的な, psychological
審理される, come
審理中の, pending
心理的な, psychological
侵略, invasion
侵略者, invader
侵略する, invade
侵略部隊, invader
診療, practice
診療所, clinic, doctor, infirmary, surgery
尽力, energy
心理療法, psychotherapy
心理療法医, psychotherapist
森林, wood
森林地, woodland
人類, human being, humanity, human race, mankind
人類学, anthropology
人類学者, anthropology
心霊の, psychic
進路, course, path
新郎, bridegroom, groom
進路を変更する, divert
神話, myth, mythology
神話上の, mythical
神話的通念, mythology
しんを取る, core
進路をふさぐ, box
巣, nest
図, diagram, fig., figure
巣穴, hole
吸い上げ管, siphon
吸い上げる, siphon, suck

成績, grade, mark, result
成績表, report card
精選された, selective
整然とした, order, orderly
精選物, pick
精巣, testicle
聖像, icon
製造, construction, production
製造会社, producer
製造業者, maker, manufacturer
清掃作業員, cleaner
盛装させる, dress
正装する, dress
盛装する, dress
製造する, manufacture, produce
製造中止する, discontinue
正装ドレス, gown
生息環境, habitat
勢ぞろい, battery
生存者, survivor
生存する, live
成体, adult
政体, regime
生態, biology
生体解剖, vivisection
生態系, ecology, ecosystem
生体組織検査, biopsy
盛大なパーティー, bash
ぜいたく, extravagance, luxury
ぜいたくな, extravagant, gracious, lavish, luxurious, luxury
贅沢な思いをさせる, pamper
ぜいたくに, richly
ぜいたく品, extravagance
生地, batter, dough, material
成長, growth
成長させる, grow
成長している, growth
成長して着られなくなる, grow
成長して～になる, grow
成長する, grow, mature
精通, mastery
精通している, familiar, way
制定, enactment, institution
制定する, establish, make
制定法, act, statute
制定法の, statutory
政敵, opponent
性的嫌がらせ, sexual harassment
性的虐待, sexual abuse
性的指向, sexuality
性的指向の, sexual
性的な, sexual
性的な倒錯, perversion
性的に刺激する, arouse, titillate
性的に挑発的な, provocative
性的魅力がある, smolder
性的魅力のある, desirable, hot
正電荷を持つ, positive
静電気, static
生徒, pupil, student
政党, party
聖堂, shrine
青銅, bronze
正当化する, justified, justify, rationalize
性倒錯者, pervert
性倒錯の, perverted
製陶所, pottery
聖堂信者席, pew
正当性, validity
正統性, orthodoxy
正統的でない, unorthodox
正当とされない, unwarranted
正当な, just, rightful, valid
正当な根拠となる, warrant
正当な理由, cause
正当に, justly
正統派的見解, orthodoxy
正統派の, orthodox

制度化する, institutionalize
制度上の, institutional
せいと見なす, ascribe
せいとんされた, neat
せいとんしてある, tidy
せいとんする, pick
成年, majority
青年, youth
生年月日, date of birth
青年時代, youth
成年男子の, virile
性の, sexual
背の高い, tall
背の低い, short
正反対, antithesis, converse
正反対だ, pole
正反対に, conversely
正反対の, opposite, polar
正反対の人, opposite
税引き前の, pretax
整備士, mechanic
製品, goods, manufacture, merchandise, product
製品ライン, portfolio, product line
政府, government, state
西部, west
政府官庁, civil service
制服, uniform
正服, gown
征服, conquest
征服者, conqueror
征服する, conquer
制服の色, color
制服を着た, uniformed
西部劇, western
生物, life, organism
静物画, still life
生物学, biology
生物学者, biology
生物学上の, biological
生物学の, biological
生物工学, biotechnology
生物ではない, lifeless
生物の, biological
生物の住まない, lifeless
政府の, governmental, state
成分, component
成文化していない, unwritten
製粉所, mill
製粉する, mill
成文の, written
性癖, propensity, tendency
性別の, sexual
制帽, cap
正方形, square
正方形の, square
西方に, west, westward
西方にある, westerly
西方の, west
製本する, bind
精密な, accurate, refined
精妙な, exquisite
声明, proclamation, statement
生命, life
生命線, lifeline
生命のある, animate
生命保険, life insurance
制約, bar, constraint, limitation
誓約, pledge, vow
誓約する, pledge
製薬の, pharmaceutical
西洋化, westernization
西洋化した, westernized
セイヨウキヅタ, ivy
静養所, retreat
西洋スモモ, plum
西洋ネギ, leek
性欲, desire
性欲をかきたてる, erotic
生理がある, menstruate

生理学, physiology
生理機能, physiology
整理する, liquidate, order, organize, tidy
成立, formation
生理の, menstrual
清涼飲料, soft drink
清涼感のある, refreshing
生理用ナプキン, sanitary napkin, sanitary towel
勢力, ground, might, muscle, strength
精力, vigor
精力的な, energetic, tireless
整列させる, marshal
精を出して, busily
精を出す, fling
税制上の優遇措置, tax break
セージ, sage
セーター, jumper, sweater
世界, universe, world
世界化する, globalize
世界観, world view
世界的規模になる, globalize
世界共通の, universal
世界中の, worldwide
世界主義的な, cosmopolitan
世界大戦, world war
世界で一流の, world-class
世界的に, universally
世界的にする, globalize
世界的に有名な, world-famous
世界の, world
世界の人々, world
世界は～の思いのままだ, oyster
世界貿易機関, WTO
世界村, global village
背が後ろに倒れる, recline
せかして～させる, railroad
せかす, hustle
せかせかする, fuss
背が立たない深さに, depth
せき, barrage, weir
席, seat
石英, quartz
責がある, blame
せき込んで話す, splutter
石材, stone
せき髄の, spinal
せきたてられた, hurried
せきたてる, hurry, urge
石炭, coal
赤道, equator
席などを詰めて空ける, move
席などを詰める, move
責任, blame, fault, onus, responsibility
責任があって, liable
責任がある, accountable
責任などを委譲する, hand
責任のある, fault, responsible
責任を負わずに, obligation
責任をとる, answer
責任を取る, account
責任をなすりつける, buck
赤熱した, red-hot
赤熱の, red-hot
せきの出る病気, cough
せき払いをする, throat
石碑, stone
責務, responsibility
赤面する, blush, color
石油, oil, petroleum
石油輸出国機構の略, OPEC
せきをして吐き出す, cough
せきをする, cough
セクシーな, gorgeous, sexy
セクシーな有名人, sex symbol
セクハラ, sexual harassment
世間知らずの, naive

世間では, popularly
世間の評判, public relations
～せざるをえない, compel
セ氏, centigrade
セ氏の, Celsius
世襲の, hereditary
～せずとも, or
～せずに, without
～せずにはいられない, compulsive
是正する, rectify, redress
世俗の, civil
世代, generation
セダン型自動車, sedan
節, clause, verse
設備過剰, overcapacity
絶縁する, insulate
絶縁体, insulation
石灰, lime
石灰岩, limestone
切開する, invasive
石化した, petrified
せっかちな, rash
赤褐色, auburn, ginger
赤褐色の, chocolate, copper
説教, sermon
説教師, preacher
説教する, lecture, preach
説教壇, pulpit
積極的差別, positive discrimination
積極的な, active, aggressive, go-ahead, proactive
接近して, quarter
セックス, sex
セックスシンボル, sex symbol
セックスする, love, sex
設計, design
設計士, designer
設計図, blueprint, design, plan
設計する, design, engineer, plan
せっけん, soap
石工, mason
接合箇所, joint
接合剤, cement
接合させる, bond
接合する, bond, knit
絶好の, golden
絶賛, acclaim
絶賛する, acclaim
絶賛の, glowing
接辞, affix
摂取量, intake
接触, contact
接触して, contact, touch
接触している, touch
接触を失う, touch
節制, abstinence
せっせとする, go
接続で, neck
接続, linkup
接続詞, conjunction
接続する, connect, hook, link, plug
接続性, connectivity
絶対, sure
絶対だめ, way
絶対的真理, gospel
絶対的な, absolute, categorical, positive, strict
絶大な影響力を持つ, dominating
絶対に, absolutely
絶対に～しない, damned
絶対に～する, never
絶対の, absolute, implicit
絶対必要ではないがあれば喜ばれるもの, icing
絶対必要な, indispensable, integral
絶対不変なもの, absolute
切断する, amputate, disconnect, sever

heartbreaking
探偵, detective
探偵の, detective
担当, responsibility
弾頭, warhead
弾道, fire
担当する, handle
単刀直入な, blunt
担当の, responsible
単独で, alone, single-handed
単独の, solitary, unilateral
だんな, mister
単なる, just, mere, simple
単なる時間の問題, time
単に〜だけ, simply
単に〜だけでも, alone
断念, abandonment
断念する, abandon, despair
たんのう, proficiency
胆嚢, gall bladder
たんのうな, proficient
堪能な, accomplished
たんぱく質, protein
ダンピングする, dump
ダンプ, dump
ダンプする, dump
単文の, simple
断片, piece, snippet
短編映画, short
断片的な, piecemeal
担保, collateral, security, surety
暖房, fire, heating
暖房機, radiator
暖房装置, heater, heating
段ボール, cardboard
段ボール箱, carton
担保付, secure
タンポポ, dandelion
タンポン, tampon
端末, terminal
断面図, cross-section
弾薬, ammunition
段落, paragraph
単利, simple interest
短絡的な, simplistic
弾力性, elasticity
弾力性のある, bouncy, resilient
弾力のある, elastic
暖炉, fireplace
治安, law and order, order
治安の悪い, rough
治安を維持する, peace
地位, grade, place, position, post, rank, rung, status
地域, area, country, district, region, zone
地域住民, community
地域でのボランティア活動, community service
地域とする, zone
地域の, regional
地域奉仕, community service
チークの木, teak
小さい, diminutive, light, little, low, small, wee
小さい機械装置, gadget
小さく仕切った部屋, cubicle
小さくなる, lower
小さく見せる, dwarf
小さすぎる, skimpy
小さな, little
小さな穴, puncture
小さな穴を開ける, prick
小さなおり, pen
小さな塊, blob, pat
小さなしみ, speck
小さな粒, particle, speck
小さな土地, patch
小さめ, modesty
チーズ, cheese
チーズバーガー, cheeseburger

地位の保有, tenure
チーム, club, side, team
チームメート, teammate
チームワーク, teamwork
地位を譲る, move
知恵, wisdom, wit
チェーン組織, chain
知恵比べをする, pit
チェス, chess
チェスのナイト, knight
チェッカー, checker, draughts
チェック, check
チェックアウトする, check
チェックインする, check
チェックする装置, checker
チェックする人, checker
チェックマーク, tick
チェックマークをつける, tick
チェックをつける, tick
知恵の遅れた, backward
チェロ, cello
チェロ奏者, cellist
知恵を絞る, puzzle
遅延, delay
地階, basement
誓い, oath, vow
近い, close, immediate
違い, difference, distinction
近いうちに, near
違いが分かる, distinguish
ちがいない, must
誓う, swear, vow
違う, different
地殻, crust
知覚, sensation
近く, toward
〜近く, near
知覚する, perceive
近くに, level, near, toward
近くの, nearby, neighboring
近ごろ, newly
地下室, basement, cellar
近々, near
近づいている, way
地下通路, subway
近づきになる, rub
近づきやすい, accessible
近づく, approach, approximate, draw, get, near
誓った, sworn
誓って, honest
違って, otherwise
誓って言う, heart
地下鉄, metro, subway, tube, underground
地下に, underground
地下の, below, subterranean
地下納骨所, vault
地下道, underpass
近道, shortcut
近寄らない, near
近寄る, draw, near
力, force, might, potency, strain, strength
力がない, powerless
力尽きる, steam
力づくで通り抜ける, break
力づける, sustain
力強い, forceful, ringing, strong
力強く, soundly
力強さ, edge
力を合わせて, shoulder
力を合わせる, force
力を入れて動かす, lever
力を入れる, brace
力を誇示する, muscle
地下牢, dungeon
誓わせる, swear
ちきちょう, Jesus
地球, earth, globe
地球儀, globe

地球の, terrestrial
地球の温暖化, global warming
地区, area, neighborhood
逐語的な, literal, word
逐語的に, literally, verbatim
畜産家, breeder
逐次知らせる, post
ちくしょう, almighty, fuck, hell
畜生, son of a bitch
蓄積, accumulation, store
蓄積する, accumulate
蓄積する, accumulate, amass
ちくちくする, prickly, tickle
チクっと痛む, sting
ちくっとした痛み, prick
チクッとした痛み, sting
乳首, nipple
チクマハッカ, catnip
ちくりと刺す, prick
地形, feature, geography
チケット, ticket
チケット売り場, box office
知事, governor
知識, knowledge, understanding
知識がある, know
知識人, intellectual
知識のある, knowledgeable
地質, geology
地質学, geology
地質学の, geological
地上待機にする, ground
地上で, ground
地上でみずからの動力によって移動させる, taxi
地上輸送郵便, surface mail
知人, acquaintance
地図, map
血筋, blood, branch
地図帳, atlas
地図を作る, chart, map
知性, intellect, intelligence
地帯, belt
乳, breast, milk
父親, father
父親であること, fatherhood
父親の育児休暇, paternity leave
父親らしい, paternal
父方, side
父方の, paternal
父となる, father
縮ませる, shrink
縮まる, narrow
縮む, contract, shrink
縮める, contract, narrow, shorten
地中海, Mediterranean
地中海沿岸, Mediterranean
乳を搾る, milk
乳を飲む, feed
膣, vagina
膣カンジダ症, thrush
秩序, order
窒素, nitrogen
窒息させる, choke, overcome
窒息死させる, smother, suffocate
窒息する, suffocate
窒息する, choke
ちっとも仕事をしない, stroke
膣の, vaginal
チップ, chip, counter, gratuity, tip
チップを渡す, tip
知的な, cerebral
知的な指導者, brain
地点, point, spot, way
血なまぐさい, bloody
ちなみに, passing
ちなんで, after
知能, intelligence
知能の, mental
知能のある, intelligent
知能や才能の優れた, gifted

知能を持った, intelligent
血の塊, clot
血の通った人間, flesh
血の気の引いた, colorless
血の気が引く, drain
血のり, gore
ちびちび飲む, sip
地表, earth
乳房, breast
地平線, horizon
地方, countryside, district, locality, province, territory
痴呆, dementia
地方議会, council
地方自治体, local authority, local government
地方政治, local government
地方的な, provincial
地方都市の生活者, Main Street
地方の, local, provincial
血まみれの, bloody
血迷った, mad
ちみつな, delicate
致命的な, deadly, fatal, mortal
茶, tea
チャイム, chime
茶色, brown
茶化すような, sardonic
着, pair
着実に, step
着手金, retainer
着手する, go
着床する, implant
着色した, colored
着色する, color
着色料, coloring
着信音, ring tone
着席する, seat
着想の基になる人/もの, inspiration
着地する, land, touch
着任, arrival
着服する, pocket
着目する, turn
着陸, landing
着陸させる, land
着陸しようとする, incoming
着陸する, land
茶さじ, teaspoon
着火, ignition
チャック, chuck, zip
チャットルーム, chat room
チャツネ, chutney
茶の葉, tea
茶番, farce, pantomime
チャペル, chapel
〜ちゃん, old
チャンス, break
ちゃんとした, decent
ちゃんとする, grow
チャンネル, channel
チャンピオン, champ, champion
注, NB
注意, attention, caution, NB
中尉, lieutenant
注意して, care, guard
注意する, look, mind, note, remind
注意するように言う, warn
注意深い, attentive, observant
注意深く見る, study
注意報, advisory
注意を促す, warning
注意を喚起する, alert
注意をそむける, turn
注意をそらす, distract, divert
注意をそらすもの, diversion
注意をそらせる, diversionary
注意を払う, attention, mark, tab
注意を引く, attention, eye, grab
中央処理装置, CPU

ぱりっとさせる, stiffen
ぱりっとした, crisp
張りつめた, tight
バリトン, baritone
ハリネズミ, hedgehog
バリバリした, crisp
バリバリと音を立てる, crunch
バリバリとかむ, crunch
バリバリにする, crisp
バリバリになる, crisp
春, spring
張る, glue, paste, post, put, stick, stiffen
バルーンモーゲージ, balloon mortgage
はるかに, far, way
バルコニー, balcony
パルス, pulse
はるばる, way
バルブ, valve
バルブ, pulp
晴れ上がる, clear
バレエ, ballet
バレエ曲, ballet
パレードカー, float
バレーボール, volleyball
はれた, swollen
晴れた, clear, fine
破裂, rupture
破裂させる, burst, bust, rupture
破裂する, burst, rupture
パレット, palette
晴れの, fair
はれもの, swelling
晴れやかになる, lighten
はれる, swell
晴れる, brighten, clear
バレル, barrel
馬ろく, bridle
パロディ, parody
パロディ化する, parody
バロメーター, barometer
ハロン, furlong
パワー, power
パワーステアリング, power steering
パワステ, power steering
歯を食いしばって頑張る, grit
歯を食いしばってこらえる, grit
歯をむき出してうなる, snarl
版, edition
バン, van
晩, evening, night
番, go
盤, board, panel
～板, board
～版, version
～番, number
パン, bread
範囲, extent, province, range, scope, span, spectrum
範囲の広い, broad
反映, reflection
繁栄した, prosperous
反映している, reflective
反映する, echo, reflect
繁栄する, prosper
半円, semicircle
半円形, semicircle
半音下がった, flat
版画, print
ハンガー, coat hanger
バンカー, bunker
挽回する, recover
半額で, half-price
半額の, half-price
反核兵器, peace
パン菓子類製造販売店, bakery
ハンカチ, handkerchief
繁華な, busy
バンガロー, bungalow

反感, antipathy, feeling, hostility
反感のある, hostile
反感を抱かせる, turn
反感を買う, turn
反感をもたせる, antagonize
反逆, rebellion
反逆児, rebel
反逆者, rebel
半球, hemisphere
半球状のもの, dome
反響, echo
反響が広がる, reverberate
反響する, echo
パンクさせる, puncture
パンクしたタイヤ, flat
パンクする, puncture
パンクの穴, puncture
番組, program, show
番組提供者となる, sponsor
番組に発表する, bill
パンクロック, punk
パンクロック愛好者, punk
半径, radius
パンケーキ, pancake
反撃する, fight
判決, decree, judgment, ruling, sentence
判決を下す, sentence
半券, stub
版権, right
番犬, watchdog
反抗, rebellion
蛮行, savagery
番号, number
反抗する, defy, react, rebel
反抗的態度, defiance
反抗的な, defiant, rebellious
番号をつける, number
番小屋, lodge
犯罪, crime, delinquency
犯罪科学, forensic
犯罪科学の, forensic
犯罪者, criminal, offender
犯罪の, criminal
犯罪容疑, rap
ハンサムな, good-looking, handsome
晩餐会, dinner
判事, bench, judge, justice
～判事, justice
万事, all, everything
破綻して, apart
反射, reflection, reflex
反射させる, bounce
反射神経, reaction, reflex
反射する, bounce
反射する, mirror, reflect, reflective
応射する, fire
反射能力, reaction
半熟練の, semiskilled
繁殖させる, breed, propagate, reproduce
繁殖する, breed, flourish, multiply, reproduce
繁殖力のある, fertile
繁殖力の強い, prolific
繁殖力のない, infertile
半信半疑の, dubious
ハンスト, hunger strike
パンスト, tights
半ズボン, short
反する, go
パンする, pan
パン製造販売人, baker
帆走, sailing
帆走権, sailing
帆走させる, sail
帆走をする, sail
伴奏, accompaniment, backup
絆創膏, plaster
伴奏をする, accompany, back

反則, foul
反則する, foul
パンダ, panda
反対, dissent, opposition, reaction, resistance, reverse
反対側の, other
反対して, against
反対者, enemy, opponent
反対尋問する, cross-examine
反対する, foot, object, oppose, rebel, resist
反体制の, dissident
反体制派, dissenter, dissident
反対で, opposed
反対に, contrary, way
反対の, against, contrary, opposing, reverse
反対の意見を言う, argue
反対派, rebel
判断, judgment, verdict
判断する, assess, decide, judge, reason
判断力, judgment, sense
判断を誤る, miscalculate, misjudge
判断を差し控える, judgment
パンチ, punch
半月ごとの, bimonthly
パンティ, brief
パンティー, knickers, panties
パンティーストッキング, pantyhose
ハンディキャップ付きの試合, handicap
斑点, fleck, spot
バンド, band, group, strap
半島, peninsula
反動, reaction
半導体, semiconductor
反動的な, reactionary
反道徳的な, obscene
半透明の, translucent
バンドエード, Band-Aid
パンと強打する, bang
判読可能な, readable
判読する, make
反時計回りに, anticlockwise
反時計回りの, anticlockwise
半年ごとの, half-yearly
ハンドセット, handset
ハンドバッグ, bag, handbag, pocketbook, purse
ハンドマイク, bullhorn
ハンドル, steering wheel, wheel
バンドルする, bundle
晩に, night
半日勤務, half-day
犯人, culprit
万人に, universally
反応, reaction, response
反応する, behave, greet, react
万能の, all-around
反応のよい, responsive
万能薬, panacea
反応を示す, react
パンの皮, crust
パンの耳, crust
バンパー, bumper
ハンバーガー, burger, hamburger
販売, sale
販売員, sales force, salesperson
販売外交員, salesman
販売業者, dealer, vendor
販売権, distributorship
販売時点, point of sale
販売時点管理, POS
販売時点情報管理, point of sale
販売する, dispense, sell
販売促進活動, promotion

販売代理店, dealership
販売人, seller
販売の促進をする, promote
販売部数, circulation
反発, backlash, reaction
反発する, react, rebel, repel
半々に, fifty-fifty
反復, repetition
反復運動過多損傷, RSI
反復する, repeat
反復の, repetitive
パンプス, pump
万物, creation
パンフレット, brochure, pamphlet, sheet
半分, half
半分にする, halve
半分に減らす, halve
半分に減る, halve
番兵, sentry
ハンマー, hammer
ハンマー投げ, hammer
反目, feud, quarrel
反目する, feud
繁茂した, bushy
繁茂する, flourish
パン屋, baker
反乱, insurgency, insurrection, mutiny, rebellion, uprising
氾濫させる, flood
はんらんする, burst
氾濫する, flood
氾濫する, overflow
反乱を起こした, rebellious
反乱を起こす, mutiny, rise
範例, paradigm
反論する, contradict, dispute
番をする, mind
火, fire
美, beauty
干上がった, dry
干上がる, dry, run
ピアス穴をあける, pierce
ピアニスト, pianist
ピアノ, piano
ビーカー, beaker
ひいき, bias
ひいきする, favor
ひいきにする, patronize
ピーク時でない, off-peak
ピークの, peak
ビーコン, beacon
ヒース, heather
ヒール, heel
ビーズ, bead
非依存, independence
ひいた, ground
ビー玉, marble
ビー玉遊び, marble
ビーチウェア, beachwear
ビーチチェア, beach chair
引いて, out
秀でる, excel
ビート, beet
ビート, peat
ビートの根, beet
ビート版, float
ピーナツ, peanut
ビーニー帽, beanie
ビーバー, beaver
ビーバーの毛皮, beaver
ビーフ, beef
ビーフステーキ, steak
ビーマー, Beemer
ピーマン, bell pepper, pepper
ヒイラギ, holly
ビール, beer
ビール醸造会社, brewer
ビール醸造業者, brewer
ビール醸造所, brewery

悲嘆にくれた, heartbroken
悲嘆にくれて, distressed
悲嘆にくれる, grieve
備蓄, stockpile
備蓄する, stockpile
非嫡出の, illegitimate
ぴちゃぴちゃ飲む, lap
微調整する, fine-tune, readjust
悲痛, woe
悲痛のあまり自分の手をもみしぼる, wring
引っかかる, catch
引っかく, scratch
引っかけて破く, snag
引っかけて破れる, snag
ひっかける, pick
ひつぎ, coffin
筆記の, written
筆記文字, script
ピックアップ・トラック, pickup
ひっくり返す, flip, invert, overturn, turn, upset
ひっくり返る, flip, overturn, turn
びっくり仰天させる, astound
びっくり仰天の, jaw-dropping
びっくりさせる, amaze, shock, surprise
びっくりした, darn
びっくりしている, heart
びっくりするような, amazing
日付, date, the
日付を書く, date
引越し, removal
引っ越す, move
引っこ抜く, uproot
引っ込みがちな人, violet
引っ込み思案, inhibition
引っ込み思案な, private
引っ込む, retract
引っ込める, retract
羊, sheep
羊飼い, shepherd
羊の肉, mutton
必修の, core
必需品, basics, necessity, supply
必須の, essential, imperative
筆跡, stroke, writing
筆舌に尽くしがたい, description
必然的な, inescapable, inevitable, logical
必然的に, inevitably, naturally, nature, necessarily
必然の, logical, necessary
ひっそりとした, quiet
ひったくられる, snatch
ぴったりな, fit, glove, mesh, snug
ぴったり合うもの, fit
ぴったりする, fit
ぴったりと合わせる, mold
ぴったりとした, tight
ぴったりの, exact, fitting, perfect, tailor-made
ぴったりの組み合わせ, match
ピッチ, pitch
ヒッチハイクする, hitch, hitchhike
ヒッチハイクをする, thumb
ピッチャー, pitcher
匹敵者, equal
匹敵する, comparable, equal, equivalent, match, rival
匹敵するものがない, rival
ヒット, hit
ビット, bit
ピット, pit
ビット/秒, bps
ヒットアンドランによる, hit-and-run
ヒット曲第1位の曲, number one
ビットマップ, bitmap
引っ張っていく, drag

引っ張ってばらばらにする, pull
引っ張る, drag, pull, tug
ヒッピー, hippie
ヒップ, hip
ひづめ, hoof
必要, use
必要以上に, unduly
必要以上に細かい区別立てをする, hair
必要以上の, undue
必要がある, need
必要最小限の, bare, bare-bones, basic, skeleton
必要最小限のもの, bone
必要時に役に立つ, useful
必要条件, prerequisite
必要条件を満たす, bill
必要性, necessity, need
必要である, do
必要であれば, need
必要としている, need
必要とする, exact, involve, necessitate, need, occupy, require, take
必要な, involved, necessary, requisite
必要ない, unnecessary
必要なだけの, enough
必要なところに金をつぎ込む, money
必要なもの, requirement, requisite
必要不可欠の, basic
必要物, want
必要を満たす, serve
否定, denial
否定して, negative
否定する, deny, negate
否定的な, negative
否定できない, undeniable
否定の, negative
否定の文の省略代用語, not
否定文でnotとともに用いる., do
ビデオ, video
ビデオカセット, video cassette, videotape
ビデオカセットレコーダー, video, video recorder
ビデオカメラ, camcorder
ビデオゲーム, video game
ビデオ装置, video
ビデオテープ, videotape
ビデオテープに録画する, video, videotape
ビデオデッキ, VCR
美的な, aesthetic
美点, beauty, virtue
秘伝の, esoteric
人, individual, man, one, person, strong, that, you
人・物が好きになる, fancy
人当たりのよい, suave
一編み, stitch
ひどい, appalling, awful, bad, bum, chronic, crap, damned, deadly, fearful, ferocious, foul, horrible, horrid, lousy, miserable, nasty, shocking, sorry, terrible
ひどい扱い, raw
一息, breather
ひどい苦痛を与える, kill
ひどい仕打ち, kick, knock
ひどい損害を与える, crippling
ひどい目, ride
ひどい目にあわせた上になお侮辱を加える, insult
ひどい目にあわせる, beat
ひどい目にあわせる, kill
非道な, evil
一泳ぎ, dip
一かえりのひな, brood
一固まりにさせる, mass

一固まりになる, mass
人が根が親切だ, heart
1切れ, slice
ひどく, bitterly, hideously, painfully, unusually
美徳, virtue
ひどく～して, mind
人食い人種, cannibal
人食いの風習, cannibalism
ひどく嫌な, abominable
ひどくおかしい, hysterical
ひどく怒らせる, incense
ひどく驚いた, astonished
ひどく驚かす, astonish
ひどくかき乱す, hell
一区画, piece
ひどく感じる, die
ひどく嫌う, loathe
ひどく興奮状態の, kite
ひどく興奮する, fit
ひどく困って, eyeball
ひどく質の悪い, dire
ひどく進行して, far
ひどく心配して, sick
ひどく退屈させる, bore
ひどくたたくこと, beating
ひと口, morsel
一口, bite, nip, sip
一口分, mouthful, slug
ひどく破壊する, ravage
ひどくばかげた, mad
ひどくばかげたこと, insanity
ひどく腹立たしい, infuriating, maddening
ひどく非難する, damn
ひどく不快な, hell
ひどく下手な, terrible
ひどく醜い, hideous
ひどく蒸し暑い, sultry
ひどく酔っ払った, plastered
ひどく悪い, abysmal, atrocious
人けがなく静かな, private
火床, grate, hearth
ひとこぎ, stroke
一言, word
一言の不平も言わずに, murmur
人込み, crush
人差し指, forefinger
人里離れた, solitary
人里はなれたところで, nowhere
1皿, course
1試合, leg, tie
等しい, equal
ひとしきりの, round
等しく, equally
人質, hostage
人質にとる, hostage
人質の状態, hostage
人好きのする, winning
ひとすじ, chink
一筋, shaft, thread
一世代, generation
人だかり, throng
人たち, folk
一束, bunch
一つ, one, piece
一つおきの, alternate
人付き合いがうまい人, mixer
ひとっこひとりとして, soul
一つしかない, unique
一つずつ調べる, go
ひと続き, chain, course, flight
一続き, streak
一続きの期間, spell
一続きの部屋, suite
一つかねて, one
一つになる, merge
一つになる, unify
一つにまとめる, unify
一つの, a

一つのことに全てをかける, egg
ひとつの場所や物に特定されない, general
一走りする., spin
一つ一つ調べる, look
1粒, grain
一つまみ, pinch
一つ屋根の下で, roof
人出, turnout
人でいっぱいの, crowded
人でなし, brute
ひととき, time
人に, us
人に遠慮なく言う, piece
一握りの, handful
人に試験をする, test
人に責任を負わせる, pin
人に頼らずに, right
人に明確な態度を取らせる, pin
人に優しい, soft
人の, your
人の嫌がることをする, dirty
人の犯した罪をきる, rap
人の感情を害すること, offense
人の関心をそらさ自分に向けさせる, upstage
人の気に入る, fancy
人の行動を妨げる, cramp
人の心を捕らえて離さない, compulsive
人の心を引き付ける, endearing
人の集団を目的地まで導く, herd
人の姿, figure
人の注意を引く, high-profile
人の手先, pawn
人の鼻先で, nose
人の費用で, expense
一飲み, drink
人のもの, hers
人の弱みに付け込む, predatory
人の例を見習う, example
ひと腹の子, litter
一針, stitch
ひと引き, pull
人々, people, person, those
人びと, public
一吹き, puff
1袋, bag
1袋の中身, bag
1人前の, public
一巻き, coil
人前で恥をさらす, dirty
ひとまとまり, clump
ひとまとめ, block
ひとみ, pupil
ひと棟の建物, block
一目で, glance
人目に晒されて, gaze
一目ぼれする, crush
人目を引く, conspicuous
人目を引く安っぽい物, kitsch
ヒト免疫不全ウィルス, HIV
一休み, breather
一休みする, foot
一山当てる, jackpot
一人当たりの, per capita
一人一票原則, vote
一人きりで, alone
一人芝居, monologue
独り占めする, hog, monopolize
ひとりだけではできない, two
一人っ子, only
ひとりで, by
独りで, isolation, own
一人で行動する人, loner
ひとりでに, accord
一人で寝るための, single
ひとりでやる, alone
一人にしておく, leave
一人につき, apiece
一人の, a, lone

分裂, breakup, split
分裂させる, fracture, split, tear
分裂する, disintegrate, fall, fracture, split
〜へ, to
ヘアスタイル, haircut
ヘアピン, bobby pin
塀, wall
嬰音, sharp
平穏, peace
平穏な, peaceful, tranquil, undisturbed, uneventful
陛下, majesty
弊害, evil
閉回路の, closed-circuit
平価を切り下げる, devalue
兵器, arm, arsenal
兵器庫, armory, arsenal
兵器類, armory
平均, average, mean
平衡, balance
平均する, average
平均で, average
平均の, mid-range
平均のとれた, balanced
平均量の, medium
平衡を失って, balance, off-balance
平衡を保つ, balance
併合, absorption
並行して, parallel
並行する, parallel
併合する, annex
平行な, parallel
米国, state
米国下院議員, representative
米国議会の, congressional
米国航空宇宙局, NASA
米国国防総省, Pentagon
米国植民地の, continental
米国の国税局, IRS
米国兵, continental
米国本土の, continental
閉鎖, closure
閉鎖する, close, seal
兵士, GI, soldier
平日, week, weekday, workday
平静, composure, equilibrium
平静さ, peace
平静さが失われる, fray
平静さを失う, fray
平静な, sedate
並足, walk
閉塞, obstruction
兵卒, private, rank
平坦な, flat
平地, ground
閉店する, shut
ペイ・パー・ビュー方式, pay-per-view
平方根, square root
平方の, sq., square
平凡, mediocrity, routine
平凡な, commonplace, conventional, gray, indifferent, mediocre, middle-of-the-road, pedestrian, routine
平凡にする, trivialize
平面, plane
平野, plain
並列, juxtaposition
並列する, juxtapose
平和, peace
平和主義, pacifism
平和主義者, pacifist
平和主義的な, pacifist
平和な, peaceful
平和を好む, peaceful
兵を駐留させる, garrison
へぇー, well

ベーコン, bacon
ページ, page, pp.
ページ順に並べる, collate
ベーシス・ポイント, basis point
ベーシック, BASIC
ベージュ色, beige
ベース, base
ベース, pace
ベースギター, bass
ペースト, paste
ペーパーバック, paperback
ベール, veil
ベールに包まれている, shroud
ベールをかぶった, veiled
壁画, mural
壁がん, niche
ヘクタール, hectare
ぺこぺこする, grovel
へこませる, dent, hollow
へこみ, dent
へこんだ部分, socket
ベジタリアンの, vegetarian
ベスト, vest, waistcoat
ベストセラー, bestseller
ベストセラーの, best-selling
ペストリー, pastry
へそ, navel
隔たって, off
隔たり, chasm, distance, gulf
隔てる, separate
へたな, lame
下手な, bad, lousy, poor
下手な仕事をする, botch
へたなまね, travesty
下手になった, rusty
べたべた張る, plaster
ペダル, pedal
ペダルを踏む, pedal
ぺちゃくちゃしゃべる, chatter
ぺチャクチャしゃべる, babble
ぺちゃんこにする, flatten
ぺちゃんこになる, flatten
別巻, supplement
別館, annex
別居, separation
別居している, absent, estranged, separated
別居する, leave
別個の, separate
別冊付録, supplement
ペッサリー, diaphragm
ヘッジファンド, hedge fund
別荘, villa
ヘッダー, header
ベッド, bed
ペット, pet
ベッド数, bed
ヘッドセット, headset
ベッドタウン, commuter belt
ベッドタウンの, bedroom
ヘッドハンター, headhunter
ヘッドフォン, headphones
ヘッドライト, bright, headlight
ヘッドレスト, headrest
ベッドわき, bedside
ベッドを整える, bed
別にして, aside
別の, another, different, other
別の医師の意見, second opinion
別の言葉で言い換える, paraphrase
別のもの, another, kettle
別のやり方で, otherwise
別々に, separately
別名〜, a. k. a.
別名は, alias
別問題, matter
別離, parting
ヘディングする, head
ベテラン, veteran
ぺてん, con

ペドフィリア, pedophilia
べとべとする, tacky
へとへとに疲れさせる, punishing
へどろ, sludge
ペナルティ, penalty
ペニー株, penny stock
ペニシリン, penicillin
ペニス, penis
ベニヤ板, veneer
〜への複占, duopoly
〜の道, road
ペパーミント, peppermint
ペパーミント・キャンディー, peppermint
ペパーミントのあめ, peppermint
へばりつく, flatten
ヘビ, serpent, snake
ベビー, baby
ベビーカー, pram, pushchair, stroller
ヘビー級のボクサー, heavyweight
ベビーシッター, nanny
ベビーバギー, stroller
ベビーベッド, crib
ヘブライ語, Hebrew
ヘブライ語の, Hebrew
ヘブライ人の, Hebrew
へまなことを言う, foot
へまをする, blunder
〜へ向かう, make
部屋, chamber, room
部屋にいる人たち, room
減らす, deplete, lose, lower, reduce, run
べらべらまくし立てる, spout
べらぼうに上がる, roof
ベランダ, porch, veranda
へり, hem, rim
ベリー, berry
ヘリコプター, chopper, helicopter
ヘリポート, helipad
減る, fall
ベル, bell
ベルト, belt
ベルトコンベヤー, conveyor belt
ヘルニア, hernia
ヘルニアになる, rupture
ヘルプ, help
ベルベット, velvet
ヘルメット, helmet
ヘロイン, heroin, smack
ぺろりと平らげる, gobble
弁, valve
ペン, pen
偏愛, weakness
変異形, variant
変温の, cold-blooded
変化, change, variation
変革させる, transform
変化する, mutate, vary
変化に富む, varied
変化に富んでいること, variety
変化のない, settled
変化をつける, vary
変換, conversion
変換する, convert
返還要求をする, reclaim
便器, toilet
便宜, convenience, expediency
ペンキ, paint
ペンキで書く, paint
ペンキ塗り, painting
便宜の, expedient
偏狭, bigotry
勉強, study
偏狭者, bigot
勉強する, do, study
偏狭な, insular, narrow-minded, parochial
辺境の植民地, outpost
勉強部屋, study

編曲, arrangement
編曲する, arrange
ペンキを塗る, decorate, paint
便宜を図るもの, facility
ペンギン, penguin
ペンキ屋, painter
偏屈な, bigoted
変形, variation
変形させる, deform
変形する, deform
変形部分, deformity
偏見, preconception, prejudice, slant
偏見のない, open-minded
偏見を抱かせる, prejudice
偏見を持った, prejudiced
変更, alteration
変更する, change, customize, move
弁護士, attorney, counsel, lawyer
弁護士事務所, practice
弁護する, defend, fight
弁護人, advocate
返済, payback, reimbursement, repayment
返済金, repayment
返済する, amortize, pay, reimburse, repay
弁済する, redeem
返事, answer, reply
偏した, biased
偏執症, paranoia
偏執症患者の, paranoid
偏執性の, paranoid
返事のない, unanswered
変種, mutant
編集者, editor
編集する, compile, edit
編集に関する, editorial
便所, can
返上する, surrender
変色させる, stain, weather
返事を書く, write
返事を出す, answer
変人, crank, freak, lunatic, oddity
返信切手を貼った封筒, stamped addressed envelope
ペンス, pence
編成, formation
編成する, put
変節, sell-out
弁舌, tongue
変節者, renegade
変節する, sell
変装, disguise
変装する, disguise
変速レバー, gearshift
編隊, formation
ペンタゴン, Pentagon
ペンダント, pendant
ベンチ, bench
ペンチ, pincer
ベンチャー, venture
ベンチャーキャピタリスト, venture capitalist
ベンチャーキャピタル, venture capital
片頭痛, migraine
返答, answer
弁当, box lunch
返答する, reply, respond
変動する, float, fluctuate, range
変動相場制にする, float
返答に困らされる, stump
ペントハウス, penthouse
変な, odd, strange
変に, oddly
編入する, incorporate
ペンネーム, pseudonym
便秘, constipation
便秘薬, laxative

最も, best, most, very
最も基本的な, essential
最も強力な, super
最も権威のある, definitive
最も重要な, cardinal, first, overriding, paramount, premier
最も重要なこと, matter, priority
最も重要なもの, flagship
最も少なく, least
最も優れたもの, ultimate
最も大切なもの, everything
最も近い, immediate
最も遠い地点の, far
最も遠くに, furthest
もっともな, good, natural, reasonable, valid
最も〜な, furthest
もっともなことを言う, sense
最も望ましくない, last
最も早くて, earliest
最もひどく, worst
最も目立つ位置, foreground
最もよい, best
最もよく, best
もっともらしい, plausible
もっともらしいことを言う, noise
最も悪いこと, worst
もっと良い時があった, day
もっと陽気にする, liven
もっと陽気になる, liven
もっとよく, better
もっぱら, exclusively, solely
モップ, mop
モップでふく, mop
もつれ, entanglement
もつれさせる, entangle
もつれた, entangled
もつれたもの, tangle
もてあそぶ, fool
モティーフ, motif
もてなし, hospitality
もてなす, entertain
モデム, modem
モデル, inspiration, model, template
モデル化する, model
モデルにする, model
モデルをする, model
元がとれる, money
元が取れる, pay
もどす, throw
戻す, get, reclaim, return
基づいた, founded
基づいて, by
基づかせる, base
基づく, go, ground
戻って, back
もとで, under
元通りになる, recover
基となる, inspire
もとに, under
基にことを進める, build
元に戻す, undo
元に戻せない, irreversible
もとの, old
もとの〜へ, back
元の位置に戻す, replace
元の状態に, back
もとの状態に戻って, again
元の状態へ, back
元の場所に, back
元の場所へ, back
元のままである, stand
求めて, hunt
求めに応じられる, available
求められて, welcome
求める, ask, seek
もともと, always
戻る, come, get, go, hark, restore, resume, return, revert, turn

戻ること, return
モニター, monitor
モニターする, monitor
もの, being, stuff, what
物, matter, thing
〜もの, as
もの憂い, languid
ものうげに話す, drone
物売り, vendor
〜もの多くの, many
物置, hut
物置小屋, shed
物音も立てない, peep
物思いにふけった, thoughtful
物影, form, shape
物語, narrative, story, tale
物語る, recount, telling
もの悲しい, plaintive
物悲しい, melancholy
もの悲しげな, moody
ものが二重に見える, double
ものぐさ, inertia
物乞い, panhandler
物腰, manner
物事が収まる, place
物事の成り立ち, scheme
物事をわかりにくくする, obscure
物差し, ruler
もの静かな, gentle, quiet
ものすごい, dreadful, horrendous, horrific
ものすごく, hell
ものすごくたくさんの, hell
物まね, imitation, impression
物まね上手な人, mimic
物まねをする, ape, mimic
モノラルの, mono
モノリシックな, monolithic
物分かりがよい, understanding
物を言わない, quiet
もはや, any, anymore
もはや使われていない, disused
模範, example, masterpiece, paragon
模範試合, exhibition game
模範的行動基準, law
模範的な, exemplary
模範となる, model
モビール, mobile
模倣, imitation
模倣された, patterned
模倣する, copy, mimic
〜もまた, too
もまた〜でない, either
もまた〜ない, nor
〜もまた〜ない, neither
もまれる, buffet
モミ, fir
もみくしゃにする, scrunch
もみ消し, cover-up
もみ消す, scotch
モミジ, maple
もむこと, rub
もめごと, friction
桃, peach
桃色, peach
もも肉, leg
もや, haze, mist
燃やす, burn
模様, design, print
模様替え, facelift
模様替えする, do
模様の付いた, patterned
催す, put, stage
もらす, talk
漏らす, give, leak
森, forest
盛り上がり, build-up, hump
盛り返させる, reassert
盛り込む, embody

盛りだくさんの, long
森の空き地, clearing
藻類, algae
モルタル, mortar
モルト, malt
モルヒネ, morphine
モルモット, guinea pig
漏れ口, leak
漏れた量, leakage
漏れ出る, escape
漏れる, filter, get, leak, seep
もろい, crumbly, flimsy, fragile, weak
もろくする, weaken
両刃の剣, sword
もろもろの, miscellaneous
門, gate
文句を言う, moan
門限, curfew
門戸を解放した, open-door
紋章, crest, emblem
門前払いする, door
問題, issue, matter, problem
問題がある, problematic
問題解決者, troubleshooter
問題点, question
問題の多い, troubled
問題を起こしている, trouble
問題を抱えた, disturbed
矢, arrow
やあ, hello, hey, there
やあ、こんにちわ, hi
ヤード, yard
焼いた, roast
野営場, campsite
野営する, camp
野営する人, camper
野営地, camp
矢面に立つ, brunt
野外活動, outdoors
野外で, outdoors
やがて, due, yet
やがて生まれる, unborn
やがて起こる, upcoming
やかん, kettle, teakettle
やかんいっぱい, kettle
夜間外出禁止令, curfew
夜間講座, evening class
ヤギ, goat
焼き網, grill
焼き網で焼く, grill
焼印を押す, brand
焼きぐし, spit
焼き尽くす, burn
焼肉器, broiler
やきもきする, suspense
やきもきする, fuss
やきもち, jealousy
やきもちをやいた, jealous
野球, baseball
野球場, ballpark
野球帽, baseball cap
野球ボール, baseball
ヤク, dope
役, part, role
焼く, bake, burn, incinerate, roast
約, about
約〜, near, neighborhood, rough
約一週間, week
役員会議室, boardroom
役員を務める, sit
薬学, pharmacy
やくざ, thug
薬剤, agent
薬剤師, chemist, druggist, pharmacist
役者, actor
役者業での, on-screen

約12個の, dozen
約12人の, dozen
役職, appointment
役職員の特典, perk
躍進する, shoot
訳せる, translate
薬草の, herbal
約束, appointment, commitment, engagement, promise, word
約束する, guarantee, pledge, promise, undertake
約束手形, promissory note
役立たずの, worthless
役立たないもの, nonsense
役立つ, assistance, handy, lend
約定期間, term
役に立たない, good, incompetent, ineffectual, unhelpful, use, useless
役に立つ, benefit, good, help, helpful, instrumental, serve, use, useful
役に立って, use
役人, officer
約〜の, order
薬品, agent, preparation
薬物, drug, medication
役目, role
役割, hat, role
役割を務める, play
役割を担う, come
役割を果たす, function, part, play, serve
役を演じること, portrayal
役を務める, act
役を割り当てる, cast
焼けつくような, baking, scorching
焼けつくように熱い, blistering
やけど, scald
やけどする, burn
やけどをする, scald
焼ける, bake
夜行性の, nocturnal
野菜, vegetable
優しい, fond, good, kind, nice, soft, sweet, tender
優しく声をかける, croon
優しくなでる, caress
優しさ, kindness
ヤシ, palm
やじ, jeer
やじ馬連, rabble
養う, cultivate, feed, keep, rear, support
野手, fielder
やじる, jeer
矢印, arrow
野心, ambition
野心的な, high flying
野心的に考える, big
野心のある, ambitious
安い, cheap, weak
安く売る, undercut
やすくて, apt
安酒場, joint
安っぽい, cheap, pulp, sleazy
休み, holiday, vacation
休み時間, recess
休みにして, off
休む, rest, take
休める, rest
やすやすと生みだす, hat
安らいだ, relaxed
安らかに, peacefully
安らぎ, ease
やすり, file
やすりをかける, file
野生状態で, wild
野生生物, wildlife
野生の, wild
やせ衰えた, gaunt, withered
やせ衰える, waste

SIMPLE PRESENT TENSE

A. With states, feelings, and perceptions

The simple present tense describes states, feelings, and perceptions that are true at the moment of speaking.

- The box *contains* six cans.   (state)
- Jenny *feels* tired.   (feeling)
- I *see* three stars in the sky.   (perception)

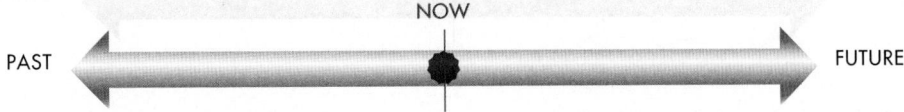

B. With situations that extend before and after the present moment

The simple present tense can also describe ongoing activities, or things that happen all the time.

- Tina *works* for a large corporation.
- She *lives* in California.
- Jim *goes* to San Francisco State College.

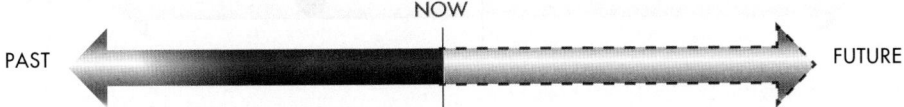

The simple present tense can also describe repeated activities that occur at regular intervals, including people's habits or customs.

- I *exercise* every morning.
- Peter usually *walks* to work.
- Anna often *cooks* dinner.

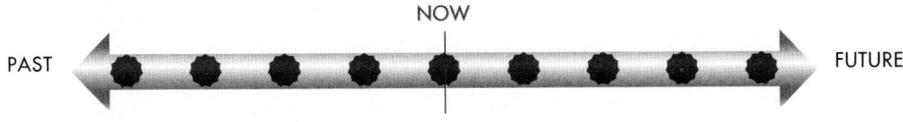

NOTE: Notice the adverbs of frequency *every morning*, *usually*, and *often* in these sentences. Other adverbs of frequency used this way include *always*, *sometimes*, *rarely*, and *never*.

C. With general facts

The simple present tense describes things that are always true.
- The Empire State Building *is* in New York City.
- The heart *pumps* blood throughout the body.
- Water *boils* at 100° Celsius.

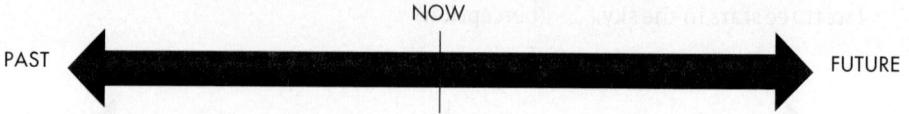

D. With future activities

The simple present tense is sometimes used to talk about scheduled events in the future.
- The train *arrives* at 8:00 tonight.
- We *leave* at 10:00 tomorrow morning.
- The new semester *begins* in September.

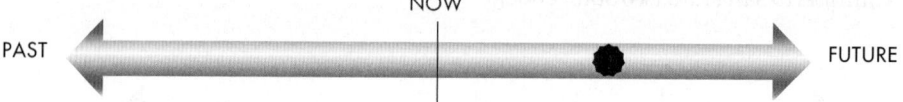

PRESENT CONTINUOUS TENSE

A. For actions that are happening right now

The present continuous tense describes an action that is happening at the moment of speaking. These activities started a short time before and will probably end in the near future.

- Ali *is watching* television right now.
- Frank and Lisa *are doing* homework in the library.
- It *is raining*.

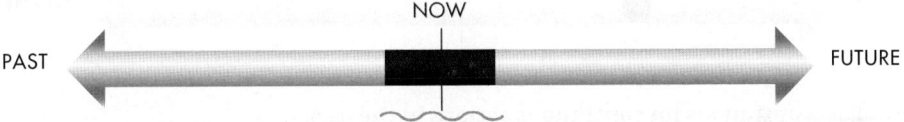

B. For ongoing activities that aren't necessarily happening at this moment

The present continuous tense can describe a continuing action that started in the past and will probably continue into the future. However, the action may not be taking place at the exact moment of speaking.

- Mr. Chong *is teaching* a Chinese cooking course.
- We *are practicing* for the soccer championships.
- My sister *is making* a quilt.

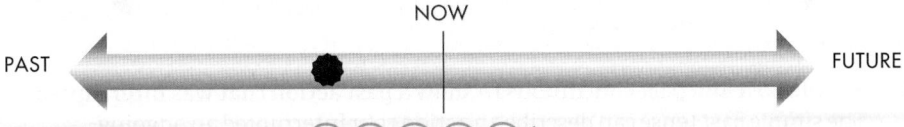

C. With situations that will happen in the future

The present continuous tense can also describe planned activities that will happen in the future.

- I *am studying* French next semester.
- We *are having* a party Friday night.
- Raquel *is taking* her driver's test on Saturday.

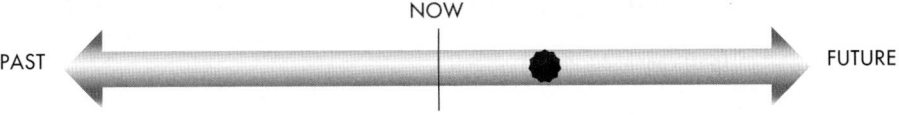

NOTE: The use of expressions like *next semester*, *Friday night*, and *on Saturday* help make it clear that the activity is planned and is not happening at the present moment, but will happen in the future.

SIMPLE PAST AND PAST CONTINUOUS

A. Simple past for one-time and repeated activities that happened in the past
The simple past tense can describe single or repeated occurrences in the past.
- I *saw* Linda at the post office yesterday.
- Alex *visited* Paris last year.
- We *played* tennis every day last summer. (repeated activity)

B. Past continuous for continuous actions in the past
The past continuous tense can describe ongoing activities that went on for a period of time in the past.
- Anna *was living* in Mexico.
- The baby *was sleeping*.
- Snow *was falling*.

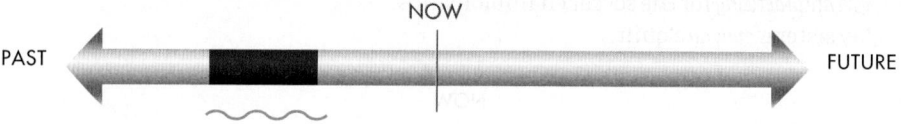

C. Simple past and past continuous to show a past action that was interrupted
The simple past tense can describe an action that interrupted an ongoing (past continuous) activity.
- I *met* Alice while I *was living* in New York.
- I *dropped* my purse while I *was crossing* the street.
- The phone *rang* while I *was studying*.

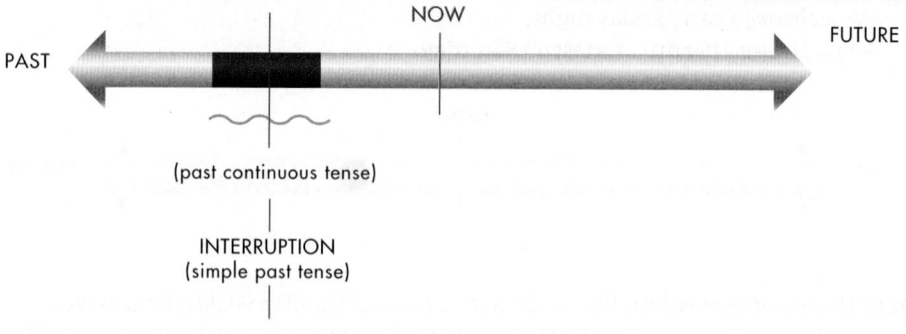

(past continuous tense)

INTERRUPTION
(simple past tense)

PRESENT PERFECT AND PRESENT PERFECT CONTINUOUS

A. Present perfect for actions or situations that started in the past and
continue in the present and possibly the future

The present perfect tense describes an action that started in the past, continues up to
the present, and may continue into the future.

- Lee *has collected* stamps for ten years.
- Carmen *has lived* in this country since 1995.
- Yukio *has played* piano since she was four years old.

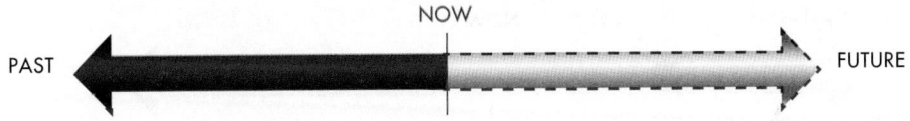

B. Present perfect for experience in general, without mentioning when
something occurred

The present perfect tense can show that something happened in the past and the
results can be seen in the present.

- We *have caught* several big fish. (they are on the table/in the boat)
- Larry *has met* my family. (they know each other)
- I *have seen* that movie twice. (I can tell you the plot)

C. Present perfect continuous for ongoing actions that started in the past and
continue in the present

The present perfect continuous tense describes an ongoing activity that went on for
a period of time in the past and is still going on.

- It *has been raining* for three days. (it's raining now)
- The baby *has been crying* for ten minutes. (she is still crying)
- We *have been waiting* for the bus since 9:00. (we're still waiting)

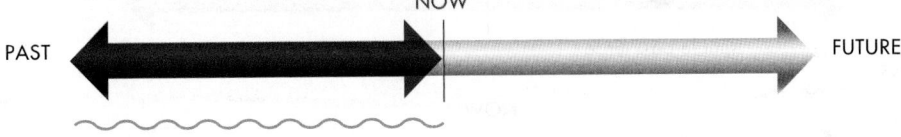

SIMPLE PAST VS. PRESENT PERFECT

A. **Simple past for situations that started and ended in the past vs. present perfect for things that started in the past but continue in the moment**
The simple past tense describes an action that started and ended in the past, while the present perfect tense describes situations that started in the past but continue up to the present and maybe into the future.

Past: John *worked* as a waiter for two years when he was in college.
Present perfect: Carol *has worked* as an engineer since 1998.

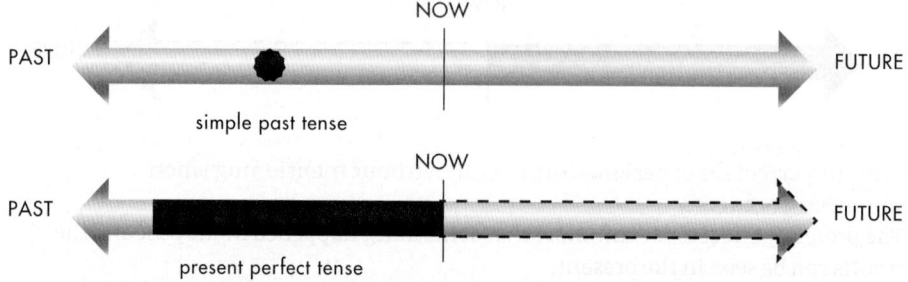

B. **Simple past to emphasize when something happened vs. present perfect to emphasize that something happened, without indicating when**
The simple past emphasizes when something happened, and the present perfect emphasizes its impact on the present.

Past: Peter *graduated* from college in 2001. (at a known point in the past: 2001)
Present perfect: Alice *has graduated* from college, and is working in the city. (exactly when is unknown)

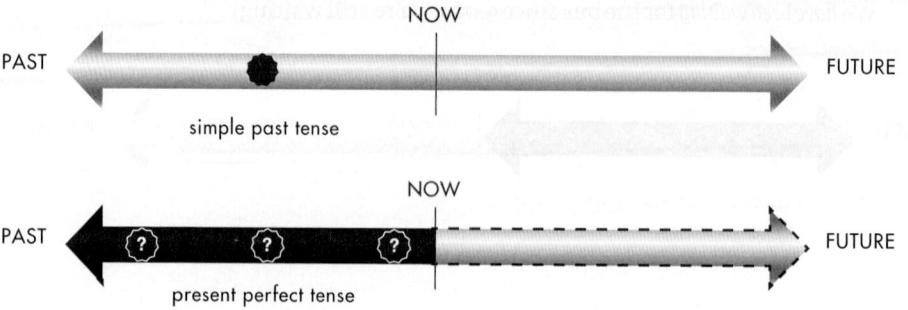

SIMPLE PAST, PAST PERFECT, AND PAST PERFECT CONTINUOUS

A. Past and past perfect tenses with an activity that occurred before another activity in the past

Two simple past tenses are used to show a sequence of events in the past.

Simple past + simple past: Ali *said* goodbye before he *left*.

                                 I *closed* the door and then *locked* it.

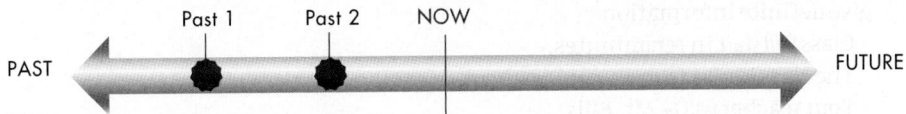

B. Past perfect continuous and simple past for a continuous activity that occurred before another event in the past

The past perfect continuous tense followed by the simple past tense shows that an ongoing activity in the past came before another past event.

- We *had been waiting* for two hours when the bus finally *arrived*.
- I *had been thinking* about the problem for days when the answer suddenly *occurred* to me.
- Terry *had been hoping* for the answer that he *got*.

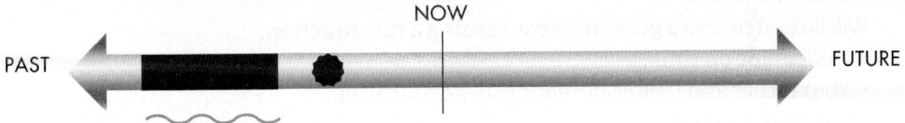

FUTURE WITH *will* AND *going to*

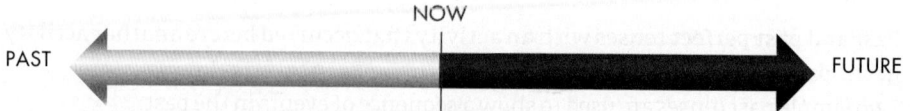

A. *Will* or *going to* **for simple facts**
Either *will* or *going to* can be used to give information about the future. *Will* is used to give definite information.
- Class *will start* in ten minutes.
- The class *is going* to use a new textbook.
- Your teacher *will be* Mr. Ellis.
- There *is going to* be a final exam.

B. *Will* or *going to* **for prediction**
Either *will* or *going to* can be used to describe things that are likely to happen in the future. *Will* is used when there is evidence that things are likely to happen.
- It *will rain* this afternoon.
- You *are going to love* that movie!
- They *are going to study* a lot the night before the exam.
- They *will* probably *stay up* all night.

C. *Will* **for promises**
Will is used to give a guarantee concerning a future action.
- I *will be there* on time.
- Your father and I *will pay for* your college education.
- I *won't tell* anyone.
- I *will save* you a seat.

D. *Will* **for decisions made at the time of speaking**
Will is used for decisions made at the time of speaking.
- I *will help* you with your homework.
- We're out of milk. I*'ll go* to the store on my way home.
- I can't talk right now, but I*'ll call* you later.
- Danny *will be* happy to wash your car.

MODALS *can*, *should/ought to*, *must*, AND *have to*

A. *Can* and *can't* **for ability, permission, and requests**
Can and *can't* are used to:
- make statements about things people are and are not able to do.
- describe what people are allowed or not allowed to do.
- make requests.

Can/can't **for ability:**   Alan *can swim* very well.
I *can't run* very fast.

Can/can't **for permission:**   You *can leave* whenever you want.
We *can't use* our dictionaries during the test.

Can/can't **for requests:**   *Can* I borrow your laptop?
Can't you turn down the TV?

B. *Should* and *ought to* **for advice and warnings**
Should and *ought to* are used to tell people what to do or what to avoid doing.

Should/shouldn't **for advice/warnings:**   What *should* I *do*?
You *should ask* questions in class.
You *shouldn't drive* so fast.

Ought to **for advice/warnings:**   You *ought to save* more money.
He *ought to buy* some new clothes.

NOTE: *Ought to* is almost never used in questions or negative statements.
~~Ought I to go?~~   ~~You ought not see that movie.~~

C. *Must* and *mustn't* **for rules and laws**
Must and *mustn't* are used in formal situations to show that something is necessary or prohibited.

Must **for necessity:**   My doctor told me that I *must lose* weight.

Must **for obligation:**   Swimmers *must shower* before entering the pool.

Mustn't **for prohibition:**   You *mustn't be* late to class.

Must and *mustn't* are not always opposites. *Needn't* (*need not*) expresses a lack of obligation to do something, whereas *mustn't* expresses an obligation not to do something.

D. *Have to* and *don't have to* **for personal obligations**
Have to and *don't have to* are used in informal or personal situations to show that something is necessary or not necessary.

Have to **for necessity:**   I *have to call* my mother tonight.
We *have to remember* to buy Jimmy a birthday present.

Don't/doesn't have to **for lack of necessity:**
You *don't have to return* the pen. You can keep it.
Grandpa *doesn't have to comb* his hair. He doesn't have any.

1347

MODALS *may*, *might*, *could*, AND *would*

A. *May* and *might* to discuss possibility and permission

May and *might* are used to describe future possibilities. *May* is used to give permission in formal situations.

May for possibility: We're not sure yet, but we *may leave* tomorrow.

The weather *may not be* good this weekend.

Might for possibility: I *might fly* to Florida this weekend, but I probably won't.

We both *might get* 100 on the test.

NOTE: Sentences with *might* are less definite than sentences with *may*.

May for permission: *May I call* you Jimmy?

You *may turn in* your paper Monday if it's not ready today.

No, you *may not have* my telephone number.

Might for permission: I wonder if I *might leave* early.

When *might* I *need* to see the doctor again?

NOTE: *Can* also works in these sentences, but *may* is more polite and formal. Sentences with *might* are often indirect questions.

B. *Could* to show possibility, past ability, and to make requests

Could is used to indicate future possibilities, past abilities, and to ask for things.

Could for future possibilities: The dog *could have* six or seven puppies.

The movie *could make* a million dollars if it's really popular.

Could for past ability: When I was six, I *could* already *speak* two languages.

Tina *could walk* when she was only eight months old.

Could for requests: *Could* you *give* me the remote control?

Could I *have* another cookie?

C. *Would* to ask permission and to make requests

Would is used to request permission and to ask for things.

Would to ask permission: *Would* you *mind* if I asked your age?

Would he *mind* if I borrowed his book?

Would to make requests: *Would* you *give* me a ride home?

I *would like* two tickets for the 7:00 show.

Used to

A. *Used to* **for statements and questions about past habits or customs**
Used to shows that something that was true in the past is no longer true.

- Years ago, children *used to be* more polite.
- I *used to hate* broccoli, but now I like it.
- Children *didn't use to have* TVs in their bedrooms.
- Did girls *use to play* on high school football teams?

NOTE: When using the negative and question forms with *used to*, drop the past tense *-d* from the word *used*.

B. *Used to* **for repeated past events**
Used to also shows that something that happened regularly in the past no longer does.

- We *used to go* to the movies every Friday night.
- Taylor *used to visit* his grandmother every Sunday.
- I didn't *use to sleep* late on Saturday, but now I do.
- Did you *use to walk* home every day?

C. *Be used to* **for statements and questions about things people have become accustomed to**
Be used to statements and questions discuss how strange or normal something feels.

- Gail has lived in Chicago and New York. She is *used to living* in big cities.
- I have six brothers and sisters. I *am used to sharing* everything with them.
- Pete *isn't used to doing* homework every night.
- *Are* you *used to* drinking black coffee yet?

NOTE: When using the negative and question forms with *be used to*, don't drop the past tense *-d* from the word *used*.

D. *Get used to* **for statements and questions about becoming accustomed to something new**
Get used to statements and questions focus on the process of becoming accustomed to something.

- After three weeks, I *got used to* the noise outside my apartment.
- I *am getting used to* living with three roommates.

NOTE: The negative form of *get used to* usually employs the modal *can't* or *couldn't*.
    I *can't get used to* getting up at 6:00 AM.
    Ellen *couldn't get used to* the cold weather in Chicago.

CONDITIONALS

A. Unreal conditions in the present
To describe a conditional situation that is unlikely to happen, use a past form in the conditional clause and the modal *would* or *could* in the main clause.

Conditional clause	Main clause
If I *had* enough money,	I *would buy* a boat.
If we *went* to Paris,	we *could visit* the Eiffel Tower.
If the traffic *got* any worse,	I *wouldn't drive* my car every day.
If Shelia *knew* the answer,	she *would tell* us.

B. Possible conditions in the future
To describe a conditional situation that is likely to happen, use a present form in the conditional clause and the future with *will* or the modal *can* in the main clause.

Conditional clause	Main clause
If I *have* enough money,	I *will buy* a boat.
If we *go* to Paris,	we *can visit* the Eiffel Tower.
If the traffic *gets* any worse,	I *won't drive* my car every day.
If Shelia *knows* the answer,	she *will tell* us.

C. Unreal conditions in the past
To describe a situation from a future point of view, use the past perfect in the conditional clause and *would have* + the past participle in the main clause.

Conditional clause	Main clause
If we *had known* it was raining,	we *would have taken* our umbrellas.
If Roberto *had been* home,	he *would have answered* the phone.
If you *had known* my grandmother,	you *would have loved* her.
If the movie *hadn't been* boring,	I *wouldn't have fallen* asleep.

D. Unreal conditions in the present
When discussing unreal conditions, the *if* clause is sometimes not stated; it is implied.

Conditional statement or question	Implied statement
I *would* never *borrow* money from a friend.	(if I had the opportunity)
Would you *want* to visit the moon?	(if you had the chance)
That *wouldn't work*.	(if you tried it)
Would he *borrow* your car without telling you?	(if he had the opportunity)

PASSIVE VOICE

A. Passive statements and questions with *be* + past participle

The passive voice is used when it is not important (or we don't know) who performs the action. The passive can be used with any tense as well as with modals.

Sentence with passive voice	Verb form
The winner *was chosen* last night.	past tense
New cures *are being discovered* every day.	present continuous
Will the renovations *be finished* by next week?	future
Aspirin *should be taken* with a full glass of water.	modal *should*

B. Passives with an agent

To put the emphasis on the subject of the sentence and also tell who performed the action, use *by* followed by the agent at the end of the sentence.

- The missing girl was finally found *by her older brother*.
- The theory of relativity was discovered *by Albert Einstein*.
- The modern movie camera was invented *by Thomas Edison*.

C. Passives with *get*

In everyday speech, *get* instead of *be* is often used to form the passive. The verb *do* (instead of the verb *be*) is used for questions and negatives with the *get* passive.

- Most hourly workers *get paid* on Thursday or Friday.
- I *got caught* going 40 miles per hour in a 25 mile per hour zone.
- *Did* anyone *get killed* in the accident?
- Roger *didn't get hired* for the job.

REPORTED SPEECH

A. Shifting verb tenses in reported speech

When reporting someone's exact words, the verb in the noun clause usually moves back one tense. Only the past perfect tense remains the same in reported speech.

Exact quote	Reported speech	Change in verb tense
I *am* tired.	He said that he *was* tired.	Simple present to simple past
We *are waiting.*	They told me that they *were waiting.*	Present continuous to past continuous
I *finished* the book last night.	She said that she *had finished* the book the night before.	Simple past to past perfect
We *are enjoying* the good weather.	They reported that they *were enjoying* the good weather.	Past continuous to past perfect continuous
I *have lived* here for two years.	He added that he *had lived* here for two years.	Present perfect to past perfect
We *had eaten* breakfast before we left the house.	They said that they *had eaten* breakfast before they left the house.	Past perfect remains the same

B. Shifting modals in reported speech

Many modals change form in reported speech.

Exact quote	Reported speech	Change in modal form
I *can speak* French.	She said that she *could speak* French.	*Can* to *could*
We *may need* help.	They said that they *might need* help.	*May* (for possibility) to *might*
You *may use* my pencil.	She said that I *could use* her pencil.	*May* (for permission) to *could*
I *must make* a phone call.	He said that he *had to make* a phone call.	*Must* to *had to*
We *will help* you.	They said that they *would help* me.	*Will* to *would*
I *should stop* smoking.	He said that he *should stop* smoking.	*Should* (no change)
We *should have left* at 9:00.	They said that they *should have left* at 9:00.	*Should have* (no change)
I *could have saved* money with a coupon.	She said that she *could have saved* money with a coupon.	*Could have* (no change)
She *must have gone* to bed early.	He said that she *must have gone* to bed early.	*Must have* (no change)

C. *Say* vs. *tell* in reported speech

The passive voice is used when it is not important (or we don't know) who performs the action. The passive can be used with any tense as well as with modals.

- When using *say* with reported speech, an object is not required. (Other verbs that work this way are *add*, *answer*, *explain*, and *reply*.)
- When using *tell* with reported speech, there is always a direct object. (Other verbs that work this way are *inform*, *notify*, *remind*, and *promise*.)

Exact quote	Reported speech	Direct object
It is raining.	He *said* that it was raining.	No
I was late to class.	She *explained* that she had been late to class.	No
I bought a camera at the mall.	He *told me* that he had bought a camera at the mall.	Yes
There is a test on Friday.	She *informed the students* that there was a test on Friday.	Yes

COMPARATIVES AND SUPERLATIVES

Comparatives and superlatives have several different forms.

A. With one-syllable adjectives and adverbs

Add -*er* or -*est*.

Adjective / Adverb	Comparative / superlative form	Example
cold	colder	December is *colder* than November.
hard	harder	The wind blows *harder* in winter than in summer.
short	shortest	December 21 is *the shortest* day of the year.
fast	fastest	Summer passes *the fastest* of any season.

B. With two-syllable adjectives ending in -*y*

Change the -*y* to -*i* and add -*er* or -*est*.

Adjective / Adverb	Comparative / superlative form	Example
easy	easier	Yesterday's assignment was *easier* than today's.
busy	busiest	This is the *busiest* shopping day of the year.

C. With most adjectives of two or more syllables not ending in -y

Use *more* + adjective for comparatives and *the most* + adjective for superlatives.

Adjective / Adverb	Comparative / superlative form	Example
famous	more famous	Amy's Pizza is *more famous* than Bennie's Pizza.
frequent	most frequent	Amy's has the *most frequent* specials of any pizzeria.
expensive	more expensive	Bennie's pizza is *more expensive* than Amy's.
delicious	most delicious	Bennie's makes the *most delicious* pizza in town.

D. Irregular comparatives and superlatives

Some adjectives and superlatives have irregular forms.

Adjective / Adverb	Comparative / superlative form	Example
bad	worse, worst	SUVs have *worse* safety records than sedans.
good	better, best	Sedans drive *better* than SUVs.
much	more, most	An SUV can carry *the most* people.
far	farther, farthest	A sedan can go *the farthest* on a tank of gas.

E. Comparisons with *as...as*

Use *as...as* + adjective or adverb to describe things that are equal, and *not as...as* + adjective or adverb to describe inequalities.

Adjective	Algebra was *as difficult as* geometry for me.
Adjective with negative	However, geometry wasn't *as interesting as* algebra.
Adverb	I worked *as hard as* anyone else, but I got a C in algebra.
Adverb with negative	I didn't do *as well as* many other students.

INFINITIVES AND GERUNDS

A verb (or sometimes an adjective) near the beginning of a sentence determines whether a second verb form should be an infinitive or a gerund. Below are lists of some common main verbs (and adjectives) and the type of verb form that follows each.

NOTE: Each list contains several high-frequency items, but the lists are not comprehensive.

A. **Verb + infinitive**
   These verbs are followed by an infinitive, not a gerund: *ask, attempt, begin, decide, expect, hope, like, plan, promise, start.*
   I *attempted* <u>to start</u> the car.
   They *decided* <u>to stay</u> home last night.
   We *hope* <u>to save</u> at least $1000 by the end of the year.

   WRONG: She plans ~~giving~~ a party this weekend.

B. **Causatives + infinitives**
   When a person causes something to happen, the causative verb is followed by a direct object plus an infinitive, not a gerund. These causative verbs are followed by an infinitive: *allow, convince, encourage, get, force, persuade, require.*
   We *convinced* the teacher <u>to postpone</u> the test until Monday.
   The teacher *encouraged* us <u>to study</u> over the weekend.
   I *got* my brother <u>to help</u> me with the grammar.

   WRONG: The teacher required us ~~leaving~~ our dictionaries at home.

C. **Verb + gerund**
   These verbs are followed by a gerund, not an infinitive: *avoid, discuss, dislike, enjoy, finish, imagine, practice, quit, recommend, suggest.*
   The couple *discussed* <u>having</u> another child.
   The children *enjoy* <u>going</u> to the park.
   The couple *can't imagine* <u>having</u> four children.

   WRONG: They avoided ~~to talk~~ about it for a few days.

D. **Preposition + infinitive and preposition + gerund**
   An infinitive is the preposition *to* and the base of a verb: *to speak.* Gerunds can be used with other prepositions such as *about, at, for, in, of,* and *on.*
   I want *to go* on vacation in August.
   I never even think *about* <u>swimming</u> in the winter.
   This organization plans *on* <u>having</u> a fundraising drive.

   WRONG: They are responsible for ~~help~~ thousands of animals.
              The guests are sorry to ~~leaving~~ the party so early.

PUNCTUATION

Apostrophe

- The apostrophe + s is used with singular and plural nouns to show possession.

  Jim's computer   the children's toys

  my boss' file   the Smiths' house [Only the apostrophe is needed when
                        a word ends in s.]

- The apostrophe + s is used to show ownership.

  Pedro and Ana's CDs [The 's on the second name shows they own the CDs together.]

  Pedro's and Ana's hats [The 's on both names shows they each own different hats.]

- The apostrophe is used in contractions.

  I'm (= I am)   they'll (= they will)

Brackets

- Brackets are used to add your own information in quoted material.

  Jason said, "This is a good time [meaning today] for us to start looking for a new apartment."

- Brackets with three dots are used when you omit words from a quotation.

  Jason said, "This is a good time [. . .] for a new apartment."

Colon

- The colon is used with clock time.

  11:30   9:45

- The colon is used to introduce a list.

  Jean enjoys all kinds of physical activity: hiking, playing tennis, and even cleaning house.

- The colon is used in the salutation of a business letter.

  Dear Ms. Mansfield:

Comma

- Commas are used with dates and addresses.

  Monday, December 1, 1964   16 Terhune Street, Teaneck, NJ 07666

- Commas are used after introductory phrases or clauses.

  After finishing school, she joined the Navy.

- Commas are used to set off items in a series.

  They served pizza, pasta, lasagna, and salad at the party.

- Commas are used to set off added information in nonrestrictive phrases or clauses.

  Mr. Karas, my sister's teacher, comes from Greece.

  Rita, who almost never misses class, is absent today.

- Commas are used in the salutation in informal correspondence and at the close of a letter.

  Dear Grace,   Sincerely yours,

Dash

- Dashes are used instead of commas when the added information contains commas.

  The school offers several math courses—algebra, geometry, and trigonometry—as well as a wide variety of science classes.

Exclamation Point

- An exclamation point is used after a word or group of words to show strong feeling.

  Stop! Don't run over that cat!

Hyphen

- Hyphens appear in compound words or numbers.

  mother-in-law   twenty-one

- Hyphens are used to divide words at the end of a line.

  After Mrs. Leander finished exploring all her options, she de-cided the best plan was to return home and start out tomorrow.

Parentheses

- Parentheses are used with nonessential information and with numbers and letters in lists.

  We left the party (which started at 7:00 P.M.) sometime after midnight.

  My requirements are (1) a room with a view and (2) a working air conditioner.

Period

- A period is used at the end of any sentence that is not a question or an exclamation.

  Rutgers University offers a wide variety of social science courses.

- A period is used after many abbreviations.

  Mr.   etc.   P.M.   Jr.   i.e.

Question Mark

- A question mark is used after a word or sentence that asks a question.

  What?   Did you say you don't have a ride home?

Quotation Marks

- Quotation marks are used to set off a direct quotation but not an indirect quotation.

  Smithers said, "Homer, you must go home now."
  Smithers said Homer must go home.

- Quotation marks are used with the titles of short written material such as poems, short stories, chapters in books, songs, and magazine articles.

  My favorite poem is "A Spider Sewed at Night" by Emily Dickinson.

Semicolon

- The semicolon is used to link independent clauses when there is no coordinating conjunction (such as *and, but, or, nor,* or *for*) between them.

  Some people like country music; some people don't.

- The semicolon is also used to link independent clauses before a conjunctive adverb (such as *however, furthermore*).

  Some people like country music; however, other people dislike it intensely.

Slash

- The slash separates alternatives.

  and/or

- The slash divides numbers in dates, and divides numerators and denominators in fractions.

  the memorable date 9/11/01   Ten and 50/100 dollars

- The slash is used when quoting lines of poetry to show where each line ends.

  My favorite lines from this poem are, "She slept beneath a tree / remembered but by me."

CAPITALIZATION

Capitalize proper nouns and proper adjectives.

- Main words in titles: Gone with the Wind
- People: John Lennon, Pélé
- Cities, nations, states, nationalities, and languages: Istanbul, Turkey, California, Brazil, American, Spanish
- Geographical items: Mekong River, Mount Olympus, Central Park
- Companies and organizations: Ford Motor Company, Harvard University, National Organization for Women
- Departments and government offices: English Department, Internal Revenue Service
- Buildings: the Empire State Building
- Trademarked products: Kleenex tissue, Scotch tape
- Days, months, and holidays: Tuesday, January, Ramadan
- Some abbreviations without periods: AT&T, UN, YMCA
- Religions and related words: Hindu, Bible, Muslim
- Historical periods, events, and documents: Civil War, Declaration of Independence
- Titles of people: Senator Clinton, President Lincoln, Ms. Tanaka, Dr. Lee
- Titles of printed matter: *Collins COBUILD Advanced Dictionary of American English, English/Japanese*

ITALICIZATION

In handwritten or typed copy, italics are shown by underlining.

Use italics for the following types of material.

- Words or phrases you wish to emphasize.

  Is this *really* your first time in an airplane?

  She feeds her dog *T-bone* steak. [It's best not to use italics for emphasis very often.]

- A publication that is not part of a larger publication.
    The Daily News (newspaper)
    The Sun Also Rises (book)
    Newsweek (magazine)
    Titanic (movie)

- Foreign words in an English sentence.
    The first four numbers in Turkish are *bir, iki, üc, dört.*
    The French have a saying: *Plus ça change . . .*

- Letters used in algebraic equations.
    $E = mc^2$

SPELLING
Frequently Misspelled Words
People sometimes confuse the spelling of the following words:

accept, except	conscience, conscious	lay, lie
access, excess	council, counsel	lead, led
advice, advise	diary, dairy	lessen, lesson
affect, effect	decent, descent, dissent	lightning, lightening
aisles, isles	desert, dessert	lose, loose
alley, ally	device, devise	marital, martial
already, all ready	discreet, discrete	maybe, may be
altar, alter	dyeing, dying	miner, minor
altogether, all together	elicit, illicit	moral, morale
always, all ways	emigrate, immigrate	of, off
amoral, immoral	envelop, envelope	passed, past
angel, angle	fair, fare	patience, patients
ask, ax	faze, phase	peace, piece
assistance, assistants	fine, find	personal, personnel
baring, barring, bearing	formerly, formally	plain, plane
began, begin	forth, fourth	pray, prey
believe, belief	forward, foreword	precede, proceed
board, bored	gorilla, guerrilla	presence, presents
break, brake	have, of	principle, principal
breath, breathe	hear, here	prophecy, prophesy
buy, by, bye	heard, herd	purpose, propose
capital, capitol	heroin, heroine	quiet, quit, quite
censor, censure, sensor	hole, whole	raise, rise
choose, chose	holy, wholly	respectfully, respectively
cite, site, sight	horse, hoarse	right, rite, write
clothes, cloths	human, humane	road, rode
coarse, course	its, it's	sat, set
complement, compliment	later, latter	sense, since

shown, shone	throne, thrown	were, wear, where, we're
stationary, stationery	to, too, two	which, witch
straight, strait	tract, track	who's, whose
than, then	waist, waste	your, you're
their, there, they're, there're	weak, week	
threw, through, thorough	weather, whether	

NOTE: The following summary will answer many spelling questions. However, there are many more rules and also many exceptions. Always check your dictionary if in doubt.

Ei and *ie*

There is an old saying that says: "I before *e*, except after *c*, or when pronounced like *ay* as in *neighbor* and *weigh*."
- I before *e*: br**ie**f, n**ie**ce, f**ie**rce
- E before *i* after the letter *c*: rec**ei**ve, conc**ei**t, c**ei**ling
- E before *i* when pronounced like *ay*: **ei**ght, w**ei**ght, th**ei**r

Prefixes

A prefix changes the meaning of a word but no letters are added or dropped.
- usual, **un**usual
- interested, **dis**interested
- use, **re**use

Suffixes
- Drop the final *e* on the base word when a suffix beginning with a vowel is added.
  drive, driv**ing**   combine, combin**ation**
- Keep the silent *e* on the base word when a suffix beginning with a consonant is added.
  live, live**ly**   safe, safe**ly** [Exceptions: truly, ninth]
- If the base word (1) ends in a final consonant, (2) is a one-syllable word or a stressed syllable, and (3) the final consonant is preceded by a vowel, double the final consonant.
  hit, hi**tt**ing   drop, dro**pp**ing
- Change a final *y* on a base word to *i* when adding any suffix except *-ing*.
  day, da**i**ly   try, tr**i**ed   BUT: play, play**ing**

GRAMMAR
Conjunctions
Conjunctions are words that connect words, phrases, or clauses.

Coordinating Conjunctions
The coordinating conjunctions are: *and, but, for, nor, or, so, yet*

- Sarah **and** Michael
- on vacation **for** three weeks
- You can borrow the book from a library **or** you can buy it at a bookstore.

Correlative Conjunctions

Correlative conjunctions are used in pairs.

The correlative conjunctions are: *both ... and, either ... or, neither ... nor, not only ... but also, whether ... or*

- **Neither** Sam **nor** Madeleine could attend the party.
- The singer was **both** out of tune **and** too loud.
- Oscar **not only** ate too much, **but also** fell asleep at the table.

Subordinating Conjunctions

Subordinating conjunctions are used to connect a subordinate clause to a main clause.

- Antonia sighed loudly **as if** she were really exhausted.
- Uri arrived late **because** his car broke down.

Here is a list of subordinating conjunctions:

after	before	no matter how	than	where
although	even if	now that	though	wherever
as far as	even though	once	till	whether
as if	how	provided that	unless	while
as soon as	if	since	until	why
as though	in as much as	so that	when	
because	in case	supposing that	whenever	

Conjunctive Adverbs

Two independent clauses can be connected using a semicolon, plus a conjunctive adverb and a comma. The conjunctive adverb often comes right after the semicolon.

- Kham wanted to buy a car; **however,** he hadn't saved up enough money.
- Larry didn't go right home; **instead,** he stopped at the health club.

Some conjunctive adverbs can appear in different positions in the second clause.

- Kham wanted to buy a car; he hadn't, **however,** saved up enough money.
- Larry didn't go right home; he stopped at the health club **instead.**

Here is a list of conjunctive adverbs:

also	finally	indeed	nevertheless	then
anyhow	furthermore	instead	next	therefore
anyway	hence	likewise	otherwise	thus
besides	however	meanwhile	similarly	
consequently	incidentally	moreover	still	

Transitional Phrases

If all the sentences in a passage begin with subject + verb, the effect can be boring. To add variety, use a transitional phrase, followed by a comma, at the beginning of some sentences.

- Rita needed to study for the test. **On the other hand,** she didn't want to miss the party.
- Yuki stayed up all night studying. **As a result,** he overslept and missed the test.

Here is a list of transitional phrases:

after all	for example
as a result	in addition
at any rate	in fact
at the same time	in other words
by the way	on the contrary
even so	on the other hand

Common Prepositions

A preposition describes a relationship to another part of speech; it is usually used before a noun or pronoun.

- Sancho was waiting **outside** the club.
- I gave the money **to** him.

Here is a list of common prepositions:

about	by	out
above	concerning	outside
across	despite	over
after	during	past
against	down	regarding
among	except	round
around	for	since
as	from	through
at	in	to
before	inside	toward
behind	into	under
below	lie	unlike
beneath	near	until
beside	of	up
between	off	upon
beyond	on	with

Phrasal Prepositions

Here is a list of phrasal prepositions:

according to	by way of	in spite of
along with	due to	instead of
apart from	except for	on account of
as for	in addition to	out of
as regards	in case of	up to
as to	in front of	with reference to
because of	in lieu of	with regard to
by means of	in place of	with respect to
by reason of	in regard to	with the exception of

DOCUMENTATION

College instructors usually require one of three formats (APA, Chicago, or MLA) to document the information you use in research papers and essays. The following pages compare and contrast the highlights of these three styles.

APA Style (American Psychological Association style)

1. General Endnote Format

   Title the page "References." Double-space the page and arrange the names alphabetically by authors' last names, the date in parentheses, followed by the rest of the information about the publication.

2. Citation for a Single Author

   Moore, (1992). *The care of the soul*. New York: HarperPerennial.

3. Citation for Multiple Authors

   List the last names first followed by initials and use the "&" sign before the last author.

   Spinosa, C., Flores, F., & Dreyfus, H.L. (1997). *Disclosing new worlds: Entrepreneurship, democratic action, and the cultivation of solidarity*. Cambridge, MA: MIT Press.

4. Citation for an Editor as Author

   Wellwood, J. (Ed.). (1992). *Ordinary magic: Everyday life as a spiritual path*. Boston: Shambhala Publications.

5. Citation for an Article in a Periodical

   List the author, last name first, the year and month (and day if applicable) of the publication. Then list the title of the article (not underlined), the name of the publication (followed by the volume number if there is one) and the page number or numbers.

   Gibson, S. (2001, November). Hanging wallpaper. *This Old House*, 77.

6. Citation of Online Materials

   Provide enough information so that readers can find the information you refer to. Try to include the date on the posting, the title, the original print source (if any), a description of where you found the information, and the date you found the material.

   Arnold, W. (April 26, 2002). "State senate announces new tax relief." *Seattle Post-Intelligencer*. Retrieved May 1, 2002, from http://seattle.pi.nwsource.com/printer2/index.asp?ploc=b

7. General In-text Citation Format

   Include two pieces of information: the last name of the author or authors of the work cited in the References and the year of publication.
   (Moore, 1992).

Chicago Style (from *The Chicago Manual of Style*)

1. General Endnote Format

   Title the page "Notes." Double-space the page. Number and indent the first line of each entry. Use full author's names, not initials. Include page references at the end of the entry.

2. Citation for a Single Author

   Thomas Moore, *The Care of the Soul* (New York: HarperPerennial, 1992), 7–9.

3. Citation for Multiple Authors

   Charles Spinosa, Ferdinand Flores, and Hubert L. Dreyfus, *Disclosing New Worlds: Entrepreneurship, Democratic Action, and the Cultivation of Solidarity* (Cambridge: MIT Press, 1997), 66.

4. Citation for an Editor as Author

   John Wellwood, ed. 1992. *Ordinary Magic: Everyday Life as Spiritual Path* (Boston: Shambhala Publications).

5. Citation for an Article in a Periodical

   List the author, last name first. Then put the title of the article in quotation marks, the name of the publication, the volume number (if one is given), the month, and the page number or numbers.

   Gibson, Stephen, "Hanging Wallpaper," *This Old House* 53 (2001): 77.

6. Citation of Online Materials

   Number and indent each entry and provide enough information so that readers can find the information you refer to. Try to include the author (first name first), the date on the posting (in parentheses), the title, the original print source (if any), a description of where you found the information, the URL, and the date you found the material (in parentheses).

1. William Arnold, "State Senate Announces New Tax Relief, "*Seattle Post-Intelligencer*, April 26, 2002, http://seattle.pi.nwsource.com/printer2/index.asp?ploc=b

7. General In-text Citation Format

Number all in-text notes. The first time you cite a work within the text, use all the information as shown in 2. above. When citing the same work again, include only the last name of the author or authors and the page or pages you refer to.

(Moore, 8)

MLA Style (Modern Language Association style)

1. General Endnote Format

Title the page "Works Cited." Double-space the page and arrange the names alphabetically by authors' last names, followed by the rest of the information about the publication as shown below.

2. Citation for a Single Author

Moore, Thomas. *The Care of the Soul*. New York: HarperPerennial, 1992.

3. Citation for Multiple Authors

List the first author's names in the same order as on the title page. List only the first author's last name first.

Spinosa, Charles, Ferdinand Flores, and Hubert L. Dreyfus. *Disclosing New Worlds: Entrepreneurship, Democratic Action, and the Cultivation of Solidarity*. Cambridge: MIT, 1997.

4. Citation for an Editor as Author

Wellwood, John, ed. *Ordinary Magic: Everyday Life as Spiritual Path*. Boston; Shambhala, 1992.

5. Citation for an Article in a Periodical

List the author (last name first), the title of the article (using quotation marks), the title of the magazine (with no period), the volume number, the date (followed by a colon), and the page number.

Gibson, Stephen. "Hanging Wallpaper." *This Old House* 53 (2001): 77.

6. Citation of On-line Materials

Provide enough information so that readers can find the information you refer to. Try to include the date on the information, the title, the original print source (if any), the date you found the material, and the URL (if possible).

Arnold, William. "State Senate Announces New Tax Relief. "*Seattle Post-Intelligencer* 26 Apr. 2002 http://seattle.pi.nwsource.com/printer2/index.asp?ploc=b

7. General In-text Citation Format

Do not number entries. When citing a work listed in the "Works Cited" section, include only the last name of the author or authors and the page or pages you refer to. (Moore 7-8)

BLOCK LETTER FORMAT

Using the block letter format, there are no indented lines.

Return address	77 Lincoln Avenue Wellesley, MA 02480
Date	May 10, 2008
Inside address	Dr. Rita Bennett Midland Hospital Senior Care Center 5000 Poe Avenue Dayton, OH 45414
Salutation	Dear Dr. Bennett:
Body of the letter	I am responding to your advertisement for a dietitian in the May 5 edition of the *New York Times*. I graduated from Boston University two years ago. Since graduation, I have been working at Brigham and Women's Hospital and have also earned additional certificates in nutritional support and diabetes education. I am interested in locating to the Midwest and will be happy to arrange for an interview at your convenience.
Complimentary close	Sincerely,
Signature	*Daniel Chin*
Typed name	Daniel Chin

INDENTED LETTER FORMAT

Using the indented format, the return address, the date, and the closing appear at the far right side of the paper. The first line of each paragraph is also indented.

Return address

77 Lincoln Avenue
Wellesley, MA 02480

Date

May 15, 2008

Inside address

Dr. Rita Bennett
Senior Care Center
5000 Poe Avenue
Dayton, OH 45414

Salutation

Dear Dr. Bennett:

Body of the letter

It was a pleasure to meet you and learn more about the programs offered at the Senior Care Center. I appreciate your taking time out to show me around and introduce me to the staff.

I am excited about the possibility of working at the Senior Care Center and I look forward to talking with you again soon.

Complimentary close

Sincerely,

Signature

Daniel Chin

Typed name

Daniel Chin

RESUMES
Successful resume strategies
- **Length:** One page
- **Honesty:** Never say something that is untrue
- **Inclusiveness:** Include information about your experience and qualifications. You do not have to include your age, religion, marital status, race, or citizenship. It is not necessary to include a photo.

Heading
Include name, address, e-mail, and phone number.

Objective
Include your goals or skills or both.

Skills
Include any skills that you have that may be helpful in the job that you are applying for.

Experience
Describe the jobs you've held. Include your accomplishments and awards. Use positive, action-oriented words with strong verbs. Use present-tense verbs for your current job and past-tense verbs for jobs you've had in the past. Include the job titles that you've held.

Education
Include schools attended. If you are a college graduate, don't include high school. List degrees with most recent first.

Interests
This is not required, but can help a potential employer see you as a well-rounded person.

Sample Resume

There are several different acceptable resume formats. Here is one example.

Maria Gonzales

9166 Main Street, Apartment 3G
Los Angeles, CA 93001
gonzales@email.com
213-555-9878

OBJECTIVE: Experienced manager seeks a management position in retail sales

EXPERIENCE:

Assistant Director of Retail

2005 – Present   Shopmart, Los Angeles, CA
Manage relationships with vendors to complete orders, create accounts, and resolve issues. Maintain inventory and generate monthly inventory reports. Plan weekly promotions. Communicate with all retail employees to improve product knowledge and selling techniques. Implemented new customer service procedures.

Server

2005 – Present   Chuy's Grill, Santa Monica, CA
Greet and seat guests. Bus tables. Answer phones and take and prepare in-house, phone, or fax orders. Train new and existing employees. Awarded Employee of the Month five times for exceeding company expectations for quality and service.

Store Supervisor

1999 – 2005   Impact Photography Systems, Waco, TX
Oversaw daily operations, including customer and employee relations, counter sales, inventory management, maintaining store appearance, banking transactions, and equipment maintenance. Managed, trained, and scheduled staff of 35.

SKILLS: Fluent in English and Spanish. Expert in MS Word and Excel.

EDUCATION:

Associate of Arts Degree

1997 – 2000   Los Angeles Community College, Los Angeles, CA
Coursework in business management, marketing, studio art, communication, psychology, and sociology.

Study Abroad

2000 – 2001   University of Valencia, Valencia, Spain
Coursework in Spanish and international business.

INTERESTS: Backpacking, playing softball, and volunteering as a tutor for Literacy First.

PROOFREADING MARKS

Teachers often use the following correction abbreviations and symbols on students' papers.

Problem area	Symbol	Example
agreement	**agr**	He **go** to work at 8:00.
capital letters	**cap**	the United states
word division or	**div**	disorientati
hyphenation	**hy**	**-on**
sentence fragment	**frag**	**Where she found the book.**
grammar	**gr**	It's the **bigger** house on the street.
need italics	**ital**	I read it in **The Daily News.**
need lower case	**lc**	I don't like Peanut Butter.
punctuation error	**p**	Where did you find that coat.
plural needed	**pl**	I bought the **grocery** on my way home.
spelling error	**sp**	Did you rec**ie**ve my letter yet?
wrong tense	**t**	I **see** her yesterday.
wrong word	**ww**	My family used to **rise** corn and wheat.
need an apostrophe	⌄	I **don⌄t** know her name.
need a comma	⌄	However⌄we will probably arrive on time.
delete something	ℓ	We had the most best meal of our lives.
start a new	¶	. . . since last Friday.
paragraph		¶ Oh, by the way . . .
transpose words	⌒	They live on the floor first.

1. GREETINGS, INTRODUCTIONS, AND LEAVE-TAKING

Greeting someone you know

Hello.

Hi.

Hey.

Morning.

How's it going?   [Informal]

What's up?   [Informal]

Greeting someone you haven't seen for a while

It's good to see you again.

It's been a long time.

How long has it been?

Long time no see!   [Informal]

You look great!   [Informal]

So what have you been up to?   [Informal]

Greeting someone you don't know

Hello.

Good morning.

Good afternoon.

Good evening.

Hi, there!   [Informal]

Saying goodbye

Goodbye.

Bye.

Bye-bye.

See you.

See you later.

Have a good day.

Take care.

Good night. [Only when saying goodbye]

Introducing yourself

Hi, I'm Tom.

Hello, my name is Tom.

Excuse me.

We haven't met.

My name is Tom.   [Formal]

I saw you in (science) class.

I met you at Jane's party.

Introducing other people

Have you two met?

Have you met Maria?

I'd like you to meet Maria.

There's someone I'd like you to meet.

Let me introduce you to Maria.

> **You:**   This is my friend Maria.
> **Ali:**   Glad to meet you, Maria.
> **You:**   Maria, this is Ali.
> **Maria:** Nice to meet you, Ali.

I've been wanting to meet you.

Tom has told me a lot about you.

Greeting guests

Welcome.

Oh, hi.

How are you?

Please come in.

Glad you could make it.

Did you have any trouble finding us?

Can I take your coat?

Have a seat.

Please make yourself at home.

> **You:**   Can I get you something to drink?
> **Guest:** Yes, please.
> **You:**   What would you like?
> **Guest:** I'll have some orange juice.

What can I get you to drink?

Would you like some . . . ?

Saying goodbye to guests

Thanks for coming.

Thanks for joining us.

I'm so glad you could come.

It wouldn't have been the same without you.

Let me get your things.

Stop by anytime.

2. HAVING A CONVERSATION

Starting a conversation
Nice weather, huh?
Aren't you a friend of Jim's?
Did you see last night's game?
What's your favorite TV show?
So, what do you think about (the situation in Europe)?
So how do you like (your new car)?
Guess what I did last night.

Showing that you are listening
Uh-huh.
Right.
Exactly.
Yeah.
OK . . .
I know what you mean.

Giving yourself time to think
Well . . .
Um . . .
Uh . . .
Let me think.
Just a minute.

> **Other:** We should ride our bikes.
> **You:** It's too far. And, I mean . . . , it's raining and we're already late.

Checking for comprehension
Do you see what I mean?
Are you with me?
Does that make sense?

Checking for agreement
Don't you agree?
So what do you think?
We have to (act fast), you know?

Expressing agreement
You're right.
I couldn't agree with you more.
Good thinking!   [Informal]
You said it!   [Informal]
You're absolutely right.
Absolutely!   [Informal]

Expressing disagreement
I'm afraid I disagree.
Yeah, but . . .
I see your point, but . . .
That's not true.
You must be joking!   [Informal]
No way!   [Informal]

Asking someone to repeat something
Excuse me?
Sorry?
I didn't quite get that.
Could you repeat that?
Could you say that again?
Say again? [Informal]

Interrupting someone
Excuse me.
Yes, but (we don't have enough time).
I know, but (that will take hours).
Wait a minute.   [Informal]
Just hold it right there!   [Impolite]

Changing the topic
By the way, what do you think about (the new teacher)?
Before I forget, (there's a free concert on Friday night).
Whatever . . . (Did you see David's new car?)
Enough about me. Let's talk about you.

Ending a conversation
It was nice talking with you.
Good seeing you.
Sorry, I have to go now.

3. USING THE TELEPHONE

Making personal calls
Hi, this is David.

Is this Alice?

Is Alice there?

May I speak with Alice, please?   [Formal]

I work with her.

We're in the same science class.

Could you tell her I called?

Would you ask her to call me?

Answering personal calls
Hello?

Who's calling, please?

Oh, hi David. How are you?

I can't hear you.

Sorry, we got cut off.

I'm in the middle of something.

Can I call you back?

What's your number again?

Listen. I have to go now.

It was nice talking to you.

Answering machine greetings
You've reached 212-555-6701.

Please leave a message after the beep.

Hi, this is Carlos.

I can't take your call right now.

Sorry I missed your call.

Please leave your name and number.

I'll call you back as soon as I can.

Answering machine messages
This is Magda. Call me back when you
   get a chance.   [Informal]

Call me back on my cell.

I'll call you back later.

Talk to you later.

If you get this message before 11:00, please
   call me back.

Making business calls
Hello. This is Andy Larson.

I'm calling about . . .

Is this an OK time?

Answering business calls
Apex Electronics. Rosa Baker speaking.
   [Formal]

Hello, Rosa Baker.

May I help you?

Who's calling, please?

Caller:	May I speak with Mr. Hafner, please?
Businessperson:	This is he.
Caller:	Mr. Hafner, please.
Businessperson:	Speaking.

Talking to an office assistant
Extension 716, please.

Customer Service, please.

May I speak with Sheila Spink, please?

She's expecting my call.

I'm returning her call.

I'd like to leave a message for Ms. Spink.

Making appointments on the phone
You:	I'd like to make an appointment to see Ms. Spink.
Assistant:	How's 11:00 on Wednesday?
You:	Wednesday is really bad for me.
Assistant:	Can you make it Thursday at 9:00?
You:	That would be perfect!
Assistant:	OK. I have you down for Thursday at 9:00.

Special explanations
I'm sorry. She's not available.

Is there something I can help you with?

Can I put you on hold?

I'll transfer you to that extension.

If you'll leave your number, I'll have Ms. Spink
   call you back.

I'll tell her you called.

4. INTERVIEWING FOR A JOB

Small talk by the interviewer
Thanks for coming in today.
Did you have any trouble finding us?
How was the drive?
Would you like a cup of coffee?
Do you happen to know (Terry Mendham)?

Small talk by the candidate
What a great view!
Thanks for arranging to see me.
I've been looking forward to meeting you.
I spent some time exploring the company's web site.
My friend, Dale, has worked here for several years.

Getting serious
OK, shall we get started?
So, anyway . . .
Let's get down to business.

General questions for a candidate
Tell me a little about yourself.
How did you get into this line of work?
How long have you been in this country?
How did you learn about the opening?
What do you know about this company?
Why are you interested in working for us?

General answers to an interviewer
I've always been interested in (finance).
I enjoy (working with numbers).
My (uncle) was (an accountant) and encouraged me to try it.
I saw your ad in the paper.
This company has a great reputation in the field.

Job-related questions for a candidate
What are your qualifications for this job?
Describe your work experience.
What were your responsibilities on your last job?
I'd like to hear more about (your supervisory experience).

Interviewer:	Have you taken any courses in (bookkeeping)?
You:	Yes, I took two courses in business school and another online course last year.

What interests you about this particular job?
Why do you think it's a good fit?
Why did you leave your last job?
Do you have any experience with (HTML)?
Would you be willing to (travel eight weeks a year)?
What sort of salary are you looking for?

Describing job qualifications to an interviewer
In (2000), I started working for (Booker's) as a (sales rep).
After (two years), I was promoted to (sales manager).
You'll notice on my resume that (I supervised six people).
I was responsible for (three territories).
I was in charge of (planning sales meetings).
I have experience in all areas of (sales).
I helped implement (online sales reports).
I had to (contact my reps) on a daily basis.
I speak (Spanish) fluently.
I think my strong points are (organization and punctuality).

Ending the interview
I'm impressed with your experience.
I'd like to arrange a second interview.
When would you be able to start?
You'll hear from us by (next Wednesday).
We'll be in touch.

5. PRESENTATIONS

Introducing yourself

Hello, everyone. I'd like to thank you all for coming.

Let me tell you a little bit about myself.

My name is (Rita Nazario).

I am president of (Catco International).

Hi. I'm (Ivan Wolf) from (Peekskill Incorporated).

Two years ago (I started out as a salesperson at Peekskill).

Today (I supervise the West Coast sales team).

Introducing someone else

This is (Tina Gorman), a (woman) who needs no introduction.

(Tina) is one of America's best-known (lawyers).

(She) is going to talk to us about (car insurance).

Let's give (her) a warm welcome.

We are lucky to have with us today (Barry Rogers).

As you know, (he) is (the president of Ranger Incorporated).

It gives me great pleasure to present (Barry Rogers).

And so without further ado, I'd like to present (Barry Rogers).

Stating the purpose

Today I'd like to talk to you about (managing your money).

Today I'm going to show you how to (save a lot of money).

I'll begin by (outlining the basics).

Then I'll (go into more detail).

I'll tell you (everything you need to know about savings accounts).

I'll provide an overview of (different types of investments).

I also hope to interest you in (some safe investments).

I'll list (the three biggest mistakes people make).

By the end, you'll (feel like an expert).

Relating to the audience

Can everyone hear me?

Raise your hand if you need me to repeat anything.

Please stop me at any point if you have a question.

How many people here (plan to continue their education)?

If you're like me, (you haven't saved up enough money).

We all know what that's like, don't we?

Does this ring a bell?

Don't you hate it when (people tell you what you should do)?

Citing sources

According to the *New York Times,* . . .

A study conducted by Harvard University showed that . . .

Recent research shows that . . .

Medical researchers have discovered that . . .

Peter Butler said, and I quote, ". . ."

I read somewhere that . . .

(The federal government) released a report stating that . . .

Making transitions

I'd like to expand on that before we move on.

The next thing I'd like to talk about is . . .

Now let's take a look at . . .

Moving right along . . .

To sum up what I've said so far, . . .

Now let's move on to the question of . . .

Now that you have an overview, let's look at some of the specifics.

Recapping the main points, . . .

I'm afraid we have to move on.

Emphasizing important points

I'd like to emphasize that . . .

Never forget that . . .

This is a key concept.

The bottom line is . . .

If you remember only one thing I've said today, . . .

I can't stress enough the importance of . . .

Using visuals

Take a look at (the chart on the screen).

I'd like to draw your attention to (the poster over there).

You'll notice that . . .

Pay special attention to the . . .

If you look closely, you'll see that . . .

So what does this tell us?

Closing

And in conclusion, . . .

Let's open the floor to questions.

It's been a pleasure being with you today.

6. AGREEING AND DISAGREEING

Agreeing
Yeah, that's right.
I know it.
I agree with you.
You're right.
That's true.
I think so, too.
That's what I think.
Me, too.
Me neither.

Agreeing strongly
You're absolutely right!
Definitely!
Certainly!
Exactly!
Absolutely!
Of course!
I couldn't agree more.
You're telling me!   [Informal]
You said it!   [Informal]

Agreeing weakly
I suppose so.
Yeah, I guess so.
It would seem that way.

Remaining neutral
I see your point.
You have a point there.
I understand what you're saying.
I see what you mean.
I'd have to think about that.
I've never thought about it that way before.
Maybe yes, maybe no.
Could be.

Disagreeing
No, I don't think so.
I agree up to a point.
I really don't see it that way.
That's not what I think.
I agree that (going by car is faster), but . . .
But what about (the expense involved)?
Yes, but . . .
I know, but . . .
No, it wasn't. / No, they don't. / etc.

> **Other person:** We could save a lot of
> money by taking the
> bus.
> **You:**   Not really. It would cost
> almost the same as
> driving.

Disagreeing strongly
I disagree completely.
That's not true.
That is not an option.
Definitely not!
Absolutely not!
You've made your point, but . . .
No way!   [Informal]
You can't be serious.   [Informal]
You've got to be kidding!   [Informal]
Where did you get that idea?   [Impolite]
Are you out of your mind!   [Impolite]

Disagreeing politely
I'm afraid I have to disagree with you.
I'm not so sure.
I'm not sure that's such a good idea.
I see what you're saying, but . . .
I'm sure many people feel that way, but . . .
But don't you think we should consider
   (other alternatives)?

7. Interrupting, Clarifying, Checking for Understanding

Informal interruptions

Ummm.

Sir? / Ma'am?

Just a minute.

Can I stop you for a minute?

Wait a minute! [Impolite]

Hold it right there! [Impolite]

Formal interruptions

Excuse me, sir / ma'am.

Excuse me for interrupting.

Forgive me for interrupting you, but . . .

I'm sorry to break in like this, but . . .

Could I interrupt you for a minute?

Could I ask a question, please?

Asking for clarification—Informal

What did you say?

I didn't catch that.

Sorry, I didn't get that.

I missed that.

Could you repeat that?

Could you say that again?

Say again?

I'm lost.

Could you run that by me one more time?

Did you say . . . ?

Do you mean . . . ?

Asking for clarification—Formal

I beg your pardon?

I'm not sure I understand what you're saying.

I can't make sense of what you just said.

Could you explain that in different words?

Could you please repeat that?

Could you go over that again?

Giving clarification—Informal

I'll go over it again.

I'll take it step by step.

I'll take a different tack this time.

Stop me if you get lost.

OK, here's a recap.

Maybe this will clarify things.

To put it another way, . . .

In other words, . . .

Giving clarification—Formal

Let me put it another way.

Let me give you some examples.

Here are the main points again.

I'm afraid you didn't understand what I said.

I'm afraid you've missed the point.

What I meant was . . .

I hope you didn't think that . . .

I didn't mean to imply that . . .

I hope that clears things up.

Checking for understanding

Do you understand now?

Is it clearer now?

Do you see what I'm getting at?

Does that help?

Is there anything that still isn't clear?

What other questions do you have?

Speaker: What else?

Listener: I'm still not clear on the difference between a preposition and a conjunction.

Now explain it to me in your own words.

8. APOLOGIZING

**Apologizing for a small accident
or mistake**
Sorry.
I'm sorry.
Excuse me.
It was an accident.
Pardon me.   [Formal]
Oops!   [Informal]
My mistake.   [Informal]
I'm terrible with (names).
I've never been good with (numbers).
I can't believe I (did) that.

**Apologizing for a serious accident
or mistake**
I'm so sorry.
I am really sorry that I (damaged your car).
I am so sorry about (damaging your car).
I feel terrible about (the accident).
I'm really sorry but (I was being very
   careful).
I'm sorry for (causing you a problem).
Please accept my apologies for . . .
   [Formal]
I sincerely apologize for . . .   [Formal]

Apologizing for upsetting someone
I'm sorry I upset you.
I didn't mean to make you feel bad.
Please forgive me.   [Formal]
I just wasn't thinking straight.
That's not what I meant to say.
I didn't mean it personally.
I'm sorry. I'm having a rough day.

Apologizing for having to say *no*
I'm sorry. I can't.
Sorry, I never (lend anyone my car).
I wish I could say *yes*.
I'm going to have to say *no*.
I can't. I have to (work that evening).
Maybe some other time.

Responding to an apology
Don't worry about it.
Oh, that's OK.
Think nothing of it.   [Formal]
Don't mention it.   [Formal]

> **Other person:** I'm afraid I lost the pen
>   you lent me.
> **You:**   No big thing.

It doesn't matter.
It's not important.
Never mind.
No problem.
It happens.
Forget it.
Don't sweat it.   [Informal]
Apology accepted.   [Formal]

Showing regret
I feel really bad.
It won't happen again.
I wish I could go back and start all over
   again.
I don't know what came over me.
I don't know what to say.
Now I know better.
Too bad I didn't . . .
It was inexcusable of me.   [Formal]
It's not like me to . . .
I hope I can make it up to you.
That didn't come out right.
I didn't mean to take it out on you.

Sympathizing
This must be very difficult for you.
I know what you mean.
I know how you're feeling.
I know how upset you must be.
I can imagine how difficult this is for you.

9. SUGGESTIONS, ADVICE, INSISTENCE

Making informal suggestions
Here's what I suggest.
I know what you should do.
Why don't you (go to the movies with Jane)?
What about (having lunch with Bob)?
Try (the French fries next time).
Have you thought about (riding your bike to work)?

Accepting suggestions
Thanks, I'll do that.
Good idea!
That's a great idea.
Sounds good to me.
That's a plan.
I'll give it a try.
Guess it's worth a try.

Refusing suggestions
No. I don't like (French fries).
That's not for me.
I don't think so.
That might work for some people, but ...
Nawww.   [Informal]
I don't feel like it.   [Impolite]

Giving serious advice—Informal
Listen!
Here's the plan.
Take my advice.
Take it from one who knows.
Take it from someone who's been there.
Here's what I think you should do.
Hey! Here's an idea.
How about (waiting until you're 30 to get married)?
Don't (settle down too quickly).
Why don't you (see the world while you're young)?
You can always (settle down later).
Don't forget—(you only live once).

Giving serious advice—formal
Have you ever thought about (becoming a doctor)?
Maybe it would be a good idea if you (went back to school).
It looks to me like (Harvard) would be your best choice.
If I were you, I'd study (medicine).
In my opinion, you should (consider it seriously).
Be sure to (get your application in early).
I always advise people to (check that it was received).
The best idea is (to study hard).
If you're really smart, you'll (start right away).

Accepting advice
You're right.
Thanks for the advice.
That makes a lot of sense.
I see what you mean.
That sounds like good advice.
I'll give it a try.
I'll do my best.
You've given me something to think about.
I'll try it and get back to you.

Refusing advice
I don't think that would work for me.
That doesn't make sense to me.
I'm not sure that would be such a good idea.
I could never (become a doctor).
Thanks for the input.
Thanks, but no thanks.   [Informal]
You don't know what you're talking about.   [Impolite]
I think I know what's best for myself.   [Impolite]
Back off!   [Impolite]

Insisting
You have to (become a doctor).
Try to see it my way.
I know what I'm talking about.
If you don't (go to medical school), I won't (pay for your college).
I don't care what you think.   [Impolite]

10. DESCRIBING FEELINGS

Happiness

I'm doing great.
This is the best day of my life.
I've never been so happy in my life.
I'm so pleased for you.
Aren't you thrilled?
What could be better?
Life is good.

Sadness

Are you OK?
Why the long face?
I'm not doing so well.
I feel awful.
I'm devastated.
I'm depressed.
I'm feeling kind of blue.
I just want to crawl in a hole.
Oh, what's the use?

Fear

I'm worried about (money).
He dreads (going to the dentist).
I'm afraid to (drive over bridges).
She can't stand (snakes).
This anxiety is killing me.
He's scared of (big dogs).
How will I ever (pass Friday's test)?
I have a phobia about (germs).

Anger

I'm really mad at (you).
They resent (such high taxes).
How could she (do) that?
I'm annoyed with (the neighbors).
(The noise of car alarms) infuriates her.
He was furious with (the children).

Boredom

I'm so bored.
There's nothing to do around here.
What a bore!
Nothing ever happens.
She was bored to tears.
They were bored to death.
I was bored stiff.
It was such a monotonous (movie).
(That TV show) was so dull.

Disgust

That's disgusting.
Eeew! Yuck!   [Informal]
I hate (raw fish).
How can you stand it?
I almost vomited.
I thought I'd puke.   [Impolite]
I don't even like to think about it.
How can you say something like that?
I wouldn't be caught dead (wearing that
    dirty old coat).

Compassion

I'm sorry.
I understand what you're going through.
Tell me about it.
How can I help?
Is there anything I can do?
She is concerned about him.
He worries about the children.
He cares for her deeply.
My heart goes out to them.
    [Old-fashioned]

Guilt

I feel terrible that I (lost your mother's
    necklace).
I never should have (borrowed it).
I feel so guilty!
It's all my fault.
I blame myself.
I make a mess of everything.
I'll never forgive myself.

abate	aim	arrival	bond
abbreviate	albeit	article	book
above	alleviate	ascend	boorish
abroad	allocation	ascertain	border
abrupt	allow	aspect	bothersome
absence	allowance	assert	bottom
absolute	alter	assimilate	boundary
absurd	amaze	assortment	brand
abuse	ambiguous	assume	break
abyss	ambivalence	assure	breakthrough
accelerate	amenity	astounding	brevity
accentuate	amiable	astute	brief
accept	amicable	atom	brilliant
acceptable	amorous	atone	brink
access	ample	attendance	broaden
accident	amplify	attest	bud
acclaim	amusement	attract	budget
accord	analogous	attractive	bulk
account	analogy	auction	burgeon
accounting	analyze	audacious	cabinet
accredited	anchor	audible	caliber
accretion	ancient	auditorium	calisthenics
accurate	animal	augment	callous
acknowledge	animate	auspicious	candid
acquiesce	animosity	author	capable
acquire	annals	authorize	capital
active	annex	autograph	captive
actually	anniversary	autonomous	capture
addict	annoying	avail	card
adept	annual	avarice	career
adhere	annuity	average	carpet
adjacent	antecedent	avoid	carry
adjust	anterior	background	categorize
admiration	anthropology	backup	caution
admit	anticipate	baffle	celebrated
admonish	antipathy	baked	cement
adopt	antiquated	balanced	certificate
advance	antisocial	bankrupt	challenge
advanced	apart	barometer	chaotic
advantage	apathy	bear	characteristic
advent	apology	become	charisma
adverse	apparel	bellicose	chiefly
advertisement	apparent	benefit	chilly
advice	appeal	benevolent	chore
affable	appealing	benign	chronic
affliction	apprehensive	bibliography	chronicle
affluent	appropriate	bill	chronological
afford	approximately	biology	circle
affordable	aptly	bisect	circulate
agenda	aqueous	blame	circumstance
agent	arbiter	bland	citizenship
aggravating	arbitrary	blind	clamor
aggregate	archaic	block	clarify
agile	arduous	bloom	classify
agitate	arid	blossom	clear
agnostic	aroma	blur	clerk
agoraphobia	arrest	bold	clever

clock
coarse
code
coherent
collateral
colleague
collect
collection
college
colloquial
colonist
command
commemorate
commonplace
compatible
compel
complex
comply
conceal
concede
conceive
concept
concoct
condense
condition
conducive
conduct
confide
confidential
confirm
conform
conjure
conscientious
conscious
consecutive
consent
conservation
consider
considerate
consideration
consistently
consortium
constant
constraint
constrict
construe
consumption
contact
contemplate
contemporary
contend
content
contentment
contingent
continue
contort
contradictory

controversial
convene
convenience
convenient
conventional
convert
convey
convince
cook
copy
core
corner
corporate
corpse
corrupt
cost
counsel
couple
courageous
courier
course
court
cowardly
crack
crate
create
credible
credit
creed
creep
crescent
critical
criticize
crop
crucial
crush
cultivate
curb
curious
currency
current
custom
cyclone
damp
dangle
dash
deadline
deceased
deceive
decent
declare
decline
decompose
decorate
deduce
deduct
deep

default
deflate
defy
degenerate
degree
dehydrate
delegate
delicate
delighted
deluge
demand
demolish
demonstration
demure
dense
dentistry
dependent
depict
deplete
depreciate
deprive
describe
description
desiccated
despise
destroy
destruction
detail
detect
determined
develop
deviate
diagnose
dial
dichotomy
dictate
dictionary
diet
difficult
diffident
dignitary
dignity
diligent
dim
diminish
diminutive
direct
disapproval
discard
discernible
discount
discourse
discreditable
discuss
disguise
disintegrate
dismiss

disorient
disparate
disparity
disperse
display
dispose
disregard
disrobe
disruptive
dissimilar
dissociate
dissuade
distinct
distinguish
distort
distribute
disturb
disturbing
diverse
docile
doctor
doctrine
document
dogma
doleful
domestic
dominant
dormant
download
downturn
drab
dramatic
drastic
draw
droop
drought
dubious
due
dumbfound
dweller
dwelling
dwindle
dynamic
dysentery
dysfunction
dyslexia
dyspepsia
dystrophy
eager
earnest
educate
efface
effect
effective
effigy
egregious
eject

elaborate	examiner	firm	grumble
elect	exceed	flaw	guess
election	exceedingly	flimsy	harass
element	exceptional	floor	harmful
elementary	exchange	florist	harmless
elevator	excite	flourish	harvest
elicit	exclaim	fluctuate	hasten
eligible	exclude	fluent	hazardous
eliminate	exclusively	fluid	haze
elucidate	excursion	forbearance	head
elude	exemplify	forbid	heave
emit	exhaust	forecast	heighten
empathy	exhibit	forfeit	henceforth
emphasize	exit	formal	heretic
employee	expand	format	hero
employment	expansion	formerly	hesitate
emulate	expel	formidable	hidden
enact	experience	formulate	highlight
enchant	explain	fortify	hit
encircle	exploit	fortune	homophone
encompass	export	found	honor
encourage	express	founder	host
endeavor	exquisite	fracture	hue
endorse	extensive	fragment	humane
endorsement	extent	frail	humid
endure	exterminate	frame	hyperactive
energetic	extol	fraud	hyperbole
engine	extract	freezing	hypersensitive
enhance	extradite	frequently	hypertension
enormous	extremely	freshly	ideal
enrich	fabricate	frigid	identical
ensue	face	frontier	illuminate
enthrall	facet	fulfillment	illustrate
enthuse	facsimile	function	illustration
entirely	fact	fundamental	immense
envision	factory	further	immigrant
equal	fail	gain	impact
equity	faint	gather	impede
equivalent	fallacy	gaudy	impediment
erode	familiar	generally	implicate
erratic	famous	generous	import
espionage	fantasy	geography	impossible
essence	fare	get	impressive
essential	fashion	ghastly	improper
establish	fathom	gigantic	inaccessible
eternal	feasible	gingerly	inactive
eugenics	feature	glove	inconvenience
eulogize	fee	goal	incorporate
euphemism	feign	good	increase
euthanasia	fertile	government	incredible
evade	fiction	grade	incredulity
evaporate	fidelity	gradually	incredulous
even	figment	graffiti	incumbent
eventually	figure	grant	indeed
evident	final	graphic	indicate
evolution	finance	gratitude	indigenous
exaggerate	finite	grimace	indiscriminate

indispensable	know	mental	novelty
indivisible	labor	mention	novice
induce	lachrymose	merchandise	nuance
induct	lack	merciless	number
inert	lasting	metropolitan	obese
inevitable	launch	microbe	oblige
infancy	lawyer	microcosm	observe
infant	layman	microfilm	obsolete
infer	lead	micrometer	obstruct
influence	league	microscope	obtain
inhabitant	lease	microsecond	obviously
initiate	leash	microwave	occasion
injury	leather	midday	occupancy
innovate	legal	mild	occur
innovative	legible	miniature	odd
inordinate	legitimate	minimal	offense
inquire	library	minimum	offensive
insensitive	likelihood	ministry	offer
insipid	limber	minor	office
inspire	limit	minuscule	omit
institution	litter	minute	ongoing
instrument	loafer	mirror	operate
intensify	lobotomy	mirth	opposition
intent	logic	misanthropy	opus
intentionally	logo	misconstrue	order
interact	loom	misogyny	orthodox
intercept	lose	missive	otherwise
interchangeable	lounge	mistake	outlandish
intermediate	lucrative	misunderstand	overcome
intermittent	luggage	mobile	overlook
interpret	lustrous	moist	owner
interrelate	macrocosm	monotone	ownership
interrupt	macroeconomics	morphology	package
intersperse	magnificent	mortgage	pad
intervene	magnitude	motion	page
intolerable	mail	motivate	paradox
intrepid	maintain	multiply	parallel
intricate	malign	must	parched
intrigue	manage	mutable	partially
intrinsic	management	naïve	participate
introduction	manhood	narrate	particle
intrude	manly	narrow	particular
inundate	manual	nascent	partisan
invent	manufacture	native	party
invention	margin	nausea	pass
investment	marvel	necessarily	passage
involuntarily	maternity	neglect	passion
involve	matriarch	negligible	patch
irate	maximum	neurology	paternal
irrelevant	mayor	nevertheless	pathetic
irritation	mean	nocturnal	pathological
isolate	meanwhile	nominal	pathology
itinerant	meddle	nonsense	patient
jeopardy	medieval	normally	patriarch
jettison	mediocre	note	pattern
judge	memory	notion	peace
junction	mend	novel	peculiar

pedal	precede	radiant	retrieve
pedestal	precedent	raise	retrospect
pedestrian	precious	range	reveal
pedicure	preconception	rate	reverberate
perceive	precondition	react	reverse
percent	predecessor	reaction	revert
perch	predict	readily	review
perennial	predictably	reason	revive
perfect	predominant	rebellion	revoke
persistent	preference	rebound	revolt
perspective	pregnant	recede	revolve
persuade	prestige	receive	rhythm
pervade	presumably	receptionist	ridge
petition	presumptuous	recess	rigid
petrified	pretense	recession	rigor
petty	prevail	recognize	rivalry
petulant	prevalent	record	robust
phantom	prevent	recover	route
pharmacist	previously	reduce	routine
phenomena	primary	refer	routinely
philanthropic	prime	refine	rudimentary
philanthropy	privacy	reflect	rupture
philharmonic	procedure	reflection	rush
philology	process	refurbish	ruthless
philosopher	proclaim	regard	sacrifice
philosophy	produce	regulate	salvage
phobia	production	reject	saturated
photograph	proficient	rejoicing	savory
pier	programmer	relate	scarce
pillage	progress	relation	scarcely
pioneer	prohibit	release	scattered
place	project	reliable	scene
placid	proliferate	relinquish	scenic
plaid	prolong	remarkable	science
plentiful	prominent	remind	scorching
ply	promise	reminisce	score
pocket	promontory	remove	scribble
podiatrist	promote	renew	script
podium	prompt	renown	scrupulous
point	prone	repel	scrutinize
policy	propel	replace	season
poll	prophetic	replay	security
pollution	propose	reply	seduce
polygamy	prospective	reportedly	seedling
polytechnic	prosperous	representative	segment
ponder	protection	requisite	selective
population	protrude	rescue	selfish
portray	provision	research	seminar
position	proximity	resident	senior
post	psychology	resilient	sensation
postpone	psychopathic	resource	sense
postscript	publication	respected	sensitive
posture	publisher	respiration	sentimental
potent	pulse	restore	sequence
practical	pungent	restrain	serve
practice	query	retain	settle
precarious	quest	reticent	settler

severe	stem	tenacious	unite
shallow	step	tentative	unlikely
shatter	stipulate	terminal	unmistakable
shed	stock	terrain	unravel
shelf	store	terrifying	unwarranted
sheltered	stream	territory	update
shift	strengthen	testify	uproar
ship	stress	theology	vacancy
shipment	stretch	theoretically	vacant
shipping	strike	thermal	vacuum
shoot	striking	thermometer	value
shortage	stringent	thrive	vanity
shrink	strive	thrust	varied
sideways	submit	ticket	vast
significance	subscribe	timid	vegetable
significant	subsequent	title	vehemence
signify	subside	topic	veil
sinecure	subsidize	torment	veracity
singular	substantiate	torpid	verbalize
site	succeed	torsion	verify
situated	successive	total	versatile
sketchy	succumb	tour	verve
skin	suffer	toxic	vibrant
soaked	suitable	tradition	viewpoint
society	sum	trail	vigorous
sociology	superficial	train	vindicate
solid	superfluous	transcend	virtual
solitary	superior	translucent	visible
soluble	supervise	transmit	vital
solve	supplement	transport	vivid
sometimes	supply	trap	vocal
somewhat	supposition	trash	vogue
sound	surmise	treacherous	volume
source	surveillance	treasury	voluptuous
spacious	suspect	treaty	wait
span	suspend	tremor	wane
specimen	swift	tremulous	wanton
spectator	switch	triangle	weak
spectrum	symbols	triple	weakness
speculate	sympathetic	tripod	wealth
spiteful	sympathy	triumph	weapon
spontaneous	synonym	trivial	weigh
sporadic	synthesis	trouble	wide
spread	taciturn	truculent	widespread
sprout	talk	tyro	wilt
spurn	tangible	ultrasonic	wisdom
square	task	unbiased	wither
stack	teacher	undeniable	withstand
stagnant	technology	undercut	witticism
stake	tedious	underestimated	woo
stance	telegram	underline	worthwhile
static	telepathy	unfavorably	wrinkle
stationary	temper	uniform	xenophobia
stature	temporize	unique	zenith
steady	tempt	unison	

Texting Abbreviations

1	used to replace "*-one*": *NE1* = anyone
2	**to** or **too**: *it's up 2 U* = it's up to you; *me 2* = me too
	used to replace "**to-**": *2day* = today
2DAY	**today**
2MORO	**tomorrow**
2NITE	**tonight**
4	**for**: *4 U* = for you
	used to replace "**-fore**": *B4* = before
411	**information**: *TNX 4 the 411*
8	used to replace "**-ate**" or "**-eat**": *GR8* = great; *C U L8R* = see you later
86	discard, get rid of
AFAIK	**as far as I know**
B	**be**: used to replace "**be-**" in other words: *B4* = before
B4	**before**
B4N	**bye for now**
BRB	**be right back**
BTW	**by the way**
C	**see**: *C U 2moro* = see you tomorrow
CID	**consider it done**
CU	**see you**
CUL8R	**call you later**
D8	**date**
EZ	**easy**
FWIW	**for what it's worth**: used for saying that someone may or may not be interested in what you have to say
FYI	**for your information**: used as a way of introducing useful information
GR8	**great**
G2G	**got to go**
HHIS	**hanging head in shame**: used for showing that you are embarassed

IB	**I'm back**
IYSS	**if you say so**
K	**OK**
L8	**late**
L8R	**later**: *CUL8R* = see you later
LOL	**laughing out loud**: used for showing that you think something is funny
MSG	**message**
MYOB	**mind your own business**: for telling people not to ask questions about something that you do not want them to know about
NE	**any**
NE1	**anyone**
NO1	**no one**
NETHING	**anything**
OIC	**Oh, I see**
OTOH	**on the other hand**
PCM	**please call me**
PLS	**please**
prolly	**probably**
R	**are**: *RU free 2nite* = Are you free tonight?
RUCMNG	**Are you coming?**
RUOK?	**Are you OK?**
SPK	**speak**
SRY	**sorry**
THNQ	**thank you**: *THNQ for visiting my home page.*
THX/TX	**thanks**: *THX 4 the info.*
TTUL/TTYL	**talk to you later**
U	**you**: *CUL8R* = see you later
URW	**You're welcome.**
W8	**wait**
WAN2	**want to**
WRK	**work**
XLNT	**excellent**
YR	**your**
ZZZZ	**sleeping**

Emoticons Horizontal →

:-)	smiling; agreeing
:-D	laughing
|-)	hee hee
|-D	ho ho
'-) or ;-)	winking; just kidding
:*)	clowning
:-(	frowning; sad
:(	sad
:'-(	crying and really sad
>:-< or :-||	angry
:-@	screaming
:-V	shouting
:-p or :-r	sticking tongue out
|-O	yawning
: *	kiss
((((name))))	hug
@-{----	rose
<3	heart
</3	broken heart

Emoticons Vertical ↓

(^_^)	smiling
(`_^) or (^_~)	winking
(>_<)	angry, or ouch
(-_-)zzz	sleeping
\(^o^)/	very excited (raising hands)
(-_-;) or (^_^')	nervous, or sweatdrop (embarrassed; semicolon can be repeated)
d-_-b title.mp3	listening to music, labelling title afterwards
\m/	rocker fingers
\m/(>_<)\m/	rocker dude

a	afford	angry	assist	based
abandon	afraid	animal	assistance	basic
abandoned	after	anniversary	assistant	basically
ability	afternoon	announce	associate	basis
able	afterward	announcement	associated	basketball
abortion	again	annual	association	bass
about	against	another	assume	bat
above	age	answer	assumption	bath
abroad	agency	antique	assured	bathroom
absence	agenda	anxiety	at	battle
absolute	agent	anxious	athlete	bay
absolutely	aggressive	any	atmosphere	be
abuse	ago	anybody	attach	beach
academic	agree	anymore	attack	bean
accept	agreement	anyone	attempt	bear
acceptable	agricultural	anything	attend	bearing
accepted	agriculture	anyway	attention	beat
access	ah	anywhere	attitude	beaten
accident	ahead	apart	attorney	beating
accompany	aid	apartment	attract	beautiful
accord	aim	apparent	attractive	beauty
according to	air	apparently	auction	because
account	air force	appeal	audience	become
accurate	aircraft	appear	audio	bed
accuse	airline	appearance	August	bedroom
achieve	airport	apple	aunt	beer
achievement	alarm	application	author	before
acid	album	apply	authority	begin
acknowledge	alcohol	appoint	auto	beginning
acquire	alert	appointment	automatic	behalf
acquisition	alive	appreciate	autumn	behave
acre	all	approach	available	behavior
across	all right	appropriate	avenue	behind
act	allegation	approval	average	being
action	alleged	approve	avoid	belief
active	alliance	April	await	believe
activist	allied	area	award	bell
activity	allow	aren't	aware	belong
actor	ally	argue	away	below
actress	almost	argument	awful	belt
actual	alone	arise	baby	bend
actually	along	arm	back	beneath
ad	alongside	armed	background	benefit
add	already	armed forces	backing	beside
addition	also	army	bad	besides
additional	alter	around	badly	best
address	alternative	arrange	bag	bet
adequate	although	arrangement	bake	better
adjust	altogether	arrest	balance	between
administration	always	arrival	ball	beyond
admire	amateur	arrive	ballot	bid
admit	amazing	art	ban	big
adopt	ambassador	article	band	bike
adult	ambition	artist	bank	bill
advance	amendment	as	banker	billion
advanced	amid	Asian	banking	bird
advantage	among	aside	bar	birth
advertise	amount	ask	bare	birthday
advice	analysis	aspect	barely	bit
advise	analyst	assault	bargain	bite
adviser	ancient	assembly	barrel	bitter
advocate	and	assess	barrier	black
affair	anger	assessment	base	blame
affect	angle	asset	baseball	blast

blind	busy	chamber	coach	concern
block	but	champion	coal	concerned
blood	butter	championship	coalition	concert
bloody	button	chance	coast	concession
blow	buy	chancellor	coat	conclude
blue	buyer	change	code	conclusion
board	by	channel	coffee	concrete
boat	bye	chaos	cold	condemn
body	cabinet	chapter	collapse	condition
boil	cable	character	colleague	conduct
bomb	cake	characteristic	collect	conference
bond	call	charge	collection	confidence
bone	calm	charity	collective	confident
book	camera	chart	college	confirm
boom	camp	charter	colonel	conflict
boost	campaign	chase	color	confront
boot	can	chat	colored	confrontation
border	cancel	cheap	column	Congress
bore	cancer	check	combat	congressional
born	candidate	cheer	combination	connection
borrow	cap	cheese	combine	conscious
boss	capable	chemical	come	consciousness
both	capacity	chest	comedy	consequence
bother	capital	chicken	comfort	conservative
bottle	captain	chief	comfortable	consider
bottom	caption	child	coming	considerable
bound	capture	childhood	command	consideration
bowl	car	chip	commander	considering
box	carbon	chocolate	comment	consist
boy	card	choice	commentator	consistent
brain	care	choose	commerce	constant
branch	career	chop	commercial	constitution
brand	careful	Christian	commission	constitutional
brave	Caribbean	Christmas	commissioner	construction
bread	caring	church	commit	consult
break	carrier	cigarette	commitment	consultant
breakfast	carry	cinema	committee	consumer
breast	case	circle	common	contact
breath	cash	circuit	communicate	contain
breathe	cast	circumstance	communication	contemporary
breed	castle	cite	communist	content
bridge	casualty	citizen	community	contest
brief	cat	city	company	context
bright	catch	civil	compare	continent
brilliant	category	civil war	compared	continue
bring	Catholic	civilian	comparison	contract
broad	cause	claim	compensation	contrast
broadcast	cautious	clash	compete	contribute
broadcasting	cave	class	competition	contribution
broker	cease	classic	competitive	control
brother	ceasefire	classical	competitor	controversial
brown	celebrate	clean	complain	controversy
brush	celebration	clear	complaint	convention
budget	cell	clever	complete	conventional
build	center	client	complex	conversation
building	central	climate	complicated	convert
bunch	century	climb	component	convict
burden	ceremony	clinic	comprehensive	conviction
burn	certain	clock	compromise	convince
burst	certainly	close	computer	convinced
bury	chain	clothes	concede	cook
bus	chair	clothing	concentrate	cooking
business	chairman	cloud	concentration	cool
businessman	challenge	club	concept	cooperate

cope	current	depend	do	effective
copy	curtain	deposit	doctor	efficient
core	customer	depression	document	effort
corner	cut	depth	doesn't	egg
corporate	cutting	deputy	dog	eight
corporation	cycle	describe	dollar	eighteen
correct	dad	description	domestic	eighteenth
correspondent	daily	desert	dominate	eighth
corruption	damage	deserve	done	eightieth
'cos	dance	design	door	eighty
cost	dancing	designer	double	either
cottage	danger	desire	doubt	elderly
cotton	dangerous	desk	down	elect
cough	dare	desperate	downtown	election
could	dark	despite	dozen	electoral
council	data	destroy	draft	electric
counsel	date	destruction	drag	electricity
count	daughter	detail	drain	electronic
counter	day	detailed	drama	elegant
counterpart	dead	detective	dramatic	element
country	deadline	determine	draw	eleven
countryside	deal	determined	dream	eleventh
county	dealer	develop	dress	eliminate
coup	dear	development	dressed	else
couple	death	device	drift	elsewhere
courage	debate	dialogue	drink	embassy
course	debt	diary	drive	emerge
court	debut	didn't	driver	emergency
cousin	decade	die	drop	emotion
cover	December	diet	drug	emotional
coverage	decide	difference	drum	emphasis
cow	decision	different	dry	emphasize
crack	deck	difficult	due	empire
craft	declaration	difficulty	dump	employ
crash	declare	dig	during	employee
crazy	decline	digital	dust	employer
cream	decorate	dinner	duty	employment
create	deep	diplomat	each	empty
creative	defeat	diplomatic	eager	enable
credit	defend	direct	ear	encounter
crew	defense	direction	earlier	encourage
cricket	deficit	director	early	end
crime	define	dirty	earn	enemy
criminal	definitely	disappear	earnings	energy
crisis	definition	disappointed	earth	enforcement
critic	degree	disaster	ease	engage
critical	delay	discipline	easily	engine
criticism	delegate	discount	east	engineer
criticize	delegation	discover	eastern	engineering
crop	deliberate	discovery	easy	English
cross	delight	discuss	eat	enhance
crowd	delighted	discussion	echo	enjoy
crown	deliver	disease	economic	enormous
crucial	delivery	dish	economics	enough
cruise	demand	dismiss	economist	ensure
cry	democracy	display	economy	enter
crystal	democrat	dispute	edge	enterprise
cue	democratic	distance	edit	entertain
cultural	demonstrate	distribution	edition	entertainment
culture	demonstration	district	editor	enthusiasm
cup	demonstrator	divide	editorial	entire
cure	deny	dividend	education	entirely
curious	department	division	educational	entitle
currency	departure	divorce	effect	entrance

entry	explain	festival	formal	genuine
environment	explanation	few	former	gesture
environmental	explode	field	formula	get
equal	exploit	fierce	forth	giant
equally	explore	fifteen	fortieth	gift
equipment	explosion	fifteenth	fortune	girl
equity	export	fifth	forty	give
equivalent	expose	fiftieth	forward	given
era	exposure	fifty	found	glad
error	express	fight	foundation	glance
escape	expression	fighter	founder	glass
especially	extend	figure	four	global
essential	extensive	file	fourteen	go
essentially	extent	fill	fourteenth	goal
establish	extra	film	fourth	god
establishment	extraordinary	final	frame	going
estate	extreme	finally	fraud	gold
estimate	extremely	finance	free	golden
ethnic	eye	financial	freedom	golf
European	fabric	find	freeze	gone
even	face	fine	frequent	good
evening	facility	finger	fresh	goods
event	fact	finish	Friday	got
eventually	faction	fire	friend	govern
ever	factor	firm	friendly	government
every	factory	first	friendship	governor
everybody	fade	fiscal	from	grab
everyone	fail	fish	front	grade
everything	failure	fishing	fruit	gradually
everywhere	fair	fit	frustrate	graduate
evidence	fairly	five	fry	grain
evil	faith	fix	fuel	grand
exact	fall	fixed	fulfill	grant
exactly	false	flag	full	grass
examination	familiar	flash	fully	grave
examine	family	flat	fun	gray
example	famous	flavor	function	great
excellent	fan	flee	fund	green
except	fancy	fleet	fundamental	grip
exception	fantasy	flexible	funding	gross
excerpt	far	flight	funny	ground
excess	fare	float	furniture	group
exchange	farm	flood	further	grow
exchange rate	farmer	floor	future	growth
exciting	fashion	flow	gain	guarantee
excuse	fast	flower	gallery	guard
execute	fat	fly	game	guerrilla
executive	fate	focus	gang	guess
exercise	father	fold	gap	guest
exhaust	fault	folk	garden	guide
exhibition	favor	follow	gas	guilty
exile	favorite	following	gate	guitar
exist	fear	food	gather	gun
existence	feature	fool	gay	guy
existing	February	foot	gear	habit
expand	federal	football	gene	hair
expansion	federation	for	general	half
expect	fee	force	general election	hall
expectation	feed	forecast	generally	halt
expense	feel	foreign	generate	hand
expensive	feeling	foreigner	generation	handle
experience	fellow	forest	generous	hang
experiment	female	forget	gentle	happen
expert	fence	form	gentleman	happy

harbor	hot	independence	involved	lady
hard	hotel	independent	involvement	lake
hardly	hour	index	iron	land
harm	house	indicate	Islam	landscape
hat	household	indication	Islamic	lane
hate	housing	individual	island	language
have	how	industrial	issue	lap
he	however	industry	IT	large
head	huge	inevitable	it	largely
headline	human	infect	item	last
headquarters	human rights	infection	its	late
heal	humor	inflation	itself	later
health	hundred	influence	jacket	latest
healthy	hundredth	inform	jail	Latin
hear	hunt	information	January	latter
hearing	hunter	ingredient	jazz	laugh
heart	hurt	initial	jersey	laughter
heat	husband	initially	Jesus	launch
heaven	I	initiative	jet	law
heavy	ice	injured	Jew	lawsuit
height	idea	injury	Jewish	lawyer
helicopter	ideal	inner	job	lay
hell	identify	innocent	join	layer
hello	identity	inquiry	joint	lead
help	if	inside	joke	leader
her	ignore	insist	journal	leadership
here	ill	inspect	journalist	leading
hero	illegal	inspector	journey	leaf
herself	illness	install	joy	league
hi	illustrate	instance	judge	leak
hide	illustration	instant	judgment	lean
high	image	instead	juice	leap
high school	imagination	institute	July	learn
highlight	imagine	institution	jump	lease
highly	immediate	instruction	June	least
highway	immediately	instrument	junior	leather
hill	immigrant	insurance	jury	leave
him	immigration	integrate	just	lecture
himself	immune	intellectual	justice	left
hint	impact	intelligence	justify	leg
hip	implement	intelligent	keen	legal
hire	implication	intend	keep	legislation
his	imply	intense	key	lend
historic	import	intention	kick	length
historical	importance	interest	kid	lens
history	important	interested	kill	lesbian
hit	impose	interesting	killer	less
hold	impossible	interim	killing	lesson
holder	impress	interior	kilometer	let
hole	impression	internal	kind	let's
holiday	impressive	international	king	letter
holy	improve	Internet	kiss	level
home	improvement	intervention	kitchen	liberal
homeless	in	interview	knee	liberate
homosexual	inch	into	knife	liberty
honest	incident	introduce	knock	library
honor	include	invasion	know	license
hook	included	invest	know-how	lie
hope	including	investigate	knowledge	life
horror	income	investment	label	lift
horse	increase	investor	labor	light
hospital	increasingly	invitation	laboratory	like
host	incredible	invite	lack	likely
hostage	indeed	involve	lad	limit

limited	march	million	Muslim	north
line	margin	millionth	must	northeast
link	marine	mind	mutual	northern
lip	mark	mine	my	northwest
list	marked	miner	myself	nose
listen	market	minimum	mystery	not
literary	marketing	minister	myth	note
literature	marriage	ministry	name	noted
little	married	minor	narrow	nothing
live	marry	minority	nation	notice
live-in	mask	minute	national	notion
living	mass	mirror	nationalist	novel
load	massive	Miss	native	November
loan	master	miss	natural	now
lobby	match	missile	naturally	nowhere
local	mate	missing	nature	nuclear
local authority	material	mission	naval	number
location	matter	mistake	navy	numerous
lock	maximum	mix	Nazi	nurse
long	May	mixed	near	object
long-term	may	mixture	nearby	objective
long-time	maybe	mobile	nearly	observe
look	mayor	model	neat	observer
loose	me	moderate	necessarily	obtain
lord	meal	modern	necessary	obvious
lose	mean	modest	neck	obviously
loss	meaning	mom	need	occasion
lost	means	moment	negative	occasional
lot	meanwhile	Monday	negotiate	occupation
loud	measure	monetary	negotiation	occupy
love	meat	money	neighbor	occur
lovely	mechanism	monitor	neighborhood	ocean
lover	medal	month	neither	o'clock
low	media	monthly	nerve	October
lower	medical	mood	nervous	odd
luck	medicine	moon	net	of
lucky	medium	moral	network	of course
lunch	meet	more	never	off
luxury	meeting	moreover	nevertheless	offense
machine	member	morning	new	offensive
mad	membership	mortgage	newly	offer
made-up	memory	most	news	offering
magazine	mental	mostly	news agency	office
magic	mention	mother	newscaster	officer
mail	merchant	motion	newspaper	official
main	mere	motivate	next	often
mainly	merely	motor	nice	oh
maintain	merger	mount	night	oil
major	mess	mountain	nightmare	okay
majority	message	mouth	nine	old
make	metal	move	nineteen	Olympic
maker	method	movement	nineteenth	on
make-up	metre	movie	ninetieth	once
male	middle	Mr.	ninety	one
man	middle class	Mrs.	ninth	one's
manage	Middle East	Ms.	no	online
management	midnight	much	no one	only
manager	might	mum	nobody	onto
manner	mild	murder	nod	open
manufacture	mile	muscle	noise	opening
manufacturer	militant	museum	none	opera
many	military	music	nor	operate
map	milk	musical	normal	operation
March	mill	musician	normally	operator

opinion	particular	pink	pp.	promote
opponent	particularly	pipe	practical	promotion
opportunity	partly	pit	practice	prompt
oppose	partner	pitch	praise	proof
opposed	partnership	place	precisely	proper
opposite	party	plain	predict	properly
opposition	pass	plan	prefer	property
opt	passage	plane	pregnancy	proportion
optimistic	passenger	planet	pregnant	proposal
option	passion	planning	premier	propose
or	past	plant	premium	prosecution
orange	path	plastic	preparation	prospect
order	patient	plate	prepare	protect
ordinary	pattern	platform	prepared	protection
organization	pause	play	presence	protein
organize	pay	player	present	protest
organized	payment	playoff	preserve	proud
organizer	peace	pleasant	presidency	prove
origin	peaceful	please	president	provide
original	peak	pleased	presidential	province
originally	peer	pleasure	press	provision
other	peg	pledge	pressure	provoke
otherwise	pen	plenty	presumably	psychological
ought	penalty	plot	pretty	pub
our	penny	plunge	prevent	public
ourselves	pension	plus	previous	publication
out	people	pocket	previously	publicity
outcome	pepper	poem	price	publish
outline	per	poet	pride	publisher
output	percent	poetry	priest	publishing
outside	percentage	point	primary	pull
outstanding	perfect	point of view	prime	pump
over	perfectly	pole	prime minister	punch
overall	perform	police	prince	pupil
overcome	performance	police officer	princess	purchase
overnight	perhaps	policeman	principal	pure
overseas	period	policy	principle	purple
overwhelming	permanent	political	print	purpose
owe	permission	politician	prior	pursue
own	permit	politics	priority	push
owner	person	poll	prison	put
ownership	personal	pollution	prisoner	qualified
pace	personality	pool	private	qualify
pack	personally	poor	privatize	quality
package	personnel	pop	prize	quantity
pact	perspective	popular	probably	quarter
page	persuade	population	problem	queen
pain	pet	port	procedure	question
painful	phase	portrait	proceed	quick
paint	philosophy	pose	process	quiet
painting	phone	position	produce	quite
pair	photo	positive	producer	quote
palace	photograph	possibility	product	race
pale	photographer	possible	production	racial
pan	phrase	possibly	profession	racing
panel	physical	post	professional	radical
panic	pick	pot	professor	radio
paper	pickup	potato	profile	rage
parent	picture	potential	profit	raid
park	piece	pound	program	rail
parliament	pile	pour	progress	railway
parliamentary	pill	poverty	project	rain
part	pilot	power	prominent	raise
participate	pin	powerful	promise	rally

range	related	retire	sample	session
rank	relation	retirement	sanction	set
rape	relationship	retreat	sand	settle
rapid	relative	return	satellite	settlement
rare	relatively	reveal	satisfied	setup
rarely	relax	revenue	Saturday	seven
rate	release	reverse	sauce	seventeen
rather	reliable	review	save	seventeenth
rating	relief	revolution	saving	seventh
raw	religion	revolutionary	say	seventieth
ray	religious	reward	scale	seventy
reach	reluctant	rhythm	scandal	several
react	rely	rice	scene	severe
reaction	remain	rich	schedule	sex
read	remaining	rid	scheme	sexual
reader	remark	ride	school	shade
reading	remarkable	rider	science	shadow
ready	remember	right	scientific	shake
real	remind	right-wing	scientist	shall
real estate	remote	ring	score	shame
reality	remove	riot	scream	shape
realize	renew	rise	screen	shaped
really	rent	risk	script	share
rear	repair	rival	sea	shareholder
reason	repeat	river	seal	sharp
reasonable	replace	road	search	she
rebel	replacement	rock	season	shed
recall	reply	rocket	seat	sheet
receive	report	role	second	shell
recent	reporter	roll	secret	shelter
recently	reporting	Roman	secretary	shift
recession	represent	romantic	Secretary of State	ship
reckon	representative	roof	secretary-general	shirt
recognition	republic	room	section	shock
recognize	republican	root	sector	shoe
recommend	reputation	rose	secure	shoot
recommendation	request	rough	security	shop
record	require	round	Security Council	shopping
recording	requirement	route	see	shore
recover	rescue	routine	seed	short
recovery	research	row	seek	shortage
recruit	reserve	royal	seem	shortly
red	resident	rugby	segment	short-term
reduce	resign	ruin	seize	shot
reduction	resignation	rule	select	should
reel	resist	ruling	selection	shoulder
refer	resistance	rumor	self	shout
reference	resolution	run	sell	show
referendum	resolve	runner	Senate	shut
reflect	resort	running	senator	sick
reform	resource	rural	send	side
refugee	respect	rush	senior	sigh
refuse	respond	sack	sense	sight
regard	response	sacrifice	sensible	sign
regime	responsibility	sad	sensitive	signal
region	responsible	safe	sentence	significant
regional	rest	safety	separate	silence
register	restaurant	sail	September	silent
regret	restore	saint	series	silver
regular	restriction	sake	serious	similar
regulation	result	salary	seriously	simple
regulator	resume	sale	servant	simply
reject	retail	salt	serve	since
relate	retain	same	service	sing

singer	sort	steel	summer	technology
single	soul	stem	summit	teenager
sink	sound	step	sun	telephone
sir	source	sterling	Sunday	television
sister	south	stick	super	tell
sit	southeast	still	superb	temperature
site	southern	stimulate	superior	temple
situation	southwest	stir	supply	temporary
six	space	stock	support	ten
sixteen	spare	stock exchange	supporter	tend
sixteenth	spark	stock market	suppose	tendency
sixth	speak	stomach	supposed	tennis
sixtieth	speaker	stone	supreme	tension
sixty	speaking	stop	sure	tenth
size	special	store	surely	term
ski	specialist	storm	surface	terrible
skill	specialize	story	surgery	territory
skin	species	straight	surplus	terror
sky	specific	strain	surprise	terrorism
sleep	specifically	strange	surprised	terrorist
slice	spectacular	strategic	surprising	test
slide	speculate	strategy	surrender	testing
slight	speech	stream	surround	text
slightly	speed	street	survey	than
slim	spell	strength	survival	thank
slip	spend	strengthen	survive	that
slow	spin	stress	suspect	the
small	spirit	stretch	suspend	theater
smart	spiritual	strict	suspicion	their
smash	spite	strike	sustain	them
smell	split	striking	sweep	theme
smile	spokesman	string	sweet	themselves
smoke	spokeswoman	strip	swim	then
smoking	sponsor	stroke	swing	theory
smooth	sport	strong	switch	therapy
snap	spot	structure	symbol	there
snow	spray	struggle	sympathy	therefore
so	spread	student	symptom	these
so-called	spring	studio	system	they
soccer	spur	study	table	thick
social	squad	stuff	tackle	thin
socialist	square	stupid	tactic	thing
society	squeeze	style	tail	think
soft	stable	subject	take	thinking
software	stadium	subsequent	takeover	third
soil	staff	subsidy	tale	Third World
soldier	stage	substance	talent	thirteen
solicitor	stake	substantial	talk	thirteenth
solid	stamp	substitute	tall	thirtieth
solution	stand	succeed	tank	thirty
solve	standard	success	tap	this
some	star	successful	tape	thorough
somebody	stare	such	target	those
somehow	start	sudden	task	though
someone	state	suddenly	taste	thought
something	State Department	suffer	tax	thousand
sometimes	statement	sufficient	tea	threat
somewhat	station	sugar	teach	threaten
somewhere	statistic	suggest	teacher	threatening
son	status	suggestion	teaching	three
song	stay	suicide	team	throat
soon	steady	suit	tear	through
sophisticated	steal	suitable	technical	throughout
sorry	steam	sum	technique	throw

Thursday	trick	upset	warm	wine
thus	trigger	urban	warn	wing
ticket	trip	urge	warning	winner
tide	triumph	urgent	wash	winning
tie	troop	us	waste	winter
tight	trouble	use	watch	wipe
till	truck	used	water	wire
time	true	useful	wave	wireless
tiny	truly	user	way	wise
tip	trust	usual	we	wish
tired	truth	usually	weak	with
tissue	try	valley	weaken	withdraw
title	tube	valuable	wealth	withdrawal
to	Tuesday	value	weapon	within
today	tune	van	wear	without
together	tunnel	variety	weather	witness
tomorrow	turn	various	web	woman
ton	TV	vary	website	wonder
tone	twelfth	vast	wedding	wonderful
tonight	twelve	vegetable	Wednesday	wood
too	twentieth	vehicle	week	wooden
tool	twenty	venture	weekend	word
tooth	twice	venue	weekly	work
top	twin	verdict	weigh	worker
torture	twist	version	weight	working
total	two	very	welcome	world
touch	type	vessel	welfare	world war
tough	typical	veteran	well	worldwide
tour	ultimate	via	well-known	worried
tourist	ultimately	vice	west	worry
tournament	U.N.	victim	western	worth
toward	unable	victimize	wet	would
tower	uncle	victory	what	wound
town	under	video	whatever	wrap
toy	underground	view	wheel	write
trace	undermine	village	when	writer
track	understand	violate	whenever	writing
trade	understanding	violence	where	written
trader	unemployment	violent	whereas	wrong
tradition	unexpected	virtually	whether	yacht
traditional	unfair	virus	which	yard
traffic	unfortunately	visible	while	yeah
tragedy	unhappy	vision	whilst	year
trail	unidentified	visit	whip	yellow
train	uniform	visitor	whisper	yen
transaction	union	vital	white	yes
transfer	unique	vitamin	White House	yesterday
transform	unit	voice	who	yet
transition	united	volume	whole	yield
transport	United Nations	voluntary	whom	you
transportation	unity	volunteer	whose	young
trap	universe	vote	why	youngster
travel	university	voter	wicket	your
traveler	unknown	vulnerable	wide	yours
treasury	unless	wage	widespread	yourself
treat	unlike	wait	wife	youth
treatment	unlikely	wake	wild	zone
treaty	until	walk	will	
tree	unusual	wall	willing	
tremendous	up	Wall Street	win	
trend	upon	want	wind	
trial	upper	war	window	

ACADEMIC WORD LIST

This list contains the head words of the families in the Academic Word List. The numbers indicate the sublist of the Academic Word List, with Sublist 1 containing the most frequent words, Sublist 2 the next most frequent and so on. For example, *abandon* and its family members are in Sublist 8 of the Academic Word List.

abandon	8	attach	6	complex	2	create	1
abstract	6	attain	9	component	3	credit	2
academy	5	attitude	4	compound	5	criteria	3
access	4	attribute	4	comprehensive	7	crucial	8
accommodate	9	author	6	comprise	7	culture	2
accompany	8	authority	1	compute	2	currency	8
accumulate	8	automate	8	conceive	10	cycle	4
accurate	6	available	1	concentrate	4	data	1
achieve	2	aware	5	concept	1	debate	4
acknowledge	6	behalf	9	conclude	2	decade	7
acquire	2	benefit	1	concurrent	9	decline	5
adapt	7	bias	8	conduct	2	deduce	3
adequate	4	bond	6	confer	4	define	1
adjacent	10	brief	6	confine	9	definite	7
adjust	5	bulk	9	confirm	7	demonstrate	3
administrate	2	capable	6	conflict	5	denote	8
adult	7	capacity	5	conform	8	deny	7
advocate	7	category	2	consent	3	depress	10
affect	2	cease	9	consequent	2	derive	1
aggregate	6	challenge	5	considerable	3	design	2
aid	7	channel	7	consist	1	despite	4
albeit	10	chapter	2	constant	3	detect	8
allocate	6	chart	8	constitute	1	deviate	8
alter	5	chemical	7	constrain	3	device	9
alternative	3	circumstance	3	construct	2	devote	9
ambiguous	8	cite	6	consult	5	differentiate	7
amend	5	civil	4	consume	2	dimension	4
analogy	9	clarify	8	contact	5	diminish	9
analyze	1	classic	7	contemporary	8	discrete	5
annual	4	clause	5	context	1	discriminate	6
anticipate	9	code	4	contract	1	displace	8
apparent	4	coherent	9	contradict	8	display	6
append	8	coincide	9	contrary	7	dispose	7
appreciate	8	collapse	10	contrast	4	distinct	2
approach	1	colleague	10	contribute	3	distort	9
appropriate	2	commence	9	controversy	9	distribute	1
approximate	4	comment	3	convene	3	diverse	6
arbitrary	8	commission	2	converse	9	document	3
area	1	commit	4	convert	7	domain	6
aspect	2	commodity	8	convince	10	domestic	4
assemble	10	communicate	4	cooperate	6	dominate	3
assess	1	community	2	coordinate	3	draft	5
assign	6	compatible	9	core	3	drama	8
assist	2	compensate	3	corporate	3	duration	9
assume	1	compile	10	correspond	3	dynamic	7
assure	9	complement	8	couple	7	economy	1

edit	6	flexible	6	infer	7	logic	5
element	2	fluctuate	8	infrastructure	8	maintain	2
eliminate	7	focus	2	inherent	9	major	1
emerge	4	format	9	inhibit	6	manipulate	8
emphasis	3	formula	1	initial	3	manual	9
empirical	7	forthcoming	10	initiate	6	margin	5
enable	5	foundation	7	injure	2	mature	9
encounter	10	found	9	innovate	7	maximize	3
energy	5	framework	3	input	6	mechanism	4
enforce	5	function	1	insert	7	media	7
enhance	6	fund	3	insight	9	mediate	9
enormous	10	fundamental	5	inspect	8	medical	5
ensure	3	furthermore	6	instance	3	medium	9
entity	5	gender	6	institute	2	mental	5
environment	1	generate	5	instruct	6	method	1
equate	2	generation	5	integral	9	migrate	6
equip	7	globe	7	integrate	4	military	9
equivalent	5	goal	4	integrity	10	minimal	9
erode	9	grade	7	intelligence	6	minimize	8
error	4	grant	4	intense	8	minimum	6
establish	1	guarantee	7	interact	3	ministry	6
estate	6	guideline	8	intermediate	9	minor	3
estimate	1	hence	4	internal	4	mode	7
ethic	9	hierarchy	7	interpret	1	modify	5
ethnic	4	highlight	8	interval	6	monitor	5
evaluate	2	hypothesis	4	intervene	7	motive	6
eventual	8	identical	7	intrinsic	10	mutual	9
evident	1	identify	1	invest	2	negate	3
evolve	5	ideology	7	investigate	4	network	5
exceed	6	ignorance	6	invoke	10	neutral	6
exclude	3	illustrate	3	involve	1	nevertheless	6
exhibit	8	image	5	isolate	7	nonetheless	10
expand	5	immigrate	3	issue	1	norm	9
expert	6	impact	2	item	2	normal	2
explicit	6	implement	4	job	4	notion	5
exploit	8	implicate	4	journal	2	notwithstanding	10
export	1	implicit	8	justify	3	nuclear	8
expose	5	imply	3	label	4	objective	5
external	5	impose	4	labor	1	obtain	2
extract	7	incentive	6	layer	3	obvious	4
facilitate	5	incidence	6	lecture	6	occupy	4
factor	1	incline	10	legal	1	occur	1
feature	2	income	1	legislate	1	odd	10
federal	6	incorporate	6	levy	10	offset	8
fee	6	index	6	liberal	5	ongoing	10
file	7	indicate	1	license	5	option	4
final	2	individual	1	likewise	10	orient	5
finance	1	induce	8	link	3	outcome	7
finite	7	inevitable	8	locate	3	output	

overall	4	protocol	9	scheme	3	team	9
overlap	9	psychology	5	scope	6	technical	3
overseas	6	publication	7	section	1	technique	3
panel	10	publish	3	sector	1	technology	3
paradigm	7	purchase	2	secure	2	temporary	9
paragraph	8	pursue	5	seek	2	tense	8
parallel	4	qualitative	9	select	2	terminate	8
parameter	4	quote	7	sequence	3	text	2
participate	2	radical	8	series	4	theme	8
partner	3	random	8	sex	3	theory	1
passive	9	range	2	shift	3	thereby	8
perceive	2	ratio	5	significant	1	thesis	7
percent	1	rational	6	similar	1	topic	7
period	1	react	3	simulate	7	trace	6
persist	10	recover	6	site	2	tradition	2
perspective	5	refine	9	so-called	10	transfer	2
phase	4	regime	4	sole	7	transform	6
phenomenon	7	region	2	somewhat	7	transit	5
philosophy	3	register	3	source	1	transmit	7
physical	3	regulate	2	specific	1	transport	6
plus	8	reinforce	8	specify	3	trend	5
policy	1	reject	5	sphere	9	trigger	9
portion	9	relax	9	stable	5	ultimate	7
pose	10	release	7	statistic	4	undergo	10
positive	2	relevant	2	status	4	underlie	6
potential	2	reluctance	10	straightforward	10	undertake	4
practitioner	8	rely	3	strategy	2	uniform	8
precede	6	remove	3	stress	4	unify	9
precise	5	require	1	structure	1	unique	7
predict	4	research	1	style	5	utilize	6
predominant	8	reside	2	submit	7	valid	3
preliminary	9	resolve	4	subordinate	9	vary	1
presume	6	resource	2	subsequent	4	vehicle	8
previous	2	respond	1	subsidy	6	version	5
primary	2	restore	8	substitute	5	via	8
prime	5	restrain	9	successor	7	violate	9
principal	4	restrict	2	sufficient	3	virtual	8
principle	1	retain	4	sum	4	visible	7
prior	4	reveal	6	summary	4	vision	9
priority	7	revenue	5	supplement	9	visual	8
proceed	1	reverse	7	survey	2	volume	3
process	1	revise	8	survive	7	voluntary	7
professional	4	revolution	9	suspend	9	welfare	5
ohibit	7	rigid	9	sustain	5	whereas	5
ct	4	role	1	symbol	5	whereby	10
te	4	route	9	tape	6	widespread	8
on	3	scenario	9	target	5		
	8	schedule	8	task	3		

USA States, Abbreviations, and Capitals

State	Capital
Alabama (AL)	Montgomery
Alaska (AK)	Juneau
Arizona (AZ)	Phoenix
Arkansas (AR)	Little Rock
California (CA)	Sacramento
Colorado (CO)	Denver
Connecticut (CT)	Hartford
Delaware (DE)	Dover
Florida (FL)	Tallahassee
Georgia (GA)	Atlanta
Hawaii (HI)	Honolulu
Idaho (ID)	Boise
Illinois (IL)	Springfield
Indiana (IN)	Indianapolis
Iowa (IA)	Des Moines
Kansas (KS)	Topeka
Kentucky (KY)	Frankfort
Louisiana (LA)	Baton Rouge
Maine (ME)	Augusta
Maryland (MD)	Annapolis
Massachusetts (MA)	Boston
Michigan (MI)	Lansing
Minnesota (MN)	Saint Paul
Mississippi (MS)	Jackson
Missouri (MO)	Jefferson City
Montana (MT)	Helena
Nebraska (NE)	Lincoln
Nevada (NV)	Carson City
New Hampshire (NH)	Concord
New Jersey (NJ)	Trenton
New Mexico (NM)	Santa Fe
New York (NY)	Albany
North Carolina (NC)	Raleigh
North Dakota (ND)	Bismarck
Ohio (OH)	Columbus
Oklahoma (OK)	Oklahoma City
Oregon (OR)	Salem
Pennsylvania (PA)	Harrisburg
Rhode Island (RI)	Providence
South Carolina (SC)	Columbia
South Dakota (SD)	Pierre
Tennessee (TN)	Nashville
Texas (TX)	Austin
Utah (UT)	Salt Lake City
Vermont (VT)	Montpelier
Virginia (VA)	Richmond
Washington (WA)	Olympia
West Virginia (WV)	Charleston
Wisconsin (WI)	Madison
Wyoming (WY)	Cheyenne

Capital of the United States of America (USA)

District of Columbia (DC)	Washingon (commonly abbreviated: Washington, D.C

This list shows the spelling and pronunciation of geographical names. If a country has different words for the country, adjective, and person, these are all shown. Inclusion in this list does not imply status as a sovereign nation.

Af|ghan|i|stan /æfgænɪstæn/; Af|ghan, Af|ghani /æfgæn/, /æfgæni, -gɑni/

Af|ri|ca /æfrɪkə/; Af|ri|can /æfrɪkən/

Al|ba|nia /ælbeɪniə/; Al|ba|ni|an /ælbeɪniən/

Al|ge|ria /ældʒɪəriə/; Al|ge|ri|an /ældʒɪəriən/

An|dor|ra /ændɔrə/; An|dor|ran /ændɔrən/

An|go|la /æŋgoʊlə/; An|go|lan /æŋgoʊlən/

Ant|arc|ti|ca /æntɑrktɪkə, -ɑrtɪ-/; Ant|arc|tic /æntɑrktɪk, -ɑrtɪk/

An|ti|gua and Bar|bu|da /æntigə ən barbudə/; An|ti|guan, Bar|bu|dan /æntigən/, /barbudən/

(the) Arc|tic Ocean /(ði) ɑrktɪk oʊʃən, ɑrtɪk/; Arc|tic /ɑrktɪk, ɑrtɪk/

Ar|gen|ti|na /ɑrdʒəntinə/; Ar|gen|tine, Ar|gen|tin|ian, or Ar|gen|tin|ean /ɑrdʒəntin, -taɪn/, /ɑrdʒəntɪniən/

Ar|me|nia /ɑrminiə/; Ar|me|nian /ɑrminiən/

A|sia /eɪʒə/; A|sian /eɪʒən/

(the) At|lan|tic Ocean /(ði) ætlæntɪk oʊʃən/

Aus|tra|lia /ɔstreɪlyə/; Aus|tral|ian /ɔstreɪlyən/

Aus|tria /ɔstriə/; Aus|tri|an /ɔstriən/

Azer|bai|jan /æzərbaɪdʒɑn, ɑzər-/; Azer|bai|ja|ni, Azeri /æzərbaɪdʒɑni, ɑzər-/, /əzgri/

(the) Ba|ha|mas /(ðə) bəhɑməz/; Ba|ha|mi|an /bəheɪmiən, -hɑ-/

Bah|rain /bɑreɪn/; Bah|raini /bɑreɪni/

Ban|gla|desh /bɑŋglədɛʃ, bæŋ-/; Ban|gla|deshi /bɑŋglədɛʃi, bæŋ-/

Bar|ba|dos /bɑrbeɪdoʊs/; Bar|ba|di|an /bɑrbeɪdiən/

Be|la|rus /bɛlərus, byɛl-/; Be|la|rus|si|an /bɛlərʌʃən, byɛl-/

Bel|gium /bɛldʒəm/; Bel|gian /bɛldʒən/

Be|lize /bəliz/; Be|liz|ean /bəliziən/

Be|nin /bənin/; Be|ni|nese /bɛnɪniz/

Bhu|tan /butɑn, -tæn/; Bhu|tani, Bhu|ta|nese /butɑni, -tæni/, /butᵊniz/

Bo|liv|ia /bəlɪviə/; Bo|liv|i|an /bəlɪviən/

ʼos|nia and Her|ze|go|vi|na /bɒzniə ən hɛrtsəgoʊvinə/; Bos|ni|an, Her|ze|go|vin|ian /bɒzniən/, /hɛrtsəgoʊviniən/

ʼwa|na /bɒtswɑnə/; Mo|tswan|a (person), ʼtswa|na (people) /mɒtswɑnə/, /batswɑnə/

ʼzɪl/; Bra|zil|ian /brəzɪlyən/

ʼrus|sa|lam /brunaɪ dɑrusɑləm/; Bru|nei, /brunaɪ/, /brunaɪən/

ʼriə/; Bul|gar|ian /bʌlgɛəriən/

Bur|ki|na Fa|so /bərkinə fɑsoʊ/; Bur|kin|abe, Bur|ki|nese /bɑrkɪnɑbeɪ/, /bɑrkɪniz/

Bur|ma--See Myanmar /bɑrmə/; Bur|mese— /bɑrmiz/

Bu|run|di /burundi/; Bu|run|di|an /burundiən/

Cam|bo|dia /kæmboʊdiə/; Cam|bo|dian /kæmboʊdiən/

Cam|er|oon /kæmərun/; Cam|eroo|nian /kæməruniən/

Can|a|da /kænədə/; Ca|na|di|an /kəneɪdiən/

Cape Verde /keɪp vɜrd/; Cape Verd|ean /keɪp vɜrdiən/

Cen|tral Af|ri|can Re|pub|lic /sɛntrəl æfrɪkən rɪpʌblɪk/; Cen|tral Af|ri|can /sɛntrəl æfrɪkən/

Chad /tʃæd/; Chad|ian /tʃædiən/

Chi|le /tʃɪli, -leɪ/; Chil|ean /tʃɪliən, tʃɪleɪ-/

Chi|na /tʃaɪnə/; Chi|nese /tʃaɪniz/

Co|lom|bia /kəlʌmbiə/; Co|lom|bi|an /kəlʌmbiən/

Co|mo|ros /kɒməroʊz/; Co|mor|an /kəmɔrən/

Co|sta Ri|ca /kɒstə rikə/; Co|sta Ri|can /kɒstə rikən/

Côte d'Ivoire /kout divwɑr/; Ivoir|i|an /ivwɑriən/

Cro|a|tia /kroʊeɪʃə/; Cro|a|tian /kroʊeɪʃən/

Cu|ba /kyubə/; Cu|ban /kyubən/

Cy|prus /saɪprəs/; Cyp|ri|ot /sɪpriət/

(the) Czech Re|pub|lic /(ðə) tʃɛk rɪpʌblɪk/; Czech /tʃɛk/

Dem|o|crat|ic Re|pub|lic of the Con|go, or (the) Con|go /dɛməkrætɪk rɪpʌblɪk əv ðə kɒngoʊ/, /(ðə) kɒngoʊ/; Con|go|lese /kɒngəliz, -lis/

Den|mark /dɛnmark/; Da|nish, Dane /deɪnɪʃ/, /deɪn/

Dji|bou|ti /dʒɪbuti/; Dji|bou|tian /dʒɪbutiən/

Dom|i|ni|ca /dɒmɪnɪkə, dəmɪnɪkə/; Do|min|i|can /dɒmɪnɪkən/

(the) Do|mi|ni|can Re|pub|lic /(ðə) dəmɪnɪkən rɪpʌblɪk; Do|mi|ni|can /dəmɪnɪkən/

East Ti|mor /ist timɔr/; East Ti|mor|ese /ist timɔriz/

Ec|ua|dor /ɛkwədɔr/; Ec|ua|dor|ian /ɛkwədɔriən/

Egypt /idʒɪpt/; Egyp|tian /ɪdʒɪpʃən/

El Sal|va|dor /ɛl sælvədɔr/; Sal|va|do|ran, Sal|va|do|rean /sælvədɔrən/, /sælvədɔriən/

Eng|land /ɪŋglənd/; Eng|lish /ɪŋglɪʃ/

Equi|to|ri|al Guin|ea /ɛkwɪtɔriəl gɪni/; Equi|to|ri|al Guin|ean, Equi|to|guin|ean /ɛkwɪtɔriəl gɪniən/, /ɛkwɪtougɪniən/

Er|i|trea /ɛrɪtriə/; Er|i|tre|an /ɛrɪtriən/

Es|to|nia /ɛstoʊniə/; Es|to|ni|an /ɛstoʊniən/

Ethi|o|pia /iθioʊpiə/; Ethi|o|pi|an /iθioʊpiən/

Eu|rope /yʊərəp/; Euro|pe|an /yʊərəpiən/

Fi|ji /ˈfiʤi/; Fi|ji|an /ˈfiʤiən, fiji-/

Fin|land /ˈfinlənd/; Fin|nish, Finn, Fin|land|er /ˈfiniʃ/, /fin/, /ˈfinləndər, -lændər/

France /frɑns/; French /frɛntʃ/

Ga|bon /gaˈboun/; Gab|o|nese /gæbəˈniz/

(the) Gam|bia /(ðə) ˈgæmbiə/; Gam|bi|an /ˈgæmbiən/

Geor|gia /ˈdʒɔrdʒə/; Geor|gian /ˈdʒɔrdʒən/

Ger|ma|ny /ˈdʒɜrməni/; Ger|man /ˈdʒɜrmən/

Gha|na /ˈgɑnə/; Gha|na|ian /ˈgɑniən, gəˈneɪən/

Greece /gris/; Greek /grik/

Gre|na|da /grɪˈneɪdə/; Gre|na|di|an /grɪˈneɪdiən/

Gua|te|ma|la /gwɑtəˈmɑlə/; Gua|te|ma|lan /gwɑtəˈmɑlən/

Guin|ea /ˈgɪni/; Guin|ean /ˈgɪniən/

Guin|ea-Bis|sau /gɪni bɪˈsɑu/; Guin|ean /ˈgɪniən/

Guy|ana /gaɪˈænə, -ˈɑnə/; Guy|a|nese /gaɪəˈniz/

Hai|ti /ˈheɪti/; Hai|tian /ˈheɪʃən/

Hon|du|ras /hɒnˈduərəs/; Hon|du|ran /hɒnˈduərən/

Hun|ga|ry /ˈhʌŋgəri/; Hun|gar|i|an /hʌŋˈgɛəriən/

Ice|land /ˈaɪslənd/; Ice|lan|dic, Ice|land|er /aɪsˈlændɪk/, /ˈaɪsləndər, -lændər/

In|dia /ˈɪndiə/; In|di|an /ˈɪndiən/

(the) In|di|an Ocean /(ði) ɪndiən ˈouʃən/

In|do|ne|sia /ɪndəˈniʒə/; In|do|ne|sian /ɪndəˈniʒən/

Iran /ɪˈrɑn, ɪˈræn, aɪˈræn/; Ira|ni|an, Iran|i /ɪˈreɪniən, ɪrɑ-, aɪreɪ-/, /ɪˈrɑni/

I|raq /ɪˈræk, ɪrak/; I|raq|i /ɪˈræki, ɪrɑki/

Ire|land /ˈaɪərlənd/; Ir|ish /ˈaɪrɪʃ/

Is|ra|el /ˈɪzriəl, -reɪəl/; Is|rae|li /ɪzˈreɪli/

I|ta|ly /ˈɪtəli/; Ital|ian /ɪˈtælyən/

Ja|mai|ca /dʒəˈmeɪkə/; Ja|mai|can /dʒəˈmeɪkən/

Ja|pan /dʒəˈpæn/; Jap|a|nese /dʒæpəˈniz/

Jor|dan /ˈdʒɔrdən/; Jor|da|ni|an /dʒɔrˈdeɪniən/

Ka|zakh|stan /kɑzakˈstɑn, -stæn/; Ka|zakh|stani, Ka|zakh /kɑzakˈstɑni, -stæni/, /kəˈzɑk, kəˈzæk/

Ken|ya /ˈkɛnyə, kin-/; Ken|yan /ˈkɛnyən, kin-/

Ki|ri|bati /kɪərəˈbɑti, -bæs/; I-Ki|ri|bati /i kɪərəˈbɑti, -bæs/

Ko|rea, South Ko|rea, North Ko|rea /kəˈriə, kɔ-/, /ˌsouθ kəriə, kɔ-/, /ˌnɔrθ kəriə, kɔ-/; Ko|rean /kəˈriən, kɔ-/, /ˌsouθ kəriən, kɔ-/, /ˌnɔrθ kəriən, kɔ/

Ku|wait /kuˈweɪt/; Ku|wait|i /kuˈweɪti/

Kyr|gyz|stan /kɪərˈgɪstɑn, -stæn/; Kyr|gyz|sta|ni /kɪərgɪsˈtɑni, -stæni/

Laos /ˈlɑous, lɑus/; Lao, Lao|tian /lɑou, lɑu/, /leɪˈouʃən/

Lat|via /ˈlætviə, lɑt-/; Lat|vi|an /ˈlætviən, lɑt-/

Leb|a|non /ˈlɛbənən, -nɒn/; Leb|a|nese /lɛbəˈniz/

Le|so|tho /ləˈsoutou, -sutu/ So|tho, Mo|so|tho (person), Ba|so|tho (people) /ˈsoutou, sutu/, /mɔˈsoutou, -sutu/, /bɑˈsoutou, -sutu/

Li|be|ria /laɪˈbɪəriə/; Li|be|ri|an /laɪˈbɪəriən/

Lib|ya /ˈlɪbiə/; Lib|y|an /ˈlɪbiən/

Liech|ten|stein /ˈlɪktənstaɪn/; Liech|ten|stein, Liech|ten|stein|er /ˈlɪktənstaɪn/, /ˈlɪktənstaɪnər/

Lith|u|a|nia /lɪθuˈeɪniə/; Lith|u|a|ni|an /lɪθuˈeɪniən/

Lux|em|bourg /ˈlʌksəmbɜrg/; Lux|em|bourg, Lux|em|bourg|er /ˈlʌksəmbɜrg/, /ˈlʌksəmbɜrgər/

Mac|e|do|nia /mæsɪˈdouniə/; Mac|e|do|ni|an /mæsɪˈdouniən/

Mad|a|gas|car /mædəˈgæskər/; Mad|a|gas|can, Mala|gasy /mædəˈgæskən/, /ˈmæləgæsi/

Ma|la|wi /məˈlɑwi/; Ma|la|wi|an /məˈlɑwiən/

Ma|lay|sia /məˈleɪʒə/; Ma|lay|sian /məˈleɪʒən/

Mal|dives /ˈmɔldɪvz, -daɪvz/; Mal|div|ian /mɔlˈdɪviən/

Ma|li /ˈmɑli/; Ma|lian /ˈmɑliən/

Mal|ta /ˈmɔltə/; Mal|tese /mɔlˈtiz/

(the) Mar|shall Is|lands /(ðə) mɑrʃəl ˈaɪləndz/; Mar|shall|ese /mɑrʃəˈliz/

Mau|ri|ta|nia /mɔrɪˈteɪniə/; Mau|ri|ta|ni|an /mɔrɪˈteɪniən/

Mau|ri|ti|us /mɔrɪˈʃəs/; Mau|ri|tian /mɔrɪˈʃən/

Mex|i|co /ˈmɛksɪkou/; Mex|i|can /ˈmɛksɪkən/

Mi|cro|ne|sia /maɪkrəˈniʒə/; Mi|cro|ne|sian /maɪkrəˈniʒən/

Mol|do|va /mɒlˈdouvə/; Mol|do|van /mɒlˈdouvən/

Mo|na|co /ˈmɒnəkou/; Mo|na|can, Mon|e|gasque /ˈmɒnəkən/, /mɒnɪˈgæsk/

Mon|go|lia /mɒŋˈgouliə/; Mon|go|li|an /mɒŋˈgouliən/

Mo|roc|co /məˈrɒkou/; Mo|roc|can /məˈrɒkən/

Mo|zam|bique /mouzæmˈbik, -zəm-/; Mo|zam|bi|can /mouzæmˈbikən, -zəm-/

Myan|mar (Burma) /myanˈmɑr (ˈbɜrmə)/; Bur|mese /bərˈmiz/

Na|mib|ia /nəˈmɪbiə/; Na|mib|ian /nəˈmɪbiən/

Na|u|ru /ˈnɑuru/; Na|u|ru|an /nɑuˈruən/

Ne|pal /nəˈpɔl/; Nep|a|lese /nɛpəˈliz/

(the) Neth|er|lands /(ðə) ˈnɛðərləndz/; Dutch /dʌtʃ/

New Zea|land /nu ˈzilənd/; New Zea|land, New Zea|land|er /nu ˈzilənd/, /nu ˈziləndər/

Nic|a|ra|gua /nɪkəˈrɑgwə/; Nic|a|ra|guan /nɪkəˈrɑgwən/

Ni|ger /ˈnaɪdʒər, niˈʒɛər/; Ni|ge|rien, Ni|ger|ois /naɪdʒɪəriən, niˈʒɛryen/, /niˈʒɛrwɑ/

Ni|ge|ria /naɪˈdʒɪəriə/; Ni|ge|ri|an /naɪˈdʒɪəriən/

Nor|way /ˈnɔrweɪ/; Nor|we|gian /nɔrˈwiʤən/

Oman /ouˈmɑn/; Omani /ouˈmɑni/

(the) Pa|cif|ic Ocean /(ðə) pəˈsɪfik ˈouʃən/

Pa|ki|stan /ˈpækɪstæn, pɑkɪˈstɑn/; Pa|ki|sta|ni /pækɪˈstæni, pɑkɪˈstɑni/

Pa|lau /ˈpɑlɑu, pə-/; Pa|lau|an /pɑˈlɑuən, pə-/

Pan|a|ma /ˈpænəmɑ, -mɔ/; Pan|a|ma|ni|an /pænəˈmeɪniər

Pap|ua New Guin|ea /pæpyuə nu gɪni, pɑpuɑ/; Pap|ua
  New Guin|ean, Pap|uan /pæpyuə nu gɪniən, pɑpuɑ/,
  pæpyuən, pɑpuən/
Par|a|guay /pærəgwaɪ, -gweɪ/; Par|a|guay|an /pærəgwaɪən,
  -gweɪən/
Pe|ru /pəru/; Pe|ru|vi|an /pəruviən/
(the) Phil|ip|pines /(ðə) fɪlɪpinz/; Phil|ip|pine, Fili|pi|no,
  Fili|pi|na /fɪlɪpin/, /fɪlɪpinoʊ/, /fɪlɪpinə/
Po|land /poʊlənd/; Po|lish, Pole /poʊlɪʃ/, /poʊl/
Por|tu|gal /pɔrchəgəl/; Por|tu|guese /pɔrchəgiz/
Qa|tar /kətɑr/; Qa|tari /kətɑri/
Ro|ma|nia /roʊmeɪniə/; Ro|ma|ni|an /roʊmeɪniən/
Rus|sia /rʌʃə/; Rus|sian /rʌʃən/
Rwan|da /ruɑndə/; Rwan|dan /ruɑndən/
Saint Kitts–Ne|vis /seɪnt kɪts nivɪs/; Kit|ti|tian, Ne|vis|ian
  /kɪtɪʃən/, /nɪvɪʒən/
Saint Lu|cia /seɪnt luʃə/; Saint Lu|cian /seɪnt luʃən/
Saint Vin|cent and the Gren|a|dines /seɪnt vɪnsənt
  ən ðə grɛnədinz/; Saint Vin|cen|tian, Vin|cen|tian
  /seɪnt vɪnsɛnʃən/, /vɪnsɛnʃən/
Sa|moa /səmoʊə/; Sa|mo|an /səmoʊən/
San Ma|ri|no /sæn mərinoʊ/; Sam|ma|ri|nese,
  San Ma|ri|nese /sæmmærɪniz/, /sæn mærɪniz/
São To|mé and Prin|ci|pe /soʊn təmeɪ ən prɪnsipi/;
  Sao To|me|an /soʊn təmeɪən/
Sau|di Ara|bi|a /soʊdi əreɪbiə/; Sau|di Ara|bi|an /soʊdi
  əreɪbiən/
Scot|land /skɒtlənd/; Scot|tish, Scot(s) /skɒtɪʃ/, /skɒts/
Sen|e|gal /sɛnɪgɔl, -gɑl/; Sen|e|gal|ese /sɛnɪgəliz/
Ser|bia and Mon|te|ne|gro /sɑrbiə ən mɒntɪnɛgroʊ/
  Ser|bi|an, Serb, Mon|te|ne|grin /sɑrbiən/, /sɑrb/,
  /mɒntɪnɛgrɪn/
(the) Sey|chelles /(ðə) seɪʃɛlz/; Sey|chel|lois /seɪʃɛlwɑ/
Sier|ra Le|one /siɛrə lioʊn/; Sier|ra Le|on|ean
  /siɛrə lioʊniən/
Sin|ga|pore /sɪŋəpɔr, sɪŋə-/; Sin|ga|por|ean /sɪŋəpɔriən,
  sɪŋə-/
Slo|va|kia /sloʊvɑkiə, -vækiə/; Slo|vak, Slo|va|ki|an
  /sloʊvæk/, /sloʊvɑkiən, -væk-/
Slo|ve|nia /sloʊviniə/; Slo|vene, Slo|ve|nian /sloʊviniən/
So|lo|mon Is|lands /sɒləmən ɑɪləndz/; Sol|o|mon Is|land|er
  /sɒləmən ɑɪləndər/
  ...lia /səmɑliə, soʊ-/; So|ma|li, So|ma|lian /səmɑli,
  /səmɑliən, soʊ-/
  ...a /soʊθ æfrɪkə/; South Af|ri|can /soʊθ æfrɪkən/
  ...ic of) Spain (ðə rɪpʌblɪk əv) /speɪn/;
  ...n|iard /spænɪʃ/, /spænyərd/

Sri Lan|ka /sri lɑŋkə, ʃri/; Sri Lan|kan /sri lɑŋkən, ʃri/
Su|dan /sudæn, -dɑn/; Su|da|nese /sudᵊniz/
Su|ri|na|me /suərɪnɑm/; Su|ri|na|mer, Su|ri|na|mese
  /suərɪnɑmər/, /suərɪnəmīz/
Swa|zi|land /swɑzilænd/; Swazi /swɑzi/
Swe|den /swidᵊn/; Swe|dish, Swede /swidɪʃ/, /swid/
Swit|zer|land /swɪtsərlənd/; Swiss /swɪs/
Syr|ia /sɪəriə/; Syr|ian /sɪəriən/
Tai|wan /tɑɪwɑn/; Tai|wan|ese /tɑɪwɑniz/
Ta|jik|i|stan /tadʒɪkɪstæn, -stan/; Ta|jik|i|stani, Ta|jik
  /tadʒɪkɪstæni, -stɑni/, /tadʒɪk, -dʒik/
Tan|za|nia /tænzəniə/; Tan|za|nian /tænzəniən/
Thai|land /tɑɪlænd, -lənd/; Thai /tɑɪ/
To|go /toʊgoʊ/; To|go|lese /toʊgəliz/
Ton|ga /tɒŋgə/; Ton|gan /tɒŋgən/
Trin|i|dad and To|ba|go /trɪnɪdæd ən təbeɪgoʊ/;
  Trin|i|da|di|an, To|ba|go|ni|an /trɪnɪdeɪdiən/,
  /toʊbəgoʊniən/
Tu|ni|sia /tunɪʒə/; Tu|ni|sian /tunɪʒən/
Tur|key /tɜrki/; Turk|ish, Turk /tɜrkɪʃ/, /tɜrk/
Turk|men|i|stan /tərkmɛnɪstæn, -stan/; Turk|men
  /tɜrkmɛn, -mən/
Tu|va|lu /tuvɑlu, tuvəlu/; Tu|va|luan /tuvəluən/
Ugan|da /yugændə, ugɑn-/; Ugan|dan /yugændən, ugɑn-/
Ukraine /yukreɪn/; Ukrai|ni|an /yukreɪniən/
(the) Unit|ed Ar|ab Emir|ates /(ðə) yunɑɪtɪd ærəb ɛmərɪts,
  -əreɪts/; Emir|ati /ɛmərɑti/
(the) Unit|ed King|dom of Great Brit|ain and
North|ern Ire|land /(ðə) yunɑɪtɪd kɪŋdəm əv greɪt brɪtᵊn
  ən nɔrðərn ɑɪərlənd/; Brit|ish /brɪtɪʃ/
(the) Unit|ed States of Amer|i|ca /(ðə) yunɑɪtɪd steɪts
  əv əmɛrɪkə/; Ameri|can /əmɛrɪkən/
Uru|guay /yuərəgweɪ, -gwɑɪ/; Uru|guay|an
  /yuərəgweɪən, -gwɑɪən/
Uz|bek|i|stan /uzbɛkɪstæn, -stan, uz-/; Uz|bek|i|stani,
  Uz|bek /uzbɛkɪstæni, -stɑni, uz-/, /uzbɛk, uz-/
Van|u|atu /vænwɑtu/; Ni-Van|u|atu /ni vænwɑtu/
Vat|i|can City /vætɪkən sɪti/
Ven|e|zu|e|la /vɛnɪzweɪlə/; Ven|ezue|lan /vɛnɪzweɪlən/
Vi|et|nam /vigtnɑm, vyɛt-/; Vi|et|nam|ese /vigtnəmiz,
  vyɛt-/
Wales /weɪlz/; Welsh /wɛlʃ/
Ye|men /ygmən/; Yem|eni, Yem|en|ite /ygməni/, /ygmənɑɪt/
Zam|bia /zæmbiə/; Zam|bi|an /zæmbiən/
Zim|ba|bwe /zɪmbɑbweɪ, -wi/; Zim|ba|bwe|an
  /zɪmbɑbweɪən, -wiən/

CREDITS

Illustrations

Photos

CREDITS